CLASSICAL VOCAL MUSIC IN PRINT

Edited By:

Thomas R. Nardone

MUSICDATA, INC.

Philadelphia, 1976

Published volumes from the "Music-In-Print" series:

Vol.   I: Sacred Choral Music In Print
Vol. II: Secular Choral Music In Print
          1976 Supplement To Choral Music In Print
Vol. III: Organ Music In Print
Vol. IV: Classical Vocal Music In Print

International Standard Book Number: 0-88478-008-2

Library of Congress Catalog Card Number: 76-29568

Manufactured in the United States of America by Port City Press

Musicdata, Inc.
18 West Chelten Avenue
Philadelphia, Pennsylvania 19144

Contents

Preface

Classical Vocal Music In Print is designed to meet the needs of vocal artists in search of music for use in recital, religious or concert stage performance. Even though "classical" appears in the title it should be understood that all stylistic periods of music have been included. The only type of vocal music that has been excluded is that which is commonly called popular music. Many folk songs and folk song collections have been included because of their frequent demand in recital programming.

We are aware of several other guides, the most well known being Sergius Kagen's *Music For The Voice,* which have been primarily designed as selective repertory guides. The Music-In-Print series serves a unique purpose of supplying the most current published guides with the most comprehensive coverage of editions available from all publishers.

This catalog contains music from international, as well as domestic, music publishers. Additional information concerning some vocal works has been culled from various sources including: BBC Song Catalogue, Bach-Werke-Verzeichnis (Thematic Catalog), Baker's Biographical Dictionary of Musicians, and Grove's Dictionary of Music and Musicians. These reference works were used to provide uniform edition titles and source titles of the vocal listings in this catalog and also to provide additional biographical information on composers.

There has been a need to clarify the listing of titles since there may be many different translations of the same musical work which appear to be separate works. We have tried to align all those titles which refer to the same work by using either the original title or an accepted English version of the title. Similarly, the need for uniform source information is important, although not as great a problem as title identification. We have tried to represent operatic source titles, especially, in a uniform manner by using the original form of the title where possible. We have also listed song cycles with uniform original titles; translated titles are indicated where included.

Another troublesome problem was the use of "high-medium-low" designations for well known operatic repertoire in a great many music catalogs we have received from music publishers. Many publishers assume that everyone knows that a particular aria is for "tenor solo", for example, and they may list "medium-high" as the only vocal indication. For operatic arias and other well known works we have tried to indicate the exact voice part needed. In cases where it was impossible to make this indication we have used a system similar to that which the publishers use.

I would like to thank the following people for their help in assembling this catalog: Nancy K. Nardone, Anne Marie Regan and Mark Resnick. Frederick J. Kent and the staff of the music department of the Free Library of Philadelphia-Main Branch have also been a great source of information and encouragement. I thank you all for your cordial assistance.

Philadelphia, Pa.   Thomas R. Nardone
December, 1976

Guide to Use

GENERAL ARRANGEMENT

Within each catalog from the "Music-In-Print" series the user will find a comprehensive listing of the works of music publishers throughout the world. The arrangement of this listing is a single alphabetic interfiling of composers' names, titles of works, and cross references. The title under the composer's name serves as the focus for major information on each composition. In the absence of a composer the title in the main list is the focal point.

For each title there are two types of information: a) generic information about the composition and b) specific information pertaining to the editions which are in print. Included in the generic information category are the uniform title of the composition, a structured title for the work (e.g., Cantata 140), a thematic catalog number or opus and number designation, the larger source from which the work was taken, and remarks. The remarks are a series of codes or abbreviations giving information on the seasonal or other usage of the piece, the type of music, and the national origin and century for folk or anonymous pieces. (These codes also make it possible to retrieve, from the data base developed for the "Music-In-Print" series, specialized listings of music for particular seasons, types, etc.)

Following the generic information about the piece is the information about the individual editions. This information includes the arranger, the published title of the edition if different from the uniform title, the language of the text, instrumentation required for performance, a difficulty rating assigned for the edition by the publisher, the format of the publication, publisher, publisher's number, price, and information on the availability of music for rental or the availability of orchestral parts.

Following is a typical entry under a composer:

(All examples in this Guide are taken from Vol. I: *Sacred Choral Music In Print*)

AHLE, JOHANN RUDOLPH (1625-1673)
Furchtet Euch Nicht *Xmas, cant
(Lillehaug, L.) "Be Not Afraid" [Eng/Ger]
dbl cor,cont,4trom sc CONCORDIA 97-6407
$1.50, cor pts CONCORDIA 97-6430 $.40,
ipa   (A316)

In this entry, the title, "Furchtet Euch Nicht" is shown in the section for the composer, Johann Rudolph Ahle. "Xmas" and "cant" are remark codes indicating that the piece is a cantata appropriate for Christmas use. (The asterisk before Xmas merely serves to set off the remarks from the title.) The piece has only one edition, arranged by L. Lillehaug. The English title is "Be Not Afraid." The text is in English and German. The piece is scored for

double chorus, continuo and four trombones. Both score and choral parts may be obtained from Concordia at the prices shown. 97-6407 and 97-6430 are the publisher's order numbers. The code "ipa" indicates that instrumental parts are available, but we have not undertaken to list the prices of these.

SACRED-SECULAR DESIGNATIONS

With few exceptions, we have relied upon the sacred-secular distinctions made for us by the publishers. Where publishers have not made the distinction, for the purpose of this index we have taken music with a scriptural text or which is appropriate for religious usage or church service to be sacred.

SEQUENCE NUMBERS

An alphanumeric number, appearing on the right margin, has been assigned to each edition represented in this catalog. These are for the purpose of easing identification and location when corrections are made in our updating service.

PRICES

We can give no assurances of the accuracy of stated prices. The prices of editions have been increasing steadily over the last few years, yet we have thought it helpful to give the user a U.S. dollar figure, where available, for comparative purposes. The publishers should be consulted directly for current prices.

CROSS REFERENCES

In order to provide the user with as many points of access as possible, the "Music-In-Print" series has been heavily cross-referenced. For example, the piece by Ahle, illustrated above, may be located under either its German or English title in the main alphabet, as well as under the composer. Therefore, the following cross references exist in the main alphabet:

FURCHTET EUCH NICHT see Ahle, Johann Rudolph

and

BE NOT AFRAID see Ahle, Johann Rudolph, Furchtet Euch Nicht

and in addition, the following cross reference will be found under the composer's name:

Be Not Afraid *see Furchtet Euch Nicht

COLLECTIONS

An attempt has been made to provide the user with access to pieces contained within collections, while still keeping the work within reasonable bounds of time and space. Accordingly, the following practices have been adopted:

If the members of a collection are published separately, they are listed individually, regardless of the number of pieces involved. If the collection is only published as a whole, the members are listed only if they do not exceed six in number. For larger collections, a code is given indicating the number of pieces and whether or not the contents are listed in the publisher's catalog. For example,

CC18L indicates a collection of 18 pieces which are *listed* in the publisher's catalog

CC101U indicates a collection of 101 pieces which are *unlisted* in the publisher's catalog

CCU indicated a collection of an unknown number of pieces

Whenever the members are listed, they are also cross-referenced to the collection. For example, consider the following entry:

BACH, JOHANN SEBASTIAN (1685-1750)
Two Bach Chorales For Christmas *Xmas, chorale oct SATB PRO ART 1440 $.30; SAB PRO ART 1816 $.30; SSA PRO ART 1106 $.30; 2pt PRO ART 1817 $.30
contains: Break Forth, O Beauteous, Heavenly Light; Child Is Born In Bethlehem, A
(B2013)

This collection contains two members, which are not published separately. Under each of the members there is a cross reference saying 'see Two Bach Chorales For Christmas'.

If the members were also published separately, the cross references in both directions would say 'see also'. If the members were *only* published separately (i.e., the collection were not published as a whole) then the cross reference under the collection would read 'see' and under the members, 'see from'. Thus, 'see' and 'see also' direct the user to information concerning publication, while 'see from' provides access to the collection of which a given publication is a part.

Another problem is the cataloging of untitled choral collections. These are collections of several pieces published as a whole, but having no overall title. In this case, the publication information is given under the first piece listed, together with the cross reference 'contains also', followed by the titles of the other members. Under each of the other members, the cross reference 'see' directs the user to the entry for the first member.

List of Abbreviations

The following is a general list of abbreviations developed for the Music-in-Print series. Therefore, all of the abbreviations do not necessarily occur in the present volume. Also, it should be noted that terms spelled out in full in the catalog, e.g., winds, tuba, Easter, Passover, folk, Swiss, do not appear in this list.

A	alto	cor-resp	choral response	Jew	Jewish
acap	a cappella	Corpus	Corpus Christi	jr cor	junior chorus
acord	accordion	cradle	cradle song	Jubil	Jubilate Deo
Adv	Advent	cym	cymbals		
Afr	African			K.	Köchel-Verzeichnis
Agnus	Agnus Dei	Dan	Danish	kbd	keyboard
Allelu	Alleluia	dbl cor	double chorus	Kor	Korean
al-sax	alto-saxophone	Ded	Dedication		
anti	antiphonal	desc	descant	L	listed
anti cor	antiphonal chorus	diff	difficult	Lat	Latin
Asc	Ascension	Doxol	Doxology	liturg	liturgical
ASD	All Saints' Day	Dut	Dutch	Lowrey	Lowrey organ
Aus	Austrian				
Austral	Australian	ea.	each	Magnif	Magnificat
		ECY	End of Church Year	mand	mandolin
		elec org	electric organ	med	medium
B	bass	Ember	Ember Days	med diff	medium difficult
Bald	Baldwin organ	Eng	English	Mediev	Medieval
Bar	baritone	Epiph	Epiphany	men cor	men's chorus
bar.hn.	baritone horn	eq voices	equal voices	Mex	Mexican
Baroq	Baroque	Eur	European	Mez	mezzo-soprano
bass clar	bass clarinet	evang	evangelistic	min sc	miniature score
bass inst	bass instruments	Eve	Evening	mix cor	mixed chorus
bass trom	bass trombone			Morav	Moravian
bds	boards	fac ed	facsimile edition	Morn	Morning
Belg	Belgian	Fest	festivals	mot	motet
Bene	Benediction, Benedictus	fing.cym.	finger cymbals		
Bibl	Biblical	Finn	Finnish	Neth	Netherlands
Boh	Bohemian	fl	flute	NJ	Name of Jesus
boy cor	boys' chorus	flugel	flügelhorn	No.	Number
Braz	Brazilian	Fr	French	Nor Am	North American
bsn	bassoon			Norw	Norwegian
bvl	bass viol	Gd.Fri.	Good Friday	Nunc	Nunc Dimittis
BVM	Blessed Virgin Mary	Gen	general		
		Ger	German	ob	oboe
camb	cambiata	girl cor	girls' chorus	oboda	oboe d'amore
cant	cantata	glock	glockenspiel	oct	octavo
Carib	Caribbean	Greg	Gregorian chant	Offer	Offertory
CC	collection	grp.	group	Op.	Opus
CCU	collection, unlisted	gtr	guitar	opt	optional, ad lib
CCUL	collection, partially listed	Gulbransen	Gulbransen organ	ora	oratorio
cel	celesta			orch	orchestra
Cen Am	Central American	Hamm	Hammond organ	org	organ
cent	century	Harv	Harvest		
chamb.	chamber	Heb	Hebrew	Palm	Palm Sunday
Chin	Chinese	hndbl	handbells	pap	paperbound
Chord	chord organ	Holywk	Holy Week	Past	Pastorale
Circum	Circumcision	horn	French horn	Pent	Pentecost
clar	clarinet	hpsd	harpsichord	perc	percussion
Class	Classical	Hung	Hungarian	pic	piccolo
cloth	clothbound			pipe	pipe organ
cmplt ed	complete edition	Impres	Impressionist	pno	piano
Cnfrm	Confirmation	Ind	Indian	Pol	Polish
Commun	Communion	inst	instruments	Polynes	Polynesian
cong	congregation	ipa	instrumental parts available	pop	popular
Conn	Conn organ	ipr	instrumental parts for rent	post	postlude
cont	continuo	Ir	Irish	Port	Portuguese
Contemp	Contemporary	Isr	Israeli	PreClass	Pre-Classical
contrabsn	contrabassoon	It	Italian	prel	prelude
cor	chorus			Proces	processional
cor pts	choral parts	Jap	Japanese	Psntd	Passiontide
cor-prel	chorale prelude			pt	part

ix

Quinqua	Quinquagesima
rec	recorder
Reces	recessional
Refm	Reformation
Rembrnc	Remembrance
Renais	Renaissance
Req	Requiem
Romant	Romantic
Royal	royal occasion
Rum	Rumanian
Russ	Russian
S	soprano
S.	Schmieder (BWV, or Bach-Werke-Verzeichnis)
s.p.	separately published
Sab	Sabbath
sac	sacred
sax	saxophone
sc	score

Scot	Scottish
sec	secular
Septua	Septuagesima
Sexa	Sexagesima
Slav	Slavic
So Am	South American
Span	Spanish
speak cor	speaking chorus
spir	spiritual
sr cor	senior chorus
study sc	study score
Swed	Swedish
SWV	Schütz-Werke-Verzeichnis
T	tenor
tamb	tambourine
Thanks	Thanksgiving
Thomas	Thomas organ
timp	timpani
treb cor	treble chorus
treb inst	treble instruments

Trin	Trinity
trom	trombone
trp	trumpet
U	unlisted
UL	partially listed
unis	unison
unis cor	unison chorus
US	United States
vcl	violoncello
vibra	vibraphone
vla	viola
vln	violin
voc pt	vocal part
voc sc	vocal score
wom cor	women's chorus
Wurlitzer	Wurlitzer organ
Xmas	Christmas
xylo	xylophone

A

A, B, C, D see Lortzing, (Gustav) Albert

A BERENICE E VOLOGESO - SOL NASCENTE see Mozart, Wolfgang Amadeus

A BETHLEEM see Motte La Croix, A.F.

A BETHLEEM, QUAND L'ENFANT DIEU see Canteloube, Joseph

A BISEL LIEBE, UN A BISELE GLICK *Jew
solo,pno KAMMEN 470 $1.00   (A1)

A BISSEL WINE *Jew
solo,pno KAMMEN 445 $1.00   (A2)

A BRIEF *Jew
solo,pno KAMMEN 413 $1.00   (A3)

A CANTIGA DA MUTUCA see Camargo Guarnieri

A CELLE QUE J'AIME see Delmet, Paul

A CELLE QUI EST TRISTE see Duteil d'Ozanne, A.

A CELLE QUI EST TROP GAIE see Busser, Henri-Paul

A CELLE QUI PART see Lacome, Paul

A CES REINES see Andriessen, Hendrik

A CETTE VOIX QUEL TROUBLE - JE CROIS ENTENDRE ENCORE see Bizet, Georges

A CEUX DE LA-BAS see Rabey, Rene

A CEUX QUI PARTENT see Doyen, Albert

A CHE MAI NELL'OMBRA see Rimsky-Korsakov, Nikolai

A CHLORIS see Delmet, Paul

A CLOE see Mozart, Wolfgang Amadeus, An Chloe

A CLYMENE see Panizza, Ettore

A CONTRE-COEUR see Ferroud, Pierre-Octave

A CONTRE-VOIX see Schmitt, Florent

A DINTOIRE MIT GOTT see Yitzchok, Levy

A DUDELE see Yitzchok, Levy

A DUE MANI see Veneziani, Vittore

A ELLE see Godard, Benjamin Louis Paul

A GEBET see Weiner, Lazar

A GRUS FON DEM NEIEM RUSSLAND *Jew
solo,pno KAMMEN 51 $1.00   (A4)

A ISIS see Larbey, V.

A KLEZMER YINGEL *Jew
solo,pno KAMMEN 449 $1.00   (A5)

A LA CLAIRE FONTAINE
"Down By The Crystal Fountain" see Crystal Fountain, The

A LA DERIVE see Blair Fairchild, Drifting

A LA FAVEUR DE LA NUIT see Casterede, Jacques

A LA FENETRE DEMICLOSE see Poise, (Jean Alexandre) Ferdinand

A LA FONTAINE see Charpentier, R.

A LA GRAND'MESSE see Lenormand, Rene

A LA-LA DEG TIRILILL see Braein, Edvard Fliflet

A LA MUSIQUE see Chabrier, Emmanuel

A LA PORTE OCCIDENTALE see Grovlez, Gabriel (Marie)

A LA RECHERCHE see Lehmann, Hans Ulrich

A LA RIVIERE see Huybrechts, Albert

A LA RONDA DEL CORRAL see Pardo

A LA "SANTE" see Honegger, Arthur

A LA TASSE, AU VERRE see Messager, Andre

A LA TRES CHERE see Erlanger, Camille

A LA VOIX D'UN AMANT FIDELE see Bizet, Georges

A L'ABSENTE see Lachaume, A.

A L'AIMEE see Vieu, Jane

A L'AMIE PERDUE see Dupre, Marcel

A L'AMOUR, RENDEZ LES ARMES see Rameau, Jean-Philippe

A LEI see Mule, Giuseppe

A L'ENVERS DE MA PORTE see Arrieu, Claude

A L'EPREUVE see Desrez

A L'ETOILE DU SOIR see Schumann, Robert (Alexander), An Den Abendstern

A L'ETRANGER, ENFANT, TON ACCUEIL see Wagner, Richard

A L'HEURE DITE see Rimsky-Korsakov, Nikolai

A L'INCONNU see Olsen, Poul Rovsing

A L'OMBRA DEL LLEDONER see Toldra, Eduardo

A L'OMBRE DES NOIRES TOURS see Saint-Saens, Camille

A L'OMBRE DU BEGUINAGE see Hermite, M.

A MA FIANCEE see Schumann, Robert (Alexander)

A MAGGIO see Cantu, M.

A MAISELE see Weiner, Lazar

A MALKE AUF PAISSACH see Gilrod, Louis

A MAMEN HOB ICH KEIN MUHL GEHAT *Jew
solo,pno KAMMEN 432 $1.00   (A6)

A MAME'S GEBET *Jew
solo,pno KAMMEN 16 $1.00   (A7)

A MAMME'S TREHREN see Meyerowitz, David

A ME RISPONDI ASTRO D'OR see Rimsky-Korsakov, Nikolai

A MEDIA LUZ see Donato

A MON AIMEE see Haring, Ch.

A MON FRERE see Middeleer, Jean De

A NANNA see Scuderi, Gaspare

A NIGUN see Weiner, Lazar

A NOS LEVRES see Raynal, F.

A ORILLAS DEL HERMOSO DANUBIO AZUL see Strauss, Johann, An Der Schonen Blauen Donau

A PAPA GIOVANNI XXIII see Lucia, Ettore

A PARTHENAY *Fr
[Fr] solo,pno DURAND 69 s.p.   (A8)

A PEINE AU SORTIR DE L'ENFANCE see Mehul, Etienne-Nicolas

A QUESTO SENO, DEH! VIENI, IDOLO MIO - OR CHE IL CIELO A ME TI RENDE see Mozart, Wolfgang Amadeus

A RIVEDERCI! see Pinsuti, Ciro

A S FA ZINQUNTANOV!
(Carlo, Musi) solo,pno (Bolognese dialect) BONGIOVANI 2094 s.p. see from El Mi Canzunett Seconda Serie   (A9)

A SA GUITARE see Poulenc, Francis

A SAINTE-BLAISE see Saint-Saens, Camille

A SAN LORENZO see Laparra, Raoul

A SEILLE see Olsen, Sparre

A SON PAGE see Leguerney, Jacques

A SUOI PIEDI see Handel, George Frideric

A SUZON see Delmet, Paul

A'. TA-LON see Holt, Simeon ten

A TE see Caltabiano, S.

A TE GRAZIE see Berlioz, Hector

A TE, O CARA see Bellini, Vincenzo

A THULE UN ROI TRES FIDELE see Bondeville, Emmanuel de

A TOI see Lebrun, Paul Henri Joseph

A TOI see Waldteufel, Emil

A TOI, IDYLLE see Lebrun, Paul Henri Joseph

A TOI J'AVAIS DONNE MA VIE see Messager, Andre

"A TRADUIRE EN ESTHONIEN" see Rivier, Jean

A TRAVERS BOIS see Chaminade, Cecile

A TRIANON see Holmes, Alfred

A TRILOGY OF SOUTHERN LYRICS see Pfohl, J.C.

A UN DOTTOR DELLA MIA SORTE see Rossini, Gioacchino

A UN JEUNE GENTILHOMME see Stalvey, Dorrance

A UNA ROSA see Cimara, Pietro

A UNE DEMOISELLE MALADE see Francaix, Jean

A UNE FIANCE see Messager, Andre

A UNE FLEUR see Durand, Jacques

A UNE FLEUR see Lacome, Paul

A UNE HIRONDELLE see Durand, Jacques

A UNE JEUNE FILLE see Desrez

A UNE MENDIANTE ROUSSE see Orthel, Leon

A UNE VIOLETTE see Brahms, Johannes, An Ein Veilchen

A VERVIERS see Leduc, Jacques

A VINGT ANS see Delmet, Paul

A VOCE SOLA see Monteverdi, Claudio

A VOUS, AMANTS see Le Flem, Paul

A VOUS, VIERGE DE DOUCOUR see Anonymous

'A VUCCHELLA see Tosti, Francesco Paolo

A WELON Y MYNYNN see Williams, Meirion

A XUSTICIA POL-A-MAN see Caamano, Roberto

AALLON KEHTOLAULU see Jarnefelt, Armas

AAMU see Kilpinen, Yrio

AAMU see Marvia, Einari

AAMULAULU "KORKEASTA VEISUSTA" see Melartin, Erkki

AAMULLA see Kilpinen, Yrio

AAMUN AUTEREESSA see Palmgren, Selim

AAN... see Reynvaan, M.C.C.

AAN DE MAAN see Schouwman, Hans

AAN DE SNEEUW see Smit Sibinga, Th. H.

AAN EEN BODE see Henkemans, Hans

AAN EEN BODE see Leeuw, Ton de

AAN FILLIS see Schouwman, Hans

AAN MARY SHELLY see Reynvaan, M.C.C.

AAN MIJN BELGEN BIJ DEN YSER see Hullebroeck, Em.

AAN MIJN BROEDER see Middeleer, Jean De, A Mon Frere

AAN U ALLEEN see Hullebroeck, Em.

AAN ZEE see Loots, Ph.

AANHEF see Masseus, Jan

AANZOEK see Zagwijn, Henri

AH, PERCHE NON POSSO ODIARTI see Bellini, Vincenzo

AH! PERFIDE! PARJURE! see Beethoven, Ludwig van, Ah! Perfido

AH! PERFIDO see Beethoven, Ludwig van

AH, POOR MARINA! see Mussorgsky, Modest

AH, QUAND JE SUIS LOIN D'ELLE see Mozart, Wolfgang Amadeus

AH! QUE J'AI MAL see Rimsky-Korsakov, Nikolai

AH! QUE ME FAITES-VOUS ENTENDRE see Rameau, Jean-Philippe

AH! QUE SON JEUNE COEUR see Rothschild, Mme W. de

AH! QUEL MALHEUR see Poise, (Jean Alexandre) Ferdinand

AH! QU'EST-CE QUE J'AI see Betove

AH RITORNA ETA DELL'ORO see Martini, Giambattista

AH! RITROVARLA NELLA SUA CAPANNA see Mascagni, Pietro

AH, SE IN CIEL, BENIGNE STELLE see Mozart, Wolfgang Amadeus

AH! S'EN ALLER see Ropartz, Joseph Guy

AH SI, BEN MIO see Verdi, Giuseppe

AH! SI LA LIBERTE see Gluck, Christoph Willibald Ritter von

AH! SI MON MOINE VOULAIT DANSER! see Folk Songs Of Eastern Canada

AH! SO PURE see Flotow, Friedrich von, Ach, So Fromm

AH! SPIETATO see Handel, George Frideric

AH! STIGIE LARVE see Handel, George Frideric

AH, STILL I HEAR IT RINGING see Bizet, Georges, Je Crois Entendre Encore

AH! TE DIRAI-JE MAMAN see Delbruck, J.

AH! TU NON HAI VOLUTO see Strauss, Richard, Ah! Du Wolltest Mich Nicht

AH! TU NON SAI see Handel, George Frideric

AH! VOTRE EMOI, JE LE PARTAGE see Cuvillier, Charles

AH! VOUS DIRAI-JE, MAMAN see Adam, Adolphe-Charles

AH, VOUS DIRAI-JE MAMAN see Mozart, Wolfgang Amadeus

AH, WHAT IS LOVE? see Russell, W.

AH! WHEN THE LAST DREAD HOUR see Bach, Johann Sebastian

AH! WITH THE GRAPE see Waterman, Constance

AHAVAS OLOM see Piket, Frederick

AHEIM, AHEIM, BRIEDERLACH AHEIM see Meyerowitz, David

AHI, AMOUR see Le Flem, Paul

AHIME CHE FAR? see Rimsky-Korsakov, Nikolai

AHIN, AHIN *folk,Jew
(Low, Leo) solo,pno HATIKVAH HCL 42
$.25   (A204)

AHLEN, WALDEMAR
Julafton *Xmas
solo,pno/org ERIKS K 148   (A205)

AHLSTROM
Sallheten
solo,pno LUNDQUIST s.p.   (A206)

AHM YISROEL CHAI see Mana-Zucca, Mme.

AHNFELDT
Hem Till Kallan
solo,pno LUNDQUIST s.p.   (A207)

AHNFELDT, O.
Kunen Dag, Et Oyeblikk Av Gangen
solo,pno MUSIKK s.p.   (A208)

AHRENS, JOSEPH (1904-   )
Angelus Silesius Liederbuch *CC12U
S solo,org (med diff) MULLER 2418
s.p.   (A209)

Regnum Dei (from Trilogia Sacra) sac,
CC7U
[Lat] (med/diff) Bar solo,fl,ob,
English horn,horn,clar,bsn,kbd sc
MULLER 2445 rental; sc MULLER
$10.00; MULLER WM68   (A210)

AHRENS, SIEGLINDE
Drei Gesange Nach Lateinischen
Psalmentexten *sac,CC3U, Psalm
B solo,org (diff) MULLER 2499 s.p.
                              (A211)
Three Songs On Latin Psalm Texts
*CC3U, Psalm
B solo,org MULLER WM116 s.p. (A212)

AHUVIA, HAIM
Nine Songs *CC9U
solo,pno OR-TAV $1.00   (A213)

AI FRATELLI CERVI see Ferrari, Giorgio

AI NOSTRI MONTI see Verdi, Giuseppe

AI VOSTRI GIUOCHI ANCH'IO PRENDER PARTE
VORREI see Thomas, Ambroise

AIDIN SILMAT see Hannikainen, Ilmari

AIGUES-MARINES see Aubert, Louis-Francois-Marie

AILEAN DUINN *Scot
solo,pno PATERSON s.p. see from
Hebridean Songs, Vol. IV   (A214)

AIM, VOJTECH BORIVOJ (1886-1972)
Es Dammert *see Stmiva Se

Stmiva Se *song cycle
Mez solo,pno PANTON 653 s.p. (A215)
"Es Dammert" Mez solo,pno PANTON
s.p.   (A216)

AIMABLE AURORE - NE VOIS-TU PAS see
Gretry, Andre Ernest Modeste

AIMANT LA ROSE, LE ROSSIGNOL see
Rimsky-Korsakov, Nikolai

AIME CELUI QUI T'AIME see Chapuis,
Auguste-Paul-Jean-Baptiste

AIME! EROS see Saint-Saens, Camille

AIMER C'EST FORGER SA PEINE see
Barbirolli, A.

AIMERAIS-JE AUTANT LES OISEAUX see
Chevreuille, Raymond

AIMEZ, AIMEZ, PENDANT LA VIE ENTIERE
see Liszt, Franz, Wie Entgehn

AIMEZ VOS MERES see Biancheri, A.

AIMONS-NOUS see Delmet, Paul

AIMONS-NOUS see Saint-Saens, Camille

AIMONS-NOUS see Sullivan, Sir Arthur
Seymour

AIMONS-NOUS ET DORMONS see Debussy,
Claude

AIMONS TOUJOURS see Godard, Benjamin
Louis Paul

AINA LAULAN see Kilpinen, Yrio

AINON AARIA KOIVULLE see Melartin,
Erkki

AINOS ARIA TILL BJORKEN see Melartin,
Erkki, Ainon Aaria Koivulle

AINSI QU'AU PAYS DES AIMEES see Poise,
(Jean Alexandre) Ferdinand

AINSI QUE LA ROSE NOUVELLE see
Chabrier, Emmanuel

AINSI QUE VOUS J'IGNORE see Lacome,
Paul

AINSI QU'UN PAPILLON LEGER see
Scarlatti, Domenico, Qual
Farfalletta Amante

AINSWORTH
Feed My Sheep *sac
high solo,pno (B flat maj) FISCHER,
C V 1545   (A217)

AIN'T IT A PRETTY NIGHT see Floyd,
Carlisle

AINUT HETKI see Merikanto, Oskar, Den
Enda Stunden

AIR see Arne, Thomas Augustine

AIR see Badings, Henk

AIR see Harrison, Lou

AIR see Haydn, (Franz) Joseph

AIR A BOIRE see Lacome, Paul

AIR CHAMPETRE see Poulenc, Francis

AIR D'AMINA see Bellini, Vincenzo

AIR DE BAUCIS see Gounod, Charles
Francois

AIR DE CARON see Lully (Lulli), Jean-
Baptiste

AIR DE CONCERT see Lenot, Jacques

AIR DE CONCOURS see Tremisot, Ed.

AIR DE DALILA see Saint-Saens, Camille

AIR DE DESPINA see Mozart, Wolfgang
Amadeus

AIR DE DIANA DE L'ENDEMIONE see Bach,
Johann Christian

AIR DE LAODICE see Scarlatti,
Alessandro

AIR DE L'ENFANT see Ravel, Maurice

AIR DE LENORE see Verdi, Giuseppe

AIR DE L'HORLOGE see Ravel, Maurice

AIR DE LIA see Debussy, Claude

AIR DE MERCURE see Beaujoyeulx,
Baltasar de

AIR DE MOMUS see Bach, Johann Sebastian

AIR DE PHEDRE see Thomson, Virgil

AIR DE POLLUX see Rameau, Jean-Philippe

AIR DE POPPEE see Handel, George
Frideric, Aria Di Poppea

AIR DE RENAUD see Gluck, Christoph
Willibald Ritter von

AIR DE REZIA see Weber, Carl Maria von

AIR DE ROCCO see Beethoven, Ludwig van

AIR DE SALUD see Falla, Manuel de, Air
Du Salut

AIR DE SANTUZZA see Mascagni, Pietro

AIR DE SERSE see Handel, George
Frideric

AIR DE SIMON see Haydn, (Franz) Joseph

AIR DE SUZANNE see Mozart, Wolfgang
Amadeus

AIR DE VENUS see Lully (Lulli), Jean-
Baptiste

AIR D'EGLISE see Stradella, Alessandro,
Aria Di Chiesa

AIR D'ELISABETH see Wagner, Richard

AIR D'ELSA see Wagner, Richard

AIR DU BARYTON see Wagner, Richard

AIR DU FEU see Ravel, Maurice

AIR DU POETE see Satie, Erik

AIR DU RAT see Satie, Erik

AIR DU ROSSIGNOL see Rameau, Jean-
Philippe

AIR DU ROSSIGNOL see Saint-Saens,
Camille

AIR DU SALUT see Falla, Manuel de

AIR D'ULRICA see Verdi, Giuseppe

AIR D'URIEL see Haydn, (Franz) Joseph

AIR EXTRAIT see Debussy, Claude

AIR GRAVE see Poulenc, Francis

AIR ROMANTIQUE see Poulenc, Francis

AIR SERIEUX [1] see Couperin (le
Grand), Francois

AARDE see Koetsier, Jan

ABANDON see Filipucci, Edm.

ABANDON see Leduc, Jacques, Birago Diop, Senegal

ABANDONNEE see Milhaud, Darius

ABBADO, MARCELLO (1926-   )
Cantata
female solo,6inst ZERBONI 4481 rental　　　　　　　　　　　(A10)

Ciapo
female solo,9inst ZERBONI 4142 rental　　　　　　　　　　　(A11)

Quindici Poesie T'ang *CC15U
Mez solo,4inst ZERBONI 5844 s.p.
　　　　　　　　　　　　　　(A12)

ABBANDONATO see Gandino, Adolfo

ABBANDONO see Respighi, Ottorino

ABBEY, H.
Four Mountain Carols *CC4U
med solo,pno MERCURY $1.25　(A13)

ABBIE'S BIRD SONG see Beeson, Jack Hamilton

ABBITTE see Pfitzner, Hans

ABBOTT, JANE
Just For Today *sac,Gen
high solo,pno (A flat maj) WILLIS $.60　　　　　　　　　　　(A14)
low solo,pno (F maj) WILLIS $.60　　　　　　　　　　　(A15)
SA soli,pno WILLIS $.75　　(A16)

ABC see Kozina, Marijan

ABEL ET CAIN see Bordewijk-Roepman, Johanna

ABEL ET CAIN see Frid, Geza

ABEND see Gilse, Jan van

ABEND see Kilpinen, Yrio, Kvallning

ABEND see Wiklund, Adolf

ABENDEMPFINDUNG see Mozart, Wolfgang Amadeus

ABENDGESANG see Mihalovici, Marcel

ABENDGESANGE see Foerster, Josef Bohuslav

ABENDHYMNE see Purcell, Henry, Evening Hymn

ABENDLAUTEN
see Russische Volkslieder

ABENDLIED see Oort, H.C.v.

ABENDLIED see Pfitzner, Hans

ABENDLIED see Reger, Max

ABENDLIED see Schumann, Robert (Alexander)

ABENDLIED see Trunk, Richard

ABENDLIEDER see Smetana, Bedrich

ABENDLIEDER see Dvorak, Antonin

ABENDLIEDER (EVENING SONGS) see Dvorak, Antonin

ABENDROT see Bijvanck, Henk

ABENDROT see Kilpinen, Yrio, Illanrusko

ABENDROTH, WALTHER (1896-   )
Drei Lieder *Op.2, CC3U
med solo,pno (med diff) MULLER 1273 s.p.　　　　　　　　　　(A17)

Drei Lieder *Op.3, CC3U
low solo,pno (med diff) MULLER 1272 s.p.　　　　　　　　　　(A18)

Funf Lieder *Op.12,No.1-5, CC5U
high solo,pno SIKORSKI 379 s.p.
　　　　　　　　　　　　　　(A19)
Holty-Trilogie *Op.25,No.1-3, CC3U
Bar solo,pno SIKORSKI 380 s.p.
　　　　　　　　　　　　　　(A20)
Trakl-Trilogie *Op.29,No.1-3, CC3U
Bar solo,pno SIKORSKI 384 s.p.
　　　　　　　　　　　　　　(A21)

ABENDS see Marx, Joseph

ABENDSEGEN see Humperdinck, Engelbert

ABENDSONNE AM MEER see Weingartner, (Paul) Felix

ABENDSTANDCHEN see Weegenhuise, Johan

ABENGLOCKEN *folk,Russ
[Ger/Russ] solo,pno ZIMMER. 1549 s.p.
　　　　　　　　　　　　　　(A22)

ABERNATHY
God Can *sac
solo,pno BENSON S5536-S $1.00 (A23)

I'm Building A Bridge *sac
solo,pno BENSON S6312-S $1.00 (A24)

ABIDE WITH ME see Fichthorn, Claude L.

ABIDE WITH ME see Liddle, Samuel

ABIDE WITH ME see Monk, William Henry

ABIDE WITH ME *sac,CC10L
(Kaiser, Kurt) solo,pno WORD 32028 $2.50　　　　　　　　　(A25)

ABIDING LOVE see Roe, Gloria [Ann]

ABIOSEH NICOL, SIERRA LEONE see Leduc, Jacques

ABLAUF DER ZEIT see Thomas, Kurt

ABLETT, NORMAN
You Never Saw My Garden
low solo,pno (C maj) CRAMER　(A26)
high solo,pno (E flat maj) CRAMER
　　　　　　　　　　　　　　(A27)

ABLOSUNG IM SOMMER see Mahler, Gustav

ABOUT A LAMB see Diercks, John H.

ABOUT LITTLE GIRLS I KNOW see Lovett, Mrs. George

ABOVE EVERY NAME see Peterson, John W.

ABRAHAM AND ISAAC see Stravinsky, Igor

ABRAHAM LINCOLN WALKS AT MIDNIGHT see Harris, R.

ABRAM, ABRAM *folk,Jew
med solo,pno HATIKVAH ED. 29 $.20
　　　　　　　　　　　　　　(A28)
ABRAMSON, ROBERT
Three Old Songs Resung *CC3U
med solo,pno MERCURY $1.50　(A29)

ABRE DE JUIN see Geraedts, Jaap

ABRIL, A.G.
Coleccion De Canciones Infantiles *CCU
(Muelas) [Span] med solo,pno UNION ESP. $6.00　　　　　　　(A30)

ABSALOM see Rorem, Ned

ABSCHEULICHER! WO EILST DU HIN? see Beethoven, Ludwig van

ABSCHIED see Bijvanck, Henk

ABSCHIED see Frid, Geza

ABSCHIED see Grieg, Edvard Hagerup, Afsked

ABSCHIED see Kremser, Edward

ABSCHIED see Marx, Joseph

ABSCHIED see Schmalstich, Clemens

ABSCHIED see Schoenberg, Arnold

ABSCHIED DER VOGEL see Hildach, Eugen

ABSCHIEDSLIED see Marx, Karl

ABSENCE see Halphen, F.

ABSENCE see Martin, Easthope

ABSENT see Metcalf, John W.

ABSENT LOVE see Allen, N.

ABSENT-MINDED see Damase, Jean-Michel

ABSENT MINDED BEGGAR, THE see Sullivan, Sir Arthur Seymour

ABSIL, JEAN (1893-1974)
Automne
see Cinq Melodies

Autre Guitare
see Cinq Melodies

Batterie *Op.12
see Deux Melodies

Cache-Cache *Op.117,No.3
see Cache-Cache

Cache-Cache
med solo,pno cmplt ed CBDM s.p.
contains: Cache-Cache, Op.117,

ABSIL, JEAN (cont'd.)
No.3; Conditionnel, Op.117, No.2; Fleur De Paris, Op.117, No.1　　　　　　　　　　　(A31)

C'est Du Soleil *Op.98,No.3
see Heure De Grace

Chanson *Op.52,No.5
see Enfantines
see Quatre Poemes De Maeterlinck

Chanson Du Chat *Op.45,No.1
see Trois Poemes De Tristan Klingsor

Cimetiere
Mez/Bar solo,pno CBDM s.p.　(A32)

Cinq Melodies
cmplt ed CBDM s.p.
contains: Automne (Mez/Bar solo, pno); Autre Guitare (Mez solo, pno); Guitare (T solo,pno) Le Nenufar (Mez/Bar solo,pno) Sur L'eau (S/T solo,pno)　(A33)

Conditionnel *Op.117,No.2
see Cache-Cache

Desirs D'hiver *Op.12,No.4
see Quatre Poemes De Maeterlinck

Deux Melodies
cmplt ed CBDM s.p.
contains: Batterie, Op.12 (S/T solo,pno); Les Pas, Op.29 (Mez solo,pno)　　　　　(A34)

Deux Poemes De Francis Jammes
S/T solo,pno cmplt ed CBDM s.p
contains: L'evier Sent Fort, Op.53,No.1; Si Un Beau Jour...; Op.53,No.2　　　　　(A35)

Enfantines
med solo,pno cmplt ed CBDM s.p.
contains: Chanson, Op.52,No.5; La Poupee Mecanique, Op.52,No.4; L'araignee, Op.52,No.1; Le Herisson, Op.52,No.2; Le Petit Garcon Malade, Op.52,No.3 (A36)

Eventail, Paravent, Potiche... *Op.64,No.3
see Le Chapeau Chinois

Fleur De Paris *Op.117,No.1
see Cache-Cache

Guitare
see Cinq Melodies

Heure De Grace
S/T solo,pno cmplt ed CBDM s.p
contains: C'est Du Soleil, Op.98, No.3; La Blanche Eglise, Op.98, No.2; Orage, Op.98,No.1　(A37)

J'ai Cherche Trente Ans *Op.12,No.3
see Quatre Poemes De Maeterlinck

La Blanche Eglise *Op.98,No.2
see Heure De Grace

La Poupee Mecanique *Op.52,No.4
see Enfantines

L'araignee *Op.52,No.1
see Enfantines

Le Chapeau Chinois
T solo,pno cmplt ed CBDM s.p.
contains: Eventail, Paravent Potiche..., Op.64,No.3; Le Vase Ou Meurt Cette Verveine, Op.64, No.2; O Ma Jolie, O Ma Caline, Op.64,No.1　　　　　(A38)

Le Herisson *Op.52,No.2
see Enfantines

Le Nenufar
see Cinq Melodies

Le Petit Garcon Malade *Op.52,No.3
see Enfantines

Le Vase Ou Meurt Cette Verveine *Op.64,No.2
see Le Chapeau Chinois

Les Pas *Op.29
see Deux Melodies

L'evier Sent Fort *Op.53,No.1
see Deux Poemes De Francis Jammes

L'infidele *Op.12,No.2
see Quatre Poemes De Maeterlinck

Ma Mere L'Oye *Op.45,No.2
see Trois Poemes De Tristan Klingsor

ABSIL, JEAN (cont'd.)

O Ma Jolie, O Ma Caline *Op.64,No.1
see Le Chapeau Chinois

Orage *Op.98,No.1
see Heure De Grace

Ou Le Coq A-T-Il La Plume? *Op.45,
No.3
see Trois Poemes De Tristan
Klingsor

Peau D'Ane *Op.26
S solo,pno cmplt ed CBDM s.p. (A39)

Quatre Poemes De Maeterlinck
cmplt ed CBDM s.p.
contains: Chanson, Op.12,No.1
(Mez/Bar solo,pno); Desirs
D'hiver, Op.12,No.4 (S/T solo,
pno); J'ai Cherche Trente Ans,
Op.12,No.3 (Mez/Bar solo,pno);
L'infidele, Op.12,No.2 (Mez/Bar
solo,pno)   (A40)

Reve De Noel *Op.80,No.1
see Reves

Reve Fantasque *Op.80,No.3
see Reves

Reve Noir *Op.80,No.2
see Reves

Reves
med solo,pno cmplt ed CBDM s.p.
contains: Reve De Noel, Op.80,
No.1; Reve Fantasque, Op.80,
No.3; Reve Noir, Op.80,No.2
(A41)

Si Un Beau Jour... *Op.53,No.2
see Deux Poemes De Francis Jammes

Sur L'eau
see Cinq Melodies

Trois Poemes De Tristan Klingsor
med solo,pno cmplt ed CBDM s.p.
contains: Chanson Du Chat, Op.45,
No.1; Ma Mere L'Oye, Op.45,
No.2; Ou Le Coq A-T-Il La
Plume?, Op.45,No.3   (A42)

ABSURDE BETRACHTUNGEN see Ostendorf,
Jens-Peter

ABT, FRANZ (1819-1885)
Agathe
"When The Swallow Homeward Flies"
solo,pno CRAMER   (A43)
"When The Swallow Homeward Flies" 2
soli,pno CRAMER   (A44)

Ave Maria *sac
[Lat/Eng/Fr] high solo,pno PRESSER
$.75   (A45)

Den Alskades Namn
solo,pno LUNDQUIST s.p.   (A46)

Erinnerung
"Still Is The Night" low solo,pno
(F maj) CRAMER   (A47)
"Still Is The Night" 2 soli,pno
LEONARD-ENG   (A48)
"Still Is The Night" high solo,pno
(B flat maj) CRAMER   (A49)

Je Pense A Toi
solo,vcl DURAND s.p.   (A50)

Le Bon Dieu Dans La Foret
solo,pno/inst DURAND s.p. (A51)

Morgonsang
solo,pno LUNDQUIST s.p.   (A52)
2 soli,pno LUNDQUIST s.p. (A53)

Nar Till Hemmet Svalan Far
solo,pno LUNDQUIST s.p.   (A54)

O, Hur Underskon Ar Ej Varens Tid
2 soli,pno LUNDQUIST s.p. (A55)

Patrie
solo,vcl DURAND s.p.   (A56)

Quatorze Melodies *CC40U
solo,pno DURAND s.p.   (A57)

Rosee Amere
[Ger] solo,pno DURAND s.p. (A58)

Somna Ljuvt Liksom Vagen Vid Strand
solo,pno LUNDQUIST s.p.   (A59)

Still Is The Night *see Erinnerung

Waldandacht *Op.211,No.3
S/T solo,pno DOBLINGER 08 551 $.60
(A60)
When The Swallow Homeward Flies *see
Agathe

ACCALMIE see Darty, Paulette

ACCLAMAZIONI DIVOTE A VOCE SOLA see
Legrenzi, Giovanni

ACCORD see Globokar, Vinko

ACCORDS see Leduc, Jacques, Birago
Diog, Senegal

ACCURITE see Bernier, Nicolas

ACCURSED WOOD, THE see Shaw, Martin

ACH, DAS LIED HAB' ICH GETRAGEN see
Cornelius, Peter

ACH, DASS ICH WASSERS G'NUG HATTE see
Bach, Johann Christoph

ACH, DE GROOTE STAD see Clercq, R. de

ACH, DU SCHONE HEIMAT see Kilpinen,
Yrio, Ohoh Kullaista Kotia

ACH! EENIG EEUWIG EEN see Sigtenhorst-
Meyer, Bernhard van den

ACH! FUHL EINMAL see Handel, George
Frideric, Ah! Tu Non Sai

ACH GOTT, WIE MANCHES HERZELEID see
Bach, Johann Sebastian

ACH HERR, LASS DEINE LIEBEN ENGELEIN
see Tunder, Franz

ACH HERR, STRAFE MICH NICHT see
Telemann, Georg Philipp

ACH, ICH BIN EIN NARR GEWESEN see
Kilpinen, Yrio, Voi Minua Mieskulua

ACH, ICH FUHL'S see Mozart, Wolfgang
Amadeus

ACH! ICH HABE SIE VERLOREN see Gluck,
Christoph Willibald Ritter von

ACH, LEGE DAS SODOM DER SUNDLICHEN
GLIEDER see Bach, Johann Sebastian

ACH LIEB', ICH MUSS SCHEIDEN see
Strauss, Richard

ACH, MAMA, ICH SAG ES DIR see Adam,
Adolphe-Charles, Ah! Vous Dirai-Je,
Maman

ACH MEIN HERZLIEBES JESULEIN see Kuhn,
M.

ACH, MEIN HERZLIEBES JESULEIN see
Schelle, Johann Hermann

ACH MEIN HERZLIEBES JESULEIN see
Schildt, Melchior

ACH MEIN SOHN see Meyerbeer, Giacomo

ACH, MEIN SOHN ABSALON see Schutz,
Heinrich, Fili Mi, Absalon

ACH MEINE AHNUNG see Mozart, Wolfgang
Amadeus, Ah, Lo Previdi

ACH, MEINE AHNUNG - HA! ENTFLIEH AUS
MEINEN AUGEN see Mozart, Wolfgang
Amadeus, Ah Lo Previdi - Ah!
T'invola Agl'occhi Miei

ACH, MEINE SEELE see Schutz, Heinrich,
Anima Mea Liquefacta Est

ACH NEEN, ACH NEEN see Sigtenhorst-
Meyer, Bernhard van den

ACH OFFNET AUG' UND OHREN see Mozart,
Wolfgang Amadeus, Aprite Un Po'
Quegl' Occhi

ACH, SIE STIRBT, MEINE HOFFNUNG see
Mozart, Wolfgang Amadeus, Mia
Speranza Adorata - Ah, Non Sai

ACH, SIE STIRBT, MEINE HOFFNUNG - ACH,
SIE SCHWANDEN, MEINE FREUDEN see
Mozart, Wolfgang Amadeus, Mia
Speranza Adorata - Ah, Non Sai

ACH, SO FROMM see Flotow, Friedrich von

ACH, SO VIELE MAGDLEIN GIBT ES see
Kilpinen, Yrio, Niin On Meita
Piikasia

ACH SOLL DIES FREIE HERZ see Gluck,
Christoph Willibald Ritter von

ACH UM DEINE FEUCHTEN SCHWINGEN see
Schubert, Franz (Peter), Suleikas
Zweiter Gesang

ACH WAS KUMMER, QUAL UND SCHMERZEN see
Strauss, Richard

ACH WAS SOLL ICH BEGINNEN see Schubert,
Franz (Peter), Delphine

ACH, WAS VERBRACH IHR STERNE - SCHON
HOFF ICH DAS UFER see Mozart,
Wolfgang Amadeus, Ma Che Vi Fece -
Sperai Vicino Al Lido

ACH, WEH' MIR see Strauss, Richard

ACH WENN ES NUN DIE MUTTER WUSZT see
Cuypers, H.

ACH, WIE SO HERRLICH ZU SCHAU'N see
Strauss, Johann

ACH, WIE SUSS ZU LIEBEN IST see
Purcell, Henry, Ah! How Sweet It Is
To Love

ACH WIR ARMEN see Humperdinck,
Engelbert

ACH, ZIEHE DIE SEELE MIT SEILEN DER
LIEBE see Bach, Johann Sebastian

ACHALEL BACHALILI see Edel, Yitzchak

ACHEYNU KOL BEYS YISROEL see Katchko,
Adolph

ACHIME see Matsumura, T.

ACHOS see Terzakis, Dimitri

ACHT ARIEN DER THETIS see Scarlatti,
Domenico

ACHT CHANSONS NACH GEDICHTEN VON ERICH
KASTNER see Wimberger, Gerhard

ACHT ERNSTE GESANGE, HEFT 1 see
Waldstein, Wilhelm

ACHT ERNSTE GESANGE, HEFT 2 see
Waldstein, Wilhelm

ACHT EUROPESE LIEDEREN see Leeuw, Ton
de

ACHT GEDICHTE VON HERMANN HESSE see
Raphael, Gunther

ACHT GESANGE see Weismann, Wilhelm

ACHT GESANGE (SMEKAL) see Kornauth,
Egon

ACHT HAFIS-LIEDER see Einem, Gottfried
von

ACHT HAIKAI DES PEDRO XISTO see
Koellreutter, Hans-Joachim

ACHT KERSTLIEDEREN see Tierie, J.F.

ACHT KINDERLIEDER see Becker, Reinhold

ACHT LIEBESLIEDER see Flury, Richard

ACHT LIEDER see Schoenberg, Arnold

ACHT LIEDER see Wolf, Hugo

ACHT LIEDER see Strauss, Richard

ACHT LIEDER see Handel, George Frideric

ACHT LIEDER see Reger, Max

ACHT LIEDER see Schoenberg, Arnold

ACHT LIEDER (EICHENDORFF) [1] see
Kornauth, Egon

ACHT LIEDER (EICHENDORFF) [2] see
Kornauth, Egon

ACHT LIEDER (GOETHE) see Knab, Armin

ACHT LIEDER, HEFT I see Schreker, Franz

ACHT LIEDER, HEFT II see Schreker,
Franz

ACHT LIEDER IM VOLKSTON see Roselius,
Ludwig

ACHT LIEDER NACH GEDICHTEN VON CHR.
MORGENSTERN HEFT I see Lothar, Mark

ACHT LIEDER NACH GEDICHTEN VON CHR.
MORGENSTERN HEFT II see Lothar,
Mark

ACHT LIEDER NACH VERSCHIEDENEN DICHTERN
see Stockmayer, Erich

ACHT LIEDEREN NAAR GEDICHTEN VAN JAN
ENGELMAN see Mulder, Herman

ACHT OUD-HOLLANDSCHE LIEDEREN see
Pijper, Willem

ACHT RINGELNATZ-CAPRICIEN see Hasse, Johann Friedrich

ACHT RUSSISCHE LIEDER see Reutter, Hermann

ACHT ZIGEUNERLIEDER see Wagner-Regeny, Rudolf

ACHT ZIGEUNERLIEDER see Brahms, Johannes

ACHT ZIGEUNERLIEDER AUS OP. 103 see Brahms, Johannes

ACHTER DE WUIVENDE DUINENLIJN see Zweers, [Bernard]

ACHTERLIJK KIND see Henkemans, Hans

ACHTUNDDREISSIG KINDERLIEDER see Reinecke, Carl

ACHTZEHN LIEDER see Dowland, John

ACK, FINGE DEN TIDEN JAG ATER see Aletter, W.

ACK, HERRE, ETT MANNISKOHJARTA see Fordell, Erik (Fritiof)

ACK HJALP MIG, DU, SOM HJALPEN AR see Nordqvist, Gustaf

ACK, HOR DU LILLA FLICKA
solo,pno GEHRMANS 151 s.p.   (A61)

ACK, JAG GAV HENNE BLOTT UPPA SKULDRAN EN KYSS see Millocker, Karl

ACK MOR, JAG VILL ETT TING HA see Brahms, Johannes

ACK, VAD VAR LEVNAD AR FLYKTIG OCH SNAR see Wohlfart, Karl

ACK, VARMELAND DU SKONA
solo,pno GEHRMANS 203 s.p. contains
also: Tanker Du Att Jag Forlorader
Ar   (A62)

ACK, VISSTE DU BLOTT
solo,pno LUNDQUIST s.p.   (A63)

ACKERMANN, DOROTHY
God Speaks To Me *sac,Gen
med solo,pno (C maj) WILLIS $.60
                                (A64)

ACKLEY, A.H.
I Never Walk Alone *sac
solo,pno WORD S-155   (A65)

If Your Heart Keeps Right *sac
(Kaiser) solo,pno WORD S-303   (A66)

ACKLEY, BENTLEY D. (1872-1958)
When I Kneel Down To Pray *sac
(Kaiser, Kurt) solo,pno WORD S-302
                                (A67)

ACQUA see Respighi, Ottorino

ACQUA CHE PASSI see Albanese, Guido

ACQUAINT THYSELF WITH HIM see Head, Michael (Dewar)

ACQUAINTED WITH THE NIGHT see Duke, John Woods

ACQUAINTED WITH THE NIGHT see Freed, Arnold

ACROSS THE VALLEY see Baxter, Maude Stewart

ACROSS THE WESTERN OCEAN see Dougherty, Celius

ACTION see Messiaen, Oliver

ACTION SCENE *sac,CC15L
solo,pno BENSON BO425 $2.00   (A68)

ACTION SONGS see Gillington, M.

ACUFF-ROSE
Praying Hands *sac
solo,pno WORD S-536   (A69)

AD ANNIE see Del Giudice, G.M.

AD ASTRA see Suchon, Eugen

AD FESTA, FIDELES see Rosetti, Francesco Antionio

AD FESTUM LETITIE see Badings, Henk

AD MENSAM COELITUS PARATAM see Morin, Jean Baptiste

AD MOSSAI *Jew
solo,pno KAMMEN 414 $1.00   (A70)

AD OR HA-BOKER
(Helfman, Max) "Till Dawn Breaks"
[Heb] med solo,pno TRANSCON. IS 501
$.45   (A71)

AD UN RUSCELLO see Fuga, Sandro

AD UNA FANCIULLA see Carabella, Ezio

ADA see Sialm, D.

ADAGIO see Stenhammar, Wilhelm

ADAGIO SOSTENUTO see Bijvanck, Henk

ADAIR, TOM
Tower Of Strength, A (composed with
Hammack, Bobby) *sac
solo,pno WORD S-502   (A72)

ADAM, ADOLPHE-CHARLES (1803-1856)
Ach, Mama, Ich Sag Es Dir *see Ah!
Vous Dirai-Je, Maman

Ah! Vous Dirai-Je, Maman *cant
"Ach, Mama, Ich Sag Es Dir" S solo,
fl,2ob,2clar,2bsn,2horn,strings
BREITKOPF-L rental   (A73)

Aria (from Alphyddan)
solo,pno LUNDQUIST s.p.   (A74)

Bravour-Variationen Uber Ein Thema
Von Mozart
(Schmidt, Gustav) high solo,fl,2ob,
2clar,2bsn,2horn,strings sc RIES
s.p.   (A75)
(Schmidt, Gustav) high solo,fl,pno
voc sc RIES s.p.   (A76)

Cantique De Noel *sac,Xmas
low solo,pno (C maj) WATERLOO $.65
                              (A77)
med solo,pno (E flat maj) WATERLOO
$.65   (A78)
high solo,pno (E flat maj) FISCHER,
C S 5398   (A79)
low solo,pno (C maj) FISCHER,C
S 5399   (A80)
"Christmas Song" [Fr/It/Eng] SA
soli,pno SCHIRM.G $.85   (A81)
"Christmas Song" [Fr/It/Eng] ST
soli,pno SCHIRM.G $1.00   (A82)
"Julsang" high solo,pno GEHRMANS
152 s.p.   (A83)
"Julsang" med solo,pno GEHRMANS 776
s.p.   (A84)
"Julsang" low solo,pno GEHRMANS 551
s.p.   (A85)
"Julsang" high solo,pno/harmonium
LUNDQUIST s.p.   (A86)
"Julsang" med solo,pno/harmonium
LUNDQUIST s.p.   (A87)
"Julsang" low solo,pno/harmonium
LUNDQUIST s.p.   (A88)
"Julsang" 2 soli,pno LUNDQUIST s.p.
                              (A89)
"O Holy Night" high solo,pno BELWIN
$1.50   (A90)
"O Holy Night" low solo,pno BELWIN
$1.50   (A91)
"O Holy Night" solo,pno (available
in 3 keys) ASHLEY $.95   (A92)
"O Holy Night" high solo,pno (E
flat maj) HARRIS $.85   (A93)
"O Holy Night" med solo,pno (D flat
maj) HARRIS $.85   (A94)
"O Holy Night" med-low solo,pno (E
maj) HARRIS $.85   (A95)
"O Holy Night" low solo,pno (B flat
maj) HARRIS $.85   (A96)
"O Holy Night" [Eng/Fr] med solo,
pno,opt vln/vcl PRESSER $.95
                              (A97)
"O Holy Night" [Eng/Fr] low solo,
pno,opt vln/vcl PRESSER $.95
                              (A98)
(Chambers) "O Holy Night" solo,pno
HARRIS $.75   (A99)
(Deis) "O Holy Night" [Fr/Eng] low
solo,pno (B flat maj) SCHIRM.G
$1.25   (A100)
(Deis) "O Holy Night" [Fr/Eng] med
solo,pno (D flat maj) SCHIRM.G
$1.25   (A101)
(Deis) "O Holy Night" [Fr/Eng] high
solo,pno (E flat maj) SCHIRM.G
$1.25   (A102)
(Deis) "O Holy Night" [Fr/Eng] med
solo,pno (C maj) SCHIRM.G $1.25
                              (A103)
(Stickles) "O Holy Night" [Fr/Eng]
high solo,org (E flat maj)
SCHIRM.G $1.00   (A104)
(Stickles) "O Holy Night" [Fr/Eng]
med solo,org (C maj) SCHIRM.G
$1.00   (A105)
(Stickles) "O Holy Night" [Fr/Eng]
med solo,org (D flat maj)
SCHIRM.G $1.00   (A106)
(Stickles) "O Holy Night" [Fr/Eng]
low solo,org (B flat maj)
SCHIRM.G $1.00   (A107)

ADAM, ADOLPHE-CHARLES (cont'd.)
Christmas Song *see Cantique De Noel

Julsang
see NY SAMLING SANGDUETTER, HEFT 2

Julsang *see Cantique De Noel

Mes Amis Ecoutez L'histoire (from Le
Postillon De Lonjumeau)
(Reger, Max) T solo,opt cor,2fl,
2ob,2clar,2bsn,4horn,2trp,3trom,
perc,strings BREITKOPF-L rental
                              (A108)

O Holy Night *see Cantique De Noel

Oh Holy Night
solo,pno CENTURY 3785   (A109)

ADAM IN BALLINGSCHAP see Roos, Robert de

ADAM KI YAMUT see Rappaport, Moshe

ADAM L'ADAM
solo,pno OR-TAV $.50   (A110)

ADAM LAY YBOUNDEN see Badings, Henk

ADAM LAY YBOUNDIN see Jenni, Donald

ADAM WAS MY GRANDFATHER see Moore, Douglas Stuart

ADAMS
All Because Of God's Amazing Grace
*sac
solo,pno BENSON S5097-S $1.00
                              (A111)
Ever Gentle, Ever Sweet *sac
solo,pno BENSON S5418-S $1.00
                              (A112)
God Said It, I Believe It, That
Settles It! *see Braun
One Of These Days *sac
solo,pno BENSON S7301-S $1.00
                              (A113)
Where The Spirit Of The Lord Is *sac
solo,pno BENSON S8465-R $1.00
                              (A114)
Young And Learning *see Zillner

ADAMS, JOHN
Ktaadn
high solo&low solo,inst
EXPERIMENTAL s.p.   (A115)

ADAMS, JOHN T.
Praise The Lord *sac
solo,pno WORD S-378   (A116)

ADAMS, STEPHEN
Den Heliga Stade *see Holy City, The

Holy City, The *sac,Xmas,gospel
low solo,pno (A flat maj) HARRIS
$1.20   (A117)
med solo,pno (B flat maj) HARRIS
$1.20   (A118)
med-high solo,pno (C maj) HARRIS
$1.20   (A119)
high solo,pno (D flat maj) HARRIS
$1.20   (A120)
solo,pno LILLENAS SM-411: RN $1.00
                              (A121)
high solo,pno (D flat maj) BOSTON
$1.50   (A122)
med-high solo,pno (C maj) BOSTON
$1.50   (A123)
med-low solo,pno (B flat maj)
BOSTON $1.50   (A124)
low solo,pno (A flat maj) BOSTON
$1.50   (A125)
high solo,pno (D maj) FISCHER,C
S 5728   (A126)
med-high solo,pno (C maj) FISCHER,C
S 5729   (A127)
med solo,pno (B flat maj) FISCHER,C
S 5730   (A128)
low solo,pno (A flat maj) FISCHER,C
S 5731   (A129)
low solo,pno (B flat maj) CENTURY
3576 $.40   (A130)
solo,pno (available in 4 keys)
ASHLEY $.95   (A131)
low solo,pno (A flat maj) BOOSEY
$1.25   (A132)
med solo,pno (B flat maj) BOOSEY
$1.25   (A133)
med-high solo,pno (C maj) BOOSEY
$1.25   (A134)
high solo,pno (D flat maj) BOOSEY
$1.25   (A135)
high solo,pno LORENZ $1.00   (A136)
med solo,pno LORENZ $1.00   (A137)
low solo,pno LORENZ $1.00   (A138)
SA soli,pno LORENZ $1.00   (A139)
ST soli,pno LORENZ $1.00   (A140)
solo,pno ABER.GRP. $1.50   (A141)
"Den Heliga Stade" high solo,pno
LUNDQUIST s.p.   (A142)
"Den Heliga Stade" low solo,pno
LUNDQUIST s.p.   (A143)
(Weatherly) solo,pno BENSON S7900-R

ADAMS, STEPHEN (cont'd.)

$1.00 (A144)
(Weatherly) high solo,pno LUDWIG
S4H $1.00 (A145)
(Weatherly) med solo,pno LUDWIG S4M
$1.00 (A146)
(Weatherly) low solo,pno LUDWIG S4L
$1.00 (A147)

Mona
high solo,pno LUNDQUIST s.p. (A148)
low solo,pno LUNDQUIST s.p. (A149)

Nirvana
low solo,pno (C maj) BOOSEY $1.50
(A150)
high solo,pno (E flat maj) BOOSEY
$1.50 (A151)

Star Of Bethlehem *sac,Xmas
low solo,pno (E flat maj) HARRIS
$1.15 (A152)
med solo,pno (F maj) HARRIS $1.15
(A153)
high solo,pno (G maj) HARRIS $1.15
(A154)
high solo,pno (F maj) SCHIRM.G $.60
(A155)
low solo,pno (F maj) BOOSEY $1.75
(A156)
high solo,pno (G maj) BOOSEY $1.75
(A157)

Thora
solo,pno (F maj) BOOSEY $1.50
(A158)

Veteran's Song
low solo,pno (C maj) BOOSEY $1.50
(A159)
high solo,pno (D maj) BOOSEY $1.50
(A160)

ADAMS, STEVE
Ever Gentle, Ever Sweet *sac,CC12L
solo,pno BENSON BO225 $2.50 (A161)

ADARIM see Chajes, Julius

ADD NEKEM A SZMEIDET see Paczolay, I.

ADDIO! see Tosti, Francesco Paolo

ADDIO ALLA MADRE see Mascagni, Pietro

ADDIO DEL PASSATO see Verdi, Giuseppe

ADDIO FIORITO ASIL see Puccini, Giacomo

ADDIO, MIGNON, FA CORE! see Thomas,
Ambroise

ADDIO, O NOSTRO PICCIOL DESCO see
Massenet, Jules, Adieu, Notre
Petite Table

ADELAIDE see Beethoven, Ludwig van

ADELE see Honegger, Arthur

ADELE'S LAUGHING SONG see Strauss,
Johann

ADELINE VERBEID see Schouwman, Hans

ADES
Quest For God *see Allen

Shorn Lamb *see Wansborough

ADESTE see Adriessen, Willem

ADESTE see Clercq, R. de

ADEUS EMA see Villa-Lobos, Heitor

ADIE FOULA! see Passani, Emile

ADIEU see Carolus-Duran, P.

ADIEU see Cuvillier, Charles

ADIEU see Denza, Luigi

ADIEU see Duprato, Jules-Laurent

ADIEU see Faure, Gabriel-Urbain

ADIEU see Godard, Benjamin Louis Paul

ADIEU see Grieg, Edvard Hagerup

ADIEU see Hahn, Reynaldo

ADIEU see Lacome, Paul

ADIEU see Mesritz Van Velthuysen, Annie

ADIEU see Milhaud, Darius

ADIEU see Ollone, Max d'

ADIEU see Ruyneman, Daniel

ADIEU see Schubert, Franz (Peter), Lebe
Wohl

ADIEU, BAISERS see De Lara, Isadore

ADIEU, BEAUTE, MA MIE see Saint-Saens,
Camille

ADIEU CELLULE, ADIEU DONJON see Ravel,
Maurice

ADIEU! C'EST DIT see Lacome, Paul

ADIEU CHERE VALLEE see Maitia Nun Zira

ADIEU CLYTIE see Busser, Henri-Paul

ADIEU DE MANON see Massenet, Jules, Je
Ne Suis Que Faiblesse

ADIEU, FAREWELL see Mc Cabe

ADIEU! FIERE CITE see Berlioz, Hector

ADIEU FORETS see Tchaikovsky, Piotr
Ilyitch

ADIEU GENTILLES HIRONDELLES see
Mendelssohn-Bartholdy, Felix

ADIEU-LIEDT see Beekhuis, Hanna

ADIEU, MA FANCHON see Messager, Andre

ADIEU, NOTRE PETITE TABLE see Massenet,
Jules

ADIEU SUZON see White, Maude Valerie

ADIEU, VOUS DY LA LARME A L'OEIL see
Roger-Ducasse, Jean-Jules Aimable

ADIEUX see Arrieu, Claude

ADIEUX A NINON see Haring, Ch.

ADIEUX A SUZON see Guiraud, Ernest

ADIEUX DE L'HOTESSE ARABE see Bizet,
Georges

ADIVINANZA DE LA GUITARRA see Cortes,
Ramiro

ADJURO VOS, FILIAE JERUSALEM see
Schutz, Heinrich

ADLER, HUGO CH.
Cantorial Responses At The Wedding
Ceremony *sac,CCU,Marriage,Jew
cantor,pno/org SAC.MUS.PR. 405
(A162)

Mah Nomar Lefonecho *sac,Jew
solo,pno/org SAC.MUS.PR. 407 (A163)

ADLER, SAMUEL (1928-)
Adonoi Moh Odom *sac
[Heb] cantor,pno TRANSCON. WJ 448
$.85 (A164)

And It Was Stormy Weather
S/T solo,pno OXFORD 96.304 $1.00
see from Four Poems Of James
Stephens (A165)

Chill Of The Eve
S/T solo,pno OXFORD 96.302 $.75 see
from Four Poems Of James Stephens
(A166)

Four Poems Of James Stephens *see
And It Was Stormy Weather; Chill
Of The Eve; Piper, The; Wind, The
(A167)

I Will Betroth Thee *sac,Marriage
[Eng] solo,pno TRANSCON. TV 567
$.75 (A168)

In Thine Own Image *sac
Mez/Bar solo,pno (med diff) OXFORD
96.200 $1.00 (A169)

Piper, The
S/T solo,pno OXFORD 96.303 $1.00
see from Four Poems Of James
Stephens (A170)

Sholom Rov *sac
[Heb] cantor,pno TRANSCON. WJ 447
$.60 (A171)

Two Songs For Three Years *CC2U
med solo,pno BOOSEY $2.25 (A172)

Wind, The
S/T solo,pno OXFORD 96.301 $.75 see
from Four Poems Of James Stephens
(A173)

Woman Of Valor, A *sac,Marriage
[Eng] solo,pno TRANSCON. TV 568
$.60 (A174)

ADMIRAL'S BROOM, THE see Bevan,
Frederick

ADMIREZ LE JOLI VAINQUEUR see Lacome,
Paul

ADMONI, I.
Music *song cycle
[Russ] MezBar soli,pno MEZ KNIGA 65
s.p. (A175)

ADOLESCENTULUS SUM see Couperin (le
Grand), Francois

ADOLPHUS, MILTON (1913-)
Lilacs
solo,clar,pno sc AM.COMP.AL. $2.75
(A176)

ADONAIS see Ronald, Sir Landon

ADONIS see Beydts, L.

ADONOI MOH ODOM see Adler, Samuel

ADONOY RO-EE see Binder, Abraham Wolfe

ADORATION see Bordewijk-Roepman,
Johanna

ADORATION see De Lara, Isadore

ADORATION see Fontenailles, H. de

ADORATION see Handel, George Frideric

ADORATION see Rabey, Rene

ADORAZIONE see Cimara, Pietro

ADORE TE DEVOTE see Mengelberg, Rudolf

ADORO TE see Mengelberg, Rudolf

ADRIAN, WALTER
Sigh No More Ladies
solo,pno CRAMER (A177)

ADRIESSEN, WILLEM (1887-1964)
Adeste
see Twee Liederen

Ave Maria *sac
Mez/A solo,pno/org DONEMUS s.p.
(A178)

De Weide Was Van Bloemen Bont
see Vier Bruidsliederen

Drie Liederen
med solo,pno ALSBACH s.p.
contains: Hei Met De Wolken Zoo
Wit; Meinacht; Zomer (A179)

Drie Liederen
Mez solo,2fl,2ob,2clar,2bsn,4horn,
2trp,timp,strings DONEMUS s.p.
contains: Hei Met De Wolken Zoo
Wit; Herinnering; O Man Van
Smarte (A180)

Druiventrossen
see Vier Liederen

Gebet Op Een Hewelijksfeest
med solo,pno/org ALSBACH (A181)

Hei Met De Wolken Zoo Wit
see Drie Liederen
see Drie Liederen

Herinnering
see Drie Liederen

Ich Lieb' Eine Blume
see Zwei Lieder

Ik Zoek Een Nieuw En Nooit Gesproken
Woord
see Vier Bruidsliederen

Lievelingskind
see Twee Liederen

Meinacht
see Drie Liederen

Mijn Troost
see Vier Liederen

Neuer Fruhling
see Zwei Lieder

O Man Van Smarte
see Drie Liederen

Oud Liedeken
see Vier Liederen

Sneeuwklokjes Luien Den Winter Uit
see Vier Bruidsliederen

Tript Lustig, Mijn Donzen Dromen
see Vier Bruidsliederen

Twee Liederen
Mez/Bar solo,pno ALSBACH s.p.
contains: Adeste; Lievelingskind
(A182)

Vier Bruidsliederen
Mez solo,pno ALSBACH s.p.
contains: De Weide Was Van
Bloemen Bont; Ik Zoek Een Nieuw
En Nooit Gesproken Woord;

ADRIESSEN, WILLEM (cont'd.)

    Sneeuwklokjes Luien Den Winter
    Uit; Tript Lustig, Mijn Donzen
    Dromen   (A183)

    Vier Liederen
    med solo,pno ALSBACH s.p.
      contains: Druiventrossen; Mijn
      Troost; Oud Liedeken; Voor De
      Liefste   (A184)

    Voor De Liefste
    see Vier Liederen

    Wiegelied
    "Wiegenlied" Mez/Bar solo,pno
    ALSBACH   (A185)

    Wiegenlied *see Wiegelied

    Zomer
    see Drie Liederen

    Zwei Lieder
    med solo,pno ALSBACH s.p.
      contains: Ich Lieb' Eine Blume;
      Neuer Fruhling   (A186)

ADRIFT see Bantock, Granville

ADVENT see Jochum, Otto

ADVENT see Jochum, Otto

ADVENT- UND WEIHNACHTSLIEDER see
    Raphael, Gunther

ADVENTS- EN KERSTLIEDEREN see Scholze,
    J.

ADVENTS- UND WEIHNACHTSMUSIK *sac,CCU,
    Adv/Xmas
    (Taubert, Karl Heinz) 4 soli,inst,
    opt. piano 4 hands RIES s.p. sc,
    solo pt   (A187)

AE FOND KISS *folk,Scot
    solo,pno (D flat maj) PATERSON FS1
    s.p.   (A188)
    (Diack, J. M.) ABar soli,pno PATERSON
    s.p.   (A189)

AE FOND KISS see Lawson, Malcolm

AE FOND KISS see Scott-Gatty, Alfred

AEBLEBLOMST see Nielsen, Carl

AEN CONSTANTINUS HUYGENS see Paap,
    Wouter

AEN DEN HEERE DUARTE see Paap, Wouter

AEN JOFFRE FRANCISCA DUARTE see Paap,
    Wouter

AEOLIAN HARP
    S solo,4inst (coedition with PWM
    Krakow) MOECK 5147 rental   (A190)

AFA see Porrino, Ennio

AFFAIRS, THE see Zur, Menachem

AFFANNO see Cantu, M.

AFFETTI AMOROSI *CCU
    (Stefani, Giovanni; Chilesotti, O.)
    solo,pno FORNI s.p.   (A191)

AFRIKAANS WIEGELIEDJE see Hullebroeck,
    Em.

AFSCHEID see Mengelberg, Rudolf

AFSCHEID see Mulder, Herman

AFSKED see Grieg, Edvard Hagerup

AFSPRAAK see Mul, Jan

AFTER see Tosti, Francesco Paolo, Dopo!

AFTER A DREAM see Faure, Gabriel-
    Urbain, Apres Un Reve

AFTER A RAIN AT MOKANSHAN see Graham,
    Robert Virgil

AFTER CALVARY see Tripp, LaVerne

AFTER THE FUNERAL see Gerber, Edward

AFTER THE TEMPEST see Franz, Robert

AFTERMATH, THE see Frankel, Benjamin

AFTERNOON, THE see Kaburagi, Mitsugu

AFTERWARDS see Mullen

AFTON I SKOGEN see Haggbom

AFTON WATER *folk,Scot
    low solo,pno (E flat maj) PATERSON
    FS2 s.p.   (A192)
    high solo,pno (G maj) PATERSON FS2
    s.p.   (A193)

AFTONBON see Skold

AFTONEN see Alfven, Hugo

AFTONEN see Dannstrom, Isidor

AFTONKLOCKAN see Myrberg, August M.

AFTONKLOCKAN see Runback, Albert

AFTONSANG
    see Vid Alvens Strand

AFTONSANG see Berg

AFTONSANG see Lago, Mario

AFTONSKY see Pesonen, Olavi (Samuel),
    Iltapilvi

AFTONSTAMNING see Alfven, Hugo

AFTONSTAMNING see Dahl

AFTONSTAMNING see Korling, August

AFTONSTAMNING see Myrberg, August M.

AFTONSTAMNING see Peterson-Berger,
    (Olof) Wilhelm

AFTONSTJARNAN see Myrberg, August M.

AFTONSTJARNAN see Sjogren, Emil

AGAFONNIKOV, V.
    Water Colours
    solo,pno MEZ KNIGA 2.84 s.p. (A194)

AGAIN see Reynolds, Roger

AGAINST IDLENESS AND MISCHIEF AND IN
    PRAISE OF LABOR see Beeson, Jack
    Hamilton

AGAMEDE'S SONG see Elwell, Herbert

AGAR ET ISMAELE ESILIATI see Scarlatti,
    Alessandro

AGATHE see Abt, Franz

AGAY, DENES (1911-   )
    Believing
    med solo,pno PRESSER $.75   (A195)

    Yankee Peddler, The
    solo,pno WEINTRB $1.50   (A196)

AGELESS THOU ART see Bryson

AGENDA see Lessard, John Ayres

AGNES see Emborg, Jens Laurson

AGNETE OG HAVMANDEN *CCU
    (Christiansen, Asger Lund;
    Sonderholm, E.) solo,pno HANSEN-DEN
    29181 s.p.   (A197)

AGNUS DEI see Bach, Johann Sebastian

AGNUS DEI see Bizet, Georges

AGNUS DEI see Faure, Jean-Baptiste

AGNUS DEI see Hahn, Reynaldo

AGNUS DEI see Hemel, Oscar van

AGNUS DEI see Mozart, Wolfgang Amadeus

AGNUS DEI see Pardo

AGONIA see Kiesewetter, Peter

AGOSTI, GUIDO (1901-   )
    Quattro Liriche *CC4U
    solo,pno ZERBONI 4358 s.p.   (A198)

    Rispetto
    solo,pno ZERBONI 4379 s.p.   (A199)

AGRIPPINA CONDOTTA A MORIRE see Handel,
    George Frideric

AGUILAR, F.
    El Bonete Del Cura
    [Span] SSA soli,opt pno UNION ESP.
    $.75   (A200)

AGUIRRE, JULIAN (1868-1924)
    El Zorzal *Op.54
    [Span] solo,pno RICORDI-ARG BA 7676
    s.p.   (A201)

    Serenata Campera *Op.42
    [Span] solo,pno RICORDI-ARG BA 6826
    s.p.   (A202)

AGUIRRE, JULIAN (cont'd.)

    Vidalita *Op.36
    [Span] solo,pno RICORDI-ARG BA 6707
    s.p.   (A203)

AH! AH! AH! LA BELLE AFFAIRE see Poise,
    (Jean Alexandre) Ferdinand

AH ARMAINEN see Giordani, Giuseppe,
    Caro Mio Ben

AH! BEAU ROSSIGNOL VOLAGE see
    Vredenburg, Max

AH! BIEN C'EST DU JOLI see Arrieu,
    Claude

AH BLUE HORIZON see Verdi, Giuseppe, O
    Cieli Azzurri

AH CHE LA MORET see Verdi, Giuseppe

AH! CHE SI GRAN MARTORO see Anonymous

AH, CHE TROPPO INEGUALI see Handel,
    George Frideric

AH! CRUDEL, NEL PIANTO MIO see Handel,
    George Frideric

AH! DISPAR VISION see Massenet, Jules

AH! DU WOLLTEST MICH NICHT see Strauss,
    Richard

AH, FORS E LUI see Verdi, Giuseppe

AH! FUYEZ, DOUCE IMAGE! see Massenet,
    Jules

AH HEAV'N! WHAT IS'T I HEAR? see Blow,
    John

AH! HOW DELIGHTFUL THE MORNING see
    Reynolds, Alfred

AH! HOW SWEET IT IS TO LOVE see
    Purcell, Henry

AH! I WOULD LINGER see Gounod, Charles
    Francois, Ah! Je Veux Vivre

AH! JE VEUX VIVRE see Gounod, Charles
    Francois

AH! JE VOUS AI TOUJOURS AIMEE see
    Duvernoy, Victor-Alphonse

AH, LA PATERNA MANO see Verdi, Giuseppe

AH! LAISSE-MOI LE VOIR see Vogel, A.

AH! LE DESTIN VA-T-IL REALISER MON REVE
    see Saint-Saens, Camille

AH, LET ME WEEP, LORD! see Handel,
    George Frideric, Lascia Ch'io
    Pianga

AH! LEUR CARNAVAL see Guiraud, Ernest

AH! LEVE-TOI, SOLEIL! see Gounod,
    Charles Francois

AH, LO PREVIDI see Mozart, Wolfgang
    Amadeus

AH LO PREVIDI - AH! T'INVOLA AGL'OCCHI
    MIEI see Mozart, Wolfgang Amadeus

AH, LO SO, PIU NON M'AVANZA see Mozart,
    Wolfgang Amadeus

AH! LOVE BUT A DAY see Protheroe,
    Daniel

AH M'ABBANDONI - IN QUESTA SELVA OSCURA
    see Mengelberg, Karel

AH! MAY THE RED ROSE see Foster,
    Stephen Collins

AH! MIO COR see Handel, George Frideric

AH! MON BEAU JARDIN see Delbruck, J.

AH! MON MARI see Guiraud, Ernest

AH, MOON OF MY DELIGHT! see Lehmann,
    Liza

AH, NON AVESSI see Kalman, Emerich

AH! NON CREDEA MIRARTI! see Bellini,
    Vincenzo

AH! NON CREDEVI TU! see Thomas,
    Ambroise

AH, NON MI RIDESTAR! see Massenet,
    Jules

AH, PER SEMPRE IO TI PERDEI see
    Bellini, Vincenzo

AIR SERIEUX [2] see Couperin (le Grand), Francois

AIR SUR UNE BLONDE see Badings, Henk

AIR TZIGANE see Winkler, Alexander Adolfovitch

AIR VARIE see Beriot, Charles-August de

AIR VARIE see Ghisi, Federico

AIR VIF see Poulenc, Francis

AIRMEN, THE see Shaw, Martin

AIRS see Lully (Lulli), Jean-Baptiste

AIRS CHANTES see Poulenc, Francis

AIRS CHANTES 1898C., THE.. see Poulenc, Francis

AIRS EXTRAITS DES OEUVRES COMPLETES VOL. I see Rameau, Jean-Philippe

AIRS EXTRAITS DES OEUVRES COMPLETES VOL. II see Rameau, Jean-Philippe

AIRS FRANCAIS see Handel, George Frideric

AITI JA KULKURIPOIKA see Merikanto, Oskar

AJNYAHITA see Zahradnik, Zdenek

AK QUE EL ALMA see Guastavino, Carlos

AKALLAN see Nordqvist, Gustaf

AKED, LINDSAY
Let Your Song Be Delicate
see Aked, Lindsay, When Kisses Are
Like Strawberries

May
see Aked, Lindsay, When Kisses Are
Like Strawberries

When Kisses Are Like Strawberries
solo,pno ALBERT AHL202 rental
contains also: May; Let Your Song
Be Delicate (A218)

AKERS, DORIS
Happiness Is God *sac
solo,pno SINGSPIR 7089 $1.00 (A219)

Lord, Give Me A Song *sac
solo,pno SINGSPIR 7087 $1.00 (A220)

Sweet, Sweet Spirit *sac
solo,pno BENSON S7636-R $1.00
(A221)

AKERS, MADDALENA H.
Rock-A-Bye Train
high solo,pno (E flat maj) WILLIS
$.60 (A222)
med solo,pno (C maj) WILLIS $.60
(A223)
low solo,pno (A maj) WILLIS $.60
(A224)

AKIBA see Vredenburg, Max

AKO HVIEZDY PADAJU see Ocenas, Andrej

AKOGARE see Nakada, Yoshinao

AKTENSKAPSFRAGAN
(A.W.) solo,pno LUNDQUIST s.p.
contains also: En Lat I Tri Toner
(A225)

AL DESIO DI CHI T'ADORA see Mozart, Wolfgang Amadeus

AL FIN MI NENA see Chueca, Federico

AL FUROR see Handel, George Frideric

AL ILEGAR AL CAMPOSANTO see Garcia Morillo, Roberto

AL PAMPERO see Andre, Jose

AL PIANTO MIO see Rimsky-Korsakov, Nikolai

AL PIE DE LA CRUZ DEL ROQUE see Sanchez, B.

AL TAL V'AL MATAR *folk,Jew
med solo,pno HATIKVAH ED. 63 $.20
(A226)

AL TEMPESTOSO VENTO INVERNALE see Ferrari-Trecate, Luigi

AL TIRA
(Helfman, Max) "Fear Not" [Heb] med
solo,pno TRANSCON. IS 502 $.45
(A227)

AL TURNARA!
(Carlo, Musi) solo,pno (Bolognese
dialect) BONGIOVANI 2083 s.p. see
from El Mi Canzunett (A228)

AL WIE TER MINNE IS ZO VROED see Strategier, Herman

ALA KUTSU KUKKASEKSI see Sonninen, Ahti

ALABAMA-SONG see Weill, Kurt

ALABIEV, ALEXANDER NICHOLAEVICH
Nightingale
med solo,pno (F sharp min) ALLANS
s.p. (A229)
high solo,pno (A min) ALLANS s.p.
(A230)
Romances And Songs, Vol. III *CCU
[Russ] solo,pno MEZ KNIGA 55 s.p.
(A231)

ALADDIN see Nielsen, Carl

ALADIN see Vieu, Jane

ALAIN, JEHAN (1911-1940)
Messe Modale En Septuor
SA soli, fl&4strings/fl&org
DOBLINGER 08 850 sc $6.00, ipa,
solo pt s.p. (A232)

Priere Pour Nous Autres Charnels
TB soli,org LEDUC s.p. (A233)

ALALEONE, DOMENICO (1881-1928)
Albe *see Mandorlo Fiorito; Nebbia;
Storia Quotidiana (A234)

Mandorlo Fiorito
[It] solo,pno SANTIS 0031 s.p. see
from Albe (A235)

Nebbia
[It] solo,pno SANTIS 0029 s.p. see
from Albe (A236)

Storia Quotidiana
[It] solo,pno SANTIS 0027 s.p. see
from Albe (A237)

ALAMO SERRANO see De Rogatis, Pascual

ALAS DE ORO see Sas, Andres

ALAS THAT SPRING see Lehmann, Liza

ALASKA see Scotto, Vincent

ALASTAIR see Hiller, Wilfred

ALBA see Ferraris, C.

ALBA FESTIVA see Gandino, Adolfo

ALBANESE, GUIDO
Acqua Che Passi
[It] solo,pno SANTIS 405 s.p.
(A238)

Canzone D'Aprile
solo,pno BONGIOVANI 1262 s.p. see
from Cinque Liriche (A239)

Cinque Liriche *see Canzone
D'Aprile; Il Cuore Di Nini;
Mattinata; Notte Di Neve; Te Lo
Voglio Dire (A240)

Core Di Mamma
[It] solo,pno SANTIS 385 s.p.
(A241)

Due Celebri Canzoni Abruzzesi
[It] solo,pno cmplt ed SANTIS 1036
s.p.
contains: L'Acquabbelle; Vola
Vola (A242)

Il Cuore Di Nini
solo,pno BONGIOVANI 1259 s.p. see
from Cinque Liriche (A243)

La Campagnola
[It] solo,pno SANTIS 895 s.p.
(A244)

La Maggiajole
[It] solo,pno SONZOGNO 2388 s.p.
(A245)

La Palummelle
[It] solo,pno SONZOGNO 2389 s.p.
(A246)

L'Acquabbelle
see Due Celebri Canzoni Abruzzesi

Lu Piante De Le Fojje
see Albanese, Guido, Povere
Ggirasole

Mattinata
solo,pno BONGIOVANI 1261 s.p. see
from Cinque Liriche (A247)

Ninna Nanna
[It] solo,pno SANTIS 399 s.p.
(A248)

Notte Di Neve
solo,pno BONGIOVANI 1258 s.p. see
from Cinque Liriche (A249)

Povere Ggirasole
[It] solo,pno SONZOGNO 2421 s.p.
contains also: Lu Piante De Le
Fojje (A250)

ALBANESE, GUIDO (cont'd.)
Te Lo Voglio Dire
solo,pno BONGIOVANI 1260 s.p. see
from Cinque Liriche (A251)

Vola Vola Vola
see Due Celebri Canzoni Abruzzesi

ALBE see Alaleone, Domenico

ALBENIZ, ISAAC (1860-1909)
Amor Summa Injuria
[Fr/Eng] med solo,pno SALABERT-US
$4.50 see from Four Songs (A252)

Crepuscule
see Zwei Lieder

Four Songs *see Amor Summa Injuria;
In Sickness And Health; Paradise
Regained; Retreat, The (A253)

Granada
(Bilbao) [Span] solo,pno RICORDI-
ARG BA 8858 s.p. (A254)

In Sickness And Health
[Fr/Eng] med solo,pno SALABERT-US
$4.50 see from Four Songs (A255)

Paradise Regained
[Fr/Eng] med solo,pno SALABERT-US
$4.50 see from Four Songs (A256)

Retreat, The
[Fr/Eng] med solo,pno SALABERT-US
$4.50 see from Four Songs (A257)

Romance (from Pepita Jimenez)
[Fr/It] high solo,pno ESCHIG $1.25
(A258)

Sei Baladas *CC6U
[It] high solo/med solo,pno UNION
ESP. $2.25 (A259)

Tango *Op.165,No.2
(Pardo) [Span] solo,pno RICORDI-ARG
BA 8726 s.p. (A260)

Tristesse
see Zwei Lieder

Zwei Lieder
[Fr] solo,pno SCHOTTS ME s.p.
contains: Crepuscule; Tristesse
(A261)

ALBERSENN
Les Boeufs
solo,pno ENOCH s.p. (A262)
solo,acap solo pt ENOCH s.p. (A263)

D'ALBERT, EUGENE FRANCIS CHARLES
(1864-1932)
Amor Und Psyche (from Die Toten
Augen)
[Ger] high solo,pno BOTE $.90
(A264)

Das Madchen Und Der Schmetterling
*Op.3,No.3
"Maiden And The Butterfly, The"
[Ger/Eng] med solo,pno BOTE $.90
(A265)
"Maiden And The Butterfly, The"
[Ger/Eng] high solo,pno BOTE $.90
(A266)

Maiden And The Butterfly, The *see
Das Madchen Und Der Schmetterling

Slumber Songs *Op.25,No.2
[Ger/Eng] med solo,pno FORBERG F103
$8.50 (A267)

ALBERT, HEINRICH (1604-1651)
Ausgewahlte Arien *sac,CCU
[Ger] 1-2 soli,cont sc CONCORDIA
97-4262 $2.50 (A268)

Elf Lieder *CC11U
high solo,pno/cembalo&lute (easy)
BAREN. 569 $2.50 (A269)

Rise, My Soul, And Praise God's
Kindness *sac
med-high solo,cont,opt fl/vln/rec
oct CONCORDIA 98-1481 $.20 (A270)

Zwolf Duette *CC12U
(Noack, Friedrich) 2 soli,cont
(med) BAREN. HM 150 $7.00 (A271)

ALBIN, ROGER (1920-)
Chantefables *CCU
S solo,fl,ob,clar,bass clar,bsn,
contrabsn,horn,trp,trom,timp,
perc,xylo,vibra,pno,cel,harp,
5strings cmplt ed RIDEAU rental;
solo,pno RIDEAU 049 s.p. (A272)

ALBINI, F. (1600?- ?)
La Primavera
solo,2fl,2ob,gtr CARISH s.p. (A273)

ALBRECHT, ALEXANDER
Noc
A solo,pno SLOV.HUD.FOND s.p.
(A274)

ALBUM, BAND I see Koschat, Thomas

ALBUM, BAND II see Koschat, Thomas

ALBUM, BAND III see Koschat, Thomas

ALBUM, BAND IV see Koschat, Thomas

ALBUM, BAND V see Koschat, Thomas

ALBUM DE CANTOS VASCONGADOS, VOL. I
*CC7U
(Martinez Villar) med solo,pno UNION
ESP. $1.25 text in Basque (A275)

ALBUM DE CANTOS VASCONGADOS, VOL. II
*CC9U
(Martinez Villar) med solo,pno UNION
ESP. $1.25 text in Basque (A276)

ALBUM DE CANTOS VASCONGADOS, VOL. III
*CC6U
(Martinez Villar) med solo,pno UNION
ESP. $2.00 text in Basque (A277)

ALBUM DE CANTOS VASCONGADOS, VOL. IV
*CC8U
(Martinez Villar) med solo,pno UNION
ESP. $1.25 text in Basque (A278)

ALBUM DE TIMBRES see Larbey, V.

ALBUM DES TSCHECHISCHEN BELCANTOS *CCU
(Branberger, J.) [Czech/It] solo,pno
SUPRAPHON s.p. (A279)

ALBUM DI DUODICI CANZONI POPOLARI
SICILIANE *CC12U
(Cali') solo,pno FORLIVESI 12289 s.p.
(A280)

ALBUM FUR SOPRAN see Purcell, Henry

ALBUM LINES see Grieg, Edvard Hagerup

ALBUM MODERNE
solo,pno DURAND s.p.
contains: Merson, Oliver, Dans Le
Parc; Roger-Ducasse, Jean-Jules
Aimable, Rondel; Roux, E.,
Dernier Souhait; Toutain-Grun,
J., Rondel (A281)

ALBUM OF DUETS *CC15L
ST soli,pno SCHIRM.G $1.75 contains
works by: Brahms; Jensen; Schumann;
Verdi and others (A282)

ALBUM OF FAVORITE GOSPEL SONGS BOOK 1
*sac,CCU
solo,pno COLE $3.00 (A283)

ALBUM OF FAVORITE GOSPEL SONGS BOOK 2
*sac,CCU
solo,pno COLE $3.00 (A284)

ALBUM OF FAVORITE STEPHEN FOSTER SONGS
see Foster, Stephen Collins

ALBUM OF FOUR SONGS see Rachmaninoff,
Sergey Vassilievitch

ALBUM OF FOURTEEN FAMOUS CHRISTMAS
CAROLS *CC14U
solo,pno LEONARD-ENG (A285)

ALBUM OF NEGRO SPIRITUALS *CCU,spir
(Burleigh, Harry T.) BELWIN high
solo,pno $2.50; low solo,pno $2.50
(A286)

ALBUM OF NINE SONGS see Nielsen, Carl

ALBUM OF SACRED SONGS *sac,CC22L
high solo,pno SCHIRM.G LIBRARY 1384
$3.50; low solo,pno SCHIRM.G
LIBRARY 1385 $3.00 contains works
by: Bizet; Gounod; Saint-Saens;
Ambrose and others (A287)

ALBUM OF SEVEN SELECTED SONGS see Bax,
Sir Arnold

ALBUM OF SIX SONGS see Debussy, Claude

ALBUM OF SIX SONGS see Faure, Gabriel-
Urbain

ALBUM OF SIXTEEN SACRED DUETS *sac,
CC16L
2 soli,pno SCHIRM.G $2.50 contains
works by: Gounod; Mendelssohn;
Bartlett; Schnecker and others
(A288)

ALBUM OF SONGS see Foster, Stephen
Collins

ALBUM OF SONGS see Speaks, Oley

ALBUM OF SONGS see Rachmaninoff, Sergey
Vassilievitch

ALBUM OF SONGS see Duparc, Henri

ALBUM OF SONGS BY ISRAELI COMPOSERS
*CCU
solo,pno OR-TAV $2.00, ea. in 2
volumes (A289)

ALBUM OF TWELVE POPULAR SONGS see
Grieg, Edvard Hagerup

ALBUM OF TWENTY-FIVE FAVORITE SONGS FOR
YOUNG GIRLS *CC25L
girl solo,pno SCHIRM.G $3.95 contains
works by: Dvorak; Haydn; Schubert;
Tchaikovsky and others (A290)

ALBUM SAMOSPEVOV see Lajovic, Anton

ALCALAY, LUNA
Plattitudes En Occasion *CC12U
12 soli,2perc,5strings MODERN
rental (A291)

ALCANDRO, LO CONFESSO see Mozart,
Wolfgang Amadeus

ALCANDRO, LO CONFESSO [KV 512] see
Mozart, Wolfgang Amadeus

ALCANDRO, LO CONFESSO - NON SO D'ONDE
VIENE see Mozart, Wolfgang Amadeus

ALCIDE AL BIVIO see Hasse, A.

ALCOCK, GILBERT A.
Treasure Flower
solo,pno,opt vln (E flat maj)
LEONARD-ENG (A292)

ALCORN, JEANNIE VEE
He Giveth Me Strength *sac
solo,pno WORD S-525 (A293)

Now Is The Time *sac
solo,pno WORD S-382 (A294)

ALCORN, JERRY
Reunion In Heaven *sac
solo,pno WORD S-387 (A295)

ALDEN
Beautiful Hands *sac
solo,pno HOPE 488 $.75 (A296)

ALDER TREE, THE see Rachmaninoff,
Sergey Vassilievitch

ALDERIGHI, DANTE (1898-1968)
Canti Militari *CCU
solo,pno ZERBONI 4069 s.p. (A297)

Cantico Delle Creature Di S.
Francesco
solo,pno FORLIVESI 11277 s.p.
(A298)

Cinque Liriche *CC5U
solo,pno ZERBONI 3688 s.p. (A299)

Villanesca
[It] solo,pno SANTIS 494 s.p.
(A300)

ALDINGTON, JOAN
Happiness
low solo,pno (D maj) CRAMER (A301)
med solo,pno (E flat maj) CRAMER
(A302)
high solo,pno (F maj) CRAMER (A303)

ALDRIDGE
He Loves You *see Short

ALEGRIA DE LA SOLEDAD see Guastavino,
Carlos

ALEMANNISCHE GEDICHTE see Nageli,
Johann (Hans) Georg

ALETTE, C.
Ashes Of Life
see Three Secular Songs

God's World
med solo,pno TRI-TEN $1.60 (A304)

Moon Has Gone, The
see Three Secular Songs

Three Secular Songs
med solo,pno TRI-TEN $2.00
contains: Ashes Of Life; Moon Has
Gone, The; What Lips Have
Kissed (A305)

What Lips Have Kissed
see Three Secular Songs

ALETTER, W.
Ack, Finge Den Tiden Jag Ater
low solo,pno GEHRMANS s.p. (A306)
high solo,pno GEHRMANS 176 s.p.
(A307)

ALFABETO A SORPRESA see Mortari,
Virgilio

ALFANO, FRANCO (1876-1954)
Antica Ninna-Ninna Partenopea
[It] A/B solo,pno RICORDI-ENG
123623 s.p. see from Tre Liriche
(A308)

Corro Come Il Cervo Muschiato
[It] S/T solo,pno RICORDI-ENG
123620 s.p. see from Nouve
Liriche Tagoriane (A309)

Dein Letztes Lied *see Finisci
L'ultimo Canto

Dio Pietoso (from Risurrezione)
[It/Fr] S solo,pno RICORDI-ENG
120675 s.p. (A310)

Due Canti Napoletani *CC2U
solo,pno ZERBONI 4178 s.p. (A311)

E Giunto Il Nostro Ultimo Autunno
[It] S/T solo,pno RICORDI-ENG
125532 s.p. (A312)

Felicita
[It] Mez/Bar solo,pno RICORDI-ENG
123621 s.p. see from Tre Liriche
(A313)

Finisci L'ultimo Canto
"Dein Letztes Lied" see Tre Liriche

Giorno Per Giorno
"Tag Fur Tag" see Tre Liriche

La Notte E L'anima
[It] solo,pno CURCI 4428 s.p. see
from Sette Liriche (A314)

Luce
solo,pno ZERBONI 4425 s.p. (A315)

Mamma, Il Giovane Principe
[It] S solo,pno RICORDI-ENG 128167
s.p. see from Tre Poemi Da Il
Giardiniere Di Rabindranath
Tagore (A316)

Melodia
[It] S solo,pno RICORDI-ENG 125748
s.p. see from Tre Nouvi Poemi
(A317)

Messaggio
[It] Mez/Bar solo,pno RICORDI-ENG
123622 s.p. see from Tre Liriche
(A318)

Ninna-Ninna Di Mezzanotte
[It] S solo,pno RICORDI-ENG 125747
s.p. see from Tre Nouvi Poemi
(A319)

Non Hai Udito I Suoi Passi
[It] solo,pno CURCI 4427 s.p. see
from Sette Liriche (A320)

Non So...
[It] solo,pno CURCI 4426 s.p. see
from Sette Liriche (A321)

Nouve Liriche Tagoriane *see Corro
Come Il Cervo Muschiato; Perche
Siedi La (A322)

Perche Allo Spuntar Del Giorno
"Warum Kam In Des Abends Dammern"
see Tre Liriche

Perche Siedi La
[It] Mez/Bar solo,pno RICORDI-ENG
123620 s.p. see from Nouve
Liriche Tagoriane (A323)

Piangi, Si, Piangi (from
Risurrezione)
[It/Fr] T solo,pno RICORDI-ENG
120676 s.p. (A324)

Preghiera Alla Madonna
[It] S solo,pno RICORDI-ENG 125749
s.p. see from Tre Nouvi Poemi
(A325)

Scendesti Dal Tuo Trono
[It] solo,pno CURCI 4424 s.p. see
from Sette Liriche (A326)

Se Taci...
[It] solo,pno CURCI 4425 s.p. see
from Sette Liriche (A327)

Sette Liriche *see La Notte E
L'anima; Non Hai Udito I Suoi
Passi; Non So...; Scendesti Dal
Tuo Trono; Se Taci...; Si
Addensano Le Nubi; Venne E Mi
Sedette Accanto (A328)

Si Addensano Le Nubi
[It] solo,pno CURCI 4422 s.p. see
from Sette Liriche (A329)

Tag Fur Tag *see Giorno Per Giorno

Tre Liriche *see Antica Ninna-Ninna
Partenopea; Felicita; Messaggio
(A330)

Tre Liriche *CC3U
solo,pno ZERBONI 4262 s.p. (A331)

ALFANO, FRANCO (cont'd.)

Tre Liriche
[It/Ger] solo,fl,ob,clar,bsn,horn,
trp,perc,cembalo,harp,pno sc
CARISH 19876 s.p., voc sc CARISH
19538 s.p.
contains: Finisci L'ultimo Canto,
"Dein Letztes Lied"; Giorno Per
Giorno, "Tag Fur Tag"; Perche
Allo Spuntar Del Giorno, "Warum
Kam In Des Abends Dammern"
(A332)

Tre Nouvi Poemi *see Melodia; Ninna-
Ninna Di Mezzanotte; Preghiera
Alla Madonna (A333)

Tre Poemi Da Il Giardiniere Di
Rabindranath Tagore *see Mamma,
Il Giovane Principe (A334)

Venne E Mi Sedette Accanto
[It] solo,pno CURCI 4423 s.p. see
from Sette Liriche (A335)

Warum Kam In Des Abends Dammern *see
Perche Allo Spuntar Del Giorno

ALFONSO EL SABIO (1221-1284)
Cuarto Cantigas *CC4U
[Span] med solo,org UNION ESP.
$1.25 (A336)

ALFVEN, HUGO (1872-1960)
Aftonen
solo,pno GEHRMANS s.p. (A337)

Aftonstamning *Op.4,No.3
solo,pno LUNDQUIST s.p. (A338)

Berceuse
"Dofta, Dofta, Vit Syren" solo,pno
GEHRMANS s.p. (A339)

Dofta, Dofta, Vit Syren *see
Berceuse

Du Ar Stilla Ro *Op.28,No.4
solo,pno LUNDQUIST s.p. (A340)

En Bat Med Blommor
solo,pno GEHRMANS s.p. (A341)

For Sverige
solo,pno GEHRMANS s.p. (A342)

Fosterlandpsalm
solo,pno LUNDQUIST s.p. (A343)

Frihetssang
solo,pno GEHRMANS s.p. (A344)

Hos Drottning Margareta
solo,pno LUNDQUIST s.p. (A345)

I Stilla Timmar
solo,pno GEHRMANS s.p. (A346)

Julsang
solo,pno LUNDQUIST s.p. (A347)

Klockorna
solo,pno LUNDQUIST s.p. (A348)

Kring Ditt Rika Och Vagiga Har Och
Andra Dikter Av Ernest Thiel
*CCU
solo,pno GEHRMANS s.p. (A349)

Lindagull, Lindagull Lilla
solo,pno GEHRMANS s.p. (A350)

O, Stode Du I Kylig Blast
solo,pno LUNDQUIST s.p. (A351)

Saa Tag Mit Hjerte
solo,pno GEHRMANS s.p. (A352)

Sju Dikter *Op.28, CC7U
solo,pno LUNDQUIST s.p. (A353)

Skogen Sover *Op.28,No.6
solo,pno LUNDQUIST s.p. (A354)

Stall Flaggan Sa Jag Ser Den
solo,pno GEHRMANS s.p. (A355)

Sveriges Flagga
solo,pno GEHRMANS s.p. (A356)

Taltrasten
solo,pno GEHRMANS s.p. (A357)

Vaggsang
solo,pno GEHRMANS s.p. (A358)

Vaggvisa
solo,pno GEHRMANS s.p. (A359)

ALGARROBO, ALGARROBAL see Ginastera,
Alberto

ALGER
Paris New-York
solo,pno RICORDI-FR s.p. solo pt,
voc sc (A360)

ALIN, PIERRE
Aupres D'un Berceau
solo,pno ENOCH s.p. (A361)
solo,acap solo pt ENOCH s.p. (A362)

La Complainte Des Pauvr's Petits Gas
solo,pno ENOCH s.p. (A363)
solo,acap solo pt ENOCH s.p. (A364)

Les Petites Momes
solo,pno ENOCH s.p. (A365)
solo,acap solo pt ENOCH s.p. (A366)

AL'INCONNUE see Chaminade, Cecile

ALISON-CROMPTON, C.
Autumn
low solo,pno (C maj) BOOSEY $1.50
(A367)
high solo,pno (E flat maj) BOOSEY
$1.50 (A368)

ALJABJEW, ALEXANDER A.
Die Nachtigall
[Czech/Russ] solo,pno SUPRAPHON
s.p. (A369)

Romanzen *CCU
[Russ] Bar solo,pno SIKORSKI R 6307
s.p. (A370)

ALL A MERRY MAY-TIME see Ronald, Sir
Landon

ALL BECAUSE OF GOD'S AMAZING GRACE see
Adams

ALL DAY I HEAR see Read, Gardner

ALL DAY I HEAR THE NOISE OF WATERS see
Grayson, Richard

ALL DAY ON THE PRAIRIE see Guion, David
Wendall Fentress

ALL FOR YOU see Bertrand

ALL FOR YOU see Martin, Easthope

ALL GOD'S CHILDREN see Gaither

ALL HAIL THOU DWELLING PURE AND LOWLY
see Gounod, Charles Francois,
Salve, Dimora Casta E Pura

ALL I CAN SAY see Crouch, Andrae

ALL IN A GARDEN GREEN see Ireland, John

ALL IN A LILY-WHITE GOWN see Martin,
Easthope

ALL IN ALL see Faye, Linda

ALL IN THE APRIL EVENING see Diack,
John Michael

ALL IN THE APRIL EVENING see Roberton,
Hugh Stevenson, Yno Yn Hwyrddydd
Ebrill

ALL-LEBEN see Bijvanck, Henk

ALL MEIN GEDANKEN *CCU,folk,Ger
(Ruhrmann) solo,pno,treb inst SCHOTTS
4129 s.p. (A371)

ALL' MEINE GEDANKEN see Strauss,
Richard

ALL MEINE GEDANKEN, MEIN HERZ UND MEIN
SINN see Strauss, Richard

ALL MOTHERS EVERYWHERE see Rodgers,
John

ALL MY LIFE
see There's Going To Be A Wedding

ALL MY LIFE see Carmichael, Ralph

ALL MY SONGS see Shemer, Naomi

ALL MY TROUBLES see Lyman, Ed.

ALL MY VERY OWN see Hope, B.M.

ALL OF ME see Lister, Mosie

ALL OF MY TOMORROWS see Cates, Bill

ALL' OMBRA DI SOSPETTO see Vivaldi,
Antonio

ALL ONCE I GLADLY OWNED see
Rachmaninoff, Sergey Vassilievitch

ALL PATHS LEAD TO YOU see Hageman,
Richard

ALL PRAISE TO THEE, ETERNAL GOD see
Lenel, Ludwig

ALL SNOW see Birch, Robert Fairfax

ALL THAT'S PAST see Berkeley, Lennox

ALL THE BIRDS ABOVE A-WINGING see
Offenbach, Jacques, Les Oiseaux
Dans La Charmille

ALL THE FUN OF THE FAIR see Martin,
Easthope

ALL THE PRETTY LITTLE HORSES see
Binder, Abraham Wolfe

ALL THE TIME IN THE WORLD see Harris,
Ron

ALL THE WAY MY SAVIOR LEADS ME
(Bartlett, Gene) 2 high soli,pro (E
flat maj) BROADMAN 4590-07 $.75
(A372)
(Bartlett, Gene) 2 low soli,pno
BROADMAN 4590-08 $.75 (A373)

ALL THE WORLD AWAKES TODAY see German,
Edward

ALL THINGS ARE POSSIBLE see Thygerson,
Robert J.

ALL THINGS DEPART see Rachmaninoff,
Sergey Vassilievitch

ALL THINGS LEAVE ME see Dello Joio,
Norman

ALL THINGS THAT HEAL see Kennedy, John
Brodbin

ALL THROUGH THE NIGHT see Somervell,
Arthur

ALL YE WHO LABOUR see Ashworth-Hope, H.

ALL YE WHO SEEK FOR SURE RELIEF see
Roberts

ALLA DEM SOM VILSE FARA see Kilpinen,
Yrio

ALLA FIERA DI MASTR'ANDREA see De
Meglio

ALLA MAMMA see Salvatori, P. Salvatore

ALLA MEMORIA DI G.B. PERGOLESI see
Vogel, Wladimir

ALLA SERA see Caltabiano, S.

ALLA VITA CHE T'ARRIDE see Verdi,
Giuseppe

ALLAH BASIT
see Internationale Volklieder, No!. 3

ALLAH MOUNAYE see Fraggi, H.

ALLAH'S HOLIDAY see Friml, Rudolf

ALL'AMORE see Veneziani, Vittore

ALLAN, LEWIS (1907-)
Long Way From Home, A
med solo,pno BROUDE BR. $.95 (A374)

ALLBRIGHT
Two Chinese Songs *sec,CC2U
solo,pno WATERLOO $1.25 (A375)

ALLE DIE, DIE SICH VERIRRTEN see
Kilpinen, Yrio, Alla Dem Som Vilse
Fara

ALLE FANGT AN
see Vier Kleine Weihnachtslieder

ALLE SINGEN MIT *CCU
(Schneider, W.) solo,pno SCHOTTS s.p.
(A376)

ALLE SONGS see Weill, Kurt

ALLE SOTTEN EN DRAGHEN GHEEN BELLEN see
Moulaert, Raymond

ALLE TERMOPILI see Margola, Franco

ALLEEN see Middeleer, Jean De, Seule

ALLEGORY: PRIDE, AN see Stout, Alan

ALLEIN see Kilpinen, Yrio, Yksin

ALLEIN GOTT IN DER HOH SEI EHR see
Schutz, Heinrich

ALLELUIA see Chaminade, Cecile

ALLELUIA see Handel, George Frideric

ALLELUIA see Hummel, Ferdinand

ALLELUIA see Moegerle

ALLELUIA see Mozart, Wolfgang Amadeus

ALLELUIA see O'Connor-Morris, G.

ALLELUJA IST EIN FROHLICH GESANG see Grimm, Heinrich

ALLELUJA, LOBET DEN HERRN see Weyrauch, Johannes

ALLELUJAH see Mozart, Wolfgang Amadeus

ALLEMAAL VRIENDJES see Muhler, P. zur

ALLEN
He Did It All For Me (composed with Powell) *sac
solo,pno BENSON S5671-S $1.00 (A377)

Quest For God (composed with Ades)
med-high solo,pno SHAWNEE IA5044 $1.00 (A378)

ALLEN, ANN
Follow After Him
(Fargason, Eddie) med solo,pno CRESPUB CP-S5051 $1.00 (A379)

ALLEN, N.
Absent Love
solo,pno BRANDEN $.50 (A380)

ALLEN, ROBERT E.
Flight, The
high solo,pno GALLEON $.75 (A381)

Sing, Soul Of Mine *sac,Easter
med solo,pno BELWIN $1.50 (A382)

ALLER AUGEN WARTEN AUF DICH see Sibelius, Jean

ALLERSEELEN see Pijper, Willem

ALLERSEELEN see Strauss, Richard

ALLERZIELEN see Bordewijk-Roepman, Johanna

ALLES see Schoenberg, Arnold

ALLES GEBEN DIE GOTTER see Giefer, Willy

ALLES HEEFT ZYN MOND see Beekhuis, Hanna

ALLES IST RICHTIG - ACH, OFFNET EURE AUGEN see Mozart, Wolfgang Amadeus, Aprite Un Po' Quegl' Occhi

ALLES, WAS WAHR IST, KANN LEISE SEIN see Matthus, Siegfried

ALLEVAR UNA BAMBINA see Charpentier, Gustave

ALLEZ AU BOIS see Rimsky-Korsakov, Nikolai

ALLEZ, O VOUS QUE J'AIME see Saint-Saens, Camille

ALLEZ POURTANT, MES CHERS ENFANTS see Saint-Saens, Camille

ALLHELGONADAG see Lassen, Eduard

ALLIER, GABRIEL
Les Pickpockets
solo,pno ENOCH s.p. (A383)

Marche Des Petits Pioupious
solo,acap solo pt ENOCH s.p. (A384)

Marche Des P'tits Pioupious
solo,pno ENOCH s.p. (A385)

Marche Lyonnaise
solo,pno ENOCH s.p. (A386)
solo,acap solo pt ENOCH s.p. (A387)

Marches Lyonnaise
solo,acap ENOCH s.p. see from CHANSONS DE TROUPE (A388)

Pickpockets
solo,acap solo pt ENOCH s.p. (A389)

ALLISON
Through The Years
high solo,pno (F maj) WILLIS $.75 (A390)
low solo,pno (A flat maj) WILLIS $.75 (A391)

ALL'ISONZO see Zafred, Mario

ALLITSEN, FRANCES
Break, Diviner Light
2 soli,pno (E flat maj) BOOSEY $1.75 (A392)

ALLITSEN, FRANCES (cont'd.)
Like As The Hart Desireth (Psalm 62) sac
low solo,pno (C maj) BOOSEY $1.50 (A393)
med solo,pno (E flat maj) BOOSEY $1.50 (A394)
high solo,pno (F maj) BOOSEY $1.50 (A395)

Lord Is My Light (Psalm 27)
2 soli,pno (B flat maj) BOOSEY $1.75 (A396)

Lord Is My Light, The (Psalm 27) sac
high solo,pno (D maj) SCHIRM.G $.85 (A397)
high solo,pno (E flat maj) SCHIRM.G $.85 (A398)
med solo,pno (C maj) SCHIRM.G $.85 (A399)
low solo,pno (B flat maj) SCHIRM.G $.85 (A400)
high solo&low solo,pno SCHIRM.G $1.00 (A401)
solo,pno (available in 4 keys) ASHLEY $.95 (A402)
low solo,pno (B flat maj) BOOSEY $1.25 (A403)
med solo,pno (C maj) BOOSEY $1.25 (A404)
med-high solo,pno (D maj) BOOSEY $1.25 (A405)
high solo,pno (E flat maj) BOOSEY $1.25 (A406)

Lute Player, The
low solo,orch (B min) ASHDOWN s.p., ipr (A407)
med solo,orch (C min) ASHDOWN s.p., ipr (A408)
high solo,orch (D min) ASHDOWN s.p., ipr (A409)

Psalm 27 *see Lord Is My Light, The

Psalm 62 *see Like As The Hart Desireth

Song Of Thanksgiving, A *sac
low solo,pno (E flat maj) BOOSEY $1.50 (A410)
high solo,pno (F maj) BOOSEY $1.50 (A411)

There's A Land *sac
low solo,pno (D maj) BOOSEY $1.50 (A412)
med solo,pno (E flat maj) BOOSEY $1.50 (A413)
high solo,pno (F maj) BOOSEY $1.50 (A414)

ALLMACHT'GE JUNGFRAU see Wagner, Richard

ALLMACHT'GER, HOCH DA DROBEN see Kilpinen, Yrio, Oi Ukko, Ylinen Herra

ALL'MEIN GEDANKEN see Bijvanck, Henk

ALLON, OSCAR
Bells Of Bray
low solo,pno (E flat maj) LEONARD-ENG (A415)
med solo,pno (F maj) LEONARD-ENG (A416)
high solo,pno (G maj) LEONARD-ENG (A417)

ALLONS PLUS VITE see Poulenc, Francis

ALLONS, SOUVENEZ-VOUS DU BAL see Wolff, A.

ALLT UNDER HIMMELENS FASTE see Gladjens Blomster

ALLTAG DER AUGEN see Schollum, Robert

ALMA GRANDE E NOBIL CORE see Mozart, Wolfgang Amadeus

ALMA MIA see Handel, George Frideric

ALMA MIA see Melichar, Wann Kommt Die Stunde?

ALMA REDEMPTORIS MATER see Baumann, Max

ALMA REDEMPTORIS MATER see Harrison, Lou

ALMA REDEMPTORIS MATER see Monferrato, Natale

ALMAN, SAMUEL
Twelve Hebrew Children's Songs *CC12U
[Heb] solo,pno TRANSCON. SP 26 $2.50 (A418)

ALMIGHTY, THE see Schubert, Franz (Peter), Die Allmacht

ALMQUIST, CARL JONAS LOVE (1793-1866)
Songes *CCU
(Mellnas, Arne) solo,pno GEHRMANS s.p. (A419)

ALNAES, EYVIND (1872-1932)
En Grav *Op.41,No.2
see Fire Sanger

En Vaggvislat *Op.41,No.3
see Fire Sanger

En Var - Et Dikt *Op.41,No.4
see Fire Sanger

Fire Sanger
solo,pno MUSIKK s.p.
contains: En Grav, Op.41,No.2; En Vaggvislat, Op.41,No.3; En Var - Et Dikt, Op.41,No.4; Smeden, Op.41,No.1 (A420)

Joy That Dwells In Two Hearts That Love *see Lykken Mellem To Mennesker

Lykken Mellem To Mennesker *Op.26, No.1
"Joy That Dwells In Two Hearts That Love" [Dan/Eng/Ger] med solo,kbd HANSEN-DEN s.p. (A421)

Sailor's Last Voyage, The *Op.17, No.2
[Eng] med solo,kbd HANSEN-DEN s.p. (A422)

Smeden *Op.41,No.1
see Fire Sanger

ALOETTE see Leeuw, Ton de

ALOETTE, VOGHEL CLEIN see Ruyneman, Daniel

ALONE see Martino, Donald

ALONE AT THE DOOR see Hurst, G.

ALONE ON THE STREET see Kusagawa, Kei

ALONG THE FIELD see Vaughan Williams, Ralph

ALONG THE STREAM see Heseltine, Philip

ALONG UNPAVED ROADS *CC8U,folk,US
(Bacon, Ernst) med solo,pno MCA $1.25 (A423)

ALORS, MA SEULE VOLUPTE see Indy, Vincent d'

ALPSKY LOVEC see Tomasek, V.J.

ALS BUBLEIN KLEIN see Nicolai, Otto

ALS DE ZONDAG KOMT see Witte, D.

ALS DIE ALTE MUTTER see Dvorak, Antonin

ALS DIE JUNGE ROSE BLUHTE see Weegenhuise, Johan

ALS EEN DROOM see Leeuw, Ton de

ALS ICH DICH GESEHEN *folk,Russ
[Ger/Russ] solo,pno ZIMMER. 1536 s.p. (A424)

ALS ICH GOTT DEN HERRN GESUCHT see Schutz, Heinrich, Exquisivi Dominum

ALS IK EEN VODELTJE WAS see Henkemans, Hans

ALS IK EEN VOGELTJE WAS see Leeuw, Ton de

ALS IK VAN UW EFFEN VOORHOOFD see Dresden, Sem

ALS IK VAN UW EFFEN VOORHOOFD see Zagwijn, Henri

ALS KIND HEB' ICH OFT see Cuypers, H.

ALS MIR DEIN LIED ERKLANG see Strauss, Richard

ALS 'T BRUINE VELD see Andriessen, K.

ALS 'T KINDJE WAKKER WORDT see Tussenbroek, H. von

ALS 'T ZONDAG IS see Hullebroeck, Em.

ALS UNSER HERR AM KREUZESSTAMM see Thiele, Siegfried

ALS WARE MEINE SEELE EINE FLOTE see Scholz, Erwin Christian

ALS WE ZINGEN ZIJN WE BLIJ see Hoogenberk-Rink, D.

ALS WIJ LATER ELKAAR WEERZIEN see Lilien, Ignace

ALSACE *Fr
(Canteloube, J.) solo,acap DURAND
s.p. see also Anthologie Des Chants
Populaires Francais Tome III (A425)

ALSINA, CARLOS ROQUE (1941-   )
Consecuenza II
solo ZERBONI 7749 s.p.   (A426)

ALSO HAT GOTT DIE WELT GELIEBET see
Buxtehude, Dietrich

ALSO SAGTE MIR DIE MUTTER see Kilpinen,
Yrio, Noin Sanoi Minun Emoni

ALT FOR NORGE see Hauger, Kristian

ALT MAANEN OPREJST STAR see Nielsen,
Carl

ALT-OTTAKRING see Lafite, C.

ALTAGYPTISCHE LIEBESLIEDER see Muller-
Medek, Tilo

ALTAR, THE see Jensen, Ludwig Irgens

ALTBAYERISCHES LIEDERBUCH *CCU
(Huber; Paul) solo,pno SCHOTTS 2599
s.p.   (A427)

ALTDEUTSCHE LIEDER see Lothar, Mark

ALTDEUTSCHES LIEBESLIED see Taubert,
Karl Heinz

ALTDEUTSCHES LIED see Kahn, Erich Itor

ALTDORFER-PASSION see Kropfreiter,
Augustinius Franz

ALTE DEUTSCHE SPRUCHWEISHEIT see
Hubschmann, Werner

ALTE DEUTSCHE WEIHNACHTSGESANGE see
Reimann, Heinrich

ALTE KOLNISCHE KARNEVALSLIEDER *CCU
(Kolle, Alaaf) solo,pno TONGER s.p.
                              (A428)

ALTE PASSIONS- UND OSTERLIEDER AUF FUNF
JAHRHUNDERTEN *CCU,5th cent
(Taubert, Karl Heinz) solo,inst RIES
s.p.   (A429)

ALTE UND NEUE WERKE *see Maitia Nun
Zira, "Adieu Chere Vallee";
Vidalita; Vive Henry IV; Encina,
Juan Del, Romerico, "Rossignol";
Milan, Luis, Toda Mi Vida Os Ame,
"Toute Ma Vie Je Vous Ai Aimee";
Scarlatti, Alessandro, O Cessate Di
Piagarmi, "O Cessez De Me Plaindre"
                              (A430)

ALTE WEIHNACHTSLIEDER see Reutter,
Hermann

ALTE WEISEN NACH G. KELLER, OP. 33,
HEFT I see Pfitzner, Hans

ALTE WEISEN NACH G. KELLER, OP. 33,
HEFT II see Pfitzner, Hans

ALTE WIEGENLIEDER *CCU
(Stern, A.) solo,pno HUG s.p. (A431)

ALTER, I.
Geshem
see Alter, I., Hallel

Hallel *sac,Jew
solo,acap SAC.MUS.PR. 412 contains
also: Tal; Geshem   (A432)

Tal
see Alter, I., Hallel

ALTES LIED see Kilpinen, Yrio, Vanha
Laulu

ALTES MINNELIED see Weegenhuise, Johan

ALTES TRINLIED see Saint-Saens,
Camille, Chanson A Boire Du Vieux
Temps

ALTISSIMA LUCE see Dallapiccola, Luigi

ALTISSIMU see Killmayer, Wilhelm

ALTITALIENISCHE ARIEN *CCU,It
(Behrend, Siegfried) solo,gtr
SIKORSKI 671 s.p.   (A433)

ALTITALIENISCHE ARIEN FUR SOPRAN *CCU
[It/Ger] S solo,pno UNIVER. 3630-31
$4.25 contains works by: Scarlatti;
Gasparini; Caldara; Durante;
Pergolesi and others   (A434)

ALTNIEDERLANDISCHE TRAUERMUSIK *CCU
A solo,fl,ob,English horn,bass clar,
bsn,2trp,2trom,harp,vla,vcl
DEUTSCHER rental contains works by:
Ockeghem; Pres and Gombert   (A435)

ALTO RHAPSODY see Brahms, Johannes

ALTO RHAPSODY see Brahms, Johannes,
Alto Rhapsody

ALTRE CINQUE LIRICHE see Pizzetti,
Ildebrando

ALVAN OCH SNIGELN see Sibelius, Jean

ALVERDEN SKAL SYNGE see Lagergren

ALVIN, ERIK
Mitt Hjarta Behover Ett Litet Barn
solo,pno LUNDQUIST s.p.   (A436)

ALYSSA see Laparra, Raoul

AM ABEND see Rovsing Olsen, Paul

AM ABEND see Scholz, Erwin Christian

AM ABEND DA ES KUHLE WAR see Bach,
Johann Sebastian

AM ALLERHEILIGENTAGE see Kilpinen,
Yrio, Pyhain Miesten Paivana

AM DORFSEE see Reger, Max

AM FELSENUFER TOBEN UNGESTUEM DIE
WELLEN see Rimsky-Korsakov, Nikolai

AM FLUSS see Bijvanck, Henk

AM HAIDEHUGEL GEHT EIN SINGEN see
Kilpinen, Yrio

AM HEILIGEN ABEND see Faisst, Clara

AM HIMMEL SKIZZIERTE LIEDER see
Tausinger, Jan, Cmaranice Po Nebi

AM I IN LOVE? see Peterson, John W.

AM LAUFENDEN BAND see Lilien, Ignace

AM MEER see Schubert, Franz (Peter)

AM MORGEN see Kilpinen, Yrio, Aamulla

AM MORGEN see Kludas, Erich

AM RHEIN, AM DEUTSCHEN RHEIN see Ries,
Franz

AM STRANDE see Brahms, Johannes

AM UFER see Strauss, Richard

AM WALDESSAUME see Bijvanck, Henk

AM WEGRAND see Schoenberg, Arnold

AM WORTHER SEE see Koschat, Thomas

AM YISRAEL CHAI
(Helfman, Max) "Israel Lives On"
[Heb] med solo,pno TRANSCON. IS 503
$.40   (A437)

AMACA see Cairone, Renato

AMADEI, A.
Forgaves
high solo,pno GEHRMANS s.p. (A438)
low solo,pno GEHRMANS s.p.   (A439)

AMALIA RODRIGUEZ see Legley, Victor

AMAMI! see Denza, Luigi

AMANDO TACENDO see Scarlatti, Domenico

AMARILLI see Brumby, Colin

AMARILLI see Caccini, Giulio

AMARILLI MIA BELLA see Caccini, Giulio

AMARILLI MY FAIR ONE see Caccini,
Giulio, Amarilli, Mia Bella

AMARYLLIS see Lessard, John Ayres

AMARYLLIS see Caccini, Giulio, Amarilli
Mia Bella

AMATO BEN see Wolf, Hugo

AMATO, BRUNO
Two Together
S solo,tuba sc SEESAW $3.00 (A440)

AMAZING GRACE *sac,folk/gospel/hymn
solo,pno OAK 060999 $1.50   (A441)
solo,pno ABER.GRP. $1.50   (A442)
(Mercer) solo,pno BENSON S5114-R
$1.00   (A443)

AMAZING GRACE DUETS AND SOLOS *sac,
CCUL
(Carmichael, Ralph) 1-2 soli,pno WORD
37532 $2.50   (A444)

AMAZING GRACE, HOW CAN IT BE? see Fox

AMAZING GRACE, HOW CAN IT BE? see
Newton, John

AMAZING GRACE - UNBOUNDED GRACE see
Newton, John

AMBER AND AMETHYST see Carse, Adam von
Ahn

AMBROSE, [PAUL] (1868-1941)
O Come To My Heart, Lord Jesus *sac
high solo,pno PRESSER $.95   (A445)

AMBROSE, R.S.
One Sweetly Solemn Thought *sac
high solo,pno (E flat maj) SCHIRM.G
$.60   (A446)
med solo,pno (D flat maj) SCHIRM.G
$.60   (A447)
high solo,pno (E flat maj) CENTURY
708 $.40   (A448)

AMBROSI, ALEARCO (1931-   )
Astra
solo,pno ZERBONI s.p.   (A449)

Voices
S,narrator,fl,ob,clar,bsn,vibra,
org,cembalo,vln,vla,vcl,bvl
SONZOGNO rental   (A450)

AMENISSIMI PRATI see Scarlatti,
Domenico

AMERCOEUR see Froidebise, Pierre

AMERICA, COMMERCE AND FREEDOM see
Reinagle, Alexander Robert

AMERICA, GEBENTCHT ZOL ZEIN DUS LAND
*Jew
solo,pno KAMMEN 444 $1.00   (A451)

AMERICA, THE BEAUTIFUL see Ward, Samuel
A.

AMERICAN BELL see Amram, David Werner

AMERICAN COUNTRY HYMN BOOK, THE *sac,
CC100U,hymn
(Brown, Aaron) solo,pno WORD 37717
$5.95   (A452)

AMERICAN FOLK SONGS AND NEGRO SPIRTUALS
*CC20U,folk/spir
solo,pno BROEKMANS B452 s.p. (A453)

AMERICAN HERO, AN see Bowles

AMERICAN LEGENDS *CCU,folk,US
(Siegmeister, Elie) med solo,pno
MARKS $1.00   (A454)

AMERICAN LULLABY see Rich, Gladys

AMERICAN MUSICAL MISCELLANY, THE
*CC111U,18th cent
DA CAPO $15.00   (A455)

AMERIKKA LAULAA *CCU,US
(Meri) solo,pno FAZER F 3162 s.p.
                              (A456)

AMERTUME see Chaminade, Cecile

AMERTUME see Cuvillier, Charles

AMES, W.T.
Minor Bird, A
med solo,pno AMP $.75 see from Two
Songs On Texts By Robert Frost
                              (A457)

Patch Of Old Snow, A
med solo,pno AMP $.75 see from Two
Songs On Texts By Robert Frost
                              (A458)

Two Songs On Texts By Robert Frost
*see Minor Bird, A; Patch Of Old
Snow, A   (A459)

AMES, WILLIAM
Among The Gods
S solo,clar,2vln,vla,vcl sc
AM.COMP.AL. $5.50, ipa   (A460)

Dust Of Snow
med solo,pno SEESAW $1.00   (A461)

Judgment
med solo,pno PRESSER $.75   (A462)

AMETHYSTES see Delage, Maurice

AMEZAGA, T.H.DE
Trois Madrigaux A Trois Voix *CC3U,
madrigal
3 soli/3 female soli/3 male soli,
acap DURAND s.p.   (A463)

AMHERST-WEBBER
La Matinee Champetre
solo,pno/inst DURAND s.p.   (A464)

AMI PRINTEMPS see Delmet, Paul

AMIRIAN, M.T.
Les Ailes Victorieuses
solo,pno/inst DURAND s.p. (A465)
[Fr] solo,acap oct DURAND s.p.
(A466)

AMIS, LE GRAND JOUR EST VENU see
Messager, Andre

AMMERS, P. VAN
'T Is Feest In Huis
solo,pno BROEKMANS 691 s.p. (A467)

AMMERSEE see Trunk, Richard

AMNIS AEVI OMNIPOTENS see Staeps, Hans
Ulrich

AMONG SHADOWS see Golde, Walter

AMONG THE BAMBOOS see Hurst, G.

AMONG THE FLOWERS see Scek, Breda, Med
Rozami

AMONG THE GODS see Ames, William

AMOR see Strauss, Richard

AMOR see Steenhuis, Francois

AMOR COMMANDA see Handel, George
Frideric

AMOR JESU see Weiland, Johannes Julius

AMOR SE PAGA see Sas, Andres

AMOR SUMMA INJURIA see Albeniz, Isaac

AMOR TI VIETA see Giordano, Umberto

AMOR TI VIETA see Verdi, Giuseppe

AMOR UND PSYCHE see d'Albert, Eugene
Francis Charles

AMOR Y ODIO see Granados, Enrique

AMORE see Faccenda, O.

AMORE FIDENTE see Veneziani, Vittore,
Amour Joyeux

AMORE TRADITORE see Bach, Johann
Sebastian

AMOROSA see De Lara, Isadore

AMOROSA see Hagg, Gustaf Wilhelm

AMOROSO see Chaminade, Cecile

AMOROUS LINE, THE see Pouhe, Joseph
Frank

AMORS, E QUE-US ES VAJAIRE? see
Ventadorn, Bernart de

AMOUR see Arrieu, Claude

AMOUR see Binet, Jean

AMOUR, AMOUR, QUEL EST DONC TON POUVOIR
see Messager, Andre

AMOUR, APPROCHE ET PRENDS MON AME see
Mozart, Wolfgang Amadeus

AMOUR AU VAINQUEUR see Filipucci, Edm.

AMOUR BRISE see Gillet, Ernest

AMOUR CACHE see Mendelssohn-Bartholdy,
Felix

AMOUR CELESTE see Liszt, Franz, Hohe
Liebe

AMOUR D'ANTAN see Chausson, Ernest

AMOUR D'AUTOMNE see Chaminade, Cecile

AMOUR DE MOY see Vaughan Williams,
Ralph

AMOUR ET DOULEUR see Gelli, E.

AMOUR ET GRAMMAIRE see Passani, Emile

AMOUR FATAL see Godard, Benjamin Louis
Paul

AMOUR INFIDELE see Delmet, Paul

AMOUR INVISIBLE see Chaminade, Cecile

AMOUR JALOUX see Fontenailles, H. de

AMOUR JOYEUX see Veneziani, Vittore

AMOUR PARTOUT see Canal, Marguerite

AMOUR POUR AMOUR see Schumann, Robert
(Alexander)

AMOUR, QUAND TU VEUX NOUS SURPRENDRE
see Rameau, Jean-Philippe

AMOUR QUE VEUX-TU see Lully (Lulli),
Jean-Baptiste

AMOUR, SORS POUR JAMAIS see Gluck,
Christoph Willibald Ritter von

AMOUR VAINQUEUR see Tremisot, Ed.

AMOUR VIENS AIDER see Saint-Saens,
Camille

AMOUR VIRIL see Saint-Saens, Camille

AMOUR VRAI, SOURCE PURE see Saint-
Saens, Camille

AMOUREUSE see Berger, Rod.

AMOUREUSES see Poulenc, Francis

AMOUREUX SEPARES see Roussel, Albert

AMOURS DE MARIE see Busser, Henri-Paul

AMOURS FLETRIES see Berger, Rod.

AMOURS LIBRES see Sureau-Bellet, J.

AMOURS LOINTAINES see Cuvillier,
Charles

AMPHION see Kox, Hans

AMPHION ANGELICUS see Blow, John

AMPHION ANGLICUS see Blow, John

AMPLE MAKE THIS BED see Horvit, Michael
M.

AMRAM, DAVID WERNER (1930-)
American Bell
narrator,fl,ob,clar,bsn,2horn,trp,
trom,tuba,strings PETERS 6678
rental (A468)

Blow Blow Thou Winter Wind
solo,pno PETERS 66593 rental (A469)

Five Shakespearean Songs (from
Twelfth Night) CC5U
solo,pno PETERS 6691A rental (A470)

Three Songs For America *CC3U
Bar solo,5winds,4strings s.p. sc
PETERS 66469, voc sc PETERS
66469A (A471)

Who Is Sylvia?
solo,pno PETERS 66592 rental (A472)

AMSTELDAM see Schouwman, Hans

AMSTERDAM see Koetsier, Jan

AMSTERDAM see Mulder, Ernest W.

AMSTERDAM see Voormolen, Alexander
Nicolas

AN ANGEL SPEAKS TO THE SHEPHERDS see
Rorem, Ned

AN CHLOE see Mozart, Wolfgang Amadeus

AN DEN ABEND see Sibelius, Jean,
Illalle

AN DEN ABENDSTERN see Schumann, Robert
(Alexander)

AN DEN SCHLAF see Wolf, Hugo

AN DEN SCHMERZ see Weingartner, (Paul)
Felix

AN DEN SONNENSCHEIN see Schumann,
Robert (Alexander)

AN DEN UFERN DES JORDAN see Schumann,
Georg

AN DEN VETTER see Haydn, (Franz) Joseph

AN DEN WASSERN ZU BABEL see Krieger,
Johann Philipp

AN DER SCHONEN BLAUEN DONAU see
Strauss, Johann

AN DIE BARONIN COLOMBINE see Bijvanck,
Henk

AN DIE ENTFERNTE see Bijvanck, Henk

AN DIE FERNE GELIEBTE see Beethoven,
Ludwig van

AN DIE GELIEBTE see Mulder, Ernest W.

AN DIE HOFFNUNG see Beethoven, Ludwig
van

AN DIE HOFFNUNG see Reger, Max

AN DIE LIEBE see Trunk, Richard

AN DIE MUSIK see Schubert, Franz
(Peter)

AN DIE NACHT see Strauss, Richard

AN DIE NACHTIGALL see Brahms, Johannes

AN DIE NACHTIGALL see Schumann, Robert
(Alexander)

AN DIE PARZEN see Rovsing Olsen, Paul

AN DIE SONNE see Schmalstich, Clemens

AN DOLOR AMOR SIT see Andriessen,
Juriaan

AN EIN VEILCHEN see Brahms, Johannes

AN EINE ROSE see Knab, Armin

AN EN VISA VILL JAG SJUNGA see
Jarnefelt, Armas, Viel' Ois Viritta
Tieossani

AN ERINNERUNGSEE'S STRAND see Nielsen,
Carl, Erindringens So

AN ESKIMO LULLABY
see Six Regional Canadian Folksongs

AN FRIGGA see Sibelius, Jean, Till
Frigga

AN I MINNET JAG ATERVANDER see
Merikanto, Oskar, Vallinkorvan
Laulu

AN JENEM TAG see Marschner, Heinrich
(August)

AN KORPENS VINGE MIN TANKE TA'R see
Peterson-Berger, (Olof) Wilhelm

AN MARIA see Holler, Karl

AN MATHILDE see Dallapiccola, Luigi

AN' O FOR ANE AND TWENTY, TAM *folk,
Scot
solo,pno (A min/B min) PATERSON FS129
s.p. (A473)

AN OLD SAGA see Hemberg, Eskil, En
Gammal Saga

AN OUTWARD SAIL see Besly, Maurice

AN SCHWYZERBUEB see Angerer, Gottfried

ANA, D'
D'un Desastre Obscure
Mez solo,clar UNIVER. 15175 $6.00
(A474)

ANA DODI see Helfman, Max

ANACREON'S DEFEAT see Purcell, Henry

ANACREON'S GRAVE see Wolf, Hugo,
Anakreon's Grab

ANACREONTICA see Toldra, Eduardo

ANAKREON'S GRAB see Wolf, Hugo

ANAKREONTIKA see Gursching, Albrecht

ANCELIN, PIERRE (1934-)
Poemes De Guerre *CC3U
Bar solo,fl,ob,clar,bsn,2horn,trp,
trom,harp,cel,perc,strings JOBERT
sc rental, voc sc s.p. (A475)

ANCHOR LINE see Beekhuis, Hanna

ANCHORS WEIGHED, THE see Braham

ANCIENT CHURCH see Kilpinen, Yrio,
Vanha Kirkko

ANCIENT GREEK SONGS see Ruyneman,
Daniel

ANCIENT VOICES OF CHILDREN see Crumb,
George

ANCIS, SOLOMON
God Of Our Fathers *see R'tzeh

R'tzeh *sac
"God Of Our Fathers" [Heb/Eng] med
solo,pno TRANSCON. WJ 418 $.60
(A476)

ANCOR SON IO TUTT'ATTONITA see
Massenet, Jules

ANCORA DUE POESIE DI APOLLINAIRE see
    Nielsen, Riccardo

...AND BE MY LOVE see Reif, Paul

AND I AM OLD TO KNOW see Binkerd,
    Gordon

AND IT WAS STORMY WEATHER see Adler,
    Samuel

AND JESUS CAME see Stolba

AND JESUS SAID: IT IS FINISHED see
    Antes, John

AND LET ME A CANIKIN CLINK see
    Castelnuovo-Tedesco, Mario

AND ONE CAME BACK ALONE see Harrhy,
    Edith

AND RUTH SAID see Avshalomov, Jacob

AND SO, GOODBYE see Charles, Ernest

AND STILL I SMILE see Gerald

AND THE STARS SHONE BRIGHTLY see
    Puccini, Giacomo, E Lucevan Le
    Stelle   /

AND THE WAVES STOOD STILL see Chajes,
    Julius

AND THERE ARE TEARS see Bantock,
    Granville

AND THERE WERE SHEPHERDS ABIDING IN THE
    FIELD see LaForge, Frank

AND THERE WILL BE SIGNS see Bender, Jan

AND THERE YOU STOOD see Weigl, Karl

AND THIS SHALL BE FOR MUSIC... see
    Cory, George

AND THOU SHALT LOVE THE LORD see
    Kaufman, H.H.

AND WITH SONGS I WILL CELEBRATE see
    Marcello, Benedetto

AND YOU HAVE GONE see Bar-Am, Benjamin

ANDA see Lagercrantz, Wilhelm

ANDALUSIA see Lecuona, Ernesto

ANDALUSIANA see Reutter, Hermann

ANDANTE RELIGIOSO see Marttinen, Tauno

ANDANTINO see Lemare

ANDAVA IL PAESE see Davico, Vincenzo

ANDERE KERNSPRUCHE see Rosenmuller,
    Johann

ANDERS, E.
    Flotenlieder Fur Sopran, Flote Und
        Klavier *Op.109, CCU
    solo,pno ZIMMER. rental   (A477)

ANDERSON
    Little Jesus Came To Town *sac,Xmas
    solo,pno HARRIS $.75   (A478)

ANDERSON, MARION
    Little Piggy Porker
    solo,pno CRAMER   (A479)

ANDERSON, THOMAS J.
    Beyond Silence
        T solo,clar,trom,vcl,vla,pno sc
        AM.COMP.AL. $7.70   (A480)

    Block Songs *CCU
        med solo, children's toys sc
        AM.COMP.AL. $4.95   (A481)

    Horizons '76
        S solo,3fl,3ob,3clar,2sax,3bsn,
        4horn,3trp,3trom,tuba,pno/cel,
        harp,strings,timp sc AM.COMP.AL.
        $39.60   (A482)

    In Memoriam Malcolm X
        med solo,pic,2fl,2ob,2clar,al-sax,
        2bsn,4horn,3trp,3trom,tuba,pno,
        2perc,strings sc AM.COMP.AL.
        $12.10   (A483)

    Variations On A Theme By M.B. Tolson
        *cant
        S solo,vln,vcl,al-sax,trp,trom,pno
        sc AM.COMP.AL. $16.50   (A484)

ANDERSON, WILLIAM H.
    Fairy Cobbler
    solo,pno (D maj) LESLIE 7007 (A485)

ANDERSON, WILLIAM H. (cont'd.)

    Hospitality *sac
        low solo,pno (C min) LESLIE 7026
                                    (A486)
        high solo,pno (D min) LESLIE 7026
                                    (A487)

    Last Year
        solo,pno (F sharp min) LESLIE 7011
                                    (A488)

    Litany, A *sac
        low solo,pno (D min) LESLIE 7009
                                    (A489)
        high solo,pno (F min) LESLIE 7010
                                    (A490)

    Little Jesus Came To Town *sac
        solo,pno (A flat maj) LESLIE 7012
                                    (A491)

    Memory, A
        low solo,pno (E maj) LESLIE 7013
                                    (A492)
        high solo,pno (G maj) LESLIE 7013
                                    (A493)

    Old Shepherd's Prayer, The *sac
        solo,pno (D min) LESLIE 7002 (A494)

    Sleep Little Jesus *sac,Xmas
        low solo,pno (C maj) LESLIE 7004
                                    (A495)
        high solo,pno (E flat maj) LESLIE
        7004   (A496)

    Song Of Mary *sac,Xmas
        solo,pno (A min) LESLIE 7031 (A497)

    Spring Magic
        solo,pno (F maj) LESLIE 7006 (A498)

    Sweet Afton
        solo,pno (D flat maj) LESLIE 7001
                                    (A499)

    To A Girl On Her Birthday
        low solo,pno (F maj) LESLIE 7025
                                    (A500)
        high solo,pno (A flat maj) LESLIE
        7025   (A501)

ANDLIGA SANGER, HEFT 1
    (Lilliestierna, Sven) solo,pno
    LUNDQUIST s.p.
    contains: Hos Gud Ar Idel Gladje;
        Jesus Av Nasaret Gar Har Fram;
        Nar Han Kommer; Nar Jag I Tron
        Min Jesus Ser; Var Jag Gar, I
        Skogar, Berg Och Dalar   (A502)

ANDLIGA SANGER, HEFT 2
    (Lilliestierna, Sven) solo,pno
    LUNDQUIST s.p.
    contains: Ar Det Sant Att Jesus Ar
        Min Broder; Blott En Dag, Ett
        Ogonblick I Sander; Hav Tro Pa
        Gud; Pa Vagen Uppat; Vit Sasom
        Sno   (A503)

ANDLIGA SANGER, HEFT 3
    (Lilliestierna, Sven) solo,pno
    LUNDQUIST s.p.
    contains: Oppna Hjartats Dorr;
        Sjalens Langtan; Trons Frid;
        Tryggare Kan Ingen Vara; Varje
        Steg Mig Jesus Leder   (A504)

ANDLIGA SANGER, HEFT 4
    (Lilliestierna, Sven) solo,pno
    LUNDQUIST s.p.
    contains: Du, Som Av Karlek Dog;
        Ga, Sion, Din Konung Att Mota;
        Jag Ar En Gast Och Framling;
        Jesus Kar, Ga Ej Forbi Mig;
        Loftena Kunna Ej Svika   (A505)

ANDONAIS see Saxe, Serge

ANDRASOVAN, TIBOR (1917-   )
    Ej, Pada, Pada Rosicka
        coloratura sop,pno SLOV.HUD.FOND
        s.p.   (A506)

    Este Raz Sa Obzriet' Mam
        coloratura sop,pno SLOV.HUD.FOND
        s.p.   (A507)

    Hviezdy Nad Prahou
        solo,pno SLOV.HUD.FOND s.p. (A508)

    Ozveny Z Povstaleckych Hor
        narrator&ST soli,pno SLOV.HUD.FOND
        s.p.   (A509)

    Spomienka Na Moskvu
        solo,pno SLOV.HUD.FOND s.p. (A510)

    Zo Slnecnej Gruzie
        high solo,pno SLOV.HUD.FOND s.p.
                                    (A511)

ANDRE, JOSE
    Al Pampero
        [Span] solo,pno RICORDI-ARG BA 3551
        s.p.   (A512)

    Hueya
        [Span] solo,pno RICORDI-ARG BA 3552
        s.p.   (A513)

ANDREAE, VOLKMAR (1879-1962)
    Inukerli
    solo,pno HUG s.p.   (A514)

ANDREE
    I Templet
    solo,pno LUNDQUIST s.p.   (A515)

    Vildfagel
    solo,pno LUNDQUIST s.p.   (A516)

ANDREE, ELFRIDA
    Svanen
    solo,pno,vln GEHRMANS s.p.   (A517)

ANDREN, ADOLF
    Reformationsaria *sac
    solo,pno GEHRMANS s.p.   (A518)

    Vid Fragornas Port
    solo,pno GEHRMANS s.p.   (A519)

ANDREN TONT DIE KIRCHENGLOCKE see
    Kilpinen, Yrio, Muut Kuuli
    Kirkonkellon

ANDREP-NORDIN, BIRGER
    I Guds Hander *sac
    solo,pno GEHRMANS s.p.   (A520)

ANDREW MINE, JASPER MINE
    see Three Moravian Carols

ANDREWS, DAVID
    Shall I Compare Thee To A Summer's
        Day?
        high solo,pno EMI s.p.   (A521)
        solo,pno ALBERT AE140 s.p. (A522)

ANDREWS, MARK (1875-1939)
    Build Thee More Stately Mansions
        *sac
        high solo,pno (E flat maj) SCHIRM.G
        $.75   (A523)

    I Heard The Bells On Christmas Day
        med solo,pno (C maj) GALAXY
        1.0984.7 $1.00   (A524)

    In Flanders' Field
        high solo,pno (E flat maj) WILLIS
        $.60   (A525)
        low solo,pno (D flat maj) WILLIS
        $.60   (A526)

    Sea Fever
        low solo,pno (D maj) SCHIRM.G $.85
                                    (A527)
    Shadow Of Thy Wings, The *sac
        high solo,pno BELWIN $1.50 (A528)

ANDRIESSEN, HENDRIK (1892-1964)
    A Ces Reines
        Mez solo,pno DONEMUS s.p. (A529)

    Ballade Van Den Merel
        narrator,fl,2ob,clar,bsn,strings
        DONEMUS s.p.   (A530)

    Bercuese Uit Philomela
        S solo,3fl,2ob,2clar,2bsn,4horn,
        2trp,2trom,timp,harp,strings
        DONEMUS   (A531)

    Cantilena Della Madre Per Il Suo
        Bimbo Malato
        Mez solo,pno DONEMUS s.p. (A532)

    Cantique Spirituel *sac
        S solo,pno/org ALSBACH s.p. (A533)
        S/T solo,strings DONEMUS   (A534)

    Chaque Heure, Ou Je Songe
        Mez solo,pno ALSBACH s.p. (A535)

    Crucem Tuam *sac
        A solo,strings DONEMUS   (A536)

    De Spiegel Uit Venetie
        "Mirror From Venice, The" solo,orch
        voc sc DONEMUS s.p.   (A537)

    Een Schepping
        S solo,pno BANK s.p.   (A538)

    Erwacht
        med solo,pno ALSBACH s.p. see also
        Zwei Lieder   (A539)

    Fiat Domine *sac
        S solo,pno/org ROSSUM s.p. (A540)
        Mez solo,strings DONEMUS   (A541)

    Gebet An Den Sonntag
        med solo,pno ALSBACH s.p. see also
        Zwei Lieder   (A542)

    Harmonie Du Soir
        Mez solo,pno ALSBACH s.p. (A543)

    L'attente Mystique
        S solo,2fl,2ob,2clar,2bsn,4horn,
        strings DONEMUS   (A544)

ANDRIESSEN, HENDRIK (cont'd.)

L'aube Spirituelle
  Mez solo,2fl,2ob,2clar,2bsn,2horn,
  strings DONEMUS   (A545)

Le Chemin De La Croix *sac
  T solo,pno DONEMUS s.p.   (A546)

Le Dormeur Du Val
  see Trois Pastorales

Les Larmes
  Mez solo,pno ALSBACH s.p.   (A547)

L'invitaion Au Voyage
  Mez solo,2fl,2ob,2clar,2bsn,2horn,
  strings DONEMUS   (A548)

Loomheid Is Op Uw Hart
  S solo,pno ALPHENAAR s.p.   (A549)
  solo,pno BROEKMANS 236 s.p. (A550)

Magna Res Est Amor
  S solo,pno/org ROSSUM s.p.   (A551)
  S solo,2fl,2ob,2clar,2bsn,4horn,
  strings DONEMUS   (A552)

Maria Schone Vrouwe *sac
  Mez solo,pno BANK s.p.   (A553)

Maria Zart Von Edler
  Mez solo,strings DONEMUS   (A554)

Maria Zart Von Edler Art *sac
  Mez solo,org ALSBACH s.p.   (A555)

Miroir De Peine
  S solo,org ROSSUM s.p.   (A556)
  S solo,strings DONEMUS   (A557)

Mirror From Venice, The *see De
  Spiegel Uit Venetie

O Sacrum Convivium *sac
  S solo,org DONEMUS s.p.   (A558)

Quand Ton Sourire Me Surprit
  S solo,pno DONEMUS s.p.   (A559)

Sensation
  see Trois Pastorales

Tete De Faune
  see Trois Pastorales

Three Romantic Songs *CC3U
  Mez solo,fl,ob,pno DONEMUS s.p.
                               (A560)

Tractus: Qui Habitat
  ST soli,org ROSSUM s.p.   (A561)

Trois Pastorales
  Mez solo,pno ROSSUM s.p.
    contains: Le Dormeur Du Val;
    Sensation; Tete De Faune   (A562)

Trois Pastorales *CC3U
  (Flothius, Marius) solo,orch
  DONEMUS s.p.   (A563)

Trois Sonnets Spirituels *sac,CC3U
  high solo,org DONEMUS s.p.   (A564)

Vijf Nageldeuntjes *CC5U
  S/T solo,pno DONEMUS s.p.   (A565)

Zwei Lieder
  med solo,pno ALSBACH s.p.
    contains & see also: Erwacht;
    Gebet An Den Sonntag   (A566)

ANDRIESSEN, JURIAAN (1925-   )
  An Dolor Amor Sit
    low solo,hpsd DONEMUS s.p. (A567)

Ariette
  see Four English Songs

Aspatia Song
  see Four English Songs

Cancion Zamora
  see Cinco Canciones Espagnoles

Cinco Canciones Espagnoles
  Bar solo,pno DONEMUS s.p.
    contains: Cancion Zamora; La
    Eremita De San Simon; Romanza
    Del Prisonero; Serenade; Si Los
    Delfines   (A568)

Epitaph For Louis Van Tulder
  ST soli,clar,pno DONEMUS s.p.
                               (A569)

Four English Songs
  T solo,pno DONEMUS s.p.
    contains: Ariette; Aspatia Song;
    Honest Fellow, The; Julia (A570)

Honest Fellow, The
  see Four English Songs

Julia
  see Four English Songs

ANDRIESSEN, JURIAAN (cont'd.)

Kerstlied *sac,canon
  2 female soli,pno/org DONEMUS s.p.
                               (A571)

La Eremita De San Simon
  see Cinco Canciones Espagnoles

Phoenix
  S solo,pno DONEMUS s.p.   (A572)

Romanza Del Prisonero
  see Cinco Canciones Espagnoles

Serenade
  see Cinco Canciones Espagnoles

Si Los Delfines
  see Cinco Canciones Espagnoles

To Wet A Widow's Eye *CC5U
  AT soli,clar,perc, viola da gamba
  DONEMUS s.p.   (A573)

Vier Gedichten Van Revius *CC4U
  med solo,pno/org/cembalo/harp
  DONEMUS s.p.   (A574)

Vijf Nageldeuntjes *CC5U
  S/T solo,4strings DONEMUS s.p.
                               (A575)

ANDRIESSEN, K.
  Als 'T Bruine Veld
    see Twaalf Gedichten, Band 1

Eerste Blik
  see Vier Liederen, Band 1

Geef Nu Ik In Twijfel Kniel
  see Twee Liederen

Het Volkslied
  see Twaalf Gedichten, Band 1

Liedje
  see Vier Liederen, Band 2

Mijn Kleen, Kleen Sochterke
  see Twaalf Gedichten, Band 1

Mijn Ventje Slaapt
  see Twaalf Gedichten, Band 1

Rosa Mystica
  see Vier Liederen, Band 1

Twaalf Gedichten, Band 1
  solo,pno ALSBACH s.p.
    contains: Als 'T Bruine Veld; Het
    Volkslied; Mijn Kleen, Kleen
    Sochterke; Mijn Ventje Slaapt;
    Wij Zingen Wij De Poeten   (A576)

Twee Liederen
  solo,pno ALSBACH s.p.
    contains: Geef Nu Ik In Twijfel
    Kniel; Werkelijkheid   (A577)

Vier Liederen, Band 1
  solo,pno ALSBACH s.p.
    contains: Eerste Blik; Rosa
    Mystica   (A578)

Vier Liederen, Band 2
  solo,pno ALSBACH s.p.
    contains: Liedje; Zomerliedje
                               (A579)

Werkelijkheid
  see Twee Liederen

Wij Zingen Wij De Poeten
  see Twaalf Gedichten, Band 1

Zomerliedje
  see Vier Liederen, Band 2

ANDRIESSEN, LOUIS (1939-   )
  Nocturnen
    S solo,2fl,2ob,2clar,2bsn,2horn,
    2trp,timp,perc,cel,harp,pno,
    strings DONEMUS   (A580)

ANDRIESSEN, N.H.
  Holland
    S/T solo,pno ALSBACH s.p. (A581)
    A/Bar solo,pno ALSBACH s.p.(A582)

ANDROMACHE'S FAREWELL see Barber,
  Samuel

ANDROZZO
  If I Can Help Somebody *sac
    solo,pno BENSON S6464-S $1.25
                               (A583)

ANDROZZO, ALMA BAZEL (1912-   )
  How I Want The Lord To Find Me *sac
    solo,pno SINGSPIR 7003 $1.00 (A584)

Live In The Sunlight
  solo,pno (E flat maj) BOOSEY $1.50
                               (A585)

ANER
  Tistel Och Lavendel
    solo,pno LUNDQUIST s.p.   (A586)

ANERCA see Garant, S.

ANERIO, GIOVANNI FRANCESCO (1567-1630)
  Drei Geistliche Konzerte *sac,CC3U,
  concerto
    (Ewerhart, Rudolf) [Lat] B solo,
    cont BIELER CS 14 s.p.   (A587)

ANFANG UND ENDE see Koetsier, Jan

ANGE ADORABLE see Gounod, Charles
  Francois

ANGE OU FEMME see Mendelssohn-
  Bartholdy, Felix

ANGEL see Lasala, Angel

ANGEL, THE see Wagner, Richard, Der
  Engel

ANGEL EROS see Harvey, Jonathan

ANGELIC SONG see Hovhaness, Alan

ANGELICA see Pizzetti, Ildebrando

ANGELO CASTO E BEL see Donizetti,
  Gaetano

ANGELS ARE STOOPING see Besly, Maurice

ANGELS EVER BRIGHT AND FAIR see Handel,
  George Frideric

ANGELS GUARD THEE see Godard, Benjamin
  Louis Paul, Cache Dans Cet Asile

ANGELS KEEP WATCHING OVER ME *sac,
  gospel
    solo,pno ABER.GRP. $1.50   (A588)

ANGELS OF PEACE see Fromm, Herbert

ANGELS OF THE LIGHT see Borowski, Felix

ANGELS OF THE MIND see Bliss, Sir
  Arthur

ANGEL'S SERENADE see Braga, Gaetana, La
  Serenata

ANGELS WITH SHINING FACES see Green,
  Dorothy M.

ANGELUS see Cuvillier, Charles

ANGELUS see Herbert, Victor

ANGELUS see Ple, Simone

ANGELUS see Saint-Saens, Camille

ANGELUS, THE see Russell, Kennedy

ANGELUS DOMINI APPARUIT see Hindemith,
  Paul

ANGELUS SILESIUS LIEDERBUCH see Ahrens,
  Joseph

ANGERER, GOTTFRIED
  An Schwyzerbueb
    solo,pno HUG s.p.   (A589)

  Schweizerschutzenlied
    solo,pno HUG s.p.   (A590)

ANGERER, PAUL (1927-   )
  Drei Narrenlieder Aus Shakespeares
  "Was Ihr Wollt" *CC3U
    Bar solo,pno DOBLINGER 08 630 $2.25
                               (A591)

ANGES, ARCHANGES see Handel, George
  Frideric

ANGES DU PARADIS see Gounod, Charles
  Francois

ANGEST see Wohlfart, Karl

ANGOISSE see Caplet, Andre

ANGRY WIFE, THE see Cannon, (Jack)
  Phillip, La Mal Mariee

ANGST see Voormolen, Alexander Nicolas

ANGSTWAGEN see Yttrehus, Rolv

ANGUISHED, THE see Birch, Robert
  Fairfax

ANI CHAVATSELOT HASHARON see Bugatch,
  Samuel

ANI LABUF, ANI LUNA see Burian, Emil
  Frantisek

ANI MRACKU NA OBZORU see Valek, Jiri

ANIMA MEA LIQUEFACTA EST see Schutz,
  Heinrich

ANIMA MIA SPERANZA see Caggiano,
    Roberto

ANIMAALINEN HYMNI see Bergman, Erik

ANIMAL CRACKERS see Hageman, Richard

ANIMALISK HYMN see Bergman, Erik,
    Sarastus

ANIME DI CAMPANE see Toschi, Pietro

ANIMUS TWO see Druckman, Jacob

ANJOU   *Fr
    (Canteloube, J.) solo,acap DURAND
    s.p. see also Anthologie Des Chants
    Populaires Francais Tome IV   (A592)

ANJOU, P. D'
    Det Brister En Strang
        solo,pno (A maj) LUNDQUIST s.p.
                                    (A593)

    Etre Jeune
        solo,pno OUVRIERES s.p.   (A594)

    Le Foyer
        solo,pno OUVRIERES s.p.   (A595)

    Sov, Sov Hjartebarn
        solo,pno LUNDQUIST s.p.   (A596)

    Tindrande
        see NY SAMLING SANGDUETTER, HEFT 1

    Tindrande Stjarnor
        MezBar soli,pno LUNDQUIST s.p. see
        from Tva Duetter   (A597)

    Tva Duetter   *see Tindrande Stjarnor
                                    (A598)

    Vita Liljor
        solo,pno LUNDQUIST s.p.   (A599)

ANNA, ARMAS, SIRPIN OLLA see Sonninen,
    Ahti

ANNA HELENES VUGGEVISE see Kjeldaas,
    Arnljot

ANNA, KIESUS, ANATAJALLE see Kilpinen,
    Yrio

ANNA MAGDALENA BACH'S MUSIC BOOK see
    Bach, Johann Sebastian

ANNA MAGDALENA NOTENBUCH see Bach,
    Johann Sebastian

ANNA-MI see Palmgren, Selim

ANNABEL LEE see Shaw, Martin

ANNABELLE LEE see Leslie, Henry David

ANNAS ET LE LEPREUX see Woronoff,
    Wladmir

ANNAS SNACKSKRIN see Lagerheim-Romare,
    Margit

ANNCHENS LIEDER see Novak, V.

ANNE, MA BIEN-AIMEE see Saint-Saens,
    Camille

ANNE-MARIE see Korling

ANNE RUTLEDGE see Raphling, Sam

ANNETTE see Godard, Benjamin Louis Paul

ANNIE see Binet, Jean

ANNIE see Michel, Ch.-H.

ANNIE LAURIE   *folk,Scot
    solo,pno (B flat maj/C maj) PATERSON
    FS4 s.p.   (A600)
    (Lehmann, Liza) low solo,pno (B flat
    maj) ASHDOWN s.p.   (A601)
    (Lehmann, Liza) med solo,pno (C maj)
    ASHDOWN s.p.   (A602)
    (Lehmann, Liza) med-high solo,pno (D
    maj) ASHDOWN s.p.   (A603)
    (Lehmann, Liza) high solo,pno (E flat
    maj) ASHDOWN s.p.   (A604)

ANNIVERSARIO see Di Martino, Aladino

ANNIVERSARY IN A COUNTRY CEMETERY see
    Diamond, David

ANNORSTADES VALS see Wiren, Dag Ivar

ANNOVAZZI, N.
    Dormi Fanciullo.. Dormi!
        solo,pno BONGIOVANI 1603 s.p.
                                    (A605)

ANN'S CRADLE SONG see Gibbs, Cecil
    Armstrong

AN'O, MY EPPIE see Kennedy-Fraser,
    Marjory

ANONIMI VARI DEI SECOLI XVII E XVIII,
    PART I   *CC7L,17-18th cent
    (Vatelli, F.) solo,pno BONGIOVANI 775
    s.p. contains works by: Del
    Violone, G.; Strozzi, B.; Marcello,
    B.; Franchi, G.P. and others   (A606)

ANONIMI VARI DEI SECOLI XVII E XVIII,
    PART II   *17-18th cent
    (Vatelli, F.) solo,pno cmplt ed
    BONGIOVANI 772 s.p.
    contains: Anonymous, Ah! Che Si
    Gran Martoro; Anonymous, Son Come
    Farfalletta; Porpora, Nicola
    Antonio, Chieggio Al Lido   (A607)

ANONYME see Middeleer, Jean De

ANONYMOUS
    A Vous, Vierge De Doucour   *sac,mot,
    14th cent
        OISEAU s.p.   (A608)

    Ah! Che Si Gran Martoro
        see ANONIMI VARI DEI SECOLI XVII E
        XVIII, PART II

    Black Eyes
        [Russ/Eng] med solo,kbd CHESTER
        s.p.   (A609)

    Brother Soldiers, All Hail!
        med solo,pno PRESSER $.75 (A610)

    Czechoslovakian Suite   *CC6U
        (Bresgen) [Czech/Ger] med solo,gtr
        WILHELM. s.p.   (A611)

    De Ce Sejour   *sac,concerto,18th cent
        (Flothius, Marius) [Fr] S solo,fl,
        pno BROEKMANS B57 s.p. contains
        also: Que Ces Lieux   (A612)

    Dindirindin   *16th cent
        (Pujol) [Fr] med solo,gtr ESCHIG
        E1301 $.90   (A613)

    En Avila Mis Ojos   *16th cent
        (Pujol) [Span] high solo,gtr ESCHIG
        E1319 $.90   (A614)

    Favorit Glee, A   *18-19th cent
        3 soli,pno HEUWEKE. 101 s.p. (A615)

    Favorit Song, A
        solo,pno HEUWEKE. 102 s.p. (A616)

    Have You Seene But A Whyte Lillie
    Grow?
        see DREI ARIEN AUS DEM SEIBZEHNTEN
        JAHRHUNDERT

    Here Amid The Shady Woods
        solo,2vln,vla,vcl,pno HEUWEKE. 104
        s.p.   (A617)

    Intonuit De Coelo   *sac,Span
        (Ewerhart, Rudolf) S/T solo,cont
        BIELER CS 35 s.p.   (A618)

    Jefferson And Liberty
        med solo,pno PRESSER $.75 (A619)

    Lamentation De La Vierge Au Pied De
    La Croix   *13th cent
        (Rokseth, Yvonne) S solo,acap
        OISEAU s.p.   (A620)

    Madonna Mia Fa   *16th cent
        (Pisador) [It] med solo,gtr ESCHIG
        E1318 $.90   (A621)

    Motets A Jouer Sur Le Pipeau   *CCU,
    13th cent
        3 soli,inst OISEAU s.p.   (A622)

    Motets Du Treizieme Siecle   *CCU,13th
    cent
        3 soli,inst OISEAU s.p.   (A623)

    Or Sus Vous Dormes Trop   *14th cent
        3 soli,inst OISEAU s.p.   (A624)

    Que Ces Lieux
        see Anonymous, De Ce Sejour

    Schweigt Stille, Plaudert Nicht
    *cant
        (Franke, E.) STB soli,2vln,vla,cont
        cmplt ed DEUTSCHER 9503 s.p., sc
        DEUTSCHER s.p., ipa   (A625)

    Son Come Farfalletta
        see ANONIMI VARI DEI SECOLI XVII E
        XVIII, PART II

    Tres Morillas Me Enamoran   *15th cent
        (Azpiazu) [Span] med solo,gtr UNION
        ESP. $1.10   (A626)

    Weihnachtliches Krippenlied   *sac,
    CCU,Xmas,18th cent
        2 soli,2vln,kbd sc VIEWEG 6115 s.p.
                                    (A627)

ANONYMOUS IN LOVE see Walton

ANORANZAS see Pahissa, Jaime

ANOTHER AMERICA see Cory, George

ANOTHER AUGUST see Flanagan, William

ANRUF see Thomas, Kurt

ANSISDAD see Luzzatti, Arturo

ANSWER see Terry

ANSWER, THE see Rachmaninoff, Sergey
    Vassilievitch

ANTENNES see Schmitt, Florent

ANTES, JOHN (1740-1811)
    And Jesus Said: It Is Finished   *sac
        solo,pno (G min) BOOSEY $1.50
                                    (A628)

    Loveliest Immanuel   *sac
        solo,pno (B flat maj) BOOSEY $1.50
                                    (A629)

ANTHEIL, GEORGE (1900-1959)
    Five Songs   *CC5U
        S solo,pno BOOSEY $1.25   (A630)

ANTHOLGIE DES CHANTS POPULAIRES FRANCO-
    CANADIENS   *CCU
    (Canteloube, J.) solo,acap cmplt ed
    DURAND s.p.   (A631)

ANTHOLOGIE DE LA CHANSON PARISIENNE AU
    SEIZIEME SIECLE   *CC48U,16th cent
    (Lesure, Francois) solo cmplt ed
    OISEAU s.p. contains works by:
    Bonnet; Certon; Costeley; Janequin;
    Sermisy and others   (A632)

ANTHOLOGIE DES CHANTS POPULAIRES
    FRANCAIS TOME I   *CC7L
    (Canteloube, J.) solo,acap cmplt ed
    DURAND s.p.
    see also: Bearn; Comte De Foix;
    Corse; Gascogne; Languedoc;
    Provence; Roussillon   (A633)

ANTHOLOGIE DES CHANTS POPULAIRES
    FRANCAIS TOME III   *CC11L,Fr
    (Canteloube, J.) solo,acap cmplt ed
    DURAND s.p.   (A634)

ANTHOLOGIE DES CHANTS POPULAIRES
    FRANCAIS TOME III   *CC11L,Fr
    (Canteloube, J.) solo,acap cmplt ed
    DURAND s.p.
    see also: Alsace; Berry;
    Bourbonnais; Bourgogne; Franche-
    Comte; Guyenne; Haut-Dauphine Et
    Bas-Dauphine; La Haute Et Basse-
    Auvergne; L'Angoumois; L'Aunis Et
    La Saintonge; Limousin; Lorraine;
    Lyonnais; Marche; Nivernais;
    Poitou; Savoie; Vendee   (A635)

ANTHOLOGIE DES CHANTS POPULAIRES
    FRANCAIS TOME IV   *CC11L,Fr
    (Canteloube, J.) solo,acap cmplt ed
    DURAND s.p.
    see also: Anjou; Artois; Bretagne;
    Champagne; Flandre; Ile-De-
    France; Maine; Normandie;
    Orleanais; Picardie; Touraine
                                    (A636)

ANTHOLOGY OF ITALIAN SONG OF THE
    SEVENTEENTH AND EIGHTEENTH
    CENTURIES, VOL. I   *CC29L,It,17th
    cent/18th cent
    (Parisotti, A.) [It/Eng] SCHIRM.G 290
    $4.00 contains works by: Gluck;
    Handel; Lotti; Paisiello and others
                                    (A637)

ANTHOLOGY OF ITALIAN SONG OF THE
    SEVENTEENTH AND EIGHTEENTH
    CENTURIES, VOL. II   *CC30L,It,17th
    cent/18th cent
    (Parisotti, A.) [It/Eng] SCHIRM.G 291
    $3.50 contains works by: Bassani;
    DeLuca; Monteverdi; Scarlatti and
    others   (A638)

ANTHOLOGY OF MODERN FRENCH SONG
    *CC29L,Fr
    [Fr/Eng] SCHIRM.G high solo,pno pap
    $4.00; high solo,pno cloth $5.50;
    low solo,pno pap $4.50; low solo,
    pno cloth $5.50 contains works by:
    Debussy; Faure; Franck; Saint-Saens
    and others   (A639)

ANTHOLOGY OF SACRED SONGS, VOLUME I
    *sac,CC40L
    S solo,pno SCHIRM.G $5.85 contains
    works by: Bach; Beethoven; Handel;
    Haydn; Mendelssohn and others
                                    (A640)

ANTHOLOGY OF SACRED SONGS, VOLUME II
    *sac,CC46L
    A solo,pno SCHIRM.G $5.85 contains
    works by: Bach; Dvorak; Handel;
    Saint-Saens and others   (A641)

ANTHOLOGY OF SACRED SONGS, VOLUME III
*sac,CC39L
T solo,pno SCHIRM.G $5.85 contains
works by: Bach; Beethoven; Gounod;
Handel; Haydn and others   (A642)

ANTHOLOGY OF SACRED SONGS, VOLUME IV
*sac,CC39L
B solo,pno SCHIRM.G $5.85 contains
works by: Bach; Dvorak; Handel;
Haydn; Mendelssohn and others
                              (A643)

ANTHONY O'DALY see Mourant, Walter

ANTICA NINNA-NINNA PARTENOPEA see
Alfano, Franco

ANTICHE GEMME ITALIANE *CC11L
(Parisotti) [It] 1-2 soli,pno cmplt
ed RICORDI-ENG ER 2287 s.p.
contains works by: Bottegari;
Rontani; Scarlatti; Marcello;
Strozzi; Stefani; Da Gagliano
                              (A644)

ANTICKE MOTIVY see Krejci, Isa

ANTICO SOLE see Malipiero, Riccardo

ANTIENNE DU SILENCE see Messiaen,
Oliver

ANTIIKIN LAULUMAAILMA, VOL. I-II
*CC20L
(Solantera) solo,pno FAZER
W 2522, 2552 s.p., ea. contains
works by: Bassani; Caccini;
Durante; Gluck; Lotti; Scarlatti;
Handel; Legrenzi; Vivaldi and
others; published in 2 editions
                              (A645)

ANTILL, JOHN HENRY (1904-   )
Five Australian Lyrics *CC5U
solo,pno BOOSEY $2.00   (A646)

In An Old Homestead
solo,pno ALLANS s.p.   (A647)

ANTINOMIA see Balassa, Sandor

ANTIPHON see Wyton, Alec

ANTIQUE see Bordewijk-Roepman, Johanna

ANTITEZA see Kowalski, Julius

ANTOINE ET CLEOPATRE see Carolus-Duran,
P.

ANTONIO JOSE
Tres Cantigas De Alphonse X *CC3U
[Span/Fr] med solo,pno ESCHIG $3.00
                              (A648)

ANTONIOU, THEODOR (1935-   )
Stimmung Der Abwesenheit
[Lat/Eng] med solo,pno/orch study
sc BAREN. 6048 $8.50, voc sc
BAREN. 6048A s.p.   (A649)

ANTONIUS VON PADUA see Mahler, Gustav

ANTREAS, E.
Femina
solo,pno ENOCH s.p.   (A650)
solo,acap solo pt ENOCH s.p. (A651)

ANTUNES, JORGE (1942-   )
Microformobiles II
Bar solo,5inst ZERBONI 7455 s.p.
                              (A652)

ANTWOORD OP EEN BRIEF see Mulder,
Herman

ANTWORTEN, BITTE see Schibler, Armin

ANU NOSIM LAPIDIM
(Helfman, Max) "Torchbearers, The"
[Heb] med solo,pno TRANSCON. IS 504
$.50   (A653)

ANVERS see Leduc, Jacques

ANY DREAM WILL DO see Webber, Andrew
Lloyd

ANY MORNING NOW see Warren, Cyril

ANYONE LIVED IN A PRETTY HOW TOWN see
Hamm, Charles

AOUA see Ravel, Maurice

APAISEMENT see Beethoven, Ludwig van

APAISEMENT see Desrez

APAISEMENT see Rabey, Rene

APAISEMENT see Rhene-Baton

APEGADO A MI see Guastavino, Carlos

APERGHIS, GEORGES (1945-   )
Concerto Grosso
narrator,MezBarB soli,3clar,2bsn,
3trom,tuba,4perc,pno,vcl,bvl,
electronic tape AMPHION A 297

APERGHIS, GEORGES (cont'd.)

s.p.   (A654)

APERITE MIHI PORTAS JUSTITIAE see
Buxtehude, Dietrich

APFELBLUTHEN see Nielsen, Carl,
Aebleblomst

APIVOR, DENIS (1916-   )
Seis Canciones De Federico Garcia
Lorca *Op.8,No.1-6, CC6U
solo,gtr BERBEN 1640 s.p.   (A655)

APOKALYPSE see Herrmann, Hugo

APOKALYPTISCHER ADVENT see Beekhuis,
Hanna

APOLLO AND DAPHNE see Handel, George
Frideric, Apollo E Dafne

APOLLO E DAFNE see Handel, George
Frideric

APOLLO UND DAPHNE see Handel, George
Frideric, Apollo E Dafne

APOLOGY, AN see Sharpe, Evelyn

APONTE-LEDEE, RAFAEL
La Ventana Abierta
AAA soli,fl,clar,trp,2perc,vln,vcl,
bvl sc SEESAW $7.00   (A656)

APOSTEL, HANS ERICH (1901-1972)
Drei Gesange Aus "Die Lieder Von
Traum Und Tod" *Op.15, CC3U
med solo,pno DOBLINGER 08 631 $2.25
                              (A657)
Funf Gesange *Op.9, CC5U
low solo,pno UNIVER. 11267 $7.00
                              (A658)
Funf Lieder *Op.22, CC5U
med solo,fl,bass clar,bsn quarto,sc
UNIVER. 12282 $3.75, ipa   (A659)

Funf Lieder *Op.3, CC5U
low solo,pno UNIVER. 5306 $4.25
                              (A660)
Vier Lieder *Op.6, CC4U
low solo,pno UNIVER. 10917 s.p.
                              (A661)
Weisse Wicken In Der Vase *Op.46a
med solo,pno DOBLINGER 08 649 s.p.
                              (A662)
Zwei Gesange *Op.40, CC2U
A solo,pno DOBLINGER 08 632 $4.25
                              (A663)

APOTHELOZ, JEAN
Voix Claires *CC9U
solo,pno HENN 109 s.p.   (A664)

APPAREILLAGE see Ponse, Luctor

APPARITION see Busser, H.

APPARITION see Debussy, Claude

APPARITIONS see Tate, Phyllis

APPASSIONATA see Cuvillier, Charles

APPEAL, THE see Goosens, Eugene

APPELBLOMMOR see Merikanto, Oskar,
Omenankukat

APPELBOOMPJES see Schuyt, Nico

APPELGARDEN see Peterson-Berger, (Olof)
Wilhelm

APPELONA see Voormolen, Alexander
Nicolas

APPELTRAD OCH PARONTRAD see Kilpinen,
Yrio

APPLE BLOSSOM see Thiman, Eric Harding

APPLE BLOSSOMS see Kellie, Lawrence

APPLE WOMAN see Blair

APPLEDOORN, DINA (1884-1934)
Drie Liederen
A/Mez solo,pno ALSBACH s.p.
contains: Harpzang Van David
(Psalm 150); Schoone Lelie;
Uitvaart Van Orpheus   (A665)

Harpzang Van David (Psalm 150)
see Drie Liederen

Psalm 150 *see Harpzang Van David

Schoone Lelie
see Drie Liederen

Uitvaart Van Orpheus
see Drie Liederen

APPORTE LES CRISTAUX DORES see Rhene-
Baton

APPROACH MY SOUL see Handel, George
Frideric

APREA, T.
Ninna Nanna
[It] solo,pno CURCI 2853 s.p.
                              (A666)

APRES CES DISCOURS MENACANTS see
Rameau, Jean-Philippe

APRES LA MORTELLE AVENTURE see Beydts,
L.

APRES L'ANGELUS see Flegier, Ange

APRES MINUIT see Ibert, Jacques

APRES UN REVE see Faure, Gabriel-Urbain

APRES UNE JOURNEE DE VENT see Orthel,
Leon

APRESLUDE see Blacher, Boris

APRI LA TUA FINESTRA see Mascagni,
Pietro

APRIL see Dunhill, Thomas Frederick

APRIL see Kennedy, John Brodbin

APRIL see Marvia, Einari, Huhtikuu

APRIL see Ruyneman, Daniel

APRIL ELEGY see Duke, John Woods

APRIL GOES A-WALKING see Dickson,
Stanley

APRIL IS IN SIGHT see Carew, Molly

APRIL MORNING see Teed, Roy

APRIL-NARRI see Bedinger, Hugo

APRIL O'CLOCK see Fox, G.

APRIL SAMT MAI see Stepan, V.

APRIL TIME see Scott, John Prindle

APRIL WEARS A SMILING FACE see Austin,
Ernest

APRILA, O BELLA see Wolf-Ferrari,
Ermanno

APRILE see Gandino, Adolfo

APRILE see Tosti, Francesco Paolo

APRITE UN PO' QUEGL' OCCHI see Mozart,
Wolfgang Amadeus

AQUAH LALUH, GHANA see Leduc, Jacques

AQUARELLE ANGLAISE see Chansarel, R.

AQUARELLES see Leduc, Jacques

AQUELLA SIERRA NEVADA see Garcia
Morillo, Roberto

AQUESTA NIT UN MATEIX VENT see Mompou,
Federico

AQUI SE ESTA QUIETO see Ficher, Jacobo

AQUI SI YO HUBIERA SIDO CABALLO see
Ficher, Jacobo

AQUILON ET ORITHIE see Rameau, Jean-
Philippe

AR DET SANT ATT JESUS AR MIN BRODER
see Andliga Sanger, Heft 2

AR DU FRIDLOS? see Dahlgren, Erland

ARAB LOVE SONG see Sutherland, Margaret

ARABESKE see Voormolen, Alexander
Nicolas

ARABIAN GIRL see Bizet, Georges, Adieux
De L'hotesse Arabe

ARABIAN LOVE SONG see R'itiha

ARABIC SONG see Ben-Haim, Paul

ARABISCHES LIED see Godard, Benjamin
Louis Paul

ARABISK SERENAD see Valentin, Karl

ARAMAZ, A.
La Maja Limonera
(Subira) [Span] ST soli,pno UNION
ESP. $2.50   (A667)

CLASSICAL VOCAL MUSIC

18

ARAMBARRI, J.
Ocho Canciones Vascas *CC8U
[Span] S solo,pno UNION ESP. $1.00
(A668)

ARAN LULLABY see Jones

ARAPOV, B.
Romances *CCU
solo,pno MEZ KNIGA 2.85 s.p. (A669)

ARAUJO, GINO DE (1890-   )
Automne
solo,pno (available in 2 keys)
ENOCH s.p. (A670)

En Septembre
solo,pno ENOCH s.p. (A671)

Les Reves
solo,pno (available in 2 keys)
ENOCH s.p. (A672)

ARBA, D'
Autmone
solo,orch HENN s.p. (A673)

Die Wasserfrau
solo,pno HENN 032 s.p. (A674)

ARC-EN-CIEL D'INNOCENCE see Messiaen,
Oliver

ARCHAISCHER TOTENHAIN see Schindler,
Gerhard

ARCHE DE NOE see Quinet, Marcel

ARCHER, VIOLET (1913-   )
Psalm 23 *see Twenty-Third Psalm

Twenty-Third Psalm (Psalm 23) sac
solo,pno BERANDOL BER 1285 $1.50
(A675)

ARCHER'S SONGBOOK, THE *sac,CCU
solo,pno BENSON BO876 $2.50 (A676)

ARCHIBALD DOUGLAS see Loewe, Carl

ARDEVOL, JOSE (1911-   )
Versos Sencillos *CC7L
[Span] S solo,pno RICORDI-ARG
BA 10907 s.p. (A677)

ARDITI, LUIGI (1822-1903)
Der Kuss *see Il Bacio

Dream Of Home *see Il Bacio

Il Bacio
[It] S/T solo,pno RICORDI-ENG 32496
s.p. (A678)
[It/Eng] S/T solo,pno RICORDI-ENG
LD.399 s.p. (A679)
low solo,pno (B flat maj) ALLANS
s.p. (A680)
med solo,pno (C maj) ALLANS s.p.
(A681)
high solo,pno (D maj) ALLANS s.p.
(A682)
"Der Kuss" [Ger/It] low solo,pno/
orch SCHOTTS s.p. (A683)
"Dream Of Home" low solo,pno (B
flat maj) ASHDOWN (A684)
"Dream Of Home" med solo,pno (C
maj) ASHDOWN (A685)
"Dream Of Home" high solo,pno (D
maj) ASHDOWN (A686)
"Kiss, The" solo,pno (available in
2 keys) ASHLEY $.95 (A687)
"Le Reve" solo,acap (in 2 keys)
DURAND s.p. (A688)
"Le Reve" [Fr] solo,acap oct DURAND
s.p. (A689)
"Love's Messenger" low solo,pno (B
flat maj) ASHDOWN (A690)
"Love's Messenger" med solo,pno (C
maj) ASHDOWN (A691)
"Love's Messenger" high solo,pno (D
maj) ASHDOWN (A692)
(Liebling) "Kiss, The" [It/Eng]
high solo,pno (D maj) SCHIRM.G
$1.00 (A693)
(Liebling) "Kiss, The" [It/Fr/Eng]
high solo,pno (C maj) SCHIRM.G
$.85 (A694)

Kiss, The *see Il Bacio

Le Reve *see Il Bacio

Love's Messenger *see Il Bacio

Parla
high solo,pno RIES s.p. (A695)
med solo,pno RIES s.p. (A696)
(Gaebel, Kurt) high solo,2fl,2ob,
2clar,2bsn,4horn,2trp,3trom,timp,
perc,harp,strings RIES s.p. (A697)
(Liebling) "Speak!" [It/Eng] high
solo,pno (C maj) SCHIRM.G $.75
(A698)

Speak! *see Parla!

ARDON GLI'INCENSI see Donizetti,
Gaetano

ARE YOU COMING TO MY GARDEN see
Wilcock, F.S.

ARE YOU IN CONTROL LORD? see Kaiser,
Kurt

ARE YOU READY? see Ellis

ARE YOU REDEEMED? see Davis

ARE YOU SAVED see Johnson, Polly

AREFRYKT FOR LIVET see Olsen, Sparre

ARENSKY, ANTON STEPANOVITCH (1861-1906)
Child And The Butterfly, The *see
L'Enfant Et Le Papillon

Cradle Song *see Petite Berceuse

Easter Day *see Jour De Paques

Fable, The *see Une Fable

Jour De Paques *Op.59,No.6
"Easter Day" [Eng/Fr] med solo,kbd
CHESTER s.p. see also Six
Children's Songs (A699)

Le Petit Oiseau Triste *Op.59,No.3
"Sad Little Bird, The" see Six
Children's Songs

Le Pinson *Op.59,No.1
"Robin, The" see Six Children's
Songs

L'Enfant Et Le Papillon *Op.59,No.4
"Child And The Butterfly, The"
[Eng/Fr] med solo,kbd CHESTER
s.p. see also Six Children's
Songs (A700)

Petite Berceuse *Op.59,No.5
"Cradle Song" [Eng/Fr] med solo,kbd
CHESTER s.p. see also Six
Children's Songs (A701)

Robin, The *see Le Pinson

Sad Little Bird, The *see Le Petit
Oiseau Triste

Six Children's Songs
[Eng/Fr] med solo,kbd CHESTER s.p.
contains: Jour De Paques, "Easter
Day", Op.59,No.6; Le Petit
Oiseau Triste, "Sad Little
Bird, The", Op.59,No.3; Le
Pinson, "Robin, The", Op.59,
No.1; L'Enfant Et Le Papillon,
"Child And The Butterfly, The",
Op.59,No.4; Petite Berceuse,
"Cradle Song", Op.59,No.5; Une
Fable, "Fable, The", Op.59,No.2
see also: Jour De Paques, "Easter
Day", Op.59,No.6; L'Enfant Et
Le Papillon, "Child And The
Butterfly, The", Op.59,No.4;
Petite Berceuse, "Cradle Song",
Op.59,No.5 (A702)

Une Fable *Op.59,No.2
"Fable, The" see Six Children's
Songs

ARESCHOUG, ANTONIE
Sympati Och Passion *sac
solo,pno,opt gtr GEHRMANS s.p.
(A703)

ARFKEN, ERNST (1925-   )
Magnificat *sac
S solo,fl/S rec,org sc HANSSLER
10.106 s.p., ipa (A704)

ARGENTO, DOMINICK
From The Diary Of Virginia Woolf
*song cycle
med solo,pno BOOSEY (A705)

Letters From Composers *CCU
solo,gtr BOOSEY $3.50 (A706)

Six Elizabethan Songs *CC5U
high solo,pno BOOSEY $2.50 (A707)

To Be Sung Upon The Waters *song
cycle
high solo,pno,clar,opt bass clar
cmplt ed BOOSEY $6.50 (A708)

ARGENTSON, R.
Three Love Letters *CC3U
solo,pno LEONARD-ENG (A709)

ARIA see Adam, Adolphe-Charles

ARIA see Bach, Johann Sebastian

ARIA see Cage, John

ARIA see Handel, George Frideric

ARIA see Ibert, Jacques

ARIA see Roman, Johan Helmich

ARIA see Stout, Alan

ARIA, THE *CCU,Renais/Baroq
(Liebling; Vine) BELWIN high solo,pno
$4.50; low solo,pno $4.50 (A710)

ARIA ALBUM FOR ALTO *sac/sec,CC52U
A solo,pno PETERS 735 $8.50 contains
works by: Bach; Beethoven; Gluck;
Handel; Haydn; Lotti; Mozart;
Pergolesi; Wagner and others (A711)

ARIA ALBUM FOR BARITONE see Verdi,
Giuseppe

ARIA ALBUM FOR BARITONE see Wagner,
Richard

ARIA ALBUM FOR BARITONE AND BASS *sac/
sec,CC54U
Bar/B solo,pno PETERS 737 $12.00
contains works by: Bach; Beethoven;
Gluck; Handel; Haydn; Lortzing; and
others (A712)

ARIA ALBUM FOR BASS see Verdi, Giuseppe

ARIA ALBUM FOR MEZZO-SOPRANO *sac/sec,
CC19U
Mez solo,pno PETERS 794 $7.50
contains works by: Bizet; Handel;
Lortzing; Mozart; Rossi; Rossini;
Weber and others (A713)

ARIA ALBUM FOR MEZZO-SOPRANO OR ALTO
see Verdi, Giuseppe

ARIA ALBUM FOR SOPRANO *sac/sec,CC58U
S solo,pno PETERS 734 $9.50 contains
works by: Auber; Bach; Beethoven;
Bellini; Bizet; Donizetti; Flotow
and others (A714)

ARIA ALBUM FOR SOPRANO see Wagner,
Richard

ARIA ALBUM FOR SOPRANO, VOL. I see
Verdi, Giuseppe

ARIA ALBUM FOR SOPRANO, VOL. II see
Verdi, Giuseppe

ARIA ALBUM FOR TENOR see Verdi,
Giuseppe

ARIA ALBUM FOR TENOR *sac/sec,CC40U
T solo,pno PETERS 736 $8.50 contains
works by: Adam; Auber; Bach;
Beethoven; Donizetti; Flotow;
Gluck; Mehul; and others (A715)

ARIA ALBUM FOR TENOR see Wagner,
Richard

ARIA ALBUM I: SOPRANO ARIAS FROM
CANTATAS see Bach, Johann Sebastian

ARIA ALBUM II: ALTO ARIAS FROM CANTATAS
see Bach, Johann Sebastian

ARIA ALBUM III: TENOR ARIAS FROM
CANTATAS see Bach, Johann Sebastian

ARIA ALBUM IV: BASS ARIAS FROM CANTATAS
see Bach, Johann Sebastian

ARIA DA HYPERION see Maderna, Bruno

ARIA DE LAS CAMPANILLAS see Delibes,
Leo, Ou Va La Jeune Indoue

ARIA DEL PAESANO see De Grand s, Renato

ARIA DEL RUISENOR see Masse

ARIA DELLA CAMPANELLE see Delibes, Leo,
Ou Va La Jeune Indoue

ARIA DES WASSERMANNS see Dvorak,
Antonin

ARIA DI CHAKLOVITZ see Mussorgsky,
Modest

ARIA DI CHIESA see Stradella,
Alessandro

ARIA DI COVIELLO see Farinelli,
Giuseppe

ARIA DI FLAMINIA see Farinelli,
Giuseppe

ARIA DI GIOVANNI: "WILLST DU DEIN HERZ
MIR SCHENKEN"
(Wolpert, Franz Alfons) S solo,pno
BREITKOPF-W EB 5942 s.p. (A716)

ARIA DI HITOMARU see De Grandis, Renato

ARIA DI KACHTCHEEVNA see Rimsky-Korsakov, Nikolai

ARIA DI LENA see Galuppi, Baldassare

ARIA DI MARINA see Mussorgsky, Modest, Ah, Poor Marina!

ARIA DI POLLISSENA see Handel, George Frideric

ARIA DI POPPEA see Handel, George Frideric

ARIA NACH WORTEN VON T.S. ELIOT see Fortner, Wolfgang

ARIA OF ERRISENA see Haydn, (Franz) Joseph

ARIA SACRA see Marcello, Benedetto

ARIADNE AUF NAXOS see Haydn, (Franz) Joseph, Arianna A Naxos

ARIANNA see Scarlatti, Alessandro

ARIANNA A NAXOS see Haydn, (Franz) Joseph

ARIAS AND SCENES see Khromushin, O.

ARIAS CELEBRES DE OPERAS: BARITONE *CC12L
[It] Bar solo,pno RICORDI-ARG BA 11826 s.p. contains works by: Bellini; Boito; Gomes; Mozart; Puccini; Rossini; Verdi (A717)

ARIAS CELEBRES DE OPERAS: TENOR *CC12L
[It] T solo,pno RICORDI-ARG BA 11825 s.p. contains works by: Boito; Donizetti; Flotow; Ponchinelli; Puccini; Rossini; Verdi (A718)

ARIAS FROM CHURCH CANTATAS see Bach, Johann Sebastian

ARIAS FROM OPERAS see Bellini, Vincenzo

ARIAS FROM OPERAS AND CANTATAS BY SOVIET COMPOSERS *CCU
[Russ] high solo,pno MEZ KNIGA 66 s.p. (A719)

ARIAS FROM OPERAS BY FOREIGN COMPOSERS *CCU
[Russ] S/coloratura sop,pno MEZ KNIGA 82 s.p. (A720)

ARIAS FROM OPERAS FOR BASS see Mozart, Wolfgang Amadeus

ARIAS FROM OPERAS FOR BASS OR BARITONE, VOL. I see Mozart, Wolfgang Amadeus

ARIAS FROM OPERAS FOR BASS OR BARITONE, VOL. II see Mozart, Wolfgang Amadeus

ARIAS FROM OPERAS FOR COLORATURA SOPRANO see Mozart, Wolfgang Amadeus

ARIAS FROM OPERAS FOR CONTRALTO see Mozart, Wolfgang Amadeus

ARIAS FROM OPERAS FOR MEZZO-SOPRANO see Mozart, Wolfgang Amadeus

ARIAS FROM OPERAS FOR SOPRANO, VOL. I see Mozart, Wolfgang Amadeus

ARIAS FROM OPERAS FOR SOPRANO, VOL. II see Mozart, Wolfgang Amadeus

ARIAS FROM OPERAS FOR SOPRANO, VOL. III see Mozart, Wolfgang Amadeus

ARIAS FROM OPERAS FOR SOPRANO, VOL. IV see Mozart, Wolfgang Amadeus

ARIAS FROM OPERAS FOR TENOR see Mozart, Wolfgang Amadeus

ARIAS FROM THE OPERAS, VOL. 1 see Haydn, (Franz) Joseph

ARIAS FROM THE OPERAS, VOL. 2 see Haydn, (Franz) Joseph

ARIAS FROM THE OPERAS, VOL. 3 see Haydn, (Franz) Joseph

ARIAS, ROMANCES AND SONGS FROM THE REPERTOIRE OF IRINA ARKHIPOVA *CCU
[Russ] Mez solo,pno MEZ KNIGA 96 s.p. (A721)

ARIAS, ROMANCES AND SONGS FROM THE REPERTOIRE OF IVAN KOZLOVSKY *CCU
[Russ] T solo,pno MEZ KNIGA 97 s.p. (A722)

ARIAS, ROMANCES AND SONGS FROM THE REPERTOIRE OF YELENA STEPANOVA *CCU
[Russ] S solo,pno MEZ KNIGA 98 s.p. (A723)

ARIAS WITH ORCHESTRA see Beethoven, Ludwig van

ARIE A ZPEVY ZE SOUCASNYCH OPER: ALT
[Czech/Ger] PANTON 862 s.p. contains Borkovec, Pavel, Pisne Madlenky (from Palecek); Fischer, Jan F., Arie Ester (from Romoe, Julie A Tma); Hanus, Jan, Pisen Sestry (from Plameny); Kapr, Jan, Zpev Matky (from Muzikantska Pohadka); Krejci, Isa, Arie Luciany (from Pozdvizeni V Efesu); Macha, Otmar, Arie Kaci (from Hratky S Certem) (A724)

ARIE A ZPEVY ZE SOUCASNYCH OPER: BAS *CC9L
[Czech/Ger] PANTON 265 s.p. contains works by: Hanus; Chlubna; Nejedly, V.; Pauer; Suchon; Vostrak (A725)

ARIE A ZPEVY ZE SOUCASNYCH OPER: SOPRAN *CC10L
[Czech/Ger] PANTON 261 s.p. contains works by: Blazek, Zd.; Cikker; Doubrava; Kalas; Kaslik; Pauer; Suchon (A726)

ARIE A ZPEVY ZE SOUCASNYCH OPER: TENOR *CC8L
[Czech/Ger] PANTON 263 s.p. contains works by: Cikker; Doubrava; Hanus; Jeremias, O.; Kapr; Kubin; Suchon (A727)

ARIE ANTICHE, VOL. I *CC30L
(Parisotti) [It] Mez/Bar solo,pno cmplt ed RICORDI-ENG 50251 s.p. contains works by: Bononcini; Caldara; Vittoria; Handel; Pergolesi; Vivaldi and others (A728)

ARIE ANTICHE, VOL. II *CC30L
(Parisotti) [It] Mez/Bar solo,pno cmplt ed RICORDI-ENG 53983 s.p. contains works by: Bassani; Cavalli; Del Leuto; Marcello; Rontano; Monteverdi and others (A729)

ARIE ANTICHE, VOL. III *CC40L
(Parisotti) [It] Mez/Bar solo,pno cmplt ed RICORDI-ENG 101918 s.p. contains works by: Blangini; Caccini; Carissimi; Cherubini; Fasolo; Dalayrac; Pergolesi and others (A730)

ARIE, CANZONETTE E BALLI A TRE, A QUATTRO E A CINQUE VOCI CON LIUTO see Vecchi, Orazio

ARIE DER LISA see Tchaikovsky, Piotr Ilyitch

ARIE DER MARINA see Mussorgsky, Modest, Ah, Poor Marina!

ARIE DES BLAZENKA see Smetana, Bedrich

ARIE DES DALIBOR see Smetana, Bedrich

ARIE DES FURSTEN GREMIN see Tchaikovsky, Piotr Ilyitch, Prince's Aria

ARIE DES GREMIN see Tchaikovsky, Piotr Ilyitch, Prince's Aria

ARIE DES LENSKY see Tchaikovsky, Piotr Ilyitch, Lensky's Aria

ARIE DES PIMEN see Mussorgsky, Modest, Pimen's Tale

ARIE DES SCHAFERS see Lothar, Mark

ARIE ESTER see Fischer, Jan F.

ARIE FUR SOPRANO see Caccini, Francesca

ARIE KACI see Macha, Otmar

ARIE LENSKIS see Tchaikovsky, Piotr Ilyitch, Lensky's Song

ARIE LUCIANY see Krejci, Isa

ARIE PER CONTRALTO see Vivaldi, Antonio

ARIE PER SOPRANO DE OPERA see Vivaldi, Antonio

ARIE SCELTE DALLE CANTATE, VOL. I see Bach, Johann Sebastian

ARIE SCELTE DALLE CANTATE, VOL. II see Bach, Johann Sebastian

ARIE SCELTE DALLE CANTATE, VOL. III see Bach, Johann Sebastian

ARIE SCELTE DALLE CANTATE, VOL. IV see Bach, Johann Sebastian

ARIE SCELTE (DALLE OPERA), VOL. I: SOPRANO LEGGERO see Mozart, Wolfgang Amadeus

ARIE SCELTE (DALLE OPERA), VOL. II: SOPRANO see Mozart, Wolfgang Amadeus

ARIE SCELTE (DALLE OPERA), VOL. III: TENORE see Mozart, Wolfgang Amadeus

ARIE SCELTE (DALLE OPERA), VOL. IV: BARITONO E BASSO see Mozart, Wolfgang Amadeus

ARIE Z ZPEVY ZE SOUCASNYCH OPER: BARYTON *CC9L
[Czech/Ger] PANTON 264 s.p. contains works by: Borkovec; Fischer, J.F.; Hanus; Macha; Pauer; Vostrak; Vyhnalek (A731)

ARIEL see Rorem, Ned

ARIEL'S FOUR SONGS FROM "THE TEMPEST" see Franco, Johan

ARIEL'S SONG see Butt, James

ARIEL'S SONG see Lessard, John Ayres

ARIEL'S SONG see Nielsen, Carl

ARIEL'S SONGS see Kiesewetter, Peter

ARIEL'S SONGS see Steen, G. v.d.

ARIEN see Haydn, (Johann) Michael

ARIEN AUS KANTATEN see Bach, Johann Sebastian

ARIEN AUS OPERN, ARIEN FUR SOPRAN BAND I see Rameau, Jean-Philippe

ARIEN AUS OPERN, ARIEN FUR TENOR BAND I see Rameau, Jean-Philippe

ARIEN UND KANZONETTEN *CC35U
(Keller, Hermann) (med diff) BAREN. 3450 cmplt ed,pap s.p., cmplt ed, cloth $18.25 contains works by: Arne; Bach; Caccini; Carisimi; Gluck; Mozart and others (A732)

ARIEN, VOL. I see Mozart, Wolfgang Amadeus

ARIEN, VOL. II see Mozart, Wolfgang Amadeus

ARIEN, VOL. III see Mozart, Wolfgang Amadeus

ARIEN, VOL. IV see Mozart, Wolfgang Amadeus

ARIETTA see Bozza, Eugene

ARIETTA see Scott, Cyril Meir

ARIETTA DI POSILLIPO see Tosti, Francesco Paolo

ARIETTE see Andriessen, Juriaan

ARIETTE see Malipiero, Gian Francesco

ARIETTE see Scarlatti, Alessandro

ARIETTES OUBLIEES see Debussy, Claude

ARIETTES OUBLIEES see Panizza, Ettore

ARIETTES OUBLIEES see Debussy, Claude

ARION see Campra, Andre

ARIOSI FUR SOPRAN see Henze, Hans Werner

ARIOSO see Messager, Andre

ARIOSO see Sibelius, Jean

ARIOSO DES EUGEN ONEGIN see Tchaikovsky, Piotr Ilyitch

ARIOSO D'EURIDICE see Monteverdi, Claudio

ARIOSO DU PREMIERE ACTE see Handel, George Frideric

ARIOSO FOR BRUDVIGSEL see Kallstenius, Edvin

ARIOSO FROM CANTATA NO. 156 see Bach, Johann Sebastian

ARIOSTI, ATTILIO (1666-ca. 1740)
  Der Ulmbaum *see L'Olmo

  Die Rose *see La Rosa

  La Rosa *cant
    (Weiss, G.; Klein, Th.) "Die Rose"
    [It/Ger] high solo,2vln,cont
    DEUTSCHER 9512 s.p.   (A733)

  L'Olmo *cant
    (Weiss, G.; Klein, Th.) "Der
    Ulmbaum" [It/Ger] high solo,2vln,
    cont DEUTSCHER 9513 s.p.   (A734)

  Vuoi Ch'io Parta
    S solo,fl,ob,clar,bsn,harp sc
    CARISH 21424 s.p., ipa   (A735)

ARISE, MY LOVE see Elmore, Robert
  [Hall]

ARISE, O SUN see Day, Maude Craske

ARISE, SHINE FOR THY LIGHT IS COME see
  Humphreys, Don

ARISE, YE SUBTERRANEAN WINDS see
  Purcell, Henry

ARIVANG
  see Internationale Volklieder, Nol. 3

ARIZAGA, RODOLFO
  Madrigal *Op.11
    [Span] solo,pno RICORDI-ARG
    BA 11995 s.p.   (A736)

  Soneto LXXI *Op.20
    [Span/Eng] low solo,pno RICORDI-ARG
    BA 11996 s.p.   (A737)

ARKADIA see Schuyt, Nico

ARKADISK FABEL see Prytz, Holger

ARKHIMANDRITOV, B.
  Diary, A *song cycle
    [Russ] Bar solo,pno MEZ KNIGA 67
    s.p.   (A738)

ARKIHUOLESI KAIKKI HEITA
  see Pieni Joulutervehdyts

ARLBERG, FRITZ
  O Tag!
    Mez/Bar solo,pno GEHRMANS s.p. see
    from SANGEN I   (A739)

  Svarmeri
    high solo,pno GEHRMANS s.p. (A740)
    low solo,pno GEHRMANS s.p.   (A741)

ARLEN
  God Remembers Everything *sac
    high solo,pno (C maj) BELWIN $1.50
                                 (A742)
    med solo,pno (E flat maj) BELWIN
    $1.50   (A743)

ARLEN, ALBERT
  Celtic Romance, A
    solo,pno ALBERT AE 59 s.p.   (A744)

  I Heard A Blackbird In A Tree
    solo,pno (G maj) BOOSEY $1.50 (A745)

  Many Things Have I Loved
    solo,pno ALBERT AE 60 s.p.   (A746)

ARM, ARM YE BRAVE see Handel, George
  Frideric

ARMA, PAUL (1904-   )
  Droit Vers Le But
    solo,pno OUVRIERES s.p.   (A747)

  Gerbe Hongroise *CC7L
    solo,pno oct OUVRIERES s.p. (A748)

  Huit Chansons (from Comment L'ane
    Gris Fut Sauve) (composed with
    Lancois, Jean) CC8L
    solo,pno OUVRIERES s.p.   (A749)

  Huit Chansons (from Trois Orgueils
    Feront Trois Vertus) (composed
    with Lancois, Jean) CC8L
    solo,pno OUVRIERES s.p.   (A750)

  La Poule Blanche (from Noces Du
    Muguet) (composed with Lancois,
    Jean)
    see Six Chansons

  Le Petit Lapin (from Noces Du Muguet)
    (composed with Lancois, Jean)
    see Six Chansons

  Les Clochetons Du Muguet (from Noces
    Du Muguet) (composed with
    Lancois, Jean)
    see Six Chansons

ARMA, PAUL (cont'd.)
  Les Fleurs Butinees (from Noces Du
    Muguet) (composed with Lancois,
    Jean)
    see Six Chansons

  Les Moineaux (from Noces Du Muguet)
    (composed with Lancois, Jean)
    see Six Chansons

  Reveil Au Bois Dormant (from Noces Du
    Muguet) (composed with Lancois,
    Jean)
    see Six Chansons

  Ruche De Reves *cant
    narrator,ob,vcl,cel,xylo,perc
    TRANSAT. s.p.   (A751)

  Six Chansons (from Noces Du Muguet)
    (composed with Lancois, Jean)
    solo,pno OUVRIERES s.p.
    contains: La Poule Blanche; Le
    Petit Lapin; Les Clochetons Du
    Muguet; Les Fleurs Butinees;
    Les Moineaux; Reveil Au Bois
    Dormant   (A752)

  Six Pieces For Solo Voice *CC6U
    solo,acap PRESSER $1.00   (A753)

ARMAGEDDON see Badings, Henk

ARMAHAN KULKU see Marvia, Einari

ARMAHIN MUISTO see Kuusisto, Taneli

ARMANDO, J.
  Closer *see Mas Cerca

  Mas Cerca
    "Closer" solo,pno CONGRESS $.60
                                 (A754)

ARMAR ARKUSSA AJAVI see Kilpinen, Yrio

ARMES, SYBIL L.
  Show Me Thy Hands, Blessed Jesus
    *sac
    solo,pno WORD S-300   (A755)

ARMIDA ABBANDONATA see Handel, George
  Frideric

ARMIDA'S GARDEN see Parry, Charles
  Hubert Hastings

ARMOTTOMAN OSA see Kilpinen, Yrio

ARMSTRONG, F.A.
  Lift Up A Song
    solo,pno (E flat maj) LEONARD-ENG
                                 (A756)

ARNALTA'S LULLABY see Monteverdi,
  Claudio

ARNE, MICHAEL (1741-1786)
  Lass Od Dee, The
    solo,vln,pno HEUWEKE. 105 s.p.
                                 (A757)

  Lass With The Delicate Air, The
    high solo,pno (G maj) SCHIRM.G $.85
                                 (A758)
    med solo,pno (E maj) SCHIRM.G $.85
                                 (A759)
    med solo,pno (F maj) ALLANS s.p.
                                 (A760)
    high solo,pno (G maj) ALLANS s.p.
                                 (A761)

  Silver Ton'd Trumpet, The
    solo,2vln,cont HEUWEKE. 106 s.p.
                                 (A762)

ARNE, THOMAS AUGUSTINE (1710-1778)
  Air (from Comus)
    med solo,pno (F maj) ALLANS s.p.
                                 (A763)
    low solo,pno (E flat maj) ALLANS
    s.p.   (A764)
    (Endicott) low solo,pno (F maj)
    FISCHER,C RS 14   (A765)
    (Endicott) med-low solo,pno (F maj)
    FISCHER,C RS 13   (A766)
    (Endicott) med-high solo,pno (G
    maj) FISCHER,C RS 12   (A767)
    (Endicott) high solo,pno FISCHER,C
    RS 11   (A768)

  Delia *cant
    (Hufstader) high solo,pno SCHIRM.G
    $1.50   (A769)

  Hail! Immortal Bacchus
    (Bevan) B solo,pno ELKIN 27.2320.04
    s.p.   (A770)

  Heart Of Oak
    solo,pno HEUWEKE. 107 s.p.   (A771)

  How Engaging, How Endearing
    (Bevan) T solo,pno ELKIN 27.2345.10
    s.p.   (A772)

  Kaunehin Keijukainen
    solo,pno FAZER F 2227 s.p.   (A773)

ARNE, THOMAS AUGUSTINE (cont'd.)
  Love Me Or Not
    see OLD ENGLISH SONG CYCLE, AN

  Morning, The *cant
    (Hufstader) high solo,pno SCHIRM.G
    $1.50   (A774)

  O Peace, Thou Fairest Child Of Heaven
    (Warrack) solo,pno/orch (G min)
    ROBERTON 2530 s.p.   (A775)

  O Ravishing Delight
    S solo,pno NOVELLO 17.0137.01 s.p.
                                 (A776)

  Pleasing Tales In Dear Romances
    (Bush) high solo,pno ELKIN
    27.2378.06 s.p.   (A777)

  Polly Willis
    high solo,pno (G maj) ALLANS s.p.
                                 (A778)
    med solo,pno (F maj) ALLANS s.p.
                                 (A779)

  Rule Britannia
    solo,pno CRAMER   (A780)
    solo,cont sc HEUWEKE. 137 s.p.
                                 (A781)

  Should You Ever Find Her Complying
    (Bush) Bar solo,pno ELKIN
    27.2376.10 s.p.   (A782)

  To All The Sex Deceitful
    (Bevan) T solo,pno ELKIN 27.2266.06
    s.p.   (A783)

  When Daisies Pied
    low solo,pno (F maj) CRAMER (A784)
    high solo,pno (E flat maj) CRAMER
                                 (A785)

  Where The Bee Sucks
    solo,pno CRAMER   (A786)

  Why So Pale And Wan, Fond Lover?
    (Bevan) B solo,pno ELKIN 27.2271.02
    s.p.   (A787)

  Ye Fauns And Ye Dryads
    low solo,pno (B flat maj) ASHDOWN
                                 (A788)
    high solo,pno (D maj) ASHDOWN
                                 (A789)

ARNELL, RICHARD (1917-   )
  Ode To The West Wind *Op.59
    S solo,3fl,2ob,2clar,2bsn,4horn,
    3trp,3trom,tuba,strings,timp
    HINRICHSEN rental   (A790)

ARNHEM see Schouwman, Hans

ARNLJOT see Peterson-Berger, (Olof)
  Wilhelm

ARNLJOT HALSAR JAMTLAND see Peterson-
  Berger, (Olof) Wilhelm

ARNLJOTS KARLEKSSANG see Peterson-
  Berger, (Olof) Wilhelm

ARNO HOLZ-SONGS see Goosen, Jacques

ARNOLD BOOK OF OLD SONGS see Quilter,
  Roger

ARNOLD, MALCOLM (1921-   )
  Five William Blake Songs *CC5U
    A solo,strings sc EMI s.p., ipa
                                 (A791)

  Only A Little Box Of Soldiers
    (composed with Leigh, F.)
    solo,pno CRAMER   (A792)

ARNOUD, J.
  Chanson Tiree Des Chatiments
    solo,pno ENOCH s.p.   (A793)

AROS MAEIR MYNDDAU MAWR see Williams,
  Meirion

ARPEGE see Dauly, G.

ARPEGE see Gui, Vittorio

ARPEGGIO see Mourant, Walter

ARRAN HOMING SONG see Noble, H.

ARRETE-TOI see Wagner, Richard, Stehe
  Still

ARRIERE-SAISON see Cras, Jean (Emile
  Paul)

ARRIETA Y CORERA, PASCUAL JUAN
  (1823-1894)
  Jota (from Llamada)
    T solo,pno RICORDI-ARG BA 1975 s.p.
                                 (A794)

ARRIEU, CLAUDE (1903-   )
  A L'envers De Ma Porte
    see Poeme De Louise De Vilmorin

  Adieux
    see Le Sable Du Sablier

ARRIEU, CLAUDE (cont'd.)

Ah! Bien C'est Du Joli
see Chansons De Philippe Soupault

Amour
see Poeme De Louise De Vilmorin

Attendez Le Prochain Bateau
see Poeme De Louise De Vilmorin

Bonjour Au Village
solo,pno AMPHION 230 $1.75   (A795)

Cadet-Roussel
solo,pno RICORDI-FR s.p. solo pt,
voc sc   (A796)

Cantate Des Sept Poemes D'amour En
Guerre
SBar soli,2fl,2ob,2clar,2bsn,2horn,
2trp,tamb,strings AMPHION s.p.
(A797)

Chanson De La Cote
solo,pno RICORDI-FR R 1575 s.p.
(A798)

Chanson Du Remouleur
see Chansons De Philippe Soupault

Chansons D'Angelterre *CCU
solo,pno RICORDI-FR R 1573-4 s.p.
(A799)

Chansons De Belise Et De Perlimplin
solo,pno AMPHION A 159 $1.75 (A800)

Chansons De Philippe Soupault
solo,pno cmplt ed AMPHION A 185-9
$3.50
contains: Ah! Bien C'est Du Joli;
Chanson Du Remouleur; Dame De
Coeur; Funebre; Pour La Liberte
(A801)

Clowneries
solo,pno/inst DURAND s.p.   (A802)

Dame De Coeur
see Chansons De Philippe Soupault

Depeche-Toi De Rire
solo,pno RICORDI-FR 1562 s.p.
(A803)

Espece De Comptine
solo,pno AMPHION A 231 $1.75 (A804)

Fete
see Le Sable Du Sablier

Funebre
see Chansons De Philippe Soupault

J'ai La Toux Dans Mon Jeu
see Poeme De Louise De Vilmorin

La Belle Qui Viendra
solo,pno AMPHION A 134 $1.50 (A805)

La Dame Bleue
solo,pno RICORDI-FR R 1412 s.p.
(A806)

La Fete Publique
see Le Sable Du Sablier

La Retraite
solo,pno AMPHION A 234 $1.75 (A807)

La Rose Et Le Reseda
solo,pno ENOCH s.p.   (A808)

L'allee Est Deserte
solo,pno AMPHION 235 $1.75   (A809)

L'Araignee
solo,pno AMPHION A 237 $1.75 (A810)

Le Capitaine Et Le Second
solo,pno ENOCH s.p.   (A811)

Le Geranium
see Le Sable Du Sablier

Le Sable Du Sablier
solo,pno AMPHION A 225-9 $6.75
contains: Adieux; Fete; La Fete
Publique; Le Geranium; Oh! Mes
Amours   (A812)

Les Chevaux Marins
solo,pno RICORDI-FR R 1411 s.p.
(A813)

Les Filles De Mayfair
solo,pno AMPHION A 236 $1.75 (A814)

Les Gueux Au Paradis *CCU
solo,pno ENOCH s.p.
see also: Saint Antoine Et Saint
Nicolas   (A815)

Les Vierges Sages
solo,pno AMPHION A 238 $1.75 (A816)

Liliom (Air De La Rousse)
solo,pno AMPHION A 149 $1.00 (A817)

L'Inconnu
see Poeme De Louise De Vilmorin

ARRIEU, CLAUDE (cont'd.)

L'orgue
solo,pno RICORDI-FR R 1576 s.p.
(A818)

Naissances
solo,pno AMPHION A 232 $1.75 (A819)

Nathalie
solo,pno ENOCH s.p.   (A820)
solo,orch ENOCH rental   (A821)

Oh! Mes Amours
see Le Sable Du Sablier

Pauvre Jean
solo,pno RICORDI-FR R 1410 s.p.
(A822)

Poeme De Louise De Vilmorin
solo,pno AMPHION A 119 $2.00
contains: A L'envers De Ma Porte;
Amour; Attendez Le Prochain
Bateau; J'ai La Toux Dans Mon
Jeu; L'Inconnu   (A823)

Pour La Liberte
see Chansons De Philippe Soupault

Priere Pour Dormir Heureux
solo,pno AMPHION A 233 $1.75 (A824)

Quand Verrai-Je Iles?
solo,pno ENOCH s.p.   (A825)

Richard II Quarante
solo,pno ENOCH s.p.   (A826)

Saint Antoine Et Saint Nicolas
solo,pno ENOCH s.p. see also Les
Gueux Au Paradis   (A827)

Un Fiacre
solo,pno ENOCH s.p.   (A828)

ARRIGO, GIROLAMO (1930-   )
E Ciascuno Saluto Nell'altro La Vita
*Bibl
[It] Mez solo,pno RICORDI-ENG
131981 s.p.   (A829)

Episodi
(Weckerlin, Jean Baptiste) S solo,
4fl HEUGEL 10981 s.p.   (A830)

Organum Jeronimus, Book I (Letter J-
E-R)
8 soli,14inst sc RICORDI-ENG 131917
s.p.   (A831)

ARRIVEDERCI... ADDIO see Petralia

ARRORRO see Ginastera, Alberto

ARRORRO see Sanchez, B.

ARROYUELO DEL MOLINO see Palau Boix, M.

ARS POETICA see Masseus, Jan

ART SONG, THE *CCU
(Howland, Alice; Zeitlin, Poldi)
[Eng] med solo,pno MUSIC 040025
$3.95   (A832)

ART-SONG ARGOSY *CC25L
(Breach, William) SCHIRM.G med-high
solo,pno $2.50; med-low solo,pno
$2.50 contains works by: Brahms;
Grieg; Moussorgsky; Schubert and
others, for use in class voice
instruction   (A833)

ART SONGS AND THEIR INTERPRETATION
*CCU
(Rich, Martin) solo,pno PRESSER $4.00
(A834)

ART SONGS: FIRST YEAR *CCU
(Glenn; Spouse) PRESSER $3.25 med-
high solo,pno; med-low solo,pno
(A835)

ART SONGS: SECOND YEAR *CCU
(Glenn; Spouse) PRESSER $3.25 med-
high solo,pno; med-low solo,pno
(A836)

ART THOU THE CHRIST? see O'Hara,
Geoffrey

ART THOU TROUBLED? see Handel, George
Frideric

ART THOU WEARY, ART THOU LADEN see
Gehring, Philip

ARTIST, THE see Reif, Paul

ARTIST'S SECRET, THE see Bosmans,
Henriette

ARTMAN
Wedding Prayer *Marriage
solo,pno SHAWNEE IA5048 $.85 (A837)

ARTOIS *Fr
(Canteloube, J.) solo,acap DURAND
s.p. see also Anthologie Des Chants
Populaires Francais Tome IV (A838)

ARUNDALE, CLAUDE

Charm Of A Child *CCU
solo,pno CRAMER available in 2 keys
(A839)

Country Cottage *CCU
solo,pno CRAMER available in 3 keys
(A840)

Dreamland City
solo,pno CRAMER   (A841)

Fisherfolk *CCU
solo,pno CRAMER available in 2 keys
(A842)

Five Short Humorous Songs *CC5U/CCU
solo,pno CRAMER   (A843)

Garden Of Memories *CCU
med solo,pno CRAMER   (A844)

Good Cider For Me
solo,pno CRAMER   (A845)

Hats Off To The Stoker
low solo,pno (B flat maj) CRAMER
(A846)
high solo,pno (C maj) CRAMER (A847)

Land Of The Almond Blossom *CCU
solo,pno CRAMER available in 2 keys
(A848)

Little Grey Friend
solo,pno CRAMER   (A849)

Little White House *CCU
solo,pno CRAMER available in 2 keys
(A850)

Night Nursery
low solo,pno (E flat maj) CRAMER
(A851)
high solo,pno (F maj) CRAMER (A852)

Oh, The Comfort Of A Garden
solo,pno CRAMER   (A853)

Old Flagged Path
low solo,pno CRAMER   (A854)
high solo,pno CRAMER   (A855)

Old Furniture *CCU
med solo,pno CRAMER   (A856)

Old Mother Sea
solo,pno CRAMER   (A857)

Old Spinet
solo,pno CRAMER   (A858)

Parson And Me
low solo,pno (C maj) CRAMER (A859)
med solo,pno (D maj) CRAMER (A860)
high solo,pno (E flat maj) CRAMER
(A861)

Peggy's Little Way
low solo,pno (C maj) CRAMER (A862)
high solo,pno (D maj) CRAMER (A863)

Poor Pantaloon
solo,pno CRAMER   (A864)

Porcelain And Pottery *CCU
low solo,pno CRAMER   (A865)

Prayers
solo,pno CRAMER   (A866)

Rain Fairy
low solo,pno (E flat maj) CRAMER
(A867)
high solo,pno (G maj) CRAMER (A868)
low solo,pno (E flat maj) ALLANS
s.p.   (A869)
med solo,pno (F maj) ALLANS s.p.
(A870)
high solo,pno (G maj) ALLANS s.p.
(A871)

Rivals
solo,pno CRAMER   (A872)

Smoking Room
low solo,pno CRAMER   (A873)
high solo,pno CRAMER   (A874)

Songs Of The North *CCU
(Lawson, Malcolm) solo,pno CRAMER
in two volumes, sold separately
(A875)

Spinning Wheel Song
solo,pno CRAMER   (A876)

Tears That Children Shed
solo,pno CRAMER   (A877)

Toby Jug
solo,pno CRAMER   (A878)

Two Little Feet
low solo,pno (E min) CRAMER (A879)
high solo,pno (G min) CRAMER (A880)

Up In The Sky
solo,pno CRAMER   (A881)

West-Away
solo,pno CRAMER   (A882)

ARUNDALE, CLAUDE (cont'd.)

When Ma Piccaninny Died
solo,pno CRAMER   (A883)

When Spring And Cherry Blossom Come
solo,pno CRAMER   (A884)

AS A FATHER WITH HIS CHILDREN see Bach,
Johann Sebastian

AS A SHEPHERD see Van Dyke, May

AS ADAM EARLY IN THE MORNING see Rorem,
Ned

AS DEW IN APRIL see Cumming, R.

AS DEW IN APRILLÉ see Gifford, Helen

AS EVER I SAW see Heseltine, Philip

AS FAIR AS DAY IN BLAZE OF NOON see
Rachmaninoff, Sergey Vassilievitch

AS FROLINAS DOS TOXOS see Toldra,
Eduardo

AS I GAED DOUN GLEMORISTON see Lawson,
Malcolm

AS I LAY IN THE EARLY SUN see Gibbs,
Cecil Armstrong

AS I LAYE A-THYNKINGE see Bullock,
Ernest

AS I RIDE BY see Kernochan, John M.

AS I WALKED FORTH see Flagello,
Nicholas

AS I WATCHED THE PLOUGHMAN PLOUGHING
see Ward, Robert

AS I WENT A-ROAMING see Brahe, May H.

AS IK HIER DIT JAAR WER see Pepping,
Ernst

AS IT FELL UPON A DAY see Copland,
Aaron

AS JOSEPH WAS A-WALKING see Kellam, Ian

AS LIFE WHAT IS SO SWEET see Diamond,
David

AS ON THE HEATH I WANDERED see
Kilpinen, Yrio, Am Haidehugel Geht
Ein Singen

AS ON THE NIGHT see Hovhaness, Alan

AS THE HART PANTETH see Blair, K.

AS THE VIOLETS CAME see Saul, George
Brandon

AS THE WINGS OF DOVES see Hovhaness,
Alan

AS THE WORK OF HUSBANDMAN see
Hovhaness, Alan

AS TIME GOES BY see Lister, Hovie

AS WE COME TO THEE IN PRAYER *sac
(Carmichael, Ralph) solo,pno WORD
S-225   (A885)

AS WELCOME AS THE FLOWERS IN MAY see
Clifton, Harry

AS WHEN THE DOVE see Handel, George
Frideric

AS YOU LIKE IT
(Stevens, Denis) [Ger] HINRICHSEN
H1564 $3.25
contains: Bartlet, Under The
Greenwood Tree (solo,pno);
Danyel, John, Blow, Blow, Thou
Winter Wind (med solo,pno,lute/
gtr); Hilton, What Shall He Have
That Killed The Deer? (BBBB soli,
pno); Holborne, Antony, Wedding
Is Great Juno's Crown (SSA soli,
pno); Morley, Thomas, It Was A
Lover And His Lass (2 high soli,
pno,lute/gtr)   (A886)

AS YOU PASS BY see Russell, Kennedy

ASCENDENTE JESU IN NAVICULAM see
Hindemith, Paul

ASH GROVE see Britten, Benjamin

ASH GROVE see Quilter, Roger

ASHES OF LIFE see Alette, C.

ASHFORD, E.L.
My Task *sac,Gen
solo,pno (available in 5 keys)
ASHLEY $.95   (A887)
high solo,pno (F maj) WILLIS $.60
(A888)
med solo,pno (E flat maj) WILLIS
$.60   (A889)
low solo,pno (D maj) WILLIS $.60
(A890)
med-high solo,pno LORENZ $1.00
(A891)
med solo,pno LORENZ $1.00   (A892)
med-low solo,pno LORENZ $1.00
(A893)
high solo,pno LORENZ $1.00   (A894)
low solo,pno LORENZ $1.00   (A895)
SA soli,pno LORENZ $1.00   (A896)
ST soli,pno LORENZ $1.00   (A897)
low solo,pno (D maj) ALLANS s.p.
(A898)
high solo,pno (F maj) ALLANS s.p.
(A899)

ASHLEY, DERICK
Call, The
see Four Sacred Songs

Four Sacred Songs *sac
A solo,pno NOVELLO s.p.
contains: Call, The (contains
also: Lowest Place, The); Hope,
A (contains also: Mother To
Babe); Lowest Place, The
(contains also: Call, The);
Mother To Babe (contains also:
Hope, A)   (A900)

Hope, A
see Four Sacred Songs

Lowest Place, The
see Four Sacred Songs

Mother To Babe
see Four Sacred Songs

ASHREI see Sheriff, Noam

ASHREY HA-GAFRUR see Helfman, Max

ASHREY HA-ISH
(Helfman, Max) "Blessed The Man"
[Heb] med solo,pno TRANSCON. IS 505
$.45   (A901)

ASHTON, BOB
Christmas Shopping
med solo,pno CRESPUB CP-23019 $.60
(A902)
How Much More *sac
low solo,pno CRESPUB CP-23030 $1.00
(A903)
high solo,pno CRESPUB CP-23031
$1.00   (A904)

Songs Of Living Faith *sac,CCUL
(Carmichael, Ralph) solo,pno WORD
$1.95   (A905)

Songs Of Living Hope *sac,CC8UL
(Carmichael, Ralph) solo,pno WORD
30058 $1.95   (A906)

ASHWORTH-HOPE, H.
All Ye Who Labour
low solo,pno (B flat maj) CRAMER
s.p.   (A907)
high solo,pno (D flat maj) CRAMER
(A908)
At Close Of Day
low solo,pno (A flat maj) CRAMER
(A909)
high solo,pno (G maj) CRAMER   (A910)

Bosun's Call
solo,pno CRAMER   (A911)

Come Along To Somerset
solo,pno CRAMER   (A912)

From Out The Long Ago
solo,pno CRAMER   (A913)

Mary O'More
low solo,pno (E flat maj) CRAMER
(A914)
high solo,pno (G maj) CRAMER   (A915)

Spring The Fiddler
solo,pno CRAMER   (A916)

Springtime In Somerset
low solo,pno (G maj) CRAMER   (A917)
high solo,pno (C maj) CRAMER   (A918)

Winds Way
solo,pno CRAMER   (A919)

ASI MORIRE! see Garcia Morillo, Roberto

ASIE see Ravel, Maurice

ASK ME NO MORE see Stevens, L.

ASKEPOTTS SANG see Bergh, Sverre

ASLAMAZOV, A.
From Armenian Poetry *CCU
[Russ] high solo,2clar MEZ KNIGA
2.86 s.p.   (A920)

ASPAKERSPOLSKA see Peterson-Berger,
(Olof) Wilhelm

ASPARNAS SUSNING see Palmgren, Selim

ASPATIA SONG see Andriessen, Juriaan

ASPERINE see Witte, D.

ASPINALL, GEORGE
Norwegian Song, A
low solo,pno (D min) CRAMER $.90
(A921)
med solo,pno (E min) CRAMER $1.15
(A922)
high solo,pno (F min) CRAMER $.90
(A923)

ASSASSINATION, THE see Dello Joio,
Norman

ASSENZA see Persico, Mario

ASSOTO see Casseus

ASSUNTA see Pizzetti, Ildebrando

ASTHORE see Trotere, Henry

ASTIQUE TON FOURNIMENT see Messager,
Andre

ASTON, PETER G. (1938-   )
Crazy Jane Grown Old Looks At The
Dancers
see Five Songs Of Crazy Jane

Crazy Jane Talks With The Bishop
see Five Songs Of Crazy Jane

Five Songs Of Crazy Jane
S solo,acap NOVELLO 17.0225.04 s.p.
contains: Crazy Jane Grown Old
Looks At The Dancers; Crazy
Jane Talks With The Bishop; I
Am Of Ireland; Those Dancing
Days Are Gone; Three Things
(A924)

I Am Of Ireland
see Five Songs Of Crazy Jane

My Dancing Day *cant
ST soli,fl,clar,2vln,vla,vcl
NOVELLO rental   (A925)

Those Dancing Days Are Gone
see Five Songs Of Crazy Jane

Three Things
see Five Songs Of Crazy Jane

ASTRA see Ambrosi, Alearco

ASTRALNA EROTIKA, BK. 1 see Ukmar,
Vilko

ASTRALNA EROTIKA, BK. 2 see Ukmar,
Vilko

ASTRO D'AMORE see Pratella, Francesco
Balilla

ASTROM
Hjarnats Saga
solo,pno LUNDQUIST s.p.   (A926)

ASTRONOMERS see Hundley, Richard

ASTRONOMISCHES BILDERBUCH see Poser,
Hans

ASTURIANA see Falla, Manuel de

AT BEDTIME see Read, Gardner

AT BLUE BELL TIME see Chappell, Stanley

AT CHRISTMASTIDE see Morgan, Orlando

AT CLOSE OF DAY see Ashworth-Hope, H.

AT COLUMBINE'S GRAVE see Shaw, Martin

AT DAWNING see Cadman, Charles
Wakefield

AT DIEPPE see Becker, John J.

AT EARLY DAWN see Ireland, John

AT EVE I HEARD A FLUTE see Strickland,
Lily Teresa

AT EVENTIDE see Loewe, Gilbert

AT EVENTIME see Austin, Grace L.

AT EVERY AGE see Tchaikovsky, Piotr
Ilyitch

AT MICHAEL'S GATE see Brooke, Harry

AT MICHAELS GATE see Kemp, David H.

AT MY WINDOW see Parker, Henry

AT NIGHT see Rachmaninoff, Sergey
Vassilievitch

AT PARTING see Rogers, James Hotchkiss

AT SUNSET see Ferguson, Edwin Earle

AT SUNSET TIME see Lora, Antonio

AT THE CROSS HER STATION KEEPING see
Graham, Robert

AT THE CROSSING see Lister, Mosie

AT THE CRY OF THE FIRST BIRD see Guion,
David Wendall Fentress

AT THE END OF THE PARADE see Yannay,
Yehuda

AT THE MID HOUR OF NIGHT see Somervell,
Arthur

AT THE NEXT HOUSE see Kaburagi, Mitsugu

AT THE ROLL CALL see Wetherington

AT THE SPRING see Thomson, Virgil

AT THE TIME OF THE BANQUET see Krapf,
Gerhard

AT THE WELL see Hageman, Richard

AT THIS SAME HOUR see Greenwood, R.

ATENARNES SANG see Sibelius, Jean

ATENARNES SANG see Sibelius, Jean,
Atenarnes Sang

ATER see Rangstrom, Ture

ATERKOMST see Peterson-Berger, (Olof)
Wilhelm

ATERVANDO TILL LIVET see Liljefors,
Ruben

ATFILE FUN A GHETTOJID see Lier, Bertus
van, Gebed Van Een Ghetto-Jood

ATKEY, OLIVE
Watermelon Man
solo,pno (B flat maj) LESLIE 7043
(A927)
Young Shepherd's Song
solo,pno BERANDOL BER 1458 $1.50
(A928)

ATMOSFERA OVATTATA I see Helmschrott,
Robert M.

ATMOSFERA OVATTATA II see Helmschrott,
Robert M.

ATOH HU YOTZROM see Chajes, Julius

ATOR, JAMES
Four Haiku Settings *CC4U
S solo,pno sc SEESAW $2.00   (A929)

Haikansona
Mez solo,ob,al-sax,vcl sc SEESAW
$4.00   (A930)

ATQUE VALE see MacNutt, Walter

ATTA JULSANGER see Maasalo, Armas

ATTA SANGER see Larsson, Lars-Erik

ATTA SETER LI *sac
solo,pno OR-TAV $.50 contains also:
Titgaddal   (A931)

ATTAIGNANT, PIERRE (? -1552)
Tant Que Vivrai (composed with
Sermisy, Claude de)
(Pujol) [Fr] med solo,gtr ESCHIG
E1314 $.90   (A932)

ATTENDEZ LE PROCHAIN BATEAU see Arrieu,
Claude

ATTENDITE, POPULE MEUS LEGEM MEAM see
Schutz, Heinrich

ATTENDS, SNEGOUROTCHKA see Rimsky-
Korsakov, Nikolai

ATTENTE see Chaminade, Cecile

ATTENTE see Vuillemin, L.

ATTENTE see Wagner, Richard

ATTORNO A LA see Jacob

ATTORNO AL NOME LUCIA see Lolini

ATTWOOD, THOMAS (1765-1838)
Land In The Ocean, The
solo,pno HEUWEKE. 108 s.p.   (A933)

When-E'er She Bade Me Cease To Plead
solo,pno HEUWEKE. 109 s.p.   (A934)

ATWOOD, TOMMY
He's Taking Good Care Of Me *sac
solo,pno WORD S-246   (A935)

Tears Of Shame *sac
solo,pno WORD S-245   (A936)

AU BOIS DE BETTANT see Busser, Henri-
Paul

AU BORD DE LA MER see Renaud, A.

AU BORD DE L'EAU see Cuvillier, Charles

AU BORD DES FLOTS see Temple, Hope

AU BOUT DES LEVRES see Hermite, M.

AU BOUT DU MONDE see Casterede, Jacques

AU BRUIT DE L'EAU QUI COULE see
Messager, Andre

AU BRUIT DES LOURDES see Gounod,
Charles Francois

AU CIMETIERE see Saint-Saens, Camille

AU CIMITIERE see Saint-Saens, Camille

AU CLAIR DE LA LUNE see Lully (Lulli),
Jean-Baptiste

AU CLAIR DE LUNE see Lully (Lulli),
Jean-Baptiste

AU COIN DE L'ATRE see Rhene-Baton

AU DELA see Holmes, Alfred

AU-DELA see Poulenc, Francis

AU DESERT see Rhene-Baton

AU DEVANT DE LA VIE see Shostakovich,
Dmitri

AU FIL DE L'EAU see Kross, Th.

AU FIRMAMENT see Chaminade, Cecile

AU FOND DES FORETS ENDORMIES see Rabey,
Rene

AU FOND DU TEMPLE see Bizet, Georges

AU FONDS DU TEMPLE see Bizet, Georges

AU GRE DES VENTS see Lonque, Georges

AU GRE DU VENT see Strimer, Joseph

AU JARDIN D'AMOUR see Cuvillier,
Charles

AU JARDIN DE L'AMOUR see Delmet, Paul

AU JARDIN DE L'INFANTE see Le
Corbeiller

AU JARDIN JOLI see Migot, Georges

AU JARDINET see Charpentier, R.

AU LOIN see Schumann, Robert
(Alexander)

AU MATIN see Marty, (Eugene) Georges

AU MATIN CLAIR see Rabey, Rene

AU MILIEU DU JARDIN see Respighi,
Ottorino

AU MUSEE see Doyen, Albert

AU NOM DU SOLEIL, ROI DU MONDE see
Indy, Vincent d'

AU PARADIS see Delmet, Paul

AU PAYS see Aubert, Louis-Francois-
Marie

AU PAYS BLEU see Chaminade, Cecile

AU PAYS D'AMOURETTE see Cuvillier,
Charles

AU PAYS DES CHANSONS see Bonnal, Ermend

AU PAYS DES VENDANGES see Vredenburg,
Max

AU PAYS D'EXIL see Lachaume, A.

AU PAYS DU REVE see Rabey, Rene

AU PAYS OU SE FAIT LA GUERRE see
Duparc, Henri

AU PAYS PARFUME see Vieu, Jane

AU PETIT LUXEMBOURG see Lapeyre,
Therese

AU PIED DE LA TERRASSE see Boussion, E.

AU PLUS PROFOND DES TERRES see Leduc,
Jacques, Abioseh Nicol, Sierra
Leone

AU PRE DE LA ROSE
see Chants De France Vol. I

AU PRINTEMPS see Gounod, Charles
Francois

AU REVOIR see Gedalge, Andre

AU ROSSIGNOL see Brahms, Johannes, An
Die Nachtigall

AU ROSSIGNOL see Gounod, Charles
Francois

AU ROSSIGNOL see Handel, George
Frideric

AU ROSSIGNOL see Schumann, Robert
(Alexander), An Die Nachtigall

AU ROYAUME DU VIN ET DES ROSES see
Rimsky-Korsakov, Nikolai

AU SOIR DE NOEL see Motte La Croix,
A.F.

AU SOMMEIL see Leguerney, Jacques

AU SOUFFLE D'UNE VOIX see Prin, Yves

AU TEMP DES FOINS see Roos, Robert de

AU TEMPS D'AUTOMNE see Lacome, Paul

AU TEMPS PASSE see Berger, Rod.

AU TROT see Rabey, Rene

AU VILLAGE DES SAINTS see Charpentier,
Jean Jacques Beauvarlet

AUBADE see Binet, Jean

AUBADE see Carion, Fern.

AUBADE see Cuvillier, Charles

AUBADE see Duteil d'Ozanne, A.

AUBADE see Erlanger, Camille

AUBADE see Farigoul, J.

AUBADE see Ferrari, Gabriella

AUBADE see Lalo, Edouard

AUBADE see Leoncavallo, Ruggiero,
Mattinata

AUBADE see Mendelssohn-Bartholdy, Felix

AUBADE see Pierne, Gabriel

AUBADE see Poise, (Jean Alexandre)
Ferdinand

AUBADE see Roberton, Hugh Stevenson

AUBADE AMOUREUSE see Delmet, Paul

AUBADE D'AVRIL see Levade, Charles
(Gaston)

AUBADE FAMILIERE see Lacome, Paul

AUBADE POUR ELLE see Delmet, Paul

AUBE DE FETE see Gandino, Adolfo, Alba
Festiva

AUBER, DANIEL-FRANCOIS-ESPRIT
(1782-1871)
L'eclat De Rire (from Manon Lescaut)
solo,pno DURAND s.p.   (A937)

AUBERT, LOUIS-FRANCOIS-MARIE
(1877-1968)
Aigues-Marines
med solo,pno/inst DURAND s.p.
(A938)
Au Pays
med solo,pno/inst DURAND s.p.
(A939)
Avril
SATB soli,orch DURAND s.p., ipr see
from Deux Poemes De J. Cheneviere
(A940)

AUBERT, LOUIS-FRANCOIS-MARIE (cont'd.)

Brodeuses
  med solo,pno/inst DURAND s.p. see
    also Crepuscules D'automne (A941)

Cache-Cache
  MezT soli,pno DURAND s.p.   (A942)

Chanson De Mer
  S/T solo,pno/inst DURAND s.p.
                                (A943)
  Mez/Bar solo,pno/inst DURAND s.p.
                                (A944)

Crepuscules D'automne
  med solo,pno/inst cmplt ed DURAND
    s.p.
    contains & see also: Brodeuses;
      Feuilles Sur L'eau; Grisaille;
      L'ame Errante; Prelude; Silence
                                (A945)

De Ceylan
  med solo,pno/inst DURAND s.p.
                                (A946)

Declaration
  S/T solo,pno/inst (F maj) DURAND
    s.p.   (A947)
  Mez/Bar solo,pno/inst (E flat maj)
    DURAND s.p.   (A948)
  A/B solo,pno/inst (D maj) DURAND
    s.p.   (A949)

Deux Poemes De J. Cheneviere *see
  Avril; Le Parc D'automne   (A950)

Douze Chants *CC12L
  [Fr/Eng] DURAND high solo,pno s.p.;
    med solo,pno s.p.   (A951)

Du Vin! Du Vin! (from La Foret Bleue)
  Bar solo,pno/inst DURAND s.p.
                                (A952)

D'un Berceau
  Mez/Bar solo,pno/inst DURAND s.p.
                                (A953)
  S/T solo,pno/inst DURAND s.p.
                                (A954)

Est-Ce Bien Vous Vraiment? (from La
  Foret Bleue)
  ST soli,pno/inst DURAND s.p. (A955)

Feuilles Sur L'eau
  med solo,pno/inst DURAND s.p. see
    also Crepuscules D'automne (A956)

Grisaille
  med solo,pno/inst DURAND s.p. see
    also Crepuscules D'automne (A957)

Helene
  S/T solo,orch DURAND s.p., ipa
                                (A958)
  Mez/Bar solo,orch DURAND s.p., ipa
                                (A959)

Invocation A Odin
  Bar solo,opt unis men cor,orch
    DURAND s.p., ipr   (A960)

J'ai Reve De Princesses Blanches
  (from La Foret Bleue)
  S solo,pno/inst DURAND s.p. (A961)

La Berceuse Du Marin
  solo,orch DURAND s.p., ipr   (A962)

La Fontaine D'Helene
  med solo,orch DURAND s.p., ipr
                                (A963)

La Lampe Du Ciel
  MezT soli,pno DURAND s.p.   (A964)

La Lettre
  Mez/Bar solo,orch DURAND s.p.
                                (A965)
  S/T solo,orch DURAND s.p.   (A966)
  solo,orch sc DURAND s.p., ipa
                                (A967)

La Mauvaise Priere
  solo,orch (G min) DURAND s.p., ipr
                                (A968)
  solo,orch (A min) DURAND s.p., ipr
                                (A969)
  solo,2pno (G min) DURAND s.p.
                                (A970)
  [Fr] solo,acap oct DURAND s.p.
                                (A971)

L'Adieu
  med solo,orch DURAND s.p., ipr see
    also Six Poemes Arabes   (A972)

L'ame Errante
  med solo,orch solo pt DURAND s.p.,
    ipr see also Crepuscules
    D'automne   (A973)

Le Destin
  med solo,orch DURAND s.p., ipa see
    also Six Poemes Arabes   (A974)

Le Mirage
  med solo,orch DURAND s.p., ipr see
    also Six Poemes Arabes   (A975)

Le Nez De Martin
  med solo,pno/inst DURAND s.p. see
    from Trois Chansons Francais

AUBERT, LOUIS-FRANCOIS-MARIE (cont'd.)
                                (A976)
  high solo,pno/inst DURAND s.p. see
    from Trois Chansons Francais
                                (A977)

Le Parc D'automne
  SATB soli,orch DURAND s.p., ipr see
    from Deux Poemes De J. Cheneviere
                                (A978)

Le Sommeil Des Colombes
  med solo,orch DURAND s.p., ipr see
    also Six Poemes Arabes   (A979)

Le Vaincu
  med solo,orch DURAND s.p., ipa see
    also Six Poemes Arabes   (A980)

Le Visage Penche
  med solo,orch DURAND s.p., ipa see
    also Six Poemes Arabes   (A981)

Les Charpentiers Du Roi
  med solo,pno/inst DURAND s.p. see
    from Trois Chansons Francais
                                (A982)
  high solo,pno/inst DURAND s.p. see
    from Trois Chansons Francais
                                (A983)

Les Souliers De L'avocat
  med solo,pno/inst DURAND s.p. see
    from Trois Chansons Francais
                                (A984)
  high solo,pno/inst DURAND s.p. see
    from Trois Chansons Francais
                                (A985)

Les Yeux
  Mez/Bar solo,orch DURAND s.p., ipr
                                (A986)
  S/T solo,orch DURAND s.p., ipr
                                (A987)

L'Heure Captive
  solo,vln DURAND s.p.   (A988)

Matin De Paques *sac,Easter
  SMezBar soli,pno ENOCH s.p. (A989)

Melancholia
  Mez/Bar solo,pno/inst DURAND s.p.
                                (A990)
  S/T solo,pno/inst DURAND s.p.
                                (A991)

Nocturne
  MezT soli,pno DURAND s.p.   (A992)
  MezBar soli,pno DURAND s.p. (A993)

Nuit Mauresque
  med solo,orch DURAND s.p., ipr
                                (A994)

Odelette
  Mez/Bar solo,pno/inst DURAND s.p.
                                (A995)
  T solo,pno/inst (E flat maj) DURAND
    s.p.   (A996)
  S solo,pno/inst (D maj) DURAND s.p.
                                (A997)

Pays Sans Nom
  med solo,orch DURAND s.p., ipr
                                (A998)

Prelude
  med solo,pno/inst DURAND s.p. see
    also Crepuscules D'automne (A999)

Premiere
  med solo,pno/inst (D flat maj)
    DURAND s.p.   (A1000)
  high solo,pno/inst (E flat maj)
    DURAND s.p.   (A1001)
  low solo,pno/inst (B flat maj)
    DURAND s.p.   (A1002)

Quand, A Tes Genoux
  see Aubert, Louis-Francois-Marie,
    Rimes Tendres
  see Aubert, Louis-Francois-Marie,
    Rimes Tendres

Rimes Tendres
  Mez/Bar/S/T solo,orch sc DURAND
    s.p., ipr contains also: Quand, A
    Tes Genoux; Si De Mon Premier
    Reve; Souvent De Nos Biens, Le
    Meilleur   (A1003)
  solo,pno oct DURAND s.p. contains
    also: Quand, A Tes Genoux; Si De
    Mon Premier Reve; Souvent De Nos
    Biens, Le Meilleur   (A1004)

Roses Du Soir
  S solo,orch DURAND s.p., ipr
                                (A1005)

Secret Aveu
  S/T solo,pno/inst DURAND s.p., ipr
                                (A1006)
  Mez/Bar solo,pno/inst DURAND s.p.,
    ipr   (A1007)

Serenade
  S/T solo,orch DURAND s.p., ipr
                                (A1008)
  Mez/Bar solo,orch DURAND s.p., ipr
                                (A1009)

Serenade Melancolique
  solo,orch (E maj) DURAND s.p.,
                                (A1010)
  solo,pno/inst (D maj) DURAND s.p.,

AUBERT, LOUIS-FRANCOIS-MARIE (cont'd.)

  ipr   (A1011)

Si De Mon Premier Reve
  see Aubert, Louis-Francois-Marie,
    Rimes Tendres
  see Aubert, Louis-Francois-Marie,
    Rimes Tendres

Silence
  med solo,orch DURAND solo pt s.p.,
    sc s.p., ipa see also Crepuscules
    D'automne   (A1012)

Six Poemes Arabes
  med solo,orch cmplt ed DURAND s.p.
    contains & see also: L'Adieu; Le
    Destin; Le Mirage; Le Sommeil
    Des Colombes; Le Vaincu; Le
    Visage Penche   (A1013)

Souvent De Nos Biens, Le Meilleur
  see Aubert, Louis-Francois-Marie,
    Rimes Tendres
  see Aubert, Louis-Francois-Marie,
    Rimes Tendres

Tendresse
  solo,pno/inst DURAND s.p.   (A1014)
  [Fr] solo,acap oct DURAND s.p.
                                (A1015)

Trois Chansons Francais *see Le Nez
  De Martin; Les Charpentiers Du
  Roi; Les Souliers De L'avocat
                                (A1016)

Trois Chants Hebraiques *CC3U
  solo,orch DURAND sc s.p., ipa, solo
    pt s.p.   (A1017)

Vieille Chanson Espagnole *CCU,Span
  (Aubert, L.) DURAND s.p. Mez/Bar
    solo,pno/inst; S/T solo,pno/inst;
    med solo,pno/inst   (A1018)

AUCH ICH WAR EIN JUNGLING see Lortzing,
  (Gustav) Albert

AUCTION BLOCK
  see Six Regional Canadian Folksongs

AUF DEM BERGE, DA GEHT DER WIND
  see In Dulci Jubilo

AUF DEM CANAL GRANDE see Gilse, Jan van

AUF DEM DNJEPR see Mussorgsky, Modest

AUF DEM FLUSSE see Jentsch, Walter

AUF DEM GEBIRGE HAT MAN EIN GESCHREI
  GEHORET see Schutz, Heinrich

AUF DEM MEER see Merikanto, Oskar,
  Merella

AUF DEM SOLLER AM MEER see Sibelius,
  Jean, Pa Verandan Vid Havet

AUF DEM STROM see Schubert, Franz
  (Peter)

AUF DEM WASSER ZU SINGEN see Schubert,
  Franz (Peter)

AUF DENN ZUM FESTE see Mozart, Wolfgang
  Amadeus

AUF DER CAMPAGNA see Marx, Joseph

AUF DER WEISE see Kludas, Erich

AUF DES LEBENS RASCHEN WOGEN see
  Lortzing, (Gustav) Albert

AUF DICH, HERR, STEHT MEIN VERTRAUEN
  see Posch, Isaac

AUF DIE FRAUEN see Haydn, (Franz)
  Joseph

AUF DIE RUHIGE NACHT-ZEIT see Huber,
  Klaus

AUF EHERNEN MAUERN see Telemann, Georg
  Philipp

AUF EIN ALTES BILD see Wolf, Hugo

AUF EIN KIND see Strauss, Richard

AUF EIN SCHLUMMERNDES KIND UND VOGLEIN
  SCHWERMUT see Winter, R.

AUF EINE HAND see Gilse, Jan van

AUF EINER GRUNEN WIESE see Gilse, Jan
  van

AUF FLUGELN DES GESANGES see
  Mendelssohn-Bartholdy, Felix

AUF GEHEIMEM WALDESPFADE see Griffes,
  Charles Tomlinson

AUF HERBSTLICHEM AST see Bijvanck, Henk

AUF INS METROPOL see Hollaender, Viktor

AUF, LASST UNS DEN HERRN LOBEN see
   Bach, Johann Michael

AUF, NUN LOBET GOTT see Rosenmuller,
   Johann

AUF REISE see Frid, Geza

AUF SCHUSTERS RAPPEN see Czernik, W.

AUF STARKEM FITTICHE see Haydn, (Franz)
   Joseph

AUF UND BLASET AM FEST DES NEUMONDS DIE
   TUBA see Schutz, Heinrich,
   Buccinate In Neomenia Tuba

AUF WIEDERSEHN see Romberg, Sigmund

AUFBRUCH see Kuiler, Cor.

AUFENTHALT see Schubert, Franz (Peter)

AUFER IMMENSAM see Schutz, Heinrich

AUFERSTEHUNG see Kelterborn, Rudolf

AUFERSTEHUNG see Orthel, Leon

AUFERSTEHUNG see Zagwijn, Henri

AUFFORDERUNG see Zipp, Friedrich

AUFGEPASST see Trunk, Richard

AUFKLANG see Borris, Siegfried

AUFLOSUNG see Verhaar, Ary

AUFTRAGE see Schumann, Robert
   (Alexander)

AUGELLETTI, CHE CANTATE see Handel,
   George Frideric

AUGEN DER LUFT see Serocki, Kazimierz

AUGEN, MEINE LIEBEN FENSTERLEIN see
   Trunk, Richard

AUGURIO see Giuranna, Barbara

AUGURIO see Pizzetti, Ildebrando

AUGUSTINATT see Linko, Ernst (Fredrik),
   Elokuun Yo

AULD FISHER, THE *folk,Scot
   low solo,pno (C maj) PATERSON FS5
   s.p.   (A1019)
   high solo,pno (D maj) PATERSON FS5
   s.p.   (A1020)

AULD JOE NICOLSON'S BONNIE NANNIE
   *folk,Scot
   solo,pno (F maj) PATERSON FS7 s.p.
                               (A1021)

AULD LANG SYNE
   "Gamla Goda Dar" solo,pno GEHRMANS
   760 s.p.   (A1022)

AULD SONGS OF HAME see Geehl, Henry
   Ernest

AULIN, TOR (1866-1914)
   Trenne Sanger *CC3U
   solo,pno GEHRMANS s.p.   (A1023)

   Tva Dikter Av August Strindberg
   *CC2U
   solo,pno GEHRMANS s.p.   (A1024)

AUNQUE ES DE NOCHE see Hively, Wells

AUPRES DA MA BLONDE
   see Chants De France Vol. I

AUPRES DE CETTE GROTTE SOMBRE see
   Debussy, Claude

AUPRES DE FEU see Pouget, Leo

AUPRES DE MA MIE see Chaminade, Cecile

AUPRES DE TOI see Bach, Johann
   Sebastian

AUPRES D'UN BERCEAU see Alin, Pierre

AUREANA DO SIL see Mompou, Federico

AURIC, GEORGES (1899-   )
   Four Songs Of A Sorrowing France
   [Eng/Fr] med solo,pno SALABERT-US
   $8.75
      contains: La Rose Et Le Reseda;
      Le Petit Bois; Nous Ne Vous
      Chantons Pas (Eluard); Richard
      II Quarante   (A1025)

AURIC, GEORGES (cont'd.)
   Huit Poemes De Jean Cocteau *CC8U
   [Fr] med solo,pno ESCHIG $8.00
                               (A1026)
   La Rose Et Le Reseda
   see Four Songs Of A Sorrowing
   France

   L'Alphabet *CC1U
   [Fr] med solo,pno ESCHIG $3.50
                               (A1027)
   Le Petit Bois
   see Four Songs Of A Sorrowing
   France

   Nous Ne Vous Chantons Pas (Eluard)
   see Four Songs Of A Sorrowing
   France

   Printemps
   [Fr] solo,pno/inst DURAND s.p.
                               (A1028)
   Quatre Poemes De Georges Gabory
   *CC4U
   [Fr] med solo,pno ESCHIG $4.00
                               (A1029)
   Richard II Quarante
   see Four Songs Of A Sorrowing
   France

   Trois Interludes *CC3U
   [Fr] high solo,pno ESCHIG $2.50
                               (A1030)
   Trois Poemes De Leon-Paul Fargue
   *CC3U
   [Fr] med solo,pno ESCHIG $5.00
                               (A1031)
   Trois Poemes De Louise De Vilmorin
   *CC3U
   [Fr] med solo,pno ESCHIG $3.25
                               (A1032)

AURINGON NOUSU see Kilpinen, Yrio

AURINGONNOUSU see Sibelius, Jean,
   Soluppgang

AURORE see Bosmans, Henriette

AURORE see Cuvillier, Charles

AURORE see Levade, Charles (Gaston)

AURORE see Tremisot, Ed.

AURORE see Wolff, A.

AUS! AUS! see Mahler, Gustav

AUS BANGER BRUST see Sibelius, Jean

AUS DEM HOHELIED SALOMONIS see Zilcher,
   Hermann

AUS DEM KAMPF MIT DER LIEBE see Handel,
   George Frideric, Dalla Guerra
   Amorosa

AUS DEM KINDERLAND see Philipp, Franz

AUS DEM TAGEBUCH EINES VERSCHOLLENEN
   see Janacek, Leos

AUS DEN GESANGEN OSSIAN'S see Mulder,
   Ernest W.

AUS DEN HIMMELSAUGEN see Reger, Max

AUS DEN LIEDERN DER TRAUER see Strauss,
   Richard

AUS DEN LIEDERN DER TRAUER [II] see
   Strauss, Richard

AUS DEN SIEBEN TAGEN see Stockhausen,
   Karlheinz

AUS DER TIEFE DES GRAMES see Bruch, Max

AUS DER TIEFE RUFE ICH, HERR, ZU DIR
   see Drischner, Max

AUS DER TIEFEN RUF ICH, HERR, ZU DIR
   see Bernhard, Christoph

AUS EINER STURMNACHT VIII see Martino,
   Donald

AUS FREMDEM LAND ZURUCKZUKEHREN
   [Russ/Fr/Ger] med solo,pno BELAIEFF
   244 s.p.   (A1033)

AUS MAHREN see Vycpalek, Ladislav

AUS STILLEN FENSTERN see Edler, Robert

AUS STILLEN FENSTERN see Vlijmen, Jan
   van

AUS TIEFER NOT SCHREI ICH ZU DIR see
   Kukuck, Felicitas

AUSGEWAHLTE ARIEN see Albert, Heinrich

AUSGEWAHLTE ARIEN FUR ALT HEFT I see
   Bach, Johann Sebastian

AUSGEWAHLTE ARIEN FUR ALT HEFT II see
   Bach, Johann Sebastian

AUSGEWAHLTE ARIEN FUR ALT HEFT III see
   Bach, Johann Sebastian

AUSGEWAHLTE ARIEN FUR BASS HEFT I see
   Bach, Johann Sebastian

AUSGEWAHLTE ARIEN FUR SOPRAN HEFT I see
   Bach, Johann Sebastian

AUSGEWAHLTE ARIEN FUR SOPRAN HEFT II
   see Bach, Johann Sebastian

AUSGEWAHLTE ARIEN FUR SOPRAN HEFT III
   see Bach, Johann Sebastian

AUSGEWAHLTE ARIEN FUR SOPRAN HEFT IV
   see Bach, Johann Sebastian

AUSGEWAHLTE ARIEN FUR TENOR HEFT I see
   Bach, Johann Sebastian

AUSGEWAHLTE ARIEN FUR TENOR HEFT II see
   Bach, Johann Sebastian

AUSGEWAHLTE ARIEN FUR TENOR HEFT III
   see Bach, Johann Sebastian

AUSGEWAHLTE DUETTE see Glinka, Mikhail
   Ivanovitch

AUSGEWAHLTE DUETTE HEFT I see Bach,
   Johann Sebastian

AUSGEWAHLTE DUETTE HEFT II see Bach,
   Johann Sebastian

AUSGEWAHLTE DUETTE HEFT III see Bach,
   Johann Sebastian

AUSGEWAHLTE LIEDER see Schubert, Franz
   (Peter)

AUSGEWAHLTE LIEDER see Telemann, Georg
   Philipp

AUSGEWAHLTE LIEDER see Siegl, Otto

AUSGEWAHLTE LIEDER see Telemann, Georg
   Philipp

AUSGEWAHLTE LIEDER see Khachaturian,
   Aram Ilyich

AUSGEWAHLTE LIEDER FUR GESANG UND
   GITARRE see Weber, Carl Maria von

AUSGEWAHLTE LIEDER HEFT 1:
   ANAKREONTISCHE FRAGMENTE,
   HOLDERLIN-FRAGMENTE see Eisler,
   Hanns

AUSGEWAHLTE LIEDER HEFT 2: LIEDER NACH
   TEXTEN VON BERTOLT BRECHT see
   Eisler, Hanns

AUSGEWAHLTE LIEDER HEFT 3: VIER
   WIEGENLIEDER-BALLADEN NACH BERTOLT
   BRECHT see Eisler, Hanns

AUSGEWAHLTE LIEDER UND GESANGE BAND I
   see Schoeck, Othmar

AUSGEWAHLTE LIEDER UND GESANGE BAND II
   see Schoeck, Othmar

AUSGEWAHLTE LIEDER UND GESANGE BAND III
   see Schoeck, Othmar

AUSGEWAHLTE LIEDER, VOLUMES I AND II
   see Brahms, Johannes

AUSGEWAHLTE ROMANZEN see Gliere,
   Reinhold Moritzovitch

AUSSCHLIESSLICH HEITER see Rubben,
   Hermannjosef

AUSSICHT AUF HIMMLISCHE FREUDEN see
   Lothar, Mark

AUSTIN, BILL
   Christ Who Lives Within, The
   (composed with Branham, Martha)
   *sac
   solo,pno SINGSPIR 7028 $1.00
                               (A1034)

AUSTIN, ERNEST (1874-1947)
   April Wears A Smiling Face
   high solo,pno (E maj) CRAMER $.95
                               (A1035)
   low solo,pno (C maj) CRAMER s.p.
                               (A1036)
   Tony The Turtle
   solo,pno CRAMER $1.15   (A1037)

AUSTIN, FREDERICK (1872-1952)
   Twelve Days Of Christmas, The
   med solo,pno NOVELLO 17.0083.09
   s.p.   (A1038)
   low solo,pno NOVELLO 17.0204.01

AUSTIN, FREDERICK (cont'd.)

     s.p.   (A1039)

AUSTIN, GRACE L.
  At Eventime
    low solo,pno BELWIN $1.50   (A1040)

AUSTIN, HARRY
  There's Someone In The Orchard
    low solo,pno (F maj) CRAMER (A1041)
    high solo,pno (G maj) CRAMER
                        (A1042)
  Throstle On The Hawthorn
    low solo,pno (F maj) CRAMER (A1043)
    high solo,pno (G maj) CRAMER
                        (A1044)

AUSTRALIAN LULLABY, AN see Harrhy, Edith

AUSWAHL DER LIEDER see Schumann, Robert (Alexander)

AUTMONE see Arba, d'

AUTOGRAPH ALBUM see Raphling, Sam

AUTOMNE see Absil, Jean

AUTOMNE see Araujo, Gino de

AUTOMNE see Chaminade, Cecile

AUTOMNE see Devreese, Godefroid

AUTOMNE see Gastinel, Leon-Gustave-Cypien

AUTOMNE see Godard, Benjamin Louis Paul

AUTOMNE see Honegger, Arthur

AUTOMNE see Mouton, H.

AUTOMNE see Quinet, Marcel

AUTOMNE see Rabey, Rene

AUTOMNE MALADE see Halffter, Ernesto

AUTONOMY OF VOICE see Mizuno, S.

AUTORI ROMANI DEL '600, VOL. I *CC7L
(Vatelli, F.) solo,pno BONGIOVANI 750
  s.p. contains works by: Rossi, L.;
  Del Leuto, A.; Dall'Auca, G.;
  Niccolino, F. Di   (A1045)

AUTORI ROMANI DEL '600, VOL. II *CC7L
(Vatelli, F.) solo,pno BONGIOVANI 764
  s.p. contains works by: Cesti, M.;
  Tenaglia, F.; Pasqualini, M.;
  Cesarini, C.; Masini, A.;
  Mazzocchi, V.   (A1046)

AUTRE CHANSON see Godard, Benjamin Louis Paul

AUTRE GUITARE see Absil, Jean

AUTREFOIS see Revel, Peter

AUTUMN see Alison-Crompton, C.

AUTUMN see Bliss, Sir Arthur

AUTUMN see Holford, Franz

AUTUMN AND THE RAINDROP'S ADVENTURE see Franco, Johan

AUTUMN DAY see Stout, Alan, Syyspaiva

AUTUMN EVE, AN see Wiren, Dag Ivar, En Hostens Kvall

AUTUMN GALE see Grieg, Edvard Hagerup

AUTUMN SETTING see Rhodes, Phillip

AUTUMN SONG see Hively, Wells

AUTUMN STORMS see Grieg, Edvard Hagerup

AUTUMN THOUGHT, AN see Massenet, Jules

AUTUMNAL LANDSCAPES see Krivitsky, D.

AUTUMNALIA see Farkas, Ferenc

AUTUMN'S LEGACY see Berkeley, Lennox

AUTUNNALE see Porrino, Ennio

AUTUNNO see Oddone, E.

AUVERGNAT see Bliss, Sir Arthur

AUX BORDS DU RHIN see Brahms, Johannes

AUX BORDS LOINTAINS see Wagner, Richard

AUX BORDS LOINTAINS DONT NUL MORTEL N'APPROCHE see Wagner, Richard

AUX CHAMPIGNONS see Mussorgsky, Modest

AUX CHENES see Gedalge, Andre

AUX CONQUERANTS DE L'AIR see Saint-Saens, Camille

AUX DAMOYSELLES PARESSEUSES D'ESCRIRE A LEURS AMYS see Enesco, Georges

AUX ENFANTS see Fontenailles, H. de

AUX HEUREUX see Holmes, Alfred

AUX LANGUEURS D'APOLLON see Rameau, Jean-Philippe

AUX OFFICIERS DE LA GARDE LANCHE see Poulenc, Francis

AUX PETITS ENFANTS see Desrez

AUX PETITS ENFANTS see Franck, Cesar

AUX PORTRES DE SEVILLE see Fourdrain, Felix

AV HIMMELSHOJD
  see En Liten Julhalsning

AV ROSOR, ROSOR RODA see Nordqvist, Gustaf

AVAK, THE HEALER see Hovhaness, Alan

AVALON see Hier, Ethel Glenn

AVANT DE MOURIR see Boulanger, G.

AVANT DE QUITTER CES LIEUX see Gounod, Charles Francois

AVANT LE CINEMA see Poulenc, Francis

AVE, DU WONNE DER FRAUEN see Senn, Karl

AVE MARIA see Abt, Franz

AVE MARIA see Adriessen, Willem

AVE MARIA see Bach, Johann Sebastian

AVE MARIA see Baumann, Max

AVE MARIA see Bijvanck, Henk

AVE MARIA see Boulay, J.

AVE MARIA see Bourguignon, Francis de

AVE MARIA see Bruch, Max

AVE MARIA see Bruckner, Anton

AVE MARIA see Cherubini, Luigi

AVE MARIA see Creston, Paul

AVE MARIA see Deshusses

AVE MARIA see D'Esposito, Salve

AVE MARIA see Diepenbrock, Alphons

AVE MARIA see Di Miniello, Crescenzio

AVE MARIA see Dubois, Theodore

AVE MARIA see Duvernoy, Victor-Alphonse

AVE MARIA see Dvorak, Antonin

AVE MARIA see Faure, Gabriel-Urbain

AVE MARIA see Filipucci, Edm.

AVE MARIA see Franck, Cesar

AVE MARIA see Goldschmidt, Adalbert von

AVE MARIA see Gounod, Charles Francois

AVE MARIA see Head, Michael (Dewar)

AVE MARIA see Heidet, le R. P.

AVE MARIA see Heiller, Anton

AVE MARIA see Kahn, Robert

AVE MARIA see Luzzi, Luigi

AVE MARIA see Mancini, Vincenzo

AVE MARIA see Mangone, Gioacchino

AVE MARIA see Mascagni, Pietro

AVE MARIA see Massenet, Jules

AVE MARIA see Mendelssohn-Bartholdy, Felix

AVE MARIA see Meyerowitz, Jan

AVE MARIA see Milanese

AVE MARIA see Millard, Harrison

AVE MARIA see Mine

AVE MARIA see Mollicone, Henry

AVE MARIA see Morgan, Frank

AVE MARIA see Neglia, Francesco Paolo

AVE MARIA see Ollone, Max d'

AVE MARIA see Ortiz De Guinea

AVE MARIA see Pardo

AVE MARIA see Peeters, Flor

AVE MARIA see Perilhou, Albert

AVE MARIA see Platamone, Stefano

AVE MARIA see Ple, Simone

AVE MARIA see Polzer, Odo

AVE MARIA see Rheinberger, Josef

AVE MARIA see Rosewig, A.H.

AVE MARIA see Samuel-Rosseau, Marcel

AVE MARIA see Scholten, J.

AVE MARIA see Schubert, Franz (Peter)

AVE MARIA see Schubert, Franz (Peter), Ave Maria

AVE MARIA see Sennes, H.

AVE MARIA see Simcus, Brian

AVE MARIA see Stanley, John

AVE MARIA see Svedbom, Vilhelm

AVE MARIA see Tausinger, Jan

AVE MARIA see Tesoriero, Gaetano

AVE MARIA see Tosti, Francesco Paolo

AVE MARIA see Valen, Fartein

AVE MARIA see Verdi, Giuseppe

AVE MARIA see Viardot-Garcia, Pauline

AVE MARIA see Voormolen, Alexander Nicolas

AVE MARIA see Vranken, Jaap

AVE MARIA see Yon, Pietro Alessandro

AVE MARIA DELL'ASSUNTA see Toschi, Pietro

AVE MARIA, GRATIA PLENA see Schutz, Heinrich

AVE MARIA PIENA DI GRAZIE see Verdi, Giuseppe

AVE MARIS STELLA see Dvorak, Antonin

AVE MARIS STELLA see Mulder, Ernest W.

AVE REGINA see Haydn, (Johann) Michael

AVE REGINA COELORUM see Pinkham, Daniel

AVE, STERN DES MEERES see Baumann, Max

AVE VERUM see Faure, Jean-Baptiste

AVE VERUM see Pergolesi, Giovanni Battista

AVE VERUM see Samuel-Rosseau, Marcel

AVE, VERUM COPRUS see Mozart, Wolfgang Amadeus

AVE, VERUM CORPUS see Mozart, Wolfgang Amadeus

AVEC LES LARMES DE MON COEUR see Lacome, Paul

AVEC SOIN, FORMEZ CHAQUE LETTRE see Messager, Andre

AVEMMARIA see Clementi, F.

AVENDGELUIDEN see Lilien, Ignace

AVENIR see Chaminade, Cecile

AVENTURES see Ligeti, Gyorgy

AVETE TORTO! see Puccini, Giacomo

AVEU see Ferrari, Gustave

AVEU see Godard, Benjamin Louis Paul

AVEU see Lacome, Paul

AVEU see Lefebvre, Channing

AVEU see Letocart, H.

AVEU see Pouget, Leo

AVIARY, THE see Bedford, David, Das
   Vogelhaus

AVIDAMENTE ALLARGO LA MIA MANO see
   Contilli, Gino

AVIDAMENTO ALLARGO LA MIA MANO see
   Caggiano, Roberto

AVIDOM, MENACHEM (1908-   )
   Four Songs Of Eilat *CC4U
      [Eng/Ger] med solo,pno ISRAELI 209
      $4.20   (A1047)

AVIS see Barraine, Elsa

AVNI, TZVI
   Collage
      solo,fl,perc,electronic tape study
      sc ISR.MUS.INST. 140 s.p. (A1048)

AVODIM HOYINU see Weiner, Lazar

AVONA see Shaw, Martin

AVOND see Bijl, Theo van der

AVOND see Colaco Osorio-Swaab, Reine

AVOND see Neirinckx, G.

AVOND see Oort, H.C.v.

AVOND see Tetterode, L. Adr. von

AVOND see Zagwijn, Henri

AVOND-GEBEDT see Horst, Anton van der

AVONDGEBEDJE see Frid, Geza

AVONDGELUIDEN see Velden, Renier Van
   der

AVONDLIED see Clercq, R. de

AVONDRUST see Rennes, Cath. v.

AVONDSTEMMING see Zagwijn, Henri

AVONDSTILTE see Oort, H.C.v.

AVONDZANG see Diepenbrock, Alphons

AVREMEL *Jew
   solo,pno KAMMEN 84 $1.00   (A1049)

AVRIL
   see La Musique, Onzieme Cahier

AVRIL see Aubert, Louis-Francois-Marie

AVRIL see Godard, Benjamin Louis Paul

AVRIL see Haring, Ch.

AVRIL see Lachaume, A.

AVRIL see Saint-Saens, Camille

AVRIL FLEURI see Levade, Charles
   (Gaston)

AVRIL S'EVEILLE see Chaminade, Cecile

AVRIR E ASSRAR
   (Carlo, Musi) solo,pno (Bolognese
   dialect) BONGIOVANI 2102 s.p. see
   from El Mi Canzunett Seconda Serie
                                 (A1050)

AVSHALOMOV, AARON (1894-1965)
   Sublimation
      high solo,pno AM.COMP.AL. $3.30
                                 (A1051)
   Willow Branch, The
      high solo,pno AM.COMP.AL. $3.30
                                 (A1052)

AVSHALOMOV, JACOB (1919-   )
   And Ruth Said
      solo,pno sc AM.COMP.AL. $1.10
                                 (A1053)
   Ch'ing T'ing Mountain, The
      low solo,pno AM.COMP.AL. $.38
                                 (A1054)
   Fed By My Labours
      low solo,pno AM.COMP.AL. $.82
                                 (A1055)
   Fu-Yi
      med solo,pno AM.COMP.AL. $.27
                                 (A1056)

AVSHALOMOV, JACOB (cont'd.)
   Glass Town
      high solo,pno HIGHGATE 7.0007.7
      $1.00   (A1057)
   Hail The "Great Land"
      med solo,pno AM.COMP.AL. $.82
                                 (A1058)
   Little Clay Cart, The
      solo,fl/pic,clar,perc,vla,vcl,
      banjo or guitar (ancient hindu)
      sc AM.COMP.AL. $11.00, ipa
                                 (A1059)
   Oedipus' Cradle Song
      T/Bar solo,pno AM.COMP.AL. $3.30
                                 (A1060)
   On The T'ung T'ing Lake
      high solo,pno AM.COMP.AL. $.55
                                 (A1061)
   Two Old Birds
      S solo,clar,pno sc AM.COMP.AL.
      $4.00, ipa   (A1062)

AVSKED see Louhivuori, Hemmo, Ero

AVSKED see Wennerburg, [Gunnar]

AWAIT THE WIND see Williams, Joan
   Franks

AWAKE see Pelissier, H.G.

AWAKE AND SING see Baxter, Maude
   Stewart

AWAKE MY HEART see Holst, Gustav

AWAKE, MY SOUL see Franco, Johan

AWAKE, MY SOUL, STRETCH EVERY NERVE see
   Hilty, Everett Jay

AWAKENED ROSE, THE see Strauss,
   Richard, Die Erwachte Rose

AWAY, DELIGHTS see Donovan, Richard
   [Frank]

AWAY ON THE HILL see Ronald, Sir Landon

AWAY TO THE MOUNTAINS see Kilpinen,
   Yrio, Tunturille

AWAY WITH PHILANDERING see Mozart,
   Wolfgang Amadeus

AXMANN, EMIL (1887-1949)
   Die Nacht
      [Czech/Ger] solo,pno SUPRAPHON s.p.
                                 (A1063)
   Kytice Pisni Ceskych *CCU
      med solo,pno SUPRAPHON s.p. (A1064)
   Kyticka Z Moravy *CCU
      solo,pno SUPRAPHON s.p.   (A1065)
   Venec Pisni Z Moravskeho Slovacka I-
   II *CCU
      solo,pno SUPRAPHON s.p., ea.
                                 (A1066)

AY, AY, AY *Span
   solo,pno ALLANS s.p.   (A1067)
   (Schipa) high solo,pno (D maj) WILLIS
   $.50   (A1068)

AY, AY, AY see Perez

AY DE MI see Enriquez de Valderrabano,
   Enrique

AY, GITANOS! see Fischer, Irwin

AY, LUNITA!... see Lasala, Angel

AY MADRE, NUNCA MAL SENTIU see Caamano,
   Roberto

AY MADRILENA! see Moreno Torroba,
   Federico

AY, MI MORENA see Moreno Torroba,
   Federico

AY MI TRIANA! see Balaguer

AYE WAUKIN', O *folk,Scot
   solo,pno (C maj/E flat maj) PATERSON
   FS105 s.p.   (A1069)

AYE WAULKING O' see Lawson, Malcolm

AYER ME DIJISTE QUE HOY see Gianneo,
   Luis

AYONT YON HILL see Lawson, Malcolm

AZEVEDO, LEX DE
   Lamb's Holy Feast, The *sac
      solo,pno WORD S-371   (A1070)

AZPIAZU, JOSE DE (1912-   )
   Cinco Canciones Populares Espanolas
   *CC5U
      [Span] med-high solo,pno UNION ESP.
      $1.50   (A1071)

AZPIAZU, JOSE DE (cont'd.)
   La Flor De La Canela
      [Span] solo,gtr RICORDI-ENG SY 408
      s.p.   (A1072)
   Noche De San Juan
      [Port] med-high solo,gtr UNION ESP.
      $.75   (A1073)
   Recuerdo
      [Span] med-high solo,gtr UNION ESP.
      $.75   (A1074)
   Zorongo Gitano
      [Span] solo,gtr RICORDI-ENG SY 407
      s.p.   (A1075)

AZUL see Campmany, Montserrat

B

B FOR BARNEY see Hughes, Herbert

BA BE BI BO BU see DuBois, Pierre Max

BAA-BAA BLACK SHEEP see Bennett, Sir
William Sterndale

BAAL T'FILLAH (COMPLETE EDITION) *sac,
CCU,Jew
(Baer, Abraham) solo,pno/org
SAC.MUS.PR. covering the year's
cycle, according to Ashkenazic and
Sephardic rituals   (B1)

BAAREN, KEES VAN (1906-1970)
Recueillement
Mez solo,pno DONEMUS   (B2)

BABADJANJAN, ARNO
Sechzehn Lieder *CC16U
[Russ] med solo,pno SIKORSKI R 6306
s.p.   (B3)

BABBIT, MILTON (1916-   )
Du *song cycle
[Ger] S solo,pno BOMART $2.50   (B4)

Sounds And Words
high solo,pno EMI s.p.   (B5)

Two Sonnets *CC2U
Bar solo,clar,vla,vcl PETERS 66610
rental   (B6)

Two Sonnets *CC2U
Bar solo,clar,vla,vcl sc BOMART
$8.50   (B7)

Vision And Prayer
S solo,electronic tape AMP $7.00
                                 (B8)
Widow's Lament In Springtime, The
S solo,pno BOMART $1.75   (B9)

BABINCIN MARSOVSKY VALCIK see Kricka,
Jaroslav

BABY BABY see Bowles, Paul Frederic

BABY JESUS IN A MANGER
see Six Polish Christmas Carols

BACARISSE, SALVADOR (1898-1963)
Cuarto Cantarcillos *Op.63, CC4U
[Span] med solo,pno UNION ESP. $.60
                                 (B10)
BACH, D.
When The Heart Is Young
low solo,pno PRESSER $.75   (B11)

BACH, ERIK
Lamentation
[Eng] S solo,perc,gtr EGTVED MF 287
s.p.   (B12)

Mattoidens Sanger
[Swed] Bar solo,gtr EGTVED MF 289
s.p.   (B13)

BACH, J.C.
Toi Que J'aime
[Fr/Ger] solo,pno/inst DURAND s.p.
                                 (B14)
BACH, JOHANN CHRISTIAN (1735-1782)
Air De Diana De L'Endemione
(Oubradous, Fernand) S solo,fl,orch
TRANSAT. s.p.   (B15)

Concert And Opera Arias *CC12U
(Landschoff) high solo,pno,opt fl/
ob/vln PETERS 4319 $5.50 with
original texts   (B16)

Meiner Allerliebsten Schonen
see Zwei Weltliche Arien

Recitative And Aria Of Arsinda (from
La Clemenza Di Scipione)
[It] S solo,fl,ob,2horn,cembalo,
vln,vcl,strings PETERS 8013
$12.50   (B17)

Sechs Italienische Duettinen *CC6U
(Reichert, Ernst) [Ger/It] SS soli,
pno BREITKOPF-W EB 6286 $5.75
                                 (B18)
Wenn Nach Der Sturme Toben
see Zwei Weltliche Arien

Zwei Weltliche Arien
(Walter, G.A.) T solo,2fl,strings,
cembalo BREITKOPF-L rental
contains: Meiner Allerliebsten
Schonen; Wenn Nach Der Sturme
Toben   (B19)

BACH, JOHANN CHRISTOPH (1642-1703)
Ach, Dass Ich Wassers G'nug Hatte
*cant
Mez/A solo,org,5strings BREITKOPF-L
rental   (B20)
(Schneider, Max) A solo,org,strings
sc BREITKOPF-W PB 4832 s.p., ipa,
voc sc BREITKOPF-W EB 6651   (B21)

Siehe, Wie Fein Und Lieblich Ist Es
*sac,cant
TTB soli,strings,org BREITKOPF-L
rental   (B22)

Wie Bist Du Denn, O Gott, In Zorn
Entbrannt *sac,cant
Bar/B solo,bsn,strings,cembalo
BREITKOPF-L rental   (B23)

BACH, JOHANN CHRISTOPH FRIEDRICH
(1732-1795)
Die Amerikanerin *song cycle
(Walter, G.A.) T solo,strings,
cembalo BREITKOPF-L rental   (B24)

BACH, JOHANN MICHAEL (1648-1694)
Auf, Lasst Uns Den Herrn Loben *sac,
cant
Mez/A solo,org,strings BREITKOPF-L
rental   (B25)

BACH, JOHANN NICOLAUS (1669-1753)
Der Jenaische Wein- Und Bierrufer
TTB soli,strings,cembalo BREITKOPF-
L rental   (B26)

BACH, JOHANN SEBASTIAN (1685-1750)
Ach Gott, Wie Manches Herzeleid
(Cantata 58) S.58, sac
SB soli,cembalo,strings, oboe
d'amore voc sc BREITKOPF-W
EB 7058 $1.75, ipr   (B27)

Ach, Lege Das Sodom Der Sundlichen
Glieder
see Ausgewahlte Arien Fur Alt Heft
III

Ach, Ziehe Die Seele Mit Seilen Der
Liebe
see Ausgewahlte Arien Fur Tenor
Heft III

Agnus Dei
solo,pno PATERSON s.p.   (B28)

Ah! When The Last Dread Hour
solo,pno PATERSON s.p. contains
also: Blessed Day (Bar solo,pno)
                                 (B29)
Air De Momus (from Der Streit
Zwischen Phoebus Und Pan)
see LA MUSIQUE, DIXIEME CAHIER
solo,pno DURAND s.p.   (B30)

Am Abend Da Es Kuhle War (from
Matthauspassion)
"'Twas In The Cool Of Eventide" B
solo,pno PATERSON s.p.   (B31)

Amore Traditore *S.203, sec,cant
[It/Ger] B solo,cembalo voc sc
BREITKOPF-W EB 7203 $1.75   (B32)
[Ger] B solo,cont voc sc KALMUS
6639 $1.50   (B33)
[It/Eng] B solo,pno/cembalo SCHOTTS
VK 8 s.p.   (B34)

Anna Magdalena Bach's Music Book
*CC42U
(Keller) [Ger] high solo/med solo,
pno cmplt ed,bds PETERS 4546
$7.50   (B35)

Anna Magdalena Notenbuch *see Aupres
De Toi   (B36)

Aria
(Bantock) high solo,pno PAXTON
P40579 s.p.   (B37)

Aria Album I: Soprano Arias From
Cantatas *CC15U
[Ger] S solo,pno PETERS 3335A $5.00
                                 (B38)
Aria Album II: Alto Arias From
Cantatas *sac,CC15U
[Ger] A solo,pno PETERS 3335B $4.50
                                 (B39)
Aria Album III: Tenor Arias From
Cantatas *sac,CC15U
T solo,pno PETERS 3335C $5.00   (B40)

Aria Album IV: Bass Arias From
Cantatas *sac,CC15U
[Ger] B solo,pno PETERS 3335D $4.50
                                 (B41)
Arias From Church Cantatas *sac,CCU
S solo,inst KALMUS 6072 $4.00   (B42)

Arie Scelte Dalle Cantate, Vol. I
*CC12U
(Zanon) [It/Ger] S solo,pno cmplt
ed RICORDI-ENG ER 2281 s.p.   (B43)

BACH, JOHANN SEBASTIAN (cont'd.)
Arie Scelte Dalle Cantate, Vol. II
*CC12U
(Zanon) [It/Ger] A solo,pno cmplt
ed RICORDI-ENG ER 2282 s.p.   (B44)

Arie Scelte Dalle Cantate, Vol. III
*CC12U
(Zanon) [It/Ger] T solo,pno cmplt
ed RICORDI-ENG ER 2283 s.p.   (B45)

Arie Scelte Dalle Cantate, Vol. IV
*CC12U
(Zanon) [It/Ger] B solo,pno cmplt
ed RICORDI-ENG ER2284 s.p.   (B46)

Arien Aus Kantaten *CCU
(Pidoux, Pierre) A solo,org (med
diff) BAREN. 86 $7.75   (B47)

Arioso From Cantata No. 156
med solo,pno AMP $.50   (B48)

As A Father With His Children
Bar solo,pno PATERSON s.p.   (B49)

Aupres De Toi
[Fr/Ger] solo,pno/inst DURAND s.p.
see from Anna Magdalena Notenbuch
                                 (B50)
[Fr] solo,acap oct DURAND s.p.
                                 (B51)
Ausgewahlte Arien Fur Alt Heft I
*sac,CC12L
(Mandyczewski, E.) A solo,inst,pno/
org BREITKOPF-L EB 7305 $6.00
                                 (B52)
Ausgewahlte Arien Fur Alt Heft II
*sac,CC12L
(Mandyczewski, E.) A solo,inst,pno/
org BREITKOPF-L EB 7306 $7.00
                                 (B53)
Ausgewahlte Arien Fur Alt Heft III
*sac
(Mandyczewski, E.) A solo,inst,pno/
org BREITKOPF-L EB 7307 $4.00
contains: Ach, Lege Das Sodom Der
Sundlichen Glieder; Die
Obrigkeit Ist Gottes Gabe;
Erbarme Dich, Mein Gott;
Hochgelobter Gottessohn; Ich
Will Nach Dem Himmel Zu; Leget
Euch Dem Heiland Unter   (B54)

Ausgewahlte Arien Fur Bass Heft I
*sac,CC12L
(Mandyczewski, E.) B solo,inst,pno/
org BREITKOPF-L EB 7311 $7.25
                                 (B55)
Ausgewahlte Arien Fur Sopran Heft I
*sac,CC12L
(Mandyczewski, E.) S solo,inst,pno/
org BREITKOPF-L EB 7301 $7.00
                                 (B56)
Ausgewahlte Arien Fur Sopran Heft II
*sac,CC12L
(Mandyczewski, E.) S solo,inst,pno/
org BREITKOPF-L EB 7302 $5.75
                                 (B57)
Ausgewahlte Arien Fur Sopran Heft III
*sec,CC12L
(Mandyczewski, E.) S solo,inst,pno/
org BREITKOPF-L EB 7303 $7.50
                                 (B58)
Ausgewahlte Arien Fur Sopran Heft IV
(Mandyczewski, E.) S solo,inst,pno/
org cmplt ed BREITKOPF-L $7.50
contains: Gelobet Sei Dir Herr,
Mein Gott; Herr, Deine Gute
Reicht So Weit; Ich Bin
Herrlich, Ich Bin Schon; Ich
Esse Mit Freunden Mein Weniges
Brot; Komm, Komm, Mein Herze
Steht Dir Offen   (B59)

Ausgewahlte Arien Fur Tenor Heft I
*sac,CC12L
(Mandyczewski, E.) T solo,inst,pno/
org BREITKOPF-L EB 7308 $6.00
                                 (B60)
Ausgewahlte Arien Fur Tenor Heft II
*sac
(Mandyczewski, E.) T solo,inst,pno/
org BREITKOPF-L EB 7309 $3.00
contains: Geliebter Jesu, Du
Allein; Gott Ist Mein Freund;
Ich Armer Mensch, Ich
Sundenknecht; O Seelen-Paradies
                                 (B61)
Ausgewahlte Arien Fur Tenor Heft III
*sac
(Mandyczewski, E.) T solo,inst,pno/
org BREITKOPF-L EB 7310 $3.25
contains: Ach, Ziehe Die Seele
Mit Seilen Der Liebe;
Erschutt're Dich Nur Nicht
Verzagte Seele; Es Dunket Mich,
Ich Seh' Dich Kommen; Frohe
Hirten, Eilt, Ach Eilet   (B62)

Ausgewahlte Duette Heft I *sac
(Mandyczewski, E.) SA soli,inst,
pno/org BREITKOPF-L EB 7312 $3.50
contains: Die Armut, So Gott Auf
Sich Nimmt; Er Kennt Die

BACH, JOHANN SEBASTIAN (cont'd.)

Rechten Freundenstunden; Wenn
Sorgen Auf Mich Dringen   (B63)

Ausgewahlte Duette Heft II *sac
(Mandyczewski, E.) SA soli,inst,
pno/org BREITKOPF-L EB 7313 $4.25
contains: Du Wahrer Gott Und
Davids Sohn; Gedenk' An Jesu
Bittern Tod; Herr, Du Siehst
Statt Guter Werke Auf Des
Herzens Des Kreuzes; Wenn Des
Kreuzes Bitterkeiten Mit Des
Fleisches Schwachheit Streiten
(B64)

Ausgewahlte Duette Heft III *sac
(Mandyczewski, E.) SA soli,inst,
pno/org BREITKOPF-L EB 7314 $5.00
contains: Beruft Gott Selbst, So
Muss Der Segen (from Cantata
88); Domine Deus, Agnus Dei;
Gottes Wort; Wir Eilen Mit
Schwachen, Doch Emsigen
Schritten   (B65)

Ave Maria *sac
med solo,pno (F maj) DOBLINGER
08 553 s.p. contains also:
Schubert, Franz (Peter), Ave
Maria   (B66)
high solo,pno (G maj) DOBLINGER
08 552 s.p. contains also:
Schubert, Franz (Peter), Ave
Maria   (B67)
med solo,pno (E flat maj) DOBLINGER
08 555 s.p. contains also:
Schubert, Franz (Peter), Ave
Maria   (B68)
low solo,pno (D maj) DOBLINGER
08 554 s.p. contains also:
Schubert, Franz (Peter), Ave
Maria   (B69)
(Gounod) Mez solo,pno (F maj)
LIENAU HOS 163 s.p.   (B70)
(Gounod) S/T solo,pno (G maj)
LIENAU HOS 162 s.p.   (B71)
(Gounod) med solo,pno (F maj)
ALLANS s.p.   (B72)
(Gounod) low solo,pno (D maj/
E flat maj) ALLANS s.p.   (B73)
(Gounod) high solo,pno (G maj)
ASHDOWN   (B74)
(Gounod) med-high solo,pno (F maj)
ASHDOWN   (B75)
(Gounod) med solo,pno (E flat maj)
ASHDOWN   (B76)
(Gounod) low solo,pno (D maj)
ASHDOWN   (B77)
(Gounod) med solo,pno (E flat maj)
CENTURY 3707 $.40   (B78)
(Gounod) high solo,pno (G maj)
CENTURY 702 $.40   (B79)
(Gounod) solo,pno (available in 3
keys) ASHLEY $.95   (B80)
(Gounod) low solo,pno (E flat maj/G
maj) FISCHER,C S 5683   (B81)
(Gounod) med solo,pno (F maj/G maj)
FISCHER,C S 5682   (B82)
(Gounod) high solo,pno (G maj)
FISCHER,C S 5681   (B83)
(Gounod) [Lat/Eng] low solo,vcl/
vln,harmonium/org,pno (E flat
maj) SCHIRM.G $1.00   (B84)
(Gounod) [Lat/Eng] med solo,vln/
vcl,harmonium/org,pno (E flat
maj) SCHIRM.G $1.00   (B85)
(Gounod) [Lat/Eng] high solo,vln/
vcl,harmonium/org,pno (F maj)
SCHIRM.G $1.00   (B86)
(Gounod) [Lat/Eng] high solo,vln/
vcl,harmonium/org,pno (G maj)
SCHIRM.G $1.00   (B87)
(Gounod) [Lat/Eng] low solo,pno (D
maj) SCHIRM.G $1.00   (B88)
(Gounod) [Lat/Eng] med solo,pno (E
flat maj) SCHIRM.G $1.00   (B89)
(Gounod) [Lat/Eng] high solo,pno (F
maj) SCHIRM.G $1.00   (B90)
(Gounod) [Lat/Eng] high solo,pno (G
maj) SCHIRM.G $1.00   (B91)
(Gounod) [Lat/Ger] med solo,pno,
org,vln/vcl sc LIENAU R81 s.p.
(B92)
(Gounod) [Lat/Fr/Ger] low solo,pno
SCHOTT-FRER SCH119 s.p.   (B93)
(Gounod) [Lat/Fr/Ger] med solo,pno
SCHOTT-FRER SCH118 s.p.   (B94)
(Gounod) [Lat/Fr/Ger] high solo,pno
SCHOTT-FRER SCH117 s.p.   (B95)
(Gounod) [Fr/Eng] high solo,pno
MARKS $1.50   (B96)
(Gounod) med solo,pno BELWIN $1.50
(B97)
(Gounod) high solo,pno BELWIN $1.50
(B98)
(Gounod) [Lat/Fr/It] Mez/Bar solo,
pno RICORDI-ENG 126835 s.p.   (B99)
(Gounod) [Lat/Fr/It] S/T solo,pno
RICORDI-ENG 126834 s.p.   (B100)
(Gounod) [Fr/It/Lat] S/T solo,pno
(F maj) RICORDI-ARG BA6545 s.p.
(B101)
(Gounod) [Fr/It/Lat] S/T solo,pno
(G maj) RICORDI-ARG BA6545 s.p.
(B102)

BACH, JOHANN SEBASTIAN (cont'd.)

(Gounod) A/Bar solo,pno (D maj)
LIENAU HOS 164 s.p.   (B103)
(Gounod) high solo,pno (G maj)
ALLANS s.p.   (B104)
(Gounod) solo,pno/org HEUGEL s.p.
see from CHANTS RELIGIEUX   (B105)
(Gounod) "Meditation" med solo,pno
PAXTON P1935 s.p.   (B106)
(Gounod, C.) [Lat/Eng] med solo,
vln&vcl/org PRESSER $.75   (B107)
(Gounod, Ch.) med-high solo,vln,org
(F maj) DOBLINGER 08 801 $1.00
(B108)
(Gounod, Ch.) solo,pno FAZER F 1923
s.p.   (B109)
(Gounod, Ch.) [Lat/Ger/Fr] low
solo,pno,vln,vcl SCHOTTS
07222-1-2 s.p., ea.   (B110)
(Gounod, Ch.) [Lat/Ger/Fr] med
solo,pno,vln,vcl SCHOTTS
07221-1-2 s.p., ea.   (B111)
(Gounod, Ch.) [Lat/Ger/Fr] high
solo,pno,vln,vcl SCHOTTS
07220-1-2 s.p., ea.   (B112)
(Gounod, Ch.) low solo,pno
LUNDQUIST s.p.   (B113)
(Gounod, Ch.) high solo,pno
LUNDQUIST s.p.   (B114)
(Gounod, Charles) S/T solo,pno
CURCI 5954 s.p.   (B115)
(Gounod, Charles) med solo,pno
CURCI 4277 s.p.   (B116)
(Gounod, Charles) Mez/Bar solo,pno
CURCI 5950 s.p.   (B117)

Bach Arias For Soprano *sac,CC19L
(Taylor, Bernard) S solo,pno
SCHIRM.G $3.00   (B118)

Bekennen Will Ich Seinen Namen (from
Cantata No. 200) sac
(Landshoff) [Ger] A solo,2vln,org,
opt vcl&bvl PETERS 4209 $4.00
(B119)

Bereite Dich, Zion, Mit Zartlichen
Trieben (from Weihnachts-
Oratorium) sac
(Keller, Hermann) A/Mez solo,vln,
cont (med diff) BAREN. 2311 $3.50
(B120)

Beruft Gott Selbst, So Muss Der Segen
(from Cantata 88)
see Ausgewahlte Duette Heft III

Beside Thy Cradle Here I Stand
see Five Sacred Songs

Beside Thy Manger Here I Stand *sac
med solo,cont oct CONCORDIA 98-1390
$.25   (B121)

Betrachte, Meine Seel, Mit
Angstlichem Vergnugen (from
Johannespassion) sac
(Scheit, K.) B solo,2vln,gtr
DOBLINGER GKM 38 $3.25   (B122)

Bist Du Bei Mir (from Anna Magdalene
Bach Notenbuch) sac
S/T solo,pno (E flat maj) LIENAU
HOS 2 s.p.   (B123)
A/Bar solo,pno (C maj) LIENAU HOS 3
s.p.   (B124)
"Wert Thou But Near" med solo,pno
(C maj) ALLANS s.p.   (B125)
"Wert Thou But Near" high solo,pno
(D maj) ALLANS s.p.   (B126)
(Deis) "Thou Art My Joy" [Eng/Ger]
high solo,pno (E flat maj)
SCHIRM.G $.85   (B127)
(Deis) "Thou Art My Joy" [Eng/Ger]
med solo,pno (C maj) SCHIRM.G
$.85   (B128)
(Deis) "Thou Art My Joy" [Eng/Ger]
low solo,pno (B flat maj)
SCHIRM.G $.85   (B129)
(Whitehead) "Come, Come, My Voice"
high solo,pno (D maj) ROBERTON
2522H s.p.   (B130)
(Whitehead) "Come, Come, My Voice"
low solo,pno (B flat maj)
ROBERTON 2552L s.p.   (B131)

Blessed Day
see Bach, Johann Sebastian, Ah!
When The Last Dread Hour

Blessed Is He That Cometh
T solo,pno PATERSON s.p.   (B132)

By Waters Of Babylon *sac
(Lovelace) med solo,org,vln BELWIN
$1.50   (B133)
(Lovelace) med solo,fl BELWIN $1.50
(B134)
(Lovelace) med solo,ob BELWIN $1.50
(B135)

Cantata 53 *see Schlage Doch,
Gewunschte Stunde

Cantata 58 *see Ach Gott, Wie
Manches Herzeleid

BACH, JOHANN SEBASTIAN (cont'd.)

Cantata 211 *see Schweigt Stille,
Plaudert Nicht

Coffee Cantata *see Schweigt Stille,
Plaudert Nicht

Come, Celebrate This Morn
see Five Spiritual Songs

Come, Christians, Greet This Day
*sac
solo,pno PATERSON s.p.   (B136)

Come, Come, My Voice *see Bist Du
Bei Mir

Come, Soothing Death
see Five Spiritual Songs

Comfort, Comfort Ye My People *sac
med solo,strings,cont oct CONCORDIA
98-2045 $.35. ipa   (B137)

Complete Works. Bach Gesellschaft
Edition *CCU
(Rust, W.; Rietz, J.; Hauptmann,
M.; Becker, C.F.; Kroll, F.;
Doerffel, A.; Naumann, E.; von
Waldersee; Kretzschmar, H.)
contains works for a variety of
instruments and vocal
combinations microfiche
UNIV.MUS.ED. reprints of
Breitkopf & Hartel Editions;
contains 47 volumes, $310.00
(B138)

Consider, O My Soul
B solo,pno PATERSON s.p.   (B139)

Consider Then, My Soul Unwary
see Five Spiritual Songs

Dearest Lord Jesus
see Five Spiritual Songs

Der Backtrog *see Quodlibet

Der Herr Denket An Uns *S.196, sec,
cant
(Mendel) [Eng/Ger] TBar soli,pno/
org PETERS 6079 $.40   (B140)

Die Armut, So Gott Auf Sich Nimmt
see Ausgewahlte Duette Heft I

Die Obrigkeit Ist Gottes Gabe
see Ausgewahlte Arien Fur Alt Heft
III

Domine Deus, Agnus Dei
see Ausgewahlte Duette Heft III

Dreiundachtzig Geistliche Lieder Und
Arien Aus Schmellis Gesangbuch
Und Dem Notenbuch Der Anna
Magdalena Bach *sac,CC83U
high solo,pno pap BREITKOPF-W
EB 2817 $4.00; high solo,pno
cloth BREITKOPF-W s.p.; low solo,
pno pap BREITKOPF-W EB 4738
$3.00; low solo,pno cloth
BREITKOPF-W s.p.   (B141)

Du Wahrer Gott Und Davids Sohn
see Ausgewahlte Duette Heft II

D'un Pas Bien Faible (from Jesu Der
Du Meine Seele)
[Fr/Ger] SA soli,pno DURAND s.p.
(B142)

Durchlaucht'ster Leopold *S.173a
SB soli,2fl,bsn,strings,cembalo sc
BREITKOPF-L PB 3081 s.p., ipr
(B143)

Eight Songs And Arias From The Anna
Magdalena Bach's Music Book
*CC8U
[Ger] high solo/med solo,pno PETERS
3392B $2.50   (B144)

Er Kennt Die Rechten Freundenstunden
see Ausgewahlte Duette Heft I

Erbarme Dich, Mein Gott (from
Matthauspassion) sac
see Ausgewahlte Arien Fur Alt Heft
III
A solo,pno (B min) LIENAU HOS 13
s.p.   (B145)

Erschutt're Dich Nur Nicht Verzagte
Seele
see Ausgewahlte Arien Fur Tenor
Heft III

Es Dunket Mich, Ich Seh' Dich Kommen
see Ausgewahlte Arien Fur Tenor
Heft III

Esurientes Implevit Bonis (from
Magnificat Es-Dur) sac
A solo,2S rec,cont sc HANSSLER
11.207 s.p., ipa   (B146)

BACH, JOHANN SEBASTIAN (cont'd.)

Five Sacred Songs *sac
  solo,org SCHIRM.EC 2521 s.p.
    contains: Beside Thy Cradle Here
    I Stand; Jehovah, Let Me Now
    Adore Thee; Jesus, Jesus, Thou
    Art Mine; Lord, My God, Be
    Praised, The; What God's
    Almighty Power Hath Made (B147)

Five Spiritual Songs *sac
  solo,pno SCHIRM.G $1.50
    contains: Come, Celebrate This
    Morn; Come, Soothing Death;
    Consider Then, My Soul Unwary;
    Dearest Lord Jesus; If Thou Art
    Near   (B148)

For The Lord Hath Magnified Me
  Bar solo,pno PATERSON s.p.   (B149)

Frohe Hirten, Eilt, Ach Eilet
  see Ausgewahlte Arien Fur Tenor
  Heft III

Gedenk' An Jesu Bittern Tod
  see Ausgewahlte Duette Heft II

Geist Und Seele Wird Verwirret *sac,
  Trin,cant
  Mez/A solo,2ob,English horn,bsn,
  strings,org,cembalo voc sc
  BREITKOPF-L EB 7035 $2.00, ipr
                              (B150)

Geistliche Lieder *CC5U,spir
  [Ger/Eng] high solo,pno FABER F0426
  $1.50   (B151)

Geistliche Lieder Und Arien *CCU
  [Ger] BREITKOPF-W high solo,pno
  $4.00; low solo,pno $3.00   (B152)

Geistliche Lieder Und Arien *sac,
  CC35L
  [Ger/Dan] CHESTER s.p. high solo,
  kbd; low solo,kbd songs from
  Schemelli's Songbook And The
  Notebook For Anna Magdalena Bach
                              (B153)

Geliebter Jesu, Du Allein
  see Ausgewahlte Arien Fur Tenor
  Heft II

Gelobet Sei Dir Herr, Mein Gott
  see Ausgewahlte Arien Fur Sopran
  Heft IV

Give Me Back My Lord
  Bar solo,pno PATERSON s.p.   (B154)

God Is Life *sac
  (Davis) med solo,pno (F maj) GALAXY
  1.2035.7 $1.00   (B155)

God Is Our Life *sac
  solo,pno PATERSON s.p.   (B156)

God, My Shepherd *sac
  (Dickinson) high solo,pno BELWIN
  $1.50   (B157)
  (Dickinson) med solo,pno BELWIN
  $1.50   (B158)
  (Dickinson) low solo,pno BELWIN
  $1.50   (B159)

Good Fellows, Be Merry
  Bar solo,pno PATERSON s.p.   (B160)

Gott Ist Mein Freund
  see Ausgewahlte Arien Fur Tenor
  Heft II

Gott, Man Lobet Dich In Der Stille
  (from Gott, Man Lobet Dich In Der
  Stille) sac
  [Ger/Eng] A solo,cembalo,strings, 2
  oboe d'amore voc sc BREITKOPF-W
  EB 7120 s.p.   (B161)

Gottes Wort
  see Ausgewahlte Duette Heft III

Green And Peaceful Are The Pastures
  *see Schafe Konnen Sicher Weiden

Guard Thy Soul
  A solo,pno PATERSON s.p.   (B162)

Hail Sabbath Day
  high solo,pno (B min) GALAXY
  1.1534.7 $1.00   (B163)
  low solo,pno (G min) GALAXY
  1.1535.7 $1.00   (B164)

Hallelujah
  A solo,pno PATERSON s.p.   (B165)

Happy Flock
  S solo,pno PATERSON s.p.   (B166)

He Hath Filled The Hungry
  A solo,pno PATERSON s.p.   (B167)

BACH, JOHANN SEBASTIAN (cont'd.)

He Hath Regarded
  S solo,pno PATERSON s.p.   (B168)

Herr, Deine Gute Reicht So Weit
  see Ausgewahlte Arien Fur Sopran
  Heft IV

Herr, Du Siehst Statt Guter Werke Auf
  Des Herzens Des Kreuzes
  see Ausgewahlte Duette Heft II

Hochgelobter Gottessohn
  see Ausgewahlte Arien Fur Alt Heft
  III

I Follow With Gladness
  S solo,pno,opt fl/vln PATERSON s.p.
                              (B169)

I Will Magnify Thee *sac
  low solo,pno (C maj) SCHIRM.G $.60
                              (B170)

Ich Armer Mensch, Ich Sundenknecht
  see Ausgewahlte Arien Fur Tenor
  Heft II

Ich Bin Herrlich, Ich Bin Schon
  see Ausgewahlte Arien Fur Sopran
  Heft IV

Ich Bin In Mir Vergnugt *S.204, sec,
  cant
  [Ger] S solo,fl,2ob,strings,cont
  voc sc KALMUS 6640 $1.50   (B171)
  (Todt, B.) S solo,fl,2ob,ob,bsn,
  strings,cembalo sc BREITKOPF-L
  PB 3073 $2.00 s.p., ipr   (B172)
  (Todt, B.) S solo,pno voc sc
  BREITKOPF-L EB 7204 $2.00   (B173)

Ich Esse Mit Freunden Mein Weniges
  Brot
  see Ausgewahlte Arien Fur Sopran
  Heft IV

Ich Geh' Und Suche Mit Verlangen
  *S.49, sac,Trin,cant
  SB soli,English horn,vcl,strings,
  org/cembalo voc sc BREITKOPF-L
  EB 7049 $2.50, ipr   (B174)
  SB soli,ob,org,strings sc
  BREITKOPF-W PB 4549 s.p., ipa
                              (B175)

Ich Habe Genug *S.82, sac,cant
  [Ger/Eng] Bar/B solo,ob,strings,
  cembalo sc BREITKOPF-L PB 2932
  s.p., ipa   (B176)
  [Ger/Eng] B solo,ob,cont,strings sc
  BREITKOPF-W PB 4582 s.p., ipa,
  voc sc BREITKOPF-W EB 7082 s.p.
                              (B177)
  [Ger] B solo,pno PETERS 2149 $4.75
                              (B178)
  (Hellmann, Diethard) [Ger/Eng] S
  solo,fl,org,strings sc BREITKOPF-
  W PB 5016 s.p., ipa, voc sc
  BREITKOPF-W EB 6969 $1.75   (B179)
  (Raphael, G.) [Ger/Eng] Bar/B solo,
  pno voc sc BREITKOPF-L EB 7082
  $2.00   (B180)

Ich Steh An Deiner Krippen Hier *sac
  A/Bar solo,pno (B min) LIENAU
  HOS 172 s.p.   (B181)
  S/T solo,pno (D min) LIENAU HOS 171
  s.p.   (B182)

Ich Weiss, Dass Mein Erloser Lebt
  *S.160, sac,Easter,cant
  [Ger/Eng] T solo,vln,bsn,cont,
  strings sc BREITKOPF-W PB 4660
  s.p., ipa, voc sc BREITKOPF-W
  EB 7160 $1.75   (B183)

Ich Will Den Kreuzstab Gerne Tragen
  (from Ich Will Den Kreuzstab
  Gerne Tragen) sac
  [Eng/Ger] B solo,pno PETERS 1664A
  $2.75   (B184)
  [Eng/Ger] B solo,orch EULENBURG
  E1008 s.p.   (B185)
  (Ropartz, Guy) B solo,orch,org
  ENOCH s.p.   (B186)

Ich Will Nach Dem Himmel Zu
  see Ausgewahlte Arien Fur Alt Heft
  III

If Thou Art Near
  see Five Spiritual Songs

In Praise Of Laughter
  Bar solo,pno PATERSON s.p.   (B187)

In Thee O Spirit *sac
  (Hamlin) med-high solo,pno (B flat
  maj) BOSTON $1.50   (B188)

Jauchzet Gott In Allen Landen *S.51,
  sac,Trin,cant
  S solo,trp,strings,cont sc HANSSLER
  10.129 s.p., ipa, voc sc HANSSLER
  s.p.   (B189)
  S solo,S,trp,strings,cembalo sc
  BREITKOPF-L PB 2901 s.p., cor pts

BACH, JOHANN SEBASTIAN (cont'd.)

  BREITKOPF-L CHB 2220 s.p., ipa
                              (B190)
  S solo,trom,strings,cont sc
  BREITKOPF-W PB 4551 s.p., ipa
                              (B191)
  [Ger] S solo,pno PETERS 1655 $4.75
                              (B192)
  [Ger/Eng] S solo,orch study sc
  EULENBURG E1038 s.p.   (B193)
  (Raphael, G.) [Ger/Eng/Fr] S solo,
  S,trp,strings,cembalo voc sc
  BREITKOPF-L EB 7051 $1.75   (B194)

Jehovah, Let Me Now Adore Thee
  see Five Sacred Songs

Jesu, Deine Gnadenblicke (from Lobet
  Gott In Seinen Reichen)
  see Bach, Johann Sebastian,
  Unschuld Kleinod Reiner Seelen

Jesu, Dir Sei Preis Gesungen (from
  Uns Ist Ein Kind Geboren) sac
  S solo,2S rec,cont HANSSLER 5.042
  s.p. see also GESANGE ZUM
  KIRCHENJAHR   (B195)

Jesu Joy Of Man's Desiring *see
  Jesus Bleibet Meine Freude

Jesu, Lass Dich Finden, Lass Doch
  Meine Sunden (from Mein Liebster
  Jesu Ist Verloren) sac
  [Ger/Fr] A solo,cembalo,strings, 2
  oboe d'amore voc sc BREITKOPF-W
  EB 7154 s.p.   (B196)

Jesus Bleibet Meine Freude (from Herz
  Und Mund Und Tat Und Leben) sac
  solo,pno BROEKMANS 424 s.p. (B197)
  (Breck) "Jesus, Joy Of Man's
  Desiring" med solo,pno (G maj)
  FISCHER,C V 2234   (B198)
  (Daymond) "Jesu Joy Of Man's
  Desiring" med solo,pno OXFORD
                              (B199)
  (Kramer) "Jesu Joy Of Man's
  Desiring" low solo,pno (F maj)
  GALAXY 1.1601.7 $1.25   (B200)
  (Kramer) "Jesu Joy Of Man's
  Desiring" high solo,pno (A flat
  maj) GALAXY 1.1600.7 $1.25 (B201)

Jesus From The Grave Is Risen *sac
  solo,pno PATERSON s.p.   (B202)

Jesus, Jesus, Thou Art Mine
  see Five Sacred Songs

Jesus, Joy Of Man's Desiring *see
  Jesus Bleibet Meine Freude

Jesus, Refuge Of The Weary *sac
  med solo,pno oct CONCORDIA 98-1765
  $.20   (B203)

Jesus, Shepherd, Be Thou Near Me
  *sac,Marriage
  high solo,pno CONCORDIA 97-9335
  $.75   (B204)
  low solo,pno CONCORDIA 97-9336 $.75
                              (B205)

Jesus, Thy Blood And Righteousness
  *sac
  med solo,cont oct CONCORDIA 98-2052
  $.25   (B206)

Jesus, Tu Es A Moi *sac
  [Fr/Ger] solo,pno/inst DURAND s.p.
                              (B207)

Jesus, Unser Trost Und Leben *sac
  S solo,2S rec,cont HANSSLER 5.052
  s.p. see also GESANGE ZUM
  KIRCHENJAHR   (B208)

Kaffee-Kantate *see Schweigt Stille,
  Plaudert Nicht

Kleines Magnificat *sac
  S solo,fl,strings,cont sc HANSSLER
  10.139 s.p., ipa   (B209)

Komm, Komm, Mein Herze Steht Dir
  Offen
  see Ausgewahlte Arien Fur Sopran
  Heft IV

Komm, Susser Tod, Komm, Sel'ge Ruh'
  *S.478, sac
  S/T solo,pno (C min) LIENAU HOS 4
  s.p.   (B210)
  A/Bar solo,pno (A min) LIENAU HOS 5
  s.p.   (B211)

Kommt, Seelem, Dieser Tag Muss Heilig
  Sein Besungen *sac
  S/T solo,pno (F maj) LIENAU HOS 173
  s.p.   (B212)
  A/Bar solo,pno (E flat maj) LIENAU
  HOS 174 s.p.   (B213)

Le Coeur Content (from Also Hat Gott
  Die Welt Geliebt) sac,Pent
  S solo,pno/org HEUGEL s.p.   (B214)

BACH, JOHANN SEBASTIAN (cont'd.)

Leget Euch Dem Heiland Unter
see Ausgewahlte Arien Fur Alt Heft
III

Let All The Multitudes Of Light *sac
med solo,pno oct CONCORDIA 98-1766
$.20 (B215)

Liebster Herr Jesu, Wo Bleibst Du So
Lange *S.484, sac
S/T solo,pno (G min) LIENAU HOS 6
s.p. (B216)
A/Bar solo,pno (E min) LIENAU HOS 7
s.p. (B217)

Lord All Holy, All Merciful
(Wheeler) solo,pno ALLANS s.p.
(B218)

Lord Bless You, The (from Der Herr
Denket An Uns) sac,Marriage
[Ger/Eng] high solo&low solo,cont
oct CONCORDIA 98-1474 $.25 (B219)

Lord Jesus Christ, Thou Prince Of
Peace *sac
med solo,fl,cont oct CONCORDIA
98-1955 $.30, ipa (B220)

Lord, My God, Be Praised, The
see Five Sacred Songs

Meditation *see Ave Maria

Mein Glaubiges Herze (from Also Hat
Gott Die Welt Geliebt) sac
S solo,pno (F maj) LIENAU HOS 18
s.p. (B221)
A solo,vln,org (D maj) LIENAU
HOS 19 s.p. (B222)
"Mon Ame Croyante Tressaille Et
Chante" [Fr/Ger] S solo,pno,vln
DURAND s.p. (B223)
"Mon Ame Croyante Tressaille Et
Chante" [Fr/Ger] S solo,pno,vcl
DURAND s.p. (B224)
"Mon Ame Croyante Tressaille Et
Chante" [Fr/Ger] S solo,pno/inst
DURAND s.p. (B225)
"My Heart Ever Faithful" S solo,pno
NOVELLO 17.0118.03 s.p. (B226)
"My Heart Ever Faithful" solo,pno
(D maj) ASHDOWN (B227)
"My Heart Ever Faithful" low solo,
pno (C maj) ALLANS s.p. (B228)
"My Heart Ever Faithful" med solo,
pno (D maj) ALLANS s.p. (B229)
"My Heart Ever Faithful" high solo,
pno (F maj) ALLANS s.p. (B230)
(Deis) "My Heart Ever Faithful"
[Eng/Ger] high solo,pno (F maj)
SCHIRM.G $.85 (B231)
(Spicker) "My Heart Ever Faithful"
[Eng/Ger] low solo,pno (C maj)
SCHIRM.G $.85 (B232)
(Spicker) "My Heart Ever Faithful"
[Eng/Ger] high solo,pno (F maj)
SCHIRM.G $.85 (B233)

Mein Herze Schwimmt Im Blut *S.199,
sac,Trin,cant
S solo,ob,bsn,cembalo,strings sc
BREITKOPF-W PB 4699 s.p., ipa
(B234)
(Schneider, M.) [Ger/Eng] S solo,
2ob,bsn,strings,cembalo voc sc
BREITKOPF-L EB 7199 $1.75, ipr
(B235)

Meine Seele Ruhmt Und Preist *S.189,
sac,cant
T solo,fl,ob,cont,3strings sc
BREITKOPF-W PB 4689 s.p., ipa,
voc sc BREITKOPF-W EB 7189 $1.75
(B236)

Melodies Et Airs Choisis *CCU
[Fr] med solo,pno BREITKOPF-W $2.25
(B237)

Mer Hahn En Neue Oberkeet *S.212,
sec,cant
SB soli,fl,horn,cembalo,strings sc
BREITKOPF-W PB 4712 s.p., ipa,
voc sc BREITKOPF-W EB 7212 $1.50,
solo pt BREITKOPF-W CHB 4712 s.p.
(B238)
[Ger] SB soli,fl,horn,cembalo,
strings sc PETERS 4627 $8.50,
ipa, study sc EULENBURG E1006
s.p. (B239)
(Cellier, Alexandre) "Nous Avons Un
Nouveau Gouverneur" solo,pno
HEUGEL 512 s.p. (B240)

Mighty He Hath Dethroned, The
T solo,pno PATERSON s.p. (B241)

Mighty Lord And King All Glorious
*sac
B solo,pno NOVELLO 17.0118.05 s.p. (B242)

Mon Ame Croyante Tressaille Et Chante
*see Mein Glaubiges Herze

Mon Doux Jesus Sera L'armure (from
Schauet Doch Und Sehet) sac
[Fr/Ger] A solo,pno/inst DURAND

s.p. (B243)

Mon Jesus Etait Mort (from Denn Du
Wirst Meine Seele Nicht In Der
Holle Lassen)
[Fr/Ger] SA soli,pno DURAND s.p.
(B244)

Mon Jesus, Ta Patience *sac
[Fr/Ger] solo,pno/inst DURAND s.p.
(B245)

My Heart Ever Faithful *see Mein
Glaubiges Herze

My Heart Rejoiceth
Mez solo,pno PATERSON s.p. (B246)

Neunundsechzig Gesange Zu Schemellis
Musicalischem Gesangbuch 1736:
BWV 439-507 *CC69U
(med) s.p.

Non Sa Che Sia Dolore *S.209, sec,
cant
[Ger] S solo,fl,strings,cont voc sc
KALMUS 6645 $1.50 (B247)
"Was Schmerz Sei Und Was Leiden"
[It/Ger] S solo,fl,strings,
cembalo sc BREITKOPF-L PB 3092
s.p., ipr, voc sc BREITKOPF-L
EB 7209 $1.75 (B248)
"Was Schmerz Sei Und Was Leiden" S
solo,fl,cont,strings sc
BREITKOPF-W PB 4709 s.p., ipa
(B249)

Nous Avons Un Nouveau Gouverneur
*see Mer Hahn En Neue Oberkeet

Now The Sheep Secure Are Grazing
*see Schafe Konnen Sicher Weiden

Nul Ne Peut Vaincre La Mort (from
Christ Lag In Todesbanden)
SA soli,pno DURAND s.p. (B250)

O Du Angenehmer Schatz (from Ehre Sei
Gott In Der Hohe) sac
A solo,2fl,bsn,cont sc HANSSLER
10.204 s.p., ipa (B251)

O Glad Dig, Mitt Hjarta *sac
S solo,pno GEHRMANS s.p. (B252)

O Holder Tag, Erwunschte Zeit
*S.210, sec,Marriage,cant
[Ger/Fr] S solo,fl,ob,strings,
cembalo sc BREITKOPF-L rental
(B253)
[Ger] S solo,fl,ob,horn,strings,
cont voc sc KALMUS 6646 $1.50
(B254)
(Todt, B.) [Ger/Fr] S solo,pno voc
sc BREITKOPF-L EB 7210 $2.00
(B255)

O Jesulein Suss *sac
S/T solo,pno (B flat maj) LIENAU
HOS 8 s.p. (B256)
A/Bar solo,pno (G maj) LIENAU HOS 9
s.p. (B257)

O, Mon Doux Jesus *sac
[Fr/Ger] solo,pno/inst DURAND s.p.
(B258)

O Sacred Head, Now Wounded (from
Matthauspassion) sac
med solo,fl,cont oct CONCORDIA
98-2053 $.25 (B259)

O Seelen-Paradies
see Ausgewahlte Arien Fur Tenor
Heft II

O Taste And See
A solo,pno PATERSON s.p. (B260)

O Yes, Just So
Mez solo,pno NOVELLO 17.0144.04
s.p. (B261)

Of Flowers The Fairest
S solo,pno PATERSON s.p. (B262)

On My Shepherd I Rely
S solo,pno,opt vln PATERSON s.p.
(B263)

One In Heart And One In Mind *sac
(Roff, J.) med solo,pno/org (easy)
GIA G-1970 $1.00 (B264)

Only Be Still
T solo,pno PATERSON s.p. (B265)

Only Son From Heaven, The *sac
med solo,strings,ob,cont oct
CONCORDIA 98-2033 $.25, ipa
(B266)

Pan Is Master Of Us All
T solo,pno PATERSON s.p. (B267)

Pardon Us, Gracious Lord
A solo,pno PATERSON s.p. (B268)

Pastoral Music
[Ger] solo,3A rec,vln,vcl,bvl,
cembalo sc VIEWEG V137 s.p., ipa

(B269)

Piccolo Magnificat *sac
(Paccagnella, E.) S solo,fl,org,
vln,vla,cont sc SANTIS 990 s.p.
(B270)

Pieta Ti Prenda Mio Dio (from
Matthauspassion)
(Respighi, O.) [It] A solo,pno
BONGIOVANI 492 s.p. (B271)

Plus De Peines, Plus De Larmes (from
Liebster Jesu, Wird Sind Hier)
[Ger/Fr] SB soli,pno DURAND s.p.
(B272)

Que Joyeux Parait Le Temps (from
Fruhling Und Liebe)
[Fr/Ger] S solo,pno/inst DURAND
s.p. (B273)

Quodlibet *S.524
"Der Backtrog" 4 soli,vcl,cont sc
BREITKOPF-L EB 7315 s.p. (B274)

Recit Et Air (from Matthauspassion)
sac
[Fr/Ger] S solo,pno/inst DURAND
s.p. (B275)

Rezitative Und Arien Aus Kantaten
Heft I *CCU
(Pidoux, Pierre) high solo,cont
(med diff) BAREN. 84 $5.75 (B276)

Rezitative Und Arien Aus Kantaten
Heft II *CCU
(Pidoux, Pierre) low solo,cont (med
diff) BAREN. 85 $5.75 (B277)

Sacred Songs And Arias, The (from
Anna Magdelena Notebook, No. 2)
sac,CCU
solo,pno study sc KALMUS 913 $1.50
(B278)

Sacred Songs From Schemelli's
Gesangbuch *sac,CC69U
[Ger/Eng] high solo,pno CONCORDIA
97-9334 $4.00; low solo,pno
CONCORDIA 97-9337 $4.00 (B279)

Saviour, Make Me All Thine Own
S solo,pno PATERSON s.p. (B280)

Schafe Konnen Sicher Weiden (from Was
Mir Behagt, Ist Nur Die Muntre
Jagd) sac
"Green And Peaceful Are The
Pastures" high solo,pno (A flat
maj) ASHDOWN (B281)
"Green And Peaceful Are The
Pastures" low solo,pno (F maj)
ASHDOWN (B282)
"Sheep May Safely Graze" low solo,
pno (F maj) ALLANS s.p. (B283)
"Sheep May Safely Graze" med solo,
pno (A flat maj) ALLANS s.p.
(B284)
"Sheep May Safely Graze" high solo,
pno (B flat maj) ALLANS s.p.
(B285)
(Davis) "Sheep May Safely Graze"
high solo,pno (A flat maj) GALAXY
1.1334.7 $1.25 (B286)
(Durr, Alfred) S solo,2fl,rec,cont
(med) BAREN. 2870 $3.25 (B287)
(Kramer) "Sheep May Safely Graze"
high solo,pno ELKIN 27.2076.00
s.p. (B288)
(Kramer) "Sheep May Safely Graze"
low solo,pno ELKIN 27.2075.02
s.p. (B289)
(Kramer) "Sheep May Safely Graze"
low solo,pno (F maj) GALAXY
1.1335.7 $1.25 (B290)
(La Forge) "Now The Sheep Secure
Are Grazing" med solo,pno
FISCHER,C V 1700 (B291)
(La Forge) "Now The Sheep Secure
Are Grazing" high solo,pno
FISCHER,C V 1403 (B292)
(Tate) "Sheep May Safely Graze"
Mez/Bar solo,pno (easy) OXFORD
62.212 $1.00 (B293)
(Tate) "Sheep May Safely Graze" S/T
solo,pno (easy) OXFORD 62.212
$1.00 (B294)

Schemelli Song Book *sac/sec,CC69U
[Ger] solo,pno PETERS $4.00 with
original clefs and unrealized
figured bass (B295)

Schemelli Song Book *sac,CC69U
[Ger] solo,pno cmplt ed PETERS 4612
$10.00 (B296)

Schlage Doch, Gewunschte Stunde
(Cantata 53) S.53, sac,cant/Req
[Ger] A solo,pno PETERS 3351 $4.75
(B297)
[Ger/Eng] A solo,orch study sc
EULENBURG E1044 s.p. (B298)
"Vieni Omai, Minuto Estremo" [It/
Ger] A solo,bells,strings,cont
RICORDI-ENG PR 634 s.p. (B299)

BACH, JOHANN SEBASTIAN (cont'd.)

Schweigt Stille, Plaudert Nicht
(Cantata 211) S.211, sec,cant
"Coffee Cantata" STB soli,fl,
strings,cont KALMUS 6064 $1.25
(B300)
"Kaffee-Kantate" [Ger/Fr] STB soli,
fl,strings,cembalo sc BREITKOPF-L
PB 3094 s.p., ipa   (B301)
"Kaffee Kantate" [Ger/Fr] STB soli,
fl,cembalo,strings sc BREITKOPF-W
PB 4711 s.p., ipa, voc sc
BREITKOPF-W EB 7211 s.p.   (B302)
"Silenzio! Zitti La!" [It/Ger] STB
soli,fl,strings,cont (Coffee
Cantata) RICORDI-ENG PR 638 s.p.
(B303)
(Todt, B.) "Kaffee-Kantate" [Ger/
Fr] STB soli,pno voc sc
BREITKOPF-L EB 7211 s.p.   (B304)

Schwingt Freudig Euch Empor *S.36,
sac
S solo,orch HENN s.p.   (B305)

Selected Arias *CCU
[Russ] S solo,pno MEZ KNIGA 83 s.p.
(B306)

Seufzer, Tranen, Kummer, Not (from
Ich Hatte Viel Bekummernis) sac
(Keller, Hermann) S solo,ob/vln,
cont (med) BAREN. 2310 $2.75
(B307)

Sheep May Safely Graze *see Schafe
Konnen Sicher Weiden

Si Ton Coeur S'abondonne *sec
[Fr/Ger] S solo,pno/inst DURAND
s.p.   (B308)

Silenzio! Zitti La! *see Schweigt
Stille, Plaudert Nicht

Slumber On
Bar solo,pno PATERSON s.p. (B309)

So Appears Thy Natal Day
low solo,pno GALAXY 1.1363.7 $1.25
(B310)

So Teach Us, Lord
S solo,pno PATERSON s.p.   (B311)

Song Of Pan
Bar solo,pno NOVELLO 17.0183.05
s.p.   (B312)

Strike, Thou Hour So Long Expected
*sac
A solo,pno NOVELLO 17.0189.04 s.p.
(B313)

Thou Art My Joy *see Bist Du Bei Mir

Though Wicked Men
T solo,pno PATERSON s.p.   (B314)

Tritt Auf Die Glaubensbahn *S.152,
sac,Xmas,cant
[Ger/Eng] SB soli,fl,ob,strings,
cembalo sc BREITKOPF-L PB 3901
s.p., ipr   (B315)
SB soli,rec,ob,cembalo,strings
BREITKOPF-W s.p.   (B316)
(Neumann, Werner) [Ger/Eng] SB
soli,rec,ob,cembalo,strings (G
min) sc BREITKOPF-W PB 4652 s.p.,
ipa, voc sc BREITKOPF-W EB 7152
$1.75   (B317)
(Raphael, G.) [Ger/Eng] SB soli,pno
voc sc BREITKOPF-L EB 7152 $1.75
(B318)

Trust In The Lord
Bar solo,pno PATERSON s.p. (B319)

'Twas In The Cool Of Eventide *see
Am Abend Da Es Kuhle War

Twelve Sacred Duets From Cantatas,
Vol. I *sac,CC4U
(Reinhart) [Ger] SA soli,inst&kbd
sc PETERS A54 s.p., ipa from
Cantatas nos. 4, 37, 78, 124
(B320)

Twelve Sacred Duets From Cantatas,
Vol. II *sac,CC2U
(Reinhart) [Ger] SA soli,inst&kbd
sc PETERS A55 s.p., ipa from
Cantatas nos.9, 184   (B321)

Twelve Sacred Duets From Cantatas,
Vol. III *sac,CC3U
(Reinhart) [Ger] SA soli,inst&kbd
sc PETERS A56 s.p., ipa from
Cantatas Nos. 88, 93, 168 (B322)

Twelve Sacred Duets From Cantatas,
Vol. IV *sac,CC3U
(Reinhart) [Ger] SA soli,inst&kbd
sc PETERS A57 s.p., ipa from
Cantatas Nos. 3, 91, 163   (B323)

Twenty-Five Sacred Songs *CC25U
(Grossman, Herbert) [Ger/Eng] solo,
pno INTERNAT. $2.50   (B324)

BACH, JOHANN SEBASTIAN (cont'd.)

Twenty-Five Sacred Songs From The
Schemelli Song Book *sac,CC25U
[Ger] high solo/med solo,pno PETERS
3392A $3.50   (B325)

Twenty Sacred Songs *sac,CC20L
(Franz, Robert) [Eng] S/T solo,pno
NOVELLO 17.0226.02 s.p.   (B326)

Twenty Sacred Songs From The
Schemelli Gesangbuch *sac,CC20U
(Franz) solo,pno BELWIN $1.50
(B327)

Unschuld Kleinod Reiner Seelen (from
Lobet Gott In Seinen Reichen) sac
(Smend, Friedrich) S solo,fl,ob,
vln,vla (med diff) BAREN. HM 1
s.p. contains also: Jesu, Deine
Gnadenblicke   (B328)

Vanish Now, Ye Gloomy Shadows *see
Weichet Nur, Betrubte Schatten

Veinte Lieder Y Arias Religiosos
*sac,CC20L
(Leuchter) [Ger/Span] T solo,pno
RICORDI-ARG BA 8922 s.p.   (B329)

Vergiss Mein Micht, Dass Ich Dein
Nicht Vergesse *S.505, sac
A/Bar solo,pno (F sharp min) LIENAU
HOS 11 s.p.   (B330)
S/T solo,pno (A min) LIENAU HOS 10
s.p.   (B331)

Vergnugte Pleissen-Stadt *S.216,
Marriage,cant
[Ger/Eng] SA soli,2fl,ob,vla,
cembalo voc sc LIENAU R29 s.p.,
ipa   (B332)
(Schumann, Georg) SA soli,2fl,ob,
pno,strings BREITKOPF-W s.p.
(B333)

Vergnugte Ruh', Beliebte Seelenlust
*S.170, sac,Trin,cant
[Ger/Eng] A solo,org,cont,strings,
oboe d'amore sc BREITKOPF-W
PB 4670 s.p., ipa, voc sc
BREITKOPF-W EB 7170 s.p.   (B334)
(Raphael, G.) [Ger/Eng] Mez/A solo,
strings&org&cembalo/fl&ob&cembalo
voc sc BREITKOPF-L EB 7170 $2.00,
ipr   (B335)

Vieni Omai, Minuto Estremo *see
Schlage Doch, Gewunschte Stunde

Viens, Douce Mort
[Fr/Ger] solo,pno/inst DURAND s.p.
(B336)

Virga Jesse Floruit (from Magnificat
Es-Dur) sac
(Durr, Alfred) SB soli,cont (D maj,
diff) BAREN. HM 80 $5.00   (B337)

Was Gott Tut, Das Ist Wohlgetan (from
Was Gott Tut, Das Ist Wohlgetan)
[Ger] T solo,opt fl,pno BOOSEY
$2.00   (B338)

Was Schmerz Sei Und Was Leiden *see
Non Sa Che Sia Dolore

Wedding Processional And Air *sac,
Marriage
(Leupold, Ulrich) high solo,pno
AUGSBURG 11-0826 $.75   (B339)

Weichet Nur, Betrubte Schatten
*S.202, sec,Marriage,cant
S solo,ob,bsn,strings,cembalo sc
BREITKOPF-L PB 3073 s.p., ipa
(B340)
S solo,ob,bsn,strings,cembalo sc
BREITKOPF-W PB 4702 s.p., ipa
(B341)
[Ger] S solo,pno PETERS 4628 $7.50
(B342)
[Ger] S solo,ob,strings,cont sc
KALMUS $3.50, voc sc KALMUS 6638
$1.50   (B343)
"Vanish Now, Ye Gloomy Shadows" S
solo,ob,strings,cembalo sc PETERS
4629 $5.00, ipa   (B344)
"Vanish Now, Ye Gloomy Shadows"
[Eng] S solo,org sc PETERS 6281
$2.75   (B345)
(Todt, B.) S solo,pno voc sc
BREITKOPF-L EB 7202 $2.25   (B346)

Wenn Des Kreuzes Bitterkeiten Mit Des
Fleisches Schwachheit Streiten
see Ausgewahlte Duette Heft II

Wenn Sorgen Auf Mich Dringen
see Ausgewahlte Duette Heft I

Wert Thou But Near *see Bist Du Bei
Mir

What God's Almighty Power Hath Made
see Five Sacred Songs

BACH, JOHANN SEBASTIAN (cont'd.)

Widerstehe Doch Der Sunde *S.54,
sac,cant
[Ger/Eng] S solo,strings,cembalo sc
BREITKOPF-L PB 2904 s.p., ipa
(B347)
A solo,cont,strings sc BREITKOPF-W
PB 4554 s.p., ipa, voc sc
BREITKOPF-W EB 7054 s.p.   (B348)
(Raphael, G.) [Ger/Eng] S solo,pno
voc sc BREITKOPF-L EB 7054 $1.50
(B349)

Wilt Thou Leave Me Thus?
T solo,pno PATERSON s.p.   (B350)

Wir Eilen Mit Schwachen, Doch Emsigen
Schritten (from Jesu Der Du Meine
Seele) sac
see Ausgewahlte Duette Heft III
SA solo,pno BREITKOPF-L EB 5474
s.p.   (B351)

With Joyful Heart I Praise My Saviour
(from Bekennen Will Ich Seinen
Namen) sac
[Eng] A solo,kbd&2vln&opt vcl&bvl/
2vln&vcl PETERS 66032 $3.00
(B352)

With Loudest Rejoicing *sac
SA soli,cont oct CONCORDIA 98-1846
$.25   (B353)

Wohl Euch, Ihr Auserwahlten Seelen
(from O Ewiges Feuer, O Ursprung
Der Liebe) sac
[Ger/Eng] A solo,2fl,cembalo,
strings voc sc BREITKOPF-W
EB 7034 s.p.   (B354)

Zwanzig Geistliche Lieder *sac,CC20U
(Franz, Robert) LEUCKART s.p. high
solo,pno/org; low solo,pno/org
(B355)

BACH, KARL PHILIPP EMANUEL (1714-1788)
Fecit Potentiam (from Magnificat) sac
Bar/B solo,3trp,timp,strings
BREITKOPF-L rental   (B356)

Ihr Tore Offnet Euch (from
Auferstehung Und Himmelfahrt) sac
Bar/B solo,2ob,2horn,2trp,strings
BREITKOPF-L rental   (B357)

Phyllis Und Thirsis *cant
S/T solo,2fl,cont sc GERIG AV 119
s.p.   (B358)
(Walter, G.A.) ST soli,2fl,cont
BREITKOPF-L rental   (B359)

Sacred Songs *sac,CC30U
high solo/med solo,pno PETERS 3748
$2.50   (B360)

BACH ARIAS FOR SOPRANO see Bach, Johann
Sebastian

BACHANAL see Dahl

BACHARACH, E.
Cuarto Canciones *CC4U
[Span] med solo,pno UNION ESP.
$1.75   (B361)

BACHELET, ALFRED (1864-1944)
Chere Nuit
S solo,orch (available in 2 keys)
LEDUC s.p.   (B362)
S solo,opt vln (available in 2
keys) LEDUC s.p.   (B363)

Noel *sac,Xmas
1-2 soli,pno/org HEUGEL s.p. (B364)

BACHELIER DE SALAMANQUE see Roussel,
Albert

BACHELORS OF DEVON, THE see Day, Maude
Craske

BACHIANAS BRASILEIRAS, NO. 5: ARIA see
Villa-Lobos, Heitor

BACIAMI see Tosti, Francesco Paolo

BACIAMI PURE IN BENARES see Kalman,
Emerich

BACK HOME see Price, Florence B.

BACK, SVEN-ERICK (1919-   )
Neither Nor
S solo,pno,perc NORDISKA 10241 s.p.
(B365)

BACK TO LOVE *sac
(Carmichael, Ralph) solo,pno WORD
S-429   (B366)

BACKER-GRONDAHL, AGATHE URSULA
(1847-1907)
Bjorken Berattar
Mez/Bar solo,pno GEHRMANS s.p. see
from SANGEN I   (B367)

BACKER-GRONDAHL, AGATHE URSULA
(cont'd.)

Fem Sanger *CC5U
solo,pno GEHRMANS s.p.   (B368)

Four Songs *Op.17, CC4U
[Ger] med solo,pno NORSK $1.00
(B369)

Fyra Sanger *CC4U
solo,pno GEHRMANS s.p.   (B370)

Priere Du Soir
solo,pno ENOCH s.p. see also CHANTS
DU NORD   (B371)

Seven Songs, Vol. I *Op.16, CC7U
[Ger/Norw] med solo,pno NORSK $1.00
(B372)

Seven Songs, Vol. II *Op.16, CC7U
[Ger/Norw] med solo,pno NORSK $1.00
(B373)

Sommerliv
solo,pno GEHRMANS s.p.   (B374)

Three Songs *Op.14, CC3U
[Eng/Norw] med solo,pno NORSK $1.00
(B375)

Three Songs *Op.18, CC3U
[Norw] med-high solo,pno NORSK
$1.00   (B376)

BACKER-LUNDE, J.
Lady Moon *Op.40,No.1
[Eng/Norw] med solo,pno NORSK $.75
(B377)

BACKMAN, HJALMAR
Fardeminnen *see Matkani Muistot

Matkani Muistot
"Fardeminnen" 2 soli,pno FAZER
W 398 s.p.   (B378)

Sondagsmorgon *see Sunnuntaiaamuna

Sunnuntaiaamuna
"Sondagsmorgon" 2 soli,pno FAZER
W 399 s.p.   (B379)

BACKSLIDIN' see Protheroe, Daniel

BACON
Quiet Airs
high solo,pno PRESSER $2.00 (B380)

BACON AND EGGS see Blyton, Carey

BACON, ERNST (1898-   )
Brady
solo,pno (B flat maj) BOOSEY $1.50
(B381)

Red Rose
solo,pno (D min) BOOSEY $1.50
(B382)

Six Songs *CC6U
low solo,pno PRESSER $1.50   (B383)

BACOVSKE PIESNE see Suchon, Eugen

BADEN, H.E.
Bells Of Hazelmere, The
low solo,pno (D flat maj) CRAMER
(B384)
high solo,pno (E flat maj) CRAMER
(B385)

BADINGS, HENK (1907-   )
Ad Festum Letitie *sac
S solo,2fl,2ob,2clar,bsn,3horn,
2trp,trom,timp,perc,cel,harp,
strings DONEMUS see from Drie
Kerstliederen   (B386)

Adam Lay Ybounden
see Drie Geeslijke Liederen Op Oude
Engelsche Teksten

Air
see Drie Geestelijke Liederen Van
Jan Luyken

Air Sur Une Blonde
see Badings, Henk, Pastorale Pour
Jeannette

Armageddon
S solo,winds,6horn,6trp,6trom,tuba,
3timp,perc,pno,cel sc PETERS
66212 $6.00   (B387)

Ballade Van Den Watersnood
narrator,pno DONEMUS s.p.   (B388)

Bandinerie
high solo/med solo,pno ALBERSEN
s.p. see from Chasonnettes (B389)

Bij Een Doode
see Liederen Van Dood En Leven

Burying Friends
med solo,pno DONEMUS s.p.   (B390)

Chanson D'hiver
see Twee Liederen Van Charles
Vildrac

BADINGS, HENK (cont'd.)

Chansonnette
high solo/med solo,pno ALBERSEN
s.p. see from Chasonnettes (B391)

Chansons Orientales
med-high solo,pno DONEMUS s.p.
contains: Derniere Promenade; La
Jeune Fille Nue;
L'indifferente; Sur Les Bords
Du Jo-Yeh   (B392)

Chant Du Desespere
see Twee Liederen Van Charles
Vildrac

Chasonnettes *see Bandinerie;
Chansonnette; Musette; Pastorale;
Rondeau; Tambourin   (B393)

Coplas
A solo,2fl,2ob,2clar,2bsn,2horn,
2trp,timp,perc,strings DONEMUS
(B394)

Coplas *CCU
solo,pno BROEKMANS 699 s.p. (B395)

Das Arme Kind
see Drei Lieder

Das Grosse Lalula
see Vijf Liederen Van Morgenstern

Das Huhn
see Vijf Liederen Van Morgenstern

Das Marchen Von Der Wolke
see Drei Lieder

Das Mondschaf
see Vijf Liederen Van Morgenstern

De Westewind
narrator,2fl,2ob,2clar,bsn,4horn,
2trp,2trom,tuba,timp,perc,cel,
harp,pno,strings DONEMUS s.p.
(B396)

Derniere Promenade
see Chansons Orientales

Dies Est Letitie *sac
S solo,2fl,2ob,2clar,bsn,3horn,
2trp,trom,timp,perc,cel,harp,
strings DONEMUS see from Drie
Kerstliederen   (B397)

Drei Lieder
med solo,pno DONEMUS s.p.
contains: Das Arme Kind; Das
Marchen Von Der Wolke; Es Ist
Lang   (B398)

Drie Dullaert Liederen *CC3U
solo,pno BROEKMANS 252 s.p. (B399)

Drie Geeslijke Liederen Op Oude
Engelsche Teksten *sac
[Eng] A solo,ob,org DONEMUS D151
s.p.
contains: Adam Lay Ybounden; I
Sing Of A Maiden; When Christ
Was Born   (B400)

Drie Geestelijke Liederen Van Jan
Luyken *sac
[Dut] A solo,org DONEMUS D444 s.p.
contains: Air; Lied Tot Alle
Vermoeijde Zielen; Van Jesus De
Ware Ruste   (B401)

Drie Kerstliederen *see Ad Festum
Letitie; Dies Est Letitie; Puer
Nobis Nascitur   (B402)

Drie Liederen Uit "Lentemaan" *CC3U
A solo,fl,clar,vln,vla,vcl voc sc
DONEMUS s.p.   (B403)

Egidius Waer Bestu Bleven
see Liederen Van Den Dood

Eindeloos
see Liederen Van Dood En Leven

Es Ist Lang
see Drei Lieder

Fisches Nachtgesang
see Vijf Liederen Van Morgenstern

Funf Lieder *CC5U
med solo,pno DONEMUS s.p.   (B404)

I Sing Of A Maiden
see Drie Geeslijke Liederen Op Oude
Engelsche Teksten

La Jeune Fille Nue
see Chansons Orientales

Les Elfes
narrator,3fl,2ob,2clar,2bsn,3horn,
3trp,3trom,timp,perc,cel,harp,
strings DONEMUS s.p.   (B405)

BADINGS, HENK (cont'd.)

Lied Tot Alle Vermoeijde Zielen
see Drie Geestelijke Liederen Van
Jan Luyken

Liederen Van Den Dood
A/Bar solo,pno DONEMUS s.p.
contains: Egidius Waer Bestu
Bleven; O, Als Ik Dood Zal
Zijn; Triomf Van Den Dood   (B406)

Liederen Van Dood En Leven
T solo,2fl,2ob,3clar,2bsn,3horn,
2trp,3trom,timp,perc,cel,harp,
vibra,strings DONEMUS s.p.
contains: Bij Een Doode;
Eindeloos; Maanlicht; Morgen
(B407)

L'indifferente
see Chansons Orientales

Lunovis
see Vijf Liederen Van Morgenstern

Maanlicht
see Liederen Van Dood En Leven

Morgen
see Liederen Van Dood En Leven

Musette
high solo/med solo,pno ALBERSEN
s.p. see from Chasonnettes (B408)

O, Als Ik Dood Zal Zijn
see Liederen Van Den Dood

Pastorale
high solo/med solo,pno ALBERSEN
s.p. see from Chasonnettes (B409)

Pastorale Pour Jeannette
high solo,pno DONEMUS s.p. contains
also: Air Sur Une Blonde;
Vaudeville   (B410)

Puer Nobis Nascitur *sac
S solo,2fl,2ob,2clar,bsn,3horn,
2trp,trom,timp,perc,cel,harp,
strings DONEMUS see from Drie
Kerstliederen   (B411)

Rondeau
high solo/med solo,pno ALBERSEN
s.p. see from Chasonnettes (B412)

Sechs Lieder Nach Gedichten Von
Othmar Lechler *CC6U
med solo,pno DONEMUS D433 s.p.
(B413)

Sur Les Bords Du Jo-Yeh
see Chansons Orientales

Tambourin
high solo/med solo,pno ALBERSEN
s.p. see from Chasonnettes (B414)

Three Old Dutch Songs *CC3U
solo,fl,harp DONEMUS s.p.   (B415)

Triomf Van Den Dood
see Liederen Van Den Dood

Twee Liederen Van Charles Vildrac
Mez solo,pno DONEMUS s.p.
contains: Chanson D'hiver; Chant
Du Desespere   (B416)

Van Jesus De Ware Ruste
see Drie Geestelijke Liederen Van
Jan Luyken

Vaudeville
see Badings, Henk, Pastorale Pour
Jeannette

Vier Wiegeliedjes *CC4U
low solo,strings DONEMUS   (B417)

Vier Wiegenliedjes *CC4U
solo,pno BROEKMANS 453 s.p. (B418)

Vijf Liederen Van Morgenstern
SATB soli,pno DONEMUS s.p.
contains: Das Grosse Lalula; Das
Huhn; Das Mondschaf; Fisches
Nachtgesang; Lunovis   (B419)

When Christ Was Born
see Drie Geeslijke Liederen Op Oude
Engelsche Teksten

BAERVOETS, RAYMOND (1930-   )
Erosions I
A solo,fl,al-sax,trp,22perc,vcl
CBDM s.p.   (B420)

BAEYENS, AUGUST-L. (1895-1966)
De Hond En Zijn Meester
see Vijf Gedichten Uit French En
Andere Cancan

De Kever
see Drie Liederen Op Gedichten Van
Victor J. Brunclair

BAEYENS, AUGUST-L. (cont'd.)

De Kip Die Gouden Eieren Legt
    see Vijf Gedichten Uit French En
    Andere Cancan

De Leeuw En De Muis
    see Vijf Gedichten Uit French En
    Andere Cancan

De Vos En De Druiven
    see Vijf Gedichten Uit French En
    Andere Cancan

Drie Liederen Op Gedichten Van Gaston
    Burssens
    cmplt ed CBDM s.p.
        contains: Hypnose (Mez/A/Bar/B
        solo,pno); Oud Liedje (med
        solo,pno); Passe-Temps (med
        solo,pno)   (B421)

Drie Liederen Op Gedichten Van Jan
    Greshoff En Justus De Harduyn
    Bar/B solo,pno cmplt ed CBDM s.p.
        contains: Een Somber Drinklied;
        Sonnet Waermede Den
        Landtman...; Thanatos'
        Avondlied   (B422)

Drie Liederen Op Gedichten Van Victor
    J. Brunclair
    cmplt ed CBDM s.p.
        contains: De Kever (med solo,
        pno); Klein Gebed Om Stilte
        (Mez/A/Bar solo,pno); Vanwaar
        Ken Ik Uw Gelaat (Mez/A/Bar
        solo,pno)   (B423)

Een Somber Drinklied
    see Drie Liederen Op Gedichten Van
    Jan Greshoff En Justus De Harduyn

Examen Troost
    med solo,pno CBDM s.p.   (B424)

Het Koren En Het Kaf
    see Vijf Gedichten Uit French En
    Andere Cancan

Hypnose
    see Drie Liederen Op Gedichten Van
    Gaston Burssens

Klein Gebed Om Stilte
    see Drie Liederen Op Gedichten Van
    Victor J. Brunclair

Oud Liedje
    see Drie Liederen Op Gedichten Van
    Gaston Burssens

Passe-Temps
    see Drie Liederen Op Gedichten Van
    Gaston Burssens

Sonnet Waermede Den Landtman...
    see Drie Liederen Op Gedichten Van
    Jan Greshoff En Justus De Harduyn

Thanatos' Avondlied
    see Drie Liederen Op Gedichten Van
    Jan Greshoff En Justus De Harduyn

Vanwaar Ken Ik Uw Gelaat
    see Drie Liederen Op Gedichten Van
    Victor J. Brunclair

Vijf Gedichten Uit French En Andere
    Cancan
    med solo,pno cmplt ed CBDM s.p.
        contains: De Hond En Zijn
        Meester; De Kip Die Gouden
        Eieren Legt; De Leeuw En De
        Muis; De Vos En De Druiven; Het
        Koren En Het Kaf   (B425)

BAG OF THE BEE, THE see Lessard, John
    Ayres

BAGGE, G.
Chant Du Vermeland
    see Trois Chants Populaires Suedois

Dans Les Pres
    see Six Chants Populaires Slaves

La Fille Allait Aux Champs
    see Trois Chants Populaires Suedois

La Vallee
    see Six Chants Populaires Slaves

L'Alouette
    see Six Chants Populaires Slaves

Le Coucou Chante
    see Six Chants Populaires Slaves

Le Rossignol De La Foret
    see Six Chants Populaires Slaves

Les Flocons De Neige Blancs
    see Six Chants Populaires Slaves

BAGGE, G. (cont'd.)

Six Chants Populaires Slaves
    solo,pno quarto OUVRIERES s.p.
    contains: Dans Les Pres; La
    Vallee; L'Alouette; Le Coucou
    Chante; Le Rossignol De La
    Foret; Les Flocons De Neige
    Blancs   (B426)

Sous Le Dome Du Ciel
    see Trois Chants Populaires Suedois

Trois Chants Populaires Suedois
    solo,pno quarto OUVRIERES s.p.
    contains: Chant Du Vermeland; La
    Fille Allait Aux Champs; Sous
    Le Dome Du Ciel   (B427)

BAGGERS, J.
Le Lecon De Tambour
    solo,acap solo pt ENOCH s.p.   (B428)

Le Petit Tambour
    solo,acap solo pt ENOCH s.p.   (B429)

BAGPIPES see Davis, Katherine K.

BAGWELL, WENDY
He Was Talking About Me (composed
    with Buckner, Jan) *sac
    solo,pno WORD S-459   (B430)

BAIGELACH see Bublitchki

BAIL AVEC MI see Messiaen, Oliver

BAILERO
    (Canteloube, J.) [Eng] med solo,pno
    PRESSER $.95 see from Songs Of
    Auvergne   (B431)

BAILEY
He Will Pilot Me *sac
    (Whitworth) solo,pno LILLENAS
    SM-911: SN $1.00   (B432)

BAILY, MRS. J.S.
Songs For My Children *CCU
    solo,pno LEONARD-ENG   (B433)

BAIN
Brother James's Air *sac
    (Tate) S/T solo,pno (very easy)
    OXFORD 62.026 $1.00   (B434)
    (Trew) Mez/Bar solo,pno/4strings/
    strings (very easy) OXFORD 61.321
    $1.00, ipr   (B435)

BAIN, MARJORIE
Island Of June
    solo,pno CRAMER $1.15   (B436)

BAINTON, EDGAR LESLIE (1880-1956)
To The Children
    solo,pno CRAMER $.95   (B437)

Twilight People
    solo,pno CRAMER $1.15   (B438)

BAIRD, TADEUSZ (1928-   )
Bozemojzmituj Sie Nade Mna
    "Lieber Gott Erbarme Dich" see Five
    Songs

Das Letze Gedicht *see Ostatnia
    Piesn

Das Schneiden Ist Ein Vogel *see
    Rozstanie Jest Ptakiem

Der Fremde *see Obcy

Five Songs
    [Pol/Ger] Mez solo,16inst voc sc
    CHESTER s.p.
    contains: Bozemojzmituj Sie Nade
    Mna, "Lieber Gott Erbarme
    Dich"; Podziel Sie Ze Mna,
    "Teile Mit Mir Das Tagliche
    Brot"; Rozcinam Pomarancze
    Boln, "Ich Zerschneide Die
    Leidesorange"; Rozstanie Jest
    Ptakiem, "Das Schneiden Ist Ein
    Vogel"; Zawsze, Kiedy Chce
    Krzycze, "Immer Wenn Ich Leben
    Will Schreie Ich"   (B439)

Four Songs
    [Pol/Ger] Mez solo,chamb.orch
    CHESTER s.p.
    contains: Obcy, "Der Fremde";
    Ostatnia Piesn, "Das Letze
    Gedicht"; Powrot, "Ruckkehr";
    Pozny Btask, "Spater Glanz"   (B440)

Ich Zerschneide Die Leidesorange
    *see Rozcinam Pomarancze Boln

Immer Wenn Ich Leben Will Schreie Ich
    *see Zawsze, Kiedy Chce Krzycze

Lieber Gott Erbarme Dich *see
    Bozemojzmituj Sie Nade Mna

BAIRD, TADEUSZ (cont'd.)

Obcy
    "Der Fremde" see Four Songs

Ostatnia Piesn
    "Das Letze Gedicht" see Four Songs

Podziel Sie Ze Mna
    "Teile Mit Mir Das Tagliche Brot"
    see Five Songs

Powrot
    "Ruckkehr" see Four Songs

Pozny Btask
    "Spater Glanz" see Four Songs

Rozcinam Pomarancze Boln
    "Ich Zerschneide Die Leidesorange"
    see Five Songs

Rozstanie Jest Ptakiem
    "Das Schneiden Ist Ein Vogel" see
    Five Songs

Ruckkehr *see Powrot

Spater Glanz *see Pozny Btask

Teile Mit Mir Das Tagliche Brot *see
    Podziel Sie Ze Mna

Zawsze, Kiedy Chce Krzycze
    "Immer Wenn Ich Leben Will Schreie
    Ich" see Five Songs

BAIRN'S PRAYER AT NIGHT, A see
    Musgrave, Thea

BAIRSTOW, EDWARD CUTHBERT (1874-1946)
Oak Tree Bough, The
    solo,pno CRAMER $.70   (B441)

When I Heard The Learned Astronomer
    solo,pno (E flat maj) ASHDOWN
                                         (B442)

BAISER D'AMANTS see Delmet, Paul

BAISER D'ENFANT see Grandjany, Marcel

BAISER SUPREME see Delmet, Paul

BAISER SUR LES YEUX see Lacombe, Paul

BAISERS see Halphen, F.

BAISS, E.
Sleep Softly Here
    solo,pno (G flat maj) BOOSEY $1.50
                                         (B443)

BAJAJA see Trojan, Vaclav

BAJKY see Pauer, Jiri

BAKER, DAVID
I Need You Every Hour *sac
    solo,pno WORD S-328   (B444)

If You Dream The Right Dream *sac
    solo,pno WORD S-334   (B445)

BAKER, M.
When The Robins Sing
    solo,pno (G maj) LESLIE 7060   (B446)

BAKER, RICHARD
Carpenter, The *sac
    med solo,pno CRESPUB CP-B138 $1.00
                                         (B447)
Everyday Is A Gift
    med solo,pno CRESPUB CP-B137 $1.00
                                         (B448)
Give Christ This Year *sac
    med solo,pno CRESPUB CP-B136 $1.00
                                         (B449)
God Speaks Today *sac
    med solo,pno CRESPUB CP-B135 $1.00
                                         (B450)
His Way-Mine *sac
    med solo,pno CRESPUB CP-S5040 $1.00
                                         (B451)
    solo,pno CRESPUB CP-B103 $.25
                                         (B452)
I Trust In God *sac
    med solo,pno CRESPUB CP-651 $1.00
                                         (B453)
It May Be Tomorrow *sac
    med solo,pno CRESPUB CP-660 $1.00
                                         (B454)
Longing For Jesus
    med solo,pno CRESPUB CP-B101 $.25
                                         (B455)
    low solo,pno CRESPUB CP-B102 $.25
                                         (B456)
Never A Man Like Him *sac
    med solo,pno CRESPUB CP-S5030 $1.00
                                         (B457)
Never The Same Again *sac
    med solo,pno CRESPUB CP-B140 $1.00
                                         (B458)
Since The Moment I Met Jesus *sac
    med solo,pno CRESPUB CP-B142 $1.00
                                         (B459)

BAKER, RICHARD (cont'd.)

Take Time For Jesus *sac
med solo,pno CRESPUB CP-S5016 $1.00
(B460)

Wonder Of God's Love, The
2 soli,pno CRESPUB CP-B139 $.25
(B461)

BAKER, RICHARD C.
Christian Friends
med solo,pno CRESPUB CP-S5050 $1.00
(B462)

BAKKERS, M.
Dors, Mon Enfant
[Fr] med solo,pno ESCHIG $.45
(B463)

BAKSA, ROBERT
Think No More, Lad
solo,pno (G maj) BOOSEY $1.50
(B464)

When I Was One-And Twenty
solo,pno BOOSEY $1.50
(B465)

When The Lad For Longing Sighs
solo,pno BOOSEY $1.50
(B466)

BAKVISCHJES see Bijl, Theo van der

BAL BLANC see Berger, Rod.

BALADA DEL JINETE MUERTO see Grisolia,
Pascual

BALADA HORSKA see Foerster, Josef
Bohuslav

BALADA LETNI see Martinu, Bohuslav

BALADA O DUSI J. NERUDY see Novak, V.

BALAGUER
Ay Mi Triana! (from Carmen La
Sevillana)
[Span] solo,pno RICORDI-ARG BA 8785
s.p.
(B467)

BALAKIREV, MILY ALEXEYEVITCH
(1837-1910)
Song Of Georgia
solo,pno (B flat min) BOOSEY $1.50
(B468)

BALANCELLE see Lacome, Paul

BALASSA, SANDOR
Antinomia
[Hung] S solo,clar,vcl BUDAPEST
6314
(B469)

BALAY, G.
Cloches D'Arvor
[Fr/Ger] solo,orch DURAND s.p., ipr
(B470)
[Fr] solo,acap oct DURAND s.p.
(B471)

BALAZS, ARPAD
Gyere Velem Akaclombos Falumba
solo,pno BUDAPEST 7421 s.p. (B472)

BALAZS, FREDERIC
For Music
S solo,pno AM.COMP.AL. $3.57 (B473)

Sonnets After Elizabeth Barrett
Browning *CCU
AM.COMP.AL. high solo,4strings sc
$8.50, ipa; high solo,fl,ob,clar,
bsn,harp,strings sc $11.00 (B474)

BALBI-BALBA see Ravize, A.

BALD MUSS ICH DICH VERLASSEN see
Mozart, Wolfgang Amadeus, Io Ti
Lascio, O Figlia

BALDACCI, GIOV. BRUNA
L'Addio
solo,pno BONGIOVANI 1652 s.p.
(B475)

Rugiada
solo,pno BONGIOVANI 1650 s.p.
(B476)

Silenzio
solo,pno BONGIOVANI 1649 s.p.
(B477)

Villa Chiusa
solo,pno BONGIOVANI 1651 s.p.
(B478)

BALES, RICHARD (1915-)
Beneath A Weeping Willow's Shade
Bar solo,fl,ob,clar,bsn,2horn,perc,
harp,strings PEER rental (B479)

Mary's Gift *Xmas,carol
solo,pno PEER $.85
(B480)

Ozymandias
S solo,fl,ob,2clar,bsn,2horn,
strings PEER sc rental, voc sc
$.85
(B481)

BALFE, MICHAEL WILLIAM (1808-1870)
Come Into The Garden Maud
low solo,pno (C maj) ASHDOWN (B482)
high solo,pno (D maj) ASHDOWN
(B483)

BALFE, MICHAEL WILLIAM (cont'd.)

Heart Bow'd Down
low solo,pno (F maj) CRAMER (B484)
high solo,pno (G maj) CRAMER (B485)

I Dreamt That I Dwelt In Marble Halls
(from Bohemian Girl, The)
S solo,pno (E flat maj) SCHIRM.G
$.75
(B486)
high solo,pno (E maj) CENTURY 582
(B487)

Killarney
solo,pno (G maj) ASHDOWN (B488)

Then You'll Remember Me (from
Bohemian Girl, The)
med solo,pno (B flat maj) SCHIRM.G
$.60
(B489)

BALL, ERNEST R. (1878-1927)
Dear Little Boy Of Mine
solo,pno ALLANS s.p. (B490)

In The Garden Of My Heart
low solo,pno (B flat maj) ALLANS
s.p.
(B491)
med solo,pno (C maj) ALLANS s.p.
(B492)
high solo,pno (E flat maj) ALLANS
s.p.
(B493)
2 low soli,pno (B flat maj) ALLANS
s.p.
(B494)
2 med soli,pno (D maj) ALLANS
s.p.
(B495)
2 high soli,pno (E flat maj) ALLANS
s.p.
(B496)

Little Bit Of Heaven, Sure They Call
It Ireland
solo,pno (E flat maj) ALLANS s.p.
(B497)

Love Me And The World Is Mine
solo,pno ALLANS s.p. (B498)

Mother Machree
low solo,pno (B flat maj) ALLANS
s.p.
(B499)
med solo,pno (C maj) ALLANS s.p.
(B500)
med-high solo,pno (D maj) ALLANS
s.p.
(B501)
high solo,pno (F maj) ALLANS s.p.
(B502)

Till The Sands Of The Desert
low solo,pno (G maj) ALLANS s.p.
(B503)
high solo,pno (B flat maj) ALLANS
s.p.
(B504)

BALLAD see Pacius, Fredrik, Balladi

BALLAD see Stenhammar, Wilhelm

BALLAD BOOK OF JOHN JACOB NILES, THE
see Niles, John Jacob

BALLAD FROM PANTALOON see Ward, Robert

BALLAD MONGER, THE see Martin, Easthope

BALLAD OF MR. AND MRS. DISCOBBOLOS see
Orr, Buxton

BALLAD OF SEMMERWATER, THE see Gibbs,
Cecil Armstrong

BALLAD OF THE RED ROCK, THE see Zarai

BALLAD OF THE TRUMPET BOY, THE see
Hoskins, William

BALLAD OF TREES AND THE MASTER see
Lekberg, Sven

BALLAD OF WILLIAM SYCAMORE see Moore,
Douglas Stuart

BALLAD ON QUEEN ANNE'S DEATH see
Hundley, Richard

BALLAD WITH EPITAPHS see Russell,
Armand

BALLADA see Lajtha, Laszlo

BALLADE see Barraud, Henry

BALLADE see Beekhuis, Hanna

BALLADE see Delage, Maurice

BALLADE see Delettre, J.

BALLADE see Henking, Bernhard

BALLADE see Lie, Harald

BALLADE see Menasce, Jacques de

BALLADE see Respighi, Ottorino, Ballata

BALLADE DE CHAMBREE see Lecocq, Charles

BALLADE DE COLOMBE see Saint-Saens,
Camille

BALLADE DE RATS ET DE SOURIS see Sakac,
Branimir, Barasou

BALLADE DE VILLON A S'AMYE see Debussy,
Claude

BALLADE DES CLOCHES see King, Harold C.

BALLADE DES FEMMES DE PARIS see
Debussy, Claude

BALLADE DES GROS DINDONS see Chabrier,
Emmanuel

BALLADE DES PAUVRES GUEUX see Schule,
B.

BALLADE DES PENDUS see Bunge, Sas

BALLADE DU DESESPERE see Legay, Marcel

BALLADE DU ROULIER see Migot, Georges

BALLADE POUR LA PAIX see Schmitt,
Florent

BALLADE PRINTANIERE see Mendelssohn-
Bartholdy, Felix

BALLADE PROVENCALE see Bonnal, Ermend

BALLADE QUE FEIT VILLON A LA REQUESTE
DE SA MERE POUR PRIER NOTRE-DAME
see Debussy, Claude

BALLADE VAN DEN BOER see Mengelberg,
Rudolf

BALLADE VAN DEN MEREL see Andriessen,
Hendrik

BALLADE VAN DEN WATERSNOOD see Badings,
Henk

BALLADE VAN EEN VERLIEFDE see Van
Streel, R.

BALLADE VAN WESTERBORK see Lilien,
Ignace

BALLADE VOM ANGENEHMEN LEBEN see Weill,
Kurt

BALLADE VOM FEST see Krenek, Ernst

BALLADE VOM KONIG LOBESAM see Krenek,
Ernst

BALLADE VON DEN SCHIFFEN see Krenek,
Ernst

BALLADE VON DER SINGENDEN FRAU IN DER
NACHT see Benguerel, Xavier

BALLADEN see Taube, Evert

BALLADEN OM BJORNEN see Nielsen, Carl

BALLADEN VON DER SEELE see Novotny, J.

BALLADI see Pacius, Fredrik

BALLADS AND SONGS, VOL. I see Loewe,
Karl Gottfried

BALLADS AND SONGS, VOL. II see Loewe,
Karl Gottfried

BALLADS OF PETRICA KEREMPUH, THE see
Lhotka-Kalinski, Ivo

BALLADS OF THE FOUR SEASONS, THE see
Bliss, Sir Arthur

BALLARD, ANN
Captain Of Sunshine, The *sac
solo,pno WORD S-532 (B505)

It'll Be Joy *sac
solo,pno WORD S-452 (B506)

No Measure Of Time *sac
solo,pno WORD S-534 (B507)

Oh, What A Sunrise *sac
(Carmichael, Ralph) solo,pno WORD
S-524 (B508)

Royal Family, The *sac
solo,pno WORD S-461 (B509)

There's Gonna Be Shoutin' *sac
solo,pno WORD S-533 (B510)

BALLATA see Castelnuovo-Tedesco, Mario

BALLATA see Farina, Guido

BALLATA see Malipiero, Gian Francesco

BALLATA see Respighi, Ottorino

BALLATA see Staffeli, Attilio

BALLATA ANTICA see Pratella, Francesco Balilla

BALLATA CAMPESTRE see Farina, Guido

BALLATA DI PRIMAVERA see De Angelis, Ruggero

BALLATA MEDIEVALE see De Lucia, Nadir

BALLATA TRISTE see Carabella, Ezio

BALLATA, ZEQUIRJA (1943-   )
    Dve Pesmi *CC2U
        solo,pno DRUSTVO DSS 322 rental
                                              (B511)

BALLET see Schouwman, Hans

BALLOONS see Harris, L.R.

BALLOONS IN THE SNOW see Boyd, Jeanne

BALLOU, ESTHER W.
    Bride
        S solo,org AM.COMP.AL. $1.37 (B512)

    Early American Portrait
        S solo,2fl,ob,clar,bsn,2horn,trp,
        trom,harp,perc,strings sc
        AM.COMP.AL. $18.70   (B513)

    Five-Four-Three
        med solo,vla,harp sc AM.COMP.AL.
        $8.25   (B514)

    Five Songs *CC5U
        S solo,pno AM.COMP.AL. $8.25 (B515)

    Song, A
        A/Mez solo,pno AM.COMP.AL. $1.37
                                      (B516)

    Street Scenes
        S solo,pno AM.COMP.AL. $3.85 (B517)

BALLROOM WHISPERS see Meyer-Helmund, Erik

BALLSPIEL IN TRIANON see Sibelius, Jean, Bollspelet Vid Trianon

BALLSPIEL IN TRIANON see Sibelius, Jean, Bollspelet Vid Trianon

BALLYNURE BALLAD see Hughes, Herbert

BALM IN GILEAD *spir
    (Burleigh, H. T.) high solo,pno
    BELWIN $1.50   (B518)
    (Burleigh, H. T.) low solo,pno BELWIN
    $1.50   (B519)

BALOGH
    Visions (composed with Sjoberg)
        high solo,pno (B flat min) GALAXY
        1.0761.7 $1.00   (B520)
        med solo/low solo,pno (G min)
        GALAXY 1.0782.7 $1.00   (B521)

BALOS, FR.
    Drei Lieder Auf Worte Franzosischer
    Poesie *CC3U
        [Czech/Fr] solo,pno SUPRAPHON s.p.
                                      (B522)

BALTIN, A.
    Concerto For Mezzo-Soprano And
    Symphony Orchestra
        Mez solo,orch sc MEZ KNIGA 2.16
        s.p.   (B523)

BALULALOW see Heseltine, Philip

BAMBINA COME TE see Casadei, S.

BAMPTON, RUTH
    In Honor Of Mother *sac
        med solo,pno BELWIN $1.50   (B524)

BANADO DEL PARANA! see Ficher, Jacobo

BANALITES see Poulenc, Francis

BANCQUART, ALAIN (1934-   )
    Erotique Voilee
        Mez solo,fl,clar,pno,2vln,vla,vcl,
        bvl sc JOBERT s.p.   (B525)

    Ombre Eclatee *CCU
        med female solo,3fl,3ob,3clar,3bsn,
        4horn,3trp,3trom,tuba,3perc,
        strings sc JOBERT rental   (B526)

    Proche *CCU
        B solo,vcl/vla sc JOBERT rental
                                      (B527)

BANDEL-TERZETT see Mozart, Wolfgang Amadeus

BANDINERIE see Badings, Henk

BANES, A.
    Les Petits Gars De 1915
        solo,acap solo pt ENOCH s.p. (B528)

BANES, A. (cont'd.)

    Les Petits Gars De 1918
        solo,pno ENOCH s.p.   (B529)

BANFFY, N.
    Banffy-Valse
    (Charmettes) solo,acap solo pt
        ENOCH s.p.   (B530)

    Ce Qui Seduit Mon Ame
        solo,pno ENOCH s.p.   (B531)

BANFFY-VALSE see Banffy, N.

BANGERT, EM.
    Queen Of The Rosary
        med solo,pno SEESAW $1.00   (B532)

BANJO SONG, A see Homer, Sidney

BANK, JACQUES (1943-   )
    Blind Boy Fuller, No. I
        solo,rec,pno, recording DONEMUS
        s.p.   (B533)

BANKA see Minami, Hiroaki

BANKS, C.O.
    Heaven And Earth Rejoice *sac
        high solo,pno BELWIN $1.50   (B534)
        low solo,pno BELWIN $1.50   (B535)

BANKS, HARRY
    O Brother Man *sac
        low solo,pno BELWIN $1.50   (B536)

    Prayer Of St. Francis *sac
        high solo,pno BELWIN $1.50   (B537)
        med solo,pno BELWIN $1.50   (B538)
        low solo,pno BELWIN $1.50   (B539)

BANKS O' DOON see Brewer, G.

BANKS OF ALLAN WATER *Scot
    solo,pno CRAMER   (B540)

BANKS OF ALLAN WATER see Shaw, Martin

BANTOCK, GRANVILLE (1868-1946)
    Adrift
        high solo,pno ELKIN 27.0999.06 s.p.
                                      (B541)
        med solo,pno ELKIN 27.0998.08 s.p.
                                      (B542)
    And There Are Tears
        solo,pno CRAMER $1.15   (B543)
    Bird Of St. Bride, The
        solo,pno CRAMER $1.15   (B544)
    Celestial Weaver
        "La Tisseuse Celeste" [Eng/Fr] med
        solo,kbd CHESTER s.p.   (B545)
    China Mandarin, The
        2 soli,pno ROBERTON 71385 s.p.
                                      (B546)
    Court Of Dreams, The
        solo,pno CRAMER $1.15   (B547)
    Dancing
        low solo,pno (D maj) CRAMER $1.00
                                      (B548)
        high solo,pno (E flat maj) CRAMER
        $1.00   (B549)
    Desolation
        [Eng] med-high solo,pno CHESTER
        s.p.   (B550)
    Down The Hwai
        solo,pno CRAMER   (B551)
    Feast Of Lanterns
        high solo,pno ELKIN 27.0964.03 s.p.
                                      (B552)
        med solo,pno ELKIN 27.0963.05 s.p.
                                      (B553)
        low solo,pno ELKIN 27.0962.07 s.p.
                                      (B554)
    Fireside Fancies
        solo,pno CRAMER $1.15   (B555)
    Great Is The Lord
        solo,pno CRAMER   (B556)
    Holy Queen Of Heaven! *see Salve
        Regina
    Island Of Pines
        [Eng] med solo,kbd CHESTER s.p.
                                      (B557)
    La Tisseuse Celeste *see Celestial
        Weaver
    Lament Of Isis
        S solo,pno BREITKOPF-W $.90 (B558)
        A/Bar solo,pno BREITKOPF-W $.90
                                      (B559)
        low solo,pno (E flat maj) ALLANS
        s.p.   (B560)
        high solo,pno (G flat maj) ALLANS
        s.p.   (B561)

BANTOCK, GRANVILLE (cont'd.)

    Le Vieux Pecheur *see Old Fisherman,
        The
    Lost One, The
        solo,pno CRAMER $.90   (B562)
    Memories With The Dusk Return
        solo,pno CRAMER   (B563)
    Morgan Le Fay
        solo,pno CRAMER   (B564)
    Night On The Mountain
        solo,pno CRAMER $1.15   (B565)
    Nocturne
        solo,pno CRAMER   (B566)
    Old Fisherman, The
        "Le Vieux Pecheur" [Eng] med-high
        solo,kbd CHESTER s.p.   (B567)
    Out Of The Depths
        solo,pno CRAMER $.90   (B568)
    Pavilion Of Abounding Joy, The
        solo,kbd CHESTER s.p.   (B569)
    Praise Ye The Lord
        solo,harp (B flat maj) CRAMER $1.15
                                      (B570)
        low solo,org (A flat maj) CRAMER
        $.95   (B571)
        high solo,org (B flat maj) CRAMER
        $1.15   (B572)
    Raindrops
        low solo,pno (G maj) ASHDOWN (B573)
        high solo,pno (B flat maj) ASHDOWN
                                      (B574)
    Salve Regina *sac
        "Holy Queen Of Heaven!" [Lat/Eng]
        med-low solo,kbd CHESTER s.p.
                                      (B575)
    Sappho *song cycle
        A solo,orch BREITKOPF-W s.p. (B576)
    Seasons, The
        solo,pno CRAMER $1.15   (B577)
    Silent Strings
        low solo,pno (D maj) BOOSEY $1.50
                                      (B578)
        high solo,pno (F maj) BOOSEY $1.50
                                      (B579)
    Singer In The Wood, The
        solo,pno CRAMER $1.15   (B580)
    Song To The Seals
        low solo,pno (E flat maj) CRAMER
        s.p.   (B581)
        med solo,pno (F maj) CRAMER $1.10
                                      (B582)
        high solo,pno (G maj) CRAMER $1.10
                                      (B583)
    Three Idylls *CC3U
        solo,fl,opt vcl CRAMER   (B584)
    Valley Of Silence, The
        solo,pno CRAMER $.70   (B585)
    Washer Of The Ford, The
        solo,pno CRAMER $.95   (B586)
    Wilderness And The Solitary Place
        (from Christ In The Wilderness)
        [Eng/Ger] S solo,pno BREITKOPF-W
        $1.25   (B587)
    Wind, The
        low solo,pno (D flat maj) ASHDOWN
                                      (B588)
        high solo,pno (E flat maj) ASHDOWN
                                      (B589)
    Youthful, Charming Chloe, The
        solo,pno CRAMER $.95   (B590)
    Yung-Yang
        med solo,pno ELKIN 27.1000.05 s.p.
                                      (B591)

BANTRY BAY see Molloy, James Lyman

BANTU AND YOU, THE see Kalanzi

BANVISE see Olsen, Sparre

BAPTISM OF JESS TAYLOR, THE see
    Frazier, Dallas

BAPTISM OF JESUS, THE see Rider, Dale
    G.

BAR see Martinu, Bohuslav

BAR-AM, BENJAMIN
    And You Have Gone
        [Heb/Eng/Ger] solo,pno ISRAELI 208
        $2.10   (B592)

BAR MITZVOH SONG see Der Neier Yid

BARAB, SEYMOUR (1921-   )
Explanation
solo,pno (G maj) BOOSEY $1.50
(B593)

Maid Me Loved
solo,pno BOOSEY $1.50
(B594)

Rivals, The *CC4U
solo,pno PRESSER $2.50   (B595)

Songs Of Perfect Propriety *CCU
med solo,pno/orch BOOSEY $2.75
(B596)

BARACHIN, P.
Sous Le Ciel Gris
solo,pno ENOCH s.p.   (B597)

BARASH, MORRIS
El Mole Rachamim
[Heb] solo,org/pno TRANSCON. WJ 438
$1.00   (B598)

BARASOU see Sakac, Branimir

BARATI, GEORGE (1913-   )
From A River Bed
S solo,pno sc AM.COMP.AL. $2.20
(B599)

BARBARA ALLAN *folk,Scot
solo,pno (B min) PATERSON FS135 s.p.
(B600)

BARBARA ALLEN see Quilter, Roger

BARBARA-SONG see Weill, Kurt

BARBARA, WHAT HAVE YOU DONE? see Mayer

BARBARIANS see Mourant, Walter

BARBE-BLEUE see Lacome, Paul

BARBE, HELMUT (1927-   )
Jeruschalajim *sac
high solo,org HANSSLER 10.306 s.p.
(B601)

Psalm 42 *sac
[Ger] S solo,org HANSSLER 10.307
s.p.   (B602)

Requiem 1965 *sac
S solo,fl,ob,bsn,vla,vcl,bvl
HANSSLER 10.277 s.p., ipa (B603)

BARBER, SAMUEL (1910-   )
Andromache's Farewell
S solo,pno SCHIRM.G $2.00   (B604)

Bessie Bobtail
med solo,pno (D min) SCHIRM.G $.75
(B605)

Collected Songs (Through 1955)
*CC31L
SCHIRM.G high solo,pno $5.00; low
solo,pno $5.00   (B606)

Daisies, The
med solo,pno (F maj) SCHIRM.G $.85
(B607)

Death Of Cleopatra
see Two Scenes From Antony And
Cleopatra

Depart
see Melodies Passageres

Despite And Still
see Despite And Still

Despite And Still
high solo&med solo,pno SCHIRM.G
$3.00
contains: Despite And Still; In
The Wilderness; Last Song, A;
My Lizard; Solitary Hotel
(B608)

Do Not Utter A Word (from Vanessa)
high solo,pno (F sharp maj)
SCHIRM.G $1.00   (B609)

Dover Beach
med solo,pno/4strings (D min) sc
SCHIRM.G $1.50, ipa   (B610)

Give Me Some Music
see Two Scenes From Antony And
Cleopatra

Hermit Songs *Op.29, CC10U
SCHIRM.G high solo,pno $2.75; low
solo,pno $2.75   (B611)

I Hear An Army *Op.10,No.3
high solo,pno SCHIRM.G $1.25 (B612)
med solo,pno SCHIRM.G $1.25 (B613)
low solo,pno SCHIRM.G $1.25 (B614)

I Love You *see Ich Liebe Dich

Ich Liebe Dich
"I Love You" [Ger/Eng] low solo,pno
(E flat maj) SCHIRM.G $1.00
(B615)
"I Love You" [Ger/Eng] high solo,
pno (G maj) SCHIRM.G $1.00 (B616)

BARBER, SAMUEL (cont'd.)
In Questa Tomba Oscura
"In This Sepulchral Darkness" [It/
Eng] med solo,pno (A flat maj)
SCHIRM.G $.85   (B617)
"In This Sepulchral Darkness" [It/
Eng] low solo,pno (F maj)
SCHIRM.G $.85   (B618)

In The Wilderness
see Despite And Still

In This Sepulchral Darkness *see In
Questa Tomba Oscura

Knoxville: Summer Of 1915
high solo,pno (A maj) SCHIRM.G
$2.50   (B619)

Last Song, A
see Despite And Still

Le Clocher Change
see Melodies Passageres

Lord Jesus Christ! (from Prayers Of
Kierkegaard) sac
high solo,pno SCHIRM.G $.85 (B620)

Melodies Passageres *Op.27
SCHIRM.G high solo,pno $1.50; low
solo,pno $1.50
contains: Depart; Le Clocher
Change; Puisque Tout Passe;
Tombeau Dans Un Parc; Un Cygne
(B621)

Monks And Raisins *Op.18,No.2
med-high solo,pno SCHIRM.G $.85
(B622)

Music For Soprano And Orchestra
*CC7L
S solo,orch SCHIRM.G $5.00 (B623)

Must The Winter Come So Soon (from
Vanessa)
Mez solo,pno SCHIRM.G $.85 (B624)

My Lizard
see Despite And Still

Nocturne *Op.13,No.4
high solo,pno SCHIRM.G $.75 (B625)
med solo,pno SCHIRM.G $.75 (B626)

Nun Takes The Veil, A *Op.13,No.1
high solo,pno SCHIRM.G $.85 (B627)
med solo,pno SCHIRM.G $.85 (B628)

Nuvoletta *Op.25
high solo,pno SCHIRM.G $.90 (B629)

Puisque Tout Passe
see Melodies Passageres

Rain Has Fallen *Op.10,No.1
high solo,pno SCHIRM.G $.85 (B630)
med solo,pno SCHIRM.G $.85 (B631)
low solo,pno SCHIRM.G $.85 (B632)

Solitary Hotel
see Despite And Still

Sure On This Shining Night *Op.13,
No.3
high solo,pno (B flat maj) SCHIRM.G
$.85   (B633)
med-low solo,pno (G maj) SCHIRM.G
$.85   (B634)

Tombeau Dans Un Parc
see Melodies Passageres

Two Scenes From Antony And Cleopatra
S solo,pno SCHIRM.G $2.50
contains: Death Of Cleopatra;
Give Me Some Music   (B635)

Un Cygne
see Melodies Passageres

Under The Willow Tree (from Vanessa)
high solo,pno (A min) SCHIRM.G $.85
(B636)
high solo&med solo,pno SCHIRM.G
$.75   (B637)

With Rue My Heart Is Laden
high solo,pno (D min) SCHIRM.G $.75
(B638)

BARBERA, G.
Sei Canti Infantili *CC6U
[It] solo,pno CURCI 6221 s.p.
(B639)

BARBIER, RENE (1890-   )
Cinq Melodies
cmplt ed CBDM s.p.
contains: Ete De Joie, Op.86 (S
solo,pno); Le Temps, Op.78 (S
solo,pno); Nuages, Op.77 (S
solo,pno); Plus...Un Croissant,
Op.79 (S solo,pno); Toujours,
Op.80 (Mez solo,pno)   (B640)

BARBIER, RENE (cont'd.)
Coucher De Soleil *Op.69
Mez/Bar solo,pno CBDM s.p. (B641)

Dieu, Pourquoi Es-Tu Cache? *Op.85
med solo,pno CBDM s.p.   (B642)

Ete De Joie *Op.86
see Cinq Melodies

Le Temps *Op.78
see Cinq Melodies

Les Coudes Dans L'herbe *Op.76
S solo,pno CBDM s.p.   (B643)

Nocturne *Op.47
A/B solo,pno CBDM s.p.   (B644)

Nuages *Op.77
see Cinq Melodies

Plus...Un Croissant *Op.79
see Cinq Melodies

Polichinelle *Op.70
med solo,pno CBDM s.p.   (B645)

Reveil *Op.8
T/S solo,pno CBDM s.p.   (B646)

Toujours *Op.80
see Cinq Melodies

BARBIROLLI, A.
Aimer C'est Forger Sa Peine
[Fr/Eng] Mez/Bar solo,pno/inst
DURAND s.p.   (B647)

Chanson D'automne
Mez/Bar solo,pno/inst DURAND s.p.
(B648)

Depart
A solo,pno/inst DURAND s.p. (B649)

E Tu Mi Fai Morir!
solo,pno FORLIVESI 10609 s.p.
(B650)

Ferveur
Mez/Bar solo,pno/inst DURAND s.p.
(B651)

La Lune
Mez/Bar solo,pno/inst DURAND s.p.
(B652)

L'Eternelle Chanson
Mez/Bar solo,pno/inst DURAND s.p.
(B653)

Mon Lied
A solo,pno/inst DURAND s.p. (B654)

Rose Messagere
Mez/Bar solo,pno/inst DURAND s.p.
(B655)

Si Je Pouvais Mourir
[Fr/Eng] Mez/Bar solo,pno/inst
DURAND s.p.   (B656)

Sorrisi E Baci
"Sourires Et Baisers" solo,pno/inst
DURAND s.p.   (B657)

Sourires Et Baisers *see Sorrisi E
Baci

BARCAROLA see Britain, Radie

BARCAROLA see Magnani, L.

BARCAROLE see Genser

BARCAROLE see Rinaldini, Dr. Joseph

BARCAROLE see Strauss, Richard

BARCAROLLA see Offenbach, Jacques,
Barcarolle

BARCAROLLE see Chaminade, Cecile

BARCAROLLE see Denza, Luigi

BARCAROLLE see Godard, Benjamin Louis
Paul

BARCAROLLE see Holmes, Alfred

BARCAROLLE see Louis, E.

BARCAROLLE see Mendelssohn-Bartholdy,
Felix

BARCAROLLE see Offenbach, Jacques

BARCAROLLE see Schubert, Franz (Peter)

BARCAROLLE AT DAWN see Bateman, Ronald

BARCAROLLE VENTIENNE see Mendelssohn-
Bartholdy, Felix

BARD OR ARMAGH see Hughes, Herbert

BARDS LEGACY see Hughes, Herbert

BAREFOOT TRAIL see Wiggers, A.S.

BARITON-BASS ALBUM *CC17U
(Werba, E.) DOBLINGER 08 503 s.p.
contains works by: Beethoven;
Flotow; Lortzing; Mozart; Verdi and
others   (B658)

BARITONE-BASS ALBUM FROM THE REPERTORY
OF HANS HOTTER *CC17U
(Werba) med solo,pno DOBLINGER $6.75
contains works by: Mozart;
Beethoven; Wagner; Verdi and
others; in German and original
language   (B659)

BARITONE SONGS see Howe, Mary

BARITONE SONGS (RADIO CITY ALBUM) *CCU
Bar solo,pno MARKS $1.50   (B660)

BARKAN, EMANUEL
Hark, My Beloved *sac,Marriage
[Eng] solo,pno TRANSCON. TV 569
$.75   (B661)

Kiddush L'yom Hashabbat
[Heb] solo,pno/org TRANSCON. WJ 443
$1.00   (B662)

Magen Avot *sac
[Heb] solo,pno TRANSCON. WJ 449
$.85   (B663)

BARKER
Mark The Perfect Man
low solo,pno (E flat maj) FISCHER,C
RS 40   (B664)

Raising Of Lazarus, The *sac
high solo,pno (F maj) FISCHER,C
RS 46   (B665)

BARLOW, F.
Die Wasserlilie
"La Fleur De L'onde" [Fr/Ger] med
solo,pno/inst DURAND s.p.   (B666)

La Fleur De L'onde *see Die
Wasserlilie

BARN DANCE see Rikud Ha-Goren

BARNARD, D'AUVERGIVE
Gallant Salamander, The
low solo,pno (D maj) ASHDOWN (B667)
high solo,pno (E maj) ASHDOWN
                                     (B668)

BARNBY, SIR JOSEPH (1838-1896)
O Perfect Love *sac,Marriage
high solo,pno (E flat maj) BOSTON
$1.50   (B669)
med-low solo,pno (D flat maj)
BOSTON $1.50   (B670)
solo,pno (available in 2 keys)
ASHLEY $.95   (B671)
low solo,pno (E flat maj) ALLANS
s.p.   (B672)
high solo,pno (F maj) ALLANS s.p.
                                     (B673)
(Simon) high solo,pno (G maj)
FISCHER,C V 2331   (B674)
(Simon) med solo,pno (E flat maj)
FISCHER,C V 2330   (B675)

BARNDOMSHEMMET I KENTUCKY see Foster,
Stephen Collins

BARNDOMSJULEN see Lagerheim-Romare,
Margit

BARNDOMSMINNEN see Dahlgren, Erland

BARNEFRONTEN see Hauger, Kristian

BARNEFRONTENS VISER see Hauger,
Kristian

BARNES, EDWARD SHIPPEN (1887-1958)
Jesus My Saviour Look On Me *sac
high solo,pno BELWIN $1.50   (B676)

Mother's Day Hymn, A *sac
high solo,pno BELWIN $1.50   (B677)
low solo,pno BELWIN $1.50   (B678)

BARNES, MARSHALL H.
Gate Of The Year, The
high solo,pno CHANTRY VOS 673H $.75
                                     (B679)
low solo,pno CHANTRY VOS 673L $.75
                                     (B680)

BARNET see Merikanto, Oskar, Lapselle

BARNET see Pesonen, Olavi (Samuel),
Lapsi

BARNET OG FAARET see Pergament, Moses

BARNEY BRALLAGHAN see Somervell, Arthur

BARNLIGE SANGE TIL JULENS PRIS see
Beck, Thomas [Ludvigsen]

BARNSTORMERS see Charles, W.

BAROKCANTATE see Bordewijk-Roepman,
Johanna

BARON MAGNUS see Sibelius, Jean, Hertig
Magnus

BARQUE D'OR see Legley, Victor

BARQUE D'OR see Mesritz Van Velthuysen,
Annie

BARQUE D'OR see Toussaint De Sutter, J.

BARRACLOUGH
Ivory Palaces *sac
solo,pno HOPE 52 $.75   (B681)

BARRAINE, ELSA (1910-   )
Avis
[Fr] solo,pno CHANT s.p.   (B682)

Il Y A Quelqu'un Auquel Je Pense
solo,pno ENOCH s.p.   (B683)
solo,orch ENOCH rental   (B684)

Je Ne Reclamais Rien De Toi
solo,pno ENOCH s.p.   (B685)
solo,orch ENOCH rental   (B686)

Je Suis Ici Pour Te Chanter Des
Chansons
solo,pno ENOCH s.p.   (B687)
solo,orch ENOCH rental   (B688)

La Lumiere
solo,pno ENOCH s.p.   (B689)
solo,orch ENOCH rental   (B690)

Pastourelle
solo,pno ENOCH s.p.   (B691)
solo,orch ENOCH rental   (B692)

BARRAUD, HENRY (1900-   )
Ballade
see Chansons De Gramadoch

Chansons De Gramadoch
solo,pno AMPHION A 117 $2.00
contains: Ballade; La Sorciere Et
Le Pirate; Quatrain   (B693)

Dieu Sanglant
see Quatre Poemes De Lanza Del
Vastro

La Nuit Du Pelerin
see Quatre Poemes De Lanza Del
Vastro

La Sorciere Et Le Pirate
see Chansons De Gramadoch

Priere De Midi
see Quatre Poemes De Lanza Del
Vastro

Priere Du Soir
see Quatre Poemes De Lanza Del
Vastro

Quatrain
see Chansons De Gramadoch

Quatre Poemes De Lanza Del Vastro
solo,pno AMPHION A 110 $2.25
contains: Dieu Sanglant; La Nuit
Du Pelerin; Priere De Midi;
Priere Du Soir   (B694)

BARRI, OCCARDO
Saved From The Storm
low solo,pno (A maj) CRAMER (B695)
med solo,pno (C maj) CRAMER (B696)
high solo,pno (E flat maj) CRAMER
                                     (B697)

BARRICADES see Newman, Anthony

BARRIE, STUART
Song Of The Wanderer
solo,pno (D maj) ASHDOWN   (B698)

BARRY, KATHERINE
I Hear A Whisper
low solo,pno (E flat maj) LEONARD-
ENG   (B699)
med solo,pno (F maj) LEONARD-ENG
                                     (B700)
high solo,pno (G maj) LEONARD-ENG
                                     (B701)
Invitation
low solo,pno (B flat maj) CRAMER
$.90   (B702)
med solo,pno (C maj) CRAMER $1.15
                                     (B703)
med-high solo,pno (E flat maj)
CRAMER $.90   (B704)
high solo,pno (D flat maj) CRAMER
$.90   (B705)

Memory, A
low solo,pno (B flat maj, contains
also: Night Has A Thousand Eyes,
The) LEONARD-ENG   (B706)
high solo,pno (D flat maj, contains

BARRY, KATHERINE (cont'd.)

also: Night Has A Thousand Eyes,
The) LEONARD-ENG   (B707)

My Happy Garden
low solo,pno (E flat maj) CRAMER
                                     (B708)
med solo,pno (F maj) CRAMER (B709)
high solo,pno (G maj) CRAMER (B710)

My Haven Of Dreams
low solo,pno (E flat maj) CRAMER
                                     (B711)
med solo,pno (F maj) CRAMER (B712)
high solo,pno (G maj) CRAMER (B713)

Night Has A Thousand Eyes, The
low solo,pno (E flat maj, contains
also: Memory, A) LEONARD-ENG
                                     (B714)
high solo,pno (F maj, contains
also: Memory, A) LEONARD-ENG
                                     (B715)
Time's Roses
med solo,pno (E maj) LEONARD-ENG
                                     (B716)
med-high solo,pno (F maj) LEONARD-
ENG   (B717)
high solo,pno (G maj) LEONARD-ENG
                                     (B718)
low solo,pno (E flat maj) LEONARD-
ENG   (B719)

BARTA, LUBOR (1928-1972)
Ctyri Pisnicky Pro Deti *CC4U
solo,pno SUPRAPHON s.p.   (B720)

BARTELINK, BERNARD (1929-   )
De Zaligsprekingen
low solo,org DONEMUS s.p.   (B721)

BARTH, HANS JOACHIM (1897-1956)
Kinderlieder *CCU
solo,pno HUG s.p.   (B722)

BARTHOLOMEW, MARSHALL (1885-   )
When We Are Parted
med-low solo,pno GALAXY 1.1870.7
$1.00   (B723)

BARTLET
Under The Greenwood Tree
see AS YOU LIKE IT

BARTLETT, GENE
Christ Lives In Me *sac
solo,pno WORD S-436   (B724)

Every Day Is A Better Day (composed
with Terrell, Beverly)
solo,pno BROADMAN 4590-17 $.75
                                     (B725)

Have A Good Day *see Terrell,
Beverly

He Will Send The Blessings If You
Pray *sac
med solo,pno BROADMAN 4590-05 $.60
                                     (B726)
Here Is My Life *sac
solo,pno BROADMAN 4590-15 $.75
                                     (B727)
You're Not Alone
high solo,pno BROADMAN 4590-01 $.60
                                     (B728)
low solo,pno BROADMAN 4590-02 $.60
                                     (B729)

BARTLETT, HOMER NEWTON (1847-1920)
O Lord, Be Merciful *sac
high solo,pno (D maj) SCHIRM.G $.75
                                     (B730)

BARTLETT, J.C.
Dream, A
low solo,orch (D maj) ASHDOWN s.p.,
ipr   (B731)
med solo,orch (F maj) ASHDOWN s.p.,
ipr   (B732)
high solo,orch (A flat maj) ASHDOWN
s.p., ipr   (B733)

BARTOK, BELA (1881-1945)
Der Junge Bartok, Band I *CC13U
solo,pno SCHOTTS 5390 s.p.   (B734)

Eight Hungarian Folksongs *CC8U,Hung
[Eng/Ger/Hung] solo,pno BOOSEY
$6.00   (B735)

Five Songs *Op.16, CC5U
[Eng/Ger] solo,pno BOOSEY $6.00
                                     (B736)

Five Village Scenes *CC5U
female solo,pno BOOSEY $8.50 (B737)

Funf Dorfszenen *CC5U
[Slav/Eng/Hung/Slav] female solo,pno
UNIVER. 8712 $5.25   (B738)

Funf Lieder *Op.15, CC5U
solo,pno UNIVER. 13150 $6.75 (B739)

Funf Lieder Der Jugend *CC5U
solo,pno BOOSEY $9.00   (B740)

BARTOK, BELA (cont'd.)

Sieben Diverse Lieder *CC7U
solo,pno BOOSEY $9.00   (B741)

Vier Lieder Der Trauer *CC4U
solo,pno BOOSEY $9.00   (B742)

Vier Tanzlieder *CC4U
solo,pno BOOSEY $9.00   (B743)

BARTOLOZZI, BRUNO (1911-   )
Tres Recuerdos Del Cielo *CC3U
female solo,10inst ZERBONI 6751
s.p.   (B744)

BARTOS, FRANTISEK (1905-1973)
Cerny *song cycle
"Der Schwarze" T solo,pno CZECH
s.p.   (B745)

Der Schwarze *see Cerny

Destive Obrazy *CC10U
solo,pno SUPRAPHON s.p.   (B746)

Tri Pisne Na Slova Francouzske Poezie
*CC3U
solo,pno SUPRAPHON s.p.   (B747)

BARTOS, JAN ZDENEK (1908-   )
Ma Pout'
solo,pno SUPRAPHON s.p.   (B748)

Pisne Mladych Textilaku *CCU
low solo,pno CZECH s.p.   (B749)

BARYBIN, YE.
In Our Native Land *song cycle
[Russ] B solo,pno MEZ KNIGA 2.87
s.p.   (B750)

BAS-SANGARENS ALBUM *CC76U
Bar/B solo,pno LUNDQUIST s.p. (B751)

BASHFUL THAMES, THE see Purcell, Henry

BASHFUL TOM see Kemp, David H.

BASIC REPERTOIRE FOR SINGERS *CC12L,
Renais/Baroq/Class
(Ottman, Robert W.; Krueger, Paul G.)
[Eng] med-high solo,pno SOUTHERN
B-180 $3.00 contains works by:
Handel; Purcell; Arne; Haydn;
Monroe and others   (B752)

BASS ALBUM *CC24L
[Ger] B solo,kbd WILHELM. s.p.
contains works by: Beethoven;
Binder; Flotow; Loewe; Mozart and
others   (B753)

BASS SONGS *CCU
(Mason, M.) B solo,pno PRESSER $3.00
                              (B754)

BASS SONGS (RADIO CITY SONGS) *CCU
B solo,pno MARKS $1.50   (B755)

BASSANI, GIOVANNI BATTISTA
(ca. 1657-1716)
Nascere, Nascere, Dive Puellule *sac
(Ewerhart, Rudolf) [Lat] A solo,
cont BIELER CS 2 s.p.   (B756)

BASSETT, KAROLYN WELLS
Dinna Forget
med solo,pno FITZSIMONS $.50   (B757)

Take Joy Home
low solo,pno (C maj) SCHIRM.G $.75
                              (B758)

BASSETT, LESLIE (1923-   )
Easter Triptych
T solo,4horn,4trp,4trom,2tuba,
bar.hn.,timp,3perc AM.COMP.AL. sc
$14.30, ipa, voc sc $2.20 (B759)

Four Songs *CC4U
high solo,pno AM.COMP.AL. $3.30
                              (B760)

Great Art Thou, O Music
high solo,pno HIGHGATE 7.0109.7
$1.50   (B761)

Slow, Slow, Fresh Fount
high solo,pno HIGHGATE 7.0041.7
$1.00   (B762)

Time And Beyond
Bar solo,clar,vcl,pno PETERS 66574
rental   (B763)

To Music
high solo,pno HIGHGATE 7.0108.7
$1.25   (B764)

BASSFORD, WILLIAM KIPP (1839-1902)
My Faith Looks Up To Thee *sac
SA soli,pno WATERLOO $.65   (B765)
(Lachner) SA soli,pno SCHIRM.G $.85
                              (B766)

BASTA COSI T'INTENDI see Martini,
Giambattista

BASTA, VINCESTI - AH NON LASCIARMI see
Mozart, Wolfgang Amadeus

BASTISAR *CCU,folk
(Clarin, Bjorn) solo,pno NORDISKA
6503 s.p.   (B767)

BAT-YONIM see Ben-Haim, Paul

BATEMAN, RONALD
Barcarolle At Dawn
high solo,pno (F maj) LEONARD-ENG
                              (B768)
2 soli,pno LEONARD-ENG   (B769)
med solo,pno (D maj) LEONARD-ENG
                              (B770)
low solo,pno (A maj) LEONARD-ENG
                              (B771)

Dream Minuet
low solo,pno (E flat maj) LEONARD-
ENG   (B772)
med solo,pno (F maj) LEONARD-ENG
                              (B773)
high solo,pno (G maj) LEONARD-ENG
                              (B774)
2 soli,pno LEONARD-ENG   (B775)

Lord Of Our Life
low solo,pno (F maj) LEONARD-ENG
                              (B776)
med solo,pno (G maj) LEONARD-ENG
                              (B777)
high solo,pno (A flat maj) LEONARD-
ENG   (B778)

Won't You Come Roving
low solo,pno (G maj) LEONARD-ENG
                              (B779)
med solo,pno (A flat maj) LEONARD-
ENG   (B780)
high solo,pno (B flat maj) LEONARD-
ENG   (B781)

BATH, THE see James, Thomas

BATH, HUBERT (1883-1945)
Cornish Rhapsody
(Stillman) solo,pno FOX,S   (B782)

BATHING IN THE SUNLIGHT OF HIS LOVE see
King

BATTEN, MRS. GEORGE
Little Brown Brother
low solo,pno (F maj) CRAMER   (B783)
high solo,pno (A flat maj) CRAMER
                              (B784)
2 soli,pno CRAMER   (B785)

Love-Song Of Har Dyal
low solo,pno (C maj) CRAMER   (B786)
high solo,pno (E maj) CRAMER (B787)

BATTERIE see Absil, Jean

BATTI, BATTI O BEL MASETTO see Mozart,
Wolfgang Amadeus

BATTLE EVE, THE see Bonheur, Theo.

BATTLE HYMN OF THE REPUBLIC
solo,pno ASHLEY $.95   (B788)

BATTLE HYMN OF THE REPUBLIC see Steffe,
William

BAUD-BOVY
Chansons Greques Du Dedocanese *CCU
solo,pno HENN 180 s.p.   (B789)

Les Muses Galantes
solo,pno HENN 907 s.p.   (B790)

BAUDRIER, YVES (1906-   )
Laisser-Courre
see Poemes De Tristan Corbiere

Paysage Mauvais
see Poemes De Tristan Corbiere

Poemes De Tristan Corbiere
solo,pno AMPHION A 170 $3.00
contains: Laisser-Courre; Paysage
Mauvais   (B791)

BAUER, JOSEF
Messe Zu Ehren Des Heilige Ulrich
*Op.10, sac
Bar solo,org BOHM s.p. sc, solo pt
                              (B792)

BAUER, MARION EUGENIE (1887-1955)
Harp, The
med solo,pno BMI $.50   (B793)

Malay To His Master, The
low solo,pno AM.COMP.AL. $2.75
                              (B794)

BAUM, A.
Lieder Aus Dem Schneckenhaus *CCU
solo,pno HUG s.p.   (B795)

BAUMANN, MAX (1917-   )
Alma Redemptoris Mater *sac
med solo,org SIRIUS s.p.   (B796)

BAUMANN, MAX (cont'd.)

Ave Maria *sac
high solo,org SIRIUS s.p.   (B797)

Ave, Stern Des Meeres
med solo,org SIRIUS s.p.   (B798)

Die Schone Seilerin *Op.61
Mez solo,fl,clar,vln,bvl SIRIUS sc
s.p., ipr, solo pt s.p.   (B799)

Psalmi *Op.67, sac,CCU,Psalm
Bar solo,pno,org SIRIUS s.p. (B800)

BAUMGARTNER
I Rosornas Dagar
2 soli,pno LUNDQUIST s.p.   (B801)

BAUMGARTNER, H. LEROY (1891-   )
Hymn Of Thanks, A *sac,Gen/Thanks
high solo,pno ABINGDON APM-457 $.50
                              (B802)

Love Is Of God *sac,Marriage
med-high solo,pno CONCORDIA 97-9327
$.75   (B803)

Thou, Who Hast Loved The Little Child
*sac
med solo,pno (Baptism) ABINGDON
APM-456 $.50   (B804)

BAUR, JURG (1918-   )
Herz, Stirb Oder Singe *song cycle
[Ger] high solo,fl,strings voc sc
PETERS 5878 $8.50   (B805)

Mit Wechselndem Schlussel *song
cycle
med solo,pno BREITKOPF-W EB 6539
$6.50   (B806)

Vom Tiefinnern Song *CC4U
[Ger] med solo,pno PETERS 5857
$6.50   (B807)

BAVICCHI, JOHN (1922-   )
Six Korean Folksongs *CC6U
S solo,pno sc SEESAW $5.00   (B808)

To The Lighthouse
S solo,horn,pno sc SEESAW $4.00
                              (B809)

Trio No. 3
A solo,vln,vcl sc SEESAW $5.00
                              (B810)

BAX, SIR ARNOLD (1883-1953)
Album Of Seven Selected Songs *CC7L
[Eng] med-high solo,pno CHESTER
s.p.   (B811)

Lullaby, A
solo,pno (E maj) ASHDOWN   (B812)

Oh Dear! What Can The Matter Be?
[Eng] med solo,kbd CHESTER s.p.
                              (B813)

BAXTER, MAUDE STEWART
Across The Valley
solo,pno CRAMER $1.15   (B814)

Awake And Sing
solo,pno CRAMER   (B815)

For Mummie And Me
solo,pno CRAMER   (B816)

Freedom
solo,pno CRAMER   (B817)

In August
solo,pno CRAMER   (B818)

In Corbar Woods
solo,pno CRAMER   (B819)

Loveliness More Fair
solo,pno CRAMER   (B820)

Lovers Sighs
solo,pno CRAMER   (B821)

One Hour Of Love
solo,pno CRAMER   (B822)

Our Lady's Bedstraw
low solo,pno (D flat maj) CRAMER
                              (B823)
high solo,pno (E flat maj) CRAMER
                              (B824)

Primeval
solo,pno CRAMER   (B825)

Soul Of The Moor
solo,pno CRAMER   (B826)

BAYNES, SIDNEY see Metra, Jules Louis
Olivier, La Serenata

BAYNON, ARTHUR
Fairies In The Glen
solo,pno CRAMER   (B827)

Little Dream Shop
solo,pno CRAMER   (B828)

BAYNON, ARTHUR (cont'd.)

Pedlar's Basket
solo,pno (C maj) CRAMER   (B829)

Three Songs Of Persia *CC3U
solo,pno LEONARD-ENG   (B830)

BAZLIK, MIRO
Les Chansons Composees Sur La Poesie
Chinoise *CCU
A solo,fl,vcl,pno SLOV.HUD.FOND
s.p.   (B831)

BAZSAROZSA *CC99U,folk,Hung
(Csenki) solo,pno BUDAPEST 1813 s.p.
     (B832)

BE JOYFUL IN THE LORD see Couperin (le
Grand), Francois

BE M'AN PERDUT see Ventadorn, Bernart
de

BE MERCIFUL, EVEN AS YOUR FATHER IS
MERCIFUL see Krapf, Gerhard

BE NEAR ME see Loewe, Gilbert

BE NOT AFRAID see Koch, Frederick

BE NOT ALWAYS TENDER, ADORING see
Handel, George Frideric, Sempre
Dolci, Ed Amorose

BE PLEASANT, BE AIRY see Stanley, John

BE STILL AND KNOW see Bitgood, Roberta

BE STILL AND KNOW THAT I AM GOD see
Dungan, Olive

BE STILL, MY SOUL (from Finlandia) sac,
gospel
solo,pno ABER.GRP. $1.50   (B833)
[Eng] solo,pno BREITKOPF-W 57 04022
$1.00 see from Sechs Lieder Nach
Texten Von J.L. Runeberg   (B834)

BE STILL MY SOUL *sac,CCUL
(Carmichael, Ralph) solo,pno WORD
35011 $2.50   (B835)

BE STILL YOU LITTLE LEAVES see
Glanville-Hicks, Peggy

BE THOU EXALTED see Huhn, Bruno

BE THOU MY GUIDE see Wheeler, Alfred

BE THOU MY LIGHT see Day, Maude Craske

BE WITH ME, LORD *sac,gospel
solo,pno ABER.GRP. $1.50   (B836)

BE YE KIND, ONE TO ANOTHER see Davis,
Katherine K.

BEACH, MRS. H.H.A. (1867-1944)
Though I Take The Wings
med solo,pno SEESAW $1.50   (B837)

Year's At The Spring, The
med solo,pno (B flat maj) WILLIS
$.75   (B838)

BEACON BARN, THE see Berkeley, Lennox

BEALE, JAMES
Lamentations *Op.35, sac,CCU,Bibl/
Psalm
S solo,fl,pno sc AM.COMP.AL. $6.60,
ipa   (B839)

Music For Soprano And Orchestra
*Op.34, CCU
S solo,2fl,2ob,English horn,2clar,
bass clar,2bsn,2horn,3trp,3trom,
tuba,2perc,cel,strings sc
AM.COMP.AL. $9.90   (B840)

Proverbs *Op.28, sac,CCU,Bibl
Bar solo,English horn,vibra,pno/vcl
sc AM.COMP.AL. $7.50, ipa   (B841)

Three Songs *Op.33, CC3U
S solo,vln,vla sc AM.COMP.AL.
$3.57, ipa   (B842)

BEAN FLOWER, THE see Moeran, Ernest J.

BEARN *Fr
(Canteloube, J.) solo,acap DURAND
s.p. see also Anthologie Des Chants
Populaires Francais Tome I   (B843)

BEAR'S SONG, THE see London, Edwin

BEAST, THE see Schmidt

BEAT! BEAT! DRUMS see Raphling, Sam

BEAT OF THE DRUM see Simpson, Nellie

BEATI OMNES, QUI TIMENT DOMINUM see
Geist, Christian

BEATITUDES see Demarest, A.

BEATITUDES see Wood, Don

BEATITUDES, THE see Humphreys

BEATITUDES, THE see Malotte, Albert Hay

BEATITUDINES see Petrassi, Goffredo

BEATRICE see Devreese, Godefroid

BEATRIC'S SONG see Walton

BEATRIJS see Voormolen, Alexander
Nicolas

BEATTY
It's Different Now *sac
solo,pno LILLENAS SM-923: SN $1.00
     (B844)

BEAU CENT-GARDE, VOTRE CUIRASSE see
Messager, Andre

BEAU PAGE see Delmet, Paul

BEAU PAGE see Godard, Benjamin Louis
Paul

BEAU PAYS, PAYS DU GAI SOLEIL see
Chabrier, Emmanuel

BEAU SOIR see Debussy, Claude

BEAUCOUP see Emer, M.

BEAUDRIE, M.
Identity
med solo,pno SEESAW $1.00   (B845)

Nights Remember, The
med solo,pno SEESAW $1.00   (B846)

You Came To Me
med solo,pno SEESAW $1.00   (B847)

Young Love
med solo,pno SEESAW $1.00   (B848)

BEAUJOYEULX, BALTASAR DE
(? -ca. 1587)
Air De Mercure (from Ballet Comique
De La Reine)
see LA MUSIQUE, QUATORZIEME CAHIER

BEAUMONT
I Look To My Lord *sac
high solo,pno PRESSER $.95   (B849)
med solo,pno PRESSER $.95   (B850)

BEAUTE DIVINE ENCHANTERESSE see
Meyerbeer, Giacomo

BEAUTIFUL BLUE DANUBE see Strauss,
Johann, An Der Schonen Blauen Donau

BEAUTIFUL DREAMER see Foster, Stephen
Collins

BEAUTIFUL GARDEN OF PRAYER, THE *sac,
gospel
solo,pno ABER.GRP. $1.50   (B851)

BEAUTIFUL HANDS see Alden

BEAUTIFUL ISLE OF SOMEWHERE *sac,
gospel
solo,pno ABER.GRP. $1.50   (B852)

BEAUTIFUL ISLE OF SOMEWHERE see Fearis,
John S.

BEAUTIFUL NEBRASKA see Fras, Jim

BEAUTIFUL SCARS see Hilliard

BEAUTIFUL SHIP FROM TOYLAND, THE see
Friml, Rudolf

BEAUTY TOUCH ME see Hindemith, Paul

BEAUX JOURS PASSES see Proch, Heinrich

BEBE CHANTE see Missa, Edmond Jean
Louis

BEBRO E IL SUO CAVALLO see Pizzetti,
Ildebrando

BECAUSE see d'Hardelot, Guy

BECAUSE HE CAME see Russell, F.

BECAUSE HE LIVES see Gaither

BECAUSE I WALK WITH THEE see Forshaw,
J. Howard

BECAUSE I WERE SHY see Johnston, Lyell

BECAUSE OF YESTERDAY see Dewey, Cleon

BECAUSE OF YOU see Haskins, Vernon C.

BECHER see Marvia, Einari, Malja

BECK, CONRAD (1901-   )
Drei Herbstgesange *CC3U
solo,pno/org SCHOTTS 2131 s.p.
     (B853)

Herbstfeuer
low solo,chamb.orch voc sc SCHOTTS
4774 s.p.   (B854)

Kammerkantate Nach Sonetten Der
Louize Labe *cant
solo,chamb.orch voc sc SCHOTTS 5399
s.p., ipa   (B855)

Sonnenfinsternis *cant
A solo,chamb.orch voc sc SCHOTTS
6102 s.p.   (B856)

BECK, JOHN NESS (1930-   )
Song Of Devotion *sac
high solo,pno (C maj) SCHIRM.G $.75
     (B857)
med solo,pno (A maj) SCHIRM.G $.75
     (B858)
low solo,pno (A maj) SCHIRM.G $.75
     (B859)

Song Of Joy *Psalm
solo,pno PETERS 6840 $2.50   (B860)

BECK, REINHOLD, I.
Legende
solo,pno RIES s.p. contains also:
Weihnachtslied, Op.45   (B861)

Weihnachtslied *Op.45
see Beck, Reinhold, I., Legende

BECK, THOMAS [LUDVIGSEN] (1899-1963)
Barnlige Sange Til Julens Pris *Xmas
solo,pno MUSIKK s.p.
contains: Et Barn Er Fodt I
Betlehem; No Koma Guds Englar;
Saele Jolekveld; Varherre Han
Hvilte I Krybben Sa Trang
     (B862)

Bon
solo,pno MUSIKK s.p.   (B863)

Danse Mi Vise, Grate Min Sang
see Vinden Blaes Synna - Vinden
Blaes Norda, Heft II

Den Fyrste Songen *Op.16,No.1
see Tri Sivlesongar

Et Barn Er Fodt I Betlehem
see Barnlige Sange Til Julens Pris

Gnier Og Gnuar
see Vinden Blaes Synna - Vinden
Blaes Norda, Heft II

Hellige Tone *Op.16,No.3
see Tri Sivlesongar

Hokken Ska'n Godblonke Tel
see Vinden Blaes Synna - Vinden
Blaes Norda, Heft II

Je Veit Om E Bygd
see Vinden Blaes Synna - Vinden
Blaes Norda, Heft I

Kjerringvise Mot Vinter'n
see Vinden Blaes Synna - Vinden
Blaes Norda, Heft II

Lerka *Op.16,No.2
see Tri Sivlesongar

No Koma Guds Englar
see Barnlige Sange Til Julens Pris

Og Alle Mine Viser
see Vinden Blaes Synna - Vinden
Blaes Norda, Heft I

Sa Dryge Berg
see Vinden Blaes Synna - Vinden
Blaes Norda, Heft I

Saele Jolekveld
see Barnlige Sange Til Julens Pris

Tri Sivlesongar
solo,pno MUSIKK s.p.
contains: Den Fyrste Songen,
Op.16,No.1; Hellige Tone,
Op.16,No.3; Lerka, Op.16,No.2
     (B864)

Varherre Han Hvilte I Krybben Sa
Trang
see Barnlige Sange Til Julens Pris

Varvise
see Vinden Blaes Synna - Vinden
Blaes Norda, Heft I

Vinden Blaes Synna - Vinden Blaes
Norda, Heft I
solo,pno MUSIKK s.p.
contains: Je Veit Om E Bygd; Og
Alle Mine Viser; Sa Dryge Berg;
Varvise; Vise Til Sjoltrost
     (B865)

BECK, THOMAS [LUDVIGSEN] (cont'd.)

Vinden Blaes Synna - Vinden Blaes
    Norda, Heft II
    solo,pno MUSIKK s.p.
        contains: Danse Mi Vise, Grate
        Min Sang; Gnier Og Gnuar;
        Hokken Ska'n Godblonke Tel;
        Kjerringvise Mot Vinter'n; Vise
        I Onna   (B866)

Vise I Onna
    see Vinden Blaes Synna - Vinden
    Blaes Norda, Heft II

Vise Til Sjoltrost
    see Vinden Blaes Synna - Vinden
    Blaes Norda, Heft I

BECKER, G.
Moirolgi
    high female solo,2clar,bass clar,
    harp ZIMMER. 1717 s.p.   (B867)

BECKER, GUNTHER (1924-   )
Four Epigrams *CC4U
    [Ger] Bar solo,fl,ob,2clar,bsn,
    horn,trp,trom,pno,harp,pno,cel,
    strings PETERS rental   (B868)

Rigolo
    high solo,fl,clar,vln,vcl,pno,treb
    inst GERIG HG 641 s.p.   (B869)

BECKER, JOHN J. (1886-1961)
At Dieppe
    ,high solo,pno AM.COMP.AL. $3.57
                                     (B870)
Monodrama I
    T solo,pno AM.COMP.AL. $6.60 (B871)

Psalms Of Love *song cycle
    med solo,org AM.COMP.AL. $3.85
                                     (B872)
BECKER, R.
Wo Du Hingehst *sac
    S/T solo,pno (C maj) LIENAU HOS 175
    s.p.   (B873)
    Mez solo,pno (B flat maj) LIENAU
    HOS 176 s.p.   (B874)
    A/Bar solo,pno (A flat maj) LIENAU
    HOS 177 s.p.   (B875)

BECKER, REINHOLD (1842-1924)
Acht Kinderlieder *Op.149,No.1-8,
    CC8L
    solo,pno LEUCKART s.p.   (B876)

BECKER-FOSS, JURGEN (1917-   )
Gelobet Sei Gott *sac,concerto
    A solo,vln,org sc HANSSLER 12.506
    s.p. see from Vier Geistliche
    Konzerte   (B877)

Kommt, Lasst Uns Anbeten *sac,
    concerto
    A solo,2vln,org sc HANSSLER 12.505
    s.p. see from Vier Geistliche
    Konzerte   (B878)

Mache Dich Auf, Werde Licht *sac,
    concerto
    A solo,S rec,org sc HANSSLER 12.507
    s.p. see from Vier Geistliche
    Konzerte   (B879)

Singet Dem Herrn Ein Neues Lied
    *sac,concerto
    A solo,org sc HANSSLER 12.508 s.p.
    see from Vier Geistliche Konzerte
                                     (B880)

Vier Geistliche Konzerte *see
    Gelobet Sei Gott; Kommt, Lasst
    Uns Anbeten; Mache Dich Auf,
    Werde Licht; Singet Dem Herrn Ein
    Neues Lied   (B881)

BECKWITH, JOHN (1927-   )
Five Lyrics Of The T'ang Dynasty
    *CC5U
    solo,pno BERANDOL BER 1295 $3.50
                                     (B882)
Four Love Songs *CC4U
    solo,pno BERANDOL BER 1296 $5.00
                                     (B883)
Four Songs From Ben Johnson's
    "Volpone" *CC4U
    solo,gtr BERANDOL BER 1339 $2.50
                                     (B884)
BECUCCI
Tesoro Mio
    [It/Eng] S solo,pno RICORDI-ENG
    LD 342 s.p.   (B885)

BEDE see Bijvanck, Henk

BEDE OM SLAAP see Koetsier, Jan

BEDE VOOR HET VADERLAND see Rontgen,
    [Julius]

BEDELL, ROBERT LEECH (1909-   )
Two Songs *sac,CC2U,Holywk/Lent
    BELWIN med solo,pno $1.50; low
    solo,pno $1.50   (B886)

BEDFORD, DAVID (1937-   )
Aviary, The *see Das Vogelhaus

Come In Here Child
    S solo,pno UNIVER. 14639 $2.50
                                     (B887)
Das Vogelhaus *song cycle
    "Aviary, The" [Eng/Ger] solo,pno
    UNIVER. 14168 $2.00   (B888)

Music For Albion Moonlight
    S solo,fl,clar,pno,vln,vcl,
    harmonica quarto,sc UNIVER. 14162
    $6.25   (B889)

Music That Her Echo Is, The
    T solo,pno UNIVER. 14615 $3.00
                                     (B890)

Star Clusters, Nebulae And Places In
    Devon
    solo,inst UNIVER. 15438 $7.00
                                     (B891)
That White And Radiant Legend
    S,narrator,8inst quarto,sc UNIVER.
    14208 $6.25   (B892)

BEDINGER, HUGO
April-Narri
    solo,pno GEHRMANS s.p.   (B893)

Belsazar
    solo,pno GEHRMANS s.p.   (B894)

Brug Ei De Oine Saa!
    solo,pno GEHRMANS s.p.   (B895)

Drommeri
    solo,pno GEHRMANS s.p.   (B896)

Du Ar
    solo,pno GEHRMANS s.p.   (B897)

En Soldat
    solo,pno GEHRMANS s.p.   (B898)

Funf Lieder *CC5U
    [Ger/Swed] solo,pno GEHRMANS s.p.
                                     (B899)
Til Mor
    solo,pno GEHRMANS 726 s.p.   (B900)

Vuggesang
    S solo,pno GEHRMANS s.p.   (B901)
    Mez solo,pno GEHRMANS s.p.   (B902)
    A solo,pno GEHRMANS s.p.   (B903)

BEDOUIN LOVE SONG, THE see Pinsuti,
    Ciro

BEDRICH, JAN (1932-   )
Stilles Lieben *see Tiche Milovani

Tiche Milovani
    "Stilles Lieben" T/S solo,pno CZECH
    s.p.   (B904)

BEE, THE see Ratcliffe, Desmond

BEECHGAARD, JULIUS (1843-1917)
Quand Le Reve A Toi
    solo,pno ENOCH s.p. see also CHANTS
    DU NORD   (B905)

BEEK, H. VAN
Wij Zijn Weer Vrij
    solo,pno BROEKMANS 302 s.p. (B906)

BEEKHUIS, HANNA (1889-   )
Adieu-Liedt
    see Drie Liederen

Alles Heeft Zyn Mond
    see Twee Oude Melodieen En Twee
    Vrije Composities

Anchor Line
    see Five Negro Songs

Apokalyptischer Advent
    A solo,pno DONEMUS s.p.   (B907)

Ballade
    see Vier Liederen Naar Aanl. Van
    Oud-Hollandsche Melodieen

Berceuse De Maitre Canard
    see Deux Melodies Populaires
    Polonaises

Berceuse D'Haiti
    see Trois Chansons Negres

Berceuse Presque Negre
    high solo,pno DONEMUS s.p.   (B908)

Chi-King
    DONEMUS Bar/Mez solo,pno s.p.; Bar/
    Mez solo,2fl,2ob,2clar,2bsn,
    4horn,2trp,3trom,tuba,timp,perc,
    cel,strings rental
    contains: Chinesisches
        Soldatenlied; Der Mude Soldat;
        Klage Der Garde   (B909)

BEEKHUIS, HANNA (cont'd.)

Chinesisches Soldatenlied
    see Chi-King

Cupidootje
    med solo,pno DONEMUS s.p.   (B910)

Cupidootje
    see MODERNE NEDERLANDSE LIED

Dans En Pastorale
    solo,fl,vla, piano 4-hands
    BROEKMANS 303 s.p.   (B911)

De Bruine Bie
    see Drie Liederen Van Gezelle

De Keizer Van Zweden
    see Vier Liederen Naar Aanl. Van
    Oud-Hollandsche Melodieen

De Nachtegael Die Sanck Een Liedt
    see Vier Liederen Naar Aanl. Van
    Oud-Hollandsche Melodieen

De Rozengaarde
    see Drie Liederen

De Winden
    see Drie Liederen Van Gezelle

De Zeven Boeven
    narrator,2fl,ob,clar,bsn,horn,pno
    DONEMUS s.p.   (B912)
    narrator,pno DONEMUS s.p.   (B913)

Der Mude Soldat
    see Chi-King

Der Sterbende Held
    see Nachtgesange

Der Trommler
    see Nachtgesange

Deux Melodies Populaires Polonaises
    Mez/A/Bar solo,pno DONEMUS s.p.
        contains: Berceuse De Maitre
        Canard; La Paresseuse   (B914)

Die Osse Ende Ooc Dat Eselkyn
    see Drie Kerstliederen

Dormeuse
    S solo,pno DONEMUS s.p.   (B915)
    3 female soli,fl,vcl,harp DONEMUS
    s.p.   (B916)

Drie Kerstliederen *sac
    med solo/high solo,pno,vcl DONEMUS
    s.p.
        contains: Die Osse Ende Ooc Dat
        Eselkyn; Een Kindekyn Is Ons
        Gheboren; Maria Die Zoude Naer
        Bethlehem Gaan   (B917)

Drie Liederen
    Bar solo,pno DONEMUS s.p.
        contains: Adieu-Liedt; De
        Rozengaarde; Jonghen Stijn (B918)

Drie Liederen Van Gezelle
    S solo,pno,vcl DONEMUS s.p.
        contains: De Bruine Bie; De
        Winden; O, Lied   (B919)

Du Bist Min
    see Twee Oude Melodieen En Twee
    Vrije Composities

D'une Qui Faisait La Longue
    see Serenades

Een Kindekyn Is Ons Gheboren
    see Drie Kerstliederen

Five Negro Songs
    high solo/low solo,pno DONEMUS s.p.
        contains: Anchor Line; Frogs,
        Frogs; I Am Not Going To Marry;
        Oh Boat, Come Back To Me;
        Turkey Buzzard, The; Where Are
        You Going?   (B920)

Frogs, Frogs
    see Five Negro Songs

I Am Not Going To Marry
    see Five Negro Songs

Ick Hebbe Ghedraghen
    see Twee Oude Melodieen En Twee
    Vrije Composities

Jonghen Stijn
    see Drie Liederen

Klage Der Garde
    see Chi-King

Kwartrijnen En Nachtstilte
    A solo,strings DONEMUS   (B921)

BEEKHUIS, HANNA (cont'd.)

Kwatrijnen En Nachstilte
A solo,4strings DONEMUS s.p. (B922)

La Paresseuse
see Deux Melodies Populaires
Polonaises

Les Deux Flutes
Mez solo,2fl,pno DONEMUS s.p.
(B923)

Les Noces Du Crocodile
see Trois Chansons Negres

Liederen
S solo,pno DONEMUS s.p.
contains: Nieltje In Het
Aquarium; Sonnet (B924)

Mamzell Zizi
see Trois Chansons Negres

Marc Groet 'S Morgens De Singen
Mez solo,pno DONEMUS s.p. (B925)

Maria Die Zoude Naer Bethlehem Gaan
see Drie Kerstliederen

M'aymerez-Vous Bien?
see Serenades

Middeleeuws Kerstliedje *CCU
solo,fl,3vln,vcl BROEKMANS 299 s.p.
(B926)

Nachtgesange
A/Mez solo,pno DONEMUS s.p.
contains: Der Sterbende Held; Der
Trommler (B927)

Nieltje In Het Aquarium
see Liederen

Nocturne
SABar soli,pno DONEMUS s.p. (B928)

O, Lied
see Drie Liederen Van Gezelle

Oh Boat, Come Back To Me
see Five Negro Songs

Op Eenen Morgenstont
see Twee Oude Melodieen En Twee
Vrije Composities

Pauv' Piti'
see Trois Chansons Negres

Psalm 5
see Tres Psalmi

Psalm 23
see Tres Psalmi

Psalm 33
see Tres Psalmi

Reflets Du Japon *CCU
[Fr] A solo,vla DONEMUS s.p. (B929)

Serenades
solo,pno DONEMUS s.p.
contains: D'une Qui Faisait La
Longue; M'aymerez-Vous Bien?;
Voici La Douce Nuit De Mai
(B930)

Sonnet
see Liederen

Tres Psalmi *sac
DONEMUS A/Bar solo,pno s.p.; A/B
solo,3fl,3ob,3clar,3bsn,2horn,
2trp,2trom,timp,perc,harp,strings
rental
contains: Psalm 5; Psalm 23;
Psalm 33 (B931)

Trois Chansons Negres
high solo,pno DONEMUS s.p.
contains: Berceuse D'Haiti; Les
Noces Du Crocodile; Mamzell
Zizi; Pauv' Piti' (B932)

Trois Chansons Pour Danser *CC3U
[Afr] high solo,pno HEUGEL s.p.
(B933)

Turkey Buzzard, The
see Five Negro Songs

Twee Oude Melodieen En Twee Vrije
Composities
med solo,fl&harp/fl&pno DONEMUS
s.p.
contains: Alles Heeft Zyn Mond;
Du Bist Min; Ick Hebbe
Ghedraghen; Op Eenen
Morgenstont (B934)

Verrassing
Mez solo,fl,pno DONEMUS s.p. (B935)

Vier Liederen *CC4UL
A solo,pno DONEMUS s.p. (B936)

BEEKHUIS, HANNA (cont'd.)

Vier Liederen Naar Aanl. Van Oud-
Hollandsche Melodieen
A solo,3fl,2ob,2clar,2bsn,4horn,
2trp,3trom,tuba,timp,perc,cel,
harp,strings DONEMUS s.p.
contains: Ballade; De Keizer Van
Zweden; De Nachtegael Die Sanck
Een Liedt; Wachterlied (B937)

Voici La Douce Nuit De Mai
see Serenades

Wachterlied
see Vier Liederen Naar Aanl. Van
Oud-Hollandsche Melodieen

Where Are You Going?
see Five Negro Songs

BEERMAN, BURTON
Consort And Song
S solo,clar,perc,vcl,pno sc
AM.COMP.AL. $7.15 (B938)

Mass *sac,Mass
T solo,fl,perc,harp,electronic tape
AM.COMP.AL. (B939)

Mixtures
soli,fl,clar,horn,vln,electronic
tape MEDIA 4811 $8.25 (B940)

BEERS, JACQUES (1902-1947)
Concerto Pour Une Voix De Soprano
S solo,fl,ob,clar,al-sax,bsn,horn,
trp,trom,pno,strings DONEMUS s.p.
(B941)

Manyanas Liebeslieder *song cycle
S solo,3fl,ob,3clar,2bsn,3horn,
2trp,2trom,timp,perc,vibra,
strings DONEMUS s.p. (B942)

Neue Geistliche Lieder *CC17U
S solo,pno (med) BAREN. 1283 $5.00
(B943)

BEE'S SONG see Keel, Frederick

BEESON, JACK HAMILTON (1921-)
Abbie's Bird Song (from Lizzie
Borden)
S solo,pno BOOSEY $1.75 (B944)

Against Idleness And Mischief And In
Praise Of Labor
solo,pno BOOSEY $1.50 (B945)

Death By Owl-Eyes
solo,pno BOOSEY $1.50 (B946)

Five Songs *CC5U
solo,pno PEER $1.50 (B947)

Indiana Homecoming
solo,pno BOOSEY $1.50 (B948)

Margret's Garden Aria (from Lizzie
Borden)
S solo,pno BOOSEY $1.75 (B949)

To A Sinister Potato
solo,pno BOOSEY $1.50 (B950)

You Should Of Done It Blues, The
solo,pno BOOSEY $1.50 (B951)

BEETHOVEN, LUDWIG VAN (1770-1827)
Abscheulicher! Wo Eilst Du Hin? (from
Fidelio)
S solo,fl,2ob,2clar,bsn,3horn,
strings BREITKOPF-W s.p. (B952)
S solo,fl,2ob,2clar,2bsn,3horn,
strings BREITKOPF-L rental (B953)

Adelaide
see Six Songs
solo,pno CRAMER (B954)
[Fr] S/T solo,pno/inst DURAND s.p.
(B955)

Ah! Perfide! Parjure! *see Ah!
Perfido

Ah! Perfido *Op.65, scena
S solo,orch HENN s.p. (B956)
A solo,fl,2clar,2bsn,2horn,strings
sc BREITKOPF-L rental (B957)
solo,pno ASHDOWN (B958)
S solo,fl,2clar,2bsn,2horn,strings
sc BREITKOPF-L PB 774 s.p., ipa,
voc sc BREITKOPF-L EB 1332 $3.50
(B959)
S solo,fl,2clar,2bsn,2horn,strings
sc KALMUS $2.50 (B960)
[Eng/It] high solo,pno PRESSER $.75
(B961)
"Ah! Perfide! Parjure!" [Fr/It] S/T
solo,pno/inst DURAND s.p. (B962)

Air De Rocco (from Fidelio)
B solo,orch HENN s.p. (B963)

An Die Ferne Geliebte *Op.98, song
cycle
solo,pno HENLE s.p. (B964)
"To The Distant Beloved" [Ger/Eng]

BEETHOVEN, LUDWIG VAN (cont'd.)

low solo,pno SCHIRM.G 617 $2.00
(B965)
"To The Distant Beloved" [Ger/Eng]
high solo,pno SCHIRM.G 616 $2.00
(B966)
(Moore, Gerald) "To The Loved One
Far Away" low solo,pno ELKIN
27.2337.09 s.p. (B967)
(Moore, Gerald) "To The Loved One
Far Away" high solo,pno ELKIN
27.2338.07 s.p. (B968)

An Die Hoffnung *Op.94
(Mottl, F.) "Ob Ein Gott Sei?" S
solo,2fl,2ob,2clar,2bsn,2horn,
strings BREITKOPF-L solo pt s.p.,
ipa, rental (B969)

Apaisement
[Fr] Mez/Bar solo,pno/inst DURAND
s.p. (B970)

Arias With Orchestra *CCUL
solo,orch study sc KALMUS 1019
$1.50 (B971)

Bitten *Op.48,No.1
see Sechs Geistliche Lieder
"Priere" see Six Melodies
Religieuses

Busslied *Op.48,No.6, sac
see Sechs Geistliche Lieder
"Cantique De Penitence" see Six
Melodies Religieuses
S/T solo,pno (A maj) LIENAU HOS 33
s.p. (B972)
A/Bar solo,pno (F maj) LIENAU
HOS 34 s.p. (B973)

Cantique De Penitence *see Busslied

Come To Me *sac
high solo,org,harp/pno (E min)
SCHIRM.G $.85 (B974)
low solo,org,harp/pno (C sharp min)
SCHIRM.G $.85 (B975)

Complete Works *CCU
(Adler, Guido; Bagge, Selmar;
David, F.; Espagne, F.;
Mandycewski, E.; Nottebohm, G.;
Reinecke, C.; Richter, E.F.;
Rietz, J.) contains works for a
variety of instruments and vocal
combinations microfiche
UNIV.MUS.ED. $170.00 reprints of
Breitkopf & Hartel Editions;
contains series 1-25 (B976)

Creation's Hymn
low solo,pno (A flat maj) ALLANS
s.p. (B977)
med solo,pno (B flat maj) ALLANS
s.p. (B978)

Delices Des Pleurs
[Fr] solo,pno/inst DURAND s.p.
(B979)
solo,pno DURAND 126 s.p. (B980)

Der Wachtelschlag *Op.237
(Mottl, F.) "Horch Wie Schallts
Dorten So Lieblich Hervor!" S
solo,2fl,2ob,2clar,2bsn,2horn,
2trp,timp,strings BREITKOPF-L
rental (B981)

Die Ehre Gottes Aus Der Natur
*Op.48,No.4, sac
see Sechs Geistliche Lieder
"La Gloire De Dieu Dans La Nature"
see Six Melodies Religieuses
A/Bar solo,pno (A maj) LIENAU
HOS 31 s.p. (B982)
S/T solo,pno (C maj) LIENAU HOS 30
s.p. (B983)
"Guds Lov I Naturen" high solo,pno
LUNDQUIST s.p. (B984)
"Guds Lov I Naturen" low solo,pno
LUNDQUIST s.p. (B985)
"Guds Lov I Naturen" solo,pno
GEHRMANS 554 s.p. (B986)
(Mottl, Felix) S solo,2fl,2ob,
2clar,2bsn,4horn,2trp,3trom,tuba,
timp,strings BREITKOPF-W see from
Sechs Lieder (B987)

Die Ehre Gottes In Der Natur *sac
"I Himlar Sjungen Den Eviges Ara"
S/T solo,pno GEHRMANS s.p. (B988)

Die Liebe Des Nachsten *Op.48,No.2
see Sechs Geistliche Lieder
"L'amour Du Prochain" see Six
Melodies Religieuses

Die Mainacht
see Funf Lieder

Die Prufung Des Kussens
"Test Of Kissing, The" [Ger/Eng] B
solo,pno INTERNAT. $1.25 see from
Two Humorous Songs For Bass And

BEETHOVEN, LUDWIG VAN (cont'd.)

Orchestra (B989)

Douze Melodies *CC12L
solo,pno oct DURAND 801B s.p. (B990)

Dream, The
(Moore) S solo,pno (med) OXFORD
62.220 $1.00 (B991)

Elegischer Gesang *see Sanft Wie Du
Lebtest

Freudvoll Und Leidvoll
"Joyful And Woeful" see Six Songs

Funf Arien *see Mit Madeln Sich
Vertragen; O Welch' Ein Leben!
Ein Ganzes Meer; Primo Amore
Piacer Del Ciel; Prufung Des
Kussens; Soll Ein Schuh Nicht
Drucken! (B992)

Funf Lieder
(Gillmann, Kurt) med solo,2fl,2ob,
2clar,2bsn,4horn,timp,harp,
strings BREITKOPF-W s.p.
contains: Die Mainacht; Immer
Leiser Wird Mein Schlummer;
Nicht Mehr Zu Dir Gehen;
Standchen "Der Mond Steht"; Wir
Wandelten (B993)

Gesange Mit Orchester, Vol. II *CCU
(Hess) solo,inst BREITKOPF-W $15.00
Vol. 2 of supplement to the
complete works (B994)

Gott, Deine Gute *Op.48,No.1, sac
A/Bar solo,pno (C maj) LIENAU
HOS 27A s.p. (B995)
S/T solo,pno (E maj) LIENAU HOS 27
s.p. (B996)

Gott! Welch Dunkel Hier (from
Fidelio)
T solo,2fl,2ob,2clar,2bsn,4horn,
timp,strings BREITKOPF-L rental
(B997)

Gottes Macht Und Vorsehung *Op.48,
No.5
see Sechs Geistliche Lieder
"Puissance De Dieu" see Six
Melodies Religieuses

Guds Lov I Naturen *see Die Ehre
Gottes Aus Der Natur

Hat Man Nicht Auch Gold Beineben
(from Fidelio)
B solo,orch HENN s.p. (B998)
B solo,2fl,2ob,2clar,2bsn,2horn,
strings BREITKOPF-L rental (B999)

He Promised Me At Parting
see Two Irish Songs

Heil'ge Nacht *sac
Mez solo,pno (D maj) LIENAU HOS 161
s.p. (B1000)

Horch Wie Schallts Dorten So Lieblich
Hervor! *see Der Wachtelschlag

I Himlar Sjungen Den Eviges Ara *see
Die Ehre Gottes In Der Natur

I Love Thee
med solo,pno (F maj) ALLANS s.p.
(B1001)

Immer Leiser Wird Mein Schlummer
see Funf Lieder

In Questa Tomba Oscura
"In This Sepulchral Darkness" see
Six Songs
[Fr/It] solo,pno DURAND 95 s.p.
(B1002)
[It] solo,pno RICCORDI-ARG BA 10878
s.p. (B1003)
low solo,pno (A flat maj) ALLANS
s.p. (B1004)
"Loin De Ma Tombe Obscure" [Fr/It]
solo,pno/inst DURAND s.p. (B1005)

In This Sepulchral Darkness *see In
Questa Tomba Oscura

Jetzt Schatzchen, Jetzt Sind Wir
Allein (from Fidelio)
ST soli,fl,2ob,2clar,2bsn,2horn,
strings BREITKOPF-L rental
(B1006)

Joyful And Woeful *see Freudvoll Und
Leidvoll

Know'st Thou The Land *see Mignon

La Gloire De Dieu Dans La Natur *sac
Bar solo,orch HENN s.p. (B1007)

La Gloire De Dieu Dans La Nature
*see Die Ehre Gottes Aus Der
Natur

BEETHOVEN, LUDWIG VAN (cont'd.)

La Mort *see Vom Tode

La Tiranna
med solo,pno NOVELLO 17.0278.05
s.p. (B1008)

L'Abence
[Fr] Mez/Bar solo,pno/inst DURAND
s.p. (B1009)

L'amour Du Prochain *see Die Liebe
Des Nachsten

Le Depart Des Patres
2 soli,pno DURAND s.p. (B1010)

Le Reveil Des Fleurs
see LA MUSIQUE, DOUZIEME CAHIER
[Fr] solo,pno/inst DURAND s.p.
(B1011)

Lieder *CCU
high solo,pno SCHOTTS 5579 s.p.
(B1012)

Loin De Ma Tombe Obscure *see In
Questa Tomba Oscura

Mignon
"Know'st Thou The Land" see Six
Songs
[Fr] solo,pno/inst DURAND s.p.
(B1013)

Mir Ist So Wunderbar (from Fidelio)
SSTB soli,2fl,2clar,2bsn,2horn,
strings BREITKOPF-L rental
(B1014)

Mit Einem Gemalten Band
"With A Painted Ribbon" see Six
Songs

Mit Madeln Sich Vertragen
see Zwei Arien
B solo,2ob,2horn,strings sc
BREITKOPF-W PB 4775 s.p., ipa see
from Funf Arien (B1015)
"To Get Along With Girls" [Ger/Eng]
B solo,pno INTERNAT. $1.25 see
from Two Humorous Songs For Bass
And Orchestra (B1016)

Nei Giorni Tuoi Felici
[It] ST soli,2fl,2ob,bsn,2horn,
strings sc PETERS 4833 $10.00,
study sc PETERS $2.50, voc sc
PETERS 4832 $5.50, ipa (B1017)
(Hess) ST soli,orch EULENBURG sc
s.p., voc sc s.p., ipa (B1018)

Neue Liebe, Neues Leben
"New Love, New Life" see Six Songs

Neues Volksliederheft *CC23U,folk
(Schunemann, Georg) solo,pno,vln,
vcl sc BREITKOPF-W EB 6974 $6.25,
ipa (B1019)

New Love, New Life *see Neue Liebe,
Neues Leben

Nicht Mehr Zu Dir Gehen
see Funf Lieder

No, Non Turbati!
[It/Ger] S solo,strings/pno sc,voc
sc MUSIKWISS. BR29 s.p. (B1020)
(Hess, Willy) [It/Ger] S solo,pno
(diff) ALKOR 245 s.p. (B1021)

Nuit D'azur
solo,pno/inst LEDUC s.p. (B1022)

O War Ich Schon Mit Dir Vereint (from
Fidelio)
S solo,fl,2ob,2clar,2bsn,2horn,
strings BREITKOPF-L rental
(B1023)

O Welch' Ein Leben! Ein Ganzes Meer
see Beethoven, Ludwig van, Soll Ein
Schuh Nicht Drucken
T solo,2ob,2bsn,2horn,strings sc
BREITKOPF-W PB 4776 s.p., ipa see
from Funf Arien (B1024)

Ob Ein Gott Sei? *see An Die
Hoffnung

Ode To Joy (from Symphony No. 9)
solo,pno ASHLEY $1.00 (B1025)

Oh, Would I Were That Sweet Linnet
see Two Irish Songs

Priere *see Bitten

Primo Amore Piacer Del Ciel
see Zwei Arien Fur Sopran
S solo,fl,2ob,2bsn,2horn,strings
BREITKOPF-L rental (B1026)
S solo,fl,2ob,2bsn,2horn,strings sc
BREITKOPF-W PB 4778 s.p., ipa see
from Funf Arien (B1027)

Prufung Des Kussens
see Zwei Arien
B solo,2fl,ob,2horn,strings sc

BEETHOVEN, LUDWIG VAN (cont'd.)

BREITKOPF-W PB 4774 s.p., ipa see
from Funf Arien (B1028)

Puissance De Dieu *see Gottes Macht
Und Vorsehung

Samtliche Lieder *CCU
high solo,pno BREITKOPF-W EB 34
$3.75; low solo,pno BREITKOPF-W
EB 296 $3.75 (B1029)

Sanft Wie Du Lebtest *Op.118
"Elegischer Gesang" SATB soli,
strings sc KALMUS $3.00 (B1030)

Scene From "Vestas Feuer"
[Ger] STTB soli,2fl,2ob,2clar,2bsn,
2horn,strings voc sc MUSIKWISS.
BR27 s.p. (B1031)

Sechs Geistliche Lieder *sac
DOBLINGER 08 556 s.p.
contains: Bitten, Op.48,No.1;
Busslied, Op.48,No.6; Die Ehre
Gottes Aus Der Natur, Op.48,
No.4; Die Liebe Des Nachsten,
Op.48,No.2; Gottes Macht Und
Vorsehung, Op.48,No.5; Vom
Tode, Op.48,No.3 (B1032)

Sechs Lieder *see Die Ehre Gottes
Aus Der Natur, Op.48,No.4 (B1033)

Sei Canti Sacri *Op.48,No.1-6, sac,
CC6U
[It] solo,pno BONGIOVANI 138 s.p.
(B1034)

Serenade
[Fr] solo,pno/inst DURAND s.p.
(B1035)

Six Melodies Religieuses *sac
solo,pno DURAND s.p.
contains: Bitten, "Priere";
Busslied, "Cantique De
Penitence"; Die Ehre Gottes Aus
Der Natur, "La Gloire De Dieu
Dans La Nature"; Die Liebe Des
Nachsten, "L'amour Du
Prochain"; Gottes Macht Und
Vorsehung, "Puissance De Dieu";
Vom Tode, "La Mort" (B1036)

Six Songs
[Ger/Eng] high solo,pno SCHIRM.G
618 $1.50
contains: Adelaide; Freudvoll Und
Leidvoll, "Joyful And Woeful";
In Questa Sepulchral Oscura, "In
This Sepulchral Darkness";
Mignon, "Know'st Thou The
Land"; Mit Einem Gemalten Band,
"With A Painted Ribbon"; Neue
Liebe, Neues Leben, "New Love,
New Life" (B1037)

Sixty-Seven Songs *CC67U
[Ger] solo,pno cmplt ed PETERS 180
$8.50 (B1038)

Soll Ein Schuh Nicht Drucken
see Zwei Arien Fur Sopran
S solo,fl,2ob,2bsn,2horn,strings
voc sc BREITKOPF-L $3.00, ipr
contains also: O Welch' Ein
Leben! Ein Ganzes Meer (T solo,
fl,2ob,2bsn,2horn,strings)
(B1039)
S solo,fl,2ob,2bsn,2horn,strings sc
BREITKOPF-W PB 4777 s.p., ipa see
from Funf Arien (B1040)

Songs *CCU
solo,pno KALMUS 6081 $4.00 (B1041)

Songs And Arias With Piano, Vols. 1-2
*CCU
solo,pno study sc KALMUS 1020-1021
$1.50, ea. (B1042)

Songs With Piano, Violin And Cello
*Op.108, CCU
solo,pno,vln,vcl study sc KALMUS
1022 $1.50 (B1043)

Songs With Piano, Violin And Cello,
Vols. 2-4 *CCU
solo,pno,vln,vcl study sc KALMUS
1023-1025 $1.50, ea. (B1044)

Standchen "Der Mond Steht"
see Funf Lieder

Test Of Kissing, The *see Die
Prufung Des Kussens

Thirty Selected Songs *CC30U
[Ger] high solo,pno PETERS 731
$6.25; med solo/low solo,pno
PETERS 732 $4.75 (B1045)

To Get Along With Girls *see Mit
Madeln Sich Vertragen

BEETHOVEN, LUDWIG VAN (cont'd.)

To The Distant Beloved *see An Die
    Ferne Geliebte

To The Loved One Far Away *see An
    Die Ferne Geliebte

Tremate, Empi, Tremate *Op.116
    STB soli,2fl,2clar,2bsn,2horn,2trp,
    timp,strings BREITKOPF-L rental
                                (B1046)
    STB soli,2fl,2clar,2bsn,2horn,2trp,
    timp,strings BREITKOPF-W s.p.
                                (B1047)

Trente Melodie Scelte *CC30U
    [It/Ger] solo,pno RICORDI-ENG
    ER 2280 s.p.   (B1048)

Twelve Scottish Songs *Op.227,No.1-
    12, CC12U
    [Eng/Ger] solo/soli,pno,vln cmplt
    ed PETERS 2524 $7.50   (B1049)

Two Humorous Songs For Bass And
    Orchestra *see Die Prufung Des
    Kussens, "Test Of Kissing, The";
    Mit Madeln Sich Vertragen, "To
    Get Along With Girls"   (B1050)

Two Irish Songs
    (Moore) S solo,pno (med) OXFORD
    63.057 $1.45
    contains: He Promised Me At
        Parting; Oh, Would I Were That
        Sweet Linnet   (B1051)

Vakteln
    Mez/Bar solo,pno GEHRMANS s.p. see
        from SANGEN I   (B1052)

Various Songs And Arias *CCU
    solo,pno/orch study sc KALMUS 1027
    $1.50   (B1053)

Vom Tode *Op.48,No.3
    see Sechs Geistliche Lieder
    "La Mort" see Six Melodies
    Religieuses

Wir Wandelten
    see Funf Lieder

With A Painted Ribbon *see Mit Einem
    Gemalten Band

Zwanzig Lieder *sac/sec,CC20L
    [Ger/Span] solo,pno RICORDI-ARG
    BA 9310 s.p.   (B1054)

Zwei Arien
    Bar/B solo,fl,2ob,2horn,strings voc
    sc BREITKOPF-L EB 6595 $4.25, ipr
    contains: Mit Madeln Sich
        Vertragen; Prufung Des Kussens
                                (B1055)

Zwei Arien Fur Sopran
    solo,pno BREITKOPF-W EB 6597 $4.25
    contains: Primo Amore Piacer Del
        Ciel; Soll Ein Schuh Nicht
        Drucken   (B1056)

BEETLEHEM, BEETLEHEM see Kahri, Jalmari

BEFORE AND AFTER SUMMER see Finzi,
    Gerald

BEFORE HE CALLS AGAIN see Jensen,
    Gordon

BEFORE HIM see Nystedt, Knut

BEFORE I FOUND THE LORD see Wolfe,
    Lanny

BEFORE SLEEPING see Thomson, Virgil

BEFORE THE CRUCIFIX see LaForge, Frank

BEFORE THE IMAGE see Rachmaninoff,
    Sergey Vassilievitch

BEFORE THE PALING OF THE STARS see
    Boda, John

BEFORE THE PALING OF THE STARS see
    Gounod, Charles Francois

BEFORE THE PALING OF THE STARS see
    Kramer, A. Walter

BEFORE THE WORLD WAS see Kendrick,
    Virginia

BEFORE THINE ALTAR see Deer

BEFORE YOU CAME see Lane-Wilson, H.

BEFREIT see Strauss, Richard

BEFREITE SEHNSUCHT see Schoeck, Othmar

BEGEBENHEIT see Blarr, Oskar Gottlieb

BEGEGNUNG see Orland, Henry

BEGEGNUNG see Strauss, Richard

BEGGAR'S SONG see Webber, Lloyd

BEGINNING OF THE END, THE see Harrison,
    Dorothy

BEGLI OCCHI LUCENTI see Falconieri,
    Andrea

BEGLUCKT, WEM RUHIG LIEBEND see
    Carriere, Paul

BEGONE, SATAN see Bender, Jan

BEGRABE DEINE TOTEN see Vletter, C.

BEHAGEN see Stenhammar, Wilhelm

BEHAR, GY.
    Two Songs *CC2U
    solo,pno BUDAPEST 7371 s.p. (B1057)

BEHOLD, HE STANDS AND KNOCKS see
    Lister, Mosie

BEHOLD, HOW FAIR AND PLEASANT see
    Vogel, Howard W.

BEHOLD HOW GOOD AND HOW PLEASANT see
    Matesky, T.

BEHOLD I SEND AN ANGEL see Head,
    Michael (Dewar)

BEHOLD I STAND AT THE DOOR see Bryant,
    Verna Mae

BEHOLD THE LAMB OF GOD see Bouman, Paul

BEHOLD THE MAN see Wilkin, Marijohn

BEHOLD THE SEA see Sharpe, Evelyn

BEHOLD, THE TABERNACLE OF GOD see
    Hoffmeister, Leon Abbott

BEHOLD, THUS IS THE MAN BLESSED see
    Ferris, William

BEHOLD THY KING see Betts, Lorne M.

BEHOLD! WHAT MANNER OF LOVE see Hatch

BEHOLD, WHAT MANNER OF LOVE see
    Humphreys, Don

BEHOLDING THEE, LORD JESUS see
    Christiansen, A.

BEHREND, A.H.
    Gift
    solo,pno (E flat maj) BOOSEY $1.50
                                (B1058)
BEHREND, SIEGFRIED (1933-   )
    Bon Jour, Ma Belle
    high solo,pno PRESSER $.95 (B1059)

    Impressionen Einer Spanischen Reise
        *CC3U
    solo,gtr SIKORSKI 373F s.p. (B1060)

    Jiddische Hochzeit *CC2U,Marriage,
        Jew
    [Ger] high solo,gtr WILHELM. s.p.
                                (B1061)
    Losst Mich Leben *song cycle
    solo,gtr SIKORSKI 775 s.p. (B1062)

    Solo Per Voce Fur Claudia
    solo,pno ZIMMER. 1905 s.p. (B1063)

    Songs By Miguel De Cervantes And
        Others For Guitar And Voice *CCU
    (Behrend) solo,gtr SCHAUR EE 2701
    s.p.   (B1064)

    Suite On Polish Folk Melodies *CCU
    [Pol] med solo,gtr BOTE $2.75
                                (B1065)
    Weihnachtsgeschichte *Xmas
    solo,perc,gtr ZIMMER. 1897 s.p.
                                (B1066)
BEI MANNERN, WELCHE LIEBE FUHLEN see
    Mozart, Wolfgang Amadeus

BEI MIR BIST DU SHAIN *Jew
    solo,pno KAMMEN 436 $1.00   (B1067)

BEI RAUSCHENDEM FESTE see Tchaikovsky,
    Piotr Ilyitch

BEIAARD see Diepenbrock, Alphons

BEIM KUCKUCKSRUF see Kilpinen, Yrio,
    Kakoa Kuullessa

BEIMEL, JACOB
    L'dor Vodor *sac
    [Heb/Eng] med solo/low solo,pno
    TRANSCON. WJ 426 $.60   (B1068)

BEING see Blank, Allan

BEING BEAUTEOUS see Henze, Hans Werner

BEIRAMAR see Nobre, Marlos

BEISPIEL see Ferroud, Pierre-Octave

BEKENNEN WILL ICH SEINEN NAMEN see
    Bach, Johann Sebastian

BEKKU, S.
    Collection Of Songs, A *CCU
    solo,pno ONGAKU s.p.   (B1069)

BEKRANSA MIG! see Lundkvist, Per

BEL AUBEPIN see Biancheri, A.

BEL AUBEPIN see Leguerney, Jacques

BEL AUBEPIN see Rivier, Jean

BEL AUTOMNE see Lefebvre, Channing

BEL CANTO ALBUM *sec,CC20U,cant,17-
    18th cent
    (Landshoff) [It] SS/TT/SA soli,pno
    PETERS 3824 $5.50   (B1070)

BEL CANTO ALBUM *CC17U,17th cent
    (Landshoff) [It] S/Mez/A/Bar solo,
    vln,vcl,pno PETERS 3481 $6.00
    contains works by: Aldovrandini,
    G.B.; Bononcini, G.M.; Caldara;
    Cesarini; Cesti; Handel; Provenzale
    and others   (B1071)

BEL CANTO ALBUM, VOL. I *CC29U,16-17th
    cent
    (Landshoff) [It] solo/soli,pno PETERS
    3348A $5.50 contains works by:
    Abbattini; Caccini; Carissimi;
    Cesti; Legrenzi; Lonati and others
                                (B1072)
BEL CANTO ALBUM, VOL. II *CC21U,17-
    18th cent
    (Landshoff) [It] solo/soli,pno PETERS
    3348C $5.50 contains works by:
    Ariosti; Bach, J.C.; Caldara;
    Cesarini; Cimarosa; Gluck; Graun;
    Hasse and others   (B1073)

BEL RAGGIO LUSINGHIER see Rossini,
    Gioacchino

BELAUD, MON PETIT CHAT GRIS see
    Francaix, Jean

BELCANTO *CC10L
    (Tomelleri, Luciano) [It] solo,pno
    cmplt ed RICORDI-ENG 129029 s.p.
    contains works by: Caccini;
    Carissimi; Cimarosa; Monteverdi;
    Paisello; Pergolesi; Peri; Rossini;
    Vivaldi   (B1074)

BELCHER, SUPPLY (1751-1836)
    While Shepherds Watched Their Flocks
        *sac,Xmas
    (Myers, Gordon) med solo,pno
    ABINGDON APM-372 $.75   (B1075)

BELFER, BEN W.
    Eyn Keloheynu *sac
    [Heb/Eng] med solo,pno TRANSCON.
    TCL 766 $.25   (B1076)

BELGODERE, V.
    Je Chante Et M'enchante *CC50U
    1-2 soli,pno OUVRIERES s.p. (B1077)

BELIEVE ME IF ALL THOSE ENDEARING YOUNG
        CHARMS *Ir
    solo,pno CRAMER   (B1078)

BELIEVE ME, IF ALL THOSE ENDEARING
    YOUNG CHARMS see Quilter, Roger

BELIEVE ME, IF ALL THOSE ENDEARING
    YOUNG CHARMS see Ronald, Sir Landon

BELIEVING see Agay, Denes

BELIEVING see Matthews

BELINA
    see Internationale Volklieder, Nol. 3

BELL, H.
    Love's Philosophy
    solo,pno BERANDOL BER 1298 $1.50
                                (B1079)
BELL, MARGARET
    Song Of The Submarines
    solo,pno CRAMER   (B1080)

    Up The Guns
    solo,pno CRAMER   (B1081)

BELL DOTH TOLL, THE see Thomson, Virgil

BELL SONG see Delibes, Leo, Ou Va La
    Jeune Indoue

BELLA E LA DONNA MIA see Caltabiano, S.

BELLA FIGLIA DELL'AMORE see Verdi,
Giuseppe

BELLA, JAN LEVOSLAV (1843-1936)
Piesne *CCU
solo,pno SLOV.HUD.FOND s.p. (B1082)

BELLA MIA FIAMMA, ADDIO see Mozart,
Wolfgang Amadeus

BELLA MIA FIAMMA - RESTA, O CARA see
Mozart, Wolfgang Amadeus

BELLA PORTA DI RUBINI see Falconieri,
Andrea

BELLA PORTA DI RUBINI see Respighi,
Ottorino

BELLA SICCOME UN ANGELO see Donizetti,
Gaetano

BELLATRIX-ALLELUIA see Sakac, Branimir

BELLE DAME SANS MERCI see Stanford,
Charles Villiers

BELLE ETOILE see Kucken, Friedrich
Wilhelm

BELLE, JE M'EN VAIS EN ALLEMAGNE see
Emmanuel, Maurice

BELLE JEUNESSE see Mendelssohn-
Bartholdy, Felix

BELLE NUIT, O NUIT D'AMOUR see
Offenbach, Jacques

BELLECOUR, MAURICE
Ma Grise Chaumiere
[Fr] med solo,pno HEUGEL 10931
(B1083)

BELLENGHI, G.
Profumi Orientali
"Voix De La Brise" solo,orch sc
DURAND s.p., ipa (B1084)
"Voix De La Brise" [Fr] solo,acap
oct DURAND s.p. (B1085)

Voix De La Brise *see Profumi
Orientali

BELLES DEESSES see Besard, Jean-
Baptiste

BELLINI, VINCENZO (1801-1835)
A Te, O Cara (from I Puritani)
T solo,pno RICORDI-ENG 119964 s.p.
(B1086)
Ah, Non Credea Mirarti! (from La
Sonnambula)
[It] S solo,pno RICORDI-ARG BA 8349
s.p. (B1087)
S solo,pno RICORDI-ENG 54327 s.p.
(B1088)
Ah, Per Sempre Io Ti Perdei (from I
Puritani)
Bar solo,pno RICORDI-ENG 126141
s.p. (B1089)
Ah, Perche Non Posso Odiarti (from La
Sonnambula)
T solo,pno RICORDI-ENG 54408 s.p.
(B1090)
Air D'Amina (from La Sonnambula)
solo,orch HENN s.p. (B1091)
Arias From Operas *CCU
[Russ] S solo,pno MEZ KNIGA 84 s.p.
(B1092)
Casta Diva (from Norma)
[It] S solo,pno RICORDI-ARG BA 8348
s.p. (B1093)
S solo,pno RICORDI-ENG 54323 s.p.
(B1094)
high solo,pno (F maj) ALLANS s.p.
(B1095)
Cinta Di Fiori (from I Puritani)
B solo,pno RICORDI-ENG 126917 s.p.
(B1096)
Come Per Me Sereno (from La
Sonnambula)
S solo,pno RICORDI-ENG 54326 s.p.
(B1097)
Deh! Con Te, Con Te Li Prendi (from
Norma)
SS soli,pno RICORDI-ENG 110271 s.p.
(B1098)
"Take Them With Thee" [It/Eng] SS
soli,pno SCHIRM.G $1.25 (B1099)
Dolente Immagine Di Fille Mia
(Segovia) [It] solo,gtr SCHOTTS
GA 152 s.p. (B1100)
Ite Sul Colle, O Druidi (from Norma)
B solo,pno RICORDI-ENG 110081 s.p.
(B1101)
La Ricordanza
(Spada, P.) solo,pno BERBEN 1968
s.p. (B1102)

BELLINI, VINCENZO (cont'd.)
Meco All'altar Di Venere (from Norma)
T solo,pno RICORDI-ENG 54406 s.p.
(B1103)
Oh! Quante Volte (from I Capuleti Ed
I Montecchi)
S solo,pno RICORDI-ENG 109813 s.p.
(B1104)
Prendi, L'anel Ti Dono (from La
Sonnambula)
ST soli,pno RICORDI-ENG 110164 s.p.
(B1105)
Qui La Voce Sua Soave (from I
Puritani)
S solo,pno RICORDI-ENG 54324 s.p.
(B1106)
Quindici Composizioni Da Camera
*CC15L
solo,pno cmplt ed RICORDI-ENG
123282 s.p. (B1107)
Son Vergin Vezzosa (from I Puritani)
S solo,pno RICORDI-ENG 96256 s.p.
(B1108)
Take Them With Thee *see Deh! Con
Te, Con Te Li Prendi
Vi Ravviso, O Luoghi Ameni (from La
Sonnambula)
B solo,pno RICORDI-ENG 54462 s.p.
(B1109)

BELLOC, HILAIRE
Tarantella
solo,pno CRAMER $.80 (B1110)

BELLONI, FR.
Krontjong Liedjes *CCU
solo,pno ALSBACH s.p. (B1111)

BELLS see Gideon, Miriam

BELLS OF BETHLEHEM, THE see Brusey

BELLS OF BRAY see Allon, Oscar

BELLS OF CHRISTMAS, THE see Shaw,
Martin

BELLS OF CHRISTMAS, THE see Thomas, Ed

BELLS OF CORDOBA see Berkeley, Lennox

BELLS OF HAZELMERE, THE see Baden, H.E.

BELLS OF LOVE, THE see Day, Maude
Craske

BELLS OF RHYMNEY AND OTHER SONGS AND
STORIES FROM THE SINGING OF PETE
SEEGER *CC80U,folk
solo,pno OAK 000003 $3.95 (B1112)

BELLS OF SORROW, THE see Kilpinen,
Yrio, Murheen Kellot

BELLS OF THE SEA see Solman

BELLS OF TIME see Weaver, Powell

BELLS THAT ARE PEALING see Gounod,
Charles Francois

BELOVED, AWAKE see Hemery, Valentine

BELOVED, LET US FLY see Rachmaninoff,
Sergey Vassilievitch

BELOVED LET US LOVE see Proulx, Richard

BELOVED MELODY see Brandl

BELOVED SAVIOUR, WILT THOU ANSWER? see
Wright, Denis

BELOVED YOU ARE MY WORLD
high solo,pno (G maj) WILLIS $.60
(B1113)
low solo,pno (E flat maj) WILLIS $.60
(B1114)

BELSAZAR see Bedinger, Hugo

BELSAZER see Bosmans, Henriette

BELZ, MEIN SHTETELE BELZ *Jew
solo,pno KAMMEN 419 $1.00 (B1115)

BEM-VINDA see Prado, Almeida

BEMBERG, HERMAN (1859-1931)
Chanson Creole
S/T solo,pno/inst DURAND s.p.
(B1116)
Chanson Tendre
solo,pno (available in 2 keys)
ENOCH s.p. (B1117)
Il Neige
"'Tis Snowing" low solo,pno (E flat
maj) ASHDOWN $1.50 (B1118)
"'Tis Snowing" med solo,pno (F maj)
ASHDOWN $1.50 (B1119)
"'Tis Snowing" high solo,pno (G
maj) ASHDOWN $1.50 (B1120)

BEMBERG, HERMAN (cont'd.)
Refrain D'amour
solo,pno ENOCH s.p. (B1121)
'Tis Snowing *see Il Neige
Twenty Songs *CC20L
cmplt ed SALABERT-US T/S solo,pno
$14.75; Bar/Mez solo,pno $14.75
(B1122)

BEN ARRIVATA see Oddone, E.

BEN DOVERRIENO see Flagello, Nicholas

BEN FU see Flagello, Nicholas

BEN VENGA AMORE! see Cimara, Pietro

BENBOW, EDWIN
In Youth Is Pleasure
solo,pno CRAMER (B1123)
Sea Song, A
solo,pno CRAMER $1.15 (B1124)

BENCHE MI SIA see Handel, George
Frideric

BEN-COHEN, Y.
Impressions Of Israel, Vol. I *CCU
solo,pno ISRAELI 225 $3.50 (B1125)
Impressions Of Israel, Vol. II *CCU
solo,pno ISRAELI 226 $3.50 (B1126)

BENDEMEER'S STREAM *Ir
solo,pno ALLANS s.p. (B1127)

BENDEMEER'S STREAM see Scott-Gatty,
Alfred

BENDER, JAN (1909-)
And There Will Be Signs *sac
med solo,pno oct CONCORDIA 98-2082
$.30 (B1128)
Begone, Satan *sac
med solo,pno oct CONCORDIA 98-1848
$.25 (B1129)
Come, O Blessed Of My Father *sac
med solo,pno oct CONCORDIA 98-1834
$.25 (B1130)
Do Not Be Amazed *sac
SA/TB soli,pno oct CONCORDIA
98-1966 $.30 (B1131)
Fear Not, For Behold, I Bring Good
Tidings Of Great Joy *sac
SA soli,pno oct CONCORDIA 98-1962
$.50 (B1132)
Go Into All The World *sac
SA/TB soli,pno oct CONCORDIA
98-1990 $.40 (B1133)
God So Loved The World *sac
SS soli,pno oct CONCORDIA 98-1641
$.25 (B1134)
Hosanna To The Son Of David *sac
SA/TB soli,pno oct CONCORDIA
98-1964 $.25 (B1135)
I Am The Good Shepherd *sac
SA/TB soli,pno oct CONCORDIA
98-1992 $.30 (B1136)
If A Man Loves Me *sac
med solo,pno oct CONCORDIA 98-1697
$.20 (B1137)
If You Ask Anything Of The Father
*sac
SA/TB soli,pno oct CONCORDIA
98-1991 $.40 (B1138)
It Is Not Fair *sac
SA soli,pno oct CONCORDIA 98-1847
$.25 (B1139)
Jesus, Son Of David, Have Mercy On Me
*sac
SA/TB soli,pno oct CONCORDIA
98-1965 $.30 (B1140)
Lord, Lord, Open To Us *sac
med solo,pno oct CONCORDIA 98-1833
$.25 (B1141)
Psalm 128 *see Wedding Song
Sir, Come Down Before My Child Dies
*sac
SA/TB soli,pno oct CONCORDIA
98-1835 $.25 (B1142)
Son, Why Have You Treated Us So?
*sac
SA soli,pno oct CONCORDIA 98-1963
$.25 (B1143)

BENDER, JAN (cont'd.)

Two Solos For Baptism *CC2U,Baptism
  solo,pno CHANTRY VOS 738 $1.00
                                        (B1144)
Wedding Song (Psalm 128) sac,Marriage
  med-high solo,pno CONCORDIA 97-4887
  $1.00   (B1145)

BENDICHO SU NOMBRE see Weiner, Lazar

BENDIX, VICTOR EMMANUEL (1851-1926)
Le Chant De La Nouvelle Annee
  solo,pno ENOCH s.p. see also CHANTS
    DU NORD   (B1146)

BENDL, KAREL (1838-1897)
Cikanske Melodie *CCU
  solo,pno SUPRAPHON s.p.   (B1147)

Notturno
  [Czech/Ger] med solo,pno SUPRAPHON
    s.p.   (B1148)

BENEATH A SOUTHERN SKY see Rich, Gladys

BENEATH A WEEPING WILLOW'S SHADE see
  Bales, Richard

BENEATH THY LEAFY SHADE see Handel,
  George Frideric, Care Selve

BENEDICAM DOMINUM see Schutz, Heinrich

BENEDICAMUS DOMINO *CC3U
  (Schmidt; Garre) soli,pno SCHOTTS
    ANT 14 s.p., ipa   (B1149)

BENEDICT, SIR JULIUS (1804-1885)
Carnival Of Venice, The
  solo,pno (E flat maj) ASHDOWN
                                        (B1150)
  high solo,pno (A flat maj) ALLANS
    s.p.   (B1151)
  (Liebling) [It/Eng] high solo,pno
    (A flat maj) SCHIRM.G $.60   (B1152)
Gipsy And The Bird, The
  solo,orch (G maj) ASHDOWN s.p., ipr
                                        (B1153)
  high solo,pno (G maj) ALLANS s.p.
                                        (B1154)
Wren, The
  high solo,pno (F maj) ALLANS s.p.
                                        (B1155)

BENEDICTO NUPTIALIS see Felciano,
  Richard

BENEDICTUS see Caamano, Roberto

BENEDICTUS see Faure, Gabriel-Urbain

BENEDICTUS see Policki, (?)

BENES, JURAJ
Monology
  A solo,4strings SLOV.HUD.FOND s.p.
                                        (B1156)

BENET, HAIM
Ranenu Ha'chassidim
  solo,pno OR-TAV $1.50   (B1157)

BENEVOLI, ORAZIO (1605-1672)
Ego Autem Pro Te, Domine *sac
  (Ewerhart, Rudolf) [Lat] S/T solo,
    cont BIELER CS 22 s.p.   (B1158)

BENEY, THERESA
Rippling River
  ST soli,pno CRAMER   (B1159)

BENGTSSON
Fyra Julsanger *CC4U,Xmas
  solo,pno LUNDQUIST s.p.   (B1160)

BENGUEREL, XAVIER (1931-   )
Ballade Von Der Singenden Frau In Der
  Nacht
  SSA soli,4vln,vla,vcl,bvl (diff) sc
    BAREN. 4436 $16.75, ipr   (B1161)

Paraules De Cada Dia
  "Worte Des Alltags" solo,3fl,2clar,
    perc,harp,pno,cel,vibra MODERN
    rental   (B1162)

Worte Des Alltags *see Paraules De
  Cada Dia

BENGZON
Fjalar *see Viola

Kung Erik
  Bar/A solo,pno LUNDQUIST s.p.
                                        (B1163)
  T/S solo,pno LUNDQUIST s.p.   (B1164)

Varjubel
  see NY SAMLING SANGDUETTER, HEFT 2

Viola
  "Fjalar" Bar/Mez solo,pno LUNDQUIST
    s.p.   (B1165)
  "Fjalar" T/S solo,pno LUNDQUIST
    s.p.   (B1166)

BEN-HAIM, PAUL (1897-   )
Arabic Song
  med solo,pno (without words)
    ISRAELI 212 $1.40   (B1167)

Bat-Yonim
  low solo,pno ISRAELI 231 $2.10
                                        (B1168)

Hatikva
  solo,pno ISRAELI 310 $1.40   (B1169)

Kochav Nafal *song cycle
  "Star Fell Down, A" med solo,pno
    ISRAELI 227 $3.50   (B1170)

Melodies From The East *CC5U,Heb
  low solo,pno ISRAELI 211 $5.60
                                        (B1171)

Myrtle Blossoms From Eden
  S/Mez/Bar solo,pno ISRAELI 621
    $5.60   (B1172)

Psalm 23 *sac
  low solo,pno ISRAELI 214 $2.80
                                        (B1173)

Star Fell Down, A *see Kochav Nafal

Three Songs Without Words *CC3U
  high solo,pno ISRAELI 125 $4.50
                                        (B1174)

BENHAMOU, MAURICE (1936-   )
Mizmor-Chir *sac,CCU,Bibl
  S solo,fl,horn,trp,trom,vibra,
    marimba,perc,strings sc JOBERT
    s.p.   (B1175)

BENI, J.
Betrayed
  solo,pno CONGRESS $.60   (B1176)

That's What Love Will Do To You
  (composed with Warren, E.)
  solo,pno CONGRESS $.60   (B1177)

BENJAMIN, ARTHUR (1893-1960)
Jamaican Rumba
  solo,pno (F maj) BOOSEY $1.50
                                        (B1178)

Linstead Market
  solo,pno (F maj) BOOSEY $1.50
                                        (B1179)

Man And Woman
  high solo,pno ELKIN 27.1438.08 s.p.
                                        (B1180)
  low solo,pno ELKIN 27.1437.10 s.p.
                                        (B1181)

Song Of The Banana Carriers
  solo,pno BOOSEY $1.50   (B1182)

Wind's Work
  low solo,pno (B flat maj) BOOSEY
    $1.50   (B1183)
  high solo,pno (C maj) BOOSEY $1.50
                                        (B1184)

BENN-EPITAPH see Linke, Norbert

BENNARD, GEORGE (1873-1958)
Old Rugged Cross, The *sac
  solo,pno WORD S-175   (B1185)
  solo,pno ALLANS s.p.   (B1186)

BENNET, T.C.S.
Leanin'
  low solo,pno (F maj) BOOSEY $1.50
                                        (B1187)
  high solo,pno (G maj) BOOSEY $1.50
                                        (B1188)

BENNETT, RICHARD RODNEY (1936-   )
Die Welt Der Insekten *see Insect
  World, The

Flower Carol
  solo,inst quarto,sc UNIVER. 14657
    $1.75   (B1189)

Insect World, The *song cycle
  "Die Welt Der Singenden Frau In Der" [Eng/Ger]
  solo,pno UNIVER. 14167 $2.75   (B1190)

Tom O'Bedlam's Song
  T solo,vcl BELWIN $3.00   (B1191)

What Sweeter Music
  solo,inst quarto,sc UNIVER. 14658
    $1.75   (B1192)

BENNETT, SIR WILLIAM STERNDALE
  (1816-1875)
Baa-Baa Black Sheep
  solo,pno CRAMER   (B1193)

Brace Of Ballads
  solo,pno CRAMER   (B1194)

Carol Singers
  low solo,pno (F maj) CRAMER (B1195)
  high solo,pno (G maj) CRAMER
                                        (B1196)

I Love Them All
  solo,pno CRAMER   (B1197)

I Need Love
  solo,pno CRAMER   (B1198)

BENNETT, SIR WILLIAM STERNDALE
  (cont'd.)

I Take Sartin Notice O' That
  solo,pno CRAMER   (B1199)

Jus' A Smile I'm Missin'
  solo,pno CRAMER   (B1200)

May Dew
  solo,pno CRAMER   (B1201)

Me And You
  solo,pno CRAMER   (B1202)

Pheobe
  solo,pno CRAMER   (B1203)

Silent Courtship
  solo,pno CRAMER   (B1204)

Sunny Land
  low solo,pno (G maj) CRAMER (B1205)
  high solo,pno (A flat maj) CRAMER
                                        (B1206)

Will She Be Waiting Up?
  solo,pno CRAMER   (B1207)

BENNETT, W.E.
May-Dew
  solo,pno ASHDOWN   (B1208)

BENSON, LIONEL S.
He That Loves A Rosy Cheek
  solo,pno CRAMER $.90   (B1209)

BENSON, WARREN
Shadow Wood
  high solo,winds MCA $3.50, ipr
                                        (B1210)

BENTON, DANIEL
Love Song
  female solo,fl,harp SEESAW   (B1211)

Two Shakespeare Songs *CC2U
  S solo,vln,fl,bass clar SEESAW
                                        (B1212)

BENVENUTI, ARRIGO (1925-   )
Cantus Gemellus
  solo,fl BRUZZI $3.50   (B1213)

Fiore D'Arancio
  [It] S solo,pno BRUZZI $5.00
                                        (B1214)

BENVENUTI, GIACOMO (1885-1943)
Cinque Liriche *see Dolce O Amici;
  La Sera; Mi Domandano; Mio Dio;
  Non Partire, Amor Mio..   (B1215)

Dolce O Amici
  solo,pno BONGIOVANI 1122 s.p. see
    from Cinque Liriche   (B1216)

La Sera
  solo,pno BONGIOVANI 1120 s.p. see
    from Cinque Liriche   (B1217)

Mi Domandano
  solo,pno BONGIOVANI 1121 s.p. see
    from Cinque Liriche   (B1218)

Mio Dio
  solo,pno BONGIOVANI 1123 s.p. see
    from Cinque Liriche   (B1219)

Non Partire, Amor Mio..
  solo,pno BONGIOVANI 1126 s.p. see
    from Cinque Liriche   (B1220)

B'ER BA-SADEH
  (Helfman, Max) "Well, The" [Heb] med
    solo,pno TRANSCON. IS 506 $.50
                                        (B1221)

BERANGER, PIERRE-JEAN DE
Cinquante Chansons Choises *CC50U
  (Levade, Ch.) solo,pno HEUGEL 249
    s.p.   (B1222)

BERBERIAN, KATHY (1925-   )
Stripsody
  solo PETERS 66164 $3.50   (B1223)

BERCEMENT see Mignan, Edouard-Charles-
  Octave

BERCEUSE see Alfven, Hugo

BERCEUSE see Biancheri, A.

BERCEUSE see Bizet, Georges

BERCEUSE see Brahms, Johannes,
  Wiegenlied

BERCEUSE see Bunge, Sas

BERCEUSE see Caplet, Andre

BERCEUSE see Chaminade, Cecile

BERCEUSE see Christian-Jollet

BERCEUSE see Clergue, J.

BERCEUSE see De Lara, Isadore

BERCEUSE see Denza, Luigi

BERCEUSE see Diepenbrock, Alphons

BERCEUSE see Ferrari, Gustave

BERCEUSE see Georges, Alexandre

BERCEUSE see Godard, Benjamin Louis
Paul, Caches Dans Cet Asile

BERCEUSE see Gretchaninov, Alexander
Tikhonovitch

BERCEUSE see Guiraud, Ernest

BERCEUSE see Jarnefelt, Armas

BERCEUSE see Lacome, Paul

BERCEUSE see Legay, Marcel

BERCEUSE see Lemaire, F.

BERCEUSE see Lilien, Ignace

BERCEUSE see Magnani, Fausto

BERCEUSE see Mariotte, Antoine

BERCEUSE see Mozart, Wolfgang Amadeus,
Wiegenlied

BERCEUSE see Mussorgsky, Modest

BERCEUSE see Pelliot, A.

BERCEUSE see Piccinelli, Nino

BERCEUSE see Piccioli, G.

BERCEUSE see Poulenc, Francis

BERCEUSE see Ravize, A.

BERCEUSE see Rhene-Baton

BERCEUSE see Rimsky-Korsakov, Nikolai

BERCEUSE see Samuel-Holeman, Eugene

BERCEUSE see Schumann, Robert
(Alexander)

BERCEUSE see Segond, Pierre

BERCEUSE see Tremisot, Ed.

BERCEUSE see Vellere, Lucie

BERCEUSE see Weber

BERCEUSE [2] see Gretchaninov,
Alexander Tikhonovitch

BERCEUSE CREOLE see Sauguet, Henri

BERCEUSE D'AMANTS see Raynal, F.

BERCEUSE D'AMORIQUE see Brucken Fock,
G.H.G. van

BERCEUSE DE GALLANE see Ibert, Jacques

BERCEUSE DE JOCELYN see Godard,
Benjamin Louis Paul, Cache Dans Cet
Asile

BERCEUSE DE LA SIRENE see Honegger,
Arthur

BERCEUSE DE LA VIE see Lane, Gerald M.

BERCEUSE DE L'OUBLI see Rabey, Rene

BERCEUSE DE MAITRE CANARD see Beekhuis,
Hanna

BERCEUSE DE REVE see Delmet, Paul

BERCEUSE DELLA PRINCIPESSA see Rimsky-
Korsakov, Nikolai

BERCEUSE D'HAITI see Beekhuis, Hanna

BERCEUSE DU GRILLON see Delannoy,
Marcel

BERCEUSE POUR LE PETIT OURS see
Strimer, Joseph

BERCEUSE PRESQUE NEGRE see Beekhuis,
Hanna

BERCEUSE PRESQUE NEGRE see Leeuw, Ton
de

BERCEUSE ROYALE see Fortner, Wolfgang

BERCEUSE TRISTE see Cuvillier, Charles

BERCEUSES A TENIR EVEILLE see Lesur,
Daniel

BERCEUSES DU CHAT see Stravinsky, Igor

BERCUESE UIT PHILOMELA see Andriessen,
Hendrik

BEREAVED MAID, THE see Walker, George

BEREAVED MOTHER, THE see Malipiero,
Gian Francesco, La Madre Folle

BEREITE DICH, ZION, MIT ZARTLICHEN
TRIEBEN see Bach, Johann Sebastian

BERELE BOSJOK *Jew
solo,pno KAMMEN 23 $1.00   (B1224)

BERELE GORILLE *Jew
solo,pno KAMMEN 461 $1.00   (B1225)

BERELE SHPIEL MIR DUS SHERELE *Jew
solo,pno KAMMEN 452 $1.00   (B1226)

BERENICE, ACH, WO BIST DU? see Gluck,
Christoph Willibald Ritter von,
Berenice, Ove Sei?

BERENICE, OVE SEI? see Gluck, Christoph
Willibald Ritter von

BERENS, HERMANN (1826-1880)
Psalm 137 *see Vid Alvarna I Babylon

Vid Alvarna I Babylon (Psalm 137) sac
Mez/Bar solo,pno GEHRMANS s.p.
(B1227)

BERENS, J.R. (1862-1928)
En Liten Visa
solo,pno GEHRMANS s.p.   (B1228)

Sveriges Skonaste Folkvisor *CCU
[Ger/Swed/Eng] solo,pno GEHRMANS
s.p.   (B1229)

BERESFORD, ARNOLD
Margery Green
low solo,pno (F maj) CRAMER (B1230)
high solo,pno (G maj) CRAMER
(B1231)

BERG
Aftonsang
low solo,pno LUNDQUIST s.p. (B1232)
med solo,pno LUNDQUIST s.p. (B1233)
high solo,pno LUNDQUIST s.p.
(B1234)

Fjarran I Skog
solo,pno LUNDQUIST s.p.   (B1235)

Uti Var Hage, Dar Vaxa Bla Bar
solo,pno LUNDQUIST s.p.   (B1236)

BERG, ALBAN (1885-1935)
Der Wein
[Ger/Fr] S solo,pno UNIVER. 9957
$8.00   (B1237)

Funf Lieder *Op.4, CC5U
[Ger/Eng] med solo,pno UNIVER.
12126 $4.75   (B1238)

Lied Der Lulu
coloratura sop,pno UNIVER. 10229
$3.25   (B1239)

Sieben Fruhe Lieder *CC7U
[Ger/Eng] high solo,pno UNIVER.
8853 $6.50   (B1240)

Vier Lieder *Op.2, CC4U
[Ger/Eng] med solo,pno UNIVER. 8813
$3.25   (B1241)

Zwei Lieder *CC2U
[Ger/Eng] solo,pno UNIVER. 12241
$4.25   (B1242)

BERG, GOTTFRID
Gud Valsigne Dessa Hjartan *Bibl
solo,org GEHRMANS s.p.   (B1243)

Mot Kvall
solo,pno/org ERIKS K 234 s.p.
(B1244)

BERG, JOSEF (1927-1971)
Pisne Noveho Werthera *CCU
Bar solo,pno SUPRAPHON s.p. (B1245)

BERG OP ZOOM see Kremser, Edward

BERGER, A.
Three Poems Of Yeats *CC3U
med solo,fl,clar,vcl sc PRESSER
$1.25   (B1246)

BERGER, B.
Liedjes En Versjes *CCU
solo,acap BROEKMANS s.p.   (B1247)

BERGER, GUSTAV
Weihnachtslied *Op.6, Xmas
solo,pno RIES s.p.   (B1248)

BERGER, JEAN (1909-   )
Carolina Cabin
see Four Songs

BERGER, JEAN (cont'd.)

Coeurs A Prendre *see Lampions
Eteints, No.7; Ombre D'Hamlet,
No.2   (B1249)

Es Ist Ein Schnitter, Heisst Der Tod
*see Faucheur Sinistre

Faucheur Sinistre
"Es Ist Ein Schnitter, Heisst Der
Tod" [Fr/Ger] solo,pno/inst
DURAND s.p.   (B1250)

Five Songs *CC5U
[Fr] med solo,fl,vla,vcl SHEPPARD
JS3001 $5.00   (B1251)

Four Songs
med solo,pno BROUDE BR. $2.25
contains: Carolina Cabin; Heart;
In Time Of Silver Rain; Lonely
People   (B1252)

Four Sonnets *CC4U
[Port/Eng] med solo,pno/4strings
SHEPPARD JS 3006 $6.00, ipr
(B1253)

Heart
see Four Songs

In Time Of Silver Rain
see Four Songs

La Belle Ilona
solo,pno/inst DURAND s.p.   (B1254)

La Fille Dans La Tour
solo,pno/inst DURAND s.p.   (B1255)

La Pernette
solo,pno/inst DURAND s.p.   (B1256)

Lampions Eteints *No.7
solo,pno/inst DURAND s.p. see also
Coeurs A Prendre   (B1257)

Les Faucheurs
"Lous Dolhaires" [Ger/Fr] solo,pno/
inst DURAND s.p.   (B1258)

Lonely People
see Four Songs

Lous Dolhaires *see Les Faucheurs

Of Love *CC5U
high solo,pno SHEPPARD JS 3005
$2.50   (B1259)

Ombre D'Hamlet *No.2
solo,pno/inst DURAND s.p. see also
Coeurs A Prendre   (B1260)

Six Rondeaux *CC6U
[Fr] med solo,vla SHEPPARD JS3003
$3.90   (B1261)

Tres Canciones *CC3U
[Span] med solo,pno/vla&vcl
SHEPPARD JS 3004 $3.00   (B1262)

Villanescas
[Span] S solo,pno SHEPPARD JS 3002
$3.50   (B1263)

BERGER, ROD.
Amoureuse
solo,acap solo pt ENOCH s.p.
(B1264)
2 female soli,pno ENOCH s.p. voc
sc, solo pt   (B1265)
solo,pno (available in 2 keys)
ENOCH s.p. see also Les
Amoureuses   (B1266)

Amours Fletries
solo,acap solo pt ENOCH s.p.
(B1267)
solo,pno ENOCH s.p.   (B1268)

Au Temps Passe
solo,acap solo pt ENOCH s.p.
(B1269)
solo,pno ENOCH s.p. see also Les
Amoureuses   (B1270)

Bal Blanc
solo,pno ENOCH s.p.   (B1271)
solo,acap solo pt ENOCH s.p.
(B1272)
2 female soli,pno ENOCH s.p. voc
sc, solo pt   (B1273)

Brise
solo,pno ENOCH s.p.   (B1274)
solo,acap solo pt ENOCH s.p.
(B1275)

Ce Que L'on Reve
solo,acap solo pt ENOCH s.p.
(B1276)
solo,pno ENOCH s.p. see also Les
Amoureuses   (B1277)

BERGER, ROD. (cont'd.)

Ce Sont Les Miss
  solo,pno ENOCH s.p.   (B1278)
  solo,acap solo pt ENOCH s.p.
              (B1279)

Chagrin D'Amour
  solo,pno ENOCH s.p.   (B1280)
  solo,acap solo pt ENOCH s.p.
              (B1281)

Chasse A Courre
  solo,pno sc ENOCH s.p. (B1282)

Dans Les Fleurs
  2 female soli,pno ENOCH s.p. voc
  sc, solo pt   (B1283)

Dans Les Larmes
  solo,pno ENOCH s.p.   (B1284)
  solo,acap solo pt ENOCH s.p.
              (B1285)

Donne Tes Yeux
  solo,acap solo pt ENOCH s.p.
              (B1286)
  solo,pno ENOCH s.p. see also Les
  Amoureuses   (B1287)

En Deux Mots
  solo,pno ENOCH s.p.   (B1288)
  solo,acap solo pt ENOCH s.p. (B1289)

Eternel Printemps
  2 female soli,pno ENOCH s.p. voc
  sc, solo pt   (B1290)

Galant Rendez-Vous
  solo,acap solo pt ENOCH s.p.
              (B1291)

Gentille Manon
  solo,acap solo pt ENOCH s.p.
              (B1292)
  solo,pno (available in 2 keys)
  ENOCH s.p. see also Les
  Amoureuses   (B1293)

Heureuse
  solo,pno ENOCH s.p.   (B1294)
  solo,acap solo pt ENOCH s.p.
              (B1295)

Hier Et Demain
  solo,acap solo pt ENOCH s.p.
              (B1296)
  solo,pno (available in 2 keys)
  ENOCH s.p. see also Les
  Amoureuses   (B1297)

Histoire D'aimer
  solo,acap solo pt ENOCH s.p.
              (B1298)
  solo,pno ENOCH s.p. see also Les
  Amoureuses   (B1299)

Isabelle
  solo,pno ENOCH s.p.   (B1300)
  solo,acap solo pt ENOCH s.p.
              (B1301)

Jeune Fille Modern Style
  solo,pno ENOCH s.p.   (B1302)
  solo,acap solo pt ENOCH s.p. (B1303)

La Bonne Place
  solo,pno ENOCH s.p.   (B1304)
  solo,acap solo pt ENOCH s.p. (B1305)

La Bouche A Berthe
  solo,pno ENOCH s.p.   (B1306)
  solo,acap solo pt ENOCH s.p. (B1307)

La Faute Des Roses
  solo,acap solo pt ENOCH s.p.
              (B1308)
  solo,pno (available in 2 keys)
  ENOCH s.p. see also Les
  Amoureuses   (B1309)

La Nuit
  solo,pno ENOCH s.p.   (B1310)
  solo,acap solo pt ENOCH s.p. (B1311)

La Vieux De La Petite
  solo,pno ENOCH s.p.   (B1312)

L'Amour Qui Passe
  solo,acap solo pt ENOCH s.p.
              (B1313)
  solo,pno ENOCH s.p. see also Les
  Amoureuses   (B1314)

Le Galant Rendez-Vous
  solo,pno ENOCH s.p.   (B1315)

Le Roman De Pierrot
  solo,pno ENOCH s.p.   (B1316)
  solo,acap solo pt ENOCH s.p. (B1317)

Le Vieux De La Petite
  solo,acap solo pt ENOCH s.p.
              (B1318)

Le Voulez-Vous
  solo,acap solo pt ENOCH s.p.
              (B1319)
  solo,pno ENOCH s.p. see also Les
  Amoureuses   (B1320)

BERGER, ROD. (cont'd.)

Les Amoureuses
  solo,pno cmplt ed ENOCH s.p.
    contains & see also: Amoureuse;
    Au Temps Passe; Ce Que L'on
    Reve; Donne Tes Yeux; Gentille
    Manon; Hier Et Demain; Histoire
    D'aimer; La Faute Des Roses;
    L'Amour Qui Passe; Le Voulez-
    Vous?; Lettre Valsee; L'Oeillet
    Rouge; Loin Du Pays; Pauvres
    Amants; Petite Annonce; Reponse
    A Amoureuse; Rien N'effacera
    Nos Caresses; Tout Pres De Moi
              (B1321)

Les Cancans
  solo,pno ENOCH s.p.   (B1322)
  solo,acap solo pt ENOCH s.p.
              (B1323)

Les Dentelles
  solo,acap solo pt ENOCH s.p.
              (B1324)

Lettre D'une Pensionnaire
  solo,pno (available in 2 keys)
  ENOCH s.p.   (B1325)
  solo,acap solo pt ENOCH s.p. (B1326)

Lettre Valsee
  solo,acap solo pt ENOCH s.p.
              (B1327)
  solo,pno ENOCH s.p. see also Les
  Amoureuses   (B1328)

L'Oeillet Rouge
  solo,acap solo pt ENOCH s.p.
              (B1329)
  solo,pno ENOCH s.p. see also Les
  Amoureuses   (B1330)

Loin Du Pays
  2 female soli,pno ENOCH s.p. voc
  sc, solo pt   (B1331)
  solo,acap solo pt ENOCH s.p.
              (B1332)
  solo,pno ENOCH s.p. see also Les
  Amoureuses   (B1333)

Marche Des Gamins De Paris
  solo,pno ENOCH s.p.   (B1334)
  solo,acap solo pt ENOCH s.p. (B1335)

Marche Des Petits Cabots
  solo,pno ENOCH s.p.   (B1336)
  solo,acap solo pt ENOCH s.p. (B1337)

Marche Du Gas Loubet
  solo,pno ENOCH s.p.   (B1338)
  solo,acap solo pt ENOCH s.p. (B1339)

Mezidon
  solo,pno ENOCH s.p.   (B1340)
  solo,acap solo pt ENOCH s.p. (B1341)

Miss Flirt
  solo,pno ENOCH s.p.   (B1342)
  solo,acap solo pt ENOCH s.p. (B1343)

Mondanite
  solo,pno ENOCH s.p.   (B1344)
  solo,acap solo pt ENOCH s.p. (B1345)

Moto-Girl
  solo,pno ENOCH s.p.   (B1346)
  solo,acap solo pt ENOCH s.p. (B1347)

Nuages Roses
  2 female soli,pno ENOCH s.p. voc
  sc, solo pt   (B1348)

Pauvres Amants
  solo,acap solo pt ENOCH s.p.
              (B1349)
  solo,pno ENOCH s.p. see also Les
  Amoureuses   (B1350)

Petite Americaine
  solo,pno ENOCH s.p.   (B1351)
  solo,acap solo pt ENOCH s.p. (B1352)

Petite Annonce
  solo,acap solo pt ENOCH s.p.
              (B1353)
  solo,pno (available in 2 keys)
  ENOCH s.p. see also Les
  Amoureuses   (B1354)

Petits Potins
  solo,pno ENOCH s.p.   (B1355)
  solo,acap solo pt ENOCH s.p. (B1356)

Pleurez Mes Yeux
  solo,pno ENOCH s.p.   (B1357)
  solo,acap solo pt ENOCH s.p. (B1358)

Poste Restante
  solo,pno ENOCH s.p.   (B1359)
  solo,acap solo pt ENOCH s.p. (B1360)

Reponse A Amoureuse
  solo,acap solo pt ENOCH s.p.
              (B1361)
  solo,pno ENOCH s.p. see also Les
  Amoureuses   (B1362)

BERGER, ROD. (cont'd.)

Reve De Trotin
  solo,pno ENOCH s.p.   (B1363)
  solo,acap solo pt ENOCH s.p. (B1364)

Rien N'effacera Nos Caresses
  solo,acap solo pt ENOCH s.p.
              (B1365)
  solo,pno ENOCH s.p. see also Les
  Amoureuses   (B1366)

Si J'avais Su
  solo,pno ENOCH s.p.   (B1367)
  solo,acap solo pt ENOCH s.p. (B1368)

Silhouette Anglaise
  solo,pno ENOCH s.p.   (B1369)
  solo,acap solo pt ENOCH s.p. (B1370)

Smart
  solo,pno ENOCH s.p.   (B1371)
  solo,acap solo pt ENOCH s.p. (B1372)

Sortie Matinale
  solo,pno ENOCH s.p.   (B1373)
  solo,acap solo pt ENOCH s.p. (B1374)

Ta Dent Du Fond
  solo,pno ENOCH s.p.   (B1375)
  solo,acap solo pt ENOCH s.p. (B1376)

Tout Passe
  solo,pno (available in 2 keys)
  ENOCH s.p.   (B1377)
  solo,acap solo pt ENOCH s.p. (B1378)

Tout Pres De Moi
  solo,acap solo pt ENOCH s.p.
              (B1379)
  solo,pno ENOCH s.p. see also Les
  Amoureuses   (B1380)

Valse Enchantee
  solo,pno ENOCH s.p.   (B1381)
  solo,acap solo pt ENOCH s.p. (B1382)

Valse Triste
  solo,pno ENOCH s.p.   (B1383)
  solo,acap solo pt ENOCH s.p. (B1384)

Verse La Goutte
  solo,pno ENOCH s.p.   (B1385)
  solo,acap solo pt ENOCH s.p. (B1386)

BERGERE see Binet, Jean

BERGERETTE see Bozza, Eugene

BERGERETTE see Martini, Jean Paul Egide

BERGERETTES *CC20L,18th cent
  (Weckerlin) [Fr/Span] solo,pno
  RICORDI-ARG BA 8974 s.p. (B1387)

BERGERETTES *CC20U,18th cent
  (Weckerlin, Jean Baptiste) [Fr] solo,
  pno HEUGEL 10964 s.p. (B1388)

BERGERETTES *CCU,folk,Fr
  (Wekerlin, J.B.) [Eng/Fr] solo,pno
  PRESSER $2.95 (B1389)

BERGERETTES *CC20L,folk,18th cent
  (Weckerlin, J. B.) [Fr/Eng] SCHIRM.G
  $1.50 (B1390)

BERGERETTES *CC6U,folk,Fr,18th cent
  (Behrend, Siegfried) solo,gtr
  SIKORSKI 543 s.p. (B1391)

BERGERONNETTE see Delbruck, J.

BERGGREEN, ANDREAS PETER (1801-1880)
  Efter Lang Sorg
    see Fyra Sanger

  Fyra Sanger
    solo,pno LUNDQUIST s.p.
      contains: Efter Lang Sorg; Over
      Dina Hander Lutad; Se, Allena
      Har Jag Vandrat; Spindelvav
              (B1392)

  Over Dina Hander Lutad
    see Fyra Sanger

  Se, Allena Har Jag Vandrat
    see Fyra Sanger

  Spindelvav
    see Fyra Sanger

BERGH, SVERRE
  Askepotts Sang (from Askepott)
    solo,pno MUSIKK s.p. (B1393)

BERGLIOT see Grieg, Edvard Hagerup

BERGMAN, ERIK (1911-)
  Animaalinen Hymni *Op.27,No.4
    solo,pno FAZER F3498 s.p. see from
    Ensamhetens Sanger (B1394)

  Animalisk Hymn *see Sarastus

BERGMAN, ERIK (cont'd.)

Der Traumer Kommt *Op.21,No.1
  solo,pno FAZER F 4039 s.p. (B1395)

Du Bist Die Auferstehung Meiner Seele
  "You Are My Soul's Awakening" see
  Mit Dir

Ensam Under Fastet *Op.4,No.2
  "Yskin Alla Taivaan" solo,pno FAZER
  F 2594 s.p. see from Seks Sanger
  (B1396)

Ensamhetens Sanger *see Animaalinen
  Hymni, Op.27,No.4; Himalajan
  Rinteella, "Gryningen", Op.27,
  No.2; Nocturne, "Pa Himalayas",
  Op.27,No.1; Sarastus, "Animalisk
  Hymn", Op.27,No.3

Falscher Madchenblick *Op.21,No.3
  solo,pno FAZER s.p. (B1398)

Gryningen *see Himalajan Rinteella

Himalajan Rinteella *Op.27,No.2
  "Gryningen" solo,pno FAZER F3496
  s.p. see from Ensamhetens Sanger
  (B1399)

I Kvallningen *Op.4,No.3
  "Illan Suussa" solo,pno FAZER
  F 2595 s.p. see from Seks Sanger
  (B1400)

Illan Suussa *see I Kvallningen

Keinulla *see Lat Vid Gungan

Kuu Nousee *see Pa Fastet Stiger
  Manen

Lat Vid Gungan *Op.4,No.5
  "Keinulla" solo,pno FAZER F 2597
  s.p. see from Seks Sanger (B1401)

Mit Dir
  [Eng/Ger/Finn] solo,pno FAZER
  W 3540 s.p.
  contains: Du Bist Die
    Auferstehung Meiner Seele, "You
    Are My Soul's Awakening";
    Mondwache, "Moon Vigil";
    Morgen, "Morning"; So Nackt
    Sind Deine Augen, "Your Eyes
    Are So Naked" (B1402)

Mondwache
  "Moon Vigil" see Mit Dir

Moon Vigil *see Mondwache

Morgen
  "Morning" see Mit Dir

Morning *see Morgen

Mot Nord *Op.4,No.6
  "Pohjolaan" solo,pno FAZER F 2598
  s.p. see from Seks Sanger (B1403)

Nocturne *Op.27,No.1
  "Pa Himalayas" solo,pno FAZER F3495
  s.p. see from Ensamhetens Sanger
  (B1404)

Pa Fastet Stiger Manen *Op.4,No.4
  "Kuu Nousee" solo,pno FAZER F 2596
  s.p. see from Seks Sanger (B1405)

Pa Himalayas *see Nocturne

Pohjolaan *see Mot Nord

Sarastus *Op.27,No.3
  "Animalisk Hymn" solo,pno FAZER
  F3497 s.p. see from Ensamhetens
  Sanger (B1406)

Seks Sanger *see Ensam Under Fastet,
  "Yskin Alla Taivaan", Op.4,No.2;
  I Kvallningen, "Illan Suussa",
  Op.4,No.3; Lat Vid Gungan,
  "Keinulla", Op.4,No.5; Mot Nord,
  "Pohjolaan", Op.4,No.6; Pa Fastet
  Stiger Manen, "Kuu Nousee", Op.4,
  No.4 (B1407)

Serenade *Op.35a,No.1
  solo,pno FAZER F4038 s.p. (B1408)

So Nackt Sind Deine Augen
  "Your Eyes Are So Naked" see Mit
  Dir

You Are My Soul's Awakening *see Du
  Bist Die Auferstehung Meiner
  Seele

Your Eyes Are So Naked *see So Nackt
  Sind Deine Augen

Yskin Alla Taivaan *see Ensam Under
  Fastet

BERGMANDEN see Sjogren, Emil

BERGMANN, R.
  Deux Poemes Rimbaldiens *see Fetes
  De La Faim; Le Dormeur Du Val
  (B1409)

Fetes De La Faim
  solo,pno/inst DURAND s.p. see from
  Deux Poemes Rimbaldiens (B1410)

La Chanson Du Moulin A Vent
  solo,pno/inst DURAND s.p. (B1411)

Le Dormeur Du Val
  solo,pno/inst DURAND s.p. see from
  Deux Poemes Rimbaldiens (B1412)

Une Nuit Qu'on Entendait La Mer Sans
  La Voir
  solo,acap quarto DURAND s.p.
  (B1413)

BERGMANNSLIED see Martinu, Bohuslav,
  Havirska

BERGSMA, WILLIAM LAURENCE (1921-   )
  Bethsabe Bathing
  solo,pno (C maj) GALAXY 1.2231.7
  $1.00 (B1414)

BERIO, LUCIANO (1925-   )
  Chamber Music *CCU
  female solo,3inst ZERBONI 5053
  rental (B1415)

BERIOT, CHARLES-AUGUST DE (1802-1870)
  Air Varie
  coloratura sop,pno HEUWEKE. 01 s.p.
  (B1416)

BERKELEY, LENNOX (1903-   )
  All That's Past *Op.65,No.3
  see Songs Of The Half-Light

Autumn's Legacy *Op.58, song cycle
  [Eng] high solo,kbd CHESTER s.p.
  (B1417)

Beacon Barn, The
  [Eng] med solo,kbd CHESTER s.p.
  (B1418)

Bells Of Cordoba
  [Eng] high solo,pno CHESTER s.p.
  (B1419)

Carry Her Over The Water *Op.53,No.5
  see Five Poems

Epitaph Of Timas
  see Three Greek Songs

Eyes Look Into The Well *Op.53,No.4
  see Five Poems

Five Poems
  [Eng] med-high solo,kbd CHESTER
  s.p.
  contains: Carry Her Over The
    Water, Op.53,No.5; Eyes Look
    Into The Well, Op.53,No.4;
    Lauds, Op.53,No.1; O Lurcher-
    Loving Collier, Op.53,No.2;
    What's In Your Mind, Op.53,No.3
    (B1420)

Five Songs
  [Eng] med solo,kbd CHESTER s.p.
  contains: Horseman, The, Op.26,
    No.1; Mistletoe, The, Op.26,
    No.2; Poor Henry, Op.26,No.3;
    Song Of The Soldiers, The,
    Op.26,No.4 (B1421)

Fleeting, The *Op.65,No.5
  see Songs Of The Half-Light

Four Poems Of St. Teresa Of Avila
  *sac
  [Eng] A solo,strings voc sc CHESTER
  s.p.
  contains: If, Lord, Thy Love For
    Me Is Strong; Let Mine Eyes See
    Thee; Shepherd, Shepherd Hark
    That Calling!; Today A Shepherd
    And Our Kin (B1422)

Full Moon *Op.65,No.2
  see Songs Of The Half-Light

Horseman, The *Op.26,No.1
  see Five Songs

If, Lord, Thy Love For Me Is Strong
  see Four Poems Of St. Teresa Of
  Avila

Lauds *Op.53,No.1
  see Five Poems

Let Mine Eyes See Thee
  see Four Poems Of St. Teresa Of
  Avila

Long Time Ago, A
  see Three Songs

Mistletoe, The *Op.26,No.2
  see Five Songs

Moth, The *Op.65,No.4
  see Songs Of The Half-Light

BERKELEY, LENNOX (cont'd.)

O Lurcher-Loving Collier *Op.53,No.2
  see Five Poems

Ode Du Premier Jour De Mai
  [Fr] med-high solo,pno CHESTER s.p.
  (B1423)

Poor Henry *Op.26,No.3
  see Five Songs

Rachel *Op.65,No.1
  see Songs Of The Half-Light

Rio Grande, The
  see Three Songs

Shepherd, Shepherd Hark That Calling!
  see Four Poems Of St. Teresa Of
  Avila

Silver *Op.26,No.5
  med solo,kbd CHESTER s.p. (B1424)

Song Of The Soldiers, The *Op.26,
  No.4
  see Five Songs

Songs Of The Half-Light
  [Eng] high solo,gtr cmplt ed
  CHESTER s.p.
  contains: All That's Past, Op.65,
    No.3; Fleeting, The, Op.65,
    No.5; Full Moon, Op.65,No.2;
    Moth, The, Op.65,No.4; Rachel,
    Op.65,No.1 (B1425)

Spring Song
  see Three Greek Songs

Stabat Mater
  [Lat] SSATBarB soli,chamb.grp. sc,
  voc sc CHESTER s.p. (B1426)

Theodore
  see Three Songs

Three Greek Songs
  [Eng] med solo,kbd CHESTER s.p.
  contains: Epitaph Of Timas;
    Spring Song; To Aster (B1427)

Three Songs
  [Eng] high solo,kbd CHESTER s.p.
  contains: Long Time Ago, A; Rio
    Grande, The; Theodore (B1428)

To Aster
  see Three Greek Songs

Today A Shepherd And Our Kin
  see Four Poems Of St. Teresa Of
  Avila

What's In Your Mind *Op.53,No.3
  see Five Poems

BERKSHIRE TRAGEDY see Broadwood, Lucy
  E.

BERLINSKI, HERMAN (1910-   )
  Kol Nidre *sac
  cantor,opt mix cor,org MERCURY
  $1.00 (B1429)

Psalm 23
  solo,fl PRESSER $1.00 (B1430)

BERLIOZ, HECTOR (1803-1869)
  A Te Grazie (from Faust)
  [It/Ger] T solo,pno COSTALL s.p.
  (B1431)

Adieu! Fiere Cite (from Les Troyens A
  Carthage)
  [Fr] Mez solo,pno CHOUDENS C203
  s.p. (B1432)

Brander's Song (from Damnation Of
  Faust, The)
  B solo,pno INTERNAT. $1.00 (B1433)

Chanson E La Puce
  solo,pno DURAND s.p. (B1434)

Complete Songs Of Berlioz, Vols. 1-10
  *CCU
  solo/soli,pno study sc KALMUS
  1227-1236 $1.50, ea. (B1435)

Cycle Of Six Songs, A *see Les Nuits
  D'Ete

Der Junge Bretagner Hirte *see Le
  Jeune Patre Breton

Hector Berlioz Works *CCU
  (Malherbe, Charles; Weingartner,
  Felix) contains works for a
  variety of instruments and vocal
  combinations microfiche
  UNIV.MUS.ED. $115.00 contains 20
  volumes (B1436)

Invocation To Nature (from Damnation
  Of Faust, The)
  [Fr/Eng] T solo,pno INTERNAT. $1.00

BERLIOZ, HECTOR (cont'd.)

(B1437)
Je Vais Mourir (from Les Troyens A
Carthage)
[Fr] Mez solo,pno CHOUDENS C56 s.p.
(B1438)
La Gloire Etait (from Benvenuto
Cellini)
[Fr] T solo,pno CHOUDENS C374 s.p.
(B1439)
Le Jeune Patre Breton *Op.13,No.4
"Der Junge Bretagner Hirte" S/T
solo,horn,pno BREITKOPF-L rental
(B1440)
Les Nuit D'Ete *song cycle
"Sommernachte" S/T solo,2fl,ob,
2clar,2bsn,3horn,harp,strings sc
BREITKOPF-W s.p.   (B1441)
Les Nuits D'Ete *Op.7, song cycle
"Cycle Of Six Songs, A" [Fr/Eng]
high solo,pno INTERNAT. $3.00
(B1442)
"Cycle Of Six Songs, A" [Fr/Eng]
low solo,pno INTERNAT. $3.00
(B1443)
"Summer Nights, The" [Fr/Eng] high
solo,pno SCHIRM.G $2.50 (B1444)
"Summer Nights, The" [Fr/Eng] low
solo,pno SCHIRM.G $2.50 (B1445)

Sommernachte *see Les Nuit D'Ete

Summer Nights, The *see Les Nuits
D'Ete

Sur Les Monts (from Benvenuto
Cellini)
[Fr] T solo,pno CHOUDENS C375 s.p.
(B1446)
Villanelle
see LA MUSIQUE, NEUVIEME CAHIER
solo,pno DURAND s.p.   (B1447)

BERMUDO, FRAY JUAN (ca. 1510-ca. 1555)
Mira Nero De Tarpeya
(Azpiazu) [Span] med solo,gtr UNION
ESP. $.50   (B1448)

BERNABEI, (GIUSEPPE) ERCOLE
(ca. 1620-1687)
Heu Me Miseram Et Infelicem *sac
(Ewerhart, Rudolf) S/T solo,cont
BIELER CS 44 s.p.   (B1449)

In Hymnis Et Canticis *sac
(Ewerhart, Rudolf) S/T solo,cont
BIELER CS 52 s.p.   (B1450)

BERNADAC, L.
Le Relais De Boissiere
solo,pno/inst DURAND s.p.   (B1451)

BERNARD, R.
Coeurs A Prendre *CC7UL
solo,pno/inst cmplt ed DURAND s.p.
(B1452)
Equinoxe
solo,pno/inst DURAND s.p.   (B1453)

J'avais Mis De L'air Parfume
see Trois Poemes De Francis Jammes

Lande Double
solo,pno/inst DURAND s.p.   (B1454)

Maintenant, O Mon Dieu
see Trois Poemes De Francis Jammes

Ombre
solo,pno/inst DURAND s.p.   (B1455)

Phares
solo,pno/inst DURAND s.p.   (B1456)

Trois Poemes De Francis Jammes
med solo,pno/inst DURAND s.p.
contains: J'avais Mis De L'air
Parfume; Maintenant, O Mon
Dieu; Une Goutte De Pluie
(B1457)
Une Goutte De Pluie
see Trois Poemes De Francis Jammes

BERNER MUNDARTLIEDLI see Schmalz, Paul

BERNERS, LORD (1883-1950)
Du Bist Wie Eine Blume
see Lieder Album

Konig Wiswamitre
see Lieder Album

La Fiancee Du Timbalier
see Trois Chansons

L'Etoile Filante
see Trois Chansons

Lieder Album
[Ger] med solo,kbd CHESTER s.p.
contains: Du Bist Wie Eine Blume;
Konig Wiswamitre;
Weihnachtslied   (B1458)

BERNERS, LORD (cont'd.)

Romance
see Trois Chansons

Trois Chansons
[Fr] med solo,kbd CHESTER s.p.
contains: La Fiancee Du
Timbalier; L'Etoile Filante;
Romance   (B1459)

Weihnachtslied
see Lieder Album

BERNHARD, CHRISTOPH (1627-1692)
Aus Der Tiefen Ruf Ich, Herr, Zu Dir
*sac,cant
(Grusnick, Bruno) S solo,2vln,cont
(med) BAREN. 3425   (B1460)

Create In Me A Clean Heart, O God
*sac
solo,pno CONCORDIA 97-5041 $2.25
(B1461)
Furchtet Euch Nicht *sac,cant
(Grusnick, Bruno) S solo,2vln,cont
(med) BAREN. 694-6468 $4.00
(B1462)
Jauchzet Dem Herrn, Alle Welt *sac,
cant
(Grusnick, Bruno) SS soli,2vln,cont
(med) BAREN. 835 $6.25   (B1463)

Jerusalem, Thou That Killest The
Prophets *sac
SAB soli,2vln,cont CONCORDIA
97-5109 $.50, ipa   (B1464)

Was Betrubst Du Dich, Meine Seele
*sac,cant
(Grusnick, Bruno) A solo,vln,vla,
vcl,cont (med) BAREN. 3423 $3.50
(B1465)

BERNICAT, F.
Couplets De La Queue De La Poele
(from Les Premieres Armes De
Louis XV)
solo,pno ENOCH s.p.   (B1466)

Enveloppe Dans Du Coton (from Les
Premieres Armes De Louis XV)
solo,pno ENOCH s.p.   (B1467)

Gai Rossignol, Viens Par Ici
solo,pno ENOCH s.p.   (B1468)
solo,acap solo pt ENOCH s.p.
(B1469)
La Pigeonne
solo,pno ENOCH s.p.   (B1470)
solo,acap solo pt ENOCH s.p.
(B1471)
Le Roi M'a Dit (from Les Premieres
Armes De Louis XV)
solo,pno ENOCH s.p.   (B1472)

L'Epingle
solo,pno ENOCH s.p.   (B1473)
solo,acap solo pt ENOCH s.p.
(B1474)
Les Passereaux
solo,pno ENOCH s.p.   (B1475)
solo,acap solo pt ENOCH s.p.
(B1476)
Un Lapin Broutant L'herbette (from
Les Premieres Armes De Louis XV)
solo,pno ENOCH s.p.   (B1477)

BERNIER, NICOLAS (1664-1734)
Accurite *mot
(Chailley, A.) solo,orch TRANSAT.
s.p.   (B1478)

C'est L'heure Aux Volets Clos
see Evasions

Evasions
solo,pno/inst LEDUC s.p.
contains: C'est L'heure Aux
Volets Clos; O Muse Dont Les
Pas Dansent   (B1479)

Kaffeekantate *see Le Cafe

Le Cafe *cant
(Hinnenthal, Johann Philipp)
"Kaffeekantate" S solo,vln/fl,
cont (med diff) BAREN. 3440 $9.75
(B1480)
Lettre D'un Ami
solo,orch LEDUC s.p.   (B1481)

N'implorez Plus (from Iris)
S solo,pno/inst DURAND s.p. (B1482)

O Muse Dont Les Pas Dansent
see Evasions

BERNIER, RENE (1905-   )
Chanson Marine
A/B solo,pno CBDM s.p.   (B1483)
A/B solo,2fl,ob,2clar,bsn,2horn,
perc,cel,triangle,vibra,harp,
5strings min sc CBDM s.p. (B1484)

BERNIER, RENE (cont'd.)

Eclaircies
CBDM S/T solo,2fl,ob,2clar,2bsn,
2horn,trp,cel,harp,triangle,xylo,
cym cmplt ed,min sc s.p.; S/T
solo,pno cmplt ed s.p.
contains: Eternite; Exultation;
Miroir; Reflets; Soliloque
(B1485)
Eclosions *CC3U
[Fr] med solo,pno ESCHIG $3.40
(B1486)
Eternite
see Eclaircies

Exultation
see Eclaircies

Miroir
see Eclaircies

Reflets
see Eclaircies

Soliloque
see Eclaircies

BERNSTEIN, LEONARD (1918-   )
Collected Songs *CC19L
solo,pno SCHIRM.G $5.00   (B1487)

Extinguish My Eyes
see Two Love Songs

I Hate Music *song cycle
S solo,pno WARNER VS0266 $1.95
(B1488)
Lamentation (from Jeremiah Symphony)
[Heb] Mez solo,pno/org WARNER
VS2380 $1.50   (B1489)

Silhouette (from Galilee)
high solo,pno SCHIRM.G $.75 (B1490)

Simple Song, A (from Mass) sac
high solo,pno (C maj) SCHIRM.G $.95
(B1491)
Two Love Songs
med solo,pno SCHIRM.G $.85
contains: Extinguish My Eyes;
When My Soul Touches Yours
(B1492)
When My Soul Touches Yours
see Two Love Songs

Word Of The Lord, The (from Mass) sac
high solo,pno (B flat maj) SCHIRM.G
$2.00   (B1493)

BERRY *Fr
(Canteloube, J.) solo,acap DURAND
s.p. see also Anthologie Des Chants
Populaires Francais Tome III
(B1494)
BERRY PICKING, THE *folk,Scot
solo,pno (A flat maj) PATERSON FS142
s.p.   (B1495)

BERSA, BLAGOJE (1873-1934)
Vocal Compositions *CCU
[Slav] solo,pno min sc CROATICA
s.p.   (B1496)

BERTELSEN, MICHAEL
Seven, The
male solo,pno, seven peawhistles sc
FOG s.p.   (B1497)

BERTHELOT, RENE
Chansons Galantes *CCU
med solo,pno OUVRIERES 5.1450.7
$4.00   (B1498)

Cinq Poesies Du Grand Siecle *CC5U
Mez solo,pno OUVRIERES 5.1433.7
$4.75   (B1499)

BERTHOMIEU, MARC
Si J'etais Charles D'Orleans
[Fr] med solo,pno HEUGEL 10921
(B1500)
Si J'etais Ronsard
[Fr] med solo,pno HEUGEL   (B1501)

BERTOUILLE, GERARD (1898-   )
Harmonie Du Soir
see Trois Poemes De Baudelaire

Le Jet D'eau
see Trois Poemes De Baudelaire

Obsession
see Trois Poemes De Baudelaire

Trois Poemes De Baudelaire
S/T solo,pno cmplt ed CBDM s.p.
contains: Harmonie Du Soir; Le
Jet D'eau; Obsession   (B1502)

BERTRAND
All For You (composed with Brown)
high solo,pno (D flat maj) SCHIRM.G
$.75   (B1503)
low solo,pno (B flat maj) SCHIRM.G
$.75   (B1504)

BERUFT GOTT SELBST, SO MUSS DER SEGEN
see Bach, Johann Sebastian

BERUHIGNUNG see Rontgen, Johannes

BESARD, JEAN-BAPTISTE (1567- ?)
Belles Deesses
(Pujol) [Fr] med solo,gtr ESCHIG
E1307 $1.75   (B1505)

Cruelle Departie
(Pujol) [Fr] med solo,gtr ESCHIG
E1308 $.90   (B1506)

Moy, Pauvre Fille
(Pujol) [Fr] med solo,gtr ESCHIG
E1309 $1.50   (B1507)

BESCHNITT, J.
Hydda Lill', Tyst Och Still'
solo,pno GEHRMANS 177 s.p. (B1508)

BESCIGNAD ANNEGNILA see Massarani,
Renzo

BESIDE STILL WATERS see Deacon, Mary

BESIDE STILL WATERS see Hamblen,
Bernard

BESIDE STILL WATERS see Silva

BESIDE THE RHINE'S NOBLE WATERS see
Schumann, Robert (Alexander), Im
Rheim, Heiligen Strome

BESIDE THY CRADLE HERE I STAND see
Bach, Johann Sebastian

BESIDE THY MANGER HERE I STAND see
Bach, Johann Sebastian

BESLY, MAURICE (1888-1945)
An Outward Sail
high solo,pno (A maj) ASHDOWN
                          (B1509)
med solo,pno (G maj) ASHDOWN
                          (B1510)
low solo,pno (F maj) ASHDOWN
                          (B1511)
Angels Are Stooping
low solo,pno (D maj) ASHDOWN
                          (B1512)
high solo,pno (F maj) ASHDOWN
                          (B1513)
med solo,pno (E maj) ASHDOWN
                          (B1514)
Epitaph, An
solo,pno (D flat maj) ROBERTON 2277
s.p.   (B1515)
Lullaby Trees
low solo,pno (E flat maj) LEONARD-
ENG   (B1516)
high solo,pno (F maj) LEONARD-ENG
                          (B1517)
Second Minuet
low solo,pno (G maj) BOOSEY $1.75
                          (B1518)
high solo,pno (B flat maj) BOOSEY
$1.75   (B1519)
2 soli,pno (G maj) BOOSEY $2.00
                          (B1520)
Sermon On The Mount *sac
solo,pno (D min) BOOSEY $1.50
                          (B1521)

BESS SONGS see Brumby, Colin

BESSER WAR' ES MIR GEGANGEN see
Kilpinen, Yrio, Parempi Syntymatta

BESSIE BELL AND MARY GRAY see Lawson,
Malcolm

BESSIE BOBTAIL see Barber, Samuel

BESSIE BOBTAIL see Mourant, Walter

BEST GEBORGEN see Clercq, R. de

BEST OF ALL see Leslie, R.

BEST OF ANDRAE see Crouch, Andrae

BEST OF RAY HILDEBRAND *sac,CCUL
solo,pno WORD 35042 $2.50   (B1522)

BEST OF SACRED SONGS, VOL. IV *sac,
CC12L
solo,pno WORD 37670 $2.95   (B1523)

BEST OF THE GOOD TWINS *sac,CCUL
solo,pno WORD 35022 $2.50   (B1524)

BEST OF THE LOWELL LUNDSTROM TEAM, THE
*sac,CC12UL
solo,pno BENSON BO925 $2.50 (B1525)

BESTER JUNGLING! MIT ENTZUCKEN see
Mozart, Wolfgang Amadeus

BETER, P.D.
Lets All Build America
solo,pno BRANDEN $.50   (B1526)

BETHLEHEM see Gounod, Charles Francois

BETHLEHEM DOWN see Heseltine, Philip

BETHLEHEM, GALILEE, GETHSEMANE see
Gaither

BETHLEHEM, TINY TOWN see Moore, Gary

BETHSABE BATHING see Bergsma, William
Laurence

BETLEHEMS STJARNA see Heilakka

BETLEM see Trojan, Vaclav

BETOVE
Ah! Qu'est-Ce Que J'ai (from Pom-Pom)
solo,pno ENOCH s.p.   (B1527)
Il Y A Des Gens (from Pom-Pom)
solo,pno ENOCH s.p.   (B1528)
J'ai Rencontre De Par Le Monde (from
Pom-Pom)
solo,pno ENOCH s.p.   (B1529)
La Mode (from Pom-Pom)
solo,pno ENOCH s.p.   (B1530)
Les Pourquoi D'Eve (from Pom-Pom)
solo,pno ENOCH s.p.   (B1531)
Pom-Pom (from Pom-Pom)
solo,pno ENOCH s.p.   (B1532)
Rondeau D'Adam (from Pom-Pom)
solo,pno ENOCH s.p.   (B1533)
Sans Avoir L'air (from Pom-Pom)
solo,pno ENOCH s.p.   (B1534)
Tango Serpentin (from Pom-Pom)
solo,pno ENOCH s.p.   (B1535)

BETRACHT DIES HERZ see Mozart, Wolfgang
Amadeus

BETRACHTE, MEINE SEEL, MIT ANGSTLICHEM
VERGNUGEN see Bach, Johann
Sebastian

BETRACHTUNG DES TODES see Haydn,
(Franz) Joseph

BETRAYED see Beni, J.

BETSY WAREING see Walker, Henry

BETTARINI, LUCIANO (1914-   )
I Due Cigni
see Quaderni Pascoliani

Il Ponte
see Quaderni Pascoliani

Nel Giardino
see Quaderni Pascoliani

Quaderni Pascoliani
[It] solo,pno cmplt ed SANTIS 953
s.p.
contains: I Due Cigni; Il Ponte;
Nel Giardino   (B1536)

Tre Liriche Di Pascoli *CC3U
female solo,orch sc ZERBONI 5183
s.p.   (B1537)

BETTER DAY, A see Wetherington

BETTER LAND see Cowen, Sir Frederic
Hymen

BETTINELLI, BRUNO (1913-   )
Cinque Liriche Di Montale
S solo,fl,clar,strings sc CARISH
21284 s.p.
contains: Debole Sistro Al Vento;
Gloria Del Disteso Mezzogiorno;
L'anima Che Dispensa; Portami
Il Girasole; Sul Muro Grafito
                          (B1538)
Dalla Forza Nasce La Forma
see Tre Liriche

Debole Sistro Al Vento
see Cinque Liriche Di Montale

Gloria Del Disteso Mezzogiorno
see Cinque Liriche Di Montale

La Natura Mi Parla
see Tre Liriche

L'anima Che Dispensa
see Cinque Liriche Di Montale

Nella Sera
see Tre Liriche

Portami Il Girasole
see Cinque Liriche Di Montale

BETTINELLI, BRUNO (cont'd.)

Sul Muro Grafito
see Cinque Liriche Di Montale

Tre Liriche
S/T solo,pno cmplt ed RICORDI-ENG
128775 s.p.
contains: Dalla Forza Nasce La
Forma; La Natura Mi Parla;
Nella Sera   (B1539)

BETTS, LORNE M.
Behold Thy King *sac
med solo,pno (C maj) WATERLOO $.75
                          (B1540)

BETWIXT MINE EYES AND HEART see Delden,
Lex van

BEUKER, H.
Ik Verlang Naar Holland
solo,pno BROEKMANS 183 s.p. (B1541)

BEUNINGEN, W.V.
Daer Staet Een Clooster In Oostenrijc
see Oud-Nederlandsche Liederen

Daer Was Een Sneeuwwit Vogeltje
see Oud-Nederlandsche Liederen

Het Daghet In Den Oosten
see Oud-Nederlandsche Liederen

Ick Hen Een Seer Traech Eselkijn
see Oud-Nederlandsche Liederen

Naer Oesterlant
see Oud-Nederlandsche Liederen

Oud-Nederlandsche Liederen
solo,pno ALSBACH s.p.
contains: Daer Staet Een Clooster
In Oostenrijc; Daer Was Een
Sneeuwwit Vogeltje; Het Daghet
In Den Oosten; Ick Hen Een Seer
Traech Eselkijn; Naer
Oesterlant; Waer Is Die Dochter
Van Seyoen   (B1542)

Waer Is Die Dochter Van Seyoen
see Oud-Nederlandsche Liederen

BEURLE, JURGEN (1943-   )
Conditional
solo,pno,3electronic tape (for
performance 5 scores are
required) sc MOECK 5081 s.p.
                          (B1543)
Diaphon
solo,perc MOECK 5075 s.p. (B1544)

Sinus
SBar soli,vln,vla,perc sc MOECK
5073 s.p.   (B1545)

Variable Realisationen
any combination of 1-4 performers -
vocal, instrumental, electronic
tape or radio noise sc MOECK 5076
s.p.   (B1546)

BEVAN, FREDERICK
Admiral's Broom, The
low solo,orch (D maj) ASHDOWN
$1.50, ipr   (B1547)
high solo,orch (F maj) ASHDOWN
$1.50, ipr   (B1548)
med solo,orch (E maj) ASHDOWN
$1.50, ipr   (B1549)

Peg Away
solo,pno CRAMER   (B1550)

BEVARINGSVISA see Peterson-Berger,
(Olof) Wilhelm

BEVERIDGE, THOMAS G. (1938-   )
St. Francis' Prayer
med solo,org FOSTER MF 752 $1.00
                          (B1551)

BEVERLY TERRELL'S FAVORITE GOSPEL SOLOS
*sac,CCU
(Terrell, Beverly) solo,pno BROADMAN
4525-04 $1.75   (B1552)

BEVERLY TERRELL'S SOLO COLLECTION, NO.
2 *sac,CC8UL
high solo,pno BROADMAN 4525-08 $2.95
                          (B1553)

BEWARE OF THE MAIDENS see Day, Maude
Craske

BEWILDERED BALLADE see Wagner, Joseph
Frederick

BEYDTS, L.
Adonis
see Le Couer Inutile

Apres La Mortelle Aventure
see Le Couer Inutile

Ceux Que Nous Aimons
see Le Couer Inutile

BEYDTS, L. (cont'd.)

Chansons Pour Les Oiseau
solo,orch cmplt ed DURAND s.p., ipr
contains: La Columbe Poignardee;
Le Petit Pigeon Bleu; Le Petit
Serin En Cage; L'oiseau Bleu
(B1554)

Dans Les Ombres De Mon Ame
see Le Couer Inutile

D'ombre Et De Soleil *CC8L
solo,orch DURAND s.p. (B1555)

En Arles
solo,pno,opt fl DURAND s.p. see
from Trois Melodies (B1556)

La Columbe Poignardee
see Chansons Pour Les Oiseau

La Saison Qui Devet Le Bois
see Le Couer Inutile

Le Couer Inutile
solo,pno DURAND s.p.
contains: Adonis; Apres La
Mortelle Aventure; Ceux Que
Nous Aimons; Dans Les Ombres De
Mon Ame; La Saison Qui Devet Le
Bois; Les Dieux Que J'appelais
(B1557)

Le Crepuscule
solo,pno,opt fl DURAND s.p. see
from Trois Melodies (B1558)

Le Petit Pigeon Bleu
see Chansons Pour Les Oiseau

Le Petit Serin En Cage
see Chansons Pour Les Oiseau

Le Present
solo,pno,opt fl DURAND s.p. see
from Trois Melodies (B1559)

Les Dieux Que J'appelais
see Le Couer Inutile

L'oiseau Bleu
see Chansons Pour Les Oiseau

Trois Melodies *see En Arles; Le
Crepuscule; Le Present (B1560)

BEYER, FRANK MICHAEL (1928-)
Biblische Szenen *sac,CC7L,Bibl
2 med soli,fl,ob,vln,vla SIRIUS
s.p. sc, solo pt (B1561)

BEYER, JOHANN SAMUEL (1669-1744)
Heilig Ist Gott *sac
ST soli,2S rec,cont HANSSLER 5.057
s.p. see also GESANGE ZUM
KIRCHENJAHR (B1562)

BEYERMAN-WALRAVEN, JEANNE (1878-)
De Ramp
see Drie Lieder Op Nederlandse
Tekst

De Zieke Buur
A solo,4fl,3ob,4clar,4bsn,4horn,
3trp,3trom,tuba,timp,perc,cel,
2harp,strings DONEMUS s.p.
(B1563)

Drie Lieder Op Nederlandse Tekst
med solo,pno DONEMUS s.p.
contains: De Ramp; In Den Stroom;
Om De Stilte (B1564)

In Den Stroom
see Drie Lieder Op Nederlandse
Tekst

Om De Stilte
see Drie Lieder Op Nederlandse
Tekst

Trois Poemes De Maurice Careme *CC3U
solo,pno BROEKMANS 203 s.p. (B1565)

BEYN N'HAR P'RAT see Chajes, Julius

BEYN N'HAR P'RAT see Weinberg, Jacob

BEYOND ALL TIME *sac
(Carmichael, Ralph) solo,pno WORD
S-108 (B1566)

BEYOND SILENCE see Anderson, Thomas J.

BEYOND THE DISTANT HILLS see Craven,
Louise

BEYOND THE RIM OF DAY see Smith, Hale

BEYOND THE STARS see Bohun, Lyle de

BEYOND THE STARS see Day, Maude Craske

BEYOND THE SUNSET see Bock, Blanch Kerr

BEYOND THE SUNSET see Brock, Blanche
[Kerr]

BEYOND TIME see Weigl, Vally

BEZANSON, PHILIP
Contrasts
med solo,pno AM.COMP.AL. $3.85
(B1567)

Songs Of Innocence *CCU
high solo,fl,ob,clar,bsn,2horn,
strings AM.COMP.AL. sc $18.70,
voc sc $8.25 (B1568)

That Time May Cease And Midnight
Never Come
Bar solo,3fl,3ob,3clar,2bsn,4horn,
3trp,3trom,tuba,3timp,perc sc
AM.COMP.AL. $16.50 (B1569)
Bar solo,pno voc sc AM.COMP.AL.
$5.50 (B1570)

Word Of Love, The
T solo,pno sc AM.COMP.AL. $8.25
(B1571)

BEZINNING see Zagwijn, Henri

BHATIA
Toy-Seller, The
S solo,pno,vln (med) OXFORD 96.001
s.p. (B1572)

BIALAS, GUNTHER (1907-)
Haiku-Folge I: Ein Mensch Und Eine
Fliege *CCU
S solo,fl BAREN. 014-6157 $6.00
(B1573)

Haiku-Folge II: Ja, Ja, Schrie
Ich.... *CCU
Bar solo,pno BAREN. 012-6158 $6.50
(B1574)

Lieder Und Balladen Nach Gedichten
Von F. Garcia Lorca *CCU
S solo,pno (diff) BAREN. 3861 $8.50
(B1575)

Preisungen
Bar solo,org (diff) cmplt ed BAREN.
4459 $14.00
contains: Psalm 90; Psalm 108;
Psalm 115 (B1576)

Psalm 90
see Preisungen

Psalm 108
see Preisungen

Psalm 115
see Preisungen

Three Songs *CC3U
Bar solo,fl,gtr sc BAREN. 014-6128
$8.00 (B1577)

BIALOSKY, MARSHALL (1923-)
Music For Soprano Solo And Acappella
Chorus
S solo,cor,acap SEESAW (B1578)

Three Songs For Soprano And Clarinet
*CC3U
S solo,clar SEESAW (B1579)

BIANCA AL PAR DI NEVE ALPINA see
Meyerbeer, Giacomo

BIANCHERI, A.
Aimez Vos Meres
solo,pno ENOCH s.p. (B1580)

Bel Aubepin
solo,pno ENOCH s.p. (B1581)

Berceuse
solo,pno ENOCH s.p. see from
Chanson Des Gueux (B1582)

Chanson Des Gueux *see Berceuse; Du
Mouron Pour Les Petits Oiseaux;
Les Petiots; Marche De Pluie;
Pauvre Aveugle; Pleine Eau; Ronde
(B1583)
Du Mouron Pour Les Petits Oiseaux
solo,pno ENOCH s.p. see from
Chanson Des Gueux (B1584)

Les Petiots
solo,pno ENOCH s.p. see from
Chanson Des Gueux (B1585)

Lever Du Jour
solo,pno ENOCH s.p. (B1586)

Marche De Pluie
solo,pno ENOCH s.p. see from
Chanson Des Gueux (B1587)

Parfum Exotique
solo,pno ENOCH s.p. (B1588)

Pauvre Aveugle
solo,pno ENOCH s.p. see from
Chanson Des Gueux (B1589)

Pleine Eau
solo,pno ENOCH s.p. see from
Chanson Des Gueux (B1590)

BIANCHERI, A. (cont'd.)

Ronde
solo,pno ENOCH s.p. see from
Chanson Des Gueux (B1591)

BIANCHINI, GUIDO
In Barcheta
[It] solo,pno SONZOGNO 2603 s.p.
(B1592)

La Perla
[It] solo,pno SONZOGNO 2560 s.p.
(B1593)

Lassime Star
[It] solo,pno SONZOGNO 2808 s.p.
(B1594)

Le Catarigole
[It] solo,pno SONZOGNO 2561 s.p.
(B1595)

Note Del Redentor
[It] solo,pno SONZOGNO 2807 s.p.
(B1596)

Redentor In Famegia
[It] solo,pno SONZOGNO 2602 s.p.
(B1597)

BIANCHINI, V.
Sept Chansons Pour Les Moins De 10
Ans *CC7U
solo,pno DURAND s.p. (B1598)

BIBB
Rondel Of Spring
solo,pno ALLANS s.p. (B1599)

BIBER, HEINRICH IGNAZ FRANZ VON
(1644-1704)
Nisi Dominus Aedificaverit Domum
(Psalm 127) sac
(Steude) [Lat] B solo,vln,cont
DEUTSCHER 9516 s.p. (B1600)

Psalm 127 *see Nisi Dominus
Aedificaverit Domum

Serenade *sac,cant
(Nettl, Paul) B solo,strings,cont
(med) NAGELS 112 $8.50, ipa
(B1601)

BIBLICAL SONGS see Dvorak, Antonin

BIBLICAL SONGS see Dvorak, Antonin

BIBLICAL SONGS see Dvorak, Antonin

BIBLICAL SONGS, VOL. I see Dvorak,
Antonin

BIBLICAL SONGS, VOL. I see Dvorak,
Antonin

BIBLICAL SONGS, VOL. II see Dvorak,
Antonin

BIBLICAL SONGS, VOL. II see Dvorak,
Antonin

BIBLICKE PISNE see Dvorak, Antonin

BIBLISCHE LIEDER see Dvorak, Antonin

BIBLISCHE LIEDER see Dvorak, Antonin

BIBLISCHE SZENEN see Beyer, Frank
Michael

BICINIEN AUS GLAREANS DODEKACHORDON
*CC12U
(Frei, Walter) 2 soli,pno (med)
BAREN. HM 187 $5.50 contains works
by: Dietrich, Sixt; Meyer, Gregor;
Obrecht, Jacob; Vacqueras, Beltram;
Desprez, Josquin (B1602)

BICINIEN HEFT I see Pepping, Ernst

BICINIEN HEFT II see Pepping, Ernst

BICINIEN HEFT III see Pepping, Ernst

BICINIUMS, VOL. 1: JAPANESE SONGS *CCU
(Szonyi, E.) solo,pno BUDAPEST 6648
s.p. (B1603)

BICINIUMS, VOL. 2: AMERICAN AND
CANADIAN FOLK SONGS *CCU
(Szonyi, E.) solo,pno BUDAPEST 6649
s.p. (B1604)

BICK, MOSHE
Jewish Wedding *CCU
solo,pno OR-TAV $1.00 (B1605)

BICKHAM, GEORGE
Musical Entertainer, The, Vols. I &
II *CCU
solo,pno BROUDE BR. $75.00 (B1606)

BID ME DISCOURSE see Bishop, Sir Henry
Rowley

BIDE YE YET *folk,Scot
solo,pno (E flat maj) PATERSON FS10
s.p. (B1607)

BIDING STILL see Willeby, Charles

BIERBAUM-LIEDER see Bordewijk-Roepman, Johanna

BIG BROWN BEAR, THE see Mana-Zucca, Mme.

BIG ROUND-UP see Harding, Harvey

BIG STEAMERS see German, Edward

BIGELOW
 Prepare To Meet Jesus *sac
  solo,pno FINE ARTS CM 1035 $.30
                              (B1608)

BIJ DEN TEMPEL see Sigtenhorst-Meyer, Bernhard van den

BIJ DEN VIJVER see Dresden, Sem

BIJ EEN DODE see Bijvanck, Henk

BIJ EEN DOODE see Badings, Henk

BIJ HET UITLEIDEN VAN ST. NICOLAAS see Loots, Ph.

BIJL, THEO VAN DER (1886-   )
 Avond
  S solo,pno ALSBACH s.p.   (B1609)

 Bakvischjes
  low solo,pno ALSBACH s.p.   (B1610)
  med solo,pno ALSBACH s.p.   (B1611)

 Die Mijns Herte Vrede Zijt
  med solo,pno ALSBACH s.p.   (B1612)
  low solo,pno ALSBACH s.p.   (B1613)

 La Douleur Chretienne
  low solo,2fl,2ob,2clar,2bsn,4horn,
   harp,strings DONEMUS s.p. (B1614)

 Le Convoi D'une Pauvre Fille
  med solo,2fl,3ob,3clar,2bsn,cel,
   harp,strings DONEMUS s.p. (B1615)

 Les Errants
  med solo,2fl,2ob,2clar,2bsn,4horn,
   harp,strings DONEMUS s.p. (B1616)

 Lied Van De Arbeid
  solo,pno ALSBACH s.p.   (B1617)

 Memorare
  med solo,org DONEMUS s.p.   (B1618)

 Moeders Liedje
  med solo,pno ALSBACH s.p.   (B1619)

 Paraat En Cordaat
  solo,pno ALSBACH s.p.   (B1620)

 Priestermorgen
  T solo,org ROSSUM s.p.   (B1621)

 Zu Wem Spreche Ich Heute?
  low solo,2fl,2ob,2clar,3bsn,4horn,
   cel,harp,org,strings DONEMUS s.p.
                              (B1622)

BIJVANCK, HENK (1909-1969)
 Abendrot
  see Drie Liederen Van Eugenie Fink

 Abschied
  see Vijf Liederen Van Bruno Ertler

 Adagio Sostenuto
  see Vier Liederen Van Grete Korber

 All-Leben
  S solo,pno DONEMUS s.p.   (B1623)

 All'mein Gedanken
  see Vijf Liederen

 Am Fluss
  see Vier Chinese Liederen Naar
   Teksten Van Li-Tai-Pe En Schin-
   Schen

 Am Waldessaume
  see Drie Liederen

 An Die Baronin Colombine
  see Drei Balladen

 An Die Entfernte
  see Vier Goethe-Liederen

 Auf Herbstlichem Ast
  see Vier Liederen Van Grete Korber

 Ave Maria
  see Vijf Liederen Van Bruno Ertler

 Bede
  see Twee Liederen Van J. V.D. Waals

 Bij Een Dode
  see Drie Liederen Van Boutens

 Bleibe Bei Mir
  see Vier Goethe-Liederen

BIJVANCK, HENK (cont'd.)
 Botschaft
  see Drie Liederen Van Eugenie Fink

 De Groene Begonia
  see Vier Liederen Van Adama Van
   Scheltema

 De Nachtegaal
  see Vier Liederen Van Adama Van
   Scheltema

 De Stem
  see Vier Liederen Van Adama Van
   Scheltema
  S/T solo,pno DONEMUS s.p.   (B1624)

 De Stilte
  see Vier Duetten

 De Ziel Spreekt
  see Drie Liederen Van Boutens

 Dem Aufgehenden Vollmonde
  see Vier Goethe-Liederen

 Dem Fruhling Zum Willkommen
  see Vier Liederen

 Der Engel
  see Drie Liederen

 Der Fruhling Naht Mit Brausen
  see Vier Duetten

 Der Summittempel
  see Vier Chinese Liederen Naar
   Teksten Van Li-Tai-Pe En Schin-
   Schen

 Die Bestandigen
  see Twee Liederen Van Li-Tai Po

 Die Einsame
  see Vier Chinese Liederen Naar
   Teksten Van Li-Tai-Pe En Schin-
   Schen

 Die Luft Ist Blau
  see Vier Duetten

 Die Mijns Herten Vrede Zijt
  see Twee Liederen Van J. V.D. Waals

 Drei Balladen
  DONEMUS s.p. B solo,pno; T solo,pno
   contains: An Die Baronin
   Colombine; Kophetua; Pierrot
   Pendu   (B1625)

 Drei Lieder (Dramatische Gebete Von
  Eugenie Fink) *CC3U
  med solo,pno DONEMUS s.p.   (B1626)

 Drie Liederen
  S solo,pno DONEMUS s.p.
   contains: Am Waldessaume; Der
   Engel; Waldeinsamkeit   (B1627)

 Drie Liederen Van Boutens
  high solo,pno DONEMUS s.p.
   contains: Bij Een Dode; De Ziel
   Spreekt; Nachtstilte   (B1628)

 Drie Liederen Van Eugenie Fink
  high solo,pno DONEMUS s.p.
   contains: Abendrot; Botschaft;
   Versohnung   (B1629)

 Druben Steht Die Kapelle
  see Vier Duetten

 Duet (Feuchtersleben)
  ST soli,pno DONEMUS s.p.   (B1630)

 Duet (Holty)
  ST soli,pno DONEMUS s.p.   (B1631)

 Dunkle Gaste
  see Twee Liederen Van Chr.
   Morgenstern

 Ehe
  see Zwei Duetten

 Einem Kinde Erzahlt
  S solo,pno DONEMUS s.p.   (B1632)

 Einsame Christnacht
  see Zwei Duetten

 Endloser Ritt
  see Vier Chinese Liederen Naar
   Teksten Van Li-Tai-Pe En Schin-
   Schen

 Es Ist Bestimmt In Gottes Rat
  see Vier Duetten

 Five Songs *CC5U
  S solo,pno DONEMUS s.p.   (B1633)

 Fruhling
  see Vijf Liederen Van Bruno Ertler

BIJVANCK, HENK (cont'd.)
 Fruhlingstag
  see Sonnette An Ead

 Funf Lieder Van Eugenie Fink
  low solo,pno DONEMUS s.p.
   contains: Gegenwart; Heimkehr;
   Spatsommernacht; Und Wisse,
   Dass Ich Tief Und Rauschend
   War; Walder Im Rauhreif   (B1634)

 Gebet
  see Twee Liederen Van Eugenie Fink

 Gegenseitig
  see Vier Goethe-Liederen

 Gegenwart
  see Funf Lieder Van Eugenie Fink

 Gekamde Koning Canteclaer
  see Twee Liederen Van Gezelle

 Gesegnete Stunde
  see Vijf Liederen Van Bruno Ertler

 Gij Badt Op Eenen Berg Alleen
  see Vier Duetten

 Harpzangen Van Koning David
  A/Mez solo,2fl,3ob,3clar,3bsn,
   4horn,3trp,3trom,2tuba,timp,perc,
   2harp,strings DONEMUS s.p.
                              (B1635)

 Heimkehr
  see Funf Lieder Van Eugenie Fink
  see Twee Liederen Van Eugenie Fink

 Ich Geb' Dir Einen Namen
  see Sonnette An Ead

 Im Ewigen Licht
  see Vier Liederen Van Grete Korber
  high solo,pno DONEMUS s.p.   (B1636)
  med solo,pno DONEMUS s.p.   (B1637)

 Ja, Was Willst Du
  see Twee Liederen Van C.
   Fleischlein

 Jung Ist Mein Herz
  S solo,pno DONEMUS s.p.   (B1638)

 Kammermusik
  B solo,pno DONEMUS s.p.   (B1639)

 Kophetua
  see Drei Balladen

 Late Zon
  see Vier Liederen Van Adama Van
   Scheltema

 Lebensdank
  see Bijvanck, Henk, Verzauberte
   Stunde

 Lenzhoffen
  see Twee Liederen Van Schaukal

 Liebe
  see Vier Duetten

 Liebe Ist Duft
  S solo,pno DONEMUS s.p.   (B1640)

 Liebe, Liebster In Der Ferne
  T solo,pno DONEMUS s.p.   (B1641)

 Madonna Van Mantegna
  Mez solo,pno DONEMUS s.p.   (B1642)

 Marchen Der Kindheit
  see Bijvanck, Henk, Verwaites Herz

 Marienstrophe *sac
  S solo,pno DONEMUS s.p.   (B1643)

 Mein Herz Schmuckt Sich Mit Dir
  see Twee Suleikaliederen

 Meine Sehnsucht
  see Bijvanck, Henk, Verwaites Herz

 Morgenstimmung
  see Bijvanck, Henk, Verzauberte
   Stunde

 Nachtstilte
  see Drie Liederen Van Boutens

 Name Gottes *sac
  med solo,pno DONEMUS s.p.   (B1644)

 Nicht Mit Engeln
  see Twee Suleikaliederen

 Nine Songs *CC9U
  Bar solo,pno DONEMUS s.p.   (B1645)

 Nur Der Steht Fest
  see Twee Liederen Van C.
   Fleischlein

BIJVANCK, HENK (cont'd.)

O Friede, Der Nun Alles Fullet
   see Vier Liederen

Pierrot Pendu
   see Drei Balladen

Ritt Durchs Leben
   S solo,pno DONEMUS s.p.   (B1646)

Schwere Tage
   see Vijf Liederen Van Bruno Ertler

Segelfahrt
   see Twee Liederen Van Chr.
   Morgenstern

Seit Du Mir Ferne Bist
   see Vijf Liederen

Sneeuw
   see Twee Liederen Van Gezelle

Sommerneige
   low solo,pno DONEMUS s.p.   (B1647)

Sonnette An Ead
   S solo,pno DONEMUS s.p.
      contains: Fruhlingstag; Ich Geb'
      Dir Einen Namen   (B1648)

Soviel Stern Am Himmel Stehen
   see Vier Duetten

Spatsommernacht
   see Funf Lieder Van Eugenie Fink

Sterne
   see Twee Liederen Van Schaukal

Stunde Der Erfullung
   S solo,pno DONEMUS s.p.   (B1649)

Tien Japanse Impressies, Bd. I *CCU
   DONEMUS s.p. high solo,pno; low
   solo,pno   (B1650)

Tien Japanse Impressies, Bd. II *CCU
   DONEMUS s.p. high solo,pno; med
   solo,pno   (B1651)

Traumwald
   A/Mez solo,pno DONEMUS s.p. (B1652)

Tristizzia
   Bar/B solo,pno DONEMUS s.p. (B1653)

Twee Liederen Van C. Fleischlein
   B/Bar solo,pno DONEMUS s.p.
      contains: Ja, Was Willst Du; Nur
      Der Steht Fest   (B1654)

Twee Liederen Van Chr. Morgenstern
   low solo,pno DONEMUS s.p.
      contains: Dunkle Gaste;
      Segelfahrt   (B1655)

Twee Liederen Van Eugenie Fink
   A solo,pno DONEMUS s.p.
      contains: Gebet; Heimkehr (B1656)

Twee Liederen Van Gezelle
   med solo,pno DONEMUS s.p.
      contains: Gekamde Koning
      Canteclaer; Sneeuw   (B1657)

Twee Liederen Van J. V.D. Waals
   A solo,ob,org DONEMUS s.p.
      contains: Bede; Die Mijns Herten
      Vrede Zijt   (B1658)

Twee Liederen Van Li-Tai Po
   Bar solo,pno DONEMUS s.p.
      contains: Die Bestandigen;
      Wanderer Erwacht In Der
      Herberge   (B1659)

Twee Liederen Van Schaukal
   S solo,pno DONEMUS s.p.
      contains: Lenzhoffen; Sterne
                                    (B1660)

Twee Suleikaliederen
   T solo,pno DONEMUS s.p.
      contains: Mein Herz Schmuckt Sich
      Mit Dir; Nicht Mit Engeln
                                    (B1661)

Two Songs (Sculptures) *CC2U
   Mez solo,pno DONEMUS s.p.   (B1662)

Uber Deine Augenlider
   med solo,pno DONEMUS s.p.   (B1663)

Um Bei Dir Zu Sein
   see Vijf Liederen

Und Wisse, Dass Ich Tief Und
   Rauschend War
   see Funf Lieder Van Eugenie Fink

Verirrt
   S solo,pno DONEMUS s.p.   (B1664)

Versohnung
   see Drie Liederen Van Eugenie Fink

BIJVANCK, HENK (cont'd.)

Verwaites Herz
   A/Mez solo,vcl,pno DONEMUS s.p.
      contains also: Meine Sehnsucht;
      Marchen Der Kindheit   (B1665)

Verzauberte Stunde
   A/Mez solo,vcl,pno DONEMUS s.p.
      contains also: Lebensdank;
      Morgenstimmung   (B1666)

Vier Chinese Liederen Naar Teksten
   Van Li-Tai-Pe En Schin-Schen
   solo,pno DONEMUS s.p.
      contains: Am Fluss; Der
      Summittempel; Die Einsame;
      Endloser Ritt   (B1667)

Vier Duetten
   SS soli,pno DONEMUS s.p.
      contains: De Stilte; Die Luft Ist
      Blau; Gij Badt Op Eenen Berg
      Alleen; Liebe; Soviel Stern Am
      Himmel Stehen   (B1668)

Vier Duetten
   SBar soli,pno DONEMUS s.p.
      contains: Der Fruhling Naht Mit
      Brausen; Druben Steht Die
      Kapelle; Es Ist Bestimmt In
      Gottes Rat   (B1669)

Vier Goethe-Liederen
   T solo,pno DONEMUS s.p.
      contains: An Die Entfernte;
      Bleibe Bei Mir; Dem Aufgehenden
      Vollmonde; Gegenseitig (B1670)

Vier Liederen
   low solo,pno DONEMUS s.p.
      contains: Dem Fruhling Zum
      Willkommen; O Friede, Der Nun
      Alles Fullet; Volksweise; Zu
      Golde Ward Die Welt   (B1671)

Vier Liederen Van Adama Van Scheltema
   high solo,pno DONEMUS s.p.
      contains: De Groene Begonia; De
      Nachtegaal; De Stem; Late Zon
                                    (B1672)

Vier Liederen Van Grete Korber
   A solo,pno DONEMUS s.p.
      contains: Adagio Sostenuto; Auf
      Herbstlichem Ast; Im Ewigen
      Licht   (B1673)

Vijf Liederen
   high solo,pno DONEMUS s.p.
      contains: All'mein Gedanken; Seit
      Du Mir Ferne Bist; Um Bei Dir
      Zu Sein; Weisst Du, Geliebter,
      Allabendlich; Wenn Sanft Du Mir
                                    (B1674)

Vijf Liederen Van Bruno Ertler
   med solo,pno DONEMUS s.p.
      contains: Abschied; Ave Maria;
      Fruhling; Gesegnete Stunde;
      Schwere Tage   (B1675)

Volksweise
   see Vier Liederen

Waldeinsamkeit
   see Drie Liederen

Walder Im Rauhreif
   see Funf Lieder Van Eugenie Fink

Wanderer Erwacht In Der Herberge
   see Twee Liederen Van Li-Tai Po

Wasserfall Bei Nacht
   A/Mez solo,pno DONEMUS s.p. (B1676)

Weisst Du, Geliebter, Allabendlich
   see Vijf Liederen

Wenn Sanft Du Mir
   see Vijf Liederen

Wie Kann Ein Tag...
   S solo,pno DONEMUS s.p.   (B1677)

Zeven Liederen Van Adama Van
   Scheltema *CC7L
   low solo,pno DONEMUS s.p.   (B1678)

Zeven Liederen Van Guido Gezelle
   *CC7L
   high solo,pno DONEMUS s.p.   (B1679)

Zu Golde Ward Die Welt
   see Vier Liederen

Zwei Duetten
   MezBar soli,pno DONEMUS s.p.
      contains: Ehe; Einsame
      Christnacht   (B1680)

BILBAO-SONG see Weill, Kurt

BILDER UND TRAUME *CC41U
   solo,pno BREITKOPF-L EB 7400 $5.00
      contains works by: Agricola; Bach,
      C.P.E.; Beethoven;

Brahms;Meyerbeer; Schumann;
Sibelius; Zechlin and others
                                    (B1681)

BILHAUD, P.
Enjolement
   solo,pno ENOCH s.p.   (B1682)
   solo,acap solo pt ENOCH s.p.
                                    (B1683)

BILL AND JACK see Newton, Ernest

BILL GAITHER TRIO see Gaither, William
J. (Bill)

BILL-STICKER JOE see Day, Maude Craske

BILLEVESEE see Wissmer, Pierre

BILLI
Madonna Fiorentina
   solo,pno FORLIVESI 11292 s.p.
                                    (B1684)
Serenata Delle Rondini
   S/T solo,pno FORLIVESI 11572 s.p.
                                    (B1685)

BILLINGS, WILLIAM (1746-1800)
When Jesus Wept *sac,Gen/Lent
   (Myers, Gordon) med solo,pno
   ABINGDON APM-436 $.75   (B1686)

BILLY see Kemp, David H.

BILLY BOY see Tate, Phyllis

BILLY IN THE DARBIES see Diamond, David

BILLY IN THE DARBIES see Evett, Robert

BILOTTI, ANTON
Old Lad, The
   high solo,pno (D maj) WILLIS $.60
                                    (B1687)
   low solo,pno (C maj) WILLIS $.60
                                    (B1688)
Serenade
   high solo,pno (G maj) WILLIS $.60
                                    (B1689)
   med solo,pno (F maj) WILLIS $.60
                                    (B1690)

BIMBA DAGLI OCCHI PIENI DI MALIA see
Puccini, Giacomo

BIMBA NON PIANGERE see Mascagni, Pietro

BIMBA VUOI TROVAR UN BEL GARZON see
Lehar, Franz

BIMBE MIE, A VENT'ANNI MI PAR DI TORNAR
see Lehar, Franz

BIMBELI BAMBELI see Roelli, H.

BIMKOM HA-ERETZ *folk,Jew
   (Roskin) solo,pno HATIKVAH HCL 32
   $.25   (B1691)

BIN EIN FAHRENDER GESELL see Busoni,
Ferruccio Benvenuto

BIND' AUF DEIN HAAR see Haydn, (Franz)
Joseph

BINDER, ABRAHAM WOLFE (1895-   )
Adonoy Ro-ee *sac,Psalm
   "Lord Is My Shepherd, The" [Heb/
   Eng] high solo,pno TRANSCON.
   TV 561 $.75   (B1692)
   "Lord Is My Shepherd, The" [Heb/
   Eng] med solo,pno TRANSCON.
   TV 562 $.75   (B1693)

All The Pretty Little Horses
   low solo,pno ELKAN-V $.95   (B1694)

Lord, Do Thou Guide Me *sac
   [Eng] med solo,pno TRANSCON. TV 558
   $.75   (B1695)
   [Eng] high solo,pno TRANSCON.
   TV 557 $.75   (B1696)

Lord Is My Shepherd, The *see Adonoy
Ro-ee

Prayer And Supplication *sac,Psalm,
   Jew
   solo,pno/org SAC.MUS.PR. 403
                                    (B1697)
Prayer For Hanukkah, A *sac,Hanakkah
   [Eng] med solo,pno TRANSCON. TV 496
   $.60   (B1698)

BINET, JEAN (1893-1960)
Amour
   solo,orch HENN s.p.   (B1699)
   solo,pno HENN 651 s.p.   (B1700)

Annie
   solo,pno HENN 655 s.p.   (B1701)

Aubade
   solo,pno HENN 657 s.p.   (B1702)

Bergere
   solo,orch HENN s.p.   (B1703)

BINET, JEAN (cont'd.)

Clotilde
solo,pno HENN 656 s.p.   (B1704)

Dix Chansons, Poemes De Jean Cuttat
*CC10U
solo,pno cmplt ed OISEAU s.p.
(B1705)

Ode A Diane Et A Apollon
solo,orch HENN s.p.   (B1706)

Quatre Chansons De Ramuz *CC4U
s.p. solo,pno HENN 652; solo,orch
HENN   (B1707)

Sermon
solo,orch HENN s.p.   (B1708)

Six Chansons Et Dix Chansons, Poemes
De Jean Cuttat *CC6U
solo,orch cmplt ed OISEAU rental
(B1709)

Six Chansons, Poemes De Jean Cuttat
*CC6U
solo,pno cmplt ed OISEAU s.p.
(B1710)

Trois Melodies (Appolinaire) *CC3U
solo,orch HENN s.p.   (B1711)

Trois Melodies De Marot *CC3U
solo,orch HENN s.p.   (B1712)

BINKERD, GORDON (1916-   )
And I Am Old To Know
solo,pno BOOSEY $1.50   (B1713)

Bygone Occasion, A
solo,pno (E maj) BOOSEY $1.50
(B1714)

Fair Morning, The
solo,pno BOOSEY $1.50   (B1715)

Her Definition
solo,pno BOOSEY $1.50   (B1716)

Her Silver Will
solo,pno BOOSEY $1.50   (B1717)

If Thou Wilt Ease Thine Heart
solo,pno BOOSEY $1.50   (B1718)

Lightly Like Music Running
solo,pno BOOSEY $1.50   (B1719)

Mermaid Remembered
solo,pno BOOSEY $1.50   (B1720)

Nursery Ode, A
solo,pno BOOSEY $1.50   (B1721)

One Foot In Eden
solo,pno BOOSEY $1.50   (B1722)

Peace
low solo,pno (G maj) BOOSEY $1.50
(B1723)
high solo,pno (C maj) BOOSEY $1.50
(B1724)

Portrait Interieur *song cycle
Mez solo,vln,vcl BOOSEY voc sc
$3.00, study sc $2.50, ipa
(B1725)

Shut Out That Moon *song cycle
low solo,pno BOOSEY $2.00   (B1726)

Somewhere I Have Never Travelled
solo,pno BOOSEY $1.50   (B1727)

Song Of Praise And Prayer
solo,pno BOOSEY $1.50   (B1728)

Three Songs *CC3U
Mez solo,4strings BOOSEY voc sc
$4.00, study sc $2.50, ipa
(B1729)

What Sweeter Musick
solo,pno BOOSEY $1.50   (B1730)

Wishing-Caps, The
solo,pno BOOSEY $1.50   (B1731)

BINNE BHEUL *Scot
solo,pno PATERSON s.p. see from
Hebridean Songs, Vol. IV   (B1732)

BINNEY, A.
Gingham Dog And Calico Cat
med solo,pno SEESAW $1.50 (B1733)

BIRAGO DIOG, SENEGAL see Leduc, Jacques

BIRAGO DIOP, SENEGAL see Leduc, Jacques

BIRCH, ROBERT FAIRFAX
All Snow *CCU
med solo,pno PRESSER $3.50 (B1734)

Anguished, The
S/Mez/A solo,pno BIRCH $.75 (B1735)

Blessed Be He Who Is Lord *sac
S solo,pno PRESSER $.75   (B1736)
T solo,pno PRESSER $.75   (B1737)
Mez solo,pno PRESSER $.75   (B1738)
A solo,pno PRESSER $.75   (B1739)

BIRCH, ROBERT FAIRFAX (cont'd.)

Bar solo,pno PRESSER $.75 (B1740)

Bugs! *CCU
med solo,pno PRESSER $3.50 (B1741)

Dawn
S solo,pno BIRCH $.75   (B1742)

Death Of The Eagle, The
S/Mez/A solo,pno BIRCH $.75 (B1743)

Desolation
Bar/B solo,pno BIRCH $.75 (B1744)

Elegy
T solo,pno BIRCH $.75   (B1745)

Entreat Me Not To Leave Thee
S/Mez/A solo,pno BIRCH $.75 (B1746)

Epitaph For A Poet
T/Mez/A solo,pno BIRCH $.75 (B1747)

Five Bhartrihari Poems *CC5U
Bar/B solo,pno BIRCH $.75 (B1748)

From The East *CCU
med solo,pno PRESSER $2.50 (B1749)

Full Life, A
Mez/A solo,pno BIRCH $.75 (B1750)
Bar/B solo,pno BIRCH $.75 (B1751)

Grassy Slopes Of Spring, The
S solo,pno BIRCH $.75   (B1752)

Green River, The
S/Mez/A/T/Bar solo,pno BIRCH $.75
(B1753)

Haiku *CCU
med solo,pno PRESSER $3.50 (B1754)

His Voice As The Sound Of The
Dulcimer
S/Mez/A/T/Bar solo,pno BIRCH $.75
(B1755)

How Sleep The Brave
Mez/A/Bar solo,pno BIRCH $.75
(B1756)

I Cannot Love Thee Less Nor More
Bar/B solo,pno BIRCH $.75 (B1757)

I Fear Thy Kisses
Bar/B solo,pno BIRCH $.75 (B1758)

I Long To See A Flower
S solo,pno BIRCH $.75   (B1759)
T solo,pno BIRCH $.75   (B1760)

I Love My Love
Bar solo,pno PRESSER $.75 (B1761)

I Shall Not Return
S/A/Mez/T solo,pno BIRCH $.75
(B1762)

I Want To Be Married
S/Mez/A solo,pno BIRCH $.75 (B1763)

I Will Worship The Lord
S/Mez/A/T/Bar solo,pno BIRCH $.75
(B1764)

If There Were Dreams
S/T solo,pno BIRCH $.75 (B1765)

If Thou Art Sleeping
T solo,pno PRESSER $.75 (B1766)

In The Fields
Mez/A/Bar solo,pno BIRCH $.75
(B1767)

It Is A Beauteous Evening
S/Mez/A/T/Bar solo,pno BIRCH $.75
(B1768)

Lake, The
Mez/A/Bar/B solo,pno BIRCH $.75
(B1769)

Lamentation
S/T solo,pno BIRCH $.75 (B1770)

Lonely Isle, The
Mez/A/T/Bar/B solo,pno BIRCH $.75
(B1771)

Love
S/Mez/A/T/Bar solo,pno BIRCH $.75
(B1772)

Memory, Come Hither
T solo,pno BIRCH $.75   (B1773)
Bar solo,pno BIRCH $.75   (B1774)

Moralist, The
A/Mez/Bar solo,pno BIRCH $.75
(B1775)

Music In Heaven
S solo,pno BIRCH $.75   (B1776)
T solo,pno BIRCH $.75   (B1777)

Music To The Soul
see Birch, Robert Fairfax, Seek Not
There

My Soul Is On My Lips
Bar/B solo,pno BIRCH $.75 (B1778)

BIRCH, ROBERT FAIRFAX (cont'd.)

O Beauty Of Beauty
Bar/B solo,pno BIRCH $.75 (B1779)

O For A Book
S/T solo,pno BIRCH $.75 (B1780)

Old Woman, The
Bar/B solo,pno BIRCH $.75 (B1781)

One More Sky, One More Sea
Mez/A/T solo,pno BIRCH $.75 (B1782)

Orison & Things Eternal
S/Mez/A/T/Bar solo,pno BIRCH $.75
(B1783)

Owl And The Pussy Cat, The
S/Mez/A/T/Bar solo,pno BIRCH $.75
(B1784)

Philosophist, The
Bar/B solo,pno BIRCH $.75 (B1785)

Prayer To Jesus *sac
Mez/A/Bar/B solo,pno BIRCH $.75
(B1786)

Put Out My Eyes
S/T solo,pno BIRCH $.75 (B1787)

Repose
S/Mez/A/T/Bar solo,pno BIRCH $.75
(B1788)

Rhapsodie
T solo,pno BIRCH $.75   (B1789)

River, The
Mez/A/Bar solo,pno BIRCH $.75
(B1790)

Rose Song, The
S solo,pno BIRCH $.75   (B1791)

Roundelay
T solo,pno BIRCH $.75   (B1792)

Seek Not There
S/Mez/A/T/Bar solo,pno BIRCH $.75
contains also: Music To The Soul
(B1793)

Shadow Of The Plum
Mez/A/Bar/B solo,pno BIRCH $.75
(B1794)

Slumber
Mez/A/Bar/B solo,pno BIRCH $.75
(B1795)

Snowfall
S/T/Mez/Bar solo,pno BIRCH $.75
(B1796)

Sonnet
S/T solo,pno BIRCH $.75 (B1797)

Summer Reverie
S/T solo,pno BIRCH $.75 (B1798)

Sweet Are The Moonbeams
S/Mez/A/Bar/T solo,pno PRESSER $.75
(B1799)

Then Falls The Miracle Of Snow
S/T solo,pno BIRCH $.75 (B1800)

There Is Sweet Music
S/Mez/A/T/Bar solo,pno BIRCH $.75
(B1801)

Tranquil Valley
S/Mez/A solo,pno BIRCH $.75 (B1802)

Tuscan Serenade
Mez/A/Bar solo,pno BIRCH $.75
(B1803)

Upon A Child That Died
Mez/A/Bar/B solo,pno BIRCH $.75
(B1804)

Voices
MezBar soli,pno BIRCH $.75 (B1805)

Waning Moon, The *CCU
med solo,pno PRESSER $1.75 (B1806)

Weep You No More
S/Mez/A/Bar solo,pno BIRCH $.75
(B1807)

When Lovely Woman Stoops To Folly
Bar/B solo,pno BIRCH $.75 (B1808)

Where Mortals Dwell
S/T solo,pno BIRCH $.75 (B1809)

White Birch
S/T solo,pno BIRCH $.75 (B1810)

Willow
S/Mez/T/Bar solo,pno BIRCH $.75
(B1811)

Winding Stream Through Yonder Glade
S/T solo,pno BIRCH $.75 (B1812)

Wisdom
S/Mez/A/T/Bar solo,pno PRESSER $.75
(B1813)

Wise Lived Yesterday, The
S/Mez/A/T/Bar solo,pno BIRCH $.75
(B1814)

Woo Not The World
S/Mez/A/Bar solo,pno BIRCH $.75
(B1815)

BIRCHAS KOHANIM see Braslavsky, Solomon G.

BIRCHES see Reif, Paul

BIRD, THE see Duke, John Woods

BIRD AND THE BEAST, THE see Dougherty, Celius

BIRD CAME DOWN THE WALK, A see Weber, Ben

BIRD IN HAND, A see Roeckel, J.L.

BIRD IN THE CHERRY TREE see Tesoriero, Gaetano

BIRD IN THE SKY see Lehmann, Liza

BIRD OF LOVE DIVINE see Wood, Haydn

BIRD OF MORN see Sharpe, Evelyn

BIRD OF ST. BRIDE, THE see Bantock, Granville

BIRD SINGS NOW, A see Mourant, Walter

BIRD-SONG see Head, Michael (Dewar)

BIRD SONG AWAY see Whipp, I.M.

BIRD SONGS see O'Neill, Norman

BIRDIES' BALL see Street, A.

BIRDS see Britten, Benjamin

BIRDS see Edwards, Clara

BIRDS, THE see Davies, Henry Walford

BIRDS, THE see Rowley, Alec

BIRDS, THE see Thiman, Eric Harding

BIRDS ARE SINGING see Roberton, Hugh Stevenson

BIRDS AT WINTER NIGHTFALL see Mallinson, (James) Albert

BIRD'S COURTING SONG see La Montaine, John

BIRDS' COURTING SONG see Sifler, Paul J.

BIRD'S PRAYER see Loam, Arthur S.

BIRD'S SONG (from Pilgrim's Progress) *sac
    S solo,pno (med) OXFORD 62.209 $1.50
                                        (B1816)

BIRD'S SONG see Delius, Frederick

BIRIBU OCCHI DI RANA see Rocca, Lodovico

BIRKE, BEILGETROFFEN see Gretchaninov, Alexander Tikhonovitch, Quand La Hache Tombe

BIRKS OF ABERFELDY, THE *folk,Scot
    solo,pno (B flat maj/D maj) PATERSON
    FS18 s.p.   (B1817)

BIRNBAUM
    Hashkivenu *Rosh Ha-Shanah/Sab-Morn
    (Roskin) [Heb] solo,pno HATIKVAH
    HCL 46 $.35   (B1818)

BIRTH OF LOVE, THE see Carrozzini, D.

BIRTH OF THE KING see Hubbard, H.

BIRTHDAY, A see Coleridge-Taylor, Samuel

BIRTHDAY, A see Woodman, Raymond Huntington

BIRTHDAY MORN, THE see Ronald, Sir Landon

BIRTHDAY OF A KING see Neidlinger, William Harold

BIRTHDAY OF A KING, THE see Neidlinger, William Harold

BIRTHRIGHT see Someran-Godfrey, M. van

BIRTWISTLE, HARRISON (1934-   )
    Cantata *cant
    S solo,inst UNIVER. 15344 $6.25
                                        (B1819)
    Entr'actes Und Sappho Fragments
    S solo,fl,ob,vln,vla,harp,perc
    quarto,sc UNIVER. 12948 $6.25
                                        (B1820)
    Monody For Corpus Christi *sac,
    Corpus
    S solo,fl,vln,horn sc,oct UNIVER.
    12928 $2.75   (B1821)

BIRTWISTLE, HARRISON (cont'd.)

    Ring A Dumb Carillon
    S solo,clar,perc sc UNIVER. 14192
    $4.00   (B1822)

BISCHOFF, PAUL (1935-   )
    If God So Clothe The Grass *sac
    med-low solo,pno (D maj) BOSTON
    $1.50   (B1823)
    solo,pno (available in 3 keys)
    ASHLEY $.95   (B1824)

BISHOP, SIR HENRY ROWLEY (1786-1855)
    Bid Me Discourse
    solo,pno CRAMER   (B1825)
    high solo,pno (G maj) ASHDOWN
                                       (B1826)
    low solo,pno (F maj) ASHDOWN
                                       (B1827)
    Echo Song
    solo,pno,fl LEONARD-ENG   (B1828)
    solo,orch (D maj) ASHDOWN s.p., ipr
                                       (B1829)
    Hogar, Dulce Hogar *see Home, Sweet
    Home

    Home Sweet Home
    low solo,pno (D maj) CRAMER (B1830)
    high solo,pno (F maj) CRAMER
                                       (B1831)
    low solo,pno (E flat maj) LEONARD-
    ENG   (B1832)
    high solo,pno (F maj) LEONARD-ENG
                                       (B1833)
    med solo,pno (E flat maj) CENTURY
    605   (B1834)
    low solo,pno (E flat maj) ASHDOWN
                                       (B1835)
    med solo,pno (E maj) ASHDOWN
                                       (B1836)
    high solo,pno (F maj) ASHDOWN
                                       (B1837)
    med solo,pno (E flat maj) ALLANS
    s.p.   (B1838)
    high solo,pno (F maj) ALLANS s.p.
                                       (B1839)
    "Hogar, Dulce Hogar" [Eng/Span]
    solo,pno RICORDI-ARG BA 8850 s.p.
                                       (B1840)
    "Ljuva Hem" solo,pno GEHRMANS 154
    s.p.   (B1841)

    Ljuva Hem *see Home Sweet Home

    Lo, Here The Gentle Lark
    solo,opt fl CRAMER   (B1842)
    solo,pno (F maj) ASHDOWN   (B1843)
    high solo,pno (F maj) ALLANS s.p.
                                       (B1844)
    (La Forge) high solo,pno (F maj)
    FISCHER,C V 1702   (B1845)

    Love Has Eyes
    high solo,pno (B flat maj) SCHIRM.G
    $.75   (B1846)

    Mocking Bird, The
    solo,pno (D maj) ASHDOWN   (B1847)

    Pilgrim Of Love
    solo,pno CRAMER   (B1848)

    Should He Upbraid
    low solo,pno (F maj) CRAMER (B1849)
    high solo,pno (G maj) CRAMER
                                       (B1850)
    high solo,pno (G maj) SCHIRM.G $.60
                                       (B1851)
    low solo,pno (F maj) ASHDOWN
                                       (B1852)
    high solo,pno (G maj) ASHDOWN
                                       (B1853)
    Tell Me My Heart
    solo,pno CRAMER   (B1854)

    When Green Leaves Come Again
    solo,pno CRAMER   (B1855)

BISKOP THOMAS FRIHETSSANG see Torlind

BISSELL, KEITH W. (1912-   )
    Hymns Of The Chinese Kings *song
    cycle
    high solo,pno WATERLOO $2.50
                                       (B1856)
    Lullaby
    solo,pno THOMP.G   (B1857)
    Overheard On A Salt Marsh
    Mez solo,fl,pno KERBY EK 36 $3.00
                                       (B1858)
    Six Maritime Folksongs, Set 1 *CC6U
    solo,pno BERANDOL BER 1299 $3.50
                                       (B1859)
    Six Maritime Folksongs, Set 2 *CC6U
    solo,pno BERANDOL BER 1300 $3.50
                                       (B1860)
    Two Songs Of Farewell *sec,CC2U
    solo,pno WATERLOO $1.50   (B1861)

BIST DU AUCH MEERE WEIT see Marx, Karl

BIST DU BEI MIR see Bach, Johann Sebastian

BIST MEIN MAZELDIGER MOISHELE *Jew
    solo,pno KAMMEN 465 $1.00   (B1862)

BITGOOD, ROBERTA (1908-   )
    Be Still And Know *sac
    low solo,pno BELWIN $1.50   (B1863)
    med solo,pno BELWIN $1.50   (B1864)
    high solo,pno BELWIN $1.50   (B1865)
    Give Me A Faith *sac
    SA soli,pno BELWIN $1.50   (B1866)
    high solo,pno BELWIN $1.50   (B1867)
    med solo,pno BELWIN $1.50   (B1868)
    low solo,pno BELWIN $1.50   (B1869)
    Greatest Of These Is Love *sac
    high solo,pno BELWIN $1.50   (B1870)
    med solo,pno BELWIN $1.50   (B1871)
    low solo,pno BELWIN $1.50   (B1872)

BITSCH, MARCEL (1921-   )
    Cantonnier Du Roi
    see Trois Chansons Sur Des Poemes
    De Maurice Fombeure

    Chanson De La Belle
    see Trois Chansons Sur Des Poemes
    De Maurice Fombeure

    La Chanson Du Roi D'Angleterre
    see Trois Chansons Sur Des Poemes
    De Maurice Fombeure

    Trois Chansons Sur Des Poemes De
    Maurice Fombeure
    solo,orch LEDUC B.L.77 s.p.
    contains: Cantonnier Du Roi;
        Chanson De La Belle; La Chanson
        Du Roi D'Angleterre   (B1873)

BITTEN see Beethoven, Ludwig van

BITTER LAKE see Zografski, Tomisalv, Gorclivo Ezero

BITTER-SWEET SONG see Kilpinen, Yrio, Das Bittersusse Lied

BITTERAUF, RICHARD
    Von Fruh Bis Spat *CC26U
    solo,pno TONOS 5402 s.p.   (B1874)

BITTERNESS OF LOVE, THE see Dunn, James Philip

BITTERSWEET see Lowthian, Caroline

BITTRA TARAR see Melartin, Erkki, Silloin Mina Itkin

BIXIO
    Torna Piccina
    low solo,pno ALLANS s.p.   (B1875)
    high solo,pno ALLANS s.p.   (B1876)

BIZET, GEORGES (1838-1875)
    A Cette Voix Quel Trouble - Je Crois
    Entendre Encore (from Les
    Pecheurs De Perles)
    [It/Ger] T solo,pno CHOUDENS C353
    s.p.   (B1877)
    [Fr] Bar solo,pno CHOUDENS C381
    s.p.   (B1878)
    [Fr] T solo,pno CHOUDENS C204 s.p.
                                       (B1879)
    A La Voix D'un Amant Fidele (from La
    Jolie Fille De Perth)
    [Fr] T solo,pno CHOUDENS C366 s.p.
                                       (B1880)
    Adieu De L'hotesse Arabe
    [Fr] high solo,pno CHOUDENS C431
    s.p.   (B1881)
    [Fr] med solo,pno CHOUDENS C239
    s.p.   (B1882)
    "Arabian Girl" high solo,pno (A
    maj) CRAMER   (B1883)
    "Arabian Girl" low solo,pno (C maj)
    CRAMER   (B1884)

    Agnus Dei *sac
    Mez solo,pno (D maj) LIENAU HOS 189
    s.p.   (B1885)
    [Lat] Mez solo,pno RICORDI-ARG
    BA 11424 s.p.   (B1886)
    [Lat] S/T solo,pno RICORDI-ARG
    BA 11425 s.p.   (B1887)
    med solo,pno (D maj) ALLANS s.p.
                                       (B1888)
    high solo,pno (F maj) CRAMER s.p.
                                       (B1889)
    low solo,pno (D maj) CRAMER s.p.
                                       (B1890)
    Mez/Bar solo,pno FORLIVESI 11730
    s.p.   (B1891)
    S/T solo,pno FORLIVESI 11729 s.p.
                                       (B1892)
    "Golden Light" low solo,pno (D maj)
    CRAMER   (B1893)
    "Golden Light" high solo,pno (F
    maj) CRAMER   (B1894)
    "Heavenly Father" solo,pno (E flat
    maj) ASHDOWN   (B1895)
    "Lamb Of God" [Lat/Eng] high solo,
    pno MARKS $1.50   (B1896)
    "Lamb Of God" [Lat/Eng] high solo,
    pno (F maj) SCHIRM.G $.85 (B1897)

BIZET, GEORGES (cont'd.)

"Lamb Of God" [Lat/Eng] low solo,
   pno (B flat maj) SCHIRM.G $.85
                                          (B1898)

"Lamb Of God" [Lat/Eng] med solo,
   pno (E flat maj) SCHIRM.G $.85
                                          (B1899)

Ah, Still I Hear It Ringing *see Je
   Crois Entendre Encore

Arabian Girl *see Adieux De
   L'hotesse Arabe

Au Fond Du Temple (from Les Pecheurs
   Du Perles)
   Bar solo,pno sc KALMUS $4.00
                                          (B1900)

Au Fonds Du Temple (from Les Pecheurs
   Du Perles)
   TB soli,2fl,2ob,2clar,2bsn,4horn,
   2trp,3trom,timp,harp,strings
   (French edition) sc CHOUDENS C92
   s.p.   (B1901)
   TB soli,pno (Italian Or German
   Edition) voc sc CHOUDENS C277
   s.p.   (B1902)

Berceuse
   "June Roses" solo,pno CRAMER
                                          (B1903)

Bohemian Love Song (from Carmen)
   solo,pno CRAMER   (B1904)

C'est Des Contrebandiers Le Refuge
   (from Carmen)
   [Fr/It] S solo,pno RICORDI-ARG
   BA 8825 s.p.   (B1905)

C'est Toi! C'est Moi! (from Carmen)
   [Fr] MezT soli,pno CHOUDENS C267
   s.p.   (B1906)

Chanson D'avril
   solo,pno CRAMER   (B1907)

Chanson Du Toreador *see Votre
   Toast, Je Peux Vous Le Rendre

De Mon Amie, Fleur Endormie (from Les
   Pecheurs De Perles)
   [Fr] T solo,pno CHOUDENS C67 s.p.
                                          (B1908)

Douce Mer
   [Fr] high solo,pno CHOUDENS C10
   s.p.   (B1909)

En Vain Pour Eviter Des Reponses
   Ameres (from Carmen)
   [Fr] Mez solo,pno CHOUDENS C64 s.p.
                                          (B1910)

Fair Maid Of Perth, The *see La
   Jolie Fille De Perth

Flower Song *see La Fleur Que Tu
   M'avais Jetee

Golden Light *see Agnus Dei

Habanera (from Carmen)
   [It] low solo,pno (D maj) CRAMER
                                          (B1911)
   [It] high solo,pno (E maj) CRAMER
                                          (B1912)
   [Fr] solo,pno CRAMER   (B1913)
   solo,pno FAZER F 2780 s.p. (B1914)
   "Love The Vagrant" [Eng/Fr] high
   solo,pno (E maj) CRAMER (B1915)
   "Love The Vagrant" [Eng/Fr] low
   solo,pno (D maj) CRAMER (B1916)
   "Love The Vagrant" [Eng] high solo,
   pno (E maj) CRAMER   (B1917)
   "Love The Vagrant" [Eng] low solo,
   pno (D maj) CRAMER   (B1918)

Habanera *see L'Amour Est Un Oiseau
   Rebelle

Heavenly Father *see Agnus Dei

Hor Ich Die Stimme *see Je Crois
   Entendre Encore

In The Woods *see Vieille Chanson

Je Crois Entendre Encore (from Les
   Pecheurs De Perles)
   "Ah, Still I Hear It Ringing" [Fr/
   Eng] T solo,pno (G min) SCHIRM.G
   $.75   (B1919)
   "Hor Ich Die Stimme" [Ger] solo,pno
   SCHAUR EE 3373 s.p.   (B1920)
   "Mi Par D'udir Ancora" [Fr/It] T
   solo,pno RICORDI-ARG BA 10887
   s.p.   (B1921)

Je Dis Que Rien Me M'Epouvante (from
   Carmen)
   [Fr/Eng] S solo,pno (E maj)
   SCHIRM.G $.85   (B1922)

Je Fremis, Je Chancelle (from Les
   Pecheurs Du Perles)
   [Fr] SBar soli,pno CHOUDENS C69
   s.p.   (B1923)

Je Suis Escamillo (from Carmen)
   [Fr] TB soli,pno CHOUDENS C65 s.p.
                                          (B1924)

June Roses *see Berceuse

La Fleur Que Tu M'avais Jetee (from
   Carmen)
   [Fr/It] T solo,pno RICORDI-ARG
   BA 8532 s.p.   (B1925)
   [Fr] T solo,pno CHOUDENS C63 s.p.
                                          (B1926)
   [It/Ger] T solo,pno CHOUDENS C354
   s.p.   (B1927)
   "Flower Song" high solo,pno (D flat
   maj) CRAMER   (B1928)
   "Flower Song" low solo,pno (B flat
   maj) CRAMER   (B1929)
   "Flower Song" high solo,pno (D flat
   maj) ALLANS s.p.   (B1930)
   "Flower Song" solo,pno/orch sc
   KALMUS $3.00   (B1931)
   "Flower Song" med solo,pno (C maj)
   ALLANS s.p.   (B1932)

La Jolie Fille De Perth
   "Fair Maid Of Perth, The" low solo,
   orch (E min) ASHDOWN s.p., ipr
                                          (B1933)
   "Fair Maid Of Perth, The" high
   solo,orch (A min) ASHDOWN s.p.,
   ipr   (B1934)

Lamb Of God *see Agnus Dei

L'amour Est Un Oiseau Rebelle (from
   Carmen)
   [Fr/It] Mez solo,pno RICORDI-ARG
   BA 8536 s.p.   (B1935)
   "Habanera" [Fr/Eng] Mez solo,pno (D
   min) SCHIRM.G $.85   (B1936)
   "Habanera" med solo,pno (D min)
   ALLANS s.p.   (B1937)
   "Habanera" high solo,pno (E min)
   ALLANS s.p.   (B1938)

Le Matin
   [Fr] high solo,pno CHOUDENS C237
   s.p.   (B1939)

Les Tringles Des Sistres Tintaient
   (from Carmen)
   [Fr] Mez solo,pno CHOUDENS C61 s.p.
                                          (B1940)

L'orage S'est Calme (from Les
   Pecheurs De Perles)
   [Fr] Bar solo,pno CHOUDENS C201
   s.p.   (B1941)

Love The Vagrant *see Habanera

Me Voila Seule Dans La Nuit (from Les
   Pecheurs De Perles)
   [Fr] S solo,pno CHOUDENS C66 s.p.
                                          (B1942)
   [Fr] Mez solo,pno CHOUDENS C382
   s.p.   (B1943)
   [It/Ger] S solo,pno CHOUDENS C368
   s.p.   (B1944)

Melons, Coupons! (from Carmen)
   [Fr] SMez soli,pno CHOUDENS C231
   s.p.   (B1945)

Mi Par D'udir Ancora *see Je Crois
   Entendre Encore

Micaelas Aria (from Carmen)
   solo,pno/orch sc KALMUS $3.00
                                          (B1946)

Michaela's Song (from Carmen)
   low solo,pno (C maj) CRAMER (B1947)
   high solo,pno (E flat maj) CRAMER
                                          (B1948)
   [Eng/Fr] solo,pno CRAMER   (B1949)

Nadir, Sprich (from Les Pecheurs De
   Perles)
   [Ger] solo,pno SCHAUR EE 3372 s.p.
                                          (B1950)

Nadirs Romans (from Carmen)
   solo,pno FAZER F 2782 s.p. (B1951)

O Dieu Brahma! (from Les Pecheurs De
   Perles)
   [Fr] S solo,pno CHOUDENS C68 s.p.
                                          (B1952)

Ouvre Ton Coeur
   [Fr] high solo,pno CHOUDENS C57
   s.p.   (B1953)
   [Fr] med solo,pno CHOUDENS C58 s.p.
                                          (B1954)

Par Cet Etoit Sentier (from Les
   Pecheurs Du Perles)
   [Fr] ST soli,pno CHOUDENS C93 s.p.
                                          (B1955)

Parle-Moi De La Mere (from Carmen)
   [Fr] ST soli,pno CHOUDENS C59 s.p.
                                          (B1956)

Pres Des Remparts De Seville (from
   Carmen)
   "Seguidilla" med solo,pno (B min)
   ALLANS s.p.   (B1957)
   "Seguidilla And Duet" solo,pno/orch
   sc KALMUS $3.00   (B1958)

Pres Des Remparts De Seville (from
   Carmen)
   [Fr/It] Mez solo,pno RICORDI-ARG
   BA 8823 s.p.   (B1959)
   "Seguedille" [Fr] Mez solo,pno
   CHOUDENS C60 s.p.   (B1960)
   "Seguedille" [Fr/It/Eng] high solo,
   pno (C sharp min) SCHIRM.G $.85
                                          (B1961)
   "Seguedille" [Eng/Fr] solo,pno
   CRAMER   (B1962)

Quand La Flamme (from La Jolie Fille
   De Perth)
   [Fr] B solo,pno CHOUDENS C435 s.p.
                                          (B1963)

Romance (from Les Pecheurs Du Perles)
   high solo,pno (G maj) ALLANS s.p.
                                          (B1964)
   med solo,pno (F maj) ALLANS s.p.
                                          (B1965)

Romance De Nadir
   solo,pno ASHDOWN   (B1966)

Scene And Habanera (from Carmen)
   solo,pno/orch sc KALMUS $3.00
                                          (B1967)

Seguedille *see Pres Des Remparts De
   Seville

Seguidilla *see Pres Des Remparts De
   Seville

Seguidilla And Duet *see Pres Des
   Ramparts De Seville

Sirs To Your Toast (from Carmen)
   [Eng] low solo,pno (E maj) CRAMER
                                          (B1968)
   [Eng] low solo,pno (E maj,
   simplified version) CRAMER
                                          (B1969)
   [Eng] med solo,pno (F maj) CRAMER
                                          (B1970)
   [Eng] high solo,pno (G maj) CRAMER
                                          (B1971)
   [Fr] low solo,pno (F maj) CRAMER
                                          (B1972)
   [Fr] high solo,pno (G maj) CRAMER
                                          (B1973)
   [Eng/Fr] solo,pno (E maj) CRAMER
                                          (B1974)

Song Of The Toreador *see Votre
   Toast, Je Peux Le Rendre

Tarantelle
   [Fr] S/Mez solo,pno CHOUDENS C20
   s.p.   (B1975)

Toreador Song *see Votre Toast, Je
   Peux Vous Le Rendre

Toreadors Aria *see Votre Toast,
   Je Peux Vous Le Rendre

Toreadorens Sang *see Votre Toast,
   Je Peux Vous Rendre

Torreador Song *see Votre Toast, Je
   Peux Vous Le Rendre

Twenty Songs *CC20U
   [Fr] s.p. high solo,pno CHOUDENS
   C348; med solo,pno CHOUDENS C94
                                          (B1976)

Vieille Chanson
   "In The Woods" high solo,pno (G
   maj) CRAMER   (B1977)
   "In The Woods" low solo,pno (F maj)
   CRAMER   (B1978)

Votre Toast, Je Peux Le Rendre (from
   Carmen)
   "Song Of The Toreador" low solo,pno
   (E maj) ALLANS s.p.   (B1979)
   "Song Of The Toreador" med solo,pno
   (E flat maj) ALLANS s.p. (B1980)
   "Song Of The Toreador" med-high
   solo,pno (F maj) ALLANS s.p.
                                          (B1981)
   "Song Of The Toreador" high solo,
   pno (G maj) ALLANS s.p.   (B1982)

Votre Toast, Je Peux Vous Le Rendre
   (from Carmen)
   [Fr/It] Bar solo,pno RICORDI-ARG
   BA 8824 s.p.   (B1983)
   "Chanson Du Toreador" [Fr/Eng] Bar
   solo,pno (F maj) SCHIRM.G $.85
                                          (B1984)
   "Toreador Song" med solo,pno (A
   min) CENTURY 1577   (B1985)
   "Toreadorens Aria" solo,pno
   LUNDQUIST s.p.   (B1986)
   "Torreador Song" solo,pno/orch sc
   KALMUS $3.00   (B1987)

Votre Toast, Je Peux Vous Rendre
   (from Carmen)
   [Fr] Bar/B solo,pno CHOUDENS C62
   s.p.   (B1988)
   [Fr] T solo,pno CHOUDENS C337 s.p.
                                          (B1989)
   "Toreadorens Sang" solo,pno FAZER

BIZET, GEORGES (cont'd.)

   F 2915 s.p.   (B1990)

BIZZELLI, ANNIBALE
  Canzone Del Sonno
   [It] solo,pno SANTIS 330 s.p.
                      (B1991)
  C'era Una Volta
   [It] solo,pno SANTIS 497 s.p.
                      (B1992)
  La Vispa Teresa
   [It] solo,pno SANTIS 400 s.p.
                      (B1993)
  Tre Canti Di Fukuko *CC3U
   [It] solo,pno SANTIS 119 s.p.
                      (B1994)

BJELINSKI, BRUNO (1909-   )
  Candomble
   S solo,pno,opt perc GERIG HG 1147
   s.p.   (B1995)

  Without Return *song cycle
   [Slav] solo,pno CROATICA s.p.
                      (B1996)

BJERKHAMMAR, SONJA
  Den Varma Viljan
   solo,pno GEHRMANS s.p.   (B1997)

BJERNO, ERLING D.
  Red Hawthorn
   [Dan/Eng] S solo,pno/org EGTVED
   MF 277 s.p.   (B1998)

BJORKANDER
  Grabergets Grona Gata
   solo,pno LUNDQUIST s.p.   (B1999)

BJORKEN BERATTAR see Backer-Grondahl,
  Agathe Ursula

BJORKENS VISA see Raab

BJORNSTRAND, GUNNAR
  Rosorna Forgar
   solo,pno,opt gtr GEHRMANS s.p.
                      (B2000)
BJORNUNGEN see Hannikainen, Vaino,
  Karhunpoika

BLACHER, BORIS (1903-1975)
  Apreslude *Op.57, CC4U
   [Ger] med solo,pno BOTE $2.50
                      (B2001)
  Drei Chansons (from Romeo Und Julia)
   CC3U
   solo,pno UNIVER. 13650 $3.25
                      (B2002)
  Drei Psalmen *CC3U
   [Ger] Bar solo,pno BOTE $5.75
                      (B2003)
  Five Negro Spirituals *CC5U,spir
   med-high solo,3clar,trom,perc,bvl
   sc BOTE $9.25, ipa   (B2004)
  Francesca Da Rimini *Op.47
   [Ger] S solo,vln BOTE $2.75 (B2005)
  Funf Sinnspruche Omars Des
   Zeltmachers *Op.3, CC5U
   [Ger] med solo,pno BOTE $1.25
                      (B2006)
  Jazz-Koloraturen *Op.1, vocalise
   S solo,al-sax,bsn sc BOTE $3.50
                      (B2007)
  Thirteen Ways Of Looking At A
   Blackbird
   [Eng/Ger] high solo,4strings BOTE
   $3.75   (B2008)
  Ungereimtes
   [Ger] med solo,pno BOTE $9.00
                      (B2009)
  Ungereimtes *CC7U
   [Ger] med solo,pno BOTE $6.50
                      (B2010)
  Vier Lieder *Op.25, CC4U
   [Ger] high solo,pno BOTE $2.00
                      (B2011)
  Vier Lieder *CC4U
   [Ger] high solo,pno BOTE $2.50
                      (B2012)
BLACK
  Red Road, The
   high solo,pno (G maj) ALLANS s.p.
                      (B2013)
   low solo,pno (A flat maj) ALLANS
   s.p.   (B2014)
   med solo,pno (E flat maj) ALLANS
   s.p.   (B2015)

BLACK AND WHITE TEARS see Kopelent,
  Marek

BLACK BEADS see DiChiera, David

BLACK CAT see Weigl, Karl

BLACK, CHARLES
  In The Sky A Wondrous Star *sac,Xmas
   high solo,pno BELWIN $1.50 (B2016)

BLACK DRESS, THE see Niles, John Jacob

BLACK EYES see Anonymous

BLACK EYES see Flothius, Marius

BLACK IS THE COLOR see Boatwright,
  Howard

BLACK IS THE COLOR OF MY TRUE LOVE'S
  HAIR
  (Shaw, C.) med solo,pno PRESSER $.95
                      (B2017)
BLACK IS THE COLOR OF MY TRUE LOVE'S
  HAIR see Niles, John Jacob

BLACK IS THE COLOR OF MY TRUE LOVE'S
  HAIR see Sifler, Paul J.

BLACK OAK TREE see Niles

BLACK POOL OF CAT see Hovhaness, Alan

BLACK SONNETT see Harvey, Jonathan

BLACK SWAN, THE see Menotti, Gian Carlo

BLACK SWANS see Musgrave, Dorothy

BLACKBIRD see Collinson

BLACKBIRD IN THE APPLE TREE see
  Lubbock, Mark H.

BLACKBIRD SINGING see Head, Michael
  (Dewar)

BLACKBIRD'S SONG see Scott, Cyril Meir

BLAHA, VACLAV (1921-1959)
  Detske Pisne *CCU
   med solo,pno SUPRAPHON s.p. (B2018)

BLAIR
  Apple Woman
   solo,pno ALLANS s.p.   (B2019)

BLAIR FAIRCHILD
  A La Derive *see Drifting

  Deux Chants Populaires Persans
   [Fr] solo,pno/inst cmplt ed DURAND
   s.p.
    contains: Errant Par La Montagne;
    O Toi Qui Pour Avoir Bu Du Vin
                      (B2020)
  Drifting
   "A La Derive" [Fr/Eng] solo,pno/
   inst DURAND s.p.   (B2021)

  Errant Par La Montagne
   see Deux Chants Populaires Persans

  Huit Poemes Chinois *CC8L
   [Fr/Eng] solo,pno/inst cmplt ed
   DURAND s.p. in 2 keys   (B2022)

  Le Message
   [Fr/Eng] solo,pno/inst DURAND s.p.
                      (B2023)
  O Toi Qui Pour Avoir Bu Du Vin
   see Deux Chants Populaires Persans

BLAIR, K.
  As The Hart Panteth *sac
   high solo,pno BELWIN $1.50 (B2024)

  Love Never Faileth *sac
   high solo/med solo,pno BELWIN $1.50
                      (B2025)
  Thou Wilt Light My Candle *sac
   high solo/med solo,pno BELWIN $1.50
                      (B2026)
BLAKE, DAVID (1936-   )
  In Praise Of Krishna
   S solo,fl,clar,bass clar,horn,harp,
   2vln,vla,vcl NOVELLO rental
                      (B2027)
BLAKE'S CRADLE SONG see Roberton, Hugh
  Stevenson

BLAKLOCKORNA see Korling, Felix

BLANATT see Gulbranson, Eilif

BLANCHARD
  Fill My Cup, Lord *sac
   solo,pno BENSON S5460-R $1.00
                      (B2028)
BLANCHARD, RICHARD
  Fill My Cup, Lord *sac
   solo,pno WORD S-25   (B2029)

  One Perfect Life *sac
   solo,pno WORD S-299   (B2030)

BLANCHARD, ROGER
  Bonjours, Bonsoir Et Bonne Nuit
   [Fr] solo,pno/inst DURAND s.p.
                      (B2031)
  C'est Dans Paris, La Grande Ville
   [Fr] solo,pno/inst DURAND s.p.
                      (B2032)
  Il N'est Dans Paris
   [Fr] solo,pno/inst DURAND s.p.
                      (B2033)

BLANCHARD, ROGER (cont'd.)
  Pour Ninon De Lenclos
   [Fr] solo,pno/inst DURAND s.p.
                      (B2034)
  Pres De Sylvie
   [Fr] solo,pno/inst DURAND s.p.
                      (B2035)
  Souvenir De Sylvie
   [Fr] solo,pno/inst DURAND s.p.
                      (B2036)
BLANCHE COM LYS... see Moulaert,
  Raymond

BLAND
  Carry Me Back To Old Virginny
   low solo,pno (A flat maj) CENTURY
   3038   (B2037)

BLAND, MRS.
  Favorite Song Of Crazy Jane, The
   solo,pno/harp HEUWEKE. 139 s.p.
                      (B2038)

BLAND FJALLEN see Heland

BLAND, HELENA M.
  Stars Are Little Children
   low solo,pno (C maj) CRAMER (B2039)
   high solo,pno (D flat maj) CRAMER
                      (B2040)
BLAND SKOGENS HOGO FURUSTAMMAR see
  Peterson-Berger, (Olof) Wilhelm

BLANDIRE PUERO see Giansetti, Giovanni
  Battista

BLANGINI, GIUSEPPE MARCO MARIA FELICE
  (1781-1841)
  Il Est Parti
   S solo,fl,clar,bsn,2horn CARISH
   s.p.   (B2041)

BLANK, A.
  Escapades *CCU
   solo,2pno PRESSER $1.50   (B2042)

BLANK, ALLAN
  Being *CC3U
   S solo,clar AM.COMP.AL. $3.30
                      (B2043)
  Brown Penny
   med solo,pno AM.COMP.AL. $1.37
                      (B2044)
  Buy Me An Ounce And I'll Sell You A
   Pound
   high solo,pno AM.COMP.AL. $1.37
                      (B2045)
  Cupid And Campaspe
   med solo,pno AM.COMP.AL. $3.30
                      (B2046)
  Don't Let That Horse Eat That Violin
   S solo,bsn sc SEESAW $1.50 (B2047)
   S solo,vln,bsn sc SEESAW $3.00
                      (B2048)
  Down By The Salley Gardens
   med solo,pno AM.COMP.AL. $1.37
                      (B2049)
  Esther's Monologue
   S solo,ob,vla,vcl sc AM.COMP.AL.
   $6.60, ipa   (B2050)
  Falling Of The Leaves, The
   med solo,pno AM.COMP.AL. $1.37
                      (B2051)
  Four Poems By Emily Dickinson *CC4U
   S solo,fl,clar sc AM.COMP.AL. $5.50
                      (B2052)
  In Just
   high solo,pno AM.COMP.AL. $3.30
                      (B2053)
  Legs, The
   med solo,pno sc AM.COMP.AL. $3.30
                      (B2054)
  Pennycandystore Behind The El-S And
   Ban, The
   solo,pno sc SEESAW $2.50   (B2055)
  Pleasures Of Merely Circulating, The
   high solo,pno AM.COMP.AL. $3.30
                      (B2056)
  Simple Day, A
   med solo,pno AM.COMP.AL. $3.30
                      (B2057)
  Six Significant Landscapes *CC6U
   S solo,fl,ob,clar,bsn,horn,trp,
   trom,harp,mand,2perc,vln,vla,vcl,
   bvl AM.COMP.AL. s.p.   (B2058)
  Somewhere I Have Never Travelled
   Mez solo,pno AM.COMP.AL. $3.30
                      (B2059)
  Song Of Huitzilopochtli
   Bar/T solo,pno AM.COMP.AL. $3.85
                      (B2060)
  To An Isle In The Water
   med solo,pno AM.COMP.AL. $1.37
                      (B2061)
BLANTER, M.
  Katioucha
   (Porret, J; Philippe-Gerard) solo,
   pno CHANT s.p.   (B2062)

  Le Soleil S'est Couche Derriere La
   Montagne
   (Kovalenkov) solo,pno CHANT s.p.
                      (B2063)

BLARR, OSKAR GOTTLIEB (1934-   )
Begebenheit
see Thema Weihnachten

Die Botschaft
see Thema Weihnachten

Thema Weihnachten *Xmas
(med diff) sc,solo pt BOSSE BE 289
s.p., ipa
contains: Begebenheit (narrator,
pno,gtr,bvl); Die Botschaft
(solo,pno,bvl); Wenn Das
Vollkommene Kommt (solo,SATB,
sax,trp,pno,bvl)   (B2064)

Wenn Das Vollkommene Kommt
see Thema Weihnachten

BLASIPPAN see Sibelius, Jean

BLASONS FUR SOPRAN see Killmayer,
Wilhelm

BLATNY, PAVEL (1931-   )
Legendy *CCU
high solo&narrator,pno CZECH s.p.
(B2065)
Pisnicky Na Slova Licove Poesie *CCU
high solo,pno CZECH s.p.   (B2066)

BLATTER, ALFRED
Dream Within A Dream, A
T solo,pno MEDIA 3102 $4.50 (B2067)

BLAUE NACHT see Weigl, Karl

BLAUER SOMMER see Strauss, Richard

BLAZEK, VILEM (1900-   )
Psalm 93 *see Zalmy 93

Psalm 100 *see Zalmy 100

Psalm 133 *see Zalmy 133

Psalm 134 *see Zalmy 134

Zalmy 93 (Psalm 93) Op.40,No.3
see Blazek, Vilem, Zalmy 134

Zalmy 100 (Psalm 100) Op.40,No.2
see Blazek, Vilem, Zalmy 134

Zalmy 133 (Psalm 133) Op.40,No.4
see Blazek, Vilem, Zalmy 134

Zalmy 134 (Psalm 134) Op.40,No.1
A solo,2fl,harp CZECH s.p. contains
also: Zalmy 100 (Psalm 100)
Op.40,No.2; Zalmy 93 (Psalm 93)
Op.40,No.3; Zalmy 133 (Psalm 133)
Op.40,No.4   (B2068)

BLAZEK, ZDENEK (1905-   )
Pisne Milostne Pro Tenor A Klavir
*Op.62, CCU
[Czech/Ger] PANTON 224 s.p. (B2069)

Pozehnani Leta *CC4U
solo,pno SUPRAPHON s.p.   (B2070)

BLAZING ROSES see David, Gyula

BLECH, LEO (1905-   )
Bonheur D'aimer
solo,pno ENOCH s.p.   (B2071)

Kinderlieder *Op.21, CCU
high solo,pno UNIVER. 8963 $4.25
(B2072)
La Chanson De Jadis
solo,pno ENOCH s.p.   (B2073)

La Victoire Du Printemps
solo,pno ENOCH s.p.   (B2074)

BLEHERIS see Finney, Ross Lee

BLEIB' BEI MIR see Liljefors, Ruben

BLEIBE see Ehrenberg, Carl Emil Theodor

BLEIBE BEI MIR see Bijvanck, Henk

BLENDINGER, HERBERT
Kammermusik
Bar solo,4strings ORLANDO s.p.
(B2075)
BLESS HIS HOLY NAME see Crouch, Andrae

BLESS, O LORD, THESE RINGS see Roff,
Joseph

BLESS OUR VOWS see Kiecker

BLESS THAT WONDERFUL NAME see Powell

BLESS THE LORD, O MY SOUL see Davis,
Katherine K.

BLESS THE LORD, O MY SOUL see Jordan,
Alice

BLESS THIS HOUSE see Brahe, May H.

BLESS US, GOD OF LOVING *sac,Scot
(Wetzler, Robert) med solo,pno
AUGSBURG 11-0721 $.75   (B2076)

BLESS US, O LORD see Hamblen, Bernard

BLESSED, THE see Peeters, Flor

BLESSED, THE see Wolfe, Jacques

BLESSED ARE THE PURE OF HEART see
Metcalf, John W.

BLESSED ARE THOSE WHO FEAR THE LORD see
Powell, Robert J.

BLESSED ARE THOSE WHO FEAR THE LORD see
Sinzheimer, Max

BLESSED BE HE WHO IS LORD see Birch,
Robert Fairfax

BLESSED DAY see Bach, Johann Sebastian

BLESSED IS HE THAT COMETH see Bach,
Johann Sebastian

BLESSED IS HE WHO WALKS NOT IN THE PATH
OF THE WICKED see Schutz, Heinrich

BLESSED IS THE MAN see Sheriff, Noam,
Ashrei

BLESSED IS THE PEOPLE see Parker,
Clifton

BLESSED JESUS see Faure, Gabriel-
Urbain, Pie Jesu

BLESSED JESUS see Gaither

BLESSED THE MAN see Ashrey Ha-Ish

BLESSED VIRGIN'S EXPOSTULATION see
Purcell, Henry

BLESSING see Curran, Pearl Gildersleeve

BLESSING, THE see Bucky, Frida Sarsen

BLESSINGS see Spross, Charles Gilbert

BLESSINGS OF THE PRIESTS see
Braslavsky, Solomon G., Birchas
Kohanim

BLEST ARE THEY see Lully (Lulli), Jean-
Baptiste

BLEST BE THOSE SWEET REGIONS see
Clarke, Jeremiah

BLEUET see Poulenc, Francis

BLEUS see Chaminade, Cecile

BLICK AUF DIE NATUR see Jez, Jakob,
Pogled Narave

BLICKE MIR NICHT see Mahler, Gustav

BLICKE MIR NICHT IN DER LIEDER see
Mahler, Gustav

BLICKHAN, TIM
Speak Softly
S solo,fl,vibra SEESAW   (B2077)

BLIJDSCHAP see Horst, Anton van der

BLIND see Ireland, John

BLIND BOY FULLER, NO. I see Bank,
Jacques

BLINDENKLAGE see Strauss, Richard

BLISS, PAUL
Come Out, Mr. Sunshine
high solo,pno (D maj) WILLIS $.50
(B2078)
BLISS, SIR ARTHUR (1891-1975)
Angels Of The Mind *song cycle
S solo,pno NOVELLO 17.0275.00 s.p.
(B2079)
Autumn
see Ballads Of The Four Seasons,
The

Auvergnat
high solo,pno NOVELLO 17.0009.10
s.p.   (B2080)

Ballads Of The Four Seasons, The
high solo,pno NOVELLO 17.0227.00
s.p.
contains: Autumn; Spring; Summer;
Winter   (B2081)

Dandelion, The
see Two Nursery Rhymes

BLISS, SIR ARTHUR (cont'd.)
Elegiac Sonnet
T solo,4strings,pno NOVELLO
17.0114.02 s.p.   (B2082)

Enchantress, The *scena
A solo,pno NOVELLO 17.0050.02 s.p.
(B2083)
A solo,2fl,pic,ob,4horn,2trp,3trom,
timp,perc,harp,strings NOVELLO
rental   (B2084)

Knot Of Riddles, A *CC7L
Bar solo,fl,ob,clar,bsn,horn,harp,
strings cmplt ed NOVELLO rental,
sc NOVELLO 17.0228.09 s.p.
(B2085)
Many A Girl Of The South Is White And
Lucent
see Women Of Yueh, The

Ragwort, The
see Two Nursery Rhymes

Sea Love
high solo,pno NOVELLO 17.0162.02
s.p.   (B2086)

Seven American Poems *CC7U
low solo,pno BOOSEY $4.50   (B2087)

She, A Tungyang Girl
see Women Of Yueh, The

She Is A Southern Girl
see Women Of Yueh, The

She Is Gathering Lotus Buds
see Women Of Yueh, The

Spring
see Ballads Of The Four Seasons,
The

Summer
see Ballads Of The Four Seasons,
The

Two Nursery Rhymes
[Eng] cmplt ed CHESTER s.p.
contains: Dandelion, The (S solo,
clar/vla); Ragwort, The (S
solo,clar/vla,pno)   (B2088)

Water Of The Mirror Lake, The
see Women Of Yueh, The

Winter
see Ballads Of The Four Seasons,
The

Women Of Yueh, The
[Eng] high solo,kbd CHESTER s.p.
contains: Many A Girl Of The
South Is White And Lucent; She,
A Tungyang Girl; She Is A
Southern Girl; She Is Gathering
Lotus Buds; Water Of The Mirror
Lake, The   (B2089)

BLISSFUL LAND see Chajes, Julius

BLITCH'S PRAYER OF REPENTANCE see
Floyd, Carlisle

BLIZKY HLAS see Podesva, Jaromir

BLOCH, AUGUSTYN (1929-   )
C'est En L'Avril
solo,pno ENOCH s.p.   (B2090)

Cloches Du Soir
solo,pno ENOCH s.p.   (B2091)

La Poule
[Fr] high solo,pno ESCHIG $2.25
(B2092)
Lai Louli
solo,pno ENOCH s.p.   (B2093)

Salmo Gioioso *sac,Psalm
S solo,5brass SCHOTTS 6059 s.p.
(B2094)
BLOCH, ERNEST (1880-1959)
Complainte
[Fr] Mez/Bar solo,pno ESCHIG $2.50
see from Historiettes Au
Crepuscule   (B2095)

Historiettes Au Crepuscule *see
Complainte; Legende; Les Fleurs;
Ronde   (B2096)

Legende
[Fr] Mez/Bar solo,pno ESCHIG $2.50
see from Historiettes Au
Crepuscule   (B2097)

Les Fleurs
[Fr] S solo,pno ESCHIG $2.25 see
from Historiettes Au Crepuscule
(B2098)
Psalm 22 *sac
[Fr/Eng] Bar/A solo,pno (D min)
SCHIRM.G $1.75   (B2099)

BLOCH, ERNEST (cont'd.)

  Psalm 114 *sac
    [Fr/Eng] high solo,pno (D maj)
      SCHIRM.G $1.00   (B2100)

  Ronde
    [Fr] Mez/Bar solo,pno ESCHIG $2.25
      see from Historiettes Au
      Crepuscule   (B2101)

BLOCH, WALDEMAR (1906-   )
  Matutin
    S solo,org DOBLINGER 08 860 s.p.
                      (B2102)

BLOCK SONGS see Anderson, Thomas J.

BLOEMPJES' ONTWAKEN see Colaco Osorio-
  Swaab, Reine

BLOESEMVAL see Devreese, Godefroid,
  Petales

BLOMMANS ODE see Sibelius, Jean

BLOMME see Mulder, Ernest W.

BLOMMORNA see Holmquist, Nils-Gustaf

BLOMMORNAS BOK see Liljefors, Ruben

BLOMSTERFLICKAN see Pergament, Moses

BLOMSTRING see Norman, Ludvig

BLOMSTRINGEN see Dannstrom, Isidor

BLONDE AUX YEUX DE PERVENCHE see
  Chabrier, Emmanuel

BLONDJE see Zagwijn, Henri

BLOOD THAT STAINED THE OLD RUGGED
  CROSS, THE *sac,gospel
  solo,pno ABER.GRP. $1.50   (B2103)

BLOOD WILL NEVER LOSE ITS POWER, THE
  see Crouch, Andrae

BLOSSOM, THE see Dukelsky, Vladimir

BLOSSOM TIME see Sharpe, Evelyn

BLOTT EN DAG, ETT OGONBLICK I SANDER
  see Andliga Sanger, Heft 2
  (Holm, Gunnar) solo,pno/org ERIKS
    s.p. contains also: Herren Star Vid
    Hjartats Dorr; Var Ar Mitt Vilsna
    Barn I Kvall; Vem Klappar Sa Sakta
    I Aftonens Frid; Tank, Nar En Gang
    Dimman Ar Forsvunnen; Nar Dagen
    Lyktat Har Sin Gang   (B2104)

BLOUNT
  It Was For Me *sac
    med solo,pno (A flat maj) ALLANS
      s.p.   (B2105)
    high solo,pno (B flat maj) ALLANS
      s.p.   (B2106)
    low solo,pno (F maj) ALLANS s.p.
                      (B2107)

BLOW BLOW THOU WINTER WIND see Amram,
  David Werner

BLOW, BLOW, THOU WINTER WIND see
  Castelnuovo-Tedesco, Mario

BLOW, BLOW, THOU WINTER WIND see
  Danyel, John

BLOW, BLOW, THOU WINTER WIND see
  Quilter, Roger

BLOW, BLOW THOU WINTER WIND see
  Russell, W.

BLOW, BLOW, THOU WINTER WIND see
  Sarjeant, J.

BLOW, JOHN (1649-1708)
  Ah Heav'n! What Is't I Hear?
    "O Himmel! Was Hort Mein Sinn?"
    [Eng/Ger] SS soli,pno SCHOTTS
    VK 30 s.p. see from Amphion
    Angelicus   (B2108)

  Amphion Angelicus *see Ah Heav'n!
    What Is't I Hear?, "O Himmel! Was
    Hort Mein Sinn?"   (B2109)

  Amphion Anglicus *CCU
    1-4 soli,inst BROUDE BR. $22.50
                      (B2110)

  O Himmel! Was Hort Mein Sinn? *see
    Ah Heav'n! What Is't I Hear?

  O Wurde Celia Mich Versteh'n
    [Eng/Ger] 2 soli,pno SCHOTTS VK 29
      s.p.   (B2111)

  Self Banished, The
    [Eng] high solo,pno SCHOTTS VK 24
      s.p.   (B2112)
    [Eng] low solo,pno SCHOTTS VK 24
      s.p.   (B2113)

BLOW, JOHN (cont'd.)

  Trois Chansons 2 (from Amphion
    Anglicus) CC3U
    solo,pno cmplt ed,cloth,min sc
      OISEAU s.p.   (B2114)

BLOW ME EYES see Malotte, Albert Hay

BLOW THE WIND SOUTHERLY *folk
  (Moore, Gerald) high solo,pno UNIVER.
    12316 $.75   (B2115)
  (Moore, Gerald) med solo,pno UNIVER.
    12316 $.75   (B2116)
  (Whittaker, W.G.) solo,pno (G maj)
    ROBERTON 2788 s.p.   (B2117)

BLOW, YE WINDS see Dougherty, Celius

BLOWER, MAURICE
  Mamble
    2 soli,pno ROBERTON 72365 s.p.
                    (B2118)

  My Early Home
    3 soli,pno ROBERTON 72648 s.p.
                    (B2119)

BLOWS THE WIND see Simpson, Donald

BLUE BELLS OF SCOTLAND, THE *folk,Scot
  solo,pno (E flat maj/F maj) PATERSON
    FS8 s.p.   (B2120)

BLUE BONNETS OVER THE BORDER *folk,
  Scot
  solo,pno (G maj) PATERSON FS11 s.p.
                    (B2121)

BLUE BOWS see Buck

BLUE DANUBE see Strauss, Johann, An Der
  Schonen Blauen Donau

BLUE DANUBE, THE see Strauss, Johann,
  An Der Schonen Blauen Donau

BLUE HILLS OF ANTRIM see Harty, Sir
  Hamilton

BLUE MOUNTAIN BALLADS see Bowles, Paul
  Frederic

BLUE NIGHT see Weigl, Karl, Blaue Nacht

BLUE TRAIN see Gorney, Jay

BLUE WATER see Rowley, Alec

BLUEBIRD see Schirmer, Rudolph [E.]

BLUES DES BETTELKINDES see Svobodo,
  Jiri, Blues Zebraveho Ditete

BLUES ZEBRAVEHO DITETE see Svobodo,
  Jiri

BLUM, ROBERT (1900-   )
  Der Streiter In Christo Jesu *sac,
    cant
    S solo,trp,perc,pno,strings MODERN
      s.p.   (B2122)

BLUME
  Ein Frischer Strauss *CC7U
    [Ger] med solo,pno,gtr NOETZEL N711
      s.p.   (B2123)

BLUMEN see Hurnik, Ilja

BLUMENFELD, HAROLD
  Lovescapes
    S solo,5winds,3strings sc SEESAW
      $19.00   (B2124)

BLUMENTHAL, JACOB (JACQUES) (1829-1908)
  In Venezia
    2 soli,pno CRAMER   (B2125)

  My Queen
    low solo,pno (C maj) CRAMER (B2126)
    med solo,pno (D maj) CRAMER (B2127)
    high solo,pno (E maj) CRAMER
                    (B2128)

  Venetian Boat Song
    low solo,pno (B flat maj) CRAMER
                    (B2129)
    high solo,pno (D maj) CRAMER
                    (B2130)
    2 soli,pno CRAMER   (B2131)

BLUMLEIN IM THAL see Godard, Benjamin
  Louis Paul, Fleur Du Vallon

BLYTHE AND MERRY WAS SHE
  (Scott) solo,pno ELKIN 27.1268.07
    s.p.   (B2132)

BLYTHE, BLYTHE AND MERRY WAS SHE
  *folk,Scot
  solo,pno (B flat maj/D maj) PATERSON
    FS12 s.p.   (B2133)

BLYTON, CAREY (1932-   )
  Bacon And Eggs
    see Three Food Songs

BLYTON, CAREY (cont'd.)

  Cormorant, The
    see Three Bird Songs

  Early Bacon
    see Three Food Songs

  Elephant, The
    see Three Bird Songs

  Poetry Of Dress - Three Songs *CC3U
    T solo,pno BELWIN $2.00   (B2134)

  Poor Fly
    see Three Insect Songs

  Sink Song
    see Three Food Songs

  Stork, The
    see Three Bird Songs

  Swat A Life
    see Three Insect Songs

  Taking The Veil
    see Three Insect Songs

  Three Bird Songs
    solo,pno ROBERTON 6503 s.p.
      contains: Cormorant, The;
      Elephant, The; Stork, The
                    (B2135)

  Three Food Songs
    solo,pno ROBERTON 6501 s.p.
      contains: Bacon And Eggs; Early
      Bacon; Sink Song   (B2136)

  Three Insect Songs
    solo,pno ROBERTON 6502 s.p.
      contains: Poor Fly; Swat A Life;
      Taking The Veil   (B2137)

BOANAS
  Daffodils From My Garden
    low solo,pno (E flat maj) ALLANS
      s.p.   (B2138)
    high solo,pno (F maj) ALLANS s.p.
                    (B2139)

BOARDMAN, E.
  Feed My Sheep *sac
    med solo,pno (G maj) BOSTON $1.50
                    (B2140)

  O'er Waiting Harp Strings Of The Mind
    *sac
    med solo,pno (C maj) BOSTON $1.50
                    (B2141)

BOARDMAN, REGINALD
  Christmas Morn *sac,Xmas,hymn
    solo,pno BRANDEN $.90   (B2142)

  Communion Hymn *sac,hymn
    solo,pno BRANDEN $.90   (B2143)

  Eden Revisited
    high solo,pno BRANDEN $.75 (B2144)
    low solo,pno BRANDEN $.75 (B2145)

  Feed My Sheep *sac,hymn
    solo,pno BRANDEN $.90   (B2146)

  Love *sac,hymn
    solo,pno BRANDEN $.90   (B2147)

  O Gentle Presence *sac,hymn
    solo,pno BRANDEN $.90   (B2148)

  Satisfied *sac,hymn
    solo,pno BRANDEN $.90   (B2149)

BOAT SONG see Cooke, S.C.

BOAT SONG see Cory, George

BOAT SONG see Redden, Finvola

BOATIE ROWS, THE *folk,Scot
  solo,pno (C maj/D maj) PATERSON FS16
    s.p.   (B2150)

BOATING SONG OF THE YO EH see
  Whitehead, Percy A.

BOATNER, EDWARD H. (1898-   )
  I Want Jesus To Walk With Me *sac
    high solo,pno GALAXY 1.1008.7 $1.00
                    (B2151)
    low solo,pno GALAXY 1.1361.7 $1.00
                    (B2152)

  Trampin
    high solo,pno GALAXY 1.1622.7 $1.00
                    (B2153)
    low solo,pno GALAXY 1.1623.7 $1.00
                    (B2154)

BOATS OF MINE see Miller

BOATWRIGHT, HOWARD (1918-   )
  Black Is The Color
    Mez solo,vln (easy) OXFORD 96.004
      s.p.   (B2155)

  Cock Robin
    Mez solo,rec (easy) OXFORD 96.002
      s.p.   (B2156)

BOATWRIGHT, HOWARD (cont'd.)

False Knight
solo,pno OXFORD s.p.   (B2157)

Grant Us Peace *sac,Jew
high solo&med solo,pno/org
SAC.MUS.PR. 411   (B2158)

Gypsie Laddie
Mez solo,2treb inst (easy) OXFORD
96.003 s.p.   (B2159)

O Waly Waly
Mez/Bar solo,pno (easy) OXFORD
96.201   (B2160)

One Morning In May
Mez solo,vln (easy) OXFORD 96.005
s.p.   (B2161)

Sinner Man
solo,pno OXFORD s.p.   (B2162)

BOBERG
Nar Jag Blir Gammal
solo,pno LUNDQUIST s.p.   (B2163)

BOCCHERINI, LUIGI (1743-1805)
Cujus Animam *sac
[Lat] S solo,strings CARISH s.p.   (B2164)

BOCK, BLANCH KERR
Beyond The Sunset *sac
solo,pno WORD S-124   (B2165)

BOCK, FRED (1939-   )
One Solitary Life *sac
solo,pno BENSON S7303-R $1.00   (B2166)

When Adam Was Created
med solo,pno MERCURY $1.25   (B2167)

BODA, JOHN (1922-   )
Before The Paling Of The Stars *sac
med solo,pno oct CONCORDIA 98-1566
$.25   (B2168)

BODDECKER, PHILIPP FRIEDRICH
(1683- ?)
Natus Est Jesus *sac,Xmas,concerto
"Weihnachtskonzert" [Lat/Ger] high
solo,pno,opt vcl NAGELS $.90   (B2169)
(Behrend, Siegfried) solo,gtr
ZIMMER. 1899 s.p.   (B2170)
(Rodemann, Albert) [Lat/Ger/Eng] S
solo,cont (med) NAGELS 57 $5.00   (B2171)
Weihnachtskonzert *see Natus Est
Jesus

BOEDIJN, GERARD H. (1893-   )
Dank *Op.101,No.3
see Drie Liederen

Drie Liederen
high solo,pno DONEMUS s.p.
contains: Dank, Op.101,No.3;
November, Op.101,No.1;
Offerande, Op.101,No.2 (B2172)

In Nachtschaduw *Op.94
Bar solo,fl,ob,clar,bsn,2horn,trp,
timp,perc,strings DONEMUS s.p.   (B2173)

November *Op.101,No.1
see Drie Liederen

Offerande *Op.101,No.2
see Drie Liederen

Twee Kerstliederen Uit Horae Belgicae
*Op.107, CC2U
S solo,pno DONEMUS s.p.   (B2174)

BOELLMANN, LEON (1862-1897)
Hear Us, Our Father
(Norden, N. L.) S/T solo,org,vln/
harp/pno BELWIN $1.50   (B2175)

BOER, JAN DEN (1932-   )
Chant D'un Fantassin
solo,pno DONEMUS s.p.   (B2176)

Rondeaux Amoureux
solo,2fl,2ob,clar,2bsn,2horn,2trp,
timp,strings DONEMUS s.p. (B2177)
solo,pno DONEMUS s.p.   (B2178)

BOERECHARLESTON see Lilien, Ignace

BOERO, FELIPE (1884-1958)
El Dia Inutil
[Span] solo,pno RICORDI-ARG
BA 10655 s.p.   (B2179)

El Mate Amargo
[Span] solo,pno RICORDI-ARG
BA 10732 s.p.   (B2180)

Funeral Coya
[Span] solo,pno RICORDI-ARG
BA 11032 s.p.   (B2181)

BOERO, FELIPE (cont'd.)

Invierno
[Span] solo,pno RICORDI-ARG
BA 11383 s.p.   (B2182)

La Pasionaria
[Span] solo,pno RICORDI-ARG BA 8501
s.p.   (B2183)

La Ruina Y El Viento
[Span] solo,pno RICORDI-ARG BA 7696
s.p.   (B2184)

Vidalita
[Span] solo,pno RICORDI-ARG BA 7465
s.p.   (B2185)

BOGENSCHUTZEN see Reutter, Hermann

BOHAC, JOSEF (1929-   )
Jasminbluten *see Kvety Jasminu

Kvety Jasminu *song cycle
"Jasminbluten" S solo,pno CZECH
s.p.   (B2186)

BOHEMIA see Ralf, Einar

BOHEMIAN LOVE SONG see Bizet, Georges

BOHM, CARL
Calm As The Night *see Still Wie Die
Nacht

Comme La Nuit *see Still Wie Die
Nacht

Din Karlek *see Still Wie Die Nacht

Lacrimae Christi
Bar solo,pno SCHAUR EE 3404A s.p.   (B2187)

B solo,pno SCHAUR EE 3404B s.p.   (B2188)

Still As The Night *see Still Wie
Die Nacht

Still Wie Die Nacht
"Calm As The Night" [Ger/Eng] med
solo,pno (D flat maj) SCHIRM.G
$.85   (B2189)
"Calm As The Night" [Ger/Eng] high
solo,pno (E flat maj) SCHIRM.G
$.85   (B2190)
"Calm As The Night" [Ger/Eng] low
solo,pno (B flat maj) SCHIRM.G
$.85   (B2191)
"Comme La Nuit" [Ger/Fr/Eng] S/T
solo,vln RICORDI-ARG BA 6579 s.p.   (B2192)
"Din Karlek" solo,pno GEHRMANS 178
s.p.   (B2193)
"Still As The Night" high solo,pno
SCHAUR EE 3401A s.p.   (B2194)
"Still As The Night" med solo,pno
SCHAUR EE 3401B s.p.   (B2195)
"Still As The Night" low solo,pno
SCHAUR EE 3401C s.p.   (B2196)
"Still As The Night" med solo,pno
(B flat maj) CENTURY 97   (B2197)
"Still As The Night" high solo,pno
(D flat maj) ALLANS s.p.   (B2198)
"Still As The Night" 2 soli,pno
ALLANS s.p.   (B2199)
"Still As The Night" low solo,pno
(B flat maj) ALLANS s.p.   (B2200)
"Still As The Night" med solo,pno
(C maj) ALLANS s.p.   (B2201)
"Still As The Night" [Ger/Eng] 2
soli,pno SCHAUR EE 3402 s.p.   (B2202)

S'Zuschaun
high solo,pno SCHAUR EE 3405A s.p.   (B2203)
low solo,pno SCHAUR EE 3405B s.p.   (B2204)

Was I Hab' *Op.326,No.12
"What I Have" solo,pno SCHAUR
EE 3406 s.p.   (B2205)

What I Have *see Was I Hab'

BOHUN, LYLE DE
Beyond The Stars
S solo,pno ARSIS   (B2206)

Celestia
S solo,pno ARSIS   (B2207)

Fantasia
solo,pno ARSIS   (B2208)

Goodnight Kiss
solo,pno ARSIS   (B2209)

Mirrored Love
solo,pno ARSIS   (B2210)

Sea Thoughts
solo,pno ARSIS   (B2211)

Slumber Song
solo,treb inst ARSIS   (B2212)

BOHUN, LYLE DE (cont'd.)

Songs Of Estrangement *song cycle
S solo,4strings cmplt ed ARSIS   (B2213)

Time Cannot Claim This Hour
solo,pno ARSIS   (B2214)

BOIKO, R.
Romances *CCU
[Russ] solo,pno MEZ KNIGA 2.88 s.p.   (B2215)

BOIS EPAIS
(Lehmann, Amelia) low solo,pno (E
flat maj) BOOSEY $1.25   (B2216)
(Lehmann, Amelia) high solo,pno (F
maj) BOOSEY $1.25   (B2217)

BOIS EPAIS see Liszt, Franz

BOIS EPAIS see Lully (Lulli), Jean-
Baptiste

BOIS, ROB DU (1934-   )
Drei Traurige Tanze *CC3U
A solo,strings DONEMUS s.p. (B2218)

Eine Rede
S solo,clar,bass clar, basset horn
DONEMUS s.p.   (B2219)

Inferno
S solo,2vln,vcl,hpsd DONEMUS s.p.   (B2220)

Les Voyages De Gulliver *CC4U
Mez solo,pno DONEMUS s.p. (B2221)

Pour Faire Chanter La Polonaise
S solo,fl,3pno DONEMUS s.p. (B2222)

Songs Of Innocence *CCU
T&countertenor,rec,bvl DONEMUS s.p.   (B2223)

Une Facon De Dire Que Les Hommes De
Cent-Vingt Ans Ne Chantent Plus
S solo,pno,2maracas,tamb, glass
chimes DONEMUS s.p.   (B2224)

Words
Mez solo,fl,vcl,pno DONEMUS s.p.   (B2225)

Zwanzig Lieder *CC20U
solo,pno DONEMUS s.p.   (B2226)

BOISDEFFRE, CHARLES-HENRI-RENE DE
(1838-1906)
L'Aube
solo,pno (available in 2 keys)
ENOCH s.p.   (B2227)
solo,acap solo pt ENOCH s.p.   (B2228)

Le Chant Du Patre
solo,pno (available in 2 keys)
ENOCH s.p.   (B2229)

Les Roses De Nazareth *sac
solo,pno ENOCH s.p.   (B2230)
[Fr] solo,pno (available in 2 keys)
ENOCH   (B2231)

Sonnet A La Vierge Marie *sac
solo,pno (available in 2 keys)
ENOCH s.p.   (B2232)
[Fr] solo,pno (available in 2 keys)
ENOCH   (B2233)

BOITO, ARRIGO (1842-1918)
Dai Campi, Dai Prati (from
Mefistofele)
[It] T solo,pno RICORDI-ARG
BA 11780 s.p.   (B2234)
T solo,pno RICORDI-ENG 44698 s.p.   (B2235)

Ecco Il Mondo (from Mefistofele)
B solo,pno RICORDI-ENG 126439 s.p.   (B2236)

Giunto Sul Passo Estremo (from
Mefistofele)
[It] T solo,pno RICORDI-ARG BA 8516
s.p.   (B2237)
T solo,pno RICORDI-ENG 44776 s.p.   (B2238)

L'altra Notte In Fondo Al Mare (from
Mefistofele)
[It] S solo,pno RICORDI-ARG BA 8515
s.p.   (B2239)
S solo,pno RICORDI-ENG 44700 s.p.   (B2240)
[It/Eng] S solo,pno INTERNAT. $1.00   (B2241)

Lontano, Lontano (from Mefistofele)
ST soli,pno RICORDI-ENG 44701 s.p.   (B2242)

Son Io Spirito Che Nega (from
Mefistofele)
B solo,pno RICORDI-ENG 44699 s.p.   (B2243)

BOIVIE
Karin Mansdotters Vaggvisa
solo,pno LUNDQUIST s.p.   (B2244)

BOJE see Prosev, Toma

BOLERAS see Ferandiere, F.

BOLJEBYVALS see Peterson-Berger, (Olof) Wilhelm

BOLLBACH, HARRY
Ring The Bells   *sac
solo,pno SINGSPIR 7082 $1.00
(B2245)

BOLLSPELET VID TRAINON see Sibelius, Jean

BOLLSPELET VID TRIANON see Sibelius, Jean

BOLOGNA, JACOPO DA
see JACOPO DA BOLOGNA

BOL'S SONG see Jensen, Ludwig Irgens

BON see Beck, Thomas [Ludvigsen]

BON see Eklof, Einar

BON see Nordqvist, Gustaf

BON see Sanner

BON see Wohlfart, Karl

BON FOR DEN ELSKEDE see Kjerulf, [Halfdan]

BON I OFREDSTID see Nordqvist, Gustaf

BON JOUR, MA BELLE see Behrend, Siegfried

BON, MAARTEN (1933-   )
Crystal Against Mirror   *see Kristal Tegen Spiegel

Kristal Tegen Spiegel
"Crystal Against Mirror" narrator, fl,clar,vcl,pno DONEMUS s.p.
(B2246)

BON VIN DONNE VIGUEUR see Vredenburg, Max

BON, WILLEM FREDERIK (1940-   )
Jadis Et Naguere   *CC3U
Mez solo,clar,vln,pno DONEMUS s.p.
(B2247)
Quatre Propheties De Nostradamus: "1999"   *CC4U
S solo,2fl,2ob,3clar,2bsn,4horn, 3trp,3trom,timp,3perc,harp,pno, strings DONEMUS s.p.   (B2248)

BONAVIST' HARBOR
see Five Canadian Folk Songs

BONAY
Priere Nuptiale   *Marriage
solo,org/pno,vln/vcl GRAS s.p.
(B2249)

BOND, ANDREWS
Vulcan
low solo,pno (D min) CRAMER $.90
(B2250)
high solo,pno (E min) CRAMER $1.15
(B2251)

BOND, CARRIE JACOBS (1862-1946)
Golden Key, The
med-high solo,pno (F maj) BOSTON $1.50
(B2252)

I Love You Truly   *Marriage
med-low solo,pno (F maj) BOSTON $1.50
(B2253)
low solo,pno (E flat maj) BOSTON $1.50
(B2254)
high solo,pno (B flat maj) BOSTON $1.50
(B2255)
med-high solo,pno (A flat maj) BOSTON $1.50
(B2256)
BarA soli,pno BOSTON $1.75 (B2257)
high solo,pno FISCHER,C S 7670
(B2258)
med-high solo,pno FISCHER,C S 7671
(B2259)
med-low solo,pno FISCHER,C S 7672
(B2260)
low solo,pno FISCHER,C S 7673
(B2261)
solo,pno,opt vln (available in 4 keys) ASHLEY $.95   (B2262)
low solo,pno,vln (E flat maj) WILLIS $.35
(B2263)
med-high solo,pno,vln (A flat maj) WILLIS $.35
(B2264)
med-low solo,pno,vln (F maj) WILLIS $.35
(B2265)
high solo,pno,vln (B flat maj) WILLIS $.35
(B2266)
med solo,pno (A flat maj) ALLANS s.p.
(B2267)
high solo,pno (E flat maj) ALLANS s.p.
(B2268)
low solo,pno (B flat maj) ALLANS s.p.
(B2269)

Just A-Wearyin' For You
low solo,pno (A flat maj) ALLANS s.p.
(B2270)
high solo,pno (D flat maj) ALLANS s.p.
(B2271)
2 low soli,pno (A flat maj) ALLANS

BOND, CARRIE JACOBS (cont'd.)
s.p.
(B2272)
2 high soli,pno (D flat maj) ALLANS s.p.
(B2273)

Perfect Day, A
ABar soli,pno BOSTON $1.75 (B2274)
high solo,pno (C maj) BOSTON $1.50
(B2275)
med-high solo,pno (A flat maj) BOSTON $1.50
(B2276)
low solo,pno (F maj) BOSTON $1.50
(B2277)

BOND OF LOVE, THE see Skillings, Otis

BOND, VICTORIA
Cornography
S solo,horn,bsn SEESAW   (B2278)

Suite Aux Troubadours   *CCU
S solo,lute,fl,ob,vla,vcl SEESAW
(B2279)

BONDESON
Urval Av De Mest Omtyckta
solo,pno LUNDQUIST s.p.   (B2280)

BONDEVILLE, EMMANUEL DE (1898-   )
A Thule Un Roi Tres Fidele
female solo,pno/inst DURAND s.p.
(B2281)

Il Etait Un Monarque
Bar solo,pno/inst DURAND s.p.
(B2282)
La Rapsodie Foraine Et Le Pardon De Saint-Anne
med solo,pno/inst DURAND s.p.
(B2283)
L'Acacia Blanc
med solo,pno/inst DURAND s.p.
(B2284)
Mon Coeur Est Lourd
female solo,pno/inst DURAND s.p.
(B2285)
Noel
med solo,pno/inst DURAND s.p.
(B2286)
Serenade
Bar solo,pno/inst DURAND s.p.
(B2287)

BONDI, VENEZIA CASA! see Wolf-Ferrari, Ermanno

BONDON, JACQUES (1927-   )
La Margelle
see Le Pain De Serpent

Le Pain De Serpent
see Le Pain De Serpent

Le Pain De Serpent
S solo,14inst cmplt ed TRANSAT. s.p.
contains: La Margelle; Le Pain De Serpent; Le Veilleur De La Lune; Petits Freres   (B2288)

Le Veilleur De La Lune
see Le Pain De Serpent

Petits Freres
see Le Pain De Serpent

BONDS, [MARGARET] (1913-   )
I Got A Home In That Rock
(Bonds, M.) med solo,pno MERCURY $.95
(B2289)

BONE
First Psalm (Psalm 1) (composed with Fenton) sac
med solo,pno (B flat min) FISCHER,C V 2054
(B2290)
low solo,pno (G min) FISCHER,C V 2055
(B2291)

Psalm 1   *see First Psalm

Thy Word Is A Lamp
high solo,pno (F maj) FISCHER,C RS 79
(B2292)
med-low solo,pno (E flat maj) FISCHER,C RS 78   (B2293)

BONE JESU, VERBUM PATRIS see Schutz, Heinrich

BONGARD, GWEN TRENEER
I Thank You God   *sac
solo,pno THOMP.G
(B2294)

BONHEUR see Rasse, Francois

BONHEUR see Ruyneman, Daniel

BONHEUR D'AIMER see Blech, Leo

BONHEUR ENVOLE see Darcieux, F.

BONHEUR IMPOSSIBLE see Schoemaker, Maurice

BONHEUR, THEO.
Battle Eve, The
TB soli,orch (D flat maj) ASHDOWN s.p., ipr
(B2295)
TB soli,orch (E flat maj) ASHDOWN s.p., ipr
(B2296)

BONIFANTI
Epitaffio Di Un Bambino
[It] solo,pno RICORDI-ARG BA 11512 s.p.
(B2297)

L'amphore
"Le Vase" [Fr] T solo,pno RICORDI-ARG BA 11513 s.p.
(B2298)

Le Vase   *see L'amphore

Pater Noster   *sac
[Lat] solo,org/pno RICORDI-ARG BA 11511 s.p.
(B2299)

BONJOUR AU VILLAGE see Arrieu, Claude

BONJOUR HIRONDELLES see Mendelssohn-Bartholdy, Felix

BONJOUR MON COEUR see Viardot-Garcia, Pauline

BONJOUR SUZON see Lacome, Paul

BONJOURS, BONSOIR ET BONNE NUIT see Blanchard, Roger

BONN see Sibelius, Jean

BONNAL, ERMEND
Au Pays Des Chansons
solo,pno OUVRIERES s.p.   (B2300)

Ballade Provencale
solo,pno OUVRIERES s.p.   (B2301)

Chansons De L'Aube Et Du Soir
solo,pno quarto OUVRIERES s.p.
contains: Fleur Des Dunes; Le Retour; Le Vieux Pommier; Les Premiers Pas; Mon Coeur Est Content; Sur Les Clochers
(B2302)

Fleur Des Dunes
see Chansons De L'Aube Et Du Soir

Le Retour
see Chansons De L'Aube Et Du Soir

Le Vieux Pommier
see Chansons De L'Aube Et Du Soir

Les Chansons D'Agnoutine   *CC12L
solo,pno quarto OUVRIERES s.p.
(B2303)

Les Premiers Pas
see Chansons De L'Aube Et Du Soir

Ma Mere Etait Une Paysanne
solo,pno OUVRIERES s.p.   (B2304)

Madalena Gure Patroina
solo,pno OUVRIERES s.p.   (B2305)

Mon Coeur Est Content
see Chansons De L'Aube Et Du Soir

Quand Les Pins Chanteront
solo,pno OUVRIERES s.p.   (B2306)

Sur Les Clochers
see Chansons De L'Aube Et Du Soir

BONNE ANNEE see Delmet, Paul

BONNE HUMEUR see Chaminade, Cecile

BONNE NUIT see Massenet, Jules

BONNE NUIT see Schubert, Franz (Peter)

BONNET VOLE see Schmitt, Florent

BONNIE BANKS O' LOCH LOMON' see Carlyle, R.

BONNIE BANKS OF LOCH LOMOND, THE see Lawson, Malcolm

BONNIE DUNDEE   *folk,Scot
solo,pno (F maj) PATERSON FS13 s.p.
(B2307)
BONNIE EARL O' MURRAY   *folk,Scot
solo,pno (B flat maj) PATERSON FS9 s.p.
(B2308)

BONNIE EARL O'MORAY, THE see Lawson, Malcolm

BONNIE GEORGE CAMPBELL see Keel, Frederick

BONNIE GEORGE CAMPBELL see Lawson, Malcolm

BONNIE STRATHYRE see Lawson, Malcolm

BONNIE WEE ROSE see Lawson, Malcolm

BONNIE WEE THING *folk,Scot
solo,pno (A maj/G maj) PATERSON FS14
s.p. (B2309)

BONNIE WEE THING see Bryant, J.

BONSET, JAC.
De Wonderbloem *Op.82
solo,pno/org/harmonium ALSBACH s.p.
(B2310)

Drie Christelijke Liederen
solo,pno/org/harmonium ALSBACH s.p.
contains: Kerstlied, Op.64,No.1;
Paaslied, Op.60,No.2;
Pinksterlied, Op.60,No.3 (B2311)

Drie Geestelijke Liederen *sac
solo,pno/org/harmonium ALSBACH s.p.
contains: Gouder Randen, Op.60,
No.2; Licht, Op.60,No.3; Onze
Vader, Op.60,No.1 (B2312)

Gouden Randen *Op.60,No.2
see Drie Geestelijke Liederen

Juicht De Vreezon Is Verrezen *Op.59
med solo,pno/org/harmonium ALSBACH
s.p. (B2313)

Kerstlied *Op.64,No.1
see Drie Christelijke Liederen

Kerstliedje *Op.212
solo,pno/org ALSBACH s.p. (B2314)

Klokkenkerstlied *Op.89, sac,CC22U
solo,pno ALSBACH s.p. (B2315)

Levenslied *Op.38
solo,pno ALSBACH s.p. (B2316)

Licht *Op.60,No.3
see Drie Geestelijke Liederen

Onze Vader *Op.60,No.1
see Drie Geestelijke Liederen

Oranje Glorie *Op.25
solo,pno ALSBACH s.p. (B2317)

Paaslied *Op.60,No.2
see Drie Christelijke Liederen

Pater Noster *Op.43, sac
solo,pno/org/harmonium ALSBACH s.p.
(B2318)

Pinksterlied *Op.60,No.3
see Drie Christelijke Liederen

Stille Nacht, Heilige Nacht *sac
solo,pno ALSBACH s.p. (B2319)

BONSOIR MIGNONNE see Lacome, Paul

BONVIN, LUDWIG (1850-1939)
Himmelsehnssucht *Op.24,No.3
solo,pno BREITKOPF-W DLV 2296 s.p.
(B2320)

BOOGAARD, BERNARD VAN DEN (1952-   )
Syntetisch Gedicht
"Synthetic Poeme" Mez&narrator,al-
sax,bass clar,pno DONEMUS s.p.
(B2321)
Synthetic Poeme *see Syntetisch
Gedicht

BOOK OF A THOUSAND SONGS *CCU
(Bona) solo,pno FISCHER,C O 3616
(B2322)

BOOK OF AYRES see Rosseter, Philip

BOOK OF ITALIAN LYRICS see Wolf, Hugo

BOOK OF SONGS see Heseltine, Philip

BOOK OF SONGS, VOLS. 1-2 see Delius,
Frederick

BOOK OF SPANISH LYRICS see Wolf, Hugo

BOONE, CHARLES (1939-   )
Vocalise *vocalise
S solo,acap SALABERT-US $6.00
(B2323)

BOOREN, JO VAN DEN (1935-   )
L'epitaphe Villon
med solo,3fl,3ob,3clar,4horn,3trp,
3trom,tuba,timp,perc,strings
DONEMUS s.p. (B2324)

BOOTH
Down From His Glory (composed with
Clibborn) *sac
solo,pno BENSON S5400-R $1.00
(B2325)

BORCHARD, ADOLPHE (1882-1967)
Dedicace
med solo,pno/inst DURAND s.p. see
from Deux Melodies (B2326)

Deux Melodies *see Dedicace;
Invocation (B2327)

BORCHARD, ADOLPHE (cont'd.)
Invocation
med solo,pno/inst DURAND s.p. see
from Deux Melodies (B2328)

BORDER CRADLE SONG see Kemp, David H.

BORDER LINE see Owens, Robert

BORDES, CHARLES (1863-1909)
Epithalame
high solo,pno SALABERT-US $3.00
(B2329)

BORDEWIJK-ROEPMAN, JOHANNA (1892-   )
Abel Et Cain
see Trois Chansons Francaises

Adoration
see Bierbaum-Lieder

Allerzielen
see Vijf Tempelzangen

Antique
see Les Illuminations

Barokcantate
see Vijf Tempelzangen

Bierbaum-Lieder
S solo,3fl,2ob,2clar,2bsn,horn,trp,
2trom,cel,harp,strings voc sc
ALBERSEN s.p.
contains: Adoration; Die Schwarze
Laute; Gigerlette; Sei Getrost
(B2330)

Bottom
see Les Illuminations

De Kroaie Enden Puyt
S solo,3fl,3ob,2clar,3bsn,2horn,
2trp,trom,harp,strings DONEMUS
s.p. (B2331)

Die Schwarze Laute
see Bierbaum-Lieder

Epiphania
see Vijf Tempelzangen

Extase
see Sechs Lieder

Fleurs
see Les Illuminations

Friede
see Sechs Lieder

Gigerlette
see Bierbaum-Lieder

Het Blanke Paard
see Vijf Tempelzangen

Het Sneeuwde Wat
see Vijf Tempelzangen

Holland
A solo,pno DONEMUS s.p. (B2332)
A solo,2fl,3ob,2clar,2bsn,4horn,
3trp,3trom,perc,harp,strings
DONEMUS s.p. (B2333)

Ik Wensche U
S solo,strings DONEMUS s.p. (B2334)

La Lune Blanche Luit Dans Les Bois
see Trois Chansons Francaises

Les Illuminations
DONEMUS s.p. S solo,2fl,3ob,2clar,
2bsn,2horn,2trp,timp,perc,
strings, 1940 arrangement; S
solo,3fl,3ob,2clar,3bsn,4horn,
3trp,3trom,tuba,timp,perc,harp,
strings, 1938 arrangement
contains: Antique; Bottom; Fleurs
(B2335)

Les Pauvres
see Trois Chansons Francaises

Oranje May Lied
S solo,3fl,3ob,2clar,2bsn,2horn,
3trp,3trom,tuba,timp,perc,strings
DONEMUS s.p. (B2336)

Schmied Schmerz
see Sechs Lieder

Sechs Lieder
A solo,pno ALSBACH s.p.
contains: Extase; Friede; Schmied
Schmerz; Traumgewalten; Zum
Ossa Sprach Der Pelion (B2337)

Sei Getrost
see Bierbaum-Lieder
S solo,pno DONEMUS s.p. (B2338)

Traumgewalten
see Sechs Lieder

BORDEWIJK-ROEPMAN, JOHANNA (cont'd.)
Trois Chansons Francaises
A solo,pno ALSBACH s.p.
contains: Abel Et Cain; La Lune
Blanche Luit Dans Les Bois; Les
Pauvres (B2339)

Uit Het Diepst Van Mijn Hart
low solo,pno BEZIGE BIJ s.p.
(B2340)

med solo,pno BEZIGE BIJ s.p.
(B2341)

Vijf Tempelzangen *sac
med solo/high solo,pno DONEMUS s.p.
contains: Allerzielen;
Barokcantate; Epiphania; Het
Blanke Paard; Het Sneeuwde Wat
(B2342)

Zum Ossa Sprach Der Pelion
see Sechs Lieder

BOREL-CLERC, CHARLES (1879-1959)
Rupture
solo,pno ENOCH s.p. (B2343)
solo,acap solo pt ENOCH s.p.
(B2344)

BORG, KIM
Harman Haat *CCU
solo,pno FAZER F 5367 s.p. (B2345)

Itakarjalaisia Lauluja *CCU
solo,pno FAZER F 5368 s.p. (B2346)

BORGULYA, A.
Sparrows
[Hung] solo,pno BUDAPEST 4191 s.p.
(B2347)

BORI see Scek, Breda

BORIS' MONOLOGUE see Mussorgsky, Modest

BORKOVEC, PAVEL (1894-   )
Heitere Lieder *CCU
[Czech/Ger] S solo,pno SUPRAPHON
s.p. (B2348)

Pisne Madlenky (from Palecek)
see ARIE A ZPEVY ZE SOUCASNYCH
OPER: ALT

Rozmarne
Bar solo,pno SUPRAPHON s.p. (B2349)

Sedm Pisni Pro Sopran *CC7U
S solo,pno SUPRAPHON s.p. (B2350)

BORLENGHI, E.
In Sogno
[It] solo,pno BONGIOVANI 2498 s.p.
(B2351)

BORMIOLI, CESARE
Salve Regina *sac
solo,pno ZERBONI 5161 s.p. (B2352)

BORN AGAIN see Skillings, Otis

BORN TO SERVE THE LORD see Chambers,
H.A.

BORNEFELD, HELMUT (1932-   )
Cantata 1 *see O Glaubig Herz,
Gebenedei

Cantata 5 *see Der Herr Ist Mein
Getreuer Hirt

Cantata 9 *see Wachet Auf, Ruft Uns
Die Stimme

Der Herr Ist Mein Getreuer Hirt
(Cantata 5) sac
S solo,fl/S rec,org (diff) BAREN.
2229 sc $5.25, solo pt $.75
(B2353)

Hirtenlieder *CCU
(Bartok, Bela) low solo,org (diff)
BAREN. 2450 $8.50 (B2354)

Lieder Am Klavier Zu Singen *CC12U
med solo,pno (med easy) BAREN. 2147
$4.75 (B2355)

Memento Mori *sac,concerto
[Ger] med solo,org (med diff)
BAREN. 2419 $5.00 (B2356)

O Glaubig Herz, Gebenedei (Cantata 1)
sac
S solo,org (med diff) BAREN. 2225
$3.50 (B2357)

Orgelchoralsatze Heft I: Advent Bis
Dreieinigkeit *sac,CC17U,Adv/
Trin
high solo,org (med diff) BAREN.
2928 $12.50 (B2358)

Orgelchoralsatze Heft II: (General
Usage) *sac,CC22U,Gen,Psalm
high solo,org (med diff) BAREN.
2929 $12.50 (B2359)

Orgelchoralsatze Heft III: Lob Und
Dank, Glaube, Tageszeiten *sac,
CC15U,Gen

BORNEFELD, HELMUT (cont'd.)

    S solo,org (med diff) BAREN. 2930
    $12.50   (B2360)

    Siona
    S solo,org (diff) BAREN. 4114
    $12.00   (B2361)

    Wachet Auf, Ruft Uns Die Stimme
    (Cantata 9)
    S solo,org (med diff) BAREN. 2444
    $12.00   (B2362)

    Wie Schon Leuchtet Der Morgenstern
    *sac,cant
    SS soli,fl,org,vln,vla,cont sc
    HANSSLER 25.018 s.p., ipa (B2363)

    Zwolf Gesange Nach Gedichten Von
    Nelly Sachs *sac,CC12U
    S solo,org HANSSLER 25.014 s.p. (B2364)

BORODIN, ALEXANDER PORFIRIEVITCH
(1833-1887)
    Cavatina Of Vladimir (from Prince
    Igor)
    [Russ/Eng/Fr] T solo,pno CHESTER
    s.p.   (B2365)

    Chanson De La Foret Sombre
    solo,orch LEDUC s.p.   (B2366)

    Cherry-Coloured Shawl, The (from
    Prince Igor)
    [Russ] med solo,pno MEZ KNIGA 118
    s.p. contains also: Listen, If
    You Please...   (B2367)

    Dissonance
    see Two Songs

    Haughtiness
    see Two Songs

    Listen, If You Please... (from Prince
    Igor)
    see Borodin, Alexander
    Porfirievitch, Cherry-Coloured
    Shawl, The

    Nicht Rast, Nicht Ruhe
    [Russ/Ger/It] Bar solo,pno voc sc
    BREITKOPF-W 61 03122 s.p. (B2368)
    [Russ/Ger/It] Bar solo,orch sc
    BREITKOPF-W 57 03039 s.p. (B2369)

    Prince Galitzky's Aria (from Prince
    Igor)
    [Russ/Eng/Fr] B solo,kbd CHESTER
    s.p.   (B2370)

    Prince Igor's Aria (from Prince Igor)
    [Russ] med solo,pno MEZ KNIGA 117
    s.p.   (B2371)
    [Russ/Eng/Fr] Bar solo,kbd CHESTER
    s.p.   (B2372)

    Romanzen Und Lieder *CCU
    [Russ] solo,pno SIKORSKI R 6309
    s.p.   (B2373)

    Two Songs
    Bar solo,pno (med) OXFORD 62.277
    $1.55
    contains: Dissonance; Haughtiness
                                        (B2374)

BOROWSKI, FELIX (1872-1956)
    Angels Of The Light *sac
    med solo,pno FITZSIMONS $.40
                                        (B2375)

BORRIS, SIEGFRIED (1906-   )
    Aufklang *Op.24,No.1
    see Drei Lieder
    see Funf Ausgewahlte Lieder Aus Op.
    12 Und Op. 24

    Der Kuss *Op.7,No.4
    see Vier Lieder

    Die Ferne Flote
    see Funf Ausgewahlte Lieder Aus Op.
    12 Und Op. 24

    Die Ferne Stadt *Op.81,No.2
    see Nocturnes

    Drei Lieder
    Bar solo,pno SIRIUS s.p.
    contains: Aufklang, Op.24,No.1;
    Einkehr, Op.24,No.3; Hoffende
    In Der Nacht, Op.24,No.2
                                        (B2376)

    Drei Lieder Aus Der "Stimmen Der
    Stille", Op. 18
    S solo,pno SIRIUS s.p.
    contains: Hohe Wolken;
    Madchenlied; Schwalben Im Abend
                                        (B2377)

    Einkehr *Op.24,No.3
    see Drei Lieder
    see Funf Ausgewahlte Lieder Aus Op.
    12 Und Op. 24

BORRIS, SIEGFRIED (cont'd.)

    Funf Ausgewahlte Lieder Aus Op. 12
    Und Op. 24
    S solo,pno SIRIUS s.p.
    contains: Aufklang; Die Ferne
    Flote; Einkehr; Hoffende In Der
    Nacht; Marzlied   (B2378)

    Hoffende In Der Nacht *Op.24,No.2
    see Drei Lieder
    see Funf Ausgewahlte Lieder Aus Op.
    12 Und Op. 24

    Hohe Wolken
    see Drei Lieder Aus Der "Stimmen
    Der Stille", Op. 18

    Im Schnee *Op.7,No.2
    see Vier Lieder

    Junge Liebe *Op.7,No.3
    see Vier Lieder

    Leih Mir Von Deinem Saitenspiel
    *Op.81,No.1
    see Nocturnes

    Madchenlied
    see Drei Lieder Aus Der "Stimmen
    Der Stille", Op. 18

    Marienkantate *Op.35,No.2, cant
    S solo,pno,4strings SIRIUS sc s.p.,
    ipa, voc sc s.p., solo pt s.p.
                                        (B2379)

    Marzlied
    see Funf Ausgewahlte Lieder Aus Op.
    12 Und Op. 24

    Nocturnes
    T solo,pno SIRIUS s.p.
    contains: Die Ferne Stadt, Op.81,
    No.2; Leih Mir Von Deinem
    Saitenspiel, Op.81,No.1;
    Schmaler Mond, Op.81,No.4;
    Traumend Singt Die Stille,
    Op.81,No.3   (B2380)

    Schmaler Mond *Op.81,No.4
    see Nocturnes

    Schwalben Im Abend
    see Drei Lieder Aus Der "Stimmen
    Der Stille", Op. 18

    Seligkeit *Op.7,No.1
    see Vier Lieder

    Sonnet
    see Three Poems For Tenor

    Springtime
    see Three Poems For Tenor

    Three Poems For Tenor
    T solo,fl,ob,bsn,horn sc SIRIUS
    s.p., ipa
    contains: Sonnet; Springtime;
    Wayfarer, The   (B2381)

    Traumend Singt Die Stille *Op.81,
    No.3
    see Nocturnes

    Vier Lieder
    T solo,pno/3strings SIRIUS s.p.
    contains: Der Kuss, Op.7,No.4; Im
    Schnee, Op.7,No.2; Junge Liebe,
    Op.7,No.3; Seligkeit, Op.7,No.1
                                        (B2382)

    Wayfarer, The
    see Three Poems For Tenor

BORSCHEL, ERICH
    Ostpreusenland!
    solo,pno ZIMMER. 1432 s.p. (B2383)

BORTE! see Grieg, Edvard Hagerup

BORTNIANSKY, DIMITRI STEPANOVITCH
(1751-1825)
    Romances And Songs *CCU
    [Russ] solo,pno MEZ KNIGA 56 s.p.
                                        (B2384)

BORUP-JORGENSEN, AXEL
    Herbsttag *Op.42, cant
    A solo,fl,clar,pno,vla,vcl,bsn sc
    FOG s.p.   (B2385)

    Sehnsucht *Op.49,No.2
    see To Sange

    To Sange
    solo,pno FOG s.p.
    contains: Sehnsucht, Op.49,No.2;
    Verirrt, Op.49,No.1   (B2386)

    Verirrt *Op.49,No.1
    see To Sange

    Winterelegie *Op.55
    SMezA soli,fl,ob,bsn,pno,vln,vla sc
    FOG s.p.   (B2387)

BOS, JANE
    Rose De Grenade
    solo,pno ENOCH s.p.   (B2388)
    solo,acap solo pt ENOCH s.p.
                                        (B2389)

BOSE WORTE IKUINEN SURU see Kilpinen,
Yrio, Sanoissa Kuluva

BOSMANS, HENRIETTE (1895-1952)
    Artist's Secret, The
    med solo,pno DONEMUS s.p. (B2390)

    Aurore
    solo,pno BROEKMANS 228 s.p. (B2391)

    Belsazer
    A solo,3fl,2ob,2clar,2bsn,4horn,
    2trp,2trom,timp,perc,cel,harp,
    strings DONEMUS s.p.   (B2392)

    Chanson
    solo,pno BROEKMANS 226 s.p. (B2393)

    Chanson Der Escargots Qui Vont A
    L'enterrement
    see Vier Liederen Op Franse Tekst

    Copla
    high solo&med solo,pno DONEMUS s.p.
                                        (B2394)

    Das Macht Den Menschen Glucklich
    solo,pno BROEKMANS 190 s.p. (B2395)

    Der Kaiser
    see Drie Liederen Op Duitse Tekst

    Die Heil'gen Drei Konige Aus
    Morgenland
    see Bosmans, Henriette, Im
    Mondenglanz Ruht Das Meer

    Dooedenmarsch
    narrator,2fl,2ob,2clar,2bsn,3horn,
    3trp,perc,strings DONEMUS s.p.
                                        (B2396)

    Drie Liederen Op Duitse Tekst
    low solo/med solo,pno DONEMUS s.p.
    contains: Der Kaiser;
    Liebestrunken; Schmied Schmerz
                                        (B2397)

    Gebed
    solo,pno BROEKMANS 217 s.p. (B2398)

    Im Mondenglanz Ruht Das Meer
    solo,pno BROEKMANS 229 s.p.
    contains also: Die Heil'gen Drei
    Konige Aus Morgenland   (B2399)

    La Chanson Du Chiffonnier
    solo,pno BROEKMANS 257 s.p. (B2400)

    La Comtesse Esmeree
    see Vier Liederen Op Franse Tekst

    Le Diable Dans La Nuit
    solo,pno BROEKMANS 256 s.p. (B2401)

    Le Sultan
    see Vier Liederen Op Franse Tekst

    Lead, Kindly Light
    [Eng] med solo,pno BROEKMANS B78
    s.p.   (B2402)

    Liebestrunken
    see Drie Liederen Op Duitse Tekst

    Mon Reve Familier
    see Vier Liederen Op Franse Tekst

    On Frappe
    solo,pno BROEKMANS 207 s.p. (B2403)

    Schmied Schmerz
    see Drie Liederen Op Duitse Tekst

    Six Melodies *CC6U
    solo,pno BROEKMANS 439 s.p. (B2404)

    Ten Melodies *CC10U
    [Fr] med solo,pno BROEKMANS B13
    s.p.   (B2405)

    Terugblick, Deel I, II, III & IV
    *CCU
    solo,pno BROEKMANS 238;238A s.p.,
    ea.   (B2406)

    Verzen
    med solo,pno DONEMUS s.p. (B2407)

    Vier Liederen Op Franse Tekst
    med solo,pno DONEMUS s.p.
    contains: Chanson Der Escargots
    Qui Vont A L'enterrement; La
    Comtesse Esmeree; Le Sultan;
    Mon Reve Familier   (B2408)

BOSSI, RENZO (1883-1965)
    Canto Nostalgico *Op.23,No.5
    see Echi Del Mare

    Echi Del Mare
    S solo,4strings,pno cmplt ed
    BONGIOVANI 1397 s.p.
    contains: Canto Nostalgico,

BOSSI, RENZO (cont'd.)

Op.23,No.5; Il Faro, Op.23,
No.6; L'Ave Maria, Op.23,No.2;
Notte Marina, Op.23,No.1; Pace
Vespertina, Op.23,No.4;
Riflessi Di Sole, Op.23,No.3
(B2409)

Era Muta La Notte
see Frammenti Lirici

Frammenti Lirici
solo,strings sc CARISH 17259 s.p.,
ipa
contains: Era Muta La Notte; Io
Son Qui; Senti, Senti; Un
Organetto Suona (B2410)

Il Faro *Op.23,No.6
see Echi Del Mare

Il Fringuello Cieco *Op.26,No.5
Bar/Mez solo,org/pno BONGIOVANI
1105 s.p. see from Prose (B2411)

Inno Italico
solo,pno voc sc BONGIOVANI 2000
s.p. (B2412)

Io Son Qui
see Frammenti Lirici

L'Ave Maria *Op.23,No.2
see Echi Del Mare

Le Rane *Op.26,No.2
Bar/Mez solo,org/pno BONGIOVANI
1102 s.p. see from Prose (B2413)

Nativita *Op.26,No.1
Bar/Mez solo,org/pno BONGIOVANI
1101 s.p. see from Prose (B2414)

Notte Marina *Op.23,No.1
see Echi Del Mare

Pace Vespertina *Op.23,No.4
see Echi Del Mare

Prose *see Il Fringuello Cieco,
Op.26,No.5; Le Rane, Op.26,No.2;
Nativita, Op.26,No.1; Rinuncia,
Op.26,No.3; Vigilia D'amore,
Op.26,No.4 (B2415)

Riflessi Di Sole *Op.23,No.3
see Echi Del Mare

Rinuncia *Op.26,No.3
Bar/Mez solo,org/pno BONGIOVANI
1103 s.p. see from Prose (B2416)

Senti, Senti
see Frammenti Lirici

Un Organetto Suona
see Frammenti Lirici

Vigilia D'amore *Op.26,No.4
Bar/Mez solo,org/pno BONGIOVANI
1104 s.p. see from Prose (B2417)

BOSSLER, KURT (1911-   )
Das Ist Ein Kostlich Ding *sac
high solo,org HANSSLER 5.158 s.p.
(B2418)
Halleluja! Lobet Den Herrn *sac
high solo,org HANSSLER 5.163 s.p.
(B2419)

BOSUN'S CALL see Ashworth-Hope, H.

BOSWELL, ERIC
Little Donkey *sac,Xmas
solo,pno HARRIS $.95 (B2420)

BOTANY BAY see Pascal

BOTHER THE MEN see Walker, Henry

BOTSCHAFT see Bijvanck, Henk

BOTSCHAFT see Brahms, Johannes

BOTSCHAFT see Marx, Karl

BOTSCHAFTEN DES REGENS see Hirsch, H.L.

BOTSFORD COLLECTION OF FOLK-SONGS, VOL
II *CCU,folk,Eur
(Botsford, Florence H.) pap SCHIRM.G
$5.00 texts in original languages
and English (B2421)

BOTSFORD COLLECTION OF FOLK-SONGS, VOL.
III *CCU,folk,Eur
(Botsford, Florence H.) pap SCHIRM.G
$5.00 texts in original languages
and English (B2422)

BOTTI, C.
Regina Bella D'amore
solo,harp BONGIOVANI 357 s.p.
(B2423)
Stornello (from Zingaresca)
solo,pno BONGIOVANI 13 s.p. (B2424)

BOTTI, C. (cont'd.)

Tu Sei Partita
solo,pno BONGIOVANI 358 s.p.
(B2425)
Un'ombra
solo,pno BONGIOVANI 431 s.p.
(B2426)
V'amo Tanto
T solo,pno BONGIOVANI 852 s.p.
(B2427)
Verso Il Mistero
solo,pno BONGIOVANI 432 s.p.
(B2428)

BOTTJE, WILL GAY
Five Songs From "Wayward Pilgrim"
*CC5U
S solo,pno AM.COMP.AL. $7.70
(B2429)
In Praise Of Music
S solo,pno AM.COMP.AL. $6.60
(B2430)
Patterns
A solo,pno AM.COMP.AL. $5.50
(B2431)
Quests Of Odysseus *CCU
T solo,pno AM.COMP.AL. $9.35
(B2432)

BOTTOM see Bordewijk-Roepman, Johanna

BOTTOM'S DREAM see Britten, Benjamin

BOULANGER, G.
Avant De Mourir *Op.17
[Ger] med solo,pno BOTE $1.00
(B2433)

BOULANGER, LILI (1893-1918)
Ils M'ont Assez Opprime Des Ma
Jeunesse (Psalm 129)
Bar solo,pno/inst DURAND s.p.
(B2434)
B solo,pno/inst DURAND s.p. (B2435)

Psalm 129 *see Ils M'ont Assez
Opprime Des Ma Jeunesse

BOULAY, J.
Ave Maria *sac
[Lat] S solo,org ENOCH s.p. (B2436)

O Salutaris *sac
[Lat] S solo,org ENOCH s.p. (B2437)

BOULEZ, PIERRE (1925-   )
Don (from Pli Selon Pli)
[Fr] S solo,inst sc,oct UNIVER.
13614 $20.50 (B2438)

Improvisation I (from Pli Selon Pli)
[Fr] S solo,inst sc,oct UNIVER.
12855 $5.75 (B2439)

Improvisation II (from Pli Selon Pli)
[Fr] S solo,inst sc,oct UNIVER.
12857 $10.50 (B2440)

Le Marteau Sans Maitre
A solo,6inst sc,oct UNIVER. 12652
$12.50 (B2441)

Tombeau V (from Pli Selon Pli)
[Fr] S solo,inst sc UNIVER. 13616
$38.50 (B2442)

BOUMAN, PAUL
Behold The Lamb Of God *sac
med solo,pno oct CONCORDIA 98-1088
$.25 (B2443)

Create In Me A Clean Heart, O God
*sac
SS/SA soli,pno oct CONCORDIA
98-1143 $.25 (B2444)

My Soul Doth Magnify The Lord *sac
med solo,pno oct CONCORDIA 98-1689
$.25 (B2445)

BOURBONNAIS *Fr
(Canteloube, J.) solo,acap DURAND
s.p. see also Anthologie Des Chants
Populaires Francais Tome III
(B2446)

BOURGEOIS, H.
Sept Complaintes *CC7U
solo,pno OUVRIERES s.p. (B2447)

BOURGEOIS, LOYS (LOUIS) (ca. 1510-1561)
La Manola
solo,orch HENN s.p. (B2448)

BOURGOGNE *Fr
(Canteloube, J.) solo,acap DURAND
s.p. see also Anthologie Des Chants
Populaires Francais Tome III
(B2449)

BOURGUIGNON, FRANCIS DE (1890-1961)
Ave Maria *sac
solo,pno BROGNEAUX s.p. (B2450)

Clairon *Op.103,No.1
see Deux Poemes De Norge

Deux Poemes D'Armand Bernier
solo,pno cmplt ed BROGNEAUX s.p.
contains: Eloge De La Terre;

BOURGUIGNON, FRANCIS DE (cont'd.)

Sifflez, Merles, Sifflez
(B2451)
Deux Poemes De Norge
S solo,pno cmplt ed CBDM s.p.
contains: Clairon, Op.103,No.1;
Le Negre-Boulanger, Op.103,No.2
(B2452)

Eloge De La Terre
see Deux Poemes D'Armand Bernier

Il Pleut *Op.28
S solo,pno CBDM s.p. (B2453)

Le Negre-Boulanger *Op.103,No.2
see Deux Poemes De Norge

Mandoline *Op.27
S solo,pno CBDM s.p. (B2454)

Sifflez, Merles, Sifflez
see Deux Poemes D'Armand Bernier

BOUSSION, E.
Au Pied De La Terrasse
see Paroles A L'Absente

Dans Le Jardin
see Paroles A L'Absente

Des Feuilles Mortes
see Paroles A L'Absente

Des Roses Dans Le Soir
see Paroles A L'Absente

Offrande
see Paroles A L'Absente

Paroles A L'Absente
solo,pno cmplt ed ENOCH s.p.
contains: Au Pied De La Terrasse;
Dans Le Jardin; Des Feuilles
Mortes; Des Roses Dans Le Soir;
Offrande (B2455)

BOUT DE CHOU see Scotto, Vincent

BOUT DE CHOU see Scotto, Vincent

BOUTIQUE JAPONAISE see Pierne, Gabriel

BOUTNIKOFF, J.
Chanson
see Le Jardin Des Caresses [2]

Le Desespoir
see Le Jardin Des Caresses [2]

Le Jardin Des Caresses [1] *Op.21
med solo,pno SALABERT-US $6.50
contains: Priere De L'aurore;
Priere De L'avant Matin; Priere
Du Coucher Du Soleil; Priere Du
Midi (B2456)

Le Jardin Des Caresses [2] *Op.22
high solo,pno SALABERT-US $6.50
contains: Chanson; Le Desespoir;
Le Tombeau D'Antar (B2457)

Le Tombeau D'Antar
see Le Jardin Des Caresses [2]

Priere De L'aurore
see Le Jardin Des Caresses [1]

Priere De L'avant Matin
see Le Jardin Des Caresses [1]

Priere Du Coucher Du Soleil
see Le Jardin Des Caresses [1]

Priere Du Midi
see Le Jardin Des Caresses [1]

BOUVAL, J.
L'Autre Soir
solo,pno ENOCH s.p. (B2458)

BOW DOWN THINE EAR see Gardner, Irene
J.

BOW DOWN THINE EAR, O LORD see
MacFadyen, A.

BOWDEN, ALFREDA
My Life's Companion *sac
solo,pno WORD S-20 (B2459)

BOWER, W.
Have You Met God's Blessed Son? *sac
solo,pno WORD S-222 (B2460)

BOWLES
American Hero, An
solo,pno SHAWNEE IA 47 $.60 (B2461)

BOWLES, PAUL FREDERIC (1910-   )
Baby Baby
med solo,pno PRESSER $.75 (B2462)

Blue Mountain Ballads *see Cabin;
Heavenly Grass (B2463)

BOWLES, PAUL FREDERIC (cont'd.)

Cabin
  med-low solo,pno (F sharp min)
  SCHIRM.G $.85 see from Blue
  Mountain Ballads   (B2464)

Heavenly Grass
  med-low solo,pno (E min) SCHIRM.G
  $.85 see from Blue Mountain
  Ballads   (B2465)

Letter To Freddy
  med solo,pno SCHIRM.G $.75 (B2466)

BOWLING
He Shall Be Like A Tree
  high solo,pno (F maj) FISCHER,C
  RS 197   (B2467)
  low solo,pno (E flat maj) FISCHER,C
  RS 198   (B2468)

BOXBERG, CHRISTIAN LUDWIG
  (1670-ca. 1730)
Machet Die Tore Weit *sac,cant
  S solo,2S rec,2vln,cont sc HANSSLER
  10.009 s.p., ipa, solo pt
  HANSSLER s.p.   (B2469)

BOYCE
I Love America
  (Wilhousky) solo,pno FISCHER,C
  V 2428   (B2470)

BOYCE, WILLIAM (1710-1779)
Rail No More, Ye Learned Asses
  (Jacob) B solo,pno (med) OXFORD
  61.706 $1.00   (B2471)

Song Of Momus To Mars, The
  (Arkwright) Bar solo,pno (med)
  OXFORD 61.729 $1.25   (B2472)

Tell Me Lovely Shepherd
  high solo,pno (D maj) ALLANS s.p.
                           (B2473)
  (Poston) S solo,pno (med easy)
  OXFORD 63.036 $1.10   (B2474)
  (Poston) A solo,pno (med easy)
  OXFORD 61.135 $1.25   (B2475)

Whether I Grow Old Or No
  (Bevan) Bar/B solo,pno ELKIN
  27.2470.07 s.p.   (B2476)

BOYD, JEANNE
Balloons In The Snow
  high solo,pno FITZSIMONS $.50
                           (B2477)

BOYD, WILLIAM S.
God Cares *sac
  (Fargason, Eddie) med solo,pno
  CRESPUB CP-S5047 $1.00   (B2478)

BOYER, DAVE
New World, A *sac,CC10UL
  solo,pno BENSON BO880 $2.50 (B2479)

BOYHOOD'S END see Tippett, Michael

BOZAY, ATTILA
Paper Slips *Op.5, song cycle
  S solo,clar,vcl BUDAPEST 4683 s.p.
                           (B2480)

BOZEMOJZMITUJ SIE NADE MNA see Baird,
  Tadeusz

BOZI, HAROLD DE
C'est La Valse A Tout Le Monde
  solo,pno ENOCH s.p.   (B2481)
  solo,acap solo pt ENOCH s.p.
                           (B2482)

Evidemment
  solo,pno ENOCH s.p.   (B2483)
  solo,acap solo pt ENOCH s.p.
                           (B2484)

La Chanson De Paname
  solo,pno ENOCH s.p.   (B2485)
  solo,acap solo pt ENOCH s.p.
                           (B2486)

La Javanette
  solo,pno ENOCH s.p.   (B2487)
  solo,acap solo pt ENOCH s.p.
                           (B2488)

Le Boston Du Passe
  solo,pno ENOCH s.p.   (B2489)
  solo,acap solo pt ENOCH s.p.
                           (B2490)

Les Nuits Du Bois
  solo,pno ENOCH s.p.   (B2491)
  solo,acap solo pt ENOCH s.p.
                           (B2492)

Ma Dziri
  solo,pno ENOCH s.p.   (B2493)
  solo,acap solo pt ENOCH s.p.
                           (B2494)

Ma Reine
  solo,pno ENOCH s.p.   (B2495)
  solo,acap solo pt ENOCH s.p.
                           (B2496)

Oh! Ma Nini, Ma Ninette
  solo,pno ENOCH s.p.   (B2497)
  solo,acap solo pt ENOCH s.p.
                           (B2498)

BOZI, HAROLD DE (cont'd.)

Recueil De Chansons Et Rondes
  Populaires *CC19L
  solo,acord DURAND s.p.   (B2499)

BOZZA, EUGENE (1905-   )
Arietta
  solo,pno/inst LEDUC s.p.   (B2500)

Bergerette *Op.43,No.3
  see Cinq Chansons Nicoises

Cinq Chansons Florentines *CC5U
  high solo,pno/inst LEDUC B.L.771
  s.p.   (B2501)

Cinq Chansons Nicoises
  solo,pno/inst LEDUC B.L.748 s.p.
    contains: Bergerette, Op.43,No.3;
    Dors, Mon Enfant Cherie, Op.43,
    No.1; La Chanson Du Ble, Op.43,
    No.5; Le Rossignol, Op.43,No.4;
    Sur Le Chemin Du Moulin, Op.43,
    No.2   (B2502)

Dors, Mon Enfant Cherie *Op.43,No.1
  see Cinq Chansons Nicoises

La Chanson Du Ble *Op.43,No.5
  see Cinq Chansons Nicoises

Le Rossignol *Op.43,No.4
  see Cinq Chansons Nicoises

Notre Amour Est Un Secret *Op.41
  solo,pno/inst LEDUC s.p.   (B2503)

Sur Le Chemin Du Moulin *Op.43,No.2
  see Cinq Chansons Nicoises

BRAAL, ANDRIES DE (1909-   )
De Grote Vogel
  Bar solo,fl,ob,clar,2horn,strings
  DONEMUS s.p.   (B2504)

In Memoriam
  Mez solo,pno DONEMUS s.p. (B2505)

Magnificat *sac
  S solo,org DONEMUS s.p.   (B2506)

Psalm 14 *sac
  Mez solo,org DONEMUS s.p. (B2507)

Psalm 132 *sac
  Mez solo,org DONEMUS s.p. (B2508)

BRABANT see Leeuw, Ton de

BRACCO
Serenata
  S/T solo,pno FORLIVESI 10942 s.p.
                           (B2509)

BRACE
O Love Divine *sac
  med solo,pno (A flat maj) WATERLOO
  $.75   (B2510)

BRACE OF BALLADS see Bennett, Sir
  William Sterndale

BRADAC, J.
Pizenske Pisne *CC16U
  solo,pno SUPRAPHON s.p.   (B2511)

BRADEN, EDWIN
I'll Sing My Song To You
  solo,pno CRAMER $1.15   (B2512)

Stay Awhile And Listen To My Song
  solo,pno CRAMER   (B2513)

BRADFORD
We're Not Home Yet, Children *sac
  solo,pno BENSON S8343-S $1.00
                           (B2514)

BRADFORD, JOHN
Just
  low solo,pno (F maj) CRAMER (B2515)
  high solo,pno (A flat maj) CRAMER
                           (B2516)

BRADLEY
My Prayer *sac
  high solo,pno (B maj) BOSTON $1.50
                           (B2517)

BRADY see Bacon, Ernst

BRAEIN, EDVARD
Song Til Nordmore
  solo,pno MUSIKK s.p.   (B2518)

BRAEIN, EDVARD FLIFLET
A La-La Deg Tirilill
  see Skjaeraasensanger

Bridge *Op.17,No.2
  see To Sanger

Du Ska Itte Tro I Graset
  solo,pno MUSIKK s.p.   (B2519)

Einsleg
  solo,pno MUSIKK s.p.   (B2520)

BRAEIN, EDVARD FLIFLET (cont'd.)

Go' Natt Da
  see Skjaeraasensanger

Hokken Ska'n Blonke Tel
  see Skjaeraasensanger

Je Veit Om En Skog Og Fem Andre
  Skjaeraasen Sanger *CC7L
  solo,pno MUSIKK s.p.   (B2521)

Juninatt
  see Skjaeraasensanger

Lang Pa Elva
  see Skjaeraasensanger

Skjaeraasensanger
  solo,pno MUSIKK s.p.
    contains: A La-La Deg Tirilill;
    Go' Natt Da; Hokken Ska'n
    Blonke Tel; Juninatt; Lang Pa
    Elva   (B2522)

Til Deg, Du Hei *Op.17,No.1
  see To Sanger

To Sanger
  solo,pno MUSIKK s.p.
    contains: Bridge, Op.17,No.2; Til
    Deg, Du Hei, Op.17,No.1 (B2523)

Ut Mot Havet
  solo,pno MUSIKK s.p.   (B2524)

BRAGA, GAETANA (1829-1907)
Angel's Serenade *see La Serenata

La Serenata *sac
  low solo,pno SCHOTTS s.p. (B2525)
  [Fr] solo,acap oct DURAND s.p.
                           (B2526)
  low solo,pno (E flat maj) ASHDOWN
                           (B2527)
  med solo,pno (F maj) ASHDOWN
                           (B2528)
  high solo,pno (G maj) ASHDOWN
                           (B2529)
  "Angel's Serenade" [Eng/Ger/It]
    high solo,vln/fl,opt vcl PRESSER
    $.75   (B2530)
  "Angel's Serenade" high solo,pno,
    opt vln (G maj) CENTURY 598 $.40
                           (B2531)
  "Serenade" solo,pno,fl/vln/vcl/mand
    (in 2 keys) DURAND s.p. (B2532)
  "Serenade" S solo,fl&gtr/vln/mand
    (G maj) DURAND s.p.   (B2533)

Mandoline
  solo,pno/inst DURAND s.p. (B2534)

Serenade *see La Serenata

BRAHAM
Anchors Weighed, The
  solo,pno CRAMER $1.15   (B2535)

BRAHE, MAY H.
As I Went A-Roaming
  high solo&low solo,pno (B flat maj)
    ASHDOWN $1.75   (B2536)
  high solo,orch (B flat maj) ASHDOWN
    $1.50, ipr   (B2537)
  med solo,orch (A flat maj) ASHDOWN
    $1.50, ipr   (B2538)
  low solo,orch (G maj) ASHDOWN
    $1.50, ipr   (B2539)

Bless This House
  2 soli,pno (E flat maj) BOOSEY
    $1.75   (B2540)
  high solo,pno (E flat maj) BOOSEY
    $1.25   (B2541)
  med solo,pno (C maj) BOOSEY $1.25
                           (B2542)
  low solo,pno (B flat maj) BOOSEY
    $1.25   (B2543)

By Road And River *CC5U
  ASHDOWN low solo,pno s.p.; med
    solo,pno s.p.; high solo,pno s.p.
                           (B2544)

Country Folk
  low solo,orch (F maj) ASHDOWN s.p.,
    ipr   (B2545)
  med solo,orch (A flat maj) ASHDOWN
    s.p., ipr   (B2546)
  high solo,orch (B flat maj) ASHDOWN
    s.p., ipr   (B2547)

Cradle Me Low
  low solo,pno (B flat maj) ASHDOWN
                           (B2548)
  med solo,pno (D flat maj) ASHDOWN
                           (B2549)
  high solo,pno (E flat maj) ASHDOWN
                           (B2550)

Dessous Ta Croisee
  solo,pno (available in 2 keys)
    ENOCH s.p.   (B2551)

Down Here
  low solo,pno (E flat maj) ASHDOWN
    $1.50   (B2552)

BRAHE, MAY H. (cont'd.)

med solo,pno (F maj) ASHDOWN $1.50
(B2553)

high solo,pno (G maj) ASHDOWN $1.50
(B2554)

Everlasting Love, The
low solo,pno (B flat maj) ASHDOWN
(B2555)
med solo,pno (C maj) ASHDOWN
(B2556)
med-high solo,pno (D flat maj)
ASHDOWN
(B2557)
high solo,pno (E flat maj) ASHDOWN
(B2558)

From The Nursery Window *CC6U
ASHDOWN s.p.
(B2559)

Guess You Know
low solo,pno (B flat maj) BOOSEY
$1.50
(B2560)
med solo,pno (C maj) BOOSEY $1.50
(B2561)
high solo,pno (E flat maj) BOOSEY
$1.50
(B2562)

I Passed By Your Window
low solo,orch (C maj) ASHDOWN
$1.50, ipr
(B2563)
med solo,orch (D maj) ASHDOWN
$1.50, ipr
(B2564)
high solo,orch (F maj) ASHDOWN
$1.50, ipr
(B2565)
med-high solo,orch (E flat maj)
ASHDOWN $1.50, ipr
(B2566)

Japanese Love Song *Jap
low solo,pno (E min) BOOSEY $1.50
(B2567)
med solo,pno (F min) BOOSEY $1.50
(B2568)
high solo,pno (G min) BOOSEY $1.50
(B2569)
low solo,pno (D maj) ALLANS s.p.
(B2570)
med solo,pno (E maj) ALLANS s.p.
(B2571)
med-high solo,pno (F maj) ALLANS
s.p.
(B2572)
high solo,pno (G maj) ALLANS s.p.
(B2573)

Meadowsweet
low solo,orch (E flat maj) ASHDOWN
s.p., ipr
(B2574)
med solo,orch (F maj) ASHDOWN s.p.,
ipr
(B2575)
high solo,orch (G maj) ASHDOWN
s.p., ipr
(B2576)

My Dear Old Town
low solo,pno (B flat maj) ASHDOWN
(B2577)
med solo,pno (C maj) ASHDOWN
(B2578)
high solo,pno (D maj) ASHDOWN
(B2579)

My Prayer For You
low solo,pno (E flat maj) ASHDOWN
(B2580)
med solo,pno (F maj) ASHDOWN
(B2581)
high solo,pno (A maj) ASHDOWN
(B2582)

None-So-Pretty
SBar/SB soli,pno ASHDOWN s.p.
(B2583)

O Western Wind!
low solo,orch (A min) ASHDOWN s.p.,
ipr
(B2584)
med solo,orch (B flat min) ASHDOWN
s.p., ipr
(B2585)
med-high solo,orch (C min) ASHDOWN
s.p., ipr
(B2586)
high solo,orch (D min) ASHDOWN
s.p., ipr
(B2587)

Off To The Greenwood
low solo,orch (C maj) ASHDOWN s.p.,
ipr
(B2588)
med solo,orch (D maj) ASHDOWN s.p.,
ipr
(B2589)
high solo,orch (E flat maj) ASHDOWN
s.p., ipr
(B2590)

Oh, Pray For Peace
solo,pno (E flat maj) BOOSEY $1.50
(B2591)

Pageant Of Summer, A *song cycle
4 soli,pno ASHDOWN s.p. (B2592)

Parting Prayer
low solo,pno (B flat maj) ALLANS
s.p.
(B2593)
med solo,pno (C maj) ALLANS s.p.
(B2594)
high solo,pno (D maj) ALLANS s.p.
(B2595)

Piper From Over The Way
low solo,pno (G maj) ALLANS s.p.
(B2596)
high solo,pno (B flat maj) ALLANS
s.p.
(B2597)

Prayer In Absence, A
low solo,orch (C maj) ASHDOWN s.p.,
ipr
(B2598)

BRAHE, MAY H. (cont'd.)

med solo,orch (E flat maj) ASHDOWN
s.p., ipr
(B2599)
high solo,orch (F maj) ASHDOWN
s.p., ipr
(B2600)

Red Roofs
low solo,orch (E flat maj) ASHDOWN
s.p., ipr
(B2601)
med solo,orch (F maj) ASHDOWN s.p.,
ipr
(B2602)
high solo,orch (G maj) ASHDOWN
s.p., ipr
(B2603)

Song Pictures *CC5U
ASHDOWN low solo,pno s.p.; med
solo,pno s.p.; high solo,pno s.p.
(B2604)

That's All
low solo,pno (B flat maj) ASHDOWN
s.p., ipr
(B2605)
med solo,pno (C maj) ASHDOWN s.p.,
ipr
(B2606)
high solo,pno (D maj) ASHDOWN
s.p., ipr
(B2607)

To A Miniature
low solo,orch (B flat maj) ASHDOWN
s.p., ipr
(B2608)
med solo,orch (C maj) ASHDOWN s.p.,
ipr
(B2609)
med-high solo,orch (D maj) ASHDOWN
s.p., ipr
(B2610)
high solo,orch (E flat maj) ASHDOWN
s.p., ipr
(B2611)
high solo&low solo,pno ASHDOWN s.p.
(B2612)

Two Little Words
low solo,pno (C maj) BOOSEY $1.50
(B2613)
high solo,pno (E flat maj) BOOSEY
$1.50
(B2614)

BRAHMS, JOHANNES (1833-1897)
A Une Violette *see An Ein Veilchen

Acht Zigeunerlieder *Op.103, CC8U
[Eng/Ger] high solo,pno SCHAUR
EE 643 $3.50; low solo,pno SCHAUR
EE 644 $3.50
(B2615)

Acht Zigeunerlieder Aus Op. 103
*CC8U
solo,pno BREITKOPF-L EB 6119 s.p.
(B2616)

Ack Mor, Jag Vill Ett Ting Ha
high solo,pno GEHRMANS s.p. (B2617)
low solo,pno GEHRMANS s.p. (B2618)

Alto Rhapsody *Op.53, sec,cant
"Alto Rhapsody" [Ger/Eng/Fr] A
solo,TTBB,2fl,2ob,2clar,2bsn,
2horn,strings study sc PETERS
3919 s.p., ipa
(B2619)
"Alto Rhapsody" [Eng/Ger] A solo,
men cor,orch BREITKOPF-W $1.25
(B2620)
"Alto Rhapsody" A solo,men cor,pno/
orch (contains also: Song Of
Destiny, Op. 54; Naenie, Op. 82)
study sc KALMUS 1160 $1.50
(B2621)
"Alto Rhapsody" [Ger] A solo,men
cor,orch voc sc KALMUS 6108 $1.25
(B2622)
"Rapsodia" [It] A solo,men cor,2fl,
2ob,2clar,2bsn,2horn CARISH s.p.
(B2623)

Alto Rhapsody *see Alto Rhapsody

Am Strande *Op.66,No.3
see Five Duets

An Die Nachtigall *Op.46,No.4
"To The Nightingale" see Metzler's
Masterpieces Vol. 11: Brahms
Lieder For Tenor
"To The Nightingale" see Metzler's
Masterpieces Vol. 12: Brahms
Lieder For Baritone Or Bass
"Au Rossignol" [Ger/Fr] solo,pno/
inst DURAND
(B2624)

An Ein Veilchen *Op.49,No.2
"To A Violet" see Metzler's
Masterpieces Vol. 12: Brahms
Lieder For Baritone Or Bass
"To A Violet" see Metzler's
Masterpieces Vol. 11: Brahms
Lieder For Tenor
"A Une Violette" [Ger/Fr] solo,pno/
inst DURAND
(B2625)
"To A Violet" solo,pno ASHDOWN s.p.
(B2626)

Au Rossignol *see An Die Nachtigall

Ausgewahlte Lieder, Volumes I And II
*CCU
(Domandl) [Ger] med solo,gtr SCHAUR
EE 1166-1167 $3.50, ea. (B2627)

Aux Bords Du Rhin
see LA MUSIQUE, SIXIEME CAHIER

BRAHMS, JOHANNES (cont'd.)

Berceuse *see Wiegenlied

Botschaft *Op.47,No.1
"Message" [Ger/Fr] solo,pno/inst
DURAND
(B2628)

Brahms-Album, Vol. I *CC51UL
(Friedlander) [Ger] $6.50 high
solo,pno PETERS 3201A; med solo,
pno PETERS 3201B; low solo,pno
PETERS 3201C
(B2629)

Brahms-Album, Vol. II *CC33UL
(Friedlander) [Eng/Ger] $6.50 high
solo,pno PETERS 3202A; med solo/
low solo,pno PETERS 3202B (B2630)

Brahms-Album, Vol. III *CC65UL
(Friedlander) [Ger] $4.75 high
solo,pno PETERS 3691A; med solo/
low solo,pno PETERS 3691B (B2631)

Brahms-Album, Vol. IV *CC48UL
(Friedlander) [Ger] $6.50 high
solo,pno PETERS 3692A; med solo/
low solo,pno PETERS 3692B (B2632)

Brahms Song Album, Vol. 1 *CCU
high solo,pno KALMUS 6113 $4.00;
med solo,pno KALMUS 6114 $4.00;
low solo,pno KALMUS 6115 $4.00
(B2633)

Brahms Song Album, Vol. 2 *CCU
high solo,pno KALMUS 6116 $4.00;
low solo,pno KALMUS 6117 $4.00
(B2634)

Brahms Song Album, Vol. 3 *CCU
high solo,pno KALMUS 6118 $4.00;
low solo,pno KALMUS 6119 $4.00
(B2635)

Brahms Song Album, Vol. 4 *CCU
high solo,pno KALMUS 6120 $4.00;
low solo,pno KALMUS 6121 $4.00
(B2636)

Cancion De Cuna *see Wiegenlied

Chant D'Amour *see Minnelied

Complete Songs Of Brahms, Vols. 1-8
*CCU
solo,pno study sc KALMUS 1168-1176
$1.50, ea.
(B2637)

Complete Works *CCU
(Gal, Hans; Mandyczewski, Eusebius)
contains works for a variety of
instruments and vocal
combinations microfiche
UNIV.MUS.ED. $185.00 reprints of
Breitkopf & Hartel Editions;
contains 26 volumes
(B2638)

Cradle Song *see Wiegenlied

D'amours Eternelles *see Von Ewiger
Liebe

Denn Es Gehet Dem Menschen *Op.121,
No.1
see Vier Ernste Gesange
"It Befalleth Both Men And Beasts"
see Vier Ernste Gesange

Der Jager Und Sein Liebchen *Op.28,
No.4
see Duets, Vol. II

Der Schmeid *Op.19,No.4
"Smith, The" see Metzler's
Masterpieces Vol. 10: Brahms
Lieder For Contralto Or Mezzo-
Soprano
"Smith, The" see Metzler's
Masterpieces Vol. 9: Brahms
Lieder For Soprano

Deutsche Volkslieder, Band I *CCU
high solo,pno BREITKOPF-L EB 6120A
s.p.; low solo,pno BREITKOPF-L
6120B s.p.
(B2639)

Deutsche Volkslieder, Band II *CCU
high solo,pno BREITKOPF-L EB 6121A
s.p.; low solo,pno BREITKOPF-L
EB 6121B s.p.
(B2640)

Deutsche Volkslieder, Vol. I *CCU,
folk,Ger
high solo,pno SCHAUR EE 647 $4.00;
low solo,pno SCHAUR EE 648 $4.00
(B2641)

Deutsche Volkslieder, Vol. I *CCU,
folk,Ger
(Zilcher) 2 soli,pno SCHAUR EE 800
s.p.
(B2642)

Deutsche Volkslieder, Vol. II *CCU,
folk,Ger
high solo,pno SCHAUR EE 649 $4.00;
low solo,pno SCHAUR EE 650 $4.00
(B2643)

Deutsche Volkslieder, Vol. II *CCU,
folk,Ger
(Zilcher) 2 soli,pno SCHAUR EE 801

BRAHMS, JOHANNES (cont'd.)

s.p.   (B2644)

Die Boten Der Liebe *Op.61,No.4
see Four Duets

Die Mainacht *Op.43,No.2
"Night In May" see Metzler's
Masterpieces Vol. 11: Brahms
Lieder For Tenor
"Night In May" see Metzler's
Masterpieces Vol. 12: Brahms
Lieder For Baritone Or Bass
"Night In May" see METZLER'S
MASTERPIECES VOL. 13: SIX SONGS
FOR SOPRANO
"Night In May" see METZLER'S
MASTERPIECES VOL. 14: SIX SONGS
FOR MEZZO-SOPRANO OR CONTRALTO
"La Nuit De Mai" [Ger/Fr] solo,pno/
inst DURAND   (B2645)
"May Night, The" [Ger/Eng] low
solo,pno (E flat maj) SCHIRM.G
$.75   (B2646)
"Night In May" [Ger/Eng] solo,pno
CRAMER   (B2647)

Die Meere *Op.20,No.3
see Three Duets

Die Nonne Und Der Ritter *Op.28,No.1
see Duets, Vol. II

Die Schwestern *Op.61,No.1
see Four Duets

Dimanche *see Sonntag

Duets, Vol. I *CC14U
[Ger] SA soli,pno PETERS 3909 $4.75
contains op. 20, 61, 66, 75
                              (B2648)
Duets, Vol. II
[Ger] ABar soli,pno PETERS 3910
$4.00
contains: Der Jager Und Sein
Liebchen, Op.28,No.4; Die Nonne
Und Der Ritter, Op.28,No.1; Es
Rauschet Das Wasser, Op.28,
No.3; Vor Der Tur, Op.28,No.2
                              (B2649)

En El Mar
(Pardo) [Span] S/T solo,pno (waltz,
op.49, no. 4) RICORDI-ARG BA 8569
s.p.   (B2650)

Enduring Love *see Von Ewiger Liebe

Es Rauschet Das Wasser *Op.28,No.3
see Duets, Vol. II

Fafang Serenad
solo,pno GEHRMANS s.p.   (B2651)

Feldeinsamkeit
"Solitude Champetre" see LA
MUSIQUE, TREIZIEME CAHIER
"Solitude Champetre" [Ger/Fr] solo,
pno/inst DURAND   (B2652)

Fidelite *see Liebestreu

Fifty Selected Songs *CC50L
[Ger/Eng] high solo,pno SCHIRM.G
1582 $10.00; low solo,pno
SCHIRM.G 1581 $10.00   (B2653)

Five Duets
[Eng/Ger/Fr] SA soli,pno SCHAUR
EE 875 $3.25
contains: Am Strande, Op.66,No.3;
Hut' Du Dich, Op.66,No.5;
Jagerlied, Op.66,No.4; Klange,
I, Op.66,No.1; Klange, II,
Op.66,No.2   (B2654)

Forty-Two Folk Songs *CC42U
[Ger/Eng] INTERNAT. low solo,pno
$2.50; high solo,pno $2.50 in two
volumes, sold separately   (B2655)

Four Duets
[Eng/Ger] SA soli,pno SCHAUR EE 838
$3.00
contains: Die Boten Der Liebe,
Op.61,No.4; Die Schwestern,
Op.61,No.1; Klosterfraulein,
Op.61,No.2; Phanomen, Op.61,
No.3   (B2656)

Four Serious Songs, Gypsy Songs And
German Folksongs *CCU
solo,pno study sc KALMUS 728 $1.50
                              (B2657)

Funf Ophelia-Lieder *CC5U
[Ger/Eng] med solo,pno BREITKOPF-W
EB 6332 $2.50   (B2658)

Geistliches Wiegenlied *Op.91,No.2
see Zwei Gesange Fur Alt
"Geistliches Wiegenlied" see Two
Songs For Contralto

Geistliches Wiegenlied *see
Geistliches Wiegenlied

Gestillte Sehnsucht *Op.91,No.1
see Zwei Gesange Fur Alt
"Gestillte Sehnsucht" see Two Songs
For Contralto

Gestillte Sehnsucht *see Gestillte
Sehnsucht

Guten Abend, Gut Nacht
Mez solo,pno (E flat maj) LIENAU
HOS 190 s.p.   (B2659)

Hut' Du Dich *Op.66,No.5
see Five Duets

I Journeyed On My Way *see Ich
Wandte Mich Und Sahe An

Ich Wandte Mich Und Sahe *Op.121,
No.2
see Vier Ernste Gesange

Ich Wandte Mich Und Sahe An
"I Journeyed On My Way" see Vier
Ernste Gesange

It Befalleth Both Men And Beasts
*see Denn Es Gehet Dem Menschen

Jagerlied *Op.66,No.4
see Five Duets

Klange, I *Op.66,No.1
see Five Duets

Klange, II *Op.66,No.2
see Five Duets

Klosterfraulein *Op.61,No.2
see Four Duets

La Nuit De Mai *see Die Mainacht

Le Forgeron
see LA MUSIQUE, PREMIER CAHIER
[Ger/Fr] solo,pno/inst DURAND
                              (B2660)

Liebeslieder Waltzes, Op. 52, And New
Liebeslieder Waltzes, Op. 65
*CCU
(Friedlander) [Ger] 1-4 soli,opt
cor, piano 4 hands cmplt ed
PETERS 3912 $6.50   (B2661)

Liebeslieder-Walzer *Op.52, CCU
SATB soli, piano 4 hands sc
BREITKOPF-L PB 3251 s.p., solo pt
BREITKOPF-L CHB 2603 s.p. (B2662)

Liebestreu
"Love's Faith" see Metzler's
Masterpieces Vol. 10: Brahms
Lieder For Contralto Or Mezzo-
Soprano
"Love's Faith" see Metzler's
Masterpieces Vol. 9: Brahms
Lieder For Soprano
"Fidelite" [Ger/Fr] solo,pno/inst
DURAND   (B2663)

Lieder-Auswahl *CCU
s.p. high solo,pno SCHOTTS 5542;
low solo,pno SCHOTTS 5543 (B2664)

Liederbuch Fur Hoch Stimme *CC34U
high solo,pno BREITKOPF-L EB 6123
$2.50   (B2665)

Liederbuch Fur Mittel Stimme *CC35U
med solo,pno BREITKOPF-L EB 6124
pap $2.50, cloth s.p.   (B2666)

Liederbuch Fur Tiefe Stimme *CC36U
low solo,pno BREITKOPF-L EB 6125
$2.50   (B2667)

Lik En Gronskande Flader
high solo,pno GEHRMANS s.p. (B2668)
low solo,pno GEHRMANS s.p.   (B2669)

Little Dustman, The *see
Sandmannchen

Little Sandman, The *see
Sandmannchen

Love's Faith *see Liebestreu

Lullaby *see Wiegenlied

May Night, The *see Die Mainacht

Meine Liebe Ist Grun
"Mon Amour Fleurit" [Ger/Fr] solo,
pno/inst DURAND   (B2670)

Melodies Textes Francais, Anglais Et
Allemand Vol. I *CC27L
[Fr/Eng/Ger] solo,pno DURAND 11801
s.p.   (B2671)

Melodies Textes Francais, Anglais Et
Allemand Vol. II *CC25L
[Fr/Eng/Ger] solo,pno DURAND 11864
s.p.   (B2672)

Melodies Textes Francais, Anglais Et
Allemand Vol. III *CC24L
[Fr/Eng/Ger] solo,pno DURAND 11906
s.p.   (B2673)

Melodies Textes Francais, Anglais Et
Allemand Vol. IV *CC25L
[Fr/Eng/Ger] solo,pno DURAND 11961
s.p.   (B2674)

Message *see Botschaft

Metzler's Masterpieces Vol. 9: Brahms
Lieder For Soprano
(Klein, Herman; Kreuz, Emil) S
solo,pno CRAMER s.p.
contains: Der Schmeid, "Smith,
The"; Liebestreu, "Love's
Faith"; Sandmannchen, "Little
Dustman, The"; Treue Lebe,
"True Love"; Von Ewiger Liebe,
"Enduring Love"; Wiegenlied,
"Cradle Song"   (B2675)

Metzler's Masterpieces Vol. 10:
Brahms Lieder For Contralto Or
Mezzo-Soprano
(Klein, Herman; Kreuz, Emil) A/Mez
solo,pno CRAMER s.p.
contains: Der Schmeid, "Smith,
The", Op.19,No.4; Liebestreu,
"Love's Faith"; Sandmannchen,
"Little Dustman, The"; Treue
Lebe, "True Love"; Von Ewiger
Liebe, "Enduring Love";
Wiegenlied, "Cradle Song" (B2676)

Metzler's Masterpieces Vol. 11:
Brahms Lieder For Tenor
(Klein, Herman; Kreuz, Emil) T
solo,pno CRAMER s.p.
contains: An Die Nachtigall, "To
The Nightingale"; An Ein
Veilchen, "To A Violet"; Die
Mainacht, "Night In May"; Ruhe
Sussliebchen Im Schatten,
"Rest, O My Dear One"; Sonntag,
"Sunday"; Wie Bist Du Meine
Konigin, "Wond'rous Art Thou,
My Lovely Queen"   (B2677)

Metzler's Masterpieces Vol. 12:
Brahms Lieder For Baritone Or
Bass
(Klein, Herman; Kreuz, Emil) Bar/B
solo,pno CRAMER s.p.
contains: An Die Nachtigall, "To
The Nightingale", Op.46,No.4;
An Ein Veilchen, "To A Violet";
Die Mainacht, "Night In May";
Ruhe Sussliebchen Im Schatten,
"Rest, O My Dear One", Op.33,
No.9; Sonntag, "Sunday"; Wie
Bist Du Meine Konigin,
"Wond'rous Art Thou, My Lovely
Queen", Op.32,No.9   (B2678)

Minnelied
"Chant D'Amour" [Ger/Fr] solo,pno/
inst DURAND   (B2679)

Mon Amour Fleurit *see Meine Liebe
Ist Grun

Mustalaislauluja *CCU
solo,pno FAZER W 2783 s.p.   (B2680)

Neue Liebeslieder-Walzer *Op.65, CCU
4 soli, piano 4 hands sc BREITKOPF-
L PB 3252 s.p., solo pt
BREITKOPF-L CHB 2657 s.p.   (B2681)

Night In May *see Die Mainacht

Ninna Nanna *see Wiegenlied

O Death, How Bitter Art Thou *see O
Tod, Wie Bitter Bist Du

O, Funne Jag Den Vag Igen
high solo,pno GEHRMANS s.p. (B2682)
low solo,pno GEHRMANS s.p.   (B2683)

O Tod, Wie Bitter Bist Du *Op.121,
No.3
see Vier Ernste Gesange
"O Death, How Bitter Art Thou" see
Vier Ernste Gesange

Oda Safica *see Sapphische Ode

Ode Saphique *see Sapphische Ode

Ou S'en Vont Mes Reves
see LA MUSIQUE, HUITIEME CAHIER

Phanomen *Op.61,No.3
see Four Duets

BRAHMS, JOHANNES (cont'd.)

Quartets, Vol. I *CC16U
[Ger] SATB soli,pno PETERS 3911
$7.50 contains Op. 31, 64, 92,
112 (B2684)

Quartets, Vol. III Gypsy Songs
*CC15U
[Ger] SATB soli,pno PETERS 3913
$8.00, ipa contains Op. 103,
Nos.1-11;Op. 112, Nos. 3-6
(B2685)

Rapsodia *see Alto Rhapsody

Rest, O My Dear One *see Ruhe
Sussliebchen Im Schatten

Ruhe Sussliebchen Im Schatten
*Op.33,No.9
"Rest, O My Dear One" see Metzler's
Masterpieces Vol. 12: Brahms
Lieder For Baritone Or Bass
"Rest, O My Dear One" see Metzler's
Masterpieces Vol. 11: Brahms
Lieder For Tenor

Sandman *see Sandmannchen

Sandmannchen
"Little Dustman, The" see Metzler's
Masterpieces Vol. 10: Brahms
Lieder For Contralto Or Mezzo-
Soprano
"Little Dustman, The" see Metzler's
Masterpieces Vol. 9: Brahms
Lieder For Soprano
"Little Sandman, The" [Ger/Eng]
high solo,pno (B flat maj)
SCHIRM.G $.50 (B2686)
"Little Sandman, The" [Ger/Eng] low
solo,pno (G maj) SCHIRM.G $.50
(B2687)
"Sandman" med solo,pno (G maj)
ALLANS s.p. (B2688)

Sapphic Ode *see Sapphische Ode

Sapphische Ode *Op.94,No.4
"Oda Safica" [Span] Mez/Bar solo,
pno RICORDI-ARG BA 8568 s.p. see
also Zehn Leider (B2689)
"Ode Saphique" [Ger/Fr] solo,pno/
inst DURAND (B2690)
"Sapphic Ode" low solo,pno (D maj)
ALLANS s.p. (B2691)
"Sapphic Ode" [Ger/Eng] low solo,
pno (D maj) SCHIRM.G $.85 (B2692)
"Sapphic Ode" [Ger/Eng] high solo,
pno (F maj) SCHIRM.G $.85 (B2693)
"Sapphic Ode" solo,pno (F maj)
ASHDOWN (B2694)

Selected Songs, Vol. I *CCU
(Domandl) solo,gtr SCHAUR EE 1166
s.p. (B2695)

Selected Songs, Vol. II *CCU
(Domandl) solo,gtr SCHAUR EE 1167
s.p. (B2696)

Serenade Inutile *see Vergebliches
Standchen

Serenata Inutil *see Vergebliches
Standchen

Seventy Songs *CC70L
(Kagen, Sergius) [Ger/Eng]
INTERNAT. low solo,pno $7.50;
high solo,pno $7.50 (B2697)

Smith, The *see Der Schmeid

Soir
see LA MUSIQUE, HUITIEME CAHIER

Solitude Champetre *see
Feldeinsamkeit

Sonntag *Op.47,No.3
"Dimanche" see LA MUSIQUE,
QUATORZIEME CAHIER
"Sunday" see Metzler's Masterpieces
Vol. 12: Brahms Lieder For
Baritone Or Bass
"Sunday" see Metzler's Masterpieces
Vol. 11: Brahms Lieder For Tenor
"Dimanche" [Ger/Fr] solo,pno/inst
DURAND (B2698)

Summer Meadows
low solo,pno (F maj) ALLANS s.p.
(B2699)

Sunday *see Sonntag

That Night In May
low solo,pno (E flat maj) ALLANS
s.p. (B2700)

Though With The Tongues Of Men And
Holy Angels *see Wenn Ich Mit
Menschen-Und Mit Engelszungen

BRAHMS, JOHANNES (cont'd.)

Three Duets
[Eng/Ger/Fr] SA soli,pno SCHAUR
EE 667 $3.00
contains: Die Meere, Op.20,No.3;
Weg Der Liebe, I, Op.20,No.1;
Weg Der Liebe, II, Op.20,No.2
(B2701)

To A Violet *see An Ein Veilchen

To The Nightingale *see An Die
Nachtigall

Treachery *see Verrath

Treue Lebe
"True Love" see Metzler's
Masterpieces Vol. 9: Brahms
Lieder For Soprano
"True Love" see Metzler's
Masterpieces Vol. 10: Brahms
Lieder For Contralto Or Mezzo-
Soprano

True Love *see Treue Lebe

Twenty-Nine Selected Songs *CC29L
[Ger] HANSEN-DEN s.p. med solo,kbd;
high solo,kbd (B2702)

Two Songs For Contralto *Op.91
[Ger/Eng] A solo,pno,opt vla/vcl
INTERNAT. $2.00
contains: Geistliches Wiegenlied,
Op.91,No.2; Gestillte
Sehnsucht, Op.91,No.1 (B2703)

Two Songs For Contralto With Viola
And Piano *Op.91, CC2U
A solo,vla,pno SCHAUR EE 845 s.p.
(B2704)

Vaggsang *see Wiegenlied

Vain Suit, The *see Vergebliches
Standchen

Vergebliches Standchen *Op.84,No.4
"Serenade Inutile" [Ger/Fr] solo,
pno/inst DURAND (B2705)
"Serenata Inutil" [Span] Mez/Bar
solo,pno (A flat maj) RICORDI-ARG
BA 8567 s.p. see also Zehn Leider
(B2706)
"Serenata Inutil" [Ger/Span/It] S/T
solo,pno (A maj) RICORDI-ARG
BA 9053 s.p. see also Zehn Leider
(B2707)
"Vain Suit, The" [Ger/Eng] med-high
solo,pno (A maj) SCHIRM.G $.75
(B2708)

Verrath *Op.15,No.5
"Treachery" [Ger/Eng] high solo,pno
(E flat min) SCHIRM.G $.60
(B2709)

Vier Ernste Gesange *sac,CC4U
(Bornefeld) low solo,org sc
HANSSLER 25.011 s.p., ipa (B2710)

Vier Ernste Gesange *Op.121,No.1-4,
CC4U
(Friedlander) [Ger] high solo,pno
PETERS 3907A $3.25; low solo,pno
PETERS 3907B $3.25 (B2711)

Vier Ernste Gesange *Op.121, CC4U
[Eng/Ger] high solo,pno SCHAUR
EE 583 $2.50; A solo,pno SCHAUR
EE 3044 $2.50; Bar solo,pno
SCHAUR EE 687 $2.50; B solo,pno
SCHAUR EE 915 $2.50 (B2712)

Vier Ernste Gesange *Op.121, sac
(Deis) [Eng/Ger] med solo/low solo,
pno SCHIRM.G 1678 $2.00
contains: Denn Es Gehet Dem
Menschen, "It Befalleth Both
Men And Beasts"; Ich Wandte
Mich Und Sahe An, "I Journeyed
On My Way"; O Tod, Wie Bitter
Bist Du, "O Death, How Bitter
Art Thou"; Wenn Ich Mit
Menschen-Und Mit Engelszungen,
"Though With The Tongues Of Men
And Holy Angels" (B2713)

Vier Ernste Gesange *Op.121,No.1-4,
CC4U
[Ger/Eng] s.p. high solo,pno
SCHOTTS 1669; low solo,pno
SCHOTTS 1670; B solo,pno SCHOTTS
1671 (B2714)

Vier Ernste Gesange
(Raphael, Gunter) B solo,2fl,2ob,
2clar,2bsn,2horn,2trp,3trom,timp,
strings voc sc BREITKOPF-W
EB 6117 s.p.
contains: Denn Es Gehet Dem
Menschen, Op.121,No.1; Ich
Wandte Mich Und Sahe, Op.121,
No.2; O Tod, Wie Bitter Bist
Du, Op.121,No.3; Wenn Ich Mit
Menschen- Und Mit Engelszungen
Redete, Op.121,No.4 (B2715)

BRAHMS, JOHANNES (cont'd.)

Vier Ernste Gesange (Four Serious
Songs) *sac,CC4U
(Sargent) A/Bar solo,orch (diff) sc
OXFORD 61.017 $3.30 (B2716)

Vierzehn Volkskinderlieder *CC14U
(Friedlander) [Ger] high solo/med
solo,pno PETERS 3696 $4.00
(B2717)

Virgin's Cradle Song, The *sac
med solo,opt vln/vla BELWIN $1.50
(B2718)

Von Ewiger Liebe *Op.43,No.1
"Enduring Love" see Metzler's
Masterpieces Vol. 10: Brahms
Lieder For Contralto Or Mezzo-
Soprano
"Enduring Love" see Metzler's
Masterpieces Vol. 9: Brahms
Lieder For Soprano
"Enduring Love" see METZLER'S
MASTERPIECES VOL. 15: SIX SONGS
FOR TENOR
"Enduring Love" see METZLER'S
MASTERPIECES VOL. 16: SIX SONGS
FOR BARITONE OR BASS
"D'amours Eternelles" [Ger/Fr]
solo,pno/inst (in 2 keys) DURAND
(B2719)

Vor Der Tur *Op.28,No.2
see Duets, Vol. II

Weg Der Liebe, I *Op.20,No.1
see Three Duets

Weg Der Liebe, II *Op.20,No.2
see Three Duets

Wenn Ich Mit Menschen-Und Mit
Engelszungen
"Though With The Tongues Of Men And
Holy Angels" see Vier Ernste
Gesange

Wenn Ich Mit Menschen- Und Mit
Engelszungen Redete *Op.121,No.4
see Vier Ernste Gesange

Wie Bist Du Meine Konigin *Op.32,
No.9
"Wond'rous Art Thou, My Lovely
Queen" see Metzler's Masterpieces
Vol. 11: Brahms Lieder For Tenor
"Wond'rous Art Thou, My Lovely
Queen" see Metzler's Masterpieces
Vol. 12: Brahms Lieder For
Baritone Or Bass

Wiegenlied *Op.49,No.4
"Cradle Song" see Metzler's
Masterpieces Vol. 9: Brahms
Lieder For Soprano
"Cradle Song" see Metzler's
Masterpieces Vol. 10: Brahms
Lieder For Contralto Or Mezzo-
Soprano
[Czech/Ger] solo,pno SUPRAPHON s.p.
(B2720)
"Berceuse" [Ger/Fr] S solo,pno/inst
DURAND s.p. (B2721)
"Berceuse" [Ger/Fr] Mez solo,pno/
inst DURAND s.p. (B2722)
"Cancion De Cuna" [Ger/It] Mez/Bar
solo,pno RICORDI-ARG BA 7850 s.p.
see also Zehn Leider (B2723)
"Cancion De Cuna" [Ger/Span] S/T
solo,pno RICORDI-ARG BA 7980 s.p.
see also Zehn Leider (B2724)
"Cradle Song" solo,pno (available
in 2 keys) ASHLEY $.95 (B2725)
"Cradle-Song" [Ger/Eng] high solo,
pno (G flat maj) SCHIRM.G $.85
(B2726)
"Cradle-Song" [Ger/Eng] med solo,
pno (F maj) SCHIRM.G $.85 (B2727)
"Cradle-Song" [Ger/Eng] low solo,
pno (E flat maj) SCHIRM.G $.85
(B2728)
"Cradle Song" med solo,pno (C maj)
CENTURY 3243 (B2729)
"Lullaby" med solo,pno (E flat maj)
ALLANS s.p. (B2730)
"Lullaby" high solo,pno (F maj)
ALLANS s.p. (B2731)
"Lullaby" solo,pno ASHDOWN s.p.
(B2732)
"Lullaby" high solo,pno (F maj)
ASHDOWN (B2733)
"Lullaby" low solo,pno (E flat maj)
ASHDOWN (B2734)
"Ninna-Nanna" Mez/Bar solo,pno
RICORDI-ENG 127896 s.p. (B2735)
"Ninna Nanna" [It] solo,pno CURCI
7463 s.p. (B2736)
"Vaggsang" solo,pno LUNDQUIST s.p.
(B2737)
(Palmer) "Cradle Song" med solo,pno
PAXTON P2254 s.p. (B2738)

Wond'rous Art Thou, My Lovely Queen
*see Wie Bist Du Meine Konigin

BRAHMS, JOHANNES (cont'd.)

Zehn Leider *CC10L
[Ger/Span] solo,pno cmplt ed
RICORDI-ARG BA 9056 s.p.
see also: Sapphische Ode, "Oda
Safica", Op.94,No.4; Serenata
Inutil; Wiegenlied, "Cancion De
Cuna", Op.49,No.4   (B2739)

Zigeunerlieder *Op.103, CCU
[Ger/Eng] INTERNAT. low solo,pno
$1.75; high solo,pno $1.75
(B2740)

Zigeunerlieder *Op.103,No.1-10,
CC10U
[Ger/Eng] s.p. high solo,pno
SCHOTTS 1667; low solo,pno
SCHOTTS 1668   (B2741)

Zwei Gesange *Op.91,No.1-2, CC2U
(Friedlander) [Eng/Ger] A solo,vla,
pno,opt vcl PETERS 3908 $3.75
(B2742)

Zwei Gesange Fur Alt
A solo,pno,opt vla cmplt ed
BREITKOPF-L EB 6109 s.p.
contains: Geistliches Wiegenlied,
Op.91,No.2; Gestillte
Sehnsucht, Op.91,No.1   (B2743)

BRAHMS-ALBUM, VOL. I see Brahms,
Johannes

BRAHMS-ALBUM, VOL. II see Brahms,
Johannes

BRAHMS-ALBUM, VOL. III see Brahms,
Johannes

BRAHMS-ALBUM, VOL. IV see Brahms,
Johannes

BRAHMS SONG ALBUM, VOL. 1 see Brahms,
Johannes

BRAHMS SONG ALBUM, VOL. 2 see Brahms,
Johannes

BRAHMS SONG ALBUM, VOL. 3 see Brahms,
Johannes

BRAHMS SONG ALBUM, VOL. 4 see Brahms,
Johannes

BRANCH
Sorry, I Never Knew You (composed
with Little) *sac
solo,pno BENSON S7572-S $1.00
(B2744)

BRANDER'S SONG see Berlioz, Hector

BRANDING see Mulder, Herman

BRANDL
Beloved Melody
low solo,pno (E flat maj) ALLANS
s.p.   (B2745)
high solo,pno (A flat maj) ALLANS
s.p.   (B2746)
med solo,pno (F maj) ALLANS s.p.
(B2747)

BRANDON, GEORGE
With One Accord *sac
med solo,pno oct CONCORDIA 98-1958
$.25   (B2748)

BRANDTS-BUYS, H.
Drie Geestelijke Liederen *sac,CC3U
solo,pno BROEKMANS 412 s.p. (B2749)

Vier Lieder Fur Bass-Stimme *Op.42,
No.1-4, CC4U
DOBLINGER s.p.   (B2750)

BRANDTS-BUYS, L.F.
Mijne Moedertaal
S/T solo,pno ALSBACH s.p.   (B2751)
A/Bar solo,pno ALSBACH s.p.   (B2752)

BRANHAM, MARTHA
Christ Who Lives Within, The *see
Austin, Bill

BRANSCOMBE, GENA (1881-   )
O Love That Guides Our Way *sac
med solo,pno BELWIN $1.50   (B2753)

BRASLAVSKY, SOLOMON G.
Birchas Kohanim *sac
"Blessings Of The Priests" [Heb]
high solo/cantor,pno TRANSCON.
WJ 425 $1.00   (B2754)
"Blessings Of The Priests" [Heb]
med solo/cantor,pno TRANSCON.
WJ 430 $1.00   (B2755)

Blessings Of The Priests *see
Birchas Kohanim

BRAUN
God Said It, I Believe It, That
Settles It! (composed with Adams)
*sac
solo,pno BENSON S5550-S $1.00
(B2756)

BRAUN, CHARLES
Ever So Far Away
low solo,pno (F maj) CRAMER (B2757)
high solo,pno (A flat maj) CRAMER
(B2758)

Sing A Song Of Purple Heather
solo,pno CRAMER   (B2759)

Three Songs Of The Heather *CC3U
solo,pno CRAMER   (B2760)

BRAUN, GENE
Music To Live By *sac,CC12UL
solo,pno BENSON BO455 $2.50 (B2761)

BRAUN, GUNTER
Kinderlieder-Suite *CCU
solo,gtr,2mand, mandola sc GERIG
HG 704 s.p., ipa   (B2762)

BRAUNFELS, BERTEL
Neues Federspiel *see Braunfels,
Walter

BRAUNFELS, WALTER (1882-1954)
Die Gott Minnende Seele *Op.53
solo,pno GERIG HG 188 s.p. (B2763)

Funf Romantische Gesange *Op.58,
CC5U
solo,pno cmplt ed GERIG HG 215 s.p.
(B2764)

Neues Federspiel (composed with
Braunfels, Bertel) *CC8L
solo,fl,ob,clar,bsn,horn,strings
RIES s.p.   (B2765)

Von Der Liebe Suss Und Bittrer Frucht
*Op.62
solo,pno GERIG HG 216 s.p. (B2766)

BRAUTIGAM, HELMUT (1916-1942)
Kleine Weihnachtskantate Nach Alten
Texten *Xmas,cant
SA soli,pno/org BREITKOPF-W EB 6231
$2.00   (B2767)

BRAUTLIEDER see Cornelius, Peter

BRAUTWERBUNG see Trunk, Richard

BRAVE NEW WORLD see Sharpe, Evelyn

BRAVNICAR, MATIJA (1897-   )
Sest Kajuhovih Pesmi *CC6U
solo,pno DRZAVNA rental   (B2768)

BRAVOUR-VARIATIONEN UBER EIN THEMA VON
MOZART see Adam, Adolphe-Charles

BRAW, BRAW LADS *folk,Scot
solo,pno (C maj/D maj) PATERSON FS15
s.p.   (B2769)

BRAY, KENNETH I.
White Butterflies
solo,pno THOMP.G   (B2770)

BREAD AND MUSIC see Spencer, J.

BREAD OF LIFE see Koch

BREAK, BREAK see Lavater

BREAK, BREAK, BREAK see Carey, Lewis

BREAK, BREAK, BREAK see Martin,
Easthope

BREAK, DIVINER LIGHT see Allitsen,
Frances

BREAK FAIREST DAWN see Handel, George
Frideric, Dank Sei Dir, Herr

BREAK O' DAY see Sanderson, Wilfred

BREAK OF DAY see Sutherland, Margaret

BREAK THE COCONUT see Guarnieri,
Camargo Mozart

BREAKFAST TIME see Mourant, Walter

BREATH OF HOME, A see Murray, Alan

BREATHES THE MAN see Laurie, Malcolm

BRECHT-EISLER SONG BOOK, THE *CC42U
(Bentley, Eric; Robinson, Earl) [Ger/
Eng] solo,pno/gtr pap OAK 000168
$6.95, cloth OAK 000062 $10.00
(B2771)

BREDON HILL see Butterworth, George
Sainton Kaye

BREEZE, EDWIN CARTER
God The Architect *sac
high solo,pno CHANTRY VOS 735H $.75
(B2772)

BREFIO see Sveinsson, Gunnar Reynir

BREIT UBER MEIN HAUPT see Strauss,
Richard

BREITKOPF, BERNHARD THEODOR (1745-1820)
Goethes Leipziger Liederbuch *CC20U
solo,pno BREITKOPF-L EB 5540 s.p.
(B2773)

BREMAN, W.F.
Eenzame Nacht
solo,pno ALSBACH s.p.   (B2774)

Egidius Waer Bestu Bleven?
Bar solo,pno ALSBACH s.p.   (B2775)
T solo,pno ALSBACH s.p.   (B2776)

Oud-Driekonigenlied *CCU
solo,pno ALSBACH s.p.   (B2777)

Schlaflied Fur Mirjam
Bar solo,pno ALSBACH s.p.   (B2778)

Venezia
Bar/Mez/A solo,pno ALSBACH s.p.
(B2779)

BRENNER, WALTER (1906-   )
Memorial Prayer *sac
[Eng] high solo,pno TRANSCON.
TV 555 $.60   (B2780)
[Eng] med solo,pno TRANSCON. TV 556
$.60   (B2781)

BRERO, CESARE (1908-   )
La Repasseuse
see Tres Poesias De Neveux

Le Poisson Gris
see Tres Poesias De Neveux

Les Soucis
see Tres Poesias De Neveux

Sous Les Arcades
[Fr] solo,pno RICORDI-ARG BA 10848
s.p.   (B2782)

Tres Poesias De Neveux
[Fr] solo,pno cmplt ed RICORDI-ARG
BA 11350 s.p.
contains: La Repasseuse; Le
Poisson Gris; Les Soucis
(B2783)

BRETAGNE *Fr
(Canteloube, J.) solo,acap DURAND
s.p. see also Anthologie Des Chants
Populaires Francais Tome IV (B2784)

BRETON, TOMAS (1850-1923)
Jota (from La "Dolores")
[Span] high solo,pno UNION ESP.
$1.50   (B2785)

BRETONNES see Rhene-Baton

BREU, S.
Sonntag Ist's
solo,pno HUG s.p.   (B2786)

BREUER, HERBERT (1945-   )
In Memoriam Hans Arp *sac,concerto
S solo,fl,sax,trp,pno,cel,perc
(diff) BAREN. 6141 s.p., ipa
(B2787)

BREVET FRAN MOR see Eken, Torleif

BREVI CANTI see Paccagnini, A.

BREVI, GIOVANNI BATTISTA
Catenae Terrenae *sac
(Ewerhart, Rudolf) [Lat] B solo,
cont BIELER CS 11 s.p.   (B2788)

Deliciae Terrenae *sac
(Ewerhart, Rudolf) [Lat] S/T solo,
cont BIELER CS 25 s.p.   (B2789)

O Spiritus Angelici *sac
(Ewerhart, Rudolf) A solo,cont
BIELER CS 34 s.p.   (B2790)

BREWER, G.
Banks O' Doon
med solo,pno SEESAW $1.00   (B2791)

BREWER, SIR ALFRED HERBERT (1865-1928)
Fairy Pipers
low solo,pno (G maj) BOOSEY $1.50
(B2792)
high solo,pno (B flat maj) BOOSEY
$1.50   (B2793)

BRICH HEREIN, SUSSER SCHEIN see Thiele,
Siegfried

B'RICH SH'MEH see Weiner, Lazar,
Bendicho Su Nombre

BRIDAL CHORUS see Wagner, Richard

BRIDAL DAWN see Martin, Easthope

BRIDAL HYMN see Malotte, Albert Hay

BRIDAL VOW, A see Madsen, Eleanor

BRIDE see Ballou, Esther W.

BRIDE AND MOTHER see Peeters, Flor

BRIDGE see Braein, Edvard Fliflet

BRIDGE, FRANK (1879-1941)
E'en As A Lovely Flower
low solo,pno (E maj) BOOSEY $1.50
(B2794)
high solo,pno (G maj) BOOSEY $1.50
(B2795)
Go Not Happy Day
low solo,pno (G maj) BOOSEY $1.50
(B2796)
high solo,pno (A maj) BOOSEY $1.50
(B2797)
Journeys End
med solo,pno GALLIARD 2.1330.7
$1.75
(B2798)
Love Went A-Riding
solo,pno (G flat maj) BOOSEY $1.50
(B2799)

BRIDGEWATER, ERNEST LESLIE
The Stratford Series Of Shakespeare
Songs, Volume I *CC9L
NOVELLO 17.0230.00 s.p. (B2800)

The Stratford Series Of Shakespeare
Songs, Volume II *CC9L
NOVELLO 17.0231.09 s.p. (B2801)

The Stratford Series Of Shakespeare
Songs, Volume III *CC15L
NOVELLO 17.0232.07 s.p. (B2802)

The Stratford Series Of Shakespeare
Songs, Volume IV *CC44L
NOVELLO 17.0233.05 s.p. (B2803)

BRIEF AN DIE GRENZE see Drejsl, Radim,
Dopis Na Hranici

BRIEF UIT CEZEMBRE see Hullebroeck, Em.

BRIEF UIT FRANKRIJK see Hullebroeck,
Em.

BRIEF UIT VLAANDEREN see Hullebroeck,
Em.

BRIEL, MARIE
Carillon *sac,Xmas
med solo,pno FITZSIMONS $.40
(B2804)

BRIEVEN UIT PORTUGAL see Legley, Victor

BRIGATI
People Got To Be Free (composed with
Cavaliere) *sac
solo,pno BENSON S7368-S $1.00
(B2805)

BRIGGS
Hold Thou My Hand *sac
high solo,pno,opt vln (G maj)
BELWIN $1.50 (B2806)
med solo,pno,opt vln (F maj) BELWIN
$1.50 (B2807)
low solo,pno,opt vln (E flat maj)
BELWIN $1.50 (B2808)
MezBar soli,pno BELWIN $1.50
(B2809)
SA soli,pno BELWIN $1.50 (B2810)
ST soli,pno BELWIN $1.50 (B2811)
med-high solo,pno,opt vln (F maj)
BOSTON $1.50 (B2812)
ST soli,pno ASHLEY $.95 (B2813)
solo,pno (available in 3 keys)
ASHLEY $.95 (B2814)
MezBar soli,pno ASHLEY $.95 (B2815)
SA soli,pno ASHLEY $.95 (B2816)

BRIGGS, C.S.
O Mary, Go Call The Cattle Home
narrator,pno PRESSER $.75 (B2817)

BRIGHT IS THE RING OF WORDS see Vaughan
Williams, Ralph

BRIGHT NEW WORLD see Price, Florence B.

BRIGHT NEW WORLD *sac,CC13UL
(Carmichael, Ralph) solo,pno WORD
30031 $1.95 contains works by:
Price, Flo and others (B2818)

BRIGHT STAR see Dello Joio, Norman

BRIGHT STAR see Maganini, Quinto

BRIGHT STAR see Meyerowitz, Jan

BRIGHTEST AND BEST
(Lipscomb) high solo,pno BELWIN $1.25
(B2819)
(Lipscomb) med solo,pno BELWIN $1.25
(B2820)

BRIGHTEST DAY, THE see Martin, Easthope

BRIGHTEST JEWEL see Burrows, Rex

BRIGID'S SONG see Diamond, David

BRILLIANT BUTTERFLY see Campra, Andre,
Charmant Papillon

BRINA see Caltabiano, S.

BRING BACK THE SPRINGTIME see Kaiser,
Kurt

BRING TO JEHOVAH see Schutz, Heinrich,
Bringt Her Dem Herren

BRING TO THE LORD GOD see Schutz,
Heinrich, Bringt Her Dem Herren

BRING YOUR BURDEN see Irwin

BRINGEN UM ZU KOMMEN see Lehmann, Hans
Ulrich

BRINGT HER DEM HERREN see Schutz,
Heinrich

BRINGUET-IDIARTBORDE, A.
Saisons
[Fr] med solo,pno ESCHIG $.35
(B2821)

BRINK, PHILIP
Elegy After Tu Fu
high solo,pno MEDIA 4108 $3.75
(B2822)

BRISE see Berger, Rod.

BRISE DE MAI see Mendelssohn-Bartholdy,
Felix

BRISE DU SOIR see Durand, Jacques

BRISE MARINE see Gui, Vittorio

BRITAIN, RADIE (1903-   )
Barcarola *vocalise
solo,pno/8vcl SEESAW (B2823)

Withered Flowers
med solo,pno SEESAW $1.00 (B2824)

BRITISH LOYALTY see Hook, James

BRITTANY see Bullock, Ernest

BRITTANY see Farrar, Ernest Bristow

BRITTEN, BENJAMIN (1913-   )
Ash Grove
low solo,pno (F maj) BOOSEY $1.75
(B2825)
high solo,pno (A flat maj) BOOSEY
$1.75 (B2826)

Birds
solo,pno (E maj) BOOSEY $1.75
(B2827)

Bottom's Dream (from Midsummer
Night's Dream, A)
Bar/B solo,pno BOOSEY $2.00 (B2828)

Canticle I *song cycle
high solo,pno BOOSEY $9.00 (B2829)

Canticle II - Abraham And Isaac
*song cycle
AT soli,pno BOOSEY $9.00 (B2830)

Canticle III - Still Falls The Rain
*song cycle
T solo,horn,pno BOOSEY $9.00
(B2831)

Canticle IV: Journey Of The Magi
*Op.86
countertenor&TBar soli,pno FABER
F0438 $12.00 (B2832)

Charm Of Lullabies *CCU
Mez solo,pno BOOSEY $6.00 (B2833)

Corpus Christi Carol *sac
A/Bar solo,pno (med easy) OXFORD
61.908 $1.15 (B2834)
S/T solo,pno (med easy) OXFORD
63.058 $1.15 (B2835)

Embroidery Aria (from Peter Grimes)
S solo,pno BOOSEY $1.75 (B2836)

Fish In The Unruffled Lakes
solo,pno (F sharp maj) BOOSEY $1.75
(B2837)

Foggy, Foggy Dew
low solo,pno (G maj) BOOSEY $1.75
(B2838)
high solo,pno (A flat maj) BOOSEY
$1.75 (B2839)

Holy Sonnets Of John Donne *sac,CCU
high solo,pno BOOSEY $7.00 (B2840)

Les Illuminations De Rimbaud *CCU
S/T solo,strings BOOSEY $9.00
(B2841)

Mother Comfort
2 soli,pno (C min) BOOSEY $2.25
(B2842)

Nocturne *song cycle
T solo,strings,opt 7inst BOOSEY
$10.00 (B2843)

Now Thro' Night's Caressing Grip
solo,pno (C sharp min) BOOSEY $1.75
(B2844)

On This Island *song cycle
[Eng/Fr] solo,pno BOOSEY $6.00
(B2845)

BRITTEN, BENJAMIN (cont'd.)
Our Hunting Fathers *song cycle
high solo,orch BOOSEY $7.50 (B2846)

Plough Boy
low solo,pno (G maj) BOOSEY $1.75
(B2847)
high solo,pno (B flat maj) BOOSEY
$1.75 (B2848)

Poet's Echo, The *Op.76, CC6U
[Russ/Eng/Ger] high solo,pno FABER
F0035 $9.50 (B2849)

Ride (from Rape Of Lucretia, The)
T solo,pno BOOSEY $1.75 (B2850)

Sechs Holderlin Fragmente *CC6U
[Eng/Ger] high solo,pno BOOSEY
$5.00 (B2851)

Serenade *song cycle
T solo,horn,strings BOOSEY $9.50
(B2852)

Seven Sonnets Of Michelangelo *CC7U
T solo,pno BOOSEY $6.00 (B2853)

Ship Of Rio
Mez solo,pno (med) OXFORD 62.226
$1.25 (B2854)

Slumber Song (from Rape Of Lucretia,
The)
[Eng/Ger] Mez solo,pno BOOSEY $1.75
(B2855)

Songs And Proverbs Of William Blake
*Op.74, song cycle
Bar solo,pno FABER F0015 $8.00
(B2856)

Songs From The Chinese *CCU
high solo,gtr BOOSEY $6.00 (B2857)

Tit For Tat *CC5U
med solo,pno FABER F0292 $10.00
(B2858)

Underneath The Abject Willow
2 soli,pno (D maj) BOOSEY $2.25
(B2859)

Who Are These Children? *Op.84, CCU
T solo,pno FABER F0394 $6.00
(B2860)

Winter Words *song cycle
high solo,pno BOOSEY $7.00 (B2861)

BRITTON
Know Ye That The Lord He Is God *sac
med solo,pno (F maj) BOSTON $1.50
(B2862)

BRO, LA CHIESETTA TRISTE see Zandonai,
Riccardo

BROADMAN SOLO COLLECTION *sac,CC7U
(Raymer, Elwyn) med solo,kbd BROADMAN
4525-05 $3.50 (B2863)

BROADNAX, EUGENE
I Heard The Voice Of Jesus Say *sac
med solo,pno GALAXY 1.2206.7 $1.00
(B2864)

BROADWOOD, LUCY E. (? -1929)
Berkshire Tragedy *Eng
solo,pno CRAMER (B2865)

Derby Ram *Eng
solo,pno CRAMER (B2866)

Farmer's Boy *Eng
solo,pno CRAMER (B2867)

Fly Is On The Turmut *Eng
solo,pno CRAMER (B2868)

Golden Vanity, The *Eng
solo,pno CRAMER (B2869)

Green Broom
solo,pno CRAMER (B2870)

Keys Of Heaven *Eng
solo,pno CRAMER (B2871)
2 soli,pno (G maj) CRAMER (B2872)
2 soli,pno (A maj) CRAMER (B2873)

King Arthur *Eng
solo,pno CRAMER (B2874)

My Johnny Was A Shoemaker *Eng
solo,pno CRAMER (B2875)

Robin-A-Thrush *Eng
solo,pno CRAMER (B2876)

Some Rival Has Stolen My True Love
Away
solo,pno (F maj) BOOSEY $1.50
(B2877)

Sweet Sally Gray *Eng
solo,pno CRAMER (B2878)

Twankydillo *Eng
solo,pno CRAMER (B2879)

Young Herchard *Eng
solo,pno CRAMER $.95 (B2880)

B'ROCHOS SHEL CHANUKOH see Marcello,
  Benedetto

BROCK, BLANCHE [KERR] (1888-1958)
  Beyond The Sunset *sac
    solo,pno ALLANS s.p.   (B2881)

BROD, MAX (1884-1968)
  Psalm 76 *sac
    high solo,pno ISRAELI 204 $2.10
                                  (B2882)

BRODER, T.
  Six Rubayyat Of Omar Khayyam *CC6U
    S solo,fl,clar ISR.MUS.INST. 111
    s.p.   (B2883)

BRODEUSES see Aubert, Louis-Francois-
  Marie

BRODRAKRETSEN see Krohn, Felix,
  Veljespiiri

BRODSZKY, FERENC (1902-   )
  I'll Walk With God *sac
    solo,pno ALLANS s.p.   (B2884)

BROEKMAN, HANS (1932-   )
  Six Roland Holst-Songs *CC6U
    med solo,pno DONEMUS s.p.   (B2885)

  Three Achterberg-Songs *CC3U
    med solo,pno DONEMUS s.p.   (B2886)

BROGI
  Fiorellin D'Amore
    solo,pno FORLIVESI 10764 s.p.
                                  (B2887)

  Pianto Nell'ombra
    solo,pno FORLIVESI 10924 s.p.
                                  (B2888)

  Sospiri Al Vento
    solo,pno FORLIVESI 10455 s.p.
                                  (B2889)

BROIT *Jew
  solo,pno KAMMEN 429 $1.00   (B2890)

BROKEN DIALOG see Kennedy, John Brodbin

BROKEN DOLL, THE see Rovics, Howard

BROKEN PIECES see Martin

BROKEN PITCHER, THE see Pontet, Henry

BROKEN VESSEL, THE see Crouch, Andrae

BROLEN, CARL A.
  Vackra Sky!
    low solo,pno GEHRMANS s.p. (B2891)
    high solo,pno GEHRMANS s.p. (B2892)
    med solo,pno GEHRMANS s.p. (B2893)

BROLLOPSDANSEN see Luolajan-Mikkola,
  Vilho, Haatanhu

BROLLOPSMARSCH see Soderman

BROOK, THE see Dolores

BROOKE, HARRY
  At Michael's Gate
    solo,pno (A flat maj) ROBERTON 2568
    s.p.   (B2894)

  Presence, The
    solo,pno CRAMER   (B2895)

BROOM O' THE COWDENKNOWES, THE *folk,
  Scot
    solo,pno (C maj/D maj) PATERSON FS17
    s.p.   (B2896)

BROOMAN
  Norrlanningens Hemlangtan
    solo,pno LUNDQUIST s.p.   (B2897)

BROONES
  Love
    high solo,pno (A flat maj) FISCHER,
    C V 2183   (B2898)
    med solo,pno (F maj) FISCHER,C
    V 2182   (B2899)

  Satisfied
    med solo,pno (A flat maj) FISCHER,C
    V 2184   (B2900)

BROQUA, ALFONSO (1876-1946)
  El Nido *So Am
    (Pujol) high solo,fl,2gtr ESCHIG
    E1509 $2.50 see from Tres Cantos
    Uruguayos   (B2901)

  El Tango *So Am
    (Pujol) high solo,fl,2gtr ESCHIG
    E1509B $2.50 see from Tres Cantos
    Uruguayos   (B2902)

  Tres Cantos Uruguayos
    (Pujol) high solo,fl,2gtr cmplt ed
    AMP $4.75
    contains & see also: El Nido; El
    Tango; Vidalita   (B2903)

BROQUA, ALFONSO (cont'd.)
  Vidalita *So Am
    (Pujol) high solo,fl,2gtr ESCHIG
    E1509A $3.00 see from Tres Cantos
    Uruguayos   (B2904)

BROSSARD, SEBASTIEN DE (1655-1730)
  Festivi Martyres *sac
    (Ewerhart, Rudolf) S/T solo,cont
    BIELER CS 62 s.p.   (B2905)

  O Plenus Irarum Dies *sac
    (Ewerhart, Rudolf) [Lat] B solo,
    cont BIELER CS 24 s.p.   (B2906)

  Quemadmodum Desiderat Cervus *sac
    (Ewerhart, Rudolf) [Lat] S/T solo,
    cont BIELER CS 13 s.p.   (B2907)

  Sonitus Armorum *sac
    (Ewerhart, Rudolf) [Lat] A solo,
    cont BIELER CS 29 s.p.   (B2908)

BROTHER JAMES'S AIR see Bain

BROTHER, LET ME TAKE YOUR HAND *sac
  (Carmichael, Ralph) solo,pno WORD
  S-94   (B2909)

BROTHER SOLDIERS, ALL HAIL! see
  Anonymous

BROTHERHOOD see Offenbach, Isaac

BROUCCI see Trojan, Vaclav

BROUILLARD BLANC see Durand, Jacques

BROUILLARDS see Respighi, Ottorino,
  Nebbie

BROUSEK PRO TVUJ JAZYCEK see Lehnert,
  Josef Robert

BROUTMAN, E.
  Night
    med solo,pno SEESAW $1.00   (B2910)

BROUWERSLIED see Hullebroeck, Em.

BROWN
  All For You *see Bertrand

  Christ My Refuge
    high solo,pno (A flat maj) FISCHER,
    C V 1812   (B2911)
    low solo,pno (F maj) FISCHER,C
    V 1813   (B2912)

  Dutch Carol
    T solo,org WESTERN AV94D $1.00
                                  (B2913)

  Feed My Sheep *sac
    high solo,pno (F maj) FISCHER,C
    V 1800   (B2914)

  Mother's Evening Prayer
    low solo,pno (D maj) FISCHER,C
    V 1805   (B2915)

  Satisfied
    high solo,pno (E flat maj) FISCHER,
    C V 1802   (B2916)
    low solo,pno (C maj) FISCHER,C
    V 1803   (B2917)

  Spanish Carol
    A solo,org WESTERN AV94S $1.00
                                  (B2918)

BROWN, AARON
  Don't Ever Let Go Of My Hand
    (composed with Faye, Linda) *sac
    solo,pno WORD S-444   (B2919)

  If I Knew Then (composed with Phelps,
    David) *sac
    solo,pno WORD S-395   (B2920)

  Jesus Cares For Me (composed with
    Richards, Shane) *sac
    solo,pno WORD S-363   (B2921)

  Show Me The Way (composed with Faye,
    Linda) *sac
    solo,pno WORD S-408   (B2922)

  What I Want You To Be *sac
    solo,pno WORD S-410   (B2923)

BROWN, BERTRAND
  On Life's Highway *sac,Gen
    low solo,pno (D maj) WILLIS $.60
                                  (B2924)
    high solo,pno (F maj) WILLIS $.60
                                  (B2925)

BROWN, CHARLES F.
  Reach Out And Touch *sac
    solo,pno WORD S-291   (B2926)

  To Be God's People *sac
    solo,pno WORD S-439   (B2927)

BROWN EYES OF MARY see King, Wilton

BROWN HAIRED MAIDEN see Lawson, Malcolm

BROWN, MARY HELEN
  Deep-Water Song
    high solo,pno (F maj) WILLIS $.60
                                  (B2928)
    med solo,pno (D flat maj) WILLIS
    $.60   (B2929)
    low solo,pno (B flat maj) WILLIS
    $.60   (B2930)

BROWN, MYRTLE HARE
  I Sing Of A Maiden *sac,Xmas
    med solo,pno (D flat maj) WATERLOO
    $.75   (B2931)

  Mary's Lullaby *sac,Xmas
    med solo,pno (G flat maj) WATERLOO
    $.75   (B2932)

  Youngest Shepherd *sac,Xmas
    med solo,pno (G maj) WATERLOO $.75
                                  (B2933)

BROWN OCTOBER ALE see De Koven, Henry
  Louis Reginald

BROWN PENNY see Blank, Allan

BROWN, R.J.
  Psalm 23 *sac
    high solo,pno BELWIN $1.50 (B2934)
    low solo,pno BELWIN $1.50 (B2935)

BROWN, S.B.
  Your Song From Paradise
    solo,pno (F maj) BOOSEY $1.50
                                  (B2936)

BROWNE
  O Daffodils
    1-2 soli,pno ALLANS s.p.   (B2937)

BROWNING, M.
  Sleep, My Laddie Sleep
    high solo,pno BELWIN $1.50 (B2938)

BRUCE COUNTY BALLAD see Johnston, R.

BRUCE, M. CAMPBELL
  Shepherdess, The
    T solo,pno NOVELLO 17.0170.03 s.p.
                                  (B2939)

BRUCH, MAX (1838-1920)
  Aus Der Tiefe Des Grames *Op.50,
    No.16 (from Achilleus)
    solo,pno SCHAUR EE 3410 s.p.
                                  (B2940)

  Ave Maria *Op.52,No.6
    solo,pno SCHAUR EE 3411 s.p.
                                  (B2941)

  Fritihof
    S solo,orch HENN s.p.   (B2942)

  Noch Lagert Dammerung *Op.50,No.8
    (from Achilleus)
    [Eng/Ger] solo,pno SCHAUR EE 3409
    $.90   (B2943)

  Penelope, Ein Gewand Wirkend *Op.41,
    No.8
    [Eng/Fr/Ger] low solo,pno SCHAUR
    EE 3408B $1.00   (B2944)
    [Eng/Fr/Ger] high solo,pno SCHAUR
    EE 3408A $1.00   (B2945)

  Penelope's Trauer *Op.41,No.5
    [Eng/Fr/Ger] low solo,pno SCHAUR
    EE 3407 $1.00   (B2946)

  Serenad
    high solo,pno GEHRMANS s.p. (B2947)
    low solo,pno GEHRMANS s.p. (B2948)

BRUCKEN FOCK, G.H.G. VAN
  Berceuse D'amorique
    solo,pno BROEKMANS 498 s.p. (B2949)

  Gebed *Op.30,No.2
    solo,pno ALSBACH s.p.   (B2950)

  Zonnedag *Op.30,No.4
    solo,pno ALSBACH s.p.   (B2951)

BRUCKNER, ANTON (1824-1896)
  Ave Maria *sac
    high solo,org BOHM s.p.   (B2952)
    A/Bar solo,pno (F maj) LIENAU
    HOS 191 s.p.   (B2953)
    A solo,5strings sc LEUCKART s.p.,
    ipa   (B2954)
    low solo,org BOHM s.p.   (B2955)

  Herr, In Demut *see Te Ergo

  Jesus, Redeemer, Our Loving Saviour
    *sac
    [Eng] high solo,pno (A flat maj)
    PETERS 6310 $1.25   (B2956)
    [Eng] low solo,pno (F maj) PETERS
    6311 $1.25   (B2957)

  Te Ergo (from Te Deum) sac
    "Herr, In Demut" Bar solo,pno (D
    min) LIENAU HOS 37 s.p.   (B2958)
    "Herr, In Demut" T solo,pno (F min)
    LIENAU HOS 36 s.p.   (B2959)

BRUDBUKETT see Gudmundsson, Ture

BRUDEFAERDEN I HARDANGER see Kjerulf,
[Halfdan]

BRUDER! see Zagwijn, Henri

BRUDER LIEDERLICH see Strauss, Richard

BRUDER LIEDERLICH
[Ger] Bar solo,pno BREITKOPF-W
EB 6458 $5.00
contains: Der Arme Schwartenhals;
Der Krumme Peter; Don Juan;
Rechenexempel   (B2960)

BRUDER SINGER *CC270U
(Baum, Richard; Gericke, Hermann
Peter) med solo,pno (easy) BAREN.
2999 cmplt ed,pap $13.25, cmplt ed,
cloth $16.75   (B2961)

BRUDERCHEN, KOMM TANZ see Humperdinck,
Engelbert

BRUDERLEIN UND SCHWESTERLEIN see
Strauss, Johann

BRUG EI DE OINE SAA! see Bedinger, Hugo

BRUGK, HANS MELCHIOR (1909-   )
Leuchtende Nacht *Op.18, CC5U
[Ger] med solo,fl,pno SCHAUR
EE 3283 $4.50   (B2962)

BRUHL, HEINRICH
Spielmusik *CCU
soli,2vln,vla sc GERIG HG 492 s.p.,
ipa   (B2963)

BRUHNS, NICHOLAUS (1665-1697)
De Profundis Clamavi *sac,concerto
(Stein) [Lat] B solo,org,2vln,vcl
PETERS 5829 $6.00   (B2964)

Der Herr Hat Seinen Stuhl Im Himmel
Bereitet *sac,concerto
(Stein) [Ger] B solo,org,2vln,
2vla,vcl PETERS 5827 $4.25, ipa
(B2965)

Erstanden Ist Der Heilige Christ
*sac,cant
(Stein) [Ger] TT/SS soli,org,2vln,
vcl PETERS 5837 $6.00   (B2966)

Hemmt Eure Tranenflut *sac,cant
(Stein) [Ger] SATB soli,bsn,org,
2vln,2vla,vcl PETERS 5836 $5.00,
ipa   (B2967)

Jauchzet Dem Herren Alle Welt *sac,
concerto
(Stein) [Ger] T/S solo,org,2vln,vcl
PETERS 5828 $6.00   (B2968)

Jauchzet Dem Herrn Alle Welt (Psalm
100) sac,cant
(Walter, Georg A.) S solo,cembalo,
strings,opt trom sc BREITKOPF-W
s.p., ipa   (B2969)

Mein Herz Ist Bereit *sac,concerto
(Stein) [Ger] B solo,org,vln,vcl
PETERS 5830 $6.00   (B2970)

Muss Nicht Der Mensch Auf Dieser
Erden *sac,cant
(Stein) [Ger] SATB soli,bsn,2trp,
org,2vln,2vla,vcl PETERS 5834
$8.00, ipa   (B2971)

Paratum Cor Meum *sac,concerto
(Stein) [Lat] TTB/SSB soli,org,vln,
2vla,vcl PETERS 5832 $6.00
(B2972)

Psalm 100 *see Jauchzet Dem Herrn
Alle Welt

Wohl Dem, Der Den Herren Furchtet
*sac,concerto
(Stein) [Ger] SSB soli,org,bsn,
2vln,2vla,vcl PETERS 5831 $4.25,
ipa   (B2973)

BRUIT D'AILES see Catherine, A.

BRULL, IGNAZ (1846-1907)
Sechse, Sieben Oder Acht *Op.85,No.2
Bar solo,pno SIKORSKI 138 s.p.
(B2974)

BRUMBY, COLIN
Amarilli
high solo,pno ALBERT AHL203 rental
(B2975)
Bess Songs *CCU
Mez solo,fl,gtr,electronic tape
ALBERT AHL204 rental   (B2976)

Christus Petra
T solo,acap ALBERT AHL214 rental
(B2977)

Easter Carol
narrator&med solo,pno ALBERT AHL212
rental   (B2978)

BRUMBY, COLIN (cont'd.)
Ein Traum Ist Unser Leben
low solo,pno ALBERT AHL210 rental
(B2979)

Go And Catch A Falling Star
med solo,pno ALBERT AHL205 rental
(B2980)

Knight Of The Holy Grail, The
solo,pno ALBERT AHL207 rental
(B2981)

Not As The Song Of Other Lands
solo,pno ALBERT AHL206 rental
(B2982)

Sons And Daughters Of Australia
solo,pno ALBERT AHL211 rental
(B2983)

Three Italian Songs *CC3U
high solo,4strings ALBERT AHL208
rental   (B2984)

White Sheep, The
solo,pno ALBERT AHL209 rental
(B2985)

BRUMLEY
Turn Your Radio On *sac
solo,pno BENSON S8270-S $1.00
(B2986)
solo,pno STAMPS 7244 $1.00   (B2987)

BRUN, G.
Dans Les Roseaux
solo,pno (available in 2 keys)
ENOCH s.p.   (B2988)

Ne Pleure Pas Quand Je Mourrai
solo,pno (available in 2 keys)
ENOCH s.p.   (B2989)

BRUNE OU BLONDE see Darty, Paulette

BRUNEAU
L'heureux Vagabond
[Fr] high solo,pno CHOUDENS C243A
s.p.   (B2990)
[Fr] low solo,pno CHOUDENS C243
s.p.   (B2991)

BRUNETTE see Durand, Jacques

BRUNI, TEDESCHI ALBERTO (1915-   )
Viaggio E Finale
T solo,orch voc sc ZERBONI 6768
s.p.   (B2992)

BRUNNER, ADOLF (1901-   )
Gesprach Jesu Mit Nikodemus *sac,
concerto
TB soli,ob,strings,org (diff)
BAREN. 2197 $5.75, ipa   (B2993)

Jesus Und Die Samariterin *sac,
concerto
STB soli,4pt mix cor,fl,strings,org
(diff) BAREN. 2143 $12.50, ipa
(B2994)

Taufkantate *cant
high solo,vln,vcl,org (med diff) sc
BAREN. 2141 $9.75   (B2995)

BRUNNER, M.
Zwanzig Kleine Lieder *CC20U
solo,pno HUG s.p.   (B2996)

BRUNO, CARLO
Tre Sonetti Di Rustico Di Filippo
*CC3U
[It] solo,fl,pic,2clar,bsn,horn,
vln,2vcl sc CURCI 8813 s.p.   (B2997)

BRUNSWICK, MARK (1902-   )
Four Songs *CC4U
T solo,pno AM.COMP.AL. $3.85
(B2998)

BRUSCHETTINI, M. (1896-   )
Giugno
S solo,fl,ob,clar,bsn,horn,timp,pno
CARISH s.p.   (B2999)

BRUSEY
Bells Of Bethlehem, The
[Eng] solo,pno BREITKOPF-W 57 04020
s.p.   (B3000)

BRUSSELMANS, MICHEL (1886-1960)
Heures D'apres-midi
med solo,pno CBDM s.p.   (B3001)

BRUSSO, G.
Herbstgold
solo,pno SCHAUR EE 3547 s.p.
(B3002)

BRUXELLAE MARIANNAE see Kersters,
Willem

BRUXELLES see Poldowski, Lady Dean Paul

BRYAN, BETTY
Songs By Betty Bryan *sac,CC14L
solo,pno MARK CP-50066 $2.00
(B3003)

BRYANT, J.
Bonnie Wee Thing
solo,pno CRAMER   (B3004)

BRYANT, VERNA MAE
Behold I Stand At The Door *sac
high solo,pno (F maj) SCHIRM.G $.60
(B3005)

BRYN, GORDON
Mary And The Kitten
low solo,pno (D maj) CRAMER (B3006)
high solo,pno (E maj) CRAMER
(B3007)

BRYSON
Ageless Thou Art
solo,pno FINE ARTS CM 1087 $.30
(B3008)

B'SHUV ADONOY see Glantz, Yehuda Leib

BUBBLE, THE see Friml, Rudolf

BUBBLE FAIRY, THE see Sherman, H.

BUBBLE SONG see Sharpe, Evelyn

BUBLITCHKI *Jew
"Baigelach" [Jew/Russ] solo,pno
KAMMEN 88 $1.00   (B3009)

BUBLITSCHKI *folk,Russ
[Ger/Russ] solo,pno ZIMMER. 1849 s.p.
(B3010)

BUCALOSSI, E.
Gitana
[Fr] solo,acap oct DURAND s.p.
(B3011)

BUCCHI, VALENTINO (1916-   )
Cinque Madrigali *CC5U,madrigal
solo,harp/pno ZERBONI 4891 s.p.
(B3012)

Lettres De La Religeuse Portugaise
solo,pno RICORDI-ENG 131701 s.p.
(B3013)

Quattro Liriche *CC4U
solo,pno ZERBONI 3925-8 s.p.
(B3014)

Tre Poesie Di Noventa *CC3U
solo,pno ZERBONI 4892 s.p.   (B3015)

BUCCINATE IN NEOMENIA TUBA see Schutz,
Heinrich

BUCH DER LIEBE see Weismann, Wilhelm

BUCHANAN, GEORGE
Ragman, The
low solo,pno (B flat maj) CRAMER
(B3016)
med solo,pno (C maj) CRAMER (B3017)
high solo,pno (D maj) CRAMER
(B3018)
Tinker Tom
solo,pno (C maj) LEONARD-ENG
(B3019)

BUCHTGER, FRITZ (1903-   )
Chansons Irrespectueuses *CCU
S/T solo,pno MODERN s.p.   (B3020)

Gott Ist Geist *CC5U,mot
SSATB soli,org/strings (diff)
BAREN. 4465 $5.50, ipa   (B3021)

BUCK
Blue Bows
low solo,pno (G maj) ALLANS s.p.
(B3022)
high solo,pno (B flat maj) ALLANS
s.p.   (B3023)

Feeding Among The Lilies
solo,pno ALLANS s.p.   (B3024)

Full Sail
solo,pno ALLANS s.p.   (B3025)

Today Is Ours *sac,Marriage
solo,pno LILLENAS SM-634: RN $1.00
(B3026)

Until The Day I Die
low solo,pno (E flat maj) ALLANS
s.p.   (B3027)
med solo,pno (F maj) ALLANS s.p.
(B3028)
high solo,pno (G maj) ALLANS s.p.
(B3029)

BUCK, DUDLEY (1839-1909)
Fear Not Ye, O Israel *sac
high solo,pno (A maj) SCHIRM.G $.85
(B3030)
med solo,pno (G maj) SCHIRM.G $.85
(B3031)
low solo,pno (E maj) SCHIRM.G $.85
(B3032)

Lord Is My Light, The *sac
AB soli,pno SCHIRM.G $.85   (B3033)

My Redeemer And My Lord *sac
high solo,pno PRESSER $.75   (B3034)

Through Peace To Light *sac
high solo,pno (D flat maj) SCHIRM.G
$.60   (B3035)

BUCK, OLE
Calligraphy
S solo,orch sc HANSEN-DEN 29224
rental   (B3036)

BUCK, VERA
Serenity
solo,pno CRAMER   (B3037)

This Is My Prayer
solo,pno CRAMER   (B3038)

To My Lady
solo,pno CRAMER   (B3039)

BUCKNER, JAN
He Was Talking About Me *see
Bagwell, Wendy

BUCKY, FRIDA SARSEN
Blessing, The *song cycle
med solo,pno PEER $2.00   (B3040)

BUDMOUTH DEARS see Finzi, Gerald

BUDS, THE see Mourant, Walter

BUDS IN SPRING see Thomas, M.

BUEN AIRE Y BELLAS CANCIONES see
Llongueras J.

BUESSER
Le Sommeil De L'enfant Jesus *Xmas
"Slumber Song Of The Child Jesus"
[Fr] high solo,pno/harp/org/vln/
vcl CHOUDENS C53 s.p.   (B3041)
"Slumber Song Of The Child Jesus"
[Fr] med solo/low solo,pno/harp/
org/vln/vcl CHOUDENS C54 s.p.
(B3042)
Slumber Song Of The Child Jesus *see
Le Sommeil De L'enfant Jesus

BUGATCH, SAMUEL (1898-   )
Ani Chavatselot Hasharon *sac
"I Am The Rose Of Sharon" [Heb/Eng]
high solo/med solo,pno TRANSCON.
TV 563 $.85   (B3043)

I Am The Rose Of Sharon *see Ani
Chavatselot Hasharon

BUGS! see Birch, Robert Fairfax

BUHLER, W.
Vierzehn Lieder *CC14U
solo,pno HUG s.p.   (B3044)

BUILD MY MANSION see Rambo

BUILD THEE MORE STATELY MANSIONS see
Andrews, Mark

BUILD THEE MORE STATELY MANSIONS see
Weaver, Powell

BUILDER, THE see Cadman, Charles
Wakefield

BULGARISCHE VOLKSLIEDER see Kuba, Lubin

BULL, OLE BORNEMANN (1810-1880)
Paimentyton Sunnuntai *CCU
solo,pno FAZER F 2844 s.p.   (B3045)

BULLOCK, ERNEST (1890-   )
As I Laye A-Thynkinge
solo,pno CRAMER $.95   (B3046)

Brittany
high solo,pno (G maj) ASHDOWN
(B3047)
med-high solo,pno (F maj) ASHDOWN
(B3048)
med solo,pno (E flat maj) ASHDOWN
(B3049)
low solo,pno (D maj) ASHDOWN
(B3050)
For Her Gait If She Be Walking
solo,pno CRAMER $.95   (B3051)

BUNCH OF ROWAN, A see Somers, Harry
Stewart

BUNGE, SAS (1924-   )
Ballade Des Pendus
A/B solo,2fl,2ob,2clar,2bsn,2horn,
timp,perc,harp,strings DONEMUS
s.p.   (B3052)

Berceuse
Mez/A solo,pno DONEMUS s.p.   (B3053)

De Speeldoos *CC5U
solo,fl,pno DONEMUS s.p.   (B3054)

Deux Poemes
med solo,pno DONEMUS s.p.
contains: Dieu Vous Gard; Sonnet
Pour Helene   (B3055)

Dieu Vous Gard
see Deux Poemes

Drink To Me Only
see Three Poems Of Ben Jonson

Four Seventh Century Poems
high solo,pno DONEMUS s.p.
contains: Go, Lovely Rose; Hag Is

BUNGE, SAS (cont'd.)

Astride, The; Never Weather-
Beaten Sail; Orpheus With His
Lute   (B3056)

Go, Lovely Rose
see Four Seventh Century Poems

Hag Is Astride, The
see Four Seventh Century Poems

Klinck-Rym
see Vier Amoureuze Liederen Uit Het
Groot Liedboeck

Liedeken
see Vier Amoureuze Liederen Uit Het
Groot Liedboeck

Never Weather-Beaten Sail
see Four Seventh Century Poems

Orpheus With His Lute
see Four Seventh Century Poems

Song To Celia
see Three Poems Of Ben Jonson

Sonnet
see Vier Amoureuze Liederen Uit Het
Groot Liedboeck

Sonnet IX
see Trois Airs

Sonnet Pour Helene
see Deux Poemes

Sonnet XIV
see Trois Airs

Sonnet XXIV
see Trois Airs

Still To Be Neat
see Three Poems Of Ben Jonson

Three Poems Of Ben Jonson
B solo,pno DONEMUS s.p.
contains: Drink To Me Only; Song
To Celia; Still To Be Neat
(B3057)
Trois Airs
Mez solo,pno DONEMUS s.p.
contains: Sonnet IX; Sonnet XIV;
Sonnet XXIV   (B3058)

Trois Poemes De Jules Supervielle
*CC3U
med solo,pno DONEMUS s.p.   (B3059)

Vier Amoureuze Liederen Uit Het Groot
Liedboeck
Bar solo,pno DONEMUS s.p.
contains: Klinck-Rym; Liedeken;
Sonnet; Wat Baet Dat U Coralen
(B3060)

Wat Baet Dat U Coralen
see Vier Amoureuze Liederen Uit Het
Groot Liedboeck

BUNIN, R.
Romances To Lyrics By English Poets
*CCU
[Russ] solo,pno MEZ KNIGA 2.89 s.p.
(B3061)
BUNTE LIEDER see Szymanowski, Karol

BUONA GENTE, PARLATE! see Spezzaferri,
Giovanni

BUONA SERA see Tesoriero, Gaetano

BURD ELLEN AND THE YOUNG TAMLANE see
Heseltine, Philip

BURDENS ARE LIFTED AT CALVARY see
Moore, John W.

BURFORD, D.
Happiest Of Hearts
solo,pno (D maj) BOOSEY $1.50
(B3062)
BURGE, D.
Song Of Sixpence, A
[Eng] S solo,pno BROUDE,A $2.00
(B3063)
BURGES, PETER
Christmas *sac
solo,pno PATERSON s.p.   (B3064)

BURGESS, DAN
By His Grace *sac
solo,pno WORD S-507   (B3065)

Thank You, Lord (from Apostle, The)
sac
solo,pno WORD S-413   (B3066)

BURGHAUSER, JARMIL (1921-   )
V Slezskem Tonu *CCU
solo,pno SUPRAPHON s.p.   (B3067)

BURGHAUSER, JARMIL (cont'd.)

Zverokruh *CCU
solo,pno SUPRAPHON s.p.   (B3068)

BURIAN, EMIL FRANTISEK (1904-1959)
Ani Labuf, Ani Luna
solo,pno SUPRAPHON s.p.   (B3069)

Detske Pisne *CCU
solo,pno SUPRAPHON s.p.   (B3070)

O Detech *Op.6
solo,pno SUPRAPHON s.p.   (B3071)

Sedm Pisni *CC7U
solo,pno SUPRAPHON s.p.   (B3072)

BURIC, MARIJAN
Mother To Son
[Slav] solo,pno CROATICA s.p.
(B3073)
BURKE
Somebody Bigger Than You And I *see
Lange

BURKHARD, PAUL (1911-   )
Das Examen *song cycle
[Ger/Eng/Fr] Mez solo,harp sc,oct
UNIVER. 11692 $6.25   (B3074)

De Schutzekonig
solo,pno HUG s.p.   (B3075)

BURKHARD, WILLY (1900-1955)
Das Ewige Brausen *cant
B solo,chamb.orch voc sc SCHOTTS
2973 s.p., ipa   (B3076)

Der Sonntag *Op.63
med solo,vln,vcl,pno (diff) BAREN.
2132 $5.75   (B3077)

Die Versuchung Jesu *Op.44, sac
B/A solo,org (med diff) BAREN. 1948
sc $4.25, solo pt $.50   (B3078)

Herbstkantate *Op.36, cant
(Morgenstern, Chr.) S solo,pno,vln,
vcl SCHOTTS 2975 s.p.   (B3079)

Magnificat *Op.64, sac
S solo,org (diff) BAREN. 2109 $5.50
(B3080)
Neun Lieder *Op.70, CC9U
med solo,pno (med diff) BAREN. 2008
$5.50   (B3081)

Und Aus Der Tag Der Pfingsten Erfullt
War *Op.43, sac
low solo,org (med diff) BAREN. 2499
sc $5.75, solo pt $.50   (B3082)

Zehn Lieder *CC10U
high solo,pno (med diff) BAREN.
2089 $7.75   (B3083)

BURKHART, FRANZ (1902-   )
Drei Adventlieder *sac,CC3U,Adv
med solo,ob,gtr DOBLINGER GKM 3
$3.25   (B3084)

O Freude Uber Freude *CC12U,Xmas
solo,org,inst DOBLINGER 07 507 voc
sc s.p., ipa, solo pt s.p.
(B3085)
BURLAKI "EI UCHNJEM" *folk,Russ
[Ger/Russ] solo,pno ZIMMER. 1544 s.p.
(B3086)
BURLAS, LADISLAV (1927-   )
Deti Z Nasho Domu
boy solo/girl solo,pno
SLOV.HUD.FOND s.p.   (B3087)

BURLEIGH, HENRY THACKER (1866-1949)
Jean
high solo,pno PRESSER $.75   (B3088)

O Perfect Love
high solo,pno PRESSER $.95   (B3089)
low solo,pno PRESSER $.95   (B3090)

BURLESKAR see Dorumsgaard, Arne

BURMESE MAID see Martin Van Lennep, H.

BURNS
I Know (composed with Rouse,
Christopher; Mann; Tripp,
LaVerne) *sac
solo,pno BENSON S6054-S $1.00
(B3091)
BURNS, ROBERT
Robert Burns Song Book, The *CCU
(McCourt, T. M.) PATERSON low solo/
med solo,pno s.p.; high solo,pno
s.p.   (B3092)

BURNS, WILLIAM K.
Meditative Songs *sac,CCU
med solo,pno ABINGDON APM-515 $1.25
(B3093)
Two Sacred Solos *sac,CC2U
low solo,pno ABINGDON APM-689 $.75;
high solo,pno ABINGDON APM-688
$.75   (B3094)

BURROWS, BEN
Dusty Miller
  solo,pno CRAMER   (B3095)

BURROWS, REX
Brightest Jewel
  high solo,pno (D maj) CRAMER
                 (B3096)

  low solo,pno (A maj) CRAMER (B3097)

Mist On The River
  solo,pno CRAMER $.95   (B3098)

One Kiss
  solo,pno CRAMER   (B3099)

BURSCHEN UND MADCHEN see Kilpinen,
  Yrio, On Kumpiaki

BURT, [FRANCIS] (1926-   )
Der Schadel *see Skull, The

Skull, The *cant
  "Der Schadel" [Eng/Ger] T solo,pno
  UNIVER. 12790 $5.25   (B3100)

BURTON, ELDIN
Lord's Prayer, The *sac
  med solo,pno MERCURY $.95 (B3101)
  low solo,pno MERCURY $.95 (B3102)

Wish, A
  high solo,pno MERCURY $.95 (B3103)

BURY
There Is A Ladye
  high solo,pno (G maj) FISCHER,C
    V 1217   (B3104)
  low solo,pno (E maj) FISCHER,C
    V 1218   (B3105)

BURY, WINIFRED
Come To Me In My Dreams
  solo,pno PATERSON s.p.   (B3106)

Deep In The Woods
  low solo,pno (F maj) PATERSON s.p.
                 (B3107)
  high solo,pno (A maj) PATERSON s.p.
                 (B3108)

Go Not, Happy Day
  solo,pno PATERSON s.p.   (B3109)

I Know A Bank
  solo,pno PATERSON s.p.   (B3110)

I Will Make You Brooches
  solo,pno PATERSON s.p.   (B3111)

It Was The Lovely Moon
  solo,pno PATERSON s.p.   (B3112)

Moon Complaining
  low solo,pno (B flat maj) PATERSON
    s.p.   (B3113)
  high solo,pno (D flat maj) PATERSON
    s.p.   (B3114)

Over The Sea
  solo,pno PATERSON s.p.   (B3115)

Sweet Nightingale
  solo,pno PATERSON s.p.   (B3116)

Tam I' The Kirk
  solo,pno PATERSON s.p.   (B3117)

There Is A Ladye
  low solo,pno (E maj) PATERSON s.p.
                 (B3118)
  high solo,pno (G maj) PATERSON s.p.
                 (B3119)

BURYING FRIENDS see Badings, Henk

BUSH
New Day
  (Dungan) med solo,pno PRESSER $.95
                 (B3120)

BUSH ABOON TRAQUAIR see Lawson, Malcolm

BUSH ABOON TRAQUAIR, THE *folk,Scot
  solo,pno (G maj) PATERSON FS136 s.p.
                 (B3121)

BUSH, GEOFFREY (1920-   )
Carol
  see Five Mediaeval Lyrics

Colloquy
  see Five Mediaeval Lyrics

Confession
  see Five Mediaeval Lyrics

Farewell Earth's Bliss
  Bar solo,strings NOVELLO rental
                 (B3122)

Fire! Fire!
  see Three Elizabethan Songs

Five Mediaeval Lyrics
  Bar solo,pno ELKIN 27.2764.01 s.p.
    contains: Carol; Colloquy;
    Confession; Rutterkin; Vanity
    Of Human Wishes, The   (B3123)

BUSH, GEOFFREY (cont'd.)
Five Songs For High Voice *CC5U
  high solo,fl,ob,2clar,bsn,2horn,
  2trp,trom,timp,strings NOVELLO
  rental   (B3124)

Four Songs From Hesperides *CC4U
  Bar solo,strings NOVELLO rental
                 (B3125)

Lay A Garland On My Hearse
  high solo,pno NOVELLO 17.0092.08
  s.p.   (B3126)

Lover's Progress *song cycle
  T solo,ob,clar,bsn NOVELLO
  17.0234.03 s.p.   (B3127)

Miracle, The
  high solo,pno SEESAW $2.00 (B3128)

Now The Lusty Spring
  high solo,pno NOVELLO 17.0129.00
  s.p.   (B3129)

Rutterkin
  see Five Mediaeval Lyrics

Sigh No More, Ladies
  see Three Elizabethan Songs

Songs Of Wonder *CCU
  S/T solo,strings NOVELLO rental
                 (B3130)

Sweet, Stay Awhile
  see Three Elizabethan Songs

There Is A Garden In Her Face
  T solo,pno ELKIN 27.2323.09 s.p.
                 (B3131)

Three Elizabethan Songs
  high solo,pno NOVELLO 17.0235.01
  s.p.
    contains: Fire! Fire!; Sigh No
    More, Ladies; Sweet, Stay
    Awhile   (B3132)

Three Songs For High Voice *CC3U
  high solo,strings NOVELLO rental
                 (B3133)

Three Songs From The Ballad Operas
  *CC3U
  Bar solo,2fl,2ob,2clar,2bsn,2horn,
  2trp,timp,strings NOVELLO rental
                 (B3134)

Vanity Of Human Wishes, The
  see Five Mediaeval Lyrics

Weep You No More
  high solo,pno NOVELLO 17.0210.06
  s.p.   (B3135)

What Thing Is Love
  high solo,pno NOVELLO 17.0211.04
  s.p.   (B3136)

When Daffodils Begin To Peer
  high solo,pno NOVELLO 17.0212.02
  s.p.   (B3137)

BUSH LYRICS see Phillips

BUSH SONGS OF AUSTRALIA *Austral
  (Meredith; Hill) solo,pno ALLANS s.p.
                 (B3138)

BUSONI, FERRUCCIO BENVENUTO (1866-1924)
Bin Ein Fahrender Gesell *Op.2,No.2
  see Zwei Lieder

Es Ist Bestimmt In Gottes Rat
  *Op.24,No.2
  low solo,pno BREITKOPF-W DLV 4898
  s.p.   (B3139)

Funf Goethe-Lieder
  voc sc BREITKOPF-W EB 6461 $5.00
    contains: Lied Des Brander (Bar
    solo,2fl,2ob,2clar,2bsn,2horn,
    2trp,3trom,timp,strings); Lied
    Des Mephistopheles (Bar solo,
    2ob,2clar,trom,timp,strings);
    Lied Des Unmuts (Bar solo,2fl,
    2ob,2clar,2bsn,2horn,timp,perc,
    strings); Schlechter Trost (Bar
    solo,fl,clar,bsn,strings);
    Zigeunerlied (Bar solo,2fl,2ob,
    2clar,2bsn,2horn,perc,strings)
    see also: Schlechter Trost
                 (B3140)

Lied Des Brander
  see Funf Goethe-Lieder

Lied Des Mephistopheles
  see Funf Goethe-Lieder

Lied Des Unmuts
  see Funf Goethe-Lieder

Monmouth *Op.24,No.1
  low solo,pno BREITKOPF-W DLV 4897
  s.p.   (B3141)

Schlechter Trost
  Bar solo,pno BREITKOPF-W 08 00185
  s.p.   (B3142)
  Bar solo,fl,clar,bsn,strings

BUSONI, FERRUCCIO BENVENUTO (cont'd.)
  BREITKOPF-W $.90 see also Funf
  Goethe-Lieder   (B3143)

Wer Hat Das Erste Lied Erdacht?
  *Op.2,No.1
  see Zwei Lieder

Zigeunerlied
  see Funf Goethe-Lieder

Zwei Lieder
  solo,pno BREITKOPF-W s.p.
    contains: Bin Ein Fahrender
    Gesell, Op.2,No.2; Wer Hat Das
    Erste Lied Erdacht?, Op.2,No.1
                 (B3144)

BUSSER, H.
Apparition *Op.109,No.2
  [Fr] high solo,pno ESCHIG $1.75 see
  from Trois Melodies   (B3145)

Soupir *Op.109,No 3
  [Fr] high solo,pno ESCHIG $1.25 see
  from Trois Melodies   (B3146)

Trois Melodies *see Apparition,
  Op.109,No.2; Soupir, Op.109,No.3;
  Watteau, Op.109,No.1   (B3147)

Watteau *Op.109,No.1
  [Fr] high solo,pno ESCHIG $1.75 see
  from Trois Melodies   (B3148)

BUSSER, HENRI-PAUL (1872-1973)
A Celle Qui Est Trop Gaie
  S/T solo,pno/inst DURAND s.p.
                 (B3149)

Adieu Clytie
  SMezA soli,orch DURAND s.p., ipr
                 (B3150)

Amours De Marie
  see Trois Quatuors Vocaux

Au Bois De Bettant
  SMezA soli,orch DURAND s.p., ipr
                 (B3151)

Chanson
  Mez/Bar solo,orch DURAND s.p., ipr
                 (B3152)
  S/T solo,orch DURAND s.p., ipr
                 (B3153)

Doucemaitresse
  see Trois Quatuors Vocaux

Evocation
  S/T solo,pno/inst DURAND s.p.
                 (B3154)
  Mez/Bar solo,pno/inst DURAND s.p.
                 (B3155)

Fille De Pandion
  SMezA soli,orch DURAND s.p., ipr
                 (B3156)

Fleur Angevine
  see Trois Quatuors Vocaux

J'ai Mis Mon Coeur A La Fenetre
  SMezA soli,pno DURAND s.p. (B3157)

J'ai Peur D'un Baiser
  S/T solo,pno/inst DURAND s.p.
                 (B3158)

Joli Baton
  SMezA soli,orch DURAND s.p., ipr
                 (B3159)

La Columbe
  Mez/Bar solo,orch DURAND s.p., ipa
                 (B3160)
  S/T solo,orch DURAND s.p., ipa
                 (B3161)

La Meilleure Pensee
  S/T solo,pno/inst DURAND s.p.
                 (B3162)
  Mez/Bar solo,pno/inst DURAND s.p.
                 (B3163)

La Nymphe De La Source
  S/T solo,orch DURAND s.p., ipr
                 (B3164)
  Mez/Bar solo,pno/inst DURAND s.p.
                 (B3165)

La Salutation Angelique
  S/T solo,pno/inst DURAND s.p.
                 (B3166)
  Mez/Bar solo,pno/inst DURAND s.p.
                 (B3167)

Le Message
  Mez/Bar solo,pno/inst DURAND s.p.
                 (B3168)
  S/T solo,orch DURAND s.p., ipr
                 (B3169)

L'Image
  solo,pno/inst (C maj) DURAND s.p.
                 (B3170)
  solo,pno/inst (A maj) DURAND s.p.
                 (B3171)

L'oiseau S'est Tu
  SMezA soli,pno DURAND s.p. (B3172)

Pantoum Neglige
  S/T solo,pno/inst DURAND s.p.
                 (B3173)

Partons, Joli Coeur
  SMezA soli,orch DURAND s.p., ipr
                 (B3174)

BUSSER, HENRI-PAUL (cont'd.)

Pour Que La Nuit Soit Douce
ST/MezT soli,pno DURAND s.p.
(B3175)

Revolte
(Bordese, Stephen) solo,pno ENOCH
s.p. see also CHANSONS DE PAGE
(B3176)

Robin Des Bois
SMezA soli,orch DURAND s.p., ipr
(B3177)

Rosees
S/T solo,orch DURAND s.p., ipr
(B3178)
Mez/Bar solo,pno/inst DURAND s.p.
(B3179)

Trois Quatuors Vocaux
SATB soli,acap cmplt ed DURAND s.p.
contains: Amours De Marie;
Doucemaitresse; Fleur Angevine
(B3180)

Viens Fanny
SMezA soli,orch DURAND s.p., ipr
(B3181)

BUSSLIED see Beethoven, Ludwig van

BUSSOTTI, SYLVANO (1931-   )
Il Nudo (from Torso) CC4U
S solo,pno,4strings sc MOECK 5021
s.p.
(B3182)

Pieces De Chair II *CCU
Bar/female solo,inst,pno RICORDI-
ENG 131667 s.p.
(B3183)

Torso
SMezBar,opt narrator,fl,ob,2clar,
2bsn,2horn,trp,trom,tuba,2harp,
cel,pno,perc,2vln,3vla,4vcl,2bvl
MOECK 5017 rental
(B3184)

BUSTOS, M.
La Necedad
med solo,pno UNION ESP. $4.75
(B3185)

BUSY DAY see Comeau, Bill

BUT LO! THE ANGEL OF THE LORD CAME UPON
THEM see Handel, George Frideric,
Und Siehe, Der Engel Des Herrn

BUT OF THE TIMES AND THE SEASONS see
Pinkham, Daniel

BUT SHALL I GO MOURN FOR THAT? see
Castelnuovo-Tedesco, Mario

BUT STARS REMAINING see LeFanu, Nicola

BUT STILL HE LOVED ME see Wyatt, John
R.

BUT THE LORD IS MINDFUL OF HIS OWN see
Mendelssohn-Bartholdy, Felix

BUTCHER
Feed My Sheep *sac
med solo,pno (D maj) FISCHER,C
V 2432
(B3186)
high solo,pno (G maj) FISCHER,C
V 2290
(B3187)

Love
med solo,pno FISCHER,C V 2429
(B3188)

Mother's Evening Prayer
med solo,pno (G min) FISCHER,C
V 2431
(B3189)
med solo,pno (F maj) FISCHER,C
V 2430
(B3190)

BUTCHER, ORVAL
So Deep To Me *sac
solo,pno WORD S-47
(B3191)

BUTE, C.J.
'K Hou Van Holland
solo,pno ALSBACH s.p.
(B3192)

BUTLER, R.
Digging Up The Road (composed with
Flynn, H.)
solo,pno LEONARD-ENG
(B3193)

Ee, By Gum! (composed with Flynn, H.)
solo,pno LEONARD-ENG
(B3194)

BUTT
They That Have Power
(Friedlander) [Eng] high solo,pno
HINRICHSEN H1564B $2.50 (B3195)

BUTT, JAMES
Ariel's Song
solo,pno CRAMER $.95
(B3196)

I Got Me Flower
med solo,pno BELWIN $1.50 (B3197)

Virtue
med solo,pno BELWIN $1.25 (B3198)

BUTTERFLIES, THE see Chausson, Ernest,
Les Papillons

BUTTERFLY CAUGHT IN THE WIND, A see
Mills, Charles

BUTTERLEY, NIGEL
Carmina *sac
Mez/Bar solo,5winds ALBERT AHL168
rental
(B3199)

Child In Nature
S solo,pno ALBERT AHL213 rental
(B3200)

Joseph And Mary *sac,Xmas
S solo,fl EMI s.p.
(B3201)
solo,fl ALBERT AE179 s.p.
(B3202)

Six Blake Songs *CC6U
med solo,pno ALBERT AHL215 rental
(B3203)

BUTTERWORTH
Four Nocturnal Songs *CC4U
S solo,pno PETERS s.p.
(B3204)

Three German Folk Songs *CC3U
T solo,pno PETERS s.p.
(B3205)

BUTTERWORTH, ARTHUR (1923-   )
Now On Land And Sea Descending
[Eng] A solo,2fl,3ob,3clar,3bsn,
4horn,3trp,3trom,timp,harp,
strings HINRICHSEN rental (B3206)

BUTTERWORTH, GEORGE SAINTON KAYE
(1885-1916)
Bredon Hill
high solo,pno (G maj) GALLIARD
2.1335.7 $1.50
(B3207)

Is My Team Ploughing
low solo,pno GALLIARD 2.1340.7
$1.75
(B3208)

Loveliest Of Trees
med solo,pno GALLIARD 2.1342.7
$1.75
(B3209)

Six Songs From A Shropshire Lad
*CC6U
solo,pno GALLIARD 2.1346.7 $5.00
(B3210)

BUTTNER, CRATO (1616-1679)
Furwahr, Er Trug Unsre Krankheit
*sac,cant
B solo,2vln,cont sc HANSSLER 10.262
s.p., ipa
(B3211)

BUXEUIL, R. DE
La Priere D'un Gueux
solo,pno OUVRIERES s.p.
(B3212)

Maman Pour Ta Fete
solo,pno OUVRIERES s.p.
(B3213)

Pas La Peine D'en Faire Un Roman
solo,pno OUVRIERES s.p.
(B3214)

BUXTEHUDE, DIETRICH (ca. 1637-1707)
Also Hat Gott Die Welt Geliebet
(Cantata 5) sac,Xmas,cant
(Matthaei, Karl) S solo,2vln,vcl,
cont (med diff) BAREN. 288 $5.50
(B3215)

Aperite Mihi Portas Justitiae (Psalm
118) sac,cant
"Open To Me Gates Of Justice" [Eng/
Lat] ATB/TTB soli,pno/org,opt
2vln PETERS 6050 $.75, ipa
(B3216)

Cantata 1 *see Singet Dem Herrn

Cantata 2 *see Herr, Auf Dich Traue
Ich

Cantata 3 *see Sicut Moses

Cantata 4 *see O Gottes Stadt

Cantata 5 *see Also Hat Gott Die
Welt Geliebet

Cantata 6 *see O Frohlich Stunden

Cantata 7 *see Jubilate Domino

Cantata 8 *see Mein Herz Ist Bereit

Cantata 9 *see Laudate Dominum

Cantata 10 *see Herr, Nun Lasst Du
Diener

Cantata 11 *see Schaffe In Mir,
Gott, Ein Rein Herz

Cantata 12 *see Herr, Wenn Ich Nur
Dich Habe

Cantate Domino *sac
(Grusnick, Bruno) SSB soli,cont
(med) BAREN. 542 $5.50 (B3217)

Cantate Domino Canticum Novum *sac,
mot
(Grusnick, Bruno) "Sing To God The
Lord" [Eng/Lat] SSB soli,org
CONCORDIA 97-6246 $.75 (B3218)

BUXTEHUDE, DIETRICH (cont'd.)

Dieu, Sauve-Moi! (from Gott Hilf Mir)
sac
[Fr/Ger] B solo,pno/inst DURAND
s.p.
(B3219)

God, Create In Me A Clean Heart *see
Schaffe Im Mir, Gott, Ein Rein
Herz

God Shall Do My Advising *sac
med solo,pno oct CONCORDIA 98-1449
$.30
(B3220)

He Lives *sac
S/T solo,vln,vla,org,opt vcl sc
CONCORDIA 97-9360 $1.50 (B3221)

Herr, Auf Dich Traue Ich (Cantata 2)
sac,cant
(Matthaei, Karl) S solo,2vln,cont
(med diff) BAREN. 126 $5.75
(B3222)

Herr, Nun Lasst Du Diener (Cantata
10) sac,cant
(Matthaei, Karl) T solo,2vln,cont
(med diff) BAREN. 1752 $5.75
(B3223)

Herr, Wenn Ich Nur Dich Habe (Cantata
12) sac,cant
(Grusnick, Bruno) S solo,2vln,vla,
cont (med diff) BAREN. 1139 $5.75
(B3224)

Herzlich Thut, Mich Verlangen *sac,
cant
[Ger] S solo,2vln,org cmplt ed
NORDISKA s.p.
(B3225)

How Can I E'er Receive *see Wie Soll
Ich Dich Empfangen

I Am The Resurrection *sac
B solo,2vln,vcl/bsn,org sc
CONCORDIA 97-4821 $2.50 (B3226)

Ich Halte Es Dafur, Dass Dieser Welt
Leiden *sac,cant
SB soli,3strings,cont sc HANSSLER
10.037 s.p., ipa, solo pt
HANSSLER s.p.
(B3227)
[Ger] SB soli,3strings,cont HANSEN-
DEN s.p.
(B3228)

In Dulci Jubilo *sac,Xmas,cant
[Lat/Ger] SSB soli,2vln,cont
HANSEN-DEN s.p.
(B3229)

In Te Domine, Speravi *sac,cant
[Lat] SAB soli,cont HANSEN-DEN s.p.
(B3230)

Jubilate Domino (Cantata 7) sac,cant
(Matthaei, Karl) A solo,vla,vcl,
cont (med diff) BAREN. 608-6462
$6.25
(B3231)

Kommst Du, Licht Der Heiden? *sac,
cant
[Ger] SSB soli,strings,cont HANSEN-
DEN s.p.
(B3232)

Lauda Sion Salvatorem *sac,cant
[Lat] SSB soli,strings,cont cmplt
ed HANSEN-DEN s.p.
(B3233)

Laudate Dominum (Cantata 9) sac,cant
(Grusnick, Bruno) S solo,2vln,cont,
opt bsn (med diff) BAREN. 1092
$5.75
(B3234)

Lord, In Thee Do I Trust *sac
high solo,pno BELWIN $1.50 (B3235)

Mein Herz Ist Bereit (Cantata 8) sac,
cant
(Matthaei, Karl) B solo,3vln,vcl,
cont (med diff) BAREN. 724-6463
$6.25
(B3236)

Mit Fried Und Freud Ich Fahr Dahin
*sac
(Fedtke, Traugott) AB soli,2vln,
vcl,opt ob&English horn&2bsn
(med) BAREN. 1735 $5.75, ipa
(B3237)

My Jesus Is My Lasting Joy *sac
(Dickinson; Alwardt) high solo,pno
BELWIN $1.50
(B3238)

Nun Freut Euch, Ihr Frommen Mit Mir
*sac,cant
(Fedtke, Traugott) SS soli,2vln,
cont (med) BAREN. 3625 $7.00
(B3239)

O Clemens, O Mitis, O Coelestis Pater
*sac,cant
[Lat] S solo,strings,org sc HANSEN-
DEN s.p.
(B3240)

O Frohlich Stunden (Cantata 6) sac,
Easter,cant
(Matthaei, Karl) S solo,2vln,vcl,
cont (med diff) BAREN. 289 $5.75
(B3241)

BUXTEHUDE, DIETRICH (cont'd.)

O Gottes Stadt (Cantata 4) sac,cant
(Matthaei, Karl) [Ger/Eng] S solo,
4strings,cont (med diff) BAREN.
128 $7.75 (B3242)

O Jesu Christe, Gottes Sohn *sac
high solo,2S rec,cont HANSSLER
5.041 s.p. (B3243)

Oh, How Blessed *sac
TB/AB soli,vcl,vln,cont oct
CONCORDIA 98-1485 $.30, ipa
(B3244)

Open To Me Gates Of Justice *see
Aperite Mihi Portas Justitiae

Psalm 118 *see Aperite Mihi Portas
Justitiae

Salve, Jesu *sac,cant
SS soli,2vln,cont sc HANSSLER
10.284 s.p., ipa, solo pt
HANSSLER s.p. (B3245)

Schaffe Im Mir, Gott, Ein Rein Herz
*sac,cant
"God, Create In Me A Clean Heart"
S/T solo,2vln,cont sc CONCORDIA
97-9359 $2.25 (B3246)

Schaffe In Mir, Gott, Ein Rein Herz
(Cantata 11) sac,cant
(Matthaei, Karl) S solo,2vln,vcl,
cont (med diff) BAREN. 1753 $5.75
(B3247)

Schonster Jesu, Liebstes Leben *sac
[Ger] S solo,2vln,org sc WILHELM.
s.p. (B3248)

Sicut Modo Geniti Infantes (from
Membra Jesu Nostri) sac,Easter,
cant
(Grusnick, Bruno) ATB soli,2vln,
vcl,cont (med) BAREN. 3460 $5.50
ipa (B3249)

Sicut Moses (Cantata 3) sac,cant
(Matthaei, Karl) S solo,2vln,vcl,
bvl (med diff) BAREN. 127 $5.25
(B3250)

Sing To God The Lord *see Cantate
Domino Canticum Novum

Sing To The Lord A New Song (Cantata
1) sac
[Ger/Eng] S solo,vln,cont sc
CONCORDIA 97-4897 $2.00 (B3251)

Singet Dem Herrn (Cantata 1) sac,cant
(Matthaei, Karl) S solo,vln,cont
(med diff) BAREN. 121 $5.75
(B3252)

Three Lovely Things There Be *sac,
cant
SB soli,2vln,cont sc CONCORDIA
97-9361 $4.00 (B3253)

Vulnerasti Cor Meum (from Membra Jesu
Nostri) sac,Easter,cant
(Grusnick, Bruno) SSB soli,2vln,
5vla,2vcl,cont (med diff) BAREN.
3461 $5.50, ipa (B3254)

Wake, Awake, For Night Is Flying
*sac,cant
[Ger/Eng] SSB soli,strings,cont sc
CONCORDIA 97-4714 $2.25, ipa
(B3255)

Was Mich Auf Dieser Welt Betrubt
*cant
[Eng/Ger] S/T solo,2vln,kbd,opt vcl
cmplt ed BOTE $2.00 (B3256)

Wie Soll Ich Dich Empfangen
"How Can I E'er Receive" SSB soli,
2vln,bsn,cont sc GERIG AV 123
s.p., ipa (B3257)

BUY ME AN OUNCE AND I'LL SELL YOU A
POUND see Blank, Allan

BUY MY STRAWBERRIES see Oliver, Herbert

BUZEK, JAN (1927-)
Je Nam Dobre Na Svete
solo,pno SUPRAPHON (B3258)

BUZZELLIS LIEDLEIN see Schmalz, Paul

BUZZI-PECCIA, ARTURO (1854-1943)
Colombetta
[It/Eng] S solo,pno RICORDI-ENG
NY 410 s.p. (B3259)

Gloria
high solo,pno SHAWNEE IA5022 $.75
(B3260)
low solo,pno SHAWNEE IA5032 $.75
(B3261)

Lolita
[It/Eng] S/T solo,pno RICORDI-ENG
111137 s.p. (B3262)
[It/Eng] Mez/Bar solo,pno RICORDI-
ENG 112929 s.p. (B3263)

BUZZI-PECCIA, ARTURO (cont'd.)

Song Of Ahez The Pale, The
high solo,pno PRESSER $.75 (B3264)
med solo,pno PRESSER $.75 (B3265)

BY A BANK I LAY see Peterkin

BY A LONELY FOREST PATHWAY see Griffes,
Charles Tomlinson, Auf Geheimem
Waldespfade

BY AN' BY *spir
(Burleigh, H. T.) low solo,pno BELWIN
$1.50 (B3266)

BY HIS GRACE see Burgess, Dan

BY MY SIDE see Petrucci, F. Lee

BY ROAD AND RIVER see Brahe, May H.

BY STILL QUIET WATERS see Fisher,
Howard

BY THE BEND OF THE RIVER see Edwards,
Clara

BY THE BIVOUAC'S FITFUL FLAME see
Harty, Sir Hamilton

BY THE CROSS see Williams, R.H.

BY THE DEE AT NIGHT see Pitfield,
Thomas Baron

BY THE FORTS OF KAZAN see Mussorgsky,
Modest, Varlamm's Song

BY THE FOUNTAIN see Chopin, Frederic

BY THE KYLE OF MOOLA *Scot
solo,pno PATERSON s.p. see from
Hebridean Songs, Vol. IV (B3267)

BY THE RIVERS OF BABYLON see Chajes,
Julius

BY THE RIVERS OF BABYLON see Dijk, Jan
van

BY THE ROADSIDE see Lang, Ivana

BY THE SEA
Bar/B solo,pno BIRCH $.75 contains
also: Olive Tree, The (B3268)

BY THE SEA see Schubert, Franz (Peter),
Am Meer

BY THE SHORT CUT TO THE ROSSES see Fox,
Charlotte Milligan

BY THE WATERS OF BABYLON see Richards,
Stephen

BY THE WATERS OF BABYLON see Speaks,
Oley

BY THE WAYSIDE
see Three Moravian Carols

BY THE WITNESS OF THE SPIRIT see
Gaither

BY WATERS OF BABYLON see Bach, Johann
Sebastian

BYE BABY BUNTING see Presser, William

BYGATAN UTFOR see Merikanto, Oskar

BYGONE DAYS see Hemery, Valentine

BYGONE OCCASION, A see Binkerd, Gordon

BYRD, WILLIAM (1543-1623)
Collected Works Of William Byrd, Vol.
15: Consort Songs *CCU
solo,pno STAINER 3.1615.7 $16.50
(B3269)

C

CA COMMENCAIT SI GENTIMENT see Lecocq,
Charles

CA' THE YOWES TO THE KNOWES *folk,Scot
solo,pno (A min/B min) PATERSON FS19
s.p. (C1)

CA' THE YOWES TO THE KNOWES see Lawson,
Malcolm

CAAMANO, ROBERTO
A Xusticia Pol-A-Man
see Dos Cantos Gallegos, Op. 3

Ay Madre, Nunca Mal Sentiu
see Dos Cantares Galaico-
Portugueses Del Siglo XIII, OP.
18

Benedictus *Op.14, sac
[Lat] solo,pno RICORDI-ARG BA 10863
s.p. (C2)

Dos Cantares Galaico-Portugueses Del
Siglo XIII, OP. 18
[Port/Span] solo,pno cmplt ed
RICORDI-ARG BA 11624 s.p.
contains: Ay Madre, Nunca Mal
Sentiu; Filha, Se Grado Edes
(C3)

Dos Cantos Gallegos, Op. 3
solo,pno cmplt ed RICORDI-ARG
BA 11174 s.p. original and
Spanish texts
contains: A Xusticia Pol-A-Man;
Vamos Bebendo (C4)

Filha, Se Grado Edes
see Dos Cantares Galaico-
Portugueses Del Siglo XIII, OP.
18

Lamento *Op.13
solo,pno (without words) RICORDI-
ARG BA 10864 s.p. (C5)

Tres Cantos De Navidad *CC3U,Xmas
low solo,pno BARRY-ARG BC 2004
$2.00 (C6)

Vamos Bebendo
see Dos Cantos Gallegos, Op. 3

CABARETLIEDJES see Witte, D.

CABARETLIEDJES see Witte, D.

CABIN see Bowles, Paul Frederic

CABOCLA DE CAXANGA see Villa-Lobos,
Heitor

CABY, R.
Carte Postale
see Poemes

Chanson De La Servante
solo,pno ENOCH s.p. (C7)

Clotilde
see Poemes

Cors De Chasse
solo,pno ENOCH s.p. (C8)

La Traversee
see Poemes

L'Adieu
see Poemes

Le Fusille
solo,pno ENOCH s.p. (C9)

Les Feux Du Bivouac
see Poemes

Par Les Portes D'Orkenise
solo,pno ENOCH s.p. (C10)

Poemes
solo,pno cmplt ed ENOCH s.p.
contains: Carte Postale;
Clotilde; La Traversee;
L'Adieu; Les Feux Du Bivouac
(C11)

Ritournelle
solo,pno ENOCH s.p. (C12)

CACCINI, FRANCESCA (1588-1640)
Arie Fur Soprano *sac
S solo,2fl/2vln,harp,cont sc FMA
FMA 33 s.p. (C13)

O Che Nuovo Stupor
(Flothius, Marius) [It] Mez solo,
vla,fl,ob,pno BROEKMANS 395-17
s.p. (C14)

CACCINI, GIULIO (1546-1618)
Amarilli
see DREI ARIEN AUS DEM SEIBZEHNTEN
JAHRHUNDERT

Amarilli Mia Bella *madrigal
[It/Fr] S/T solo,pno RICORDI-ARG
BA 8161 s.p.   (C15)
"Amarilli My Fair One" [It/Eng] low
solo,pno (F min) SCHIRM.G $.50
(C16)
(Parisotti) "Amaryllis" [It/Fr] S/T
solo,pno RICORDI-ENG 121036 s.p.
(C17)
(Parisotti) "Amaryllis" [It/Fr]
Mez/Bar solo,pno RICORDI-ENG
113448 s.p.   (C18)

Amarilli My Fair One *see Amarilli,
Mia Bella

Amaryllis *see Amarilli Mia Bella

Le Nuove Musiche *CCU
(Hitchcock, H. Wiley) solo,pno A-R
ED s.p.   (C19)

Le Nuove Musiche *CCU
solo,pno BROUDE BR. $25.00   (C20)

Nuove Musiche E Nuova Maniera Di
Scriverle *CC29U
(Hitchcock, H. Wiley) T/B solo,cont
A-R ED s.p.   (C21)

CACHE-CACHE see Absil, Jean

CACHE-CACHE see Aubert, Louis-Francois-
Marie

CACHE-CACHE see Absil, Jean

CACHE DANS CET ASILE see Godard,
Benjamin Louis Paul

CACHES DANS CET ASILE see Godard,
Benjamin Louis Paul

CACILIE see Strauss, Richard

CACIOPPO, G.
Time On Time In Miracles
S solo,2horn,trom,bass trom,pno,
perc,vcl BERANDOL BER 1109 $5.00
(C22)

CADENZA MICHELANGIOLESCHE see Vlad,
Roman

CADET-COQUELIN see Petit, A.

CADET-ROUSSEL see Arrieu, Claude

CADIER, M.
Les Moineaux
solo,pno/inst DURAND s.p.   (C23)

CADIX see Durand, Jacques

CADMAN, CHARLES WAKEFIELD (1881-1946)
At Dawning *Op.29,No.1
med solo&low solo,pno PRESSER $.95
(C24)
high solo,pno PRESSER $.95   (C25)
high solo&med solo,pno PRESSER $.95
(C26)
low solo,pno PRESSER $.95   (C27)
med-low solo,pno PRESSER $.95   (C28)
med solo,pno PRESSER $.95   (C29)

Builder, The *Op.78,No.1
med solo,pno SHAWNEE IA5007 $.60
(C30)
high solo,pno SHAWNEE IA5010 $.60
(C31)
low solo,pno SHAWNEE IA5001 $.75
(C32)
med-low solo,pno SHAWNEE IA5003
$.75   (C33)

Driving With A Lady
med solo,pno (B flat maj) MUSICUS
$1.25   (C34)
low solo,pno (G maj) MUSICUS $1.25
(C35)
Mistah Shakespeah
med solo,pno (D min) MUSICUS $1.25
(C36)

O Ye Who Seek The Lord *sac
high solo,pno BELWIN $1.50   (C37)

Snowflakes At My Window
med solo,pno FITZSIMONS $.40   (C38)

CADON LE STELLE see Davico, Vincenzo

CADUNT UMBRAE see Eder, Helmut

CADZOW, D.
Golden Dawn
solo,pno BERANDOL BER 1301 $1.50
(C39)

Lord's Prayer, The *sac
med solo,pno (F sharp min) CENTURY
3933 $.40   (C40)

CAGE D'OISEAU see Garant, S.

CAGE, JOHN (1912-   )
Aria
solo PETERS 6701 $12.50   (C41)

Experiences II
solo PETERS 6708B $5.00   (C42)

Five Songs For Contralto *CC5U
A solo,pno PETERS 6710 $9.00   (C43)

Flower, A
solo,pno PETERS 6711 $4.00   (C44)

Forever And Sunsmell
solo,2perc PETERS 6715 $5.00   (C45)

She Is Asleep I
4solo,12drums sc PETERS 6746 $12.00
(C46)
She Is Asleep II
solo PETERS 6747 $5.00   (C47)

Sixty-Two Mesostics Re Merce
Cunningham *CC62U
solo,acap, microphone needed PETERS
6807 $27.50   (C48)

Solo For Voice 1
solo PETERS 6750 $2.00   (C49)

Solo For Voice 2
solo PETERS 6751 $13.50   (C50)

Song Books, Vol. 1: Solos For Voice
3-58 *CCU
solo,pno PETERS 6806A $80.00   (C51)

Song Books, Vol. II: Solos For Voice
59-92 *CCU
solo,pno PETERS 6806B $80.00   (C52)

Wonderful Widow Of Eighteen Springs,
The
solo,pno PETERS 6297 $2.50   (C53)

CAGED BIRD see Joubert, John

CAGGIANO, ROBERTO
Anima Mia Speranza
see Tre Poesie Di R. Carrieri

Avidamento Allargo La Mia Mano
see Tre Poesie Mistiche Di S.
Quasimodo

El Canto
see Tre Poesie Di F. Garcia Lorca

Il Cielo E Deserto
see Tre Poesie Di R. Carrieri

La Balada Del Agua Del Mar
see Tre Poesie Di F. Garcia Lorca

Malaguena
see Tre Poesie Di F. Garcia Lorca

Mamma Fammi La Pappa
[It] solo,pno SANTIS 332 s.p. (C54)

Morti
see Tre Poesie Di R. Carrieri

Nessuno
see Tre Poesie Mistiche Di S.
Quasimodo

Si China Il Giorno
see Tre Poesie Mistiche Di S.
Quasimodo

Tre Poesie Di F. Garcia Lorca
[It] solo,pno cmplt ed SANTIS 821
s.p.
contains: El Canto; La Balada Del
Agua Del Mar; Malaguena   (C55)

Tre Poesie Di R. Carrieri
[It] solo,pno cmplt ed SANTIS 820
s.p.
contains: Anima Mia Speranza; Il
Cielo E Deserto; Morti   (C56)

Tre Poesie Mistiche Di S. Quasimodo
[It] solo,pno cmplt ed SANTIS 802
s.p.
contains: Avidamento Allargo La
Mia Mano; Nessuno; Si China Il
Giorno   (C57)

CAHOOTS see Swanson, Howard

CAIN, NOBLE (1896-   )
Loving Me
low solo,pno (B flat maj) BOOSEY
$1.50   (C58)
high solo,pno (E flat maj) BOOSEY
$1.50   (C59)

CAIRONE, RENATO
Amaca
see Sei Piccole Liriche

CAIRONE, RENATO (cont'd.)

Il Guindolo
see Sei Piccole Liriche

Lili
see Sei Piccole Liriche

Momento D'amore A Una Corolla
see Sei Piccole Liriche

O Confortante Voce
see Sei Piccole Liriche

Rondo
see Sei Piccole Liriche

Sei Piccole Liriche
[It] solo,pno cmplt ed SANTIS 757
s.p.
contains: Amaca; Il Guindolo;
Lili; Momento D'amore A Una
Corolla; O Confortante Voce;
Rondo   (C60)

CAJA CHAYERA see Quaratino, Pascual

CALABRO, LOUIS
Cantilena
solo,strings ELKAN-V $1.25, ipr
(C61)
Macabre Reflections *song cycle
Mez solo,pno ELKAN-V $2.50   (C62)

CALAFATO, SALVATORE (1933-   )
Guerra A La Guerra Por La Guerra
Bar solo,6inst sc ZERBONI 6893 s.p.
(C63)

CALAMITES see Heiss, Hermann

CALATANAZOR see Gombau, G.

CALATO IN ARNO see Giordano, Umberto

CALCAGNO, ELSA
La Parra Quebrada
[Span] solo,pno RICORDI-ARG BA 9637
s.p.   (C64)

Madre Vidalitay
[Span] solo,pno RICORDI-ARG
BA 10946 s.p.   (C65)

CALDARA, ANTONIO (1670-1736)
Come Raggio Di Sol
[It/Fr] Mez/Bar solo,pno RICORDI-
ARG BA 11850 s.p.   (C66)
(Parisotti) [It/Fr] S/T solo,pno
RICORDI-ENG 121037 s.p.   (C67)

Haec Est Regina Virginum *sac,cant
(Ewerhart, Rudolf) [Lat] S solo,
2vln,cont sc BIELER DK 11 s.p.,
ipa   (C68)

Laudate, Pueri, Dominum (Psalm 112)
sac,cant
S solo,mix cor,2vln,vcl/bvl sc
GERIG AV 131 s.p., ipa   (C69)

Psalm 112 *see Laudate, Pueri,
Dominum

Quell' Usignuolo (from Sancta Ferma)
[Ger/Eng/It] S solo,fl,pno ZIMMER.
1113 $2.00   (C70)

Sebben, Crudele
(Parisotti) [It/Fr] Mez/Bar solo,
pno RICORDI-ENG 113462 s.p. (C71)

Veni, Dilecte, Veni *sac
(Ewerhart, Rudolf) [Lat] S/T solo,
cont BIELER CS 27 s.p.   (C72)

CALDER, LEE
God Is My Salvation *sac
med solo,pno (F maj) GALAXY
1.2182.7 $1.00   (C73)

CALDO SANGUE see Scarlatti, Alessandro

CALDWELL, MARY ELIZABETH (1909-   )
Carol Of The Little King *sac,Xmas
med solo/low solo,pno BELWIN $1.50
(C74)
I Know A Lovely Garden *sac,Easter
high solo,pno BELWIN $1.50   (C75)
low solo,pno BELWIN $1.50   (C76)

Lute Caroll, A *sac,Xmas
med solo,opt fl/vln BELWIN $1.50
(C77)

Sweet Holy Child *sac,Xmas
high solo,pno BELWIN $1.50   (C78)
low solo,pno BELWIN $1.50   (C79)

CALENDAPRILE see Gandino, Adolfo

CALES OTERO, F.
Tres Canciones *CC3U
[Span] high solo,pno UNION ESP.
$1.50   (C80)

CALI'
E Vui Durmiti Ancora
solo,pno FORLIVESI 12266 s.p.   (C81)

CALICO PIE see Koch, Johannes H.E.

CALINO see Lacome, Paul

CALL, THE see Ashley, Derick

CALL, THE see Oliver, Herbert

CALL, THE see Vaughan Williams, Ralph

CALL OF LOVE see Mana-Zucca, Mme.

CALL OF THE PROPHET, THE see Kayden, M.

CALLEJEO see Granados, Enrique

CALLER HERRIN *Scot
low solo,pno (E flat maj) CRAMER
(C82)
high solo,pno (F maj) CRAMER   (C83)
solo,pno LEONARD-ENG   (C84)

CALLIGRAMMES see Poulenc, Francis

CALLIGRAPHY see Buck, Ole

CALLING TO ME see Di Veroli, Manilio

CALLING TO THEE see Wyatt, E.

CALLUM O' GLEN *folk,Scot
solo,pno (A min) PATERSON FS25 s.p.
(C85)

CALM AS THE NIGHT see Bohm, Carl, Still
Wie Die Nacht

CALM IS THE NIGHT see Niles, John Jacob

CALM ME, O FATHER see Verdi, Giuseppe,
Pace, Pace, Mio Dio

CALME NOCTURNE see Pennequin, J.-G.

CALMES AUX QUAIS DESERTS see Mulot, M.

CALTABIANO, S.
A Te
solo,pno BONGIOVANI 2155 s.p. (C86)

Alla Sera
see Due Sonetti Del Foscolo

Bella E La Donna Mia
see Tre Liriche Carducciane

Brina
solo,pno BONGIOVANI 1809 s.p. (C87)

Chitarra Di Notte
solo,pno BONGIOVANI 1885 s.p. (C88)

Cinque Liriche Su Poesie Greche
solo,pno cmplt ed BONGIOVANI 1963
s.p.
contains: Desiderio; Il Figlio
Alla Madre Severa; Invocazione;
Preghiera D'un Clefta;
Rimprovero   (C89)

Desiderio
see Cinque Liriche Su Poesie Greche

Domani
solo,pno BONGIOVANI 1811 s.p. (C90)

Due Sonetti Del Foscolo
solo,pno cmplt ed BONGIOVANI 2313
s.p.
contains: Alla Sera; In Morte Del
Fratello   (C91)

I Pini
solo,pno BONGIOVANI 1884 s.p. (C92)

Il Figlio Alla Madre Severa
see Cinque Liriche Su Poesie Greche

In Morte Del Fratello
see Due Sonetti Del Foscolo

Invocazione
see Cinque Liriche Su Poesie Greche

Passa La Nave Mia
see Tre Liriche Carducciane

Pianto Antico
see Tre Liriche Carducciane

Preghiera Dell'Alba
solo,pno BONGIOVANI 2154 s.p. (C93)

Preghiera D'un Clefta
see Cinque Liriche Su Poesie Greche

Profumo
solo,pno BONGIOVANI 1810 s.p. (C94)

Rimprovero
see Cinque Liriche Su Poesie Greche

CALTABIANO, S. (cont'd.)
Tre Canti Saffici *CC3U
A solo,pno BONGIOVANI 2207 s.p.
(C95)

Tre Liriche Carducciane
[It] solo,pno cmplt ed BONGIOVANI
2477 s.p.
contains: Bella E La Donna Mia;
Passa La Nave Mia; Pianto
Antico   (C96)

CALVARY see Lee, Don

CALVARY see Rodney, Paul

CALVARY ROAD, THE see Lillenas, Haldor

CALYPSO see Carolus-Duran, P.

CAMARGO GUARNIERI
A Cantiga Da Mutuca
see Quatro Cantigas

Cantiga
see Quatro Cantigas

Cinco Poemas De Alice
[Port] solo,pno cmplt ed RICORDI-
ARG BA 11642 s.p.
contains: E Agora...So Me Resta A
Minha Voz; Nao Posso Mais
Esconder Que Te Amo; Pedido;
Promesa; Recolhi No Meu Coracao
A Tua Voz   (C97)

E Agora...So Me Resta A Minha Voz
see Cinco Poemas De Alice

Nao Posso Mais Esconder Que Te Amo
see Cinco Poemas De Alice

Nao Sei
see Quatro Cantigas

Para Acordar Teu Coracao *CC8L
[Port] solo,pno cmplt ed RICORDI-
ARG BA 11095 s.p.   (C98)

Pedido
see Cinco Poemas De Alice

Promesa
see Cinco Poemas De Alice

Quatro Cantigas
[Port] solo,pno cmplt ed RICORDI-
ARG BA 11621 s.p.
contains: A Cantiga Da Mutuca;
Cantiga; Nao Sei; Vamos A Dar A
Despedida   (C99)

Recolhi No Meu Coracao A Tua Voz
see Cinco Poemas De Alice

Vamos A Dar A Despedida
see Quatro Cantigas

CAMBIERI, EMILIO (1907-1967)
Canti Della Primavera *sac/sec,CCU
ACORD s.p.   (C100)

CAMEL'S HUMP, THE see German, Edward

CAMEOS FOR KIDDIES see Gourley, Ronald

CAMILLERI, CHARLES
Three Songs From Omar Khayyam *sec,
CC3U
med solo,pno (C maj) WATERLOO $1.25
(C101)

CAMMINA, CAMMINA see Margola, Franco

CAMPAIGN see Reif, Paul

CAMPANA
La Malinconia
[It] solo,pno DURAND 24 s.p. (C102)

Maria Och Rizzio
2 soli,pno LUNDQUIST s.p.   (C103)

CAMPANAS see Guastavino, Carlos

CAMPANE DI FESTA see Veneziani, Vittore

CAMPANELLA see Recli, Giulia

CAMPBELL
He'll Understand And Say "Well Done"
*sac
solo,pno BENSON S5752-RS $1.00
(C104)
I've Got More To Go To Heaven For
*sac
solo,pno BENSON S6437-S $1.00
(C105)
Less Of Me *sac
solo,pno BENSON S6842-R $1.25
(C106)
Next Step, The *sac
solo,pno BENSON S7992-S $1.00
(C107)

CAMPBELL, ALEX
Songs *CCU
solo,pno GALLIARD 2.9022.7 $2.25
(C108)

CAMPBELL, DAVID
Search *CCU
solo,pno GALLIARD 2.9021.7 $2.25
(C109)

CAMPBELL, HILDA M.
Orain Na Clarsaich
"Songs Of The Harp" solo,pno
PATERSON s.p.   (C110)

Songs Of The Harp *see Orain Na
Clarsaich

CAMPBELL, JACK
Hold My Coat *sac
solo,pno WORD S-411   (C111)

I'm Living In A Happy World *sac
solo,pno WORD S-393   (C112)

I've Got More To Go To Heaven For
*sac
solo,pno WORD S-431   (C113)

Jesus *sac
solo,pno GOSPEL 05 TM 0368 $1.00
(C114)

CAMPBELL-TIPTON, LOUIS (1877-1921)
Crying Of Water, The *see Le Cri Des
Eaux

Hymn To The Night
high solo,pno BELWIN $1.50   (C115)
low solo,pno BELWIN $1.50   (C116)

Le Cri Des Eaux
"Crying Of Water, The" [Fr/Eng]
high solo,pno (B maj) SCHIRM.G
$.75   (C117)

Spirit Flower
low solo,pno (D maj) ALLANS s.p.
(C118)
med solo,pno (E maj) ALLANS s.p.
(C119)
high solo,pno (G flat maj) ALLANS
s.p.   (C120)

Spirit Flower, A
[Ger/Eng] med solo,pno (E maj)
SCHIRM.G $.85   (C121)

CAMPENHOUT, FRANCOIS VAN (1779-1848)
La Brabanconne
solo,pno/inst DURAND s.p.   (C122)

CAMPIAN, THOMAS (1567-1620)
Songs From Rosseter's Book Of Ayres
(1601) *CCU
solo,pno STAINER 3.1346.7 $5.50
(C123)
Third Book Of Ayres (C1617) *CCU
solo,pno GALLIARD 3.1345.7 $6.25
(C124)

CAMPION, EDWARD
Ninety And Nine, The *sac
med solo,pno (F min) SCHIRM.G $.85
(C125)
low solo,pno (D min) SCHIRM.G $.85
(C126)

CAMPMANY, MONTSERRAT
Azul
[Span] solo,pno RICORDI-ARG
BA 11051 s.p.   (C127)

Canto De Amor
[Span] solo,pno RICORDI-ARG
BA 11044 s.p.   (C128)

CAMPOGALLIANI, E.
Castello In Aria
solo,pno BONGIOVANI 1957 s.p.
(C129)

L'Arrivo
solo,pno BONGIOVANI 1919 s.p.
(C130)

Piangete Occhi
solo,pno BONGIOVANI 1920 s.p.
(C131)

CAMPOLIETI
Serenade
solo,pno RICORDI-FR R1874 s.p.
(C132)

CAMPOS-PARSI, HECTOR
Columnas Y Circulos
solo,pno BARRY-ARG BC 2008 s.p.
(C133)

CAMPRA, ANDRE (1660-1744)
Arion *cant
(Feuillie, J.) S solo,fl,cont
HEUGEL s.p.   (C134)

Brilliant Butterfly *see Charmant
Papillon

Chanson Du Papillon (from Les Fetes
Venitiennes)
S solo,orch DURAND s.p., ipa (C135)

Charmant Papillon
"Brilliant Butterfly" [Fr/Eng] med-
high solo,pno (G min) SCHIRM.G
$.75   (C136)

CAMPRA, ANDRE (cont'd.)

Domine, Dominus Noster *sac,cant
(Ewerhart, Rudolf) [Lat] S solo,fl/
vln,cont sc BIELER DK 3 s.p., ipa
(C137)

Exaltabo Te, Deus Meus, Rex *sac
(Ewerhart, Rudolf) [Lat] B solo,
cont BIELER CS 9 s.p.   (C138)

Jubilate Deo *sac
(Ewerhart, Rudolf) [Lat] S/T solo,
cont BIELER CS 32 s.p.   (C139)

Les Femmes *cant
(Winter) [Fr/Ger] B solo,strings,
cont SIKORSKI 641 s.p.   (C140)

O Dulcis Amor *sac
(Ewerhart, Rudolf) [Lat] S/T solo,
cont BIELER CS 17 s.p.   (C141)

Quam Dulce Est, Inhaerere Tibi *sac
(Ewerhart, Rudolf) [Lat] A solo,
cont BIELER CS 6 s.p.   (C142)

Quemadmodum Desiderat Cervus *sac
(Ewerhart, Rudolf) S/T solo,cont
BIELER CS 56 s.p.   (C143)

Zwei Elevations *sac,CC2U
(Ewerhart, Rudolf) S/T solo,cont
BIELER CS 63 s.p.   (C144)

CAMPTOWN RACES see Foster, Stephen
Collins

CAN L'HERBA FRESCH' see Ventadorn,
Bernart de

CAN LIFE BE A BLESSING see Nordoff,
Paul

CAN THIS BE TATIANA? see Tchaikovsky,
Piotr Ilyitch, Onegin's Song

CAN VEI LA LAUZETA see Ventadorn,
Bernart de

CANAL BANK, THE see Strilko, Anthony

CANAL, MARGUERITE (1890-   )
Amour Partout
[Fr] med solo,pno ESCHIG $.85 see
from Cuarto Berceuses   (C145)

Chanson De Route
solo,pno ENOCH s.p.   (C146)
solo,acap solo pt ENOCH s.p. (C147)

Cuarto Berceuses *see Amour Partout;
Dormeuse; Fileuse; Pour Endormir
L'enfant   (C148)

Dormeuse
[Fr] med solo,pno ESCHIG $.75 see
from Cuarto Berceuses   (C149)

Fileuse
[Fr] med solo,pno ESCHIG $1.00 see
from Cuarto Berceuses   (C150)

J'ai Penetre O Mon Epouse (from
Cantique Des Cantiques)
see Trois Chants Extraits Du
Cantique Des Cantiques
solo,orch ENOCH rental   (C151)

Le Bonheur Est Dans Le Pre
solo,pno ENOCH s.p.   (C152)
solo,acap solo pt ENOCH s.p. (C153)
solo,orch ENOCH rental   (C154)

L'Image
solo,pno ENOCH s.p.   (C155)
solo,acap solo pt ENOCH s.p. (C156)

Little Maid Of Mine *see Ma Petit
Fille Est Si Blonde

Ma Petit Fille Est Si Blonde
"Little Maid Of Mine" [Fr/Eng] med
solo,pno ESCHIG $.75   (C157)

Mon Epousee Ma Soeur (from Cantique
Des Cantiques)
see Trois Chants Extraits Du
Cantique Des Cantiques
solo,orch ENOCH rental   (C158)

Pour Endormir L'enfant
[Fr] med solo,pno ESCHIG $.85 see
from Cuarto Berceuses   (C159)

Qu'il Est Exquis Ton Amour (from
Cantique Des Cantiques)
see Trois Chants Extraits Du
Cantique Des Cantiques
solo,orch ENOCH rental   (C160)

Trois Chants Extraits Du Cantique Des
Cantiques
solo,pno cmplt ed ENOCH s.p.
contains: J'ai Penetre O Mon
Epouse; Mon Epousee Ma Soeur;
Qu'il Est Exquis Ton Amour

CANAL, MARGUERITE (cont'd.)

(C161)

CANARD see Stravinsky, Igor

CANCAO DAS AGUAS CLARAS see Villa-
Lobos, Heitor

CANCAO DE CRISTAL see Villa-Lobos,
Heitor

CANCION see Falla, Manuel de

CANCION see Olazabal, Zirso de

CANCION A LA LUNA LUNANCA see
Ginastera, Alberto

CANCION AL ARBOL DEL OLVIDO see
Ginastera, Alberto

CANCION DE AUSENCIA see Lopez-Buchardo,
Carlos

CANCION DE CUNA see Brahms, Johannes,
Wiegenlied

CANCION DE CUNA see De Rogatis, Pascual

CANCION DE CUNA see Garcia Estrada,
Juan Agustin

CANCION DE CUNA see Mozart, Wolfgang
Amadeus, Wiegenlied

CANCION DE CUNA see Napolitano, Emilio

CANCION DE CUNA DE LA VIRGEN see Reger,
Max, Maria Wiegenlied

CANCION DE CUNA INDIA see Gilardi,
Gilardo

CANCION DE ESTUDIANTE see Pahissa,
Jaime

CANCION DE FORTUNIO see Tosti,
Francesco Paolo, Chanson De
Fortunio

CANCION DE LA BANDERA see Panizza,
Ettore

CANCION DE LA ESPADA see Guerrero

CANCION DE LA MADRE see Dvorak,
Antonin, Als Die Alte Mutter

CANCION DE LA NINA GAUCHA see Jurafsky,
Abraham

CANCION DE LA PEPA GALANA see Pahissa,
Jaime

CANCION DE LA PRIMAVERA see D'Esposito,
Salve

CANCION DE LA VENDIMIA see Espoile,
Raoul H.

CANCION DE LA VIRGEN see Hively, Wells

CANCION DE LUNA PARA DORMIR A UN
NEGRITO see Lilien, Ignace

CANCION DE NAVIDAD see Guastavino,
Carlos

CANCION DE NAVIDAD, NO. 2 see
Guastavino, Carlos

CANCION DE PERICO see Lopez-Buchardo,
Carlos

CANCION DE SOLVEJG see Grieg, Edvard
Hagerup, Solveigs Sang

CANCION DE VENDIMIA see Pahissa, Jaime

CANCION DE VILIA see Lehar, Franz

CANCION DEL AMOR DOLIDO see Falla,
Manuel de

CANCION DEL CAPITAN see Luna, P.

CANCION DEL CARRETERO see Lopez-
Buchardo, Carlos

CANCION DEL "CORDON BLEU" see Chueca,
Federico

CANCION DEL FUEGO FATUO see Falla,
Manuel de

CANCION DEL GRUMETE see Rodrigo,
Joaquin

CANCION DEL NINO PEQUENITO see Lopez-
Buchardo, Carlos

CANCION DEL PANUELO see Pahissa, Jaime

CANCION DEL TROVERO PEDRO DE VIDAL see
D'Esposito, Salve

CANCION HINDU see Rimsky-Korsakov,
Nikolai

CANCION MORESCA see Piccinelli, Nino

CANCION PARA EL NINO EN LA CUNA see
Quaratino, Pascual

CANCION ZAMORA see Andriessen, Juriaan

CANCIONERO see Gerhard, Roberto

CANCIONERO ESPANOL *CC30L,15-16th cent
(Grau) [It] T solo,pno RICORDI-ARG
BA 9853 s.p. contains works by:
Anchieta, Contreras; De La Torre;
Encina; Escobar and others   (C162)

CANCIONES see Peyretti, Alberto

CANCIONES AMATORIAS see Granados,
Enrique

CANCIONES ARABESCAS see Pedrell, F.

CANCIONES ARGENTINAS see Lasala, Angel

CANCIONES CALLEJERAS see Morera,
Enrique

CANCIONES CASTELLANAS see Salas, Juan
Orrego

CANCIONES CLASICAS ESPANOLAS, VOL. I
*CC7U,Span
(Obradors) [Span] med solo,pno UNION
ESP. $3.50   (C163)

CANCIONES CLASICAS ESPANOLAS, VOL. II
*CC5U,Span
(Obradors) [Span] med solo,pno UNION
ESP. $4.50   (C164)

CANCIONES CLASICAS ESPANOLAS, VOL. III
*CC6U,Span
(Obradors) [Span] med solo,pno UNION
ESP. $3.50   (C165)

CANCIONES CLASICAS ESPANOLAS, VOL. IV
*CC5U,Span
(Obradors) [Span] med solo,pno UNION
ESP. $2.75   (C166)

CANCIONES DE ESPANA see Cases

CANCIONES DE LA ANDALUCIA MEDIEVAL Y
RENACENTISTA *CCU,Span,13th cent/
14th cent/15th cent/16th cent
(Lamana) [Span] med solo,pno UNION
ESP. $4.50   (C167)

CANCIONES DE NANA Y DESVELO see
Salvador, M.

CANCIONES DEL TEATRO DE FEDERICO GARCIA
LORCA see Pittaluga, Gustavo

CANCIONES EPIGRAMATICAS see Vives,
Amadeo

CANCIONES ESPANOLAS see Torroba, F.M.

CANCIONES ESPANOLAS ANTIGUAS *CCU,Span
(Garcia Lorca) [Span] med solo,pno
UNION ESP. $3.50   (C168)

CANCIONES ESPANOLAS ANTIGUAS see Lorca,
F.G.

CANCIONES ESPANOLAS DEL RENACIMIENTO
*CC18U,Span,Renais
(Tarrago) [Span] med solo,pno UNION
ESP. $4.50   (C169)

CANCIONES FOLKLORICAS ESPANOLAS *CCU,
folk,Span
(Benedito) med solo,acap UNION ESP.
$6.00   (C170)

CANCIONES IBERICAS see Manen, Joan

CANCIONES PARA NINOS see Montsalvatge,
Xavier

CANCIONES PLAYERAS see Espla, Oscar

CANCIONES POPULARES *CCU
(Garcia Lorca) [Span] med solo,gtr
UNION ESP. $1.50   (C171)

CANCIONES POPULARES CATALANES see
Pahissa, Jaime

CANCIONES POPULARES DE EXTREMADURA
*CC6U,folk,Span
(Gil) [Span] med solo,pno UNION ESP.
$1.25   (C172)

CANCIONES POPULARES ESPANOLAS see
Tarrago, G.

CANCIONES POPULARES ESPANOLAS *CCU,
Span
(Tarrago) [Span] med solo,pno UNION
ESP. $6.50   (C173)

CANCIONES POPULARES ESPANOLAS, VOL. I
*CCU,Span
(Tarrago) [Span] med solo,gtr UNION
ESP. $5.50 (C174)

CANCIONES POPULARES ESPANOLAS, VOL. II
*CCU,Span
(Tarrago) [Span] med solo,gtr UNION
ESP. $4.50 (C175)

CANCIONES POPULARES ESPANOLAS, VOL. III
*CCU,Span
(Tarrago) [Span] med solo,gtr UNION
ESP. $4.75 (C176)

CANCIONES POPULARES ESPANOLAS, VOL. IV
*CC6U,Span
(Benedito) [Span] med solo,pno UNION
ESP. $.65 (C177)

CANCIONES POPULARES ESPANOLAS, VOL. V
*CC6U,Span
(Benedito) [Span] med solo,pno UNION
ESP. $.75 (C178)

CANCIONES POPULARES POPULARES
ESPANOLAS, VOL. III *CC6U,Span
(Benedito) [Span] med solo,pno UNION
ESP. $.75 (C179)

CANCIONES POPULARES RUSAS *CC20L
(Gaymar) [Russ/Span] solo,pno
RICORDI-ARG BA 9967 s.p. (C180)

CANCIONES TAURINAS *CC8U,Span
(Gil) [Span] med solo,pno UNION ESP.
$1.75 (C181)

CANCO AMOROSA see Montsalvatge, Xavier

CANCO CATALANA NO. 1 see Casals, Pablo

CANCO DE LA FIRA see Mompou, Federico

CANCO DE PASSAR CANTANT see Toldra,
Eduardo

CANCO DEL TEULADI see Rodrigo, Joaquin

CANDIDA MIA COLOMBA see Ghedini,
Giorgio Federico

CANDLE, THE see Melecci

CANDLE LIGHTS OF CHRISTMAS see Repper,
Charles

CANDOMBLE see Bjelinski, Bruno

CANINO
Cantata 2 *see Fortis

Fortis (Cantata 2) cant
[It/Ger] Mez solo,fl,harp,
harmonium,perc,vla sc RICORDI-ENG
131014 s.p. (C182)

CANNING, THOMAS
How Beautiful Upon The Mountains
SS soli,4strings,org sc AM.COMP.AL.
$11.00 (C183)

Nature's Playmates
med solo,pno AM.COMP.AL. $5.50
(C184)

CANNON, (JACK) PHILLIP (1929-   )
Angry Wife, The *see La Mal Mariee

Cinq Chansons De Femme
[Fr/Eng] S solo,pno NOVELLO s.p.
contains: La Bien Aimee, "Girl
Whose Love Shines Fair, A"; La
Bien Mariee, "Merry Wife, The";
La Mal Mariee, "Angry Wife,
The"; La Veuve, "Widow, The";
L'amoureuse, "Girl In Love, A"
(C185)

Girl In Love, A *see L'amoureuse

Girl Whose Love Shines Fair, A *see
La Bien Aimee

La Bien Aimee
"Girl Whose Love Shines Fair, A"
see Cinq Chansons De Femme

La Bien Mariee
"Merry Wife, The" see Cinq Chansons
De Femme

La Mal Mariee
"Angry Wife, The" see Cinq Chansons
De Femme

La Veuve
"Widow, The" see Cinq Chansons De
Femme

L'amoureuse
"Girl In Love, A" see Cinq Chansons
De Femme

Merry Wife, The *see La Bien Mariee

CANNON, (JACK) PHILLIP (cont'd.)

Widow, The *see La Veuve

CANOE SONG see En Roulant Ma Boule

CANON A TROIS see Couperin (le Grand),
Francois

CAN'T HELP TALKING ABOUT MY LORD *sac,
gospel
solo,pno ABER.GRP. $1.50 (C186)

CAN'T REMEMBER see Goatley, Alma

CAN'T WAIT 'TIL HE'S HERE see Matthews

CANTA IN PRATO see Vivaldi, Antonio

CANTA LA SPONDA see Prandi, A.

CANTA TU CANTO, RUISENOR Y VUELA see
Lopez-Buchardo, Carlos

CANTA UNO AUGELLO IN VOCE DI SOAVE see
Ghedini, Giorgio Federico

CANTABO DOMINO see Schutz, Heinrich

CANTAMUS see Starer, Robert

CANTAN LAS NINAS DE ESPANA see Gil, B.

CANTANDO VAN LOS PASTORES see Romero,
M.

CANTAR A UN SAUCE see Valenti Costa,
Pedro

CANTAR DE AMORES see Valenti Costa,
Pedro

CANTAR DE UNA SERRANA see Valenti
Costa, Pedro

CANTAR DEL ALMA see Mompou, Federico

CANTARES see Turina, Joaquin

CANTARES see Lasala, Angel

CANTARES ANDALUCES see Farga, O.

CANTATA see Abbado, Marcello

CANTATA see Birtwistle, Harrison

CANTATA see Fellegara, Vittorio

CANTATA see Pradas, Josep

CANTATA DOMESTICA see Mohler, Philipp

CANTATA FOR VOICE AND ORCHESTRA see
Carter, John

CANTATA I see Riley, Dennis

CANTATA III see Westergaard, Peter

CANTATA ON MELANCHOLY, A see Pennisi,
Francesco

CANTATA PICCOLA see Finke, Fidelio
Fritz

CANTATA PRO DEFUNCTIS see Hambraeus,
Bengt

CANTATA SACRA see Lewkovitch, Bernhard

CANTATA SECONDA see Testi, Flavio

CANTATA THREE, 1961 see Sims, Ezra

CANTATAS see Pergolesi, Giovanni
Battista

CANTATAS AND CANZONETS FOR SOLO VOICE
see Legrenzi, Giovanni

CANTATAS FOR ONE AND TWO VOICES, BOOK
III see Monteclair, Michel Pignolet
de

CANTATE see Hasse, Johann Adolph

CANTATE DE LA ROSE ET DE L'AMOUR see
Durey, Louis

CANTATE DES SEPT POEMES D'AMOUR EN
GUERRE see Arrieu, Claude

CANTATE DOMINO see Buxtehude, Dietrich

CANTATE DOMINO see Heidet, le R. P.

CANTATE DOMINO see Krieger, Johann
Philipp

CANTATE DOMINO CANTICUM NOVUM see
Buxtehude, Dietrich

CANTATE MORALI E SPIRITUALI A VOCE SOLA
see Cazzati, Maurizio

CANTELOUBE, JOSEPH
A Bethleem, Quand L'Enfant Dieu
*sac,Xmas
SAT soli,pno DURAND s.p., ipr
(C187)

CANTERBURY FAIR see Leslie-Smith, K.

CANTERVILLE GHOST, THE see Knaifel, A.

CANTI CEREMISSI see Veress, Sandor

CANTI DA "ESTRAVAGARIO" see Gentilucci,
A.

CANTI D'AMORE see Fuga, Sandro

CANTI D'AMORE see Toni, Alceo

CANTI DELLA FANCIULLEZZA see Ferraris,
C.

CANTI DELLA LONTANANZA see Menotti,
Gian Carlo

CANTI DELLA LONTANANZA (DEDICATI A
ELISABETH SCHWARZKOPF) see Menotti,
Gian Carlo

CANTI DELLA MIA PRIGIONIA see Guerrini,
Guido

CANTI DELLA MONTAGNA see Malatesta,
Luigi

CANTI DELLA NEBBIA E DEL SOLE see
Guarino, C.

CANTI DELLA PRIMAVERA see Cambieri,
Emilio

CANTI DELLA SICILIA VENTI CANZONI
SICILIANE *CCU
(Frontini) solo,pno/mand FORLIVESI
10267 s.p. (C188)

CANTI DI NATALE *CC8U,Xmas
(Breguet, J.) [Fr/Ger/It/Eng] solo,
gtr BERBEN 1126 s.p. (C189)

CANTI DI NOVEMBRE see Zafred, Mario

CANTI DI RILKE see Rossellini, Renzo

CANTI DI STAGIONE see Porrino, Ennio

CANTI DRAMMATICI DAL RUSSO see
Spezzaferri, Giovanni

CANTI MILITARI see Alderighi, Dante

CANTI MINIMI see Davico, Vincenzo

CANTI NUOVI PER LA NUOVA LITURGIA see
Varnava', S.

CANTI POETICI (3 VOLS.) see Gerstel,
Oswald

CANTI POPOLARI DI VARIE NAZIONI, VOL. 1
*CC19U
solo,pno BERBEN 1582 s.p. contains
songs from the romance language
countries (C190)

CANTI POPOLARI DI VARIE NAZIONI, VOL. 2
*CC25U
solo,pno BERBEN 1804 s.p. contains
songs from the germanic and slavic
speaking countries (C191)

CANTI POPOLARI EBRAICI see Milhaud,
Darius

CANTI POPOLARI RUSSI see Lyanova,
Adriana

CANTICA see Dalby, Martin

CANTICA I see Lechner, Konrad

CANTICA II see Lechner, Konrad

CANTICEL see Toldra, Eduardo

CANTICLE see Hovhaness, Alan

CANTICLE FOR BROTHERS APART see Tewson,
William

CANTICLE I see Britten, Benjamin

CANTICLE II - ABRAHAM AND ISAAC see
Britten, Benjamin

CANTICLE III - STILL FALLS THE RAIN see
Britten, Benjamin

CANTICLE IV: JOURNEY OF THE MAGI see
Britten, Benjamin

CANTICLE NO. 1 see Leichtling, Alan

CANTICLE OF THE SUN, THE see Mills,
Charles

CANTICLE TO APOLLO see Strilko, Anthony

CANTICO DELLE CREATURE DI FRANCESCO D'ASSISI see Heppener, Robert

CANTICO DELLE CREATURE DI S. FRANCESCO see Alderighi, Dante

CANTICO DI VITTORIA see Guerrini, Guido

CANTICUM CANTICORUM see Stout, Alan

CANTICUM PSALMI RESURRECTIONIS see Schoenbach, D.

CANTIGA see Camargo Guarnieri

CANTIGAS DE AMIGO see Sciammarella, Valdo

CANTILENA see Calabro, Louis

CANTILENA DELLA MADRE PER IL SUO BIMBO MALATO see Andriessen, Hendrik

CANTILENA PRO ADVENTU see Haydn, (Johann) Michael

CANTILENE A COLOMBINA see Pratella, Francesco Balilla

CANTILENE DE L'OISEAU MAGICIEN: A L'AMOUR see Desrez

CANTILIENA see Guastavino, Carlos

CANTIQUE see Decruck, F.

CANTIQUE A L'EPOUSE see Chausson, Ernest

CANTIQUE D'AMOUR see Georges, Alexandre

CANTIQUE DE NOEL see Adam, Adolphe-Charles

CANTIQUE DE PENITENCE see Beethoven, Ludwig van, Busslied

CANTIQUE DE RACINE see Hahn, Reynaldo

CANTIQUE DE SAINTE CECILE A LA VIERGE IMMACULEE see Chausson, Ernest

CANTIQUE SPIRITUEL see Andriessen, Hendrik

CANTO A SEVILLA see Turina, Joaquin

CANTO ARABO see Giuranna, Barbara

CANTO DE AMOR see Campmany, Montserrat

CANTO DE AMOR see Chopin, Frederic

CANTO DE PRIMAVERA see Mendelssohn-Bartholdy, Felix, Fruhlingslied

CANTO DELL'OSPITE see Sinigaglia, Leone

CANTO DI PRIMAVERA see Cimara, Pietro

CANTO DI TROVATORE see Veneziani, Vittore, Chant De Troubadour

CANTO FUNEBRE see Respighi, Ottorino

CANTO GENERAL see Schat, Peter

CANTO GITANO see Granados, Enrique

CANTO NOSTALGICO see Bossi, Renzo

CANTO NOTTURNO DEL VIANDANTE see Siciliani, Francesco

CANTO OLIMPICO see Franceschini, Sandro

CANTO TOSCANO
    (Brogi) MezBar soli,pno/mand
    FORLIVESI 10765 s.p.   (C192)

CANTO TRISTE see Pauer, Jiri

CANTONNIER DU ROI see Bitsch, Marcel

CANTORIAL RESPONSES AT THE WEDDING CEREMONY see Adler, Hugo Ch.

CANTOS A LA NOCHE see Ruiz Pipo', Antonio

CANTOS DE AMOR Y DE GUERRA see Rodrigo, Joaquin

CANTOS DEL TUCUMAN see Ginastera, Alberto

CANTOS ESPANOLES *CC29U,Span
    (Ocon) [Span] med solo,pno/gtr UNION
    ESP. $9.00   (C193)

CANTU, M.
  A Maggio
    see Imagini Di Velluto

  Affanno
    see Due Liriche

  Canzone Vespertina
    T solo,pno BONGIOVANI 1317 s.p.
                                  (C194)
  Correspondances
    see Deux Lyriques

  Cosi
    see Imagini Di Velluto

  Deux Lyriques
    S solo,pno cmplt ed BONGIOVANI 1071
    s.p.
    contains: Correspondances; La
        Cloche Felee   (C195)

  Due Liriche
    S solo,pno cmplt ed BONGIOVANI 1323
    s.p.
    contains: Affanno; Rimpianto
                                  (C196)
  Due Sonetti
    S solo,pno cmplt ed BONGIOVANI 1324
    s.p.
    contains: La Lune; Sonetto
        D'ottobre   (C197)

  Il Sonno Dei Dimenticati
    see Imagini Di Velluto

  Imagini Di Velluto
    S solo,pno cmplt ed BONGIOVANI 1511
    s.p.
    contains: A Maggio; Cosi; Il
        Sonno Dei Dimenticati; In Fondo
        Al Prato; Notturno   (C198)

  Immacolata *ora
    [It/Fr] solo,pno RICORDI-ENG s.p.
                                  (C199)
  In Fondo Al Prato
    see Imagini Di Velluto

  La Cloche Felee
    see Deux Lyriques

  La Lune
    see Due Sonetti

  Le Litanie D'amore
    S/T solo,pno BONGIOVANI 1510 s.p.
                                  (C200)
  Notte D'agosto
    S solo,pno BONGIOVANI 1318 s.p.
                                  (C201)
  Notturno
    see Imagini Di Velluto

  Rimpianto
    see Due Liriche

  Sonetto D'ottobre
    see Due Sonetti

  Tramonto Montano
    S solo,pno BONGIOVANI 1319 s.p.
                                  (C202)

CANTUS GEMELLUS see Benvenuti, Arrigo

CANTUS MYSTICUS see Mulder, Ernest W.

CANTUS PSALMORUM see Pololanik, Zdenek

CANZONE A BALLO DEL POLIZIANO see Rosi, Gino

CANZONE D'APRILE see Albanese, Guido

CANZONE DEL BIMBO see Liviabella, Lino

CANZONE DEL SALICE see Verdi, Giuseppe

CANZONE DEL SONNO see Bizzelli, Annibale

CANZONE DI ADDIO see Vandor, Ivan

CANZONE DI MARTA see Mussorgsky, Modest

CANZONE DI PARASSIA see Mussorgsky, Modest

CANZONE DI RE ENZO see Respighi, Ottorino

CANZONE DI VARLAAM see Mussorgsky, Modest

CANZONE NO. 1 see Farina, Guido

CANZONE NO. 2 see Farina, Guido

CANZONE PE 'L BIMBO see Veneziani, Vittore

CANZONE PER BALLO see Pizzetti, Ildebrando

CANZONE VESPERTINA see Cantu, M.

CANZONE-VOCALIZZO see Mortari, Virgilio

CANZONE XXVI see Scheidt, Samuel

CANZONETTA see Davico, Vincenzo

CANZONETTA see Guerrini, Guido

CANZONETTA see Lewkovitch, Bernhard

CANZONETTA see Lilien, Ignace

CANZONETTA see Massarani, E.

CANZONETTA see Tirindelli, Pier Adolfo

CANZONETTA D'ALTRI TEMPI see Tocchi, Gian-Luca

CANZONETTE E BALLATE see Satra, Antonin

CANZONETTE E CANTATE A DUE VOCI see Mazzaferrata, G.B.

CANZONETTE PER CAMERA A VOCE SOLA *CCU
    solo,pno FORNI s.p. contains works by
    various composers   (C203)

CANZONETTEN HEFT I see Monteverdi, Claudio

CANZONETTEN HEFT II see Monteverdi, Claudio

CANZONI AMOROSE DE DUECENTE see Henkemans, Hans

CANZONI E SCHERZI see Regt, Hendrik de

CANZONI TROBADORICHE see Sesini, U.

CANZONIERE see Ferrari-Trecate, Luigi

CANZONIERE DEI FANCIULLI, VOL. I: CANTI RELIGIOSI see Schinelli, Achille

CANZONIERE DEI FANCIULLI, VOL. II: CANTI PATRIOTTICI see Schinelli, Achille

CANZONIERE DEI FANCIULLI, VOL. III: CANTI DI ARGOMENTO DIVERSO see Schinelli, Achille

CANZONIERE DEI FANCIULLI, VOL. IV: BRANI DI OPERE TEATRALI see Schinelli, Achille

CANZUNETTA DL'ESPUSIZION
    (Carlo, Musi) solo,pno (Bolognese
    dialect) BONGIOVANI 2087 s.p. see
    from El Mi Canzunett   (C204)

CANZUNETTA PRUIBE
    (Carlo, Musi) solo,pno (Bolognese
    dialect) BONGIOVANI 2090 s.p. see
    from El Mi Canzunett   (C205)

CAPANNA BIANCA see De Lucia, Nadir

CAPE ANN see Thomas, A.

CAPLET, ANDRE (1878-1925)
  Angoisse
    solo,pno/inst DURAND s.p. see from
    Trois Poemes   (C206)

  Berceuse
    see Quatre Poemes
    solo,pno/inst DURAND s.p. see also
    Le Vieux Coffret   (C207)

  Ce Sable Fin Et Fuyant
    solo,pno/orch DURAND s.p., ipr see
    from Trois Poemes   (C208)

  Chanson D'automne
    Mez/Bar solo,pno/inst DURAND s.p.
                                  (C209)
  Cinq Ballades Francais De Paul Fort
    med solo,orch cmplt ed DURAND s.p.,
    ipr
    contains & see also: Cloche
        D'Aube; La Ronde; L'adieu En
        Barque; Notre Chaumiere En
        Yveline; Songe D'une Nuit D'ete
                                  (C210)
  Cloche D'Aube
    med solo,orch (contains also: La
    Ronde) DURAND s.p., ipr see also
    Cinq Ballades Francais De Paul
    Fort   (C211)

  Detresse
    solo,orch DURAND s.p., ipr   (C212)

  Deux Sonnets
    med solo,harp cmplt ed DURAND s.p.
    contains: Doux Fut Le Trait;
        Quand Reverrai-Je Helas   (C213)

  Doux Fut Le Trait
    see Deux Sonnets
    solo,pno/inst DURAND s.p.   (C214)

CAPLET, ANDRE (cont'd.)

Ecoute, Mon Coeur!
solo,fl DURAND s.p.   (C215)

En Regardant Ces Belles Fleurs
S solo,pno/inst DURAND s.p.
contains also: Quand Reverrai-Je,
Helas   (C216)

Foret
solo,orch DURAND s.p., ipr see also
Le Vieux Coffret   (C217)

Hymne A La Naissance Du Matin
solo,orch DURAND s.p., ipr   (C218)

In Una Selva Oscura
see Quatre Poemes
solo,orch DURAND s.p., ipr see also
Le Vieux Coffret   (C219)

La Cigale Et La Fourmi
see Trois Fables De Jean De La
Fontaine

La Cloche Felee
med solo,pno/inst DURAND s.p.
                                   (C220)

La Croix Douloureuse
solo,orch DURAND s.p., ipr   (C221)

La Foret
see Quatre Poemes

La Mort Des Pauvres
med solo,pno/inst DURAND s.p.
                                   (C222)

La "Part A Dieu"
med solo,pno/inst DURAND s.p.
                                   (C223)

La Ronde
med solo,orch (contains also:
Cloche D'Aube) DURAND s.p., ipr
see also Cinq Ballades Francais
De Paul Fort   (C224)

L'adieu En Barque
med solo,orch (conatins also: Notre
Chaumiere En Yveline; Songe D'une
Nuit D'ete) DURAND s.p., ipr see
also Cinq Ballades Francais De
Paul Fort   (C225)

Le Corbeau Et Le Renard
see Trois Fables De Jean De La
Fontaine

Le Loup Et L'Agneau
see Trois Fables De Jean De La
Fontaine

Le Vieux Coffret
solo,pno/inst cmplt ed DURAND s.p.,
ipr
contains & see also: Berceuse;
Foret; In Una Selva Oscura;
Songe   (C226)

Notre Chaumiere En Yveline
med solo,orch (contains also: Songe
D'une Nuit D'ete; L'adieu En
Barque) DURAND s.p., ipr see also
Cinq Ballades Francais De Paul
Fort   (C227)

Nuit D'automne
med solo,pno/inst DURAND s.p.
                                   (C228)

Preludes
Mez/Bar solo,orch DURAND s.p., ipr
                                   (C229)

Priere Normande
high solo,pno/inst DURAND s.p.
                                   (C230)
Mez solo,pno/inst (D maj) DURAND
s.p.   (C231)

Quand Reverrai-Je, Helas
see Caplet, Andre, En Regardant Ces
Belles Fleurs
see Deux Sonnets

Quatre Poemes
solo,pno DURAND s.p.
contains: Berceuse; In Una Selva
Oscura; La Foret; Songe   (C232)

Songe
see Quatre Poemes
solo,orch DURAND s.p., ipr see also
Le Vieux Coffret   (C233)

Songe D'une Nuit D'ete
med solo,orch (contains also:
L'adieu En Barque; Notre
Chaumiere En Yveline) DURAND
s.p., ipr see also Cinq Ballades
Francais De Paul Fort   (C234)

Trois Fables De Jean De La Fontaine
solo,pno/inst cmplt ed DURAND s.p.
contains: La Cigale Et La Fourmi;
Le Corbeau Et Le Renard; Le
Loup Et L'Agneau   (C235)

CAPLET, ANDRE (cont'd.)

Trois Poemes *see Angoisse; Ce Sable
Fin Et Fuyant   (C236)

Viens, Une Flute Invisible
med solo,pno/inst DURAND s.p.
                                   (C237)

CAPOUL, V.
La Noctuelle
solo,pno ENOCH s.p.   (C238)

Meha
[It] solo,pno (available in 2 keys)
ENOCH s.p.   (C239)
[Fr] solo,pno (available in 2 keys)
ENOCH s.p.   (C240)
solo,acap solo pt ENOCH s.p.   (C241)

CAPRICCIO see Liebermann, Rolf

CAPRICORNUS, SAMUEL (1628-1665)
Der Gerechten Seelen Sind In Gottes
Hand *sac,concerto
(Grusnick, Bruno) SATB soli,2vln,
vcl,cont (med) BAREN. 957 $5.00
                                   (C242)

Mein Gott Und Herr *sac
SSB soli,2vln,cont sc BAREN. 6226
$8.50, ipa   (C243)

CAPRIOLI, GIOVANNI PAOLO
Drei Geistliche Konzerte *sac,CC3U,
concerto
(Ewerhart, Rudolf) S/T solo,cont
BIELER CS 46 s.p.   (C244)

CAPSHAW, BETTY
Circle Incomplete, A
med solo,pno CRESPUB CP-S5053 $1.00
                                   (C245)

Just A Little While From Now *sac
med solo,pno CRESPUB CP-S5057 $1.00
                                   (C246)

CAPTAIN MAC' see Sanderson, Wilfred

CAPTAIN MACKINTOSH AND COLONEL ANNE
*Scot
(Diack, J. M.) ABar soli,pno PATERSON
s.p.   (C247)

CAPTAIN OF SUNSHINE, THE see Ballard,
Ann

CAPTAIN SAM see Orr, J.

CAPTIVE, THE see Edwards, George

CAPTIVE, THE see Medtner, Nikolai
Karlovitch

CAPUA, EDUARDO DI
see DI CAPUA, EDUARDO

CAPUCCI, L.
Voci Di Fontane
[It] solo,pno CURCI 428 s.p. (C248)

CAR JE NE SUIS QU'UNE ETRANGERE see
Saint-Saens, Camille

CARA, M.
Io Non Compro
(Pujol) [It] med solo,gtr ESCHIG
E1315 $1.10   (C249)

CARA MIA see Russell, Kennedy

CARA, SE LE MIE PENE see Mozart,
Wolfgang Amadeus

CARA SIGNORINA see Hajos, Karl

CARA SPOSA see Handel, George Frideric

CARABELLA, EZIO (1891-   )
Ad Una Fanciulla
Mez solo,pno BONGIOVANI 464 s.p.
                                   (C250)
S solo,pno BONGIOVANI 463 s.p.
                                   (C251)

Ballata Triste
[It] solo,pno SANTIS 202 s.p.
                                   (C252)

CARAVAN, THE see Shaw, Martin

CARCELERAS see Chapi

CARDEW, CORNELIUS (1936-   )
High Heaven Is Not Just
see Three Bourgeois Songs

Our Joy
see Three Bourgeois Songs

Soon
solo,pno EXPERIMENTAL s.p. (C253)

Three Bourgeois Songs
high solo,pno EXPERIMENTAL s.p.
contains: High Heaven Is Not
Just; Our Joy; Turtle-Dove, The
                                   (C254)
Turtle-Dove, The
see Three Bourgeois Songs

CARDILLO
Core 'Ngrato
[It] solo,pno RICORDI-ARG BA 6285
s.p.   (C255)
[It] S/T solo,pno RICORDI-ENG
127448 s.p.   (C256)
(Donaldson) "Faithless Heart" solo,
pno BELWIN $1.50   (C257)

Faithless Heart *see Core' Ngrato

CARE-CHARMING SLEEP see Plessis, Hubert
du

CARE LUCI BEN MIO see Scarlatti,
Domenico

CARE SELVE
(Lehmann, Amelia) low solo,pno (F
maj) BOOSEY $1.50   (C258)
(Lehmann, Amelia) high solo,pno (A
maj) BOOSEY $1.50   (C259)

CARE SELVE see Handel, George Frideric

CAREFREE see Hunter, Winifred

CAREW, MOLLY
April Is In Sight
solo,pno CRAMER   (C260)

CAREY
Lord's Prayer, The *sac,gospel
med solo,pno ABER.GRP. $1.50 (C261)
high solo,pno ABER.GRP. $1.50
                                   (C262)

Psalm 23 *sac,gospel
low solo,pno ABER.GRP. $1.50 (C263)
med solo,pno ABER.GRP. $1.50 (C264)
high solo,pno ABER.GRP. $1.50
                                   (C265)

CAREY, HENRY (1692-1743)
Friendly Adviser, The
(Cockshott, G.) solo,pno NOVELLO
17.0060.10 s.p.   (C266)

Sally In Our Alley
solo,pno (D maj) BOOSEY $1.50
                                   (C267)

CAREY, LEWIS
Break, Break, Break
low solo,pno (F maj) BOOSEY $1.50
                                   (C268)
high solo,pno (B flat maj) BOOSEY
$1.50   (C269)
med solo,pno (G maj) BOOSEY $1.50
                                   (C270)

Nearer, My God, To Thee *sac
low solo,pno (F maj) BOOSEY $1.50
                                   (C271)
high solo,pno (G maj) BOOSEY $1.50
                                   (C272)

CARGOES see Dobson, Tom

CARGOES see Shaw, Martin

CARILLON see Briel, Marie

CARILLONS BLANCS see Vieu, Jane

CARION, FERN.
Aubade
T solo,pno BROGNEAUX s.p.   (C273)

Trois Poemes D'Emile Verhaeren *CC3U
solo,pno (med diff) BROGNEAUX s.p.
                                   (C274)

CARISSIMI, GIACOMO (1605?-1674)
Chamber Duets *CC6U
(Landshoff) [It] SS/TT soli,pno
PETERS 3824B $7.50   (C275)

Domine, Deus Meus *sac
(Ewerhart, Rudolf) [Lat] S/T solo,
cont BIELER CS 8 s.p.   (C276)

Lucifer *sac
(Ewerhart, Rudolf) B solo,cont
BIELER CS 37 s.p.   (C277)

O Quam Pulchra Es *sac
(Ewerhart, Rudolf) S/T solo,cont
BIELER CS 57 s.p.   (C278)

O Vulnera Doloris *sac
(Ewerhart, Rudolf) [Lat] B solo,
cont BIELER CS 16 s.p.   (C279)

Piangete, Ohime, Piangete
solo,pno FORLIVESI 12080 s.p.
                                   (C280)

Salve, Salve, Puellule *sac
(Ewerhart, Rudolf) S/T solo,cont
BIELER CS 48 s.p.   (C281)

Six Solo Cantatas *CC6U,cant
[It/Eng] high solo,kbd,cont cmplt
ed FABER FO114 $24.00   (C282)

Vittoria, Vittoria
solo,pno FORLIVESI 10872 s.p.
                                   (C283)
(Parisotti) [It/Fr] Mez/Bar solo,
pno RICORDI-ENG 113452 s.p.
                                   (C284)

CARITAS see Stout, Alan

CARL LOEWES WERKE see Loewe, Karl Gottfried

CARL SANDBURG'S NEW AMERICAN SONGBAG
*CC59U,folk,US
med solo,pno/gtr BMI pap $1.25, cloth
$2.95   (C285)

CARLBERG
Dryckesvisa
solo,pno LUNDQUIST s.p.   (C286)

CARLETON
My Christmas Prayer *sac,Xmas
SA soli,pno LORENZ $1.00   (C287)

CARLSON, BENGT (IVAR) (1890-1953)
Odas Sang
solo,pno FAZER F 933 s.p.   (C288)

CARLSON, DOSIA
Wedding Blessing, A *sac,Marriage
med solo,pno (F maj) SCHIRM.G $.85
                                         (C289)
low solo,pno (D maj) SCHIRM.G $.85
                                         (C290)

CARLYLE, R.
Bonnie Banks O' Loch Lomon'
low solo,pno (F maj) LEONARD-ENG
                                         (C291)
high solo,pno (G maj) LEONARD-ENG
                                         (C292)

CARMAN, M.
La Semaille
solo,pno ENOCH s.p.   (C293)
solo,acap solo pt ENOCH s.p.   (C294)

CARME *It
(Charles, Ernest) [It/Eng] low solo,
pno (D maj) SCHIRM.G $.60   (C295)

CARMELA see Tosti, Francesco Paolo

CARMEN see Jarnefelt, Armas

CARMENA see Wilson, H. Lane

CARMENCITA see Lane, Gerald M.

CARMENCITA see Repper, Charles

CARMICHAEL, MARY GRANT (1851-1935)
Come And Trip It
low solo,pno (A min) ASHDOWN (C296)
high solo,pno (B min) ASHDOWN
                                         (C297)

CARMICHAEL, RALPH
All My Life *sac
solo,pno WORD S-53   (C298)

For Pete's Sake! *sac,CCUL
solo,pno WORD 35001 $2.50   (C299)

He's Everything To Me *sac
solo,pno WORD S-34   (C300)
solo,pno WORD S-211   (C301)
solo,pno BENSON S5768-R $1.00
                                         (C302)

Love Is Surrender *sac
solo,pno WORD S-100   (C303)
(The Carpenters) solo,pno WORD
S-258   (C304)

Quiet Place, A *sac
solo,pno WORD S-112   (C305)

Reach Out To Jesus *sac
solo,pno WORD S-90   (C306)
solo,pno WORD S-210   (C307)
solo,pno BENSON S7412-R $1.00
                                         (C308)

Something Good Is Going To Happen To
You *sac
solo,pno BENSON S7555-R $1.00
                                         (C309)

Vocal Solos From One Hundred And Two
Strings, Vol. 2 *sac,CC10UL
solo,pno WORD 35012 $2.50   (C310)

CARMINA see Butterley, Nigel

CARMINA PACIFICA see Clarke, Henry
Leland

CARMINA PRINCETONIA
solo,pno SCHIRM.G $5.00   (C311)

CARMINA SACRA *sac,CCU
(Solantera, K. & L.) solo,pno FAZER
F 4568 s.p.   (C312)

CARNATIONS see Valverde, Joaquin,
Clavelitos

CARNAVAL see Delannoy, Marcel

CARNAVAL see Pierret, P.

CARNEVALI, VITO
Come, Love With Me
high solo,pno BELWIN $1.50   (C313)

CARNICER, RAMON (1789-1855)
El Musico Y El Poeta
(Subira) [Span] 2 soli,pno UNION
ESP. $4.75   (C314)

CARNIVAL OF VENICE, THE see Benedict,
Sir Julius

CARO, IO VOGLIO UN BOA DI STRUZZO see
Kalman, Emerich

CARO MIO BEN see Giordani, Giuseppe

CARO NOME see Verdi, Giuseppe

CAROL see Bush, Geoffrey

CAROL see Kechley, [Gerald]

CAROL see Kerr, Harrison

CAROL see Rawsthorne, Alan

CAROL FOR A CHOIR BOY see Jillett,
David

CAROL, M.
Cinco Canciones *CC5U
[Span] med solo,pno UNION ESP.
$1.50   (C315)

Seguidillas Murcianas
[Span] med-high solo,pno UNION ESP.
$.75   (C316)

CAROL OF JESUS CHILD see Hughes,
Herbert

CAROL OF THE BELLS *folk,Czech
(Wilhousky) solo,pno FISCHER,C V 2440
                                         (C317)

CAROL OF THE BIRDS see Thiman, Eric
Harding

CAROL OF THE BIRDS, THE see Niles, John
Jacob

CAROL OF THE DRUM see Davis, Katherine
K.

CAROL OF THE LITTLE KING see Caldwell,
Mary Elizabeth

CAROL OF THE SKIDDAW YOWES see Gurney,
Ivor

CAROL SINGERS see Bennett, Sir William
Sterndale

CAROLINA CABIN see Berger, Jean

CAROLS FOR CHRISTMAS *CCU,Xmas,carol
(Anthony, G.W.) med solo,pno PRESSER
$.75   (C318)

CAROLUS-DURAN, P.
Adieu
solo,pno ENOCH s.p.   (C319)

Antoine Et Cleopatre
solo,pno ENOCH s.p.   (C320)

Calypso
solo,pno ENOCH s.p.   (C321)

Chanson De Barberine
solo,pno (available in 2 keys)
ENOCH s.p.   (C322)

Chauves-Souris
solo,pno ENOCH s.p.   (C323)

Envoi
solo,pno ENOCH s.p.   (C324)

Impression
solo,pno ENOCH s.p.   (C325)

Instant
solo,pno ENOCH s.p.   (C326)

La Plaine
solo,pno ENOCH s.p.   (C327)

Le Soleil Reste
solo,pno ENOCH s.p.   (C328)

Les Cloches
solo,pno ENOCH s.p.   (C329)

Les Etoiles
solo,pno ENOCH s.p.   (C330)

L'Etang
solo,pno ENOCH s.p.   (C331)

Reve
solo,pno ENOCH s.p.   (C332)
low solo,cor,orch, humming chorus
sc ENOCH s.p., ipa   (C333)

Souvenir D'un Soir
solo,pno ENOCH s.p.   (C334)

CARON-LEGRIS, A.
Soir D'Hiver
solo,pno BERANDOL BER 1302 $1.50
                                         (C335)

CAROSIO, N.
Primavera Garibaldina
[It] solo,pno CURCI 5607 s.p.
                                         (C336)

CAROUSEL OF LIFE see McClintic, Gerry

CAROVNA LASKA see Doubrava, Jaroslav

CAROVNY KVET see Vignati, Milos

CAROVNY SVET see Vignati, Milos

CARPENTER, THE see Baker, Richard

CARPENTER, THE see Fox, George

CARPENTER, JOHN ALDEN (1876-1951)
Day Is No More, The
med solo,pno (G sharp min) SCHIRM.G
$.75   (C337)

Four Negro Songs *see That Soothin'
Song   (C338)

Gitanjali
med solo,pno SCHIRM.G $3.50
contains: I Am Like A Remnant Of
A Cloud Of Autumn (B flat maj);
Light, My Light (C maj); On The
Day When Death Will Knock At
Thy Door (D min); On The
Seashore Of Endless Worlds (A
flat maj); Sleep That Flits On
Baby's Eyes, The (D maj); When
I Bring To You Colour'd Toys (F
sharp maj)   (C339)

Home Road, The
med solo,pno (E flat maj) SCHIRM.G
$.60   (C340)

I Am Like A Remnant Of A Cloud Of
Autumn
see Gitanjali

Light, My Light
see Gitanjali

On The Day When Death Will Knock At
Thy Door
see Gitanjali

On The Seashore Of Endless Worlds
see Gitanjali
med solo,pno (A flat maj) SCHIRM.G
$1.00   (C341)

Sleep That Flits On Baby's Eyes, The
see Gitanjali
med solo,pno (D maj) SCHIRM.G $.85
                                         (C342)

That Soothin' Song
med-low solo,pno SCHIRM.G $.60 see
from Four Negro Songs   (C343)

When I Bring To You Colour'd Toys
see Gitanjali
med-high solo,pno (F sharp maj)
SCHIRM.G $.85   (C344)
low solo,pno (E flat maj) SCHIRM.G
$.85   (C345)

CARPENTER'S SON, THE see Orr, Charles
Wilfred

CARR
Oriental Miniatures *CCU
high solo,pno WESTERN AR11 $1.75
                                         (C346)

CARRIERE, PAUL
Begluckt, Wem Ruhig Liebend
see Sechs Lieder

Der Soldat
see Sechs Lieder

Lied Der Soldaten
see Sechs Lieder

Schliesse Mir Die Augen Beide
see Sechs Lieder

Sechs Lieder
med solo,pno LEUCKART s.p.
contains: Begluckt, Wem Ruhig
Liebend; Der Soldat; Lied Der
Soldaten; Schliesse Mir Die
Augen Beide; Spruch; Willkomm
                                         (C347)

Spruch
see Sechs Lieder

Willkomm
see Sechs Lieder

CARRION CROW see Pitfield, Thomas Baron

CARROLL, J. ROBERT
Lord May Their Lives *sac,Marriage
med solo,pno/org (easy) GIA G-1601
$1.00   (C348)

CARROLL, J. ROBERT (cont'd.)

Wedding Song, A *sac,Marriage
    med solo,pno/org (easy) GIA G-1917
    $1.00   (C349)

CARROLL, PETER
My Own Dear Love
    solo,pno (C maj) BOOSEY $1.50
                                       (C350)

CARROZZINI, D.
Birth Of Love, The
    med solo,pno PARAGON $.85   (C351)

Inspiration Waltz
    med solo,pno PARAGON $.85   (C352)

CARRY HER OVER THE WATER see Berkeley,
Lennox

CARRY ME BACK TO OLD VIRGINNY see Bland

CARRY ME 'LONG see Foster, Stephen
Collins

CARRYIN' COALS see Glick, F.

CARSE, ADAM VON AHN (1878-1958)
Amber And Amethyst
    solo,pno CRAMER   (C353)

Opal
    low solo,pno (D flat maj) CRAMER
                                   (C354)
    high solo,pno (F maj) CRAMER (C355)

CARTE POSTALE see Caby, R.

CARTER
Crippled Boy's Prayer, A *sac
    solo,pno BENSON S5012-S $1.00
                                   (C356)

CARTER, E.
Dust Of Snow
    med solo,pno AMP $.70   (C357)

Rose Family, The
    med solo,pno AMP $.60   (C358)

Tell Me Where Is Fancy Bred
    (Silverman) low solo,gtr AMP $.85
                                   (C359)
Voyage
    med solo,pno AMP $.85   (C360)

CARTER, ELLIOTT COOK, JR. (1908-   )
Warble For Lilac Time
    S solo,fl,2clar,bsn,harp,strings
    PEER sc rental, voc sc $2.00
                                   (C361)

CARTER, JOHN
Cantata For Voice And Orchestra
    *cant
    solo,2fl,2ob,2clar,2bsn,4horn,3trp,
    3trom,timp,perc,harp,strings PEER
    sc rental, voc sc $2.25   (C362)

CARTES POSTALES see Jacob, Dom Clement

CARTOMANCIE see Rivier, Jean

CARUSO ALBUM *CC8L
    [It/Eng] T solo,pno cmplt ed RICORDI-
    ENG LD 178 s.p. contains works by:
    Puccini; Tosti; Donaudy; Verdi and
    others   (C363)

CARYLL, IVAN (1861-1921)
Chanson Des Heures (from Son Altesse
    Royale)
    solo,pno ENOCH s.p.   (C364)

Chanson Sur Le Prince Consort (from
    Son Altesse Royale)
    solo,pno ENOCH s.p.   (C365)

Couplets De La Desillusion (from Son
    Altesse Royale)
    solo,pno ENOCH s.p.   (C366)

Couplets De La Timidite (from Son
    Altesse Royale)
    solo,pno ENOCH s.p.   (C367)

Couplets De L'arbre Genealogique
    (from Son Altesse Royale)
    solo,pno ENOCH s.p.   (C368)

Couplets Des Recriminations (from Son
    Altesse Royale)
    solo,pno ENOCH s.p.   (C369)

Couplets Du Mana Militari (from Son
    Altesse Royale)
    solo,pno ENOCH s.p.   (C370)

Couplets Du Portrait De La Reine
    (from Son Altesse Royale)
    solo,pno (available in 2 keys)
    ENOCH s.p.   (C371)

Couplets Du Telephone (from Son
    Altesse Royale)
    solo,pno ENOCH s.p.   (C372)

CARYLL, IVAN (cont'd.)

Duo De La Premiere Entreuvue (from
    Son Altesse Royale)
    solo,pno ENOCH s.p.   (C373)

Duo De L'Intimite (from Son Altesse
    Royale)
    solo,pno ENOCH s.p.   (C374)

Duo Des Bonnes Intentions (from Son
    Altesse Royale)
    2 soli,pno ENOCH s.p.   (C375)

La Valse Du Prince (from Son Altesse
    Royale)
    solo,orch ENOCH s.p., ipa   (C376)

Que Ne Suis-Je Plutot (from Son
    Altesse Royale)
    solo,pno (available in 2 keys)
    ENOCH s.p.   (C377)

Scene De L'arrivee Du Prince (from
    Son Altesse Royale)
    solo,pno ENOCH s.p.   (C378)

Valse De Cyril (from Son Altesse
    Royale)
    solo,pno ENOCH s.p.   (C379)

CASADEI, S.
Bambina Come Te
    [It] solo,pno BONGIOVANI 2490 s.p.
                                   (C380)

CASADESUS, HENRI GUSTAVE (1879-1947)
Dans Tes Jardins, Noble Versailles
    see Quatre Chansons Francaises

Gentil Coquelicot Mesdames
    see Quatre Chansons Francaises

La Sommeilleuse
    see Quatre Chansons Francaises

Quatre Chansons Francaises
    med solo,pno SALABERT-US $5.00
    contains: Dans Tes Jardins, Noble
    Versailles; Gentil Coquelicot
    Mesdames; La Sommeilleuse;
    Retournons Dans Les Bois   (C381)

Retournons Dans Les Bois
    see Quatre Chansons Francaises

CASADESUS, ROBERT MARCEL (1899-1972)
La Tarentelle
    solo,pno ENOCH s.p.   (C382)

CASADITA see Halffter, Rodolfo

CASAGRANDE, A. (1922-1964)
Ninna Nanna
    [It] solo,pno CURCI 6902 s.p.
                                   (C383)
CASALONGA, M.
Reponse Au Sonnet D'Arvers
    solo,pno ENOCH s.p.   (C384)

CASALS, PABLO (1876-1973)
Canco Catalana No. 1
    S solo,pno (Catalan and English
    text) BROUDE,A $1.00   (C385)

De Cara Al Mar
    S solo,pno (Catalan and English
    text) BROUDE,A $1.00   (C386)

El Angel Travieso
    [Eng/Span] S solo,pno BROUDE,A
    $1.00   (C387)

Tres Estrofas De Amor *CC3U
    [Eng/Span] S solo,pno BROUDE,A
    $1.00   (C388)

CASANOVA, ANDRE (1919-   )
Cavalier Seul
    Bar solo,4strings/orch sc,quarto
    AMPHION R 2044 s.p.   (C389)

Divertimento
    Mez solo,fl,ob,clar,bsn,pno,vln,vla
    sc JOBERT s.p.   (C390)

Le Chant D'Aube
    S solo,orch voc sc JOBERT s.p.
                                   (C391)

Le Livre De La Foi Juree
    narrator&3 soli,3fl,3ob,3clar,2bsn,
    2horn,2trp,trom,cel,timp,perc,
    strings JOBERT rental   (C392)

CASELLA, ALFREDO (1883-1947)
La Sera Fiesolana
    [It/Fr] S solo,pno RICORDI-ENG
    119549 s.p.   (C393)

Ninna Nanna, Corbellina
    [It] solo,pno SANTIS 539 s.p.
                                   (C394)

Tre Canti Sacri *sac,CC3U
    Bar solo,orch voc sc ZERBONI 4173
    s.p.   (C395)

CASELLA, ALFREDO (cont'd.)

Tre Canzoni Trecentesche *CC3U
    [It/Fr] S solo,pno RICORDI-ENG
    119505 s.p.   (C396)

CASEMAJOR, L.
Les Saisons
    solo,pno ENOCH s.p.   (C397)
    solo,acap solo pt ENOCH s.p. (C398)

CASES
Canciones De Espana *CC8L
    [Span] solo,pno RICORDI-ARG
    BA 10791 s.p.   (C399)

CASNER, MYRON D.
O Jesus, I Have Promised *sac
    med solo,pno oct CONCORDIA 98-1459
    $.25   (C400)

CASOLA, FRANCESCO
Quam Candidus Es *sac
    (Ewerhart, Rudolf) S/T solo,cont
    BIELER CS 53 s.p.   (C401)

CASS COUNTY
see Long Wharf Songs

CASSANDRA see Williams, Joan Franks

CASSERMAN, HJALMAR
Sanger Och Visor Heft II & III *CCU
    solo,pno GEHRMANS s.p., ea. (C402)

CASSEUS
Assoto
    see Haitenesques

Farewell To Fancy
    see Haitenesques

Girl In The Woods
    see Haitenesques

Haitenesques
    [Fr/Eng] solo,gtr cmplt ed RICORDI-
    ENG FC 2751 s.p.
    contains: Assoto; Farewell To
    Fancy; Girl In The Woods; Such
    A Lively Morning   (C403)

Such A Lively Morning
    see Haitenesques

CASSLER, G. WINSTON
Crown With Thy Benediction *sac
    med solo,pno AUGSBURG 11-0712 $.75
                                   (C404)

Whither Thou Goest *sac
    med solo,pno AUGSBURG 11-0700 $.75
                                   (C405)
    low solo,pno AUGSBURG 11-0701 $.75
                                   (C406)

CASTA DIVA see Bellini, Vincenzo

CASTEL, J.
La Gitanilla En El Coliseo
    [Span] high solo,pno UNION ESP.
    $4.00   (C407)

CASTELBERG, M.
Sieben Geistliche Lieder *sac,CC7U
    solo,pno HUG s.p.   (C408)

CASTELLO IN ARIA see Campogalliani, E.

CASTELNUOVO-TEDESCO, MARIO (1895-1968)
And Let Me A Canikin Clink
    see Shakespeare Songs For Baritone,
    Set 2

Ballata
    [It] solo,pno CURCI 433 s.p. (C409)

Blow, Blow, Thou Winter Wind
    see Shakespeare Songs For Baritone,
    Set 1

But Shall I Go Mourn For That?
    see Shakespeare Songs For Baritone,
    Set 2

Cinque Poesie Romanesche *CC5U
    solo,pno FORLIVESI 12031 s.p.
                                   (C410)

Come Away, Come Away Death
    see Shakespeare Songs For Baritone,
    Set 1

Come Unto These Yellow Sands
    see Shakespeare Songs For Tenor,
    Set 1

Coplas *CC11U
    solo,pno FORLIVESI 10752 s.p.
                                   (C411)

Die Drei Konige *sac,Xmas
    "I Re Magi" solo,pno FORLIVESI
    11747 s.p.   (C412)

Divan Of Moses-Ibn-Ezra, The *Op.207
    solo,gtr BERBEN 1713 s.p.   (C413)

CASTELNUOVO-TEDESCO, MARIO (cont'd.)

Due Preghiere Per I Bimbi D'Italia
  *CC2U
  solo,pno FORLIVESI 11258 s.p.
                                    (C414)

Fear No More The Heat Of The Sun
  see Shakespeare Songs For Contralto
  Or Baritone, Set 2

Fie On Sinful Fantasy!
  see Shakespeare Songs For Soprano

Fool, The *song cycle
  [Eng] high solo,kbd CHESTER s.p.
                                    (C415)

Full Fathom Five
  see Shakespeare Songs For Tenor,
  Set 1

Get You Hence, For I Must Go
  see Shakespeare Songs For Contralto
  Or Baritone, Set 2

Girotondo Dei Golosi
  solo,pno FORLIVESI 10854 s.p.
                                    (C416)

Hark! Hark! The Lark
  see Shakespeare Songs For Contralto
  Or Baritone, Set 1

How Should I Your True Love Know?
  see Shakespeare Songs For Contralto
  Or Baritone, Set 2

I Re Magi *see Die Drei Konige

I Shall No More To Sea
  see Shakespeare Songs For Baritone,
  Set 2

Immortal Gods, I Crave No Pelf
  see Shakespeare Songs For Baritone,
  Set 1

In Youth When I Did Love
  see Shakespeare Songs For Baritone,
  Set 2

Indian Serenade
  solo,pno FORLIVESI 11259 s.p.
                                    (C417)

It Was A Lover And His Lass
  see Shakespeare Songs For Contralto
  Or Baritone, Set 1

Lawn As White As Driven Snow
  see Shakespeare Songs For Tenor,
  Set 1

L'infinito
  solo,pno FORLIVESI 10906 s.p.
                                    (C418)

My Betrothed
  high solo,pno BELWIN $1.50   (C419)

Ninna Nanna
  Mez/Bar solo,pno FORLIVESI 10768
  s.p.   (C420)
  S/T solo,pno FORLIVESI 10767 s.p.
                                    (C421)

No More Dams I'll Make
  see Shakespeare Songs For Baritone,
  Set 2

Oh Mistress Mine
  see Shakespeare Songs For Tenor,
  Set 2

Orpheus With His Lute
  see Shakespeare Songs For Soprano

Pardon, Goddess Of The Night
  see Shakespeare Songs For Contralto
  Or Baritone, Set 2

Poor Soul Sat Sighing, The
  see Shakespeare Songs For Contralto
  Or Baritone, Set 1

Seal My Heart
  high solo,pno BELWIN $1.50   (C422)

Sera
  [It] solo,pno CURCI 434 s.p. (C423)

Shakespeare Songs For Baritone, Set 1
  [Eng] Bar solo,kbd CHESTER s.p.
    contains: Blow, Blow, Thou Winter
    Wind; Come Away, Come Away
    Death; Immortal Gods, I Crave
    No Pelf; Under The Green-Wood
    Tree   (C424)

Shakespeare Songs For Baritone, Set 2
  [Eng] Bar solo,kbd CHESTER s.p.
    contains: And Let Me A Canikin
    Clink; But Shall I Go Mourn For
    That?; I Shall No More To Sea;
    In Youth When I Did Love; No
    More Dams I'll Make   (C425)

Shakespeare Songs For Contralto Or
  Baritone, Set 1
  [Eng] A/Bar solo,pno CHESTER s.p.
    contains: Hark! Hark! The Lark;

CASTELNUOVO-TEDESCO, MARIO (cont'd.)

    It Was A Lover And His Lass;
    Poor Soul Sat Sighing, The;
    Tell Me Where Is Fancy Bred;
    When Daisies Pied; When Icicles
    Hang By The Wall   (C426)

Shakespeare Songs For Contralto Or
  Baritone, Set 2
  [Eng] A/Bar solo,kbd CHESTER s.p.
    contains: Fear No More The Heat
    Of The Sun; Get You Hence, For
    I Must Go; How Should I Your
    True Love Know?; Pardon,
    Goddess Of The Night; Sigh No
    More, Ladies   (C427)

Shakespeare Songs For Soprano
  [Eng] S solo,kbd CHESTER s.p.
    contains: Fie On Sinful Fantasy!;
    Orpheus With His Lute; Where
    The Bee Sucks; You Spotted
    Snakes   (C428)

Shakespeare Songs For Tenor, Set 1
  [Eng] T solo,kbd CHESTER s.p.
    contains: Come Unto These Yellow
    Sands; Full Fathom Five; Lawn
    As White As Driven Snow; Take,
    O Take Those Lips Away; Who Is
    Sylviau   (C429)

Shakespeare Songs For Tenor, Set 2
  [Eng] T solo,kbd CHESTER s.p.
    contains: Oh Mistress Mine; What
    Shall He Have That Killed The
    Deer?; When Daffodils Begin To
    Peer; When That I Was And A
    Little Tiny Boy   (C430)

Sigh No More, Ladies
  see Shakespeare Songs For Contralto
  Or Baritone, Set 2

Take, O Take Those Lips Away
  see Shakespeare Songs For Tenor,
  Set 1

Tell Me Where Is Fancy Bred
  see Shakespeare Songs For Contralto
  Or Baritone, Set 1

Three Sephardic Songs *CC3U
  [Heb/Eng/Fr] med solo,pno ISRAELI
  205 $4.20 also with Sephardic
  text   (C431)

Under The Green-Wood Tree
  see Shakespeare Songs For Baritone,
  Set 1

Vogelweide *Op.186, song cycle
  Bar solo,gtr SCHAUR EE 2703 s.p.
                                    (C432)

What Shall He Have That Killed The
  Deer?
  see Shakespeare Songs For Tenor,
  Set 2

When Daffodils Begin To Peer
  see Shakespeare Songs For Tenor,
  Set 2

When Daisies Pied
  see Shakespeare Songs For Contralto
  Or Baritone, Set 1

When Icicles Hang By The Wall
  see Shakespeare Songs For Contralto
  Or Baritone, Set 1

When That I Was And A Little Tiny Boy
  see Shakespeare Songs For Tenor,
  Set 2

Where The Bee Sucks
  see Shakespeare Songs For Soprano

Who Is Sylviau
  see Shakespeare Songs For Tenor,
  Set 1

You Spotted Snakes
  see Shakespeare Songs For Soprano

CASTEREDE, JACQUES
A La Faveur De La Nuit
  see Quatre Poemes De Robert Desnos

Au Bout Du Monde
  see Quatre Poemes De Robert Desnos

J'ai Reve Tellement Fort De Toi
  see Quatre Poemes De Robert Desnos

Ombres Des Arbres Dans L'eau
  see Quatre Poemes De Robert Desnos

Quatre Poemes De Robert Desnos
  Bar solo,pno cmplt ed RIDEAU 043
  s.p.
    contains: A La Faveur De La Nuit;
    Au Bout Du Monde; J'ai Reve
    Tellement Fort De Toi; Ombres
    Des Arbres Dans L'eau   (C433)

CASTIGLIONI, NICCOLO (1932-   )
Elegia
  S solo,18inst sc ZERBONI 5425 s.p.
                                    (C434)

Figure
  solo,orch voc sc SCHOTTS s.p.
                                    (C435)

Sinfonia No. 1
  S solo,orch sc ZERBONI 5333 s.p.
                                    (C436)

CASTILLO, M.
Dos Canciones Para La Navidad *CC2U
  [Span] med-high solo,pno UNION ESP.
  $1.00   (C437)

CASTLE OF DROMORE see Somervell, Arthur

CASTRO, JOSE MARIA (1892-1964)
El Sueno
  "Il Sogno" [Span/It] solo,pno
  RICORDI-ARG BA 7369 s.p.   (C438)

Il Sogno *see El Sueno

CASTRO, JUAN JOSE (1895-1968)
La Casada Infiel
  [Span] solo,pno RICORDI-ARG BA 9338
  s.p.   (C439)

CAT CAME FIDDLING, A see Kapp, Paul

CATALANI, ALFREDO (1854-1893)
Ebben, N'andro Lontana (from La
  Wally)
  [It] S solo,pno RICORDI-ENG 122419
  s.p.   (C440)

Ebben, Ne Andro Lontana (from La
  Wally)
  [It/Eng] S solo,pno INTERNAT. $1.00
                                    (C441)

Ebben, Ne Andro Lontana *see Pues
  Bien...Ire Lejana

Pues Bien...Ire Lejana (from La
  Wally)
  "Ebben, Ne Andro Lontana" [It/Span]
  S solo,pno RICORDI-ARG BA 8144
  s.p.   (C442)

CATBIRD, THE see Clokey, Joseph Waddell

CATE, H.
Two Little Birdlings
  med solo,pno SEESAW $1.00   (C443)

CATECHISME DE NUIT see Komives, Janos

CATENA MUSICALE see Dresden, Sem

CATENAE TERRENAE see Brevi, Giovanni
  Battista

CATES, BILL
All Of My Tomorrows (from Joy) sac
  solo,pno BROADMAN 4590-29 $1.00
                                    (C444)

Do You Really Care? (from Good News)
  sac
  solo,pno BROADMAN 4590-13 $.75
                                    (C445)
  solo,pno SINGSPIR 7084-SN $1.00
                                    (C446)

God Sent His Son *sac
  med solo,pno (easy) BROADMAN
  4590-27 $1.00   (C447)

Not Someday, But Now *sac
  solo,pno BROADMAN 4590-36 $1.00
                                    (C448)

Presence Of Christ, The (from
  Encounter) sac
  solo,pno BROADMAN 4590-30 $1.00
                                    (C449)

Push Me, Lord (from Joy) sac
  solo,pno BROADMAN 4590-39 $1.00
                                    (C450)

To The Ends Of The Earth (from Common
  Cup, The) sac
  solo,pno BROADMAN 4590-36 $1.00
                                    (C451)
  solo,pno BROADMAN 4590-37 $1.00
                                    (C452)

CATHERINE, A.
Bruit D'ailes
  solo,pno ENOCH s.p.   (C453)

CATHOLIC WEDDING FOLIO *sac,CCU,
  Marriage
  (Vene) BELWIN high solo,pno $1.25;
  low solo,pno $1.25   (C454)

CATTINI, U. (1922-   )
Cinque Carmi Di Catullo
  [It] CARISH s.p.
    contains: Lugete O Veneres
    Cupidinesque (solo,2fl,2ob,
    2clar,2bsn,timp,harp,strings);
    Malest Cornifici (solo,
    strings); Passer Deliciae Meae
    Puellae (solo,fl); Quid Est,
    Catulle (solo,2fl,2ob,2clar,
    2bsn,vla,vcl,bvl); Vivamus
    (solo,2clar,2ob,2bsn,2horn,
    2trp)   (C455)

CATTINI, U. (cont'd.)

Lugete O Veneres Cupidinesque
see Cinque Carmi Di Catullo

Malest Cornifici
see Cinque Carmi Di Catullo

Passer Deliciae Meae Puellae
see Cinque Carmi Di Catullo

Quid Est, Catulle
see Cinque Carmi Di Catullo

Vivamus
see Cinque Carmi Di Catullo

CATULLUS: ON THE BURIAL OF HIS BROTHER
see Rorem, Ned

CAUGHT UP TOGETHER see Horne

CAUGHT UP TOGETHER see Horne, Roger

CAUSE US, O LORD, OUR GOD see Rozin,
Albert

CAVALIER SEUL see Casanova, Andre

CAVALIERE
People Got To Be Free *see Brigati

CAVALIERS see Friml, Rudolf

CAVALLI, (PIETRO) FRANCESCO (1602-1676)
Five Operatic Arias *CC5U
[It/Eng] high solo,kbd FABER F0010
$2.50   (C456)

Hillo, Il Mio Bene E Morto (from
Ercole Amante)
S solo,strings CARISH s.p.   (C457)

Prison Scene (from L'Ormindo)
[It/Eng] ST soli,kbd FABER F0027
$2.00   (C458)

CAVATINA DI PULCINELLA see Farinelli,
Giuseppe

CAVATINA OF VLADIMIR see Borodin,
Alexander Porfirievitch

CAVATINE see Gounod, Charles Francois

CAVATINE see Rossini, Gioacchino

CAZZATI, MAURIZIO (1620-1677)
Cantate Morali E Spirituali A Voce
Sola *sac,CCU,cant
solo,pno FORNI s.p.   (C459)

Dulcis Amor *sac
(Ewerhart, Rudolf) B solo,cont
BIELER CS 55 s.p.   (C460)

Factum Est Praelium Magnum *sac
(Ewerhart, Rudolf) B solo,cont
BIELER CS 60 s.p.   (C461)

In Calvaria Rupe *sac
(Ewerhart, Rudolf) [Lat] B solo,
cont BIELER CS 19 s.p.   (C462)

Motetti A Voce Sola *CCU,mot
solo,pno FORNI s.p.   (C463)

CE COEUR PLAINTIF see Ropartz, Joseph
Guy

CE DOUX PETIT VISAGE see Poulenc,
Francis

CE MONDE DE ROSEE see Delvincourt,
Claude

CE N'EST PAS COMME VOUS see Saint-
Saens, Camille

CE N'EST PAS LE FAUTE A NOUS DEUX see
Wolff, A.

CE QU'ADAM DIT A EVE see Daniel-Lesur

CE QUE CHANTAIT DELMET see Chaubet, P.

CE QUE DIT LA CHANSON see Collin, L.

CE QUE J'AIMAIS LE MIEUX EN TOI see
Rabey, Rene

CE QUE J'AIME see Rhene-Baton

CE QUE JE SUIS SANS TOI see Gounod,
Charles Francois

CE QUE L'ON REVE see Berger, Rod.

CE QUI ME PLAIT see David, J.

CE QUI SEDUIT MON AME see Banffy, N.

CE QU'IL A LE CHAT see Stravinsky, Igor

CE SABLE FIN ET FUYANT see Caplet,
Andre

C'E SEMPRE see De Rubertis, Victor

CE SOIR ON ME DEDAIGNE see Saint-Saens,
Camille

CE SONT LES MISS see Berger, Rod.

CE SONT NOS PETITS SOLDATS see Scotto,
Vincent

CECCHERINI, T
Inno Pontificio
[It] solo,pno CURCI 2767 s.p.
(C464)

CECILE see Honegger, Arthur

CECILIA see Sinigaglia, Leone

CECILIA see Voormolen, Alexander
Nicolas

CECILIA VOLGI UN SGUARDO see Handel,
George Frideric

CECILY see Strauss, Richard, Cacilie

CEDANT A D'INDGNES see Duvernoy,
Victor-Alphonse

CELEBRATED SACRED SOLOS *sac,CC11L
BOSTON high solo,pno $2.50; low solo,
pno $2.50   (C465)

CELEBRATED SONGS, VOL. 1 see Hirai,
Kozaburo

CELEBRATED SONGS, VOL. 2 see Hirai,
Kozaburo

CELEBRATION OF DIVINE LOVE see
Williamson, Malcolm

CELEBRE MENUET see Exaudet

CELEBRE SERANADE see Gounod, Charles
Francois

CELEBRE SICILIANA see Pergolesi,
Giovanni Battista

CELEBRITAT see Diepenbrock, Alphons

CELESTE AIDA see Verdi, Giuseppe

CELESTIA see Bohun, Lyle de

CELESTIAL WEAVER see Bantock, Granville

CELIA
(Lehmann, Amelia) high solo,pno (F
min) ASHDOWN $1.50   (C466)
(Lehmann, Amelia) med solo,pno (G
min) ASHDOWN $1.50   (C467)
(Lehmann, Amelia) low solo,pno (A
min) ASHDOWN $1.50   (C468)

CELLE QUE J'AIME see Lacome, Paul

CELLE QUE NOUS AIMONS see Cuvillier,
Charles

CELLE QUI PASSE see Gedalge, Andre

CELTIC LULLABY, A *folk,Ir
(Roberton, Hugh S.) 3 soli,pno
ROBERTON 71545 s.p.   (C469)

CELTIC ROMANCE, A see Arlen, Albert

C'EN EST FAIT, CE COEUR BRULE see
Maurat, Edmond

CENDRE ROUGE (LA) see Saint-Saens,
Camille

CENDRES see Larbey, V.

CENDRILLON see Lacome, Paul

CENTIPEDE AND OTHER RHYMES see Dale,
Mervyn

CENTO CANTI NAZIONALI RUSSI, VOL. 1
*CC40U
(Rimsky-Korsakov, Nicolai) [Russ/Ger/
Fr/Eng] BESSEL 10963 A s.p.   (C470)

CENTO CANTI NAZIONALI RUSSI, VOL. 2
*CC30U
(Rimsky-Korsakov, Nicolai) [Russ/Ger/
Fr/Eng] BESSEL 10963 B s.p.   (C471)

CENTO CANTI NAZIONALI RUSSI, VOL. 3
*CC30U
(Rimsky-Korsakov, Nicolai) [Russ/Ger/
Fr/Eng] BESSEL 10963 C s.p.   (C472)

CENTRAL PARK AT DUSK see Duke, John
Woods

CEOL MARA *CC17L,folk
med-high solo,pno CHESTER s.p. all
songs in Gaelic, 8 are in English,

also   (C473)

CEPHALE ET PROCRIS see Guerre,
Elizabeth Jacquet de la

C'ERA UN RE, UN RE DI THULE see Gounod,
Charles Francois

C'ERA UNA VOLTA see Bizzelli, Annibale

CERCHIA, A.
Voix Ancienne
solo,pno ENOCH s.p.   (C474)

CERHA, FRIEDRICH (1926-   )
Sept Rubaijat Des Omar Khajjam *CC7U
S/T solo,pno MODERN s.p.   (C475)

CERNIK, JOSEF (1880-   )
Slezske Pisne Na Slova P. Bezruce
*CCU
solo,pno SUPRAPHON s.p.   (C476)

Zpevy Moravskych Kopanicaru *CCU
solo,pno SUPRAPHON s.p.   (C477)

CERNOCH see Karhu, Edwin T.

CERNY see Bartos, Frantisek

CERRO, LUNA Y AIRE see Quaratino,
Pascual

CERVENY MAK see Hrusovsky, Ivan

CES AIRS JOYEUX, CES CHANTS DE FETE see
Debussy, Claude

CESKE A SLOVENSKE LIDOVE PISNE see
Trojan, Vaclav

CESKE A SLOVENSKE LIDOVE PISNE see
Trojan, Vaclav

CESKE OPERNI ARIE PRO ALT *CCU
A solo,pno SUPRAPHON   (C478)

CESKE OPERNI ARIE PRO BARYTON *CCU
Bar solo,pno SUPRAPHON   (C479)

CESKE OPERNI ARIE PRO BAS *CCU
B solo,pno SUPRAPHON   (C480)

CESKE OPERNI ARIE PRO TENOR *CCU
T solo,pno SUPRAPHON   (C481)

CESKE OPERNI PRO SOPRAN *CCU
S solo,pno SUPRAPHON   (C482)

CESKOSLOVENSKA STATNI HYMNA *CCU
solo,pno SUPRAPHON s.p.   (C483)

CESSATE, DEH, CESSATE see Foggia,
Francesco

CESSATE, OMAI CESSATE see Vivaldi,
Antonio

C'EST A MOI DE MARGARITA see Saint-
Saens, Camille

C'EST AINSI QUE TU EST see Poulenc,
Francis

C'EST BIEN FINI, JE DOIS COMPTE A DIEU
see Saint-Saens, Camille

C'EST DANS PARIS, LA GRANDE VILLE see
Blanchard, Roger

C'EST DES CONTREBANDIERS LE REFUGE see
Bizet, Georges

C'EST DU SOLEIL see Absil, Jean

C'EST DU VIN DE GASCOGNE see Messager,
Andre

C'EST ELLE see Fragerolle, G.

C'EST ELLE see Mozart, Wolfgang Amadeus

C'EST ELLE see Saint-Saens, Camille

C'EST EN L'AVRIL see Bloch, Augustyn

C'EST FRANCOIS LES BAS-BLEUS see
Messager, Andre

C'EST ICI QU'HABITE PHRYNE see Saint-
Saens, Camille

C'EST ICI QU'ON AIME TOUJOURS see
Filipucci, Edm.

C'EST LA BRISE DU SOIR see Laparra,
Raoul

C'EST LA BRUNE see Guiraud, Ernest

C'EST LA FILLE A JEAN-PIERRE see
Lacome, Paul

C'EST LA LOI MILITAIRE see Vasseur,
Leon (-Felix-Augustin-Joseph)

C'EST LA PAIX see Faure, Gabriel-Urbain

C'EST LA PLUIE DOUCE see Sancan, P.

C'EST LA QUE JE VAIS LE REVOIR see
Guiraud, Ernest

C'EST LA QUE NOUS AIMONS see Schumann,
Robert (Alexander)

C'EST LA VALSE A TOUT LE MONDE see
Bozi, Harold de

C'EST LE JOYEUX SERGENT see Vasseur,
Leon (-Felix-Augustin-Joseph)

C'EST LE MEME QU'HIER, JE CHERCHAIS see
Levade, Charles (Gaston)

C'EST LE SOIR see Migot, Georges

C'EST LE TANGO D'AMOUR see Filipucci,
Edm.

C'EST LE VENT
(Emmerechts; Joulain, Emile) solo,pno
GRAS s.p.   (C484)

C'EST LES GENS DE BOUZE
see La Musique, Quatorzieme Cahier

C'EST L'ESPAGNE see Offenbach, Jacques

C'EST L'HEURE see Schmitt, Florent

C'EST L'HEURE AUX VOLETS CLOS see
Bernier, Nicolas

C'EST TOI! C'EST MOI! see Bizet,
Georges

C'EST TOI QUE JE REVOIS see Messager,
Andre

C'EST UN AMANT see Fredly, A.

C'EST UN P'TIT RAMONEUR see
Delvincourt, Claude

C'EST UN REVE see Wellings, M.

C'EST UN TORRENT IMPETREUX see Gluck,
Christoph Willibald Ritter von

C'EST UN VIEUX VIN DE MALVOISIE see
Levade, Charles (Gaston)

C'EST UNE CHANSON D'AMOUR see
Offenbach, Jacques

CESTA see Moyzes, Alexander

CESTA ZIVYCH see Hlobil, Emil

CESTI, MARC' ANTONIO (1623-1669)
Four Chamber Duets *CC4U
(Burrows, David L.) 2 soli,inst A-R
ED $8.95   (C485)

Intorno All'idol Mio
[It/Fr] Mez/Bar solo,pno RICORDI-
ARG BA 11851 s.p.   (C486)
solo,pno FORLIVESI 10873 s.p.
                                  (C487)

CET INSTANT-LA see Leduc, Jacques, Dei
Anang, Ghana

C'ETAIT A L'AUBE DERNIERE see Nougues,
Jean

C'ETAIT EN AVRIL see Chaminade, Cecile

C'ETAIT EN AVRIL see Ronald, Sir Landon

C'ETAIT UN SOIR see Cuvillier, Charles

C'ETAIT UN SOIR DE FEERIES see
Huybrechts, Albert

CETTE GRANDE CHAMBRE see Ibert, Jacques

CETTE LIGNE EST UN SIGNE see Lacome,
Paul

CEUX QUE NOUS AIMONS see Beydts, L.

CHABRIER, EMMANUEL (1841-1894)
A La Musique
(Samazeuilh) solo,pno ENOCH s.p.
                                  (C488)
Ainsi Que La Rose Nouvelle (from
L'Etoile)
solo,pno ENOCH s.p.   (C489)
Ballade Des Gros Dindons
solo,pno ENOCH s.p.   (C490)
solo,orch ENOCH rental   (C491)
solo,acap solo pt ENOCH s.p. (C492)
Beau Pays, Pays Du Gai Soleil (from
Le Roi Malgre Lui)
solo,pno ENOCH s.p.   (C493)
Blonde Aux Yeux De Pervenche (from
Gwendoline)
female solo,pno ENOCH s.p.   (C494)

CHABRIER, EMMANUEL (cont'd.)

Mez solo,pno ENOCH s.p.   (C495)

Chanson Pour Jeanne
solo,pno (available in 2 keys)
ENOCH s.p.   (C496)
solo,orch ENOCH rental   (C497)

Credo D'amour
solo,pno (available in 2 keys)
ENOCH s.p.   (C498)

Duo Du Deuxieme Acte (from
Gwendoline)
2 soli,pno ENOCH s.p.   (C499)

Duo Du Troisieme Acte (from
Gwendoline)
2 soli,pno ENOCH s.p.   (C500)

Enfants, Je Vous Benis (from
Gwendoline)
3 soli,pno ENOCH s.p.   (C501)

Epithalame (from Gwendoline)
solo,pno ENOCH s.p.   (C502)
solo,pno oct ENOCH s.p.   (C503)

Espana
S solo,pno ENOCH s.p.   (C504)
T/S solo,pno ENOCH s.p.   (C505)
Bar/Mez solo,pno ENOCH s.p.   (C506)
MezA/BarB soli,pno (D maj) voc sc,
solo pt ENOCH s.p.   (C507)
2 soli,pno (E maj) voc sc ENOCH
s.p.   (C508)
2 soli,pno (D maj) voc sc ENOCH
s.p.   (C509)
solo,acap solo pt ENOCH s.p. (C510)
(Vieuxble, R.) boy solo/girl solo,
acap solo pt ENOCH s.p.   (C511)

Gwendoline: Fileuse
solo,orch ENOCH rental   (C512)

Il Est Parti Celui Que J'aime (from
Le Roi Malgre Lui)
2 soli,pno ENOCH s.p.   (C513)

Il Est Un Vieux Chant De Boheme (from
Le Roi Malgre Lui)
solo,pno ENOCH s.p.   (C514)

Je Suis Du Pays Des Gondoles (from Le
Roi Malgre Lui)
solo,pno ENOCH s.p.   (C515)

Je Suis Le Roi, Je Suis Le Roi (from
Le Roi Malgre Lui)
solo,pno ENOCH s.p.   (C516)

Je T'aime De Toute Mon Ame (from Le
Roi Malgre Lui)
solo,pno ENOCH s.p.   (C517)

Je Vis Dans La Bourrasque Amere (from
Gwendoline)
male solo,pno ENOCH s.p.   (C518)
T solo,pno ENOCH s.p.   (C519)

La Sulamite
solo,pno ENOCH s.p.   (C520)

L'amour, Ce Divin Maitre (from Le Roi
Malgre Lui)
solo,pno ENOCH s.p.   (C521)

Le Polonais Est Triste Et Grave (from
Le Roi Malgre Lui)
solo,pno ENOCH s.p.   (C522)

Le Roi Malgre Lui
solo,orch ENOCH rental   (C523)

Legende
solo,pno ENOCH s.p.   (C524)

Les Cigales
solo,pno (original edition) ENOCH
s.p.   (C525)
solo,pno (simplified edition) ENOCH
s.p.   (C526)
solo,acap solo pt ENOCH s.p. (C527)
solo,orch ENOCH rental   (C528)

Lied
solo,pno ENOCH s.p.   (C529)

L'Ile Heureuse
solo,pno (available in 2 keys)
ENOCH s.p.   (C530)
solo,acap solo pt ENOCH s.p. (C531)
solo,orch ENOCH rental   (C532)

Little Star
solo,pno (E flat maj) ASHDOWN
                              (C533)

Melodies *CC13L
solo,pno cmplt ed ENOCH s.p.
available in 2 keys   (C534)

Moi, Je N'ai Pas Une Ame (from
L'Etoile)
solo,pno ENOCH s.p.   (C535)

CHABRIER, EMMANUEL (cont'd.)

Ne Riez Pas (from Gwendoline)
solo,pno ENOCH s.p.   (C536)

Nos Lances Sont Des Aiguilles (from
Gwendoline)
female solo,pno ENOCH s.p.   (C537)
Mez solo,pno ENOCH s.p.   (C538)

Nous Avons Frappe Des Epees (from
Gwendoline)
solo,pno ENOCH s.p.   (C539)

Oh! Petite Etoile (from L'Etoile)
solo,pno ENOCH s.p.   (C540)

On Cherche Qui Vous A Nui (from Le
Roi Malgre Lui)
solo,pno ENOCH s.p.   (C541)

Pastorale Des Cochons Roses
solo,pno ENOCH s.p.   (C542)
solo,acap solo pt ENOCH s.p. (C543)
solo,orch ENOCH rental   (C544)

Quand On Aime (from L'Etoile)
solo,pno ENOCH s.p.   (C545)

Scene Et Legende (from Gwendoline)
solo,orch ENOCH rental   (C546)

Sur Le Flot Bleu Nous Glissions En
Revant (from Le Roi Malgre Lui)
2 soli,pno ENOCH s.p.   (C547)

Toutes Les Fleurs
solo,pno (available in 2 keys)
ENOCH s.p.   (C548)

Viens Ici! (from Gwendoline)
2 soli,pno ENOCH s.p.   (C549)

Villanelle Des Petits Canards
solo,pno (original edition) ENOCH
s.p.   (C550)
solo,pno (easy) ENOCH s.p.   (C551)
solo,acap solo pt ENOCH s.p. (C552)
solo,orch ENOCH rental   (C553)

CHACARERA see De Rogatis, Pascual

CHACARERA see Ginastera, Alberto

CHACAYALERA see Espoile, Raoul H.

CHACAYALERAS see Espoile, Raoul H.

CHACONNE see Vogel, Wladimir

CHACUN, MADAME, A SON ASPECT see
Messager, Andre

CHADAL, M.
Chanson Du Gai Meunier (from Si
L'amour Passe)
solo,pno/inst DURAND s.p.   (C554)

Couplets De Francinette (from Si
L'amour Passe)
solo,pno/inst DURAND s.p.   (C555)

Duo Des Fraises (from Pas De Fumee
Sans Feu)
solo,pno DURAND s.p.   (C556)

Duo-Valse (from Si L'amour Passe)
2 soli,pno/inst DURAND s.p.   (C557)

L'Araignee
solo,pno/inst DURAND s.p.   (C558)
[Fr] solo,acap oct DURAND s.p.
                              (C559)

Romance A Francinette (from Si
L'amour Passe)
solo,pno/inst DURAND s.p.   (C560)

CHADWICK, GEORGE WHITEFIELD (1854-1931)
Come Unto Me *sac
(Bartley) ST soli,pno SCHIRM.G $.75
                              (C561)
Songs To Poems By Arlo Bates *CC100U
solo,pno DA CAPO $12.50   (C562)

CHAGEI ISRAEL see Hadar, Joseph

CHAGRIN see Schumann, Robert
(Alexander)

CHAGRIN D'AMOUR see Berger, Rod.

CHAGRINS ROSES see Delmet, Paul

CHAILLEY, JACQUES (1910-   )
Chanson Pour La Route
see Le Pelerin D'Assise

L'Alouette
see Le Pelerin D'Assise

Le Jardin De Notre Soeur Claire
see Le Pelerin D'Assise

Le Pelerin D'Assise
solo,pno quarto OUVRIERES s.p.
contains: Chanson Pour La Route;

CHAILLEY, JACQUES (cont'd.)

L'Alouette; Le Jardin De Notre
Soeur Claire; Priere Pour
Demander Pardon   (C563)

Priere Pour Demander Pardon
see Le Pelerin D'Assise

CHAILLY, LUCIANO (1920-   )
Lamento Di Danae
[It] S solo,pno RICORDI-ENG 129247
s.p.   (C564)

L'appello
[It] solo,pno SONZOGNO 2927 s.p.
                         (C565)
Bar solo,fl,ob,clar,bsn,horn,trp,
trom,timp,perc,vibra,electronic
tape,harp,strings SONZOGNO rental
                         (C566)
Liriche Della Resistenza Vietnamita
*CCU
Bar solo,11inst sc ZERBONI 7966
s.p.   (C567)

Tre Liriche *CC3U
[It] B solo,pno SONZOGNO 2889 s.p.
                         (C568)
Tre Liriche Su Testo Cinese *CC3U
solo,pno FORLIVESI 12368 s.p.
                         (C569)

CHAIX
Poeme Funebre
solo,orch HENN s.p.   (C570)

CHAJES, JULIUS (1910-   )
Adarim
"In The Mountains" [Heb] med solo/
low solo,pno TRANSCON. SP 5 $.85
                         (C571)
"In The Mountains" [Heb] high solo,
pno/orch TRANSCON. SP 25 $.85,
ipa   (C572)

And The Waves Stood Still
med solo,pno TRANSCON. TV 574 $.75
                         (C573)

Atoh Hu Yotzrom *sac
"Thou Art The Creator" [Heb] high
solo/cantor,pno TRANSCON. WJ 431
$1.00   (C574)
"Thou Art The Creator" [Heb] med
solo/cantor,pno TRANSCON. WJ 432
$1.00   (C575)

Beyn N'har P'rat
"Where The Tigris Flows" [Heb] high
solo,pno TRANSCON. SP 14 $.60
                         (C576)

Blissful Land
high solo,pno/orch TRANSCON. TV 573
$1.00, ipa   (C577)

Evening Song
high solo/med solo,pno/orch
TRANSCON. TV 450 $.75, ipa (C579)

Galil
[Heb] high solo/med solo,pno
TRANSCON. SP 11 $.75   (C580)

Gamal, G'mali
"Song Of The Camel Driver" [Heb]
high solo,pno TRANSCON. SP 20
$.75   (C581)

Hineh Bar'chu
"Old Jerusalem" [Heb] high solo/med
solo,pno TRANSCON. SP 3 $.75
                         (C582)
"Old Jerusalem" high solo,pno/org/
orch TRANSCON. SP 22 $1.00, ipr
                         (C583)

How Can I Reveal
high solo,pno/orch TRANSCON. TV 571
$1.00, ipa   (C584)

In The Mountains *see Adarim

L'chu V'nivneh
"Walls Of Zion" [Heb] high solo/med
solo,pno TRANSCON. SP 9 $.60
                         (C585)

Mah Yafim
"Palestinian Nights" [Heb] high
solo,pno TRANSCON. SP 24 $.60
                         (C586)
"Palestinian Nights" [Heb] med
solo,pno TRANSCON. SP 4 $.60
                         (C587)
"Palestinian Nights" [Heb] high
solo/med solo,strings TRANSCON.
rental   (C588)

Old Jerusalem *see Hineh Bar'chu

Palestinian Nights *see Mah Yafim

CHAJES, JULIUS (cont'd.)

Psalm 137 *see By The Rivers Of
Babylon

Shir V'nivneh
"Song Of Love" [Heb] high solo,pno
TRANSCON. SP 13 $.75   (C589)

Song Of Love *see Shir V'nivneh

Song Of The Camel Driver *see Gamal,
G'mali

Thou Art The Creator *see Atoh Hu
Yotzrom

Walls Of Zion *see L'chu V'nivneh

Where The Tigris Flows *see Beyn
N'har P'rat

CHALAYEV, S.
Those Green Tresses Of Sadness *song
cycle
[Russ] B solo,pno MEZ KNIGA 79 s.p.
                         (C590)

CHALEUR see Roos, Robert de

CHALK, C.
I Told My Love To The Roses
see Two Songs

Love Was A Wanderer
low solo,pno (E flat maj, contains
also: What Is In Your Eyes?)
LEONARD-ENG   (C591)
med solo,pno (F maj, contains also:
What Is In Your Eyes?) LEONARD-
ENG   (C592)
high solo,pno (G maj, contains
also: What Is In Your Eyes?)
LEONARD-ENG   (C593)

Scythe Song
see Two Songs

Two Songs
solo,pno LEONARD-ENG s.p.
contains: I Told My Love To The
Roses; Scythe Song   (C594)

What Is In Your Eyes?
high solo,pno (F maj, contains
also: Love Was A Wanderer)
LEONARD-ENG   (C595)
low solo,pno (D maj, contains also:
Love Was A Wanderer) LEONARD-ENG
                         (C596)
med solo,pno (E flat maj, contains
also: Love Was A Wanderer)
LEONARD-ENG   (C597)

CHAMBER DUETS see Carissimi, Giacomo

CHAMBER MUSIC see Mengelberg, Rudolf

CHAMBER MUSIC see Berio, Luciano

CHAMBER MUSIC BY JAMES JOYCE see
Reutter, Hermann

CHAMBERS, H.A.
Born To Serve The Lord *sac
solo,pno BENSON S5216-S $1.00
                         (C598)

True Love's The Gift *sac,Marriage
low solo,pno (C maj) LESLIE 7046
                         (C599)
high solo,pno (E flat maj) LESLIE
7046   (C600)

CHAMINADE, CECILE (1857-1944)
A Travers Bois
ST/SBar soli,pno ENOCH s.p. voc sc,
solo pt   (C601)

Al'Inconnue
solo,pno (available in 2 keys)
ENOCH s.p. see also Vingt
Melodies, Vol. II   (C602)

Alleluia *sac
solo,acap solo pt ENOCH s.p. (C603)
solo,pno (available in 2 keys)
ENOCH s.p. see also Vingt
Melodies, Vol. IV   (C604)

Amertume
solo,acap solo pt ENOCH s.p. (C605)
solo,pno (available in 2 keys)
ENOCH s.p. see also Vingt
Melodies, Vol. III   (C606)

Amoroso
solo,pno (available in 2 keys)
ENOCH s.p. see also Vingt
Melodies, Vol. I   (C607)

Amour D'automne
solo,acap solo pt ENOCH s.p. (C608)
Mez solo,orch (E flat maj) ENOCH
rental   (C609)
solo,pno (available in 2 keys)
ENOCH s.p. see also Vingt
Melodies, Vol. I   (C610)

CHAMINADE, CECILE (cont'd.)

Amour Invisible
solo,acap solo pt ENOCH s.p. (C611)

Attente
solo,acap solo pt ENOCH s.p. (C612)
solo,pno (available in 2 keys)
ENOCH s.p.   (C613)

Au Firmament
solo,acap solo pt ENOCH s.p. (C614)
solo,pno (available in 2 keys)
ENOCH s.p.   (C615)

Au Pays Bleu
solo,acap solo pt ENOCH s.p. (C616)
solo,pno (available in3 keys) ENOCH
s.p.   (C617)

Aupres De Ma Mie
solo,pno (available in 2 keys)
ENOCH s.p. see also Vingt
Melodies, Vol. I   (C618)

Automne
"September Serenade" solo,orch (F
maj) ASHDOWN s.p., ipr   (C619)

Avenir
solo,acap solo pt ENOCH s.p. (C620)
solo,pno (available in 2 keys)
ENOCH s.p.   (C621)

Avril S'eveille
solo,acap solo pt ENOCH s.p. (C622)
solo,pno (available in 2 keys)
ENOCH s.p. see also Vingt
Melodies, Vol. III   (C623)

Barcarolle
MezBar soli,pno ENOCH s.p. voc sc,
solo pt   (C624)
MezBar soli,orch ENOCH rental
                         (C625)

Berceuse
solo,acap solo pt ENOCH s.p. (C626)
solo,pno (available in 2 keys)
ENOCH s.p. see also Vingt
Melodies, Vol. II   (C627)

Bleus
solo,acap solo pt ENOCH s.p. (C628)
solo,pno (available in 2 keys)
ENOCH s.p. see also Vingt
Melodies, Vol. III   (C629)

Bonne Humeur
solo,acap solo pt ENOCH s.p. (C630)
solo,pno (available in 2 keys)
ENOCH s.p. see also Vingt
Melodies, Vol. IV   (C631)

C'etait En Avril
solo,acap solo pt ENOCH s.p. (C632)
solo,pno (available in 2 keys)
ENOCH s.p.   (C633)

Chanson De Mer
solo,pno (available in 2 keys)
ENOCH s.p.   (C634)
solo,acap solo pt ENOCH s.p. (C635)

Chanson De Neige
solo,acap solo pt ENOCH s.p. (C636)
solo,pno (available in 2 keys)
ENOCH s.p. see also Vingt
Melodies, Vol. IV   (C637)

Chanson Espagnole
solo,acap solo pt ENOCH s.p. (C638)
solo,pno (available in 3 keys)
ENOCH s.p. see also Vingt
Melodies, Vol. II   (C639)

Chanson Forestiere
solo,pno (available in 2 keys)
ENOCH s.p.   (C640)
solo,acap solo pt ENOCH s.p. (C641)

Chanson Naive
solo,pno ENOCH s.p.   (C642)
solo,acap solo pt ENOCH s.p. (C643)

Chanson Slave
solo,acap solo pt ENOCH s.p. (C644)
Mez solo,orch (F min) ENOCH rental
                         (C645)
solo,pno (available in 2 keys)
ENOCH s.p. see also Vingt
Melodies, Vol. I   (C646)

Chanson Triste
solo,acap solo pt ENOCH s.p. (C647)
solo,pno (available in 2 keys)
ENOCH s.p. see also Vingt
Melodies, Vol. III   (C648)

Colette
solo,pno (available in 2 keys)
ENOCH s.p. see also Vingt
Melodies, Vol. I   (C649)

Console-Moi
solo,pno (available in 2 keys)
ENOCH s.p.   (C650)

CHAMINADE, CECILE (cont'd.)

    solo,acap solo pt ENOCH s.p. (C651)

Contes De Fees
    solo,pno (available in 2 keys)
      ENOCH s.p.   (C652)
    solo,acap solo pt ENOCH s.p. (C653)

Couplets Bachiques
    solo,acap solo pt ENOCH s.p. (C654)
    solo,pno (available in 3 keys)
      ENOCH s.p. see also Vingt
      Melodies, Vol. III   (C655)

Depart
    solo,pno (available in 2 keys)
      ENOCH s.p.   (C656)
    solo,acap solo pt ENOCH s.p. (C657)

Dites-Lui
    solo,acap solo pt ENOCH s.p. (C658)
    solo,pno (available in 2 keys)
      ENOCH s.p. see also Vingt
      Melodies, Vol. IV   (C659)

Duo D'Etoiles
    SMez soli,pno ENOCH s.p. voc sc,
      solo pt   (C660)

Ecrin
    solo,acap solo pt ENOCH s.p. (C661)
    solo,pno (available in 2 keys)
      ENOCH s.p. see also Vingt
      Melodies, Vol. IV   (C662)

Espoir
    solo,acap solo pt ENOCH s.p. (C663)
    solo,pno (available in 2 keys)
      ENOCH s.p. see also Vingt
      Melodies, Vol. II   (C664)

Exil
    solo,acap solo pt ENOCH s.p. (C665)
    solo,pno (available in 2 keys)
      ENOCH s.p. see also Vingt
      Melodies, Vol. IV   (C666)

Extase
    solo,acap solo pt ENOCH s.p. (C667)
    solo,pno (available in 2 keys)
      ENOCH s.p. see also Vingt
      Melodies, Vol. IV   (C668)

Fleur Du Matin
    solo,acap solo pt ENOCH s.p. (C669)
    solo,pno (available in 2 keys)
      ENOCH s.p. see also Vingt
      Melodies, Vol. III   (C670)

Fleur Jetee
    solo,pno ENOCH s.p. see also Vingt
      Melodies, Vol. I   (C671)

Fragilite
    solo,pno ENOCH s.p.   (C672)

I Would Believe
    low solo,pno (E flat maj) ASHDOWN
                                    (C673)
    med solo,pno (F maj) ASHDOWN (C674)
    high solo,pno (A flat maj) ASHDOWN
                                    (C675)

Immortalite!
    solo,acap solo pt ENOCH s.p. (C676)
    solo,pno (available in 2 keys)
      ENOCH s.p. see also Vingt
      Melodies, Vol. III   (C677)

Infini
    solo,pno (available in 2 keys)
      ENOCH s.p.   (C678)
    solo,vcl (available in 2 keys)
      ENOCH s.p.   (C679)
    solo,acap solo pt ENOCH s.p. (C680)

Invocation
    solo,pno ENOCH s.p. see also Vingt
      Melodies, Vol. II   (C681)

Jadis
    solo,acap solo pt ENOCH s.p. (C682)
    solo,pno (available in 2 keys)
      ENOCH s.p. see also Vingt
      Melodies, Vol. III   (C683)

Je Voudrais
    solo,pno (available in 2 keys)
      ENOCH s.p.   (C684)
    solo,acap solo pt ENOCH s.p. (C685)

Joie D'aimer
    MezBar soli,pno ENOCH s.p. voc sc,
      solo pt   (C686)

La Damoiselle
    solo,acap solo pt ENOCH s.p. (C687)
    solo,pno (available in 2 keys)
      ENOCH s.p. see also Vingt
      Melodies, Vol. IV   (C688)

La Fiancee Du Soldat
    solo,acap solo pt ENOCH s.p. (C689)
    solo,pno ENOCH s.p. see also Vingt
      Melodies, Vol. I   (C690)
    solo,orch ENOCH rental see also

CHAMINADE, CECILE (cont'd.)

Vingt Melodies, Vol. I   (C691)

La Lune Paresseuse
    solo,acap solo pt ENOCH s.p. (C692)
    solo,pno (available in 2 keys)
      ENOCH s.p. see also Vingt
      Melodies, Vol. IV   (C693)

La Plus Jolie
    solo,pno (available in 2 keys)
      ENOCH s.p.   (C694)
    solo,acap solo pt ENOCH s.p. (C695)

La Reine De Mon Coeur
    solo,acap solo pt ENOCH s.p. (C696)
    solo,pno (available in 2 keys)
      ENOCH s.p. see also Vingt
      Melodies, Vol. IV   (C697)

L'Absente
    solo,pno (available in 2 keys)
      ENOCH s.p. see also Vingt
      Melodies, Vol. I   (C698)

L'Allee D'emeraude Et D'or
    solo,acap solo pt ENOCH s.p. (C699)
    solo,pno (available in 2 keys)
      ENOCH s.p. see also Vingt
      Melodies, Vol. IV   (C700)

L'Amour Captif
    solo,acap solo pt ENOCH s.p. (C701)
    solo,pno (available in 3 keys)
      ENOCH s.p. see also Vingt
      Melodies, Vol. II   (C702)

L'Amour Invisible
    solo,pno (available in 2 keys)
      ENOCH s.p.   (C703)

L'Angelus
    MezBar soli,pno ENOCH s.p. voc sc,
      solo pt   (C704)
    MezBar soli,orch ENOCH rental
                                    (C705)

L'Anneau D'Argent
    solo,pno (available in 3 keys)
      ENOCH s.p.   (C706)
    solo,acap solo pt ENOCH s.p. (C707)

L'Anneau Du Soldat
    solo,pno (available in 2 keys)
      ENOCH s.p. see also Vingt
      Melodies, Vol. I   (C708)

Le Beau Chanteur
    solo,pno (available in 2 keys)
      ENOCH s.p.   (C709)
    solo,acap solo pt ENOCH s.p. (C710)

Le Charme D'amour
    solo,acap solo pt ENOCH s.p. (C711)
    solo,pno (available in 2 keys)
      ENOCH s.p. see also Vingt
      Melodies, Vol. IV   (C712)

Le Ciel Est Bleu
    solo,acap solo pt ENOCH s.p. (C713)
    solo,pno (available in 2 keys)
      ENOCH s.p. see also Vingt
      Melodies, Vol. II   (C714)

Le Deux Menetriers
    B/Bar solo,orch ENOCH rental (C715)

Le Noel Des Oiseaux
    solo,acap solo pt ENOCH s.p. (C716)
    solo,pno (available in 2 keys)
      ENOCH s.p. see also Vingt
      Melodies, Vol. II   (C717)

Le Pecheur Et L'Ondine
    ST/SBar soli,pno ENOCH s.p. voc sc,
      solo pt   (C718)

Le Rendez-Vous
    solo,pno (available in 2 keys)
      ENOCH s.p. see also Vingt
      Melodies, Vol. III   (C719)

Le Threne Du Vieux Roi
    solo,pno (available in 2 keys)
      ENOCH s.p.   (C720)

Le Village
    solo,pno (available in 2 keys)
      ENOCH s.p.   (C721)
    solo,acap solo pt ENOCH s.p. (C722)

Les Amazones
    solo,pno ENOCH s.p.   (C723)

Les Deux Coeurs
    solo,acap solo pt ENOCH s.p. (C724)
    solo,pno ENOCH s.p. see also Vingt
      Melodies, Vol. II   (C725)

Les Deux Menetriers *scena
    B solo,pno ENOCH s.p.   (C726)

Les Fiances
    MezBar soli,pno ENOCH s.p. voc sc,
      solo pt   (C727)

CHAMINADE, CECILE (cont'd.)

Les Heureuses
    solo,pno (available in 2 keys)
      ENOCH s.p.   (C728)
    solo,acap solo pt ENOCH s.p. (C729)

Les Presents
    solo,acap solo pt ENOCH s.p. (C730)
    solo,pno (available in 3 keys)
      ENOCH s.p. see also Vingt
      Melodies, Vol. III   (C731)

Les Reves
    solo,pno (available in 2 keys)
      ENOCH s.p. see also Vingt
      Melodies, Vol. I   (C732)
    solo,orch ENOCH rental see also
      Vingt Melodies, Vol. I   (C733)

Les Trois Baisers
    (Bordese, Stephen) solo,pno
      (available in 2 keys) ENOCH s.p.
      see also CHANSONS DE PAGE (C734)

Lettres D'amour
    solo,pno (available in 2 keys)
      ENOCH s.p.   (C735)
    solo,acap solo pt ENOCH s.p. (C736)

L'Ideal
    solo,pno (available in 2 keys)
      ENOCH s.p. see also Vingt
      Melodies, Vol. I   (C737)

L'Ondine Du Leman
    solo,pno ENOCH s.p.   (C738)
    solo,acap solo pt ENOCH s.p. (C739)

L'Orgue
    solo,pno ENOCH s.p.   (C740)
    solo,acap solo pt ENOCH s.p. (C741)

Love's Garden
    low solo,pno (F maj) ASHDOWN (C742)
    high solo,pno (A flat maj) ASHDOWN
                                    (C743)

Ma Premiere Lettre
    solo,pno ENOCH s.p. see also Vingt
      Melodies, Vol. II   (C744)

Ma Primiere Lettre
    solo,acap solo pt ENOCH s.p. (C745)

Madeleine
    solo,pno ENOCH s.p.   (C746)

Madrigal
    solo,acap solo pt ENOCH s.p. (C747)
    S solo,orch (D maj) ENOCH rental
                                    (C748)
    low solo,pno (B flat maj) ASHDOWN
                                    (C749)
    med solo,pno (C maj) ASHDOWN (C750)
    med-high solo,pno (D maj) ASHDOWN
                                    (C751)
    high solo,pno (E flat maj) ASHDOWN
                                    (C752)
    solo,pno (available in 2 keys)
      ENOCH s.p. see also Vingt
      Melodies, Vol. I   (C753)
    solo,orch ENOCH rental see also
      Vingt Melodies, Vol. I   (C754)

Malgre Nous
    solo,pno (available in 2 keys)
      ENOCH s.p. see also Vingt
      Melodies, Vol. II   (C755)

Mandoline
    solo,pno ENOCH s.p.   (C756)
    solo,acap solo pt ENOCH s.p. (C757)

Marthe Et Marie
    SMez/SA soli,pno ENOCH s.p. voc sc,
      solo pt   (C758)

Menuet
    solo,vcl ENOCH s.p.   (C759)
    solo,pno ENOCH s.p.   (C760)
    solo,acap solo pt ENOCH s.p. (C761)
    solo,orch ENOCH rental   (C762)

Mirage
    solo,pno (available in 2 keys)
      ENOCH s.p.   (C763)
    solo,acap solo pt ENOCH s.p. (C764)

Mon Coeur Chante
    solo,acap solo pt ENOCH s.p. (C765)
    solo,pno (available in 2 keys)
      ENOCH s.p. see also Vingt
      Melodies, Vol. III   (C766)

Mots D'amour
    solo,acap solo pt ENOCH s.p. (C767)
    solo,pno (available in 2 keys)
      ENOCH s.p. see also Vingt
      Melodies, Vol. III   (C768)

N'est-Ce-Pas?
    solo,acap solo pt ENOCH s.p. (C769)
    solo,pno (available in 2 keys)
      ENOCH s.p. see also Vingt
      Melodies, Vol. IV   (C770)

CHAMINADE, CECILE (cont'd.)

Nice La Belle
solo,pno (available in 2 keys)
ENOCH s.p. see also Vingt
Melodies, Vol. I   (C771)

Nocturne Pyreneen
AB soli,pno ENOCH s.p. voc sc, solo
pt   (C772)

Nous Nous Aimions
solo,pno (available in 2 keys)
ENOCH s.p.   (C773)
solo,acap solo pt ENOCH s.p. (C774)

Nuit D'ete
solo,acap solo pt ENOCH s.p. (C775)
solo,pno (available in 2 keys)
ENOCH s.p. see also Vingt
Melodies, Vol. III   (C776)

Nuit Etoilee
solo,acap solo pt ENOCH s.p. (C777)
solo,pno (available in 2 keys)
ENOCH s.p. see also Vingt
Melodies, Vol. III   (C778)

Partout!
solo,acap solo pt ENOCH s.p. (C779)
solo,pno (available in 2 keys)
ENOCH s.p. see also Vingt
Melodies, Vol. II   (C780)

Petits Coeurs
solo,pno (available in 2 keys)
ENOCH s.p.   (C781)
solo,acap solo pt ENOCH s.p. (C782)

Plaintes D'amour
solo,pno (available in 2 keys)
ENOCH s.p. see also Vingt
Melodies, Vol. I   (C783)

Portrait
solo,fl ENOCH s.p.   (C784)
solo,acap solo pt ENOCH s.p. (C785)
solo,pno (available in 2 keys)
ENOCH s.p. see also Vingt
Melodies, Vol. IV   (C786)

Pourquoi?
solo,pno (available in 2 keys)
ENOCH s.p.   (C787)
solo,acap solo pt ENOCH s.p. (C788)

Ravana
solo,pno ENOCH s.p.   (C789)

Refrain De Novembre
solo,acap solo pt ENOCH s.p. (C790)
solo,pno (available in 2 keys)
ENOCH s.p. see also Vingt
Melodies, Vol. IV   (C791)

Ressemblance
solo,pno (available in 2 keys)
ENOCH s.p. see also Vingt
Melodies, Vol. II   (C792)

Reste!
solo,acap solo pt ENOCH s.p. (C793)
solo,pno (available in 2 keys)
ENOCH s.p. see also Vingt
Melodies, Vol. III   (C794)

Reve D'un Soir
solo,vcl (available in 2 keys)
ENOCH s.p.   (C795)
solo,acap solo pt ENOCH s.p. (C796)
solo,pno (available in 2 keys)
ENOCH s.p. see also Vingt
Melodies, Vol. I   (C797)

Reves Defunts
solo,acap solo pt ENOCH s.p. (C798)
solo,pno (available in 2 keys)
ENOCH s.p. see also Vingt
Melodies, Vol. III   (C799)

Ritournelle
solo,acap solo pt ENOCH s.p. (C800)
low solo,pno (D flat maj) ASHDOWN
                          (C801)
med solo,pno (E flat maj) ASHDOWN
                          (C802)
high solo,pno (F maj) ASHDOWN
                          (C803)
solo,pno (available in 2 keys;
available in 3 keys) ENOCH s.p.
see also Vingt Melodies, Vol. I
                          (C804)

Ronde D'amour
solo,acap solo pt ENOCH s.p. (C805)
solo,pno (available in 2 keys)
ENOCH s.p. see also Vingt
Melodies, Vol. II   (C806)
solo,orch ENOCH rental see also
Vingt Melodies, Vol. II   (C807)

Roulis Des Greves
solo,pno (available in 2 keys)
ENOCH s.p.   (C808)
solo,acap solo pt ENOCH s.p. (C809)

CHAMINADE, CECILE (cont'd.)

Sans Amour
solo,acap solo pt ENOCH s.p. (C810)
solo,pno (available in 3 keys)
ENOCH s.p. see also Vingt
Melodies, Vol. II   (C811)
solo,orch ENOCH rental see also
Vingt Melodies, Vol. II   (C812)

September Serenade *see Automne

Serenata
solo,pno ENOCH s.p. see also Vingt
Melodies, Vol. III   (C813)

Ses Yeux
solo,pno (available in 2 keys)
ENOCH s.p.   (C814)
solo,acap solo pt ENOCH s.p. (C815)

Si J'etais Jardinier
solo,acap solo pt ENOCH s.p. (C816)
solo,pno (available in 2 keys)
ENOCH s.p. see also Vingt
Melodies, Vol. II   (C817)

Silver Ring, The
high solo,orch (F maj) ASHDOWN
s.p., ipr   (C818)
low solo,orch (D flat maj) ASHDOWN
s.p., ipr   (C819)
med solo,orch (E flat maj) ASHDOWN
s.p., ipr   (C820)

Sommeil D'enfant
solo,acap solo pt ENOCH s.p. (C821)
solo,pno (available in 2 keys)
ENOCH s.p. see also Vingt
Melodies, Vol. IV   (C822)

Son Nom
solo,pno (available in 2 keys)
ENOCH s.p.   (C823)
solo,acap solo pt ENOCH s.p. (C824)

Sonne Clairon
solo,pno (available in 2 keys)
ENOCH s.p.   (C825)
solo,acap solo pt ENOCH s.p. (C826)
Mez solo,orch (F maj) ENOCH rental
                          (C827)

Souhait
solo,pno ENOCH s.p. see also Vingt
Melodies, Vol. I   (C828)

Sur La Plage
solo,pno (available in 2 keys)
ENOCH s.p. see also Vingt
Melodies, Vol. I   (C829)

Toi!
solo,pno (available in 2 keys)
ENOCH s.p. see also Vingt
Melodies, Vol. II   (C830)

Ton Sourire
solo,acap solo pt ENOCH s.p. (C831)
solo,pno (available in 2 keys)
ENOCH s.p. see also Vingt
Melodies, Vol. IV   (C832)

Trois Baisers
solo,acap solo pt ENOCH s.p. (C833)

Tu Me Dirais
solo,acap solo pt ENOCH s.p. (C834)
solo,pno (available in 2 keys)
ENOCH s.p. see also Vingt
Melodies, Vol. I   (C835)
solo,orch ENOCH rental see also
Vingt Melodies, Vol. I   (C836)

Un Souffle A Passe
solo,acap solo pt ENOCH s.p. (C837)
solo,pno (available in 2 keys)
ENOCH s.p. see also Vingt
Melodies, Vol. IV   (C838)

Veux-Tu?
solo,acap solo pt ENOCH s.p. (C839)
solo,pno (available in 2 keys)
ENOCH s.p. see also Vingt
Melodies, Vol. III   (C840)

Viatique
solo,pno (available in 2 keys)
ENOCH s.p. see also Vingt
Melodies, Vol. II   (C841)

Viens Mon Bien-Aime!
solo,acap solo pt ENOCH s.p. (C842)
S solo,orch (G flat maj) ENOCH
rental   (C843)
solo,pno (available in 2 keys)
ENOCH s.p. see also Vingt
Melodies, Vol. II   (C844)

Vieux Portrait
solo,pno ENOCH s.p.   (C845)

Vingt Melodies, Vol. I
solo,pno cmplt ed ENOCH s.p.
available in 2 keys
contains & see also: Amoroso;
Amour D'Automne; Aupres De Ma

CHAMINADE, CECILE (cont'd.)

Mie; Chanson Slave; Colette;
Fleur Jetee; La Fiancee Du
Soldat; L'Absente; L'Anneau Du
Soldat; Les Reves; L'Ideal;
Madrigal; Nice La Belle;
Plaintes D'amour; Reve D'un
Soir; Ritournelle; Souhait; Sur
La Plage; Tu Me Dirais;
Voisinage   (C846)

Vingt Melodies, Vol. II
solo,pno cmplt ed ENOCH s.p.
available in 2 keys
contains & see also: Al'Inconnue;
Berceuse; Chanson Espagnole;
Espoir; Invocation; L'Amour
Captif; Le Ciel Est Bleu; Le
Noel Des Oiseaux; Les Deux
Coeurs; Ma Premiere Lettre;
Malgre Nous; Partout;
Ressemblance; Ronde D'amour;
Sans Amour; Si J'etais
Jardinier; Toi!; Viatique;
Viens Mon Bien-Aime   (C847)

Vingt Melodies, Vol. III
solo,pno cmplt ed ENOCH s.p.
available in 2 keys
contains & see also: Amertume;
Avril S'eveille; Bleus; Chanson
Triste; Couplets Bachiques;
Fleur Du Matin; Immortalite;
Jadis; Le Rendez-Vous; Les
Presents; Mon Coeur Chante;
Mots D'amour; Nuit D'Ete; Nuit
Etoilee; Reste; Reves Defunts;
Serenata; Veux-Tu?   (C848)

Vingt Melodies, Vol. IV
solo,pno cmplt ed ENOCH s.p.
available in 2 keys
contains & see also: Alleluia;
Bonne Humeur; Chanson De Neige;
Dites-Lui; Ecrin; Exil; Extase;
La Damoiselle; La Lune
Paresseuse; La Reine De Mon
Coeur; L'Allee D'Emeraude Et
D'Or; Le Charme D'amour; N'est-
Ce Pas?; Portrait; Refrain De
Novembre; Sommeil D'Enfant; Ton
Sourire; Un Souffle A Passe;
Voix Du Large   (C849)

Voeu Supreme
solo,pno ENOCH s.p.   (C850)
solo,acap solo pt ENOCH s.p. (C851)

Voisinage
solo,acap solo pt ENOCH s.p. (C852)
solo,orch ENOCH rental see also
Vingt Melodies, Vol. I   (C853)
solo,pno (available in 2 keys)
ENOCH s.p. see also Vingt
Melodies, Vol. I   (C854)

Voix Du Large
solo,acap solo pt ENOCH s.p. (C855)
solo,pno (available in 2 keys)
ENOCH s.p. see also Vingt
Melodies, Vol. IV   (C856)

CHAMPAGNE *Fr
(Canteloube, J.) solo,acap DURAND
s.p. see also Anthologie Des Chants
Populaires Francais Tome IV (C857)

CHAMPAGNE see Hullebroeck, Em.

CHAMPS PATERNELS see Mehul, Etienne-Nicolas

CHANCE, NANCY
Darksong
S solo,2fl,2ob,2horn,harp,gtr,
5perc,pno sc SEESAW $16.00 (C858)

Edensong
S solo,fl,clar,vcl,harp,2perc sc
SEESAW $6.00   (C859)

Three Poems By Rilke *CC3U
S solo,fl,English horn,vcl sc
SEESAW $4.00   (C860)

CHANDLER, T.
Lamb, The
med solo,pno AMP $.75   (C861)

CHANDNI CHITAKNA see Rouse, Christopher

CHANGEONS PROPOS see Enesco, Georges

CHANLER, THEODORE WARD (1902-   )
Children, The *CC9U
med solo,pno SCHIRM.G $2.00 (C862)

O Mistress Mine
solo,pno (D flat maj) BOOSEY $1.50
                          (C863)

Three Husbands
solo,pno (C maj) BOOSEY $1.50
                          (C864)

CHANNEL FIRING see Heilner, Irwin

CHANSAREL, R.
    Aquarelle Anglaise
        solo,pno (available in 2 keys)
        ENOCH s.p.   (C865)

    Mandoline
        solo,pno (available in 2 keys)
        ENOCH s.p.   (C866)

    Serenade
        solo,pno (available in 2 keys)
        ENOCH s.p.   (C867)

    Sous L'epais Sycomore
        solo,pno (available in 2 keys)
        ENOCH s.p.   (C868)

CHANSON see Absil, Jean

CHANSON see Bosmans, Henriette

CHANSON see Boutnikoff, J.

CHANSON see Busser, Henri-Paul

CHANSON see Fellegara, Vittorio

CHANSON see Ferrari, Gustave

CHANSON see Francaix, Jean

CHANSON see Gallois Montbrun

CHANSON see Godard, Benjamin Louis Paul

CHANSON see Ibert, Jacques

CHANSON see Lacome, Paul

CHANSON see Levade, Charles (Gaston)

CHANSON see Menasce, Jacques de

CHANSON see Middeleer, Jean De

CHANSON see Migot, Georges

CHANSON see Pillois, Jacques

CHANSON see Poulenc, Francis

CHANSON see Rabaud, Henri

CHANSON see Ravize, A.

CHANSON see Ruyneman, Daniel

CHANSON see Satie, Erik

CHANSON see Vellones, P.

CHANSON see Y'Ener

CHANSON see Le Jeune, H.

CHANSON A BERCER see Schule, B.

CHANSON A BOIRE see Delmet, Paul

CHANSON A BOIRE see Jongen, Leon

CHANSON A BOIRE see Larmanjat, J.

CHANSON A BOIRE see Poot, Marcel

CHANSON A BOIRE see Ravel, Maurice

CHANSON A BOIRE see Street, G.

CHANSON A BOIRE see Vredenburg, Max

CHANSON A BOIRE DU MEDECIN MALGRE LUI
    see Charpentier, Marc-Antoine

CHANSON A BOIRE DU VIEUX TEMPS see
    Saint-Saens, Camille

CHANSON A DULCINEE see Ibert, Jacques

CHANSON ALBUMS OF MARGUERITE OF
    AUSTRIA, THE *CCU
    (Picker, Martin) solo,pno UNIV.CAL
    $30.00   (C869)

CHANSON ARABE see Lacome, Paul

CHANSON AUTRICHIENNE *Ger
    [Ger] solo,pno DURAND 92 s.p. (C870)

CHANSON BOHEME see Lachaume, A.

CHANSON BOHEME see Rasse, Francois

CHANSON BRETONNE see Durand, Jacques

CHANSON BRETONNE see Guerrini, Guido

CHANSON BREVE see Rabey, Rene

CHANSON BREVE see Vieu, Jane

CHANSON CALINE see Delmet, Paul

CHANSON CHINOISE see Cuvillier, Charles

CHANSON CREOLE see Bemberg, Herman

CHANSON CREPUSCULAIRE see Delmet, Paul

CHANSON D'AMOUR see Chausson, Ernest

CHANSON D'AMOUR see Wiggers, W.

CHANSON D'ANTAN see Gedalge, Andre

CHANSON D'AUTOMNE see Barbirolli, A.

CHANSON D'AUTOMNE see Caplet, Andre

CHANSON D'AUTOMNE see Komter, Jan
    Maarten

CHANSON D'AUTOMNE see Milhaud, Darius

CHANSON D'AUTOMNE see Panizza, Ettore

CHANSON D'AUTOMNE see Toussaint De
    Sutter, J.

CHANSON D'AVENTURE see Sims, Ezra

CHANSON D'AVRIL see Bizet, Georges

CHANSON D'AVRIL see Fontenailles, H. de

CHANSON D'AVRIL see Godard, Benjamin
    Louis Paul

CHANSON D'AVRIL see Rabey, Rene

CHANSON D'AVRIL see Schumann, Robert
    (Alexander), Fruhlingslied

CHANSON DE BARBERINE see Carolus-Duran,
    P.

CHANSON DE BARBERINE see Rossellini,
    Renzo

CHANSON DE BLONDEL see Gretry, Andre
    Ernest Modeste

CHANSON DE BOHEME see Migot, Georges

CHANSON DE CLOWN see Chausson, Ernest

CHANSON DE COLOMBINE see Poise, (Jean
    Alexandre) Ferdinand

CHANSON DE CRISTAL see Villa-Lobos,
    Heitor, Cancao De Cristal

CHANSON DE FLOREAL see Legay, Marcel

CHANSON DE FLORIAN see Godard, Benjamin
    Louis Paul

CHANSON DE FLORIAN see Ives, Charles

CHANSON DE FOL see Honegger, Arthur

CHANSON DE FORTUNIO see Devries, Ivan

CHANSON DE FORTUNIO see Ibert, Jacques

CHANSON DE FORTUNIO see Tosti,
    Francesco Paolo

CHANSON DE JUIN see Godard, Benjamin
    Louis Paul

CHANSON DE LA BELLE see Bitsch, Marcel

CHANSON DE LA BERGERE see Hirschmann,
    H.

CHANSON DE LA COTE see Arrieu, Claude

CHANSON DE LA FORET SOMBRE see Borodin,
    Alexander Porfirievitch

CHANSON DE LA-HAUT see Varese, Edgar

CHANSON DE LA MARGUERITE see Lacome,
    Paul

CHANSON DE LA MARIEE
    see La Musique, Quatorzieme Cahier

CHANSON DE LA MORT see Ibert, Jacques

CHANSON DE LA MUSIQUE MILITAIRE see
    Messager, Andre

CHANSON DE LA NOURRICE see Schmitt,
    Florent

CHANSON DE LA NUIT DURABLE see De
    Severac, Deodat

CHANSON DE LA PATRIE see Lippacher, Cl.

CHANSON DE LA PLUIE see Viardot-Garcia,
    Pauline

CHANSON DE LA PLUS HAUTE TOUR see
    Denis, Didier

CHANSON DE LA POIRE see Honegger,
    Arthur

CHANSON DE LA PUCE see Mussorgsky,
    Modest

CHANSON DE LA ROSE see DuBois, Pierre
    Max

CHANSON DE LA SERVANTE see Caby, R.

CHANSON DE L'AVEUGLE see Milhaud,
    Darius

CHANSON DE L'EMIGRANT see Honegger,
    Arthur

CHANSON DE L'OR see Roget, H.

CHANSON DE LUNE see Hermite, M.

CHANSON DE MA MIE see Messager, Andre

CHANSON DE MAI see Schumann, Robert
    (Alexander), Mailied

CHANSON DE MARS SOUS LA NEIGE see
    Vellones, P.

CHANSON DE MELISSANDE see Fabre, G.

CHANSON DE MER see Aubert, Louis-
    Francois-Marie

CHANSON DE MER see Chaminade, Cecile

CHANSON DE MER see Viardot-Garcia,
    Pauline

CHANSON DE MOISSON see Delmet, Paul

CHANSON DE NEIGE see Chaminade, Cecile

CHANSON DE PIERROT see Lacome, Paul

CHANSON DE PRINTEMPS see Denza, Luigi,
    Fruhlingslied

CHANSON DE PRINTEMPS see Lacome, Paul

CHANSON DE PRINTEMPS see Mendelssohn-
    Bartholdy, Felix, Fruhlingslied

CHANSON DE PRISCA see Pierne, Gabriel

CHANSON DE QUATRE SAISONS see Quinet,
    Marcel

CHANSON DE REITRE see Filipucci, Edm.

CHANSON DE RONSARD see Duprato, Jules-
    Laurent

CHANSON DE ROUTE see Canal, Marguerite

CHANSON DE SCOZZONE see Saint-Saens,
    Camille

CHANSON DE VEILLEE see Chaumont,
    Lambert

CHANSON DE VIEILLARD see Ellis, E.S.

CHANSON DE YANTHIS see Pierne, Gabriel

CHANSON DE ZULEIKA see Rimsky-Korsakov,
    Nikolai

CHANSON D'ECOLIER see Perronnet, Amelie

CHANSON DER ESCARGOTS QUI VONT A
    L'ENTERREMENT see Bosmans,
    Henriette

CHANSON DES CUEILLEUSES DE LENTISQUES
    see Ravel, Maurice

CHANSON DES GUEUX see Biancheri, A.

CHANSON DES HEURES see Caryll, Ivan

CHANSON DES JOUEUX DE BOULE
    (Joulain, Emile) solo,pno GRAS s.p.
                                   (C871)

CHANSON DES LOUPS (LE PETIT POUCET) see
    Messager, Andre

CHANSON DES OISEAUX see Geloso, C.

CHANSON DES PRES see Godard, Benjamin
    Louis Paul

CHANSON DES SIRENES see Honegger,
    Arthur

CHANSON D'ETE see Jongen, Leon

CHANSON D'ETE see Lacome, Paul

CHANSON D'ETE see Toutain-Grun, J.

CHANSON D'EXIL see Tremisot, Ed.

CHANSON D'HIVER see Badings, Henk

CHANSON D'HIVER see King, Harold C.

CHANSON D'HIVER see Lacome, Paul

CHANSON D'HIVER see Lippacher, Cl.

CHANSON DISSIDENT see Stravinsky, Igor

CHANSON DOULOUREUSE see Delmet, Paul

CHANSON DU CHAGRIN D'AMOUR see Falla, Manuel de, Cancion Del Amor Dolido

CHANSON DU CHAT see Absil, Jean

CHANSON DU CHAT see Satie, Erik

CHANSON DU COUTEAU see Dufresne, C.

CHANSON DU DEPART see Ibert, Jacques

CHANSON DU DUC see Ibert, Jacques

CHANSON DU FEU FOLLET see Falla, Manuel de, Cancion Del Fuego Fatuo

CHANSON DU FLORERO see Tremisot, Ed.

CHANSON DU GAI MEUNIER see Chadal, M.

CHANSON DU MATIN see Schumann, Robert (Alexander)

CHANSON DU PAPILLON see Campra, Andre

CHANSON DU PAPILLON DE CAMPRA see Wekerlin, Jean Baptiste

CHANSON DU PRINTEMPS see Delbruck, J.

CHANSON DU PRINTEMPS see Milhaud, Darius

CHANSON DU REMOULEUR see Arrieu, Claude

CHANSON DU REMOULEUR see DuBois, Pierre Max

CHANSON DU REVEIL see Delmet, Paul

CHANSON DU RIEN see Ibert, Jacques

CHANSON DU SENECHAL see Saint-Saens, Camille

CHANSON DU SPECTRE see Gedalge, Andre

CHANSON DU TEMPS PASSE see Falkenberg, G.

CHANSON DU TOREADOR see Bizet, Georges, Votre Toast, Je Peux Vous Le Rendre

CHANSON DU TRAIVAIL see Delbruck, J.

CHANSON D'UN JOUR DE PRINTEMPS see Cuvillier, Charles

CHANSON E LA PUCE see Berlioz, Hector

CHANSON EPIQUE see Ravel, Maurice

CHANSON ESPAGNOLE see Chaminade, Cecile

CHANSON ESPAGNOLE see Ravel, Maurice

CHANSON FLEURIE see Lachaume, A.

CHANSON FORESTIERE see Chaminade, Cecile

CHANSON FRANCAISE see Ravel, Maurice

CHANSON FRELE see Delmet, Paul

CHANSON FUNEBRE see Migot, Georges

CHANSON GALANTE see Panizza, Ettore

CHANSON HEBRAIQUE see Ravel, Maurice

CHANSON HINDOUE see Rimsky-Korsakov, Nikolai

CHANSON INDOUE see Rimsky-Korsakov, Nikolai

CHANSON INTERCALEE DANS LES MAUCROIX see Durand, Jacques

CHANSON ITALIENNE see Ravel, Maurice

CHANSON JALOUSE see Cuvillier, Charles

CHANSON LAPONNE see Tremisot, Ed.

CHANSON LASSE see Vuillemin, L.

CHANSON LIBERTINE see Delmet, Paul

CHANSON LORRAINE see Lacome, Paul

CHANSON MARINE see Bernier, Rene

CHANSON MEDIEVALE see Satie, Erik

CHANSON MELANCOLIQUE see Messager, Andre

CHANSON MIGNARDE see Sivry, Ch. de

CHANSON MONOTONE see Ranta, Sulho

CHANSON MORAVE see Malipiero, Gian Francesco

CHANSON NAIVE see Chaminade, Cecile

CHANSON NAIVE see Rabey, Rene

CHANSON NAPOLITAINE see Paray, Paul

CHANSON NORVEGIENNE see Fourdrain, Felix

CHANSON PARESSEUSE see Delmet, Paul

CHANSON PERPETUELLE see Chausson, Ernest

CHANSON PERSANE see Gilson, Paul

CHANSON PERSANE see Sanderson, G.

CHANSON POPULAIRES DU VIVARAIS VOL. I see Indy, Vincent d'

CHANSON POPULAIRES DU VIVARAIS VOL. II see Indy, Vincent d'

CHANSON POUR COMPTER see Stravinsky, Igor

CHANSON POUR HELENE see Halphen, F.

CHANSON POUR JEAN see Chizat

CHANSON POUR JEANNE see Chabrier, Emmanuel

CHANSON POUR LA BIEN-AIMEE see Chretien, H.

CHANSON POUR LA ROUTE see Chailley, Jacques

CHANSON POUR LUI see Cuvillier, Charles

CHANSON POUR MA BELLE see Delmet, Paul

CHANSON POUR MA MERE see Delmet, Paul

CHANSON POUR MA MIE see Privas, Xavier

CHANSON POUR MARIA CHAPDELAINE see Rasse, Francois

CHANSON POUR UN PETIT BATEAU see Dere, Jean

CHANSON PROVENCALE see Dell'Acqua, Eva

CHANSON ROMANESQUE see Ravel, Maurice

CHANSON ROSE see Fragerolle, G.

CHANSON ROUGE see Colomb, A.

CHANSON RUSSE see Glazounov, Alexander Konstantinovitch

CHANSON SLAVE see Chaminade, Cecile

CHANSON SOLDATESQUE DU TEMPS DE CHARLES VIII see La Musique, Dixieme Cahier

CHANSON SUR LE PRINCE CONSORT see Caryll, Ivan

CHANSON TENDRE see Bemberg, Herman

CHANSON TIMIDE see Cuvillier, Charles

CHANSON TIREE DES CHATIMENTS see Arnoud, J.

CHANSON TRISTE see Chaminade, Cecile

CHANSON TRISTE see Delmet, Paul

CHANSON TRISTE see Duparc, Henri

CHANSON TRISTE see Lacombe, Paul

CHANSON TRISTE see Saint-Saens, Camille

CHANSON TRISTE see Scholz, Erwin Christian

CHANSON VENITIENNE see Delmet, Paul

CHANSON VIOLETTE see Paray, Paul

CHANSONNETTE see Badings, Henk

CHANSONS see Chevreuille, Raymond

CHANSONS BAS see Milhaud, Darius

CHANSONS BOURGUIGNONNES see Emmanuel, Maurice

CHANSONS BOURGUIGNONNES see Emmanuel, Maurice

CHANSONS BRETONNES see Rhene-Baton

CHANSONS BRETONNES see Filipucci, Edm.

CHANSONS BREVES see Filipucci, Edm.

CHANSONS CAMBODGIENNES see Lesur, Daniel

CHANSONS CANADIENNES, VOLUME I *CC17L (Sevrane; Verdun, Henry) med solo,pno SALABERT-US $14.00 (C872)

CHANSONS CANADIENNES, VOLUME II *CC14L (Sevrane; Verdun, Henry) med solo,pno SALABERT-US $14.00 (C873)

CHANSONS D'ALAGHIAZ *CC5U (Berberian, Onnik) solo,pno/inst DURAND s.p. Armenian (C874)

CHANSONS D'AMOUR see Lecocq, Charles

CHANSONS D'AMOUR see Jacob, Dom Clement

CHANSONS D'AMOUR DE LA VEILLE CHINE see Vellones, P.

CHANSONS D'ANGELTERRE see Arrieu, Claude

CHANSONS DE BELISE ET DE PERLIMPLIN see Arrieu, Claude

CHANSONS DE BILITIS see Koechlin, Charles

CHANSONS DE BILITIS see Debussy, Claude

CHANSONS DE GRAMADOCH see Barraud, Henry

CHANSONS DE GRAND'MERE see Perronnet, Amelie

CHANSONS DE LA ROULETTE see Ferny, Jacques

CHANSONS DE LA VILLE ET DES CHAMPS see Delvincourt, Claude

CHANSONS DE L'AUBE ET DU SOIR see Bonnal, Ermend

CHANSONS DE L'OURS see Stravinsky, Igor

CHANSONS DE NEGRESSE see Milhaud, Darius

CHANSONS DE PAGE
(Bordese, Stephen) solo,pno cmplt ed ENOCH s.p.
contains & see also: Busser, Henri-Paul, Revolte; Chaminade, Cecile, Les Trois Baisers; Delmet, Paul, Liberte; Dubois, Theodore, Le Vittrail; Duvernoy, Victor-Alphonse, Doux Larcin; Fontenailles, H. de, Legende Des Fleurs; Ganne, Louis Gaston, Lamento; Hahn, Reynaldo, Adieu; Lefebvre, Channing, Aveu; Levade, Charles (Gaston), Enlevement; Marechal, Henri-Charles, Le Reve; Puget, Paul-Charles-Marie, Le Luth (C875)

CHANSONS DE PHILIPPE SOUPAULT see Arrieu, Claude

CHANSONS DE RONSARD see Milhaud, Darius

CHANSONS DE TROUPE *see Allier, Gabriel, Marches Lyonnaise; Ganne, Louis Gaston, Marches D'Auvergne; Gauwin, Ad., Marche Bretonne; Laffitte, J., Marche Bourguignonne; Marie, Gabriel, Marche Flamande; Ratez, Emile-Pierre, Marches Franc-Comtoise (C876)

CHANSONS DOUCES see Rhene-Baton

CHANSONS DU CARNAVAL DE LONDRES see Milhaud, Darius

CHANSONS DU MONSIEUR BLEU see Rosenthal, Manuel

CHANSONS DU PAYS-LORRAIN *see Compagnon Boulanger; Folle Enchere; La Fiancee Captive; Le Bedeau De Saint-Gilles; Le Cavalier Et La Bergere; Le Retour; Les Armes Du Baron; Les Rosiers Blancs; Perdrai-Je Ma Peine; Quand On Marie Les Filles (C877)

CHANSONS ENFANTINES see Landry, Al.

CHANSONS ENFANTINES, VOL. I see Grovlez, Gabriel (Marie)

CHANSONS ENFANTINES, VOL. II see Grovlez, Gabriel (Marie)

CHANSONS ESPAGNOLES see Schumann, Robert (Alexander)

CHANSONS ET REVERIES see Schumann, Robert (Alexander)

CHANSONS ET ROMANCE see Egk, Werner

CHANSONS FRANCAISES POUR DEBUTANTES *CCU,folk,Fr (Stephan; Foss) solo,pno OXFORD (C878)

CHANSONS GALANTES see Berthelot, Rene

CHANSONS GREQUES DU DEDOCANESE see Baud-Bovy

CHANSONS INNOCENTES see Martirano, S.

CHANSONS IRRESPECTUEUSES see Buchtger, Fritz

CHANSONS LOINTAINES see Hue, [Georges-Adolphe]

CHANSONS MADECASSES see Ravel, Maurice

CHANSONS MADECASSES (EDITION ORIGINALE) see Ravel, Maurice

CHANSONS MARTINIQUAISES see Passani, Emile

CHANSONS ORIENTALES see Badings, Henk

CHANSONS POLYPHONIQUES see Jannequin, Clement

CHANSONS POPULAIRES DE CRETE OCCIDENTALE *CCU,folk,Greek (Baud-Bovy, Samuel) male solo,acap MINKOFF s.p. (C879)

CHANSONS POPULAIRES DES PROVINCES BELGES, VOL. I *CC206U,Fr (Closson) solo,pno SCHOTT-FRER SCH107 s.p. (C880)

CHANSONS POPULAIRES DES PROVINCES BELGES, VOL. II *CC102U (Closson) solo,pno SCHOTT-FRER SCH108 $7.50 (C881)

CHANSONS POPULAIRES DU VIVARAIS, VOL. I see Indy, Vincent d'

CHANSONS POPULAIRES ESPAGNOLES see Koeckert

CHANSONS POPULAIRES POLONAISES see Opienski, Henryk

CHANSONS POPULAIRES TCHECOSLOVAQUES, VOL. I see Kricka, Jaroslav

CHANSONS POPULAIRES TCHECOSLOVAQUES, VOL. II see Kricka, Jaroslav

CHANSONS POUR LES OISEAU see Beydts, L.

CHANSONS POUR MARYCINTHE see Rhene-Baton

CHANSONS PRINTANIERES see Hue, [Georges-Adolphe]

CHANSONS VILLAGEOISES see Poulenc, Francis

CHANT D'ALSACE see Duvernoy, Victor-Alphonse

CHANT D'AMOUR see Brahms, Johannes, Minnelied

CHANT D'AMOUR see Haydn, (Franz) Joseph, Liebeslied

CHANT D'AMOUR see Hermans, Nico

CHANT D'AMOUR see Messager, Andre

CHANT D'AMOUR see Schumann, Robert (Alexander), Liebeslied

CHANT D'AMOUR see Wagner, Richard

CHANT D'AMOUR INCA see Stubbs du Perron, Ed.

CHANT D'APRES-MIDI see Cuvillier, Charles

CHANT D'AUTOMNE see Huybrechts, Albert

CHANT D'AVRIL see Oskam, Izaak J.

CHANT DE FACHEUR see Ravize, A.

CHANT DE LA FIANCEE (I) see Schumann, Robert (Alexander), Lied Der Braut [1]

CHANT DE LA FIANCEE (II) see Schumann, Robert (Alexander), Lied Der Braut [2]

CHANT DE LABOUR see Ravize, A.

CHANT DE MARGARITA see Saint-Saens, Camille

CHANT DE MARIAGE see Franck, Cesar, Panis Angelicus

CHANT DE MARRIAGE see Pileur

CHANT DE MER see Dufresne, C.

CHANT DE NAKAMTI see Roussel, Albert

CHANT DE NOEL see Schlosser, Paul

CHANT DE NOEL see Schlosser, Paul

CHANT DE TROUBADOUR see Veneziani, Vittore

CHANT DE WOLFRAM see Wagner, Richard

CHANT DES BATELIERS DU VOLGA see Koeneman, T.

CHANT DES COMMUNIANTES see Stevens, M.

CHANT DES HALEURS DE LA VOLGA *Russ (Doyen, Alb.) solo,pno/inst LEDUC s.p. (C882)

CHANT DES RECRUTEURS see Lajtha, Laszlo

CHANT DU BERCEAU see Stievenard, M.

CHANT DU BRAHMANE see Roussel, Albert

CHANT DU CAVALIER see Holmes, Alfred

CHANT DU CYNGE see Schubert, Franz (Peter), Swannengesang

CHANT DU DESESPERE see Badings, Henk

CHANT DU MARIN see Wagner, Richard

CHANT DU SOIR see Schumann, Robert (Alexander), Nachtlied

CHANT DU VERMELAND see Bagge, G.

CHANT D'UN FANTASSIN see Boer, Jan den

CHANT FUNEBRE see Koechlin, Charles

CHANT JUIF see Mussorgsky, Modest

CHANTE L'ALOUETTE see Strimer, Joseph

CHANTE, ROSSIGNOL! see Saint-Requier, Leon

CHANTE SI DOUCEMENT see Ropartz, Joseph Guy

CHANTEFABLES see Stravinsky, Soulima

CHANTEFABLES see Albin, Roger

CHANTEZ, JOUEZ see Peyrot

CHANTEZ PETITS ENFANTS see Cocheux, Rene

CHANTONS see Truillet-Soyer, M.

CHANTONS LES VIELLES CHANSONS D'EUROPE *CC232U (Arma, Paul) solo,pno OUVRIERES s.p. (C883)

CHANTRIER, A.
   La Chanson Des Galets
      (Charmettes) solo,pno ENOCH s.p. (C884)
      (Charmettes) solo,acap solo pt ENOCH s.p. (C885)

   L'Adieu
      solo,pno ENOCH s.p. (C886)

   L'Angelus D'Amour
      (Charmettes) solo,pno ENOCH s.p. (C887)
      (Charmettes) solo,acap solo pt ENOCH s.p. (C888)

   Le Retour
      solo,pno ENOCH s.p. (C889)

   Madame Est Servie
      (Charmettes) solo,pno ENOCH s.p. (C890)
      (Charmettes) solo,acap solo pt ENOCH s.p. (C891)

CHANTRIER, A. (cont'd.)

   Serenade Parisienne
      (Charmettes) solo,pno ENOCH s.p. (C892)
      (Charmettes) solo,acap solo pt ENOCH s.p. (C893)

   Viens Tout Pres
      solo,pno ENOCH s.p. (C894)
      solo,acap solo pt ENOCH s.p. (C895)

CHANTS CORSES see Tomasi, H.

CHANTS DE FLANDRE see Georges, Alexandre

CHANTS DE FRANCE VOL. I (Canteloube, J.) solo,pno DURAND s.p. contains: Au Pre De La Rose; Aupres Da Ma Blonde; Delicieuses Cimes; D'ou Venez-Vous, Fillette; Ou Irai-Je Me Plaindre; Reveillez-Vous (C896)

CHANTS DE FRANCE VOL. II (Canteloube, J.) solo,pno DURAND s.p. contains: Dodo Nanette; Il Etait Une Fregate; L'autre Jour En Voulant Danser; Lorsque J'etais Tant Amoureuse; Moue, Quand J'etais Chez Mon Pere; Quand La Marie S'en Va-t'a L'iau (C897)

CHANTS DE JOIE see Perrot-Huret

CHANTS DE LA REVOLUTION RUSSE ET DE LA GUERRE CIVILE *CC8L [Russ] solo,pno cmplt ed CHANT s.p. (C898)

CHANTS DE PAIX see Perrot-Huret

CHANTS DE RHENANIE see Georges, Alexandre

CHANTS DE TERRE ET DE CIEL see Messiaen, Oliver

CHANTS DE WALLONIE see Georges, Alexandre

CHANTS D'ESPAGNE see Palacio

CHANTS DU DESIR see Escher, Rudolf George

CHANTS DU NORD *CC12L solo,pno cmplt ed ENOCH s.p. see also: Backer-Grondahl, Agathe Ursula, Priere Du Soir; Beechgaard, Julius, Quand Le Reve A Toi; Bendix, Victor Emmanuel, Le Chant De La Nouvelle Annee; Gade, Niels Wilhelm, Dans Le Foret; Gade, Niels Wilhelm, Le Chasseur Du Bois D'Ete; Grieg, Edvard Hagerup, L'Oiseau D'Amour; Heise, Peter Arnold, La Chanson De L'Amie Du Roi; Lange-Muller, Peter Erasmus, La Seule Pensee; Sinding, Christian, Perles; Sjogren, Emil, Dors, Chere Prunelle; Stenhammar, Wilhelm, Le Hanap De L'Ancestre (C899)

CHANTS ET CHANSONS POPULAIRES DE LA FRANCE *CCU (Delloye, H.L.) FORNI s.p. (C900)

CHANTS ET DANSES DE LA MORT see Mussorgsky, Modest, Song And Dances Of Death

CHANTS POPULAIRES see Ravel, Maurice

CHANTS POPULAIRES RUSSES *CC9L [Russ] solo,pno cmplt ed CHANT s.p. (C901)

CHANTS RELIGIEUX *see Bach, Johann Sebastian, Ave Maria; Faure, Jean-Baptiste, Charite; Faure, Jean-Baptiste, Credo; Faure, Jean-Baptiste, Crucifix; Faure, Jean-Baptiste, Notre Pere; Faure, Jean-Baptiste, O Salutaris; Faure, Jean-Baptiste, Sancta Maria; Gounod, Charles Francois, Notre-Dame De France; Lefebure-Wely, Louis James Alfred, O Salutaris; Mascagni, Pietro, Ave Maria; Massenet, Jules, Ave Maria; Massenet, Jules, Souvenez-Vous Vierge Marie; Niedermeyer, Louis, Pater Noster; Stradella, Alessandro, Aria Di Chiesa, "Air D'Eglise" (C902)

CHANUKA SONGS see Nardi, Nachum

CHANUKAH, OY CHANUKAH *Jew solo,pno KAMMEN 498 $1.00 (C903)

CHAPEL BELLS see DeSylva

CHAPI
Carceleras (from Las Hijas Del
Zebedeo)
[Span] solo,pno RICORDI-ARG
BA 10934 s.p.   (C904)

Zaragozana (from Las Tentaciones De
San Antonio)
[Span] ST soli,pno RICORDI-ARG
BA 2003 s.p.   (C905)

CHAPI, R.
Las Hijas Del Zebedeo
[Span] med solo,pno UNION ESP.
$1.25   (C906)
(Azpiazu) [Span/Port] med solo,gtr
UNION ESP. $.75   (C907)

CHAPPELL, STANLEY
At Blue Bell Time
solo,pno CRAMER   (C908)

Forgotten Road
solo,pno CRAMER   (C909)

CHAPUIS, AUGUSTE-PAUL-JEAN-BAPTISTE
(1858-1933)
Aime Celui Qui T'aime
Mez solo,vln DURAND s.p.   (C910)

Complainte De La Glu
solo,pno/inst DURAND s.p.   (C911)

En Avril, Dans Les Bois
solo,pno/inst DURAND s.p.   (C912)

Hymne A La Beaute
solo,pno/inst DURAND s.p.   (C913)

La Quenouille
Mez/Bar solo,pno/inst DURAND s.p.
(C914)

Le Tombeau De Zuleika
Mez/Bar solo,pno/inst DURAND s.p.
(C915)

Mythologie
Mez/Bar solo,pno/inst DURAND s.p.
(C916)

Quand Sur L'eau Changeante
solo,pno/inst DURAND s.p. see from
Quatre Melodies   (C917)

Quatre Melodies *see Quand Sur L'eau
Changeante; Serenade; Si J'ai
Parle De Mon Amour; Un Petit
Roseau M'a Suffit   (C918)

Serenade
solo,pno/inst DURAND s.p. see from
Quatre Melodies   (C919)

Si J'ai Parle De Mon Amour
solo,pno/inst DURAND s.p. see from
Quatre Melodies   (C920)

Si Mes Vers Avaient Des Ailes
Mez/Bar solo,pno/inst DURAND s.p.
(C921)

Un Petit Roseau M'a Suffit
solo,pno/inst DURAND s.p. see from
Quatre Melodies   (C922)

CHAQUE HEURE, OU JE SONGE see
Andriessen, Hendrik

CHAQUE PAYS A SA MANIERE see Lacome,
Paul

CHARACTERISTIC BRAZILIAN SONGS see
Villa-Lobos, Heitor

CHARIOT OF CLOUDS see Peterson, John W.

CHARITE see Faure, Jean-Baptiste

CHARITE see Vieu, Jane

CHARITY see Hageman, Richard

CHARITY see Hartley, Evaline

CHARLES, ERNEST (1895-   )
And So, Goodbye
low solo,pno (A flat maj) SCHIRM.G
$.60   (C923)

Clouds
high solo,pno (D flat maj) SCHIRM.G
$1.00   (C924)
med solo,pno (B flat maj) SCHIRM.G
$1.00   (C925)
low solo,pno (A flat maj) SCHIRM.G
$1.00   (C926)
low solo,pno (A flat maj) ALLANS
s.p.   (C927)
med solo,pno (B flat maj) ALLANS
s.p.   (C928)
high solo,pno (D flat maj) ALLANS
s.p.   (C929)

House On A Hill, The
low solo,pno (C maj) SCHIRM.G $.75
(C930)

Let My Song Fill Your Heart
high solo,pno (D flat maj) SCHIRM.G
$.85   (C931)

CHARLES, ERNEST (cont'd.)
low solo,pno (B flat maj) SCHIRM.G
$.85   (C932)
ST soli,pno SCHIRM.G $.75   (C933)
SA soli,pno SCHIRM.G $.75   (C934)

Love Is Of God *sac
high solo,pno (F maj) SCHIRM.G $.85
(C935)

My Lady Walks In Loveliness
high solo,pno (F maj) SCHIRM.G
$1.00   (C936)
low solo,pno (D flat maj) SCHIRM.G
$1.00   (C937)

O Lovely World
med-low solo,pno (E flat maj)
SCHIRM.G $.75   (C938)

Over The Land Is April
high solo,pno (A maj) WILLIS $.60
(C939)
low solo,pno (F maj) WILLIS $.60
(C940)

Psalm 27 *see Psalm Of Exultation

Psalm Of Exultation (Psalm 27) sac
med solo,pno (C maj) SCHIRM.G $.75
(C941)

Save Me, O God *sac
med-low solo,pno (B min) SCHIRM.G
$.75   (C942)

Spendthrift
low solo,pno (E maj) ALLANS s.p.
(C943)
high solo,pno (A flat maj) ALLANS
s.p.   (C944)

Sweet Song Of Long Ago
med solo,pno (E flat maj) SCHIRM.G
$.75   (C945)
low solo,pno (C maj) SCHIRM.G $.75
(C946)

When I Have Sung My Songs
high solo,pno (F maj) SCHIRM.G $.85
(C947)
low solo,pno (D flat maj) SCHIRM.G
$.85   (C948)
low solo,pno (D flat maj) ALLANS
s.p.   (C949)
high solo,pno (F maj) ALLANS s.p.
(C950)

CHARLES GUITEAU see Sims, Ezra

CHARLES TRENET A NEW YORK see Trenet,
Charles

CHARLES, W.
Barnstormers *song cycle
solo,pno BOOSEY $2.50   (C951)

Green-Eyed Dragon
low solo,pno (F sharp min) BOOSEY
$1.50   (C952)
high solo,pno (A min) BOOSEY $1.50
(C953)

CHARLIE IS MY DARLING *folk,Scot
solo,pno (D min) PATERSON FS20 s.p.
(C954)

(Roberton, Hugh S.) 2 soli,pno
ROBERTON 72181 s.p.   (C955)

CHARM OF A CHILD see Arundale, Claude

CHARM OF LULLABIES see Britten,
Benjamin

CHARMANT PAPILLON see Campra, Andre

CHARME DE PRINTEMPS see Schumann,
Robert (Alexander)

CHARME, REVE, IMAGE see Messager, Andre

CHARMING CHLOE see German, Edward

CHARON AND PHILOMEL see Lawes, William

CHARPENTIER
Depuis Le Jour
"Ever Since That Day" solo,pno
ASHLEY $.95   (C956)

Ever Since That Day *see Depuis Le
Jour

CHARPENTIER, GUSTAVE (1860-1956)
Allevar Una Bambina (from Luisa)
[It] Bar solo,pno HEUGEL 4449 s.p.
(C957)
Da Quel Giorno (from Luisa)
[Fr] S solo,pno HEUGEL 4446 B s.p.
(C958)
[It] S solo,pno HEUGEL 4446 s.p.
(C959)

Depuis Le Jour (from Louise)
[Fr/Eng] S solo,pno INTERNAT. $1.25
(C960)
"Since That Fair Day" [Fr/Eng] Mez
solo,pno (G maj) SCHIRM.G $.85
(C961)

Resta... E Ti Riposa (from Luisa)
[It] Bar solo,pno HEUGEL 4450 s.p.
(C962)

CHARPENTIER, GUSTAVE (cont'd.)
Since That Fair Day *see Depuis Le
Jour

CHARPENTIER, JEAN JACQUES BEAUVARLET
(1734-1794)
Au Village Des Saints
see Quatre Psaumes De Toukaram

Pres Du Lit Ou Tu Chantes
see Quatre Psaumes De Toukaram

Quatre Psaumes De Toukaram *sac
S solo,orch LEDUC s.p.
contains: Au Village Des Saints;
Pres Du Lit Ou Tu Chantes; Que
Jamais Mes Yeux; Quelle Main
Fait Mouvoir Mon Corps   (C963)

Que Jamais Mes Yeux
see Quatre Psaumes De Toukaram

Quelle Main Fait Mouvoir Mon Corps
see Quatre Psaumes De Toukaram

Trois Poemes De Henry Clairvaux
*CC3U
S solo,pno LEDUC s.p.   (C964)

CHARPENTIER, MARC-ANTOINE (1634?-1704)
Chanson A Boire Du Medecin Malgre Lui
see LA MUSIQUE, TREIZIEME CAHIER

Glory To God In The Highest
see Three Hymns Of The Church

Jesu Corona Virginium *sac
SMez soli,fl,cont BROEKMANS 1025
s.p.   (C965)

Now, My Tongue, The Mystery Telling
see Three Hymns Of The Church

O Come, Creator Spirit, Come
see Three Hymns Of The Church

Sieben Motetten *sac,CC7U,mot
(Ewerhart, Rudolf) [Lat] S/T solo,
cont BIELER CS 30 s.p.   (C966)

Three Hymns Of The Church *sac
med-high solo,pno oct CONCORDIA
98-1779 $.25
contains: Glory To God In The
Highest; Now, My Tongue, The
Mystery Telling; O Come,
Creator Spirit, Come   (C967)

Trio Des Femmes Mores (from Le Malade
Imaginaire)
SSA soli,pno/inst DURAND s.p.
(C968)

CHARPENTIER, R.
A La Fontaine
SMezA soli,orch DURAND s.p., ipr
see from Trois Chansons A Dire
(C969)

Au Jardinet
SMezA soli,orch DURAND s.p., ipr
see from Trois Chansons A Dire
(C970)

Dans Un Pre
SMezA soli,orch DURAND s.p., ipr
see from Trois Chansons A Dire
(C971)

Trois Chansons A Dire *see A La
Fontaine; Au Jardinet; Dans Un
Pre   (C972)

CHARTON, G.
J'suis Bete
solo,pno ENOCH s.p.   (C973)
solo,acap solo pt ENOCH s.p.   (C974)

CHASIDISH *folk,Jew
(Low, Leo) solo,pno HATIKVAH HCL 27
$.30   (C975)

CHASING THE BREEZE *folk,Scot
solo,pno (E maj/G maj) PATERSON FS132
s.p.   (C976)

CHASONNETTES see Badings, Henk

CHASSAIGNE, F.
Le Compartiment Des Fumeurs
solo,pno ENOCH s.p.   (C977)
solo,acap solo pt ENOCH s.p.   (C978)

CHASSE A COURRE see Berger, Rod.

CHASSE A L'ENFANT see Kosma, J.

CHASSES LASSES see Samazeuilh, Gustave

CHATAU, H.
Les Bretelles
solo,pno ENOCH s.p.   (C979)
solo,acap solo pt ENOCH s.p.   (C980)

CHATEAU D'ORGUEIL see Georges,
Alexandre

CHATTERTON see Diamond, David

CHATZOS see Wolf, Artur

CHAUBET, P.
  Ce Que Chantait Delmet
    solo,acap solo pt ENOCH s.p.   (C981)
    solo,pno ENOCH s.p.   (C982)

CHAUMONT, LAMBERT (1630-1712)
  Chanson De Veillee
    solo,acap solo pt ENOCH s.p.   (C983)
    solo,pno ENOCH s.p.   (C984)

  Laus Mea Dominus *sac,CC2U
    solo,org ENOCH voc sc, solo pt
                                    (C985)

CHAUN, FRANTISEK (1921-   )
  Lieder *see Pisne

  Pisne
    "Lieder" male solo,pno PANTON s.p.
                                    (C986)
  Pisne Na Slova Rainera Marii Rilka
    *CCU
    solo,pno PANTON 997 s.p.   (C987)

CHAUSSON, ERNEST (1855-1899)
  Amour D'antan *Op.8,No.2
    med solo,pno SALABERT-US $2.25
                                    (C988)
  Butterflies, The *see Les Papillons

  Cantique A L'epouse *Op.36,No.1
    med solo,pno SALABERT-US $2.25
                                    (C989)
  Cantique De Sainte Cecile A La Vierge
    Immaculee
    solo,org,opt vcl SALABERT-US $2.25
                                    (C990)
  Chanson D'Amour *Op.28,No.2
    med solo,pno SALABERT-US $2.25 see
    from Songs From Shakespeare
                                    (C991)
  Chanson De Clown *Op.28,No.1
    med solo,pno SALABERT-US $2.25 see
    from Songs From Shakespeare
                                    (C992)
  Chanson Perpetuelle
    S solo,orch DURAND s.p., ipa (C993)
    S solo,pno,4strings DURAND s.p.
                                    (C994)
  Dans La Foret Du Charme Et De
    L'enchantement *Op.36,No.2
    med solo,pno SALABERT-US $2.25
                                    (C995)
  Fauves Las *Op.24,No.4
    med solo,pno SALABERT-US $2.25 see
    from Serres Chaudes   (C996)
  Lassitude *Op.24,No.3
    med solo,pno SALABERT-US $2.25 see
    from Serres Chaudes   (C997)
  Le Temps Des Lilas (from Poeme De
    L'Amour Et De La Mer)
    [Fr/Eng] high solo,pno INTERNAT.
    $1.00   (C998)
    [Fr/Eng] low solo,pno INTERNAT.
    $1.00   (C999)
    high solo/med solo,pno/orch
    SALABERT-US $2.25, ipr   (C1000)
  Les Heures *Op.27,No.1
    med solo,pno SALABERT-US $2.25
                                    (C1001)
  Les Papillons
    "Butterflies, The" [Fr/Eng] med
    solo,pno (G maj) SCHIRM.G $.50
                                    (C1002)
  Oraison *Op.24,No.5
    med solo,pno SALABERT-US $2.25 see
    from Serres Chaudes   (C1003)
  Poeme De L'Amour Et De La Mer
    [Fr/Eng] high solo,pno INTERNAT.
    $2.50   (C1004)
    high solo/med solo,pno/orch voc sc
    SALABERT-US $15.00, ipr   (C1005)
  Serre Chaude *Op.24,No.1
    med solo,pno SALABERT-US $2.25 see
    from Serres Chaudes   (C1006)
  Serre D'Ennui *Op.24,No.2
    med solo,pno SALABERT-US $2.25 see
    from Serres Chaudes   (C1007)
  Serres Chaudes *see Fauves Las,
    Op.24,No.4; Lassitude, Op.24,
    No.3; Oraison, Op.24,No.5; Serre
    Chaude, Op.24,No.1; Serre
    D'Ennui, Op.24,No.2   (C1008)
  Songs From Shakespeare *see Chanson
    D'Amour, Op.28,No.2; Chanson De
    Clown, Op.28,No.1   (C1009)
  Twenty Songs *CC20L
    (Kagen, Sergius) [Fr/Eng] INTERNAT.
    high solo,pno $4.00; low solo,pno
    $4.00   (C1010)
  Twenty Songs *CC20L
    med solo,pno SALABERT-US $16.50
                                    (C1011)

CHAUTAGNE, MARC
  Le Bonheur D'etre Vieux
    solo,pno ENOCH s.p.   (C1012)
    solo,acap solo pt ENOCH s.p.
                                    (C1013)
  Soyons Republicains
    solo,pno ENOCH s.p.   (C1014)
    solo,acap solo pt ENOCH s.p.
                                    (C1015)

CHAUVES-SOURIS see Carolus-Duran, P.

CHAVAGNAT, ED.
  Douze Melodies *CC12U
    solo,pno ENOCH s.p.   (C1016)

CHAVEZ, CARLOS (1899-   )
  Dos Canciones *CC2U
    [Span/Eng] Mez/Bar solo,pno BOOSEY
    $3.00   (C1017)
  Hoy No Lucio La Estrella De Tus Ojos
    "Now From Your Eyes No Longer
    Shines The Starlight" [Span/Eng]
    med-low solo,pno SCHIRM.G $.75
                                    (C1018)
  Nocturna Rosa
    "Nocturnal Rose" [Span/Eng] med
    solo,pno SCHIRM.G $.90   (C1019)
  Nocturna Rose *see Nocturna Rosa

  Now From Your Eyes No Longer Shines
    The Starlight *see Hoy No Lucio
    La Estrella De Tus Ojos

  Reaper, The *see Segador

  Segador
    "Reaper, The" [Span/Eng] med solo,
    pno SCHIRM.G $.75   (C1020)

CHAYALEY HA-SHALOM see Weinberg, Jacob

CHAYECHA VE'CHAYAI
  solo,pno OR-TAV $.50   (C1021)

CHAZAK V'EMATS see Weinberg, Jacob

CHAZARRETA
  Lopez Pereyra
    solo,2gtr RICORDI-ENG BA 11546 s.p.
                                    (C1022)

CHE BELL NAS!
  (Carlo, Musi) solo,pno (Bolognese
  dialect) BONGIOVANI 2061 s.p. see
  from El Mi Canzunett   (C1023)

CHE C-COSA E STATO? see Oddone, E.

CHE FARO SENZA EURIDICE see Gluck,
  Christoph Willibald Ritter von

CHE GELIDA MANINA see Puccini, Giacomo

CHE GLI DIRAI QUEL GIORNO see Menotti,
  Gian Carlo

CHE PIU POTREI see Di Martino, Aladino

CHE PIU SI TARDA OMAI see Handel,
  George Frideric

CHE SERENA CHE PLACIDA CALMA.. see
  Martini, Giambattista

CHE SPERI, BAMBOLA? see Guarino, C.

CHE TUA MADRE DOVRA see Puccini,
  Giacomo

CHECK see Mourant, Walter

CH'ELLA MI CREDA LIBERO E LONTANO see
  Puccini, Giacomo

CHEMIN D'AVRIL see Delmet, Paul

CHEMIN DE CROIX see Georges, Alexandre

CHEMIN DE RONDE see Siohan, Robert

CHEMIN QUI TOURNE see Orthel, Leon

CHEMINEAU see Lachaume, A.

CHENNAULT, JUDY
  I Bring My Life *sac
    med solo,pno CRESPUB CP-S5027 $1.00
                                    (C1024)
  Proof Is Calvary, The *sac
    med solo,pno CRESPUB CP-S5052 $1.00
                                    (C1025)

CHENOWETH, WILBUR (1899-   )
  Love, I Come To You *sac,Marriage
    med solo,pno SCHIRM.G $.85   (C1026)
  Noel, Noel, Bells Are Ringing *sac
    low solo,pno (C maj) SCHIRM.G $.75
                                    (C1027)

CHERCHANT D'AMOUR see Trabadelo, A. de

CHERE AME see Saint-Saens, Camille

CHERE ANNE QUE J'ADORE see Saint-Saens,
  Camille

CHERE DAME see Mozart, Wolfgang
  Amadeus, Madamina! Il Catalogo E
  Questo

CHERE NUIT see Bachelet, Alfred

CHERE PATRIE
  solo,pno DURAND 186 s.p.   (C1028)

CHERRY-COLOURED SHAWL, THE see Borodin,
  Alexander Porfirievitch

CHERRY HUNG WITH SNOW, THE see Ross,
  Colin

CHERRY RIPE
  low solo,pno (E maj) CRAMER   (C1029)
  high solo,pno (C maj) CRAMER   (C1030)
  (Scott) high solo,pno ELKIN
  27.1263.06 s.p.   (C1031)

CHERRY RIPE see Horn, Charles Edward

CHERRY RIPE see Roberton, Hugh
  Stevenson

CHERRY TREE, THE see Gibbs, Cecil
  Armstrong

CHERRY TREE, THE see Musgrave, Thea,
  Gean, The

CHERRY TREE, THE see Rowley, Alec

CHERUBINI, LUIGI (1760-1842)
  Ave Maria *sac
    solo,pno/org (available in 2 keys)
    HEUGEL s.p.   (C1032)
    solo,pno,vln (available in 2 keys)
    HEUGEL s.p.   (C1033)
    [It] high solo,pno (F maj) CRAMER
                                    (C1034)
    [It] low solo,pno (E flat maj)
    CRAMER   (C1035)
    [Lat/Ger] high solo&med solo,pno/
    org,vln LIENAU R82 s.p.   (C1036)
    Mez/Bar solo,pno FORLIVESI 11262
    s.p.   (C1037)
    "Gruss Dir, Maria" A/Bar solo,pno
    (D maj) LIENAU HOS 39 s.p.
                                    (C1038)
    "Gruss Dir, Maria" S/T solo,pno (F
    maj) LIENAU HOS 38 s.p.   (C1039)
  Ecce Panis *sac
    solo,pno/org (available in 2 keys)
    HEUGEL s.p.   (C1040)
  Four Duets *CC4U
    [It/Ger] SS soli,pno/harp PETERS
    2108 $4.75   (C1041)
  Gruss Dir, Maria *see Ave Maria

  O Salutaris *sac
    solo,pno/org (available in 2 keys)
    HEUGEL s.p.   (C1042)

CHESHAM, EDWARD M.
  Longshoreman, The
    low solo,pno (E maj) CRAMER $.95
                                    (C1043)
    high solo,pno (F maj) CRAMER $.90
                                    (C1044)
  Soldier Jim
    low solo,pno (F maj) CRAMER   (C1045)
    high solo,pno (G maj) CRAMER
                                    (C1046)

CHESHIRE, MATTIE
  I'm In Love Wi' Susan
    solo,pno CRAMER   (C1047)

CHESTNUT CASTS HIS FLAMBEAUX, THE see
  Heilner, Irwin

CHEU NOUS ON EST COMME CA see Lachaume,
  A.

CHEVILLARD, (PAUL ALEXANDRE) CAMILLE
  (1859-1923)
  L'Attente
    Mez/Bar solo,pno/inst DURAND s.p.
                                    (C1048)
    S/T solo,pno/inst DURAND s.p.
                                    (C1049)

CHEVREUILLE, RAYMOND (1901-   )
  Aimerais-Je Autant Les Oiseaux
    *Op.36,No.3
    see Chansons

  Chansons
    T/Bar solo,pno cmplt ed CBDM s.p.
    contains: Aimerais-Je Autant Les
    Oiseaux, Op.36,No.3; Dors, Ma
    Caprine, Dors, Op.36,No.5; Le
    Printemps, Le Long Des
    Buissons..., Op.36,No.1;
    Pendant Que La Pluie Aux
    Carreaux, Op.36,No.4; Ris, Vent
    D'ete, Sur La Girouette...,
    Op.36,No.2   (C1050)

  Dors, Ma Caprine, Dors *Op.36,No.5
    see Chansons

CHEVREUILLE, RAYMOND (cont'd.)

Le Printemps, Le Long Des Buissons...
*Op.36,No.1
see Chansons

Pendant Que La Pluie Aux Carreaux
*Op.36,No.4
see Chansons

Ris, Vent D'ete, Sur La Girouette...
*Op.36,No.2
see Chansons

CHEZ NOUS see Christian-Jollet

CHI DISSE CHE LA FEMMENA see Pergolesi, Giovanni Battista

CHI IL BEL SOGNO see Puccini, Giacomo

CHI-KING see Beekhuis, Hanna

CHI NON ODE E CHI NON VEDE see Pergolesi, Giovanni Battista

CHI SA, CHI SA, QUAL SIA see Mozart, Wolfgang Amadeus

CHI T'INTENDE see Handel, George Frideric

CHI VUOL LA ZINGARELLA? see Paisiello, Giovanni

CHIAPANECAS *Mex
(King) high solo,pno (G maj) WILLIS $.60 (C1051)

CHIARE ONDE see Vivaldi, Antonio

CHIEGGIO AL LIDO see Porpora, Nicola Antonio

CHIEMSEE-TERZETTE see Zilcher, Hermann

CHIEN ET CHAT see Delbruck, J.

CHILD AND THE BUTTERFLY, THE see Arensky, Anton Stepanovitch, L'Enfant Et Le Papillon

CHILD IN NATURE see Butterley, Nigel

CHILD JESUS see Hatch, Owen A.

CHILD RETURNS HOME, A see Strandsjo, Olivebring

CHILDE, ROBERT
Crystal Cup, The
high solo,pno (G maj) WILLIS $.60 (C1052)
low solo,pno (E flat maj) WILLIS $.60 (C1053)

CHILDHOOD FABLES FOR GROWNUPS see Fine, Irving

CHILDREN, THE see Chanler, Theodore Ward

CHILDREN OF EXILE see Vigoda, Samuel, Golus Kinder

CHILDREN OF MEN see Russell, Kennedy

CHILDREN OF THE MOON see Warren

CHILDREN'S CORNER see Russell, Kennedy

CHILDREN'S DREAMS see Cowen, Sir Frederic Hymen

CHILDREN'S HOME, THE see Cowen, Sir Frederic Hymen

CHILDRENS HOUR, THE see Clarke, Robert Coningsby

CHILDREN'S LETTER TO THE UNITED NATIONS, THE see Dougherty, Celius

CHILDREN'S PRAYER, THE see Reger, Max, Des Kindes Gebet

CHILDREN'S SONGS see Weigl, Karl

CHILDREN'S SONGS OF CZECHOSLOVAKIA *CC12U,folk
(Gray, Vera) solo,pno voc sc OXFORD 68.220 $1.90 (C1054)

CHILDREN'S SONGS OF DENMARK *CC12U, folk,Dan
(MacMahon, Desmond) solo,pno OXFORD 68.218 $.75 (C1055)

CHILDREN'S SONGS OF FRANCE *CC12U, folk,Fr
(Gray, Vera) solo,pno OXFORD 68.217 $1.50 (C1056)

CHILDREN'S SONGS OF ITALY *CC10U,folk, It
(Gray, Vera) solo,pno OXFORD 68.231

$2.15 (C1057)

CHILDREN'S SONGS OF RUSSIA *CC11U, folk,Russ
(Wiseman, Herbert) solo,pno OXFORD 68.222 $1.80 (C1058)

CHILDREN'S SONGS OF SPAIN *CC12U,folk, Span
(Brown, S.H.) solo,pno OXFORD 68.229 $2.50 (C1059)

CHILDS, BARNEY (1926-   )
Music For Singer
solo,2pno BERANDOL BER 1111 $4.00 (C1060)

Seven Epigrams *CC7U
S solo,clar,pno TRI-TEN $2.10 (C1061)

CHILD'S CAROL *sac,carol,Belg
(Naylor, Bernard) solo,pno (C maj) LESLIE 7035 (C1062)

CHILD'S CHRISTMAS SONG, A see Walter, C.

CHILDS, DAVID
Seven Psalms *sac,CC7U
low solo,pno ABINGDON APM-385 $2.50; high solo,pno ABINGDON APM-390 $2.50 (C1063)

CHILD'S PRAYER see Weinberg, Jacob

CHILD'S PRAYER, A see Klemm, Gustav

CHILD'S PRAYER, A see Sifler, Paul J.

CHILD'S PRAYER AT NIGHT, A see Musgrave, Thea, Bairn's Prayer At Night, A

CHILD'S SONG OF PRAISE, A see Dunhill, Thomas Frederick

CHILDS THOUGHTS, A see Douglas, A.

CHILL OF THE EVE see Adler, Samuel

CHILL OF THE EVE see Mourant, Walter

CHINA MANDARIN, THE see Bantock, Granville

CHINEESCHE LIEDEREN see Ruyneman, Daniel

CHINESE LOVE POEM see Wood, Joseph

CHINESE MINIATURES see Kozina, Marijan, Kitajske Miniature

CHINESE MOTHER GOOSE RHYMES *CCU
(Crist) solo,pno FISCHER,C 0 139 (C1064)

CHINESE SONGS see Heilner, Irwin

CHINESE SONGS, NO. 1 see Kosa, Gyorgy

CHINESE SONGS, NO. 2 see Kosa, Gyorgy

CHINESISCHE LIEBESLIEDER see Liebermann, Rolf

CHINESISCHE LIEDER see Strategier, Herman

CHINESISCHE SUITE NACH GEDICHTEN VON HANS BETHGES CHINESISCHER FLOTE see Herrmann, Hugo

CHINESISCHES SOLDATENLIED see Beekhuis, Hanna

CH'ING T'ING MOUNTAIN, THE see Avshalomov, Jacob

CHINOISERIE see Falla, Manuel de

CHINTZ AND CHIPPENDALE see McGeoch, Daisy

CH'IO MI SCORDI DI TE see Mozart, Wolfgang Amadeus

CHIOMA D'ORO see Monteverdi, Claudio

CHISSA CHI AMERO DOMAN see Lehar, Franz

CHISTT see Pardo

CHITARRA DI NOTTE see Caltabiano, S.

CHIUDI!!
(Carlo, Musi) solo,pno (Bolognese dialect) BONGIOVANI 2069 s.p. see from El Mi Canzunett (C1065)

CHIUDI GLI OCCHI see Lehar, Franz

CHIUDO GLI OCCHI see Massenet, Jules

CHIZAT
Chanson Pour Jean
high solo,med solo,pno/inst,opt vln LEDUC s.p., ipa (C1066)
med solo&low solo,pno/orch (E flat maj) LEDUC s.p. (C1067)

CHLAIDZE, G.
Psalms Of Love *song cycle
[Russ] T solo,pno MEZ KNIGA 2.109 s.p. (C1068)

CHLAPCI A CHLAPI see Felix, Vaclav

CHLAPEC see Zelinka, Jan Evangelista

CHLOE see Zagwijn, Henri

CHLORIS see Dolin, S.

CHLUBNA, OSWALD (1893-1971)
Melancholicke Serenady O Lasce
"Melancholische Serenaden Uber Liebe" high solo,pno CZECH s.p. (C1069)

Melancholische Serenaden Uber Liebe *see Melancholicke Serenady O Lasce

CHO-TUNG TANG, JORDAN
World, The
solo,acap SEESAW (C1070)

CHOEUR DES PATRES see Ravel, Maurice

CHOICE SACRED DUETS *sac,CCU
[Ger] 2 soli,pno PRESSER $4.95 (C1071)

CHOICE SACRED SONGS *sac,CCU
(Wilmans, W.) PRESSER high solo,pno $4.95; low solo,pno $4.95 (C1072)

CHOIX DE ROMANCES ET CHANSONS see Glinka, Mikhail Ivanovitch

CHOMED CHINDE, MIR WAND SINGE *CC50U
(Vogel) solo,pno HUG s.p. (C1073)

CHOOSE GOD TODAY see Holm, Dallas

CHOOSE LIFE see Zilch, Margot

CHOOSING SHOES see Drynan, Margaret

CHOPCHERRY see Heseltine, Philip

CHOPIN, FREDERIC (1810-1849)
By The Fountain
solo,pno ASHDOWN s.p. (C1074)

Canto De Amor
(Pardo) [Span] solo,pno (transcribed from: Waltz, op. 69, no. 1) RICORDI-ARG BA 8570 s.p. (C1075)

Chopin Songs *CCU
(Paderewski) [Pol/Eng] solo,pno MARKS $6.50 (C1076)

Flickans Onskan
solo,pno GEHRMANS s.p. (C1077)

Frederic Chopin's Works - First Critical Edition *CCU
(Bargiel, W.; Brahms, J.; Franchomme, A.; Liszt, F.; Reinecke, C.; Rudorff, E.) contains works for a variety of instruments and vocal combinations microfiche UNIV.MUS.ED. $45.00 reprints of Breitkopf & Hartel Editions; contains 14 volumes with a supplement and revisions (C1078)

Lithanisk Visa
solo,pno GEHRMANS s.p. (C1079)

Madchen's Wunsch
"Maiden's Wish, The" [Ger/Eng] med solo,pno (A maj) SCHIRM.G $.50 (C1080)
"Maiden's Wish, The" solo,pno ASHDOWN s.p. (C1081)

Maiden's Wish, The *see Madchen's Wunsch

Noche De Ensuenos
(Pardo) [Span] solo,pno (transcribed from: Nocturne, op. 9, no. 2) RICORDI-ARG BA 8723 s.p. (C1082)

Polish Songs *Op.74, CC16U,Pol
[Ger] high solo,pno PETERS 1925A $6.00; med solo,pno PETERS 1925B $6.00 (C1083)

Songs *CCU
[Hung] solo,pno BUDAPEST 3521 s.p. (C1084)

Tristesse
low solo,pno (C maj) ALLANS s.p. (C1085)
high solo,pno (E flat maj) ALLANS

CHOPIN, FREDERIC (cont'd.)

s.p.   (C1086)
(Martini) "Tristeza" [Fr/Span]
solo,pno (transcribed from: Grand
Studies, op. 10, no. 3) RICORDI-
ARG BA 8312 s.p.   (C1087)

Tristeza *see Tristesse

CHOPIN SONGS see Chopin, Frederic

CHORALBUCH *CC90U,Xmas
(Doerffel) [Ger] solo,pno PETERS 1423
$3.50   (C1088)

CHORALSINGBUCH *sac,CCU
(Brodde, Otto) med solo,org (med)
BAREN. 671 s.p.   (C1089)

CHOREIA I see Kounadis, Arghyris

CHORISTER, THE see Sullivan, Sir Arthur
Seymour

CHORUS see Ricketts, L.

CHOU, WEN-CHUNG (1923-   )
Seven Poems Of T'Ang Dynasty *CC7U
T solo,7winds,perc sc PRESSER $3.00
(C1090)

CHRENNIKOW, TICHON
Lied Des Betrunkenen
[Russ/Ger] Bar solo,pno SIKORSKI
2173 s.p. see from Viel Larm Um
Nichts   (C1091)

Lieder Und Romanzen *CCU
[Russ] solo,pno SIKORSKI R 6385
s.p.   (C1092)

Viel Larm Um Nichts *see Lied Des
Betrunkenen   (C1093)

CHRETIEN, H.
Chanson Pour La Bien-Aimee
solo,pno ENOCH s.p.   (C1094)

La-Bas
solo,pno (available in 2 keys)
ENOCH s.p.   (C1095)

Le Printemps, C'est Toi
solo,pno ENOCH s.p.   (C1096)

Les Ailes Du Reve
solo,pno ENOCH s.p.   (C1097)

CHRISANDER, NILS
Dar Sorlar Svagt En Kalla
solo,pno GEHRMANS s.p.   (C1098)

Mot Det Hoga!
solo,pno GEHRMANS s.p.   (C1099)

Varfor?
solo,pno GEHRMANS s.p.   (C1100)

CHRIST CHILD see Pull, Edwin

CHRIST CHILD see Van De Water, B.

CHRIST CHILD, THE see Mills, Charles

CHRIST-CHILD LIVES, THE see Davis,
Muriel K.

CHRIST IS A WONDERFUL SAVIOUR *sac,
gospel
solo,pno ABER.GRP. $1.50   (C1101)

CHRIST IS ARISEN see Couperin (le
Grand), Francois

CHRIST IS BORN
see Six Polish Christmas Carols

CHRIST IS RISEN see Dressler, L.R.

CHRIST IS RISEN see Rachmaninoff,
Sergey Vassilievitch

CHRIST IS RISEN see Rachmaninoff,
Sergey Vassilievitch, Christ Is
Risen

CHRIST IS RISEN TODAY see Davis,
Katherine K.

CHRIST IS THE KING OF ALL KINGS see
Holiday, Mickey

CHRIST LIVES IN ME see Bartlett, Gene

CHRIST MY REFUGE see Brown

CHRIST MY REFUGE see Farrar

CHRIST MY REFUGE see Fischer, Irwin

CHRIST MY REFUGE see MacDermid

CHRIST MY REFUGE see Root

CHRIST, THE LIVING WAY see Roesch

CHRIST THE LORD IS RISEN AGAIN see
Couperin (le Grand), Francois

CHRIST THE VICTOR see Rossini, Carlo

CHRIST WENT UP INTO THE HILLS see
Hageman

CHRIST WENT UP INTO THE HILLS see
Hageman, Richard

CHRIST WHO LIVES WITHIN, THE see
Austin, Bill

CHRISTBAUM see Cornelius, Peter

CHRISTCHILD'S LULLABY see Weigl, Vally

CHRISTE, DER DU BIST TAG UND LICHT see
Schein, Johann Hermann

CHRISTENSEN, HENNING
Dieppe, Encore Le Dernier Reflux
*Op.14,No.2
see Drie Beckett-Sange

Drie Beckett-Sange
Bar solo,perc,harp,cel,vibra,vln
FOG III, 190 s.p.
contains: Dieppe, Encore Le
Dernier Reflux, Op.14,No.2;
Elles Viennent, Op.14,No.3; Je
Voudrais Que Mon Amour, Op.14,
No.1   (C1102)

Elles Viennent *Op.14,No.3
see Drie Beckett-Sange

Je Voudrais Que Mon Amour *Op.14,
No.1
see Drie Beckett-Sange

CHRISTGEBURT- UND MARIENLIEDER *CC15U,
Xmas,14-17th cent
[Ger] high solo/med solo,pno&lute/
pno&gtr/pno PETERS 4361 $4.00
(C1103)

CHRISTIAN CAROLS FROM MANY COUNTRIES
*sac,Xmas,carol
(Coleman, Satis N.; Jorgensen, Elin
K.) boy solo,pno SCHIRM.G $1.50
(C1104)

CHRISTIAN FRIENDS see Baker, Richard C.

CHRISTIAN-JOLLET
Berceuse
solo,pno OUVRIERES s.p.   (C1105)

Chez Nous
2 soli,pno OUVRIERES s.p.   (C1106)

CHRISTIAN SCIENCE SERVICE SONGS *sac,
CC23L
med solo,pno SCHIRM.G $4.00 (C1107)

CHRISTIAN WAY, THE see Lucas

CHRISTIANS TRIBULATION see Hubbard, H.

CHRISTIANSEN, A.
Beholding Thee, Lord Jesus (composed
with Rasley, John M.) *sac
solo,pno SINGSPIR 7101 $1.00
(C1108)

CHRISTIE, K.
Journey
med solo,pno PRESSER $.75   (C1109)

CHRISTKIND see Cornelius, Peter

CHRISTKINDLEINS WIEGENLIED see Jaeger,
Willy

CHRISTMAS see Burges, Peter

CHRISTMAS see Josten, Werner

CHRISTMAS ALBUM *CC24U,Xmas
[Ger] solo,pno,opt vln&vcl PETERS
2800A $4.75   (C1110)

CHRISTMAS ALBUM *CCU,Xmas
(Farkas; Szekeres) [Hung] solo,pno
BUDAPEST 6334 s.p.   (C1111)

CHRISTMAS ALLELUIA, A see Gustafson,
Dwight

CHRISTMAS ANTIPHON see Stout, Alan

CHRISTMAS AT THE CLOISTERS see
Corigliano, John

CHRISTMAS CALYPSO see Patterson

CHRISTMAS CANDLE see Warren

CHRISTMAS CANDLE see Warren, Elinor
Remick

CHRISTMAS CANTATA see Scarlatti,
Alessandro

CHRISTMAS CAROL see Franco, Johan

CHRISTMAS CAROL see Keel, Frederick

CHRISTMAS CAROL, A see Dello Joio,
Norman

CHRISTMAS CAROL, A see Weigl, Vally

CHRISTMAS CAROL, A see Williamson,
Malcolm

CHRISTMAS CAROL ENSEMBLES *sac,CC18UL,
Xmas
(Whitsett, Eleanor) 3 soli,pno
LILLENAS MC-4 $1.50   (C1112)

CHRISTMAS CAROL FOR THE HOMELESS
CHILDREN see Debussy, Claude, Noel
Des Enfants Qui N'ont Plus De
Maisons

CHRISTMAS CAROLS FOR SOLO VOICE *CCU,
Xmas,carol
(Cassler, G. Winston) solo,pno
AUGSBURG 11-9151 $1.75   (C1113)

CHRISTMAS CAROLS FROM MANY COUNTRIES
*sac,CCU,Xmas,carol/folk
(Coleman, Satis N.; Jorgensen, Elin
K.) boy solo,pno SCHIRM.G $.75
(C1114)

CHRISTMAS, CHRISTMAS *sac,gospel
solo,pno ABER.GRP. $1.50   (C1115)

CHRISTMAS DAY see Roberts, Mervyn

CHRISTMAS ENSEMBLE *sac,CCUL,Xmas
(DeCou, Harold; Johnson, Norman) SSA/
TTBB soli,pno SINGSPIR $1.50
(C1116)

CHRISTMAS EVE see Hageman, Richard

CHRISTMAS FOR LOW VOICE, NO. I *sac,
CCUL,Xmas
low solo,pno LILLENAS MC-8 $1.50
(C1117)

CHRISTMAS FOR LOW VOICE, NO. II *sac,
CCUL,Xmas
low solo,pno LILLENAS MC-16 $1.50
(C1118)

CHRISTMAS IS A FEELING see Sleeth,
Natalie

CHRISTMAS IS FOR CHILDREN see Peterson,
John W.

CHRISTMAS IS HERE see Marier

CHRISTMAS LULLABY see Pitfield, Thomas
Baron

CHRISTMAS LULLABY, A see Weigl, Vally

CHRISTMAS MESSAGE see Fischer, Irwin

CHRISTMAS MESSAGE, A see Weigl, Vally

CHRISTMAS MORN see Boardman, Reginald

CHRISTMAS MORN see Eakin

CHRISTMAS MORN see Fischer, Irwin

CHRISTMAS MORN see MacDermid

CHRISTMAS MORN see Root

CHRISTMAS MORN see Way

CHRISTMAS MORN see Young

CHRISTMAS PAST...CHRISTMAS PRESENT
*sac,CC10L,Xmas
solo,pno WORD 37661 $2.50 contains
works by: Kaiser, Kurt; Caldwell,
Mary; Brown, Charles and others
(C1119)

CHRISTMAS SHOPPING see Ashton, Bob

CHRISTMAS SING ALONG *sac/sec,CCU,Xmas
solo,pno MUSIC 020107 $3.95 contains
works by: Bach; Mozart; Handel and
others   (C1120)

CHRISTMAS SONG see Adam, Adolphe-
Charles, Cantique De Noel

CHRISTMAS SONG see Voormolen, Alexander
Nicolas

CHRISTMAS SONGS *CC29U,Xmas
(Steigenberger) [Ger] solo,gtr
NOETZEL N1211 s.p.   (C1121)

CHRISTMAS SONGS see Cornelius, Peter

CHRISTMAS SONGS *CC29U,Xmas
(Steigenberger) [Ger] solo,gtr
NOETZEL N1211 s.p.   (C1122)

CHRISTMAS SPIRIT, THE see Fox, Baynard

CHRISTMAS SPIRIT, THE see Loes, Harry
Dixon

CHRISTMAS TIME IS A HAPPINESS TIME see
Rice, Ruth

CHRISTMAS TREE see Diamond, David

CHRISTOU, JANI
Sinfonia No. I Con Lirica Sul Poema
Di T.S. Eliot "Eyes That Last I
Saw In Tears"
female solo,orch sc SANTIS 887
s.p., ipr   (C1123)

CHRISTUJENNA *sac,Xmas,carol
(Watkinson, G.) solo,org CHRIS 50571
s.p.   (C1124)

CHRISTUS DER KINDERFREUND see
Cornelius, Peter

CHRISTUS HAT DEM TODE DIE MACHT
GENOMMEN see Kretzschmar, Gunther

CHRISTUS PETRA see Brumby, Colin

CHRISTUSLIEDER see Haas, Joseph

CHROMATIC TUNES see Danyel, John

CHRYSALIDE see Depecker, Rose

CHU YEH see Heilner, Irwin

CHUCK OLSON SINGS *sac,CC11UL
solo,pno LILLENAS MB-325 $1.95
                             (C1125)

CHUECA, FEDERICO (1846-1908)
Al Fin Mi Nena (from La Corria De
Toros)
[Span] 4 soli,pno RICORDI-ARG
BA 2061 s.p.   (C1126)
[Span] ST soli,pno RICORDI-ARG
BA2060 s.p.   (C1127)

Cancion Del "Cordon Bleu" (from La
Caza Del Oso)
[Span] solo,pno RICORDI-ARG BA 2012
s.p.   (C1128)

Jota (from La Alegria De La Heurta)
[Span] 3 soli,pno RICORDI-ARG
BA 7695 s.p.   (C1129)

Jota De Los Ratas (from La Gran Via)
(composed with Valverde, Joaquin)
[Span] soli,pno RICORDI-ARG BA 6550
s.p.   (C1130)

Mazurca (from De Madrid A Paris)
(composed with Valverde, Joaquin)
[Span] solo,pno RICORDI-ARG BA 3509
s.p.   (C1131)

Mazurca De La Perdiz (from La Caza
Del Oso)
2 soli,pno RICORDI-ARG BA 500 s.p.
                        (C1132)

Mazurca De Los Paraguas (from Un Ano
Pasado Por Agua) (composed with
Valverde, Joaquin)
[Span] ST soli,pno RICORDI-ARG
BA 3458 s.p.   (C1133)

Vals De Caballero De Gracia (from La
Gran Via) (composed with
Valverde, Joaquin)
[Span] soli,pno RICORDI-ARG BA 6635
s.p.   (C1134)

Vals Y Cuple De Los Obreros (from La
Borracha)
[Span] solo,pno RICORDI-ARG BA 2016
s.p.   (C1135)

CHUENCH'I see Schurmann, Gerard

CHURCH, HARDEN
Longing
high solo,pno (A flat maj) WILLIS
$.60   (C1136)
low solo,pno (F min) WILLIS $.60
                        (C1137)

CHURCH IS FINALLY OVER *sac
(Carmichael, Ralph) solo,pno WORD
S-86   (C1138)

CHURCH SOLOIST *sac,CCU
low solo,pno BELWIN $3.00   (C1139)

CHURCH SOLOISTS FAVORITES *sac,CCU
(Fredrickson) high solo,pno FISCHER,C
RB 65; low solo,pno FISCHER,C RB 66
                             (C1140)

CHURCH TRIUMPHANT, THE see Gaither

CHURCH YEAR IN SONGS *sac,CC60U
[Ger] high solo,pno/org PETERS 4229A
$10.00; med solo/low solo,pno/org
PETERS 4229B $10.00   (C1141)

CHVILE SLAVY JSEM MEL see Jeremias,
Otakar

CIACCHER E NARZISAT
(Carlo, Musi) solo,pno (Bolognese
dialect) BONGIOVANI 2048 s.p. see
from El Mi Canzunett   (C1142)

CIAPO see Abbado, Marcello

CIASCUN S'ALLEGRI see Dallapiccola,
Luigi

CICLAMINO D'AUTUNNO see Gandino, Adolfo

CICLAMINO DI PRIMAVERA see Gandino,
Adolfo

CIEL OER ET VENS see Roussel, Albert

CIELITO LINDO see Fernandez

CIELO D'ARGENTO see Ferrari-Trecate,
Luigi

CIELO E MAR see Ponchielli, Amilcare

CIELO STELLATO see Hazon, Roberto

CIGAN see Kozina, Marijan

CIGAN HVALI SVOJEGA KONJA see Kozina,
Marijan

CIGARETTES see Papirossen

CIGLIC, ZVONIMIR (1921-   )
Dve Pesmi
med solo,pno DRUSTVO DSS 288 rental
contains: Topoli V Jeseni; Usoda
                             (C1143)

Topoli V Jeseni
see Dve Pesmi

Tri Pesmi *CC3U
high solo,pno DRZAVNA rental
                             (C1144)

Usoda
see Dve Pesmi

CIKANSKE MELODIE see Dvorak, Antonin

CIKANSKE MELODIE see Bendl, Karel

CIKKER, JAN (1911-   )
O Mamicke
low solo,pno SLOV.HUD.FOND s.p.
                             (C1145)

Pat Ludovych Piesni *CC5U
solo,pno SLOV.HUD.FOND s.p. (C1146)

CILEA, FRANCESCO (1866-1950)
Come Due Tizzi Accesi (from
L'Arlesiana)
[It] Bar solo,pno SONZOGNO 1013
$1.25   (C1147)

E La Solita Storia Del Pastore (from
L'Arlesiana)
[It/Eng/Ger] T solo,pno SONZOGNO
1009 $1.25   (C1148)

Ecco Il Monologo (from Adriana
Lecouvreur)
[It] Bar solo,pno SONZOGNO 1103
$1.25   (C1149)

Era Un Giorno Di Festa (from
L'Arlesiana)
[It] Mez solo,pno SONZOGNO 2900
$1.25   (C1150)

Essere Madre E Un Inferno (from
L'Arlesiana)
[It/Eng] Mez solo,pno SONZOGNO 2805
$1.25   (C1151)

Io Sono L'umile Ancella (from Adriana
Lecouvreur)
[It/Eng/Ger] S solo,pno SONZOGNO
1102 $1.25   (C1152)
[It/Eng] S solo,pno INTERNAT. $.90
                        (C1153)

La Dolchissima Effigie (from Adriana
Lecouvreur)
[It/Eng] T solo,pno SONZOGNO 1127
$1.25   (C1154)

Lamento Di Federico (from
L'Arlesiana)
[It/Eng] T solo,pno INTERNAT. $1.00
                        (C1155)

L'anima Ho Stanca (from Adriana
Lecouvreur)
[It/Eng/Ger] T solo,pno SONZOGNO
1106 $1.25   (C1156)

Nel Ridestarmi
[It] solo,pno CURCI 258 s.p.
                        (C1157)
[It] S solo,2fl,2ob,2clar,2bsn,
2horn,harp,strings sc CURCI 7326
rental   (C1158)

O Mia Cuna Fiorita (from Gloria)
S solo,pno SONZOGNO 2762 s.p.
                        (C1159)

O Vagabonda Stella D'Oriente (from
Adriana Lecouvreur)
[It/Eng] Mez solo,pno SONZOGNO 1104
$1.25   (C1160)

CILEA, FRANCESCO (cont'd.)
Poveri Fiori (from Adriana
Lecouvreur)
[It] S solo,pno RICORDI-ARG BA 9757
s.p.   (C1161)
[It/Eng/Ger] S solo,pno SONZOGNO
1108 $1.25   (C1162)
[It/Eng] solo,pno INTERNAT. $.90
                        (C1163)

Pur Dolente Son Io (from Gloria)
T solo,pno SONZOGNO 2846 s.p.
                        (C1164)

Vita Breve
[It] S solo,2fl,2ob,2clar,2bsn,
2horn,harp,strings sc CURCI 7327
rental   (C1165)
[It] solo,pno CURCI 259 s.p.
                        (C1166)

CIMARA, PIETRO
A Una Rosa
solo,pno BONGIOVANI 728 s.p. see
from Cinque Liriche (Seconda
Serie)   (C1167)

Adorazione
Mez solo,pno BONGIOVANI 571 s.p.
see from Cinque Liriche (Prima
Serie)   (C1168)

Ben Venga Amore!
[It] solo,pno BONGIOVANI 833 s.p.
                        (C1169)

Canto Di Primavera
solo,pno FORLIVESI 10793 s.p.
                        (C1170)

Cinque Canti
[It] solo,pno cmplt ed BONGIOVANI
1923 s.p.
contains: Dolce Sonno; Sia
Benedetta; Siete Piu Bella; Una
Fontana; Vo' Cantare   (C1171)

Cinque Liriche (Prima Serie) *see
Adorazione; Dormi!, "La
Serenata"; Mattinata; Nostalgia;
Stelle Chiare   (C1172)

Cinque Liriche (Seconda Serie) *see
A Una Rosa; Notte D'estate;
Paesaggio; Paranzelle; Presso Una
Fontana   (C1173)

Dal Vostro Verziere
[It] solo,pno BONGIOVANI 884 s.p.
                        (C1174)

Dolce Sonno
see Cinque Canti

Dormi!
"La Serenata" S/T solo,pno
BONGIOVANI 575 s.p. see from
Cinque Liriche (Prima Serie)
                        (C1175)

Dovunque
"Everywhere" [Eng/It] solo,pno
BONGIOVANI 953 s.p.   (C1176)

E' Tornata Primavera
[Eng] solo,pno BONGIOVANI 1637 s.p.
                        (C1177)
[It] solo,pno BONGIOVANI 882 s.p.
see from Tre Ballate Di
Calendimaggio   (C1178)

Everywhere *see Dovunque

Fiocca La Neve
[It] A solo,pno BONGIOVANI 515 s.p.
                        (C1179)
[It] Mez solo,pno BONGIOVANI 516
s.p.   (C1180)
[It] S solo,pno BONGIOVANI 519 s.p.
                        (C1181)
"La Neige Tombe" [Fr/It] Mez/Bar
solo,pno BONGIOVANI 858 s.p.
                        (C1182)
"Snow Is Falling, The" [Eng] A
solo,pno BONGIOVANI 859 s.p.
                        (C1183)
"Snow Is Falling, The" [Eng] Mez
solo,pno BONGIOVANI 1632 s.p.
                        (C1184)
"Snow Is Falling, The" [Eng] S
solo,pno BONGIOVANI 1633 s.p.
                        (C1185)

Invito Alla Danza
[It] solo,pno BONGIOVANI 1854 s.p.
                        (C1186)

La Neige Tombe *see Fiocca La Neve

La Serenata *see Dormi!

Le Campane Di Malines
[It] solo,pno BONGIOVANI 879 s.p.
                        (C1187)

L'infinito
[It] solo,pno BONGIOVANI 1855 s.p.
                        (C1188)

Maggiolata
solo,pno BONGIOVANI 644 s.p.
                        (C1189)

Mattinata
S/Mez solo,pno BONGIOVANI 574 s.p.
see from Cinque Liriche (Prima
Serie)   (C1190)

CIMARA, PIETRO (cont'd.)

Mentre Cade La Neve
[It] solo,pno BONGIOVANI 954 s.p.
(C1191)

Mysticite
[Fr] solo,pno BONGIOVANI 867 s.p.
(C1192)

Non Piu
solo,pno FORLIVESI s.p. (C1193)

Nostalgia
S/Mez solo,pno BONGIOVANI 572 s.p.
see from Cinque Liriche (Prima
Serie) (C1194)

Notte D'estate
solo,pno BONGIOVANI 725 s.p. see
from Cinque Liriche (Seconda
Serie) (C1195)

O Dolce Notte
[It] solo,pno BONGIOVANI 868 s.p.
(C1196)

Offerta
[It] solo,pno BONGIOVANI 881 s.p.
see from Tre Ballate Di
Calendimaggio (C1197)

Paesaggio
solo,pno BONGIOVANI 727 s.p. see
from Cinque Liriche (Seconda
Serie) (C1198)

Paranzelle
solo,pno BONGIOVANI 724 s.p. see
from Cinque Liriche (Seconda
Serie) (C1199)

Presso Una Fontana
solo,pno BONGIOVANI 276 s.p. see
from Cinque Liriche (Seconda
Serie) (C1200)

Primavera
solo,pno FORLIVESI 11740 s.p.
(C1201)

Scherzo
[It] solo,pno BONGIOVANI 729 s.p.
(C1202)
[Eng] solo,pno BONGIOVANI 1638 s.p.
(C1203)

Sia Benedetta
see Cinque Canti

Siete Piu Bella
see Cinque Canti

Snow Is Falling, The *see Fiocca La
Neve

Spiando Ai Vetri
[It] solo,pno BONGIOVANI 1788 s.p.
(C1204)

Stelle Chiare
S/Mez solo,pno BONGIOVANI 573 s.p.
see from Cinque Liriche (Prima
Serie) (C1205)

Stornello
[It] S/T solo,pno BONGIOVANI 408
s.p. (C1206)
[It] Mez/Bar solo,pno BONGIOVANI
409 s.p. (C1207)
[It/Fr] S/T solo,pno BONGIOVANI 856
s.p. (C1208)
"Velvety Red Like" [Eng] Bar/Mez
solo,pno BONGIOVANI 1634 s.p.
(C1209)
"Velvety Red Like" [Eng] T/S solo,
pno BONGIOVANI 857 s.p. (C1210)

Tornan Le Stelle
[It] Bar/Mez solo,pno BONGIOVANI
452 s.p. (C1211)

Tre Ballate Di Calendimaggio *see E'
Tornata Primavera; Offerta
(C1212)

Una Fontana
see Cinque Canti

Vecchia Chitarra
solo,pno FORLIVESI 11741 s.p.
(C1213)

Velvety Red Like *see Stornello

Vo' Cantare
see Cinque Canti

CIMAROSA, DOMENICO (1749-1801)
Dieci Arie Inedite *CC10U
solo,pno ZERBONI 3731 s.p. (C1214)

Ove Fuggo (from I Traci Amanti)
2 soli,2ob,2horn CARISH s.p.
(C1215)

Perdonate, Signor Mio (from Il
Matrimonio Segreto)
[It] S solo,pno RICORDI-ENG 54328
s.p. (C1216)

Resta In Pace Idolo Mio (from Orazi E
Curiazi)
T solo,2ob,2clar,bsn,2horn CARISH
s.p. (C1217)

CIMETIERE see Absil, Jean

CIMITIERE see Poulenc, Francis

CINCO CANCIONES see Carol, M.

CINCO CANCIONES ANTIGUAS *CCU,Carib
(Tarrago) [Span] med solo,gtr UNION
ESP. $1.75 (C1218)

CINCO CANCIONES ARGENTINAS see De
Rogatis, Pascual

CINCO CANCIONES ARGENTINAS AL ESTILO
POPULAR see Lopez-Buchardo, Carlos

CINCO CANCIONES ESPAGNOLES see
Andriessen, Juriaan

CINCO CANCIONES POPULARES ARGENTINAS
see Ginastera, Alberto

CINCO CANCIONES POPULARES ESPANOLAS see
Azpiazu, Jose de

CINCO COPLAS ANDALOUSES see Schveitzer,
M.

CINCO MELODIAS see Hahn, Reynaldo

CINCO MELODIES see Gavito, J.S.

CINCO POEMAS DE ALICE see Camargo
Guarrieri

CINCO SIGLOS DE CANCIONES ESPANOLAS
(1300-1800) *CCU,Span
(Lamana) [Span] med solo,pno UNION
ESP. $4.50 (C1219)

CINDERELLA see Provost, W.

CINQ BALLADES FRANCAIS DE PAUL FORT see
Caplet, Andre

CINQ CHANSONS see Francaix, Jean

CINQ CHANSONS DANS LE STYLE POPULAIRE
see Schule, B.

CINQ CHANSONS DE CROISADE see Le Flem,
Paul

CINQ CHANSONS DE FEMME see Cannon,
(Jack) Phillip

CINQ CHANSONS FLORENTINES see Bozza,
Eugene

CINQ CHANSONS FRANCAISES see Coppola,
Piero

CINQ CHANSONS NICOISES see Bozza,
Eugene

CINQ CHANTS ET UNE VOCALISE see
Constant, Marius

CINQ EPITAPHES see Vellones, Pierre

CINQ MELODIES see Tansman, Alexander

CINQ MELODIES see Absil, Jean

CINQ MELODIES see Barbier, Rene

CINQ MELODIES see Schumann, Robert
(Alexander)

CINQ MELODIES see Veneziani, Vittore

CINQ MELODIES see Ruyneman, Daniel

CINQ MELODIES FRANCAISES see Legley,
Victor

CINQ MELODIES POPULAIRES GRECQUES see
Ravel, Maurice

CINQ MELODIES SUR DES POESIES DE JEAN
LAHOR see Rhene-Baton

CINQ NOELS FRANCAIS see Klerk, Albert
de

CINQ PETITES FILLES see Middeleer, Jean
De

CINQ POEMES CHANTES see DuBois, Pierre
Max

CINQ POEMES CHRETIENS see Decruck, F.

CINQ POEMES DE BAUDELAIRE see Debussy,
Claude

CINQ POEMES DE BAUDELAIRE see Debussy,
Claude

CINQ POEMES DE FRANCOIS VILLON see
Franken, Wim

CINQ POEMES DE P.-J. TOULET see
Ferroud, Pierre-Octave

CINQ POEMES DE PAUL ELUARD see Poulenc,
Francis

CINQ POEMES DE PAUL ELUARD see Poulenc,
Francis

CINQ POEMES DE PHILIPPE MONNIER see
Wissmer, Pierre

CINQ POEMES DE RUBINO see Coppola,
Piero

CINQ POESIES DU GRAND SIECLE see
Berthelot, Rene

CINQ PRIERES see Milhaud, Darius

CINQ QUATRAINS PORTUGAIS see Peyrot

CINQ QUATRAINS VON FR, JAMMES, SERIES I
see Roos, Robert de

CINQ QUATRIANS VON FR. JAMMES, SERIES
II see Roos, Robert de

CINQ ROMANCES see Shostakovich, Dmitri

CINQ SONNETS DE LOUISE LABE see Lenot,
Jacques

CINQUAIN see Jenni, Donald

CINQUANDO CANTI POPOLARI UNGHERESI see
Demeny, Dezso

CINQUANTE CHANSONS CHOISES see
Beranger, Pierre-Jean de

CINQUANTE MELODIES, CHOISIES see
Schumann, Robert (Alexander)

CINQUANTE MELODIES CHOISIES see
Schubert, Franz (Peter)

CINQUE
Del Salon En El Angulo Oscuro
see Tres Liricas Sobre Rimas De
Becquer

El Amor Que Pasa
see Tres Liricas Sobre Rimas De
Becquer

La Jeune Fille Et Le Ramier
solo,pno RICORDI-FR R 1858 s.p.
(C1220)

Las Ropas Descenidas
see Tres Liricas Sobre Rimas De
Becquer

Mattinata Veneziana
[It] solo,pno RICORDI-ARG BA 10725
s.p. (C1221)

Tres Liricas Sobre Rimas De Becquer
[Span] med solo,pno cmplt ed
RICORDI-ARG BA 11108 s.p.
contains: Del Salon En El Angulo
Oscuro; El Amor Que Pasa; Las
Ropas Descenidas (C1222)

CINQUE CANTI see Cimara, Pietro

CINQUE CANTI see Dallapiccola, Luigi

CINQUE CANTI ALL'ANTICA see Respighi,
Ottorino

CINQUE CANTI POPOLARI DELLA LIGURIA see
Cortese, Luigi

CINQUE CANZONI DEI TROVATORI see
Farkas, Ferenc

CINQUE CARMI DI CATULLO see Cattini, U.

CINQUE ELEGIE BIBLICI see Vlad, Roman

CINQUE FAVOLE see Malipiero, Gian
Francesco

CINQUE FRAMMENTI DI SAFFO see
Dallapiccola, Luigi

CINQUE LIRICHE see Respighi, Ottorino

CINQUE LIRICHE see Albanese, Guido

CINQUE LIRICHE see Benvenuti, Giacomo

CINQUE LIRICHE see Gandino, Adolfo

CINQUE LIRICHE see Alderighi, Dante

CINQUE LIRICHE see Pizzetti, Ildebrando

CINQUE LIRICHE DI MONTALE see
Bettinelli, Bruno

CINQUE LIRICHE (PRIMA SERIE) see
Cimara, Pietro

CINQUE LIRICHE (SECONDA SERIE) see
Cimara, Pietro

CINQUE LIRICHE SU POESIE GRECHE see
    Caltabiano, S.

CINQUE MADRIGALI see Bucchi, Valentino

CINQUE MOMENTI MUSICALI see Cortese,
    Luigi

CINQUE NOTTURNI see Davico, Vincenzo

CINQUE POESIE ROMANESCHE see
    Castelnuovo-Tedesco, Mario

CINQUE STROFE DAL GRECO see Prosperi,
    Carlo

CINQUE STROFE DAL GRECO see Prosperi,
    Carlo

CINQUE, VINCENZO
    L'Italia Torna
    [It] solo,pno SONZOGNO 2902 s.p.
                                    (C1223)

CINQUNDQUATRE-VENT BERCEUSES DE TOUS
    LES PEUPLES *CC85U
    (Arma, Paul) [Fr] OUVRIERES s.p.
                                    (C1224)

CINTA DI FIORI see Bellini, Vincenzo

CIRCLE INCOMPLETE, A see Capshaw, Betty

CIRCLE OF THE KEYS, THE see Repper,
    Charles

CIRCUS, THE see Reif, Paul

CIRIBIRIBIN see Pestalozza, Heinrich

CISTE JITRO see Foerster, Josef
    Bohuslav

CITA see Guastavino, Carlos

CITHAR, LAD MIN BON DIG NORE see
    Nielsen, Carl

CITKOWITZ, ISRAEL (1909-   )
    Five Songs *CC5U
    solo,pno BOOSEY $2.00   (C1225)

CITY BIRDS see Weigl, Vally

CITY OF GOLD see Cohron

CITY OF SLEEP see Kernochan, Marshall

CIVIL WAR SONGS *CCU
    (Hitchcock, H. Wiley) DA CAPO s.p.
    contains works by: Clay, Henry;
    Root, George; Emmett, Dan; Gilmore,
    Patrick and others   (C1226)

CLAERE see Sigtenhorst-Meyer, Bernhard
    van den

CLAFLIN, AVERY (1898-   )
    Finale
    A solo,4strings sc AM.COMP.AL.
    $5.50, ipr   (C1227)

    Two Arias (from Uncle Tom's Cabin)
    CC2U
    S solo,pno AM.COMP.AL. $5.50
                                    (C1228)

CLAIR COMME LE JOUR see Daniel-Lesur

CLAIR DE LUNE see Debussy, Claude

CLAIR DE LUNE see Diepenbrock, Alphons

CLAIR DE LUNE see Saint-Saens, Camille

CLAIR DE LUNE see Truillet-Soyer, M.

CLAIR DE LUNE see Voormolen, Alexander
    Nicolas

CLAIR DE LUNE [1] see Debussy, Claude

CLAIR DE LUNE DE NOVEMBRE see Sauguet,
    Henri

CLAIRON see Bourguignon, Francis de

CLAIRS DE LUNE see Fragerolle, G.

CLANG OF THE WOODEN SPOON, THE see
    Molloy, James Lyman

CLARIBEL see Gerschefski, Edwin

CLARK
    Let Us Climb The Hill Together
    solo,pno GENTRY $1.00   (C1229)

    Pious Selinda
    Bar solo,pno MUSICUS $1.25 (C1230)

CLARK, HAROLD
    Come, Asleep
    high solo,pno ELKIN 27.2100.07 s.p.
                                    (C1231)

CLARK, HENRY A.
    Hear My Prayer, O Lord (Psalm 143)
    sac
    low solo,pno (E flat maj) LESLIE
    7056   (C1232)
    high solo,pno (F maj) LESLIE 7057
                                    (C1233)
    Psalm 143 *see Hear My Prayer, O
    Lord

CLARKE, EMILE
    Sincerity
    med solo,pno (E flat maj) CRAMER
                                    (C1234)
    med-high solo,pno (F maj) CRAMER
                                    (C1235)
    high solo,pno (G maj) CRAMER
                                    (C1236)
    low solo,pno (D maj) CRAMER (C1237)
    2 soli,pno (E flat maj) CRAMER
                                    (C1238)
    2 soli,pno (F maj) CRAMER   (C1239)

    Three Little Birds
    solo,pno CRAMER   (C1240)

CLARKE, HENRY LELAND (1907-   )
    Carmina Pacifica
    med solo,pno AM.COMP.AL. $1.38
                                    (C1241)

    Domestic Motto
    med solo,pno AM.COMP.AL. $.27
                                    (C1242)

    Emily Dickinson Canons *CCU
    med solo,vla/vln/vcl AM.COMP.AL.
    $2.20   (C1243)

    Four Elements *CC4U
    S solo,vcl AM.COMP.AL. $2.20
                                    (C1244)
    Four Songs For A Young Lady *CC4U
    high solo,pno AM.COMP.AL. $2.75
                                    (C1245)

    Freedom
    low solo,pno AM.COMP.AL. $.55
                                    (C1246)

    I Died For Beauty
    med solo,pno AM.COMP.AL. $.82
                                    (C1247)

    Lark
    S solo,acap AM.COMP.AL. $.27
                                    (C1248)

    Le Soleil Ni La Mort
    med solo,pno AM.COMP.AL. $.27
                                    (C1249)

    Life In Ghana
    med solo,fl,pno sc AM.COMP.AL.
    $2.75, ipa   (C1250)

    Lord Is My Shepherd, The (Psalm 23)
    sac
    high solo,fl,timp/bvl sc
    AM.COMP.AL. $2.20   (C1251)

    Lullaby For A Reluctant Sleeper
    high solo,pno AM.COMP.AL. $.55
                                    (C1252)

    Mercy, Pity, Peace, And Love
    SA soli,fl,ob,perc sc AM.COMP.AL.
    $2.20, ipa   (C1253)

    Overhead
    high solo,pno AM.COMP.AL. $1.10
                                    (C1254)
    low solo,pno AM.COMP.AL. $1.10
                                    (C1255)

    Psalm 23 *see Lord Is My Shepherd,
    The

    Puget Sound Cinquain
    med solo,inst AM.COMP.AL. $.27
                                    (C1256)

    Quality Of Mercy, The
    SA soli,fl,ob,perc sc AM.COMP.AL.
    $2.20, ipa   (C1257)

    Robin Answers, The
    med solo,pno AM.COMP.AL. $.27
                                    (C1258)

    Rondeau Redouble
    Mez solo,clar,bsn,vcl sc
    AM.COMP.AL. $2.75, ipa   (C1259)
    Bar solo,clar,bsn,vcl sc
    AM.COMP.AL. $2.75, ipa   (C1260)

    Sanctus For St. Cecelia's Day
    S/T solo,pno/org AM.COMP.AL. $2.20
                                    (C1261)

    Soliloquy, The
    med solo,pno AM.COMP.AL. $3.57
                                    (C1262)

    Song To A Young Pianist
    med solo,fl AM.COMP.AL. $1.10
                                    (C1263)

    Spirit Of Delight
    med solo,pno AM.COMP.AL. $2.75
                                    (C1264)

    These Are The Times
    med solo,pno AM.COMP.AL. $1.10
                                    (C1265)

    Thine Own Heart Makes The World
    med solo,pno AM.COMP.AL. $.27
                                    (C1266)

    When Any Mortal
    med solo,pno AM.COMP.AL. $.55
                                    (C1267)

CLARKE, HENRY LELAND (cont'd.)

    William Penn Fruits Of Solitude
    med solo,pno AM.COMP.AL. $5.50
                                    (C1268)

    Winter Is A Cold Thing
    med-high solo,pno AM.COMP.AL. $1.10
                                    (C1269)

    Woman Of Virtue, A
    solo,winds,perc sc AM.COMP.AL. $.55
                                    (C1270)

CLARKE, JEREMIAH (ca. 1673-1707)
    Blest Be Those Sweet Regions *hymn
    [Eng] high solo,pno SCHOTTS 10933
    s.p.   (C1271)

CLARKE, THOMAS (ca. 1700)
    I Will Magnify Thee, O Lord *sac
    med-high solo,pno oct CONCORDIA
    98-1796 $.20   (C1272)

CLARKE, ROBERT CONINGSBY (1879-1934)
    Childrens Hour, The *CCU
    solo,pno CRAMER   (C1273)

CLASSIC ITALIAN SONGS, VOL. I *CCU
    (Glenn; Taylor) [Eng/It] PRESSER
    $3.25 high solo,pno; med solo,pno;
    low solo,pno   (C1274)

CLASSIC ITALIAN SONGS, VOL. II *CCU
    (Glenn; Taylor) [Eng/It] PRESSER
    $3.25 high solo,pno; med solo,pno;
    low solo,pno   (C1275)

CLASSIC ITALIAN SONGS, VOL. III *CCU
    (Glenn; Taylor) [Eng/It] PRESSER
    $3.25 high solo,pno; med solo,pno;
    low solo,pno   (C1276)

CLASSIC SONGS *CCU
    (Taylor) SUMMY high solo,pno $3.95;
    low solo,pno $3.95   (C1277)

CLASSICAL SONGS, VOLUME 5 *CC26L
    [Eng] solo,pno NOVELLO 17.0238.06
    s.p. contains works by: Brahms;
    Handel; Schubert; Purcell and
    others   (C1278)

CLASSICAL SPANISH SONGS see Obrados,
    Fernando

CLASSICS OF GERMAN SONG, VOL. I *CC45U
    $7.50 high solo,pno PETERS 4545A; med
    solo,pno PETERS 4578A; low solo,pno
    PETERS 4575A contains works by:
    Albert; Bach, J.S.; Krieger;
    Beethoven and others   (C1279)

CLASSICS OF GERMAN SONG, VOL. II
    *CC55U
    $7.50 high solo,pno PETERS 4545B; med
    solo,pno PETERS 4578B; low solo,pno
    PETERS 4575B contains works by:
    Brahms; Cornelius; Franz; Jensen;
    Liszt; Mendelssohn and others
                                    (C1280)

CLAUDE RHEA'S FAVORITE GOSPEL SOLOS
    *CCU
    solo,pno BROADMAN 4525-03 $1.50
                                    (C1281)

CLAUSETTI, P.
    E Nel Mio Sogno
    [It] solo,pno BONGIOVANI 1033 s.p.
                                    (C1282)

    La Canzone Di Pierrot
    [It] solo,pno BONGIOVANI 1032 s.p.
                                    (C1283)

    La Nonna Fila
    [It] solo,pno BONGIOVANI 1031 s.p.
                                    (C1284)

    Nei Meriggi
    [It] solo,pno BONGIOVANI 1030 s.p.
                                    (C1285)

CLAVELITOS see Valverde, Joaquin

CLAY, FREDERIC (1838-1889)
    I'll Sing Thee Songs Of Araby
    low solo,pno (E flat maj) ALLANS
    s.p.   (C1286)
    med solo,pno (F maj) ALLANS s.p.
                                    (C1287)
    high solo,pno (G maj) ALLANS s.p.
                                    (C1288)
    She Wandered Down The Mountain Side
    solo,pno (C maj) BOOSEY $1.50
                                    (C1289)

CLAYTON, NORMAN
    For All My Sin *sac
    solo,pno WORD S-137   (C1290)

    If We Could See Beyond Today *sac
    solo,pno WORD S-157   (C1291)

    Long Years Ago In Bethlehem *sac
    solo,pno WORD S-162   (C1292)

    New Songs From Norman Clayton *sac,
    CC9L
    solo,pno WORD 37518 $1.95   (C1293)

CLAYTON WEDDING MELODIES, VOL. 1 *sac,
    CC10UL,Marriage
    (Clayton, Norman) solo,org WORD 32018
    $2.00   (C1294)

CLAYTON WEDDING MELODIES, VOL.2 *sac,
CCU,Marriage
  solo,org WORD 32019 $2.00   (C1295)

CLAYTON'S FAVORITES, VOL. 1 *sac,CCUL,
gospel
  (Clayton, Norman) solo,pno WORD 10019
  $1.00   (C1296)

CLAYTON'S SOLOS AND DUETS, VOL. 2
  *sac,CC96U
  1-2 soli,pno WORD 10023 $1.00
  contains works by: Peterson, John
  and others   (C1297)

CLEANSING FIRES see Gabriel, Virginia

CLEAR MIDNIGHT, A
  see Three Poems Of Walt Whitman

CLEMATIS see Schouwman, Hans

CLEMENTI, ALDO (1925-   )
  Due Poesie *CC2U
    S solo,pno ZERBONI 7244 s.p.
                                   (C1298)
  Silben
    female solo,4inst ZERBONI 6772
    rental   (C1299)

CLEMENTI, F.
  Avemmaria
    [It] solo,pno BONGIOVANI 897 s.p.
                                   (C1300)
  Triste Primavera
    [It] solo,pno BONGIOVANI 898 s.p.
                                   (C1301)

CLEMENTS, JOHN (1910-   )
  Crossing The Bar
    solo,pno CRAMER   (C1302)

  Early One Morning
    solo,pno CRAMER   (C1303)

  Gibberish
    solo,pno CRAMER   (C1304)

CLEOPATRA'S DREAM see Mollicone, Henry

CLEOPATRA'S FAREWELL see Krebs, S.

CLEOPATRE see Fragerolle, G.

CLEOPATRE I see Mulder, Ernest W.

CLEOPATRE II see Mulder, Ernest W.

CLERAMBAULT, LOUIS-NICOLAS (1676-1749)
  La Muse De L'Opera
    see Two Cantatas For Soprano And
    Instruments

  La Musette *cant
    "O Cruel And Inimical Absence!" S
    solo,strings,cont sc GERIG AV 128
    s.p.   (C1305)

  Le Fameux Chantre De La Thrace (from
    Orphee)
    solo,pno/inst DURAND s.p.   (C1306)

  L'ile De Delos
    see Two Cantatas For Soprano And
    Instruments

  O Cruel And Inimical Absence! *see
    La Musette

  O Gloire Qui M'alarme (from Jupiter
    Et Europe)
    Mez solo,pno/inst DURAND s.p.
                                   (C1307)

  Orphee *cant
    [Fr/Eng] high solo,fl,vln,kbd,cont
    cmplt ed FABER F0479 $14.00
                                   (C1308)
  Pluton Surpris D'entendre (from
    Orphee)
    solo,pno/inst DURAND s.p.   (C1309)

  Two Cantatas For Soprano And
    Instruments *cant
    (Foster, Donald H.) A-R ED s.p.
    contains: La Muse De L'Opera (S
    solo,fl,ob,bsn,trp,timp,vln,
    cont); L'ile De Delos (S solo,
    fl,vln,cont)   (C1310)

CLERCQ, R. DE
  Ach, De Groote Stad
    see Liederen, Vol. 3

  Adeste
    see Liederen, Vol. 2

  Avondlied
    see Liederen, Vol. 3

  Best Geborgen
    see Liederen, Vol. 5

  De Leeuwerik
    see Liederen, Vol. 2

CLERCQ, R. DE (cont'd.)
  De Meidoorn
    see Liederen, Vol. 5

  De Mulder
    see Liederen, Vol. 3

  De Oogst
    see Liederen, Vol. 6

  De Regenboog
    see Liederen, Vol. 7

  De Vogel Die Naar 'T Zuiden Trekt
    see Liederen, Vol. 4

  De Wiedsters
    see Liederen, Vol. 2

  De Zwingel
    see Liederen, Vol. 1

  Diep In Het Koren
    see Liederen, Vol. 2

  Duitsche Hoornen
    see Liederen, Vol. 6

  Gelijk De Boom
    see Liederen, Vol. 7

  Herfstlied
    see Liederen, Vol. 6

  Koninkventjes
    see Liederen, Vol. 5

  Kus Mijn Hart Op Mijnen Mond
    see Liederen, Vol. 4

  Lapper Krispijn
    see Liederen, Vol. 7

  Liederen, Vol. 1
    solo,pno ALSBACH s.p.
    contains: De Zwingel; Naar Geen
    Ander; Op Het Stuk; Van Den
    Zanger; Vlaamse Kermis; Zagers
                                   (C1311)
  Liederen, Vol. 2
    solo,pno ALSBACH s.p.
    contains: Adeste; De Leeuwerik;
    De Wiedsters; Diep In Het
    Koren; Oude Koppel; Ring-Ring
                                   (C1312)
  Liederen, Vol. 3
    solo,pno ALSBACH s.p.
    contains: Ach, De Groote Stad;
    Avondlied; De Mulder; Moederke
    Alleen; Molenaars Dochterke;
    Van Den Boever   (C1313)

  Liederen, Vol. 4
    solo,pno ALSBACH s.p.
    contains: De Vogel Die Naar 'T
    Zuiden Trekt; Kus Mijn Hart Op
    Mijnen Mond; Met Een Zoet, Zoet
    Liedje; Scheiden Beiden;
    Sneeuwvlokjes; Zoet Sterreken
                                   (C1314)
  Liederen, Vol. 5
    solo,pno ALSBACH s.p.
    contains: Best Geborgen; De
    Meidoorn; Koninkventjes; Rood
    Pioeneke; Treed In Mijn Huis;
    Zijt Gij Dood De Beste Borg
                                   (C1315)
  Liederen, Vol. 6
    solo,pno ALSBACH s.p.
    contains: De Oogst; Duitsche
    Hoornen; Herfstlied; Nachtlied;
    Plaveiers; Wanneer Gedenkt Ge
    Mijn   (C1316)

  Liederen, Vol. 7
    solo,pno ALSBACH s.p.
    contains: De Regenboog; Gelijk De
    Boom; Lapper Krispijn; Mijn
    Kleen Dochterken;
    Regendroppels; Scharesliep
                                   (C1317)
  Met Een Zoet, Zoet Liedje
    see Liederen, Vol. 4

  Mijn Kleen Dochterken
    see Liederen, Vol. 7

  Moederke Alleen
    see Liederen, Vol. 3

  Molenaars Dochterke
    see Liederen, Vol. 3

  Naar Geen Ander
    see Liederen, Vol. 1

  Nachtlied
    see Liederen, Vol. 6

  Op Het Stuk
    see Liederen, Vol. 1

  Oude Koppel
    see Liederen, Vol. 2

CLERCQ, R. DE (cont'd.)
  Plaveiers
    see Liederen, Vol. 6

  Regendroppels
    see Liederen, Vol. 7

  Ring-Ring
    see Liederen, Vol. 2

  Rood Pioeneke
    see Liederen, Vol. 5

  Scharesliep
    see Liederen, Vol. 7

  Scheiden Beiden
    see Liederen, Vol. 4

  Sneeuwvlokjes
    see Liederen, Vol. 4

  Treed In Mijn Huis
    see Liederen, Vol. 5

  Van Den Boever
    see Liederen, Vol. 3

  Van Den Zanger
    see Liederen, Vol. 1

  Vlaamse Kermis
    see Liederen, Vol. 1

  Wanneer Gedenkt Ge Mijn
    see Liederen, Vol. 6

  Zagers
    see Liederen, Vol. 1

  Zijt Gij Dood De Beste Borg
    see Liederen, Vol. 5

  Zoet Sterreken
    see Liederen, Vol. 4

CLERGUE, J.
  Berceuse
    see Deux Melodies

  Deux Melodies
    solo,pno/inst LEDUC s.p.
    contains: Berceuse; Fete Foraine
                                   (C1318)
  Fete Foraine
    see Deux Melodies

CLERICE, J.
  Le Mistral
    solo,pno ENOCH s.p.   (C1319)
    solo,acap solo pt ENOCH s.p.
                                   (C1320)
  Monsieur Boude
    solo,pno ENOCH s.p.   (C1321)
    solo,acap solo pt ENOCH s.p.
                                   (C1322)
  Reviens Nysa
    solo,pno ENOCH s.p.   (C1323)

  Serenade
    solo,pno ENOCH s.p.   (C1324)

CLIBBORN
  Down From His Glory *sac
    solo,pno STAMPS 7259-SN $1.00
                                   (C1325)
  Down From His Glory *see Booth

CLICK GO THE SHEARS *Austral
  solo,pno ALLANS s.p.   (C1326)

CLICK O' THE LATCH see Hier, Ethel
  Glenn

CLIFTON, HARRY
  As Welcome As The Flowers In May
    solo,pno CRAMER   (C1327)

CLIMAX ALBUM NO. 8 see Dalmaine, Cyril
  C.

CLIMB EV'RY MOUNTAIN - THE
  INSPIRATIONAL SONGBOOK *sac,
  CC147UL,Xmas/Gen
  (Tillett, Beverly) solo,pno CHAPPELL
  0083162-123 $8.95   (C1328)

CLIQUETON, CLIQUETIS see Verhaar, Ary

CLOCHARD see Pelemans, Willem

CLOCHARDS see Pelemans, Willem

CLOCHE see Leeuw, Ton de

CLOCHE D'AUBE see Caplet, Andre

CLOCHE DU SOIR see Honegger, Arthur

CLOCHE ET TAMBOUR see Godard, Benjamin
  Louis Paul

CLOCHES D'ARVOR see Balay, G.

CLOCHES DE PAQUES see Renie

CLOCHES DU SOIR see Bloch, Augustyn

CLOCK, THE see Gerschefski, Edwin

CLOCK, THE see Hilliam, B.C.

CLOCK SHOP, THE see Haufrecht, Herbert

CLODAGH see Franco, Johan

CLOISTERS, THE see Corigliano, John

CLOKEY, JOSEPH WADDELL (1890-1960)
Catbird, The
    high solo,pno BELWIN $1.50 (C1329)

God Is In Everything *sac
    high solo,pno BELWIN $1.50 (C1330)
    low solo,pno BELWIN $1.50 (C1331)

No Lullaby Need Mary Sing *sac,Xmas
    high solo,pno BELWIN $1.50 (C1332)
    low solo,pno BELWIN $1.50 (C1333)

Set Me As A Seal *sac,Marriage
    med solo,pno BELWIN $1.50 (C1334)

Storke, The *sac,Xmas
    med solo,pno BELWIN $1.50 (C1335)

CLORI, TIRSI E FILENO see Handel,
    George Frideric

CLORINDA see Morgan, Orlando

CLOS TA PAUPIERE see Fourdrain, Felix

CLOS TA PAUPIERE see Schumann, Robert
    (Alexander)

CLOSE EVERY DOOR see Webber, Andrew
    Lloyd

CLOSE THINE EYES see Plumstead, Mary

CLOSE TO MY HEART see Guastavino,
    Carlos, Apegado A Mi

CLOSER see Armando, J., Mas Cerca

CLOSER THAN A BROTHER *sac
    (Carmichael, Ralph) solo,pno WORD
    S-499 (C1336)

CLOSER TO JESUS see Fox, Baynard

CLOSER TO THEE see Steele

CLOSING DUET see Strauss, Richard

CLOTHS OF HEAVEN see Dunhill, Thomas
    Frederick

CLOTILDE see Binet, Jean

CLOTILDE see Caby, R.

CLOTILDE see Honegger, Arthur

CLOTILDE see Leguerney, Jacques

CLOUD-SHADOWS see Rogers, James
    Hotchkiss

CLOUDBERRY FLOWER, THE see Kilpinen,
    Yrio, Hillankukka

CLOUDS see Charles, Ernest

CLOUGH-LEIGHTER, HENRY (1874-1956)
O Perfect Love *sac,Marriage
    (Barnaby) high solo,pno PRESSER
    $.95 (C1337)
    (Barnaby) med solo,pno PRESSER $.95
    (C1338)

CLOWN see Ketting, Otto

CLOWNERIES see Arrieu, Claude

CLUTSAM, GEORGE H. (1866-1951)
I Dreamt Of A King's Fair Daughter
    low solo,pno (D min) ASHDOWN
    (C1339)
    high solo,pno (F min) ASHDOWN
    (C1340)

I Know Of Two Bright Eyes
    low solo,orch (E flat maj) ASHDOWN
    s.p., ipr (C1341)
    med-low solo,orch (F maj) ASHDOWN
    s.p., ipr (C1342)
    med solo,orch (G flat maj) ASHDOWN
    s.p., ipr (C1343)
    med solo,orch (G maj) ASHDOWN s.p.,
    ipr (C1344)
    med-high solo,orch (A flat maj)
    ASHDOWN s.p., ipr (C1345)
    high solo,orch (A maj) ASHDOWN
    s.p., ipr (C1346)

If I Were A Lark
    low solo,pno (C maj) ASHDOWN
    (C1347)
    med solo,pno (E flat maj) ASHDOWN
    (C1348)

CLUTSAM, GEORGE H. (cont'd.)

high solo,pno (F maj) ASHDOWN
    (C1349)
Min Kruslockiga Baby *see My Curly
    Headed Baby

My Curly Headed Babby
    low solo,orch (C maj) ASHDOWN s.p.,
    ipr (C1350)
    med solo,orch (D maj) ASHDOWN s.p.,
    ipr (C1351)
    med-high solo,orch (E maj) ASHDOWN
    s.p., ipr (C1352)
    high solo,orch (F maj) ASHDOWN
    s.p., ipr (C1353)

My Curly Headed Baby
    high solo&low solo,pno ASHDOWN s.p.
    (C1354)
    "Min Kruslockiga Baby" solo,pno,opt
    gtr GEHRMANS s.p. (C1355)

CMARANICE PO NEBI see Tausinger, Jan

CO VECER ZPIVA see Foerster, Josef
    Bohuslav

COBBLERS' SONG see Norton

COCARDES see Poulenc, Francis

COCCHI, GIACHIMO (1720-ca. 1773)
Favorite Air In The Pastoral Of
    Daphnis And Amaryllis, The
    solo,cont HEUWEKE. 110 s.p. (C1356)

COCHEUX, RENE
Chantez Petits Enfants *CC10L
    solo,pno DURAND s.p. (C1357)

COCK-A-DOODLE-DOO! see Kapp, Paul

COCK ROBIN see Boatwright, Howard

COCORICO see Lachaume, A.

COELESTIS DUM SPIRAT AURA see Handel,
    George Frideric

COENEN, WILLEM (1837-1918)
Come Unto Me *sac
    med solo,pno NOVELLO 17.0033.02
    s.p. (C1358)
    med-low solo,pno (D maj) SCHIRM.G
    $.60 (C1359)
    low solo,pno NOVELLO 17.0034.00
    s.p. (C1360)
    high solo,pno (F maj) SCHIRM.G $.60
    (C1361)

COEUR DE MOUSME see Cuvillier, Charles

COEUR EN PERIL see Roussel, Albert

COEURS A PRENDRE see Bernard, R.

COFFEE CANTATA see Bach, Johann
    Sebastian, Schweigt Stille,
    Plaudert Nicht

COHAN, GEORGE MICHAEL (1878-1942)
So Long Mary
    med solo,pno (D maj) WILLIS $.60
    (C1362)

COHEN, M.J.
Drie Liederen *Op.14, CC3U
    solo,pno BROEKMANS 231 s.p. (C1363)

Twee Liederen *Op.12, CC2U
    solo,pno BROEKMANS 146 s.p. (C1364)

Twee Liederen *Op.13, CC2U
    solo,pno BROEKMANS 147 s.p. (C1365)

COHNREICH, L.
I Thought Of You
    low solo,pno (B flat maj) LEONARD-
    ENG (C1366)
    med solo,pno (C maj) LEONARD-ENG
    (C1367)
    high solo,pno (D maj) LEONARD-ENG
    (C1368)

COHRON
City Of Gold *sac
    solo,pno BENSON S5268-S $1.00 (C1369)

COL SANGUE SOL CANCELLASI see Verdi,
    Giuseppe

COLACO OSORIO-SWAAB, REINE (1889-   )
Avond
    A solo,pno DONEMUS s.p. (C1370)

Bloempjes' Ontwaken
    S solo,pno DONEMUS s.p. (C1371)

Das Roseninnere
    Mez solo,pno DONEMUS s.p. (C1372)

De Opwekking Van Lazarus *sac,Bibl
    narrator,pno DONEMUS s.p. (C1373)

De Tocht Door De Hemelen
    narrator,pno DONEMUS s.p. (C1374)

COLACO OSORIO-SWAAB, REINE (cont'd.)

Dorpsdans
    A/Mez solo,pno DONEMUS s.p. (C1375)

Ezechiel 37 *sac,Bibl
    narrator,harp DONEMUS s.p. (C1376)

Fetes Galantes
    low solo,pno DONEMUS s.p. (C1377)

Genezing Van Den Blinde *sac,Bibl
    narrator,3fl,2ob,3clar,2bsn,2horn,
    2trp,2trom,perc,cel,harp,strings
    DONEMUS s.p. (C1378)
    narrator,2fl,2ob,2clar,bsn,horn,
    timp,perc,cel,strings DONEMUS
    s.p. (C1379)

Jesaja 40 *sac,Bibl
    narrator,pno DONEMUS s.p. (C1380)

Jesaja 60 *Bibl
    narrator,pno DONEMUS s.p. (C1381)

Johannes 10 *sac,Bibl
    narrator,pno DONEMUS s.p. (C1382)

Laat De Luiken Gesloten Zijn
    narrator,pno DONEMUS s.p. (C1383)

Mein Volk
    narrator,harp/pno DONEMUS s.p.
    (C1384)

Sange Eines Fahrenden Spielmanns
    med solo,pno DONEMUS s.p. (C1385)

Twee Duetten Op Tekst Uit "Het
    Koningsgraf"
    SA soli,pno DONEMUS s.p. (C1386)

Zij Komt
    S solo,pno DONEMUS s.p. (C1387)

COLAS, H.
En Remuant Des Vieux Papiers
    solo,pno OUVRIERES s.p. (C1388)

COLBY see Passani, Emile

COLDING-JORGENSEN, HENRIK
Enfance IV
    "Je Suis Le Saint En Priere" A
    solo,pno voc sc FOG III, 218 s.p.
    (C1389)

Je Suis Le Saint En Priere *see
    Enfance IV

Pa Din Taerskel
    A solo,fl,pic,2ob,English horn,
    3clar,3bsn,2horn,trp,2trom,tuba,
    harp,2perc,strings sc FOG
    III, 233 s.p. (C1390)

COLD'S THE WIND see Shaw, Geoffrey
    [Turton]

COLE
Rock Of Ages
    4 soli,pno (F maj) CENTURY 92
    (C1391)

Something I Can Feel *sac
    solo,pno BENSON S7557-S $1.00
    (C1392)

Ten Thousand Years *sac
    solo,pno BENSON S7691-S $1.00
    (C1393)

COLE, ELMER
Old Time Way, The *sac
    solo,pno WORD S-454 (C1394)

Something I Can Feel *sac
    solo,pno WORD S-451 (C1395)

COLECCION DE CANCIONES INFANTILES see
    Garcia Abril, A.

COLECCION DE CANCIONES INFANTILES see
    Abril, A.G.

COLECCION DE CANTOS Y BAILES POPULARES
    ESPANOLES, VOL. I *CC22U,Span
    (Romero) med solo,pno UNION ESP.
    $3.00 (C1396)

COLECCION DE CANTOS Y BAILES POPULARES
    ESPANOLES, VOL. II *CC22U,Span
    (Romero) med solo,pno UNION ESP.
    $4.00 (C1397)

COLECHIN
Forest Fire
    solo,pno ALLANS s.p. (C1398)

COLECTED WORKS see Liszt, Franz

COLEMAN, HENRY
O Little One Sleep
    solo,pno CRAMER (C1399)

COLEMAN, JACK
Forth He Came *sac
    solo,pno WORD S-259 (C1400)

COLEMAN, JACK (cont'd.)

Jesus Never Forgets *sac
solo,pno WORD S-505   (C1401)

Your Tender Love
see THERE'S GOING TO BE A WEDDING

COLERIDGE-TAYLOR, SAMUEL (1875-1912)
Birthday, A
high solo,pno (B flat maj) CRAMER
*(C1402)
low solo,pno (A flat maj) CRAMER
(C1403)
Fall On Me Like A Silent Dew
2 soli,pno ROBERTON 71376 s.p.
(C1404)
Lovely Little Dream
low solo,pno (A maj) CRAMER $.95
(C1405)
med solo,pno (D maj) CRAMER $.95
(C1406)
high solo,pno (G maj) CRAMER $.95
(C1407)
Oh, The Summer
2 soli,pno ROBERTON 71308 s.p.
(C1408)
Willow Song, The (from Othello)
low solo,pno (E min) CRAMER $.95
(C1409)
med solo,pno (F min) CRAMER $.95
(C1410)
high solo,pno (G min) CRAMER $1.00
(C1411)

COLES, JACK
My Design, For A Dream
solo,pno CRAMER   (C1412)

COLETTE see Chaminade, Cecile

COLIAS, G.
Histoire D'un Tres Grand Et D'une
Toute Petite
solo,pno ENOCH s.p.   (C1413)
solo,acap solo pt ENOCH s.p.
(C1414)
Histoire D'une Jupe Amarante Et D'un
Pantalon De Drap Gris
solo,pno ENOCH s.p.   (C1415)
solo,acap solo pt ENOCH s.p.
(C1416)

COLINDES *CC16U
solo,pno cloth OISEAU s.p.   (C1417)

COLINS CATTLE see Lawson, Malcolm

COLIN'S SUCCESS see Defesch, William

COLIS POSTAL see Delmet, Paul

COLLAGE see Avni, Tzvi

COLLAN, KARL (1828-1871)
Du Ar Min Ro
high solo,pno GEHRMANS 156 s.p.
(C1418)
low solo,pno GEHRMANS 156 s.p.
(C1419)
solo,pno LUNDQUIST s.p.   (C1420)

Fafang Onskan
high solo,pno GEHRMANS 157 s.p.
(C1421)
low solo,pno GEHRMANS 556 s.p.
(C1422)
solo,pno LUNDQUIST s.p.   (C1423)

Pa Roines Strand
solo,pno GEHRMANS 180 s.p. (C1424)
solo,pno LUNDQUIST s.p.   (C1425)

Rose-Marie
solo,pno GEHRMANS 158 s.p. (C1426)
solo,pno LUNDQUIST s.p.   (C1427)

Sylvian Joululaulu *Xmas
(Marvia) "Sylvias Julvisa" solo,pno
FAZER F 3447 s.p.   (C1428)

Sylvias Julvisa *see Sylvian
Joululaulu

Torpflickan
solo,pno LUNDQUIST s.p.   (C1429)

COLLARES DE PERLAS see Espoile, Raoul
H.

COLLECCION DE TONADILLAS see Granados,
Enrique

COLLECTED EDITION see Mendelssohn-
Bartholdy, Felix

COLLECTED SONGS see Bernstein, Leonard

COLLECTED SONGS see Dan, Ikuma

COLLECTED SONGS 1950-1954 see Taylor,
Clifford

COLLECTED SONGS (THROUGH 1955) see
Barber, Samuel

COLLECTED SONGS, VOL. 2 see Grieg,
Edvard Hagerup

COLLECTED SONGS, VOL. 5 see Grieg,
Edvard Hagerup

COLLECTED SONGS, VOL. 6 see Grieg,
Edvard Hagerup

COLLECTED SONGS, VOL. 7 see Grieg,
Edvard Hagerup

COLLECTED SONGS, VOL. 9 see Grieg,
Edvard Hagerup

COLLECTED SONGS, VOL. 10 see Grieg,
Edvard Hagerup

COLLECTED WORKS see Lassus, Roland de
(Orlandus)

COLLECTED WORKS see Schein, Johann
Hermann

COLLECTED WORKS see Schutz, Heinrich

COLLECTED WORKS see Sweelinck, Jan
Pieterszoon

COLLECTED WORKS OF WILLIAM BYRD, VOL.
15: CONSORT SONGS see Byrd, William

COLLECTED WORKS, VOL. IV see
Dolukhanyan, A.

COLLECTION OF FESTIVE HYMNS *CCU
(Knight, V.) solo,pno LEONARD-ENG
(C1430)
COLLECTION OF SACRED SONGS see
Rodeheaver

COLLECTION OF SONGS, A see Ishiketa, M.

COLLECTION OF SONGS, A see Bekku, S.

COLLECTION OF SONGS, VOL. 1: LIGHT
SOPRANO see Handel, George Frideric

COLLECTION OF SONGS, VOL. 2: DRAMATIC
SOPRANO see Handel, George Frideric

COLLECTION OF SONGS, VOL. 3: MEZZO-
SOPRANO see Handel, George Frideric

COLLECTION OF SONGS, VOL. 4: CONTRALTO
see Handel, George Frideric

COLLECTION OF SONGS, VOL. 5: TENOR see
Handel, George Frideric

COLLECTION OF SONGS, VOL. 6: BARITONE
see Handel, George Frideric

COLLECTION OF SONGS, VOL. 7: BASS see
Handel, George Frideric

COLLEGIAN'S PRAYER *sac
(Carmichael, Ralph) solo,pno WORD
S-109   (C1431)

COLLIN, L.
Ce Que Dit La Chanson
solo,pno ENOCH s.p.   (C1432)
solo,acap solo pt ENOCH s.p.
(C1433)
Les Bains De Mer
solo,pno ENOCH s.p.   (C1434)
solo,acap solo pt ENOCH s.p.
(C1435)

COLLINSON
Blackbird
solo,pno ALLANS s.p.   (C1436)

COLLOQUE see Mercure, Pierre

COLLOQUE SENTIMENTAL see Cuvillier,
Charles

COLLOQUE SENTIMENTAL see Debussy,
Claude

COLLOQUE SENTIMENTAL see Orland, Henry

COLLOQUE SENTIMENTAL see Panizza,
Ettore

COLLOQUY see Bush, Geoffrey

COLOMB, A.
Chanson Rouge
(Montoya) solo,acap solo pt ENOCH
s.p.   (C1437)
(Montoya, G.) solo,pno ENOCH s.p.
(C1438)
(Montoya, G.) solo,acap ENOCH s.p.
(C1439)
Le Secret
(Montoya) solo,acap solo pt ENOCH
s.p.   (C1440)
(Montoya, G.) solo,pno ENOCH s.p.
(C1441)
(Montoya, G.) solo,acap ENOCH s.p.
(C1442)
Mariage D'ames
(Montoya) solo,acap solo pt ENOCH
s.p.   (C1443)

COLOMB, A. (cont'd.)

(Montoya, G.) solo,pno ENOCH s.p.
(C1444)
(Montoya, G.) solo,acap ENOCH s.p.
(C1445)
COLOMBETTA see Buzzi-Peccia, Arturo

COLONNA, LUIGI
Quattro Liriche Per I Versi Di
Leopardi, Shakespeare, Goethe E
Malarme *CC4U
[It] solo,pno SANTIS 807 s.p.
(C1446)
COLOR HIM LOVE *sac,CCUL
(McKay, John) solo,kbd SINGSPIR $1.00
(C1447)

COLORATURA ALBUM *CC22U
coloratura sop,pno PETERS 2074 $7.50
with original and German texts;
contains works by: Auber; Arditi;
Bellini; Donizetti; Marchesi;
Mozart and others   (C1448)

COLORATURA ARIAS see Mozart, Wolfgang
Amadeus

COLORI DEL TEMPO see Petrassi, Goffredo

COLOURS see Prosev, Toma, Boje

COLUMBIA, THE GEM OF THE OCEAN see Shaw

COLUMBINE see Harrhy, Edith

COLUMBINES see Hazelhurst, Cecil

COLUMNAS Y CIRCULOS see Campos-Parsi,
Hector

COLVILLE, VAL
Home On The Range
solo,pno (G maj) LEONARD-ENG
(C1449)
COM' E GENTIL see Donizetti, Gaetano

COMBAT DEL SOMNI see Mompou, Federico

COMBATTIMENTO DI TANCREDI E CLORINDA
see Monteverdi, Claudio

COMBIEN DE FOIS, LAS DE SOUFFRIR see
Wagner, Richard

COME AGAIN, SWEET LOVE see Dowland,
John

COME ALL YE FAIR AND TENDER LADIES
see Schirmer's American Folk-Song
Series, Set XXI (American-English
Folk-Songs From The Southern
Appalachian Mountains)

COME ALONG AND DANCE see Pennington,
Chester

COME ALONG TO SOMERSET see Ashworth-
Hope, H.

COME ALONG WITH ME see Skillings, Otis

COME AND SEE ME *sac
solo,pno STAMPS 7240 $1.00   (C1450)

COME AND SEE THE MAN see Lister, Mosie

COME AND TRIP IT see Carmichael, Mary
Grant

COME AND TRIP IT see Handel, George
Frideric

COME AS YOU ARE see Harris, Ron

COME, ASLEEP see Clark, Harold

COME AWAY, COME AWAY DEATH see
Castelnuovo-Tedesco, Mario

COME AWAY, COME AWAY, DEATH see Davies,
Henry Walford

COME AWAY, COME AWAY, DEATH see Finzi,
Gerald

COME AWAY, COME AWAY DEATH see Russell,
W.

COME AWAY, COME SWEET LOVE see
Mollicone, Henry

COME AWAY DEATH see Cook, John

COME AWAY, DEATH see Dale, Benjamin J.

COME AWAY DEATH see Holford, Franz

COME AWAY, DEATH see Montgomery, Bruce

COME BACK TO SORRENTO see De Curtis

COME, BELOVED see Handel, George
Frideric, Care Selve

COME, CELEBRATE THIS MORN see Bach, Johann Sebastian

COME, CHRISTIANS, GREET THIS DAY see Bach, Johann Sebastian

COME, COME, MY VOICE see Bach, Johann Sebastian, Bist Du Bei Mir

COME DAL CIEL PRECIPITA see Verdi, Giuseppe

COME DOWN TO KEW see Deis, Carl

COME DUE TIZZI ACCESI see Cilea, Francesco

COME, EVERY MAN NOW GIVE HIS TOAST see Dibdin, Charles

COME GENTLE DARK see Niles, John Jacob

COME, GENTLE NIGHT see Franck, Cesar, O Fraiche Nuit

COME HITHER, YOU THAT LOVE see Russell, Welford

COME, HOLY SPIRIT see Gaither

COME, HOLY SPIRIT see Peterson, John W.

COME IN HERE CHILD see Bedford, David

COME INTO THE ARK see Jensen, Gordon

COME INTO THE GARDEN MAUD see Balfe, Michael William

COME LET US SING UNTO THE LORD see Lekberg, Sven

COME LET'S BE MERRY
  (Wilson, H.L.) solo,pno (B flat maj) BOOSEY $1.50   (C1451)

COME, LITTLE LEAVES see Weigl, Vally

COME LIVE WITH ME see Handel, George Frideric

COME LIVE WITH ME AND BE MY LOVE see Russell, Welford

COME, LOVE WITH ME see Carnevali, Vito

COME LOVELY SLEEP see Smith, Herbert Arnold

COME MY BELOVED see Overby, Rolf Peter

COME MY DEAR ONE see Steffani, Agostino, Vieni O Cara, Amata Sposa

COME MY SWEET PRETTY MAID see Harding, Phyllis

COME, O BLESSED OF MY FATHER see Bender, Jan

COME, O COME, MY LIFE'S DELIGHT see Gurney, Ivor

COME O'ER THE STREAM, CHARLIE *folk, Scot
  solo,pno (E flat maj/F maj) PATERSON FS21 s.p.   (C1452)

COME, OH WAWE see Kilpinen, Yrio, Kirkkorannassa

COME ON DOWN see Hayford

COME ON, LET'S PRAISE HIM! see Wolfe, Lanny

COME OUT, MR. SUNSHINE see Bliss, Paul

COME PER ME SERENO see Bellini, Vincenzo

COME RAGGIO DI SOL see Caldara, Antonio

COME RAGGIO DI SOL see Diepenbrock, Alphons

COME RUGIADA AL CESPITE see Verdi, Giuseppe

COME SING TO ME see Thompson, Jack

COME SLEEP see Glanville-Hicks, Peggy

COME, SOOTHING DEATH see Bach, Johann Sebastian

COME, SPIRIT OF THE LIVING GOD see Speaks, Oley

COME, SWEET MORNING
  (Lehmann, Amelia) low solo,pno (D maj) ASHDOWN $1.50   (C1453)
  (Lehmann, Amelia) med solo,pno (E maj) ASHDOWN $1.50   (C1454)
  (Lehmann, Amelia) high solo,pno (G maj) ASHDOWN $1.50   (C1455)

COME, TAKE THE WATER OF LIFE see Fischer, Irwin

COME THOU LONG EXPECTED JESUS see Hill, Eugene

"COME, THOU REDEEMER OF THE EARTH" see Willan, Healey

COME TO ME see Beethoven, Ludwig van

COME TO ME IN MY DREAMS see Bury, Winifred

COME TO ME SOOTHING SLEEP see Handel, George Frideric, Vieni O Figlio

COME TO THE FAIR see Martin, Easthope

COME TO THE REALM OF ROSES AND WINE see Rimsky-Korsakov, Nikolai, Au Royaume Du Vin Et Des Roses

COME TO THE STABLE WITH JESUS see O'Hara, Geoffrey

COME, TOUCH MY HAND see Rottura, Joseph James

COME UN BEL DI DI MAGGIO see Giordano, Umberto

COME UN ROMITO FIOR see Thomas, Ambroise

COME UNTO HIM see Dunn, James Philip

COME UNTO HIM see Handel, George Frideric

COME UNTO ME see Chadwick, George Whitefield

COME UNTO ME see Coenen, Willem

COME UNTO ME see Fischer, Irwin

COME UNTO ME see Giordani, Giuseppe, Caro Mio Ben

COME UNTO ME see King

COME UNTO ME AND REST see Pull, Edwin

COME UNTO THESE YELLOW SANDS see Castelnuovo-Tedesco, Mario

COME UNTO THESE YELLOW SANDS see LaForge, Frank

COME WITH US, O BLESSED JESUS see Elmore, Robert [Hall]

COME WITH YOUR HEARTACHE see Harper

COME, YE BLESSED see Scott, John Prindle

COME, YE CHILDREN, AND HEARKEN TO ME see Steffani, Agostino

COME, YE SINNERS see Vick

COMEAU, BILL
  Busy Day *sac
  solo,pno,opt gtr VANGUARD V546 $1.00   (C1456)

COMENTARIOS see Pablo, Luis de

COMFIRMATION PRAYER see Kessler, Minuetta

COMFORT, COMFORT YE MY PEOPLE see Bach, Johann Sebastian

COMFORT OF HAIR, THE see Lang, Ivana

COMFORT YE MY PEOPLE see Handel, George Frideric

COMIC DUET FOR TWO CATS see Rossini, Gioacchino, Duetto Buffo Di Due Gatti

COMIN' THRO' THE RYE *folk,Scot
  solo,pno (A maj/G maj) PATERSON FS23 s.p.   (C1457)
  (Winlaw, Maurice) low solo,pno (F maj) CRAMER   (C1458)
  (Winlaw, Maurice) high solo,pno (A maj) CRAMER   (C1459)

COMIN' THROUGH THE RYE
  solo,pno (G maj) LEONARD-ENG   (C1460)

COMING AGAIN see Lister, Mosie

COMING HOME TO YOU see Rose, Michael

COMING OF SPRING, THE see Holford, Franz

COMING OF THE KING, THE see Gillis, Don

COMME AUX SAINTES MARIES see Orthel, Leon

COMME ELLE A LES YEUX BANDES see Ibert, Jacques

COMME ILS ONT FUI see Mendelssohn-Bartholdy, Felix

COMME J'ALLAIS see Ibert, Jacques

COMME J'ALLAIS COUVERT DE LA POUSSIERE DU VOYAGE see Migot, Georges

COMME JE T'AIME see Ghislaine, Elsa

COMME LA FLEUR see Lacome, Paul

COMME LA NUIT see Bohm, Carl, Still Wie Die Nacht

COMME L'EAU see Lacombe, Paul

COMME LES LYS see Levade, Charles (Gaston)

COMME UN NAVIRE SANS BOUSSOLE see Lacome, Paul

COMME VA? see Giazotto, Remo

COMMENT, CHER LEL, AS TU LE COEUR... see Rimsky-Korsakov, Nikolai

COMMENT DIRE BIEN see Saint-Saens, Camille

'COMMENT' DISAIENT-ILS see Liszt, Franz, O Lieb, So Lang Du Lieben Kannst

COMMENTARY see Mc Bride, Robert Guyn

COMMENTARY ON T'UNG JEN see Stout, Alan

COMMIATO see Dallapiccola, Luigi

COMMITTED UNTO THEE see Walley, Steven

COMMUNICATIONS see Kasemets, U.

COMMUNIOMUSIK see Nilsson, Torsten

COMMUNION see O'Connor-Morris, G.

COMMUNION HYMN see Boardman, Reginald

COMO QUIERES QUE ADIVINE see Guridi, Jesus

COMPAGNON BOULANGER
  (Fragerolle, G.) solo,acap ENOCH s.p. see from Chansons Du Pays-Lorrain   (C1461)
  (Fragerolle, G.) solo,pno ENOCH s.p. see from Chansons Du Pays-Lorrain   (C1462)

COMPAGNONS DE LA CHANSON *CCU
  [Fr] med solo,pno FRANCE $1.25   (C1463)

COMPLAINTE see Bloch, Ernest

COMPLAINTE D'AMOUR see Hue, [Georges-Adolphe]

COMPLAINTE DE FLORINDE see Ibert, Jacques

COMPLAINTE DE FRANCE see Jacob, Dom Clement

COMPLAINTE DE LA GLU see Chapuis, Auguste-Paul-Jean-Baptiste

COMPLAINTE DE L'OISEAU see Perissas, M.

COMPLAINTE DE PETITE LUMIERE ET DE L'OURSE see Ravize, A.

COMPLAINTE DE ST. NICOLAS see Perilhou, Albert

COMPLETE EDITION see Mozart, Wolfgang Amadeus

COMPLETE SONG CYCLES see Schubert, Franz (Peter)

COMPLETE SONGS OF BERLIOZ, VOLS. 1-10 see Berlioz, Hector

COMPLETE SONGS OF BRAHMS, VOLS. 1-8 see Brahms, Johannes

COMPLETE SONGS OF MENDELSSOHN, VOLS. 1-4 see Mendelssohn-Bartholdy, Felix

COMPLETE SONGS OF MOZART, VOL. 5 see Mozart, Wolfgang Amadeus

COMPLETE SONGS OF MOZART, VOLS. 1-4 see Mozart, Wolfgang Amadeus

COMPLETE SONGS OF SCHUBERT, THE see Schubert, Franz (Peter)

COMPLETE SONGS OF SCHUMANN, VOLS. 1-8
see Schumann, Robert (Alexander)

COMPLETE WORKS see Beethoven, Ludwig
van

COMPLETE WORKS see Brahms, Johannes

COMPLETE WORKS see Rameau, Jean-
Philippe

COMPLETE WORKS see Schumann, Robert
(Alexander)

COMPLETE WORKS see Glinka, Mikhail
Ivanovitch

COMPLETE WORKS see Schubert, Franz
(Peter)

COMPLETE WORKS. BACH GESELLSCHAFT
EDITION see Bach, Johann Sebastian

THE COMPLETE WORKS OF FRANZ SCHUBERT,
VOL. 14 (PTS. III, IV): LIEDER:
AUGUST 1815 THROUGH 1816 see
Schubert, Franz (Peter)

THE COMPLETE WORKS OF FRANZ SCHUBERT,
VOL. 15 (PTS. V, VI): LIEDER: 1817
TO 1821 see Schubert, Franz (Peter)

THE COMPLETE WORKS OF FRANZ SCHUBERT,
VOL. 16 (PTS. VII, VIII): LIEDER:
1822 TO "DIE WINTERREISE", 1827 see
Schubert, Franz (Peter)

THE COMPLETE WORKS OF FRANZ SCHUBERT,
VOL. 17 (PTS. IX, X): LIEDER: FROM
"DIE WINTERREISE" TO
"SCHWANENGSANG", 1828 see Schubert,
Franz (Peter)

COMPOSIZIONI DA CAMERA see Verdi,
Giuseppe

COMPOSIZIONI DA CAMERA VOL. I see
Donizetti, Gaetano

COMPOSIZIONI DA CAMERA VOL. II see
Donizetti, Gaetano

COMPTINES, BOOK I see Mompou, Federico

COMPTINES, BOOK II see Mompou, Federico

COMPTINES POUR ENFANTS SINISTRES see
Souris, Andre

COMTE DE FOIX *Fr
(Canteloube, J.) solo,acap DURAND
s.p. see also Anthologie Des Chants
Populaires Francais Tome I   (C1464)

CON AMORE see Moody, James

CON ANTONIO MACHADO see Rodrigo,
Joaquin

CON GLI ANGIOLI see Persico, Mario

CON IL ANGIOLI see Gandino, Adolfo

CON OSSEQUIO, CON RISPETTO see Mozart,
Wolfgang Amadeus

CON QUE LA LAVARE see Narvaez, Luis de

CON QUE LA LAVARE? see Rodrigo, Joaquin

CON UN OCC'
(Carlo, Musi) solo,pno (Bolognese
dialect) BONGIOVANI 2054 s.p. see
from El Mi Canzunett   (C1465)

CON UNA MANZANA VERDE see Lopez De La
Rosa, Horatio

CONCENTRICITIES see Sivic, Pavle,
Sosredja

CONCERT AND OPERA ARIAS see Bach,
Johann Christian

CONCERT ARIA AFTER SOLOMON see Weber,
Ben

CONCERT ARIAS see Mozart, Wolfgang
Amadeus

CONCERT PIECE FOR SEVEN, NO. 2 see
Steiner, Gitta

CONCERT PIECE FOR SEVEN, NO. I see
Steiner, Gitta

CONCERTI SACRI see Driessler, Johannes

CONCERTI SACRI see Driessler, Johannes

CONCERTO see Tharichen, W.

CONCERTO FOR COLORATURA SOPRANO AND
ORCHESTRA see Gliere, Reinhold
Moritzovitch, Konzert Fur
Koloratursopran Und Orchester

CONCERTO FOR MEZZO-SOPRANO AND SYMPHONY
ORCHESTRA see Baltin, A.

CONCERTO FOR SOPRANO AND ORCHESTRA see
Parchman, Gen

CONCERTO FUNEBRE see Ghedini, Giorgio
Federico

CONCERTO GROSSO see Aperghis, Georges

CONCERTO PER LA NOTTE DI NATALE see
Dallapiccola, Luigi

CONCERTO POUR SOPRANO COLORATURE ET
ORCHESTRE see Gliere, Reinhold
Moritzovitch, Konzert Fur
Koloratursopran Und Orchester

CONCERTO POUR UNE VOIX DE SOPRANO see
Beers, Jacques

CONDEMNED PLAYGROUND, THE see Gideon,
Miriam

CONDITIONAL see Beurle, Jurgen

CONDITIONNEL see Absil, Jean

CONDOTTA ELL'ERA IN CEPPI see Verdi,
Giuseppe

CONE, EDWARD T. (1917-   )
Silent Noon
high solo,pno EMI s.p.   (C1466)

CONFESSA DUNQUE see Rimsky-Korsakov,
Nikolai

CONFESSION see Bush, Geoffrey

CONFESSION see Delmet, Paul

CONFESSION, THE see Revel, Peter

CONFESSION STONE, THE see Dodson

CONFIDENCES DE FLEURS see Mendelssohn-
Bartholdy, Felix

CONFORM see Kaiser, Kurt

CONGRATULATIONS ARE IN ORDER see
Jensen, Gordon

CONJURATION see Davidson, Malcolm

CONJURATION, THE see Shaw, Martin

CONNAIS-TU LE PAYS see Thomas, Ambroise

CONNAIS-TU MON BEAU VILLAGE see
Truillet-Soyer, M.

CONNOLLY, JUSTIN [RIVEAGH] (1933-   )
M-Piriform *Op.10
S solo,3clar,perc,pno NOVELLO
rental   (C1467)

CONS, A.
John Peel
solo,pno LEONARD-ENG   (C1468)

CONSCIENTIOUS OBJECTOR see Weigl, Vally

CONSECRATION HYMN see Jude, William
Herbert

CONSECUENZA II see Alsina, Carlos Roque

CONSEILS see Duteil d'Ozanne, A.

CONSEILS D'UNE GRAND'MERE see Wellings,
M.

CONSERVATE, RADDOPPIATE see Handel,
George Frideric

CONSERVATI FEDELE see Mozart, Wolfgang
Amadeus

CONSERVEZ BIEN LA PAIX DU COEUR see
Gaveaux, Pierre

CONSIDER see Heseltine, Philip

CONSIDER AND HEAR ME see Harker, F.
Flaxington

CONSIDER AND HEAR ME see Wooler, A.

CONSIDER, LORD see Thomson, Virgil

CONSIDER NOW THE LILY *sac
(Carmichael, Ralph) solo,pno WORD
S-97   (C1469)

CONSIDER, O MY SOUL see Bach, Johann
Sebastian

CONSIDER THE LILIES see Scott, John
Prindle

CONSIDER THE LILIES see Topliff, Robert

CONSIDER THEN, MY SOUL UNWARY see Bach,
Johann Sebastian

CONSIDER YE see Handel, George Frideric

CONSOLAMINI, CONSOLAMINI, POPULE MEUS
see Nilsson, Torsten

CONSOLATION see Fontenailles, H. de

CONSOLATION see Lacome, Paul

CONSOLATION see Nelson

CONSOLE-MOI see Chaminade, Cecile

CONSOLI, MARC-ANTONIO
Equinox I
Mez solo,fl,vcl,pno,perc sc
AM.COMP.AL. $9.90   (C1470)

Equinox II
solo,fl,clar,vln,vcl,pno,perc,
vibra,cel sc AM.COMP.AL. $12.10
                             (C1471)

Isonic I
S solo,fl,2pno,vibra,xylo,chimes,
2perc sc AM.COMP.AL. $16.50
                             (C1472)

CONSORT AND SONG see Beerman, Burton

CONSTANT FLAME see Murray, Alan

CONSTANT LOVER, THE see Sampson,
Godfrey

CONSTANT, MARIUS (1925-   )
Cinq Chants Et Une Vocalise *CC6U
S solo,orch voc sc SALABERT-US
$32.00, ipr   (C1473)

CONSTRASTO see Respighi, Ottorino

CONTADINO see Peragallo, Mario

CONTEMPLATION see Godard, Benjamin
Louis Paul

CONTEMPORARY AMERICAN SONGS *CCU,
Contemp
(Taylor) high solo,pno SUMMY $3.95
                             (C1474)

CONTEMPORARY ART SONG ALBUM, BK. 1
*CCU
high solo,pno GALAXY 1.2449.7 $2.50
                             (C1475)

CONTEMPORARY ART SONG ALBUM, BK. 2
*CCU
med solo,pno GALAXY 1.2504.7 $3.00
                             (C1476)

CONTEMPORARY ART SONGS *CC28L,Eng/US
solo,pno SCHIRM.G $5.00 contains
works by: Barber; Dunhill; Vaughan
Williams; Symons and others (C1477)

CONTEMPORARY CHRISTMAS CAROLS see
McAfee, Don

CONTEMPORARY SONGS IN ENGLISH *CCU,
Contemp
(Taylor) med-high solo,pno FISCHER,C
O 3819; med-low solo,pno FISCHER,C
O 3820   (C1478)

CONTENTED see Gaither

CONTENTED AM I *sac,gospel
solo,pno ABER.GRP. $1.50   (C1479)

CONTENTMENT see Nelson

CONTES DE FEES see Chaminade, Cecile

CONTES DIVINS see Holmes, Alfred

CONTILLI, GINO (1907-   )
Avidamente Allargo La Mia Mano
see Due Liriche Di Quasimodo

Due Canti *CC2U
solo,pno ZERBONI 5449 s.p.   (C1480)

Due Liriche Di Quasimodo
[It] solo,pno cmplt ed SANTIS 861
s.p.
contains: Avidamente Allargo La
Mia Mano; Latomie   (C1481)

Immagini Sonore
S solo,11inst sc ZERBONI 6260 s.p.
                             (C1482)

Latomie
see Due Liriche Di Quasimodo

Offerta Musicale
S solo,5inst voc sc ZERBONI 5769
s.p.   (C1483)

CONTRABAND see Geehl, Henry Ernest

CONTRABANDIEREN see Sjogren, Emil

CONTRALTO SONGS (RADIO CITY ALBUM)
*CCU
A solo,pno MARKS $1.50   (C1484)

CONTRARIA ROMANA see Kapr, Jan

CONTRAST, THE see Walton, William

CONTRASTE see Labey, Marcel

CONTRASTS see Bezanson, Philip

CONTRE-POINT DU JOUR see DuBois, Pierre
Max

CONVERSATION see Rorem, Ned

CONVERSATION PIECE see Somers, Harry
Stewart

CONVERSE
What A Friend We Have In Jesus
solo,pno ASHLEY $.95   (C1485)

CONVERSE, FREDERICK SHEPHERD
(1871-1940)
Three Songs From Sanctuary *sac,CC3U
med solo,pno BELWIN $1.25 (C1486)

CONVIEN PARTIR see Donizetti, Gaetano

COOK
Glory Road *sac
solo,pno BENSON S5529-S $1.00
(C1487)
COOK, A.
November Thrush
med solo,pno SEESAW $1.00   (C1488)

COOK, JOHN
Come Away Death
see Two Songs From Twelfth Night

O Mistress Mine
see Two Songs From Twelfth Night

Two Songs From Twelfth Night *sec
WATERLOO $1.25
contains: Come Away Death (med
solo,pno) (B flat maj); O
Mistress Mine (high solo,pno)
(C maj)   (C1489)

COOKE, EDITH
I Dream'd A Dream
low solo,pno (G maj) CRAMER (C1490)
high solo,pno (A flat maj) CRAMER
(C1491)
COOKE, HERBERT L.
Our House Is Full Of Fairies
low solo,pno (D flat maj) CRAMER
(C1492)
high solo,pno (C maj) CRAMER
(C1493)
When Mother Was Married
solo,pno (A flat maj) LEONARD-ENG
(C1494)
COOKE, S.C.
Boat Song
see Nocturnes

Echoing Green, The
see Three Songs Of Innocence

Moon, The
see Nocturnes

Nocturnes
S solo,pno,horn (med) OXFORD 63.061
$3.30
contains: Boat Song; Moon, The;
Owl; Returning, We Hear The
Larks; River Roses   (C1495)

Owl
see Nocturnes

Piping Down The Valleys Wild
see Three Songs Of Innocence

Returning, We Hear The Larks
see Nocturnes

River Roses
see Nocturnes

Shepherd, The
see Three Songs Of Innocence

Three Songs Of Innocence
S solo,pno,clar (med easy) OXFORD
63.054 $2.15
contains: Echoing Green, The;
Piping Down The Valleys Wild;
Shepherd, The   (C1496)

COOL AND SILENT IS THE LAKE see
Davenport, Gladys

COOL HILL PASTURES *Scot
solo,pno PATERSON s.p. see from
Hebridean Songs, Vol. IV   (C1497)

COOL TOMBS see Raphling, Sam

COOLIN, THE see Mourant, Walter

COOPER O' FIFE, THE see Lawson, Malcolm

COPERARIO, GIOVANNI (ca. 1575-1626)
Funeral Teares, Songs Of Mourning,
Masque Of Squires *CCU
solo,pno STAINER 3.1335.7 $5.50
(C1498)

COPLA see Bosmans, Henriette

COPLA see D'Esposito, Salve

COPLA see Jurafsky, Abraham

COPLA CRIOLLA see Lopez-Buchardo,
Carlos

COPLAND, AARON (1900-   )
As It Fell Upon A Day
solo,pno,fl,clar BOOSEY $4.00
(C1499)
Dear March, Come In
solo,pno (F sharp maj) BOOSEY $1.50
(C1500)
Dirge In Woods
solo,pno (E flat maj) BOOSEY $1.50
(C1501)
Going To Heaven
solo,pno (B flat maj) BOOSEY $1.75
(C1502)
Heart, We Will Forget Him
solo,pno (E flat maj) BOOSEY $1.50
(C1503)
I Bought Me A Cat
solo,pno (F maj) BOOSEY $1.50
(C1504)
I've Heard An Organ Talk Sometimes
solo,pno (B flat maj) BOOSEY $1.50
(C1505)
Laurie's Song (from Tender Land, The)
S solo,pno BOOSEY $1.75   (C1506)
Nature, The Gentlest Mother
solo,pno (E flat maj) BOOSEY $1.50
(C1507)
Old American Songs, Vol. 1 *CCU
solo,pno/orch BOOSEY $3.50 (C1508)
Old American Songs, Vol. 2 *CCU
solo,pno/orch BOOSEY $3.50 (C1509)
Old Poem
[Eng/Fr] med solo,pno SALABERT-US
$1.50   (C1510)
Poet's Song
solo,pno BOOSEY $1.50   (C1511)
Selected Songs *CCU
[Russ] solo,pno MEZ KNIGA 88 s.p.
(C1512)
Simple Gifts
solo,pno BOOSEY $1.50   (C1513)
Twelve Poems Of Emily Dickinson
*CC12U
solo,pno BOOSEY $5.00   (C1514)
Vocalise
solo,pno BOOSEY $1.50   (C1515)

COPLAS see Badings, Henk

COPLAS see Lasala, Angel

COPLAS see Luzzatti, Arturo

COPLAS see Jurafsky, Abraham

COPLAS see Gianneo, Luis

COPLAS see Badings, Henk

COPLAS see Mul, Jan

COPLAS see Castelnuovo-Tedesco, Mario

COPLEY, IAN A.
Twelfth Night
solo,pno (B min) ROBERTON 2615 s.p.
(C1516)
solo,pno (E min) ROBERTON 2615 s.p.
(C1517)

COPPELIA-WALTZ see Delibes, Leo

COPPER SUN *CCU
(Clark, R.) solo,pno PRESSER $1.50
(C1518)
COPPOLA, PIERO (1888-1971)
Cinq Chansons Francaises *see Dans
L'univers; Laissez Jouer, Jeunes
Gens; Ma Belle Si Ton Ame; Quand
Vous Voudrez Faire Une Amie;
Voici La Douce Nuit De Mai
(C1519)
Cinq Poemes De Rubino
[Fr/It] solo,orch DURAND s.p., ipa
contains: Intermede Gal; La Danse
Des Mains Amputees; Le
Chemineau Maigre; Les Faunes;
Musique "In-Horto"   (C1520)
Dans L'univers
solo,pno/inst DURAND s.p. see from
Cinq Chansons Francaises (C1521)
Intermede Gal
see Cinq Poemes De Rubino

COPPOLA, PIERO (cont'd.)
J'ai Besion De Toi
solo,pno/inst DURAND s.p. (C1522)
La Danse Des Mains Amputees
see Cinq Poemes De Rubino
Laissez Jouer, Jeunes Gens
solo,pno/inst DURAND s.p. see from
Cinq Chansons Francaises (C1523)
Le Chemineau Maigre
see Cinq Poemes De Rubino
Les Faunes
see Cinq Poemes De Rubino
Ma Belle Si Ton Ame
solo,pno/inst DURAND s.p. see from
Cinq Chansons Francaises (C1524)
Musique "In-Horto"
see Cinq Poemes De Rubino
Quand Vous Voudrez Faire Une Amie
solo,pno/inst DURAND s.p. see from
Cinq Chansons Francaises (C1525)
Voici La Douce Nuit De Mai
solo,pno/inst DURAND s.p. see from
Cinq Chansons Francaises (C1526)
COQUARD, ARTHUR (1846-1910)
Le Chanvre *Op.96,No.5
SA soli,pno DURAND s.p.   (C1527)
Le Renouveau *Op.96,No.4
SA soli,pno DURAND s.p.   (C1528)
L'Hirondelle *Op.96,No.2
SA soli,pno DURAND s.p.   (C1529)
Nocturne *Op.96,No.1
SA soli,pno DURAND s.p.   (C1530)

COQUETTES SONG see Storace, J.

CORAL, GIAMPAOLO (1944-   )
Magnificat *sac
S solo,orch sc,quarto ZERBONI 7337
s.p.   (C1531)

CORALS see Treharne, Bryceson

CORDARA
Pater Noster *sac
solo,pno FORLIVESI 11505 s.p.
(C1532)
CORDERITO see Guastavino, Carlos

CORE DI MAMMA see Albanese, Guido

CORE' NGRATO see Cardillo

CORGHI, AZIO (1937-   )
Gli Uomini Vuoti
6 soli,fl,clar,horn,perc,vibra,pno,
vla,bvl,gtr SONZOGNO rental
(C1533)
Symbola
solo,orch ZERBONI 7396 s.p. (C1534)
Tactus
solo,orch ZERBONI 7863 s.p. (C1535)

CORIGLIANO, JOHN (1938-1975)
Christmas At The Cloisters
med solo,pno SCHIRM.G $.75 see from
Cloisters, The   (C1536)
Cloisters, The *see Christmas At The
Cloisters; Fort Tryon Park:
September; Song To The Witch Of
The Cloisters; Unicorn, The
(C1537)
Fort Tryon Park: September
med solo,pno SCHIRM.G $.75 see from
Cloisters, The   (C1538)
Song To The Witch Of The Cloisters
med solo,pno SCHIRM.G $.75 see from
Cloisters, The   (C1539)
Unicorn, The
med solo,pno SCHIRM.G $.75 see from
Cloisters, The   (C1540)

CORMORANT, THE see Blyton, Carey

CORN RIGS *folk,Scot
solo,pno (A maj) PATERSON FS22 s.p.
(C1541)
CORNELIUS-ALBUM see Cornelius, Peter

CORNELIUS, PETER (1824-1874)
Ach, Das Lied Hab' Ich Getragen (from
Der Barbier Von Bagdad)
T solo,2fl,2ob,2clar,2bsn,4horn,
trom,timp,strings BREITKOPF-W
s.p.   (C1542)
Brautlieder *Marriage,song cycle
[Ger/Eng] high solo,pno INTERNAT.
$2.00   (C1543)

CORNELIUS, PETER (cont'd.)

Christbaum *Op.8,No.1
see Sechs Weihnachtslieder

Christkind *Op.8,No.6
see Sechs Weihnachtslieder

Christmas Songs *CCU,Xmas
[Eng/Ger] high solo,pno PETERS
3105AA $3.25; med solo/low solo,
pno PETERS 3105BB $3.25 (C1544)

Christus Der Kinderfreund *Op.8,No.5
see Sechs Weihnachtslieder

Cornelius-Album *CC23U
(Friedlander) [Ger] solo,pno PETERS
3106 $8.00 (C1545)

Die Hirten *Op.8,No.2
see Sechs Weihnachtslieder

Die Konige *Op.8,No.3
see Sechs Weihnachtslieder

Peter Cornelius Musical Works *CCU
(Hasse, Max; Baussnern, Waldemar
von) contains works for a variety
of instruments and vocal
combinations microfiche
UNIV.MUS.ED. $50.00 reprints of
Breitkopf & Hartel Editions;
contains 5 large volumes (C1546)

Salem Aleikum (from Der Barbier Von
Bagdad)
solo,pno DOBLINGER 08 557 s.p.
(C1547)

Sechs Weihnachtslieder
[Ger/Dan] med solo,kbd NORDISKA
s.p.
contains: Christbaum, Op.8,No.1;
Christkind, Op.8,No.6; Christus
Der Kinderfreund, Op.8,No.5;
Die Hirten, Op.8,No.2; Die
Konige, Op.8,No.3; Simeon,
Op.8,No.4 (C1548)

Selected Duets *CC11U
(Friedlander) [Ger] SS/SBar/SB
soli,pno PETERS 3718 $4.75
(C1549)

Simeon *Op.8,No.4
see Sechs Weihnachtslieder

So Leb' Ich Noch (from Der Barbier
Von Bagdad)
T solo,2fl,2ob,2clar,2bsn,4horn,
trom,strings BREITKOPF-W s.p.
(C1550)

Weihnachtslieder *CCU,Xmas
(med easy) s.p. med solo,pno BAREN.
567; high solo,pno BAREN. 567A;
low solo,pno BAREN. 567B (C1551)

Weihnachtslieder *Op.8, CCU,Xmas
med solo,pno BAREN. 19304 $4.25
(C1552)

Weihnachtslieder *Op.8, CCU,Xmas
[Ger/Eng] high solo,pno BREITKOPF-L
EB 2082 $1.50; med solo,pno
BREITKOPF-L EB 2078 $1.50; low
solo,pno BREITKOPF-L EB 2115
$1.50 (C1553)

Weihnachtslieder *Op.8, CCU,Xmas
[Ger/Eng] med solo,pno SCHOTTS 610
s.p. (C1554)

Weihnachtslieder *Op.8, CCU,Xmas
HUG s.p. high solo,pno; med solo,
pno (C1555)

CORNET DE BONBONS see Gillet, Ernest

CORNISH LAND see Hope, H. Ashworth

CORNISH RHAPSODY see Bath, Hubert

CORNOGRAPHY see Bond, Victoria

CORPUS CHRISTI CAROL see Britten,
Benjamin

CORPUS CHRISTI CAROL see Crosse

CORREA NEL SENO AMATO see Scarlatti,
Alessandro

CORRESPONDANCES see Cantu, M.

CORRESPONDANCES see Pezzati, Romano

CORRIDORS see Moryl, Richard

CORRIE, J.
Down Glanna Way
low solo,pno (C maj) LEONARD-ENG
(C1556)
high solo,pno (E flat maj) LEONARD-
ENG (C1557)

CORRO COME IL CERVO MUSCHIATO see
Alfano, Franco

CORS DE CHASSE see Caby, R.

CORSE *Fr
(Canteloube, J.) solo,acap DURAND
s.p. see also Anthologie Des Chants
Populaires Francais Tome I (C1558)

CORTEGE see Pijper, Willem

CORTES, RAMIRO (1933-   )
Adivinanza De La Guitarra
"Riddle Of The Guitar, The" [Span/
Eng] solo,pno PEER $.95 see from
Three Spanish Songs (C1559)

Falcon, The
S solo,pno PETERS 6062 $1.75
(C1560)

Guitar, The *see La Guitarra

La Guitarra
"Guitar, The" [Span/Eng] solo,pno
PEER $.95 see from Three Spanish
Songs (C1561)

Las Seis Cuerdas
"Six Strings, The" [Span/Eng] solo,
pno PEER $.95 see from Three
Spanish Songs (C1562)

Riddle Of The Guitar, The *see
Adivinanza De La Guitarra

Six Strings, The *see Las Seis
Cuerdas

Three Spanish Songs *see Adivinanza
De La Guitarra, "Riddle Of The
Guitar, The"; La Guitarra,
"Guitar, The"; Las Seis Cuerdas,
"Six Strings, The" (C1563)

CORTESE, LUIGI (1899-   )
Cinque Canti Popolari Della Liguria
*CC5U
solo,pno ZERBONI 8026 s.p. (C1564)

Cinque Momenti Musicali *CC5U
solo,pno ZERBONI 4024 s.p. (C1565)

Due Canti Persiani *CC2U
Mez solo,2inst ZERBONI 3993 rental
(C1566)

Psalm 8 *see Salmo VIII

Quatre Odes De Ronsard *CC4U
female solo,pno voc sc ZERBONI 4527
s.p. (C1567)

Salmo VIII (Psalm 8) sac
female solo,3inst ZERBONI 4503
rental (C1568)

Tre Poemi Di Rilke *CC3U
solo,pno ZERBONI 5160 s.p. (C1569)

CORTIGIANI, VIL RAZZA DANNATA see
Verdi, Giuseppe

CORTINA DE FULLATGE see Mompou,
Federico

CORTOPASSI, D.
Rusticanella
solo,pno SCHAUR EE 3542 s.p.
(C1570)

CORY, ELEANOR
Waking
S solo,clar,bsn,trp,pno,perc,vln,
vla,vcl,bvl, tenor saxophone sc
AM.COMP.AL. $26.40, ipa (C1571)

CORY, GEORGE
And This Shall Be For Music...
solo,pno GENERAL 291 $1.25 (C1572)

Another America
solo,pno GENERAL 655 $2.00 (C1573)

Boat Song
solo,pno GENERAL 549 $1.25 (C1574)

Equinox
solo,pno GENERAL 552 $1.50 (C1575)

Good Night
solo,pno GENERAL 551 $1.25 (C1576)

Lord's Prayer, The *sac
solo,pno GENERAL 76 $1.00 (C1577)

Music I Heard With You
solo,pno GENERAL 494 $1.50 (C1578)

Peace Of Mind
solo,pno GENERAL 14 $1.25 (C1579)

So We'll Go No More A-Roving
solo,pno GENERAL 550 $1.25 (C1580)

CORYDON see Pepusch, John Christopher

CORYLOPSIS!
(Carlo, Musi) solo,pno (Bolognese
dialect) BONGIOVANI 2084 s.p. see
from El Mi Canzunett (C1581)

CORS DE CHASSE see Caby, R.

COS COB SONG VOLUME *CCU
(Copland) solo,pno BOOSEY $5.00
(C1582)

COSI see Cantu, M.

COSI DUNQUE TRADISCI see Mozart,
Wolfgang Amadeus

COSI DUNQUE TRADISCI - ASPIRI RIMORSI
ATROCI see Mozart, Wolfgang Amadeus

COSI ORGOGLIOSA see Scarlatti, Domenico

COSMIC CHRIST, THE see Haubiel, Charles

COSSETTO, EMIL (1918-   )
Lyrics *song cycle
[Slav] solo,pno CROATICA s.p.
(C1583)

Pit, The *song cycle
[Slav] solo,pno CROATICA s.p.
(C1584)

COST see Ireland, John

COSTA, G.
Villanelle
solo,pno ENOCH s.p. (C1585)

COSTIN, HAROLD
When Love Goes Through The Valley
low solo,pno (F maj) CRAMER (C1586)
high solo,pno (A flat maj) CRAMER
(C1587)

COTE D'AZUR see Escher, Rudolf George

COTTON, GENE
Power To Be *sac,CC13UL
solo,pno BENSON BO830 $2.50 (C1588)

COTTRAU, TEODORO (1827-1879)
Santa Lucia
solo,pno CRAMER (C1589)

COUCHER DE SOLEIL see Barbier, Rene

COUCHER DE SOLEIL see Pandelides, S.

COULD I BUT FEEL MY SORROW see
Malashkin, Leonid Dimitrievitch

COULD I HAVE HELD HIS NAIL-PIERCED
HANDS see O'Hara, Geoffrey

COULD MAN BE DRUNK FOREVER see Heilner,
Irwin

COULD MY SONGS THEIR WAY BE WINGING see
Hahn, Reynaldo, Si Mes Vers Avaient
Des Ailes!

COULDN'T HEAR NOBODY PRAY *spir
(Burleigh, H. T.) low solo,pno BELWIN
$1.50 (C1590)

COULEURS JUXTAPOSEES see Guezec, Jean-
Pierre

COULTHARD, JEAN (1908-   )
Ecstasy
solo,pno BERANDOL BER 1303 $2.50
(C1591)

COUNT YOUR BLESSINGS see O'Hara,
Geoffrey

COUNTING SHEEP see Rowley, Alec

COUNTING THE BEATS see Searle, Humphrey

COUNTRY COTTAGE see Arundale, Claude

COUNTRY FOLK see Brahe, May H.

COUNTRY GARDENS
low solo,orch (C maj) ASHDOWN s.p.,
ipr (C1592)
med solo,orch (D maj) ASHDOWN s.p.,
ipr (C1593)
high solo,orch (F maj) ASHDOWN s.p.,
ipr (C1594)

COUNTRY GIRLS see Williams, W.S.Gwynn

COUNTRY TUNE see English, George
Phillip

COUNTRYMAN, THE see Heseltine, Philip

COUPERIN (LE GRAND), FRANCOIS
(1668-1733)
Adolescentulus Sum *mot
S solo,2fl,vln,org OISEAU s.p.
(C1595)

Air Serieux [1]
MezMez soli,pno OISEAU s.p. (C1596)

Air Serieux [2]
SBar soli,strings,cont sc OISEAU
s.p. (C1597)

Be Joyful In The Lord *sac
SA soli,pno oct CONCORDIA 98-1734
$.25 (C1598)

Canon A Trois
3 soli,acap OISEAU s.p. (C1599)

COUPERIN (LE GRAND), FRANCOIS (cont'd.)

Christ Is Arisen *sac
SS/TT soli,pno oct CONCORDIA
98-1733 $.30 (C1600)

Christ The Lord Is Risen Again *sac
SA soli,pno oct CONCORDIA 98-1893
$.25 (C1601)

Epitaphe D'un Paresseux
SBar soli,pno OISEAU s.p. (C1602)

In Thee, O Lord, Is Fullness Of Joy
*sac
SA soli,pno oct CONCORDIA 98-2059
$.30 (C1603)

Lecons De Tenebres *sac
1-2 soli,cont HEUGEL s.p. (C1604)

Lecons De Tenebres, Premiere Lecon
*sac,CCU
(Ewerhart, Rudolf) [Lat] S/T solo,
cont BIELER CS 3 s.p. (C1605)

Lecons De Tenebres, Second Lecon
*sac,CCU
(Ewerhart, Rudolf) [Lat] S/T solo,
cont BIELER CS 4 s.p. (C1606)

Lecons De Tenebres, Troisieme Lecon
*sac,cant
(Ewerhart, Rudolf) SS soli,cont sc
BIELER DK 10 s.p., ipa (C1607)

O Clap Your Hands *sac
SA soli,pno oct CONCORDIA 98-1821
$.30 (C1608)
SABar soli,cont oct CONCORDIA
98-1822 $.30 (C1609)

Quatre Versets D'un Motet *CC4U
SS soli,org OISEAU s.p. (C1610)

Sept Versets D'un Motet (1704) *CC7U
2 soli OISEAU s.p. (C1611)

Sing Unto The Lord A New Song *sac
SA soli,pno oct CONCORDIA 98-1709
$.25 (C1612)

Trois Chansons *CC3U
solo,pno min sc OISEAU s.p. (C1613)

Trois Lecons De Tenebres *sac,CC7U
1-2 soli,org OISEAU s.p. (C1614)

Trois Vestales Champetres Et Trois
Policons *sac,CC6U
solo,acap OISEAU s.p. (C1615)

COUPERIN, GERVAIS-FRANCOIS (1759-1826)
La Chaumiere
solo,pno OISEAU s.p. (C1616)

COUPLETS see Gretry, Andre Ernest
Modeste

COUPLETS BACHIQUES see Chaminade,
Cecile

COUPLETS DE BERTHA see Cuvillier,
Charles

COUPLETS DE FRANCINETTE see Chadal, M.

COUPLETS DE GASPARD see Weber, Carl
Maria von

COUPLETS DE GRETCHEN see Cuvillier,
Charles

COUPLETS DE JACQUET see Messager, Andre

COUPLETS DE LA CASQUETTE see Messager,
Andre

COUPLETS DE LA DESILLUSION see Caryll,
Ivan

COUPLETS DE LA GOURMANDE see
Planquette, Robert

COUPLETS DE LA QUEUE DE LA POELE see
Bernicat, F.

COUPLETS DE LA ROSE ET DU MUGUET see
Lecocq, Charles

COUPLETS DE LA TIMIDITE see Caryll,
Ivan

COUPLETS DE L'ARBRE GENEALOGIQUE see
Caryll, Ivan

COUPLETS DES RECRIMINATIONS see Caryll,
Ivan

COUPLETS DIALOGUES see Messager, Andre

COUPLETS DU KOUSS KOUSS see Cuvillier,
Charles

COUPLETS DU MANA MILITARI see Caryll,
Ivan

COUPLETS DU PORTRAIT DE LA REINE see
Caryll, Ivan

COUPLETS DU TELEPHONE see Caryll, Ivan

COURBOIS, J.-P.
Don Quichotte *cant
(Oubradous, Fernand) T solo,orch
voc sc TRANSAT. s.p. (C1617)

COURIERS SING, THE *sac,CC10UL
solo,pno LILLENAS MB-250 $1.95 (C1618)

COURT OF DREAMS, THE see Bantock,
Granville

COVENT GARDEN see Gibbs, Cecil
Armstrong

COWAN
Waltzing Matilda
solo,pno (E flat maj) ALLANS s.p. (C1619)

COWARD'S LAMENT, THE see Duke, John
Woods

COWELL
Pasture, The
high solo,pno EMI s.p. (C1620)

St. Agnes Morning
solo,pno PRESSER $.95 (C1621)

COWELL, HENRY DIXON (1897-1965)
Daybreak
solo,pno PEER $.95 (C1622)

Firelight And Lamp
solo,pno PETERS 6673 $1.25 (C1623)

Little Black Boy, The
solo,pno PETERS 6674 $1.50 (C1624)

Spring Comes Singing
S solo,pno AMP $.60 (C1625)

Toccanta *song cycle
S solo,fl,vcl,pno BOOSEY $5.00 (C1626)

Vocalise *vocalise
S solo,fl,pno PETERS 6675 $3.00 (C1627)

COWEN, SIR FREDERIC HYMEN (1852-1935)
Better Land
high solo,pno (C maj) BOOSEY $1.50 (C1628)
low solo,pno (A flat maj) BOOSEY
$1.50 (C1629)

Children's Dreams
med solo,pno (D min) LEONARD-ENG (C1630)
low solo,pno (C min) LEONARD-ENG (C1631)
high solo,pno (E min) LEONARD-ENG (C1632)
Children's Home, The
low solo,pno (B flat maj) LEONARD-
ENG (C1633)
med solo,pno (D maj) LEONARD-ENG (C1634)
med-low solo,pno (C maj) LEONARD-
ENG (C1635)
2 soli,pno LEONARD-ENG (C1636)
high solo,pno (F maj) LEONARD-ENG (C1637)
med-high solo,pno (E flat maj)
LEONARD-ENG (C1638)

Gift Of Rest
low solo,pno (C maj) LEONARD-ENG (C1639)
med solo,pno (D maj) LEONARD-ENG (C1640)
high solo,pno (F maj) LEONARD-ENG (C1641)
Light In Darkness
low solo,pno (D flat maj) CRAMER (C1642)
high solo,pno (F maj) CRAMER (C1643)
Maytide In My Garden *CCU
solo,pno CRAMER pap s.p., cloth
s.p. (C1644)

Onaway, Awake, Beloved
low solo,pno (B maj) CRAMER (C1645)
med solo,pno (C maj) CRAMER (C1646)
med-high solo,pno (D maj) CRAMER (C1647)
high solo,pno (E maj) CRAMER (C1648)
TB soli,pno CRAMER (C1649)
low solo,pno (B flat maj) ALLANS
s.p. (C1650)
med solo,pno (C maj) ALLANS s.p. (C1651)
med-high solo,pno (E maj) ALLANS
s.p. (C1652)
high solo,pno (F maj) ALLANS s.p. (C1653)

COWEN, SIR FREDERIC HYMEN (cont'd.)

Sea Hath Its Pearls, The
solo,pno CRAMER (C1654)

Swallows
low solo,pno (F maj) BOOSEY $1.50 (C1655)
high solo,pno (A maj) BOOSEY $1.50 (C1656)

COWLES, EUGENE
Forgotten
low solo,pno (F maj) ASHDOWN (C1657)
high solo,pno (A flat maj) ASHDOWN (C1658)
med-low solo,pno PRESSER $.75 (C1659)

COWLES, WALTER RUEL (1881-1959)
Forgotten
solo,pno (available in 3 keys)
ASHLEY $.95 (C1660)

COX, ALLAN
That Name Is Jesus *sac
med solo,pno CRESPUB CP-S5023 $1.00 (C1661)

COX, DAVID (1916-)
Humours Of Love
med solo,pno BELWIN $2.50 (C1662)

COX, RALPH
To A Hilltop
low solo,pno (B maj) CRAMER (C1663)
med solo,pno (D maj) CRAMER (C1664)
high solo,pno (C maj) CRAMER (C1665)

CRAB, A see Kaburagi, Mitsugu

CRABBED AGE AND YOUTH see Parry,
Charles Hubert Hastings

CRABTREE, RALPH
Little Things That Matter
solo,pno CRAMER (C1666)

CRACOVIAK see Moniuszko, Stanislaw

CRADLE CAROL see Ouchterlony, David

CRADLE IN BETHLEHEM, THE see Quilter,
Roger

CRADLE ME LOW see Brahe, May H.

CRADLE OF CATS, A see Wright, Geoffrey

CRADLE SONG see Arensky, Anton
Stepanovitch, Petite Berceuse

CRADLE SONG see Brahms, Johannes,
Wiegenlied

CRADLE SONG see Delius, Frederick

CRADLE SONG see Fromm, Herbert

CRADLE SONG see Mozart, Wolfgang
Amadeus

CRADLE SONG see Nieland, H.

CRADLE SONG see Rimsky-Korsakov,
Nikolai, Berceuse

CRADLE SONG see Rorem, Ned

CRADLE SONG see Schubert, Franz
(Peter), Wiegenlied

CRADLE SONG see Stout, Alan

CRADLE SONG see Sutherland, Margaret

CRADLE SONG see Thordarson, Sigurdur

CRADLE SONG, A see Hind, John

CRADLE SONG, A see Sinding, Christian

CRADLE SONG, A see Weigl, Karl

CRADLE SONG FOR A DEAD HORSEMAN see
Sallinen, Aulis

CRAIGIE-BURN WOOD see Gover, Gerald

CRAINTE see Pouget, Leo

CRAMPTON, ERNEST
If We Marry For Love
2 soli,pno CRAMER (C1667)

Ye Olde Hall *CCU
solo,pno CRAMER (C1668)

Your Step Upon The Stair
solo,pno LEONARD-ENG (C1669)

Zobeide
solo,pno CRAMER (C1670)

CRAPPIUS, ANDREAS
  Musik Im Hauslichen Leben
    solo,2A rec,T rec sc UNIVER. 12616
    $3.75, ipa   (C1671)

CRAS, JEAN (EMILE PAUL) (1879-1932)
  Arriere-Saison
    see Elegies

  Dans Le Parc
    see Elegies

  Desir
    see Elegies

  Elegies
    DURAND high solo,pno quarto s.p.;
      high solo,orch s.p., ipr
      contains: Arriere-Saison; Dans Le
      Parc; Desir; Soir   (C1672)

  Soir
    see Elegies

CRAVEN, LOUISE
  Beyond The Distant Hills
    solo,pno (E maj) LEONARD-ENG
                                      (C1673)
  My Life Is Yours
    low solo,pno (E flat maj) ALLANS
    s.p.   (C1674)
    high solo,pno (G maj) ALLANS s.p.
                                      (C1675)
  Whither Thou Goest
    solo,pno (B flat maj) LEONARD-ENG
                                      (C1676)

CRAXTON, HAROLD
  Snowdrop, The
    low solo,pno (D flat maj) CRAMER
    $.95   (C1677)
    high solo,pno (E flat maj) CRAMER
                                      (C1678)

CRAZY JANE GROWN OLD LOOKS AT THE
  DANCERS see Aston, Peter G.

CRAZY JANE TALKS WITH THE BISHOP see
  Aston, Peter G.

CREATE IN ME see Powers, George

CREATE IN ME A CLEAN HEART, O GOD see
  Bernhard, Christoph

CREATE IN ME A CLEAN HEART, O GOD see
  Bouman, Paul

CREATE IN ME A CLEAN HEART O GOD see
  Miller

CREATE IN ME A CLEAN HEART, O GOD see
  Mueller, Carl F.

CREATION see Hinchcliffe, Irvin

CREATION, THE see Fortner, Wolfgang

CREATION'S HYMN see Beethoven, Ludwig
  van

CREATOR SPIRIT, BY WHOSE AID see
  Kindermann, Johann Erasmus

CREDI, CARINA, E GRACE ERROR see
  Kalman, Emerich

CREDIMI O CORE see Scarlatti, Domenico

CREDO see Faure, Jean-Baptiste

CREDO see Redman, Reginald

CREDO D'AMOUR see Chabrier, Emmanuel

CREDO IN UN DIO CRUDEL see Verdi,
  Giuseppe

CREDO POUR TOUS see Delmet, Paul

CREMESINI, M.
  Mistero
    [It] solo,pno BONGIOVANI 2166 s.p.
                                      (C1679)
  Notte
    [It] solo,pno BONGIOVANI 2165 s.p.
                                      (C1680)

CREPUSCOLO see Recli, Giulia

CREPUSCOLO see Respighi, Ottorino

CREPUSCULE see Albeniz, Isaac

CREPUSCULE see Devreese, Godefroid

CREPUSCULE see Rabaud, Henri

CREPUSCULE see Rhene-Baton

CREPUSCULE D'AMOUR see Duval, A.

CREPUSCULE DE MI-JUILLET see Sauguet,
  Henri

CREPUSCULE D'OR see Tremisot, Ed.

CREPUSCULE EN PROVINCE see Leduc,
  Jacques

CREPUSCULE PLUVIEUX see Mulder, Ernest
  W.

CREPUSCULES D'AUTOMNE see Aubert,
  Louis-Francois-Marie

CRESPUSCULE see Cuvillier, Charles

CRESTON, PAUL (1906-   )
  Ave Maria *sac,Xmas
    [Lat/Fr] med-high solo,pno BELWIN
    $1.50   (C1681)

  Psalm 23 *Op.37, sac
    med solo,pno (D maj) SCHIRM.G $1.00
                                      (C1682)
    high solo,pno (F maj) SCHIRM.G
    $1.00   (C1683)

  Serenade, A
    high solo,pno BELWIN $1.50 (C1684)

  Song Of Joys, A
    high solo,pno BELWIN $1.50 (C1685)

CRI see Cugley, Ian

CRICKET ON THE HEART, THE see Herbert,
  Victor

CRIES OF LONDON, THE see Dering,
  Richard

CRIMOND see Grant

CRIPPLED BOY'S PRAYER, A see Carter

CRISTOFARO, A. DE
  Valse Venitienne
    solo,pno ENOCH s.p.   (C1686)

  Valse Ventienne
    solo,acap solo pt ENOCH s.p.
                                      (C1687)

CRISWICK, MARY
  Elizabethan And Jacobean Songs *CCU
    med solo,gtr STAINER 3.8147.7 $3.75
                                      (C1688)

CROCKER
  I Don't Need To Understand *sac
    solo,pno LILLENAS SM-913: SN $1.00
                                      (C1689)
    solo,pno BENSON S5996-RS $1.00
                                      (C1690)

CROFT, COLBERT
  First Million Years, The (composed
    with Croft, Joyce) *sac
    solo,pno WORD S-468   (C1691)

  He Just Loved Me More And More
    (composed with Croft, Joyce)
    *sac
    solo,pno WORD S-349   (C1692)
    solo,pno WORD S-354   (C1693)

  Heaven Only Knows (composed with
    Croft, Joyce) *sac
    solo,pno WORD S-396   (C1694)

  I Believe He Died For Me (composed
    with Croft, Joyce) *sac
    solo,pno WORD S-369   (C1695)
    solo,pno BENSON S5953-S $1.00
                                      (C1696)
  I Can't Even Walk Without You Holding
    My Hand (composed with Croft,
    Joyce) *sac
    solo,pno WORD S-523   (C1697)

  It's Closer Than It's Ever Been
    (composed with Croft, Joyce)
    *sac
    solo,pno WORD S-419   (C1698)

  Jesus, I Love You (composed with
    Croft, Joyce) *sac
    solo,pno WORD S-416   (C1699)

  Lily Of The Valley Is My Lord, The
    (composed with Croft, Joyce)
    *sac
    solo,pno WORD S-457   (C1700)

  Lord, Take The Hand Of This Child
    (composed with Croft, Joyce)
    *sac
    solo,pno WORD S-435   (C1701)

  Love Reached Down (composed with
    Croft, Joyce) *sac
    solo,pno WORD S-394   (C1702)

  Obey The Spirit Of The Lord (composed
    with Croft, Joyce) *sac
    solo,pno WORD S-330   (C1703)

  Something Special (composed with
    Croft, Joyce) *sac
    solo,pno WORD S-535   (C1704)

  Things Are Not The Same (composed
    with Croft, Joyce) *sac
    solo,pno WORD S-391   (C1705)

CROFT, COLBERT (cont'd.)
  When Heaven's Gates Are Open Wide
    (composed with Croft, Joyce)
    *sac
    solo,pno WORD S-403   (C1706)

  Who's Gonna Hold Your Hand? (composed
    with Croft, Joyce) *sac
    solo,pno WORD S-412   (C1707)

CROFT, JOYCE
  First Million Years, The *see Croft,
    Colbert

  He Just Loved Me More And More *see
    Croft, Colbert

  Heaven Only Knows *see Croft,
    Colbert

  I Believe He Died For Me *see Croft,
    Colbert

  I Can't Even Walk Without You Holding
    My Hand *see Croft, Colbert

  It's Closer Than It's Ever Been *see
    Croft, Colbert

  Jesus, I Love You *see Croft,
    Colbert

  Lily Of The Valley Is My Lord, The
    *see Croft, Colbert

  Lord, Take The Hand Of This Child
    *see Croft, Colbert

  Love Reached Down *see Croft,
    Colbert

  Obey The Spirit Of The Lord *see
    Croft, Colbert

  Something Special *see Croft,
    Colbert

  Things Are Not The Same *see Croft,
    Colbert

  When Heaven's Gates Are Open Wide
    *see Croft, Colbert

  Who's Gonna Hold Your Hand? *see
    Croft, Colbert

CROFT, WILLIAM (1678-1727)
  My Heart Is Ev'ry Beauty's Prey
    (Johnstone, H. Diack) solo,pno,opt
    vcl (A maj) ROBERTON 1016 s.p.
                                      (C1708)

CROIS-MOI see Schlosser, Paul

CROIS MON CONSEIL, CHERE CLIMENE see
  Debussy, Claude

CROME, FRITZ
  Drei Soldaten *see Tre Soldater

  For Dag *Op.29,No.2
    "Vor Dem Tag" see Zwei Lieder

  Tre Soldater *Op.29,No.1
    "Drei Soldaten" see Zwei Lieder

  Vor Dem Tag *see For Dag

  Zwei Lieder
    [Dan/Ger] solo,pno FOG III, 25 s.p.
    contains: For Dag, "Vor Dem Tag",
    Op.29,No.2; Tre Soldater, "Drei
    Soldaten", Op.29,No.1   (C1709)

CRONE'S CREEL *Scot
    solo,pno PATERSON s.p. see from
    Hebridean Songs, Vol. IV   (C1710)

CROON FOR THE CHRIST CHILD see
  Posamanick, Beatrice

CROQUEMITAINE see Lacome, Paul

CROQUIS see Vellere, Lucie

CROS, CHARLES
  Paquita
    solo,pno ENOCH s.p.   (C1711)
    solo,acap solo pt ENOCH s.p.
                                      (C1712)

CROSS, THE see Ware, Harriet

CROSS AND THE SWITCHBLADE, THE *sac,
  CCUL
    (Carmichael, Ralph) solo,pno WORD
    35051 $2.50   (C1713)

CROSS WAS HEWN FROM A TREE, A see
  Liddell, R.

CROSSE
  Corpus Christi Carol
    Mez/Bar solo,clar,horn,4strings
    (diff) sc OXFORD 62.228 $2.80,
    ipr   (C1714)

CROSSE (cont'd.)

For The Unfallen
T solo,horn,strings (diff) OXFORD
63.066 $14.20   (C1715)

Medieval French Songs *CCU
solo,clar,perc,pno OXFORD rental
(C1716)

Memories Of Morning: Night
solo,pno OXFORD 62.232 $15.50
(C1717)

CROSSES OF CROSSED COLORS see Pousseur,
Henri

CROSSING THE BAR see Clements, John

CROSSING THE BAR see Gerschefski, Edwin

CROUCH, ANDRAE
All I Can Say *sac
solo,pno WORD S-476   (C1718)

Best Of Andrae *sac,CC19L
solo,pno WORD 37731 $4.95   (C1719)

Bless His Holy Name *sac
solo,pno WORD S-503   (C1720)

Blood Will Never Lose Its Power, The
*sac
solo,pno BENSON S7774-R $1.00
(C1721)

Broken Vessel, The *sac
solo,pno BENSON S7775-R $1.00
(C1722)

Heaven *sac
solo,pno WORD S-373   (C1723)

I Didn't Think It Could Be *sac
solo,pno WORD S-484   (C1724)

I Don't Know Why *sac
solo,pno WORD S-271   (C1725)
solo,pno BENSON S5994-R $1.00
(C1726)

I Find No Fault In Him *sac
solo,pno BENSON S6010-R $1.00
(C1727)

I'll Still Love You *sac
solo,pno WORD S-478   (C1728)

I'm Gonna Keep On Singing *sac
solo,pno WORD S-264   (C1729)
solo,pno BENSON S6338-R $1.00
(C1730)

It Ain't No New Thing *sac
solo,pno WORD S-483   (C1731)

It Won't Be Long *sac
solo,pno WORD S-272   (C1732)
solo,pno BENSON S6622-R $1.00
(C1733)

I've Got Confidence *sac
solo,pno WORD S-233   (C1734)
solo,pno BENSON S6434-R $1.00
(C1735)

Jesus *sac
solo,pno WORD S-265   (C1736)
solo,pno BENSON S6701-R $1.00
(C1737)

Jesus Is The Answer *sac
solo,pno WORD S-374   (C1738)
solo,pno BENSON S6728-S $1.00
(C1739)

Just Like He Said He Would *sac
solo,pno WORD S-482   (C1740)

My Tribute *sac
solo,pno WORD S-267   (C1741)
solo,pno BENSON S7119-R $1.00
(C1742)

Oh, I Need Him *sac
solo,pno WORD S-375   (C1743)

Oh, Savior *sac
solo,pno WORD S-477   (C1744)

Praises *sac
solo,pno WORD S-479   (C1745)

Sweet Love Of Jesus, The *sac
solo,pno WORD S-475   (C1746)

Take Me Back *sac
solo,pno WORD S-498   (C1747)

Take Me Back *sac,CC11L
solo,pno WORD 37727 $2.50   (C1748)

Tell Them *sac
solo,pno WORD S-497   (C1749)

They Shall Be Mine *sac
solo,pno WORD S-481   (C1750)

Through It All *sac
solo,pno BENSON S8182-R $1.00
(C1751)

What Ya Gonna Do *sac
solo,pno WORD S-266   (C1752)

You Can Depend On Me *sac
solo,pno WORD S-480   (C1753)

CROUCH, F. NICHOLS
Kathleen Mavourneen
low solo,pno (D flat maj) ASHDOWN
(C1754)
med solo,pno (E flat maj) ASHDOWN
(C1755)
high solo,pno (F maj) ASHDOWN
(C1756)

CROWE, A.C.
Fairie Voices, Waltz-Song
solo,pno CRAMER   (C1757)

CROWN, THE see Rae, Kenneth

CROWN OF THE YEAR, THE see Martin,
Easthope

CROWN OF VICTORY, THE see Davis

CROWN WITH THY BENEDICTION see Cassler,
G. Winston

CRUCEM TUAM see Andriessen, Hendrik

CRUCIFIX see Faure, Jean-Baptiste

CRUCIFIXION, THE see Curran, Pearl
Gildersleeve

CRUCIFIXUS see Faure, Jean-Baptiste

CRUDA, FUNESTA SMANIA see Donizetti,
Gaetano

CRUDEL TIRANNO, AMOR see Handel, George
Frideric

CRUDELE? AH NO, MIO BENE see Mozart,
Wolfgang Amadeus

CRUEL BROTHER, THE
see Schirmer's American Folk-Song
Series, Set XXII (American-English
Folk-Ballads From The Southern
Appalachian Mountains)

CRUEL PEGGY see Hook, James

CRUELLE DEPARTIE see Besard, Jean-
Baptiste

CRUELLE MERE DES AMOURS see Rameau,
Jean-Philippe

CRUELLE? SUIS-JE CRUELLE? see Mozart,
Wolfgang Amadeus, Crudele? Ah No,
Mio Bene

CRUGER, JOHANN (1598-1662)
Nun Jauchzet All, Ihr Frommen *sac
SA soli,2S rec,cont HANSSLER 5.037
s.p. see also GESANGE ZUM
KIRCHENJAHR   (C1758)

Nun Lasst Uns Gehn Und Treten *sac
SA soli,2S rec,cont HANSSLER 5.043
s.p. see also GESANGE ZUM
KIRCHENJAHR   (C1759)

O Jesu Christ, Dein Kripplein Ist
*sac
SA soli,2S rec,cont HANSSLER 5.040
s.p. see also GESANGE ZUM
KIRCHENJAHR   (C1760)

Tauet, Himmel, Den Gerechten *sac
SA soli,2S rec,cont HANSSLER 5.038
s.p. see also GESANGE ZUM
KIRCHENJAHR   (C1761)

CRUICKSHANK, R.
He Is There *sac
(Wild) solo,pno BERANDOL DC 4 $1.50
(C1762)
Little People's Prayer *sac
(Wild) solo,pno BERANDOL DC 3 $1.50
(C1763)

CRUMB, GEORGE (1929-   )
Ancient Voices Of Children
S&boy solo,ob,harp,3perc,mand,
electric piano, toy piano PETERS
66303 $12.50   (C1764)

Lux Aeterna For Five Masked Musicians
S solo,2perc, bass flute, sitar
PETERS 66495 $7.50   (C1765)

Madrigals, Book I *CCU,madrigal
S solo,bvl,vibra PETERS 66458 $7.50
(C1766)
Madrigals, Book II *CCU,madrigal
S solo,fl,perc PETERS 66459 $7.50
(C1767)
Madrigals, Book III *CCU,madrigal
S solo,harp,perc PETERS 66460 $7.50
(C1768)
Madrigals, Book IV *CCU,madrigal
S solo,fl,pic,harp,perc,bvl, alto
flute PETERS 66461 $7.50 (C1769)

Night Of The Four Moons
A solo,pic,perc, alto flute, banjo,
electric cello PETERS 66462
$12.00   (C1770)

CRUMB, GEORGE (cont'd.)

Songs, Drones And Refrains Of Death
*CCU
Bar solo,2perc, electric guitar,
electric bass, electric piano &
harpsichord PETERS 66463 $15.00
(C1771)

CRUSADE FAVORITES FROM AROUND THE WORLD
*sac,CCUL
solo,pno WORD 30023 $2.00   (C1772)

CRUSADE SOLOIST, THE *sac,CC16UL
solo,pno,gtr/acord LILLENAS MB-033
$1.95   (C1773)

CRUSELL
Frithiof Och Bjorn
2 soli,pno LUNDQUIST s.p.   (C1774)

CRUX FIDELIS see Stout, Alan

CRYES OF OLDE LONDON, BOOK I *CCU
(Thomas) solo,pno PAXTON G36009 s.p.
(C1775)
CRYES OF OLDE LONDON, BOOK II *CCU
(Thomas) solo,pno PAXTON G36016 s.p.
(C1776)

CRYING OF WATER, THE see Campbell-
Tipton, Louis, Le Cri Des Eaux

CRYING WATER see Hamblen, Bernard

CRYPTOGAMEN see Schat, Peter

CRYSTAL AGAINST MIRROR see Bon,
Maarten, Kristal Tegen Spiegel

CRYSTAL CUP, THE see Childe, Robert

CRYSTAL FOUNTAIN, THE *folk
(Widdicombe, Trevor) [Eng/Fr] solo,
pno ROBERTON 72664 s.p. French-
Canadian
contains: A La Claire Fontaine,
"Down By The Crystal Fountain";
En Roulant Ma Boule, "Canoe
Song"; Isabeau S'y Promene,
"Isabelle"; Mon Pere A Fait Batir
Maison, "Down In The Meadow"; Une
Perdriole, "To-Day The First Of
May"; Vive La Canadienne!,
"Marianna"   (C1777)

CRZELLITZER, FRITZ
Twenty-One Songs *CC21U
[Ger] solo,pno OR-TAV s.p.   (C1778)

CSARDAS see Strauss, Johann, Klange Der
Heimat

CTYRI MONOLOGY see Macha, Otmar

CTYRI PISNE see Dvorak, Antonin

CTYRI PISNE see Mikoda, Borivoj

CTYRI PISNE see Palenicek, Josef

CTYRI PISNE see Rezac, Ivan

CTYRI PISNE NA SLOVA DETSKE POEZIE see
Vrba, F.

CTYRI PISNE PRO BARYTON see Valek, Jiri

CTYRI PISNICKY PRO DETI see Barta,
Lubor

CTYRI UKOLEBAVKY see Novak, V.

CUANDO EL REY NIMROD
(Neumann, Richard) "When King Nimrod"
solo,pno/org (Ladino text)
TRANSCON. WJ 401 $1.00   (C1779)

CUANDO SALI DE MARBELLA see Maravilla,
L.

CUARTO BERCEUSES see Canal, Marguerite

CUARTO CANCIONES see Bacharach, E.

CUARTO CANCIONES see Lavilla, F.

CUARTO CANCIONES see Rodriguez Albert,
R.

CUARTO CANCIONES ARGENTINAS see
Pedrell, F.

CUARTO CANCIONES ESPANOLAS see Lavilla,
F.

CUARTO CANCIONES LEONESAS see Halffter,
C.

CUARTO CANCIONES POPULARES CATALANAS
*CC4U,Span
(Tarrago) med solo,pno UNION ESP.
$2.00   (C1780)

CUARTO CANCIONES POPULARES CATALANAS
*CC4U,Span
(Tarrago) [Span] med solo,gtr UNION
ESP. $2.00   (C1781)

CUARTO CANCIONES POPULARES DE ANDALUCIA
see Nin-Culmell, Joaquin

CUARTO CANCIONES POPULARES DE CATALANA
see Nin-Culmell, Joaquin

CUARTO CANCIONES POPULARES MALLORQUINAS
see Thomas, J.M.

CUARTO CANCIONES SEFARDIES see Pla, R.

CUARTO CANCIONES VASCAS see Lavilla, F.

CUARTO CANTARCILLOS see Bacarisse,
Salvador

CUARTO CANTIGAS see Alfonso El Sabio

CUARTO MADRIGALES AMATORIOS see
Rodrigo, Joaquin

CUARTO MELODIES CATALANES see Donostia,
R.P.

CUARTO POPULARES DE SALAMANCA see Nin-
Culmell, Joaquin

CUATRO CANCIONES AL ESTILO POPULAR
ARGENTINO see Jurafsky, Abraham

CUATRO MADRIGALES AMATORIOS see
Rodrigo, Joaquin

CUAUHTEMOC see Velazquez, Leonardo

CUCKOO see Lehmann, Liza

CUCKOO, THE
see Three Slovak Songs

CUCKOO, THE see Dvorak, Antonin, Der
Kukuk

CUCKOO, THE see Kilpinen, Yrio, Der
Kuckuck

CUCKOO AND CHESTNUT TIME see Pitfield,
Thomas Baron

CUCKOO CLOCK see Grant-Schaefer, G.A.

CUCKOO SONG see Hely-Hutchinson,
(Christian) Victor

CUEILLETTE see Gedalge, Andre

CUENTOS DEL BOSQUE DE VIENA see
Strauss, Johann, G'schichten Aus
Dem Wienerwald

CUGLEY, IAN
    Cri
        A solo,2vla ALBERT AHL218 rental
                                        (C1782)
    This Is The Truth Sent From Above
        Bar solo,rec,ob,vcl ALBERT AHL216
        rental   (C1783)

    Zum
        solo,fl,vibra,perc ALBERT AHL217
        rental   (C1784)

CUI, CESAR ANTONOVITCH (1835-1918)
    Dans La Plaine Blonde
        S/T solo,pno/inst DURAND s.p.
                                        (C1785)
    Ici-Bas *Op.54,No.5
        [Russ/Fr] med solo,pno BELAIEFF 254
        s.p.   (C1786)
    Je N'en Ai Jamais Aime Qu'une
        *Op.54,No.4
        [Russ/Fr] med solo,pno BELAIEFF 253
        s.p.   (C1787)

    La Pauvre Fleur Disait
        S/T solo,pno/inst DURAND s.p.
                                        (C1788)
    L'echo
        Mez/Bar solo,pno/inst DURAND s.p.
                                        (C1789)
CUIUS ANIMAM see Rossini, Gioacchino

CUJUS ANIMAM see Boccherini, Luigi

CUM DECENDISSET JESUS see Hindemith,
Paul

CUM FACTUS ESSET JESUS see Hindemith,
Paul

CUM NATUS ESSET see Hindemith, Paul

CUMMING, R.
    As Dew In April
        solo,pno,ob,opt vln/clar (D maj)
        BOOSEY $1.50   (C1790)

    Go, Lovely Rose
        solo,pno (F maj) BOOSEY $1.50
                                        (C1791)
    Little Black Boy
        solo,pno (D maj) BOOSEY $1.50
                                        (C1792)

CUMMING, R. (cont'd.)

    Memory, Hither Come
        solo,pno (E maj) BOOSEY $1.50
                                        (C1793)
    We Happy Few *song cycle
        med solo,pno BOOSEY $3.50   (C1794)

CUOPRE TAL VOLTA IL CIELO see Handel,
George Frideric

CUOR D'AMANTE RICHIEDE GRAN COSA LO SAI
see Lehar, Franz

CUORE, COME UN FIORE see Mascagni,
Pietro

CUPID AND CAMPASPE see Blank, Allan

CUPID, CUPID BEND THY BOW see Pepusch,
John Christopher

CUPIDOOTJE see Beekhuis, Hanna

CUPIDOTJE see Beekhuis, Hanna

CUPIDS GARDEN see Somervell, Arthur

CUPID'S POWER I DESPISE see Stanley,
John

CURIOUS THING see Klemm, Gustav

CURRAN, PEARL GILDERSLEEVE (1875-1941)
    Blessing *sac
        low solo,pno (B flat maj) SCHIRM.G
        $.75   (C1795)
    Crucifixion, The *sac
        high solo,pno (G maj) SCHIRM.G
        $1.00   (C1796)
    Dawn
        low solo,pno (A flat maj) SCHIRM.G
        $.75   (C1797)
    Gratitude *sac
        high solo,pno (A flat maj) SCHIRM.G
        $.75   (C1798)
    Ho! Mr. Piper
        low solo,pno (D maj) SCHIRM.G $.85
                                        (C1799)
        low solo,pno (D maj) ALLANS s.p.
                                        (C1800)
        high solo,pno (F maj) ALLANS s.p.
                                        (C1801)
    Hold Thou My Hand *sac
        high solo,pno (F maj) SCHIRM.G $.85
                                        (C1802)
    Life
        high solo,pno (F maj) SCHIRM.G $.85
                                        (C1803)
        med solo,pno (E flat maj) SCHIRM.G
        $.85   (C1804)
        low solo,pno (C maj) SCHIRM.G $.85
                                        (C1805)
        low solo,pno (F maj) ALLANS s.p.
                                        (C1806)
        med solo,pno (E flat maj) ALLANS
        s.p.   (C1807)
        high solo,pno (C maj) ALLANS s.p.
                                        (C1808)
    Nocturne
        low solo,pno (B maj) SCHIRM.G $.75
                                        (C1809)
        med solo,pno (D flat maj) ALLANS
        s.p.   (C1810)
        high solo,pno (F maj) ALLANS s.p.
                                        (C1811)
        low solo,pno (B maj) ALLANS s.p.
                                        (C1812)
    Nursery Rhymes
        high solo,pno (G maj) SCHIRM.G $.75
                                        (C1813)
        low solo,pno (E flat maj) SCHIRM.G
        $.75   (C1814)
    Prayer *sac
        med-high solo,pno (E flat maj)
        SCHIRM.G $.85   (C1815)
    Rain
        low solo,pno (C maj) SCHIRM.G $.75
                                        (C1816)
    Resurrection, The *sac
        low solo,pno (A maj) SCHIRM.G $.75
                                        (C1817)
CURRY, W. LAWRENCE
    Nightingale
        med solo,pno FITZSIMONS $.50
                                        (C1818)
CURSCHMANN, F.
    Till Bruden
        high solo,pno GEHRMANS s.p. (C1819)
        low solo,pno GEHRMANS s.p.   (C1820)
CURTIS
    Gondolsang
        solo,pno LUNDQUIST s.p.   (C1821)

CURVA MINORE see Esposito, E.

CURWIN, CLIFFORD
    Early Morning
        solo,pno CRAMER   (C1822)
CUSTER, ARTHUR (1923-   )
    Songs Of The Seasons *CCU
        S solo,fl,ob,clar/al-sax,2horn,trp,
        timp,strings AM.COMP.AL. sc
        $31.90, voc sc $9.35   (C1823)
CUVILLIER, CHARLES (1877-1955)
    Adieu
        solo,pno ENOCH s.p. see also Vingt
        Melodies   (C1824)
    Ah! Votre Emoi, Je Le Partage (from
        La Reine Joyeuse)
        solo,pno ENOCH s.p.   (C1825)
    Amertume
        solo,pno (available in 2 keys)
        ENOCH s.p.   (C1826)
    Amours Lointaines
        solo,pno (available in 2 keys)
        ENOCH s.p.   (C1827)
    Angelus *sac
        [Lat] solo,pno/org ENOCH s.p.
                                        (C1828)
    Appassionata
        solo,pno (available in 2 keys)
        ENOCH s.p.   (C1829)
    Au Bord De L'eau
        solo,pno (available in 2 keys)
        ENOCH s.p.   (C1830)
    Au Jardin D'amour
        solo,pno (available in 2 keys)
        ENOCH s.p. see also Vingt
        Melodies   (C1831)
    Au Pays D'amourette
        solo,acap solo pt ENOCH s.p.
                                        (C1832)
        solo,pno (available in 2 keys)
        ENOCH s.p. see also Vingt
        Melodies   (C1833)
    Aubade
        solo,pno (available in 2 keys)
        ENOCH s.p.   (C1834)
    Aurore
        2 soli,pno ENOCH s.p. see from Nuit
        D'Isaphan   (C1835)
    Berceuse Triste
        solo,pno (available in 2 keys)
        ENOCH s.p.   (C1836)
    Celle Que Nous Aimons
        solo,pno (available in 2 keys)
        ENOCH s.p.   (C1837)
    C'etait Un Soir
        solo,pno (available in 2 keys)
        ENOCH s.p.   (C1838)
    Chanson Chinoise
        solo,pno (available in 2 keys)
        ENOCH s.p.   (C1839)
    Chanson D'un Jour De Printemps
        solo,pno ENOCH s.p. see also Vingt
        Melodies   (C1840)
    Chanson Jalouse
        solo,pno (available in 2 keys)
        ENOCH s.p.   (C1841)
    Chanson Pour Lui
        solo,pno (available in 2 keys)
        ENOCH s.p.   (C1842)
    Chanson Timide
        solo,pno (available in 2 keys)
        ENOCH s.p.   (C1843)
    Chant D'Apres-Midi
        solo,pno ENOCH s.p.   (C1844)
        solo,orch ENOCH rental   (C1845)
    Coeur De Mousme
        solo,pno ENOCH s.p.   (C1846)
    Colloque Sentimental
        Mez solo,orch (E min) ENOCH rental
                                        (C1847)
        solo,vcl ENOCH s.p.   (C1848)
        solo,pno (available in 2 keys)
        ENOCH s.p.   (C1849)
    Couplets De Bertha (from Les Rendez-
        Vous Strasbourgeois)
        solo,pno ENOCH s.p.   (C1850)
    Couplets De Gretchen (from Les
        Rendez-Vous Strasbourgeois)
        solo,pno ENOCH s.p.   (C1851)
    Couplets Du Kouss Kouss (from Afgar)
        solo,pno ENOCH s.p.   (C1852)

CUVILLIER, CHARLES (cont'd.)

Crespuscule
    solo,pno (available in 2 keys)
    ENOCH s.p. see from Nuit
    D'Ispahan   (C1853)

Cypris
    solo,pno ENOCH s.p. see also Vingt
    Melodies   (C1854)

Dans Mon Coeur
    solo,pno (available in 2 keys)
    ENOCH s.p.   (C1855)

Doit-On Le Dire
    solo,pno ENOCH s.p.   (C1856)
    solo,acap solo pt ENOCH s.p.
                                 (C1857)

Il Etait Une Fois
    solo,pno (available in 2 keys)
    ENOCH s.p. see also Vingt
    Melodies   (C1858)

J'ai Tout Oublie (from Son Petit
    Frere)
    solo,pno ENOCH s.p.   (C1859)

John Bull Vient S'habiller En France
    (from Les Muscadines)
    solo,pno (available in 2 keys)
    ENOCH s.p.   (C1860)

La Collerette De Pierrot
    solo,pno ENOCH s.p.   (C1861)

La Gerbe
    solo,pno ENOCH s.p. see also Vingt
    Melodies   (C1862)

La Rose Au Rosier Blanc
    solo,pno (available in 2 keys)
    ENOCH s.p.   (C1863)

La Vie Est Grise
    solo,pno (available in 2 keys)
    ENOCH s.p.   (C1864)

L'adorable Symphonie
    solo,pno (available in 2 keys)
    ENOCH s.p.   (C1865)

Larmes Refoulees
    solo,pno (available in 2 keys)
    ENOCH s.p.   (C1866)

L'Aurore
    2 soli,pno ENOCH s.p. voc sc, solo
    pt   (C1867)

Le Berceau
    solo,pno (available in 2 keys)
    ENOCH s.p.   (C1868)

Le Chien
    solo,pno ENOCH s.p.   (C1869)
    solo,acap solo pt ENOCH s.p. (C1870)

Le Coq Du Clocher
    solo,pno (available in 2 keys)
    ENOCH s.p.   (C1871)

Le Godillots
    solo,pno solo pt ENOCH s.p. (C1872)

Le Passe Qui File
    solo,pno ENOCH s.p. see also Vingt
    Melodies   (C1873)

Le Printemps
    solo,pno (available in 2 keys)
    ENOCH s.p. see also Vingt
    Melodies   (C1874)

Le Retour Du Printemps
    solo,acap solo pt ENOCH s.p.
                                 (C1875)
    solo,pno ENOCH s.p. see also Vingt
    Melodies   (C1876)

Le Vendredi
    solo,pno ENOCH s.p. see also Vingt
    Melodies   (C1877)

L'Eglise Du Village
    solo,pno (available in 2 keys)
    ENOCH s.p. see also Vingt
    Melodies   (C1878)

Les Godillots
    solo,pno oct ENOCH s.p.   (C1879)

Les Hirondelles
    solo,pno ENOCH s.p.   (C1880)

Les Loups Blancs
    solo,pno ENOCH s.p.   (C1881)
    solo,acap solo pt ENOCH s.p.
                                 (C1882)

Les Mouettes
    solo,pno (available in 2 keys)
    ENOCH s.p.   (C1883)

Les Pecheuses
    solo,pno ENOCH s.p.   (C1884)

CUVILLIER, CHARLES (cont'd.)

Les Petits Elfes
    solo,pno ENOCH s.p. see also Vingt
    Melodies   (C1885)

Les Triolets De La Marquise
    solo,pno (available in 2 keys)
    ENOCH s.p.   (C1886)

L'Ete De La Saint-Martin (from Afgar)
    solo,pno ENOCH s.p.   (C1887)

L'Eventail
    solo,pno ENOCH s.p. see also Vingt
    Melodies   (C1888)

L'Oiseleur
    solo,pno (available in 2 keys)
    ENOCH s.p.   (C1889)

Lorsque Je Partis De Metro-Bazar
    (from La Reine Joyeuse)
    solo,pno ENOCH s.p.   (C1890)

Ma Belle M'a Dit
    solo,pno ENOCH s.p. see also Vingt
    Melodies   (C1891)

Ma Vigne Et Ma Mie
    solo,pno (available in 2 keys)
    ENOCH s.p.   (C1892)

Melancolie
    solo,pno (available in 2 keys)
    ENOCH s.p.   (C1893)

Menuets De Vade
    solo,pno (available in 2 keys)
    ENOCH s.p.   (C1894)

Musique D'antan
    solo,pno (available in 2 keys)
    ENOCH s.p.   (C1895)

Nocturne
    solo,pno (available in 2 keys)
    ENOCH s.p. see from Nuit
    D'Ispahan   (C1896)

Non
    solo,pno ENOCH s.p.   (C1897)

Nous Ne Connaissions Jusqu'ici (from
    Afgar)
    solo,pno ENOCH s.p.   (C1898)

Nuit D'Isaphan *see Aurore   (C1899)

Nuit D'Ispahan *see Crespuscule;
    Nocturne   (C1900)

Oh! La Troublante Volupte (from La
    Reine Joyeuse)
    solo,pno ENOCH s.p.   (C1901)

Ophelie
    solo,pno ENOCH s.p.   (C1902)

Oui, C'est L'amour (from Son Petit
    Frere)
    solo,pno ENOCH s.p.   (C1903)

Ouvrez Aux Enfants
    solo,pno (available in 2 keys)
    ENOCH s.p.   (C1904)

Papillon Blanc
    solo,pno ENOCH s.p. see also Vingt
    Melodies   (C1905)

Paques Fleuries
    solo,pno ENOCH s.p. see also Vingt
    Melodies   (C1906)

Petit Tout Petit (from Son Petit
    Frere)
    2 soli,pno ENOCH s.p.   (C1907)

Plaintes Sur La Mort De Sylvie
    solo,pno (available in 2 keys)
    ENOCH s.p.   (C1908)

Primevere
    solo,pno (available in 2 keys)
    ENOCH s.p.   (C1909)

Prophetie
    solo,pno (available in 2 keys)
    ENOCH s.p.   (C1910)
    Mez solo,orch (C min) ENOCH rental
                                 (C1911)

Que Ne Puis-Je Comme Elleviou? (from
    Les Muscadines)
    solo,pno (available in 2 keys)
    ENOCH s.p.   (C1912)

Ronde Du Bois Dore
    solo,acap solo pt ENOCH s.p. (C1913)
    solo,pno ENOCH s.p. see also Vingt
    Melodies   (C1914)

Rondeau
    solo,pno ENOCH s.p.   (C1915)

CUVILLIER, CHARLES (cont'd.)

Rose D'amour
    solo,pno (available in 2 keys)
    ENOCH s.p.   (C1916)

Seize Ans
    solo,pno (available in 2 keys)
    ENOCH s.p. see also Vingt
    Melodies   (C1917)

Si Tu Veux
    solo,pno (available in 2 keys)
    ENOCH s.p.   (C1918)

Siasons Moroses
    solo,pno ENOCH s.p. see also Vingt
    Melodies   (C1919)

Sonnet De Joachim Du Bellay
    solo,pno (available in 2 keys)
    ENOCH s.p.   (C1920)

Sous La Ramure
    solo,pno (available in 2 keys)
    ENOCH s.p.   (C1921)

Tout A L'heure
    solo,pno (available in 2 keys)
    ENOCH s.p.   (C1922)

Tu Fais Le Castillan Superbe (from
    Afgar)
    2 soli,pno ENOCH s.p.   (C1923)

Va Mon Adore (from Son Petit Frere)
    solo,pno ENOCH s.p.   (C1924)

Valse D'amour
    solo,pno (available in 2 keys)
    ENOCH s.p.   (C1925)

Vieux Madrigal
    solo,pno (available in 2 keys)
    ENOCH s.p.   (C1926)

Vingt Melodies
    solo,pno cmplt ed ENOCH s.p.
    available in 2 keys
    contains & see also: Adieu; Au
        Jardin D'amour; Au Pays
        D'amourette; Chanson D'un Jour
        De Printemps; Cypris; Il Etait
        Une Fois; La Gerbe; Le Passe
        Qui File; Le Printemps; Le
        Retour Du Printemps; Le
        Vendredi; L'Eglise Du Village;
        Les Petits Elfes; L'Eventail;
        Ma Belle M'a Dit; Papillon
        Blanc; Paques Fleuries; Ronde
        Du Bois Dore; Seize Ans;
        Siasons Moroses   (C1927)

CUYANA see Lasala, Angel

CUYPERS, H.
    Ach Wenn Es Nun Die Mutter Wuszt
        see Vier Madchenlieder

    Als Kind Heb' Ich Oft
        see Vier Madchenlieder

    De Bietbauw
        see Liederen, Serie 1

    Kind Van Mijn Liefde
        see Liederen, Serie 1

    Liederen, Serie 1
        solo,pno ALSBACH s.p.
        contains: De Bietbauw; Kind Van
            Mijn Liefde; Of Hij Zal Komen
                                     (C1928)
    Liederen, Serie 2: Van 'T Spinsterke
        solo,pno ALSBACH   (C1929)

    Liederen, Serie 3
        solo,pno ALSBACH s.p.
        contains: Op Den Weefstoel;
            Sarlotteken; Vlaamse Kermis
                                     (C1930)
    Of Hij Zal Komen
        see Liederen, Serie 1

    Op Den Weefstoel
        see Liederen, Serie 3

    Sarlotteken
        see Liederen, Serie 3

    Sehnsucht
        see Vier Madchenlieder

    Vier Madchenlieder
        solo,pno ALSBACH s.p.
        contains: Ach Wenn Es Nun Die
            Mutter Wuszt; Als Kind Heb' Ich
            Oft; Sehnsucht; Von Deinem
            Heiszen Kusse   (C1931)

    Vlaamse Kermis
        see Liederen, Serie 3

    Von Deinem Heiszen Kusse
        see Vier Madchenlieder

CYCLAMEN see Mulder, Herman

CYCLE OF HOLY SONGS see Rorem, Ned

CYCLE OF LIFE, A see Ronald, Sir Landon

CYCLE OF NOVELTIES see Parchman, Gen

CYCLE OF SIX SONGS, A see Berlioz,
   Hector, Les Nuits D'Ete

CYCLE OF SONNETS, A see Dahl, Ingolf

CYCLUS ANTIQUUS see Kardos, Istvan

CYGNE BLANC see Migot, Georges

CYGNES SUR L'EAU see Faure, Gabriel-
   Urbain

CYGNOLOGY see Tanenbaum, Elias

CYKLUS PISNI O LASCE NA TEXT J.V.
   SLADKA see Toman, Josef

CYMRU FACH see Richards, David

CYNARA see Delius, Frederick

CYNARA see Maganini, Quinto

CYPRIAN SONGS see Lees, Benjamin

CYPRIS see Cuvillier, Charles

CYTHERE   *Op.42,No.5
   [Ger/Eng] solo,pno ZIMMER. s.p. see
   from Zwolf Gesange Nach Gedichten
   Von Paul Verlaine   (C1932)

CYTHERE see Kowalski, Max

CZARDAS see Lacome, Paul

CZARDAS see Nicklass-Kempner, S.

CZARNIKOW
   God Walks The Dark Hills *sac
   solo,pno BENSON S5566-S $1.00
                                 (C1933)

CZECH SONGS FOR YOUNG CHILDREN
   *CC12U, folk,Czech
   (Offer, Charles) solo,pno OXFORD
   68.227 $.75   (C1934)

CZECHOSLOVAKIAN SUITE see Anonymous

CZERNIK, W.
   Auf Schusters Rappen
   solo,pno/orch ZIMMER. 1434 s.p.,
      ipr   (C1935)

   Mon Reve Familier
   see Zwei Lieder Nach Gedichten Von
      Paul Verlaine

   Und Es Wird Kommen Eon Sommertag
   see Zwei Lieder Nach Gedichten Von
      Paul Verlaine

   Venezianische Nacht
   [Ger/It] solo,pno/orch ZIMMER. 1435
      s.p., ipr   (C1936)

   Willst Du Mit Mir In Die Sonne Gehn?
   solo,pno/orch ZIMMER. 1436 s.p.,
      ipr   (C1937)

   Zwei Lieder Nach Gedichten Von Paul
      Verlaine
   solo,pno/orch ZIMMER. 1437 s.p.,
      ipr
      contains: Mon Reve Familier; Und
      Es Wird Kommen Eon Sommertag
                                 (C1938)

D

D' 'A MALASCIORTA MIA VACO P' 'O MARE
   see Giazotto, Remo

DA CHRISTUS GEBOREN WAR see Marx, Karl

DA DUE VENTI see Vivaldi, Antonio

DA ER MICH ANSAH see Kuiler, Cor.

DA GEH ICH ZU MAXIM see Lehar, Franz

DA ICH NUN IN IHR AUGE SAH see
   Donizetti, Gaetano

DA-OZ, RAM
   Kumu Ve'nashir
   solo,pno OR-TAV $1.00   (D1)

DA PRISEN KOM see Hauger, Kristian

DA QL' ALTRA PART!
   (Carlo, Musi) solo,pno (Bolognese
   dialect) BONGIOVANI 2057 s.p. see
   from El Mi Canzunett   (D2)

DA QUEL GIORNO see Charpentier, Gustave

DA SCHLAGT DIE ABSCHIEDSSTUNDE see
   Mozart, Wolfgang Amadeus

DA STIEG EIN BAUM see Rautavaara,
   Einojuhani

DA TAR JAG MIN GITARR see Lagerheim-
   Romare, Margit

DA TAUTS DE GRAUTS see Kolz, E.

DAAR STOND EEN STER TE GLOREN see Oort,
   H.C.v.

DABER ELAI BE'SHIRIM *CCU
   solo,pno OR-TAV $3.50   (D3)

DADDY'S ANGEL see Hemery, Valentine

DAER STAET EEN CLOOSTER IN OOSTENRIJC
   see Beuningen, W.v.

DAER WAS EEN SNEEUWWIT VOGELTJE see
   Beuningen, W.v.

DAFFINS see Musgrave, Thea

DAFFODIL GOLD see Hodgson, A.R.

DAFFODILS see Gyring, Elizabeth

DAFFODILS see Musgrave, Thea, Daffins

DAFFODILS FROM MY GARDEN see Boanas

DAG AAN DAG KOMT HIJ EN GAAT see
   Mengelberg, Karel

DAG, SOM JAG LEVAT! see Peterson-
   Berger, (Olof) Wilhelm

DAGAR KOMMA, DAGAR SER JAG LYKTA see
   Nordqvist, Gustaf

DAGEN FLYR see Peterson-Berger, (Olof)
   Wilhelm

DAGEN SVALNAR see Snare, Sigurd

DAGS VISOR see Reimers, Ivar

DAHINTER WIRD STILLE see Wagner-Regeny,
   Rudolf

DAHL
   Aftonstamning
   solo,pno LUNDQUIST s.p.   (D4)

   Bachanal
   high solo,pno LUNDQUIST s.p.   (D5)
   low solo,pno LUNDQUIST s.p.   (D6)

   Invocation
   [Fr/Swed] solo,pno LUNDQUIST s.p.
                                  (D7)

   Lovsang
   high solo,pno,vln LUNDQUIST s.p.
                                  (D8)
   low solo,pno,vln LUNDQUIST s.p.
                                  (D9)

   Midsommar
   solo,pno LUNDQUIST s.p.   (D10)

   Tonerna
   SBar soli,pno LUNDQUIST s.p.   (D11)

DAHL, INGOLF (1912-1970)
   Cycle Of Sonnets, A *song cycle
   Bar solo,pno BOONIN $12.00   (D12)

DAHL, INGOLF (cont'd.)
   Three Songs To Poems By Albert
      Ehrismann *CC3U
   S solo,pno BOONIN $6.00   (D13)

DAHLGREN, ERLAND
   Ar Du Fridlos?
   solo,pno,opt gtr GEHRMANS s.p. (D14)

   Barndomsminnen
   solo,pno,opt gtr GEHRMANS s.p. (D15)

   Du Ar Min Herre *sac
   solo,pno,opt gtr GEHRMANS s.p. (D16)

   Guds Gavor *sac
   solo,pno,opt gtr GEHRMANS s.p. (D17)

   Han Kommer
   solo,pno,opt gtr GEHRMANS s.p. (D18)

   Harlighetens Morgon
   solo,pno,opt gtr (E maj) GEHRMANS
      s.p.   (D19)
   solo,pno,opt gtr (F maj) GEHRMANS
      s.p.   (D20)
   2 soli,pno GEHRMANS s.p.   (D21)

   Herlighetens Morgon
   solo,pno MUSIKK s.p.   (D22)

   Hor, Helga Klockor Kalla
   solo,pno,opt gtr GEHRMANS s.p. (D23)

   Jag En Gast Och Pilgrim Ar
   solo,pno,opt gtr GEHRMANS s.p. (D24)

   Jag Langtar Hem
   solo,pno,opt gtr GEHRMANS s.p. (D25)

   Vand Ater Till Hemmet Idag
   solo,pno,opt gtr GEHRMANS s.p. (D26)

DAI CAMPI, DAI PRATI see Boito, Arrigo

DAI DAL GESS!!
   (Carlo, Musi) solo,pno (Bolognese
   dialect) BONGIOVANI 2089 s.p. see
   from El Mi Canzunett   (D27)

DAINTIE DAVIE *folk,Scot
   solo,pno (C maj) PATERSON FS115 s.p.
                                  (D28)

DAINTY, E.
   My Ladye's Glove
   solo,pno BERANDOL BER 1304 $1.50
                                  (D29)

DAISIES see Hawley, Charles Beach

DAISIES, THE see Barber, Samuel

DAISIES, THE see Mourant, Walter

DAISY'S SONG see Sveinbjornsson,
   Sveinbjorn

DAISY'S SONG see Taylor, H. Stanley

DAL LABBRO IL CANTO see Verdi, Giuseppe

DAL QUADERNO DI FRANCINE see Vogel,
   Wladimir

DAL TUO STELLATO SOGLIO see Rossini,
   Gioacchino

DAL VOSTRO VERZIERE see Cimara, Pietro

DALAYRAC, [NICOLAS] (1753-1809)
   Notre Meunier
   see LA MUSIQUE, PREMIER CAHIER

   Quand Le Bien-Aime Reviendra
   solo,pno/inst DURAND s.p.   (D30)

DALBOLAT see Nordqvist, Gustaf

DALBY, MARTIN (1942-   )
   Cantica
   S/T solo,clar,pno,vla NOVELLO
      rental   (D31)

   Keeper Of The Pass, The
   S solo,3clar,2bass clar,perc,pno
      NOVELLO rental   (D32)

   Muse Of Love *song cycle
   high solo,pno BOOSEY $4.50   (D33)

DALCROZE, JACQUES
   J'ai Des P'tites Fleurs Bleues
   2 soli,orch HENN s.p.   (D34)

   La Noce
   2 soli,orch HENN s.p.   (D35)

   L'Amour
   2 soli,orch HENN s.p.   (D36)

   Le Vent
   2 soli,orch HENN s.p.   (D37)

   Matin Pastoral
   S solo,orch HENN s.p.   (D38)

DALCROZE, JACQUES (cont'd.)

Notre Geneve *CC16U
  solo,pno HENN 605 s.p.   (D39)

Ronde
  2 soli,orch HENN s.p.   (D40)

Valse Des Mouettes
  solo,pno ALSBACH s.p.   (D41)

DALE, BENJAMIN J. (1885-1943)
  Come Away, Death
    high solo,pno NOVELLO 17.0029.04
    s.p.   (D42)
    low solo,pno NOVELLO 17.0030.08
    s.p.   (D43)

  O Mistress Mine
    T solo,pno NOVELLO 17.0135.05 s.p.
                                  (D44)
    Bar solo,pno NOVELLO 17.0136.03
    s.p.   (D45)

DALE, MERVYN
  Centipede And Other Rhymes *CCU
    ASHDOWN s.p.   (D46)

  Fie Diddle Dee
    solo,pno (F maj) ASHDOWN   (D47)

  Footsteps In The Snow
    solo,pno (F maj) ASHDOWN   (D48)

  Four English Lyrics *CC4U
    ASHDOWN s.p.   (D49)

  Sixteen Silly Songs For Kids *CC16U
    solo,pno ASHDOWN s.p.   (D50)

  Snowie The Snowman
    solo,pno (F maj) ASHDOWN   (D51)

  Sweet To Me
    solo,pno (F maj) ASHDOWN   (D52)

DALEKY HLAS see Jirko, Ivo

DALLA FORZA NASCE LA FORMA see
  Bettinelli, Bruno

DALLA GUERRA AMOROSA see Handel, George
  Frideric

DALLA SUA PACE see Mozart, Wolfgang
  Amadeus

DALLA SUA PACE LA MIA DIPENDE see
  Mozart, Wolfgang Amadeus

DALLAPICCOLA, LUIGI (1904-1975)
  Altissima Luce
    see Tre Laudi

  An Mathilde
    female solo,orch voc sc ZERBONI
    5300 s.p.   (D53)

  Ciascun S'allegri
    see Tre Laudi

  Cinque Canti *CC5U
    Bar solo,8inst voc sc ZERBONI 5339
    s.p.   (D54)

  Cinque Frammenti Di Saffo *CC5U
    S solo,orch voc sc ZERBONI 4041
    s.p.   (D55)

  Commiato
    S solo,15inst voc sc ZERBONI 7528
    s.p.   (D56)

  Concerto Per La Notte Di Natale
    *sac,Xmas
    S solo,orch min sc ZERBONI 5433
    s.p.   (D57)

  Divertimento In Quattro Esercizi
    S solo,fl,ob,clar,bsn,vla,vcl sc
    CARISH 17132 s.p.   (D58)

  Due Liriche Di Anacreonte *CC2U
    S solo,4inst ZERBONI 5926 rental
                                  (D59)

  Goethe Lieder *CCU
    female solo,3clar ZERBONI 5848
    rental   (D60)

  Madonna Sancta Maria
    see Tre Laudi

  Parole Di San Paolo
    Mez solo,9inst voc sc ZERBONI 6310
    s.p.   (D61)

  Preghiere
    Bar solo,orch voc sc ZERBONI 5981
    s.p.   (D62)

  Quattro Liriche Di Machado *CC4U
    female solo,16inst voc sc ZERBONI
    4582 s.p.   (D63)

DALLAPICCOLA, LUIGI (cont'd.)

  Rencesvals
    solo,pno ZERBONI 4267 s.p.   (D64)

  Sex Carmina Alcaei
    S solo,11inst.voc sc ZERBONI 4181
    s.p.   (D65)

  Sicut Umbra
    Mez solo,12inst voc sc ZERBONI 7079
    s.p.   (D66)

  Tre Laudi *sac
    solo,fl,ob,clar,bsn,horn,trp,sax,
    harp,pno,4strings min sc CARISH
    18906 s.p.
    contains: Altissima Luce; Ciascun
      S'allegri; Madonna Sancta Maria
                                  (D67)

  Tre Poemi *CC3U
    S solo,chamb.orch study sc ARS VIVA
    AV 62 s.p., ipa   (D68)

DALLAS HOLM-SONGBOOK see Holm, Dallas

DALLAS HOLM SONGS see Holm, Dallas

DALMAINE, CYRIL C.
  Climax Album No. 8 *CCU
    solo,pno PAXTON P15368 s.p.   (D69)

DALMARSCH see Peterson-Berger, (Olof)
  Wilhelm

DALTON, LARRY
  Genesis Song, The *sac
    solo,pno WORD S-486   (D70)

  Lord, I'm Coming Home Today *sac
    (Heady) solo,pno WORD S-487   (D71)

DALVISA see Olsson, Otto Emmanuel

DALWAY
  Killiney Strand
    see Three Irish Airs

  Love Entrapped Me
    see Three Irish Airs

  Love Repaid
    see Three Irish Airs

  Three Irish Airs
    Bar solo,pno (very easy) OXFORD
    62.201 $1.75
    contains: Killiney Strand; Love
      Entrapped Me; Love Repaid (D72)

DAMALS see Ehrenberg, Carl Emil Theodor

DAMASE, JEAN-MICHEL (1928-   )
  Absent-Minded
    see No Exit

  Deux Poemes
    Bar solo,pno cmplt ed RIDEAU 050
    s.p.
    contains: Masques; Neige   (D73)

  Faire-Part
    see No Exit

  Jeux De L'Amour *CC3U
    solo,pno TRANSAT. s.p.   (D74)

  Masques
    see Deux Poemes

  Neige
    see Deux Poemes

  No Exit *Op.26
    [Fr] med solo,pno SALABERT-US $5.50
    contains: Absent-Minded; Faire-
      Part; O Nightingale; Post-Card;
      Remembrance; San Francisco
      Night   (D75)

  O Nightingale
    see No Exit

  Post-Card
    see No Exit

  Remembrance
    see No Exit

  San Francisco Night
    see No Exit

D'AMBROSI, DANTE (1902-1965)
  Fogli D'Album Per Soprano
    [It] S solo,pno cmplt ed SANTIS 856
    s.p.
    contains: Madrigale; Morticino;
      Profumo; Solo   (D76)

  Madrigale
    see Fogli D'Album Per Soprano

  Morticino
    see Fogli D'Album Per Soprano

D'AMBROSI, DANTE (cont'd.)

  Profumo
    see Fogli D'Album Per Soprano

  Solo
    see Fogli D'Album Per Soprano

DAME AINSI EST see Le Flem, Paul

DAME DE COEUR see Arrieu, Claude

DAME SOURIS see Truillet-Soyer, M.

DAME THERESE see Ryelandt, Joseph

DAME VOR DEM SPIEGEL see Orthel, Leon

DAMES OF PARIS, THE see Debussy,
  Claude, Ballade Des Femmes De Paris

DAMM, SVENERIK
  En Vintervisa
    see Jag Hor Klockor Ringa

  Jag Hor Klockor Ringa
    solo,pno,opt gtr GEHRMANS s.p.
    contains: En Vintervisa; Nar Du
      Sluter Mina Ogon; Varfor Hor
      Jag Klockor Ringa   (D77)

  Nar Du Sluter Mina Ogon
    see Jag Hor Klockor Ringa

  Varfor Hor Jag Klockor Ringa
    see Jag Hor Klockor Ringa

DAMMERUNG see Jarnefelt, Armas,
  Skymning

DAMMI I TUOI OCCHI see Paczolay, I.,
  Add Nekem A Szmeidet

DAMMRUNG SENKTE SICH VON OBEN see
  Trapp, Max

DAMON UND DAPHNE see Poser, Hans

D'AMOR SULL'ALI ROSEE see Verdi,
  Giuseppe

D'AMOURS ETERNELLES see Brahms,
  Johannes, Von Ewiger Liebe

DAMUNT DE TU NOMES LES FLORS see
  Mompou, Federico

DAN, IKUMA (1924-   )
  Collected Songs *CCU
    solo,pno ONGAKU s.p.   (D78)

DANA
  Flee As A Bird *sac
    low solo,pno (D min) CENTURY 704
    $.40   (D79)

DANCE, THE see Rossini, Gioacchino, La
  Danza

DANCE DUET see Humperdinck, Engelbert

DANCE OF THE CRYSTAL FAIRY see Revel,
  Peter

DANCE TO YOUR DADDY *folk,Scot
  solo,pno (B flat maj/C maj) PATERSON
    FS140 s.p.   (D80)
  (Roberton, Hugh S.) 2 soli,pno
    ROBERTON 72426 s.p.   (D81)

DANCE WHILE THE WORLD IS YOUNG see
  Oliver, Herbert

DANCING see Bantock, Granville

DANCING LESSON, THE see Oliver, Herbert

DANCING WILL KEEP YOU YOUNG see
  Romberg, Sigmund

DANDELION, THE see Bliss, Sir Arthur

DANDELOT, [GEORGES] (1895-   )
  Quatre-Vingt Dictees Musicales
    *CC80U
    solo,pno ESCHIG $3.50   (D82)

  Quinze Chansons De Bilitis, Vol. I
    *CC15U
    [Fr] high solo,pno ESCHIG $3.75
                                  (D83)
  Quinze Chansons De Bilitis, Vol. II
    *CC15U
    [Fr] high solo,pno ESCHIG $3.40
                                  (D84)
  Quinze Chansons De Bilitis, Vol. III
    *CC15U
    [Fr] high solo,pno ESCHIG $2.00
                                  (D85)

DANICAN-PHILIDOR, ANNE (1681-1728)
  see PHILIDOR, ANNE

DANIEL see Miller, James

DANIEL BOONE see Stringfield, Lamar

DANIEL-LESUR (1908-   )
  Ce Qu'Adam Dit A Eve
    see Clair Comme Le Jour

  Clair Comme Le Jour
    solo,pno AMPHION A 122 $2.50
      contains: Ce Qu'Adam Dit A Eve;
      Jeunes Filles; Plage   (D86)

  Hotel Du Souvenir
    see L'Enfance De L'art

  Jeunes Filles
    see Clair Comme Le Jour

  L'Empreinte
    see Trois Poemes De Cecile Sauvage

  L'Enfance De L'art
    solo,pno AMPHION A 116 $2.00
      contains: Hotel Du Souvenir;
      Nocturne; Petit Matin   (D87)

  L'Idiot Du Village
    see Trois Poemes De Cecile Sauvage

  Neige
    see Trois Poemes De Cecile Sauvage

  Nocturne
    see L'Enfance De L'art

  Petit Matin
    see L'Enfance De L'art

  Plage
    see Clair Comme Le Jour

  Trois Poemes De Cecile Sauvage
    solo,pno AMPHION A 112 $2.00
      contains: L'Empreinte; L'Idiot Du
      Village; Neige   (D88)

DANK see Boedijn, Gerard H.

DANK see Schoenberg, Arnold

DANK AN DIE HAUSFRAU see Kilpinen,
  Yrio, Kiitos Emannasta

DANK SEI DIR, HERR see Handel, George
  Frideric

DANKET DEM HERRN UND PREDIGET SEINEN
  NAMEN see Rosenmuller, Johann

DANKGEBED see Rontgen, [Julius]

DANKGEBET see Kremser, Edward

DANN SINGE ICH see Kilpinen, Yrio,
  Silloin Laulan

DANNAZIONE E PREGHIERA see Procaccini,
  T.

D'ANNE JOUANT DE L'ESPINETTE see Ravel,
  Maurice

D'ANNE QUE ME JECTA DE LA NEIGE see
  Ravel, Maurice

D'ANNE QUI ME JECTA DE LA NEIGE see
  Ravel, Maurice

DANNO BUDHUNGE
  see Internationale Volslieder, Vol 1

DANNSTROM, ISIDOR
  Aftonen
    see Sex Andliga Sanger

  Blomstringen
    see Sex Andliga Sanger

  Det Ar Sa Underliga Stallen
    solo,pno LUNDQUIST s.p.   (D89)

  Deullanterna
    2 soli,pno LUNDQUIST s.p.   (D90)

  For Fosterlandet
    see Sex Andliga Sanger

  Hur Ljuvt Det Ar Att Komma
    see Sex Andliga Sanger
    high solo,pno LUNDQUIST s.p. (D91)
    low solo,pno LUNDQUIST s.p.   (D92)

  O, Fadershem, Mot Dig Jar Ser
    see Sex Andliga Sanger

  Sex Andliga Sanger *sac
    solo,pno LUNDQUIST s.p.
      contains: Aftonen; Blomstringen;
      For Fosterlandet; Hur Ljuvt Det
      Ar Att Komma; O, Fadershem, Mot
      Dig Jar Ser; Sommaren   (D93)

  Sex Polskor *CC6U
    solo,pno LUNDQUIST s.p.   (D94)

DANNSTROM, ISIDOR (cont'd.)

  Sommaren
    see Sex Andliga Sanger

DANNY BOY see Weatherly, F.E.

DANNY TAYLOR SINGS *sac,CC10UL
  solo,pno,gtr LILLENAS MB-313 $1.95
                                    (D95)
DANS CE PARC PEUPLE DE MARBRES see
  Levade, Charles (Gaston)

DANS DER MAEGDEKENS see Schouwman, Hans

DANS EN PASTORALE see Beekhuis, Hanna

DANS LA BRUME see Lenormand, Rene

DANS LA BRUME ARGENTEE see Samazeuilh,
  Gustave

DANS LA FORET see Schumann, Robert
  (Alexander), Waldesgesprach

DANS LA FORET DU CHARME ET DE
  L'ENCHANTEMENT see Chausson, Ernest

DANS LA GANTERIE see Lecocq, Charles

DANS LA NUIT see Geloso, C.

DANS LA NUIT see Levade, Charles
  (Gaston)

DANS LA NUIT OU SEUL JE VEILLE see
  Meyerbeer, Giacomo

DANS LA NYMPHEE see Faure, Gabriel-
  Urbain

DANS LA PLAINE BLONDE see Cui, Cesar
  Antonovitch

DANS LA RUE see Veneziani, Vittore

DANS LA VERTE RAMURE see Rousseau,
  Jean-Jacques

DANS LE CALME, LA BARQUE SE BALANCE see
  Migot, Georges

DANS LE FORET see Gade, Niels Wilhelm

DANS LE FORET see Gedalge, Andre

DANS LE JARDIN see Boussion, E.

DANS LE JARDIN D'ANNA see Poulenc,
  Francis

DANS LE MATIN BLEU see Favre, Georges

DANS LE PARC see Cras, Jean (Emile
  Paul)

DANS LE PARC see Merson, Oliver

DANS LE POTAGER see Veneziani, Vittore

DANS LE ROYAUME DU CANCAN see Messager,
  Andre

DANS LE SABLE see Rush, Loren

DANS LE SERRE see Wagner, Richard, Im
  Treibhaus

DANS LE SILENCE PUR see Gaubert,
  Philippe

DANS LE SOMMEIL (from Si J'Etais Roi)
  B solo LEDUC s.p.   (D96)

DANS LES ARBRES BLANCS DE GIVRE see
  Messager, Andre

DANS LES BOIS D'ANDILLY see Godard,
  Benjamin Louis Paul

DANS LES COINS BLEUS see Saint-Saens,
  Camille

DANS LES FLEURS see Berger, Rod.

DANS LES HERBES... see Quinet, Marcel

DANS LES LARMES see Berger, Rod.

DANS LES OMBRES DE MON AME see Beydts,
  L.

DANS LES PRES see Bagge, G.

DANS LES ROSEAUX see Brun, G.

DANS LES RUES DE PARIS see Scotto,
  Vincent

DANS LES RUINES D'UNE ABBAYE see
  Gedalge, Andre

DANS L'HERBE see Poulenc, Francis

DANS L'UNIVERS see Coppola, Piero

DANS MA RAISON see Lacome, Paul

DANS MON COEUR see Cuvillier, Charles

DANS MON COEUR see Holmes, Alfred

DANS NOS JEUX see Rameau, Jean-Philippe

DANS QUELS PARJURES see Mozart,
  Wolfgang Amadeus

DANS ROPTE FELEN see Soderman, (Johan)
  August

DANS TES JARDINS, NOBLE VERSAILLES see
  Casadesus, Henri Gustave

DANS TOUTE CIRCONSTANCE see Lecocq,
  Charles

DANS UN CHAMP DE BLES D'OR see
  Messager, Andre

DANS UN COIN DE VIOLETTES see Rhene-
  Baton

DANS UN PARC ABANDONNE see Holmes,
  Alfred

DANS UN PARFUM DE ROSES BLANCHES see
  Rasse, Francois

DANS UN PRE see Charpentier, R.

DANS UN VILLAGE D'AVEYRON see Migot,
  Georges

DANS UNE GRANGE CHAMPETRE see Klerk,
  Albert de

DANS UNE PAUVRE ETABLE see Klerk,
  Albert de

DANS VOTRE BERCEAU see Lachaume, A.

DANSE see Doyen, Albert

DANSE see Larbey, V.

DANSE see Leeuw, Ton de

DANSE DES BAMBOUS see Gillet, Ernest

DANSE DU BEBE-PILULE see Messiaen,
  Oliver

DANSE DU GLAIVE see Favre, Georges,
  Korol Ar C'hleze

DANSE MACABRE see Saint-Saens, Camille

DANSE MI VISE, GRATE MIN SANG see Beck,
  Thomas [Ludvigsen]

DANSE MIGNONNE see Durante, Francesco

DANSEN see Sonninen, Ahti, Tanssit

DANSERVISE see Nielsen, Carl

DANSEUSE see Faure, Gabriel-Urbain

DANSLEK see Korling

DANSONS see Denza, Luigi

DANSONS LA RONDE see Fabre, G.

DANTESCA see Nacamuli, Guido

DANVISA see Korling, Felix

DANYEL, JOHN
  Blow, Blow, Thou Winter Wind
    see AS YOU LIKE IT

  Chromatic Tunes *CCU
    (Warlock; Wilson) [Eng] med solo,
    kbd CHESTER s.p.   (D97)

  Songs For The Lute, Viol And Voice
    *CCU
    solo,lute, viol STAINER 3.1330.7
    $4.50   (D98)

DANZA, DANZA, FANCIULLA see Durante,
  Francesco

DANZA ESPANOLA, NO. 5 see Granados,
  Enrique

DANZAS Y CANTOS REGIONALES DEL NORTE
  AGENTINO, VOL. I see Gomez
  Carrillo, Manuel

DANZAS Y CANTOS REGIONALES DEL NORTE
  ARGENTINO, VOL. II see Gomez
  Carrillo, Manuel

DAPHENEO see Satie, Erik

DAPHNE see Walton, William

DAPHNE AND STREPHON see Lawes, William

DAPHNENS EINZIGER FEHLER see Haydn, (Franz) Joseph

DAR BJORKARNA SUSA see Merikanto, Oskar

DAR HJORTRONEN BLOMMA see Peterson-Berger, (Olof) Wilhelm

DAR SORLAR SVAGT EN KALLA see Chrisander, Nils

DARCIEUX, F.
Bonheur Envole
solo,acap solo pt ENOCH s.p. (D99)
solo,pno ENOCH s.p. (D100)

Les Cygnes
solo,pno/inst DURAND s.p. (D101)

Les Libellules
solo,pno/inst DURAND s.p. (D102)

DARF EINE NIEDRE MAGD ES WAGEN see Lortzing, (Gustav) Albert

DARGOMYZHSKY, [ALEXANDER SERGEYEVITCH] (1813-1869)
Der Alte Korporal
[Russ/Fr/Ger/Eng] solo,pno
BREITKOPF-W 57 03040 s.p. (D103)

Der Muller
[Russ/Fr/Ger/Eng] solo,pno
BREITKOPF-W 57 03041 s.p. (D104)

Selected Romances And Songs *CCU
[Russ] solo,pno MEZ KNIGA 59 s.p. (D105)

DARK EYES *Russ
solo,pno ALLANS s.p. (D106)

DARK UPON THE HARP see Druckman, Jacob

DARKE, ROBERT
Little Billy Buttercup
solo,pno LEONARD-ENG (D107)

DARKNESS see Hayakawa, Masaaki

DARKNESS AND DAWN see Loughborough, Raymond

DARKSONG see Chance, Nancy

DARTT
Last Sunday, The *sac
solo,pno BENSON S7937-S $1.00 (D108)

DARTY, PAULETTE
Accalmie
solo,acap solo pt ENOCH s.p. (D109)
solo,pno ENOCH s.p. (D110)

Brune Ou Blonde
solo,acap solo pt ENOCH s.p. (D111)
solo,pno ENOCH s.p. (D112)

En Me Montrant Des Roses
solo,pno ENOCH s.p. (D113)

En Me Montrant Les Roses
solo,acap solo pt ENOCH s.p. (D114)

DAS ANTLITZ see Mikoda, Borivoj, Tvar

DAS ARME KIND see Badings, Henk

DAS ATTELIED see Grieg, Edvard Hagerup, Den Gamle Vise

DAS BACHLEIN see Strauss, Richard

DAS BANDEL see Mozart, Wolfgang Amadeus, Liebes Mandel, Wo Is 'S Bandel

DAS BITTERSUSSE LIED see Kilpinen, Yrio

DAS BLUT JESU CHRISTI MACHET UNS REIN see Schutz, Heinrich

DAS DORF SINGT see Zelinka, Jan Evangelista, Vesnice Zpiva

DAS EINHORN see King, Harold C.

DAS ENDE DES GESETZES see Jacob, Werner, Telos Nomou

DAS ENTBRENNEN see Goldbach, Stanislav, Vzplanuti

DAS ERBE DEUTSCHER MUSIK, BAND 58: GOETHES LIEDER, ODEN, BALLADEN UND ROMANZEN MIT MUSIK TEIL I see Reichardt, Johann Friedrich

DAS ERLOSCHENE ALTARBILD see Zagwijn, Henri

DAS EWIGE BRAUSEN see Burkhard, Willy

DAS EXAMEN see Burkhard, Paul

DAS FERNE LIED see Weismann, Wilhelm

DAS FISCHERMADCHEN see Schubert, Franz (Peter)

DAS GANZE JAHR IM KINDERLIED *CCU
(Goedel; Dreising) 1-2 soli,fl
SCHOTTS 3582 s.p. (D115)

DAS GEBET see Fibich, Zdenko, Modlitba

DAS GEHEIMNIS see Strauss, Richard

DAS GEKREUZIGTE HERZ see Jirasek, Ivo, Ukrizovane Srdce

DAS GELBE LAUB ERZITTERT see Weegenhuise, Johan

DAS GESPRACH MIT NICODEMUS see Hasse, Johann Friedrich

DAS GRAB DES HAFIS see Szymanowski, Karol

DAS GROSSE LALULA see Badings, Henk

DAS GRUNE BLATT see Rinaldini, Dr. Joseph

DAS GUSTAV-LIED DER WASCHFRAU GUSTE see Dittersdorf, Karl Ditters von

DAS HECKENLIED see Roselius, Ludwig

DAS HEMD see Trunk, Richard

DAS HERZ IST NUR EIN UHRWERK see Ziehrer, Carl Michael

DAS HIMMLISCHE MENUETT see Lothar, Mark

DAS HIMMLISCHE MENUETT see Taubert, Karl Heinz

DAS HOHE TOR see Erdlen, Hermann

DAS HOHELIED DER LIEBE see Kropfreiter, Augustinius Franz

DAS HOHELIED SALOMOS see Erbse, Heimo

DAS HOLDE BESCHEIDEN, OP. 62, PART I see Schoeck, Othmar

DAS HOLDE BESCHEIDEN, OP. 62, PART II see Schoeck, Othmar

DAS HUHN see Badings, Henk

DAS INSELCHEN see Rachmaninoff, Sergey Vassilievitch, Little Island, The

DAS IRDISCHE LEBEN see Mahler, Gustav

DAS IST DIE ERSTE LIEBELEI see Eysler, Edmund S.

DAS IST DORT, WO DIE LETZTEN HUTTEN SIND see Franken, Wim

DAS IST EIN KOSTLICH DING see Bossler, Kurt

DAS IST EIN KOSTLICH DING see Rosenmuller, Johann

DAS IST MEINE FREUDE see Rosenmuller, Johann

DAS JAHR IM ROSTIGEN WALD see Jirasek, Ivo, Rok V Rezavem Lese

DAS JUNGFRAULEIN see Trunk, Richard

DAS KAROLISSER HEFT *CCU,Xmas
(Stern) solo,pno HUG s.p. (D116)

DAS KARUSSELL see Zagwijn, Henri

DAS KARUSSELL UND ANDERE RILKE-GEDICHTE see Marx, Karl

DAS KIND DER ARMEN see Kilpinen, Yrio, Koyhan Lapset

DAS KINDERJAHR *CC24U
solo,pno cmplt ed GERIG HG 545 s.p. (D117)

DAS KIRCHENLIED IN KLEINER BESETZUNG, HEFT I *sac,CC34U
(Stern, Hermann) med solo,inst,org
HANSSLER 19.801 s.p. (D118)

DAS KIRCHENLIED IN KLEINER BESETZUNG, HEFT II *sac,CC51U
med solo,inst,org HANSSLER 19.802
s.p. settings by: Friedel; Koch;
Kukuck; Kretzschmar; Ruppel; Lotz;
Schwartz and others (D119)

DAS KLAMPFENLIED *CCU
(Zschiesche) solo,gtr SCHOTTS 4462
s.p. (D120)

DAS KONIGSLIED see Gilse, Jan van

DAS KREUZ IM SCHNEE see Pylkkanen, Tauno Kullervo, Risti Lumessa

DAS LEBEN GLEICHT DEM SPIEL see Tchaikovsky, Piotr Ilyitch

DAS LETZE GEDICHT see Baird, Tadeusz, Ostatnia Piesn

DAS LICHT see Hanus, Jan, Svetlo

DAS LIEBSTE LIED *CCU
solo,pno SCHOTTS 3799; 4000 s.p., ea.
in 2 books (D121)

DAS LIED DER BILDSAULE see Jentsch, Walter

DAS LIED DER VOLKER I: RUSSISCHE VOLKSLIEDER *CCU,folk,Russ
(Moller, H.) solo,pno SCHOTTS 551
s.p. (D122)

DAS LIED DER VOLKER II: SKANDINAVISCHE VOLKSLIEDER *CCU,folk
(Moller, H.) solo,pno SCHOTTS 552
s.p. Scandinavian (D123)

DAS LIED DER VOLKER III: ENGLISCHE UND NORDAMERIKANISCHE VOLKSLIEDER *CCU,folk
(Moller, H.) solo,pno SCHOTTS 553
s.p. (D124)

DAS LIED DER VOLKER IV: KELTISCHE VOLKSLIEDER *CCU,folk
(Moller, H.) solo,pno SCHOTTS 554
s.p. (D125)

DAS LIED DER VOLKER V: FRANZOSISCHE VOLKSLIEDER *CCU,folk
(Moller, H.) solo,pno SCHOTTS 555
s.p. (D126)

DAS LIED DER VOLKER VI: VOLKSLIEDER AUS SPANIEN UND PORTUGAL *CCU,folk
(Moller, H.) solo,pno SCHOTTS 556
s.p. (D127)

DAS LIED DER VOLKER VII: ITALIENISCHE VOLKSLIEDER *CCU,folk
(Moller, H.) solo,pno SCHOTTS 557
s.p. (D128)

DAS LIED DER VOLKER VIII: SUDSLAWISCHE VOLKSLIEDER *CCU,folk
(Moller, H.) solo,pno SCHOTTS 558
s.p. (D129)

DAS LIED DER VOLKER IX: GRIECHISCHE, ALBANISCHE UND RUMANISCHE VOLKSLIEDER *CCU,folk
(Moller, H.) solo,pno SCHOTTS 559
s.p. (D130)

DAS LIED DER VOLKER X: WESTSLAWISCHE VOLKSLIEDER *CCU,folk
(Moller, H.) solo,pno SCHOTTS 1228
s.p. (D131)

DAS LIED DER VOLKER XI: WESTSLAWISCHE VOLKSLIEDER *CCU,folk
(Moller, H.) solo,pno SCHOTTS 1229
s.p. (D132)

DAS LIED DER VOLKER XII: UNGARISCHE VOLKSLIEDER *CCU,folk
(Moller, H.) solo,pno SCHOTTS 560
s.p. (D133)

DAS LIED DER VOLKER XIII: BALTISCHE VOLKSLIEDER *CCU,folk
(Moller, H.) solo,pno SCHOTTS 1230
s.p. (D134)

DAS LIED DES VOLLIG ARGLOSEN see Trexler, Georg

DAS LIED TONT FORT see Staeps, Hans Ulrich

DAS LIED VOM KINDE see Kronsteiner, Hermann

DAS LIED VON DER KREUZSPINNE see Sibelius, Jean

DAS LIED VON FERNE see Rontgen, Johannes

DAS MACHT DEN MENSCHEN GLUCKLICH see Bosmans, Henriette

DAS MADCHEN AM TEICHE SINGT see Rontgen, Johannes

DAS MADCHEN UND DER SCHMETTERLING see d'Albert, Eugene Francis Charles

DAS MAGNIFICAT see Schutz, Heinrich

DAS MARCHEN VON DER WOLKE see Badings, Henk

DAS MARIENLEBEN see Hindemith, Paul

DAS MAUSCHEN see Trunk, Richard

DAS MITLEIDIGE MADEL see Rontgen, Johannes

DAS MITLEIDIGE MADEL see Schilling, M. von

DAS MONDSCHAF see Badings, Henk

DAS MUTTERHERZ see Jeremias, Jaroslav

DAS NEST see Rontgen, Johannes

DAS NEUE OPERETTEN-BUCH *CC92U
  solo,pno SCHOTTS
  2525; 2850; 3700; 4300; 4500 s.p.,
  ea. in 5 volumes   (D135)

DAS OLGENAHRTE LAMPLEIN see Wolpert

DAS OSTEREI see Haas, Joseph

DAS PFAND see Schmalstich, Clemens

DAS REGENLIED see Lothar, Mark

DAS REH see Roselius, Ludwig

DAS ROSENBAND see Saladin, O.

DAS ROSENINNERE see Colaco Osorio-
  Swaab, Reine

DAS SCHICKSAL see Kuula, Toivo, Kohtalo

DAS SCHLAFENDE GLUCK see Kilpinen,
  Yrio, Makaaja-Onni

DAS SCHNEIDEN IST EIN VOGEL see Baird,
  Tadeusz, Rozstanie Jest Ptakiem

DAS SOLOLIED IM CHORKONZERT, HEFT I
  *CC13L
  solo,pno LEUCKART $4.00 contains
  works by: Lang, Hans; Siegl, Otto;
  Zipp, Friedrich; Zoll, Paul (D136)

DAS STADTCHEN see Trunk, Richard

DAS STANDCHEN see D'Ysot, E.

DAS STILLE LEUCHTEN see Schoeck, Othmar

DAS STRAUSSCHEN see Dvorak, Antonin

DAS SUSSE LIED VERHALT see Wagner,
  Richard

DAS TRAURIGE HERZ see Poser, Hans

DAS TURNIER see Saint-Saens, Camille,
  Le Pas D'armes Du Roi Jean

DAS VATER UNSER see Knab, Armin

DAS VATER UNSER see Knierer, Hermann

DAS VATERUNSER see Gulbins, Max

DAS VEILCHEN see Mozart, Wolfgang
  Amadeus

DAS VERKLARTE JAHR see Marx, Joseph

DAS VERLASSENE MAGDELEIN see Pfitzner,
  Hans

DAS VERLASSENE MAGDLEIN see Pfitzner,
  Hans

DAS VERSCHLOSSENE PARADIES see Wolpert

DAS VOGELHAUS see Bedford, David

DAS VOLKSLIEDERALBUM FUR GITARRE, HEFT
  1 UND 2 *CCU,folk
  (Schwarz-Reiflingen, Erwin) solo,gtr
  SIKORSKI 225A; 225B s.p., ea.
                              (D137)

DAS VORBILD see Eisler, Hanns

DAS WAISENKIND see Dvorak, Antonin,
  Sirotek

DAS WANDSBEKER LIEDERBUCH see Schoeck,
  Othmar

DAS WAPPENSCHILD see Schoenberg, Arnold

DAS WAR SEHR GUT! see Strauss, Richard

DAS WEIHNACHTSBAUMLEIN see Lothar, Mark

DAS WEIHNACHTSEVANGELIUM see Mayer, M.

DAS WEIHNACHTSLIEDERBUCH *CC40U,Xmas
  (Strobach, Siegfried) [Ger] solo,pno
  BREITKOPF-W EB 6440 $2.00   (D138)

DAS WEISS ICH UND HAB ES ERLEBT see
  Edler, Robert

DAS WESSOBRUNNER GEBET see Knab, Armin

DAS WIESENLIED see Godard, Benjamin
  Louis Paul, Chanson Des Pres

DAS WUNDERGLOCKENSPIEL see Zollner,
  Heinrich

DAS ZAUBERLIED see Meyer-Helmund, Erik

DAS ZAUBERWORT see Ravel, Maurice

DAS ZEITGENOSSISCHE LIED, BAND I *CCU,
  20th cent
  (Reutter, Hermann) S solo,pno SCHOTTS
  5745 s.p.   (D139)

DAS ZEITGENOSSISCHE LIED, BAND II
  *CCU,20th cent
  (Reutter, Hermann) Mez/A solo,pno
  SCHOTTS 5746 s.p.   (D140)

DAS ZEITGENOSSISCHE LIED, BAND III
  *CCU,20th cent
  (Reutter, Hermann) T solo,pno SCHOTTS
  5747 s.p.   (D141)

DAS ZEITGENOSSISCHE LIED, BAND IV
  *CCU,20th cent
  (Reutter, Hermann) Bar/B solo,pno
  SCHOTTS 5748 s.p.   (D142)

DAS ZITTERNDE GLANZEN DER SPIELENDEN
  WELLEN see Handel, George Frideric

DASST AUS DIESEM ENGEN HAUS see Edler,
  Robert

DAT JAAR see Mulder, Herman

DATIME A PIENA MANO E ROSE E ZIGLI see
  Ghedini, Giorgio Federico

DAUBNEY, BRIAN
  She Hath An Art
  med solo,pno NOVELLO 17.0169.10
  s.p.   (D143)

DAULY, G.
  Arpege
  solo,pno ENOCH s.p.   (D144)

  Larmes
  solo,pno ENOCH s.p.   (D145)

  Viens, Une Flute Invisible
  solo,pno ENOCH s.p.   (D146)

DAUS, A.
  Songs Of Rochel *CCU
  med solo,fl,vla ISRAELI 504 $3.50,
  ipr   (D147)

D'AUTRES CHANSONS, VOL. II see Kosma,
  J.

DAVENPORT, GLADYS
  Cool And Silent Is The Lake
  solo,pno (E flat maj) LESLIE 7019
                              (D148)
  Remembrance
  solo,pno (E flat maj) LESLIE 7042
                              (D149)
DAVICO, VINCENZO (1899-1969)
  Andava Il Paese
  see Cinque Notturni

  Cadon Le Stelle
  see Canti Minimi

  Canti Minimi
  [It] solo,pno cmplt ed BONGIOVANI
  960 s.p.
    contains: Cadon Le Stelle;
    Canzonetta; Spes Ultima Dea
                              (D150)
  Canzonetta
  see Canti Minimi

  Cinque Notturni
  [It] solo,pno cmplt ed SANTIS 749
  s.p.
    contains: Andava Il Paese; E Di
    Silenzi Placidi; Limpida Fresca
    Notte; Mormorio Di Foglie;
    Notte, Chinato Il Volto (D151)

  E Di Silenzi Placidi
  see Cinque Notturni

  Limpida Fresca Notte
  see Cinque Notturni

  Liriche Giapponesi
  [It/Fr] solo,pno cmplt ed
  BONGIOVANI 1265 s.p.
    contains: Luna D'estate; Pioggia
                              (D152)
  Luna D'estate
  see Liriche Giapponesi

  Mormorio Di Foglie
  see Cinque Notturni

DAVICO, VINCENZO (cont'd.)
  Ninna Nanna Abruzzese
  [It] solo,pno CURCI 5039 s.p.
                              (D153)
  Notte, Chinato Il Volto
  see Cinque Notturni

  Novembre
  see Tre Liriche

  O Luna Che Fai Lume
  S solo,strings,harp,cembalo CARISH
  s.p.   (D154)

  Offrande *CC2U
  [Fr] solo,pno BONGIOVANI 377 s.p.
                              (D155)
  Passione
  see Tre Liriche

  Pioggia
  see Liriche Giapponesi

  Plenilunio Estivo
  [It] solo,pno BONGIOVANI 2254 s.p.
                              (D156)
  Sonno
  see Tre Liriche

  Spes Ultima Dea
  see Canti Minimi

  Tre Liriche
  [It] solo,pno cmplt ed CURCI 5040
  s.p.
    contains: Novembre; Passione;
    Sonno   (D157)

  Tre Ninne Nanne Popolari *CC3U
  [It] solo,pno BONGIOVANI 2253 s.p.
                              (D158)
DAVID AND GOLIATH *sac,gospel
  solo,pno ABER.GRP. $1.50   (D159)

DAVID AND GOLIATH see Malotte, Albert
  Hay

DAVID, GYULA (1913-   )
  Blazing Roses
  female solo,fl,vla BUDAPEST 5528
  s.p.   (D160)

  Five Csokonai Songs *CC5U
  [Hung] solo,pno BUDAPEST 2918 s.p.
                              (D161)
  Four Songs *CC4U
  [Hung] solo,pno BUDAPEST 2919 s.p.
                              (D162)
DAVID, J.
  Ce Qui Me Plait
  solo,pno/inst DURAND s.p.   (D163)

DAVID, JOHANN NEPOMUK (1895-   )
  Frohlich Wir Nun All Fangen An *cant
  3 soli,ob,org sc BREITKOPF-W
  PB 3753 s.p.   (D164)

  Ich Sturbe Gern Aus Minne
  S solo,org BREITKOPF-W EB 5776 s.p.
                              (D165)
DAVID, KARL HEINRICH (1884-1951)
  Quatre Chants *CC4U
  solo,pno HUG s.p.   (D166)

DAVID MOURNS FOR ABSALOM see Diamond,
  David

DAVID, THOMAS CHRISTIAN (1925-   )
  Vier Lieder Nach Chinesischen
  Gedichten *CC4U
  solo,pno DOBLINGER 08 633 s.p.
                              (D167)
DAVID'S HARP see Strilko, Anthony

DAVIDS PSALMER I-II see Wennerburg,
  [Gunnar]

DAVIDSON, CHARLES (1929-   )
  Eshet Chayil *sac
  [Heb] high solo,pno TRANSCON.
  WJ 440 $.85   (D168)
  [Heb] med solo,pno TRANSCON. WJ 441
  $.85   (D169)

  Lord Is My Shepherd, The (Psalm 23)
  sac
  [Eng] high solo,pno TRANSCON.
  TV 575 $.85   (D170)

  Psalm 23 *see Lord Is My Shepherd,
  The

DAVIDSON, M.T.
  Hills Of Dan
  high solo,pno PARAGON $.85 (D171)

  Lullaby To A Doll
  med solo,pno PARAGON $.85   (D172)

  Songs For Young Songbirds *CC12L
  solo,pno PARAGON $2.50   (D173)

DAVIDSON, MALCOLM
Conjuration
  high solo,pno (G min) CRAMER (D174)
  low solo,pno (E min) CRAMER (D175)

DAVIDSON, MARK
One Master *sac
  solo,pno WORD S-75 (D176)

DAVIES, HENRY WALFORD (1869-1941)
Birds, The
  high solo,pno NOVELLO s.p. (D177)

Come Away, Come Away, Death
  T solo,pno NOVELLO s.p. (D178)

Follow Your Saint
  med solo,pno NOVELLO s.p. (D179)

I Love All Beauteous Things
  med solo,pno NOVELLO s.p. (D180)

I Vow To Thee My Country
  solo,pno CRAMER (D181)

Never Weather-Beaten Sail
  low solo,pno NOVELLO s.p. (D182)

O Mistress Mine
  T solo,pno NOVELLO s.p. (D183)

Orpheus With His Lute
  med solo,pno NOVELLO s.p. (D184)

Peace Waits Among The Hills
  high solo,pno NOVELLO s.p. (D185)

Softly Along The Road
  med solo,pno NOVELLO s.p. (D186)

Tune Thy Music To Thy Heart
  med solo,pno NOVELLO s.p. (D187)

When That I Was And A Little Tiny Boy
  T solo,pno NOVELLO s.p. (D188)

DAVIES, [WILLIAM] HENRY
Teach Me To Forgive
  solo,pno (D maj) BOOSEY $1.50 (D189)

DAVIK, INGEBRIGT
Det Star Eit Lys Over Betlehem
  see No Ma Julen Skunde Seg

Forste Skuledagen Min
  solo,pno MUSIKK s.p. (D190)

No Ma Julen Skunde Seg *Xmas
  solo,pno MUSIKK s.p.
  contains: Det Star Eit Lys Over
    Betlehem; No Na Julen Skunde
    Seg; Vesle Julestjerna (D191)

No Na Julen Skunde Seg
  see No Ma Julen Skunde Seg

Vesle Julestjerna
  see No Ma Julen Skunde Seg

DAVIS
Are You Redeemed? *sac
  solo,pno LILLENAS SM-632: RN $1.00 (D192)

Crown Of Victory, The *sac
  (Heady) solo,pno WORD S-83 (D193)

Faith Is The Key *sac
  (Heady) solo,pno WORD S-276 (D194)

God Still Lives *sac
  (Heady) solo,pno WORD S-84 (D195)

He Loves The Passer-By *sac
  (Heady) solo,pno WORD S-69 (D196)

Heaven Seems Much Nearer *sac
  (Heady) solo,pno WORD S-248 (D197)

I Stand Amazed *sac
  (Heady) solo,pno WORD S-64 (D198)

I'm On The Highway Home *sac
  (Heady) solo,pno WORD S-247 (D199)

Little Drummer Boy *sac,Xmas
  solo,pno (simplified version)
    HARRIS $.90 (D200)
  solo,pno HARRIS $1.20 (D201)

Lord, Don't Let Me Fail You *sac
  (Heady) solo,pno WORD S-68 (D202)

One More Valley *see Rambo

Sheltered In The Arms Of God *see
  Rambo

Someday (composed with Williams)
  *sac
  solo,pno BENSON S7532-S $1.00 (D203)

They Call His Name Jesus *sac
  (Heady) solo,pno WORD S-277 (D204)

DAVIS (cont'd.)
Though Men Call Us Free
  S solo,clar,pno sc,cmplt ed WESTERN
  AV207 $10.00 (D205)

Three Moods *CC3U
  S solo,vln,vcl,pno WESTERN AV209 (D206)

Three Nails, The *see Harrah

Till He Wipes Away My Tears *sac
  (Heady) solo,pno WORD S-65 (D207)

When I Wait Before His Throne *sac
  (Heady) solo,pno WORD S-278 (D208)

Wildflower Suite *CCU
  S solo,fl,ob,vln,vcl,pno sc,cmplt
  ed WESTERN AV208 $15.00 (D209)

DAVIS, KATHERINE K. (1892-   )
Bagpipes
  low solo,pno (G maj) GALAXY
  1.1764.7 $1.00 (D210)

Be Ye Kind, One To Another
  low solo,pno GALAXY 1.1696.7 $1.00 (D211)

Bless The Lord, O My Soul *sac
  low solo,pno GALAXY 1.1924.7 $1.25 (D212)

Carol Of The Drum *sac,Xmas
  med solo,pno BELWIN $1.50 (D213)

Christ Is Risen Today *sac,Easter
  med solo,pno GALAXY 1.1628.7 $1.00 (D214)

Deaf Old Woman
  med solo/low solo,pno GALAXY
  1.1627.7 $1.25 (D215)

He's Gone Away
  med solo/low solo,pno GALAXY
  1.1602.7 $1.25 (D216)

How Lovely Are Thy Dwellings
  high solo,pno (D maj) GALAXY
  1.1872.7 $1.25 (D217)

I Have A Fawn
  med solo,pno GALAXY 1.2337.7 $1.00 (D218)

Little Drummer Boy *sac,Xmas
  (Onorati; Simeone) med solo,pno
  BELWIN $1.50 (D219)

Lord Is God *sac
  med solo,pno (D maj) GALAXY
  1.2009.7 $1.00 (D220)

Mill Wheel
  low solo,pno (A min) GALAXY
  1.1739.7 $1.25 (D221)

My God Hath Sent His Angel *sac
  high solo,pno GALAXY 1.2085.7 $1.00 (D222)

Nancy Hanks
  high solo,pno GALAXY 1.1158.7 $1.25 (D223)

Pitcher
  med solo,pno GALAXY 1.1827.7 $1.00 (D224)

Soldier, The
  med solo/low solo,pno GALAXY
  1.1626.7 $1.00 (D225)

Star At Christmas
  med solo,pno GALAXY 1.2131.7 $1.00 (D226)

Trust In The Lord *sac
  high solo,pno (D maj) GALAXY
  1.1551.7 $1.00 (D227)
  med solo,pno (C maj) GALAXY
  1.1552.7 $1.00 (D228)

DAVIS, MURIEL K.
Christ-Child Lives, The *sac
  high solo,pno (E flat maj) SCHIRM.G
  $.60 (D229)
  low solo,pno (C maj) SCHIRM.G $.60 (D230)

DAVIS, ROY
Songs And Epilogues *CCU
  solo,pno OXFORD $4.50 (D231)

DAVOSAS SPIGIAS see Sialm, D.

DAWN see Birch, Robert Fairfax

DAWN see Curran, Pearl Gildersleeve

DAWN see Griffes, Charles Tomlinson, Le
  Reveillon

DAWN see Milner, Anthony

DAWN AT LAONA see Hovhaness, Alan

DAWN OF CREATION see Liddell, R.

DAWN OF LOVE, THE see Friml, Rudolf,
  L'Alba D'Amore

DAWN SPRITE see Turner, Olive

DAWNING OF A NEW DAY, THE see Wolfe,
  Lanny

DAWNING OF THAT DAY, THE see Hallett,
  John C.

DAWSON
Lasseter's Last Ride
  solo,pno ALLANS s.p. (D232)

Out In The Fields
  high solo,pno KJOS TH130 $.75 (D233)
  med solo,pno KJOS TM130 $.75 (D234)

There Is A Balm In Gilead
  high solo,pno KJOS TH105 $.75 (D235)
  low solo,pno KJOS TL105 $.75 (D236)

Whalin' Up The Lachlan
  solo,pno ALLANS s.p. (D237)

DAY AFTER DAY see Puccini, Giacomo,
  Quando M'en Vo Soletta

DAY AT THE FAIR, A see Martin, Easthope

DAY FOR LOVE, A see Desmond, Charles

DAY I FIRST SAW GOD see Floering

DAY IS NO MORE, THE see Carpenter, John
  Alden

DAY LIKE TODAY, A see Drobish, Douglas

DAY, MAUDE CRASKE
Arise, O Sun
  low solo,pno (D flat maj) CRAMER
  $1.10 (D238)
  med solo,pno (E flat maj) CRAMER (D239)
  2 soli,pno (E flat maj) CRAMER
  $1.10 (D240)
  2 soli,pno (D flat maj) CRAMER
  $1.10 (D241)
  high solo,pno (G flat maj) CRAMER (D242)
  med-high solo,pno (F maj) CRAMER
  $1.10 (D243)

Bachelors Of Devon, The
  high solo,pno (E flat maj) CRAMER (D244)
  low solo,pno (D flat maj) CRAMER (D245)

Be Thou My Light
  high solo,pno (B flat maj) CRAMER (D246)
  low solo,pno (A flat maj) CRAMER (D247)

Bells Of Love, The
  solo,pno CRAMER (D248)

Beware Of The Maidens
  low solo,pno (D flat maj) CRAMER
  $.90 (D249)
  high solo,pno (E flat maj) CRAMER (D250)

Beyond The Stars
  low solo,pno (G flat maj) CRAMER (D251)
  high solo,pno (A flat maj) CRAMER (D252)

Bill-Sticker Joe
  low solo,pno (C maj) CRAMER (D253)
  high solo,pno (D maj) CRAMER (D254)

Fairy Shoon, The
  low solo,pno (E flat maj) CRAMER (D255)
  high solo,pno (F maj) CRAMER (D256)

Fairy Shopping
  solo,pno CRAMER (D257)

Fiddler Fairies
  low solo,pno (G maj) CRAMER (D258)
  high solo,pno (A flat maj) CRAMER (D259)

Fisher Lad
  low solo,pno (D min) CRAMER (D260)
  high solo,pno (F min) CRAMER (D261)

Glory Of The Dawn
  low solo,pno (F maj) CRAMER (D262)
  high solo,pno (A flat maj) CRAMER (D263)

Harvest
  solo,pno CRAMER (D264)

Heart Of Mine
  solo,pno CRAMER (D265)

Here's To The Ladies
  solo,pno CRAMER (D266)

Kitchen Fire
  solo,pno CRAMER (D267)

Love Pipes Of June
  high solo,pno (F maj) CRAMER (D268)
  low solo,pno (D flat maj) CRAMER

DAY, MAUDE CRASKE (cont'd.)
                                              (D269)
     med solo,pno (E flat maj) CRAMER
                                              (D270)
Mighty Builder, The
     low solo,pno (D min) CRAMER   (D271)
     high solo,pno (F min) CRAMER   (D272)

Music Of The Trees
     solo,pno CRAMER   (D273)

Perfect Prayer
     low solo,pno (B flat min) CRAMER
                                              (D274)
     med solo,pno (C min) CRAMER   (D275)
     med-high solo,pno (D flat min)
     CRAMER   (D276)
     high solo,pno (E flat min) CRAMER
                                              (D277)
Pixies Picnic, The
     solo,pno CRAMER   (D278)

Ring, Bells Ring
     med solo,pno (E min) CRAMER   (D279)
     high solo,pno (F min) CRAMER   (D280)
     low solo,pno (D min) CRAMER   (D281)

Shine Out O Stars
     low solo,pno (D flat maj) CRAMER
                                              (D282)
     med solo,pno (E flat maj) CRAMER
                                              (D283)
     high solo,pno (F maj) CRAMER   (D284)

Spring Tapped At My Window
     high solo,pno (A sharp maj) CRAMER
                                              (D285)
     low solo,pno (G maj) CRAMER   (D286)

Spring's A Dancer
     high solo,pno (F maj) CRAMER   (D287)
     low solo,pno (E flat maj) CRAMER
                                              (D288)
Tell Me Gipsy
     low solo,pno (D flat maj) CRAMER
     $1.15   (D289)
     med solo,pno (E flat maj) CRAMER
     $1.15   (D290)
     high solo,pno (F maj) CRAMER $.90
                                              (D291)
Unknown Land
     high solo,pno (F maj) CRAMER (D292)
     low solo,pno (B flat maj) CRAMER
                                              (D293)
     med solo,pno (E flat maj) CRAMER
                                              (D294)
We Never Do That At Sea
     low solo,pno (G maj) LEONARD-ENG
                                              (D295)
     high solo,pno (A flat maj) LEONARD-
     ENG   (D296)

White Horses
     solo,pno CRAMER   (D297)

DAY OF CALM SEA see Smolanoff, Michael

DAY OF MIRACLES, THE see Lister, Mosie

DAY OF PALMS, THE see Moeran, Ernest J.

DAY OF TRIUMPH *sac,gospel
     solo,pno ABER.GRP. $1.50   (D298)

DAY, RUTH E.
Love Came To Me
     high solo,pno (F min) WILLIS $.40
                                              (D299)
DAY WILL COME, THE see Sharpe, Evelyn

DAY WILL FIND US, A see Nystroem,
     Gosta, Ute I Skaren

DAYBREAK see Cowell, Henry Dixon

DAYBREAK see King, Harold C.

DAYBREAK see Mamlock, Ursula

DAYS PASS ON, THE see Thordarson,
     Sigurdur

DAZA, E.
Enfermo Estaba Antioco
     (Azpiazu) [Span] med solo,gtr UNION
     ESP. $.75   (D300)

DCERENKA MOJA see Holoubek, Ladislav

DE AEGYPYO see Johansson, Bengt

DE AKELEI see Masseus, Jan

DE ANTIQUERA SALE EL MORO see
     Guastavino, Carlos

DE BAGGE GRENADJARERNA see Schumann,
     Robert (Alexander), Die Beiden
     Grenadiere

DE BAGGE ROSORNA see Sibelius, Jean

DE BATTLE OB JERICHO *spir
     (Roberton, Hugh S.) 3 soli,pno
     ROBERTON 72115 s.p.   (D301)

DE BEELDEN EN DE GAMELAN see
     Sigtenhorst-Meyer, Bernhard van den

DE BESCHEIDEN HERDER see Mul, Jan

DE BIETBAUW see Cuypers, H.

DE BLAUWVOET see Hullebroeck, Em.

DE BLIN' MAN STOOD ON DE ROAD AN' CRIED
     *spir
     (Burleigh, H. T.) high solo,pno
     BELWIN $1.50   (D302)
     (Burleigh, H. T.) low solo,pno BELWIN
     $1.50   (D303)

DE BOEREN see Schouwman, Hans

DE BOEVEN VAN FRESNES see Hullebroeck,
     Em.

DE BORO-BOEDOER see Sigtenhorst-Meyer,
     Bernhard van den

DE BRIEF VAN DEN SCHACHT see
     Hullebroeck, Em.

DE BRUID see Mulder, Ernest W.

DE BRUINE BIE see Beekhuis, Hanna

DE CAMPASSIONE MATRIS AD FILIUM see
     Mortari, Virgilio

DE CARA AL MAR see Casals, Pablo

DE CE SEJOUR see Anonymous

DE CEYLAN see Aubert, Louis-Francois-
     Marie

DE CI, DE LA, CAHIN, CAHA see Messager,
     Andre

DE COMPASSIONE MATREM TEMPORA PASSONIS
     SUE see Mortari, Virgilio

DE DAHLIA see Hullebroeck, Em.

DE DAMRAKKERTJES see Jong, H. de

DE DANS DER GODEN see Pluister, Simon

DE DARTELE SATER see Ketting, Otto

DE DEERNE see Ruyneman, Daniel

DE DIJK see Lier, Bertus van

DE DONDE VENIS, AMORE? see Rodrigo,
     Joaquin

DE DOOD see Dijk, Jan van

DE DRUKKUNST see Paap, Wouter

DE FIJNPROEVERS see Hullebroeck, Em.

DE FLEURS see Debussy, Claude

DE FLUITSPELER see Dresden, Sem

DE FLUITSPELER see Zagwijn, Henri

DE FUNERE AD VITAM see Geist, Christian

DE GEHEIME ZEE see Zagwijn, Henri

DE GILDE VIERT see Hullebroeck, Em.

DE GLORY ROAD *spir
     (Wolfe) solo,pno ALLANS s.p.   (D304)

DE GLORY ROAD see Wolfe, Jacques

DE GOEDE DOOD see Delden, Lex van

DE GOSPEL TRAIN *spir
     (Burleigh, H. T.) high solo,pno
     BELWIN $1.50   (D305)
     (Burleigh, H. T.) low solo,pno BELWIN
     $1.50   (D306)

DE GRAAFBUIKSPREKER see Rontgen,
     Johannes

DE GRAND MATIN ME SUIS LEVE
     see La Musique, Sixieme Cahier

DE GREVE see Debussy, Claude

DE GROENE BEGONIA see Bijvanck, Henk

DE GROTE VOGEL see Braal, Andries de

DE HEILGA KLOCKOR MANA TIL BON see
     Josephson, Jacob Axel

DE HERDERTJES LAGEN BIJ NACHTE see
     Oort, H.C.v.

DE HOLLANDER EN DE ZEEUW see Rontgen,
     [Julius]

DE HOND EN ZIJN MEESTER see Baeyens,
     August-L.

DE HOREN see Hullebroeck, Em.

DE JONGENS ZEGGEN 'T AAN DE MEISJES see
     Hullebroeck, Em.

DE KEIZER VAN ZWEDEN see Beekhuis,
     Hanna

DE KERKERBALLADE see Zagwijn, Henri

DE KEVER see Baeyens, August-L.

DE KINDERTREIN see Lilien, Ignace

DE KIP DIE GOUDEN EIEREN LEGT see
     Baeyens, August-L.

DE KLARE DAG see Diepenbrock, Alphons

DE KLEINE SOUBRETTE see Witte, D.

DE KLEUREN VAN MIJN VADERLAND see
     Hoeven, L.

DE KOELTE NEIGT see Zagwijn, Henri

DE KROAIE ENDEN PUYT see Bordewijk-
     Roepman, Johanna

DE KWIKSTAART see Hullebroeck, Em.

DE LA JUSTITIA E FALSITA see Ugolini,
     G.

DE LA MUCHACHA DORADA see Garcia
     Morillo, Roberto

DE LA ROSA see Garcia Morillo, Roberto

DE LEEUW EN DE MUIS see Baeyens,
     August-L.

DE LEEUWERIK see Clercq, R. de

DE LENTEREGEN see Pluister, Simon

DE LEYE see Dijk, Jan van

DE LIEFDEGIFT see Mulder, Herman

DE LIEREMAN see Zweers, [Bernard]

DE LOOME VLERK GEBROKEN see Zagwijn,
     Henri

DE LOS ALAMOS VENGO see Vazquez, J.

DE LOS ALAMOS VENGO, MADRE see Rodrigo,
     Joaquin

DE LOS RAMOS see Garcia Morillo,
     Roberto

DE LUD ACHTERN DIEK see Janssen, Gunnar

DE MEIDOORN see Clercq, R. de

DE MEREL see Zweers, [Bernard]

DE MI PATRIA see Sammartino, Luis

DE' MIEI BOLLENTI SPIRITI see Verdi,
     Giuseppe

DE MINNEBODE see Schouwman, Hans

DE MOI QU'ATTENDEZ-VOUS see Duvernoy,
     Victor-Alphonse

DE MON AMIE, FLEUR ENDORMIE see Bizet,
     Georges

DE MUIS, DIE KNAAGT see Lilien, Ignace

DE MULDER see Clercq, R. de

DE NACHTEGAAL see Bijvanck, Henk

DE NACHTEGAEL DIE SANCK EEN LIEDT see
     Beekhuis, Hanna

DE NACHTEN see Zagwijn, Henri

DE NARE SCHADUW see Sigtenhorst-Meyer,
     Bernhard van den

DE ONTROUWE LIEFSTE see Henkemans, Hans

DE ONTROUWE LIEFSTE see Leeuw, Ton de

DE OOGST see Clercq, R. de

DE OOIEVAAR see Hullebroeck, Em.

DE OPWEKKING VAN LAZARUS see Colaco
     Osorio-Swaab, Reine

DE OUDE VIOOL see Mulder, Herman

DE OUDE WIJSHEID see Schouwman, Hans

DE PEREN see Witte, D.

DE PISANGBLAREN see Sigtenhorst-Meyer,
Bernhard van den

DE PLEURS S'EGRENE see Schmitt, Florent

DE POEDELMAN see Nieland, H.

DE PROFUNDIS see Hufschmidt, Wolfgang

DE PROFUNDIS see Martin, Easthope

DE PROFUNDIS see Sifler, Paul J.

DE PROFUNDIS see Leskovic, Bogomir

DE PROFUNDIS CLAMAVI see Bruhns,
Nicholaus

DE PROFUNDIS CLAMAVI see Kayser, Leif

DE RAMP see Beyerman-Walraven, Jeanne

DE REGENBOOG see Clercq, R. de

DE REGENVLAAG see Hullebroeck, Em.

DE REVE see Debussy, Claude

DE ROOS see Zweers, [Bernard]

DE ROZEN DROOMEN see Zagwijn, Henri

DE ROZENGAARDE see Beekhuis, Hanna

DE SCHALMEI see Franken, Wim

DE SCHALMEI see Godron, Hugo

DE SCHALMEI see Vredenburg, Max

DE SCHIPPER see Ketting, Otto

DE SCHUTZEKONIG see Burkhard, Paul

DE SOIR see Debussy, Claude

DE SOKTE SITT see Svedlund, Karl-Erik

DE SPEELDOOS see Bunge, Sas

DE SPIEGEL UIT VENETIE see Andriessen,
Hendrik

DE SPIN see Michielsen, A.

DE STEM see Bijvanck, Henk

DE STERREZIENSTER see Ridder, C. de

DE STILTE see Bijvanck, Henk

DE STRIJDER see Mulder, Herman

DE STRIJDZANG DER HOUTHAKKERS see
Hullebroeck, Em.

DE TOCHT DOOR DE HEMELEN see Colaco
Osorio-Swaab, Reine

DE TON REGARD LA DOUCEUR ME PENETRE see
Saint-Saens, Camille

DE TON REGARD LA DOUCHEUR ME PENETRE
see Saint-Saens, Camille

DE TOOVERFLUIT see Henkemans, Hans

DE TORENS VAN AMSTERDAM see Lambrechts,
F.

DE TOUT MON COEUR, CAHIER 1 & 2 see
Mathil

DE TOVERFLUIT see Leeuw, Ton de

DE TROUBADOUR see Vredenburg, Max

DE UEREN VAN DE BITTERE PASSIE JESU
CHRISTI see Leeuw, Ton de

DE UITVERKORENE see Lilien, Ignace

DE UNGES SANG see Nielsen, Carl

DE VACKRASTE SOLOSANGER, VOL. 1 see
Merikanto, Oskar

DE VACKRASTE SOLOSANGER, VOL. 2 see
Merikanto, Oskar

DE VALLE LACRIMARUM see Foggia,
Francesco

DE VARE ELLEVE SVENDE see Sjogren, Emil

DE VERHUIZENDE MEID see Hullebroeck,
Em.

DE VERSTOOTEN VRIENDIN VAN DEN KEIZER
see Ruyneman, Daniel

DE VERWORPELINGEN VAN DEN YZER see
Hullebroeck, Em.

DE VINKJES see Faddegon-Keene, E.

DE VLAAMSCHE TALE see Mortelmans,
Lodewijk

DE VLAGGEN UIT see Spoel, A.

DE VOGEL DIE NAAR 'T ZUIDEN TREKT see
Clercq, R. de

DE VOORSPELLING see Hullebroeck, Em.

DE VOS EN DE DRUIVEN see Baeyens,
August-L.

DE WATERLELIE see Oskam, Izaak J.

DE WEEZANG VAN AUVOURS see Hullebroeck,
Em.

DE WEIDE WAS VAN BLOEMEN BONT see
Adriessen, Willem

DE WESTEWIND see Badings, Henk

DE WIEDSTERS see Clercq, R. de

DE WIEGENDE MIJNWERKER see Hullebroeck,
Em.

DE WILGEN see Koetsier, Jan

DE WIM-WAM REUS see Nieland, H.

DE WINDEN see Beekhuis, Hanna

DE WINDEN LACHEN ZACHT see Mulder,
Herman

DE WONDERBLOEM see Bonset, Jac.

DE WONDERFLUIT see Ruyneman, Daniel

DE ZALIGSPREKINGEN see Bartelink,
Bernard

DE ZEGEN DES VROUWENKIESRECHTS see
Witte, D.

DE ZEVEN BOEVEN see Beekhuis, Hanna

DE ZIEKE BUUR see Beyerman-Walraven,
Jeanne

DE ZIEL SPREEKT see Bijvanck, Henk

DE ZIEL SPREEKT see Schouwman, Hans

DE ZOMERAVOND OP HET LAND see
Voormolen, Alexander Nicolas

DE ZON see Mulder, Herman

DE ZON SCHIJNT IN MIJN ZIEL see
Nieland, H.

DE ZONNE see Dijk, Jan van

DE ZONNE ZEGENT DE WERELD see Nees, G.

DE ZOTTE STUDENT see Zagwijn, Henri

DE ZWINGEL see Clercq, R. de

DEACON, MARY
Beside Still Waters *sac
low solo,pno BELWIN $1.50 (D307)

Your Cross *sac
low solo,pno BELWIN $1.50 (D308)

DEAF OLD WOMAN see Davis, Katherine K.

DEANE, UEL
Please Do Not Pass Me By
T solo,pno ELKIN 27.2759.00 s.p.
(D309)

DE ANGELIS, RUGGERO
Ballata Di Primavera
[It] solo,pno BONGIOVANI 1353 s.p.
see from Due Canti Duecenteschi
(D310)
Due Canti Duecenteschi *see Ballata
Di Primavera; Visione (D311)

Schizzo
see Tre Acqueforti

Serenata
see Tre Acqueforti

Sonetto E Ballata
[It] S solo,pno BONGIOVANI 631 s.p.
(D312)
Tre Acqueforti
[It] solo,pno cmplt ed BONGIOVANI
869 s.p.
contains: Schizzo; Serenata;
Visione (D313)

Visione
see Tre Acqueforti
[It] solo,pno BONGIOVANI 1352 s.p.
see from Due Canti Duecenteschi
(D314)

DE ANGELIS, UGALBERTO
La Terra Nuda *Op.26
narrator,fl,timp,perc,bells,vibra,
xylo,cel,pno,harp,2vln,vla,vcl
SONZOGNO rental (D315)

Long Time Ago, A *Op.37
Bar solo,fl,ob,clar,4horn,4trp,
3trom,tuba,timp,perc,bells,pno,
org,harp,strings, ondes martinot
SONZOGNO rental (D316)

Tre Canti *Op.35, CC3U
S solo,fl,clar,cembalo,vln,vla,vcl
SONZOGNO rental (D317)

Tre Canti Per Voce E Chitarra
*Op.31, CC3U
solo,gtr SONZOGNO 2901 s.p. (D318)

DEANNA DURBIN'S FAVORITE SONGS AND
ARIAS, BOOK I *CC10L
(Segurola, Andres De) solo,pno
SCHIRM.G $3.95 contains works by:
Mozart; Bizet; Gounod; Verdi and
others (D319)

DEANNA DURBIN'S FAVORITE SONGS AND
ARIAS, BOOK II *CC10L
(Segurola, Andres De) solo,pno
SCHIRM.G $3.95 contains works by:
Lotti; Schubert; Purcell;
Rachmaninoff and others (D320)

DEAR CHRISTIANS, ONE AND ALL REJOICE
see Schein, Johann Hermann

DEAR CHRISTIANS, PRAISE GOD EVERMORE
see Kindermann, Johann Erasmus

DEAR COMPANION, THE
see Schirmer's American Folk-Song
Series, Set XXI (American-English
Folk-Songs From The Southern
Appalachian Mountains)

DEAR DARK HEAD see Moore, Douglas
Stuart

DEAR DAVID see York, Sybil

DEAR DELIGHT see Head, Michael (Dewar)

DEAR EARTH: A QUINTET OF POEMS see
Weigl, Vally

DEAR FRIENDS AND GENTLE HEARTS see
Maxwell

DEAR HEART see Sterne, Colin

DEAR HOME-LAND, THE see Slaughter,
Walter A.

DEAR LAND OF HOME see Valmore, G.

DEAR LITTLE BOY OF MINE see Ball,
Ernest R.

DEAR LITTLE HAND see Giannini, Vittorio

DEAR LITTLE JAMMY FACE see Russell,
Kennedy

DEAR LITTLE SHAMROCK see Hughes,
Herbert

DEAR LORD AND FATHER see Steere,
William C.

DEAR LORD AND FATHER OF MANKIND see
Keedy

DEAR LORD, REMEMBER ME *sac,gospel
solo,pno ABER.GRP. $1.50 (D321)

DEAR MARCH, COME IN see Copland, Aaron

DEAR OLD DUBLIN see Friml, Rudolf

DEAR RING UPON MY FINGER see Schubert,
Franz (Peter), Du Ring An Meinem
Finger

DEAR RING UPON MY FINGER see Schumann,
Robert (Alexander), Du Ring An
Meinem Finger

DEAREST, BELIEVE see Giordani,
Giuseppe, Caro Mio Ben

DEAREST BELOVED see Winecoff, V.D.

DEAREST, DEAREST, SLEEPEST THOU? see
Weigl, Vally

DEAREST LORD JESUS see Bach, Johann
Sebastian

DEAREST LOVER see Handel, George
Frideric, Cara Sposa

DEAREST MAIDEN, COME TO ME see Haydn,
(Franz) Joseph

DEARING, DOROTHY
Memory Of Your Song
  solo,pno CRAMER   (D322)

DEARLY BELOVED *CCU,Marriage
  (Agay, Denes) solo,pno MUSIC 040162
  $3.95   (D323)

DEATH AND THE MAIDEN see Schubert,
  Franz (Peter), Der Tod Und Das
  Madchen

DEATH BY OWL-EYES see Beeson, Jack
  Hamilton

DEATH IS THE CHILLY NIGHT see Van De
  Water, B.

DEATH-IT IS STILL COLD NIGHT see
  Heller, A.

DEATH OF A YOUNG MAN see Josephs,
  Wilfred

DEATH OF BORIS, THE see Mussorgsky,
  Modest

DEATH OF CLEOPATRA see Barber, Samuel

DEATH OF JUGOVIC MOTHER, THE see
  Komadina, Vojin, Smrt Majke
  Jugovica

DEATH OF THE EAGLE, THE see Birch,
  Robert Fairfax

DEATH OF TSAR BORIS, THE see
  Mussorgsky, Modest, Death Of Boris,
  The

DEATH SNIPS PROUD MEN BY THE NOSE see
  Weigl, Vally

DEATH THE RELEASER see Strauss,
  Richard, Befreit

DEBALLI
Himno Nacional Uruguayo
  (Grasso) [Span] solo,pno RICORDI-
  ARG BA 9339 s.p.   (D324)

DE BANFIELD, RAFFAELLO (1922-   )
For Ophelia
  S solo,3fl,3ob,2clar,2bsn,4horn,
  3trp,3trom,tuba,timp,perc,xylo,
  cel,harp,strings SONZOGNO rental
                                     (D325)

DEBLOCQ, G.
Le Chant Du Welfare
  (Souffriau, A.) solo,pno BROGNEAUX
  s.p.   (D326)

DEBOLE SISTRO AL VENTO see Bettinelli,
  Bruno

DEBORAH see Lacome, Paul

DEBOUT LA-DEDANS see Scotto, Vincent

DEBUSSY, CLAUDE (1862-1918)
Aimons-Nous Et Dormons
  "Sleep Dear Love" [Fr/Eng] high
    solo,pno PRESSER $.75   (D327)
  "Sleep Dear Love" [Fr/Eng] med
    solo,pno PRESSER $.75   (D328)

Air De Lia (from L'Enfant Prodigue)
  high solo,pno ELKAN-V $1.75 (D329)
  med solo,pno ELKAN-V $1.75 (D330)

Air Extrait (from Damoiselle Elue)
  solo,pno/inst DURAND s.p.   (D331)

Album Of Six Songs *sac,CC6U
  high solo,pno BOSTON $2.50 (D332)

Apparition
  see Quatre Chansons De Jeunesse

Ariettes Oubliees *CCU
  [Fr/Eng] INTERNAT. high solo,pno
  $2.00; low solo,pno $2.00   (D333)

Ariettes Oubliees *CC7L
  solo,pno JOBERT s.p.   (D334)

Aupres De Cette Grotte Sombre
  [Fr/Eng] S/T solo,pno/inst DURAND
  s.p. see also Le Promenoir Des
  Deux Amants   (D335)
  [Fr/Eng] Mez/Bar solo,pno/inst
  DURAND s.p. see also Le Promenoir
  Des Deux Amants   (D336)

Ballade De Villon A S'Amye
  "From Villon To His Love" [Fr/Eng]
  solo,orch DURAND s.p., ipa see
  also Trois Ballades De Francois
  Villon   (D337)

Ballade Des Femmes De Paris
  solo,pno ELKAN-V $2.30   (D338)
  "Dames Of Paris, The" [Fr/Eng]
  solo,orch DURAND s.p., ipa see
  also Trois Ballades De Francois
  Villon   (D339)

DEBUSSY, CLAUDE (cont'd.)

Ballade Que Feit Villon A La Requeste
  De Sa Mere Pour Prier Notre-Dame
  "Made By Villon At His Mother's
  Request As A Prayer To The Virgin
  Mary" [Fr/Eng] solo,orch DURAND
  s.p., ipa see also Trois Ballades
  De Francois Villon   (D340)

Beau Soir
  solo,pno JOBERT s.p.   (D341)
  "Evening Fair" [Fr/Eng] med solo,
  pno (D maj) SCHIRM.G $.75   (D342)
  "Evening Fair" [Eng/Fr] high solo,
  pno PRESSER $.75   (D343)

Ces Airs Joyeux, Ces Chants De Fete
  (from L'Enfant Prodigue)
  [Fr/Ger] solo,orch DURAND s.p., ipa
                            (D344)

Chansons De Bilitis *CCU
  [Fr/Eng] solo,pno INTERNAT. $1.75
                            (D345)

Christmas Carol For The Homeless
  Children *see Noel Des Enfants
  Qui N'ont Plus De Maisons

Cinq Poemes De Baudelaire
  S/T solo,pno/inst cmplt ed DURAND
  s.p.
    contains & see also: Harmonie Du
    Soir; La Mort Des Amants; Le
    Balcon; Le Jet D'eau;
    Recueillement   (D346)

Cinq Poemes De Baudelaire *CCU
  [Fr/Eng] low solo,pno INTERNAT.
  $2.00   (D347)

Clair De Lune
  see Fetes Galantes, Vol. 1

Clair De Lune [1]
  see Quatre Chansons De Jeunesse

Colloque Sentimental (from Fetes
  Galantes)
  S/T solo,orch DURAND s.p., ipa
                            (D348)
  Mez/Bar solo,orch DURAND s.p., ipa
                            (D349)

Crois Mon Conseil, Chere Climene
  [Fr/Eng] Mez/Bar solo,pno/inst
  DURAND s.p. see also Le Promenoir
  Des Deux Amants   (D350)
  [Fr/Eng] S/T solo,pno/inst DURAND
  s.p. see also Le Promenoir Des
  Deux Amants   (D351)

Dames Of Paris, The *see Ballade Des
  Femmes De Paris

De Fleurs
  see Proses Lyriques

De Greve
  see Proses Lyriques

De Reve
  see Proses Lyriques

De Soir
  see Proses Lyriques

Deux Melodies Sur Des Poemes De Paul
  Verlaine
  solo,pno JOBERT s.p.
    contains: Le Son Du Cor
    S'afflige; L'echelonnement Des
    Haies   (D352)

Dieu Qu'il La Fait Bon Regarder
  see Trois Chansons De Charles
  D'Orleans

Diez Canciones *CC10L
  [Fr/Span] solo,pno RICORDI-ARG
  BA 10068 s.p.   (D353)

Douze Chants *CC12L
  DURAND high solo,pno s.p.; low
  solo,pno s.p.   (D354)

En Sourdine
  see Fetes Galantes, Vol. 1

Evening Fair *see Beau Soir

Eventail
  med solo,pno/inst DURAND s.p. see
  also Trois Poemes De Stephane
  Mallarme   (D355)

Fantoches
  see Fetes Galantes, Vol. 1

Fetes Galantes, Series I *CCU
  [Fr/Eng] INTERNAT. high solo,pno
  $1.75; low solo,pno $1.75 (D356)

Fetes Galantes, Series II *CCU
  [Fr/Eng] INTERNAT. high solo,pno
  $1.75; low solo,pno $1.75 (D357)

DEBUSSY, CLAUDE (cont'd.)

Fetes Galantes, Vol. 1
  solo,pno JOBERT s.p.
    contains: Clair De Lune; En
    Sourdine; Fantoches   (D358)

Fleurs Des Bles
  solo,pno/inst LEDUC s.p.   (D359)

Forty-Three Songs *CC43L
  (Kagen, Sergius) [Fr/Eng] INTERNAT.
  high solo,pno $7.50; med-low
  solo,pno $7.50   (D360)

From Villon To His Love *see Ballade
  De Villon A S'Amye

Harmonie Du Soir
  S/T solo,pno/inst DURAND s.p. see
  also Cinq Poemes De Baudelaire
                            (D361)

Je Tremble En Voyant Ton Visage
  [Fr/Eng] Mez/Bar solo,pno/inst
  DURAND s.p. see also Le Promenoir
  Des Deux Amants   (D362)
  [Fr/Eng] S/T solo,pno/inst DURAND
  s.p. see also Le Promenoir Des
  Deux Amants   (D363)

La Belle Au Bois Dormant
  [Fr/Eng/Ger] med solo,pno ESCHIG
  $2.50 see from Trois Melodies
                            (D364)

La Chambre Magique (from Le Martyre
  De Saint Sebastien)
  S solo,orch DURAND s.p. contains
  also: La Voix De La Vierge
  Erigone   (D365)

La Chevelure
  see Trois Chansons De Bilitis

La Damoiselle Elue (from La
  Damoiselle Elue)
  [Fr] solo,pno/inst DURAND s.p.
                            (D366)

La Flute De Pan
  see Trois Chansons De Bilitis

La Grotte
  [Fr/Eng] Mez/Bar solo,pno/inst
  DURAND s.p. see also Trois
  Chansons De France   (D367)
  [Fr/Eng] S/T solo,pno/inst DURAND
  s.p. see also Trois Chansons De
  France   (D368)

La Lettre Voici Ce Qu'il Ecrit A Son
  Frere Pelleas (from Pelleas Et
  Melisande)
  Mez solo,pno/inst DURAND s.p.
                            (D369)

La Mort Des Amants
  S/T solo,pno/inst DURAND s.p. see
  also Cinq Poemes De Baudelaire
                            (D370)

La Voix De La Vierge Erigone (from Le
  Martyre De Saint Sebastien)
  see Debussy, Claude, La Chambre
  Magique
  S solo,pno/inst DURAND s.p., ipa
                            (D371)

L'annee En Vain Chasse L'annee (from
  L'Enfant Prodigue)
  [Fr/Eng] S solo,orch DURAND s.p.,
  ipa   (D372)
  [Fr/Ger] Mez solo,orch DURAND s.p.,
  ipa   (D373)

Le Balcon
  S/T solo,orch DURAND s.p., ipr see
  also Cinq Poemes De Baudelaire
                            (D374)

Le Faune (from Fetes Galantes)
  S/T solo,orch DURAND s.p., ipa
                            (D375)
  Mez/Bar solo,orch DURAND s.p., ipa
                            (D376)

Le Jet D'eau
  Mez/Bar solo,orch DURAND s.p., ipa
  see also Cinq Poemes De
  Baudelaire   (D377)
  S/T solo,orch DURAND s.p., ipa see
  also Cinq Poemes De Baudelaire
                            (D378)
  [Fr/Ger] Mez/Bar solo,pno DURAND
  s.p.   (D379)
  [Eng/Ger] S solo,pno DURAND s.p.
                            (D380)

Le Promenoir Des Deux Amants
  [Fr/Eng] cmplt ed DURAND s.p. Mez/
  Bar solo,pno/inst; S/T solo,pno/
  inst
    contains & see also: Aupres De
    Cette Grotte Sombre; Crois Mon
    Conseil, Chere Climene; Je
    Tremble En Voyant Ton Visage
                            (D381)

Le Son Du Cor S'afflige
  see Deux Melodies Sur Des Poemes De
  Paul Verlaine
  solo,pno JOBERT s.p.   (D382)

DEBUSSY, CLAUDE (cont'd.)

Le Temps A Laissie Son Manteau
[Fr/Eng] S/T solo,pno/inst DURAND
s.p. see also Trois Chansons De
France (D383)
[Fr/Eng] Mez/Bar solo,pno/inst
DURAND s.p. see also Trois
Chansons De France (D384)

Le Tombeau Des Naiades
see Trois Chansons De Bilitis

L'echelonnement Des Haies
see Deux Melodies Sur Des Poemes De
Paul Verlaine

Les Chansons De Bilitis *CC12U
narrator,2fl,2harp,cel sc JOBERT
s.p. (D385)

Les Cheveux (from Pelleas Et
Melisande)
T solo,pno/inst DURAND s.p.
contains also: Oh! Oh! Qu'est-ce
Que C'est (D386)

Les Cloches
[Fr] Mez solo,pno DURAND s.p. (D387)
[Fr] S/T solo,pno DURAND s.p. (D388)

Les Ingenus (from Fetes Galantes)
[Fr/Ger] S/T solo,pno/inst DURAND
s.p. (D389)
[Fr/Ger] Mez/Bar solo,pno/inst
DURAND s.p. (D390)

Lia's Recitative And Aria (from
L'Enfant Prodigue)
[Fr/Eng] S solo,pno INTERNAT. $1.25
(D391)
[Fr/Eng] Mez solo,pno INTERNAT.
$1.25 (D392)

Made By Villon At His Mother's
Request As A Prayer To The Virgin
Mary *see Ballade Que Feit
Villon A La Requeste De Sa Mere
Pour Prier Notre-Dame

Maintenant Que Le Pere De Pelleas Est
Sauve (from Pelleas Et Melisande)
B solo,pno/inst DURAND s.p. (D393)

Mandoline
Mez/Bar solo,orch DURAND s.p., ipa
(D394)
S/T solo,pno/inst DURAND s.p. (D395)
[Fr] solo,acap oct DURAND s.p. (D396)

Noel Des Enfants Qui N'ont Plus De
Maisons
"Christmas Carol For The Homeless
Children" med solo,orch DURAND
s.p., ipr (D397)

Nuit D'Etoiles
"Under Starlight" [Fr/Eng] high
solo,pno MARKS $1.50 (D398)
"Under Starlight" [Fr/Eng] med
solo,pno MARKS $1.50 (D399)

Oh! Oh! Qu'est-ce Que C'est (from
Pelleas Et Melisande)
see Debussy, Claude, Les Cheveux

Pantomine
see Quatre Chansons De Jeunesse

Paysage Sentimental
[Fr/Eng/Ger] high solo,pno ESCHIG
$2.25 see from Trois Melodies
(D400)

Pierrot
see Quatre Chansons De Jeunesse

Placet Futile
med solo,pno/inst DURAND s.p. see
also Trois Poemes De Stephane
Mallarme (D401)

Pour Ce Que Plaisance Est Morte
[Fr/Eng] Mez/Bar solo,pno/inst
DURAND s.p. see also Trois
Chansons De France (D402)
[Fr/Eng] S/T solo,pno/inst DURAND
s.p. see also Trois Chansons De
France (D403)

Proses Lyriques *CCU
[Fr/Eng] INTERNAT. high solo,pno
$2.00; low solo,pno $2.00 (D404)

Proses Lyriques
solo,pno JOBERT s.p.
contains: De Fleurs; De Greve; De
Reve; De Soir (D405)

Quand J'ai Ouy Le Tabourin
see Trois Chansons De Charles
D'Orleans

DEBUSSY, CLAUDE (cont'd.)

Quatre Chansons De Jeunesse
solo,pno JOBERT s.p.
contains: Apparition; Clair De
Lune [1]; Pantomine; Pierrot
(D406)

Que Vois-Je? Un Pavre Voyeur (from
L'Enfant Prodigue)
ST soli,orch DURAND s.p. (D407)

Recit Et Air D'Azael (from L'Enfant
Prodigue)
solo,orch (available in 2 keys)
DURAND s.p., ipa (D408)

Recit Et Air De Lia (from L'Enfant
Prodigue)
solo,orch (available in two keys)
DURAND s.p., ipa (D409)

Recueillement
S/T solo,pno/inst DURAND s.p. see
also Cinq Poemes De Baudelaire
(D410)

Romance
[Fr/Ger] S/T solo,pno/inst DURAND
s.p. (D411)
[Fr/Ger] Mez/Bar solo,pno/inst
DURAND s.p. (D412)
low solo,pno (C maj) BOSTON $1.50
(D413)

Selected Romances *CCU
[Russ] solo,pno MEZ KNIGA 86 s.p.
(D414)

Sleep Dear Love *see Aimons-Nous Et
Dormons

Soupir
med solo,pno/inst DURAND s.p. see
also Trois Poemes De Stephane
Mallarme (D415)

Thirty Songs *CC30L
[Fr/Eng] low solo,pno SCHIRM.G 1783
$4.00 (D416)

Trois Ballades De Francois Villon
*CC3U
[Fr/Eng] solo,orch DURAND s.p., ipa
see also: Ballade De Villon A
S'Amye, "From Villon To His
Love"; Ballade Des Femmes De
Paris, "Dames Of Paris, The";
Ballade Que Feit Villon A La
Requeste De Sa Mere Pour Prier
Notre-Dame, "Made By Villon At
His Mother's Request As A
Prayer To The Virgin Mary"
(D417)

Trois Chansons De Bilitis
solo,pno JOBERT s.p.
contains: La Chevelure; La Flute
De Pan; Le Tombeau Des Naiades
(D418)

Trois Chansons De Charles D'Orleans
[Fr] solo,pno/inst cmplt ed DURAND
s.p.
contains: Dieu Qu'il La Fait Bon
Regarder; Quand J'ai Ouy Le
Tabourin; Yver Vous N'estes
Qu'un Villain (D419)

Trois Chansons De France
[Fr/Eng] DURAND s.p. Mez/Bar solo,
pno/inst; S/T solo,pno/inst
contains & see also: La Grotte;
Le Temps A Laissie Son Manteau;
Pour Ce Que Plaisance Est Morte
(D420)

Trois Melodies *see La Belle Au Bois
Dormant; Paysage Sentimental;
Voici Que Le Printemps (D421)

Trois Poemes De Stephane Mallarme
med solo,pno/inst cmplt ed DURAND
s.p.
contains & see also: Eventail;
Placet Futile; Soupir (D422)

Twelve Songs *CC12U
PRESSER $2.00 high solo,pno; low
solo,pno (D423)

Under Starlight *see Nuit D'Etoiles

Voici Que Le Printemps
[Fr/Eng/Ger] med solo,pno ESCHIG
$2.50 see from Trois Melodies
(D424)

Vous Ne Savez Pasou Je Vous Ai Menee?
(from Pelleas Et Melisande)
2 soli,pno/inst DURAND s.p. (D425)

Yver Vous N'estes Qu'un Villain
see Trois Chansons De Charles
D'Orleans

DECEPTION see Haring, Ch.

DECIMAS EN TONO MENOR see Lapuente,
P.G.

DECLARATION see Aubert, Louis-Francois-
Marie

DECLARATION see Dufresne, C.

DECLARATION see Schumann, Robert
(Alexander)

DECLARATION OF INDEPENDENCE see
Dougherty, Celius

DE CRESCENZO
Messidoro
[It] S/T solo,pno RICORDI-ENG
123974 s.p. (D426)

Notte D'amore
[It] solo,pno RICORDI-ENG NY 1074
s.p. (D427)

Quann'a Femmena Vo!
[It] solo,pno RICORDI-ARG BA 9971
s.p. (D428)

Rondine Al Nido
[It] S/T solo,pno RICORDI-ARG
BA 9874 s.p. (D429)

DECRUCK, F.
Cantique *sac
[Fr/Eng] DURAND s.p. see from Cinq
Poemes Chretiens (D430)

Cinq Poemes Chretiens *see Cantique;
Jesus Tombe Pour La Seconde Fois;
La Couronne Effeuillee; La
Epiphanie; Le Crucifix (D431)

Jesus Tombe Pour La Seconde Fois
*sac
[Fr/Eng] DURAND s.p. see from Cinq
Poemes Chretiens (D432)

La Couronne Effeuillee *sac
[Fr/Eng] DURAND s.p. see from Cinq
Poemes Chretiens (D433)

La Epiphanie *sac
[Fr/Eng] DURAND s.p. see from Cinq
Poemes Chretiens (D434)

Le Crucifix *sac
[Fr/Eng] DURAND s.p. see from Cinq
Poemes Chretiens (D435)

DE CURTIS
Come Back To Sorrento
med solo,pno (D maj) CENTURY 3617
(D436)
solo,pno (available in 3 keys)
ASHLEY $.95 (D437)
med-high solo,pno (D maj) BOSTON
$1.50 (D438)
high solo,pno (E maj) BOSTON $1.50
(D439)

DEDANS PARIS, VILLE JOLIE see Rivier,
Jean

DEDEKIND, CONSTANTINE CHRISTIAN
(1628-1725)
Vier Geistliche Konzerte *CC4U,
concerto
[Ger] A solo,pno NAGELS $2.00
(D440)

DEDICACE see Borchard, Adolphe

DEDICACE see Godard, Benjamin Louis
Paul

DEDICATION see Edwards, Clara

DEDICATION see Franz, Robert, Widmung

DEDICATION see Schumann, Robert
(Alexander), Widmung

DEDICATION, A see Franz, Robert,
Widmung

DEDICATION AND FOUR SONGS see Sharpe,
Evelyn

DEEP ABIDING PEACE, A *sac,gospel
solo,pno ABER.GRP. $1.50 (D441)

DEEP, DEEP WATERS see Wilson, Al

DEEP GROUND, LONG WATERS see Symonds,
Norman

DEEP IN THE QUIET FOREST see Henley,
Peter J.

DEEP IN THE WOODS see Bury, Winifred

DEEP IN YOUR EYES see Loewe, Gilbert

DEEP RIVER *sac,gospel/spir
solo,pno (available in 2 keys) ASHLEY
$.95 (D442)
solo,pno ABER.GRP. $1.50 (D443)
(Burleigh, H. T.) high solo,pno
BELWIN $1.50 (D444)
(Burleigh, H. T.) med solo,pno BELWIN
$1.50 (D445)
(Burleigh, H. T.) low solo,pno BELWIN
$1.50 (D446)
(Roberton, Hugh S.) 3 soli,pno
ROBERTON 72105 s.p. (D447)

(Rolfe) low solo,pno (E flat maj)
      CENTURY 3476   (D448)

DEEP SEA SHANTIES *CCU
   (Trevine, Owen) solo,pno CRAMER
                                     (D449)

DEEP-WATER SONG see Brown, Mary Helen

DEER
   Before Thine Altar *sac,Marriage
      med-high solo,pno (E flat maj)
      BOSTON $1.50   (D450)

DEES HELE LIEFDE IS HEENGEGAAN see
   Zagwijn, Henri

DEFESCH, WILLIAM
   Colin's Success
      (Poston) solo,pno (D maj) ROBERTON
      2594 s.p.   (D451)

DEFONTAINE, M.
   La Marjolaine Et Ses Compagnons
      see Six Chansons Pour Enfants

   La Perruche Au Miroir
      see Six Chansons Pour Enfants

   La Princesse Du Printemps
      see Six Chansons Pour Enfants

   La Reine Au Verger
      see Six Chansons Pour Enfants

   Le Duvet Du Pissenlit
      see Six Chansons Pour Enfants

   Les Coquelicots
      see Six Chansons Pour Enfants

   Six Chansons Pour Enfants
      cmplt ed JOBERT solo,pno s.p.;
      solo,acap s.p.
      contains: La Marjolaine Et Ses
         Compagnons; La Perruche Au
         Miroir; La Princesse Du
         Printemps; La Reine Au Verger;
         Le Duvet Du Pissenlit; Les
         Coquelicots   (D452)

DEFOSSE, H.
   Heure D'ete
      [Fr/Eng] solo,pno/inst DURAND s.p.
                                     (D453)

DEFOSSEZ, RENE (1905-   )
   L'infidele
      A/B solo,pno CBDM s.p.   (D454)

DEFUNCTO HERODE see Hindemith, Paul

DEFUNE
   see Internationale Volklieder, Nol. 3

DEGEL see Schubert, Franz (Peter)

DE GRANDIS, RENATO (1927-   )
   Aria Del Paesano (from Il Cieco Di
      Hyuga)
      B solo,inst TONOS 7296 s.p. (D455)

   Aria Di Hitomaru (from Il Cieco Di
      Hyuga)
      S solo,inst TONOS 7295 s.p. (D456)

   Mille Fili Di Pioggia (from Il Cieco
      Di Hyuga)
      T solo,inst TONOS 7294 s.p.
      contains also: Vole Vo Nasconder
         Mi   (D457)

   Salterio Popolare I: Sette Poesie
      Popolari - Due Cantate *CC9U
      solo,pno TONOS 7231 s.p.   (D458)

   Salterio Popolare II: Nove Poesie
      Popolari - El Kalendario Del
      Popolo *CCU
      solo,pno TONOS 7232 s.p.   (D459)

   Serenata Prima
      T solo,6inst sc ZERBONI 7249 s.p.
                                     (D460)

   Vole Vo Nasconder Mi (from Il Cieco
      Di Hyuga)
      see De Grandis, Renato, Mille Fili
      Di Pioggia

DEH! CON TE, CON TE LI PRENDI see
   Bellini, Vincenzo

DEH! LASCIA O FANCIULLA see Pratella,
   Francesco Balilla

DEH! NON GIURARE.. see Pratella,
   Francesco Balilla

DEH, PER QUESTO ISTANTE SOLO see
   Mozart, Wolfgang Amadeus

DEH, RENDETEMI OMBRE CARE see
   Provenzale, Francesco

DEH! TORNA MIO BENE see Proch,
   Heinrich, Woher Dieses Sehnen

DEH, VIENI ALLA FINESTRA! see Mozart,
   Wolfgang Amadeus

DEH VIENI, NON TARDAR see Mozart,
   Wolfgang Amadeus

DEHMEL LIEDER see Reynvaan, M.C.C.

DEI ANANG, GHANA see Leduc, Jacques

DEIDRE'S FAREWELL *Scot
   low solo,pno (E flat maj) PATERSON
      s.p. see from Hebridean Songs, Vol.
      IV   (D461)
   high solo,pno (G maj) PATERSON s.p.
      see from Hebridean Songs, Vol. IV
                                     (D462)

DEIL'S AWA' WI' THE EXCISEMAN, THE
      *folk,Scot
   solo,pno (D maj/F maj) PATERSON FS24
      s.p.   (D463)

DEIN ANGESICHT see Schumann, Robert
   (Alexander)

DEIN BIN ICH see Mozart, Wolfgang
   Amadeus, L'amero Saro Costante

DEIN, DAN, DON
   (Carlo, Musi) solo,pno (Bolognese
      dialect) BONGIOVANI 2070 s.p. see
      from El Mi Canzunett   (D464)

DEIN IST MEIN GANZES HERZ see Lehar,
   Franz

DEIN LETZTES LIED see Alfano, Franco,
   Finisci L'ultimo Canto

DEINE STIMME see Mikoda, Borivoj, Tvuj
   Hlas

DEINE TOTEN WERDEN LEBEN see Telemann,
   Georg Philipp

DEINGEDENKEN see Marx, Karl

DEIS, CARL (1883-1960)
   Come Down To Kew
      high solo,pno (G maj) SCHIRM.G $.75
                                     (D465)

DEITA SILVANE see Respighi, Ottorino

DEJA DE CANTAR JILGUERO see Gianneo,
   Luis

DEJA SE PERD LEUR VOIX see Wagner,
   Richard

DEJAME ESTA VOZ see Guastavino, Carlos

DEJEUNER see Dufresne, C.

DE JONG, CONRAD (1934-   )
   Hist Whist
      high solo,fl,vla,perc SCHIRM.G
      $1.25   (D466)

DEKKER, DIRK (1945-   )
   Little John's Morning After
      solo,fl,vcl,pno DONEMUS s.p. (D467)

DE KOVEN, HENRY LOUIS REGINALD
      (1859-1920)
   Brown October Ale (from Robin Hood)
      B solo,pno (E flat maj) SCHIRM.G
      $.60   (D468)

   Oh, Promise Me (from Robin Hood)
      high solo,pno MARKS $1.50   (D469)
      med solo,pno MARKS $1.50   (D470)
      high solo,pno (A flat maj) SCHIRM.G
      $.85   (D471)
      med solo,pno (G maj) SCHIRM.G $.85
                                     (D472)
      med solo,pno (F maj) SCHIRM.G $.85
                                     (D473)
      low solo,pno (E flat maj) SCHIRM.G
      $.85   (D474)
      high solo,pno (A flat maj) FISCHER,
      C S 7632   (D475)
      med solo,pno (F maj) FISCHER,C
      S 7633   (D476)
      solo,pno CENTURY 3788   (D477)
      solo,pno (available in 4 keys)
      ASHLEY $.95   (D478)
      (Deis) ST/SBar/SA soli,pno SCHIRM.G
      $.75   (D479)
      (Deis) TB/TBar soli,pno SCHIRM.G
      $.75   (D480)

   Recessional *sac,Gen
      high solo,pno (F maj) WILLIS $.50
                                     (D481)
      low solo,pno (D maj) WILLIS $.50
                                     (D482)
      low solo,pno PRESSER $.95   (D483)

DEL AMOR CON CIEN ANOS see Garcia
   Morillo, Roberto

DEL AMOR MARAVILLOSO see Garcia
   Morillo, Roberto

DEL ORIENTE LEJANO see Palau Boix, M.

DEL SALON EN EL ANGULO OSCURO see
   Cinque

DELA, M.
   La Lettre
      solo,pno BERANDOL BER 1305 $1.50
                                     (D484)
   Ronde
      solo,pno BERANDOL BER 1311 $1.50
                                     (D485)
   Spleen
      solo,pno BERANDOL BER 1306 $1.50
                                     (D486)

DELABRE, L.G.
   France! C'est Pour Toi
      solo,pno/inst DURAND s.p.   (D487)
      [Fr] solo,acap oct DURAND s.p.
                                     (D488)
   Jean-Pierre
      solo,pno/inst DURAND s.p.   (D489)
      [Fr] solo,acap oct DURAND s.p.
                                     (D490)
   La Querelle
      solo,pno/inst DURAND s.p.   (D491)

DELAGE, MAURICE (1879-1961)
   Amethystes
      see Trois Melodies

   Ballade
      see Trois Poemes

   Deux Fables De La Fontaine
      solo,pno/inst DURAND s.p.
      contains: La Cigale Et La Fourmi;
         Le Corbeau Et Le Renard   (D492)

   Du Livre De Monelle
      see Trois Melodies

   Guitare
      see Trois Poemes Desenchantes

   In Morte Di Un Samurai
      [Fr] med solo,pno ESCHIG $1.30 (D493)

   Intermezzo
      see Trois Melodies

   La Chanson De Ma Vie
      high solo,pno sc JOBERT s.p. (D494)

   La Cigale Et La Fourmi
      see Deux Fables De La Fontaine

   L'Alouette
      see Trois Poemes
      solo,fl DURAND s.p.   (D495)

   Le Corbeau Et Le Renard
      see Deux Fables De La Fontaine

   L'Enfant
      solo,pno/inst DURAND s.p.   (D496)

   Les Colombes
      high solo,pno sc JOBERT s.p. (D497)

   Les Demoiselles D'Avignon
      high solo,pno sc JOBERT s.p. (D498)

   Naissanve De Bouddha
      see Quatre Poemes Hindous

   Quatre Poemes Hindous
      solo,orch cmplt ed DURAND s.p., ipa
      contains: Naissanve De Bouddha;
         Si Vous Pensez; Un Sapin Isole;
         Une Belle   (D499)

   Ragamalika
      med solo,orch (Hindu text only)
      DURAND s.p., ipr   (D500)

   Roses D'octobre
      see Trois Poemes

   Sept Hai-Kais *CC7U
      S/T solo,fl,ob,clar,pno,strings
      JOBERT sc s.p., voc sc s.p.
                                     (D501)

   Si Ton Esprit
      see Trois Poemes Desenchantes

   Si Vous Pensez
      see Quatre Poemes Hindous

   Sobre Las Olas
      med solo,pno sc JOBERT s.p.   (D502)
      high solo,pno sc JOBERT s.p. (D503)

   Toute Allegresse
      high solo,pno sc JOBERT s.p. (D504)
      med solo,pno sc JOBERT s.p.   (D505)

   Trois Melodies
      solo,pno/inst cmplt ed DURAND s.p.
      contains: Amethystes; Du Livre De
         Monelle; Intermezzo   (D506)

   Trois Poemes
      solo,orch cmplt ed DURAND s.p., ipr
      contains: Ballade; L'Alouette;
         Roses D'octobre   (D507)

DELAGE, MAURICE (cont'd.)

Trois Poemes Desenchantes
solo,pno/inst cmplt ed DURAND s.p.
contains: Guitare; Si Ton Esprit;
Tu Passais   (D508)

Tu Passais
see Trois Poemes Desenchantes

Un Sapin Isole
see Quatre Poemes Hindous

Une Belle
see Quatre Poemes Hindous

DELAMONT
King Jesus *sac
solo,pno BENSON S6818-S $1.00
(D509)

DELANNOY, MARCEL
Berceuse Du Grillon (from Ginevra)
[Fr] Mez/Bar solo,pno ESCHIG $1.00
(D510)

Carnaval
med solo,orch DURAND s.p., ipr see
from Quatre Regrets De Joachim Du
Bellay   (D511)

Dernier Chant De La Sulamite *Op.63,
cant
A solo,vla,pno voc sc TRANSAT. s.p.
(D512)

Deux Poemes *see Neige; Tombeau
D'Amour   (D513)

Dialogue De La Rose Et Du Rossignol
(from Ginevra)
[Fr] coloratura sop/T solo,pno
ESCHIG $1.25   (D514)

Fetes Romanesque
med solo,orch DURAND s.p., ipr see
from Quatre Regrets De Joachim Du
Bellay   (D515)

Heureux
med solo,orch DURAND s.p., ipr see
from Quatre Regrets De Joachim Du
Bellay   (D516)

Il Niege De La Joie
[Fr] high solo,pno ESCHIG $1.60 see
from Trois Poemes   (D517)

Je Ne Chante
med solo,orch DURAND s.p., ipr see
from Quatre Regrets De Joachim Du
Bellay   (D518)

Neige
[Fr] high solo,pno ESCHIG $1.10 see
from Deux Poemes   (D519)

Quatre Regrets De Joachim Du Bellay
*see Carnaval; Fetes Romanesque;
Heureux; Je Ne Chante (D520)

Sept Pairs De Souliers (from Ginevra)
[Fr] S solo,pno ESCHIG $.75 (D521)

Suite A Chanter
[Fr] med solo,pno,strings,cel
ESCHIG $4.25   (D522)

Tombeau D'Amour
[Fr] low solo,pno ESCHIG $1.35 see
from Deux Poemes   (D523)

Trois Poemes *see Il Niege De La
Joie   (D524)

DE LARA, ISADORE (1858-1935)
Adieu, Baisers
solo,pno (available in 2 keys)
ENOCH s.p.   (D525)

Adoration
solo,pno ENOCH s.p.   (D526)

Amorosa
solo,pno ENOCH s.p.   (D527)

Berceuse
solo,pno ENOCH s.p. see from
Strophes Et Interludes (D528)

Delivrance
solo,pno ENOCH s.p.   (D529)

Interlude
solo,pno (available in 2 keys)
ENOCH s.p. see from Strophes Et
Interludes   (D530)

Le Long Du Chemin
solo,pno ENOCH s.p.   (D531)

Les Sources
solo,pno (available in 2 keys)
ENOCH s.p. see from Strophes Et
Interludes   (D532)

Que Me Fait Toute La Terre?
solo,pno ENOCH s.p. see from
Strophes Et Interludes (D533)

DE LARA, ISADORE (cont'd.)

Rondel De L'Adieu
solo,pno (available in 3 keys)
ENOCH s.p.   (D534)
solo,acap (available in 3 keys)
ENOCH s.p.   (D535)

Si Vous Vouliez
solo,pno ENOCH s.p.   (D536)

Soir D'amertune
solo,pno (available in 2 keys)
ENOCH s.p.   (D537)
solo,acap (available in 2 keys)
ENOCH s.p.   (D538)

Strophes
solo,pno (available in 2 keys)
ENOCH s.p. see from Strophes Et
Interludes   (D539)

Strophes Et Interludes *see
Berceuse; Interlude; Les Sources;
Que Me Fait Toute La Terre?;
Strophes   (D540)

DELARUE-MARDRUS, LUCIE
Tes Yeux
solo,pno ENOCH s.p.   (D541)

DELAS, JOSE LUIS DE (1928-   )
Frons
S solo,brass,perc GERIG HG 941 s.p.
(D542)

DELBOS, CL.
Primevere *song cycle
solo,pno/inst LEDUC B.L.700 s.p.
(D543)

DELBRUCK, A.
La Revanche
solo,pno ENOCH s.p.   (D544)

DELBRUCK, J.
Ah! Mon Beau Jardin
solo,pno ENOCH s.p. see also Rondes
Et Chansonettes Enfantines (D545)

Ah! Te Dirai-Je Maman
solo,pno ENOCH s.p. see also Rondes
Et Chansonettes Enfantines (D546)

Bergeronnette
solo,pno ENOCH s.p. see also Rondes
Et Chansonettes Enfantines (D547)

Chanson Du Printemps
solo,pno ENOCH s.p. see also Rondes
Et Chansonettes Enfantines (D548)

Chanson Du Traivail
solo,pno ENOCH s.p. see also Rondes
Et Chansonettes Enfantines (D549)

Chien Et Chat
solo,pno ENOCH s.p. see also Rondes
Et Chansonettes Enfantines (D550)

Deux Joyeux Enfants
solo,pno ENOCH s.p. see also Rondes
Et Chansonettes Enfantines (D551)

Enfants! Savez-Vous Qui
solo,pno ENOCH s.p. see also Rondes
Et Chansonettes Enfantines (D552)

Il Etait Une Bergere
solo,pno ENOCH s.p. see also Rondes
Et Chansonettes Enfantines (D553)

La Bonne Aventure Enfantine
solo,pno ENOCH s.p. see also Rondes
Et Chansonettes Enfantines (D554)

La France Est Belle
solo,pno ENOCH s.p. see also Rondes
Et Chansonettes Enfantines (D555)

Le Clair De Lune
solo,pno ENOCH s.p. see also Rondes
Et Chansonettes Enfantines (D556)

Le Corbeau Et Le Renard
solo,pno ENOCH s.p. see also Rondes
Et Chansonettes Enfantines (D557)

Le Fer
solo,pno ENOCH s.p. see also Rondes
Et Chansonettes Enfantines (D558)

Le Feu
solo,pno ENOCH s.p. see also Rondes
Et Chansonettes Enfantines (D559)

Le Lievre Et La Tortue
solo,pno ENOCH s.p. see also Rondes
Et Chansonettes Enfantines (D560)

Le Petit Oiseau
solo,pno ENOCH s.p. see also Rondes
Et Chansonettes Enfantines (D561)

Le Petite Marie
solo,pno ENOCH s.p. see also Rondes
Et Chansonettes Enfantines (D562)

DELBRUCK, J. (cont'd.)

Les Betises Que Dit Nicolas
solo,pno ENOCH s.p. see also Rondes
Et Chansonettes Enfantines (D563)

Mere Sois Mes Amours
solo,pno ENOCH s.p. see also Rondes
Et Chansonettes Enfantines (D564)

Petit Jean
solo,pno ENOCH s.p. see also Rondes
Et Chansonettes Enfantines (D565)

Pourvu Que L'on Travaille
solo,pno ENOCH s.p. see also Rondes
Et Chansonettes Enfantines (D566)

Priere
2 soli,pno ENOCH s.p. see also
Rondes Et Chansonettes Enfantines
(D567)

Repose Enfant
solo,pno ENOCH s.p. see also Rondes
Et Chansonettes Enfantines (D568)

Rondes Et Chansonettes Enfantines
*CC39L
solo,pno cmplt ed ENOCH s.p.
see also: Ah! Mon Beau Jardin;
Ah! Te Dirai-Je Maman;
Bergeronnette; Chanson Du
Printemps; Chanson Du Traivail;
Chien Et Chat; Deux Joyeux
Enfants; Enfants! Savez-Vous
Qui; Il Etait Une Bergere; La
Bonne Aventure Enfantine; La
France Est Belle; Le Clair De
Lune; Le Corbeau Et Le Renard;
Le Fer; Le Feu; Le Lievre Et La
Tortue; Le Petit Oiseau; Le
Petite Marie; Les Betises Que
Dit Nicolas; Mere Sois Mes
Amours; Petit Jean; Pourvu Que
L'on Travaille; Priere; Repose
Enfant; Vive L'eau   (D569)

Vive L'eau
solo,pno ENOCH s.p. see also Rondes
Et Chansonettes Enfantines (D570)

DEL CORONA, RODOLFO
Filastrocca
[It] solo,pno BONGIOVANI 2180 s.p.
(D571)

Pieta
[It] solo,pno BONGIOVANI 2179 s.p.
(D572)

Rispetto Toscano
[It] solo,pno BONGIOVANI 2217 s.p.
(D573)

DELDEN, LEX VAN (1919-   )
Betwixt Mine Eyes And Heart *Op.72,
No.2
see Drie Sonnetten Van Shakespeare

De Goede Dood *Op.47,No.1
Mez solo,pno DONEMUS s.p. contains
also: Lied Om Den Blijen En
Onvoorzienen Dood, Op.47,No.2
(D574)

Drie Sonnetten Van Shakespeare
A solo,pno DONEMUS s.p.
contains: Betwixt Mine Eyes And
Heart, Op.72,No.2; If The Dull
Substance Of My Flesh, Op.72,
No.3; When Most I Wink, Op.72,
No.1   (D575)

Elegie *Op.1,No.1
see L'amour

If The Dull Substance Of My Flesh
*Op.72,No.3
see Drie Sonnetten Van Shakespeare

L'amour
S solo,fl,clar,vln,vla,vcl voc sc
DONEMUS s.p.
contains: Elegie, Op.1,No.1; Les
Roses De Saadi, Op.1,No.4;
Sonnet IX, Op.1,No.3; Sonnet
XXIV, Op.1,No.2   (D576)

Les Roses De Saadi *Op.1,No.4
see L'amour

Lied Om Den Blijen En Onvoorzienen
Dood *Op.47,No.2
see Delden, Lex van, De Goede Dood

Melopee *Op.25,No.1
see Twee Liederen Van P. Van
Ostayen

Polonaise *Op.25,No.2
see Twee Liederen Van P. Van
Ostayen

Sonnet IX *Op.1,No.3
see L'amour

Sonnet XXIV *Op.1,No.2
see L'amour

DELDEN, LEX VAN (cont'd.)

Twee Liederen Van P. Van Ostayen
Bar solo,pno DONEMUS s.p.
contains: Melopee, Op.25,No.1;
Polonaise, Op.25,No.2   (D577)

Vocalise *Op.29a
Mez solo,pno DONEMUS s.p.   (D578)

When Most I Wink *Op.72,No.1
see Drie Sonnetten Van Shakespeare

Zingende Soldaten *Op.13
B solo,pno DONEMUS s.p.   (D579)

DELETTRE, J.
Ballade
[Fr] med solo,pno ESCHIG $.60
(D580)

Parle-Moi D'autre Chose
[Fr] med solo,pno ESCHIG $.60
(D581)

DE LEVA, ENRICO (1867-1955)
'E Spingole Frangese
[It] Mez/Bar solo,pno RICORDI-ENG
53152 s.p.   (D582)

DELGADINA see Sciammarella, Valdo

DEL GIUDICE, G.M.
Ad Annie
[It] solo,pno BONGIOVANI 2014 s.p.
(D583)

Il Paese
[It] solo,pno BONGIOVANI 2013 s.p.
(D584)

DELIA see Arne, Thomas Augustine

DELIBES, LEO (1836-1891)
Aria De Las Campanillas *see Ou Va
La Jeune Indoue

Aria Della Campanelle *see Ou Va La
Jeune Indoue

Bell Song *see Ou Va La Jeune Indoue

Coppelia-Waltz
[Fr/Eng] high solo,pno (E flat maj)
SCHIRM.G $.60   (D585)

Die Nachtigall *see Le Rossignol

Fair Maidens *see Les Filles De
Cadix

Girls Of Cadiz *see Les Filles De
Cadix

Indian Bell Song *see Ou Va La Jeune
Indoue

Le Rossignol
"Die Nachtigall" [Ger/Eng/Fr] solo,
fl ZIMMER. 1128 $2.00   (D586)

Les Filles De Cadix
[Fr/It] S/T solo,pno RICORDI-ARG
BA 7689 s.p.   (D587)
"Fair Maidens" high solo,orch (F
sharp maj) ASHDOWN s.p., ipr
(D588)
"Fair Maidens" low solo,orch (D
maj) ASHDOWN s.p., ipr   (D589)
"Girls Of Cadiz" high solo,pno (F
sharp min) ALLANS s.p.   (D590)
(Liebling) "Maids Of Cadiz, The"
[Fr/Eng] high solo,pno (F sharp
min) SCHIRM.G $.85   (D591)

Les Filles Des Cadix
(Bantock) "Maids Of Cadiz" high
solo,pno PAXTON P40586 s.p.
(D592)

Maids Of Cadiz *see Les Filles Des
Cadix

Maids Of Cadiz, The *see Les Filles
De Cadix

O Gentil Menzogna (from Lakme)
[Fr] T solo,pno HEUGEL 4448 B s.p.
(D593)

Ou Va La Jeune Indoue (from Lakme)
"Aria De Las Campanillas" [Fr/It] S
solo,pno RICORDI-ARG BA 8600 s.p.
(D594)
"Aria Della Campanelle" [It] S
solo,pno HEUGEL 4447 s.p.   (D595)
"Aria Della Campanelle" [Fr] S
solo,pno HEUGEL 4447 B s.p.
(D596)
"Bell Song" high solo,pno (G maj)
ALLANS s.p.   (D597)
"Bell Song" med solo,pno (F maj)
ALLANS s.p.   (D598)
"Indian Bell Song" [Fr/Eng] S solo,
pno (E min) SCHIRM.G $.85 (D599)

Passepied
(Aslanoff) [Fr/Eng] high solo,pno
(C sharp min) SCHIRM.G $.60
(D600)

DELICE DU VIVANT see Thiriet, A.

DELICES DES PLEURS see Beethoven,
Ludwig van

DELICIAE TERRENAE see Brevi, Giovanni
Battista

DELICIEUSES CIMES
see Chants De France Vol. I

DELIE OBJECT DE PLUS HAULTE VERTU see
Roland-Manuel, Alexis

DE' LIGUORI, S. ALFONSO MARIA
Il Canto Della Passione *sac
(Gubitosi, E.) [It] STB soli,
cembalo,strings sc CURCI 7632
rental   (D601)

DELIRE see Levade, Charles (Gaston)

DELIUS, FREDERICK (1862-1934)
Bird's Song
see Twilight Fancies

Book Of Songs, Vols. 1-2 *CCU
solo,pno OXFORD s.p., ea.   (D602)

Cradle Song
T solo,pno (easy) OXFORD 61.803
$1.25 see from Three Ibsen Songs
(D603)

Cynara
[Eng/Ger] solo,pno (C maj) BOOSEY
$1.75   (D604)

In The Garden Of The Seraglio
[Eng/Ger] solo,pno (E flat maj)
BOOSEY $1.75   (D605)

Late Lark
[Eng/Ger] solo,pno BOOSEY $1.75
(D606)

Let Springtime Come
see Twilight Fancies

Love's Philosophy
S/T solo,pno (med) OXFORD 63.406
$1.50   (D607)

Morning Star
[Fr/Eng] solo,pno (C maj) BOOSEY
$1.75   (D608)

Nightingale
high solo,pno (G maj) GALLIARD
2.1374.7 $1.75   (D609)

So White, So Soft, So Sweet Is She
solo,pno BOOSEY $1.75   (D610)

Spring, The Sweet Spring
solo,pno (D maj) BOOSEY $1.75
(D611)

Summer Landscape
see Twilight Fancies

Ten Songs *CC10U
solo,pno STAINER 3.1101.7 $3.50
(D612)

Three Ibsen Songs *see Cradle Song
(D613)

To Daffodils
solo,pno (C maj) BOOSEY $1.75
(D614)

Twilight Fancies
(med) Mez solo,pno OXFORD 62.060
$1.25; A solo,pno OXFORD 61.177
$1.25; solo,orch OXFORD rental
contains: Bird's Song; Let
Springtime Come; Summer
Landscape   (D615)

DELIVRANCE see De Lara, Isadore

DELL' ARIA AMICA see Martini,
Giambattista

DELL'ACQUA, EVA
Chanson Provencale
high solo,orch (E flat maj) ASHDOWN
s.p., ipr   (D616)
low solo,orch (C maj) ASHDOWN s.p.,
ipr   (D617)

Villanelle
low solo,orch (B flat maj) ASHDOWN
s.p., ipr   (D618)
med solo,orch (C maj) ASHDOWN s.p.,
ipr   (D619)
med-high solo,orch (D maj) ASHDOWN
s.p., ipr   (D620)
high solo,orch (E flat maj) ASHDOWN
s.p., ipr   (D621)
low solo,orch (B flat maj, contains
cadenzas) ASHDOWN s.p., ipr
(D622)
med solo,orch (C maj, contains
cadenzas) ASHDOWN s.p., ipr
(D623)
med-high solo,orch (D maj, contains
cadenzas) ASHDOWN s.p., ipr

DELL'ACQUA, EVA (cont'd.)
(D624)
high solo,orch (E flat maj,
contains cadenzas) ASHDOWN
s.p., ipr   (D625)
low solo,vln (C maj) ASHDOWN
s.p., ipr   (D626)
high solo,vln (D maj) ASHDOWN
s.p., ipr   (D627)
solo,vln/vcl (E flat maj, contains
cadenzas) ASHDOWN s.p., ipr
(D628)
[Fr/Ger] S solo,pno SCHOTT-FRER
s.p.   (D629)

DELL'ALCOVA NEL TEPOR see Lehar, Franz

DELLO JOIO, NORMAN (1913-   )
All Things Leave Me
med solo,pno (F maj) FISCHER,C
V 2238   (D630)

Assassination, The
low solo,pno (G min) FISCHER,C
V 2076   (D631)

Bright Star *sac,Xmas
med solo,pno MARKS $1.50   (D632)
high solo,pno MARKS $1.50   (D633)

Christmas Carol, A *sac,Xmas
med solo,pno MARKS $1.50   (D634)
high solo,pno MARKS $1.50   (D635)

Holy Infant's Lullaby, The *sac,Xmas
high solo,pno MARKS $1.50   (D636)
med solo,pno MARKS $1.50   (D637)

How Do I Love Thee
high solo,pno FISCHER,C 2230 (D638)

New Born
med solo,pno FISCHER,C V 1957
(D639)

Note Left On A Doorstep
med solo,pno MARKS $1.50   (D640)

There Is A Lady Sweet And Kind
med solo,pno FISCHER,C V 1982
(D641)

Three Songs Of Adieu *song cycle
high solo,pno MARKS $2.00   (D642)

Un Sonetto Di Petrarca
[It/Eng] high solo,pno MARKS $1.50
(D643)
high solo,pno EMI s.p.   (D644)

DELMET, PAUL
A Celle Que J'aime
solo,pno ENOCH s.p.   (D645)
solo,acap solo pt ENOCH s.p. (D646)

A Chloris
solo,pno ENOCH s.p.   (D647)
solo,acap solo pt ENOCH s.p. (D648)

A Suzon
solo,pno ENOCH s.p.   (D649)
solo,acap solo pt ENOCH s.p. (D650)

A Vingt Ans
solo,pno ENOCH s.p.   (D651)
solo,acap solo pt ENOCH s.p. (D652)

Aimons-Nous (from La Cinquantaine)
2 soli,pno ENOCH s.p.   (D653)

Ami Printemps
solo,acap solo pt ENOCH s.p. (D654)
solo,pno ENOCH s.p.   (D655)

Amour Infidele
solo,acap solo pt ENOCH s.p. (D656)
solo,pno ENOCH s.p.   (D657)

Au Jardin De L'Amour
solo,acap solo pt ENOCH s.p. (D658)
solo,pno ENOCH s.p.   (D659)

Au Paradis
solo,acap solo pt ENOCH s.p. (D660)
solo,pno ENOCH s.p.   (D661)

Aubade Amoureuse
solo,acap solo pt ENOCH s.p. (D662)
solo,pno ENOCH s.p.   (D663)

Aubade Pour Elle
solo,acap solo pt ENOCH s.p. (D664)
solo,pno ENOCH s.p.   (D665)

Baiser D'amants
solo,acap solo pt ENOCH s.p. (D666)
solo,pno ENOCH s.p.   (D667)

Baiser Supreme
solo,acap solo pt ENOCH s.p. (D668)
solo,pno ENOCH s.p.   (D669)

Beau Page
solo,acap solo pt ENOCH s.p. (D670)
solo,pno ENOCH s.p.   (D671)

DELMET, PAUL (cont'd.)

Berceuse De Reve
    solo,acap solo pt ENOCH s.p. (D672)
    solo,pno ENOCH s.p.   (D673)

Bonne Annee
    solo,acap solo pt ENOCH s.p. (D674)
    solo,pno ENOCH s.p.   (D675)

Chagrins Roses
    solo,acap solo pt ENOCH s.p. (D676)

Chanson A Boire
    solo,acap solo pt ENOCH s.p. (D677)
    solo,pno (available in 2 keys)
        ENOCH s.p. see also Les Plus
        Jolies Chansons, Vol. I   (D678)

Chanson Caline
    solo,acap solo pt ENOCH s.p. (D679)
    solo,pno ENOCH s.p.   (D680)

Chanson Crepusculaire
    solo,acap solo pt ENOCH s.p. (D681)
    solo,pno ENOCH s.p. see also Les
        Plus Jolies Chansons, Vol. II
                                  (D682)

Chanson De Moisson
    solo,pno ENOCH s.p.   (D683)
    solo,acap solo pt ENOCH s.p. (D684)

Chanson Douloureuse
    solo,pno ENOCH s.p.   (D685)
    solo,acap solo pt ENOCH s.p. (D686)

Chanson Du Reveil
    solo,acap solo pt ENOCH s.p. (D687)
    solo,pno ENOCH s.p. see also Quinze
        Chansons, Vol. I   (D688)

Chanson Frele
    solo,acap solo pt ENOCH s.p. (D689)
    solo,pno ENOCH s.p. see also Quinze
        Chansons, Vol. I   (D690)

Chanson Libertine
    solo,pno ENOCH s.p.   (D691)
    solo,acap solo pt ENOCH s.p. (D692)

Chanson Paresseuse
    solo,pno ENOCH s.p.   (D693)
    solo,acap solo pt ENOCH s.p. (D694)

Chanson Pour Ma Belle
    solo,pno ENOCH s.p.   (D695)
    solo,acap solo pt ENOCH s.p. (D696)

Chanson Pour Ma Mere
    solo,acap solo pt ENOCH s.p. (D697)
    solo,pno ENOCH s.p. see also Les
        Plus Jolies Chansons, Vol. I
                                  (D698)

Chanson Triste
    solo,acap solo pt ENOCH s.p. (D699)
    solo,pno ENOCH s.p.   (D700)

Chanson Venitienne
    solo,acap solo pt ENOCH s.p. (D701)
    solo,pno ENOCH s.p. see also Quinze
        Chansons, Vol. I   (D702)

Chemin D'avril
    solo,pno ENOCH s.p.   (D703)
    solo,acap solo pt ENOCH s.p. (D704)

Colis Postal
    solo,pno ENOCH s.p.   (D705)
    solo,acap solo pt ENOCH s.p. (D706)

Confession
    solo,pno ENOCH s.p.   (D707)
    solo,acap solo pt ENOCH s.p. (D708)

Credo Pour Tous
    solo,pno ENOCH s.p.   (D709)
    solo,acap solo pt ENOCH s.p. (D710)

Dormez
    solo,pno ENOCH s.p.   (D711)
    solo,acap solo pt ENOCH s.p. (D712)

Dors En Paix (from La Cinquantaine)
    solo,pno ENOCH s.p.   (D713)
    solo,pno ENOCH s.p.   (D714)
    solo,acap solo pt ENOCH s.p. (D715)

Duo Des Pecheurs De Bremes
    2 soli,pno ENOCH s.p. voc sc, solo
        pt   (D716)

Elle!
    solo,acap solo pt ENOCH s.p. (D717)
    solo,pno ENOCH s.p. see also Quinze
        Chansons, Vol. II   (D718)

Ensorcellement
    solo,pno ENOCH s.p.   (D719)
    solo,acap solo pt ENOCH s.p. (D720)

Envoi De Fleurs
    solo,acap solo pt ENOCH s.p. (D721)
    solo,orch ENOCH rental   (D722)
    solo,pno ENOCH s.p. see also Quinze
        Chansons, Vol. I   (D723)

DELMET, PAUL (cont'd.)

Evocation
    solo,acap solo pt ENOCH s.p. (D724)
    solo,pno ENOCH s.p. see also Quinze
        Chansons, Vol. I   (D725)

Fable Eternelle
    solo,pno ENOCH s.p.   (D726)
    solo,acap solo pt ENOCH s.p. (D727)

Fanfreluches
    solo,acap solo pt ENOCH s.p. (D728)
    solo,pno ENOCH s.p. see also Quinze
        Chansons, Vol. II   (D729)

Fermons Nos Rideaux
    solo,acap solo pt ENOCH s.p. (D730)
    solo,pno ENOCH s.p. see also Quinze
        Chansons, Vol. II   (D731)

Fiancee Aux Etoiles
    solo,acap solo pt ENOCH s.p. (D732)
    solo,pno ENOCH s.p. see also Les
        Plus Jolies Chansons, Vol. IV
                                  (D733)

Fin De Bail
    solo,pno ENOCH s.p.   (D734)
    solo,acap solo pt ENOCH s.p. (D735)

Fleurettes
    solo,pno ENOCH s.p.   (D736)
    solo,acap solo pt ENOCH s.p. (D737)

Fleurs De France
    solo,pno ENOCH s.p.   (D738)
    solo,acap solo pt ENOCH s.p. (D739)

Folie D'amour
    solo,pno ENOCH s.p.   (D740)
    solo,acap solo pt ENOCH s.p. (D741)

Gai Pinson
    solo,pno ENOCH s.p.   (D742)
    solo,acap solo pt ENOCH s.p. (D743)

Idylle Lointaine
    solo,pno ENOCH s.p.   (D744)
    solo,acap solo pt ENOCH s.p. (D745)

Incertitude
    solo,pno ENOCH s.p.   (D746)
    solo,acap solo pt ENOCH s.p. (D747)

Inquietude
    solo,pno ENOCH s.p.   (D748)
    solo,acap solo pt ENOCH s.p. (D749)

J'ai Dit A Ma Belle
    solo,acap solo pt ENOCH s.p. (D750)
    solo,pno ENOCH s.p. see also Quinze
        Chansons, Vol. I   (D751)

J'ai Voulu Fuir
    solo,acap solo pt ENOCH s.p. (D752)
    solo,pno ENOCH s.p. see also Quinze
        Chansons, Vol. II   (D753)

Je Croyais Encor
    solo,pno ENOCH s.p.   (D754)
    solo,acap solo pt ENOCH s.p. (D755)

Je Doute
    solo,pno ENOCH s.p.   (D756)
    solo,acap solo pt ENOCH s.p. (D757)

Je Viens A Vous
    solo,pno ENOCH s.p.   (D758)
    solo,acap solo pt ENOCH s.p. (D759)

Jusqu'a Demain!
    solo,acap solo pt ENOCH s.p. (D760)
    solo,pno ENOCH s.p. see also Quinze
        Chansons, Vol. I   (D761)

La Camarade
    solo,pno ENOCH s.p.   (D762)
    solo,acap solo pt ENOCH s.p. (D763)

La Cinquantaine (from La
        Cinquantaine)
    solo,pno ENOCH s.p.   (D764)
    solo,pno sc,oct ENOCH s.p.   (D765)
    solo,acap solo pt ENOCH s.p. (D766)
    solo,orch ENOCH rental   (D767)

La Coeur Du Poete
    solo,pno ENOCH s.p.   (D768)

La Fee Aux Cheveux D'or
    solo,acap solo pt ENOCH s.p. (D769)
    solo,pno ENOCH s.p. see also Les
        Plus Jolies Chansons, Vol. II
                                  (D770)

La Main Dans La Main
    solo,acap solo pt ENOCH s.p. (D771)

La Mode
    solo,pno ENOCH s.p.   (D772)
    solo,acap solo pt ENOCH s.p. (D773)

La Moisson Du Poete
    solo,pno ENOCH s.p.   (D774)
    solo,acap solo pt ENOCH s.p. (D775)

DELMET, PAUL (cont'd.)

La Nichonnette
    solo,pno ENOCH s.p.   (D776)
    solo,acap solo pt ENOCH s.p. (D777)

La Noisette
    solo,pno ENOCH s.p.   (D778)
    solo,acap solo pt ENOCH s.p. (D779)

La Petite Eglise
    solo,acap solo pt ENOCH s.p. (D780)
    solo,pno ENOCH s.p. see also Les
        Plus Jolies Chansons, Vol. IV
                                  (D781)

La Rose Noire
    solo,acap solo pt ENOCH s.p. (D782)

La Tristesse Des Levres
    solo,acap solo pt ENOCH s.p. (D783)
    solo,pno ENOCH s.p. see also Les
        Plus Jolies Chansons, Vol. III
                                  (D784)

L'Amant Au Tombeau De Sa Maitresse
    solo,pno ENOCH s.p.   (D785)
    solo,acap solo pt ENOCH s.p. (D786)

L'Amour Est Mon Tresor
    solo,pno ENOCH s.p.   (D787)
    solo,acap solo pt ENOCH s.p. (D788)

L'Ancienne
    solo,pno ENOCH s.p.   (D789)
    solo,acap solo pt ENOCH s.p. (D790)

Lassitude
    solo,acap solo pt ENOCH s.p. (D791)
    solo,pno ENOCH s.p. see also Quinze
        Chansons, Vol. I   (D792)

Le Baiser Qui Fuit
    solo,acap solo pt ENOCH s.p. (D793)
    solo,pno ENOCH s.p. see also Les
        Plus Jolies Chansons, Vol. I
                                  (D794)

Le Chanteur Des Bois
    solo,acap solo pt ENOCH s.p. (D795)
    solo,orch ENOCH rental   (D796)
    solo,pno ENOCH s.p. see also Quinze
        Chansons, Vol. II   (D797)

Le Coeur Du Poete
    solo,acap solo pt ENOCH s.p. (D798)

Le Mai D'amour
    solo,acap solo pt ENOCH s.p. (D799)
    solo,pno ENOCH s.p. see also Les
        Plus Jolies Chansons, Vol. III
                                  (D800)

Le Main Dans La Main
    solo,pno ENOCH s.p.   (D801)

Le Pain De L'Amour
    solo,pno ENOCH s.p.   (D802)
    solo,acap solo pt ENOCH s.p. (D803)

Le Petit Navire
    solo,pno/inst LEDUC s.p.   (D804)

Le Petite Eglise
    2 soli,pno ENOCH s.p. voc sc, solo
        pt   (D805)

Le Pre D'amour
    solo,pno ENOCH s.p.   (D806)
    solo,acap solo pt ENOCH s.p. (D807)

Le Printemps A Pleins Verres
    solo,acap solo pt ENOCH s.p. (D808)
    solo,pno ENOCH s.p. see also Les
        Plus Jolies Chansons, Vol. I
                                  (D809)

Le Reliquaire
    solo,pno ENOCH s.p.   (D810)
    solo,acap solo pt ENOCH s.p. (D811)

Le Renouveau
    solo,acap solo pt ENOCH s.p. (D812)

Le Vieux Banc
    solo,acap solo pt ENOCH s.p. (D813)
    solo,pno ENOCH s.p. see also Les
        Plus Jolies Chansons, Vol. III
                                  (D814)

Le Vieux Mendiant
    solo,pno/inst LEDUC s.p.   (D815)

Legende Du Papillon
    solo,pno ENOCH s.p.   (D816)
    solo,acap solo pt ENOCH s.p. (D817)

Les Bleuets
    solo,acap solo pt ENOCH s.p. (D818)
    solo,pno ENOCH s.p. see also Quinze
        Chansons, Vol. II   (D819)

Les Chagrins Roses
    solo,pno ENOCH s.p.   (D820)

Les Femmes De France
    solo,pno (available in 2 keys)
        ENOCH s.p.   (D821)
    2 soli,pno (F maj) ENOCH s.p. voc
        sc, solo pt   (D822)
    solo,acap solo pt ENOCH s.p. (D823)

DELMET, PAUL (cont'd.)

Les Levres
  solo,acap solo pt ENOCH s.p. (D824)
  solo,pno ENOCH s.p. see also Quinze
  Chansons, Vol. II   (D825)

Les Maitresses
  solo,pno ENOCH s.p.   (D826)
  solo,acap solo pt ENOCH s.p. (D827)

Les Plus Jolies Chansons, Vol. I
  *CC10L
  solo,pno cmplt ed ENOCH s.p.
    see also: Chanson A Boire;
    Chanson Pour Ma Mere; Le Baiser
    Qui Fuit; Le Printemps A Pleins
    Verres; L'Etoile Du Berger; Mon
    Moulin; Sonnez Musettes (D828)

Les Plus Jolies Chansons, Vol. II
  *CC10L
  solo,pno cmplt ed ENOCH s.p.
    see also: Chanson Crepusculaire;
    La Fee Aux Cheveux D'Or; Ohe!
    Les Amoureux; Que Ne Veux-Tu
                               (D829)

Les Plus Jolies Chansons, Vol. III
  *CC10L
  solo,pno cmplt ed ENOCH s.p.
    see also: La Tristesse Des
    Levres; Le Mai D'Amour; Le
    Vieux Banc; Madame, Je
    Voudrais; Par Les Pres   (D830)

Les Plus Jolies Chansons, Vol. IV
  *CC10L
  solo,pno cmplt ed ENOCH s.p.
    see also: Fiancee Aux Etoiles; La
    Petite Eglise; Ma Douce
    Annette; Reine Blonde; Sur
    L'herbe Follette; Vous Avez Ri
                               (D831)

Les Trois Ages De L'amour
  solo,acap solo pt ENOCH s.p. (D832)
  solo,pno ENOCH s.p. see also Quinze
  Chansons, Vol. II   (D833)

L'Escalier
  solo,pno ENOCH s.p.   (D834)
  solo,acap solo pt ENOCH s.p. (D835)

L'Etang
  solo,pno ENOCH s.p.   (D836)
  solo,acap solo pt ENOCH s.p. (D837)

L'Etoile D'amour
  solo,acap solo pt ENOCH s.p. (D838)
  solo,orch ENOCH rental   (D839)
  solo,pno (available in 2 keys)
    ENOCH s.p. see also Quinze
    Chansons, Vol. II   (D840)

L'Etoile Du Berger
  solo,acap solo pt ENOCH s.p. (D841)
  solo,pno ENOCH s.p. see also Les
  Plus Jolies Chansons, Vol. I
                             (D842)

Lettre A Ninon
  solo,acap solo pt ENOCH s.p. (D843)
  solo,pno (available in 2 keys)
    ENOCH s.p. see also Quinze
    Chansons, Vol. II   (D844)

Liberte
  solo,acap solo pt ENOCH s.p. (D845)
  (Bordese, Stephen) solo,pno ENOCH
  s.p. see also CHANSONS DE PAGE
                             (D846)

L'Ile Des Baisers
  solo,acap solo pt ENOCH s.p. (D847)
  solo,pno ENOCH s.p. see also Quinze
  Chansons, Vol. I   (D848)

Ma Bien-Aimee
  solo,pno ENOCH s.p.   (D849)
  solo,acap solo pt ENOCH s.p. (D850)

Ma Douce Annette
  solo,acap solo pt ENOCH s.p. (D851)
  solo,pno ENOCH s.p. see also Les
  Plus Jolies Chansons, Vol. IV
                             (D852)

Ma Jolie
  solo,pno ENOCH s.p.   (D853)
  solo,acap solo pt ENOCH s.p. (D854)

Ma Tendre Amie
  solo,pno ENOCH s.p.   (D855)
  solo,acap solo pt ENOCH s.p. (D856)

Madame Je Voudrais!
  solo,acap solo pt ENOCH s.p. (D857)
  solo,pno ENOCH s.p. see also Les
  Plus Jolies Chansons, Vol. III
                             (D858)

Madrigal D'Antan
  solo,pno ENOCH s.p.   (D859)
  solo,acap solo pt ENOCH s.p. (D860)

Marinette
  solo,acap solo pt ENOCH s.p. (D861)
  solo,pno ENOCH s.p. see also Quinze
  Chansons, Vol. I   (D862)

DELMET, PAUL (cont'd.)

Melancolie
  solo,acap solo pt ENOCH s.p. (D863)
  solo,pno ENOCH s.p. see also Quinze
  Chansons, Vol. II   (D864)

Mi-Closes
  solo,pno ENOCH s.p.   (D865)
  solo,acap solo pt ENOCH s.p. (D866)

Mon Coeur A Reve
  solo,pno ENOCH s.p.   (D867)
  solo,acap solo pt ENOCH s.p. (D868)

Mon Moulin
  solo,pno ENOCH s.p.   (D869)
  solo,pno ENOCH s.p. see also Les
  Plus Jolies Chansons, Vol. I
                             (D870)

Noces D'or
  solo,pno ENOCH s.p.   (D871)
  solo,acap solo pt ENOCH s.p. (D872)

Nouvel Evangile
  solo,pno ENOCH s.p.   (D873)
  solo,acap solo pt ENOCH s.p. (D874)

O Salutaris! *sac
  [Lat] Bar solo,pno/org ENOCH s.p.
                             (D875)

Ohe! Les Amoureux
  solo,acap solo pt ENOCH s.p. (D876)
  solo,pno ENOCH s.p. see also Les
  Plus Jolies Chansons, Vol. II
                             (D877)

Par Les Pres
  solo,acap solo pt ENOCH s.p. (D878)
  solo,pno ENOCH s.p. see also Les
  Plus Jolies Chansons, Vol. III
                             (D879)

Pensee D'hiver
  solo,pno ENOCH s.p.   (D880)
  solo,acap solo pt ENOCH s.p. (D881)

Petit Mari
  solo,pno ENOCH s.p.   (D882)
  solo,acap solo pt ENOCH s.p. (D883)

Philosophie
  solo,pno ENOCH s.p.   (D884)
  solo,acap solo pt ENOCH s.p. (D885)

Portrait Sans Modele
  solo,pno ENOCH s.p.   (D886)
  solo,acap solo pt ENOCH s.p. (D887)

Pour Un Sourire
  solo,pno ENOCH s.p.   (D888)
  solo,acap solo pt ENOCH s.p. (D889)

Pour Vos Seize Ans
  solo,pno ENOCH s.p.   (D890)

Pour Votre Fete
  solo,pno ENOCH s.p.   (D891)
  solo,acap solo pt ENOCH s.p. (D892)

Quand Nous Serons Vieux!
  solo,acap solo pt ENOCH s.p. (D893)
  solo,pno ENOCH s.p. see also Quinze
  Chansons, Vol. II   (D894)

Qu'avez-vous Fait
  solo,pno ENOCH s.p.   (D895)
  solo,acap solo pt ENOCH s.p. (D896)

Que Ne Veux-Tu?
  solo,acap solo pt ENOCH s.p. (D897)
  solo,pno ENOCH s.p. see also Les
  Plus Jolies Chansons, Vol. II
                             (D898)

Qu'importe
  solo,pno ENOCH s.p.   (D899)
  solo,acap solo pt ENOCH s.p. (D900)

Quinze Chansons, Vol. I
  solo,pno cmplt ed ENOCH s.p.
    contains & see also: Chanson Du
    Reveil; Chanson Frele; Chanson
    Venitienne; Envoi De Fleurs;
    Evocation; J'ai Dit A Ma Belle;
    Jusqu'a Demain; Lassitude;
    L'Ile Des Baisers; Marinette;
    Romance Fanee; Rose D'amour; Tu
    M'apparus; Une Femme Qui Passe;
    Vous Etes Jolie   (D901)

Quinze Chansons, Vol. II
  solo,pno cmplt ed ENOCH s.p.
    contains & see also: Elle;
    Fanfreluches; Fermons Nos
    Rideaux; J'ai Voulu Fuir; Le
    Chanteur Des Bois; Les Bleuets;
    Les Levres; Les Trois Ages De
    L'Amour; L'Etoile D'Amour;
    Lettre A Ninon; Melancolie;
    Quand Nous Serons Vieux; Ton
    Nez; Toujours Vous; Volupte
                             (D902)

Quinze Chansons, Vols. I & II *CC30L
  solo,pno cmplt ed ENOCH s.p. (D903)

Regrets Pour Elle
  solo,pno ENOCH s.p.   (D904)
  solo,acap solo pt ENOCH s.p. (D905)

DELMET, PAUL (cont'd.)

Reine Blonde
  solo,acap solo pt ENOCH s.p. (D906)
  solo,pno ENOCH s.p. see also Les
  Plus Jolies Chansons, Vol. IV
                             (D907)

Renouveau
  solo,pno ENOCH s.p.   (D908)

Reve D'Amant
  solo,pno ENOCH s.p.   (D909)
  solo,acap solo pt ENOCH s.p. (D910)

Reveuse Demoiselle
  solo,pno ENOCH s.p.   (D911)
  solo,acap solo pt ENOCH s.p. (D912)

Ritournelle
  solo,pno ENOCH s.p.   (D913)
  solo,acap solo pt ENOCH s.p. (D914)

Romance Fanee
  solo,acap solo pt ENOCH s.p. (D915)
  solo,pno ENOCH s.p. see also Quinze
  Chansons, Vol. I   (D916)

Rose D'amour
  solo,acap solo pt ENOCH s.p. (D917)
  solo,pno ENOCH s.p. see also Quinze
  Chansons, Vol. I   (D918)

Rose Noire
  solo,pno ENOCH s.p.   (D919)

Rosine
  solo,pno ENOCH s.p.   (D920)
  solo,acap solo pt ENOCH s.p. (D921)

Rupture D'automne
  solo,pno ENOCH s.p.   (D922)
  solo,acap solo pt ENOCH s.p. (D923)

Separons-Nous
  solo,pno ENOCH s.p.   (D924)
  solo,acap solo pt ENOCH s.p. (D925)

Serment D'Amant
  solo,pno ENOCH s.p.   (D926)
  solo,acap solo pt ENOCH s.p. (D927)

Sonnez, Musettes
  solo,acap solo pt ENOCH s.p. (D928)
  solo,pno ENOCH s.p. see also Les
  Plus Jolies Chansons, Vol. I
                             (D929)

Souffrance D'aimer
  solo,pno ENOCH s.p.   (D930)
  solo,acap solo pt ENOCH s.p. (D931)

Stances A Manon
  solo,pno/inst LEDUC s.p.   (D932)
  solo,pno/inst LEDUC s.p.   (D933)

Supreme Aveu
  solo,pno ENOCH s.p.   (D934)
  solo,acap solo pt ENOCH s.p. (D935)

Sur L'herbe Follette
  solo,acap solo pt ENOCH s.p. (D936)
  solo,pno ENOCH s.p. see also Les
  Plus Jolies Chansons, Vol. IV
                             (D937)

Suzette
  solo,pno ENOCH s.p.   (D938)
  solo,acap solo pt ENOCH s.p. (D939)

Ton Nez
  solo,acap solo pt ENOCH s.p. (D940)
  solo,orch ENOCH rental   (D941)
  solo,pno ENOCH s.p. see also Quinze
  Chansons, Vol. II   (D942)

Toujours Vous
  solo,acap solo pt ENOCH s.p. (D943)
  solo,pno ENOCH s.p. see also Quinze
  Chansons, Vol. II   (D944)

Tu M'apparus
  solo,acap solo pt ENOCH s.p. (D945)
  solo,pno ENOCH s.p. see also Quinze
  Chansons, Vol. I   (D946)

Une Femme Qui Passe
  solo,acap solo pt ENOCH s.p. (D947)
  solo,pno ENOCH s.p. see also Quinze
  Chansons, Vol. I   (D948)

Valet De Coeur
  solo,pno ENOCH s.p.   (D949)
  solo,acap solo pt ENOCH s.p. (D950)

Valse Fleurie
  solo,pno ENOCH s.p.   (D951)
  solo,acap solo pt ENOCH s.p. (D952)

Vers Le Ciel
  solo,pno ENOCH s.p.   (D953)
  solo,acap solo pt ENOCH s.p. (D954)

Vision D'Amant
  solo,pno ENOCH s.p.   (D955)
  solo,acap solo pt ENOCH s.p. (D956)

DELMET, PAUL (cont'd.)

Volupte
solo,acap solo pt ENOCH s.p. (D957)
solo,pno ENOCH s.p. see also Quinze
Chansons, Vol. II   (D958)

Vos Petits Pieds
solo,pno ENOCH s.p.   (D959)
solo,acap solo pt ENOCH s.p. (D960)

Vous Avez Ri!
solo,acap solo pt ENOCH s.p. (D961)
solo,pno ENOCH s.p. see also Les
Plus Jolies Chansons, Vol. IV
(D962)

Vous Etes Jolie!
solo,acap solo pt ENOCH s.p. (D963)
solo,pno (available in 2 keys)
ENOCH s.p. see also Quinze
Chansons, Vol. I   (D964)

DELPHINE see Schubert, Franz (Peter)

DEL RIEGO
Star Was His Candle, A *sac,Xmas
med solo,pno (C maj) FISCHER,C
V 1321   (D965)
low solo,pno (B flat maj) FISCHER,C
V 1322   (D966)
high solo,pno (C maj) ALLANS s.p.
(D967)
low solo,pno (B flat maj) ALLANS
s.p.   (D968)

DELSBOVALSEN see Schenell, Per

DEL TREDICI, DAVID (1937-   )
Four Songs On Poems Of James Joyce
*CC4U
high solo,pno BOOSEY $4.50   (D969)

I Hear An Army *song cycle
S solo,4strings study sc BOOSEY
$4.00, ipa   (D970)

DE LUCIA, NADIR
Ballata Medievale
[It] solo,pno SANTIS 0022 s.p.
(D971)
Capanna Bianca
[It] solo,pno SANTIS 0065 s.p.
(D972)
Il Marinaro Canta
[It] solo,pno SANTIS 0010 s.p.
(D973)
Invito-Gavotte
[It] solo,pno SANTIS 0002 s.p.
(D974)
La Canzone Dell'amore
[It] solo,pno SANTIS 0004 s.p.
(D975)
Spagnolata
[It] solo,pno SANTIS 0006 s.p.
(D976)

DELVINCOURT, CLAUDE (1888-1954)
Ce Monde De Rosee *CC40U
med solo,orch LEDUC s.p.   (D977)

C'est Un P'tit Ramoneur
solo,pno/inst DURAND s.p. see from
Chansons De La Ville Et Des
Champs   (D978)

Chansons De La Ville Et Des Champs
*see C'est Un P'tit Ramoneur;
Entre Les Deux; La Bergere
Indulgente; La Delaisee; Le
Berger Collinet; L'enlevement En
Mer   (D979)

Entre Les Deux
solo,pno/inst DURAND s.p. see from
Chansons De La Ville Et Des
Champs   (D980)

J'ay Contente Ma Volonte Suffisamment
solo,pno/inst DURAND s.p. see from
Quatre Chansons De Clement Marot
(D981)

Je Ne Fay Rien Que Requerir
solo,pno/inst DURAND s.p. see from
Quatre Chansons De Clement Marot
(D982)

Je Suis Ayme De La Plus Belle
solo,pno/inst DURAND s.p. see from
Quatre Chansons De Clement Marot
(D983)

La Bergere Indulgente
solo,pno/inst DURAND s.p. see from
Chansons De La Ville Et Des
Champs   (D984)

La Delaisee
solo,pno/inst DURAND s.p. see from
Chansons De La Ville Et Des
Champs   (D985)

Le Berger Collinet
solo,pno/inst DURAND s.p. see from
Chansons De La Ville Et Des
Champs   (D986)

L'enlevement En Mer
solo,pno/inst DURAND s.p. see from
Chansons De La Ville Et Des

DELVINCOURT, CLAUDE (cont'd.)

Champs   (D987)

Quand Vous Voudrez Faire Une Amye
solo,pno/inst DURAND s.p. see from
Quatre Chansons De Clement Marot
(D988)
Quatre Chansons De Clement Marot
*see J'ay Contente Ma Volonte
Suffisamment; Je Ne Fay Rien Que
Requerir; Je Suis Ayme De La Plus
Belle; Quand Vous Voudrez Faire
Une Amye   (D989)

DEM AUFGEHENDEN VOLLMONDE see Bijvanck,
Henk

DEM EINZIGEN see Haas, Joseph

DEM FRUHLING ZUM WILLKOMMEN see
Bijvanck, Henk

DEM GENIUS DES AUGENBLICKS see Marx,
Joseph

DEM MIHLNERS TREHRN *folk,Jew
high solo,pno HATIKVAH ED. 43 $.35
(D990)

DEM UNENDLICHEN see Schubert, Franz
(Peter)

DEM WEIBE see Tomasek, Jaroslav

DEMAIN see Dufresne, C.

DEMAIN, DES L'AUBE see Ferrari, Gustave

DEMANDE see Dufresne, C.

DEMANDEZ-MOI POURQUOI see Lefort, G.

DEMANTEN PA MARSSNON see Sibelius, Jean

DEMAREST, A.
Beatitudes *sac
med solo,pno (G maj) BOSTON $1.50
(D991)
Whither Shall I Go From Thy Spirit
high solo,pno BOONIN C5105 $.80
(D992)
low solo,pno BOONIN C5106 $.80
(D993)

DE MEGLIO
Alla Fiera Di Mastr'Andrea
[It/Eng] S/T solo,pno RICORDI-ENG
LD 387 s.p.   (D994)

DEMENY, DEZSO
Cinquando Canti Popolari Ungheresi
*CC50U,Hung
solo,pno ZERBONI 4761 s.p.   (D995)

DEMOCRACY see Heilner, Irwin

DEMON, J.
Golondrina
[Span] high solo,pno UNION ESP.
$.75   (D996)

DEN ALSKADES NAMN see Abt, Franz

DEN-BAU see Guarnieri, Camargo Mozart

DEN BERGTAGNA
solo,pno,opt gtr GEHRMANS 208 s.p.
(D997)

DEN BRUTNE see Kotilainen, Otto,
Sortunut

DEN BUSEN BEWEGT MIR see Mozart,
Wolfgang Amadeus, Un Moto Di Gioia

DEN CLIVO DOHARA see Novak, Milan

DEN DANSKE ROMANCE: HIGH ROMANTICS:
GADE, HARTMANN, RUNG   *CC13L
[Dut] solo,kbd HANSEN-DEN s.p. (D998)

DEN DANSKE ROMANCE: LATE ROMANTICS see
Heise, Peter Arnold

DEN, DER GIBT, O HERR, GIB WIEDER see
Kilpinen, Yrio, Anna, Kiesus,
Anatajalie

DEN DIE HIRTEN LOBETEN SEHRE see
Metzger, Hans-Arnold

DEN DJUPA KALLAN see Kilpinen, Yrio

DEN ENDA STUNDEN see Merikanto, Oskar

DEN FORAELDRELOSE see Grieg, Edvard
Hagerup

DEN FORSTA GANG JAG SA DIG see Sjoberg,
Birger

DEN FORSTA GANGEN DIN BLICK JAG SAG see
Kun Ensi Kerran Silmas Nain

DEN FORSTA KYSSEN see Sibelius, Jean

DEN FORSTE LAERKE see Nielsen, Carl

DEN FREUNDEN SAGT VON MIR see Geissler,
Fritz

DEN FYRSTE SONGEN see Beck, Thomas
[Ludvigsen]

DEN GAMLE see Lindblad, Adolf Fredrik

DEN GAMLE VISE see Grieg, Edvard
Hagerup

DEN GLADE TRUMPETAREN see Korling,
Felix

DEN GYLLENE STUNDEN see Nordqvist,
Gustaf

DEN GYLNE KRO see Hauger, Kristian

DEN HELIGA JULNATTEN see Myrberg,
August M.

DEN HELIGA NATTEN see Korling

DEN HELIGA STADE see Adams, Stephen,
Holy City, The

DEN HOOGEN HEMEL see Sigtenhorst-Meyer,
Bernhard van den

DEN HVIDE, RODE ROSE see Soderman,
(Johan) August

DEN JAG ALSKAR AR EN FISKARE see
Strickland, Lily Teresa, My Lover
Is A Fisherman

DEN KARASTE SAGAN see Korling, Felix

DEN LANGTANDE see Melartin, Erkki,
Kaipaava

DEN LJUSA NATTENS LJUSA FAGELDRILLAR
see Kilpinen, Yrio

DEN LYCKLIGE see Valentin, Karl

DEN MUTIGEN ACHTZEHN see Dessau, Paul

DEN RESANDE STUDENTEN see Josephson,
Jacob Axel

DEN SISTA KVALLEN see Lidholm, Ingvar

DEN SISTA STUNDEN see Tuuri, Jaako,
Viimeinen Hetki

**DEN TAG HINDURCH NUR EINMAL MAG ICH
SPRECHEN** see Schubert, Franz
(Peter), Memnon

DEN TIDIGA SORGEN see Stenhammar,
Wilhelm

DEN VARMA VILJAN see Bjerkhammar, Sonja

DEN VITA HUSTRUNS SANG see Pylkkanen,
Tauno Kullervo, Valkean Vaimon
Laulu

DE NINNO, ALFREDO
Il Corvo E La Volpe
[It] solo,pno SANTIS 973 s.p.
(D999)
Ninna Nanna
[It] solo,pno SANTIS 972 s.p.
(D1000)

DENIS, DIDIER (1947-   )
Chanson De La Plus Haute Tour
S solo,pno RIDEAU rental   (D1001)

Des Gants Blancs
S solo,pno RIDEAU rental   (D1002)

La Vieille Danse
S solo,fl,pic,clar,perc,vln,vla,vcl
RIDEAU rental   (D1003)

T'y, Qui Dit, Bah! D'a Bout D'ou?
S solo,pno RIDEAU rental   (D1004)

DENISE
(Fragerolle, G.) solo,acap ENOCH s.p.
see from Vieux Noels De France
(D1005)
(Fragerolle, G.) solo,pno ENOCH s.p.
see from Vieux Noels De France
(D1006)

DENISOV, EDISON VASILIEVITCH
(1929-   )
Funf Geschichten Vom K. Herrn *song
cycle
[Ger] T solo,7inst SIKORSKI 805
s.p.   (D1007)

Italienische Lieder *song cycle
[Russ/Ger] S solo,fl,vln,cembalo
SIKORSKI 803 s.p.   (D1008)

Klagelieder Nach Judischer
Volkspoesie *CCU
[Russ/Ger] S solo,3perc,pno
SIKORSKI 804 s.p.   (D1009)

DENISOV, EDISON VASILIEVITCH (cont'd.)

Sonne Der Inkas *song cycle
[Russ/Span/Ger] S solo,11inst
SIKORSKI 802 s.p.   (D1010)

DENK ES, O SEELE see Wolf, Hugo

DENK ES, OH SEELE see Pfitzner, Hans

DENKMAELER DER TONKUNST IN OESTERREICH
*CCUL
contains works for a variety of
instruments and vocal combinations
microfiche UNIV.MUS.ED. reprints of
Breitkopf & Hartel Editions;
reprint of the Graz edition;
contains 83 volumes; includes vocal
works by: Fux, J.J.; Wolkenstein,
Oswald von; Peurl, Paul; Posch,
Isaak; Reuental, Neidhart von;
Caldara, Antonio and others;
$495.00   (D1011)

DENKMAELER DEUTSCHER TONKUNST, ERSTE
FOLGE (NEWLY REVISED EDITION)
*CCUL
(Moser, Hans Joachim; Crosby, C.
Russel, Jr.) contains vocal,
choral, operatic and instrumental
works microfiche UNIV.MUS.ED.
reprints of Breitkopf & Hartel
Editions; contains 65 volumes;
includes vocal works by: Tunder,
Franz; Ahle, Johann Rudolf; Albert,
Heinrich; Krieger, Adam; Rhau,
Georg; Elmenhorst, Heinrich;
Telemann, Georg Philipp and others;
$425.00   (D1012)

DENMARK SINGS *CC26U,folk,Dan
[Dan/Eng] med solo,kbd HANSEN-DEN
s.p.   (D1013)

DENN ES GEHET DEM MENSCHEN see Brahms,
Johannes

DENNE AR MIN KARE SON see Stenhammar

DENNY'S DAUGHTER see Harty, Sir
Hamilton

DENSMORE, JOHN H. (1880-1943)
I Must Down To The Seas Again
med-low solo,pno (B flat maj)
BOSTON $1.50   (D1014)

Voice And The Flute, The
high solo,pno,opt fl PRESSER $1.50
                                 (D1015)

DENZA, LUIGI (1846-1922)
Adieu
2 soli,pno ENOCH s.p. voc sc, solo
pt   (D1016)

Amami!
[It] S/T solo,pno RICORDI-ARG
BA 47175 s.p.   (D1017)
[It] Mez/Bar solo,pno RICORDI-ARG
BA 47176 s.p.   (D1018)

Barcarolle
2 soli,pno ENOCH s.p. voc sc, solo
pt   (D1019)

Berceuse
2 soli,pno ENOCH s.p. voc sc, solo
pt   (D1020)

Chanson De Printemps *see
Fruhlingslied

Dansons
2 soli,pno ENOCH s.p. voc sc, solo
pt   (D1021)

Fruhlingslied
"Chanson De Printemps" 2 soli,pno
ENOCH s.p. voc sc, solo pt   (D1022)

Fuggimi!
[It] S/T solo,pno RICORDI-ARG
BA 47339 s.p.   (D1023)

Funiculi-Funicula
[It] S/T solo,pno RICORDI-ENG
126791 s.p.   (D1024)
[It] Mez/Bar solo,pno RICORDI-ENG
126792 s.p.   (D1025)

Had You But Known
low solo,pno (C min) ASHDOWN
                                 (D1026)
med solo,pno (D min) ASHDOWN
                                 (D1027)
high solo,pno (E min) ASHDOWN
                                 (D1028)

Julia!
[It/Span] Mez/Bar solo,pno RICORDI-
ARG BA 46388 s.p.   (D1029)

Les Cloches
2 soli,pno ENOCH s.p. voc sc, solo
pt   (D1030)

DENZA, LUIGI (cont'd.)

Mattinata Di Maggio
[It] S/T solo,pno RICORDI-ARG
BA 99776 s.p.   (D1031)

Non T'amo Piu
[It] S/T solo,pno RICORDI-ARG
BA104582 s.p.   (D1032)
[It] Mez/Bar solo,pno RICORDI-ARG
BA 104583 s.p.   (D1033)

Occhi Di Fata
[It] S/T solo,pno RICORDI-ENG 49402
s.p.   (D1034)
[It] Mez/Bar solo,pno RICORDI-ENG
49403 s.p.   (D1035)
[It] A/B solo,pno RICORDI-ENG 49404
s.p.   (D1036)

Rosa
[It] Mez/Bar solo,pno RICORDI-ARG
BA 111960 s.p.   (D1037)

Se...
[It] S/T solo,pno RICORDI-ENG 46673
s.p.   (D1038)

Si Tu M'aimais
[Fr/It] S/T solo,pno RICORDI-ARG
RF 3160 s.p.   (D1039)

Torna
[It] Mez/Bar solo,pno RICORDI-ARG
RF 3123 s.p.   (D1040)

Vieni!
[It] S/T solo,pno RICORDI-ENG
110229 s.p.   (D1041)

DE PABLO, LUIS (1930-   )
Visto De Cerca
3 male soli,orch sc ZERBONI 7912
s.p.   (D1042)

DEPART see Barber, Samuel

DEPART see Barbirolli, A.

DEPART see Chaminade, Cecile

DEPART ET RETOUR see Kucken, Friedrich
Wilhelm, L'Hirondelle

DEPARTED see Grieg, Edvard Hagerup,
Borte!

DEPECHE-TOI DE RIRE see Arrieu, Claude

DEPECKER, ROSE
Chrysalide
solo,pno (available in 2 keys)
ENOCH s.p.   (D1043)

Reveuse
solo,pno (available in 2 keys)
ENOCH s.p.   (D1044)

DEPLORATION DE TONTON see Francaix,
Jean

DEPOUILLEMENT see Roos, Robert de

DEPUIS LE JOUR see Charpentier

DEPUIS LE JOUR see Charpentier, Gustave

DEPUIS LONGTEMPS see Lacome, Paul

DER ABEND see Diepenbrock, Alphons

DER ADLER see Nielsen, Carl, Hogen

DER ALEF BES *folk,Jew
high solo,pno HATIKVAH ED. 35 $.25
                                 (D1045)

DER ALTE see Reger, Max

DER ALTE GARTEN see Petersen, Wilhelm

DER ALTE KORPORAL see Dargomyzhsky,
[Alexander Sergeyevitch]

DER ALTE STEINKLOPFER see Nielsen,
Carl, Jens Vejmand

DER ALTER TZEGEINER *Jew
solo,pno KAMMEN 451 $1.00   (D1046)

DER ANACHRONISTISCHE ZUG see Dessau,
Paul

DER APFELBAUM AM WEGRAND see Finke,
Fidelio Fritz

DER ARBEITSMANN see Pfitzner, Hans

DER ARBEITSMANN see Strauss, Richard

DER ARME SCHWARTENHALS
see Bruder Liederlich

DER AUSSATZIGE see Lilien, Ignace

DER BACKTROG see Bach, Johann
Sebastian, Quodlibet

DER BLINDE see Lilien, Ignace

DER BLUTENZWEIG see Edler, Robert

DER BOTE see Pfitzner, Hans

DER BUTZEMANN *CC35U
solo,pno SCHOTTS 5350 s.p.   (D1047)

DER CHINESISCHE SPIEGEL see Marez
Oyens, Tera de

DER DIAMANT AUF DEM MARZSCHNEE see
Sibelius, Jean, Demanten Pa
Marssnon

DER DICHTER see Marx, Joseph

DER DICHTER SPRICHT see Herrmann, Hans

DER DISH WASHER *Jew
solo,pno KAMMEN 408 $1.00   (D1048)

DER DOPPELGANGER see Schubert, Franz
(Peter)

DER DORNBUSCH see Sibelius, Jean,
Tornet

DER DRIVER EN DUG see Sjogren, Emil

DER DU, HERR JESU, RUH UND RAST see
Raphael, Gunther

DER DU VON DEM HIMMEL BIST see Liszt,
Franz

DER DU VON DEM HIMMEL BIST see Newlin,
Dika

DER EINSAME see Grieg, Edvard Hagerup

DER EINSIEDLER see Geiser, Walther

DER ENGEL see Bijvanck, Henk

DER ENGEL see Gretchaninov, Alexander
Tikhonovitch, L'ange

DER ENGEL see Wagner, Richard

DER ENGLISCHE GRUSS see Knab, Armin

DER ENTWURZELTE see Zipp, Friedrich

DER ER EN BROND see Lewkovitch,
Bernhard

DER ERSTE BALL see Kuiler, Cor.

DER ERSTE KUSS see Sibelius, Jean, Den
Forsta Kyssen

DER EWIGE WEG see Roos, Robert de

DER FAUN see Kowalski, Max

DER FEIND see Trunk, Richard

DER FELDHERR see Mussorgsky, Modest

DER FEUERANBETER see Strategier, Herman

DER FILOSOF *folk,Jew
med solo,pno HATIKVAH ED 54 $.30
                                 (D1049)

DER FISCHERKNABE see Liszt, Franz

DER FRAGEBOGEN DES HERZENS see Podesva,
Jaromir, Dotaznik Srdce

DER FREMDE see Baird, Tadeusz, Obcy

DER FREMDE GAST see Ostrcil, Otakor

DER FREUND see Godard, Benjamin Louis
Paul, Chanson De Florian

DER FREUND see Wolf, Hugo

DER FRUHLING see Mikoda, Borivoj, Jaro

DER FRUHLING NAHT MIT BRAUSEN see
Bijvanck, Henk

DER FUHRMAN *folk,Jew
high solo,pno HATIKVAH ED. 26 $.25
                                 (D1050)

DER GANZE WALD IST SILBERWEISS see
Jochum, Otto

DER GARTNER see Knab, Armin

DER GARTNER see Wolf, Hugo

DER GAST see Marx, Joseph

DER GEFANGENE see Gretchaninov,
Alexander Tikhonovitch, Le Captif

DER GELAHMTE see Lilien, Ignace

DER GERECHTEN SEELEN SIND IN GOTTES HAND see Capricornus, Samuel

DER GOLDVOGEL *CCU
(Bresgen, C.) solo,pno SCHOTTS 4875 s.p.   (D1051)

DER GOTT UND DIE BAJADERE see Eisler, Hanns

DER GOTT UND DIE BAJADERE see Schoeck, Othmar

DER HAHN see Lothar, Mark

DER HANDWERKSBURSCHE see Trunk, Richard

DER HARFENSPIELER UND SEIN SOHN see Sibelius, Jean, Harpolekaren Och Hans Son

DER HARMONISCHE TEIL I, NEUJAHR-REMINISCERE see Telemann, Georg Philipp

DER HARMONISCHE TEIL II, OCULI-PFINGSTEN see Telemann, Georg Philipp

DER HARMONISCHE TEIL III, TRINITATIS see Telemann, Georg Philipp

DER HARMONISCHE TEIL IV, SONNTAG NACH TRINITATIS - WEIHNACHTEN see Telemann, Georg Philipp

DER HASE UND DER IGEL see Reuter, Fritz

DER HERR DENKET AN UNS see Bach, Johann Sebastian

DER HERR ERSTAND see Rachmaninoff, Sergey Vassilievitch, Christ Is Risen

DER HERR HAT SEINEN STUHL IM HIMMEL BEREITET see Bruhns, Nicholaus

DER HERR IST GROSS see Schutz, Heinrich

DER HERR IST MEIN GETREUER HIRT see Bornefeld, Helmut

DER HERR IST MEIN HIRTE see Drischner, Max

DER HERR IST MEIN HIRTE see Hellmann, Diethard

DER HERR IST MEIN HIRTE see Wiemer, Wolfgang

DER HERR IST MEIN LICHT see Schutz, Heinrich

DER HERR IST MEIN LICHT UND MEIN HEIL see Ruppel, Paul Ernst

DER HERR IST MEINE STARKE see Schutz, Heinrich

DER HERR SCHAUET VOM HIMMEL see Schutz, Heinrich

DER HIMMEL HAT see Reger, Max

DER HIRT AUF DEM FELSEN see Schubert, Franz (Peter)

DER HOCHZEITSBRATEN see Schubert, Franz (Peter)

DER HOLLE RACHE KOCKT IN MEINEM HERZEN see Mozart, Wolfgang Amadeus

DER HOLLE RACHEN KOCHT IN MEINEM HERZEN see Mozart, Wolfgang Amadeus

DER HUTEJUNGE see Roselius, Ludwig

DER JAGER UND SEIN LIEBCHEN see Brahms, Johannes

DER JAGERKNABE see Sibelius, Jean, Jagargossen

DER JAKOBINER see Dvorak, Antonin

DER JENAISCHE WEIN- UND BIERRUFER see Bach, Johann Nicolaus

DER JENSEITSTRAUM see Gretchaninov, Alexander Tikhonovitch

DER JUNGE BARTOK, BAND I see Bartok, Bela

DER JUNGE BRETAGNER HIRTE see Berlioz, Hector, Le Jeune Patre Breton

DER JUNGGESELLE see Kilpinen, Yrio, Mikas On Poikana Elea

DER KAISER see Bosmans, Henriette

DER KASBEK *folk,Russ
[Ger/Russ] solo,pno ZIMMER. 1519 s.p.
                              (D1052)

DER KIRSCHDIEB see Wiemer, Wolfgang

DER KLEINE FRITZ AN SEINE JUNGEN FREUNDE see Weber, Carl Maria von

DER KLEINE MOZART see Schmalz, Paul

DER KLEINE SANDMANN see Humperdinck, Engelbert

DER KNABE see Zelinka, Jan Evangelista

DER KONIG IN THULE see Diepenbrock, Alphons

DER KONIG VON THULE see Liszt, Franz

DER KRUMME PETER
   see Bruder Liederlich

DER KUCKUCK see Kilpinen, Yrio

DER KUCKUCK see Roselius, Ludwig

DER KUKUK see Dvorak, Antonin

DER KUSS see Arditi, Luigi, Il Bacio

DER KUSS see Borris, Siegfried

DER KUSS see Sibelius, Jean, Kyssen

DER LAUTENMUSIKANT, BAND I-III *CC250U
(Gotze) solo,gtr cmplt ed,pap SCHOTTS 2392; 3585; 4065 s.p., ea., cmplt ed,cloth SCHOTTS 4850 s.p.   (D1053)

DER LIEBESGARTEN see Schmalstich, Clemens

DER LIEBESWUNSCH see Godard, Benjamin Louis Paul, Voudrais-Tu

DER LINDENBAUM see Schubert, Franz (Peter)

DER LOBGESANG DER MARIA see Zentner, Johannes

DER LUSTIGE EHEMANN see Dresden, Sem

DER MAI TRITT EIN MIT FREUDEN see Schoenberg, Arnold

DER MAME'S ZINDELE *Jew
   solo,pno KAMMEN 428 $1.00   (D1054)

DER MANN IN MOND see Trunk, Richard

DER MASS DES MANNES see Marvia, Einari

DER MENSCH see Zimmermann, Udo

DER MOND GLUHT see Reger, Max

DER MOND IST AUFGEGANGEN see Schulz, Joh. Abraham Peter

DER MONDFLECK see Lothar, Mark

DER MORGEN *Op.90,No.3
[Swed/Ger] solo,pno BREITKOPF-W DLV 5633 s.p. see from Sechs Lieder Nach Texten Von J.L. Runeberg
                              (D1055)

DER MORGEN see Sibelius, Jean, Morgonen

DER MORGEN SHTERN see Rumshinsky, Jos. M.

DER MORGEN WAR VON DIR ERFULLT see Flothius, Marius

DER MORGENSTERN IST AUFGEDRUNGEN see Stoll, Helene Marianne

DER MUDE SOLDAT see Beekhuis, Hanna

DER MULLER see Dargomyzhsky, [Alexander Sergeyevitch]

DER MYSTISCHE TROMPETER see Wildgans, Friedrich

DER NACHTLICHE RITT see Godard, Benjamin Louis Paul, Le Voyageur

DER NEIER YID *Bar mitzvah,Jew
"Bar Mitzvoh Song" solo,pno KAMMEN 453 $1.00   (D1056)

DER NEUE ALLADDIN see Kilpinen, Yrio, Uusi Alladdin

DER NEUE AMADIS see Krenek, Ernst

DER NEUGIERIGE see Schubert, Franz (Peter)

DER NORDEN *Op.90,No.1
[Swed/Ger] solo,pno BREITKOPF-W DLV 5631 s.p. see from Sechs Lieder Nach Texten Von J.L. Runeberg

DER NORDEN see Norden
                              (D1057)

DER NORDEN see Sibelius, Jean, Norden

DER NOVEMBER IST DIE HEIMAT see Herrmann, Peter

DER NUSSBAUM see Schumann, Robert (Alexander)

DER ODEM DER LIEBE see Mozart, Wolfgang Amadeus, Un' Aura Amorosa

DER OUSWURF FON DER NATUR *Jew
solo,pno KAMMEN 442 $1.00   (D1058)

DER PALMGALGEN see Ziems, H.

DER PANTHER UND ANDERE RILKE-GEDICHTE see Marx, Karl

DER PAVILLON AUS PORZELLAN see Lothar, Mark

DER PFARRER VON CLEVERSULZBACH see Korn, Peter Jona

DER PFLAUMENBAUM see Wiemer, Wolfgang

DER PIROL see Lothar, Mark

DER PROZESS SCHON GEWONNEN - ICH SOLL EIN GLUCK ENTBEHREN see Mozart, Wolfgang Amadeus

DER RATTENFANGER see Wolf, Hugo

DER RAUCH see Marx, Joseph

DER RAUCH see Wiemer, Wolfgang

DER REBI HOT GEHEISEN FREILACH ZEIN *folk,Jew
solo,pno KAMMEN 34 $1.00   (D1059)

DER REIHER DES VERGESSENS see Lothar, Mark

DER REISEBECHER see Gilse, Jan van

DER ROTE SARAFAN *folk,Russ
[Ger/Russ] solo,pno ZIMMER. 1548 s.p.
                              (D1060)

DER SANGER, OP. 57, PART I see Schoeck, Othmar

DER SANGER, OP. 57, PART II see Schoeck, Othmar

DER SCHADEL see Burt, [Francis], Skull, The

DER SCHILDWACHE NACHTLIED see Mahler, Gustav

DER SCHLESISCHE WANDERER *CCU
(Speer; Pankalla) solo,pno TONGER s.p.   (D1061)

DER SCHMEID see Brahms, Johannes

DER SCHONSTE PLATZ see Kilpinen, Yrio

DER SCHWAN see Franken, Wim

DER SCHWAN DES TODES see Pylkkanen, Tauno Kullervo

DER SCHWAN DES TODES see Pylkkanen, Tauno Kullervo, Kuoleman Jousten

DER SCHWARZE see Bartos, Frantisek, Cerny

DER SIDER'L see Gilrod, Louis

DER SINGAUF *CC82U
(Draths; Lutz) solo,acord,gtr SCHOTTS 4828 s.p.   (D1062)

DER SKILAUFER see Kilpinen, Yrio, Yli Hohtavan Hangen

DER SOLDAT see Carriere, Paul

DER SOMMERFADEN see Trunk, Richard

DER SONNTAG see Burkhard, Willy

DER SPAN AUF DEN WELLEN see Sibelius, Jean, Lastu Lainehilla

DER SPOTTVOGEL see Mussorgsky, Modest

DER SPUK see Kilpinen, Yrio

DER STACHLIGE HIMMEL see Matej, Jozka, Ostnate Nebe

DER STERBENDE HELD see Beekhuis, Hanna

DER STIERKAMPFER see Marvia, Einari

DER STREITER IN CHRISTO JESU see Blum, Robert

DER STRUWWELPETER see Kohler, Siegfried

DER SUMMITTEMPEL see Bijvanck, Henk

DER SYLPHE DES FRIEDENS see Mozart, Wolfgang Amadeus, Ridente La Calma

DER TAG, DER IST SO FREUNDENREICH see Grimm, Heinrich

DER TAG, DER IST SO FREUNDENREICH *CCU,Adv/Xmas
(Hessen Berg, K.) solo,treb inst SCHOTTS 4241 s.p.   (D1063)

DER TAMBOUR see Wolf, Hugo

DER TAMBOURSG'SELL see Mahler, Gustav

DER TANZ see Kilpinen, Yrio, Tanssi

DER TANZ DER GOTTER see Fussan, Werner

DER TANZBAR see Lothar, Mark

DER TIERKREIS see Jirasek, Ivo, Zviretnik

DER TOD DES GELIEBTEN see Orthel, Leon

DER TOD ENKIDUS see Schibler, Armin

DER TOD UND DAS MADCHEN see Schubert, Franz (Peter)

DER TON see Marx, Joseph

DER TRAUM see Sibelius, Jean, Drommen

DER TRAUMER KOMMT see Bergman, Erik

DER TRAUMGOTT see Weingartner, (Paul) Felix

DER TRAURIGE GARTEN see Reznicek, Emil Nikolaus von

DER TREUE SCHAFER see Rameau, Jean-Philippe, Le Berger Fidele

DER TRINKER UND DIE SPIEGEL see Hartig, Heinz Friedrich

DER TROMMLER see Beekhuis, Hanna

DER ULMBAUM see Ariosti, Attilio, L'Olmo

DER UNS DIE STUNDEN ZAHLTE see Erbse, Heimo

DER VERLORENE HAUFEN see Schoenberg, Arnold

DER VERZWEIFELTE LIEBHABER see Kuhn, Siegfried

DER VOGELFANGER BIN ICH JA see Mozart, Wolfgang Amadeus

DER VOGELSTALLER see Sibelius, Jean, Fagelfangaren

DER VOGELSTELLER *Op.90,No.4
[Swed/Ger] solo,pno BREITKOPF-W DLV 5634 s.p. see from Sechs Lieder Nach Texten Von J.L. Runeberg
(D1064)
DER VOGELSTELLER see Fogelfangaren

DER VOLKSMUSIKANT *CCU
(Draths; Lechner) solo,pno SCHOTTS 5050 s.p.   (D1065)

DER VOLLMOND SCHEINT see Kilpinen, Yrio

DER VOLLMOND STRAHLT AUF BERGESHOHN see Schubert, Franz (Peter)

DER WACHTELSCHLAG see Beethoven, Ludwig van

DER WANDERER see Schoenberg, Arnold

DER WANDERER see Schubert, Franz (Peter)

DER WANDERER AN DEN TOD see Edler, Robert

DER WANDERER UND DAS BLUMENMADCHEN see Emborg, Jens Laurson

DER WANDERER UND DER BACH see Sibelius, Jean

DER WANDERNDE MUSIKANT see Schwarz-Schilling, Reinhard

DER WEG see Petrzelka, Vilem

DER WEIBERORDEN see Telemann, Georg Philipp

DER WEIHNACHTSKREIS *sac,CCU,Xmas
(Lohr) solo,pno HUG s.p.   (D1066)

DER WEIN see Berg, Alban

DER WELLE WIEGENLIED see Jarnefelt, Armas, Aallon Kehtolaulu

DER WELT LOHN see King, Harold C.

DER WIDERHALL see Haas, Joseph

DER WIMPEL *CCU
(Lutz) solo,gtr SCHOTTS 5225 s.p.   (D1067)

DER WUNDERGARTEN *CC170U,folk
(Rein; Lang) 1-2 soli,pno SCHOTTS 4375 s.p.   (D1068)

DER YIDDISHER WANDERER *Jew
solo,pno KAMMEN 418 $1.00   (D1069)

DER ZEITUNGSLESER see Vlijmen, Jan van

DER ZUPFGEIGENHANSL *CCU
(Scherrer) s.p. solo,gtr cloth SCHOTTS 4055; solo,acord cloth SCHOTTS 3586   (D1070)

DER ZUPFGEIGENHANSL *CCU
(Salzmann) solo,pno SCHOTTS 4650 s.p.   (D1071)

DERBY RAM see Broadwood, Lucy E.

DERBY RAM, THE see Hurlestone, William T.

DERE, JEAN (1886-1970)
Chanson Pour Un Petit Bateau
solo,pno JOBERT s.p. see also Jeux Et Chansons A La Mode De Chez Nous   (D1072)

Jeux Et Chansons A La Mode De Chez Nous
solo,pno cmplt ed JOBERT s.p. contains & see also: Chanson Pour Un Petit Bateau; Le Petit Canard; Le Rossignol; Les Bleuets, Les Marguerites, Les Coquelicots; Les Cailloux; Les Liserons; Les Lupins; Les Noces De La Messange; Les Nounous Vaches; Les Petits Champignons; Les Vilaines Puces   (D1073)

Le Petit Canard
solo,pno JOBERT s.p. see also Jeux Et Chansons A La Mode De Chez Nous   (D1074)

Le Rossignol
solo,pno JOBERT s.p. see also Jeux Et Chansons A La Mode De Chez Nous   (D1075)

Les Bleuets, Les Marguerites, Les Coquelicots
solo,pno JOBERT s.p. see also Jeux Et Chansons A La Mode De Chez Nous   (D1076)

Les Cailloux
solo,pno JOBERT s.p. see also Jeux Et Chansons A La Mode De Chez Nous   (D1077)

Les Liserons
solo,pno JOBERT s.p. see also Jeux Et Chansons A La Mode De Chez Nous   (D1078)

Les Lupins
solo,pno JOBERT s.p. see also Jeux Et Chansons A La Mode De Chez Nous   (D1079)

Les Noces De La Messange
solo,pno JOBERT s.p. see also Jeux Et Chansons A La Mode De Chez Nous   (D1080)

Les Nounous Vaches
solo,pno JOBERT s.p. see also Jeux Et Chansons A La Mode De Chez Nous   (D1081)

Les Petits Champignons
solo,pno JOBERT s.p. see also Jeux Et Chansons A La Mode De Chez Nous   (D1082)

Les Vilaines Puces
solo,pno JOBERT s.p. see also Jeux Et Chansons A La Mode De Chez Nous   (D1083)

DERING, RICHARD
Cries Of London, The
(Stevens, Denis) SATTB soli,2vln, 2vla,vcl (med) PENN STATE PSM 5 s.p., ipa   (D1084)

DERING, RICHARD (cont'd.)

Secular Vocal Music *CCU
solo,pno STAINER 3.8925.8 $20.00   (D1085)

DERNIER CHANT DE LA SULAMITE see Delannoy, Marcel

DERNIER CHRYSANTHEME see Trabadelo, A. de

DERNIER POEME see Poulenc, Francis

DERNIER POEME see Vermeulen, Matthijs

DERNIER RAYON see Pouget, Leo

DERNIER SOUHAIT see Roux, E.

DERNIERE BEUVERIE see Georges, Alexandre

DERNIERE DANSE see Migot, Georges

DERNIERE PAGE see Levade, Charles (Gaston)

DERNIERE PROMENADE see Badings, Henk

DERNIERE PROMENADE see Steenhuis, Francois

DERNIERES FEUILLES see Lonque, Georges

DERNIERS ADIEUX DE LA FILLE DE JEPTHE see Handel, George Frideric

DE ROGATIS, PASCUAL
Alamo Serrano
[Span] solo,pno RICORDI-ARG BA 9160 s.p.   (D1086)

Cancion De Cuna
see Cinco Canciones Argentinas

Chacarera
see Cinco Canciones Argentinas

Cinco Canciones Argentinas
[Span] solo,pno cmplt ed RICORDI-ARG BA 6093 s.p. contains: Cancion De Cuna; Chacarera; Gato; La Sombra. Yaravi; Vidala   (D1087)

Gato
see Cinco Canciones Argentinas

Gueya
[Span] solo,pno RICORDI-ARG BA 11064 s.p.   (D1088)

La Sombra. Yaravi
see Cinco Canciones Argentinas

Miel
[Span] solo,pno RICORDI-ARG BA 11384 s.p.   (D1089)

Rayos De Luna
[Span] solo,pno RICORDI-ARG BA 9048 s.p.   (D1090)

Vidala
see Cinco Canciones Argentinas

DERRICKS, CLEAVANT
Have A Little Talk With Him *sac
solo,pno WORD S-467   (D1091)

Keep Watching And Praying *sac
solo,pno WORD S-472   (D1092)

Let Your Heart Do The Walking *sac
solo,pno WORD S-473   (D1093)

My Soul Has Been Set Free *sac
solo,pno WORD S-469   (D1094)

Prescription For Salvation *sac
solo,pno WORD S-471   (D1095)

Save Our Blest America *sac
solo,pno STAMPS 7270-SN $1.00   (D1096)

Sweetest Music This Side Of Heaven *sac
solo,pno WORD S-470   (D1097)

DERRIERE MURCIE EN FLEURS see Honegger, Arthur

DE RUBERTIS, VICTOR
C'e Sempre
[It] T solo,pno RICORDI-ARG BA 6121 s.p.   (D1098)

DES ENGELS ANREGUNG AN DIE SEELE see Huber, Klaus

DES FAHRMANNS BRAUTE see Sibelius, Jean, Koskenlaskian Morsiamet

DES FEUILLES MORTES see Boussion, E.

DES FLEURS DE CE JARDIN see Nougues, Jean

DES FLEURS FONT UNE BRODERIE see Ropartz, Joseph Guy

DES FLEURS FONT UNE BRODERIE see Roussel, Albert

DES FLUTES SUR LA PELOUSE see Schumann, Robert (Alexander)

DES GANTS BLANCS see Denis, Didier

DES HAFIS LIEBESLIEDER, SET I see Szymanowski, Karol

DES HERZENS MORGEN see Sibelius, Jean, Hjartats Morgon

DES KINDES GEBET see Reger, Max

DES LASST UNS ALLE FROHLICH SEIN *CCU, Xmas
(Hellmann) [Ger] med solo,pno
BREITKOPF-W $2.75   (D1099)

DES LE PREMIER AGE DU MONDE see Indy, Vincent d'

DES MADCHEN'S KLAGE see Schubert, Franz (Peter)

DES MENSCHEN LOS see Kilpinen, Yrio

DES NACHTS AUF MEINEM LAGER see Schutz, Heinrich, In Lectulo Per Noctes

DES OEILLETS JAPONAIS see Grovlez, Gabriel (Marie)

DES PAS DANS L'ALLEE see Saint-Saens, Camille

DES PAS DE SABOTS see Laparra, Raoul

DES ROSES DANS LE SOIR see Boussion, E.

DES TODES TOD see Hindemith, Paul

DES WALDES WIPFEL RAUSCHEN see Svedbom, Vilhelm

DESANTIS
Learning To Live *sac
med solo,pno (E flat maj) BOSTON
$1.50   (D1100)

DESCH, RUDOLF (1911-   )
Naheliederbuch *CC43U
solo,pno TONOS 5401 s.p.   (D1101)

DESCHECHA DE ROMANCE QUE CANTARON LOS SERAPHINES see Montsalvatge, Xavier

DESCORT see Maros, Miklos

DESCRIBE ME see Hovhaness, Alan

DESDE QUE TE CONOCI see Guastavino, Carlos

DESDEMONA'S SONG see Pitfield, Thomas Baron

DESDICHAS DE MI PASION see Lopez-Buchardo, Carlos

DESEO see Guastavino, Carlos

DESERT, THE see Emanuel, Louis

DESERT SHALL BLOOM LIKE A ROSE, THE see Lister, Mosie

DESERT STARS see Repper, Charles

DESERTO SULLA TERRA see Verdi, Giuseppe

DESESPERANCE see Levade, Charles (Gaston)

DESESPOIR see Viardot-Garcia, Pauline

DESET NARODNIH, VOL. I see Svara, Danilo

DESET NARODNIH, VOL. II see Svara, Danilo

DESET OTROSKIH SALJIVK see Scek, Ivan

DESET POHADEK NA MOTIVY CESKYCH PISNI see Valek, Jiri

DE SEVERAC, DEODAT
Chanson De La Nuit Durable
[Eng/Fr] high solo,pno SALABERT-US
$3.75   (D1102)

Ma Poupee Cherie
med solo,pno SALABERT-US $3.75
(D1103)

Twelve Songs *CC12L
[Eng/Fr] med solo/high solo,pno
SALABERT-US $9.00   (D1104)

DESHUSSES
Ave Maria *sac
solo,org HENN 840 s.p.   (D1105)

DESIDERARE see Pratella, Francesco Balilla

DESIDERIO see Caltabiano, S.

DESIR see Cras, Jean (Emile Paul)

DESIR D'AMOUR see Saint-Saens, Camille

DESIR DE L'ORIENT see Saint-Saens, Camille

DESIR FOU see Trabadelo, A. de

DESIRE see Lora, Antonio

DESIRE see Owens, Robert

DESIRE IN SPRING see Gurney, Ivor

DESIRS D'HIVER see Absil, Jean

DESMONAS SANG see Kilpinen, Yrio

DESMOND, CHARLES
Day For Love, A
solo,orch (A flat maj) ASHDOWN
s.p., ipr   (D1106)

Sitting By The Window
low solo,orch (G maj) ASHDOWN s.p.,
ipr   (D1107)
high solo,orch (B flat maj) ASHDOWN
s.p., ipr   (D1108)

Things So Dear To My Heart
solo,pno CRAMER   (D1109)

DESNUDO BAJO LA ILUVIA see Lilien, Ignace

DESOLACION see Siccardi, Honorio, Desolazione

DESOLATE CITY, THE see Porter, Quincy

DESOLATION see Bantock, Granville

DESOLATION see Birch, Robert Fairfax

DESOLAZIONE see Siccardi, Honorio

DESORMES, L.
L'Amour D'une Rose
solo,pno (available in 2 keys)
ENOCH s.p.   (D1110)
solo,acap solo pt ENOCH s.p.
(D1111)

DESPEDIDA see Mamorsky, Morris

DESPITE AND STILL see Barber, Samuel

DESPITE AND STILL see Barber, Samuel

D'ESPOSITO, SALVE
Ave Maria (from Lin Calel)
[Span] solo,pno RICORDI-ARG BA 8225
s.p.   (D1112)

Cancion De La Primavera (from Pedro, Pedrito Y Pedrin)
[Span] solo,pno RICORDI-ARG BA 9170
s.p.   (D1113)

Cancion Del Trovero Pedro De Vidal
(from Cuento De Abril)
[Span] solo,pno RICORDI-ARG BA 9137
s.p.   (D1114)

Copla
see Tres Piezas

El Arroyuela
see Tres Piezas

Lloraba La Nina
see Tres Piezas

Tres Piezas
[Span] solo,pno cmplt ed RICORDI-
ARG BA 8784 s.p.
contains: Copla; El Arroyuela;
Lloraba La Nina   (D1115)

DESREZ
A L'epreuve
solo,pno/inst LEDUC s.p.   (D1116)

A Une Jeune Fille
B solo,pno/inst LEDUC s.p.   (D1117)

Apaisement
"Elle Est Venue" solo,pno/inst
LEDUC s.p.   (D1118)

Aux Petits Enfants
solo,pno/inst LEDUC s.p.   (D1119)

Cantilene De L'Oiseau Magicien: A
L'Amour
solo,pno/inst LEDUC s.p. see from
Poemes Salomniques   (D1120)

DESREZ (cont'd.)

Deux Melodies De Printemps *see
Extase; Le Retour Du Printemps
(D1121)

Elle Est Venue *see Apaisement

Extase
solo,pno/inst LEDUC s.p. see from
Deux Melodies De Printemps
(D1122)

Ici-Bas
solo,pno/inst LEDUC s.p.   (D1123)

Il A Donc Tressailli
solo,pno/inst LEDUC s.p.   (D1124)

Ils Ne Sont Plus, Les Jours De Notre
Enfance
solo,pno/inst LEDUC s.p.   (D1125)

La Chansin Du Rossignol
solo,pno/inst LEDUC s.p.   (D1126)

La Nuit Du Destin
solo,pno/inst LEDUC s.p. see from
Poemes Salomniques   (D1127)

La Priere Du Poete
solo,pno/inst LEDUC s.p.   (D1128)

Le Retour Du Printemps
solo,pno/inst LEDUC s.p. see from
Deux Melodies De Printemps
(D1129)

Pluie D'ete
solo,pno/inst LEDUC s.p.   (D1130)

Poemes Salomniques
solo,pno/inst cmplt ed LEDUC s.p.
contains & see also: Cantilene De
L'Oiseau Magicien: A L'Amour;
La Nuit Du Destin; Prelude:
Hymne Au Soleil   (D1131)

Prelude: Hymne Au Soleil
solo,pno/inst LEDUC s.p. see from
Poemes Salomniques   (D1132)

Roses Et Papillons
solo,pno/inst LEDUC s.p.   (D1133)

Si J'etais Dieu
solo,pno/inst LEDUC s.p.   (D1134)

Si La Mort Est Le But
A solo,pno/inst LEDUC s.p.   (D1135)

Si Vous N'avez Rien Me Dire
solo,pno/inst LEDUC s.p.   (D1136)

Soirs D'Hiver
solo,pno/inst LEDUC s.p.   (D1137)

DESSAU, PAUL (1894-   )
Den Mutigen Achtzehn
solo,pno BREITKOPF-L EB 5876 s.p.
(D1138)

Der Anachronistische Zug
solo,pno,perc PETERS 5316 s.p.
(D1139)

Funf Lieder *CC5U
(Strittmatter) low solo,gtr
DEUTSCHER 9042 s.p.   (D1140)

Funf Lieder Nach Texten Von
Ringelnatz, Claudius Und Goethe
*CC5U
BREITKOPF-L EB 5881 s.p.   (D1141)

DESSOUS TA CROISEE see Brahe, May H.

DESTIVE OBRAZY see Bartos, Frantisek

DESYLVA
Chapel Bells *sac
(Carmichael, Ralph) solo,pno WORD
S-55   (D1142)

Take Me Home *sac
(Carmichael, Ralph) solo,pno WORD
S-56   (D1143)

DET AR EN ROS UTSPRUNGEN see Melartin, Erkki

DET AR HARLIGT ATT VANDRA GANGLAT see Haggbom

DET AR MIN VANS ROST see Stenhammar, Per Ulrik

DET AR SA UNDERLIGA STALLEN see Dannstrom, Isidor

DET BLIR EJ TILL STOFT see Peterson-Berger, (Olof) Wilhelm

DET BODES DER FOR see Nielsen, Carl

DET BORDE VARIT STJARNOR see Nordqvist, Gustaf

DET BORDE VARIT STJARNOR see Wideen, Ivar

DET BRINNER EN STJARNA I OSTERLAND see
Wikander, David

DET BRISTER EN STRANG see Anjou, P. d'

DET ENDA see Nystroem, Gosta

DET FORSTE MODE see Grieg, Edvard
Hagerup

DET FORSTE MODE see Sjogren, Emil

DET GALLER see Hannikainen, Ilmari

DET HENDTE I DEN GAMLE BY see Madsen,
Erik

DET KARASTE MINNET see Kuusisto,
Taneli, Armahin Muisto

DET KLAPPAR SA SAKTA see Myrberg,
August M.

DET KLINGAR EN TON OVER FRUSEN SJO see
Heilakka

DET SAGS, DET BLOTT KARLEK AR see
Kirchner, T.

DET SJUNGANDE FINLAND *CCU
(Maasalo; Strahle) solo,pno FAZER
s.p.   (D1144)

DET STAR EIT LYS OVER BETLEHEM see
Davik, Ingebrigt

DET STAR ETT LJUS I OSTERLAND
solo,pno,opt gtr GEHRMANS 212 s.p.
contains also: Jag Unnar Dig Anda
Allt Gott   (D1145)

DET STIGER, DET STIGER EN BOLJA see
Nordqvist, Gustaf

DET STOD EN JUNGFRU see Gullberg, Olof

DET STORE GLEDESBUD see Mathisen,
Halvaan

DET SVENSKA LANDET see Koch, Sigurd
Christian Erlund von

DET TACKA KONET JAG STUDERAT see
Millocker, Karl

DET VAR DANS BORT I VAGEN see Lambert,
Helfrid

DET VAR EN GANG see Nordqvist, Gustaf

DET VAR EN GANG EN JUNGFRU see Wideen,
Ivar

DET VAR EN GANG EN KONGE see Krane,
Kjell

DET VAR EN LORDAGSAFTEN
solo,pno,opt gtr GEHRMANS 225 s.p.
contains also: Pigen Synger (D1146)

DET VAR LARKSANG OCH GLANS OVER LIDEN
see Fougstedt, Nils-Eric

DET VARE NOG! see Mendelssohn-
Bartholdy, Felix, Es Ist Genug

DETENEOS see Falla, Manuel de

DETENTE! see Wagner, Richard, Stehe
Still!

DETI Z NASHO DOMU see Burlas, Ladislav

DETONI, DUBRAVKO (1937-   )
Katavasija
solo,fl,ob,clar,bsn,pno,cembalo,
org,perc,gtr MUSIC INFO rental
(D1147)
Tropar Za Bogorodica
solo,fl,ob,clar,bsn,pno,cembalo,
org,perc,gtr MUSIC INFO rental
(D1148)

DETRESSE see Caplet, Andre

DETSKE NALADY see Haba, Alois

DETSKE PESNICKY see Moyzes, Alexander

DETSKE PISNE see Blaha, Vaclav

DETSKE PISNE see Burian, Emil Frantisek

DETSKE PISNICKY see Urks, I.J.

DETSKE RADOSTI see Laborecky, Jozef

DETSKE UKOLEBAVKY see Pauer, Jiri

DETSKY KOUTEK see Sauer, Frantisek

DETSKYM SRDCIAM see Freso, Tibor

DEULLANTERNA see Dannstrom, Isidor

DEUNTJE see Schouwman, Hans

DEUS MEUS see Dubois, Theodore

DEUTLICH LIEGT VOR MIR see Rimsky-
Korsakov, Nikolai

DEUTSCH DE LA MEURTHE, H.
Quand Vous Passez
solo,pno (available in 2 keys)
ENOCH s.p.   (D1149)

Stances A Victor-Hugo
solo,pno (available in 2 keys)
ENOCH s.p.   (D1150)

DEUTSCHE LIEBESLIEDER *CCU
(Walcha) 2 soli,pno SCHOTTS 3596 s.p.
(D1151)
DEUTSCHE VOLKSLIEDER see Trunk, Richard

DEUTSCHE VOLKSLIEDER, BAND I see
Brahms, Johannes

DEUTSCHE VOLKSLIEDER, BAND II see
Brahms, Johannes

DEUTSCHE VOLKSLIEDER, VOL. I see
Brahms, Johannes

DEUTSCHE VOLKSLIEDER, VOL. I see
Brahms, Johannes

DEUTSCHE VOLKSLIEDER, VOL. I see
Herrmann, William

DEUTSCHE VOLKSLIEDER, VOL. II see
Brahms, Johannes

DEUTSCHE VOLKSLIEDER, VOL. II see
Brahms, Johannes

DEUTSCHE VOLKSLIEDER, VOL. II see
Herrmann, William

DEUTSCHE ZWIEGESANGE see Rhau, Johannes

DEUTSCHER LIEDERSCHATZ *CC215U,Xmas/
Gen,folk,Ger
(Erk; Friedlander) solo,pno cmplt ed
PETERS 395 $12.50   (D1152)

DEUTSCHES LIED see Weill, Kurt

DEUTSCHES VOLKSLIEDERSPIEL, HEFT 2 see
Zilcher, Hermann

DEUTSCHLAND see Trunk, Richard

DEUTSCHLAND IM VOLKSLIED *CC700U,folk,
Ger
[Ger] solo,acap cloth PETERS 4879
$20.00   (D1153)

DEUTTO FINALE (LAURA E PULCINELLA) see
Farinelli, Giuseppe

DEUX BALLADES see Wiszniewski, Zbigniew

DEUX CHANSONS see Francaix, Jean

DEUX CHANSONS D'AMOUR ET UNE AUTRE GAIE
see Lazar, Filip

DEUX CHANSONS DE MEZZETIN see Jacob,
Dom Clement

DEUX CHANSONS D'EXIL see Lachaume, A.

DEUX CHANSONS DU FILM: MADAME BOVARY
see Milhaud, Darius

DEUX CHANSONS DU PECHEUR JAPONAIS see
Koptagel, Y.

DEUX CHANSONS EXTRAIT DE "LA TEMPETE ET
DEUX AUTRES CHANSONS *CC4U
cmplt ed,cloth,min sc OISEAU s.p.
contains works by: Shakespeare,
William And Johnson, Robert (D1154)

DEUX CHANTS see Migot, Georges

DEUX CHANTS POPULAIRES DE BRETAGNE see
Favre, Georges

DEUX CHANTS POPULAIRES PERSANS see
Blair Fairchild

DEUX CHANTS SPIRITUELS see Mirandolle,
Ludovicus

DEUX FABLES DE LA FONTAINE see Delage,
Maurice

DEUX IDYLLES see Roussel, Albert

DEUX IMPLORATIONS SACREES see Maurat,
Edmond

DEUX JOYEUX ENFANTS see Delbruck, J.

DEUX LETTRES D'ENFANTS see Menasce,
Jacques de

DEUX LIEDS see Vuillemin, L.

DEUX LYRIQUES see Cantu, M.

DEUX MELODIES see Diepenbrock, Alphons

DEUX MELODIES see Clergue, J.

DEUX MELODIES see Ibert, Jacques

DEUX MELODIES see Migot, Georges

DEUX MELODIES see Migot, Georges

DEUX MELODIES see Absil, Jean

DEUX MELODIES see Borchard, Adolphe

DEUX MELODIES see Leguerney, Jacques

DEUX MELODIES see Rhene-Baton

DEUX MELODIES see Tcherepnin, Alexander

DEUX MELODIES see Orthel, Leon

DEUX MELODIES see Poulenc, Francis

DEUX MELODIES D'AUTOMNE see Kelkel,
Manfred

DEUX MELODIES DE PRINTEMPS see Desrez

DEUX MELODIES HEBRAIQUES see Ravel,
Maurice

DEUX MELODIES POPULAIRES FRANCAISES see
Saint-Requier, Leon

DEUX MELODIES POPULAIRES POLONAISES see
Beekhuis, Hanna

DEUX MELODIES POUR UNE VOIX DE SOPRANO
see Diepenbrock, Alphons

DEUX MELODIES SUR DES POEMES DE PAUL
VERLAINE see Debussy, Claude

DEUX MELODIES SUR DES POESIES DE RENEE
VIVIEN see Rhene-Baton

DEUX MOTETS POUR LA CHAPELLE DU ROY see
Robert, Pierre

DEUX ODES CHINOISES see Grovlez,
Gabriel (Marie)

DEUX PETITS AIRS see Milhaud, Darius

DEUX POEMES see Milhaud, Darius

DEUX POEMES see Ropartz, Joseph Guy

DEUX POEMES see Wagner, Richard

DEUX POEMES see Bunge, Sas

DEUX POEMES see Damase, Jean-Michel

DEUX POEMES see Delannoy, Marcel

DEUX POEMES CHANTES see Samazeuilh,
Gustave

DEUX POEMES CHINOIS, OP. 47 see
Roussel, Albert

DEUX POEMES D'ARMAND BERNIER see
Bourguignon, Francis de

DEUX POEMES DE FRANCIS JAMMES see
Absil, Jean

DEUX POEMES DE J. CHENEVIERE see
Aubert, Louis-Francois-Marie

DEUX POEMES DE MAURICE CAREME see
Rasse, Francois

DEUX POEMES DE NORGE see Bourguignon,
Francis de

DEUX POEMES DE P. FORT see Vellones, P.

DEUX POEMES DE RONSARD see Roussel,
Albert

DEUX POEMES DE RONSARD see Durand,
Jacques

DEUX POEMES DE SHAKESPEARE see Sauguet,
Henri

DEUX POEMES DE TRISTAN DEREME see
Jacob, Dom Clement

DEUX POEMES D'HO-CHI-MINH see Durey,
Louis

DEUX POEMES RIMBALDIENS see Bergmann,
R.

DEUX POEMS see Mesritz Van Velthuysen,
Annie

DEUX POEMS DE J. PASSERAT see Mul, Jan

DEUX PRIERES POUR LES TEMPS MALHEUREUX
see Rosenthal, Manuel

DEUX RONDELS see Roger-Ducasse, Jean-
Jules Aimable

DEUX RONDELS DE PERONNELLE
D'ARMENTIERES see Roland-Manuel,
Alexis

DEUX SONNETS see Caplet, Andre

DEUX SONNETS DE JEAN CASSOU see
Rosenthal, Manuel

DEUX STELES DE VICTOR SEGALEN see
Migot, Georges

DEUXIEME AIR DE L'ARCHANGE see Franck,
Cesar

DEV PISNE see Ostrcil, Otakor

DEVANT MOI S'ETEND LA VUE see Handel,
George Frideric

DEVANT SATAN, SUIVANT L'USAGE see
Serpette, Gaston

DEVATY, ANTONIN (1903-   )
Die Mutter *see Matka

Matka *song cycle
"Die Mutter" T solo,pno CZECH s.p.
(D1155)

DEVAUX, M.
Au Fil De L'eau *see Kross, Th.

DEVCIC, NATKO (1914-   )
Konzert Fur Tenor Und Kammerensemble
T solo,perc sc GERIG HG 815 s.p.
(D1156)

Vokali I
S solo,pno GERIG HG 696 s.p.
(D1157)

Vokali II
Bar solo,pno GERIG HG 798 s.p.
(D1158)

DEVEEN, T.
Who's That Calling So Sweet?
low solo,pno (F maj) CRAMER (D1159)
high solo,pno (G maj) CRAMER
(D1160)

DEVET SAMOSPEVOV see Lipovsek, Marijan

DE VICTORIA, TOMAS LUIS
see VICTORIA, TOMAS LUIS DE

DE VITO, ALBERT
Long Ago In Bethlehem *sac,Xmas
high solo,pno (C maj) KENYON $.95
(D1161)
low solo,pno (A flat maj) KENYON
$.95 (D1162)

Sea Fever
high solo,pno (G maj) KENYON $.95
(D1163)
low solo,pno (E flat maj) KENYON
$.95 (D1164)

DEVREESE, GODEFROID (1893-1972)
Automne
"Herfst" med solo,pno CBDM s.p.
(D1165)

Beatrice
"Zilver" med solo,pno CBDM s.p.
(D1166)

Bloesemval *see Petales

Crepuscule
"Het Avondt" med solo,pno CBDM s.p.
(D1167)

Faune
Mez/Bar solo,pno CBDM s.p. (D1168)

Herfst *see Automne

Het Avondt *see Crepuscule

Il Passa
S solo,pno CBDM s.p. (D1169)
med solo,pno CBDM s.p. (D1170)

La Sieste Interrompue
"'T Dutje" med solo,pno CBDM s.p.
(D1171)

Offergave *see Offrande

Offrande
"Offergave" [Dut/Fr] solo,pno CBDM
s.p. (D1172)

Petales
"Bloesemval" med solo,pno CBDM s.p.
(D1173)

'T Dutje *see La Sieste Interrompue

Zilver *see Beatrice

DEVRIES, IVAN
Chanson De Fortunio
Bar solo,fl,bsn AMPHION A 138 $1.00
(D1174)

Elle Se Refuse Toujours A Comprendre
see Trois Poemes De Paul Eluard

Inconnue, Elle Etait Ma Forme
Preferee
see Trois Poemes De Paul Eluard

La Courbe De Tes Yeux
see Trois Poemes De Paul Eluard

Trois Poemes De Paul Eluard
solo,pno AMPHION A 114 $1.75
contains: Elle Se Refuse Toujours
A Comprendre; Inconnue, Elle
Etait Ma Forme Preferee; La
Courbe De Tes Yeux (D1175)

DEW UPON THE LILY, THE see German,
Edward

DEWDROPS see Guastavino, Carlos, Rocio

DEWEY, CLEON
Because Of Yesterday (composed with
Dewey, Levoy) *sac
solo,pno WORD S-409 (D1176)

DEWEY, LEVOY
Because Of Yesterday *see Dewey,
Cleon

DEY CAN'T COTCH ME TO BURY ME see
Protheroe, Daniel

DEZEMBER see Marx, Joseph

D'HAENE, RAFAEL LODEWIJK (1943-   )
Five Lyrics For Orchestre
Mez/Bar solo,orch ANDEL s.p.
(D1177)

Vocalise *vocalise
solo,pno ANDEL s.p. (D1178)

Works From Roemanie *song cycle
Bar solo,pno ANDEL s.p. (D1179)

DI DUE RAI see Vivaldi, Antonio

DI LANGIT see Hullebroeck, Em.

DI LUGLIO see Pagliuca, C.

DI MAISE MIT DER VELT see Weiner, Lazar

DI', MARIA DOLCE... see Ghedini,
Giorgio Federico

DI NOTTE see Gubitosi, Emilia

DI PIACER MI BALZA IL COR see Rossini,
Gioacchino

DI PIU COSE see Flagello, Nicholas

DI PROVENZA IL MAR, IL SUOL see Verdi,
Giuseppe

DI QUELLA PIRA see Verdi, Giuseppe

DI RIGORI ARMATO IL SENO see Strauss,
Richard

DI, RIO... see Ficher, Jacobo

DI SUN see Weiner, Lazar

DI' TU SE FEDELE IL FLUTTO M'ASPETTA
see Verdi, Giuseppe

DIA DE GRACA see Nobre, Marlos

DIABLERIE see Leeuw, Ton de

DIABLERIE see Rontgen, Johannes

DIACK, JOHN MICHAEL (1869-1946)
All In The April Evening
low solo,pno (C min) BOOSEY $1.50
(D1180)
high solo,pno (F min) BOOSEY $1.50
(D1181)
med solo,pno (D min) BOOSEY $1.50
(D1182)

Doctor Faustus
solo,pno PATERSON s.p. (D1183)

In Love, If Love Be Love
low solo,pno (G maj) PATERSON s.p.
(D1184)
high solo,pno (B maj) PATERSON s.p.
(D1185)

Johnnie Drum
solo,pno PATERSON s.p. (D1186)

Lady, When I Behold
see Two Old English Love Lyrics

Little Boy Blue
low solo,pno (D maj) PATERSON s.p.
(D1187)
high solo,pno (F maj) PATERSON s.p.
(D1188)

DIACK, JOHN MICHAEL (cont'd.)
Little Jack Horner
low solo,pno (G maj) PATERSON s.p.
(D1189)
high solo,pno (C maj) PATERSON s.p.
(D1190)

Little Polly Flinders
low solo,pno (E flat maj) PATERSON
s.p. (D1191)
high solo,pno (F maj) PATERSON s.p.
(D1192)

My Little Nut Tree
solo,pno PATERSON s.p. (D1193)

One Morning, Oh! So Early
low solo,pno (B flat maj) LEONARD-
ENG (D1194)
high solo,pno (E flat maj) LEONARD-
ENG (D1195)

She Is Not Fair
low solo,pno (D maj) PATERSON s.p.
(D1196)
high solo,pno (F maj) PATERSON s.p.
(D1197)

Son Of Mary
low solo,pno (F maj) PATERSON s.p.
(D1198)
high solo,pno (A maj) PATERSON s.p.
(D1199)

Sweet And Kind
see Two Old English Love Lyrics

Two Old English Love Lyrics
solo,pno PATERSON s.p.
contains: Lady, When I Behold;
Sweet And Kind (D1200)

Wee Willie Winkie *CCU
solo,pno PATERSON s.p. (D1201)

DIAGNOSIS '69 see Sarai, Tibor

DIAKVNISHVILI, M.
Three Poems By G. Tabidze *CC3U
[Russ] Bar solo,pno MEZ KNIGA 2.91
s.p. (D1202)

DIALOGO see Toni, Alceo

DIALOGO CON JACOPONE DA TODI see
Malipiero, Gian Francesco

DIALOGO DI MARIONETTE see Gubitosi,
Emilia

DIALOGO DI MARIONETTE see Massarani, E.

DIALOGO DI MARIONETTE see Sangiorgio,
A.

DIALOGUE DE LA ROSE ET DU ROSSIGNOL see
Delannoy, Marcel

DIALOGUE FROM "A CENTURY OF ROUNDELS",
A see King, Harold C.

DIALOGUE OF ABRAHAM AND ISAAC, THE see
Lockwood, Normand

DIALOGUES DES CARMELITES see Poulenc,
Francis

DIALOGUES FOR TWO VOICES AND CONTINUO
see Lawes, William

DIAMETRIA see Prosev, Toma, Dijametrija

DIAMOND, DAVID (1915-   )
Anniversary In A Country Cemetery
solo,pno (E min) BOOSEY $1.50
(D1203)

As Life What Is So Sweet
solo,pno (B min) BOOSEY $1.50
(D1204)

Billy In The Darbies
solo,pno ELKAN-V $.95 see from
Seven Songs (D1205)

Brigid's Song
med solo,pno MERCURY $.95 (D1206)

Chatterton
solo,pno PEER $.95 (D1207)

Christmas Tree *Xmas
solo,pno ELKAN-V $1.25 (D1208)

David Mourns For Absalom *sac
high solo,pno MERCURY $.95 (D1209)

Do I Love You?
solo,pno PEER $1.75 (D1210)

Epitaph
med solo,pno AMP $.60 (D1211)

Epitaph, The
solo,pno ELKAN-V $.95 see from Five
Songs (D1212)

Five Songs *see Epitaph, The;
Monody; Portrait, A; Somewhere;
This World Is Not My Home (D1213)

DIAMOND, DAVID (cont'd.)

Flower Given To My Daughter
   solo,pno BOOSEY $1.50   (D1214)

For An Old Man
   solo,pno PEER $.95   (D1215)

Four Ladies
   solo,pno PEER $.95   (D1216)

Four Uncles
   solo,pno ELKAN-V $.95 see from
   Seven Songs   (D1217)

Homage To Paul Klee
   solo,pno ELKAN-V $.95   (D1218)

I Am Rose
   solo,pno ELKAN-V $.95   (D1219)

I Have Longed To Move Away
   solo,pno PEER $.95   (D1220)

I Shall Imagine Life
   solo,pno PEER $.95   (D1221)

Let Nothing Disturb Thee
   med solo,pno AMP $.60   (D1222)

Life And Death
   solo,pno PEER $1.00   (D1223)

Lift Not The Painted Veil
   solo,pno PEER $.95   (D1224)

Love And Time *song cycle
   solo,pno PEER $.95   (D1225)

Love Is More
   solo,pno PEER $.95   (D1226)

Lover As Mirror, The
   solo,pno ELKAN-V $.95 see from
   Seven Songs   (D1227)

Mad Maid's Song, The
   solo,fl,hpsd/pno PEER $1.65   (D1228)

Midnight Meditation, The *song cycle
   Bar solo,pno PEER $1.85   (D1229)

Millennium, The
   solo,pno PEER $1.00   (D1230)

Monody
   solo,pno ELKAN-V $.95 see from Five
   Songs   (D1231)

Music When Soft Voices Die
   med solo,pno AMP $.75   (D1232)

My Little Mother
   solo,pno ELKAN-V $.95 see from
   Seven Songs   (D1233)

My Papa's Waltz
   solo,pno PEER $.95   (D1234)

My Spirit Will Not Haunt The Mound
   solo,pno PEER $.95   (D1235)

Ode
   solo,pno PEER $1.25   (D1236)

On Death
   med solo,pno AMP $.75   (D1237)

Portrait, A
   solo,pno ELKAN-V $.95 see from Five
   Songs   (D1238)

Prayer
   solo,pno PEER $.95   (D1239)

Seven Songs *see Billy In The
   Darbies; Four Uncles; Lover As
   Mirror, The; My Little Mother;
   Sister Jane; Souvent J'ai Dit A
   Mon Mari; Twisted Trinity, The
                                    (D1240)
Shepherd Boy Sings In The Valley Of
   Humiliation
   solo,pno PEER $.95   (D1241)

Sister Jane
   solo,pno ELKAN-V $.95 see from
   Seven Songs   (D1242)

Somewhere
   solo,pno ELKAN-V $.95 see from Five
   Songs   (D1243)

Souvent J'ai Dit A Mon Mari
   solo,pno ELKAN-V $.95 see from
   Seven Songs   (D1244)

This World Is Not My Home
   solo,pno ELKAN-V $.95 see from Five
   Songs   (D1245)

To Lucasta On Going To The Wars
   med solo,pno AMP $.60   (D1246)

DIAMOND, DAVID (cont'd.)

Twisted Trinity, The
   solo,pno ELKAN-V $.95 see from
   Seven Songs   (D1247)

Vocalises *CCU,vocalise
   solo,vla PEER $1.25   (D1248)

We Two *song cycle
   solo,pno PEER $5.00   (D1249)

DIANA AND HER DARLINGS DEARE see
   Voormolen, Alexander Nicolas

DIANE ET ACTEON see Rameau, Jean-
   Philippe

DIAPHON see Beurle, Jurgen

DIARY, A see Arkhimandritov, B.

DIBDIN, CHARLES (1745-1814)
   Come, Every Man Now Give His Toast
   (Bush) T solo,pno ELKIN 27.2474.10
   s.p.   (D1250)

Tom Tough
   solo,pno CRAMER   (D1251)

Ye Gloomy Thoughts
   (Reynolds) high solo,pno ELKIN
   27.1551.01 s.p.   (D1252)

DIBIASE, E.
   Return, The
   med solo,pno PRESSER $.75   (D1253)

DI CAPUA, [EDUARDO] (1864-1917)
   Du Ar Min Sol
   solo,pno LUNDQUIST s.p.   (D1254)

My Sunshine *see O Sole Mio

O Sole Mio
   "My Sunshine" [It/Eng] high solo,
   pno (G maj) SCHIRM.G $.60 (D1255)
   "My Sunshine" med solo,pno (F maj)
   CENTURY 2151   (D1256)

DICEBAT JESUS SCRIBIS ET PHARISAEIS see
   Hindemith, Paul

DICEN see Lerma, P.

DICEN QUE ANDAN DICIENDO.. see Lasala,
   Angel

DICEN QUE ME CASE YO see Salas, Juan
   Orrego

DICH BITT ICH, TRAUTES JESULEIN see
   Helder, Bartholomaeus

DICH THEURE HALLE see Wagner, Richard

DICH WOLLT ICH VERGESSEN see Schumann,
   Georg

DICHIERA, DAVID
   Black Beads *CC3U
   Mez solo,pno PEER $3.00   (D1257)

DICHMONT, WILLIAM
   If You Ain't Dere
   solo,pno (E flat maj) LESLIE 7023
                                    (D1258)
   Ma Little Banjo
   low solo,pno (E maj) SCHIRM.G $.75
                                    (D1259)
   Peace I Leave With You
   high solo,pno PRESSER $.75 (D1260)
   low solo,pno PRESSER $.75   (D1261)

DICHTERLEVEN see Zagwijn, Henri

DICHTERLIEBE see Schumann, Robert
   (Alexander)

DICHTERS ABENDGANG see Strauss, Richard

DICHTERWIJDING see Zagwijn, Henri

DICIASETTE VECCHIE CANZONI POPOLARI
   EMILIANE see Grimaldi, C.

DICITE, MORTALES see Pellegrini,
   Domenico

DICK, EDITH
   When Daffodils Unfold
   low solo,pno (E flat maj) CRAMER
                                    (D1262)
   high solo,pno (F maj) CRAMER
                                    (D1263)
DICKINSON, CLARENCE (1873-1969)
   God Ever Near *sac
   2 soli,pno BELWIN $1.50   (D1264)

Shepherds' Story, The *sac,Xmas
   high solo,pno BELWIN $1.50   (D1265)

Song Of Christmas, A *sac,Xmas
   med solo,pno BELWIN $1.50   (D1266)

DICKINSON, CLARENCE (cont'd.)

Song Of The Angels *sac
   solo,pno BELWIN $1.50   (D1267)

Still There Is Bethlehem *sac
   med solo,pno BELWIN $1.50   (D1268)

DICKINSON, PETER (1934-   )
   Extravaganzas *song cycle
   med solo,pno NOVELLO s.p.   (D1269)

DICKSON, STANLEY
   April Goes A-Walking
   low solo,pno (E flat maj) ASHDOWN
                                    (D1270)
   high solo,pno (G maj) ASHDOWN
                                    (D1271)
   med solo,pno (F maj) ASHDOWN
                                    (D1272)
   God Bless You
   low solo,orch (C maj) ASHDOWN s.p.,
   ipr   (D1273)
   med solo,orch (E flat maj) ASHDOWN
   s.p., ipr   (D1274)
   high solo,orch (F maj) ASHDOWN
   s.p., ipr   (D1275)
   Little Brown Cottage
   low solo,orch (B flat maj) ASHDOWN
   s.p., ipr   (D1276)
   med solo,orch (C maj) ASHDOWN s.p.,
   ipr   (D1277)
   high solo,orch (E flat maj) ASHDOWN
   s.p., ipr   (D1278)
   Thanks Be To God
   low solo,orch (B flat maj) ASHDOWN
   $1.25, ipr   (D1279)
   med solo,orch (C maj) ASHDOWN
   $1.25, ipr   (D1280)
   med-high solo,orch (D flat maj)
   ASHDOWN $1.25, ipr   (D1281)
   high solo,orch (E flat maj) ASHDOWN
   $1.25, ipr   (D1282)
   high solo&low solo,pno (E flat maj)
   ASHDOWN $1.75   (D1283)

DICTA ANTIQUORUM see Pinos-Simandel,
   Alois

DID YOU STOP TO PRAY THIS MORNING
   *sac,gospel
   solo,pno ABER.GRP. $1.50   (D1284)

DIDN'T HE see Matthews, Randy

DIDN'T HE SHINE? see Reynolds

DIDN'T IT RAIN'
   (Bonds, M.) med solo,pno MERCURY $.95
                                    (D1285)
DIDN'T MY LORD D'LIVER DANIEL?
   (Waring) solo,pno SHAWNEE IA 12 $.60
                                    (D1286)
DI DOMENICA
   First Kiss Of Love, The
   solo,pno MUSICUS $1.25   (D1287)

DIDO'S LAMENT see Purcell, Henry, When
   I Am Laid In Earth

DIE ALLEE see Trunk, Richard

DIE ALLMACHT see Schubert, Franz
   (Peter)

DIE ALLMACHTIGE see Strauss, Richard

DIE ALTE KIRCHE see Mesritz Van
   Velthuysen, Annie

DIE ALTEN STRASSEN NOCH see Redl, F.

DIE ALTIJD DROOMLOOS SLIEP see Dresden,
   Sem

DIE AMERIKANERIN see Bach, Johann
   Christoph Friedrich

DIE AMSEL see Tiessen, Heinz

DIE ANEMONE see Sibelius, Jean,
   Blasippan

DIE ARMUT, SO GOTT AUF SICH NIMMT see
   Bach, Johann Sebastian

DIE AUFGEREGTEN see Schoenberg, Arnold

DIE BALLADE VOM WASSERRAD see Eisler,
   Hanns

DIE BALLADE VON DEN EISENBAHNEN see
   Krenek, Ernst

DIE BAR see Martinu, Bohuslav, Bar

DIE BAUME WURDEN GELB see Pfitzner,
   Hans

DIE BEIDEN GRENADIERE see Schumann,
   Robert (Alexander)

DIE BEIDEN ROSEN see Sibelius, Jean, De Bagge Rosorna

DIE BESCHWORUNG see Frid, Geza

DIE BESTANDIGEN see Bijvanck, Henk

DIE BIDEN ROSEN see Sibelius, Jean, De Bagge Rosorna

DIE BLINDE see Horvath, Josef Maria

DIE BLOCKFLOTE ZUM KLAVIER HEFT II: MAIENZEIT UND SOMMERLUST *CCU solo,rec,pno BREITKOPF-L EB 5681 s.p. (D1288)

DIE BLUME see Sibelius, Jean, Blommans Ode

DIE BLUMEN *folk,Russ [Ger/Russ] solo,pno ZIMMER. 1542 s.p. (D1289)

DIE BLUMEN see Hurnik, Ilja, Kvetiny

DIE BLUMME see Sibelius, Jean, Blommans Ode

DIE BOBBE MIT'N ZEIDIN *Jew solo,pno KAMMEN 426 $1.00 (D1290)

DIE BOTEN DER LIEBE see Brahms, Johannes

DIE BOTSCHAFT see Blarr, Oskar Gottlieb

DIE BRAUTFAHRT see Godard, Benjamin Louis Paul, Embarquez-Vous

DIE BURGSCHAFT see Eisler, Hanns

DIE CHINESISCHE FLOTE see Fussan, Werner

DIE CHINESISCHE FLOTE see Fussan, Werner

DIE DREI KONIGE see Castelnuovo-Tedesco, Mario

DIE DREI SHWESTER see Lavenda, Pincus

DIE DREI SPATZEN see Lothar, Mark

DIE DREI- UND VIERSTIMMIGEN GESANGE see Haydn, (Franz) Joseph

DIE DREI ZIGEUNER see Liszt, Franz

DIE DREIZEHNJAHRIGE see Linnala, Eino

DIE EBENE see Kilpinen, Yrio, Lakeus

DIE EBENE II see Kilpinen, Yrio, Lakeus II

DIE EBENE III see Kilpinen, Yrio, Lakeus III

DIE EBENE IV see Kilpinen, Yrio, Lakeus IV

DIE EBENE V see Kilpinen, Yrio, Lakeus V

DIE ECHONYMPHE see Sibelius, Jean, Kaiutar

DIE EHRE GOTTES AUS DER NATUR see Beethoven, Ludwig van

DIE EHRE GOTTES IN DER NATUR see Beethoven, Ludwig van

DIE EIFERSUCHT IST EINE PLAGE see Lortzing, (Gustav) Albert

DIE EIGENSINNIGE see Gilse, Jan van

DIE EINSAME see Bijvanck, Henk

DIE EINSAME see Jentsch, Walter

DIE EINSAMKEIT see Handel, George Frideric, La Solitudine

DIE EISKONIGIN see Risinger, Karel, Ledova Kralovna

DIE ENTFUHRING see Orthel, Leon

DIE ENTFUHRUNG see Saint-Saens, Camille, L'Enlevement

DIE ERDBEEREN see Dvorak, Antonin

DIE ERDE see Schubert, Franz (Peter)

DIE ERINNERUNG see Godard, Benjamin Louis Paul, Te Souviens-Tu

DIE ERSTE LERCHE see Nielsen, Carl, Den Forste Laerke

DIE ERSTE NAG see Mulder, Ernest W.

DIE ERTWARTUNG see Saint-Saens, Camille, L'Attente

DIE ERWACHTE ROSE see Strauss, Richard

DIE FERNE FLOTE see Borris, Siegfried

DIE FERNE STADT see Borris, Siegfried

DIE FLEDERMAUS see Straesser, Joep

DIE FORELLE see Schubert, Franz (Peter)

DIE FREUNDIN DES HAFIS see Zipp, Friedrich

DIE FRIST IST UM see Wagner, Richard

DIE FRUHEN KRANZE see Rontgen, Johannes

DIE FRUHNEN GRABER see Saladin, O.

DIE FURCHT DES HERREN IST DER WEISHEIT ANFANG see Schutz, Heinrich

DIE FUSSWASCHUNG see Zagwijn, Henri

DIE GANSE see Trunk, Richard

DIE GEFANGENEN see Gretchaninov, Alexander Tikhonovitch, Les Forets

DIE GEGENDEN see Mikoda, Borivoj, Krajiny

DIE GEHEIMNISVOLLE FLOTE see Fussan, Werner

DIE GELIEBTEN see Haba, Alois, Milenci

DIE GEOGE SANG see Kuiler, Cor.

DIE GETAUSCHTE LIEBE see Vivaldi, Antonio, All' Ombra Di Sospetto

DIE GLOCKE see Saint-Saens, Camille, La Cloche

DIE GLOCKEN SIND AUF FALSCHER SPUR see Gielen, Michael

DIE GOLDFISCHE see Ranta, Sulho, Kultakalat

DIE GOLDNE GARBE see Jode, Fritz

DIE GOTT MINNENDE SEELE see Braunfels, Walter

DIE GOTTSELIGKEIT IST ZU ALLEN DINGEN NUTZE see Schutz, Heinrich

DIE GREENE KOSEENE *Jew solo,pno KAMMEN 439 $1.00 (D1291)

DIE GUTEN GABEN see Lothar, Mark

DIE HEILE WELT see Krol, Bernhard

DIE HEIL'GEN DREI KONIGE AUS MORGENLAND see Bosmans, Henriette

DIE HEILIGEN DREI KONIGE see Mommers, H.G.

DIE HEILIGEN DREI KONIGE see Strauss, Richard

DIE HERRLICHKEIT AUF ERDEN see Weyrauch, Johannes

DIE HINDUMADCHEN see Reinecke, Carl

DIE HIRTEN see Cornelius, Peter

DIE HOCHSTE MACHT IST MEIN see Mussorgsky, Modest

DIE HOFFNUNG IST MEIN LEBEN see Telemann, Georg Philipp

DIE HOLLE FLIEHT see Homilius, Gottfried August

DIE HUPFENDE ELSTER see Mussorgsky, Modest

DIE IHR DES UNERMESSLICHEN WELTALLS SCHOPFER EHRT see Mozart, Wolfgang Amadeus

DIE IHR IM HADES HERRSCHT see Gluck, Christoph Willibald Ritter von, Divinites Du Styx

DIE JAHRESZEITEN see Reutter, Hermann

DIE JUNGE HEXE see Roselius, Ludwig

DIE JUNGE MAGD see Hindemith, Paul

DIE JUNGE NONNE see Schubert, Franz (Peter)

DIE KAROLISSER-LAUTE *CCU,Xmas (Stern) solo,pno HUG s.p. (D1292)

DIE KATZE see Roselius, Ludwig

DIE KINDLEIN WISSEN'S see Mirandolle, Ludovicus

DIE KLEINE MUHLE see Strauss, Josef

DIE KLEINE STADT see Lothar, Mark

DIE KLEINE VLAM IN HET DUISTER see Mulder, Ernest W.

DIE KLEINE VLAM IN HET DUISTER see Mulder, Herman

DIE KONIGE see Cornelius, Peter

DIE KRAHE see Schubert, Franz (Peter)

DIE KURTISANE see Orthel, Leon

DIE LAUTE see Martino, Donald

DIE LAUTE see Orthel, Leon

DIE LEIERFRAU see Lilien, Ignace

DIE LERCHE *folk,Russ [Ger/Russ] solo,pno ZIMMER. 1545 s.p. (D1293)

DIE LERCHE see Dvorak, Antonin

DIE LERCHE see Kilpinen, Yrio, Leivonen

DIE LERCHE see Palmgren, Selim, Leivonen

DIE LERCHE "ZWISCHEN ERD' UND HIMMEL" see Glinka, Mikhail Ivanovitch

DIE LETZTE NACHT see Peterson-Berger, (Olof) Wilhelm

DIE LETZTE NOT see Roos, Robert de

DIE LIBELLE "SCHONE LIBELLE, SCHWIRRTEST MIR HEREIN" see Sibelius, Jean

DIE LIEBE DES NACHSTEN see Beethoven, Ludwig van

DIE LIEBENDE SCHREIBT see Diepenbrock, Alphons

DIE LINDENBAUM see Schubert, Franz (Peter)

DIE LORELEY see Liszt, Franz

DIE LOTOSBLUME see Schumann, Robert (Alexander)

DIE LUFT IST BLAU see Bijvanck, Henk

DIE MAGDEBURGER WEIHNACHTSFEIER see King, Harold C.

DIE MAINACHT see Beethoven, Ludwig van

DIE MAINACHT see Brahms, Johannes

DIE MASKE DES BOSEN see Wiemer, Wolfgang

DIE MEERE see Brahms, Johannes

DIE MEERFAHRT see Saint-Saens, Camille, Soiree En Mer

DIE MIJNS HERTE VREDE ZIJT see Bijl, Theo van der

DIE MIJNS HERTEN VREDE ZIJT see Bijvanck, Henk

DIE MINNE BIDDE IC see Moulaert, Raymond

DIE MITTAGSSCHLAF see Godard, Benjamin Louis Paul, La Sieste

DIE MONDBRUCKE see Pylkkanen, Tauno Kullervo

DIE MONDBRUCKE see Pylkkanen, Tauno Kullervo, Kuun Silta

DIE MOWE see Funf Beruhmte Russische Lieder

DIE MUTTER see Devaty, Antonin, Matka

DIE NACHT see Axmann, Emil

DIE NACHT see Diepenbrock, Alphons

DIE NACHT see Mussorgsky, Modest

DIE NACHT see Strauss, Richard

DIE NACHT see Purcell, Henry

DIE NACHT DES ZWIEFELS see Lilien, Ignace

DIE NACHT VAN ZELFVERNEDERING see Zagwijn, Henri

DIE NACHTE see Schreiber, Josef, Noci

DIE NACHTEGAAL see Lilien, Ignace

DIE NACHTIGALL see Aljabjew, Alexander A.

DIE NACHTIGALL see Delibes, Leo, Le Rossignol

DIE NACHTIGALL see Krenek, Ernst

DIE NACHTIGALL see Pylkkanen, Tauno Kullervo, Satakieli

DIE NACHTIGALL UND DIE ROSE see Wolpert

DIE NAHERIN see Lilien, Ignace

DIE NEUE HARFE see Laitenen, Arvo, Koske, Herra, Kielihin

DIE NONNE UND DER RITTER see Brahms, Johannes

DIE OBRIGKEIT IST GOTTES GABE see Bach, Johann Sebastian

DIE OREME YESOIMELE see Kammen, Joseph

DIE OSSE ENDE OOC DAT ESELKYN see Beekhuis, Hanna

DIE POST see Schubert, Franz (Peter)

DIE PRIMEL see Sibelius, Jean, Sippan

DIE PROPHEZEIUNG DER MARFA see Mussorgsky, Modest, Martha's Divination

DIE PRUFUNG DES KUSSENS see Beethoven, Ludwig van

DIE ROSE see Ariosti, Attilio, La Rosa

DIE ROSE see Dvorak, Antonin

DIE ROSE see Schubert, Franz (Peter)

DIE ROUMANISHE KRETCHME see Rumshinsky, Jos. M.

DIE RUHE KEHRET MIR ZURUCK see Gluck, Christoph Willibald Ritter von

DIE SCHENKE AM SEE see Siegl, Otto

DIE SCHMIEDE see Lilien, Ignace

DIE SCHONE MULLERIN see Schubert, Franz (Peter)

DIE SCHONE SEILERIN see Baumann, Max

DIE SCHWARZE LAUTE see Bordewijk-Roepman, Johanna

DIE SCHWESTERN see Brahms, Johannes

DIE SEEJUNGFER see Haydn, (Franz) Joseph

DIE SEELE CHRISTI HEILIGE MICH see Schutz, Heinrich

DIE SEEROSE see Marvia, Einari

DIE SERENADEN see Hindemith, Paul

DIE SHAINE YUGEND see Schwartz, Abe

DIE SIEBEN WORTE DES ERLOSERS AM KREUZ see Pergolesi, Giovanni Battista, Septum Verba

DIE SIEBEN WORTE JESU CHRISTI AM KREUZ see Schutz, Heinrich

DIE SO IHR DEN HERREN FURCHTET see Schutz, Heinrich

DIE SOMMERNACHT *Op.90,No.5
[Swed/Ger] solo,pno BREITKOPF-W DLV 5635 s.p. see from Sechs Lieder Nach Texten Von J.L. Runeberg
(D1294)

DIE SOMMERNACHT see Saladin, O.

DIE SOMMERNACHT see Sibelius, Jean, Sommarnatten

DIE SOMMERNACHT see Sommernatten

DIE SONNE SCHAUE see Zagwijn, Henri

DIE SONNE SIE LACHTE see Saint-Saens, Camille, Printemps Qui Commence

DIE SPINNERIN see Trunk, Richard

DIE SPRODE see Taylor, H. Stanley

DIE SPRUCHE DES PETER BORNEMISZA see Kurtag, Gyorgy

DIE STADT see Hageman, Richard

DIE STADT see Trunk, Richard

DIE STEM VAN SUID-AFRICA see Mengelberg, Rudolf

DIE STERNBLUME see Sibelius, Jean, Vit Sippan

DIE STERNBLUME see Sibelius, Jean, Vitsippan

DIE STERNE UBERM MEER see Kraft

DIE STERNSINGER see Gorner, H.G.

DIE STERRETJIE see Hullebroeck, Em.

DIE STILLA STADT see Sibelius, Jean

DIE STILLE STADT see Pfitzner, Hans

DIE STILLE STADT see Zagwijn, Henri

DIE STIMM DES HERREN see Schutz, Heinrich

DIE STIMME DES VATERLANDS see Picha, Frantisek, Rodne Hroudy Hlas

DIE STUNDE NAHT see Purcell, Henry

DIE STURZWELLE see Kilpinen, Yrio, Hyokyaalto

DIE SUN HOT FAR MIR NOCH KEIN MUHL NIT GESHEINT see Lillian, Isadore

DIE TEPPICHWEBER VON KUJAN-BULAK see Eisler, Hanns

DIE TIEFSTEN WUNDEN see Laitenen, Arvo, Syvimmat Haavat

DIE TIROLER SEIND OFTEN SO LUSTIG see Haibel, Jakob J.

DIE TOTE NACHTIGALL see Liszt, Franz

DIE TREPPE see Rietz, Johannes

DIE UHR see Loewe, Carl

DIE UMKEHR see Roos, Robert de

DIE UNTERHOSE see Straesser, Joep

DIE VAGANTENBALLADE see Koerppen, Alfred

DIE VATERGRUFT see Liszt, Franz

DIE VATERGRUFT see Taylor, H. Stanley

DIE VEREHRUNG see Kilpinen, Yrio

DIE VERLASSENE see Verhaar, Ary

DIE VERLASSENS see Dvorak, Antonin

DIE VERLEUMDUNG, SIE IST EIN LUFTCHEN see Rossini, Gioacchino

DIE VERSUCHUNG JESU see Burkhard, Willy

DIE VERWAISTE see Kilpinen, Yrio, Armottoman Osa

DIE WAGE DES GLUCKS see Salieri, Antonio

DIE WAISE see Grieg, Edvard Hagerup, Den Foraeldrelose

DIE WALLFAHRT NACH KEVLAAR see Weingartner, (Paul) Felix

DIE WASSERFRAU see Arba, d'

DIE WASSERLILIE see Barlow, F.

DIE WEIDENFLOTE see Lothar, Mark

DIE WEISE VON LIEBE UND TOD see Leeuw, Ton de

DIE WEISE VON LIEBE UND TOD see Reutter, Hermann

DIE WEISE VON LIEBE UND TOD DES KORNETS CHRISTOPH RILKE see Ruyneman, Daniel

DIE WEISSBROTKANTATE see Eisler, Hanns

DIE WEISSEN MORGEN see Marvia, Einari, Valkeat Aamut

DIE WELT DER INSEKTEN see Bennett, Richard Rodney, Insect World, The

DIE WELT STEHT AUF KEIN FALL MEHR LANG see Muller, A.

DIE WELT VERANDERN WIR see Eisler, Hanns

DIE WINDJIE see Mulder, Ernest W.

DIE WINTER IS VERGANGEN see Ruyneman, Daniel

DIE WINTER IS VERGANGHEN see Nieland, Jan

DIE WINTERREISE see Schubert, Franz (Peter)

DIE WITWE SCHICKEDANZ see Lothar, Mark

DIE WOLKEN see Zechlin, Ruth, Orchesterstuck No. 1

DIE WORTER see Kelemen, Milko

DIE YIDDISHE POLKA *Jew
solo,pno KAMMEN 478 $1.00   (D1295)

DIE ZEHN NEUEN FIEDELLIEDER, HEFT 1 see Schmid, Reinhold

DIE ZEHN NEUEN FIEDELLIEDER, HEFT 2 see Schmid, Reinhold

DIE ZEHN NEUEN FIEDELLIEDER, HEFT 3 see Schmid, Reinhold

DIE ZUCHTHAUS-KANTATE see Eisler, Hanns

DIE ZWOLF RAUBER
see Funf Beruhmte Russische Lieder

DIECI ARIE INEDITE see Cimarosa, Domenico

DIECI ARIE ITALIANE DEL SEI E SETTECENTO *CC10L,16-17th cent (Bryks, Negri) [It] solo,pno cmplt ed RICORDI-ENG 129005 s.p. contains works by: Albinoni; Aldrovandini; Caccini; Veracini Gasparini and others   (D1296)

DIECKMANN, JOHANNES (1893-1969) *CCU,
Kinder- Und Weihnachtslieder   Xmas
(Dessau, Paul; Medek, Thilo) solo, pno BREITKOPF-W EB 4185 s.p.
(D1297)

DIEMENTE, EDWARD
Hosanna III
solo,3inst sc SEESAW $10.00 (D1298)

March 31, 1970
solo/soli,trp,trom,sax,gtr,bvl, 5perc sc SEESAW $6.00   (D1299)

Some Faces Of Love
narrator,electronic tape sc SEESAW $2.00   (D1300)

DIEMER, LOUIS (1843-1919)
L'Attente
solo,pno (available in 2 keys) ENOCH s.p.   (D1301)

DIEP IN HET DENNENBOSCH see Zweers, [Bernard]

DIEP IN HET KOREN see Clercq, R. de

DIEP RIVIER see Mulder, Ernest W.

DIEP VAN MIJZELF see Schuyt, Nico

DIEPENBROCK, ALPHONS (1862-1921)
Ave Maria *sac
Mez solo,pno/org ALSBACH s.p.
(D1302)
Avondzang
high solo,pno ALSBACH s.p. (D1303)
T/S solo,2fl,2ob,3clar,2bsn,4horn, strings DONEMUS s.p. see also Drie Sonnetten   (D1304)

Beiaard
Mez solo,pno ALSBACH s.p. (D1305)

Berceuse
Mez solo,vcl,harp,strings DONEMUS s.p.   (D1306)
Mez solo,vcl,pno ALSBACH s.p.
(D1307)

Celebritat
Bar solo,pno ALSBACH s.p. (D1308)

Clair De Lune
SS soli,pno/orch DONEMUS s.p. see also Deux Melodies   (D1309)

DIEPENBROCK, ALPHONS (cont'd.)

S solo,2fl&2ob&2clar&2bsn&strings/
3fl&3ob&3clar&2bsn&4horn&strings
DONEMUS s.p. see also Deux
Melodies Pour Une Voix De Soprano
S solo,pno ALSBACH s.p.   (D1311)

Come Raggio Di Sol
see Due Canzoni
S solo,fl,ob,clar,bsn,horn ALSBACH
s.p.   (D1312)

De Klare Dag
T solo,pno ALSBACH s.p.   (D1313)

Der Abend
high solo,pno ALSBACH s.p.   (D1314)
S solo,pno/orch ALSBACH s.p. see
also Drei Lieder Fur Sopranstimme
(D1315)

Der Konig In Thule
A solo,2ob,3clar,2bsn,4horn,timp,
perc,strings,opt trp&3trom
DONEMUS s.p. see also Zwei
Balladen Von Goethe   (D1316)

Deux Melodies
DONEMUS s.p. S solo,3fl,3ob,3clar,
2bsn,4horn,strings; S solo,2fl,
2ob,2clar,2bsn,strings
contains & see also: Clair De
Lune; Ecoutez La Chanson Bien
Douce   (D1317)

Deux Melodies Pour Une Voix De
Soprano
S solo,2fl&2ob&2clar&2bsn&strings/
3fl&3ob&3clar&2bsn&4horn&strings
DONEMUS s.p.
contains & see also: Clair De
Lune; Ecoutez La Chanson Bien
Douce   (D1318)

Die Liebende Schreibt
S solo,pno ALSBACH s.p.   (D1319)

Die Nacht
A/Mez solo,2fl,2ob,2clar,2bsn,
4horn,trp,2trom,tuba,timp,perc,
harp,inst ALSBACH s.p. min sc,
voc sc   (D1320)

Drei Lieder Fur Sopranstimme
ALSBACH s.p. S solo,ob,vln,vla; S
solo,2fl,2ob,3clar,2bsn,4horn,
timp,harp,strings; S solo,2fl,
3ob,3clar,2bsn,4horn,strings
contains & see also: Der Abend;
Hinuber Wall' Ich; Lied Der
Spinnerin   (D1321)

Drie Sonnetten
T/S solo,2fl,2ob,3clar,2bsn,4horn,
strings DONEMUS s.p.
contains: Avondzang; Ik Ben In
Eenzaamheid Niet Meer Alleen;
Zij Sluimert
see also: Avondzang; Zij Sluimert
(D1322)

Due Canzoni
T/S solo,pno ALSBACH s.p.
contains: Come Raggio Di Sol;
Preghiera Alla Madonna (sac)
(D1323)

Ecoutez La Chanson Bien Douce
SS soli,pno/orch DONEMUS s.p. see
also Deux Melodies   (D1324)
S solo,2fl&2ob&2clar&2bsn&strings/
3fl&3ob&3clar&2bsn&4horn&strings
DONEMUS s.p. see also Deux
Melodies Pour Une Voix De Soprano
(D1325)
S solo,pno ALSBACH s.p.   (D1326)

En Sourdine
med solo,pno ALSBACH s.p.   (D1327)
low solo,pno ALSBACH s.p.   (D1328)
(Andriessen, Hendrik) low solo,fl,
horn,strings DONEMUS s.p.   (D1329)

Es War Ein Alter Konig
Bar/A solo,pno ALSBACH s.p. (D1330)
(Andriessen, Hendrik) A/Bar solo,
2fl,ob,horn,strings DONEMUS s.p.
(D1331)

Hinuber Wall' Ich
S/T solo,pno ALSBACH s.p.   (D1332)
S solo,pno/orch ALSBACH s.p. see
also Drei Lieder Fur Sopranstimme
(D1333)

Hymne An Die Nacht: Gehoben Ist Der
Stein
S solo,2fl,2ob,3clar,2bsn,4horn,
3trp,3trom,tuba,timp,perc,harp,
strings voc sc ALSBACH s.p.
(D1334)

Hymne An Die Nacht: Muss Immer Der
Morgen
A/Mez solo,3fl,3ob,3clar,3bsn,
4horn,2trp,3trom,tuba,timp,perc,
2harp,strings ALSBACH s.p. min
sc, voc sc   (D1335)

DIEPENBROCK, ALPHONS (cont'd.)

Ik Ben In Eenzaamheid Niet Meer
Alleen
see Drie Sonnetten
high solo,pno ALSBACH s.p.   (D1336)

Im Grossen Schweigen
Bar solo,2fl,3ob,4clar,2bsn,4horn,
4trp,3trom,tuba,timp,perc,2harp,
strings voc sc ALSBACH s.p.
(D1337)
Bar solo,3fl,3ob,4clar,2bsn,4horn,
4trp,3trom,tuba,timp,perc,2harp,
strings DONEMUS s.p.   (D1338)

Jesu Dulcis Memoria *sac
Bar solo,org ALSBACH s.p.   (D1339)

Kann Ich Im Busen Heisse Wunsche
Tragen?
A solo,pno ALSBACH s.p.   (D1340)
(Andriessen, Hendrik) A/Mez solo,
2fl,ob,2clar,2bsn,2horn,strings
DONEMUS s.p.   (D1341)

Les Chats
low solo,pno ALSBACH s.p.   (D1342)
A/Mez solo,pno/orch DONEMUS s.p.
see also Trois Melodies Pour Une
Voix Grave   (D1343)

Liebesklage
Bar/Mez solo,pno ALSBACH s.p.
(D1344)

Lied Der Spinnerin
S solo,pno ALSBACH s.p.   (D1345)
S solo,pno/orch ALSBACH s.p. see
also Drei Lieder Fur Sopranstimme
(D1346)

Lied Van Den Hop (from De Vogels)
T solo,pno ALSBACH s.p.   (D1347)
T solo,3fl,3ob,3clar,2bsn,3horn,
3trp,3trom,timp,perc,harp,strings
voc sc ALSBACH s.p.   (D1348)

L'invitation Au Voyage
Bar/Mez solo,pno ALSBACH s.p.
(D1349)

Lydische Nacht
Bar solo,2fl,3ob,3clar,2bsn,4horn,
3trp,3trom,timp,perc,harp,strings
voc sc ALSBACH s.p.   (D1350)

Mandoline
med solo/high solo,pno ALSBACH s.p.
(D1351)

Memorare
T solo,org ALSBACH s.p.   (D1352)

Mignon
A solo,2ob,3clar,2bsn,4horn,timp,
perc,strings,opt trp&3trom
DONEMUS s.p. see also Zwei
Balladen Von Goethe   (D1353)

O Jesu Ego Amo Te *sac
Bar/Mez solo,pno/org ALSBACH s.p.
(D1354)

Preghiera Alla Madonna
see Due Canzoni

Puisque L'aube Grandit
med solo,pno ALSBACH s.p.   (D1355)
A/Mez solo,pno/orch DONEMUS s.p.
see also Trois Melodies Pour Une
Voix Grave   (D1356)

Recueille
A/Mez solo,pno/orch DONEMUS s.p.
see also Trois Melodies Pour Une
Voix Grave   (D1357)

Trois Melodies Pour Une Voix Grave
cmplt ed DONEMUS s.p. A/Mez solo,
2fl,2ob,2clar,2bsn,2horn,harp,
strings; A solo,2fl,2ob,3clar,
bsn,4horn,strings; Mez solo,fl,
2ob,2clar,2bsn,2horn,strings
contains & see also: Les Chats;
Puisque L'aube Grandit;
Recueille   (D1358)

Verzamelde Liederen *CCU
ALSBACH s.p. Bar/Mez solo,pno; T/S
solo,pno   (D1359)

Vondel's Vaart Naar Agrippina
Bar solo,2fl,3ob,3clar,2bsn,4horn,
3trp,3trom,tuba,timp,perc,harp,
strings ALSBACH s.p.   (D1360)

Wenige Wissen *sac
S/T solo,org ALSBACH s.p.   (D1361)
S solo,2fl,3ob,3clar,2bsn,4horn,
2trp,3trom,timp,strings DONEMUS
s.p. see also Zwei Geistliche
Lieder   (D1362)

Wenn Ich Ihn Nur Habe *sac
S solo,org ALSBACH s.p.   (D1363)
S solo,fl,ob,clar,bsn,horn,bvl voc
sc ALSBACH s.p.   (D1364)
S solo,2fl,3ob,3clar,2bsn,4horn,
strings DONEMUS s.p. see also
Zwei Geistliche Lieder   (D1365)

DIEPENBROCK, ALPHONS (cont'd.)

Zij Sluimert
T/S solo,2fl,2ob,3clar,2bsn,4horn,
strings DONEMUS s.p. see also
Drie Sonnetten   (D1366)

Zwei Balladen Von Goethe
A solo,2ob,3clar,2bsn,4horn,timp,
perc,strings,opt trp&3trom
DONEMUS s.p.
contains & see also: Der Konig In
Thule; Mignon   (D1367)

Zwei Geistliche Lieder *sac
S solo,orch DONEMUS s.p.
contains & see also: Wenige
Wissen; Wenn Ich Ihn Nur Habe
(D1368)

DIEPPE, ENCORE LE DERNIER REFLUX see
Christensen, Henning

DIERCKS, JOHN H.
About A Lamb *song cycle
high solo,pno TRI-TEN $2.50 (D1369)

DIERS, ANN MAC DONALD
Stopping By Woods On A Snowy Evening
med solo,pno (E min) GALAXY
1.1976.7 $1.00   (D1370)

DIES ALLA
(Herbage, Julian) solo,pno CRAMER
(D1371)

DIES BILDNIS IST BEZAUBERND SCHON see
Mozart, Wolfgang Amadeus

DIES EST LETITIE see Badings, Henk

DIES IST DER TAG, DEN DER HERR MACHT
see Kretzschmar, Gunther

DIES IST EIN GIESSBACH see Gluck,
Christoph Willibald Ritter von,
C'est Un Torrent Impetreux

DIES NATALIS see Finzi, Gerald

DIETERICH, M.
God Of Love
solo,pno (D maj) BOOSEY $1.50
(D1372)

DIETSCHMANN
He's On His Way *see Meyers

DIETTERICH, PHILIP R.
Now Will I Praise The Lord *sac
low solo,pno ABINGDON APM-904 $1.00
(D1373)
high solo,pno ABINGDON APM-905
$1.00   (D1374)

DIEU D'ISRAEL see Mariotte, Antoine

DIEU DU BONHEUR see Gaveaux, Pierre

DIEU GOUVERNE L'ORIENT see Schumann,
Robert (Alexander)

DIEU, POURQUOI ES-TU CACHE? see
Barbier, Rene

DIEU! POURQUOI SEPARER DEUX COEURS see
Rameau, Jean-Philippe

DIEU! QUELLE FAIBLESSE see Lacome, Paul

DIEU QUI SOURIT ET QUI DONNE see
Godard, Benjamin Louis Paul

DIEU QU'IL LA FAIT BON REGARDER see
Debussy, Claude

DIEU! QU'IL LA FAIT BON REGARDER see
Millot, E.

DIEU SANGLANT see Barraud, Henry

DIEU, SAUVE-MOI! see Buxtehude,
Dietrich

DIEU TUTELAIRE see Wagner, Richard,
Gerechter Gott

DIEU VOUS GARD see Bunge, Sas

DIEWEIL AUCH HEUER NACH ADVENT see
Thiele, Siegfried

DIEZ CANCIONES see Debussy, Claude

DIEZ CANCIONES POPULARES
NORTEAMERICANAS see Foster, Stephen
Collins

DIFFENDERFER
I Thank You, God *sac
solo,pno LILLENAS SM-640: RN $1.00
(D1375)
Welcome Home *sac
solo,pno LILLENAS SM-951: SN $1.00
(D1376)

DIG A LITTLE DEEPER IN GOD'S LOVE
*sac,gospel
solo,pno ABER.GRP. $1.50   (D1377)

DIGGING UP THE ROAD see Butler, R.

DIGTE OCH SANGE see Soderman, (Johan) August

DIGUEDONDAINE *CC100U
(Kampp, Ejnar) [Fr] solo,kbd HANSEN-DEN s.p.   (D1378)

DIHAU, DESIRE
Les Rois Mages
solo,pno GENERAL 54 $5.00   (D1379)

DIJAMETRIJA see Prosev, Toma

DIJK, JAN VAN (1918-   )
By The Rivers Of Babylon (Psalm 137) sac
female solo,2fl,ob,bsn,al-sax,horn, trp,perc,org,strings DONEMUS s.p.
(D1380)
De Dood
see Vijf Kleengedichtjes Van Guido Gezelle
De Leye
see Vijf Kleengedichtjes Van Guido Gezelle
De Zonne
see Vijf Kleengedichtjes Van Guido Gezelle
see Vijf Gezelleliederen
Drie Duetten
SA soli,acap DONEMUS s.p.
contains: Gebedt; Gebenedijd; Nacht-Stilte   (D1381)
Elf Kurzlieder *CC11U
S solo,pno DONEMUS s.p.   (D1382)
Eurydike
see Twee Liederen Van Maarten Mourik
Gebedt
see Drie Duetten
see Vijf Liederen
see Zes Liederen
Gebenedijd
see Drie Duetten
see Vijf Liederen
see Zes Liederen
Het Masker Van Den Rooden Dood
narrator,2fl,2ob,horn,pno,strings DONEMUS s.p.   (D1383)
Ik Die Bij Sterren Sliep
Bar solo,2fl,2ob,3clar,3bsn,4horn, 2trp,3trom,tuba,harp,strings DONEMUS s.p.   (D1384)
Jesu, Wijs En Wondermachtig
see Vijf Liederen
see Zes Liederen
Kerstliedje
see Vijf Liederen
see Zes Liederen
Levensloop
see Twee Liederen Van Maarten Mourik
Missa
S solo,orch DONEMUS s.p.   (D1385)
Nacht-Stilte
see Drie Duetten
see Vijf Liederen
see Zes Liederen
Nu Sijt Wellekome
narrator,pno DONEMUS s.p.   (D1386)
Psalm
see Zes Liederen
Psalm 137 *see By The Rivers Of Babylon
Septet
[Fr/Dan/Eng] S solo,fl,clar,horn, vln,vla,vcl,bvl DONEMUS s.p.
(D1387)
'T Begijnhofsklokske
see Vijf Gezelleliederen
see Vijf Kleengedichtjes Van Guido Gezelle
'T Is Stille
see Vijf Gezelleliederen
med solo,pno DONEMUS s.p. see also Tien Gezelleliederen   (D1388)
low solo,pno DONEMUS s.p. see also Tien Gezelleliederen   (D1389)
'T Is Voorbij
see Vijf Gezelleliederen
see Vijf Kleengedichtjes Van Guido Gezelle

DIJK, JAN VAN (cont'd.)
Tien Gezelleliederen *sac/sec,CC10L
A solo,pno DONEMUS s.p.
see also: 'T Is Stille   (D1390)
Twee Liederen Van Maarten Mourik
B/Bar solo,pno DONEMUS s.p.
contains: Eurydike; Levensloop
(D1391)
Vijf Gezelleliederen
A solo,fl,ob,clar,horn,strings DONEMUS s.p.
contains: De Zonne; 'T Begijnhofsklokske; 'T Is Stille; 'T Is Voorbij; Waar Gaat Gij   (D1392)
Vijf Kleengedichtjes Van Guido Gezelle
A solo,pno DONEMUS s.p.
contains: De Dood; De Leye; De Zonne; 'T Begijnhofsklokske; 'T Is Voorbij   (D1393)
Vijf Liederen
Bar solo,fl,4strings DONEMUS s.p.
contains: Gebedt; Gebenedijd; Jesu, Wijs En Wondermachtig; Kerstliedje; Nacht-Stilte
(D1394)
Waar Gaat Gij
see Vijf Gezelleliederen
Wat Ben Ik, Dan Een Vogel In De Schemering?
Bar solo,fl,3clar,2bsn,4horn, strings DONEMUS s.p.   (D1395)
Wijding Aan Mijn Vader
B solo,3fl,2ob,2clar,3bsn,3horn, harp,strings DONEMUS s.p. (D1396)
Zes Liederen *sac
A solo,ob,org DONEMUS s.p.
contains: Gebedt; Gebenedijd; Jesu, Wijs En Wondermachtig; Kerstliedje; Nacht-Stilte; Psalm   (D1397)

DIKTAREN OCH TIDEN see Taube, Evert

DIKTER AV F. NIETZSCHE, HEFT 1 see Peterson-Berger, (Olof) Wilhelm

DIKTER AV F. NIETZSCHE, HEFT 2 see Peterson-Berger, (Olof) Wilhelm

DILEMMANIANA VOOR MARRIE see Knap, Rolf

DILETTO E SPAVENTO DEL MARE see Ghedini, Giorgio Federico

DILETTO SPIRTUALE see Verovio, S.

DILLE CH'IL VIVIR MIO see Vivaldi, Antonio

DILLER-PAGE CAROL-BOOK, THE *CC34U, Xmas,carol
solo,pno SCHIRM.G $1.75   (D1398)

DILLER-PAGE CAROLBOOK, THE *sac,CC34U, Xmas
(Diller, Angela; Page, Kate Stearns) 1-2 soli,pno SCHIRM.G $1.75 (D1399)

DILLER-PAGE SONG-BOOK, VOL. I, THE *CCU,folk,Eur/US
solo,pno SCHIRM.G $1.50   (D1400)

DILLER-PAGE SONG-BOOK, VOL. II, THE *CCU,Eng/US
solo,pno SCHIRM.G $1.50   (D1401)

DILLIGER, JOHANN (1593-1647)
Eighteen Vocal Concertos *CC18U, concerto
(Eby, Margarette) solo,inst A-R ED s.p.   (D1402)

DILLON, FANNIE CHARLES (1881-1947)
Wild Rover
(Collinson) med solo,pno PAXTON P40613 s.p.   (D1403)

DIMANCHE see Brahms, Johannes, Sonntag

DIMANCHE D'AVRIL see Poldowski, Lady Dean Paul

DI MARTINO, ALADINO
Anniversario
see Due Liriche
Che Piu Potrei
see Due Liriche
Due Liriche
[It] solo,pno cmplt ed SANTIS 893 s.p.
contains: Anniversario; Che Piu Potrei   (D1404)

DI MINIELLO, CRESCENZIO
Ave Maria *sac
solo,pno SANTIS 337 s.p.   (D1405)

DIMITRI'S MONOLOG see Mussorgsky, Modest

DIMMI, CARA see Handel, George Frideric

DIMMI DI SI! see Kalman, Emerich

DIMMLER, L.
Meine Kleinen Lieder *CCU
(Wolki) solo,gtr SCHOTTS 4843 s.p.
(D1406)

DIMOV, BOJIDAR (1935-   )
Incantationes I *CCU
S solo,fl,trp,harp,vla MODERN rental   (D1407)
Incantationes II *CCU
S solo,fl,trp,2perc,harp,2vla, electric sound system MODERN rental   (D1408)
Raumspiel Teil 1 *CCU
S solo,5brass,4strings,pno GERIG HG 803 s.p.   (D1409)
Raumspiel Teil 2 *CCU
S solo,5brass,4strings,pno GERIG HG 824 s.p.   (D1410)

DIMPLED CHEEK see Somervell, Arthur

DIN BLICK EJ AV KARLEKEN SKYMMES see Hallnas, Hilding

DIN KARLEK see Bohm, Carl, Still Wie Die Nacht

DIN ROST see Sjogren, Emil

DIN TRADGARD BLOMMAR AN EN GANG see Hallnas, Hilding

DINA BLA OGON see Lewerth

DINA OGON ARO ELDAR see Peterson-Berger, (Olof) Wilhelm

DINA OGON ARO ELDAR see Soderstrom, Nils

DINA OGON OCH MINA OGON see Melartin, Erkki, Sinun Silmas Ja Minun Silmat

DINDIRINDIN see Anonymous

DINERSTEIN, N.
Four Settings *CC4U
S solo,4strings cmplt ed BOOSEY $4.50   (D1411)

DINNA FORGET see Bassett, Karolyn Wells

DINT' 'O SUONNO see Giazotto, Remo

D'INVERNO see Gandino, Adolfo

DIO DELL'OR see Gounod, Charles Francois

DIO DI GUIDA! see Verdi, Giuseppe

DIO! MI POTEVI SCAGLIAR TUTTI I MALI see Verdi, Giuseppe

DIO PIETOSO see Alfano, Franco

DIO POSSENTE, DIO D'AMOR see Gounod, Charles Francois

DIOGENES see Schouwman, Hans

DIONYSOS see Peterson-Berger, (Olof) Wilhelm

DIOUGAN GWENC' HLAN see Favre, Georges

DIR A NICKEL, MIR A NICKEL see Rumshinsky, Jos. M.

DIR, O HERR, GILT ALL MEIN HOFFEN see Schutz, Heinrich, In Te, Domine, Speravi

DIRALA D' SE?
(Carlo, Musi) solo,pno (Bolognese dialect) BONGIOVANI 2063 s.p. see from El Mi Canzunett   (D1412)

DIRGE see Hoag, Charles K.

DIRGE see Plessis, Hubert du

DIRGE see Rosemarin, Samson

DIRGE see Thomson, Virgil

DIRGE see Wishart

DIRGE IN WOODS see Copland, Aaron

DIRGE IN WOODS see Parry, Charles
Hubert Hastings

DIRIGADUR, DOMINE. ORATIO MEA see
Mancini, Vincenzo

DIRKSON, DAN
Reach Out, Take The Hand *sac
solo,pno BRIDGE Z 647 s.p. (D1413)

Shadow Of The Cross *sac
solo,pno BRIDGE Z 648 s.p. (D1414)

DIS-MOI DE TON COEUR see Poise, (Jean
Alexandre) Ferdinand

DIS-MOI PAUVRE HIRONDELLE see Schumann,
Robert (Alexander)

DIS-MOI, POURQUOI see Mussorgsky,
Modest

DIS-MOI POURQUOI see Scotto, Vincent

DISCIPLE'S PRAYER, A see O'Brien, Bill

DISCOVERY see Guastavino, Carlos,
Hallazgo

DISCOVERY see Owens

DISCOVOLO, M.
Favoletta
[It] solo,pno BONGIOVANI 2319 s.p.
(D1415)

DISCRETION see Ezaki, K.

DISCRETION see Godard, Benjamin Louis
Paul

DISMOI QUE JE SUIS BELLE see Massenet,
Jules

DISPERATA see Gubitosi, Emilia

DISPERATA see Morelli, A.

DISSONANCE see Borodin, Alexander
Porfirievitch

DISTANT FLUTE, THE see Sternberg, Erich
Walter

DISTLER, HUGO (1908-1942)
Drei Geistliche Konzerte *sac,
concerto
S solo,org (diff) cmplt ed BAREN.
1231 $4.25
contains: Es Ist Ein Kostlich
Ding, Op.17,No.1; Freuet Euch
In Dem Herrn, Op.17,No.2;
Lieben Bruder, Schicket Euch In
Die Zeit, Op.17,No.3 (D1416)

Drei Lieder *CC3U
A solo,pno (med) BAREN. 4116 $5.75
(D1417)
Es Ist Ein Kostlich Ding *Op.17,No.1
see Drei Geistliche Konzerte

Freuet Euch In Dem Herrn *Op.17,No.2
see Drei Geistliche Konzerte

It Is A Precious Thing
see Three Sacred Concertos

Kleine Sommerkantate *cant
SS soli,4strings (med easy) BAREN.
1064 $4.25 (D1418)

Lieben Bruder, Schicket Euch In Die
Zeit *Op.17,No.3
see Drei Geistliche Konzerte

Lied Am Herde
(Grabner, Hermann) med solo,pno
(diff) BAREN. 1979 $7.75 (D1419)

My Dear Brethren, Meet The Demands Of
This Time
see Three Sacred Concertos

O Rejoice In The Lord At All Times
see Three Sacred Concertos

Three Sacred Concertos *Op.17, sac
S/T solo,org,hpsd CONCORDIA 97-4925
$2.00
contains: It Is A Precious Thing;
My Dear Brethren, Meet The
Demands Of This Time; O Rejoice
In The Lord At All Times
(D1420)

DISTRACTED MAID, THE see Heseltine,
Philip

DISTURNA DI RISPETTI TOSCANI see
Petralia

DIT IS UW DEEL see King, Harold C.

DIT MIN TANKE GAR see Linko, Ernst
(Fredrik), Sinne

DITE ALMENO, IN CHE MANIERA see Mozart,
Wolfgang Amadeus

DITES-LUI see Chaminade, Cecile

DITHYRAMB EJ LANGRE TORSTA DU SKALL see
Peterson-Berger, (Olof) Wilhelm

DITSON TREASURY OF SACRED SONGS *sac,
CCU
low solo,pno PRESSER $2.50 (D1421)

DITT NAMM JAG HADE SKRIVIT see
Peterson-Berger, (Olof) Wilhelm

DITTENHAVER, SARAH LOUISE
Lady Of The Amber Wheat
high solo,pno GALAXY 1.1440.7 $1.00
(D1422)
DITTERSDORF, KARL DITTERS VON
(1739-1799)
Das Gustav-Lied Der Waschfrau Guste
(from Ein Roman In Der
Waschkuche)
[Ger] med-high solo,pno BOTE $1.00
(D1423)
Drei Italienische Konzertarien
(Rhau, Gunter) S solo,2ob,2horn,
strings voc sc BREITKOPF-W
EB 5952 $2.75
contains: Quanto Mai Felici
Siete; Quegli Orchietti; Quel
Contino E Un Po Furbetto
(D1424)
Quanto Mai Felici Siete
see Drei Italienische Konzertarien

Quegli Orchietti
see Drei Italienische Konzertarien

Quel Contino E Un Po Furbetto
see Drei Italienische Konzertarien

DITTRICH, PAUL-HEINZ (1930-   )
Qua-Sie
2 narrators,clar,pno,treb inst,vcl
GERIG HG 916 s.p. (D1425)

DITTY see Finzi, Gerald

DITTY see Koch, Johannes H.E.

DIVAN OF MOSES-IBN-EZRA, THE see
Castelnuovo-Tedesco, Mario

DIVCI PISNE see Hurnik, Ilja

DI VEROLI, MANILIO
Calling To Me
low solo,pno (F maj) CRAMER (D1426)
high solo,pno (A maj) CRAMER
(D1427)
It Isn't Raining There
solo,pno CRAMER (D1428)

DIVERSE SETTINGS see Simons, Netty

DIVERTIMENTO see Casanova, Andre

DIVERTIMENTO see Otten, Ludwig

DIVERTIMENTO I see Merku, Pavle

DIVERTIMENTO IN QUATTRO ESERCIZI see
Dallapiccola, Luigi

DIVERTISSEMENTS ET AIRS A DANSER see
Ravize, A.

DIVIDERCI DOBBIAM see Massenet, Jules

DIVINA KAREL *CCU,Xmas
[Czech/Eng] med solo,pno,strings
CZECH s.p. (D1429)

DIVINATION DE MARTHE see Mussorgsky,
Modest, Martha's Divination

DIVINITES DU STYX see Gluck, Christoph
Willibald Ritter von

DIX CHANSONS D'ENFANTS see Ravize, A.

DIX CHANSONS, POEMES DE JEAN CUTTAT see
Binet, Jean

DIX CHANSONS POPULAIRES see Ravize, A.

DIX CHANTS POUR LA JEUNESSE see
Schlosser, Paul

DIX, J. AIRLIE
Miller Of Winchelsea
low solo,pno (D maj) LEONARD-ENG
(D1430)
high solo,pno (E flat maj) LEONARD-
ENG (D1431)

Ould Side Car, The
low solo,pno (D flat maj) CRAMER
(D1432)
med solo,pno (E flat maj) CRAMER
(D1433)
high solo,pno (F maj) CRAMER
(D1434)
2 soli,pno (E flat maj) LEONARD-ENG

DIX, J. AIRLIE (cont'd.)
(D1435)
2 soli,pno (F maj) LEONARD-ENG
(D1436)
Sergeant Of Horse
low solo,pno (B flat maj) CRAMER
(D1437)
high solo,pno (C maj) CRAMER
(D1438)
Trumpeter
low solo,pno (F maj) BOOSEY $1.50
(D1439)
med solo,pno (G maj) BOOSEY $1.50
(D1440)
high solo,pno (A maj) BOOSEY $1.50
(D1441)
Trumpeter, The
high solo,pno (C maj) WILLIS $.75
(D1442)
low solo,pno (G maj) WILLIS $.75
(D1443)
DIX NOELS BOURGUIGNONS *CC10L,Fr,18th
cent
(Ravize, A.) solo,pno/inst DURAND
s.p. (D1444)
DIX NOELS ESPAGNOLS *CC10U,Xmas,Span
(Nin) [Span/Fr] med solo,pno ESCHIG
$8.75 (D1445)
DIX ROMANCES FRANCAISES see Noske, W.

DIX SONNETS DE SHAKESPEARE see
Kabalevsky, Dmitri Borisovitch

DIXIE NIGHT see Repper, Charles

DIXIT JESUS PETRO see Hindemith, Paul

DJUPT TILL STILLHETENS LJUSA VILA see
Tolonen, Jouko (Paavo Kalervo),
Syvan Aanettomyyden Syliin

DNES see Mikula, Zdenko

DO I LOVE YOU? see Diamond, David

DO IT AGAIN, LORD see Harrison, Dorothy

DO KOLECKA, DOKOLA see Novak, Milan

DO, LORD *sac,gospel
solo,pno ABER.GRP. $1.50 (D1446)

DO NOT AWAKE ME see Weigl, Vally

DO NOT BE AMAZED see Bender, Jan

DO NOT GO GENTLE see Mc Cabe

DO NOT GO, MY LOVE see Hageman, Richard

DO NOT UTTER A WORD see Barber, Samuel

DO, RE, MI, FA, SOL
(Carlo, Musi) solo,pno (Bolognese
dialect) BONGIOVANI 2075 s.p. see
from El Mi Canzunett (D1447)

DO THINE EYES IN WONDERMENT *folk,Jew
(Roskin) high solo&low solo,pno
HATIKVAH $.50 (D1448)

DO YOU CARE see Koechlin, Charles, Si
Tu Le Veux

DO YOU EVER THINK TO PRAY? *sac,gospel
solo,pno ABER.GRP. $1.50 (D1449)

DO YOU HEAR WHAT I HEAR? see Regney,
Noel

DO YOU KNOW JESUS? see Whittle

DO YOU KNOW MY JESUS? see Ellis

DO YOU KNOW THE CHRIST OF CHRISTMAS see
Peterson, John W.

DO YOU REALLY CARE? see Cates, Bill

DOBIAS, VACLAV (1909-   )
Kdoz Jste Bozi Bojovnici
solo,pno SUPRAPHON s.p. (D1450)

Prag Mein Einziges *song cycle
[Czech/Ger] solo,pno SUPRAPHON s.p.
(D1451)
Praho Jedina
solo,pno SUPRAPHON s.p. (D1452)

DOBOS, K.
Flashes
[Hung/Eng] S solo,vln,vcl,pno
BUDAPEST 5128 s.p. (D1453)

DOBSON, TOM
Cargoes
high solo,pno (F maj) SCHIRM.G $.75
(D1454)
DOCE ARIAS DE OPERAS see Mozart,
Wolfgang Amadeus

DOCE CANCIONES ESPANOLAS ANTIGUAS
  *CC12L
  (Lorcia, Garcia) [Span] solo,pno
  cmplt ed RICORDI-ARG BA 12128 s.p.
                                    (D1455)
DOCE CANCIONES INFANTILES see Mingote,
  A.

DOCE CANCIONES POPULARES ESPANOLAS
  *CC12U,Span
  (Toldra) [Span] med solo,pno UNION
  ESP. $3.75   (D1456)

DOCH MEIN VOGEL KEHRT NICHT WIEDER see
  Sibelius, Jean, Men Nin Fagel Marks
  Dock Inte

DOCKHORN, LOTTE
  Schalk Und Scherz
  solo,lute/gtr LEUCKART s.p. (D1457)

DOCTOR FAUSTUS see Diack, John Michael

DOCTOR FELL see Lessard, John Ayres

DODD, RUTH
  Share The Blessings *sac
  solo,pno WORD S-24   (D1458)

DODEN TANKTE JAG MIG SA see Hallnas,
  Hilding

DODGE, JOHN
  Gossiping (composed with Dodge, May)
  high solo,pno (D flat maj) WILLIS
    $.50   (D1459)
  low solo,pno (B flat maj) WILLIS
    $.50   (D1460)

DODGE, MAY
  Gossiping *see Dodge, John

DODICI CANTE ROMAGNOLE *CC12U
  (Pratella, G.B.) solo,pno BONGIOVANI
  1735 s.p.   (D1461)

DODICI DUETTI DA CAMERA see Martini,
  Giambattista

DODICI! GIROTONDO see Tocchi, Gian-Luca

DODICI NUOVE MELODIE see Gandino,
  Adolfo

DODINETTE see Marcelles, P.

DODO see Stravinsky, Igor

DODO NANETTE
  see Chants De France Vol. II

DODSFORNIMMELSEN see Marvia, Einari,
  Kuoleman Tantu

DODSON
  Confession Stone, The *sac
  (Fleming) solo,pno MCA $3.00 see
    from Songs Of Mary   (D1462)

  I Want To Stroll Over Heaven With You
    *sac
  solo,pno BENSON S6148-S $1.00
                                  (D1463)
  Songs Of Mary *see Confession Stone,
    The   (D1464)

DODSON, CAROLYN
  One Gift *sac
  med solo,pno CRESPUB CP-S5024 $1.00
                                  (D1465)

DODSPOLKA see Skold

DODUN
  see La Musique, Douzieme Cahier

DOE JE MEE see Smit, H.J.

DOEBLER, CURT (1896-   )
  Es Lebe Der Heilige Dreieinige Gott
  S solo,org SIRIUS s.p.   (D1466)

DOES JESUS CARE? *sac,gospel
  solo,pno ABER.GRP. $1.50   (D1467)

DOFTA, DOFTA, VIT SYREN see Alfven,
  Hugo, Berceuse

DOG-WOOD see Hively, Wells

DOGA, E.
  Here Is Our Motherland *CC5U
  [Russ] solo,pno MEZ KNIGA 71 s.p.
                                  (D1468)

DOG'S LIFE see Head, Michael (Dewar)

DOHL, FRIEDHELM (1936-   )
  Epitaph "Tich Yuang Tuc"
  S solo,clar,chamb.grp. GERIG HG 627
    s.p.   (D1469)

  Fragment "Sybille"
  Bar solo,fl,vla,vcl,pno sc GERIG
    s.p., ipa   (D1470)

DOHL, FRIEDHELM (cont'd.)
  Sieben Haiku *CC7U
  S solo,fl,pno GERIG HG 619 s.p.
                                  (D1471)
  Wenn Aber *CC9U
  Bar solo,pno GERIG HG 801 s.p.
                                  (D1472)

DOIT ET AVOIR see DuBois, Pierre Max

DOIT-ON LE DIRE? see Cuvillier, Charles

DOLANSKY, L.
  Pisne *CCU
  solo,pno SUPRAPHON s.p.   (D1473)

DOLCE FAR NIENTE see Sibelius, Jean

DOLCE O AMICI see Benvenuti, Giacomo

DOLCE SONNO see Cimara, Pietro

DOLD FORENING see Sibelius, Jean

DOLENTE IMMAGINE DI FILLE MIA see
  Bellini, Vincenzo

DOLIN, S.
  Chloris
  solo,pno BERANDOL BER 1307 $1.50
                                  (D1474)

DOLL'S SONG see Offenbach, Jacques

DOLLY'S REVENGE see Pontet, Henry

DOLMETSCH, ARNOLD (1858-1940)
  Have You Seen But A Whyte Lilie Grow
  solo,pno (F maj) BOOSEY $1.50
    contains also: My Lytell Pretty
    One (B flat maj)   (D1475)

  My Lytell Pretty One
  see Dolmetsch, Arnold, Have You
    Seen But A Whyte Lilie Grow

DOLORES
  Brook, The
  high solo,pno (D maj) LEONARD-ENG
                                  (D1476)
  low solo,pno (C maj) LEONARD-ENG
                                  (D1477)

DOLORES see Waldteufel, Emil

DOLPH
  Onward For God And My Country
  (composed with Waring, Tom)
  solo,pno SHAWNEE IA 43 $.60 (D1478)

DOLUKHANYAN, A.
  Collected Works, Vol. IV *CCU
  [Russ] solo,pno MEZ KNIGA 2.92 s.p.
                                  (D1479)

DOMANI see Caltabiano, S.

DOMANI VADO VIA see Gandino, Adolfo

D'OMBRE ET DE SOLEIL see Beydts, L.

DOMESTIC MOTTO see Clarke, Henry Leland

DOMINATOR, DOMINE see Giansetti,
  Giovanni Battista

DOMINE DEUS, AGNUS DEI see Bach, Johann
  Sebastian

DOMINE, DEUS MEUS see Carissimi,
  Giacomo

DOMINE, DOMINUS NOSTER see Campra,
  Andre

DOMINE, EXAUDI ORATIONEM MEAM see
  Selle, Thomas

DOMINE, LABIA MEA APERIES see Schutz,
  Heinrich

DOMINICAL see Ladmirault, Paul (Emile)

DOMINUS REGNAT see Kayser, Leif

DOMMANGE, L.
  Regnavit Dominus *sac
  solo,pno DURAND $.95   (D1480)

DON see Boulez, Pierre

DON BOSCO-JUGENDMESSE see Flury, A.

DON JUAN
  see Bruder Liederlich

DON QUICHOTTE see Courbois, J.-P.

DON QUICHOTTE see Lacome, Paul

DON QUICHOTTE A DULCINEE see Ravel,
  Maurice

DON QUIXOTE AND THE SHEEP see Lessard,
  John Ayres

DONATH, J.
  Hail Mary *sac
  high solo,pno PRESSER $.75 (D1481)
  low solo,pno PRESSER $.75   (D1482)

DONATI
  Due Liriche
  solo,pno cmplt ed FORLIVESI 12265
    s.p.
    contains: In Ogni Sera; Notturno
                                  (D1483)
  In Ogni Sera
  see Due Liriche

  Notturno
  see Due Liriche

  Preghiera A San Sergio *sac
  solo,pno FORLIVESI 11569 s.p.
                                  (D1484)

DONATI, PINO (1907-1975)
  Notte, Divina Notte *sac
  solo,fl,ob,clar,bsn,horn,trp,trom,
    harp sc CARISH 21781 s.p. (D1485)

  Pastorale
  solo,fl,ob,2clar,bsn,2horn,trp,
    tuba,harp CARISH s.p.   (D1486)

DONATO
  A Media Luz
  low solo,pno (C maj) CENTURY 3635
                                  (D1487)

DONATONI, FRANCO (1927-   )
  Serenata
  S solo,orch min sc ZERBONI 5605
    s.p.   (D1488)

DONAUDY, STEFANO (1879-1925)
  O Del Mio Amato Ben
  [It] S/T solo,pno RICORDI-ARG
    BA 8533 s.p.   (D1489)
  [It] Mez/Bar solo,pno RICORDI-ENG
    117226 s.p.   (D1490)
  "O, Vanished Loneliness" solo,pno
    BELWIN $1.50   (D1491)

  O, Likeness, Dim And Faded *see
    Vaghissima Sembianza

  O, Vanished Loneliness *see O Del
    Mio Amato Ben

  Spirate Pur, Spirate
  [It] S/T solo,pno RICORDI-ARG
    BA 8534 s.p.   (D1492)
  solo,pno BELWIN $1.50   (D1493)

  Vaghissima Sembianza
  [It] S/T solo,pno RICORDI-ENG
    117222 s.p.   (D1494)
  "O, Likeness, Dim And Faded" solo,
    pno BELWIN $1.50   (D1495)

DONC, CE SERA PAR UN CLAIR JOUR D'ETE
  see Gaubert, Philippe

DONDE HABITE EL OLVIDO see Guastavino,
  Carlos

DONDE LIETA USCI see Puccini, Giacomo

DONES SENCILLOS see Guastavino, Carlos

DONETTA see Pratella, Francesco Balilla

DONIZETTI, GAETANO (1797-1848)
  Angelo Casto E Bel (from Il Duca
    D'Alba)
  T solo,pno RICORDI-ENG 54411 s.p.
                                  (D1496)

  Ardon Gli'incensi (from Lucia Di
    Lammermoor)
  [It] S solo,pno RICORDI-ARG BA 8237
    s.p.   (D1497)
  S solo,pno RICORDI-ENG 54333 s.p.
                                  (D1498)
  (Liebling) "Mad Scene, The" [It/
    Eng] S solo,pno,fl (C min)
    SCHIRM.G $1.00   (D1499)

  Bella Siccome Un Angelo (from Don
    Pasquale)
  [It] Bar solo,pno RICORDI-ARG
    BA 11781 s.p.   (D1500)
  Bar solo,pno RICORDI-ENG 54441 s.p.
                                  (D1501)

  Com' E Gentil (from Don Pasquale)
  [It] T solo,pno RICORDI-ARG
    BA 11782 s.p.   (D1502)
  T solo,pno RICORDI-ENG 54409 s.p.
                                  (D1503)

  Composizioni Da Camera Vol. I *CC12L
  (Mingardo) [It/Fr] solo,pno
    RICORDI-ENG 130330 s.p.   (D1504)

  Composizioni Da Camera Vol. II
    *CC12L
  (Mingardo) [It/Fr/Ger] solo,pno
    RICORDI-ENG 130331 s.p.   (D1505)

  Convien Partir (from La Figlia Del
    Reggimento)
  [It] S solo,pno RICORDI-ARG BA 8517
    s.p.   (D1506)
  S solo,pno RICORDI-ENG 96261 s.p.

DONIZETTI, GAETANO (cont'd.)

(D1507)
Cruda, Funesta Smania (from Lucia Di
Lammermoor)
Bar solo,pno RICORDI-ENG 96284 s.p.
(D1508)
Da Ich Nun In Ihr Auge Sah (from
L'elisir D'amore)
T solo,fl,2ob,2clar,2bsn,horn,harp,
strings DEUTSCHER rental   (D1509)

Fra Poco A Me Ricovero (from Lucia Di
Lammermoor)
T solo,pno RICORDI-ENG 54415 s.p.
(D1510)
Mad Scene, The *see Ardon
Gli'incensi

Merce Dilette Amichi (from I Vespri
Siciliani)
high solo,pno (A min) ALLANS s.p.
(D1511)
O Luce Di Quest'anima (from Linda Di
Chamounix)
S solo,pno RICORDI-ENG 54331 s.p.
(D1512)
O Mio Fernando (from La Favorita)
S/Mez solo,pno RICORDI-ENG 54330
s.p.   (D1513)

Quanto E Bella, Quanto E Cara (from
L'Elsir D'Amore)
T solo,pno RICORDI-ENG 125874 s.p.
(D1514)
Regnava Nel Silenzio (from Lucia Di
Lammermoor)
[It] S solo,pno RICORDI-ARG BA 8518
s.p.   (D1515)
S solo,pno RICORDI-ENG 54332 s.p.
(D1516)
Sei Arie *CC6U
(Pestalozza, C.) [It] solo,pno
RICORDI-ENG 132182 s.p.   (D1517)

So Anch'io La Virtu Magica (from Don
Pasquale)
S solo,pno RICORDI-ENG 54329 s.p.
(D1518)
Spirto Gentil (from La Favorita)
[It] T solo,pno RICORDI-ARG BA 8531
s.p.   (D1519)
T solo,pno RICORDI-ENG 54414 s.p.
(D1520)
Terra Adorata De' Padri Miei (from
Don Sebastiano)
Mez solo,pno RICORDI-ENG 54381 s.p.
(D1521)
Tornami A Dir Che M'ami (from Don
Pasquale)
[It] ST soli,pno RICORDI-ARG
BA 11751 s.p.   (D1522)
S/T solo,pno RICORDI-ENG 127800
s.p.   (D1523)

Tu Che A Dio Spiegasti L'ali (from
Lucia Di Lammermoor)
[It] T solo,pno RICORDI-ARG
BA 11752 s.p.   (D1524)
T solo,pno RICORDI-ENG 128171 s.p.
(D1525)
Udite, Udite, O Rustici (from
L'Elisir D'Amore)
B solo,pno RICORDI-ENG 54472 s.p.
(D1526)
Una Furtiva Lagrima (from Don
Pasquale)
[It] T solo,pno RICORDI-ARG BA 8145
s.p.   (D1527)
T solo,pno RICORDI-ENG 54412 s.p.
(D1528)
high solo,pno (B flat min) ALLANS
s.p.   (D1529)

Una Vergin, Un Angel Di Dio (from La
Favorita)
T solo,pno RICORDI-ENG 54413 s.p.
(D1530)
Vi Skiljas At (from La Fille Du
Regiment)
solo,pno LUNDQUIST s.p.   (D1531)

Vien, Leonora, A' Piedi Tuoi (from La
Favorita)
Bar solo,pno RICORDI-ENG 54443 s.p.
(D1532)
Vieni, La Mia Vendetta (from Lucrezia
Borgia)
B solo,pno RICORDI-ENG 54463 s.p.
(D1533)
solo,pno (A flat maj) ASHDOWN
(D1534)

DONKEY RIDING
see Six Regional Canadian Folksongs

DONKEY RIDING see Pitfield, Thomas
Baron

DONKEY SERENADE, THE see Friml, Rudolf

DONNA BIANCA see Sinigaglia, Leone

DONNA, CHE IN CIEL see Handel, George
Frideric

DONNA LOMBARDA see Pizzetti, Ildebrando

DONNA NON VIDI MAI see Puccini, Giacomo

DONNE MIE, LA FATTE A TANTI see Mozart,
Wolfgang Amadeus

DONNE-MOI TON COEUR see Ganne, Louis
Gaston

DONNE, PIANSI see Zandonai, Riccardo

DONNE TES YEUX see Berger, Rod.

DONNE VAGHE see Paisiello, Giovanni

DONOSTIA, R.P.
Cuarto Melodies Catalanes *CC4U
[Fr/Span] med solo,pno ESCHIG $2.25
(D1535)
DONOVAN, RICHARD [FRANK] (1891-   )
Away, Delights
see Four Songs

Down By The Sally Gardens
med solo,pno GALAXY 1.1631.7 $1.00
(D1536)
Five Elizabethan Lyrics *CC5U
high solo,4strings AM.COMP.AL. sc
$8.25, ipa, voc sc $6.60 (D1537)

Four Songs
solo,pno NEW VALLEY $2.50
contains: Away, Delights; Here
Comes A Lusty Wooer; O Love,
How Thou Art Tired Out With
Rhyme!; Song For A Dance
(D1538)
Here Comes A Lusty Wooer
see Four Songs

O Love, How Thou Art Tired Out With
Rhyme!
see Four Songs

Song For A Dance
see Four Songs

DON'T BE WEARY TRAVELER *spir
(Burleigh, H. T.) high solo,pno
BELWIN $1.50   (D1539)
(Burleigh, H. T.) low solo,pno BELWIN
$1.50   (D1540)

DON'T COME IN SIR, PLEASE! see Scott,
Cyril Meir

DON'T EVER LET GO OF MY HAND see Brown,
Aaron

DON'T GO AWAY WITHOUT JESUS see Taylor,
L.

DON'T GO TO HEAVEN ALONE see Jensen,
Gordon

DON'T LET ME BE THE ONE *sac
solo,pno STAMPS 7263-RN $1.00 (D1541)

DON'T LET THAT HORSE EAT THAT VIOLIN
see Blank, Allan

DON'T LET THE SUN GO DOWN see Strachey,
J.

DON'T TAKE MY CROSS AWAY see Rambo

DON'T TALK TO ME OF SPRING see Young,
Victor

DON'T YOU WEEP WHEN I'M GONE *spir
(Burleigh, H. T.) med solo,pno BELWIN
$1.50   (D1542)

DOODE STEDEN see Sigtenhorst-Meyer,
Bernhard van den

DOOEDENMARSCH see Bosmans, Henriette

DOOR IN THE WALL, THE see Wuorinen,
Charles

DOOR WEL EN WEE see Hullebroeck, Em.

DOORNROOSJE see Mortelmans, Lodewijk

DOPIS NA HRANICI see Drejsl, Radim

DOPO! see Tosti, Francesco Paolo

DOPPELBAUER, JOSEF FRIEDRICH
(1918-   )
Drei Gesange (George) *CC3U
S solo,fl,vla,vcl sc DOBLINGER
08 818 $10.50   (D1543)

Salve Regina *sac
[Lat] S solo,org DOBLINGER 08 852
$2.00   (D1544)

DOPPELGLEICHNIS see Trunk, Richard

DORATI, ANTAL (1906-   )
Two Enchantments Of Li Tai Pe *CC2U
Bar solo,orch voc sc ZERBONI 6318
s.p.   (D1545)
DOREL, F.
Garden Of Your Heart
2 soli,pno (A flat maj) BOOSEY
$1.75   (D1546)

When My Ships Come Sailing Home
solo,pno (B flat maj) BOOSEY $1.50
(D1547)
DORET
Fleuris Dans Mon Esprit
solo,orch HENN s.p.   (D1548)

Je Chanterai Toujours
solo,orch HENN s.p.   (D1549)

Je Voudrais Quand Tous Deux
solo,orch HENN s.p.   (D1550)

DORFBILDER see Rubin, Marcel

DORFMUSIK see Fryberg, M.

DORFSCHWALBEN AUS OSTERREICH see
Strauss, Josef

DORFTANZ see Lothar, Mark

DORINE see Schmalstich, Clemens

DORMEUSE see Beekhuis, Hanna

DORMEUSE see Canal, Marguerite

DORMEUSE see Marinier, P.

DORMEZ see Delmet, Paul

DORMI! see Cimara, Pietro

DORMI, DORMI see Melichar

DORMI FANCIULLA CARA see Petralia

DORMI FANCIULLO.. DORMI! see Annovazzi,
N.

DORMI JESU see Scheel, J.G.

DORMIDITO LE VI YO see Santonja, O.

DORPSDANS see Colaco Osorio-Swaab,
Reine

DORS, CHER PETIT see Lacome, Paul

DORS, CHERE PRUNELLE see Sjogren, Emil

DORS EN PAIX see Delmet, Paul

DORS, MA CAPRINE, DORS see Chevreuille,
Raymond

DORS, MA PENSEE TE BERCE see Lacombe,
Paul

DORS, MA POUPEE see Rabey, Rene

DORS, MON ENFANT see Bakkers, M.

DORS MON ENFANT see Wagner, Richard

DORS, MON ENFANT CHERIE see Bozza,
Eugene

DORS MON PETIT ANGE see Strimer, Joseph

DORS MON SOLEIL see Philippart-
Gonzalez, Renee

DORSCHEN see Mulder, Herman

DORSEY
My Desire *sac,gospel
solo,pno ABER.GRP. $1.50   (D1551)

Today *sac,gospel
solo,pno ABER.GRP. $1.50   (D1552)

DORT, WO DIE KLAREN BACHLEIN see
Muller, Rudolf

DORT WU DIE ZEDER *Jew
solo,pno KAMMEN 3 $1.00   (D1553)

DORUMSGAARD, ARNE
Burleskar
solo,pno MUSIKK s.p.
contains: Eg Kryp, Op.13,No.1;
Skreddarsveinen, Op.13,No.2;
Trur Eg, Op.13,No.3   (D1554)

Dusk In The Enchanted Wood *Op.8,
CC10U
[Eng/Norw/Ger] Bar/B solo,pno NORSK
$2.75
see also: There's A Fjord, Op.8,
No.3   (D1555)

Eg Kryp *Op.13,No.1
see Burleskar

DORUMSGAARD, ARNE (cont'd.)

En Hustavle *Op.5,No.1
  see Overlandssanger

I Blahaug
  see Tre Songar

Kvelding
  see Tre Songar

Natt
  see Tre Songar

Overlandssanger
  solo,pno MUSIKK s.p.
    contains: En Hustavle, Op.5,No.1;
    Sovnen, Op.6,No.1   (D1556)

Skreddarsveinen *Op.13,No.2
  see Burleskar

Sovnen *Op.6,No.1
  see Overlandssanger

There's A Fjord *Op.8,No.3
  [Eng/Norw/Ger] S solo,pno NORSK
  $.65 see also Dusk In The
  Enchanted Wood   (D1557)

Tre Songar
  solo,pno MUSIKK s.p.
    contains: I Blahaug; Kvelding;
    Natt   (D1558)

Trur Eg *Op.13,No.3
  see Burleskar

DOS CANCIONES see Halffter, Ernesto

DOS CANCIONES see Turina, Joaquin

DOS CANCIONES see Garcia Leoz, J.

DOS CANCIONES see Chavez, Carlos

DOS CANCIONES CASTELLANAS DE GARCILASO
  DE LA VEGA see Olazabal, Zirso de

DOS CANCIONES PARA CANTAR A LOS NINOS
  see Rodrigo, Joaquin

DOS CANCIONES PARA LA NAVIDAD see
  Castillo, M.

DOS CANTARES GALAICO-PORTUGUESES DEL
  SIGLO XIII, OP. 18 see Caamano,
  Roberto

DOS CANTOS GALLEGOS, OP. 3 see Caamano,
  Roberto

DOS GEBET *folk,Jew
  (Roskin) Bar solo,vln,pno HATIKVAH
  $.75   (D1559)

DOS LID FUN YERUSHOLAYIM *folk,Jew
  high solo,pno HATIKVAH ED. 65 $.30
    (D1560)

DOS LID VUN DER ERD see Shir Ha-Adamah

DOS LIRICAS see Pardo

DOS PASACALLES see Marin, J.

DOS PAYSAGES see Villa-Lobos, Heitor

DOS PIEZAS see Siccardi, Honorio

DOS POEMAS see Rodrigo, Joaquin

DOS POEMAS DE JORGE MANRIQUE see Nin-
  Culmell, Joaquin

DOS SONETOS see Halffter, Rodolfo

DOS TONADOS LEVANTINAS see Espla, Oscar

DOS VILLANCICOS NAVIDENOS see Tarrago,
  G.

DOST THOU KNOW THAT FAIR LAND? see
  Thomas, Ambroise, Connais-Tu Le
  Pays

DOTAZNIK SRDCE see Podesva, Jaromir

DOTH NOT WISDOM CRY see Salomon, Karel

DOTTERN SADE see Stenhammar, Wilhelm

DOTTIE RAMBO-SONGBOOK see Rambo, Dottie

DOTTRINA IN MUSICA
  (Carlo, Musi) solo,pno (Bolognese
  dialect) BONGIOVANI 2043 s.p. see
  from El Mi Canzunett   (D1561)

D'OU VENEZ-VOUS? see Guiraud, Ernest

D'OU VENEZ-VOUS, FILLETTE
  see Chants De France Vol. I

D'OU VIENS-TU BERGER
  (Fragerolle, G.) solo,acap ENOCH s.p.
  see from Vieux Noels De France

    (D1562)
  (Fragerolle, G.) solo,pno ENOCH s.p.
  see from Vieux Noels De France
    (D1563)

DOUAY, G.
  Les Baisers D'Autrefois
    solo,pno ENOCH s.p.   (D1564)
    solo,acap solo pt ENOCH s.p.
    (D1565)

DOUBLE, THE see Schubert, Franz
  (Peter), Der Doppelganger

DOUBLE THE TROUBLE see Mana-Zucca, Mme.

DOUBRAVA, JAROSLAV (1909-1960)
  Carovna Laska *song cycle
  "Zauberliebe" low solo,pno
    SUPRAPHON s.p.   (D1566)

  Epigramme *see Epigramy

  Epigramy
  "Epigramme" med solo,pno CZECH s.p.
    (D1567)
  Gesang Der Heimat *see Zpev Rodneho
    Kraje

  Paradies Der Heimat *see Raj Domova

  Raj Domova
  "Paradies Der Heimat" med solo,pno
    SUPRAPHON s.p.   (D1568)

  Zauberliebe *see Carovna Laska

  Zpev Rodneho Kraje
  "Gesang Der Heimat" ST soli,pno
    CZECH s.p.   (D1569)

DOUBTING OR DREAMING see Thomas, Arthur
  Goring

DOUCE CHANSON see Messager, Andre

DOUCE FIEVRE see Y'Ener

DOUCE MER see Bizet, Georges

DOUCEMAITRESSE see Busser, Henri-Paul

DOUCEUR see Migot, Georges

DOUCEUR DE MON PAYS
  (Beziade; Beldent) solo,pno GRAS s.p.
    (D1570)

DOUCEUR DU SOIR DANS LE VILLAGE see
  Rhene-Baton

DOUG LAWRENCE *sac,CC11L
  solo,pno WORD 37737 $2.95   (D1571)

DOUG OLDHAM SONGBOOK *sac,CCUL
  med solo,pno,opt gtr SINGSPIR 4336
  $2.95   (D1572)

DOUGHERTY, CELIUS (1902-   )
  Across The Western Ocean
  med solo,pno (D maj) SCHIRM.G $.85
    see from Five Sea Chanties
    (D1573)

  Bird And The Beast, The
  med-low solo,pno (F maj) SCHIRM.G
  $.80   (D1574)

  Blow, Ye Winds
  med solo,pno (F maj) SCHIRM.G $.85
    see from Five Sea Chanties
    (D1575)

  Children's Letter To The United
    Nations, The
  med solo,pno SCHIRM.G $.60 (D1576)

  Declaration Of Independence
  med-low solo,pno (F maj) SCHIRM.G
  $.60   (D1577)

  First Christmas, The *sac
  high solo,pno (G maj) SCHIRM.G $.75
    (D1578)
  Five Sea Chanties *see Across The
    Western Ocean; Blow, Ye Winds;
    Rio Grande; Shenandoah   (D1579)

  Green Meadows
  med solo,pno (A maj) SCHIRM.G $.60
    (D1580)
  K'E, The *Chin
  med solo,pno (C maj) SCHIRM.G $.75
    (D1581)

  Listen! The Wind
  solo,pno BOOSEY $1.50   (D1582)

  Little Four Paws
  med-high solo,pno (F maj) SCHIRM.G
  $.75 see from Songs By E.E.
    Cummings   (D1583)

  Loveliest Of Trees
  solo,pno (D min) BOOSEY $1.50
    (D1584)
  Madonna Of The Evening Flowers
  solo,pno BOOSEY $1.50   (D1585)

  Minor Bird, A
  med solo,pno (F min) SCHIRM.G $.85
    (D1586)

DOUGHERTY, CELIUS (cont'd.)

  New England Pastoral
  solo,pno (F maj) BOOSEY $1.50
    (D1587)
  O By The By
  high solo,pno (F maj) SCHIRM.G $.75
    see from Songs By E.E. Cummings
    (D1588)

  Pianissimo
  med-high solo,pno (E maj) SCHIRM.G
  $.60   (D1589)

  Primavera
  high solo,pno (A flat maj) SCHIRM.G
  $.75   (D1590)

  Rio Grande
  med solo,pno (E flat maj) SCHIRM.G
  $.85 see from Five Sea Chanties
    (D1591)
  Shenandoah
  low solo,pno (D maj) SCHIRM.G $.85
    see from Five Sea Chanties
    (D1592)

  Sonatina
  med solo,pno (A maj) SCHIRM.G $.75
    (D1593)
  Song For Autumn
  med solo,pno (E min) SCHIRM.G $.75
    (D1594)

  Song Of Liberty
  solo,pno (E flat maj) BOOSEY $1.50
    (D1595)
  Song Of The Jasmine
  solo,pno (G flat maj) BOOSEY $1.50
    (D1596)
  Songs By E.E. Cummings *see Little
    Four Paws; O By The By; Thy
    Fingers Make Early Flowers
    (D1597)

  Sound The Flute
  med solo,pno (F maj) SCHIRM.G $.75
    (D1598)
  Stranger, The *sac
  high solo,pno (A flat maj) SCHIRM.G
  $.60   (D1599)

  Sweet Spring Is Your Time
  ST soli,pno SCHIRM.G $1.00 (D1600)
  SS soli,pno SCHIRM.G $1.00 (D1601)

  Thy Fingers Make Early Flowers
  high solo,pno (E flat maj) SCHIRM.G
  $.75 see from Songs By E.E.
    Cummings   (D1602)

  Until And I Heard
  high solo,pno (F maj) SCHIRM.G $.75
    (D1603)
  Upstream
  med solo,pno (B flat maj) SCHIRM.G
  $.75   (D1604)

DOUGLAS, A.
  Childs Thoughts, A *CCU
  solo,pno LEONARD-ENG   (D1605)

DOUGLAS GORDON see Kellie, Lawrence

DOULEUR D'AIMER see Trabadelo, A. de

DOULEURS see Wagner, Richard, Schmerzen

DOUN, E.
  Father In Heaven
  2 soli,pno (B flat maj) BOOSEY
  $1.75   (D1606)

DOUN IN YON BANK see Somervell, Arthur

DOUN THE BURN see Hook

DOUTE see Hermite, M.

D'OUTREMER see Scott, Cyril Meir, From
  Afar

DOUWDEUNTJE see Pijper, Willem

DOUX FOYER, SOIS BENI see Reissiger

DOUX FUT LE TRAIT see Caplet, Andre

DOUX LARCIN see Duvernoy, Victor-
  Alphonse

DOUX PLAISIR see Mana-Zucca, Mme.

DOUZE CHANSONS CANADIENNES *CC12U
  (Coutts, George) solo,pno WATERLOO
  $2.50   (D1607)

DOUZE CHANSONS POPULAIRES RUSSES D'HIER
  ET D'AUJOURD'HUI *CC12L
  [Fr] solo,pno CHANT s.p.   (D1608)

DOUZE CHANTS see Aubert, Louis-
  Francois-Marie

DOUZE CHANTS see Debussy, Claude

DOUZE CHANTS see Faure, Gabriel-Urbain

DOUZE CHANTS see Ravel, Maurice

DOUZE CHANTS see Saint-Saens, Camille

DOUZE CHANTS POUR VOIX MOYENNES see Poulenc, Francis

DOUZE DOUS *see Mendelssohn-Bartholdy, Felix, L'automne; Mendelssohn-Bartholdy, Felix, Le Bal Des Fleurs; Mendelssohn-Bartholdy, Felix, Les Bles; Mendelssohn-Bartholdy, Felix, Les Oiseaux Voyageurs; Mendelssohn-Bartholdy, Felix, Vogue, Leger Zephir; Mozart, Wolfgang Amadeus, C'est Elle (from Le Nozze Di Figaro); Mozart, Wolfgang Amadeus, Le Portrait (from Cosi Fan Tutte); Rameau, Jean-Philippe, Les Amants Trahis; Rameau, Jean-Philippe, Tambourin; Renaud, A., Au Bord De La Mer; Renaud, A., Habenera; Saint-Saens, Camille, Aux Conquerants De L'Air; Saint-Saens, Camille, El Desdichado; Saint-Saens, Camille, La Brise; Saint-Saens, Camille, Pastorale; Saint-Saens, Camille, Venus   (D1609)

DOUZE DOUS see Schumann, Robert (Alexander)

DOUZE DUOS see Mendelssohn-Bartholdy, Felix

DOUZE DUOS see Schumann, Robert (Alexander)

DOUZE MELODIES see Beethoven, Ludwig van

DOUZE MELODIES see Godard, Benjamin Louis Paul

DOUZE MELODIES see Chavagnat, Ed.

DOUZE POEMES see Poulenc, Francis

DOVE see Landers, Bill

DOVE, THE see Ronald, Sir Landon

DOVE, J.
  Glorious Time Of The Year
    solo,pno (D flat maj) BOOSEY $1.50
                                    (D1610)
DOVE SAYS COO, THE see Fiske, R.

DOVE SONG, THE see Moore, Douglas Stuart

DOVE SONO see Mozart, Wolfgang Amadeus

DOVE STA AMORE see Perera, Ronald

DOVER BEACH see Barber, Samuel

DOVUNQUE see Cimara, Pietro

DOWLAND, JOHN (1563-1626)
  Achtzehn Lieder *CC18U
    (Behrend, Siegfried) [Eng] solo,gtr
    SIKORSKI 558 s.p.   (D1611)

  Come Again, Sweet Love
    (Pujol) med solo,gtr ESCHIG E1315
    $2.50   (D1612)

  Drei Lieder Mit Gitarre *CC3U
    [Ger/Eng] med solo,gtr sc,oct
    UNIVER. 12403 $2.75   (D1613)

  Fifty Songs, Bk. 1 *CCU
    high solo,pno STAINER 3.3334.7
    $3.50; low solo,pno STAINER
    3.3336.7 $3.50   (D1614)

  Fifty Songs, Bk. 2 *CCU
    high solo,pno STAINER 3.3335.7
    $3.50; low solo,pno STAINER
    3.3337.7 $3.50   (D1615)

  First Book Of Ayres *CCU
    solo,pno STAINER 3.1343.7 $5.50
                                 (D1616)
  Pilgrimes Solace And Three Songs From
    A Musicall Banquet *CCU
    solo,pno STAINER 3.1341.7 $7.50
                                 (D1617)
  Second Book Of Ayres *CCU
    solo,pno STAINER 3.1340.7 $5.50
                                 (D1618)
  Sieben Lieder Aus Der Lautentabulatur
    *CC7U
    (Scheit, K.) [Ger/Eng] solo,pno
    UNIVER. 11842 $3.75   (D1619)

  Third Book Of Songs *CCU
    solo,pno STAINER 3.1337.7 $5.50
                                 (D1620)
  Two Songs *CC2U
    (Behrend) S solo,A rec,gtr BOTE
    $2.25   (D1621)

DOWLAND, ROBERT (1586-1641)
  Musical Banquet, A (1610) *CCU
    solo,pno STAINER 3.1334.7 $7.50
                                 (D1622)
DOWN AT THE DOCKS see Thomson, Virgil

DOWN BY THE CRYSTAL FOUNTAIN see A La Claire Fontaine

DOWN BY THE SALLEY GARDENS see Blank, Allan

DOWN BY THE SALLY GARDENS see Donovan, Richard [Frank]

DOWN BY THE SALLY GARDENS see Hughes, Herbert

DOWN BY THE SALLY GARDENS see Methold, Diana

DOWN BY THE SIDE OF THE RIVER *sac, gospel
    solo,pno ABER.GRP. $1.50   (D1623)

DOWN FROM HIS GLORY see Booth

DOWN FROM HIS GLORY see Clibborn

DOWN GLANNA WAY see Corrie, J.

DOWN HERE see Brahe, May H.

DOWN IN THE FOREST see Ronald, Sir Landon

DOWN IN THE MEADOW see Mon Pere A Fait Batir Maison

DOWN THE FLOWING STREAM see Newton, Ernest

DOWN THE HWAI see Bantock, Granville

DOWN THE VALE see Moir, F.L.

DOWN VAUXHALL WAY see Oliver, Herbert

DOWNINGS-SONGBOOK, THE *sac,CC12UL
    solo,pno BENSON BO955 $2.50   (D1624)

DOYEN, ALBERT (1882-1935)
  A Ceux Qui Partent
    see Poeme Lyrique

  Au Musee
    see Poeme Lyrique

  Danse
    see Sur Des Poemes D'Andre Spire

  Invective
    see Poeme Lyrique

  La Tristesse
    see Poeme Lyrique

  Le Chant De Zarathoustra
    see Poeme Lyrique

  Le Ciel Est Par-Desses Le Toit
    see Poeme Lyrique

  Le Foyer
    solo,pno/inst LEDUC s.p.   (D1625)

  L'Heure Du Berger
    solo,pno/inst LEDUC s.p.   (D1626)

  Ne...
    see Sur Des Poemes D'Andre Spire

  Nuit
    see Sur Des Poemes D'Andre Spire

  Poeme Lyrique
    med solo,pno/inst LEDUC s.p.
    contains: A Ceux Qui Partent; Au
      Musee; Invective; La Tristesse;
      Le Chant De Zarathoustra; Le
      Ciel Est Par-Desses Le Toit
                                  (D1627)
  Possession
    see Sur Des Poemes D'Andre Spire

  Sur Des Poemes D'Andre Spire
    high solo,pno/inst LEDUC s.p.
    contains: Danse; Ne...; Nuit;
      Possession; Traversee; Vacanes
                                  (D1628)
  Traversee
    see Sur Des Poemes D'Andre Spire

  Vacanes
    see Sur Des Poemes D'Andre Spire

DR. CLASH AND SIGNOR FALASOLE see Flagello, Nicholas

DRAAG NU DEN OLIJFTAK AAN see Pomper, A.

DRAEGER, WALTER
  Zwiegesang *CC6U
    s.p. S solo,vln,pno BREITKOPF-L
    EB 5888; S solo,pno BREITKOPF-L
    EB 5888   (D1629)

DRAKE, THE see Stravinsky, Igor

DRAKE'S DRUM see Hedgecock, Walter William

DRAKE'S DRUM see Stanford, Charles Villiers

DRAKE'S DRUM see Wheeler, J.R.

DRAUMAR I STJERNESNO see Egge, Klaus

DRAUSSEN BRICHT DAS EIS see Kilpinen, Yrio, Ei Sula Syan Suruinen

DRAZAN, JOSEF (1909-   )
  Noci *CC2U
    med solo,pno CZECH s.p.   (D1630)

DREAM see Grieg, Edvard Hagerup, Ein Traum

DREAM see Lora, Antonio

DREAM, A see Bartlett, J.C.

DREAM, A see Grieg, Edvard Hagerup, Ein Traum

DREAM, THE see Beethoven, Ludwig van

DREAM, THE see Rachmaninoff, Sergey Vassilievitch

DREAM, THE see Sibelius, Jean, Drommen

DREAM CLOUD see Hill

DREAM DIALOGUE FOR SOPRANO AND PERCUSSION see Steiner, Gitta

DREAM FACES see Hutchison, William M.

DREAM MINUET see Bateman, Ronald

DREAM OF CHRISTMAS, A see Holst, Gustav

DREAM OF DELIGHT see Rubinstein, Anton

DREAM OF HOME see Arditi, Luigi, Il Bacio

DREAM OF LOVE see Liszt, Franz, Liebestraum

DREAM OF OLWEN see Williams, C.

DREAM OF OLWEN, THE see Rosenmuller, Johann

DREAM OF PARADISE, A see Gray, Hamilton

DREAM PEDLARY see Parry, Charles Hubert Hastings

DREAM PEDLARY see Williams, W.S.Gwynn

DREAM SELLER, THE see Lee, E. Markham

DREAM VALLEY see Quilter, Roger

DREAM VESSELS see Tunks, Ada

DREAM VILLAGE see Rowley, Alec

DREAM WITHIN A DREAM, A see Blatter, Alfred

DREAMING see Hamblen, Bernard

DREAMING LAKE see Head, Michael (Dewar)

DREAMLAND see Mulder, Herman

DREAMLAND CITY see Arundale, Claude

DREAMS see Hope, H. Ashworth

DREAMS see Strelezki, Anton

DREAMS see Wagner, Richard, Traume

DREAMS see Warren, Elinor Remick

DREAMS OF THE SEA see Naylor, Bernard

DREI ABENDLIEDER NACH WORTEN VON WOLFRAM BROCKMEIER see Thomas, Kurt

DREI ADVENTLIEDER see Burkhart, Franz

DREI ALTAGYPTISCHE GEDICHTE see Reutter, Hermann

DREI ALTTESTAMENTLICHE SPRUCHE see Hufschmidt, Wolfgang

DREI ARIEN see Staromieyski, J.

DREI ARIEN see Haydn, (Johann) Michael

DREI ARIEN AUF TEXTE VON FRIEDRICH G. KLOPSTOCK see Oboussier, Robert

DREI ARIEN AUS DEM SEIBZEHNTEN JAHRHUNDERT *17th cent (Runge) high solo,gtr SCHOTTS 10164 s.p.
   contains: Anonymous, Have You Seene But A Whyte Lillie Grow?; Caccini, Giulio, Amarilli; Monteverdi, Claudio, Lasciatemi Morire   (D1631)

DREI ARIEN DER DEIDAMIA see Scarlatti, Domenico

DREI BALLADEN see Bijvanck, Henk

DREI BAROCK-LIEDER see Petersen, Wilhelm

DREI CHANSONS see Jelinek, Hanns

DREI CHANSONS see Blacher, Boris

DREI CHINESISCHE LIEDER see Kox, Hans

DREI CHORALKONZERTE see Schein, Johann Hermann

DREI COPLAS see Kox, Hans

DREI DEUTSCHE VOLKSLIEDER AUS "DES KNABEN WUNDERHORN" see Reznicek, Emil Nikolaus von

DREI DINGE VERSUSSEN DAS LEBEN see Eysler, Edmund S.

DREI DUETTE see Philipp, Franz

DREI DUETTE see Emborg, Jens Laurson

DREI EICHENDORFF-LIEDER see Taubert, Karl Heinz

DREI EVANGELIEN-KONZERTE see Graap, Lothar

DREI FABELN see Kricka, Jaroslav

DREI FRAGMENTE NACH HOLDERLIN UND DREI TENTOS AUS "KAMMERMUSIK 1958" see Henze, Hans Werner

DREI GEDICHTE VON R. DEHMEL see Gilse, Jan van

DREI GEISHA LIEDER, O-SEN see Verhaar, Ary

DREI GEISTLICHE GESANGE see Raphael, Gunther

DREI GEISTLICHE GESANGE see Kropfreiter, Augustinius Franz

DREI GEISTLICHE GESANGE see Raphael, Gunther

DREI GEISTLICHE GESANGE see Dvorak, Antonin

DREI GEISTLICHE GESANGE (1931) see Raphael, Gunther

DREI GEISTLICHE KONZERTE see Hammerschmidt, Andreas

DREI GEISTLICHE KONZERTE see Distler, Hugo

DREI GEISTLICHE KONZERTE see Viadana, Lodovico Grossi da

DREI GEISTLICHE KONZERTE see Grandi, Alessandro

DREI GEISTLICHE KONZERTE see Viadana, Lodovico Grossi da

DREI GEISTLICHE KONZERTE see Viadana, Lodovico Grossi da

DREI GEISTLICHE KONZERTE see Anerio, Giovanni Francesco

DREI GEISTLICHE KONZERTE see Caprioli, Giovanni Paolo

DREI GEISTLICHE LIEDER see Schwarz-Schilling, Reinhard

DREI GEISTLICHE LIEDER see Mitterhofer, Alfred

DREI GEISTLICHE LIEDER see Haas, Joseph

DREI GEISTLICHE VOLKSTEXTE see Webern, Anton von

DREI GESANGE see Webern, Anton von

DREI GESANGE see Krenek, Ernst

DREI GESANGE see Gilse, Jan van

DREI GESANGE see Hermann, H.

DREI GESANGE see Reutter, Hermann

DREI GESANGE AUS "DIE LIEDER VON TRAUM UND TOD" see Apostel, Hans Erich

DREI GESANGE AUS R. TAGORE'S "DER GARTNER" see Gilse, Jan van

DREI GESANGE AUS R. TAGORE'S "GITANJALI" see Gilse, Jan van

DREI GESANGE (GEORGE) see Doppelbauer, Josef Friedrich

DREI GESANGE NACH GEDICHTEN VON ANDREAS GRYPHIUS see Motte, Diether de la

DREI GESANGE NACH GEDICHTEN VON HOLDERLIN see Weismann, Wilhelm

DREI GESANGE NACH HOLDERLIN see Killmayer, Wilhelm

DREI GESANGE NACH LATEINISCHEN PSALMENTEXTEN see Ahrens, Sieglinde

DREI GESANGE NACH MITTELHOCHDEUTSCHEN DICHTUNGEN see Hausegger, Siegmund von

DREI GESANGE VON PAUL VERLAINE see Trexler, Georg

DREI GOETHE-LIEDER see Ehrenberg, Carl Emil Theodor

DREI GOETHELIEDER see Trapp, Max

DREI HAUSLICHE LIEDER NACH GEDICHTEN VON JO EHLERS see Heiss, Hermann

DREI HEITERE LIEDER see Roselius, Ludwig

DREI HEITERE LIEDER see Lothar, Mark

DREI HERBSTGESANGE see Beck, Conrad

DREI HOHELIEDMOTETTEN *sac,CC3U,mot (Ewerhart, Rudolf) [Lat] S/T solo, cont BIELER CS 23 s.p. contains works by: Monteverdi, Claudio; Bernardi, Steffano; Grandi, Alessandro   (D1632)

DREI HYMNISCHE GESANGE see Sibelius, Jean

DREI ITALIENISCHE KONZERTARIEN see Dittersdorf, Karl Ditters von

DREI KLAVIERLIEDER see Wildgans, Friedrich

DREI KLEINE GEISTLICHE KONZERTE see Hufschmidt, Wolfgang

DREI LIEBESLIEDER see Nedbal, Manfred J.M.

DREI LIEBESLIEDER see Marx, Karl

DREI LIEBESLIEDER see Zechlin, Ruth

DREI LIEBESLIEDER see Landre, Willem

DREI LIEDER see Westerman, G. von

DREI LIEDER see Haass, Hans

DREI LIEDER see Petzold, Rudolf

DREI LIEDER see Abendroth, Walther

DREI LIEDER see Abendroth, Walther

DREI LIEDER see Strauss, Richard

DREI LIEDER see Webern, Anton von

DREI LIEDER see Webern, Anton von

DREI LIEDER see Distler, Hugo

DREI LIEDER see Skorzeny, Fritz

DREI LIEDER see Rinaldini, Dr. Joseph

DREI LIEDER see Schiske, Karl

DREI LIEDER see Haydn, (Franz) Joseph

DREI LIEDER see Badings, Henk

DREI LIEDER see Landre, Willem

DREI LIEDER see Rontgen, Johannes

DREI LIEDER see Giltay, Berend

DREI LIEDER see Reimann, Aribert

DREI LIEDER see Roselius, Ludwig

DREI LIEDER see Pfitzner, Hans

DREI LIEDER see Reutter, Hermann

DREI LIEDER see Reutter, Hermann

DREI LIEDER see Reutter, Hermann

DREI LIEDER see Sibelius, Jean

DREI LIEDER see Pfanner, Adolf

DREI LIEDER see Borris, Siegfried

DREI LIEDER see Schumann, Georg

DREI LIEDER see Schumann, Georg

DREI LIEDER see Schumann, Georg

DREI LIEDER see Schoeck, Othmar

DREI LIEDER see Mixa, Franz

DREI LIEDER see Mixa, Franz

DREI LIEDER see Saladin, O.

DREI LIEDER AUF GEDICHTE VON EMIL HECKER see Micheelsen, Hans-Friedrich

DREI LIEDER AUF GEDICHTE VON F.TH. CSOKORA see Reiner, Karel

DREI LIEDER AUF WORTE FRANZOSISCHER POESIE see Balos, Fr.

DREI LIEDER AUS DER "STIMMEN DER STILLE", OP. 18 see Borris, Siegfried

DREI LIEDER AUS LILOFEE see Roselius, Ludwig

DREI LIEDER AUS SCHILLERS WILHELM TELL see Liszt, Franz

DREI LIEDER BY POLITZER see Orland, Henry

DREI LIEDER DER ANDACHT see Roselius, Ludwig

DREI LIEDER DER MIGNON see Tolonen, Jouko (Paavo Kalervo)

DREI LIEDER (DRAMATISCHE GEBETE VON EUGENIE FINK) see Bijvanck, Henk

DREI LIEDER FUR BARITON see Steffen, Wolfgang

DREI LIEDER FUR EINE SINGSTIMME UND KLAVIER see Kurzbach, Paul

DREI LIEDER FUR HOHE STIMME see Mirandolle, Ludovicus

DREI LIEDER FUR SOPRAN UND ORCHESTER see Edler, Robert

DREI LIEDER FUR SOPRANSTIMME see Diepenbrock, Alphons

DREI LIEDER MIT GITARRE see Dowland, John

DREI LIEDER NACH EICHENDORFF UND HEBBEL see Oboussier, Robert

DREI LIEDER NACH GEDICHTEN VON EICHENDORFF see Schwarz-Schilling, Reinhard

DREI LIEDER ON POEMS BY E. HECKER see Micheelsen, Hans-Friedrich

DREI LYRISCHE CHANSONS see Wimberger, Gerhard

DREI MARIEN-LEGENDEN AUS DEN WUNDERHORN-LIEDERN see Handel, George Frideric

DREI MARIENLIEDER see Lothar, Mark

DREI MARIENMOTETTEN see Nivers, Guillaume Gabriel

DREI MONOLOGE DES EMPEDOKLES see Reutter, Hermann

DREI MORGENSTERNLIEDER see Seiber, Matyas

DREI MOTETTEN see Milans, Tomas

DREI MOTETTEN *sac,CC3U,mot,Span,18th
cent
(Ewerhart, Rudolf) [Lat] S/A/T/B
solo,cont BIELER CS 21 s.p. (D1633)

DREI MYSTISCHE GESANGE see Lafite, C.

DREI NARRENLIEDER AUS SHAKESPEARES "WAS
IHR WOLLT" see Angerer, Paul

DREI NEUGRIECHISCHE GEDICHTE see
Dvorak, Antonin

DREI NOCTURNES NACH SAPPHO see
Kounadis, Arghyris

DREI PERSISCHE LIEDER see Ruyneman,
Daniel

DREI PSALMEN see Blacher, Boris

DREI PSALMFRAGMENTE see Lohr, Ina

DREI RILKE-GESANGE see Fromm-Michaels,
Ilse

DREI RILKELIEDER see Zagwijn, Henri

DREI SCHONE DINGE SEIND see Schutz,
Heinrich

DREI SEEMANNSLIEDER see Girnatis,
Walter

DREI SHAKESPEARE-LIEDER see Kochan,
Gunter

DREI SOLDATEN see Crome, Fritz, Tre
Soldater

DREI SONETTE VON SHAKESPEARE see
Vostrak, Zbynek

DREI SONETTE VON W. SHAKESPEARE see
Reimann, Aribert

DREI SPANISCHE LIEDER see Reimann,
Aribert

DREI TIERLIEDER see Eder, Helmut

DREI TRAURIGE TANZE see Bois, Rob du

DREI TRAUTE GESANGE see Ferroud,
Pierre-Octave

DREI WEIHNACHTSGESANGE see Schollum,
Robert

DREI WEIHNACHTSLIEDER see Martin, Frank

DREI WEIHNACHTSLIEDER see Schroeder,
Hermann

DREI ZIGEUNERROMANZEN see Reutter,
Hermann

DREISSIG AUSGEWAHLTE LIEDER see
Schumann, Robert (Alexander)

DREISTIMMIGE CANZONETTEN, HEFT I see
Monteverdi, Claudio

DREISTIMMIGE CANZONETTEN, HEFT II see
Monteverdi, Claudio

DREISTIMMIGE CANZONETTEN, HEFT III see
Monteverdi, Claudio

DREIUNDACHTZIG GEISTLICHE LIEDER UND
ARIEN AUS SCHMELLIS GESANGBUCH UND
DEM NOTENBUCH DER ANNA MAGDALENA
BACH see Bach, Johann Sebastian

DREIUNDDREISSIG BALLADEN UND LIEDER,
BAND I & II see Loewe, Carl

DREIUNDDREISSIG PSALMLIEDER DES KASPAR
ULENBERG *sac,CCU
(Lohmann, A.) solo,org CHRIS 50857
s.p. (D1634)

DREIUNDDREISSIG VOLKSLIEDER see
Neumeyer, Fritz

DREIUNDZWANZIG GESANGE IN NEUER AUSWAHL
see Wolf, Hugo

DREIUNDZWANZIG KINDERLIEDER see Knab,
Armin

DREIZEHN ARIEN AUS MOZARTS MESSEN,
VESPERN, MOTETTEN UND KANTATEN see
Mozart, Wolfgang Amadeus

DREIZEHN GESANGE NACH WORTEN VON FRANZ
KAFKA see Heiss, Hermann

DREIZEHN KLEINE LIEDER see Jelinek,
Hanns

DREIZEHN MOTTETEN see Hindemith, Paul

DREJSL, RADIM (1923-1953)
Brief An Die Grenze *see Dopis Na
Hranici

Dopis Na Hranici
"Brief An Die Grenze" med female
solo,pno CZECH s.p. (D1635)

Gegenden Der Kindheit *see Krajiny
Detstvi

Krajiny Detstvi
"Gegenden Der Kindheit" med solo,
pno CZECH s.p. (D1636)

Lied Uber Dem Kind *see Pisen Nad
Ditetem

Pijacke Pisne *CCU
B solo,pno CZECH s.p. (D1637)

Pisen Nad Ditetem
"Lied Uber Dem Kind" med solo,pno
CZECH s.p. (D1638)

DRESDEN, SEM (1881-1957)
Als Ik Van Uw Effen Voorhoofd
see Drie Liedjes Van Jacques Perk

Bij Den Vijver
med solo,pno ALSBACH s.p. (D1639)

Catena Musicale
S solo,4fl,3ob,2clar,2bsn,4horn,
3trp,3trom,timp,perc,cel,harp,
xylo,strings DONEMUS s.p. (D1640)

De Fluitspeler
med solo,pno ALSBACH s.p. (D1641)

Der Lustige Ehemann
med solo,pno ALSBACH s.p. (D1642)

Die Altijd Droomloos Sliep
see Vier Liederen

Drie Liedjes Van Jacques Perk
med solo,pno ALSBACH s.p.
contains: Als Ik Van Uw Effen
Voorhoofd; 'K Wil U Eens Wat
Zeggen Blondje; Leg Uw Beide
Blanke Handjes (D1643)

En Ied'ren Nacht
see Vier Liederen

Gefunden
low solo,pno ALSBACH s.p. (D1644)

'K Wil U Eens Wat Zeggen Blondje
see Drie Liedjes Van Jacques Perk

Kerstlied *sac
med solo,3trom,perc,strings DONEMUS
s.p. (D1645)

Leg Uw Beide Blanke Handjes
see Drie Liedjes Van Jacques Perk

Liebster! Nur Dich Seh'n
low solo,pno ALSBACH s.p. (D1646)
solo,pno ALSBACH s.p. (D1647)

Mijn Vrienden
see Vier Liederen

O Merel
see Vier Liederen

Oud Spinet
med solo,pno ALSBACH s.p. (D1648)

Rembrandt's "Saul En David"
S solo,3fl,3ob,2clar,3bsn,4horn,
3trp,3trom,timp,perc,cel,harp,
xylo,strings DONEMUS s.p. (D1649)

Treurig, Treurig
med solo,pno ALSBACH s.p. (D1650)

Vier Liederen
med solo,pno DONEMUS s.p.
contains: Die Altijd Droomloos
Sliep; En Ied'ren Nacht; Mijn
Vrienden; O Merel (D1651)

Vier Vocalises *CC4U,vocalise
Mez solo,fl,clar,bsn,perc,pno,vln,
vla voc sc DONEMUS s.p. (D1652)

DRESSEL, ERWIN (1909-)
Tierlieder *CCU
solo,pno RIES s.p. (D1653)

DRESSLER, L.R.
Christ Is Risen
high solo,pno,opt vln PRESSER $.75
(D1654)

DREVENY KRISTUS see Hanus, Jan

DREY MINNELIEDER see Martin, Frank

DREYFUS!
(Carlo, Musi) solo,pno (Bolognese
dialect) BONGIOVANI 2052 s.p. see
from El Mi Canzunett (D1655)

DRIE BECKETT-SANGE see Christensen,
Henning

DRIE CHINEESCHE LIEDEREN see Pluister,
Simon

DRIE CHRISTELIJKE LIEDEREN see Bonset,
Jac.

DRIE DANSWIJZEN see Schouwman, Hans

DRIE DANSWIJZEN OP OUD-NEDERLANDSE
GEDICHTEN see Schouwman, Hans

DRIE DUETTEN see Dijk, Jan van

DRIE DULLAERT LIEDEREN see Badings,
Henk

DRIE FABELEN VAN R.M. RILKE see King,
Harold C.

DRIE GEDICHTEN VAN A. DONKER see
Lilien, Ignace

DRIE GEDICHTEN VAN J. LUYKEN see
Voormolen, Alexander Nicolas

DRIE GEDICHTEN VAN P.C. BOUTENS see
Schouwman, Hans

DRIE GEDICHTEN VAN R.M. RILKE see
Voormolen, Alexander Nicolas

DRIE GEESLIJKE LIEDEREN OP OUDE
ENGELSCHE TEKSTEN see Badings, Henk

DRIE GEESTELIJKE LIEDEREN see Horst,
Anton van der

DRIE GEESTELIJKE LIEDEREN see Bonset,
Jac.

DRIE GEESTELIJKE LIEDEREN see Brandts-
Buys, H.

DRIE GEESTELIJKE LIEDEREN VAN JAN
LUYKEN see Badings, Henk

DRIE GEZELLE LIEDEREN see Wijker, H.

DRIE KERSTLIEDEREN see Beekhuis, Hanna

DRIE KERSTLIEDEREN see Badings, Henk

DRIE LATIJNSE MINNELIEDEREN see Mul,
Jan

DRIE LATIJNSE MINNELIEDEREN see Mul,
Jan

DRIE LIEDER OP NEDERLANDSE TEKST see
Beyerman-Walraven, Jeanne

DRIE LIEDEREN see Adriessen, Willem

DRIE LIEDEREN see Beekhuis, Hanna

DRIE LIEDEREN see Boedijn, Gerard H.

DRIE LIEDEREN see Bijvanck, Henk

DRIE LIEDEREN see Henkemans, Hans

DRIE LIEDEREN see Mengelberg, Rudolf

DRIE LIEDEREN see Vredenburg, Max

DRIE LIEDEREN see Adriessen, Willem

DRIE LIEDEREN see Niel, Matty

DRIE LIEDEREN see Mulder, Herman

DRIE LIEDEREN see Appeldoorn, Dina

DRIE LIEDEREN see Zagwijn, Henri

DRIE LIEDEREN see Cohen, M.J.

DRIE LIEDEREN see Iordens, J.D.R.

DRIE LIEDEREN see Sanders, Paul F.

DRIE LIEDEREN see Post, Piet

DRIE LIEDEREN OP DUITSE TEKST see
Bosmans, Henriette

DRIE LIEDEREN OP GEDICHTEN VAN GASTON
BURSSENS see Baeyens, August-L.

DRIE LIEDEREN OP GEDICHTEN VAN JAN
GRESHOFF EN JUSTUS DE HARDUYN see
Baeyens, August-L.

DRIE LIEDEREN OP GEDICHTEN VAN VICTOR
J. BRUNCLAIR see Baeyens, August-L.

DRIE LIEDEREN UIT "LENTEMAAN" see
Badings, Henk

DRIE LIEDEREN UIT P. MERKMANS GEZANGEN
see Nozeman, Jacob

DRIE LIEDEREN VAN BOUTENS see Bijvanck,
Henk

DRIE LIEDEREN VAN C. WOLFSON see
Zagwijn, Henri

DRIE LIEDEREN VAN E.L. SMELIK see
Orthel, Leon

DRIE LIEDEREN VAN EUGENIE FINK see
Bijvanck, Henk

DRIE LIEDEREN VAN GEZELLE see Beekhuis,
Hanna

DRIE LIEDEREN VAN H. SWARTH see
Pluister, Simon

DRIE LIEDEREN VAN ISOUDE see Voormolen,
Alexander Nicolas

DRIE LIEDEREN VAN J. SCHURMANN see
Mulder, Herman

DRIE LIEDEREN VAN J. SLAUERHOFF see
Godron, Hugo

DRIE LIEDEREN VAN M. LUKA see Mesritz
Van Velthuysen, Annie

DRIE LIEDEREN VAN M. VASALIS UIT "DE
VOGEL PHOENIX" see Schuyt, Nico

DRIE LIEDEREN VAN RAINER MARIA RILKE
see Orthel, Leon

DRIE LIEDEREN VAN RAINER MARIA RILKE
see Orthel, Leon

DRIE LIEDJES see Zagwijn, Henri

DRIE LIEDJES UIT "DE LAATSTE REIS VAN
DON ANDREES" see Schouwman, Hans

DRIE LIEDJES VAN J. PERK see Zagwijn,
Henri

DRIE LIEDJES VAN JACQUES PERK see
Dresden, Sem

DRIE MORGENSTERLIEDEREN see Vlijmen,
Jan van

DRIE NACHTLIEDEREN VAN F. BASTIAANSE
see Mulder, Herman

DRIE OUD-NEDERLANDSCHE LIEDEREN see
Horst, Anton van der

DRIE OUD-NEDERLANDSCHE LIEDEREN see
Horst, Anton van der

DRIE OUD-NEDERLANDSE LIEDEREN see
Klerk, Albert de

DRIE OUD-NEDERLANDSE LIEDEREN see
Horst, Anton van der

DRIE OUD-PERZISCHE KWATRIJNEN see Lier,
Bertus van

DRIE OUD-VLAAMSCHE LIEDEREN EN DRIE
KINDERLIEDJES see Lilien, Ignace

DRIE REDOLZE DUETTEN see Rontgen,
Johannes

DRIE ROMANCES VAN H. HEINE see Frid,
Geza

DRIE ROMANTISCHE MINIATUREN VAN STARING
see Schouwman, Hans

DRIE SHAKESPEARE-LIEDEREN UIT
"DRIEKONINGENAVOND" see Frid, Geza

DRIE SMIDSLIEDEREN see Zagwijn, Henri

DRIE SONNETTEN see Diepenbrock, Alphons

DRIE SONNETTEN VAN SHAKESPEARE see
Delden, Lex van

DRIE WERKJES see Nieland, H.

DRIESSLER, JOHANNES (1921-   )
Concerti Sacri *sac,CCU,concerto
[Lat] S solo,org BREITKOPF-W
EB 6436 $7.25   (D1656)

Concerti Sacri *Op.47,No.2, sac,CCU,
concerto
[Lat] Bar solo,org BREITKOPF-W
EB 6437 $6.25   (D1657)

Engadin-Kantate *Op.53, concerto
Bar solo,ob,cembalo,strings voc sc
BREITKOPF-W EB 6439 $4.00 (D1658)

Et Resurrexit Tertia Die *sac,
concerto
Bar solo,org BREITKOPF-W EB 6463
$3.75   (D1659)

DRIESSLER, JOHANNES (cont'd.)

Liebesreime *Op.10,No.3, CC10U
Mez/A solo,pno (diff) BAREN. 2427
$4.75   (D1660)

Sieben Lieder *Op.10,No.1, CC7U
med solo,pno (diff) BAREN. 2425
$5.00   (D1661)

DRIFTING see Blair Fairchild

DRIFTING see Grieg, Edvard Hagerup, Im
Kahne

DRIGO, RICCARDO (1846-1930)
Notturno D'amore (from I Milioni
D'Arlecchino)
[It] solo,pno RICORDI-ARG BA 6722
s.p.   (D1662)

Serenade (from Les Millions
D'Arlequin)
solo,pno ZIMMER. 1407 s.p. (D1663)
[Eng] high solo,pno CHESTER s.p.
                        (D1664)
(Marcato, U.) [It] solo,pno ZIMMER.
s.p.   (D1665)

DRINK TO ME ONLY see Bunge, Sas

DRINK TO ME ONLY WITH THINE EYES *Eng
low solo,pno (E flat maj) CRAMER
                        (D1666)
high solo,pno (F maj) CRAMER (D1667)
low solo,orch (D maj) ASHDOWN s.p.,
ipr   (D1668)
med solo,orch (E flat maj) ASHDOWN
s.p., ipr   (D1669)
high solo,orch (F maj) ASHDOWN s.p.,
ipr   (D1670)
(Cohen) solo,pno SHAWNEE IA 48 $.50
                        (D1671)

DRINK TO ME ONLY WITH THINE EYES see
Mozart, Wolfgang Amadeus

DRINK TO ME ONLY WITH THINE EYES see
Quilter, Roger

DRINKING SONG see Monteverdi, Claudio

DRINKING SONG see Nicolai, Otto

DRINKING SONG see Rappaport, Eda

DRINKING SONG see Verdi, Giuseppe,
Libiamo Ne' Lieti Calici

DRINKLIED see Mengelberg, Rudolf

DRISCHNER, MAX
Aus Der Tiefe Rufe Ich, Herr, Zu Dir
(Psalm 130)
see Tubinger Psalmen

Der Herr Ist Mein Hirte (Psalm 23)
sac,concerto
2 soli,org/pno SCHUL 191 s.p. voc
sc, solo pt   (D1672)

Herr, Du Erforschest Mich (Psalm 139)
see Tubinger Psalmen

Herr Gott, Du Bist Unsere Zuflucht
(Psalm 90) sac,concerto
2 soli,org/pno SCHUL 176 s.p. voc
sc, solo pt   (D1673)

Ich Liege Und Schlafe Ganz Mit
Frieden
see Tubinger Psalmen

Psalm 23 *see Der Herr Ist Mein
Hirte

Psalm 90 *see Herr Gott, Du Bist
Unsere Zuflucht

Psalm 130 *see Aus Der Tiefe Rufe
Ich, Herr, Zu Dir

Psalm 139 *see Herr, Du Erforschest
Mich

Tubinger Psalmen *sac,concerto
solo,vln,org sc,solo pt SCHUL 189
s.p., ipa
contains: Aus Der Tiefe Rufe Ich,
Herr, Zu Dir (Psalm 130); Herr,
Du Erforschest Mich (Psalm
139); Ich Liege Und Schlafe
Ganz Mit Frieden   (D1674)

DRIVING WITH A LADY see Cadman, Charles
Wakefield

DRIVSNO see Nordqvist, Gustaf

DROBISH, DOUGLAS
Day Like Today, A *sac
solo,pno WORD S-229   (D1675)

DROBNE KVETY see Schneider-Trnavsky,
Mikulas

DROBNE PESMI see Jirim, Frantisek

DROIT VERS LE BUT see Arma, Paul

DROJ HOS MIG see Liljefors, Ruben,
Bleib' Bei Mir

DROMD LYCKA see Peterson-Berger, (Olof)
Wilhelm

DROMMEN see Hallen, Andreas

DROMMEN see Sibelius, Jean

DROMMENS LAND see Kaski, Heino, Unen
Maa

DROMMERI see Bedinger, Hugo

DROMVISA see Rangstrom, Ture

DROOM IS 'T LEVEN, ANDERS NIET see
Voormolen, Alexander Nicolas

DROOMLAND see Mulder, Herman

DROOP NOT YOUNG LOVER see Handel,
George Frideric

DROP, DROP, SLOW TEARS see France,
William E.

DROP, DROP, SLOW TEARS see Warren,
Raymond

DROP ME A FLOWER see Stanford, Charles
Villiers

DROUET, L.F.PH. (1792-1873)
O Dolce Concento
solo,pno/harp,opt fl HEUWEKE. 013
s.p.   (D1676)

DRUBEN STEHT DIE KAPELLE see Bijvanck,
Henk

DRUCKMAN, JACOB
Animus Two
Mez solo,2perc,electronic tape sc
MCA $4.50, ipa   (D1677)

Dark Upon The Harp *sac,Psalm
Mez solo,brass,perc sc PRESSER
$4.00, ipr   (D1678)

DRUIVENTROSSEN see Adriessen, Willem

DRUM see Kagen, Sergius

DRY BONES
(Burleigh, H.T.) low solo,pno (G min)
GALAXY 1.0535.7 $1.00   (D1679)

DRY YOUR EYES see Zeller

DRYCKESVISA see Carlberg

DRYCKESVISA see Sjogren, Emil

DRYE, S.L.
Evening
solo,pno BRODT $.75   (D1680)

DRYNAN, MARGARET
Choosing Shoes
see Songs For Judith

Includin' Me *spir
solo,pno THOMP.G   (D1681)

Little
see Songs For Judith

Lullaby
see Songs For Judith

"Sh"
see Songs For Judith

Songs For Judith
solo,pno THOMP.G s.p.
contains: Choosing Shoes; Little;
Lullaby; "Sh"   (D1682)

D'SANGERREIS see Horler, A.

DU see Babbit, Milton

DU see Jarnefelt, Armas

DU see Landre, Willem

DU AHNST NICHT, WAS DIES SCHWERT BALD
VERMAG see Handel, George Frideric

DU AR see Bedinger, Hugo

DU AR MIN HERRE see Dahlgren, Erland

DU AR MIN RO see Collan, Karl

DU AR MIN SOL see Di Capua, [Eduardo]

DU AR SA VACKAR FOR MINA OGON see
Ekman, Karl Ekman, sen.

DU AR STILLA RO see Alfven, Hugo

DU BIST see Verhaar, Ary

DU BIST DIE AUFERSTEHUNG MEINER SEELE
see Bergman, Erik

DU BIST DIE RUH see Schubert, Franz
(Peter)

DU BIST EIN ARBEITSAMER MENSCH see
Lortzing, (Gustav) Albert

DU BIST MEIN ENTZIGE LIEBE *Jew
solo,pno KAMMEN 457 $1.00   (D1683)

DU BIST MIN see Beekhuis, Hanna

DU BIST TREU UND BESTANDIG? see Handel,
George Frideric, Tu Fedel, Tu
Costante?

DU BIST WIE EINE BLUME see Berners,
Lord

DU BIST WIE EINE BLUME see Liszt, Franz

DU BIST WIE EINE BLUME see Schumann,
Robert (Alexander)

DU BIST WIEDER GEKOMMEN see Marsik,
Emanuel, Ty's Prisel Zase

DU CONFLICT EN DOULEUR see Enesco,
Georges

DU, DER DU WEISST see Verhaar, Ary

DU DIEU AMOUR see Rameau, Jean-Philippe

DU DROMMER EN DROM see Hallnas, Hilding

DU FRAGTEST MICH see Ehrenberg, Carl
Emil Theodor

DU GAMLA DU FRIA
high solo,pno GEHRMANS 210 s.p.
contains also: Mandom Mod Och
Morske Man
low solo,pno GEHRMANS 557 s.p.
(D1684)   (D1685)
(Hagg, G.) med solo,pno GEHRMANS 159
s.p.   (D1686)

DU GAMLA, DU FRIA, DU FJALLHOGA NORD
solo,pno LUNDQUIST s.p.   (D1687)

DU GIBST DIE LIEBE HIN see Schmalstich,
Clemens

DU HAST UNS GERUFEN see Woll, E.

DU KAN ALDRIG FANGA MEJ see Lagerheim-
Romare, Margit

DU KOM see Torjussen, Trygve

DU LER see Peterson-Berger, (Olof)
Wilhelm

DU, LIEBE NACHTIGALL see Haibel, Jakob
J.

DU LIKNAR SKARA BLOMMAN see Liszt,
Franz, Du Bist Wie Eine Blume

DU LIVRE DE MONELLE see Delage, Maurice

DU MEIN GEDANKE see Grieg, Edvard
Hagerup

DU MITT KLARA HJARTEGULL see Merikanto,
Oskar, Kullan Murunen

DU MOURON POUR LES PETITS OISEAUX see
Biancheri, A.

DU, NOR DU ALEIN *Jew
solo,pno KAMMEN 455 $1.00   (D1688)

...DU PAUVRE SCARRON, PAR LUI-MEME see
Vellones, Pierre

DU PLUS LOIN see Vibert, Mathieu

DU PRINTEMPS see Durand, Jacques

DU PRINTEMPS see Vredenburg, Max

DU P'TIT TONNEAU D'LA VIVANDIERE see
Vasseur, Leon (-Felix-Augustin-
Joseph)

DU RING AN MEINEM FINGER see Schubert,
Franz (Peter)

DU RING AN MEINEM FINGER see Schumann,
Robert (Alexander)

DU SCHALKSKNECHT see Schutz, Heinrich

DU SCHAUST MICH AN MIT STUMMEN FRAGEN
see Sjogren, Emil

DU SER PA MIG MED HEMLIG FRAGA see
Sjogren, Emil, Du Schaust Mich An
Mit Stummen Fragen

DU SIDDER I BAADEN SOM SVOMMER see
Sjogren, Emil

DU SKA ITTE TRO I GRASET see Braein,
Edvard Fliflet

DU SOLEIL POUR TOUT LE MONDE see
Ostrovski, A.

DU, SOM AV KARLEK DOG
see Andliga Sanger, Heft 4

DU SOM BLAND JASMINER see Hedar, Josef

DU SOM I ROSIG FAGRINGS VAR see Lassen,
Eduard

DU STANDIGT FRAGAR see Meyer-Helmund,
Erik

DU STUMMER WEGGENOSSE MEIN see
Kilpinen, Yrio, Sa Mykka
Matkalainen Maan

DU SVENSKA LAND see Wideen, Ivar

DU TRODDE MIG BETRAKTA see Madetoja,
Leevi, Luulit Ma Katselin Sua

DU UND DU see Strauss, Johann,
Bruderlein Und Schwesterlein

DU VIN! DU VIN! see Aubert, Louis-
Francois-Marie

DU WAHRER GOTT UND DAVIDS SOHN see
Bach, Johann Sebastian

DU WAHRER MENSCH UND GOTT see Mozart,
Leopold

DU WUNDERSCHONE TOVE see Schoenberg,
Arnold

DUARTE, JOHN W. (1919-   )
Five Quiet Songs *Op.37,No.1-5, CC5U
[Eng] solo,gtr BERBEN 1520 s.p.
(D1689)

DUBINUSHKA *folk,Russ
[Russ] low solo,pno MEZ KNIGA 121
s.p.   (D1690)

DUBLANC, EMILIO
Milagro
solo,pno RICORDI-ARG BA 11016 s.p.
(D1691)
Trigo Limpio
[Span] solo,pno RICORDI-ARG
BA 11478 s.p.   (D1692)

DUBOIS, PIERRE MAX
Ba Be Bi Bo Bu
solo,pno/inst LEDUC s.p.   (D1693)

Chanson De La Rose
T solo,orch LEDUC s.p. see from
Etoiles Brulees   (D1694)

Chanson Du Remouleur
solo,orch LEDUC s.p. see from Six
Chansons   (D1695)

Cinq Poemes Chantes *see Contre-
Point Du Jour; La Mome Neant; Les
Erreurs; Rengaine A Pleurer;
Rengaine Pour Piano Mecanique
(D1696)
Contre-Point Du Jour
B solo,pno RIDEAU 047 s.p. see from
Cinq Poemes Chantes   (D1697)

Doit Et Avoir
solo,orch LEDUC s.p. see from Six
Chansons   (D1698)

Etoiles Brulees *see Chanson De La
Rose; Poussivite; Variations Pour
Une Trompette De Cavalerie;
Vieilles Chansons; Voyage En
Tortillard   (D1699)

Imitation Des Fleurs
solo,orch LEDUC s.p. see from Six
Chansons   (D1700)

La Galette
solo,orch LEDUC s.p. see from Six
Chansons   (D1701)

La Mome Neant
B solo,pno RIDEAU 048 s.p. see from
Cinq Poemes Chantes   (D1702)

Le Zodiaque
[Fr] med solo,pno ESCHIG $5.00
(D1703)
Les Erreurs
B solo,pno RIDEAU 046 s.p. see from
Cinq Poemes Chantes   (D1704)

DUBOIS, PIERRE MAX (cont'd.)

Monsieur Pepinet
solo,orch LEDUC s.p. see from Six
Chansons   (D1705)

Ne Derangez Pas Le Monde
solo,pno/inst LEDUC s.p.   (D1706)

Pour Les Mauvais Jours
solo,orch LEDUC s.p. see from Six
Chansons   (D1707)

Poussivite
T solo,orch LEDUC s.p. see from
Etoiles Brulees   (D1708)

Rengaine A Pleurer
B solo,pno RIDEAU 044 s.p. see from
Cinq Poemes Chantes   (D1709)

Rengaine Pour Piano Mecanique
B solo,pno RIDEAU 045 s.p. see from
Cinq Poemes Chantes   (D1710)

Six Chansons *see Chanson Du
Remouleur; Doit Et Avoir;
Imitation Des Fleurs; La Galette;
Monsieur Pepinet; Pour Les
Mauvais Jours   (D1711)

Variations Pour Une Trompette De
Cavalerie
T solo,orch LEDUC s.p. see from
Etoiles Brulees   (D1712)

Vieilles Chansons
T solo,orch LEDUC s.p. see from
Etoiles Brulees   (D1713)

V'la C'que C'est Qu'd'aller Au Bois
solo,pno/inst LEDUC s.p.   (D1714)

Voyage En Tortillard
T solo,orch LEDUC s.p. see from
Etoiles Brulees   (D1715)

DUBOIS, THEODORE (1837-1924)
Ave Maria *sac
high solo,pno/org (A maj) HEUGEL
s.p.   (D1716)
S solo,pno/org (E flat maj) HEUGEL
s.p.   (D1717)
solo,ob,vln,vcl (available in 2
keys) HEUGEL s.p.   (D1718)
solo,pno/org (available in 3 keys)
HEUGEL s.p.   (D1719)

Deus Meus (from Sept Paroles Du
Christ) sac
B solo,pno/org HEUGEL s.p. (D1720)

Ecce Panis *sac
SBar soli,pno BELWIN $1.50   (D1721)

Le Vittrail
(Bordese, Stephen) solo,pno
(available in 2 keys) ENOCH s.p.
see also CHANSONS DE PAGE (D1722)

O Salutaris *sac
B solo,ob,clar,vln (A maj) HEUGEL
s.p.   (D1723)

O Vos Omnes (from Sept Paroles Du
Christ) sac
S solo,pno/org HEUGEL s.p. (D1724)

Panis Angelicus *sac
Mez solo,ob,vcl (A min) HEUGEL s.p.
(D1725)
Puer Natus Est Nobis *sac,mot
SA soli,org HEUGEL s.p.   (D1726)

Tantum Ergo *sac
high solo,pno/org (E maj) HEUGEL
s.p.   (D1727)

DUBREUILH, G.
Lettre A La Marquise
solo,pno (available in 2 keys)
ENOCH s.p.   (D1728)
solo,acap solo pt ENOCH s.p.
(D1729)

DUC ALMA LUX see Mana-Zucca, Mme.

DUCHOW, M.
For A Rose's Sake
solo,pno BERANDOL BER 1308 $1.50
(D1730)

DUCK AND THE KANGAROO, THE see Hely-
Hutchinson, (Christian) Victor

DUE ARIE see Galuppi, Baldassare

DUE ARIE PER SOPRANO see Mannino,
Franco

DUE BALLATE see Malipiero, Riccardo

DUE BALLATE see Fuga, Sandro

DUE BICINIA see Pleskow, Raoul

DUE CACCE QUATTROCENTESCHE *CC2U,It,
14th cent
(Desderi, Ettore) solo,gtr BERBEN
1112 s.p.   (D1731)

DUE CANTI see Contilli, Gino

DUE CANTI DI KABIR see Platamone,
Stefano

DUE CANTI DI LEOPARDI see Melby, John

DUE CANTI DUECENTESCHI see De Angelis,
Ruggero

DUE CANTI NAPOLETANI see Alfano, Franco

DUE CANTI PERSIANI see Cortese, Luigi

DUE CANZONI see Diepenbrock, Alphons

DUE CANZONI ABRUZZESI see Guerrini,
Guido

DUE CELEBRI CANZONI ABRUZZESI see
Albanese, Guido

DUE LAUDE see Mortari, Virgilio

DUE LIRICHE see Mortari, Virgilio

DUE LIRICHE see Fasullo, P.

DUE LIRICHE see Cantu, M.

DUE LIRICHE see Pratella, Francesco
Balilla

DUE LIRICHE see Esposito, E.

DUE LIRICHE see Liguori, E.

DUE LIRICHE see Di Martino, Aladino

DUE LIRICHE see Platamone, Stefano

DUE LIRICHE see Terni, Enrico

DUE LIRICHE see Donati

DUE LIRICHE DI ANACREONTE see
Dallapiccola, Luigi

DUE LIRICHE DI QUASIMODO see Contilli,
Gino

DUE LIRICHE DI SAFFO see Petrassi,
Goffredo

DUE LIRICHE INFANTILI see Farina, Guido

DUE LIRICHE NAPOLETANE see Pizzetti,
Ildebrando

DUE LIRICHE SACRE see Tommasini,
Vincenzo

DUE LIRICHE SU TESTI POPOLARI TOSCANI
see Fiume, Orazio

DUE LIRICHE TEDESCHE E UN CONGEDO DI
GIOSUE CARDUCCI see Mannino, Franco

DUE PAGINE D'ALBUM see Porrino, Ennio

DUE POEMETTI see Rosa, M.

DUE POEMI DI COVENTRY PATMORE see
Milhaud, Darius

DUE POESIE see Clementi, Aldo

DUE POESIE DI APOLLINAIRE see Nielsen,
Riccardo

DUE POESIE DI QUASIMODO see Turchi,
Guido

DUE PREGHIERE PER I BIMBI D'ITALIA see
Castelnuovo-Tedesco, Mario

DUE PUPILLE AMABILI see Mozart,
Wolfgang Amadeus

DUE SONETTI see Cantu, M.

DUE SONETTI DEL BERNI see Malipiero,
Gian Francesco

DUE SONETTI DEL FOSCOLO see Caltabiano,
S.

DUERMETE YA see Lerma, P.

DUET see Mana-Zucca, Mme.

DUET ALBUM *CCU
(Morris; Anderson) high solo&med
solo,pno BOOSEY $5.00   (D1732)

DUET (FEUCHTERSLEBEN) see Bijvanck,
Henk

DUET (HOLTY) see Bijvanck, Henk

DUETS *CCU
[Russ] SMez/MezB soli,pno MEZ KNIGA
105 s.p. contains works by:
Artyomov, V.; Ziv, M.   (D1733)

DUETS FOR TWO FEMALE VOICES, VOL. 1:
CARISSIMI TO BEETHOVEN *CCU
(Forrai) 2 soli,pno BOOSEY $4.50
                               (D1734)

DUETS FOR TWO FEMALE VOICES, VOL. 2:
BEETHOVEN TO KODALY *CCU
2 female soli,pno BOOSEY $4.50
original and Hungarian texts
                               (D1735)

DUETS FROM THE GREAT OPERAS I *CC18L
(Adler, Kurt) SBar soli,pno SCHIRM.G
$5.00 contains works by: Mozart;
Pucini; Verdi; Wagner and others
                               (D1736)

DUETS FROM THE GREAT OPERAS II *CC22L
(Adler, Kurt) ST soli,pno SCHIRM.G
$5.00 contains works by: Beethoven;
Bizet; Gounod; Verdi and others
                               (D1737)

DUETS, VOL. I see Brahms, Johannes

DUETS, VOL. II see Brahms, Johannes

DUETT MARINA - DIMITRI see Mussorgsky,
Modest

DUETTE AUS OPERETTEN, HEFT 1 *CCU
2 soli,pno DOBLINGER 88 501 s.p.
                               (D1738)

DUETTE AUS OPERETTEN, HEFT 2 *CCU
2 soli,pno DOBLINGER 88 502 s.p.
                               (D1739)

DUETTE AUS OPERETTEN, HEFT 3 *CCU
2 soli,pno DOBLINGER 88 503 s.p.
                               (D1740)

DUETTENKRANZ, VOL. I: EIGHTEEN SECULAR
DUETS *CC18U
(Martienssen) [Ger/It] SS/SA soli,pno
PETERS 3838A $8.50 contains works
by: Albert; Brahms; Cherubini;
Loewe; Marcello; Schumann and
others   (D1741)

DUETTENKRANZ, VOL. II: FOURTEEN DUETS
*CC14U
(Martienssen) [Ger/It] ST/SBar/SB/
ABar/AB soli,pno PETERS 3838B $7.50
contains works by: Albert; Brahms;
Handel; Cornelius; Schubert and
others   (D1742)

DUETTENKRANZ, VOL. III: FIFTEEN OPERA
DUETS *CC15U
(Martienssen) [Ger/It] ST/SBar/SB/AT
soli,pno PETERS 3839A $8.50
contains works from: Carmen; Barber
Of Bagdad; Alceste; Julius Caesar;
Rodelinda; Tales Of Hoffmann and
others   (D1743)

DUETTENKRANZ, VOL. IV: TWELVE OPERA
DUETS *CC12L
(Martienssen) [Ger/It] SS/SMez/SA
soli,pno PETERS 3839B $7.50
contains works from: Nozze D'Ercol
E D'Ebe; Orpheus; Flavio;
Radamisto; Undine; Cosi Fan Tutte
and others   (D1744)

DUETTER 1964 see Nielsen, Svend

DUETTO BUFFO DI DUE GATTI see Rossini,
Gioacchino

DUETTO DELL'OASI see Massenet, Jules

DUETTO FINALE see Monteverdi, Claudio

DUFRESNE, C.
Chanson Du Couteau
solo,pno ENOCH s.p. see also Vingt
Melodies   (D1745)

Chant De Mer
solo,pno ENOCH s.p. see also Vingt
Melodies   (D1746)

Declaration
solo,pno ENOCH s.p. see also Vingt
Melodies   (D1747)

Dejeuner
solo,pno ENOCH s.p. see also Vingt
Melodies   (D1748)

Demain
solo,pno ENOCH s.p. see also Vingt
Melodies   (D1749)

Demande
solo,pno ENOCH s.p. see also Vingt
Melodies   (D1750)

Flirt Des Papillons
solo,pno ENOCH s.p. see also Vingt
Melodies   (D1751)

Jeanneton
solo,pno ENOCH s.p. see also Six
Chansons Provencales   (D1752)

DUFRESNE, C. (cont'd.)
La Galline Noire
solo,pno ENOCH s.p. see also Six
Chansons Provencales   (D1753)

La Repetiere
solo,pno ENOCH s.p. see also Six
Chansons Provencales   (D1754)

L'Adieu
solo,pno ENOCH s.p. see also Vingt
Melodies   (D1755)

Le Brick Perdu
solo,pno ENOCH s.p. see also Vingt
Melodies   (D1756)

Le Marche Du Poete
solo,pno ENOCH s.p. see also Vingt
Melodies   (D1757)

Le Mistral
solo,pno ENOCH s.p. see also Six
Chansons Provencales   (D1758)
solo,orch ENOCH rental see also Six
Chansons Provencales   (D1759)

Le Romerage
solo,pno ENOCH s.p. see also Six
Chansons Provencales   (D1760)
solo,orch ENOCH rental see also Six
Chansons Provencales   (D1761)

Les Eloignes
solo,pno ENOCH s.p. see also Vingt
Melodies   (D1762)

Les Magnans
solo,pno ENOCH s.p. see also Six
Chansons Provencales   (D1763)
solo,orch ENOCH rental see also Six
Chansons Provencales   (D1764)

Les Pecheuses De Crevettes
solo,pno ENOCH s.p. see also Vingt
Melodies   (D1765)

Nuages D'amour
solo,pno ENOCH s.p. see also Vingt
Melodies   (D1766)

Regrets
solo,pno ENOCH s.p. see also Vingt
Melodies   (D1767)

Romance Du Fou
solo,pno ENOCH s.p. see also Vingt
Melodies   (D1768)

Six Chansons Provencales
solo,pno cmplt ed ENOCH s.p.
contains & see also: Jeanneton;
La Galline Noire; La Repetiere;
Le Mistral; Le Romerage; Les
Magnans   (D1769)

Tout Un Soir
solo,pno ENOCH s.p. see also Vingt
Melodies   (D1770)

Viens
solo,pno ENOCH s.p.   (D1771)

Vingt Melodies *CC20L
solo,pno cmplt ed ENOCH s.p.
see also: Chanson Du Couteau;
Chant De Mer; Declaration;
Dejeuner; Demain; Demande;
Flirt Des Papillons; L'Adieu;
Le Brick Perdu; Le Marche Du
Poete; Les Eloignes; Les
Pecheuses De Crevettes; Nuages
D'amour; Regrets; Romance Du
Fou; Tout Un Soir; Vision
                            (D1772)

Vision
solo,pno ENOCH s.p. see also Vingt
Melodies   (D1773)

DUFVOBAD see Kotilainen, Otto,
Kyyhkynen Kylpee

DUGOUT, THE see Flanagan, William

DUISTERNIS see Mulder, Herman

DUITSCHE HOORNEN see Clercq, R. de

DUKAS, PAUL (1865-1935)
Les Cinq Filles D'Orlamonde (from
Ariane Et Barbe-Bleue)
solo,pno/inst DURAND s.p.   (D1774)

Les Diamants (from Ariane Et Barbe-
Bleue)
S solo,orch DURAND s.p., ipr
                            (D1775)

Sonnet De Ronsard
solo,orch DURAND s.p., ipr (D1776)

DUKE
In The Fields
low solo,pno FISCHER,C V 2243
                            (D1777)

DUKE (cont'd.)

Just Spring
  high solo,pno (B maj) FISCHER,C
  V 2217   (D1778)

Mountains Are Dancing, The
  high solo,pno FISCHER,C V 2261
                            (D1779)

DUKE, JOHN WOODS (1899-   )
Acquainted With The Night
  solo,pno PEER $.95   (D1780)

April Elegy
  med-high solo,pno SCHIRM.G $.75
                            (D1781)

Bird, The
  see Two Songs

Central Park At Dusk
  solo,pno BOOSEY $1.50   (D1782)

Coward's Lament, The
  solo,pno PEER $.95 see from Three
  Gothic Ballads   (D1783)

End Of The World, The
  solo,pno NEW VALLEY $1.25 (D1784)

For A Dead Kitten
  solo,pno PEER $.85   (D1785)

Hist...Whist
  solo,pno PEER $.95   (D1786)

I Can't Be Talkin' Of Love
  med solo,pno (F sharp maj) SCHIRM.G
  $.85   (D1787)

I Carry Your Heart
  high solo,pno SCHIRM.G $1.00
                            (D1788)

I Ride The Great Black Horses
  med solo,pno SCHIRM.G $.75 (D1789)

I Watched The Lady Caroline
  med-low solo,pno SCHIRM.G $.75
                            (D1790)

Little Elegy
  see Two Songs

Loveliest Of Trees
  low solo,pno (F maj) SCHIRM.G $1.25
                            (D1791)

Love's Secret
  solo,pno (D min) BOOSEY $1.50
                            (D1792)

Mad Knight's Song, The
  solo,pno PEER $1.00 see from Three
  Gothic Ballads   (D1793)

My Soul Is An Enchanted Boat
  solo,pno NEW VALLEY $1.00 (D1794)

Old King, The
  solo,pno PEER $.95 see from Three
  Gothic Ballads   (D1795)

Peggy Mitchell
  med-high solo,pno (G maj) SCHIRM.G
  $.75   (D1796)

Rapunzel
  high solo,pno MERCURY $.95 (D1797)

Remembrance
  solo,pno PEER $1.00   (D1798)

Shelling Peas
  high solo,pno (E flat maj) SCHIRM.G
  $.60   (D1799)

Three Gothic Ballads *see Coward's
  Lament, The; Mad Knight's Song,
  The; Old King, The   (D1800)

To The Thawing Wind
  solo,pno PEER $.95   (D1801)

Twentieth Century
  see Two Songs

Two Songs
  med solo,pno NEW VALLEY $2.25
  contains: Twentieth Century;
  White In The Moon   (D1802)

Two Songs
  high solo,pno SCHIRM.G $.85
  contains: Bird, The; Little Elegy
                            (D1803)

When I Was One And Twenty
  med-high solo,pno (A min) SCHIRM.G
  $.85   (D1804)

When Slim Sophia Mounts Her Horse
  high solo,pno MERCURY $.95 (D1805)

White Dress, The
  med solo,pno SCHIRM.G $.75 (D1806)

White In The Moon
  see Two Songs

DUKE, VERNON (1903-1969)
  see DUKELSKY, WLADMIR

DUKELSKY, VLADIMIR (1903-1969)
Blossom, The
  see Four Songs (William Blake)

Fifty Russian Art Songs, Volume III
  *CC50U,Russ
  [Eng/Russ] solo,pno MCA $3.50
                            (D1807)

Fly, The
  see Four Songs (William Blake)

Four Songs (William Blake)
  med solo,pno BROUDE BR. $2.50
  contains: Blossom, The; Fly, The;
  How Sweet I Roam'd; Nurse's
  Song   (D1808)

How Sweet I Roam'd
  see Four Songs (William Blake)

Into My Heart
  see Six Songs (A.E.Housman)

La Boheme Et Mon Coeur *CC7L
  solo,pno cmplt ed AMPHION A 145
  $2.50   (D1809)

Loveliest Of Trees
  see Six Songs (A.E.Housman)

Musical Zoo *CCU
  solo,pno GENERAL 499 $3.50 (D1810)

Now Hollow Fires
  see Six Songs (A.E.Housman)

Nurse's Song
  see Four Songs (William Blake)

Oh, When I Was In Love
  see Six Songs (A.E.Housman)

Six Songs (A.E.Housman)
  med solo,pno BROUDE BR. $2.50
  contains: Into My Heart;
  Loveliest Of Trees; Now Hollow
  Fires; Oh, When I Was In Love;
  When I Watch The Living; With
  Rue My Heart Is Laden   (D1811)

When I Watch The Living
  see Six Songs (A.E.Housman)

With Rue My Heart Is Laden
  see Six Songs (A.E.Housman)

DULCIS AMOR see Cazzati, Maurizio

DULGT KAEJRLIGHED see Grieg, Edvard
  Hagerup

DUMAYNE, JEAN
Heatherland
  low solo,pno (D flat maj) CRAMER
                            (D1812)
  med solo,pno (E flat maj) CRAMER
                            (D1813)
  high solo,pno (F maj) CRAMER
                            (D1814)

DUMAYNE, JOHN
Elizabethan Love Song
  low solo,pno (B flat maj) CRAMER
                            (D1815)
  high solo,pno (C maj) CRAMER
                            (D1816)

DUMKA O NALEPKOVI see Novak, Milan

D'UN BERCEAU see Aubert, Louis-
  Francois-Marie

D'UN DESASTRE OBSCURE see Ana, d'

...D'UN GRAND MEDECIN see Vellones,
  Pierre

D'UN JARDIN ABANDONNE see Goeyens,
  Fern.

D'UN LIVRE D'IMAGES see Perissas, M.

D'UN MILLE-PATTES AMOUREUX see Schmitt,
  Florent

...D'UN PARESSEUX see Vellones, Pierre

D'UN PAS BIEN FAIBLE see Bach, Johann
  Sebastian

DUNA see McGill, Josephine

DUNCAN
  I Asked The Lord *see Lange

DUNE see Hoch, Francesco

...D'UNE DEVOTE see Vellones, Pierre

...D'UNE FEMME PAR SON MARI see
  Vellones, Pierre

D'UNE FONTAINE see Tesson, P.

D'UNE FONTAINE see Woronoff, Wladmir

D'UNE PRISON see Hahn, Reynaldo

D'UNE QUI FAISAIT LA LONGUE see
  Beekhuis, Hanna

DUNGAN, OLIVE
Be Still And Know That I Am God *sac
  high solo,pno PRESSER $.95 (D1817)

Eternal Life *sac
  low solo,pno (B flat maj) PRESSER
  $.95   (D1818)
  high solo,pno (D maj) PRESSER $.95
                            (D1819)
  (Bock, F.) low solo,org PRESSER
  $.95   (D1820)
  (Bock, F.) high solo,org PRESSER
  $.95   (D1821)

Make Prayer Your Partner *sac
  solo,pno WORD S-237   (D1822)

Thy Loving Kindness
  med solo,pno PRESSER $.95 (D1823)

When I Sing Your Songs
  med solo,pno PRESSER $.95 (D1824)

When In My Heart
  (Morley) solo,pno BELWIN $1.50
                            (D1825)

White Jade
  med solo,pno GALAXY 1.1111.7 $1.00
                            (D1826)

DUNHILL, THOMAS FREDERICK (1877-1946)
April
  solo,pno CRAMER $1.15   (D1827)

Child's Song Of Praise, A
  solo,pno CRAMER $1.15   (D1828)

Cloths Of Heaven
  low solo,pno (C maj) STAINER
  3.1302.7 $1.50   (D1829)
  high solo,pno (E flat maj) GALAXY
  1.5092.7 $1.25   (D1830)

Evening
  solo,pno CRAMER $.95   (D1831)

Gifts
  solo,pno CRAMER   (D1832)

Go Pretty Birds
  solo,pno CRAMER $.70   (D1833)

Holy Babe, The
  solo,pno CRAMER $.90   (D1834)

How Soft, Upon The Ev'ning Air
  solo,pno (E maj) ROBERTON 2603 s.p.
                            (D1835)
  solo,pno (A maj) ROBERTON 2603 s.p.
                            (D1836)
  (Jacobson) 2 soli,pno ROBERTON
  72505 s.p.   (D1837)

I Can Hear A Cuckoo
  solo,pno CRAMER   (D1838)

I Remember
  solo,pno CRAMER $1.15   (D1839)

I Think Of You (from Tantivy Towers)
  solo,pno CRAMER   (D1840)

If Ever I Marry At All
  solo,pno CRAMER $1.15   (D1841)

If I'd Been Mrs. Noah
  solo,pno CRAMER $.95   (D1842)

In The Dawn
  solo,pno CRAMER $1.15   (D1843)

Little Road To Bethlehem *sac,Xmas
  high solo,pno (E flat maj) HARRIS
  $1.20   (D1844)
  low solo,pno (C maj) HARRIS $1.20
                            (D1845)

Little Town Of Bethlehem
  low solo,pno (C maj) CRAMER $.90
                            (D1846)
  high solo,pno (E flat maj) CRAMER
  $1.15   (D1847)

Quiet Night, The
  solo,pno CRAMER   (D1848)

Ride Straight (from Tantivy Towers)
  solo,pno CRAMER   (D1849)

Suffolk Owl, The
  low solo,pno (A flat maj) CRAMER
                            (D1850)
  high solo,pno (B flat maj) CRAMER
                            (D1851)

Sweet July
  solo,pno CRAMER $.70   (D1852)

Three Fine Ships
  low solo,pno (C maj) CRAMER $.90
                            (D1853)
  high solo,pno (D maj) CRAMER $.90

DUNHILL, THOMAS FREDERICK (cont'd.)
                                        (D1854)
    To Dance And Sing (from Tantivy
      Towers)
      solo,pno CRAMER   (D1855)

    Visit From The Moon, A
      solo,pno CRAMER $.95   (D1856)

DUNI, R.
    L'amour Se Plait (from Le Peintre
      Amoureux De Son Modele)
      (Flothius, Marius) [Fr] S solo,fl,
      vla BROEKMANS 395-13 s.p. (D1857)

DUNKEL IST DIE KLEINE KAMMER see
    Kilpinen, Yrio, Pimea Isoton Pirtti

DUNKLE BLATTER see Madetoja, Leevi,
    Yrtit Tummat

DUNKLE GASTE see Bijvanck, Henk

DUNLAP, FERN GLASGOW
    Jesus, Thou Art My Shepherd *sac
      med solo,pno (E flat maj) SCHIRM.G
      $.75   (D1858)

    Our Father Cares *sac
      med solo,pno (D maj) SCHIRM.G $.75
                                   (D1859)
    Wedding Prayer *sac,Marriage
      high solo,pno (G maj) SCHIRM.G $.85
                                   (D1860)
      med solo,pno (E flat maj) SCHIRM.G
      $.85   (D1861)
      low solo,pno (C maj) SCHIRM.G $.85
                                   (D1862)
      high solo,org (G maj) SCHIRM.G $.85
                                   (D1863)
      med solo,org (E flat maj) SCHIRM.G
      $.85   (D1864)
      low solo,org (C maj) SCHIRM.G $.85
                                   (D1865)
      SA/SBar soli,pno SCHIRM.G $1.25
                                   (D1866)

DUNLOP, MERRILL
    Lonely I Can Never Be *sac
      solo,pno SINGSPIR 7105 $1.00
                                   (D1867)

DUNN, JAMES PHILIP (1884-1936)
    Bitterness Of Love, The
      high solo,pno BELWIN $1.50 (D1868)
      high solo,pno (C sharp min) CRAMER
      $.90   (D1869)
      low solo,pno (G min) CRAMER $.90
                                   (D1870)
      med solo,pno BELWIN $1.50   (D1871)

    Come Unto Him *sac
      high solo,pno BELWIN $1.50 (D1872)
      low solo,pno BELWIN $1.50   (D1873)

DUNSTABLE, JOHN (ca. 1385-1453)
    Veni Sancte Spiritus *sac,mot
      [Lat] SAT soli,org/trom HINRICHSEN
      H1453 s.p.   (D1874)

DUO see MacBride, David

DUO DE LA PREMIERE ENTREUVUE see
    Caryll, Ivan

DUO DE LA THEIERE ET DE LA TASSE see
    Ravel, Maurice

DUO DE L'INTIMITE see Caryll, Ivan

DUO DE MARGARITA ET TEBALDO see Saint-
    Saens, Camille

DUO DES BONNES INTENTIONS see Caryll,
    Ivan

DUO DES CHAMELIERS see Messager, Andre

DUO DES FRAISES see Chadal, M.

DUO DES PECHEURS DE BREMES see Delmet,
    Paul

DUO D'ETOILES see Chaminade, Cecile

DUO D'HELENE ET DE PARIS see Saint-
    Saens, Camille

DUO DU DEUXIEME ACTE see Chabrier,
    Emmanuel

DUO DU MARIAGE see Messager, Andre

DUO DU TROISIEME ACTE see Chabrier,
    Emmanuel

DUO LIRICHE see Ghedini, Giorgio
    Federico

DUO PREMIER ACTE see Verdi, Giuseppe

DUO TURC see Perpignan, F.

DUO-VALSE see Chadal, M.

DUODICI CANTI A DUE VOCI see
    Mendelssohn-Bartholdy, Felix

DUODICI COMPOSIZIONI VOCALI PROFANE E
    SACRE see Monteverdi, Claudio

DUODIECI ARIE ITALIANE DEI SECOLI XVII
    E XVIII *CC12L,17-18th cent
    (Zanon) [It/Ger/Eng] solo,pno cmplt
    ed RICORDI-ENG 130307 s.p. contains
    works by: Cesarini; Cesi; Ciampi;
    Giardini; Rossi; Sarri; Vinci;
    Chelleri and others   (D1875)

DUOS see Schumann, Robert (Alexander)

DUPARC, HENRI (1848-1933)
    Album Of Songs *sac,CCU
      BOSTON high solo,pno $2.50; low
      solo,pno $2.50   (D1876)

    Au Pays Ou Se Fait La Guerre
      med solo,pno/orch SALABERT-US
      $2.25, ipr   (D1877)

    Chanson Triste
      high solo,pno/orch SALABERT-US
      $2.25, ipr   (D1878)

    Elegie
      high solo,pno SALABERT-US $2.25
                                   (D1879)
    La Mamoir De Rosemonde
      high solo/med solo,pno/orch
      SALABERT-US $2.25, ipr   (D1880)

    La Vague Et La Cloche
      low solo,pno/orch SALABERT-US
      $3.00, ipr   (D1881)

    Lamento
      high solo/med solo,pno SALABERT-US
      $2.25   (D1882)

    Le Gallop
      solo,pno/inst DURAND s.p.   (D1883)

    Serenade Florentine
      high solo,pno/orch
      SALABERT-US $2.25, ipr   (D1884)

    Songs *CC12L
      (Kagen, Sergius) [Fr/Eng] INTERNAT.
      high solo,pno, contains songs 1-
      11 only $3.50; med solo,pno
      $4.00; low solo,pno $4.00 (D1885)

    Soupir
      high solo,pno/orch SALABERT-US
      $2.25, ipr   (D1886)

    Testament
      med solo,pno/orch SALABERT-US
      $2.25, ipr   (D1887)

    Thirteen Songs *CC13L
      high solo/med solo,pno SALABERT-US
      $11.00   (D1888)

DUPERIER, J.
    Trois Sonnets Pour Helene *CC3U
      solo,orch HENN s.p.   (D1889)

DUPIN, PAUL (1865-1949)
    La Payse A Jean
      solo,vln DURAND s.p.   (D1890)

    La Saga Du Bersekir
      see Trois Legendes

    L'Abri
      see Trois Legendes

    Le Vieux Menestrier (Trial)
      med solo,pno/inst DURAND s.p. see
      also Trois Chansons Dans Le
      Caractere Populaire   (D1891)

    Les "Pourquoi" De Solange
      med solo,pno/inst DURAND s.p. see
      also Trois Chansons Dans Le
      Caractere Populaire   (D1892)

    L'Eternelle Berceuse
      see Trois Legendes

    L'homme De La Terre
      med solo,pno/inst DURAND s.p. see
      also Trois Chansons Dans Le
      Caractere Populaire   (D1893)

    Trois Chansons Dans Le Caractere
      Populaire
      med solo,pno/inst cmplt ed DURAND
      s.p.
      contains & see also: Le Vieux
        Menestrier (Trial); Les
        "Pourquoi" De Solange; L'homme
        De La Terre   (D1894)

    Trois Legendes
      cmplt ed DURAND s.p.
      contains: La Saga Du Bersekir
        (high solo,pno/inst); L'Abri
        (med solo,pno/inst);
        L'Eternelle Berceuse (Mez solo,

DUPIN, PAUL (cont'd.)
      pno/inst)   (D1895)

DUPRATO, JULES-LAURENT (1827-1892)
    Adieu
      solo,pno (available in 2 keys)
      ENOCH s.p.   (D1896)

    Chanson De Ronsard
      solo,pno ENOCH s.p.   (D1897)

    Ici-Bas
      solo,pno (available in 2 keys)
      ENOCH s.p.   (D1898)
      solo,acap solo pt ENOCH s.p. (D1899)

    Le Chanteur Florentin
      solo,pno ENOCH s.p.   (D1900)

DUPRE, MARCEL (1886-1971)
    A L'amie Perdue *CC7L
      solo,orch cmplt ed LEDUC s.p.
                                   (D1901)
    Chansons De Bilitis *see Roses Dans
      La Nuit; Sous La Pluie   (D1902)

    Fantasio
      Mez/Bar solo,pno/inst DURAND s.p.
      see from Quatre Melodies   (D1903)

    Feerie Au Clair De Lune
      Mez/Bar solo,pno/inst DURAND s.p.
      see from Quatre Melodies   (D1904)

    La Geole
      Mez/Bar solo,pno/inst DURAND s.p.
                                   (D1905)
    Les Deux Soeurs
      solo,orch LEDUC s.p.   (D1906)

    Marquise
      solo,orch LEDUC s.p.   (D1907)

    Noel De France
      solo,pno/inst LEDUC s.p.   (D1908)

    Pour Une Amie Perdue
      S/T solo,pno/inst DURAND s.p. see
      from QUATRE MELODIES   (D1909)
      Mez/Bar solo,pno/inst DURAND s.p.
      see from Quatre Melodies   (D1910)

    Quatre Melodies *see Fantasio;
      Feerie Au Clair De Lune; Regards
      Sur L'Infini   (D1911)

    Regards Sur L'Infini
      Mez/Bar solo,pno/inst DURAND s.p.
      see from Quatre Melodies   (D1912)

    Roses Dans La Nuit
      solo,orch LEDUC s.p. see also
      Chansons De Bilitis   (D1913)

    Sous La Pluie
      solo,orch LEDUC s.p. see also
      Chansons De Bilitis   (D1914)

DURAND
    Som I Ungdomens Ar
      solo,pno LUNDQUIST s.p.   (D1915)

DURAND, E.
    Le Retour Des Hirondelles
      2 soli,pno DURAND s.p.   (D1916)

DURAND, JACQUES
    A Une Fleur
      Mez/Bar solo,pno/inst DURAND s.p.
                                   (D1917)
    A Une Hirondelle
      see Deux Poemes De Ronsard

    Brise Du Soir
      S/T solo,pno/inst DURAND s.p.
                                   (D1918)
    Erouillard Blanc
      Mez/Bar solo,pno/inst DURAND s.p.
                                   (D1919)
    Brunette
      Mez/Bar solo,pno/inst DURAND s.p.
                                   (D1920)
    Cadix
      Mez/Bar solo,pno/inst DURAND s.p.
                                   (D1921)
    Chanson Bretonne
      solo,pno/inst DURAND s.p.   (D1922)

    Chanson Intercalee Dans Les Maucroix
      Mez/Bar solo,pno/inst DURAND s.p.
                                   (D1923)
    Deux Poemes De Ronsard
      solo,pno/inst cmplt ed DURAND s.p.
      contains: A Une Hirondelle;
        Esperance   (D1924)

    Du Printemps
      MezBar soli,pno DURAND s.p. (D1925)
      MezBar soli,pno DURAND s.p. (D1926)

    Esperance
      see Deux Poemes De Ronsard

DURAND, JACQUES (cont'd.)

Laurette
   solo,pno/inst DURAND s.p.   (D1927)

Leve-Toi
   Mez/Bar solo,pno/inst DURAND s.p.
                        (D1928)
   S/T solo,pno/inst DURAND s.p.
                        (D1929)

Margot, Prends Garde!
   Mez/Bar solo,pno/inst DURAND s.p.
                        (D1930)

Marine
   Mez/Bar solo,pno/inst DURAND s.p.
                        (D1931)

Ninette
   solo,pno/inst DURAND s.p.   (D1932)

Nocturne
   solo,pno/inst DURAND s.p.   (D1933)

Non, Tu Ne M'aimes Pas, Brunette
   Mez/Bar solo,pno/inst DURAND s.p.
                        (D1934)

Nuit Sereine
   Mez/Bar solo,pno/inst DURAND s.p.
                        (D1935)

Pantomime
   solo,pno/inst DURAND s.p.   (D1936)

Quelques Quatrains Extraits Du
    Chansonnier Des Graces De 1828
    *CCU
   solo,orch DURAND s.p., ipr   (D1937)

Roses De Mai
   Mez/Bar solo,pno/inst DURAND s.p.
                        (D1938)

Serenade Langoureuse
   solo,pno/inst DURAND s.p.   (D1939)

S'il Avait Su
   solo,orch DURAND s.p., ipr   (D1940)

Sur La Falaise
   S/T solo,pno/inst DURAND s.p.
                        (D1941)

DURAND, (MARIE-)AUGUSTE (1830-1909)
La Lecon D'amour
   Mez/Bar solo,pno/inst DURAND s.p.
                        (D1942)

Pater   *sac,Bibl
   solo,pno/org DURAND s.p.   (D1943)

DURANTE, FRANCESCO (1684-1755)
Danse Mignonne
   [Fr/It] med solo,pno/inst DURAND
   s.p.   (D1944)

Danza, Danza, Fanciulla
   (Alboniz) solo,gtr RICORDI-ENG
    129883 s.p.   (D1945)
   (Parisotti) [It/Fr] Mez/Bar solo,
    pno RICORDI-ARG BA 11852 s.p.
                        (D1946)

Vergin Tutt'amor
   solo,pno FORLIVESI 10874 s.p.
                        (D1947)
   "Virgin, Fount Of Love" [It/Eng]
    med solo,pno (C min) SCHIRM.G
    $.75   (D1948)
   (Parisotti) [It/Fr] Mez/Bar solo,
    pno RICORDI-ARG BA 11853 s.p.
                        (D1949)
   (Parisotti) [It/Fr] Mez/Bar solo,
    pno RICORDI-ENG 113465 s.p.
                        (D1950)

Virgin, Fount Of Love *see Vergin,
   Tutt'amor

DURCH DEN WALD EIN RAUSCHEN ZIEHT see
   Rimsky-Korsakov, Nikolai

DURCH DIE NACHT see Krenek, Ernst

DURCH DIE WALDER, DURCH DIE AUEN see
   Weber, Carl Maria von

DURCH DIESEN KUSS see Millocker, Karl

DURCH ZARTLICHKEIT UND SCHMEICHELN see
   Mozart, Wolfgang Amadeus

DURCHLAUCHT'STER LEOPOLD see Bach,
   Johann Sebastian

DUREY, LOUIS (1888-   )
Cantate De La Rose Et De L'Amour
   *cant
   [Fr] solo,pno CHANT s.p.   (D1951)

Deux Poemes D'Ho-Chi-Minh *CCU
   [Fr] solo,pno CHANT s.p.   (D1952)

Les Constructeurs
   [Fr] solo,pno CHANT s.p.   (D1953)

Trois Poemes De Petrone *CC3U
   med solo,pno/inst DURAND s.p.
                        (D1954)

Vergers *CCU
   [Fr] solo,pno CHANT s.p.   (D1955)

DURHAM
I Won't Have To Cross Jordon Alone
   *see Ramsey

DURINGER
Ombres Adoree
   solo,pno/inst DURAND s.p.   (D1956)

DUS CHUPE KLEID see Lowenwrith, Sam

DUS KEN ICH NIT see Rund, Morris

DUS PINTELE YID *Jew
   solo,pno KAMMEN 477 $1.00   (D1957)

DUS RAIDELE DRAIT SICH see Lillian,
   Isadore

DUSK see Repper, Charles

DUSK IN THE ENCHANTED WOOD see
   Dorumsgaard, Arne

DUSK OF DREAMS see Martin, Easthope

DUST OF SNOW see Ames, William

DUST OF SNOW see Carter, E.

DUSTY MILLER see Burrows, Ben

DUTCH CAROL see Brown

DUTEIL D'OZANNE, A.
A Celle Qui Est Triste
   solo,pno ENOCH s.p. see from Six
    Melodies   (D1958)

Aubade
   solo,pno ENOCH s.p. see from Six
    Melodies   (D1959)

Conseils
   solo,pno ENOCH s.p. see from Six
    Melodies   (D1960)

Le Temps D'aimer
   solo,pno ENOCH s.p. see from Six
    Melodies   (D1961)

Paysage
   solo,pno ENOCH s.p. see from Six
    Melodies   (D1962)

Saison D'amour
   solo,pno ENOCH s.p. see from Six
    Melodies   (D1963)

Six Melodies *see A Celle Qui Est
   Triste; Aubade; Conseils; Le
   Temps D'aimer; Paysage; Saison
   D'amour   (D1964)

DUVAL, A.
Crepuscule D'amour
   solo,pno ENOCH s.p.   (D1965)
   solo,acap solo pt ENOCH s.p.
                        (D1966)

Fete D'amour
   solo,pno ENOCH s.p.   (D1967)
   solo,acap solo pt ENOCH s.p.
                        (D1968)

La Parisienne
   solo,pno ENOCH s.p.   (D1969)
   solo,acap solo pt ENOCH s.p.
                        (D1970)

Marche Des Petites Bonnes
   solo,pno ENOCH s.p.   (D1971)
   solo,acap solo pt ENOCH s.p.
                        (D1972)

DUVAN see Yradier, Sebastian, La Paloma

DUVERNOY, VICTOR-ALPHONSE (1842-1907)
Ah! Je Vous Ai Toujours Aimee (from
   Helle)
   male solo,pno ENOCH   (D1973)
   Bar solo,pno ENOCH   (D1974)

Ave Maria *sac
   [Lat] solo,vln ENOCH s.p.   (D1975)

Cedant A D'indgnes (from Helle)
   Mez solo,pno ENOCH   (D1976)
   female solo,pno ENOCH   (D1977)

Chant D'Alsace
   solo,orch ENOCH rental   (D1978)
   solo,pno (available in 2 keys)
    ENOCH s.p.   (D1979)

De Moi Qu'attendez-vous (from Helle)
   2 soli,pno ENOCH   (D1980)

Doux Larcin
   (Bordese, Stephen) solo,pno
    (available in 2 keys) ENOCH s.p.
    see also CHANSONS DE PAGE (D1981)

Elle Va Venir (from Helle)
   solo,pno ENOCH   (D1982)

Leve-Toi
   solo,pno (available in 2 keys)
    ENOCH s.p.   (D1983)

DUVERNOY, VICTOR-ALPHONSE (cont'd.)

Nuit Etoilee
   solo,pno (available in 2 keys)
    ENOCH s.p.   (D1984)

O Mon Fils Que J'adore (from Helle)
   solo,pno ENOCH   (D1985)

Scene (Helle Et Gautier) (from Helle)
   2 soli,pno ENOCH   (D1986)

Voici Le Soir (from Helle)
   S solo,pno ENOCH   (D1987)
   Mez solo,pno ENOCH   (D1988)
   A solo,pno ENOCH   (D1989)

Vous A Qui Le Flot Obeit (from Helle)
   2 soli,pno ENOCH   (D1990)

Vous Qui Me Fuyez (from Helle)
   S solo,pno ENOCH   (D1991)
   Mez solo,pno ENOCH   (D1992)

DVA REVOLUCNI POCHODY see Jezek,
   Jaroslav

DVA SAMOSPEVA see Mirk, Vasilij

DVA ZALMOVE ZPEVY see Hanus, Jan

DVA ZPEVY see Plavec, Josef

DVACET LIDOVYCH PISNI V UPRAVE V.
   NEJEDLEHO *CC20U
   solo,pno SUPRAPHON s.p.   (D1993)

DVACET PET CHODSKYCH PISNI see Zich,
   Jaroslav

DVANACT CHODSKYCH PISNI see Jindrich,
   Jindrich

DVANACT LIDOVYCH PISNI Z HOLESOVSKA see
   Schneeweiss, Jan

DVE BALADY A PISEN see Vomacka,
   Boleslav

DVE MELODIE see Jindrich, Jindrich

DVE PESMI see Ballata, Zequirja

DVE PESMI see Ciglic, Zvonimir

DVE PISNE see Hajek, Maxmilian

DVE PISNE see Tomasek, V.J.

DVE PISNE PRO SOPRAN see Ostrcil,
   Otakor

DVE PISNE PRO TENOR see Ostrcil, Otakor

DVORACEK, JIRI (1928-   )
Jitrni Monology
   [Czech/Ger] Bar solo,pno PANTON 229
   s.p.   (D1994)

Ring Of Grass *CC4U
   S solo,pno PANTON s.p.   (D1995)

Take Mnou Zije Amerika! *CCU
   female solo*male solo,trp,pno CZECH
   s.p.   (D1996)

DVORAK, ANTONIN (1841-1904)
Abendlieder *Op.31, CCU
   [Ger/Eng] solo,pno SUPRAPHON s.p.
                        (D1997)

Abendlieder (Evening Songs) *CCU
   [Czech/Ger] med solo,pno ARTIA
   $3.00 Op. 3, Op. 9   (D1998)

Als Die Alte Mutter *Op.55,No.4
   "Cancion De La Madre" [Span] S/T
    solo,pno RICORDI-ARG BA 8839 s.p.
                        (D1999)
   "Songs My Mother Taught Me" high
    solo,pno (D maj) FISCHER,C S 5192
                        (D2000)
   "Songs My Mother Taught Me" low
    solo,pno (G maj) CENTURY 3477
                        (D2001)
   "Songs My Mother Taught Me" med
    solo,pno SCHAUR EE 1065A s.p.
                        (D2002)
   "Songs My Mother Taught Me" 2 low
    soli,pno (B flat maj) ALLANS s.p.
                        (D2003)
   "Songs My Mother Taught Me" 2 med-
    high soli,pno (C maj) ALLANS s.p.
                        (D2004)
   "Songs My Mother Taught Me" 2 high
    soli,pno (D maj) ALLANS s.p.
                        (D2005)
   "Songs My Mother Taught Me" 2 med
    soli,pno (B maj) ALLANS s.p.
                        (D2006)
   "Songs My Mother Taught Me" [Eng/
    Ger] high solo,pno PRESSER $.75
                        (D2007)
   "Songs My Mother Taught Me" [Ger/
    Eng] high solo,pno (D maj)
    SCHIRM.G $.85   (D2008)
   "Songs My Mother Taught Me" [Ger/

DVORAK, ANTONIN (cont'd.)

Eng] med solo,pno (B maj)
    SCHIRM.G $.85   (D2009)

Aria Des Wassermanns (from Rusalka) s.p.
    [Czech/Ger] solo,pno SUPRAPHON s.p.
                                     (D2010)
    [Czech/Eng] solo,pno SUPRAPHON s.p.
                                     (D2011)

Ave Maria *Op.19,No.2
    see Drei Geistliche Gesange

Ave Maris Stella *Op.19,No.1
    see Drei Geistliche Gesange

Biblical Songs *Op.99, CCU
    high solo,pno SCHIRM.G 1824 $1.50;
    low solo,pno SCHIRM.G 1825 $1.50
                                     (D2012)
Biblical Songs *Op.99, CCU
    [Czech/Ger/Eng] high solo/low solo,
    orch ARTIA $4.00   (D2013)
Biblical Songs *CCU,Bibl
    high solo,pno FISCHER,C RB 31; low
    solo,pno FISCHER,C RB 32 (D2014)
Biblical Songs, Vol. I *Op.99,No.1-
    5, CC5U
    INTERNAT. high solo,pno $2.00; low
    solo,pno $2.00   (D2015)
Biblical Songs, Vol. I *Op.99, CCU,
    Bibl
    [Eng/Ger/Czech] high solo,pno
    SCHAUR EE 850A $1.50; low solo,
    pno SCHAUR EE 850B $1.50 (D2016)
Biblical Songs, Vol. II *Op.99,No.6-
    10, CC5U
    INTERNAT. high solo,pno $2.00; low
    solo,pno $2.00   (D2017)
Biblical Songs, Vol. II *Op.99, CCU,
    Bibl
    [Eng/Ger/Czech] high solo,pno
    SCHAUR EE 851A $1.50; low solo,
    pno SCHAUR EE 851B $1.50 (D2018)
Biblicke Pisne *CCU,Bibl
    [Czech/Eng/Ger] SUPRAPHON s.p. high
    solo,pno; A solo,pno   (D2019)
Biblische Lieder *Op.99, CCU,Bibl
    (Fischer-Dieskau) s.p. high solo,
    pno SCHAUR EE 3222; low solo,pno
    SCHAUR EE 3223   (D2020)
Biblische Lieder *Op.99,No.1-10,
    sac,CC10U,Bibl
    [Czech/Ger/Eng] SUPRAPHON s.p. high
    solo,pno; low solo,pno   (D2021)

Cancion De La Madre *see Als Die
    Alte Mutter

Cikanske Melodie *CC7U
    SUPRAPHON s.p. high solo,pno; low
    solo,pno see also Gypsy Songs
                                     (D2022)
Ctyri Pisne *Op.82, CC4U
    med solo,pno SUPRAPHON s.p. (D2023)

Cuckoo, The *see Der Kukuk

Das Strausschen *Op.7,No.1
    see Four Songs
    "Nosegay, The" see Lieder Aus Der
    Koniginhofer Handschrift

Das Waisenkind *see Sirotek

Der Jakobiner *see In Weiter Fremde
    Irrten Wir   (D2024)

Der Kukuk *Op.7,No.3
    see Four Songs
    "Cuckoo, The" see Lieder Aus Der
    Koniginhofer Handschrift

Die Erdbeeren *Op.7,No.6
    "Strawberries, The" see Lieder Aus
    Der Koniginhofer Handschrift

Die Lerche *Op.7,No.4
    see Four Songs
    "Lark, The" see Lieder Aus Der
    Koniginhofer Handschrift

Die Rose *Op.7,No.2
    see Four Songs
    "Rose, The" see Lieder Aus Der
    Koniginhofer Handschrift

Die Verlassens *Op.7,No.5
    "Forsaken, The" see Lieder Aus Der
    Koniginhofer Handschrift

Drei Geistliche Gesange *sac
    [Lat] solo,org SUPRAPHON s.p.
    contains: Ave Maria, Op.19,No.2;
    Ave Maris Stella, Op.19,No.1; O
    Sanctissima, "Hymnus Ad Laudes
    In Festo Ss. Trinitatis",
    Op.19,No.3   (D2025)

Drei Neugriechische Gedichte
    [Czech] solo,pno SUPRAPHON s.p.
    contains: Koljas, Op.50,No.1;
    Lament For A City, Op.50,No.3;
    Naiads, Op.50,No.2   (D2026)

Eine Kleine Fruhlingsweise *Op.101,
    No.7
    "Eine Kleine Fruhlingsweise" med
    solo,pno SCHAUR 3422B s.p.
                                     (D2027)
    "Eine Kleine Fruhlingsweise" high
    solo,pno SCHAUR EE 3422A s.p.
                                     (D2028)
    "Eine Kleine Fruhlingsweise" low
    solo,pno SCHAUR EE 3422C s.p.
                                     (D2029)
    "Humoreske" med solo,pno (C maj)
    CENTURY 1689   (D2030)
    "Humoreske" low solo,pno (D flat
    maj) ALLANS s.p.   (D2031)
    "Humoreske" high solo,pno (E flat
    maj) ALLANS s.p.   (D2032)
    (Pardo) "Humoresca" [Span] solo,pno
    RICORDI-ARG BA 8571 s.p. (D2033)

Eine Kleine Fruhlingsweise *see Eine
    Kleine Fruhlingsweise

Flowery Omens *Op.6,No.3
    see Vier Lieder Nach Serbischer
    Volkspoesie

Forsaken, The *see Die Verlassens

Four Moravian Duets *Op.38, CC4U
    [Eng/Czech/Ger] SA soli,pno SCHAUR
    EE 93 $3.00   (D2034)
Four Serbian Songs *Op.6, CC4U
    med solo,pno SCHAUR EE 280 $3.75
                                     (D2035)
Four Songs
    [Ger] med-high solo,pno SCHAUR 1180
    $3.75
    contains: Das Strausschen, Op.7,
    No.1; Der Kukuk, Op.7,No.3; Die
    Lerche, Op.7,No.4; Die Rose,
    Op.7,No.2   (D2036)
Four Songs *Op.82, CC4U
    [Czech/Ger/Eng] high solo/low solo,
    pno ARTIA $3.00   (D2037)
Gipsy Songs *Op.55, CCU
    [Eng/Ger/Czech] high solo,pno
    SCHAUR EE 582 $3.00; low solo,pno
    SCHAUR EE 1065 $3.00   (D2038)
God Is My Shepherd *Op.99,No.4, sac
    low solo,pno (B maj) FISCHER,C
    HO 523   (D2039)
    high solo,pno (E maj) FISCHER,C
    HO 522   (D2040)
Goin' Home *Op.95
    med solo,pno SCHAUR EE 3424 s.p.
                                     (D2041)
    low solo,pno SCHAUR EE 3424 s.p.
                                     (D2042)
    high solo,pno SCHAUR EE 3424 s.p.
                                     (D2043)
    low solo,pno (C maj) ALLANS
    s.p.   (D2044)
    med solo,pno (D flat maj) ALLANS
    s.p.   (D2045)
    high solo,pno (E flat maj) ALLANS
    s.p.   (D2046)
    (Fisher) med solo,pno PRESSER $.95
                                     (D2047)
    (Fisher) low solo,pno PRESSER $.95
                                     (D2048)
    (Fisher) high solo,pno PRESSER $.95
                                     (D2049)
Gypsy Songs *Op.55,No.1-7, song
    cycle
    [Ger/Eng] high solo,pno INTERNAT.
    $2.50   (D2050)
    [Ger/Eng] low solo,pno INTERNAT.
    $2.50   (D2051)
Gypsy Songs *Op.55, CCU
    [Czech/Ger/Eng] high solo/low solo,
    pno ARTIA $3.00   (D2052)

Humoresca *see Eine Kleine
    Fruhlingsweise

Humoreske *see Eine Kleine
    Fruhlingsweise

Hymnus Ad Laudes In Festo Ss.
    Trinitatis *see O Sanctissima

Im Volkston *see V Narodnim Tonu

Im Volkston *Op.73, CC4U
    [Czech] SUPRAPHON s.p. high solo,
    pno; low solo,pno   (D2053)

In Weiter Fremde Irrten Wir (from Der
    Jakobiner)
    [Czech/Ger] solo,pno SUPRAPHON s.p.
    see from Der Jakobiner   (D2054)

DVORAK, ANTONIN (cont'd.)

[Czech/Eng] solo,pno SUPRAPHON s.p.
                                     (D2055)
Inflammatus Et Accensus (from Stabat
    Mater) sac
    A solo,pno NOVELLO 17.0079.00 s.p.
                                     (D2056)
Kinderlied Fur Zwei Kinderstimmen
    Ohne Begleitung *CCU
    [Czech/Ger/Eng] 2 boy soli/2 girl
    soli,acap SUPRAPHON s.p.   (D2057)
Klange Aus Mahren, Op. 20, 32, 38
    *CCU
    solo,pno SUPRAPHON s.p.   (D2058)
Klange Aus Mahren, Vol. I *Op.32,
    CCU
    [Eng/Ger/Czech] SA soli,pno SCHAUR
    EE 1793A $3.25   (D2059)
Klange Aus Mahren, Vol. II *Op.32,
    CCU
    [Eng/Ger/Czech] SA soli,pno SCHAUR
    EE 1793B $3.25   (D2060)
Koljas *Op.50,No.1
    see Drei Neugriechische Gedichte

Lament For A City *Op.50,No.3
    see Drei Neugriechische Gedichte

Largo
    low solo,pno (C maj) CENTURY 3624
                                     (D2061)
Lark, The *see Die Lerche

Lieder Auf Worte Von Eliska
    Krasnohorska *CCU
    [Czech/Ger/Eng] solo,pno SUPRAPHON
    s.p.   (D2062)
Lieder Auf Worte Von Pfleger-Moravsky
    *Op.2, CCU
    [Czech/Ger/Eng] solo,pno SUPRAPHON
    s.p.   (D2063)
Lieder Aus Der Koniginhofer
    Handschrift
    [Czech/Ger/Eng] solo,pno SUPRAPHON
    s.p.
    contains: Cuckoo, The, Op.7,No.3;
    Das Strausschen, "Nosegay,
    The", Op.7,No.1; Die Erdbeeren,
    "Strawberries, The", Op.7,No.6;
    Die Lerche, "Lark, The", Op.7,
    No.4; Die Rose, "Rose, The",
    Op.7,No.2; Die Verlassens,
    "Forsaken, The", Op.7,No.5
                                     (D2064)
Liedeslieder *Op.83, CCU
    [Eng/Ger/Czech] high solo,pno
    SCHAUR EE 769 $3.25   (D2065)
Little May-Time Song
    low solo,pno (D flat maj) ALLANS
    s.p.   (D2066)
    high solo,pno (E flat maj) ALLANS
    s.p.   (D2067)
Naiads *Op.50,No.2
    see Drei Neugriechische Gedichte

No Escape *Op.6,No.4
    see Vier Lieder Nach Serbischer
    Volkspoesie

Nosegay, The *see Das Strausschen

O Sanctissima *Op.19,No.3, sac
    "Hymnus Ad Laudes In Festo Ss.
    Trinitatis" see Drei Geistliche
    Gesange
    boy solo/girl solo,pno SUPRAPHON
    s.p.   (D2068)
    [Lat] ABar soli,org SUPRAPHON s.p.
                                     (D2069)
Once Fell A Maid Asleep *Op.6,No.1
    see Vier Lieder Nach Serbischer
    Volkspoesie

Psalm 23 *sac
    high solo,pno GALAXY 1.1194.7 $1.00
                                     (D2070)
    low solo,pno GALAXY 1.1195.7 $1.00
                                     (D2071)
Psalmen (from Biblical Songs, Op. 99)
    sac,CC6U,Bibl
    (Bornefeld, Helmut) med solo,org
    (med diff) BAREN. 2426 $9.75
                                     (D2072)
Rose, The *see Die Rose

Rosmarin *see Rozmaryna

Rozmaryna
    "Rosmarin" see Dvorak, Antonin,
    Sirotek

Rusalkas Lied An Den Mond (from
    Rusalka)
    [Czech/Ger/Eng] solo,pno SUPRAPHON
    s.p.   (D2073)
    "Rusalka's Song To The Moon" high
    solo,pno (G flat maj) ALLANS s.p.

DVORAK, ANTONIN (cont'd.)

Rusalka's Song To The Moon   *see
    Rusalkas Lied An Den Mond   (D2074)

Russische Lieder   *CCU
    [Czech/Russ] 2 soli,pno SUPRAPHON
    s.p.   (D2075)

Sirotek   *Op.5
    "Das Waisenkind" [Czech/Ger/Eng]
    solo,pno SUPRAPHON s.p. contains
    also: Rozmaryna, "Rosmarin"   (D2076)

Song Of The Water Gnome (from
    Rusalka)
    [Czech/Ger] B solo,pno BOOSEY $1.75
                                     (D2077)

Song To The Moon (from Rusalka)
    [Czech/Ger/Eng] S solo,pno BOOSEY
    $1.50   (D2078)

Songs My Mother Taught Me   *see Als
    Die Alte Mutter

Strawberries, The   *see Die Erdbeeren

Tri Novorecke Basne   *CC3U
    med solo,pno SUPRAPHON s.p. (D2079)

V Narodnim Tonu
    "Im Volkston" high solo,pno
    SUPRAPHON s.p.   (D2080)
    "Im Volkston" low solo,pno
    SUPRAPHON s.p.   (D2081)

Vecerni Pisne   *CCU
    med solo,pno SUPRAPHON s.p. (D2082)

Vier Lieder   *Op.82, CC4U
    [Czech] SUPRAPHON s.p. high solo,
    pno; low solo,pno   (D2083)

Vier Lieder Nach Serbischer
    Volkspoesie
    [Czech/Ger/Eng] solo,pno SUPRAPHON
    s.p.
    contains: Flowery Omens, Op.6,
    No.3; No Escape, Op.6,No.4;
    Once Fell A Maid Asleep, Op.6,
    No.1; Warning, Op.6,No.2   (D2084)

Warning   *Op.6,No.2
    see Vier Lieder Nach Serbischer
    Volkspoesie

DYCK, VLADIMIR
    Vos Vet Sain Mit Isroel?
    high solo,pno,vln (Yiddish and
    French texts) SALABERT-US $4.50
                                     (D2085)

D'YE KEN JOHN PEEL see Metcalfe,
    William

DYING OF THE LIGHT, THE see Riegger,
    Wallingford

DYKES, JOHN BACCHUS (1823-1876)
    Lead Kindly Light   *sac
    low solo,pno (G maj) CENTURY 3619
    $.40   (D2086)

DYNINGEN see Kilpinen, Yrio

DYSON, GEORGE (1883-1964)
    Night Piece
    see Three Songs To Julia

    Poet's Hymn, A
    solo,pno CRAMER $.95   (D2087)

    Sea Music
    2 soli,pno CRAMER   (D2088)

    Sweet, Be Not Proud
    see Three Songs To Julia

    Three Songs To Julia
    med solo,pno NOVELLO 17.0241.06
    s.p.
    contains: Night Piece; Sweet, Be
    Not Proud; When I Behold   (D2089)

    When I Behold
    see Three Songs To Julia

D'YSOT, E.
    Das Standchen
    [It/Fr] solo,pno SANTIS 560 s.p.
                                     (D2090)

E

E AGORA...SO ME RESTA A MINHA VOZ see
    Camargo Guarnieri

E CIASCUNO SALUTO NELL'ALTRO LA VITA
    see Arrigo, Girolamo

E DESTIN! DEBBO ANDARMENE see
    Leoncavallo, Ruggiero

E DI SILENZI PLACIDI see Davico,
    Vincenzo

E GIUNTO IL NOSTRO ULTIMO AUTUNNO see
    Alfano, Franco

E HEHU KERITO see Jillett, David

E HERZIGS MEITELI see Luthold, E.

E IL MIO DOLORE IO CANTO see Pizzetti,
    Ildebrando

E LA SOLITA STORIA DEL PASTORE see
    Cilea, Francesco

E LIEKE see Maes, L.

E LO MIO AMORE see Tirindelli, Pier
    Adolfo

E L'UCCELLINO see Puccini, Giacomo

E LUCEVAN LE STELLE see Puccini,
    Giacomo

E NEL MIO SOGNO see Clausetti, P.

E SE UN GIORNO TORNASSE... see
    Respighi, Ottorino

E SO PADER LI MANDA A DIR
    (Carlo, Musi) solo,pno (Bolognese
    dialect) BONGIOVANI 2047 s.p. see
    from El Mi Canzunett   (E1)

E SOGNO? O REALTA? see Verdi, Giuseppe

'E SPINGOLE FRANGESE see De Leva,
    Enrico

E' TORNATA PRIMAVERA see Cimara, Pietro

E TU MI FAI MORIR! see Barbirolli, A.

E UN RISO GENTIL see Leoncavallo,
    Ruggiero

E VUI DURMITI ANCORA see Cali'

EACH MAN see Tautenhahn, Gunther

EACH STEP I TAKE see Mercer

EACH STEP OF THE WAY see Harper

EAKIN
    Christmas Morn   *sac,Xmas
    med solo,pno (B flat maj) FISCHER,C
    V 2333   (E2)

EARL OF BRISTOL'S FAREWELL, THE see
    Orr, Charles Wilfred

EARLIE'S SON see Lawson, Malcolm

EARLS, PAUL
    Lord's Prayer, The
    S solo,org SCHIRM.EC 2598 s.p. (E3)

EARLY AMERICAN PORTRAIT see Ballou,
    Esther W.

EARLY AMERICAN SONGS   *CC64U,folk,US
    (Johnson, M.; Johnson, T.) 1-2 med
    soli,pno AMP $.40   (E4)

EARLY BACON see Blyton, Carey

EARLY IN THE MORNING see Rorem, Ned

EARLY MORNING see Curwin, Clifford

EARLY MORNING IN LONDON see Griffes,
    Charles Tomlinson, Impression Du
    Matin

EARLY MUSIC IN FACSIMILE, VOL. I: A
    FIFTEENTH CENTURY SONG BOOK   *CCU,
    15th cent
    solo,pno BOETHIUS $10.40   (E5)

EARLY MUSIC IN FACSIMILE, VOL. II: THE
    TURPYN BOOK OF LUTE SONGS   *CCU
    solo,pno BOETHIUS $19.60   (E6)

EARLY MUSIC SERIES, VOL. 1: HARMONIA
    CONCERTANS, PART I see Posch, Isaac

EARLY MUSIC SERIES, VOL. 2: MUSICHE,
    PART I see Gagliano, Giovanni
    Battista da

EARLY MUSIC SERIES, VOL. 3: SIX
    CANTATAS see Savioni, Mario

EARLY MUSIC SERIES, VOL. 4: HARMONIA
    CONCERTANS, PART II see Posch,
    Isaac

EARLY MUSIC SERIES, VOL. 5: MUSICHE,
    PART II see Gagliano, Giovanni
    Battista da

EARLY MUSIC SERIES, VOL. 6: HARMONIA
    CONCERTANS, PART III see Posch,
    Isaac

EARLY ONE MORNING see Clements, John

EARLY ONE MORNING see Tarrasch

EARTH AND AIR AND RAIN see Finzi,
    Gerald

EARTH IS THE LORD'S, THE see
    Freudenthal, Josef

EARTH TREMBLED, THE see Purcell, Henry

EARTH WILL SING, THE see Owens

EAST PAGODA OF THE TEMPLE YAKUSHIJI,
    THE see Hayashi, Azusa, Yakushiji
    Azuma-To

EAST RIDING, THE see Ireland, John

EASTER BELLS   *sac,gospel
    solo,pno ABER.GRP. $1.50   (E7)

EASTER CAROL see Brumby, Colin

EASTER CAROL see Shaw, Martin

EASTER CAROLS NEW AND OLD   *sac,CC68UL,
    Easter
    1-4 soli,pno LILLENAS ME-8 $1.00 (E8)

EASTER DAY see Arensky, Anton
    Stepanovitch, Jour De Paques

EASTER FOR LOW VOICE   *sac,CC32UL,
    Easter
    low solo,pno LILLENAS ME-32 $1.50
                                     (E9)

EASTER HYMN   *Easter
    (Bantock, Granville) [Eng/Fr] high
    solo,kbd CHESTER s.p.   (E10)

EASTER PRAYER, AN see Thiman, Eric
    Harding

EASTER TRIPTYCH see Bassett, Leslie

EASTER TRIUMPH see Hildach, Eugen

EASTERLING, MARION W.
    When I Wake Up To Sleep No More   *sac
    solo,pno WORD S-407   (E11)
    solo,pno BENSON S8433-S $1.00   (E12)

EASTERN GATE, THE see Heilner, Irwin

EASTERN GATE, THE see Martin

EASY GERMAN CLASSIC SONGS   *CCU
    (Golde, W.) [Eng/Ger] med solo,pno
    PRESSER $1.50   (E13)

EATING SONG see Taylor, Deems (Joseph)

EATON
    Holy Sonnets Of John Donne   *sac,CCU
    solo,pno SHAWNEE IA 64 $2.50   (E14)

    Songs For R P B   *CCU
    solo,pno SHAWNEE IA 67 $10.00   (E15)

EBART, SAMUEL (1655-1684)
    Jesu Christe, Hab' Erbarmen   *see
    Miserere, Christe, Mei

    Miserere, Christe, Mei   *sac,concerto
    T/S solo,vln,vcl,org KISTNER cmplt
    ed s.p., voc sc s.p., ipa
    "Jesu Christe, Hab' Erbarmen" [Lat/
    Ger] T/S solo,vln,vcl,cont sc
    CONCORDIA 97-4240 $2.00   (E17)

EBBEN, N'ANDRO LONTANA see Catalani,
    Alfredo

EBBEN, NE ANDRO LONTANA see Catalani,
    Alfredo

EBBEN, NE ANDRO LONTANA see Catalani,
    Alfredo, Pues Bien...Ire Lejana

EBBENHORST-TENGBERGEN, M.E. VON
    Zeven Kinderliedjes   *CC7U
    solo,pno BROEKMANS 144 s.p.   (E18)

EBEL, ARNOLD (1883-1963)
Zehn Lieder Aus Dem Quickborn
*Op.20, CC10U
solo,pno SCHAUR EE 1182 s.p.   (E19)

EBEN, PETR (1929-   )
Heimliche Lieder
[Czech/Ger] solo,pno SUPRAPHON s.p.
(E20)

Jarni Popevky *CCU
solo,pno SUPRAPHON   (E21)

Male Smutky *CC5U
high solo,pno SUPRAPHON   (E22)

Pisne Nelaskave *CCU
[Czech/Ger] A solo,vla/pno PANTON
414 s.p.   (E23)

Pisne Nelaskave *CCU
[Czech/Ger] A solo,vla,opt pno
PANTON s.p.   (E24)

Sechs Lieder *CC6U
med solo,pno DEUTSCHER 9001 s.p.
(E25)

Sechs Minnelieder *CC6U
[Czech/Ger/Eng/It/Fr] solo,pno
SUPRAPHON s.p.   (E26)

Sestero Piesni Milostnych *CC6U
[Czech/Ger/Eng/Fr/It] med solo,pno/
harp SUPRAPHON s.p.   (E27)

Tri Tiche Pisne *CC3U
[Czech/Ger] S solo,fl,pno CZECH
s.p.   (E28)

EBERLE, F.
Unterm Lindenbaum
solo,pno SCHAUR EE 3540 s.p.   (E29)

EBREZZA see Veneziani, Vittore

ECCE HOMO see Peterson-Berger, (Olof)
Wilhelm

ECCE HOMO see Trunk, Richard

ECCE NUNC see Klerk, Albert de

ECCE PANIS see Cherubini, Luigi

ECCE PANIS see Dubois, Theodore

ECCE PANIS see Samuel-Rosseau, Marcel

ECCO DI DOLCI RAGGI see Monteverdi,
Claudio

ECCO DUNQUE L'ORRIBIL CITTA see
Massenet, Jules

ECCO, ECCO, L'INFAUSTO LIDO see
Porpora, Nicola Antonio

ECCO IL MONDO see Boito, Arrigo

ECCO IL MONOLOGO see Cilea, Francesco

ECCO IL PUNTO - NON, PIU DI FIORI see
Mozart, Wolfgang Amadeus

ECCO LA NOTTE see Mannino, Franco

ECCO, QUEL FIERO ISTANTE see Mozart,
Wolfgang Amadeus

ECCO, RIDENTE IN CIELO see Rossini,
Gioacchino

ECCO SETTEMBRE see Pick-Mangiagalli,
Riccardo

ECHANGES see Ferroud, Pierre-Octave

ECHI DEL MARE see Bossi, Renzo

ECHO see Hindemith, Paul

ECHO see Rovics, Howard

ECHO SONG see Bishop, Sir Henry Rowley

ECHOES FROM POEMS BY PATRICIA BENTON
see Weigl, Vally

ECHOES IN THE ORCHARD see Slater, David
D.

ECHOES OF GOD'S GREATNESS see Good,
Dwayne

ECHOING GREEN, THE see Cooke, S.C.

ECHOS D'ALLEMAGNE, VOL. I *CC24L
solo,pno DURAND 80 s.p. contains
works by: Mendelssohn; Spohr;
Kucken; Beethoven and others   (E30)

ECHOS D'ALLEMAGNE, VOL. III *CC28L
solo,pno DURAND 2270 s.p. contains
works by: Beethoven; Schumann;
Mendelssohn; Schubert and others
(E31)

ECHOS DE FRANCE, VOL. I *CC42L
1-3 soli,pno DURAND 89 s.p. contains
works by: Dalayrac; Gluck; Piccini;
Mehul; Lully and others   (E32)

ECHOS DE FRANCE, VOL. II *CC46L
1-3 soli,pno DURAND 401 s.p. contains
works by: Monsigny; Gretry;
Dalayrac;Philidor; Albanese;
Martini and others   (E33)

ECHOS DE FRANCE, VOL. III (1650 TO
1850) *CC45L
solo,pno DURAND 7004 s.p. conatins
works by: Lully; Rameau; Cherubini;
Kreutzer; Piccini and others   (E34)

ECHOS DU TEMPS PASSE, VOL. I *CC41L
solo,pno DURAND 111 s.p. contains
works by: Machault; Jannequin;
Stuart; Durand; Campra and others
(E35)

ECHOS DU TEMPS PASSE, VOL. II *CC45L
solo,pno DURAND 225 s.p. contains
works by: Guedron; Ballard;
L'Attaingnant; Rameau; Boisset and
others   (E36)

ECHOS DU TEMPS PASSE, VOL. III *CC45L
solo,pno DURAND 2461 s.p. contains
works by: Lulli; Lemaire; Couperin;
Rebel and others   (E37)

ECHOS II DE VOTRE FAUST see Pousseur,
Henri

ECHO'S SONG see Rorem, Ned

ECKERT, KARL ANTON FLORIAN (1820-1879)
Er Liebt Nur Mich Allein
(Liebling) "None He Loves But Me"
[Ger/Fr/Eng] med solo,pno (B flat
maj) SCHIRM.G $.60   (E38)

None He Loves But Me *see Er Liebt
Nur Mich Allein

Swiss Echo Song
high solo,pno (D maj) ALLANS s.p.
(E39)

ECLAIRCIES see Bernier, Rene

ECLOSIONS see Bernier, Rene

ECO DI NAPOLI, VOL. I *CC50L
(De Meglio) [It] solo,pno RICORDI-ENG
44980 s.p.   (E40)

ECO DI NAPOLI, VOL. II *CC50L
(De Meglio) [It] solo,pno RICORDI-ENG
45980 s.p.   (E41)

ECO DI NAPOLI, VOL. III *CC50L
(De Meglio) [It] solo,pno RICORDI-ENG
93530 s.p.   (E42)

ECOUTE, MON COEUR! see Caplet, Andre

ECOUTER ET NE RIEN ENTENDRE see
Pillois, Jacques

ECOUTEZ LA CHANSON BIEN DOUCE see
Diepenbrock, Alphons

ECOUTEZ, TOUT SE TAIT see Saint-Saens,
Camille

ECRIN see Chaminade, Cecile

ECSTASIS MANE EBURNEI see Rouse,
Christopher

ECSTASY see Coulthard, Jean

ECSTASY see Rummel, Walter Morse

ECSTASY OF SPRING see Rosenmuller,
Johann

ECSTATIC, THE see Naylor, Bernard

ED ANCHE BEPPE AMO see Mascagni, Pietro

ED E PUR DUNGUE VERO see Monteverdi,
Claudio

ED E SUBITO SERA see Jensch, Lothar

ED IO NON NE GODEVO see Giordano,
Umberto

EDEJI
Jag Sjunger Om Karlek
solo,pno LUNDQUIST s.p.   (E43)

EDEL, YITZCHAK (1896-   )
Achalei Bachalili
"Shepherd's Song" [Heb] high solo,
pno TRANSCON. SP 6 $.75   (E44)

Shepherd's Song *see Achalei
Bachalili

EDEN REVISITED see Boardman, Reginald

EDEN, ROBERT
What's In The Air Today
high solo,pno ELKIN 27.0461.07 s.p.
(E45)

EDENSONG see Chance, Nancy

EDER, HELMUT (1916-   )
Cadunt Umbrae *Op.61
A solo,orch study sc DOBLINGER
STP 342 s.p.   (E46)

Drei Tierlieder *Op.5,No.1-3, CC3U
high solo,orch DOBLINGER 08 629
$2.25   (E47)

EDGE OF DREAMS see Sowerby, Leo

EDLER, ROBERT (1912-   )
Aus Stillen Fenstern
see Vier Morgenstern Lieder

Das Weiss Ich Und Hab Es Erlebt
*Op.1,No.3
see Gesange An Gott

Dasst Aus Diesem Engen Haus *Op.1,
No.2
see Gesange An Gott

Der Blutenzweig
see Vier Lieder Fur Bariton

Der Wanderer An Den Tod
see Vier Lieder Fur Bariton

Drei Lieder Fur Sopran Und Orchester
S solo,2fl,2ob,2clar,2bsn,2horn,
2trp,timp,strings TONOS s.p.
contains: Im Blick Des Mondes,
Op.3,No.1; Mich Ruft Dein Bild,
Op.3,No.2; Zu Spat, Op.3,No.3
(E48)

Erster Schnee
see Vier Morgenstern Lieder

Gesange An Gott *sac
med-high solo,fl,ob,2clar,bsn,
2horn,strings TONOS s.p.
contains: Das Weiss Ich Und Hab
Es Erlebt, Op.1,No.3; Dasst Aus
Diesem Engen Haus, Op.1,No.2;
Mitten In Der Nacht, Op.1,No.1
(E49)

Im Blick Des Mondes *Op.3,No.1
see Drei Lieder Fur Sopran Und
Orchester

Mich Ruft Dein Bild *Op.3,No.2
see Drei Lieder Fur Sopran Und
Orchester

Mitten In Der Nacht *Op.1,No.1
see Gesange An Gott

Nacht
see Vier Lieder Fur Bariton

Nebel Hangt
see Vier Morgenstern Lieder

Sei Bereit!
see Vier Morgenstern Lieder

Vier Lieder Fur Bariton
Bar solo,pno TONOS 5411 s.p.
contains: Der Blutenzweig; Der
Wanderer An Den Tod; Nacht; Weg
Nach Innen   (E50)

Vier Morgenstern Lieder
S solo,pno TONOS 5412 s.p.
contains: Aus Stillen Fenstern;
Erster Schnee; Nebel Hangt; Sei
Bereit!   (E51)

Weg Nach Innen
see Vier Lieder Fur Bariton

Zu Spat *Op.3,No.3
see Drei Lieder Fur Sopran Und
Orchester

EDMUND, J.
Milkmaids
med solo,pno PRESSER $.75   (E52)

EDMUNDS
Five Arias *CC5U
high solo,pno FISCHER,C RB 35; low
solo,pno FISCHER,C RB 36   (E53)

Jesus, Jesus, Rest Your Head
high solo,pno (G maj) FISCHER,C
RS 291   (E54)
med solo,pno (E flat maj) FISCHER,C
RS 290   (E55)
low solo,pno (C maj) FISCHER,C
RS 292   (E56)

Praise We The Lord *sac
low solo,pno FISCHER,C RS 273   (E57)
high solo,pno FISCHER,C RS 272
(E58)

EDMUNDS, JOHN (1913-   )
Have These For Yours
solo,pno PEER $.95   (E59)

Isle Of Portland
solo,pno BOOSEY $1.50   (E60)

O Death, Rock Me Asleep
solo,pno PEER $.95   (E61)

EDRIC CONNOR COLLECTION OF WEST INDIAN
SPIRITUALS AND FOLK TUNES *CCU,
folk
(Saunders, M.; Evans, H.) solo,pno
BOOSEY $4.50   (E62)

EDWARD
see Schirmer's American Folk-Song
Series, Set XXII (American-English
Folk-Ballads From The Southern
Appalachian Mountains)

EDWARD GRAY see Sullivan, Sir Arthur
Seymour

EDWARD MACDOWELL SONGS see MacDowell,
Edward Alexander

EDWARDS, CLARA (? -1974)
Birds
solo,pno ALLANS s.p.   (E63)
high solo,pno (A flat maj) SCHIRM.G
$.60   (E64)

By The Bend Of The River *sac
med solo,pno (E flat maj) ALLANS
s.p.   (E65)
low solo,pno (C maj) ALLANS s.p.
(E66)
low solo,pno (C maj) SCHIRM.G $.85
(E67)
med solo,pno (E flat maj) SCHIRM.G
$.85   (E68)
high solo,pno (G flat maj) ALLANS
s.p.   (E69)
(Deis) SA soli,pno SCHIRM.G $.85
(E70)
(Deis) SBar soli,pno SCHIRM.G $.85
(E71)
Dedication *sac
med-high solo,pno (B flat maj)
SCHIRM.G $.85   (E72)

Evening Song
low solo,pno (D maj) SCHIRM.G $.85
(E73)
Fisher's Widow, The
med-high solo,pno (C min) SCHIRM.G
$.60   (E74)
high solo,pno (C min) ALLANS s.p.
(E75)
low solo,pno (A min) ALLANS s.p.
(E76)
Into The Night
med solo,pno (F maj) SCHIRM.G $1.00
(E77)
low solo,pno (E flat maj) SCHIRM.G
$1.00   (E78)
high solo,pno (G maj) SCHIRM.G
$1.00   (E79)
high solo,pno (G maj) ALLANS s.p.
(E80)
low solo,pno (E flat maj) ALLANS
s.p.   (E81)
med solo,pno (F maj) ALLANS s.p.
(E82)
Lord Is Exalted, The *sac
med-high solo,pno (D maj) SCHIRM.G
$.60   (E83)

Lord Is My Light, The (Psalm 27) sac
high solo,pno (G maj) SCHIRM.G $.75
(E84)
Love Song, A
med solo,pno PRESSER $.75   (E85)

My Task *see Ashford, E.L.

Psalm 27 *see Lord Is My Light, The

Snow, The
high solo,pno (A maj) SCHIRM.G $.75
(E86)
To Thee, Divine Redeemer *sac
low solo,pno (A min) SCHIRM.G $.60
(E87)
When Jesus Walked On Galilee *sac
med-high solo,pno (F maj) SCHIRM.G
$.75   (E88)
low solo,pno (D flat maj) SCHIRM.G
$.75   (E89)

EDWARDS, GEORGE
Captive, The
S solo,fl,ob,clar,bass clar,vibra,
hpsd,2vln,2vla,vcl,bvl sc
AM.COMP.AL. $26.50   (E90)

Three Hopkins Songs *CC3U
SS soli,2pno sc AM.COMP.AL. $7.70
(E91)

EDWARDS, ROSS
Kan-Touk *sac
female solo,harp,2pno,2perc,
electronic tape ALBERT AHL183
s.p.   (E92)

EDWIN, ROBERT
Keep The Rumor Going *sac,CCUL
solo,pno,opt gtr VANGUARD V541
$2.00   (E93)

EE, BY GUM! see Butler, R.

EEN ALLEEN IS MAAR VERDRIETIG *CC171U
(Weiss; Andreae) solo,pno ALSBACH
s.p.   (E94)

EEN ALRE LIEFFELICKEN EEN see Horst,
Anton van der

EEN AMSTERDAMSCH LIED see Flothius,
Marius

E'EN AS A LOVELY FLOWER see Bridge,
Frank

EEN BEETJE INSPRAAK see Janssen, Guus

EEN DING HEB IK BEGEERD see Schouwman,
Hans

EEN DISSONANT see Mulder, Herman

EEN GOED LYEDEKEN see Schouwman, Hans

EEN HAND see Middeleer, Jean De, Une
Main

EEN HOLLANDSCH LIED see Tetterode, L.
Adr. von

EEN JONGE DICHTER DENKT AAN DE GELIEFDE
see Pluister, Simon

EEN JONGE DICHTER DENKT AAN ZIJN
GELIEFDE see Ruyneman, Daniel

EEN KINDEKYN IS ONS GHEBOREN see
Beekhuis, Hanna

EEN KLAAGZANG see Reynvaan, M.C.C.

EEN KRUIS MET ROZEN see Hutschenruyter,
Wouter

EEN KRUIS MET ROZEN see Pomper, A.

EEN LENTEKIND see Loots, Ph.

EEN LIED DER BLIJDSCHAP see Legley,
Victor

EEN LIED VAN DEN DOOD see Zagwijn,
Henri

EEN LIED VAN DEN WIJN see Strategier,
Herman

EEN LIED VAN HERTOG JAN I VAN BARBANT
see Weegenhuise, Johan

EEN LIEDJE VAN DE ZEE see Rontgen,
[Julius]

EEN LIEDJE VAN VERLANGEN see Witte, D.

EEN MAHARADJA IN MALAKKA see Rontgen,
Johannes

EEN MIDDELEEUWSCH MEILIED see
Felderhof, Jan

EEN NIEUWE LENTE OP HOLLANDS ERF see
Voormolen, Alexander Nicolas

EEN OUD LIED see Zweers, [Bernard]

EEN SCHEPPING see Andriessen, Hendrik

EEN SOMBER DRINKLIED see Baeyens,
August-L.

EENMAAL HEB IK U AANSCHOUWD see Zweers,
[Bernard]

EENS MEIEN MORGENS VROEGE see
Schouwman, Hans

EENZAME NACHT see Breman, W.F.

EENZAME NACHT see Voormolen, Alexander
Nicolas

EENZAME WAKE see Zagwijn, Henri

E'ER SINCE THINE EYE TOWARDS MINE WAS
WENDED see Strauss, Richard,
Seitdem Dein Aug'in Meines Schaute

EERRIJCKJEN see Sigtenhorst-Meyer,
Bernhard van den

EERSTE AANBLIK see Zagwijn, Henri

EERSTE BLIK see Andriessen, K.

EERSTE COMMUNIELIED see Hullebroeck,
Em.

EERSTE MISSIELIED see Hullebroeck, Em.

EFENT, REBETSIN!
see Six Folk Songs

EFFINGER, CECIL (1914-   )
Mary's Soliloquy (from St. Luke
Christmas Story, The) sac
med solo,pno (A min) SCHIRM.G $.75
(E95)

EFFINGER, J.C.
I Shall Not Pass Again This Way
high solo,pno PRESSER $.95   (E96)
low solo,pno PRESSER $.95   (E97)

EFFLEUREMENT see Ratz, Ludo

EFTER LANG SORG see Berggreen, Andreas
Peter

EFTERSKORD see Stenhammar, Wilhelm

EG KRYP see Dorumsgaard, Arne

EGAN O'RAHILLY see Mourant, Walter

EGENOLF
Gassenhawerlin Und Reutterliedlin
[Ger] S solo,2A rec,T rec,B rec
PETERS N995   (E98)

EGERTON, ARTHUR
Immortal Love *sac,Gen/Marriage
solo,pno (D flat maj) LESLIE 7040
(E99)

EGGE, KLAUS (1906-   )
Draumar I Stjernesno
solo,pno MUSIKK s.p.
contains: Eit Lite Sumarkvede,
Op.18,No.3; Helgsog Fra Rymdi,
Op.18,No.1; Ut Slaer Seg Din
Sjeleblom, Op.18,No.2   (E100)

Eit Lite Sumarkvede *Op.18,No.3
see Draumar I Stjernesno

Elskhugskvede
solo,pno MUSIKK s.p.   (E101)

Helgsog Fra Rymdi *Op.18,No.1
see Draumar I Stjernesno

Ut Slaer Seg Din Sjeleblom *Op.18,
No.2
see Draumar I Stjernesno

EGGE, RAGNVALD
Fader Var
solo,pno MUSIKK s.p.   (E102)

EGIDIUS see Praag, Henri C. van

EGIDIUS see Voormolen, Alexander
Nicolas

EGIDIUS WAER BESTU BLEVEN see Badings,
Henk

EGIDIUS WAER BESTU BLEVEN? see Breman,
W.F.

EGIDIUS, WAER BESTU BLEVEN see Hemel,
Oscar van

EGIDIUS, WAER BESTU BLEVEN? see
Weegenhuise, Johan

EGK, WERNER (1901-   )
Chansons Et Romance *CCU
[Fr] S solo,pno/orch SCHOTTS 4217
s.p.   (E103)

La Tentation De St. Antoine
[Fr] A solo,4strings/strings voc sc
SCHOTTS 4543 s.p., study sc
SCHOTTS 4559 s.p., sc SCHOTTS
s.p., ipr   (E104)

Natur - Liebe - Tod *cant
B solo,chamb.orch voc sc SCHOTTS
2921 rental   (E105)

Quattro Canzoni *CC4U
[Ger/It] high solo,pno/orch SCHOTTS
4344 s.p.   (E106)

Variationen Uber Ein Altes Wiener
Strophenlied
coloratura sop,pno/orch SCHOTTS
3788 s.p.   (E107)

EGLE see Respighi, Ottorino

EGO AUTEM see Vlad, Roman

EGO AUTEM PRO TE, DOMINE see Benevoli,
Orazio

EGON, RODRIGO
Three Village Songs *CC3U
solo,pno BOOSEY $2.25   (E108)

Tres Canciones Aldeanas *CC3U
solo,pno BARRY-ARG BC 2007 s.p.
(E109)

EGYPTIAN FOLK SONGS *CC56U
(Rasheed, Baheega Sidky) solo,pno OAK
000071 $2.95 Arabic and English

texts   (E110)

EGYPT'S MIGHT IS TUMBLED DOWN see
Fleming, Christopher le

EH BIEN! MONSIEUR, NE SERAIT-CE PAS
CHARMANT see Messager, Andre

EH BIEN! PARLEZ, MONSIEUR see Messager,
Andre

EH VERGILBT DEIN HAG see Rietz,
Johannes

EHATYSSAVU see Sonninen, Ahti

EHE see Bijvanck, Henk

EHEU FUGACES see Kilpinen, Yrio

EHRE SEI GOTT IN DER HOHE! see Reger,
Max

EHRENBERG, CARL EMIL THEODOR
(1878-1962)
Bleibe *Op.31,No.1
see Drei Goethe-Lieder

Damals *Op.16,No.3
S solo,pno LEUCKART s.p. see also
Vier Gesange   (E111)

Drei Goethe-Lieder
solo,pno RIES s.p.
contains: Bleibe, Op.31,No.1; Ein
Gleiches, Op.31,No.3;
Elfenliedchen, Op.31,No.2
(E112)

Du Fragtest Mich *Op.17,No.2
[Fr/Ger] S solo,pno LEUCKART s.p.
see also Liebeshymnen   (E113)

Ein Gleiches *Op.31,No.3
see Drei Goethe-Lieder

Eines Weibes Bitte *Op.18,No.2
[Fr/Ger] med solo,pno LEUCKART s.p.
see also Zwei Ernste Gesange
(E114)

Elfenliedchen *Op.31,No.2
see Drei Goethe-Lieder

Es Schwellt Mir Die Brust *Op.17,
No.4
[Fr/Ger] S solo,pno LEUCKART s.p.
see also Liebeshymnen   (E115)

Fallendes Laub *Op.16,No.2
S solo,pno LEUCKART s.p. see also
Vier Gesange   (E116)

Gebet *Op.18,No.1
[Fr/Ger] med solo,pno LEUCKART s.p.
see also Zwei Ernste Gesange
(E117)

Im Walde *Op.21,No.2
see Zwei Lieder Nach Gedichten Von
Theodor Storm

Indes Einst Der Todbleiche Mond
*Op.17,No.3
[Fr/Ger] S solo,pno LEUCKART s.p.
see also Liebeshymnen   (E118)

Liebesgluck *Op.16,No.1
S solo,pno LEUCKART s.p. see also
Vier Gesange   (E119)

Liebeshymnen
[Fr/Ger] LEUCKART S solo,pno cmplt
ed,voc sc s.p.; S solo,2fl,2ob,
2clar,2bsn,4horn,2trp,3trom,timp,
perc,harp,5strings rental
contains & see also: Du Fragtest
Mich, Op.17,No.2; Es Schwellt
Mir Die Brust, Op.17,No.4;
Indes Einst Der Todbleiche
Mond, Op.17,No.3; Schweigen,
Op.17,No.1   (E120)

Schliesse Mir Die Augen Beide
*Op.21,No.1
see Zwei Lieder Nach Gedichten Von
Theodor Storm

Schweigen *Op.17,No.1
[Fr/Ger] S solo,pno LEUCKART s.p.
see also Liebeshymnen   (E121)

Vier Gesange
LEUCKART S solo,pno cmplt ed,voc sc
s.p.; S solo,2fl,2ob,2clar,2bsn,
4horn,2trp,3trom,timp,perc,harp,
5strings cmplt ed,sc rental
contains & see also: Damals,
Op.16,No.3; Fallendes Laub,
Op.16,No.2; Liebesgluck, Op.16,
No.1; Zuversicht, Op.16,No.4
(E122)

Zuversicht *Op.16,No.4
S solo,pno LEUCKART s.p. see also
Vier Gesange   (E123)

Zwei Ernste Gesange
[Fr/Ger] LEUCKART med solo,pno
cmplt ed,voc sc s.p.; med solo,

EHRENBERG, CARL EMIL THEODOR (cont'd.)
2fl,2ob,2clar,2bsn,4horn,2trp,
3trom,timp,harp,5strings cmplt
ed,sc rental
contains & see also: Eines Weibes
Bitte, Op.18,No.2; Gebet,
Op.18,No.1   (E124)

Zwei Lieder Nach Gedichten Von
Theodor Storm
solo,pno RIES s.p.
contains: Im Walde, Op.21,No.2;
Schliesse Mir Die Augen Beide,
Op.21,No.1   (E125)

EHRLICH, ABEL
Writing Of Hezekiah, The
S solo,vln,ob,bsn (3 copies needed
for performance) ISR.MUS.INST.
061 s.p.   (E126)

EHRSTROM, (JARL) OTTO (SIGURD)
(1891-   )
Fyra Visor *CC4U
solo,gtr FAZER F 4697 s.p.   (E127)

EHTOO see Linko, Ernst (Fredrik)

EI KUKAAN TAI'A ARVATA see Haapalainen,
Vaino

EI MINUSTA LIENEKANA see Kilpinen, Yrio

EI RUNO RAHATTA LAULA see Kilpinen,
Yrio

EI SULA SYAN SURUINEN see Kilpinen,
Yrio

EI, WAS TUT ES, WENN ICH SINGE see
Kilpinen, Yrio, Mita Tuosta, Jos Ma
Laulan

EICHENDORFF-LIEDER see Knab, Armin

EICHENDORFF LIEDER I see Mengelberg,
Rudolf

EICHENDORFF SONGS, VOL. I: NOS. 1-10
see Wolf, Hugo

EICHENDORFF SONGS, VOL. II: NOS. 11-20
see Wolf, Hugo

EICHENSTADT UND ABENSTERN see
Straesser, Joep

EICHENWALD, PHILIPP (1915-   )
Suoni Estremi
narrator,4strings MODERN s.p.
(E128)

EICHHORN, HERMENE WARLICK (1906-   )
Prayer To The Trinity
solo,pno BRODT $.75   (E129)

EIGHT CHORALE SETTINGS see Schein,
Johann Hermann

EIGHT ENGELMAN-SONGS see Tal, Marjo

EIGHT HUNGARIAN FOLKSONGS see Bartok,
Bela

EIGHT PETOFI SONGS see Szervanszky,
Endre

EIGHT POEMS FROM THE JAPANESE see
Stout, Alan

EIGHT POEMS OF GERARD MANLEY HOPKINS
see Pinkham, Daniel

EIGHT POEMS OF GUILLAUME APOLLINAIRE
see Satie, Erik

EIGHT RUSSIAN FOLKSONGS *CC8U
(Liadov, Anatol K.) solo,pno KALMUS
95 study sc $2.50, sc $7.00   (E130)

EIGHT SONGS see Frankel, Benjamin

EIGHT SONGS see Sibelius, Jean

EIGHT SONGS see Hovhaness, Alan

EIGHT SONGS see Grieg, Edvard Hagerup

EIGHT SONGS AND ARIAS FROM THE ANNA
MAGDALENA BACH'S MUSIC BOOK see
Bach, Johann Sebastian

EIGHT VOCAL DUETS see Marzials, Thomas

EIGHTEEN DUETS see Rubinstein, Anton

EIGHTEEN DUETS see Mendelssohn-
Bartholdy, Felix

EIGHTEEN SONGS *CC18L
(Uppling) solo,pno LUNDQUIST s.p.
contains works by: Boivie;
Hallstrom; Lassen; Helmund; Ries
and others   (E131)

EIGHTEEN VOCAL CONCERTOS see Dilliger,
Johann

EIGHTY-FIVE SONGS see Schumann, Robert
(Alexander)

EIKO TOTTA see Kilpinen, Yrio

EILE GOTT, MICH ZU ERRETTEN see Wiemer,
Wolfgang

EILE, MICH, GOTT, ZU ERRETTEN see
Schutz, Heinrich

EILI, EILI!
(Schindler) "Invocation" high solo,
pno (B min, English and Yiddish
texts) SCHIRM.G $.75   (E132)
(Schindler) "Invocation" low solo,pno
(A min, English and Yiddish texts)
SCHIRM.G $.75   (E133)

EILI EILI see Saminsky, Lazare

EIN BRIEF see Trunk, Richard

EIN BUNDEL CHANSONS VON FRECH BIS POCO
TRISTE see Zehm, Friedrich

EIN FESTE BURG see Schein, Johann
Hermann

EIN FICHTENBAUM see Marx, Joseph

EIN FICHTENBAUM STEHT EINSAM see Liszt,
Franz

EIN FRAUENSCHICKSAL see Orthel, Leon

EIN FRISCHER STRAUSS see Blume

EIN FRUHLINGSLIED see Niggeling, Willi

EIN FULLEN WARD GEBOREN see Reutter,
Hermann

EIN GEDANKE see Trunk, Richard

EIN GLEICHES see Ehrenberg, Carl Emil
Theodor

EIN GLEICHES see Weigl, Karl

EIN GOTT VERMAGS see Rautavaara,
Einojuhani

EIN GRAB see Weegenhuise, Johan

EIN GRAUSES DUNKEL see Schumann, Georg

EIN JEDER LAUFT, DER IN DEN SCHRANKEN
LAUFT see Telemann, Georg Philipp

EIN JEDER VON DEM SEINEN see Schollum,
Robert

EIN JUNGER FREUND see Vlijmen, Jan van

EIN KIND IST UNS GEBOREN see Schutz,
Heinrich

EIN KINDERMARCHEN see Hess, W.

EIN KINDERMARCHEN AM KAMINFEUER see
Merikanto, Oskar, En Barnsaga Vid
Brasen

EIN KINDERTAG see Kludas, Erich

EIN KLEINES KINDELEIN see Tunder, Franz

EIN KLEINES LIED see Gilse, Jan van

EIN KLEINES REQUIEM see Reutter,
Hermann

EIN MADCHEN ODER WEIBCHEN WUNSCHT
PAPAGENO SICH see Mozart, Wolfgang
Amadeus

EIN' MAGD, EIN' DIENERIN see Haydn,
(Johann) Michael, Cantilena Pro
Adventu

EIN MELODIE see Jentsch, Walter

EIN SCHUTZ BIN ICH see Kreutzer,
Konradin

EIN SCHWAN see Grieg, Edvard Hagerup,
En Svane

EIN SCHWEIGEN LIEGT OB WINTERWEISSEM
LAND see Jochum, Otto

EIN SCHWIPSERL see Straus, Oscar

EIN SONNTAG AUF DER ALM see Koschat,
Thomas

EIN STRAUSS, FUR DICH GEPFLUCKT see
Knorr, Ernst Lother von

EIN TAG IN UNSERER STADT see Lesser,
Wolfgang

EIN TOTENTANZ see Reimann, Aribert

EIN TRAUM see Grieg, Edvard Hagerup

EIN TRAUM IST UNSER LEBEN see Brumby, Colin

EIN VOGLEIN SINGT SO SUSSE see Frauchiger, Ch.

EIN WEIB see Frid, Geza

EIN WORT see Pablo, Luis de

EINDELOOS see Badings, Henk

EINE BRAUTMESSE see Jochum, Otto

EINE KLEINE FRUHLINGSWEISE see Dvorak, Antonin

EINE KLEINE FRUHLINGSWEISE see Dvorak, Antonin, Eine Kleine Fruhlingsweise

EINE REDE see Bois, Rob du

EINE RUNE see Kilpinen, Yrio, En Rune

EINE SINGSTIMME UND EIN CELLO MUSIZIEREN see Graener, Paul

EINE WELKE see Orthel, Leon

EINE WINTERWEISE see Palmgren, Selim, En Vintervisa

EINEM, GOTTFRIED VON
Acht Hafis-Lieder *Op.5, CC8U
high solo,pno UNIVER. 11569 $5.25
(E134)

Five Songs *Op.25,No.1-5, CC5U
[Ger] high solo,pno PETERS 5855
$5.25
(E135)

Funf Lieder Aus Dem Chinesischen
*Op.8, CC5U
[Ger] med solo,pno BOTE $5.00
(E136)

Japanische Blatter *Op.15, CCU
solo,pno SCHOTTS 4344 s.p.
published with Universal Musik
Verlag
(E137)

Rosa Mystica *CC8U
[Ger] med solo,orch BOOSEY $13.00
(E138)

Sieben Lieder *Op.19, CC7U
[Ger] med solo,pno BOTE $3.25
(E139)

Von Der Liebe *song cycle
high solo,orch BOOSEY $7.50 (E140)

EINEM KINDE ERZAHLT see Bijvanck, Henk

EINES SCHATTENS TRAUM see Giefer, Willy

EINES TRAUMERS SANG AN DAS LEBEN see Jarnefelt, Armas, En Drommares Sang Till Livet

EINES WEIBES BITTE see Ehrenberg, Carl Emil Theodor

EINGELEGTE RUDER see Gilse, Jan van

EINGELEGTE RUDER see Pfitzner, Hans

EINGEPAKT *Jew
solo,pno KAMMEN 467 $1.00 (E141)

EINHEITSLIEDER *sac,CCU
solo,org SCHOTTS 3825 voc sc s.p.,
solo pt s.p.
(E142)

EINHUNDERTELF KINDERLIEDER ZUR BIBEL
*sac,CC111U,Bibl
(Watkinson, G.) solo,perc CHRIS
50580-82 s.p.
(E143)

EINKEHR see Borris, Siegfried

EINS BITTE ICH VOM HERREN see Schutz, Heinrich

EINSAM see Kilpinen, Yrio, Kaikissa Yksin

EINSAM IN TRUBEN TAGEN see Wagner, Richard

EINSAM KLINGT DAS GLOCKCHEN *folk,Russ
see Funf Beruhmte Russische Lieder
[Ger/Russ] solo,pno ZIMMER. 1550 s.p.
(E144)

EINSAM SING' ICH see Kilpinen, Yrio, Ikava Omia Maita

EINSAME see Strauss, Richard

EINSAME CHRISTNACHT see Bijvanck, Henk

EINSAME NACHT see Kox, Hans

EINSAMKEIT see Ferroud, Pierre-Octave

EINSAMKEITEN DER SEELE see Petrzelka, Vilem

EINSCHONER MANN IST DELIKAT see Haibel, Jakob J.

EINSLEG see Braein, Edvard Fliflet

EINST DEM GRAU see Kruyf, Ton de

EINST TRAUMTE MEINER SEL'GEN BASE see Weber, Carl Maria von

EINU SINNI
see Fimm Numer I Islenzkum
Pjoobuningum

EINUNDDREISSIG LIEDER NACH GEDICHTEN
VON HUUGO JALKASEN, VOL. I see
Kilpinen, Yrio

EINUNDDREISSIG LIEDER NACH GEDICHTEN
VON HUUGO JALKASEN, VOL. III see
Kilpinen, Yrio

EINUNDDREISSIG LIEDER NACH GEDICHTEN
VON HUUGO JALKASEN, VOL. IV see
Kilpinen, Yrio

EISDELL, HUBERT
Loughareema
low solo,pno (C maj) CRAMER (E145)
high solo,pno (D maj) CRAMER (E146)

Wherefores And Whys *CCU
solo,pno CRAMER
(E147)

EISENMANN, W.
Rubaiyat, Zyklus 1 *song cycle
solo,pno HUG s.p.
(E148)

Rubaiyat, Zyklus 2 *song cycle
solo,pno HUG s.p.
(E149)

EISENSTEIN
Terror
[Span] solo,pno RICORDI-ARG
BA 11063 s.p.
(E150)

EISLER, HANNS (1898-1962)
Ausgewahlte Lieder Heft 1:
Anakreontische Fragmente,
Holderlin-Fragmente *CCU
solo,pno DEUTSCHER 9081 s.p. (E151)

Ausgewahlte Lieder Heft 2: Lieder
Nach Texten Von Bertolt Brecht
*CCU
solo,pno DEUTSCHER 9082 s.p. (E152)

Ausgewahlte Lieder Heft 3: Vier
Wiegenlieder-Balladen Nach
Bertolt Brecht *CCU
DEUTSCHER 9083 s.p.
(E153)

Das Vorbild
A solo,fl,ob,clar,bsn,2horn,strings
sc DEUTSCHER 1076 s.p., ipr
(E154)

Der Gott Und Die Bajadere
solo,clar,bass clar BREITKOPF-L
rental see also Lieder Und
Kantaten Band I
(E155)

Die Ballade Vom Wasserrad
solo,fl,clar,perc,pno,bvl, banjo
BREITKOPF-L rental see also
Lieder Und Kantaten Band I (E156)

Die Burgschaft
solo,clar,bass clar BREITKOPF-L
rental see also Lieder Und
Kantaten Band I
(E157)

Die Teppichweber Von Kujan-Bulak
*cant
S solo,fl,ob,2clar,2bsn,3horn,trp,
timp,perc,strings sc DEUTSCHER
1079 s.p., ipr
(E158)

Die Weissbrotkantate *cant
solo,2clar,vla,vcl DEUTSCHER rental
(E159)

Die Welt Verandern Wir
solo,unis,strings,gtr,cembalo,
2clar,bsn BREITKOPF-L rental see
also Lieder Und Kantaten Band I
(E160)

Die Zuchthaus-Kantate *cant
solo,2clar,vla,vcl BREITKOPF-L
rental see also Lieder Und
Kantaten Band I
(E161)

Ernste Gesange Fur Bariton-Solo *CCU
Bar solo,strings BREITKOPF-L
EB 4051 s.p., ipr
(E162)

Es Lachelt Der See
MezTBar soli,2fl,2ob,2clar,2bsn,
4horn,3trp,3trom,tuba,timp,perc,
strings BREITKOPF-L rental see
also Lieder Und Kantaten Band X
(E163)

Funf Lieder *CC5U
med solo,pno PETERS 5077 s.p.
(E164)

EISLER, HANNS (cont'd.)

Funf Palmstrom *Op.5, sac,CC5U,Psalm
solo,fl,pno,vla,vcl sc UNIVER. 8322
$3.75
(E165)

Lied Uber Den Frieden
MezBar soli,mix cor,2fl,2ob,2clar,
2bsn,2horn,2trp,trom,perc,strings
BREITKOPF-L rental see also
Lieder Und Kantaten Band X (E166)

Lied Von Der Belebenden Wirkung Des
Geldes
solo,fl,2clar,al-sax,sax,2trp,trom,
perc,gtr,pno,bvl BREITKOPF-L
rental see also Lieder Und
Kantaten Band I
(E167)

Lieder, Songs, Kantaten *CCU
solo,inst BREITKOPF-L EB 4072 s.p.
(E168)

Lieder Und Kantaten Band I *CC75UL
solo,inst cloth BREITKOPF-L s.p.
see also: Der Gott Und Die
Bajadere; Die Ballade Vom
Wasserrad; Die Burgschaft; Die
Welt Verandern Wir; Die
Zuchthaus-Kantate; Lied Von Der
Belebenden Wirkung Des Geldes;
Ulm 1592
(E169)

Lieder Und Kantaten Band X *CCUL
solo,cor,inst cloth BREITKOPF-L
s.p.
see also: Es Lachelt Der See;
Lied Uber Den Frieden (E170)

Sechs Lieder *Op.2, CC6U
high solo,pno UNIVER. 7778 $4.25
(E171)

Soldaritatslied *Op.27,No.1
med solo,pno UNIVER. 10073 $2.25
(E172)

Tagebuch *cant
SMezAT soli,winds,pno sc,oct
UNIVER. 8882 $4.25
(E173)

Ulm 1592
solo,4strings BREITKOPF-L rental
see also Lieder Und Kantaten Band
I
(E174)

Vier Kantaten *CC4U,cant
solo,pno UNIVER. 11664 $5.25 Op.
60, 62, 64, 65
(E175)

Zeitungsausschnitte *Op.11
solo,pno UNIVER. 9647 $5.25 (E176)

Zwei Elegien *CC2U
med solo,pno UNIVER. 11631 $2.75
(E177)

Zwei Elegien *CC2U
med solo,pno PETERS 5078 s.p.
(E178)

EISMA, WILL (1929-   )
Le Gibet
Bar solo,inst, live-elctronics
DONEMUS s.p.
(E179)

Rugiada
Mez solo,pno DONEMUS s.p. (E180)

EIT LITE SUMARKVEDE see Egge, Klaus

EITLE WUNSCHE see Sibelius, Jean

EJ EN BLOMMA MA JAG KALLAS see
Sonninen, Ahti, Ala Kutsu
Kukkaseksi

EJ, PADA, PADA ROSICKA see Andrasovan,
Tibor

EJ, SRDENKO MOJE I see Slavicky,
Klement

EJ, UHORNY, EJ, LANY see Reiner, Karel

EK, GUNNAR (1900-   )
En Pastoral
solo,pno,opt gtr GEHRMANS s.p.
(E181)

Stockholm
solo,pno,opt gtr GEHRMANS s.p.
(E182)

EKBERG
Sex Dikter *CC6U
solo,pno LUNDQUIST s.p. (E183)

EKEN, TORLEIF
Brevet Fran Mor
solo,pno MUSIKK s.p. (E184)

EKENBERG
Rida Ranka
solo,pno LUNDQUIST s.p. (E185)

EKLOF, EINAR (1886-1954)
Bon
solo,pno LUNDQUIST s.p. (E186)

Hembygdens Sang
solo,pno LUNDQUIST s.p. (E187)

EKLOF, EINAR (cont'd.)

    Lovsang
        solo,pno/org ERIKS K248 s.p. (E188)

    Morgon
        high solo,pno ERIKS K 246 s.p.
                            (E189)
        low solo,pno ERIKS K 247 s.p.
                            (E190)
        (Hellman, I.) high solo/low solo,
          fl,2clar,horn,trp,trom,strings
          ERIKS rental, ea.   (E191)

    Varsang
        solo,pno LUNDQUIST s.p.   (E192)

EKMAN, KARL EKMAN, SEN. (1869-1947)
    Du Ar Sa Vackar For Mina Ogon
    [Finn] solo,pno FAZER F 426 s.p.
                            (E193)

EKONYMFEN see Sibelius, Jean, Kaiutar

EKSYKSISSA see Sibelius, Jean, Vilse

EL ABETO *Xmas
    (Martini) [Span] solo,pno (G maj)
    RICORDI-ARG BA 11656 s.p.   (E194)

EL ADIOS DE LAS HADAS see Pahissa,
    Jaime

EL ALMA ME HAS ROBADO see Gianneo, Luis

EL AMOR see Pradas, Josep

EL AMOR QUE PASA see Cinque

EL AMOR Y LOS OJOS see Vives, Amadeo

EL ANGEL see Wagner, Richard, Der Engel

EL ANGEL TRAVIESO see Casals, Pablo

EL ARROYUELA see D'Esposito, Salve

EL BARBIR E LA TOCA!
    (Carlo, Musi) solo,pno (Bolognese
    dialect) BONGIOVANI 2056 s.p. see
    from El Mi Canzunett   (E195)

EL BONETE DEL CURA see Aguilar, F.

EL CANAPE see Palomino, J.

EL CANTO see Caggiano, Roberto

EL CANTO DE LOS PAJAROS see Pahissa,
    Jaime

EL CARNAVAL
    (Carlo, Musi) solo,pno (Bolognese
    dialect) BONGIOVANI 2105 s.p. see
    from El Mi Canzunett Seconda Serie
                             (E196)
EL CINEMATOGROF
    (Carlo, Musi) solo,pno (Bolognese
    dialect) BONGIOVANI 2101 s.p. see
    from El Mi Canzunett Seconda Serie
                             (E197)
EL CORRO DE LAS NINAS *CC60U,folk,Span
    (Montalban) [Span] med solo,pno UNION
    ESP. $1.75   (E198)

EL-DABH, HALIM (1921-   )
    Eye Of Horus, The
        B solo,perc PETERS 66292 rental
                            (E199)

    Ghost, The *see Yulei

    Tahmeela *song cycle
        [Eng] S solo,fl,ob,clar,bsn,horn,
        vln PETERS 6536 rental (E200)

    Yulei
        "Ghost, The" S solo,ob,clar,horn,
        trp,strings PETERS 6301 rental (E201)
EL DESDICHADO see Saint-Saens, Camille

EL DESPERTAR DE LAS FLORES see
    Llongueras J.

EL DIA INUTIL see Boero, Felipe

EL DOU TORR DLA MERCANZI ARTENSIS E
    RICCADONNA
    (Carlo, Musi) solo,pno (Bolognese
    dialect) BONGIOVANI 2107 s.p. see
    from El Mi Canzunett Seconda Serie
                             (E202)
EL ECUADOR see Gomez Carrillo, Manuel

EL FIACCARESTA
    (Carlo, Musi) solo,pno (Bolognese
    dialect) BONGIOVANI 2067 s.p. see
    from El Mi Canzunett   (E203)

EL FLECHAZO see Quaratino, Pascual

EL GALAN Y LA CALAVERA see
    Sciammarella, Valdo

EL GANADICO see Salas, Juan Orrego

EL GENASI
    (Carlo, Musi) solo,pno (Bolognese
    dialect) BONGIOVANI 2100 s.p. see
    from El Mi Canzunett Seconda Serie
                             (E204)
EL GNACCHER!
    (Carlo, Musi) solo,pno (Bolognese
    dialect) BONGIOVANI 2055 s.p. see
    from El Mi Canzunett   (E205)

EL JUCIO DEL ANO see Esteve, Pablo

EL LABRADOR Y EL POBRE see Guastavino,
    Carlos

EL LONEDE DI BARBIR
    (Carlo, Musi) solo,pno (Bolognese
    dialect) BONGIOVANI 2098 s.p. see
    from El Mi Canzunett Seconda Serie
                             (E206)
EL MAESTRO see Milan, Luis

EL MAGICO JARDIN see Garcia Mansilla,
    Eduardo

EL MAJO DISCRETO see Granados, Enrique

EL MAJO OLVIDADO see Granados, Enrique

EL MAJO TIMIDO see Granados, Enrique

EL MAJO Y LA ITALIANA FINGIDA see
    Laserna, Blas de

EL MAJO Y LA MAJA see Garcia, M.

EL MAR LEJANO see Garcia Leoz, J.

EL MATE AMARGO see Boero, Felipe

EL MESTER SQUASS!
    (Carlo, Musi) solo,pno (Bolognese
    dialect) BONGIOVANI 2074 s.p. see
    from El Mi Canzunett   (E207)

EL MI CANZUNETT *see Al Turnara!;
    Canzunetta Dl'Espusizion;
    Canzunetta Pruibe; Che Bell Nas!;
    Chiudi!!; Ciaccher E Narzisat; Con
    Un Occ'; Corylopsis!; Da Ql' Altra
    Part!; Dai Dal Gess!!; Dein, Dan,
    Don; Dirala D' Se?; Do, Re, Mi, Fa,
    Sol; Dottrina In Musica; Dreyfus!;
    E So Pader Li Manda A Dir; El
    Barbir E La Toca!; El Fiaccaresta;
    El Gnaccher!; El Mester Squass!; El
    Mond L'e Fatt Acse!; El San Michel,
    La Ca E La Rata D'affet; I Zalett;
    I Zever; L' A-J Passaria!; La Mi
    Premma Mrousa!; La Muntura Di
    Impiega Dla Posta; La Pison!; La
    Quadreglia; La Scheccia Angot!; La
    Scuffiareina; La Tassa Souvra Ai
    Tlon!; La Zeinta Daziaria;
    L'accademia De "La Lira";
    L'Acquedott; L'era Fasol!; Mo Che,
    Pickmann?!; Oh! Ch'al Scusa!; Oh!
    Che Miraquel!; Oh! Che Zucca; Piron
    El Furnar; Pr' Un Lativ!; Pst!
    Pst! Pst!; Sulfanein E Luster!;
    Sussezza, Cudghein E Zampon; Ta-Ta;
    Trei Mnester; Un' Avventura A
    Veglion!; Una Bona Medseina; Very
    Smart!   (E208)

EL MI CANZUNETT SECONDA SERIE *see A S
    Fa Zinquntanov!; Avrir E Assrar; El
    Carnaval; El Cinematogrof; El Dou
    Torr Dla Mercanzi Artensis E
    Riccadonna; El Genasi; El Lonede Di
    Barbir; El Mi Ritratt; El Redder;
    El Tango; El Vagabond; La
    Muntagnola; La Purtinara; La
    "Sonambula"; San Martein; Tripoli
    Se, Tripoli No; Turnand Indri Da
    Paderen!   (E209)

EL MI RITRATT
    (Carlo, Musi) solo,pno (Bolognese
    dialect) BONGIOVANI 2099 s.p. see
    from El Mi Canzunett Seconda Serie
                             (E210)
EL MIRAR DE LA MAJA see Granados,
    Enrique

EL MOLE RACHAMIM see Barash, Morris

EL MOND L'E FATT ACSE!
    (Carlo, Musi) solo,pno (Bolognese
    dialect) BONGIOVANI 2073 s.p. see
    from El Mi Canzunett   (E211)

EL MUSICO Y EL POETA see Carnicer,
    Ramon

EL NIDO see Broqua, Alfonso

EL NINO JUDIO see Luna, P.

EL NOI DE LA MARE see Pahissa, Jaime

EL OMBU see Gianneo, Luis

EL PAJONAL see Sas, Andres

EL PALITO see Espoile, Raoul H.

EL PANO MORUNO see Falla, Manuel de

EL PARAISO see Maiztegui, Isidro

EL REDDER
    (Carlo, Musi) solo,pno (Bolognese
    dialect) BONGIOVANI 2097 s.p. see
    from El Mi Canzunett Seconda Serie
                            (E212)
EL RETRATO DE ISABELA see Vives, Amadeo

EL RUISENOR see Saint-Saens, Camille

EL SAN MICHEL, LA CA E LA RATA D'AFFET
    (Carlo, Musi) solo,pno (Bolognese
    dialect) BONGIOVANI 2062 s.p. see
    from El Mi Canzunett   (E213)

EL SIRIRI see Giacobbe, Juan Francisco

EL SOL see Gianneo, Luis

EL SOLDADO see Pla, M.

EL SUENO see Castro, Jose Maria

EL TANGO
    (Carlo, Musi) solo,pno (Bolognese
    dialect) BONGIOVANI 2093 s.p. see
    from El Mi Canzunett Seconda Serie
                            (E214)
EL TANGO see Broqua, Alfonso

EL TRALALA Y EL PUNTEADO see Granados,
    Enrique

EL VAGABOND
    (Carlo, Musi) solo,pno (Bolognese
    dialect) BONGIOVANI 2106 s.p. see
    from El Mi Canzunett Seconda Serie
                            (E215)
EL VASO see Guastavino, Carlos

EL YIVNE HA-GALIL see Weinberg, Jacob

EL ZORONGO
    see La Musique, Deuxieme Cahier

EL ZORZAL see Aguirre, Julian

EL ZORZAL see Gianneo, Luis

ELAMA see Marvia, Einari

ELBENREIGEN see Lothar, Mark

ELCKERLYC'S BEDE see King, Harold C.

ELDORADO see Griffis, E.

ELDORADO see Huybrechts, Albert

ELECTED, THE see Peeters, Flor

ELEGANT SONGS TO CONFESS LOVE see
    Nakada, Yoshinao

ELEGIA see Castiglioni, Niccolo

ELEGIA see Guerrini, Guido

ELEGIA see Massenet, Jules, Elegie

ELEGIA see Veress, Sandor

ELEGIA AN DIE NACHTIGALL see Kilpinen,
    Yrio, Elegie Satakielelle

ELEGIA DI MARCO see Neglia, Francesco
    Paolo

ELEGIA ETERNA see Granados, Enrique

ELEGIA KAUNEUDELLE see Kilpinen, Yrio

ELEGIA, NO. 2 see Massenet, Jules

ELEGIA ROMANTICA see Nordio, C.

ELEGIA YKSINAISYYDELLE see Kilpinen,
    Yrio

ELEGIA YOLLE see Kilpinen, Yrio

ELEGIAC SONNET see Bliss, Sir Arthur

ELEGIE *folk,Russ
    [Ger/Russ] solo,pno ZIMMER. 1552 s.p.
                            (E216)
ELEGIE see Delden, Lex van

ELEGIE see Duparc, Henri

ELEGIE see Kelterborn, Rudolf

ELEGIE see Massenet, Jules

ELEGIE see Orland, Henry

ELEGIE see Purcell, Henry, Queen's
    Epicedium, The

ELEGIE see Satie, Erik

ELEGIE see Sheikewitz, Wolf

ELEGIE see Sjogren, Emil

ELEGIE see Schoeck, Othmar

ELEGIE A CLYMENE see Migot, Georges

ELEGIE AN DIE EINSAMKEIT see Kilpinen, Yrio, Elegia Yksinaisyydelle

ELEGIE AN DIE NACHT see Kilpinen, Yrio, Elegia Yolle

ELEGIE AN DIE SCHONHEIT see Kilpinen, Yrio, Elegia Kauneudelle

ELEGIE SATAKIELELLE see Kilpinen, Yrio

ELEGIE SUR LA MORT D'UNE PRINCESSE ENCHANTEE see Lilien, Ignace

ELEGIES see Cras, Jean (Emile Paul)

ELEGISCHER GESANG see Beethoven, Ludwig van, Sanft Wie Du Lebtest

ELEGY see Birch, Robert Fairfax

ELEGY see Jacobi, Frederick

ELEGY see Medtner, Nikolai Karlovitch

ELEGY see Milford, Robin

ELEGY see Roff, Joseph

ELEGY see Sydeman, William

ELEGY see Thordarson, Sigurdur

ELEGY AFTER TU FU see Brink, Philip

ELEGY AND DANCE see Salomon, Karel

ELEGY FOR J.F.K. see Stravinsky, Igor

ELEGY OF EQUINOX see Maegaard Jan, Jaevndognselegi I

ELEIOTT, MAX
He Came, He'll Come Again *sac
(Krogstad, Bob) solo,pno GOSPEL
05 TM 0403 $1.00   (E217)

ELEONORA see Tocchi, Gian-Luca

ELEPHANT, THE see Blyton, Carey

ELEVEN SCRIPTURAL SONGS OF THE
TWENTIETH CENTURY *sac,CC11L,Bibl
med solo,pno/org COBURN $3.00
contains works by: Flowers,
Geoffrey; Swift, Robert; Fischer,
Irwin; Robinson, McNeil; Lane,
Richard; Kendrick, Virginia; Lepke,
Charma Davies   (E218)

ELEVEN SONGS see Granados, Enrique

ELEVEN SONGS see Rochberg, George

ELEVEN SONGS see Ireland, John

ELEVEN SONGS AND TWO HARMONIZATIONS see
Ives, Charles

ELEVEN SONGS FROM "A SHROPSHIRE LAD"
see Leichtling, Alan

ELF AND THE CHESTNUT TREE, THE see
Sharpe, Evelyn

ELF AND THE DOORMOUSE, THE see Weigl,
Vally

ELF DIERKUNDIGE DICTOEFENINGEN VAN
TRIJNTE FOP see Rontgen, Johannes

ELF KURZLIEDER see Dijk, Jan van

ELF LIEDER see Albert, Heinrich

ELFENLIED see Wolf, Hugo

ELFENLIEDCHEN see Ehrenberg, Carl Emil
Theodor

ELFKING, THE see Sibelius, Jean, Nacken

ELGAR, EDWARD (1857-1934)
Fate's Discourtesy
low solo,orch (B flat maj) ASHDOWN
s.p., ipr   (E219)
high solo,orch (C maj) ASHDOWN
s.p., ipr   (E220)

Fringes Of The Fleet, The *CC4U
ASHDOWN low solo,pno s.p.; high
solo,pno s.p.   (E221)

Haste Ye Feathered Songsters (from
Chanson De Matin)
med solo,pno NOVELLO 17.0065.00

ELGAR, EDWARD (cont'd.)
s.p.   (E222)

In Moonlight
high solo,pno NOVELLO 17.0072.03
s.p.   (E223)
med solo,pno NOVELLO 17.0073.01
s.p.   (E224)

Land Of Hope And Glory
low solo,pno (B flat maj) BOOSEY
$1.75   (E225)
med solo,pno (C maj) BOOSEY $1.75
(E226)
high solo,pno (D maj) BOOSEY $1.75
(E227)

Lowestoft Boat, The
low solo,orch (C maj) ASHDOWN s.p.,
ipr   (E228)
high solo,orch (D maj) ASHDOWN
s.p., ipr   (E229)

O Soft Was The Song
low solo,pno NOVELLO 17.0142.08
s.p.   (E230)

Pleading
high solo,pno NOVELLO 17.0152.05
s.p.   (E231)
med solo,pno NOVELLO 17.0153.03
s.p.   (E232)
low solo,pno NOVELLO 17.0154.01
s.p.   (E233)

Salut D'amour
"Violer" solo,pno,opt gtr GEHRMANS
658 s.p.   (E234)

Sea Pictures *CCU
A solo,pno/orch BOOSEY $5.00 (E235)

Sea Slumber Song
solo,pno (E maj) BOOSEY $1.50
(E236)

Submarines
low solo,orch (C min) ASHDOWN s.p.,
ipr   (E237)
high solo,orch (D min) ASHDOWN
s.p., ipr   (E238)

Sweepers, The
low solo,orch (B flat maj) ASHDOWN
s.p., ipr   (E239)
high solo,orch (C maj) ASHDOWN
s.p., ipr   (E240)

To The Children
Bar solo,pno ELKIN 27.0881.07 s.p.
(E241)

Torch, The
high solo,pno NOVELLO 17.0198.03
s.p.   (E242)
med solo,pno NOVELLO 17.0199.01
s.p.   (E243)
low solo,pno NOVELLO 17.0200.09
s.p.   (E244)

Violer *see Salut D'amour

Was It Some Golden Star?
med solo,pno NOVELLO 17.0209.02
s.p.   (E245)

Where Corals Lie
low solo,pno (D min) BOOSEY $1.75
(E246)
high solo,pno (F min) BOOSEY $1.75
(E247)

ELI, ELI *sac,Jew
solo,pno ASHLEY $.95   (E248)
solo,pno KAMMEN 1 $1.00   (E249)
(Hitzel) [Eng/Heb] med solo,pno (A
min) CENTURY 2037 $.40   (E250)

ELILAND see Fielitz, Alexander von

ELISABETH see Hessenberg, Kurt

ELISABETH SCHUMANN: LIEDERBUCH *CC30U
[Ger/Eng] S solo,pno cmplt ed UNIVER.
9559 $8.00 Songs From Her
Repertoire   (E251)

ELISABETH'S ARIE see Wagner, Richard

ELITROPIO D'AMOR see Scarlatti,
Alessandro

ELIXIR see Lora, Antonio

ELIZABETH see Harrhy, Edith

ELIZABETHAN AND JACOBEAN SONGS see
Criswick, Mary

ELIZABETHAN LOVE SONG see Dumayne, John

ELIZABETHAN LOVE SONGS see Keel,
Frederick

ELIZABETHAN SONG BAG, AN see Raebeck

ELIZABETH'S GREETING see Wagner,
Richard, Dich Theure Halle

ELIZABETH'S PRAYER see Wagner, Richard,
Allmacht'ge Jungfrau

ELIZABETH'S SONG see Head, Michael
(Dewar)

ELLA GIAMMAI M'AMO see Verdi, Giuseppe

ELLE! see Delmet, Paul

ELLE see Godard, Benjamin Louis Paul

ELLE see Saint-Saens, Camille

ELLE A FUI see Offenbach, Jacques

ELLE EST A TOI see Schumann, Robert
(Alexander)

ELLE EST SANS FACON, LISETTE see Poise,
(Jean Alexandre) Ferdinand

ELLE EST VENUE see Desrez, Apaisement

ELLE ET LUI see Schumann, Robert
(Alexander)

ELLE ETAIT PRES DE MOI see Vogel, A.

ELLE ETAIT VENNE see Schmitt, Florent

ELLE ETAIT VENUE see Ibert, Jacques

ELLE SE NOMME: CHAIR! see Laparra,
Raoul

ELLE SE REFUSE TOUJOURS A COMPRENDRE
see Devries, Ivan

ELLE VA VENIR see Duvernoy, Victor-
Alphonse

ELLENS FATE DESERVES A TEAR see Hook,
James

ELLES SONT VENUES see Lattes, M.

ELLES VIENNENT see Christensen, Henning

ELLETT, ROY
Flight
solo,pno CRAMER   (E252)

ELLIOT, DENNIS
Touched By His Nail-Scarred Hand
*sac
solo,pno GOSPEL 05 TM 0239 $1.00
(E253)

ELLIOTT
Pixie Piper Mam
low solo,pno (C maj) ALLANS s.p.
(E254)
high solo,pno (D maj) ALLANS s.p.
(E255)
Spring's A Lovable Lady
low solo,pno (E flat maj) ALLANS
s.p.   (E256)
high solo,pno (G maj) ALLANS s.p.
(E257)

ELLIOTT, ANNE
Five Rhythmic Songs *CC5U
solo,pno CRAMER   (E258)

ELLIOTT, J.W.
Song Of Hybrias The Cretan
low solo,pno (F maj) ASHDOWN (E259)
high solo,pno (G maj) ASHDOWN
(E260)

ELLIOTT, KENNETH
Musa Jocosa Mihi
solo,pno STAINER 3.0845.7 $1.50
(E261)

ELLIOTT, MALCOLM
Songs Of Australia *CCUL
solo,pno EMI s.p.   (E262)

ELLIOTT, PERCY
Red Roofs Of Bendon, The
low solo,pno (D maj) CRAMER (E263)
med solo,pno (E flat maj) CRAMER
(E264)
high solo,pno (F maj) CRAMER (E265)

ELLIS
Are You Ready? *sac
solo,pno LILLENAS SM-949: SN $1.00
(E266)
Do You Know My Jesus? *sac
solo,pno LILLENAS SM-494 $1.00
(E267)
solo,pno BENSON S5352-S $1.00
(E268)
Go With Jesus *sac
solo,pno LILLENAS SM-854: SN $1.00
(E269)
God's Way Is True *sac
solo,pno LILLENAS SM-950: SN $1.00
(E270)
Heavenly Love *sac
solo,pno LILLENAS SM-816: SN $1.00
(E271)
How Sweet It Is *sac
solo,pno LILLENAS SM-480: SN $1.00
(E272)

ELLIS (cont'd.)

I'll Sing Of My Redeemer *sac
  solo,pno LILLENAS SM-808: SN $1.00
                                    (E273)

I'm In A New World *sac
  solo,pno LILLENAS SM-884: SN $1.00
                                    (E274)

Jesus Heard My Prayer *sac
  solo,pno LILLENAS SM-855: SN $1.00
                                    (E275)

Jesus Is Still The Same *sac
  solo,pno LILLENAS SM-948: SN $1.00
                                    (E276)

Jesus Loves Me *sac
  solo,pno LILLENAS SM-817: SN $1.00
                                    (E277)

Leave It With Him *sac
  high solo,pno (F maj) BOSTON $1.50
                                    (E278)
  med-high solo,pno (D flat maj)
  BOSTON $1.50   (E279)
  low solo,pno (B flat maj) BOSTON
  $1.50   (E280)

Let Me Touch Him *sac
  solo,pno LILLENAS SM-470 $1.00
                                    (E281)

Lift It Up To Jesus *sac
  solo,pno LILLENAS SM-870: SN $1.00
                                    (E282)

Love Is Why *sac
  solo,pno LILLENAS SM-496: SN $1.00
                                    (E283)
  solo,pno LILLENAS SM-807: RN $1.00
                                    (E284)
  solo,pno BENSON S6976-S $1.00
                                    (E285)

Love Of God, The *sac,gospel
  solo,pno ABER.GRP. $1.50   (E286)

Love Of God Is Real, The *sac
  solo,pno LILLENAS SM-851: SN $1.00
                                    (E287)

My God Can Do Anything *sac
  solo,pno LILLENAS SM-495: SN $1.00
                                    (E288)

My Saviour And My Guide *sac
  solo,pno LILLENAS SM-828: SN $1.00
                                    (E289)

Where Is Your Faith? *sac
  solo,pno LILLENAS SM-805: SN $1.00
                                    (E290)

Where There Is Love *sac
  solo,pno LILLENAS SM-853: SN $1.00
                                    (E291)

ELLIS, E.S.
Chanson De Vieillard
  solo,pno (C maj) BOOSEY $1.50
                                    (E292)

ELLIS, O.
Sunset Poem
  med solo,pno BELWIN $1.50   (E293)

ELLSTEIN, ABE
Oi Mamme! Bin Ich Farliebt!! *Jew
  solo,pno KAMMEN 449 $1.00 see also
  FAVORITE JEWISH SONGS, VOL. 2
                                    (E294)

Zug Es Mir Noch Amuhl *Jew
  solo,pno KAMMEN 474 $1.00 see also
  JEWISH THEATRE SONGS, VOL. 1
                                    (E295)

Zug Far Vus *Jew
  solo,pno KAMMEN 469 $1.00 see also
  JEWISH THEATRE SONGS, VOL. 1
                                    (E296)

ELMORE, ROBERT [HALL] (1913-   )
Arise, My Love
  high solo,pno SEESAW $1.50   (E297)

Come With Us, O Blessed Jesus
  see FIVE WEDDING SONGS

ELOGE DE LA TERRE see Bourguignon,
  Francis de

ELOGE DES CHAPONS see Schmitt, Florent

ELOGE, POEME DE ST-LEGER-LEGER see
  Milhaud, Darius

ELOKAS, OSSI
Komm I Kvall *see Tule Illalla

Tule Illalla *Op.9,No.3
  "Komm I Kvall" solo,pno FAZER
  W 1947 s.p.   (E298)

ELOKUUN YO see Linko, Ernst (Fredrik)

ELOPERS, THE see Oliver, Herbert

ELOVAARA, TOIVO
Nyt Herran Kansa Laula *CC10U
  solo,pno FAZER W 3773 s.p.   (E299)

ELPENOR see Roussel, Albert

ELS OBERCOCS I LES PETITES COLLIDORES
  see Toldra, Eduardo

ELSEWHERE see Roberts, Mervyn

ELSKHUGSKVEDE see Egge, Klaus

ELVEN ZINGEN BIJ EEN ALLEEN GELATEN
  KIND see Henkemans, Hans

ELVES' DANCE, THE see Handel, George
  Frideric

ELWELL, HERBERT (1898-   )
Agamede's Song
  solo,pno NEW VALLEY $1.00   (E300)

Suffolk Owl
  solo,pno NEW VALLEY $1.00   (E301)

Three Poems Of Robert Liddell Lowe
  *CC3U
  solo,pno CRESCENDO $2.50   (E302)

ELYSIUM see Waldstein, Wilhelm

EMANUEL, LOUIS
Desert, The
  solo,pno (D min) LEONARD-ENG (E303)

EMBARQUEZ-VOUS see Godard, Benjamin
  Louis Paul

EMBARRASSED MAIDEN *Scot
  solo,pno PATERSON s.p. see from
  Hebridean Songs, Vol. IV   (E304)

EMBLEM, AN see Thompson, Jack

EMBORG, JENS LAURSON
Agnes *Op.30,No.3
  [Ger/Eng] SBar soli,pno LEUCKART
  s.p. see from Drei Duette (E305)

Der Wanderer Und Das Blumenmadchen
  *Op.30,No.1
  [Ger/Eng] SBar soli,pno LEUCKART
  s.p. see from Drei Duette (E306)

Drei Duette *see Agnes, Op.30,No.3;
  Der Wanderer Und Das
  Blumenmadchen, Op.30,No.1;
  Vollmond Am See, Op.30,No.2
                                    (E307)

Vollmond Am See *Op.30,No.2
  [Ger/Eng] SBar soli,pno LEUCKART
  s.p. see from Drei Duette (E308)

EMBROIDERY ARIA see Britten, Benjamin

EMER, M.
Beaucoup
  [Fr] med solo,pno ESCHIG $.65
                                    (E309)

J'ai Lasse Mon Coeur
  [Fr] med solo,pno ESCHIG $1.00
                                    (E310)

EMIGRANTI see Tocchi, Gian-Luca

EMILY DICKINSON CANONS see Clarke,
  Henry Leland

EMMANUEL, MAURICE (1862-1938)
Belle, Je M'en Vais En Allemagne
  solo,pno/inst DURAND s.p. see from
  Chansons Bourguignonnes   (E311)

Chansons Bourguignonnes *see Belle,
  Je M'en Vais En Allemagne;
  Guignolet De Saint-Lazare; Il
  Etait Une Fille D'honneur; J'ai
  Vu Le Loup; La Complainte De
  Notre-Dame; Noel   (E312)

Chansons Bourguignonnes *CC28L
  [Span/Fr] solo,pno DURAND 9111 s.p.
                                    (E313)

Guignolet De Saint-Lazare
  solo,pno/inst DURAND s.p. see from
  Chansons Bourguignonnes   (E314)

Il Etait Une Fille D'honneur
  solo,pno/inst DURAND s.p. see from
  Chansons Bourguignonnes   (E315)

In Memoriam
  [Fr] high solo,pno,vln,vcl DURAND
  s.p.   (E316)

J'ai Vu Le Loup
  solo,pno/inst DURAND s.p. see from
  Chansons Bourguignonnes   (E317)

La Complainte De Notre-Dame
  solo,pno/inst DURAND s.p. see from
  Chansons Bourguignonnes   (E318)

Noel
  solo,pno/inst DURAND s.p. see from
  Chansons Bourguignonnes   (E319)

Trois Odelettes Anacreontiques *CC3U
  solo,fl,pno DURAND s.p.   (E320)

EMMEL
Philosophy
  solo,pno (E flat maj) ALLANS s.p.
                                    (E321)

EMOIS D'AMOUR see Goublier, G.

EMOTION see Middeleer, Jean De

EMPEDOKLES LIED see Panni, Marcello

EMPEROR OF ICE CREAM, THE see Reynolds,
  Roger

EMPEROR WALTZ see Strauss, Johann

EMPTY-HANDED TRAVELER, THE see Menotti,
  Gian Carlo

EN ALAS DE MI CANTO see Mendelssohn-
  Bartholdy, Felix, Auf Flugeln Des
  Gesanges

EN ARLES see Beydts, L.

EN AVANT! see Schumann, Robert
  (Alexander)

EN AVILA MIS OJOS see Anonymous

EN AVRIL see Letocart, H.

EN AVRIL, DANS LES BOIS see Chapuis,
  Auguste-Paul-Jean-Baptiste

EN BARNSAGA VID BRASAN see Merikanto,
  Oskar

EN BARNSAGA VID BRASEN see Merikanto,
  Oskar

EN BAT MED BLOMMOR see Alfven, Hugo

EN BAT MED BLOMMOR see Rangstrom, Ture

EN BEGHEEFT MI NIET see Weegenhuise,
  Johan

EN BLANC see Miyoshi, Akira

EN BLOMMA see Runback, Albert

EN BLOMMA STAD VID VAGEN see Sibelius,
  Jean

EN BONNES VOIX see Schmitt, Florent

EN BORDE INTE SOVA see Scholander,
  Torkel

EN CAUSANT D'AMOUR see Varques, F.

EN CONTEMPLANT CETTE ASSEMBLEE IMENSE
  see Wagner, Richard

EN DAG HAR GATT see Korling

EN DALMASTRALL see Wiklund, Adolf

EN DEUX MOTS see Berger, Rod.

EN DROM AR LIVET see Korling

EN DROMMARES SANG TILL LIVET see
  Jarnefelt, Armas

EN DYSTER GREN see Kuusisto, Taneli,
  Tumma Ritva

EN EL BOSQUE see Garcia Estrada, Juan
  Agustin

EN EL INVERNACULO see Wagner, Richard,
  Im Treibhaus

EN EL MAR see Brahms, Johannes

EN EL PALACIO LOS SOLDADOS see Garcia
  Morillo, Roberto

EN FADERS BON see Palm, Hermann

EN FALLEN STAJARNA see Engstrom,
  Theofil

EN FLOTS TUMULTUEUX see Middeleer, Jean
  De, Op 'T Wilde Golven

EN FORET see Rasse, Francois

EN GALANT MILITAIRE see Lacome, Paul

EN GAMMAL DANSRYTM see Peterson-Berger,
  (Olof) Wilhelm

EN GAMMAL NYARSVISA see Rangstrom, Ture

EN GAMMAL SAGA see Hemberg, Eskil

EN GAMMAL VARVISA see Wohlfart, Karl

EN GANG BLIR ALLTING STILLA see
  Frumerie, (Per) Gunnar (Fredrik)
  de

EN GANG BLIR ALLTING STILLA see Lambert

EN GLAD TRALL see Korling, Felix

EN GLAD VISA see Svedbom, Vilhelm

EN GLADJE JAG GICK ATT MOTA see
Nordqvist, Gustaf

EN GRAV see Alnaes, Eyvind

EN HOSTENS KVALL see Wiren, Dag Ivar

EN HUSTAVLE see Dorumsgaard, Arne

EN IED'REN NACHT see Dresden, Sem

EN LA FUENTE DEL ROSEL see Vasquez,
Juan

EN LA PUNTA DE AQUEL CERRO see
Jurafsky, Abraham

EN LAS FUENTES DE ARANJUEZ see Romero,
A.

EN LAT I TRI TONER
see Aktenskapsfragan

EN LITEN JULHALSNING *Xmas
solo,pno FAZER F 3852 s.p.
contains: Av Himmelshojd; Hej
Tomtegubbar; Julen Ar Kommen; O
Du Saliga; Raska Fotter Springa
(E322)

EN LITEN VISA see Berens, J.R.

EN LITEN VISA see Hallstrom, Ivar

EN LOS SURCOS DEL AMOR see Guastavino,
Carlos

EN MA HUOLI HUITUKOILLE see Klemetti,
Heikki

EN MADRID LA BELLA see Garcia Mansilla,
Eduardo

EN MADRIGAL see Peterson-Berger, (Olof)
Wilhelm

EN ME MONTRANT DES ROSES see Darty,
Paulette

EN ME MONTRANT LES ROSES see Darty,
Paulette

EN MI CAMA HAY UN DOSEL see Lehar,
Franz, Hab' Ein Blaues Himmelbett!

EN NEJD I SKONSTA FAGRING see Home,
Sweet Home

EN NYARSLAT see Kjellander

EN OLE SYOTAVA SORIA see Luolajan-
Mikkola, Vilho

EN ONSKAN see Snare, Sigurd

EN PASSANT see Pouget, Leo

EN PASTORAL see Ek, Gunnar

EN POSITIVVISA see Stenhammar, Wilhelm

EN REGARDANT CES BELLES FLEURS see
Caplet, Andre

EN REMUANT DES VIEUX PAPIERS see Colas,
H.

EN ROULANT MA BOULE
"Canoe Song" see Crystal Fountain,
The

EN ROUTE see Georges, Alexandre

EN RUNA see Nordqvist, Gustaf

EN RUNE see Kilpinen, Yrio

EN SAMLING SOLOSANGER FOR UNGDOM, VOLS.
I-IV *CCU
solo,pno FAZER
W 1407, W 2095, W 1674, W 2564
s.p., ea.   (E323)

EN SANG, ETT VAPEN *CC6U,Span
(Bjorlin, Ulf) [Swed] solo,pno/gtr
GEHRMANS s.p.   (E324)

EN SANG FOR VARJE ARSTID see Marvia,
Einari

EN SEPTEMBRE see Araujo, Gino de

EN SJOMAN ALSKAR HAVETS VAG
solo,pno,opt gtr GEHRMANS 467 s.p.
(E325)

EN SKEPPAREVISA see Lambert, Helfrid

EN SKUGGA see Pylkkanen, Tauno
Kullervo, Varjo

EN SKYMNINGENS VISA see Korling, Felix

EN SNES DANSKE VISER, VOL. 1 *CC21U
(Nielsen, C.; Laub, T.) [Dan] med
solo,kbd HANSEN-DEN s.p.   (E326)

EN SNES DANSKE VISER, VOL. 2 see
Nielsen, Carl

EN SOLDAT see Bedinger, Hugo

EN SOMMARDAG see Lindblad, Adolf
Fredrik

EN SOMMARLAT I SEGELBAT
solo,pno LUNDQUIST s.p.   (E327)

EN SOMMARMELODI see Nordqvist, Gustaf

EN SOMMARPOLKETT see Korling

EN SOURDINE see Debussy, Claude

EN SOURDINE see Diepenbrock, Alphons

EN SOURDINE see Gaubert, Philippe

EN SOURDINE see Panizza, Ettore

EN SPELEMAN see Korling

EN SPELMANSSAGA see Korling, Felix

EN SPELMANSVISA see Peterson-Berger,
(Olof) Wilhelm

EN STJARNA BRANN see Tirindelli, Pier
Adolfo

EN STRIMMA HAV see Snare, Sigurd

EN SUA UNHOITA see Haapalainen, Vaino

EN SVANE see Grieg, Edvard Hagerup

EN TIEDA, MUISTATKO MUA see Pylkkanen,
Tauno Kullervo

EN TOCH... see Witte, D.

EN UN JOLI VOYAGE see Rabey, Rene

EN UN SOURIRE DE CLEMENCE see Saint-
Saens, Camille

EN UNG MOR see Kilpinen, Yrio

EN VAGGVISLAT see Alnaes, Eyvind

EN VAIN POUR EVITER DES REPONSES AMERES
see Bizet, Georges

EN VALSMELODI see Taube, Evert

EN VAR - ET DIKT see Alnaes, Eyvind

EN VARDAG see Lindblad, Adolf Fredrik

EN VARNATT FROSTEN FOLL see Soderman,
(Johan) August

EN VARVINTERVISA see Sjogren, Emil

EN VARVISA see Morley, Thomas

EN VARVISA see Salonen, Sulo

EN VINTERVISA see Damm, Svenerik

EN VINTERVISA see Kjellander

EN VINTERVISA see Nordqvist, Gustaf

EN VINTERVISA see Palmgren, Selim

EN VINTERVISA see Peterson-Berger,
(Olof) Wilhelm

EN VINTERVISA see Wennerberg, Gunnar

EN VISA OM KARLEK see Peterson-Berger,
(Olof) Wilhelm

EN VISA TILL KARIN NAR HON HADE DANSAT
see Hallen, Andreas

EN VISA VILL JAG SJUNGA
(Skold, Sven) solo,pno,lute LUNDQUIST
s.p.   (E328)

ENCANTAMIENTO see Guastavino, Carlos

ENCHAINEMENT see Mouton, H.

ENCHANTED HOUR, THE see Hahn, Reynaldo,
L'Heure Exquise

ENCHANTED STRINGS see Turner, J.G.

ENCHANTMENT see Geehl, Henry Ernest

ENCHANTMENT see Guastavino, Carlos,
Encantamiento

ENCHANTMENT see Hope, H. Ashworth

ENCHANTRESS, THE see Bliss, Sir Arthur

ENCHANTRESS, THE see Hatton, John
Liptrot

ENCINA, JUAN DEL (1468-1529)
Romerico
(Lavie) [Fr/Span] med solo,gtr
ESCHIG $1.00   (E329)
(Lavie, Ferandez) "Rossignol"
[Span/Fr/It] solo,gtr SCHOTTS
GA 194 s.p. see from ALTE UND
NEUE WERKE   (E330)

Rossignol *see Romerico

ENCINAR, RAMON (1954-   )
Homenaje A J. Cortazar
Mez solo,4inst ZERBONI 7687 s.p.
(E331)

ENCORE, ENCORE see Filipucci, Edm.

ENCORE UN SOIR see Lachaume, A.

END OF THE WORLD, THE see Duke, John
Woods

ENDERS, HARVEY
Russian Picnic
low solo,pno (A maj) SCHIRM.G $.60
(E332)

ENDLICH NAHT SICH DIE STUNDE see
Mozart, Wolfgang Amadeus, Giunse
Alfin Il Momento - Non Tardar Amato
Bene

ENDLICH NAHT SICH DIE STUNDE - O SAUME
LANGER NICHT see Mozart, Wolfgang
Amadeus, Giunse Alfin Il Momento -
Non Tardar Amato Bene

ENDLOSER RITT see Bijvanck, Henk

ENDURING LOVE see Brahms, Johannes, Von
Ewiger Liebe

ENDYMION see Kilpinen, Yrio

ENDYMION see Zagwijn, Henri

ENEKSZO see Kodaly, Zoltan

ENESCO, GEORGES (1881-1955)
Aux Damoyselles Paresseuses D'escrire
A Leurs Amys
solo,pno ENOCH s.p. see also Sept
Chansons De Clement Marot (E333)

Changeons Propos
solo,pno ENOCH s.p. see also Sept
Chansons De Clement Marot (E334)

Du Conflict En Douleur
solo,pno ENOCH s.p. see also Sept
Chansons De Clement Marot (E335)

Estrene A Anne
solo,pno ENOCH s.p. see also Sept
Chansons De Clement Marot (E336)

Estrene A La Rose
solo,pno ENOCH s.p. see also Sept
Chansons De Clement Marot (E337)

Languir Me Fais
solo,pno ENOCH s.p. see also Sept
Chansons De Clement Marot (E338)

Le Desert
solo,pno ENOCH s.p.   (E339)

Le Galop
solo,pno (available in 2 keys)
ENOCH s.p.   (E340)
solo,pno (available in 2 keys)
ENOCH s.p.   (E341)

Present De Couleur Blanche
solo,pno ENOCH s.p. see also Sept
Chansons De Clement Marot (E342)

Sept Chansons De Clement Marot
solo,pno cmplt ed ENOCH s.p.
contains & see also: Aux
Damoyselles Paresseuses
D'escrire A Leurs Amys;
Changeons Propos; Du Conflict
En Douleur; Estrene A Anne;
Estrene A La Rose; Languir Me
Fais; Present De Couleur
Blanche   (E343)

Soupir
solo,pno (available in 2 keys)
ENOCH s.p.   (E344)

ENFANCE IV see Colding-Jorgensen,
Henrik

ENFANT AUX AIRS D'IMPERATRICE see
Offenbach, Jacques

ENFANT, JE TE DONNE L'EXEMPLE see
Saint-Saens, Camille

ENFANTINES see Absil, Jean

ENFANTINES see Mussorgsky, Modest

ENFANTS, JE NE VOUS EN VEUX PAS see
Saint-Saens, Camille

ENFANTS, JE VOUS BENIS see Chabrier,
Emmanuel

ENFANTS-POETES see Smit Sibinga, Th. H.

ENFANTS! SAVEZ-VOUS QUI see Delbruck,
J.

ENFERMO ESTABA ANTIOCO see Daza, E.

ENFIN LES NOIRS NUAGES see Rimsky-
Korsakov, Nikolai

ENGADIN-KANTATE see Driessler, Johannes

ENGEL, EWIG LICHT UND SCHON see Handel,
George Frideric

ENGEL, JOEL (1868-1927)
Omrim Yeshna Eretz *sac
"There Is A Land" [Heb/Eng] med
solo,pno (also with Yiddish text)
TRANSCON. SP 12 $.85   (E345)

There Is A Land *see Omrim Yeshna
Eretz

ENGELSGRUSS see Knab, Armin

ENGELTERZETT see Mendelssohn-Bartholdy,
Felix

ENGFUHRUNG see Reimann, Aribert

ENGLERT, GIUSEPPE GIORGIO (1925-   )
Le Roman De Kapitagolei
STB soli,3fl,3ob,3clar,3bsn,4horn,
3trp,2trom,tuba,timp,perc,strings
HINRICHSEN rental   (E346)

ENGLISH COUNTRY SONGS *CCU
(Broadwood, Lucy; Maitland, Fuller)
solo,pno CRAMER pap s.p., cloth
s.p.   (E347)

ENGLISH FOLK SONGS FROM THE SOUTHERN
APPALACHIANS *CC273U,folk
(Sharp, Cecil J.) solo,pno OXFORD two
vols. bound in one   (E348)

ENGLISH, GEORGE PHILLIP
Country Tune
solo,pno ALBERT AE274 s.p.   (E349)

Wings Of A Dove
med solo,pno SEESAW $1.50   (E350)

ENGLISH LYRICS, FIRST SET see Parry,
Charles Hubert Hastings

ENGLISH SONGS: PART 1 see Howe, Mary

ENGLISH SONGS: PART 2 see Howe, Mary

ENGLISH SONGS: PART 3 see Howe, Mary

ENGLISH USAGE see Thomson, Virgil

ENGSTROM, THEOFIL
En Fallen Stajarna
solo,pno,opt gtr GEHRMANS s.p.
(E351)
ENID BLYTON'S HAPPY YEAR SONG BOOK see
Johnson, Noel

ENIGME ETERNELLE see Ravel, Maurice

ENJOLEMENT see Bilhaud, P.

ENKELI TAIVAAN
see Pieni Joulutervehdyts

ENLEVEMENT see Levade, Charles (Gaston)

ENLOE, NEIL
Statue Of Liberty, The *sac
solo,pno WORD S-460   (E352)
solo,pno BENSON S7587-S $1.00
(E353)
ENNEA see Tamba, A.

ENOCH ARDEN see Strauss, Richard

ENOS, J.
I Have A Rendez-Vous With Death
solo,pno (B maj) BOOSEY $1.50
(E354)
Sea Fever
solo,pno (D flat maj) BOOSEY $1.50
(E355)
ENOUGH TO KNOW see Ross

ENRICHI
Quatre Chansons *Op.58,No.1-4, CC4U
[Fr] S solo,gtr,pno ZANIBON ZA4895
s.p.   (E356)

ENRIQUEZ DE VALDERRABANO, ENRIQUE
Ay De Mi
(Azpiazu) [Span] med solo,gtr UNION
ESP. $.75   (E357)

ENRIQUEZ DE VALDERRABANO, ENRIQUE
(cont'd.)

Ya Cabalga Calainos
(Azpiazu) [Span] med solo,gtr UNION
ESP. $.50   (E358)

ENSAM UNDER FASTET see Bergman, Erik

ENSAMHET see Runback, Albert

ENSAMHETENS SANGER see Bergman, Erik

ENSI SUUDELMA see Sibelius, Jean, Den
Forsta Kyssen

ENSORCELLEMENT see Delmet, Paul

ENSUENO see Schumann, Robert
(Alexander), Traumerei

ENSUENOS see Wagner, Richard, Traume

ENTELECHIE II see Schat, Peter

ENTENDS CONTRE LE VIEUX PEUPLIER see
Sancan, P.

ENTER IN O CHRIST see Kempinski, Leo A.

ENTHOVEN
Lyrische Suite *Op.21, CCU
S solo,orch BROEKMANS 234 s.p.
(E359)
ENTRA L'UOMO ALLOR CHE NASCE see
Martini, Giambattista

ENTR'ACTES UND SAPPHO FRAGMENTS see
Birtwistle, Harrison

ENTRE CORTINAS VERDES see Gianneo, Luis

ENTRE LE BOEUF ET L'ANE GRIS see
Tiersot, (Jean Baptiste Elisee)
Julien

ENTRE LES DEUX see Delvincourt, Claude

ENTREAT ME NOT TO LEAVE THEE see Birch,
Robert Fairfax

ENTREAT ME NOT TO LEAVE THEE see Gore,
Richard T.

ENTREAT ME NOT TO LEAVE THEE see
Gounod, Charles Francois

ENTREAT ME NOT TO LEAVE THEE see Young,
Gordon

ENTRUCKUNG see Schoenberg, Arnold

ENTWEIHUNG see Gilse, Jan van

ENVELOPPE DANS DU COTON see Bernicat,
F.

ENVOI see Carolus-Duran, P.

ENVOI see Lacome, Paul

ENVOI see Street, G.

ENVOI [1] (FROM "I PROMISE") see
Schouwman, Hans

ENVOI [2] (FROM "WHAT WE SHALL TEACH")
see Schouwman, Hans

ENVOI DE FLEURS see Delmet, Paul

ENVOI DE ROSES see Pouget, Leo

ENVOY see Hindemith, Paul

EPANOUISSEMENT see Gedalge, Andre

EPHEU see Strauss, Richard

EPICEDIUM see Mimaroglu, Ilhan
Kamaleddin

EPIGRAMME see Doubrava, Jaroslav,
Epigramy

EPIGRAMME DE SOY MEME see Menasce,
Jacques de

EPIGRAMY see Doubrava, Jaroslav

EPILOG see Kuula, Toivo, Epilogi

EPILOG see Redel, Martin Christoph

EPILOGI see Kuula, Toivo

EPIPHANIA see Bordewijk-Roepman,
Johanna

EPIPHANIE see Finkbeiner, Reinhold

EPIPHANY ADORATION see Seagard, John

EPISODI see Arrigo, Girolamo

EPISTOLA DI PULCINELLA A COLUMBINA see
Oddone, E.

EPITAFFIO DI UN BAMBINO see Bonifanti

EPITAPH see Diamond, David

EPITAPH see Kelemen, Milko

EPITAPH see Kohs, Ellis B.

EPITAPH see Reimann, Aribert

EPITAPH see Thompson, David Cleghorn

EPITAPH, AN see Besly, Maurice

EPITAPH, AN see Koch, Johannes H.E.

EPITAPH, THE see Diamond, David

EPITAPH AUF RIMBAUD see Steffens,
Walter

EPITAPH FOR A POET see Birch, Robert
Fairfax

EPITAPH FOR LOUIS VAN TULDER see
Andriessen, Juriaan

EPITAPH FUR EINEN DICHTER see Reutter,
Hermann

EPITAPH OF TIMAS see Berkeley, Lennox

EPITAPH ON THE AUTHOR see Gideon,
Miriam

EPITAPH "TICH YUANG TUC" see Dohl,
Friedhelm

EPITAPH UPON A CHILD THAT DIED see
Presser, William

EPITAPH UPON A MAID see Presser,
William

EPITAPH UPON A VIRGIN see Presser,
William

EPITAPHE see Frank, Marcel [Gustave]

EPITAPHE see Lazarus, Daniel

EPITAPHE see Poulenc, Francis

EPITAPHE DE BILITIS see Koechlin,
Charles

EPITAPHE D'UN PARESSEUX see Couperin
(le Grand), Francois

EPITAPHE EN FORME DE BALLADE see
Zafred, Mario

EPITAPHIUM JOANNIS HUNYADI see Kodaly,
Zoltan

EPITAPHS FROM ROBERT BURNS see Gideon,
Miriam

EPITHALAME see Bordes, Charles

EPITHALAME see Chabrier, Emmanuel

EPITHALAME see Saint-Saens, Camille

EPITHAPE see Fellegara, Vittorio

EPOUSAILLES see Frapier-Roncin

EPOUVANTE see Messiaen, Oliver

EPSTEIN, [DAVID M.] (1930-   )
Four Songs *song cycle
S solo,horn,strings sc PRESSER
$2.50, ipr   (E360)

EQUINOX see Cory, George

EQUINOX I see Consoli, Marc-Antonio

EQUINOX II see Consoli, Marc-Antonio

EQUINOXE see Bernard, R.

ER, DER HERRLICHSTE VON ALLEN see
Schumann, Robert (Alexander)

ER IST ALLES see Tucapsky, Antonin, On
Je Vse

ER IST DER RICHTIGE NICHT FUR MICH see
Strauss, Richard

ER IST'S see Wolf, Hugo

ER KENNT DIE RECHTEN FREUNDENSTUNDEN
see Bach, Johann Sebastian

ER LIEBT NUR MICH ALLEIN see Eckert,
Karl Anton Florian

ER SCHLAFT, WIR ALLE SIND IN ANGST UND
NOT see Lortzing, (Gustav) Albert

ER SOR CAPANNA see Petrolini

ER WIEDET SEINE HERDE see Handel, George Frideric, He Shall Feed His Flock

ERA-M COSSELHATZ SENHOR see Ventadorn, Bernart de

ERA MUTA LA NOTTE see Bossi, Renzo

ERA UN GIORNO DI FESTA see Cilea, Francesco

ERAKKOMAJA see Hannikainen, Ilmari

ERAS see Kilpinen, Yrio

ERAT JOSEPH ET MARIA see Hindemith, Paul

ERATO see Zagwijn, Henri

ERBARM DICH MEIN, O HERRE GOTT see Schutz, Heinrich

ERBARME DICH, MEIN GOTT see Bach, Johann Sebastian

ERBARMEN see Nicode, Jean Louis

ERBSE, HEIMO (1924-   )
    Das Hohelied Salomos *Op.26
    [Ger] SBar soli,2fl,2ob,2clar,2bsn,
    2horn,2trp,3trom,timp,harp,
    strings voc sc PETERS 8114 $15.00
                                    (E361)

    Der Uns Die Stunden Zahlte *Op.21,
    No.1-3, CC3U
    (Celan) [Ger] low solo,pno PETERS
    5955 $6.50   (E362)

    Five Orchestra Songs After Trakl
    *Op.27
    [Ger] Bar solo,2fl,2ob,2clar,2bsn,
    4horn,3trp,3trom,timp,perc,harp,
    pno,strings sc PETERS 8112 $10.00
                                    (E363)

    Nachklange *Op.33
    high solo,gtr GERIG HG 1082 s.p.
                                    (E364)

    Three Eichendorff Songs *Op.12,No.1-
    3, CC3U
    [Ger] high solo,pno PETERS 5848
    $4.00   (E365)

    Three Morike Songs *Op.17,No.1-3,
    CC3U
    [Ger] med solo,pno PETERS 5862
    $5.75   (E366)

ERD' UND HIMMEL MAG SICH WAPPNEN see Handel, George Frideric

ERDLEN, HERMANN (1893-1972)
    Das Hohe Tor *CC26U,Adv/Xmas
    solo,pno TONOS 5480 s.p.
    see also: Wie So Still Es
    Geworden   (E367)

    Lo, How A Rose E'er Blooming *sac
    med solo,pno oct CONCORDIA 98-1828
    $.25   (E368)

    Wie So Still Es Geworden
    solo,pno TONOS s.p. see also Das
    Hohe Tor   (E369)

ERE BRIGHT ROSINA MET MY EYES see Shield, William

ERES MARINERITA see Velez Camarero, E.

ERES TU see Oteo

ERFULLUNG see Messner, Joseph

ERGETZ VAIT see Weiner, Lazar

ERGO INTEREST - QUAERE SUPERNA see Mozart, Wolfgang Amadeus

ERHEBE DICH, GENOSSIN MEINER SCHMACH see Wagner, Richard

ERHEBE DIE HANDE see Roos, Robert de

ERHEBUNG see Schoenberg, Arnold

ERHEBUNG (SINFONIE NO. 3) see Gilse, Jan van

ERHORE MICH, WENN ICH RUFE see Schutz, Heinrich

ERI GIA TUTTA MIA see Monteverdi, Claudio

ERI TU CHE MACCHIAVI see Verdi, Giuseppe

ERIC WILD FOLIO OF SACRED MUSIC, VOL. 2 see Wild, Eric

ERIKSSON, JOSEF
    Kvelden Lister Seg Pa Ta Over
    Kloverengen
    solo,pno GEHRMANS s.p.   (E370)

    Sanger Om Blommor Och Fjarilar *CCU
    solo,pno GEHRMANS s.p.   (E371)

ERIN THE TEAR AND THE SMILE see Hughes, Herbert

ERINDRINGENS SO see Nielsen, Carl

ERINNERUNG see Abt, Franz

ERINNERUNG see Mahler, Gustav

ERINNERUNG see Marx, Joseph

ERISKAY LOVE LILT
    (Kennedy-Fraser, M.; MacLeod, K.) low
    solo,pno (E flat maj) BOOSEY $1.75
                                    (E372)
    (Kennedy-Fraser, M.; MacLeod, K.) med
    solo,pno (G maj) BOOSEY $1.75
                                    (E373)
    (Kennedy-Fraser, M.; MacLeod, K.)
    high solo,pno (A maj) BOOSEY $1.75
                                    (E374)

ERKLING, THE see Schubert, Franz (Peter), Erlkonig

ERL KING see Schubert, Franz (Peter), Erlkonig

ERLANGER, CAMILLE (1863-1919)
    A La Tres Chere
    solo,pno ENOCH s.p.   (E375)

    Aubade
    [Fr] high solo,pno ESCHIG $1.50
                                    (E376)

    Recueillement
    solo,pno (available in 2 keys)
    ENOCH s.p.   (E377)

    Sous La Tonnelle
    solo,pno ENOCH s.p.   (E378)

ERLEBACH, PHILIPP HEINRICH (1657-1714)
    Heute Ist Der Siegestag *sac
    high solo,2rec,cont HANSSLER 5.051
    s.p. see also GESANGE ZUM
    KIRCHENJAHR   (E379)

    Ich Lasse Gott In Allem Walten *sac
    high solo,2S rec,cont HANSSLER
    5.065 s.p. see also GESANGE ZUM
    KIRCHENJAHR   (E380)

    Ihr Gedanken
    [Ger/Eng] S/T solo,2vln,kbd,opt vln
    cmplt ed BOTE $2.50   (E381)

ERLKING, THE see Schubert, Franz (Peter), Erlkonig

ERLKONIG see Schubert, Franz (Peter)

ERLOSCHEN see Sibelius, Jean

ERLOSCHENE GLUT see Merikanto, Oskar, Kuin Hiipuva Hiillos Tummentuu

ERMITEN see Hannikainen, Ilmari, Erakkomaja

ERNANI, ERNANI, INVOLAMI see Verdi, Giuseppe

ERNSTE GESANGE see Laitenen, Arvo

ERNSTE GESANGE FUR BARITON-SOLO see Eisler, Hanns

ERNSTE STUNDE see Orthel, Leon

ERO see Louhivuori, Hemmo

ERO E LEANDRO see Veretti, Antonio

ERORTERUNG see Godard, Benjamin Louis Paul, Contemplation

EROS see Finke, Fidelio Fritz

EROS see Grieg, Edvard Hagerup

EROSIONS I see Baervoets, Raymond

EROTIC MUSE, THE *CCU
    (Cray, Edward) solo,pno cloth OAK
    000105 $12.50   (E382)

EROTICA see Pizzetti, Ildebrando

EROTICKE PISNE see Soukup, Vladimir

EROTIKON see Foerster, Josef Bohuslav

EROTIQUE VOILEE see Bancquart, Alain

EROTISCH LANDSCHAP see Frid, Geza

EROTUS MIELILLA see Kilpinen, Yrio

ERQUICKTES HERZ see Telemann, Georg Philipp

ERRANT PAR LA MONTAGNE see Blair Fairchild

ERRER A TRAVERS LES MERS see Nougues, Jean

ERRICHTET KEINEN DENKSTEIN see Rautavaara, Einojuhani

ERSCHEINUNG see Trunk, Richard

ERSCHIENEN IST DER HERRLICH TAG see Schein, Johann Hermann

ERSCHUTT'RE DICH NUR NICHT VERZAGTE SEELE see Bach, Johann Sebastian

ERSTANDEN IST DER HEILIGE CHRIST see Bruhns, Nicholaus

ERSTANDEN IST DER HERRE CHRIST see Selle, Thomas

ERSTE SYMPHONIE see Hartmann, Karl Amadeus

ERSTER SCHNEE see Edler, Robert

ERSTER VERLUST see Ferroud, Pierre-Octave

ERSTES OFFERTORIUM see Schubert, Franz (Peter)

ERWACHEN see Vycpalek, Ladislav

ERWACHT see Andriessen, Hendrik

ERWARTUNG see Schoenberg, Arnold

ERWARTUNG see Wiklund, Adolf

ES BLINKEN IN DER SONNE see Zipp, Friedrich

ES BRENT see Gelbart, M.

ES DAMMERT see Aim, Vojtech Borivoj, Stmiva Se

ES DANKEN DIR, GOTT, DIE VOLKER see Hammerschmidt, Andreas

ES DUFTET LIND DIE FRUHLINGSNACHT see Schumann, Georg

ES DUNKET MICH, ICH SEH' DICH KOMMEN see Bach, Johann Sebastian

ES GEHT AUF MITTERNACHT see Tchaikovsky, Piotr Ilyitch

ES GEHT JETZT UM DIE VESPERZEIT see Weismann, Wilhelm

ES GIBT DINGT, DIE MUSS MAN VERGESSEN see Straus, Oscar

ES GINGEN ZWEI GESPIELEN GUT see Schoenberg, Arnold

ES HAMPFELI LIEDLI see Zullig, E.

ES IS DOCH DU A GOTT IN HIMMEL *Jew
    solo,pno KAMMEN 447 $1.00   (E383)

ES IST BESTIMMT IN GOTTES RAT see Bijvanck, Henk

ES IST BESTIMMT IN GOTTES RAT see Busoni, Ferruccio Benvenuto

ES IST EIN KOSTLICH DING see Distler, Hugo

ES IST EIN ROS' ENTSPRUNGEN see Holler, Karl

ES IST EIN SCHNITTER, HEISST DER TOD see Berger, Jean, Faucheur Sinistre

ES IST GENUG see Mendelssohn-Bartholdy, Felix

ES IST LANG see Badings, Henk

ES IST NACHT see Flothius, Marius

ES IST NACHT see Zagwijn, Henri

ES LACHELT DER SEE see Eisler, Hanns

ES LEBE DER HEILIGE DREIEINIGE GOTT see Doebler, Curt

ES LOCKTE SCHONE WARME see Schubert, Franz (Peter), Die Rose

ES MUSS EIN WUNDERBARES SEIN see Liszt, Franz

ES MUSS EIN WUNDERBARES SEIN see Oort,
H.C.v.

ES RAUSCHET DAS WASSER see Brahms,
Johannes

ES SCHWELLT MIR DIE BRUST see
Ehrenberg, Carl Emil Theodor

ES STEH GOTT AUF see Schutz, Heinrich

ES SUNGEN DREI ENGEL see Mahler, Gustav

ES VET KEIN MOL KEIN TZVEITE NIT ZEIN
*Jew
solo,pno KAMMEN 458 $1.00   (E384)

ES VILT SICH MIR   *Jew
solo,pno KAMMEN 87 $1.00   (E385)

ES WAR EIN ALTER KONIG see Diepenbrock,
Alphons

ES WAR IM HERBST   *folk,Russ
[Ger/Russ] solo,pno ZIMMER. 1540 s.p.
(E386)

ESA CANCION see Saenz, Pedro

ESCAPADES see Blank, A.

ESCAPE AT BEDTIME see Keel, Frederick

ESCENA DE LA FLOR see Guerrero

ESCENAS CANTADAS Y DANZADAS see
Llongueras J.

ESCHER, RUDOLF GEORGE (1912-   )
Chants Du Desir   *Op.22a, CC4U
Mez solo,pno DONEMUS s.p.   (E387)

   Cote D'Azur   *Op.21,No.2
   see Nostalgies

   Nostalgies
   T solo,2fl,2clar,bsn,horn,timp,
   perc,cel,harp,strings DONEMUS
   s.p.
      contains: Cote D'Azur, Op.21,
      No.2; Outwards, Op.21,No.4;
      Possession Francaise, Op.21,
      No.1; Republique Argentine,
      Op.21,No.3   (E388)

   Outwards   *Op.21,No.4
   see Nostalgies

   Possession Francaise   *Op.21,No.1
   see Nostalgies

   Republique Argentine   *Op.21,No.3
   see Nostalgies

   Strange Meeting   *Op.25a
   Bar solo,pno DONEMUS s.p.   (E389)

   Univers De Rimbaud   *song cycle
   T solo,3fl,4ob,3clar,2bsn,sax,
   2horn,2trp,trom,5perc,2harp,
   strings DONEMUS s.p.   (E390)

ESCOGIENDO NOVIA see Sciammarella,
Valdo

ESHET CHAYIL see Davidson, Charles

ESKON HAALAULU see Marttinen, Tauno

ESO ENAI see Piket, Frederick

ESORCISMI I see Laneri, Roberto

ESPANA see Chabrier, Emmanuel

ESPECE DE COMPTINE see Arrieu, Claude

ESPERA see Sanchez de Fuentes, Eduardo

ESPERANCE see Durand, Jacques

ESPERANCE EN D'HEUREUX JOURS see
Messager, Andre

ESPINES see Riba, P.R. de la

ESPLA, OSCAR (1886-   )
Canciones Playeras   *CCU
[Span] med solo,pno UNION ESP.
$2.00   (E391)

   Dos Tonados Levantinas   *CC2U
   [Span] med solo,pno UNION ESP. $.60
(E392)

ESPOILE, RAOUL H.
Cancion De La Vendimia
[Span] solo,pno RICORDI-ARG BA 7629
s.p.   (E393)

   Chacayalera
   see Chacayaleras

   Chacayaleras
   [Span] solo,pno cmplt ed RICORDI-
   ARG BA 6874 s.p.
      contains: Chacayalera; Huaynu; La
      Tabaquerita; Llankirai; Si

ESPOILE, RAOUL H. (cont'd.)

      Quieres Que Yo Te Diga; Yaravi
(E394)

   Collares De Perlas
   [Span] solo,pno cmplt ed RICORDI-
   ARG BA 6973 s.p.
      contains: Perlas Blancas; Perlas
      Negras   (E395)

   El Palito
   [Span] solo,pno RICORDI-ARG BA 6879
   s.p.   (E396)

   Huainito
   [Span] solo,pno RICORDI-ARG BA 6033
   s.p.   (E397)

   Huaynu
   see Chacayaleras

   La Tabaquerita
   see Chacayaleras

   Laudes De Cristo Rey
   [Span] solo,pno RICORDI-ARG BA 7470
   s.p.   (E398)

   Lied No. 14
   [Span] solo,pno RICORDI-ARG
   BA 11542 s.p. see from Rimos Y
   Abrojos   (E399)

   Llankirai
   see Chacayaleras

   Novia Y Hermana (from La Ciudad Roja)
   "Romanza De Enrique" [Span] T solo,
   pno RICORDI-ARG BA 7230 s.p. (E400)

   Oh Querer Que Me Tiendes Las Alas
   (from La Ciudad Roja)
   [Span] S solo,pno RICORDI-ARG
   BA 7231 s.p.   (E401)

   Parole E Fatti
   [It] solo,pno SANTIS 117 s.p. (E402)

   Patria En El Mar
   [Span] solo,pno RICORDI-ARG BA 6880
   s.p.   (E403)

   Perlas Blancas
   see Collares De Perlas

   Perlas Negras
   see Collares De Perlas

   Rimos Y Abrojos   *see Lied No. 14
(E404)

   Romanza De Enrique   *see Novia Y
   Hermana

   Rondel
   [Span] solo,pno RICORDI-ARG
   BA 10883 s.p.   (E405)

   Si Quieres Que Yo Te Diga
   see Chacayaleras

   Tu Pie   *madrigal
   [Span] solo,pno RICORDI-ARG BA 6974
   s.p.   (E406)

   Yaravi
   see Chacayaleras

   Zorzal
   [Span] solo,pno RICORDI-ARG BA 7032
   s.p.   (E407)

L'ESPOIR
New Born King, The
solo,pno SHAWNEE IA 19 $.50   (E408)

ESPOIR see Chaminade, Cecile

ESPOIR EN DIEU see Rhene-Baton

ESPOSITO, E.
Curva Minore
see Due Liriche

   Due Liriche
   [It] solo,pno cmplt ed CURCI 8247
   s.p.
      contains: Curva Minore; L'Angelo
(E409)

   L'Angelo
   see Due Liriche

ESSERE MADRE E UN INFERNO see Cilea,
Francesco

ESSYAD, AHMED
Identite
S&narrator,perc,13strings sc JOBERT
s.p.   (E410)

EST-CE BIEN VOUS VRAIMENT? see Aubert,
Louis-Francois-Marie

EST-CE LE PRESTIGE DU CASQUE see
Messager, Andre

EST-CE TOI DONT JE SENS LA DIVINE
PRESENCE see Lefebvre, Channing

EST-IL VRAI? see Mendelssohn-Bartholdy,
Felix

ESTA IGLESIA NO TIENE see Guastavino,
Carlos

ESTA NOCHE see Ruzicka, Peter

ESTABLISH A HOUSE see Rider, Dale G.

ESTANG see Roos, Robert de

ESTE RAZ SA OBZRIET' MAM see
Andrasovan, Tibor

ESTERHAZY, PAL (1635-1713)
Harmonia Caelestis
S solo,cor,inst sc BAREN. 6401
$6.25, ipa   (E411)

ESTEVE, PABLO (? -1794)
El Jucio Del Ano
[Span] med solo,pno UNION ESP.
$4.00   (E412)

   Fortunita, Fortunita
   (Subira) [Span] ST soli,pno UNION
   ESP. $2.75   (E413)

ESTHER'S MONOLOGUE see Blank, Allan

ESTNISCHE LIEDER see Rakow, Nikolaj

ESTOY EN UN VERDE PRADO see Lasala,
Angel

ESTRELLA E LUA NOVA see Villa-Lobos,
Heitor

ESTRELLITA see Ponce, Manuel Maria

ESTRENE A ANNE see Enesco, Georges

ESTRENE A LA ROSE see Enesco, Georges

ESTUARY see Head, Michael (Dewar)

ESTUDIANTINA see Lacome, Paul

ESURIENTES IMPLEVIT BONIS see Bach,
Johann Sebastian

ET BARN ER FODT I BETLEHEM see Beck,
Thomas [Ludvigsen]

ET C'EST A MOI QUE L'ON DIT see
Laparra, Raoul

ET CUR NON TE AMO see Stamegna, Nicolo

ET INCARNATUS EST see Mozart, Wolfgang
Amadeus

ET MOI AUSSI see Sauvageot, M.

ET QUAND NOUS SERONS VIEUX, CHERE AME
see Laparra, Raoul

ET RESURREXIT TERTIA DIE see Driessler,
Johannes

ET TOC ET TOC PAN PAN see Scotto,
Vincent

ET VOUS NE VEREZ PAS NOS LARMES see
Pouget, Leo

ET YOU, YOU, YOU see Gaubert, Philippe

ETE see Quinet, Marcel

ETE DE JOIE see Barbier, Rene

ETELAPOHJALAISIA KANSANLAULUJA, VOLS.
I-II see Kuula, Toivo

ETELAPOHJALAISIA KANSANLAULUJA, VOLS.
I-III see Jalas, Jussi

ETERNAL LIFE see Dungan, Olive

ETERNEL PRINTEMPS see Berger, Rod.

ETERNELLE CHANSON see Wolff, A.

ETERNITE see Bernier, Rene

ETHIOPIA SALUTING THE COLOURS see Wood,
Charles

ETHOS B' see Terzakis, Dimitri

ETHOS GAMMA see Terzakis, Dimitri

ETOILE DU MATIN see Saint-Saens,
Camille

ETOILES BRULEES see DuBois, Pierre Max

ETRE JEUNE see Anjou, P. d'

ETRE POETE see King, Harold C.

ETRE POETE see King, Harold C.

ETT DROMACKORD see Sjogren, Emil

ETT FANG AV RODA ROSOR see Nordkvist, Martin

ETT HAR JAG BEGART AV HERRAN see Korling

ETT KARLEKSLOFTE see Schumann, Robert (Alexander)

ETTRICK see Peel, Graham

EUCH HOLDE FRAUEN see Mozart, Wolfgang Amadeus, Non So Piu Sosa Son

EUCH, IHR EINSAMEN SCHATTEN - ZEPHIRETTEN LEICHT GEFIEDERT see Mozart, Wolfgang Amadeus

EUCH LUFTEN, DIE MEINE KLAGEN see Wagner, Richard

EULENBERG, P.
    Rosenlieder *CC5U
        [Eng/Ger] med solo,pno BOTE $1.50
            (E414)

EUNUNDDREISSIG LIEDER NACH GEDICHTEN VON HUUGO JALKASEN, VOL. II see Kilpinen, Yrio

EUPHONIUM DANCE see Roe, Betty

EUROPAISCHE KINDERLIEDER *CC49U,Eur
    [Ger] solo,pno SCHOTTS s.p.   (E415)

EUROPAISCHE VOLKSLIEDER HEFT I *CCU, folk,Eur
    DEUTSCHER 9051 s.p. original text and German text   (E416)

EUROPAISCHE VOLKSLIEDER HEFT II *CCU, folk,Eur
    DEUTSCHER 9052 s.p. original text and German text   (E417)

EUROPAISCHE WEIHNACHTSLIEDER *CC24U, Xmas,Eur
    (Karl; Taubert, Heinz) solo,pno SCHAUR EE 3250 s.p.   (E418)

EUROPAISCHE WEIHNACHTSLIEDER *CC15U, Xmas,Eur
    (Behrend, Siegfried) solo,gtr SIKORSKI 488 s.p.   (E419)

EURYDICE TO ORPHEUS see Mollicone, Henry

EURYDIKE see Dijk, Jan van

EVA see Orthel, Leon

EVANGELIE DER NATUUR see Zweers, [Bernard]

EVANGELIENMUSIK see Reda, Siegfried

EVANS
    Honeybird
        high solo,pno (B flat maj) ALLANS s.p.   (E420)
        low solo,pno (G maj) ALLANS s.p.   (E421)
    Tale Of A Fairy
        low solo,pno (B flat maj) ALLANS s.p.   (E422)
        high solo,pno (C maj) ALLANS s.p.   (E423)

EVANS, H.
    Virgin Mary Had A Baby Boy
        solo,pno (F maj) BOOSEY $1.50   (E424)

EVANS, HAL
    Lakes Of Ould Ireland
        solo,pno (D flat maj) LEONARD-ENG   (E425)

EVASION see Rasse, Francois

EVASIONS see Bernier, Nicolas

EVEIL see Gedalge, Andre

EVEILLE-TOI see Lemaire, F.

EVEN AS I FIRST LOVED YOU see Street, James

EVEN BRAVEST HEART MAY SWELL see Gounod, Charles Francois, Avant De Quitter Ces Lieux

EVEN THOUGH THE WORLD KEEPS CHANGING see Whittenberg, Charles

EVENING see Drye, S.L.

EVENING see Dunhill, Thomas Frederick

EVENING see Niles, John Jacob

EVENING see North, Michael

EVENING FAIR see Debussy, Claude, Beau Soir

EVENING FALLS, AN see Mourant, Walter

EVENING HYMN see Purcell, Henry

EVENING IN LILAC TIME see Thiman, Eric Harding

EVENING PRAYER see Humperdinck, Engelbert, Abendsegen

EVENING PRAYER, AN see Gabriel, Sr., Charles H.

EVENING SONG see Chajes, Julius

EVENING SONG see Edwards, Clara

EVENING STAR see Wagner, Richard, O Du Mein Holder Abendstern

EVENSONG see Schumann, Robert (Alexander), Abendlied

EVENTAIL see Debussy, Claude

EVENTAIL, PARAVENT, POTICHE... see Absil, Jean

EVER GENTLE, EVER SWEET see Adams, Steve

EVER GENTLE, EVER SWEET see Adams

EVER SINCE THAT DAY see Charpentier, Depuis Le Jour

EVER SO FAR AWAY see Braun, Charles

EVERLASTING ARMS see Noe, J.T.

EVERLASTING CONTENDERS, THE see Mills, Charles

EVERLASTING LOVE, THE see Brahe, May H.

EVERLASTING VOICES, THE see Ruyneman, Daniel

EVERY DAY, EVERY HOUR *sac,gospel
    solo,pno ABER.GRP. $1.50   (E426)

EVERY DAY IS A BETTER DAY see Bartlett, Gene

EVERY DAY IS FRIDAY TO A SEAL see Heilner, Irwin

EVERY DAY WILL BE SUNDAY, BY AND BY *sac,gospel
    solo,pno ABER.GRP. $1.50   (E427)

EVERY FLOWER see Puccini, Giacomo, Tutti I Fiori

EVERY GOOD AND PERFECT GIFT IS FROM ABOVE see Rider, Dale G.

EVERY STAR IS A DREAM see Rizzi, Alba

EVERY STEP OF THE WAY *sac,gospel
    solo,pno ABER.GRP. $1.50   (E428)

EVERYBODY'S FAVORITE SONGS *sac/sec, CC200U,folk
    solo,pno MUSIC 020001 $3.95   (E429)

EVERYDAY IS A GIFT see Baker, Richard

EVERYONE SANG see Wells, Howard

EVERYTHING THAT I CAN SPY see Mourant, Walter

EVERYTHING WILL BE ALL RIGHT see Hubbard, H.

EVERYTHING'S UNDER CONTROL see Stallings

EVERYTIME I FEEL THE SPIRIT *spir
    low solo,pno (D maj) ALLANS s.p.   (E430)
    high solo,pno (F maj) ALLANS s.p.   (E431)

EVERYWHERE see Cimara, Pietro, Dovunque

EVERYWHERE see Wolfe, Lanny

EVERYWHERE I GO see Martin, Easthope

EVETT, ROBERT (1922-   )
    Billy In The Darbies
        Bar solo,clar,4strings AM.COMP.AL. sc $6.60, ipa, voc sc $4.40   (E432)

EVIDEMMENT see Bozi, Harold de

EVIG VILA see Schubert, Franz (Peter)

EVIGT SVALLET EMOT see Madetoja, Leevi, Ljat Hyrskyja Pain

EVIL TEMPT ME NOT *sac,gospel
    solo,pno ABER.GRP. $1.50   (E433)

EVILLE, V.
    I Will Dwell In The House Of The Lord (Psalm 23) sac
        solo,pno (F maj) BOOSEY $1.50   (E434)
    I Will Lift Up Mine Eyes (Psalm 121) sac
        solo,pno (F maj) BOOSEY $1.50   (E435)
    Psalm 23 *see I Will Dwell In The House Of The Lord
    Psalm 121 *see I Will Lift Up Mine Eyes

EVOCATION see Busser, Henri-Paul

EVOCATION see Delmet, Paul

EVOCATION see Hlobil, Emil

EVOCATION see Pouget, Leo

EVOCATIONS see Somers, Harry Stewart

EVOCATIONS DE GUINEE see Fraggi, H.

EV'RY MAIL DAY see Work, John [Wesley]

EV'RY PRAYER IS A FLOWER *sac,gospel
    solo,pno ABER.GRP. $1.50   (E436)

EV'RY TIME I FEEL THE SPIRIT see Still, William Grant

EWE-BUGHTS, THE *folk,Scot
    solo,pno (D min) PATERSON FS26 s.p.   (E437)

EW'GE QUELLE, MILDER STROM see Telemann, Georg Philipp

EWIG, SO SPRICHT DIE SEELE see Handel, George Frideric

EWIGE TRAUER see Kilpinen, Yrio, Ikuinen Suru

EWIGE WALZERMELODIE see Strauss, Josef

EWING, M.
    Heart Of A Butterfly
        low solo,pno (F maj) LEONARD-ENG   (E438)
        high solo,pno (G maj) LEONARD-ENG   (E439)
    How Did Everybody Know
        low solo,pno (C maj) LEONARD-ENG   (E440)
        high solo,pno (D flat maj) LEONARD-ENG   (E441)
    I'm Calling Love For You
        solo,pno (E flat maj) LEONARD-ENG   (E442)
    Jonathan Jollybun
        low solo,pno (D maj) LEONARD-ENG   (E443)
        high solo,pno (E maj) LEONARD-ENG   (E444)

EWING, PORTEOUS
    This England
        solo,pno (C maj) ASHDOWN   (E445)

EX MINIMIS PATET IPSE DEUS see Voormolen, Alexander Nicolas, Lofsang

EXALTABO TE, DEUS MEUS, REX see Campra, Andre

EXAMEN TROOST see Baeyens, August-L.

EXAMPLES see Lacy, Steve

EXAUCANT TA PRIERE see Saint-Saens, Camille

EXAUDET
    Celebre Menuet
        solo,pno/inst DURAND s.p.   (E446)
    Menuet
        see LA MUSIQUE, NEUVIEME CAHIER

EXAUDI DEUS see Gabrieli, Giovanni

EXCELSIOR see Torjussen, Trygve

EXCELSIOR *CC32U
    solo,pno FAZER W 1850 s.p.   (E447)

EXCEPT I LOVE see Musgrave, Thea

EXEMPLE see Ferroud, Pierre-Octave

EXIL see Chaminade, Cecile

EXIT EDICTUM see Hindemith, Paul

EXPERIENCES II see Cage, John

EXPIRATION, THE see Mills, Charles

EXPLANATION see Barab, Seymour

EXQUISIVI DOMINUM see Schutz, Heinrich

EXSULTATE JUBILATE see Mozart, Wolfgang
    Amadeus

EXTASE see Bordewijk-Roepman, Johanna

EXTASE see Chaminade, Cecile

EXTASE see Desrez

EXTASE see Ganne, Louis Gaston

EXTASE see Jongen, Leon

EXTASE see Saint-Saens, Camille

EXTASE LANGOUREUSE see Trabadelo, A. de

EXTINGUISH MY EYES see Bernstein,
    Leonard

EXTRA SPECIAL CONSTABLES see Newton,
    Ernest

EXTRAVAGANZAS see Dickinson, Peter

EXULTA FILIA see Monteverdi, Claudio

EXULTATE IN DEO FIDELES see Stradella,
    Alessandro

EXULTATION see Bernier, Rene

EXULTAVIT COR MEUM see Schutz, Heinrich

EY-SHAM
    solo,pno OR-TAV $.50   (E448)

EYE HATH NOT SEEN see Gaul, Alfred
    Robert

EYE OF HORUS, THE see El-Dabh, Halim

EYES LOOK INTO THE WELL see Berkeley,
    Lennox

EYES THAT LAST I SAW IN TEARS see Mc
    Cabe

EYKEN, HEINRICH VAN
    Ikarus *Op.26
      solo,2fl,2ob,2clar,2bsn,4horn,2trp,
      3trom,tuba,timp,perc,strings
      BIRNBACH sc rental, voc sc s.p.
                                       (E449)
    Judiths Liebeslied *Op.20
      solo,2fl,2ob,2clar,2bsn,4horn,3trp,
      3trom,tuba,timp,perc,harp,strings
      BIRNBACH sc rental, voc sc s.p.
                                       (E450)
    Lied Der Walkure *Op.16,No.2
      high solo/low solo,2fl,2ob,2clar,
      2bsn,4horn,2trp,3trom,tuba,timp,
      perc,harp,strings BIRNBACH sc
      rental, voc sc s.p.   (E451)

EYKEN, JAN ALBERT VAN (1823-1868)
    Rust Mijn Ziel Uw God Is Koning *sac
      solo,pno ALSBACH s.p.   (E452)

EYN KELOHEYNU see Belfer, Ben W.

EYN KELOHEYNU see Krasnoff, Israel

EYN KI-Y'RUSHALAYIM
    (Helfman, Max) "Jerusalem - The One
      And Only" [Heb] med solo,pno
      TRANSCON. IS 507 $.40   (E453)

EYSLER, EDMUND S. (1874-1949)
    Das Ist Die Erste Liebelei
      [Ger] med solo,pno BOTE $1.00 see
      from Zwei Wiener Lieder   (E454)

    Drei Dinge Versussen Das Leben
      [Ger] med solo,pno BOTE $1.00 see
      from Zwei Wiener Lieder   (E455)

    Zwei Wiener Lieder *see Das Ist Die
      Erste Liebelei; Drei Dinge
      Versussen Das Leben   (E456)

EZAKI, K.
    Discretion
      see Ezaki, K., Moving Pulses

    Moving Pulses
      3 soli,perc ONGAKU s.p. contains
      also: Discretion (female solo,
      inst)   (E457)

EZECHIEL 37 see Colaco Osorio-Swaab,
    Reine

EZEK'EL SAW THE WHEEL *spir
    (Bonds, M.) low solo,pno MERCURY $.95
                                       (E458)

EZEKIEL see Weiner, Lazar

F

FA LA NANA BAMBIN see Sadero, G.

FA-SO-LA see House, Jerry

FABLE
    see Long Wharf Songs

FABLE see Gyring, Elizabeth

FABLE, THE see Arensky, Anton
    Stepanovitch, Une Fable

FABLE ETERNELLE see Delmet, Paul

FABLES DE FLORIAN see Vellones, Pierre

FABLES IN SONG see Kubik, Gail

FABLIAU see Ganne, Louis Gaston

FABRE, G.
    Chanson De Melissande
      solo,pno ENOCH s.p.   (F1)

    Dansons La Ronde
      solo,pno ENOCH s.p.   (F2)

    L'Elue
      solo,pno ENOCH s.p.   (F3)

FACCENDA, O.
    Amore
      [It] solo,pno BONGIOVANI 2136 s.p.
                                       (F4)
    Primavera
      [It] solo,pno BONGIOVANI 2137 s.p.
                                       (F5)

FACE TO FACE see Johnson

FACTUM EST PRAELIUM MAGNUM see Cazzati,
    Maurizio

FADDEGON-KEENE, E.
    De Vinkjes
      solo,pno BROEKMANS 232 s.p.   (F6)

    Lente Trioletten
      solo,pno BROEKMANS 269 s.p.   (F7)

FADER VAR see Egge, Ragnvald

FADER VAR see Hannikainen, Ilmari

FADER VAR see Melartin, Erkki, Isa
    Meidan

FADERNAS ARV see Malmstrom

FAERIE FROLIC see Lora, Antonio

FAFANG ONSKAN see Collan, Karl

FAFANG SERENAD see Brahms, Johannes

FAGEL BLA see Madetoja, Leevi, Lintu
    Sininen

FAGELFANGAREN see Sibelius, Jean

FAGELSANG see Myrberg, August M.

FAHRT ZUM AUFGEBOT see Marvia, Einari,
    Kuulutusmatka

FAIN WOULD I CHANGE THAT NOTE see
    Joubert, John

FAIN WOULD I CHANGE THAT NOTE see
    Thiman, Eric Harding

FAIR ANNETTE'S SONG see Nordoff, Paul

FAIR HELEN see Montgomery, Bruce

FAIR HELEN OF KIRKCONNEL *folk,Scot
    low solo,pno (F maj) PATERSON FS28
    s.p.   (F8)
    high solo,pno (A flat maj) PATERSON
    FS28 s.p.   (F9)

FAIR HOUSE OF JOY see Quilter, Roger

FAIR IS THE ROSE see Russell, Welford

FAIR JESSIE see Fielitz, Alexander von,
    Schon Gretlein

FAIR MAID OF PERTH, THE see Bizet,
    Georges, La Jolie Fille De Perth

FAIR MAIDENS see Delibes, Leo, Les
    Filles De Cadix

FAIR MORNING, THE see Binkerd, Gordon

FAIR OF BRITAINS ISLE, THE see Hook,
    James

FAIR ROSALIND see Morgan, Orlando

FAIR YOUNG MARY see Lawson, Malcolm

FAIRCHILD
  Memory, A
    med-high solo,pno (E flat maj)
      BOSTON $1.50   (F10)

FAIRE-PART see Damase, Jean-Michel

FAIREST LORD JESUS see Willan, Healey

FAIREST OF ALL see Mana-Zucca, Mme.,
  Piu Bello Del Sole

FAIRIE VOICES, WALTZ-SONG see Crowe,
  A.C.

FAIRIES HAVE NEVER A PENNY TO SPEND,
  THE see Weigl, Vally

FAIRIES IN THE GLEN see Baynon, Arthur

FAIRINGS see Martin, Easthope

FAIRY COBBLER see Anderson, William H.

FAIRY FOLK see Geehl, Henry Ernest

FAIRY LOUGH see Stanford, Charles
  Villiers

FAIRY LURES see Stafford, C.V.

FAIRY PATH, THE see Rowley, Alec

FAIRY PEDLAR, THE see Rowley, Alec

FAIRY PIPERS see Brewer, Sir Alfred
  Herbert

FAIRY SHOON, THE see Day, Maude Craske

FAIRY SHOPPING see Day, Maude Craske

FAIRY STORY BY THE FIRE see Merikanto,
  Oskar

FAIRY STORY BY THE FIRE, A see
  Merikanto, Oskar

FAIRY TALES see Harrison, Sidney

FAIRY TAYLOR see Head, Michael (Dewar)

FAIRY TREE, THE see O'Brien, Vincent

FAIRY WAYS see Macmurrough, Dermot

FAIS NONO see Messager, Andre

FAISST, CLARA (1872-1948)
  Am Heiligen Abend *sac
    med solo,pno MULLER 480 s.p. (F11)

  Ruth *sac
    med solo,pno MULLER 26 s.p.   (F12)

  Trauungslied Von Dir Gestiftet Ist
    Die Ehe
    med solo,pno/org (med) MULLER 52
    s.p.   (F13)

FAITES-LUI MES AVEUX see Gounod,
  Charles Francois

FAITH AND PRAYER see Slaughter, Henry

FAITH CAN DO ANYTHING see Giesking,
  Shirley

FAITH CAN MOVE MOUNTAINS *sac,gospel
  solo,pno ABER.GRP. $1.50   (F14)

FAITH IN SPRING see Schubert, Franz
  (Peter), Fruhlingsglaube

FAITH IS THE KEY *sac,gospel
  solo,pno ABER.GRP. $1.50   (F15)

FAITH IS THE KEY see Davis

FAITH UNLOCKS THE DOOR see Scott

FAITHFUL HEART ENRAPTURED see Morley,
  Thomas, L'Amero, Saro Costante

FAITHFUL OF ALLAH see Sharpe, Evelyn

FAITHLESS HEART see Cardillo, Core'
  Ngrato

FALCON, THE see Cortes, Ramiro

FALCON, THE see Ives, Grayston

FALCONIERI, ANDREA (1586-1656)
  Begli Occhi Lucenti
    solo,pno FORLIVESI 10875 s.p. (F16)

  Bella Porta Di Rubini
    solo,pno FORLIVESI 12077 s.p. (F17)

FALCONIERI, ANDREA (cont'd.)

  Pupillette
    solo,pno FORLIVESI 10888 s.p. (F18)

FALKENBERG, G.
  Chanson Du Temps Passe *canon
    2 soli,pno DURAND s.p.   (F19)

  Le Papillon
    solo,pno (available in 2 keys)
      ENOCH s.p.   (F20)
    2 female soli,pno ENOCH s.p. voc
      sc, solo pt   (F21)

FALKS SANG UR KARLEKENS KOMEDI see
  Sjogren, Emil

FALL, LEO (1873-1925)
  Kind, Du Kannst Tanzen (from Die
    Geschiedene Frau)
    solo,pno DOBLINGER 88 522 s.p.
                                   (F22)

FALL ON ME LIKE A SILENT DEW see
  Coleridge-Taylor, Samuel

FALLA, MANUEL DE (1876-1946)
  Air De Salud *see Air Du Salut

  Air Du Salut (from La Vida Breve)
    [Span/Fr] med-high solo,kbd CHESTER
    s.p.   (F23)
    "Air De Salud" [Span/Fr] high solo,
    pno ESCHIG $3.75   (F24)

  Asturiana
    [Span/Fr] med solo,pno ESCHIG $1.00
    see also Siete Canciones
      Populares Espanolas   (F25)
    (Llobet-Pujol) [Span/Fr] med solo,
    gtr ESCHIG E1503 $2.00 see also
    Siete Canciones Populares
      Espanolas   (F26)

  Cancion
    [Span/Fr] med solo,pno ESCHIG $2.50
    see also Siete Canciones
      Populares Espanolas   (F27)
    (Llobet-Pujol) [Span/Fr] med solo,
    gtr ESCHIG E1506 $2.00 see also
    Siete Canciones Populares
      Espanolas   (F28)

  Cancion Del Amor Dolido (from El Amor
    Brujo)
    "Chanson Du Chagrin D'Amour" [Span/
    Fr] med-low solo,kbd CHESTER s.p.
                                   (F29)

  Cancion Del Fuego Fatuo (from El Amor
    Brujo)
    "Chanson Du Feu Follet" [Span/Fr]
    med-low solo,kbd CHESTER s.p.
                                   (F30)

  Chanson Du Chagrin D'Amour *see
    Cancion Del Amor Dolido

  Chanson Du Feu Follet *see Cancion
    Del Fuego Fatuo

  Chinoiserie
    see Three Songs
    see Tres Melodies
    med solo,pno SALABERT-US $3.75 see
    from Three Songs   (F31)

  Deteneos (from El Retablo De Maese
    Pedro)
    "Stop, You Scoundrels!" [Span/Eng/
    Fr] med-low solo,kbd CHESTER s.p.
                                   (F32)

  El Pano Moruno
    [Span/Fr] med solo,pno ESCHIG $3.75
    see also Siete Canciones
      Populares Espanolas   (F33)
    (Llobet-Pujol) [Span/Fr] med solo,
    gtr ESCHIG E1501 $2.25 see also
    Siete Canciones Populares
      Espanolas   (F34)

  Jota
    [Span/Fr] med-high solo,pno ESCHIG
    $3.75 see also Siete Canciones
      Populares Espanolas   (F35)
    (Llobet, M.) [Span/Fr] med solo,gtr
    CHESTER s.p. see also Siete
      Canciones Populares Espanolas
                                   (F36)
    (Llobet-Pujol) [Span/Fr] med solo,
    gtr ESCHIG E1504 $3.00 see also
    Siete Canciones Populares
      Espanolas   (F37)

  Les Colombes
    see Three Songs
    see Tres Melodies
    med solo,pno SALABERT-US $3.75 see
    from Three Songs   (F38)

  Nana
    [Span/Fr] med solo,pno ESCHIG $1.00
    see also Siete Canciones
      Populares Espanolas   (F39)
    (Llobet, M.) [Span/Fr] med solo,gtr
    CHESTER s.p. see also Siete
      Canciones Populares Espanolas
                                   (F40)

FALLA, MANUEL DE (cont'd.)

    (Llobet-Pujol) [Span/Fr] med solo,
    gtr ESCHIG E1505 $1.75 see also
    Siete Canciones Populares
      Espanolas   (F41)

  Polo
    [Span/Fr] med solo,pno ESCHIG $2.50
    see also Siete Canciones
      Populares Espanolas   (F42)
    (Llobet-Pujol) [Span/Fr] med solo,
    gtr ESCHIG E1507 $2.25 see also
    Siete Canciones Populares
      Espanolas   (F43)

  Seguidilla Murciana
    (Llobet, M.) [Span/Fr] med solo,gtr
    CHESTER s.p. see also Siete
      Canciones Populares Espanolas
                                   (F44)
  Seguidilla Muriciana
    [Span/Fr] med solo,pno ESCHIG $3.75
    see also Siete Canciones
      Populares Espanolas   (F45)
    (Llobet-Pujol) [Span/Fr] med solo,
    gtr ESCHIG E1502 $2.50 see also
    Siete Canciones Populares
      Espanolas   (F46)

  Seguidille
    see Three Songs
    see Tres Melodies
    med solo,pno SALABERT-US $3.75 see
    from Three Songs   (F47)

  Siete Canciones Populares Espanolas
    [Span/Eng/Fr] cmplt ed high solo,
    pno ESCHIG E3052 $4.00; med solo,
    pno ESCHIG E3053 $4.00
    contains & see also: Asturiana;
      Cancion; El Pano Moruno; Jota;
      Nana; Polo; Seguidilla
      Muriciana   (F48)

  Siete Canciones Populares Espanolas
    *CC7L
    [Span/Fr] CHESTER s.p. med solo,
    kbd; high solo,kbd
    see also: Jota; Nana; Seguidilla
      Muriciana   (F49)

  Soneto A Cordoba
    [Span/Eng] high solo,harp CHESTER
    s.p.   (F50)

  Stop, You Scoundrels! *see Deteneos

  Three Songs
    [Fr/Eng] high solo,pno INTERNAT.
    $1.75
    contains: Chinoiserie; Les
      Colombes; Seguidille   (F51)

  Three Songs *see Chinoiserie; Les
    Colombes; Seguidille   (F52)

  Tres Melodies
    [Fr] high solo,kbd CHESTER s.p.
    contains: Chinoiserie; Les
      Colombes; Seguidille   (F53)

  Tus Ojillos Negros
    [Span] high solo,pno UNION ESP.
    $1.75
    (Azpaizu) [Span] med solo,gtr UNION
    ESP. $1.25   (F55)

  Vocal Works *CCU
    [Russ] solo,pno MEZ KNIGA 94 s.p.
                                   (F56)

FALLEN POPLAR, THE see Naylor, Bernard

FALLENDES LAUB see Ehrenberg, Carl Emil
  Theodor

FALLING ASLEEP IN AN ORCHARD see
  Flothius, Marius

FALLING BLOSSOM see Sawyer, Yvonne

FALLING OF THE LEAVES, THE see Blank,
  Allan

FALSCHER MADCHENBLICK see Bergman, Erik

FALSE KNIGHT see Boatwright, Howard

FALSE KNIGHT UPON THE ROAD, THE
  see Schirmer's American Folk-Song
    Series, Set XXII (American-English
    Folk-Ballads From The Southern
    Appalachian Mountains)

FALSE PROPHET see Scott, John Prindle

FALSE PROPHET, THE see Scott, John
  Prindle

FALSE YOUNG MAN, THE
  see Schirmer's American Folk-Song
    Series, Set XXI (American-English
    Folk-Songs From The Southern
    Appalachian Mountains)

FAMA E FOME see Grunauer, Ingomar

FAMILIALE see Kosma, J.

FAMILY MUSIC BOOK, THE *CC300U
    solo,pno,org (med diff) SCHIRM.G
    $9.95   (F57)

FAMILY OF GOD, THE see Gaither

FAMME MURI see Guerrini, Guido

FAMOUS CLASSICAL SONGS *CC6U
    [Lat/It] solo,pno LYCHE LY10 s.p.
    contains works by: Bach-Gounod;
    Caccini; Giordani; Gluck; Handel
                                 (F58)

FAMOUS IRISH SONGS *CCU
    (Neir) solo,pno PAXTON P15346 s.p.
                                 (F59)

FAMOUS NEGRO SPIRITUALS *CC16U,spir
    [Eng] med solo,pno LYCHE LY136 s.p.
                                 (F60)

FAMOUS OPERA ARIAS, VOL. 1 *CCU
    (Vargas) coloratura sop,pno BOOSEY
    $4.50 original and Hungarian texts
                                 (F61)

FAMOUS OPERA ARIAS, VOL. 2 *CCU
    (Vargas) Bar solo,pno BOOSEY $4.50
    original and Hungarian texts
                                 (F62)

FAMOUS OPERA DUETS, VOL. 1 *CCU
    (Vargas) SBar soli,pno BUDAPEST $4.50
                                 (F63)

FAMOUS OPERA DUETS, VOL. 2 *CCU
    (Vargas) ST soli,pno BUDAPEST $4.50
                                 (F64)

FAMOUS SACRED SONGS *sac,CCU
    solo,pno PAXTON P15325 s.p.   (F65)

FAMOUS SCOTTISH SONGS *CCU,Scot
    solo,pno PAXTON P15350 s.p.
                                 (F66)

FAMOUS SONGS *CCU
    (Krehbiel, H.E.) S solo,pno PRESSER
    $5.00   (F67)

FANCIULLA, SBOCCIATO E L'AMORE see
    Puccini, Giacomo

FANFARE see Schumann, Robert
    (Alexander)

FANFARE TRIONFALE see Heppener, Robert

FANFRELUCHES see Delmet, Paul

FANGENS AFTENSANG see Hall, Pauline

FANGESONGAR FRA KIRKENES see Kjeldaas,
    Gunnar

FANJUNKAR BERG see Korling, Felix

FANJUNKAR BERG see Peterson-Berger,
    (Olof) Wilhelm

FANS OF BLUE see Hovhaness, Alan

FANTASIA see Bohun, Lyle de

FANTASIA QUASI UN CANTATA see Flothius,
    Marius

FANTASIE see Zagwijn, Henri

FANTASIE VON UBERMORGEN see Jelinek,
    Hanns

FANTASIO see Dupre, Marcel

FANTASTICARE see Pratella, Francesco
    Balilla

FANTASY see Mana-Zucca, Mme.

FANTOCHES see Debussy, Claude

FAR ABOVE THE PURPLE HILLS see
    Giannini, Vittorio

FAR AWAY see Lindsay, M.

FAR AWAY ISLES see Repper, Charles

FAR FROM MY LOVE I LANGUISH see Sarti,
    Giuseppe, Lungi Dal Caro Bene

FAR GREATER IN HIS LOWLY STATE see
    Gounod, Charles Francois

FARADAY, MICHAEL
    Little Princess, Look Up!
    solo,pno CRAMER   (F68)

FARAHERDEN see Sonninen, Ahti,
    Lammaspaimen

FARANDOLE NOCTURNE see Varney, Pierre
    Joseph Alphonse

FARANDOLE PRINTANIERE see Lacome, Paul

FARAUT, B.
    J'ai Repris Mon Sourire
    solo,pno OUVRIERES s.p.   (F69)

    Ne Joue Pas Avec Mon Coeur
    solo,pno OUVRIERES s.p.   (F70)

FARBERMAN, HAROLD (1930-   )
    New York Times: August 30, 1964, The
    *song cycle
    med solo,pno,perc GENERAL 413 $3.00
                                 (F71)

FARDEMANNENS PSALM see Hannikainen,
    Ilmari, Matkamiehen Virsi

FARDEMINNEN see Backman, Hjalmar,
    Matkani Muistot

FARWEEL TO MY HAME *folk,Scot
    solo,pno (F maj) PATERSON FS103 s.p.
                                 (F72)

FAREWELL see Geehl, Henry Ernest

FAREWELL see Guarnieri, Camargo Mozart,
    Vou-Me Embora

FAREWELL see Liddle, Samuel

FAREWELL see Roussel, Albert

FAREWELL, A see Fisher, Howard

FAREWELL, A see Mechem, Kirke

FAREWELL CARNIVAL see Kodaly, Zoltan

FAREWELL EARTH'S BLISS see Bush,
    Geoffrey

FAREWELL GLENALBIN see Lawson, Malcolm

FAREWELL, ONCE MY DELIGHT see Woollen,
    Russell

FAREWELL TABLET TO AGATHOCLES see
    Gideon, Miriam

FAREWELL TO FANCY see Casseus

FAREWELL TO FIUNARY see Lawson, Malcolm

FAREWELL TO SUMMER see Johnson, Noel

FAREWELL TO YESTERDAY see Foster, F.

FAREWELL TOAST, A see Schumann, Robert
    (Alexander), Wanderlied

FAREWELL, YE MOUNTAINS see Tchaikovsky,
    Piotr Ilyitch, Adieu, Forets

FARGA, O.
    Cantares Andaluces
    [Span/Fr] high solo,pno ESCHIG $.65
                                 (F73)
    Ojos Claros, Serenos
    [Span/Fr] high solo,pno ESCHIG $.65
                                 (F74)

FARGASON, EDDIE
    Joy Only He Can Give, The *sac
    med solo,pno CRESPUB CP-S5026 $1.00
                                 (F75)

FARIGOUL, J.
    Aubade
    solo,pno ENOCH s.p.   (F76)

FARINA, GUIDO (1903-   )
    Ballata
    [It] solo,pno BONGIOVANI 1759 s.p.
                                 (F77)
    Ballata Campestre
    [It] solo,pno BONGIOVANI 1529 s.p.
                                 (F78)
    Canzone No. 1
    [It] solo,pno BONGIOVANI 1760 s.p.
                                 (F79)
    Canzone No. 2
    [It] solo,pno BONGIOVANI 1761 s.p.
                                 (F80)
    Due Liriche Infantili *see Giro
    Tondo; La Befana   (F81)
    Filastrocca Del Gatto Nero
    [It] solo,pno BONGIOVANI 1734 s.p.
                                 (F82)
    Giro Tondo
    [It] solo,pno BONGIOVANI 1527 s.p.
    see from Due Liriche Infantili
                                 (F83)
    La Befana
    [It] solo,pno BONGIOVANI 1526 s.p.
    see from Due Liriche Infantili
                                 (F84)
    Notturnino
    [It] solo,pno BONGIOVANI 1763 s.p.
                                 (F85)
    Ricciolina Trotta Trotta
    [It] solo,pno BONGIOVANI 1733 s.p.
                                 (F86)
    Strambotto
    [It] solo,pno BONGIOVANI 1528 s.p.
                                 (F87)
    Tre Liriche *CC3U
    solo,strings CARISH s.p.   (F88)

FARINELLI, GIUSEPPE (1769-1836).
    Aria Di Coviello (from Il Dottorato
    Di Pulcinella)
    (Gargiulo, T.) solo,pno CURCI
    rental   (F89)

    Aria Di Flaminia (from Il Dottorato
    Di Pulcinella)
    (Gargiulo, T.) solo,pno CURCI
    rental   (F90)

    Cavatina Di Pulcinella (from Il
    Dottorato Di Pulcinella)
    (Gargiulo, T.) solo,pno CURCI
    rental   (F91)

    Deutto Finale (Laura E Pulcinella)
    (from Il Dottorato Di Pulcinella)
    (Gargiulo, T.) solo,pno CURCI
    rental   (F92)

FARIZADE AU SOURIRE DE ROSE see Roland-
    Manuel, Alexis

FARJEON, HARRY (1878-1948)
    Presents From Heaven
    solo,pno (G maj) LESLIE 7024 (F93)

FARKAS, FERENC (1905-   )
    Autumnalia
    [Hung] solo,pno BUDAPEST 7431 s.p.
                                 (F94)
    Cinque Canzoni Dei Trovatori *CC5U
    [Fr] solo,gtr BERBEN 1521 s.p.
                                 (F95)
    Fruit Basket
    [Hung] solo,pno BUDAPEST 1054 s.p.
                                 (F96)
    Let Us Sing For Cypria
    [Hung] solo,pno BUDAPEST 1162 s.p.
                                 (F97)
    Pastorali
    [Hung/It] solo,pno BUDAPEST 6262
    s.p.   (F98)
    Petofi Songs *CCU
    [Hung] solo,pno BUDAPEST 6650 s.p.
                                 (F99)
    Selected Songs *CCU
    [Hung/Ger] solo,pno BUDAPEST 2744
    s.p.   (F100)
    Three Eulau Songs *CC3U
    [Hung/Ger] solo,pno BUDAPEST 4408
    s.p.   (F101)
    Three Guillevic Songs *CC3U
    [Hung/Fr] solo,pno BUDAPEST 4409
    s.p.   (F102)
    Tibicinium *CC2U
    [Hung/Ger] solo,fl BUDAPEST 5294
    s.p.   (F103)
    Waiting For The Spring *cant
    solo,pno BUDAPEST 10103 s.p. (F104)
    Wanderer's Songs *CCU
    [Hung/Ger] solo,pno BUDAPEST 3882
    s.p.   (F105)
    Zold A Kokeny *CCU,folk,Hung
    [Hung] solo,pno BUDAPEST 1581 s.p.
                                (F106)

FARLORENE YUGEND *Jew
    solo,pno KAMMEN 60 $1.00   (F107)

FARMER'S BOY see Broadwood, Lucy E.

FARR, IAN
    Pictures
    solo,pno ALBERT AHL219 rental
                                (F108)
    Rimbaud Songs *CC5U
    A solo,pno ALBERT AHL220 rental
                                (F109)

FARRAND, NOEL
    Spring Song
    med solo,pno AM.COMP.AL. $1.37
                                (F110)

FARRAR
    Christ My Refuge
    high solo,pno (E flat maj) FISCHER,
    C V 2334   (F111)

FARRAR, ERNEST BRISTOW (1885-1918)
    Brittany
    high solo,pno NOVELLO 17.0013.08
    s.p.   (F112)
    low solo,pno NOVELLO 17.0015.04
    s.p.   (F113)

FARTHER ALONG *sac,gospel
    solo,pno ABER.GRP. $1.50   (F114)

FARVAL! see Nordholm, H.

FASCINATION see Marchetti

FAST GRUNN see Tonnessen, Peder

FASULLO, P.
    Due Liriche
    [It] solo,pno cmplt ed BONGIOVANI
    2446 s.p.
    contains: Germina Luce; Uccelli

FASULLO, P. (cont'd.)

Germina Luce (F115)
see Due Liriche

Uccelli
see Due Liriche

Viva Lu Suli Mie
[It] solo,pno BONGIOVANI 2336 s.p.
(F116)

FATAL AMOUR see Rameau, Jean-Philippe

FATAL DIVINITA see Gluck, Christoph
Willibald Ritter von

FATAL INTERVIEW see Kohs, Ellis B.

FATE THE FIDDLER see Sharpe, Evelyn

FATE'S DISCOURTESY see Elgar, Edward

FATHER see O'Hara, Geoffrey

FATHER ABRAHAM, HAVE MERCY ON ME see
Krapf, Gerhard

FATHER ABRAHAM, HAVE MERCY ON ME see
Schutz, Heinrich

FATHER IN HEAVEN see Doun, E.

FATHER LOVES YOU, THE see Salsbury,
Sonny

FATHER-MOTHER see O'Connor-Morris, G.

FATHER O'FLYNN see Stanford, Charles
Villiers

FAUBOURG GITANE see Legley, Victor

FAUCHEUR SINISTRE see Berger, Jean

FAUCHEY, PAUL
Panis Angelicus *sac
med solo,pno/org (G maj) HEUGEL
s.p. (F117)

FAULKNER
Feed My Sheep *sac
high solo,pno (E maj) FISCHER,C
V 2113 (F118)

FAUNE see Devreese, Godefroid

FAUNE see Lonque, Georges

FAURE, GABRIEL-URBAIN (1845-1924)
Adieu *Op.21,No.3
[Fr] solo,acap oct DURAND s.p. see
from Poeme D'un Jour (F119)
S/T solo,pno/inst DURAND s.p. see
also Poeme D'un Jour (F120)
Mez/Bar solo,pno/inst DURAND s.p.
see also Poeme D'un Jour (F121)

After A Dream *see Apres Un Reve

Album Of Six Songs *sac,CC6U
high solo,pno BOSTON $2.50 (F122)

Apres Un Reve
"After A Dream" [Fr/Eng] high solo,
pno (D min) SCHIRM.G $.85 (F123)

Ave Maria *Op.93, sac
SS soli,vln,vcl,harmonium,org
HEUGEL s.p. (F124)

Benedictus *sac
Mez solo,opt cor,pno/org HEUGEL
s.p. (F125)

Blessed Jesus *see Pie Jesu

C'est La Paix *Op.114
solo,pno/inst DURAND s.p. (F126)

Cygnes Sur L'eau *Op.113,No.1
solo,pno DURAND s.p. see also
Mirages (F127)

Dans La Nymphee
med solo,pno/inst DURAND s.p. see
also Le Jardin Clos (F128)

Danseuse *Op.113,No.4
solo,pno DURAND s.p. see also
Mirages (F129)

Douze Chants *CC12L
med solo,pno DURAND s.p. (F130)

Gabriel Faure Album Of Twenty Songs,
Volume I *CCU
MARKS S/T solo,pno $3.00; Mez/Bar
solo,pno $3.00 (F131)

Gabriel Faure Album Of Twenty Songs,
Volume II *CCU
MARKS S/T solo,pno $3.00; Mez/Bar
solo,pno $3.00 (F132)

FAURE, GABRIEL-URBAIN (cont'd.)

Gabriel Faure Album Of Twenty Songs,
Volume III *CCU
MARKS S/T solo,pno $3.00; Mez/Bar
solo,pno $3.00 (F133)

Jardin Nocturne *Op.113,No.3
solo,pno DURAND s.p. see also
Mirages (F134)

Kyrie *sac
S solo,opt cor,pno/org HEUGEL s.p.
(F135)

La Bonne Chanson *Op.61,No.1-9, CC9U
HAMELLE high solo,pno $8.75; med
solo,pno $8.75 (F136)

La Bonne Chanson *song cycle
high solo,pno INTERNAT. $3.00
(F137)

low solo,pno INTERNAT. $3.00 (F138)

Le Jardin Clos *CC8L
med solo,pno DURAND s.p.
see also: Dans La Nymphee (F139)

L'Horizon Chimerique *Op.118, song
cycle
med solo,orch DURAND s.p., ipr
(F140)

Mirages
solo,pno DURAND s.p.
contains & see also: Cygnes Sur
L'eau, Op.113,No.1; Danseuse,
Op.113,No.4; Jardin Nocturne,
Op.113,No.3; Reflets Dans
L'eau, Op.113,No.2 (F141)

Pie Jesu (from Requiem) sac
"Blessed Jesus" med-high solo,pno
FITZSIMONS $.60 (F142)

Poeme D'un Jour *see Adieu (F143)

Poeme D'un Jour
[Fr/Ger/Eng] cmplt ed DURAND s.p.
contains & see also: Adieu,
Op.21,No.3; Rencontre, Op.21,
No.1; Toujours, Op.21,No.2
(F144)

Reflets Dans L'eau *Op.113,No.2
solo,pno DURAND s.p. see also
Mirages (F145)

Rencontre *Op.21,No.1
S/T solo,pno/inst DURAND s.p. see
also Poeme D'un Jour (F146)
Mez/Bar solo,pno/inst DURAND s.p.
see also Poeme D'un Jour (F147)

Serenade Du Bourgeois Gentilhomme
[Fr/Eng] solo,pno HEUGEL 10925 s.p.
(F148)

Thirty Songs *CC30L
(Kagen, Sergius) [Fr/Eng] INTERNAT.
high solo,pno $5.00; med solo,pno
$5.00; med-high solo,pno $5.00
(F149)

Toujours *Op.21,No.2
S/T solo,pno/inst DURAND s.p. see
also Poeme D'un Jour (F150)
Mez/Bar solo,pno/inst DURAND s.p.
see also Poeme D'un Jour (F151)

Twenty-Five Selected Songs *CC25L
[Fr/Eng] high solo,pno SCHIRM.G
1713 $4.00; low solo,pno SCHIRM.G
1714 $4.00 (F152)

Vingt Melodies, Vol. 1 *CCU
HAMELLE $15.50 high solo,pno; med
solo,pno (F153)

Vingt Melodies, Vol. 2 *CCU
HAMELLE $15.50 high solo,pno; med
solo,pno (F154)

Vingt Melodies, Vol. 3 *CCU
HAMELLE $15.50 high solo,pno; med
solo,pno (F155)

FAURE, JEAN-BAPTISTE (1830-1914)
Agnus Dei *sac
solo,pno/org (available in 2 keys)
HEUGEL s.p. (F156)

Ave Verum *sac
2 high soli,pno/org HEUGEL s.p. (F157)

Charite *sac
solo,pno/org HEUGEL s.p. see from
CHANTS RELIGIEUX (F158)
2 high soli,pno/org HEUGEL s.p.
(F159)

Credo *sac
solo,pno/org HEUGEL s.p. see from
CHANTS RELIGIEUX (F160)
solo,pno/org (available in 2 keys)
HEUGEL s.p. (F161)

Crucifix *sac
solo,pno/org HEUGEL s.p. see from
CHANTS RELIGIEUX (F162)
2 soli,pno/org (available in 2
keys) HEUGEL s.p. see from CHANTS

FAURE, JEAN-BAPTISTE (cont'd.)

RELIGIEUX (F163)
solo,pno/org (available in 2 keys)
HEUGEL s.p. (F164)
[Fr/Eng] high solo&low solo,pno
SCHIRM.G $.85 (F165)

Crucifixus *sac
[Fr/Eng] high solo,pno (E min)
SCHIRM.G $.85 (F166)

Les Rameaux *sac,Palm
[Fr] Mez/Bar solo,pno RICORDI-ARG
BA 1887 s.p. (F167)
"Palms, The" [Eng/Fr] high solo,pno
(C maj) SCHIRM.G $.85 (F168)
"Palms, The" [Eng/Fr] med solo,pno
(B flat maj) SCHIRM.G $.85 (F169)
"Palms, The" [Eng/Fr] low solo,pno
(A flat maj) SCHIRM.G $.85 (F170)
"Palms, The" high solo,pno FISCHER,
C S 4858 (F171)
"Palms, The" med solo,pno FISCHER,C
S 4859 (F172)
"Palms, The" low solo,pno FISCHER,C
S 4860 (F173)
"Palms, The" med solo,pno (A flat
maj) CENTURY 85 $.40 (F174)
"Palms, The" solo,pno (available in
3 keys) ASHLEY $.95 (F175)
"Palms, The" med solo,pno LORENZ
$1.00 (F176)
"Palms, The" SA soli,pno LORENZ
$1.00 (F177)

Notre Pere *sac
solo,pno/org HEUGEL s.p. see from
CHANTS RELIGIEUX (F178)
TB solo,pno/org HEUGEL s.p. see
from CHANTS RELIGIEUX (F179)
2 soli,pno/org (available in 3
keys) HEUGEL s.p. (F180)

O Salutaris *sac
solo,pno/org HEUGEL s.p. see from
CHANTS RELIGIEUX (F181)
2 soli,pno/org (available in 2
keys) HEUGEL s.p. (F182)

Palms, The *see Les Rameaux

Pie Jesu *sac
med solo,opt cor,pno/org (F maj)
HEUGEL s.p. (F183)

Sancta Maria *sac
solo,pno/org HEUGEL s.p. see from
CHANTS RELIGIEUX (F184)
solo,pno/org (available in 2 keys)
HEUGEL s.p. (F185)

Stella
[Fr/It] Mez/Bar solo,pno RICORDI-
ARG BA 1840 s.p. (F186)

FAUT DE LA MEFIANCE see Lecocq, Charles

FAUVES LAS see Chausson, Ernest

FAUVETTE ET RONDE DE LA CHAUVE-SOURIS
see Migot, Georges

FAVOLA ANTICA see Veneziani, Vittore

FAVOLETTA see Discovolo, M.

FAVOLETTA see Veneziani, Vittore

FAVORIT GLEE, A see Anonymous

FAVORIT SONG, A see Anonymous

FAVORITE ABANDONNEE see Roussel, Albert

FAVORITE AIR IN THE PASTORAL OF DAPHNIS
AND AMARYLLIS, THE see Cocchi,
Giachimo

FAVORITE ARIAS FROM THE OPERA *CC10U
T solo,pno LYCHE LY60 s.p. contains
works by: Gounod; Meyerbeer and
others (F187)

FAVORITE FRENCH FOLK SONGS *CC60U,Fr
(Mills, Alan) [Fr/Eng] solo,pno OAK
000072 $2.95 (F188)

FAVORITE JEWISH SONGS, VOL. 2 *CC18L,
Jew
solo,pno KAMMEN $2.50
see also: Oif'n Pripetchok;
Ellstein, Abe, Oi Mamme! Bin Ich
Farliebt!!; Gilrod, Louis, Der
Sider'l; Gilrod, Louis, Samit Und
Seid; Gilrod, Louis, Shmendrik's
Kalle; Goldstein, Gus, Men Kon
Leben Nor Men Lost Nit; Lillian,
Isadore, In A Klein Shtiebele;
Lillian, Isadore, Schwartze
Karshelach; Lowenwrith, Sam, Dus
Chupe Kleid; Meyerowitz, David, A
Mamme's Trehren; Meyerowitz,
David, Gam'se L'Toivoh; Mysell,
Bella, Glick - Du Bist Gekummen
Tzu Shpait; Picon, Molly, Liebes

Schmertzen; Rumshinsky, Jos. M.,
Der Morgen Shtern; Rund, Morris,
Dus Ken Ich Nit; Sheikewitz,
Wolf, Elegie; Shorr, Anshel, Mein
Yiddishe Meidele; Stuchkoff, N.,
Warshe   (F189)

FAVORITE SACRED SONGS *sac,CC65U
solo,pno WORD 10013 $1.25   (F190)

FAVORITE SONG OF CRAZY JANE, THE see
Bland, Mrs.

FAVORITE SPANISH FOLKSONGS *CC45U,
folk,Cen Am/Span
(Paz, Elena) [Span/Eng] solo,pno OAK
000073 $2.95   (F191)

FAVOURITE SONGS IN THE OPERA CALL'D
ADRIANO, THE see Veracini,
Francesco Maria

FAVOURITE SONGS IN THE OPERA CALL'D
ARTAXERSES, THE see Hasse, A.

FAVOURITE SONGS IN THE OPERA DEMOFONTE,
THE see Vento, Mattia

FAVRE, GEORGES (1905-   )
Dans Le Matin Bleu
see Poemes Marins

Danse Du Glaive *see Korol Ar
C'hleze

Deux Chants Populaires De Bretagne
SMezA soli,orch cmplt ed DURAND
s.p., ipr
contains: Diougan Gwenc' Hlan,
"La Prephetie De Gwenc' Hlan";
Korol Ar C'hleze, "Danse Du
Glaive"   (F192)

Diougan Gwenc' Hlan
"La Prephetie De Gwenc' Hlan" see
Deux Chants Populaires De
Bretagne

Korol Ar C'hleze
"Danse Du Glaive" see Deux Chants
Populaires De Bretagne

La Prephetie De Gwenc' Hlan *see
Diougan Gwenc' Hlan

O Toi Qui Sais Aimer
see Poemes Marins

Poemes Marins
cmplt ed DURAND s.p.
contains: Dans Le Matin Bleu; O
Toi Qui Sais Aimer; Sous Le
Ciel Pale Du Soir   (F193)

Printemps Breton
2 soli,pno DURAND s.p.   (F194)

Sous Le Ciel Pale Du Soir
see Poemes Marins

FAYE, LINDA
All In All *sac
solo,pno WORD S-389   (F195)

Don't Ever Let Go Of My Hand *see
Brown, Aaron

Show Me The Way *see Brown, Aaron

Today's Gonna Be A Brighter Day *sac
(Brown, Aaron) solo,pno WORD S-443
(F196)
FEAR NO MORE THE HEAT OF THE SUN see
Castelnuovo-Tedesco, Mario

FEAR NOT see Al Tira

FEAR NOT, FOR BEHOLD, I BRING GOOD
TIDINGS OF GREAT JOY see Bender,
Jan

FEAR NOT, I AM WITH THEE see Foster,
Will

FEAR NOT, O CHILD OF GOD see Hallett,
John C.

FEAR NOT YE, O ISRAEL see Buck, Dudley

FEAR THE ALMIGHTY see Schutz, Heinrich

FEAR THOU NOT see Pearson, Albie

FEAR THOU NOT, FOR I AM WITH THEE see
Fischer, Irwin

FEARING, JOHN
Sonnet
solo,pno (E flat maj) LESLIE 7061
(F197)
When Jesus Christ Was Four Years Old
*sac
solo,pno (C min) LESLIE 7058 (F198)

FEARIS, JOHN S.
Beautiful Isle Of Somewhere *sac
solo,pno (A flat maj) ALLANS s.p.
(F199)
SA soli,pno LORENZ $1.00   (F200)
med solo,pno (A flat maj) WILLIS
$.50   (F201)

FEAST OF LANTERNS see Bantock,
Granville

FECIT POTENTIAM see Bach, Karl Philipp
Emanuel

FED BY MY LABOURS see Avshalomov, Jacob

FEDERLEIN
From Cross To Crown *sac,Easter
SA soli,pno BOSTON $1.75   (F202)

FEED MY LAMBS see Koch, Frederick

FEED MY SHEEP see Ainsworth

FEED MY SHEEP see Boardman, E.

FEED MY SHEEP see Boardman, Reginald

FEED MY SHEEP see Brown

FEED MY SHEEP see Butcher

FEED MY SHEEP see Faulkner

FEED MY SHEEP see Fischer, Irwin

FEED MY SHEEP see Handel, George
Frideric

FEED MY SHEEP see Hinchcliffe, Irvin

FEED MY SHEEP see Joy, Virginia

FEED MY SHEEP see MacDermid

FEED MY SHEEP see Souers, Mildred

FEED MY SHEEP see Whipp, I.M.

FEED MY SHEEP see Wrightson

FEED MY SHEEP see Young

FEEDING AMONG THE LILIES see Buck

FEELING AT HOME IN THE PRESENCE OF
JESUS see Gaither

FEERIE AU CLAIR DE LUNE see Dupre,
Marcel

FEES see Migot, Georges

FEEST IN HUIS see Pelt, R.A. van

FEINSLIEBCHEN, KOMM ANS FENSTER see
Mozart, Wolfgang Amadeus, Deh Vieni
Alla Finestra

FEKETE SZOLO see Ranki, Gyorgy

FELCIANO, RICHARD (1930-   )
Benedicto Nuptialis
med solo/med male solo,org
SCHIRM.EC 2318 s.p.   (F203)

FELDEINSAMKEIT see Brahms, Johannes

FELDERHOF, JAN (1907-   )
Een Middeleeuwsch Meilied
Mez/Bar solo,pno DONEMUS s.p.
(F204)
Jezus En Maria *sac
med solo,org DONEMUS s.p.   (F205)

Kerstlied
Mez/Bar solo,pno DONEMUS s.p.
(F206)
Na Jaren
T solo,pno DONEMUS s.p.   (F207)

O La La
Mez/Bar solo,pno DONEMUS s.p.
(F208)
Paarlende Webben
S solo,pno DONEMUS s.p.   (F209)

Puer Natus Est *sac
high solo,pno DONEMUS s.p. (F210)

Venite Adoramus *sac
high solo,pno DONEMUS s.p. (F211)

Voor Een Dag Van Morgen
low solo,pno DONEMUS s.p.   (F212)

FELDMAN, MORTON (1926-   )
For Franz Kline
S solo,vln,vcl,clar,pno (six scores
needed for performance) sc PETERS
6948 $3.00   (F213)

Four Songs To E.E. Cummings *CC4U
S solo,vcl,pno PETERS 6936 $2.50 3
scores needed for performance
(F214)

FELDMAN, MORTON (cont'd.)

Intervals
Bar solo,vcl,trom,vibra,perc (5
scores needed for performance) sc
PETERS 6908 $7.50   (F215)

Journey To The End Of The Night
S solo,fl,clar,bass clar,bsn sc
PETERS 6927 $7.50, ipa   (F216)

O'Hara Songs, The *CCU
Bar solo,chimes,pno,vln,vla sc
PETERS 6949 $4.00 6 scores needed
for performance   (F217)

Rabbi Akiba
S solo,fl,English horn,horn,trp,
trom,tuba,perc,pno,cel,vcl,bvl
(11 scores needed for
performance) sc PETERS 6957 $9.00
(F218)
Vertical Thoughts III
S solo,fl,horn,trp,trom,tuba,pno,
cel,2perc,vln,vcl,bvl (12 scores
needed for performance) sc PETERS
6954 $3.00   (F219)

Vertical Thoughts V
S solo,tuba,perc,cel,vln (5 scores
needed for performance) sc PETERS
6956 $2.00   (F220)

FELICITA see Alfano, Franco

FELICTA-GIOVINEZZA see Pratella,
Francesco Balilla

FELIX, VACLAV (1928-   )
Chlapci A Chlapi
"Knaben Und Kerle" med solo,pno
CZECH s.p.   (F221)

Knaben Und Kerle *see Chlapci A
Chlapi

Offenes Haus *see Otevreny Dum

Otevreny Dum *Op.13, cant
[Czech/Ger] AT soli,pno PANTON 062
s.p.   (F222)
"Offenes Haus" AT soli,pno CZECH
s.p.   (F223)

Tkalcovska Srdce
"Weberherzen" S solo,pno CZECH s.p.
(F224)
Weberherzen *see Tkalcovska Srdce

FELLEGARA, VITTORIO (1927-   )
Cantata
2 female soli,orch sc ZERBONI 6577
s.p.   (F225)

Chanson
S solo,orch sc ZERBONI 7957 s.p.
(F226)
Epithape
2 female soli,5strings min sc
ZERBONI 6287 s.p.   (F227)

FELLOWSHIP SONG OF SIGMA CHI see
Vernor, F. Dudleigh

FELLS, G.
Le Prisonnier
solo,pno ENOCH s.p.   (F228)

FELTNER
I'll See You In The Rapture *sac
solo,pno BENSON S6279-S $1.00
(F229)
FEM SANGER see Backer-Grondahl, Agathe
Ursula

FEM SANGER see Mascagni, Pietro

FEM SANGER see Salonen, Sulo

FEM SANGER see Snare, Sigurd

FEM SANGER see Stenhammar, Wilhelm

FEM SANGER FOR TVENNE ROSTER see
Myrberg, August M.

FEM SANGER FRA OP. 52 see Olsen, Sparre

FEM SANGER I see Sibelius, Jean

FEM SANGER TILL DIKTER AV RYDBERG see
Sibelius, Jean

FEM VISOR see Stenhammar, Wilhelm

FEM VISOR see Nordqvist, Gustaf

FEM VISOR see Wideen

FEM VISOR I FOLKTON see Reimers, Ivar

FEMINA see Antreas, E.

FEMME SENSIBLE see Lecocq, Charles

FEMMES SI BELLES, REPONDEZ-MOI see
Mozart, Wolfgang Amadeus

FEN, THE see Kilpinen, Yrio, Janka

FENESTA CHE LUCIVE
[It] Mez/Bar solo,pno RICORDI-ENG
126832 s.p. (F230)

FENNELLEY, BRIAN
Songs With Improvisation *CCU
med solo,clar,pno sc AM.COMP.AL.
$7.15 (F231)

FENNER
When Children Pray
low solo,pno (C maj) ALLANS s.p.
(F232)
high solo,pno (E flat maj) ALLANS
s.p. (F233)

FENSTAD
Stein Song
med solo,pno (A flat maj) FISCHER,C
V 1117 (F234)

FENTON
First Psalm *see Bone

FERANDIERE, F.
Boleras
[Span] med-high solo,gtr UNION ESP.
$.60 (F235)

La Consulta
(Subira) [Span] high solo,pno UNION
ESP. $3.75 (F236)

FERAUDY, M. DE
Un Peu De Bonheur
solo,pno ENOCH s.p. (F237)
solo,acap ENOCH s.p. (F238)

FERENCZY, OTO (1921-   )
Kytica Lesna
med solo,pno SLOV.HUD.FOND s.p.
(F239)
Spievana Abeceda *CCU
boy solo/girl solo,pno
SLOV.HUD.FOND s.p. (F240)

Tri Sonety Na Shakespeara *CC3U
Bar solo,pno SLOV.HUD.FOND s.p.
(F241)

FERGUSON
Wings Of A Dove *sac
solo,pno BENSON S8524-S $1.00
(F242)

FERGUSON, EDWIN EARLE
At Sunset
med solo,pno BELWIN $1.50 (F243)

Luna Que Reluces
"Moon With Thy Loveliness Beaming"
[Eng/Span] med solo,2pno AMP
$1.00 see from Two Spanish Songs
(F244)
Moon With Thy Loveliness Beaming
*see Luna Que Reluces

Quiero Dormir Y No Puedo
"'Tis Love That Keeps Me From
Sleeping" [Eng/Span] med solo,
2pno AMP $1.00 see from Two
Spanish Songs (F245)

'Tis Love That Keeps Me From Sleeping
*see Quiero Dormir Y No Puedo

Two Spanish Songs *see Luna Que
Reluces, "Moon With Thy
Loveliness Beaming"; Quiero
Dormir Y No Puedo, "'Tis Love
That Keeps Me From Sleeping"

FERMATE OMAI FERMATE see Scarlatti,
Alessandro

FERMONS NOS RIDEAUX see Delmet, Paul

FERNANDEZ
Cielito Lindo
solo,pno ALLANS s.p. (F247)

FERNE, KENNETH
Gather Ye Rosebuds
solo,pno (A flat maj) LEONARD-ENG
(F248)

FERNY, JACQUES
Chansons De La Roulette *CC100U
solo,pno cmplt ed JOBERT s.p.
(F249)

FERRANTE
Fleurs De France *CC6U
solo,pno HENN 110 s.p. (F250)

FERRARI, GABRIELLA (1851-1921)
Aubade
solo,pno (available in 2 keys)
ENOCH s.p. (F251)

Larmes En Songe
solo,pno (available in 3 keys)
ENOCH s.p. (F252)

FERRARI, GABRIELLA (cont'd.)

Runes
solo,pno ENOCH s.p. (F253)

Sous Bois
solo,pno (available in 2 keys)
ENOCH s.p. (F254)

FERRARI, GIORGIO (1925-   )
Ai Fratelli Cervi *cant
[It] Mez/Bar solo,pno SONZOGNO 2872
s.p. (F255)
Bar/Mez solo,fl,ob,clar,horn,trp,
trom,perc,harp,vln,vla,vcl
SONZOGNO rental (F256)

FERRARI, GUSTAVE (1872-1948)
Aveu
solo,pno ENOCH s.p. (F257)
solo,acap ENOCH s.p. (F258)

Berceuse
solo,pno ENOCH s.p. (F259)

Chanson
solo,pno ENOCH s.p. (F260)

Demain, Des L'Aube
solo,pno (available in 2 keys)
ENOCH s.p. (F261)

Floraison
solo,pno (available in 2 keys)
ENOCH s.p. (F262)

Jour.. Soir
solo,pno ENOCH s.p. (F263)

Les Premiers Mots D'amour
solo,pno (available in 2 keys)
ENOCH s.p. (F264)

Mirror, The
[Eng/Fr] med solo,pno SALABERT-US
$3.75 (F265)

Peut-Etre
solo,pno ENOCH s.p. (F266)

FERRARI-TRECATE, LUIGI (1884-1964)
Al Tempestoso Vento Invernale
see Quattro Liriche

Canzoniere *CC7U
[It] solo,pno BONGIOVANI 2447 s.p.
(F267)
Cielo D'argento
[It] solo,pno BONGIOVANI 694 s.p.
see from Stornelli Nello Stile
Popolare (F268)

Filastrocca Del Si E No
[It] solo,pno BONGIOVANI 1723 s.p.
(F269)
Fiorin Di Terra
[It] solo,pno BONGIOVANI 696 s.p.
see from Stornelli Nello Stile
Popolare (F270)

La Notte D'ottobre
see Quattro Liriche

Le Bambolette
[It] solo,pno BONGIOVANI 1985 s.p.
(F271)
L'ultimo Carro
see Quattro Liriche

O Mia Casetta
[It] solo,pno BONGIOVANI 695 s.p.
see from Stornelli Nello Stile
Popolare (F272)

Quattro Liriche
[It] solo,pno cmplt ed CURCI 6222
s.p.
contains: Al Tempestoso Vento
Invernale; La Notte D'ottobre;
L'ultimo Carro; Un Giorno Amaro
(F273)
Rustic Song *see Strambotto In
Serenata

Sette Brevi Canzoni Romantiche *CC7U
[It] solo,pno BONGIOVANI 1615 s.p.
(F274)
Stornelli Nello Stile Popolare *see
Cielo D'argento; Fiorin Di Terra;
O Mia Casetta (F275)

Strambotto In Serenata
"Rustic Song" [Eng] solo,pno
BONGIOVANI 1691 s.p. (F276)
"Rustic Song" [It] solo,pno
BONGIOVANI 1613 s.p. (F277)

Tutto Ritorna
[It] solo,pno BONGIOVANI 1724 s.p.
(F278)
Un Giorno Amaro
see Quattro Liriche

FERRARIS, C.
Alba
[It] solo,pno BONGIOVANI 2434 s.p.
(F279)
Canti Della Fanciullezza *CCU
[It] solo,pno BONGIOVANI 2322 s.p.
(F280)

FERRARIS, P.
Les Oiseaux Et Les Baisers
solo,pno ENOCH s.p. (F281)

FERRATA, GIUSEPPE (1865-1928)
Night And The Curtains Drawn
high solo,pno (F maj) BELWIN $1.50
(F282)
high solo,pno (E flat maj) BELWIN
$1.50 (F283)
med solo,pno BELWIN $1.50 (F284)

FERRERS, HERBERT (? -1958)
Roister Doister
solo,pno (A flat maj) BOOSEY $1.50
(F285)

FERRIS, WILLIAM
Behold, Thus Is The Man Blessed
(Psalm 127) sac,Marriage
T/S solo,org (easy) GIA G-1475
$1.00 (F286)

My Heart Is Ready, O God *sac
high solo,pno BELWIN $1.50 (F287)

Psalm 127 *see Behold, Thus Is The
Man Blessed

FERRITTO, JOHN
Five Madrigals *CC5U,madrigal
Mez solo,acap AM.COMP.AL. $2.75
(F288)

Oggi *Op.9
S solo,clar,pno sc AM.COMP.AL.
$6.60, ipa (F289)

Sogni *Op.12
S solo,3fl,3ob,3clar,2bsn,4horn,
3trp,3trom,tuba,timp,4perc,pno,
harp,strings, offstage solo viola
sc AM.COMP.AL. $19.25 (F290)

FERRO, P.
Il Gran Cerchio D'ombra
[It] solo,pno CURCI 1165 s.p.
(F291)

Invocazione
[It] solo,pno CURCI 453 s.p. (F292)

Ninna-Nanna Strapaesana
[It] solo,pno CURCI 599 s.p. (F293)

FERRO, STEFANO
Suite Agreste *CCU
[It/Ger] female solo,fl,English
horn,clar,harp,vla RICORDI-ENG
PR 727 s.p. (F294)

FERROUD, PIERRE-OCTAVE (1900-1936)
A Contre-Coeur *see Odile;
Sollicitude; Theo (F295)

Beispiel
see Drei Traute Gesange

Cinq Poemes De P.-J. Toulet *CC5U
solo,orch DURAND s.p., ipr (F296)

Drei Traute Gesange
solo,pno cmplt ed DURAND s.p.
contains: Beispiel; Einsamkeit;
Erster Verlust (F297)

Echanges
see Trois Chansons De Jules
Supervielle

Einsamkeit
see Drei Traute Gesange

Erster Verlust
see Drei Traute Gesange

Exemple
see Trois Poemes Intimes De Goethe

L'abeille
see Trois Poemes De Paul Valery

Le Vin Perdu
see Trois Poemes De Paul Valery

Les Pas
see Trois Poemes De Paul Valery

Observatoire
see Trois Chansons De Jules
Supervielle

Odile
solo,pno/inst DURAND s.p. see from
A Contre-Coeur (F298)

Pont Superieur
see Trois Chansons De Jules
Supervielle

FERROUD, PIERRE-OCTAVE (cont'd.)

Premier Chagrin
see Trois Poemes Intimes De Goethe

Solitude
see Trois Poemes Intimes De Goethe

Sollicitude
solo,pno/inst DURAND s.p. see from
A Contre-Coeur   (F299)

Theo
solo,pno/inst DURAND s.p. see from
A Contre-Coeur   (F300)

Trois Chansons De Fous *CCU
Bar/T solo,orch DURAND s.p., ipr
(F301)

Trois Chansons De Jules Supervielle
solo,pno/inst cmplt ed DURAND s.p.
contains: Echanges; Observatoire;
Pont Superieur   (F302)

Trois Poemes De Paul Valery
solo,pno/inst cmplt ed DURAND s.p.
contains: L'abeille; Le Vin
Perdu; Les Pas   (F303)

Trois Poemes Intimes De Goethe
solo,orch cmplt ed DURAND s.p.
s.p., ipr
contains: Exemple; Premier
Chagrin; Solitude   (F304)

FERRY, THE see Sternberg, Erich Walter

FERRY ME ACROSS THE WATER see Peel,
Graham

FERVEUR see Barbirolli, A.

FEST PA SKANSEN see Olson, Daniel

FESTEIG see Toldra, Eduardo

FESTIVAL OF SPRING see Strauss,
Richard, Fruhlingsfeier

FESTIVALS AND HOLY DAYS see
Stutschevsky, Joachim

FESTIVE DAWN, A see Gandino, Adolfo,
Alba Festiva

FESTIVE EVENING, A see Gandino, Adolfo,
Sera Festiva

FESTIVI MARTYRES see Brossard,
Sebastien de

FETE see Arrieu, Claude

FETE D'AMOUR see Duval, A.

FETE FORAINE see Clergue, J.

FETE NUPTIALE see Georges, Alexandre

FETES DE LA FAIM see Bergmann, R.

FETES ENFANTINES see Renie

FETES GALANTES see Colaco Osorio-Swaab,
Reine

FETES GALANTES see Pijper, Willem

FETES GALANTES, SERIES I see Debussy,
Claude

FETES GALANTES, SERIES II see Debussy,
Claude

FETES GALANTES, VOL. 1 see Debussy,
Claude

FETES ROMANESQUE see Delannoy, Marcel

FETLER, DAVID
O Father, All Creating *sac,Marriage
CONCORDIA 97-9325 $.75   (F305)

FEUER, JOSEPH
Mah Tovu *sac
[Heb] high solo,pno TRANSCON.
TCL 297 $.40   (F306)

FEUERREITER see Wolf, Hugo

FEUILLAGE DU COEUR see Samazeuilh,
Gustave

FEUILLES SUR L'EAU see Aubert, Louis-
Francois-Marie

FEVRIER, HENRI (1875-   )
Noel *sac
high solo,pno/org HEUGEL s.p.
(F307)

FEW WORDS ABOUT JESUS, A see Haney, J.

FIABA see Mompello, Federico

FIALA, GEORGE
Four Russian Poems *CC4U
solo,pno WATERLOO $3.00   (F308)

FIANCAILLES POUR RIRE see Poulenc,
Francis

FIANCEE AUX ETOILES see Delmet, Paul

FIAT DOMINE see Andriessen, Hendrik

FIAT NOX see Kilpinen, Yrio

FIAT VOLUNTAS TUA see Heiller, Anton

FIBICH
Poem
med solo,pno (C maj) CENTURY 3629
(F309)

FIBICH, ZDENKO (1850-1900)
Das Gebet *see Modlitba

Fruhjahrsstrahlen *Op.36,No.1
[Czech/Ger] solo,pno SUPRAPHON s.p.
(F310)

Modlitba *Op.41,No.36
(Herle J.) "Das Gebet" S solo,org
SUPRAPHON s.p.   (F311)

Patero Zpevu
solo,pno SUPRAPHON s.p.   (F312)

Sestero Pisni Pro Stredni Hlas *CCU
med solo,pno SUPRAPHON s.p.   (F313)

Zwei Gesange *Op.3, CC2U
[Ger/Czech] solo,pno SUPRAPHON s.p.
(F314)

FICHER, JACOBO (1896-   )
Aqui Se Esta Quieto
see Seis Canciones Del Parana, Op.
77

Aqui Si Yo Hubiera Sido Caballo
see Seis Canciones Del Parana, Op.
77

Banado Del Parana!
see Seis Canciones Del Parana, Op.
77

Di, Rio...
see Seis Canciones Del Parana, Op.
77

Los Barcos Pasan Tan Cerca De La
Orilla
see Seis Canciones Del Parana, Op.
77

Palabras A Mama *Op.34,No.2
"Parole Alla Mamma" [Span/It] solo,
pno RICORDI-ARG BA 7370 s.p.
(F315)

Paloma Deseperada
see Seis Canciones Del Parana, Op.
77

Parole Alla Mamma *see Palabras A
Mama

Seis Canciones Del Parana, Op. 77
[Span] solo,pno cmplt ed RICORDI-
ARG BA 11181 s.p.
contains: Aqui Se Esta Quieto;
Aqui Si Yo Hubiera Sido
Caballo; Banado Del Parana!;
Di, Rio...; Los Barcos Pasan
Tan Cerca De La Orilla; Paloma
Deseperada   (F316)

FICHTHORN, CLAUDE L. (1885-   )
Abide With Me
high solo,pno PRESSER $.75   (F317)

FIDDLE AND I see Goodeve, Mrs. Arthur

FIDDLE FAIRIES see Day, Maude Craske

FIDDLER OF DOONEY, THE see Kauder, Hugo

FIDDLERS, THE see Shepherd, Arthur

FIDDLER'S COIN, THE see Strilko,
Anthony

FIDELIA OMNIA see Staromieyski, J.

FIDELITE see Brahms, Johannes,
Liebestreu

FIDES see Persico, Mario

FIDES see Stout, Alan

FIDGETY BAIRN, THE
(Roberton, Hugh S.) solo,pno (E flat
maj) ROBERTON 2741 s.p. see also
Songs Of The Isles   (F318)

FIE DIDDLE DEE see Dale, Mervyn

FIE ON SINFUL FANTASY! see Castelnuovo-
Tedesco, Mario

FIEDELLIEDER see Krenek, Ernst

FIELD IS THE WORLD, THE *sac
high solo,pno CRESPUB CP-R 659 $1.00
(F319)

FIELD IS THE WORLD, THE see Ware,
Broadman

FIELDS ARE FULL see Gibbs, Cecil
Armstrong

FIELDS O' BALLYCLARE see Turner-Maley,
Florence

FIELDS OF THE EMEK see Sadot She-Ba-
Emek

FIELITZ, ALEXANDER VON (1860-1930)
Eliland
"Song Of Chiemsee" [Eng/Ger] med
solo,pno BREITKOPF-W $1.25 (F320)

Fair Jessie *see Schon Gretlein

Schon Gretlein
"Fair Jessie" [Eng/Ger] low solo,
pno BREITKOPF-W $1.80   (F321)

Song Of Chiemsee *see Eliland

FIERE BEAUTE see Saint-Saens, Camille

FIERTE, PARDONNE-MOI see Schlosser,
Paul

FIESTA see Humphreys

FIESTA ESPANOLA, VOL. I *CCU
(Grecos) [Span] med solo,gtr UNION
ESP. $1.75   (F322)

FIEVET, P.
Les Roses
Mez solo,pno/inst DURAND   (F323)

FIFINELLA see Tchaikovsky, Piotr
Ilyitch, Pimpinella

FIFTEEN ARIAS FOR COLORATURA SOPRANO
*CC15L
(Liebling) coloratura sop,pno
SCHIRM.G $6.00 contains works by:
Bellini; Gounod; Mozart; Verdi and
others   (F324)

FIFTEEN ARIAS FOR HIGH VOICE see
Handel, George Frideric

FIFTEEN DUOS see Gounod, Charles
Francois

FIFTEEN NEAPOLITAN SONGS OF THE
SIXTEENTH CENTURY *CC15U,It,16th
cent
(Gorzanis) [Fr] med solo,gtr NOETZEL
6080 s.p.   (F325)

FIFTEEN SONGS AND AIRS, SET 1 see
Purcell, Henry

FIFTEEN SONGS AND AIRS, SET 2 see
Purcell, Henry

FIFTEENTH CENTURY CAROL see Hammond,
Gladys

FIFTY ADDITIONAL SONGS see Schubert,
Franz (Peter)

FIFTY ART SONGS FROM THE MODERN
REPERTOIRE *CC50L
solo,pno SCHIRM.G $3.95 contains
works by: Bartok; Debussy; Ravel;
Strauss and others   (F326)

FIFTY-FIVE ART SONGS *CC55L
(Spaeth, Sigmund; Thompson, Carl O.)
solo,pno SUMMY contains works by:
Bach; Brahms; Cornelius; Gounod;
Lalo; Mozart and others   (F327)

FIFTY MODERN ENGLISH SONGS *CC50U
BOOSEY $7.50   (F328)

FIFTY RUSSIAN ART SONGS, VOLUME III see
Dukelsky, Vladimir

FIFTY SELECTED SONGS see Franz, Robert

FIFTY SELECTED SONGS see Brahms,
Johannes

FIFTY SELECTED SONGS BY SCHUBERT,
SCHUMANN, BRAHMS, WOLF, AND STRAUSS
*CC50L
high solo,pno SCHIRM.G 1754 $7.00;
low solo,pno SCHIRM.G 1755 $7.00
(F329)

FIFTY-SIX SONGS YOU LIKE TO SING *sac/
sec,CC56L
solo,pno SCHIRM.G $3.95 contains
works by: Brahms; Dvorak; Grieg;
Saint-Saens and others   (F330)

FIFTY SONGS see Schumann, Robert
(Alexander)

FIFTY SONGS see Franz, Robert

FIFTY SONGS see Grieg, Edvard Hagerup

FIFTY SONGS see Schubert, Franz (Peter)

FIFTY SONGS see Takata, Saburo

FIFTY SONGS, BK. 1 see Dowland, John

FIFTY SONGS, BK. 2 see Dowland, John

FIFTY SONGS, W. SHAKESPEARE *CC50U
PRESSER high solo,pno $5.00; low
solo,pno $5.00   (F331)

FIFTY SVENSKA FOLKVISOR see Hagg,
Gustaf Wilhelm

FIFTY-TWO SACRED SONGS YOU LIKE TO SING
*sac,CC52L
solo,pno SCHIRM.G $3.00 contains
works by: Bach; Bizet; Gaul;
Gounod; Tchaikovsky and others
(F332)

FIFTY-TWO SELECTED SONGS see Schubert,
Franz (Peter)

FIFTY-TWO SONGS ON POMS BY MORICKE see
Wolf, Hugo

FIGLIA! MIO PADRE! see Verdi, Giuseppe

FIGLIO DEL CIELO see Puccini, Giacomo

FIGURAS see Lamuraglia, Nicolas

FIGURE see Castiglioni, Niccolo

FIGUS-BYSTRY, VILLIAM (1875-1937)
Mati Moja
solo,pno SLOV.HUD.FOND s.p. (F333)

Sny I, II, III
solo,pno SLOV.HUD.FOND s.p., ea.
(F334)

Tzuby
solo,pno SLOV.HUD.FOND s.p. (F335)

Ziale A Radosti
solo,pno SLOV.HUD.FOND s.p. (F336)

FILASTROCCA see Del Corona, Rodolfo

FILASTROCCA DEL GATTO NERO see Farina,
Guido

FILASTROCCA DEL SI E NO see Ferrari-
Trecate, Luigi

FILEUSE see Canal, Marguerite

FILEUSE see Pennequin, J.-G.

FILHA, SE GRADO EDES see Caamano,
Roberto

FILI MI, ABSALON see Schutz, Heinrich

FILIPUCCI, EDM.
Abandon
solo,pno ENOCH s.p.   (F337)
solo,acap ENOCH s.p.   (F338)

Amour Au Vainqueur
solo,pno ENOCH s.p.   (F339)
solo,acap ENOCH s.p.   (F340)

Ave Maria *sac
[Lat/Fr] solo,org/harmonium,opt vln
ENOCH s.p.   (F341)

C'est Ici Qu'on Aime Toujours
solo,pno ENOCH s.p.   (F342)
solo,acap ENOCH s.p.   (F343)

C'est Le Tango D'amour
solo,pno ENOCH s.p.   (F344)
solo,acap ENOCH s.p.   (F345)

Chanson De Reitre
solo,pno ENOCH s.p. see from
Chansons Breves   (F346)

Chansons Bretonnes *see La Brise Est
Douce; La Chanson Du Matelot; Le
Goeland   (F347)

Chansons Breves *see Chanson De
Reitre; Hymne A La Mort; Hymne A
L'amour; L'ironique Serenade;
Veux-Tu Mon Reve   (F348)

Encore, Encore
solo,acap ENOCH s.p.   (F349)
solo,pno ENOCH s.p.   (F350)

Hymne A La Mort
solo,pno ENOCH s.p. see from
Chansons Breves   (F351)

FILIPUCCI, EDM. (cont'd.)

Hymne A L'amour
solo,pno (available in 2 keys)
ENOCH s.p. see from Chansons
Breves   (F352)

La Brise Est Douce
solo,pno ENOCH s.p. see from
Chansons Bretonnes   (F353)
solo,acap ENOCH s.p. see from
Chansons Bretonnes   (F354)

La Chanson Du Matelot
solo,pno ENOCH s.p. see from
Chansons Bretonnes   (F355)
solo,acap ENOCH s.p. see from
Chansons Bretonnes   (F356)

La Marchande De Tout
solo,pno ENOCH s.p.   (F357)

La Mauvaise Chanson
solo,pno ENOCH s.p.   (F358)

Le Goeland
solo,acap (available in 2 keys)
ENOCH s.p. see from Chansons
Bretonnes   (F359)
solo,pno (available in 2 keys)
ENOCH s.p. see from Chansons
Bretonnes   (F360)

Lentement, Lentement
solo,pno ENOCH s.p.   (F361)
solo,acap ENOCH s.p.   (F362)
solo,orch ENOCH rental   (F363)

Lentement Tu Me Prends Ma Vie
solo,pno ENOCH s.p.   (F364)
solo,acap ENOCH s.p.   (F365)

L'ironique Serenade
solo,pno ENOCH s.p. see from
Chansons Breves   (F366)

Marche De La Cite Glorieuse
solo,pno ENOCH s.p.   (F367)
solo,acap ENOCH s.p.   (F368)

Pourquoi Tarder
solo,pno (available in 2 keys)
ENOCH s.p.   (F369)

Rondel Galant
solo,pno (available in 2 keys)
ENOCH s.p.   (F370)

Serenade Printaniere
solo,pno (available in 2 keys)
ENOCH s.p.   (F371)

Ses Yeux
solo,pno (available in 2 keys)
ENOCH s.p.   (F372)

Si Tu Voulais
solo,pno ENOCH s.p.   (F373)
solo,acap ENOCH s.p.   (F374)

Simple Romance
solo,pno (available in 2 keys)
ENOCH s.p.   (F375)

Tu Reviendras
solo,pno ENOCH s.p.   (F376)
solo,acap ENOCH s.p.   (F377)

Une Page D'amour
solo,pno ENOCH s.p.   (F378)
solo,acap ENOCH s.p.   (F379)

Valse Ensorceleuse
solo,pno ENOCH s.p.   (F380)
solo,acap ENOCH s.p.   (F381)

Veux-Tu Mon Reve
solo,pno (available in 2 keys)
ENOCH s.p. see from Chansons
Breves   (F382)

FILL MY CUP, LORD see Blanchard

FILL MY CUP, LORD see Blanchard,
Richard

FILL THOU MY LIFE, O LORD see O'Connor-
Morris, G.

FILL UP YOUR GLASS see Hope, H.
Ashworth

FILL YOUR LIFE WITH LOVE see Moore,
Gene

FILLE A LA BLONDE CHEVELURE see Godard,
Benjamin Louis Paul

FILLE D'ANJOU
(Emmereshts; Beldent) solo,pno GRAS
s.p.   (F383)

FILLE DE PANDION see Busser, Henri-Paul

FILLI DI GIOIA VUOI FARMI MORIR see
Verdi, Giuseppe

FILS DE LA VIERGE see Schmitt, Florent

FIMM NUMER I ISLENZKUM PJOOBUNINGUM
(Sveinsson, Gunnar R.) solo,pno
ICELAND s.p.
contains: Einu Sinni;
Hreppstjorasnyta; Keisari Nokkur
Maetur Mann; Kysstu Mig Hin Mjuka
Maer; Oll Natturan Fer Enn Ao
Deyja   (F384)

FIN DE BAIL see Delmet, Paul

FIN DU JOUR see Richepin, T.

FINAL LOVE DUET see Monteverdi,
Claudio, Duetto Finale

FINAL SCENE FROM "EUGENE ONEGIN" see
Tchaikovsky, Piotr Ilyitch

FINALE see Claflin, Avery

FINDLAY, S.
Five Shakespearean Songs *CC5U
med solo,pno BOOSEY $2.25   (F385)

FINE, IRVING (1914-1962)
Childhood Fables For Grownups *CCU
med solo,pno BOOSEY $3.75, ea.
published in two sets   (F386)

Mutability *song cycle
med solo,pno BELWIN $2.50   (F387)

FINE, VIVIAN (1913-   )
Four Songs *see She Weeps Over
Rahoon   (F388)

She Weeps Over Rahoon
solo,4strings PRESSER $2.00 see
from Four Songs   (F389)

FINGE AN EN GANG see Soderman, (Johan)
August

FINISCI L'ULTIMO CANTO see Alfano,
Franco

FINK, MICHAEL
Rain Comes Down
high solo,pno SCHIRM.EC 129 s.p.
(F390)

What Lips My Lips Have Kissed
high solo,pno SCHIRM.EC s.p. (F391)

FINKBEINER, REINHOLD (1929-   )
Epiphanie
SABar soli,3perc,org BREITKOPF-W
s.p.   (F392)

Herr, Deine Gute Reicht, Soweit Der
Himmel Ist
S solo,org BREITKOPF-W EB 6311
$3.00   (F393)

Perlen..Vor Die Saue *sac,Bibl
Bar,narrator,2fl,2ob,3bass clar,
2contrabsn,4horn,4trp,4trom,tuba,
timp,perc,org,9strings BREITKOPF-
W s.p.   (F394)

FINKE, FIDELIO FRITZ (1891-1968)
Cantata Piccola *cant
med solo,pno DEUTSCHER 9035 s.p.
(F395)

Der Apfelbaum Am Wegrand *CC4U
solo,pno BREITKOPF-L EB 4100 s.p.
(F396)

Eros *cant
ST soli,3fl,3ob,3clar,3bsn,4horn,
3trp,3trom,timp,perc,harp,strings
BREITKOPF-L rental   (F397)

Lob Des Sommers *CC4U
solo,pno BREITKOPF-L EB 5749 $1.75
(F398)

Lob Des Sommers *CC4U
[Ger] low solo,pno BREITKOPF-W
$1.75   (F399)

Schein Und Sein *CC10U
A/Bar solo,3fl,3ob,3clar,3bsn,
4horn,2trp,2trom,tuba,timp,perc,
cel,harp,strings voc sc
BREITKOPF-L EB 5860 s.p., ipr
(F400)

FINLANDIA-HYMN see Sibelius, Jean,
Finlandia-Hymnen

FINLANDIA-HYMNEN see Sibelius, Jean

FINLANDIA VI *CCU,Finn
solo,pno FAZER W 2729 s.p.   (F401)

FINLANDIAHYMNEN see Sibelius, Jean,
Finlandia-Hymnen

FINLANDS VARTRAD see Madetoja, Leevi,
Suomen Puu

FINNBORG
　Frojdens Vart Sinne
　　see Tva Julsanger

　Se, Natten Flyr For Dagens Frojd
　　see Tva Julsanger

　Tva Julsanger　*Xmas
　　solo,pno LUNDQUIST s.p.
　　contains: Frojdens Vart Sinne;
　　　Se, Natten Flyr For Dagens
　　　Frojd　　　　　　　　　　(F402)

FINNESSY, MICHAEL (1946-　　)
　Jeanne D'Arc
　　ST soli,fl,pic,A rec,sax,horn,trp,
　　gtr,harp,4perc,3vln,vla,vcl,bvl
　　MODERN rental　　　　　　　(F403)

　Light Matter
　　S solo,ob,gtr,inst MODERN rental (F404)

　Orfeo
　　SSSMezTB soli,3trom,2lute,bvl,perc
　　MODERN rental　　　　　　　(F405)

　World
　　SSATBarB soli,2fl,2ob,clar,sax,
　　horn,2trp,trom,tuba,cym,cembalo,
　　harp,2pno,3perc,strings MODERN
　　rental　　　　　　　　　　(F406)

FINNEY, ROSS LEE (1906-　　)
　Bleheris
　　TA soli,fl,pic,ob,English horn,
　　clar,bass clar,bsn,contrabsn,
　　4horn,2trp,3trom,tuba,timp,2perc,
　　harp,strings PETERS 66114 rental (F407)

　Forbidding Mourning
　　see Three Love Songs

　Look How The Floor Of Heaven
　　see Three Seventeenth Century
　　　Lyrics

　Love's Growth
　　see Three Love Songs

　Of Weeping
　　see Three Love Songs

　On May Morning
　　see Three Seventeenth Century
　　　Lyrics

　On The Life Of Man
　　see Three Seventeenth Century
　　　Lyrics

　Three Love Songs
　　solo,pno NEW VALLEY $3.00
　　contains: Forbidding Mourning;
　　　Love's Growth; Of Weeping
　　　　　　　　　　　　　　(F408)

　Three Seventeenth Century Lyrics
　　solo,pno NEW VALLEY $3.00
　　contains: Look How The Floor Of
　　　Heaven; On May Morning; On The
　　　Life Of Man　　　　　　(F409)

FINSK BON see Kuusisto, Taneli,
　Suomalainen Rukous

FINSKA FOLKVISOR see Melartin, Erkki

FINSKA SANGKOMPOSITIONER II see
　Merikanto, Oskar

FINSKA SANGKOMPOSITIONER IV see
　Merikanto, Oskar

FINSKA SANGKOMPOSITIONER V see
　Merikanto, Oskar

FINSKA SANGKOMPOSITIONER VII see
　Merikanto, Oskar

FINZI, GERALD (1901-1956)
　Before And After Summer　*song cycle
　　Bar solo,pno BOOSEY $9.00　(F410)

　Budmouth Dears
　　solo,pno (F sharp min) BOOSEY $1.50
　　　　　　　　　　　　　　(F411)

　Come Away, Come Away, Death
　　solo,pno (B min) BOOSEY $1.50
　　　　　　　　　　　　　　(F412)

　Dies Natalis　*song cycle
　　S/T solo,strings BOOSEY $9.00 (F413)

　Ditty
　　solo,pno (G maj) BOOSEY $1.75
　　　　　　　　　　　　　　(F414)

　Earth And Air And Rain　*song cycle
　　Bar solo,pno BOOSEY $10.00　(F415)

　Her Temple
　　solo,pno (E flat maj) BOOSEY $1.50
　　　　　　　　　　　　　　(F416)

　I Said To Love　*song cycle
　　low solo,pno BOOSEY $5.75　(F417)

　Let Us Garlands Bring　*song cycle
　　Bar solo,pno,strings BOOSEY $8.00
　　　　　　　　　　　　　　(F418)

FINZI, GERALD (cont'd.)

　Music For "Love's Labour's Lost"
　　*song cycle
　　med solo,pno BOOSEY $5.00　(F419)

　O Mistress Mine
　　solo,pno (E flat maj) BOOSEY $1.50
　　　　　　　　　　　　　　(F420)

　Oh Fair To See　*song cycle
　　high solo,pno BOOSEY $6.00　(F421)

　Rollicum-Rorum
　　solo,pno (D maj) BOOSEY $1.50
　　　　　　　　　　　　　　(F422)

　Sigh
　　solo,pno (G maj) BOOSEY $1.50
　　　　　　　　　　　　　　(F423)

　Till Earth Outwears　*song cycle
　　high solo,pno BOOSEY $6.00　(F424)

　To A Poet　*song cycle
　　low solo,pno BOOSEY $6.00　(F425)

　Young Man's Exhortation　*song cycle
　　T solo,pno BOOSEY $10.00　(F426)

FIOCCA LA NEVE see Cimara, Pietro

FIOCCO, JOSEPH-HECTOR (1703-1741)
　Lamentatio Prima　*sac,cant
　　(Ewerhart, Rudolf) [Lat] S solo,
　　2vcl,cont sc BIELER DK 13 s.p.,
　　ipa　　　　　　　　　　　(F427)

　Lamentatio Secunda　*sac,cant
　　(Ewerhart, Rudolf) [Lat] S solo,
　　vcl,cont sc BIELER DK 6 s.p., ipa
　　　　　　　　　　　　　　(F428)

　Lamentatio Tertia　*sac
　　(Ewerhart, Rudolf) S/T solo,cont
　　BIELER CS 33 s.p.　　　　(F429)

FIOLEN see Wohlfart, Karl

FIONNPHORT FERRY see Sharpe, Evelyn

FIONN'S KEENING　*Scot
　solo,pno PATERSON s.p. see from
　Hebridean Songs, Vol. IV　(F430)

FIOR DI GIAGGIOLO see Mascagni, Pietro

FIOR DI LOTO SBOCCI see Kalman, Emerich

FIORDA, GIUSEPPE NUCCIO (1894-　　)
　Partita
　　STBar soli,3fl,3ob,3clar,4bsn,
　　4horn,4trp,3trom,tuba,timp,perc,
　　vibra,xylo,cel,pno,harp,strings
　　SONZOGNO rental　　　　　(F431)
　　[It] 3 soli,pno SONZOGNO 2932 s.p.
　　　　　　　　　　　　　　(F432)

FIORE D'ARANCIO see Benvenuti, Arrigo

FIORELLA-MIA see Scotto, Vincent

FIORELLIN D'AMORE see Brogi

FIORENTINELLE! AH! QUI M'APELLE? see
　Saint-Saens, Camille

FIORILE see Pick-Mangiagalli, Riccardo

FIORILLO, V.
　L'Adieu Du Marin
　　solo,pno ENOCH s.p.　　　(F433)

FIORIN DI TERRA see Ferrari-Trecate,
　Luigi

FIPS see Lothar, Mark

FIRE AND ICE see Moritz, Edvard

FIRE ENGELSKE SONETTER see Hogenhaven,
　Knud

FIRE! FIRE! see Bush, Geoffrey

FIRE FOLKELIGE MELODIER see Nielsen,
　Carl

FIRE ORHEIMSONGAR see Nystedt, Knut

FIRE SANGE see Hochella

FIRE SANGER see Alnaes, Eyvind

FIRELIGHT AND LAMP see Cowell, Henry
　Dixon

FIRENZE see Spadaro

FIRESIDE FANCIES see Bantock, Granville

FIRESTONE, IDABELLE
　If I Could Tell You
　　high solo,pno (A flat maj) SCHIRM.G
　　$.75　　　　　　　　　　(F434)
　　med solo,pno (F maj) SCHIRM.G $.75
　　　　　　　　　　　　　　(F435)
　　low solo,pno (E flat maj) SCHIRM.G
　　$.75　　　　　　　　　　(F436)

FIRESTONE, IDABELLE (cont'd.)

　In My Garden
　　high solo,pno (D maj) SCHIRM.G $.75
　　　　　　　　　　　　　　(F437)
　　med solo,pno (C maj) SCHIRM.G $.75
　　　　　　　　　　　　　　(F438)
　　low solo,pno (A maj) SCHIRM.G $.75
　　　　　　　　　　　　　　(F439)
　　solo,pno ALLANS s.p.　　(F440)
　　(Dews) SA soli,pno SCHIRM.G $.85
　　　　　　　　　　　　　　(F441)

　You Are The Song In My Heart
　　high solo,pno (G maj) SCHIRM.G $.75
　　　　　　　　　　　　　　(F442)
　　med solo,pno (F maj) SCHIRM.G $.75
　　　　　　　　　　　　　　(F443)

FIRST BOOK OF AYRES see Dowland, John

FIRST BOOK OF AYRES see Morley, Thomas

FIRST BOOK OF FOLK SONGS　*CC25U
　(Lund, Engel; Rauter, Ferdinand)
　solo,pno OXFORD 68.701 $2.50 (F444)

FIRST BOOK OF SONGS see Pilkington,
　Francis

FIRST CHRISTMAS, THE see Dougherty,
　Celius

FIRST CHRISTMAS MORN, THE see Newton,
　Ernest

FIRST CRITICAL EDITION OF THE WORKS OF
　PALESTRINA see Palestrina, Giovanni

FIRST EASTER MORN, THE see Scott, John
　Prindle

FIRST KISS OF LOVE, THE see Di Domenica

FIRST LOOK, THE see Knight

FIRST LOVE see Mana-Zucca, Mme., On
　Revient Toujours

FIRST MERCY, THE see Heseltine, Philip

FIRST MILLION YEARS, THE see Croft,
　Colbert

FIRST NOEL, THE see Gounod, Charles
　Francois

FIRST PLACE see Spurr, Thurlow

FIRST PRIMROSE see Grieg, Edvard
　Hagerup, Med En Vandlilje

FIRST PSALM see Bone

FIRST VOCAL ALBUM see Schubert, Franz
　(Peter)

FISCHER, GLADYS W.
　To Us In Bethlehem　*sac,Xmas
　　high solo,pno BELWIN $1.50　(F445)

FISCHER, IRWIN
　Ay, Gitanos!
　　low solo,pno sc AM.COMP.AL. $1.37
　　　　　　　　　　　　　　(F446)
　　med solo,pno sc AM.COMP.AL. $1.37
　　　　　　　　　　　　　　(F447)

　Christ My Refuge
　　low solo,pno sc AM.COMP.AL. $1.10
　　　　　　　　　　　　　　(F448)
　　high solo,pno sc AM.COMP.AL.
　　$1.10　　　　　　　　　　(F449)

　Christmas Message　*Xmas
　　med solo,pno sc AM.COMP.AL. $1.10
　　　　　　　　　　　　　　(F450)

　Christmas Morn　*Xmas
　　med solo,pno sc AM.COMP.AL. $1.37
　　　　　　　　　　　　　　(F451)
　　low solo,pno sc AM.COMP.AL. $1.37
　　　　　　　　　　　　　　(F452)

　Come, Take The Water Of Life　*Bibl
　　med solo,pno AM.COMP.AL. $1.10
　　　　　　　　　　　　　　(F453)
　　high solo,org AM.COMP.AL. $1.10
　　　　　　　　　　　　　　(F454)

　Come Unto Me　*sac,Bibl
　　solo,pno/org COBURN　　　(F455)
　　low solo,pno AM.COMP.AL. $1.10
　　　　　　　　　　　　　　(F456)
　　high solo,pno AM.COMP.AL. $1.10
　　　　　　　　　　　　　　(F457)

　Delight Thyself In The Lord
　　S solo,org AM.COMP.AL. $1.10 (F458)
　　low solo,pno AM.COMP.AL. $1.10
　　　　　　　　　　　　　　(F459)

　Fear Thou Not, For I Am With Thee
　　*Bibl
　　med solo,pno AM.COMP.AL. $1.10
　　　　　　　　　　　　　　(F460)

　Feed My Sheep
　　high solo,pno sc AM.COMP.AL. $1.10
　　　　　　　　　　　　　　(F461)
　　low solo,pno sc AM.COMP.AL. $1.10
　　　　　　　　　　　　　　(F462)

　Go From Me
　　high solo,pno AM.COMP.AL. $1.10
　　　　　　　　　　　　　　(F463)

FISCHER, IRWIN (cont'd.)

God Is Our Refuge
  S solo,org AM.COMP.AL. $1.10 (F464)

God Shall Wipe Away All Tears
  med solo,pno AM.COMP.AL. $1.37
    (F465)

God So Loved The World *sac
  low solo,pno (E min) AM.COMP.AL.
    $1.37   (F466)
  high solo,pno (F sharp min)
    AM.COMP.AL. $1.37   (F467)

Horseman, The
  med solo,pno sc AM.COMP.AL. $.82
    (F468)

Hour Is Come, The
  med solo,org AM.COMP.AL. $1.92
    (F469)

How Beautiful Upon The Mountains
  *Bibl
  med solo,pno AM.COMP.AL. $1.37
    (F470)

I Saw The Moon
  high solo,pno sc AM.COMP.AL. $.55
    (F471)
  low solo,pno sc AM.COMP.AL. $.55
    (F472)

If I Take The Wings Of The Morning
  *Bibl
  med solo,pno AM.COMP.AL. $1.10
    (F473)
  high solo,pno sc AM.COMP.AL. $1.10
    (F474)

If Ye Love Me, Keep My Commandments
  *sac,Bibl
  solo,pno/org COBURN   (F475)
  low solo,pno AM.COMP.AL. $1.10
    (F476)
  med solo,pno AM.COMP.AL. $1.10
    (F477)
  high solo,pno AM.COMP.AL. $1.10
    (F478)

Increase *sac
  solo,pno/org COBURN   (F479)
  S solo,org AM.COMP.AL. $1.10 (F480)

Let The Beauty Of The Lord Be Upon Us
  *sac
  high solo,pno AM.COMP.AL. $1.10
    (F481)
  low solo,pno AM.COMP.AL. $1.10
    (F482)

Lord By Wisdom Hath Founded The
    Earth, The *sac
  med solo,pno AM.COMP.AL. $1.10
    (F483)

Lord Is My Shepherd, The (Psalm 23)
  high solo,pno/org sc AM.COMP.AL.
    $1.10   (F484)

Lord, Teach Me Thy Statutes *sac
  med solo,pno AM.COMP.AL. $1.10
    (F485)

Love
  high solo,pno sc AM.COMP.AL. $1.65
    (F486)
  low solo,pno sc AM.COMP.AL. $1.10
    (F487)

Love One Another *sac
  high solo,pno (F sharp min)
    AM.COMP.AL. $1.37   (F488)
  low solo,pno (E min) AM.COMP.AL.
    $1.37   (F489)

Lullaby, A
  Mez solo,pno sc AM.COMP.AL. $1.10
    (F490)

Make A Joyful Noise Unto The Lord
  *sac
  med solo,pno/org AM.COMP.AL. $1.10
    (F491)

Mother's Evening Prayer
  high solo,pno sc AM.COMP.AL. $1.65
    (F492)
  low solo,pno sc AM.COMP.AL. $1.10
    (F493)

Nocturne
  med solo,pno AM.COMP.AL. $1.37
    (F494)

O Lord, How Manifold Are Thy Works
  *sac
  high solo,pno AM.COMP.AL. $1.10
    (F495)

Praise Ye The Lord *sac
  S solo,pno AM.COMP.AL. $1.10 (F496)

Psalm 23 *see Lord Is My Shepherd,
    The

Psalm Of Praise *sac,Psalm
  med solo,pno AM.COMP.AL. $1.37
    (F497)

Quicken Me, O Lord *sac
  med solo,pno AM.COMP.AL. $1.10
    (F498)

Satisfied
  high solo,pno sc AM.COMP.AL. $1.37
    (F499)
  low solo,pno sc AM.COMP.AL. $1.10
    (F500)

Season Of Star-Song
  med solo,pno AM.COMP.AL. $1.10
    (F501)

FISCHER, IRWIN (cont'd.)

Song Of Shadows
  med solo,pno sc AM.COMP.AL. $1.65
    (F502)

Song Of The Willow Branches
  high solo,pno AM.COMP.AL. $1.37
    (F503)

Still There Is Bethlehem
  high solo,pno sc AM.COMP.AL. $1.10
    (F504)
  low solo,pno sc AM.COMP.AL. $1.10
    (F505)

Suffer The Children To Come Unto Me
  *sac
  med solo,pno AM.COMP.AL. $1.10
    (F506)

Taste And See That The Lord Is Good
  high solo,pno AM.COMP.AL. $1.37
    (F507)
  low solo,pno AM.COMP.AL. $1.37
    (F508)

There Is No Time
  high solo,pno sc AM.COMP.AL. $1.10
    (F509)
  low solo,pno sc AM.COMP.AL. $1.10
    (F510)

Vista
  med solo,pno AM.COMP.AL. $1.37
    (F511)

Walk In The Wilderness, The
  med solo,pno sc AM.COMP.AL. $.82
    (F512)

What You Are
  med solo,pno sc AM.COMP.AL. $.55
    (F513)

When From The Lips Of Truth *sac
  solo,pno/org COBURN   (F514)
  med solo,pno AM.COMP.AL. $1.10
    (F515)

Winter Winds
  med solo,pno sc AM.COMP.AL. $1.10
    (F516)
  low solo,pno sc AM.COMP.AL. $1.10
    (F517)

World Of Dream, The
  med solo,pno sc AM.COMP.AL. $2.20
    (F518)

You Were Glad Tonight
  med solo,pno sc AM.COMP.AL. $.82
    (F519)

FISCHER, JAN F. (1921-   )
  Arie Ester (from Romoe, Julie A Tma)
    see ARIE A ZPEVY ZE SOUCASNYCH
    OPER: ALT

FISCHER-MAIDEN, THE see Schubert, Franz
  (Peter), Das Fischermadchen

FISCHERKNABE, HIRT ALPENJAGER see
  Liszt, Franz, Der Fischerknabe

FISCHER'S ALBUM OF SACRED SOLOS *sac,
  CCU
  solo,pno BELWIN $4.00   (F520)

FISCHES NACHTGESANG see Badings, Henk

FISCHHOF, R.
  Ombre Et Lueur
    solo,pno ENOCH s.p.   (F521)

FISH, THE see Shapiro, Norman

FISH IN THE UNRUFFLED LAKES see
  Britten, Benjamin

FISHELACH IN WASSER *Jew
  solo,pno KAMMEN 424 $1.00 (F522)

FISHER
  King And The Beggar, The *sac
    solo,pno BENSON S7928-R $1.00
      (F523)

FISHER, H.
  Old Violin
    solo,pno,opt vln (G maj) BOOSEY
      $1.50   (F524)

  Sittin' Thinkin'
    low solo,pno (E flat maj) BOOSEY
      $1.50   (F525)
    high solo,pno (F maj) BOOSEY $1.50
      (F526)

FISHER, HOWARD
  By Still Quiet Waters
    solo,pno (G maj) LEONARD-ENG (F527)

  Farewell, A (from Grave And Gay)
    high solo,pno (A maj, contains
      also: Song Of The Button, The)
      LEONARD-ENG   (F528)
    med-high solo,pno (A flat maj,
      contains also: Song Of The
      Button, The) LEONARD-ENG (F529)
    med solo,pno (G maj, contains also:
      Song Of The Button, The) LEONARD-
      ENG   (F530)
    low solo,pno (F maj, contains also:
      Song Of The Button, The) LEONARD-
      ENG   (F531)

  Frills And Fancies *CCU
    solo,pno LEONARD-ENG   (F532)

FISHER, HOWARD (cont'd.)

From Inverness To Fell
  low solo,pno (C min) LEONARD-ENG
    (F533)
  high solo,pno (D min) LEONARD-ENG
    (F534)

Kiss And A Smile, A (from Grave And
    Gay)
  low solo,pno (G maj, contains also:
    Mignonette) LEONARD-ENG (F535)
  med solo,pno (A flat maj, contains
    also: Mignonette) LEONARD-ENG
      (F536)
  high solo,pno (B flat maj, contains
    also: Mignonette) LEONARD-ENG
      (F537)

Look Down Dear Eyes
  high solo,pno (G maj) LEONARD-ENG
    (F538)
  low solo,pno (F maj) LEONARD-ENG
    (F539)
  2 soli,pno (F maj) LEONARD-ENG
    (F540)
  2 soli,pno (B flat maj) LEONARD-ENG
    (F541)

Mignonette (from Grave And Gay)
  med solo,pno (B flat maj, contains
    also: Kiss And A Smile, A)
    LEONARD-ENG   (F542)
  high solo,pno (C maj, contains
    also: Kiss And A Smile, A)
    LEONARD-ENG   (F543)
  low solo,pno (A flat maj, contains
    also: Kiss And A Smile, A)
    LEONARD-ENG   (F544)

Rollicking, Rolling Stone, A
  low solo,pno (F maj) CRAMER (F545)
  high solo,pno (G maj) CRAMER (F546)

Side Car
  solo,pno CRAMER   (F547)

Song Of The Button, The (from Grave
    And Gay)
  high solo,pno (A flat maj, contains
    also: Farewell, A) LEONARD-ENG
      (F548)
  med solo,pno (F maj, contains also:
    Farewell, A) LEONARD-ENG (F549)
  med-high solo,pno (G maj, contains
    also: Farewell, A) LEONARD-ENG
      (F550)
  low solo,pno (E flat maj, contains
    also: Farewell, A) LEONARD-ENG
      (F551)

Thoughts
  low solo,pno (F maj) LEONARD-ENG
    (F552)
  high solo,pno (A flat maj) LEONARD-
    ENG   (F553)

FISHER LAD see Day, Maude Craske

FISHER, LEE
  Songs Of Lee Fisher, The *sac,CC9L
    solo,pno WORD 35049 $2.50 (F554)

FISHER-MAIDEN, THE see Schubert, Franz
  (Peter), Das Fischermadchen

FISHER, WILLIAM ARMS (1861-1948)
  Seek Ye First The Kingdom Of God
    med solo,pno PRESSER $.75 (F555)

FISHERFOLK see Arundale, Claude

FISHERMAN AND HIS WIFE, THE see Hyde

FISHER'S WIDOW, THE see Edwards, Clara

FISHES AND THE POET'S HANDS, THE see
  Reif, Paul

FISHING see Oldham, Arthur

FISKE, R.
  Dove Says Coo, The
    see Six Nursery Tunes

  Hoddley, Poddley, Puddle And Frogs
    see Six Nursery Tunes

  I Won't Be My Father's Jack
    see Six Nursery Tunes

  Lilies Are White
    see Six Nursery Tunes

  O My Kitten A Kitten
    see Six Nursery Tunes

  Six Nursery Tunes
    [Eng] med solo,kbd CHESTER s.p.
      contains: Dove Says Coo, The;
      Hoddley, Poddley, Puddle And
      Frogs; I Won't Be My Father's
      Jack; Lilies Are White; O My
      Kitten A Kitten; Suky, You
      Shall Be My Wife   (F556)

  Suky, You Shall Be My Wife
    see Six Nursery Tunes

FIUME, ORAZIO
    Due Liriche Su Testi Popolari Toscani
    *CC2U
    [It] solo,pno SANTIS 758 s.p.
                                        (F557)

FIVE ARIAS see Wolf, Hugo

FIVE ARIAS see Edmunds

FIVE AUSTRALIAN LYRICS see Antill, John
    Henry

FIVE BHARTRIHARI POEMS see Birch,
    Robert Fairfax

FIVE CANADIAN FOLK SONGS *folk
    (Gibbs, C. Armstrong) solo,pno OXFORD
    60.811 $.50
    contains: Bonavist' Harbor; I'se
    The B'y That Builds The Boat;
    Morning Dew, The; My Canadian
    Bride; Stormy Scenes Of Winter,
    The   (F558)

FIVE CANCIONES OF THE SEVENTEETH
    CENTURY *CC5U,17th cent
    (Tarrago) [Span] med solo,gtr UNION
    ESP. $1.25   (F559)

FIVE CANZONETS see Ronald, Sir Landon

FIVE CHINESE LYRICS see Oldham, Arthur

FIVE CHINESE MINIATURES see Redman,
    Reginald

FIVE CSOKONAI SONGS see David, Gyula

FIVE DUETS see Brahms, Johannes

FIVE DUETS see Weigl, Karl

FIVE ELEGIES see Mc Cabe

FIVE ELIZABETHAN LYRICS see Donovan,
    Richard [Frank]

FIVE ELIZABETHAN SONGS see Rieti,
    Vittorio

FIVE EPIC SONGS FROM THE ISLAND OF
    HIJUMAA see Otsa, H.

FIVE EYES see Gibbs

FIVE EYES see Gibbs, Cecil Armstrong

FIVE EYES see Kent, Mrs. Ada Twohy

FIVE FINGER EXERCISES see Reif, Paul

FIVE FOLK SONGS see Pisk, Paul Amadeus

FIVE-FOUR-THREE see Ballou, Esther W.

FIVE FRENCH FOLK SONGS *folk,Fr
    (Hopkins, A.) [Fr] med solo,kbd
    HANSEN-DEN s.p.
    contains: Gai Lon La; Hollaika; Les
    Trois Rubans; Me Suis Mise En
    Dance; Quand Mon Mari Se Fachera
                                        (F560)

FIVE GAMBLING SONGS see Niles, John
    Jacob

FIVE GREEK FOLK SONGS see Ravel,
    Maurice

FIVE INVOCATIONS see Plessis, Hubert du

FIVE ISTRIAN SONGS see Lang, Ivana

FIVE JAPANESE SONGS see Lewis, Peter
    Tod

FIVE JEWISH ART SONGS *CC5U
    (Weiner, L.) solo,pno MERCURY $2.50
    Yiddish and English texts   (F561)

FIVE JEWISH ART SONGS see Weiner, Lazar

FIVE JOLLY SONGS see Hutchinson, Hely

FIVE LITTLE SONGS OF OLD JAPAN see
    Whitehead, Percy A.

FIVE LOVE SONGS see Musgrave, Thea

FIVE LYRICS see Reuland, Jacques

FIVE LYRICS FOR ORCHESTRE see D'Haene,
    Rafael Lodewijk

FIVE LYRICS FROM "THE PROPHET" see
    Stearns, Peter Pindar

FIVE LYRICS OF THE T'ANG DYNASTY see
    Beckwith, John

FIVE MADRIGALS see Ferritto, John

FIVE MEDIAEVAL LYRICS see Bush,
    Geoffrey

FIVE MOUNTAIN-TCHEREMISSIAN FOLK SONGS
    see Kodaly, Zoltan

FIVE MOVEMENTS FOR CHAMBER GROUP AND
    TENOR see Pignon, Paul

FIVE NEGRO SONGS see Beekhuis, Hanna

FIVE NEGRO SONGS *CC5U
    (Brown, L.) [Eng] solo,pno SCHOTTS
    10004 s.p.   (F562)

FIVE NEGRO SPIRITUALS see Blacher,
    Boris

FIVE OPERATIC ARIAS see Cavalli,
    (Pietro) Francesco

FIVE ORCHESTRA SONGS AFTER TRAKL see
    Erbse, Heimo

FIVE POEMS see Berkeley, Lennox

FIVE POEMS BY HARDY see Ireland, John

FIVE POEMS BY ROBERT HERRICK see
    Lessard, John Ayres

FIVE POEMS OF MAX JACOB see Poulenc,
    Francis

FIVE POEMS OF WALT WHITMAN see Rorem,
    Ned

FIVE QUIET SONGS see Duarte, John W.

FIVE RHYTHMIC SONGS see Elliott, Anne

FIVE ROMANCES TO LYRICS BY SERGEI
    YESENIN see Liepins, A.

FIVE RONDELS see O'Neill, Norman

FIVE ROWS BACK see Peterson, John W.

FIVE RUMANIAN SONGS *CC5U
    [Rum] A solo,gtr WILHELM. s.p. (F563)

FIVE SACRED SOLOS see Koch

FIVE SACRED SONGS see Schutz, Heinrich

FIVE SACRED SONGS see Bach, Johann
    Sebastian

FIVE SEA CHANTIES see Dougherty, Celius

FIVE SHAKESPEARE SONGS see Quilter,
    Roger

FIVE SHAKESPEAREAN SONGS see Amram,
    David Werner

FIVE SHAKESPEAREAN SONGS see Findlay,
    S.

FIVE SHORT HUMOROUS SONGS see Arundale,
    Claude

FIVE SHORT SACRED CONCERTOS (ENGLISH
    VERSION) see Schutz, Heinrich

FIVE SHORT SACRED CONCERTOS (GERMAN
    VERSION) see Schutz, Heinrich

FIVE SHORT SONGS ON AMERICAN POEMS see
    Gerber, Steven

FIVE SINGING MINIATURES see
    Haussermann, R.

FIVE SONGS *CC5U
    (Beckwith, John) solo,pno WATERLOO
    $2.50   (F564)

FIVE SONGS see Lutoslawski, Witold

FIVE SONGS see Berger, Jean

FIVE SONGS see Bijvanck, Henk

FIVE SONGS see Schipper, Dirk

FIVE SONGS see Beeson, Jack Hamilton

FIVE SONGS see Einem, Gottfried von

FIVE SONGS see Strauss, Richard

FIVE SONGS see Gretchaninov, Alexander
    Tikhonovitch

FIVE SONGS see Diamond, David

FIVE SONGS see Monteverdi, Claudio

FIVE SONGS see Glanville-Hicks, Peggy

FIVE SONGS see Malipiero, Gian
    Francesco

FIVE SONGS see Hopekirk, Helen

FIVE SONGS see Lohr, Hanns

FIVE SONGS see Wagner, Richard

FIVE SONGS see Ballou, Esther W.

FIVE SONGS see Weber, Ben

FIVE SONGS see Weigl, Karl

FIVE SONGS see Nowak, Lionel

FIVE SONGS see Purcell, Henry

FIVE SONGS see Strauss, Richard

FIVE SONGS see Antheil, George

FIVE SONGS see Bartok, Bela

FIVE SONGS see Citkowitz, Israel

FIVE SONGS see Scarlatti, Domenico

FIVE SONGS see Mayer, Milan

FIVE SONGS see Nielsen, Carl

FIVE SONGS see Baird, Tadeusz

FIVE SONGS see Berkeley, Lennox

FIVE SONGS see Nielsen, Carl

FIVE SONGS see Kardos, Istvan

FIVE SONGS see Liszt, Franz

FIVE SONGS see Krumpholtz, Johann
    Baptist

FIVE SONGS see Thordarson, Sigurdur

FIVE SONGS FOR CONTRALTO see Cage, John

FIVE SONGS FOR DARK VOICE see Somers,
    Harry Stewart

FIVE SONGS FOR HIGH VOICE see Bush,
    Geoffrey

FIVE SONGS FOR MEDIUM VOICE see
    Strauss, Richard

FIVE SONGS FOR MEDIUM VOICE AND
    PREPARED PIANO see Koch, Frederick

FIVE SONGS FROM "PHANTASUS" see Weigl,
    Karl

FIVE SONGS FROM "STRAY BIRDS" see
    Mamlock, Ursula

FIVE SONGS FROM "WAYWARD PILGRIM" see
    Bottje, Will Gay

FIVE SONGS FROM WILLIAM BLAKE see
    Thomson, Virgil

FIVE SONGS OF CRAZY JANE see Aston,
    Peter G.

FIVE SONGS OF REMEMBRANCE see Weigl,
    Vally

FIVE SONGS OF WORSHIP (REVISED EDITION)
    see Fromm, Herbert

FIVE SONGS ON ENGLISH POEMS see
    Manneke, Daniel

FIVE SONGS ON JAPANESE HAIKU see Riley,
    Dennis

FIVE SONGS TO TEXTS BY POUL BORUM see
    Trede, Yngre Jan

FIVE SONNETS see Mallinson, (James)
    Albert

FIVE SPIRITUAL SONGS see Bach, Johann
    Sebastian

FIVE STUDIES ON TEXTS BY PRUDENTIUS see
    Schafer, M.

FIVE VILLAGE SCENES see Bartok, Bela

FIVE WEDDING SONGS *sac,Marriage
    med-high solo,pno AMSI $3.00
    contains: Elmore, Robert [Hall],
    Come With Us, O Blessed Jesus;
    Rickard, Jeffrey, Lead Us,
    Heavenly Father; Sateren, Leland
    Bernhard, God Of Earth And
    Heaven; Wetzler, Robert Paul,
    Holy Jesus, Send Your Blessing;
    Wood, Dale, O God Of Love (F565)

FIVE WESENDONK SONGS see Wagner,
    Richard

FIVE WILLIAM BLAKE SONGS see Arnold,
    Malcolm

FIVE YIDDISH SONGS see Weiner, Lazar

FJALAR see Bengzon, Viola

FJALLVANDRING see Peterson-Berger,
(Olof) Wilhelm

FJARRAN I SKOG see Berg

FJARRAN OVAN STJARNOR ALLA see
Soderman, (Johan) August

FJARRAN PA ENSLIG STIG see Korling,
August

FJARRAN TONER see Myrberg, August M.

FJORTON SANGDUETTER, HEFT 1-2 *CC14L
(Lundberg) 2 soli,pno LUNDQUIST s.p.,
ea. contains works by: Haggbom;
Berg; Farval; Mendelssohn;
Rubinstein; Pacius; Lundberg and
others   (F566)

FLACKRE, EWIGES LICHT see Trunk,
Richard

FLAG OF EMPIRE see Gillington, M.

FLAG SONG see Ives, Charles

FLAGELLO, NICHOLAS (1928-   )
As I Walked Forth
solo,pno GENERAL 329 $1.00   (F567)

Ben Doverrieno
solo,pno GENERAL 325 $2.00   (F568)

Ben Fu
solo,pno GENERAL 327 $2.50   (F569)

Di Piu Cose
solo,pno GENERAL 328 $2.00   (F570)

Dr. Clash And Signor Falasole
solo,pno GENERAL 334 $1.50   (F571)

Good English Hospitality
solo,pno GENERAL 332 $1.50   (F572)

Land, The *song cycle
solo,pno GENERAL 10 $5.00   (F573)

Leave, O Leave Me To My Sorrows
solo,pno GENERAL 333 $1.50   (F574)

L'infinito
solo,pno GENERAL 50 $2.50   (F575)

O Father, O Father
solo,pno GENERAL 331 $1.25   (F576)

This Frog He Would A-Wooing Ride
solo,pno GENERAL 330 $1.00   (F577)

FLAIOLET *13th cent
(Bonnal, Ermend) solo,pno OUVRIERES
s.p.   (F578)

FLAME OF GOD'S REDEEMING LOVE, THE
*sac
(Carmichael, Ralph) solo,pno WORD
S-224   (F579)

FLAMENCO MEDITATIONS see Surinach,
Carlos

FLAMME BEI NACHT see Thomas, Kurt

FLAMME ETERNELLE see Schumann, Robert
(Alexander)

FLAMMEN PERDONAMI see Mascagni, Pietro

FLAMMEN PIETA see Mascagni, Pietro

FLAMMENDE ROSE see Handel, George
Frideric

FLANAGAN, WILLIAM (1926-1969)
Another August
S solo,fl,2ob,2clar,2bsn,2horn,
2trp,timp,cembalo,pno,strings
PETERS 66429 rental   (F580)

Dugout, The
solo,pno PEER $.85   (F581)

Go And Catch A Falling Star
solo,pno PEER $.95   (F582)

Good-Bye, My Fancy
S solo,fl,gtr/pno PEER $1.50   (F583)

Heaven Haven
solo,pno PEER $.85   (F584)

Horror Movie
solo,pno PETERS 6847 $1.75   (F585)

If You Can
see Two Songs

Plants Cannot Travel
see Two Songs

FLANAGAN, WILLIAM (cont'd.)
See How They Love Me
solo,pno PETERS 6846 $1.75   (F586)

Send Home My Long Strayed Eyes
solo,pno PEER $.95   (F587)

Song For A Winter Child
solo,pno PEER $.85   (F588)

Two Songs
high solo,pno PETERS $1.75
contains: If You Can; Plants
Cannot Travel   (F589)

Upside-Down Man, The
solo,pno PEER $1.00   (F590)

Valentine To Sherwood Anderson
solo,pno PEER $.95   (F591)

Weeping Pleiads, The *song cycle
Bar solo,fl,clar,pno,vln,vcl PEER
rental   (F592)

FLANDRE *Fr
(Canteloube, J.) solo,acap DURAND
s.p. see also Anthologie Des Chants
Populaires Francais Tome IV   (F593)

FLASHES see Dobos, K.

FLAX see Lang, Ivana

FLEA, THE see Krenek, Ernst

FLECHA see Manen, Joan

FLECHA, MATEO (1530-1604)
La Girigonza (composed with
Fuenllana, Miguel de)
(Pujol) [Span] high solo,gtr ESCHIG
E1304 $.90   (F594)

FLEE AS A BIRD see Dana

FLEETING, THE see Berkeley, Lennox

FLEGIER, ANGE (1846-1927)
Apres L'Angelus
solo,pno (available in 2 keys)
ENOCH s.p.   (F595)
solo,acap (available in 2 keys)
ENOCH s.p.   (F596)

Horn, The *see Le Cor

La Barque D'amour
solo,pno (available in 2 keys)
ENOCH s.p.   (F597)
solo,acap (available in 2 keys)
ENOCH s.p.   (F598)

Le Cor
"Horn, The" [Fr/Eng] med solo,pno
(F maj) SCHIRM.G $.75   (F599)
"Horn, The" [Eng/Fr] B solo,pno
PRESSER $.75   (F600)
"Horn, The" [Fr/Eng] low solo,pno
(D maj) SCHIRM.G $.75   (F601)

Le Rendez-Vous
MezBar soli,pno ENOCH s.p. voc sc,
solo pt   (F602)

Les Enfants Et Les Amoureux
solo,pno (available in 2 keys)
ENOCH s.p.   (F603)
solo,acap (available in 2 keys)
ENOCH s.p.   (F604)

Les Hirondelles De Mer
solo,pno ENOCH s.p.   (F605)

Oubli
solo,pno (available in 2 keys)
ENOCH s.p.   (F606)
solo,acap (available in 2 keys)
ENOCH s.p.   (F607)

Renouveau
solo,pno (available in 2 keys)
ENOCH s.p.   (F608)
solo,acap (available in 2 keys)
ENOCH s.p.   (F609)

Tout Est Fini
solo,pno (available in 2 keys)
ENOCH s.p.   (F610)
solo,acap (available in 2 keys)
ENOCH s.p.   (F611)

Toutes Les Roses
solo,pno (available in 2 keys)
ENOCH s.p.   (F612)

Voyageurs Celestes
solo,pno (available in 2 keys)
ENOCH s.p.   (F613)
solo,acap (available in 2 keys)
ENOCH s.p.   (F614)

FLEISCHMANN, O.
Fruhlingsreigen
high solo,pno SCHAUR EE 3425A s.p.
(F615)
med solo,pno SCHAUR EE 3425B s.p.
(F616)

FLEMING, CHRISTOPHER LE
Egypt's Might Is Tumbled Down
[Eng] med solo,kbd CHESTER s.p.
(F617)

Hymnes *sac
[Eng] med solo,kbd CHESTER s.p.
(F618)

If It's Ever Spring Again
[Eng] med solo,kbd CHESTER s.p.
(F619)

FLETCHER, PERCY EASTMAN (1879-1932)
Shafts Of Cupid, The
high solo,pno NOVELLO 17.0166.05
s.p.   (F620)
med solo,pno NOVELLO 17.0167.03
s.p.   (F621)
low solo,pno NOVELLO 17.0168.01
s.p.   (F622)

Smile Of Spring, The
S solo,pno NOVELLO 17.0175.04 s.p.
(F623)
Mez solo,pno NOVELLO 17.0176.02
s.p.   (F624)
A solo,pno NOVELLO 17.0177.00
s.p.   (F625)

Songster's Awakening
high solo,pno NOVELLO 17.0184.03
s.p.   (F626)
low solo,pno NOVELLO 17.0185.01
s.p.   (F627)

FLEUR ANGEVINE see Busser, Henri-Paul

FLEUR DE NEIGE see Holmes, Alfred

FLEUR DE PARIS see Absil, Jean

FLEUR DES DUNES see Bonnal, Ermend

FLEUR D'EXIL, NO. 1 see Godard,
Benjamin Louis Paul

FLEUR D'EXIL, NO. 2 see Godard,
Benjamin Louis Paul

FLEUR DU MATIN see Chaminade, Cecile

FLEUR DU VALLON see Godard, Benjamin
Louis Paul

FLEUR JETEE see Chaminade, Cecile

FLEUR MEURTRIE see Lacombe, Paul

FLEURETTES see Delmet, Paul

FLEURIS DANS MON ESPRIT see Doret

FLEURIS, PAYS DES SOVIETS *CC40UL
[Russ] solo,pno solo pt,cmplt ed
CHANT s.p.   (F628)

FLEURS see Bordewijk-Roepman, Johanna

FLEURS D'ADIEU see Tremisot, Ed.

FLEURS D'AJONC see Rhene-Baton

FLEURS DE FRANCE see Ferrante

FLEURS DE FRANCE see Delmet, Paul

FLEURS DE MAI see Mendelssohn-
Bartholdy, Felix

FLEURS DE MON JARDIN see Gey, Jeo

FLEURS DES BLES see Debussy, Claude

FLEURS FANEES see Lemaire, F.

FLEURS PARISIENNES see Lecocq, Charles

FLEURY, H.
Matutina
solo,pno (available in 2 keys)
ENOCH s.p.   (F629)

FLICKA MED DEN RODA MUNNEN see
Soderman, (Johan) August

FLICKA, SJUNG see Jalkanen, Teppo,
Laula Tytto

FLICKAM KOM IFRAN SIN ALSKLINGS MOTE
see Sibelius, Jean

FLICKAN FRAN DROMMARANS BY see
Soderlundh, Lille Bror

FLICKAN I MARSEILLE see Lagerheim-
Romare, Margit

FLICKAN KNYTER I JOHANNENATTEN see
Stenhammar, Wilhelm

FLICKAN KOM IFRAN SIN ALSKLINGS MOTE
see Sibelius, Jean

FLICKAN KOM IFRAN SIN ALSKLINGS MOTE
    see Stenhammar, Wilhelm

FLICKAN UNDER NYMANEN see Korling

FLICKANS LANGTAN see Norman, Ludvig

FLICKANS ONSKAN see Chopin, Frederic

FLIEDER IM MONDLICHT see Trunk, Richard

FLIEG DAHIN see Weismann, Julius

FLIEGERLIED see Strniste, Jiri, Letecka

FLIEH MICH NICHT, HERZENSLIEB
    [Russ/Fr/Ger] med solo,pno BELAIEFF
    245 s.p.   (F630)

FLIEHENDE HINDINNEN see Mikoda,
    Borivoj, Prchajici Lane

FLIES, J. BERNHARD (1770- ?)
    Schlafe Mein Prinzchen
      (Mottl, F.) S solo,fl,strings voc
      sc BREITKOPF-L rental   (F631)

    Wiegenlied
      solo,pno FAZER F 2761 s.p.   (F632)

FLIGHT see Ellett, Roy

FLIGHT, THE see Allen, Robert E.

FLIGHT FOR HEAVEN see Rorem, Ned

FLIGHT OF THE LARK, THE see Serly,
    Tibor

FLIRT DES PAPILLONS see Dufresne, C.

FLIRTATION INTERMEZZO see Strauss,
    Johann

FLO see Mills, Charles

FLOERING
    Day I First Saw God *sac
      high solo,pno (G min) ALLANS s.p.
                                    (F633)
      low solo,pno (E flat min) ALLANS
      s.p.   (F634)

FLOODES OF TEARS see Somervell, Arthur

FLOODS OF SPRING see Rachmaninoff,
    Sergey Vassilievitch, Spring Waters

FLOR DE CARDON see Napolitano, Emilio

FLOR DE CEIBO see Gaito, Constantino

FLORAISON see Ferrari, Gustave

FLORENZ HAT SCHONE FRAUEN see Suppe,
    Franz von

FLORES DE ESPANA *CC38U,folk,Span
    (Hernandez) [Span] med solo,pno UNION
    ESP. $3.50   (F635)

FLORET SILVA see Mul, Jan

FLORIA, CAM
    He That Overcomes *sac
      solo,pno WORD S-372   (F636)

FLORIAN'S SONG see Godard, Benjamin
    Louis Paul, Chanson De Florian

FLORIDA LOVE SONG see Woodforde-Finden,
    Amy

FLOTENLIEDER FUR SOPRAN, FLOTE UND
    KLAVIER see Anders, E.

FLOTHIUS, MARIUS (1914-   )
    Black Eyes *Op.33,No.3
      see Four Trifles

    Der Morgen War Von Dir Erfullt
      *Op.3,No.1
      see Vier Liederen Van Chr.
      Morgenstern

    Een Amsterdamsch Lied *Op.40
      SBar soli,fl,clar,2vln,vla,vcl,bvl,
      pno DONEMUS s.p.   (F637)

    Es Ist Nacht *Op.3,No.2
      see Vier Liederen Van Chr.
      Morgenstern

    Falling Asleep In An Orchard *Op.33,
      No.1
      see Four Trifles

    Fantasia Quasi Un Cantata *Op.71
      Mez solo,cembalo,11strings DONEMUS
      s.p.   (F638)

    Four Trifles
      DONEMUS high solo/low solo,pno
      s.p.; high solo,fl,ob,2clar,bsn,
      al-sax,horn,trp,timp,perc,strings
      rental

FLOTHIUS, MARIUS (cont'd.)

      contains: Black Eyes, Op.33,No.3;
      Falling Asleep In An Orchard,
      Op.33,No.1; Look, The, Op.33,
      No.2; Seal Woman, The, Op.33,
      No.4   (F639)

    Hij Droech Onse Smerten *Op.10,No.1
      see Twee Sonnetten

    Hymnus *Op.67
      S solo,3fl,3ob,3clar,2bsn,4horn,
      3trp,3trom,2tuba,timp,perc,vibra,
      strings DONEMUS s.p.   (F640)

    Kleine Ouverture *Op.14
      S solo,2fl,2ob,3clar,3bsn,3horn,
      3trp,3trom,tuba,timp,perc,cel,
      harp,vibra,strings DONEMUS s.p.
                                    (F641)
    Kleine Suite *Op.47, CCU,vocalise
      S solo,pno DONEMUS s.p.   (F642)

    Look, The *Op.33,No.2
      see Four Trifles

    Love And Strife *Op.34, song cycle
      [Eng] A solo,fl,ob,vla,vcl s.p. sc
      DONEMUS D175, min sc DONEMUS D174
                                    (F643)
    Negro Lament *Op.49
      A solo,ob/A rec/al-sax/vla,pno
      DONEMUS s.p.   (F644)

    O Als Ik Dood Zal Zijn
      Mez/Bar solo,fl,English horn,clar,
      bass clar,bsn,horn DONEMUS s.p.
                                    (F645)
    O Nacht... *Op.3,No.3
      see Vier Liederen Van Chr.
      Morgenstern

    Odysseus And Nausikaa *Op.60,
      madrigal
      SATBar soli,harp DONEMUS s.p.
                                    (F646)
    Quatter Miniatures Rumantschas
      *Op.68, CC4U
      S solo,fl DONEMUS s.p.   (F647)

    Rebel, Mijn Hart *Op.10,No.2
      see Twee Sonnetten

    Rondel
      S solo,pno DONEMUS s.p.   (F648)

    Seal Woman, The *Op.33,No.4
      see Four Trifles

    Sonnet *Op.9
      Mez solo,2fl,2ob,3clar,2bsn,3horn,
      3trp,3trom,timp,perc,pno,strings
      DONEMUS s.p.   (F649)

    To An Old Love *Op.32
      Mez solo,fl,3clar,2bsn,al-sax,
      2horn,3trp,3trom,timp,harp,
      strings DONEMUS s.p.   (F650)

    Twee Sonnetten
      DONEMUS med solo,pno s.p.; Mez/Bar
      solo,2ob,2clar,2bsn,trp,timp,
      perc,strings rental
      contains: Hij Droech Onse
      Smerten, Op.10,No.1; Rebel,
      Mijn Hart, Op.10,No.2   (F651)

    Vier Liederen Van Chr. Morgenstern
      DONEMUS S solo,pno s.p.; S solo,
      2fl,ob,2clar,bsn,2horn,2trp,timp,
      perc,cel,harp,vibra,strings
      rental
      contains: Der Morgen War Von Dir
      Erfullt, Op.3,No.1; Es Ist
      Nacht, Op.3,No.2; O Nacht...,
      Op.3,No.3; Wasserfal Bei Nacht,
      Op.3,No.4   (F652)

    Vorfruhling *Op.15,No.1-3, CC3U
      Mez solo,pno DONEMUS s.p.   (F653)

    Wasserfal Bei Nacht *Op.3,No.4
      see Vier Liederen Van Chr.
      Morgenstern

FLOTOW, FRIEDRICH VON (1812-1883)
    Ach, So Fromm (from Martha)
      T solo,2fl,2ob,2clar,2bsn,4horn,
      2trp,2trom,tuba,timp,drums,
      strings BREITKOPF-L rental (F654)
      "Ah! So Pure" med solo,pno (E flat
      maj) ALLANS s.p.   (F655)
      "Ah! So Pure" low solo,pno (C maj)
      ALLANS s.p.   (F656)
      "Ah! So Pure" high solo,pno (F maj)
      ALLANS s.p.   (F657)
      "Lyonelin Romanssi" solo,pno FAZER
      F 3422 s.p.   (F658)
      "M'appari Tutt'amor" [It/Fr] T
      solo,pno RICORDI-ARG BA 8347 s.p. (F659)
      "M'appari Tutt'amor" [It] T solo,
      pno RICORDI-ENG 54418 s.p. (F660)

FLOTOW, FRIEDRICH VON (cont'd.)

    Ah! So Pure *see Ach, So Fromm

    La Ultima Rosa De Verano *see Letzte
      Rose

    Letzte Rose (from Martha)
      S solo,2fl,2ob,2clar,2bsn,4horn,
      2trp,2trom,tuba,timp,harp,strings
      BREITKOPF-L rental   (F661)
      "La Ultima Rosa De Verano" [It/Eng/
      Span] solo,pno RICORDI-ARG
      BA 9097 s.p.   (F662)

    Lezte Rose (from Martha)
      "Qui Sola Vergin Rosa" [It/Fr/Ger/
      Eng] S solo,pno (G maj) SCHIRM.G
      $.75   (F663)

    Lyonelin Romanssi *see Ach! So Fromm

    M'appari Tutt'amor *see Ach, So
      Fromm

    Qui Sola Vergin Rosa *see Lezte Rose

FLOW, MY TEARS see Jacob

FLOWER, A see Cage, John

FLOWER, A see Schouwman, Hans

FLOWER CAROL see Bennett, Richard
    Rodney

FLOWER GIRL, THE see Pergament, Moses,
    Blomsterflickan

FLOWER GIVEN TO MY DAUGHTER see
    Diamond, David

FLOWER GIVEN TO MY DAUGHTER see
    Strickland, William

FLOWER OF HEAVEN, THE see Thiman, Eric
    Harding

FLOWER SONG see Bizet, Georges, La
    Fleur Que Tu M'avais Jetee

FLOWER SONG see Gounod, Charles
    Francois, Faites-Lui Mes Aveux

FLOWERS OF THE FOREST, THE , KEF-KAF
    *folk,Scot
    solo,pno PATERSON FS30 s.p.   (F664)

FLOWERY OMENS see Dvorak, Antonin

FLOYD, CARLISLE (1926-   )
    Ain't It A Pretty Night (from
      Susannah)
      S solo,pno BOOSEY $1.50 contains
      also: Trees On The Mountain
                                    (F665)
    Blitch's Prayer Of Repentance (from
      Susannah)
      Bar/B solo,pno BOOSEY $1.50 (F666)

    It Must Make The Good Lord Sad (from
      Susannah)
      T solo,pno BOOSEY $1.50   (F667)

    Mystery *song cycle
      high solo,orch BOOSEY $3.00 (F668)

    Pilgrimage *song cycle
      low solo,pno/orch BOOSEY $3.50
                                    (F669)
    Trees On The Mountain (from Susannah)
      see Floyd, Carlisle, Ain't It A
      Pretty Night

FLUCH EUCH! EW'GER FLUCH EUREM STAMME
    see Saint-Saens, Camille, Maudite A
    Jamais Soit La Race

FLUISTERINGEN see Sigtenhorst-Meyer,
    Bernhard van den

FLURY, A.
    Don Bosco-Jugendmesse *sac,Mass
      solo,org CHRIS 50697-98 s.p. (F670)

FLURY, RICHARD (1896-1967)
    Acht Liebeslieder *CC8U
      solo,pno HUG s.p.   (F671)

    Funf Lieder *CC5U
      solo,pno HUG s.p.   (F672)

    Nachtlieder *CCU
      solo,pno HUG s.p.   (F673)

    Neunundzwanzig Lieder *CC29U
      solo,pno HUG s.p.   (F674)

    Siebzehn Lieder *CC17U
      solo,pno HUG s.p.   (F675)

FLY, THE see Dukelsky, Vladimir

FLY, THE see Sydeman, William

FLY IS ON THE TURMUT see Broadwood,
Lucy E.

FLYNN, H.
Digging Up The Road *see Butler, R.

Ee, By Gum! *see Butler, R.

FLYTTFAGLARNA see Kaski, Heino,
Muuttolinnut

FOCK, A.
Les Soldats De Bois
solo,pno ENOCH s.p.   (F676)
solo,acap ENOCH s.p.   (F677)

FOERSTER, JOSEF BOHUSLAV (1859-1951)
Abendgesange *Op.126, song cycle
[Czech/Ger] solo,pno SUPRAPHON s.p.
(F678)
Balada Horska
solo,pno SUPRAPHON s.p.   (F679)

Ciste Jitro *Op.107, CC3U
solo,orch SUPRAPHON s.p.   (F680)

Co Vecer Zpiva *Op.116
solo,pno SUPRAPHON s.p.   (F681)

Erotikon
solo,pno SUPRAPHON s.p.   (F682)

Jaro A Touha
solo,pno SUPRAPHON s.p.   (F683)

Laska *Op.46, song cycle
solo,pno (published in 2 volumes)
SUPRAPHON s.p., ea.   (F684)

Opustena
solo,pno SUPRAPHON s.p.   (F685)

Pasiflora
solo,pno SUPRAPHON s.p.   (F686)

Pisen Saskova
solo,pno SUPRAPHON s.p.   (F687)

Pisne Cernovych Dnu *Op.189, CCU
solo,pno SUPRAPHON s.p.   (F688)

Pisne Soumraku *Op.42, CCU
high solo,pno SUPRAPHON s.p.   (F689)

Posledni Pisne F.X. Svobody *Op.180,
CCU
high solo,pno SUPRAPHON s.p.   (F690)

Rozmarne Pisne
solo,pno SUPRAPHON s.p.   (F691)

Sest Pisne Na Slova Ceskych Basniku
*CC6U
solo,pno SUPRAPHON s.p.   (F692)

Sest Pisni Na Slova A.S. Puskina
*Op.161, CC6U
Bar solo,pno SUPRAPHON s.p.   (F693)

Tri Notturna Pro Solovy Hlas
*Op.163, CC3U
solo,vcl,pno SUPRAPHON s.p.   (F694)

U Bran Stesti *Op.186, CC6U
high solo,pno SUPRAPHON s.p.   (F695)

FOG see Harris, Roy

FOG see Haubiel, Charles

FOG see Raphling, Sam

FOGELFANGAREN *Op.90,No.4
"Der Vogelsteller" [Swed/Ger] med-
high solo,kbd HANSEN-DEN s.p. see
from Six Songs   (F696)

FOGG, ERIC (1903-1939)
Spindrift
high solo,pno ELKIN 27.1639.09 s.p.
(F697)
low solo,pno ELKIN 27.1638.00 s.p.
(F698)

FOGGIA, ANTONIO
O Quam Fulgido Splendore *sac
(Ewerhart, Rudolf) [Lat] S/T solo,
cont BIELER CS 10 s.p.   (F699)

FOGGIA, FRANCESCO (ca. 1604-1688)
Cessate, Deh, Cessate *sac
(Ewerhart, Rudolf) S/T solo,cont
BIELER CS 38 s.p.   (F700)

De Valle Lacrimarum *sac
(Ewerhart, Rudolf) [Lat] S/T solo,
cont BIELER CS 28 s.p.   (F701)

FOGGY, FOGGY DEW see Britten, Benjamin

FOGLI D'ALBUM PER SOPRANO see
D'Ambrosi, Dante

FOLEY
Just A Closer Walk With Thee *sac,
gospel
solo,pno ABER.GRP. $1.50   (F702)

FOLIE D'AMOUR see Delmet, Paul

FOLK DANCES *CC111U,folk,Hung
(Lajtha; Rajeczky) solo,pno BUDAPEST
668 s.p.   (F703)

FOLK LULLABIES *CCU,folk
(Cass-Beggs, Michael; Cass-Beggs,
Barbara) solo,pno OAK 000104 $3.95
(F704)
FOLK MUSIC FESTIVAL IN HAWAII *sac,CCU
(Kelly) solo,pno BOSTON $4.50 (F705)

FOLK MUSICAL THEMES *sac,CCUL,folk
(Dino) solo,pno WORD 37722 $2.95
(F706)
FOLK SONG CANTATA see Kadosa, [Paul]

FOLK SONG FROM THE GREEK see Mills,
Charles

FOLK SONGS *CCU,folk
high solo,pno FISCHER,C RB 51; low
solo,pno FISCHER,C RB 52   (F707)

FOLK SONGS AND BALLADS OF LANCASHIRE
*CC35U,folk,Eng
(Boardman, Harry; Boardman, Lesley)
solo,pno OAK 000147 $2.95   (F708)

FOLK SONGS AND BALLADS OF SCOTLAND
*CC70U,Scot
(MacColl, Ewan) solo,pno OAK 000057
$3.95   (F709)

FOLK SONGS FOR MEXICO AND SOUTH AMERICA
*CCU
(Hague) solo,pno BELWIN $1.25 (F710)

FOLK SONGS FROM SUSSEX *CCU,folk
(Butterworth, George) solo,pno
GALLIARD 2.1338.7 $2.25   (F711)

FOLK SONGS OF EASTERN CANADA *folk
(Ridout, Godfrey) S solo,pno/orch
THOMP.G s.p., ipr
contains: Ah! Si Mon Moine Voulait
Danser!; I'll Give My Love An
Apple; Jai Cueilli La Belle Rose;
She's Like The Swallow   (F712)

FOLK SONGS OF EUROPE *CC138U,Eur
(Karpeles, Maud) solo,pno OAK 000074
$3.95   (F713)

FOLK SONGS OF FRANCE *CCU,Fr
(Scott, Barbara) [Fr/Eng] solo,pno
OAK 000075 $2.95   (F714)

FOLK SONGS OF GHANA *CCU,folk,Afr
(Nketia, J.H. Kwabena) solo,pno
OXFORD   (F715)

FOLK SONGS OF GREECE *CC53U,Greek
(Alevizos, Susan; Alevizos, Ted)
solo,pno OAK 000002 $3.95   (F716)

FOLK SONGS OF JAMAICA *CC30U,folk,
Carib
(Murray, Tom) solo,pno OXFORD 68.706
$3.25   (F717)

FOLK SONGS OF JAPAN *CCU,Jap
(Berger, Donald) [Jap/Eng] solo,gtr,
opt fl&perc OAK 000132 $3.95 (F718)

FOLK SONGS OF PEGGY SEEGER *CC88U
(Seeger, Peggy) solo,pno OAK 000038
$2.95   (F719)

FOLK SONGS OF THE AMERICAS *CC150U,Nor
Am/So Am
(Lloyd, A. L.; Artez De Ramon Y
Rivera, Isabel) solo,pno OAK 000056
$3.95   (F720)

FOLK SONGS OF THE SOUTHERN APPALACHIANS
*CC77U,folk
(Ritchie, Jean) solo,pno OAK 000039
$3.95   (F721)

FOLK SONGS OF THE WORLD *CCU,folk
solo,pno MUSIC 020133 $5.95 (F722)

FOLK TUNE see Kansansavelma

FOLKELIGE MORGENSANGE *CCU
(Warming, Per; Bengtsson, Gustav)
solo,pno HANSEN-DEN 29252 s.p.
(F723)
FOLKEVISE see Lewkovitch, Bernhard

FOLKLORE ECOSSAIS *CCU,folk,Scot
(Holst, Imogen) solo,rec,pno cmplt ed
OISEAU s.p.   (F724)

FOLKLORE RUSSE *CCU,folk,Russ
(Strimer, Joseph) [Fr/Russ] solo,rec
cmplt ed OISEAU s.p.   (F725)

FOLKSANG see Merikanto, Oskar

FOLKSONG ARRANGEMENTS, VOL. 1: BRITISH
ISLES *CCU,folk
(Britten, Benjamin) high solo/med
solo,pno BOOSEY $5.00   (F726)

FOLKSONG ARRANGEMENTS, VOL. 2: FRANCE
*CCU,folk
(Britten, Benjamin) high solo/med
solo,pno BOOSEY $5.00   (F727)

FOLKSONG ARRANGEMENTS, VOL. 3: BRITISH
ISLES *CCU,folk
(Britten, Benjamin) high solo/med
solo,pno BOOSEY $5.00   (F728)

FOLKSONG ARRANGEMENTS, VOL. 4: MOORE'S
IRISH MELODIES *CCU,folk
(Britten, Benjamin) high solo,pno
BOOSEY $5.00   (F729)

FOLKSONG ARRANGEMENTS, VOL. 5: BRITISH
ISLES *CCU,folk
(Britten, Benjamin) high solo,pno
BOOSEY $5.00   (F730)

FOLKSONG ARRANGEMENTS, VOL. 6: ENGLAND
*CCU,folk
(Britten, Benjamin) high solo,gtr
BOOSEY $5.00   (F731)

FOLKSONGS FROM THE CATSKILLS see
Haufrecht, Herbert

FOLKSONGS OF TRINIDAD AND TOBAGO *CCU,
folk
(Walke; Walters) solo,pno BOOSEY
$3.25   (F732)

FOLKVISA see Merikanto, Oskar,
Kansanlaulu

FOLLE CARESSE see Lachaume, A.

FOLLE E COLUI - NASCE AL BOSCO see
Handel, George Frideric

FOLLE ENCHERE
(Fragerolle, G.) solo,pno ENOCH s.p.
see from Chansons Du Pays-Lorrain
(F733)
(Fragerolle, G.) solo,acap ENOCH s.p.
see from Chansons Du Pays-Lorrain
(F734)

FOLLOW AFTER HIM see Allen, Ann

FOLLOW, I WILL FOLLOW THEE *sac,gospel
solo,pno ABER.GRP. $1.50   (F735)

FOLLOW JESUS see Lee, Don

FOLLOW ME see Stanphill, Ira F.

FOLLOW YOUR SAINT see Davies, Henry
Walford

FOLLOWING SUIT see Wheeler

FOND MEMORIES see Garland, Hugh

FONTANA see Guarino, C.

FONTENAILLES, H. DE
Adoration
med solo,pno/inst (D flat maj)
DURAND s.p.   (F736)
high solo,pno/inst (E flat maj)
DURAND s.p.   (F737)
low solo,pno/inst (C maj) DURAND
s.p.   (F738)

Amour Jaloux
S/T solo,pno/inst DURAND   (F739)
Mez/Bar solo,pno/inst DURAND   (F740)

Aux Enfants
low solo,pno/inst (F maj) DURAND
(F741)
high solo,pno/inst (B flat maj)
DURAND   (F742)
med solo,pno/inst (G maj) DURAND
(F743)
Chanson D'avril
2 soli,pno DURAND s.p.   (F744)

Consolation
Mez/Bar solo,pno/inst DURAND (F745)
S/T solo,pno/inst DURAND   (F746)

La Messe De Minuit
high solo,pno/inst (D maj) DURAND
s.p.   (F747)
med solo,pno/inst (C maj) DURAND
s.p.   (F748)
low solo,pno/inst (B flat maj)
DURAND s.p.   (F749)

Legende Des Fleurs
(Bordese, Stephen) solo,pno
(available in 2 keys) ENOCH s.p.
see also CHANSONS DE PAGE (F750)

Les Baisers Sont Des Fleurs
[Fr] solo,acap oct DURAND s.p.
(F751)

FONTENAILLES, H. DE (cont'd.)

Les Deux Coeurs
[Fr] solo,acap oct DURAND s.p.
(F752)

L'heure D'aimer
low solo,pno/inst (F maj) DURAND
s.p.   (F753)
high solo,pno/inst (A flat maj)
DURAND s.p.   (F754)
med solo,pno/inst (G maj) DURAND
s.p.   (F755)

Mon Coeur Veut S'endormir
Mez/Bar solo,pno/inst DURAND s.p.
(F756)
S/T solo,pno/inst DURAND s.p.
(F757)

Obstination
[Fr] solo,acap oct DURAND s.p.
(F758)

Pensee D'autrefois
S/T solo,pno/inst DURAND s.p.
(F759)
Mez/Bar solo,pno/inst DURAND s.p.
(F760)

Prends Mon Coeur
solo,pno (available in 2 keys)
ENOCH s.p.   (F761)

Si J'etais Dieu
S/T solo,pno/inst DURAND s.p.
(F762)
Mez/Bar solo,pno/inst DURAND s.p.
(F763)

Trianon
S/T solo,pno/inst DURAND s.p.
(F764)
Mez/Bar solo,pno/inst DURAND s.p.
(F765)

Un Baiser
S/T solo,pno/inst DURAND s.p.
(F766)
Mez/Bar solo,pno/inst DURAND s.p.
(F767)

FONTENLA, JORGE
Madrigal
[Span] solo,pno/harp RICORDI-ARG
BA 11005 s.p.   (F768)

FONTRIER, GABRIEL
Sleep Now, Dream Now
solo,pno GENERAL 18 $1.00   (F769)

FOOD OF LOVE, THE see Grant, W. Parks

FOOL, THE see Castelnuovo-Tedesco,
Mario

FOOLISH QUESTIONS see Taylor, D.

FOOT NOTE see Franco, Johan

FOOT-PRINTS OF JESUS *sac,gospel
solo,pno ABER.GRP. $1.50   (F770)

FOOTSTEPS IN THE SNOW see Dale, Mervyn

FOR A DEAD KITTEN see Duke, John Woods

FOR A ROSE'S SAKE see Duchow, M.

FOR ALL ETERNITY see Mascheroni, Angelo

FOR ALL MY SIN see Clayton, Norman

FOR ALL OF THESE (WE THANK THEE, LORD)
see Smith, Herbert Arnold

FOR AN OLD MAN see Diamond, David

FOR AULD LANG SYNE see Harrhy, Edith

FOR COLORATURA, CLARINET, VIOLA, CELLO
see Huggler, John

FOR DAG see Crome, Fritz

FOR DIG ALLEN see Geehl, Henry Ernest,
For You Alone

FOR FIVE PLAYERS AND BARITONE see
Pleskow, Raoul

FOR FOSTERLANDET see Dannstrom, Isidor

FOR FRANZ KLINE see Feldman, Morton

FOR HER GAIT IF SHE BE WALKING see
Bullock, Ernest

FOR I AM HIS see Slater

FOR LANGE SE'N see Myrberg, August M.

FOR MUMMIE AND ME see Baxter, Maude
Stewart

FOR MUSIC see Balazs, Frederic

FOR MY LADY see Helm, Everett

FOR MY SAKE THOU HAST DIED see Moore,
Donald Lee

FOR MY TRANSGRESSIONS see Grimm, Johann
D.

FOR OPHELIA see De Banfield, Raffaello

FOR PETE'S SAKE! see Carmichael, Ralph

FOR POULENC see Rorem, Ned

FOR SUCH A TIME AS THIS see Oldham,
Doug

FOR SVERIGE see Alfven, Hugo

FOR THE LORD HATH MAGNIFIED ME see
Bach, Johann Sebastian

FOR THE UNFALLEN see Crosse

FOR THOSE TEARS I DIED see Stevens

FOR US TWO see Mana-Zucca, Mme., Im
Lenz

FOR VILSNA FOTTER SJUNGER GRASET see
Lidholm, Ingvar

FOR YOU ALONE *sac
low solo,pno (D flat maj) ASHLEY
$1.00   (F771)
med solo,pno (E flat maj) ASHLEY
$1.00   (F772)
med-high solo,pno (F maj) ASHLEY
$1.00   (F773)
high solo,pno (G maj) ASHLEY $1.00
(F774)

FOR YOU ALONE see Geehl, Henry Ernest

FOR YOU WITH LOVE see Warren, Elinor
Remick

FOR YOUR DEAR SAKE see Trotere, Henry

FOR YOUR DELIGHT see Hundley, Richard

FORARSVISE see Jersild, Jorgen

FORBES-SMITH, NETTA
There Are Fairies In The Garden
low solo,pno (G maj) CRAMER (F775)
high solo,pno (A flat maj) CRAMER
(F776)

FORBIDDEN MUSIC see Gastaldon,
Stanislas, Musica Proibita

FORBIDDING MOURNING see Finney, Ross
Lee

FORBJUDEN MUSIK see Gastaldon,
Stanislas, Musica Proibita

FORD
O Praise The Lord *sac
solo,pno LILLENAS SM-642: RN $1.00
(F777)

FORD, DONALD
Song Of Homecoming
solo,pno CRAMER   (F778)

Thanks To You
solo,pno CRAMER $.95   (F779)

FORD, THOMAS (ca. 1580-1648)
Ten Airs From Musicke Of Sundrie
Kindes *CCU
solo,pno STAINER 3.1342.7 $5.50
(F780)

FORDELL, ERIK (FRITIOF) (1917-   )
Ack, Herre, Ett Manniskohjarta
"Oi Herra, Ihmisen Sydan" see Fyra
Sanger

Fyra Sanger
solo,pno FAZER F 3675 s.p.
contains: Ack, Herre, Ett
Manniskohjarta, "Oi Herra,
Ihmisen Sydan"; Lat I Skogen,
"Huhuilu Metsassa"; Som Ett
Blommande Mandeltrad, "Niinkuin
Kukkiva Mantelipuu"; Toner,
"Savelet"   (F781)

Huhuilu Metsassa *see Lat I Skogen

Lat I Skogen
"Huhuilu Metsassa" see Fyra Sanger

Niinkuin Kukkiva Mantelipuu *see Som
Ett Blommande Mandeltrad

Oi Herra, Ihmisen Sydan *see Ack,
Herre, Ett Manniskohjarta

Psalm 108 *sac
[Finn] solo,pno FAZER F 5110 s.p.
(F782)
Psalm 128 *sac
[Finn] solo,pno FAZER F 5111 s.p.
(F783)
Psalm 133 *sac
[Finn] solo,pno FAZER F 5112 s.p.
(F784)
Psalm 134 *sac
[Finn] solo,pno FAZER F 5113 s.p.
(F785)

FORDELL, ERIK (FRITIOF) (cont'd.)

Savelet *see Toner

Som Ett Blommande Mandeltrad
"Niinkuin Kukkiva Mantelipuu" see
Fyra Sanger

Toner
"Savelet" see Fyra Sanger

FOREST FIRE see Colechin

FOREST WIND see Stiasny

FORET see Caplet, Andre

FORETS PAISIBLES see Rameau, Jean-
Philippe

FOREVER AND SUNSMELL see Cage, John

FOREVER IS A LONG, LONG TIME see
Jensen, Gordon

FORGAVES see Amadel, A.

FORGAVES UPPA STIGEN see Mehler,
Friedrich

FORGET HER see Korte, Karl

FORGIVE ME LORD, TRY ME ONE MORE TIME
*sac,gospel
solo,pno ABER.GRP. $1.50   (F786)

FORGOTTEN see Cowles, Eugene

FORGOTTEN see Cowles, Walter Ruel

FORGOTTEN ROAD see Chappell, Stanley

FORLEDDE VAN see Kilpinen, Yrio

FORLORN QUEEN see Hughes, Herbert

FORM OF WOOING see Schirmer, Rudolph
[E.]

FORR AGDE JAG INTET see Kilpinen, Yrio

FORSAKEN see Koschat, Thomas, Verlassen
Bin I

FORSAKEN, THE see Dvorak, Antonin, Die-
Verlassens

FORSBERG, ROLAND
Jag Ar Livets Brod
see Verbum Christi

Jag Ar Uppstandelsen Och Livet
see Verbum Christi

Se, Vi Ga Upp Till Jerusalem
see Verbum Christi

Verbum Christi *sac,Bibl
Bar solo,org ERIKS K 242 s.p.
contains: Jag Ar Livets Brod; Jag
Ar Uppstandelsen Och Livet; Se,
Vi Ga Upp Till Jerusalem (F787)

FORSHAW, J. HOWARD
Because I Walk With Thee *sac,Gen
high solo,pno (D flat maj) WILLIS
$.60   (F788)
low solo,pno (B flat maj) WILLIS
$.60   (F789)

FORSMADD
see Karaste Gok, Som Gal Uti Fjarran

FORSTE SKULEDAGEN MIN see Davik,
Ingebrigt

FORSYTH, CECIL (1870-1941)
Tell Me Not Of A Lovely Lass
low solo,pno BELWIN $1.50   (F790)

FORSYTH, JOSEPHINE (1889-1940)
Lord's Prayer, The *sac
med-high solo,pno (D flat maj)
SCHIRM.G $.85   (F791)

FORSYTHIS see Otto, E.

FORT EMMANUEL see Hoogenberk-Rink, D.

FORT TRYON PARK: SEPTEMBER see
Corigliano, John

FORT ZIEHT DER FRUHLING see Kilpinen,
Yrio

FORTH HE CAME see Coleman, Jack

FORTIS see Canino

FORTNER, JACK (1935-   )
SprING *CCU
S solo,fl,sax,bsn,vibra,harp,pno,
vla,vcl,bvl sc JOBERT s.p. (F792)

FORTNER, WOLFGANG (1907-   )
Aria Nach Worten Von T.S. Eliot
Mez/A solo,fl,vla,chamb.orch
SCHOTTS rental   (F793)

Berceuse Royale
[Fr] S solo,vln,strings voc sc
SCHOTTS 4990 s.p., ipr   (F794)

Creation, The
[Eng/Ger] med solo,orch voc sc
SCHOTTS 4612 s.p., ipa   (F795)

Mitte Des Lebens *cant
S solo,fl,bass clar,horn,harp,vln
sc SCHOTTS 6594 s.p., ipa, voc sc
SCHOTTS 6595 s.p.   (F796)

Shakespeare-Songs *CCU
[Ger/Eng] med solo,pno SCHOTTS 1605
s.p.   (F797)

Terzinen
male solo,pno SCHOTTS 5834 s.p.
                                  (F798)

Vier Gesange *CC4U
low solo,pno SCHOTTS 3639 s.p.
                                  (F799)

FORTROSTAN see Thierfelder

FORTUNE, VOILA DONC see Guiraud, Ernest

FORTUNITA, FORTUNITA see Esteve, Pablo

FORTY-EIGHT SONGS ON POEMS BY GOETHE
see Wolf, Hugo

FORTY-FIVE ARIAS FROM OPERAS AND
ORATORIOS, VOL. I see Handel,
George Frideric

FORTY-FIVE ARIAS FROM OPERAS AND
ORATORIOS, VOL. II see Handel,
George Frideric

FORTY-FIVE ARIAS FROM OPERAS AND
ORATORIOS, VOL. III see Handel,
George Frideric

FORTY-FOUR FRENCH FOLK-SONGS AND
VARIANTS FROM CANADA, NORMANDY, AND
BRITTANY *CC44L,folk,Fr
(Tiersot, Julie) [Fr/Eng] solo,pno
SCHIRM.G $2.00   (F800)

FORTY FRENCH SONGS, VOL. I *CC20L
(Kagen, Sergius) [Fr] INTERNAT. high
solo,pno $5.00; med solo,pno $5.00;
low solo,pno $5.00 contains works
by: Berlioz; Franck; Gounod; Saint-
Saens and others   (F801)

FORTY FRENCH SONGS, VOL. II *CC20L
(Kagen, Sergius) [Fr] INTERNAT. high
solo,pno $5.00; med solo,pno $5.00;
low solo,pno $5.00 contains works
by: Bizet; Liszt; Bruneau; D'Indy
and others   (F802)

FORTY SONG (FROM ELIZABETHAN AND
JACOBEAN SONG BOOKS), BK. 1 *CCU
(Fellowes, Edmund H.) $2.50 high
solo,pno STAINER 3.4003.7; low
solo,pno STAINER 3.3999.7 (F803)

FORTY SONGS see Strauss, Richard

FORTY SONGS see Tchaikovsky, Piotr
Ilyitch

FORTY SONGS (FROM ELIZABETHAN AND
JACOBEAN SONG BOOKS), BK. 2 *CCU
(Fellowes, Edmund H.) $2.50 high
solo,pno STAINER 3.4004.7; low
solo,pno STAINER 3.4000.7 (F804)

FORTY SONGS (FROM ELIZABETHAN AND
JACOBEAN SONG BOOKS), BK. 3 *CCU
(Fellowes, Edmund H.) $2.50 high
solo,pno STAINER 3.4005.7; low
solo,pno STAINER 3.4001.7 (F805)

FORTY SONGS (FROM ELIZABETHAN AND
JACOBEAN SONG BOOKS), BK. 4 *CCU
(Fellowes, Edmund H.) $2.50 high
solo,pno STAINER 3.4006.7; low
solo,pno STAINER 3.4002.7 (F806)

FORTY SONGS, VOL. I see Puccini,
Giacomo

FORTY SONGS, VOL. II see Puccini,
Giacomo

FORTY SONGS, VOL. III see Puccini,
Giacomo

FORTY SONGS, VOL. IV see Puccini,
Giacomo

FORTY-THREE SONGS see Debussy, Claude

FORTY-TWO FOLK SONGS see Brahms,
Johannes

FOSS, HUBERT JAMES (1899-1953)
Winter Chant
solo,pno CRAMER   (F807)

FOSS, LUKAS (1922-   )
Song For A Wanderer *see Wanders
Gemutsruhe

Three Airs For Frank O'Hara's Angel
*CC3U
S/countertenor,vcl/vla,hpsd/pno
SALABERT-US $10.00   (F808)

Wanders Gemutsruhe
"Song For A Wanderer" [Ger/Eng]
solo,pno PEER $.95   (F809)

FOSSILE see Pennisi, Francesco

FOSTER, F.
Farewell To Yesterday
solo,pno (D flat maj) BOOSEY $1.50
                            (F810)

FOSTER, FAY (1886-1960)
My Journey's End
low solo,pno (B min) SCHIRM.G $.75
                            (F811)

FOSTER, MYLES BIRKET (1851-1922)
Oh! For A Closer Walk With God *sac
high solo,pno NOVELLO 17.0130.04
s.p.   (F812)
med solo,pno NOVELLO 17.0131.02
s.p.   (F813)

Souls Of The Righteous, The *sac
med solo,pno BELWIN $1.50   (F814)

FOSTER, STEPHEN COLLINS (1826-1864)
Ah! May The Red Rose
solo,pno ALLANS s.p.   (F815)

Album Of Favorite Stephen Foster
Songs *CCU
solo,pno COLE $3.50   (F816)

Album Of Songs *CC20L
(Milligan, H. V.) solo,pno SCHIRM.G
1439 $2.00   (F817)

Barndomshemmet I Kentucky
(Meri) solo,pno FAZER F 2969 s.p.
                            (F818)

Beautiful Dreamer
med solo,pno (D maj) CENTURY 3244
                            (F819)
med solo,pno MARKS $1.50   (F820)
high solo,pno (E flat maj) ALLANS
s.p.   (F821)
low solo,pno (D maj) ALLANS s.p.
                            (F822)
solo,pno ASHLEY $.95   (F823)

Camptown Races
(Nevin) med solo,pno BELWIN $1.25
                            (F824)

Carry Me 'Long
(Nevin) low solo,pno BELWIN $1.25
                            (F825)

Diez Canciones Populares
Norteamericanas *CC10L
(Sammartino) [Eng/Span] solo,pno
RICORDI-ARG BA 8815 s.p.   (F826)

Household Songs *CC150U
solo,pno DA CAPO $12.50   (F827)

I Dream Of Jeanie With The Light
Brown Hair
low solo,pno (E flat maj) BOSTON
$1.50   (F828)
solo,pno ASHDOWN   (F829)
"Jeanie With The Light Brown Hair"
med solo,pno (F maj) CENTURY 3247
                            (F830)
"Jeanie With The Light Brown Hair"
solo,pno (available in 2 keys)
ASHLEY $.95   (F831)
"Jeanie With The Light Brown Hair"
low solo,pno (E flat maj) ALLANS
s.p.   (F832)
"Jeanie With The Light Brown Hair"
med solo,pno (F maj) ALLANS s.p.
                            (F833)
"Jeanie With The Light Brown Hair"
high solo,pno (G maj) ALLANS s.p.
                            (F834)

Jeanie With The Light Brown Hair
*see I Dream Of Jeanie With The
Light Brown Hair

Memories Of Stephen Foster *CCU
solo,pno MARKS $2.00   (F835)

Minstrel Show Songs *CCU
solo,opt cor,pno DA CAPO s.p.
                            (F836)

My Journey's End
high solo,pno ALLANS s.p.   (F837)
low solo,pno ALLANS s.p.   (F838)

Old Black Joe
2 med soli,pno (D maj) CENTURY 1119
                            (F839)

Old Folks At Home
med solo,pno (G maj) CENTURY 509
                            (F840)

FOSTER, STEPHEN COLLINS (cont'd.)

Song Album *sac,CC15U
solo,pno BOSTON $2.50   (F841)

Stephen Foster Song Book *CC40L
solo,pno pap DOVER 23048-1 $3.95,
cloth DOVER 23086-4 $8.95   (F842)

Sweetly She Sleeps My Alice Fair
low solo,pno (A flat maj) ALLANS
s.p.   (F843)
high solo,pno (B flat maj) ALLANS
s.p.   (F844)

Unknown Foster, The *CC7U
(Behrend, J.) solo,pno PRESSER
$2.00   (F845)

Vanha Kotini Kentuckyssa
(Meri) solo,pno FAZER F 2969 s.p.
                            (F846)

FOSTER, WILL
Fear Not, I Am With Thee *sac
low solo,pno (E flat min) SCHIRM.G
$.60   (F847)

FOSTERLANDPSALM see Alfven, Hugo

FOSTERLANDSHYMN see Nordqvist, Gustaf

FOSTERLANDSSANG see Korling

FOTSPAREN I SNON see Hannikainen,
Ilmari

FOU D'AMOUR see Marty, (Eugene) Georges

FOUGSTEDT, NILS-ERIC (1910-   )
Det Var Larksang Och Glans Over Liden
*Op.14,No.2
"Oli Leivosen Helketta Haassa"
solo,pno FAZER W 1816 s.p. see
from Tva Varsangar   (F848)

Laulema *see Visa

Oli Leivosen Helketta Haassa *see
Det Var Larksang Och Glans Over
Liden

Romanssi Elokuvasta (from Katariina
Ja Munkkiniemen Kreivi)
solo,pno FAZER W 1926 s.p. (F849)

Tva Varsangar *see Det Var Larksang
Och Glans Over Liden, "Oli
Leivosen Helketta Haassa", Op.14,
No.2; Visa, "Laulema", Op.14,No.1
                            (F850)

Visa *Op.14,No.1
"Laulema" solo,pno FAZER W 1815
s.p. see from Tva Varsangar
                            (F851)

FOUND see Strauss, Richard, Gefunden

FOUNTAIN, THE see Medtner, Nikolai
Karlovitch

FOUNTAIN, THE see Rachmaninoff, Sergey
Vassilievitch

FOUQUET, V.
Schutterslied
solo,pno ALSBACH s.p.   (F852)

FOUR AMERICAN SONGS see Matesky, T.

FOUR ANCIENT SONGS OF SOLOMON see
Morgenstern, L.

FOUR AND TWENTY SNOWFLAKES see
Stickles, William

FOUR ARIAS see Vivaldi, Antonio

FOUR BIBULOUS SONGS see Webber, Lloyd

FOUR BLAKE SONGS see Sutherland,
Margaret

FOUR BOUTENS SONGS see Weegenhuise,
Johan

FOUR CHAMBER DUETS see Cesti, Marc'
Antonio

FOUR CHILDREN'S SONGS see Franco, Johan

FOUR CHINESE MINIATURES see Kozina,
Marijan, Stiri Kitajske Miniature

FOUR D.H. LAWRENCE SONGS see Rieti,
Vittorio

FOUR DIALOGUES see Rorem, Ned

FOUR DO-IT-YOURSELF PIECES see
Johnston, Ben

FOUR DREAM SONGS see Sallinen, Aulis

FOUR DUCKS ON A POND see Needham,
Alicia Adelaide

FOUR DUETS see Cherubini, Luigi

FOUR DUETS see Brahms, Johannes

FOUR ELEMENTS see Clarke, Henry Leland

FOUR EMILY DICKINSON SONGS see
Persichetti, Vincent

FOUR ENGLISH LYRICS see Dale, Mervyn

FOUR ENGLISH SONGS see Andriessen,
Juriaan

FOUR EPIGRAMS see Becker, Gunther

FOUR FIFTEENTH-CENTURY CHANSONS *CC4U,
15th cent
(Katz) [Fr] opt S solo,3rec sc AMP
$.60   (F853)

FOUR FOLK SONGS see Ravel, Maurice

FOUR FRAGMENTS FROM THE CANTERBURY
TALES see Trimble, Lester

FOUR GERMAN FOLK SONGS see Schoenberg,
Arnold

FOUR GLIMPSES OF NIGHT see Heider,
Werner

FOUR GREEK FOLKSONGS see Seiber, Matyas

FOUR HAIKU SETTINGS see Ator, James

FOUR HAIKU SONGS see Smolanoff, Michael

FOUR HYMNS see Vaughan Williams, Ralph

FOUR IMPRESSIONS see Griffes, Charles
Tomlinson

FOUR INDIAN LOVE LYRICS see Woodforde-
Finden, Amy

FOUR INVENTIONS AND A FUGUE see
Karlins, M. William

FOUR ITALIAN VILLANELLAS *CC4U,It
(Katz) [It] opt S solo,4rec sc AMP
$.60   (F854)

FOUR JAPANESE LYRICS see Josephs,
Wilfred

FOUR JAPANESE SONGS see Sydeman,
William

FOUR LADIES see Diamond, David

FOUR LAST SONGS see Vaughan Williams,
Ralph

FOUR LAST SONGS see Strauss, Richard

FOUR LITTLE JOHNNY CAKES see Lavater

FOUR LITTLE POEMS BY CHILDREN WITH
PROGRESSIVE MUSCULAR DYSTROPHY see
Hayakawa, Masaaki

FOUR LITTLE SONGS see Strauss, Richard

FOUR LOVE SONGS see Beckwith, John

FOUR MEDIEVAL FRENCH SONGS *CC4U
(Selber, Matyas) female solo,3inst
ZERBONI 5972 rental   (F855)

FOUR MORAVIAN DUETS see Dvorak, Antonin

FOUR MOTETS see Smit, Leo

FOUR MOTIVATIONS FOR VOICE see Owens,
Robert

FOUR MOUNTAIN CAROLS see Abbey, H.

FOUR NEGRO SONGS see Carpenter, John
Alden

FOUR NIGHTS see Vaughan Williams, Ralph

FOUR NOCTURNAL SONGS see Butterworth

FOUR NOCTURNES see Kahn, Erich Itor

FOUR NORTH COUNTRY SONGS see
Williamson, Malcolm

FOUR NURSERY RHYMES see Presser,
William

FOUR OLD FRENCH SONGS see Seiber,
Matyas

FOUR ORCHESTRAL SONGS see Maganini,
Quinto

FOUR ORCHESTRAL SONGS see Kohs, Ellis
B.

FOUR-PART SONGS see Haydn, (Franz)
Joseph

FOUR PIECES ON MEDIEVAL GERMAN POEMS
see Kahn, Erich Itor

FOUR POEMS BY EMILY DICKINSON see
Blank, Allan

FOUR POEMS BY HAMILTON WILLIAMS see
Franco, Johan

FOUR POEMS OF GUILLAUME APOLLINAIRE see
Poulenc, Francis

FOUR POEMS OF JAMES STEPHENS see Adler,
Samuel

FOUR POEMS OF RENE CHALUPT see Rivier,
Jean

FOUR POEMS OF RONSARD AND MAROT see
Rivier, Jean

FOUR POEMS OF ST. TERESA OF AVILA see
Berkeley, Lennox

FOUR POEMS OF TENNYSON see Rorem, Ned

FOUR POEMS OF THOMAS see Holloway,
Robin

FOUR PRELUDES see Swanson, Howard

FOUR PSALMS see Fromm, Herbert

FOUR ROMANCES, OP. 46; FOUR MONOLOGUES,
OP. 91 see Shostakovich, Dmitri

FOUR RUSSIAN POEMS see Fiala, George

FOUR SACRED SONGS see Ashley, Derick

FOUR SACRED SONGS see Purcell, Henry

FOUR SACRED SONGS see Knab, Armin

FOUR SACRED SONGS see Pisk, Paul
Amadeus

FOUR SCENES FOR SOPRANO AND BRASS
QUINTET see Plog

FOUR SCOTTISH SONGS see Rankl

FOUR SERBIAN SONGS see Dvorak, Antonin

FOUR SERIOUS SONGS, GYPSY SONGS AND
GERMAN FOLKSONGS see Brahms,
Johannes

FOUR SETTINGS see Dinerstein, N.

FOUR SEVENTH CENTURY POEMS see Bunge,
Sas

FOUR SHAKESPEARE SONGS see Moeran,
Ernest J.

FOUR SHAKESPEARE SONGS see Griesbach,
Karl-Rudi

FOUR SHAKESPEARE SONGS SET 1 see
Montgomery, Bruce

FOUR SHAKESPEARE SONGS SET 2 see
Montgomery, Bruce

FOUR SHORT SOLOS see Jones, Marjorie

FOUR SONGS see Fine, Vivian

FOUR SONGS see Epstein, [David M.]

FOUR SONGS see Donovan, Richard [Frank]

FOUR SONGS see Sanderson, Wilfred

FOUR SONGS see Berger, Jean

FOUR SONGS see Orthel, Leon

FOUR SONGS see Gretchaninov, Alexander
Tikhonovitch

FOUR SONGS see Ives, Charles

FOUR SONGS see Weber, B.

FOUR SONGS see Weisgall, Hugo

FOUR SONGS see Albeniz, Isaac

FOUR SONGS see Honegger, Arthur

FOUR SONGS see Mompou, Federico

FOUR SONGS see Backer-Grondahl, Agathe
Ursula

FOUR SONGS see Dvorak, Antonin

FOUR SONGS see Bassett, Leslie

FOUR SONGS see Brunswick, Mark

FOUR SONGS see Mills, Charles

FOUR SONGS see Strauss, Richard

FOUR SONGS see Dvorak, Antonin

FOUR SONGS see Mayer, Milan

FOUR SONGS see Goosens, Eugene

FOUR SONGS see Rimsky-Korsakov, Nikolai

FOUR SONGS see Baird, Tadeusz

FOUR SONGS see Holst, Gustav

FOUR SONGS see Stravinsky, Igor

FOUR SONGS see Saul, George Brandon

FOUR SONGS see David, Gyula

FOUR SONGS see Hajdu, Mihaly

FOUR SONGS see Lorand, Istvan

FOUR SONGS see Kadosa, [Paul]

FOUR SONGS ABOUT LOVE see Lessard, John
Ayres

FOUR SONGS AFTER HOLDERLIN see Horvath,
Josef Maria

FOUR SONGS AFTER HOPKINS see Krenek,
Ernst

FOUR SONGS FOR A YOUNG LADY see Clarke,
Henry Leland

FOUR SONGS FOR BARITONE see Mechem,
Kirke

FOUR SONGS FOR MEDIUM VOICE AND
VIBRAPHONE see Steiner, Gitta

FOUR SONGS FOR SOPRANO see Sifler, Paul
J.

FOUR SONGS FROM BEN JOHNSON'S "VOLPONE"
see Beckwith, John

FOUR SONGS FROM HERRICK'S 'HESPERIDES'
Bar solo,pno ELKIN 27.2198.08 s.p.
contains: Impatient Lover, The; To
Electra; Upon Julia's Clothes;
Upon The Loss Of His Mistress
(F856)

FOUR SONGS FROM HESPERIDES see Bush,
Geoffrey

FOUR SONGS I see Yannatos, James

FOUR SONGS II see Yannatos, James

FOUR SONGS OF A SORROWING FRANCE see
Auric, Georges

FOUR SONGS OF DEVOTION see Kosakoff,
Reuven

FOUR SONGS OF EILAT see Avidom,
Menachem

FOUR SONGS OF THE HILL see Ronald, Sir
Landon

FOUR SONGS ON POEMS BY ESZRA POUND see
Heppener, Robert

FOUR SONGS ON POEMS OF JAMES JOYCE see
Del Tredici, David

FOUR SONGS ON THE POEMS BY NELLY SACHS
see Kadosa, [Paul]

FOUR SONGS TO E.E. CUMMINGS see
Feldman, Morton

FOUR SONGS TO THE POEMS OF THOMAS
CAMPION see Thomson, Virgil

FOUR SONGS (WILLIAM BLAKE) see
Dukelsky, Vladimir

FOUR SONNETS see Berger, Jean

FOUR SONNETS OF LOUIZE LABE see
Roetscher, Konrad

FOUR SPIRITUAL LAWS, THE see Johnson,
Paul

FOUR STOCKHOLM POEMS see Stenhammar,
Wilhelm

FOUR TRIFLES see Flothius, Marius

FOUR UNCLES see Diamond, David

FOURDRAIN, FELIX (1880-1923)
Aux Portres De Seville
solo,pno RICORDI-FR R 1263 s.p.
(F857)

Chanson Norvegienne
solo,pno RICORDI-FR R 134 s.p.
(F858)
S/T solo,pno BELWIN $1.50   (F859)

FOURDRAIN, FELIX (cont'd.)

Clos Ta Paupiere
solo,pno ENOCH s.p.   (F860)

La Belle Au Bois Dormant
solo,pno RICORDI-FR R 23 s.p.   (F861)

Le Romarin
solo,pno (available in 2 keys)
ENOCH s.p.   (F862)

L'isba En Flammes
solo,pno RICORDI-FR R 1262 s.p.   (F863)

Ma Maison
solo,pno RICORDI-FR R 925 s.p.   (F864)

Mon Jardin
solo,pno RICORDI-FR R 924 s.p.   (F865)

Petite Flamme
solo,pno (available in 2 keys)
ENOCH s.p.   (F866)

Vieille Chanson Du Jeune Temps
solo,pno ENOCH s.p.   (F867)

FOURNIER, P.
Nocturne A Deux Voix
MezT soli,pno DURAND s.p.   (F868)

FOURTEEN CHRISTMAS SONGS FOR SOPRANO,
RECORDER, AND OTHER INSTRUMENTS see
Poser, Hans

FOURTEEN SACRED SONGS see Wolf, Hugo

FOURTEEN SONGS see Ives, Charles

FOWLER
Wasted Years *sac
solo,pno BENSON S8332-S $1.00
                                       (F869)
FOX
Amazing Grace, How Can It Be? *sac
solo,pno BENSON S5115-R $1.00
                                       (F870)
Gone *sac
solo,pno BENSON S5587-S $1.00
                                       (F871)
Hills Of Home, The
high solo,pno (C min) FISCHER,C
V 900   (F872)
med-high solo,pno (A min) FISCHER,C
V 901   (F873)
med-low solo,pno (G min) FISCHER,C
V 959   (F874)
low solo,pno (F min) FISCHER,C
V 914   (F875)
high solo,pno (C min) ALLANS s.p.
                                       (F876)
low solo,pno (F min) ALLANS s.p.
                                       (F877)
med solo,pno (G min) ALLANS s.p.
                                       (F878)
med-high solo,pno (A min) ALLANS
s.p.   (F879)

I'll Tell The World *sac
solo,pno BENSON S6284-R $1.00
                                       (F880)
What Love *sac
solo,pno LILLENAS SM-945: SN $1.00
                                       (F881)
FOX, THE see Heseltine, Philip

FOX, ALBERT
Just To Be Near You
solo,pno (B flat maj) LEONARD-ENG
                                       (F882)
2 soli,pno LEONARD-ENG   (F883)

FOX, BAYNARD
Christmas Spirit, The
med solo,pno FOX $1.00   (F884)

Closer To Jesus *sac
med solo,pno FOX $1.00   (F885)

I Have A Friend
solo,pno FOX $1.00   (F886)

I Wonder Why He Should Love
med solo,pno FOX $1.00   (F887)

I'll Tell The World That I'm A
Christian
med solo,pno FOX $1.00   (F888)

Isn't It A Joy To Be A Christian?
solo,pno FOX $1.00   (F889)

Like A Thief In The Night
solo,pno GENTRY $1.00   (F890)

Well Done Thou Good And Faithful
Servant
med solo,pno FOX $1.00   (F891)

When God Steps In
solo,pno GENTRY $1.00   (F892)

With Love
solo,pno GENTRY $1.00   (F893)

FOX, CHARLOTTE MILLIGAN (1860-1916)
By The Short Cut To The Rosses
solo,pno (E flat maj) BOOSEY $1.50
                                       (F894)
FOX, ELDRIDGE
Gone *sac
solo,pno WORD S-362   (F895)

FOX, G.
April O'Clock
solo,pno BERANDOL BER 1309 $1.50
                                       (F896)
Love's Caution
solo,pno BERANDOL BER 1310 $1.50
                                       (F897)
FOX, GEORGE
Carpenter, The *sac
med solo,pno BELWIN $1.50   (F898)

Lord, It Belongs Not To My Care *sac
med solo,pno (C maj) WATERLOO $.75
                                       (F899)
FOX, J.B.
Tragic Tale, A
high solo,pno PRESSER $.75 (F900)

FOX, OSCAR
My Heart Is A Silent Violin
solo,pno (G maj) PATERSON s.p.
                                       (F901)
solo,pno (B flat maj) PATERSON s.p.
                                       (F902)
solo,pno (D maj) PATERSON s.p.
                                       (F903)
FOX-TROT DE LAS "GIGLETTES" see Lehar,
Franz

FOXGLOVES see Head, Michael (Dewar)

FRA LE SPICHE see Recli, Giulia

FRA MONTE PINCIO see Grieg, Edvard
Hagerup

FRA POCO A ME RICOVERO see Donizetti,
Gaetano

FRAG ICH MEIN BEKLOMMEN HERZ see
Rossini, Gioacchino

FRAGE see Mana-Zucca, Mme.

FRAGE UND ANTWORT see Marx, Joseph

FRAGEROLLE, G.
C'est Elle
solo,acap ENOCH s.p.   (F904)
solo,pno ENOCH s.p.   (F905)

Chanson Rose
solo,acap ENOCH s.p.   (F906)
solo,pno ENOCH s.p.   (F907)

Clairs De Lune
solo,pno ENOCH s.p.   (F908)

Cleopatre (from Le Spinx)
solo,pno ENOCH s.p.   (F909)
solo,pno ENOCH s.p. see from Le
Sphinx   (F910)

Hymne A L'amour
solo,pno ENOCH s.p.   (F911)
solo,acap ENOCH s.p.   (F912)

Jeanne D'Arc
solo,pno ENOCH s.p.   (F913)

La Canadienne
solo,pno ENOCH s.p.   (F914)

La Chanson Des Larmes
solo,pno ENOCH s.p.   (F915)
solo,acap ENOCH s.p.   (F916)

La Chasse Fantastique
solo,pno ENOCH s.p.   (F917)

La Glu
solo,pno ENOCH s.p.   (F918)
solo,acap ENOCH s.p.   (F919)

La Marche A L'Etoile *ora
solo,pno ENOCH s.p.   (F920)

La Marche Au Soleil
solo,pno ENOCH s.p.   (F921)

La Vierge (from Le Spinx)
solo,pno ENOCH s.p.   (F922)
solo,pno ENOCH s.p. see from Le
Sphinx   (F923)

L'Amour Mouille
solo,acap ENOCH s.p.   (F924)
solo,pno ENOCH s.p.   (F925)

Le Capiston Marchand
solo,pno ENOCH s.p.   (F926)
solo,acap ENOCH s.p.   (F927)

Le Chat Botte
solo,pno (available in 2 keys)
ENOCH s.p.   (F928)

FRAGEROLLE, G. (cont'd.)

Le Droit Du Seigneur
solo,pno ENOCH s.p.   (F929)
solo,acap ENOCH s.p.   (F930)

Le Gas Du Moustoir
solo,pno ENOCH s.p.   (F931)
solo,acap ENOCH s.p.   (F932)

Le Juif Errant
solo,pno ENOCH s.p.   (F933)

Le Page Lancelot
solo,pno ENOCH s.p.   (F934)
solo,acap ENOCH s.p.   (F935)

Le Retour De La Croisade
solo,pno ENOCH s.p.   (F936)
solo,acap ENOCH s.p.   (F937)

Le Reve De Joel
solo,pno ENOCH s.p.   (F938)

Le Seigneur De Bondy
solo,pno ENOCH s.p.   (F939)
solo,acap ENOCH s.p.   (F940)

Le Sphinx
solo,pno ENOCH s.p.   (F941)

Le Sphinx *see Cleopatre; La Vierge;
Moise   (F942)

Le Tonnelier
solo,pno ENOCH s.p.   (F943)
solo,acap ENOCH s.p.   (F944)

Les Alpins
solo,acap ENOCH s.p.   (F945)
solo,pno ENOCH s.p.   (F946)

Les Nuits Consolent
solo,pno ENOCH s.p.   (F947)
solo,acap ENOCH s.p.   (F948)

Les Rosiers Blancs
2 soli,pno ENOCH s.p. voc sc, solo
pt   (F949)

Les Vieux Papillons
solo,pno (available in 2 keys)
ENOCH s.p.   (F950)
solo,acap (available in 2 keys)
ENOCH s.p.   (F951)

Lourdes *ora
solo,pno ENOCH s.p.   (F952)

L'Ouverture De La Chasse
solo,pno ENOCH s.p.   (F953)
solo,acap ENOCH s.p.   (F954)

Mariage Bleu
solo,pno ENOCH s.p.   (F955)
solo,acap ENOCH s.p.   (F956)

Moise (from Le Spinx)
solo,pno ENOCH s.p.   (F957)
solo,pno ENOCH s.p. see from Le
Sphinx   (F958)

Nounou
solo,pno ENOCH s.p.   (F959)
solo,acap ENOCH s.p.   (F960)

Par Saint-Jacques
solo,pno ENOCH s.p.   (F961)
solo,acap ENOCH s.p.   (F962)

FRAGGI, H.
Allah Mounaye
see Evocations De Guinee

Evocations De Guinee
solo,orch cmplt ed ENOCH s.p.
contains: Allah Mounaye; Guinea;
O Mami Ouama   (F963)

Guinea
see Evocations De Guinee

O Mami Ouama
see Evocations De Guinee

FRAGILITE see Chaminade, Cecile

FRAGMENT see Krenek, Ernst

FRAGMENT FROM CALAMUS see Harrison, Lou

FRAGMENT: ODE TO THE WEST WIND see
King, Harold C.

FRAGMENT OF HEAVEN, A see Spencer, J.

FRAGMENT OF ORESTES see Ruyneman,
Daniel

FRAGMENT "SYBILLE" see Dohl, Friedhelm

FRAGMENTO II see Raxach, Enrique

FRAGMENTS D'OPERAS, VOLS. I & II see
Wagner, Richard

FRAGMENTS FROM THE SONG OF SONGS see
   Sifler, Paul J.

FRALIX
   They Tore The Old Country Church Down
     *sac
     solo,pno BENSON S8136-S $1.00
                        (F964)

FRAMMENTI LIRICI see Bossi, Renzo

FRAMMENTO DI BALLATA see Recli, Giulia

FRAN GRANDER OCH GLANTOR see Lagerheim-
   Romare, Margit

FRAN VAR TILL HOST see Runback, Albert

FRANCAIX, JEAN (1912-   )
   A Une Demoiselle Malade
     see Trois Epigrammes

   Belaud, Mon Petit Chat Gris
     see Trois Epigrammes

   Chanson
     see Deux Chansons

   Cinq Chansons *CC5U
     [Fr/Ger] med solo,pno ESCHIG $3.75
                        (F965)

   Deploration De Tonton *cant
     Mez solo,strings (humorous)
     TRANSAT. s.p.   (F966)

   Deux Chansons
     [Fr] solo,gtr SCHOTTS 4189 s.p.
      contains: Chanson; Priere Du Soir
                        (F967)
   La Chatte Blanche
     T solo,orch voc sc TRANSAT. s.p.
                        (F968)
   La Grenouille Qui Veut Se Faire Aussi
     Grosse Que Le Boeuf
     S/T solo,pno TRANSAT. s.p.   (F969)

   L'Adolescence Clementine *CC5U
     [Fr] med solo,pno ESCHIG $4.50
                        (F970)

   Le Coq Et Le Renard
     solo,pno TRANSAT. s.p.   (F971)

   Les Inestimables Chroniques Du Bon
     Geant Gargantua
     narrator,strings solo pt TRANSAT.
     s.p.   (F972)

   Levez Ces Couvre-Chefs Plus Haut
     see Trois Epigrammes

   Priere Du Soir
     see Deux Chansons

   Trois Epigrammes
     solo,pno cmplt ed TRANSAT. s.p.
      contains: A Une Demoiselle
      Malade; Belaud, Mon Petit Chat
      Gris; Levez Ces Couvre-Chefs
      Plus Haut   (F973)

FRANCE! C'EST POUR TOI see Delabre,
   L.G.

FRANCE, WILLIAM E.
   Drop, Drop, Slow Tears *sac
     solo,pno BERANDOL BER 1286 $1.50
                        (F974)
   Wedding Hymn *Marriage
     solo,pno THOMP.G   (F975)

FRANCESCA DA RIMINI see Blacher, Boris

FRANCESCHINI, SANDRO
   Canto Olimpico
     [It/Fr/Ger/Eng] solo,pno BERBEN 496
     s.p.   (F976)

FRANCHE-COMTE *Fr
   (Canteloube, J.) solo,acap DURAND
     s.p. see also Anthologie Des Chants
     Populaires Francais Tome III (F977)

FRANCHE RIBAUDE see Varney, Pierre
   Joseph Alphonse

FRANCISCI, ONDREJ
   Nova Piesen Znie *CCU
     boy solo/girl solo,pno
     SLOV.HUD.FOND s.p.   (F978)

FRANCK, CESAR (1822-1890)
   Aux Petits Enfants
     SA soli,pno ENOCH s.p. voc sc, solo
     pt see also Six Duos   (F979)
     (Mariotte, A.) solo,pno (available
     in 2 keys) ENOCH s.p. see from
     Quatre Melodies   (F980)
     (Mariotte, A.) solo,acap (available
     in 2 keys) ENOCH s.p. see from
     Quatre Melodies   (F981)

   Ave Maria *sac,Xmas
     [Lat] low solo,pno (E min) ASHDOWN
                        (F982)
     [Lat] med solo,pno/org SCHOTT-FRER
     SCH112 s.p.   (F983)
     [Lat] high solo,pno/org SCHOTT-FRER

FRANCK, CESAR (cont'd.)
     SCH111 s.p.   (F984)
     [Lat] solo,pno/org (available in 2
     keys) ENOCH s.p.   (F985)
     [Lat] high solo,pno (G min) ASHDOWN
                        (F986)
     solo,pno (available in 2 keys)
     ENOCH s.p. see also Melodies
                        (F987)
   Chant De Mariage *see Panis
     Angelicus

   Come, Gentle Night *see O Fraiche
     Nuit

   Deuxieme Air De L'Archange (from
     Redemption) sac
     Mez solo,pno/org HEUGEL s.p. (F988)

   La Chanson Du Vannier
     SA soli,pno ENOCH s.p. voc sc, solo
     pt see also Six Duos   (F989)

   La Procession
     solo,orch LEDUC s.p.   (F990)
     solo,vln,vcl (D maj) LEDUC s.p.
                        (F991)
     solo,pno (D maj) ASHDOWN   (F992)

   La Vase Brise
     solo,acap solo pt ENOCH s.p. (F993)

   La Vierge A La Creche *sac
     [Fr] solo,pno (available in 2 keys)
     ENOCH   (F994)
     SA soli,pno ENOCH s.p. voc sc, solo
     pt see also Six Duos   (F995)
     "Mary At The Cradle" solo,pno (E
     min) ASHDOWN $1.50   (F996)
     (Mariotte, A.) solo,pno (available
     in 2 keys) ENOCH s.p. see from
     Quatre Melodies   (F997)
     (Mariotte, A.) solo,acap (available
     in 2 keys) ENOCH s.p. see from
     Quatre Melodies   (F998)

   L'Ange Garden *sac
     [Fr] solo,pno (avilable in 2 keys)
     ENOCH   (F999)
     SA soli,pno ENOCH s.p. see also Six
     Duos   (F1000)
     (Mariotte, A.) solo,acap (available
     in 2 keys) ENOCH s.p. see from
     Quatre Melodies   (F1001)
     (Mariotte, A.) solo,pno (available
     in 2 keys) ENOCH s.p. see from
     Quatre Melodies   (F1002)

   Le Mariage Des Roses
     solo,acap solo pt ENOCH s.p. (F1003)

   Le Marriage Des Roses
     solo,orch ENOCH rental   (F1004)
     solo,pno (available in 4 keys)
     ENOCH s.p. see also Melodies
                       (F1005)
     "Wooing Of The Rose, The" low solo,
     pno (A maj) ASHDOWN   (F1006)
     "Wooing Of The Rose, The" high
     solo,pno (B maj) ASHDOWN   (F1007)

   Le Vase Brise
     solo,pno (available in 2 keys)
     ENOCH s.p. see also Melodies
                       (F1008)

   Les Cloches Du Soir
     solo,pno/inst LEDUC s.p.   (F1009)

   Les Danses De Lormont
     SA soli,pno ENOCH s.p. voc sc, solo
     pt see also Six Duos   (F1010)
     (Mariotte, A.) solo,acap (available
     in 2 keys) ENOCH s.p. see from
     Quatre Melodies   (F1011)
     (Mariotte, A.) solo,pno (available
     in 2 keys) ENOCH s.p. see from
     Quatre Melodies   (F1012)

   Lied
     solo,pno ENOCH s.p. see also
     Melodies   (F1013)

   Mary At The Cradle *see La Vierge A
     La Creche

   Melodies *CC11L
     solo,pno cmplt ed ENOCH s.p.
     available in 2 keys
     see also: Ave Maria; Le Marriage
     Des Roses; Le Vase Brise; Lied;
     Nocturne; Roses Et Papillons;
     S'il Est Un Charmant Gazon   (F1014)

   Nocturne
     solo,acap solo pt ENOCH s.p.
                        (F1015)
     solo,orch (E flat min) ENOCH s.p.
     see also Melodies   (F1016)
     solo,pno (available in 2 keys)
     ENOCH s.p. see also Melodies (F1017)

   Nocturne *see O Fraiche Nuit

FRANCK, CESAR (cont'd.)
   O Fraiche Nuit
     "Come, Gentle Night" solo,pno (D
     maj) ASHDOWN   (F1018)
     "Nocturne" solo,orch (E flat min)
     sc ENOCH s.p., ipa   (F1019)

   O Lord Most Holy *see Panis
     Angelicus

   Panis Angelicus (from Missa Solemne)
     sac,Marriage
     Mez solo,pno (A maj) LIENAU HOS 192
     s.p.   (F1020)
     [Lat] solo,org/pno (F maj) RICORDI-
     ARG BA 9143 s.p.   (F1021)
     [Lat] solo,pno (A maj) RICORDI-ARG
     BA 9162 s.p.   (F1022)
     [Lat] S/T solo,pno RICORDI-ENG
     127663 s.p.   (F1023)
     [Lat] Mez/Bar solo,pno RICORDI-ENG
     127664 s.p.   (F1024)
     S/T solo,pno FORLIVESI 11263 s.p.
                       (F1025)
     low solo,pno,opt vln&vcl (F maj)
     ASHDOWN $1.75, ipr   (F1026)
     med solo,pno,opt vln&vcl (G maj)
     ASHDOWN $1.75, ipr   (F1027)
     med-high solo,pno,opt vln&vcl (A
     maj) ASHDOWN $1.75, ipr   (F1028)
     high solo,pno,opt vln&vcl (B maj)
     ASHDOWN $1.75, ipr   (F1029)
     Mez/Bar solo,pno FORLIVESI 11264
     s.p.   (F1030)
     [Lat] high solo,pno/org (B maj)
     SCHOTT-FRER SCH113 s.p.   (F1031)
     [Lat] low solo,pno/org (F maj)
     SCHOTT-FRER SCH116 s.p.   (F1032)
     [Lat] high solo,pno/org (A maj)
     SCHOTT-FRER SCH114 s.p.   (F1033)
     [Lat] med solo,pno/org (G maj)
     SCHOTT-FRER SCH115 s.p.   (F1034)
     low solo,pno/org (easy) GIA G-1723
     $1.00   (F1035)
     med solo,pno/org (easy) GIA G-1724
     $1.00   (F1036)
     high solo,pno/org (easy) GIA G-1725
     $1.00   (F1037)
     "Chant De Mariage" solo,pno HENN
     534 s.p.   (F1038)
     "O Lord Most Holy" [Eng/Lat] med
     solo,pno (G maj) SCHIRM.G $.85
                       (F1039)
     "O Lord Most Holy" [Eng/Lat] low
     solo,pno (F maj) SCHIRM.G $.85
                       (F1040)
     "O Lord Most Holy" [Eng/Lat] high
     solo,pno (A maj) SCHIRM.G $.85
                       (F1041)
     "O Lord Most Holy" [Eng/Lat] med
     solo,pno (F maj) FISCHER,C S 5686
                       (F1042)
     "O Lord Most Holy" [Eng/Lat] high
     solo,pno (A flat maj) FISCHER,C
     S 5685   (F1043)
     "O Lord Most Holy" [Eng/Lat] low
     solo,pno (D flat maj) FISCHER,C
     S 5687   (F1044)
     "O Lord Most Holy" solo,pno
     (available in 3 keys) ASHLEY $.95
                       (F1045)
     "O Lord Most Holy" low solo&low
     solo,pno (G maj) ALLANS s.p.
                       (F1046)
     "O Lord Most Holy" low solo,pno (F
     maj) ALLANS s.p.   (F1047)
     "O Lord Most Holy" med solo,pno (G
     maj) ALLANS s.p.   (F1048)
     "O Lord Most Holy" high solo,pno (A
     maj) ALLANS s.p.   (F1049)
     "O Lord Most Holy" low solo,org (F
     maj) BOSTON $1.50   (F1050)
     "O Lord Most Holy" med-high solo,
     vcl&harp/vln&harp/vcl&pno/vln&pno
     (G maj) BOSTON $1.50   (F1051)
     "O Lord Most Holy" high solo&low
     solo,pno BOSTON $1.75   (F1052)
     "O Lord Most Holy" high solo,org (A
     maj) BOSTON $1.50   (F1053)
     "O Lord Most Holy" med-high solo,
     org (G maj) BOSTON $1.50   (F1054)
     (Hill, Harry) "O Lord Most Holy"
     low solo,pno (F maj) WATERLOO
     $.90   (F1055)
     (Hill, Harry) "O Lord Most Holy"
     med solo,pno (G maj) WATERLOO
     $.90   (F1056)
     (Hill, Harry) "O Lord Most Holy"
     high solo,pno (A maj) WATERLOO
     $.90   (F1057)

   Premier Air De L'Archange (from
     Redemption) sac
     Mez solo,pno/org HEUGEL s.p.
                        (F1058)

   Procession
     med-high solo,pno (D maj) BOSTON
     $1.50   (F1059)

   Quatre Melodies *see Aux Petits
     Enfants; La Vierge A La Creche;
     L'Ange Garden; Les Danses De
     Lormont   (F1060)

FRANCK, CESAR (cont'd.)

Roses Et Papillons
    solo,acap solo pt ENOCH s.p.
                                    (F1061)
    solo,orch ENOCH rental
                                    (F1062)
    solo,pno (available in 2 keys)
    ENOCH s.p. see also Melodies
                                    (F1063)

S'il Est Un Charmant Gazon
    solo,acap solo pt ENOCH s.p.
                                    (F1064)
    solo,orch ENOCH rental
                                    (F1065)
    solo,pno (available in 2 keys)
    ENOCH s.p. see also Melodies
                                    (F1066)

Six Duos
    SA soli,pno cmplt ed ENOCH s.p.
    contains & see also: Aux Petits
    Enfants; La Chanson Du Vannier;
    La Vierge A La Creche; L'Ange
    Garden; Les Danses De Lormont;
    Soleil   (F1067)

Six Songs *sac,CC6U
    BOSTON high solo,pno $2.50; low
    solo,pno $2.50   (F1068)

Soleil
    SA soli,pno ENOCH s.p. voc sc, solo
    pt see also Six Duos   (F1069)

Wooing Of The Rose, The *see Le
    Marriage Des Roses

FRANCO, JOHAN (1908-   )
Ariel's Four Songs From "The Tempest"
    *CC4U
    high solo,gtr/marimba sc
    AM.COMP.AL. $1.10   (F1070)

Autumn And The Raindrop's Adventure
    med solo,pno AM.COMP.AL. $1.10 (F1071)

Awake, My Soul
    med solo,pno/org AM.COMP.AL. $.82
                                    (F1072)

Christmas Carol *Xmas,carol
    med solo,pno AM.COMP.AL. $1.37 (F1073)

Clodagh
    Mez solo,pno AM.COMP.AL. $3.30
                                    (F1074)
    Mez solo,fl,2ob,2clar,2bsn,2horn,
    2trp,2trom,timp,harp,perc,strings
    sc AM.COMP.AL. $8.25   (F1075)

Foot Note
    med solo,pno AM.COMP.AL. $1.37 see
    also Three Poems By Hamilton
    Williams   (F1076)

Four Children's Songs *CC4U
    3 soli,acap sc AM.COMP.AL. $1.37
                                    (F1077)

Four Poems By Hamilton Williams
    med solo,pno cmplt ed AM.COMP.AL.
    $3.85
    contains & see also: His Low
    Door; Husheen, Little Ones,
    Husho; Mary, What Do You See In
    The Sky?; There's A Garden In
    Antrim Is Lonely Tonight
                                    (F1078)

Green Rushes
    med solo,pno AM.COMP.AL. $3.30 see
    also Three Poems By Hamilton
    Williams   (F1079)

His Low Door
    med solo,pno AM.COMP.AL. $1.37 see
    also Four Poems By Hamilton
    Williams   (F1080)

Husheen, Little Ones, Husho
    med solo,pno AM.COMP.AL. $1.37 see
    also Four Poems By Hamilton
    Williams   (F1081)

I Want To Play Strom
    med solo,pno AM.COMP.AL. $.27   (F1082)

Introduction And The Virgin Queen's
    Dream Monologue
    S solo,pno AM.COMP.AL. $.82   (F1083)
    S solo,2fl,2ob,2clar,3bsn,2horn,
    3trp,4trom,xylo,perc,strings
    AM.COMP.AL. sc $13.20, voc sc
    $5.50   (F1084)

Invocation Of Light
    med solo,pno AM.COMP.AL. $1.37 (F1085)

Leaves' Secret, The
    med solo,pno AM.COMP.AL. $.27
                                    (F1086)

Locksley Hall
    med solo,pno AM.COMP.AL. $1.37 (F1087)

Lord Cometh, The
    high solo,English horn,clar,bass
    clar sc AM.COMP.AL. $1.37, ipa
                                    (F1088)

Lord's Prayer, The *sac
    S solo,pno AM.COMP.AL. $.82 (F1089)

FRANCO, JOHAN (cont'd.)

Marching Song
    high solo,pno AM.COMP.AL. $.82
                                    (F1090)

Mary, What Do You See In The Sky?
    med solo,pno AM.COMP.AL. $.82 see
    also Four Poems By Hamilton
    Williams   (F1091)

Music *see Muziek   (F1092)

Music
    med solo,pno AM.COMP.AL. $1.37
                                    (F1093)

Muziek
    med solo,pno sc AM.COMP.AL. $1.37
    see from Music   (F1094)

My New Day Is Dawning *Psalm
    med solo,pno AM.COMP.AL. $3.30
                                    (F1095)

Night Of The Full Moon, The
    low solo,pno AM.COMP.AL. $.82
                                    (F1096)

Prayer At The Portal
    med solo,pno AM.COMP.AL. $.82
                                    (F1097)

Prayer For Realization, A
    med solo,pno AM.COMP.AL. $1.37
                                    (F1098)

Professional Toast
    med solo,pno AM.COMP.AL. $.27
                                    (F1099)

Prophecy From "Locksley Hall"
    Mez solo,fl,ob,clar,bsn,horn,trp,
    strings AM.COMP.AL.   (F1100)

Sayings Of The Word *song cycle
    Mez solo,pno AM.COMP.AL. $3.85
                                    (F1101)

Seven Poems Under A Tree *CC7U
    A solo,pno AM.COMP.AL. $3.30
                                    (F1102)

Song Of Life, The
    high solo,pno AM.COMP.AL. $2.75
                                    (F1103)
    S solo,clar,English horn,bass clar
    sc AM.COMP.AL. $2.75, ipa (F1104)
    T solo,clar,English horn,bass clar
    sc AM.COMP.AL. $2.75, ipa (F1105)

Song To Be Sung In A June Twilight
    med solo,pno AM.COMP.AL. $.82 see
    also Three Poems By Hamilton
    Williams   (F1106)

Songs Of The Spirit
    AM.COMP.AL. high solo,pno

Sonnet
    S solo,4strings sc AM.COMP.AL.
    $4.40, ipa   (F1107)

Spirit Quickeneth, The
    Mez solo,pno AM.COMP.AL. $1.37
                                    (F1108)

Symphony No. 4
    T solo,3fl,3ob,3clar,3bsn,2horn,
    2trp,3trom,cel,strings
    AM.COMP.AL. sc $19.80, voc sc
    $5.50   (F1109)

Tempest, The
    S solo,hpsd,cel,marimba,perc,
    electronic tape sc AM.COMP.AL.
    $6.60   (F1110)

There's A Garden In Antrim Is Lonely
    Tonight
    med solo,pno AM.COMP.AL. $1.37 see
    also Four Poems By Hamilton
    Williams   (F1111)

Three Poems By Hamilton Williams
    med solo,pno cmplt ed AM.COMP.AL.
    $3.85
    contains & see also: Foot Note;
    Green Rushes; Song To Be Sung
    In A June Twilight   (F1112)

Till The Old Cat Dies
    med solo,pno AM.COMP.AL. $.55
                                    (F1113)

Twelve Words
    Bar solo,pno AM.COMP.AL. $5.50
                                    (F1114)
    A solo,pno AM.COMP.AL. $5.50
                                    (F1115)

Two Duets *CC2U
    BarBar/MezMez soli,fl sc
    AM.COMP.AL. $1.10   (F1116)

Two Shakespeare Sonnets *CC2U
    AM.COMP.AL. A/Bar solo,pno $3.30;
    S/T solo,pno $3.85   (F1117)

Under The Shade Of The Sycamore Tree
    Mez solo,pno AM.COMP.AL. $1.37
                                    (F1118)
    A solo,pno AM.COMP.AL. $1.37
                                    (F1119)

Vier Liederen *CC4U
    solo,pno BROEKMANS 201 s.p. (F1120)

FRANCO, JOHAN (cont'd.)

When Friendly Death Shall Grasp My
    Hand
    Bar solo,pno AM.COMP.AL. $1.37
                                    (F1121)

When I Was Born *Chin
    S solo,pno AM.COMP.AL. $1.37
                                    (F1122)
    Bar solo,pno AM.COMP.AL. $1.37
                                    (F1123)

FRANCO MENDES, H.
In De Stad
    see Twee Liederen

Nachtliegje
    see Twee Liederen

Twee Liederen
    solo,pno ALSBACH s.p.
    contains: In De Stad; Nachtliegje
                                    (F1124)

Was Mir Gefallt
    solo,pno ALSBACH s.p.   (F1125)

FRANK, A.
Verjaardaglied Prins Bernhard
    solo,pno BROEKMANS 108 s.p. (F1126)

FRANK, J.W.
O Du Mein Trost *sac
    Mez solo,pno (B flat maj) LIENAU
    HOS 180 s.p.   (F1127)
    A/Bar solo,pno (G maj) LIENAU
    HOS 181 s.p.   (F1128)

FRANK, MARCEL [GUSTAVE] (1909-   )
Epitaphe
    solo,pno/inst DURAND s.p.   (F1129)

Va, Corsaire
    solo,pno/inst DURAND s.p.   (F1130)

FRANKEL, BENJAMIN (1906-   )
Aftermath, The *Op.17, song cycle
    T solo,trp,timp,strings NOVELLO
    rental   (F1131)

Eight Songs *Op.32, CC8L
    NOVELLO 17.0242.04 s.p.   (F1132)

FRANKEN, WIM (1922-   )
Cinq Poemes De Francois Villon *CC5U
    T solo,pno DONEMUS s.p.   (F1133)

Das Ist Dort, Wo Die Letzten Hutten
    Sind
    see Vijf Liederen Van R.M. Rilke

De Schalmei
    see Franken, Wim, Volkswijze

Der Schwan
    see Vijf Liederen Van R.M. Rilke

Herbst
    see Vijf Liederen Van R.M. Rilke

Herbsttag
    see Vijf Liederen Van R.M. Rilke

Het Einde
    see Franken, Wim, Volkswijze

Kindervrage
    see Franken, Wim, Volkswijze

Marschlied
    see Franken, Wim, Volkswijze

Six Slauerhoff Songs *CC6U
    solo,pno DONEMUS s.p.   (F1134)

Vijf Liederen Van R.M. Rilke
    low solo,pno DONEMUS s.p.
    contains: Das Ist Dort, Wo Die
    Letzten Hutten Sind; Der
    Schwan; Herbst; Herbsttag; Zum
    Einschlafen Zu Sagen   (F1135)

Volkswijze
    med solo,pno DONEMUS s.p. contains
    also: Kindervrage; De Schalmei;
    Marschlied; Het Einde   (F1136)

Yoeng Poe Tsjoeng *CC8L
    high solo,pno DONEMUS s.p. (F1137)

Zum Einschlafen Zu Sagen
    see Vijf Liederen Van R.M. Rilke

FRANZ, ROBERT (1815-1892)
After The Tempest
    solo,pno ASHDOWN s.p.   (F1138)

Dedication *see Widmung

Dedication, A *see Widmung

Fifty Selected Songs *CC50U
    (Weismann) [Ger] high solo,pno
    LYCHE 9085A $12.00; med solo/low
    solo,pno LYCHE 9085B $12.00
                                    (F1139)

FRANZ, ROBERT (cont'd.)

Fifty Songs *CC50U
[Eng/Ger] PRESSER high solo,pno
$5.00; low solo,pno $5.00   (F1140)

Good Night!
solo,pno ASHDOWN s.p.   (F1141)

Hark! How Still
med solo,pno (C maj) ALLANS s.p.
(F1142)
high solo,pno (D maj) ALLANS s.p.
(F1143)

Ich Hab' In Deinem Auge
"Within Thine Eye" [Ger/Eng] med
solo,pno (G flat maj) SCHIRM.G
$.50   (F1144)

Ich Lieb' Eine Blume
"My Love Is A Flower" [Ger/Eng]
high solo,pno (D flat maj)
SCHIRM.G $.50   (F1145)

Lovely Rose, The
solo,pno ASHDOWN s.p.   (F1146)

My Love Is A Flower *see Ich Lieb'
Eine Blume

Vocal Album *CC62L
[Ger/Eng] high solo,pno SCHIRM.G
1572 $3.50   (F1147)

Widmung
"Dedication" [Ger/Eng] med solo,pno
(F maj) SCHIRM.G $1.25   (F1148)
"Dedication" [Ger/Eng] low solo,pno
(E flat maj) SCHIRM.G $1.25
(F1149)
"Dedication" med solo,pno (A flat
maj) ALLANS s.p.   (F1150)
"Dedication, A" solo,pno ASHDOWN
s.p.   (F1151)

Within Thine Eye *see Ich Hab' In
Deinem Auge

FRANZOSISCHE BALLADEN see Hippman, S.

FRANZSON, BJORN
Zehn Lieder *CC10L
solo,pno ICELAND s.p.   (F1152)

FRAPIER-RONCIN
Epousailles
solo,pno OUVRIERES s.p.   (F1153)

FRAPPE, FRAPPE UNE INNOCENTE see
Mozart, Wolfgang Amadeus, Batti,
Batti, O Bel Masetto

FRAS, JIM
Beautiful Nebraska
high solo,pno (F maj) WILLIS $.75
(F1154)

FRASER
Love Will Find A Way
(Simson) 2 soli,pno ALLANS s.p.
(F1155)
(Simson) low solo,pno (E flat maj)
ALLANS s.p.   (F1156)
(Simson) med solo,pno (F maj)
ALLANS s.p.   (F1157)
(Simson) high solo,pno (G maj)
ALLANS s.p.   (F1158)

FRASER, DENNISE
Life's Story
low solo,pno (C maj) ASHDOWN
(F1159)
med solo,pno (D maj) ASHDOWN
(F1160)
high solo,pno (E flat maj) ASHDOWN
(F1161)

When London Was A Garden
low solo,orch (C maj) ASHDOWN s.p.,
ipr   (F1162)
med solo,orch (E flat maj) ASHDOWN
s.p., ipr   (F1163)
high solo,orch (F maj) ASHDOWN
s.p., ipr   (F1164)

FRAU SPINNE see Haas, Joseph

FRAUCHIGER, CH.
Ein Voglein Singt So Susse *Op.42
(composed with Hess, W.), song
cycle
"Little Bird Keeps Calling, A"
[Ger/Eng] solo,pno EULENBURG 530
s.p.   (F1165)

Little Bird Keeps Calling, A *see
Ein Voglein Singt So Susse

FRAUENHOLTZ, JOHANN CHRISTOPH
(1684-1754)
Jesus, Thanks To Thee We Offer *sac
med-high solo,pno oct CONCORDIA
98-1827 $.25   (F1166)

Verbirg Nicht Deine Holden Strahlen
*sac,cant
S solo,vln,cont sc CONCORDIA
97-4252 $2.25   (F1167)

FRAUENHOLTZ, JOHANN CHRISTOPH (cont'd.)

S solo,strings,org voc sc CONCORDIA
97-4252 $3.50, cmplt ed CONCORDIA
s.p., ipa   (F1168)

FRAUENLIEBE UND LEBEN see Schumann,
Robert (Alexander)

FRAYTAG OYF DER NACHT *folk,Jew
med solo,pno HATIKVAH ED. 110 $.25
(F1169)

FRAZIER, DALLAS
Baptism Of Jess Taylor, The (composed
with Shafer, Sanger) *sac
solo,pno WORD S-398   (F1170)

FREDEGONDE see Ollone, Max d'

FREDERIC CHOPIN'S WORKS - FIRST
CRITICAL EDITION see Chopin,
Frederic

FREDERICH, OTTO
Nachtlied *Op.10
low solo,2fl,2English horn,2bass
clar,2bsn,2horn,2trp,3trom,3timp,
harp,strings RIES s.p.   (F1171)

FREDERICK II OF PRUSSIA (1712-1786)
Nota Ve Questa Dea (from Il Re
Pastore)
S solo,strings,cembalo/pno sc
VIEWEG 1703 s.p., ipa   (F1172)
S solo,pno voc sc VIEWEG 1704 s.p.
(F1173)

Sulle Piu Belle Piante (from Il Re
Pastore)
S solo,strings,cembalo/pno sc
VIEWEG 1591 s.p., ipa   (F1174)
S solo,pno voc sc VIEWEG 1591A s.p.
(F1175)

FREDERICKSON, CARL
O Child Divine *sac,Xmas
high solo,pno BELWIN $1.50   (F1176)
low solo,pno BELWIN $1.50   (F1177)

FREDLY, A.
C'est Un Amant
solo,pno ENOCH s.p.   (F1178)

FREDLYS DIN JORD, DU DANSKE MAND see
Nielsen, Carl

FREE TO GO HOME see Gaither

FREEBOOTER SONGS see Wallace, William

FREED, ARNOLD
Acquainted With The Night
solo,pno (F min) BOOSEY $1.50
(F1179)

FREED, ISADORE (1900-1960)
November
solo,pno PEER $.95   (F1180)

Psalm 8 *sac
solo,pno PEER $.95   (F1181)

When I Was One-And-Twenty
solo,pno PEER $.95   (F1182)

FREEDMAN, HARRY (1922-   )
Toccata
S solo,fl KERBY 2150 $3.00   (F1183)

FREEDOM see Baxter, Maude Stewart

FREEDOM see Clarke, Henry Leland

FREEDOM! see Lister, Mosie

FREEDOM IS A CONSTANT STRUGGLE *CCU
(Carawan, Guy; Carawan, Candie) solo,
pno pap OAK 000040 $4.95, cloth OAK
000095 $7.95   (F1184)

FREIA, LA BLONDE AUX YEUX D'AZUR see
Saint-Saens, Camille

FREIHOLD see Schoenberg, Arnold

FREITAGABEND see Lechthaler, Josef

FRELE COMME UN HARMONICA see Rhene-
Baton

FRENCH ART SONGS *CCU
(Glemm; Taylor) [Eng/Fr] PRESSER med-
high solo,pno $3.25; med-low solo,
pno $3.25   (F1185)

FRENCH-CANADIAN FOLK SONGS *CCU
(Creston) solo,pno BELWIN $1.75
(F1186)

FRENCH, G.
Pirate Gold
solo,pno (B min) BOOSEY $1.50   (F1187)

FRENCH SONGS see Howe, Mary

FRENET HA' *folk,Scot
solo,pno (D min/F sharp maj) PATERSON
FS31 s.p.   (F1188)

FRESCAS SOMBRAS DE SAUCES see Lopez-
Buchardo, Carlos

FRESCOBALDI, GIROLAMO (1583-1643)
Maddalena Alla Croce
see Two Sacred Songs

Sonetto Spirtuale In Stile Recitativo
see Two Sacred Songs

Two Sacred Songs *sac
(Dallapiccola, Luigi) [It/Eng]
INTERNAT. high solo,pno $1.50;
low solo,pno $1.50
contains: Maddalena Alla Croce;
Sonetto Spirtuale In Stile
Recitativo   (F1189)

FRESO, TIBOR (1918-   )
Detskym Srdciam *CCU
boy solo/girl solo,pno
SLOV.HUD.FOND s.p.   (F1190)

Nova Jar
med solo,pno SLOV.HUD.FOND s.p.
(F1191)

Stupnica Piesni *CCU
boy solo/girl solo,pno
SLOV.HUD.FOND s.p.   (F1192)

FREUDE SOLL IN DEINEN WERKEN SEIN see
Schilling, M. von

FREUDE UND GLUCK see Schutz, Heinrich,
Exultavit Cor Meum

FREUDENTHAL, JOSEF (1903-1964)
Earth Is The Lord's, The (Psalm 24)
sac,Bar mitzvah/Cnfrm/Gen
high solo,pno TRANSCON. TV 489 $.75
(F1193)
med solo,pno TRANSCON. TV 490 $.75
(F1194)

Lamp Unto My Feet, A (Psalm 119) sac,
Bar mitzvah/Cnfrm/Gen
high solo,pno TRANSCON. TV 499 $.75
(F1195)
med solo,pno TRANSCON. TV 500 $.75
(F1196)

Last Words Of David, The *sac,Bibl
med solo,pno TRANSCON. TV 566 $.75
(F1197)
high solo,pno TRANSCON. TV 565 $.75
(F1198)

Let Us Sing Unto The Lord (Psalm 95)
sac
high solo,pno TRANSCON. TV 474 $.75
(F1199)
med solo,pno TRANSCON. TV 475 $.75
(F1200)

Lied Fun A Chaver
"Song Of Comradeship" [Eng] high
solo/med solo,pno (also with
Yiddish text) TRANSCON. WJ 415
$.40   (F1201)

Lord Is My Shepherd, The (Psalm 23)
sac
med solo,pno TRANSCON. TV 498 $.75
(F1202)
high solo,pno TRANSCON. TV 497 $.75
(F1203)

Lord's Blessing, The (Psalm 67) sac
med solo,pno TRANSCON. TV 480 $.75
(F1204)
high solo,pno TRANSCON. TV 479 $.75
(F1205)

Precepts Of Micah, The *sac,Bar
mitzvah/Cnfrm/Gen
high solo,pno TRANSCON. TV 559 $.75
(F1206)
med solo,pno TRANSCON. TV 560 $.75
(F1207)

Psalm 23 *see Lord Is My Shepherd,
The

Psalm 24 *see Earth Is The Lord's,
The

Psalm 67 *see Lord's Blessing, The

Psalm 95 *see Let Us Sing Unto The
Lord

Psalm 119 *see Lamp Unto My Feet, A

Singing Israel, The
[Heb] med solo,pno TRANSCON. SP 48
$.25   (F1208)

Song Of Comradeship *see Lied Fun A
Chaver

V'Shomru *sac
[Heb] med solo,pno TRANSCON. WJ 429
$.60   (F1209)

FREUDVOLL UND LEIDVOLL see Beethoven,
Ludwig van

FREUDVOLL UND LIEDVOLL see Liszt, Franz

FREUET EUCH DES HERREN, IHR GERECHTEN
see Schutz, Heinrich

FREUET EUCH IN DEM HERRN see Distler,
Hugo

FREUNDLICHE VISION see Strauss, Richard

FREY, MARTIN
Rosen Aus Dem Rosengarten, Band II
*CCU
LEUCKART solo,pno s.p.; solo,lute
s.p.   (F1210)

FRIAR OF ORDERS GREY see Reeve

FRID see Hallstrom, Ivar

FRID see Runback, Albert

FRID, GEZA (1904-   )
Abel Et Cain *Op.15
low solo,3fl,2ob,3clar,3bsn,4horn,
3trp,3trom,tuba,timp,perc,2harp,
strings DONEMUS s.p.   (F1211)

Abschied *Op.59, song cycle
low solo,pno DONEMUS s.p.   (F1212)
high solo,pno DONEMUS s.p.   (F1213)

Auf Reise *Op.60, song cycle
S solo,pno DONEMUS s.p.   (F1214)

Avondgebedje *Op.26,No.2
see Vox Amantium

Die Beschworung *Op.41,No.1
see Drie Romances Van H. Heine

Drie Romances Van H. Heine
DONEMUS S solo,pno s.p.; S solo,
2fl,2ob,2clar,2bsn,horn,timp,
perc,harp,strings rental
contains: Die Beschworung, Op.41,
No.1; Ein Weib, Op.41,No.2;
Fruhlingsfeier, Op.41,No.3
(F1215)

Drie Shakespeare-Liederen Uit
"Driekoningenavond" *Op.65a,
CC3U
Bar solo,pno DONEMUS s.p.   (F1216)

Ein Weib *Op.41,No.2
see Drie Romances Van H. Heine

Erotisch Landschap *Op.26,No.1
see Vox Amantium

Fruhlingsfeier *Op.41,No.3
see Drie Romances Van H. Heine
SA soli,fl,clar,ob,vln,vcl DONEMUS
s.p.   (F1217)

Fuj A Szel *Op.19,No.4
see Quatre Chansons Avec Textes
Hongrois

Havasok Es Riviera *Op.19,No.2
see Quatre Chansons Avec Textes
Hongrois

Kato A Misen *Op.19,No.1
see Quatre Chansons Avec Textes
Hongrois

Kinderliedjes, Bd I *Op.53, CCU
Mez solo,pno DONEMUS s.p.   (F1218)

Kinderliedjes, Bd. II *Op.56, CCU
Mez solo,pno DONEMUS s.p.   (F1219)

Meg Akarlak Tartanti *Op.19,No.3
see Quatre Chansons Avec Textes
Hongrois

Mon Coeur Balance *Op.26,No.3
see Vox Amantium

Quatre Chansons Avec Textes Hongrois
[Hung] med-high solo,pno DONEMUS
s.p.
contains: Fuj A Szel, Op.19,No.4;
Havasok Es Riviera, Op.19,No.2;
Kato A Misen, Op.19,No.1; Meg
Akarlak Tartanti, Op.19,No.3
(F1220)
Schopenhauer Cantate *Op.22, cant
Mez solo,2fl,2ob,2clar,2bsn,horn,
trp,timp,perc,strings DONEMUS
s.p.   (F1221)

Venedig *Op.83, song cycle
Bar solo,pno DONEMUS s.p.   (F1222)

Verraad *Op.26,No.4
see Vox Amantium

Vox Amantium
med solo/high solo,pno DONEMUS s.p.
contains: Avondgebedje, Op.26,
No.2; Erotisch Landschap,
Op.26,No.1; Mon Coeur Balance,
Op.26,No.3; Verraad, Op.26,No.4
(F1223)

FRIEBERG, F.A.
Ljungby Horn
T solo,pno GEHRMANS s.p.   (F1224)
Bar solo,pno GEHRMANS s.p.   (F1225)
B solo,pno GEHRMANS s.p.   (F1226)

FRIEDE see Bordewijk-Roepman, Johanna

FRIEDE see Oort, H.C.v.

FRIEDELL, HAROLD W.
Shepherdess, The
high solo,pno BELWIN $1.50   (F1227)
med solo,pno BELWIN $1.50   (F1228)

FRIEDEN see Gilse, Jan van

FRIEDEN see Pfitzner, Hans

FRIEDLICHE NACHT see Thomas, Kurt

FRIEND
Little Boy From The Carpenter Shop,
The *sac
solo,pno BENSON S7946-S $1.00
(F1229)
Night Before Easter, The (composed
with Sumner) *sac
solo,pno BENSON S7996-S $1.00
(F1230)

FRIEND O' MINE see Sanderson, Wilfred

FRIEND OF THE FATHER see Harris, Ron

FRIENDLY ADVISER, THE see Carey, Henry

FRIENDSHIP see Marzials, Theo

FRIENDSHIP see Sibelius, Jean,
Vanskapens Blomma

FRIERSON
O Lil Lamb *sac
solo,pno HOPE 58 $1.00   (F1231)

FRIESEN, DICK
Straw Carol, The *sac
(Eklund, Harry) solo,pno WORD S-290
(F1232)

FRIESLAND see Schouwman, Hans

FRIHETSSANG see Alfven, Hugo

FRILLS AND FANCIES see Fisher, Howard

FRIML, RUDOLF (1879-   )
Allah's Holiday (from Katinka)
high solo,pno (E min) SCHIRM.G $.60
(F1233)
low solo,pno (C min) SCHIRM.G $.60
(F1234)
Beautiful Ship From Toyland, The
(from Firefly, The)
B solo,pno (B flat maj) SCHIRM.G
$.60   (F1235)
Bubble, The (from High Jinks)
low solo,pno (E flat maj) SCHIRM.G
$.60   (F1236)
high solo,pno (G maj) SCHIRM.G $.60
(F1237)
Cavaliers (from Music Hath Charms)
med-high solo,pno SCHIRM.G $.60
(F1238)
Dawn Of Love, The *see L'Alba
D'Amore

Dear Old Dublin (from Kitty Darlin')
med solo,pno (E flat maj) SCHIRM.G
$.60   (F1239)

Donkey Serenade, The (from Firefly,
The)
low solo,pno (G maj) SCHIRM.G $.75
(F1240)
med solo,pno (B flat maj) SCHIRM.G
$.75   (F1241)

Giannina Mia (from Firefly, The)
high solo,pno (E maj) SCHIRM.G $.85
(F1242)
med solo,pno (C maj) SCHIRM.G $.85
(F1243)
low solo,pno (B flat maj) SCHIRM.G
$.85   (F1244)

He Who Loves And Runs Away (from
Firefly, The)
med solo,pno (E flat maj) SCHIRM.G
$.60   (F1245)

I Love You, Dear (from Glorianna)
low solo,pno (C maj) SCHIRM.G $.60
(F1246)
ST soli,pno SCHIRM.G $.60   (F1247)

I Want The World To Know (from Music
For Madame)
med-high solo,pno (D maj) SCHIRM.G
$.60   (F1248)
low solo,pno (B flat maj) SCHIRM.G
$.60   (F1249)

I'm Only Dreaming (from You're In
Love)
high solo,pno (E flat maj) SCHIRM.G
$.60   (F1250)
low solo,pno (C maj) SCHIRM.G $.60
(F1251)

Katinka (from Katinka)
high solo,pno (D maj) SCHIRM.G $.60
(F1252)

FRIML, RUDOLF (cont'd.)
low solo,pno (B flat maj) SCHIRM.G
$.60   (F1253)

Kitty Darlin' (from Kitty Darlin')
med solo,pno (E flat maj) SCHIRM.G
$.60   (F1254)

L'Alba D'Amore (from Firefly, The)
"Dawn Of Love, The" [Eng/It] S
solo,pno SCHIRM.G $.60   (F1255)

Land Where Dreams Come True, The
(from Kitty Darlin')
ABar soli,pno SCHIRM.G $.60 (F1256)
ST/MezT soli,pno SCHIRM.G $.60
(F1257)

Love (from Music Hath Charms)
med-high solo,pno (D maj) SCHIRM.G
$.60   (F1258)

Love Is Like A Firefly (from Firefly,
The)
high solo,pno (F maj) SCHIRM.G $.60
(F1259)
low solo,pno (D maj) SCHIRM.G $.60
(F1260)

Love-Land (from You're In Love)
high solo,pno (F maj) SCHIRM.G $.60
(F1261)

Love's Own Kiss (from High Jinks)
high solo,pno (D maj) SCHIRM.G $.60
(F1262)
low solo,pno (B flat maj) SCHIRM.G
$.60   (F1263)

My Heart Is Yours (from Music Hath
Charms)
high solo,pno (E flat maj) SCHIRM.G
$.60   (F1264)
med-low solo,pno (C maj) SCHIRM.G
$.60   (F1265)

My Sweet Bambina (from Music For
Madame)
med solo,pno (A flat maj) SCHIRM.G
$.60   (F1266)

Rachety Coo! (from Katinka)
high solo,pno (G maj) SCHIRM.G $.60
(F1267)
low solo,pno (E flat maj) SCHIRM.G
$.60   (F1268)

Romance (from Music Hath Charms)
high solo,pno (E flat maj) SCHIRM.G
$.60   (F1269)
low solo,pno (C maj) SCHIRM.G $.60
(F1270)

Some Time (from Some Time)
high solo,pno (A maj) SCHIRM.G $.60
(F1271)
low solo,pno (F maj) SCHIRM.G $.60
(F1272)

Something Seems Tingle-Ingleing (from
High Jinks)
low solo,pno (D maj) SCHIRM.G $.60
(F1273)
high solo,pno (F maj) SCHIRM.G $.60
(F1274)

Sweet Dreams (from Little Whopper,
The)
high solo,pno (F maj) SCHIRM.G $.60
(F1275)
low solo,pno (C maj) SCHIRM.G $.60
(F1276)

Sympathy (from Firefly, The)
high solo,pno (A flat maj) SCHIRM.G
$.60   (F1277)
low solo,pno (F maj) SCHIRM.G $.60
(F1278)
SBar soli,pno SCHIRM.G $.60 (F1279)

'Tis The End, So Farewell! (from
Katinka)
high solo,pno (G maj) SCHIRM.G $.60
(F1280)
low solo,pno (D maj) SCHIRM.G $.60
(F1281)

When A Maid Comes Knocking At Your
Heart (from Firefly, The)
high solo,pno (F maj) SCHIRM.G $.60
(F1282)
low solo,pno (D maj) SCHIRM.G $.60
(F1283)

When She Gives Him A Shamrock Bloom
(from Kitty Darlin')
med-low solo,pno (D maj) SCHIRM.G
$.60   (F1284)

Woman's Kiss, A (from Firefly, The)
high solo,pno (F maj) SCHIRM.G $.60
(F1285)
med-low solo,pno (E flat maj)
SCHIRM.G $.60   (F1286)

Your Photo (from Katinka)
med-high solo,pno (D maj) SCHIRM.G
$.60   (F1287)

You're In Love (from You're In Love)
high solo,pno (F maj) SCHIRM.G $.60
(F1288)
med-low solo,pno (E flat maj)
SCHIRM.G $.60   (F1289)

FRINGES OF THE FLEET, THE see Elgar,
Edward

FRISCHENSCHLAGER, FRIEDRICH (1885-1970)
Sieben Kammerlieder *CC7U
B solo,4kbd DOBLINGER s.p.   (F1290)

FRISSON D'EAU VIVE see Middeleer, Jean
De

FRITHIOF OCH BJORN see Crusell

FRITIHOF see Bruch, Max

FRODING
Later Om Janter A Friing
solo,pno LUNDQUIST s.p.   (F1291)

Mina Levnadstimmar Stupa
high solo,pno LUNDQUIST s.p.
(F1292)
low solo,pno LUNDQUIST s.p. (F1293)

Studentsang
solo,pno LUNDQUIST s.p.   (F1294)

FROG, THE see Iida, Takashi

FROGS, FROGS see Beekhuis, Hanna

FROHE HIRTEN, EILT, ACH EILET see Bach,
Johann Sebastian

FROHLICH, O.
Lotos Flower *see Lotosblume

Lotosblume
"Lotos Flower" solo,pno CONGRESS
$.60   (F1295)

FROHLICH WIR NUN ALL FANGEN AN see
David, Johann Nepomuk

FROHLICHE WEIHNACHT UBERALL *CC39U,
Xmas
1-2 soli,gtr SCHOTTS 5400 s.p.
(F1296)

FROHLOCKET, IHR SELIGEN KINDER DER
FREIEN see Telemann, Georg Philipp

FROHLOCKET MIT HANDEN see Schutz,
Heinrich

FROHSINN see Genzmer, Harald

FROHSINN IM RANZEL see Lehner, Leo

FROIDEBISE, PIERRE (1914-1962)
Amercoeur *cant
S solo,fl,ob,English horn,clar,bsn,
horn,pno CBDM s.p.   (F1297)

Stele Pour Sei Shonagon *Op.1,No.4
S solo,fl,2clar,bsn,horn,trp,trom,
tuba,xylo,vibra,cel,harp,pno,
perc,5strings CBDM s.p.   (F1298)

FROJDENS VART SINNE see Finnborg

FROKEN CHIC see Lincke, Paul

FROLIC see Glanville-Hicks, Peggy

FROM A CHILD'S GARDEN see Williamson,
Malcolm

FROM A LOVER'S LETTER see Kodaly,
Zoltan

FROM A LUTE OF JADE see Read, Gardner

FROM A RIVER BED see Barati, George

FROM AFAR see Scott, Cyril Meir

FROM AN UNKNOWN PAST see Rorem, Ned

FROM ARMENIAN POETRY see Aslamazov, A.

FROM AUTUMN'S THRILLING TOMB see
Strilko, Anthony

FROM CROSS TO CROWN see Federlein

FROM DEPTHS OF WOE I CRY TO THEE see
Schein, Johann Hermann

FROM GOD SHALL NAUGHT DIVIDE ME see
Schutz, Heinrich

FROM HARMONIUM see Lybbert, Donald

FROM INVERNESS TO FELL see Fisher,
Howard

FROM LINCOLN THE GREAT COMMONER see
Ives, Charles

FROM MY WINDOW see Kendrick, Virginia

FROM OUT HERE see Kaiser, Kurt

FROM OUT THE LONG AGO see Ashworth-
Hope, H.

FROM PATERSON see Williams, Joan Franks

FROM PUSHKIN'S TIMES see Samonov, A.

FROM THE CANTICLE OF THE SUN see
Thomson, Virgil

FROM THE DARK TOWER see Moore, Dorothy
Rudd

FROM THE DIARY OF VIRGINIA WOOLF see
Argento, Dominick

FROM THE EAST see Birch, Robert Fairfax

FROM THE MANGER TO THE CROSS *sac,
gospel
solo,pno ABER.GRP. $1.50   (F1299)

FROM THE NURSERY WINDOW see Brahe, May
H.

FROM THE ORIENT see Smolanoff, Michael

FROM THE PSALMS see Mc Cabe

FROM THE SONG OF SONGS see Van Etten,
Jane

FROM THE SONGS OF SORROW see Strauss,
Richard, Aus Den Liedern Der Trauer

FROM THE SONGS OF SORROW [II] see
Strauss, Richard, Aus Den Liedern
Der Trauer [II]

FROM THE UNKNOWN ISLAND OF A HEART see
Mallinson, (James) Albert

FROM THE YOUTH see Lajovic, Anton, Iz
Mladih Dni

FROM THIS DAY ON see Melton, Carol

FROM THOREAU see Whear, Paul William

FROM VILLON TO HIS LOVE see Debussy,
Claude, Ballade De Villon A S'Amye

FROM WHERE HAVE YOU COME BELOVED? see
Rodrigo, Joaquin, De Donde Venis,
Amore?

FROMM see Linnala, Eino

FROMM, HERBERT (1905-   )
Angels Of Peace
see Five Songs Of Worship (Revised
Edition)

Cradle Song
see Three Palestine Poems

Five Songs Of Worship (Revised
Edition) *sac
[Heb/Eng] med solo,pno cmplt ed
TRANSCON. $2.25
contains: Angels Of Peace;
Invocation; Lamentation Of
David; Sabbath Joy; Sabbath
Queen   (F1300)

Four Psalms *sac,CC4U,Psalm
[Eng] high solo,pno/org TRANSCON.
TV 577 $2.75   (F1301)

Grant Us Peace *sac
high solo,pno TRANSCON. TV 477 $.75
(F1302)
med solo,pno TRANSCON. TV 478 $.75
(F1303)
Invocation
see Five Songs Of Worship (Revised
Edition)

Lamentation Of David
see Five Songs Of Worship (Revised
Edition)

Legend
see Three Palestine Poems

Maise Fun A Pastuch'l
"Shepherd's Story" [Heb/Eng] med
solo,pno (also with Yiddish text)
TRANSCON. SP 2 $.75   (F1304)

Sabbath Joy
see Five Songs Of Worship (Revised
Edition)

Sabbath Queen
see Five Songs Of Worship (Revised
Edition)

Seven Prayers *sac,CC7U,prayer
[Heb/Eng] med solo/cantor,pno
TRANSCON. WJ 442 $2.50   (F1305)

Shepherd's Story *see Maise Fun A
Pastuch'l

There I Saw Her
see Three Palestine Poems

FROMM, HERBERT (cont'd.)

Three Palestine Poems
[Heb/Eng] med solo,pno TRANSCON.
SP 15 $1.50
contains: Cradle Song; Legend;
There I Saw Her   (F1306)

FROMMEL, GERHARD (1906-   )
Neun Gedichte Aus "Sange Eines
Fahrenden Spielmanns" *CC9U
solo,fl,clar,bsn,horn,strings RIES
s.p.   (F1307)

FROMM-MICHAELS, ILSE
Drei Rilke-Gesange *CC3U
Bar solo,pno SIKORSKI 706 s.p.
(F1308)

FRONS see Delas, Jose Luis De

FROST-BOUND WOOD, THE see Heseltine,
Philip

FRU SOMMAR see Lundborg, Gosta

FRUH
Geistlieder Gesang *sac
solo,pno HENN 326 s.p.   (F1309)

Maori-Lieder
solo,pno HENN 325 s.p.   (F1310)

FRUHER FRUHLING see Kilpinen, Yrio,
Kevat Keralla

FRUHER RIEF MEIN TRAUTER KUCKUCK see
Kilpinen, Yrio, Muinainen Kakeni

FRUHJAHRSSTRAHLEN see Fibich, Zdenko

FRUHLING see Bijvanck, Henk

FRUHLING see Haas, Joseph

FRUHLING see Marvia, Einari, Kevat

FRUHLING see Weigl, Vally

FRUHLING AM BERGESHANG see Robrecht, C.

FRUHLING SCHWINDET EILIG see Sibelius,
Jean, Varen Flyktar Hastigt

FRUHLINGNACHT see Schumann, Robert
(Alexander)

FRUHLINGS-SONNENSCHEIN see Walter,
Fried

FRUHLINGSFEIER see Frid, Geza

FRUHLINGSFEIER see Strauss, Richard

FRUHLINGSFLUTEN see Rachmaninoff,
Sergey Vassilievitch, Spring Waters

FRUHLINGSGLAUBE see Schubert, Franz
(Peter)

FRUHLINGSLIED see Denza, Luigi

FRUHLINGSLIED see Mendelssohn-
Bartholdy, Felix

FRUHLINGSLIED see Schumann, Robert
(Alexander)

FRUHLINGSMORGEN see Mahler, Gustav

FRUHLINGSMORGEN see Reger, Max

FRUHLINGSNACHT see Schumann, Robert
(Alexander)

FRUHLINGSREIGEN see Fleischmann, O.

FRUHLINGSSONNE see Trunk, Richard

FRUHLINGSSTIMMEN see Strauss, Johann

FRUHLINGSTAG see Bijvanck, Henk

FRUHLINGSTAG see Schinhan, J.P.

FRUHLINGSTAU, IN DEINEN AUGEN see Marx,
Karl

FRUHLINGSZAUBER see Sibelius, Jean,
Vartagen

FRUHSTUCK see Steffen, Wolfgang

FRUHZEITIGER FRUHLING see Trapp, Max

FRUIT BASKET see Farkas, Ferenc

FRUKTTID see Peterson-Berger, (Olof)
Wilhelm

FRULINGSSTIMMEN see Strauss, Johann

FRUMERIE, (PER) GUNNAR (FREDRICK) DE
(1908-   )
En Gang Blir Allting Stilla
low solo,pno ERIKS K 136 s.p.
(F1311)

FRUMERIE, (PER) GUNNAR (FREDRICK) DE
(cont'd.)

    high solo,pno ERIKS K 119 s.p.
                          (F1312)

FRYBERG, M.
  Dorfmusik
    "Village Band, The" solo,pno SCHAUR
    s.p.   (F1313)

  Village Band, The *see Dorfmusik

FRYXELL, REGINA HOLMEN
  Vision, A *sac,Xmas
    med solo,pno BELWIN $1.50   (F1314)

FU-YI see Avshalomov, Jacob

FUCHSIA TREE see Quilter, Roger

FUENLLANA, MIGUEL DE
  La Girigonza *see Flecha, Mateo

  Vos Me Matastes *see Vasquez, Juan

DE FUENTES
  see SANCHEZ DE FUENTES, EDUARDO

FUGA DI BARNABO VISCONTI see Orefice,
  Giacomo

FUGA, SANDRO (1906-   )
  Ad Un Ruscello
    [It] solo,pno BONGIOVANI 1082 s.p.
                        (F1315)
  Canti D'amore
    [It] solo,pno RICORDI-ENG 129408
    s.p.   (F1316)
  Due Ballate *CC2U
    solo,pno ZERBONI 4143 s.p. (F1317)
  L'isola Dei Sogni
    [It] solo,pno BONGIOVANI 1083 s.p.
                        (F1318)
  Sera Sui Monti
    [It] solo,pno BONGIOVANI 1081 s.p.
                        (F1319)
  Tre Liriche *CC3U
    solo,pno ZERBONI 4239 s.p. (F1320)

FUGGIMI! see Denza, Luigi

FUGIT AMOR see Marsick, M.-P.

FUGUE ON MONEY see Raphling, Sam

FUJ A SZEL see Frid, Geza

FULEIHAN, ANIS (1900-   )
  My Ahmed Has Gone To Give Battle
    solo,pno PEER $.95   (F1321)

  Suite Sur Des Airs De La Vieille
    France *CCU
    S solo,2fl,ob,2clar,2bsn,2horn,
    strings PEER rental   (F1322)

FULFILMENT see O'Connor-Morris, G.

FULL CIRCLE see Sydeman, William

FULL FATHOM FIVE see Castelnuovo-
  Tedesco, Mario

FULL FATHOM FIVE see Lessard, John
  Ayres

FULL FATHOM FIVE see Montgomery, Bruce

FULL FATHOM FIVE see Shaw, Martin

FULL LIFE, A see Birch, Robert Fairfax

FULL MOON see Berkeley, Lennox

FULL MOON SHINES, THE see Kilpinen,
  Yrio, Der Vollmond Scheint

FULL OF DESPAIR see Verdi, Giuseppe, Il
  Lacerato Spirito

FULL SAIL see Buck

FULLY CLOTHED IN ARMOR, WITH HER SHIELD
  AND SPEAR, ATHENA EMERGED FROM THE
  FOREHEAD OF ZEUS see Rice, Thomas

FULMORE
  I Got Jesus *sac
    solo,pno BENSON S6015-R $1.00
                        (F1323)
  We're All God's Children *sac
    solo,pno BENSON S8345-R $1.00
                        (F1324)

FULTON, F.
  Oh, Love!
    solo,pno PARAGON $.85   (F1325)

FULTON, NORMAN
  Two Christmas Songs *CC2U,Xmas
    solo,pno OXFORD s.p.   (F1326)

FUMEE see Privas, Xavier

FUMEES see Rhene-Baton

FUNEBRE see Arrieu, Claude

FUNERAL COYA see Boero, Felipe

FUNERAL OF A NAGO KING see Tavares,
  Hekel

FUNERAL TEARES, SONGS OF MOURNING,
  MASQUE OF SQUIRES see Coperario,
  Giovanni

FUNF AIRS AUS "THE BEGGAR'S OPERA" see
  Gay, John

FUNF ALTE WEIHNACHTSLIEDER *Op.32,
  No.1-5, CC5U,Xmas
  (Hallwachs, Karl) solo,pno RIES s.p.
                        (F1327)

FUNF ALTJAPANISCHE GEISHALIEDER *CC5U
  (Behrend, Siegfried) solo,gtr
  SIKORSKI 248 s.p.   (F1328)

FUNF ANTIKE ODEN see Reutter, Hermann

FUNF ARIEN see Beethoven, Ludwig van

FUNF ARIEN DER ANTIOPE see Scarlatti,
  Domenico

FUNF AUSGEWAHLTE LIEDER AUS OP. 12 UND
  OP. 24 see Borris, Siegfried

FUNF BERUHMTE RUSSISCHE LIEDER *folk,
  Russ
  [Ger/Russ] solo,pno ZIMMER. 1357 s.p.
    contains: Die Mowe; Die Zwolf
    Rauber; Einsam Klingt Das
    Glockchen; Schwarze Augen; Zwei
    Gitarren   (F1329)

FUNF CANONS see Webern, Anton von

FUNF DORFSZENEN see Bartok, Bela

FUNF DUETTE FUR SOPRAN UND ALT see
  Reger, Max

FUNF FRAGMENTE NACH FR. HOLDERLIN see
  Reutter, Hermann

FUNF GEDICHTE see Wagner, Richard

FUNF GEDICHTE VON MATHILDE WESENDONK
  see Wagner, Richard

FUNF GEDICHTE VON PAUL CELAN see
  Reimann, Aribert

FUNF GEISTLICHE LIEDER see Webern,
  Anton von

FUNF GESANGE see Apostel, Hans Erich

FUNF GESANGE see Trexler, Georg

FUNF GESANGE FUR BARITON UND
  KAMMERORCHESTER see Zimmermann, Udo

FUNF GESANGE NACH FRIEDRICH HOLDERLIN
  UND STEFAN GEORGE see Petersen,
  Wilhelm

FUNF GESCHICHTEN VOM K. HERRN see
  Denisov, Edison Vasilievitch

FUNF GOETHE-LIEDER see Busoni,
  Ferruccio Benvenuto

FUNF HEITERE GESANGE see Schumann,
  Robert (Alexander)

FUNF LIEDER see Bedinger, Hugo

FUNF LIEDER see Schreker, Franz

FUNF LIEDER see Webern, Anton von

FUNF LIEDER see Apostel, Hans Erich

FUNF LIEDER see Webern, Anton von

FUNF LIEDER see Weigl, Karl

FUNF LIEDER see Bartok, Bela

FUNF LIEDER see Berg, Alban

FUNF LIEDER see Apostel, Hans Erich

FUNF LIEDER see Dessau, Paul

FUNF LIEDER see Geissler, Fritz

FUNF LIEDER see Kochan, Gunter

FUNF LIEDER see Kobler, Robert

FUNF LIEDER see Uray, Ernst Ludwig

FUNF LIEDER see Waldstein, Wilhelm

FUNF LIEDER see Rontgen, Johannes

FUNF LIEDER see Badings, Henk

FUNF LIEDER see Eisler, Hanns

FUNF LIEDER see Klebe, Giselher

FUNF LIEDER see Sheinkman, M.

FUNF LIEDER see Korngold, Erich
  Wolfgang

FUNF LIEDER see Reutter, Hermann

FUNF LIEDER see Strauss, Richard

FUNF LIEDER see Beethoven, Ludwig van

FUNF LIEDER see Weigl, Karl

FUNF LIEDER see Strauss, Richard

FUNF LIEDER see Spinner, Leopold

FUNF LIEDER see Flury, Richard

FUNF LIEDER see Semmler, R.

FUNF LIEDER see Schwickert, Gustav

FUNF LIEDER see Pfitzner, Hans

FUNF LIEDER see Abendroth, Walther

FUNF LIEDER AUS DEM CHINESISCHEN see
  Einem, Gottfried von

FUNF LIEDER AUS DEM JAHR DER SEELE see
  Zillig, Winfried

FUNF LIEDER AUS DEM PAUL-GERHARDT-
  LIEDERBUCH see Pepping, Ernst

FUNF LIEDER (CAMOES) see Genzmer,
  Harald

FUNF LIEDER DER JUGEND see Bartok, Bela

FUNF LIEDER IM HERBST see Ronnefeld,
  Peter

FUNF LIEDER IN SCHWEIZER MUNDART see
  Langer, Richard

FUNF LIEDER MIT KLAVIER see Trunk,
  Richard

FUNF LIEDER NACH BIERBAUM see Gerster,
  Ottmar

FUNF LIEDER NACH GEDICHTEN AUS WOLFRAM
  BROCKMEIER see Thomas, Kurt

FUNF LIEDER NACH GEDICHTEN VON BERT
  BRECHT see Wiemer, Wolfgang

FUNF LIEDER NACH GEDICHTEN VON
  CHRISTIAN MORGENSTERN see Lutz,
  Oswald

FUNF LIEDER NACH GEDICHTEN VON M.L.
  KASCHNITZ see Reutter, Hermann

FUNF LIEDER NACH KAFKA see Krenek,
  Ernst

FUNF LIEDER NACH TEXTEN VON RINGELNATZ,
  CLAUDIUS UND GOETHE see Dessau,
  Paul

FUNF LIEDER SOBRE TEXTOS DE WESENDONK
  see Wagner, Richard

FUNF LIEDER VAN EUGENIE FINK see
  Bijvanck, Henk

FUNF MARIENLIEDER see Kowalski, Max

FUNF NEAPOLITANISCHE LIEDER see Henze,
  Hans Werner

FUNF OPHELIA-LIEDER see Brahms,
  Johannes

FUNF PALMSTROM see Eisler, Hanns

FUNF ROMANTISCHE GESANGE see Braunfels,
  Walter

FUNF SINNSPRUCHE OMARS DES ZELTMACHERS
  see Blacher, Boris

FUNF SONETTE AN OPRHEUS see Rautavaara,
  Einojuhani

FUNF SPATE LIEDER see Holmboe, Vagn

FUNF TRUNKENE LIEDER see Lilien, Ignace

FUNF VOKLSLIEDER AUS TAVASTLAND, VOL. I
  see Hannikainen, Ilmari

FUNF VOLKSLIEDER AUS TAVASTLAND, VOL.
  II see Hannikainen, Ilmari

FUNF WANDERLIEDER see Lehner, Leo

FUNF WILHELM-BUSCH-LIEDER see Kobler,
Robert

FUNFTAUSEND TALER see Lortzing,
(Gustav) Albert

FUNFUNDZWANZIG KINDERLIEDER see
Pudelko, Walter

FUNFZEHN AUSGEWAHLTE LIEDER see
Sibelius, Jean

FUNFZEHN GEDICHTE AUS "BUCH DER
HANGENDEN GARTEN" see Schoenberg,
Arnold

FUNFZEHN LIEDER see Schubert, Franz
(Peter)

FUNFZEHN LIEDER see Wolf, Hugo

FUNFZEHN RUSSISCHE LIEDER UND ROMANZEN
*CC15U,Russ
(Malukoff, A.) [Ger/Russ] solo,gtr
ZIMMER. 1321 $3.50   (F1330)

FUNFZIG AUSGEWAHLTE LIEDER see Mozart,
Wolfgang Amadeus

FUNFZIG AUSGEWAHLTE LIEDER see Zelter,
Carl Friedrich

FUNFZIG GESANGE ZU MESSFEIER UND
WORTGOTTESDIENST MIT KINDERN see
Rohr, H.

FUNFZIG RUSSISCHE VOLKSLIEDER *CC50U,
folk,Russ
(Swerkoff, E.L.) [Ger/Russ] solo,pno
ZIMMER. 1391 s.p.   (F1331)

FUNICULI-FUNICULA see Denza, Luigi

FUNNY FELLOW see Head, Michael (Dewar)

FUR DICH see Landre, Willem

FUR DICH ALLEIN see Geehl, Henry
Ernest, For You Alone

FUR FUNFZEHN PFENNIG see Strauss,
Richard

FUR KINDER see Gerhard

FURCHTE DICH NICHT see Schutz, Heinrich

FURCHTET EUCH NICHT see Bernhard,
Christoph

FURCHTET EUCH NICHT see Hammerschmidt,
Andreas

FURIE D'AVERNO see Sacchini, Antonio
(Maria Gasparo Gioacchino)

FURRER, FRANZ (1924-   )
Insides
A/Bar solo,pno,vcl,gtr MODERN s.p.
(F1332)
FURWAHR, ER TRUG UNSERE KRANKHEIT see
Schein, Johann Hermann

FURWAHR, ER TRUG UNSRE KRANKHEIT see
Buttner, Crato

FUSIANS see Tremisot, Ed.

FUSSAN, WERNER (1913-   )
Der Tanz Der Gotter
see Die Chinesische Flote

Die Chinesische Flote
S solo,fl,4strings sc BREITKOPF-W
s.p.
contains: Der Tanz Der Gotter;
Die Geheimnisvolle Flote; In
Der Fremde   (F1333)

Die Chinesische Flote *CC3U
S solo,fl,4strings BREITKOPF-W s.p.
(F1334)
Die Geheimnisvolle Flote
see Die Chinesische Flote

In Der Fremde
see Die Chinesische Flote

FUSSL, K.H.
Miorita
TS soli,5inst sc,quarto UNIVER.
13916 $9.00   (F1335)

FUSSREISE see Wolf, Hugo

FUSTE, E.
Sabor De Espana
solo,pno ENOCH s.p.   (F1336)

FYLL TILL RANDEN see Korling, August

FYRA ANDLIGA SANGER see Rautavaara,
Einojuhani

FYRA DIKTER see Liljefors, Ruben

FYRA DIKTER see Nordqvist, Gustaf

FYRA DIKTER see Peterson-Berger, (Olof)
Wilhelm

FYRA DIKTER see Skold

FYRA DUETTER see Merikanto, Oskar

FYRA GOTLANDSKA VISOR see Mehler,
Friedrich

FYRA JULSANGER see Bengtsson

FYRA NYA SANGER see Sjogren, Emil

FYRA SANGER see Liljefors, Ruben

FYRA SANGER see Wiklund, Adolf

FYRA SANGER see Backer-Grondahl, Agathe
Ursula

FYRA SANGER see Josephson, Jacob Axel

FYRA SANGER see Lindblad, Otto

FYRA SANGER see Fordell, Erik (Fritiof)

FYRA SANGER see Merikanto, Oskar

FYRA SANGER see Berggreen, Andreas
Peter

FYRA SANGER see Nordqvist, Gustaf

FYRA SANGER I FOLKTON *sac
solo,pno GEHRMANS s.p.
contains: Strandsjo, Gote, Jag Ser
Guds Spar; Svedlund, Karl-Erik,
Han Klappar Pa; Svedlund, Karl-
Erik, I Himmelen, I Himmelen;
Svedlund, Karl-Erik, Nu Ar Din
Segertimma   (F1337)

FYRA SANGER VID PIANO see Stenhammar,
Per Ulrik

FYRA SMA VISOR see Svedbom, Vilhelm

FYRA VISOR see Ehrstrom, (Jarl) Otto
(Sigurd)

FYRA VISOR see Milveden, Ingemar

FYRA VISOR AV FRODING see Wohlfart,
Karl

FYRA VISOR I SVENSK FOLKTON see
Peterson-Berger, (Olof) Wilhelm

G

GA, SION, DIN KONUNG ATT MOTA
see Andliga Sanger, Heft 4

GABER, HARLEY
Voce II
med solo,fl,perc sc AM.COMP.AL.
$3.85   (G1)

GABRIEL, SR., CHARLES H. (1856-1932)
Evening Prayer, An *sac
solo,pno WORD S-337   (G2)
(Felts, W. Roland) solo,pno WORD
S-226   (G3)

His Eye Is On The Sparrow
solo,pno ASHLEY $.95   (G4)
med solo,pno PRESSER $.75   (G5)

GABRIEL, VIRGINIA
Cleansing Fires
high solo,pno (D maj) LEONARD-ENG
(G6)
med solo,pno (C maj) LEONARD-ENG
(G7)
low solo,pno (B flat maj) LEONARD-
ENG   (G8)

GABRIEL FAURE ALBUM OF TWENTY SONGS,
VOLUME I see Faure, Gabriel-Urbain

GABRIEL FAURE ALBUM OF TWENTY SONGS,
VOLUME II see Faure, Gabriel-Urbain

GABRIEL FAURE ALBUM OF TWENTY SONGS,
VOLUME III see Faure, Gabriel-
Urbain

GABRIELI, GIOVANNI (1557-1612)
Exaudi Deus *sac,mot
TTBBBBB soli,inst sc HANSSLER 1.489
s.p. see from Sacrae Symphoniae I
(G9)
Sacrae Symphoniae I *see Exaudi Deus
(G10)

GAB'S EIN EINZIG BRUNNELEIN see Reger,
Max

GABURO, KENNETH (1927-   )
Two
Mez solo,bvl, alto flute PRESSER
$2.00   (G11)

GABUS, MONIQUE
Ivre D'insouciance
see Quatre Melodies Sur Des Textes
D'Andre Gide

La Brise Vagabonde
see Quatre Melodies Sur Des Textes
D'Andre Gide

Quatre Melodies Sur Des Textes
D'Andre Gide
solo,pno cmplt ed TRANSAT. s.p.
contains: Ivre D'insouciance; La
Brise Vagabonde; Seuil De La
Vraie Jeunesse; Voici Que Se
Fait Si Furtive   (G12)

Seuil De La Vraie Jeunesse
see Quatre Melodies Sur Des Textes
D'Andre Gide

Voici Que Se Fait Si Furtive
see Quatre Melodies Sur Des Textes
D'Andre Gide

GADDY, CAROL
Shepherd Of Love *sac
solo,pno oct MASTER CP-MM 2002
1.25   (G13)

GADE, NIELS WILHELM (1817-1890)
Dans Le Foret
solo,pno ENOCH s.p. see also CHANTS
DU NORD   (G14)

Le Chasseur Du Bois D'Ete
solo,pno ENOCH s.p. see also CHANTS
DU NORD   (G15)

Oluf's Ballade (from Elverskud)
[Dan/Ger] med-low solo,kbd HANSEN-
DEN s.p.   (G16)

GAGIC, BOGDAN (1931-   )
L'ete De Nuit *CC4U
A solo,fl,bsn,trom,trp,pno,vla,bvl
MUSIC INFO rental   (G17)

GAGLIANO, GIOVANNI BATTISTA DA
(ca. 1585-ca. 1650)
Early Music Series, Vol. 2: Musiche,
Part I *CCU
(Geiringer, Karl) 1-2 soli,inst
PRESSER $6.00   (G18)

GAGLIANO, GIOVANNI BATTISTA DA
  (cont'd.)
    Early Music Series, Vol. 5: Musiche,
      Part II *CCU
      (Geiringer, Karl) 1-3 soli PRESSER
      $6.00   (G19)

GAGLIARDI, GEORGE
    Life Forever
      solo,pno FINE ARTS S469L $.80 (G20)

    Without, Within
      solo,pno FINE ARTS S669W $.80 (G21)

GAGNEBIN, HENRI (1886-   )
    Trois Chansons Spirtuelles *sac,CC3U
      solo,pno HENN 164 s.p.   (G22)

    Trois Melodies *CC3U
      solo,pno HENN 163 s.p.   (G23)

GAI LON LA
    see Five French Folk Songs

GAI PINSON see Delmet, Paul

GAI ROSSIGNOL, VIENS PAR ICI see
    Bernicat, F.

GAIETE AND ORIOR see Head, Michael
    (Dewar)

GAILHARD, ANDRE (1885-   )
    Six Chants Exotiques *CC6U
      [Fr] high solo,pno CHOUDENS C258
      s.p.   (G24)

GAILY SINGING see Medtner, Nikolai
    Karlovitch

GAINES, SAMUEL RICHARDS (1869-1945)
    My Heart Hath A Mind
      high solo,pno (E flat maj) GALAXY
      1.1518.7 $1.00   (G25)

GAITHER
    All God's Children *sac
      solo,pno BENSON S5098-RS $1.00
                                     (G26)

    Because He Lives *sac
      solo,pno BENSON S5157-R $1.00 (G27)
      solo,pno BENSON S5158-S $1.00 (G28)

    Bethlehem, Galilee, Gethsemane *sac
      solo,pno BENSON S5182-S $1.00 (G29)

    Blessed Jesus *sac
      solo,pno BENSON S5202-S $1.00 (G30)

    By The Witness Of The Spirit *sac
      solo,pno BENSON S5235-S $1.00 (G31)

    Church Triumphant, The *sac
      solo,pno BENSON S7793-S $1.00 (G32)

    Come, Holy Spirit *sac
      solo,pno BENSON S5298-S $1.00 (G33)

    Contented *sac
      solo,pno BENSON S5312-S $1.00 (G34)

    Family Of God, The *sac
      solo,pno BENSON S7842-S $1.00 (G35)

    Feeling At Home In The Presence Of
      Jesus *sac
      solo,pno BENSON S5450-S $1.00 (G36)

    Free To Go Home *sac
      solo,pno BENSON S5489-S $1.00 (G37)

    Gentle Shepherd *sac
      solo,pno BENSON S5510-S $1.00 (G38)

    Get All Excited *sac
      solo,pno BENSON S5507-S $1.00 (G39)

    Getting Used To The Family Of God
      *sac
      solo,pno BENSON S5508 $1.00 (G40)

    God Gave The Song *see Huff, Ronn

    Going Home *sac
      solo,pno BENSON S5584-S $1.00 (G41)

    Happiness *sac
      solo,pno BENSON S5616-RS $1.00
                                     (G42)

    Have You Had A Gethsemane *sac
      solo,pno BENSON S5644-S $1.00 (G43)

    He Touched Me *sac
      solo,pno BENSON 5718-R $1.00 (G44)
      solo,pno BENSON S5716-S $1.00 (G45)

    He's Still The King Of Kings *sac
      solo,pno BENSON S5798-S $1.00 (G46)

    Hill Called Mt. Calvary, A *sac
      solo,pno BENSON S5020-S $1.00 (G47)
      solo,pno BENSON S5022-R $1.00 (G48)

GAITHER (cont'd.)
    I Came To Praise The Lord *sac
      solo,pno BENSON S5976-S $1.00 (G49)

    I Could Never Outlove The Lord *sac
      solo,pno BENSON S5986-S $1.00 (G50)

    I Just Feel Like Something Good Is
      About To Happen *sac
      solo,pno BENSON S6051-S $1.00 (G51)

    I Will Serve Thee *sac
      solo,pno BENSON S6184-RS $1.00
                                     (G52)

    If It Keeps Gettin' Better *sac
      solo,pno BENSON S6478-S $1.00 (G53)

    I'm Almost Home *sac
      solo,pno BENSON S6292-S $1.00 (G54)

    I'm Free *sac
      solo,pno BENSON S6328-S $1.00 (G55)

    I'm Gonna Keep On *sac
      solo,pno BENSON S6339-S $1.00 (G56)

    It Will Be Worth It All *sac
      solo,pno BENSON S6620-S $1.00 (G57)

    I've Been To Calvary *sac
      solo,pno BENSON S6420-S $1.00 (G58)

    Jesus *sac
      solo,pno BENSON S6700-S $1.00 (G59)

    Jesus Is Lord Of All *sac
      solo,pno BENSON S6722-S $1.00 (G60)

    Jesus, We Just Want To Thank You
      *sac
      solo,pno BENSON S6709-S $1.00 (G61)

    Joy Comes In The Morning *sac
      solo,pno BENSON S6759-S $1.00 (G62)

    King Is Coming, The *sac
      solo,pno BENSON S7930-S $1.00 (G63)
      solo,pno BENSON S7931-R $1.00 (G64)

    Let's Just Praise The Lord *sac
      solo,pno BENSON S6858-S $1.00 (G65)

    Longer I Serve Him, The *sac
      solo,pno BENSON S7948-S $1.00 (G66)

    Lovest Thou Me *sac
      solo,pno BENSON S6996-S $1.00 (G67)

    My Faith Still Holds *sac
      solo,pno BENSON S7074-S $1.00 (G68)

    No Greater Love *sac
      solo,pno BENSON S7149-S $1.00 (G69)

    Old Rugged Cross Made The Difference,
      The *sac
      solo,pno BENSON S8012-S $1.00 (G70)
      solo,pno BENSON S8014-R $1.00 (G71)

    Oldham Sings Gaither, Vol. I *sac,
      CCUL
      solo,pno BENSON BO447 $2.50   (G72)

    Oldham Sings Gaither, Vol. II *sac,
      CCUL
      solo,pno BENSON BO448 $2.50   (G73)

    Plenty Of Room In The Family *sac
      solo,pno BENSON S7377-S $1.00 (G74)

    Rejoice, You're A Child Of The King
      *sac
      solo,pno BENSON S7419-S $1.00 (G75)

    Since Jesus Passed By *sac
      solo,pno BENSON S7500-S $1.00 (G76)

    Something Beautiful *sac
      solo,pno BENSON S7554-S $1.00 (G77)

    Something Worth Living For *sac
      solo,pno BENSON S7560-S $1.00 (G78)

    Spirit Of Jesus Is In This Place, The
      *sac
      solo,pno BENSON S8038-S $1.00 (G79)

    Thanks For Sunshine *sac
      solo,pno BENSON S7710-S $1.00 (G80)

    Thanks To Calvary *sac
      solo,pno BENSON S7712-RS $1.00
                                     (G81)

    That's Worth Everything *sac
      solo,pno BENSON S7749-S $1.00 (G82)

    There's Something About That Name
      *sac
      solo,pno BENSON S8113-R $1.00 (G83)
      solo,pno BENSON S8114-S $1.00 (G84)

    They That Sow In Tears *sac
      solo,pno BENSON S8132-S $1.00 (G85)

GAITHER (cont'd.)
    This Could Be The Dawning Of That Day
      *sac
      solo,pno BENSON S8146-S $1.00 (G86)

    Walk On The Water *sac
      solo,pno BENSON S8318-S $1.00 (G87)

    Waters Are Troubled, The *sac
      solo,pno BENSON S8079-S $1.00 (G88)

    Worthy The Lamb *sac
      solo,pno BENSON S8566-S $1.00 (G89)

GAITHER, GLORIA
    King Is Coming, The *see Gaither,
      William J. (Bill)

GAITHER, WILLIAM J. (BILL)
    Bill Gaither Trio *sac,CC12UL
      3 soli,pno BENSON BO460 $2.50 (G90)

    He Touched Me And Other Songs *CC9UL
      (DeCou, Harold) high solo,pno
      SINGSPIR 5416 $2.95; low solo,pno
      SINGSPIR 5415 $2.95; med solo,pno
      SINGSPIR 5414 $2.95; 3 female
      soli,pno SINGSPIR 5413 $2.95
                                     (G91)

    King Is Coming, The (composed with
      Gaither, Gloria) *sac,CC12UL
      solo,pno BENSON BO461 $2.95   (G92)

GAITO, CONSTANTINO (1878-1945)
    Flor De Ceibo
      [Span] solo,pno RICORDI-ARG BA 8886
      s.p.   (G93)

GALANT KWARTET see Mul, Jan

GALANT RENDEZ-VOUS see Berger, Rod.

GALANTE CONVERSATION see Goldberg, L.

GALATEA see Lora, Antonio

GALBRAITH, J.
    Lead Us, O Father *sac
      AB soli,pno BOSTON $1.75   (G94)
      ST soli,pno BOSTON $1.75   (G95)

GALEOTTI, CESARE (1872-1929)
    Si L'on Te Disait
      solo,pno ENOCH s.p.   (G96)

    Sur Un Nuage
      solo,pno ENOCH s.p.   (G97)

GALGEN see Lilien, Ignace

GALGENLIEDER NACH CHRISTIAN MORGENSTERN
    see Heiss, Hermann

GALGENLIEDER VON CHR. MORGENSTERN see
    Zagwijn, Henri

GALIL see Chajes, Julius

GALILEI see Matthus, Siegfried

GALINDO, BLAS (1910-   )
    Three Songs *CC3U
      [Span/Eng] solo,pno BARRY-ARG $2.00
                                     (G98)

GALL, JAN
    Madchen Mit Dem Roten Mundchen
      *Op.1,No.3
      A/Bar solo,pno LEUCKART s.p. (G99)

GALLAND, E.
    Monsieur Printemps
      2 soli,pno DURAND s.p.   (G100)

GALLANT SALAMANDER, THE see Barnard,
    D'Auvergive

GALLANT WEAVER, THE *folk,Scot
    low solo,pno (B flat maj) PATERSON
      FS107 s.p.   (G101)
    high solo,pno (C maj) PATERSON FS107
      s.p.   (G102)

GALLIARD, JOHANN ERNST (1687-1749)
    Wie Suss Ertont Des Vogels Sang
      S solo,S rec,A rec,vln,vla,cont sc
      UNIVER. 12629 $1.00, ipa   (G103)

GALLOIS, CH.
    La Source
      2 soli,pno DURAND s.p.   (G104)

    Les Papillons
      2 soli,pno DURAND s.p.   (G105)

GALLOIS MONTBRUN
    Chanson
      solo,orch LEDUC s.p. see from Trois
      Melodies   (G106)

    Les Sept Peches Capitaux *CC7L
      high solo,pno/inst LEDUC B.L.792
      s.p.   (G107)

GALLOIS MONTBRUN (cont'd.)

Lorsque Tu Dors
solo,orch LEDUC s.p. see from Trois
Melodies   (G108)

Souvenir
solo,orch LEDUC s.p. see from Trois
Melodies   (G109)

Trois Melodies *see Chanson; Lorsque
Tu Dors; Souvenir   (G110)

GALLON, NOEL (1891-1966)
La Marne
solo,pno ENOCH s.p. contains also:
L'Yser; Verdun   (G111)

L'Yser
see Gallon, Noel, La Marne

Verdun
see Gallon, Noel, La Marne

GALLOWAY, T.B.
Gypsy Trail
high solo,pno PRESSER $.75   (G112)

GALLOWS TREE, THE see Scott, Tom

GALM see Schierbeck, Poul

GALOS
Le Chant Du Berger
solo,pno/inst LEDUC s.p.   (G113)
solo,vln/vcl LEDUC s.p.   (G114)

Noel Sur Le Lac De Come
solo,pno/inst LEDUC s.p.   (G115)

GALUPPI, BALDASSARE (1706-1785)
Aria Di Lena (from Il Filosofo Di
Campagna)
S solo,strings CARISH s.p.   (G116)

Due Arie *CC2U
high solo,pno ISRAELI 320S $2.80
                                        (G117)

Rapida Cerva, Fuge *sac,cant
(Ewerhart, Rudolf) [Lat] S solo,
strings,cont sc BIELER DK 12
s.p., ipa   (G118)

GAMAL, G'MALI see Chajes, Julius

GAMBLER, DON'T YOU LOSE YOUR PLACE see
Niles, John Jacob

GAMBLER'S LAMENT, THE see Niles, John
Jacob

GAMBLER'S WIFE, THE see Niles, John
Jacob

GAMIN, CONSCRIT, SOLDAT see Gauwin, Ad.

GAMLA GODA DAR see Auld Lang Syne

GAMMAL BONDE see Nordqvist, Gustaf

GAMMAL NEDERLANDARE see Stenhammar,
Wilhelm

GAMMAL RAMSA see Peterson-Berger,
(Olof) Wilhelm

GAMMAL SORG see Nordqvist, Gustaf

GAM'SE L'TOIVOH see Meyerowitz, David

GANDINO, ADOLFO
Abbandonato
[It] solo,pno BONGIOVANI 342 s.p.
see from Ventiquattro Melodie
                                        (G119)

Alba Festiva
[It] solo,pno BONGIOVANI 441 s.p.
see from Dodici Nuove Melodie
                                        (G120)
"Aube De Fete" [Fr/It] solo,pno
BONGIOVANI 864 s.p. see from
Dodici Nuove Melodie   (G121)
"Festive Dawn, A" [Eng] solo,pno
BONGIOVANI 865 s.p. see from
Dodici Nuove Melodie   (G122)

Aprile
[It] solo,pno BONGIOVANI 341 s.p.
see from Ventiquattro Melodie
                                        (G123)

Aube De Fete *see Alba Festiva

Calendaprile
[It] solo,pno BONGIOVANI 435 s.p.
see from Dodici Nuove Melodie
                                        (G124)

Ciclamino D'autunno
[It] solo,pno BONGIOVANI 1684 s.p.
see also Quattro Fiori   (G125)

Ciclamino Di Primavera
[It] solo,pno BONGIOVANI 1683 s.p.
see also Quattro Fiori   (G126)

GANDINO, ADOLFO (cont'd.)

Cinque Liriche
[It] solo,pno cmplt ed BONGIOVANI
1717 s.p.
contains & see also: Il Brivido;
La Messa; La Tessitrice; Le
Ciaramelle; L'or Di Notte   (G127)

Con Il Angioli
[It] solo,pno BONGIOVANI 329 s.p.
see from Ventiquattro Melodie
                                        (G128)

D'Inverno
[It] solo,pno BONGIOVANI 436 s.p.
see from Dodici Nuove Melodie
                                        (G129)

Dodici Nuove Melodie *see Alba
Festiva; Calendaprile; D'Inverno;
Invito Alla Caccia; Le Nove Son
Suonate; Morto; Ninna Nanna;
Notturno; O Falce Di Luna; Rondo;
Vagito; Veneziana; Viole Pallide
                                        (G130)

Domani Vado Via
[It] solo,pno BONGIOVANI 323 s.p.
see from Ventiquattro Melodie
                                        (G131)

Festive Dawn, A *see Alba Festiva

Festive Evening, A *see Sera Festiva

Ho Pianto In Sogno
[It] solo,pno BONGIOVANI 327 s.p.
see from Ventiquattro Melodie
                                        (G132)

Il Brivido
[It] solo,pno BONGIOVANI 1718 s.p.
see also Cinque Liriche   (G133)

Il Canto Si Levo
see Quattro Paesaggi Abruzzesi

Il Melagrano
[It] solo,pno BONGIOVANI 1686 s.p.
see also Quattro Fiori   (G134)

Il Verno
[It] solo,pno BONGIOVANI 1681 s.p.
see also Quattro Paesaggi
Abruzzesi   (G135)

Invito Alla Caccia
[It] solo,pno BONGIOVANI 444 s.p.
see from Dodici Nuove Melodie
                                        (G136)

Io Sono Stanca
[It] solo,pno BONGIOVANI 325 s.p.
see from Ventiquattro Melodie
                                        (G137)

La Figlia Del Re Degli Elfi
[It] solo,pno BONGIOVANI 337 s.p.
see from Ventiquattro Melodie
                                        (G138)

La Lavandaia
[It] solo,pno BONGIOVANI 336 s.p.
see from Ventiquattro Melodie
                                        (G139)

La Mano Tua Mi Posa
[It] solo,pno BONGIOVANI 322 s.p.
see from Ventiquattro Melodie
                                        (G140)

La Messa
[It] solo,pno BONGIOVANI 1719 s.p.
see also Cinque Liriche   (G141)

La Tessitrice
[It] solo,pno BONGIOVANI 1721 s.p.
see also Cinque Liriche   (G142)

La Vendemmia
[It] solo,pno BONGIOVANI 1680 s.p.
see also Quattro Paesaggi
Abruzzesi   (G143)

Lai
[It] solo,pno BONGIOVANI 332 s.p.
see from Ventiquattro Melodie
                                        (G144)

Le Ciaramelle
[It] solo,pno BONGIOVANI 1722 s.p.
see also Cinque Liriche   (G145)

Le Nove Son Suonate
[It/Eng] solo,pno BONGIOVANI 1688
s.p. see from Dodici Nuove
Melodie   (G146)

L'or Di Notte
[It] solo,pno BONGIOVANI 1720 s.p.
see also Cinque Liriche   (G147)

Lungi Lungi
[It] solo,pno BONGIOVANI 321 s.p.
see from Ventiquattro Melodie
                                        (G148)

Minuetto
[It] solo,pno BONGIOVANI 335 s.p.
see from Ventiquattro Melodie
                                        (G149)

Miranda
[It] solo,pno BONGIOVANI 333 s.p.
see from Ventiquattro Melodie
                                        (G150)

GANDINO, ADOLFO (cont'd.)

Morto
[It] solo,pno BONGIOVANI 442 s.p.
see from Dodici Nuove Melodie
                                        (G151)

Ninna Nanna
[It] solo,pno BONGIOVANI 438 s.p.
see from Dodici Nuove Melodie
                                        (G152)

Notte
[It] solo,pno BONGIOVANI 344 s.p.
see from Ventiquattro Melodie
                                        (G153)

Notturno
[It] solo,pno BONGIOVANI 443 s.p.
see from Dodici Nuove Melodie
                                        (G154)

O Falce Di Luna
[It] solo,pno BONGIOVANI 445 s.p.
see from Dodici Nuove Melodie
                                        (G155)

Olaf, Il Vecchio Re
[It] solo,pno BONGIOVANI 338 s.p.
see from Ventiquattro Melodie
                                        (G156)

Orfano
[It] solo,pno BONGIOVANI 328 s.p.
see from Ventiquattro Melodie
                                        (G157)

Pianto
[It] solo,pno BONGIOVANI 331 s.p.
see from Ventiquattro Melodie
                                        (G158)

Quattro Fiori
[It] solo,pno cmplt ed BONGIOVANI
1682 s.p.
contains & see also: Ciclamino
D'autunno; Ciclamino Di
Primavera; Il Melagrano; Una
Rosetta   (G159)

Quattro Paesaggi Abruzzesi
[It] solo,pno cmplt ed BONGIOVANI
1677 s.p.
contains: Il Canto Si Levo; Il
Verno; La Vendemmia; San
Vincenzo
see also: Il Verno; La Vendemmia;
San Vincenzo   (G160)

Rondo
[It] solo,pno BONGIOVANI 446 s.p.
see from Dodici Nuove Melodie
                                        (G161)

San Vincenzo
[It] solo,pno BONGIOVANI 1678 s.p.
see also Quattro Paesaggi
Abruzzesi   (G162)

Selva E Mare
[It] solo,pno BONGIOVANI 334 s.p.
see from Ventiquattro Melodie
                                        (G163)

Sera Festiva
[Fr/It] solo,pno BONGIOVANI 860
s.p. see from Ventiquattro
Melodie   (G164)
[It] solo,pno BONGIOVANI 330 s.p.
see from Ventiquattro Melodie
                                        (G165)
"Festive Evening, A" [Eng] solo,pno
BONGIOVANI 861 s.p. see from
Ventiquattro Melodie   (G166)

Serenata
[It] solo,pno BONGIOVANI 343 s.p.
see from Ventiquattro Melodie
                                        (G167)

Similitudine
[It] solo,pno BONGIOVANI 326 s.p.
see from Ventiquattro Melodie
                                        (G168)

Spes, Ultima Dea
[It] solo,pno BONGIOVANI 339 s.p.
see from Ventiquattro Melodie
                                        (G169)

Splende Il Sole
[It] solo,pno BONGIOVANI 324 s.p.
see from Ventiquattro Melodie
                                        (G170)

Una Rosetta
[It] solo,pno BONGIOVANI 1685 s.p.
see also Quattro Fiori   (G171)

Vagito
[It] solo,pno BONGIOVANI 437 s.p.
see from Dodici Nuove Melodie
                                        (G172)

Veneziana
[It] solo,pno BONGIOVANI 439 s.p.
see from Dodici Nuove Melodie
                                        (G173)

Ventiquattro Melodie *see
Abbandonato; Aprile; Con Il
Angioli; Domani Vado Via; Ho
Pianto In Sogno; Io Sono Stanca;
La Figlia Del Re Degli Elfi; La
Lavandaia; La Mano Tua Mi Posa;
Lai; Lungi Lungi; Minuetto;
Miranda; Notte; Olaf, Il Vecchio
Re; Orfano; Pianto; Selva E Mare;
Sera Festiva; Serenata;
Similitudine; Spes, Ultima Dea;
Splende Il Sole   (G174)

GANDINO, ADOLFO (cont'd.)

Viole Pallide
[It] solo,pno BONGIOVANI 440 s.p.
see from Dodici Nuove Melodie
(G175)

GANGLOFF, L.
Passez-Moi L'madere
solo,pno ENOCH s.p.   (G176)
solo,acap ENOCH s.p.   (G177)

GANNE, LOUIS GASTON (1862-1923)
Donne-Moi Ton Coeur
solo,pno ENOCH s.p.   (G178)
solo,acap ENOCH s.p.   (G179)

Extase
solo,pno ENOCH s.p.   (G180)
solo,acap ENOCH s.p.   (G181)

Fabliau
solo,pno ENOCH s.p.   (G182)
solo,acap ENOCH s.p.   (G183)

Hymne De La Jeunesse Chretienne *sac
solo,pno ENOCH s.p.   (G184)
solo,acap ENOCH s.p.   (G185)
[Fr] solo,pno ENOCH   (G186)

La Czarine
solo,pno ENOCH s.p.   (G187)
solo,acap ENOCH s.p.   (G188)

La Housarde
solo,pno ENOCH s.p.   (G189)
solo,acap ENOCH s.p.   (G190)

La Mousme
solo,pno ENOCH s.p.   (G191)
solo,acap ENOCH s.p.   (G192)

La Noce Du Violoniste
solo,pno ENOCH s.p.   (G193)
solo,acap ENOCH s.p.   (G194)

Lamento
(Bordese, Stephen) solo,pno
(available in 2 keys) ENOCH s.p.
see also CHANSONS DE PAGE   (G195)

Le Cocher
solo,pno ENOCH s.p.   (G196)
solo,acap ENOCH s.p.   (G197)

Les Trois Heures De La Vie
solo,pno ENOCH s.p.   (G198)
solo,acap ENOCH s.p.   (G199)

Marche D'Auvergne
solo,pno ENOCH s.p.   (G200)
solo,acap ENOCH s.p.   (G201)

Marche Des Amoureux
solo,pno ENOCH s.p.   (G202)
solo,acap ENOCH s.p.   (G203)

Marche Grecque
solo,pno ENOCH s.p.   (G204)
solo,acap ENOCH s.p.   (G205)

Marche Lorraine
solo,pno ENOCH s.p.   (G206)
solo,acap ENOCH s.p.   (G207)

Marche Russe
solo,acap ENOCH s.p.   (G208)

Marches D'Auvergne
solo,acap ENOCH s.p. see from
CHANSONS DE TROUPE   (G209)

Meneut Rose
solo,pno ENOCH s.p.   (G210)
solo,acap ENOCH s.p.   (G211)

Nos Petits Matelots
solo,pno ENOCH s.p.   (G212)
solo,acap ENOCH s.p.   (G213)

Serenade Paienne
solo,pno (available in 2 keys)
ENOCH s.p.   (G214)
solo,acap (available in 2 keys)
ENOCH s.p.   (G215)

GANSEBLUMCHEN UND SCHMETTERLING see
Lehner, Leo

GANYMED see Nielsen, Riccardo

GANYMED see Schubert, Franz (Peter)

GANZ, RUDOLPH (1877-   )
If Roses Never Bloomed Again
high solo,pno BELWIN $1.50   (G216)

Memory, A
high solo,pno (G maj) SCHIRM.G $.85
(G217)

Vad Ar Karlek
low solo,pno GEHRMANS s.p.   (G218)
high solo,pno GEHRMANS s.p. (G219)

GANZ, WILHELM (1833-1914)
I Seek For Thee In Every Flower
low solo,pno (E flat maj) ASHDOWN
(G220)
med solo,pno (F maj) ASHDOWN
(G221)
med-high solo,pno (G maj) ASHDOWN
(G222)
high solo,pno (A flat maj) ASHDOWN
(G223)

Sing Sweet Bird
low solo,pno (B flat maj) ASHDOWN
(G224)
med solo,pno (C maj) ASHDOWN (G225)
high solo,pno (D flat maj) ASHDOWN
(G226)

GARANT, S.
Anerca
S solo,8inst BERANDOL BER 1113
$8.00   (G227)

Cage D'Oiseau
solo,pno BERANDOL BER 1114 $5.00
(G228)

Phrases I *CCU
A solo,pno,cel,perc BERANDOL
BER 1115 $15.00   (G229)

GARBAROCHE, G.
Valse Merveilleuse
solo,pno ENOCH s.p.   (G230)
solo,acap ENOCH s.p.   (G231)

GARCIA, M.
El Majo Y La Maja
(Subira) 2 soli,pno UNION ESP.
$7.00   (G232)

GARCIA ABRIL, A.
Coleccion De Canciones Infantiles
*CCU
[Span] med solo,pno UNION ESP.
$1.50   (G233)

Tres Canciones Espanolas *CC3U
[Span] med solo,pno UNION ESP.
$1.50   (G234)

GARCIA ESTRADA, JUAN AGUSTIN
(1895-   )
Cancion De Cuna
[Ger/Span/Eng/It] solo,pno RICORDI-
ARG BA 7323 s.p.   (G235)

En El Bosque
"In The Forest" [Span/Eng/It] solo,
pno RICORDI-ARG BA 7368 s.p.
(G236)

In The Forest *see En El Bosque

GARCIA LEOZ, J.
Dos Canciones
[Span] med-high solo,pno UNION ESP.
$1.25
contains: El Mar Lejano; Verde
Verderol   (G237)

El Mar Lejano
see Dos Canciones

Seis Canciones *CC6U
[Span] med-high solo,pno UNION ESP.
$2.50   (G238)

Triptico De Canciones
[Span] med-high solo,pno UNION ESP.
$1.10   (G239)

Verde Verderol
see Dos Canciones

GARCIA MANSILLA, EDUARDO
El Magico Jardin (from La Angelical
Manuelita)
[Span] S solo,pno RICORDI-ARG
BA 5481 s.p.   (G240)

En Madrid La Bella (from La Angelical
Manuelita)
[Span] S solo,pno RICORDI-ARG
BA 5482 s.p.   (G241)

GARCIA MORILLO, ROBERTO (1911-   )
Al Ilegar Al Camposanto *Op.28,No.3
see Romances Del Amor Y La Muerte

Aquella Sierra Nevada *Op.18,No.5
(from Marin)
[Span] solo,pno RICORDI-ARG
BA 11402 s.p.   (G242)

Asi Morire! *Op.18,No.9 (from Marin)
[Span] solo,pno RICORDI-ARG
BA 11404 s.p.   (G243)

De La Muchacha Dorada (from El
Tamarit)
see Garcia Morillo, Roberto, Del
Amor Con Cien Anos

De La Rosa (from El Tamarit)
see Garcia Morillo, Roberto, Del
Amor Con Cien Anos

De Los Ramos (from El Tamarit)
see Garcia Morillo, Roberto, Del
Amor Con Cien Anos

GARCIA MORILLO, ROBERTO (cont'd.)

Del Amor Con Cien Anos (from El
Tamarit)
[Span] solo,pno cmplt ed RICORDI-
ARG BA 11584 s.p. contains also:
Del Amor Maravilloso; De La
Muchacha Dorada; De La Rosa; De
Los Ramos   (G244)

Del Amor Maravilloso (from El
Tamarit)
see Garcia Morillo, Roberto, Del
Amor Con Cien Anos

En El Palacio Los Soldados *Op.28,
No.2
see Romances Del Amor Y La Muerte

Que Bien Canta Un Ruisenor *Op.18,
No.7 (from Marin)
[Span] solo,pno RICORDI-ARG
BA 11403 s.p.   (G245)

Romances Del Amor Y La Muerte
[Span] solo,pno cmplt ed RICORDI-
ARG BA 12206 s.p.
contains: Al Ilegar Al
Camposanto, Op.28,No.3; En El
Palacio Los Soldados, Op.28,
No.2; Yo Me Patiera De Burgus,
Op.28,No.1   (G246)

Ya No Puedo Mas, Senora *Op.18,No.3
(from Marin)
[Span] solo,pno RICORDI-ARG
BA 11401 s.p.   (G247)

Yo Me Patiera De Burgus *Op.28,No.1
see Romances Del Amor Y La Muerte

GARDEN, THE see Griffes, Charles
Tomlinson, Le Jardin

GARDEN EASTWARD see Weisgall, Hugo

GARDEN I LOVE see Nutting, Godfrey

GARDEN IS A LOVESOME THING see Hill

GARDEN IS A LOVESOME THING, A see
Mallinson, (James) Albert

GARDEN OF HAPPINESS see Wood, Daniel

GARDEN OF MEMORIES see Arundale, Claude

GARDEN OF YOUR HEART see Dorel, F.

GARDEN WHERE THE PRATIES GROW see
Liddle, Samuel

GARDENS BY THE SEA see Repper, Charles

GARDNER, IRENE J.
Bow Down Thine Ear *sac,Gen
high solo,pno (F maj) WILLIS $.60
(G248)
low solo,pno (D flat maj) WILLIS
$.60   (G249)

GARLAND, THE see Mendelssohn-Bartholdy,
Felix

GARLAND, HUGH
Fond Memories
solo,pno (G min) LESLIE 7029 (G250)

GARLAND OF MOUNTAIN SONG, A *CC24U,
folk,US
(Ritchie) med solo,pno BMI $3.50
(G251)

GARLICK, ANTHONY
Psalm 23 *sac
T solo,pno sc SEESAW $3.00   (G252)

GARNALENWALS see Rontgen, Johannes

GARTAN MOTHER'S LULLABY see Hughes,
Herbert

GARTLAN
Lilac Tree
high solo,pno (A maj) ALLANS s.p.
(G253)
low solo,pno (F maj) ALLANS s.p.
(G254)
med solo,pno (G maj) ALLANS s.p.
(G255)

GARTNER, CLARENCE
Love Is Mine
low solo,pno (B flat maj) LEONARD-
ENG   (G256)
med solo,pno (C maj) LEONARD-ENG
(G257)
high solo,pno (E flat maj) LEONARD-
ENG   (G258)

Out Of The Crimson West
low solo,pno (A flat maj) CRAMER
(G259)
high solo,pno (C maj) CRAMER (G260)

Trusting Eyes
low solo,pno (B flat maj) LEONARD-
ENG   (G261)

GARTNER, CLARENCE (cont'd.)

    high solo,pno (C maj) LEONARD-ENG
                     (G262)

GASCOGNE *Fr
  (Canteloube, J.) solo,acap DURAND
  s.p. see also Anthologie Des Chants
  Populaires Francais Tome I   (G263)

GASELEN see Schoeck, Othmar

GASLINI, GIORGIO (1929-   )
  Magnificat *sac
  [Lat] S solo,al-sax,pno,bvl UNIVER.
  13589 $4.25   (G264)

GASS, IRENE
  On A Holiday
  solo,pno CRAMER   (G265)

GASSENHAWERLIN UND REUTTERLIEDLIN see
  Egenolf

GASSNER, MOSHE
  Hayareach Hatsahov
  solo,pno OR-TAV $1.00   (G266)

GAST, LOTHAR (1928-   )
  Wir Ruhmen Uns Allein Des Kreuzes
  *sac
  med solo,org HANSSLER 12.218 s.p.
                     (G267)

GASTALDON, STANISLAS
  Forbidden Music *see Musica Proibita

  Forbjuden Musik *see Musica Proibita

  Musica Proibita
  "Forbidden Music" [It/Eng] high
    solo,pno (A maj) SCHIRM.G $.75
                     (G268)
  "Forbidden Music" [It/Eng] med
    solo,pno (G maj) SCHIRM.G $.75
                     (G269)
  "Forbjuden Musik" A/B solo,pno
    GEHRMANS s.p.   (G270)
  "Forbjuden Musik" S/T solo,pno
    GEHRMANS s.p.   (G271)
  "Forbjuden Musik" Mez/Bar solo,pno,
    opt gtr GEHRMANS s.p.   (G272)

GASTINEL, LEON-GUSTAVE-CYPIEN
  (1823-1906)
  Automne
  2 soli,pno DURAND s.p.   (G273)

  Le Ruisseau
  2 soli,pno DURAND s.p.   (G274)

  Le Village
  2 soli,pno DURAND s.p.   (G275)

  Les Deux Colombes
  2 soli,pno DURAND s.p.   (G276)

GATE OF THE YEAR, THE see Barnes,
  Marshall H.

GATE OF THE YEAR, THE see Heaton,
  Leonard

GATE OF THE YEAR (NEW YEAR'S) see Pull,
  Edwin

GATHER YE ROSEBUDS see Ferne, Kenneth

GATHER YE ROSEBUDS see Sanderson,
  Wilfred

GATHERING DAFFODILS see Somervell,
  Arthur

GATHERING FLOWERS FOR THE MASTER'S
  BOUQUET *sac,gospel
  solo,pno ABER.GRP. $1.50   (G277)

GATHERING OF THE CLANS see Gourley,
  Ronald

GATLIN, LARRY
  Help Me *sac
  solo,pno BENSON S5829-S $1.00
                     (G278)
  It Must Have Rained In Heaven *sac
  solo,pno WORD S-421   (G279)

GATO see De Rogatis, Pascual

GATO see Ginastera, Alberto

GATO see Sammartino, Luis

GATTY, A. SCOTT
  O That We Two Were Maying
  2 soli,pno LEONARD-ENG   (G280)

GAUBERT, PHILIPPE (1879-1941)
  Dans Le Silence Pur
  solo,pno/inst DURAND s.p. see also
    Six Melodies   (G281)

  Donc, Ce Sera Par Un Clair Jour D'ete
  solo,pno/inst DURAND s.p. see also
    Six Melodies   (G282)

GAUBERT, PHILIPPE (cont'd.)

  En Sourdine
  solo,pno/inst DURAND s.p. see also
    Six Melodies   (G283)

  Et You, You, You
  see Trois Nouvelles Ballades
    Francaises De Paul Fort

  La Foret Ardente
  solo,pno ENOCH s.p. see from Poemes
    D'Automne   (G284)

  La Lune Blanche
  solo,pno/inst DURAND s.p. see also
    Six Melodies   (G285)

  Le Ciel Est Gai, C'est Joli Mai
  see Quatre Balades Francaises De
    Paul Fort

  Le Depart Du Matelot
  see Quatre Balades Francaises De
    Paul Fort

  Le Jardin Mouille
  solo,pno/inst DURAND s.p. see also
    Six Melodies   (G286)

  Le Repos En Egypte
  solo,pno (available in 2 keys)
    ENOCH s.p.   (G287)

  Le Secret
  solo,pno/inst DURAND s.p.   (G288)

  Le Val Harmonieux
  solo,pno/inst DURAND s.p. see also
    Six Melodies   (G289)

  Les Deux Ames
  see Trois Nouvelles Ballades
    Francaises De Paul Fort

  Les Paroles Que Tu M'as Dites
  see Trois Nouvelles Ballades
    Francaises De Paul Fort

  Mon Desir
  solo,pno ENOCH s.p.   (G290)

  Parfum
  solo,pno ENOCH s.p.   (G291)

  Paysage
  solo,pno ENOCH s.p.   (G292)
  solo,orch ENOCH rental   (G293)

  Poemes D'Automne *see La Foret
    Ardente; Soir Empourpre   (G294)

  Pour L'Absente
  solo,pno ENOCH s.p.   (G295)

  Quatre Balades Francaises De Paul
    Fort
  DURAND high solo,orch cmplt ed
    s.p., ipr; low solo,pno/inst
    cmplt ed s.p.
    contains: Le Ciel Est Gai, C'est
      Joli Mai; Le Depart Du Matelot;
      S'ils Gagnent Bataille; Sur La
      Mer, Au Pale Soleil   (G296)

  S'ils Gagnent Bataille
  see Quatre Balades Francaises De
    Paul Fort

  Six Melodies
  solo,pno/inst cmplt ed DURAND s.p.
    contains & see also: Dans Le
      Silence Pur; Donc, Ce Sera Par
      Un Clair Jour D'ete; En
      Sourdine; La Lune Blanche; Le
      Jardin Mouille; Le Val
      Harmonieux   (G297)

  Soir Empourpre
  solo,orch ENOCH rental   (G298)
  solo,pno ENOCH s.p. see from Poemes
    D'Automne   (G299)

  Soir Paien
  solo,fl,pno ENOCH s.p.   (G300)

  Sur La Mer, Au Pale Soleil
  see Quatre Balades Francaises De
    Paul Fort

  Trois Nouvelles Ballades Francaises
    De Paul Fort
  solo,pno/inst cmplt ed DURAND s.p.
    contains: Et You, You, You; Les
      Deux Ames; Les Paroles Que Tu
      M'as Dites   (G301)

  Une Fee
  solo,pno (available in 2 keys)
    ENOCH s.p.   (G302)

GAUDIA, PASTORES, OPTATE see Gratiani,
  Bonifatio

GAUKLE, GAUKLE, MADCHENFALTER see
  Mirandolle, Ludovicus

GAUL
  Shepherds And The Inn
  med solo,pno PRESSER $.95   (G303)

GAUL, ALFRED ROBERT (1837-1913)
  Eye Hath Not Seen (from Holy City,
    The) sac
  med solo,pno (B flat maj) SCHIRM.G
    $.85   (G304)

GAUL, HARVEY BARTLET (1881-1945)
  Joy
  high solo,pno BELWIN $1.50   (G305)
  low solo,pno BELWIN $1.50   (G306)

  Zions Children, Comin Along
  low solo,pno GALAXY 1.1690.7 $1.00
                     (G307)

GAUWIN, AD.
  Gamin, Conscrit, Soldat
  solo,pno ENOCH s.p.   (G308)
  solo,acap ENOCH s.p.   (G309)

  Marche Bretonne
  solo,acap ENOCH s.p. see from
    CHANSONS DE TROUPE   (G310)
  solo,pno ENOCH s.p.   (G311)

GAVAZZENI, GIANANDREA (1909-   )
  Notturni Di Bevoitori Bergamaschi
  *CCU
  T solo,orch voc sc ZERBONI 3794
    s.p.   (G312)

GAVEAUX, PIERRE (1761-1825)
  Conservez Bien La Paix Du Coeur
  solo,pno DURAND 190 s.p.   (G313)

  Dieu Du Bonheur (from Le Trompeur
    Trompe)
  (Flothius, Marius) [Fr] S solo,
    clar,pno BROEKMANS 395-16 s.p.
                     (G314)

GAVITO, J.S.
  Cinco Melodies *CC5U
  [Span/Fr] med solo,pno ESCHIG $4.25
                     (G315)

GAVOTTE see Lacome, Paul

GAVOTTE see Schouwman, Hans

GAVOTTE CHANTEE, A L'AMOUR RENDEZ LES
  ARMES see Rameau, Jean-Philippe

GAY, JOHN (1685-1732)
  Funf Airs Aus "The Beggar's Opera"
    (from Beggar's Opera, The) CC5U
  (Pepusch, J. Chr.) [Ger/Eng]
    DOBLINGER 08 558 $1.50   (G316)

GAYATRI see Marvia, Einari

GAZAROSSIAN, COHARIK A.
  Trois Chansons Populaires Armeniennes
  *CC3U
  [Fr] solo,pno/inst DURAND s.p.
    Armenian text also   (G317)

GAZELLE LIEDEREN see Masseus, Jan

GAZTAMBIDE, JOAQUIN (1822-1870)
  Gracias, Fortuna Mia (from Juramento)
  [Span] Bar solo,pno RICORDI-ARG
    BA 2020 s.p.   (G318)

GEAN, THE see Musgrave, Thea

GEBED see Bosmans, Henriette

GEBED see Brucken Fock, G.H.G. van

GEBED VAN EEN GHETTO-JOOD see Lier,
  Bertus van

GEBED VAN STELLA see Mortelmans,
  Lodewijk

GEBEDT see Dijk, Jan van

GEBENEDIJD see Dijk, Jan van

GEBET see Bijvanck, Henk

GEBET see Ehrenberg, Carl Emil Theodor

GEBET see Knab, Armin

GEBET see Maasalo, Armas, Rukous

GEBET see Wolf, Hugo

GEBET AN DEN SONNTAG see Andriessen,
  Hendrik

GEBET OBDACH! see Nielsen, Carl,
  Husvild

GEBET OP EEN HEWELIJKSFEEST see
  Adriessen, Willem

GEBET VON BAHA 'U'N9LIAH see Wolcott,
  Ch

GEBURTSAKT DER PHILOSOPHIE see
    Straesser, Joep

GEBURTSTAG see Kludas, Erich

GEDACHTNISLIEDER see Kox, Hans

GEDAINK, ICH HOB MEIN HARTZ GEGEBEN DIR
    *Jew
    solo,pno KAMMEN 463 $1.00   (G319)

GEDALGE, ANDRE (1856-1926)
    Au Revoir
        solo,pno (available in 2 keys)
        ENOCH s.p. see also Dans Le Foret
                                          (G320)
    Aux Chenes
        solo,pno (available in 2 keys)
        ENOCH s.p. see also Dans Le Foret
                                          (G321)
    Celle Qui Passe
        solo,pno (available in 2 keys)
        ENOCH s.p.   (G322)
    Chanson D'Antan
        solo,pno (available in 2 keys)
        ENOCH s.p.   (G323)
    Chanson Du Spectre
        solo,acap ENOCH s.p.   (G324)
        solo,pno ENOCH s.p.   (G325)
    Cueillette
        solo,pno (available in 2 keys)
        ENOCH s.p.   (G326)
    Dans Le Foret *CC15L
        solo,pno cmplt ed ENOCH s.p.
        see also: Au Revoir; Aux Chenes;
            Epanouissement; Eveil; L'Amour
            Lointain; Le Charme Est Rompu;
            Le Sentier; Lilas; Ma Bien-
            Aimee; Matin De Mai; Mon Coeur
            Dort; Pour Ma Mignonne;
            Pourquoi; Reves; Serenade
                                          (G327)
    Dans Les Ruines D'une Abbaye
        solo,pno (available in 2 keys)
        ENOCH s.p.   (G328)
    Epanouissement
        solo,pno (available in 2 keys)
        ENOCH s.p. see also Dans Le Foret
                                          (G329)
    Eveil
        solo,pno (available in 2 keys)
        ENOCH s.p. see also Dans Le Foret
                                          (G330)
    La Belle Fille
        solo,pno (available in 2 keys)
        ENOCH s.p.   (G331)
    L'Amour Lointain
        solo,pno (available in 2 keys)
        ENOCH s.p. see also Dans Le Foret
                                          (G332)
    Le Charme Est Rompu
        solo,pno (available in 2 keys)
        ENOCH s.p. see also Dans Le Foret
                                          (G333)
    Le Chemin Des Ecolieres
        solo,acap (available in 2 keys)
        ENOCH s.p.   (G334)
        solo,pno (available in 2 keys)
        ENOCH s.p.   (G335)
    Le Sentier
        solo,pno (available in 2 keys)
        ENOCH s.p. see also Dans Le Foret
                                          (G336)
    Lilas
        solo,pno (available in 2 keys)
        ENOCH s.p. see also Dans Le Foret
                                          (G337)
    Ma Bien-Aimee
        solo,pno (available in 2 keys)
        ENOCH s.p. see also Dans Le Foret
                                          (G338)
    Matin De Mai
        solo,pno (available in 2 keys)
        ENOCH s.p. see also Dans Le Foret
                                          (G339)
    Mon Coeur Dort
        solo,pno (available in 2 keys)
        ENOCH s.p. see also Dans Le Foret
                                          (G340)
    Pour Ma Mignonne
        solo,pno (available in 2 keys)
        ENOCH s.p. see also Dans Le Foret
                                          (G341)
    Pourquoi
        solo,pno (available in 2 keys)
        ENOCH s.p. see also Dans Le Foret
                                          (G342)
    Reves
        solo,pno (available in 2 keys)
        ENOCH s.p. see also Dans Le Foret
                                          (G343)
    Sept Chansons De Robert Burns *CC7L
        solo,pno ENOCH s.p.   (G344)
    Serenade
        solo,pno (available in 2 keys)
        ENOCH s.p. see also Dans Le Foret
                                          (G345)

GEDANKENNAHE see Trunk, Richard

GEDANKENSTILLE see Reznicek, Emil
    Nikolaus von

GEDENK' AN JESU BITTERN TOD see Bach,
    Johann Sebastian

GEDENKE, HERR, AN DEINE BARMHERZIGKEIT
    see Kretzschmar, Gunther

GEDENKEN see Schmalstich, Clemens

GEDENKT MIJ IN UW GEBEDEN see Mulder,
    Ernest W.

GEDENKT MIJ IN UW GEBEDEN see Mulder,
    Herman

GEDICHT see Mulder, Herman

GEEF NU IK IN TWIJFEL KNIEL see
    Andriessen, K.

GEEHL, HENRY ERNEST (1881-   )
    Auld Songs Of Hame
        low solo,pno (C maj) ASHDOWN (G346)
        high solo,pno (F maj) ASHDOWN
                                          (G347)
        med solo,pno (E flat maj) ASHDOWN
                                          (G348)
    Contraband
        high solo,pno (D maj) LEONARD-ENG
                                          (G349)
        low solo,pno (C maj) LEONARD-ENG
                                          (G350)
    Enchantment
        high solo,pno (F maj) LEONARD-ENG
                                          (G351)
        low solo,pno (C maj) LEONARD-ENG
                                          (G352)
    Fairy Folk
        high solo,pno (G maj) ASHDOWN
                                          (G353)
        med solo,pno (F maj) ASHDOWN (G354)
        low solo,pno (E flat maj) ASHDOWN
                                          (G355)
    Farewell
        solo,pno ASHDOWN see from Two Songs
                                          (G356)
    For Dig Allen *see For You Alone
    For You Alone
        med solo,pno,opt vln (E flat maj)
            LEONARD-ENG   (G357)
        2 soli,pno (E flat maj) LEONARD-ENG
                                          (G358)
        low solo,pno,opt vln (D flat maj)
            LEONARD-ENG   (G359)
        high solo,pno,opt vln (G maj)
            LEONARD-ENG   (G360)
        med-high solo,pno,opt vln (F maj)
            LEONARD-ENG   (G361)
        2 soli,pno (F maj) LEONARD-ENG
                                          (G362)
        "For Dig Allen" solo,pno LUNDQUIST
            s.p.   (G363)
        "Fur Dich Allein" solo,pno HUG s.p.
                                          (G364)
    Fur Dich Allein *see For You Alone

    "Good-Day!" Said The Blackbird
        low solo,pno (C maj) ASHDOWN (G365)
        med solo,pno (D flat maj) ASHDOWN
                                          (G366)
        high solo,pno (E flat maj) ASHDOWN
                                          (G367)
    If All The Stars Were Diamonds
        low solo,pno (C maj) LEONARD-ENG
                                          (G368)
        high solo,pno (F maj) LEONARD-ENG
                                          (G369)
    Island Of The Purple Sea
        2 soli,pno LEONARD-ENG   (G370)
    Lily, The
        solo,pno ASHDOWN see from Two Songs
                                          (G371)
    May Time
        2 soli,pno (F maj) LEONARD-ENG
                                          (G372)
        2 soli,pno (G maj) LEONARD-ENG
                                          (G373)
    Mountains Of Allah, The *CCU
        solo,pno LEONARD-ENG
        see also: Mountains Of Allah,
            The; Rose Of Ispahan   (G374)
    Mountains Of Allah, The
        low solo,pno (B flat maj) LEONARD-
            ENG see also Mountains Of Allah,
            The   (G375)
        med solo,pno (C maj) LEONARD-ENG
            see also Mountains Of Allah, The
                                          (G376)
        high solo,pno (E maj) LEONARD-ENG
            see also Mountains Of Allah, The
                                          (G377)
    My World
        low solo,pno (C maj) LEONARD-ENG
                                          (G378)
        med solo,pno (D flat maj) LEONARD-
            ENG   (G379)
        high solo,pno (E flat maj) LEONARD-
            ENG   (G380)

GEEHL, HENRY ERNEST (cont'd.)
    Old House, The
        solo,pno (G maj) ASHDOWN   (G381)
    Road That Leads To You, The
        low solo,pno (D maj) ASHDOWN (G382)
        med solo,pno (E flat maj) ASHDOWN
                                          (G383)
        high solo,pno (F maj) ASHDOWN
                                          (G384)
    Rose Of Ispahan
        solo,pno (F maj) CRAMER see also
            Mountains Of Allah, The   (G385)
    Two Songs *see Farewell; Lily, The
                                          (G386)
    What Of Thy Flocks O Shepherd!
        low solo,pno (B flat maj) ASHDOWN
                                          (G387)
        med solo,pno (C maj) ASHDOWN (G388)
        high solo,pno (E flat maj) ASHDOWN
                                          (G389)
    When Spring Goes Shopping
        low solo,pno (D maj) ASHDOWN (G390)
        med solo,pno (E flat maj) ASHDOWN
                                          (G391)
        high solo,pno (F maj) ASHDOWN
                                          (G392)
    Yeoman's Yarn, A
        low solo,pno (B flat maj) LEONARD-
            ENG   (G393)
        high solo,pno (C maj) LEONARD-
            ENG   (G394)
    Youth, The Fiddler
        low solo,pno (D maj) ASHDOWN (G395)
        med solo,pno (E flat maj) ASHDOWN
                                          (G396)
        high solo,pno (F maj) ASHDOWN
                                          (G397)
    Zinetta
        low solo,pno (B flat maj) LEONARD-
            ENG   (G398)
        med solo,pno (D maj) LEONARD-ENG
                                          (G399)
        high solo,pno (E flat maj) LEONARD-
            ENG   (G400)

GEEN OVERPAD see Oort, H.C.v.

GEEN TIJD IS BUITEN see Horst, Anton
    van der

GEESE AND SWANS see Stravinsky, Igor

GEESTELIJK LIED see Zagwijn, Henri

GEFUNDEN see Dresden, Sem

GEFUNDEN see Strauss, Richard

GEGENDEN DER KINDHEIT see Drejsl,
    Radim, Krajiny Detstvi

GEGENSEITIG see Bijvanck, Henk

GEGENWART see Bijvanck, Henk

GEGRUSSET SEIST DU, HOLDSELIGE see
    Weckmann, Matthais

GEHEIMES see Schubert, Franz (Peter)

GEHEIMNIS see Gilse, Jan van

GEHRING, PHILIP (1925-   )
    Art Thou Weary, Art Thou Laden *sac
        med solo,pno oct CONCORDIA 98-1945
        $.25   (G401)

GEHT NUN ZUR RUH see Zacharias, H.

GEIBEL, ADAM (1855-1933)
    In Old Judea
        med solo,pno,opt vln PRESSER $.75
                                          (G402)

GEIGERIN see Lechthaler, Josef

GEIJER
    Sanger, Heft 1 *CC25L
        solo,pno LUNDQUIST s.p.   (G403)
    Sanger, Heft 2 *CC25L
        solo,pno LUNDQUIST s.p.   (G404)

GEIJER, ERIK GUSTAF
    Kolargossen
        see Geijer, Erik Gustaf, Pa
            Nyarsdagen
    Natthimmeln
        solo,pno GEHRMANS 727 s.p.   (G405)
    Pa Nyarsdagen
        solo,pno GEHRMANS s.p. contains
            also: Kolargossen   (G406)

GEISER, WALTHER (1897-   )
    Der Einsiedler *Op.37,No.2, sac
        T solo,org (diff) BAREN. 2413 $4.25
                                          (G407)

GEISHA LIEDER see Strategier, Herman

GEISLER, WILLY
    Kinderlieder, Heft I, II, & III *CCU
    solo,pno RIES s.p., ea.   (G408)

GEISSLER, FRITZ (1921-   )
    Den Freunden Sagt Von Mir
    solo,pno/harmonium/org BREITKOPF-L
        EB 4008 s.p.   (G409)

    Funf Lieder *CC5U
    solo,5brass study sc DEUTSCHER 1350
        s.p., ipa   (G410)

    Nachtelegien
    high solo,bass clar,cembalo,vibra,
    strings, alto flute DEUTSCHER
        rental   (G411)

    Vier Liebeslieder Nach Hebraischen
    Texten *CC4U
    [Ger] S solo,2fl,bsn,perc,timp,
    harp,4strings voc sc BREITKOPF-L
        EB 5868 $2.00, ipr   (G412)

GEIST, CHRISTIAN (1640-1711)
    Beati Omnes, Qui Timent Dominum
    *sac,concerto
    (Lundgren; Sorensen) [Lat] B solo,
    2vln,vcl,org PETERS 5897 $4.25
                                     (G413)
    De Funere Ad Vitam *sac,concerto
    (Lundgren; Sorensen) [Lat] A solo,
    org,vln,vcl PETERS 5898 $4.25
                                     (G414)
    Vater Unser, Der Du Bist Im Himmel
    *sac,concerto
    (Lundgren; Sorensen) [Ger] med
    solo,org,2vln,vcl PETERS 5899
        $4.25   (G415)

GEIST UND SEELE WIRD VERWIRRET see
    Bach, Johann Sebastian

GEISTLICHE ARIEN, TEIL I see Schubert,
    Franz (Peter)

GEISTLICHE ARIEN, TEIL II see Schubert,
    Franz (Peter)

GEISTLICHE CHORMUSIK 1648 see Schutz,
    Heinrich

GEISTLICHE GESANGE see Holler, Karl

GEISTLICHE GESANGE I see Gletle, Johann
    Melchoir

GEISTLICHE GESANGE II see Gletle,
    Johann Melchoir

GEISTLICHE LIEDER see Bach, Johann
    Sebastian

GEISTLICHE LIEDER MIT ORGELBEGLEITUNG
    see Reinhart, W.

GEISTLICHE LIEDER UND ARIEN see Bach,
    Johann Sebastian

GEISTLICHE LIEDER UND ARIEN see Bach,
    Johann Sebastian

GEISTLICHE SOLOGESANGE UND DUETTE, HEFT
    I & II *sac,CCU
    1-2 soli,pno/org HUG s.p., ea. (G416)

GEISTLICHE SOLOLIEDER DES BAROCK HEFT I
    *sac,CC13U
    (Isenberg, Karl) med solo,cont/pno/
    org (med easy) BAREN. 1461 $3.50
    contains works by: Neander, Joachim
    and Strattner, Georg Christoph
                                     (G417)
GEISTLICHE SOLOLIEDER DES BAROCK HEFT
    III *sac,CCU
    (Isenberg, Karl) med solo,cont/pno/
    org (med easy) BAREN. 1561 s.p.
    contains works by: Cruger, Johann;
    Schop, Johann; Sohr, Peter and
    others   (G418)

GEISTLICHE ZWIEGESANGE see Othmayr,
    Kaspar

GEISTLICHES LIED see Zagwijn, Henri

GEISTLICHES WIEGENLIED see Brahms,
    Johannes

GEISTLICHES WIEGENLIED see Brahms,
    Johannes, Geistliches Wiegenlied

GEISTLIEDER GESANG see Fruh

GEITVIK, S.H.
    Himmelske Fader *sac
    solo,pno,trp MUSIKK s.p.   (G419)

GEKAMDE KONING CANTECLAER see Bijvanck,
    Henk

GELBART, M.
    Es Brent
    high solo/med solo,pno (Yiddish
    text) TRANSCON. WJ 421 $.60
                                     (G420)

GELBART, M. (cont'd.)

    Roite Bletlech
    med solo,pno (Yiddish text)
    TRANSCON. WJ 420 $.60   (G421)

GELIEBTER JESU, DU ALLEIN see Bach,
    Johann Sebastian

GELIJK DE BOOM see Clercq, R. de

GELIJK EEN WATERDROP see Sigtenhorst-
    Meyer, Bernhard van den

GELLI, E.
    Amour Et Douleur
    Mez/Bar solo,pno/inst DURAND s.p.
                                     (G422)
    S/T solo,vln/vcl DURAND s.p.   (G423)
    S/T solo,pno/inst DURAND s.p.
                                     (G424)
    Mez/Bar solo,vln/vcl DURAND s.p. (G425)
    La Farfalla
    [Fr] solo,acap oct DURAND s.p.
                                     (G426)
    "Le Pappillon" S/T solo,orch DURAND
        s.p., ipa   (G427)
    "Le Pappillon" Mez/Bar solo,orch
        DURAND s.p., ipa   (G428)

    Le Pappillon *see La Farfalla

    Vision
    [Fr] solo,acap oct DURAND s.p.
                                     (G429)

GELOBET SEI DIR HERR, MEIN GOTT see
    Bach, Johann Sebastian

GELOBET SEI GOTT see Becker-Foss,
    Jurgen

GELOSO, C.
    Chanson Des Oiseaux
    solo,pno ENOCH s.p.   (G430)

    Dans La Nuit
    solo,pno (available in 2 keys)
        ENOCH s.p.   (G431)

GELSA see Pratella, Francesco Balilla

GELT *Jew
    solo,pno KAMMEN 407 $1.00   (G432)

GELUK see Zagwijn, Henri

GENDARMES see Offenbach, Jacques

GENDARMES' DUET see Offenbach, Jacques,
    Gendarmes

GENERAL MUNROE see Hughes, Herbert

GENESIS DREAM see Smith-Brindle,
    Reginald

GENESIS SONG, THE see Dalton, Larry

GENEY, MICHEL
    La Valse De La Neige
    solo,pno/acord LEUCKART s.p.   (G433)

GENEZING VAN DEN BLINDE see Colaco
    Osorio-Swaab, Reine

GENIEVRES HERISSES see Leguerney,
    Jacques

GENREBILLEDE see Nielsen, Carl

GENSER
    Barcarole
    2 soli,pno LUNDQUIST s.p.   (G434)

GENTIL COQUELICOT MESDAMES see
    Casadesus, Henri Gustave

GENTILLE MANON see Berger, Rod.

GENTILUCCI, A.
    Canti Da "Estravagario"
    Bar solo,ob,vln,vla,vcl SONZOGNO
        rental   (G435)

    Siamo Prossimi Al Risveglio *cant
    [It/Ger] Bar solo,pno,perc,bvl
    quarto RICORDI-ENG 131483 s.p.
                                     (G436)

GENTLE DOVE see Meyerowitz, Jan

GENTLE HOLY SAVIOUR see Gounod, Charles
    Francois

GENTLE LADY see Sterne, Colin

GENTLE MAIDEN see Somervell, Arthur

GENTLE MARY see McFeeters, Raymond

GENTLE SHEPHERD *sac,gospel
    solo,pno ABER.GRP. $1.50   (G437)

GENTLE SHEPHERD see Gaither

GENTLE SLEEP see Naylor, Bernard

GENTLE STRANGER, THE see Lister, Mosie

GENTLE THE NIGHT WINDS see Schubert,
    Franz (Peter)

GENTLE WATER-BIRD, THE see Sutherland,
    Margaret

GENTLE WIND, A see Oldham, Arthur

GENUG, ICH BIN ENTSCHLOSSEN - LASS, O
    FREUND, UNS STANDHAFT SCHEIDEN see
    Mozart, Wolfgang Amadeus, Non Piu!
    Tutto Ascoltai - Non, Temer, Amato
    Bene

GENUG, ICH BIN ENTSCHLOSSEN - LASS, O
    FREUND, UNS STANDHAFT SCHEIDEN
    2CLAR, 2BSN, 2HORN, STR see Mozart,
    Wolfgang Amadeus, Non Piu, Tutto
    Ascoltai - Non Temer, Amato Bene

GENZMER, HARALD (1909-   )
    Frohsinn
    see Vier Lieder

    Funf Lieder (Camoes) *CC5U
    Bar solo,pno PETERS 8031 $9.00
                                     (G438)
    Liederbuch *CCU
    S solo,pno SCHOTTS 3797 s.p.   (G439)

    Lilie Der Auen
    see Vier Lieder

    Mistral Cantata
    [Ger] S solo,2fl,2ob,2clar,2bsn,
    2horn,2trp,2trom,tuba,timp,perc,
    harp,strings voc sc PETERS 8071
    $12.50   (G440)

    Sehnsucht Nach Der Heimat
    see Vier Lieder

    Vier Lieder
    solo,pno RIES s.p.
    contains: Frohsinn; Lilie Der
    Auen; Sehnsucht Nach Der
    Heimat; Voglein Schwermut
                                     (G441)
    Voglein Schwermut
    see Vier Lieder

GEOCOCCYX CALIFORNIANUS see Madden,
    Charles

GEOMETRY see Mollicone, Henry

GEORG FRIEDRICH HANDEL'S WORKS see
    Handel, George Frideric

GEORGE BEVERLY SHEA GOSPEL SOLOS *sac,
    CCUL
    solo,kbd SINGSPIR 5433 $1.95   (G442)

GEORGE BEVERLY SHEA SINGS HIS FAVORITES
    *sac,CCUL
    (Shea, George Beverly) med solo,pno
    WORD 30042 $2.50   (G443)

GEORGE BEVERLY SHEA SOLOS *sac,CCUL
    (Shea, George Beverly) solo,kbd
    SINGSPIR 5432 $1.95   (G444)

GEORGE LIEDER see Stout, Alan

GEORGES, ALEXANDRE
    Berceuse
    solo,pno ENOCH s.p.   (G445)
    solo,acap ENOCH s.p.   (G446)

    Cantique D'amour (from Miarka)
    solo,pno (available in 2 keys)
        ENOCH s.p.   (G447)
    solo,pno (available in 2 keys)
        ENOCH s.p. see also Les Chansons
        De Miarka   (G448)
    solo,orch (available in 2 keys)
        ENOCH s.p., ipa see also Les
        Chansons De Miarka   (G449)

    Chants De Flandre *see Derniere
        Beuverie; En Route; Les Moulins;
        Les Trois Plaies; Une Femme; Une
        Heure Viendra   (G450)

    Chants De Rhenanie *see Chateau
        D'orgueil; Gretchen; Lecon
        D'histoire; Les Bateliers; Les
        Ponts De Vigilance; Trois Grands
        Empereurs   (G451)

    Chants De Wallonie *see Ils Ont
        Brule Ma Wallonie; L'ame De
        Wallonie; Le Coq Wallon.U Vierges
        Et Meres; Les Enfants; Pleurez!
        Priez!   (G452)

    Chateau D'orgueil
    solo,pno ENOCH see from Chants De
        Rhenanie   (G453)

GEORGES, ALEXANDRE (cont'd.)

Chemin De Croix *sac,CC12U
  solo,pno cmplt ed ENOCH s.p.   (G454)

Derniere Beuverie
  solo,pno ENOCH see from Chants De
    Flandre   (G455)

En Route
  solo,pno ENOCH see from Chants De
    Flandre   (G456)

Fete Nuptiale (from Miarka)
  solo,pno ENOCH s.p.   (G457)
  solo,orch ENOCH s.p., ipa see also
    Les Chansons De Miarka   (G458)
  solo,pno ENOCH s.p. see also Les
    Chansons De Miarka   (G459)

Gretchen
  solo,pno ENOCH see from Chants De
    Rhenanie   (G460)

Hymne A La Riviere (from Miarka)
  solo,pno ENOCH s.p.   (G461)
  solo,pno ENOCH s.p. see also Les
    Chansons De Miarka   (G462)

Hymne Au Soleil (from Miarka)
  solo,pno ENOCH s.p.   (G463)
  solo,pno ENOCH s.p. see also Les
    Chansons De Miarka   (G464)

Hymne Des Morts (from Miarka)
  solo,pno ENOCH s.p.   (G465)
  solo,pno ENOCH s.p. see also Les
    Chansons De Miarka   (G466)
  solo,orch ENOCH s.p., ipa see also
    Les Chansons De Miarka   (G467)

Ils Ont Brule Ma Wallonie
  solo,pno ENOCH see from Chants De
    Wallonie   (G468)

Juillet
  solo,pno ENOCH s.p.   (G469)
  solo,acap ENOCH s.p.   (G470)

La Feuille De Bouleau
  solo,pno ENOCH s.p.   (G471)

La Flibustier
  solo,pno ENOCH s.p.   (G472)

La Parole (from Miarka)
  solo,pno (available in 2 keys)
    ENOCH s.p.   (G473)
  solo,pno (available in 2 keys)
    ENOCH s.p. see also Les Chansons
    De Miarka   (G474)
  solo,orch (available in 2 keys)
    ENOCH s.p., ipa see also Les
    Chansons De Miarka   (G475)

La Pieuvre
  solo,pno ENOCH s.p.   (G476)
  solo,acap ENOCH s.p.   (G477)

La Pluie (from Miarka)
  solo,pno ENOCH s.p.   (G478)
  solo,orch (available in 2 keys)
    ENOCH s.p., ipa see also Les
    Chansons De Miarka   (G479)
  solo,pno (available in 2 keys)
    ENOCH s.p. see also Les Chansons
    De Miarka   (G480)

La Poussiere (from Miarka)
  solo,pno (available in 2 keys)
    ENOCH s.p.   (G481)
  solo,pno (available in 2 keys)
    ENOCH s.p. see also Les Chansons
    De Miarka   (G482)

L'ame De Wallonie
  solo,pno ENOCH see from Chants De
    Wallonie   (G483)

Le Bapteme De Miarka (from Miarka)
  solo,pno ENOCH s.p.   (G484)

Le Baptieme De Miarka (Hymne A La
    Riviere Et Hymne Au Soleil)
  solo,pno ENOCH s.p.   (G485)
  solo,orch ENOCH s.p., ipa   (G486)

Le Coq Wallon.U Vierges Et Meres
  solo,pno ENOCH see from Chants De
    Wallonie   (G487)

Le Savoir
  solo,pno (available in 2 keys)
    ENOCH s.p. see also Les Chansons
    De Miarka   (G488)
  solo,orch (available in 2 keys)
    ENOCH s.p., ipa see also Les
    Chansons De Miarka   (G489)

L'Eau Qui Court
  solo,pno (available in 2 keys)
    ENOCH s.p. see also Les Chansons
    De Miarka   (G490)
  solo,acap (available in 2 keys)
    ENOCH s.p. see also Les Chansons
    De Miarka   (G491)

GEORGES, ALEXANDRE (cont'd.)

  solo,orch (available in 2 keys)
    ENOCH s.p., ipa see also Les
    Chansons De Miarka   (G492)

Lecon D'histoire
  solo,pno ENOCH see from Chants De
    Rhenanie   (G493)

Legende Bretonne
  solo,pno ENOCH s.p.   (G494)
  solo,orch sc ENOCH s.p., ipa   (G495)

Les Bateliers
  solo,pno ENOCH see from Chants De
    Rhenanie   (G496)

Les Chansons De Miarka *CC14L
  solo,pno cmplt ed ENOCH s.p.
    available in 2 keys
    see also: Cantique D'amour; Fete
      Nuptiale; Hymne A La Riviere;
      Hymne Au Soleil; Hymne Des
      Morts; La Parole; La Pluie; La
      Poussiere; Le Savoir; L'Eau Qui
      Court; Les Deux Baisers; Marche
      Romane; Miarka S'en Va; Nuages
                                   (G497)

Les Deux Baisers
  solo,pno (available in 2 keys)
    ENOCH s.p. see also Les Chansons
    De Miarka   (G498)

Les Enfants
  solo,pno ENOCH see from Chants De
    Wallonie   (G499)

Les Moulins
  solo,pno ENOCH see from Chants De
    Flandre   (G500)

Les Ponts De Vigilance
  solo,pno ENOCH see from Chants De
    Rhenanie   (G501)

Les Trois Plaies
  solo,pno ENOCH see from Chants De
    Flandre   (G502)

Marche Romane (from Miarka)
  solo,pno (available in 2 keys)
    ENOCH s.p.   (G503)
  solo,pno (available in 2 keys)
    ENOCH s.p. see also Les Chansons
    De Miarka   (G504)

Miarka S'en Va
  solo,pno ENOCH s.p. see also Les
    Chansons De Miarka   (G505)
  solo,acap ENOCH s.p., ipa see also
    Les Chansons De Miarka   (G506)

Noel
  solo,pno ENOCH s.p.   (G507)

Nuages
  solo,pno (available in 2 keys)
    ENOCH s.p. see also Les Chansons
    De Miarka   (G508)
  solo,orch (available in 2 keys)
    ENOCH s.p., ipa see also Les
    Chansons De Miarka   (G509)

Pleurez! Priez!
  solo,pno ENOCH see from Chants De
    Wallonie   (G510)

Trois Grands Empereurs
  solo,pno ENOCH see from Chants De
    Rhenanie   (G511)

Une Femme
  solo,pno ENOCH see from Chants De
    Flandre   (G512)

Une Heure Viendra
  solo,pno ENOCH see from Chants De
    Flandre   (G513)

GERAEDTS, JAAP (1924-   )
Abre De Juin
  high solo,pno DONEMUS s.p. contains
    also: Une Minute   (G514)

Het Vlaamsche Meisje En Den Franschen
    Heer
  ST soli,pno DONEMUS s.p.   (G515)

Lied
  S solo,pno DONEMUS s.p.   (G516)

Ronde
  S solo,pno DONEMUS s.p.   (G517)

Tortelduve
  S/Mez solo,pno DONEMUS s.p.   (G518)

Tota Pulchra Es Maria *sac
  S solo,org DONEMUS s.p.   (G519)

Une Minute
  see Geraedts, Jaap, Abre De Juin

GERAEDTS, JAAP (cont'd.)

Vier Kinderliedjes *CC4U
  S solo,pno DONEMUS s.p.   (G520)

World, The
  Bar solo,pno DONEMUS s.p.   (G521)

GERALD
And Still I Smile (composed with
    Smith)
  med solo,pno PARAGON $.85   (G522)

If I Could Hear My Mother Pray Again
    (composed with Vaughn; Rowe;
    Gordon) *sac
  solo,pno CHAPLET $.35   (G523)

Valley Of My Dreams (composed with
    Kmetz, T.)
  solo,pno PARAGON $.85   (G524)

You Laughed Me Out Of Your Heart
    (composed with Smith)
  solo,pno PARAGON $.85   (G525)

GERALD, ED.
Un Rendez-Vous D'oiseaux
  solo,pno ENOCH s.p.   (G526)
  solo,acap ENOCH s.p.   (G527)

GERALD, THOMAS J.
Keep Me Faithful *see Peters, W.F.

GERBAUD, G.
Voila L'plaisir, Mesdames
  solo,pno ENOCH s.p.   (G528)
  solo,acap ENOCH s.p.   (G529)

GERBE HONGROISE see Arma, Paul

GERBER, EDWARD
After The Funeral
  Bar solo,vln,vla,vcl sc AM.COMP.AL.
    $6.60, ipa   (G530)

GERBER, STEVEN
Five Short Songs On American Poems
    *CC5U,US
  S solo,pno sc AM.COMP.AL. $5.50
                                   (G531)

Three French Songs *CC3U,Fr
  T solo,pno AM.COMP.AL. $3.85   (G532)

Three Poems Of Ezra Pound *CC3U
  S solo,pno sc AM.COMP.AL. $5.50
                                   (G533)

GERECHTER GOTT see Wagner, Richard

GERHARD
Fur Kinder *CC10U
  [Ger/Fr/Eng] solo,pno TONGER s.p.
                                   (G534)

Ohr Der Fruhe
  med solo,pno TONGER s.p.   (G535)

Vier Rezitative *CC4U
  low solo,pno TONGER s.p.   (G536)

GERHARD, ROBERTO (1896-1970)
Cancionero *CC8U,Span
  med solo,pno MODERN s.p.   (G537)

Seven Haiku *CC7U
  Bar solo,pno,strings BELWIN $10.50
                                   (G538)

GERMAN
Rolling Down To Rio
  med solo,pno BELWIN $1.50   (G539)
  low solo,pno BELWIN $1.50   (G540)

GERMAN ART SONGS *CCU
  (Taylor, B.) [Eng/Ger] PRESSER med-
    high solo,pno $3.25; med-low solo,
    pno $3.25   (G541)

GERMAN, EDWARD (1862-1936)
All The World Awakes Today
  solo,pno CRAMER $.95   (G542)

Big Steamers
  high solo,pno (D maj) CRAMER   (G543)
  low solo,pno (C maj) CRAMER   (G544)

Camel's Hump, The
  low solo,pno NOVELLO 17.0016.02
    s.p.   (G545)

Charming Chloe
  med solo,pno NOVELLO 17.0019.07
    s.p.   (G546)
  high solo,pno NOVELLO 17.0018.09
    s.p.   (G547)

Dew Upon The Lily, The
  solo,pno CRAMER $.95   (G548)

Glorious Devon
  low solo,pno (C maj) BOOSEY $1.75
                                   (G549)
  high solo,pno (D maj) BOOSEY $1.75
                                   (G550)

It Was A Lover And His Lass
  high solo,pno NOVELLO 17.0084.07
    s.p.   (G551)
  low solo,pno NOVELLO 17.0085.05

GERMAN, EDWARD (cont'd.)

   s.p.   (G552)

   London Town
     T solo,pno NOVELLO 17.0096.00 s.p.
                          (G553)
     Bar solo,pno NOVELLO 17.0097.09
      s.p.   (G554)
     B solo,pno NOVELLO 17.0098.07 s.p.
                          (G555)

   My Song Is Of The Sturdy North
     low solo,pno (C min) CRAMER $1.10
                          (G556)
     high solo,pno (D min) CRAMER $.95
                          (G557)

   Orpheus With His Lute
     low solo,pno NOVELLO 17.0147.09
      s.p.   (G558)

   Rolling Down To Rio
     med solo,pno NOVELLO 17.0158.04
      s.p.   (G559)
     low solo,pno NOVELLO 17.0159.02
      s.p.   (G560)
     high solo,pno (A min) WILLIS $.75
                          (G561)
     low solo,pno (G min) WILLIS $.75
                          (G562)

   Who'll Buy My Lavender
     solo,pno (available in 2 keys)
      ASHLEY $.95   (G563)
     low solo,pno (C maj) BOOSEY $1.75
                          (G564)
     med solo,pno (D maj) BOOSEY $1.75
                          (G565)
     high solo,pno (E maj) BOOSEY $1.75
                          (G566)
     high solo,pno (D maj) WILLIS $.75
                          (G567)
     low solo,pno (C maj) WILLIS $.75
                          (G568)

GERMAN FOLK SONGS *CC266U
  [Ger] solo,pno MARKS $2.50   (G569)

GERMAN FOLK SONGS *CC20U
  (Brahms, Johannes) [Ger] high solo,
  pno PETERS 3927A $4.75; low solo,
  pno PETERS 3927B $4.75   (G570)

GERMAN FOLK SONGS *CC50U,folk,Ger
  (Kevess, Arthur) [Ger/Eng] solo,pno
  OAK 000114 $3.95   (G571)

GERMAN FOR AMERICANS see Reif, Paul

GERMAN SONGS see Howe, Mary

GERMANIA ALBUM *CCU
  [Ger/Eng] solo,pno MARKS $2.00 (G572)

GERMINA LUCE see Fasullo, P.

GERMONTIN ROMANSSI see Verdi, Giuseppe,
  Di Provenza Il Mar, Il Suol

GERN HAB' ICH DIE FRAU'N GEKUSST see
  Lehar, Franz

GEROVITSCH, ELIEZER (1844-1913)
  Songs Of Prayer *sac,CCU,Sab-Eve,Jew
  (Hecker, W.; Piket, F.) solo,pno/
  org SAC.MUS.PR.   (G573)

GERSCHEFSKI, EDWIN (1909-   )
  Claribel *Op.3,No.1
    high solo,pno AM.COMP.AL. $3.30
                        (G574)
  Clock, The
    med-high solo,pno AM.COMP.AL. $1.37
                        (G575)
  Crossing The Bar
    low solo,pno AM.COMP.AL. $3.30
                        (G576)
  Lai
    Bar solo,pno AM.COMP.AL. $2.75
                        (G577)
  Lord's Controversy With His People,
    The *Op.34,No.1c
    S solo,pno sc AM.COMP.AL. $4.95
                        (G578)
  Meeting At Night, Parting At Morning
    high solo,pno AM.COMP.AL. $1.37
                        (G579)
    low solo,pno AM.COMP.AL. $1.37
                        (G580)
  On His Blindness
    med solo,pno AM.COMP.AL. $1.37
                        (G581)
  Sonnet Number One To Jean Reti
    med solo,pno sc AM.COMP.AL. $1.92
                        (G582)
  To Belshazzar
    low solo,pno AM.COMP.AL. $1.37
                        (G583)
    high solo,pno AM.COMP.AL. $1.37
                        (G584)
  Voice Of The Wind
    med-high solo,pno AM.COMP.AL. $1.37
                        (G585)
  Wanting Is What?
    high solo,pno AM.COMP.AL. $1.37
                        (G586)

GERSTEL, OSWALD
  Canti Poetici (3 Vols.) *CCU
    solo,pno OR-TAV rental   (G587)

  Reaven, The
    Bar solo,inst,opt electronic tape
    OR-TAV rental   (G588)

GERSTER, OTTMAR (1897-1969)
  Funf Lieder Nach Bierbaum *CC5U
    med solo,pno SCHOTTS 3795 s.p.
                          (G589)

GESAMMELTE LIEDER see Kuula, Toivo

GESANG see Kupka, Karel, Zpev

GESANG DER ATHENER see Sibelius, Jean,
  Atenarnes Sang

GESANG DER ERZENGEL see Raphael,
  Gunther

GESANG DER HEIMAT see Doubrava,
  Jaroslav, Zpev Rodneho Kraje

GESANG DES LEBENS see Marx, Joseph

GESANG MARGITS see Wolf, Hugo

GESANG WEYLAS see Wolf, Hugo

GESANG ZUR NACHT see Togni, Camillo

GESANGE see Othegraven, August J. von

GESANGE AN GOTT see Haas, Joseph

GESANGE AN GOTT see Edler, Robert

GESANGE DER FERNE see Oboussier, Robert

GESANGE DES ORIENTS see Strauss,
  Richard

GESANGE DES SPATEN JAHRES, OP. 71 see
  Krenek, Ernst

GESANGE MIT ORCHESTER, VOL. II see
  Beethoven, Ludwig van

GESANGE NACH P. STURMBUSCH see Siegl,
  Otto

GESANGE (RUCKERT), OP. 87 see Strauss,
  Richard

GESANGE ZUM KIRCHENJAHR *sac,CC27L
  1-2 soli,2treb inst,cont HANSSLER
  2.007 sc,pap s.p., sc,cloth s.p.,
  solo pt s.p., ipa
  see also: Bach, Johann Sebastian,
  Jesu, Dir Sei Preis Gesungen
  (from Uns Ist Ein Kind Geboren);
  Bach, Johann Sebastian, Jesus,
  Unser Trost Und Leben; Beyer,
  Johann Samuel, Heilig Ist Gott;
  Cruger, Johann, Nun Jauchzet All,
  Ihr Frommen; Cruger, Johann, Nun
  Lasst Uns Gehn Und Treten;
  Cruger, Johann, O Jesu Christ,
  Dein Kripplein Ist; Cruger,
  Johann, Tauet, Himmel, Den
  Gerechten; Erlebach, Philipp
  Heinrich, Heute Ist Der
  Siegestag; Erlebach, Philipp
  Heinrich, Ich Lasse Gott In Allem
  Walten; Haller, Hans Christoph,
  Hochpreiset Meine Seele; Haller,
  Hans Christoph, Nehmt Wahr Das
  Licht; Helder, Bartholomaeus,
  Dich Bitt Ich, Trautes Jesulein;
  Hellmann, Diethard, Nun Bitten
  Wir Den Heiligen Geist; Petz
  (Pez), Johann Christoph, Guter
  Geber, Lob Und Preis Sei Dir;
  Raphael, Gunther, Herr Christ,
  Hilf Uns; Raphael, Gunther, In
  Dem Herren Freuet Euch; Raphael,
  Gunther, Schmucket Das Fest;
  Stern, Hermann, Hinunter Ist Der
  Sonnen Schein; Thiele, Siegfried,
  Als Unser Herr Am Kreuzesstamm;
  Thiele, Siegfried, Brich Herein,
  Susser Schein; Thiele, Siegfried,
  Dieweil Auch Heuer Nach Advent;
  Weismann, Wilhelm, Es Geht Jetzt
  Um Die Vesperzeit; Wenzel,
  Eberhard, Jesus Christus, Konig
  Und Herr; Wenzel, Eberhard, Nun
  Ist Der Himmel Aufgetan;
  Weyrauch, Johannes, Zeit Ist Wie
  Ewigkeit; Zagatti, Francesco,
  Gloria Patri   (G590)

GESANGSSZENE see Hartmann, Karl Amadeus

GESEGNET IST DIE ZUVERSICHT see
  Telemann, Georg Philipp

GESEGNETE STUNDE see Bijvanck, Henk

GESELLIGE GESANGE see Mozart, Wolfgang
  Amadeus

GESHEM●see Alter, I.

GESICHT UND ANTLITZ see Reutter,
  Hermann

GESICHT UND ANTLITZ see Reutter,
  Hermann

GESICHTE see Gumbel, Martin

GESPRACH JESU MIT NIKODEMUS see
  Brunner, Adolf

GESTATTET IHR, DEM UNSCHEINBAREN
  KNECHTE GOTTES see Mussorgsky,
  Modest

GESTERN WAR ICH ATLAS see Strauss,
  Richard

GESTILLTE SEHNSUCHT see Brahms,
  Johannes

GESTILLTE SEHNSUCHT see Brahms,
  Johannes, Gestillte Sehnsucht

GESU BAMBINO see Yon, Pietro Alessandro

GET ALL EXCITED see Gaither

GET IN TOUCH WITH THE SAVIOR see Lee,
  Don

GET ON THE ROAD see Gilder, Eric

GET YOU HENCE, FOR I MUST GO see
  Castelnuovo-Tedesco, Mario

GETTING USED TO THE FAMILY OF GOD see
  Gaither

GEUBTES HERZ see Schoenberg, Arnold

GEVANGEN see Utermohlen, C.F.

GEVEN EN NEMEN see Mul, Jan

GEWEIHTE NACHT see Weismann, Julius

GEY, JEO
  Fleurs De Mon Jardin *CC12L
    solo,pno DURAND s.p.   (G591)

GEYMULLER, MARGHERITA
  Tre Liriche *CC3U
    solo,pno ZERBONI 3722 s.p.   (G592)

GEZEITEN see Kuusisto, Ilkka

GEZICHT see Schouwman, Hans

GHASEL see Schoenberg, Arnold

GHASEL see Zagwijn, Henri

GHEDINI, GIORGIO FEDERICO (1892-1965)
  Candida Mia Colomba
    [It] S/T solo,pno RICORDI-ENG
    127119 s.p. see from Duo Liriche
                        (G593)
  Canta Uno Augello In Voce Di Soave
    [It] S/T solo,pno RICORDI-ENG
    123901 s.p.   (G594)
  Concerto Funebre *concerto
    TB soli,orch voc sc ZERBONI 4489
    s.p.   (G595)
  Datime A Piena Mano E Rose E Zigli
    [It] S/T solo,pno RICORDI-ENG
    123902 s.p.   (G596)
  Di', Maria Dolce... *sac
    [It] Mez/Bar solo,pno RICORDI-ENG
    120585 s.p.   (G597)
  Diletto E Spavento Del Mare
    [It] S/T solo,pno RICORDI-ENG
    120582 s.p.   (G598)
  Duo Liriche *see Candida Mia
    Colomba; Tu Te Ne Vai   (G599)
  La Quiete Della Notte
    [It] A/B solo,pno RICORDI-ENG
    120583 s.p.   (G600)
  Lectio Libri Sapientiae
    female solo,orch voc sc ZERBONI
    4402 s.p.   (G601)
  Quattro Canti Napoletani *CC4U
    solo,pno ZERBONI 4192 s.p.   (G602)
  Quattro Duetti Su Testi Sacri *sac,
    CC4U
    2 female soli,pno ZERBONI 4400 s.p.
                        (G603)
  Quattro Strambotti Di Giustiniani
    *CC4U
    solo,pno ZERBONI 4188 s.p.   (G604)
  Tre Canti Di Shelley *CC3U
    solo,pno ZERBONI 4189 s.p.   (G605)

GHEDINI, GIORGIO FEDERICO (cont'd.)

Tu Te Ne Vai
[It] Mez/Bar solo,pno RICORDI-ENG
127120 s.p. see from Duo Liriche
(G606)

Vocalizzo Da Concerto *concerto
[It] Bar solo,orch sc CURCI 7132
s.p.   (G607)

GHEQUETST BEN IC VAN BINNEN see Leeuw,
Ton de

GHEQUETST BEN IC VAN BINNEN see Lilien,
Ignace

GHEQUETST BEN IC VAN BINNEN see
Moulaert, Raymond

GHEQUETST BEN ICK VAN BINNEN see Klerk,
Albert de

GHISI, FEDERICO (1901-   )
Air Varie *CCU
Mez solo,2inst ZERBONI 4635 rental
(G608)

GHISLAINE, ELSA
Comme Je T'aime
solo,pno (available in 2 keys)
ENOCH s.p.   (G609)
solo,acap (available in 2 keys)
ENOCH s.p.   (G610)

GHOST, THE see El-Dabh, Halim, Yulei

GHOST, THE see Kilpinen, Yrio, Der Spuk

GHOST, THE see Sharpe, Evelyn

GHOSTS IN LOVE see Swanson, Howard

GIA IL SOLE DEL GANGE see Scarlatti,
Alessandro

GIACOBBE, JUAN FRANCISCO
El Siriri
see Pajaritos Criollos

La Paloma Torcaza
see Pajaritos Criollos

La Viudita
see Pajaritos Criollos

Pajaritos Criollos
[Span] solo,pno cmplt ed RICORDI-
ARG BA 9087 s.p.
contains: El Siriri; La Paloma
Torcaza; La Viudita   (G611)

GIANNEO, LUIS (1897-   )
Ayer Me Dijiste Que Hoy
see Coplas

Coplas
[Span] solo,pno cmplt ed RICORDI-
ARG BA 10518 s.p.
contains: Ayer Me Dijiste Que
Hoy; Deja De Cantar Jilguero;
El Alma Me Has Robado; Entre
Cortinas Verdes; No Ando Porque
Te Quiero; Yo Me Arrime A Un
Pino Verde   (G612)

Deja De Cantar Jilguero
see Coplas

El Alma Me Has Robado
see Coplas

El Ombu
see Pampeanas

El Sol
see Pampeanas

El Zorzal
see Pampeanas

Entre Cortinas Verdes
see Coplas

Llora El Gaucho
see Pampeanas

No Ando Porque Te Quiero
see Coplas

Pampeanas
[Span] solo,pno cmplt ed RICORDI-
ARG BA 6198 s.p.
contains: El Ombu; El Sol; El
Zorzal; Llora El Gaucho   (G613)

Yo Me Arrime A Un Pino Verde
see Coplas

GIANNINA MIA see Friml, Rudolf

GIANNINI, VITTORIO (1903-1966)
Dear Little Hand
"Manella Mia" solo,pno BELWIN $1.50
(G614)

Far Above The Purple Hills
high solo,pno BELWIN $1.50   (G615)

GIANNINI, VITTORIO (cont'd.)

I Shall Think Of You
med solo,pno BELWIN $1.50   (G616)

If I Had Known
high solo,pno BELWIN $1.50   (G617)

It Is A Spring Night
high solo,pno BELWIN $1.50   (G618)

Manella Mia *see Dear Little Hand

Ohie Meneche
high solo,pno BELWIN $1.50   (G619)

Sea Dream
high solo,pno BELWIN $1.50   (G620)

Tell Me, Oh Blue, Blue Sky
high solo,pno BELWIN $1.50   (G621)

Waiting
high solo,pno BELWIN $1.50   (G622)
med solo,pno BELWIN $1.50   (G623)

Zompa Llari Llira!
solo,pno BELWIN $1.50   (G624)

GIANSETTI, GIOVANNI BATTISTA
Blandire Puero *sac
(Ewerhart, Rudolf) S solo,cont
BIELER CS 43 s.p.   (G625)

Dominator, Domine *sac
(Ewerhart, Rudolf) S/T solo,cont
BIELER CS 64 s.p.   (G626)

GIASSON, PAUL E.
Vocalise
high solo,pno GALLEON $.75   (G627)

GIAZOTTO, REMO (1910-   )
Comme Va?
[It] solo,pno CURCI 6602 s.p. see
from Sei Canzoni Napoletane Da
Camera   (G628)
solo,fl,2clar,2bsn,2horn,timp,harp,
strings sc CURCI 7261 rental see
from Sei Canzoni Napoletane Da
Camera [2]   (G629)

D' 'A Malasciorta Mia Vaco P' 'O Mare
solo,2fl,ob,2clar,bsn,2horn,timp,
vibra,harp,strings sc CURCI 7256
rental see from Sei Canzoni
Napoletane Da Camera [2]   (G630)
[It] solo,pno CURCI 6603 s.p. see
from Sei Canzoni Napoletane Da
Camera   (G631)

Dint' 'O Suonno
[It] solo,pno CURCI 6599 s.p. see
from Sei Canzoni Napoletane Da
Camera   (G632)
solo,2clar,2bass clar,bsn,2horn,
timp,cel,harp,strings sc CURCI
7258 rental see from Sei Canzoni
Napoletane Da Camera [2]   (G633)

Notte 'E Luna
solo,fl,ob,2clar,bsn,2horn,timp,
harp,strings,2mand sc CURCI 7260
rental see from Sei Canzoni
Napoletane Da Camera [2]   (G634)
[It] solo,pno CURCI 6601 s.p. see
from Sei Canzoni Napoletane Da
Camera   (G635)

Pianefforte 'E Notte
[It] solo,pno CURCI 6598 s.p. see
from Sei Canzoni Napoletane Da
Camera   (G636)
solo,fl,2clar,2bsn,2horn,trp,timp,
triangle,cel,harp,strings sc
CURCI 7257 rental see from Sei
Canzoni Napoletane Da Camera [2]
(G637)

Sei Canzoni Napoletane Da Camera [2]
*see Comme Va?; D' 'A Malasciorta
Mia Vaco P' 'O Mare; Dint' 'O
Suonno; Notte 'E Luna;
Pianefforte 'E Notte; Vurria
Scrivere Nu Libbro   (G638)

Sei Canzoni Napoletane Da Camera
*see Comme Va?; D' 'A Malasciorta
Mia Vaco P' 'O Mare; Dint' 'O
Suonno; Notte 'E Luna;
Pianefforte 'E Notte; Vurria
Scrivere Nu Libbro   (G639)

Vurria Scrivere Nu Libbro
[It] solo,pno CURCI 6600 s.p. see
from Sei Canzoni Napoletane Da
Camera   (G640)
solo,fl,pic,ob,2clar,bsn,2horn,
timp,harp,strings,2mand sc CURCI
7259 rental see from Sei Canzoni
Napoletane Da Camera [2]   (G641)

GIB MIR DEIN HERZE see Melartin, Erkki

GIB MIR TZURIK DIE MAMENIU *Jew
solo,pno KAMMEN 13 $1.00   (G642)

GIB UNSERN FURSTEN see Schutz, Heinrich

GIBBERISH see Clements, John

GIBBS
Five Eyes
low solo,pno (G min) BOSTON $1.50
(G643)
high solo,pno (B flat min) BOSTON
$1.50   (G644)

GIBBS, CECIL ARMSTRONG (1889-1960)
Ann's Cradle Song
solo,pno (C sharp min) ROBERTON
2379 s.p.   (G645)

As I Lay In The Early Sun
solo,pno (F maj) BOOSEY $1.50
(G646)

Ballad Of Semmerwater, The
solo,pno (G min) ROBERTON 2497 s.p.
(G647)

Cherry Tree, The
solo,pno (B min) ROBERTON 2565 s.p.
(G648)

Covent Garden
med solo,orch (D maj) ASHDOWN s.p.;
ipr   (G649)
low solo,orch (C maj) ASHDOWN s.p.;
ipr   (G650)
high solo,orch (E maj) ASHDOWN
s.p., ipr   (G651)

Fields Are Full
solo,pno (E flat min) BOOSEY $1.50
(G652)

Five Eyes
low solo,pno (B flat min) BOOSEY
$1.50   (G653)
low solo,pno (G min) BOOSEY $1.50
(G654)

Immortality
solo,pno (A min) BOOSEY $1.50
(G655)

In The Highlands
solo,pno (E flat maj) ROBERTON 2433
s.p.   (G656)

Midnight
solo,pno (B flat min) BOOSEY $1.50
(G657)

Nod
solo,pno (D maj) BOOSEY $1.50
(G658)

Silver
solo,pno (E min) BOOSEY $1.50
(G659)

To One Who Passed Whistling Through
The Night
high solo,pno (F maj) SCHIRM.G $.75
(G660)
solo,pno (C maj) ROBERTON 2229 s.p.
(G661)

When I Was One-And-Twenty
solo,pno (G maj) ROBERTON 2331 s.p.
(G662)

When Music Sounds
solo,pno (D maj) BOOSEY $1.50
(G663)

GIDEON, MIRIAM (1906-   )
Bells
low solo,pno AM.COMP.AL. $.82
(G664)

Condemned Playground, The
ST soli,fl,bsn,4strings AM.COMP.AL.
sc $9.35, ipa, voc sc $5.50
(G665)

Epitaph On The Author
med solo,pno sc AM.COMP.AL. $.55
(G666)

Epitaphs From Robert Burns *CCU
low solo,pno AM.COMP.AL. $3.30
(G667)

Farewell Tablet To Agathocles
med solo,pno sc AM.COMP.AL. $3.30
(G668)

Little Ivory Figures Pulled With
String
med-low solo,gtr AM.COMP.AL. $.82
(G669)

Mixco
low solo,pno AM.COMP.AL. $4.40
(G670)
med solo,pno AM.COMP.AL. $4.40
(G671)

Questions Of Nature
med solo,ob,pno,perc sc AM.COMP.AL.
$9.90   (G672)

Rhymes From The Hill
solo,clar,vcl,marimba AM.COMP.AL.
sc $5.50, voc sc $5.50   (G673)

Songs Of Voyage *CCU
AM.COMP.AL. high solo,pno $5.50;
low solo,pno $5.50   (G674)

Sonnets From Fatal Interview *CCU
AM.COMP.AL. high solo,vln,vla,vcl
sc $5.50, ipa; high solo,pno voc
sc $4.40   (G675)

Sonnets From Shakespeare *CCU
AM.COMP.AL. high solo,trp,4strings/
strings sc $6.60, ipa; low solo,
trp,4strings/strings sc $6.60,

GIDEON, MIRIAM (cont'd.)

    ipa; high solo,pno voc sc $4.40;
    low solo,pno voc sc $4.40 (G676)

    Spiritual Madrigals *CCU
    AM.COMP.AL. 2 male soli,pno sc
    $8.25, ipa; 3 male soli,vln,vcl,
    bsn sc $8.25, ipa   (G677)

    To Music
    low solo,pno AM.COMP.AL. $3.30
                (G678)
    high solo,pno AM.COMP.AL. $3.30
                (G679)
    med solo,pno sc AM.COMP.AL. $3.30
                (G680)

GIEFER, WILLY (1930-   )
    Alles Geben Die Gotter   *CC4U
    A solo,chamb.grp. GERIG HG 1064
    s.p.   (G681)

    Eines Schattens Traum
    Mez solo,fl,vcl GERIG HG 955 s.p.
                (G682)

GIELEN, MICHAEL (1927-   )
    Die Glocken Sind Auf Falscher Spur
    S,narrator,pno,perc,vcl,gtr sc
    GERIG HG 813 s.p.   (G683)

GIESKING, SHIRLEY
    Faith Can Do Anything
    med solo,pno CRESPUB CP-S5054 $1.00
                (G684)

GIFFORD, HELEN
    As Dew In Aprille *sac,carol
    med solo,pno EMI s.p.   (G685)
    solo,pno ALBERT AE 13 s.p. (G686)

GIFT see Behrend, A.H.

GIFT OF CHRISTMAS, THE see Schirmer,
    Rudolph [E.]

GIFT OF FIRE, THE see Heilner, Irwin

GIFT OF REST see Cowen, Sir Frederic
    Hymen

GIFTS see Dunhill, Thomas Frederick

GIFTS see Gold, Ernest

GIGERLETTE see Bordewijk-Roepman,
    Johanna

GIGLI ALBUM *CCUL
    [It/Eng] T solo,pno RICORDI-ENG
    LD 322 s.p. contains works by:
    Puccini; Cottrau; Rossini; Handel;
    Tosti and others   (G687)

GIJ BAD OP ENEN BERG see Nieland, H.

GIJ BADT OP EENEN BERG ALLEEN see
    Bijvanck, Henk

GIL, B.
    Cantan Las Ninas De Espana *CCU,Span
    [Span] med solo,pno UNION ESP.
    $2.25   (G688)

GIL, JOSE
    Morera De Mi Tierra
    [Span] solo,pno RICORDI-ARG RF 6693
    s.p.   (G689)

GILARDI, GILARDO (1889-1963)
    Cancion De Cuna India
    [Span] solo,pno RICORDI-ARG BA 8605
    s.p.   (G690)

    Vidala Santiaguena
    [Span] solo,pno RICORDI-ARG BA 7344
    s.p.   (G691)

GILBERT AND SULLIVAN see Sullivan, Sir
    Arthur Seymour

GILBERT AND SULLIVAN AT HOME see
    Sullivan, Sir Arthur Seymour

GILBERT, HARRY
    Word Of God Incarnate *sac
    high solo,pno BELWIN $1.50 (G692)

GILBERT, NORMAN
    Lord Is My Shepherd, The
    ST soli,pno NOVELLO 17.0103.07 s.p.
                (G693)

GILBERT, WILLIAM SCHWENCK (1836-1911)
    Gilbert And Sullivan *see Sullivan,
    Sir Arthur Seymour

GILDER, ERIC
    Get On The Road
    solo,pno CRAMER   (G694)

    Lady Mine
    solo,pno CRAMER   (G695)

    To My Lady Singing
    solo,pno CRAMER   (G696)

GILLET, ERNEST (1856-1940)
    Amour Brise
    solo,pno ENOCH s.p.   (G697)
    solo,acap ENOCH s.p.   (G698)

    Cornet De Bonbons
    solo,pno ENOCH s.p.   (G699)
    solo,acap ENOCH s.p.   (G700)

    Danse Des Bambous
    solo,pno ENOCH s.p.   (G701)
    solo,acap ENOCH s.p.   (G702)

    La Derniere Letre De Manon
    solo,pno ENOCH s.p.   (G703)
    solo,acap ENOCH s.p.   (G704)

    La Lettre De Manon
    solo,pno ENOCH s.p.   (G705)
    solo,acap ENOCH s.p.   (G706)

    Sainte-Marie *sac
    solo,pno ENOCH s.p.   (G707)
    solo,acap ENOCH s.p.   (G708)
    [Fr] solo,pno ENOCH   (G709)

    Salut Au Drapeau
    solo,pno ENOCH s.p.   (G710)
    solo,acap ENOCH s.p.   (G711)

    Serenade
    solo,pno ENOCH s.p.   (G712)
    solo,acap ENOCH s.p.   (G713)

GILLINGTON, M.
    Action Songs *CCU
    solo,pno LEONARD-ENG s.p., ea. in
    three books, sold separately
                (G714)

    Flag Of Empire (composed with
    Godfrey)
    solo,pno LEONARD-ENG   (G715)

    Willow Pattern Plate
    solo,pno LEONARD-ENG   (G716)

GILLIS, DON
    Coming Of The King, The *sac,Xmas
    med solo,pno BELWIN $1.50 (G717)

    Hymn And Prayer For Peace
    solo,pno CRESCENDO $1.00 (G718)

GILLON, D.
    Heart To Heart *sac
    solo,pno WORD S-531   (G719)

GILROD, LOUIS
    A Malke Auf Paissach *Jew
    solo,pno KAMMEN 45 $1.00 see also
    JEWISH THEATRE SONGS, VOL. 1
                (G720)

    Der Sider'l *Jew
    solo,pno KAMMEN 409 $1.00 see also
    FAVORITE JEWISH SONGS, VOL. 2
                (G721)

    Samit Und Seid *Jew
    solo,pno KAMMEN 68 $1.00 see also
    FAVORITE JEWISH SONGS, VOL. 2
                (G722)

    Shmendrik's Kalle *Jew
    solo,pno KAMMEN 48 $1.00 see also
    FAVORITE JEWISH SONGS, VOL. 2
                (G723)

GILSE, JAN VAN (1881-1944)
    Abend
    see Gilse, Jan van, Zwei
    Abendlieder

    Auf Dem Canal Grande
    see Vier Gedichte Von C.F. Meyer

    Auf Eine Hand
    see Vier Liederen Van Detlev Von
    Liliencron

    Auf Einer Grunen Wiese
    see Vier Liederen Van Detlev Von
    Liliencron

    Das Konigslied
    see Drei Gesange

    Der Reisebecher
    see Vier Gedichte Von C.F. Meyer

    Die Eigensinnige
    see Twee Liederen Op Duitse Tekst

    Drei Gedichte Von R. Dehmel
    high solo,pno DONEMUS s.p.
    contains: Entweihung; Geheimnis;
    Waldnacht   (G724)

    Drei Gesange
    med solo,2fl,2ob,2clar,2bsn,4horn,
    3trp,3trom,tuba,timp,harp,strings
    DONEMUS s.p.
    contains: Das Konigslied;
    Frieden; Herbststurm   (G725)

    Drei Gesange Aus R. Tagore's "Der
    Gartner" *CC3U
    S solo,3fl,3ob,2clar,2bsn,4horn,
    3trp,3trom,timp,cel,2harp,strings
    DONEMUS s.p.   (G726)

GILSE, JAN VAN (cont'd.)

    Drei Gesange Aus R. Tagore's
    "Gitanjali" *CC3U
    S solo,2fl,3ob,2clar,2bsn,4horn,
    3trp,3trom,timp,perc,cel,harp,
    strings DONEMUS s.p.   (G727)

    Ein Kleines Lied
    see Twee Liederen Op Duitse Tekst

    Eingelegte Ruder
    see Vier Gedichte Von C.F. Meyer

    Entweihung
    see Drei Gedichte Von R. Dehmel

    Erhebung (Sinfonie No. 3)
    S solo,3fl,3ob,4clar,3bsn,6horn,
    4trp,3trom,tuba,timp,perc,harp,
    strings DONEMUS s.p.   (G728)

    Frieden
    see Drei Gesange

    Geheimnis
    see Drei Gedichte Von R. Dehmel

    Hans Der Schwarmer
    see Vier Liederen Van Detlev Von
    Liliencron

    Herbststurm
    see Drei Gesange

    Lied Auf Dem Flusse
    high solo,pno DONEMUS s.p. (G729)

    Lied Der Heiligen Jungfrau *sac
    med solo,pno DONEMUS s.p. (G730)

    Neergebrand
    med solo,pno DONEMUS s.p. (G731)

    Requiem
    see Gilse, Jan van, Zwei
    Abendlieder

    Santis
    see Vier Liederen Van Detlev Von
    Liliencron

    Schnitterlied
    see Vier Gedichte Von C.F. Meyer

    Twee Liederen Op Duitse Tekst
    high solo/med solo,pno DONEMUS s.p.
    contains: Die Eigensinnige; Ein
    Kleines Lied   (G732)

    Vier Gedichte Von C.F. Meyer
    med solo,pno ALSBACH s.p.
    contains: Auf Dem Canal Grande;
    Der Reisebecher; Eingelegte
    Ruder; Schnitterlied   (G733)

    Vier Liederen Van Detlev Von
    Liliencron
    high solo/med solo,pno DONEMUS s.p.
    contains: Auf Eine Hand; Auf
    Einer Grunen Wiese; Hans Der
    Schwarmer; Santis   (G734)

    Waldnacht
    see Drei Gedichte Von R. Dehmel

    Zwei Abendlieder
    med solo,pno DONEMUS s.p. contains
    also: Requiem; Abend   (G735)

GILSON, PAUL (1865-1942)
    Chanson Persane
    solo,pno (available in 2 keys)
    ENOCH s.p.   (G736)

GILTAY, BEREND (1910-   )
    Drei Lieder *CC3U
    A solo,4strings/strings DONEMUS
    s.p.   (G737)

GIMIENDO POR VER EL MAR see Halffter,
    Rodolfo

GINASTERA, ALBERTO (1916-   )
    Algarrobo, Algarrobal
    see Cantos Del Tucuman

    Arrorro
    see Cinco Canciones Populares
    Argentinas

    Cancion A La Luna Lunanca
    [Span] solo,pno RICORDI-ARG
    BA 10517 s.p.   (G738)

    Cancion Al Arbol Del Olvido
    [Span] solo,pno RICORDI-ARG BA 8226
    s.p.   (G739)

    Cantos Del Tucuman
    solo,fl,vln,harp cmplt ed RICORDI-
    ARG BA 11034 s.p.
    contains: Algarrobo, Algarrobal;
    Solita Su Alma; Vida, Vidita,
    Vidala; Yo Naci En El Valle
                (G740)

GINASTERA, ALBERTO (cont'd.)

Chacarera
see Cinco Canciones Populares
Argentinas

Cinco Canciones Populares Argentinas
[Span] solo,pno cmplt ed RICORDI-
ARG BA 8891 s.p.
contains: Arrorro; Chacarera;
Gato; Triste; Zamba   (G741)

Gato
see Cinco Canciones Populares
Argentinas

Solita Su Alma
see Cantos Del Tucuman

Triste
see Cinco Canciones Populares
Argentinas

Vida, Vidita, Vidala
see Cantos Del Tucuman

Yo Naci En El Valle
see Cantos Del Tucuman

Zamba
see Cinco Canciones Populares
Argentinas

GING AN EINEM WINTERMORGEN see
Sibelius, Jean, Arioso

GINGER CAT, THE see Protheroe, Daniel

GINGHAM DOG AND CALICO CAT see Binney,
A.

GIORDANI, GIUSEPPE (ca. 1753-1798)
Ah Armainen *see Caro Mio Ben

Caro Mio Ben *sac
[It] solo,pno (D maj) DURAND 227
s.p.   (G742)
[It/Eng] solo,pno CRAMER   (G743)
med solo,pno (E flat maj) ALLANS
s.p.   (G744)
low solo,pno (D maj) ALLANS s.p.
                              (G745)
[Swed] solo,pno LUNDQUIST s.p.
                              (G746)
[It] low solo,pno SCHOTTS s.p.
                              (G747)
high solo,pno (E flat maj) ALLANS
s.p.   (G748)
"Ah Armainen" solo,pno FAZER W 2792
s.p.   (G749)
(Deis) "Come Unto Me" low solo,pno
(C maj) SCHIRM.G $.60   (G750)
(Deis) "Dearest, Believe" [It/Eng]
low solo,pno (C maj) SCHIRM.G
$1.00   (G751)
(Deis) "Dearest, Believe" [It/Eng]
med solo,pno (E flat maj)
SCHIRM.G $1.00   (G752)
(Deis) "Dearest, Believe" [It/Eng]
high solo,pno (F maj) SCHIRM.G
$1.00   (G753)
(Parisotti) [It/Fr] S/T solo,pno
RICORDI-ARG BA 8162 s.p.   (G754)
(Segovia) solo,gtr SCHOTTS GA 175
s.p.   (G755)

Come Unto Me *see Caro Mio Ben

Dearest, Believe *see Caro Mio Ben

Herr, Du Und Gott *sac
"Trauungsgesang Nach Der Arie "Caro
Mio Ben"" high solo,pno/org
SCHOTTS s.p.   (G756)
"Trauungsgesang Nach Der Arie "Caro
Mio Ben"" low solo,pno/org
SCHOTTS s.p.   (G757)
"Trauungsgesang Nach Der Arie "Caro
Mio Ben"" med solo,opt fl,pno/
org,vln/vcl SCHOTTS s.p.   (G758)

Trauungsgesang Nach Der Arie "Caro
Mio Ben" *see Herr, Du Und Gott

GIORDANO, UMBERTO (1867-1948)
Amor Ti Vieta (from Fedora)
high solo,pno (C maj) SCHIRM.G $.85
                              (G759)
[It/Eng] T solo,pno INTERNAT. $1.00
                              (G760)
[It/Eng/Ger] T solo,pno SONZOGNO
992 $1.25   (G761)

Calato In Arno (from La Cena Delle
Beffe)
[It] T solo,pno SONZOGNO 2522 $1.25
                              (G762)
Come Un Bel Di Di Maggio (from Andrea
Chenier)
[It/Eng/Ger] T solo,pno SONZOGNO
962 $1.25   (G763)
[It/Eng] T solo,pno INTERNAT. $1.00
                              (G764)
Ed Io Non Ne Godevo (from La Cena
Delle Beffe)
[It] S solo,pno SONZOGNO 2521 $1.25

GIORDANO, UMBERTO (cont'd.)
                              (G765)
Gli Avrei Detto: Tenetevele (from
Madame Sans-Gene)
[It] S solo,pno SONZOGNO $1.25
                              (G766)
La Mamma Morta (from Andrea Chenier)
[It] S solo,pno RICORDI-ARG BA 9753
s.p.   (G767)
[It/Eng/Ger] S solo,pno SONZOGNO
961 $1.25   (G768)
[It/Eng] S solo,pno INTERNAT. $1.00
                              (G769)
Mio Padre E Tra I Forzati (from
Siberia)
[It] S solo,pno SONZOGNO 1169 $1.25
                              (G770)
Nemico Della Patria (from Andrea
Chenier)
[It] Bar solo,pno RICORDI-ARG
BA 9752 s.p.   (G771)
[It/Eng/Ger] Bar solo,pno SONZOGNO
960 $1.25   (G772)
[It/Eng] Bar solo,pno INTERNAT.
$1.00   (G773)
Non E La Vita (from La Cena Delle
Beffe)
[It] T solo,pno SONZOGNO 2523 $1.25
                              (G774)
O Grandi Occhi Lucenti Di Fede (from
Fedora)
[It] S solo,pno SONZOGNO 995 $1.25
                              (G775)
Si, Fui Soldato (from Andrea Chenier)
[It/Eng/Ger] T solo,pno SONZOGNO
2373 $1.25   (G776)
Son La Vecchia Madelon (from Andrea
Chenier)
[It] Mez solo,pno SONZOGNO 963
$1.25   (G777)
Su Questa Santa Croce (from Fedora)
[It] S solo,pno SONZOGNO 996 $1.25
                              (G778)
Un Di All'azzurro Spazio (from Andrea
Chenier)
[It/Eng/Ger] T solo,pno SONZOGNO
958 $1.25   (G779)
[It/Eng] T solo,pno INTERNAT. $1.25
                              (G780)
Vicino A Te S'acqueta (from Andrea
Chenier)
[It/Eng/Ger] ST soli,pno SONZOGNO
2374 $1.25   (G781)

GIORNO PER GIORNO see Alfano, Franco

GIPSY see Kozina, Marijan, Cigan

GIPSY AND THE BIRD, THE see Benedict,
Sir Julius

GIPSY COUNTESS, THE see Glover, Stephen

GIPSY MELODIES see Novak, Vitezslav

GIPSY PRAISES HIS HORSE, THE see
Kozina, Marijan, Cigan Hvali
Svojega Konja

GIPSY SONGS see Dvorak, Antonin

GIPSY SONGS AND DANCES *CCU
(Grabocz; Csenki) solo,pno BUDAPEST
5358 s.p.   (G782)

GIPSY SPRING see Oliver, Herbert

GIRAN PURE IN CIEL LE SFERE see
Pasquini, Bernardo

GIRL AND THE DUCK, THE see Newton,
Ernest

GIRL IN GREEN see Holford, Franz

GIRL IN LOVE, A see Cannon, (Jack)
Phillip, L'amoureuse

GIRL IN THE WOODS see Casseus

GIRL WHOSE LOVE SHINES FAIR, A see
Cannon, (Jack) Phillip, La Bien
Aimee

GIRL WITH THE BUCKLES ON HER SHOES
*folk,Ir
(Nelson) 2 soli,pno ROBERTON 72655
s.p.   (G783)
(Nelson) 3 soli,pno ROBERTON 72468
s.p.   (G784)

GIRL WITH YELLOW HAIR see Strauss,
Johann

GIRLS OF CADIZ see Delibes, Leo, Les
Filles De Cadix

GIRNATIS, WALTER (1894-   )
Drei Seemannslieder
med solo,pno SIKORSKI 137 s.p.
contains: Irgendwo Im Hafen;
Piratenlied; Weit Hinter Rio

GIRNATIS, WALTER (cont'd.)
                              (G785)
Irgendwo Im Hafen
see Drei Seemannslieder

Marien-Konzert *sac,concerto
med solo,2vln,vcl,org (med diff)
MULLER 1753   (G786)

Piratenlied
see Drei Seemannslieder

Weit Hinter Rio
see Drei Seemannslieder

GIRO GIRO TONDO see Mortari, Virgilio

GIRO TONDO see Farina, Guido

GIROTONDO DEI GOLOSI see Castelnuovo-
Tedesco, Mario

GIT MIR OP MEIN HARTZ TZURIK *Jew
solo,pno KAMMEN 427 $1.00   (G787)

GITANA see Bucalossi, E.

GITANJALI see Carpenter, John Alden

GITARRELIEDER see Weber, Carl Maria von

GITARRELIEDER FUR ALLE *CCU,folk
(Burkhart, Fr.; Scheit, K.) solo,gtr
DOBLINGER 05 920 $1.50   (G788)

GITARREN SPIELT AUF, HEFT I-VII
(Buhe) solo,gtr SCHOTTS
4356-4357; 4830-4835 s.p., ea.
                              (G789)

GIUGNO see Bruschettini, M.

GIULIETTA SONO IO! see Zandonai,
Riccardo

GIULLARESCA see Guarino, C.

GIUNSE ALFIN IL MOMENTO see Mozart,
Wolfgang Amadeus

GIUNSE ALFIN IL MOMENTO - NON TARDAR
AMATO BENE see Mozart, Wolfgang
Amadeus

GIUNTO SUL PASSO ESTREMO see Boito,
Arrigo

GIURANNA, BARBARA
Augurio
[It] Mez/Bar solo,pno RICORDI-ENG
124500 s.p.   (G790)

Canto Arabo
[It] Mez/Bar solo,pno RICORDI-ENG
123139 s.p.   (G791)

La Guerriera
[It] S/T solo,pno RICORDI-ENG
120926 s.p.   (G792)

Ninna-Nanna
[It] S/T solo,pno RICORDI-ENG
123191 s.p.   (G793)

Stornello
[It] S/T solo,pno RICORDI-ENG
120925 s.p.   (G794)

GIV see Torlind

GIVE A MAN A HORSE HE CAN RIDE see
Lambert

GIVE A MAN A HORSE HE CAN RIDE see
O'Hara, Geoffrey

GIVE ALL YOUR LOVE TO ME see Harrison,
W.

GIVE AND TAKE see Sterndale-Bennett

GIVE CHRIST THIS YEAR see Baker,
Richard

GIVE ME A DOUBLE PORTION see Polk,
Videt

GIVE ME A FAITH see Bitgood, Roberta

GIVE ME A VISION see Terrell, Beverly

GIVE ME BACK MY LORD see Bach, Johann
Sebastian

GIVE ME JESUS *sac,spir
(Burleigh, H. T.) high solo,pno
BELWIN $1.50   (G795)
(Burleigh, H. T.) low solo,pno BELWIN
$1.50   (G796)
(Johnson, T. Rosamond) high solo,pno
FISCHER,C V 1520   (G797)

GIVE ME MY SCALLOP SHELL OF QUIET see
Russell, Welford

GIVE ME SOME MUSIC see Barber, Samuel

GIVE ME THAT OLD TIME RELIGION *sac,
    gospel
    solo,pno ABER.GRP. $1.50   (G798)

GIVE ME YOUR HAND see Stewart

GIVE THANKS AND SING see Harris

GIVE THE LORD A CHANCE see Reynolds,
    William Jensen

GIVE THEM A LIFT *sac
    solo,pno STAMPS 7239 $1.00   (G799)

GIVE UP see Goodman

GLAD HEARTS ADVENTURING see Shaw,
    Martin

GLADJENS BLOMSTER
    solo,pno GEHRMANS 211 s.p. contains
    also: Allt Under Himmelens Faste
                                    (G800)

GLADYS SWARTHOUT ALBUM OF CONCERT SONGS
    AND ARIAS *CC16L
    solo,pno SCHIRM.G $3.95 text in
    English and original languages,
    contains works by: Bach; Handel;
    Brahms; Rachmaninoff and others
                                    (G801)

GLANS OVER SJO OCH STRAND see
    Nordqvist, Gustaf, Julsang

GLANTZ, YEHUDA LEIB
    B'shuv Adonoy (Psalm 126) sac
    [Heb] high solo,pno TRANSCON.
    WJ 413 $.85   (G802)

    Ich Bin A Yisroel
    high solo,pno (Yiddish text)
    TRANSCON. WJ 411 $.60   (G803)

    Matai
    "When?" [Heb] high solo,pno
    TRANSCON. WJ 412 $.60   (G804)

    Psalm 126 *see B'shuv Adonoy

    Songs *CCU
    solo,pno ISR.MUS.INST. 506 s.p.
                                    (G805)

    When? *see Matai

GLANVILLE-HICKS, PEGGY (1912-   )
    Be Still You Little Leaves
    solo,pno OISEAU s.p.   (G806)

    Come Sleep
    solo,pno OISEAU s.p.   (G807)

    Five Songs *CC5U
    solo,pno WEINTRB $3.00   (G808)

    Frolic
    solo,pno OISEAU s.p.   (G809)

    Letters From Morocco
    [It/Ger] T solo,fl,ob,bsn,trp,
    3perc,harp,strings PETERS 66127
    rental   (G810)

    Looking At A Blackbird
    see Glanville-Hicks, Peggy,
    Thirteen Ways

    Profiles From China
    solo,pno WEINTRB $2.00   (G811)

    Rest
    solo,pno OISEAU s.p.   (G812)

    Thirteen Ways
    solo,pno WEINTRB $3.00 contains
    also: Looking At A Blackbird
                                    (G813)

GLASS, DUDLEY
    My Country Love
    solo,pno CRAMER   (G814)

GLASS TOWN see Avshalomov, Jacob

GLATTIGHET, GYLLENE, KOM! see Peterson-
    Berger, (Olof) Wilhelm

GLAZOUNOV, ALEXANDER KONSTANTINOVITCH
    (1865-1936)
    Chanson Russe
    [Russ/Fr/Eng/Ger] med solo,pno
    BELAIEFF 257 s.p.   (G815)

    Romance Of Nina *Op.102
    [Russ/Fr] med solo,pno BELAIEFF 256
    s.p.   (G816)

    Romance Orientale *Op.27,No.2
    [Russ/Fr] med solo,pno BELAIEFF 255
    s.p.   (G817)

GLEE MAIDEN see Solomon, Edward

GLEESON, HORACE
    Little Hills, The
    high solo,pno (A flat maj) WILLIS
    $.60   (G818)
    low solo,pno (F maj) WILLIS $.60
                                    (G819)
    low solo,pno (F maj) ALLANS s.p.
                                    (G820)
    high solo,pno (A flat maj) ALLANS
    s.p.   (G821)

    My Little Feathered Friend
    low solo,pno (A flat maj) ALLANS
    s.p.   (G822)
    high solo,pno (C maj) ALLANS s.p.
                                    (G823)

GLEICHNISSE see Serocki, Kazimierz

GLENLYON LAMENT *folk,Scot
    (Roberton, Hugh S.) 2 soli,pno
    ROBERTON 72043 s.p.   (G824)

GLETLE, JOHANN MELCHOIR (1626-1683)
    Geistliche Gesange I *sac
    (Schanzlin, Hans Peter) ATB soli,
    cont (med) BAREN. 3454 $2.75
    contains: Salve Regina; Tota
    Pulchra Est   (G825)

    Geistliche Gesange II *sac,CCU
    (Schanzlin, Hans Peter) S/T solo,
    2vln,cont (med) BAREN. 3455 $9.75
                                    (G826)

    Salve Regina
    see Geistliche Gesange I

    Tota Pulchra Est
    see Geistliche Gesange I

GLI ANGUI D'INFERNO see Mozart,
    Wolfgang Amadeus

GLI AVREI DETTO: TENETEVELE see
    Giordano, Umberto

GLI UOMINI VUOTI see Corghi, Azio

GLICK - DU BIST GEKUMMEN TZU SHPAIT see
    Mysell, Bella

GLICK, F.
    Carryin' Coals
    med solo,pno PRESSER $.75   (G827)

GLIDE GENTLY see Walton, William

GLIERE, REINHOLD MORITZOVITCH
    (1875-1956)
    Ausgewahlte Romanzen *CCU
    [Russ/Ger] solo,pno SIKORSKI R 6310
    s.p.   (G828)

    Concerto For Coloratura Soprano And
    Orchestra *see Konzert Fur
    Koloratursopran Und Orchester

    Concerto Pour Soprano Colorature Et
    Orchestre *see Konzert Fur
    Koloratursopran Und Orchester

    Konzert Fur Koloratursopran Und
    Orchester *Op.82, concerto
    coloratura sop,orch voc sc SIKORSKI
    2158 s.p., sc SIKORSKI rental
                                    (G829)
    "Concerto Pour Soprano Coloratura
    Et Orchestre" [Fr] coloratura
    sop,orch/pno voc sc CHANT s.p.
                                    (G830)
    (Frank) "Concerto For Coloratura
    Soprano And Orchestra" coloratura
    sop,orch MCA $5.00, ipr   (G831)

GLIMES, J.DE
    L'Oiseau Bleu
    2 soli,pno DURAND s.p.   (G832)

GLIMPSE OF HOPE see Weigl, Vally

GLINKA, MIKHAIL IVANOVITCH (1804-1857)
    Ausgewahlte Duette *CCU
    [Russ] 2 soli,pno SIKORSKI R 6311
    s.p.   (G833)

    Choix De Romances Et Chansons *CCU
    [Fr] solo,pno cmplt ed CHANT s.p.
                                    (G834)
    Complete Works *CCUL
    (Schwarz, Boris) [Russ/Eng]
    contains works for a variety of
    instruments and vocal
    combinations microfiche
    UNIV.MUS.ED. reprinted with
    permission of Mezhdunarodnaja
    Kniga, Moscow; contains 18
    volumes; $250.00   (G835)

    Die Lerche "Zwischen Erd' Und Himmel"
    [Russ/Fr/Ger/Eng] solo,pno
    BREITKOPF-W 57 03044 s.p.   (G836)

    Leuchtest Mir Zum Letzten Mal (from
    Life For The Tsar, A)
    B solo,pno/orch BREITKOPF-W
    57 03043 s.p.   (G837)

GLINKA, MIKHAIL IVANOVITCH (cont'd.)
    Nachtliche Heerschau "Des Nachts Um
    Die Zwolfte Stunde"
    [Russ/Fr/Ger/Eng] Bar solo,pno
    BREITKOPF-W 57 03042 s.p.   (G838)

    Romances For Two Voices *CCU
    [Russ] 2 soli,pno MEZ KNIGA 107
    s.p.   (G839)

    Romanzen Und Lieder, Band 2 *CCU
    solo,pno SIKORSKI R 6341 s.p.
                                    (G840)

GLOBOKAR, VINKO (1934-   )
    Accord *sac,concerto
    [Lat] S solo,fl,trom,vcl,perc,org
    voc sc PETERS 5976 $9.00   (G841)

GLOM MIG EJ see Lundkvist, Per

GLOMBIG, E.
    Mein Ganzes Leben Liebe
    "Promesse Eternelle" solo,pno
    SCHAUR s.p.   (G842)

    Promesse Eternelle *see Mein Ganzes
    Leben Liebe

    Weisse Orchideen
    solo,pno SCHAUR s.p.   (G843)

GLOMKANS LAND see Marvia, Einari, Unhon
    Maa

GLORIA see Buzzi-Peccia, Arturo

GLORIA see Rorem, Ned

GLORIA DEL DISTESO MEZZOGIORNO see
    Bettinelli, Bruno

GLORIA IN EXCELSIS see Perusio, Matheus
    de

GLORIA IN EXCELSIS DEO see White, Louie
    L.

GLORIA JEZUKE, GLORIA see Loots, Ph.

GLORIA PATRI see Zagatti, Francesco

GLORIOUS DEVON see German, Edward

GLORIOUS FOREVER see Rachmaninoff,
    Sergey Vassilievitch

GLORIOUS HOBO, THE see Weigl, Karl

GLORIOUS TIME OF THE YEAR see Dove, J.

GLORY, GLORY CLEAR THE ROAD *sac,
    gospel
    solo,pno ABER.GRP. $1.50   (G844)

GLORY OF CALVARY'S CROSS, THE see Paris

GLORY OF MY GARDEN, THE see Wood,
    Daniel

GLORY OF THE DAWN see Day, Maude Craske

GLORY ROAD see Cook

GLORY TO GOD IN THE HIGHEST see
    Charpentier, Marc-Antoine

GLORY TO THEE, MY GOD see Gounod,
    Charles Francois

GLORY, WHAT A DAY see Harris

GLOSA see Pablo, Luis de

GLOSE see Komadina, Vojin

GLOSSES see Komadina, Vojin, Glose

GLOVER, CHARLES W. (1806-1863)
    Rose Of Tralee, The
    low solo,pno (B flat maj) CENTURY
    3702   (G845)
    solo,pno (B flat maj) ALLANS s.p.
                                    (G846)
    (Spencer) high solo,pno FOX,S
                                    (G847)
    (Spencer) med solo,pno FOX,S   (G848)
    (Spencer) low solo,pno FOX,S   (G849)

GLOVER, STEPHEN
    Gipsy Countess, The
    2 soli,pno LEONARD-ENG   (G850)

    Hoort Gij De Wilde Golven? *see What
    Are The Wild Waves Saying?

    Lily And The Rose
    2 soli,pno LEONARD-ENG   (G851)

    Music And Her Sister Song
    2 soli,pno LEONARD-ENG   (G852)

    Nightingale And The Rose
    2 soli,pno LEONARD-ENG   (G853)

GLOVER, STEPHEN (cont'd.)

Tell Us Oh Tell Us Where Shall We
 Find
 2 soli,pno LEONARD-ENG   (G854)

What Are The Wild Waves Saying?
 solo,pno (E flat maj) LEONARD-ENG
                               (G855)
 2 soli,pno LEONARD-ENG   (G856)
 "Hoort Gij De Wilde Golven?" 2
 soli,pno ALSBACH s.p.   (G857)

GLUCK AUF', GUDS FRED see Olsen, Sparre

GLUCK, CHRISTOPH WILLIBALD RITTER VON
 (1714-1787)
Ach! Ich Habe Sie Verloren (from
 Orfeo Ed Euridice)
 A/Bar solo,strings BREITKOPF-L
 rental   (G858)

Ach Soll Dies Freie Herz (from
 Armida)
 S solo,ob,strings BREITKOPF-L
 rental   (G859)

Ah! Si La Liberte (from Armide)
 S solo,orch HENN s.p.   (G860)

Air De Renaud (from Armide)
 see LA MUSIQUE, TREIZIEME CAHIER

Amour, Sors Pour Jamais (from Armide)
 [Fr] S solo,pno CHOUDENS C268 s.p.
                               (G861)

Berenice, Ach, Wo Bist Du? *see
 Berenice, Ove Sei?

Berenice, Ove Sei? (from Antigono)
 (Reinecke, Carl) "Berenice, Ach, Wo
 Bist Du?" S solo,fl,2ob,2clar,
 2bsn,2horn,2trp,timp,strings
 BREITKOPF-W s.p.   (G862)

C'est Un Torrent Impetreux (from Les
 Pelerins De La Mecque)
 "Dies Ist Ein Giessbach" Bar solo,
 2fl,2ob,strings BREITKOPF-W s.p.
                               (G863)
Che Faro Senza Euridice? (from Orfeo)
 low solo,pno (B flat maj) ALLANS
 s.p.   (G864)
 [It] high solo,pno (D maj) CRAMER
                               (G865)
 [It] low solo,pno (C maj) CRAMER
                               (G866)
 solo,pno FORLIVESI s.p.   (G867)
 [It] A solo,pno RICORDI-ENG 54387
 s.p.   (G868)
 [It] A solo,pno RICORDI-ARG
 BA 11697 s.p.   (G869)
 "Live Without My Fair Euridice?"
 [It/Eng] Mez solo,pno (C maj)
 SCHIRM.G $.85   (G870)
 "Live Without My Fair Euridice?"
 [It/Eng] A solo,pno (B flat maj)
 SCHIRM.G $.85   (G871)

Die Ihr Im Hades Herrscht *see
 Divinites Du Styx

Die Ruhe Kehret Mir Zurück (from
 Iphigenie En Tauride)
 Bar solo,ob,strings BREITKOPF-L
 rental   (G872)

Dies Ist Ein Giessbach *see C'est Un
 Torrent Impetreux

Divinites Du Styx (from Alceste)
 scena
 [Fr/Eng] S solo,pno (B flat maj)
 SCHIRM.G $.75   (G873)
 [Fr/Eng] Mez solo,pno (A flat maj)
 SCHIRM.G $.75   (G874)
 "Die Ihr Im Hades Herrscht" S solo,
 2ob,2clar,2bsn,2horn,3trom,
 strings BREITKOPF-L rental (G875)

Fatal Divinita (from Alceste)
 [It/Fr] S solo,pno RICORDI-ENG
 BA 8830 s.p.   (G876)

J'ai Perdu Mon Eurydice (from Orpheo
 Ed Euridice)
 see LA MUSIQUE, TROISIEME CAHIER
 solo,pno DURAND s.p.   (G877)

Live Without My Fair Euridice? *see
 Che Faro Senza Euridice?

O Del Mio Dolce Ardor (from Paride Ed
 Elena)
 solo,pno FORLIVESI 10877 s.p.
                               (G878)
 "O Thou Belov'd" [It/Eng] high
 solo,pno (E min) SCHIRM.G $.85
                               (G879)
 "O Thou Belov'd" [It/Eng] low solo,
 pno (D min) SCHIRM.G $.85   (G880)
 (Parisotti) [It/Fr] S/T solo,pno
 RICORDI-ARG BA 8238 s.p.   (G881)
 (Parisotti) [It/Fr] Mez/Bar solo,
 pno RICORDI-ENG 113473 s.p.
                               (G882)

GLUCK, CHRISTOPH WILLIBALD RITTER VON
 (cont'd.)

 (Parisotti) [It/Fr] S/T solo,pno
 RICORDI-ENG 121039 s.p.   (G883)

O Du, Die Mir Das Leben Gab *see O
 Toi, Qui Prolongaes Mes Jours

O Malheureuse Iphigenie (from
 Iphigenie En Tauride)
 [Fr] S solo,pno CHOUDENS C206 s.p.
                               (G884)

O Saviour, Hear Me *sac,Offer
 (Buck) high solo,vln/fl/vcl,pno (F
 maj) SCHIRM.G $.75   (G885)
 (Buck) high solo,pno (F maj)
 SCHIRM.G $.85   (G886)
 (Buck) low solo,pno (D flat maj)
 SCHIRM.G $.85   (G887)

O Thou Belov'd *see O Del Mio Dolce
 Ardor

O Toi Qui Prologeas Mes Jours (from
 Iphigenie En Tauride)
 solo,orch HENN s.p.   (G888)

O Toi, Qui Prolongaes Mes Jours (from
 Iphigenie En Tauride)
 "O Du, Die Mir Das Leben Gab" S
 solo,2ob,strings BREITKOPF-W s.p.
                               (G889)

O Toi Qui Prolongeas Mes Jours (from
 Iphigenie En Tauride)
 [Fr] S solo,pno CHOUDENS C70 s.p.
                               (G890)

Songs, Odes And Arias *CC9U
 [Ger] high solo/med solo,pno PETERS
 2250 $4.75   (G891)

Spiagge Amate (from Paride Ed Elena)
 solo,pno FORLIVESI 10878 s.p.
                               (G892)

Vardrottningen
 2 soli,pno LUNDQUIST s.p.   (G893)

Vieni Che Poi
 [It] solo,pno CRAMER   (G894)

Von Jugend Auf Im Treusten Bunde
 (Iphigenie En Tauride) T solo,bsn,
 strings BREITKOPF-L rental (G895)

Vous Ressemblez A La Rose Naissante
 (from La Rencontre Imprevue)
 (Flothius, Marius) T solo,fl,pno
 BROEKMANS 395-8 s.p.   (G896)

Wo Bin Ich? Nein, Nicht Ein Opfer
 Werd Ich's Nennen (from Alceste)
 S solo,2fl,2ob,2clar,2horn,strings
 BREITKOPF-L rental   (G897)

GLUCK UND HULD, MEIN HERR, ZUM GRUSSE
 see Rossini, Gioacchino

GLUCKES GENUG see Strauss, Richard

GLUCKLICHER TAG see Thomas, Kurt

GLUCKSELIGKEITS-ODE see Sibelius, Jean

GLUNTARNE see Wennerburg, [Gunnar]

GNATTALI, RADAMES (1906-   )
 Ninando
 [Port/Span] solo,pno RICORDI-ARG
 BA 8065 s.p.   (G898)

GNIER OG GNUAR see Beck, Thomas
 [Ludvigsen]

GNOME AND THE PENGUIN see Holford,
 Franz

GNORA CREDITEMI see Pergolesi, Giovanni
 Battista

GO AND CATCH A FALLING STAR see Brumby,
 Colin

GO AND CATCH A FALLING STAR see
 Flanagan, William

GO AND CATCH A FALLING STAR see Hoiby,
 Lee

GO DOWN IN THE LONESOME VALLEY *spir
 (Burleigh, H.T.) high solo,pno BELWIN
 $1.50   (G899)
 (Burleigh, H.T.) low solo,pno BELWIN
 $1.50   (G900)

GO DOWN MOSES *spir
 (Burleigh, H. T.) high solo,pno
 BELWIN $1.50   (G901)
 (Burleigh, H. T.) low solo,pno BELWIN
 $1.50   (G902)

GO DOWN TO KEW IN LILAC TIME see Peel,
 Graham

GO FROM ME see Fischer, Irwin

GO FROM MY WINDOW, GO see Somervell,
 Arthur

GO INTO ALL THE WORLD see Bender, Jan

GO, LOVELY ROSE see Bunge, Sas

GO, LOVELY ROSE see Cumming, R.

GO, LOVELY ROSE see Lee, E. Markham

GO' NATT DA see Braein, Edvard Fliflet

GO NOT HAPPY DAY see Bridge, Frank

GO NOT, HAPPY DAY see Bury, Winifred

GO PLACIDLY... see Malipiero, Riccardo

GO, PLOUGHMAN, PLOUGH! see Haufrecht,
 Herbert

GO PRETTY BIRDS see Dunhill, Thomas
 Frederick

GO TELL EVERYONE *sac,CC12U
 solo,pno,opt gtr VANGUARD V547 $1.95
                               (G903)

GO TELL IT ON DE MOUNTAINS *spir
 (Burleigh, H. T.) med solo,pno BELWIN
 $1.50   (G904)

GO TELL IT ON THE MOUNTAIN *spir
 solo,pno ASHLEY $.95   (G905)
 (Bonds, M.) med solo,pno MERCURY $.95
                               (G906)

GO TELL IT ON THE MOUNTAIN see Work,
 John [Wesley]

GO THY WAY, EAT THY BREAD WITH JOY see
 Pinkham, Daniel

GO TO THE MARKET, DAUGHTER FAIR
 see Three Songs Of Old Quebec

GO 'WAY FROM MY WINDOW see Niles, John
 Jacob

GO WITH JESUS see Ellis

GOAT PATHS, THE see Mourant, Walter

GOATHEMALA see Goeyvaerts, Karel

GOATLEY, ALMA
 Can't Remember
 low solo,pno (D maj) ASHDOWN (G907)
 med solo,pno (E flat maj) ASHDOWN
                               (G908)
 high solo,pno (F maj) ASHDOWN
                               (G909)

GOBER, BELLE BAIRD
 I Will Lift Up Mine Eyes (Psalm 121)
 sac
 Mez solo,pno FITZSIMONS $.40 (G910)

 Psalm 121 *see I Will Lift Up Mine
 Eyes

GOD BE IN MY HEART see Warren, Elinor
 Remick

GOD BE WITH YOU TILL WE MEET AGAIN
 *sac
 (Rolfe) low solo,pno (G maj) CENTURY
 3699 $.40   (G911)

GOD BLESS CANADA see Roff, Joseph

GOD BLESS ME see Harding, Phyllis

GOD BLESS THE HILLS see Murray, Alan

GOD BLESS THE MORNING see Oliver,
 Herbert

GOD BLESS THIS DAY see Lesser, Rena S.

GOD BLESS YOU see Dickson, Stanley

GOD BLESS YOU; GO WITH GOD see Roberts

GOD BREAKETH THE BATTLE see Parry,
 Charles Hubert Hastings

GOD CAN see Abernathy

GOD CAN SEE US *sac
 (Carmichael, Ralph) solo,pno WORD
 S-256   (G912)

GOD CARES see Boyd, William S.

GOD, CREATE IN ME A CLEAN HEART see
 Buxtehude, Dietrich, Schaffe In
 Mir, Gott, Ein Rein Herz

GOD DID A WONDERFUL THING FOR ME see
 Peterson, John W.

GOD EVER NEAR see Dickinson, Clarence

GOD GAVE ME LOVE see Rawls, R. Maines

GOD GAVE ME YOU see Kaiser, Ralph L.

GOD GAVE THE SONG see Huff, Ronn

GOD-GIVEN LOVE see Hawkins

GOD HAS NOT CHANGED see Jensen, Gordon

GOD, HURRAH! see Wetzler, Robert Paul

GOD I NEED THEE see Work, John [Wesley]

GOD IS EVERYWHERE see Williams

GOD IS GOD *sac,gospel
   solo,pno ABER.GRP. $1.50   (G913)

GOD IS HERE RIGHT NOW see Kaiser, Kurt

GOD IS IN EVERYTHING see Clokey, Joseph
   Waddell

GOD IS LIFE see Bach, Johann Sebastian

GOD IS LOVE see Morse, Charles Henry

GOD IS LOVE see Shelley, Harry Rowe

GOD IS MY SALVATION see Calder, Lee

GOD IS MY SHEPHERD see Dvorak, Antonin

GOD IS OUR LIFE see Bach, Johann
   Sebastian

GOD IS OUR REFUGE see Fischer, Irwin

GOD IS SO WONDERFUL see Marshall,
   Virginia

GOD IS THE ANSWER see Slaughter, Henry

GOD LIT HIS STARS see Nutting, Godfrey

GOD LIVES IN MY HEART see O'Hara,
   Geoffrey

GOD LOVES YOU *sac
   (Carmichael, Ralph) solo,pno WORD
   S-232   (G914)

GOD LYAEUS see Plessis, Hubert du

GOD MAKES DUCKS see Mollicone, Henry

GOD, MY SHEPHERD see Bach, Johann
   Sebastian

GOD NATT see Knutsen, Torbjorn

GOD NATT see Madetoja, Leevi, Hyvaa
   Yota

GOD NATT see Merikanto, Oskar, Hyvaa
   Yota

GOD NATT see Olsen, Sparre

GOD OF EARTH AND HEAVEN see Sateren,
   Leland Bernhard

GOD OF LOVE see Dieterich, M.

GOD OF LOVE MY SHEPHERD IS, THE see
   Thiman, Eric Harding

GOD OF MIRACLES, THE *sac
   (Carmichael, Ralph) solo,pno WORD
   S-232   (G915)

GOD OF OUR FATHERS see Ancis, Solomon,
   R'tzeh

GOD PUT A RAINBOW IN THE CLOUD *sac,
   gospel
   solo,pno ABER.GRP. $1.50   (G916)

GOD REMEMBERS EVERYTHING see Arlen

GOD SAID IT, I BELIEVE IT, THAT SETTLES
   IT! see Braun

GOD SAVE THE QUEEN
   (Bantock) med solo,pno PAXTON P141
   s.p.   (G917)

GOD SENT HIS SON see Cates, Bill

GOD SHALL DO MY ADVISING see Buxtehude,
   Dietrich

GOD SHALL WIPE AWAY ALL TEARS
   (Roma) 2 soli,pno WARNER VD0004 $1.50
                                      (G918)

GOD SHALL WIPE AWAY ALL TEARS see
   Fischer, Irwin

GOD SHALL WIPE AWAY ALL TEARS see
   Harker, F. Flaxington

GOD SHALL WIPE AWAY ALL TEARS see
   Sullivan, Albert

GOD SO LOVED THE WORLD see Bender, Jan

GOD SO LOVED THE WORLD see Fischer,
   Irwin

GOD SO LOVED THE WORLD see Stainer,
   John

GOD SPEAKING TO YOU see Salsbury, Sonny

GOD SPEAKS TO ME see Ackermann, Dorothy

GOD SPEAKS TODAY see Baker, Richard

GOD SPOKE *sac,CC10UL
   solo,pno,gtr LILLENAS MB-275 $1.95
                                      (G919)

GOD SPOKE TO ME ONE DAY *sac,gospel
   solo,pno ABER.GRP. $1.50   (G920)

GOD SPOKE TO ME TODAY see Hughes

GOD STILL LIVES see Davis

GOD THAT WAS REAL see Walvoord, John

GOD THE ARCHITECT see Breeze, Edwin
   Carter

GOD WALKS THE DARK HILLS see Czarnikow

GOD WHO MADEST EARTH AND HEAVEN see
   Newton, Ernest

GOD WILL TAKE CARE OF YOU *sac,gospel
   solo,pno ABER.GRP. $1.50   (G921)

GODARD, BENJAMIN LOUIS PAUL (1849-1895)
   A Elle
      solo,pno/inst DURAND s.p.   (G922)

   Adieu
      solo,pno/inst DURAND s.p.   (G923)

   Aimons Toujours
      solo,pno/inst DURAND s.p.   (G924)

   Amour Fatal
      solo,pno/inst DURAND s.p.   (G925)

   Angels Guard Thee *see Cache Dans
      Cet Asile

   Annette
      see Six Villanelles
      solo,pno/inst DURAND s.p.   (G926)

   Arabisches Lied
      solo,pno (in 2 keys) DURAND s.p.
                                      (G927)

   Automne
      solo,pno/inst DURAND s.p.   (G928)

   Autre Chanson
      solo,pno/inst DURAND s.p.   (G929)

   Aveu
      solo,pno/inst DURAND s.p.   (G930)

   Avril
      see Six Villanelles
      solo,pno/inst DURAND s.p.   (G931)

   Barcarolle
      solo,pno (available in 2 keys)
      ENOCH s.p.   (G932)

   Beau Page
      S/T solo,pno/inst DURAND s.p.
                                      (G933)
      Mez/Bar solo,pno/inst DURAND s.p.
                                      (G934)

   Berceuse *see Caches Dans Cet Asile

   Berceuse De Jocelyn *see Cache Dans
      Cet Asile

   Blumlein Im Thal *see Fleur Du
      Vallon

   Cache Dans Cet Asile (from Jocelyn)
      "Angels Guard Thee" med solo,pno (C
      maj) CRAMER   (G935)
      "Angels Guard Thee" med-high solo,
      pno (D flat maj) CRAMER   (G936)
      "Angels Guard Thee" high solo,pno
      (E flat maj) CRAMER   (G937)
      "Angels Guard Thee" low solo,pno (B
      flat maj) CRAMER   (G938)
      "Angels Guard Thee" low solo,pno (C
      maj) ALLANS s.p.   (G939)
      "Angels Guard Thee" 2 soli,pno
      CRAMER   (G940)
      "Angels Guard Thee" med solo,pno (D
      flat maj) ALLANS s.p.   (G941)
      "Angels Guard Thee" med-high solo,
      pno (B flat maj) ALLANS s.p.
                                      (G942)
      "Angels Guard Thee" high solo,pno
      (E flat maj) ALLANS s.p.   (G943)
      "Berceuse De Jocelyn" solo,pno (A
      flat maj) ASHDOWN   (G944)

   Caches Dans Cet Asile (from Jocelyn)
      "Berceuse" med solo,pno (A flat
      maj) CENTURY 1323   (G945)
      "Berceuse" [Fr/Eng] high solo,pno
      (F maj) SCHIRM.G $.85   (G946)

GODARD, BENJAMIN LOUIS PAUL (cont'd.)

   Chanson
      solo,pno/inst DURAND s.p.   (G947)

   Chanson D'avril
      "Song Of April" solo,pno CRAMER
                                      (G948)

   Chanson De Florian
      [Eng/Fr] low solo,pno (D maj)
      CENTURY 16   (G949)
      [Fr] solo,acap oct DURAND s.p.
                                      (G950)
      "Der Freund" S/T solo,pno DURAND
      s.p.   (G951)
      "Der Freund" Mez/Bar solo,pno
      DURAND s.p.   (G952)
      "Florian's Song" [Fr/Eng] med-high
      solo,pno (D maj) SCHIRM.G $.85
                                      (G953)
      "Florian's Song" [Fr/Eng] low solo,
      pno (C maj) SCHIRM.G $.85   (G954)

   Chanson De Juin
      [Fr] high solo,pno CHOUDENS C9 s.p.
                                      (G955)

   Chanson Des Pres
      "Das Wiesenlied" solo,pno (in 2
      keys) DURAND s.p.   (G956)

   Cloche Et Tambour
      solo,pno/inst DURAND s.p.   (G957)

   Contemplation
      A/B solo,pno/inst DURAND s.p.
                                      (G958)
      Mez/Bar solo,pno/inst DURAND s.p.
                                      (G959)
      "Erorterung" S/T solo,pno DURAND
      s.p.   (G960)
      "Erorterung" Mez/Bar solo,pno
      DURAND s.p.   (G961)

   Dans Les Bois D'Andilly
      solo,pno/inst DURAND s.p.   (G962)

   Das Wiesenlied *see Chanson Des Pres

   Dedicace
      solo,pno/inst DURAND s.p.   (G963)

   Der Freund *see Chanson De Florian

   Der Liebeswunsch *see Voudrais-Tu

   Der Nachtliche Ritt *see Le Voyageur

   Die Brautfahrt *see Embarquez-Vous

   Die Erinnerung *see Te Souviens-Tu

   Die Mittagsschlaf *see La Sieste

   Dieu Qui Sourit Et Qui Donne
      solo,pno/inst DURAND s.p.   (G964)

   Discretion
      solo,pno/inst DURAND s.p.   (G965)

   Douze Melodies *CC20L
      solo,pno DURAND s.p.   (G966)

   Elle
      solo,pno/inst DURAND s.p.   (G967)

   Embarquez-Vous
      "Die Brautfahrt" S/T solo,pno
      DURAND s.p.   (G968)
      "Die Brautfahrt" Mez/Bar solo,pno
      DURAND s.p.   (G969)

   Erorterung *see Contemplation

   Fille A La Blonde Chevelure
      solo,pno/inst DURAND s.p.   (G970)

   Fleur D'Exil, No. 1
      solo,pno DURAND s.p.   (G971)

   Fleur D'Exil, No. 2
      solo,harmonium/pno,vcl DURAND s.p.
                                      (G972)

   Fleur Du Vallon
      "Blumlein Im Thal" Mez/Bar solo,pno
      DURAND s.p.   (G973)

   Florian's Song *see Chanson De
      Florian

   Guitare
      solo,pno/inst DURAND s.p.   (G974)

   Ich Liebe Dich *see L'Amour

   Invitation Au Voyage
      Mez/Bar solo,pno/inst DURAND s.p.
                                      (G975)

   Jacotte
      solo,pno/inst DURAND s.p.   (G976)

   J'ai Dans L'ame
      solo,pno/inst DURAND s.p.   (G977)

   Je Ne Veux Pas D'autres Choses
      Mez/Bar solo,pno/inst DURAND s.p.
                                      (G978)

GODARD, BENJAMIN LOUIS PAUL (cont'd.)

[Fr] solo,acap oct DURAND s.p.
(G979)

Komm! *see Viens!

La Belle Saison D'Amour
solo,pno/inst DURAND s.p. (G980)

La Fleur Et Le Papillon
solo,pno/inst DURAND s.p. (G981)

La Plus Belle
see Six Villanelles
solo,pno/inst DURAND s.p. (G982)

La Sieste
"Die Mittagsschlaf" solo,pno DURAND
s.p. (G983)

L'Abeille
see Six Villanelles
solo,pno/inst DURAND s.p. (G984)

L'Amour
"Ich Liebe Dich" Mez/Bar solo,pno
DURAND s.p. (G985)
"Ich Liebe Dich" S/T solo,pno
DURAND s.p. (G986)

L'Attente
solo,pno/inst DURAND s.p. (G987)

Le Banc De Pierre
solo,pno/inst DURAND s.p. (G988)

Le Menetrier
solo,pno/inst DURAND s.p. (G989)

Le Portrait
solo,pno/inst DURAND s.p. (G990)

Le Retour Du Printemps
see Six Villanelles
solo,pno/inst DURAND s.p. (G991)

Le Sentier
Mez/Bar solo,pno/inst DURAND s.p.
(G992)

Le Soir Vient
solo,pno/inst DURAND s.p. (G993)

Le Voyageur
"Der Nachtliche Ritt" Mez/Bar solo,
pno DURAND s.p. (G994)

Leonora's Aria (from Tasso)
[Fr/Eng] S solo,pno INTERNAT. $1.00
(G995)

Les Larmes
solo,pno DURAND s.p. (G996)
solo,vln DURAND s.p. (G997)

Les Papillons
solo,pno (available in 2 keys)
ENOCH s.p. (G998)

Les Syiphes
solo,pno/inst DURAND s.p. (G999)

L'Etoile
solo,pno/inst DURAND s.p. (G1000)

L'heureux Berger
solo,pno/inst DURAND s.p. (G1001)

Lise
solo,pno/inst DURAND s.p. (G1002)

Lullaby
[Eng/Fr] med solo,pno PRESSER $.75
(G1003)

Marie
solo,pno/inst DURAND s.p. (G1004)

Mon Ami
solo,pno/inst DURAND s.p. (G1005)

Ou Donc?
solo,pno/inst DURAND s.p. (G1006)

Pourquoi
solo,pno/inst DURAND s.p. (G1007)

Printemps
(DuCamp, M.) S/T solo,pno/inst
DURAND s.p. (G1008)
(Guinard, Ed.) Mez/Bar solo,pno/
inst DURAND s.p. (G1009)
(Guinard, Ed.) S/T solo,pno/inst
DURAND s.p. (G1010)

Qui Donc Vous A Donne Vos Yeux?
Mez/Bar solo,pno/inst DURAND s.p.
(G1011)

Ronde
see Six Villanelles
solo,pno/inst DURAND s.p. (G1012)

Rondeau
solo,pno/inst DURAND s.p. (G1013)

Six Villanelles
solo,pno DURAND s.p.
contains: Annette; Avril; La Plus
Belle; L'Abeille; Le Retour Du

GODARD, BENJAMIN LOUIS PAUL (cont'd.)

Printemps; Ronde (G1014)

Song Of April *see Chanson D'avril

Sous Les Arbres
solo,pno/inst DURAND s.p. (G1015)

Te Souviens-Tu
[Fr] solo,acap oct DURAND s.p.
(G1016)
"Die Erinnerung" solo,pno DURAND
s.p. (G1017)

Trente Morceaux De Chant *CC30L
S/T solo,pno DURAND s.p. (G1018)

Venise
solo,pno/inst DURAND s.p. (G1019)

Veux-Tu?
Mez/Bar solo,pno/inst DURAND s.p.
(G1020)

Viens!
"Komm!" solo,pno,fl/ob/vln/vcl/
harmonium DURAND s.p. (G1021)

Viens Avec Nous (from La Vivandiere)
[Fr] med female solo,pno CHOUDENS
C208 s.p. (G1022)

Voudrais-Tu
"Der Liebeswunsch" solo,pno DURAND
s.p. (G1023)

Zwolf Lieder *CC12L
[Ger/Fr] solo,pno cmplt ed DURAND
s.p. (G1024)

GODEN EN ZANGERS see Leeuw, Ton de

GODFREY
Flag Of Empire *see Gillington, M.

GODNAT see Nielsen, Carl

GODNATT see Halvorsen, Leif

GODRON, HUGO (1900-)
De Schalmei
see Drie Liederen Van J. Slauerhoff

Drie Liederen Van J. Slauerhoff
Bar solo,pno DONEMUS s.p.
contains: De Schalmei;
Sterrenkind; Voor De Verre
Prinses (G1025)

Sterrenkind
see Drie Liederen Van J. Slauerhoff

Voor De Verre Prinses
see Drie Liederen Van J. Slauerhoff

GOD'S EDUCATION see Heilner, Irwin

GOD'S GRACE IS EHOUGH FOR ME see Red,
Buryl

GOD'S GRACE MAKES UP THE DIFFERENCE FOR
ME see Jensen, Gordon

GOD'S HALLOWED PLACE see Moore, Donald
Lee

GOD'S LITTLE CANDLES *sac,gospel
solo,pno ABER.GRP. $1.50 (G1026)

GOD'S LOVE see Masters

GOD'S MESSENGER see Kemper

GOD'S MIGHTY PEACE see Lee, Don

GOD'S NEWEST ANGEL see Moore, Gene

GOD'S PEOPLE see Kite, D.L.

GOD'S THOUGHT OF HIMSELF see Schouwman,
Hans

GOD'S VOICE HAS SOFTLY CALLED see Mana-
Zucca, Mme.

GOD'S WAY IS TRUE see Ellis

GOD'S WONDERFUL PEOPLE see Wolfe, Lanny

GOD'S WORLD see Alette, C.

GODVRUCHTIG DRINKLIED see Strategier,
Herman

GOEDE DOOD see Mulder, Herman

GOEDEN NACHT see Rennes, Cath. v.

GOEMANNE, NOEL
Ode To Love
high solo/low solo,pno FOSTER
MF 754 $1.25 (G1027)

GOETHE AMPHORISMEN see Vogel, Wladimir

GOETHE-LIEDER see Petersen, Wilhelm

GOETHE LIEDER see Dallapiccola, Luigi

GOETHE SONGS see Schubert, Franz
(Peter)

GOETHE SONGS, VOL. I: NOS. 1-11 see
Wolf, Hugo

GOETHE SONGS, VOL. II: NOS. 12-18, 49-
51 see Wolf, Hugo

GOETHE SONGS, VOL. III: NOS. 19-33 see
Wolf, Hugo

GOETHE SONGS, VOL. IV: NOS. 34-48 see
Wolf, Hugo

GOETHES LEIPZIGER LIEDERBUCH see
Breitkopf, Bernhard Theodor

GOETHES LIEDER, ODEN, BALLADEN UND
ROMANZEN see Reichardt, Johann
Friedrich

GOEYENS, FERN.
D'Un Jardin Abandonne
solo,pno (diff) BROGNEAUX s.p.
(G1028)
J'ai Besoin De Votre Tendresse
solo,pno BROGNEAUX s.p. (G1029)
Le Jour Du Seigneur *sac
solo,pno (diff) BROGNEAUX s.p.
(G1030)
Mon Enfant
solo,pno BROGNEAUX s.p. (G1031)
Ouvre Ta Fenetre
solo,pno BROGNEAUX s.p. (G1032)

GOEYVAERTS, KAREL (1923-)
Goathemala
Mez solo,fl CBDM s.p. (G1033)

GOGO see Stahuljak, Dubravko

GOIN' EASY see Yantis, David

GOIN' HOME see Dvorak, Antonin

GOING HOME see Gaither

GOING TO HEAVEN see Copland, Aaron

GOING TO KILDARE see Newton, Ernest

GOING TO ST. IVES see Lessard, John
Ayres

GOKKES, S.
Sjire Kodesj *CCU
solo,pno s.p. cloth BROEKMANS 170,
pap BROEKMANS 351 (G1034)

GOLD, ERNEST (1921-)
Gifts
high solo,pno SCHIRM.G $.75 see
from Songs Of Love And Parting
(G1035)
Music, When Soft Voices Die
high solo,pno SCHIRM.G $.75 see
from Songs Of Love And Parting
(G1036)
Parting
high solo,pno SCHIRM.G $.75 see
from Songs Of Love And Parting
(G1037)
Peace
high solo,pno SCHIRM.G $.75 see
from Songs Of Love And Parting
(G1038)
Red, Red Rose, A
high solo,pno SCHIRM.G $.75 see
from Songs Of Love And Parting
(G1039)
Shall I Compare Thee
high solo,pno SCHIRM.G $.75 see
from Songs Of Love And Parting
(G1040)
Songs Of Love And Parting *see
Gifts; Music, When Soft Voices
Die; Parting; Peace; Red, Red
Rose, A; Shall I Compare Thee;
Time Does Not Bring Relief
(G1041)
Time Does Not Bring Relief
high solo,pno SCHIRM.G $.75 see
from Songs Of Love And Parting
(G1042)

GOLDBACH, STANISLAV (1896-)
Das Entbrennen *see Vzplanuti
Pisne Potulneho Pevce *CCU
med solo,pno CZECH s.p. (G1043)
Vzplanuti
"Das Entbrennen" med solo,pno CZECH
s.p. (G1044)

GOLDBERG, L.
Galante Conversation
[Fr] solo,acap oct DURAND s.p.
(G1045)
solo,pno/inst DURAND s.p. (G1046)

GOLDE, WALTER (1887-1910)
  Among Shadows
    high solo/med solo,pno SEESAW $1.00
                                    (G1047)

  I Will Lift Up Mine Eyes
    high solo,pno BRODT $.75   (G1048)
    low solo,pno BRODT $.75   (G1049)

  Love Was With Me Yesterday
    high solo,pno BELWIN $1.50   (G1050)
    med solo,pno BELWIN $1.50   (G1051)
    low solo,pno BELWIN $1.50   (G1052)

  O Beauty, Passing Beauty
    solo,pno BRODT $.60   (G1053)

GOLDEN BIRD, THE see Reger, Max, Zum
  Schlafen

GOLDEN DAWN see Cadzow, D.

GOLDEN HOUR OF NOON, THE see O'Neill,
  Norman

GOLDEN KEY, THE see Bond, Carrie Jacobs

GOLDEN LADY, THE see Lockwood, Normand

GOLDEN LIGHT see Bizet, Georges, Agnus
  Dei

GOLDEN PEACOCK, THE, VOLS. 1 & 2 *CCU,
  folk,Jew
  solo,pno OR-TAV s.p., ea.   (G1054)

GOLDEN SERIES LOW VOICE COLLECTION,
  VOL. 1 *sac,CCUL
  low solo,pno WORD 10105 $1.00   (G1055)

GOLDEN SERIES LOW VOICE COLLECTION,
  VOL. 2 *sac,CCUL
  low solo,pno WORD 10106 $1.00   (G1056)

GOLDEN SONG see Kilpinen, Yrio,
  Goldenes Lied

GOLDEN SONGS *CC10U,Eng,16-17th cent
  (Komter) [Eng] solo,gtr PETERS HU2041
  s.p.   (G1057)

GOLDEN SONGS OF GLORY *sac,CCU,gospel
  solo,pno STAMPS 4852-SN $1.00
    contains works by: Presley, Luther;
    Polk, Videt; Brock, Dwight;
    Cravens, Rupert and others   (G1058)

GOLDEN STOCKINGS see Shepherd, Arthur

GOLDEN TRESSES see Monteverdi, Claudio,
  Chioma D'Oro

GOLDEN VANITY, THE see Broadwood, Lucy
  E.

GOLDENES LIED see Kilpinen, Yrio

GOLDFARB, SAMUEL E.
  V'shomru *sac
    [Heb] med solo,pno TRANSCON. WJ 427
    $.50   (G1059)

GOLDMAN, MAURICE
  Song Of Ruth *sac,Marriage
    high solo,pno/orch TRANSCON. TV 473
    $.75, ipa   (G1060)
    med solo,pno TRANSCON. TV 476 $.75
                                    (G1061)
    [Heb] high solo,strings,pno
    TRANSCON. rental   (G1062)
    [Heb] high solo,ob,clar,strings,pno
    TRANSCON. rental   (G1063)

GOLDMAN, RICHARD FRANKO (1911-   )
  My Kingdom
    med solo,pno PRESSER $.75   (G1064)

  Two Poems Of William Blake *CC2U
    med solo,pno PRESSER $.75   (G1065)

  Weary Yeare, The
    high solo,pno PRESSER $.75   (G1066)

GOLDMARK, KARL (1830-1915)
  Zwolf Gesange *Op.18,No.1-12, CC12U
    DOBLINGER s.p. high solo,pno; med
    solo,pno; low solo,pno   (G1067)

GOLDNE BRUCKEN SEIEN ALLE LIEDER MIR
  see Svedbom, Vilhelm

GOLDNE WIEGEN see Rothschuh, Fritz

GOLDSCHMIDT, ADALBERT VON (1848-1906)
  Ave Maria *sac
    [Lat] solo,pno/org (available in 2
    keys) ENOCH s.p.   (G1068)

GOLDSTEIN, GUS
  Men Kon Leben Nor Men Lost Nit *Jew
    solo,pno KAMMEN 12 $1.00 see also
    FAVORITE JEWISH SONGS, VOL. 2
                                    (G1069)

GOLDSTEIN, MORRIS
  Hot A Yid A Weibele *Jew
    solo,pno KAMMEN 485 $1.00 see also
    JEWISH THEATRE SONGS, VOL. 1
                                    (G1070)

GOLLOHAN
  This Day Is Yours (composed with
    Marvin)
    med solo,pno (B flat maj) WILLIS
    $.60   (G1071)

GOLLWELL, JOHN (1893-1953)
  Novy Den *CC4U
    high solo,pno CZECH s.p.   (G1072)

GOLONDRINA see Demon, J.

GOLUBEV, E.
  Three Poems By S. Gorodetsky *song
    cycle
    [Russ] B solo,pno MEZ KNIGA 69 s.p.
                                    (G1073)

GOLUS KINDER see Vigoda, Samuel

GOMBAU, G.
  Calatanazor
    [Span] med solo,pno UNION ESP. $.60
                                    (G1074)

  Romance Del Duero
    [Span] med solo,pno UNION ESP. $.60
                                    (G1075)

GOMEZ CARRILLO, MANUEL (1883-   )
  Danzas Y Cantos Regionales Del Norte
    Argentino, Vol. I *CC16L
    [Span] solo,pno RICORDI-ARG BA 6708
    s.p.
    see also: El Ecuador; Huainito;
    La Ofrenda Del Trovador; Pobre
    Mi Negra; Que Linda Sois!;
    Trova: "Quiero Entonar A Tu
    Oido"; Yerba Buena; Zamba De
    Vargas   (G1076)

  Danzas Y Cantos Regionales Del Norte
    Argentino, Vol. II *CC20L
    [Span] solo,pno cmplt ed RICORDI-
    ARG BA 7093 s.p.
    see also: La Negrita   (G1077)

  El Ecuador
    [Span] solo,pno RICORDI-ARG
    BA 10275 s.p. see also Danzas Y
    Cantos Regionales Del Norte
    Agentino, Vol. I   (G1078)

  Huainito
    [Span] solo,pno RICORDI-ARG BA 8783
    s.p. see also Danzas Y Cantos
    Regionales Del Norte Agentino,
    Vol. I   (G1079)

  La Negrita
    [Span] solo,pno RICORDI-ARG BA 7452
    s.p. see also Danzas Y Cantos
    Regionales Del Norte Argentino,
    Vol. II   (G1080)

  La Ofrenda Del Trovador
    [Span] solo,pno RICORDI-ARG BA 9776
    s.p. see also Danzas Y Cantos
    Regionales Del Norte Agentino,
    Vol. I   (G1081)

  La Telesita
    [Span] solo,opt cor,pno RICORDI-ARG
    BA 10456 s.p.   (G1082)

  Mis Ojos Tienen La Culpa
    [Span] solo,pno RICORDI-ARG BA 9222
    s.p.   (G1083)

  Nostalgia Indigena
    [Span] S/T solo,pno sc RICORDI-ARG
    BA 12044 s.p.   (G1084)

  Pobre Mi Negra
    [Span] solo,pno RICORDI-ARG BA 8807
    s.p. see also Danzas Y Cantos
    Regionales Del Norte Agentino,
    Vol. I   (G1085)

  Que Linda Sois!
    [Span] solo,pno RICORDI-ARG BA 8808
    s.p. see also Danzas Y Cantos
    Regionales Del Norte Agentino,
    Vol. I   (G1086)

  Trova: "Quiero Entonar A Tu Oido"
    [Span] solo,pno RICORDI-ARG BA 8855
    s.p. see also Danzas Y Cantos
    Regionales Del Norte Agentino,
    Vol. I   (G1087)

  Vidala Del Regreso
    [Span] solo,pno RICORDI-ARG BA 9224
    s.p.   (G1088)

  Yerba Buena
    [Span] solo,pno RICORDI-ARG BA 8901
    s.p. see also Danzas Y Cantos
    Regionales Del Norte Agentino,
    Vol. I   (G1089)

  Zamba De Vargas
    [Span] solo,pno RICORDI-ARG BA 8781
    s.p. see also Danzas Y Cantos

GOMEZ CARRILLO, MANUEL (cont'd.)

    Regionales Del Norte Agentino,
    Vol. I   (G1090)

GONDOLSANG see Curtis

GONE see Fox

GONE see Fox, Eldridge

GONE see Raphling, Sam

GONERIL'S LULLABY see Keats, Horace

GONFIO TU VEDI IL FIUME see Martini,
  Giambattista

GONNA LOVE see Van Dyke, Vonda

GONNA WAKE UP SINGIN' see Price,
  Florence B.

GOOD BOY, A see Williamson, Malcolm

GOOD-BY! see Tosti, Francesco Paolo,
  Addio!

GOOD-BYE, MY FANCY see Flanagan,
  William

GOOD BYE, MY FANCY see Williams, David
  H.

GOOD-BYE, WORLD, GOOD-BYE see Lister,
  Mosie

GOOD CIDER FOR ME see Arundale, Claude

"GOOD-DAY!" SAID THE BLACKBIRD see
  Geehl, Henry Ernest

GOOD, DWAYNE
  Echoes Of God's Greatness *sac
    solo,pno WORD S-10   (G1091)

  Have Gospel, Must Travel *sac
    solo,pno WORD S-7   (G1092)

  I'm Glad I'm A Christian *sac
    solo,pno WORD S-17   (G1093)

  Lest I Forget *sac
    solo,pno WORD S-14   (G1094)

  Savior Knows, The *sac
    solo,pno WORD S-19   (G1095)

  Wise Men Still Adore Him *sac
    solo,pno WORD S-263   (G1096)

GOOD ENGLISH HOSPITALITY see Flagello,
  Nicholas

GOOD FELLOWS, BE MERRY see Bach, Johann
  Sebastian

GOOD LUCK, GOOD CHEER see Wolfsohn,
  Georg

GOOD LUCK, MR. FISHERMAN see Scott,
  John Prindle

GOOD NIGHT see Cory, George

GOOD NIGHT! see Franz, Robert

GOOD-NIGHT see Parry, Charles Hubert
  Hastings

GOOD OLD DAYS see Kaiser, Kurt

GOOD OLD GOSPEL SINGING see Lister,
  Mosie

GOOD ROARIN' FIRE, A
  see Three Irish Folk Songs

GOOD SHEPHERD see Van De Water, B.

GOOD TIDINGS see Wetzler, Robert Paul

GOODE, GEORGE
  When I Survey
    solo,pno CRAMER   (G1097)

GOODE, JACK C.
  Seven Sacred Solos *sac,CC7U
    solo,pno ABINGDON APM-484 $2.50
                                    (G1098)

GOODENOUGH, FORREST
  How Do I Love Thee?
    med solo,pno AM.COMP.AL. $2.75
                                    (G1099)

GOODEVE, MRS. ARTHUR
  Fiddle And I
    high solo,pno (B flat maj) ASHDOWN
                                    (G1100)
    low solo,pno (A maj) ASHDOWN
                                    (G1101)

GOODMAN
  Give Up *sac
    solo,pno BENSON S5520-S $1.00
                                    (G1102)

GOODMAN (cont'd.)

Had It Not Been *sac
solo,pno BENSON S5612-S $1.00
(G1103)

How Much More *sac
solo,pno BENSON S5925-S $1.00
(G1104)

Until You've Known *sac
solo,pno BENSON S8288-S $1.00
(G1105)

Who Am I? *sac
solo,pno BENSON S8492-S $1.00
(G1106)

GOODNIGHT, GOD BLESS YOU see Wild, Eric

GOODNIGHT KISS see Bohun, Lyle de

GOODNIGHT MISTER MOON see Murray, Alan

GOODRICH, THELMA
Somebody's Calling My Name *sac
solo,pno WORD S-314 (G1107)

GOODSON
We've Come This Far By Faith *sac
solo,pno BENSON S8344-R $1.00 (G1108)

GOODWIN, PAUL
Sweet Jesus *sac
solo,pno GOSPEL 05 TM 0478 $1.00
(G1109)

GOOSEN, JACQUES (1952-)
Arno Holz-Songs *CCU
A solo,2fl,2ob,2clar,bsn,sax,al-
sax,horn,2trp,trom,timp,perc,
vibra,cel,cembalo,harmonium,harp,
8vln,4vla,4vcl,gtr DONEMUS s.p.
(G1110)

GOOSENS, EUGENE (1893-1962)
Appeal, The *Op.26,No.1
[Eng] med solo,kbd CHESTER s.p. see
from Three Songs (G1111)

Four Songs
[Eng] high solo,kbd CHESTER s.p.
contains: Seascape; Threshold;
Winter Night Idyll, A; Woodland
Dell, A (G1112)

Melancholy *Op.26,No.2
[Eng] med solo,kbd CHESTER s.p. see
from Three Songs (G1113)

Philomel *Op.26,No.3
[Eng] med solo,kbd CHESTER s.p. see
from Three Songs (G1114)

Seascape
see Four Songs

Three Songs *see Appeal, The, Op.26,
No.1; Melancholy, Op.26,No.2;
Philomel, Op.26,No.3 (G1115)

Threshold
see Four Songs

Winter Night Idyll, A
see Four Songs

Woodland Dell, A
see Four Songs

GOOSSEN, FREDERIC
Ode
Mez solo,2fl,2ob,2clar,2bsn,4horn,
2trp,3trom,3timp,perc,strings
AM.COMP.AL. (G1116)

GOPAK see Mussorgsky, Modest

GORCLIVO EZERO see Zografski, Tomisalv

GORDIGIANI, LUIGI (1806-1860)
Ogni Sabato Avrete Il Lume Acceso
solo,pno FORLIVESI 10430 s.p.
(G1117)

GORDON
If I Could Hear My Mother Pray Again
*see Gerald

GORDON FOR ME
solo,pno ALLANS s.p. (G1118)

GORDON JENSEN-SONGBOOK see Jensen,
Gordon

GORDON, W.
Haven Of Tenderness
med solo,pno (E flat maj) BOOSEY
$1.50 (G1119)
high solo,pno (F maj) BOOSEY $1.50
(G1120)
low solo,pno (C maj) BOOSEY $1.50
(G1121)

GORE, RICHARD T.
Entreat Me Not To Leave Thee *sac,
Marriage
high solo,pno CONCORDIA 97-9345
$.75 (G1122)
low solo,pno CONCORDIA 97-9346 $.75
(G1123)
O Sing Unto The Lord A New Song *sac
high solo,pno BELWIN $1.50 (G1124)
low solo,pno BELWIN $1.50 (G1125)

GORM GRYM see Maurice, Pierre

GORNER, H.G.
Die Sternsinger *Op.14
solo,pno SCHAUR EE 3066 s.p.
(G1126)

GORNEY, JAY
Blue Train (from Blue Train, The)
solo,pno CRAMER (G1127)

GOSH, BOBBY
Reach Up *see Van Dyke, Vonda

GOSPEL ACCORDING TO OLE JOHN, THE see
Lister, Mosie

GOSPEL FROM THE HOUSE OF CASH *sac,
CC16L,gospel
(Brown, Aaron) solo,pno WORD 37676
$3.95 (G1128)

GOSPEL HITS OF THE 70'S, VOL. I *sac,
CC12UL
solo,pno BENSON BO235 $2.50 (G1129)

GOSPEL HITS OF THE 70'S, VOL. II *sac,
CC15L
solo,pno BENSON BO236 $2.50 (G1130)

GOSPEL QUARTET FAVORITES *sac,CCU,
gospel
4 soli,pno STAMPS 4817-SN $1.00
(G1131)

GOSPEL QUARTETS *sac,CC205U,gospel
4 male soli,pno STAMPS 4836-SN $1.95
(G1132)

GOSPEL SINGER, THE *sac,CCU
(Reynolds, William J.) S/T solo,pno
BROADMAN 4525-02 $.80; A/Bar/B
solo,pno BROADMAN 4525-01 $.80
(G1133)

GOSPEL SOLOIST, THE *sac,CCU,gospel
med solo,kbd BROADMAN 4525-07 $2.75
(G1134)

GOSPEL SONGS BY GLORIA ROE, VOL. 2
*sac,CCUL,gospel
solo,pno WORD 10032 $1.00 contains
works by: Roe, Gloria; Carle, Bill
(G1135)

GOSPEL SONGS BY GLORIA ROE, VOL. 3
*sac,CCUL,gospel
solo,pno WORD 10033 $1.00 contains
works by: Roe, Gloria; Kerr, Phil
(G1136)

GOSPEL TRAIN, THE *spir
(Widdicombe) 2 soli,pno/orch ROBERTON
72494 s.p. (G1137)

GOSPEL TRAIN IS COMING, THE *sac,
gospel
solo,pno ABER.GRP. $1.50 (G1138)

GOSPEL'S BEST WORDS AND MUSIC, VOL. 1
*sac,CC12L,gospel
(Brown, Aaron) solo,pno WORD 37662
$2.95 (G1139)

GOSPEL'S BEST WORDS AND MUSIC, VOL. 2
*sac,CC12L,gospel
(Brown, Aaron) solo,pno WORD 37693
$2.95 (G1140)

GOSPEL'S BEST WORDS AND MUSIC, VOL. 3
*sac,CC14L,gospel
(Brown, Aaron) solo,pno WORD 37740
$2.95 (G1141)

GOSS
I Won't Have To Worry Any More *see
Jones

GOSSIPING see Dodge, John

GOSSLER, G.
Sweeter For The Wait, The
med solo,pno SEESAW $1.00 (G1142)

GOTOVAC, JAKOV (1895-)
Intimity *song cycle
[Slav] solo,pno CROATICA s.p.
(G1143)

GOTT, DEINE GUTE see Beethoven, Ludwig
van

GOTT DER VATER WOHN UNS BEI see Schein,
Johann Hermann

GOTT ICH FALLE DIR ZU FUSSEN see Haydn,
(Johann) Michael

GOTT IS A TATE *Jew
solo,pno KAMMEN 425 $1.00 (G1144)

GOTT IST GEIST see Buchtger, Fritz

GOTT IST LIEBE see Thiele, Siegfried

GOTT IST MEIN FREUND see Bach, Johann
Sebastian

GOTT, MAN LOBET DICH IN DER STILLE see
Bach, Johann Sebastian

GOTT RAD see Hinrichs, F.

GOTT! WELCH DUNKEL HIER see Beethoven,
Ludwig van

GOTT WILL MENSCH UND STERBLICH WERDEN
see Telemann, Georg Philipp

GOTT! WIRF MICH NICHT ZU DEINEN STEINEN
see Pesonen, Olavi (Samuel)

GOTTES MACHT UND VORSEHUNG see
Beethoven, Ludwig van

GOTTES WORT see Bach, Johann Sebastian

GOTTLIEB, JACK (1930-)
May We Lie Down (from Gates Of
Prayer)
[Eng] solo,pno/org TRANSCON. TV 544
$1.00 (G1145)

GOTTSCHALK
Last Hope, The *sac
med solo,pno (B flat maj) CENTURY
1063 $.40 (G1146)

GOTZE
Tyst Som En Natt, Djup Som Ett Hav
2 soli,pno LUNDQUIST s.p. (G1147)

GOUBLIER, G.
Emois D'amour
solo,pno ENOCH s.p. (G1148)
solo,pno ENOCH s.p. (G1149)

Il A Suffi
solo,pno ENOCH s.p. (G1150)
solo,acap ENOCH s.p. (G1151)

J'ai Reve De T'aimer
solo,pno ENOCH s.p. (G1152)
solo,acap ENOCH s.p. (G1153)

Journee D'amour
solo,pno ENOCH s.p. (G1154)
solo,acap ENOCH s.p. (G1155)

Laissez Glaner
solo,pno ENOCH s.p. (G1156)
solo,acap ENOCH s.p. (G1157)

L'Angelus De La Mer
solo,pno (available in 4 keys)
ENOCH s.p. (G1158)
solo,orch (D maj) ENOCH s.p., ipa
(G1159)
MezBar soli,pno ENOCH s.p. voc sc,
solo pt (G1160)

Le Chaplet D'amour
solo,acap ENOCH s.p. (G1161)
solo,pno ENOCH s.p. (G1162)

Les Baisers
solo,acap ENOCH s.p. (G1163)
solo,pno ENOCH s.p. (G1164)

Les Voeux
solo,pno ENOCH s.p. (G1165)
solo,acap ENOCH s.p. (G1166)

Reve
solo,acap (available in 2 keys)
ENOCH s.p. (G1167)
solo,pno (available in 2 keys)
ENOCH s.p. (G1168)

GOUDEN RANDEN see Bonset, Jac.

GOULDING, EDMUND (1891-1959)
Lovely Song My Heart Is Singing, The
high solo,pno (D flat maj) SCHIRM.G
$.75 (G1169)

GOUNOD, CHARLES FRANCOIS (1818-1893)
Ah! I Would Linger *see Ah! Je Veux
Vivre

Ah! Je Veux Vivre! (from Romeo Et
Juliette)
[Fr/It] S solo,pno RICORDI-ARG
BA 8998 s.p. (G1170)
"Waltz Song" high solo,pno (G maj)
ALLANS s.p. (G1171)
"Waltz Song" low solo,pno (E flat
maj) ALLANS s.p. (G1172)
"Waltz Song" med solo,pno (F maj)
ALLANS s.p. (G1173)
(Liebling) "Ah! I Would Linger"
[Fr/It/Eng] S solo,pno (G maj)
SCHIRM.G $.85 (G1174)

Ah! Leve-Toi, Soleil! (from Romeo Et
Juliette)
[Fr] T solo,pno CHOUDENS C236 s.p.
(G1175)

Air De Baucis (from Philemon Et
Baucis)
2 soli,orch HENN s.p. (G1176)

All Hail Thou Dwelling Pure And Lowly
*see Salve, Dimora Casta E Pura

Ange Adorable (from Romeo Et
Juliette)
[Fr] ST soli,pno CHOUDENS C77 s.p.
(G1177)

GOUNOD, CHARLES FRANCOIS (cont'd.)

Anges Du Paradis (from Mireille)
[Fr] T solo,pno CHOUDENS C233 s.p.
(G1178)

Au Bruit Des Lourdes
"Vulcan's Song" low solo,pno (B
flat maj) CRAMER   (G1179)
"Vulcan's Song" high solo,pno (C
maj) CRAMER   (G1180)

Au Printemps
[Fr] high solo,pno CHOUDENS C30
s.p.   (G1181)
[Fr] low solo,pno CHOUDENS C32 s.p.
(G1182)
[Fr] med solo,pno CHOUDENS C31 s.p.
(G1183)
"To Spring" low solo,pno (C maj)
CRAMER   (G1184)
"To Spring" high solo,pno (D flat
maj) CRAMER   (G1185)

Au Rossignol
[Fr] high solo,pno CHOUDENS C232
s.p.   (G1186)
"To The Nightingale" solo,pno
CRAMER   (G1187)

Avant De Quitter Ces Lieux (from
Faust)
"Even Bravest Heart May Swell" Bar
solo,pno (E flat maj) SCHIRM.G
$.75   (G1188)
"Even Bravest Heart May Swell" T
solo,pno (F maj) SCHIRM.G $.75
(G1189)
"Even Bravest Heart May Swell" B
solo,pno (D flat maj) SCHIRM.G
$.75   (G1190)

Ave Maria *sac
solo,pno/org (available in 3 keys)
HEUGEL s.p.   (G1191)

Before The Paling Of The Stars *sac,
Xmas
med solo,pno BELWIN $1.50   (G1192)

Bells That Are Pealing
2 soli,pno CRAMER   (G1193)

Bethlehem
solo,pno CRAMER   (G1194)

Cavatine (from Romoe Et Juliette)
solo,orch HENN s.p.   (G1195)

Ce Que Je Suis Sans Toi
[Fr] high solo,pno CHOUDENS C235
s.p.   (G1196)
"Without Thee" low solo,pno (E maj)
CRAMER   (G1197)
"Without Thee" high solo,pno (F
maj) CRAMER   (G1198)

Celebre Seranade
solo,pno/inst (available in 3 keys,
one with orchestral acc.) LEDUC
s.p.   (G1199)
solo,pno/inst (for school use)
LEDUC s.p.   (G1200)

C'era Un Re, Un Re Di Thule (from
Faust)
[It] S solo,pno RICORDI-ENG 54339
s.p.   (G1201)

Dio Dell'or (from Faust)
[It] B solo,pno RICORDI-ENG 54464
s.p.   (G1202)

Dio Possente, Dio D'amor (from Faust)
[It] Bar solo,pno RICORDI-ARG
BA 11783 s.p.   (G1203)
[It] Bar solo,pno RICORDI-ENG 54446
s.p.   (G1204)
"Valentinin Rukous (Invocation)"
solo,pno FAZER F 2917 s.p.
(G1205)
"Valentins Gebet" [Ger/Fr] high
solo,pno BOTE $.75   (G1206)
"Valentins Gebet" [Ger/Fr] med
solo,pno BOTE $.75   (G1207)
"Valentins Gebet" [Ger/Fr] low
solo,pno BOTE $.75   (G1208)
"Valentins Gebet" [Ger/Fr] med-high
solo,pno BOTE $.75   (G1209)

Entreat Me Not To Leave Thee *sac
low solo,pno (C maj) SCHIRM.G $.85
(G1210)
med solo,pno (D maj) SCHIRM.G $.85
(G1211)
high solo,pno (E maj) SCHIRM.G $.85
(G1212)
med solo,pno PRESSER $.75   (G1213)
solo,pno (available in 3 keys)
ASHLEY $.95   (G1214)
low solo,pno (C maj) BOSTON $1.50
(G1215)
high solo,pno (E maj) BOSTON $1.50
(G1216)
low solo,pno (C maj) SCHIRM.G $1.25
(G1217)
med solo,org (D maj) SCHIRM.G $1.25

GOUNOD, CHARLES FRANCOIS (cont'd.)

(G1218)
high solo,org (E maj) SCHIRM.G
$1.25   (G1219)

Even Bravest Heart May Swell *see
Avant De Quitter Ces Lieux

Faites-Lui Mes Aveux (from Faust)
"Flower Song" med solo,pno (B flat
maj) ALLANS s.p.   (G1220)
"Flower Song" high solo,pno (C maj)
ALLANS s.p.   (G1221)
"Flower Song" low solo,pno (B flat
maj) ASHDOWN   (G1222)
"Flower Song" high solo,pno (C maj)
ASHDOWN   (G1223)
"Flower Song" med solo,pno (C maj)
CENTURY 1565   (G1224)
"Lilla Blomma Du Ar" solo,pno
LUNDQUIST s.p.   (G1225)
"Lovely Flowers, Will Ye" [Fr/It/
Eng] S solo,pno (C maj) SCHIRM.G
$.75   (G1226)
"Lovely Flowers, Will Ye" [Fr/It/
Eng] Mez solo,pno (B flat maj)
SCHIRM.G $.75   (G1227)

Far Greater In His Lowly State
low solo,pno (C maj) CRAMER (G1228)
high solo,pno (D maj) CRAMER
(G1229)

Fifteen Duos *CC15U
(Martienssen) [Fr] ST soli,pno
CHOUDENS C338 s.p.   (G1230)

First Noel, The *sac
(Stickles) low solo,pno (C maj)
SCHIRM.G $.60   (G1231)
(Stickles) high solo,pno (E flat
maj) SCHIRM.G $.60   (G1232)

Flower Song *see Faites-Lui Mes
Aveux

Gentle Holy Saviour *sac,Easter
MezBar soli,pno BOSTON $1.75
(G1233)
SA soli,pno BOSTON $1.75   (G1234)

Glory To Thee, My God
med solo,pno (C maj) CRAMER (G1235)
low solo,pno (B flat maj) CRAMER
(G1236)
2 soli,pno CRAMER   (G1237)
high solo,pno (E flat maj) CRAMER
(G1238)
med-high solo,pno (D maj) CRAMER
(G1239)

Guardian Angel, The *see L'ange
Gardien

Helas! Moi, Le Hair (from Romeo Et
Juliette)
[Fr] ST soli,pno CHOUDENS C367 s.p.
(G1240)

Il A Perdu Ma Trace! (from Philemon
Et Baucis)
[Fr] S solo,pno CHOUDENS C75 s.p.
(G1241)

Il Etait Un Roi De Thule (from Faust)
"King Of Thule, The" see Gounod,
Charles Francois, Jewel Song
"Jewel Song" solo,pno/orch sc
KALMUS $3.25 contains also: King
Of Thule, The   (G1242)
"Jewel Song" high solo,pno PRESSER
$.85   (G1243)
"Jewel Song" high solo,pno
(abridged version) PRESSER $.75
(G1244)
"King Of Thule, The" S solo,pno (A
min) SCHIRM.G $.60   (G1245)

Inspirez Moi! (from La Reine De Saba)
"Lend Me Your Aid" med-high solo,
pno (B flat maj) CRAMER   (G1246)
"Lend Me Your Aid" high solo,pno (C
maj) CRAMER   (G1247)
"Lend Me Your Aid" low solo,pno (G
maj) CRAMER   (G1248)
"Lend Me Your Aid" med solo,pno (A
maj) CRAMER   (G1249)
"Lend Me Your Aid" TBar soli,pno
CRAMER   (G1250)

Je Te Rends Grace, O Dieu D'amour
*sac
solo,pno/inst (available in 2 keys)
LEDUC s.p.   (G1251)
SMez soli,pno/inst LEDUC s.p.
(G1252)

Je Veux Vivre (from Romeo Et
Juliette)
[Fr] S solo,pno CHOUDENS C76 s.p.
(G1253)

Jesus A La Creche *see Noel

Jesus De Nazareth *see Nazareth

Jesus Of Nazareth *see Nazareth

Jewel Song *see Il Etait Un Roi De
Thule

GOUNOD, CHARLES FRANCOIS (cont'd.)

King Of Love My Shepherd Is, The
*see Le Roi D'amour Est Mon
Pasteur

King Of Thule, The *see Il Etait Un
Roi De Thule

La Brise Est Douce Et Parfumee (from
Mireille)
[Fr] ST soli,pno CHOUDENS C73 s.p.
(G1254)

La Reine De Saba
"She Alone Charmeth My Sadness" low
solo,pno (E maj) CRAMER   (G1255)
"She Alone Charmeth My Sadness"
high solo,pno (G sharp maj)
CRAMER   (G1256)

L'ange Gardien
"Guardian Angel, The" high solo,pno
(E flat maj) CRAMER   (G1257)
"Guardian Angel, The" low solo,pno
(C maj) CRAMER   (G1258)

Le Calvaire *sac
"There Is A Green Hill" med solo,
pno (E flat maj) ALLANS s.p.
(G1259)
"There Is A Green Hill" high solo,
pno (F maj) ALLANS s.p.   (G1260)
"There Is A Green Hill" low solo,
pno (D maj) ALLANS s.p.   (G1261)
"There Is A Green Hill" high solo,
pno NOVELLO 17.0191.06 s.p.
(G1262)
"There Is A Green Hill" low solo,
pno NOVELLO 17.0193.02 s.p.
(G1263)
"There Is A Green Hill" med solo,
pno (E min) CENTURY 1477 $.40
(G1264)
"There Is A Green Hill Far Away"
[Fr/Eng] low solo,pno (D min)
SCHIRM.G $.75   (G1265)
"There Is A Green Hill Far Away"
[Fr/Eng] low solo,pno (D min)
SCHIRM.G $.75   (G1266)
"There Is A Green Hill Far Away"
low solo,pno (D maj) ASHDOWN
(G1267)
"There Is A Green Hill Far Away"
med solo,pno (E maj) ASHDOWN
(G1268)
"There Is A Green Hill Far Away"
high solo,pno (F maj) ASHDOWN
(G1269)

Le Roi D'amour Est Mon Pasteur *sac
solo,pno/inst (available in 3 keys)
LEDUC s.p.   (G1270)
"King Of Love My Shepherd Is, The"
med solo,pno (D maj) SCHIRM.G
$.85   (G1271)
"King Of Love My Shepherd Is, The"
low solo,pno (C maj) SCHIRM.G
$.85   (G1272)

Le Temp S'envole (from Mireille)
[Fr] S solo,pno CHOUDENS C241 s.p.
(G1273)

Lend Me Your Aid *see Inspirez Moi!

Let Us Break Bread Together *sac
solo,pno (available in 3 keys)
ASHLEY $.95   (G1274)

Lilla Blomma Du Ar *see Faites-Lui
Mes Aveux

Lovely Flowers, Will Ye *see Faites-
Lui Mes Aveux

Mais Ce Dieu Que Peut-Il? (from
Faust)
[Fr] TB soli,pno CHOUDENS C207 s.p.
(G1275)

Mandolin, The
[Eng/Fr] high solo,pno PRESSER $.75
(G1276)

Medje
solo,pno CRAMER   (G1277)

Mignon
low solo,pno (D maj) CRAMER (G1278)
med solo,pno (E maj) CRAMER (G1279)
high solo,pno (F maj) CRAMER
(G1280)

Mon Coeur Ne Peut Changer! (from
Mireille)
[Fr] S solo,pno CHOUDENS C242 s.p.
(G1281)

Nazareth *sac,Xmas
low solo,pno NOVELLO 17.0128.02
s.p.   (G1282)
solo,pno HARRIS $.75   (G1283)
"Jesus De Nazareth" solo,pno/inst
(available in 4 keys, 2 have
orchestral acc.) LEDUC s.p.
(G1284)
"Jesus Of Nazareth" low solo,pno (D
maj) WATERLOO $.65   (G1285)
"Jesus Of Nazareth" med solo,pno (E
flat maj) WATERLOO $.65   (G1286)
"Jesus Of Nazareth" high solo,pno
(F maj) WATERLOO $.65   (G1287)

GOUNOD, CHARLES FRANCOIS (cont'd.)

"Jesus Of Nazareth" [Fr/Eng] med
  solo,pno (E flat maj) SCHIRM.G
  $.75
                                   (G1288)

Noel *sac,Xmas
  low solo,pno (B flat maj) CRAMER
                                   (G1289)
  high solo,pno (C maj) CRAMER
                                   (G1290)
"Jesus A La Creche" solo/2 soli,
  pno/inst LEDUC s.p.   (G1291)

Notre-Dame De France *sac
  solo,pno/org HEUGEL s.p. see from
  CHANTS RELIGIEUX   (G1292)
  solo,pno/org (available in 5 keys)
  HEUGEL s.p.   (G1293)

O Divine Redeemer *see Repentir

O Douce Nuit D'amour! (from Romeo Et
  Juliette)
  [Fr] ST soli,pno CHOUDENS C279 s.p.
                                   (G1294)

O Legere Hirondelle (from Mireille)
  [Fr] Mez solo,pno (E maj) CHOUDENS
  C74 s.p.   (G1295)
  [Fr] coloratura sop,pno (G maj)
  CHOUDENS C205 s.p.   (G1296)

O Ma Belle Rebelle
  [Fr] high solo,pno CHOUDENS C274
  s.p.   (G1297)
  [Fr] med solo,pno CHOUDENS C273
  s.p.   (G1298)

O Ma Lyre Immortelle (from Sapho)
  [Fr] Mez solo,pno CHOUDENS C270B
  s.p.   (G1299)
  [Fr] S solo,pno CHOUDENS C270A s.p.
                                   (G1300)
  [Fr] A solo,pno CHOUDENS C270 s.p.
                                   (G1301)

O Riante Nature! (from Philemon Et
  Baucis)
  [Fr] S solo,pno CHOUDENS C210 s.p.
                                   (G1302)

Priere
  [Eng] solo,pno (C maj) CRAMER
                                   (G1303)
  [Fr] solo,pno (C sharp maj) CRAMER
                                   (G1304)

Repentir *sac
  "O Divine Redeemer" solo,pno (E
  flat maj) ASHDOWN   (G1305)
  "O Divine Redeemer" 2 soli,pno (C
  maj) CRAMER   (G1306)
  "O Divine Redeemer" 2 soli,pno (A
  maj) CRAMER   (G1307)
  "O Divine Redeemer" high solo,pno
  (C maj) FISCHER,C S 7660   (G1308)
  "O Divine Redeemer" med solo,pno (B
  flat maj) FISCHER,C S 7659
                                   (G1309)
  "O Divine Redeemer" low solo,pno (A
  maj) FISCHER,C S 7659   (G1310)
  "O Divine Redeemer" solo,pno
  (available in 3 keys) ASHLEY $.95
                                   (G1311)
  "O Divine Redeemer" low solo,pno (G
  maj) CRAMER   (G1312)
  "O Divine Redeemer" med solo,pno (A
  flat maj) CRAMER   (G1313)
  "O Divine Redeemer" med-high solo,
  pno (B flat maj) CRAMER   (G1314)
  "O Divine Redeemer" high solo,pno
  (C maj) CRAMER   (G1315)
  "O Divine Redeemer" [Eng/Fr/Lat]
  med solo,pno (B flat maj)
  SCHIRM.G $.75   (G1316)
  "O Divine Redeemer" [Eng/Fr/Lat]
  high solo,pno (C maj) SCHIRM.G
  $.75   (G1317)
  "O Divine Redeemer" [Eng/Fr/Lat]
  low solo,pno (A maj) SCHIRM.G
  $.75   (G1318)
  "O Divine Redeemer" [Fr/Lat/Eng]
  MezBar soli,pno SCHIRM.G $.85
                                   (G1319)

Ring On Sweet Angelus
  solo,pno CRAMER   (G1320)
  2 soli,pno CRAMER   (G1321)

Ring Out, Wild Bells *sac
  low solo,pno (A min) SCHIRM.G $.60
                                   (G1322)
Rondo Du Veau D'or (from Faust)
  [Fr] B solo,pno CHOUDENS C71 s.p.
                                   (G1323)
  "Rondo Vom Goldenen Kalb" [Ger/Fr]
  B solo,pno BOTE $1.75   (G1324)

Rondo Vom Goldenen Kalb *see Rondo
  Du Veau D'or

Salve, Dimora Casta E Pura (from
  Faust)
  [It] T solo,pno RICORDI-ARG
  BA 11539 s.p.   (G1325)
  [It] T solo,pno RICORDI-ENG 54419
  s.p.   (G1326)
  "All Hail Thou Dwelling Pure And
  Lowly" [Eng/Fr/It] high solo,pno
  PRESSER $.75   (G1327)

GOUNOD, CHARLES FRANCOIS (cont'd.)

Serenade (from Faust)
  [Ger/Fr] B solo,pno BOTE $.75
                                   (G1328)
  low solo,pno (E flat maj) ASHDOWN
                                   (G1329)
  med solo,pno (F maj) ASHDOWN
                                   (G1330)
  high solo,pno (G maj) ASHDOWN
                                   (G1331)
  med solo,pno (F maj) ALLANS s.p.
                                   (G1332)
  high solo,pno (G maj) ALLANS s.p.
                                   (G1333)
  low solo,pno (E flat maj) ALLANS
  s.p.   (G1334)
  (Deis) "Sing, Smile, Slumber" [Fr/
  Eng] med solo,pno (F maj)
  SCHIRM.G $.60   (G1335)
  (Deis) "Sing, Smile, Slumber" [Fr/
  Eng] low solo,pno (E flat maj)
  SCHIRM.G $.60   (G1336)

She Alone Charmeth My Sadness *see
  La Reine De Saba

Sing Again
  solo,pno CRAMER   (G1337)

Sing, Smile, Slumber *see Serenade

Soldier's Chorus (from Faust)
  med solo,pno (G maj) CENTURY 1575
                                   (G1338)
There Is A Green Hill *see Le
  Calvaire

There Is A Green Hill Far Away *see
  Le Calvaire

To Spring *see Au Printemps

To The Nightingale *see Au Rossignol

Toujours A Toi, Seigneur *hymn
  solo,pno/inst (available in 2 keys)
  LEDUC s.p.   (G1339)
  SMez/SA soli,pno/inst LEDUC s.p.
                                   (G1340)
Valentinin Rukous (Invocation) *see
  Dio Possente, Dio D'amor

Valentins Gebet *see Dio Possente,
  Dio D'amor

Veiled Picture
  high solo,pno (A flat maj) CRAMER
                                   (G1341)
  low solo,pno (F maj) CRAMER   (G1342)

Venise
  [Fr] high solo,pno CHOUDENS C249
  s.p.   (G1343)

Vous Qui Faites L'endormie (from
  Faust)
  [Fr] B solo,pno CHOUDENS C72 s.p.
                                   (G1344)
Vulcan's Song *see Au Bruit Des
  Lourdes

Waltz Song *see Ah! Je Veux Vivre!

Watchman, What Of The Night?
  solo,pno CRAMER   (G1345)

When In The Early Morn
  med solo,pno (C maj) CRAMER (G1346)
  high solo,pno (D flat maj) CRAMER
                                   (G1347)
  low solo,pno (B flat maj) CRAMER
                                   (G1348)
Without Thee *see Ce Que Je Suis
  Sans Toi

GOURLEY, RONALD
  Cameos For Kiddies *CCU
  solo,pno LEONARD-ENG   (G1349)

  Gathering Of The Clans
  solo,pno ALLANS s.p.   (G1350)

GOVER, GERALD
  Craigie-Burn Wood
  solo,pno PATERSON s.p.   (G1351)

  I See His Blood Upon The Rose
  solo,pno (A flat maj) BOOSEY $1.50
                                   (G1352)
  Our Lord And Our Lady
  solo,pno (F min) BOOSEY $1.50
                                   (G1353)
GOW, DAVID (1924-   )
  West Sussex Drinking Song
  solo,pno (A flat maj) BOOSEY $1.50
                                   (G1354)
GRAAP, LOTHAR (1933-   )
  Drei Evangelien-Konzerte *sac,CC3U,
  concerto
  med solo,org DEUTSCHER 9061 s.p.
                                   (G1355)
GRABERGETS GRONA GATA see Bjorkander

GRABESNACHT MEIN LIEBCHEN VERHULLT see
  Kilpinen, Yrio, Maassa Marjani
  Makavi

GRABGESANG see Maasalo, Armas,
  Hautalaulu

GRABS, MANFRED (1938-   )
  Holderlin-Gesange
  S solo,2fl,2ob,2clar,2bsn,3horn,
  2trp,2trom,tuba,perc,harp,
  cembalo,strings DEUTSCHER rental
                                   (G1356)

GRABSTEIN see Kilpinen, Yrio

GRACE IS SUFFICIENT *sac,gospel
  solo,pno ABER.GRP. $1.50   (G1357)

GRACE OF HEAVEN see Royle, F.

GRACIAS, FORTUNA MIA see Gaztambide,
  Joaquin

GRADSTEIN, ALFRED (1904-1954)
  Trois Chansons Enfantines *CC3U
  [Fr/Pol] high solo,pno ESCHIG $1.60
                                   (G1358)
GRAEFF, J.G.
  Six Canzonets *Op.13, CC6U
  solo,pno HEUWEKE. 040 s.p. (G1359)

GRAENER, PAUL
  Eine Singstimme Und Ein Cello
  Musizieren *Op.113, CC3U
  [Ger] med solo,vcl sc BOTE $4.75
                                   (G1360)
  Nacht- Und Spukgesange
  (Morgenstern) [Ger] med solo,pno
  (in two books) BOTE $2.50, ea.
                                   (G1361)
  Neue Galgenlieder Von Christian
  Morgenstern *Op.43b,No.1-7, CC7L
  med solo,pno BREITKOPF-W EB 6870
  $2.50   (G1362)
  Palmstrom Singt *Op.43a,No.1-7, CC7L
  med-low solo,pno BREITKOPF-W
  EB 6869 $2.50   (G1363)
  Zehn Lons-Lieder *Op.71, CC10U
  [Ger] BOTE high solo,pno $2.25; low
  solo,pno $2.25   (G1364)

GRAF, M.
  Lied Der Jungen Schweizer
  solo,pno HUG s.p.   (G1365)

GRAFSTROM
  Klockan Tickar
  see Sanger Till Dig

  Latt Som En Fjader
  see Sanger Till Dig

  Min Tankes Duva
  see Sanger Till Dig

  Musik, Musik Ar Du
  see Sanger Till Dig

  Sanger *CC9L
  solo,pno LUNDQUIST s.p.   (G1366)

  Sanger Om Doden *CCU
  solo,pno LUNDQUIST s.p.   (G1367)

  Sanger Till Dig
  solo,pno LUNDQUIST s.p.
  contains: Klockan Tickar; Latt
  Som En Fjader; Min Tankes Duva;
  Musik, Musik Ar Du; Till Dig;
  Vill Du Dela Min Gladje (G1368)

  Till Dig
  see Sanger Till Dig

  Tre Sanger *CC3U
  solo,pno LUNDQUIST s.p.   (G1369)

  Vill Du Dela Min Gladje
  see Sanger Till Dig

GRAHAM
  Wee Fiddle Moon (composed with
  Hoffmeister, Leon Abbott)
  high solo,pno (A flat maj) WILLIS
  $.60   (G1370)

GRAHAM, ROBERT
  At The Cross Her Station Keeping
  *sac
  low solo,pno BELWIN $1.50 (G1371)
  med solo,pno BELWIN $1.50 (G1372)

GRAHAM, ROBERT VIRGIL (1912-   )
  After A Rain At Mokanshan
  med solo,pno AMP $.60   (G1373)

GRAMLE ANDERS ROGSTERS SANG see
  Nielsen, Carl

GRANADA see Albeniz, Isaac

GRANADOS, ENRIQUE (1867-1916)
Amor Y Odio (from Goyescas)
[Span] med solo,pno UNION ESP. $.50
(G1374)

(Azpiazu) [Span] high solo,gtr
UNION ESP. $1.25   (G1375)

Callejeo
(Azpiazu) [Span] med solo,gtr UNION
ESP. $1.10   (G1376)

Canciones Amatorias *CCU
(Ferrer) [Span] high solo,pno UNION
ESP. $5.25   (G1377)

Canto Gitano
[Span] med solo,pno UNION ESP. $.75
(G1378)

Colleccion De Tonadillas *CCU
[Span] med solo,pno UNION ESP.
$4.50   (G1379)

Danza Espanola, No. 5
(Wolff, E.) [Span] solo,pno
RICORDI-ARG BA 9738 s.p. (G1380)

El Majo Discreto
[Span] high solo,pno UNION ESP.
$1.50   (G1381)
[Span] solo,pno RICORDI-ARG BA 8428
s.p.   (G1382)
(Azpiazu) [Span] med solo,gtr UNION
ESP. $1.50   (G1383)

El Majo Olvidado
[Span] solo,pno RICORDI-ARG BA 8421
s.p.   (G1384)
[Span] Bar solo,gtr UNION ESP.
$1.25   (G1385)

El Majo Timido
(Azpiazu) [Span] med solo,gtr UNION
ESP. $.90   (G1386)

El Mirar De La Maja
[Span] high solo,pno UNION ESP.
$1.00   (G1387)
(Azpiazu) [Span] high solo,gtr
UNION ESP. $1.10   (G1388)

El Tralala Y El Punteado
[Span] med solo,pno UNION ESP.
$1.25   (G1389)
[Span] solo,pno RICORDI-ARG BA 8429
s.p.   (G1390)
(Azpiazu) [Span] med solo,gtr UNION
ESP. $1.10   (G1391)

Elegia Eterna
[Span] high solo,pno UNION ESP.
$1.25   (G1392)

Eleven Songs *CC11L
[Span/Eng] solo,pno INTERNAT. $2.50
(G1393)

La Maja De Goya
(Azpiazu) [Span] med solo,gtr UNION
ESP. $1.50   (G1394)

La Maja Dolorosa *CC3U
[Span] med solo,pno,opt English
horn UNION ESP. $1.00   (G1395)

La Maja Dolorosa *CC3U
(Azpiazu) Mez solo,gtr UNION ESP.
$1.75   (G1396)

La Maya Y Ruisenor
"Lover And The Nightingale" low
solo,pno (E min) ALLANS s.p.
(G1397)
"Lover And The Nightingale" high
solo,pno (F sharp min) ALLANS
s.p.   (G1398)

Las Currutacas Modestas
(Azpiazu) [Span] SA soli,gtr UNION
ESP. $1.25   (G1399)

L'Ocell Profeta
[Span] high solo,pno UNION ESP.
$1.00   (G1400)

Lover And The Nightingale *see La
Maya Y Ruisenor

Poet And The Nightingale
low solo,pno (E min) ALLANS s.p.
(G1401)
high solo,pno (F sharp min) ALLANS
s.p.   (G1402)

Si Al Retiro Me Llevas
[Span] med solo,pno UNION ESP.
$1.10   (G1403)

GRAND OPERA *CC75U
solo,pno MUSIC 0200015 $3.95 contains
works by: Verdi; Gounod; Wagner and
others   (G1404)

GRAND-PERE see Schlosser, Paul

GRANDFORT, M. DE
La Marion
solo,pno ENOCH s.p.   (G1405)
solo,acap ENOCH s.p.   (G1406)

GRANDI, ALESSANDRO (? -1630)
Drei Geistliche Konzerte *sac,CC3U,
concerto
(Ewerhart, Rudolf) [Lat] S/T solo,
cont BIELER CS 18 s.p.   (G1407)

O Fair Art Thou *sac
(Clokey) med solo,pno BELWIN $1.50
(G1408)

GRANDJANY, MARCEL (1891-   )
Baiser D'enfant
S solo,pno/inst DURAND s.p. (G1409)

Le Vanneur
Mez solo,pno/inst DURAND s.p.
(G1410)

GRANDMA see Sachs

GRANDMA'S THANKSGIVING see Simeone

GRAND'MERE see Truillet-Soyer, M.

GRANDS OISEAUX BLANCS see Viardot-
Garcia, Pauline

GRANIER, J.
Hosanna *sac
med solo,pno BELWIN $1.50   (G1411)

GRANT
Crimond (Psalm 23)
(Howe) med solo,pno PAXTON P40611
s.p.   (G1412)

Psalm 23 *see Crimond

GRANT, CECIL
Take Up Thy Cross
low solo,pno (B flat maj) ASHDOWN
(G1413)
high solo,pno (D maj) ASHDOWN
(G1414)

GRANT, D.
Greeting Of The Day
solo,pno (F maj) BOOSEY $1.50
(G1415)

GRANT, DAVID (1833-1893)
Lord Is My Shepherd, The
low solo,pno (F maj) ASHDOWN
(G1416)
high solo,pno (A flat maj) ASHDOWN
(G1417)

GRANT, DOUGLAS
Paddy's Wedding
low solo,pno (C maj) CRAMER (G1418)
high solo,pno (D maj) CRAMER
(G1419)

GRANT, W. PARKS
Food Of Love, The
med solo,pno AM.COMP.AL. $1.37
(G1420)
Hangman's Song *Op.12,No.1
med solo,pno AM.COMP.AL. $1.92
(G1421)
Rose Und Tod *Op.4,No.1
A/Bar solo,pno sc AM.COMP.AL. $1.10
(G1422)
When The Wind Sighs Round The House
*Op.1
high solo,pno AM.COMP.AL. $.50
(G1423)

GRANT ME, DEAR LORD, DEEP PEACE OF MIND
see Stickles, William

GRANT-SCHAEFER, G.A.
Cuckoo Clock
solo,pno (E flat maj) ALLANS s.p.
(G1424)

GRANT TO US O GRACIOUS LORD see Handel,
George Frideric

GRANT US PEACE see Boatwright, Howard

GRANT US PEACE see Fromm, Herbert

GRANT US PEACE see Grieb, Herbert [C.]

GRANT US PEACE see Handel, George
Frideric

GRANT US PEACE see Helfman, Max

GRASS see Hart, Fritz (Bennicke)

GRASS, THE see Persichetti, Vincent

GRASSELETTE ET MAIGRELETTE see Saint-
Saens, Camille

GRASSY SLOPES OF SPRING, THE see Birch,
Robert Fairfax

GRATEFUL OH LORD AM I
2 soli,pno WARNER VD2006 $1.50
(G1425)

GRATIANI, BONIFATIO
Gaudia, Pastores, Optate *sac
(Ewerhart, Rudolf) [Lat] S/T solo,
cont BIELER CS 1 s.p.   (G1426)

GRATIANI, BONIFATIO (cont'd.)

Pastores, Dum Custodistis *sac
(Ewerhart, Rudolf) S/T solo,cont
BIELER CS 41 s.p.   (G1427)

Salve, Regina *sac
(Ewerhart, Rudolf) S/T solo,cont
BIELER CS 39 s.p.   (G1428)

Venite, Pastores *sac
(Ewerhart, Rudolf) S/T solo,cont
BIELER CS 61 s.p.   (G1429)

GRATITUDE see Curran, Pearl
Gildersleeve

GRATULATION see Peterson-Berger, (Olof)
Wilhelm

GRAU, EDUARDO
Nana
[Span] solo,pno RICORDI-ARG
BA 10896 s.p.   (G1430)

Nina, En Mi Cielo
[Span] solo,pno RICORDI-ARG BA 9773
s.p.   (G1431)

Romance De La Conquista De Alhama
[Span] solo,pno RICORDI-ARG
BA 10988 s.p.   (G1432)

GRAUES LAND see Rontgen, Johannes

GRAUN, KARL HEINRICH (1704-1759)
Sokrates *cant
(Winschermann) T solo,strings,cont
SIKORSKI 665 s.p.   (G1433)

GRAVE OF LOVE, THE see Tollefsen,
Augusta

GRAVSKRIFT OVER ETT LITET BARN see
Kilpinen, Yrio

GRAY
Praying Hands *sac
solo,pno LILLENAS SM-932: SN $1.00
(G1434)

GRAY, HAMILTON
Dream Of Paradise, A *sac
low solo,pno,opt vln/vcl PRESSER
$.75   (G1435)
high solo,pno (A flat maj) ASHDOWN
(G1436)
med-high solo,pno (G maj) ASHDOWN
(G1437)
med solo,pno (F maj) ASHDOWN
(G1438)
low solo,pno (E flat maj) ASHDOWN
(G1439)
med solo,pno (F maj) CENTURY 597
$.40   (G1440)

Heavenly Song, The *sac
med solo,pno (E flat maj) CENTURY
995 $.40   (G1441)
low solo,pno (G maj) ASHDOWN
(G1442)
high solo,pno (C maj) ASHDOWN
(G1443)
med solo,pno (A flat maj) ASHDOWN
(G1444)
med-high solo,pno (B flat maj)
ASHDOWN   (G1445)

GRAYSON, RICHARD
All Day I Hear The Noise Of Waters
high solo,pno HIGHLAND $1.00
(G1446)

Passionate Shepherd To His Love, The
T solo,pno HIGHLAND $1.50 (G1447)

With Rue My Heart Is Laden
med solo,pno HIGHLAND $1.00 (G1448)

GRBEC, IVAN (1889-1966)
Samospevi Zvezek 1 *CCU
high solo,pno DRUSTVO DSS 312
rental   (G1449)

Samospevi Zvezek 2 *CCU
high solo,pno DRUSTVO DSS 342
rental   (G1450)

GREAT AND MARVELOUS see Humphreys

GREAT ART SONGS OF THREE CENTURIES
*CC59L
(Taylor) SCHIRM.G high solo,pno
$6.00; low solo,pno $6.00 contains
works by: Beethoven; Brahms;
Handel; Schumann and others (G1451)

GREAT ART THOU, O MUSIC see Bassett,
Leslie

GREAT ATLANTIC AND PACIFIC SONG BOOK,
THE *CCU,folk,US
(Silber, Irwin) solo,pno,gtr, banjo
MUSIC 020127 $3.95   (G1452)

GREAT AWAKENING, THE see Kramer, A.
Walter

GREAT COMMISSION, THE see Wiant, Bliss

GREAT DUETS FROM THE MASTERS, VOL. I
  *CC20L
  (Wilkins, Marie; Wilkins, Joseph) S&
  solo,pno SCHIRM.G $4.00 contains
  works by: Handel; Mendelssohn;
  Mozart; Schubert and others (G1453)

GREAT DUETS FROM THE MASTERS, VOL. II
  *CC15L
  (Wilkins, Marie; Wilkins, Joseph)
  Mez&solo,pno SCHIRM.G $4.00
  contains works by: Handel;
  Offenbach; Verdi; Mendelssohn and
  others   (G1454)

GREAT DUETS FROM THE MASTERS, VOL. IV
  *CC12L
  (Wilkins, Marie; Wilkins, Joseph)
  Bar&solo/B&solo,pno SCHIRM.G $3.00
  contains works by: Gounod; Mozart;
  Verdi; Puccini and others   (G1455)

GREAT HILLS REMAIN see Williams,
  Meirion

GREAT IS THE LORD see Bantock,
  Granville

GREAT IS THY FAITHFULNESS *sac,gospel
  solo,pno ABER.GRP. $1.50   (G1456)

GREAT IS THY FAITHFULNESS see Runyan

GREAT JOY see Merriweather, Roy

GREAT JUDGMENT MORNING, THE *sac,
  gospel
  solo,pno ABER.GRP. $1.50   (G1457)

GREAT LAND OF MINE see Howe, Mary

GREAT MUSIC FROM BILLY GRAHAM FILMS
  *sac,CC6UL
  (Carmichael, Ralph) solo,pno WORD
  10008 $1.95   (G1458)

GREAT PEACE HAVE THEY WHICH LOVE THY
  LAW see Rogers, James Hotchkiss

GREAT SPACES see Koch, Frederick

GREAT TO BE ALIVE see Skillings, Otis

GREATER see Wolfe, Lanny

GREATER IS HE THAT IS IN ME see Wolfe,
  Lanny

GREATER LOVE HATH NO MAN see
  Wetherington

GREATEST GIFT, THE see Roff, Joseph

GREATEST OF THESE, THE see Ware

GREATEST OF THESE IS LOVE see Bitgood,
  Roberta

GREATEST OF THESE IS LOVE, THE see Moe,
  Daniel

GREATEST OF THESE IS LOVE, THE see Roe,
  Gloria [Ann]

GREAVES, RALPH
  Tinker, Tailor *CC8U
  Mez/Bar solo,pno (easy) OXFORD
  68.054 $.65   (G1459)

GREEN
  He Died On The Cross *sac
  solo,pno LILLENAS SM-621: RN $1.00
                                (G1460)

GREEN see Mulder, Ernest W.

GREEN see Panizza, Ettore

GREEN AIR see Lora, Antonio

GREEN AND PEACEFUL ARE THE PASTURES see
  Bach, Johann Sebastian, Schafe
  Konnen Sicher Weiden

GREEN-BLOODED FISH, THE see Mechem,
  Kirke

GREEN BROOM see Broadwood, Lucy E.

GREEN BUSHES see Keel, Frederick

GREEN CATHEDRAL see Hahn, [Carl]

GREEN CORNFIELD see Head, Michael
  (Dewar)

GREEN, DOROTHY M.
  Angels With Shining Faces *sac
  solo,pno WORD S-27   (G1461)

GREEN-EYED DRAGON see Charles, W.

GREEN IS THE WILLOW see Kendrick,
  Virginia

GREEN ISLE OF ERIN see Roeckel, J.L.

GREEN MEADOWS see Dougherty, Celius

GREEN PASTURES *CCU
  (Johnson) solo,pno FISCHER,C O 2068
                                (G1462)

GREEN PASTURES see Sanderson, Wilfred

GREEN, PHILIP
  Scots Girl
  solo,pno (G maj) BOOSEY $1.50
                                (G1463)

  Story Of The Sparrows
  low solo,pno (F maj) BOOSEY $1.50
                                (G1464)
  high solo,pno (G maj) BOOSEY $1.50
                                (G1465)

GREEN RAIN see Head, Michael (Dewar)

GREEN RIVER, THE see Birch, Robert
  Fairfax

GREEN RUSHES see Franco, Johan

GREEN SINGER, THE see Sutherland,
  Margaret

GREEN STILLNESS see Saminsky, Lazare

GREEN STONES see Hovhaness, Alan

GREENE
  Sing Me To Sleep
  high solo,pno,opt vln/vcl (E flat
  maj) BOSTON $1.50   (G1466)
  med-high solo,pno,opt vln/vcl (E
  flat maj) BOSTON $1.50   (G1467)

  Until You Find The Lord *sac
  solo,pno LILLENAS SM-943: SN $1.00
                                (G1468)

GREENE, MAURICE (1695-1775)
  Thou Visitest The Earth *sac
  med solo,pno oct CONCORDIA 98-1817
  $.25   (G1469)

GREENE, PLUNKET
  I Will Give You The Keys Of Heaven
  med solo,pno (G maj) WILLIS $.25
                                (G1470)

GREENFIELD, ALFRED M.
  Hem Of His Garment, The *sac
  med-high solo,pno (E flat maj)
  SCHIRM.G $.85   (G1471)
  low solo,pno (C maj) SCHIRM.G $.85
                                (G1472)

GREENHILL, HAROLD
  Silver
  2 soli,pno ROBERTON 71887 s.p.
                                (G1473)

GREENSLEEVES *sac,Xmas,carol/folk,Eng
  med solo,pno (A maj) ALLANS s.p.
                                (G1474)
  "What Child Is This" solo,pno ASHLEY
  $.95   (G1475)
  (Bantock) med solo,pno PAXTON P2222
  s.p.   (G1476)
  (Collins) med solo,pno PAXTON P40602
  s.p.   (G1477)
  (Ridout, Godfrey) "What Star Is
  This?" solo,pno THOMP.G   (G1478)
  (Wolff, Ernst V.) "What Child Is
  This?" med solo,pno (A flat maj)
  SCHIRM.G $.85   (G1479)

GREENSLEEVES see Stickles, William

GREENSLEEVES see Vaughan Williams,
  Ralph

GREENWAY
  Visiting With Jesus
  (Bock, F.) solo,pno GENTRY $1.00
                                (G1480)

GREENWOOD, R.
  At This Same Hour
  solo,pno (F maj) BOOSEY $1.50
                                (G1481)

GREETING see Schumann, Robert
  (Alexander), Widmung

GREETING OF THE DAY see Grant, D.

GREETINGS see Mana-Zucca, Mme., Sholom
  Alechem

GREGOR, CESTMIR (1926-   )
  Liedchen Der Arbeitsreserven *see
  Pisnicki Pracovnich Zaloh

  Pisnicki Pracovnich Zaloh
  "Liedchen Der Arbeitsreserven" 2
  med soli,pno CZECH s.p.   (G1482)

GREGOR, V.
  Zazni Pisni Vznesena II *CCU
  solo,pno SUPRAPHON   (G1483)

GREGORC, JURIJ (1916-   )
  Tri Zenske Pesmi *CC3U
  female solo,strings DRUSTVO DSS 118
  rental   (G1484)

GREISENGESANG see Schubert, Franz
  (Peter)

GREMIN'S ARIA see Tchaikovsky, Piotr
  Ilyitch, Prine's Aria

GRETCHANINOV, ALEXANDER TIKHONOVITCH
  (1864-1956)
  Berceuse *Op.1,No.5
  "Wiegenlied" see Five Songs

  Berceuse [2] *Op.7,No.4
  [Russ/Fr/Ger] med solo,pno BELAIEFF
  269 s.p.   (G1485)

  Birke, Beilgetroffen *see Quand La
  Hache Tombe

  Der Engel *see L'ange

  Der Gefangene *see Le Captif

  Der Jenseitstraum *Op.135,No.1-3,
  CC3UL
  [Russ/Fr/Ger] high solo,pno
  BELAIEFF 273 s.p.   (G1486)

  Die Gefangenen *see Les Forets

  Five Songs
  [Russ/Fr/Ger] med solo,pno BELAIEFF
  258 s.p.
  contains: Berceuse, "Wiegenlied",
  Op.1,No.5; Les Forets, "Die
  Gefangenen", Op.1,No.3; "Mon
  Pays!", "Heimat Mein", Op.1,
  No.4; Quand La Hache Tombe,
  "Birke, Beilgetroffen", Op.1,
  No.2; Voix Nocturnes, "Stimmen
  Der Nacht", Op.1,No.1
  see also: Les Forets, "Die
  Gefangenen", Op.1,No.3; Mon
  Pays!, "Heimat Mein", Op.1,
  No.4; Quand La Hache Tombe,
  "Birke, Beilgetroffen", Op.1,
  No.2; Voix Nocturnes, "Stimmen
  Der Nacht", Op.1,No.1   (G1487)

  Four Songs *Op.5,No.1-4, CC4UL
  [Russ/Fr/Ger] med solo,pno cmplt ed
  BELAIEFF 263 s.p.
  see also: Nacht, Op.5,No.2;
  Pourquoi Se Fanent Tes
  Feuilles?, "Weide, Was
  Neigest", Op.5,No.3; Triste Est
  La Steppe   (G1488)

  Heimat Mein *see Mon Pays!

  Il S'est Tu, Le Charmant Rossignol
  *Op.20,No.2
  "Tief Im Haine" [Russ/Fr/Ger] med
  solo,pno BELAIEFF 270 s.p.
                                (G1489)

  Jadis Tu M'as Aime *Op.7,No.1
  "Sie War Dein Eigen" [Russ/Fr/Ger]
  med solo,pno BELAIEFF 268 s.p.
                                (G1490)

  L'ange *Op.135,No.2
  "Der Engel" [Russ/Fr/Ger] med solo,
  pno BELAIEFF 274 s.p.   (G1491)

  Le Captif *Op.20,No.4
  "Der Gefangene" [Russ/Fr/Ger] med
  solo,pno BELAIEFF 272 s.p.
                                (G1492)

  Les Forets *Op.1,No.3
  "Die Gefangenen" [Russ/Fr/Ger] med
  solo,pno BELAIEFF 261 s.p. see
  also Five Songs   (G1493)

  Les Rameaux *Op.47,No.2, sac,Palm
  "Palm Sunday" solo,pno (C maj)
  BOOSEY $1.50   (G1494)

  Lullaby
  [Russ] high solo,pno MEZ KNIGA 115
  s.p.   (G1495)

  Mon Pays! *Op.1,No.4
  "Heimat Mein" [Russ/Fr/Ger] med
  solo,pno BELAIEFF 262 s.p. see
  also Five Songs   (G1496)

  Nacht *Op.5,No.2
  [Russ/Fr/Ger] med solo,pno BELAIEFF
  266 s.p. see also Four Songs
                                (G1497)

  Nacht [2] *Op.20,No.3
  [Russ/Fr/Ger] med solo,pno BELAIEFF
  271 s.p.   (G1498)

  O God Of Love *sac
  high solo,pno BELWIN $1.50   (G1499)

  Over The Steppe *see Triste Est La
  Steppe

  Palm Sunday *see Les Rameaux

  Polka Vocalise
  S solo,pno/inst DURAND s.p. (G1500)

  Pourquoi Se Fanent Tes Feuilles?
  *Op.5,No.3
  "Weide, Was Neigest" [Russ/Fr/Ger]

GRETCHANINOV, ALEXANDER TIKHONOVITCH
(cont'd.)

med solo,pno BELAIEFF 267 s.p.
see also Four Songs   (G1501)

Quand La Hache Tombe *Op.1,No.2
"Birke, Beilgetroffen" [Russ/Fr/
Ger] med solo,pno BELAIEFF 260
s.p. see also Five Songs   (G1502)

Schneeflockchen *Op.47, CC10U
solo,pno BREITKOPF-L EB 4217 s.p. (G1503)

Sie War Dein Eigen *see Jadis Tu
M'as Aime

Slumber Song
med-high solo,pno (E maj) BOSTON
$1.50   (G1504)

Sonetti Romani *Op.160,No.1-5, CC5U
[Russ/Eng] high solo,pno BELAIEFF
276 s.p.   (G1505)

Stimmen Der Nacht *see Voix
Nocturnes

Three Elegies *Op.152,No.1-3, CC3U
[Russ/Fr/Ger] high solo,pno
BELAIEFF 275 s.p.   (G1506)

Tief Im Haine *see Il S'est Tu, Le
Charmant Rossignol

Triste Est La Steppe *Op.5,No.1
[Russ/Fr/Ger] med solo,pno BELAIEFF
264 s.p. see also Four Songs   (G1507)
[Eng/Fr] med solo,pno BELAIEFF 265
s.p. see also Four Songs   (G1508)
"Over The Steppe" low solo,pno (A
min) SCHIRM.G $.75   (G1509)

Voix Nocturnes *Op.1,No.1
"Stimmen Der Nacht" [Russ/Fr/Ger]
med solo,pno BELAIEFF 259 s.p.
see also Five Songs   (G1510)

Weide, Was Neigest *see Pourquoi Se
Fanent Tes Feuilles?

Wiegenlied *see Berceuse

GRETCHEN see Georges, Alexandre

GRETCHEN AM SPINNRADE see Schubert,
Franz (Peter)

GRETCHEN AT THE SPINNING WHEEL see
Schubert, Franz (Peter), Gretchen
Am Spinnrade

GRETRY, ANDRE ERNEST MODESTE
(1741-1813)
Aimable Aurore - Ne Vois-Tu Pas (from
Cephale Et Procris)
[Fr/Eng/Ger] S solo,fl,pno ZIMMER.
1115 s.p.   (G1511)

Chanson De Blondel (from Richard
Coeur De Lion)
see LA MUSIQUE, ONZIEME CAHIER

Couplets (from Richard Coeur De Lion)
see LA MUSIQUE, DOUZIEME CAHIER

Romance (from Richard Coeur De Lion)
see LA MUSIQUE, QUATRIEME CAHIER
solo,pno DURAND s.p.   (G1512)

Serenade
(Behrend) [Fr] med solo,gtr BOTE
$1.25   (G1513)

Tandis Que Tout Sommeille (from
L'Amant Jaloux)
[Fr] solo,pno DURAND 17 s.p.   (G1514)

Veillons Mes Soeurs (from Zemire Et
Azor)
SSA soli,pno DURAND s.p.   (G1515)

Zemir Et Azor
see LA MUSIQUE, DIXIEME CAHIER

GREY, F.H.
Just Count The Stars
low solo,pno (C maj) BOOSEY $1.50 (G1516)
med solo,pno (E flat maj) BOOSEY
$1.50   (G1517)
high solo,pno (F maj) BOOSEY $1.50 (G1518)

GREY RECUMBENT TOMBS see Voormolen,
Alexander Nicolas

GREY YEARS see Weigl, Karl

GRIDA DI VENDITORI NAPOLETANI see
Napoli, Jacopo

GRIEB, HERBERT [C.] (1898-   )
Grant Us Peace *sac
solo,pno TRANSCON. TV 570 $.75
contains also: May The Words   (G1519)

May The Words
see Grieb, Herbert [C.], Grant Us
Peace

GRIEG, EDVARD HAGERUP (1843-1907)
Abschied *see Afsked

Adieu
[Eng] high solo/med solo,pno PETERS
2764E $1.75   (G1520)

Afsked *Op.4,No.3
"Abschied" see Six Songs

Album Lines
[Eng/Ger] med solo,pno PETERS 467L
$1.75 contains also: Med En
Vandlilje, "First Primrose"   (G1521)

Album Of Twelve Popular Songs *CC12L
[Ger] high solo,pno PETERS 4924A
$4.75; med solo/low solo,pno
PETERS 4924B $4.75   (G1522)

Autumn Gale
solo,pno (D min) ASHDOWN $1.50   (G1523)

Autumn Storms
[Eng/Ger] high solo/med solo,pno
PETERS 466G $1.75   (G1524)

Bergliot *Op.42, declamation
[Norw/Ger] narrator,pno PETERS
2263A $4.50   (G1525)

Borte! *Op.25,No.5
"Departed" [Eng/Ger] med solo,pno
PETERS 467M $1.75 contains also:
To Brune Ojne, "Two Brown Eyes"   (G1526)

Cancion De Solveig *see Solveigs
Sang

Collected Songs, Vol. 2 *CC15L
[Norw] med-high solo,kbd HANSEN-DEN
s.p.   (G1527)

Collected Songs, Vol. 5 *CC12L
[Norw] med-high solo,kbd HANSEN-DEN
s.p.   (G1528)

Collected Songs, Vol. 6 *CC11L
[Norw] med-high solo,kbd HANSEN-DEN
s.p.   (G1529)

Collected Songs, Vol. 7 *CC10L
[Norw] med solo,kbd HANSEN-DEN s.p. (G1530)

Collected Songs, Vol. 9 *CC10L
[Norw] med solo,kbd HANSEN-DEN s.p. (G1531)

Collected Songs, Vol. 10 *CC9L
[Norw] med-high solo,kbd HANSEN-DEN
s.p.   (G1532)

Das Attelied *see Den Gamle Vise

Den Foraeldrelose *Op.4,No.1
"Die Waise" see Six Songs

Den Gamle Vise *Op.4,No.5
"Das Attelied" see Six Songs

Departed *see Borte!

Der Einsame *Op.32
Bar solo,2horn,strings PETERS
rental   (G1533)

Det Forste Mode
solo,pno/org ERIKS K 208 s.p.   (G1534)

Die Waise *see Den Foraeldrelose

Dream *see Ein Traum

Dream, A *see Ein Traum

Drifting *see Im Kahne

Du Mein Gedanke
see Grieg, Edvard Hagerup, Ich
Liebe Dich

Dulgt Kaejrlighed *Op.39,No.2
see Six Romances

Eight Songs *CC8U
[Hung] solo,pno BUDAPEST 3518 s.p.
with Hungarian and original
texts   (G1535)

Ein Schwan *see En Svane

Ein Traum *Op.48,No.6
"Dream" [Eng/Ger/Fr] med solo/low
solo,pno PETERS 2622B $2.00   (G1536)
"Dream" [Eng/Ger/Fr] high solo,pno
PETERS 2622A $2.50   (G1537)
"Dream, A" [Ger/Eng] high solo,pno
(D flat maj) SCHIRM.G $.85

GRIEG, EDVARD HAGERUP (cont'd.)

(G1538)
"Dream, A" solo,pno (F sharp min)
ASHDOWN $1.50   (G1539)

En Svane *Op.25,No.2
solo,pno/org ERIKS K 210   (G1540)
"Ein Schwan" [Ger/Eng] high solo,
pno (F maj) SCHIRM.G $.75   (G1541)
"Swan, A" [Eng/Ger] med solo/low
solo,pno PETERS 2623B $1.75   (G1542)
"Swan, A" [Eng/Ger] high solo,pno
PETERS 2633A $1.75   (G1543)
"Swan, The" low solo,pno (E flat
maj) ASHDOWN $1.50   (G1544)
"Swan, The" high solo,pno (F maj)
ASHDOWN $1.50   (G1545)

Eros *Op.70,No.1
solo,2fl,2ob,2clar,2bsn,4horn,2trp,
timp,strings PETERS rental   (G1546)

Fifty Songs *CC50U
[Eng/Ger] low solo,pno PRESSER
$5.00   (G1547)

First Primrose *see Med En Vandlilje

Fra Monte Pincio *Op.39,No.1
see Six Romances

Grieg-Album *CC12L
[Eng/Ger] high solo/med solo,pno
PETERS 466C $4.25   (G1548)

Grieg-Album Pisni *CCU
SUPRAPHON s.p. high solo,pno; med
solo,pno   (G1549)

Haugtussa *Op.67, song cycle
solo,pno/org ERIKS K 205 s.p.   (G1550)
"Mountain Maid, The" [Eng/Ger] Mez
solo,pno PETERS 2863 $3.25   (G1551)

Henrik Wergeland *Op.58,No.3
solo,3fl,2ob,2clar,2bsn,4horn,2trp,
3trom,tuba,timp,perc,harp,strings
PETERS rental   (G1552)

Hope
[Eng] med solo,pno PETERS 2456B
$1.75   (G1553)

Hore Jeg Sangen Klinge *Op.39,No.6
see Six Romances

Hvor Er' De Nu? *Op.4,No.6
"Wo Sind Sie Hin?" see Six Songs

I Liden Hojt Deroppe *Op.39,No.3
see Six Romances

I Love Thee *see Ich Liebe Dich

Ich Liebe Dich *Op.5,No.3
S/Mez solo,pno SCHOTTS 09598;09599
s.p., ea. contains also: Du Mein
Gedanke   (G1554)
"I Love Thee" high solo,pno (E flat
maj) ASHDOWN $1.50   (G1555)
"I Love Thee" low solo,pno (B flat
maj) ASHDOWN $1.50   (G1556)
"I Love Thee" [Eng/Ger/Fr] low
solo,pno (B flat maj) PETERS
2162D $2.00   (G1557)
"I Love Thee" [Eng/Ger/Fr] med
solo/high solo,pno (D maj) PETERS
2162A $2.00   (G1558)
"I Love Thee" [Eng/Ger/Fr] med
solo,pno (C maj) PETERS 2162B
$2.00   (G1559)
"I Love Thee" [Eng/Ger/Fr] high
solo,pno (E flat maj) PETERS
2162C $2.00   (G1560)
"I Love Thee" [Ger/Eng] med solo,
pno (C maj) SCHIRM.G $.85   (G1561)
"I Love Thee" [Ger/Eng] low solo,
pno (B flat maj) SCHIRM.G $.85   (G1562)
"I Love Thee" [Ger/Eng] high solo,
pno (D maj) SCHIRM.G $.85   (G1563)
"I Love Thee" high solo,pno (D maj)
FISCHER,C S 4644   (G1564)
"I Love Thee" [Span/It] high solo,
pno (D maj) PETERS 2162E $2.00   (G1565)
"I Love Thee" [Span/It] med solo,
pno (C maj) PETERS 2162F $2.00   (G1566)
"I Love Thee" solo,pno (available
in 2 keys) ASHLEY $.95   (G1567)
"I Love Thee" med solo,pno (C maj)
ASHDOWN $1.50   (G1568)
"I Love Thee" med solo,pno (C maj)
FISCHER,C S 7639   (G1569)
"I Love Thee" low solo,pno (B flat
maj) FISCHER,C S 4645   (G1570)
"Te Amo Ya" [Span] solo,pno
RICORDI-ARG BA 12014 s.p.   (G1571)

Im Kahne *Op.60,No.3
"Drifting" [Eng/Ger/Fr] med solo/
low solo,pno PETERS 2625B $2.00

GRIEG, EDVARD HAGERUP (cont'd.)

                    (G1572)
"In The Boat" [Ger/Eng] high solo,
  pno (G maj) SCHIRM.G $.60 (G1573)

Immortal Love *sac
  (Park, Dorothy Allan; Bissell,
  Keith W.) med solo,pno (F maj)
  WATERLOO $.75   (G1574)

In The Boat *see Im Kahne

Jaegersang *Op.4,No.4
  "Jagerlied" see Six Songs

Jagerlied *see Jaegersang

Jeg Elsker Dig
  solo,pno/org ERIKS K 207 s.p.
                   (G1575)

L'Arbre De Noel *sac,Xmas
  solo,pno/org HEUGEL s.p. (G1576)

Last Spring *see Letzter Fruhling

Letzter Fruhling *Op.33,No.2
  "Last Spring" [Eng/Ger/Fr] high
  solo,pno (F sharp maj) PETERS
  2624A $2.00   (G1577)
  "Last Spring" [Eng/Ger/Fr] med
  solo/low solo,pno (E flat maj)
  PETERS 2624B $2.00   (G1578)
  "Last Spring" [Eng/Ger/Fr] high
  solo,pno (G maj) PETERS 2624C
  $2.00   (G1579)

L'Oiseau D'Amour
  solo,pno ENOCH s.p. see also CHANTS
  DU NORD   (G1580)

Lovely Evening In Summer *Op.26,No.2
  [Eng/Ger] med solo,pno PETERS 467I
  $1.75   (G1581)

Margaret's Cradle Song
  [Eng/Ger] high solo,pno PETERS 466F
  $1.75   (G1582)
  [Eng/Ger] med solo/low solo,pno
  PETERS 467F $1.75   (G1583)
  solo,pno ASHDOWN see from Two
  Selected Songs   (G1584)

Med En Primula Veris *Op.26,No.4
  solo,pno/org ERIKS K 211 s.p.
                  (G1585)

Med En Vandlilje *Op.25,No.4
  "First Primrose" see Grieg, Edvard
  Hagerup, Album Lines
  "Water Lily, The" solo,pno (A maj)
  ASHDOWN $1.50   (G1586)
  "With A Water-Lily" high solo,pno
  (A maj, In Norwegian And English
  Texts) SCHIRM.G $.60 (G1587)
  "With A Water-Lily" med-low solo,
  pno (G maj, In Norwegian And
  English Texts) SCHIRM.G $.60
                  (G1588)
  "With A Water Lily" [Eng/Ger] med
  solo/low solo,pno PETERS 467H
  $1.75   (G1589)
  "With A Water-Lily" med solo,pno
  NOVELLO 17.0223.08 s.p. (G1590)
  "With A Water Lily" [Eng/Ger] high
  solo,pno PETERS 466H $1.75
                  (G1591)

Millom Rosor *Op.39,No.4
  see Six Romances

Min Tanke Er Et Maegtigt Fjeld
  *Op.5,No.4
  "My Mind Is Like A Mountain Steep"
  [Eng/Ger] med solo,pno PETERS
  467N $1.75   (G1592)

Minstrel's Song *see Spillemaend

Morgan Thau *see Morgendug

Morgendug *Op.4,No.2
  "Morgan Thau" see Six Songs

Mountain Maid, The *see Haugtussa

My Johann *Norw
  (Aslanoff) high solo,pno (G maj)
  SCHIRM.G $.85   (G1593)

My Mind Is Like A Mountain Steep
  *see Min Tanke Er Et Maegtigt
  Fjeld

Nightingale *Op.48,No.4
  [Eng/Fr] high solo/med solo,pno
  PETERS 2435C $1.75   (G1594)

Og Jeg Vil Ha Meg En Hjertenskjaer
  *Op.60,No.5
  solo,pno/org ERIKS K 274 s.p.
                  (G1595)
Peer Gynt *see Peer Gynt's Serenade;
  Solveigs Sang; Solveigs
  Vuggevise, Op.23,No.23 (G1596)

GRIEG, EDVARD HAGERUP (cont'd.)

Peer Gynt's Serenade
  [Norw] high solo,kbd HANSEN-DEN
  s.p. see from Peer Gynt (G1597)

Poema Erotico *Op.43,No.5
  (Pardo) [Span] solo,pno RICORDI-ARG
  BA 8724 s.p.   (G1598)

Praise Ye The Lord *sac
  (Park, Dorothy Allan; Bissell,
  Keith W.) med solo,pno (A maj)
  WATERLOO $.75   (G1599)

Prayer For Grace *sac
  (Park, Dorothy Allan; Bissell,
  Keith W.) high solo,pno (F maj)
  WATERLOO $.75   (G1600)

Princess *see Prinsessen

Prinsessen
  "Princess" [Eng/Ger/Fr] high solo,
  pno PETERS 2452A $2.00 (G1601)
  "Princess" [Eng/Ger/Fr] med solo/
  low solo,pno PETERS 2452B $2.00
                  (G1602)

Ragna *Op.44,No.5
  low solo,pno (E flat maj) ASHDOWN
                  (G1603)
  high solo,pno (G maj) ASHDOWN
                  (G1604)

Selected Songs *CC60U
  [Ger] high solo,pno PETERS 3208A
  $10.50; med solo/low solo,pno
  PETERS 3208B $12.50   (G1605)

Selected Songs *CC36L
  [Ger/Eng] high solo,pno SCHIRM.G
  1592 $3.00; low solo,pno SCHIRM.G
  1593 $3.00   (G1606)

Selected Songs *CCU
  [Russ] solo,pno MEZ KNIGA 85 s.p.
                  (G1607)

Six Romances
  [Norw] med-high solo,kbd HANSEN-DEN
  s.p.
    contains: Dulgt Kaejrlighed,
    Op.39,No.2; Fra Monte Pincio,
    Op.39,No.1; Hore Jeg Sangen
    Klinge, Op.39,No.6; I Liden
    Hojt Deroppe, Op.39,No.3;
    Millom Rosor, Op.39,No.4; Ved
    En Ung Hustrus Bare, Op.39,No.5
                (G1608)

Six Songs
  [Ger/Dan] med solo,kbd HANSEN-DEN
  s.p.
    contains: Afsked, "Abschied",
    Op.4,No.3; Den Foraeldrelose,
    "Die Waise", Op.4,No.1; Den
    Gamle Vise, "Das Attelied",
    Op.4,No.5; Hvor Er' De Nu?, "Wo
    Sind Sie Hin?", Op.4,No.6;
    Jaegersang, "Jagerlied", Op.4,
    No.4; Morgendug, "Morgan Thau",
    Op.4,No.2   (G1609)

Solveig's Lullaby *see Solveigs
  Vuggevise

Solveigs Sang *Op.23,No.18
  [Norw] high solo,kbd HANSEN-DEN
  s.p. see from Peer Gynt (G1610)
  "Cancion De Solvejg" [Span] S/T
  solo,pno RICORDI-ARG BA 8022 s.p.
                  (G1611)
  "Solveig's Song" [Eng/Ger/Fr] high
  solo,pno PETERS 2453A $2.00
                  (G1612)
  "Solveig's Song" [Eng/Ger/Fr] med
  solo/low solo,pno PETERS 2453B
  $2.00   (G1613)
  "Solveig's Song" low solo,pno (F
  maj) ASHDOWN $1.50   (G1614)
  "Solveig's Song" med solo,pno (G
  maj) ASHDOWN $1.50   (G1615)
  "Solveig's Song" high solo,pno (A
  maj) ASHDOWN $1.50   (G1616)
  "Sunshine Song" [Ger/Eng] high
  solo,pno (A maj) SCHIRM.G $.85
                  (G1617)

Solveig's Song *see Solveigs Sang

Solveigs Vuggevise *Op.23,No.23
  [Norw] high solo,kbd HANSEN-DEN
  s.p. see from Peer Gynt (G1618)
  "Solveig's Lullaby" [Ger] high
  solo/med solo,pno PETERS 3708
  $1.75   (G1619)

Solvejgs Lied
  [Czech/Ger] solo,pno SUPRAPHON s.p.
                  (G1620)

Solvejzina Pisen (from Peer Gynt
  Suite)
  S solo,pno SUPRAPHON   (G1621)

Spillemaend *Op.25,No.1
  "Minstrel's Song" [Eng/Ger] med
  solo/low solo,pno PETERS 466K
  $1.75   (G1622)

GRIEG, EDVARD HAGERUP (cont'd.)

Spring *see Varen

Sunshine Song *see Solveigs Sang

Swan, A *see En Svane

Swan, The *see En Svane

Te Amo Ya *see Ich Liebe Dich

To Brune Ojne *Op.5,No.1
  "Two Brown Eyes" see Grieg, Edvard
  Hagerup, Borte!
  solo,pno/org ERIKS K 206 s.p.
                  (G1623)
  "Two Hazel Eyes" ASHDOWN
  see from Two Selected Songs
                  (G1624)

Twenty Selected Songs, Vol. 1 *CCU
  solo,pno BOOSEY $6.00   (G1625)

Two Brown Eyes *see To Brune Ojne

Two Hazel Eyes *see To Brune Ojne

Two Selected Songs *see Margaret's
  Cradle Song; To Brune Ojne, "Two
  Hazel Eyes", Op.5,No.1 (G1626)

Varen *Op.33,No.2
  solo,pno/org ERIKS K 212 s.p.
                  (G1627)
  [Norw] low solo,kbd HANSEN-DEN s.p.
                  (G1628)
  [Norw] med solo,kbd HANSEN-DEN s.p.
                  (G1629)
  "Spring" high solo,pno (F maj)
  ASHDOWN $1.50   (G1630)
  "Spring" low solo,pno (D maj)
  ASHDOWN $1.50   (G1631)

Ved En Ung Hustrus Bare *Op.39,No.5
  see Six Romances

Ved Rundarne *Op.33,No.9
  solo,pno/org ERIKS K 273 s.p.
                  (G1632)

Vom Monte Pincio *Op.39,No.1
  solo,2fl,2clar,2bsn,2horn,perc,
  harp,strings PETERS rental
                  (G1633)

Water Lily, The *see Med En
  Vandlilje

With A Water-Lily *see Med En
  Vandlilje

Wo Sind Sie Hin? *see Hvor Er' De
  Nu?

GRIEG-ALBUM see Grieg, Edvard Hagerup

GRIEG-ALBUM PISNI see Grieg, Edvard
  Hagerup

GRIESBACH, KARL-RUDI (1916-   )
  Four Shakespeare Songs *CC4U
  [Ger] low solo,pno PETERS 5174
  $7.50   (G1634)

  Hoher Himmel *song cycle
  high solo,pno BREITKOPF-L EB 7701
  s.p.   (G1635)

  Nacht Der Farben
  S solo,5strings,harp BREITKOPF-L
  rental   (G1636)

GRIETJE see Hullebroeck, Em.

GRIEVE NOT THE HOLY SPIRIT see Noble,
  Thomas Tertius

GRIFFES, CHARLES TOMLINSON (1884-1920)
  Auf Geheimem Waldespfade
  "By A Lonely Forest Pathway" [Ger/
  Eng] med solo,pno (D flat maj)
  SCHIRM.G $.85   (G1637)

  By A Lonely Forest Pathway *see Auf
  Geheimem Waldespfade

  Dawn *see Le Reveillon

  Early Morning In London *see
  Impression Du Matin

  Four Impressions
  [Eng] med-high solo,pno PETERS
  66310B $4.00
    contains: Impression Du Matin,
    "Early Morning In London"; La
    Mer, "Sea, The"; Le Jardin,
    "Garden, The"; Le Reveillon,
    "Dawn"   (G1638)

  Garden, The *see Le Jardin

  Impression Du Matin
  "Early Morning In London" see Four
  Impressions

GRIFFES, CHARLES TOMLINSON (cont'd.)

In A Myrtle Shade
high solo,pno SCHIRM.G $.75 (G1639)

La Fuite De La Lune
med solo,pno (D flat maj) SCHIRM.G
$.75   (G1640)

La Mer
"Sea, The" see Four Impressions

Le Jardin
"Garden, The" see Four Impressions

Le Reveillon
"Dawn" see Four Impressions

Old Song Re-Sung, An
low solo,pno (F maj) SCHIRM.G $.75
(G1641)

Sea, The *see La Mer

Symphony In Yellow
med solo,pno (B maj) SCHIRM.G $.75
(G1642)

Thy Dark Eyes To Mine
high solo,pno (A flat maj) SCHIRM.G
$.60   (G1643)

GRIFFIS, E.
Eldorado
med solo,pno SEESAW $1.50   (G1644)

To Helen
med solo,pno SEESAW $1.00   (G1645)

To The River
med solo,pno SEESAW $1.00   (G1646)

GRIFFITHS, H.
Wayside Flowers
solo,pno CRAMER   (G1647)

GRIMALDI, C.
Diciasette Vecchie Canzoni Popolari
Emiliane *CC17U
solo,pno BONGIOVANI 800 s.p.
(G1648)

GRIMM, CARL HUGO (1890-   )
Prayer For Mother's Day, A *sac
med solo,pno BELWIN $1.50   (G1649)

GRIMM, HEINRICH (ca. 1593-1637)
Alleluja Ist Ein Frohlich Gesang
see Zwei Kleine Osterkonzerte

Der Tag, Der Ist So Freundenreich
see Zwei Kleine Geistliche Konzerte

In Dieser Osterlichen Zeit
see Zwei Kleine Osterkonzerte

Machet Die Tore Weit
see Zwei Kleine Geistliche Konzerte

Zwei Kleine Geistliche Konzerte
*sac,concerto
(Lorenzen, Hermann) 2 med soli,cont
(med) BAREN. 460 $7.00
contains: Der Tag, Der Ist So
Freundenreich; Machet Die Tore
Weit   (G1650)

Zwei Kleine Osterkonzerte *sac,
Easter,concerto
(Lorenzen, Hermann) 2 med soli,cont
(med) BAREN. 461 $2.75
contains: Alleluja Ist Ein
Frohlich Gesang; In Dieser
Osterlichen Zeit   (G1651)

Zwei Kleine Weihnachtskonzerte *sac,
CC2U,Xmas,concerto
(Lorenzen, Hermann) SS/ST soli,cont
(med) BAREN. 6460 $4.25   (G1652)

GRIMM, JOHANN D.
For My Transgressions
see Two Holy Week Arias

Lamb Of God! Thou Shalt Remain
Forever *sac
(Nolte, Ewald V.) low solo,pno
ABINGDON APM-547 $.85   (G1653)
(Nolte, Ewald V.) high solo,pno
ABINGDON APM-546 $.85   (G1654)

O What Love Is Here Displayed
see Two Holy Week Arias

Two Holy Week Arias
solo,pno BRODT $1.00
contains: For My Transgressions;
O What Love Is Here Displayed
(G1655)

GRIMSRUD, SOLVEIG
I Look Not Back *sac
high solo,pno (E flat maj) SCHIRM.G
$.75   (G1656)
low solo,pno (C maj) SCHIRM.G $.75
(G1657)

GRINDELWALDER LIED see Krenger, J.R.

GRINPOJKEN see Nyblom, C.G.

GRISAILLE see Aubert, Louis-Francois-
Marie

GRISOLIA, PASCUAL
Balada Del Jinete Muerto
[Span] solo,pno RICORDI-ARG
BA 11712 s.p.   (G1658)

Los Alamos Bajo La Luna
[Span] solo,pno RICORDI-ARG BA 9805
s.p.   (G1659)

Nocturno
[Span] solo,pno RICORDI-ARG BA 9804
s.p.   (G1660)

GRISONNE, LA BONNE JUMENT see
Schlosser, Paul

GROET DER MARTELAREN see Landre,
Guillaume

GRONDAHL, AGATHE (URSULA) BACKER
see BACKER-GRONDAHL, AGATHE URSULA

GRONINGEN see Schouwman, Hans

GRONNEBERG, HANNA
Mens Jeg Lever (composed with
Gronneberg, Moe)
solo,pno MUSIKK s.p.   (G1661)

GRONNEBERG, MOE
Mens Jeg Lever *see Gronneberg,
Hanna

GROOT, COR (CORNELIUS WILHELMUS) DE
(1914-   )
Sieben Goethe-Lieder *CC7L
med solo,pno ALBERSEN s.p.   (G1662)

GROOTMOEDERS RUST see Smit Sibinga, Th.
H.

GROSS IST JEHOVA see Schubert, Franz
(Peter), Die Allmacht

GROVEN, EIVIND (1901-   )
I Denne Sode Juletid *Xmas
(Groven, Aslaug) solo,pno MUSIKK
s.p.   (G1663)

Norske Folketoner Til Norske
Folkeviser Og Arnulf Overlands
"Om Kvelden" *CC9L
solo,pno MUSIKK s.p.   (G1664)

GROVER, MAYNARD J.
I Love All Lovely Things
solo,pno (B flat maj) PATERSON s.p.
(G1665)
solo,pno (D maj) PATERSON s.p.
(G1666)

GROVLEZ, GABRIEL (MARIE) (1879-1944)
A La Porte Occidentale
see Deux Odes Chinoises

Chansons Enfantines, Vol. I *CCU
[Fr] med solo,pno ESCHIG $4.00
(G1667)
Chansons Enfantines, Vol. II *CCU
[Fr] med solo,pno ESCHIG $4.75
(G1668)

Des Oeillets Japonais
see Trois Melodies Sur Des Poemes
De J. Dominique

Deux Odes Chinoises
solo,pno/inst cmplt ed DURAND s.p.
contains: A La Porte Occidentale;
La Fleur De Pecher   (G1669)

Guitares Et Mandolines
S solo,pno/inst DURAND s.p. (G1670)

La Fleur De Pecher
see Deux Odes Chinoises

Le Don Silencieux
see Trois Melodies Sur Des Poemes
De J. Dominique

Paroles A L'Absente *CC2U
[Fr/Eng] high solo,kbd CHESTER s.p.
(G1671)
Serenade
see Trois Melodies Sur Des Poemes
De J. Dominique

Trois Melodies Sur Des Poemes De J.
Dominique
med solo,pno/inst cmplt ed DURAND
s.p.
contains: Des Oeillets Japonais;
Le Don Silencieux; Serenade
(G1672)

GRUBER, FRANZ XAVER (1787-1863)
Sante Notte *see Stille Nacht
Heil'ge Nacht

Silent Night *see Stille Nacht,
Heil'ge Nacht

GRUBER, FRANZ XAVER (cont'd.)

Silent Night, Holy Night *see Stille
Nacht, Heil'ge Nacht

Stille Nacht Heil'ge Nacht *sac
"Sante Notte" [It/Ger] Mez/Bar
solo,pno RICORDI-ENG s.p. (G1673)
"Silent Night" solo,pno ASHLEY $.95
(G1674)
"Silent Night" [Eng/Ger] med solo,
pno AMP $.40   (G1675)
"Silent Night, Holy Night" med
solo,pno (C maj) CENTURY 2159
$.40   (G1676)

GRUNAUER, INGOMAR (1938-   )
Fama E Fome
T solo,fl,clar,perc,pno,vla MODERN
rental   (G1677)

GRUND
Way, The Truth, The Life, The *sac
solo,pno BENSON S8084-R $1.00
(G1678)

GRUNT EIN TANNENBAUM see Wolters

GRUSS see Lothar, Mark

GRUSS see Nielsen, Carl, Hilsen

GRUSS DIR, MARIA see Cherubini, Luigi,
Ave Maria

GRUSSE AM DIE HEIMAT see Kromer, Karl

GRY see Nielsen, Carl

GRYNINGEN see Bergman, Erik, Himalajan
Rinteella

G'SCHICHTEN AUS DEM WIENERWALD see
Strauss, Johann

G'SCHICTEN AUS DEM WIENERWALD see
Strauss, Johann

GUADIANA see Quaratino, Pascual

GUARD THY SOUL see Bach, Johann
Sebastian

GUARDA QUI CHE LO VEDRAI see Haydn,
(Franz) Joseph

GUARDATE, PAZZO IO SON see Puccini,
Giacomo

GUARDIAN ANGEL, THE see Gounod, Charles
Francois, L'ange Gardien

GUARDIAN ANGELS see Handel, George
Frideric

GUARINO, C.
Canti Della Nebbia E Del Sole *CCU
solo,pno BONGIOVANI 2356 s.p.
(G1679)
Che Speri, Bambola?
solo,pno BONGIOVANI 1780 s.p.
(G1680)
Fontana
solo,pno BONGIOVANI 1814 s.p.
(G1681)
Giullaresca
solo,pno BONGIOVANI 1713 s.p.
(G1682)
La Leggenda Di Mine
solo,pno BONGIOVANI 1864 s.p.
(G1683)
Mamma, Il Tuo Cuore
solo,pno BONGIOVANI 1781 s.p.
(G1684)
Mani D'autunno
solo,pno BONGIOVANI 1976 s.p.
(G1685)
Stornelli
solo,pno BONGIOVANI 1714 s.p.
(G1686)

GUARNIERI, CAMARGO MOZART (1907-   )
Break The Coconut
med solo,pno PRESSER $.75   (G1687)

Den-Bau
[Port] med solo,pno PRESSER $.75
(G1688)
Farewell *see Vou-Me Embora

Haunted *see Quando Embalada

Quando Embalada
"Haunted" [Port/Eng] med solo,pno
AMP $.60   (G1689)

There Is So Much To Tell You
[Eng/Port] med solo,pno PRESSER
$.75   (G1690)

Vou-Me Embora
"Farewell" [Port/Eng] med solo,pno
AMP $.60   (G1691)

When I First Saw You
[Eng/Port] med solo,pno PRESSER
$.75   (G1692)

GUARTE, GUARTE EL REY DON SANCHO see
  Pisador, Diego

GUASTAVINO, CARLOS (1912-   )
  Ak Que El Alma
    solo,gtr RICORDI-ENG BA 12442 s.p.
                                    (G1693)
  Alegria De La Soledad
    see Las Nubes
  Apegado A Mi
    "Close To My Heart" see Seis
      Canciones De Cuna De Gabriela
      Mistral
  Campanas
    [Span] solo,pno RICORDI-ARG BA 9866
    s.p.   (G1694)
  Cancion De Navidad *Xmas
    [Span] solo,pno RICORDI-ARG BA 9924
    s.p.   (G1695)
  Cancion De Navidad, No. 2
    [Span] solo,pno RICORDI-ARG
    BA 11261 s.p.   (G1696)
  Cantiliena
    see Tres Canciones Sobre Poesias De
      Iglesias De La Casa
  Cita
    [Span] solo,pno RICORDI-ARG BA 9869
    s.p.   (G1697)
  Close To My Heart *see Apegado A Mi
  Corderito
    "Little Lambkin" see Seis Canciones
      De Cuna De Gabriela Mistral
  De Antiquera Sale El Moro *CCU
    [Span] solo,gtr RICORDI-ENG
    BA 11665 s.p. contains works by:
      Morales & Fuenllana   (G1698)
  Dejame Esta Voz
    [Span] solo,pno RICORDI-ARG
    BA 11437 s.p.   (G1699)
  Desde Que Te Conoci
    see Guastavino, Carlos, K Cuarto
      Canciones Argentinas
  Deseo
    see Las Nubes
  Dewdrops *see Rocio
  Discovery *see Hallazgo
  Donde Habite El Olvido
    see Tres Canciones Sobre Poesias De
      Cernuda
  Dones Sencillos
    see Tres Canciones Sobre Poesias De
      Iglesias De La Casa
  El Labrador Y El Pobre
    [Span] solo,pno RICORDI-ARG
    BA 11091 s.p.   (G1700)
  El Vaso
    [Span] solo,pno RICORDI-ARG
    BA 11994 s.p.   (G1701)
  En Los Surcos Del Amor
    see Guastavino, Carlos, K Cuarto
      Canciones Argentinas
  Encantamiento
    "Enchantment" see Seis Canciones De
      Cuna De Gabriela Mistral
  Enchantment *see Encantamiento
  Esta Iglesia No Tiene
    [Span] solo,pno RICORDI-ARG
    BA 10172 s.p.   (G1702)
  Hallazgo
    "Discovery" see Seis Canciones De
      Cuna De Gabriela Mistral
  Jardin Antiguo
    see Las Nubes
  K Cuarto Canciones Argentinas
    [Span] solo,pno cmplt ed RICORDI-
    ARG BA 10217 s.p. contains also:
      Desde Que Te Conoci; En Los
      Surcos Del Amor; Mi Garganta;
      Viniendo De Chilecito   (G1703)
  La Palomita
    see Tres Canciones Sobre Poesias De
      Iglesias De La Casa
  La Primera Pregunta
    [Span] solo,pno RICORDI-ARG
    BA 11446 s.p.   (G1704)
  La Rosa Y El Sauce
    "Rose And The Willow, The" [Span/
    Eng] solo,pno RICORDI-ARG BA 9770

GUASTAVINO, CARLOS (cont'd.)
    s.p.   (G1705)
  Las Nubes
    [Span] solo,pno cmplt ed RICORDI-
    ARG BA 10971 s.p.
      contains: Alegria De La Soledad;
        Deseo; Jardin Antiguo (G1706)
  Little Lambkin *see Corderito
  Los Dias Perdidos
    [Span] solo,pno RICORDI-ARG
    BA 12204 s.p.   (G1707)
  Meciendo
    "Rock-A-By" see Seis Canciones De
      Cuna De Gabriela Mistral
  Mi Garganta
    see Guastavino, Carlos, K Cuarto
      Canciones Argentinas
  Paisaje
    [Span] solo,pno RICORDI-ARG BA 9771
    s.p.   (G1708)
  Pajaro Muerto
    see Tres Canciones Sobre Poesias De
      Cernuda
  Piececitos
    [Span] solo,pno RICORDI-ARG
    BA 11953 s.p.   (G1709)
  Por Los Campos Verdes
    "Thru The Emerald Meadows" [Span/
    Eng/Fr] solo,pno RICORDI-ARG
    BA 9870 s.p.   (G1710)
  Pueblto, Mi Pueblo
    [Span] solo,pno RICORDI-ARG BA 8565
    s.p.   (G1711)
    solo,gtr RICORDI-ENG BA 12443 s.p.
                                    (G1712)
  Riqueza
    [Span] solo,pno RICORDI-ARG
    BA 11438 s.p.   (G1713)
  Rocio
    "Dewdrops" see Seis Canciones De
      Cuna De Gabriela Mistral
  Rock-A-By *see Meciendo
  Rose And The Willow, The *see La
    Rosa Y El Sauce
  Se Equivoco La Paloma
    [Span] solo,pno RICORDI-ARG BA 8278
    s.p.   (G1714)
  Seis Canciones De Cuna De Gabriela
    Mistral
    [Span/Eng] solo,pno RICORDI-ARG
    BA 11970 s.p.
      contains: Apegado A Mi, "Close To
      My Heart"; Corderito, "Little
      Lambkin"; Encantamiento,
      "Enchantment"; Hallazgo,
      "Discovery"; Meciendo, "Rock-A-
      By"; Rocio, "Dewdrops" (G1715)
  Severa Villafane
    solo,gtr RICORDI-ENG BA 12444 s.p.
                                    (G1716)
  Siesta
    [Span] solo,pno RICORDI-ARG
    BA 10913 s.p.   (G1717)
  Soneto A La Armonia
    [Span] solo,pno RICORDI-ARG
    BA 12203 s.p.   (G1718)
  Thru The Emerald Meadows *see Por
    Los Campos Verdes
  Tres Canciones Sobre Poesias De
    Cernuda
    [Span] solo,pno cmplt ed RICORDI-
    ARG BA 10987 s.p.
      contains: Donde Habite El Olvido;
        Pajaro Muerto; Violetas (G1719)
  Tres Canciones Sobre Poesias De
    Iglesias De La Casa
    [Span] solo,pno cmplt ed RICORDI-
    ARG BA 10544 s.p.
      contains: Cantiliena; Dones
        Sencillos; La Palomita (G1720)
  Viniendo De Chilecito
    see Guastavino, Carlos, K Cuarto
      Canciones Argentinas
  Violetas
    see Tres Canciones Sobre Poesias De
      Cernuda

GUBAIDULINA, S.
  Phacelia *song cycle
    [Russ] solo,pno MEZ KNIGA 70 s.p.
                                    (G1721)

GUBITOSI, EMILIA (1887-1972)
  Di Notte
    [It] solo,pno CURCI 1823 s.p.
                                    (G1722)
  Dialogo Di Marionette
    [It] solo,pno CURCI 679 s.p.
                                    (G1723)
  Disperata
    [It] solo,pno CURCI 1821 s.p.
                                    (G1724)
  Il Flauto Nottorno
    [It] S solo,fl,orch CURCI sc
    rental, voc sc rental   (G1725)
  Le Illusioni
    [It] solo,pno CURCI 678 s.p.
                                    (G1726)
  L'ultimo Sogno
    [It] solo,pno CURCI 680 s.p.
                                    (G1727)
  Nera Nerella
    [It] solo,pno CURCI 685 s.p.
                                    (G1728)
  Ninna-Nanna Cosacca
    [It] solo,pno CURCI 600 s.p.
                                    (G1729)

GUD VALSIGNE DESSA HJARTAN see Berg,
  Gottfrid

GUD VET DET, VAR HAN VANKAR see
  Kjerulf, [Halfdan]

GUD VET DET VAR HAN VANKAR see Korling,
  August

GUDMUNDS ERSTE GESANG see Wolf, Hugo

GUDMUNDS ZWEITE GESANG see Wolf, Hugo

GUDMUNDSSON, TURE
  Brudbukett *CC7U,Marriage
    solo,pno GEHRMANS s.p.   (G1730)

GUDS GAVOR see Dahlgren, Erland

GUDS LOV see Norrman, John

GUDS LOV I NATUREN see Beethoven,
  Ludwig van, Die Ehre Gottes Aus Der
  Natur

GUDSTJANSTRINGNING see Runback, Albert

GUEPE see Ponse, Luctor

GUERRA A LA GUERRA POR LA GUERRA see
  Calafato, Salvatore

GUERRE, ELIZABETH JACQUET DE LA
  Cephale Et Procris
    S solo,fl,pno OISEAU s.p.   (G1731)

GUERRERO
  Cancion De La Espada (from El Huesped
    Del Sevillano)
    [Span] solo,pno RICORDI-ARG BA 7390
    s.p.   (G1732)
  Escena De La Flor (from Los
    Gavilanes)
    [Span] solo,pno RICORDI-ARG
    BA 10775 s.p.   (G1733)
  Pasacalle De Las Escaleras (from La
    Rosa Del Azafran)
    [Span] solo,pno RICORDI-ARG BA 6330
    s.p.   (G1734)
  Tango-Milonga (from Los Gavilanes)
    [Span] solo,pno RICORDI-ARG BA 7385
    s.p.   (G1735)
  Tango-Milonga (from La Monteria)
    [Span] solo,pno RICORDI-ARG BA7027
    s.p.   (G1736)

GUERRINI, GUIDO (1890-1965)
  Canti Della Mia Prigionia *CCU
    solo,pno BONGIOVANI 2279 s.p.
                                    (G1737)
  Cantico Di Vittoria
    B solo,2fl,2ob,2clar,2bsn,2horn,pno
    CARISH s.p.   (G1738)
  Canzonetta
    S/T solo,pno BONGIOVANI 520 s.p.
                                    (G1739)
  Chanson Bretonne
    [It] solo,pno CURCI 2383 s.p.
                                    (G1740)
  Due Canzoni Abruzzesi
    [It] solo,pno cmplt ed BONGIOVANI
    1464 s.p.
      contains & see also: Famme Muri;
        St'amore   (G1741)
  Elegia
    [Fr] solo,pno BONGIOVANI 1289 s.p.
                                    (G1742)
  Famme Muri
    [It] solo,pno BONGIOVANI 1466 s.p.
      see also Due Canzoni Abruzzesi
                                    (G1743)
  Le Fiamme Su L'altare
    solo,pno BONGIOVANI 1237 s.p.
                                    (G1744)

GUERRINI, GUIDO (cont'd.)

St'amore
  [It] solo,pno BONGIOVANI 1465 s.p.
    see also Due Canzoni Abruzzesi
                                   (G1745)

Tre Canti Armeni *CC3U
  [It] solo,pno CURCI 2382 s.p.
                                   (G1746)

GUESS YOU KNOW see Brahe, May H.

GUEYA see De Rogatis, Pascual

GUEZEC, JEAN-PIERRE
  Couleurs Juxtaposees
    ST soli,pno SALABERT-US $6.50
                                   (G1747)

GUGLIELMI, PIETRO ALESSANDRO
    (1728-1804)
  Terzetto Adalinda - Lelio - D.
    Mercurio (from La Virtuosa In
    Mergellina)
    2 soli,2clar CARISH s.p.   (G1748)

GUI, VITTORIO (1885-1975)
  Arpege
    solo,pno BONGIOVANI 978 s.p.
                                   (G1749)

  Brise Marine
    [Fr] solo,pno BONGIOVANI 1151 s.p.
      see from Quattro Liriche Di St.
      Mallarme   (G1750)

  Heure D'ete
    solo,pno BONGIOVANI 977 s.p.
                                   (G1751)

  Les Colombes
    solo,pno BONGIOVANI 981 s.p.
                                   (G1752)

  O Si Chere
    [Fr] solo,pno BONGIOVANI 1152 s.p.
      see from Quattro Liriche Di St.
      Mallarme   (G1753)

  Oubli
    solo,pno BONGIOVANI 980 s.p.
                                   (G1754)

  Quattro Canti Della Morte *CC4U
    solo,pno BONGIOVANI 1149 s.p.
                                   (G1755)

  Quattro Liriche Di St. Mallarme *see
      Brise Marine; O Si Chere;
      Renouveau; Rondel   (G1756)

  Renouveau
    [Fr] solo,pno BONGIOVANI 1150 s.p.
      see from Quattro Liriche Di St.
      Mallarme   (G1757)

  Rondel
    [Fr] solo,pno BONGIOVANI 1153 s.p.
      see from Quattro Liriche Di St.
      Mallarme   (G1758)

  Soror Dolorosa
    solo,pno BONGIOVANI 979 s.p.
                                   (G1759)

GUIDON, J.
  Toujours L'aimer
    solo,pno ENOCH s.p.   (G1760)

GUIGNOLET DE SAINT-LAZARE see Emmanuel,
  Maurice

GUILLOU, JEAN (1930-   )
  Judith Symphonie
    Mez solo,orch AMPHION s.p.   (G1761)

GUINEA see Fraggi, H.

GUION, DAVID WENDALL FENTRESS
    (1895-   )
  All Day On The Prairie
    solo,pno ALLANS s.p.   (G1762)

  At The Cry Of The First Bird *sac
    med solo,pno (B min) SCHIRM.G $.85
                                   (G1763)

  Home On The Range
    low solo,pno (E flat maj) ALLANS
      s.p.   (G1764)
    high solo,pno (F maj) ALLANS s.p.
                                   (G1765)

  I Talked To God Last Night *sac
    high solo,pno (E flat min) SCHIRM.G
      $.85   (G1766)
    med solo,pno (C min) SCHIRM.G $.85
                                   (G1767)
    low solo,pno (B flat min) SCHIRM.G
      $.85   (G1768)

  My Lord And My God *sac
    med solo,pno CRESPUB CP-T2001 $1.00
                                   (G1769)

  Prayer *sac
    med-high solo,pno (E flat maj)
      SCHIRM.G $.85   (G1770)
    low solo,pno (C maj) SCHIRM.G $.85
                                   (G1771)

GUIRAUD, ERNEST (1837-1892)
  Adieux A Suzon
    solo,pno (available in 2 keys)
      ENOCH s.p.   (G1772)

GUIRAUD, ERNEST (cont'd.)

  Ah! Leur Carnaval (from Piccolino)
    [Fr] solo,acap oct DURAND s.p.
                                   (G1773)

  Ah! Mon Mari (from Galante Aventure)
    Mez solo,pno/inst DURAND s.p.
                                   (G1774)
    S solo,pno/inst DURAND s.p.   (G1775)

  Berceuse
    Mez/Bar solo,pno/inst DURAND s.p.
                                   (G1776)

  C'est La Brune (from Piccolino)
    [Fr] solo,acap oct DURAND s.p.
                                   (G1777)

  C'est La Que Je Vais Le Revoir (from
      Galante Aventure)
    S solo,pno/inst DURAND s.p.   (G1778)

  D'ou Venez-Vous?
    solo,pno/inst DURAND s.p.   (G1779)

  Fortune, Voila Donc (from Galante
      Aventure)
    T solo,pno/inst DURAND s.p.   (G1780)

  Le Compliment Du Petit Jost (from
      Piccolino)
    [Fr] solo,acap oct DURAND s.p.
                                   (G1781)

  Mentir, Mentir (from Galante
      Aventure)
    Bar solo,pno/inst DURAND s.p.
                                   (G1782)

  Mortelle Souffrance (from Galante
      Aventure)
    T solo,pno/inst DURAND s.p.   (G1783)
    Bar solo,pno/inst DURAND s.p.
                                   (G1784)

  Ne Suis-Je Pas (from Piccolino)
    [Fr] solo,acap oct DURAND s.p.
                                   (G1785)

  Noel! Deja (from Piccolino)
    Mez solo,orch DURAND s.p., ipa
                                   (G1786)
    S solo,orch DURAND s.p.   (G1787)

  Parais A Ta Fenetre (from Piccolino)
    [Fr] solo,acap oct DURAND s.p.
                                   (G1788)

  Paris, Voila Paris (from Galante
      Aventure)
    T solo,pno/inst DURAND s.p.   (G1789)

  Que D'aventures (from Galante
      Aventure)
    Mez solo,pno/inst DURAND s.p.
                                   (G1790)
    S solo,pno/inst DURAND s.p.   (G1791)

  Sorrentine, Sorrente, Sorrente (from
      Piccolino)
    Mez/Bar solo,orch DURAND s.p., ipa
                                   (G1792)
    S/T solo,orch DURAND s.p.   (G1793)
    [Fr] solo,acap oct DURAND s.p.
                                   (G1794)

  Suis-Tu Le Mouvement (from Piccolino)
    [Fr] solo,acap oct DURAND s.p.
                                   (G1795)

  Sur Mon Ame (from Galante Aventure)
    S solo,pno/inst DURAND s.p.   (G1796)
    Mez solo,pno/inst DURAND s.p.
                                   (G1797)

  Toi La Plus Chere (from Galante
      Aventure)
    Bar solo,pno/inst DURAND s.p.
                                   (G1798)
    T solo,pno/inst DURAND s.p.   (G1799)

  Tous Les Bois (from Piccolino)
    [Fr] solo,acap oct DURAND s.p.
                                   (G1800)

GUITAR, THE see Cortes, Ramiro, La
  Guitarra

GUITARE see Absil, Jean

GUITARE see Delage, Maurice

GUITARE see Godard, Benjamin Louis Paul

GUITARES ET MANDOLINE see Saint-Saens,
  Camille

GUITARES ET MANDOLINES see Grovlez,
  Gabriel (Marie)

GUITARRE see Ranken, Ruth

GULBINS, MAX
  Das Vaterunser *Op.29, sac,CC7U
    [Ger/Eng] med solo,org LEUCKART
      s.p.   (G1801)

GULBRANSON, EILIF
  Blanatt
    solo,pno MUSIKK s.p.   (G1802)

GULESIAN, M.H.
  House By The Side Of The Road
    high solo,pno PRESSER $.75   (G1803)

GULLBERG, OLOF
  Det Stod En Jungfru *CC7U
    solo,pno GEHRMANS s.p.   (G1804)

GULLS see Hier, Ethel Glenn

GULLVIVAN see Kilpinen, Yrio

GUMBEL, MARTIN
  Gesichte *sac,Bibl
    Bar,3 narrators,fl,trom,vcl,perc sc
      HANSSLER 10.320 s.p.   (G1805)

GUMS see Willis

GUNGA, GUNGA see Madetoja, Leevi,
  Heijaa, Heijaa

GURIDI, JESUS (1886-1961)
  Como Quieres Que Adivine
    med solo,pno UNION ESP. $1.75 see
      also Seis Canciones Castellanas
                                   (G1806)

  No Quiero Tus Avellanas
    [Span] med-high solo,pno UNION ESP.
      $1.00 see also Seis Canciones
      Castellanas   (G1807)
    (Tarrago) [Span] med solo,pno UNION
      ESP. $1.10 see also Seis
      Canciones Castellanas   (G1808)

  Seis Canciones Castellanas *CC6UL
    [Span] med-high solo,pno UNION ESP.
      $4.00
      see also: Como Quieres Que
        Adivine; No Quiero Tus
        Avellanas   (G1809)

  Seis Canciones Infantiles *CC6U
    [Span] med solo,pno UNION ESP.
      $2.50   (G1810)

GURNEY, IVOR (1890-1937)
  Carol Of The Skiddaw Yowes
    solo,pno (A min) BOOSEY $1.50
                                   (G1811)

  Come, O Come, My Life's Delight
    solo,pno (A flat maj) BOOSEY $1.50
                                   (G1812)

  Desire In Spring
    Bar solo,pno (med) OXFORD 61.014
      $1.00   (G1813)
    T solo,pno (med) OXFORD 62.916
      $1.10   (G1814)

  Sleep
    solo,pno (B flat maj) BOOSEY $1.50
                                   (G1815)

  Twenty Songs, Vol. 1 *CC10U
    solo,pno (med easy) OXFORD 60.001
      $2.85   (G1816)

  Twenty Songs, Vol. 2 *CC10U
    solo,pno (med easy) OXFORD 60.002
      $3.00   (G1817)

  Twenty Songs, Vol. 3 *CC10U
    solo,pno (med) OXFORD 68.705 $3.00
                                   (G1818)

  Twenty Songs, Vol. 4 *CC10U
    solo,pno (med) OXFORD 60.012 $3.00
                                   (G1819)

GURRELIEDER see Schoenberg, Arnold

GURSCHING, ALBRECHT (1934-   )
  Anakreontika *cant
    Bar solo,fl,bsn,vln,bvl,cembalo,
      perc MODERN rental   (G1820)

GUSTAFSON, DWIGHT
  Christmas Alleluia, A *sac,Xmas
    low solo,pno BELWIN $1.50   (G1821)
    high solo,pno BELWIN $1.50   (G1822)

GUSTAVE DE SUEDE, (PRINCE) (1827-1852)
  Plus D'amour, Plus De Roses
    Mez/Bar solo,pno/inst DURAND s.p.
                                   (G1823)
    [Fr] solo,acap oct DURAND s.p.
                                   (G1824)

  Sjung Om Studentens Lyckliga Dag
    solo,pno GEHRMANS 729 s.p.   (G1825)

GUT NACHT see Kuiler, Cor.

GUTE NACHT see Nielsen, Carl, Godnat

GUTE NACHT see Reger, Max

GUTE NACHT see Trunk, Richard

GUTEN ABEND, GUT NACHT see Brahms,
  Johannes

GUTEN ABEND, VOGELEIN see Hannikainen,
  Ilmari

GUTER GEBER, LOB UND PREIS SEI DIR see
  Petz (Pez), Johann Christoph

GUTIERREZ-PONCE, M.
  Sol Tropical
    [Span/Fr] med solo,pno ESCHIG $.60
                                   (G1826)

GUTIERREZ-PONCE, M. (cont'd.)

Ventana Florida
[Span/Fr] high solo,pno ESCHIG $.60
(G1827)

GUYENNE *Fr
(Canteloube, J.) solo,acap DURAND
s.p. see also Anthologie Des Chants
Populaires Francais Tome III
(G1828)

GWENDOLINE: FILEUSE see Chabrier,
Emmanuel

GWENLLIAN see Sullivan, Sir Arthur
Seymour

GWILYM AND ELLEN see Sullivan, Sir
Arthur Seymour

G'WINE TO HEBBN' *spir
(Wolfe) solo,pno ALLANS s.p. (G1829)

GWYNNE, UNA
January
solo,pno CRAMER $.95 (G1830)

GYERE VELEM AKACLOMBOS FALUMBA see
Balazs, Arpad

GYONGYVIRAG *CC92U,folk,Hung
(Bardos) solo,pno BUDAPEST 943 s.p.
(G1831)

GYPSIE LADDIE see Boatwright, Howard

GYPSY LOVE SONG see Herbert, Victor

GYPSY NIGHTS *CCU
(de Butzow) [Russ/Fr/Eng] med solo,
pno BOOSEY $5.50 (G1832)

GYPSY RIVER see Russell, Kennedy

GYPSY SONG see Romberg, Sigmund

GYPSY SONGS see Dvorak, Antonin

GYPSY SONGS see Dvorak, Antonin

GYPSY TRAIL see Galloway, T.B.

GYPSY VARIATIONS see Prister, Bruno

GYPSY'S SONG see Verdi, Giuseppe

GYRING, ELIZABETH
Daffodils
S solo,pno AM.COMP.AL. $3.30
(G1833)

Fable
S solo,pno AM.COMP.AL. $2.20
(G1834)

Hymn
S solo,pno AM.COMP.AL. $2.20
(G1835)

H

HA, HA! WO WILL WI HUT NOCH DANZEN see
Telemann, Georg Philipp

HA-KOTZRIM
(Helfman, Max) "Reapers, The" [Heb]
med solo,pno TRANSCON. IS 509 $.45
(H1)

HA-RU-NO YO-NI see Murai, Tsuguji

HAAPALAINEN, VAINO
Ei Kukaan Tai'a Arvata
see Nelja Suomalaista
Kansanlauluduettoa

En Sua Unhoita
see Nelja Suomalaista
Kansanlauluduettoa

Nelja Suomalaista Kansanlauluduettoa
2 soli,pno FAZER F 2720 s.p.
contains: Ei Kukaan Tai'a Arvata;
En Sua Unhoita; Pappa Lupas;
Suo Ei Kasva Kivia (H2)

Pappa Lupas
see Nelja Suomalaista
Kansanlauluduettoa

Suo Ei Kasva Kivia
see Nelja Suomalaista
Kansanlauluduettoa

HAAPASALO, KREETA
Kanteleeni *CCU
solo,pno FAZER W 929 s.p. (H3)

HAAS, JOSEPH (1879-1960)
Christuslieder *Op.74, CCU
high solo,pno SCHOTTS 2021 s.p.
(H4)

Das Osterei *Op.33,No.7
1-2 soli,pno LEUCKART s.p. see also
Rum Bidi Bum (H5)

Dem Einzigen *Op.13,No.3
see Drei Geistliche Lieder

Der Widerhall *Op.33,No.8
1-2 soli,pno LEUCKART s.p. see also
Rum Bidi Bum (H6)

Drei Geistliche Lieder
med solo,org LEUCKART s.p.
contains: Dem Einzigen, Op.13,
No.3; Hor' Mein Flehen, Op.13,
No.1; Pilgerspruch, Op.13,No.2
(H7)

Frau Spinne *Op.33,No.9
1-2 soli,pno LEUCKART s.p. see also
Rum Bidi Bum (H8)

Fruhling *Op.59
solo,pno SCHOTTS 2642 s.p. (H9)

Gesange An Gott *Op.68, CCU
high solo,pno SCHOTTS 2020 s.p.
(H10)

Heimliche Lieder Der Nacht *Op.54,
CCU
solo,pno SCHOTTS 2016 s.p. (H11)

Hor' Mein Flehen *Op.13,No.1
see Drei Geistliche Lieder

Kinderreigen *Op.33,No.1
1-2 soli,pno LEUCKART s.p. see also
Rum Bidi Bum (H12)

Kuckuckslieder *Op.38, CCU
solo,pno SCHOTTS 2640 s.p. (H13)

Lieder Der Reife Und Ernte *CCU
high solo,pno SCHOTTS 3791 s.p.
(H14)

Lieder Des Glucks *Op.52, CCU
s.p. high solo,pno SCHOTTS 2014;
med solo,pno SCHOTTS 2015 (H15)

Lieder Vom Leben *Op.76, CCU
high solo,pno SCHOTTS 2022 s.p.
(H16)

Lieder Von Baum Und Wald *CCU
s.p. high solo,pno SCHOTTS 4020;
low solo,pno SCHOTTS 4021 (H17)

Nachtgang
solo,pno SCHOTTS 2019 s.p. see also
Unterwegs (H18)

Nur Eine Kleine Geige *Op.33,No.3
1-2 soli,pno LEUCKART s.p. see also
Rum Bidi Bum (H19)

Ob Ich Mich Wehre *Op.33,No.6
1-2 soli,pno LEUCKART s.p. see also
Rum Bidi Bum (H20)

HAAS, JOSEPH (cont'd.)

Pilgerspruch *Op.13,No.2
see Drei Geistliche Lieder

Rum Bidi Bum
1-2 soli,pno cmplt ed LEUCKART s.p.
contains & see also: Das Osterei,
Op.33,No.7; Der Widerhall,
Op.33,No.8; Frau Spinne, Op.33,
No.9; Kinderreigen, Op.33,No.1;
Nur Eine Kleine Geige, Op.33,
No.3; Ob Ich Mich Wehre, Op.33,
No.6; Unser Liebes Franzel,
Op.33,No.5; Wenn Ich Mein
Huhnchen Locke, Op.33,No.2;
Wiegenlied, Op.33,No.4; Zum
Erntekranz, Op.33,No.10 (H21)

Sechs Gedichte *Op.48,No.1-6, CC6U
solo,pno SCHOTTS 2641 s.p. (H22)

Unser Liebes Franzel *Op.33,No.5
1-2 soli,pno LEUCKART s.p. see also
Rum Bidi Bum (H23)

Unterwegs *Op.65, CCU
high solo,pno SCHOTTS 2018 s.p.
see also: Nachtgang (H24)

Wenn Ich Mein Huhnchen Locke *Op.33,
No.2
1-2 soli,pno LEUCKART s.p. see also
Rum Bidi Bum (H25)

Wiegenlied *Op.33,No.4
1-2 soli,pno LEUCKART s.p. see also
Rum Bidi Bum (H26)

Zum Erntekranz *Op.33,No.10
1-2 soli,pno LEUCKART s.p. see also
Rum Bidi Bum (H27)

HAASS, HANS (1899-1955)
Drei Lieder *CC3U
low solo,pno GERIG HG 149 s.p. (H28)

HAATANHU see Luolajan-Mikkola, Vilho

HAB' DAHEIM GELERNT DIE LIEDER see
Kilpinen, Yrio, Otettiin Minusta
Outo

HAB' EIN BLAUES HIMMELBETT! see Lehar,
Franz

HAB ICH LIEB see Kubizek, Augustinian

HABA, ALOIS (1893-1973)
Detske Nalady
"Kinderstimmungen" med solo, with
guitar tuned in quarter steps
CZECH s.p. (H29)

Die Geliebten *see Milenci

Kinderstimmungen *see Detske Nalady

Milenci
"Die Geliebten" S solo,pno CZECH
s.p. (H30)

Od Unora 1948
"Vom Februar 1948" med solo,pno
CZECH s.p. (H31)

Pet Milostnych Pisni Lidovych Z
Moravy *CC5U
med solo,pno CZECH s.p. (H32)

Vom Februar 1948 *see Od Unora 1948

HABA, KAREL (1898-1972)
Herbstimmungen *see Podzimni Nalady

Letni Nalady *Op.23, song cycle
solo,pno SUPRAPHON s.p. (H33)

Podzimni Nalady *song cycle
"Herbstimmungen" Mez solo,pno/orch
CZECH s.p. (H34)

Valasske Pisne *CCU
solo,pno SUPRAPHON s.p. (H35)

HABANERA see Bizet, Georges

HABANERA see Bizet, Georges, L'Amour
Est Un Oiseau Rebelle

HABATAKI see Nakada, Yoshinao

HABE DEINE LUST AN DEM HERRN see
Schutz, Heinrich

HABE MITLEID MIT MIR *folk,Russ
[Ger/Russ] solo,pno ZIMMER. 1505 s.p.
(H36)

HABE MOCHTE SINGEN see Kilpinen, Yrio,
Onpa Tietty Tietyssani

HABENERA see Renaud, A.

D'HACK, A.
    Le Rossignol Et Le Petit Soldat
        solo,pno ENOCH s.p.   (H37)
        solo,acap solo pt ENOCH s.p.   (H38)

HACKEN, EMANUEL
    Songs To Jewish Poetry *CCU
        solo,pno OR-TAV $3.00   (H39)

HAD I A GOLDEN POUND see Head, Michael
    (Dewar)

HAD I BUT MET YOU see Johnston, Lyell

HAD ICK VLOGHELEN see Voormolen,
    Alexander Nicolas

HAD IT NOT BEEN see Goodman

HAD SIN IN MY LIFE see Paris

HAD YOU BUT KNOWN see Denza, Luigi

HADAR, JOSEPH
    Chagei Israel *CCU
        solo,pno OR-TAV $1.50   (H40)

HADDOCK, B.
    Oh My Wild Rose
        solo,pno BERANDOL BER 1312 $1.50
                                       (H41)

HADLEY
    To A Chelsea China Lady
        low solo,pno (F maj) ALLANS s.p.
                                       (H42)
        high solo,pno (A maj) ALLANS s.p.
                                       (H43)

HAEC DIES see Mengelberg, Rudolf

HAEC EST REGINA VIRGINUM see Caldara,
    Antonio

HAEGI, A.
    Kling Klang Kling Di Wing *CC20U
        solo,pno HUG s.p.   (H44)

    Schneewittchen Und Andere
            Kinderlieder *CCU
        solo,pno HUG s.p.   (H45)

HAESJEN see Sigtenhorst-Meyer, Bernhard
    van den

HAEUSSLER, P.
    Just As I Am
        solo,pno (E flat maj) BOOSEY $1.50
                                       (H46)
    Let Not Your Heart Be Troubled
        low solo,pno (D flat maj) BOOSEY
            $1.50   (H47)
        high solo,pno (E flat maj) BOOSEY
            $1.50   (H48)

HAFIS SONGS see Zipp, Friedrich

HAG, THE see Mc Cabe

HAG IS ASTRIDE, THE see Bunge, Sas

HAGANAH see Weinberg, Jacob

HAGEMAN
    Christ Went Up Into The Hills *sac
        low solo,pno (C min) FISCHER,C
            V 891   (H49)
        high solo,org (E flat min) FISCHER,
            C V 820   (H50)
        high solo,pno (E flat min) FISCHER,
            C V 819   (H51)

HAGEMAN, RICHARD
    All Paths Lead To You
        high solo,pno GALAXY 1.1954.7 $1.00
                                       (H52)
    Animal Crackers
        med-high solo,pno SCHIRM.G $.85
                                       (H53)
    At The Well
        high solo,pno (G flat maj) ALLANS
            s.p.   (H54)
        low solo,pno (D flat maj) ALLANS
            s.p.   (H55)
    Charity
        low solo,pno (A flat maj) ALLANS
            s.p.   (H56)
        med-high solo,pno (D flat maj)
            SCHIRM.G $.75   (H57)
        high solo,pno (D flat maj) ALLANS
            s.p.   (H58)
        med solo,pno (B flat maj) ALLANS
            s.p.   (H59)
    Christ Went Up Into The Hills *sac
        solo,pno ALLANS s.p.   (H60)
    Christmas Eve
        high solo,pno (G maj) GALAXY
            1.0733.7 $1.25   (H61)
        med solo,pno (E maj) GALAXY
            1.0796.7 $1.25   (H62)
    Die Stadt
        "Town, The" [Eng/Ger] high solo,pno
            (A maj) SCHIRM.G $.75   (H63)

HAGEMAN, RICHARD (cont'd.)
    Do Not Go, My Love
        low solo,pno (D min) SCHIRM.G $1.00
                                       (H64)
        high solo,pno (F sharp min)
            SCHIRM.G $1.00   (H65)
        high solo,pno (F sharp min) ALLANS
            s.p.   (H66)
        low solo,pno (D min) ALLANS s.p.
                                       (H67)
    He Passed By *see Il Passa
    Hush
        high solo,pno (F maj) GALAXY
            1.1821.7 $1.00   (H68)
    Il Passa
        "He Passed By" [Fr/Eng] high solo,
            pno BELWIN $1.50   (H69)
    Lift Thou The Burdens, Father
        high solo/med solo,pno (G maj)
            GALAXY 1.1467.7 $1.50   (H70)
    Miranda
        high solo,pno ELKIN 27.2288.07 s.p.
                                       (H71)
        low solo,pno ELKIN 27.2287.09 s.p.
                                       (H72)
        high solo,pno (A maj) GALAXY
            1.1116.7 $1.25   (H73)
        low solo,pno (F maj) GALAXY
            1.1148.7 $1.25   (H74)
    Music I Heard With You
        Mez solo,pno ELKIN 27.2022.01 s.p.
                                       (H75)
        high solo,pno GALAXY 1.0877.7 $1.00
                                       (H76)
        low solo,pno GALAXY 1.0878.7 $1.00
                                       (H77)
    Night Has A Thousand Eyes
        solo,pno (E flat maj) BOOSEY $1.50
                                       (H78)
    Rich Man
        low solo,pno GALAXY 1.0795.7 $1.00
                                       (H79)
    Town, The *see Die Stadt

HAGER, JOAN
    Shepherd's Song, The *see Richard,
        Leone

HAGG, GUSTAF WILHELM (1867-1925)
    Amorosa
        solo,pno GEHRMANS s.p.   (H80)
    Fifty Svenska Folkvisor *CC50U
        [Swed] solo,pno GEHRMANS s.p. (H81)

HAGG, TORSTEN
    I Herrens Hand
        solo,pno GEHRMANS s.p.   (H82)

HAGGBOM
    Afton I Skogen
        see NY SAMLING SANGDUETTER, HEFT 2

    Det Ar Harligt Att Vandra Ganglat
        solo,pno LUNDQUIST s.p.   (H83)
    I Skog Och Pa Sjo
        2 soli,pno LUNDQUIST s.p.   (H84)

HAHA, DU STOLTA JANTA see Scholtz, S.

HAHN, [CARL] (1874-1929)
    Green Cathedral
        med solo,pno PRESSER $.95   (H85)
        high solo,pno PRESSER $.95   (H86)
        low solo,pno PRESSER $.95   (H87)

HAHN, REYNALDO (1875-1947)
    Adieu
        (Bordese, Stephen) solo,pno
            (available in 2 keys) ENOCH s.p.
            see also CHANSONS DE PAGE (H88)
    Agnus Dei *sac
        SB soli,pno/org HEUGEL s.p.   (H89)
    Cantique De Racine *sac
        S solo,pno/org HEUGEL s.p.   (H90)
    Cinco Melodias
        [Fr] solo,pno cmplt ed RICORDI-ARG
            BA 11148 s.p.
            contains: D'une Prison; L'heure
            Exquise; Paysage; Reverie; Si
            Mes Vers Avaient Des Ailes!
                                       (H91)
    Could My Songs Their Way Be Winging
        *see Si Mes Vers Avaient Des
        Ailes!
    D'une Prison
        see Cinco Melodias
    Enchanted Hour, The *see L'Heure
        Exquise
    If My Songs Were Only Winged *see Si
        Mes Vers Avaient Des Ailes!

HAHN, REYNALDO (cont'd.)
    L'heure Exquise
        see Cinco Melodias
        "Enchanted Hour, The" [Fr/Eng] high
            solo,pno (D flat maj) SCHIRM.G
            $.85   (H92)
        "Enchanted Hour, The" [Fr/Eng] low
            solo,pno (B maj) SCHIRM.G $.85
                                       (H93)
    Nine Songs *CC9L
        high solo,pno SALABERT-US $7.50
                                       (H94)
    Noel *sac,Xmas
        S solo,pno/org HEUGEL s.p.   (H95)
    O Salutaris *sac
        high solo,pno/org HEUGEL s.p. (H96)
    Paysage
        see Cinco Melodias
    Reverie
        see Cinco Melodias
    Si Mes Vers Avaient Des Ailes!
        see Cinco Melodias
        "Could My Songs Their Way Be
            Winging" med solo,pno PRESSER
            $.75   (H97)
        "If My Songs Were Only Winged" low
            solo,pno (C maj) ASHDOWN   (H98)
        "If My Songs Were Only Winged" med
            solo,pno (D maj) ASHDOWN   (H99)
        "If My Songs Were Only Winged" high
            solo,pno (E maj) ASHDOWN   (H100)
        "Were My Song With Wings Provided"
            [Fr/Eng] med solo,pno (D maj)
            SCHIRM.G $.75   (H101)
        "Were My Song With Wings Provided"
            [Fr/Eng] low solo,pno (C maj)
            SCHIRM.G $.75   (H102)
    Twelve Songs *CC12L
        (Kagen, Sergius) [Fr/Eng] INTERNAT.
            high solo,pno $3.00; low solo,pno
            $3.00   (H103)
    Were My Song With Wings Provided
        *see Si Mes Vers Avaient Des
        Ailes

HAIBEL, JAKOB J. (1761-1826)
    Die Tiroler Seind Often So Lustig
        (from Der Tiroler Wastel)
        MezBar soli,2ob,2bsn,2horn,strings
            sc DOBLINGER DM 161 s.p., ipa,
            voc sc DOBLINGER DM 161A s.p.
                                      (H104)
    Du, Liebe Nachtigall (from Der
        Tiroler Wastel)
        S solo,2fl,2bsn,2horn,strings sc
            DOBLINGER DM 159 s.p., ipa, voc
            sc DOBLINGER DM 159A s.p. (H105)
    Einschoner Mann Ist Delikat (from Der
        Tiroler Wastel)
        S solo,2fl,2clar,2bsn,2horn,2trp,
            strings sc DOBLINGER DM 158 s.p.,
            ipa, voc sc DOBLINGER DM 158A
            s.p.   (H106)
    Manner, Wenn Die Madeln Schmeicheln
        (from Der Tiroler Wastel)
        ST soli,2fl,2horn,strings sc
            DOBLINGER DM 162 s.p., ipa, voc
            sc DOBLINGER DM 162A s.p. (H107)
    Schaffen Sie Was Gut's, Ihr Gnaden
        (from Der Tiroler Wastel)
        T solo,2ob,2bsn,2horn,strings sc
            DOBLINGER DM 160 s.p., ipa, voc
            sc DOBLINGER DM 160A s.p., ipa
                                      (H108)
    Wer Nicht Dem Bugerstande (from Der
        Tiroler Wastel)
        B solo,2ob,2bsn,2horn sc DOBLINGER
            DM 163 s.p., ipa, voc sc
            DOBLINGER DM 163A s.p.   (H109)

HAIKANSONA see Ator, James

HAIKU see Birch, Robert Fairfax

HAIKU see Leeuw, Ton de

HAIKU-FOLGE I: EIN MENSCH UND EINE
    FLIEGE see Bialas, Gunther

HAIKU-FOLGE II: JA, JA, SCHRIE ICH....
    see Bialas, Gunther

HAIKU II see Leeuw, Ton de

HAIKU SETTINGS see Powell, M.

HAIKU SETTINGS see Mamlock, Ursula

HAIL! IMMORTAL BACCHUS see Arne, Thomas
    Augustine

HAIL MARY see Donath, J.

HAIL MARY see Peeters, Flor, Ave Maria

HAIL SABBATH DAY see Bach, Johann
Sebastian

HAIL THE "GREAT LAND" see Avshalomov,
Jacob

HAIL TO MAINE see Shirley, P.

HAINE D'AMOUR see Sureau-Bellet, J.

HAINS, S.B.
Prayer For Peace *sac
solo,pno BERANDOL BER 1670 $1.50
(H110)

HAIRSTON
Mary's Little Boy Jesus *sac,Xmas
solo,pno HARRIS $1.15 (H111)

HAITENESQUES see Casseus

HAJDU, MIHALY
Four Songs *CC4U
[Hung] solo,pno BUDAPEST 5097 s.p.
(H112)

Songs On Budapest *song cycle
[Hung/Ger] Bar solo,pno BUDAPEST
6863 s.p. (H113)

Three Ady Songs *CC3U
[Hung] solo,pno BUDAPEST 4183 s.p.
(H114)

HAJEK, MAXMILIAN (1909-1969)
Dve Pisne *CC2U
high solo,pno CZECH s.p. (H115)

HAJOS, KARL
Cara Signorina (from Il Pierrot Nero)
[It] solo,pno BONGIOVANI 948 s.p.
(H116)

Il Gatto Rosso (from Il Pierrot Nero)
[It] solo,pno BONGIOVANI 969 s.p.
(H117)

Il Saluto Del Marinaio (from Il
Pierrot Nero)
[It] solo,pno BONGIOVANI 952 s.p.
(H118)

Il Sogno Dice Ecc. (from Il Pierrot
Nero)
[It] solo,pno BONGIOVANI 950 s.p.
(H119)

Ma Perche Arrossir (from Il Pierrot
Nero)
[It] solo,pno BONGIOVANI 949 s.p.
(H120)

Questo Simbolo Di Fior (from Il
Pierrot Nero)
[It] solo,pno BONGIOVANI 951 s.p.
(H121)

HAKANSSON, KNUT ALGOT (1887-1929)
Hemmet
solo,pno LUNDQUIST s.p. (H122)

HALET, L.
La Chanteuse Des Cours
solo,acap solo pt ENOCH s.p. (H123)

HALEVY, [JACQUES-FRANCOIS-FROMENTAL-
ELIE] (1799-1862)
Rachel, Quand Du Seigneur La Grace
Tutelaire (from La Juive)
[Fr] T solo,pno CHOUDENS C202 s.p.
(H124)

Si La Rigueur Et La Vengeance (from
La Juive)
[Fr] A solo,pno CHOUDENS C282 s.p.
(H125)

HALFFTER, C.
Cuarto Canciones Leonesas *CC4U
[Span] S solo,pno UNION ESP. $1.25
(H126)

Vier Brecht-Lieder *CC4U
med solo,2pno UNIVER. 14934 $4.25
two copies needed for performance
(H127)

HALFFTER, ERNESTO (1905-   )
Automne Malade
[Fr] high solo,orch ESCHIG $1.75
(H128)

Dos Canciones *CC2U
[Fr/Span] high solo,pno ESCHIG
$1.75 (H129)

Le Lit Laque Blanc
[Fr] high solo,pno ESCHIG $1.10
(H130)

HALFFTER, RODOLFO (1900-   )
Casadita
see Marinero En Tierra, Op. 27

Dos Sonetos *Op.15, CC2U
[Span] med solo,pno UNION ESP.
$1.25 (H131)

Gimiendo Por Ver El Mar
see Marinero En Tierra, Op. 27

Marinero En Tierra, Op. 27
[Span] solo,pno cmplt ed RICORDI-
ARG BA 12199 s.p.
contains: Casadita; Gimiendo Por
Ver El Mar; Que Altos Los
Balcones; Siempre Que Sueno Las
Playas; Verano (H132)

HALFFTER, RODOLFO (cont'd.)

Que Altos Los Balcones
see Marinero En Tierra, Op. 27

Siempre Que Sueno Las Playas
see Marinero En Tierra, Op. 27

Verano
see Marinero En Tierra, Op. 27

HALFTE DES LEBENS see Rovsing Olsen,
Paul

HALICHA L'KEYSARYA see Zahavi, David

HALL
Song Of Innocence, A
[Eng] high solo,pno HINRICHSEN H82A
$1.75 (H133)
[Eng] med solo/low solo,pno
HINRICHSEN H82B $1.75 (H134)

HALL, L.W.
Love Sleeps In A Rose
med solo,pno BMI $.50 (H135)

HALL, PAULINE (1890-1969)
Fangens Aftensang
solo,pno MUSIKK s.p. (H136)

HALLAZGO see Guastavino, Carlos

HALLEL see Alter, I.

HALLELUJA! *CCU,Xmas
(Steinbrecher, A.) solo,pno UNIVER.
10550 $3.00 (H137)

HALLELUJA! see Hummel, Ferdinand,
Alleluia

HALLELUJA! LOBET DEN HERRN see Bossler,
Kurt

HALLELUJAH see Bach, Johann Sebastian

HALLELUJAH see Hummel, Ferdinand,
Alleluia

HALLELUJAH! *sac,CCU
solo,pno,gtr LILLENAS MB-060 $1.50
(H138)

HALLELUJAH, BROTHER! see Matthews,
Randy

HALLELUJAH DAY *sac,gospel
solo,pno ABER.GRP. $1.50 (H139)

HALLELUJAH SQUARE see Overhalt

HALLELUYA see Wyner, Yehudi

HALLEN, ANDREAS (1846-1925)
Drommen
solo,pno GEHRMANS s.p. (H140)

En Visa Till Karin Nar Hon Hade
Dansat
solo,pno GEHRMANS s.p. (H141)

Hymn Till Fosterjorden
solo,pno LUNDQUIST s.p. (H142)

Junker Nils Sjunger Till Lutan
low solo,pno LUNDQUIST s.p. (H143)

Norrland *Op.55
2 soli,pno GEHRMANS s.p. (H144)

Stenbocks Kurir
solo,pno GEHRMANS s.p. (H145)

Tre Duetter *Op.27, CC3U
2 soli,pno GEHRMANS s.p. (H146)

Visor
solo,pno GEHRMANS s.p. (H147)

HALLER, HANS CHRISTOPH (1572-1617)
Hochpreiset Meine Seele *sac
SA soli,2S rec,cont HANSSLER 5.063
s.p. see also GESANGE ZUM
KIRCHENJAHR (H148)

Nehmt Wahr Das Licht *sac
SA soli,2S rec,cont HANSSLER 5.064
s.p. see also GESANGE ZUM
KIRCHENJAHR (H149)

Requiem *sac
A solo,vla,org sc HANSSLER 10.181
s.p. (H150)

HALLETT, JOHN C.
Dawning Of That Day, The *sac
solo,pno WORD S-128 (H151)

Fear Not, O Child Of God *sac
solo,pno WORD S-133 (H152)

He Made The Blind To See *sac
solo,pno WORD S-149 (H153)

HALLETT, JOHN C. (cont'd.)

I Heard The Voice Of Jesus Say *sac
solo,pno WORD S-154 (H154)

My Song Of Songs *sac
solo,pno WORD S-171 (H155)

HALLILA, UTI STORM OCH REGN see
Sibelius, Jean

HALLNAS, HILDING (1903-   )
Din Blick Ej Av Karleken Skymmes
solo,pno/org ERIKS K 265 s.p.
(H156)

Din Tradgard Blommar An En Gang
solo,pno/org ERIKS K 271 s.p.
(H157)

Doden Tankte Jag Mig Sa
solo,pno/org ERIKS K 279 (H158)

Du Drommer En Drom
see I Skogen Om Natten

Hemlig Serenad
solo,pno/org ERIKS K 268 s.p.
(H159)

Hur Langesen Var Det?
see I Skogen Om Natten

I Skogen Om Natten
solo,pno GEHRMANS s.p.
contains: Du Drommer En Drom; Hur
Langesen Var Det?; Malarna
Fladdrar; Manskensvit Och
Midnattsbla; Slocknad Stjarnas
Sken Nar Hit (H160)

Malarna Fladdrar
see I Skogen Om Natten

Manskensvit Och Midnattsbla
see I Skogen Om Natten

Regnet Slar Och Slar
solo,pno/org ERIKS K 277 s.p.
(H161)

Saliga Vantan
see Tre Sanger

Sang
solo,pno/org ERIKS K 267 s.p.
(H162)

Ser Du
see Tre Sanger

Slocknad Stjarnas Sken Nar Hit
see I Skogen Om Natten

Sporjer Du Broder
solo,pno/org ERIKS K 269 s.p.
(H163)

Torso
solo,pno/org ERIKS K 266 s.p.
(H164)

Tre Dagar
solo,pno/org ERIKS K270 s.p. (H165)

Tre Sanger
solo,pno GEHRMANS s.p.
contains: Saliga Vantan; Ser Du;
Undinen (H166)

Under Vintergatan
solo,pno/org ERIKS K 276 s.p.
(H167)

Undinen
see Tre Sanger

HALLNASS, GUN
Sju Visor *CC7U
solo,pno GEHRMANS s.p. (H168)

HALLOWED A-BE THY NAME
(Saunders, M.) solo,pno (E flat maj)
BOOSEY $1.50 (H169)

HALLSTROM, IVAR (1826-1901)
En Liten Visa
solo,pno LUNDQUIST s.p. (H170)

Frid
solo,pno LUNDQUIST s.p. (H171)

Ich Bin Jung
high solo,pno LUNDQUIST s.p. (H172)
low solo,pno LUNDQUIST s.p. (H173)

Isola Bella
2 soli,pno LUNDQUIST s.p. (H174)

Kvallstankar
solo,pno LUNDQUIST s.p. (H175)
2 soli,pno LUNDQUIST s.p. (H176)

Min Sang
solo,pno GEHRMANS 659 s.p. (H177)

Motsatser
2 soli,pno LUNDQUIST s.p. (H178)

Sangen
2 soli,pno LUNDQUIST s.p. (H179)

HALLSTROM, IVAR (cont'd.)

Spinnaria
solo,pno LUNDQUIST s.p.   (H180)

Svarta Svanor
solo,pno LUNDQUIST s.p.   (H181)

Visa "Nar Vikingen For Vida"
Mez/Bar solo,pno GEHRMANS s.p. see
from SANGEN I   (H182)

HAL'LU ET ADONAI see Kohn, Karl

HALPHEN, F.
Absence
solo,pno ENOCH s.p.   (H183)

Baisers
solo,pno (available in 2 keys)
ENOCH s.p.   (H184)

Chanson Pour Helene
solo,pno ENOCH s.p.   (H185)

Nuit
solo,pno (available in 2 keys)
ENOCH s.p.   (H186)

HALT see Witte, D.

HALT EICH ALLE TZUSAMMEN, CHAVERIM KOL
YISRUHL *Jew
solo,pno KAMMEN 448 $1.00   (H187)

HALUNKENSONGS see Strohbach, Siegfried

HALVORSEN, LEIF (1887-1959)
Godnatt
solo,pno MUSIKK s.p.   (H188)

HAMALAINEN, LAURI
Kuhun Taidin Verrata
solo,pno FAZER F 2097 s.p.   (H189)

HAMARAN AANIA see Kaski, Heino

HAMBLEN
I Believe *sac,gospel
solo,pno ABER.GRP. $1.50   (H190)

O Troubled Heart Be Still *sac
high solo,pno (G maj) BOSTON $1.50
(H191)

Until Then *sac
solo,pno BENSON S8280-R $1.00
(H192)

HAMBLEN, BERNARD (1877-1962)
Beside Still Waters
low solo,pno (F maj) ASHDOWN $1.50
(H193)
SBar soli,pno ASHDOWN $1.75   (H194)
high solo,pno (A flat maj) ASHDOWN
$1.50   (H195)

Bless Us, O Lord
high solo,pno (E flat maj) BOOSEY
$1.50   (H196)
low solo,pno (B flat maj) BOOSEY
$1.50   (H197)

Crying Water
med solo,pno (E maj) ASHDOWN   (H198)
low solo,pno (D maj) ASHDOWN   (H199)
high solo&low solo,pno ASHDOWN s.p.
(H200)
high solo,pno (G maj) ASHDOWN
(H201)

Dreaming
solo,pno (C maj) BOOSEY $1.50 (H202)

Hear Thou My Prayer *sac,Gen
high solo,pno (F min) WILLIS $.60
(H203)
low solo,pno (D min) WILLIS $.60
(H204)

Nomad, The
low solo,pno (C maj) WILLIS $.60
(H205)
high solo,pno (F maj) WILLIS $.60
(H206)
med solo,pno (D maj) WILLIS $.60
(H207)

Trust In Him *sac
high solo,pno (D min) SCHIRM.G $.75
(H208)
low solo,pno (B flat min) SCHIRM.G
$.75   (H209)

When Singing Birds Were Mute
low solo,pno (A maj) CRAMER   (H210)
high solo,pno (F maj) CRAMER   (H211)

HAMBRAEUS, BENGT (1928-   )
Cantata Pro Defunctis *cant
[Lat] Bar solo,org NORDISKA s.p.
(H212)

Psalm 123 *sac
[Lat/Swed/Eng] S solo,org ERIKS
K 258 s.p.   (H213)

Spectogram *Op.34
S solo,inst (without words)
NORDISKA s.p.   (H214)

HAMBURGER LIEDER, BAND I *CC13U
med solo,pno SIKORSKI 545A s.p.
conatins works by: Klussmann, Ernst
Gernot; Oertzen, Rudolf Von; Poser,
Hans   (H215)

HAMBURGER LIEDER, BAND II *CC9U
Bar solo,pno SIKORSKI s.p. contains
works by: Ihlenfeld, Eckart;
Roetscher, Konrad; Trede, Yngve Jan
(H216)

HAME, HAME, HAME *folk,Scot
solo,pno (A min) PATERSON FS32 s.p.
(H217)

HAMEL, PETER MICHAEL
So Ahnlich Wie
high female solo,fl,harp study sc
ORLANDO s.p.   (H218)

HAMERTON, ANN
Shepherd's Carol
solo,pno (D min) ROBERTON 2601 s.p.
(H219)

HAMILL, JIM
Something To Hold On To *sac
solo,pno WORD S-453   (H220)

HAMILTON, ALISDAIR
Plumes Of Time, The *song cycle
med solo,pno ROBERTON 1504 s.p.
(H221)

HAMM, CHARLES
Anyone Lived In A Pretty How Town
solo,pno NEW VALLEY $1.25   (H222)

Round
soli MEDIA 1703 $4.00   (H223)

HAMMACK, BOBBY
Tower Of Strength, A *see Adair, Tom

HAMMERSCHMIDT, ANDREAS (1612-1675)
Drei Geistliche Konzerte *sac
SS/TT soli,cont HANSSLER s.p.
contains: Furchtet Euch Nicht;
Lobe Den Herren, Meine Seele;
Verleih Uns Frieden Genadiglich
(H224)

Es Danken Dir, Gott, Die Volker
*cant
(Pidoux, Pierre) T solo,2vln,cont
(med) BAREN. 459-6467 $4.00
(H225)

Furchtet Euch Nicht
see Drei Geistliche Konzerte

I Am The Resurrection *sac,cant
[Ger/Eng] T solo,strings,cont
CONCORDIA 97-6317 $2.00, ipa
(H226)

Let The People Praise Thee, O God
*sac,Marriage,cant
T/S solo,2vln/2fl,cont CONCORDIA
98-1858 $1.00   (H227)
T/S solo,2vln/2fl,cont oct
CONCORDIA 98-1826 $.35, ipa
(H228)

Lobe Den Herren, Meine Seele
see Drei Geistliche Konzerte

My Soul, Now Bless Thy Maker *sac
high solo,6brass,cont sc CONCORDIA
97-5044 $3.00, ipa, solo pt
CONCORDIA 97-5173 $3.50   (H229)

Verleih Uns Frieden Genadiglich
see Drei Geistliche Konzerte

HAMMOND, GLADYS
Fifteenth Century Carol
solo,pno CRAMER   (H230)

HAMOIR, A.
Kindje
solo,pno ALSBACH s.p.   (H231)

HAN KLAPPAR PA see Svedlund, Karl-Erik

HAN KOMMER see Dahlgren, Erland

HAN KULKEVI KUIN YLI KUKKIEN see
Merikanto, Oskar

HANA see Kumaki, Mamoru

HA'NACKER MILL see Plumstead, Mary

HANCOCKS, B.J.
Proverbs *CCU
solo,pno CRAMER   (H232)

Twelve Wise Sayings *CC12U
solo,pno CRAMER   (H233)

HANDEL, GEORGE FRIDERIC (1685-1759)
A Suoi Piedi (from Tamerlano)
(Somervell) "Lost Love" solo,pno/
orch (G min) ROBERTON 2768 s.p.
(H234)

Ach! Fuhl Einmal *see Ah! Tu Non Sai

Acht Lieder *CC8U
low solo,pno BREITKOPF-L EB 5747
s.p.   (H235)

HANDEL, GEORGE FRIDERIC (cont'd.)
Adoration
high solo,pno (A maj) ALLANS s.p.
(H236)
med solo,pno (G maj) ALLANS s.p.
(H237)
low solo,pno (F maj) ALLANS s.p.
(H238)

Agrippina Condotta A Morire (Cantata
14)
[It] S solo,cembalo,strings
BREITKOPF-W s.p.   (H239)

Ah, Che Troppo Ineguali *sac,cant
(Ewerhart, Rudolf) [It] S solo,
strings,cont sc BIELER DK 7 s.p.,
ipa   (H240)

Ah! Crudel, Nel Pianto Mio *cant
S solo,2ob,bsn,strings,cembalo
BREITKOPF-L rental   (H241)

Ah, Let Me Weep, Lord! *see Lascia
Ch'io Pianga

Ah! Mio Cor (from Alcina)
(Gunther) [It/Ger] high solo,pno
BOTE $1.50   (H242)
(Gunther) [It/Ger] low solo,pno
BOTE $1.50   (H243)

Ah! Spietato (from Amadigi)
[It/Ger] low solo,pno BOTE $1.50
(H244)
[It/Ger] high solo,pno BOTE $1.50
(H245)

Ah! Stigie Larve (from Orlando)
[Ger/Eng/It] A solo,pno SCHOTTS
10613 s.p.   (H246)

Ah! Tu Non Sai (from Otto Und
Theophano)
"Ach! Fuhl Einmal" Mez/A solo,
strings BREITKOPF-L rental   (H247)

Air De Poppee *see Aria Di Poppea

Air De Serse (from Xerxes)
(F maj) DURAND s.p.   (H248)

Airs Francais *CCU
[Fr/Eng/Ger] S solo,cont BAREN.
012-6454 $6.50   (H249)

Al Furor (from Arminio)
see Six Italian Arias, Vol. I

Alleluia (from Esther II)
see Handel, George Frideric, O King
Of Kings

Alma Mia (from Floridante)
med solo,pno (E flat maj) ALLANS
s.p.   (H250)
high solo,pno (F maj) ALLANS s.p.
(H251)
(Kroll) [Eng/It] high solo,pno BOTE
$1.50   (H252)
(Kroll) [Eng/It] low solo,pno BOTE
$1.50   (H253)

Amor Commanda (from Floridante)
[It/Ger] high solo,pno BOTE $1.50
(H254)

Angels Ever Bright And Fair (from
Theodora) sac
med solo,pno (F maj) ALLANS s.p.
(H255)
S solo,pno (F maj) SCHIRM.G $.85
(H256)
high solo,pno (F maj) CRAMER   (H257)
low solo,pno (E flat maj) CRAMER
(H258)
high solo,pno (G maj) ALLANS s.p.
(H259)

Anges, Archanges (from Samson)
S solo,pno/inst DURAND s.p.   (H260)

Apollo And Daphne *see Apollo E
Dafne

Apollo E Dafne *cant
(Lewis, A.) "Apollo And Daphne"
[It/Eng] SB soli,orch CHESTER
s.p.   (H261)
(Seiffert, M.) "Apollo Und Daphne"
SB soli,fl,2ob,bsn,strings,
cembalo BREITKOPF-L rental   (H262)

Apollo Und Daphne *see Apollo E
Dafne

Approach My Soul *sac
(Park, Dorothy Allan; Bissell,
Keith W.) med solo,pno (G maj)
WATERLOO $.75   (H263)

Aria (from Atlanta)
high solo,pno (A maj) WILLIS $.75
(H264)
low solo,pno (F maj) WILLIS $.75
(H265)

Aria Di Pollissena (from Radamisto)
(Bibb) [It/Eng] Mez solo,pno (C
min) SCHIRM.G $.75   (H266)

HANDEL, GEORGE FRIDERIC (cont'd.)

Aria Di Poppea (from Agrippina)
  "Air De Poppee" [Fr/It] solo,pno/
  inst DURAND s.p.   (H267)
  (Bibb) [It/Eng] S solo,pno (G flat
  maj) SCHIRM.G $.60   (H268)

Arioso Du Premiere Acte (from
  Deidamia)
  [Fr/It] solo,pno/inst DURAND s.p.
                                      (H269)

Arm, Arm Ye Brave (from Judas
  Maccabeus)
  solo,pno CRAMER   (H270)

Armida Abbandonata *cant
  S solo,vln,vcl,bvl,cembalo
  BREITKOPF-L rental   (H271)

Art Thou Troubled (from Rodelinda)
  med solo,pno (F maj) FISCHER,C
  HO 503   (H272)
  low solo,pno BELWIN $1.50   (H273)
  high solo,pno BELWIN $1.50   (H274)
  med solo,pno NOVELLO 17.0007.03
  s.p.   (H275)
  high solo,pno NOVELLO 17.0006.05
  s.p.   (H276)

As When The Dove (from Acis And
  Galatea)
  S solo,pno NOVELLO 17.0008.01 s.p.
                                      (H277)

Au Rossignol (from Roland)
  Mez solo,opt fl DURAND s.p.   (H278)

Augelletti, Che Cantate (from
  Rinaldo)
  S solo,pic,2rec,strings,cont
  SIKORSKI 539-P s.p., ipa sc, solo
  pt contains also: Il Volo Cosi
  Fido (from Ricardo)   (H279)

Aus Dem Kampf Mit Der Liebe *see
  Dalla Guerra Amorosa

Be Not Always Tender, Adoring *see
  Sempre Dolci, Ed Amorose

Benche Mi Sia (from Ottone)
  see Six Italian Arias, Vol. I

Beneath Thy Leafy Shade *see Care
  Selve

Break Fairest Dawn *see Dank Sei
  Dir, Herr

But Lo! The Angel Of The Lord Came
  Upon Them *see Und Siehe, Der
  Engel Des Herrn

Cantata 14 *see Agrippina Condotta A
  Morire

Cara Sposa (from Rinaldo)
  "Dearest Lover" A solo,pno PATERSON
  s.p.   (H280)
  (Gunther) [It/Ger] med solo,ob/vln,
  pno BOTE $1.75   (H281)

Care Selve (from Atalanta)
  solo,pno FORLIVESI 12141 s.p.
                                      (H282)
  high solo,pno (A flat maj) ALLANS
  s.p.   (H283)
  med solo,pno (F maj) ALLANS s.p.
                                      (H284)
  low solo,pno (E flat maj) ALLANS
  s.p.   (H285)
  [It] med solo,pno MARKS $1.50
                                      (H286)
  [It] high solo,pno MARKS $1.50
                                      (H287)
  "Beneath Thy Leafy Shade" solo,pno
  (A flat maj) ASHDOWN   (H288)
  "Come Beloved" high solo,pno (A
  maj) FISCHER,C V 2344   (H289)
  "Come, Beloved" solo,pno (available
  in 2 keys) ASHLEY $.95   (H290)
  "Come Beloved" med solo,pno (F maj)
  FISCHER,C V 2343   (H291)
  (Gunther) [It/Ger] low solo,pno
  BOTE $1.00   (H292)
  (Gunther) [It/Ger] high solo,pno
  BOTE $1.00   (H293)

Cecilia Volgi Un Sguardo *cant
  ST soli,strings,cont DEUTSCHER
  rental   (H294)

Che Piu Si Tarda Omai (from Tolomeo)
  T solo,strings,cembalo BREITKOPF-L
  rental   (H295)

Chi T'intende (from Berenice)
  (Flothius, Marius) [It] S solo,ob,
  pno BROEKMANS 395-18 s.p.   (H296)

Clori, Tirsi E Fileno *cant
  3 soli,2fl,2ob,2bsn,strings,cont
  DEUTSCHER rental   (H297)

Coelestis Dum Spirat Aura *sac,cant
  (Ewerhart, Rudolf) [Lat] S solo,
  2vln,cont sc BIELER DK 2 s.p.,
  ipa   (H298)

Collection Of Songs, Vol. 1: Light
  Soprano *CCU
  (Ford) S solo,pno BOOSEY $12.00
                                      (H299)
Collection Of Songs, Vol. 2: Dramatic
  Soprano *CCU
  (Ford) S solo,pno BOOSEY $12.00
                                      (H300)
Collection Of Songs, Vol. 3: Mezzo-
  Soprano *CCU
  (Ford) Mez solo,pno BOOSEY $12.00
                                      (H301)
Collection Of Songs, Vol. 4:
  Contralto *CCU
  (Ford) A solo,pno BOOSEY $12.00
                                      (H302)
Collection Of Songs, Vol. 5: Tenor
  *CCU
  (Ford) T solo,pno BOOSEY $12.00
                                      (H303)
Collection Of Songs, Vol. 6: Baritone
  *CCU
  (Ford) Bar solo,pno BOOSEY $12.00
                                      (H304)
Collection Of Songs, Vol. 7: Bass
  *CCU
  (Ford) B solo,pno BOOSEY $12.00
                                      (H305)

Come And Trip It (from L'Allegro, Il
  Pensieroso Ed Il Moderato)
  high solo,pno (B min) BOOSEY $1.50
                                      (H306)
  low solo,pno (A min) BOOSEY $1.50
                                      (H307)

Come Beloved *see Care Selve

Come Live With Me (from Semele)
  Bar solo,pno PATERSON s.p.   (H308)

Come To Me Soothing Sleep *see Vieni
  O Figlio

Come Unto Him (from Messiah, The) sac
  med solo,pno (G maj) SCHIRM.G $.85
                                      (H309)
  high solo,pno (B flat maj) SCHIRM.G
  $.85   (H310)

Comfort Ye My People (from Messiah)
  solo,pno CRAMER   (H311)

Conservate, Raddoppiate *cant
  "O Bewahret Und Befeuert" SA soli,
  cont GERIG AV 127 s.p.   (H312)

Consider Ye
  B solo,pno PATERSON s.p.   (H313)

Crudel Tiranno, Amor *sac,cant
  (Zenck, Hermann) "O Amor, Du
  Tyrann" [Ger/It] S solo,2vln,vla,
  cont (diff) BAREN. 1974 $7.00   (H314)

Cuopre Tal Volta Il Cielo *sac,cant
  (Zenck, Hermann) "Oft Decken
  Wolken" [Ger/It] B solo,2vln,cont
  (diff) BAREN. 1976 $5.75   (H315)

Dalla Guerra Amorosa *sac,cant
  "Aus Dem Kampf Mit Der Liebe" [It/
  Ger] B solo,cont BAREN. 6469
  $5.00   (H316)
  (Zenck, Hermann) "Aus Dem Kampf Mit
  Der Liebe" [Ger/It] B solo,cont
  (diff) BAREN. 1972 $5.50   (H317)

Dank Sei Dir, Herr *sac
  [Ger] high solo,pno BOTE $1.25   (H318)
  solo,pno/orch SCHOTTS 09676 1-2
  s.p.   (H319)
  [Ger] low solo,pno BOTE $1.25
                                      (H320)
  "Break Fairest Dawn" high solo,pno
  (C maj) ALLANS s.p.   (H321)
  "Break Fairest Dawn" low solo,pno
  (A maj) ALLANS s.p.   (H322)
  "Thanks Be To Thee" high solo,pno
  BELWIN $1.50   (H323)
  "Thanks Be To Thee" low solo,pno
  BELWIN $1.50   (H324)
  "Thanks Be To Thee" low solo,pno (A
  maj) BOSTON $1.50   (H325)

Das Zitternde Glanzen Der Spielenden
  Wellen *sac
  S solo,vln,cont KISTNER cmplt ed
  s.p., voc sc s.p., ipa   (H326)
  S solo,vln,kbd CONCORDIA 97-4438
  $3.50   (H327)

Dearest Lover *see Cara Sposa

Derniers Adieux De La Fille De Jepthe
  (from Jephte)
  [Fr/Eng] solo,pno/inst DURAND s.p.
                                      (H328)

Devant Moi S'etend La Vue (from
  L'Allegro, Il Penseroso Ed Il
  Moderato)
  S solo,pno/inst DURAND s.p.   (H329)

Die Einsamkeit *see La Solitudine

Dimmi, Cara (from Scipione)
  [It/Ger] high solo,pno BOTE $1.10   (H330)
  [It/Ger] med solo,pno BOTE $1.10   (H331)

Donna, Che In Ciel *cant
  "Herrin, Du Strahlst Im Himmel" S
  solo,mix cor,2vln,vla,cont sc
  GERIG AV 130 s.p., ipa   (H332)

Drei Marien-Legenden Aus Den
  Wunderhorn-Liedern *CC3U
  s.p. high solo,pno BREITKOPF-L
  EB 5576; med solo,pno BREITKOPF-L
  EB 5577   (H333)

Droop Not Young Lover (from Ezio)
  solo,pno CRAMER   (H334)

Du Ahnst Nicht, Was Dies Schwert Bald
  Vermag (from Poros)
  B solo,2ob,strings,cont DEUTSCHER
  rental   (H335)

Du Bist Treu Und Bestandig? *see Tu
  Fedel, Tu Costante?

Elves' Dance, The (from Triumph Of
  Time And Truth, The)
  S solo,pno PATERSON s.p.   (H336)

Engel, Ewig Licht Und Schon (from
  Alexander Balus)
  see Handel, George Frideric,
  Schalkhaft Spielt Mit Schlauen
  Blicken

Er Wiedet Seine Herde *see He Shall
  Feed His Flock

Erd' Und Himmel Mag Sich Wappnen
  (from Tamerlano)
  T solo,4ob,2bsn,3trp,timp,strings,
  cembalo BREITKOPF-L rental   (H337)

Ewig, So Spricht Die Seele (from
  Poros)
  BS soli,strings,cont DEUTSCHER
  rental   (H338)

Feed My Sheep *sac
  (Schnewlin) low solo,pno (E maj)
  FISCHER,C V 2340   (H339)

Fifteen Arias For High Voice *CC15L
  (Wolff) high solo,pno SCHIRM.G 1745
  $2.50   (H340)

Flammende Rose *sac
  S solo,vln,cembalo,bvl sc CONCORDIA
  97-4260 $2.75   (H341)
  S solo,vln,cont KISTNER cmplt ed
  s.p., voc sc s.p., ipa   (H342)

Folle E Colui - Nasce Al Bosco (from
  Ezio)
  Bar/B solo,ob,bsn,strings,cembalo
  BREITKOPF-L rental   (H343)

Forty-Five Arias From Operas And
  Oratorios, Vol. I *CC15L
  (Kagen, Sergius) INTERNAT. high
  solo,pno $3.75; low solo,pno
  $3.75   (H344)

Forty-Five Arias From Operas And
  Oratorios, Vol. II *CC15L
  (Kagen, Sergius) INTERNAT. high
  solo,pno $3.75; low solo,pno
  $3.75   (H345)

Forty-Five Arias From Operas And
  Oratorios, Vol. III *CC15L
  (Kagen, Sergius) INTERNAT. high
  solo,pno $3.75; low solo,pno
  $3.75   (H346)

Georg Friedrich Handel's Works *CCUL
  (Chrysander, Friedrich) contains
  works for a variety of
  instruments and vocal
  combinations microfiche
  UNIV.MUS.ED. reprints of
  Breitkopf & Hartel Editions;
  contains 96 volumes and 6
  supplements; $375.00   (H347)

Grant To Us O Gracious Lord *sac
  (Park, Dorothy Allan; Bissell,
  Keith W.) med solo,pno (F maj)
  WATERLOO $.90   (H348)

Grant Us Peace *sac
  (Park, Dorothy Allan; Bissell,
  Keith W.) low solo,pno (F maj)
  WATERLOO $.90   (H349)

HANDEL, GEORGE FRIDERIC (cont'd.)

Guardian Angels (from Triumph Of Time
    And Truth, The)
    see Handel, George Frideric, She's
    Gone

Have Mercy, Lord (from Te Deum) sac
    (Matthews) high solo,pno ELKAN-V
    $.95   (H350)

He Shall Feed His Flock (from
    Messiah, The) sac
    high solo,pno (B flat maj) SCHIRM.G
    $.85   (H351)
    med-low solo,pno (F maj) SCHIRM.G
    $.85   (H352)
    "Er Wiedet Seine Herde" Mez solo,
    pno (G maj) LIENAU HOS 66 s.p.
                                            (H353)
    "Er Wiedet Seine Herde" S solo,pno
    (B flat maj) LIENAU HOS 65 s.p.
                                            (H354)

He Was Despised And Rejected (from
    Messiah)
    solo,pno CRAMER   (H355)

Heilig, Heilig *sac
    S/T solo,pno (G maj) LIENAU HOS 55
    s.p.   (H356)

Hence Iris, Hence Away (from Semele)
    A solo,pno NOVELLO 17.0067.07 s.p.
                                            (H357)

Herrin, Du Strahlst Im Himmel *see
    Donna, Che In Ciel

Honor And Arms (from Samson) sac
    solo,pno/orch sc KALMUS $3.00
                                            (H358)

Honour And Arms (from Samson) sac
    B solo,pno NOVELLO 17.0068.05 s.p.
                                            (H359)
    B solo,pno (B flat maj) SCHIRM.G
    $.85   (H360)

Horch, Er Schlagt Das Goldne Spiel
    (from Alexander Balus)
    S solo,2fl,2bsn,strings,harp,mand,
    org BREITKOPF-L rental   (H361)

How Beautiful Are The Feet (from
    Messiah)
    solo,pno CRAMER   (H362)

Huldigungskantate *cant
    solo,cont GERIG AV 122 s.p.   (H363)

Hur Ljuvliga De Badskap (from
    Messiah) sac
    Mez solo,pno GEHRMANS s.p.   (H364)

I Know That My Redeemer Liveth (from
    Messiah) sac
    S solo,pno NOVELLO 17.0069.03 s.p.
                                            (H365)
    S solo,pno BELWIN $1.50   (H366)
    solo,pno CRAMER   (H367)
    [Ger/Eng] high solo,pno (E maj)
    SCHIRM.G $1.00   (H368)
    [Ger/Eng] med solo,pno (D maj)
    SCHIRM.G $1.00   (H369)
    high solo,pno (E maj) CENTURY 608
    $.40   (H370)
    low solo,pno (E maj) ASHDOWN (H371)
    high solo,pno (E maj) ASHDOWN
                                            (H372)
    med solo,pno (D maj/F sharp maj)
    ALLANS s.p.   (H373)
    high solo,pno (E maj) ALLANS s.p.
                                            (H374)
    "Ich Weiss, Dass Mein Erloser
    Lebet" S solo,pno (E maj) LIENAU
    HOS 67 s.p.   (H375)
    "Ich Weiss, Dass Mein Erloser
    Lebet" A solo,pno (C maj) LIENAU
    HOS 68 s.p.   (H376)
    "Ich Weiss, Dass Mein Erloser
    Lebet" S solo,fl,clar,bsn,strings
    BREITKOPF-W s.p.   (H377)

I Will Magnify Thee
    A solo,pno PATERSON s.p.   (H378)

Ich Lieb' Euch, Ihr Augen (from
    Julius Caesar)
    S solo,ob,harp,strings,cont
    DEUTSCHER rental   (H379)

Ich Weiss, Dass Mein Erloser Lebet
    *see I Know That My Redeemer
    Liveth

Il Mio Crudel Martoro (from
    Ariodante)
    see Six Italian Arias, Vol. II

Il Volo Cosi Fido (from Ricardo)
    see Handel, George Frideric,
    Augelletti, Che Cantate

Ingratitude's The Queen Of Crimes
    (Howe) low solo,pno PAXTON P40475
    s.p.   (H380)

HANDEL, GEORGE FRIDERIC (cont'd.)

Italiens Erwachen *cant
    (Seiffert, M; Moser, H.J.) SSA/STB
    soli,chamb.orch,cembalo
    BREITKOPF-L rental   (H381)

Jag Vet Att Min Forlossare Lever
    (from Messiah) sac
    Mez solo,pno GEHRMANS s.p.   (H382)

Jetzt Muss Ich Mit Ihm Brechen (from
    Radamisto)
    T solo,2ob,strings,cont DEUTSCHER
    rental   (H383)

Jetzt Ruhe, Jetzt Schlafe (from
    Radamisto)
    B solo,2ob,strings,cont DEUTSCHER
    rental   (H384)

La Fete D'Alexandre
    see LA MUSIQUE, NEUVIEME CAHIER

La Lucrezia: O Numi Eterni *cant
    [It/Eng] S solo,pno SCHOTTS VK 7
    s.p.   (H385)

La Mia Pace (from Der Tiroler Wastel)
    S solo,fl,2ob,2bsn,2horn,strings
    DOBLINGER sc s.p., ipa, voc sc
    s.p. contains also: L'Amore
    Artigiano   (H386)

La Solitudine *cant
    (Boyd) [Lat/Ger] AB soli,cont
    DEUTSCHER 4105 s.p.   (H387)
    (Boyd, Malcolm) "Die Einsamkeit"
    [It/Ger] A solo,cont (med) sc
    BAREN. 4105 s.p.   (H388)

La Speranza E Giunta (from Ottone)
    (Jacobson) "Spring" 2 soli,cont
    ROBERTON 72386 s.p.   (H389)
    (Somervell) "Spring" high solo,pno/
    orch (E maj) ROBERTON 2480H s.p.
                                            (H390)
    (Somervell) "Spring" low solo,pno/
    orch (D maj) ROBERTON 2480L s.p.
                                            (H391)

L'Amore Artigiano (from Der Tiroler
    Wastel)
    see Handel, George Frideric, La Mia
    Pace

Largo *see Ombra Mai Fu

Lascia Ch'io Pianga (from Rinaldo)
    sac
    solo,orch HENN s.p.   (H392)
    [It] A solo,pno RICORDI-ARG
    BA 11698 s.p.   (H393)
    S/T solo,pno FORLIVESI 11937 s.p.
                                            (H394)
    Mez/Bar solo,pno FORLIVESI 11938
    s.p.   (H395)
    [It/Ger] med solo,pno BOTE $1.10
                                            (H396)
    "Ah, Let Me Weep, Lord!" [It/Eng] A
    solo,pno (D maj) SCHIRM.G $.75
                                            (H397)
    "Lass Mich Mit Tranen" A solo,pno
    (D maj) LIENAU HOS 73 s.p.   (H398)
    "Lass Mich Mit Tranen" S solo,pno
    (F maj) LIENAU HOS 72 s.p.   (H399)
    "Lass Mich Mit Tranen Mein Los
    Beklagen" S solo,strings,cont
    DEUTSCHER rental   (H400)
    "O Lord, Correct Me" solo,pno (E
    flat maj) LEONARD-ENG   (H401)
    (Hamlin) "O Lord Correct Me" high
    solo,pno (E flat maj) BOSTON
    $1.50   (H402)
    (Hamlin) "O Lord Correct Me" low
    solo,pno (C maj) BOSTON $1.50
                                            (H403)

Lass Den Vorsatz Dir Nicht Truben
    (from Poros)
    SB soli,2ob,strings,cont DEUTSCHER
    rental   (H404)

Lass Mich Mit Tranen *see Lascia
    Ch'io Pianga

Lass Mich Mit Tranen Mein Los
    Beklagen *see Lascia Ch'io
    Pianga

Leave Me
    B solo,pno PATERSON s.p.   (H405)

Let The Bright Seraphim (from Samson)
    sac
    S solo,pno NOVELLO 17.0094.04 s.p.
                                            (H406)

Liebliche Walder (from Almira)
    (Gunther) [Ger] S solo,ob/vln,pno
    BOTE $1.75   (H407)

Look Down, Harmonius Saint *sac,cant
    "Preis Der Tonkunst" [Eng/Ger] S/T
    solo,strings,cembalo sc PETERS
    4631 $6.00, ipa   (H408)
    "Preis Der Tonkunst" [Eng/Ger] S/T
    solo,strings,cembalo sc CONCORDIA
    97-4263 $3.50   (H409)

HANDEL, GEORGE FRIDERIC (cont'd.)

    (Stevens, Denis) [Eng] T solo,
    4strings,cont (med) PENN STATE
    PSM 1 s.p., ipa   (H410)
    (Stevens, Denis) T solo,2vln,vla,
    cont PENN STATE PSMS 1 $3.00
                                            (H411)

Lost Love *see A Suoi Piedi

Love's Homage
    low solo,pno (F maj) ASHDOWN (H412)
    high solo,pno (A flat maj) ASHDOWN
                                            (H413)

Meine Liebliche Platane - So
    Schatt'gen Raum (from Xerxes)
    (Mottl, F.) S solo,ob,2clar,2bsn,
    2horn,harp,strings BREITKOPF-L
    rental   (H414)

Meine Seele Hort Im Sehen *sac
    [Ger] S solo,fl/vln,cont sc
    CONCORDIA 97-4268 $2.75, voc sc
    CONCORDIA s.p., ipa   (H415)

Minuet From Berenice
    low solo,pno (C maj) ALLANS s.p.
                                            (H416)
    med solo,pno (D maj) ALLANS s.p.
                                            (H417)
    high solo,pno (E flat maj) ALLANS
    s.p.   (H418)

Mistress Mine (from Jephtha)
    Bar solo,pno PATERSON s.p.   (H419)

Mon Lo Diro Col Labbro (from Tolomeo)
    (Somervell) "Silent Worship" low
    solo,pno/orch (G maj) ROBERTON
    2502L s.p.   (H420)
    (Somervell) "Silent Worship" high
    solo,pno/orch (A maj) ROBERTON
    2502H s.p.   (H421)

Nachtigallenarie (from L'Allegro, Il
    Pensieroso Ed Il Moderato)
    [Ger/Eng] S solo,fl,5strings,cont
    LEUCKART rental   (H422)
    (Seydel, Hans-Jakob) [Ger/Eng] S
    solo,fl,cont LEUCKART $2.25
                                            (H423)

Ne Men Con L'ombre (from Serse)
    see Six Italian Arias, Vol. II

Neue Kinderlieder *CCU
    solo,pno BREITKOPF-L EB 5748 s.p.
                                            (H424)

Neun Deutsche Arien *CC9L
    (Roth, H.) S solo,pno,vln,vcl voc
    sc BREITKOPF-L EB 5458 $5.00,
    study sc BREITKOPF-L EB 5480
    $1.80   (H425)

Nie Soll Des Schiffes Steuermann Dem
    Stillen Meer Vertrauen (from
    Poros)
    B solo,2fl,2horn,strings,cont
    DEUTSCHER rental   (H426)

No Se Emendera Jamas *cant
    (Behrend, Siegfried) S solo,gtr,
    viola da gamba SIKORSKI 575 s.p.
                                            (H427)

No Shade So Rare *see Ombra Mai Fu

Nun Schweiget Winde *see Silete
    Venti

Nur Eins Erbitte Ich *sac
    high solo,2S rec,cont HANSSLER
    5.066 s.p.   (H428)

O Amor, Du Tyrann *see Crudel
    Tiranno, Amor

O Bewahret Und Befeuert *see
    Conservate, Raddoppiate

O, Come Chiare E Belle *cant
    3 soli,trp,strings,cont DEUTSCHER
    rental   (H429)

O Doux Sommeil (from Semele)
    DURAND s.p.   (H430)

O Hatt' Ich Jubals Harf (from Joshua)
    sac
    S solo,pno (A maj) LIENAU HOS 57
    s.p.   (H431)
    A solo,pno (F maj) LIENAU HOS 58
    s.p.   (H432)
    T solo,strings BREITKOPF-L rental
                                            (H433)

O King Of Kings (from Esther II) sac
    [Eng] high solo,kbd CHESTER s.p.
    contains also: Alleluia   (H434)

O Lord, Correct Me *see Lascia Ch'io
    Pianga

O Lord, We Pray For Daily Grace *sac
    solo,pno PATERSON s.p.   (H435)

O Lord Whose Mercies Numberless (from
    Saul)
    solo,pno CRAMER   (H436)

HANDEL, GEORGE FRIDERIC (cont'd.)

O Magnify The Lord (from Chandos
  Anthems)
  solo,pno CRAMER   (H437)

O Mon Pere, Si Tu Voulais (from La
  Resurrezione)
  [Fr/Ger] solo,pno/inst DURAND s.p.
                                     (H438)

O Never, Never Bow We Down (from
  Judas Maccabeus)
  solo,pno CRAMER   (H439)

O Qualis De Coelo Sonus *sac,cant
  (Ewerhart, Rudolf) [Lat] S solo,
  2vln,cont sc BIELER DK 1 s.p.,
  ipa   (H440)

O Sacred Oracles Of Truth (from
  Belshazzar)
  solo,pno CRAMER   (H441)

O Schmach, O Wut - O Rosig Wie Die
  Pfirsiche (from Acis And
  Galathea)
  B solo,fl,strings,cembalo
  BREITKOPF-L rental   (H442)

O Sleep, Why Dost Thou Leave Me?
  (from Semele)
  S solo,pno NOVELLO 17.0141.10 s.p.
                                     (H443)
  high solo,pno (E maj) SCHIRM.G $.85
                                     (H444)
  med solo,pno (E flat maj) ALLANS
  s.p.   (H445)
  high solo,pno (E maj) ALLANS s.p.
                                     (H446)
  "O Sommeil, Doux Sommeil!" [Fr/Ger]
  solo,pno/inst DURAND s.p.   (H447)

O Sommeil, Doux Sommeil! *see O
  Sleep, Why Dost Thou Leave Me?

Oft Decken Wolken *see Cuopre Tal
  Volta Il Cielo

Oh! Had I Jubal's Lyre (from Joshua)
  sac
  high solo,pno (A maj) SCHIRM.G $.85
                                     (H448)
  [Eng/Ger] high solo,pno BOTE $1.10 (H449)

Ombr Des Bois *see Ombra Mai Fu

Ombra Cara (from Radamisto)
  [It/Ger] med solo,pno BOTE $1.10
                                     (H450)

Ombra Mai Fu (from Xerxes) sac
  [It/Eng] Mez/Bar solo,pno RICORDI-
  ENG 127487 s.p.   (H451)
  S/T solo,pno FORLIVESI 11927 s.p.
                                     (H452)
  Mez/Bar solo,pno FORLIVESI 11928
  s.p.   (H453)
  "Largo" [It/Ger/Fr] S/T solo,pno (G
  maj) RICORDI-ARG BA 7587 s.p.   (H454)
  "Largo" solo,pno FAZER F 2150 s.p. (H455)
  "Largo" med solo,pno (F maj) ALLANS
  s.p.   (H456)
  "Largo" high solo,pno (G maj)
  ALLANS s.p.   (H457)
  "Largo" low solo,pno (E flat maj)
  ALLANS s.p.   (H458)
  "Largo" low solo,pno LUNDQUIST s.p. (H459)
  "Largo" S/T solo,pno (G maj, Three
  Texts: Sacred, Secular And
  Italian) LIENAU HOS 78 s.p.   (H460)
  "Largo" Mez solo,pno (F maj, Three
  Texts: Sacred, Secular And
  Italian) LIENAU HOS 79 s.p.   (H461)
  "Largo" A/Bar solo,pno (E flat maj,
  Three Texts: Sacred, Secular And
  Italian) LIENAU HOS 79A s.p.   (H462)
  "Largo" [It/Ger] med solo,pno,vln/
  vcl LIENAU R84 s.p.   (H463)
  "Largo" high solo,pno LUNDQUIST
  s.p.   (H464)
  "No Shade So Rare" [It/Eng] high
  solo,pno (G maj) SCHIRM.G $.85   (H465)
  "Ombr Des Bois" [Fr] solo,acap oct
  DURAND s.p.   (H466)
  "Rest" low solo,pno (D flat maj)
  ASHDOWN   (H467)
  "Rest" med solo,pno (E flat maj)
  ASHDOWN   (H468)
  "Rest" med-high solo,pno (F maj)
  ASHDOWN   (H469)
  "Rest" high solo,pno (G maj)
  ASHDOWN   (H470)
  "Rest" MezA soli,pno ASHDOWN s.p. (H471)
  (Buck, D.) "Trust In The Lord" high
  solo,pno (G maj) SCHIRM.G $.75   (H472)
  (Eddy) high solo,pno (E maj)
  FISCHER,C V 1884   (H473)
  (Eddy) low solo,pno (E flat maj)

HANDEL, GEORGE FRIDERIC (cont'd.)

  FISCHER,C V 1885   (H474)

Our Limped Streams With Freedom Flow
  (from Joshua)
  solo,pno CRAMER   (H475)

Pack Clouds Away
  see OLD ENGLISH SONG CYCLE, AN

Pastorella, Vagha Bella *sac,cant
  [Ger/It] S/T solo,cont sc CONCORDIA
  97-4267 $3.00   (H476)
  [It/Ger] S/T solo,cembalo,vcl
  KISTNER cmplt ed s.p., sc s.p.,
  ipa   (H477)

Patenza *cant
  (Roth, H.) S solo,vcl,cembalo
  BREITKOPF-L rental   (H478)

Pena Tiranna (from Amadigi)
  "Qualen Ohne Ende" Mez/A solo,ob,
  bsn,strings BREITKOPF-L rental   (H479)

Pensieri Notturni Di Filli: Nel Dolce
  Dell' Oblio *cant
  [It/Ger] S solo,fl,pno,opt vcl
  ZIMMER. 1114 s.p.   (H480)
  "Sweet Forgetting" high solo,pno/
  hpsd,A rec/fl SCHIRM.G $1.00   (H481)
  (Behrend) [It] S solo,fl,gtr BOTE
  $2.75   (H482)
  (Bergmann; Hunt) [It/Eng] S solo,
  fl,pno SCHOTTS 10372 s.p.   (H483)

Pensieri Notturni Di Filli: Nel Dolce
  Dell'oblio *cant
  (Schaller, E.) S solo,A rec/treb
  inst,gtr,vcl DOBLINGER GKM 28
  $4.25   (H484)

People That Walked In Darkness (from
  Messiah)
  solo,pno CRAMER   (H485)

Pious Orgies (from Judas Maccabeus)
  low solo,pno (F maj) CRAMER   (H486)
  high solo,pno (G maj) CRAMER   (H487)

Praise The Lord With A Cheerful Noise
  S solo,pno PATERSON s.p.   (H488)

Praise The Lord With Cheerful Noise
  (from Esther)
  solo,pno CRAMER   (H489)

Preis Der Tonkunst *see Look Down,
  Harmonius Saint

Qualen Ohne Ende *see Pena Tiranna

Quell'amor (from Teseo)
  see Six Italian Arias, Vol. I

Recitativ Und Arie (from Messiah) sac
  (Klemetti) [Finn/Ger] solo,pno
  FAZER W 3189 s.p.   (H490)

Rejoice Greatly, O Daughter Of Zion!
  (from Messiah) sac
  solo,pno CRAMER   (H491)
  "Tochter Zions, Freue Dich" Mez
  solo,pno (F maj) LIENAU HOS 70
  s.p.   (H492)

Rejoice O Judah (from Judas
  Maccabeus)
  solo,pno CRAMER   (H493)

Rest *see Ombra Mai Fu

Return Oh God (from Samson)
  [Eng/Ger] med solo,pno BOTE $1.10
                                     (H494)

Salve Regina *sac,cant
  (Seiffert, M.) [Lat] S solo,org,
  strings sc BREITKOPF-L EB 4149
  $2.50   (H495)

Schalkhaft Spielt Mit Schlauen
  Blicken (from Alexander Balus)
  solo,strings,pno BREITKOPF-L rental
  contains also: Engel, Ewig Licht
  Und Schon   (H496)

Schattige Ruh (Largo) (from Xerxes)
  T solo,strings,cont DEUTSCHER
  rental   (H497)

Schmilz, O Harter Sinn (from Otto Und
  Theophano)
  A solo,strings,cont DEUTSCHER
  rental   (H498)

Se Fedel Vuoci Ch'io Ti Creda (from
  Orlando)
  [It/Ger] high solo,pno BOTE $1.50 (H499)

Se Il Timore (from Deidamia)
  see Six Italian Arias, Vol. II

HANDEL, GEORGE FRIDERIC (cont'd.)

Secular Solos For Bass *sec,CC11L
  B solo,pno NOVELLO 17.0245.09 s.p.
                                     (H500)

Sei Mia Gioia (from Parthenope)
  (Gunther) [It/Ger] high solo,pno
  BOTE $1.10   (H501)

Sempre Dolci, Ed Amorose (from
  Berenice)
  "Be Not Always Tender, Adoring"
  [It/Eng] S solo,pno (A maj)
  SCHIRM.G $.75   (H502)

Shall I In Mamre's Fertile Plain
  (from Joshua)
  solo,pno CRAMER   (H503)

She's Gone (from Triumph Of Time And
  Truth, The)
  (Flothius, Marius) [Eng] S solo,ob,
  pno BROEKMANS 395-1 s.p. contains
  also: Guardian Angels   (H504)

Sibillar Gli Angui D'Aletto (from
  Rinaldo)
  Bar/B solo,ob,bsn,2trp,timp,
  strings,cembalo BREITKOPF-L
  rental   (H505)

Silent Worship *see Mon Lo Diro Col
  Labbro

Silete Venti *mot
  "Nun Schweiget Winde" S solo,2ob,
  bsn,strings,cembalo BREITKOPF-L
  rental   (H506)

Sing Songs Of Praise (from Esther)
  solo,pno CRAMER   (H507)

Six Italian Arias, Vol. I
  [It] S solo,pno/pno&vln HINRICHSEN
  H1759A $3.75
  contains: Al Furor (from
  Arminio); Benche Mi Sia (from
  Ottone); Quell'amor (from
  Teseo)   (H508)

Six Italian Arias, Vol. II
  [It] S solo,pno/pno&vln HINRICHSEN
  H1759B $3.75
  contains: Il Mio Crudel Martoro
  (from Ariodante); Ne Men Con
  L'ombre (from Serse); Se Il
  Timore (from Deidamia)   (H509)

Six Italian Chamber Duets *CC6U
  (Brahms, Johannes) [It/Ger] SS/SA
  soli,pno PETERS 2070 $12.00   (H510)

Smiling Hours, The (from Hercules)
  A solo,pno NOVELLO 17.0178.09 s.p.
                                     (H511)

So Sei's - Herz, Der Liebe Susser
  Born (from Acis Und Galathea)
  S solo,2fl,strings,cembalo
  BREITKOPF-L rental   (H512)

So Wie Die Taube (from Acis Und
  Galathea)
  S solo,ob,strings,cembalo
  BREITKOPF-L rental   (H513)

Songs From The Oratorios For Baritone
  Or Bass *sac,CC12L
  Bar/B solo,pno NOVELLO 17.0249.01
  s.p.   (H514)

Songs From The Oratorios For
  Contralto *sac,CC12L
  A solo,pno NOVELLO 17.0247.05 s.p.
                                     (H515)

Songs From The Oratorios For Soprano
  *sac,CC12L
  S solo,pno NOVELLO 17.0246.07 s.p.
                                     (H516)

Songs From The Oratorios For Tenor
  *sac,CC12L
  T solo,pno NOVELLO 17.0248.03 s.p.
                                     (H517)

Sound An Alarm (from Judas Maccabeus)
  solo,pno CRAMER   (H518)

Spacious Firmament, The
  Bar solo,pno PATERSON s.p.   (H519)

Spanish Cantata *cant
  [Span] med solo,gtr BROEKMANS 25
  s.p.   (H520)

Spring *see La Speranza E Giunta

Supplication *sac
  (Park, Dorothy Allan; Bissell,
  Keith W.) med solo,pno (E flat
  maj) WATERLOO $.90   (H521)

Susse Stille, Sanfte Quelle *sac
  S/T solo,fl,bvl sc CONCORDIA
  97-4261 $2.00   (H522)
  (Flothius, Marius) S solo,fl,pno
  BROEKMANS 395-20 s.p.   (H523)

HANDEL, GEORGE FRIDERIC (cont'd.)

Sweet Bird
  solo,pno (A flat maj) ASHDOWN
                                    (H524)

Sweet Forgetting *see Pensieri
  Notturni Di Filli: Nel Dolce
  Dell' Oblio

Sweet One And Twenty (from
  Floridante)
  Bar solo,pno PATERSON s.p. (H525)

Ten Songs *CC10U
  (Somervell) med solo,pno FABER
  C02974 $1.00   (H526)

Thanks Be To Thee *see Dank Sei Dir,
  Herr

That God Is Great
  (Howe) Bar solo,pno PAXTON P40516
  s.p.   (H527)

Then Will I Jehovah's Praise (from
  Occasional Oratorio)
  solo,pno CRAMER   (H528)

Thirty Arias For A Female Voice
  *CC30U
  [Eng/Ger] S/Mez/A solo,pno PETERS
  3493 $10.50 Arias From Oratorios
  And Operas, In Original Language
                              (H529)

Thou Didst Blow With The Wind (from
  Israel In Egypt)
  (Howe) S solo,pno PAXTON P40604
  s.p.   (H530)

Thou Shalt Bring Them In (from Israel
  In Egypt)
  solo,pno CRAMER   (H531)

Thy Mercy, Lord
  S solo,pno PATERSON s.p.   (H532)

To God Sing Praise
  T solo,pno PATERSON s.p.   (H533)

To God, Who Made The Radiant Sun
  see Handel, George Frideric, Total
  Eclipse

Tochter Zions, Freue Dich *see
  Rejoice Greatly, O Daughter Of
  Zion!

Total Eclipse (from Samson)
  solo,pno CRAMER   (H534)
  T solo,pno PATERSON s.p. contains
  also: To God, Who Made The
  Radiant Sun   (H535)

Tra Le Fiamme *sac,cant
  (Zenck, Hermann) "Um Die Flamme"
  [Ger/It] S solo,2fl,ob,bsn,2vln,
  cont (diff) BAREN. 1977 $14.00
                              (H536)

Trumpet Is Calling, The *see Un
  Ombra Di Pace

Trust In The Lord *see Ombra Mai Fu

Tu Fedel, Tu Costante? *sac,cant
  (Zenck, Hermann) "Du Bist Treu Und
  Bestandig?" [Ger/It] S solo,2vln,
  cont (diff) BAREN. 1973 $10.50
                              (H537)

Tune Your Harps To Cheerful Strains
  (from Esther)
  solo,pno CRAMER   (H538)

Turn Thee O Lord *see Verdi Prati

Twelve Songs *CC12U
  (Rondegger) BELWIN S solo,pno
  $2.00; A solo,pno $2.00; Bar/B
  solo,pno $2.00   (H539)

Um Die Flamme *see Tra Le Fiamme

Un Ombra Di Pace (from Calphurnia)
  (Somervell) "Trumpet Is Calling,
  The" solo,pno/orch (B flat maj)
  ROBERTON 2762 s.p.   (H540)

Und Siehe, Der Engel Des Herrn (from
  Messiah) sac,Xmas
  (Steglich) "But Lo! The Angel Of
  The Lord Came Upon Them" [Eng/
  Ger] S solo,opt vcl NAGELS $1.50
                              (H541)
  (Steglich, Rudolf) "But Lo! The
  Angel Of The Lord Came Upon Them"
  [Ger/Eng] S solo,cont (med easy)
  NAGELS 104 $4.25   (H542)

V'Adoro, Pupille (from Julius Caesar)
  [It/Ger] high solo,pno BOTE $1.50
                              (H543)
  [It/Ger] med solo,pno BOTE $1.50
                              (H544)

Vartan Du Gar *see Where'er You Walk

HANDEL, GEORGE FRIDERIC (cont'd.)

Verdi Prati (from Alcina)
  "Turn Thee O Lord" solo,pno CRAMER
                              (H545)

Vieni O Figlio (from Ottone)
  (Somervell) "Come To Me Soothing
  Sleep" solo,pno/orch (E flat maj)
  ROBERTON 2550 s.p.   (H546)

Vierge Marie
  [Fr/Ger] S solo,pno/inst DURAND
  s.p.   (H547)

Voglio Dire (from Parthenope)
  [It/Ger] med solo,pno BOTE $1.00
                              (H548)

War Is Toil And Trouble
  T solo,pno PATERSON s.p.   (H549)

Wedding Hymn *sac,Marriage
  (MacNutt) med solo,pno BERANDOL
  BER 1287 $1.50   (H550)
  (MacNutt) low solo,pno BERANDOL
  BER 1288 $1.50   (H551)

Weep No More (from Hercules)
  Mez solo,pno PATERSON s.p. (H552)
  A solo,pno PATERSON s.p.   (H553)

Wenn Segelnd Auf Den Wogen (from
  Poros)
  S solo,strings,cont DEUTSCHER
  rental   (H554)

Wer Einmal Vom Damon Der Liebe
  Verwundet (from Poros)
  B solo,strings,cont DEUTSCHER
  rental   (H555)

Wer Fand In Diesem Walde So Liebliche
  Beute (from Admetos)
  B solo,2ob,2horn,strings,cont
  DEUTSCHER rental   (H556)

Wer Kennt Des Menschen Herz (from
  Radamisto)
  S solo,strings,cont DEUTSCHER
  rental   (H557)

What Though I Trace Each Herb A
  Flower (from Solomon)
  Bar solo,pno PATERSON s.p. (H558)

What's Sweeter Than A New Blown Rose
  2 soli,pno CRAMER   (H559)
  (Howe) S solo,pno PAXTON P40473
  s.p.   (H560)

When You Marry Me (from Semele)
  S/Bar solo,pno PATERSON s.p. (H561)
  A/B solo,pno PATERSON s.p. (H562)

Where E'er You Walk (from Semele)
  low solo,pno (G maj) CRAMER (H563)
  med solo,pno (A flat maj) CRAMER
                              (H564)
  high solo,pno (B flat maj) CRAMER
                              (H565)
Where'er You Walk (from Semele)
  T solo,pno NOVELLO 17.0218.01 s.p.
                              (H566)
  high solo,pno (B flat maj) WATERLOO
  $.75   (H567)
  low solo,pno (F maj) WATERLOO $.75
                              (H568)
  med solo,pno (G maj) WATERLOO $.75
                              (H569)
  high solo,pno (B flat maj) SCHIRM.G
  $1.00   (H570)
  med solo,pno (G maj) SCHIRM.G $1.00
                              (H571)
  low solo,pno (F maj) SCHIRM.G $1.00
                              (H572)
  high solo,pno (B flat maj) FISCHER,
  C S 4648   (H573)
  low solo,pno (G maj) FISCHER,C
  S 4649   (H574)
  high solo,pno (B flat maj) WILLIS
  $.75   (H575)
  low solo,pno (F maj) WILLIS $.75
                              (H576)
  low solo,pno (G maj) ALLANS s.p.
                              (H577)
  med solo,pno (A flat maj) ALLANS
  s.p.   (H578)
  high solo,pno (B flat maj) ALLANS
  s.p.   (H579)
  "Vartan Du Gar" solo,pno/org ERIKS
  K 280   (H580)

Why Do The Nations So Furiously Rage
  Together?
  solo,pno CRAMER   (H581)

With Thee Th' Unsheltered Moor I'd
  Tread (from Solomon)
  solo,pno CRAMER   (H582)

Zwei Gesange Aus Den "Deutschen
  Arien" *CC2U
  (Scheit, K.) S solo,vln,fl,gtr,opt
  vcl DOBLINGER GKM 27 $4.00 (H583)

HANDEL, GEORGE FRIDERIC (cont'd.)

Zwolf Alt-Arien Aus Opern Und
  Oratorien *CC12U
  A solo,pno BREITKOPF-L EB 1339
  $3.50   (H584)

Zwolf Sopran-Arien Aus Opern Und
  Oratorien *CC12U
  S solo,pno BREITKOPF-L EB 1338
  $3.50   (H585)

Zwolf Wunderhorn-Lieder *CC12U
  solo,pno BREITKOPF-L EB 5195 s.p.
                              (H586)

HANDLE, JOHNNY
  High Level Ranters Song And Tune Book
  *CCU
  solo,pno GALLIARD 2.8151.7 $2.50
                              (H587)

HANDMAN, DOREL
  Sept Melodies *CC7L
  solo,pno DURAND s.p.   (H588)

HANDS, EYES AND HEART see Vaughan
  Williams, Ralph

HANDSOME NELL see Reuland, Jacques

HANEY, J.
  Few Words About Jesus, A (composed
  with Thompson, S.) *sac,gospel
  solo,pno SAUL AVE   (H589)

HANFF, JOHANN NICOLAUS (1665-1711)
  Ich Will Den Herrn Loben *cant
  (Grusnick, Bruno) [Ger/Swed] S
  solo,vln,cont (med) BAREN. 3424
  $7.75   (H590)

HANGMAN'S SONG see Grant, W. Parks

HANISCH, EDUARD
  Spray Selbdritt'
  narrator,gtr,perc SCHAUR EE 2706
  s.p.   (H591)

HANKS
  I'll Pray For You *sac
  solo,pno LILLENAS SM-915: SN $1.00
                              (H592)

  In My Father's House Are Many
  Mansions *sac
  solo,pno BENSON S6524-S $1.00
                              (H593)

  Lonely Voices *sac
  solo,pno HOPE 53 $1.00   (H594)

HANNEKEMAN see Hoendevanger, W.

HANNIKAINEN, ILMARI (1892-1955)
  Aidin Silmat
  "Mors Ogon" solo,pno FAZER W 2281
  s.p.   (H595)

  Det Galler
  "Kylva" solo,pno FAZER W 2280 s.p.
                              (H596)

  Erakkomaja *Op.8,No.3
  "Ermiten" solo,pno FAZER F 897 s.p.
                              (H597)

  Ermiten *see Erakkomaja

  Fader Var *Op.24, sac
  "Vater Unser" solo,pno FAZER F 2404
  s.p.   (H598)

  Fardemannens Psalm *see Matkamiehen
  Virsi

  Fotsparen I Snon
  "Jalanjaljet Lumessa" solo,pno
  FAZER F 4124 s.p.   (H599)

  Funf Vokslieder Aus Tavastland, Vol.
  I *Finn
  [Finn/Ger/Fr] solo,pno FAZER F 2128
  s.p.
  contains: Guten Abend, Vogelein,
  Op.30,No.1; Tanzlied I, Op.30,
  No.2   (H600)

  Funf Volkslieder Aus Tavastland, Vol.
  II *Finn
  [Finn/Ger/Fr] solo,pno FAZER F 2130
  s.p.
  contains: In Meines Gluckes
  Garten, Op.30,No.3; Seit Ich
  Die Heimat Musste Lassen, Op.30,
  No.4; Tanzlied II, Op.30,
  No.5   (H601)

  Guten Abend, Vogelein *Op.30,No.1
  see Funf Vokslieder Aus
  Tavastland, Vol. I

  In Meines Gluckes Garten *Op.30,No.3
  see Funf Volkslieder Aus
  Tavastland, Vol. II

  Jalanjaljet Lumessa *see Fotsparen I
  Snon

  Kayskelen Kukkatarhassain *Op.16,
  No.2
  "There Has Fallen A Splendid Tear"

HANNIKAINEN, ILMARI (cont'd.)

   see Two Songs

Kom Til Mig, Jesus *see Tule
  Luokseni Herra Jeesus

Kylva *see Det Galler

Liettualualainen Laulu *Op.13,No.1
  see Three Songs

Lumitunnelma *Op.13,No.2
  see Three Songs

Matkamiehen Virsi *Op.18,No.1, Psalm
  "Fardemannens Psalm" solo,pno FAZER
  F 1864 s.p.   (H602)

Mors Ogon *see Aidin Silmat

Rosary, The *see Rukousnauha

Rukousnauha *Op.16,No.1
  "Rosary, The" see Two Songs

Seit Ich Die Heimat Musste Lassen
  *Op.30,No.4
  see Funf Volkslieder Aus
  Tavastland, Vol. II

Syv Laulua Kivijarven
  Laulunaytelmasta Talkootanssit
  *CC7U
  solo,pno FAZER W 2924 s.p.   (H603)

Tanzlied I *Op.30,No.2
  see Funf Vokslieder Aus
  Tavastland, Vol. I

Tanzlied II *Op.30,No.5
  see Funf Volkslieder Aus
  Tavastland, Vol. II

There Has Fallen A Splendid Tear
  *see Kayskelen Kukkatarhassain

Three Songs
  [Finn/Dan] med solo,kbd HANSEN-DEN
  s.p.
    contains: Liettualualainen Laulu,
    Op.13,No.1; Lumitunnelma,
    Op.13,No.2; Tuulikin
    Kehtolaulu, Op.13,No.3   (H604)

Toinen Sarja Hamalaisia
  Kansanlauluja, Vols. I-II
  *Op.36, CCU
  [Finn] solo,pno FAZER F 2371; F2374
  s.p., ea.   (H605)

Tule Luokseni Herra Jeesus *Op.29,
  No.5, sac
  "Kom Til Mig, Jesus" solo,pno FAZER
  F 1791 s.p.   (H606)

Tuulikin Kehtolaulu *Op.13,No.3
  see Three Songs

Two Songs
  [Eng/Finn/Dan] med solo,kbd HANSEN-
  DEN s.p.
    contains: Kayskelen
    Kukkatarhassain, "There Has
    Fallen A Splendid Tear", Op.16,
    No.2; Rukousnauha, "Rosary,
    The", Op.16,No.1   (H607)

Vater Unser *see Fader Var

HANNIKAINEN, VAINO (1900-1960)
  Bjornungen *see Karhunpoika

Karelische Volkslieder Aus
  Kiihtelysvaara, Vols. I-III *CCU
  solo,pno FAZER
  W 2369; W 2370; W 3166 s.p., ea.
                               (H608)

Karhunpoika *Op.10
  "Bjornungen" solo,pno FAZER F 2494
  s.p.   (H609)

HANS DER SCHWARMER see Gilse, Jan van

HANS OG GRETE see Hauger, Kristian

HANS UND GRETHE see Mahler, Gustav

HANSJE see Mortelmans, Lodewijk

HANUS, JAN (1915-   )
  Das Licht *see Svetlo

Dreveny Kristus *sac,CCU
  low solo,pno CZECH s.p.   (H610)

Dva Zalmove Zpevy *CC2U,Psalm
  Bar solo,orch/pno SUPRAPHON s.p.
                               (H611)

Pisen Sestry (from Plameny)
  see ARIE A ZPEVY ZE SOUCASNYCH
  OPER: ALT

Sonette Auf Texten Von Dichtern Der
  Renaissance *Op.48, CCU
  [Czech/Ger] solo,pno SUPRAPHON s.p.

HANUS, JAN (cont'd.)

Sonety   (H612)
  low solo,pno SUPRAPHON s.p. (H613)

Svetlo
  "Das Licht" S solo,pno,tamb CZECH
  s.p.   (H614)

HAPPIEST OF HEARTS see Burford, D.

HAPPINESS see Aldington, Joan

HAPPINESS see Gaither

HAPPINESS see Schubert, Franz (Peter)

HAPPINESS IS GOD see Akers, Doris

HAPPINESS IS THE LORD *sac,CCUL
  SAT soli,pno SINGSPIR 5616 $1.50
                               (H615)

HAPPINESS IS THE LORD see Stanphill,
  Ira F.

HAPPY AM I see Holiday, Mickey

HAPPY FLOCK see Bach, Johann Sebastian

HAPPY GOODMAN FAMILY SONG BOOK *sac,
  CCUL
  solo,pno WORD 35017-SN $2.95   (H616)

HAPPY HOLIDAYS see Irving, W.W.S.

HAPPY IS THE MAN see Thiman, Eric
  Harding

HAPPY JUBILEE, THE see Pace, Millie Lou

HAPPY MILK MAID, THE see Hook, James

HAPPY ROAD AND OTHER SONGS *sac,CC22UL
  solo,pno WORD 37734 $3.95   (H617)

HAPPY SIDE OF LIFE, THE see Smith

HAPPY SUMMER SONG see Kahn, Gerald

HAPPY YOUNG HEART see Sullivan, Sir
  Arthur Seymour

HAR AR DEN SKONA SOMMAR see Taube,
  Evert

HAR DAGEN SANKET AL SIN SORG see
  Nielsen, Carl

HAR DU EN VAN see Knorring, M. von

HAR JAG SOMNAT I DOFT AV KLOVER see
  Wohlfart, Karl

HARAWI see Messiaen, Oliver

HARD HITTING SONGS FOR HARD-HIT PEOPLE
  *CC150U,folk
  (Lomax, Alan; Guthrie, Woody; Seeger,
  Pete) solo,pno pap OAK 000177
  $6.95, cloth OAK 000041 $12.50
                               (H618)

HARD TIMES see Kozina, Marijan, Iz
  Tezkih Dni

HARD TRIALS *spir
  (Burleigh, H. T.) med solo,pno BELWIN
  $1.50   (H619)
  (Burleigh, H. T.) solo,pno BELWIN
  $1.50   (H620)

D'HARDELOT, GUY (1858-1936)
  Because *Marriage
  med-high solo,org (B flat maj)
  BOSTON $1.50   (H621)
  med-high solo,pno (B flat maj)
  BOSTON $1.50   (H622)
  solo,pno (available in 3 keys)
  ASHLEY $.95   (H623)
  med solo,pno FISCHER,C S 7675
                               (H624)
  high solo,pno FISCHER,C S 7676
                               (H625)
  low solo,pno FISCHER,C S 7674
                               (H626)
  high solo,pno (C maj) BOSTON $1.50
                               (H627)
  low solo,pno (A flat maj) BOSTON
  $1.50   (H628)
  (Teschemacher) low solo,pno (A flat
  maj) LUDWIG S-3 $.75   (H629)
  (Teschemacher) high solo,pno (C
  maj) LUDWIG S-5 $.75   (H630)
  (Teschemacher) med solo,pno (B flat
  maj) LUDWIG S-4 $.75   (H631)

L'Amour Cache
  solo,pno (available in 2 keys)
  ENOCH s.p.   (H632)

Le Jour Et La Nuit
  solo,pno (available in 2 keys)
  ENOCH s.p.   (H633)

D'HARDELOT, GUY (cont'd.)

L'Eventail
  solo,acap ENOCH s.p.   (H634)
  solo,pno ENOCH s.p.   (H635)

HARDERWIJK see Sigtenhorst-Meyer,
  Bernhard van den

HARDING, B.
  Vocal Selections From "Daisy"
  (composed with Smith, J.) *CCU
  solo,pno JRB $2.95   (H636)

HARDING, HARVEY
  Big Round-Up
  low solo,pno (C maj) WILLIS $.60
                               (H637)

O Be Joyful *sac,Gen
  low solo,pno (A maj) WILLIS $.75
                               (H638)

Po' Li'l Lam'
  med solo,pno (C maj) WILLIS $.60
                               (H639)

HARDING, PHYLLIS
  Come My Sweet Pretty Maid
  solo,orch (A flat maj) ASHDOWN
  s.p., ipr   (H640)

God Bless Me
  low solo,orch (E flat maj) ASHDOWN
  s.p., ipr   (H641)
  high solo,orch (G maj) ASHDOWN
  s.p., ipr   (H642)

In This Sweet Loveliness
  solo,pno (E flat maj) ASHDOWN s.p.,
  ipr   (H643)

Leafy Lanes Of England, The
  low solo,orch (A flat maj) ASHDOWN
  s.p., ipr   (H644)
  high solo,orch (C maj) ASHDOWN
  s.p., ipr   (H645)

Sittin' In The Cornfields
  solo,pno (G maj) ASHDOWN s.p., ipr
                               (H646)

HARDT, RICHARD
  Musical Alphabet, The
  solo,pno GENERAL 725 $1.25   (H647)

HARFENSPIELER I see Wolf, Hugo

HARFENSPIELER II see Wolf, Hugo

HARFENSPIELER III see Wolf, Hugo

HARHOREY LAILA see Rappaport, Eda

HARING, CH.
  A Mon Aimee
  solo,pno ENOCH s.p.   (H648)

Adieux A Ninon
  solo,pno (available in 2 keys)
  ENOCH s.p.   (H649)

Avril
  SA soli,pno voc sc ENOCH s.p.
                               (H650)

Deception
  solo,pno ENOCH s.p.   (H651)
  solo,acap ENOCH s.p.   (H652)

Il Vous En Souveindra
  solo,pno ENOCH s.p.   (H653)

L'amour Qui Passe
  solo,pno (available in 2 keys)
  ENOCH s.p.   (H654)

Le Drapeau Des Ecoliers Francais
  solo,pno ENOCH s.p.   (H655)
  solo,acap ENOCH s.p.   (H656)

Le Ramier
  solo,pno (available in 2 keys)
  ENOCH s.p.   (H657)
  solo,acap (available in 2 keys)
  ENOCH s.p.   (H658)

Le Temps Des Amours
  solo,pno ENOCH s.p.   (H659)
  solo,acap ENOCH s.p.   (H660)

Peine D'amour
  solo,pno (available in 2 keys)
  ENOCH s.p.   (H661)

Spleen
  solo,pno (available in 2 keys)
  ENOCH s.p.   (H662)

HARK! HARK, MY SOUL see Shelley, Harry
  Rowe

HARK! HARK! THE LARK see Castelnuovo-
  Tedesco, Mario

HARK! HARK! THE LARK see Quilter, Roger

HARK! HARK! THE LARK see Schubert,
  Franz (Peter)

HARK! HOW STILL see Franz, Robert

HARK, MY BELOVED see Barkan, Emanuel

HARK, NOW EVERYTHING IS STILL see
Plessis, Hubert du

HARK! THE ECHOING AIR see Purcell,
Henry

HARK! THE GOAT BELLS RINGING see Smart,
Henry Thomas

HARK TO THE MANDOLINE see Parker, Henry

HARKER, F. FLAXINGTON (1876-1936)
Consider And Hear Me *sac
high solo,pno (D min) SCHIRM.G $.75
(H663)
med solo,pno (B flat min) SCHIRM.G
$.75   (H664)

God Shall Wipe Away All Tears *sac
high solo,pno (F maj) SCHIRM.G $.85
(H665)
low solo,pno (D flat maj) SCHIRM.G
$.85   (H666)

He Shall Feed His Flock *sac,Xmas
ST soli,pno SCHIRM.G $.85   (H667)

How Beautiful Upon The Mountains
*sac
high solo,pno (C sharp min)
SCHIRM.G $1.00   (H668)
med solo,pno (B min) SCHIRM.G $1.00
(H669)
low solo,pno (G sharp min) SCHIRM.G
$1.00   (H670)
high solo&low solo,pno SCHIRM.G
$1.15   (H671)

I Will Lift Up Mine Eyes To The Hills
SA soli,pno SHAWNEE IB5001 $.75
(H672)

Like As The Hart Desireth The
Waterbrooks *sac
high solo,pno (A flat maj) SCHIRM.G
$.75   (H673)

O Love That Wilt Not Let Me Go *sac
med solo,pno (A flat maj) SCHIRM.G
$.75   (H674)

O Perfect Love *sac,Marriage
high solo,pno (F maj) SCHIRM.G $.75
(H675)
low solo,pno (D flat maj) SCHIRM.G
$.75   (H676)

HARKINS
It's In Your Hands *sac
solo,pno BENSON S6656-S $1.00
(H677)

HARLEQUIN'S ROSE see Smith, F.S.
Breville

HARLIGHETENS MORGON see Dahlgren,
Erland

HARLING, WILLIAM FRANKE (1887-1958)
Song Of Thanksgiving, A *sac
high solo,pno BELWIN $1.50   (H678)

That Rose - Your Love
high solo,pno (D flat maj) SCHIRM.G
$.60   (H679)

HARMAN HAAT see Borg, Kim

HARMON, B.
I've Come Too Far *sac
solo,pno BENSON S6426-S $1.00
(H680)

HARMONIA CAELESTIS see Esterhazy, Pal

HARMONICE MUSICES ODHECATON A see
Petrucci, Ottaviano

HARMONIE see Lefebvre, Channing

HARMONIE DU SOIR see Andriessen,
Hendrik

HARMONIE DU SOIR see Bertouille, Gerard

HARMONIE DU SOIR see Debussy, Claude

HARMONISCHEN GOTTESDIENST see Telemann,
Georg Philipp

HARMONIUM see Persichetti, Vincent

HARP see Joubert, John

HARP, THE see Bauer, Marion Eugenie

HARP OF THE WOODLAND see Martin,
Easthope

HARPER
Come With Your Heartache *sac
solo,pno STAMPS 7261-SN $1.00
(H681)

HARPER (cont'd.)
Each Step Of The Way *sac
solo,pno STAMPS 7252-SN $1.00
(H682)
solo,pno BENSON S5412-RS $1.00
(H683)

He'll Hold My Hand
see Harper, When I've Traveled My
Last Mile

I'm Singing For My Lord *sac
solo,pno STAMPS 7253-SN $1.00
(H684)

What Would I Do Without Jesus *sac
solo,pno STAMPS 7256-SN $1.00
(H685)

When I've Traveled My Last Mile *sac
solo,pno cmplt ed STAMPS 7248-RN
$1.00, cmplt ed STAMPS 7238-SN
$1.00 contains also: He'll Hold
My Hand   (H686)

HARPIST'S SONGS see Wolf, Hugo

HARPOLEKAREN OCH HANS SON see Sibelius,
Jean

HARPOLEKARENS KARLEKSSANG see Raebel,
M.

HARPUNSOITTAJA JA HANEN POIKANSA see
Sibelius, Jean, Harpolekaren Och
Hans Son

HARPZANG VAN DAVID see Appledoorn, Dina

HARPZANGEN VAN KONING DAVID see
Bijvanck, Henk

HARRAH
Three Nails, The (composed with
Davis) *sac
solo,pno BENSON S8058-S $1.00
(H687)

HARRE, MEINE SEELE *sac
Mez solo,pno (E flat maj) LIENAU
HOS 49 s.p.   (H688)

HARREX, P.
Sonata Fur Frauenstimme, Flote Und
Schlagzeug *sonata
female solo,fl,perc ARS VIVA AV 201
s.p.   (H689)

HARRHY, EDITH
And One Came Back Alone
high solo,pno (F maj) ALLANS s.p.
(H690)
low solo,pno (E flat maj) ALLANS
s.p.   (H691)

Australian Lullaby, An
solo,pno ALLANS s.p.   (H692)

Columbine
solo,pno ALLANS s.p.   (H693)

Elizabeth
solo,pno ALLANS s.p.   (H694)

For Auld Lang Syne
low solo,pno (C maj) PATERSON s.p.
(H695)
high solo,pno (F maj) PATERSON s.p.
(H696)

Little Brown Thing
solo,pno (D maj) ALLANS s.p. (H697)

Prayer *sac
low solo,pno (F maj) ALLANS s.p.
(H698)
high solo,pno (A flat maj) ALLANS
s.p.   (H699)

Songs Of The Season *song cycle
solo,pno ALLANS s.p.   (H700)

Thrush, The
low solo,pno (B flat maj) ALLANS
s.p.   (H701)
high solo,pno (C maj) ALLANS s.p.
(H702)

Wonga Dale
solo,pno (F maj) ALLANS s.p. (H703)

You Came To Me In May
high solo,pno (A flat maj) ALLANS
s.p.   (H704)
low solo,pno (F maj) ALLANS s.p.
(H705)

HARRIS
Give Thanks And Sing *sac
low solo,pno (B flat maj) BOSTON
$1.50   (H706)
med-high solo,pno (C maj) BOSTON
$1.50   (H707)
high solo,pno (D maj) BOSTON $1.50
(H708)

Glory, What A Day
high solo/low solo,pno oct SCHMITT
1875 $.30   (H709)

I've Got Jesus In My Heart *sac
solo,pno GENTRY $1.00   (H710)

HARRIS, BRYN
These Dancing Days Are Gone
Bar solo,perc EXPERIMENTAL s.p.
(H711)

HARRIS, CHARLES A.E.
I Heard The Voice Of Jesus Say *sac
high solo,pno (E maj) SCHIRM.G $.85
(H712)
low solo,pno (C maj) SCHIRM.G $.85
(H713)

HARRIS, EDWARD
Sea Charm
low solo,pno (G sharp min) BOOSEY
$1.50   (H714)
high solo,pno (B flat min) BOOSEY
$1.50   (H715)

HARRIS, L.R.
Balloons
high solo,pno PRESSER $.75   (H716)

HARRIS, R.
Abraham Lincoln Walks At Midnight
*cant
Mez solo,vln,vcl,pno AMP $5.00
(H717)

HARRIS, RON
All The Time In The World *sac
solo,pno WORD S-517   (H718)

Come As You Are *sac
solo,pno WORD S-526   (H719)

Friend Of The Father *sac
solo,pno WORD S-527   (H720)

I Do And Can And I Will *sac
solo,pno WORD S-516   (H721)

Jesus Was There All The Time *sac
solo,pno WORD S-522   (H722)

Just Because I Asked *sac
solo,pno WORD S-518   (H723)

Keep That Moment Alive *sac
solo,pno WORD S-528   (H724)

Over And Over And Over Again *sac
solo,pno WORD S-541   (H725)

Praise The Lord, He Never Changes
*sac
solo,pno WORD S-519   (H726)

Put Jesus First In Your Life *sac
solo,pno WORD S-520   (H727)

Someone Who Can *sac
solo,pno WORD S-521   (H728)

HARRIS, ROY (1898-   )
Fog
med solo,pno FISCHER,C V 1960 (H729)

HARRIS, RUSSELL G.
Litany, The *Op.19
SABar soli,4fl,3ob,3clar,2sax,2bsn,
4horn,2trp,3trom,tuba,harp,timp,
perc,strings sc AM.COMP.AL.
$11.00   (H730)

HARRISON
In The Gloaming
med solo,pno (F maj) CENTURY 1483
(H731)

HARRISON, DOROTHY
Beginning Of The End, The *sac
solo,pno oct MASTER CP-MM 2003
$1.25   (H732)

Do It Again, Lord *sac
solo,pno oct MASTER CP-MM 2000
$1.25   (H733)

John McKay Sings Dorothy Harrison
*sac,CCUL
solo,kbd SINGSPIR 5017 $1.00 (H734)

HARRISON, JULIUS ALLEN GREENWAY
(1885-1963)
King Charles
solo,pno (C min) BOOSEY $1.50
(H735)

Marching Along
solo,pno (F min) BOOSEY $1.50
(H736)

To Chloe
low solo,pno (F maj) ASHDOWN (H737)
high solo,pno (G maj) ASHDOWN
(H738)

Wanderer's Song, The
low solo,orch (C maj) ASHDOWN s.p.,
ipr   (H739)
med solo,orch (D maj) ASHDOWN s.p.,
ipr   (H740)
high solo,orch (E maj) ASHDOWN
s.p., ipr   (H741)

HARRISON, LOU (1917-   )
Air (from Rapunzel)
solo,fl,harp,pno,3strings sc PEER
$2.00, ipa   (H742)

HARRISON, LOU (cont'd.)

Alma Redemptoris Mater *sac
Bar solo,trom,pno,vln sc PEER $2.50
(H743)

Fragment From Calamus
(Whitman) low solo,pno BOMART $1.00
(H744)

HARRISON, SIDNEY (1903-   )
Fairy Tales
solo,pno CRAMER   (H745)

I Hear An Army
solo,pno CRAMER $1.15   (H746)

HARRISON, W.
Give All Your Love To Me
solo,pno (G maj) BOOSEY $1.50
(H747)

HART
Orpheus
solo,pno ALLANS s.p.   (H748)

What Doth The Lord Require Of Thee
*sac
med solo,pno FISCHER,C V 2411
(H749)

HART, FRITZ (BENNICKE) (1874-1949)
Grass
med solo,pno PRESSER $.75   (H750)

HART VAN VLAANDEREN see Mengelberg,
Rudolf

HARTAUS see Linnala, Eino, Fromm

HARTIG, HEINZ FRIEDRICH
Der Trinker Und Die Spiegel *Op.16,
CC5U
[Ger] Bar solo,inst BOTE $3.00
(H751)

Three Songs *Op.40a, CC3U
[Ger] Bar solo,pno BOTE $6.00
(H752)

HARTLEY, EVALINE
Charity *sac,Gen
high solo,pno (F maj) WILLIS $.60
(H753)

low solo,pno (D flat maj) WILLIS
$.60   (H754)

HARTLEY, WALTER S. (1927-   )
Psalm Cycle, A *sac,song cycle
med-high solo,pno,fl TRI-TEN $5.00
(H755)

Two Songs After William Blake *CC2U
S solo,pno CRESCENDO $3.00   (H756)

HARTLIEB
Schaue, Male, Singe *CCU
solo,pno PETERS s.p.   (H757)

HARTMANN, JOHAN PEDER EMILIUS
(1805-1900)
Mes Pensers
solo,pno ENOCH s.p.   (H758)

HARTMANN, KARL AMADEUS (1905-1963)
Erste Symphonie
"Symphony No. 1" A solo,orch voc sc
SCHOTTS rental, study sc SCHOTTS
4577 s.p.   (H759)

Gesangsszene
Bar solo,pno/orch SCHOTTS 5464 s.p.
(H760)

Lamento
S solo,pno SCHOTTS 4906 s.p. (H761)

Symphony No. 1 *see Erste Symphonie

HARTMANN, LUIGI
Jag Dromde Om Ett Kungabarn
low solo,pno GEHRMANS s.p. (H762)
high solo,pno GEHRMANS s.p. (H763)

Svanesang
high solo,pno GEHRMANS s.p. (H764)
low solo,pno GEHRMANS s.p. (H765)

HARTMANN, THOMAS ALEXANDROVICH DE
(1885-1956)
Poet's Love, A *Op.59, song cycle
[Russ/Eng/Fr] solo,pno BELAIEFF
349A s.p.   (H766)

HARTSUIKER, ANDRIES
Sancta Caecilia
see MODERNE NEDERLANDSE LIED

HARTY, SIR HAMILTON (1879-1941)
Blue Hills Of Antrim
solo,pno (B flat maj) BOOSEY $1.50
(H767)

By The Bivouac's Fitful Flame
solo,pno (E flat maj) BOOSEY $1.50
(H768)

Denny's Daughter
solo,pno (G flat maj) BOOSEY $1.50
(H769)

Lane O' The Thrushes
solo,pno (E maj) BOOSEY $1.50
(H770)

Mayo Love Song
solo,pno (D maj) BOOSEY $1.50
(H771)

HARTY, SIR HAMILTON (cont'd.)

My Lagan Love
low solo,pno (C maj) BOOSEY $1.75
(H772)

high solo,pno (E maj) BOOSEY $1.75
(H773)

Spring
solo,pno (E maj) BOOSEY $1.75
(H774)

HARVEST see Day, Maude Craske

HARVEST IS ABUNDANT, THE see Matthews,
Harvey Alexander

HARVEST OF SORROW, THE see
Rachmaninoff, Sergey Vassilievitch

HARVEST OF SORROW, THE see
Rachmaninoff, Sergey Vassilievitch,
Harvest Of Sorrow, The

HARVEY, BILL
I Want That Mountain *sac
solo,pno SINGSPIR 7070 $1.00 (H775)

HARVEY, JONATHAN (1939-   )
Angel Eros
high solo,2vln,vla,vcl NOVELLO
rental   (H776)

Black Sonnett (Cantata 5)
SMezBarB soli,fl,ob,clar,bsn,horn
NOVELLO rental   (H777)

Cantata 5 *see Black Sonnett

HARVEY, RICHARD W.
It Was So Quiet *sac
low solo,pno ABINGDON APM-691 $.75
(H778)

high solo,pno ABINGDON APM-690 $.75
(H779)

HARWOOD-JONES, H.F.
Light A Star For Me *sec
med solo,pno (F maj) WATERLOO $.75
(H780)

Magic Moments Pass A'Wing *sec
med solo,pno (C maj) WATERLOO $.75
(H781)

HASHIRIM SHELANU *CCU
solo,pno OR-TAV $3.50   (H782)

HASHKIVENU see Birnbaum

HASHKIVENU see Nowakowsky, David

HASKINS, VERNON C.
Because Of You
low solo,pno (G maj) WILLIS $.60
(H783)

high solo,pno (B flat maj) WILLIS
$.60   (H784)

Love Never Faileth *sac
med solo,pno (D maj) SCHIRM.G $.75
(H785)

HASSE
Majnatt
2 soli,pno LUNDQUIST s.p. (H786)

HASSE, A.
Alcide Al Bivio
solo,pno FORNI s.p.   (H787)

Favourite Songs In The Opera Call'd
Artaxerses, The *CCU
solo,pno FORNI s.p.   (H788)

HASSE, JOHANN ADOLPH (1699-1783)
Cantate
S/A solo,orch HEUGEL 11009 s.p.
(H789)

In This Last Caress
solo,pno (E flat maj) ASHDOWN
(H790)

Pallido Il Sole
A solo,vla,cont BROEKMANS 1009 s.p.
(H791)

HASSE, JOHANN FRIEDRICH (1902-   )
Acht Ringelnatz-Capricien *CC8L
Bar solo,pno SIRIUS s.p. (H792)

Das Gesprach Mit Nicodemus *sac
med solo,fl,clar,5strings voc sc
SIRIUS s.p., ipa   (H793)

HASSELBACHER'S SCENA see Williamson,
Malcolm

HASSIDIC TUNES see Stutschevsky,
Joachim

HAST DU VON DEN FISCHERKINDERN see
Pfitzner, Hans

HASTE THEE, LORD GOD, HASTE TO SAVE ME
see Schutz, Heinrich, Eile, Mich,
Gott, Zu Erretten

HASTE YE FEATHERED SONGSTERS see Elgar,
Edward

HASTEN, O LORD, TO REDEEM ME see
Schutz, Heinrich

HAT GESAGT see Strauss, Richard

HAT MAN NICHT AUCH GOLD BEINEBEN see
Beethoven, Ludwig van

HATCH
Behold! What Manner Of Love
high solo,pno SHAWNEE IA5046 $1.00
(H794)

Secret Room, The
med-high solo,pno SHAWNEE IA5043
$.85   (H795)

HATCH, OWEN A.
Child Jesus *sac
low solo,pno (E flat maj) SCHIRM.G
$.60   (H796)

HATFIELD BELLS see Martin, Easthope

HATHCOCK
I Present You To Jesus *sac
solo,pno LILLENAS SM-615: RN $1.00
(H797)

HATIKVA see Ben-Haim, Paul

HATIKVAH
"Song Of Hope" [Heb/Eng] med solo,pno
MARKS $1.50   (H798)

HATIKVOH *Jew
solo,pno ASHLEY $.95   (H799)
solo,pno KAMMEN 3 $1.00 (H800)

HATO see Kumaki, Mamoru

HATS OFF TO THE STOKER see Arundale,
Claude

HATSOADIM BE'ROSH *CCU
solo,pno OR-TAV $3.50   (H801)

HATT ICH EINMAL see Kilpinen, Yrio, Kun
Ma Kerran

HATTE EINEN KNABEN see Kurzbach, Paul

HATTEY, P.
Seven Poems Of Robert Graves *CC7U
solo,pno BUDAPEST $3.50 (H802)

HATTON, JOHN LIPTROT (1809-1886)
Enchantress, The
low solo,pno (A maj) ASHDOWN (H803)
high solo,pno (B flat maj) ASHDOWN
(H804)
To Anthea
low solo,pno (E flat maj) CRAMER
(H805)

high solo,pno (F maj) CRAMER (H806)

HATTORI, T.
Home Song Album *CCU
solo,pno ONGAKU s.p.   (H807)

HATZE, JOSIP (1879-1959)
Selected Songs *CCU
[Slav] solo,pno CROATICA s.p.
(H808)

HATZVI ISRAEL see Orgad, Ben-Zion

HAUBENSTOCK-RAMATI, ROMAN (1919-   )
Mobile For Shakespeare
S/Mez solo,pno,cel,vibra,3perc sc
UNIVER. 13421 $5.25   (H809)

HAUBIEL, CHARLES (1892-   )
Cosmic Christ, The
high solo,pno SEESAW $3.00 (H810)
low solo,pno SEESAW $3.00 (H811)

Fog
high solo,pno SEESAW $1.50 (H812)
low solo,pno SEESAW $1.50 (H813)

Kiss, The
high solo,pno SEESAW $1.00 (H814)
low solo,pno SEESAW $1.00 (H815)

Love Hath Ever Wrought
high solo,pno SEESAW $1.00 (H816)
low solo,pno SEESAW $1.00 (H817)

Madonna
high solo,pno SEESAW $1.00 (H818)
low solo,pno SEESAW $1.00 (H819)

Mother Goose Songs *CCU
high solo,pno SEESAW $7.00 (H820)

O Love Me Not
high solo,pno SEESAW $1.00 (H821)
low solo,pno SEESAW $1.00 (H822)

Sea Gulls
high solo,pno SEESAW $1.50 (H823)
low solo,pno SEESAW $1.50 (H824)

Sea Wind
high solo,pno SEESAW $1.50 (H825)
low solo,pno SEESAW $1.50 (H826)

Terry, My Son
med solo,pno SEESAW $1.00 (H827)
low solo,pno SEESAW $1.00 (H828)

HAUBIEL, CHARLES (cont'd.)

Three Love Songs *CC3U
  high solo,pno SEESAW $4.00   (H829)

Three Nature Songs *CC3U
  high solo,pno SEESAW $4.00   (H830)

Three Philosphical Songs *CC3U
  high solo,pno SEESAW $5.00   (H831)

To You
  high solo/med solo/low solo,pno
  SEESAW $1.50   (H832)

Wedding Ring, The
  high solo,pno SEESAW $1.00   (H833)
  low solo,pno SEESAW $1.00   (H834)

HAUER, JOSEF MATTHIAS (1883-1959)
Holderlin-Lieder, Band I: Op.6 And
  Op.12 *CCU
  med solo,pno UNIVER. 9443 s.p.
                                    (H835)
Holderlin-Lieder, Band II: Op.23
  *CCU
  Bar solo,pno UNIVER. 9444 $3.75
                                    (H836)
Holderlin-Lieder, Band III: Op.32
  *CCU
  Bar solo,pno UNIVER. 9445 $4.25
                                    (H837)
Holderlin-Lieder, Band IV: Op.40
  *CCU
  Bar solo,pno UNIVER. 9446 $4.25
                                    (H838)

HAUFRECHT, HERBERT (1909-   )
Clock Shop, The *CC8L
  med solo,pno BROUDE BR. $2.50
                                    (H839)
Folksongs From The Catskills *CCU,
  folk,US
  med solo,pno AM.COMP.AL. $9.90
                                    (H840)
Go, Ploughman, Plough!
  low solo,pno AM.COMP.AL. $1.10
                                    (H841)
  high solo,pno AM.COMP.AL. $1.10
                                    (H842)
Let's Play Maccabees
  med solo,ob,clar,harp,perc
  AM.COMP.AL. sc $9.25, ipa, voc sc
  $3.57   (H843)
Life
  high solo,pno AM.COMP.AL. $1.10
                                    (H844)
  low solo,pno AM.COMP.AL. $1.10
                                    (H845)
O Li'l Lamb!
  med solo,pno AM.COMP.AL. $1.10
                                    (H846)
Old Woman, The
  med solo,pno AM.COMP.AL. $.55
                                    (H847)
Petticoat Lane *folk
  med solo,pno AM.COMP.AL. $2.75
                                    (H848)
  med solo,pno sc AM.COMP.AL. $2.75
                                    (H849)
Strange Lullaby
  med solo,pno AM.COMP.AL. $2.20
                                    (H850)
Wild Americay
  med solo,pno AM.COMP.AL. $1.10
                                    (H851)

HAUGE, ALBERT M.
I Blow My Bugle
  Bar solo,pno (B flat maj) WILLIS
  $.60   (H852)

HAUGER, KRISTIAN
Alt For Norge
  see Barnefrontens Viser

Barnefronten
  see Barnefrontens Viser

Barnefrontens Viser
  solo,pno MUSIKK s.p.
    contains: Alt For Norge;
    Barnefronten; Da Prisen Kom;
    Prinsebarna; Speidersang;
    Velkommen   (H853)

Da Prisen Kom
  see Barnefrontens Viser

Den Gylne Kro
  solo,pno MUSIKK s.p.   (H854)

Hans Og Grete
  solo,pno MUSIKK s.p.   (H855)

Prinsebarna
  see Barnefrontens Viser

Speidersang
  see Barnefrontens Viser

Velkommen
  see Barnefrontens Viser

HAUGHTINESS see Borodin, Alexander
Porfirievitch

HAUGTUSSA see Grieg, Edvard Hagerup

HAUNTED see Guarnieri, Camargo Mozart,
Quando Embalada

HAUNTED OBJECTS (IN MEMORIUM STEFAN
WOLPE) see Rovics, Howard

HAUPSTADT see Injado

HAUPT, WALTER
Monolog Einer Alternden Frau
  A solo,fl,2perc study sc ORLANDO
  s.p.   (H856)

HAUS IN BONN see Newlin, Dika

HAUS- UND TROSTBUCH TEIL I see Pepping,
Ernst

HAUS- UND TROSTBUCH TEIL II see
Pepping, Ernst

HAUS- UND TROSTBUCH TEIL III see
Pepping, Ernst

HAUS- UND TROSTBUCH TEIL IV see
Pepping, Ernst

HAUS- UND TROSTBUCH TEIL I-IV see
Pepping, Ernst

HAUSEGGER, SIEGMUND VON (1872-1948)
Drei Gesange Nach Mittelhochdeutschen
  Dichtungen *CC3U
  med female solo,vla,pno RIES s.p.
                                    (H857)

HAUSSERMANN, R.
Five Singing Miniatures *CC5U
  high solo/med solo,pno SEESAW $3.00
                                    (H858)
On The River
  high solo/med solo,pno SEESAW $4.00
                                    (H859)
Three Moods
  high solo/med solo,pno SEESAW $3.00
                                    (H860)

HAUSSPRUCH see Taubert, Karl Heinz

HAUT-DAUPHINE ET BAS-DAUPHINE *Fr
(Canteloube, J.) solo,acap DURAND
  s.p. see also Anthologie Des Chants
  Populaires Francais Tome III (H861)

HAUTALAULU see Maasalo, Armas

HAV TACK see Nordqvist, Gustaf

HAV TRO PA GUD
  see Andliga Sanger, Heft 2

HAVA NASHIRA *CCU
  solo,pno OR-TAV $3.50   (H862)

HAVASOK ES RIVIERA see Frid, Geza

HAVE A GOOD DAY see Terrell, Beverly

HAVE A LITTLE TALK WITH HIM see
Derricks, Cleavant

HAVE FAITH IN GOD see Thompson, Gordon
V.

HAVE FUN SINGING *CC100U
(Lindsay, Charles, Jr.) solo,pno
  MUSIC 040045 $3.95   (H863)

HAVE GOSPEL, MUST TRAVEL see Good,
Dwayne

HAVE MERCY, LORD see Handel, George
Frideric

HAVE THESE FOR YOURS see Edmunds, John

HAVE THINE OWN WAY, LORD *sac,gospel
  solo,pno ABER.GRP. $1.50   (H864)

HAVE YOU ANY RIVERS *sac,gospel
  solo,pno ABER.GRP. $1.50   (H865)

HAVE YOU HAD A GETHSEMANE see Gaither

HAVE YOU HEARD...GOD LOVES YOU see
Oldham, Doug

HAVE YOU MET GOD'S BLESSED SON? see
Bower, W.

HAVE YOU SEEN BUT A BRIGHT LILY GROW?
see Russell, W.

HAVE YOU SEEN BUT A WHITE LILY see
Southam

HAVE YOU SEEN BUT A WHITE LILY GROW?
(Grew, Syanes) solo,pno (E maj)
  ROBERTON 2756 s.p.   (H866)

HAVE YOU SEEN BUT A WHITE LILY GROW?
see Heseltine, Philip

HAVE YOU SEEN BUT A WHYTE LILIE GROW
see Dolmetsch, Arnold

HAVE YOU SEEN BUT A WHYTE LILLIE GROW
  *Eng
  high solo,pno (F maj) ALLANS s.p.
                                    (H867)
(Dolmetsch) med solo,pno (F maj)
  SCHIRM.G $.50   (H868)

HAVE YOU SEENE BUT A WHYTE LILLIE GROW?
see Anonymous

HAVE YOU TRIED THE LORD TODAY? see Ott,
J.

HAVELKA, SVATOPLUK (1925-   )
Heptameron
  [Ger/Czech] narrator&SATBar soli,
  orch PANTON 529 s.p.   (H869)

HAVEN OF REST FAVORITES *sac,CCU,
  gospel
  solo,pno WORD 20031 $1.95   (H870)

HAVEN OF TENDERNESS see Gordon, W.

HAVETS VISA see Nystroem, Gosta

HAVIRSKA see Martinu, Bohuslav

HAVSKUNGENS DOTTER see Sonninen, Ahti,
Merenkuninkaan Tytar

HAWAIIANS SING, THE *sac,CC10UL
(Skillings, Otis) solo,pno LILLENAS
  MB-321 $2.50   (H871)

HAWKINS
God-Given Love *sac
  solo,pno LILLENAS SM-450: RN $1.00
                                    (H872)
I've Discovered The Way Of Gladness
  *sac
  solo,pno LILLENAS SM-465: RN $1.00
                                    (H873)
Let Thy Mantle Fall On Me *sac
  solo,pno LILLENAS SM-445: RN $1.00
                                    (H874)

HAWKINS, J.
Three Cavatinas *CC3U
  S solo,cel,vibra,vln,vcl BERANDOL
  BER 1118 $5.00   (H875)

HAWLEY, CHARLES BEACH (1858-1915)
Daisies
  low solo,pno (E flat maj) SCHIRM.G
  $.60   (H876)

HAWTHORNE, ALICE
Whispering Hope
  med solo,pno BELWIN $1.25   (H877)
  high solo,pno (E flat maj) SCHIRM.G
  $.85   (H878)
  med-low solo,pno (C maj) SCHIRM.G
  $.85   (H879)
  high solo&low solo,pno (E flat maj)
  FISCHER,C S 5936   (H880)
  2 soli,pno (C maj) CENTURY 2361
                                    (H881)
  solo,pno ASHLEY $.95   (H882)
  solo,pno (E flat maj) ASHDOWN
                                    (H883)
  high solo&low solo,pno ASHDOWN s.p.
                                    (H884)
  solo,pno ALLANS s.p.   (H885)

HAXA see Schierbeck, Poul

HAY, G.
Three Moon Songs *CC3U
  solo,pno LEONARD-ENG   (H886)

HAYAKAWA, MASAAKI
Darkness
  see Four Little Poems By Children
  With Progressive Muscular
  Dystrophy

Four Little Poems By Children With
  Progressive Muscular Dystrophy
  [Jap/Eng] S/Mez solo,4sax,perc,harp
  JAPAN 7511 s.p.
    contains: Darkness; I Will Give
    You Dreams; Someday, Somewhere;
    Sunset   (H887)

I Will Give You Dreams
  see Four Little Poems By Children
  With Progressive Muscular
  Dystrophy

Someday, Somewhere
  see Four Little Poems By Children
  With Progressive Muscular
  Dystrophy

Sunset
  see Four Little Poems By Children
  With Progressive Muscular
  Dystrophy

HAYAMA, M
Trois Pieces Pour Soprano Et Piano
  *CC3U
  S solo,pno ONGAKU s.p.   (H888)

HAYAREACH HATSAHOV see Gassner, Moshe

HAYASHI, AZUSA (1936-   )
East Pagoda Of The Temple Yakushiji,
The *see Yakushiji Azuma-To

Yakushiji Azuma-To *song cycle
"East Pagoda Of The Temple
Yakushiji, The" [Jap] Mez solo,
pno JAPAN 7303 s.p.   (H889)

HAYASHI, H.
Sky
S solo,fl ONGAKU s.p.   (H890)

HAYDN, (FRANZ) JOSEPH (1732-1809)
Air (from Die Jahreszeiten)
see LA MUSIQUE, SEPTIEME CAHIER

Air De Simon (from Die Jahreszeiten)
Bar solo,orch HENN s.p.   (H891)

Air D'Uriel (from Die Schopfung)
T solo,orch HENN s.p.   (H892)

An Den Vetter
see Three-Part Songs

Aria Of Errisena
see Haydn, (Franz) Joseph, Scene Of
Berenice

Ariadne Auf Naxos *see Arianna A
Naxos

Arianna A Naxos *cant
(Flothius) [It] S solo,pno UNIVER.
HMP 197 $5.25   (H893)
(Frank, E.) Mez solo,2fl,2ob,2clar,
2bsn,2horn,2trp,timp,strings
BREITKOPF-L rental   (H894)
(Link) "Ariadne Auf Naxos" solo,
orch RIES s.p.   (H895)

Arias From The Operas, Vol. 1 *CCU
[It/Hung] S/Mez solo,pno BUDAPEST
2552 $3.75   (H896)

Arias From The Operas, Vol. 2 *CCU
[It/Hung] T solo,pno BUDAPEST 3039
$3.75   (H897)

Arias From The Operas, Vol. 3 *CCU
[It] Bar/B solo,pno BUDAPEST 3040
$3.75   (H898)

Auf Die Frauen
see Three-Part Songs

Auf Starkem Fittiche (from Die
Schopfung)
[Ger/Eng/Fr] S solo,2fl,2clar,2bsn,
2horn,strings EB 118 s.p., ipr
contains also: Mit Wurd' Und
Hoheit Angetan (T solo,2fl,2ob,
2bsn,2horn,2trp,timp,strings);
Nun Beut Die Flur (S solo,2fl,
clar,bsn,2horn,strings) (H899)

Betrachtung Des Todes
see Three-Part Songs

Bind' Auf Dein Haar
"My Mother Bids Me Bind" low solo,
pno (G maj) CRAMER   (H900)
"My Mother Bids Me Bind" high solo,
pno (A maj) CRAMER   (H901)
"My Mother Bids Me Bind My Hair"
[Ger/Eng] med solo,pno
SCHIRM.G $.85   (H902)
"My Mother Bids Me Bind My Hair"
med solo,pno ALLANS s.p.   (H903)

Chant D'Amour *see Liebeslied

Daphnens Einziger Fehler
see Three-Part Songs

Dearest Maiden, Come To Me
[Eng] med solo,pno HINRICHSEN
H1351B $1.25   (H904)

Die Drei- Und Vierstimmigen Gesange
*CC11U,concerto
(Paumgartner, Bernhard) SSB/SATB
soli,pno (med) BAREN. 901 $11.25
(H905)

Die Seejungfer
"Mermaids Song, The" solo,pno
CRAMER   (H906)

Drei Lieder *CC3U
(Scheit, K.) med solo,gtr DOBLINGER
GKM 22 $3.25   (H907)

Four-Part Songs *CC9U
[Ger] SATB soli,pno PETERS 1354
$5.50   (H908)

Guarda Qui Che Lo Vedrai
(Landon, R.) [It] ST soli,pno
DOBLINGER DM 35 $5.25 contains
also: Saper Vorrei Se M'ami
(H909)

HAYDN, (FRANZ) JOSEPH (cont'd.)
Hier Steht Der Wandrer Nun (from Die
Jahreszeiten)
[Ger/Eng/Fr] T solo,fl,2ob,bsn,
2horn,strings voc sc EB 116 s.p.
contains also: Schon Eilet Froh
Der Ackersmann (B solo,fl,2ob,
2bsn,2horn,strings)   (H910)

How Marvelous Is The Power Of God
(Davis) high solo,pno (B flat maj)
GALAXY 1.1914.7 $1.00   (H911)

I All Sin Glans Nu Himlen Blanker
*sac
B solo,pno GEHRMANS s.p.   (H912)

Idylle
Mez/Bar solo,pno/inst DURAND s.p.
(H913)
solo,pno DURAND 129 s.p.   (H914)

Joesph Haydn Werke, Reihe XXXI:
Kanons *CCU
solo,pno cloth HENLE s.p.   (H915)

Joseph Haydn Werke, Reihe XXIX, Band
1: Lieder Fur Eine Singstimme
*CCU
solo,pno cloth HENLE s.p.   (H916)

Joseph Haydn Werke, Reihe XXX:
Mehrstimmige Gesange *CCU
soli,pno cloth HENLE s.p.   (H917)

Joseph Haydn Werke, Reihe XXXII, Band
1: Volksliedbearbeitungen -
Schottische Lieder No. 1-100
*CCU
solo,pno cloth HENLE s.p.   (H918)

Liebeslied
"Chant D'Amour" solo,pno DURAND 130
s.p.   (H919)
"Chant D'amour" solo,pno/inst
DURAND s.p.   (H920)

Lieder *CCU
(Leuchter) [Span] solo,pno RICORDI-
ARG BA 11805 s.p. complete
collection in original and
Spanish texts   (H921)

Mermaids Song, The *see Die
Seejungfer

Miseri Noi, Misera Patria *cant
(Landon, R.) S solo,2fl,2ob,2bsn,
2horn,strings sc DOBLINGER DM 17
s.p., ipa, voc sc DOBLINGER
DM 17A $4.25   (H922)

Mit Wurd' Und Hoheit Angetan (from
Die Schopfung)
see Haydn, (Franz) Joseph, Auf
Starkem Fittiche
T solo,2fl,2ob,2bsn,2horn,2trp,
timp,strings BREITKOPF-L rental
(H923)

My Mother Bids Me Bind *see Bind'
Auf Dein Haar

My Mother Bids Me Bind My Hair *see
Bind' Auf Dein Haar

Nun Beut Die Flur (from Die
Schopfung) sac
see Haydn, (Franz) Joseph, Auf
Starkem Fittiche
Mez solo,pno (G maj) LIENAU HOS 84
s.p.   (H924)
S solo,pno (B flat maj) LIENAU
HOS 83 s.p.   (H925)

Nun Scheint In Vollem Glanze (from
Die Schopfung)
Bar/B solo,2fl,2ob,3bsn,2horn,2trp,
timp,strings BREITKOPF-L rental
(H926)

On Mighty Pens (from Creation) sac
S solo,pno NOVELLO 17.0146.00 s.p.
(H927)

Pieta Di Me
(Landon, R.) SST soli,English horn,
bsn,2horn,strings sc DOBLINGER
DM 250 s.p., ipa, voc sc
DOBLINGER DM 250A s.p.   (H928)

Sag' An, Wird Sich Dein Lieben
[Ger/It] SS soli,pno BREITKOPF-W
DLV 4019 s.p.   (H929)

Sailors Song
solo,pno CRAMER   (H930)

Saper Vorrei Se M'ami
see Haydn, (Franz) Joseph, Guarda
Qui Che Lo Vedrai

Scena Di Berenice *scena
(Landon, R.) [It] S solo,2fl,2ob,
2clar,2bsn,2horn,strings sc
DOBLINGER DM 129 s.p., ipa, voc
sc DOBLINGER DM 129A $4.75, study
sc DOBLINGER STP 154 s.p.   (H931)

HAYDN, (FRANZ) JOSEPH (cont'd.)
Scene Of Berenice
[It/Ger] S solo,2fl,2ob,2bsn,2horn,
strings sc,voc sc MUSIKWISS.
rental contains also: Aria Of
Errisena   (H932)

Schon Eilet Froh Der Ackersmann (from
Die Jahreszeiten)
see Haydn, (Franz) Joseph, Hier
Steht Der Wandrer Nun
B solo,fl,2ob,2bsn,2horn,strings
BREITKOPF-L rental   (H933)

She Never Told Her Love
solo,pno CRAMER   (H934)
med solo,pno (A flat maj) SCHIRM.G
$.85   (H935)
(Howe) A solo,pno PAXTON P40495
s.p.   (H936)

Son Pietosa, Son Bonina (from La
Circe)
(Landon, R.) S solo,fl,2ob,2bsn,
2horn,strings sc DOBLINGER DM 19
s.p., ipa, voc sc DOBLINGER
DM 19A $3.25, study sc DOBLINGER
STP. 162 s.p.   (H937)

Spirit's Song, The
low solo,pno (D min) CRAMER (H938)
high solo,pno (F min) CRAMER (H939)
low solo,pno (D min) ASHDOWN (H940)
high solo,pno (F min) ASHDOWN
(H941)

Stabat Mater *sac,Mass
SATB soli,2ob,strings BREITKOPF-L
rental   (H942)

Thirty-Five Canzonettas And Songs
*CC35U
(Landshoff) [Eng/Ger] high solo,pno
PETERS 1351A $4.50   (H943)

Three-Part Songs
(Weismann) [Ger] PETERS 4936 $6.50
contains: An Den Vetter (SAT
soli,pno); Auf Die Frauen (TTB
soli,pno); Betrachtung Des
Todes (STB soli,pno); Daphnens
Einziger Fehler (TTB soli,pno)
(H944)

Twelve Canzonets *CC12U
solo,pno GALLIARD 2.8840.7 $3.50
(H945)

Twenty-Four Canons *sac,CC24U,canon
2-8 soli,pno, English edition
PETERS 6999 $.60; 2-8 soli,pno,
German edition PETERS 2965A $4.75
second part entitled: The Ten
Commandments   (H946)

With Verdure Clad (from Creation) sac
S solo,pno NOVELLO 17.0224.06 s.p.
(H947)
solo,pno CRAMER   (H948)
S solo,pno (B flat maj) SCHIRM.G
$.85   (H949)

HAYDN, (JOHANN) MICHAEL (1737-1806)
Arien *CCU
solo,pno UNIVER. HMP 192 $6.00
(H950)

Ave Regina *sac
[Lat] B solo,vla&strings/org PETERS
GM30 rental, ipa   (H951)
(Munster) B solo,vla,strings
EULENBURG GM 30 s.p., ipa (H952)

Cantilena Pro Adventu
(Landon) "Ein' Magd, Ein' Dienerin"
S solo,pno UNIVER. HMP 37 $3.75
(H953)

Drei Arien *CC3U
[It] Bar solo,pno UNIVER. HMP 83
$5.25   (H954)

Ein' Magd, Ein' Dienerin *see
Cantilena Pro Adventu

Gott Ich Falle Dir Zu Fussen *sac
S solo,org,vln sc BOHM s.p. (H955)

Lauft, Ihr Hirten, Allzugleich *sac,
cant
"Run, Ye Shepherds, To The Light" S
solo,mix cor,2vln,cont sc GERIG
AV 139 s.p., ipa   (H956)

Libera
solo,pno sc UNIVER. HMP211 $5.25
(H957)

Run, Ye Shepherds, To The Light *see
Lauft, Ihr Hirten, Allzugleich

Vier Arien *CC4U
[It] T solo,pno UNIVER. HMP 82
$7.25   (H958)

Vierzehn Arien, Band I *CCU
[It] S solo,pno UNIVER. HMP 81A
$7.75   (H959)

HAYDN, (JOHANN) MICHAEL (cont'd.)

Vierzehn Arien, Band II *CCU
[It] S solo,pno UNIVER. HMP 81B
$7.75   (H960)

Wir Bitten Dich Unendlich Wesen
(Kirchberger, A.) SA soli,strings,
cont sc EULENBURG GM 207 s.p.,
ipa   (H961)

HAYFORD
Come On Down (composed with Stone)
*sac
solo,pno BENSON S5300-R $1.25
    (H962)
solo,pno BENSON S5302-S $1.25
    (H963)

Nobody Cared *sac
solo,pno LILLENAS SM-485: RN $1.00
    (H964)

HAYLOFT HOEDOWN *CC19U
med solo,pno BMI $.60   (H965)

HAYNES, WALTER BATTISON (1859-1900)
Ould Plaid Shawl, The
low solo,pno NOVELLO 17.0150.09
s.p.   (H966)
high solo,pno NOVELLO 17.0148.07
s.p.   (H967)
med solo,pno NOVELLO 17.0149.05
s.p.   (H968)

HAZELHURST, CECIL (1880-   )
Columbines
solo,pno CRAMER   (H969)

O Leave Your Sheep *see Quittez
Pasteurs

Quittez Pasteurs
"O Leave Your Sheep" med solo,pno
(F maj) ASHDOWN $1.50 (H970)
"O Leave Your Sheep" high solo,pno
(G maj) ASHDOWN $1.50 (H971)
"O Leave Your Sheep" low solo,pno
(E flat maj) ASHDOWN $1.50 (H972)
"O Leave Your Sheep" high solo&low
solo,pno ASHDOWN $1.75 (H973)

Wood Fires
solo,pno CRAMER   (H974)

HAZON, ROBERTO
Cielo Stellato *CC5U,Psalm
med solo,pno,4perc SONZOGNO rental
    (H975)

HAZZARD, PETER
Massage
SAB soli,fl,clar,trp,sax,trom,3perc
sc SEESAW $4.00   (H976)

Praise Book, A
SATB soli,2trp,tuba,3perc sc SEESAW
$4.00   (H977)

HE AIN'T COMING HERE TO DIE NO MORE see
Singer, W.

HE BOUGHT MY SOUL AT CALVARY *sac,
gospel
solo,pno ABER.GRP. $1.50 (H978)

HE CAME BACK see Keller, Joan

HE CAME, HE'LL COME AGAIN see Eleiott,
Max

HE COMFORTS ME see Matthews

HE DID IT ALL FOR ME see Allen

HE DIED FOR US see Owens

HE DIED ON THE CROSS see Green

HE GIVETH ME STRENGTH see Alcorn,
Jeannie Vee

HE GIVETH MORE GRACE see Mitchell

HE HATH FILLED THE HUNGRY see Bach,
Johann Sebastian

HE HATH REGARDED see Bach, Johann
Sebastian

HE IS AN ENGLISHMAN see Sullivan, Sir
Arthur Seymour

HE IS GOD see Zilch, Margot

HE IS MINE AND I AM HIS see Speer, G.T.

HE IS NEAR see Milham, Richard

HE IS THE ONE see Roe, Gloria [Ann]

HE IS THE WAY, HE IS THE TRUTH, HE IS
THE LIFE see Skillings, Otis

HE IS THERE see Cruickshank, R.

HE JUST LOVED ME MORE AND MORE see
Croft, Colbert

HE KEPT ON LOVING ME see Horne, Roger

HE KNOWS JUST HOW MUCH YOU CAN BEAR
*sac,gospel
solo,pno ABER.GRP. $1.50   (H979)

HE KNOWS JUST WHAT I NEED see Lister,
Mosie

HE LIVES see Buxtehude, Dietrich

HE LOVES THE PASSER-BY see Davis

HE LOVES YOU see Short

HE MADE THE BLIND TO SEE see Hallett,
John C.

HE MET ME THERE see Nelson

HE NEVER WILL LEAVE ME *sac,gospel
solo,pno ABER.GRP. $1.50 (H980)

HE OF ALL TRUE MEN THE NOBLEST see
Schumann, Robert (Alexander), Er,
Der Herrlichste Von Allen

HE PASSED BY see Hageman, Richard, Il
Passa

HE PILOTS MY SHIP see Hinson, D.

HE PROMISED ME AT PARTING see
Beethoven, Ludwig van

HE RANSOMED ME *sac,gospel
solo,pno ABER.GRP. $1.50 (H981)

HE RESTORETH MY SOUL see Rambo

HE SAID HE WOULD DELIVER ME see Redd,
G.C.

HE SHALL BE LIKE A TREE see Bowling

HE SHALL FEED HIS FLOCK see Handel,
George Frideric

HE SHALL FEED HIS FLOCK see Harker, F.
Flaxington

HE SHALL GIVE HIS ANGELS CHARGE see
Scott, John Prindle

HE SMILED ON ME see O'Hara, Geoffrey

HE THAT DWELLETH IN THE SECRET PLACE
see Humphreys, Don

HE THAT LOVES A ROSY CHEEK see Benson,
Lionel S.

HE THAT LOVES A ROSY CHEEK see Norman,
Lorna

HE THAT OVERCOMES see Floria, Cam

HE TOUCHED ME see Gaither

HE TOUCHED ME AND OTHER SONGS see
Gaither, William J. (Bill)

HE TURNED THE WATER INTO WINE see
Stearman

HE WALKED THAT LONESOME ROAD see
Peterson, John W.

HE WAS ALONE see Paxson, Theodore

HE WAS DESPISED AND REJECTED see
Handel, George Frideric

HE WAS TALKING ABOUT ME see Bagwell,
Wendy

HE WAS THERE *sac,gospel
solo,pno ABER.GRP. $1.50   (H982)

HE WASHED MY EYES WITH TEARS see
Stanphill, Ira F.

HE WHO LOVES AND RUNS AWAY see Friml,
Rudolf

HE WILL NEVER LET ME DOWN see
Wetherington

HE WILL NOT FAIL see Wurm, Louise

HE WILL PILOT ME see Bailey

HE WILL SEND THE BLESSINGS IF YOU PRAY
see Bartlett, Gene

HE WON'T LET YOU DOWN see Matthews

HEAD, H.
Song Of The North Wind
solo,pno CRAMER   (H983)

HEAD, MICHAEL (DEWAR) (1900-   )
Acquaint Thyself With Him
(Koch) high solo,pno (G maj) BOOSEY
$1.50   (H984)
(Koch) low solo,pno (E flat maj)

HEAD, MICHAEL (DEWAR) (cont'd.)

BOOSEY $1.50   (H985)

Ave Maria
high solo,pno (C min) BOOSEY $1.50
    (H986)
low solo,pno (A min) BOOSEY $1.50
    (H987)

Behold I Send An Angel *sac
(Koch) solo,pno (G maj) BOOSEY
$1.50   (H988)

Bird-Song
solo,pno,opt fl (F maj) BOOSEY
$2.00   (H989)

Blackbird Singing
high solo,pno (A flat maj) BOOSEY
$1.75   (H990)
low solo,pno (E maj) BOOSEY $1.75
    (H991)

Dear Delight
solo,pno (A flat maj) BOOSEY $1.50
    (H992)

Dog's Life
solo,pno (D min) BOOSEY $1.50
    (H993)

Dreaming Lake
solo,pno (E maj) BOOSEY $1.50
    (H994)

Elizabeth's Song
solo,pno (G maj) BOOSEY $1.50
    (H995)

Estuary
solo,pno (E flat maj) BOOSEY
$1.50   (H996)

Fairy Taylor
solo,pno (G maj) BOOSEY $1.75
    (H997)

Foxgloves
high solo,pno (C maj) BOOSEY $1.75
    (H998)
low solo,pno (A flat maj) BOOSEY
$1.75   (H999)

Funny Fellow
solo,pno (F maj) BOOSEY $1.50
    (H1000)

Gaiete And Orior
solo,pno (F min) BOOSEY $1.50
    (H1001)

Green Cornfield
high solo,pno (F maj) BOOSEY $1.50
    (H1002)
low solo,pno (E flat maj) BOOSEY
$1.50   (H1003)

Green Rain
solo,pno (D flat maj) BOOSEY $1.50
    (H1004)

Had I A Golden Pound
solo,pno (C maj) BOOSEY $1.50
    (H1005)

Homecoming Of The Sheep
solo,pno (C sharp min) BOOSEY $1.50
    (H1006)

How Sweet The Moonlight Sleeps
solo,pno (D flat maj) BOOSEY $1.50
    (H1007)

Limehouse Reach
solo,pno (G maj) BOOSEY $1.75
    (H1008)

Little Road To Bethlehem *sac,Xmas
high solo,pno (A flat maj) HARRIS
$1.15   (H1009)
low solo,pno (F maj) HARRIS $1.15
    (H1010)
low solo,pno (F maj) BOOSEY $1.50
    (H1011)
high solo,pno (A flat maj) BOOSEY
$1.50   (H1012)

Lone Dog
solo,pno (C min) BOOSEY $1.50
    (H1013)

Lord's Prayer
solo,pno (E flat maj) BOOSEY $1.75
    (H1014)

Love's Lament
solo,pno (F min) BOOSEY $1.50
    (H1015)

Ludlow Town
solo,pno (G maj) BOOSEY $1.50
    (H1016)

Matron Cat's Song
solo,pno (A min) BOOSEY $1.50
    (H1017)

O Gloriosa Domina *sac
solo,pno (G maj) BOOSEY $1.50
    (H1018)

O Money
low solo,pno (G min) BOOSEY $1.75
    (H1019)
high solo,pno (B min) BOOSEY $1.75
    (H1020)

O To Be In England
solo,pno (F maj) BOOSEY $1.50
    (H1021)

Oh For A March Wind
solo,pno (A maj) BOOSEY $1.50
    (H1022)

On The Wings Of The Wind
solo,pno (E flat maj) BOOSEY $1.50
    (H1023)

HEAD, MICHAEL (DEWAR) (cont'd.)

Over The Rim Of The Moon *song cycle
high solo/low solo,pno BOOSEY $5.00
(H1024)
Piper
low solo,pno,opt fl (D min) BOOSEY
$2.00 (H1025)
high solo,pno,opt fl (F min) BOOSEY
$2.00 (H1026)
Plague Of Love
low solo,pno (C maj) BOOSEY $1.50
(H1027)
high solo,pno (E maj) BOOSEY $1.50
(H1028)
Robin's Carol
solo,pno (A flat maj) BOOSEY $1.50
(H1029)
Sancta Et Immaculata Virginitas
solo,pno (E maj) BOOSEY $1.50
(H1030)
Ships Of Arcady
low solo,pno (B flat maj) BOOSEY
$1.75 (H1031)
high solo,pno (D maj) BOOSEY $1.75
(H1032)
Singer
solo,acap (F min) BOOSEY $1.50
(H1033)
Slumber Song Of The Madonna
low solo,pno (B flat maj) BOOSEY
$1.50 (H1034)
high solo,pno (C maj) BOOSEY $1.50
(H1035)
Small Christmas Tree
solo,pno (A flat maj) BOOSEY $1.50
(H1036)
Star Candles
solo,pno (D min) BOOSEY $1.50
(H1037)
Sweet Chance That Led My Steps
low solo,pno (D maj) BOOSEY $1.50
(H1038)
high solo,pno (F maj) BOOSEY $1.50
(H1039)
Sweethearts And Wives
solo,pno (G maj) BOOSEY $1.50
(H1040)
There's Many Will Love A Maid
low solo,pno (D maj) BOOSEY $1.50
(H1041)
high solo,pno (G maj) BOOSEY $1.50
(H1042)
Three Mummers
solo,pno (A flat maj) BOOSEY $1.50
(H1043)
Thus Spake Jesus
low solo,pno (G min) BOOSEY $1.50
(H1044)
high solo,pno (B min) BOOSEY $1.50
(H1045)
Twins
solo,pno (C maj) BOOSEY $1.50
(H1046)
Vagabond Song
solo,pno (C sharp min) BOOSEY $1.50
(H1047)
What Christmas Means To Me
low solo,pno (F maj) BOOSEY $1.50
(H1048)
high solo,pno (A flat maj) BOOSEY
$1.50 (H1049)
When I Think Upon The Maidens
low solo,pno (D flat maj) BOOSEY
$1.50 (H1050)
high solo,pno (E flat maj) BOOSEY
$1.50 (H1051)
When Sweet Ann Sings
low solo,pno (E flat maj) BOOSEY
$1.50 (H1052)
high solo,pno (F maj) BOOSEY $1.50
(H1053)
Why Have You Stolen My Delight
solo,pno (A flat maj) BOOSEY $1.50
(H1054)
HEALER, THE *sac
solo,pno STAMPS 7254-SN $1.00 (H1055)

HEALER OF BROKEN HEARTS see Stiffler,
Georgia

HEALTH AND JOY BE WITH YOU
(Roberton, Hugh S.) solo,pno (E flat
maj) ROBERTON 2777 s.p. (H1056)

HEALTH AND JOY BE WITH YOU see Lawson,
Malcolm

HEAR! BETHLEHEM
see Six Polish Christmas Carols

HEAR DE LAMBS A-CRYING *spir
(Burleigh, H. T.) med solo,pno BELWIN
$1.50 (H1057)

HEAR DEM BELLS
(McCosh) low solo,pno (G maj) WILLIS
$.50 (H1058)

HEAR ME YE WINDS AND WAVES
(Lehmann, Amelia) low solo,pno (G
min) BOOSEY $1.50 (H1059)
(Lehmann, Amelia) high solo,pno (A

min) BOOSEY $1.50 (H1060)

HEAR MY CRY see Sowerby, Leo

HEAR MY PRAYER see Mendelssohn-
Bartholdy, Felix

HEAR MY PRAYER, O LORD see Clark, Henry
A.

HEAR MY PRAYER, O LORD see Norris,
Harry

HEAR O ISRAEL see Klein, Jonathan

HEAR O ISRAEL see Smolanoff, Michael

HEAR OUR VOICE, O LORD see Helfman,
Max, Sh'ma Koleynu

HEAR THEM CRYIN' see Repp, Ray

HEAR THOU MY PRAYER see Hamblen,
Bernard

HEAR US, OUR FATHER see Boellmann, Leon

HEAR YE, ISRAEL see Mendelssohn-
Bartholdy, Felix, Hore Israel

HEARING see Rorem, Ned

HEART see Berger, Jean

HEART AND MIND, POSSESSIONS, LORD see
Hilty, Everett Jay

HEART BOW'D DOWN see Balfe, Michael
William

HEART IS A REBEL, THE *sac
(Carmichael, Ralph) solo,pno WORD
S-29 (H1061)

HEART OF A BUTTERFLY see Ewing, M.

HEART OF HEAVEN see Weaver, Mary

HEART OF MINE see Day, Maude Craske

HEART OF OAK see Arne, Thomas Augustine

HEART ON THE WALL see Owens, Robert

HEART THAT WARM'D MY GUILELESS BREAST,
THE see Phelps, Ellsworth

HEART THAT'S FREE see Robyn

HEART TO HEART see Gillon, D.

HEART, WE WILL FORGET HIM see Copland,
Aaron

HEART WORSHIPS see Holst, Gustav

HEART'S ASSURANCE, THE see Tippett,
Michael

HEART'S HAVEN see Vaughan Williams,
Ralph

HEART'S SECRET see Rachmaninoff, Sergey
Vassilievitch

HEATH
Somebody Bigger Than You And I *see
Lange

HEATHER ROSE see Schubert, Franz
(Peter), Heidenroslein

HEATHERLAND see Dumayne, Jean

HEATON, LEONARD
Gate Of The Year, The *sac
solo,pno (C min) LESLIE 7028
(H1062)
Infinite, The *sac
solo,pno (E min) LESLIE 7027
(H1063)

HEAVEN see Crouch, Andrae

HEAVEN AND EARTH REJOICE see Banks,
C.O.

HEAVEN CAME DOWN AND GLORY FILLED MY
SOUL see Peterson, John W.

HEAVEN FOR ME see Wolfe, Lanny

HEAVEN HAS ALREADY BEGUN see Lister,
Mosie

HEAVEN HAVEN see Flanagan, William

HEAVEN IS MY HOME *sac
solo,pno STAMPS 7267-SN $1.00 (H1064)

HEAVEN ONLY KNOWS see Croft, Colbert

HEAVEN SEEMS MUCH NEARER see Davis

HEAVEN TO GO TO HEAVEN IN see Jensen,
Gordon

HEAVEN WILL BE MY HOME see Hubbard, H.

HEAVEN WILL SURELY BE WORTH IT ALL
*sac,gospel
solo,pno ABER.GRP. $1.50 (H1065)

HEAVENLY FATHER see Bizet, Georges,
Agnus Dei

HEAVENLY GRASS see Bowles, Paul
Frederic

HEAVENLY LOVE see Ellis

HEAVENLY SONG, THE see Gray, Hamilton

HEAVING OF THE LEAD, THE see Shield,
William

HEAV'N HEAV'N *spir
(Burleigh, H. T.) high solo,pno
BELWIN $1.50 (H1066)
(Burleigh, H. T.) low solo,pno BELWIN
$1.50 (H1067)

HEBET EURE AUGEN AUF GEN HIMMEL see
Rosenmuller, Johann

HEBREW AND YIDDISH FOLK-SONGS *sac/
sec,CC10L
(Bonin, Mary) solo,pno ELKIN
27.2588.06 s.p. Hebrew, Yiddish and
English Texts (H1068)

HEBREW MELODIES *CCU
(Diamond, David) solo,pno PEER $2.50
(H1069)

HEBREW SONGS, VOL. I see Weinberg,
Jacob

HEBREW SONGS, VOL. II see Weinberg,
Jacob

HEBRIDEAN SHANTY
(Roberton, Hugh S.) solo,pno (E flat
maj) ROBERTON 2747 s.p. (H1070)

HEBRIDEAN SONGS, VOL. IV *see Ailean
Duinn; Binne Bheul; By The Kyle Of
Moola; Cool Hill Pastures; Crone's
Creel; Deidre's Farewell;
Embarrassed Maiden; Fionn's
Keening; Iona Boat Song; Land Of
The Little People; Leaping Galley;
Macleod's Galley; Moorland Lilt;
Potato Liftin'; Sea Feast; Seabird,
Flying Hither; Silent Crane; To
Iona; To The Isle Of Skye; Uncanny
Mannikin, The; We Will Go A-Sailing
(H1071)

HECTOR BERLIOZ WORKS see Berlioz,
Hector

HEDAR, JOSEF
Du Som Bland Jasminer
see Medan Natten Gar

Jag Har Gatt Inunder Stjarnor
see Medan Natten Gar

Medan Natten Gar
solo,pno GEHRMANS s.p.
contains: Du Som Bland Jasminer;
Jag Har Gatt Inunder Stjarnor;
Regnet Slar Och Slar Och Slar
Ett Litet Hus (H1072)

Regnet Slar Och Slar Och Slar Ett
Litet Hus
see Medan Natten Gar

HEDENBLAD, IVAR
Tre Sanger *Op.11, CC3U
solo,pno GEHRMANS s.p. (H1073)

HEDGE-ROSES see Schubert, Franz
(Peter), Heidenroslein

HEDGECOCK, WALTER WILLIAM (1864-1932)
Drake's Drum
low solo,pno (C maj) CRAMER (H1074)
high solo,pno (D maj) CRAMER
(H1075)
When Bright Eyes Glance
low solo,pno (B flat maj) CRAMER
(H1076)
high solo,pno (C maj) CRAMER
(H1077)

HEEL MIJN LEVEN see Mulder, Herman

HEERENVEEN see Schouwman, Hans

HEERLIJK OUD HUIS see Tierie, J.F.

HEFFLE CUCKOO FAIR see Shaw, Martin

HEFT OP MIJN CRUYS see Horst, Anton van
der

HEGER, ROBERT (1886-   )
Vier Alte Marienlieder *Op.31, CC4U
S solo,pno UNIVER. 13829 $7.50
(H1078)

HEHKUVA HENKI see Nyberg, Mikael

HEI, GRUASS DIE GOTT LANDLE see Laval,
   D.

HEI JA HOI, MITEN MYRSKY SE SOI see
   Sibelius, Jean, Hallila, Uti Storm
   Och Regn

HEI MET DE WOLKEN ZOO WIT see
   Adriessen, Willem

HEI TONTTU-UKOT HYPPIKAA
   see Pieni Joulutervehdyts

HEIDENROSLEIN see Schubert, Franz
   (Peter)

HEIDENROSLEIN see Soderman

HEIDER, WERNER (1930-   )
   Four Glimpses Of Night
      [Eng] S solo,pno,pic,ob,clar,bsn,
      horn,trp,trom,timp,perc,harp,
      strings sc PETERS 5809 $6.00
                                    (H1079)
   Picasso-Musik
      Mez solo,clar,vln,pno sc PETERS
      8281LI s.p.   (H1080)

HEIDESTEMMINGEN see Schouwman, Hans

HEIDET, LE R. P.
   Ave Maria *sac
      [Lat] A/B solo,pno/org ENOCH s.p.
                                    (H1081)
   Cantate Domino *sac
      [Lat] Bar/Mez solo,pno/org ENOCH
      s.p.   (H1082)
   O Cor Amoris *sac
      [Lat] T/S solo,pno/org ENOCH s.p.
                                    (H1083)

HEIJAA, HEIJAA see Madetoja, Leevi

HEIJKORN
   Liten Karins Vaggvisa
      solo,pno LUNDQUIST s.p.   (H1084)
   Vallflickans Visa
      solo,pno LUNDQUIST s.p.   (H1085)

HEIL U, MOEDER see Mortelmans, Lodewijk

HEILAKKA
   Betlehems Stjarna
      see Tva Julsanger

   Det Klingar En Ton Over Frusen Sjo
      see Tva Julsanger

   Tva Julsanger
      solo,pno LUNDQUIST s.p.
         contains: Betlehems Stjarna; Det
         Klingar En Ton Over Frusen Sjo
                                    (H1086)

HEILBUT, P.
   Vier Neue Lieder Zum Advent *CC4U,
      Adv
      solo,pno HUG s.p.   (H1087)

HEIL'GE NACHT see Beethoven, Ludwig van

HEILGE NACHT, DU SINKEST NIEDER see
   Schubert, Franz (Peter), Nacht Und
   Traume

HEILIG, HEILIG see Handel, George
   Frideric

HEILIG IST GOTT see Beyer, Johann
   Samuel

HEILIGENSTADTER RENDEZVOUS see Strauss,
   Johann

HEILINI SOITTELI see Melartin, Erkki

HEILLER, ANTON (1923-   )
   Ave Maria
      see Heiller, Anton, Pater Noster

   Fiat Voluntas Tua
      A solo,pno DOBLINGER 08 634 $1.25
                                    (H1088)
   Pater Noster *sac
      A solo,pno DOBLINGER 08 635 $3.50
         contains also: Ave Maria   (H1089)
   Sub Tuum Praesidium *sac
      A solo,pno DOBLINGER 08 636 $1.00
                                    (H1090)
   Zwei Geistliche Gesange *sac,CC2U
      (Optavi; Gaudete) [Lat] S solo,org
      DOBLINGER 08 851 $5.25   (H1091)

HEILMANN, HARALD (1924-   )
   Psalm 23 *sac
      high solo,pno SIRIUS s.p.   (H1092)

HEILNER, IRWIN
   Channel Firing
      med solo,pno AM.COMP.AL. $2.75
                                    (H1093)
   Chestnut Casts His Flambeaux, The
      med solo,pno AM.COMP.AL. $3.57
                                    (H1094)

HEILNER, IRWIN (cont'd.)
   Chinese Songs *CCU,Chin
      med solo,fl,ob,clar,bsn,horn,trp,
      trom,pno,perc,strings sc
      AM.COMP.AL. $13.75   (H1095)
   Chu Yeh
      med solo,pno sc AM.COMP.AL. $1.10
                                    (H1096)
   Could Man Be Drunk Forever
      med solo,pno AM.COMP.AL. $.55
                                    (H1097)
   Democracy
      med solo,gtr AM.COMP.AL. $.27
                                    (H1098)
   Eastern Gate, The *Chin
      med solo,pno AM.COMP.AL. $2.20
                                    (H1099)
   Every Day Is Friday To A Seal
      med solo,pno/gtr, or banjo or
      ukelele sc AM.COMP.AL. $1.10
                                    (H1100)
   Gift Of Fire, The
      solo,gtr AM.COMP.AL. $.55   (H1101)
   God's Education
      med solo,pno AM.COMP.AL. $2.75
                                    (H1102)
   Henry At The Grating
      solo,gtr AM.COMP.AL. $1.10   (H1103)
   I Rose Up As My Custom Is
      med solo,pno AM.COMP.AL. $3.57
                                    (H1104)
   Letter From The Draft Board
      solo,gtr AM.COMP.AL. $.55   (H1105)
   Lo-Yang
      med solo,pno sc AM.COMP.AL. $1.10
                                    (H1106)
   Long Roads, The
      med solo,pno sc AM.COMP.AL. $1.10
                                    (H1107)
   Mammy Sings
      med solo,pno AM.COMP.AL. $.27
                                    (H1108)
   My Little Son
      med solo,pno sc AM.COMP.AL. $2.75
                                    (H1109)
   Now Dreary Dawns The Eastern Light
      med solo,pno AM.COMP.AL. $.55
                                    (H1110)
   Old Harp, The
      ST soli,pno sc AM.COMP.AL. $2.75
                                    (H1111)
   On The Birth Of His Son *Chin
      med solo,pno AM.COMP.AL. $1.10
                                    (H1112)
   Peace Is A Lovely Word
      med solo,pno/gtr sc AM.COMP.AL.
      $.55   (H1113)
   Plucking The Rushes *Chin
      med solo,pno AM.COMP.AL. $2.75
                                    (H1114)
   Red Cockatoo, The *Chin
      med solo,pno AM.COMP.AL. $.55
                                    (H1115)
   Regret
      med solo,pno sc AM.COMP.AL. $1.37
                                    (H1116)
   Rock-'N-Roll Session
      solo,gtr AM.COMP.AL. $.55   (H1117)
   Scholar In The Narrow Street, The
      *Chin
      med solo,pno AM.COMP.AL. $2.75
                                    (H1118)
   Starlings On The Roof
      med solo,pno AM.COMP.AL. $2.75
                                    (H1119)
   Stars Have Not Dealt Me The Worst
      They Could Do, The
      med solo,pno AM.COMP.AL. $.55
                                    (H1120)
   Stevenson
      med solo,gtr AM.COMP.AL. $.27
                                    (H1121)
   What Were They Like?
      med solo,gtr AM.COMP.AL. $3.57
                                    (H1122)
   When I Set Out For Lyonnesse
      med solo,pno AM.COMP.AL. $2.20
                                    (H1123)
   Wild Anemone, The
      solo,gtr AM.COMP.AL. $1.10   (H1124)

HEIMAT MEIN see Gretchaninov, Alexander
   Tikhonovitch, Mon Pays!

HEIMAT, SIEH DES MORGENS HELLE
   SCHWINGEN (from Finlandia)
   [Finn/Swed] solo,pno BREITKOPF-W
   EB 5993 s.p. see from Sechs Lieder
   Nach Texten Von J.L. Runeberg
                                    (H1125)

HEIMATLAND see Trunk, Richard

HEIMKEHR see Bijvanck, Henk

HEIMKEHR see Othegraven, August J. von

HEIMKEHR see Strauss, Richard

HEIMLENGSLA see Nystedt, Knut

HEIMLICHE AUFFORDERUNG see Strauss,
   Richard

HEIMLICHE LIEDER see Eben, Petr

HEIMLICHE LIEDER DER NACHT see Haas,
   Joseph

HEIMWEH see Wolf, Hugo

HEINE LIEDER see Wolf, Hugo

HEINICHEN, JOHANN DAVID (1683-1729)
   Mia Climene Adorata *cant
      S solo,cont GERIG AV 118 s.p.
                                    (H1126)
   Nisi Dominus Aedificaverit Domum
      (Psalm 127) sac,mot
      (Janetzky; Stolzenbach) [Lat] high
      solo,ob,cont DEUTSCHER 9505 s.p.
                                    (H1127)
   Psalm 127 *see Nisi Dominus
      Aedificaverit Domum

HEINRICH-HEINE-LIEDER see Schumann,
   Robert (Alexander)

HEINZELMANNCHEN-BALLADE see Kraft,
   Walter

HEIRESS see Lawson, Malcolm

HEISE, PETER ARNOLD (1830-1879)
   Den Danske Romance: Late Romantics
      *CC13L
      [Dut] solo,kbd HANSEN-DEN s.p.
                                    (H1128)
   La Chanson De L'Amie Du Roi
      solo,pno ENOCH s.p. see also CHANTS
      DU NORD   (H1129)

HEISS, HERMANN (1897-1966)
   Calamites
      S/T solo,2clar,bass clar,2trp,trom,
      perc,vibra,marimba,pno,strings
      MODERN rental   (H1130)
   Drei Hausliche Lieder Nach Gedichten
      Von Jo Ehlers *CC3U
      S solo,pno BREITKOPF-W EB 6225 s.p.
                                    (H1131)
   Dreizehn Gesange Nach Worten Von
      Franz Kafka *CC13U
      med-high solo,pno BREITKOPF-W
      EB 6219 $3.00   (H1132)
   Galgenlieder Nach Christian
      Morgenstern *CCU
      S solo,fl (diff) MULLER 1863 s.p.
                                    (H1133)
   Heiter Bis Wolkig *CC5U
      solo,pno BREITKOPF-W EB 6224 s.p.
                                    (H1134)
   Lieder Der Liebe *CC9U
      [Ger/Jap/Chin] S solo,pno
      BREITKOPF-W EB 5954 $2.00   (H1135)
   Logatome
      narrator,inst MODERN rental   (H1136)
   Requiem *sac,Req
      SA soli,4strings/4strings&org/org
      s.p. sc BREITKOPF-W EB 6994, voc
      sc BREITKOPF-W EB 6995   (H1137)
   Salutatio
      solo&narrator, electronic inst
      MODERN s.p.   (H1138)
   Sieben Dreistimmige Sentenzen Nach
      Worten Von Gunther Michel *CC7U
      SABar soli,kbd/3strings sc
      BREITKOPF-W PB 3773 s.p., ipa
                                    (H1139)
   Zum Neuen Jahr *CC7U
      S solo,clar,pno voc sc BREITKOPF-W
      EB 6218 $3.25   (H1140)

HEISSA, HOPSA, BEI REGEN UND WIND see
   Sibelius, Jean

HEISSA, HOPSA, BEI REGEN UND WIND see
   Sibelius, Jean, Hallila, Uti Storm
   Och Regn

HEISSA TROIKA *folk,Russ
   [Ger/Russ] solo,pno ZIMMER. 1501 s.p.
                                    (H1141)

HEITER BIS WOLKIG see Heiss, Hermann

HEITERE LIEDER see Borkovec, Pavel

HEITERES HERBARIUM see
   Mittergradnegger, Gunther

HEITERES HERBARIUM see Salmhofer, Franz

HEITERKEIT UND FROHLICHKEIT see
   Lortzing, (Gustav) Albert

HEJ DUNKOM!
   solo,pno GEHRMANS 163 s.p.   (H1142)

HEJ TOMTEGUBBAR
see En Liten Julhalsning

HEKSTER, WALTER (1937-   )
Snow Man, The
S solo,bass clar,perc DONEMUS s.p.
(H1143)

HELAND
Bland Fjallen
see Sanger Med Piano

I Hennes Hem
see Sanger Med Piano

Larkan
see Sanger Med Piano

Sanger Med Piano
solo,pno LUNDQUIST s.p.
contains: Bland Fjallen; I Hennes
Hem; Larkan; Steeple-Chase;
Trumslagaren   (H1144)

Steeple-Chase
see Sanger Med Piano

Trumslagaren
see Sanger Med Piano

HELAS! CETTE NUIT S'ACHEVE, ET MON REVE
S'ENFUIT see Levade, Charles
(Gaston)

HELAS, JE NE DOIS PLUS ENTENDRE see
Messager, Andre

HELAS! MOI, LE HAIR see Gounod, Charles
Francois

HELDER, BARTHOLOMAEUS (1585-1635)
Dich Bitt Ich, Trautes Jesulein *sac
high solo,2S rec,cont HANSSLER
5.035 s.p. see also GESANGE ZUM
KIRCHENJAHR   (H1145)

HELE, JAK NADHERNE see Tucapsky,
Antonin

HELEN OF KIRKCONNEL see Lawson, Malcolm

HELENE see Aubert, Louis-Francois-Marie

HELFMAN, MAX (1901-1963)
Ana Dodi *sac,Marriage
"Song Of Songs" [Heb] solo,pno
TRANSCON. WJ 445 $.85   (H1146)

Ashrey Ha-Gafrur
see Two Hannah Szenesh Poems

Grant Us Peace *sac
med solo,pno TRANSCON. TV 483 $.85
(H1147)
high solo,pno TRANSCON. TV 484 $.85
(H1148)
Hear Our Voice, O Lord *see Sh'ma
Koleynu

Kol Kara
see Two Hannah Szenesh Poems

May The Words *sac
S/T solo,pno TRANSCON. TV 550 $.60
(H1149)
R'tze *sac
[Heb] solo,pno TRANSCON. WJ 446
$1.00   (H1150)

Set Me As A Seal Upon Thy Heart *see
Simeni Chachotam

Sh'ma Koleynu *sac
"Hear Our Voice, O Lord" [Heb] med
solo/cantor,pno TRANSCON. WJ 434
$1.00   (H1151)
"Hear Our Voice, O Lord" [Heb] high
solo/cantor,pno TRANSCON. WJ 433
$1.00   (H1152)

Simeni Chachotam
"Set Me As A Seal Upon Thy Heart"
[Heb/Eng] solo,pno/org TRANSCON.
WJ 444 $1.00   (H1153)

Song Of Songs *see Ana Dodi

Two Hannah Szenesh Poems *sac
[Heb] TRANSCON. SP 23 $1.50
contains: Ashrey Ha-Gafrur; Kol
Kara   (H1154)

Voice Of My Beloved, The *sac,
Marriage
high solo,pno TRANSCON. TV 549
$1.00   (H1155)

HELGSOG FRA RYMDI see Egge, Klaus

HELIAN DI TRAKL see Togni, Camillo

HELIER, IVY ST.
You Didn't Ask Me First
solo,pno CRAMER   (H1156)

HE'LL BREAK THROUGH THE BLUE see
Wyrtzen, Don

HE'LL GO WITH ME ALL THE WAY see Jayne,
Mary

HE'LL HOLD MY HAND see Harper

HE'LL NEVER LET YOU FALL *sac
(Carmichael, Ralph) solo,pno WORD
S-16   (H1157)

HE'LL UNDERSTAND AND SAY "WELL DONE"
*sac,gospel
solo,pno ABER.GRP. $1.50   (H1158)

HE'LL UNDERSTAND AND SAY "WELL DONE"
see Campbell

HELLA, MARTTI (1890-1965)
Joululauluja *CCU,Xmas
solo,pno FAZER W 3524 s.p.   (H1159)

HELLE NACHT see Reger, Max

HELLE NACHT see Trunk, Richard

HELLER, A.
Death-It Is Still Cold Night
see Two Heine Songs

Lord's Prayer, The *sac
(Andreson, R.) med solo,pno MERCURY
$.95   (H1160)

Pine Tree Towers Lonely, A
see Two Heine Songs

Two Heine Songs
[Eng/Ger] med solo,pno MERCURY
$1.00
contains: Death-It Is Still Cold
Night; Pine Tree Towers Lonely,
A   (H1161)

HELLER, STEPHEN (1813-1888)
Sieben Deutsche Lieder *CC7U
solo,pno EULENBURG GM 544 s.p.
(H1162)

HELLERMANN, HERBERT
Poem For Soprano And Four Instruments
S solo,fl,bass clar,trom,vcl sc
AM.COMP.AL. $6.60, ipa   (H1163)

HELLIDENS SANG see Nielsen, Carl

HELLIGE TONE see Beck, Thomas
[Ludvigsen]

HELLMANN, DIETHARD (1928-   )
Der Herr Ist Mein Hirte *sac
high solo,2S rec,org HANSSLER 5.068
s.p.   (H1164)

Nun Bitten Wir Den Heiligen Geist
*sac
SA soli,2S rec,cont HANSSLER 5.056
s.p. see also GESANGE ZUM
KIRCHENJAHR   (H1165)

HELM, EVERETT (1913-   )
For My Lady
see Two Love Songs

It Is So Long
see Two Love Songs

Two Love Songs
med solo,pno PRESSER $.75
contains: For My Lady; It Is So
Long   (H1166)

HELM, THEODORE OTTO
Tres Cantos Sobre Textos Del Siglo
XIII *CC3U
[It] solo,pno RICORDI-ARG BA 9209
s.p.   (H1167)

HELMSCHROTT, ROBERT M.
Atmosfera Ovattata I
S solo,fl study sc ORLANDO s.p.
(H1168)
Atmosfera Ovattata II
S solo,fl,trp,vibra,bvl study sc
ORLANDO s.p.   (H1169)

HELOISE AND ABELARD see Pasatieri,
Thomas

HELP ME see Gatlin, Larry

HELP ME TO BE KIND see Moore, Donald
Lee

HELPS, ROBERT (1928-   )
Running Sun, The
S solo,pno AM.COMP.AL. $5.50 (H1170)

Two Songs *CC2U
S solo,pno AM.COMP.AL. $5.50 (H1171)

HELY-HUTCHINSON, (CHRISTIAN) VICTOR
(1901-1947)
Cuckoo Song
S solo,pno ELKIN 27.1960.06 s.p.
(H1172)

HELY-HUTCHINSON, (CHRISTIAN) VICTOR
(cont'd.)

Duck And The Kangaroo, The
see Three Of Edward Lear's Nonsense
Songs

Old Mother Hubbard
low solo,pno (E maj) PATERSON s.p.
(H1173)
high solo,pno (G maj) PATERSON s.p.
(H1174)
Owl And The Pussy Cat, The
see Three Of Edward Lear's Nonsense
Songs

Song Of Soldiers, The
high solo,pno ELKIN 27.1857.10 s.p.
(H1175)
low solo,pno ELKIN 27.1866.09 s.p.
(H1176)
Table And The Chair, The
see Three Of Edward Lear's Nonsense
Songs

Three Of Edward Lear's Nonsense Songs
solo,pno PATERSON s.p.
contains: Duck And The Kangaroo,
The; Owl And The Pussy Cat,
The; Table And The Chair, The
(H1177)
Trees
med solo,pno ELKIN 27.1643.07 s.p.
(H1178)

HEM OF HIS GARMENT, THE see Greenfield,
Alfred M.

HEM TILL KALLAN see Ahnfeldt

HEMBERG, ESKIL
An Old Saga *see En Gammal Saga

En Gammal Saga *Op.30
"An Old Saga" S solo,harp,hpsd
NORDISKA 2477 s.p.   (H1179)

HEMBYGDEN see Korling

HEMBYGDENS SANG see Eklof, Einar

HEMBYGDSSANG see Wideen, Ivar

HEMEL, OSCAR VAN (1892-   )
Agnus Dei
see Trittico Liturgico Per Soprano

Egidius, Waer Bestu Bleven
see Twee Liedern Uit "Krans Der
Middeleeuwen"

Kyrie
see Trittico Liturgico Per Soprano

Le Tombeau De Kathleen Ferrier
A solo,3fl,3ob,3clar,3bsn,4horn,
3trp,3trom,tuba,timp,perc,cel,
strings DONEMUS s.p.   (H1180)

Sanctus
see Trittico Liturgico Per Soprano

Trittico Liturgico Per Soprano *sac
S/Mez solo,org/strings DONEMUS s.p.
contains: Agnus Dei; Kyrie;
Sanctus   (H1181)

Twee Liedern Uit "Krans Der
Middeleeuwen"
Bar solo,pno DONEMUS s.p.
contains: Egidius, Waer Bestu
Bleven; Zondaarslied   (H1182)

Zondaarslied
see Twee Liedern Uit "Krans Der
Middeleeuwen"

HEMELSCHE LIEFDE see Hullebroeck, Em.

HEMERY, VALENTINE
Beloved, Awake
low solo,pno (C maj) LEONARD-ENG
(H1183)
high solo,pno (F maj) LEONARD-ENG
(H1184)
med solo,pno (D maj) LEONARD-ENG
(H1185)
Bygone Days
low solo,pno,opt vln (B flat maj)
LEONARD-ENG   (H1186)
high solo,pno,opt vln (E flat maj)
LEONARD-ENG   (H1187)
med-high solo,pno,opt vln (D maj)
LEONARD-ENG   (H1188)
med solo,pno,opt vln (C maj)
LEONARD-ENG   (H1189)

Daddy's Angel
med solo,pno (E flat maj) LEONARD-
ENG   (H1190)
low solo,pno (C maj) LEONARD-ENG
(H1191)
high solo,pno (F maj) LEONARD-ENG
(H1192)

In Memory's Garden
low solo,pno (C maj) LEONARD-ENG
(H1193)

HEMERY, VALENTINE (cont'd.)

   high solo,pno (D maj) LEONARD-ENG
                           (H1194)
  Loves Tomorrow
   low solo,pno (B flat maj) LEONARD-
    ENG   (H1195)
   med solo,pno (D maj) LEONARD-ENG
                           (H1196)
   high solo,pno (E flat maj) LEONARD-
    ENG   (H1197)
  Soldiers Of Fortune
   2 soli,pno LEONARD-ENG   (H1198)

  Thine
   high solo,pno (F maj) CRAMER
                          (H1199)
   low solo,pno (D flat maj) CRAMER
                          (H1200)

HEMLANGTAN see Peterson-Berger, (Olof)
  Wilhelm

HEMLANGTAN see Wolf, Hugo

HEMLIG SERENAD see Hallnas, Hilding

HEMMARSCHEN, GANGLAT see Stenhammar,
  Wilhelm

HEMMET see Hakansson, Knut Algot

HEMMET DEN EIFER, VERBANNET DIE RACHE
  see Telemann, Georg Philipp

HEMMETS SANGER see Norrman, John

HEMMETS SANGER, HEFT 1 *CC20L
  (Lundberg) solo,pno LUNDQUIST s.p.
   contains works by: Alfven;
   Haquinius; Rangstrom; Sjogren and
   others   (H1201)

HEMMETS SANGER, HEFT 2 *CC26L
  (Lundberg) solo,pno LUNDQUIST s.p.
   contains works by: Nordqvist;
   Sjogren; Norberg; Mendelssohn;
   Schumann and others   (H1202)

HEMMT EURE TRANENFLUT see Bruhns,
  Nicholaus

HEMPHILL
  I'll Soon Be Gone *sac
   solo,pno BENSON S6282-S $1.00
                         (H1203)
  Pity The Man *sac
   solo,pno BENSON S7376-S $1.00
                         (H1204)
  Ready To Leave *sac
   solo,pno BENSON S7414-S $1.00
                         (H1205)

HENCE IRIS, HENCE AWAY see Handel,
  George Frideric

HENCE WITH YOUR TRIFLING DEITY see
  Purcell, Henry

HENDERSON
  He's Gone Away
   solo,pno FISCHER,C V 2427 (H1206)

HENDERSON, W.G.
  Highland Maid, A
   see Two Hebridean Love Songs

  My Love Is As The Dawn
   see Two Hebridean Love Songs

  Two Hebridean Love Songs
   solo,pno THOMP.G s.p.
    contains: Highland Maid, A; My
    Love Is As The Dawn   (H1207)

HENGEVELD, G.
  Moonlight
   solo,pno BROEKMANS 762A s.p.
                         (H1208)
  Nun Bist Du Hin
   solo,pno BROEKMANS 205 s.p. (H1209)
  Pippeloentje Uit Logeren
   solo,pno BROEKMANS 776 s.p. (H1210)
  Schlummerlied
   solo,pno BROEKMANS 698 s.p. (H1211)
  Sprinkhanenconcert
   solo,pno BROEKMANS 649 s.p. (H1212)
  Twilight
   solo,pno BROEKMANS 755 s.p. (H1213)
  Twintig Kerstliederen *sac,CC20U
   solo,pno BROEKMANS 813 s.p. (H1214)

HENKEMANS, HANS (1913-   )
  Aan Een Bode
   see De Tooverfluit

  Achterlijk Kind
   see Drie Liederen

  Als Ik Een Vodeltje Was
   see De Tooverfluit

HENKEMANS, HANS (cont'd.)

  Canzoni Amorose De Duecente *CCU
   SBar soli,3fl,3ob,2clar,3bsn,4horn,
   timp,perc,pno,harp,strings
   DONEMUS s.p.   (H1215)

  De Ontrouwe Liefste
   see De Tooverfluit

  De Tooverfluit
   T solo,pno DONEMUS s.p.
    contains: Aan Een Bode; Als Ik
    Een Vodeltje Was; De Ontrouwe
    Liefste; Nachtmuzikanten;
    Onbeschrijfelijke Vreugde
                         (H1216)

  Drie Liederen
   med solo,pno DONEMUS s.p.
    contains: Achterlijk Kind; Elven
    Zingen Bij Een Alleen Gelaten
    Kind; Het Verdronken Kind
                         (H1217)

  Elven Zingen Bij Een Alleen Gelaten
   Kind
   see Drie Liederen

  Het Verdronken Kind
   see Drie Liederen

  Nachtmuzikanten
   see De Tooverfluit

  Onbeschrijfelijke Vreugde
   see De Tooverfluit

HENKING, BERNHARD (1897-   )
  Ballade
   A solo,2fl,ob,2clar,2horn,timp,
   harp,strings DONEMUS s.p. (H1218)

  Villonnerie
   Bar solo,3fl,3ob,3clar,3bsn,4horn,
   3trp,3trom,tuba,timp,perc,2harp,
   pno,strings DONEMUS s.p. (H1219)

HENLEY, PETER J.
  Deep In The Quiet Forest
   low solo,pno (F maj) CRAMER (H1220)
   high solo,pno (A flat maj) CRAMER
                         (H1221)
  Morning Sun, The
   low solo,pno (B flat maj) CRAMER
   $.90   (H1222)
   high solo,pno (D maj) CRAMER $1.15
                        (H1223)

HENNES BUDSKAP *Op.90,No.2
  "Ihre Botschaft" [Swed/Ger] med-high
  solo,kbd HANSEN-DEN s.p. see from
  Six Songs   (H1224)

HENNES BUDSKAP see Sibelius, Jean

HENNES LJUVA ROST MIG RORDE see
  Nordqvist, Gustaf

HENNESSY, SWAN (1866-1929)
  Trois Chansons Celtiques *CC3U
  [Fr] med solo,pno ESCHIG $1.60
                         (H1225)

HENRIC VAN VELDEKE see Strategier,
  Herman

HENRIK WERGELAND see Grieg, Edvard
  Hagerup

HENRY AND HAZEL SLAUGHTER-SONGBOOK see
  Slaughter, Hazel

HENRY AND HAZEL SLAUGHTER-SONGBOOK,
  VOL. II see Slaughter, Hazel

HENRY AT THE GRATING see Heilner, Irwin

HENRY CLAY WORK SONGS see Work, Henry
  Clay

HENRY VIII, KING OF ENGLAND (1491-1547)
  Trois Chansons De Sa Composition
  *CC3U
   solo,pno min sc OISEAU s.p. (H1226)

HENSCHEL, ISADORE GEORGE (1850-1934)
  Morgenhymne
   "Morning Hymn" [Ger/Eng] low solo,
   pno (D flat maj) SCHIRM.G $.60 (H1227)
  Morning Hymn *see Morgenhymne

HENSEN, GLORIA
  Holding To The Hand Of God *sac
   solo,pno WORD S-335   (H1228)

  Right By My Side *sac
   solo,pno WORD S-336   (H1229)

HENSON
  Keep A Happy Heart *sac
   (Whitworth) solo,pno LILLENAS
   SM-924: SN $1.00   (H1230)

HENTY, DICK
  Sweeper
   low solo,pno (C min) CRAMER (H1231)
   high solo,pno (D min) CRAMER
                        (H1232)

HENZE, HANS WERNER (1926-   )
  Ariosi Fur Sopran *CCU
   [It/Ger] S solo,pno,vln, piano 4-
   hands voc sc SCHOTTS 5454 s.p.
                        (H1233)

  Being Beauteous *cant
   [Fr] coloratura sop,harp,4vcl voc
   sc SCHOTTS 5269 s.p. (H1234)

  Drei Fragmente Nach Holderlin Und
   Drei Tentos Aus "Kammermusik
   1958" *CC6U
   (Bream) solo,gtr SCHOTTS 4886 s.p.
                        (H1235)

  Funf Neapolitanische Lieder *CC5U
   med solo,chamb.orch voc sc SCHOTTS
   4766 s.p.   (H1236)

  Kammermusik 1958 Uber Die Hymne "In
   Lieblicher Blaue" Von Holderlin
   T solo,8inst,gtr voc sc SCHOTTS
   4897 s.p., ipr   (H1237)

HEPPENER, ROBERT (1925-   )
  Cantico Delle Creature Di Francesco
   D'Assisi
   high solo,harp,strings DONEMUS s.p.
                        (H1238)

  Fanfare Trionfale
   soli,orch DONEMUS s.p. (H1239)

  Four Songs On Poems By Eszra Pound
   *CC4U
   med solo,pno DONEMUS s.p. (H1240)

HEPTAMERON see Havelka, Svatopluk

HER BRIGHT SMILE HAUNTS ME STILL see
  Wrighton, W.T.

HER DEFINITION see Binkerd, Gordon

HER I'LL LOVE see Mozart, Wolfgang
  Amadeus

HER SILVER WILL see Binkerd, Gordon

HER SONG see Ireland, John

HER STAR DE GRONNE STAMMER see
  Lewkovitch, Bernhard

HER TEMPLE see Finzi, Gerald

HERACLEITUS see Heseltine, Philip

HERALDS OF GREEN YOUTH, THE see
  Smolanoff, Michael

HERBERIGS, ROBERT (1886-1974)
  La Chanson D'Eve *CC11L
   med solo,pno cmplt ed CBDM s.p.
                        (H1241)

HERBERT
  When You're Away
   high solo,pno (G maj) ALLANS s.p.
                        (H1242)
   low solo,pno (D maj) ALLANS s.p.
                        (H1243)
   med solo,pno (F maj) ALLANS s.p.
                        (H1244)

HERBERT, MURIEL
  Lake Isle Of Innisfree, The
   med solo,pno ELKIN 27.1662.03 s.p.
                        (H1245)
   low solo,pno ELKIN 27.1661.05 s.p.
                        (H1246)
  Sing Unto The Lord, All The Earth
   *sac
   med solo,pno ELKIN 27.2464.02 s.p.
                        (H1247)

HERBERT, VICTOR (1859-1924)
  Angelus (from Sweethearts)
   ST soli,pno SCHIRM.G $.60 (H1248)

  Cricket On The Heart, The (from
   Sweethearts)
   med-high solo,pno (E maj) SCHIRM.G
   $.60   (H1249)

  Gypsy Love Song
   med-high solo,pno (C maj) BOSTON
   $1.50
   high solo,pno (E flat maj) BOSTON
   $1.50   (H1251)
   high solo,pno (A maj) ALLANS s.p.
                        (H1252)
   med solo,pno (C maj) ALLANS s.p.
                        (H1253)
   low solo,pno (E flat maj) ALLANS
   s.p.   (H1254)
   low solo,pno (B flat maj) BOSTON
   $1.50   (H1255)
   2 high soli,pno (A maj) ALLANS s.p.
                        (H1256)
   2 low soli,pno (E flat maj) ALLANS
   s.p.   (H1257)

  Ivy And The Oak, The (from
   Sweethearts)
   high solo,pno (F maj) SCHIRM.G $.60
                        (H1258)

  Jeannette And Her Little Wooden Shoes
   (from Sweethearts)
   med-high solo,pno (E flat maj)
   SCHIRM.G $.60   (H1259)

HERBERT, VICTOR (cont'd.)

Kiss Me Again
solo,pno ASHLEY $.95 (H1260)

Moonbeams
solo,pno ALLANS s.p. (H1261)

Sweethearts (from Sweethearts)
high solo,pno (B flat maj) SCHIRM.G
$.75 (H1262)
med solo,pno (A flat maj) SCHIRM.G
$.75 (H1263)
low solo,pno (F maj) SCHIRM.G $.75
(H1264)
SBar/SA soli,pno SCHIRM.G $1.00
(H1265)

Toyland
solo,pno (available in 2 keys)
ASHLEY $.95 (H1266)

HERBST see Franken, Wim

HERBST see Kilpinen, Yrio

HERBST see Kurzbach, Paul

HERBST see Lilien, Ignace

HERBST, E.
Zwischen Abend Und Morgen *Op.7,
sac,CC4U
solo,fl,pno BOHM s.p. (H1267)

HERBSTABEND see Sibelius, Jean,
Hostkvall

HERBSTFEUER see Beck, Conrad

HERBSTGOLD see Brusso, G.

HERBSTHAUCH see Pfitzner, Hans

HERBSTIMMUNGEN see Haba, Karel,
Podzimni Nalady

HERBSTKANTATE see Burkhard, Willy

HERBSTREGEN see Kilpinen, Yrio,
Kaupungilla Sataa

HERBSTSONETT see Kilpinen, Yrio,
Syyssonetti

HERBSTSTIMMUNG see Kuula, Toivo,
Syystunnelma

HERBSTSTURM see Gilse, Jan van

HERBSTTAG see Borup-Jorgensen, Axel

HERBSTTAG see Franken, Wim

HERBSTZEITLOSE see Marx, Joseph

HERCULES see Hovhaness, Alan

HERD BOY'S SONG, THE see Oldham, Arthur

HERDEFLICKANS VAGGSANG see Tuuri,
Jaako, Paimentyton Kehtolaulu

HERDING SONG see Lawson, Malcolm

HERE AMID THE SHADY WOODS see Anonymous

HERE AND NOW, I BELIEVE *sac
(Carmichael) solo,pno WORD S-504
(H1268)

HERE BEAUTY DWELLS see Rachmaninoff,
Sergey Vassilievitch

HERE COMES A LUSTY WOOER
see Songs Of Wonder

HERE COMES A LUSTY WOOER see Donovan,
Richard [Frank]

HERE COMES THE BRIDE see Munsey

HERE IN THESE WORDS see Peter

HERE IN THIS SILKEN WORLD OF MINE see
Puccini, Giacomo, In Quelle Trine
Morbide

HERE IS MY LIFE see Bartlett, Gene

HERE IS MY SONG see Squire, W.H.

HERE IS OUR MOTHERLAND see Doga, E.

HERE LET MY LIFE see Purcell, Henry

HERE, LORD, WE MEET see Rowley, Alec

HERE ON MY THRONE see Vaughan Williams,
Ralph

HERE'S A HEALTH TO ANE I LO'E DEAR
*folk,Scot
solo,pno (B flat maj) PATERSON FS33
s.p. (H1269)

HERE'S TO A SOLDIER HERO see Peterson,
John W.

HERE'S TO THE HEALTH see Reuland,
Jacques

HERE'S TO THE LADIES see Day, Maude
Craske

HERFST see Devreese, Godefroid, Automne

HERFST IN FRIESLAND see Schouwman, Hans

HERFSTBOSCH see Wap van Pesch, L.

HERFSTLIED see Clercq, R. de

HERFSTMORGEN see Mulder, Ernest W.

HERINNERING see Adriessen, Willem

HERINNERING see Masseus, Jan

HERINNERING see Schellekens, G.

HERINNERING AAN HOLLAND see Voormolen,
Alexander Nicolas

HERLIGHETENS MORGEN see Dahlgren,
Erland

HERMANN, H.
Drei Gesange *Op.78, CC3U
[Ger] med solo,pno BOTE $2.00
(H1270)

HERMANN LONS LIEDER, VOL. I see
Kilpinen, Yrio

HERMANN LONS LIEDER, VOL. II see
Kilpinen, Yrio

HERMANN LONS LIEDER, VOL. III see
Kilpinen, Yrio

HERMANN LONS LIEDER, VOL. IV see
Kilpinen, Yrio

HERMANS, NICO (1919-)
Chant D'amour *Op.13,No.1
see La Flute De Jade

La Flute De Jade
A solo,fl,harp DONEMUS s.p.
contains: Chant D'amour, Op.13,
No.1; L'Indifferente, Op.13,
No.2 (H1271)

L'Indifferente *Op.13,No.2
see La Flute De Jade

Nacht *Op.10,No.1
see Twee Nocturnes
see Twee Nocturnes Van P.C. Boutens

Nachtstilte *Op.10,No.2
see Twee Nocturnes Van P.C. Boutens
see Twee Nocturnes

Twee Nocturnes
Mez solo,fl,strings DONEMUS s.p.
contains: Nacht, Op.10,No.1;
Nachtstilte, Op.10,No.2 (H1272)

Twee Nocturnes Van P.C. Boutens
Mez solo,fl,pno DONEMUS s.p.
contains: Nacht, Op.10,No.1;
Nachtstilte, Op.10,No.2 (H1273)

HERMIT SONGS see Barber, Samuel

HERMITE, M.
A L'ombre Du Beguinage
solo,pno ENOCH s.p. (H1274)
solo,acap ENOCH s.p. (H1275)

Au Bout Des Levres
solo,pno ENOCH s.p. (H1276)
solo,acap ENOCH s.p. (H1277)

Chanson De Lune
solo,pno ENOCH s.p. (H1278)

Doute
solo,pno ENOCH s.p. (H1279)

Lentement, Doucement, Tendrement
solo,pno ENOCH s.p. (H1280)
solo,acap ENOCH s.p. (H1281)

Les Fleurs Ne Mentent Jamais
solo,acap ENOCH s.p. (H1282)
solo,pno ENOCH s.p. (H1283)

Les Reves Sont Des Bulles De Savon
solo,pno ENOCH s.p. (H1284)
solo,acap ENOCH s.p. (H1285)

Les Roses De Mon Balcon
solo,pno ENOCH s.p. (H1286)
solo,acap ENOCH s.p. (H1287)

Un Chant D'amour
solo,pno ENOCH s.p. (H1288)
solo,acap ENOCH s.p. (H1289)

HERO, THE see Menotti, Gian Carlo

HERODE, NE ME REFUSE PAS see Massenet,
Jules

HEROIC SONG see Sugar, Rezso

HERON-MAXWELL, K.
Keep On Hopin'
solo,pno (E flat maj) BOOSEY $1.50
(H1290)

HERR, AUF DICH TRAUE ICH see Buxtehude,
Dietrich

HERR CHRIST, DER EINIG GOTTS SOHN see
Poos, Heinrich

HERR CHRIST, HILF UNS see Raphael,
Gunther

HERR, DEINE GUTE REICHT SO WEIT see
Bach, Johann Sebastian

HERR, DEINE GUTE REICHT, SOWEIT DER
HIMMEL IST see Finkbeiner, Reinhold

HERR, DEN ICH TIEF IM HERZEN TRAGE see
Hiller, Ferdinand

HERR, DEN ICH TIEF IM HERZEN TRAGE see
Simon, Hermann

HERR DER GNADE, GOTT DES LICHTS see
Telemann, Georg Philipp

HERR, DU ERFORSCHEST MICH see
Drischner, Max

HERR, DU HAST WORTE DES EWIGEN LEBENS
see Thiele, Siegfried

HERR, DU SIEHST STATT GUTER WERKE AUF
DES HERZENS DES KREUZES see Bach,
Johann Sebastian

HERR, DU UND GOTT see Giordani,
Giuseppe

HERR GLOMME see Roselius, Ludwig

HERR GOTT, DU BIST UNSERE ZUFLUCHT see
Drischner, Max

HERR, ICH HOFFE DARAUF see Schutz,
Heinrich

HERR, ICH TRAUE AUF DICH see Schoof,
Armin

HERR, IN DEMUT see Bruckner, Anton, Te
Ergo

HERR, KEHRE DICH WIEDER ZU UNS see
Praetorius, Michael

HERR, LASS MEIN LEBEN WIE EINE KERZE
SEIN see Jochum, Otto

HERR LOFFEL UND FRAU GABEL see Lothar,
Mark

HERR, NEIG' DEIN OHR ZU MIR see
Hofmann, Wolfgang

HERR, NEIGE DEINE HIMMEL see Schutz,
Heinrich

HERR, NEIGE DEINE OHREN see
Kretzschmar, Gunther

HERR, NUN LASSEST DU DEINEN DIENER IM
FRIEDE FAHREN see Schutz, Heinrich

HERR, NUN LASST DU DEINEN DIENER see
Schein, Johann Hermann

HERR, NUN LASST DU DEINEN DIENER IM
FRIEDEN FAHREN see Schein, Johann
Hermann

HERR, NUN LASST DU DIENER see
Buxtehude, Dietrich

HERR OLLONDAL see Peterson-Berger,
(Olof) Wilhelm

HERR OLUF see Loewe, Carl

HERR OLUFS SANG see Nielsen, Carl

HERR, SCHICKE WAS DU WILLT see Wolf,
Hugo

HERR, UNSER HERRSCHER see Schutz,
Heinrich

HERR, VOR DEIN ANTLITZ TRETEN ZWEI
*sac,CC13U
(Brodde, Otto) med solo,org (med
diff) BAREN. 1945 $5.00 (H1291)

HERR, WANN ICH NUR DICH HABE see
Schutz, Heinrich

HERR, WENN ICH NUR DICH HABE see
    Buxtehude, Dietrich

HERR, WENN ICH NUR DICH HABE see
    Rosenmuller, Johann

HERR, WIE LANGE WILLST DU MEIN
    VERGESSEN? see Kretzschmar, Gunther

HERR, WIE SIND DEINE WERKE see
    Micheelsen, Hans-Friedrich

HERR, WOHIN SOLLEN WIR GEHEN? see
    Sibelius, Jean

HERRA ON MINUN PAIMENENI see Sonninen,
    Ahti

HERRA, SINUN ARMOSI ULOTTUU TAIVAISIIN
    see Sonninen, Ahti

HERRE, JAG TAKKER DIG! see Nordqvist,
    Gustaf

HERRE NU LATER DU DIN TJANARE FARA I
    FRID see Wennerberg, Gunnar

HERREN STAR VID HJARTATS DORR
    see Blott En Dag Ett Ogonblick I
    Sander

HERRIN, DU STRAHLST IM HIMMEL see
    Handel, George Frideric, Donna, Che
    In Ciel

HERRMANN, GEORG
    Sag' Mir Nur Einmal Ja *Op.4
        solo,pno RIES s.p.   (H1292)

HERRMANN, HANS
    Der Dichter Spricht
        solo,pno voc sc BIRNBACH s.p.
                                  (H1293)
    Lyrischer Prolog
        high solo,pno voc sc BIRNBACH s.p.
                                  (H1294)
        low solo,pno voc sc BIRNBACH s.p.
                                  (H1295)
    Psalm 126 *Op.43, sac
        solo,org BREITKOPF-W s.p. (H1296)
    Salomo *Op.23,No.1
        high solo,pno voc sc BIRNBACH s.p.
                                  (H1297)
        low solo,pno voc sc BIRNBACH s.p.
                                  (H1298)
    Warst Du Von Stein
        solo,pno voc sc BIRNBACH s.p.
                                  (H1299)

HERRMANN, HUGO (1896-1967)
    Apokalypse *song cycle
        Bar/S solo,strings,perc TONOS 7050
        s.p.   (H1300)
    Chinesische Suite Nach Gedichten Von
        Hans Bethges Chinesischer Flote
        *Op.38, CCU
        S solo,vcl BREITKOPF-W EB 5443 s.p.
                                  (H1301)
    Hymnische Gesange
        solo,pno TONOS 5406 s.p.
        contains: Hyperions
            Schicksalslied; Pastorale
            Religioso   (H1302)
    Hyperions Schicksalslied
        see Hymnische Gesange
    Lieder Einer Mutter *CCU
        med solo,pno SIKORSKI 315 s.p.
                                  (H1303)
    Minnespiel *Op.4, CCU
        SSA soli,pno/harp sc BREITKOPF-W
        PB 3176 s.p., solo pt BREITKOPF-W
        CHB 2565 s.p.   (H1304)
    Pastorale Religioso
        see Hymnische Gesange

HERRMANN, PETER (1941-   )
    Der November Ist Die Heimat *cant
        Bar solo,2fl,2ob,2clar,2bsn,4horn,
        3trp,timp,perc,strings DEUTSCHER
        rental   (H1305)

HERRMANN, WILLIAM
    Deutsche Volkslieder, Vol. I
        *Op.143, CCU,folk,Ger
        2 soli,pno SCHAUR EE 636 s.p.
                                  (H1306)
    Deutsche Volkslieder, Vol. II
        *Op.143, CCU,folk,Ger
        2 soli,pno SCHAUR EE 637 s.p.
                                  (H1307)

HERTIG MAGNUS see Sibelius, Jean

HERTOG, H.J. DEN
    Kerstlied *sac
        solo,pno ALSBACH s.p.   (H1308)

HERTZMAN
    Varsang
        2 soli,pno LUNDQUIST s.p. (H1309)

HERVE (1825-1892)
    Mamze'lle Nitouche
        solo,pno SUPRAPHON s.p.   (H1310)

HERVORMINGSLIED see Rijp, A.W.

HERZ see Lilien, Ignace

HERZ DER NACHT see Serocki, Kazimierz

HERZ, STIRB ODER SINGE see Baur, Jurg

HERZENS KRONELEIN see Strauss, Richard

HERZGEWACHSE see Schoenberg, Arnold

HERZLICH LIEB HAB ICH DICH, O HERR see
    Schutz, Heinrich

HERZLICH THUT, MICH VERLANGEN see
    Buxtehude, Dietrich

HE'S ALREADY DONE see Sims

HE'S BEEN MY DEAREST FRIEND see Jensen,
    Gordon

HE'S COMING BACK--AND SOON see Lister,
    Mosie

HE'S EVERYTHING TO ME see Carmichael,
    Ralph

HE'S EVERYTHING TO ME see Lister, Mosie

HE'S FILLING UP HEAVEN WITH SINNERS see
    Peterson, John W.

HE'S GOIN' AWAY see Niles

HE'S GONE AWAY
    (Shaw, C.) med solo,pno PRESSER $.95
                                  (H1311)

HE'S GONE AWAY see Davis, Katherine K.

HE'S GONE AWAY see Henderson

HE'S GOT THE WHOLE WORLD IN HIS HAND
    *sac,gospel
    solo,pno ABER.GRP. $1.50   (H1312)

HE'S GOT THE WHOLE WORLD IN HIS HANDS
    *sac,spir
    solo,pno ASHLEY $.95   (H1313)
    (Benson) solo,pno BENSON S5784-RS
        $1.00   (H1314)
    (Bonds, M.) high solo,pno MERCURY
        $.95   (H1315)
    (Burleigh, H. T.) med solo,pno BELWIN
        $1.50   (H1316)

HE'S JUST DE SAME TODAY *spir
    (Burleigh, H. T.) high solo,pno
        BELWIN $1.50   (H1317)
    (Burleigh, H. T.) low solo,pno BELWIN
        $1.50   (H1318)

HE'S LISTENING see Price, Florence B.

HE'S MY SAVIOUR, LORD, AND KING *sac,
    gospel
    solo,pno ABER.GRP. $1.50   (H1319)

HE'S ON HIS WAY see Meyers

HE'S ONLY A PRAYER AWAY see Lange

HE'S ONLY A PRAYER AWAY see Lister,
    Mosie

HE'S STILL THE KING OF KINGS see
    Gaither

HE'S TAKING GOOD CARE OF ME see Atwood,
    Tommy

HE'S THE LORD OF GLORY see Spiers, P.

HE'S THERE WAITING *sac
    (Carmichael, Ralph) solo,pno WORD
        S-101   (H1320)

HESELTINE, PHILIP (1894-1930)
    Along The Stream
        see Saudades
    As Ever I Saw
        low solo,pno (D flat maj) BOOSEY
        $1.50   (H1321)
        high solo,pno (E flat maj) BOOSEY
        $1.50   (H1322)
    Balulalow *sac,Xmas
        S/T solo,pno/4strings (easy) OXFORD
        63.310 $1.00   (H1323)
    Bethlehem Down
        solo,org (D min) BOOSEY $1.50
                                  (H1324)
    Book Of Songs *CC12L
        Mez/Bar solo,pno (med) OXFORD
        68.704 $2.50   (H1325)
    Burd Ellen And The Young Tamlane
        see Lillygay

HESELTINE, PHILIP (cont'd.)
    Chopcherry
        see Peterisms Set 1
    Consider
        S/T solo,pno (med) OXFORD 63.101
        $1.00   (H1326)
    Countryman, The
        [Eng/Fr] solo,pno (A flat maj)
        BOOSEY $1.50   (H1327)
    Distracted Maid, The
        see Lillygay
    First Mercy, The
        [Eng/Fr] solo,pno (G min) BOOSEY
        $1.50   (H1328)
    Fox, The
        T solo,pno (med) OXFORD 63.723
        $1.25   (H1329)
    Frost-Bound Wood, The *sac
        Bar solo,pno (med) OXFORD 61.304
        $1.10   (H1330)
    Have You Seen But A White Lily Grow?
        Bar solo,pno (very easy) OXFORD
        63.724 $.75   (H1331)
    Heracleitus
        see Saudades
    In An Arbour Green
        solo,pno PATERSON s.p.   (H1332)
    Johnny Wi' The Tye
        see Lillygay
    Lillygay
        [Eng] high solo,kbd CHESTER s.p.
        contains: Burd Ellen And The
            Young Tamlane; Distracted Maid,
            The; Johnny Wi' The Tye; Rantum
            Tantum; Shoemaker, The (H1333)
    Milkmaids
        high solo,orch (G maj) ASHDOWN
        $1.50, ipr   (H1334)
        low solo,orch (E maj) ASHDOWN
        $1.50, ipr   (H1335)
    My Own Country
        Bar solo,pno (med easy) OXFORD
        61.722 $1.20   (H1336)
        T solo,pno (med easy) OXFORD 63.060
        $1.05   (H1337)
    Passionate Shepherd, The
        high solo,pno ELKIN 27.1691.07 s.p.
                                  (H1338)
    Peterisms Set 1
        [Eng] high solo,kbd CHESTER s.p.
        contains: Chopcherry; Rutterkin;
            Sad Song, A   (H1339)
    Rantum Tantum
        see Lillygay
    Rutterkin
        see Peterisms Set 1
    Sad Song, A
        see Peterisms Set 1
    Saudades
        [Eng] med solo,kbd CHESTER s.p.
        contains: Along The Stream;
            Heracleitus; Take, O Take Those
            Lips Away   (H1340)
    Second Book Of Songs *CC12L
        S/T/Bar solo,pno (med) OXFORD
        68.055 $3.30   (H1341)
    Shoemaker, The
        see Lillygay
    Sleep
        Bar solo,pno (med easy) OXFORD
        61.175 $1.25   (H1342)
    Song Album *CCU
        med solo,pno BOOSEY $4.25 (H1343)
    Sweet-And-Twenty
        T solo,pno (easy) OXFORD 63.316
        $1.00   (H1344)
    Sweet O' The Year, The
        low solo,pno ELKIN 27.2215.01 s.p.
                                  (H1345)
    Take, O Take Those Lips Away
        see Saudades
    Thirteen Songs *CC13U
        med-high solo,pno GALLIARD 2.9018.7
        $3.50   (H1346)
    Yarmouth Fair
        T solo,pno (G maj,easy) OXFORD
        63.745 $1.25   (H1347)
        Bar solo,pno (E maj,easy) OXFORD
        61.728 $1.25   (H1348)

HESELTINE, PHILIP (cont'd.)

B solo,pno (D maj,easy) OXFORD
61.904 $1.25 (H1349)

HESPERIA see Torjussen, Trygve

HESPERIS see Peterson-Berger, (Olof)
Wilhelm

HESPOS, HANS-JOACHIM (1938-)
Palimpsest
solo,perc MODERN rental (H1350)

HESS
Kommt, Wir Wollen Blumen Binden
*Op.13
2 female soli,pno BREITKOPF-W
08 00326 s.p. (H1351)

HESS, W.
Ein Kindermarchen *Op.34
med solo,fl,pno EULENBURG GM 117
s.p. (H1352)

Ein Voglein Singt So Susse *see
Frauchiger, Ch.

Zwolf Gesange *CC12U
solo,pno HUG s.p. (H1353)

HESSE-LIEDER, GESANGE DES ABSCHIEDS see
Wagner-Regeny, Rudolf

HESSENBERG, KURT (1908-)
Elisabeth
Mez solo,vln,pno PETERS 4499 $4.75
(H1354)
Lieder Eines Lumpen *Op.51
T solo,pno (med diff) BAREN. 2135
$9.75 (H1355)
Sieben Leben Mocht Ich Haben *Op.64,
song cycle
A solo,fl,A rec,vln,vla,vcl (med
diff) BAREN. 3421 $5.75 (H1356)
Wenn Ich, O Kindlein *Op.30,No.1-6,
CC6U
med solo,pno SCHOTTS 1331 s.p.
(H1357)
Zehn Lieder *Op.32, CC10U
Mez/Bar solo,pno,vln,vla SCHOTTS
4299 s.p. (H1358)

HESSISCHE LIEDER UND TANZE see Kelling,
Hajo

HET ANGELUS see Rennes, Cath. v.

HET ANGELUS KLEPT IN DE VERTE see
Rennes, Cath. v.

HET AVONDGEBED see Zagwijn, Henri

HET AVONDT see Devreese, Godefroid,
Crepuscule

HET BLANKE PAARD see Bordewijk-Roepman,
Johanna

HET BOORLINGSKEN-MOEDERTAAL see
Hullebroeck, Em.

HET DAGHET IN DEN OOSTEN see Beuningen,
W.v.

HET DAGHET IN DEN OOSTEN see Moulaert,
Raymond

HET DIDDLE DIDDLE see Presser, William

HET EILAND DER BEMINDEN see Zagwijn,
Henri

HET EINDE see Franken, Wim

HET EZELTJE see Mulder, Herman

HET GEBED DES HEEREN see Pomper, A.

HET GEBREK IN CHLORIS see Schouwman,
Hans

HET GEITENWEITJE see Lilien, Ignace

HET GEVECHT see Kersters, Willem

HET HEMELSCH JERUSALEM see Schouwman,
Hans

HET HERT see Orthel, Leon

HET HOOGLIED VAN SALOMO see Zagwijn,
Henri

HET IS DE LIEFDE see Hullebroeck, Em.

HET JONGE JAAR see Mortelmans, Lodewijk

HET KEMPISCH OSSEBOERKEN see
Hullebroeck, Em.

HET KLOKGEBED see Zagwijn, Henri

HET KOREN EN HET KAF see Baeyens,
August-L.

HET LAND VAN NOORD SCHARWOU see Witte,
D.

HET LAND VAN UTOPEIA see Zagwijn, Henri

HET LANDJE VAN BELOFTE see Hullebroeck,
Em.

HET LANDJE VAN KOKANJE see Zagwijn,
Henri

HET LIED DAT FLUISTERT see Mulder,
Herman

HET LIED VAN DE JEUGD see Rontgen,
Johannes

HET LIED VAN DE REGEN see Mulder,
Herman

HET LIED VAN NELE see Hullebroeck, Em.

HET LIED VOOR DE CHRISTELIJKE
FEESTDAGEN see Tierie, J.F.

HET LIEDJE VAN DE BELAARDIER see
Hullebroeck, Em.

HET LOOZE MOOLENARINNETJE see Nieland,
H.

HET MASKER VAN DEN ROODEN DOOD see
Dijk, Jan van

HET MEISJE VAN AMSTERDAM see
Hullebroeck, Em.

HET MEISJE VAN DEN BUITEN see
Hullebroeck, Em.

HET NAARDERMEER see Sigtenhorst-Meyer,
Bernhard van den

HET ONGELUK see Middeleer, Jean De, Le
Malheur

HET ONZE VADER see Nieland, H.

HET SNEEUWDE WAT see Bordewijk-Roepman,
Johanna

HET STERVENDE KIND see Hinderdael, C.

HET STROOIEN DAK see Mortelmans,
Lodewijk

HET UURWERK see Middeleer, Jean De, La
Montre

HET VERDRONKEN KIND see Henkemans, Hans

HET VERWAEND KWEZELTJE see Schouwman,
Hans

HET VIEL EEN HEMELS DOUWE see Horst,
Anton van der

HET VIEL EEN HEMELS DOUWE see Ruyneman,
Daniel

HET VLAAMSCHE MEISJE EN DEN FRANSCHEN
HEER see Geraedts, Jaap

HET VOLKSLIED see Andriessen, K.

HET WAREN TWEE CONINCKINDEREN see
Moulaert, Raymond

HET WIEGELIED DER VLAAMSCH GEZINDE
MOEDER see Hullebroeck, Em.

HET WUF DIE SPON see Schouwman, Hans

HET ZIJN GEEN JONGENS see Hullebroeck,
Em.

HEU, ME MISERAM! see Jeffries, George

HEU ME MISERAM ET INFELICEM see
Bernabei, (Giuseppe) Ercole

HEULETT, M.
In After Days
med solo,pno SEESAW $1.00 (H1359)

HEURE BLANCHE see Santesteban, J. de

HEURE DE GRACE see Absil, Jean

HEURE D'ETE see Defosse, H.

HEURE D'ETE see Gui, Vittorio

HEURE DU RETOUR see Roussel, Albert

HEURES D'APRES-MIDI see Brusselmans,
Michel

HEURES DOUCES see Toutain-Grun, J.

HEUREUSE see Berger, Rod.

HEUREUX see Delannoy, Marcel

HEUSSENSTAMM, GEORGE
With Jesus Will I Go *sac
SA soli,pno oct CONCORDIA 98-1778
$.25 (H1360)

HEUT ABEND see Nielsen, Carl, I Aften

HEUT' ES KEIN ABEND WERDEN WILL see
Jentsch, Walter

HEUT SINGT DIE LIEBE CHRISTENHEIT see
Krieger, Johann Philipp

HEUTE IST ALLES TEUER' WORDEN see
Kilpinen, Yrio, Nyt On Kaikki
Kallistunna

HEUTE IST CHRISTUS, DER HERR, GEBOREN
see Schutz, Heinrich

HEUTE IST DER SIEGESTAG see Erlebach,
Philipp Heinrich

HEY THE DUSTY MILLER *folk,Scot
solo,pno (D flat maj/E flat maj)
PATERSON FS134 s.p. (H1361)

HIBBARD, WILLIAM
Reflexa
S solo,trom,vcl,perc,harp sc
AM.COMP.AL. $8.25 (H1362)

HIBI-ITE-YUKO see Kumaki, Mamoru

HIDDEN WONDER see Peeters, Flor

HIDE ME, ROCK OF AGES *sac,gospel
solo,pno ABER.GRP. $1.50 (H1363)

HIDING PLACE, THE see Leech

HIELAND LADDIE *folk,Scot
solo,pno (F maj) PATERSON FS125 s.p.
(H1364)

HIER see Poulenc, Francis

HIER ET DEMAIN see Berger, Rod.

HIER, ETHEL GLENN (1889-)
Avalon
high solo/med solo,pno SEESAW $1.00
(H1365)
Click O' The Latch
high solo/med solo,pno SEESAW $1.50
(H1366)
Gulls
high solo/med solo,pno SEESAW $1.50
(H1367)
Hour, The
high solo,pno SEESAW $1.50 contains
also: Return, The (H1368)
Lonely Cabin, The
med solo,pno SEESAW $1.50 (H1369)
Return, The
see Hier, Ethel Glenn, Hour, The

HIER IM IRDSCHEN JAMMERTAL see Weber,
Carl Maria von

HIER STEHT DER WANDRER NUN see Haydn,
(Franz) Joseph

HIGH HEAVEN IS NOT JUST see Cardew,
Cornelius

HIGH LEAP THE FIRETONGUES see Verdi,
Giuseppe, Stride La Vampa

HIGH LEVEL RANTERS SONG AND TUNE BOOK
see Handle, Johnny

HIGH VOICE SERIES, NOS. 1-6 *CCUL
high solo,kbd SINGSPIR
5021-5025; 5170 $1.50, ea. (H1370)

HIGH VOICE SOLOS NO. I *sac,CCUL
T/S solo,pno LILLENAS MB-065 $1.50
(H1371)
HIGH VOICE SOLOS NO. II *sac,CCUL
T/S solo,pno LILLENAS MB-066 $1.50
(H1372)
HIGH VOICE SOLOS NO. III *sac,CCUL
T/S solo,pno LILLENAS MB-067 $1.50
(H1373)
HIGH VOICE SOLOS NO. IV *sac,CCUL
T/S solo,pno LILLENAS MB-354 $1.50
(H1374)
HIGH VOICE SOLOS, VOL. 1 *sac,CCU
(Mann, Bill; Bock, Fred) high solo,
pno WORD 10005 $1.00 (H1375)
HIGH VOICE SOLOS, VOL. 2 *sac,CCU
(Mann, Bill; Evan, Clark) high solo,
pno WORD 20021 $1.50 (H1376)
HIGH VOICE SPECIALS, VOL. 1 *sac,CCU
high solo,pno HOPE 516 $1.25 (H1377)

HIGHER HANDS *sac
solo,pno SINGSPIR 7046-SN $1.00
(H1378)

HIGHER HANDS see Peterson, John W.

HIGHEST HILL, THE see Lister, Mosie

HIGHLAND CRADLE SONG
   (Roberton, Hugh S.) solo,pno (C maj)
   ROBERTON 2785 s.p. see also Songs
   Of The Isles   (H1379)

HIGHLAND FRAGMENTS see Kaburagi,
   Mitsugu

HIGHLAND MAID, A see Henderson, W.G.

HIGHLAND PASTORAL see McLeod, Robert

HIGHLAND QUEEN, THE see Hook, James

HIGHLAND SONG see Sacco

HIJ DIE GEEN LIEDJE ZINGEN KAN see
   Hullebroeck, Em.

HIJ DROECH ONSE SMERTEN see Flothius,
   Marius

HIJ KOMT see Verrees, E.

HIJMAN, JULIUS (1901-   )
   Zes Liederen *CC6U
   solo,pno BROEKMANS 300 s.p. (H1380)

HILDACH, EUGEN (1849-1924)
   Abschied Der Vogel
   "Passage-Birds' Farewell" [Ger/Eng]
   high solo&med solo,pno SCHIRM.G
   $.75   (H1381)

   Easter Triumph *sac
   (McKinney) low solo,pno BELWIN
   $1.50   (H1382)
   (McKinney) high solo,pno,opt vln/
   vcl BELWIN $1.50   (H1383)

   Passage-Birds' Farewell *see
   Abschied Der Vogel

   Where'er Thou Goest *see Wo Du
   Hingehst

   Wo Du Hingehst *Marriage
   "Where'er Thou Goest" [Eng/Ger] med
   solo,pno/org/harmonium NOETZEL
   N253B s.p.   (H1384)
   "Where'er Thou Goest" [Eng/Ger]
   high solo,pno/org/harmonium
   NOETZEL N253A s.p.   (H1385)
   "Where'er Thou Goest" [Eng/Ger] low
   solo,pno/org/harmonium NOETZEL
   N253C   (H1386)
   "Where'er Thou Goest" [Eng/Ger]
   SBar soli,pno/org/harmonium
   NOETZEL N357 s.p.   (H1387)

HILDEBRAND, RAY
   I Need You Every Hour *sac,CC10L
   solo,pno WORD 37517 $2.50   (H1388)

   Say I Do *sac
   solo,pno WORD S-327   (H1389)

HILDENBRAND, SIEGFRIED
   Ich Schrie Zum Herrn *sac
   S solo,vln,org sc HANSSLER 10.175
   s.p., ipa   (H1390)

HILL
   Dream Cloud
   low solo,pno (F maj) ALLANS s.p.
                                     (H1391)
   high solo,pno (A flat maj) ALLANS
   s.p.   (H1392)

   Garden Is A Lovesome Thing
   solo,pno ALLANS s.p.   (H1393)

   Hinemoa's Song
   high solo,pno (F maj) ALLANS s.p.
                                     (H1394)
   low solo,pno (D maj) ALLANS s.p.
                                     (H1395)

   Mopoke
   solo,pno ALLANS s.p.   (H1396)

   Wake My Tender Thrilling Flute
   low solo,pno (B flat maj) ALLANS
   s.p.   (H1397)
   high solo,pno (D flat maj) ALLANS
   s.p.   (H1398)

   What A Day That Will Be *sac
   solo,pno BENSON S8360-S $1.00   (H1399)

HILL CALLED MT. CALVARY, A see Gaither

HILL, EUGENE
   Come Thou Long Expected Jesus *sac,
   Xmas
   high solo,pno (G maj) WATERLOO $.90
                                     (H1400)
   med solo,pno (E flat maj) WATERLOO
   $.90   (H1401)

   Jesus The Very Thought Of Thee *sac
   low solo,pno (G maj) WATERLOO $.90
                                     (H1402)

HILL, EUGENE (cont'd.)

   med solo,pno (F maj) WATERLOO $.90
                                     (H1403)
   My Prayer *sac
   med solo,pno (E maj) WATERLOO $.75
                                     (H1404)
   high solo,pno (G maj) WATERLOO $.75
                                     (H1405)

HILL, LADY ARTHUR
   In The Gloaming
   low solo,pno (F maj) LEONARD-ENG
                                     (H1406)
   med solo,pno (G maj) LEONARD-ENG
                                     (H1407)
   high solo,pno (A flat maj) LEONARD-
   ENG   (H1408)
   2 soli,pno LEONARD-ENG   (H1409)

HILLANKUKKA see Kilpinen, Yrio

HILLER
   Majsang
   2 soli,pno LUNDQUIST s.p.   (H1410)

   Sechs Lieder Zum Singen Mit Gitarre
   *CC6U
   solo,gtr/pno TONGER s.p.   (H1411)

HILLER, FERDINAND (1811-1885)
   Herr, Den Ich Tief Im Herzen Trage
   *Op.46,No.1, sac
   S/T solo,pno (F maj) LIENAU HOS 153
   s.p.   (H1412)
   [Ger] med solo,vln&pno/vln&org
   LIENAU R85 s.p.   (H1413)
   A/Bar solo,pno (C maj) LIENAU
   HOS 155 s.p.   (H1414)
   Mez solo,pno (E flat maj) LIENAU
   HOS 154 s.p.   (H1415)
   "Prayer" [Eng/Ger] high solo,pno
   PETERS 2584A $2.25   (H1416)
   "Prayer" [Eng/Ger] low solo,pno
   PETERS 2584C $2.25   (H1417)
   "Prayer" [Eng/Ger] med solo,pno
   PETERS 2584B $2.25   (H1418)

   Prayer *see Herr, Den Ich Tief Im
   Herzen Trage

HILLER, WILFRED (1941-   )
   Alastair *CC7U
   S solo,fl,vla study sc ORLANDO s.p.
                                     (H1419)
   Let Thy Song Be Love
   S solo,pno ORLANDO s.p.   (H1420)

HILLIAM, B.C.
   Clock, The
   solo,pno CRAMER   (H1421)

   Old Sea Dog
   solo,pno (B flat maj) BOOSEY $1.50
                                     (H1422)
   Sailor's Life, A
   solo,pno CRAMER $1.15   (H1423)

HILLIARD
   Beautiful Scars *sac
   solo,pno BENSON S5153-R $1.00
                                     (H1424)

HILLO, IL MIO BENE E MORTO see Cavalli,
   (Pietro) Francesco

HILLS see LaForge, Frank

HILLS OF DAN see Davidson, M.T.

HILLS OF DONEGAL see Sanderson, Wilfred

HILLS OF HOME, THE see Fox

HILLS VISOR *CCU
   (Lundkvist, P.) [Eng/Swed] solo,pno
   LUNDQUIST s.p.   (H1425)

HILSEN see Nielsen, Carl

HILTON
   What Shall He Have That Killed The
   Deer?
   see AS YOU LIKE IT

HILTY, EVERETT JAY
   Awake, My Soul, Stretch Every Nerve
   *sac
   med solo,pno oct CONCORDIA 98-1922
   $.25   (H1426)

   Heart And Mind, Possessions, Lord
   *sac
   med solo,pno oct CONCORDIA 98-1918
   $.25   (H1427)

HIMALAJAN RINTEELLA see Bergman, Erik

HIMFYS KARLEKSSANGER see Nordqvist,
   Gustaf

HIMLENS BLA see Liljefors, Ruben

HIMMEL UND ERDE VERGEHEN see Schutz,
   Heinrich

HIMMELSEHNSSUCHT see Bonvin, Ludwig

HIMMELSKE FADER see Geitvik, S.H.

HIMMLISCHE SCHLITTENFAHRT see
   Pylkkanen, Tauno Kullervo,
   Taivainen Rekiretki

HIMNO NACIONAL URUGUAYO see Deballi

HIMNOS NACIONALES AMERICANOS *CC22U,US
   [Eng] T solo,pno RICORDI-ARG BA 9043
   s.p.   (H1428)

HINCHCLIFFE, IRVIN
   Creation
   solo,pno PATERSON s.p.   (H1429)

   Feed My Sheep *sac
   low solo,pno (E flat maj) FISCHER,C
   V 1573   (H1430)

   Tranquility
   solo,pno PATERSON s.p.   (H1431)

HIND, JOHN
   Cradle Song, A
   med solo,pno NOVELLO 17.0037.05
   s.p.   (H1432)

   I Loved A Lass
   Bar solo,pno NOVELLO 17.0070.07
   s.p.   (H1433)

   Mad Maid's Song, The
   med solo,pno NOVELLO 17.0116.09
   s.p.   (H1434)

   Wakening, The
   med solo,pno NOVELLO 17.0208.04
   s.p.   (H1435)

HINDEMITH, PAUL (1895-1963)
   Angelus Domini Apparuit *sac,Bibl/
   mot
   [Lat] S/T solo,pno SCHOTTS 5088
   s.p. see from Dreizehn Motteten
                                     (H1436)
   Ascendente Jesu In Naviculam *sac,
   Bibl/mot
   [Lat] S/T solo,pno SCHOTTS 5094
   s.p. see from Dreizehn Motteten
                                     (H1437)
   Beauty Touch Me
   see Two Songs

   Cum Decendisset Jesus *sac,Bibl/mot
   [Lat] S/T solo,pno SCHOTTS 5093
   s.p. see from Dreizehn Motteten
                                     (H1438)
   Cum Factus Esset Jesus *sac,Bibl/mot
   [Lat] S/T solo,pno SCHOTTS 5091
   s.p. see from Dreizehn Motteten
                                     (H1439)
   Cum Natus Esset *sac,Bibl/mot
   [Lat] S/T solo,pno SCHOTTS 4392
   s.p. see from Dreizehn Motteten
                                     (H1440)
   Das Marienleben *Op.27, song cycle
   S solo,pno (revised edition)
   SCHOTTS 2026 s.p.   (H1441)
   S solo,pno SCHOTTS 2025 s.p.
                                     (H1442)
   Defuncto Herode *sac,Bibl/mot
   [Lat] S/T solo,pno SCHOTTS 5090
   s.p. see from Dreizehn Motteten
                                     (H1443)
   Des Todes Tod *Op.23,No.1
   S solo,2vla,2vcl sc SCHOTTS 5422
   s.p., ipa, voc sc SCHOTTS 4493
   s.p.   (H1444)
   Dicebat Jesus Scribis Et Pharisaeis
   *sac,Bibl/mot
   [Lat] S/T solo,pno SCHOTTS 5086
   s.p. see from Dreizehn Motteten
                                     (H1445)
   Die Junge Magd *Op.23,No.2
   A solo,fl,clar,strings voc sc
   SCHOTTS 2024 s.p., sc SCHOTTS
   3404 s.p., ipa   (H1446)
   Die Serenaden *Op.35, cant
   S solo,ob,vla,vcl sc,voc sc SCHOTTS
   2027 s.p., ipa   (H1447)
   Dixit Jesus Petro *sac,Bibl/mot
   [Lat] S/T solo,pno SCHOTTS 5087
   s.p. see from Dreizehn Motteten
                                     (H1448)
   Dreizehn Motteten *see Angelus
   Domini Apparuit; Ascendente Jesu
   In Naviculam; Cum Decendisset
   Jesus; Cum Factus Esset Jesus;
   Cum Natus Esset; Defuncto Herode;
   Dicebat Jesus Scribis Et
   Pharisaeis; Dixit Jesus Petro;
   Erat Joseph Et Maria; Exit
   Edictum; Nuptiae Factae Sunt;
   Pastores Loquebantur; Vidit
   Joannes Jesum   (H1449)

   Echo
   [Eng] S/Mez solo,pno SCHOTTS 10321
   s.p. see from Nine English Songs
                                     (H1450)

HINDEMITH, PAUL (cont'd.)

Envoy
[Eng] S/Mez solo,pno SCHOTTS 10325
s.p. see from Nine English Songs
(H1451)

Erat Joseph Et Maria *sac,Bibl/mot
[Lat] S/T solo,pno SCHOTTS 5089
s.p. see from Dreizehn Motteten
(H1452)

Exit Edictum *sac,Bibl/mot
[Lat] S/T solo,pno SCHOTTS 5085
s.p. see from Dreizehn Motteten
(H1453)

Image
see Two Songs

La Belle Dame Sans Merci
[Eng] high solo/med solo,pno
SCHOTTS s.p.
(H1454)

Lieder Fur Sopran *Op.18,No.1-8, CCU
solo,pno SCHOTTS 2023 s.p. (H1455)

Moon, The
[Eng] S/Mez solo,pno SCHOTTS 10322
s.p. see from Nine English Songs
(H1456)

Nine English Songs *see Echo; Envoy;
Moon, The; On A Fly Drinking Out
Of His Cup; On Hearing 'The Last
Rose Of Summer'; Sing On There In
The Swamp; To Music, To Becalm
His Fever; Whistlin' Thief, The;
Wild Flower's Song, The (H1457)

Nuptiae Factae Sunt *sac,Bibl/mot
[Lat] S/T solo,pno SCHOTTS 4391
s.p. see from Dreizehn Motteten
(H1458)

On A Fly Drinking Out Of His Cup
[Eng] S/Mez solo,pno SCHOTTS 10323
s.p. see from Nine English Songs
(H1459)

On Hearing 'The Last Rose Of Summer'
[Eng] S/Mez solo,pno SCHOTTS 10320
s.p. see from Nine English Songs
(H1460)

Pastores Loquebantur *sac,Bibl/mot
[Lat] S/T solo,pno SCHOTTS 4390
s.p. see from Dreizehn Motteten
(H1461)

Sechs Lieder Nach Gedichten Von
Friedrich Holderlin *CC6U
[Eng] s.p. T solo,pno SCHOTTS 5462;
low solo,pno SCHOTTS 5752 (H1462)

Sing On There In The Swamp
[Eng] S solo,pno SCHOTTS 10682 s.p.
see from Nine English Songs
(H1463)
[Eng] Mez solo,pno SCHOTTS 10327
s.p. see from Nine English Songs
(H1464)

To Music, To Becalm His Fever
[Eng] S/Mez solo,pno SCHOTTS 10480
s.p. see from Nine English Songs
(H1465)

Two Songs
[Eng] high solo,pno SCHOTTS 4441
s.p.
contains: Beauty Touch Me; Image
(H1466)

Vidit Joannes Jesum *sac,Bibl/mot
[Lat] S/T solo,pno SCHOTTS 5092
s.p. see from Dreizehn Motteten
(H1467)

Whistlin' Thief, The
[Eng] S/Mez solo,pno SCHOTTS 10324
s.p. see from Nine English Songs
(H1468)

Wild Flower's Song, The
[Eng] S solo,pno SCHOTTS 10681 s.p.
see from Nine English Songs
(H1469)
[Eng] Mez solo,pno SCHOTTS 10326
s.p. see from Nine English Songs
(H1470)

HINDERDAEL, C.
Het Stervende Kind
solo,pno ALSBACH s.p. (H1471)

HINDU SONG see Rimsky-Korsakov,
Nikolai, Chanson Hindoue

HINE, STUART
How Great Thou Art *sac
solo,pno BENSON S5900-R $1.00
(H1472)
solo,pno BENSON S5904-S $1.00
(H1473)
solo,pipe/Hamm BENSON S5912-R $1.25
(H1474)

HINEH BAR'CHU see Chajes, Julius

HINEMOA'S SONG see Hill

HINENI (HERE AM I) *sac,CC11UL,Jew
(Dauermann, Stuart) solo,pno,gtr
LILLENAS MB-370 $2.50 (H1475)

HINES
I Would Rather Sing Of Jesus *sac
solo,pno HOPE 551 $.75 (H1476)

HINES (cont'd.)

O Will He Yet Draw Near Again *sac
solo,pno HOPE $.75 (H1477)

HINNE MA TOV!
see Six Folk Songs

HINRICHS, F.
Gott Rad
2 soli,pno LUNDQUIST s.p. (H1478)

Prinsessan
high solo,pno GEHRMANS s.p. (H1479)
low solo,pno GEHRMANS s.p. (H1480)

HINSON, D.
He Pilots My Ship *sac
solo,pno BENSON S5709-S $1.00
(H1481)

Lighthouse, The *sac
solo,pno BENSON S7938-S $1.00
(H1482)

Orchids
high solo/med solo,pno SEESAW $1.00
(H1483)

HINTER EINER GRUNEN WEIDE see Rontgen,
Johannes

HINUBER WALL' ICH see Diepenbrock,
Alphons

HINUNTER IST DER SONNEN SCHEIN see
Stern, Hermann

HIPPMAN, S.
Franzosische Balladen *Op.4, CCU
[Czech/Ger/Fr] solo,pno SUPRAPHON
s.p. (H1484)

HIRAI, KOZABURO (1910-   )
Celebrated Songs, Vol. 1 *CCU
solo,pno ONGAKU s.p. (H1485)

Celebrated Songs, Vol. 2 *CCU
solo,pno ONGAKU s.p. (H1486)

Nihon No Hana *CC39U
solo,pno ONGAKU s.p. (H1487)

HIRNER, TEODOR (1910-   )
Hore Grunom, Dolu Grunom
boy solo/girl solo,pno
SLOV.HUD.FOND s.p. (H1488)

HIRONDELLE QUI PART AUX INDES see
Migot, Georges

HIRSCH, H.L.
Botschaften Des Regens *CC4U
[Ger] S solo,pno PETERS 5969 $4.50
(H1489)

HIRSCHMANN, H.
Chanson De La Bergere
solo,pno (available in 2 keys)
ENOCH s.p. (H1490)

Serenade Florentine
solo,pno (available in 2 keys)
ENOCH s.p. (H1491)

HIRTENLIED see Kilpinen, Yrio,
Paimenlaulu

HIRTENLIEDER see Bornefeld, Helmut

HIS AND HERS see Madsen, Eleanor

HIS EYE IS ON THE SPARROW see Gabriel,
Sr., Charles H.

HIS EYES WITH FIRE WERE FLAMING see
Leoncavallo, Ruggiero, Qual Fiamma
Avea Nel Guardo

HIS GENTLE LOOK see Red, Buryl

HIS GRACE IS SUFFICIENT FOR ME see
Lister, Mosie

HIS GRACE WILL SEE US THROUGH see
Poglietti, Alessandro

HIS HAND IN MINE see Lister, Mosie

HIS LAND *sac
(Carmichael, Ralph) solo,pno WORD
S-230 (H1492)

HIS LAND *sac,CCUL
(Carmichael, Ralph) solo,pno WORD
30059 $2.50 (H1493)

HIS LOW DOOR see Franco, Johan

HIS NAME IS WONDERFUL see Mieir

HIS NAME SO SWEET see Johnson

HIS SHEEP AM I see Johnson, Orien

HIS VOICE AS THE SOUND OF THE DULCIMER
see Birch, Robert Fairfax

HIS WAY-MINE see Baker, Richard

HIST WHIST see De Jong, Conrad

HIST...WHIST see Duke, John Woods

HISTOIRE D'AIMER see Berger, Rod.

HISTOIRE DE CHASSE see Vellones, P.

HISTOIRE D'UN TRES GRAND ET D'UNE TOUTE
PETITE see Colias, G.

HISTOIRE D'UNE JUPE AMARANTE ET D'UN
PANTALON DE DRAP GRIS see Colias,
G.

HISTOIRE D'UNE POMME see Michiels, G.

HISTOIRES NATURELLES see Ravel, Maurice

HISTORIETTES AU CREPUSCULE see Bloch,
Ernest

HIVA see Wagner, Richard

HIVELY, WELLS
Aunque Es De Noche
high solo,pno AM.COMP.AL. $2.75
(H1494)

Autumn Song
med solo,pno AM.COMP.AL. $.55
(H1495)

Cancion De La Virgen
med solo,pno AM.COMP.AL. $1.10
(H1496)

Dog-Wood
Bar solo,pno AM.COMP.AL. $5.50
(H1497)
Mez solo,pno AM.COMP.AL. $5.50
(H1498)

If Music Be The Food Of Love
med solo,pno AM.COMP.AL. $1.10
(H1499)

La Croix De La Lorraine
med solo,pno AM.COMP.AL. $2.75
(H1500)

Le Bon Pasteur
med solo,pno AM.COMP.AL. $1.10
(H1501)

Merry May, The
med solo,pno AM.COMP.AL. $1.10
(H1502)

Nicolette
med solo,pno AM.COMP.AL. $.55
(H1503)

Orphee, Orphelin
S solo,pno AM.COMP.AL. $1.37
(H1504)

Pastores
med solo,pno AM.COMP.AL. $.55
(H1505)

Romance De La Luna, Luna
high solo,pno AM.COMP.AL. $4.95
(H1506)
S/T solo,2fl,2ob,2clar,2bsn,2horn,
2trp,3trom,timp,harp,tamb,strings
sc AM.COMP.AL. $14.85 (H1507)

Sandals
med solo,pno AM.COMP.AL. $.55
(H1508)

Song Of The Rainchant
high solo,pno AM.COMP.AL. $1.10
(H1509)

Song On A May Morning
high solo,pno AM.COMP.AL. $1.10
(H1510)

Songs For A Little Son *CCU
med solo,pno AM.COMP.AL. $4.95
(H1511)

Three Shakespeare Songs *CC3U
high solo,pno AM.COMP.AL. $4.95
(H1512)

Twilight In Paris
med solo,pno AM.COMP.AL. $1.10
(H1513)

HIVER see Quinet, Marcel

HJARNATS SAGA see Astrom

HJARTAT see Nordqvist, Gustaf

HJARTAT SJUNGER see Nordqvist, Gustaf

HJARTATS MORGON see Sibelius, Jean

HJARTATS SOMMAR see Nordqvist, Gustaf

HJARTEROVET *CCU
(Hahn; Setterlind) solo,pno NORDISKA
6488 s.p. (H1514)

HJORLEIFSSON, SIGGURINGI E. (1902-   )
Sound Of Spring, The
solo,pno ICELAND s.p. (H1515)

Wanderings
solo,pno ICELAND s.p. (H1516)

HLASY NOCI see Picha, Frantisek

HLOBIL, EMIL (1901-   )
  Cesta Zivych *CC4U
  med solo,pno CZECH s.p.   (H1517)

  Evocation
  S solo,2fl CZECH s.p.   (H1518)

HO! MR. PIPER see Curran, Pearl
  Gildersleeve

HO PIANTO IN SOGNO see Gandino, Adolfo

HO-REE, HO-RO, MY LITTLE WEE GIRL!
  (Roberton, Hugh S.) solo,pno (E flat
  maj) ROBERTON 2783 s.p. see also
  Songs Of The Isles   (H1519)

HO RO MY NUT BROWN MAIDEN see Lawson,
  Malcolm

HO, WHO COMES HERE see Jacob

HOAG, CHARLES K.
  Dirge
  solo,pno BOOSEY $1.50   (H1520)

  Love's Snare
  see Three Songs

  Three Songs
  solo,pno NEW VALLEY $2.50
    contains: Love's Snare; What
    Menys Thys; Words   (H1521)

  What Menys Thys
  see Three Songs

  Words
  see Three Songs

HOB ICH MIR A MANTL see Neumann,
  Richard J.

HOBBS, CHRISTOPHER
  Song 1
  solo,pno EXPERIMENTAL s.p.   (H1522)

  Song 2
  solo,pno EXPERIMENTAL s.p.   (H1523)

  Voicepiece
  soli (includes suggestions for
    performance) EXPERIMENTAL s.p.
                                 (H1524)

HOCH, FRANCESCO (1943-   )
  Dune
  2 soli,4strings voc sc ZERBONI 8013
  s.p.   (H1525)

HOCHELLA
  Fire Sange *Op.10, CC4U
  solo,pno GEHRMANS s.p.   (H1526)

HOCHGEBIRGSWINTER see Kilpinen, Yrio

HOCHGELOBTER GOTTESSOHN see Bach,
  Johann Sebastian

HOCHMANN, KLAUS (1932-   )
  Requiem Fur Einen Unbekannten *Req
  B solo,org (diff) BAREN. 4111
  $10.50   (H1527)

HOCHPREISET MEINE SEELE see Haller,
  Hans Christoph

HOCHSOMMERNACHT see Marx, Joseph

HOCHSTES VERTRAUN see Wagner, Richard

HOCHZEITLICH LIED see Strauss, Richard

HOCHZEITS-SPRUCH see Werba, E.

HOCHZEITSLIED see Schoenberg, Arnold

HODDINOTT, ALUN (1929-   )
  Medieval Carol *sac,carol
  Mez/Bar solo,pno (med easy) OXFORD
  62.229 $1.30   (H1528)

HODDLEY, PODDLEY, PUDDLE AND FROGS see
  Fiske, R.

HODGSON, A.R.
  Daffodil Gold
  high solo,orch (A maj) ASHDOWN
    $1.50, ipr   (H1529)
  med solo,orch (G maj) ASHDOWN
    $1.50, ipr   (H1530)
  low solo,orch (F maj) ASHDOWN
    $1.50, ipr   (H1531)

HODIE CHRISTUS NATUS EST see Schutz,
  Heinrich

HODSON, J.A.
  Tell Me Mary How To Woo Thee
  solo,pno CRAMER   (H1532)

HOE GARIEL MARIA VOND see Moulaert,
  Raymond

HOE JONG-HENDRIK UIT VRIJEN GING see
  Spoel, A.

HOE LANK NOG, HERR see Mulder, Ernest
  W.

HOE SCHOON DE MORGENDAUW see
  Mortelmans, Lodewijk

HOE VER OOK WEG see Lilien, Ignace

HOENDEVANGER, W.
  Hannekeman
  solo,pno BROEKMANS 106 s.p.   (H1533)

HOEVEN, L.
  De Kleuren Van Mijn Vaderland
  solo,pno BROEKMANS 84B s.p.   (H1534)

HOFFENDE IN DER NACHT see Borris,
  Siegfried

HOFFMANN, GEORG MELCHOIR
  Meine Seele Ruhmt Und Preist *sac,
    cant
  T solo,fl,ob,strings,cembalo
    (formerly attributed to J.S.Bach
    - BWV 189) voc sc BREITKOPF-L
    EB 7189 s.p., ipr   (H1535)

  Schlage Doch, Gewunschte Stunde
    *sac,cant
  Mez/A solo,strings,org,cembalo,
    campanella (formally attributed
    to J.S. Bach - BWV 53) sc
    BREITKOPF-L PB 2903 s.p., ipa
                                 (H1536)

  (Raphael, G.) Mez/A solo,pno
    (formally attributed to J.S. Bach
    - BWV 53) voc sc BREITKOPF-L
    EB 7053 $2.00   (H1537)

HOFFMEISTER, LEON ABBOTT
  Behold, The Tabernacle Of God *sac
  low solo,pno (F maj) SCHIRM.G $.60
                                 (H1538)
  How Long Wilt Thou Forget Me, O Lord?
    *sac,Gen
  high solo,pno (A min) WILLIS $.60
                                 (H1539)
  low solo,pno (F min) WILLIS $.60
                                 (H1540)
  I Will Lift Up Mine Eyes *sac,Gen
  high solo,pno (A flat maj) WILLIS
    $.60   (H1541)
  low solo,pno (F maj) WILLIS $.60
                                 (H1542)
  Lord's Prayer, The *sac,Gen
  high solo,pno (A flat maj) WILLIS
    $.60   (H1543)
  low solo,pno (F maj) WILLIS $.60
                                 (H1544)

  Wee Fiddle Moon *see Graham

HOFFNUNG see Reichardt, Luise

HOFMANN, WOLFGANG (1922-   )
  Herr, Neig' Dein Ohr Zu Mir (Psalm
    85) sac
  S/T solo,org SIRIUS s.p.   (H1545)

  Psalm 85 *see Herr, Neig' Dein Ohr
    Zu Mir

HOGA MADONNA see Stradella, Alessandro

HOGAR, DULCE HOGAR see Bishop, Sir
  Henry Rowley, Home, Sweet Home

HOGEN see Nielsen, Carl

HOGEN GARA
  see Internationale Volkslieder, Vol.
  2

HOGENHAVEN, KNUD
  Fire Engelske Sonetter
  S solo,pno FOG III, 215 s.p.
    contains: How Oft, When Thou My
    Music; Music To Hear; When I
    Have Fears; When In The
    Cronicle   (H1546)

  How Oft, When Thou My Music
  see Fire Engelske Sonetter

  Music To Hear
  see Fire Engelske Sonetter

  When I Have Fears
  see Fire Engelske Sonetter

  When In The Cronicle
  see Fire Engelske Sonetter

HOGNER, FRIEDRICH (1897-   )
  Zwei Trauungsgesange Und Tauflied
    *CC2U
  solo,vln,org PETERS 8078 $8.50
                                 (H1547)

HOGT PA FALLETS ORMBUNKSSNAR see
  Peterson-Berger, (Olof) Wilhelm

HOGUE! CELTES HOGUE C'EST LE JOUR
  ATTENDU see Indy, Vincent d'

HOHE LIEBE see Liszt, Franz

HOHE WOLKEN see Borris, Siegfried

HOHENFLUG see Oort, H.C.v.

HOHER HIMMEL see Griesbach, Karl-Rudi

HOIBY, LEE (1926-   )
  Go And Catch A Falling Star
  solo,pno (D flat maj) BOOSEY $1.50
                                 (H1548)

HOKANSON, MARGRETHE (1893-   )
  Seven Devotional Songs *sac,CC7U
  med solo,pno HOPE 503 $2.50   (H1549)

HOKKEN SKA'N BLONKE TEL see Braein,
  Edvard Fliflet

HOKKEN SKA'N GODBLONKE TEL see Beck,
  Thomas [Ludvigsen]

HOLBORNE, ANTONY
  Wedding Is Great Juno's Crown
  see AS YOU LIKE IT

HOLBROOKE, JOSEPH (1878-1958)
  Killary
  solo,pno CRAMER   (H1550)

  Where Be You Going?
  low solo,pno (F maj) CRAMER (H1551)
  high solo,pno (A maj) CRAMER
                                 (H1552)

HOLD MY COAT see Campbell, Jack

HOLD ON *spir
  (Bonds, M.) med solo,pno PRESSER $.75
                                 (H1553)

HOLD THOU MY HAND see Briggs

HOLD THOU MY HAND see Curran, Pearl
  Gildersleeve

HOLDEN, DAVID
  Land Dirge, A
  solo,pno NEW VALLEY $1.00   (H1554)

HOLDER DU AV MIG see Sjogren, Emil

HOLDERLIN see Zilcher, Hermann

HOLDERLIN-GESANGE see Grabs, Manfred

HOLDERLIN-LIEDER, BAND I: OP.6 AND
  OP.12 see Hauer, Josef Matthias

HOLDERLIN-LIEDER, BAND II: OP.23 see
  Hauer, Josef Matthias

HOLDERLIN-LIEDER, BAND III: OP.32 see
  Hauer, Josef Matthias

HOLDERLIN-LIEDER, BAND IV: OP.40 see
  Hauer, Josef Matthias

HOLDING TO THE HAND OF GOD see Hensen,
  Gloria

HOLENIA, HANNS
  Zwanzig Lieder *CC20U
  solo,pno KRENN 1.3 s.p.   (H1555)

HOLFORD, FRANZ
  Autumn
  see Three Lyric Songs

  Come Away Death
  solo,pno ALBERT AE 35 s.p.   (H1556)
  Bar solo,pno EMI s.p.   (H1557)

  Coming Of Spring, The
  solo,pno ALBERT AE 36 s.p.   (H1558)
  T solo,pno EMI s.p.   (H1559)

  Girl In Green
  solo,pno ALLANS s.p.   (H1560)

  Gnome And The Penguin
  see Three Lyric Songs

  I Have A Bonnet Trimmed With Blue
  med solo,pno EMI s.p.   (H1561)

  Keel Row
  med solo,pno EMI s.p.   (H1562)

  Madrigal
  solo,pno ALBERT AE227 s.p.   (H1563)

  Mangers
  med solo,pno EMI s.p.   (H1564)
  solo,pno ALBERT AE176 s.p.   (H1565)

  Molly
  see Three Lyric Songs

  Moonlit Apples
  solo,pno ALBERT AE234 s.p.   (H1566)

  Music When Soft Voices Die
  med solo,pno EMI s.p.   (H1567)
  solo,pno ALBERT AE182 s.p.   (H1568)

  Three Lyric Songs
  solo,pno ALBERT AE 17 s.p.
    contains: Autumn; Gnome And The
    Penguin; Molly   (H1569)

HOLFORD, FRANZ (cont'd.)

Toll Gate, The
solo,pno ALBERT AE350 s.p.   (H1570)

Two Australian Folksongs *CC2U
solo,pno EMI s.p.   (H1571)

Whitethroat And The Holly, The
solo,pno ALBERT AE358 s.p.   (H1572)

Wily Cupid
solo,pno ALBERT AE225 s.p.   (H1573)

HOLIDAY, MICKEY
Christ Is The King Of All Kings *sac
solo,pno SINGSPIR 7016 $1.00   (H1574)

Happy Am I *sac
solo,pno SINGSPIR 7098 $1.00   (H1575)

HOLIDAY SONG see Zemer Chag

HOLLAENDER, VIKTOR (1866-1940)
Auf Ins Metropol
[Ger] high solo,pno BOTE $2.25   (H1576)

La Montmartroise
solo,pno ENOCH s.p.   (H1577)
solo,acap ENOCH s.p.   (H1578)

HOLLAIKA
see Five French Folk Songs

HOLLAND see Andriessen, N.H.

HOLLAND see Bordewijk-Roepman, Johanna

HOLLAND see Mulder, Ernest W.

HOLLAND, KENNETH
Sky Roses
solo,pno ALLANS s.p.   (H1579)

HOLLANDSCH LIEDJE see Tussenbroek, H. von

HOLLER, JOHN (1904-   )
Now The Day Is Over *sac
med solo,pno BELWIN $1.50   (H1580)

HOLLER, KARL (1907-   )
An Maria *Op.17,No.2
see Geistliche Gesange

Es Ist Ein Ros' Entsprungen *Op.17, No.1
see Geistliche Gesange

Geistliche Gesange *sac
[Ger/Eng] LEUCKART S solo,pno/org
cmplt ed $5.25; S solo,orch cmplt ed s.p.
contains: An Maria, Op.17,No.2;
Es Ist Ein Ros' Entsprungen,
Op.17,No.1; Nachtwachterlied,
Op.17,No.3; O Liebes Jesulein,
Op.17,No.5; Pater Noster,
Op.17,No.6; Wendisches
Marienlied, Op.17,No.4   (H1581)

Nachtwachterlied *Op.17,No.3
see Geistliche Gesange

O Liebes Jesulein *Op.17,No.5
see Geistliche Gesange

Pater Noster *Op.17,No.6
see Geistliche Gesange

Wendisches Marienlied *Op.17,No.4
see Geistliche Gesange

HOLLOWAY, ROBIN
Four Poems Of Thomas *CC4U
solo,pno OXFORD s.p.   (H1582)

Seven Poems Of Sturiss *CC7U
solo,pno OXFORD s.p.   (H1583)

Three Georgian Songs *CC3U
Bar solo,pno OXFORD s.p.   (H1584)

Two Songs For Mezzosoprano And Guitar *CC2U
Mez solo,gtr OXFORD $5.10   (H1585)

HOLM
If I Had It To Do All Over Again *sac
solo,pno BENSON S6473-R $1.00   (H1586)

Let My Light Shine *sac
solo,pno BENSON S6851-R $1.00   (H1587)

Make Me A New Creature *sac
solo,pno BENSON S7003-R $1.00   (H1588)

Peace, Joy And Love *sac
solo,pno BENSON S7365-R $1.00   (H1589)

HOLM, DALLAS
Choose God Today *sac
solo,pno SINGSPIR 7079 $1.00   (H1590)

HOLM, DALLAS (cont'd.)
Dallas Holm-Songbook *sac,CC12L
solo,pno BENSON B0536 $2.50   (H1591)

Dallas Holm Songs *sac,CCUL
solo,kbd SINGSPIR 5140 $2.50   (H1592)

I'm Telling Them Today *sac
solo,pno SINGSPIR 7078 $1.00   (H1593)

HOLM, MOGENS WINKEL (1936-   )
Nightmare
S solo,kbd HANSEN-DEN s.p.   (H1594)

HOLMBOE, VAGN (1909-   )
Funf Spate Lieder *CC5U
solo,pno HANSEN-DEN 29175 s.p.   (H1595)

HOLMES, ALFRED (1837-1876)
A Trianon
Mez/Bar solo,pno/inst DURAND   (H1596)
S/T solo,pno/inst DURAND   (H1597)

Au Dela
solo,pno (available in 2 keys)
ENOCH s.p.   (H1598)

Aux Heureux
S/T solo,pno/inst DURAND   (H1599)
Mez/Bar solo,pno/inst DURAND   (H1600)

Barcarolle
solo,pno (available in 3 keys)
ENOCH s.p.   (H1601)

Chant Du Cavalier
solo,pno/inst DURAND   (H1602)

Contes Divins *see La Belle
Madeleine; La Legende De Saint
Amour; L'Aubepine De Saint-
Patrick; Le Chemin Du Ciel; Les
Lys Bleus; Les Moutons Des Anges   (H1603)

Dans Mon Coeur
solo,pno (available in 3 keys)
ENOCH s.p.   (H1604)

Dans Un Parc Abandonne
Mez/Bar solo,pno/inst DURAND s.p.   (H1605)
S/T solo,pno/inst DURAND s.p.   (H1606)

Fleur De Neige
[Fr] solo,acap oct DURAND s.p.   (H1607)
Mez/Bar solo,pno/inst DURAND s.p.   (H1608)

Invocation
solo,pno DURAND s.p.   (H1609)

La Belle Madeleine *sac
S/T solo,pno/inst DURAND s.p. see
from Contes Divins   (H1610)
Mez/Bar solo,pno/inst DURAND s.p.
see from Contes Divins   (H1611)

La Chanson Du Page
A solo,pno/inst DURAND   (H1612)

La Legende De Saint Amour *sac
Mez/Bar solo,pno/inst DURAND s.p.
see from Contes Divins   (H1613)
S/T solo,pno/inst DURAND s.p. see
from Contes Divins   (H1614)

La Priere Au Drapeau
solo,pno ENOCH s.p.   (H1615)
solo,acap ENOCH s.p.   (H1616)

La Princesse
solo,pno DURAND s.p. see from
Quatre Chansons Populaires   (H1617)

La Sirene
solo,pno (in 2 keys) DURAND s.p.   (H1618)

L'Amour Qui Chante
solo,pno/inst (in 3 keys) DURAND   (H1619)

L'Appel Du Printemps
S/T solo,pno/inst DURAND   (H1620)
Mez/Bar solo,pno/inst DURAND   (H1621)

L'Aubepine De Saint-Patrick *sac
solo,pno/inst DURAND s.p. see from
Contes Divins   (H1622)

Le Chemin Du Ciel *sac
Mez/Bar solo,pno/inst DURAND s.p.
see from Contes Divins   (H1623)
S/T solo,pno/inst DURAND s.p. see
from Contes Divins   (H1624)
[Fr] solo,acap oct DURAND s.p.   (H1625)

Les Chevaliers Du Ciel
solo,pno (available in 2 keys)
ENOCH s.p.   (H1626)

Les Deux Enfants De Rois
solo,pno (in 2 keys) DURAND s.p.
see from Quatre Chansons
Populaires   (H1627)

HOLMES, ALFRED (cont'd.)
Les Exiles
solo,pno (available in 2 keys)
ENOCH s.p.   (H1628)

Les Lys Bleus *sac
S/T solo,pno/inst DURAND s.p. see
from Contes Divins   (H1629)
Mez/Bar solo,pno/inst DURAND s.p.
see from Contes Divins   (H1630)

Les Moutons Des Anges *sac
Mez/Bar solo,pno/inst DURAND s.p.
see from Contes Divins   (H1631)
S/T solo,pno/inst DURAND s.p. see
from Contes Divins   (H1632)

Les Sept Ivresses *CC7L
T solo,pno/inst DURAND s.p.   (H1633)

Les Trois Pages
solo,pno DURAND s.p. see from
Quatre Chansons Populaires   (H1634)

Message D'amour
Mez/Bar solo,pno/inst DURAND s.p.   (H1635)
S/T solo,pno/inst DURAND s.p.   (H1636)

Mignonne
solo,pno DURAND s.p. see from
Quatre Chansons Populaires   (H1637)

Nocturne
S/T solo,pno/inst DURAND s.p.   (H1638)
Mez/Bar solo,pno/inst DURAND s.p.   (H1639)

Nox...Amor
Mez/Bar solo,pno/inst DURAND s.p.   (H1640)

Nox...Silentium
solo,pno DURAND s.p.   (H1641)

Ogier Le Danois
solo,pno (available in 2 keys)
ENOCH s.p.   (H1642)
solo,acap (available in 2 keys)
ENOCH s.p.   (H1643)

Quatre Chansons Populaires *see La
Princesse; Les Deux Enfants De
Rois; Les Trois Pages; Mignonne   (H1644)

HOLMQUIST, NILS-GUSTAF
Blommorna
solo,pno,opt gtr GEHRMANS s.p.   (H1645)

Nar Vi Bli Gamla
solo,pno,opt gtr GEHRMANS s.p.   (H1646)

HOLOUBEK, LADISLAV (1913-   )
Dcerenka Moja *song cycle
Mez solo,pno SLOV.HUD.FOND s.p.   (H1647)

K L'udu *song cycle
Mez solo,pno SLOV.HUD.FOND s.p.   (H1648)

Mladost *song cycle
S solo,pno SLOV.HUD.FOND s.p.   (H1649)

Spevy Jesene *song cycle
B solo,pno SLOV.HUD.FOND s.p.   (H1650)

Vyznania *song cycle
S solo,pno SLOV.HUD.FOND s.p.   (H1651)

HOLST, GUSTAV (1874-1934)
Awake My Heart
high solo,pno (D maj) ASHDOWN   (H1652)
low solo,pno (B flat maj) ASHDOWN   (H1653)

Dream Of Christmas, A
1-2 soli,pno/orch ROBERTON 71517
s.p.   (H1654)

Four Songs
[Eng] high solo,vln CHESTER s.p.
contains: I Sing Of A Maiden;
Jesu Sweet, Now Will I Sing; My
Leman Is So True; My Soul Has
Nought But Fire And Ice   (H1655)

Heart Worships *sac
low solo,pno (D min) GALAXY
1.5096.7 $1.50   (H1656)
low solo,pno FISCHER,C V 2360   (H1657)
high solo,pno FISCHER,C V 2359   (H1658)
high solo,pno (E min) STAINER
3.1301.7 $1.50   (H1659)

I Sing Of A Maiden
see Four Songs

Jesu Sweet, Now Will I Sing
see Four Songs

My Leman Is So True
see Four Songs

HOLST, GUSTAV (cont'd.)

My Soul Has Nought But Fire And Ice
  see Four Songs

Sergeant's Song
  low solo,pno (G min) ASHDOWN $1.50
                                    (H1660)
  high solo,pno (A min) ASHDOWN $1.50
                                    (H1661)
She Who Is Dear To Me
  low solo,pno (D maj) ASHDOWN
                                    (H1662)
  high solo,pno (F maj) ASHDOWN
                                    (H1663)
Twelve Humbert Wolfe Songs *CC12U
  solo,pno GALLIARD 2.9017.7 $3.50
                                    (H1664)
Vedic Hymns *CC9L
  [Eng] med-high solo,kbd CHESTER
  s.p.   (H1665)

HOLT, P.
  Three Songs Of Contemplation *CC3U
    solo,pno BERANDOL BER 1313 $3.50
                                    (H1666)
HOLT, SIMEON TEN (1923-   )
  A'. Ta-Lon
    Mez solo,3fl,3ob,5clar,bsn,2horn,
    3trp,trom,harp,marimba,pno,vibra,
    3vln,3vla,3vcl,3bvl,gtr,mand
    DONEMUS s.p.   (H1667)

HOLTY-TRILOGIE see Abendroth, Walther

HOLY BABE, THE see Dunhill, Thomas
  Frederick

HOLY BIBLE, THE see Malotte, Albert Hay

HOLY BOY see Ireland, John

HOLY CHILD, THE see Martin, Easthope

HOLY CITY, THE see Adams, Stephen

HOLY HILL, A see Lora, Antonio

HOLY HOLY see Mana-Zucca, Mme., Kodosh-
  Kodosh

HOLY, HOLY see Owens, Jimmy

HOLY, HOLY, HOLY see Lossius, Lukas

HOLY HOUR, THE see Nevin, Ethelbert
  Woodbridge

HOLY INFANT'S LULLABY, THE see Dello
  Joio, Norman

HOLY JESUS, SEND YOUR BLESSING see
  Wetzler, Robert Paul

HOLY LAND see Taylor, Charles H.

HOLY MOTHER SINGS see McKinney, Howard
  D.

HOLY NIGHT *folk,Ger
  (Roberton, Hugh S.) 2 soli,pno
  ROBERTON 71972 s.p.   (H1668)

HOLY NIGHT see Rheinberger, Josef

HOLY NIGHT, SILENT NIGHT
  (Geehl, Henry) low solo,pno (B flat
  maj) ASHDOWN s.p.   (H1669)
  (Geehl, Henry) high solo,pno (D flat
  maj) ASHDOWN s.p.   (H1670)

HOLY QUEEN OF HEAVEN! see Bantock,
  Granville, Salve Regina

HOLY REDEEMER see Schein, Johann
  Hermann

HOLY SONNETS OF JOHN DONNE see Britten,
  Benjamin

HOLY SONNETS OF JOHN DONNE see Eaton

HOLY SPIRIT, FLOW THROUGH ME see Mills

HOLY THURSDAY see Teed, Roy

HOLY THURSDAY see Walton, William

HOLY WEEK AT GENOA see Sharpe, Evelyn

HOLY WORD *sac,CCU
  high solo/low solo,pno BOOSEY $4.00
                                    (H1671)
HOMAGE TO PAUL KLEE see Diamond, David

HOMBERG, JOHANNES (1931-   )
  Mensagem
    S solo,clar,bsn,trp,trom,vln,bvl
    GERIG HG 712 s.p.   (H1672)

HOME see Rosing, J.

HOME OF MINE see O'Neill, Norman

HOME ON THE RANGE see Colville, Val

HOME ON THE RANGE see Guion, David
  Wendall Fentress

HOME ROAD, THE see Carpenter, John
  Alden

HOME SONG ALBUM see Hattori, T.

HOME, SWEET HOME
  "En Nejd I Skonsta Fagring" solo,pno
  LUNDQUIST s.p.   (H1673)

HOME SWEET HOME see Bishop, Sir Henry
  Rowley

HOME TO OUR MOUNTAINS see Verdi,
  Giuseppe, Ai Nostri Monti

HOMECOMING OF THE SHEEP see Head,
  Michael (Dewar)

HOMENAJE A J. CORTAZAR see Encinar,
  Ramon

HOMENAJE A LOPE DE VEGA see Turina,
  Joaquin

HOMER
  Requiem
    low solo,pno (G flat maj) ALLANS
    s.p.   (H1674)
    high solo,pno (A maj) ALLANS s.p.
                                    (H1675)
  Uncle Rome
    low solo,pno (E flat maj) ALLANS
    s.p.   (H1676)
    high solo,pno (F maj) ALLANS s.p.
                                    (H1677)
HOMER, SIDNEY (1864-1953)
  Banjo Song, A
    high solo,pno (C maj) ALLANS s.p.
                                    (H1678)
    low solo,pno (A maj) ALLANS s.p.
                                    (H1679)
    low solo,pno (A maj) SCHIRM.G $.75
                                    (H1680)
  Sheep And Lambs *sac
    high solo,pno (A flat maj) SCHIRM.G
    $.85   (H1681)
    low solo,pno (G flat maj) SCHIRM.G
    $.85   (H1682)

HOMEWARD see Strauss, Richard, Heimkehr

HOMILIUS, GOTTFRIED AUGUST (1714-1785)
  Die Holle Flieht (from Was Suchet
  Ihr)
    Bar/B solo,2harp,strings BREITKOPF-
    L rental   (H1683)

HOMING SHIP, THE see Loughborough,
  Raymond

HOMMAGE A THIBAUT DE CHAMPAGNE see
  Migot, Georges

HOMMAGE A VALERY-LARBAUD see Rivier,
  Jean

HONEGGER, ARTHUR (1892-1955)
  A La "Sante"
    see Six Poems Of Apollinaire

  Adele
    see Petit Cours De Morale

  Automne
    see Six Poems Of Apollinaire

  Berceuse De La Sirene
    see Three Songs

  Cecile
    see Petit Cours De Morale

  Chanson De Fol
    see Three Poems Of Paul Fort

  Chanson De La Poire
    see Three Songs

  Chanson De L'Emigrant
    med solo,pno SALABERT-US $1.50
                                    (H1684)
  Chanson Des Sirenes
    see Three Songs

  Cloche Du Soir
    see Three Poems Of Paul Fort

  Clotilde
    see Six Poems Of Apollinaire

  Derriere Murcie En Fleurs
    see Four Songs

  Four Songs
    [Fr] low solo,pno SALABERT-US $3.00
      contains: Derriere Murcie En
      Fleurs; La Douceur De Tes Yeux;
      La Terre, Les Eaux Va Buvant;
      Un Grand Sommeil Noir   (H1685)

HONEGGER, ARTHUR (cont'd.)

  Il Faut Que De Tous Mes Esprits
  J'exalte (Psalm 88)
    see Three Psalms

  Irene
    see Petit Cours De Morale

  Jamais Ne Cesserai De Magnifier Le
  Seigneur (Psalm 34)
    see Three Psalms

  Jeanne
    see Petit Cours De Morale

  La Douceur De Tes Yeux
    see Four Songs

  La Terre, Les Eaux Va Buvant
    see Four Songs

  L'Adieu
    see Six Poems Of Apollinaire

  Le Chausseur Perdu En Foret
    see Three Poems Of Paul Fort

  Le Delphinim
    see Three Poems Of Claudel

  Le Rendez-Vous
    see Three Poems Of Claudel

  Les Cloches
    see Six Poems Of Apollinaire

  Mimaamaquim (Psalm 130) sac
    "Out Of The Depths" [Heb] low solo,
    pno/orch SALABERT-US $2.25
                                    (H1686)
  Mon Dieu Vous M'avez Appele Parmi Les
  Hommes
    see Quatre Poemes

  O Dieu, Donne-Moi Delivrance De Cet
  Homme Pernicieux (Psalm 160)
    see Three Psalms

  O Salutaris *sac
    S solo,opt harmonium HEUGEL s.p.
                                    (H1687)
  Out Of The Depths *see Mimaamaquim

  Petit Cours De Morale
    med solo,pno SALABERT-US $3.00
      contains: Adele; Cecile; Irene;
      Jeanne; Rosemonde   (H1688)

  Peuple Du Christ
    see Quatre Poemes

  Psalm 34 *see Jamais Ne Cesserai De
    Magnifier Le Seigneur

  Psalm 88 *see Il Faut Que De Tous
    Mes Esprits J'exalte

  Psalm 130 *see Mimaamaquim

  Psalm 160 *see O Dieu, Donne-Moi
    Delivrance De Cet Homme
    Pernicieux

  Quatre Poemes
    [Fr] med-high solo,kbd HANSEN-DEN
    s.p.
      contains: Mon Dieu Vous M'avez
      Appele Parmi Les Hommes; Peuple
      Du Christ; Sur Le Basalte;
      Toute Seule Silence Les Yeux
      Eteints   (H1689)

  Rosemonde
    see Petit Cours De Morale

  Saltimbanques
    see Six Poems Of Apollinaire

  Sieste
    see Three Poems Of Claudel

  Six Poems Of Apollinaire
    med solo,pno/orch SALABERT-US
    $6.00, ipr
      contains: A La "Sante"; Automne;
      Clotilde; L'Adieu; Les Cloches;
      Saltimbanques   (H1690)

  Song
    med solo,pno SALABERT-US $1.50
                                    (H1691)
    med solo,fl,4strings SALABERT-US
    $3.00   (H1692)

  Sur Le Basalte
    see Quatre Poemes

  Three Poems Of Claudel
    med solo,pno SALABERT-US $4.50
      contains: Le Delphinim; Le
      Rendez-Vous; Sieste   (H1693)

  Three Poems Of Paul Fort
    med solo,pno SALABERT-US $3.75
      contains: Chanson De Fol; Cloche

HONEGGER, ARTHUR (cont'd.)

Du Soir; Le Chausseur Perdu En
Foret   (H1694)

Three Psalms
med solo,pno SALABERT-US $3.00
contains: Il Faut Que De Tous Mes
Esprits J'exalte (Psalm 88);
Jamais Ne Cesserai De Magnifier
Le Seigneur (Psalm 34); O Dieu,
Donne-Moi Delivrance De Cet
Homme Pernicieux (Psalm 160)
(H1695)

Three Songs
SALABERT-US med solo,pno $4.50; med
solo,fl,strings $6.00
contains: Berceuse De La Sirene;
Chanson De La Poire; Chanson
Des Sirenes   (H1696)

Toute Seule Silence Les Yeux Eteints
see Quatre Poemes

Un Grand Sommeil Noir
see Four Songs

HONEST FELLOW, THE see Andriessen,
Juriaan

HONEY SHUN see Schirmer, Rudolph [E.]

HONEYBIRD see Evans

HONNEUR A L'AMERIQUE see Saint-Saens,
Camille

HONOR AND ARMS see Handel, George
Frideric

HONOR! HONOR! see Johnson

HONOUR AND ARMS see Handel, George
Frideric

HOO-TZA-TZA see Kanapoff, F.

HOOGENBERK-RINK, D.
Als We Zingen Zijn We Blij
solo,acap BROEKMANS 476 s.p.
(H1697)

Fort Emmanuel
solo,pno BROEKMANS 950 s.p. (H1698)

Kerstlicht
solo,pno BROEKMANS 693 s.p. (H1699)

HOOK
Doun The Burn
low solo,pno (A maj) ALLANS s.p.
(H1700)
high solo,pno (B flat maj) ALLANS
s.p.   (H1701)

HOOK, JAMES (1746-1827)
British Loyalty
"King, Lord And Commons" solo,pno
HEUWEKE. 111 s.p.   (H1702)

Cruel Peggy
solo,pno HEUWEKE. 112 s.p.   (H1703)

Ellens Fate Deserves A Tear
solo,pno HEUWEKE. 113 s.p.   (H1704)

Fair Of Britains Isle, The
solo,pno HEUWEKE. 118 s.p.   (H1705)

Happy Milk Maid, The
solo,pno HEUWEKE. 119 s.p.   (H1706)

Highland Queen, The
solo,pno HEUWEKE. 120 s.p.   (H1707)

I Sigh For The Girl I Adore
solo,2fl,2horn,2vln,2vla,cont
HEUWEKE. 115 s.p.   (H1708)

I'd Rather Be Excus'd
solo,pno HEUWEKE. 114 s.p.   (H1709)

King And The Constitution, The
solo,pno/hpsd HEUWEKE. 121 s.p.
(H1710)
King, Lord And Commons *see British
Loyalty

Lash'd To The Helm
solo,pno HEUWEKE. 116 s.p.   (H1711)

Lass Of Richmond Hill, The
solo,2fl,bsn,2horn,cembalo,2vln,vla
HEUWEKE. 122 s.p.   (H1712)

Softly Lulling, Sweetly Thrilling
(Bush) A solo,pno ELKIN 27.2471.05
s.p.   (H1713)

Sweet Robinette
solo,pno HEUWEKE. 117 s.p.   (H1714)

Then I Fly To Meet My Love
solo,pno HEUWEKE. 123 s.p.   (H1715)

HOOK, JAMES (cont'd.)

Then Say My Sweet Girl Can You Love
Me
solo,pno HEUWEKE. 124 s.p.   (H1716)

Upon My Word I Did
solo,pno HEUWEKE. 125 s.p.   (H1717)

HOORN see Sigtenhorst-Meyer, Bernhard
van den

HOORT GIJ DE WILDE GOLVEN? see Glover,
Stephen, What Are The Wild Waves
Saying?

HOPAK see Mussorgsky, Modest

HOPE see Grieg, Edvard Hagerup

HOPE, A see Ashley, Derick

HOPE, B.M.
All My Very Own
high solo,pno (E flat maj) BOOSEY
$1.50   (H1718)
low solo,pno (G maj) BOOSEY $1.50
(H1719)

HOPE, H. ASHWORTH
Cornish Land
solo,pno LEONARD-ENG   (H1720)

Dreams
low solo,pno (E flat maj) LEONARD-
ENG   (H1721)
2 soli,pno (C maj) LEONARD-ENG
(H1722)
high solo,pno (C maj) LEONARD-ENG
(H1723)
2 soli,pno (E flat maj) LEONARD-ENG
(H1724)
Enchantment
solo,pno LEONARD-ENG   (H1725)

Fill Up Your Glass
solo,pno LEONARD-ENG   (H1726)

I Cry Your Mercy Mistress
see Two Old World Songs

I Thank You, Life
high solo,pno (G maj) LEONARD-ENG
(H1727)
low solo,pno (E flat maj) LEONARD-
ENG   (H1728)

In Grandma's Days
solo,pno LEONARD-ENG   (H1729)

Irish Love Song
solo,pno (E flat maj) LEONARD-ENG
(H1730)
Kildare
low solo,pno (E flat maj) LEONARD-
ENG   (H1731)
high solo,pno (G maj) LEONARD-ENG
(H1732)
Life's Shadows
low solo,pno (F maj) LEONARD-ENG
(H1733)
high solo,pno (G maj) LEONARD-ENG
(H1734)
Little Coloured Coon
solo,pno LEONARD-ENG   (H1735)

Long Beat Home
solo,pno LEONARD-ENG   (H1736)

My Party Frock
solo,pno (G maj) LEONARD-ENG
(H1737)
Nobody Knows
solo,pno (F maj) LEONARD-ENG
(H1738)
Road Thro' The Valley
low solo,pno (C maj) CRAMER (H1739)
high solo,pno (E flat maj) CRAMER
(H1740)
Soldiers Of The Cross, Arise
solo,pno (A flat maj) CRAMER
(H1741)
Somerset Bachelor
solo,pno (F maj) CRAMER   (H1742)

Song Of Devon
solo,pno CRAMER   (H1743)

Song Of The Blackmore Vale
solo,pno CRAMER   (H1744)

Sparkford Harriers
solo,pno CRAMER   (H1745)

Tell Me Mistress This I Pray
see Two Old World Songs

That's Happy Home
solo,pno CRAMER   (H1746)

To You
high solo,pno (C maj) LEONARD-ENG
(H1747)
low solo,pno (A flat maj) LEONARD-
ENG   (H1748)

HOPE, H. ASHWORTH (cont'd.)

Two Old World Songs
solo,pno LEONARD-ENG s.p.
contains: I Cry Your Mercy
Mistress; Tell Me Mistress This
I Pray   (H1749)

Two Short Songs *CC2U
solo,pno LEONARD-ENG   (H1750)

HOPE IN THE LORD *sac
high solo,pno ASHLEY $1.00   (H1751)
low solo,pno ASHLEY $1.00   (H1752)

HOPE IS A THING WITH FEATHERS see
Sydeman, William

HOPE ON! see Strauss, Richard, Nur Mut!

HOPEKIRK, HELEN
Five Songs *CC5UL
med-high solo,pno SCHIRM.G $1.25
(H1753)

HOPKELE *Jew
solo,pno KAMMEN 466 $1.00   (H1754)

HOPKINS
Till The Whole World Knows *sac
solo,pno LILLENAS SM-620: RN $1.00
(H1755)

HOPKINS, ANTHONY (1921-)
Humble Song To The Birds, A *cant
[Eng/Fr] high solo,pno HANSEN-DEN
s.p.   (H1756)

Melancholy Song, A
[Eng] med solo,kbd HANSEN-DEN s.p.
(H1757)

Recueillement
[Fr] med-high solo,kbd HANSEN-DEN
s.p.   (H1758)

HOPKINS, B.
Two Poems *CC2U
S solo,bass clar,trp,harp,vla sc
UNIVER. 14204 s.p.   (H1759)

HOPKINS, J.M.
How Do I Love Thee?
high solo,pno PRESSER $.75   (H1760)

HOR' AMOR FLEHN, O GOTT DER LIEBE see
Mozart, Wolfgang Amadeus, Porgi
Amor

HOR CHE'L CIEL E LA TERRA see
Monteverdi, Claudio

HOR DU AUGUSTI SOMMARREGN see
Rangstrom, Ture

HOR, HELGA KLOCKOR KALLA see Dahlgren,
Erland

HOR HUR STILLA VINDEN SUSAR see Wrangel

HOR ICH DIE STIMME see Bizet, Georges,
Je Crois Entendre Encore

HOR' MEIN FLEHEN see Haas, Joseph

HOR MEIN FLEHN, O GOTT DER LIEBE see
Mozart, Wolfgang Amadeus

HORA see Rappaport, Moshe

HORA TELEM see Sambursky, D.

HORATI DE VINO CARMINA see Krol,
Bernhard

HORCH, ER SCHLAGT DAS GOLDNE SPIEL see
Handel, George Frideric

HORCH WIE SCHALLTS DORTEN SO LIEBLICH
HERVOR! see Beethoven, Ludwig van,
Der Wachtelschlag

HORE GRUNOM, DOLU GRUNOM see Hirner,
Teodor

HORE ISRAEL see Mendelssohn-Bartholdy,
Felix

HORE JEG SANGEN KLINGE see Grieg,
Edvard Hagerup

HORET MICH AN, GEHEIME MACHTE see
Mussorgsky, Modest

HORIZONS '76 see Anderson, Thomas J.

HORLER, A.
D'Sangerreis
solo,pno HUG s.p.   (H1761)

Loffelschliifi
solo,pno HUG s.p.   (H1762)

O Heiri, Mach Mer Jo Kei Schand
solo,pno HUG s.p.   (H1763)

Vier Konig Sind Machtig
solo,pno HUG s.p.   (H1764)

HORN, THE see Flegier, Ange, Le Cor

HORN, CHARLES EDWARD (1786-1849)
Cherry Ripe
high solo,pno (E flat maj) ALLANS
s.p.   (H1765)
med solo,pno (E flat maj) SCHIRM.G
$.75   (H1766)

I Know A Bank
2 soli,pno (E flat maj) LEONARD-ENG
(H1767)
2 soli,pno (C maj) LEONARD-ENG
(H1768)
I've Been Roaming
med solo,pno PRESSER $.75   (H1769)
low solo,pno PRESSER $.75   (H1770)
med solo,pno (D maj) ALLANS s.p.
(H1771)
high solo,pno (E flat maj) ALLANS
s.p.   (H1772)

HORNE
Caught Up Together *sac
solo,pno BENSON S5255-S $1.00
(H1773)

HORNE, ROGER
Caught Up Together *sac
solo,pno WORD S-434   (H1774)

He Kept On Loving Me *sac
solo,pno WORD S-540   (H1775)

I'm Going To Meet You In Heaven
Someday *sac
solo,pno WORD S-529   (H1776)

I'm One Of His Own *sac
solo,pno WORD S-464   (H1777)

Seek The Lord Today *sac
solo,pno WORD S-458   (H1778)

Tomorrow He May Come *sac
solo,pno WORD S-485   (H1779)

When I'm Gone *sac
solo,pno WORD S-442   (H1780)

HORNUNG
O Dream, O Dreaming
solo,gtr RICORDI-ENG SY 2204 s.p.
(H1781)

HOROVITZ, JOSEPH
Lady Macbeth *scena
Mez solo,pno NOVELLO 20.0155.01
s.p.   (H1782)

HORROR MOVIE see Flanagan, William

HORSEMAN, THE see Berkeley, Lennox

HORSEMAN, THE see Fischer, Irwin

HORST, ANTON VAN DER (1899-1965)
Avond-Gebedt *Op.29a
see Drie Geestelijke Liederen

Blijdschap *Op.22a, hymn
S solo,opt pno/org DONEMUS s.p.
(H1783)
Drie Geestelijke Liederen *sac
low solo,pno/org DONEMUS s.p.
contains: Avond-Gebedt, Op.29a;
Geen Tijd Is Buiten, Op.29b;
Mijn Lant Wil Niet Meer
Treuren, Op.29c   (H1784)

Drie Oud-Nederlandsche Liederen
high solo,pno/org ALSBACH s.p.
contains: Heft Op Mijn Cruys,
Op.18,No.1; Het Viel Een Hemels
Douwe, Op.18,No.2; Wat Vreugd'
Hoor Ik Uyt 'S Hemels Zaelen,
Op.18,No.3   (H1785)

Drie Oud-Nederlandsche Liederen
S solo,fl,2ob,2clar,bsn,perc,cel,
strings DONEMUS s.p.
contains: Een Alre Lieffelicken
Een, Op.17b,No.2; Nu Laet Ons
Allen Gode Loven, Op.17b,No.3;
Och Voor Den Doot, Op.17b,No.1
(H1786)
Drie Oud-Nederlandse Liederen
*Op.17a, CC3U
high solo,fl,org ALSBACH s.p.
(H1787)
Een Alre Lieffelicken Een *Op.17b,
No.2
see Drie Oud-Nederlandsche Liederen

Geen Tijd Is Buiten *Op.29b
see Drie Geestelijke Liederen

Heft Op Mijn Cruys *Op.18,No.1
see Drie Oud-Nederlandsche Liederen

Het Viel Een Hemels Douwe *Op.18,
No.2
see Drie Oud-Nederlandsche Liederen

Le Ciel En Nuit S'est Deplie *Op.81a
low solo,pno DONEMUS s.p. (H1788)

HORST, ANTON VAN DER (cont'd.)
Mijn Lant Wil Niet Meer Treuren
*Op.29c
see Drie Geestelijke Liederen

Nu Laet Ons Allen Gode Loven
*Op.17b,No.3
see Drie Oud-Nederlandsche Liederen

Och Voor Den Doot *Op.17b,No.1
see Drie Oud-Nederlandsche Liederen

Oratio *Op.19a
S solo,2fl,3ob,3clar,3bsn,3horn,
3trp,3trom,timp,2harp,strings
DONEMUS s.p.   (H1789)

Psalm 121 *Op.16a, sac
low solo,pno DONEMUS s.p. (H1790)

Wat Vreugd' Hoor Ik Uyt 'S Hemels
Zaelen *Op.18,No.3
see Drie Oud-Nederlandsche Liederen

Zeven Italiaanse Liederen *Op.21a,
CC7U
S solo,3fl,3ob,4clar,2bsn,4horn,
2trp,3trom,timp,perc,2harp,
strings DONEMUS s.p.   (H1791)

HORT, WAS EINST IN DER STADT KASAN
GESCHEHEN see Mussorgsky, Modest

HORUSITZKY, Z.
Songs On Chinese Poems *CCU
[Hung] solo,pno BUDAPEST 2857 s.p.
(H1792)
Three Shakespeare Sonnets *CC3U
[Hung/Eng] solo,pno BUDAPEST 2765
s.p.   (H1793)

Three Songs *CC3U
[Hung/Ger] solo,pno BUDAPEST 3926
s.p.   (H1794)

HORVATH, JOSEF MARIA (1931-   )
Die Blinde
[Ger] A,2 narrators,fl,trp,pno,vln
study sc PETERS 5824 $4.00
(H1795)
Four Songs After Holderlin *CC4U
[Ger] S/T solo,fl,clar,vla,vcl
study sc PETERS 5823 $4.00
(H1796)

HORVIT, MICHAEL M.
Ample Make This Bed
see Three Songs Of Elegy

I Felt A Cleavage In My Mind
see Three Songs Of Elegy

I Felt A Funeral In My Brain
see Three Songs Of Elegy

Three Songs Of Elegy
S solo,pno SCHIRM.EC 116 s.p.
contains: Ample Make This Bed; I
Felt A Cleavage In My Mind; I
Felt A Funeral In My Brain
(H1797)
HORY A SRDCE see Novak, Milan

HOS DROTTNING MARGARETA see Alfven,
Hugo

HOS GUD AR IDEL GLADJE
see Andliga Sanger, Heft 1

HOSANNA see Granier, J.

HOSANNA III see Diemente, Edward

HOSANNA TO THE SON OF DAVID see Bender,
Jan

HOSKINS, WILLIAM
Ballad Of The Trumpet Boy, The
Bar solo,2fl,2ob,2clar,2bsn,2horn,
timp,4perc,strings sc AM.COMP.AL.
$39.60   (H1798)

Jerusalem From The Mountain
ST soli,trp,trom,2pno voc sc
AM.COMP.AL. $1.37   (H1799)

Lost Lands, The
Mez solo,strings sc AM.COMP.AL.
$12.10   (H1800)

Romance, Who Loves To Nod And Sing
Mez solo,vla,pno sc AM.COMP.AL.
$5.50, ipa   (H1801)

Stopping By Woods On A Snowy Evening
Mez solo,pno AM.COMP.AL. $3.85
(H1802)
Two Songs *CC2U
Bar solo,pno AM.COMP.AL. $4.67
(H1803)
HOSPITALITY see Anderson, William H.

HOST see Madetoja, Leevi, Syksy

HOSTAGES see Scek, Breda, Talci

HOSTDAG see Marvia, Einari, Syyspaiva

HOSTENS VAR see Liljefors, Ruben

HOSTHORN see Peterson-Berger, (Olof)
Wilhelm

HOSTKVALL see Sibelius, Jean

HOSTSANG see Kuula, Toivo, Vanha
Syyslaulu

HOSTSANG see Mendelssohn-Bartholdy,
Felix

HOSTVISA see Myrberg, August M.

HOT A YID A WEIBELE see Goldstein,
Morris

HOT DAY AT THE SEASHORE, A see Thomson,
Virgil, Jour De Chaleur Aux Bains
De Mer

HOTEL DU SOUVENIR see Daniel-Lesur

HOUR, THE see Hier, Ethel Glenn

HOUR COMETH, THE see Mourant, Walter

HOUR DARK AND SOLEMN, THE see Verdi,
Giuseppe, Solenne In Quest'ora

HOUR GLASS, THE see Pinkham, Daniel

HOUR IS COME, THE see Fischer, Irwin

HOUR OF CALVARY, THE see O'Hara,
Geoffrey

HOURGLASS see Mc Cabe

HOUSE BY THE SIDE OF THE ROAD see
Gulesian, M.H.

HOUSE, JERRY
Fa-So-La *sac
solo,pno WORD S-379   (H1804)

HOUSE OF CLAY, THE see Naylor, Bernard

HOUSE OF LIFE, THE see Vaughan
Williams, Ralph

HOUSE OF THE DYING, THE see Lessard,
John Ayres

HOUSE ON A HILL, THE see Charles,
Ernest

HOUSEHOLD SONGS see Foster, Stephen
Collins

HOUSER
River Of Jordan, The *sac
(Hall) solo,pno LILLENAS SM-939: SN
$1.00   (H1805)

HOVERING LANDSCAPE see Vass, L.

HOVHANESS, ALAN (1911-   )
Angelic Song *Op.19, cant
S/T solo,horn,strings PETERS 6589
rental   (H1806)

As On The Night *Op.100,No.1b, Xmas
S solo,strings,cel AMP $3.00 see
from Triptych   (H1807)
(Wither) S solo,strings,cel AMP
$1.50 see from Triptych   (H1808)

As The Wings Of Doves *Op.5,No.3
see Three Odes Of Solomon

As The Work Of Husbandman *Op.5,No.2
see Three Odes Of Solomon

Avak, The Healer *cant
S solo,trp,strings study sc PEER
$4.25, ipr   (H1809)

Black Pool Of Cat
med solo,pno PETERS 6032 $1.75
(H1810)
Canticle *Op.115
S solo,ob,xylo,harp,cel,strings sc
PETERS 6549 $7.50, ipr, voc sc
PETERS 6549A $3.50   (H1811)

Dawn At Laona *Op.153, cant
low solo,pno PETERS 6449 $3.50
(H1812)
Describe Me *Op.95,No.1
see Three Songs

Eight Songs *CC8L
low solo,pno PETERS 66442 $10.00
contains songs in English and
Armenian texts; op. 238, nos. 1-
4, op. 242, nos. 1-4   (H1813)

Fans Of Blue *Op.95,No.3
see Three Songs

HOVHANESS, ALAN (cont'd.)

Green Stones *Op.95,No.2
see Three Songs

Hercules *Op.56,No.4
S solo,vln PETERS 66025 $3.25
(H1814)

How I Adore Thee *Op.7
med solo,pno PETERS P6479 $2.00
(H1815)

I Heard Thee Singing
high solo,pno PETERS 6218 $1.50
(H1816)

Innisfallen *Op.84,No.2
solo,pno PETERS 6033 $1.50 (H1817)

Layla *Op.29
med solo,pno PETERS 6483 $2.50
(H1818)

Live In The Sun *Op.169
med solo,pno/cel PETERS 6468 $1.50
(H1819)

Love Songs Of Hafiz *Op.33, CC8U
med solo,pno PETERS 6484 $5.00
(H1820)

Lullaby Of The Lake *Op.74,No.4
solo,pno PETERS 6219 $1.25 (H1821)

Moon Has A Face, The *Op.156
med solo,pno PETERS 6467 $1.25
(H1822)

No Way Is Hard *Op.5,No.1
see Three Odes Of Solomon

O Goddess Of The Sea *Op.151
low solo,pno PETERS 6448 $2.50
(H1823)

O Lady Moon
high solo,pno EMI s.p. (H1824)

O World *Op.32,No.4
B solo,pno PETERS 66186A $1.75
(H1825)
T/Bar solo,pno,opt trom PETERS
66186B $1.75 (H1826)

Out Of The Depths *Op.142,No.3
solo,pno/org PETERS 6045 $1.75
(H1827)

Pagan Saint *Op.74,No.1
solo,pno PETERS 6220 $1.50 (H1828)

Persephone *Op.154
low solo,pno PETERS 6451 $3.00
(H1829)

Raven River *Op.74,No.8
low solo,pno PETERS 6221 $1.50
(H1830)

Saturn *Op.243
S solo,clar,pno sc PETERS 66440
$9.00 (H1831)

Starlight Of Noon *Op.32,No.1
med solo,pno PETERS 6621 $1.50
(H1832)

Three Odes Of Solomon
med solo,pno PETERS 6477 $2.50
contains: As The Wings Of Doves,
Op.5,No.3; As The Work Of
Husbandman, Op.5,No.2; No Way
Is Hard, Op.5,No.1 (H1833)

Three Songs
med solo,pno PETERS 6026 $2.50
contains: Describe Me, Op.95,
No.1; Fans Of Blue, Op.95,No.3;
Green Stones, Op.95,No.2
(H1834)

Triptych *see As On The Night,
Op.100,No.1b (H1835)

Two Shakespeare Sonnets
solo,pno PETERS 66222 s.p.
contains: When In Disgrace With
Fortune And Men's Eyes; When To
The Sessions Of Sweet Silent
Thought (H1836)

Watchman, Tell Us Of The Night *Xmas
S solo,pno/org PETERS 6465 $1.75
(H1837)

When In Disgrace With Fortune And
Men's Eyes
see Two Shakespeare Sonnets

When To The Sessions Of Sweet Silent
Thought
see Two Shakespeare Sonnets

Yar Nazani *Op.24
solo,pno (Armenian text) PETERS
66018 $2.00 (H1838)

HOVLAND, EGIL. (1924-)
Lamenti *Op.43
S solo,3fl,3ob,3clar,3bsn,4horn,
3trp,3trom,tuba,timp,perc,harp,
pno,cel,strings study sc LYCHE
LY555 s.p. (H1839)

Magnificat *Op.44
[Lat] A solo,harp, alto flute sc
NORSK s.p. (H1840)

HOW ABOUT YOUR HEART *sac,gospel
solo,pno ABER.GRP. $1.50
(H1841)

HOW BEAUTIFUL ARE THE FEET see Handel,
George Frideric

HOW BEAUTIFUL ARE THE FEET see Perry,
Julia

HOW BEAUTIFUL HEAVEN MUST BE *sac,
gospel
solo,pno ABER.GRP. $1.50 (H1842)

HOW BEAUTIFUL UPON THE MOUNTAINS see
Canning, Thomas

HOW BEAUTIFUL UPON THE MOUNTAINS see
Fischer, Irwin

HOW BEAUTIFUL UPON THE MOUNTAINS see
Harker, F. Flaxington

HOW BEAUTIFULLY THEY PLAY see Jaj, De
Szepen Muzsikalnak

HOW CAN I E'ER RECEIVE see Buxtehude,
Dietrich, Wie Soll Ich Dich
Empfangen

HOW CAN I REVEAL see Chajes, Julius

HOW CAN MY LIPS DENY IT? see Menotti,
Gian Carlo, Che Gli Dirai Quel
Giorno

HOW CAN THE TREE BUT WITHER see Vaughan
Williams, Ralph

HOW COLD YOUR LITTLE HAND IS see
Puccini, Giacomo, Che Gelida Manina

HOW COME see Murray

HOW DID EVERYBODY KNOW see Ewing, M.

HOW DO I KNOW see Paisley, William M.

HOW DO I LOVE THEE see Dello Joio,
Norman

HOW DO I LOVE THEE? see Goodenough,
Forrest

HOW DO I LOVE THEE? see Hopkins, J.M.

HOW DO I LOVE THEE see Lippe

HOW DO I LOVE THEE see Mills, Charles

HOW DO I LOVE THEE? see Surinach,
Carlos

HOW ENGAGING, HOW ENDEARING see Arne,
Thomas Augustine

HOW EXCELLENT IS THY LOVING KINDNESS
see Humphreys, Don

HOW FAIR THIS SPOT see Rachmaninoff,
Sergey Vassilievitch

HOW GLORIOUS IS THY NAME see Slogedal,
Bjarne, Hvor Herlig Klinger Ditt
Navn

HOW GREAT THOU ART see Hine, Stuart

HOW HAST THOU OFFENDED? see Schutz,
Heinrich, Was Hast Du Verwirket?

HOW I ADORE THEE see Hovhaness, Alan

HOW I WANT THE LORD TO FIND ME see
Androzzo, Alma Bazel

HOW LONG? see Lewis

HOW LONG, GREAT GOD see Purcell, Henry

HOW LONG HAS IT BEEN? see Lister, Mosie

HOW LONG WILT THOU? see Sowerby, Leo

HOW LONG WILT THOU FORGET ME? see
Pflueger, Carl

HOW LONG WILT THOU FORGET ME, O LORD?
see Hoffmeister, Leon Abbott

HOW LOVELY ARE THY DWELLINGS see Davis,
Katherine K.

HOW LOVELY ARE THY DWELLINGS see
Liddle, Samuel

HOW LOVELY IS THE HAND OF GOD see
Loughborough, Raymond

HOW LOVELY IT IS see Walters, G.

HOW MANY NIGHTS see Weigl, Vally

HOW MARVELOUS IS THE POWER OF GOD see
Haydn, (Franz) Joseph

HOW MUCH MORE see Ashton, Bob

HOW MUCH MORE see Goodman

HOW NEAR TO GOD see Kent, Mrs. Ada
Twohy

HOW OFT, WHEN THOU MY MUSIC see
Hogenhaven, Knud

HOW PLEASANT IS THIS FLOWERY PLAIN AND
GROUND see Purcell, Henry

HOW PLEASANT IT IS TO HAVE MONEY see
Kagen, Sergius

HOW PLEASANT TO KNOW MR. LEAR see
Roxburgh, Edwin

HOW SHALL A MORTAL SONG ASPIRE see
Latrobe, Christian I.

HOW SHOULD I YOUR TRUE LOVE KNOW? see
Castelnuovo-Tedesco, Mario

HOW SLEEP THE BRAVE see Birch, Robert
Fairfax

HOW SOFT, UPON THE EV'NING AIR see
Dunhill, Thomas Frederick

HOW SWEET I ROAM'D see Dukelsky,
Vladimir

HOW SWEET IT IS see Ellis

HOW SWEET THE MOONLIGHT SLEEPS see
Head, Michael (Dewar)

HOW TO SING NATURALLY see Long, H.

HOW WONDERFUL *sac,CC11L
(Carmichael, Ralph) low solo,pno WORD
30021 $1.95 (H1843)

HOWARD
Love In Thy Youth
see OLD ENGLISH SONG CYCLE, AN

HOWARD, JOHN TASKER (1890-1964)
Soft Invader Of My Soul
(Bevan) T solo,pno ELKIN 27.2373.05
s.p. (H1844)

HOWARD, L.
Our Garden *CCU
solo,pno LEONARD-ENG (H1845)

Six Little Songs For Somebody *CC6U
solo,pno LEONARD-ENG (H1846)

Songs For You And Me *CCU
solo,pno LEONARD-ENG (H1847)

Songs I Can Sing Myself *CCU
solo,pno LEONARD-ENG (H1848)

HOW'D YOU LIKE TO BE A BABY GIRL see
O'Reilly

HOWE, MARY (1882-1964)
Baritone Songs *CCU
Bar solo,pno GALAXY 1.2149.7 $3.00
(H1849)

English Songs: Part 1 *CCU
solo,pno GALAXY 1.2148.7 $3.00
(H1850)

English Songs: Part 2 *CCU
solo,pno GALAXY 1.2152.7 $3.00
(H1851)

English Songs: Part 3 *CCU
solo,pno GALAXY 1.2172.7 $3.00
(H1852)

French Songs *CCU
solo,pno GALAXY 1.2150.7 $3.00
(H1853)

German Songs *CCU
solo,pno GALAXY 1.2151.7 $3.00
(H1854)

Great Land Of Mine
med solo,pno PRESSER $.75 (H1855)

Seven Goethe Songs *CC7U
solo,pno GALAXY 1.2147.7 $3.00
(H1856)

Three Hokku *CC3U
high solo,pno GALAXY 1.2157.7 $1.00
(H1857)

HOWELL, DOROTHY (1898-)
Little Prince
solo,pno CRAMER $.90 (H1858)

To Sine In Winter
solo,pno CRAMER $1.15 (H1859)

Tortoiseshell Cat
solo,pno CRAMER $1.15 (H1860)

HOWELLS, HERBERT NORMAN (1892-)
King David
solo,pno BOOSEY $1.50 (H1861)

HOY NO LUCIO LA ESTRELLA DE TUS OJOS
see Chavez, Carlos

HRAME SA HRAME see Novak, Milan

HREPPSTJORASNYTA
see Fimm Numer I Islenzkum
Pjoobuningum

HRISANIDE, ALEXANDRE (1936-   )
I-Ro-La-Hai
S solo,fl,ob,clar,al-sax,bsn,horn,
trp,trom,3perc,pno,strings GERIG
HG 890 s.p.   (H1862)

HRUSKA, J.
Pisne Pro Sopran *CCU
S solo,pno PANTON 931 s.p. (H1863)

HRUSOVSKY, IVAN (1927-   )
Cerveny Mak *song cycle
S solo,pno SLOV.HUD.FOND s.p.
                                   (H1864)

HUAINITO see Espoile, Raoul H.

HUAINITO see Gomez Carrillo, Manuel

HUAYNU see Espoile, Raoul H.

HUBANS, CH.
L'Ami Printemps
solo,pno ENOCH s.p.   (H1865)
solo,acap ENOCH s.p.   (H1866)

HUBBARD
Thing Called Love, A *sac
solo,pno BENSON S5072-S $1.00
                                   (H1867)

HUBBARD, H.
Birth Of The King *sac,gospel
solo,pno SAUL AVE   (H1868)

Christians Tribulation (composed with
Redd, G.C.; Merriweather, Roy)
*sac,gospel
solo,pno SAUL AVE   (H1869)

Everything Will Be All Right
(composed with Redd, G.C.) *sac,
gospel
solo,pno SAUL AVE   (H1870)

Heaven Will Be My Home (composed with
Redd, G.C.) *sac,gospel
solo,pno SAUL AVE   (H1871)

I Am Thine (composed with Redd, G.C.;
Merriweather, Roy) *sac,gospel
solo,pno SAUL AVE   (H1872)

I Done Got Over (composed with
Stevens, Sammy) *sac,gospel
solo,pno SAUL AVE   (H1873)

I Dreamed I Went To Heaven (composed
with Stevens, Sammy) *sac,gospel
solo,pno SAUL AVE   (H1874)

I Wish That I Had Been There
(composed with Redd, G.C.) *sac,
gospel
solo,pno SAUL AVE   (H1875)

I'm Sheltered In His Arms (composed
with Redd, G.C.; Merriweather,
Roy) *sac,gospel
solo,pno SAUL AVE   (H1876)

Jesus Died (composed with Redd, G.C.)
*sac,gospel
solo,pno SAUL AVE   (H1877)

Jesus Will Move Every (composed with
Redd, G.C.) *sac,gospel
solo,pno SAUL AVE   (H1878)

Loved Ones Are Waiting (composed with
Redd, G.C.) *sac,gospel
solo,pno SAUL AVE   (H1879)

New Way Of Life, A (composed with
Redd, G.C.; Merriweather, Roy)
*sac,gospel
solo,pno SAUL AVE   (H1880)

Only (composed with Stevens, Sammy)
*sac,gospel
solo,pno SAUL AVE   (H1881)

There's Nothing Like The Holy Ghost
(composed with Redd, G.C.) *sac,
gospel
solo,pno SAUL AVE   (H1882)

They Shall Be Mine (composed with
Merriweather, Roy) *sac,gospel
solo,pno SAUL AVE   (H1883)

Think Of The Goodness Of God
(composed with Redd, G.C.) *sac,
gospel
solo,pno SAUL AVE   (H1884)

Walk On The Pathway (composed with
Redd, G.C.) *sac,gospel
solo,pno SAUL AVE   (H1885)

HUBBARD, H. (cont'd.)
Where Were You Going (composed with
Redd, G.C.) *sac,gospel
solo,pno SAUL AVE   (H1886)

Yes I'll Know Him (composed with
Redd, G.C.) *sac,gospel
solo,pno SAUL AVE   (H1887)

HUBER, KLAUS (1924-   )
Auf Die Ruhige Nacht-Zeit
S solo,fl,vla,vcl (diff) BAREN.
3480 $12.00, ipa   (H1888)

Des Engels Anregung An Die Seele
T solo,fl,clar,horn,harp sc,oct
UNIVER. 13059 $5.75   (H1889)

Psalm Of Christ *sac,Psalm
[Eng] Bar solo,clar,bass clar,horn,
trp,trom,vln,vla,vcl sc ARS VIVA
AV 305 s.p.   (H1890)

HUBERTIN LAULU see Pacius, Fredrik

HUBERTS SANG see Pacius, Fredrik,
Hubertin Laulu

HUBSCHMANN, WERNER (1901-1969)
Alte Deutsche Spruchweisheit
T solo,gtr DEUTSCHER 9044 s.p.
                                   (H1891)

HUDBA PRO SOPRAN, FLETNU A HARFU see
Jirasek, Ivo

HUE, [GEORGES-ADOLPHE] (1858-1948)
Chansons Lointaines
SALABERT-US $9.00
contains: Complainte D'amour (med
solo,pno); Les Barques
Eternelles (med solo,pno);
Litanies Passionees (med solo,
pno); Soir Paien (med solo,fl)
                                   (H1892)

Chansons Printanieres *CC7L
high solo/med solo,pno SALABERT-US
$9.00   (H1893)

Complainte D'amour
see Chansons Lointaines

I Wept Beloved
high solo,pno (F min) BOSTON $1.50
                                   (H1894)
low solo,pno (E flat min) BOSTON
$1.50   (H1895)

Les Barques Eternelles
see Chansons Lointaines

Litanies Passionees
see Chansons Lointaines

Soir Paien
see Chansons Lointaines

HUE! HO! TONNERE! see Lefort, G.

HUERTER, CHARLES (1885-   )
My Prayer *sac,Gen
low solo,pno (D flat maj) WILLIS
$.60   (H1896)
high solo,pno (G flat maj) WILLIS
$.60   (H1897)
med solo,pno (B flat maj) WILLIS
$.60   (H1898)

HUEYA see Andre, Jose

HUFF, RONN
God Gave The Song (composed with
Gaither) *sac
solo,pno BENSON S5539-R $2.00
                                   (H1899)
New World, A *sac
solo,pno BENSON S5040-R $1.00
                                   (H1900)

HUFFMAN, PAUL
He Came Back *see Keller, Joan

HUFSCHMIDT, WOLFGANG (1934-   )
De Profundis *sac
Bar solo,org (diff) BAREN. 4124
                                   (H1901)
Drei Alttestamentliche Spruche *sac,
CC3U
S solo,fl,vla (diff) BAREN. 4119
s.p.   (H1902)

Drei Kleine Geistliche Konzerte
*CC3U
S solo,org (med diff) BAREN. 4120
                                   (H1903)
Ich Steh An Deiner Krippen Hier *sac
ST soli,2vln,vcl (med diff) BAREN.
4121 $7.75   (H1904)

HUGGLER, JOHN (1928-   )
For Coloratura, Clarinet, Viola,
Cello *Op.20
coloratura sop,clar,vla,vcl sc
AM.COMP.AL. $9.90, ipa   (H1905)

HUGGLER, JOHN (cont'd.)
Sculptures *Op.39
S solo,4fl,3clar,4horn,6trp,6trom,
timp,4perc,pno,strings PETERS
6869 rental   (H1906)

Seven Songs *Op.74, CC7U
S solo,2fl,2ob,2clar,2bsn,4horn,
3trp,3trom,timp,perc,harp,strings
PETERS 66504 rental   (H1907)

HUGHES
God Spoke To Me Today *sac
SA soli,pno LORENZ $1.00   (H1908)

Keep Christ In Christmas *sac,Xmas
med solo,pno LORENZ $1.00   (H1909)

One Way *sac
med solo,pno LORENZ $1.00   (H1910)

HUGHES, BOB
Jesus Is Real *sac
med solo,pno CRESPUB CP-T2002 $1.00
                                   (H1911)

HUGHES, HERBERT (1882-1937)
B For Barney
see Hughes, Herbert, I Will Walk
With My Love

Ballynure Ballad
solo,pno (C min) BOOSEY $1.50
                                   (H1912)

Bard Or Armagh
solo,pno (B flat maj) BOOSEY $1.50
                                   (H1913)

Bards Legacy
solo,pno CRAMER   (H1914)

Carol Of Jesus Child
low solo,pno (E flat maj) ASHDOWN
$1.75   (H1915)
high solo,pno (G maj) ASHDOWN $1.75
                                   (H1916)
med solo,pno (F maj) ASHDOWN $1.75
                                   (H1917)

Dear Little Shamrock
high solo,pno (B flat maj) CRAMER
                                   (H1918)
low solo,pno (G maj) CRAMER (H1919)

Down By The Sally Gardens
solo,pno (E flat maj) BOOSEY $1.50
                                   (H1920)

Erin The Tear And The Smile
low solo,pno (A flat maj) CRAMER
                                   (H1921)
high solo,pno (C maj) CRAMER
                                   (H1922)
med solo,pno (B flat maj) CRAMER
                                   (H1923)

Forlorn Queen
solo,pno (B maj) BOOSEY $1.50
                                   (H1924)

Gartan Mother's Lullaby
solo,pno (D maj) BOOSEY $1.50
                                   (H1925)

General Munroe
solo,pno CRAMER   (H1926)

I Have A Bonnet Trimmed With Blue
solo,pno (F maj) BOOSEY $1.50
                                   (H1927)

I Know Where I'm Goin'
solo,pno (A flat maj) BOOSEY $1.50
                                   (H1928)

I Will Walk With My Love
solo,pno (A flat maj) BOOSEY $1.50
contains also: B For Barney
                                   (H1929)

If I Had A-Knew
solo,pno (G maj) ASHDOWN   (H1930)

Kitty, My Love, Will You Marry Me
solo,pno (E flat maj) BOOSEY $1.50
                                   (H1931)

Kitty Of Coleraine
high solo,pno (B flat maj) CRAMER
                                   (H1932)
low solo,pno (G maj) CRAMER (H1933)

Low Backed Car
low solo,pno (E flat maj) CRAMER
                                   (H1934)
med solo,pno (F maj) CRAMER (H1935)
high solo,pno (G maj) CRAMER
                                   (H1936)

Meeting Of The Waters
solo,pno CRAMER $1.15   (H1937)

My Father Has Some Very Fine Sheep
solo,pno (G maj) ASHDOWN   (H1938)

Oft In The Stilly Night
solo,pno CRAMER $1.15   (H1939)

Open The Door Softly
low solo,pno (E flat maj) ASHDOWN
$1.75   (H1940)
med solo,pno (F maj) ASHDOWN $1.75
                                   (H1941)
high solo,pno (G maj) ASHDOWN $1.75
                                   (H1942)

HUGHES, HERBERT (cont'd.)

Palatine's Daughter, The
solo,pno (A flat maj) ASHDOWN
(H1943)

Rory O'More
solo,pno CRAMER   (H1944)

She Is Far From The Land
solo,pno CRAMER   (H1945)

She Moved Thro' The Fair
solo,pno (G maj) BOOSEY $1.50
(H1946)

Shockheaded Peter   *CCU
solo,pno CRAMER   (H1947)

Silent O'Moyle
low solo,pno (G min) CRAMER (H1948)
high solo,pno (A min) CRAMER
(H1949)

Spanish Lady
solo,pno (A maj) BOOSEY $1.50
(H1950)

Star Of The County Down
solo,pno (F sharp min) BOOSEY $1.50
(H1951)

Winding Banks Of Erne
solo,pno CRAMER   (H1952)

HUGHES, J. SCOTT
Your Voice
low solo,pno,opt vln (F maj)
LEONARD-ENG   (H1953)
med solo,pno,opt vln (A flat maj)
LEONARD-ENG   (H1954)
high solo,pno,opt vln (C maj)
LEONARD-ENG   (H1955)

HUGH'S SONG OF THE ROAD see Vaughan
Williams, Ralph

HUGO WOLF ALBUM see Wolf, Hugo

HUGO WOLF-ALBUM FOR BARITONE OR BASS
see Wolf, Hugo

HUHN, BRUNO (1871-1950)
Be Thou Exalted   *sac
AB soli,pno SCHIRM.G $.85   (H1956)

Invictus
low solo,pno (A flat maj) WILLIS
$.60   (H1957)
high solo,pno (D maj) WILLIS $.60
(H1958)
med solo,pno (B flat maj) WILLIS
$.60   (H1959)

HUHTIKUU see Marvia, Einari

HUHUILU METSASSA see Fordell, Erik
(Fritiof), Lat I Skogen

HUIT CHANSONS see Arma, Paul

HUIT CHANSONS see Arma, Paul

HUIT CHANSONS POLONAISES see Poulenc,
Francis

HUIT MELODIES JAPONAISE see Tansman,
Alexander

HUIT POEMES CHINOIS see Blair Fairchild

HUIT POEMES DE JEAN COCTEAU see Auric,
Georges

HUIT POEMES DE M. DESBORDES-VALMORE see
Schlosser, Paul

HUKVALDER VOLKSPOESIE IN LIEDERN see
Janacek, Leos

HULDAS KARIN see Taube, Evert

HULDIGUNG see Strauss, Richard

HULDIGUNGSKANTATE see Handel, George
Frideric

HULL, MOLLY
Sprig Of Boronia
low solo,pno (E flat maj) ALLANS
s.p.   (H1960)
high solo,pno (G maj) ALLANS s.p.
(H1961)

HULLEBROECK, EM.
Aan Mijn Belgen Bij Den Yser
see Liederen, Vol. 15

Aan U Alleen
see Liederen, Vol. 2

Afrikaans Wiegeliedje
see Liederen, Vol. 16

Als 'T Zondag Is
see Liederen, Vol. 2

Brief Uit Cezembre
see Liederen, Vol. 17: De Liederen
Der Vlaamsche Marteling

HULLEBROECK, EM. (cont'd.)

Brief Uit Frankrijk
see Liederen, Vol. 11

Brief Uit Vlaanderen
see Liederen, Vol. 7

Brouwerslied
see Liederen, Vol. 14

Champagne
see Liederen, Vol. 10

De Blauwvoet
see Liederen, Vol. 18

De Boeven Van Fresnes
see Liederen, Vol. 17: De Liederen
Der Vlaamsche Marteling

De Brief Van Den Schacht
see Liederen, Vol. 18

De Dahlia
see Liederen, Vol. 11

De Fijnproevers
see Liederen, Vol. 10

De Gilde Viert
see Liederen, Vol. 10

De Horen
see Liederen, Vol. 19

De Jongens Zeggen 'T Aan De Meisjes
see Liederen, Vol. 2

De Kwikstaart
see Liederen, Vol. 7

De Ooievaar
see Liederen, Vol. 12

De Regenvlaag
see Liederen, Vol. 19

De Strijdzang Der Houthakkers
see Liederen, Vol. 17: De Liederen
Der Vlaamsche Marteling

De Verhuizende Meid
see Liederen, Vol. 7

De Verworpelingen Van Den Yzer
see Liederen, Vol. 17: De Liederen
Der Vlaamsche Marteling

De Voorspelling
see Liederen, Vol. 13

De Weezang Van Auvours
see Liederen, Vol. 17: De Liederen
Der Vlaamsche Marteling

De Wiegende Mijnwerker
see Liederen, Vol. 3

Di Langit
see Maleische Liederen, Bd.1

Die Sterretjie
see Liederen, Vol. 16

Door Wel En Wee
see Liederen, Vol. 4

Eerste Communielied
see Liederen, Vol. 8

Eerste Missielied
see Liederen, Vol. 8

Grietje
see Liederen, Vol. 11

Hemelsche Liefde
see Liederen, Vol. 3

Het Boorlingsken-Moedertaal
see Liederen, Vol. 4

Het Is De Liefde
see Hullebroeck, Em., Knokkelbeen

Het Kempisch Osseboerken
see Liederen, Vol. 18

Het Landje Van Belofte
see Liederen, Vol. 15

Het Lied Van Nele
see Liederen, Vol. 19

Het Liedje Van De Belaardier
see Liederen, Vol. 13

Het Meisje Van Amsterdam
see Liederen, Vol. 19

Het Meisje Van Den Buiten
see Liederen, Vol. 13

HULLEBROECK, EM. (cont'd.)

Het Wiegelied Der Vlaamsch Gezinde
Moeder
see Liederen, Vol. 18

Het Zijn Geen Jongens
see Liederen, Vol. 10

Hij Die Geen Liedje Zingen Kan
see Liederen, Vol. 3

Huwelijkslied
see Liederen, Vol. 8

In Mijn Liefkens Hoveken
see Liederen, Vol. 2

Jan En Annemie
see Liederen, Vol. 11

Jezus' Moeder
see Liederen, Vol. 7

Jubellied
see Liederen, Vol. 8

Kalme Rust
see Kostschoolbundel
see Liederen, Vol. 13

Karlijntje
see Liederen, Vol. 14

Kermislied
see Liederen, Vol. 3

Klaes De Sprak Zijn Moeder Aen
see Liederen, Vol. 15

Klompenliedeke
see Liederen, Vol. 12

Knokkelbeen
solo,pno ALSBACH s.p. contains
also: Het Is De Liefde (H1962)

Koningin Der Belgen
solo,pno ALSBACH s.p.   (H1963)

Konninginnelied
see Zes Liederen

Kostschoolbundel
solo,pno ALSBACH s.p.
contains: Kalme Rust; Moederke
Alleen; Op Kerstdag; Spelde
Werksterlied; Verjaringslied;
Voor Het Kantkusse   (H1964)

Krontjong Padan
see Maleische Liederen, Bd.1

Lied Der Vlaamsche Hogeschool
see Liederen, Vol. 11

Liederen, Vol. 2
solo,pno ALSBACH s.p.
contains: Aan U Alleen; Als 'T
Zondag Is; De Jongens Zeggen 'T
Aan De Meisjes; In Mijn
Liefkens Hoveken; Marieke;
Wiegeliedje   (H1965)

Liederen, Vol. 3
solo,pno ALSBACH s.p.
contains: De Wiegende Mijnwerker;
Hemelsche Liefde; Hij Die Geen
Liedje Zingen Kan; Kermislied;
Marleentje; Op Kerstdag (H1966)

Liederen, Vol. 4
solo,pno ALSBACH s.p.
contains: Door Wel En Wee; Het
Boorlingsken-Moedertaal; Mijn
Kleen Kleen Dochterke; Ring-
King; Speldewerksterslied
(H1967)

Liederen, Vol. 7
solo,pno ALSBACH s.p.
contains: Brief Uit Vlaanderen;
De Kwikstaart; De Verhuizende
Meid; Jezus' Moeder; 'T Kindeke
Slaapt; Vlaamse Kermis (H1968)

Liederen, Vol. 8
solo,pno ALSBACH s.p.
contains: Eerste Communielied;
Eerste Missielied;
Huwelijkslied; Jubellied;
Liefdadigheidslied;
Verjaringslied   (H1969)

Liederen, Vol. 10
solo,pno ALSBACH s.p.
contains: Champagne; De
Fijnproevers; De Gilde Viert;
Het Zijn Geen Jongens;
Schachtenliefde; Testament Van
Een Student   (H1970)

Liederen, Vol. 11
solo,pno ALSBACH s.p.
contains: Brief Uit Frankrijk; De
Dahlia; Grietje; Jan En
Annemie; Lied Der Vlaamsche

HULLEBROECK, EM. (cont'd.)

   Hogeschool; Van 'T Schoone
   Wiedsterke   (H1971)

Liederen, Vol. 12
  solo,pno ALSBACH s.p.
    contains: De Ooievaar;
    Klompenliedeke; Van Jan De
    Mosselman; Vrijersliedje; Wij
    Willen; Zendelingsbede (H1972)

Liederen, Vol. 13
  solo,pno ALSBACH s.p.
    contains: De Voorspelling; Het
    Liedje Van De Belaardier; Het
    Meisje Van Den Buiten; Kalme
    Rust; Paschen; Stantje En
    Wantje   (H1973)

Liederen, Vol. 14
  solo,pno ALSBACH s.p.
    contains: Brouwerslied;
    Karlijntje; Peetje's Brief;
    Sprookjesweelde; Van Den Witten
    Ezel; Vlaanderens Maagd (H1974)

Liederen, Vol. 15
  solo,pno ALSBACH s.p.
    contains: Aan Mijn Belgen Bij Den
    Yser; Het Landje Van Belofte;
    Klaes De Sprak Zijn Moeder Aen;
    Mijn Fientje; Naar
    Scherpenheuvel; Wat Moeder
    Schreef   (H1975)

Liederen, Vol. 16
  solo,pno ALSBACH s.p.
    contains: Afrikaans Wiegeliedje;
    Die Sterretjie; Sonnedaal;
    Studentenlied; Trouw; Uit Pure
    Pret   (H1976)

Liederen, Vol. 17: De Liederen Der
  Vlaamsche Marteling
  solo,pno ALSBACH s.p.
    contains: Brief Uit Cezembre; De
    Boeven Van Fresnes; De
    Strijdzang Der Houthakkers; De
    Verworpelingen Van Den Yzer; De
    Weezang Van Auvours; Morgenrood
                (H1977)

Liederen, Vol. 18
  solo,pno ALSBACH s.p.
    contains: De Blauwvoet; De Brief
    Van Den Schacht; Het Kempisch
    Osseboerken; Het Wiegelied Der
    Vlaamsch Gezinde Moeder; Mijn
    Paradijsje; Vrijheidslied
                (H1978)

Liederen, Vol. 19
  solo,pno ALSBACH s.p.
    contains: De Horen; De
    Regenvlaag; Het Lied Van Nele;
    Het Meisje Van Amsterdam;
    Padvinders Vooruit; Schaap Of
    Leeuw   (H1979)

Liefdadigheidslied
  see Liederen, Vol. 8

Lieve Vrouw Der Lage Landen
  solo,pno ALSBACH s.p.   (H1980)

Maleische Liederen, Bd.1
  solo,pno ALSBACH s.p.
    contains: Di Langit; Krontjong
    Padan; Nina Bobo   (H1981)

Marieke
  see Liederen, Vol. 2

Marionettenlied
  solo,pno ALSBACH s.p.   (H1982)

Marleentje
  see Liederen, Vol. 3

Mijn Fientje
  see Liederen, Vol. 15

Mijn Kleen Kleen Dochterke
  see Liederen, Vol. 4

Mijn Paradijsje
  see Liederen, Vol. 18

Moederke Alleen
  see Kostschoolbundel
  see Zes Liederen

Morgenrood
  see Liederen, Vol. 17: De Liederen
  Der Vlaamsche Marteling

Naar Scherpenheuvel
  see Liederen, Vol. 15

Nina Bobo
  see Maleische Liederen, Bd.1

O Swastika
  solo,pno ALSBACH s.p.   (H1983)

HULLEBROECK, EM. (cont'd.)

Op Kerstdag
  see Kostschoolbundel
  see Liederen, Vol. 3
  see Zes Liederen

Padvinders Vooruit
  see Liederen, Vol. 19

Paschen
  see Liederen, Vol. 13

Peetje's Brief
  see Liederen, Vol. 14

Ring-King
  see Liederen, Vol. 4

Schaap Of Leeuw
  see Liederen, Vol. 19

Schachtenliefde
  see Liederen, Vol. 10

Smederslied
  solo,pno ALSBACH s.p.   (H1984)

Sonnedaal
  see Liederen, Vol. 16

Spelde Werksterlied
  see Kostschoolbundel

Speldewerksterslied
  see Liederen, Vol. 4
  see Zes Liederen

Sprookjesweelde
  see Liederen, Vol. 14

Stantje En Wantje
  see Liederen, Vol. 13

Studentenlied
  see Liederen, Vol. 16

'T Kindeke Slaapt
  see Liederen, Vol. 7

Testament Van Een Student
  see Liederen, Vol. 10

Trouw
  see Liederen, Vol. 16

Uit Pure Pret
  see Liederen, Vol. 16

Van Den Witten Ezel
  see Liederen, Vol. 14

Van Jan De Mosselman
  see Liederen, Vol. 12

Van 'T Schoone Wiedsterke
  see Liederen, Vol. 11
  see Zes Liederen

Verjaringslied
  see Kostschoolbundel
  see Liederen, Vol. 8

Vlaamse Kermis
  see Liederen, Vol. 7

Vlaanderens Maagd
  see Liederen, Vol. 14

Voor Het Kantkusse
  see Kostschoolbundel

Voor Het Kantkussen
  see Zes Liederen

Vrijersliedje
  see Liederen, Vol. 12

Vrijheidslied
  see Liederen, Vol. 18

Wat Moeder Schreef
  see Liederen, Vol. 15

Wiegeliedje
  see Liederen, Vol. 2

Wij Willen
  see Liederen, Vol. 12

Zendelingsbede
  see Liederen, Vol. 12

Zes Liederen
  2 soli,pno ALSBACH s.p.
    contains: Konninginnelied;
    Moederke Alleen; Op Kerstdag;
    Speldewerksterslied; Van 'T
    Schoone Wiedsterke; Voor Het
    Kantkussen   (H1985)

Zeven Liederen *CC7L
  solo,pno ALSBACH s.p.   (H1986)

HULLEBROECK, EM. (cont'd.)

Zonne Slapegaan *CC2U
  soli,pno ALSBACH s.p.   (H1987)

HULST, G. V.D.
  Mijn Land
    solo,pno BROEKMANS 250 s.p. (H1988)

HULTNER
  Min Tos
    solo,pno LUNDQUIST s.p. (H1989)

HUMBLE PRIERE see Jacob, Dom Clement

HUMBLE PRIERE see Strimer, Joseph

HUMBLE SONG TO THE BIRDS, A see
  Hopkins, Anthony

HUMFREY, PELHAM (1647-1674)
  Trois Chansons (from Treasury Of
    Musick) CC3U
    cmplt ed,cloth,min sc OISEAU s.p.
                (H1990)

HUMLEVISA see Peterson-Berger, (Olof)
  Wilhelm

HUMLOR see Peterson-Berger, (Olof)
  Wilhelm

HUMMEL, FERDINAND (1855-1928)
  Alleluia *Op.73, sac
    "Halleluja!" high solo,pno BELWIN
    $1.50   (H1991)
    "Halleluja!" low solo,pno BELWIN
    $1.50   (H1992)
    "Halleluja!" med solo,pno BELWIN
    $1.50   (H1993)
    "Hallelujah" [Lat/Eng] high solo,
    kbd HANSEN-DEN s.p.   (H1994)

  Halleluja! *see Alleluia

  Hallelujah *see Alleluia

HUMORESCA see Dvorak, Antonin, Eine
  Kleine Fruhlingsweise

HUMORESKE see Dvorak, Antonin, Eine
  Kleine Fruhlingsweise

HUMOROUS SCOTTISH SONGS, BOOK I *CCU
  solo,pno PATERSON s.p.   (H1995)

HUMOROUS SCOTTISH SONGS, BOOK II *CCU
  solo,pno PATERSON s.p.   (H1996)

HUMOROUS SCOTTISH SONGS, BOOK III *CCU
  solo,pno PATERSON s.p.   (H1997)

HUMOURS OF LOVE see Cox, David

HUMPERDINCK, ENGELBERT (1854-1921)
  Abendsegen (from Hansel Und Gretel)
    [Ger/Eng] med solo,pno SCHOTTS s.p.
             (H1998)
    [Ger/Eng] 2 soli,pno SCHOTTS s.p.
             (H1999)
    "Evening Prayer" low solo,pno (B
    flat maj) FISCHER,C S 7665
             (H2000)
    "Evening Prayer" high solo,pno (D
    maj) FISCHER,C S 7664 (H2001)
    "Evening Prayer" med solo,pno (C
    maj) CENTURY 3402   (H2002)

  Ach Wir Armen (from Hansel Und
    Gretel)
    [Ger/Eng] Bar solo,pno SCHOTTS s.p.
             (H2003)

  Bruderchen, Komm Tanz (from Hansel
    Und Gretel)
    [Ger/Eng] 2 soli,pno SCHOTTS s.p.
             (H2004)

  Dance Duet (from Hansel And Gretel)
    2 soli,pno ALLANS s.p. (H2005)

  Der Kleine Sandmann (from Hansel Und
    Gretel)
    [Ger/Eng] low solo,pno SCHOTTS s.p.
             (H2006)
    [Ger/Eng] high solo,pno SCHOTTS
    s.p.   (H2007)

  Evening Prayer *see Abendsegen

  Knusperhauschen-Duett (from Hansel
    Und Gretel)
    [Ger/Eng] 2 soli,pno SCHOTTS s.p.
             (H2008)

  Lied Des Taumannchens (from Hansel
    Und Gretel)
    [Ger/Eng] S solo,pno SCHOTTS s.p.
             (H2009)

  Little Man, The (from Hansel Und
    Gretel)
    med solo,pno (F maj) CENTURY 3435
             (H2010)

  Suse, Liebe Suse (from Hansel Und
    Gretel)
    [Ger/Eng] med solo,pno SCHOTTS s.p.
             (H2011)
    "Susy Little Susy" med solo,pno (F
    maj) CENTURY 3433   (H2012)

HUMPERDINCK, ENGELBERT (cont'd.)

Susy Little Susy *see Suse, Liebe
  Suse

There Stands A Little Man
  med solo,pno (F maj) CENTURY 3435
                                    (H2013)

HUMPHREYS
  Beatitudes, The *sac
    high solo,pno (E flat maj) FISCHER,
    C RS 156   (H2014)
    low solo,pno (C maj) FISCHER,C
    RS 157   (H2015)

  Fiesta
    high solo,pno (E flat maj) BOSTON
    $1.50   (H2016)

  Great And Marvelous
    low solo,pno (F maj) FISCHER,C
    RS 114   (H2017)
    high solo,pno (A flat maj) FISCHER,
    C RS 113   (H2018)

  I Will Lift Up Mine Eyes *sac
    high solo,pno (F maj) BOSTON $1.50
                                    (H2019)

  Man
    high solo,pno (A flat maj) FISCHER,
    C RS 159   (H2020)

  Song Of Exaltation *sac
    low solo,pno (C maj) BOSTON $1.50
                                    (H2021)
    high solo,pno (E flat maj) BOSTON
    $1.50   (H2022)

  Vocalitis
    high solo,pno (E flat maj) BOSTON
    $1.50   (H2023)

HUMPHREYS, DON
  Arise, Shine For Thy Light Is Come
    *sac,Gen
    med solo,pno (B flat maj) WILLIS
    $.75   (H2024)
    low solo,pno (G maj) WILLIS $.75
                                    (H2025)

  Behold, What Manner Of Love *sac
    med-high solo,pno (B flat maj)
    SCHIRM.G $.85   (H2026)

  He That Dwelleth In The Secret Place
    *sac,Gen
    med solo,pno (A flat maj) WILLIS
    $.75   (H2027)

  How Excellent Is Thy Loving Kindness
    *sac,Gen
    high solo,pno (B flat maj) WILLIS
    $.75   (H2028)
    low solo,pno (A flat maj) WILLIS
    $.75   (H2029)

  I Know He Cares For Me *sac,Gen
    high solo,pno (F maj) WILLIS $.60
                                    (H2030)

  I Sought The Lord *sac,Gen
    high solo,pno (C maj) WILLIS $.75
                                    (H2031)
    low solo,pno (B flat maj) WILLIS
    $.75   (H2032)

  Let This Mind Be In You *sac,Gen
    high solo,pno (F maj) WILLIS $.75
                                    (H2033)
    low solo,pno (E flat maj) WILLIS
    $.75   (H2034)

  Lord Is My Shepherd, The *sac,Gen
    high solo,pno (A flat maj) WILLIS
    $.60   (H2035)
    low solo,pno (F maj) WILLIS $.60
                                    (H2036)

  My Prayer *sac,Gen
    high solo,pno (B flat maj) WILLIS
    $.60   (H2037)
    low solo,pno (A flat maj) WILLIS
    $.60   (H2038)

  Praise Ye The Lord *sac,Gen
    low solo,pno (F maj) WILLIS $.75
                                    (H2039)
    high solo,pno (A flat maj) WILLIS
    $.75   (H2040)

  Ransomed Of The Lord, The *sac,Gen
    high solo,pno (D min) WILLIS $.60
                                    (H2041)
    low solo,pno (F flat min) WILLIS
    $.60   (H2042)

  Rejoice In The Lord *sac,Gen
    med solo,pno (E flat maj) WILLIS
    $.75   (H2043)

  Seek Ye The Lord *sac,Gen
    high solo,pno (F maj) WILLIS $.75
                                    (H2044)
    low solo,pno (E flat maj) WILLIS
    $.75   (H2045)

HUMPTY DUMPTY see Murrill, Herbert
  (Henry John)

HUMPTY DUMPTY see Presser, William

HUNDERT RUSSISCHE VOLKSLIEDER, OP. 24,
  BAND I see Rimsky-Korsakov, Nikolai

HUNDERT RUSSISCHE VOLKSLIEDER, OP. 24,
  BAND II see Rimsky-Korsakov,
  Nikolai

HUNDERT RUSSISCHE VOLKSLIEDER, OP. 24,
  BAND III see Rimsky-Korsakov,
  Nikolai

HUNDERT WEGE see Sibelius, Jean, Hundra
  Vagar

HUNDLEY, RICHARD
  Astronomers
    solo,pno (F sharp min) BOOSEY $1.50
                                    (H2046)

  Ballad On Queen Anne's Death
    solo,pno GENERAL 4 s.p.   (H2047)

  For Your Delight
    solo,pno GENERAL 6 $1.00   (H2048)

  Maiden Snow
    solo,pno GENERAL 13 $1.00   (H2049)

  Postcard From Spain
    solo,pno GENERAL 16 $1.00   (H2050)

  Softly The Summer
    solo,pno GENERAL 19 $1.00   (H2051)

  Spring
    solo,pno GENERAL 20 $1.00   (H2052)

  Wild Plum
    solo,pno GENERAL 26 $1.00   (H2053)

HUNDRA VAGAR see Sibelius, Jean

HUNDRED BEST SHORT SONGS BOOK I, THE
  *CC24L
  S/Mez/T solo,pno PATERSON s.p.
    contains works by: Bach; Berlioz;
    Liszt; Schumann and others   (H2054)

HUNDRED BEST SHORT SONGS BOOK II, THE
  *CC24L
  S/Mez/T solo,pno PATERSON s.p.
    contains works by: Brahms; Haydn;
    Schubert; Schumann and others
                                    (H2055)

HUNDRED BEST SHORT SONGS BOOK III, THE
  *CC24L
  A/Bar/B solo,pno PATERSON s.p.
    contains works by: Arne; Brahms;
    Mozart; Tschaikowsky and others
                                    (H2056)

HUNDRED BEST SHORT SONGS BOOK IV, THE
  *CC28L
  A/Bar/B solo,pno PATERSON s.p.
    contains works by: Brahms; Liszt;
    Purcell; Schubert and others
                                    (H2057)

HUNDRED BEST SHORT SONGS, VOL. 1 *CCU
  S/Mez/T solo,pno FISCHER,C PT 281
                                    (H2058)

HUNDRED BEST SHORT SONGS, VOL. 2 *CCU
  S/Mez/T solo,pno FISCHER,C PT 282
                                    (H2059)

HUNDRED BEST SHORT SONGS, VOL. 3 *CCU
  A/Bar/B solo,pno FISCHER,C PT 283
                                    (H2060)

HUNDRED BEST SHORT SONGS, VOL. 4 *CCU
  A/Bar/B solo,pno FISCHER,C PT 284
                                    (H2061)

HUNDRED PIPERS, THE *folk,Scot
  solo,pno (F maj) PATERSON FS34 s.p.
                                    (H2062)

HUNDRED YEARS HENCE see Laird, W.

HUNGARIA ALBUM *CCU,folk
  [Hung/Eng] solo,pno MARKS $1.50
                                    (H2063)

HUNGARIAN FOLK SONGS *CC53U
  [Hung/Ger] FORBERG F81 s.p.   (H2064)

HUNGARIAN FOLK SONGS *CCU,folk,Hung
  (Bartok, B.; Kodaly, Z.) [Hung] solo,
  pno BUDAPEST 5766   (H2065)

HUNGRY FOR THE SEA see McLeod, Robert

HUNTER, THE see Rovics, Howard

HUNTER, WINIFRED
  Carefree
    solo,pno LEONARD-ENG   (H2066)

  I Dreamed A Dream
    solo,pno (D flat maj) LEONARD-ENG
                                    (H2067)

HUNTSMAN, THE see Kilpinen, Yrio, Die
  Verehrung

HUNTSMEN, THE see Weigl, Vally

HUR LANGESEN VAR DET? see Hallnas,
  Hilding

HUR LJUVLIGA DE BADSKAP see Handel,
  George Frideric

HUR LJUVT DET AR ATT KOMMA see
  Dannstrom, Isidor

HUR MANGEN GANG see Palmgren, Selim

HURD, MICHAEL (1928-   )
  Shore Leave *song cycle
    Bar solo,strings NOVELLO 17.0272.06
    s.p.   (H2068)
    Bar solo,strings NOVELLO rental
                                    (H2069)

HURE, JEAN (1877-1930)
  Te Deum
    solo,pno SALABERT-US $5.50   (H2070)

HURLESTONE, WILLIAM T.
  Derby Ram, The
    solo,pno (E flat maj) ASHDOWN
                                    (H2071)

HURNIK, ILJA (1922-   )
  Blumen *Op.3, song cycle
    [Czech/Ger] solo,pno SUPRAPHON s.p.
                                    (H2072)

  Die Blumen *see Kvetiny

  Divci Pisne *CCU
    med solo,pno SUPRAPHON s.p.   (H2073)

  Kvetiny *song cycle
    "Die Blumen" high solo,pno
    SUPRAPHON s.p.   (H2074)

  Meditace *CC3U
    low solo,pno CZECH s.p.   (H2075)

  Slezske Pisne *CCU
    med solo,pno SUPRAPHON s.p.   (H2076)

  Sulamit *song cycle
    [Czech/Ger] solo,pno SUPRAPHON s.p.
                                    (H2077)

HURST, G.
  Alone At The Door
    solo,pno BERANDOL BER 1315 $1.50
    see from Two Chinese Love Songs
                                    (H2078)

  Among The Bamboos
    solo,pno BERANDOL BER 1316 $1.50
    see from Two Chinese Love Songs
                                    (H2079)

  Music When Soft Voices Die
    solo,pno BERANDOL BER 1314 $1.50
                                    (H2080)

  Two Chinese Love Songs *see Alone At
    The Door; Among The Bamboos
                                    (H2081)

HURU DYRBAR AR EJ DIN NAD see Ostling

HURU LANGE VILL DU SORJA see
  Stenhammar, Per Ulrik

HUSH see Hageman, Richard

HUSH-A-BA BIRDIE *folk,Scot
  (Roberton, Hugh S.) 3 soli,pno
  ROBERTON 72119 s.p.   (H2082)

HUSH-A-BA, BIRDIE, CROON, CROON see Mc
  Cabe, John

HUSH ME TO DREAMS see Russell, Kennedy

HUSH, THE BABY IS SLEEPING see Kaiser,
  Kurt

HUSHEEN HUSHO see Sharpe, Evelyn

HUSHEEN, LITTLE ONES, HUSHO see Franco,
  Johan

HUSS, HENRY HOLDEN (1862-1953)
  Shed No Tear
    med solo,pno SEESAW $1.00   (H2083)

HUSSENS KERKER see Pfitzner, Hans

HUSTAD, DONALD P.
  If Jesus Had Not Come *sac
    solo,pno HOPE 486 $.75   (H2084)

  Name Of Joy, A *sac
    solo,pno HOPE 528 $.75   (H2085)

  There Is My Dwelling *sac
    solo,pno HOPE 556 $.75   (H2086)

HUSTON, JOHN
  Hymn To God The Father *sac
    med solo,pno BELWIN $1.50   (H2087)

HUSVILD see Nielsen, Carl

HUT' DU DICH see Brahms, Johannes

HUTCHESON, JERE
  Shadows Of A Floating Life
    MezT soli,fl,vln,bvl,vibra SEESAW
                                    (H2088)

HUTCHINSON
  Old Mother Hubbard
    high solo,pno FISCHER,C V 1350
                                    (H2089)
    low solo,pno FISCHER,C V 1351
                                    (H2090)

HUTCHINSON, HELY
  Five Jolly Songs *CC5U
    solo,pno CRAMER   (H2091)

HUTCHISON, W.
  Sous Les Etoiles
    solo,pno (available in 2 keys)
      ENOCH s.p.   (H2092)
    solo,acap (available in 2 keys)
      ENOCH s.p.   (H2093)

  Vision
    solo,pno (available in 2 keys)
      ENOCH s.p.   (H2094)
    solo,acap (available in 2 keys)
      ENOCH s.p.   (H2095)

HUTCHISON, WARNER
  Sacrilege Of Alan Kent, The
    Bar solo,orch,electronic tape sc
      SEESAW $50.00   (H2096)

HUTCHISON, WILLIAM M.
  Dream Faces
    high solo,pno (B flat maj) LEONARD-
      ENG   (H2097)
    2 soli,pno LEONARD-ENG   (H2098)
    med-high solo,pno (A flat maj)
      LEONARD-ENG   (H2099)
    med solo,pno (G maj) LEONARD-ENG
                               (H2100)
    low solo,pno (F maj) LEONARD-
      ENG   (H2101)

  Pierrot
    low solo,pno (F maj) CRAMER (H2102)
    high solo,pno (G maj) CRAMER
                               (H2103)
    2 soli,pno LEONARD-ENG   (H2104)

  Side By Side To The Better Land
    high solo,pno (E flat maj) CRAMER
                               (H2105)
    low solo,pno (D maj) CRAMER (H2106)

  Silver Rhine
    2 soli,pno LEONARD-ENG   (H2107)

HUTET EUCH see Schutz, Heinrich

HUTH, GUSTAV (1902-1969)
  Pet Pisni *CC5U
    med solo,pno CZECH s.p.   (H2108)

HUTJE BIJ DE ZEE *CCU
  2 soli,pno ALSBACH s.p.   (H2109)

HUTSCHENRUYTER, WOUTER (1796-1878)
  Een Kruis Met Rozen
    solo,pno ALSBACH s.p.   (H2110)

HUWELIJKSLIED see Hullebroeck, Em.

HUWELIJKSLIED see Noble, Felix de

HUWELIJKSZANG see Lambrechts-Vos, A.

HUYBRECHTS, ALBERT (1879-1938)
  A La Riviere
    see Trois Poemes D'Edgard Poe

  C'etait Un Soir De Feeries
    S solo,pno CBDM s.p.   (H2111)

  Chant D'automne
    S solo,pno CBDM s.p.   (H2112)

  Eldorado
    see Trois Poemes D'Edgard Poe

  Je Ne Prends Point Garde
    see Trois Poemes D'Edgard Poe

  Les Roses De Saadi
    S solo,pno CBDM s.p.   (H2113)

  Mirliton
    S solo,pno CBDM s.p.   (H2114)

  Priere Pour Avoir Une Femme Simple
    T solo,pno CBDM s.p.   (H2115)

  Trois Poemes D'Edgard Poe
    S/Mez solo,pno cmplt ed CBDM s.p.
      contains: A La Riviere; Eldorado;
      Je Ne Prends Point Garde
                               (H2116)

HUZELLA, E.
  Miser Catulle
    ST soli,10inst BUDAPEST 10123 s.p.
                               (H2117)

HVAD SYNGER DU OM see Nielsen, Carl

HVE EINFALT ER BITT FYRIRHEIT see
  Sveinsson, Gunnar Reynir

HVEM STYRDE HIT DIN VAG? *Op.90,No.6
  "Wer Hat Dich Hergefuhrt?" [Swed/Ger]
    med-high solo,kbd HANSEN-DEN s.p.
    see from Six Songs   (H2118)

HVIEZDY NAD PRAHOU see Andrasovan,
  Tibor

HVIL OVER VERDEN, DU DYBE FRED see
  Sjogren, Emil

HVILE I SKOVEN "I GRANEHOLTET VID
  MIDDAGSTID" see Kjerulf, [Halfdan]

HVOR ER' DE NU? see Grieg, Edvard
  Hagerup

HVOR HERLIG KLINGER DITT NAVN see
  Slogedal, Bjarne

HWAINGERDD see Williams, Meirion

HYDDA LILL', TYST OCH STILL' see
  Beschnitt, J.

HYDE
  Fisherman And His Wife, The
    S&narrator,fl,ob,clar,bsn,bass
      clar,perc,harp,pno WESTERN $1.00
                               (H2119)

HYDE PARK see Poulenc, Francis

HYLAND, CYRIL
  Windy Day, A
    solo,pno (E flat maj) ASHDOWN
                               (H2120)

HYMAN, RICHARD R. (1927-   )
  Songs From The Plays Of Shakespeare
    *CCU
    solo,pno GENERAL 163 $3.50 (H2121)

HYMENEE see Larbey, V.

HYMN see Gyring, Elizabeth

HYMN see Josephson, Jacob Axel

HYMN see Mulder, Ernest W.

HYMN AND PRAYER FOR PEACE see Gillis,
  Don

HYMN BEFORE SLEEP see Orr, Charles
  Wilfred

HYMN "FJARRAN, ACK FJARRAN" see
  Soderman, (Johan) August

HYMN FROM THE ROMAN BREVIARY see
  Poulenc, Francis, Sombre Nuit,
  Aveugles Tenebres

HYMN OF CREATION see Thybo, Leif

HYMN OF LIBERATION see Shir La-Moledat

HYMN OF THANKS, A see Baumgartner, H.
  Leroy

HYMN TILL FOSTERJORDEN see Hallen,
  Andreas

HYMN TO GOD THE FATHER see Huston, John

HYMN TO THAIS see Sibelius, Jean

HYMN TO THE HOLY TRINITY see Lawes

HYMN TO THE NIGHT see Campbell-Tipton,
  Louis

HYMN TO THE SUN see Rimsky-Korsakov,
  Nikolai

HYMNE see Mirandolle, Ludovicus

HYMNE see Pijper, Willem

HYMNE see Satie, Erik

HYMNE see Vermeulen, Matthijs

HYMNE A ASTARTE see Koechlin, Charles

HYMNE A EROS see Saint-Saens, Camille

HYMNE A LA BEAUTE see Chapuis, Auguste-
  Paul-Jean-Baptiste

HYMNE A LA MORT see Filipucci, Edm.

HYMNE A LA NAISSANCE DU MATIN see
  Caplet, Andre

HYMNE A LA NUIT see Koechlin, Charles

HYMNE A LA PAIX see Saint-Saens,
  Camille

HYMNE A LA RIVIERE see Georges,
  Alexandre

HYMNE A L'AMOUR see Filipucci, Edm.

HYMNE A L'AMOUR see Fragerolle, G.

HYMNE, AERE DET EVIGE FORAR I LIVET see
  Olsen, Sparre

HYMNE AN DEUTSCHLAND see Reutter,
  Hermann

HYMNE AN DIE GOTTIN EOS see Weismann,
  Wilhelm

HYMNE AN DIE LIEBE see Strauss, Richard

HYMNE AN DIE NACHT: GEHOBEN IST DER
  STEIN see Diepenbrock, Alphons

HYMNE AN DIE NACHT: MUSS IMMER DER
  MORGEN see Diepenbrock, Alphons

HYMNE AU SOLEIL see Georges, Alexandre

HYMNE DE A LEGION D'HONNEUR see Pares,
  Ph.

HYMNE "DE BRENTE VARE GARDER see
  Rangstrom, Ture

HYMNE DE LA JEUNESSE CHRETIENNE see
  Ganne, Louis Gaston

HYMNE DE LA LEGION D'HONNEUR see Pares,
  Ph.

HYMNE DE LA LIBERATION see Limann

HYMNE DES MORTS see Georges, Alexandre

HYMNE NATIONAL A JEHANNE D'ARC see
  Mignan, Edouard-Charles-Octave

HYMNE SOVIETIQUE
  (Alexandrov, A.; Mikhalov, I.;
  Reguistan, E.) [Fr] solo,pno CHANT
  s.p.   (H2122)

HYMNE TO GOD THE FATHER, A see Presser,
  William

HYMNE "WESEN REIHT SICH AN WESEN" see
  Zagwijn, Henri

HYMNES see Fleming, Christopher le

HYMNI see Kilpinen, Yrio

HYMNI THAIS'LLE see Sibelius, Jean,
  Hymn To Thais

HYMNISCHE GESANGE see Herrmann, Hugo

HYMNISCHES KONZERT see Schubert, Heinz

HYMNS FOR LOW VOICE *sac,CC115UL
  (Stringfield, R. W.; Whitsett,
  Eleanor) A/Bar/B solo,pno LILLENAS
  MB-080 $2.50   (H2123)

HYMNS FROM THE CROSSROADS *CCU,hymn
  (Robertson) solo,pno,org,inst
  FISCHER,C O 4516 s.p., ipa (H2124)

HYMNS OF THE CHINESE KINGS see Bissell,
  Keith W.

HYMNS OF THE OLD CHURCH CHOIR *sac,
  CCU,hymn
  (Lamb; Solman) med solo,pno PAXTON
  P35027 s.p.   (H2125)

HYMNUS see Flothius, Marius

HYMNUS AD LAUDES IN FESTO SS.
  TRINITATIS see Dvorak, Antonin, O
  Sanctissima

HYMNUS DER LIEBE see Reger, Max

HYOKYAALTO see Kilpinen, Yrio

HYPERIONS SCHICKSALSLIED see Herrmann,
  Hugo

HYPERIONS SCHICKSALSLIED see Rovsing
  Olsen, Paul

HYPNOSE see Baeyens, August-L.

HYVAA YOTA see Madetoja, Leevi

HYVAA YOTA see Merikanto, Oskar

I

I ADORE THEE see Tchaikovsky, Piotr
Ilyitch

I AFTEN see Nielsen, Carl

I AFTEN see Nordqvist, Gustaf

I ALL SIN GLANS NU HIMLEN BLANKER see
Haydn, (Franz) Joseph

I AM A ROAMER see Mendelssohn-
Bartholdy, Felix

I AM CONFIRM'D see Voormolen, Alexander
Nicolas

I AM LIKE A REMNANT OF A CLOUD OF
AUTUMN see Carpenter, John Alden

I AM NOT GOING TO MARRY see Beekhuis,
Hanna

I AM OF IRELAND see Aston, Peter G.

I AM PROUD TO BE AN AMERICAN see
Malotte, Albert Hay

I AM ROSE see Diamond, David

I AM ROSE see Rorem, Ned

I AM SEEKING FOR A CITY see Miller,
James

I AM THE CAPTAIN OF THE PINAFORE see
Sullivan, Sir Arthur Seymour

I AM THE GOOD SHEPHERD see Bender, Jan

I AM THE RESURRECTION see Buxtehude,
Dietrich

I AM THE RESURRECTION see
Hammerschmidt, Andreas

I AM THE ROSE OF SHARON see Bugatch,
Samuel, Ani Chavatselot Hasharon

I AM THE RULER OF THE QUEEN'S NAVEE see
Sullivan, Sir Arthur Seymour

I AM THINE see Hubbard, H.

I AM WITH YOU ALWAYS see Innis, M.

I ARISE FROM DREAMS OF THEE see
Quilter, Roger

I ASK NONE ELSE OF THEE see Matthews,
David

I ASKED THE LORD see Lange

I ASSURE YOU see Panetti, Joan

I ATTEMPT FROM LOVE'S SICKNESS TO FLY
see Purcell, Henry

I BELIEVE see Hamblen

I BELIEVE see Reynolds, William Jensen

I BELIEVE GOD IS REAL *sac
(Carmichael, Ralph) solo,pno WORD
S-96   (I1)

I BELIEVE HE DIED FOR ME see Croft,
Colbert

I BELIEVE IN GOD see Lanier, Gary

I BELIEVE IN MIRACLES see Peterson,
John W.

I BELIEVE IN THE MAN IN THE SKY *sac,
gospel
solo,pno ABER.GRP. $1.50   (I2)

I BELIEVE JESUS see Smith, Tab

I BELIEVE THAT MY REDEEMER LIVES see
Peloquin, C. Alexander

I BI TEMP D-LA PURTINARA see Patuelli,
G.

I BLAHAUG see Dorumsgaard, Arne

I BLOW MY BUGLE see Hauge, Albert M.

I BOUGHT ME A CAT see Copland, Aaron

I BOWED ON MY KNEES AND CRIED HOLY
*sac,gospel
solo,pno ABER.GRP. $1.50   (I3)

I BRING MY LIFE see Chennault, Judy

I BUILT A HOME NEAR WIDE SEAS see
Nystroem, Gosta, Jag Har Ett Hem
Vid Havet

I CAME TO PRAISE THE LORD see Gaither

I CAMPANI see Rosi, Gino

I CAN HEAR A CUCKOO see Dunhill, Thomas
Frederick

I CANNOT HIDE FROM GOD *sac
(Carmichael, Ralph) solo,pno WORD
S-425   (I4)

I CANNOT LOVE THEE LESS NOR MORE see
Birch, Robert Fairfax

I CAN'T BE TALKIN' OF LOVE see Duke,
John Woods

I CAN'T EVEN WALK WITHOUT YOU HOLDING
MY HAND see Croft, Colbert

I CANTI DEI CAMPI see Oddone, E.

I CANTI DELLA PACE see Zanettovich,
Daniele

I CANTI DELL'ESILIO see Porrino, Ennio

I CARRIED BOTH LORD AND KING see
O'Hara, Geoffrey

I CARRY YOUR HEART see Duke, John Woods

I COME BEFORE THY THRONE see Moore,
Donald Lee

I COULD NEVER OUTLOVE THE LORD see
Gaither

I COULDN'T COULD I? see Roeckel, J.L.

I CRY YOUR MERCY MISTRESS see Hope, H.
Ashworth

I DE SIDSTE OIJEBLIKKE see Sjogren,
Emil

I DENNE SODE JULETID see Groven, Eivind

I DID NOT KNOW see Trotere, Henry

I DIDN'T THINK IT COULD BE see Crouch,
Andrae

I DIED FOR BEAUTY see Clarke, Henry
Leland

I DINA HANDERS MJUKA FAGELBO see
Kilpinen, Yrio

I DO AND CAN AND I WILL see Harris, Ron

I DODENS TYSTA TEMPELGARDAR see
Sjogren, Emil

I DODENS TYSTA TEMPLGARDAR see Sjogren,
Emil

I DONE GOT OVER see Hubbard, H.

I DON'T KNOW see Mozart, Wolfgang
Amadeus, Non So Piu Cosa Son

I DON'T KNOW WHY see Crouch, Andrae

I DON'T NEED TO UNDERSTAND see Crocker

I DON'T SUPPOSE see Trotere, Henry

I DREAM OF JEANIE WITH THE LIGHT BROWN
HAIR see Foster, Stephen Collins

I DREAM OF NAOMI
solo,pno OR-TAV $.50   (I5)

I DREAM'D A DREAM see Cooke, Edith

I DREAMED A DREAM see Hunter, Winifred

I DREAMED I WENT TO HEAVEN see Hubbard,
H.

I DREAMED ONCE OF A YOUNG PRINCESS FAIR
see Trunk, Richard, Mir Traumte Von
Einem Konigskind

I DREAMT OF A KING'S FAIR DAUGHTER see
Clutsam, George H.

I DREAMT THAT I DWELT IN MARBLE HALLS
see Balfe, Michael William

I DROMMANDE NATTENS STILLHET see
Rangstrom, Ture

I DROMMARNES LAND see Korling

I DROMMEN DU AR MIG NARA see Sjogren,
Emil

I DUE CIGNI see Bettarini, Luciano

I DUE GRANATIERI see Schumann, Robert
(Alexander), Die Beiden Grenadiere

I DUE TARLI see Zandonai, Riccardo

I DUNNO see Nichol, H. Ernest

I EN SKOG PA BERGET IDA see Offenbach,
Jacques

I EN SKOGSBACKE see Stenhammar, Wilhelm

I ENSAMHET see Wolf, Hugo

I EVIGHET see Mascheroni, Angelo, For
All Eternity

I EXPECT A MIRACLE *sac
(Carmichael, Ralph) solo,pno WORD
S-89   (I6)

I FAGARDEN see Kuula, Toivo,
Karjapihassa

I FAIN WOULD REST see Jensen, Ludwig
Irgens

I FALCIATORI see Sinigaglia, Leone

I FAUNI see Respighi, Ottorino

I FEAR NO FOE see Pinsuti, Ciro

I FEAR THY KISSES see Birch, Robert
Fairfax

I FEEL ME NEAR TO SOME HIGH THING see
Moritz, Edvard

I FEEL SO GOOD ABOUT IT see Redman,
Reginald

I FELL IN LOVE WITH A DRAGON see Mills,
Charles

I FELT A CLEAVAGE IN MY MIND see
Horvit, Michael M.

I FELT A FUNERAL IN MY BRAIN see
Horvit, Michael M.

I FIND MY ALL IN JESUS *sac,gospel
solo,pno ABER.GRP. $1.50   (I7)

I FIND MY LOVE see Mamorsky, Morris

I FIND NO FAULT IN HIM see Crouch,
Andrae

I FOLLOW WITH GLADNESS see Bach, Johann
Sebastian

I FONSTRET STAR ETT LJUS see Snare,
Sigurd

I FOUND A FRIEND *sac,gospel
solo,pno ABER.GRP. $1.50   (I8)

I FOUND A FRIEND see Van Dyke, Vonda

I FOUND IT ALL IN JESUS see Mercer

I FOUND THE ANSWER see Lange

I FOUND WHAT I WANTED *sac
(Carmichael, Ralph) solo,pno WORD
S-427   (I9)

I GAED A WAEFU' GATE *folk,Scot
solo,pno (A min/G min) PATERSON FS109
s.p.   (I10)

I GAVE HER CAKES AND I GAVE HER ALE see
Russell, W.

I GO MY WAY see Puccini, Giacomo,
Quando Me'n Vo Soletta

I GOT A HOME IN-A-DAT ROCK *spir
(Burleigh, H. T.) low solo,pno BELWIN
$1.50   (I11)
(Burleigh, H. T.) low solo,pno BELWIN
$1.50   (I12)

I GOT A HOME IN THAT ROCK see Bonds,
[Margaret]

I GOT A ROBE *spir
(Roberton, H.S.) 3 soli,pno ROBERTON
72106 s.p.   (I13)
(Widdicombe) 2 soli,pno ROBERTON
72560 s.p.   (I14)

I GOT JESUS see Fulmore

I GOT ME FLOWER see Butt, James

I GUDS HANDER see Andrep-Nordin, Birger

I GUESS THAT I'VE CHANGED see Matthews,
Randy

I HAD A DARLING DOVE
see Three Bohemian Songs

I HAD A FLOWER see Kellie, Lawrence

I HATE MUSIC see Bernstein, Leonard

I HAVE A BONNET TRIMMED WITH BLUE
(Holford, Franz) solo,pno ALBERT
AE148 s.p.   (I15)

I HAVE A BONNET TRIMMED WITH BLUE see
Holford, Franz

I HAVE A BONNET TRIMMED WITH BLUE see
Hughes, Herbert

I HAVE A DREAM see Reed, Phyllis
Luidens

I HAVE A FAWN see Davis, Katherine K.

I HAVE A FLAUNTING AIR see O'Neill,
Norman

I HAVE A FRIEND see Fox, Baynard

I HAVE A HOME   *sac,gospel
solo,pno ABER.GRP. $1.50   (I16)

I HAVE A LONGING IN MY HEART *sac,
gospel
solo,pno ABER.GRP. $1.50   (I17)

I HAVE A MELODY see Lyman, Ed.

I HAVE A RENDEZ-VOUS WITH DEATH see
Enos, J.

I HAVE BEEN BY THE POPLARS see Rodrigo,
Joaquin, De Los Alamos Vengo, Madre

I HAVE BUT ONE GOAL *sac,gospel
solo,pno ABER.GRP. $1.50   (I18)

I HAVE LONGED TO MOVE AWAY see Diamond,
David

I HAVE MY HAND IN THE HAND OF THE LORD
*sac,gospel
solo,pno ABER.GRP. $1.50   (I19)

I HAVE RETURNED see Wilkin, Marijohn

I HAVE TROD THE UPWARD AND THE DOWNWARD
SLOPE see Vaughan Williams, Ralph

I HAVE TWELVE OXEN see Ireland, John

I HEAR A WHISPER see Barry, Katherine

I HEAR AN ARMY see Barber, Samuel

I HEAR AN ARMY see Del Tredici, David

I HEAR AN ARMY see Harrison, Sidney

I HEAR YOU CALLING ME see Marshall, C.

I HEARD A BLACKBIRD IN A TREE see
Arlen, Albert

I HEARD A FLY BUZZ WHEN I DIED see
Sydeman, William

I HEARD A PIPER PIPING see Peterkin

I HEARD A ROBIN SINGING see Leonard

I HEARD THE BELLS ON CHRISTMAS DAY see
Andrews, Mark

I HEARD THE VOICE OF JESUS SAY see
Broadnax, Eugene

I HEARD THE VOICE OF JESUS SAY see
Hallett, John C.

I HEARD THE VOICE OF JESUS SAY see
Harris, Charles A.E.

I HEARD THE VOICE OF JESUS SAY see
Rathbun, F.G.

I HEARD THE VOICE OF JESUS SAY see
Steane, Bruce

I HEARD THEE SINGING see Hovhaness,
Alan

I HEARD YOU GO BY see Wood, Daniel

I HEIMSENS HJARTA see Tonnessen, Peder

I HENNES HEM see Heland

I HERRENS HAND see Hagg, Torsten

I HIMLAR SJUNGEN DEN EVIGES ARA see
Beethoven, Ludwig van, Die Ehre
Gottes In Der Natur

I HIMMELEN, I HIMMELEN see Svedlund,
Karl-Erik

I JOURNEYED ON MY WAY see Brahms,
Johannes, Ich Wandte Mich Und Sahe
An

I JUDGE THEE NOT see Schumann, Robert
(Alexander), Ich Grolle Nicht

I JUST CAME TO TALK WITH YOU, LORD see
Rambo

I JUST FEEL LIKE SOMETHING GOOD IS
ABOUT TO HAPPEN see Gaither

I JUST WANT TO KNOW see Wolfe, Lanny

I KNEEL TO PRAY see Wilson, Harry
[Robert]

I KNEW IT LONG AGO see Verdi, Giuseppe,
Ella Giammai M'Amo

I KNOW   *sac,gospel
solo,pno ABER.GRP. $1.50   (I20)

I KNOW see Burns

I KNOW A BANK see Bury, Winifred

I KNOW A BANK see Horn, Charles Edward

I KNOW A BANK see Shaw, Martin

I KNOW A LOVELY GARDEN see Caldwell,
Mary Elizabeth

I KNOW DE LORD'S LAID HIS HANDS ON ME
*spir
(Burleigh, H. T.) low solo,pno BELWIN
$1.50   (I21)
(Burleigh, H. T.) low solo,pno BELWIN
$1.50   (I22)

I KNOW HE CARES FOR ME see Humphreys,
Don

I KNOW HE'S MINE see Wells, Howard

I KNOW HE'S MINE see Younce, George

I KNOW OF TWO BRIGHT EYES see Clutsam,
George H.

I KNOW STARLIGHT see Lockwood, Normand

I KNOW THAT MY REDEEMER LIVETH see
Handel, George Frideric

I KNOW THE SECRET see Winter, Sister
Miriam Therese

I KNOW, WHERE I'M GOIN'
see Internationale Volslieder, Vol 1

I KNOW WHERE I'M GOIN' see Hughes,
Herbert

I KNOW WHO HOLDS TOMORROW *sac,gospel
solo,pno ABER.GRP. $1.50   (I23)

I KVALLNINGEN see Bergman, Erik

I LAY MY SINS ON JESUS see Speaks, Oley

I LEFT MY DEARIE LYING HERE *folk,Scot
solo,pno (A maj/G maj) PATERSON FS124
s.p.   (I24)

I LIDEN HOJT DEROPPE see Grieg, Edvard
Hagerup

I LIE AWAKE AND LISTEN see Moore,
Douglas Stuart

I LIFT UP MY EYES see Jennings, Kenneth
L.

I LO'E NA A LADDIE BUT ANE *folk,Scot
solo,pno (E flat maj) PATERSON FS114
s.p.   (I25)
(Diack, J. M.) MezT soli,pno PATERSON
s.p.   (I26)

I LONG TO SEE A FLOWER see Birch,
Robert Fairfax

I LOOK NOT BACK see Grimsrud, Solveig

I LOOK TO MY LORD see Beaumont

I LOOKED FOR LOVE *sac
(Carmichael, Ralph) solo,pno WORD
S-79   (I27)

I LOV'D A LASS, A FAIR ONE see Keel,
Frederick

I LOVE A LITTLE COTTAGE see O'Hara,
Geoffrey

I LOVE ALL BEAUTEOUS THINGS see Davies,
Henry Walford

I LOVE ALL GRACEFUL THINGS see Thiman,
Eric Harding

I LOVE ALL LOVELY THINGS see Grover,
Maynard J.

I LOVE AMERICA see Boyce

I LOVE AMERICA see Peterson, John W.

I LOVE HIM TOO MUCH see Wolfe, Lanny

I LOVE LIFE see Mana-Zucca, Mme.

I LOVE MY LADYE see Russell, Kennedy

I LOVE MY LOVE see Birch, Robert
Fairfax

I LOVE ORDINARY THINGS see York, Sybil

I LOVE THE JOCUND DANCE see Morawetz,
Oskar

I LOVE THEE see Beethoven, Ludwig van

I LOVE THEE see Grieg, Edvard Hagerup,
Ich Liebe Dich

I LOVE THEM ALL see Bennett, Sir
William Sterndale

I LOVE THIS LAND see Sveinbjornsson,
Sveinbjorn

I LOVE YOU see Barber, Samuel, Ich
Liebe Dich

I LOVE YOU, DEAR see Friml, Rudolf

I LOVE YOU, MA CHERIE see Rubens, Paul
Alfred

I LOVE YOU TRULY see Bond, Carrie
Jacobs

I LOVED A LASS see Hind, John

I MIDNATTSTUND see Valentin, Karl

I MIND THE DAY see Willeby, Charles

I MURMUR NOT see Schumann, Robert
(Alexander), Ich Grolle Nicht

I MUST AWAY see Mana-Zucca, Mme.

I MUST DOWN TO THE SEAS AGAIN see
Densmore, John H.

I MUST GO FORTH INTO THE MORNING see
Milkey, E.T.

I MUST TELL JESUS *sac,gospel
solo,pno ABER.GRP. $1.50   (I28)

I NATT SKALL JAG DO see Pergament,
Moses

I NATTEN see Merikanto, Oskar, Yolla

I NATTEN see Sibelius, Jean

I NEED LOVE see Bennett, Sir William
Sterndale

I NEED YOU EVERY HOUR see Baker, David

I NEED YOU EVERY HOUR see Hildebrand,
Ray

I NEVER KNEW LOVE see Smith

I NEVER KNEW LOVE see Smith, Tab

I NEVER WALK ALONE see Ackley, A.H.

I PASSED BY THE BEACH AT TAGO see
Sydeman, William

I PASSED BY YOUR WINDOW see Brahe, May
H.

I PASTORI see Pizzetti, Ildebrando

I PINI see Caltabiano, S.

I PRESENT YOU TO JESUS see Hathcock

I QUIETLY TURNED TO YOU see Red, Buryl

I RE MAGI see Castelnuovo-Tedesco,
Mario, Die Drei Konige

I REACHED UP see Lister, Mosie

I REMEMBER see Dunhill, Thomas
Frederick

I REMEMBER see Kmetz, T.

I RIDE THE GREAT BLACK HORSES see Duke,
John Woods

I-RO-LA-HAI see Hrisanide, Alexandre

I ROSE UP AS MY CUSTOM IS see Heilner,
Irwin

I ROSORNAS DAGAR see Baumgartner

I SAID TO LOVE see Finzi, Gerald

I SAW A MAN see Smith

I SAW A MAN PURSUING THE HORIZON see
Owen, Richard

I SAW IN LOUISIANA A LIVE OAK GROWING
see Newlin, Dika

I SAW THE MOON see Fischer, Irwin

I SAW THE ROSE see Lora, Antonio

I SEE HIS BLOOD UPON THE ROSE see
Gover, Gerald

I SEEK FOR THEE IN EVERY FLOWER see
Ganz, Wilhelm

I SEEK SOME COMELY MAIDEN see Mozart,
Wolfgang Amadeus

I SERAILLETS HAVE see Nielsen, Carl

I SERALJENS LUSTGARD see Sjogren, Emil

I SETTE PECCATI CAPITALI see Weill,
Kurt

I SHALL IMAGINE LIFE see Diamond, David

I SHALL NO MORE TO SEA see Castelnuovo-
Tedesco, Mario

I SHALL NOT PASS AGAIN THIS WAY see
Effinger, J.C.

I SHALL NOT RETURN see Birch, Robert
Fairfax

I SHALL PASS THIS WAY AGAIN see
Russell, Kennedy

I SHALL THINK OF YOU see Giannini,
Vittorio

I SHOULD HAVE BEEN CRUCIFIED see
Jensen, Gordon

I SIGH FOR THE GIRL I ADORE see Hook,
James

I SIN VAGGA I FAGER DROM see Wideen,
Ivar

I SING OF A MAIDEN see Badings, Henk

I SING OF A MAIDEN see Brown, Myrtle
Hare

I SING OF A MAIDEN see Holst, Gustav

I SING OF A MAIDEN see Kechley,
[Gerald], Carol

I SING TO THE LORD see Schutz, Heinrich

I SKOG OCH PA SJO see Haggbom

I SKOGEN see Josephson, Jacob Axel

I SKOGEN see Stenhammar, Wilhelm

I SKOGEN see Wrangel

I SKOGEN OM NATTEN see Hallnas, Hilding

I SKOVEN "JEG GIK MIG I SKOVEN SA ENSOM
EN GANG" see Kjerulf, [Halfdan]

I SOMMARNATT see Soderman

I SOUGHT THE LORD see Humphreys, Don

I STAND AMAZED see Davis

I STILL REMEMBER THINGS GOD HAS
FORGOTTEN see Jensen, Gordon

I STILLA TIMMAR see Alfven, Hugo

I STOOD ON DE RIBBER OB JORDON *spir
(Burleigh, H. T.) low solo,pno BELWIN
$1.50   (I29)

I STROVE WITH NONE see Sutherland,
Margaret

I SYSTRAR, I BRODER, I ALSKANDE PAR see
Sibelius, Jean

I TAKE SARTIN NOTICE O' THAT see
Bennett, Sir William Sterndale

I TALKED TO GOD LAST NIGHT see Guion,
David Wendall Fentress

I TASTE A LIQUOR NEVER BREWED see
Sydeman, William

I TEMPI, ASSAI LONTANI see Respighi,
Ottorino

I TEMPLET see Andree

I TETTI see Petralia

I THANK YOU GOD see Bongard, Gwen
Treneer

I THANK YOU, GOD see Diffenderfer

I THANK YOU, LIFE see Hope, H. Ashworth

I THANK YOU LORD *sac,gospel
solo,pno ABER.GRP. $1.50   (I30)

I THINK see Panetti, Joan

I THINK I COULD TURN see Kagen, Sergius

I THINK OF YOU see Dunhill, Thomas
Frederick

I THOUGHT OF YOU see Cohnreich, L.

I TOLD MY LOVE TO THE ROSES see Chalk,
C.

I TRUST IN GOD see Baker, Richard

I TYST KONVALJESKOG see Wennerberg,
Gunnar

I UNGDOMS AR see Nystedt, Knut

I VANTAN PA FAR see Lambert

I VARENS UNDERSKONA MAJ see Soderman,
(Johan) August

I VARLDEN AR JAG BLOTT EN GAST see
Noren

I VASSEN see Palmgren, Selim

I VOW TO THEE MY COUNTRY see Davies,
Henry Walford

I WAITED FOR THE LORD see Mendelssohn-
Bartholdy, Felix, Ich Harrette Des
Herrn

I WALK WITH HIS HAND IN MINE see
Stanphill, Ira F.

I WALKED INTO THE GARDEN *sac
high solo,pno (A flat maj) ASHLEY
$1.00   (I31)
low solo,pno (E flat maj) ASHLEY
$1.00   (I32)
med solo,pno (F maj) ASHLEY $1.00
                                 (I33)

I WALKED TODAY WHERE JESUS WALKED see
O'Hara, Geoffrey

I WALKED TODAY WHERE JESUS WALKED see
Rotoli

I WALKED TODAY WHERE JESUS WALKED see
Twoig

I WANDERED LONELY see Werther, Rudolf

I WANT JESUS MORE THAN ANYTHING see
Marsh

I WANT JESUS TO WALK WITH ME see
Boatner, Edward H.

I WANT THAT MOUNTAIN see Harvey, Bill

I WANT THE WORLD TO KNOW see Friml,
Rudolf

I WANT THE WORLD TO KNOW see Smith

I WANT TO BE MARRIED see Birch, Robert
Fairfax

I WANT TO BE READY *spir
(Burleigh, H. T.) med solo,pno BELWIN
$1.50   (I34)

I WANT TO CAPTURE see Weinberg, Jacob

I WANT TO PLAY STROM see Franco, Johan

I WANT TO SEE JESUS see Sexton

I WANT TO STROLL OVER HEAVEN WITH YOU
see Dodson

I WANT YOU TO KNOW see Mayfield, Larry

I WANTED TO COME HOME see Korte, Karl

I WAS IN HIS MIND see La Rowe, Jane

I WAS NOT SORROWFUL see Ireland, John

I WAS THE TREE see O'Hara, Geoffrey

I WATCHED THE LADY CAROLINE see Duke,
John Woods

I WENT TO HEAVEN see Walker, George

I WEPT BELOVED see Hue, [Georges-
Adolphe]

I WILL BETROTH THEE see Adler, Samuel

I WILL BUILD MY HOUSE IN THE WATER see
Keats, Horace

I WILL DWELL IN THE HOUSE OF THE LORD
see Eville, V.

I WILL GIVE MY LOVE AN APPLE *folk
(Moore, Gerald) high solo,pno UNIVER.
12318 $.75   (I35)
(Moore, Gerald) med solo,pno UNIVER.
12318 $.75   (I36)

I WILL GIVE THANKS TO GOD ETERNALLY see
Schutz, Heinrich

I WILL GIVE YOU DREAMS see Hayakawa,
Masaaki

I WILL GIVE YOU THE KEYS OF HEAVEN see
Greene, Plunket

I WILL GO WITH MY FATHER A-PLOUGHING
see Quilter, Roger

I WILL LIE DOWN IN AUTUMN see Swanson,
Howard

I WILL LIFT UP see Sowerby, Leo

I WILL LIFT UP MINE EYES see Eville, V.

I WILL LIFT UP MINE EYES see Gober,
Belle Baird

I WILL LIFT UP MINE EYES see Golde,
Walter

I WILL LIFT UP MINE EYES see
Hoffmeister, Leon Abbott

I WILL LIFT UP MINE EYES see Humphreys

I WILL LIFT UP MINE EYES TO THE HILLS
see Harker, F. Flaxington

I WILL LIFT UP MINE EYES UNTO THE HILLS
see Kendrick, Virginia

I WILL LIFT UP MINE EYES UNTO THE HILLS
see Parker, Clifton

I WILL MAGNIFY THEE see Bach, Johann
Sebastian

I WILL MAGNIFY THEE see Handel, George
Frideric

I WILL MAGNIFY THEE, O GOD see
Mosenthal, Joseph

I WILL MAGNIFY THEE, O LORD see Clarke,
Thomas

I WILL MAKE YOU BROOCHES see Bury,
Winifred

I WILL NOT LEAVE YOU COMFORTLESS see
Pinkham, Daniel, Non Vos Relinquam
Orphanos

I WILL PRAISE THEE WITH MY WHOLE HEART
see Matesky, T.

I WILL SERVE THEE see Gaither

I WILL WALK WITH MY LOVE
(Moore, Gerald) high solo,pno UNIVER.
12314 $.75   (I37)
(Moore, Gerald) med solo,pno UNIVER.
12314 $.75   (I38)

I WILL WALK WITH MY LOVE see Hughes,
Herbert

I WILL WORSHIP THE LORD see Birch,
Robert Fairfax

I WISH I WAS BY THAT DIM LAKE
B solo,pno BIRCH $.75   (I39)

I WISH THAT I HAD BEEN THERE see
Hubbard, H.

I WISH WE'D ALL BEEN READY see Norman,
Larry

I WISH WE'D ALL BEEN READY see Norman,
Lucille

I WISH YOU ALL COULD KNOW HIM see
Johnson, P.

I WONDER AS I WANDER see Niles, John
Jacob

I WONDER HOW JOHN FELT see Wilson

I WONDER IF EVER THE ROSE see Slater,
David D.

I WONDER IF IT'S HAPPENED YET TO YOU
   see Wyrtzen, Don

I WONDER WHEN I SHALL BE MARRIED
   *folk,Ir
   (Nelson) 3 soli,pno ROBERTON 75037
   s.p.   (I40)

I WONDER WHY see Pfautsch, Lloyd

I WONDER WHY HE SHOULD LOVE see Fox,
   Baynard

I WON'T BE MY FATHER'S JACK see Fiske,
   R.

I WON'T HAVE TO CROSS JORDAN ALONE
   *sac,gospel
   solo,pno ABER.GRP. $1.50   (I41)

I WON'T HAVE TO CROSS JORDON ALONE see
   Ramsey

I WON'T HAVE TO WORRY ANY MORE see
   Jones

I WON'T TURN BACK see Lister, Mosie

I WOULD BELIEVE see Chaminade, Cecile

I WOULD FAIN FORGET see Mana-Zucca,
   Mme., Je Voudrais Oublier

I WOULD RATHER SING OF JESUS see Hines

I ZALETT
   (Carlo, Musi) solo,pno (Bolognese
   dialect) BONGIOVANI 2046 s.p. see
   from El Mi Canzunett   (I42)

I ZEVER
   (Carlo, Musi) solo,pno (Bolognese
   dialect) BONGIOVANI 2045 s.p. see
   from El Mi Canzunett   (I43)

IACOBI GALLI DISTICHA see Jirim,
   Frantisek

IAMBES ET ANAPESTES see Kalomiris,
   Manolis

IANTHE see Schirmer, Rudolph [E.]

IBERT, JACQUES (1890-1962)
   Apres Minuit
   med solo,orch LEDUC s.p. see from
   Trois Chansons De Charles Vildrac
                               (I44)

   Aria *vocalise
   solo,fl LEDUC s.p.   (I45)

   Berceuse De Gallane
   solo,orch LEDUC s.p.   (I46)

   Cette Grande Chambre
   see La Verdure Doree

   Chanson
   solo,pno/inst LEDUC s.p. see from
   Deux Melodies   (I47)

   Chanson A Dulcinee (from Don
   Quichotte)
   solo,orch LEDUC s.p.   (I48)

   Chanson De Fortunio (from Chandelier)
   solo,orch LEDUC s.p.   (I49)

   Chanson De La Mort (from Don
   Quichotte)
   solo,orch LEDUC s.p.   (I50)

   Chanson Du Depart (from Don
   Quichotte)
   solo,orch LEDUC s.p.   (I51)

   Chanson Du Duc (from Don Quichotte)
   solo,orch LEDUC s.p.   (I52)

   Chanson Du Rien
   solo,orch LEDUC s.p.   (I53)

   Comme Elle A Les Yeux Bandes
   med solo,orch LEDUC s.p. see from
   Trois Chansons De Charles Vildrac
                               (I54)

   Comme J'allais
   see La Verdure Doree

   Complainte De Florinde
   solo,orch LEDUC s.p.   (I55)

   Deux Melodies *see Chanson; Jardin
   Du Ciel   (I56)

   Elle Etait Venue
   med solo,orch LEDUC s.p. see from
   Trois Chansons De Charles Vildrac
                               (I57)

   Jardin Du Ciel
   solo,pno/inst LEDUC s.p. see from
   Deux Melodies   (I58)

   La Verdure Doree
   solo,orch cmplt ed LEDUC B.L.652
   s.p.

IBERT, JACQUES (cont'd.)

   contains: Cette Grande Chambre;
   Comme J'allais; Personne Ne
   Saura Jamais; Tiede Azur
   see also: Personne Ne Saura
   Jamais   (I59)

   Le Petit Ane Blanc
   solo,orch LEDUC s.p.   (I60)

   Personne Ne Saura Jamais
   solo,orch LEDUC s.p. see also La
   Verdure Doree   (I61)

   Tiede Azur
   see La Verdure Doree

   Trois Chansons De Charles Vildrac
   *see Apres Minuit; Comme Elle A
   Les Yeux Bandes; Elle Etait Venue
                               (I62)

IBLAND MYRTEN OCH JASMINER see
   Peterson-Berger, (Olof) Wilhelm

IC EN WEET GHEEN SCHOONDER VROUWE see
   Weegenhuise, Johan

IC SECH ADIEU see Weegenhuise, Johan

ICH ARMER MENSCH, ICH SUNDENKNECHT see
   Bach, Johann Sebastian

ICH ATMET EINEN LINDEN DUFT see Mahler,
   Gustav

ICH BENK NOCH DER EAST SIDE FIN AMUHL
   see Olshanetsky, Alex

ICH BETE AN DIE MACHT DER LIEBE *sac
   Mez solo,pno (D flat maj) LIENAU
   HOS 50 s.p.   (I63)

ICH BEUGE MEINE KNIE see Schutz,
   Heinrich

ICH BIN A YISROEL see Glantz, Yehuda
   Leib

ICH BIN AN OUSWURF FON DER NATUR *Jew
   solo,pno KAMMEN 442 $1.00   (I64)

ICH BIN DAS BROT DES LEBENS see
   Rosenmuller, Johann

ICH BIN DAS FAKTOTUM see Rossini,
   Gioacchino, Largo Al Factotum Della
   Citta

ICH BIN DER WELT see Mahler, Gustav

ICH BIN DER WELT ABHANDEN GEKOMMEN see
   Mahler, Gustav

ICH BIN DIE AUFERSTEHUNG see Schutz,
   Heinrich

ICH BIN DIE AUFERSTEHUNG UND DAS LEBEN
   see Schutz, Heinrich

ICH BIN HERRLICH, ICH BIN SCHON see
   Bach, Johann Sebastian

ICH BIN IN MIR VERGNUGT see Bach,
   Johann Sebastian

ICH BIN JUNG see Hallstrom, Ivar

ICH BIN JUNG GEWESEN see Schutz,
   Heinrich

ICH DANKE DEM HERRN see Schutz,
   Heinrich

ICH DANKE DEM HERRN VON GANZEM HERZEN
   see Schutz, Heinrich

ICH DANKE DIR, HERR see Schutz,
   Heinrich

ICH DARF NICHT see Schoenberg, Arnold

ICH ERKLOMM DIESE FELSEN see Saint-
   Saens, Camille, J'ai Gravi La
   Montagne

ICH ERWAHLE MIR DEN BRAUNEN see Mozart,
   Wolfgang Amadeus, Prendero Quel
   Brunnettio

ICH ESSE MIT FREUNDEN MEIN WENIGES BROT
   see Bach, Johann Sebastian

ICH FLEHE EUCH AN see Schutz, Heinrich,
   Adjuro Vos, Filiae Jerusalem

ICH FRAGE NICHT WIE SOLL ES ENDEN see
   Oort, H.C.v.

ICH FUHR AHEIM - TZU PALESTINA *Jew
   solo,pno KAMMEN 78 $1.00   (I65)

ICH GEB' DIR EINEN NAMEN see Bijvanck,
   Henk

ICH GEH JETZT IMMER DEN GLEICHEN PFAD
   see Voormolen, Alexander Nicolas

ICH GEH' UND SUCHE MIT VERLANGEN see
   Bach, Johann Sebastian

ICH GING MIT LUST see Mahler, Gustav

ICH GLAUB see Reger, Max

ICH GLAUBE, DASS ICH NICHT see Kukuck,
   Felicitas

ICH GROLLE NICHT see Schumann, Robert
   (Alexander)

ICH HAB see Reger, Max

ICH HAB' IN DEINEM AUGE see Franz,
   Robert

ICH HAB IN PENNA EINEN LIEBSTEN WOHNEN
   see Wolf, Hugo

ICH HAB MEIN SACH GOTT HEIMGESTELLT see
   Schutz, Heinrich

ICH HABE GENUG see Bach, Johann
   Sebastian

ICH HABE NUR EINEN GEDANKEN see
   Schumann, Georg

ICH HALTE ES DAFUR, DASS DIESER WELT
   LEIDEN see Buxtehude, Dietrich

ICH HARRETTE DES HERRN see Mendelssohn-
   Bartholdy, Felix

ICH HATTE EINST EIN SCHONES VATERLAND
   see Lassen, Eduard

ICH HEB MEIN AUGEN SEHNLICH AUF see
   Schutz, Heinrich

ICH HOB DICH *Jew
   solo,pno KAMMEN 435 $1.00   (I66)

ICH HOB KEIN MUHL A MAMEN GEHAT *Jew
   solo,pno KAMMEN 432 $1.00   (I67)

ICH HOB MEIN HARTZ FARLOIRN, VEN ICH
   HOB GEFINEN DICH *Jew
   solo,pno KAMMEN 456 $1.00   (I68)

ICH KEN ES DIR NIT ZUGEN, NOR ICH VEIS
   VUS ICH VIL *Jew
   solo,pno KAMMEN 481 $1.00   (I69)

ICH KOMME see Kilpinen, Yrio, Jo
   Tulenki

ICH KUSSE DEINE LIPPEN see Rudolpe, M.

ICH LASSE GOTT IN ALLEM WALTEN see
   Erlebach, Philipp Heinrich

ICH LIEB' EINE BLUME see Adriessen,
   Willem

ICH LIEB' EINE BLUME see Franz, Robert

ICH LIEB' EUCH, IHR AUGEN see Handel,
   George Frideric

ICH LIEBE DICH *folk,Russ
   [Ger/Russ] solo,pno ZIMMER. 1541 s.p.
                               (I70)

ICH LIEBE DICH see Barber, Samuel

ICH LIEBE DICH see Godard, Benjamin
   Louis Paul, L'Amour

ICH LIEBE DICH see Grieg, Edvard
   Hagerup

ICH LIEBE DICH see Liszt, Franz

ICH LIEBE DICH see Strauss, Richard

ICH LIEGE UND SCHLAFE see Schutz,
   Heinrich

ICH LIEGE UND SCHLAFE GANZ MIT FRIEDEN
   see Drischner, Max

ICH LIESS DICH ACHTLOS see Kilpinen,
   Yrio, Sun Tuskin Huomasin

ICH MOCHTE HINGEHN see Liszt, Franz

ICH MOCHTE, ICH WARE IM INDIERLAND see
   Sibelius, Jean

ICH MOCHTE SCHWEBEN see Sjogren, Emil

ICH RUF ZU DIR see Schein, Johann
   Hermann

ICH RUF ZU DIR, HERR JESU CHRIST see
   Reda, Siegfried

ICH RUF ZU DIR, HERR JESU CHRIST see
   Schutz, Heinrich

ICH SCHLEICHE BANG UND STILL HERUM see Schubert, Franz (Peter)

ICH SCHRIE ZUM HERRN see Hildenbrand, Siegfried

ICH SCHWEBE see Strauss, Richard

ICH SEHE DICH IN TAUSEND BILDERN see Reger, Max

ICH SEHE DICH IN TAUSEND BILDERN see Weegenhuise, Johan

ICH SEHE WIE IN EINEM SPIEGEL see Strauss, Richard

ICH SINGE DEM HERRN see Schutz, Heinrich, Cantabo Domino

ICH SINGE WIE DIE VOGELEIN SINGEN see Kilpinen, Yrio, Laulan Ilman Lainehilta

ICH STEH AN DEINER KRIPPEN HIER see Bach, Johann Sebastian

ICH STEH AN DEINER KRIPPEN HIER see Hufschmidt, Wolfgang

ICH STURBE GERN AUS MINNE see David, Johann Nepomuk

ICH TRAGE MEINE MINNE see Strauss, Richard

ICH VERKUNDIGE EUCH GROSSE FREUDE see Vierdanck, Johann

ICH VERLOR DIE KRAFT UND DAS LEBEN see Liszt, Franz

ICH VERMAHNE EUCH ABER see Schwartz, Gerhard von

ICH VIL ZICH SHPIELEN *Jew
  solo,pno KAMMEN 471 $1.00   (I71)

ICH WANDTE MICH UND SAHE see Brahms, Johannes

ICH WANDTE MICH UND SAHE AN see Brahms, Johannes

ICH WAR EIN KIND UND TRAUMTE VIEL see Voormolen, Alexander Nicolas

ICH WAR IN MEINEN JUNGEN JAHREN see Lortzing, (Gustav) Albert

ICH WEISS, DASS MEIN ERLOSER LEBET see Handel, George Frideric, I Know That My Redeemer Liveth

ICH WEISS, DASS MEIN ERLOSER LEBT see Bach, Johann Sebastian

ICH WEISS, DASS MEIN ERLOSER LEBT see Micheelsen, Hans-Friedrich

ICH WEISS, DASS MEIN ERLOSER LEBT see Telemann, Georg Philipp

ICH WEISS DEN TAG NOCH see Scholz, Erwin Christian

ICH WEISS EIN FASS IN EINEM TIEFEN KELLER see May, Ed.

ICH WEISS EIN HERRLICH AUGENPAAR
  *folk,Russ
  [Ger/Russ] solo,pno ZIMMER. 1534 s.p.
                                   (I72)

ICH WEISS NICHT, WO ICH BIN see Mozart, Wolfgang Amadeus, Non So Piu Cosa Son

ICH WERDE NICHT STERBEN, SONDERN LEBEN see Schutz, Heinrich

ICH WILL DEN HERREN LOBEN ALLEZEIT see Schutz, Heinrich

ICH WILL DEN HERRN LOBEN see Hanff, Johann Nicolaus

ICH WILL DEN HERRN LOBEN ALLEZEIT see Schutz, Heinrich

ICH WILL DEN KREUZSTAB GERNE TRAGEN see Bach, Johann Sebastian

ICH WILL MICH IM GRUNEN WLAD see Pfitzner, Hans

ICH WILL MICH ZUR LIEBEN, MARIA VERMEITEN see Kowalski, Max

ICH WILL NACH DEM HIMMEL ZU see Bach, Johann Sebastian

ICH WOLLT' EIN STRAUSSLEIN BINDEN see Strauss, Richard

ICH ZERSCHNEIDE DIE LEIDESORANGE see Baird, Tadeusz, Rozcinam Pomarancze Boln

ICI-BAS see Cui, Cesar Antonovitch

ICI-BAS see Desrez

ICI-BAS see Duprato, Jules-Laurent

ICK HEBBE GHEDRAGHEN see Beekhuis, Hanna

ICK HEN EEN SEER TRAECH ESELKIJN see Beuningen, W.v.

ICK MEENDE OOCK DE GOTHEYT WOONDE VERRE see Sigtenhorst-Meyer, Bernhard van den

ICK SAGH DE SCHOONHEYT see Sigtenhorst-Meyer, Bernhard van den

ICK SEG ADIEU see Klerk, Albert de

ICK SEG ADIEU see Moulaert, Raymond

ICONE DI UNA GRANDE CITTA see Pesko, Zoltan

I'D RATHER BE EXCUS'D see Hook, James

I'D RATHER HAVE JESUS see Miller

I'D RATHER HAVE JESUS AND OTHER SONGS
  *sac,CCUL,gospel
  solo,pno STAMPS 4853-SN $1.00
  contains works by: Presley, Luther;
    Wilson, Wilbur   (I73)

IDEALE see Tosti, Francesco Paolo

IDENTITE see Essyad, Ahmed

IDENTITY see Beaudrie, M.

IDILIO see Saenz, Pedro

IDYLLE see Haydn, (Franz) Joseph

IDYLLE FANEE see Legay, Marcel

IDYLLE LEGERE see Rabey, Rene

IDYLLE LOINTAINE see Delmet, Paul

IDYLLE PARISIENNE see Levade, Charles (Gaston)

IDYLLEN see Trunk, Richard

IF A MAN LOVES ME see Bender, Jan

IF ALL THE STARS WERE DIAMONDS see Geehl, Henry Ernest

IF CHRIST CAME BACK see O'Hara, Geoffrey

IF EVER I MARRY AT ALL see Dunhill, Thomas Frederick

IF GOD SO CLOTHE THE GRASS see Bischoff, Paul

IF I BUT HAD A LITTLE COAT see Walton, K.

IF I BUT TOUCH HIS GARMENT'S HEM see Moore, Donald Lee

IF I CAN HELP SOMEBODY see Androzzo

IF I CAN JUST HOLD OUT see Younce, George

IF I COULD HEAR MY MOTHER PRAY AGAIN see Gerald

IF I COULD PRAY LIKE A CHILD AGAIN
  *sac,gospel
  solo,pno ABER.GRP. $1.50   (I74)

IF I COULD SING A THOUSAND MELODIES see Mercer

IF I COULD TELL YOU see Firestone, Idabelle

IF I FORGET TO PRAY see Norman, Pierre

IF I FREELY MAY DISCOVER see Russell, Welford

IF I HAD A-KNEW see Hughes, Herbert

IF I HAD BUT TWO LITTLE WINGS see Lehmann, Liza

IF I HAD IT TO DO ALL OVER AGAIN see Holm

IF I HAD KNOWN see Giannini, Vittorio

IF I HAD TWENTY CHERRIES see Rowley, Alec

IF I KNEW THEN see Brown, Aaron

IF I MIGHT COME TO YOU see Squire, W.H.

IF I MIGHT LOVE YOU see Ronald, Sir Landon

IF I TAKE THE WINGS OF THE MORNING see Fischer, Irwin

IF I WERE A LARK see Clutsam, George H.

IF I'D BEEN MRS. NOAH see Dunhill, Thomas Frederick

IF IT KEEPS GETTIN' BETTER see Gaither

IF IT'S EVER SPRING AGAIN see Fleming, Christopher le

IF I'VE FORGOTTEN see Stanphill, Ira F.

IF JESUS CAME TO YOUR HOUSE *sac, gospel
  solo,pno ABER.GRP. $1.50   (I75)

IF JESUS HAD NOT COME see Hustad, Donald P.

IF, LORD, THY LOVE FOR ME IS STRONG see Berkeley, Lennox

IF MUSIC BE THE FOOD OF LOVE see Hively, Wells

IF MUSIC BE THE FOOD OF LOVE see Purcell, Henry

IF MY PEOPLE see Wyrtzen, Don

IF MY PEOPLE WILL PRAY see Owens, Jimmy

IF MY SONGS WERE ONLY WINGED see Hahn, Reynaldo, Si Mes Vers Avaient Des Ailes!

IF NO ONE EVER MARRIES ME see Lehmann, Liza

IF O'ER THE FLOOR see Wiren, Dag Ivar, Om Till Din Badd

IF ROSES NEVER BLOOMED AGAIN see Ganz, Rudolph

IF THAT ISN'T LOVE see Rambo, Dottie

IF THAT ISN'T LOVE see Rambo

IF THE DULL SUBSTANCE OF MY FLESH see Delden, Lex van

IF THE LORD ISN'T WALKING BY MY SIDE see Slaughter, Henry

IF THERE BE ECSTASY see Shaw, C.

IF THERE BE HEART OF GOLD see Wilson, R. Barclay

IF THERE WERE DREAMS see Birch, Robert Fairfax

IF THERE WERE DREAMS TO SELL see Ireland, John

IF THOU A REASON DOST DESIRE TO KNOW see Thomson, Virgil

IF THOU ART NEAR see Bach, Johann Sebastian

IF THOU ART SLEEPING see Birch, Robert Fairfax

IF THOU LOV'ST ME see Pergolesi, Giovanni Battista, Se Tu M'Ami

IF THOU MUST LOVE ME see Surinach, Carlos

IF THOU PREPARE THINE HEART see Parker, Clifton

IF THOU WILT EASE THINE HEART see Binkerd, Gordon

IF WE COULD SEE BEYOND TODAY see Clayton, Norman

IF WE MARRY FOR LOVE see Crampton, Ernest

IF WISHES WERE HORSES see Rowley, Alec

IF WITH ALL YOUR HEARTS see Mendelssohn-Bartholdy, Felix, So Ihr Mich Von Ganzen Herzen

IF YE LOVE ME, KEEP MY COMMANDMENTS see Fischer, Irwin

IF YOU AIN'T DERE see Dichmont, William

IF YOU ARE THERE see North, Michael

IF YOU ASK ANYTHING OF THE FATHER see Bender, Jan

IF YOU CAN see Flanagan, William

IF YOU DREAM THE RIGHT DREAM see Baker, David

IF YOU HAD DIED see Lora, Antonio

IF YOU KNOW THE LORD see Reichner, Bickley

IF YOUR HEART KEEPS RIGHT see Ackley, A.H.

IHME see Kilpinen, Yrio

IHR GEDANKEN see Erlebach, Philipp Heinrich

IHR HABT NICHT EINEN KNECHTISCHEN GEIST see Schwartz, Gerhard von

IHR HEILIGEN, LOBSINGET DEM HERRN see Schutz, Heinrich

IHR MACHTIGEN see Mozart, Wolfgang Amadeus

IHR TORE OFFNET EUCH see Bach, Karl Philipp Emanuel

IHR TRANEN, FLIESST (from Prince Igor) [Russ/Fr/Ger] S solo,pno BELAIEFF 250 s.p.   (I76)

IHR VOLKER HORT see Telemann, Georg Philipp

IHR WISST, DASS ER EUCH LIEBT see Lortzing, (Gustav) Albert

IHRE AUGEN see Strauss, Richard

IHRE BOTSCHAFT *Op.90,No.2 [Swed/Ger] solo,pno BREITKOPF-W DLV 5632 s.p. see from Sechs Lieder Nach Texten Von J.L. Runeberg (I77)

IHRE BOTSCHAFT see Hennes Budskap

IHRE BOTSCHAFT see Sibelius, Jean, Hennes Budskap

IIDA, TAKASHI
    Frog, The *song cycle
    solo,pno JAPAN 7505 s.p.   (I78)

IK BEN GENOODIGD TOT HET FEEST DEZER WERELD see Ruyneman, Daniel

IK BEN IN EENZAAMHEID NIET MEER ALLEEN see Diepenbrock, Alphons

IK BEN TREURIG see Middeleer, Jean De, Je Suis Triste

IK DIE BIJ STERREN SLIEP see Dijk, Jan van

IK HEB GEZIEN see Loots, Ph.

IK HOOR DE NACHT see Mulder, Herman

IK VERLANG NAAR HOLLAND see Beuker, H.

IK VOEL MIJN LEVEN see Middeleer, Jean De

IK WEET NIET VAN UIT WELKEN VERREN TIJD see Ruyneman, Daniel

IK WENSCHE U see Bordewijk-Roepman, Johanna

IK ZAG CECILIA KOMEN see Lilien, Ignace

IK ZOEK EEN NIEUW EN NOOIT GESPROKEN WOORD see Adriessen, Willem

IKA
    Tva Rosenblad *CC2U
    solo,pno LUNDQUIST s.p.   (I79)

IKARUS see Eyken, Heinrich van

IKARUS see Kilpinen, Yrio

IKAVA OMIA MAITA see Kilpinen, Yrio

IKAVISSA see Merikanto, Oskar

IKAVYYS see Marttinen, Tauno

IKONEN, LAURI (1888-   )
    Kleiner Pfad *see Polku Pieni

    Pirtissani Pimenee *Op.33,No.2
    solo,pno FAZER W 1740 s.p.   (I80)

IKONEN, LAURI (cont'd.)

    Polku Pieni
    "Kleiner Pfad" solo,pno FAZER
    W 2256 s.p.   (I81)

IKUINEN SURU see Kilpinen, Yrio

IL A DONC TRESSAILLI see Desrez

IL A NEIGE see Marinier, P.

IL A PERDU MA TRACE! see Gounod, Charles Francois

IL A SUFFI see Goublier, G.

IL AVAIT CINQ PIEDS see Lecocq, Charles

IL BACIO see Arditi, Luigi

IL BALEN DEL SUO SORRISO see Verdi, Giuseppe

IL BARCHEGGIO see Stradella, Alessandro

IL BIMBO see Rocca, Lodovico

IL BRIGIDINO see Verdi, Giuseppe

IL BRIVIDO see Gandino, Adolfo

IL BRIVIDO see Scuderi, Gaspare

IL CACCIATORE DEL BOSCO see Sinigaglia, Leone

IL CALVARIO see Tortone, A.

IL CANTASTORIE see Malipiero, Gian Francesco

IL CANTICO DEI CANTICI II see LeFanu, Nicola

IL CANTO DEI CANTICI see Veretti, Antonio

IL CANTO DELLA PASSIONE see De' Liguori, S. Alfonso Maria

IL CANTO SI LEVO see Gandino, Adolfo

IL CIELO E DESERTO see Caggiano, Roberto

IL CLEFTA PRIGIONE see Pizzetti, Ildebrando

IL CORVO E LA VOLPE see De Ninno, Alfredo

IL CROIT ENTENDRE PLEURER SON COEUR DANS LA PLAINTE DU RUISSEAU see Vuillemin, L.

IL CUORE DI NINI see Albanese, Guido

IL EST BRILLANT COMME L'AURORE see Messager, Andre

IL EST D'ETRANGES SOIRS see Paray, Paul

IL EST DEUX NOBLES COEURS QUE J'AIME see Saint-Saens, Camille

IL EST DOUX DE SE COUCHER see Ravel, Maurice

IL EST PARTI see Blangini, Giuseppe Marco Maria Felice

IL EST PARTI CELUI QUE J'AIME see Chabrier, Emmanuel

IL EST UN VIEUX CHANT DE BOHEME see Chabrier, Emmanuel

IL ETAIT TEMPS, VOICI GONZALVE see Ravel, Maurice

IL ETAIT UN JOLI DRAGON see Messager, Andre

IL ETAIT UN MONARQUE see Bondeville, Emmanuel de

IL ETAIT UN OISEAU GRIS see Monsigny, Pierre-Alexandre

IL ETAIT UN PETIT NAVIRE see Inghelbrecht, Desire Emile

IL ETAIT UN ROI DE THULE see Gounod, Charles Francois

IL ETAIT UNE BERGERE see Delbruck, J.

IL ETAIT UNE FEMME see Tremisot, Ed.

IL ETAIT UNE FILLE D'HONNEUR see Emmanuel, Maurice

IL ETAIT UNE FOIS see Cuvillier, Charles

IL ETAIT UNE FOIS see Offenbach, Jacques

IL ETAIT UNE FREGATE see Chants De France Vol. II

IL FAIT TOUT LUI-MEME MONSIEUR SANS SOUCI see Poulenc, Francis

IL FARO see Bossi, Renzo

IL FAUT NOUS AIMER SUR TERRE see Roget, H.

IL FAUT QUE DE TOUS MES ESPRITS J'EXALTE see Honegger, Arthur

IL FAUT TE FAIRE SOLDAT see Perissas, M.

IL FAUT VOUS APPRENDRE see Lecocq, Charles

IL FIGLIO ALLA MADRE SEVERA see Caltabiano, S.

IL FIGLIO DEL RE see Sinigaglia, Leone

IL FIORELLINO BUCANEVE see Novikoff, Sergio

IL FLASO PELLEGRINO see Sabino, A.

IL FLAUTO NOTTORNO see Gubitosi, Emilia

IL FRINGUELLO CIECO see Bossi, Renzo

IL GABBIANO see Vlad, Roman

IL GATTO ROSSO see Hajos, Karl

IL GIARDINO DI AMORE see Scarlatti, Alessandro

IL GIOVANE WERTHER see Tosatti, Vieri

IL GIUDICE SOMERS see Peragallo, Mario

IL GRAN CERCHIO D'OMBRA see Ferro, P.

IL GRILLO E LA FORMICA see Sinigaglia, Leone

IL GUINDOLO see Cairone, Renato

IL IMPLORE LA MELANCOLIQUE ROSE see Vuillemin, L.

IL LA PREND DANS SES BRAS see Poulenc, Francis

IL LACERATO SPIRITO see Verdi, Giuseppe

IL M'AIME, J'EN SUIS BIEN CERTAINE see Messager, Andre

IL MARINARO CANTA see De Lucia, Nadir

IL MARITINO see Sinigaglia, Leone

IL ME L'A DIT QU'A LA MOISSON see Migot, Georges

IL MELAGRANO see Gandino, Adolfo

IL MIO BEN QUANDO VERRA see Paisiello, Giovanni

IL MIO CRUDEL MARTORO see Handel, George Frideric

IL MIO TESORO INTANTO see Mozart, Wolfgang Amadeus

IL MIO UCCELO NEL DESERTO see Mortari, Virgilio

IL MOSE see Perti, Giacomo Antonio

IL NEIGE see Bemberg, Herman

IL NEIGE see Levade, Charles (Gaston)

IL NEIGE DE LA JOIE see Petit, P.

IL NEIGE DES SECRETS see Petit, P.

IL N'EST DANS PARIS see Blanchard, Roger

IL NIEGE DE LA JOIE see Delannoy, Marcel

IL NOME VOSTRO IO SO see Massenet, Jules

IL NUDO see Bussotti, Sylvano

IL NUNZIO see Scuderi, Gaspare

IL N'Y A PAS DE MOTS ASSEZ PROFONDS see Pillois, Jacques

IL PAESE see Del Giudice, G.M.

IL PAESE see Mompello, Federico

IL PASSA see Devreese, Godefroid

IL PASSA see Hageman, Richard

IL PASTORE see Pratella, Francesco
  Balilla

IL PELLEGRINO DI S. GIACOMO see
  Sinigaglia, Leone

IL PETTIROSSO see Mompello, Federico

IL PIANTO CHE SI VUOL FRENARE see
  Massenet, Jules

IL PICCOLO BAR see Kalman, Emerich

IL PLEURE DANS MON COEUR see Schmitt,
  Florent

IL PLEUT see Bourguignon, Francis de

IL PLEUT DES PETALES DE FLEURS see
  Lacombe, Paul

IL PLEUT DES PETALES DE FLEURS see
  Rhene-Baton

IL PLEUT DOUCEMENT SUR LA VILLE see
  Ruyneman, Daniel

IL PLEUVAIT see Planquette, Robert

IL PONTE see Bettarini, Luciano

IL PRIMO LIBRO DELLE CANZONETTE A TRE
  VOCI DI S. ROSSI see Rossi,
  Salomone

IL QUADRO DELLE MERAVIGLIE see Mannino,
  Franco

IL RACCONTO DEL SIGNORE MAILLARD (DALLA
  SUITE) see Tosatti, Vieri

IL RAGNO SALTIMBANCO see Sabino, A.

IL REGNO MIO see Morelli, A.

IL RIFUGIO see Sinigaglia, Leone

IL SALUTO DEL MARINAIO see Hajos, Karl

IL SALUTO DI BEATRICE see Neglia,
  Francesco Paolo

IL SERA BANNI
  see La Musique, Quatorzieme Cahier

IL S'EST TU, LE CHARMANT ROSSIGNOL see
  Gretchaninov, Alexander
  Tikhonovitch

IL SOGNO see Castro, Jose Maria, El
  Sueno

IL SOGNO CHE T'INNAMORA see Respighi,
  Ottorino

IL SOGNO DICE ECC. see Hajos, Karl

IL SONGE QUE NUL NE SAURAIT NAITRE POUR
  LA PREMIERE FOIS see Vuillemin, L.

IL SONNO DEI DIMENTICATI see Cantu, M.

IL SUICIDA see Peragallo, Mario

IL TRAMONTO see Respighi, Ottorino

IL VAGGIO DEFINITIVO see Platamone,
  Stefano

IL VERNO see Gandino, Adolfo

IL VIAGGIATORE see Lorenzini, Danilo

IL VIAGGIO DELLA LUNA see Rocca,
  Lodovico

IL VIANDANTE see Pratella, Francesco
  Balilla

IL VIGGIATORE CHIMERICO see Platamone,
  Stefano

IL VOLE see Poulenc, Francis

IL VOLO COSI FIDO see Handel, George
  Frideric

IL VOUS EN SOUVEINDRA see Haring, Ch.

IL Y A DES GENS see Betove

IL Y A QUELQU'UN AUQUEL JE PENSE see
  Barraine, Elsa

ILE-DE-FRANCE *Fr
  (Canteloube, J.) solo,acap DURAND
  s.p. see also Anthologie Des Chants
  Populaires Francais Tome IV   (I82)

I'LL AYE CA' IN BY YON TOUN *folk,Scot
  solo,pno (C maj/E flat maj) PATERSON
  FS127 s.p.   (I83)

I'LL BE HAPPY *sac
  solo,pno STAMPS 7246 $1.00   (I84)

I'LL BE IN THE RAPTURE see Knight

I'LL BELIEVE FOREVERMORE see Squire,
  Fred

I'LL BID MY HEART BE STILL *folk,Scot
  (Roberton, Hugh S.) 3 soli,pno
  ROBERTON 72085 s.p.   (I85)

I'LL FOLLOW JESUS see Lister, Mosie

I'LL GET MY REWARD see Tripp, LaVerne

I'LL GIVE MY LOVE AN APPLE
  see Folk Songs Of Eastern Canada

I'LL GLORY IN THE CROSS see Jensen,
  Gordon

I'LL GO OVER JORDAN SOME DAY *sac
  solo,pno STAMPS 7264 $1.00   (I86)

I'LL GO OVER JORDAN SOME DAY see
  Shrader, John L.

I'LL HOLD YOUR HAND see Puccini,
  Giacomo, Che Gelida Manina

I'LL HOLD YOUR HAND IN MY HAND see
  Puccini, Giacomo, Che Gelida Manina

I'LL LEAVE IT ALL BEHIND *sac,gospel
  solo,pno ABER.GRP. $1.50   (I87)

I'LL LIVE FOR JESUS *sac
  solo,pno STAMPS 7258 $1.00   (I88)

I'LL LIVE FOR JESUS see Schultz

I'LL MEET YOU IN THE MORNING *sac,
  gospel
  solo,pno ABER.GRP. $1.50   (I89)

I'LL NEVER BE LONELY IN HEAVEN see
  Wetherington

I'LL PRAY FOR YOU see Hanks

I'LL SAIL UPON THE DOG-STAR see
  Purcell, Henry

I'LL SEE YOU IN THE RAPTURE see Feltner

I'LL SET MY LOVE TO MUSIC see Russell,
  Kennedy

I'LL SING MY SONG TO YOU see Braden,
  Edwin

I'LL SING OF MY REDEEMER see Ellis

I'LL SING THEE SONGS OF ARABY see Clay,
  Frederic

I'LL SING TO YOU see Thompson, Jack

I'LL SOON BE GONE see Hemphill

I'LL STILL LOVE YOU see Crouch, Andrae

I'LL TAKE YOU HOME AGAIN KATHLEEN see
  Westendorf

I'LL TELL IT WHEREVER I GO *sac,gospel
  solo,pno ABER.GRP. $1.50   (I90)

I'LL TELL THE WORLD see Fox

I'LL TELL THE WORLD THAT I'M A
  CHRISTIAN see Fox, Baynard

I'LL WAIT A LITTLE LONGER *sac,gospel
  solo,pno ABER.GRP. $1.50   (I91)

I'LL WALK WITH GOD
  2 soli,pno WARNER VD0006 $1.50 (I92)

I'LL WALK WITH GOD see Brodszky, Ferenc

ILLALLE see Sibelius, Jean

ILLAN SUUSSA see Bergman, Erik, I
  Kvallningen

ILLANRUSKO see Kilpinen, Yrio

ILLO, MARIA
  Revolution Come The Spring
  solo,pno GALLIARD 2.2026.7 $2.50
                                 (I93)

ILLUSTRES CHEFS GUERRIERS see Indy,
  Vincent d'

ILMENAU see Ives, Charles

ILS CHANTENT, TOUS CES MASQUES see
  Wolff, A.

ILS M'ONT ASSEZ OPPRIME DES MA JEUNESSE
  see Boulanger, Lili

ILS M'ONT DIT, POUR PARER TON CORPS see
  Mariotte, Antoine

ILS NE SONT PLUS, LES JOURS DE NOTRE
  ENFANCE see Desrez

ILS ONT BRULE MA WALLONIE see Georges,
  Alexandre

ILS PARTENT TOUS see Middeleer, Jean De

ILTA see Kuusisto, Taneli

ILTA see Luolajan-Mikkola, Vilho

ILTAPILVI see Pesonen, Olavi (Samuel)

I'M A' DOUN FOR LACK O' JOHNNIE *folk,
  Scot
  solo,pno (F maj/G maj) PATERSON FS126
  s.p.   (I94)

I'M A POOR LIL ORPHAN IN THIS WORLD see
  Perry, Julia

I'M A TIN SOLDIER see Jessel, Leon

IM ABENDROT see Jansen, F. Gustav

IM ABENDROT see Schubert, Franz (Peter)

IM ABENDROTH see Schubert, Franz
  (Peter)

I'M ALMOST HOME see Gaither

I'M ALWAYS CALLED MIMI see Puccini,
  Giacomo, Mi Chiamano Mimi

I'M BEGINNING TO UNDERSTAND see
  Lindberg, Russ

IM BLASSGELBEN KLEIDCHEN see Kuiler,
  Cor.

IM BLICK DES MONDES see Edler, Robert

IM BOOT see Pylkkanen, Tauno Kullervo,
  Venheessa

I'M BOUND FOR THE KINGDOM see Lister,
  Mosie

I'M BUILDING A BRIDGE see Abernathy

I'M CALLING LOVE FOR YOU see Ewing, M.

I'M CLIMBING HIGHER AND HIGHER *sac,
  gospel
  solo,pno ABER.GRP. $1.50   (I95)

I'M CLIMBING UP THE MOUNTAIN see
  Lister, Mosie

IM EWIGEN LICHT see Bijvanck, Henk

I'M FEELING FINE see Lister, Mosie

IM FELD EIN MADCHEN SINGT see Sibelius,
  Jean

I'M FREE see Gaither

I'M FREE AGAIN *sac,gospel
  solo,pno ABER.GRP. $1.50   (I96)

I'M GETTING MORE LIKE JESUS EVERY DAY
  *sac,gospel
  solo,pno ABER.GRP. $1.50   (I97)

I'M GLAD I'M A CHRISTIAN see Good,
  Dwayne

I'M GOIN' TO THANK GOD *spir
  (Dett, R. Nathaniel) high solo,pno
  BELWIN $1.50   (I98)

I'M GOING HOME *sac,gospel
  solo,pno ABER.GRP. $1.50   (I99)

I'M GOING THERE see Wetherington

I'M GOING TO MEET YOU IN HEAVEN SOMEDAY
  see Horne, Roger

I'M GONNA KEEP ON see Gaither

I'M GONNA KEEP ON SINGING see Crouch,
  Andrae

I'M GONNA MAKE IT THROUGH SOMEHOW see
  Stanphill, Ira F.

I'M GONNA TELL THE WORLD see Matthews

IM GROSSEN SCHWEIGEN see Diepenbrock,
  Alphons

I'M HAPPY WAY DOWN IN MY SOUL *sac,
  gospel
  solo,pno ABER.GRP. $1.50   (I100)

IM HIMMELREICH EIN HAUS STEHT see Knab,
Armin

I'M HIS TO COMMAND see Kerr

I'M IN A NEW WORLD see Ellis

I'M IN LOVE WI' SUSAN see Cheshire,
Mattie

I'M JUST A FLAG WAVING AMERICAN see
Peterson, John W.

IM KAHNE see Grieg, Edvard Hagerup

IM LENZ see Mana-Zucca, Mme.

IM LIEBESLUST see Liszt, Franz

I'M LIVING IN A HAPPY WORLD see
Campbell, Jack

I'M LIVING IN HIS LOVE *sac
(Carmichael, Ralph) solo,pno WORD
S-355   (I101)

I'M LOOKING FOR JESUS see Lee, Don

IM MAI see Jansen, F. Gustav

IM MARZWIND see Lothar, Mark

IM MONDENGLANZ RUHT DAS MEER see
Bosmans, Henriette

IM MONDSCHEIN see Kilpinen, Yrio,
Kuutamolla

IM NEBEL see Schoeck, Othmar

I'M NOBODY see Kagen, Sergius

I'M NOBODY see Persichetti, Vincent

I'M ON THE HIGHWAY HOME see Davis

I'M ONE OF HIS OWN see Horne, Roger

I'M ONLY DREAMING see Friml, Rudolf

I'M OWRE YOUNG TO MARRY YET *folk,Scot
solo,pno (D flat maj/E flat maj)
PATERSON FS104 s.p.   (I102)

I'M READY, LORD *sac,gospel
solo,pno ABER.GRP. $1.50   (I103)

IM RHEIM, HEILIGEN STROME see Schumann,
Robert (Alexander)

IM RHEIN, IM SCHONEN STROME see Liszt,
Franz

IM SCHMERZEN ERSCHAUERUND see Kilpinen,
Yrio, Olit Tuskasta Varisten
Herannyt Syon

IM SCHNEE see Borris, Siegfried

IM SCHNEE see Rinaldini, Dr. Joseph

IM SEELENAUG see Zagwijn, Henri

I'M SHELTERED IN HIS ARMS see Hubbard,
H.

I'M SINGING FOR MY LORD see Harper

I'M SO HAPPY see Paris

I'M SO UNWORTHY see Jensen, Gordon

IM SPATBOOT see Strauss, Richard

IM STILLEN REICH see Wetzel, Justus
Hermann

IM STRAHL DER HELLENISCHEN SONNE see
Karel, Rudolf

IM STROM see Micheelsen, Hans-Friedrich

I'M TELLING THEM TODAY see Holm, Dallas

IM TREIBHAUS see Wagner, Richard

IM VOLKSTON see Dvorak, Antonin, V
Narodnim Tonu

IM VOLKSTON see Scholz, Erwin Christian

IM VOLKSTON see Dvorak, Antonin

IM WALDE see Ehrenberg, Carl Emil
Theodor

IM WEINBLATTDAMMER see Lilien, Ignace

IM WUNDERSCHONEN MONAT MAI see
Schumann, Robert (Alexander)

IM WUNDERSCHONEN MONAT MAI see Soderman

IMAGE see Hindemith, Paul

IMAGES see Tanenbaum, Elias

IMAGES III see Migot, Georges

IMAGES PALESTINIENNES, VOL. II see
Schlionsky, Verdina

IMAGINARY ISLANDS see Mills, Charles

IMAGINI DI VELLUTO see Cantu, M.

IMITATION DES FLEURS see DuBois, Pierre
Max

IMMACOLATA see Cantu, M.

IMMAGINI SONORE see Contilli, Gino

IMMER DENK' ICH JENES ABENDS see
Ippolitov-Ivanov, Mikhail
Mikhailovitch

IMMER LEISER WIRD MEIN SCHLUMMER see
Beethoven, Ludwig van

IMMER SING' ICH see Kilpinen, Yrio,
Aina Laulan

IMMER WENN ICH LEBEN WILL SCHREIE ICH
see Baird, Tadeusz, Zawsze, Kiedy
Chce Krzycze

IMMER WIEDER see Vlad, Roman

IMMORALITY, AN see Koch, Johannes H.E.

IMMORTAL GODS, I CRAVE NO PELF see
Castelnuovo-Tedesco, Mario

IMMORTAL LOVE see Egerton, Arthur

IMMORTAL LOVE see Grieg, Edvard Hagerup

IMMORTALITE! see Chaminade, Cecile

IMMORTALITY see Gibbs, Cecil Armstrong

IMMORTALITY see Joubert, John

IMPARA A COMPATIR L'ALTRUI MARTIR see
Scarlatti, Domenico

IMPATIENCE see Schubert, Franz (Peter),
Ungeduld

IMPATIENCE see Schumann, Robert
(Alexander)

IMPATIENT LOVER, THE
see Four Songs From Herrick's
'Hesperides'

IMPERIALS-SONGBOOK *sac,CCUL
solo,pno BENSON BO953 $2.50   (I104)

IMPETUOUS HEART see Kauder, Hugo

IMPLORAZIONE see Setaccioli, Giacomo

IMPRESSION see Carolus-Duran, P.

IMPRESSION DU MATIN see Griffes,
Charles Tomlinson

IMPRESSIONEN EINER SPANISCHEN REISE see
Behrend, Siegfried

IMPRESSIONI see Pratella, Francesco
Balilla

IMPRESSIONS OF ISRAEL, VOL. I see Ben-
Cohen, Y.

IMPRESSIONS OF ISRAEL, VOL. II see Ben-
Cohen, Y.

IMPROMPTU see Pergament, Moses

IMPROMPTU IN MARCH see Moeran, Ernest
J.

IMPROVISATIES UIT HET LABYRINT see
Schat, Peter

IMPROVISATION see Moritz, Edvard

IMPROVISATION I see Boulez, Pierre

IMPROVISATION II see Boulez, Pierre

IMPROVISATION ON A POEM BY E.E.
CUMMINGS see Randall, J.K.

IMPROVVISAZIONE III see Razzi, Fausto

IMPULSE, THE see Owen, Richard

IN A CONSERVATORY see Wagner, Richard,
Im Treibhaus

IN A GONDOLA see Komter, Jan Maarten

IN A GONDOLA see Rorem, Ned

IN A GUST OF WIND see Sydeman, William

IN A KLEIN SHTIEBELE see Lillian,
Isadore

IN A MONASTERY GARDEN see Ketelbey,
Albert William

IN A MYRTLE SHADE see Griffes, Charles
Tomlinson

IN A PALACE GARDEN see MacCunn, Hamish

IN A PERSIAN GARDEN see Lehmann, Liza

IN A SILENT WORLD see Lyman, Ed.

IN A STABLE MEAN AND LOWLY *sac
(Dickinson, C.) solo,pno BELWIN $1.50
(I105)

IN AFTER DAYS see Heulett, M.

IN ALIUM see Taverner, John

IN ALL I DO TODAY see Moore

IN ALL THE LOVELY GARDENS see
Sanderson, Wilfred

IN ALTO MARE see Respighi, Ottorino

IN AN ARBOUR GREEN see Heseltine,
Philip

IN AN EASTERN ALLEY see Noe, J.T.

IN AN OLD-FASHIONED TOWN see Squire,
W.H.

IN AN OLD HOMESTEAD see Antill, John
Henry

IN AUGUST see Baxter, Maude Stewart

IN BARCHETA see Bianchini, Guido

IN BLESSED CONTENTMENT see Mozart,
Wolfgang Amadeus, Ridente La Calma

IN BOYHOOD see Ireland, John

IN CALVARIA RUPE see Cazzati, Maurizio

IN CELEBRATION see Williams, Joan
Franks

IN CELLAR COOL
(Winlaw, Maurice) solo,pno CRAMER
(I106)

IN CLAGHEN see Ruyneman, Daniel

IN CORBAR WOODS see Baxter, Maude
Stewart

IN DE STAD see Franco Mendes, H.

IN DEEZ' DAGEN VAN DEN JARE see
Strategier, Herman

IN DEM HERREN FREUET EUCH see Raphael,
Gunther

IN DEN NACHT see Voormolen, Alexander
Nicolas

IN DEN STROOM see Beyerman-Walraven,
Jeanne

IN DER CAMPAGNA see Strauss, Richard

IN DER FREMDE see Fussan, Werner

IN DER FREMDE see Weegenhuise, Johan

IN DER FREMDE see Zagwijn, Henri

IN DER FREMDE see Zipp, Friedrich

IN DER FRUHE see Wolf, Hugo

IN DER NACHT see Sibelius, Jean

IN DER NACHT see Trunk, Richard

IN DER SOMMERNACHT see Kilpinen, Yrio,
Kesayossa

IN DIE TIJD DAT BINNEN, BUITEN see
Strategier, Herman

IN DIESEN HEIL'GEN HALLEN see Mozart,
Wolfgang Amadeus

IN DIESEN WINTERTAGEN see Schoenberg,
Arnold

IN DIESER OSTERLICHEN ZEIT see Grimm,
Heinrich

IN DUISTERNIS see Mulder, Ernest W.

IN DUISTERNIS see Mulder, Herman

IN DUISTERNIS see Schouwman, Hans

IN DULCI JUBILO *CC98U,Xmas
(Kuusisto; Solantera) solo,pno FAZER
W 2746 s.p.   (I107)

IN DULCI JUBILO
see In Dulci Jubilo

IN DULCI JUBILO see Buxtehude, Dietrich

IN DULCI JUBILO see Krol, Bernhard

IN DULCI JUBILO *Xmas
(Pillney, Karl Hermann) med solo,fl,
strings,cembalo voc sc BREITKOPF-W
EB 6306 $3.50
contains: Auf Dem Berge, Da Geht
Der Wind; In Dulci Jubilo; Lobt
Gott, Ihr Christen, Allzugleich;
O Jesulein Suss; O Jesulein Zart;
Salzburger Weihnachtslied
"Schlaf, Mein Liebes Kindlein"
(I108)

IN EINEM KUHLEN GRUNDE
"Mill In The Valley" [Ger/Eng] med
solo,pno (F maj) SCHIRM.G $.50
(I109)

IN FAITH AND HOPE see Johnson, Noel

IN FELD see Weiner, Lazar

IN FERNEM LAND, UNNAHBAR EUREN
SCHRITTEN see Wagner, Richard

IN FIJNE VINGERTOPPEN see Mulder,
Herman

IN FLANDERS' FIELD see Andrews, Mark

IN FONDO AL PRATO see Cantu, M.

IN GEDEMPTEN TOON see Mulder, Herman

IN GLORIOUS SONG NO. I *sac,CC53UL
1-4 soli,pno LILLENAS MB-083 $1.50
(I110)

IN GLORIOUS SONG NO. II *sac,CC47UL
(Lister, Mosie) 1-4 soli,pno LILLENAS
MB-340 $1.50   (I111)

IN GOLDENER FULLE see Strauss, Richard

IN GOTTES HUT see Vycpalek, Ladislav

IN GRANDMA'S DAYS see Hope, H. Ashworth

IN GRANITE FOR EVER see Utkin, V.

IN HEAVENLY LOVE ABIDING see
Mendelssohn-Bartholdy, Felix

IN HIS CARE see Sateren, Leland
Bernhard

IN HONOR OF MOTHER see Bampton, Ruth

IN HYMNIS ET CANTICIS see Bernabei,
(Giuseppe) Ercole

IN JUST see Blank, Allan

IN LECTULO PER NOCTES see Schutz,
Heinrich

IN LOVE, IF LOVE BE LOVE see Diack,
John Michael

IN LOVE WITH JESUS see York, Sybil

IN LOVE WITH TIME see Lora, Antonio

IN MAIEN see Marx, Joseph

IN MAY see Schumann, Robert (Alexander)

IN MEINER TRAUME HEIMAT see Marx,
Joseph

IN MEINES GLUCKES GARTEN see
Hannikainen, Ilmari

IN MEMORIAM see Braal, Andries de

IN MEMORIAM see Emmanuel, Maurice

IN MEMORIAM see Koerbler, Milivoj

IN MEMORIAM see Masseus, Jan

IN MEMORIAM see Novak, V.

IN MEMORIAM see Weegenhuise, Johan

IN MEMORIAM ALICE HAWTHORNE see Sims,
Ezra

IN MEMORIAM DYLAN THOMAS see
Stravinsky, Igor

IN MEMORIAM GERRIT WILLEMS see Knap,
Rolf

IN MEMORIAM HANS ARP see Breuer,
Herbert

IN MEMORIAM MALCOLM X see Anderson,
Thomas J.

IN MEMORIAN see Kropfreiter,
Augustinius Franz

IN MEMORY'S GARDEN see Hemery,
Valentine

IN MEZZO AL MARE see Pratella,
Francesco Balilla

IN MIJN LIEFKENS HOVEKEN see
Hullebroeck, Em.

IN MOONLIGHT see Elgar, Edward

IN MORTE DEL FRATELLO see Caltabiano,
S.

IN MORTE DI UN SAMURAI see Delage,
Maurice

IN MY DISTRESS see Lanier, Gary

IN MY END IS MY BEGINNING see
Wildberger, Jacques

IN MY FATHER'S HOUSE ARE MANY MANSIONS
see Hanks

IN MY GARDEN see Firestone, Idabelle

IN NACHTSCHADUW see Boedijn, Gerard H.

IN OGNI SERA see Donati

IN OLD JUDEA see Geibel, Adam

IN OLD MADRID see Trotere, Henry

IN OLDEN SPAIN see Lalo, Edouard,
Aubade

IN OUR NATIVE LAND see Barybin, Ye.

IN PRAISE OF CIDER see Woodgate, Leslie

IN PRAISE OF KRISHNA see Blake, David

IN PRAISE OF LAUGHTER see Bach, Johann
Sebastian

IN PRAISE OF MUSIC see Bottje, Will Gay

IN PRAISE OF SORROW see Strauss,
Richard, Lob Des Leidens

IN QUELLE TRINE MORBIDE see Puccini,
Giacomo

IN QUESTA NOTTE CARICA DI STELLE see
Pizzetti, Ildebrando

IN QUESTA REGGIA see Puccini, Giacomo

IN QUESTA TOMBA OSCURA see Barber,
Samuel

IN QUESTA TOMBA OSCURA see Beethoven,
Ludwig van

IN REMEMBRANCE see Kilpinen, Yrio, Zur
Erinnerung

IN RIVA ALL'ARNO see Petralia

IN SHADOW see Silverman, Faye-Ellen

IN SHOP AUF DER ELTER *Jew
solo,pno KAMMEN 416 $1.00   (I112)

IN SICKNESS AND HEALTH see Albeniz,
Isaac

IN SILENT COUNTRYSIDE see Lane, Lewis

IN SOGNO see Borlenghi, E.

IN SPRING see Wilson, R. Barclay

IN SPRINGTIME see Weigl, Vally

IN STILLER DAMMERUNG see Trunk, Richard

IN STRANGE MYSTERIOUS FASHION see
Puccini, Giacomo, Recondita Armonia

IN SUMMER WOODS see Ireland, John

IN 'T AVONDDUISTER DWAAL IK see
Mortelmans, Lodewijk

IN TE DOMINE, SPERAVI see Buxtehude,
Dietrich

IN TE, DOMINE, SPERAVI see Schutz,
Heinrich

IN TE SPERO, O SPOSO AMATO see Mozart,
Wolfgang Amadeus

IN THE ARMS OF SWEET DELIVERANCE see
Lister, Mosie

IN THE BEGINNING *sac,gospel
solo,pno ABER.GRP. $1.50   (I113)

IN THE BLACK, DISMAL DUNGEON OF DESPAIR
see Purcell, Henry

IN THE BLEAK MIDWINTER see Thiman, Eric
Harding

IN THE BLEAK MIDWINTER see Williams,
David H.

IN THE BOAT see Grieg, Edvard Hagerup,
Im Kahne

IN THE CROSS OF CHRIST I GLORY see
Murray

IN THE DAWN see Dunhill, Thomas
Frederick

IN THE DUSK OF THE TWILIGHT see Parker,
Henry

IN THE DUSKY PATH OF A DREAM see
Mallinson, (James) Albert

IN THE END OF THE SABBATH see Speaks,
Oley

IN THE EYES OF THE LORD see Lister,
Mosie

IN THE FIELDS see Birch, Robert Fairfax

IN THE FIELDS see Duke

IN THE FOREST see Garcia Estrada, Juan
Agustin, En El Bosque

IN THE FOREST see Medtner, Nikolai
Karlovitch

IN THE GARB OF OLD GAUL *folk,Scot
solo,pno (G maj) PATERSON FS35 s.p.
(I114)

IN THE GARDEN OF MY HEART see Ball,
Ernest R.

IN THE GARDEN OF THE SERAGLIO see
Delius, Frederick

IN THE GARDEN OF THE WORLD see Repper,
Charles

IN THE GLOAMING see Harrison

IN THE GLOAMING see Hill, Lady Arthur

IN THE HIGHLANDS see Gibbs, Cecil
Armstrong

IN THE IMAGE OF GOD see Peterson, John
W.

IN THE INN see Mc Bradd

IN THE LATE BOAT see Strauss, Richard,
Im Spatboot

IN THE MEADOW see Weigl, Vally

IN THE MOONLIGHT see Pitfield, Thomas
Baron

IN THE MOUNTAINS see Chajes, Julius,
Adarim

IN THE QUIETNESS OF MY LIFE see Lanier,
Gary

IN THE SHADOW OF THE CROSS *sac,gospel
solo,pno ABER.GRP. $1.50   (I115)

IN THE SHADY GREEN PASTURES see
Minkler, Ross

IN THE SILENCE OF THE NIGHT
see Six Polish Christmas Carols

IN THE SILENT NIGHT see Rachmaninoff,
Sergey Vassilievitch

IN THE SKY A WONDROUS STAR see Black,
Charles

IN THE WILDERNESS see Barber, Samuel

IN THE WOODS see Bizet, Georges,
Vieille Chanson

IN THE WOODS see MacDowell, Edward
Alexander

IN THEE, O LORD, IS FULLNESS OF JOY see
Couperin (le Grand), Francois

IN THEE O SPIRIT see Bach, Johann
Sebastian

IN THESE SOFT SILKEN CURTAINS see
Puccini, Giacomo, In Quelle Trine
Morbide

IN THINE OWN IMAGE see Adler, Samuel

IN THIS LAST CARESS see Hasse, Johann
Adolph

IN THIS SEPULCHRAL DARKNESS see Barber,
Samuel, In Questa Tomba Oscura

IN THIS SEPULCHRAL DARKNESS see
Beethoven, Ludwig van, In Questa
Tomba Oscura

IN THIS SWEET LOVELINESS see Harding,
Phyllis

IN TIME OF DAFFODILS see Malipiero,
Riccardo

IN TIME OF SILVER RAIN see Berger, Jean

IN TIME OF SILVER RAIN see Swanson,
Howard

IN TIMES LIKE THESE see Jones, Ruth
Caye

IN UNA SELVA OSCURA see Caplet, Andre

IN VALLEYS GREEN AND STILL see Orr,
Charles Wilfred

IN VENEZIA see Blumenthal, Jacob
(Jacques)

IN WEITER FREMDE IRRTEN WIR see Dvorak,
Antonin

IN YOUR DEAR EYES see Trotere, Henry

IN YOUTH IS PLEASURE see Benbow, Edwin

IN YOUTH IS PLEASURE see Pinkham,
Daniel

IN YOUTH WHEN I DID LOVE see
Castelnuovo-Tedesco, Mario

INCANDESCENCES see Zbar, Michel

INCANTATIO see Verhaar, Ary

INCANTATIONES I see Dimov, Bojidar

INCANTATIONES II see Dimov, Bojidar

INCANTATIONS see Sivic, Pavle,
Zaklinjanja

INCANTATIONS see Yannay, Yehuda

INCERTITUD see Mompou, Federico

INCERTITUDE see Delmet, Paul

INCLINE YOUR EAR see Strickland, Lily
Teresa

INCLINEZ-VOUS, MON LIS! see Saint-
Saens, Camille

INCLUDIN' ME see Drynan, Margaret

INCONNUE, ELLE ETAIT MA FORME PREFEREE
see Devries, Ivan

INCREASE see Fischer, Irwin

INDES EINST DER TODBLEICHE MOND see
Ehrenberg, Carl Emil Theodor

INDEX see Radic, Dusan, Spisak

INDIAN BELL SONG see Delibes, Leo, Ou
Va La Jeune Indoue

INDIAN LULLABY see Mana-Zucca, Mme.,
Puva

INDIAN SERENADE see Castelnuovo-
Tedesco, Mario

INDIAN SERENADE see Sanderson, Wilfred

INDIAN SERENADE, THE see Mourant,
Walter

INDIAN SUMMER DAY see Weinberg, Jacob

INDIANA HOMECOMING see Beeson, Jack
Hamilton

INDISCHES LIED see Melartin, Erkki

INDISK SANG see Melartin, Erkki,
Indisches Lied

INDY, VINCENT D' (1851-1931)
Alors, Ma Seule Volupte (from
Fervaal)
Mez solo,pno/inst DURAND s.p.
(I116)
Au Nom Du Soleil, Roi Du Monde (from
Fervaal)
Mez solo,pno/inst DURAND s.p.
(I117)

INDY, VINCENT D' (cont'd.)
Chanson Populaires Du Vivarais Vol. I
*CC78L
solo,pno DURAND oct s.p., sc s.p.
(I118)
Chanson Populaires Du Vivarais Vol.
II *CC50L
solo,pno DURAND s.p. (I119)
Chansons Populaires Du Vivarais, Vol.
I *see La-Bas, Dans La Prairie;
La Belle, Si Tu Me Delaisses; La
Belle Ysabeau; La Bergere Aux
Champs; La Fillette Et Le Demon;
Ma Lisette; Marche Des Conscrits
Dans La Montagne; Nous Entrerons
Dans Ce Joli Mois; Rossignolet Du
Bois; Sont Trois Jeunes Garcons,
Tous Trois Allant En Guerre
(I120)
Des Le Premier Age Du Monde (from
Fervaal)
Bar solo,pno/inst DURAND s.p.
(I121)
Hogue! Celtes Hogue C'est Le Jour
Attendu (from Fervaal)
T solo,pno/inst DURAND s.p. (I122)
Bar solo,pno/inst DURAND s.p.
(I123)
Illustres Chefs Guerriers (from
Fervaal)
Bar solo,pno/inst DURAND s.p.
(I124)
Invocation A La Mer (from L'Etranger)
S solo,orch DURAND s.p., ipa (I125)
Jadis, Enfievre Parles Chants Des
Bardes (from Fervaal)
T solo,pno/inst DURAND s.p. (I126)
Je Veux Garder Ma Liberte (from
Attendez-Moi Sous L'Orme)
solo,pno ENOCH s.p. (I127)
La-Bas, Dans La Prairie
Mez/Bar solo,pno/inst DURAND s.p.
see from Chansons Populaires Du
Vivarais, Vol. I (I128)
La Belle, Si Tu Me Delaisses
Mez/Bar solo,pno/inst DURAND s.p.
see from Chansons Populaires Du
Vivarais, Vol. I (I129)
La Belle Ysabeau
Mez/Bar solo,pno/inst DURAND s.p.
see from Chansons Populaires Du
Vivarais, Vol. I (I130)
La Bergere Aux Champs
Mez/Bar solo,pno/inst DURAND s.p.
see from Chansons Populaires Du
Vivarais, Vol. I (I131)
La Bonne Terre
see LA MUSIQUE, CINQUIEME CAHIER
La Fillette Et Le Demon
Mez/Bar solo,pno/inst DURAND s.p.
see from Chansons Populaires Du
Vivarais, Vol. I (I132)
La Premier Dent
solo,pno DURAND s.p. (I133)
Ma Lisette
Mez/Bar solo,pno/inst DURAND s.p.
see from Chansons Populaires Du
Vivarais, Vol. I (I134)
Marche Des Conscrits Dans La
Montagne
Mez/Bar solo,pno/inst DURAND s.p.
see from Chansons Populaires Du
Vivarais, Vol. I (I135)
Nous Entrerons Dans Ce Joli Mois
Mez/Bar solo,pno/inst DURAND s.p.
see from Chansons Populaires Du
Vivarais, Vol. I (I136)
Recit De L'emeraude (from L'Etranger)
Bar solo,pno/inst DURAND s.p.
(I137)
Recit De L'etranger (from L'Etranger)
Bar solo,orch DURAND s.p., ipa
(I138)
Ronde Poitevine
solo,pno ENOCH s.p. (I139)
Rossignolet Du Bois
Mez/Bar solo,pno/inst DURAND s.p.
see from Chansons Populaires Du
Vivarais, Vol. I (I140)
Serment La Vita (from L'Etranger)
S solo,orch DURAND s.p., ipr (I141)
Sont Trois Jeunes Garcons, Tous Trois
Allant En Guerre
Mez/Bar solo,pno/inst DURAND s.p.
see from Chansons Populaires Du
Vivarais, Vol. I (I142)

INDY, VINCENT D' (cont'd.)
Terrible Nuit (from Fervaal)
T solo,pno/inst DURAND s.p.
(I143)
Vita Et Les Jeunes Filles (from
L'Etranger)
S solo,orch DURAND s.p., ipr (I144)

INEBBRIARSI see Pratella, Francesco
Balilla

INEXORABLE see Middeleer, Jean De, Ik
Voel Mijn Leven

INFELICE! E TUO CREDEVI see Verdi,
Giuseppe

INFERIORITY COMPLEX see Mechem, Kirke

INFERNO see Bois, Rob du

INFIDELIBUS see Planquette, Robert

INFINI see Chaminade, Cecile

INFINITE, THE see Heaton, Leonard

INFINITO see Polin, Claire

INFIRMATA VULNERATA see Scarlatti,
Alessandro

INFLAMMATUS ET ACCENSUS see Dvorak,
Antonin

INGALILL see Lejdstrom

INGALILL see Nordqvist, Gustaf

INGAS VISA see Soderman, (Johan) August

INGEMISCO see Verdi, Giuseppe

INGEN VAG AR FOR LANG see Raff, Joseph
Joachim

INGENIO see Sanchez, B.

INGENTING FAR STORA VAR STUND MED
VARANDRA see Milveden, Ingemar

INGERID I ROSENGARD see Soderman,
(Johan) August

INGHELBRECHT, DESIRE EMILE (1880-1965)
Il Etait Un Petit Navire
solo,orch LEDUC B.L.678 s.p. see
from Quatre Chansons Populaires
Francaises (I145)
Mon Pere M'a Donne Un Mari
solo,orch LEDUC B.L.675 s.p. see
from Quatre Chansons Populaires
Francaises (I146)
Quatre Chansons Populaires Francaises
*see Il Etait Un Petit Navire;
Mon Pere M'a Donne Un Mari (I147)

INGLES
Now I Have Everything *sac
solo,pno BENSON S7216-S $1.00
(I148)

INGRATE LYDIA see Verdi, Giuseppe

INGRATITUDE'S THE QUEEN OF CRIMES see
Handel, George Frideric

INGRID SJUNGER I KLOSTRET see
Nordqvist, Gustaf

INGRIDS VISE "OG RAEVEN LA UNDER
BIRKEROD" see Kjerulf, [Halfdan]

INHEMSKA SOLOSANGER, VOLS. I-II *CCU
solo,pno FAZER F 2561; F 2988 s.p.,
ea. (I149)

INJADO
Haupstadt
solo,inst, sitar MODERN rental
(I150)

INN, THE see Toye, (John) Francis

INNAN DET SKYMMER see Nordqvist, Gustaf

INNES, GERTRUDE
Lo, Quhat It Is To Love
solo,pno (D maj) LESLIE 7051 (I151)
Love Is A Sickness
solo,pno (G maj) LESLIE 7052 (I152)
Sister Awake!
solo,pno (E flat maj) LESLIE 7053
(I153)

INNIS, M.
I Am With You Always *sac,Gen
high solo,pno (F maj) WILLIS $.75
(I154)
low solo,pno (D maj) WILLIS $.75
(I155)

INNISFALLEN see Hovhaness, Alan

INNO A MARIA NOSTRA DONNA see Malipiero, Gian Francesco

INNO A ROMA see Puccini, Giacomo

INNO ITALICO see Bossi, Renzo

INNO PONTIFICIO see Ceccherini, T

INO see Telemann, Georg Philipp

INQUIETUDE see Delmet, Paul

INQUIETUDE see Levade, Charles (Gaston)

INSANI see Rouse, Christopher

INSCRIPTION FOR AN OLD TOMB see Stiasny

INSECT WORLD, THE see Bennett, Richard Rodney

INSEGUO LA NOTTE see Liguori, E.

INSELGEBURT see Steffen, Wolfgang

INSIDE THOSE PEARLY GATES *sac,gospel solo,pno ABER.GRP. $1.50 (I156)

INSIDES see Furrer, Franz

INSPIRATION WALTZ see Carrozzini, D.

INSPIREZ MOI! see Gounod, Charles Francois

INSPIRING GOSPEL SOLOS AND DUETS NO. I
*sac,CC150UL
(Lillenas, Haldor) 1-2 soli,pno
LILLENAS MB-084 $1.50 (I157)

INSPIRING GOSPEL SOLOS AND DUETS NO. II
*sac,CC152UL
(Lillenas, Haldor) 1-2 soli,pno
LILLENAS MB-085 $1.50 (I158)

INSPIRING TRIOS SERIES, NO. 1 *sac,
CCUL
SSA soli,pno SINGSPIR 5700 $1.00
(I159)

INSPIRING TRIOS SERIES, NOS. 2-3 *sac,
CCUL
3 male soli,pno SINGSPIR 5701-5702
$1.00 (I160)

INSTANT see Carolus-Duran, P.

INSTRUCTIVE SONGS, VOL. I: SONGS BY FAMOUS AND LESS-KNOWN COMPOSERS, ALSO FOLK SONGS *CC60U
(Friedlander) [Ger] $7.50 high solo, pno PETERS 2882A; med solo,pno PETERS 2882B; low solo,pno PETERS 2882C arranged in progressive order (I161)

INSTRUCTIVE SONGS, VOL. II: NEW SELECTION OF SONGS *CC60U
(Losse) [Ger] $7.50 high solo,pno PETERS 4458A; med solo,pno PETERS 4458B; low solo,pno PETERS 4458C arranged chronologically (I162)

INSTRUCTIVE SONGS, VOL. III: CONTEMPORARY SONGS *CC40U
(Losse) [Ger] high solo,pno PETERS 4672A $11.50; med solo,pno PETERS 4672B $11.50; low solo,pno PETERS 4672C $11.50 (I163)

INTE AR JAD ENSAM see Skold, Sven

INTERCOLLEGIATE SONG BOOK *CC82U,US
(Hansen) med solo,pno BMI $1.50 (I164)

INTERCOLLEGIATE SONG BOOK FOR HAMMOND ORGAN *CC20U,US
(Buhrman) med solo,org BMI $1.50 (I165)

INTERIEUR see Stravinsky, Igor

INTERIOR see Lessard, John Ayres

INTERLUDE see De Lara, Isadore

INTERLUDES FOR VOICE AND VIBRAPHONE see Steiner, Gitta

INTERMEDE GAL see Coppola, Piero

INTERMEZZO see Delage, Maurice

INTERMEZZO see Kalik, Vaclav

INTERMEZZO see Nacamuli, Guido

INTERMEZZO see Schumann, Robert (Alexander)

INTERMEZZO see Schumann, Robert (Alexander), Intermezzo

INTERMEZZO (A LOVE STORY) see Provost, Heinz

INTERMEZZO MELANCOLIQUE see Lacome, Paul

INTERMEZZO MELICO see Veretti, Antonio

INTERNATIONALE VOLKLIEDER, NOL. 3
*folk
(Behrend, Siegfried) solo,gtr
SIKORSKI 668C s.p.
contains: Allah Basit; Arivang; Belina; Defune; Wenn Der Regen Fallt (I166)

INTERNATIONALE VOLKSLIEDER, VOL. 2
*folk
(Behrend, Siegfried) solo,gtr
SIKORSKI 668B s.p.
contains: Hogen Gara; Malaguena De Antequera; Moskauer Nachte; Zwei In Einer Grossen Stadt (I167)

INTERNATIONALE VOLKSLIEDER, VOL. 4:
LIEDER AUS CAMBODIA, ISRAEL, KONGO, PHILIPPINEN *CCU,folk
(Behrend, Siegfried) solo,gtr
SIKORSKI 668D s.p. (I168)

INTERNATIONALE VOLSLIEDER, VOL 1
(Behrend, Siegfried) solo,gtr
SIKORSKI 668A s.p.
contains: Danno Budhunge; I Know, Where I'm Goin'; Pastechl; Suliram (I169)

INTERVALS see Feldman, Morton

INTET AR FORGAVES see Mellander, Oskar

INTET AR SOM VANTANS TIDER see Peterson-Berger, (Olof) Wilhelm

INTIMA see Svara, Danilo

INTIMITES see Mariotte, Antoine

INTIMITY see Gotovac, Jakov

INTO MY HEART see Dukelsky, Vladimir

INTO MY HEART AN AIR THAT KILLS see Orr, Charles Wilfred

INTO THE NIGHT see Edwards, Clara

INTO THE WOODS MY MASTER WENT see Nevin, Ethelbert Woodbridge

INTONUIT DE COELO see Anonymous

INTORNO ALL'IDOL MIO see Cesti, Marc' Antonio

INTOXICATION see Tcherepnin, Alexander

INTRODUCTION see Vogel, Wladimir

INTRODUCTION AND THE VIRGIN QUEEN'S DREAM MONOLOGUE see Franco, Johan

INTRUDER, THE see Lambert, Constant

INUKERLI see Andreae, Volkmar

INVANO see Tosti, Francesco Paolo

INVECTIVE see Doyen, Albert

INVENCIONS MOVILS II see Mestres-Quadreny, Josep Maria

INVENERUNT ME CUSTODES see Schutz, Heinrich

INVERNO see Maini, Manlio

INVERNO see Platamone, Stefano

INVICTI BELLATE see Vivaldi, Antonio

INVICTUS see Huhn, Bruno

INVIERNO see Boero, Felipe

INVIOLATA see Levade, Charles (Gaston)

INVISIBLE HANDS *sac,gospel
solo,pno ABER.GRP. $1.50 (I170)

INVISIBLE LIGHT, THE see Weigl, Karl

INVITACION AL VALS see Weber, Carl Maria von, Invitation To The Dance

INVITATION see Barry, Katherine

INVITATION AU VOYAGE see Godard, Benjamin Louis Paul

INVITATION IN AUTUMN see Moeran, Ernest J.

INVITATION TO LATE LOVE see Saul, George Brandon

INVITATION TO THE DANCE see Weber, Carl Maria von

INVITO see Venticinque, R.S.

INVITO ALLA CACCIA see Gandino, Adolfo

INVITO ALLA DANZA see Cimara, Pietro

INVITO ALLA DANZA see Respighi, Ottorino

INVITO-GAVOTTE see De Lucia, Nadir

INVITO RESPINTO see Sinigaglia, Leone

INVOCATION see Borchard, Adolphe

INVOCATION see Chaminade, Cecile

INVOCATION see Dahl

INVOCATION see Eili, Eili!

INVOCATION see Fromm, Herbert

INVOCATION see Holmes, Alfred

INVOCATION see Monnikendam, Marius

INVOCATION see Sifler, Paul J.

INVOCATION A LA LUNE see Tomasi, H.

INVOCATION A LA MER see Indy, Vincent d'

INVOCATION A LA VIERGE see Pouget, Leo

INVOCATION A ODIN see Aubert, Louis-Francois-Marie

INVOCATION ET HYMNE AU SOLEIL see Rameau, Jean-Philippe

INVOCATION OF LIGHT see Franco, Johan

INVOCATION POUR LE FETE D'ARISTOTE see Schmitt, Florent

INVOCATION TO NATURE see Berlioz, Hector

INVOCAZIONE see Caltabiano, S.

INVOCAZIONE see Ferro, P.

IO CH'ARMATO SIN HOR see Monteverdi, Claudio

IO CONOSCO UN GIARDINO see Pietri, Giuseppe

IO CREDEA see Scarlatti, Domenico

IO MORIREI CONTENTO see Scarlatti, Alessandro

IO NON COMPRO see Cara, M.

IO NON HO CHE UNA POVERA STANZETTA see Leoncavallo, Ruggiero

IO NON PRETENDO O STELLE see Martini, Giambattista

IO NON SO PIU see Nielsen, Riccardo

IO PER L'ANTICO DIRITTO see Porrino, Ennio

IO SON QUI see Bossi, Renzo

IO SON TITANIA LA BIONDA see Thomas, Ambroise, Je Suis Titania

IO SONO LA MADRE see Respighi, Ottorino

IO SONO L'UMILE ANCELLA see Cilea, Francesco

IO SONO STANCA see Gandino, Adolfo

IO TI LASCIO see Mozart, Wolfgang Amadeus

IO TI LASCIO, O FIGLIA see Mozart, Wolfgang Amadeus

IONA BOAT SONG *Scot
solo,pno (contains also: To Iona)
PATERSON s.p. see from Hebridean Songs, Vol. IV (I171)

IONE, DEAD THE LONG YEAR see Strickland, William

IORDENS, J.D.R.
Drie Liederen *CC3U
solo,pno BROEKMANS 202 s.p. (I172)

IPPOLITOV-IVANOV, MIKHAIL MIKHAILOVITCH (1859-1935)
Immer Denk' Ich Jenes Abends see Vier Romanzen

IPPOLITOV-IVANOV, MIKHAIL MIKHAILOVITCH
(cont'd.)

Mein Liebling, Du Sollst Hier
Verweilen
see Vier Romanzen

O Konntest Du Einmal Vergessen
see Vier Romanzen

Rauschender Blatter Hold Gefluster
see Vier Romanzen

Vier Romanzen
[Russ/Fr/Ger] solo,pno BREITKOPF-W
57 03045 s.p.
contains: Immer Denk' Ich Jenes
Abends; Mein Liebling, Du
Sollst Hier Verweilen; O
Konntest Du Einmal Vergessen;
Rauschender Blatter Hold
Gefluster   (I173)

IRELAND, JOHN (1879-1962)
All In A Garden Green
solo,pno (F maj) BOOSEY $1.50
                                   (I174)
At Early Dawn
2 soli,pno ROBERTON 71333 s.p.
                                   (I175)
Blind
solo,pno (D maj) BOOSEY $1.50
contains also: Cost (F min)
                                   (I176)
Cost
see Ireland, John, Blind

East Riding, The
low solo,pno (G min) ASHDOWN (I177)
high solo,pno (C min) ASHDOWN
                                   (I178)
med solo,pno (A min) ASHDOWN (I179)

Eleven Songs *CC11U
med solo,pno GALLIARD 2.9016.7
$3.50   (I180)

Five Poems By Hardy *CC5U
solo,pno OXFORD s.p.   (I181)

Her Song
med solo,pno (G maj) CRAMER $1.10
                                   (I182)
low solo,pno (F maj) CRAMER $.95
                                   (I183)
high solo,pno (A maj) CRAMER $.95
                                   (I184)
Holy Boy
low solo,pno (E flat maj) BOOSEY
$1.50   (I185)
high solo,pno (F maj) BOOSEY $1.50
                                   (I186)
I Have Twelve Oxen
low solo,pno (F maj) BOOSEY $1.50
                                   (I187)
high solo,pno (G maj) BOOSEY $1.50
                                   (I188)
I Was Not Sorrowful
solo,pno BOOSEY $1.50   (I189)

If There Were Dreams To Sell
high solo,pno (F maj) BOOSEY $1.50
                                   (I190)
med solo,pno (E flat maj) BOOSEY
$1.50   (I191)
low solo,pno (D flat maj) BOOSEY
$1.50   (I192)

In Boyhood
see Two Songs

In Summer Woods
2 soli,pno ROBERTON 71334 s.p.
                                   (I193)
Journey, The
low solo,pno (B flat maj) ASHDOWN
                                   (I194)
med solo,pno (C maj) ASHDOWN (I195)
high solo,pno (E flat maj) ASHDOWN
                                   (I196)
Sea Fever
med-high solo,pno (G min) GALLIARD
2.1499.7 $1.50   (I197)
low solo,pno (E min) GALLIARD
2.1497.7 $1.50   (I198)
high solo,pno (A min) GALLIARD
2.1500.7 $1.50   (I199)
med solo,pno (F min) GALLIARD
2.1498.7 $1.50   (I200)

Songs Of The Wayfarer *CCU
med solo,pno BOOSEY $6.00   (I201)

Spring Sorrow
low solo,pno (F maj) BOOSEY $1.50
                                   (I202)
high solo,pno (A flat maj) BOOSEY
$1.50   (I203)

Summer Schemes
low solo,pno (G maj) CRAMER $.95
                                   (I204)
high solo,pno (A maj) CRAMER $.95
                                   (I205)

IRELAND, JOHN (cont'd.)

Thanksgiving *Thanks
solo,pno (D maj) BOOSEY $1.50
                                   (I206)
Two Songs
Bar solo,pno OXFORD 62.221 $1.60
contains: In Boyhood; We'll To
The Woods No More   (I207)

Weathers
low solo,pno (C maj) CRAMER (I208)
med solo,pno (D maj) CRAMER (I209)
high solo,pno (E maj) CRAMER (I210)

We'll To The Woods No More
see Two Songs

IRELAND, MOTHER IRELAND see
Loughborough, Raymond

IRENE see Honegger, Arthur

IRGENDWO IM HAFEN see Girnatis, Walter

IRGENDWO SPIELT MUSIK see Strauss,
Josef

IRIS see Wolf

IRISH BOOK see Johnston, Richard

IRISH COUNTRY SONGS, VOLS. 1-4 *CCU,Ir
(Hughes, H.) high solo/low solo,pno
BOOSEY $7.50, ea.   (I211)

IRISH FAIRIES IN JUNE see Loam, Arthur
S.

IRISH FOLK SINGER'S ALBUM, AN *CC8L
(Clifford, Teresa; Nelson, Havelock)
solo,pno ROBERTON 2984 s.p. (I212)

IRISH FOLKSONGS *CCU,folk,Ir
(Ferguson, H.) solo,pno BOOSEY $3.50
                                   (I213)
IRISH IDYLL IN SIX MINIATURES see
Stanford, Charles Villiers

IRISH LOVE SONG see Hope, H. Ashworth

IRISH LOVE-SONG, AN see Smoldon, W.L.

IRISH LOVER see Stanford, Charles
Villiers

IRISH LULLABY see Noble, Felix de

IRISH SLUMBER SONG see Newton, Ernest

IRISH SONGS OF RESISTANCE *CC50U,Ir
(Galvin, Patrick) solo,pno OAK 000080
$2.45   (I214)

IRMELIN ROSE see Nielsen, Carl

IRMELIN ROSE see Peterson-Berger,
(Olof) Wilhelm

IRVING, W.W.S.
Happy Holidays
solo,pno CRAMER   (I215)

Love's Dawn
solo,pno CRAMER   (I216)

Oh, Yoicks! Tally Ho!
solo,pno CRAMER   (I217)

Rose, On An Autumn Day
solo,pno CRAMER   (I218)

IRWIN
Bring Your Burden *sac
solo,pno BENSON S5231-S $1.00
                                   (I219)
IRWIN, LOIS
It Was Jesus *sac
solo,pno STAMPS 7251-SN $1.00
                                   (I220)
Try Jesus *sac
solo,pno STAMPS 7255-SN $1.00
                                   (I221)
IS HE SATISFIED *sac,gospel
solo,pno ABER.GRP. $1.50   (I222)

IS HE THE ONE see Verdi, Giuseppe, Ah,
Fors E Lui

IS IT ANY WONDER? see Owens

IS IT THOU? see Verdi, Giuseppe, Eri Tu
Che Macchiavi

IS MY LORD SATISFIED WITH ME? see Suggs

IS MY TEAM PLOUGHING see Butterworth,
George Sainton Kaye

IS NOT HIS WORD LIKE A FIRE see
Mendelssohn-Bartholdy, Felix

IS THERE NOT A CAUSE *sac
(Carmichael, Ralph) solo,pno WORD
S-262   (I223)

IS YOUR NAME WRITTEN THERE? see
Wetherington

ISA MEIDAN see Melartin, Erkki

ISABEAU S'Y PROMENE
"Isabelle" see Crystal Fountain, The

ISABEL, PERDISTE LA TU FAXA see
Mudarra, Alonso de

ISABELLE see Berger, Rod.

ISABELLE see Isabeau S'y Promene

ISAIAH see Weiner, Lazar

I'SE THE B'Y THAT BUILDS THE BOAT
see Five Canadian Folk Songs

ISHII, KAN (1921-   )
Tale Of Green Reed And Gentian
solo,pno ONGAKU s.p.   (I224)

ISHIKETA, M.
Collection Of Songs, A *CCU
solo,pno ONGAKU s.p.   (I225)

Twofold Tale, The
solo,pno ONGAKU s.p.   (I226)

ISLAND IN A ROOM see Kupferman, Meyer

ISLAND OF JUNE see Bain, Marjorie

ISLAND OF PINES see Bantock, Granville

ISLAND OF THE PURPLE SEA see Geehl,
Henry Ernest

ISLAND SHEILING SONG
(Kennedy-Fraser, M.; MacLeod, K.)
solo,pno (G maj) BOOSEY $1.50
                                   (I227)
ISLAND SPINNING SONG
(Roberton, Hugh S.) solo,pno (F sharp
min) ROBERTON 2748 s.p. see also
Songs Of The Isles   (I228)

ISLAY LOVE LILT, THE see Kennedy-
Fraser, Marjory

ISLE OF LEGEND, THE see Tanaka, T.

ISLE OF PORTLAND see Edmunds, John

ISLE OF PORTLAND, THE see Orr, Charles
Wilfred

ISLE OF THE HEATHER see Somervell,
Arthur

ISMAH'H HATAN BECALA
see Six Folk Songs

ISN'T IT A JOY TO BE A CHRISTIAN? see
Fox, Baynard

ISOLA BELLA see Hallstrom, Ivar

ISOLATED MOMENT see Red, Buryl

ISOLDE'S LIEBESTOD see Wagner, Richard

ISONIC I see Consoli, Marc-Antonio

ISRAEL EN BATAILLE see Mariotte,
Antoine

ISRAEL LEBT see Milhaud, Darius

ISRAEL LIVES see Mana-Zucca, Mme., Ahm
Yisroel Chai

ISRAEL LIVES ON see Am Yisrael Chai

ISRAEL! ROMPS TA CHAINE see Saint-
Saens, Camille

ISRAEL! WERDE FREI see Saint-Saens,
Camille, Israel! Romps Ta Chaine

ISRAELI AND JEWISH SONG HITS *CCUL,Jew
(Jaffe, Ben; Kammen, Jack) solo,pno
KAMMEN $1.95   (I229)

ISRAELI SONGBOOK *CCU
(Omer, Avraham; Ravina, Menashe)
solo,pno OR-TAV $1.00   (I230)

ISS DEIN BROT MIT FREUDEN see Schutz,
Heinrich

IST EIN SCHLOSS see King, Harold C.

IST EIN SCHLOSS see Orthel, Leon

IST GOTT FUR UNS see Rosenmuller,
Johann

IST GOTT FUR UNS, WER MAG WIDER UNS
SEIN? see Schutz, Heinrich

I'STA CANZONA NUN'A SACCIO FA see
Piccinelli, Nino

IT AIN'T NO NEW THING see Crouch, Andrae

IT ALL DEPENDS see Nelson

IT BEFALLETH BOTH MEN AND BEASTS see Brahms, Johannes, Denn Es Gehet Dem Menschen

IT CAME UPON THE MIDNIGHT CLEAR see Speaks, Oley

IT COSTS SO LITTLE see Liddell, R.

IT-ENG see Puccini, Giacomo

IT HAPPENED TO ME see Jensen, Gordon

IT IS A BEAUTEOUS EVENING see Birch, Robert Fairfax

IT IS A PRECIOUS THING see Distler, Hugo

IT IS A SPRING NIGHT see Giannini, Vittorio

IT IS ALMOST TIME see Petrucci, F. Lee

IT IS ENOUGH see Mendelssohn-Bartholdy, Felix, Es Ist Genug

IT IS FATE see Mana-Zucca, Mme.

IT IS FINISHED see Waermo, Einar

IT IS I, BE NOT AFRAID see Pull, Edwin

IT IS NA, JEAN, THY BONNIE FACE see White, Maude Valerie

IT IS NOT FAIR see Bender, Jan

IT IS PRETTY IN THE CITY see Read, Gardner

IT IS SO LONG see Helm, Everett

IT ISN'T RAINING THERE see Di Veroli, Manilio

IT MAY BE TOMORROW see Baker, Richard

IT MUST HAVE RAINED IN HEAVEN see Gatlin, Larry

IT MUST MAKE THE GOOD LORD SAD see Floyd, Carlisle

IT SEEMS I'VE ALWAYS LOVED YOU *sac, Marriage
   see There's Going To Be A Wedding
   (Carmichael, Ralph) solo,pno WORD
   S-376 $1.00   (I231)

IT STRIKES ME THAT see Ives, Charles

IT TOOK A MIRACLE *sac,gospel
   solo,pno ABER.GRP. $1.50   (I232)

IT WAS A LOVER AND HIS LASS see Castelnuovo-Tedesco, Mario

IT WAS A LOVER AND HIS LASS see German, Edward

IT WAS A LOVER AND HIS LASS see Morley, Thomas

IT WAS A LOVER AND HIS LASS see Vaughan Williams, Ralph

IT WAS FOR ME see Blount

IT WAS JESUS see Irwin, Lois

IT WAS SO QUIET see Harvey, Richard W.

IT WAS THE LOVELY MOON see Bury, Winifred

IT WAS THE TIME OF ROSES see Sharpe, Cedric

IT WILL BE WORTH IT ALL see Gaither

IT WON'T BE LONG see Crouch, Andrae

ITAKARJALAISIA LAULUJA see Borg, Kim

ITALIAANSE VOLKSLIEDEREN *CC20U,folk, It
   (Vries, L. De) solo,pno BROEKMANS 385
   s.p.   (I233)

ITALIAN CHAMBER DUETS *CC18U
   (Landshoff) [It] PETERS 3824C $9.50
   contains works by: D'Astorga;
   Bonocini; Gagliano; Grandi;
   Marcello and others   (I234)

ITALIAN LYRICS, VOL. I: NOS. 1-15 see Wolf, Hugo

ITALIAN LYRICS, VOL. II: NOS. 16-30 see Wolf, Hugo

ITALIAN LYRICS, VOL. III: NOS. 31-46 see Wolf, Hugo

ITALIAN SONGS OF THE EIGHTEENTH CENTURY *CC20L,It,18th cent
   (Fuchs, Albert) med solo,pno
   INTERNAT. $3.50 contains works by:
   Scarlatti; Manzi; Torelli; Mancini
   and others   (I235)

ITALIAN VOCAL DUETS FROM THE EARLY EIGHTEENTH CENTURY *CC10L,18th cent
   (Saville, Eugenia) 2 soli,pno
   SCHIRM.G $2.50   (I236)

ITALIENISCHE LIEDER see Denisov, Edison Vasilievitch

ITALIENISCHES LIEDERBUCH see Zillig, Winfried

ITALIENISCHES LIEDERBUCH see Wolf, Hugo

ITALIENISHE ARIEN UND LIEDER *CC9L
   [It/Ger] med solo,kbd HANSEN-DEN s.p.
   contains works by: Giordani;
   Caccini; Handel; Luzzi; Gluck;
   Lotti; Mozart; Pergolesi   (I237)

ITALIENS ERWACHEN see Handel, George Frideric

ITE see Johansson, Bengt

ITE SUL COLLE, O DRUIDI see Bellini, Vincenzo

ITKISIT JOSKUS ILLOIN see Madetoja, Leevi

IT'LL BE JOY see Ballard, Ann

IT'S A HAPPY DAY see Phieffer, Don

IT'S A LONG, LONESOME ROAD see Matthews

IT'S ALL RIGHT see Younce, George

IT'S ALRIGHT NOW see Lister, Mosie

IT'S CLOSER THAN IT'S EVER BEEN see Croft, Colbert

IT'S DIFFERENT NOW see Beatty

IT'S IN MY HEART see Slater, Arthur

IT'S IN YOUR HANDS see Harkins

IT'S ME AGAIN, LORD see Rambo

IT'S NOT AN EASY ROAD see Peterson, John W.

IT'S OUR WORLD *sac,CC10L
   (Carmichael, Ralph) solo,pno WORD
   37620 $2.50   (I238)

IT'S OUR WORLD see Kaiser, Kurt

IT'S REAL *sac,gospel
   solo,pno ABER.GRP. $1.50   (I239)

IT'S STILL REAL TODAY see Jensen, Gordon

IT'S THE END OF MY LIFE see Puccini, Giacomo, Donde Lieta Usci

IT'S TIME TO PRAY see Peterson, John W.

IT'S WEDDING TIME SERIES, NOS. 1-2
   *sac,CCUL,Marriage
   solo,org SINGSPIR $2.50, ea.   (I240)

IT'S WORTH IT ALL see Tripp, LaVerne

ITSU-NI-NATTARA see Kumaki, Mamoru

ITZT BLICKEN DURCH DES HIMMELS SAAL see Schutz, Heinrich

IVANOVA, LIDIA
   L'inverno
      see Tre Canti Di Shakespeare Per
      Soprano Leggero

   Mattinata
      see Tre Canti Di Shakespeare Per
      Soprano Leggero

   Primavera D'amore
      see Tre Canti Di Shakespeare Per
      Soprano Leggero

   Tre Canti Di Shakespeare Per Soprano Leggero
      [It] S solo,pno cmplt ed SANTIS 648
      s.p.
      contains: L'inverno; Mattinata;
      Primavera D'amore   (I241)

IVANOVA, LIDIA (cont'd.)

   Ventun Canti Ad Una, Due E Tre Voci
   Pari *sac/sec,CC21U
   1-3 soli SANTIS 848 s.p.   (I242)

I'VE BEEN CHANGED see Lister, Mosie

I'VE BEEN IN DE STORM SO LONG *spir
   (Burleigh, H. T.) med solo,pno BELWIN
   $1.50   (I243)

I'VE BEEN ROAMING see Horn, Charles Edward

I'VE, BEEN ROAMING see Rutter, Ida

I'VE BEEN TO CALVARY see Gaither

I'VE BROUGHT SOME SONGS see McGeoch, Daisy

I'VE COME TOO FAR see Harmon, B.

I'VE DISCOVERED THE WAY OF GLADNESS see Hawkins

I'VE FOUND A NEW WAY see Ott, J.

I'VE GOT A RAM see Moore, Douglas Stuart

I'VE GOT A REASON TO SING see Skillings, Otis

I'VE GOT CONFIDENCE see Crouch, Andrae

I'VE GOT JESUS IN MY HEART see Harris

I'VE GOT MORE TO GO TO HEAVEN FOR see Campbell

I'VE GOT MORE TO GO TO HEAVEN FOR see Campbell, Jack

I'VE GOT THE CORNERS TURNED DOWN see Snider

I'VE HAD A VISION OF JESUS see Jones, H.B.

I'VE HEARD AN ORGAN TALK SOMETIMES see Copland, Aaron

I'VE KISSED AND I'VE PRATTLED see Shield, William

I'VE PUT MY ALL IN YOUR CARE *sac, gospel
   solo,pno ABER.GRP. $1.50   (I244)

IVERI see Sivic, Pavle

IVES, CHARLES (1874-1954)
   Chanson De Florian
   med solo,pno PRESSER $.75   (I245)

   Eleven Songs And Two Harmonizations
   *CC13U
   (Kirkpatrick) med solo,pno AMP
   $3.00   (I246)

   Flag Song
   solo,pno PEER $1.00   (I247)

   Four Songs *CC4U
   solo,pno PRESSER $1.25   (I248)

   Fourteen Songs *CC14L
   solo,pno PEER $5.00   (I249)

   From Lincoln The Great Commoner
   solo,pno PEER $1.25   (I250)

   Ilmenau
   "Over All The Treetops" [Ger/Eng]
   solo,pno PEER $.95   (I251)

   It Strikes Me That
   med solo,pno MERCURY $1.25   (I252)

   Light That Is Felt, The
   low solo,pno MERCURY $1.25   (I253)

   Nine Songs *CC9L
   solo,pno PEER $3.00   (I254)

   Nineteen Songs *CC19U
   med solo,pno PRESSER $3.95   (I255)

   Over All The Treetops *see Ilmenau

   Sacred Songs *sac,CC11L
   solo,pno PEER $4.00   (I256)

   Serenity
   (Whittier) med solo,pno AMP A377
   $.25   (I257)

   Seven Songs *CC7U
   med solo,pno AMP $2.00   (I258)

   Sunrise
   solo,vln,pno PETERS rental   (I259)

IVES, CHARLES (cont'd.)

Ten Songs   *CC10L
solo,pno PEER $3.50   (I260)

Thirteen Songs   *CC13L
solo,pno PEER $4.50   (I261)

Thirty-Four Songs   *CC34U
high solo,pno PRESSER $4.50   (I262)

Three Songs   *CC3U
med solo,pno AMP $1.50   (I263)

Twelve Songs   *CC12L
solo,pno PEER $4.00   (I264)

Vote For Names
solo,pno PEER $1.00   (I265)
solo/soli,3pno PEER $2.00   (I266)

IVES, GRAYSTON
Falcon, The
solo,pno/orch (D maj) ROBERTON 1001
s.p.   (I267)

IVORY PALACES see Barraclough

IVORY TOWER see Peeters, Flor

IVRE D'INSOUCIANCE see Gabus, Monique

IVY AND THE OAK, THE see Herbert,
Victor

IZ MLADIH DNI see Lajovic, Anton

IZ TEZKIH DNI see Kozina, Marijan

IZ ZAPUSCINE (POSTHUMOUS COLLECTION)
see Kozina, Marijan

IZBRANE PESMI see Kozina, Marijan

J

JA, DET ER FORAR see Lewkovitch,
Bernhard

JA ICH LIEB SIE see Tchaikovsky, Piotr
Ilyitch, I Adore Thee

JA, SO SINGT UND TANZT MAN NUR IN WIEN
see Strauss, Johann

JA, WAS WILLST DU see Bijvanck, Henk

JAA HYVASTI JA NAKEMIIN see Kilpinen,
Yrio

JABBERWOCKY see Sydeman, William

JABLICKO S POSELSTVIM see Sodomka, K.

JACHINO, CARLO (1889-   )
Santa Orazione Alla Vergine Maria
*sac
[It/Ger] solo,strings quarto
RICORDI-ENG 131280 s.p.   (J1)

JACK L'EVENTREUR see Rorem, Ned

JACK OVERDUE see Shaw, Martin

JACK PRICE SONGBOOK, VOL. I see Price,
Jack

JACK PRICE SONGBOOK, VOL. II see Price,
Jack

JACKELE, SHIK MIR A CHEKELE   *Jew
solo,pno KAMMEN 462 $1.00   (J2)

JACKIE AND BRIDIES SONG BOOK 1   *CCU
(Mc Donald, Jackie; O'Donnell,
Bridie) solo,pno GALLIARD 2.2030.7
$1.75   (J3)

JACKIE AND BRIDIES SONG BOOK 2   *CCU
(Mc Donald, Jackie; O'Donnell,
Bridie) solo,pno GALLIARD 2.2027.7
$1.75   (J4)

JACOB
Attorno A La
high solo,org BREITKOPF-W EB 8017
s.p.   (J5)

Flow, My Tears
see Three Songs

Ho, Who Comes Here
see Three Songs

Musik Der Trauer   *CCU
narrator,fl,treb inst BREITKOPF-W
EB 8015 s.p.   (J6)

Of All The Birds
see Three Songs

Three Songs
S solo,clar,pno (med) OXFORD 60.004
$1.70, ipa
contains: Flow, My Tears; Ho, Who
Comes Here; Of All The Birds
(J7)

JACOB, DOM CLEMENT (1906-   )
Cartes Postales
high solo,pno sc JOBERT s.p.   (J8)

Chansons D'amour   *CCU
high solo,pno sc JOBERT s.p.   (J9)

Complainte De France
med solo,pno sc JOBERT s.p.   (J10)

Deux Chansons De Mezzetin   *CC2U
high solo,pno sc JOBERT s.p.   (J11)

Deux Poemes De Tristan Dereme   *CC3U
high solo,pno sc JOBERT s.p.   (J12)

Humble Priere
med solo,pno sc JOBERT s.p.   (J13)
med solo,pno sc JOBERT s.p.   (J14)

Le Depot Est Obligatoire
high solo,pno sc JOBERT s.p.   (J15)

Promenades
high solo,pno sc JOBERT s.p.   (J16)

Six Chansons De Sainte Therese
D'Avila   *CC6U
solo,pno sc JOBERT s.p.   (J17)

Six Poemes De Jean Cocteau   *CC6U
high solo,pno sc JOBERT s.p.   (J18)

Six Sonnets De Michel-Ange   *CC6U
solo,pno sc JOBERT s.p.   (J19)

JACOB, DOM CLEMENT (cont'd.)

Trois Poemes D'Alfred De Musset
*CC3U
high solo,pno sc JOBERT s.p.   (J20)

JACOB, GORDON (1895-   )
Mother I Will Have A Husband
high solo,pno GALLIARD 2.1520.7
$1.25   (J21)

JACOB, WERNER (1938-   )
Das Ende Des Gesetzes   *see Telos
Nomou

Telos Nomou
"Das Ende Des Gesetzes" narrator,
rec,English horn,horn,trom,perc,
cembalo,pno,org s.p.   (J22)

JACOBI, FREDERICK (1891-1952)
Elegy
see Three Songs

Ode To Freedom
see Three Songs

On The Sleep Of Plants
see Three Songs

Three Songs
solo,pno NEW VALLEY $2.50
contains: Elegy; Ode To Freedom;
On The Sleep Of Plants   (J23)

JACOBITE LAMENT see Lawson, Malcolm

JACOB'S LADDER   *sac,gospel
solo,pno ABER.GRP. $1.50   (J24)

JACOB'S VOICE see Wolf, Artur, Kol
Yaakov

JACOBSSON
Varsang
high solo,pno LUNDQUIST s.p.   (J25)
low solo,pno LUNDQUIST s.p.   (J26)

JACOPO DA BOLOGNA
Lux Purpurata Radiis. Diligite
Justiciam   *sac,mot
3 soli OISEAU s.p.   (J27)

Non Al Suo Amante   *madrigal
2 soli OISEAU s.p.   (J28)

Reverie-Barcarolle
solo,pno/inst DURAND s.p.   (J29)
[Fr] solo,acap oct DURAND s.p.
(J30)

JACOTIN see Klerk, Albert de

JACOTTE see Godard, Benjamin Louis Paul

JADIS see Chaminade, Cecile

JADIS, ENFIEVRE PARLES CHANTS DES
BARDES see Indy, Vincent d'

JADIS ET NAGUERE see Bon, Willem
Frederik

JADIS QUAND TU LUTTAIS see Wagner,
Richard

JADIS TU M'AS AIME see Gretchaninov,
Alexander Tikhonovitch

J'ADORE LES FEMMES see Scotto, Vincent

JAEGER, WILLY
Christkindleins Wiegenlied
solo,org,vln,vcl RIES s.p.   (J31)

JAEGERSANG see Grieg, Edvard Hagerup

JAEVNDOGNSELEGI I see Maegaard Jan

JAG AR EN GAST OCH FRAMLING
see Andliga Sanger, Heft 4

JAG AR EN GAST OCH FRAMLING see
Lundborg, Gosta

JAG AR LIVETS BROD see Forsberg, Roland

JAG AR UPPSTANDELSEN OCH LIVET see
Forsberg, Roland

JAG DROMDE OM ETT KUNGABARN see
Hartmann, Luigi

JAG EN GAST OCH PILGRIM AR see
Dahlgren, Erland

JAG GAR I TUSEN TANKAR
solo,pno GEHRMANS 164 s.p.   (J32)

JAG GICK MIG UT EN AFTONSTUND
solo,pno GEHRMANS 204 s.p. contains
also: Vad Jag Har Lovat Det Skall
Jag Halla   (J33)

JAG HAR DROMT see Rangstrom, Ture

JAG HAR ETT HEM VID HAVET see Nystroem, Gosta

JAG HAR GATT INUNDER STJARNOR see Hedar, Josef

JAG HAR HAFT EN STOR, TYST SORG see Kilpinen, Yrio

JAG HAR I DROMMEN GRATIT see Lassen, Eduard

JAG HOR EN STAMMA SA KAND OCH KAR see Nordqvist, Gustaf

JAG HOR KLOCKOR RINGA see Damm, Svenerik

JAG HORDE DIN ROST see Nordqvist, Gustaf

JAG KANDE EN TRAST see Wideen

JAG LANGTAR HEM see Dahlgren, Erland

JAG LEVER see Merikanto, Oskar, Ma Elan

JAG SER GUDS SPAR see Strandsjo, Gote

JAG SER UPPA DINA OGON
solo,pno GEHRMANS 209 s.p.   (J34)

JAG SJUNGER OM KARLEK see Edeji

JAG TACKAR DIG, HERRE GUD see Mendelssohn-Bartholdy, Felix

JAG TROR JAG FAR BORJA OVERGE ATT SORJA
solo,pno GEHRMANS 214 s.p. contains also: Och Hor Du Unga Dora   (J35)

JAG UNNAR DIG ANDA ALLT GOTT
see Det Star Ett Ljus I Osterland

JAG VANTAR INGEN LYCKA see Kilpinen, Yrio

JAG VANTAR MANEN see Nystroem, Gosta

JAG VET ATT MIN FORLOSSARE LEVER see Handel, George Frideric

JAG VET EJ OM DU MIG MINNES see Pylkkanen, Tauno Kullervo, En Tieda, Muistatko Mua

JAG VILL DIG TACKA OCH LOVA see Torlind, Tore

JAG VILL GE MIN HJARTANS LILLE BRODER see Skold

JAG VILLE VARA TARAR see Kilpinen, Yrio

JAGARGOSSEN see Sibelius, Jean

JAGDLIED see Kreutzer, C.

JAGERLIED see Brahms, Johannes

JAGERLIED see Grieg, Edvard Hagerup, Jaegersang

JAHRESRINGE HEFT I: BERGENGRUEN-DUETTE see Lothar, Mark

JAHRESRINGE HEFT II: MORGENSTERN-DUETTE see Lothar, Mark

JAHRLANG MOCHT' ICH SO DICH HALTEN see Sjogren, Emil

J'AI ATTENDU see Rimsky-Korsakov, Nikolai

J'AI BESION DE TOI see Coppola, Piero

J'AI BESOIN DE VOTRE TENDRESSE see Goeyens, Fern.

J'AI BU DE CETTE BOISSON see Serpette, Gaston

J'AI CHAUD see Wolff, A.

J'AI CHERCHE TRENTE ANS see Absil, Jean

JAI CUEILLI LA BELLE ROSE
see Folk Songs Of Eastern Canada

J'AI DANS L'AME see Godard, Benjamin Louis Paul

J'AI DE LA FIGURE see Messager, Andre

J'AI DES P'TITES FLEURS BLEUES see Dalcroze, Jacques

J'AI DES REFRAINS see Messager, Andre

J'AI DESCENDU see Seiber, Matyas

J'AI DEUX AMOUREUX see Lacome, Paul

J'AI DIT A MA BELLE see Delmet, Paul

J'AI GRAVI LA MONTAGNE see Saint-Saens, Camille

J'AI LA TOUX DANS MON JEU see Arrieu, Claude

J'AI LASSE MON COEUR see Emer, M.

J'AI LE POUVOIR SUPREME see Mussorgsky, Modest, My Pow'r Is Now Supreme

J'AI LE REBOURS see Le Roy, A.

J'AI MIS MON COEUR A LA FENETRE see Busser, Henri-Paul

J'AI PARDONNE see Schumann, Robert (Alexander)

J'AI PASSE PAR LA see Okolowicz, E.

J'AI PENETRE, O MON EPOUSE see Canal, Marguerite

J'AI PERDU MON EURYDICE see Gluck, Christoph Willibald Ritter von

J'AI PERDU MYRTILLE see Lacome, Paul

J'AI PEUR D'UN BAISER see Busser, Henri-Paul

J'AI RENCONTRE DE PAR LE MONDE see Betove

J'AI REPRIS MON SOURIRE see Faraut, B.

J'AI REVE DE PRINCESSES BLANCHES see Aubert, Louis-Francois-Marie

J'AI REVE DE T'AIMER see Goublier, G.

J'AI REVE TELLEMENT FORT DE TOI see Casterede, Jacques

J'AI SCELLE MON COEUR see Sureau-Bellet, J.

J'AI TOUT OUBLIE see Cuvillier, Charles

J'AI UNE PETITE FEMME see Yresne M. d'

J'AI VOULU FUIR see Delmet, Paul

J'AI VU LE LOUP see Emmanuel, Maurice

J'AI VU NOS CHAMPS see Wagner, Richard

J'AIMAIS MON COUSIN see Messager, Andre

J'AIME, DANS SON LOINTAIN MYSTERE see Saint-Saens, Camille

J'AIME DOULOUREUSEMENT see Lacome, Paul

J'AIME LA FEMME see Messager, Andre

J'AIME LES CLOCHES see Wangermez, Ed.

J'AIME PAS LA LUNE see Pelemans, Willem

JAJ, DE SZEPEN MUZSIKALNAK
(Ranki) "How Beautifully They Play" solo,pno BUDAPEST 2196 $2.25 (J36)

JALANJALJET LUMESSA see Hannikainen, Ilmari, Fotsparen I Snon

JALAS, JUSSI (1908-   )
Etelapohjalaisia Kansanlauluja, Vols. I-III *CCU
solo,pno FAZER
W 2381; W 2382; W 2537 s.p., ea.
(J37)

JALKANEN, TEPPO
Flicka, Sjung *see Laula Tytto

Kanervan Kukka
"Ljung" solo,pno FAZER F 1482 s.p.
(J38)

Laula Tytto
"Flicka, Sjung" solo,pno FAZER F 1483 s.p.   (J39)

Ljung *see Kanervan Kukka

JAM LUCIS ORTO SIDERE see Klerk, Albert de

JAM MORIAR, MI FILI see Monteverdi, Claudio

JAMA, AGNES (1921-   )
Vocatio
Mez solo,clar,pno DONEMUS s.p.
(J40)

JAMAICAN RUMBA see Benjamin, Arthur

JAMAIS NE CESSERAI DE MAGNIFIER LE SEIGNEUR see Honegger, Arthur

JAMAIS ON NE SAURA see Laparra, Raoul

JAMES JOYCE SONGS see Persichetti, Vincent

JAMES, PHILIP (1890-1975)
Jesus, Fount Of Love *sac
high solo,pno BELWIN $1.50   (J41)

King Of Love, The *sac
high solo,pno BELWIN $1.50   (J42)

Stranger, The *sac
med solo,pno MCA $1.50   (J43)
med solo,pno BELWIN $1.50   (J44)

JAMES, THOMAS
Bath, The
med solo,pno sc AM.COMP.AL. $.82
(J45)

JAMTLANDSMINNEN see Peterson-Berger, (Olof) Wilhelm

JAMUNDER CANTIONAL see Rossler, Ernst Karl

JAN BROEDER see Lilien, Ignace

JAN EN ANNEMIE see Hullebroeck, Em.

JAN HINNERK see Olsson, Otto Emmanuel

JANACEK, LEOS (1854-1928)
Aus Dem Tagebuch Eines Verschollenen *CCU
[Czech/Ger] solo,pno SUPRAPHON s.p.
(J46)

Hukvalder Volkspoesie In Liedern *CCU
[Czech] solo,pno SUPRAPHON s.p.
(J47)

Mahrische Volkspoesie In Liedern *CCU
[Czech/Ger] solo,pno SUPRAPHON s.p.
(J48)

Sechsundzwanzig Volksballaden *CC26U
[Czech] solo,pno SUPRAPHON s.p.
(J49)

JANE see Levade, Charles (Gaston)

JANE GREY see Schoenberg, Arnold

JANE'S BIG UMBRELLA see Russell, Kennedy

JANINKA ZPIVA see Macha, Otmar

JANKA see Kilpinen, Yrio

JANKO, JANKO, BETTER BEWARE!
see Three Slovak Songs

JANNEQUIN, CLEMENT (ca. 1475-ca. 1560)
Chansons Polyphoniques *CCU
(Tillman Merritt, A.; Lesure, Francois) solo,pno cmplt ed OISEAU s.p.   (J50)

JANSEN, F. GUSTAV
Im Abendrot *Op.31,No.4
see Vier Duette

Im Mai *Op.31,No.1
see Vier Duette

So Wahr Die Sonne Scheinet *Op.31, No.2
see Vier Duette

Vier Duette
MezT/AT soli,pno LEUCKART s.p.
contains: Im Abendrot, Op.31, No.4; Im Mai, Op.31,No.1; So Wahr Die Sonne Scheinet, Op.31, No.2; Wer Gott Das Herze Gibet, Op.31,No.3   (J51)

Wer Gott Das Herze Gibet *Op.31,No.3
see Vier Duette

JANSSEN, GUNNAR
De Lud Achtern Diek
solo,pno SIKORSKI 709 s.p.   (J52)

Lapuster
solo,pno SIKORSKI 708 s.p.   (J53)

Sunnschien Op'n Weg
Bar solo,pno SIKORSKI 707 s.p.
(J54)

JANSSEN, GUUS (1951-   )
Een Beetje Inspraak
narrator,fl,perc,electronic tape DONEMUS s.p.   (J55)

JANUARY see Gwynne, Una

JAPAN see Marx, Joseph, Regenlied

JAPANESE LOVE SONG see Brahe, May H.

JAPANESE LULLABY see Stanford, Charles Villiers

JAPANISCHE BLATTER see Einem, Gottfried von

JAPANISCHE LIEDER see Zieritz, Grete von

JAPONNERIE see Samazeuilh, Gustave

JAR V UDOLI see Zimmer, Jan

JARDANYI, [PAL] (1920-1966)
Ropulj Pava *CCU,folk,Hung
[Hung] solo,pno BUDAPEST 777 s.p.
(J56)

JARDIM FANADO see Villa-Lobos, Heitor

JARDIN ANTIGUO see Guastavino, Carlos

JARDIN D'AMOUR see Lachaume, A.

JARDIN D'AMOUR see Vuillermoz, Emile

JARDIN DU CIEL see Ibert, Jacques

JARDIN NOCTURNE see Faure, Gabriel-Urbain

JARDIN PRES DE LA MER see Pillois, Jacques

JARNEFELT, ARMAS (1869-1958)
Aallon Kehtolaulu
"Der Welle Wiegenlied" solo,pno
FAZER W 933 s.p.   (J57)

An En Visa Vill Jag Sjunga *see
Viel' Ois Viritta Tieossani

Berceuse
solo,pno LUNDQUIST s.p.   (J58)
"Kehtolaulu" solo,pno FAZER F 1894
s.p.   (J59)

Carmen
solo,pno LUNDQUIST s.p.   (J60)

Dammerung *see Skymning

Der Welle Wiegenlied *see Aallon
Kehtolaulu

Du
solo,pno LUNDQUIST s.p.   (J61)
"Sina" solo,pno FAZER F 2496 s.p.
(J62)

Eines Traumers Sang An Das Leben
*see En Drommares Sang Till Livet

En Drommares Sang Till Livet
"Eines Traumers Sang An Das Leben"
solo,pno FAZER F 121 s.p.   (J63)

Kehtolaulu *see Berceuse

Kehtolaulu
"Vaggsang" solo,pno FAZER W 936
s.p.   (J64)

Lina
"Line" solo,pno FAZER F 728 s.p.
(J65)

Line *see Lina

Sina *see Du

Skymning
solo,pno LUNDQUIST s.p.   (J66)
"Dammerung" solo,pno FAZER F 122
s.p.   (J67)

Sommarnatt Pa Stranden
solo,pno LUNDQUIST s.p.   (J68)

Sommarnatt Pa Stranden *see
Suvirannalla

Sonntag *see Sunnuntaina

Sunnuntaina
"Sonntag" solo,pno FAZER F 220 s.p.
(J69)

Suvirannalla
"Sommarnatt Pa Stranden" solo,pno
FAZER F 2498 s.p.   (J70)

Titania
solo,pno FAZER F 63 s.p.   (J71)

Tretton Ar
solo,pno LUNDQUIST s.p.   (J72)

Vaggsang *see Kehtolaulu

Viel' Ois Viritta Tieossani
"An En Visa Vill Jag Sjunga" solo,
pno FAZER F 381 s.p.   (J73)

JARNI POPEVKY see Eben, Petr

JARO see Mikoda, Borivoj

JARO A TOUHA see Foerster, Josef Bohuslav

JARO PACHOLATKO see Kricka, Jaroslav

J'ARROSE MES GALONS see Oberfeld, C.

JASMINBLUTEN see Bohac, Josef, Kvety Jasminu

JATTEN see Wennerburg, [Gunnar]

JAUBERT, MAURICE (1900-1940)
Quatre Romances *CC4U
high solo,pno sc JOBERT s.p. (J74)

Trois Chansons De Bord *CC3U
solo,pno ENOCH s.p.   (J75)

JAUCHZET DEM HERREN ALLE WELT see
Bruhns, Nicholaus

JAUCHZET DEM HERRN ALLE WELT (Psalm
100) sac
(Walter, G.A.) S/T solo,bsn,2vla,
cembalo,opt trp BREITKOPF-L rental
(J76)

JAUCHZET DEM HERRN, ALLE WELT see
Bernhard, Christoph

JAUCHZET DEM HERRN ALLE WELT see
Bruhns, Nicholaus

JAUCHZET DEM HERRN, ALLE WELT see
Schauss-Flake, Magdalene

JAUCHZET, FROHLOCKET see Telemann,
Georg Philipp

JAUCHZET GOTT, ALLE LANDE see Koch,
Johannes H.E.

JAUCHZET GOTT, ALLE LANDE see Weiland,
Johannes Julius

JAUCHZET GOTT IN ALLEN LANDEN see Bach,
Johann Sebastian

JAUCHZT, IHR CHRISTEN, SEID VERGNUGT
see Telemann, Georg Philipp

J'AURAIS TANT DE CHOSES A DIRE see
Rabey, Rene

J'AVAIS MIS DE L'AIR PARFUME see
Bernard, R.

J'AVAIS REVE see Lacome, Paul

J'AVAIS UNE AMOUREUSE see Lacome, Paul

J'AY CONTENTE MA VOLONTE SUFFISAMMENT
see Delvincourt, Claude

JAYHAWK SONG, THE see Naramore, Arch

JAYNE, MARY
Are You Saved *see Johnson, Polly

He'll Go With Me All The Way *sac
solo,pno WORD S-209   (J77)

JAZZ DANS LA NUIT see Ropartz, Joseph
Guy

JAZZ DANS LA NUIT see Roussel, Albert

JAZZ-KOLORATUREN see Blacher, Boris

JAZZ SONGS see Roe, Betty

JAZZ SONGS FOR SOPRANO AND DOUBLE BASS
see Roe, Betty

JE CHANTE ET M'ENCHANTE see Belgodere,
V.

JE CHANTE POUR TOI see Lehar, Franz

JE CHANTERAIS TOUJOURS see Doret

JE CONNAIS MA MERE see Rimsky-Korsakov,
Nikolai

JE CROIS ENTENDRE ENCORE see Bizet,
Georges

JE CROIS, J'ATTENDS, J'ESPERE see
Saint-Saens, Camille

JE CROYAIS ENCOR! see Delmet, Paul

JE DIS QUE RIEN ME M'EPOUVANTE see
Bizet, Georges

JE DOUTE! see Delmet, Paul

JE FAISAIS UN REVE INSENSE see Saint-
Saens, Camille

JE FIS UN REVE see Rabey, Rene

JE FLANE see Perronnet, Amelie

JE FREMIS, JE CHANCELLE see Bizet,
Georges

JE LUI DIRAI: BON CHEVALIER see Lacome,
Paul

JE MARCHAIS AU MILIEU DES FLEURS see
Saint-Saens, Camille

JE M'BALADE DANS MOSCAU see Petrov, A.

JE ME LAMENTE see Leguerney, Jacques

JE ME METS EN VOTRE MERCI see Millot,
E.

JE M'EN SOUVIENS TOUJOURS see
Villebichot, A. de

JE N'AI PAS OUBLIE see Lonque, Georges

JE N'AI RIEN QUE TROIS FEUILLES D'OR
see Ropartz, Joseph Guy

JE NAM DOBRE NA SVETE see Buzek, Jan

JE NAM DOBRE NA ZEMI see Sommer,
Vladimir

JE NE CHANTE see Delannoy, Marcel

JE NE FAY RIEN QUE REQUERIR see
Delvincourt, Claude

JE NE ME SOUVIENS PLUS see Rhene-Baton

JE NE PRENDS POINT GARDE see
Huybrechts, Albert

JE NE RECLAMAIS RIEN DE TOI see
Barraine, Elsa

JE NE SAIS see Mouton, H.

JE NE SAIS PAS DE FLEUR see Lacombe,
Paul

JE NE SAIS VRAIMENT MADAME COMMENT VOUS
DIRE see Offenbach, Jacques

JE NE SUIS MOINS AIMABLE see Le Roy, A.

JE NE SUIS QUE FAIBLESSE see Massenet,
Jules

JE NE TE REVERRAI JAMAIS see Saint-
Saens, Camille

JE NE VEUX PAS D'AUTRES CHOSES see
Godard, Benjamin Louis Paul

JE NE VEUX PLUS AIMER QUE MA MERE MARIE
see Mulder, Ernest W.

JE N'EN AI JAMAIS AIME QU'UNE see Cui,
Cesar Antonovitch

JE NOMMERAI TON FRONT see Poulenc,
Francis

JE N'OSE see Lioncourt, Guy de

JE N'OSE PAS see Staub, V.

JE PENSE A TOI see Abt, Franz

JE PENSE A TOI see Schumann, Robert
(Alexander)

JE REVE A TOI see Rodney, Paul

JE SAIS LA SOURCE... see Santoliquido,
Francesco

JE SAIS QUE JE L'AIME PLUS QUE LA TERRE
see Laparra, Raoul

JE SENS DANS MON COEUR see Lecocq,
Charles

JE SUIS AYME DE LA PLUS BELLE see
Delvincourt, Claude

JE SUIS DU PAYS DES GONDOLES see
Chabrier, Emmanuel

JE SUIS ESCAMILLO see Bizet, Georges

JE SUIS FEMME ET CABARETIERE see
Lacome, Paul

JE SUIS ICI POUR TE CHANTER DES
CHANSONS see Barraine, Elsa

JE SUIS LA SOURCE see Terni, Enrico

JE SUIS LE ROI, JE SUIS LE ROI see
Chabrier, Emmanuel

JE SUIS LE SAINT EN PRIERE see Colding-
Jorgensen, Henrik, Enfance IV

JE SUIS LINDOR see Paisiello, Giovanni

JE SUIS SERGENT INSTRUCTEUR see
Serpette, Gaston

JE SUIS TITANIA see Thomas, Ambroise

JE SUIS TOUJOURS OUVRIERE see Lacome,
Paul

JE SUIS TRISTE see Middeleer, Jean De

JE SUIS UNE PAUVRE FILLE see Messager, Andre

JE SUIS VOTRE FEAL see Saint-Saens, Camille

JE T'AIME see Mouton, H.

JE T'AIME DE TOUTE MON AME see Chabrier, Emmanuel

JE TE JURE, O MON AMOUR see Serpette, Gaston

JE TE RENDS GRACE, O DIEU D'AMOUR see Gounod, Charles Francois

JE TE VEUX see Satie, Erik

JE TREMBLE EN VOYANT TON VISAGE see Debussy, Claude

JE VAIS MOURIR see Berlioz, Hector

JE VAIS SEULETTE see Philidor, Francois Andre Danican

JE VEIT OM E BYGD see Beck, Thomas [Ludvigsen]

JE VEIT OM EN SKOG OG FEM ANDRE SKJAERAASEN SANGER see Braein, Edvard Fliflet

JE VEUX see Rhene-Baton

JE VEUX GARDER MA LIBERTE see Indy, Vincent d'

JE VEUX PLEURER see Wolff, A.

JE VEUX VIVRE see Gounod, Charles Francois

JE VIENS A VOUS see Delmet, Paul

JE VIENS D'ETRE COMPROMISE see Messager, Andre

JE VIS see Rasse, Francois

JE VIS DANS LA BOURRASQUE AMERE see Chabrier, Emmanuel

JE VOUDRAIS see Chaminade, Cecile

JE VOUDRAIS see Lattes, M.

JE VOUDRAIS ETRE VOLTIGEUR see Messager, Andre

JE VOUDRAIS OUBLIER see Mana-Zucca, Mme.

JE VOUDRAIS QUAND TOUS DEUX see Doret

JE VOUDRAIS QUE MON AMOUR see Christensen, Henning

JE VOUS AI TELLEMENT MELE see Wolff, A.

JE VOUS AIME see Tcherepnin, Alexander

JE VOUS ENVOIE see Leguerney, Jacques

JE VOUS SALUE MARIE see Yung, Alfred

JEALOUS LOVER see Quilter, Roger

JEALOUSY see Maganini, Quinto

JEAN see Burleigh, Henry Thacker

JEAN LORIOT see Lachaume, A.

JEAN-PIERRE see Delabre, L.G.

JEANIE WITH THE LIGHT BROWN HAIR see Foster, Stephen Collins, I Dream Of Jeanie With The Light Brown Hair

JEANNE see Honegger, Arthur

JEANNE D'ARC see Finnessy, Michael

JEANNE D'ARC see Fragerolle, G.

JEANNE D'ARC A DOMREMY see Ollone, Max d'

JEANNETON see Dufresne, C.

JEANNETON QUI N'A PAS DE MAMAN see Strimer, Joseph

JEANNETTE see Rontgen, Johannes

JEANNETTE AND HER LITTLE WOODEN SHOES see Herbert, Victor

JEDE NORGEN GEHT DIE SONNE AUF see Marx, Karl

JEDINOU VTERINU JESTE see Zahradnik, Zdenek

JEESUS SANA ELAMAN see Linnala, Eino

JEFFERSON AND LIBERTY see Anonymous

JEFFRIES
    My Old Black Billy And Other Songs
      *CCU
      solo,pno ALLANS s.p.   (J78)

JEFFRIES, GEORGE (? -1685)
    Heu, Me Miseram!
      (Aston, Peter) SB soli,pno NOVELLO
      17.0277.07 s.p.   (J79)

JEG ELSKER DIG see Grieg, Edvard Hagerup

JEG GIVER MIT DIGT TIL VAAREN see Sjogren, Emil

JEG SER FOR MIT OJE SOM DET FINESTE SPIND see Sjogren, Emil

JEHOVAH, LET ME NOW ADORE THEE see Bach, Johann Sebastian

JEHRING, J.
    Zwei Verlassene Italiener
      solo,pno HUG s.p.   (J80)

JELINEK, HANNS (1901-1969)
    Drei Chansons *see Fantasie Von
      Ubermorgen; Maskenball Im
      Hochgebirge; Monolog Des Blinden
                                    (J81)
    Dreizehn Kleine Lieder *Op.13,No.1-
      7, CC7U
      med solo,pno UNIVER. 11914 $3.75
                                    (J82)
    Fantasie Von Ubermorgen
      solo,pno UNIVER. 10026 $2.75 see
      from Drei Chansons   (J83)
    Maskenball Im Hochgebirge
      solo,pno UNIVER. 10027 $2.75 see
      from Drei Chansons   (J84)
    Monolog Des Blinden
      solo,pno UNIVER. 10025 $2.75 see
      from Drei Chansons   (J85)
    Selbstbildnis Des Marc Aurel *Op.24
      narrator,fl,bass clar,pno,vcl
      MODERN s.p.   (J86)
    Unterwegs *Op.28, cant
      S solo,vibra,bvl MODERN s.p. (J87)
    Vier Songs Fur Mittlere Stimme *CC4U
      med solo,pno MODERN s.p.   (J88)

JEMNITZ, S.
    Six Songs *Op.62, CC6U
      [Hung/Ger] solo,pno BUDAPEST 3925
      s.p.   (J89)
    Two Songs *CC2U
      [Hung/Ger] solo,pno BUDAPEST 2859
      s.p.   (J90)

JEN V NAS JE JARO see Plavec, Josef

JENKINS, MARGARET AIKENS
    Lord, Don't Let Me Fail *sac
      solo,pno WORD S-80   (J91)
    Tell It All To Jesus *sac
      solo,pno WORD S-81   (J92)

JENNI, DONALD
    Adam Lay Yboundin
      med solo,pno AM.COMP.AL. $.82 (J93)
    Cinquain
      see Jenni, Donald, Snow Toward
      Evening
    Short Psalm, A *sac,Psalm
      med-high solo,org AM.COMP.AL. $1.10
                                    (J94)
    Snow Toward Evening
      high solo,pno AM.COMP.AL. $1.37
      contains also: Cinquain   (J95)

JENNIE KISSED ME see Peter, L.

JENNINGS, KENNETH L.
    I Lift Up My Eyes *sac
      high solo,pno AUGSBURG 11-0729 $.75
                                    (J96)
      med solo,pno AUGSBURG 11-0728 $.75
                                    (J97)

JENNY AND THE GOLDSMITH see Mallinson, (James) Albert

JENNY KISSED ME see Sutherland, Margaret

JENNY WREN see Rowley, Alec

JENNY'S BAWBEE *folk,Scot
      solo,pno (F maj) PATERSON FS37 s.p.
                                    (J98)

JENNY'S MANTLE see Somervell, Arthur

JENS VEJMAND see Nielsen, Carl

JENSCH, LOTHAR (1916-   )
    Ed E Subito Sera
      S solo,2pic,fl,English horn,bass
      clar,horn,2trp,trom,tuba,3timp,
      perc,harp,cel,pno,strings sc
      GERIG HG 713 s.p.   (J99)
    Notturno Scordato
      solo,fl,vcl GERIG HG 1135 s.p.
                                    (J100)

JENSEN, ADOLF (1837-1879)
    Till Vastanvinden
      high solo,pno GEHRMANS s.p.   (J101)
      low solo,pno GEHRMANS s.p.   (J102)

JENSEN, GORDON
    Before He Calls Again *sac
      solo,pno BENSON S5172-S $1.00
                                    (J103)
    Come Into The Ark *sac
      solo,pno BENSON S5299-S $1.00
                                    (J104)
    Congratulations Are In Order *sac
      solo,pno BENSON S5309-S $1.00
                                    (J105)
    Don't Go To Heaven Alone *sac
      solo,pno BENSON S5373-S $1.00
                                    (J106)
    Forever Is A Long, Long Time *sac
      solo,pno BENSON S5485-R $1.00
                                    (J107)
    God Has Not Changed *sac
      solo,pno BENSON S5542-S $1.00
                                    (J108)
    God's Grace Makes Up The Difference
      For Me *sac
      solo,pno BENSON S5569-S $1.00
                                    (J109)
    Gordon Jensen-Songbook *sac,CC10L
      solo,pno BENSON BO484 $2.50 (J110)
    Heaven To Go To Heaven In *sac
      solo,pno BENSON S5807-R $1.00
                                    (J111)
    He's Been My Dearest Friend *sac
      solo,pno BENSON S5764-R $1.00
                                    (J112)
    I Should Have Been Crucified *sac
      solo,pno BENSON S6132-S $1.00
                                    (J113)
      solo,pno BENSON S6131-R $1.00
                                    (J114)
    I Still Remember Things God Has
      Forgotten *sac
      solo,pno BENSON S6133-R $1.00
                                    (J115)
    I'll Glory In The Cross *sac
      solo,pno BENSON S6241-R $1.00
                                    (J116)
    I'm So Unworthy *sac
      solo,pno BENSON S6382-S $1.00
                                    (J117)
    It Happened To Me *sac
      solo,pno BENSON S6586-S $1.00
                                    (J118)
    It's Still Real Today *sac
      solo,pno BENSON S6690-S $1.00
                                    (J119)
    Jesus Will Outshine Them All *sac
      solo,pno BENSON S6758-R $1.00
                                    (J120)
      solo,pno BENSON S6755-S $1.00
                                    (J121)
    Justified By Faith *sac
      solo,pno BENSON S6809-R $1.00
                                    (J122)
    Leave A Well In The Valley *sac
      solo,pno BENSON S6833-S $1.00
                                    (J123)
    Over And Over *sac
      solo,pno BENSON S7334-S $1.00
                                    (J124)
    Redemption Draweth Nigh *sac
      solo,pno BENSON S7418-S $1.00
                                    (J125)
    Song Holy Angels Cannot Sing, A *sac
      solo,pno BENSON S5058-S $1.00
                                    (J126)
    Sunrise *sac
      solo,pno BENSON S7605-S $1.00
                                    (J127)
    Take A Look At Calvary *sac
      solo,pno BENSON S7651-S $1.00
                                    (J128)
    Take It All *sac
      solo,pno BENSON S7650-S $1.00
                                    (J129)
    Tears Are A Language *sac
      solo,pno BENSON S7686-R $1.00
                                    (J130)
      solo,pno BENSON S7687-S $1.00
                                    (J131)
    There's Enough Of God's Love *sac
      solo,pno BENSON S8115-S $1.00
                                    (J132)
    We'll Cast Our Crowns At His Feet
      *sac
      solo,pno BENSON S8341-S $1.00
                                    (J133)
    Whisper Jesus *sac
      solo,pno BENSON S8487-R $1.00
                                    (J134)

JENSEN, GORDON (cont'd.)

Will You Be Among The Missing? *sac
solo,pno BENSON S8518-S $1.00
(J135)

JENSEN, LUDWIG IRGENS (1894-1969)
Altar, The
med solo,pno NOVELLO 17.0002.02
s.p.   (J136)
med solo,pno NORSK $.75   (J137)

Bol's Song
[Eng/Norw] med solo,pno BOTE $.75
(J138)

I Fain Would Rest
solo,pno ASHDOWN s.p.   (J139)

O Linger Yet
solo,pno ASHDOWN s.p.   (J140)

J'ENTENDS LE MOULIN see Saint-Requier,
Leon

J'ENTENDS MON COEUR see Middeleer, Jean
De, Mijn Hart Klopt Hoorbaar

JENTSCH, WALTER
Auf Dem Flusse *Op.2,No.4
see Vier Lieder

Das Lied Der Bildsaule *Op.24,No.5
see Sechs Lieder

Die Einsame *Op.2,No.2
see Vier Lieder

Ein Melodie *Op.2,No.3
see Vier Lieder

Heut' Es Kein Abend Werden Will
*Op.24,No.2
see Sechs Lieder

Sechs Lieder
RIES high solo,pno s.p.; low solo,
pno s.p.
contains: Das Lied Der Bildsaule,
Op.24,No.5; Heut' Es Kein Abend
Werden Will, Op.24,No.2; Singt
Mein Schatz Wie Ein Fink,
Op.24,No.3; Spate Gedanken
Einer Bacchantin, Op.24,No.1;
Unterschied Im Antworten,
Op.24,No.6; Vertrauen, Op.24,
No.4   (J141)

Singt Mein Schatz Wie Ein Fink
*Op.24,No.3
see Sechs Lieder

Spate Gedanken Einer Bacchantin
*Op.24,No.1
see Sechs Lieder

Unterschied Im Antworten *Op.24,No.6
see Sechs Lieder

Vertrauen *Op.24,No.4
see Sechs Lieder

Vier Lieder
solo,pno RIES s.p.
contains: Auf Dem Flusse, Op.2,
No.4; Die Einsame, Op.2,No.2;
Ein Melodie, Op.2,No.3;
Vigilien, Op.2,No.1   (J142)

Vier Lieder Nach Texten Von Peter
Huchel Und Carmen Bernos De
Gasztold *CCU
solo,pno SIKORSKI 782 s.p.   (J143)

Vigilien *Op.2,No.1
see Vier Lieder

JEREMIAS, JAROSLAV (1889-1919)
Das Mutterherz
[Czech/Ger] solo,pno SUPRAPHON s.p.
(J144)

JEREMIAS, OTAKAR (1892-1962)
Chvile Slavy Jsem Mel
Mez solo,orch PANTON 350 s.p.
(J145)

Pisne *CCU
high solo,pno PANTON s.p.   (J146)

Pisne Pro Vyssi Hlas *CCU
high solo,pno PANTON 800 s.p.
(J147)

JEREMIAS I TROSTLOSA
Tattare-Emma
solo,pno LUNDQUIST s.p.   (J148)

JEREMY TAYLOR, BOOK 1 see Taylor,
Jeremy

JEREMY TAYLOR, BOOK 2 see Taylor,
Jeremy

JERSILD, JORGEN (1913-   )
Forarsvise
see Three Songs

Kilden
see Three Songs

JERSILD, JORGEN (cont'd.)

Lo
see Three Songs

Three Songs
[Dan] high solo,kbd HANSEN-DEN s.p.
contains: Forarsvise; Kilden; Lo
(J149)

JERUSALEM! see Mendelssohn-Bartholdy,
Felix

JERUSALEM see Parker, Henry

JERUSALEM see Parker, Horatio William

JERUSALEM see Parry, Charles Hubert
Hastings

JERUSALEM FROM THE MOUNTAIN see
Hoskins, William

JERUSALEM, MY HAPPY HOME see Thomson,
Virgil

JERUSALEM - THE ONE AND ONLY see Eyn
Ki-Y'rushalayim

JERUSALEM, THOU THAT KILLEST THE
PROPHETS see Bernhard, Christoph

JERUSCHALAJIM see Barbe, Helmut

JERUSHOLAYIM *folk,Jew
med solo,pno HATIKVAH ED. 52 $.35
(J150)

JESAJA 40 see Colaco Osorio-Swaab,
Reine

JESAJA 60 see Colaco Osorio-Swaab,
Reine

JESEN see Tylnak, Ivan

JESEN I MAJ see Krizkovsky, Karel
(Pavel)

JESI, ADA (1912-   )
Sei Vocalizzi Da Concerto *CC6U,
vocalise
solo,pno ZERBONI 7771 s.p.   (J151)

JESSEL, LEON (1871-1942)
I'm A Tin Soldier
high solo,pno (D maj) ASHDOWN s.p.,
ipr   (J152)
low solo,pno (C maj) ASHDOWN s.p.,
ipr   (J153)

JESU ALLERLIEFST KIND see Nieland, Jan

JESU CHRISTE, HAB' ERBARMEN see Ebart,
Samuel, Miserere, Christe, Mei

JESU CORONA VIRGINIUM see Charpentier,
Marc-Antoine

JESU, DEINE GNADENBLICKE see Bach,
Johann Sebastian

JESU, DIR SEI PREIS GESUNGEN see Bach,
Johann Sebastian

JESU DULCIS MEMORIA see Diepenbrock,
Alphons

JESU, GOOD ABOVE ALL OTHERS see Willan,
Healey

JESU JOY OF MAN'S DESIRING see Bach,
Johann Sebastian, Jesus Bleibet
Meine Freude

JESU, LASS DICH FINDEN, LASS DOCH MEINE
SUNDEN see Bach, Johann Sebastian

JESU SWEET, NOW WILL I SING see Holst,
Gustav

JESU, THE VERY THOUGHT see Silvester,
Frederick C.

JESU! THOU DEAR BABE DIVINE *sac
(Dickinson, C.) solo,pno BELWIN $1.50
(J154)

JESU, WIJS EN WONDERMACHTIG see Dijk,
Jan van

JESULEIN SCHON'S KINDELEIN see
Kowalski, Max

JESUS see Campbell, Jack

JESUS see Crouch, Andrae

JESUS see Gaither

JESUS see Weigl, Karl

JESUS A LA CRECHE see Gounod, Charles
Francois, Noel

JESUS AV NASARET GAR HAR FRAM
see Andliga Sanger, Heft 1

JESUS BLEIBET MEINE FREUDE see Bach,
Johann Sebastian

JESUS CARES FOR ME see Brown, Aaron

JESUS CHRISTUS, KONIG UND HERR see
Wenzel, Eberhard

JESUS DE NAZARETH see Gounod, Charles
Francois, Nazareth

JESUS DID IT FOR ME see Wolfe, Lanny

JESUS DIED see Hubbard, H.

JESUS, FOUNT OF LOVE see James, Philip

JESUS FROM THE GRAVE IS RISEN see Bach,
Johann Sebastian

JESUS GOT AHOLD OF MY LIFE see Wolfe,
Lanny

JESUS, HE IS THE SON OF GOD see Lee,
Don

JESUS HEARD MY PRAYER see Ellis

JESUS, I LOVE YOU see Croft, Colbert

JESUS IS A ROCK IN A WEARY LAND *sac,
gospel
solo,pno ABER.GRP. $1.50   (J155)

JESUS IS COMING see Peterson, John W.

JESUS IS COMING AGAIN see Peterson,
John W.

JESUS IS COMING BACK AGAIN see Rushford

JESUS IS COMING SOON see Winsett

JESUS IS LORD OF ALL see Gaither

JESUS IS REAL see Hughes, Bob

JESUS IS STILL THE ANSWER see Wolfe,
Lanny

JESUS IS STILL THE SAME see Ellis

JESUS IS STILL WONDERFUL see Peterson,
John W.

JESUS IS THE ANSWER see Crouch, Andrae

JESUS IS THE ANSWER see Watters, Bob

JESUS, JESUS, REST YOUR HEAD
(Niles) high solo,pno (G maj)
SCHIRM.G $.85   (J156)
(Niles) low solo,pno (D maj) SCHIRM.G
$.85   (J157)

JESUS, JESUS, REST YOUR HEAD see
Edmunds

JESUS, JESUS, REST YOUR HEAD see Niles,
John Jacob

JESUS, JESUS, THOU ART MINE see Bach,
Johann Sebastian

JESUS, JOY OF MAN'S DESIRING see Bach,
Johann Sebastian, Jesus Bleibet
Meine Freude

JESUS KAR, GA EJ FORBI MIG
see Andliga Sanger, Heft 4

JESUS, LAT MEG LIKJAST DEG see
Tonnessen, Peder

JESUS LIVETS HELGA ORD see Linnala,
Eino, Jeesus Sana Elaman

JESUS LOVES ME see Ellis

JESUS MADE A BELIEVER OUT OF ME see
Wolfe, Lanny

JESUS MADE ME HIGHER see Omartian

JESUS MY SAVIOUR LOOK ON ME see Barnes,
Edward Shippen

JESUS NEVER FORGETS see Coleman, Jack

JESUS OF NAZARETH see Gounod, Charles
Francois, Nazareth

JESUS ONLY see Rotoli

JESUS, OUR SAVIOR, FOR US WAS BORN see
Schutz, Heinrich, Heute Ist
Christus, Der Herr, Geboren

JESUS, REDEEMER, OUR LOVING SAVIOUR see
Bruckner, Anton

JESUS, REFUGE OF THE WEARY see Bach,
Johann Sebastian

JESUS SAID IT *sac,CCUL,Bibl
(Burroughs, Bob) med solo,pno PRESSER
$2.50   (J158)

JESUS SAID TO THE WIDOW, "DO NOT WEEP"
see Krapf, Gerhard

JESUS, SHEPHERD, BE THOU NEAR ME see
Bach, Johann Sebastian

JESUS, SON OF DAVID, HAVE MERCY ON ME
see Bender, Jan

JESUS SONGS *sac,CCU
solo,pno MEL BAY MB93315 $1.95 (J159)

JESUS, STAND BESIDE THEM see Lovelace,
Austin C.

JESUS, THANKS TO THEE WE OFFER see
Frauenholtz, Johann Christoph

JESUS, THE MASTER see Pace, Millie Lou

JESUS THE VERY THOUGHT OF THEE see
Hill, Eugene

JESUS, THE VERY THOUGHT OF THEE see
Thiman, Eric Harding

JESUS, THE VERY THOUGHT OF THEE see
Williams, David H.

JESUS, THOU ART MY SHEPHERD see Dunlap,
Fern Glasgow

JESUS, THOU WHO KNOWEST DEATH see
Wright, Denis

JESUS, THY BLOOD AND RIGHTEOUSNESS see
Bach, Johann Sebastian

JESUS TOMBE POUR LA SECONDE FOIS see
Decruck, F.

JESUS, TU ES A MOI see Bach, Johann
Sebastian

JESUS UND DIE SAMARITERIN see Brunner,
Adolf

JESUS, UNSER TROST UND LEBEN see Bach,
Johann Sebastian

JESUS WAS THERE ALL THE TIME see
Harris, Ron

JESUS, WE JUST WANT TO THANK YOU see
Gaither

JESUS WEPT *sac,gospel
solo,pno ABER.GRP. $1.50   (J160)

JESUS WILL MOVE EVERY see Hubbard, H.

JESUS WILL OUTSHINE THEM ALL see
Jensen, Gordon

JETZT MUSS ICH MIT IHM BRECHEN see
Handel, George Frideric

JETZT REDE DU see Schumann, Georg

JETZT RUHE, JETZT SCHLAFE see Handel,
George Frideric

JETZT SCHATZCHEN, JETZT SIND WIR ALLEIN
see Beethoven, Ludwig van

JETZT SINGEN WIR! *CC21U,Ger
[Ger] solo,pno cmplt ed HINRICHSEN
H41 $4.50, solo pt HINRICHSEN H40
$2.50   (J161)

JETZT, VITELLIA! SCHLAGT DIE STUNDE -
NIE SOLL MIT ROSEN see Mozart,
Wolfgang Amadeus, Ecco Il Punto -
Non, Piu Di Fiori

JEUNE FILLE see Wissmer, Pierre

JEUNE FILLE MODERN STYLE see Berger,
Rod.

JEUNES FILLES see Daniel-Lesur

JEUNES FILLES, VOS SONGES HEUREUX see
Mozart, Wolfgang Amadeus

JEUX DE L'AMOUR see Damase, Jean-Michel

JEUX ET CHANSONS A LA MODE DE CHEZ NOUS
see Dere, Jean

JEVA see Melartin, Erkki

JEWEL SONG see Gounod, Charles
Francois, Il Etait Un Roi De Thule

JEWETT
Teach Me To Pray *sac
low solo,pno (E flat maj) ALLANS
s.p.   (J162)
med solo,pno (F maj) ALLANS s.p.
(J163)
med-high solo,pno (G maj) ALLANS

JEWETT (cont'd.)

s.p.   (J164)
high solo,pno (A flat maj) ALLANS
s.p.   (J165)

JEWISH FOLK SONGS *CC40U,folk,Jew
(Rubin, Ruth) solo,pno OAK 000082
$3.95 Yiddish and English Texts
(J166)

JEWISH FOLKSONGS *CCU,folk,Jew
(Stutschewsky, Y.) solo,pno OR-TAV
$2.00   (J167)

JEWISH FOLKSONGS *CC95U,folk,Jew
(Seculetz, Emil) solo,pno OR-TAV
$4.00 with Yiddish and Hebrew text
(J168)

JEWISH SONG HITS BOOK *CCUL,Jew
(Estella, Joseph M.) solo,pno KAMMEN
$1.95   (J169)

JEWISH THEATRE SONGS, VOL. 1 *CC24L,
Jew
solo,pno KAMMEN $2.50
see also: Ellstein, Abe, Zug Es Mir
Noch Amuhl; Ellstein, Abe, Zug
Far Vus; Gilrod, Louis, A Malke
Auf Paissach; Goldstein, Morris,
Hot A Yid A Weibele; Kammen,
Joseph, Die Oreme Yesoimele;
Kammen, Joseph, Moishe, Mach Es
Noch Amuhl; Kanapoff, F., Hoo-
Tza-Tza; Lavenda, Pincus, Die
Drei Shwester; Lillian, Isadore,
Die Sun Hot Far Mir Noch Kein
Muhl Nit Gesheint; Lillian,
Isadore, Dus Raidele Drait Sich;
Meyerowitz, David, Aheim, Aheim,
Briederlach Aheim; Meyerowitz,
David, Oisgeshpielt; Meyerowitz,
David, Wen Es Fehlt Uns A Mame's
Gebet; Meyerowitz, David, Wu Nemt
Men Parnusse; Meyerowitz, David,
Wu Sannen Meine Sieben Gute Yohr;
Meyerowitz, David, Zion's
Liedele; Olshanetsky, Alex, Ich
Benk Noch Der East Side Fin
Amuhl; Rumshinsky, Jos. M., Die
Roumanishe Kretchme; Rumshinsky,
Jos. M., Dir A Nickel, Mir A
Nickel; Rumshinsky, Jos. M.,
Meidlach, Weiblach; Rumshinsky,
Jos. M., Mein Goldele; Schwartz,
Abe, Die Shaine Yugend; Secunda,
Sholom, Shabes Tzu Nacht; Small,
Solomon, Zion, Zion Heilige,
Bleibst Shoin   (J170)

JEWISH WEDDING see Bick, Moshe

JEZ, JAKOB (1928-   )
Blick Auf Die Natur *see Pogled
Narave

Pogled Narave
"Blick Auf Die Natur" 2 soli,clar,
horn,perc solo pt GERIG HG 1111
s.p.   (J171)

Spomin
"Vergiss Mein Nicht" solo,glock,pno
GERIG HG 1044 s.p.   (J172)

Vergiss Mein Nicht *see Spomin

JEZEK, JAROSLAV (1906-1942)
Dva Revolucni Pochody *CC2U
solo,pno SUPRAPHON s.p.   (J173)

Laska Ma Pravo
"Liebe Hat Recht" med solo,pno
CZECH s.p.   (J174)

Liebe Hat Recht *see Laska Ma Pravo

Sest Pisni Pro Zpev Na Texty Jeana
Cocteau, Nezvala A Seiferta
*CC6U
solo,pno PANTON 236 s.p.   (J175)

Svet Patri Nam *CCU
solo,pno SUPRAPHON s.p.   (J176)

Tri Straznici *CC3U
solo,pno SUPRAPHON s.p.   (J177)

JEZUS EN MARIA see Felderhof, Jan

JEZUS' MOEDER see Hullebroeck, Em.

JIDDISCHE HOCHZEIT see Behrend,
Siegfried

J'IGNORE SON NOM (from Si J'Etais Roi)
T solo LEDUC s.p.   (J178)

JIHOCESKE see Novak, V.

JIHOCESKE PISNE A PISNICKY see Rychlik,
Jan

JILLETT, DAVID
Carol For A Choir Boy *sac,Xmas
boy solo/S solo,org ALBERT AE323
s.p.   (J179)

E Hehu Kerito
"Strong Is Your Love" see Jillett,
David, Mo Maria

Mo Maria *sac
"Mo Maria You Are Near" [Eng] solo,
gtr ALBERT AE257 s.p. contains
also: E Hehu Kerito, "Strong Is
Your Love"   (J180)

Mo Maria You Are Near *see Mo Maria

Strong Is Your Love *see E Hehu
Kerito

JIM MILLER SINGS see Miller, James

JIMMY OWENS SONGS see Owens, Jimmy

JIMMY SWAGGART-SONGBOOK see Swaggart,
Jimmy

JINDRICH, JINDRICH (1876-1967)
Dvanact Chodskych Pisni *CC12U
solo,pno SUPRAPHON s.p.   (J181)

Dve Melodie *CCU
solo,pno SUPRAPHON s.p.   (J182)

Kvapilovy Pisne I-II *CCU
solo,pno SUPRAPHON s.p., ea. (J183)

Letme Okamziky *CC3U
low solo,pno SUPRAPHON s.p. (J184)

Pamatce Nerudove *song cycle
med solo,pno (published in 2 vols.)
SUPRAPHON s.p., ea.   (J185)

Pisne Heydukovy *song cycle
med solo,pno SUPRAPHON s.p.   (J186)

Pisne Krasnohorske *CC5U
solo,pno SUPRAPHON s.p.   (J187)

Pisne, Ses. 1-2 *CCU
high solo,pno SUPRAPHON s.p., ea.
(J188)

Proste Motivy *CCU
med solo,pno SUPRAPHON s.p.   (J189)

Sest Lidovych Pisni *CC6U
solo,pno SUPRAPHON s.p.   (J190)

Sladkovy Pisne, Ses. 1-2 *CC20U
solo,pno SUPRAPHON s.p., ea. (J191)

Sovovy Pisne *CCU
solo,pno SUPRAPHON s.p.   (J192)

Theerovy Pisne, Ses. 1-2 *CC20U
solo,pno SUPRAPHON s.p., ea. (J193)

Vyber Z Pisni *CCU
high solo&med solo,pno SUPRAPHON
s.p.   (J194)

Wolkerovy Pisne *CC10U
high solo,pno SUPRAPHON s.p. (J195)

JIRAK, KAREL BOLESLAV (1891-1972)
Liebesblumen *see Milodejne Kviti

Lyrisches Intermezzo *CCU
[Czech/Ger] solo,pno SUPRAPHON s.p.
(J196)

Meditation *Op.8
[Czech/Ger] solo,pno SUPRAPHON s.p.
(J197)

Milodejne Kviti *song cycle
solo,pno PANTON 684 s.p.   (J198)
"Liebesblumen" high solo,pno PANTON
s.p.   (J199)

Rok
solo,pno SUPRAPHON s.p.   (J200)

Tragikomodien *Op.6, song cycle
[Czech/Ger] solo,pno SUPRAPHON s.p.
(J201)

JIRANEK, A.
Slovenske Spevy *CCU
solo,pno SUPRAPHON s.p.   (J202)

JIRASEK, IVO (1920-   )
Das Gekreuzigte Herz *see Ukrizovane
Srdce

Das Jahr Im Rostigen Wald *see Rok V
Rezavem Lese

Der Tierkreis *see Zviretnik

Hudba Pro Sopran, Fletnu A Harfu
*CCU
S solo,fl,harp PANTON 799 s.p.
(J203)

Rok V Rezavem Lese *song cycle
"Das Jahr Im Rostigen Wald" low
male solo,clar,vibra,harp,pno,vln
CZECH s.p.   (J204)

JIRASEK, IVO (cont'd.)

Schlesische Lieder *see Slezske
  Pisne

Slezske Pisne *song cycle
  "Schlesische Lieder" female solo&
  male solo,pno CZECH s.p.   (J205)

Ukolebavky *song cycle
  "Wiegenlieder" high solo,pno CZECH
  s.p.   (J206)

Ukrizovane Srdce *song cycle
  "Das Gekreuzigte Herz" low male
  solo,pno CZECH s.p.   (J207)

Wiegenlieder *see Ukolebavky

Zviretnik *song cycle
  "Der Tierkreis" 2 female soli,pno
  CZECH s.p.   (J208)

JIRIM, FRANTISEK (1837-1914)
Drobne Pesmi *CCU
  solo,pno DRUSTVO DSS 128 rental
                              (J209)

Iacobi Galli Disticha
  solo,cym,triangle,lute DRUSTVO
  DSS 503 rental   (J210)

Odsevi Hajamovih Stihov
  "Reflections On Haiam Poetry" S
  solo,chamb.grp./clar&bsn&trp&
  harp&vln&vla&vcl sc DRUSTVO
  DSS 500 rental   (J211)

Reflections On Haiam Poetry *see
  Odsevi Hajamovih Stihov

Tri Baladne Pesmi *CC3U
  Bar/B solo,pno DRUSTVO DSS 441
  rental   (J212)

Tri Murnove Pesmi *CC3U
  solo,fl,vla DRUSTVO rental (J213)

Trije Samospevi *CC3U
  solo,pno DRUSTVO DSS 55 rental
                              (J214)

JIRKO, IVO (1926-   )
Daleky Hlas *CC4U
  S solo,fl, alto flute CZECH s.p.
                              (J215)

JITRNI MONOLOGY see Dvoracek, Jiri

JO ET PRESSENTIA COM LA MAR see Mompou,
  Federico

JO ON JOULU TAALLA see Sibelius, Jean,
  Nu Sa Kommer Julen

JO TULENKI see Kilpinen, Yrio

JOB'S CURSE see Purcell, Henry

JOC D'INFANT see Vives, Amadeo

JOCHUM, OTTO (1898-1969)
Advent *sac,CC5U,Adv
  med solo,pno (med diff) MULLER 2059
  s.p.   (J216)

Advent *sac,Adv
  2058 s.p. high solo,pno MULLER
  2058A; med solo,pno MULLER 2058B
  contains: Der Ganze Wald Ist
    Silberweiss, Op.87,No.3; Ein
    Schweigen Liegt Ob
    Winterweissem Land, Op.87,No.2;
    Herr, Lass Mein Leben Wie Eine
    Kerze Sein, Op.87,No.5; Wenn
    Weisse Flocken Wald Und Feld
    Verschonen, Op.87,No.4; Wieder
    Glanzt Der Abendstern, Op.87,
    No.1   (J217)

Der Ganze Wald Ist Silberweiss
  *Op.87,No.3
  see Advent

Ein Schweigen Liegt Ob Winterweissem
  Land *Op.87,No.2
  see Advent

Eine Brautmesse *Op.21, sac,Mass
  S solo,org,vln BOHM rental (J218)

Herr, Lass Mein Leben Wie Eine Kerze
  Sein *Op.87,No.5
  see Advent

Marienlegende *Op.41, sac
  high solo,pno BOHM rental   (J219)

Wenn Weisse Flocken Wald Und Feld
  Verschonen *Op.87,No.4
  see Advent

Wieder Glanzt Der Abendstern *Op.87,
  No.1
  see Advent

JOCI VERNALES see Novak, Jan

JOCK O' HAZELDEAN *folk,Scot
  low solo,pno (E flat maj) PATERSON
  FS39 s.p.   (J220)
  high solo,pno (F maj) PATERSON FS39
  s.p.   (J221)

JOCUND DANCE, THE see Quilter, Roger

JODE, FRITZ
  Die Goldne Garbe *CCU
  solo,pno SIKORSKI 159 s.p. pap,
  cloth   (J222)

JOESPH HAYDN WERKE, REIHE XXXI: KANONS
  see Haydn, (Franz) Joseph

JOHANNA'S ARIA see Tchaikovsky, Piotr
  Ilyitch

JOHANNES 10 see Colaco Osorio-Swaab,
  Reine

JOHANNES HERBST COLLECTION, THE *sac,
  CCU
  contains works for a variety of
    instruments and vocal combinations
    microfiche UNIV.MUS.ED. reprint
    from the Archives of the Moravian
    Music Foundation, North Carolina;
    contains works by: Herbst,
    Johannes; Antes; Haydn; Hasse;
    Bach, C.P.E.; Freydt; Geisler,
    J.C.; Gregor; Latrobe; Naumann;
    Peter; Rolle;Schulz; $600.00 (J223)

JOHANNI see Niggeling, Willi

JOHANSEN, DAVID MONRAD (1888-   )
Nordlands Trompet *Op.13, CC8L
  solo,pno MUSIKK s.p.   (J224)

Syv Sanger *Op.6, CC7L
  solo,pno MUSIKK s.p.   (J225)

Ti Norske Barnerim *Op.14, CC10L
  solo,pno MUSIKK s.p.   (J226)

JOHANSSON, BENGT (1914-   )
De Aegypyo
  see Three Songs

Ite
  see Three Songs

Three Songs
  [Eng/Finn] solo,pno FAZER F 5176
  s.p.
    contains: De Aegypyo; Ite; Tree,
    The   (J227)

Tree, The
  see Three Songs

JOHN ANDERSON, MY JO *folk,Scot
  solo,pno (D min/G min) PATERSON FS40
  s.p.   (J228)

JOHN BULL VIENT S'HABILLER EN FRANCE
  see Cuvillier, Charles

JOHN CHARLES THOMAS ALBUM OF FAVORITE
  SONGS AND ARIAS *CC20L
  solo,pno SCHIRM.G $3.95 contains
  works by: Brahms; Rossini; Wagner;
  Beethoven and others   (J229)

JOHN GRUMLIE *folk,Scot
  solo,pno (A maj) PATERSON FS41 s.p.
                              (J230)

JOHN JAMES AUDUBON see Raphling, Sam

JOHN MCKAY SINGS AL WILSON *sac,CCUL
  solo,kbd SINGSPIR 5016 $1.00 (J231)

JOHN MCKAY SINGS DOROTHY HARRISON see
  Harrison, Dorothy

JOHN MCKAY SINGS JOYCE MOTT see Mott,
  Joyce Lock

JOHN MCKAY SOLOS *sac,CCUL
  (McKay, John) solo,kbd SINGSPIR $1.00
                              (J232)
JOHN PEEL
  (Dunhill, Thomas F.) solo,pno CRAMER
                              (J233)
JOHN PEEL see Cons, A.

JOHN PEEL see Mc Cabe, John

JOHN PEEL see Thomson, Virgil

JOHN PETERSON'S FOLIO OF FAVORITES see
  Peterson, John W.

JOHN W. PETERSON SONG FAVORITES FOR LOW
  VOICE *sac,CCUL
  (Peterson, John W.) A/B solo,pno
  SINGSPIR 4285 $1.95   (J234)

JOHN W. PETERSON SONG FAVORITES FOR
  TRIOS *sac,CCUL
  SSA soli,pno SINGSPIR 4289 $1.95
                              (J235)

JOHN W. PETERSON'S SONG FAVORITES see
  Peterson, John W.

JOHNEEN see Stanford, Charles Villiers

JOHNNIE COPE *folk,Scot
  solo,pno (E min/F sharp min) PATERSON
  FS42 s.p.   (J236)

JOHNNIE DRUM see Diack, John Michael

JOHNNY CASH - PRECIOUS MEMORIES *sac,
  CC32UL,gospel/hymn
  solo,pno STAMPS 4851-RN $2.95 (J237)

JOHNNY HAS GONE FOR A SOLDIER see Mc
  Cabe, John

JOHNNY SANDS see Sinclair, J.

JOHNNY SHALL HAVE A NEW BONNET see
  Rowley, Alec

JOHNNY WI' THE TYE see Heseltine,
  Philip

JOHNNYS TRIUMPHLIED see Krenek, Ernst

JOHN'S GONE DOWN ON DE ISLAND *spir
  (Burleigh, H. T.) high solo,pno
  BELWIN $1.50   (J238)
  (Burleigh, H. T.) low solo,pno BELWIN
  $1.50   (J239)

JOHNSON
Face To Face *sac
  med-high solo,pno (F maj) BOSTON
  $1.50   (J240)
  high solo,pno (G maj) BOSTON $1.50
                              (J241)
  low solo,pno (E flat maj) BOSTON
  $1.50   (J242)
  high solo,pno (G maj) ALLANS s.p.
                              (J243)
  med solo,pno (F maj) ALLANS s.p.
                              (J244)
  low solo,pno (E flat maj) ALLANS
  s.p.   (J245)
  solo,pno (available in 3 keys)
  ASHLEY $.95   (J246)

His Name So Sweet
  high solo,pno (G maj) FISCHER,C
  V 1222   (J247)

Honor! Honor!
  high solo,pno (B flat maj) FISCHER,
  C V 1220   (J248)
  low solo,pno (G maj) FISCHER,C
  V 1502   (J249)

Lift Ev'ry Voice And Sing
  high solo,pno (B flat maj) MARKS
  $1.50   (J250)
  med solo,pno (A flat maj) MARKS
  $1.50   (J251)
  solo,pno (available in 2 keys)
  ASHLEY $.95   (J252)

Ride On, King Jesus *sac
  high solo,pno (F maj) FISCHER,C
  V 2223   (J253)
  med solo,pno (E flat maj) FISCHER,C
  V 2131   (J254)
  low solo,pno (D flat maj) FISCHER,C
  V 2224   (J255)

There Is A Land *sac
  low solo,pno (F maj) ALLANS s.p.
                              (J256)
  med solo,pno (G maj) ALLANS s.p.
                              (J257)
  high solo,pno (A flat maj) ALLANS
  s.p.   (J258)

Witness
  high solo,pno (F min) FISCHER,C
  V 1478   (J259)
  med solo,pno (D min) FISCHER,C
  V 1479   (J260)

JOHNSON, HALL (1887-1970)
Le's Have A Union
  high solo,pno (G flat maj) SCHIRM.G
  $.75   (J261)

Po Moner Got A Home At Las'
  high solo,pno (F maj) SCHIRM.G $.75
                              (J262)

Swing Dat Hammer
  med solo,pno (G maj) SCHIRM.G $.75
                              (J263)
JOHNSON, NOEL
Enid Blyton's Happy Year Song Book
  *CCU
  solo,pno CRAMER   (J264)

Farewell To Summer
  high solo,pno,opt vln (D maj)
  LEONARD-ENG   (J265)
  med solo,pno,opt vln (B flat maj)
  LEONARD-ENG   (J266)
  low solo,pno,opt vln (A maj)
  LEONARD-ENG   (J267)
  2 soli,pno LEONARD-ENG   (J268)
  med-high solo,pno,opt vln (C maj) .

JOHNSON, NOEL (cont'd.)

LEONARD-ENG   (J269)

In Faith And Hope
solo,pno (F maj) LEONARD-ENG (J270)

Song Of Aiche
high solo,pno (G min) CRAMER (J271)
low solo,pno (F min) CRAMER (J272)

JOHNSON, ORIEN
His Sheep Am I *sac
solo,pno WORD S-54   (J273)

JOHNSON, P.
I Wish You All Could Know Him *sac
solo,pno BENSON S6182-R $1.00 (J274)

Life Never Came Easily *sac
solo,pno BENSON S6867-R $1.00
                           (J275)

More Than You'll Ever Know *sac
solo,pno BENSON S7047-R $1.00
                           (J276)

There Is A Light *sac
solo,pno BENSON S8111-R $1.00
                           (J277)

This Is Just What I've Been Looking
For *sac
solo,pno BENSON S8155-R $1.00
                           (J278)

When I Say Jesus *sac
solo,pno BENSON S8431-R $1.00
                           (J279)

You're Gonna Love Your New Life With
The Lord *sac
solo,pno BENSON S8589-R $1.00
                           (J280)

JOHNSON, PAUL
Four Spiritual Laws, The *sac
solo,pno WORD S-269   (J281)

JOHNSON, POLLY
Are You Saved (composed with Jayne,
Mary) *sac
solo,pno WORD S-45   (J282)

JOHNSON, T.
Trio
S solo,vcl,vibra AMP   (J283)

JOHNSON, WENDY
Property In Heaven *sac
solo,pno WORD S-447   (J284)

JOHNSTON, BEN
Four Do-It-Yourself Pieces *CC4U
any combination of singers and
performers MEDIA 2705 $4.50
                           (J285)

JOHNSTON, LYELL
Because I Were Shy
solo,pno CRAMER $1.10   (J286)

Had I But Met You
low solo,pno (G maj) LEONARD-ENG
                           (J287)
high solo,pno (B flat maj) LEONARD-
ENG   (J288)

Ould John Braddleum
solo,pno CRAMER   (J289)

Three Northern County Folk Songs
*CC3U,folk
solo,pno CRAMER   (J290)

Thro' Copse And Vale
low solo,pno (C maj) CRAMER (J291)
high solo,pno (D maj) CRAMER (J292)

Tinker Tim
solo,pno CRAMER   (J293)

JOHNSTON, R.
Bruce County Ballad
solo,pno BERANDOL BER 1317 $1.50
                           (J294)

JOHNSTON, RICHARD
Irish Book *CCU
high solo,pno WATERLOO $3.00 (J295)

JOIE see Massenet, Jules

JOIE D'AIMER see Chaminade, Cecile

JOLI BATON see Busser, Henri-Paul

JOLI JOKER see Richepin, T.

JOLI MAI see Leduc, Jacques

JOLI MAI see Symiane, Magdeleine

JOLI SEIGNEUR see Messager, Andre

JOLIVET, ANDRE (1905-1974)
Les Trois Complaintes Du Soldat
*song cycle
solo,orch DURAND s.p., ipr (J296)

Poemes Intimes *CC5U
[Fr] med solo,pno HEUGEL 10677 s.p.
                           (J297)

JOLIVET, ANDRE (cont'd.)
Suite Liturique *sac,CCU
S/T solo,English horn,vcl,harp
DURAND s.p., ipa   (J298)

JOLLY ROGER, THE see Robertson, R.
Ritchie

JOLLY TINKER
(Newton, Ernest) low solo,pno (B flat
maj) CRAMER   (J299)
(Newton, Ernest) high solo,pno (C
maj) CRAMER   (J300)

JOMMELLI, NICCOLO (1714-1774)
Miserere A Due Canti Soli *sac
[It/Ger] 2 soli,2vln,vla,bvl FORNI
s.p.   (J301)

JONATHAN JOLLYBUN see Ewing, M.

JONES
Aran Lullaby
solo,pno ALLANS s.p.   (J302)

I Won't Have To Worry Any More
(composed with Goss) *sac
solo,pno BENSON S6194-S $1.00
                           (J303)

JONES, EDWARD (1752-1824)
Shepherds Of Souls (from Sign Of The
Cross)
solo,pno CRAMER   (J304)

JONES, H.B.
I've Had A Vision Of Jesus *sac
solo,pno GOSPEL 05 TM 0430 $1.00
                           (J305)

JONES, JAMES EDMUND
My Shepherd Of Galilee *sac
low solo,pno (C maj) THOMP.G s.p.
                           (J306)
high solo,pno (E flat maj) THOMP.G
s.p.   (J307)

JONES, MARJORIE
Four Short Solos *CC4U
med solo,pno GENTRY $1.00 (J308)

Marjorie Jones Songbook, Vol. 1 *CCU
solo,pno GENTRY $3.50   (J309)

Songs Of Marjorie Jones, Vol. 1
*sac,CCUL
(Bock, Fred) high solo,pno WORD
35013 $2.50; low solo,pno WORD
35014 $2.50   (J310)

Songs Of Marjorie Jones, Vol. 2
*sac,CCUL
(Bock, Fred) high solo,pno WORD
35020 $2.50; low solo,pno WORD
35021 $2.50   (J311)

Two Encore Solos By Marjorie Jones
*CC2U
solo,pno GENTRY $1.50   (J312)

JONES, RUTH CAYE
In Times Like These *sac
solo,pno SINGSPIR 7054 $1.00 (J313)

JONG, H. DE
De Damrakkertjes *CCU
solo,pno BROEKMANS 761 s.p. (J314)

JONGE, DE.
Lievelingslied
solo,org ALSBACH s.p.   (J315)

JONGEN, JOSEPH-MARIE-ALPHONSE-NICHOLAS
(1873-1953)
Le Carnaval Des Tranchees *Op.57,
No.2
see Les Fetes Rouges

L'epiphanie Des Exiles *Op.57,No.1
see Les Fetes Rouges

Les Fetes Rouges
S solo,pno cmplt ed CBDM s.p.
contains: Le Carnaval Des
Tranchees, Op.57,No.2;
L'epiphanie Des Exiles, Op.57,
No.1; Les Languages De Feu,
Op.57,No.3   (J316)

Les Languages De Feu *Op.57,No.3
see Les Fetes Rouges

Rouge *Op.85
S solo,pno CBDM s.p.   (J317)

JONGEN, LEON (1885-   )
Chanson A Boire
B solo,pno CBDM s.p.   (J318)

Chanson D'ete
solo,pno/inst DURAND s.p. see from
Trois Poemes   (J319)

Extase
solo,pno/inst DURAND s.p. see from
Trois Poemes   (J320)

JONGEN, LEON (cont'd.)
Musique Sur L'eau
solo,pno/inst DURAND s.p. see from
Trois Poemes   (J321)

Provinciales *CC10L
med solo,pno cmplt ed CBDM s.p.
                           (J322)

Trois Poemes *see Chanson D'ete;
Extase; Musique Sur L'eau (J323)

JONGH, GEORGE DE
Willow Tree, The
low solo,pno (B flat maj) CRAMER
s.p.   (J324)
high solo,pno (D flat maj) CRAMER
$.95   (J325)

JONGHEN STIJN see Beekhuis, Hanna

JONSSON, THORARINN (1900-   )
Songs *CCU
solo,pno ICELAND s.p.   (J326)

JORDAN, ALICE
Bless The Lord, O My Soul *sac
med solo,pno ABINGDON APM-800 $1.00
                           (J327)

JORDENS ONSKAN see Nordqvist, Gustaf

JORUM see Peterson-Berger, (Olof)
Wilhelm

JOS MA LAULULLE RUPEAN see Kilpinen,
Yrio

JOS YSTAVA SULL' ON see Knorring, M.
von, Har Du En Van

JOSEPH see Mehul, H.

JOSEPH AND MARY see Butterley, Nigel

JOSEPH, DEAREST JOSEPH see Lockwood,
Normand

JOSEPH, DU SOHN DAVID see Schutz,
Heinrich

JOSEPH HAYDN WERKE, REIHE XXIX, BAND 1:
LIEDER FUR EINE SINGSTIMME see
Haydn, (Franz) Joseph

JOSEPH HAYDN WERKE, REIHE XXX:
MEHRSTIMMIGE GESANGE see Haydn,
(Franz) Joseph

JOSEPH HAYDN WERKE, REIHE XXXII, BAND
1: VOLKSLIEDBEARBEITUNGEN -
SCHOTTISCHE LIEDER NO. 1-100 see
Haydn, (Franz) Joseph

JOSEPHINE'S SONG see Sullivan, Sir
Arthur Seymour

JOSEPHS, WILFRED (1927-   )
Death Of A Young Man *Op.76b
Bar solo,3fl,2ob,2clar,2bsn,3horn,
perc,harp,cel,strings NOVELLO
rental   (J328)

Four Japanese Lyrics *song cycle
high solo,clar,pno NOVELLO s.p.
                           (J329)

Nightmusic *Op.71
A solo,2fl,2ob,2clar,2bsn,2horn,
2trp,perc,harp,cel,strings
NOVELLO rental   (J330)

JOSEPHSON, JACOB AXEL (1818-1880)
De Heilga Klockor Mana Til Bon *sac
Mez/Bar solo,pno GEHRMANS s.p.
                           (J331)

Den Resande Studenten *Op.24,No.4
see Fyra Sanger
high solo,pno GEHRMANS s.p. (J332)
low solo,pno GEHRMANS s.p.   (J333)

Fyra Sanger
solo,pno GEHRMANS s.p.
contains: Den Resande Studenten,
Op.24,No.4; Hymn, Op.24,No.2;
Se Glad Ut, Op.24,No.3; Varme
Och Ljus, Op.24,No.1   (J334)

Hymn *Op.24,No.2
see Fyra Sanger

I Skogen
high solo,pno GEHRMANS s.p. (J335)
med solo,pno GEHRMANS s.p.   (J336)

Langtan Fran Havet
high solo,pno GEHRMANS s.p. (J337)
med solo,pno GEHRMANS s.p.   (J338)

Lovoffer
low solo,pno GEHRMANS 782 s.p.
                           (J339)
high solo,pno GEHRMANS 789 s.p.
                           (J340)
med solo,pno GEHRMANS 775 s.p.
                           (J341)

JOSEPHSON, JACOB AXEL (cont'd.)

Se Glad Ut   *Op.24,No.3
see Fyra Sanger

Sjung, Sjung Du Underdara Sang
low solo,pno GEHRMANS s.p.   (J342)

Stjarnklart
high solo,pno GEHRMANS 778 s.p.
(J343)
med solo,pno GEHRMANS s.p.   (J344)
low solo,pno GEHRMANS s.p.   (J345)

Varme Och Ljus   *Op.24,No.1
see Fyra Sanger
high solo,pno GEHRMANS s.p.   (J346)
med solo,pno GEHRMANS s.p.   (J347)

Ved Nattetid
med solo,pno GEHRMANS s.p.   (J348)
high solo,pno GEHRMANS s.p.   (J349)

JOSHUA FIT DE BATTLE OB JERICHO   *spir
(Burleigh, H. T.) solo,pno BELWIN
$1.50   (J350)

JOSHUA FIT DE BATTLE OF JERICHO
(Bonds, M.) med solo,pno MERCURY $.95
(J351)

JOSHUA FIT THE BATTLE OF JERICHO   *sac,
gospel
solo,pno ABER.GRP. $1.50   (J352)

JOSTEN, WERNER (1885-1963)
Christmas
solo,pno NEW VALLEY $1.25   (J353)

Through The Silver Mist
med solo,pno PRESSER $.75   (J354)

JOTA see Arrieta y Corera, Pascual Juan

JOTA see Breton, Tomas

JOTA see Chueca, Federico

JOTA see Falla, Manuel de

JOTA DE LOS RATAS see Chueca, Federico

JOUBERT, JOHN (1927-   )
Caged Bird
see Six Poems Of Emily Bronte,
Op.63

Fain Would I Change That Note
T solo,pno NOVELLO 17.0055.03 s.p.
(J355)

Harp
see Six Poems Of Emily Bronte,
Op.63

Immortality
see Six Poems Of Emily Bronte,
Op.63

Love Me Not For Comely Grace
T solo,pno NOVELLO 17.0107.10 s.p.
(J356)

My Love In Her Attire
T solo,pno NOVELLO 17.0122.03 s.p.
(J357)

O Come, Soft Rest Of Cares
T solo,pno NOVELLO 17.0132.00 s.p.
(J358)

Oracle
see Six Poems Of Emily Bronte,
Op.63

Six Poems Of Emily Bronte, Op.63
high solo,pno NOVELLO 17.0279.03
s.p.
contains: Caged Bird; Harp;
Immortality; Oracle; Sleep;
Storm   (J359)

Sleep
see Six Poems Of Emily Bronte,
Op.63

Stay, O Sweet, And Do Not Rise
T solo,pno NOVELLO 17.0187.08 s.p.
(J360)

Storm
see Six Poems Of Emily Bronte,
Op.63

To Spring
see Two Invocations

To Winter
see Two Invocations

Two Invocations
T solo,pno NOVELLO 17.0205.10 s.p.
contains: To Spring; To Winter
(J361)

JOUEUR DU BUGLE see Poulenc, Francis

JOUIS! C'EST AU FLEUVE see Saint-Saens,
Camille

JOULUDUETTOJA   *CCU,Xmas
(Hannikainen) 2 soli,pno FAZER F 3789
s.p.   (J362)

JOULULAULUJA see Hella, Martti

JOULULAULUJA III   *CCU,Xmas
(Sarlin, Anna) 1-2 soli,pno FAZER
W 943 s.p.   (J363)

JOULULAULUJA VI   *CCU,Xmas
(Sarlin, Anna) solo,pno FAZER W 944
s.p.   (J364)

JOULULAULUJA VIII   *CCU,Xmas
(Sarlin, Anna) solo,pno FAZER W 945
s.p.   (J365)

JOULUPUKKI KOLKUTTAA see Sibelius,
Jean, Nu Star Jul Vid Snoig Port

JOULUPUKKI KOLTUTTAA see Sibelius,
Jean, Nu Star Jul Vid Snoig Port

JOULUVIRSI see Sibelius, Jean

JOUR DE CHALEUR AUX BAINS DE MER see
Thomson, Virgil

JOUR DE JOIE see Shostakovich, Dmitri

JOUR DE PAQUES see Arensky, Anton
Stepanovitch

JOUR DE PLUIE see Saint-Saens, Camille

JOUR DE RECONNAISSANCE see
Shostakovich, Dmitri

JOUR DE RENCONTRE see Shostakovich,
Dmitri

JOUR DE SOUVENIR see Shostakovich,
Dmitri

JOUR D'OFFENSE see Shostakovich, Dmitri

JOUR FATAL OU DES DIEUX MEMES see
Lefebvre, Channing

JOUR.. SOIR see Ferrari, Gustave

JOURNEE D'AMOUR see Goublier, G.

JOURNEY see Christie, K.

JOURNEY, THE see Ireland, John

JOURNEY TO THE END OF THE NIGHT see
Feldman, Morton

JOURNEYS END see Bridge, Frank

JOUTSENLAULU see Pylkkanen, Tauno
Kullervo

JOY see Gaul, Harvey Bartlet

JOY see Mills, Charles

JOY COMES IN THE MORNING see Gaither

JOY COMETH IN THE MORNING see Wilson,
Al

JOY IS LIKE THE RAIN see Winter, Sister
Miriam Therese

JOY IS THE CENTER OF HIS WILL   *sac
(Carmichael, Ralph) solo,pno WORD
S-356   (J366)

JOY OF HEAVEN COME DOWN, THE see
Lister, Mosie

JOY OF MY HEART
(Roberton, Hugh S.) solo,pno (A maj)
ROBERTON 2532 s.p. see also Songs
Of The Isles   (J367)

JOY OF SONG, THE   *CCU
solo,pno MUSIC 080003 $2.95   (J368)

JOY ONLY HE CAN GIVE, THE see Fargason,
Eddie

JOY, SHIPMATE, JOY
see Three Poems Of Walt Whitman

JOY THAT DWELLS IN TWO HEARTS THAT LOVE
see Alnaes, Eyvind, Lykken Mellem
To Mennesker

JOY THAT JESUS GIVES, THE see Wolfe,
Lanny

JOY, VIRGINIA
Feed My Sheep   *sac
high solo,pno (E flat maj) FISCHER,
C V 2337   (J369)

JOYFUL AND WOEFUL see Beethoven, Ludwig
van, Freudvoll Und Leidvoll

JOYFUL HYMN OF TOIL see Shir Ha-Avoda

JOYS OF LOVE, THE see Martini, Jean
Paul Egide, Plaisir D'Amour

J'SUIS BETE see Charton, G.

JUBAL see Sibelius, Jean

JUBELLIED see Hullebroeck, Em.

JUBILATE DEO see Campra, Andre

JUBILATE DEO see Schutz, Heinrich

JUBILATE DEO OMNIS TERRA see Schutz,
Heinrich

JUBILATE DOMINO see Buxtehude, Dietrich

JUBILATION!   *sac,CC100UL
solo,pno WORD 37751 $6.95   (J370)

JUBILEE SPIRITUALS   *sac,CC196UL,
gospel/spir
solo,pno STAMPS 4837-SN $1.95   (J371)

JUBILENT OMNES see Riccio, Giovanni
Battista

JUDE, WILLIAM HERBERT (1851-1922)
Consecration Hymn   *sac
solo,pno WORD S-73   (J372)

Skipper, The
low solo,pno (B flat maj) ASHDOWN
(J373)
med solo,pno (C maj) ASHDOWN   (J374)
high solo,pno (D maj) ASHDOWN
(J375)

Tar's Lass
low solo,pno (C maj) CRAMER   (J376)
high solo,pno (D maj) CRAMER   (J377)

JUDGMENT see Ames, William

JUDITH SYMPHONIE see Guillou, Jean

JUDITHA TRIUMPHANS see Vivaldi, Antonio

JUDITHS LIEBESLIED see Eyken, Heinrich
van

JUEL-FREDERIKSEN, EMIL
Moderens Sang
solo,pno MUSIKK s.p.   (J378)

JUG OF PUNCH, THE see Wood, Charles

JUHANNUSTULILLA see Merikanto, Oskar

JUICHT DE VREEZON IS VERREZEN see
Bonset, Jac.

JUILLET see Georges, Alexandre

JUIN: ROSES, CERISES, PARFUMS see
Privas, Xavier

JUJENA see Lopez-Buchardo, Carlos

JUL see Munktell

JUL see Raebel, M.

JUL, JUL, STRALANDE JUL see Nordqvist,
Gustaf

JULAFTON see Ahlen, Waldemar

JULDUETTER   *CCU,Xmas
(Hannikainen, V.) 2 soli,pno FAZER
F 3789 s.p.   (J379)

JULEN AR KOMMEN
see En Liten Julhalsning

JULENS ALLA VACKRA KLOCKOR RINGEN see
Sjogren, Emil

JULESALME see Tonnessen, Peder

JULESANG see Nielsen, Carl

JULIA see Andriessen, Juriaan

JULIA! see Denza, Luigi

JULIAN'S GARDEN see Thompson, Ann
Harding

JULINACHT see Schilling, M. von

JULINDER   *CC3U,Xmas
solo,pno,lute LUNDQUIST s.p.   (J380)

JULOTTESANG see Riccius, August
Ferdinand

JULSANG see Adam, Adolphe-Charles

JULSANG see Adam, Adolphe-Charles,
Cantique De Noel

JULSANG see Alfven, Hugo

JULSANG see Nordqvist, Gustaf

JULY RAIN see Mechem, Kirke

JUMP, JIM CROW see Romberg, Sigmund

JUNE see Quilter, Roger

JUNE DAY, A see Kagen, Sergius

JUNE IS IN MY HEART see Vaughan

JUNE MAGIC see Spencer, Marquerita

JUNE ROSES see Bizet, Georges, Berceuse

JUNE TWILIGHT see Wishart, Peter

JUNG HEXENLIED see Strauss, Richard

JUNG IST MEIN HERZ see Bijvanck, Henk

JUNGE LIEBE see Borris, Siegfried

JUNGE LYRIK see Ranta, Sulho

JUNGFRU MARIA see Liljefors, Ruben

JUNGFRULIN see Lidholm, Ingvar

JUNGFRUN UNDER LIND see Peterson-
    Berger, (Olof) Wilhelm

JUNGGESELLENSCHWUR see Strauss, Richard

JUNIDAGEN LEKTE see Nordqvist, Gustaf

JUNINATT see Braein, Edvard Fliflet

JUNKER NILS SJUNGER TILL LUTAN see
    Hallen, Andreas

JUNKERNS SERENAD see Rangstrom, Ture

JUNKMAN, THE see Swanson, Howard

JURAFSKY, ABRAHAM
    Cancion De La Nina Gaucha
        see Cuatro Canciones Al Estilo
        Popular Argentino

    Copla
        see Tres Canciones

    Coplas
        [Span] solo,pno cmplt ed RICORDI-
        ARG BA 8506 s.p.
        contains: En La Punta De Aquel
        Cerro; Que Me Has Hecho, Que Me
        Has Hecho!; Sin Poder Con Esta
        Lengua   (J381)

    Cuatro Canciones Al Estilo Popular
    Argentino
        [Span] solo,pno cmplt ed RICORDI-
        ARG BA 11038 s.p.
        contains: Cancion De La Nina
        Gaucha; La Tapera; Nostalgia;
        Se Casa El Boyero   (J382)

    En La Punta De Aquel Cerro
        see Coplas

    La Tapera
        see Cuatro Canciones Al Estilo
        Popular Argentino

    Nostalgia
        see Cuatro Canciones Al Estilo
        Popular Argentino

    Poema Para Una Muerta Voz
        see Tres Melodias

    Que Me Has Hecho, Que Me Has Hecho!
        see Coplas

    Romance De La Muerte Temprana
        see Tres Melodias

    Se Casa El Boyero
        see Cuatro Canciones Al Estilo
        Popular Argentino

    Sin Poder Con Esta Lengua
        see Coplas

    Tarde
        see Tres Melodias

    Tres Canciones
        [Span] solo,pno cmplt ed RICORDI-
        ARG BA8502 s.p.
        contains: Copla; Vidala; Vidalita
                                 (J383)

    Tres Melodias
        [Span] solo,pno cmplt ed RICORDI-
        ARG BA 10995 s.p.
        contains: Poema Para Una Muerta
        Voz; Romance De La Muerte
        Temprana; Tarde   (J384)

    Vidala
        see Tres Canciones

    Vidalita
        see Tres Canciones

JUROVSKY, SIMON (1912-1963)
    Muskat *song cycle
    S solo,pno SLOV.HUD.FOND s.p.
                                 (J385)

JUS' A SMILE I'M MISSIN' see Bennett,
    Sir William Sterndale

JUSQU'A DEMAIN! see Delmet, Paul

JUST see Bradford, John

JUST A BIT see Sandstrom, Sven-David

JUST A CLOSER WALK WITH THEE *sac
    solo,pno ASHLEY $.95   (J386)
    (Jarrett) solo,pno BENSON S6780-S
    $1.00   (J387)

JUST A CLOSER WALK WITH THEE see Foley

JUST A CLOSER WALK WITH THEE see
    Winsett

JUST A LITTLE TALK WITH JESUS *sac,
    gospel
    solo,pno ABER.GRP. $1.50   (J388)

JUST A LITTLE WHILE FROM NOW see
    Capshaw, Betty

JUST A MOTHER WITH A BABY see Wilson,
    John F.

JUST A ROSE WILL DO *sac,gospel
    solo,pno ABER.GRP. $1.50   (J389)

JUST A-WEARYIN' FOR YOU see Bond,
    Carrie Jacobs

JUST ACROSS THE STREET see Stewart,
    Bromley

JUST AS I AM (from Purpose) sac
    solo,pno BROADMAN 4590-14 $.75 (J390)

JUST AS I AM see Haeussler, P.

JUST BECAUSE I ASKED see Harris, Ron

JUST BECAUSE THE VIOLETS see Russell,
    Kennedy

JUST COUNT THE STARS see Grey, F.H.

JUST FOR TODAY see Abbott, Jane

JUST FOR TODAY see Seaver

JUST FOR YOU *sac,CCUL
    3 female soli,pno,opt gtr SINGSPIR
    5836 $1.50   (J391)

JUST LIKE HE SAID HE WOULD see Crouch,
    Andrae

JUST ONE DAY AT A TIME see Orton, Irv

JUST SPRING see Duke

JUST TAKE HIM AT HIS WORD see
    Richardson, Betsy

JUST TO BE NEAR YOU see Fox, Albert

JUST TO HAVE YOU, DEAR JESUS *sac
    solo,pno STAMPS 7262-SN $1.00 (J392)

JUSTIFIED BY FAITH see Jensen, Gordon

JUSTUS GERMINAVIT see Sieprawski, Pawel

K

K CUARTO CANCIONES ARGENTINAS see
    Guastavino, Carlos

'K HOORE TUITEND' HOORNEN see
    Mortelmans, Lodewijk

'K HOU VAN HOLLAND see Bute, C.J.

K L'UDU see Holoubek, Ladislav

'K WIL U EENS WAT ZEGGEN see Zagwijn,
    Henri

'K WIL U EENS WAT ZEGGEN see Zweers,
    [Bernard]

'K WIL U EENS WAT ZEGGEN BLONDJE see
    Dresden, Sem

'K WIL U EENS WAT ZEGGEN, BLONDJE see
    Zagwijn, Henri

'K ZAL MIJ VAN TE DICHTEN ZWICHTEN see
    Mul, Jan

KABALEVSKY, DMITRI BORISOVITCH
    (1904-   )
    Dix Sonnets De Shakespeare *CC10U
    [Fr] solo,pno cmplt ed CHANT s.p.
                                 (K1)

KABURAGI, MITSUGU (1926-   )
    Afternoon, The
        see Highland Fragments

    At The Next House
        see Highland Fragments

    Crab, A
        see Highland Fragments

    Highland Fragments
        [Eng/Jap] solo,pno JAPAN 7103 s.p.
        contains: Afternoon, The; At The
        Next House; Crab, A; Road, A;
        Rock, A   (K2)

    Poems Of The Sea *song cycle
        [Eng/Jap] solo,pno JAPAN 7203 s.p.
                                 (K3)

    Road, A
        see Highland Fragments

    Rock, A
        see Highland Fragments

KACHA-KACH see Weinberg, Jacob

KADDISCH see Ravel, Maurice

KADDISH see Stein, Leon

KADOSA, [PAUL] (1903-   )
    Folk Song Cantata *Op.30
    [Hung/Ger] solo,clar,vln,pno
    BUDAPEST 3663 s.p.   (K4)

    Four Songs *Op.4, CC4U
    solo,pno BUDAPEST 7131 s.p. (K5)

    Four Songs On The Poems By Nelly
    Sachs *CC4U
    [Hung/Ger] solo,pno BUDAPEST 6572
    s.p.   (K6)

    Seven Petofi Songs *Op.44a, CC7U
    [Hung] solo,pno BUDAPEST 470 s.p.
                                 (K7)

    Seven Songs *CC7U
    [Hung/Ger] solo,pno BUDAPEST 4677
    s.p.   (K8)

    Still Songs *Op.46b, CCU
    [Hung] solo,pno BUDAPEST 2854 s.p.
                                 (K9)

    Three Radnoti Songs *CC3U
    [Hung/Ger] solo,pno BUDAPEST 4184
    s.p.   (K10)

    Three Songs *CC3U
    [Hung] solo,pno BUDAPEST 2714 s.p.
                                 (K11)

KAEN KUKKUESSA see Kauppi, Emil

KAFENDA, FRICO (1883-1963)
    Oda Na Mladost'
    S solo,pno SLOV.HUD.FOND s.p. (K12)

    Styri Piesne *CC4U
    male solo,pno SLOV.HUD.FOND s.p.
                                 (K13)

    Tri Miniaturne Piesne *CC3U
    high solo,pno SLOV.HUD.FOND s.p.
                                 (K14)

KAFFEE-KANTATE see Bach, Johann
    Sebastian, Schweigt Stille,
    Plaudert Nicht

KAFFEEKANTATE see Bernier, Nicolas, Le
Cafe

KAFFEGRUT OG FANTASI see Ludt, Finn

KAGEL, MAURICIO (1931-   )
Recitativarie
solo,cembalo UNIVER. 15620 $5.75
(K15)

KAGEN, SERGIUS (1909-1964)
Drum
med solo,pno PRESSER $.75   (K16)

How Pleasant It Is To Have Money
high solo,pno MERCURY $.95   (K17)

I Think I Could Turn
B solo,pno PRESSER $.75   (K18)

I'm Nobody
solo,pno WEINTRB $1.50   (K19)

June Day, A
solo,pno WEINTRB $1.50   (K20)

Let It Be Forgotten
solo,pno WEINTRB $1.50   (K21)

London
med solo,pno PRESSER $.75   (K22)

Mag
solo,pno WEINTRB $1.50   (K23)

Maybe
solo,pno WEINTRB $1.50   (K24)

Memory, Hither Come
med solo,pno PRESSER $.75   (K25)

Miss T
solo,pno WEINTRB $1.50   (K26)

Three Satires *CC3U
med solo,pno PRESSER $1.50   (K27)

Upstream
solo,pno WEINTRB $1.50   (K28)

KAHN-ALBUM, BAND I: AUSERLESENE LIEDER
see Kahn, Robert

KAHN-ALBUM, BAND II: "LIEBESFRUHLING",
OP. 34 see Kahn, Robert

KAHN, ERICH ITOR (1905-1956)
Altdeutsches Lied
med solo,pno AM.COMP.AL. $.82 (K29)

Four Nocturnes *CC4U
S solo,pno AM.COMP.AL. $9.90   (K30)

Four Pieces On Medieval German Poems
*CC4U
S solo,pno AM.COMP.AL. $6.60   (K31)

Music For Ten Instruments And Soprano
S solo,2fl,2ob,3clar,horn,vcl,bvl
AM.COMP.AL. sc $13.20, voc sc
$3.85   (K32)

Trois Chansons Populaires *CC3U,Fr
Mez solo,pno AM.COMP.AL. $3.85
(K33)

Trost
high solo,pno AM.COMP.AL. $.82
(K34)

Two Psalms *CC2U,Psalm
Mez solo,pno AM.COMP.AL. $3.85
(K35)

KAHN, GERALD
Happy Summer Song
low solo,pno (C maj) ASHDOWN (K36)
high solo,pno (F maj) ASHDOWN (K37)
med-high solo,pno (E flat maj)
ASHDOWN   (K38)
med solo,pno (D maj) ASHDOWN (K39)

KAHN, PERCY B. (PERCIVAL BENEDICT)
(1880-   )
Song Of The Chase
solo,pno CRAMER $.95   (K40)

KAHN, ROBERT (1865-1951)
Ave Maria *sac
low solo,pno (F maj) ALLANS s.p.
(K41)
high solo,pno (G maj) ALLANS s.p.
(K42)
Kahn-Album, Band I: Auserlesene
Lieder *CCU
[Ger/Eng] high solo,pno LEUCKART
s.p.   (K43)

Kahn-Album, Band II:
"Liebesfruhling", Op. 34 *CCU
LEUCKART s.p. high solo,pno; med
solo,pno; low solo,pno   (K44)

KAHOWEZ, GUNTER (1940-   )
Sommerpoesie - Winterpoesie
S solo,ob,clar,trom,perc,pno,vla
MODERN rental   (K45)

KAHRI, JALMARI
Beetlehem, Beetlehem *sac
solo,pno FAZER W 3777 s.p.   (K46)

KAIKISSA YKSIN see Kilpinen, Yrio

KAINAR BEIM WASSER see Rezac, Ivan,
Kainar U Vody

KAINAR U VODY see Rezac, Ivan

KAIPAAVA see Melartin, Erkki

KAIPAUS see Kaski, Heino

KAISER, KURT
Are You In Control Lord? *sac
solo,pno WORD S-512   (K47)

Bring Back The Springtime *sac
solo,pno WORD S-295   (K48)
solo,pno WORD S-296   (K49)

Conform *sac
solo,pno WORD S-103   (K50)

From Out Here *sac
solo,pno WORD S-253   (K51)

God Is Here Right Now *sac
solo,pno WORD S-510   (K52)

Good Old Days *sac
solo,pno WORD S-104   (K53)

Hush, The Baby Is Sleeping *sac
solo,pno WORD S-392   (K54)

It's Our World *sac
solo,pno WORD S-255   (K55)

Master Designer *sac
solo,pno WORD S-95   (K56)

Moment Of Truth, The *sac
solo,pno WORD S-254   (K57)

Nothing But Amazing *sac
solo,pno WORD S-513   (K58)

Oh How He Loves You And Me *sac
solo,pno WORD S-463   (K59)

Pass It On *sac
solo,pno WORD S-102   (K60)
solo,pno BENSON S7350-R $1.00 (K61)

Reach Your Hand *sac
solo,pno WORD S-351   (K62)

Sunday Mornin' *sac
solo,pno WORD S-440   (K63)

That's For Me *sac
solo,pno WORD S-105   (K64)

That's The Way It Is *sac
solo,pno WORD S-99   (K65)

KAISER, RALPH L.
God Gave Me You
high solo,pno FOX,S   (K66)
high solo&low solo,pno FOX,S (K67)
med solo&low solo,pno FOX,S (K68)
ST soli,pno FOX,S   (K69)
low solo,pno FOX,S   (K70)
med solo,pno FOX,S   (K71)

KAISERWALZER see Strauss, Johann

KAIUTAR see Sibelius, Jean

KAKOA KUULLESSA see Kilpinen, Yrio

KAKONEN SE KUKKUU see Simila, Arpo

KAKS' OLI MEITA KAUNOKAISTA see
Kilpinen, Yrio

KAKSI HENGELLISTA LAULUA see Kuusisto,
Taneli

KAKSI KARJALAISTA KANSANLAULUA see
Linnala, Eino

KAKSI LAULUA see Klemetti, Heikki

KAKSI LAULUA see Kauppi, Emil

KAKSI LAULUA see Kuula, Toivo

KALABIS, VIKTOR (1923-   )
Ptaci Svatby *CCU
T solo,pno CZECH s.p.   (K72)

KALANZI
Bantu And You, The *CCU,Afr
solo,pno EULENBURG GM 3 s.p. (K73)

KALAS, JULIUS (1902-1967)
Spanelsky Kruh *CC5U
Bar solo,pno CZECH s.p.   (K74)

KALEIDOSKOP see Pauer, Jiri

KALIK, VACLAV (1891-1951)
Intermezzo
solo,pno SUPRAPHON s.p.   (K75)

KALINENKO, K.
Lullaby
[Russ] MezBar soli,orch sc MEZ
KNIGA 15 s.p.   (K76)

KALINKA *folk,Russ
[Ger/Russ] solo,pno ZIMMER. 1726 s.p.
(K77)
[Ger/Russ] solo,acord ZIMMER. 1826
s.p.   (K78)

KALLAN see Lagercrantz, Wilhelm

KALLAN see Svedbom, Vilhelm

KALLAUSCH, KURT
Mittagswelt *cant
S solo,2fl,2ob,2clar,2bsn,4horn,
2trp,3trom,timp,perc,strings,pno
BREITKOPF-L rental   (K79)

KALLELSEROK see Sonninen, Ahti,
Ehatyssavu

KALLIOPE see Zagwijn, Henri

KALLSTENIUS, EDVIN (1881-   )
Arioso For Brudvigsel
solo,pno GEHRMANS s.p.   (K80)

KALMAN
Love's Own Sweet Song
high solo,pno MARKS $1.50   (K81)
med solo,pno MARKS $1.50   (K82)

KALMAN, EMERICH (1882-1953)
Ah, Non Avessi (from La Baiadera)
[It] solo,pno BONGIOVANI 924 s.p.
(K83)

Baciami Pure In Benares (from La
Baiadera)
[It] solo,pno BONGIOVANI 920 s.p.
(K84)

Caro, Io Voglio Un Boa Di Struzzo
(from La Baiadera)
[It] solo,pno BONGIOVANI 921 s.p.
(K85)

Credi, Carina, E Grace Error (from La
Baiadera)
[It] solo,pno BONGIOVANI 913 s.p.
(K86)

Dimmi Di Si! (from Contessa Mariza)
[It] solo,pno BONGIOVANI 974 s.p.
(K87)

Fior Di Loto Sbocci (from La
Baiadera)
[It] solo,pno BONGIOVANI 916 s.p.
(K88)

Il Piccolo Bar (from La Baiadera)
[It] solo,pno BONGIOVANI 919 s.p.
(K89)

Komm' Zigany (from La Condesa Mariza)
"Ven Gitano" [Ger/Span] solo,pno
RICORDI-ARG BA10045 s.p.   (K90)

O Bajadera (from La Baiadera)
[It] solo,pno BONGIOVANI 914 s.p.
(K91)

O Piccol Bel Cavalier (from La
Baiadera)
[It] solo,pno BONGIOVANI 918 s.p.
(K92)

Occhi Fondi Neri (from La Baiadera)
[It] solo,pno BONGIOVANI 922 s.p.
(K93)

Quand' In Cielo Brillan Le Stelle
(from La Baiadera)
[It] solo,pno BONGIOVANI 917 s.p.
(K94)

Se Poteste Sol Pensare (from La
Baiadera)
[It] solo,pno BONGIOVANI 915 s.p.
(K95)

Signorina Vuol (from La Baiadera)
[It] solo,pno BONGIOVANI 923 s.p.
(K96)

Ti Guardi Il Ciel (from Contessa
Mariza)
[It] solo,pno BONGIOVANI 972 s.p.
(K97)

Ven Gitano *see Komm' Zigany

Vieni A Varasdin! (from Contessa
Mariza)
[It] solo,pno BONGIOVANI 973 s.p.
(K98)

Vorrei Sognare Di Te (from Contessa
Mariza)
[It] solo,pno BONGIOVANI 971 s.p.
(K99)

KALMANOFF, MARTIN (1920-   )
Lion And The Lamb, The
solo,pno ELKAN-V $.95   (K100)

KALME RUST see Hullebroeck, Em.

KALOMIRIS, MANOLIS
Iambes Et Anapestes *CC7L
[Fr/Greek] high solo,pno SALABERT-
US $13.50   (K101)

KAM' ZU MIR DER GELIEBTE MEIN see
   Kilpinen, Yrio, Kun Mun Kultani
   Tulisi

KAMAAL see Michael, Edward

KAMINSKI, HEINRICH (1886-1946)
   Lied Eines Gefangenen
      med solo,pno/org (med easy) BAREN.
      2137 $2.75   (K102)

KAMMEN, JOSEPH
   Die Oreme Yesoimele *Jew
      solo,pno KAMMEN 30 $1.00 see also
      JEWISH THEATRE SONGS, VOL. 1
                                    (K103)

   Moishe, Mach Es Noch Amuhl (composed
      with Kanapoff, F.) *Jew
      solo,pno KAMMEN 58 $1.00 see also
      JEWISH THEATRE SONGS, VOL. 1
                                    (K104)

KAMMERKANTATE NACH SONETTEN DER LOUIZE
   LABE see Beck, Conrad

KAMMERMUSIK see Bijvanck, Henk

KAMMERMUSIK see Blendinger, Herbert

KAMMERMUSIK 1958 UBER DIE HYMNE "IN
   LIEBLICHER BLAUE" VON HOLDERLIN see
   Henze, Hans Werner

KAMRAT! see Korling, August

KAN DET TROSTE see Kjerulf, [Halfdan]

KAN-TOUK see Edwards, Ross

KANA see Kelterborn, Rudolf

KANAPOFF, F.
   Hoo-Tza-Tza *Jew
      solo,pno KAMMEN 57 $1.00 see also
      JEWISH THEATRE SONGS, VOL. 1
                                    (K105)

   Moishe, Mach Es Noch Amuhl *see
      Kammen, Joseph

KANARIENVOGEL-KANTATE see Telemann,
   Georg Philipp

KANERVAN KUKKA see Jalkanen, Teppo

KANJAG VAL GLOMMA see Merikanto, Oskar,
   Muistellessa

KANN ICH IM BUSEN HEISSE WUNSCHE
   TRAGEN? see Diepenbrock, Alphons

KANN MICH AUCH AN EIN MADEL ERINNERN
   see Strauss, Richard

KANNEL see Simila, Arpo

KANNER DU VAL DET LAND see Thomas,
   Ambroise, Connais-Tu Le Pays

KANNER NI FIA JANSSON see Norlander,
   Emil

KANONENSONG see Weill, Kurt

KANSAN VIRSI KANSAN SUUSSA see Strahle,
   L.J.G.

KANSANLAULU see Merikanto, Oskar

KANSANLAULUJA KAKISALMELTA I-III see
   Melartin, Erkki

KANSANSAVELMA
   (Ranta, Sulho) "Folk Tune" solo,pno
   FAZER F 3346 s.p.   (K106)

KANSKE FINGE DU RO see Nordqvist,
   Gustaf

KANTAT II see Matousek, Lukas

KANTATE see Moeschinger, Albert

KANTELEENI see Haapasalo, Kreeta

KANTELETAR-LIEDER, OP. 100 see
   Kilpinen, Yrio

KANZONETTEN UND ARIE see Zambona, H.G.

KAPP, PAUL
   Cat Came Fiddling, A *CCU
      solo,pno GENERAL 157 $2.95   (K107)

   Cock-A-Doodle-Doo! *CCU
      solo,pno GENERAL 208 $2.95   (K108)

KAPPEL, FRITZ
   Volkalwerke (Aus Dem Nachlass) *CCU
      solo,pno KRENN 1.9 s.p.   (K109)

KAPR, JAN (1914-   )
   Contraria Romana *CC8U
      solo,pno GENERAL 729 $5.00   (K110)

   Krystal *song cycle
      T solo,pno SUPRAPHON s.p.   (K111)

KAPR, JAN (cont'd.)
   Milostne Pisne *CCU
      Bar solo,pno SUPRAPHON s.p.   (K112)

   Nove Ceskoslovensko *CCU
      solo,pno SUPRAPHON s.p.   (K113)

   Quartet No. 6
      Bar solo,strings GENERAL 724SU
      $10.00   (K114)

   Ubungen Fur Koloratursopran *CCU
      [Czech/Ger] coloratura sop,fl,harp
      SUPRAPHON s.p.   (K115)

   Zpev Matky (from Muzikantska Pohadka)
      see ARIE A ZPEVY ZE SOUCASNYCH
      OPER: ALT

KAPRAL, VACLAV (1889-1947)
   Milodejne Kviti *CC5U
      high solo,pno SUPRAPHON s.p.   (K116)

KAPRALOVA, VITESLAZA (1915-1940)
   Navzdy *CC3U
      high solo,pno SUPRAPHON s.p.   (K117)

   Sbohem A Satecek *CCU
      solo,orch SUPRAPHON s.p.   (K118)

KARA, LAT DU SKARAN VARA see Sonninen,
   Ahti, Anna, Armas, Sirpin Olla

KARASTE GOK, SOM GAL UTI FJARRAN
   Mez/Bar solo,pno GEHRMANS 222 s.p.
      contains also: Forsmadd   (K119)

KARDOS, DEZIDER (1914-   )
   Piesne O Laske *CCU
      high solo,pno SLOV.HUD.FOND s.p.
                                     (K120)

   Pomozeme Slavikovi *CCU
      boy solo/girl solo,pno,acord
      SLOV.HUD.FOND s.p.   (K121)

   Spevy Z Vychodneho Slovenska *CCU
      med solo,pno SLOV.HUD.FOND s.p.
                                     (K122)

   Vychodoslovenske Spevy *CCU
      med solo,pno SLOV.HUD.FOND s.p.
                                     (K123)

KARDOS, ISTVAN
   Cyclus Antiquus *song cycle
      [Eng] solo,pno GENERAL 732 $7.50
                                     (K124)

   Five Songs *CC5U
      [Hung/Ger] solo,pno BUDAPEST 3328
      s.p.   (K125)

KAREL, RUDOLF (1880-1945)
   Im Strahl Der Hellenischen Sonne
      *CC5U
      [Czech/Ger] high solo,pno SUPRAPHON
      s.p.   (K126)

   Laska *Op.35
      solo,pno SUPRAPHON s.p.   (K127)

KARELISCHE VOLKSLIEDER AUS
   KIIHTELYSVAARA, VOLS. I-III see
   Hannikainen, Vaino

KARESTOR TRETTON NYSS JAG AGDE see
   Sonninen, Ahti, Mull' On Kultaa
   Kolmetoista

KARG-ELERT, SIGFRID (1877-1933)
   Nun Ruhen Alle Walder *Op.87,No.3
      (from Symphonischer Choral)
      med solo,org,vln BREITKOPF-W
      57 04039 s.p.   (K128)

   Three Symphonic Chorales *Op.87,
      No.1, CC3U,chorale
      [Ger] med solo,org/vln BREITKOPF-W
      $2.00   (K129)

KARHU, EDWIN T.
   Cernoch *Op.34
      solo,pno SUPRAPHON s.p.   (K130)

   To Thine Ownself Be True
      med solo,pno CENTURY PR $.60   (K131)

KARHUNPOIKA see Hannikainen, Vaino

KARIN MANSDOTTERS VAGGVISA see Boivie

KARIN MANSDOTTERS VAGGVISA FOR ERIK XIV
   see Lindblad, Adolf Fredrik

KARJAPIHASSA see Kuula, Toivo

KARJINSKY, N.
   Trois Melodies *CC3U
      [Fr] med solo,pno ESCHIG $.95
                                     (K132)

KARKOFF, MAURICE INGVAR (1927-   )
   Tre Sma Kineser Och Nio Andra
      Barnvisor *CC12U
      solo,pno GEHRMANS s.p.   (K133)

KARL EXSULTATE see Lenot, Jacques

KARLEK see Norman, Ludvig

KARLEK see Stange, Max

KARLEK PER TELEFON see Lagerheim-
   Romare, Margit

KARLEK, VIN OCH SANG
   solo,pno LUNDQUIST s.p.   (K134)

KARLEKEN AR EN ROSENLUND see Nordqvist,
   Gustaf

KARLEKENS VISA see Milveden, Ingemar

KARLIJNTJE see Hullebroeck, Em.

KARLINS, M. WILLIAM
   Four Inventions And A Fugue *CC5U
      A solo,bsn,pno sc AM.COMP.AL. $5.50
                                     (K135)
   Quartet
      S solo,strings sc AM.COMP.AL. $7.70
                                     (K136)
   Song For Soprano
      S solo,fl,vcl sc AM.COMP.AL. $3.30
                                     (K137)
   Three Songs *CC3U
      S solo,fl,pno MEDIA 3103 $3.75
                                     (K138)
   Three Songs From Sixteenth And
      Seventeenth Century Poems *CC3U
      S solo,fl,vln/vla,vcl sc
      AM.COMP.AL. $8.80, ipa   (K139)

KARLOWICZ, MIECZYSLAW (1876-1909)
   Songs (Second Edition) *CCU
      (Belza, I.) [Russ] solo,pno MEZ
      KNIGA 87 s.p.   (K140)

KARNEVAL see Svedbom, Vilhelm

KARNEVALE see Kuusisto, Ilkka

KARNTNER LIEDER, BAND II: AM WORTHER
   SEE, OP. 26 see Koschat, Thomas

KARNTNER LIEDER, BAND VIII: SECHS
   LIEDER see Koschat, Thomas

KARWOCHE see Wolf, Hugo

KASEMETS, U.
   Communications *CCU
      solo,narrator,perc BERANDOL
      BER 1124 $7.00   (K141)

   Three Miniatures *CC3U
      solo,pno BERANDOL BER 1319 $2.50
                                     (K142)

   Variations On Variations *CCU
      solo,inst,electronic tape BERANDOL
      BER 1131 $5.00   (K143)

KASHIWAGI, TOSHIO (1912-   )
   Selected Poems Of Chinese Poetesses
      From The Han To Qing Dynasties
      *CC12L
      [Jap] med-high solo,pno JAPAN 7304
      s.p. English translation of poems
                                     (K144)

KASHMIRI SONG see Woodforde-Finden, Amy

KASKI, HEINO
   Drommens Land *see Unen Maa

   Flyttfaglarna *see Muuttolinnut

   Hamaran Aania
      see Kolme Laulua

   Kaipaus
      see Kolme Laulua

   Kolme Laulua
      solo,pno FAZER F 3416 s.p.
         contains: Hamaran Aania; Kaipaus;
         Soutaa Pilvet Valkeat   (K145)

   Lahdettyas *Op.26,No.3
      solo,pno FAZER F 1450 s.p.   (K146)

   Latu *Op.54,No.2
      solo,pno FAZER F 2784 s.p.   (K147)

   Muuttolinnut
      "Flyttfaglarna" solo,pno FAZER
      F 4069 s.p.   (K148)

   Soutaa Pilvet Valkeat
      see Kolme Laulua

   Talviaamu *Op.54,No.1
      "Vintermorgon" solo,pno FAZER
      W 1832 s.p.   (K149)

   Unen Maa *Op.54,No.5
      "Drommens Land" solo,pno FAZER
      F 2846 s.p.   (K150)

   Vintermorgon *see Talviaamu

KASSANDRA see Mamangakis, Nikos

KATARINA see Peterson, John W.

KATAVASIJA see Detoni, Dubravko

KATCHKO, ADOLPH
    Acheynu Kol Beys Yisroel *sac
    [Heb/Eng] high solo,pno TRANSCON.
    WJ 414 $.85   (K151)

KATHLEEN MAVOURNEEN see Crouch, F.
    Nichols

KATHLEEN NI HOOLHAUN see Somervell,
    Arthur

KATINKA see Friml, Rudolf

KATIOUCHA see Blanter, M.

KATJIES see Mulder, Ernest W.

KATJUSCHA *folk,Russ
    [Ger/Russ] solo,pno ZIMMER. 1858 s.p.
                                         (K152)

KATO A MISEN see Frid, Geza

KATSURA see Matsudaira, Yoritsune

KATTER, VIVIAN
    Souls, Lord *sac
    solo,pno GOSPEL 05 TM 0140 $1.00
                                         (K153)

KATTFOTTERNAS VISA see Korling, Felix

KATTY GOLLAGHER see Mourant, Walter

KATZ, E.
    Six Cantus Firmus Settings *CC6U
    med solo,S rec,S rec/A rec,A rec/T
    rec AMP $.60   (K154)

KATZEN-DUETT see Rossini, Gioacchino,
    Duetto Buffo Di Due Gatti

KAUDER, HUGO (1888-   )
    Fiddler Of Dooney, The
    solo,vln sc SEESAW $2.00   (K155)

    Impetuous Heart
    solo,horn,harp sc SEESAW $2.00
                                         (K156)

    Song From "Deirdre"
    solo,fl,harp sc SEESAW $2.00 (K157)

    Who Goes With Fergus?
    solo,horn,harp sc SEESAW $2.00
                                         (K158)

KAUFMAN, H.H.
    And Thou Shalt Love The Lord
    (composed with Luskin, Samuel)
    *sac,Bar mitzvah/Cnfrm/Gen
    high solo,pno TRANSCON. TV 481 $.75
                                         (K159)
    med solo,pno TRANSCON. TV 482 $.75
                                         (K160)

KAUNEHIN KEIJUKAINEN see Arne, Thomas
    Augustine

KAUPPI, EMIL
    Kaen Kukkuessa
    see Kaksi Laulua

    Kaksi Laulua
    solo,pno FAZER F 682 s.p.
        contains: Kaen Kukkuessa; Sairas
        Soittaja   (K161)

    Kehtolaulu Naytelmasta Laivan
    Kannella *Op.29, CCU
    solo,pno FAZER F 985 s.p.   (K162)

    Laulan Lasta Nukkumahan *Op.51,No.1
    solo,pno FAZER F 1173 s.p.   (K163)

    Sairas Soittaja
    see Kaksi Laulua

    Suomalaisia Kansanlauluduettoja,
    Vols. I-II *CCU
    2 soli,pno FAZER F 3567;F 3611
    s.p., ea.   (K164)

KAUPUNGILLA SATAA see Kilpinen, Yrio

KAVATINE DES FIGARO see Rossini,
    Gioacchino, Cavatine

KAVITA 1 see Sohal, Naresh

KAVITA 2 see Sohal, Naresh

KAVITA 3 see Sohal, Naresh

KAY SEIMEN LUO see Maasalo, Armas

KAYDEN, M.
    Call Of The Prophet, The *Bibl
    high solo,pno PRESSER $.75   (K165)

    Psalm 121 *sac
    high solo,pno MERCURY $.95   (K166)

KAYN, ROLAND (1933-   )
    Phasen
    female solo,8-16perc sc ZERBONI
    7113 s.p.   (K167)

KAYSER, LEIF (1919-   )
    De Profundis Clamavi (Psalm 129)
    see Tre Salmi Per Contralto E
    Organo

    Dominus Regnat (Psalm 98)
    see Tre Salmi Per Contralto E
    Organo

    Laetata Sum (Psalm 121)
    see Tre Salmi Per Contralto E
    Organo

    Psalm 98 *see Dominus Regnat

    Psalm 121 *see Laetata Sum

    Psalm 129 *see De Profundis Clamavi

    Tre Salmi Per Contralto E Organo
    [Lat] FOG III, 137 s.p.
        contains: De Profundis Clamavi
        (Psalm 129); Dominus Regnat
        (Psalm 98); Laetata Sum (Psalm
        121)   (K168)

KAYSKELEN KUKKATARHASSAIN see
    Hannikainen, Ilmari

KAZACSAY, T.
    Lorca Songs *CCU
    [Hung] solo,pno BUDAPEST 5162 s.p.
                                         (K169)

    Pro Memoria *Op.124
    [Hung] solo,pno BUDAPEST 3928 s.p.
                                         (K170)

KDOZ JSTE BOZI BOJOVNICI see Dobias,
    Vaclav

KDYZ KVETLY STROMY NEJKRASNEJI see
    Marsik, Emanuel

KDYZ SE DVA SETKAJI see Seidel, Jan

K'E, THE see Dougherty, Celius

KEARTON, T. WILFRED
    Wanton Gales
    low solo,pno (F maj) CRAMER (K171)
    high solo,pno (A maj) CRAMER (K172)

    When The Shadows Of Evening Fall
    solo,pno CRAMER   (K173)

KEATS, HORACE
    Goneril's Lullaby
    solo,pno CRAMER   (K174)

    I Will Build My House In The Water
    solo,pno CRAMER   (K175)

    Little Birdling In A Tree
    solo,pno CRAMER $.95   (K176)

KEBY VSETKY DETI see Novak, Milan

KECHLEY, [GERALD] (1919-   )
    Carol
    "I Sing Of A Maiden" solo,pno
    PRESSER $.95   (K177)

    I Sing Of A Maiden *see Carol

KEEDY
    Dear Lord And Father Of Mankind *sac
    high solo,pno BOSTON $1.50
                                         (K178)
    Love Of God *sac
    high solo,pno (D flat maj) BOSTON
    $1.50   (K179)

KEEGAN, PATRICK
    My Soul Shall Be Joyful *sac,CC10L
    solo,pno ALBERT AE145 s.p. (K180)

KEEL, FREDERICK
    Bee's Song
    low solo,pno (B flat min) CRAMER
    $.90   (K181)
    high solo,pno (C min) CRAMER $1.00
                                         (K182)

    Bonnie George Campbell
    low solo,pno (D min) CRAMER $1.00
                                         (K183)
    high solo,pno (F min) CRAMER (K184)
    med solo,pno (E min) CRAMER $.95
                                         (K185)

    Christmas Carol
    high solo,pno (A min) CRAMER $1.15
                                         (K186)
    low solo,pno (F sharp min) CRAMER
    $1.15   (K187)

    Elizabethan Love Songs *CCU
    high solo/low solo,pno BOOSEY
    $10.00, ea. published in two
    volumes   (K188)

    Escape At Bedtime
    solo,pno CRAMER $.70   (K189)

KEEL, FREDERICK (cont'd.)
    Green Bushes
    low solo,pno (F maj) CRAMER (K190)
    high solo,pno (A maj) CRAMER (K191)

    I Lov'd A Lass, A Fair One
    solo,pno CRAMER $.95   (K192)

    Lament For Fidele
    solo,pno CRAMER $.95   (K193)

    Merry Month Of May
    solo,pno (F maj) BOOSEY $1.50
                                         (K194)
    Mocking Fairy
    low solo,pno (G maj) CRAMER s.p.
                                         (K195)
    high solo,pno (A maj) CRAMER $1.10
                                         (K196)
    Music When Soft Voices Die
    solo,pno CRAMER $.95   (K197)

    Nocturne
    solo,pno CRAMER $.95   (K198)

    Owl, The
    solo,pno CRAMER $1.10   (K199)

    Remembrance
    low solo,pno (D min) CRAMER $.95
                                         (K200)
    high solo,pno (E min) CRAMER $.95
                                         (K201)
    Sea Burthen, A
    solo,pno CRAMER $.95   (K202)

    Sergeant's Song, The
    solo,pno CRAMER $1.15   (K203)

    Ship Of Rio
    low solo,pno (E flat maj) CRAMER
                                         (K204)
    high solo,pno (F maj) CRAMER (K205)

    Song Of The Thrush
    solo,pno CRAMER   (K206)

    There Sits A Bird On Yonder Tree
    low solo,pno (E flat maj) CRAMER
    $.95   (K207)
    high solo,pno (F maj) CRAMER (K208)

    Three Salt Water Ballads *CC3U
    solo,pno BOOSEY $3.75   (K209)

    Trade Winds
    low solo,pno (E flat maj) BOOSEY
    $1.75   (K210)
    high solo,pno (F maj) BOOSEY $1.75
                                         (K211)
    Twilight
    solo,pno CRAMER $.95   (K212)

    When Icicles Hang By The Wall
    solo,pno CRAMER $.95   (K213)

KEEL ROW
    (Holford, Franz) solo,pno ALBERT
    AE147 s.p.   (K214)

KEEL ROW see Holford, Franz

KEEP A HAPPY HEART see Henson

KEEP AMERICA FREE see Moore, Judy

KEEP CHRIST IN CHRISTMAS see Hughes

KEEP ME FAITHFUL see Peters, W.F.

KEEP ON HOLDING TO THOSE NAIL-SCARRED
    HANDS see Slaughter, Henry

KEEP ON HOPIN' see Heron-Maxwell, K.

KEEP SINGIN' THAT LOVE SONG see Lee,
    Don

KEEP THAT MOMENT ALIVE see Harris, Ron

KEEP THE RUMOR GOING see Edwin, Robert

KEEP WATCHING AND PRAYING see Derricks,
    Cleavant

KEEPER OF THE PASS, THE see Dalby,
    Martin

KEEPSAKE see Malipiero, Gian Francesco

KEHTOLAULU see Jarnefelt, Armas,
    Berceuse

KEHTOLAULU see Kilpinen, Yrio

KEHTOLAULU see Jarnefelt, Armas

KEHTOLAULU NAYTELMASTA LAIVAN KANNELLA
    see Kauppi, Emil

KEINU see Kilpinen, Yrio

KEINULLA see Bergman, Erik, Lat Vid
    Gungan

KEISARI NOKKUR MAETUR MANN
  see Fimm Numer I Islenzkum
    Pjoobuningum

KEJSAR KARLS VISA see Rangstrom, Ture

KEKOBA see Tremblay, George

KELEMEN, MILKO (1924-   )
  Die Worter *cant
    [Ger] Mez solo,2fl,2clar,ob,horn,
    trp,trom,timp,perc,pno,cel,
    cembalo,harp,strings study sc
    PETERS 8041   (K215)

  Epitaph
    [Slav/Ger] Mez solo,vla,3perc,vibra
    study sc PETERS 5817 $3.50 (K216)

  Musik Fur Heissenbuttel *CCU
    Mez solo,clar,vln,vcl,pno PETERS
    8277LI s.p.   (K217)

  O Primavera *cant
    [It] T solo,strings study sc PETERS
    $4.00   (K218)

KELKEL, MANFRED (1929-   )
  Deux Melodies D'Automne *Op.1, CC2U
    high solo,pno TRANSAT. s.p. (K219)

  Le Coeur Froid
    solo,pno RICORDI-FR R 1579 s.p.
                                     (K220)
    solo,pno RICORDI-ENG 1579 s.p.
                                     (K221)

KELLAM, IAN
  As Joseph Was A-Walking *sac
    med solo,pno ELKIN 27.2525.08 s.p.
                                     (K222)

KELLER
  Organa Domestica *CC7U
    [Ger] solo,pno/inst NOETZEL N764
    s.p.   (K223)

KELLER, JOAN
  He Came Back (composed with Huffman,
    Paul) *sac
    solo,pno WORD S-466   (K224)

KELLIE, LAWRENCE (1862-1932)
  Apple Blossoms
    low solo,pno (D flat maj) CRAMER
                                     (K225)
    high solo,pno (E flat maj) CRAMER
                                     (K226)
  Douglas Gordon
    low solo,pno (E flat maj) CRAMER
                                     (K227)
    high solo,pno (C maj) CRAMER (K228)

  I Had A Flower
    low solo,pno (B flat maj) LEONARD-
    ENG   (K229)
    high solo,pno (E flat maj) LEONARD-
    ENG   (K230)

  Now Will I Sing To God
    high solo,pno (G flat maj) CRAMER
                                     (K231)
    low solo,pno (E flat maj) CRAMER
                                     (K232)
    med solo,pno (F maj) CRAMER (K233)

  She Dwelt Among The Untrodden Ways
    low solo,pno (F maj) CRAMER (K234)
    high solo,pno (A flat maj) CRAMER
                                     (K235)

KELLIGREWS SOIRREE
  see Six Regional Canadian Folksongs

KELLING, HAJO (1907-   )
  Hessische Lieder Und Tanze *CCU
    solo,fl,ob,clar,bsn,rec,2horn,2trp,
    trom,glock,xylo,2drums,2vln,vla,
    vcl,bvl sc GERIG HG 300 s.p., ipa
                                     (K236)

KELLY, BRYAN (1934-   )
  Shield Of Achilles
    T solo,timp,perc,strings NOVELLO
    rental   (K237)

  Shield Of Achilles, The
    T solo,strings,timp,perc NOVELLO
    17.0269.06 s.p.   (K238)

  Sweetest Love
    Bar solo,pno NOVELLO 17.0190.08
    s.p.   (K239)

KELLY, EARL
  Rue Francois Premier
    med solo,pno SEESAW $1.00   (K240)

KELLY, ROBERT (1916-   )
  Raindrops
    med solo,2pno sc AM.COMP.AL. $.55
                                     (K241)
  Song Cycle *song cycle
    S solo,pno AM.COMP.AL. $6.60 (K242)

KELTERBORN, RUDOLF (1931-   )
  Auferstehung
    see Kelterborn, Rudolf, Kana

KELTERBORN, RUDOLF (cont'd.)

  Elegie *cant
    Mez solo,ob,perc,cembalo,vla MODERN
    s.p.   (K243)

  Kana *sac
    Bar solo,2vln,org (diff) BAREN.
    4456 $9.75 contains also:
    Auferstehung   (K244)

KELVIN GROVE *folk,Scot
    solo,pno (A maj/G maj) PATERSON FS123
    s.p.   (K245)

KEMP, DAVID H.
  At Michaels Gate
    low solo,pno (F maj) CRAMER (K246)
    high solo,pno (A flat maj) CRAMER
                                     (K247)
  Bashful Tom
    low solo,pno (C maj) CRAMER (K248)
    high solo,pno (D maj) CRAMER (K249)

  Billy
    low solo,pno (E flat maj) CRAMER
                                     (K250)
    high solo,pno (F maj) CRAMER (K251)

  Border Cradle Song
    low solo,pno (G maj) CRAMER (K252)
    high solo,pno (A flat maj) CRAMER
                                     (K253)
KEMPER
  God's Messenger *sac
    solo,pno ALLANS s.p.   (K254)

KEMPINSKI, LEO A. (1891-1958)
  Enter In O Christ *sac
    med solo,pno BELWIN $1.50   (K255)

KENDRICK, VIRGINIA
  Before The World Was *sac,Bibl
    high solo,pno SCHMITT $1.50 (K256)
    low solo,pno SCHMITT $1.50   (K257)
    med solo,pno SCHMITT 104 $1.50
                                     (K258)
  From My Window
    solo,pno FOX,S   (K259)

  Green Is The Willow
    med solo,pno BELWIN $1.50   (K260)

  I Will Lift Up Mine Eyes Unto The
    Hills (Psalm 121) sac
    med-high solo,pno SCHMITT 112 $1.75
                                     (K261)
  Psalm 121 *see I Will Lift Up Mine
    Eyes Unto The Hills

  White Sky
    med solo,pno BELWIN $1.50   (K262)

KENDRICKS, VIRGINIA
  Music Is Beauty
    solo,pno CRESCENDO $1.00   (K263)

KENNEDY
  Star Of The East *sac,Xmas
    solo,pno HARRIS $.75   (K264)
    high solo,pno (D flat maj) FISCHER,
    C S 7648   (K265)
    med solo,pno (F maj) FISCHER,C
    S 7646   (K266)
    low solo,pno (E flat maj) FISCHER,C
    S 7647   (K267)
    med solo,pno (F maj) CENTURY 3871
    $.40   (K268)
    solo,pno (available in 3 keys)
    ASHLEY $.95   (K269)
    SA soli,pno LORENZ $1.00   (K270)

KENNEDY, DION W.
  Song Of Consecration *sac
    high solo,pno BELWIN $1.50   (K271)

KENNEDY, JAMES I.
  Where The River Shannon Flows
    solo,pno (C maj) ALLANS s.p. (K272)

KENNEDY, JOHN BRODBIN
  All Things That Heal
    solo,pno BOOSEY $1.50   (K273)

  April
    solo,pno (B flat maj) BOOSEY $1.50
    contains also: May   (K274)

  Broken Dialog
    solo,pno (C maj) BOOSEY $1.50
                                     (K275)
  May
    see Kennedy, John Brodbin, April

KENNEDY-FRASER, MARJORY (1857-1930)
  An'O, My Eppie
    solo,pno (E maj) PATERSON s.p.
                                     (K276)
    low solo,pno (C maj) PATERSON s.p.
                                     (K277)
  Islay Love Lilt, The
    low solo,pno (C maj) PATERSON s.p.
                                     (K278)
    high solo,pno (D maj) PATERSON s.p.
                                     (K279)

KENNEDY-FRASER, MARJORY (cont'd.)

  Nancy's Hair Is Yellow Like Gowd
    low solo,pno (E flat maj) PATERSON
    s.p.   (K280)
    med solo,pno (F maj) PATERSON
    s.p.   (K281)
    high solo,pno (G maj) PATERSON s.p.
                                     (K282)
  Twelve Songs From The Fourth Volume
    *CC12U
    solo,pno (easy) PATERSON s.p.
                                     (K283)
  Whistle, The
    low solo,pno (C maj) PATERSON s.p.
                                     (K284)
    high solo,pno (D maj) PATERSON s.p.
                                     (K285)

KENNST DU DAS LAND? see Schumann,
  Robert (Alexander)

KENT, MRS. ADA TWOHY
  Five Eyes *sec
    med solo,pno (A maj) WATERLOO $.75
                                     (K286)
  How Near To God *sac
    low solo,pno (C maj) WATERLOO $.75
                                     (K287)
    med solo,pno (E flat maj) WATERLOO
    $.75   (K288)

  Royal Mounted *sec
    med solo,pno (F maj) WATERLOO $.75
                                     (K289)

KENWARD, MAURICE
  Paddy's Perplexity
    solo,pno (C maj) CRAMER   (K290)

KERKEIN KEVAT RIENTAA see Sibelius,
  Jean, Varen Flyktar Hastigt

KERMISLIED see Hullebroeck, Em.

KERMISLIED see Klerk, Albert de

KERNOCHAN, JOHN M.
  As I Ride By
    low solo,pno GALAXY 1.1512.7 $1.00
                                     (K291)

KERNOCHAN, MARSHALL
  City Of Sleep
    low solo,pno GALAXY 1.0881.7 $1.00
                                     (K292)
  Lilacs
    high solo,pno GALAXY 1.0614.7 $1.00
                                     (K293)
    med solo,pno GALAXY 1.1147.7 $1.00
                                     (K294)
  Portrait
    solo,pno (E maj) GALAXY 1.0587.7
    $1.00   (K295)

  Smugglers Songs
    low solo,pno GALAXY 1.0626.7 $1.00
                                     (K296)
    high solo,pno GALAXY 1.0625.7 $1.00
                                     (K297)

KERNSPRUCHE see Rosenmuller, Johann

KERNSPRUCHEN see Rosenmuller, Johann

KEROB-SHAL see Schmitt, Florent

KERR
  I'm His To Command *sac
    solo,pno STAMPS 7261-SN $1.00
                                     (K298)
  Touch Of His Hand, The *sac
    solo,pno STAMPS 7249-SN $1.00
                                     (K299)

KERR, HARRISON (1897-   )
  Carol *carol
    high solo,4strings AM.COMP.AL. sc
    $3.30, ipa, voc sc $1.25   (K300)

KERRY DANCE see Molloy, James Lyman

KERSTERS, WILLEM (1929-   )
  Bruxellae Mariannae *Op.3,No.2
    see Zes Liederen

  Het Gevecht *Op.58
    "Le Combat" solo,pno CBDM s.p.
                                     (K301)
  Koel Is De Wereld *Op.3,No.6
    see Vier Liederen
    see Zes Liederen

  Le Combat *see Het Gevecht

  Lied *Op.3,No.3
    see Vier Liederen
    see Zes Liederen

  Salome *Op.3,No.1
    see Zes Liederen

  Tussen De Lantaaren *Op.3,No.5
    see Vier Liederen

  Tussen De Lantaarnen *Op.3,No.5
    see Zes Liederen

  Vier Liederen
    A/B solo,pno cmplt ed CBDM s.p.
    contains: Koel Is De Wereld,

KERSTERS, WILLEM (cont'd.)

    Op.3,No.6; Lied, Op.3,No.3;
    Tussen De Lantaaren, Op.3,No.5;
    Virgo, Op.3,No.4   (K302)

  Virgo *Op.3,No.4
    see Vier Liederen
    see Zes Liederen

  Zes Liederen
    S/T solo,pno cmplt ed CBDM s.p.
    contains: Bruxellae Mariannae,
      Op.3,No.2; Koel Is De Wereld,
      Op.3,No.6; Lied, Op.3,No.3;
      Salome, Op.3,No.1; Tussen De
      Lantaarnen, Op.3,No.5; Virgo,
      Op.3,No.4   (K303)

KERSTHYMNE EN OUD-JAAR see Tierie, J.F.

KERSTLICHT see Hoogenberk-Rink, D.

KERSTLIED see Andriessen, Juriaan

KERSTLIED see Bonset, Jac.

KERSTLIED see Dresden, Sem

KERSTLIED see Felderhof, Jan

KERSTLIED see Hertog, H.J. den

KERSTLIED see Weegenhuise, Johan

KERSTLIEDEREN see Noble, Felix de

KERSTLIEDJE see Wertheim, R.

KERSTLIEDJE see Bonset, Jac.

KERSTLIEDJE see Dijk, Jan van

KERSTLIEDJE see Voormolen, Alexander
  Nicolas

KERSTMIS see Klerk, Jos. de

KERSTZANG see Vladeracken, G. von

KESAAAMU see Ranta, Sulho

KESAN ONNI see Pesonen, Olavi (Samuel)

KESAYO see Kilpinen, Yrio

KESAYO KIRKKOMAALLA see Kuula, Toivo

KESAYOSSA see Kilpinen, Yrio

KESSLER, MINUETTA
  Comfirmation Prayer *sac,Bar
    mitzvah/Cnfrm/Gen
    high solo/med solo,pno TRANSCON.
    TV 495 $.75   (K304)

KETELBEY, ALBERT WILLIAM (1875-1959)
  In A Monastery Garden
    high solo,orch (G maj) ASHDOWN
    s.p., ipr   (K305)
    med solo,orch (F maj) ASHDOWN s.p.,
    ipr   (K306)
    low solo,orch (E flat maj) ASHDOWN
    s.p., ipr   (K307)

KETTING, OTTO (1935-   )
  Clown
    see Vier Gedichten Von M. Nijhoff

  De Dartele Sater
    see Minnedeuntjes

  De Schipper
    see Vier Gedichten Von M. Nijhoff

  Koridon
    see Minnedeuntjes

  Little Love-God, The
    see Three Sonnets By W. Shakespeare

  Minnedeuntjes
    Bar solo,pno DONEMUS s.p.
    contains: De Dartele Sater;
      Koridon   (K308)

  Music To Hear
    see Three Sonnets By W. Shakespeare

  Shakespeare's Winteravondsprookje
    see Vier Gedichten Von M. Nijhoff

  Since I Left You
    see Three Sonnets By W. Shakespeare

  Three Sonnets By W. Shakespeare
    low solo/med solo,pno DONEMUS s.p.
    contains: Little Love-God, The;
      Music To Hear; Since I Left You
                             (K309)

  Twee Reddelozen
    see Vier Gedichten Von M. Nijhoff

  Vier Gedichten Von M. Nijhoff
    Mez solo,2fl,2ob,3clar,acord,pno,
    perc,vln,2vla,vcl DONEMUS s.p.

KETTING, OTTO (cont'd.)

    contains: Clown; De Schipper;
      Shakespeare's
      Winteravondsprookje; Twee
      Reddelozen   (K310)

KEVAT see Marvia, Einari

KEVAT KERALLA see Kilpinen, Yrio

KEVATLAUANTAI see Linko, Ernst
  (Fredrik)

KEVATLAULU see Merikanto, Oskar

KEVATLAULU see Salonen, Sulo, En
  Varvisa

KEVATLINNUILE ETELASSA see Merikanto,
  Oskar

KEVATLINTU see Ranta, Sulho

KEVATTA see Kilpinen, Yrio

KEYS OF HEAVEN see Broadwood, Lucy E.

KEYS TO THE KINGDOM, THE *sac,gospel
  solo,pno ABER.GRP. $1.50   (K311)

KHACHATURIAN, ARAM ILYICH (1903-   )
  Ausgewahlte Lieder *CCU
  [Russ] solo,pno SIKORSKI R 6129
    s.p.   (K312)

KHACHATURIAN, KAREN
  Lieder Fur Gesang Und Klavier Und
    Lieder Fur Chor Und Klavier *CCU
  [Russ] solo,cor,pno SIKORSKI R 6325
    s.p.   (K313)

KHROMUSHIN, O.
  Arias And Scenes (from Francoise) CCU
  [Russ] solo,pno MEZ KNIGA 2.108
    s.p.   (K314)

KI MI-TZIYON
  (Helfman, Max) "Torah Dance" [Heb]
    med solo,pno TRANSCON. IS 511 $.45
                             (K315)

KIDDIES see McGeoch, Daisy

KIDDUSH L'YOM HASHABBAT see Barkan,
  Emanuel

KIDS OF THE STREET see Peterson, John
  W.

KIECKER
  Bless Our Vows *Marriage
    (Wick) solo,pno SCHMITT $.50 (K316)

KIENZL, WILHELM (1857-1941)
  O Schone Jugendtage (from Der
    Evangelimann)
    [Eng/Ger/Swed] high solo,pno BOTE
    $1.75   (K317)
    [Eng/Ger/Swed] low solo,pno BOTE
    $1.75   (K318)

  Selig Sind, Die Verfolgung Leiden
    (from Der Evangelimann)
    [Eng/Ger/Swed] high solo,pno BOTE
    $1.00   (K319)
    [Eng/Ger/Swed] low solo,pno BOTE
    $1.00   (K320)

  Sieben Lieder *Op.106,No.1-7, CC7U
    solo,pno DOBLINGER s.p.   (K321)

KIESEWETTER, PETER (1945-   )
  Agonia *scena
    female solo,2perc study sc ORLANDO
    s.p.   (K322)

  Ariel's Songs *CCU
    S solo,cembalo ORLANDO s.p.
    available in high or low editions
                             (K323)

KIITOS EMANNASTA see Kilpinen, Yrio

KILDARE see Hope, H. Ashworth

KILDEN see Jersild, Jorgen

KILISEE KULKUNEN
  see Pieni Joulutervehdyts

KILKEEL see Parke, Dorothy

KILLARNEY
  (Lehmann, Liza) low solo,pno (E flat
    maj) CRAMER   (K324)
  (Lehmann, Liza) high solo,pno (G maj)
    CRAMER   (K325)

KILLARNEY see Balfe, Michael William

KILLARY see Holbrooke, Joseph

KILLEBUKKEN see Soderman, (Johan)
  August

KILLINEY STRAND see Dalway

KILLMAYER, WILHELM (1927-   )
  Altissimu
    S solo,T rec,5inst study sc ORLANDO
    s.p.   (K326)

  Blasons Fur Sopran *CCU
    S solo,clar,pno,vln,vcl SCHOTTS
    6114 s.p.   (K327)

  Drei Gesange Nach Holderlin *CC3U
    Bar solo,pno SCHOTTS 5831 s.p.
                             (K328)

  Le Petit Savoyard *CCU
    S solo,fl,pic,4perc,cembalo,vln,
    vcl,bvl MODERN s.p.   (K329)

  Salvum Me Fac *cant
    Bar solo,pno SCHOTTS 6411 s.p.
                             (K330)

KILNER, HELEN
  Wert Thou A Slave
    low solo,pno (E flat maj) LEONARD-
    ENG   (K331)
    high solo,pno (G maj) LEONARD-ENG
                             (K332)

KILPINEN, YRIO (1892-1959)
  Aamu *Op.18,No.2
    "Morgen" see Einunddreissig Lieder
    Nach Gedichten Von Huugo
    Jalkasen, Vol. IV

  Aamulla
    "Am Morgen" [Finn/Dan/Ger] high
    solo,kbd HANSEN-DEN s.p.   (K333)

  Abend *see Kvallning

  Abendrot *see Illanrusko

  Ach, Du Schone Heimat *see Ohoh
    Kullaista Kotia

  Ach, Ich Bin Ein Narr Gewesen *see
    Voi Minua Mieskulua

  Ach, So Viele Magdlein Gibt Es *see
    Niin On Meita Piikasia

  Aina Laulan *Op.100,No.9
    "Immer Sing' Ich" solo,pno FAZER
    F 3248 see from Lauluja
    Kantelettaren Runoihin, Vol. II
                             (K334)

  Alla Dem Som Vilse Fara *Op.42,No.6
    "Alle Die, Die Sich Verirrten" see
    Six Songs

  Alle Die, Die Sich Verirrten *see
    Alla Dem Som Vilse Fara

  Allein *see Yksin

  Allmacht'ger, Hoch Da Droben *see Oi
    Ukko, Ylinen Herra

  Also Sagte Mir Die Mutter *see Noin
    Sanoi Minun Emoni

  Altes Lied *see Vanha Laulu

  Am Allerheiligentage *see Pyhain
    Miesten Paivana

  Am Haidehugel Geht Ein Singen
    "As On The Heath I Wandered" solo,
    pno FAZER F 4639 see from Hermann
    Lons Lieder, Vol. III   (K335)

  Am Morgen *see Aamulla

  Ancient Church *see Vanha Kirkko

  Andren Tont Die Kirchenglocke *see
    Muut Kuuli Kirkonkellon

  Anna, Kiesus, Anatajalle *Op.100,
    No.30
    "Den, Der Gibt, O Herr, Gib Wieder"
    solo,pno FAZER F 3269 see from
    Lauluja Kantelettaren Runoihin,
    Vol. IV   (K336)

  Appeltrad Och Parontrad *Op.49,No.4
    see Siebenundzwanzig Lieder Nach
    Gedichten Von Erik Blomberg, Vol.
    II

  Armar Arkussa Ajavi *Op.100,No.57
    "Mein Geliebter Schlaft Im Sarge"
    solo,pno FAZER F 3296 see from
    Lauluja Kantelettaren Runoihin,
    Vol. VIII   (K337)

  Armottoman Osa *Op.100,No.27
    "Die Verwaiste" solo,pno FAZER
    F 3266 see from Lauluja
    Kantelettaren Runoihin, Vol. IV
                             (K338)

  As On The Heath I Wandered *see Am
    Haidehugel Geht Ein Singen

  Auringon Nousu *Op.26,No.5
    "Sonnenaufgang" solo,pno FAZER
    F 2308 see from Siebenunddreissig

KILPINEN, YRIO (cont'd.)

Lieder Nach Gedichten Von V.A.
Koskenniemi, Vol. VII   (K339)

Away To The Mountains *see
Tunturille

Beim Kuckucksruf *see Kakoa
Kuullessa

Bells Of Sorrow, The *see Murheen
Kellot

Besser War' Es Mir Gegangen *see
Parempi Syntymatta

Bitter-Sweet Song *see Das
Bittersusse Lied

Bose Worte Ikuinen Suru *see
Sanoissa Kuluva

Burschen Und Madchen *see On
Kumpiaki

Cloudberry Flower, The *see
Hillankukka

Come, Oh Wawe *see Kirkkorannassa

Cuckoo, The *see Der Kuckuck

Dank An Die Hausfrau *see Kiitos
Emannasta

Dann Singe Ich *see Silloin Laulan

Das Bittersusse Lied
"Bitter-Sweet Song" solo,pno FAZER
F 4632 see from Hermann Lons
Lieder, Vol. I   (K340)

Das Kind Der Armen *see Koyhan
Lapset

Das Schlafende Gluck *see Makaaja-
Onni

Den, Der Gibt, O Herr, Gib Wieder
*see Anna, Kiesus, Anatajalle

Den Djupa Kallan *Op.49,No.5
see Siebenundzwanzig Lieder Nach
Gedichten Von Erik Blomberg, Vol.
II

Den Ljusa Nattens Ljusa Fageldrillar
*Op.49,No.3
see Siebenundzwanzig Lieder Nach
Gedichten Von Erik Blomberg, Vol.
II

Der Junggeselle *see Mikas On
Poikana Elea

Der Kuckuck
"Cuckoo, The" solo,pno FAZER F 4634
see from Hermann Lons Lieder,
Vol. I   (K341)

Der Neue Alladdin *see Uusi Alladdin

Der Schonste Platz
"There Where White Ringdoves
Flutter" solo,pno FAZER F 4645
see from Hermann Lons Lieder,
Vol. IV   (K342)

Der Skilaufer *see Yli Hohtavan
Hangen

Der Spuk
"Ghost, The" solo,pno FAZER F 4637
see from Hermann Lons Lieder,
Vol. II   (K343)

Der Tanz *see Tanssi

Der Vollmond Scheint
"Full Moon Shines, The" solo,pno
FAZER F 4635 see from Hermann
Lons Lieder, Vol. II   (K344)

Des Menschen Los *Op.16,No.15
[Finn/Ger] med solo,2fl,2rec,2bsn,
2horn,timp,strings voc sc
BREITKOPF-W s.p.   (K345)

Desmonas Sang *Op.51,No.1
see Siebenundzwanzig Lieder Nach
Gedichten Von Erik Blomberg, Vol.
IV

Die Ebene *see Lakeus

Die Ebene II *see Lakeus II

Die Ebene III *see Lakeus III

Die Ebene IV *see Lakeus IV

Die Ebene V *see Lakeus V

KILPINEN, YRIO (cont'd.)

Die Lerche *see Leivonen

Die Sturzwelle *see Hyokyaalto

Die Verehrung
"Huntsman, The" solo,pno FAZER
F 4644 see from Hermann Lons
Lieder, Vol. IV   (K346)

Die Verwaiste *see Armottoman Osa

Draussen Bricht Das Eis *see Ei Sula
Syan Suruinen

Du Stummer Weggenosse Mein *see Sa
Mykka Matkalainen Maan

Dunkel Ist Die Kleine Kammer *see
Pimea Isoton Pirtti

Dyningen *Op.48,No.1
see Siebenundzwanzig Lieder Nach
Gedichten Von Erik Blomberg, Vol.
I

Eheu Fugaces *Op.18,No.4
see Einunddreissig Lieder Nach
Gedichten Von Huugo Jalkasen,
Vol. IV

Ei Minusta Lienekana *Op.100,No.12
"Nein, Ich Kann Nicht" solo,pno
FAZER F 3251 see from Lauluja
Kantelettaren Runoihin, Vol. II
(K347)

Ei Runo Rahatta Laula *Op.100,No.28
"Mochte Singen" solo,pno FAZER
F 3267 see from Lauluja
Kantelettaren Runoihin, Vol. IV
(K348)

Ei Sula Syan Suruinen *Op.100,No.25
"Draussen Bricht Das Eis" solo,pno
FAZER F 3264 see from Lauluja
Kantelettaren Runoihin, Vol. IV
(K349)

Ei, Was Tut Es, Wenn Ich Singe *see
Mita Tuosta, Jos Ma Laulan

Eiko Totta
solo,pno FAZER F 2777 see from Syv
Laulua Eila Kivikk'ahon Runoihin
(K350)

Eine Rune *see En Rune

Einsam *see Kaikissa Yksin

Einsam Sing' Ich *see Ikava Omia
Maita

Einunddreissig Lieder Nach Gedichten
Von Huugo Jalkasen, Vol. I
*Op.15,No.1-7, CC7L
solo,pno FAZER F 3148 s.p.   (K351)

Einunddreissig Lieder Nach Gedichten
Von Huugo Jalkasen, Vol. III
*Op.17,No.1-9, CC9L
solo,pno FAZER F 3150   (K352)

Einunddreissig Lieder Nach Gedichten
Von Huugo Jalkasen, Vol. IV
solo,pno FAZER F 3151 s.p.
contains: Aamu, "Morgen", Op.18,
No.2; Eheu Fugaces, Op.18,No.4;
Illanrusko, "Abendrot", Op.18,
No.1; Pyhain Miesten Paivana,
"Am Allerheiligentage", Op.18,
No.5; Uusi Alladdin, "Der Neue
Alladdin"; Yli Hohtavan Hangen,
"Der Skilaufer", Op.18,No.6
(K353)

Elegia An Die Nachtigall *see Elegie
Satakielelle

Elegia Kauneudelle *Op.20,No.1
"Elegie An Die Schonheit" solo,pno
FAZER F 2273 see from
Siebenunddreissig Lieder Nach
Gedichten Von V.A. Koskenniemi,
Vol. I   (K354)

Elegia Yksinaisyydelle *Op.25,No.4
"Elegie An Die Einsamkeit" solo,pno
FAZER F2302 see from
Siebenunddreissig Lieder Nach
Gedichten Von V.A. Koskenniemi,
Vol. VI   (K355)

Elegia Yolle *Op.20,No.5
"Elegie An Die Nacht" solo,pno
FAZER F 2277 see from
Siebenunddreissig Lieder Nach
Gedichten Von V.A. Koskenniemi,
Vol. I   (K356)

Elegie An Die Einsamkeit *see Elegia
Yksinaisyydelle

Elegie An Die Nacht *see Elegia
Yolle

Elegie An Die Schonheit *see Elegia
Kauneudelle

KILPINEN, YRIO (cont'd.)

Elegie Satakielelle *Op.21,No.1
"Elegia An Die Nachtigall" solo,pno
FAZER F 2278 see from
Siebenunddreissig Lieder Nach
Gedichten Von V.A.Koskenniemi,
Vol. II   (K357)

En Rune *Op.42,No.1
"Eine Rune" see Six Songs

En Ung Mor *Op.50,No.2
see Siebenundzwanzig Lieder Nach
Gedichten Von Erik Blomberg, Vol.
III

Endymion *Op.20,No.2
solo,pno FAZER F 2274 see from
Siebenunddreissig Lieder Nach
Gedichten Von V.A. Koskenniemi,
Vol. I   (K358)

Eras
solo,pno FAZER F 2775 see from Syv
Laulua Eila Kivikk'ahon Runoihin
(K359)

Erotus Mielilla *Op.100,No.24
"Wie Ist Ein Frohes Herz" solo,pno
FAZER F 3263 see from Lauluja
Kantelettaren Runoihin, Vol. III
(K360)

Eununddreissig Lieder Nach Gedichten
Von Huugo Jalkasen, Vol. II
*Op.16,No.1-8, CC8L
solo,pno FAZER F 3149   (K361)

Ewige Trauer *see Ikuinen Suru

Fen, The *see Janka

Fiat Nox *Op.25,No.5
solo,pno FAZER F 2303 see from
Siebenunddreissig Lieder Nach
Gedichten Von V.A. Koskenniemi,
Vol. VI   (K362)

Forledde Van *Op.51,No.8
see Siebenundzwanzig Lieder Nach
Gedichten Von Erik Blomberg, Vol.
V

Forr Agde Jag Intet *Op.49,No.1
see Siebenundzwanzig Lieder Nach
Gedichten Von Erik Blomberg, Vol.
II

Fort Zieht Der Fruhling *Op.17,No.23
[Finn/Ger] med solo,2English horn,
2rec,2horn,3trom,strings voc sc
BREITKOPF-W s.p.   (K363)

Fruher Fruhling *see Kevat Keralla

Fruher Rief Mein Trauter Kuckuck
*see Muinainen Kakeni

Full Moon Shines, The *see Der
Vollmond Scheint

Ghost, The *see Der Spuk

Golden Song *see Goldenes Lied

Goldenes Lied
"Golden Song" solo,pno FAZER F 4640
see from Hermann Lons Lieder,
Vol. III   (K364)

Grabesnacht Mein Liebchen Verhullt
*see Maassa Marjani Makavi

Grabstein *Op.80, CC4U
[Ger] med solo,pno BOTE $4.50
(K365)

Gravskrift Over Ett Litet Barn
*Op.51,No.2
see Siebenundzwanzig Lieder Nach
Gedichten Von Erik Blomberg, Vol.
IV

Gullvivan *Op.51,No.6
see Siebenundzwanzig Lieder Nach
Gedichten Von Erik Blomberg, Vol.
V

Hab' Daheim Gelernt Die Lieder *see
Otettiin Minusta Outo

Habe Mochte Singen *see Onpa Tietty
Tietyssani

Hatt Ich Einmal *see Kun Ma Kerran

Herbst *Op.98, song cycle
[Ger] med solo,pno BOTE $3.50
(K366)

Herbstregen *see Kaupungilla Sataa

Herbstsonett *see Syyssonetti

Hermann Lons Lieder, Vol. I *see Das
Bittersusse Lied, "Bitter-Sweet
Song"; Der Kuckuck, "Cuckoo,
The"; Mannertreu, "There Was A
Wind That Blew"   (K367)

KILPINEN, YRIO (cont'd.)

Hermann Lons Lieder, Vol. II *see
    Der Spuk, "Ghost, The"; Der
    Vollmond Scheint, "Full Moon
    Shines, The"; Kussekraut, "Love
    Song"; Liebessuche, "Search, The"
                                    (K368)

Hermann Lons Lieder, Vol. III *see
    Am Haidehugel Geht Ein Singen,
    "As On The Heath I Wandered";
    Goldenes Lied, "Golden Song"; Zur
    Erinnerung, "In Remembrance"
                                    (K369)

Hermann Lons Lieder, Vol. IV *see
    Der Schonste Platz, "There Where
    White Ringdoves Flutter"; Die
    Verehrung, "Huntsman, The";
    Rosenbusche, "Roses";
    Schaferlied, "Shepherd's Song"
                                    (K370)

Heute Ist Alles Teuer' Worden *see
    Nyt On Kaikki Kallistunna

Hillankukka *Op.53,No.1
    "Cloudberry Flower, The" [Eng/Ger/
    Finn] solo,pno FAZER F 2156 see
    from Tunturilauluja, Vol. II
                                    (K371)

Hirtenlied *see Paimenlaulu

Hochgebirgswinter *Op.99
    [Ger] med solo,pno BOTE $3.00
                                    (K372)

Huntsman, The *see Die Verehrung

Hymni *CCU
    solo,pno FAZER F 2614 s.p.   (K373)

Hyokyaalto *Op.23,No.6
    "Die Sturzwelle" solo,pno FAZER
    F 2293 see from Siebenunddreissig
    Lieder Nach Gedichten Von V.A.
    Koskenniemi, Vol. IV   (K374)

I Dina Handers Mjuka Fagelbo *Op.50,
    No.1
    see Siebenundzwanzig Lieder Nach
    Gedichten Von Erik Blomberg, Vol.
    III

Ich Komme *see Jo Tulenki

Ich Liess Dich Achtlos *see Sun
    Tuskin Huomasin

Ich Singe Wie Die Vogelein Singen
    *see Laulan Ilman Lainehilta

Ihme *Op.21,No.6
    "Wunder" solo,pno FAZER see from
    Siebenunddreissig Lieder Nach
    Gedichten Von V.A.Koskenniemi,
    Vol. II   (K375)

Ikarus *Op.24,No.5
    solo,pno FAZER F 2298 see from
    Siebenunddreissig Lieder Nach
    Gedichten Von V.A. Koskenniemi,
    Vol. V   (K376)

Ikava Omia Maita *Op.100,No.26
    "Einsam Sing' Ich" solo,pno FAZER
    F 3265 see from Lauluja
    Kantelettaren Runoihin, Vol. IV
                                    (K377)

Ikuinen Suru *Op.100,No.60
    "Ewige Trauer" solo,pno FAZER 3299
    see from Lauluja Kantelettaren
    Runoihin, Vol. VIII   (K378)

Illanrusko *Op.18,No.1
    "Abendrot" see Einunddreissig
    Lieder Nach Gedichten Von Huugo
    Jalkasen, Vol. IV

Im Mondschein *see Kuutamolla

Im Schmerzen Erschauerund *see Olit
    Tuskasta Varisten Herannyt Syon

Immer Sing' Ich *see Aina Laulan

In Der Sommernacht *see Kesayossa

In Remembrance *see Zur Erinnerung

Jaa Hyvasti Ja Nakemiin *Op.25,No.3
    "Lebewohl Und Auf Wiedersehn" solo,
    pno FAZER F 2301 see from
    Siebenunddreissig Lieder Nach
    Gedichten Von V.A. Koskenniemi,
    Vol. VI   (K379)

Jag Har Haft En Stor, Tyst Sorg
    *Op.49,No.2
    see Siebenundzwanzig Lieder Nach
    Gedichten Von Erik Blomberg, Vol.
    II

Jag Vantar Ingen Lycka *Op.48,No.6
    see Seibenundzwanzig Lieder Nach
    Gedichten Von Erik Blomberg, Vol.
    I

KILPINEN, YRIO (cont'd.)

Jag Ville Vara Tarar *Op.50,No.4
    see Siebenundzwanzig Lieder Nach
    Gedichten Von Erik Blomberg, Vol.
    III

Janka *Op.52,No.1
    "Fen, The" [Eng/Ger/Finn] solo,pno
    FAZER F 2152 see from
    Tunturilauluja, Vol. I   (K380)

Jo Tulenki *Op.100,No.37
    "Ich Komme" solo,pno FAZER F 3276
    see from Lauluja Kantelettaren
    Runoihin, Vol. V   (K381)

Jos Ma Laululle Rupean *Op.100,No.13
    "Wenn Men Lied Ich Beginne" solo,
    pno FAZER F 3252 see from Lauluja
    Kantelettaren Runoihin, Vol. II
                                    (K382)

Kaikissa Yksin *Op.100,No.42
    "Einsam" solo,pno FAZER F 3281 see
    from Lauluja Kantelettaren
    Runoihin, Vol. VI   (K383)

Kakoa Kuullessa *Op.7,No.2
    "Beim Kuckucksruf" solo,pno FAZER
    W 375 s.p.   (K384)

Kaks' Oli Meita Kaunokaista *Op.100,
    No.49
    "Wie Zwei Vogelein Waren Wir Beide"
    solo,pno FAZER F 3288 see from
    Lauluja Kantelettaren Runoihin,
    Vol. VII   (K385)

Kam' Zu Mir Der Geliebte Mein *see
    Kun Mun Kultani Tulisi

Kanteletar-Lieder, Op. 100 *CC64U
    [Finn/Ger] solo,pno BREITKOPF-W
    57 05004-11 available for high,
    medium and low voice in 8 volumes
                                    (K386)

Kaupungilla Sataa *Op.24,No.1
    "Herbstregen" solo,pno FAZER F 2294
    see from Siebenunddreissig Lieder
    Nach Gedichten Von V.A.
    Koskenniemi, Vol. V   (K387)

Kehtolaulu *Op.23,No.4
    "Wiegenlied" solo,pno FAZER F 2291
    see from Siebenunddreissig Lieder
    Nach Gedichten Von V.A.
    Koskenniemi, Vol. IV   (K388)

Keinu *CCU
    solo,pno FAZER F 4869 s.p.   (K389)

Kesayo *Op.23,No.3
    "Sommernacht" solo,pno FAZER F 2290
    see from Siebenunddreissig Lieder
    Nach Gedichten Von V.A.
    Koskenniemi, Vol. IV   (K390)

Kesayossa *Op.21,No.4
    "In Der Sommernacht" solo,pno FAZER
    F 2281 see from Siebenunddreissig
    Lieder Nach Gedichten Von
    V.A.Koskenniemi, Vol. II   (K391)

Kevat Keralla *Op.20,No.3
    "Fruher Fruhling" solo,pno FAZER
    F 2275 see from Siebenunddreissig
    Lieder Nach Gedichten Von V.A.
    Koskenniemi, Vol. I   (K392)

Kevatta
    solo,pno FAZER F 2776 see from Syv
    Laulua Eila Kivikk'ahon Runoihin
                                    (K393)

Kiitos Emannasta *Op.100,No.62
    "Dank An Die Hausfrau" solo,pno
    FAZER F 3301 see from Lauluja
    Kantelettaren Runoihin, Vol. VIII
                                    (K394)

Kirkkorannassa *Op.54,No.2
    "Come, Oh Wawe" [Eng/Ger/Finn]
    solo,pno FAZER F2161 see from
    Tunturilauluja, Vol. III   (K395)

Klein Und Kleiner Wird Der Freunde
    Kreis *see Ystavien Piiri
    Pienentyy

Komm, O Komm *see Kuti, Kuti
    Kultaseni

Komm, O Komme *see Tule Tanne

Korsbar *Op.51,No.5
    see Siebenundzwanzig Lieder Nach
    Gedichten Von Erik Blomberg, Vol.
    IV

Koyhan Lapset *Op.100,No.18
    "Das Kind Der Armen" solo,pno FAZER
    F 3257 see from Lauluja
    Kantelettaren Runoihin, Vol. III
                                    (K396)

Kuckuck Rief Im Fichtenwalde *see
    Vaha Ilo Emottomalle Kaesta

KILPINEN, YRIO (cont'd.)

Kukkalatva Kuusi *Op.100,No.3
    "Shon Maria, Meine Beere" solo,pno
    FAZER F 3242 see from Lauluja
    Kantelettaren Runoihin, Vol. I
                                    (K397)

Kummalstako Kuuleminen *Op.100,No.14
    "Reifen Einst" solo,pno FAZER
    F 3253 see from Lauluja
    Kantelettaren Runoihin, Vol. II
                                    (K398)

Kun Ma Kerran *Op.100,No.23
    "Hatt Ich Einmal" solo,pno FAZER
    F 3262 see from Lauluja
    Kantelettaren Runoihin, Vol. III
                                    (K399)

Kun Mun Kultani Tulisi *Op.100,No.43
    "Kam' Zu Mir Der Geliebte Mein"
    solo,pno FAZER F 3282 see from
    Lauluja Kantelettaren Runoihin,
    Vol. VI   (K400)

Kussekraut
    "Love Song" solo,pno FAZER F 4638
    see from Hermann Lons Lieder,
    Vol. II   (K401)

Kuti, Kuti Kultaseni *Op.100,No.44
    "Komm, O Komm" solo,pno FAZER
    F 3283 see from Lauluja
    Kantelettaren Runoihin, Vol. VI
                                    (K402)

Kuusen Juuret Kuivettuvat *Op.100,
    No.53
    "Laub Und Gras, Die Trocken Alle"
    solo,pno FAZER F 3292 see from
    Lauluja Kantelettaren Runoihin,
    Vol. VII   (K403)

Kuusi Ja Lintunen
    "Tannenbaumchen Und Voglein" [Finn/
    Dan/Ger] med solo,kbd HANSEN-DEN
    s.p.   (K404)

Kuusi Laulu *see Mitt Sagoland,
    "Mein Marchenland", Op.47,No.1;
    Rosa Lill', "Roselein", Op.47,
    No.5; Sa Dansa, "So Tanze",
    Op.47,No.6; Sjung Mitt Hjarta,
    "Sing Mein Herze", Op.47,No.3;
    Solstralen, "Sonnenstrahlen",
    Op.47,No.2; Stamningsvisa,
    "Stimmungslied", Op.47,No.4
                                    (K405)

Kuutamolla *Op.21,No.2
    "Im Mondschein" solo,pno FAZER
    F 2279 see from Siebenunddreissig
    Lieder Nach Gedichten Von
    V.A.Koskenniemi, Vol. II   (K406)

Kvallning *Op.42,No.4
    "Abend" see Six Songs

Lakeus *Op.22,No.1
    "Die Ebene" solo,pno FAZER F 2283
    see from Siebenunddreissig Lieder
    Nach Gedichter Von V.A.
    Koskenniemi, Vol. III   (K407)

Lakeus II *Op.22,No.2
    "Die Ebene II" solo,pno FAZER
    F 2284 see from Siebenunddreissig
    Lieder Nach Gedichten Von V.A.
    Koskenniemi, Vol. III   (K408)

Lakeus III *Op.22,No.3
    "Die Ebene III" solo,pno FAZER
    F 2285 see from Siebenunddreissig
    Lieder Nach Gedichten Von V.A.
    Koskenniemi, Vol. III   (K409)

Lakeus IV *Op.22,No.4
    "Die Ebene IV" solo,pno FAZER
    F 2286 see from Siebenunddreissig
    Lieder Nach Gedichten Von V.A.
    Koskenniemi, Vol. III   (K410)

Lakeus V *Op.22,No.5
    "Die Ebene V" solo,pno FAZER F 2287
    see from Siebenunddreissig Lieder
    Nach Gedichten Von V.A.
    Koskenniemi, Vol. III   (K411)

Landschaft *see Landskap

Landskap *Op.42,No.3
    "Landschaft" see Six Songs

Lang' Ersehnt Ich *see Viikon
    Vuottelin Kakea

Larksang *Op.51,No.9
    see Siebenundzwanzig Lieder Nach
    Gedichten Von Erik Blomberg, Vol.
    V

Lass Fahren *see Lat Vara

Lat Vara *Op.42,No.2
    "Lass Fahren" see Six Songs

Laub Und Gras, Die Trocken Alle *see
    Kuusen Juuret Kuivettuvat

KILPINEN, YRIO (cont'd.)

Laulan Ilman Lainehilta *Op.100,
   No.48
   "Ich Singe Wie Die Vogelein Singen"
   solo,pno FAZER F 3287 see from
   Lauluja Kantelettaren Runoihin,
   Vol. VI   (K412)

Lauluja Kantelettaren Runoihin, Vol.
   I *see Kukkalatva Kuusi, "Shon
   Maria, Meine Beere", Op.100,No.3;
   Missa Armahin, "Wo Mag Mein
   Schatzlein Weilen", Op.100,No.2;
   Oisi Mulla Vallan Miekka, "Wenn
   Ich Macht Und Gelde Hatte",
   Op.100,No.8; On Kumpiaki,
   "Burschen Und Madchen", Op.100,
   No.6; Paimenlaulu, "Hirtenlied",
   Op.100,No.1; Silloin Laulan,
   "Dann Singe Ich", Op.100,No.5;
   Sopivaisia, "Solches Hort' Ich",
   Op.100,No.7; Tule Tanne, "Komm, O
   Komme", Op.100,No.4   (K413)

Lauluja Kantelettaren Runoihin, Vol.
   II *see Aina Laulan, "Immer
   Sing' Ich", Op.100,No.9; Ei
   Minusta Lienekana, "Nein, Ich
   Kann Nicht", Op.100,No.12; Jos Ma
   Laululle Rupean, "Wenn Mein Lied
   Ich Beginne", Op.100,No.13;
   Kummalstako Kuuleminen, "Reifen
   Einst", Op.100,No.14; Mikas On
   Poikana Elea, "Der Junggeselle",
   Op.100,No.16; Niin On Meita
   Piikasia, "Ach, So Viele Magdlein
   Gibt Es", Op.100,No.10; Tanssi,
   "Der Tanz", Op.100,No.15; Viikon
   Vuottelin Kakea, "Lang' Ersehnt
   Ich", Op.100,No.11   (K414)

Lauluja Kantelettaren Runoihin, Vol.
   III *see Erotus Mielilla, "Wie
   Ist Ein Frohes Herz", Op.100,
   No.24; Koyhan Lapset, "Das Kind
   Der Armen", Op.100,No.18; Kun Ma
   Kerran, "Hatt Ich Einmal",
   Op.100,No.23; Mitapa Suren
   Sanoista, "Was Kummert Mich",
   Op.100,No.21; Paista Paivanen
   Jumala, "Scheine Hell, O Sonne",
   Op.100,No.17; Parempi Syntymatta,
   "Besser War' Es Mir Gegangen",
   Op.100,No.22; Tuutulaulu,
   "Wiegenlied", Op.100,No.20; Voi,
   Jos Mie Tok' Miehen Saisin, "Wenn
   Ich", Op.100,No.19   (K415)

Lauluja Kantelettaren Runoihin, Vol.
   IV *see Anna, Kiesus,
   Anatajalle, "Den, Der Gibt, O
   Herr, Gib Wieder", Op.100,No.30;
   Armottoman Osa, "Die Verwaiste",
   Op.100,No.27; Ei Runo Rahatta
   Laula, "Mochte Singen", Op.100,
   No.28; Ei Sula Syan Suruinen,
   "Draussen Bricht Das Eis",
   Op.100,No.25; Ikava Omia Maita,
   "Einsam Sing' Ich", Op.100,No.26;
   Nyt On Kaikki Kallistunna, "Heute
   Ist Alles Teuer' Worden", Op.100,
   No.31; Onpa Tietty Tietyssani,
   "Habe Mochte Singen", Op.100,
   No.29; Tule Meille, Tuomas-Kulta,
   "Sei Willkommen, Lieber Thomas",
   Op.100,No.32   (K416)

Lauluja Kantelettaren Runoihin, Vol.
   V *see Jo Tulenki, "Ich Komme",
   Op.100,No.37; Milla Maksan
   Maammon Maion, "Wie Entgelt' Ich
   Meiner Mutter", Op.100,No.39;
   Mita Tuosta, Jos Ma Laulan, "Ei,
   Was Tut Es, Wenn Ich Singe",
   Op.100,No.36; Muinainen Kakeni,
   "Fruher Rief Mein Trauter
   Kuckuck", Op.100,No.35; Noin
   Sanoi Minun Emoni, "Also Sagte
   Mir Die Mutter", Op.100,No.33;
   Ohoh Kullaista Kotia, "Ach, Du
   Schone Heimat", Op.100,No.38;
   Otettiin Minusta Outo, "Hab'
   Daheim Gelernt Die Lieder",
   Op.100,No.34; Soitapas, "Singe,
   Mein Schones Madchen", Op.100,
   No.40   (K417)

Lauluja Kantelettaren Runoihin, Vol.
   VI *see Kaikissa Yksin,
   "Einsam", Op.100,No.42; Kun Mun
   Kultani Tulisi, "Kam' Zu Mir Der
   Geliebte Mein", Op.100,No.43;
   Kuti, Kuti Kultaseni, "Komm, O
   Komm", Op.100,No.44; Laulan Ilman
   Lainehilta, "Ich Singe Wie Die
   Vogelein Singen", Op.100,No.48;
   Makaaja-Onni, "Das Schlafende
   Gluck", Op.100,No.47; Mont' On
   Mulla Morsianta, "Viele Madchen
   Kann Ich Zahlen", Op.100,No.45;
   Muut Kuuli Kirkonkellon, "Andren
   Tont Die Kirchenglocke", Op.100,
   No.41; Voi Minua Mieskulua, "Ach,
   Ich Bin Ein Narr Gewesen",
   Op.100,No.46   (K418)

Lauluja Kantelettaren Runoihin, Vol.
   VII *see Kaks' Oli Meita
   Kaunokaista, "Wie Zwei Vogelein
   Waren Wir Beide", Op.100,No.49;
   Kuusen Juuret Kuivettuvat, "Laub
   Und Gras, Die Trocken Alle",
   Op.100,No.53; Oi Ukko, Ylinen
   Herra, "Allmacht'ger, Hoch Da
   Droben", Op.100,No.56; Pah' On
   Orjana Elea, "O Wie Bitter Ein
   Knecht Zu Sein", Op.100,No.54;
   Saisinko Kaelta Kielen, "Wie Der
   Kuckuck Mocht' Ich Rufen",
   Op.100,No.50; Soria Sotahan
   Kuolla, "Schon Ist Es Zu Sterben
   Im Kampfe", Op.100,No.55; Tuuti,
   Tuuti Tummaistani, "Schlaf, Nur
   Schlaf", Op.100,No.51; Vaha Ilo
   Emottomalle Kaesta, "Kuckuck Rief
   Im Fichtenwalde", Op.100,No.52
                                (K419)

Lauluja Kantelettaren Runoihin, Vol.
   VIII *see Armar Arkussa Ajavi,
   "Mein Geliebter Schlaft Im
   Sarge", Op.100,No.57; Ikuinen
   Suru, "Ewige Trauer", Op.100,
   No.60; Kiitos Emannasta, "Dank An
   Die Hausfrau", Op.100,No.62;
   Miksi En Vasyisi, "Sollt' Auch
   Ich Nicht Ermuden", Op.100,No.63;
   Mista Sinne Tie Menevi, "Sollen
   Diesen Weg Nun Gehen", Op.100,
   No.64; Omat On Virret Oppimiani,
   "Selbst Gelernt Hab' Ich Meine
   Lieder", Op.100,No.61; Pimea
   Isoton Pirtti, "Dunkel Ist Die
   Kleine Kammer", Op.100,No.58;
   Sanoissa Kuluva, "Bose Worte
   Ikuinen Suru", Op.100,No.59
                                (K420)

Laululle *Op.52,No.3
   "To The Song" [Eng/Ger/Finn] solo,
   pno FAZER F 2154 see from
   Tunturilauluja, Vol. I   (K421)

Lebewohl Und Auf Wiedersehn *see Jaa
   Hyvasti Ja Nakemiin

Lehdokki *Op.21,No.3
   "Nachtviole" solo,pno FAZER F 2280
   see from Siebenunddreissig Lieder
   Nach Gedichten Von
   V.A.Koskenniemi, Vol. II   (K422)

Leivonen *Op.26,No.4
   "Die Lerche" solo,pno FAZER F 2307
   see from Siebenunddreissig Lieder
   Nach Gedichten Von V.A.
   Koskenniemi, Vol. VII   (K423)

Liebessuche
   "Search, The" solo,pno FAZER F 4636
   see from Hermann Lons Lieder,
   Vol. II   (K424)

Lieder Nach Gedichten Von Huugo
   Jalkanen, Op. 15 *CC31U
   [Finn/Ger] high solo/med solo,pno
   BREITKOPF-W 57 05012 s.p.   (K425)

Lieder Nach Gedichten Von Huugo
   Jalkanen, Op. 16 *CC31U
   [Finn/Ger] high solo/med solo,pno
   BREITKOPF-W 57 05013 s.p.   (K426)

Lieder Nach Gedichten Von Huugo
   Jalkanen, Op. 17 *CC31U
   [Finn/Ger] high solo/med solo,pno
   BREITKOPF-W 57 05014 s.p.   (K427)

Lieder Nach Gedichten Von Huugo
   Jalkanen, Op. 18 *CC31U
   [Finn/Ger] high solo/med solo,pno
   BREITKOPF-W 57 05015 s.p.   (K428)

Lieder Um Eine Kleine Stadt *Op.95,
   CCU
   [Ger] med solo,pno BOTE $4.50, ea.
   in two volumes   (K429)

Liederfolge *Op.97, song cycle
   [Ger] med solo,pno BOTE $4.50
                                (K430)

Love Song *see Kussekraut

Maassa Marjani Makavi *Op.3,No.3
   "Grabesnacht Mein Liebchen
   Verhullt" solo,pno FAZER W 379
   s.p.   (K431)

Makaaja-Onni *Op.100,No.47
   "Das Schlafende Gluck" solo,pno
   FAZER F 3286 see from Lauluja
   Kantelettaren Runoihin, Vol. VI
                                (K432)

Mannertreu
   "There Was A Wind That Blew" solo,
   pno FAZER F 4633 see from Hermann
   Lons Lieder, Vol. I   (K433)

Manniskans Hem *Op.48,No.5
   see Seibenundzwanzig Lieder Nach
   Gedichten Von Erik Blomberg, Vol.
   I

Mein Geliebter Schlaft Im Sarge *see
   Armar Arkussa Ajavi

Mein Marchenland *see Mitt Sagoland

Memnonin Laulu
   solo,pno FAZER F 2774 see from Syv
   Laulua Eila Kivikk'ahon Runoihin
                                (K434)

Migrant, The *see Muuttilintu

Mikas On Poikana Elea *Op.100,No.16
   "Der Junggeselle" solo,pno FAZER
   F 3255 see from Lauluja
   Kantelettaren Runoihin, Vol. II
                                (K435)

Miksi En Vasyisi *Op.100,No.63
   "Sollt' Auch Ich Nicht Ermuden"
   solo,pno FAZER F 3302 see from
   Lauluja Kantelettaren Runoihin,
   Vol. VIII   (K436)

Milla Maksan Maammon Maion *Op.100,
   No.39
   "Wie Entgelt' Ich Meiner Mutter"
   solo,pno FAZER F 3278 see from
   Lauluja Kantelettaren Runoihin,
   Vol. V   (K437)

Missa Armahin *Op.100,No.2
   "Wo Mag Mein Schatzlein Weilen"
   solo,pno FAZER F 3241 see from
   Lauluja Kantelettaren Runoihin,
   Vol. I   (K438)

Mista Sinne Tie Menevi *Op.100,No.64
   "Sollen Diesen Weg Nun Gehen" solo,
   pno FAZER F 3303 see from Lauluja
   Kantelettaren Runoihin, Vol. VIII
                                (K439)

Mita Tuosta, Jos Ma Laulan *Op.100,
   No.36
   "Ei, Was Tut Es, Wenn Ich Singe"
   solo,pno FAZER F 3275 see from
   Lauluja Kantelettaren Runoihin,
   Vol. V   (K440)

Mitapa Suren Sanoista *Op.100,No.21
   "Was Kummert Mich" solo,pno FAZER
   F 3260 see from Lauluja
   Kantelettaren Runoihin, Vol. III
                                (K441)

Mitt Sagoland *Op.47,No.1
   "Mein Marchenland" solo,pno FAZER
   F 2264 see from Kuusi Laulu   (K442)

Mochte Singen *see Ei Runo Rahatta
   Laula

Modern *Op.50,No.3
   see Siebenundzwanzig Lieder Nach
   Gedichten Von Erik Blomberg, Vol.
   III

Mondschein-Ode *Op.62,No.7
   Mez/A solo,2clar,2bsn,3horn,harp,
   3strings BREITKOPF-L rental   (K443)

Mont' On Mulla Morsianta *Op.100,
   No.45
   "Viele Madchen Kann Ich Zahlen"
   solo,pno FAZER F 3284 see from
   Lauluja Kantelettaren Runoihin,
   Vol. VI   (K444)

Morgen *see Aamu

Morgenlied *Op.15,No.5
   [Finn/Ger] med solo,2fl,2clar,2bsn,
   3horn,timp,perc,harp,strings voc
   sc BREITKOPF-W s.p.   (K445)

Mountain Brook, The *see
   Tunturilahde

Muinainen Kakeni *Op.100,No.35
   "Fruher Rief Mein Trauter Kuckuck"
   solo,pno FAZER F 3274 see from
   Lauluja Kantelettaren Runoihin,
   Vol. V   (K446)

Muisto
   solo,pno FAZER F 2773 see from Syv
   Laulua Eila Kivikk'ahon Runoihin
                                (K447)

Murheen Kellot *Op.53,No.2
   "Bells Of Sorrow, The" [Eng/Ger/
   Finn] solo,pno FAZER F 2157 see
   from Tunturilauluja, Vol. II (K448)

Muut Kuuli Kirkonkellon *Op.100,
   No.41
   "Andren Tont Die Kirchenglocke"
   solo,pno FAZER F 3280 see from
   Lauluja Kantelettaren Runoihin,
   Vol. VI   (K449)

Muuttilintu *Op.53,No.3
   "Migrant, The" [Eng/Ger/Finn] solo,
   pno FAZER F 2158 see from
   Tunturilauluja, Vol. II   (K450)

KILPINEN, YRIO (cont'd.)

Nachtviole *see Lehdokki

Nein, Ich Kann Nicht *see Ei Minusta
Lienekana

Niin On Meita Piikasia *Op.100,No.10
"Ach, So Viele Magdlein Gibt Es"
solo,pno FAZER F 3249 see from
Lauluja Kantelettaren Runoihin,
Vol. II   (K451)

Nocturne
solo,pno FAZER F 2772 see from Syv
Laulua Eila Kivikk'ahon Runoihin
(K452)

Noin Sanoi Minun Emoni *Op.100,No.33
"Also Sagte Mir Die Mutter" solo,
pno FAZER F 3272 see from Lauluja
Kantelettaren Runoihin, Vol. V
(K453)

Notturno *Op.16,No.13
(Fougstedt, Nils Erik) [Finn/Ger]
med solo,2fl,2ob,2clar,2bsn,
2horn,harp,strings BREITKOPF-W
s.p.   (K454)
(Parmet, Simon) [Finn/Ger] med
solo,fl,ob,clar,bsn,3horn,strings
voc sc BREITKOPF-W s.p.   (K455)

Nyt On Kaikki Kallistunna *Op.100,
No.31
"Heute Ist Alles Teuer' Worden"
solo,pno FAZER F 3270 see from
Lauluja Kantelettaren Runoihin,
Vol. IV   (K456)

O Wie Bitter Ein Knecht Zu Sein *see
Pah' On Orjana Elea

Och Stod Du I Den Kalla Blast
*Op.51,No.7
see from Siebenundzwanzig Lieder Nach
Gedichten Von Erik Blomberg, Vol.
V

Ohoh Kullaista Kotia *Op.100,No.38
"Ach, Du Schone Heimat" solo,pno
FAZER F 3277 see from Lauluja
Kantelettaren Runoihin, Vol. V
(K457)

Oi Ukko, Ylinen Herra *Op.100,No.56
"Allmacht'ger, Hoch Da Droben"
solo,pno FAZER F 3295 see from
Lauluja Kantelettaren Runoihin,
Vol. VII   (K458)

Oisi Mulla Vallan Miekka *Op.100,
No.8
"Wenn Ich Macht Und Gelde Hatte"
solo,pno FAZER F 3247 see from
Lauluja Kantelettaren Runoihin,
Vol. I   (K459)

Olit Tuskasta Varisten Herannyt Syon
*Op.26,No.1
"Im Schmerzen Erschauerund" solo,
pno FAZER F 2304 see from
Siebenunddreissig Lieder Nach
Gedichten Von V.A. Koskenniemi,
Vol. VII   (K460)

Omat On Virret Oppimiani *Op.100,
No.61
"Selbst Gelernt Hab' Ich Meine
Lieder" solo,pno FAZER F 3300 see
from Lauluja Kantelettaren
Runoihin, Vol. VIII   (K461)

On Kaikki Syksyn Tahdet Syttyneet
*Op.24,No.2
"Sind Alie Herbstes Sterne
Aufgegluht" solo,pno FAZER F 2295
see from Siebenunddreissig Lieder
Nach Gedichten Von V.A.
Koskenniemi, Vol. V   (K462)

On Kumpiaki *Op.100,No.6
"Burschen Und Madchen" solo,pno
FAZER F 3245 see from Lauluja
Kantelettaren Runoihin, Vol. I
(K463)

Onnelliset *CC2U
solo,pno FAZER F 4868 s.p.   (K464)

Onpa Tietty Tietyssani *Op.100,No.29
"Habe Mochte Singen" solo,pno FAZER
F 3268 see from Lauluja
Kantelettaren Runoihin, Vol. IV
(K465)

Otettiin Minusta Outo *Op.100,No.34
"Hab' Daheim Gelernt Die Lieder"
solo,pno FAZER F 3273 see from
Lauluja Kantelettaren Runoihin,
Vol. V   (K466)

Pah' On Orjana Elea *Op.100,No.54
"O Wie Bitter Ein Knecht Zu Sein"
solo,pno FAZER F 3293 see from
Lauluja Kantelettaren Runoihin,
Vol. VII   (K467)

Paimenlaulu *Op.100,No.1
"Hirtenlied" solo,pno FAZER F 3240
see from Lauluja Kantelettaren

KILPINEN, YRIO (cont'd.)

Runoihin, Vol. I   (K468)

Paista Paivanen Jumala *Op.100,No.17
"Scheine Hell, O Sonne" solo,pno
FAZER F 3256 see from Lauluja
Kantelettaren Runoihin, Vol. III
(K469)

Parempi Syntymatta *Op.100,No.22
"Besser War' Es Mir Gegangen" solo,
pno FAZER F 3261 see from Lauluja
Kantelettaren Runoihin, Vol. III
(K470)

Pimea Isoton Pirtti *Op.100,No.58
"Dunkel Ist Die Kleine Kammer"
solo,pno FAZER F 3297 see from
Lauluja Kantelettaren Runoihin,
Vol. VIII   (K471)

Pyhain Miesten Paivana *Op.18,No.5
"Am Allerheiligentage" see
Einunddreissig Lieder Nach
Gedichten Von Huugo Jalkasen,
Vol. IV

Rakastan Kauneutta
solo,pno FAZER F 2771 see from Syv
Laulua Eila Kivikk'ahon Runoihin
(K472)

Rannalta I *Op.23,No.1
"Vom Strande I" solo,pno FAZER
F 2288 see from Siebenunddreissig
Lieder Nach Gedichten Von V.A.
Koskenniemi, Vol. IV   (K473)

Rannalta II *Op.23,No.2
"Vom Strande II" solo,pno FAZER
F 2289 see from Siebenunddreissig
Lieder Nach Gedichten Von V.A.
Koskenniemi, Vol. IV   (K474)

Reifen Einst *see Kummalstako
Kuuleminen

Rosa Lill' *Op.47,No.5
"Roselein" solo,pno FAZER F 2268
see from Kuusi Laulu   (K475)

Roselein *see Rosa Lill'

Rosenbusche
"Roses" solo,pno FAZER F 4643 see
from Hermann Lons Lieder, Vol. IV
(K476)

Roses *see Rosenbusche

Sa Dansa *Op.47,No.6
"So Tanze" solo,pno FAZER F 2269
see from Kuusi Laulu   (K477)

Sa Menit *Op.53,No.4
"You Went Away, My Love" [Eng/Ger/
Finn] solo,pno FAZER F 2159 see
from Tunturilauluja, Vol. II
(K478)

Sa Mykka Matkalainen Maan *Op.25,
No.2
"Du Stummer Weggenosse Mein" solo,
pno FAZER F 2300 see from
Siebenunddreissig Lieder Nach
Gedichten Von V.A. Koskenniemi,
Vol. VI   (K479)

Sag', Wo Weilst Du, Mein Lieb?
*Op.16,No.9
(Fougstedt, Nils Erik) [Finn/Ger]
med solo,2fl,2ob,2clar,2bsn,
2horn,strings BREITKOPF-W s.p.
(K480)
(Parmet, Simon) [Finn/Ger] med
solo,fl,English horn,rec,2bsn,
4horn,timp,harp,strings voc sc
BREITKOPF-W s.p.   (K481)

Saisinko Kaelta Kielen *Op.100,No.50
"Wie Der Kuckuck Mocht' Ich Rufen"
solo,pno FAZER F 3289 see from
Lauluja Kantelettaren Runoihin,
Vol. VII   (K482)

Sanoissa Kuluva *Op.100,No.59
"Bose Worte Ikuinen Suru" solo,pno
FAZER F 3298 see from Lauluja
Kantelettaren Runoihin, Vol. VIII
(K483)

Schaferlied
"Shepherd's Song" solo,pno FAZER
F 4642 see from Hermann Lons
Lieder, Vol. IV   (K484)

Scheine Hell, O Sonne *see Paista
Paivanen Jumala

Schlaf, Nur Schlaf *see Tuuti, Tuuti
Tummaistani

Schon Ist Es Zu Sterben Im Kampfe
*see Soria Sotahan Kuolla

Search, The *see Liebessuche

Sechs Lieder *Op.59, CC6U
[Ger] med solo,pno BOTE $4.50
(K485)

KILPINEN, YRIO (cont'd.)

Sechs Lieder Um Den Tod *Op.62, CC6U
[Eng/Ger] med solo,pno BOTE $4.50
(K486)

Sechs Sommersegen *Op.75, CC6U
[Ger] med-high solo,pno BOTE $4.50
(K487)

Sei Willkommen, Lieber Thomas *see
Tule Meille, Tuomas-Kulta

Seibenundzwanzig Lieder Nach
Gedichten Von Erik Blomberg, Vol.
I
solo,pno FAZER W 2571 s.p.
contains: Dyningen, Op.48,No.1;
Jag Vantar Ingen Lycka, Op.48,
No.6; Manniskans Hem, Op.48,
No.5; Snoblommor, Op.48,No.2;
Stjarnorna Aro Sa Stilla,
Op.48,No.3; Vem Ar Du?, Op.48,
No.4   (K488)

Selbst Gelernt Hab' Ich Meine Lieder
*see Omat On Virret Oppimiani

Septembersonett *see Syyskuun
Sonetti

Shepherd's Song *see Schaferlied

Shon Maria, Meine Beere *see
Kukkalatva Kuusi

Sieben Lieder *Op.79, CC7U
[Ger] med-high solo,pno BOTE $4.00
(K489)

Siebenunddreissig Lieder Nach
Gedichten Von V.A. Koskenniemi,
Vol. I *see Elegia Kauneudelle,
"Elegie An Die Schonheit", Op.20,
No.1; Elegia Yolle, "Elegie An
Die Nacht", Op.20,No.5; Endymion,
Op.20,No.2; Kevat Keralla,
"Fruher Fruhling", Op.20,No.3;
Sonetti Sadun Linnusta, "Sonett
Auf Den Marchenvogel", Op.20,No.4
(K490)

Siebenunddreissig Lieder Nach
Gedichten Von V.A.Koskenniemi,
Vol. II *see Elegie
Satakielelle, "Elegia An Die
Nachtigall", Op.21,No.1; Ihme,
"Wunder", Op.21,No.6; Kesayossa,
"In Der Sommernacht", Op.21,No.4;
Kuutamolla, "Im Mondschein",
Op.21,No.2; Lehdokki,
"Nachtviole", Op.21,No.3;
Syyskuun Sonetti,
"Septembersonett", Op.21,No.5
(K491)

Siebenunddreissig Lieder Nach
Gedichten Von V.A. Koskenniemi,
Vol. III *see Lakeus, "Die
Ebene", Op.22,No.1; Lakeus II,
"Die Ebene II", Op.22,No.2;
Lakeus III, "Die Ebene III",
Op.22,No.3; Lakeus IV, "Die Ebene
IV", Op.22,No.4; Lakeus V, "Die
Ebene V", Op.22,No.5   (K492)

Siebenunddreissig Lieder Nach
Gedichten Von V.A. Koskenniemi,
Vol. IV *see Hyokyaalto, "Die
Sturzwelle", Op.23,No.6;
Kehtolaulu, "Wiegenlied", Op.23,
No.4; Kesayo, "Sommernacht",
Op.23,No.3; Rannalta I, "Vom
Strande I", Op.23,No.1; Rannalta
II, "Vom Strande II", Op.23,No.2;
Vanha Laulu, "Altes Lied", Op.23,
No.5   (K493)

Siebenunddreissig Lieder Nach
Gedichten Von V.A. Koskenniemi,
Vol. V *see Ikarus, Op.24,No.5;
Kaupungilla Sataa, "Herbstregen",
Op.24,No.1; On Kaikki Syksyn
Tahdet Syttyneet, "Sind Alie
Herbstes Sterne Aufgegluht",
Op.24,No.2; Syyssonetti,
"Herbstsonett", Op.24,No.3;
Yksin, "Allein", Op.24,No.4
(K494)

Siebenunddreissig Lieder Nach
Gedichten Von V.A. Koskenniemi,
Vol. VI *see Elegia
Yksinaisyydelle, "Elegie An Die
Einsamkeit", Op.25,No.4; Fiat
Nox, Op.25,No.5; Jaa Hyvasti Ja
Nakemiin, "Lebewohl Und Auf
Wiedersehn", Op.25,No.3; Sa Mykka
Matkalainen Maan, "Du Stummer
Weggenosse Mein", Op.25,No.2;
Ystavien Piiri Pienentyy, "Klein
Und Kleiner Wird Der Freunde
Kreis", Op.25,No.1   (K495)

Siebenunddreissig Lieder Nach
Gedichten Von V.A. Koskenniemi,
Vol. VII *see Auringon Nousu,
"Sonnenaufgang", Op.26,No.5;
Leivonen, "Die Lerche", Op.26,
No.4; Olit Tuskasta Varisten
Herannyt Syon, "Im Schmerzen
Erschauerund", Op.26,No.1; Sun

KILPINEN, YRIO (cont'd.)

Tuskin Huomasin, "Ich Liess Dich
Achtlos", Op.26,No.2; Valkeat
Kaupungit, "Weisse Stadte",
Op.26,No.3   (K496)

Siebenundzwanzig Lieder Nach
Gedichten Von Erik Blomberg, Vol.
II
solo,pno FAZER W 2572 s.p.
contains: Appeltrad Och
Parontrad, Op.49,No.4; Den
Djupa Kallan, Op.49,No.5; Den
Ljusa Nattens Ljusa
Fageldrillar, Op.49,No.3; Forr
Agde Jag Intet, Op.49,No.1; Jag
Har Haft En Stor, Tyst Sorg,
Op.49,No.2; Var Stilla Hjarta,
Op.49,No.6   (K497)

Siebenundzwanzig Lieder Nach
Gedichten Von Erik Blomberg, Vol.
III
solo,pno FAZER W 2573 s.p.
contains: En Ung Mor, Op.50,No.2;
I Dina Handers Mjuka Fagelbo,
Op.50,No.1; Jag Ville Vara
Tarar, Op.50,No.4; Modern,
Op.50,No.3; Till En Diktare,
Op.50,No.6; Visa, Op.50,No.5
                                    (K498)

Siebenundzwanzig Lieder Nach
Gedichten Von Erik Blomberg, Vol.
IV
solo,pno FAZER W 2582 s.p.
contains: Desmonas Sang, Op.51,
No.1; Gravskrift Over Ett Litet
Barn, Op.51,No.2; Korsbar,
Op.51,No.5; Till Elektra,
Op.51,No.4; Till Nagra
Paskliljor, Op.51,No.3   (K499)

Siebenundzwanzig Lieder Nach
Gedichten Von Erik Blomberg, Vol.
V
solo,pno FAZER W 2583 s.p.
contains: Forledde Van, Op.51,
No.8; Gullvivan, Op.51,No.6;
Larksang, Op.51,No.9; Och Stod
Du I Den Kalla Blast, Op.51,
No.7   (K500)

Silloin Laulan *Op.100,No.5
"Dann Singe Ich" solo,pno FAZER
F 3244 see from Lauluja
Kantelettaren Runoihin, Vol. I
                                    (K501)

Sind Alle Herbstes Sterne Aufgegluht
*see On Kaikki Syksyn Tahdet
Syttyneet

Sing Mein Herze *see Sjung Mitt
Hjarta

Singe, Mein Schones Madchen *see
Soitapas

Six Songs
[Finn/Dan/Ger] med solo,kbd HANSEN-
DEN s.p.
contains: Alla Dem Som Vilse
Fara, "Alle Die, Die Sich
Verirrten", Op.42,No.6; En
Rune, "Eine Rune", Op.42,No.1;
Kvallning, "Abend", Op.42,No.4;
Landskap, "Landschaft", Op.42,
No.3; Lat Vara, "Lass Fahren",
Op.42,No.2; Sol, Sol!, "Sonn',
Sonn!", Op.42,No.5   (K502)

Sjung Mitt Hjarta *Op.47,No.3
"Sing Mein Herze" solo,pno FAZER
F 2266 see from Kuusi Laulu
                                    (K503)

Snoblommor *Op.48,No.2
see Seibenundzwanzig Lieder Nach
Gedichten Von Erik Blomberg, Vol.
I

So Tanze *see Sa Dansa

Soitapas *Op.100,No.40
"Singe, Mein Schones Madchen" solo,
pno FAZER F 3279 see from Lauluja
Kantelettaren Runoihin, Vol. V
                                    (K504)

Sol, Sol! *Op.42,No.5
"Sonn', Sonn!" see Six Songs

Solches Hort' Ich *see Sopivaisia

Sollen Diesen Weg Nun Gehen *see
Mista Sinne Tie Menevi

Sollt' Auch Ich Nicht Ermuden *see
Miksi En Vasyisi

Solstralen *Op.47,No.2
"Sonnenstrahlen" solo,pno FAZER
F 2265 see from Kuusi Laulu
                                    (K505)

Sommernacht *see Kesayo

KILPINEN, YRIO (cont'd.)

Sonett Auf Den Marchenvogel *see
Sonetti Sadun Linnusta

Sonetti Sadun Linnusta *Op.20,No.4
"Sonett Auf Den Marchenvogel" solo,
pno FAZER F 2276 see from
Siebenunddreissig Lieder Nach
Gedichten Von V.A. Koskenniemi,
Vol. I   (K506)

Song Of The Fells *see Tunturilaulu

Sonn', Sonn! *see Sol, Sol!

Sonnenaufgang *see Auringon Nousu

Sonnenstrahlen *see Solstralen

Sopivaisia *Op.100,No.7
"Solches Hort' Ich" solo,pno FAZER
F 3246 see from Lauluja
Kantelettaren Runoihin, Vol. I
                                    (K507)

Soria Sotahan Kuolla *Op.100,No.55
"Schon Ist Es Zu Sterben Im Kampfe"
solo,pno FAZER F 3294 see from
Lauluja Kantelettaren Runoihin,
Vol. VII   (K508)

Spielmanns-Lieder *Op.77, CCU
[Ger] med solo,pno BOTE $4.50
                                    (K509)

Stamningsvisa *Op.47,No.4
"Stimmungslied" solo,pno FAZER
F 2267 see from Kuusi Laulu
                                    (K510)

Stimmungslied *see Stamningsvisa

Stjarnorna Aro Sa Stilla *Op.48,No.3
see Seibenundzwanzig Lieder Nach
Gedichten Von Erik Blomberg, Vol.
I

Summer Song *see Suvilaulu

Sun Tuskin Huomasin *Op.26,No.2
"Ich Liess Dich Achtlos" solo,pno
FAZER F 2305 see from
Siebenunddreissig Lieder Nach
Gedichten Von V.A. Koskenniemi,
Vol. VII   (K511)

Suvilaulu *Op.54,No.3
"Summer Song" [Eng/Ger/Finn] solo,
pno FAZER F 2162 see from
Tunturilauluja, Vol. III   (K512)

Syv Laulua Eila Kivikk'ahon Runoihin
*see Eiko Totta; Eras; Kevatta;
Memnonin Laulu; Muisto; Nocturne;
Rakastan Kauneutta   (K513)

Syyskuun Sonetti *Op.21,No.5
"Septembersonett" solo,pno FAZER
F 2282 see from Siebenunddreissig
Lieder Nach Gedichten Von
V.A.Koskenniemi, Vol. II   (K514)

Syyssonetti *Op.24,No.3
"Herbstsonett" solo,pno FAZER
F 2296 see from Siebenunddreissig
Lieder Nach Gedichten Von V.A.
Koskenniemi, Vol. V   (K515)

Tannenbaumchen Und Voglein *see
Kuusi Ja Lintunen

Tanssi *Op.100,No.15
"Der Tanz" solo,pno FAZER F 3254
see from Lauluja Kantelettaren
Runoihin, Vol. II   (K516)

There Was A Wind That Blew *see
Mannertreu

There Where White Ringdoves Flutter
*see Der Schonste Platz

Till Elektra *Op.51,No.4
see Siebenundzwanzig Lieder Nach
Gedichten Von Erik Blomberg, Vol.
IV

Till En Diktare *Op.50,No.6
see Siebenundzwanzig Lieder Nach
Gedichten Von Erik Blomberg, Vol.
III

Till Nagra Paskliljor *Op.51,No.3
see Siebenundzwanzig Lieder Nach
Gedichten Von Erik Blomberg, Vol.
IV

To The Song *see Laululle

Tule Meille, Tuomas-Kulta *Op.100,
No.32
"Sei Willkommen, Lieber Thomas"
solo,pno FAZER F 3271 see from
Lauluja Kantelettaren Runoihin,
Vol. IV   (K517)

KILPINEN, YRIO (cont'd.)

Tule Tanne *Op.100,No.4
"Komm, O Komme" solo,pno FAZER
F 3243 see from Lauluja
Kantelettaren Runoihin, Vol. I
                                    (K518)

Tunturilahde *Op.52,No.2
"Mountain Brook, The" [Eng/Ger/
Finn] solo,pno FAZER F 2153 see
from Tunturilauluja, Vol. I
                                    (K519)

Tunturilaulu *Op.54,No.4
"Song Of The Fells" [Eng/Ger/Finn]
solo,pno FAZER F 2163 see from
Tunturilauluja, Vol. III   (K520)

Tunturilauluja, Vol. I *see Janka,
"Fen, The", Op.52,No.1; Laululle,
"To The Song", Op.52,No.3;
Tunturilahde, "Mountain Brook,
The", Op.52,No.2; Tunturille,
"Away To The Mountains", Op.52,
No.4   (K521)

Tunturilauluja, Vol. II *see
Hillankukka, "Cloudberry Flower,
The", Op.53,No.1; Murheen Kellot,
"Bells Of Sorrow, The", Op.53,
No.2; Muuttilintu, "Migrant,
The", Op.53,No.3; Sa Menit, "You
Went Away, My Love", Op.53,No.4
                                    (K522)

Tunturilauluja, Vol. III *see
Kirkkorannassa, "Come, Oh Wawe",
Op.54,No.2; Suvilaulu, "Summer
Song", Op.54,No.3; Tunturilaulu,
"Song Of The Fells", Op.54,No.4;
Vanha Kirkko, "Ancient Church",
Op.54,No.1   (K523)

Tunturille *Op.52,No.4
"Away To The Mountains" [Eng/Ger/
Finn] solo,pno FAZER F 2155 see
from Tunturilauluja, Vol. I
                                    (K524)

Tuuti, Tuuti Tummaistani *Op.100,
No.51
"Schlaf, Nur Schlaf" solo,pno FAZER
F 3290 see from Lauluja
Kantelettaren Runoihin, Vol. VII
                                    (K525)

Tuutulaulu *Op.100,No.20
"Wiegenlied" solo,pno FAZER F 3259
see from Lauluja Kantelettaren
Runoihin, Vol. III   (K526)

Twenty Songs, Vol. 3, Op. 41 *CC8L
[Finn/Dan/Ger] med solo,kbd HANSEN-
DEN s.p.   (K527)

Uusi Alladdin
"Der Neue Alladdin" see
Einunddreissig Lieder Nach
Gedichten Von Huugo Jalkasen,
Vol. IV

Vaha Ilo Emottomalle Kaesta *Op.100,
No.52
"Kuckuck Rief Im Fichtenwalde"
solo,pno FAZER F 3291 see from
Lauluja Kantelettaren Runoihin,
Vol. VII   (K528)

Valkeat Kaupungit *Op.26,No.3
"Weisse Stadte" solo,pno FAZER
F 2306 see from Siebenunddreissig
Lieder Nach Gedichten Von V.A.
Koskenniemi, Vol. VII   (K529)

Vanha Kirkko *Op.54,No.1
"Ancient Church" [Eng/Ger/Finn]
solo,pno FAZER F2160 see from
Tunturilauluja, Vol. III   (K530)

Vanha Laulu *Op.23,No.5
"Altes Lied" solo,pno FAZER F 2292
see from Siebenunddreissig Lieder
Nach Gedichten Von V.A.
Koskenniemi, Vol. IV   (K531)

Var Stilla Hjarta *Op.49,No.6
see Siebenundzwanzig Lieder Nach
Gedichten Von Erik Blomberg, Vol.
II

Vem Ar Du? *Op.48,No.4
see Seibenundzwanzig Lieder Nach
Gedichten Von Erik Blomberg, Vol.
I

Viele Madchen Kann Ich Zahlen *see
Mont' On Mulla Morsianta

Viikon Vuottelin Kakea *Op.100,No.11
"Lang' Ersehnt Ich" solo,pno FAZER
F 3250 see from Lauluja
Kantelettaren Runoihin, Vol. II
                                    (K532)

Visa *Op.50,No.5
see Siebenundzwanzig Lieder Nach
Gedichten Von Erik Blomberg, Vol.
III

KILPINEN, YRIO (cont'd.)

Voi, Jos Mie Tok' Miehen Saisin
  *Op.100,No.19
  "Wenn Ich" solo,pno FAZER F 3258
    see from Lauluja Kantelettaren
    Runoihin, Vol. III   (K533)

Voi Minua Mieskulua *Op.100,No.46
  "Ach, Ich Bin Ein Narr Gewesen"
  solo,pno FAZER F 3285 see from
    Lauluja Kantelettaren Runoihin,
    Vol. VI   (K534)

Vom Strande I *see Rannalta I

Vom Strande II *see Rannalta II

Was Kummert Mich *see Mitapa Suren
  Sanoista

Weisse Stadte *see Valkeat Kaupungit

Wenn Ich *see Voi, Jos Mie Tok'
  Miehen Saisin

Wenn Ich Macht Und Gelde Hatte *see
  Oisi Mulla Vallan Miekka

Wenn Mein Lied Ich Beginne *see Jos
  Ma Laululle Rupean

Wie Der Kuckuck Mocht' Ich Rufen
  *see Saisinko Kaelta Kielen

Wie Entgelt' Ich Meiner Mutter *see
  Milla Maksan Maammon Maion

Wie Ist Ein Frohes Herz *see Erotus
  Mielilla

Wie Zwei Vogelein Waren Wir Beide
  *see Kaks' Oli Meita Kaunokaista

Wiegenlied *see Kehtolaulu

Wiegenlied *see Tuutulaulu

Wo Mag Mein Schatzlein Weilen *see
  Missa Armahin

Wunder *see Ihme

Yksin *Op.24,No.4
  "Allein" solo,pno FAZER F 2297 see
    from Siebenunddreissig Lieder
    Nach Gedichten Von V.A.
    Koskenniemi, Vol. V   (K535)

Yli Hohtavan Hangen *Op.18,No.6
  "Der Skilaufer" see Einunddreissig
    Lieder Nach Gedichten Von Huugo
    Jalkasen, Vol. IV

You Went Away, My Love *see Sa Menit

Ystavien Piiri Pienentyy *Op.25,No.1
  "Klein Und Kleiner Wird Der Freunde
    Kreis" solo,pno FAZER F 2299 see
    from Siebenunddreissig Lieder
    Nach Gedichten Von V.A.
    Koskenniemi, Vol. VI   (K536)

Zehn Lieder Der Liebe *Op.60-61,
  CC10U
  [Ger] med solo,pno BOTE $3.50. ea.
    in two volumes   (K537)

Zur Erinnerung
  "In Remembrance" solo,pno FAZER
    F 4641 see from Hermann Lons
    Lieder, Vol. III   (K538)

Zwolf Fjeldlieder, Op. 52 *CCU
  [Finn/Swed/Ger/Eng] solo,pno
    BREITKOPF-W 57 05041 s.p.   (K539)

Zwolf Fjeldlieder, Op. 53 *CCU
  [Finn/Swed/Ger/Eng] solo,pno
    BREITKOPF-W 57 05042 s.p.   (K540)

Zwolf Fjeldlieder, Op. 54 *CCU
  [Finn/Swed/Ger/Eng] solo,pno
    BREITKOPF-W 57 05043 s.p.   (K541)

KIM, ANDY
  Letters Found Near A Suicide
    Mez solo,pno EMI s.p.   (K542)

KIND see Mengelberg, Rudolf

KIND DEATH see Merku, Pavle, Prijazna
  Smrt

KIND DER AARDE see Zweers, [Bernard]

KIND, DU KANNST TANZEN see Fall, Leo

KIND VAN MIJN LIEFDE see Cuypers, H.

KINDER MIR HOBN SIMCHAS TOYRE *folk,
  Jew
  med solo,pno HATIKVAH ED. 42 $.25
                                (K543)

KINDER SPIELEN ZUR WEIHNACHT *CCU,Xmas
  (Pohl, Lotta; Buschbaum, Rainer-Glen)
  solo,2pno (easy) NAGELS 803 s.p.
                                (K544)
KINDER SPIELEN ZUR WEIHNACHT *CC19U,
  Xmas
  (Pohl; Buschbaum) [Ger] med solo,pno
    NAGELS $1.75   (K545)

KINDER- UND WEIHNACHTSLIEDER see
  Dieckmann, Johannes

KINDERLIED FUR ZWEI KINDERSTIMMEN OHNE
  BEGLEITUNG see Dvorak, Antonin

KINDERLIEDER see Blech, Leo

KINDERLIEDER see Schafer, M.

KINDERLIEDER see Barth, Hans Joachim

KINDERLIEDER see Prokofiev, Serge

KINDERLIEDER, HEFT I, II, & III see
  Geisler, Willy

KINDERLIEDER I see Reinecke, Carl

KINDERLIEDER I see Trunk, Richard

KINDERLIEDER II see Reinecke, Carl

KINDERLIEDER II see Trunk, Richard

KINDERLIEDER NACH TEXTEN VON CHR.
  MORGENSTERN see Skorzeny, Fritz

KINDERLIEDER-SUITE see Braun, Gunter

KINDERLIEDJES, BD I see Frid, Geza

KINDERLIEDJES, BD. II see Frid, Geza

KINDERMANN, JOHANN ERASMUS (1616-1655)
  Creator Spirit, By Whose Aid *sac
    SA/TB soli,2vln/2fl,cont oct
    CONCORDIA 98-1482 $.25   (K546)

  Dear Christians, Praise God Evermore
    *sac
    med solo,2vln,cont oct CONCORDIA
    98-1503 $.20   (K547)

KINDERREIGEN see Haas, Joseph

KINDERREIME see Scholz, Erwin Christian

KINDERREIME see Metzler, Friedrich

KINDERSANG SCHAFFT FROHE HERZEN see
  Lehner, Leo

KINDERSTIMMUNGEN see Haba, Alois,
  Detske Nalady

KINDERSTUBE see Mussorgsky, Modest

KINDERSTUBE see Mussorgsky, Modest

KINDERTOTENLIEDER see Mahler, Gustav

KINDERTOTENLIEDER see Mahler, Gustav

KINDERTOTENLIEDER see Mahler, Gustav

KINDERTOTENLIEDER see Mahler, Gustav

KINDERVRAGE see Franken, Wim

KINDESGEBET see Schumann, Georg

KINDHEIT see Orthel, Leon

KINDJE see Hamoir, A.

KINDJE WAT BEN JE TOCH ZACHT see
  Mortelmans, Lodewijk

KINDLICHE FRAGE see Kox, Hans

KING
  Bathing In The Sunlight Of His Love
    *sac
    solo,pno BENSON S5150-R $1.00
                                (K548)

  Come Unto Me *sac
    med solo,pno (C maj) CENTURY 1115
    $.40   (K549)

  Rosary, The *sac
    med solo,pno (A flat maj) CENTURY
    1114 $.40   (K550)

  Welcome Home, Children *sac
    solo,pno BENSON S8357-R $1.00
                                (K551)

KING AND I, THE see Lister, Mosie

KING AND THE BEGGAR, THE see Fisher

KING AND THE CONSTITUTION, THE see
  Hook, James

KING ARTHUR see Broadwood, Lucy E.

KING ARTHUR'S FAREWELL see Warren,
  Elinor Remick

KING ASCENDETH INTO HEAVEN, THE see
  Willan, Healey

KING CHARLES see Harrison, Julius Allen
  Greenway

KING DAVID see Howells, Herbert Norman

KING, HAROLD C. (1895-   )
  Ballade Des Cloches
    see Etre Poete

  Chanson D'hiver
    see Etre Poete

  Das Einhorn
    see Drie Fabelen Van R.M. Rilke

  Daybreak
    see Three Poems Bij H.W. Longfellow

  Der Welt Lohn
    see Vier Lieder Von W. Von Der
    Vogelweide

  Dialogue From "A Century Of
    Roundels", A
    Bar solo,bsn/vcl,pno DONEMUS s.p.
                                (K552)

  Die Magdeburger Weihnachtsfeier
    see Vier Lieder Von W. Von Der
    Vogelweide

  Dit Is Uw Deel
    Bar solo,pno DONEMUS s.p.   (K553)

  Drie Fabelen Van R.M. Rilke
    med solo/high solo,fl/ob/clar,pno
    voc sc DONEMUS s.p.
    contains: Das Einhorn; Ist Ein
      Schloss; Sankt Georg   (K554)

  Elckerlyc's Bede (from Den Spyegel
    Der Salicheyt Van Elckerlyc)
    S/T solo,pno DONEMUS s.p.   (K555)
    Mez/Bar solo,pno DONEMUS s.p.
                                (K556)

  Etre Poete
    see Etre Poete

  Etre Poete
    S solo,fl,clar,pno DONEMUS s.p.
    contains: Ballade Des Cloches;
      Chanson D'hiver; Etre Poete; La
      Lune Jaune; Les Chrysanthemes;
      Ondee Printaniere   (K557)

  Fragment: Ode To The West Wind
    Bar solo,pno DONEMUS s.p.   (K558)

  Ist Ein Schloss
    see Drie Fabelen Van R.M. Rilke

  La Lune Jaune
    see Etre Poete

  Les Chrysanthemes
    see Etre Poete

  Liebesbetorung
    see Vier Lieder Von W. Von Der
    Vogelweide

  Lof Van Nederland, Vol. I *CCU
    solo,pno BROEKMANS 181 s.p. (K559)

  Lof Van Nederland, Vol. II *CCU
    solo,pno BROEKMANS 182 s.p. (K560)

  Milton
    see Three Poems Bij H.W. Longfellow

  Ondee Printaniere
    see Etre Poete

  Sankt Georg
    see Drie Fabelen Van R.M. Rilke

  Three Poems Bij H.W. Longfellow
    low solo/med solo,pno DONEMUS s.p.
    contains: Daybreak; Milton; Tide
      Rises, The Tide Falls, The (K561)

  Tide Rises, The Tide Falls, The
    see Three Poems Bij H.W. Longfellow

  Traumdeutung
    see Vier Lieder Von W. Von Der
    Vogelweide

  Vergers *CCU
    med solo,pno DONEMUS s.p.   (K562)

  Vier Lieder Von W. Von Der Vogelweide
    med solo,pno DONEMUS s.p.
    contains: Der Welt Lohn; Die
      Magdeburger Weihnachtsfeier;
      Liebesbetorung; Traumdeutung
                                (K563)
  Zegen, Een Bundel Liederen *CC9L
    med solo,pno DONEMUS s.p.   (K564)

KING HENRY'S SONG see Sullivan, Sir
Arthur Seymour

KING IS COMING, THE see Gaither

KING IS COMING, THE see Gaither,
William J. (Bill)

KING IS COMING AND OTHER SONGS, THE
*sac,CCUL
(Gaither, Bill) solo,kbd SINGSPIR
5417 $2.95   (K565)

KING JESUS see Delamont

KING JESUS WILL ROLL ALL BURDEN'S AWAY
*sac,gospel
solo,pno ABER.GRP. $1.50   (K566)

KING, LORD AND COMMONS see Hook, James,
British Loyalty

KING MIDAS see Rorem, Ned

KING OF LOVE, THE see James, Philip

KING OF LOVE MY SHEPHERD IS, THE see
Gounod, Charles Francois, Le Roi
D'amour Est Mon Pasteur

KING OF LOVE MY SHEPHERD IS, THE see
Shelley, Harry Rowe

KING OF LOVE MY SHEPHERD IS, THE see
Speaks, Oley

KING OF THULE, THE see Gounod, Charles
Francois, Il Etait Un Roi De Thule

KING PHILIP'S ARIA see Verdi, Giuseppe

KING REBE'S ARIA see Tchaikovsky, Piotr
Ilyitch

KING RENE'S ARIA see Tchaikovsky, Piotr
Ilyitch

KING, WILTON
Brown Eyes Of Mary
solo,pno LEONARD-ENG   (K567)

Rose Will Blow, The
low solo,pno (F maj) CRAMER   (K568)
med solo,pno (G maj) CRAMER   (K569)
high solo,pno (A flat maj) CRAMER
(K570)

KINGDOM BY THE SEA see Somervell,
Arthur

KINGSLEY, GERSHON
Prayer For Peace *sac
high solo,pno TRANSCON. TV 551 $.75
(K571)
med solo,pno TRANSCON. TV 552 $.75
(K572)
Psalm 86 *see Teach Me, O Lord

Teach Me, O Lord (Psalm 86) sac,Bar
mitzvah/Cnfrm/Gen
med solo,pno TRANSCON. TV 554 $.75
(K573)
high solo,pno TRANSCON. TV 553 $.75
(K574)
Three Sacred Songs *sac,CC3U,Gen/
Marriage
[Heb/Eng] cantor/med solo,pno,opt
vcl TRANSCON. TV 545 $2.75 (K575)

KINNERSLEY, ELIZABETH
Rose In My Garden Dreaming
low solo,pno (E flat maj) CRAMER
(K576)
high solo,pno (G maj) CRAMER   (K577)

KIRALY, ERNO (1919-   )
Refleksija Br. 6
"Reflexion No. VI" solo,strings
MUSIC INFO rental   (K578)

Reflexion No. VI *see Refleksija Br.
6

KIRCHENLIED TEIL I *sac,CCU
(Diewald, J.; Lohmann, A.; Thurmair,
G.) solo,org CHRIS 50143 s.p.
(K579)

KIRCHENLIED TEIL II *sac,CCU
(Diewald, J.; Lohmann, A.; Thurmair,
G.) solo,org CHRIS 50144 s.p.
(K580)

KIRCHNER, T.
Det Sags, Det Blott Karlek Ar
high solo,pno GEHRMANS s.p.   (K581)
low solo,pno GEHRMANS s.p.   (K582)

KIRK
New Life, A *sac
solo,pno LILLENAS SM-875: SN $1.00
(K583)

KIRKKOLAULUJA *sac,CC50UL
solo,pno FAZER F3393 s.p. contains
works by: Carlsson; Elokas; Franck
and others   (K584)

KIRKKORANNASSA see Kilpinen, Yrio

KIRKLAND, TERRY
Until You Were There *sac
(McNabb) solo,pno LILLENAS
SM-952: SN $1.00   (K585)

KIRLIN, JUNE C.
Think On These Things *sac
low solo,pno (F maj) SCHIRM.G $.85
(K586)

KIRSCHBLUTENLIEDER see Walzel, L.M.

KIRSTY FORSYTH see McLeod, Robert

KISHI, KOICHI
Sieben Japanische Lieder *CC7L
solo,pno voc sc BIRNBACH s.p.   (K587)

KISHMUL'S GALLEY
(Kennedy-Fraser, M.; MacLeod, K.)
solo,pno (E maj) BOOSEY $1.50
(K588)

KISS, THE see Arditi, Luigi, Il Bacio

KISS, THE see Haubiel, Charles

KISS, THE see Rouse, Christopher

KISS AND A SMILE, A see Fisher, Howard

KISS ME AGAIN see Herbert, Victor

KISTENMACHER, ARTHUR
Trinklied
high solo,pno RIES s.p.   (K589)
med solo,pno RIES s.p.   (K590)
low solo,pno RIES s.p.   (K591)
(Satow, Karl) solo,2fl,ob,2clar,
2bsn,4horn,2trp,3trom,timp,perc,
harp,strings (E flat maj) RIES
s.p.   (K592)
(Schlemm, G.A.) solo,fl,ob,clar,
bsn,3horn,2trp,trom,timp,harp,
strings (F sharp maj) RIES s.p.
(K593)

KITAJSKE MINIATURE see Kozina, Marijan

KITCHEN
Broken Pieces *see Martin

KITCHEN FIRE see Day, Maude Craske

KITE, D.L.
God's People *sac
med solo,pno CRESPUB CP-S5058 $1.00
(K594)

KITTEL, CHRISTOPH (ca. 1620-ca. 1680)
O Susser Jesu Christ *sac
S/T solo,2vln,cont sc HANSSLER
20.604 s.p., ipa   (K595)

KITTY-CAT BIRD, THE see Kubik, Gail

KITTY DARLIN' see Friml, Rudolf

KITTY MAGEE see Somervell, Arthur

KITTY, MY LOVE, WILL YOU MARRY ME?
*folk
(Moore, Gerald) high solo,pno UNIVER.
12313 $.75   (K596)
(Moore, Gerald) med solo,pno UNIVER.
12313 $.75   (K597)

KITTY, MY LOVE, WILL YOU MARRY ME see
Hughes, Herbert

KITTY OF COLERAINE see Hughes, Herbert

KIURUN TIE see Luolajan-Mikkola, Vilho

KJELDAAS, ARNLJOT
Anna Helenes Vuggevise
see To Sanger

Lekende Barn
see To Sanger

To Sanger
solo,pno MUSIKK s.p.
contains: Anna Helenes Vuggevise;
Lekende Barn   (K598)

KJELDAAS, GUNNAR
Fangesongar Fra Kirkenes *CC8L
solo,pno MUSIKK s.p.   (K599)

KJELLANDER
En Nyarslat
solo,pno LUNDQUIST s.p. contains
also: En Vintervisa   (K600)

En Vintervisa
see Kjellander, En Nyarslat

Lilla Blomma, Hur Ensam Du Ar
solo,pno LUNDQUIST s.p.   (K601)

Nar Alla Faglar Tiga
solo,pno LUNDQUIST s.p.   (K602)

KJELLSBY, ERLING
Ten Norwegian Folk Songs *CC10U
[Norw] med solo,pno LYCHE LY457
s.p.   (K603)

KJERRINGVISE MOT VINTER'N see Beck,
Thomas [Ludvigsen]

KJERULF, [HALFDAN] (1815-1868)
Bon For Den Elskede
see Kjerulf, [Halfdan], Prinsessen
Sad Hojt I Sit Jomfrubur

Brudefaerden I Hardanger
solo,pno GEHRMANS 626 s.p.   (K604)

Gud Vet Det, Var Han Vankar
solo,pno GEHRMANS 365 s.p.   (K605)

Hvile I Skoven "I Graneholtet Vid
Middagstid"
solo,pno GEHRMANS 630 s.p.   (K606)

I Skoven "Jeg Gik Mig I Skoven Sa
Ensom En Gang"
solo,pno GEHRMANS 643 s.p.   (K607)

Ingrids Vise "Og Raeven La Under
Birkerod"
solo,pno GEHRMANS 632 s.p.   (K608)

Kan Det Troste
solo,pno LUNDQUIST s.p.   (K609)
low solo,pno HIRSCHS s.p.   (K610)
high solo,pno GEHRMANS 640 s.p.
(K611)

Laengsel
solo,pno LUNDQUIST s.p.   (K612)

Laengsel "Jeg Kunde Slet Ikke Sove"
solo,pno GEHRMANS 629 s.p.   (K613)

Laengsel "Vildeste Fugl I Flugt
solo,pno GEHRMANS 642 s.p.   (K614)

Min Elskte, Jeg Er Bunden
solo,pno GEHRMANS 627 s.p.   (K615)
solo,pno LUNDQUIST s.p.   (K616)

Min Skat
solo,pno GEHRMANS 648 s.p.   (K617)

Mit Hjerte Og Min Lyre
solo,pno LUNDQUIST s.p.   (K618)

Nokken "Jeg Lagde Mit Ore Til Kildens
Bred
solo,pno GEHRMANS 641 s.p. contains
also: Serenade "Natten Er Sa
Stille   (K619)

O, Vidste Du Bare!
solo,pno GEHRMANS 646 s.p.   (K620)

Over De Hoje Fjelde
solo,pno GEHRMANS 634 s.p.   (K621)

Prinsessen Sad Hojt I Sit Jomfrubur
solo,pno GEHRMANS 638 s.p. contains
also: Bon For Den Elskede (K622)

Quand Tu Dors
"Sov Och Drom" solo,pno GEHRMANS
647 s.p.   (K623)

Sanger Och Visor II-III *CCU
solo,pno GEHRMANS s.p., ea.   (K624)

Serenade "Av Manestraler Natten
Vaever"
solo,pno GEHRMANS 644 s.p.   (K625)

Serenade "Natten Er Sa Stille
see Kjerulf, [Halfdan], Nokken "Jeg
Lagde Mit Ore Til Kildens Bred

Serenade Ved Stranbredden "Hytten Er
Lukket"
solo,pno GEHRMANS 650 s.p.   (K626)

Serenade Ved Strandbredden
solo,pno LUNDQUIST s.p.   (K627)

Solvirkning "Til Fjelds Under
Granelien"
solo,pno GEHRMANS 639 s.p.   (K628)

Sov Och Drom *see Quand Tu Dors

Sovnen "Da Barnet Sov Ind"
solo,pno GEHRMANS 636 s.p.   (K629)

Synnoves Sang
solo,pno LUNDQUIST s.p.   (K630)

Ved Sjoen Den Morke
solo,pno GEHRMANS 645 s.p.   (K631)

Ved Sjoen "Hun Gik Langs Med
Stranden"
solo,pno GEHRMANS 637 s.p.   (K632)

Vejviseren Synger
solo,pno GEHRMANS 631 s.p.   (K633)

KJERULF, [HALFDAN] (cont'd.)

Vidste Du Vej
    solo,pno GEHRMANS 649 s.p.   (K634)

KLAARTJE see Voormolen, Alexander
    Nicolas

KLADSKE PISNICKY see Vycpalek, Ladislav

KLAES DE SPRAK ZIJN MOEDER AEN see
    Hullebroeck, Em.

KLAGE see Kremser, Edward

KLAGE DER ARIADNE see Monteverdi,
    Claudio, Lasciatemi Morire

KLAGE DER GARDE see Beekhuis, Hanna

KLAGELIEDER NACH JUDISCHER VOLKSPOESIE
    see Denisov, Edison Vasilievitch

KLAGEN see Merikanto, Oskar, Soi
    Vienosti Murheeni Soitto

KLAGEN IM WIND see Trunk, Richard

KLANGE AUS MAHREN, OP. 20, 32, 38 see
    Dvorak, Antonin

KLANGE AUS MAHREN, VOL. I see Dvorak,
    Antonin

KLANGE AUS MAHREN, VOL. II see Dvorak,
    Antonin

KLANGE DER HEIMAT see Strauss, Johann

KLANGE, I see Brahms, Johannes

KLANGE, II see Brahms, Johannes

KLARA STJARNOR MED OGON SNALLE
    solo,pno GEHRMANS 165 s.p.   (K635)

KLARNAD MORGON see Palmgren, Selim,
    Aamun Autereessa

KLART see Milveden, Ingemar

KLATSCHHANDCHENSPIEL see Mussorgsky,
    Modest

KLAVIERCHORALBUCH *sac,CC206U
    (Baum, Richard; Hofmann, Friedrich)
    solo,pno (med easy) cloth BAREN.
    3499 s.p.   (K636)

KLEBE, GISELHER (1925-   )
    Funf Lieder *Op.38,CC5U
    [Ger] med solo,pno BOTE $3.00
        (K637)

    Romische Elegien *Op.15
    narrator,pno,cembalo,bvl sc SCHOTTS
    rental, study sc SCHOTTS 4576
    s.p.   (K638)

KLEENLIEDJES OP KLEENDICHTJES see
    Zagwijn, Henri

KLEIN GEBED OM STILTE see Baeyens,
    August-L.

KLEIN, IVY FRANCES
    Primrose
    solo,pno CRAMER   (K639)

    Windless Day
    solo,pno CRAMER   (K640)

    Wood Of Flowers, The
    solo,pno CRAMER   (K641)

KLEIN, JONATHAN
    Hear O Israel *Sab-Eve
    SA soli,fl,sax,horn,pno,perc,bvl sc
    SEESAW $15.00, ipa   (K642)

KLEIN UND KLEINER WIRD DER FREUNDE
    KREIS see Kilpinen, Yrio, Ystavien
    Piiri Pienentyy

KLEINE BALLADE VON DEN DREI FLUSSEN see
    Reutter, Hermann

KLEINE GEISTLICHE KONZERTE see Schutz,
    Heinrich

KLEINE GEISTLICHE KONZERTE HEFT I see
    Schutz, Heinrich

KLEINE GEISTLICHE KONZERTE HEFT II see
    Schutz, Heinrich

KLEINE GEISTLICHE KONZERTE HEFT III see
    Schutz, Heinrich

KLEINE GEISTLICHE KONZERTE HEFT IV see
    Schutz, Heinrich

KLEINE GEISTLICHE KONZERTE HEFT V see
    Schutz, Heinrich

KLEINE GEISTLICHE KONZERTE HEFT VI see
    Schutz, Heinrich

KLEINE GEISTLICHE KONZERTE HEFT VII see
    Schutz, Heinrich

KLEINE GEISTLICHE KONZERTE HEFT VIII
    see Schutz, Heinrich

KLEINE GEISTLICHE KONZERTE HEFT IX see
    Schutz, Heinrich

KLEINE GEISTLICHE KONZERTE HEFT X see
    Schutz, Heinrich, Ich Hab Mein Sach
    Gott Heimgestellt

KLEINE GEISTLICHE KONZERTE HEFT XI see
    Schutz, Heinrich

KLEINE GEISTLICHE KONZERTE HEFT XII see
    Schutz, Heinrich

KLEINE GEISTLICHE KONZERTE HEFT XIV see
    Schutz, Heinrich

KLEINE GEISTLICHE KONZERTE HEFT XV see
    Schutz, Heinrich

KLEINE GEISTLICHE KONZERTE HEFT XVII
    see Schutz, Heinrich

KLEINE GEISTLICHE KONZERTE HEFT XVIII
    see Schutz, Heinrich, Jubilate Deo

KLEINE GEISTLICHE KONZERTE HEFT XIX see
    Schutz, Heinrich

KLEINE GEISTLICHE KONZERTE HEFT XX see
    Schutz, Heinrich, Wohl Dem, Der
    Nicht Wandelt Im Rate Der Gottlosen

KLEINE GESCHICHTE see Siebert, F.

KLEINE GESCHICTE see Siebert, F.

KLEINE KANTATE VON WALD UND AU see
    Telemann, Georg Philipp

KLEINE OUVERTURE see Flothius, Marius

KLEINE PHILOSOPHIE see Krebs, H.

KLEINE PRELUDE VAN RAVEL see Smit, Leo

KLEINE SOMMERKANTATE see Distler, Hugo

KLEINE SUITE see Flothius, Marius

KLEINE SUITE see Verhaar, Ary

KLEINE URSULA see Rudloff, P.

KLEINE WEIHNACHTSGESCHICHTE see Lothar,
    Mark

KLEINE WEIHNACHTSKANTATE NACH ALTEN
    TEXTEN see Brautigam, Helmut

KLEINER LASSE see Sibelius, Jean, Lasse
    Liten

KLEINER LASSE see Sibelius, Jean, Lasse
    Litten

KLEINER PFAD see Ikonen, Lauri, Polku
    Pieni

KLEINER, S.
    Mondsec
    "Nuit Etoilee" S/T solo,pno/inst
    DURAND s.p.   (K643)

    Nuit Etoilee *see Mondsec

KLEINER UND LEICHTER MESSGESANG see
    Rheinberger, Josef

KLEINES GEITLICHES KONZERT see Reutter,
    Hermann

KLEINES MAGNIFICAT see Bach, Johann
    Sebastian

KLEINSINGER, GEORGE (1914-   )
    Pee-Wee The Piccolo
    narrator,pno SCHIRM.G $.75   (K644)

KLEMETTI, HEIKKI (1876-1953)
    En Ma Huoli Huitukoille
    see Kolme Laulua

    Kaksi Laulua
    solo,pno FAZER F 2436 s.p.
        contains: Koditon; Parempi Olisi
        Ollut   (K645)

    Koditon
    see Kaksi Laulua

    Kolme Laulua
    solo,pno FAZER F 2432 s.p.
        contains: En Ma Huoli
        Huitukoille; Kultanukki;
        Rientoni   (K646)

KLEMETTI, HEIKKI (cont'd.)

    Kultanukki
    see Kolme Laulua

    Laps Suomen *CCU
    solo,pno FAZER F 2435 s.p.   (K647)

    Oi Kallis Suomenmaa *Op.41,No.3
    solo,pno FAZER F 2621 s.p.   (K648)

    Parempi Olisi Ollut
    see Kaksi Laulua

    Rientoni
    see Kolme Laulua

KLEMM, GUSTAV (1897-1947)
    Child's Prayer, A *sac
    low solo,pno (C maj) SCHIRM.G $.75
        (K649)
    low solo,pno (C maj) SCHIRM.G $.75
        (K650)
    med solo,pno (E flat maj) SCHIRM.G
    $.75   (K651)

    Curious Thing
    med solo,pno GALAXY 1.1142.7 $1.00
        (K652)

    Soft Are Your Arms
    solo,pno (F maj) BOOSEY $1.50
        (K653)

KLENAU, PAUL VON (1883-1946)
    Vier Lieder Nach Gedichten Von
    Friedrich Holderlin *CC4U
    low solo,pno (med easy) MULLER 1402
    s.p.   (K654)

KLERK, ALBERT DE (1917-   )
    Cinq Noels Francais *Xmas
    A solo,2fl,2ob,2clar,2bsn,2horn voc
    sc DONEMUS s.p.
        contains: Dans Une Grange
        Champetre; Dans Une Pauvre
        Etable; Jacotin; Tous Les
        Bourgeois De Chatre; Une Jeune
        Pucelle   (K655)

    Dans Une Grange Champetre
    see Cinq Noels Francais

    Dans Une Pauvre Etable
    see Cinq Noels Francais

    Drie Oud-Nederlandse Liederen
    low solo/med solo,pno DONEMUS s.p.
        contains: Ghequetst Ben Ick Van
        Binnen; Ick Seg Adieu; Syt
        Vrolyc Groot En Kleyne   (K656)

    Ecce Nunc (Psalm 133)
    see Klerk, Albert de, Laetatus Sum

    Ghequetst Ben Ick Van Binnen
    see Drie Oud-Nederlandse Liederen

    Ick Seg Adieu
    see Drie Oud-Nederlandse Liederen

    Jacotin
    see Cinq Noels Francais

    Jam Lucis Orto Sidere
    high solo,2fl,2ob,2clar,2bsn,2horn,
    2trp,3trom,timp,harp,strings
    DONEMUS s.p.   (K657)

    Kermislied
    med solo,pno TOORTS s.p.   (K658)

    Laetatus Sum (Psalm 121) sac
    S solo,pno DONEMUS s.p. contains
    also: Ecce Nunc (Psalm 133)
        (K659)

    Minnelied
    med solo,pno TOORTS s.p.   (K660)

    Psalm 121 *see Laetatus Sum

    Psalm 133 *see Ecce Nunc

    Syt Vrolyc Groot En Kleyne
    see Drie Oud-Nederlandse Liederen

    Tous Les Bourgeois De Chatre
    see Cinq Noels Francais

    Une Jeune Pucelle
    see Cinq Noels Francais

KLERK, JOS. DE
    Kerstmis
    solo,pno HEUWEKE. 280 s.p.   (K661)

KLETTURINN see Sveinsson, Gunnar Reynir

KLEURIG TWAALFTAL see Klunne, C.

KLINCK-RYM see Bunge, Sas

KLING see Strauss, Richard

KLING KLANG KLING DI WING see Haegi, A.

KLING LEISE, MEIN LIED see Liszt, Franz

KLINGENDE FAHRT *CCU
(Zschiesche) solo,gtr SCHOTTS 4840
s.p.   (K662)

KLINGENDE HEIMAT *CCU,folk
(Schwarz-Reiflingen, Erwin) solo,gtr
SIKORSKI 377 s.p.   (K663)

KLINGENDE LYRIK *CCU
(Reichert, E.) high solo,pno
DOBLINGER 08 504 s.p.   (K664)

KLINGENDORF
Tio Nya Visor Om Varen Och Sommaren
*CC10U
solo,pno LUNDQUIST s.p.   (K665)

KLINGSOR-LIEDER see Thomass, Eugen C.

KLIP, KLAP, EFEN MIR *folk,Jew
med solo,pno HATIKVAH ED. 47 $.20
(K666)

KLOCKAN TICKAR see Grafstrom

KLOCKORNA see Alfven, Hugo

KLOKKENKERSTLIED see Bonset, Jac.

KLOKKENZANG see Mortelmans, Lodewijk

KLOMPENLIEDEKE see Hullebroeck, Em.

KLOSTERFRAULEIN see Brahms, Johannes

KLOTZMAN, D.
Ocho Canciones Hebreas Modernas
*CC8L
[Span] solo,pno cmplt ed RICORDI-
ARG BA 10915 s.p. texts in Hebrew
and Yiddish   (K667)

KLUDAS, ERICH
Am Morgen
see Ein Kindertag

Auf Der Weise
see Ein Kindertag

Ein Kindertag
(Schreiter, Heinz) solo,fl,ob,
2clar,bsn,2horn,trp,timp,perc,
harp,strings RIES s.p.
contains: Am Morgen; Auf Der
Weise; Geburtstag; Laterne;
Rummelplatz   (K668)

Geburtstag
see Ein Kindertag

Laterne
see Ein Kindertag

Rummelplatz
see Ein Kindertag

KLUNNE, C.
Kleurig Twaalftal
solo,pno BROEKMANS 223 s.p. (K669)

KMETZ, T.
I Remember
med solo,pno PARAGON $1.00   (K670)

Valley Of My Dreams *see Gerald

KNAB
Knechtsballade
T solo,4strings sc TONGER s.p., ipa
(K671)

KNAB, ARMIN (1881-1951)
Acht Lieder (Goethe) *CC8U
high solo,4strings voc sc SCHOTTS
s.p.   (K672)

An Eine Rose *CC4U
[Ger] med solo,pno PETERS 5031
$4.75   (K673)

Das Vater Unser
see Knab, Armin, Der Englische
Gruss

Das Wessobrunner Gebet
see Vier Lieder Fur Sopran

Der Englische Gruss *sac
med solo,org BAREN. 2085
$5.75 contains also: Das Vater
Unser   (K674)

Der Gartner
see Eichendorff-Lieder

Dreiundzwanzig Kinderlieder *CC23U
solo,pno BREITKOPF-L EB 5233 s.p.
(K675)

Eichendorff-Lieder
A/Bar solo,pno LEUCKART s.p.
contains: Der Gartner;
Morgendammerung; Nacht; Nachts;
Was Ist Mir Denn So Wehe (K676)

KNAB, ARMIN (cont'd.)

Engelsgruss
see Zwei Solo-Kantaten

Four Sacred Songs *sac,CC4U
[Ger] med solo,org PETERS 5032
$6.00   (K677)

Gebet
see Vier Lieder Fur Sopran

Im Himmelreich Ein Haus Steht
see Vier Lieder Fur Sopran

Morgendammerung
see Eichendorff-Lieder

Nachgelassene Lieder, Heft 1 *CC7U
solo,pno PETERS 5311 s.p.   (K678)

Nachgelassene Lieder, Heft 2 *CC4U
solo,pno PETERS 5312 s.p.   (K679)

Nacht
see Eichendorff-Lieder

Nachts
see Eichendorff-Lieder

Sternseherin Lieder *CC3U
high solo,pno PETERS 5034 s.p.
(K680)

Three Songs *CC3U
[Ger] low solo,pno PETERS 5035
$6.00   (K681)

Vanitas Mundi
see Zwei Solo-Kantaten

Vier Lieder Fur Sopran
S solo,org LEUCKART s.p.
contains: Das Wessobrunner Gebet;
Gebet; Im Himmelreich Ein Haus
Steht; Wurzeln Des Waldes
(K682)

Was Ist Mir Denn So Wehe
see Eichendorff-Lieder

Wurzeln Des Waldes
see Vier Lieder Fur Sopran

Zwei Solo-Kantaten
S solo,fl,strings voc sc SCHOTTS
4038 s.p., ipa
contains: Engelsgruss; Vanitas
Mundi   (K683)

Zwolf Lieder Nach Goethe *CC12U
solo,pno SCHOTTS 3931 s.p.   (K684)

KNABEN UND KERLE see Felix, Vaclav,
Chlapci A Chlapi

KNAIFEL, A.
Canterville Ghost, The
SB soli,chamb.orch MEZ KNIGA 2.28
s.p.   (K685)

KNAP, ROLF (1937-   )
Dilemmaniana Voor Marrie
narrator,vcl, electronics DONEMUS
s.p.   (K686)

In Memoriam Gerrit Willems
narrator,2orch, electric saw, hand
saw and four thick planks DONEMUS
s.p.   (K687)

Le Couple(t)
solo,pno, electronics DONEMUS s.p.
(K688)

KNAPP, (MRS.) JOSEPH F.
Open The Gates Of The Temple *sac,
Easter
low solo,pno (D maj) WATERLOO $.65
(K689)
solo,pno (available in 5 keys)
ASHLEY $.95   (K690)
high solo,pno (F maj) ALLANS s.p.
(K691)
low solo,pno (D maj) ALLANS s.p.
(K692)
med solo,pno (E flat maj) ALLANS
s.p.   (K693)
med solo,pno (E flat maj) WATERLOO
$.65   (K694)
high solo,pno (F maj) WATERLOO $.65
(K695)
high solo,pno (G maj) BOSTON $1.50
(K696)
med-high solo,pno (F maj) BOSTON
$1.50   (K697)
med-low solo,pno (E flat maj)
BOSTON $1.50   (K698)
low solo,pno (D maj) BOSTON $1.50
(K699)
low solo,pno (C maj) BOSTON $1.50
(K700)
high solo&low solo,pno (F maj)
FISCHER,C V 1954   (K701)

KNECHT RUPRECHT-VOLKSLIEDER see
Taubert, Karl Heinz

KNECHTSBALLADE see Knab

KNEEL AT THE CROSS *sac,gospel
solo,pno ABER.GRP. $1.50   (K702)

KNELLWOLF, J.
Sennis Alp
solo,pno HUG s.p.   (K703)

KNIERER, HERMANN (1875-1957)
Das Vater Unser *sac
high solo,pno MULLER 36 s.p. (K704)
low solo,pno MULLER 37 s.p. (K705)

KNIGHT
First Look, The *sac
solo,pno BENSON S7841-S $1.00
(K706)

I'll Be In The Rapture *sac
solo,pno BENSON S6233-S $1.00
(K707)

Rocked In The Cradle Of The Deep
*sac
low solo,pno BELWIN $1.25   (K708)
low solo,pno (G maj) CENTURY 91
$.40   (K709)

KNIGHT, THE see Walton, Kenneth

KNIGHT OF BETHLEHEM, THE see Thompson,
David Cleghorn

KNIGHT OF THE HOLY GRAIL, THE see
Brumby, Colin

KNIGHT'S SONG, A see Shaw, Martin

KNOCK, KNOCK see Winter, Sister Miriam
Therese

KNOKKELBEEN see Hullebroeck, Em.

KNORR, ERNST LOTHER VON (1896-1973)
Ein Strauss, Fur Dich Gepfluckt
*CC15U
med solo,pno (med) BAREN. 2424
$5.75   (K710)

Sechs Kinderlieder Nach Gedichten Von
Christian Morgenstern *CC6U
med solo,pno (med) MULLER 1860 s.p.
(K711)

KNORRING, M. VON
Har Du En Van
"Jos Ystava Sull' On" solo,pno
FAZER F 766 s.p.   (K712)

Jos Ystava Sull' On *see Har Du En
Van

KNOT OF RIDDLES, A see Bliss, Sir
Arthur

KNOW YE THAT THE LORD HE IS GOD see
Britton

KNOWN ONLY TO HIM *sac,gospel
solo,pno ABER.GRP. $1.50   (K713)

KNOW'ST THOU NOT THAT FAIR LAND? see
Thomas, Ambroise, Connais Tu Le
Pays?

KNOW'ST THOU THE LAND see Beethoven,
Ludwig van, Mignon

KNOXVILLE: SUMMER OF 1915 see Barber,
Samuel

KNUSPERHAUSCHEN-DUETT see Humperdinck,
Engelbert

KNUTSEN, TORBJORN
God Natt
solo,pno MUSIKK s.p.   (K714)

KOBLER, ROBERT (1912-   )
Funf Lieder *CC5U
solo,vln,pno BREITKOPF-L EB 4017
s.p.   (K715)

Funf Wilhelm-Busch-Lieder *CC5U
S solo,vln,pno BREITKOPF-L EB 4017
$2.50   (K716)

KOBMANDS-VISE see Nielsen, Carl

KOCH
Bread Of Life *sac
high solo,pno (E flat maj) BOSTON
$1.50   (K717)

Five Sacred Solos *CC5U
med solo,pno FISCHER,C O 4944
(K718)

KOCH, FREDERICK
Be Not Afraid
solo,pno (C maj) BOOSEY $1.50
(K719)

Feed My Lambs *sac
solo,pno BOOSEY $1.50   (K720)

Five Songs For Medium Voice And
Prepared Piano *CC5U
med solo,pno sc SEESAW $5.00 (K721)

KOCH, FREDERICK (cont'd.)

Great Spaces
S solo,pno SEESAW   (K722)

Monadnock Cadenzas And Variations
*CCU
solo,trp,clar,perc,5strings,
electronic tape sc SEESAW $8.00
(K723)

River Night
med solo,pno TRI-TEN $1.20 (K724)

String Quartet No. 2
S solo,4strings sc SEESAW $10.00
(K725)

Trio Of Praise
A solo,vla,pno sc SEESAW $3.00
(K726)

KOCH, JOHANNES H.E. (1918-   )
Calico Pie
solo,pno GENERAL 177 $1.25 (K727)

Ditty
solo,pno GENERAL 185 $1.25 (K728)

Epitaph, An
solo,pno GENERAL 175 $1.25 (K729)

Immorality, An
solo,pno GENERAL 173 $1.25 (K730)

Jauchzet Gott, Alle Lande *sac
med solo,org HANSSLER 12.221 s.p.
(K731)

New Songs Of Old Mother Goose *CCU
solo,pno GENERAL 282 $2.75 (K732)

Nun Juble Laut, All Kreatur *sac,
concerto
SSATB soli,2rec,strings (diff)
BAREN. 3983 $9.75, ipa (K733)

Silver
solo,pno GENERAL 180 $1.25 (K734)

Tame Cat
solo,pno GENERAL 181 $1.25 (K735)

Tea Shop, The
solo,pno GENERAL 179 $1.25 (K736)

KOCH, SIGURD CHRISTIAN ERLUND VON
(1910-   )
Det Svenska Landet
solo,pno GEHRMANS s.p.   (K737)

KOCHAN, GUNTER (1930-   )
Drei Shakespeare-Lieder *CC3U
A solo,pno PETERS 9141 $9.00 (K738)

Funf Lieder *CC5U
med solo,pno DEUTSCHER 9002 s.p.
(K739)

KOCHAV NAFAL see Ben-Haim, Paul

KODALY, ZOLTAN (1882-1967)
Enekszo *Op.1, CCU,folk,Hung
[Hung/Eng] solo,pno BUDAPEST 1745
s.p.   (K740)

Epitaphium Joannis Hunyadi
[Hung] solo,pno BUDAPEST 5042 s.p.
(K741)

Farewell Carnival
[Eng/Ger/Hung] solo,pno (D maj)
BOOSEY $1.75 see from Seven
Songs, Op. 6   (K742)

Five Mountain-Tcheremissian Folk
Songs *CC5U
[Hung/Ger] solo,pno BUDAPEST 2646
s.p.   (K743)

From A Lover's Letter
[Eng/Ger/Hung] solo,pno (F sharp
min) BOOSEY $1.75 see from Seven
Songs, Op. 6   (K744)

Sadly Rustle The Leaves
[Eng/Ger/Hung] solo,pno (C sharp
min) BOOSEY $1.75 see from Seven
Songs, Op. 6   (K745)

Seven Songs, Op. 6 *see Farewell
Carnival; From A Lover's Letter;
Sadly Rustle The Leaves;
Solitude; Weeping   (K746)

Solitude
[Eng/Ger/Hung] solo,pno (C sharp
min) BOOSEY $1.75 see from Seven
Songs, Op. 6   (K747)

Three Songs *Op.14, CC3U
[Eng/Hung/Ger] S solo,pno BOOSEY
$5.00   (K748)

Weeping
[Eng/Ger/Hung] solo,pno BOOSEY
$1.75 see from Seven Songs, Op. 6
(K749)

KODITON see Klemetti, Heikki

KODOSH-KODOSH see Mana-Zucca, Mme.

KOECHLIN, CHARLES (1867-1950)
Chansons De Bilitis
high solo,pno SALABERT-US $8.00
contains: Chant Funebre; Epitaphe
De Bilitis; Hymne A Astarte;
Hymne A La Nuit; Pluie Au Matin
(K750)

Chant Funebre
see Chansons De Bilitis

Do You Care *see Si Tu Le Veux

Epitaphe De Bilitis
see Chansons De Bilitis

Hymne A Astarte
see Chansons De Bilitis

Hymne A La Nuit
see Chansons De Bilitis

La Chasse
see Rondels

La Nuit
see Rondels

Le Printemps
see Rondels

Le Renouveau
see Rondels

Le The
see Rondels

L'ete
see Rondels

Pluie Au Matin
see Chansons De Bilitis

Rondels
SALABERT-US $4.50
contains: La Chasse (high solo/
med solo,pno); La Nuit (high
solo/med solo,pno); Le
Printemps (high solo/med solo,
pno); Le Renouveau (SATB soli,
pno); Le The (high solo/med
solo,pno); L'ete (high solo/med
solo,pno)   (K751)

Si Tu Le Veux
"Do You Care" high solo,pno (A maj)
BOSTON $1.50   (K752)

KOECKERT
Chansons Populaires Espagnoles *CCU
solo,pno HENN 150 s.p.   (K753)

KOEKOEK see Praag, Henri C. van

KOEL IS DE WERELD see Kersters, Willem

KOELLREUTTER, HANS-JOACHIM (1915-   )
Acht Haikai Des Pedro Xisto *CC8U
B solo,fl,pno,gtr,perc MODERN s.p.
(K754)

Kulka - Gesange *CCU
S solo,pno MODERN s.p.   (K755)

Mudai
solo,acap MODERN rental (K756)

KOENEMAN, T.
Chant Des Bateliers Du Volga
(Chaliapine) "Song Of The Volga
Boatmen, The" [Russ/Eng/Fr] B
solo,kbd CHESTER s.p.   (K757)

Quand Le Roi Part Aux Combats
"When The King Went Forth To War"
[Eng/Fr] B solo,kbd (G maj)
CHESTER s.p.   (K758)
"When The King Went Forth To War"
[Eng/Fr] B solo,kbd (A maj)
CHESTER s.p.   (K759)

Song Of The Volga Boatmen, The *see
Chant Des Bateliers Du Volga

When The King Went Forth To War *see
Quand Le Roi Part Aux Combats

KOERBLER, MILIVOJ
In Memoriam
[Slav] solo,pno CROATICA s.p.
(K760)

Ten Songs For Children *CC10U
[Slav] solo,pno CROATICA s.p.
(K761)

KOERPPEN, ALFRED (1926-   )
Die Vagantenballade
B solo,fl,pno,perc voc sc
BREITKOPF-W EB 6989-91 s.p., ipa
(K762)
A solo,fl,timp,perc,pno BREITKOPF-W
s.p.   (K763)

Wie Freundliche Strahlt (from Der
Wildschutz)
Bar solo,2fl,2ob,2clar,2bsn,4horn,
2trp,3trom,timp,strings

KOERPPEN, ALFRED (cont'd.)

BREITKOPF-W s.p.   (K764)

KOESIUTAZ E' JESAKABAN see Paczolay, I.

KOETSIER, JAN (1911-   )
Aarde
see Zwervers Verzen

Amsterdam *Op.38, cant
S/T solo,fl,clar,pno,2vln,vla,vcl
DONEMUS s.p.   (K765)

Anfang Und Ende *Op.1,No.1
A solo,vla,pno DONEMUS s.p.
contains also: Nacht, Op.1,No.2;
Madchen Am Fenster, Op.1,No.3;
Nocturn I, Op.1,No.4; Nocturn II,
Op.1,No.5; Schluszstuck, Op.1,
No.6   (K766)

Bede Om Slaap
see Zwervers Verzen

De Wilgen
B/Bar solo,pno DONEMUS s.p. (K767)

Madchen Am Fenster *Op.1,No.3
see Koetsier, Jan, Anfang Und Ende

Merel
see Zwervers Verzen

Morgenstond
see Zwervers Verzen

Nacht *Op.1,No.2
see Koetsier, Jan, Anfang Und Ende

Nocturn I *Op.1,No.4
see Koetsier, Jan, Anfang Und Ende

Nocturn II *Op.1,No.5
see Koetsier, Jan, Anfang Und Ende

Schluszstuck *Op.1,No.6
see Koetsier, Jan, Anfang Und Ende

Vor Bildern Lyonel Feiningers, Heft I
*CC6U
med solo,pno DONEMUS s.p. (K768)

Vor Bildern Lyonel Feiningers, Heft
II *CC6U
med solo,pno DONEMUS s.p. (K769)

Wakker
see Zwervers Verzen

Zwervers Verzen *Op.9,No.1
med solo/high solo,pno DONEMUS s.p.
contains: Aarde; Bede Om Slaap;
Merel; Morgenstond; Wakker
(K770)

KOGOJ, MARIJ (1895-1956)
Poslednji Spevi *CCU
solo,pno DRUSTVO DSS 206 rental
(K771)

Samospevi *CCU
solo,pno PROSVETNI rental (K772)

KOHELETH see Weinberg, Jacob

KOHLER, SIEGFRIED (1927-   )
Der Struwwelpeter *Op.31
med solo,pno PETERS 5204 s.p.
(K773)

KOHN, KARL
Hal'lu Et Adonai
[Heb] solo,pno/org TRANSCON.
WJ 1404 $1.00   (K774)

KOHOTTAKAA RIEMUHUUTO *sac,CC27L
(Bashmakov) solo,pno FAZER F 5151
s.p. contains works by Russian
composers   (K775)

KOHOUT, J.
Milenci *song cycle
high solo,pno SUPRAPHON s.p. (K776)

KOHS, ELLIS B. (1916-   )
Epitaph
high solo,pno AM.COMP.AL. $3.30
(K777)

Fatal Interview
low solo,pno AM.COMP.AL. $7.70
(K778)

Four Orchestral Songs *CC4U
AT soli,2fl,2ob,2clar,2bsn,2horn,
2trp,3trom,tuba,harp,perc,strings
sc AM.COMP.AL. $8.25   (K779)

Psalm 23 *sac,mot
ST soli,pno sc AM.COMP.AL. (K780)

Three Elegaic Airs *CC3U
low solo,pno AM.COMP.AL. $3.30
(K781)

KOHTALO see Kuula, Toivo

KOIF MIR SHICHEILACH *Jew
solo,pno KAMMEN 403 $1.00 (K782)

KOIFT BAIGELACH *Jew
   solo,pno KAMMEN 88 $1.00   (K783)

KOIRUOHO, RUUSUKUKKA see Luolajan-
   Mikkola, Vilho

KOKKONEN, JOONAS (1921-   )
   Loululauluja Lapsille *Xmas
   solo,pno FAZER F 5046 s.p. (K784)

KOKOELMA YKSINLAULUJA NUORISOLLE, VOLS.
   I-IV *CCU
   solo,pno FAZER
   W 1407; W 2095; W 1674; W 2564
   s.p., ea.   (K785)

KOL KARA see Helfman, Max

KOL NIDRE *sac,Yom Kippur,Jew
   [Heb/Eng] solo,pno (traditional)
   MARKS $1.50   (K786)
   solo,pno ASHLEY $.95   (K787)
   solo,pno KAMMEN 2 $1.00   (K788)

KOL NIDRE see Berlinski, Herman

KOL YAAKOV see Wolf, Artur

KOLARGOSSEN see Geijer, Erik Gustaf

KOLEDA MILOSTNA see Martinu, Bohuslav

KOLENDRAGERS VAN SUEZ see Wall, C. v.d.

KOLER, MARTIN (1620-   )
   Unser Herr Jesus Christus *cant
   (Haacke, Walter) SSB soli,2vln,
   2vla,bsn,org (diff) BAREN. 956
   $5.25, ipa   (K789)

KOLINSKI, M.
   Six French Folksongs *CC6U
   S solo,fl,pno BERANDOL BER 1076
   $3.50   (K790)

KOLJAS see Dvorak, Antonin

KOLME LAULUA see Kaski, Heino

KOLME LAULUA see Klemetti, Heikki

KOLME LAULUA see Kotilainen, Otto

KOLME LAULUA see Kuusisto, Taneli

KOLUMBINE see Marx, Joseph

KOLZ, E.
   Da Tauts De Grauts
   [Ger] med solo,pno DOBLINGER $2.00
                              (K791)

KOM, JUL, MED KLARA, VITA LJUS see
   Skold

KOM MED MIG see Merikanto, Oskar, Tule
   Kanssani

KOM NU HIT, DOD see Sibelius, Jean

KOM TIL MIG, JESUS see Hannikainen,
   Ilmari, Tule Luokseni Herra Jeesus

KOMADINA, VOJIN (1933-   )
   Death Of Jugovic Mother, The *see
      Smrt Majke Jugovica

   Glose
   "Glosses" SBar soli,fl,perc,vla,bvl
   MUSIC INFO rental   (K792)

   Glosses *see Glose

   Smrt Majke Jugovica
   "Death Of Jugovic Mother, The"
   SBar,narrator,bvl,perc, folk
   instruments MUSIC INFO rental
                              (K793)

KOMATSU, KIYOSHI (1900-   )
   Neuf Tankas *CC9L
   [Fr] S solo,pno JAPAN 7113 s.p.
                              (K794)

KOMIVES, JANOS (1932-   )
   Catechisme De Nuit
   S solo,3fl,3ob,3clar,3bsn,4horn,
   3trp,3trom,tuba,timp,4perc,harp,
   pno,cel,strings JOBERT sc s.p.,
   voc sc s.p.   (K795)

KOMM! see Godard, Benjamin Louis Paul,
   Viens!

KOMM AN MEIN HERZ, O LIEBLING MEINER
   SEELE - ALL DES LEBENS SELIGKEITEN
   see Mozart, Wolfgang Amadeus, A
   Questo Seno Deh Vieni, Idolo Mio -
   Or Che Il Cielo A Me Ti Rende

KOMM AN MEIN HERZ, O LIEBLING MEINER
   SEELE - ALL DES LEBENS SELIKEITEN
   see Mozart, Wolfgang Amadeus, A
   Questo Seno Deh Vieni, Idolo Mio -
   Or Che Il Cielo A Me Ti Rende

KOMM DOCH, GELIEBTER MEIN see Schutz,
   Heinrich, Veni, Dilecte Mi

KOMM HERBEI, TOD see Sibelius, Jean,
   Kom Nu Hit, Dod

KOMM I KVALL see Elokas, Ossi, Tule
   Illalla

KOMM IN DEN KLEINEN PAVILLON see Lehar,
   Franz

KOMM, KOMM, HELD MEINER TRAUME see
   Straus, Oscar

KOMM, KOMM, MEIN HERZE STEHT DIR OFFEN
   see Bach, Johann Sebastian

KOMM, O KOMM see Kilpinen, Yrio, Kuti,
   Kuti Kultaseni

KOMM, O KOMME see Kilpinen, Yrio, Tule
   Tanne

KOMM, SUSSER TOD, KOMM, SEL'GE RUH' see
   Bach, Johann Sebastian

KOMM' ZIGANY see Kalman, Emerich

KOMMA, KARL MICHAEL
   Liederbuch Aus Bohmen *CC8L
   med-high solo,pno LEUCKART $3.00
                              (K796)

KOMMEN TILL EN FADER ATER see
   Nordqvist, Gustaf

KOMMER I SNART, I HUSMAEND see Nielsen,
   Carl

KOMMET HER, IHR FRECHEN SUNDER see
   Mozart, Wolfgang Amadeus

KOMMET IHR HIRTEN see Metzger, Hans-
   Arnold

KOMMST DU, LICHT DER HEIDEN? see
   Buxtehude, Dietrich

KOMMT ALLE ZU MIR see Schutz, Heinrich,
   Venite Ad Me

KOMMT EIN SCHLANKER BURSCH GEGANEN see
   Weber, Carl Maria von

KOMMT, LASST UNS ANBETEN see Becker-
   Foss, Jurgen

KOMMT, SEELEM, DIESER TAG MUSS HEILIG
   SEIN BESUNGEN see Bach, Johann
   Sebastian

KOMMT, WIR WOLLEN BLUMEN BINDEN see
   Hess

KOMORI, AKIHIRO (1931-   )
   Stories Of A Day *CC2U
   [Jap] S solo,pno JAPAN 7012 s.p.
                              (K797)

KOMPONISTEN AUF ABWEGEN HEFT I: LIEDER
   *CCU
   (Volkmann) [Ger] solo,pno BREITKOPF-W
   EB 6727 s.p.   (K798)

KOMPONISTEN AUF ABWEGEN HEFT II: ARIEN
   *CCU
   (Volkmann) [Ger] solo,pno BREITKOPF-W
   EB 6728 s.p.   (K799)

KOMPONISTEN AUF ABWEGEN ODER DIE
   SELTSAMEN VERWANDLUNGEN VON
   "HANSCHEN KLEIN", HEFT I & II *CCU
   (Volkmann, Joachim) solo,2fl,2ob,
   2clar,2bsn,2horn,2trp,trom,tuba,
   timp,perc,harp,cembalo,strings
   study sc BREITKOPF-W PB 4883 s.p.
                              (K800)

KOMTER, JAN MAARTEN (1905-   )
   Chanson D'Automne
   Mez solo,fl DONEMUS s.p. contains
   also: La Lune Blanche   (K801)

   In A Gondola
   S solo,gtr DONEMUS s.p.   (K802)

   La Lune Blanche
   see Komter, Jan Maarten, Chanson
      D'Automne

KONIG WISWAMITRE see Berners, Lord

KONINGIN DER BELGEN see Hullebroeck,
   Em.

KONINKVENTJES see Clercq, R. de

KONNINGINNELIED see Hullebroeck, Em.

KONSTELACE CYKLUS see Tausinger, Jan,
   Konstellationen Zyklus

KONSTELLATIONEN ZYKLUS see Tausinger,
   Jan

KONUNGARS KONUNG see Noren

KONVALINKA, MILOS (1919-   )
   Slunecka, Ses. 1-2 *CCU
   boy solo/girl solo,pno SUPRAPHON
   s.p., ea.   (K803)

KONZERT-ARIEN FUR BASS see Mozart,
   Wolfgang Amadeus

KONZERT-ARIEN FUR HOHE STIMME BAND I
   see Mozart, Wolfgang Amadeus

KONZERT-ARIEN FUR HOHE STIMME BAND II
   see Mozart, Wolfgang Amadeus

KONZERT FUR KOLORATURSOPRAN UND
   ORCHESTER see Gliere, Reinhold
   Moritzovitch

KONZERT FUR TENOR UND KAMMERENSEMBLE
   see Devcic, Natko

KOOL, B.
   Vier Liederen *CC4U
   solo,pno BROEKMANS 75 s.p. (K804)

KOPELENT, MAREK (1932-   )
   Black And White Tears
   solo,pno GERIG HG 1008 s.p. (K805)

   Snehah
   SA soli,4winds,perc,vln,vla,vcl
   solo pt GERIG HG 675 s.p. (K806)
   solo,pno SUPRAPHON s.p.   (K807)

KOPHETUA see Bijvanck, Henk

KOPORC, SRECKO (1900-1965)
   Osem Otroskih Pesmi *CC8U
   solo,pno DRUSTVO DSS 105 rental
                              (K808)

   Tri Pesmi *CC3U
   solo,pno DRUSTVO DSS 1 rental
                              (K809)

KOPPARFLOJELN see Peterson-Berger,
   (Olof) Wilhelm

KOPTAGEL, Y.
   Deux Chansons Du Pecheur Japonais
   *CC2U
   [Fr] med solo,pno ESCHIG $3.50
                              (K810)

KORAL see Korling, Sven

KORIDON see Ketting, Otto

KORLING
   Anne-Marie
   solo,pno LUNDQUIST s.p.   (K811)

   Danslek
   see Sanger Ur Egna Torvan

   Den Heliga Natten
   solo,pno LUNDQUIST s.p. see from
      Tre Sanger   (K812)

   En Dag Har Gatt
   solo,pno LUNDQUIST s.p. see from
      Tre Sanger   (K813)

   En Drom Ar Livet
   solo,pno LUNDQUIST s.p.   (K814)

   En Sommarpolkett
   solo,pno LUNDQUIST s.p.   (K815)

   En Speleman
   solo,pno LUNDQUIST s.p. see from
      Tre Sanger   (K816)

   Ett Har Jag Begart Av Herran
   solo,pno LUNDQUIST s.p.   (K817)

   Flickan Under Nymanen
   solo,pno LUNDQUIST s.p.   (K818)

   Fosterlandssang
   see Sanger Ur Egna Torvan

   Hembygden
   solo,pno LUNDQUIST s.p.   (K819)

   I Drommarnes Land
   solo,pno LUNDQUIST s.p.   (K820)

   Lockfageln
   see Sanger Ur Egna Torvan

   Pelle, Stackers Gosse
   see Sanger Ur Egna Torvan

   Sanger Ur Egna Torvan
   solo,pno LUNDQUIST s.p.
   contains: Danslek;
      Fosterlandssang; Lockfageln;
      Pelle, Stackers Gosse;
      Vandringstrall   (K821)

   Skepparvisa
   solo,pno LUNDQUIST s.p.   (K822)

   Tre Sanger *see Den Heliga Natten;
      En Dag Har Gatt; En Speleman
                              (K823)

KORLING (cont'd.)

Tre Sanger   *CC3U
    solo,pno LUNDQUIST s.p.   (K824)

Vaga Vinn!
    solo,pno LUNDQUIST s.p.   (K825)

Vandringstrall
    see Sanger Ur Egna Torvan

KORLING, AUGUST (1842-1919)
  Aftonstamning
    med solo,pno GEHRMANS s.p.   (K826)
    high solo,pno GEHRMANS s.p.   (K827)

  Fjarran Pa Enslig Stig
    med solo,pno GEHRMANS s.p.   (K828)
    high solo,pno GEHRMANS s.p.   (K829)

  Fyll Till Randen
    solo,pno GEHRMANS s.p.   (K830)

  Gud Vet Det Var Han Vankar
    solo,pno GEHRMANS s.p.   (K831)

  Kamrat!
    solo,pno GEHRMANS s.p.   (K832)

  Nar Stjarneharen Blanker
    high solo,pno GEHRMANS s.p.   (K833)
    med solo,pno GEHRMANS s.p.   (K834)

  Nar Varen Star I Blom
    solo,pno GEHRMANS 186 s.p.   (K835)

  Sangarkonst
    solo,pno GEHRMANS s.p.   (K836)

  Sjomansflickan
    solo,pno GEHRMANS s.p.   (K837)

  Slumra, Bolja Bla
    solo,pno GEHRMANS s.p.   (K838)

  Snart Synker Solen
    solo,pno GEHRMANS s.p.   (K839)

  Tre Dikter   *CC3U
    solo,pno GEHRMANS s.p.   (K840)

  Tre Sanger   *CC3U
    solo,pno GEHRMANS s.p.   (K841)

  Tva Sanger For Mezzosopran *CC2U
    Mez solo,pno GEHRMANS s.p.   (K842)

KORLING, FELIX
  Blaklockorna
    solo,pno GEHRMANS s.p.   (K843)

  Danvisa
    solo,pno GEHRMANS 572 s.p.   (K844)

  Den Glade Trumpetaren
    solo,pno GEHRMANS 187 s.p.   (K845)

  Den Karaste Sagan
    solo,pno GEHRMANS 661 s.p.   (K846)

  En Glad Trall
    solo,pno GEHRMANS 662 s.p.   (K847)

  En Skymningens Visa
    S solo,pno GEHRMANS s.p.   (K848)
    A solo,pno GEHRMANS s.p.   (K849)

  En Spelmanssaga
    solo,pno GEHRMANS 237 s.p.   (K850)

  Fanjunkar Berg
    solo,pno GEHRMANS s.p.   (K851)

  Kattfotternas Visa
    solo,pno GEHRMANS 663 s.p.   (K852)

  Liten, Min Sjal Ar Sjuk
    solo,pno GEHRMANS s.p.   (K853)

  Ljuvt Var Det Dock!
    solo,pno GEHRMANS s.p.   (K854)

  Maskrosornas Visa
    solo,pno GEHRMANS 664 s.p.   (K855)

  Sen Har Jag Ej Fragat Mera
    solo,pno GEHRMANS s.p.   (K856)

  Serenad
    solo,pno GEHRMANS s.p.   (K857)

  Tuppen
    solo,pno GEHRMANS 188 s.p.   (K858)

  Under De Ljusa Lindar
    solo,pno GEHRMANS s.p.   (K859)

  Varjubel
    solo,pno GEHRMANS s.p.   (K860)

  Vindringssang
    solo,pno GEHRMANS s.p.   (K861)

KORLING, SVEN
  Koral
    solo,pno GEHRMANS s.p. see from
      Sanger Och Visor   (K862)

  Musik
    solo,pno GEHRMANS s.p. see from
      Sanger Och Visor   (K863)

  Sanger Och Visor *see Koral; Musik;
    Valborgsmassavisa; Vinden Och
    Backen   (K864)

  Valborgsmassavisa
    solo,pno GEHRMANS s.p. see from
      Sanger Och Visor   (K865)

  Vinden Och Backen
    solo,pno GEHRMANS s.p. see from
      Sanger Och Visor   (K866)

KORN, PETER JONA
  Der Pfarrer Von Cleversulzbach
    *Op.24, CC6U
    med solo,pno SCHAUR EE 3230 s.p.
                                   (K867)
  Pfarrer Von Cleversulzbach *CC6U
    [Eng/Ger] med solo,pno BOOSEY $5.00
                                   (K868)

KORNAUTH, EGON (1891-1959)
  Acht Gesange (Smekal) *Op.12,No.1-8,
    CC8U
    solo,pno DOBLINGER s.p., ea. (K869)

  Acht Lieder (Eichendorff) [1]
    *Op.36,No.1-8, CC8U
    low solo,pno DOBLINGER s.p. (K870)

  Acht Lieder (Eichendorff) [2]
    *Op.38,No.1-8, CC8U
    DOBLINGER s.p. med solo,pno; high
      solo,pno   (K871)

  Sechs Lieder *Op.1,No.1-6, CC6U
    solo,pno DOBLINGER s.p., ea. (K872)

  Sechs Lieder *Op.21,No.1-6, CC6U
    solo,pno DOBLINGER s.p., ea. (K873)

  Sechs Lieder (Eichendorff) *Op.37,
    No.1-6, CC6U
    high solo,pno DOBLINGER s.p. (K874)

  Sechs Lieder (Hesse) *Op.22,No.1-6,
    CC6U
    solo,pno DOBLINGER s.p., ea. (K875)

  Vier Gesange *Op.8,No.1-4, CC4U
    solo,pno DOBLINGER s.p., ea. (K876)

  Vier Lieder (Brentano) *Op.34,No.1-
    4, CC4U
    high solo,pno DOBLINGER s.p. (K877)

KORNBLUMEN see Strauss, Richard

KORNGOLD, ERICH WOLFGANG (1897-1957)
  Funf Lieder *Op.38,No.1-5, CC5U
    solo,pno SCHOTTS 4533 s.p.   (K878)

  Mariettas Lied Zum Laute (from Die
    Tote Stadt)
    high solo,pno SCHOTTS s.p.   (K879)

  Sonett Fur Wien *Op.41
    Mez solo,pno SCHOTTS s.p.   (K880)

  Tanzlied Des Pierrot (from Die Tote
    Stadt)
    med solo,pno SCHOTTS s.p.   (K881)

KOROL AR C'HLEZE see Favre, Georges

KOROMOGAE see Matsudaira, Yoritsune

KORSBAR see Kilpinen, Yrio

KORTE, KARL (1928-   )
  Forget Her
    see Songs Of Wen I-To

  I Wanted To Come Home
    see Songs Of Wen I-To

  Laundry Song, The
    see Songs Of Wen I-To

  Songs Of Wen I-To
    high solo,pno SCHIRM.EC 148 s.p.
      contains: Forget Her; I Wanted To
      Come Home; Laundry Song, The
                                   (K882)
  Wine Of The Grape
    T solo,pno SCHIRM.EC 2309 s.p.
                                   (K883)

KORTE, OLDRICH FRANTISEK (1926-   )
  Trubadorske Zpevy *CCU
    solo,pno PANTON 939 s.p.   (K884)

KOSA, GYORGY (1897-   )
  Chinese Songs, No. 1 *CCU
    [Hung] solo,pno BUDAPEST 1891 s.p.
                                   (K885)
  Chinese Songs, No. 2 *CCU
    [Hung] solo,pno BUDAPEST 2711 s.p.
                                   (K886)

KOSA, GYORGY (cont'd.)

  Selected Songs *CCU
    [Hung] solo,pno BUDAPEST 2743 s.p.
                                   (K887)

  Twelve Songs *CC12U
    [Hung] solo,pno BUDAPEST 2449 s.p.
                                   (K888)

KOSAKOFF, REUVEN (1898-   )
  Four Songs Of Devotion *CC4U
    [Eng] solo,pno/org TRANSCON. TV 582
    $2.50   (K889)

  Life Is A Passing Shadow
    see Songs From The Bible

  My Beloved And I *sac,Marriage
    high solo,pno TRANSCON. TV 493 $.75
                                   (K890)
    med solo,pno TRANSCON. TV 494 $.75
                                   (K891)

  Psalm 23
    see Songs From The Bible

  Psalm 121
    see Songs From The Bible

  Psalm 130
    see Songs From The Bible

  Songs From The Bible *sac,Bibl
    med solo,org TRANSCON. TV 472 $2.25
      contains: Life Is A Passing
      Shadow; Psalm 23; Psalm 121;
      Psalm 130; Woman Of Valor, A
                                   (K892)

  Woman Of Valor, A
    see Songs From The Bible

KOSCHAT IM RUCKSACK see Koschat, Thomas

KOSCHAT, THOMAS (1845-1914)
  Album, Band I *CCU
    LEUCKART s.p. high solo,pno, opt.
      zither; low solo,pno, opt. zither
                                   (K893)
  Album, Band II *CCU
    (Wobersin, W.) LEUCKART s.p. low
      solo,pno, opt. zither; low solo,
      lute/gtr   (K894)
  Album, Band III *CCU
    (Wobersin, W.) LEUCKART s.p. high
      solo,pno, opt. zither; low solo,
      pno, opt. zither; solo,lute/gtr
                                   (K895)
  Album, Band IV *CCU
    LEUCKART s.p. high solo,pno; low
      solo,pno   (K896)
  Album, Band V *CCU
    LEUCKART s.p. high solo,pno; low
      solo,pno   (K897)

  Am Worther See
    solo,pno LEUCKART s.p.   (K898)

  Ein Sonntag Auf Der Alm
    solo,pno LEUCKART s.p.   (K899)

  Forsaken *see Verlassen Bin I

  Karntner Lieder, Band II: Am Worther
    See, Op. 26 *CCU
    (Gutmann, Fr.; Messner, O.) solo,
      zither LEUCKART s.p.   (K900)

  Karntner Lieder, Band VIII: Sechs
    Lieder *CC6U
    (Gutmann, Fr; Messner, O.) solo,
      zither LEUCKART s.p.   (K901)

  Koschat Im Rucksack *CCU
    (Muller-Eisenach, C.H.) med solo,
      lute/gtr LEUCKART s.p.   (K902)

  Verlassen Bin I *Op.4,No.1
    low solo,pno LEUCKART s.p.   (K903)
    high solo,pno LEUCKART s.p.   (K904)
    solo, zither LEUCKART s.p.   (K905)
    "Forsaken" high solo,pno (B flat
      maj) ALLANS s.p.   (K906)
    "Forsaken" low solo,pno (A flat
      maj) ALLANS s.p.   (K907)

  Walzeralbum, Band I *CCU
    med-high solo,pno LEUCKART s.p.
                                   (K908)

KOSKA MEILLA ON JOULU *CC79U,Xmas
  (Marvia) solo,pno FAZER F 5211 s.p.
                                   (K909)

KOSKA VALAISSEE KOINTAHTONEN see
  Sonninen, Ahti

KOSKE, HERRA, KIELIHIN see Laitenen,
  Arvo

KOSKENLASKIAN MORSIAMET see Sibelius,
  Jean

KOSMA, J.
  Chasse A L'enfant
    solo,pno ENOCH s.p.   (K910)
    solo,acap ENOCH s.p.   (K911)

KOSMA, J. (cont'd.)

D'autres Chansons, Vol. II *CCU
solo,pno ENOCH s.p. (K912)

Familiale
solo,pno ENOCH s.p. (K913)
solo,acap ENOCH s.p. (K914)

La Menagerie De Tristan
[Fr] med solo,pno ESCHIG $8.00
(K915)

Le Cauchemar Du Chauffeur De Taxi
solo,pno ENOCH s.p. (K916)

Le Parterre D'hyacinthe
[Fr] med solo,pno ESCHIG $4.75
(K917)

L'Enfance
solo,acap ENOCH s.p. (K918)
solo,pno ENOCH s.p. (K919)

Les Bruits De La Nuit
solo,acap ENOCH s.p. (K920)
solo,pno ENOCH s.p. (K921)

Les Enfants Qui S'aiment
solo,pno ENOCH s.p. see also
Premier Receueil De Chansons
(K922)

Les Feuilles Mortes
solo,pno ENOCH s.p. see also
Premier Receueil De Chansons
(K923)

Premier Receueil De Chansons *CC7L
solo,acap cmplt ed ENOCH s.p.
see also: Les Enfants Qui
S'aiment; Les Feuilles Mortes
(K924)

Vingt-Et-Un Chansons, Vol. I *CC21U
solo,pno ENOCH s.p. (K925)

KOSTSCHOOLBUNDEL see Hullebroeck, Em.

KOTILAINEN, OTTO (1868-1936)
Den Brutne *see Sortunut

Dufvobad *see Kyyhkynen Kylpee

Kolme Laulua
solo,pno FAZER s.p.
contains: Kyyhkynen Kylpee,
"Dufvobad"; Nauti, "Njut";
Sortunut, "Den Brutne" (K926)

Kyyhkynen Kylpee
"Dufvobad" see Kolme Laulua

Nauti
"Njut" see Kolme Laulua

Njut *see Nauti

Sortunut
"Den Brutne" see Kolme Laulua

KOTIMAANI OMPI SUOMI see Simila, Arpo

KOTIMAISIA YKSINLAULUJA, VOLS. I-II
*CCU
solo,pno FAZER 2561; 2988 s.p., ea.
(K927)

KOTTARAINEN see Merikanto, Oskar

KOUNADIS, ARGHYRIS (1924-   )
Choreia I
S solo,fl,cel,gtr,vcl,pno TONGER
s.p. (K928)

Drei Nocturnes Nach Sappho *CC3U
S solo,fl,cel,vibra,vln,vla,vcl
MODERN s.p. (K929)

Quattro Pezzi *CC4U
S solo,fl,vcl,pno TONGER s.p.
(K930)

KOUNTZ, RICHARD (1896-1950)
Little Bells Through Dark Of Night
high solo,pno (A flat maj) GALAXY
1.1282.7 $1.00 (K931)
low solo,pno (F maj) GALAXY
1.1283.7 $1.00 (K932)

Little French Clock
high solo,pno (F maj) GALAXY
1.1787.7 $1.00 (K933)
med solo,pno (E flat maj) GALAXY
1.0718.7 $1.00 (K934)
low solo,pno (C maj) GALAXY
1.0719.7 $1.00 (K935)
low solo,pno ALLANS s.p. (K936)
high solo,pno ALLANS s.p. (K937)

Mountain Brook
high solo,pno (G maj) GALAXY
1.2092.7 $1.00 (K938)

Palm Sunday
high solo,pno (E maj) GALAXY
1.1684.7 $1.00 (K939)
low solo,pno (B flat maj) GALAXY
1.1685.7 $1.00 (K940)

Prayer Of The Norwegian Child *sac
med-high solo,pno (A min) SCHIRM.G
$1.00 (K941)

KOUNTZ, RICHARD (cont'd.)

low solo,pno (F min) SCHIRM.G $1.00
(K942)

Sleigh, The
med-high solo,pno (F min) SCHIRM.G
$.85 (K943)
low solo,pno (D min) SCHIRM.G $.85
(K944)

What Shall I Ask
low solo,pno (D maj) GALAXY
1.1820.7 $1.00 (K945)

KOVAN KOMMER, KOVAN GAR see Norlander,
Emil

KOVARICEK, FRANTISEK (1924-   )
Pisnicky *CCU
med solo,pno CZECH s.p. (K946)

Zlata Vlna Cervna
solo,pno SUPRAPHON s.p. (K947)

KOVAROVIC, KAREL (1862-1920)
Slovacka Pisen *CCU
high solo,pno SUPRAPHON s.p. (K948)

Svitani Pro Vyssi Hlas *CCU
high solo,pno SUPRAPHON s.p. (K949)

KOWALSKI, JULIUS
Antiteza *song cycle
high solo,pno SLOV.HUD.FOND s.p.
(K950)

O Slobode *song cycle
Bar solo,pno SLOV.HUD.FOND s.p.
(K951)

Zverincek
boy solo/girl solo,pno
SLOV.HUD.FOND s.p. (K952)

KOWALSKI, MAX (1882-1956)
Cythere *Op.13,No.3
see Sechs Gedichte Von Paul
Verlaine

Der Faun *Op.13,No.5
see Sechs Gedichte Von Paul
Verlaine

Funf Marienlieder
med-high solo,pno LEUCKART s.p.
contains: Ich Will Mich Zur
Lieben, Maria Vermeiten, Op.12,
No.5; Jesulein Schon's
Kindelein, Op.12,No.4; Maria
Mein Im Rosenhag, Op.12,No.1;
Waldvogelein, Op.12,No.2;
Wiegenlied, Op.12,No.3 (K953)

Ich Will Mich Zur Lieben, Maria
Vermeiten *Op.12,No.5
see Funf Marienlieder

Jesulein Schon's Kindelein *Op.12,
No.4
see Funf Marienlieder

Mandoline *Op.13,No.2
see Sechs Gedichte Von Paul
Verlaine

Maria Mein Im Rosenhag *Op.12,No.1
see Funf Marienlieder

Mondschein *Op.13,No.6
see Sechs Gedichte Von Paul
Verlaine

Pantomime *Op.13,No.4
see Sechs Gedichte Von Paul
Verlaine

Sechs Gedichte Von Paul Verlaine
med solo,pno LEUCKART s.p.
contains: Cythere, Op.13,No.3;
Der Faun, Op.13,No.5;
Mandoline, Op.13,No.2;
Mondschein, Op.13,No.6;
Pantomime, Op.13,No.4;
Serenade, Op.13,No.1 (K954)

Serenade *Op.13,No.1
see Sechs Gedichte Von Paul
Verlaine

Twelve Poems From Pierrot Lunaire,
Volumes I And II *Op.4, CC12U
[Eng/Ger] med solo,pno SCHAUR
EE 1118-1119 $1.75, ea. (K955)

Waldvogelein *Op.12,No.2
see Funf Marienlieder

Wiegenlied *Op.12,No.3
see Funf Marienlieder

KOX, HANS (1930-   )
Amphion
2 narrators,2horn,2trp,2trom,timp,
perc DONEMUS s.p. (K956)

Drei Chinesische Lieder
Bar solo,pno DONEMUS s.p.;
contains: Einsame Nacht;
Kindliche Frage; Weisses Haar

KOX, HANS (cont'd.)

Im Spiegel (K957)

Drei Coplas
Mez solo,pno DONEMUS s.p. (K958)

Einsame Nacht
see Drei Chinesische Lieder

Gedachtnislieder *CCU
solo,2ob,bass clar,3horn,strings
DONEMUS s.p. (K959)

Kindliche Frage
see Drei Chinesische Lieder

L'Allegria
solo,orch DONEMUS s.p. (K960)

Vues Des Anges
Bar solo,vln DONEMUS s.p. (K961)

Weisses Haar Im Spiegel
see Drei Chinesische Lieder

KOYHAN LAPSET see Kilpinen, Yrio

KOZINA, MARIJAN (1907-1965)
ABC *CCU
boy solo/girl solo,pno DRZAVNA
(K962)

Chinese Miniatures *see Kitajske
Miniature

Cigan
"Gipsy" solo,pno DRUSTVO DSS 448
(K963)

Cigan Hvali Svojega Konja
"Gipsy Praises His Horse, The" see
Iz Zapuscine (Posthumous
Collection)

Four Chinese Miniatures *see Stiri
Kitajske Miniature

Gipsy *see Cigan

Gipsy Praises His Horse, The *see
Cigan Hvali Svojega Konja

Hard Times *see Iz Tezkih Dni

Iz Tezkih Dni
"Hard Times" see Iz Zapuscine
(Posthumous Collection)

Iz Zapuscine (Posthumous Collection)
cmplt ed SLOV.AKA. SAZU 30 s.p.
contains: Cigan Hvali Svojega
Konja, "Gipsy Praises His
Horse, The" (solo,2pic,2ob,
2clar,2bsn,4horn,3trp,3trom,
tuba,perc,strings); Iz Tezkih
Dni, "Hard Times" (solo,2fl,
2ob,clar,bass clar,bsn,
contrabsn,4horn,perc,strings);
O Domovina, "Oh, My Native
Country" (soli,mix cor,brass);
Oreh, "Nut, The" (S solo,2pic,
2ob,2clar,2bsn,4horn,3trp,
3trom,tuba,perc,harp,strings);
Pesem Od Lepe Vide, "Song About
Lepa Vida, The" (cor,acap);
Stiri Kitajske Miniature, "Four
Chinese Miniatures" (solo,fl,
ob,clar,2trp,3perc,strings)
(song cycle) (K964)

Izbrane Pesmi *CCU
solo,pno SLOV.AKA. SAZU 22 (K965)

Kitajske Miniature *song cycle
"Chinese Miniatures" high solo,pno
DRUSTVO DSS 376 (K966)

Meetings *see Srecanja

Nut, The *see Oreh

O Domovina
"Oh, My Native Country" see Iz
Zapuscine (Posthumous Collection)

Oh, My Native Country *see O
Domovina

Oreh
"Nut, The" see Iz Zapuscine
(Posthumous Collection)

Pesem Od Lepe Vide
"Song About Lepa Vida, The" see Iz
Zapuscine (Posthumous Collection)

Song About Lepa Vida, The *see Pesem
Od Lepe Vide

Srecanja
"Meetings" solo,pno DRUSTVO DSS 375
(K967)

Stiri Kitajske Miniature
"Four Chinese Miniatures" see Iz
Zapuscine (Posthumous Collection)

KOZINA, MARIJAN (cont'd.)

    Tri Pesmi *CC3U
    solo,pno DRUSTVO DSS 92A   (K968)

    Tri Vesele Pesmi *CC3U
    cmplt ed DRUSTVO DSS 29B   (K969)

KRAFT
    Die Sterne Uberm Meer *CCU
    solo,pno/acord TONGER s.p.   (K970)

KRAFT, KARL (1908-   )
    Missa Unisona *Op.97, sac,Mass
    solo,org BOHM s.p. sc, solo pt
                                  (K971)
    Von Der Verganglichkeit *Op.76, sac
    A solo,org BOHM rental   (K972)

KRAFT, WALTER (1905-   )
    Heinzelmannchen-Ballade
    S solo,fl,3strings (diff) sc BAREN.
    2133 $9.75, voc sc BAREN. 2134
    $5.50, BAREN. 2134   (K973)

    O Lux Beata Trinitas
    SSSS soli,4vln,fl,bsn,vcl,bvl,org
    (diff) BAREN. 2195 $5.50, ipr
                                  (K974)

KRAHMER, HERBERT
    That Is Why
    high solo,pno (C maj) WILLIS $.60
                                  (K975)
    low solo,pno (G maj) WILLIS $.60
                                  (K976)

KRAJINY see Mikoda, Borivoj

KRAJINY DETSTVI see Drejsl, Radim

KRAMER, A. WALTER (1890-   )
    Before The Paling Of The Stars *sac,
    Xmas
    high solo,pno BELWIN $1.50   (K977)
    med solo,pno BELWIN $1.50   (K978)

    Great Awakening, The
    (Walter) high solo,pno (F maj)
    BELWIN $1.50   (K979)
    (Walter) med solo,pno (C maj)
    BELWIN $1.50   (K980)

    Minnelied
    high solo,pno BELWIN $1.50   (K981)

    O, Haul The Water
    [Norw/Eng] med solo,pno PRESSER
    $.75   (K982)

    Pleading
    high solo,pno BELWIN $1.50   (K983)
    low solo,pno BELWIN $1.50   (K984)

    When I Was Seventeen
    high solo,pno BELWIN $1.50   (K985)

KRAMERSPIEGEL see Strauss, Richard

KRANAOS see Mignan, Edouard-Charles-
    Octave

KRANE, KJELL
    Det Var En Gang En Konge
    solo,pno MUSIKK s.p.   (K986)

KRANENDONK
    No Other Name
    med solo,pno SHAWNEE IA5042 $1.00
                                  (K987)

KRANZ, ALBERT
    Mein Liederbuch *CCU
    (Kramer) solo,gtr PRO MUSICA 51
    s.p.   (K988)

KRAPF, GERHARD (1924-   )
    At The Time Of The Banquet *sac
    med solo,pno oct CONCORDIA 98-1977
    $.30   (K989)

    Be Merciful, Even As Your Father Is
    Merciful *sac
    med solo,pno oct CONCORDIA 98-1979
    $.25   (K990)

    Father Abraham, Have Mercy On Me
    *sac
    med solo,pno oct CONCORDIA 98-1976
    $.25   (K991)

    Jesus Said To The Widow, "Do Not
    Weep" *sac
    med solo,pno oct CONCORDIA 98-2031
    $.30   (K992)

    Master, We Toiled All Night *sac
    med solo,pno oct CONCORDIA 98-1980
    $.30   (K993)

    Morning Prayer
    solo,pno CHANTRY VOS 739 s.p. (K994)

    O Lord, I Will Praise Thee *sac
    med solo,pno oct CONCORDIA 98-1853
    $.30   (K995)

KRAPF, GERHARD (cont'd.)

    Rejoice With Me, For I Have Found My
    Sheep *sac
    med solo,pno oct CONCORDIA 98-1978
    $.30   (K996)

    Truly, Truly, I Say To You *sac
    med solo,pno oct CONCORDIA 98-1975
    $.30   (K997)

    You Have Heard That It Was Said *sac
    med solo,pno oct CONCORDIA 98-1981
    $.25   (K998)

KRASNOFF, ISRAEL
    Eyn Keloheynu *sac
    [Heb] med solo,pno TRANSCON.
    TCL 296 $.25   (K999)

KRASNOW
    Lullaby Of The Zoo
    (Darion) solo,pno FOX,S   (K1000)

KRATZ, RAY
    Nita
    high solo,pno (C maj) WILLIS $.50
                                  (K1001)
    low solo,pno (G maj) WILLIS $.50
                                  (K1002)

KRAUZE, ZYGMUNT (1938-   )
    Wir Besitzen Keinerlei Fahigkeit, Aus
    Der Klosterneuburgerstrasse
    Werzugehen
    Mez solo,English horn,bsn,al-sax,
    trp,trom,vcl,bvl MOECK 5163 s.p.
                                  (K1003)

KREBS, H.
    Kleine Philosophie *Op.1
    [Ger] S/T solo,orch BOTE $2.50
                                  (K1004)
    Rodin-Kantate *Op.14
    [Ger] T solo,pno BOTE $2.25   (K1005)

KREBS, JOHANN LUDWIG (1713-1780)
    Vater Unser *sac
    [Ger/Eng] S/T solo,pno (G flat maj)
    LIENAU HOS 88 s.p.   (K1006)
    [Ger/Eng] Mez solo,pno (F maj)
    LIENAU HOS 89 s.p.   (K1007)
    [Ger/Eng] A/Bar solo,pno (E flat
    maj) LIENAU HOS 90 s.p.   (K1008)

KREBS, S.
    Cleopatra's Farewell
    high solo,pno SEESAW $1.00   (K1009)

KREISLER
    Old Refrain, The
    med solo,pno (F maj) FISCHER,C
    F 2564   (K1010)

KREJCI, ISA (1904-1968)
    Anticke Motivy *CC3U
    low male solo,pno SUPRAPHON s.p.
                                  (K1011)
    Arie Luciany (from Pozdvizeni V
    Efesu)
    see ARIE A ZPEVY ZE SOUCASNYCH
    OPER: ALT

    Pet Pisni Na Texty J.A. Komenskeho
    *CC5U
    med solo,pno SUPRAPHON s.p.   (K1012)

KREK, UROS (1922-   )
    Pet Narodni Pesmi *CC5U
    high solo,pno DRUSTVO
    DSS 193-HG 573   (K1013)

KREMSER, EDWARD (1838-1914)
    Abschied
    see Sechs Altniederlandische
    Volkslieder

    Berg Op Zoom
    see Sechs Altniederlandische
    Volkslieder

    Dankgebet
    see Sechs Altniederlandische
    Volkslieder
    "Wir Treten Zum Beten" med solo,pno
    LEUCKART s.p.   (K1014)

    Klage
    see Sechs Altniederlandische
    Volkslieder

    Kriegslied
    see Sechs Altniederlandische
    Volkslieder

    Sechs Altniederlandische Volkslieder
    solo,pno LEUCKART s.p.
    contains: Abschied; Berg Op Zoom;
    Dankgebet; Klage; Kriegslied;
    Wilhelmus Von Nassauen (K1015)

    Wilhelmus Von Nassauen
    see Sechs Altniederlandische
    Volkslieder

    Wir Treten Zum Beten *see Dankgebet

KRENEK, ERNST (1900-   )
    Ballade Vom Fest
    med solo,pno UNIVER. 10091 $4.25
    see also Gesange Des Spaten
    Jahres, Op. 71   (K1016)

    Ballade Vom Konig Lobesam *Op.9,No.7
    med solo,pno UNIVER. 7573 $3.25
                                  (K1017)

    Ballade Von Den Schiffen
    med solo,pno UNIVER. 10090 $2.75
    see also Gesange Des Spaten
    Jahres, Op. 71   (K1018)

    Der Neue Amadis *Op.56,No.2
    solo,pno UNIVER. 9569 s.p. see from
    Drei Gesange   (K1019)

    Die Ballade Von Den Eisenbahnen
    [Ger/Eng] med solo,pno (diff)
    BAREN. 3956 $16.75   (K1020)

    Die Nachtigall *Op.68
    solo,pno UNIVER. 7122   (K1021)

    Drei Gesange *see Der Neue Amadis,
    Op.56,No.2; Fragment, Op.56,No.3;
    Zerstorung Magdeburgs, Op.56,No.1
                                  (K1022)

    Durch Die Nacht *Op.67
    solo,pno UNIVER. 9410 s.p.   (K1023)

    Fiedellieder *Op.64, CCU
    med solo,pno UNIVER. 9685 s.p.
                                  (K1024)

    Flea, The
    high solo,pno EMI s.p.   (K1025)

    Four Songs After Hopkins *CC4U
    [Eng] S solo,pno (med) BAREN. 4125
    $9.75   (K1026)

    Fragment *Op.56,No.3
    solo,pno UNIVER. 9570 s.p. see from
    Drei Gesange   (K1027)

    Funf Lieder Nach Kafka *Op.82, CC5U
    solo,pno UNIVER. 12658 $3.75 A
    Universal - Schott Joint Venture
                                  (K1028)

    Gesange Des Spaten Jahres, Op. 71
    *CCU
    med solo,pno cmplt ed UNIVER. 14149
    $12.00
    see also: Ballade Vom Fest;
    Ballade Von Den Schiffen;
    Liebeslieder; Trinklied; Und
    Herbstlaub Und Regenschauer;
    Vor Dem Tod   (K1029)

    Johnnys Triumphlied (from Johnny
    Spielt Auf)
    solo,pno UNIVER. 8997 $2.75   (K1030)

    La Corona *Op.91
    MezBar soli,perc,org (diff) BAREN.
    3991 rental   (K1031)

    Liebeslieder
    med solo,pno UNIVER. 10089 $2.75
    see also Gesange Des Spaten
    Jahres, Op. 71   (K1032)

    Monolog Der Stella *Op.57
    solo,pno UNIVER. 9556 s.p.   (K1033)

    Neun Lieder (Aus Op. 9, 15, 19)
    *CC9U
    high solo,pno UNIVER. 6005 $4.75
                                  (K1034)

    O Lacrimosa *Op.48
    med solo,pno UNIVER. 8729 $3.25
                                  (K1035)

    Reisebuch Aus Den Osterreichischen
    Alpen, Op 62, Books I-IV *CCU
    med solo,pno UNIVER. 9931-34 $5.25,
    ea.   (K1036)

    Selections From "Reisebuch Aus Den
    Osterreichischen Alpen" *CCU
    [Eng] med solo,pno UNIVER. 12877
    $7.25   (K1037)

    Sestina
    S solo,vln,gtr,fl,pno,trp,perc
    (diff) BAREN. 3824 rental   (K1038)

    Swanee-River-Song (from Johnny Spielt
    Auf)
    solo,pno UNIVER. 8996 $2.75   (K1039)

    Trinklied
    med solo,pno UNIVER. 10488 $2.75
    see also Gesange Des Spaten
    Jahres, Op. 71   (K1040)

    Und Herbstlaub Und Regenschauer
    med solo,pno UNIVER. 10087 $2.75
    see also Gesange Des Spaten
    Jahres, Op. 71   (K1041)

    Vier Gesange *Op.53, CC4U
    solo,pno UNIVER. 8924 s.p.   (K1042)

KRENEK, ERNST (cont'd.)

Vor Dem Tod
med solo,pno UNIVER. 10088 $2.75
see also Gesange Des Spaten
Jahres, Op. 71 (K1043)

Wechsellied Zum Tanz *Op.43a
high solo,pno UNIVER. 10086 $3.25
(K1044)

Wechselrahmen *CC6U
high solo,pno (diff) BAREN. 4113
$7.75 (K1045)

Zerstorung Magdeburgs *Op.56,No.1
solo,pno UNIVER. 9568 s.p. see from
Drei Gesange (K1046)

Zwei Geistliche Gesange *sac,CC2U
[Eng/Ger] med solo,pno (diff)
BAREN. 3862 $8.50 (K1047)

KRENGER, J.R.
Grindelwalder Lied
solo,pno HUG s.p. (K1048)

KRESANEK, JOZEF (1913-   )
Styri Piesne *CC4U
T solo,pno SLOV.HUD.FOND s.p.
(K1049)

To Je Vojna
S solo,pno SLOV.HUD.FOND s.p.
(K1050)

KRETZSCHMAR, GUNTHER (1929-   )
Christus Hat Dem Tode Die Macht
Genommen *sac
med solo,org HANSSLER 12.219 s.p.
(K1051)

Dies Ist Der Tag, Den Der Herr Macht
*sac
med solo,org HANSSLER 12.223 s.p.
(K1052)

Gedenke, Herr, An Deine
Barmherzigkeit *sac
med solo,org HANSSLER 12.216 s.p.
(K1053)

Herr, Neige Deine Ohren *sac
med solo,org HANSSLER 12.224 s.p.
(K1054)

Herr, Wie Lange Willst Du Mein
Vergessen? *sac
high solo,org HANSSLER 5.122 s.p.
(K1055)

KREUTZ, ROBERT E.
Memorare, The *sac
med solo,pno/org (easy) GIA G-1897
$1.00 (K1056)

Sacred Trust *sac,Marriage
med solo,pno/org (easy) GIA G-1870
$1.00 (K1057)

KREUTZER, C.
Jagdlied
med-high solo,pno DOBLINGER 08 559
$.90 (K1058)

KREUTZER, KONRADIN
Ein Schutz Bin Ich (from Das
Nachtlager Von Granada)
Bar solo,fl,2ob,2clar,2bsn,4horn,
2trp,timp,strings BREITKOPF-L
rental (K1059)

KRICKA, JAROSLAV (1882-1969)
Babincin Marsovsky Valcik
solo,pno SUPRAPHON s.p. (K1060)

Chansons Populaires Tchecoslovaques,
Vol. I *CCU
solo,pno HENN 446 s.p. (K1061)

Chansons Populaires Tchecoslovaques,
Vol. II *CCU
solo,pno HENN 482 s.p. (K1062)

Drei Fabeln *Op.21, CC3U
[Ger/Fr] solo,pno SUPRAPHON s.p.
(K1063)

Jaro Pacholatko *Op.29
solo,pno SUPRAPHON s.p. (K1064)

Milostne Pisne *CCU
solo,pno SUPRAPHON s.p. (K1065)

Nas Baryk
boy solo/girl solo,pno SUPRAPHON
s.p. (K1066)

Nase Pani Bozena Nemcova *Op.112
solo,pno SUPRAPHON s.p. (K1067)

Po Cesku *CCU
B/Bar solo,pno CZECH s.p. (K1068)

Podzimni Toulky *CC4U
solo,pno SUPRAPHON s.p. (K1069)

Prvni Touhy, Ses. 1-2 *CCU
solo,pno SUPRAPHON s.p., ea.
(K1070)

Sipkova Ruze
solo,pno SUPRAPHON s.p. (K1071)

KRICKA, JAROSLAV (cont'd.)

Stinohra *CC6U
low solo,pno PANTON 1007 s.p.
(K1072)

Vanocni Koledy *CCU,Xmas
high solo,pno SUPRAPHON s.p.
(K1073)

Zmoudreni Dona Quichota
solo,pno SUPRAPHON s.p. (K1074)

Zviratka
solo,pno SUPRAPHON s.p. (K1075)

KRIEGER, JOHANN PHILIPP (1649-1725)
An Den Wassern Zu Babel *sac,
concerto
(Osthoff, Helmut) STB soli,2vln,
cont (med) BAREN. 448 $7.75
(K1076)

Cantate Domino *sac,cant
S solo,2vln,cont sc HANSSLER 10.050
s.p., ipa (K1077)

Heut Singt Die Liebe Christenheit
*sac,cant
SB soli,trp,2vln,cont sc HANSSLER
10.288 s.p., ipa, solo pt
HANSSLER s.p. (K1078)

Vierundzwanzig Lieder Und Arien, Heft
I *CC12U
(Moser, Hans Joachim) S/A/T solo,
cont (med easy) NAGELS 174 $6.25
(K1079)

Vierundzwanzig Lieder Und Arien, Heft
II *CC12U
(Moser, Hans Joachim) S/A/T/B solo,
cont (med easy) NAGELS 175 $6.25
(K1080)

Wo Wilt Du Hin, Weil's Abend Ist
*sac
(Seiffert, Max) [Ger] SS/TT soli,
cont CONCORDIA 97-4152 $3.25
(K1081)

KRIEGSLIED see Kremser, Edward

KRIETSCH, GEORG (1904-1969)
Tierlieder *CC8L
solo,pno TONOS 5404 s.p. (K1082)

KRING DITT RIKA OCH VAGIGA HAR OCH
ANDRA DIKTER AV ERNEST THIEL see
Alfven, Hugo

KRIPPENLIED see Staeps, Hans Ulrich

KRISHNA WITH HIS FLUTE
solo,pno LEONARD-ENG (K1083)

KRISTAL TEGEN SPIEGEL see Bon, Maarten

KRISTALLEN DEN FINA
see Om Dagen Vid Mitt Arbete

KRISTI KORS see Tonnessen, Peder

KRISTOFFERSON, KRIS
One Day At A Time *see Wilkin,
Marijohn

Why Me? *sac
solo,pno BENSON S8507-S $1.00
(K1084)

KRITIK DES HERZENS see Poser, Hans

KRIVINKA, GUSTAV (1928-   )
Marchen Von Dem Krokodil Aus Brunn
*see Pohadka O Brnenskem
Krokodylovi

Pohadka O Brnenskem Krokodylovi
"Marchen Von Dem Krokodil Aus
Brunn" med solo,pno CZECH s.p.
(K1085)

KRIVITSKY, D.
Autumnal Landscapes *song cycle
S solo,clar,harp,vla sc MEZ KNIGA
2.71 s.p. (K1086)

KRIZKOVSKY, KAREL (PAVEL) (1820-1885)
Jesen I Maj *CCU
solo,pno SUPRAPHON s.p. (K1087)

KROGSTAD, BOB
Song For Christmas, A *sac,Xmas
solo,pno,opt ob GOSPEL s.p. (K1088)

KROHN, FELIX (1898-   )
Brodrakretsen *see Veljespiiri

Veljespiiri
"Brodrakretsen" solo,pno FAZER
F 3463 s.p. (K1089)

KROL, BERNHARD (1934-   )
Die Heile Welt *Op.14
med solo,pno SCHAUR EE 3210 $2.00
(K1090)

Horati De Vino Carmina *Op.30
[Lat] S/T solo,horn,pno SCHAUR
EE 1187 $3.50 (K1091)

In Dulci Jubilo *Op.25, Xmas,cant
[Ger] SBar soli,pno,opt inst SCHAUR
EE 1185 $2.50 (K1092)

KROL, BERNHARD (cont'd.)

Maria Klar *sac
S solo,gtr,bvl,perc (diff) BOSSE
BE 265 s.p. (K1093)

Tagzeiten *Op.43, CC3U
S solo,vln SCHAUR EE 3318 s.p.
(K1094)

KROLL, GEORG
Magnificat *sac
S solo,ob,clar,al-sax,bass clar,
vcl,bvl (diff) study sc BOSSE
BE 411 s.p., ipr (K1095)

KROMER, KARL
Grusse Am Die Heimat
low solo,pno SIKORSKI 139 s.p.
(K1096)

high solo,pno SIKORSKI 139 s.p.
(K1097)

KRONSTEINER, HERMANN (1914-   )
Das Lied Vom Kinde *song cycle
Mez solo,pno/org DOBLINGER 08 627
$2.50 (K1098)

KRONSTEINER, JOSEF (1910-   )
Vier Rilke-Lieder *CC4U
[Ger] A solo,vla OSTER $1.25
(K1099)

KRONTJONG LIEDJES see Belloni, Fr.

KRONTJONG LIEDJES see Ruyneman, Daniel

KRONTJONG PADAN see Hullebroeck, Em.

KROPFREITER, AUGUSTINIUS FRANZ
(1936-   )
Altdorfer-Passion *Bibl/ora
[Ger/Eng] ABar soli,fl,ob,clar,bsn,
horn,org,2vln,2vcl,bvl voc sc
DOBLINGER 08 822 $5.00, sc
DOBLINGER 08 820 s.p., ipa
(K1100)

Das Hohelied Der Liebe
A solo,vcl,org DOBLINGER 08 855
s.p. (K1101)

Drei Geistliche Gesange *sac,CC3U
Bar solo,org DOBLINGER 08 854 $5.75
(K1102)

In Memorian *CC5U
S solo,fl,vla,vcl DOBLINGER 08 823
$5.00 (K1103)

Zwei Geistliche Gesange *sac,CC2U
S solo,org DOBLINGER 08 853 $5.25
(K1104)

KROSS, TH.
Au Fil De L'eau (composed with
Devaux, M.)
solo,acap ENOCH s.p. (K1105)
solo,pno ENOCH s.p. (K1106)

KRUISWEG see Kuiler, Cor.

KRULS, A.
Tien Nieuwe Nederlandse Liederen
*CC10U
solo,pno BROEKMANS 284 s.p. (K1107)

KRUMPHOLTZ, JOHANN BAPTIST (1742-1790)
Five Songs *CC5U
solo,harp HARP PUB $3.75 (K1108)

Late Eighteenth Century Songs *CCU
solo,harp HARP PUB $3.75 from Op.
10 (K1109)

KRUYF, TON DE (1926-   )
Einst Dem Grau
Mez solo,fl,ob,clar,trom,perc,harp,
vcl,bvl DONEMUS s.p. (K1110)

Pour Faire Le Portrait D'un Oiseau
Mez solo,fl,ob,clar,bsn,horn,trp,
perc,cel,harp,pno,vibra,xylo,vcl,
bvl DONEMUS s.p. (K1111)

KRYSTAL see Kapr, Jan

KTAADN see Adams, John

KUBA, LUBIN (1863-1956)
Bulgarische Volkslieder *CCU
solo,pno SUPRAPHON s.p. with Czech
and Bulgarian texts (K1112)

KUBIK, GAIL (1914-   )
Fables In Song *see Kitty-Cat Bird,
The; Lamb, The; Serpent, The;
Sloth, The (K1113)

Kitty-Cat Bird, The
med solo,pno BELWIN $1.50 see from
Fables In Song (K1114)

Lamb, The
med solo,pno BELWIN $1.50 see from
Fables In Song (K1115)

Like A Clear, Deep Pool
solo,pno PEER $.85 see from Songs
About Women (K1116)

KUBIK, GAIL (cont'd.)

Serpent, The
    med solo,pno BELWIN $2.00 see from
    Fables In Song   (K1117)

She Who Was All Piety
    solo,pno PEER $.95 see from Songs
    About Women   (K1118)

Sloth, The
    med solo,pno BELWIN $1.50 see from
    Fables In Song   (K1119)

Songs About Women *see Like A Clear,
    Deep Pool; She Who Was All Piety;
    Woman's Armor, A   (K1120)

Woman's Armor, A
    solo,pno PEER $.85 see from Songs
    About Women   (K1121)

KUBIK, LADISLAV
Lament Of A Warrior's Wife
    S&narrator,bass clar,pno,perc,vla
    PANTON s.p.   (K1122)

KUBIN, RUDOLF (1900-1973)
Perly Slezske
    "Schlesische Perlen" med solo,pno
    CZECH s.p.   (K1123)

Schlesische Perlen *see Perly
    Slezske

Zpevy Anglickych Haviru *CCU
    [Czech/Eng] solo,pno PANTON 051
    s.p.   (K1124)

KUBIZEK, AUGUSTINIAN (1918-   )
Hab Ich Lieb *CC4U
    S solo,vln&strings/vln&pno voc sc
    DOBLINGER s.p.   (K1125)

Mater Castissima *Op.22c,No.2
    [Lat] med solo,pno DOBLINGER 08 628
    $3.00   (K1126)
    [Lat] solo,3treb inst sc DOBLINGER
    08 824 $3.00, ipa   (K1127)

KUCKEN, FRIEDRICH WILHELM (1810-1882)
Belle Etoile
    2 soli,pno DURAND s.p.   (K1128)

Depart Et Retour *see L'Hirondelle

La Captive
    [Ger] solo,pno DURAND s.p.   (K1129)

La Fleur Du Vallon
    [Ger] solo,pno DURAND s.p.   (K1130)

Le Mois De Mai
    2 soli,pno DURAND s.p.   (K1131)

L'Hirondelle
    "Depart Et Retour" 2 soli,pno
    DURAND s.p.   (K1132)

Ton Nom
    [Ger] solo,pno DURAND 36 s.p.
                                      (K1133)

KUCKUCK RIEF IM FICHTENWALDE see
    Kilpinen, Yrio, Vaha Ilo
    Emottomalle Kaesta

KUCKUCKSLIEDER see Haas, Joseph

KUHN, M.
Ach Mein Herzliebes Jesulein *sac,
    Xmas
    solo,pno HUG s.p.   (K1134)

KUHN, SIEGFRIED
Der Verzweifelte Liebhaber
    high solo,pno RIES s.p.   (K1135)

Kurze Fahrt
    high solo,pno RIES s.p.   (K1136)

Minnelied
    high solo,pno RIES s.p.   (K1137)

Nachtwandler
    med solo,pno RIES s.p.   (K1138)

Schlummerlied
    low solo,pno RIES s.p.   (K1139)

KUHUN TAIDIN VERRATA see Hamalainen,
    Lauri

KUILER, COR.
Aufbruch *Op.32,No.4
    see Der Erste Ball

Da Er Mich Ansah *Op.32,No.2
    see Der Erste Ball

Der Erste Ball
    solo,pno ALSBACH s.p.
    contains: Aufbruch, Op.32,No.4;
    Da Er Mich Ansah, Op.32,No.2;
    Die Geoge Sang, Op.32,No.3; Gut
    Nacht, Op.32,No.6; Im
    Blassgelben Kleidchen, Op.32,

KUILER, COR. (cont'd.)

    No.1; Nachhauseweg, Op.32,No.5
                                      (K1140)

Die Geoge Sang *Op.32,No.3
    see Der Erste Ball

Gut Nacht *Op.32,No.6
    see Der Erste Ball

Im Blassgelben Kleidchen *Op.32,No.1
    see Der Erste Ball

Kruisweg
    solo,pno ALSBACH s.p.   (K1141)

Nachhauseweg *Op.32,No.5
    see Der Erste Ball

O Jubel Mijn Hart
    solo,pno ALSBACH s.p.   (K1142)

Schneewittchen *Op.14
    solo,pno ALSBACH s.p.   (K1143)

KUIN HIIPUVA HIILLOS TUMMENTUU see
    Merikanto, Oskar

KUIN LINNUT TUMMAN VEEN see Kuusisto,
    Taneli

KUKKALATVA KUUSI see Kilpinen, Yrio

KUKUCK, FELICITAS (1914-   )
Aus Tiefer Not Schrei Ich Zu Dir
    *sac,concerto
    B solo,vla,org sc HANSSLER 13.005
    s.p., ipa   (K1144)

Ich Glaube, Dass Ich Nicht *sac
    Bar solo,org HANSSLER 5.046 s.p.
                                      (K1145)

KULERVON VALITUS see Sibelius, Jean

KULKA - GESANGE see Koellreutter, Hans-
    Joachim

KULKURIN KOSINTA see Pesonen, Olavi
    (Samuel)

KULLAN MURUNEN see Merikanto, Oskar

KULLERVON KEHTOLAULU see Launis, Armas
    (Emmanuel)

KULLERVON VALITUS see Sibelius, Jean

KULLERVOS KLAGAN see Sibelius, Jean,
    Kullervon Valitus

KULLERVOS KLAGE see Sibelius, Jean,
    Kullervon Valitus

KULTAKALAT see Ranta, Sulho

KULTANUKKI see Klemetti, Heikki

KUMAKI, MAMORU (1935-   )
Hana
    see Songs From Poem Of Dyukichi
    Yagi

Hato
    see Songs From Poem Of Dyukichi
    Yagi

Hibi-Ite-Yuko
    see Songs From Poem Of Dyukichi
    Yagi

Itsu-Ni-Nattara
    see Songs From Poem Of Dyukichi
    Yagi

Soboku-Na-Koto
    see Songs From Poem Of Dyukichi
    Yagi

Songs From Poem Of Dyukichi Yagi
    [Jap] S solo,pno JAPAN 7106 s.p.
    contains: Hana; Hato; Hibi-Ite-
    Yuko; Itsu-Ni-Nattara; Soboku-
    Na-Koto   (K1146)

KUMMALSTAKO KUULEMINEN see Kilpinen,
    Yrio

KUMMER, A.
Uit Een Bron, Vol. I *CCU
    solo,pno BROEKMANS 163 s.p. (K1147)

Uit Een Bron, Vol. II *CCU
    solo,pno BROEKMANS 164 s.p. (K1148)

KUMU VE'NASHIR see Da-Oz, Ram

KUN ENSI KERRAN SILMAS NAIN *folk,Finn
    (Pacius, Fredrik) "Den Forsta Gangen
    Din Blick Jag Sag" solo,pno FAZER
    W 1298 s.p.   (K1149)

KUN HELMIN HEIJASTAAPI see Linnala,
    Eino

KUN MA KERRAN see Kilpinen, Yrio

KUN MINA MOKOMAN SAISIN see Marvia,
    Einari

KUN MUN KULTANI TULISI see Kilpinen,
    Yrio

KUN MUN KULTANI TULISI see Maasalo,
    Armas

KUN NUKAHDAN KATSOEN TAHTIIN see
    Merikanto, Oskar, Somnar Jag Med
    Blicken Fast

KUN PAIVA PAISTAA see Merikanto, Oskar

KUN VAAN LAULAA SAAN see Merikanto,
    Oskar

KUNAD, RAINER (1936-   )
Melodie, Die Ich Verloren Hatte
    S solo,fl,2vln,2vcl sc DEUTSCHER
    9402 s.p., ipr   (K1150)

Schattenland Strome *CCU
    T solo,gtr DEUTSCHER 9041 s.p.
                                      (K1151)

KUNC, JAN (1883-   )
Kyticka Lidovych Pisni *CC22U
    solo,pno SUPRAPHON   (K1152)

Molinbursky Pesnicky *CCU
    solo,pno SUPRAPHON s.p.   (K1153)

Smutky *Op.2
    solo,pno SUPRAPHON s.p.   (K1154)

KUNDE JAG DIKTA EN VISA see Nordqvist,
    Gustaf

KUNEN DAG, ET OYEBLIKK AV GANGEN see
    Ahnfeldt, O.

KUNG ERIK see Bengzon

KUNG HEIMER OCH ASLOG see Soderman,
    (Johan) August

KUNG LILJEKONVALJE see Liljefors, Ruben

KUNG LILJEKONVALJE AV DUNGEN see
    Wideen, Ivar

KUNSTERLEBEN see Strauss, Johann

KUNSTLERLEBEN see Strauss, Johann

KUNZ, ERNST (1891-   )
Sechs Lieder *CC6U
    solo,pno HUG s.p.   (K1155)

KUOLEMA KANNELTA LOI see Merikanto,
    Oskar

KUOLEMAN JOUSTEN see Pylkkanen, Tauno
    Kullervo

KUOLEMAN TANTU see Marvia, Einari

KUPFERMAN, MEYER (1926-   )
Island In A Room
    solo,pno GENERAL 9 $2.00   (K1156)

KUPKA, KAREL (1927-   )
Gesang *see Zpev

Pisnicky Pro Nizsi Hlas *CCU
    low solo,pno SUPRAPHON s.p. (K1157)

Tri Canzony Pro Bas *CC3U
    B solo,clar,pno,vln CZECH s.p.
                                      (K1158)
Zpev
    "Gesang" B solo,clar,pno,3perc
    CZECH s.p.   (K1159)

KURIOSE GESCHICHTE see Pfitzner, Hans

KURTAG, GYORGY (1926-   )
Die Spruche Des Peter Bornemisza
    *CCU
    solo,pno UNIVER. 14493 $21.00
                                      (K1160)

KURTZ, EUGENE (1923-   )
La Derniere Contrebasse A Las Vegas
    female solo&male solo,bvl sc JOBERT
    rental   (K1161)

Three Songs From Medea *CC3U
    [Eng/Fr] JOBERT s.p. S solo,3fl,
    3ob,3clar,3bsn,4horn,3trp,3trom,
    tuba,perc,2vibra,harp,cel,timp,
    strings sc,voc sc; A solo,pno voc
    sc   (K1162)

KURZBACH, PAUL (1902-   )
Drei Lieder Fur Eine Singstimme Und
    Klavier
    solo,pno cmplt ed BREITKOPF-L
    EB 5899 s.p.
    contains: Hatte Einen Knaben;
    Herbst; Lied Von Der Bleibe
                                      (K1163)

KURZBACH, PAUL (cont'd.)

Hatte Einen Knaben
see Drei Lieder Fur Eine Singstimme
Und Klavier

Herbst
see Drei Lieder Fur Eine Singstimme
Und Klavier

Lied Von Der Bleibe
see Drei Lieder Fur Eine Singstimme
Und Klavier

KURZE FAHRT see Kuhn, Siegfried

KURZER TAG see Thomas, Kurt

KUS MIJN HART OP MIJNEN MOND see
Clercq, R. de

KUSAGAWA, KEI
Alone On The Street *song cycle
[Jap] solo,pno JAPAN 7003 s.p.
(K1164)

KUSSE MICH *folk,Russ
[Ger/Russ] solo,pno ZIMMER. 1510 s.p.
(K1165)

KUSSEKRAUT see Kilpinen, Yrio

KUSSES HOFFNUNG see Sibelius, Jean,
Kyssens Hopp

KUTI, KUTI KULTASENI see Kilpinen, Yrio

KUU NOUSEE see Bergman, Erik, Pa Fastet
Stiger Manen

KUULA, TOIVO (1883-1918)
Das Schicksal *see Kohtalo

Epilog *see Epilogi

Epilogi
"Epilog" see Kaksi Laulua

Etelapohjalaisia Kansanlauluja, Vols.
I-II *CCU
solo,pno FAZER W 2122; W 2220 s.p.,
ea. (K1166)

Gesammelte Lieder *CCU
solo,pno FAZER F 4871 s.p. (K1167)

Herbststimmung *see Syystunnelma

Hostsang *see Vanha Syyslaulu

I Fagarden *see Karjapihassa

Kaksi Laulua
solo,pno FAZER W 2121 s.p.
contains: Epilogi, "Epilog";
Kesayo Kirkkomaalla,
"Sommernacht Auf Einem
Friedhof" (K1168)

Karjapihassa *Op.31a,No.2
"I Fagarden" solo,pno FAZER W 144
s.p. (K1169)

Kesayo Kirkkomaalla
"Sommernacht Auf Einem Friedhof"
see Kaksi Laulua

Kohtalo *Op.23,No.4
"Das Schicksal" solo,pno FAZER s.p.
(K1170)

Natt *see Yo

Sielut *Op.27,No.3
"Sjalarna" solo,pno FAZER W 1946
s.p. (K1171)

Sjalarna *see Sielut

Sommernacht Auf Einem Friedhof *see
Kesayo Kirkkomaalla

Suutelo *Op.8,No.1
solo,pno FAZER W 2135 s.p. (K1172)

Syystunnelma *Op.2,No.1
"Herbststimmung" solo,pno FAZER
W 2249 s.p. (K1173)

Vanha Syyslaulu *Op.24,No.3
"Hostsang" solo,pno FAZER W 972
s.p. (K1174)

Yo
"Natt" solo,pno FAZER W 593 s.p.
(K1175)

KUULUTUSMATKA see Marvia, Einari

KUUN SILTA see Pylkkanen, Tauno
Kullervo

KUUSEN JUURET KUIVETTUVAT see Kilpinen,
Yrio

KUUSI JA LINTUNEN see Kilpinen, Yrio

KUUSI LAULU see Kilpinen, Yrio

KUUSISTO, ILKKA (1933-   )
Gezeiten
see Vier Lieder Zu Worten Von Aale
Tynni

Karnevale
see Vier Lieder Zu Worten Von Aale
Tynni

Mond Und Sonne
see Vier Lieder Zu Worten Von Aale
Tynni

Primavera
see Vier Lieder Zu Worten Von Aale
Tynni

Vier Lieder Zu Worten Von Aale Tynni
[Finn/Ger] solo,pno FAZER s.p.
contains: Gezeiten; Karnevale;
Mond Und Sonne; Primavera
(K1176)

KUUSISTO, TANELI (1905-   )
Armahin Muisto *Op.44,No.2
(Pimia) "Det Karaste Minnet" 2
soli,pno FAZER F 2885 s.p.
(K1177)

Det Karaste Minnet *see Armahin
Muisto

En Dyster Gren *see Tumma Ritva

Finsk Bon *see Suomalainen Rukous

Ilta *Op.5,No.3
solo,pno FAZER 2446 s.p. see from
Kolme Laulua (K1178)

Kaksi Hengellista Laulua
solo,pno FAZER F 2447 s.p.
contains: Sun Etehens Lapsi
Betlehemin, Op.6,No.1; Sun
Ristis Juurehen, Op.6,No.2
(K1179)

Kolme Laulua *see Ilta, Op.5,No.3;
Kuin Linnut Tumman Veen, Op.5,
No.1; Tahtilaulu, Op.5,No.2
(K1180)

Kuin Linnut Tumman Veen *Op.5,No.1
solo,pno FAZER F 2444 s.p. see from
Kolme Laulua (K1181)

Ratsumies *Op.40,No.5
"Ryttaren" solo,pno FAZER F 2852
s.p. (K1182)

Ryttaren *see Ratsumies

Saunakamari, Laulusarja *Op.59, CCU
solo,pno FAZER W 3699 s.p. (K1183)

Savolaisia Kansanlauluja II *Op.56a,
CCU
solo,pno FAZER F 3536 s.p. (K1184)

Sun Etehens Lapsi Betlehemin *Op.6,
No.1
see Kaksi Hengellista Laulua

Sun Ristis Juurehen *Op.6,No.2
see Kaksi Hengellista Laulua

Suomalainen Rukous *Op.27,No.2
"Finsk Bon" solo,pno FAZER W 1869
s.p. (K1185)

Tahtilaulu *Op.5,No.2
solo,pno FAZER 2445 s.p. see from
Kolme Laulua (K1186)

Tumma Ritva *Op.39,No.1
"En Dyster Gren" solo,pno FAZER
F 4910 s.p. (K1187)

KUUTAMOLLA see Kilpinen, Yrio

KUYAS see Somers, Harry Stewart

KVALL see Linko, Ernst (Fredrik), Ehtoo

KVALL I KLARA see Stenhammar, Wilhelm

KVALL I SKOGEN see Nordqvist, Gustaf

KVALL I SKOGEN see Pergament, Moses

KVALL I SKOGEN see Rangstrom, Ture

KVALLEN see Wibergh, Olof

KVALLNING see Kilpinen, Yrio

KVALLSTANKAR see Hallstrom, Ivar

KVALLSVISA see Rangstrom, Ture

KVANDAL, JOHAN
Syv Sanger *CC7L
solo,pno MUSIKK s.p. (K1188)

KVAPIL, JAROSLAV (1892-1958)
Lieder Fur Hohe Stimme Und Klavier
*CCU
high solo,pno SUPRAPHON s.p.
(K1189)

KVAPILOVY PISNE I-II see Jindrich,
Jindrich

KVARNEN see Pergament, Moses

KVARNHJULET see Sibelius, Jean

KVELDEN LISTER SEG PA TA OVER
KLOVERENGEN see Eriksson, Josef

KVELDING see Dorumsgaard, Arne

KVETINY see Hurnik, Ilja

KVETY JASMINU see Bohac, Josef

KVI TRALAR DET IKKJE LENGER I SKOGEN
see Olsen, Sparre

KVOLDVISA see Stefansson, Fjolnir

KWARTRIJNEN EN NACHTSTILTE see
Beekhuis, Hanna

KWATRIJNEN EN NACHSTILTE see Beekhuis,
Hanna

KWINTET see Otten, Ludwig

KYLVA see Hannikainen, Ilmari, Det
Galler

KYRIE see Faure, Gabriel-Urbain

KYRIE see Hemel, Oscar van

KYRIE ELEISON see Mollicone, Henry

KYRIE, GOTT VATER IN EWIGKEIT see
Weyrauch, Johannes

KYRKOSANGARENS ALBUM see Wibergh, Olof

KYSS MEJ PAA OJNENE, SOL see Nordqvist,
Gustaf

KYSSEN see Sibelius, Jean

KYSSENS HOPP see Sibelius, Jean

KYSSTU MIG HIN MJUKA MAER
see Fimm Numer I Islenzkum
Pjoobuningum

KYTICA LESNA see Ferenczy, Oto

KYTICE PISNI CESKYCH see Axmann, Emil

KYTICE PISNI PRO DETI A PIONYRY *CC11L
solo,pno SUPRAPHON contains works by:
Fischer; Kalabis; Strasek; Valek
(K1190)

KYTICKA LIDOVYCH PISNI see Kunc, Jan

KYTICKA Z MORAVY see Axmann, Emil

KYYHKYNEN KYLPEE see Kotilainen, Otto

L

L' A-J PASSARIA!
(Carlo, Musi) solo,pno (Bolognese
dialect) BONGIOVANI 2050 s.p. see
from El Mi Canzunett   (L1)

LA BACHELETTE see Varney, Pierre Joseph
Alphonse

LA BAGATELLE see Varney, Pierre Joseph
Alphonse

LA BALADA DEL AGUA DEL MAR see
Caggiano, Roberto

LA BALANCELLE see Migot, Georges

LA BARCA see Recli, Giulia

LA BARQUE see Samazeuilh, Gustave

LA BARQUE D'AMOUR see Flegier, Ange

LA-BAS see Chretien, H.

LA-BAS see Saint-Saens, Camille

LA-BAS see Schubert, Franz (Peter)

LA-BAS, DANS LA PRAIRIE see Indy,
Vincent d'

LA-BAS SUR LA MER see Maeder

LA-BAS VERS L'EGLISE see Ravel, Maurice

LA BEATA see Laserna, Blas de

LA BEAUTE QUE JE SERS EST TELLE see
Saint-Saens, Camille

LA BEFANA see Farina, Guido

LA BELLE AU BOIS DORMANT see Debussy,
Claude

LA BELLE AU BOIS DORMANT see Fourdrain,
Felix

LA BELLE AU BOIS DORMANT see Lacome,
Paul

LA BELLE AU BOIS DORMANT see Vieu, Jane

LA BELLE DAME SANS MERCI see Hindemith,
Paul

LA BELLE DE PARIS see Van Parys, G.

LA BELLE EN DORMANT see Thomson, Virgil

LA BELLE FILLE see Gedalge, Andre

LA BELLE ILONA see Berger, Jean

LA BELLE JEUNE FILLE DU MIDI see
Lacome, Paul

LA BELLE MADELEINE see Holmes, Alfred

LA BELLE MEUNIERE see Schubert, Franz
(Peter)

LA BELLE QUI VIENDRA see Arrieu, Claude

LA BELLE SAISON D'AMOUR see Godard,
Benjamin Louis Paul

LA BELLE, SI TU ME DELAISSES see Indy,
Vincent d'

LA BELLE YSABEAU see Indy, Vincent d'

LA BELTA PRESTO FINISCE see Lewkovitch,
Bernhard

LA BERCEUSE see Schubert, Franz
(Peter), Wiegenlied

LA BERCEUSE see Truillet-Soyer, M.

LA BERCEUSE DU MARIN see Aubert, Louis-
Francois-Marie

LA BERGERE AUX CHAMPS
see Two French Folk Songs

LA BERGERE AUX CHAMPS see Indy, Vincent
d'

LA BERGERE INDULGENTE see Delvincourt,
Claude

LA BERGERONNETTE see Truillet-Soyer, M.

LA BETE NOIRE see Levade, Charles
(Gaston)

LA BIEN AIMEE see Cannon, (Jack)
Phillip

LA BIEN-AIMEE see Wachs, Paul Etienne
Victor

LA BIEN MARIEE see Cannon, (Jack)
Phillip

LA BLANCHE EGLISE see Absil, Jean

LA BOHEME ET MON COEUR see Dukelsky,
Vladimir

LA BONNE AVENTURE ENFANTINE see
Delbruck, J.

LA BONNE CHANSON see Faure, Gabriel-
Urbain

LA BONNE CHANSON see Faure, Gabriel-
Urbain

LA BONNE CHANSON see Mulder, Ernest W.

LA BONNE CHANSON see Shibata, Minao

LA BONNE FORTUNE see Wissmer, Pierre

LA BONNE MANTE see Lacombe, Paul

LA BONNE PLACE see Berger, Rod.

LA BONNE TERRE see Indy, Vincent d'

LA BOUCHE A BERTHE see Berger, Rod.

LA BRABANCONNE see Campenhout, Francois
van

LA BRISE see Saint-Saens, Camille

LA BRISE EST DOUCE see Filipucci, Edm.

LA BRISE EST DOUCE ET PARFUMEE see
Gounod, Charles Francois

LA BRISE VAGABONDE see Gabus, Monique

LA CALESITA see Pahissa, Jaime

LA CALME PLAT see Schubert, Franz
(Peter)

LA CALUNNIA E UN VENTICELLO see
Rossini, Gioacchino

LA CAMARADE see Delmet, Paul

LA CAMPAGNOLA see Albanese, Guido

LA CAMPANA see Lopez De La Rosa,
Horatio

LA CAMPANA see Setaccioli, Giacomo

LA CANADIENNE see Fragerolle, G.

LA CANCION DEL SALDAN see Napolitano,
Emilio

LA CANZONE DEI RICORDI see Martucci,
Giuseppe

LA CANZONE DELL'AMORE see De Lucia,
Nadir

LA CANZONE DI CHERUBINO see Rossellini,
Renzo

LA CANZONE DI DORETTA see Puccini,
Giacomo

LA CANZONE DI FORTUNIO see Rossellini,
Renzo

LA CANZONE DI PIERROT see Clausetti, P.

LA CAPTIVE see Kucken, Friedrich
Wilhelm

LA CARAVANE DU MONDE see Toussaint De
Sutter, J.

LA CARPE see Steenhuis, Francois

LA CASADA INFIEL see Obrados, Fernando

LA CASADA INFIEL see Castro, Juan Jose

LA CENICIENTA see Napolitano, Emilio

LA CHAMBRE MAGIQUE see Debussy, Claude

LA CHAMBRE VIDE see Rossellini, Renzo

LA CHANSIN DU ROSSIGNOL see Desrez

LA CHANSON DE BRUMAIRE see Legay,
Marcel

LA CHANSON DE CELLES QUI RESTENT see
Rhene-Baton

LA CHANSON DE CONSOLATION see Legay,
Marcel

LA CHANSON DE FLOREAL see Legay, Marcel

LA CHANSON DE FRIMAIRE see Legay,
Marcel

LA CHANSON DE FRUCTIDOR see Legay,
Marcel

LA CHANSON DE GERMINAL see Legay,
Marcel

LA CHANSON DE JADIS see Blech, Leo

LA CHANSON DE LA FILEUSE see Legay,
Marcel

LA CHANSON DE LA FLEUR ROUGE see Rhene-
Baton

LA CHANSON DE LA MAISON TRISTE see
Rhene-Baton

LA CHANSON DE LA MUSE see Legay, Marcel

LA CHANSON DE LA PAIX see Legay, Marcel

LA CHANSON DE LA ROSE BLANCHE see
Legay, Marcel

LA CHANSON DE LA TERRE see Legay,
Marcel

LA CHANSON DE LA VOILETTE see Legay,
Marcel

LA CHANSON DE L'AMIE DU ROI see Heise,
Peter Arnold

LA CHANSON DE L'EXILE see Rhene-Baton

LA CHANSON DE L'HYMENEE see Legay,
Marcel

LA CHANSON DE MA VIE see Delage,
Maurice

LA CHANSON DE MESSIDOR see Legay,
Marcel

LA CHANSON DE MON VILLAGE see Legay,
Marcel

LA CHANSON DE NIVOSE see Legay, Marcel

LA CHANSON DE NOEL see Rhene-Baton

LA CHANSON DE PANAME see Bozi, Harold
de

LA CHANSON DE PLUVOISE see Legay,
Marcel

LA CHANSON DE PRAIRIAL see Legay,
Marcel

LA CHANSON DE THERMIDOR see Legay,
Marcel

LA CHANSON DE TYLTYL see Wolff, A.

LA CHANSON DE VENDEMIAIRE see Legay,
Marcel

LA CHANSON DE VENTOSE see Legay, Marcel

LA CHANSON DES CATHERINES see Legay,
Marcel

LA CHANSON DES CERISES see Messager,
Andre

LA CHANSON DES CHANSONS see Tesson, P.

LA CHANSON DES COUPES see Legay, Marcel

LA CHANSON DES FLEURS NOUVELLES see
Rhene-Baton

LA CHANSON DES GALETS see Chantrier, A.

LA CHANSON DES LARMES see Fragerolle,
G.

LA CHANSON DES PETITES DANEUSES see
Legay, Marcel

LA CHANSON DES PETITS MENDIANTS see
Legay, Marcel

LA CHANSON DES PLEURS see Legay, Marcel

LA CHANSON D'EVE see Herberigs, Robert

LA CHANSON D'EVE see Rasse, Francois

LA CHANSON DU BATTOIR see Street, G.

LA CHANSON DU BLE see Bozza, Eugene

LA CHANSON DU BOIS D'AMOUR see Rhene-
Baton

LA CHANSON DU BOUQUET D'ANJONCS see Rhene-Baton

LA CHANSON DU CAPITAINE see Serpette, Gaston

LA CHANSON DU CHEMIN see Legay, Marcel

LA CHANSON DU CHIFFONNIER see Bosmans, Henriette

LA CHANSON DU CHRYSANTHEME see Legay, Marcel

LA CHANSON DU COUCOU see Legay, Marcel

LA CHANSON DU JEUNE ARCHER see Schumann, Robert (Alexander)

LA CHANSON DU MARIN see Roget, H.

LA CHANSON DU MATELOT see Filipucci, Edm.

LA CHANSON DU MOULIN A VENT see Bergmann, R.

LA CHANSON DU MYOSOTIS see Legay, Marcel

LA CHANSON DU PAGE see Holmes, Alfred

LA CHANSON DU ROI D'ANGLETERRE see Bitsch, Marcel

LA CHANSON DU ROUET see Michel, Ch.-H.

LA CHANSON DU SOLEIL see Roques, J.

LA CHANSON DU VANNIER see Franck, Cesar

LA CHANSON DU VERGER FLEURI see Rhene-Baton

LA CHANSON FATALE see Roget, H.

LA CHANTEUSE DES COURS see Halet, L.

LA CHARMANTE AVENTURE see Lacome, Paul

LA CHASSE see Koechlin, Charles

LA CHASSE AU FURET see Laparra, Raoul

LA CHASSE FANTASTIQUE see Fragerolle, G.

LA CHATELAINE see Margis, A.

LA CHATTE BLANCHE see Francaix, Jean

LA CHAUMIERE see Couperin, Gervais-Francois

LA CHEVELURE see Debussy, Claude

LA CHRONIQUE MEDISANTE see Lacome, Paul

LA CI DAREM see Mozart, Wolfgang Amadeus

LA CI DAREM LA MANO see Mozart, Wolfgang Amadeus

LA CIGALE ET LA FOURMI see Caplet, Andre

LA CIGALE ET LA FOURMI see Delage, Maurice

LA CINQUANTAINE see Delmet, Paul

LA CITERNE DES MILLE COLONNES see Schmitt, Florent

LA CLAIRE FONATINE see Levade, Charles (Gaston)

LA CLOCHE see Saint-Saens, Camille

LA CLOCHE FELEE see Cantu, M.

LA CLOCHE FELEE see Caplet, Andre

LA COCCINELLE see Saint-Saens, Camille

LA COCCINELLE see Schumann, Robert (Alexander)

LA COEUR DU POETE see Delmet, Paul

LA COLLERETTE DE PIERROT see Cuvillier, Charles

LA COLOMBA see Tocchi, Gian-Luca

LA COLUMBE see Busser, Henri-Paul

LA COLUMBE DESCEND see Saint-Saens, Camille

LA COLUMBE POIGNARDEE see Beydts, L.

LA COMPARSA DEL FAROL see Lilien, Ignace

LA COMPARSITA see Matos, Rodriquez

LA COMPLAINTE DE NOTRE-DAME see Emmanuel, Maurice

LA COMPLAINTE DES PAUVR'S PETITS GAS see Alin, Pierre

LA COMPLAINTE DU PETIT ANE see Strimer, Joseph

LA COMTESSE ESMEREE see Bosmans, Henriette

LA CONSULTA see Ferandiere, F.

LA CONTRADA SENZA SOLE see Massarani, E.

LA CORONA see Krenek, Ernst

LA CORONA see Rice, Thomas

LA COURBE DE TES YEUX see Devries, Ivan

LA COURONNE EFFEUILLEE see Decruck, F.

LA COURTE PAILLE see Poulenc, Francis

LA CRECHE see Motte La Croix, A.F.

LA CROCEFISSIONE see Tortone, A.

LA CROIX DE LA LORRAINE see Hively, Wells

LA CROIX DOULOUREUSE see Caplet, Andre

LA CROIX DU SUD see Varese, Edgar

LA CUMPARSITA see Rodriguez, Augusto

LA CUZQUENITA see Sas, Andres

LA CZARINE see Ganne, Louis Gaston

LA DAME BLEUE see Arrieu, Claude

LA DAME D'ANDRE see Poulenc, Francis

LA DAME DE MONTECARLO see Poulenc, Francis

LA DAMOISELLE see Chaminade, Cecile

LA DAMOISELLE ELUE see Debussy, Claude

LA DANSE AU BORD DU LAC see Labey, Marcel

LA DANSE DE TAIA see Tremisot, Ed.

LA DANSE DES EPEES see Lacome, Paul

LA DANSE DES MAINS AMPUTEES see Coppola, Piero

LA DANZA
(Rossini) solo,pno FORLIVESI 11960 s.p. (L2)

LA DANZA see Rossini, Gioacchino

LA DEL PANUELO ROJO see Tabuyo, I.

LA DELAISEE see Delvincourt, Claude

LA DERNIERE BERCEUSE see Rhene-Baton

LA DERNIERE CHANSON see Varney, Pierre Joseph Alphonse

LA DERNIERE CONTREBASSE A LAS VEGAS see Kurtz, Eugene

LA DERNIERE FLAMME see Rabey, Rene

LA DERNIERE LETRE DE MANON see Gillet, Ernest

LA DIVA DE "L'EMPIRE" see Satie, Erik

LA DOLCHISSIMA EFFIGIE see Cilea, Francesco

LA DONNA E MOBILE see Verdi, Giuseppe

LA DOUBLE (LE SOSIE) see Schubert, Franz (Peter), Der Doppelganger

LA DOUCEUR DE TES YEUX see Honegger, Arthur

LA DOULEUR CHRETIENNE see Bijl, Theo van der

LA EPIPHANIE see Decruck, F.

LA EREMITA DE SAN SIMON see Andriessen, Juriaan

LA FABLE DU VILLAGE see Rivier, Jean

LA FAMILLE POLICHINELLE see Lacome, Paul

LA FARANDOLE see Lacome, Paul

LA FARFALLA see Gelli, E.

LA FARFALLETTA see Wolf, Hugo

LA FAUTE DES ROSES see Berger, Rod.

LA FAUVETTE see Schumann, Robert (Alexander)

LA FEE see Schubert, Franz (Peter)

LA FEE AUX CHEVEUX D'OR see Delmet, Paul

LA FELICITA see Scuderi, Gaspare

LA FEMME A L'ACCORDEON see Lilien, Ignace

LA FEMME DU CHEF see Schumann, Robert (Alexander)

LA FEMME QUI FUT see Tremisot, Ed.

LA FETE D'ALEXANDRE see Handel, George Frideric

LA FETE PUBLIQUE see Arrieu, Claude

LA FEUILLE DE BOULEAU see Georges, Alexandre

LA FEUILLE DE PEUPLIER see Saint-Saens, Camille

LA FEUILLE DU PEUPLIER see Saint-Saens, Camille

LA FIANCEE CAPTIVE
(Fragerolle, G.) solo,pno ENOCH s.p. see from Chansons Du Pays-Lorrain (L3)
(Fragerolle, G.) solo,acap ENOCH s.p. see from Chansons Du Pays-Lorrain (L4)

LA FIANCEE DU SOLDAT see Chaminade, Cecile

LA FIANCEE DU TIMBALIER see Berners, Lord

LA FIANCEE DU TIMBALIER see Saint-Saens, Camille

LA FIANCEE PERDUE see Messiaen, Oliver

LA FIGLIA DEL RE DEGLI ELFI see Gandino, Adolfo

LA FILLE ALLAIT AUX CHAMPS see Bagge, G.

LA FILLE AU SABOTIER see Lacome, Paul

LA FILLE DANS LA TOUR see Berger, Jean

LA FILLE DE JEPHTE see Lacome, Paul

LA FILLE DE JEPHTE see Maurice, Pierre

LA FILLE DU PECHEUR see Schubert, Franz (Peter), Das Fischermadchen

LA FILLE DU PORT see Wiener, Jean

LA FILLE DU ROI DE TARTARIE see Voormolen, Alexander Nicolas

LA FILLETTE ET LE DEMON see Indy, Vincent d'

LA FINE see Respighi, Ottorino

LA FINE DELLA VOLPE see Rocca, Lodovico

LA FLAMME CHANTE see Rhene-Baton

LA FLECHA Y LA CANCION see Lasala, Angel

LA FLEUR DE L'ONDE see Barlow, F., Die Wasserlilie

LA FLEUR DE PECHER see Grovlez, Gabriel (Marie)

LA FLEUR DU VALLON see Kucken, Friedrich Wilhelm

LA FLEUR ET LE PAPILLON see Godard, Benjamin Louis Paul

LA FLEUR QUE TU M'AVAIS JETEE see Bizet, Georges

LA FLIBUSTIER see Georges, Alexandre

LA FLOR DE LA CANELA see Azpiazu, Jose de

LA FLORA, VOL. 1 *CC43L,16-18th cent [It] med-high solo,pno HANSEN-DEN s.p. contains works by: Caccini; Monteverdi; Frescobaldi; Carissimi;

Scarlatti and others   (L5)

LA FLORA, VOL. 2 *CC43L,16-18th cent
[It] med-high solo,pno HANSEN-DEN
s.p. contains works by: Peri;
Rontani; Vitali; Berti; Albinoni
and others   (L6)

LA FLORA, VOL. 3 *CC43L,16-18th cent
[It] med-high solo/high solo&med
solo,kbd HANSEN-DEN s.p. contains
works by: Caccini; Cifra;
Falconieri; Vitali; Handel and
others   (L7)

LA FLUTE DE BAMBOU see Vieu, Jane

LA FLUTE DE JADE see Hermans, Nico

LA FLUTE DE PAN see Debussy, Claude

LA FLUTE ENCHANTEE see Ravel, Maurice

LA FOLLETTA see Marchesi

LA FONTAINE see Perissas, M.

LA FONTAINE D'HELENE see Aubert, Louis-
Francois-Marie

LA FORET see Caplet, Andre

LA FORET ARDENTE see Gaubert, Philippe

LA FORTUNE see Schumann, Robert
(Alexander), Spinnelied

LA FRAICHEUR ET LE FEU see Poulenc,
Francis

LA FRANCE EST BELLE see Delbruck, J.

LA FUITE DE LA LUNE see Griffes,
Charles Tomlinson

LA GAGGIA see Pratella, Francesco
Balilla

LA GALETTE see DuBois, Pierre Max

LA GALLINE NOIRE see Dufresne, C.

LA GANDOLA see Liviabella, Lino

LA GARBURE BEARNAISE see Vogel, A.

LA GEOLE see Dupre, Marcel

LA GERBE see Cuvillier, Charles

LA GIRIGONZA see Flecha, Mateo

LA GIROMETTA see Sibella, Gabrielle

LA GITANILLA EN EL COLISEO see Castel,
J.

LA GLOIRE DE DIEU DANS LA NATUR see
Beethoven, Ludwig van

LA GLOIRE DE DIEU DANS LA NATURE see
Beethoven, Ludwig van, Die Ehre
Gottes Aus Der Natur

LA GLOIRE ETAIT see Berlioz, Hector

LA GLORIA E IMENEO see Vivaldi, Antonio

LA GLU see Fragerolle, G.

LA GOLONDRINA *folk,Span
(Serrandell, Narciso) "Swallow, The"
high solo&med solo,pno SCHIRM.G
$.60   (L8)

LA GOLONDRINA see Serradell, Narciso

LA GOUTTE DE PLUIE see Middeleer, Jean
De

LA GRENOUILLE AMERICAINE see Satie,
Erik

LA GRENOUILLE QUI VEUT SE FAIRE AUSSI
GROSSE QUE LE BOEUF see Francaix,
Jean

LA GRENOUILLERE see Poulenc, Francis

LA GREVE DES BAISERS see Michiels, G.

LA GROTTE see Debussy, Claude

LA GUERISON DU POETE see Schumann,
Robert (Alexander)

LA GUERRIERA see Giuranna, Barbara

LA GUITARRA see Cortes, Ramiro

LA GUITARRA DE LOS NEGROS see Lilien,
Ignace

LA HALTE see Tincler, G.

LA HALTE DES HEURES see Schmit, Camille

LA-HAUT PARMI CES CHAMPS
see La Musique, Dixieme Cahier

LA-HAUT SUR LA MONTAGNE
see La Musique, Cinquieme Cahier

LA HAUTE ET BASSE-AUVERGNE *Fr
(Canteloube, J.) solo,acap DURAND
s.p. see also Anthologie Des Chants
Populaires Francais Tome III   (L9)

LA HOUSARDE see Ganne, Louis Gaston

LA JAVANETTE see Bozi, Harold de

LA JEANNETON POUR DOT see Vogel, A.

LA JEUNE FILLE ET LA MORT see Schubert,
Franz (Peter)

LA JEUNE FILLE ET LA VIOLETTE see
Mozart, Wolfgang Amadeus

LA JEUNE FILLE ET LE RAMIER see Cinque

LA JEUNE FILLE NUE see Badings, Henk

LA JEUNE MERE see Schubert, Franz
(Peter)

LA JEUNE RELIGIEUSE see Schubert, Franz
(Peter)

LA JOLIE FILLE DE PERTH see Bizet,
Georges

LA JOUEUR DE VIELLE see Schubert, Franz
(Peter)

LA JOURNEE D'UNE DANSEUSE see
Planquette, Robert

LA LAMPE DU CIEL see Aubert, Louis-
Francois-Marie

LA LAVANDAIA see Gandino, Adolfo

LA LECHUZA see Lamuraglia, Nicolas

LA LECON D'AMOUR see Durand, (Marie-
)Auguste

LA LEGENDE DE SAINT AMOUR see Holmes,
Alfred

LA LEGENDE DES PEAGERS see Tremisot,
Ed.

LA LEGGENDA DI MINE see Guarino, C.

LA LETTRE see Aubert, Louis-Francois-
Marie

LA LETTRE see Dela, M.

LA LETTRE D'AMOUR see Stewart, Robert
[Prescott]

LA LETTRE DE MANON see Gillet, Ernest

LA LETTRE DU JARDINIER see Tournier,
Marcel

LA LETTRE VOICI CE QU'IL ECRIT A SON
FRERE PELLEAS see Debussy, Claude

LA LIBELLULE see Saint-Saens, Camille

LA LONGEVA see Peragallo, Mario

LA LORELEY see Liszt, Franz, Die
Loreley

LA LUCREZIA: O NUMI ETERNI see Handel,
George Frideric

LA LUMIERE see Barraine, Elsa

LA LUNA E L'USIGNOLO see Sonzogno,
Giulio Cesare

LA LUNE see Barbirolli, A.

LA LUNE see Cantu, M.

LA LUNE see Vellere, Lucie

LA LUNE BLANCHE see Gaubert, Philippe

LA LUNE BLANCHE see Komter, Jan Maarten

LA LUNE BLANCHE see Melartin, Erkki

LA LUNE BLANCHE see Ruyneman, Daniel

LA LUNE BLANCHE LUIT DANS LES BOIS see
Bordewijk-Roepman, Johanna

LA LUNE EGRENE EN PERLES BLONDES see
Messager, Andre

LA LUNE ETAIT TRES HAUTE... see Quinet,
Marcel

LA LUNE JAUNE see King, Harold C.

LA LUNE PARESSEUSE see Chaminade,
Cecile

LA MADERECITA see Massa

LA MADRE see Liviabella, Lino

LA MADRE AL FIGLIO LONTANO see
Pizzetti, Ildebrando

LA MADRE DONCELLA see Llongueras J.

LA MADRE FOLLE see Malipiero, Gian
Francesco

LA MADRE PIANGE see Piccioli, G.

LA MAGGIAJOLE see Albanese, Guido

LA MAIN DANS LA MAIN see Delmet, Paul

LA MAISON see Messiaen, Oliver

LA MAISON DANS LE COEUR see Vermeulen,
Matthijs

LA MAISON DE PLAISANCE see Voormolen,
Alexander Nicolas

LA MAITRISE MODERNE, VOL. I see
Tritant, G.

LA MAITRISE MODERNE, VOL. II see
Tritant, G.

LA MAJA DE GOYA see Granados, Enrique

LA MAJA DOLOROSA see Granados, Enrique

LA MAJA DOLOROSA see Granados, Enrique

LA MAJA LIMONERA see Aramaz, A.

LA MAL MARIEE see Cannon, (Jack)
Phillip

LA MALINCONIA see Campana

LA MAMMA see Toni, Alceo

LA MAMMA E COME IL PANE CALDO see
Respighi, Ottorino

LA MAMMA MORTA see Giordano, Umberto

LA MAMOIR DE ROSEMONDE see Duparc,
Henri

LA MANANA DE SAN JUAN see Pisador,
Diego

LA MANO TUA MI POSA see Gandino, Adolfo

LA MANOLA see Bourgeois, Loys (Louis)

LA MAR ESTAVA ALEGRA see Toldra,
Eduardo

LA MARCHANDE DE TOUT see Filipucci,
Edm.

LA MARCHE A L'ETOILE see Fragerolle, G.

LA MARCHE AU SOLEIL see Fragerolle, G.

LA MARGELLE see Bondon, Jacques

LA MARION see Grandfort, M. de

LA MARIPOSA see Napolitano, Emilio

LA MARJOLAINE ET SES COMPAGNONS see
Defontaine, M.

LA MARNE see Gallon, Noel

LA MARSEILLAISE see Rouget de L'Isle,
Claude Joseph

LA MATINEE CHAMPETRE see Amherst-Webber

LA MAUVAISE CHANSON see Filipucci, Edm.

LA MAUVAISE PRIERE see Aubert, Louis-
Francois-Marie

LA MAYA Y RUISENOR see Granados,
Enrique

LA MEILLEURE PENSEE see Busser, Henri-
Paul

LA MELODIE DES BAISERS see Massenet,
Jules

LA MEMORIA E L'OBLIO see Margola,
Franco

LA MENAGERIE DE TRISTAN see Kosma, J.

LA MER see Griffes, Charles Tomlinson

LA MESSA see Gandino, Adolfo

LA MESSE DE MINUIT see Fontenailles, H. de

LA MI PREMMA MROUSA!
  (Carlo, Musi) solo,pno (Bolognese
  dialect) BONGIOVANI 2085 s.p. see
  from El Mi Canzunett   (L10)

LA MIA CANZONE see Tosti, Francesco Paolo

LA MIA LETIZIA INFONDERE see Verdi, Giuseppe

LA MIA PACE see Handel, George Frideric

LA MIA TURCA see Monteverdi, Claudio

LA MINIATURE DE SABLES see Zbar, Michel

LA MINUTE HEUREUSE see Rabey, Rene

LA MODE see Betove

LA MODE see Delmet, Paul

LA MODE COMMODE see Schmitt, Florent

LA MOISSON DES ROSES see Lachaume, A.

LA MOISSON DU POETE see Delmet, Paul

LA MOME NEANT see DuBois, Pierre Max

LA MONTMARTROISE see Hollaender, Viktor

LA MONTRE see Middeleer, Jean De

LA MORT see Beethoven, Ludwig van, Vom Tode

LA MORT see Legley, Victor

LA MORT see Smit, Leo

LA MORT DE PIERROT see Porena, Boris

LA MORT DES AMANTS see Debussy, Claude

LA MORT DES AMANTS see Smit, Leo

LA MORT DES ARTISTES see Smit, Leo

LA MORT DES PAUVRES see Caplet, Andre

LA MORT DES PAUVRES see Smit, Leo

LA MORT D'OPHELIE see Saint-Saens, Camille

LA MORT DU NOMBRE see Messiaen, Oliver

LA MORT DU ROSSIGNOL see Schmitt, Florent

LA MORTE see Levade, Charles (Gaston)

LA MORTE DI ANITA see Pratella, Francesco Balilla

LA MORTE DI SOCRATE see Malipiero, Gian Francesco

LA MOUSME see Ganne, Louis Gaston

LA MUNTAGNOLA
  (Carlo, Musi) solo,pno (Bolognese
  dialect) BONGIOVANI 2104 s.p. see
  from El Mi Canzunett Seconda Serie
                                  (L11)

LA MUNTURA DI IMPIEGA DLA POSTA
  (Carlo, Musi) solo,pno (Bolognese
  dialect) BONGIOVANI 2044 s.p. see
  from El Mi Canzunett   (L12)

LA MUSE DE L'OPERA see Clerambault, Louis-Nicolas

LA MUSETTE see Clerambault, Louis-Nicolas

LA MUSETTE see Rameau, Jean-Philippe

LA MUSIQUE see Orthel, Leon

LA MUSIQUE, PREMIER CAHIER
  (Musson, A.) solo,acap cmplt ed
  DURAND s.p.
    contains: Le Renouveau; Brahms,
    Johannes, Le Forgeron; Dalayrac,
    [Nicolas], Notre Meunier;
    Pergolesi, Giovanni Battista, La
    Servante Maitresse; Schumann,
    Robert (Alexander), Le Pays De
    Cocagne   (L13)

LA MUSIQUE, DEUXIEME CAHIER
  (Musson, A.) solo,acap cmplt ed
  DURAND s.p.
    contains: El Zorongo; Le Bon Vieux
    Temps; Schubert, Franz (Peter),
    La Truite; Schumann, Robert
    (Alexander), En Avant!; de
    Travenet, Pauvre Jacques   (L14)

LA MUSIQUE, TROISIEME CAHIER
  (Musson, A.) solo,acap cmplt ed
  DURAND s.p.
    contains: Le Mai; Le Retour Du
    Rossignol; Le Vigneron; Gluck,
    Christoph Willibald Ritter von,
    J'ai Perdu Mon Eurydice (from
    Orpheo Ed Euridice); Schubert,
    Franz (Peter), Voyages   (L15)

LA MUSIQUE, QUATRIEME CAHIER
  (Musson, A.) solo,acap cmplt ed
  DURAND s.p.
    contains: Nous Sommes Tous Venus;
    Quand J'etais Chez Mon Pere;
    Gretry, Andre Ernest Modeste,
    Romance (from Richard Coeur De
    Lion); Mehul, H., Joseph;
    Schumann, Robert (Alexander), La
    Coccinelle   (L16)

LA MUSIQUE, CINQUIEME CAHIER
  (Musson, A.) solo,acap cmplt ed
  DURAND s.p.
    contains: La-Haut Sur La Montagne;
    Les Trois Corbeaux; Indy, Vincent
    d', La Bonne Terre; Schubert,
    Franz (Peter), La Source;
    Schumann, Robert (Alexander), La
    Chanson Du Jeune Archer   (L17)

LA MUSIQUE, SIXIEME CAHIER
  (Musson, A.) solo,acap cmplt ed
  DURAND s.p.
    contains: De Grand Matin Me Suis
    Leve; Brahms, Johannes, Aux Bords
    Du Rhin; Mendelssohn-Bartholdy,
    Felix, Villanelle; Rameau, Jean-
    Philippe, Le Grillon; Schumann,
    Robert (Alexander), Berceuse
                                 (L18)

LA MUSIQUE, SEPTIEME CAHIER
  (Musson, A.) solo,acap cmplt ed
  DURAND s.p.
    contains: Seguidillas; Haydn,
    (Franz) Joseph, Air (from Die
    Jahreszeiten); Schumann, Robert
    (Alexander), Personne; Vidal, Le
    Cordier; Weber, Carl Maria von,
    Couplets De Gaspard (from Der
    Freischutz)   (L19)

LA MUSIQUE, HUITIEME CAHIER
  (Musson, A.) solo,acap cmplt ed
  DURAND s.p.
    contains: Sont Trois Jeunes
    Garcons; Brahms, Johannes, Ou
    S'en Vont Mes Reves; Brahms,
    Johannes, Soir; Mehul, H.,
    Romance (from Joseph);
    Mendelssohn-Bartholdy, Felix, Ou
    S'en Vont Mes Reves; Wagner,
    Richard, Chant D'Amour (from Die
    Walkure)   (L20)

LA MUSIQUE, NEUVIEME CAHIER
  (Musson, A.) solo,acap cmplt ed
  DURAND s.p.
    contains: Le Mois D'avril S'en Est
    Alle; Berlioz, Hector,
    Villanelle; Exaudet, Menuet;
    Handel, George Frideric, La Fete
    D'Alexandre; Saint-Saens,
    Camille, Sommeil Des Fleurs (L21)

LA MUSIQUE, DIXIEME CAHIER
  (Musson, A.) solo,acap cmplt ed
  DURAND s.p.
    contains: Chanson Soldatesque Du
    Temps De Charles VIII; La-Haut
    Parmi Ces Champs; Bach, Johann
    Sebastian, Air De Momus (from Der
    Streit Zwischen Phoebus Und Pan);
    Gretry, Andre Ernest Modeste,
    Zemir Et Azor; Saint-Saens,
    Camille, Etoile Du Matin   (L22)

LA MUSIQUE, ONZIEME CAHIER
  (Musson, A.) solo,acap cmplt ed
  DURAND s.p.
    contains: Avril; Mettez La Main Au
    Corbeillon; Gretry, Andre Ernest
    Modeste, Chanson De Blondel (from
    Richard Coeur De Lion); Schumann,
    Robert (Alexander), Dis-Moi
    Pauvre Hirondelle; Wagner,
    Richard, Dors Mon Enfant   (L23)

LA MUSIQUE, DOUZIEME CAHIER
  (Musson, A.) solo,acap cmplt ed
  DURAND s.p.
    contains: Dodun; La Peche Des
    Moules; Beethoven, Ludwig van, Le
    Reveil Des Fleurs; Gretry, Andre
    Ernest Modeste, Couplets (from
    Richard Coeur De Lion); Saint-
    Saens, Camille, La Feuille Du
    Peuplier   (L24)

LA MUSIQUE, TREIZIEME CAHIER
  (Musson, A.) solo,acap cmplt ed
  DURAND s.p.
    contains: La Perronnelle; L'etoile
    Du Matin; Brahms, Johannes,
    Solitude Champetre; Charpentier,
    Marc-Antoine, Chanson A Boire Du

Medecin Malgre Lui; Gluck,
    Christoph Willibald Ritter von,
    Air De Renaud (from Armide) (L25)

LA MUSIQUE, QUATORZIEME CAHIER
  (Musson, A.) solo,acap cmplt ed
  DURAND s.p.
    contains: C'est Les Gens De Bouze;
    Chanson De La Mariee; Il Sera
    Banni; Beaujoyeulx, Baltasar de,
    Air De Mercure (from Ballet
    Comique De La Reine); Brahms,
    Johannes, Dimanche   (L26)

LA NAISSANCE DE LA LYRE see Ropartz, Joseph Guy

LA NAJADE see Respighi, Ottorino

LA NATURA MI PARLA see Bettinelli, Bruno

LA NECEDAD see Bustos, M.

LA NEGRITA see Gomez Carrillo, Manuel

LA NEIGE TOMBE see Cimara, Pietro, Fiocca La Neve

LA NICHONNETTE see Delmet, Paul

LA NIEGE see Viannet, R.

LA NINA DE LA REJA see Romero, A.

LA NOCE see Dalcroze, Jacques

LA NOCE DU VIOLONISTE see Ganne, Louis Gaston

LA NOCTUELLE see Capoul, V.

LA NOEL DES ANGES see Lecocq, Charles

LA NOEL DES COUCOUS see Lecocq, Charles

LA NOEL DES MATELOTS see Tremisot, Ed.

LA NOEL DES VAGABONDS see Tremisot, Ed.

LA NOISETTE see Delmet, Paul

LA NONNA FILA see Clausetti, P.

LA NOTTE
  Mez solo,bass clar,drums,glock,harp,
  bvl sc GERIG HG 637 s.p.   (L27)

LA NOTTE see Wildberger, Jacques

LA NOTTE D'OTTOBRE see Ferrari-Trecate, Luigi

LA NOTTE E L'ANIMA see Alfano, Franco

LA NOTTE ILLUMINATA see Perti, Giacomo Antonio

LA NUIT see Berger, Rod.

LA NUIT see Koechlin, Charles

LA NUIT see Rimsky-Korsakov, Nikolai

LA NUIT DE MAI see Brahms, Johannes, Die Mainacht

LA NUIT DU DESTIN see Desrez

LA NUIT DU PELERIN see Barraud, Henry

LA NYMPHE DE LA SOURCE see Busser, Henri-Paul

LA OFRENDA DEL TROVADOR see Gomez Carrillo, Manuel

LA OU TU RESPIRES, BIEN AIME(E) see Pillois, Jacques

LA PAIX, LE PAIN, LA LIBERTE see Yatove, J.

LA PALERMA see Palau Boix, M.

LA PALOMA see Yradier, Sebastian

LA PALOMA TORCAZA see Giacobbe, Juan Francisco

LA PALOMITA see Guastavino, Carlos

LA PALUMMELLE see Albanese, Guido

LA PARAPLUIE DE MA GRAND'MERE
  (Emmereshts; Beldent) solo,pno GRAS
  s.p.   (L28)

LA PARESSEUSE see Beekhuis, Hanna

LA PARIHUANA see Sas, Andres

LA PARISIENNE see Duval, A.

LA PAROLE see Georges, Alexandre

LA PARRA QUEBRADA see Calcagno, Elsa

LA "PART A DIEU" see Caplet, Andre

LA PARTENZA DELLA PRIMAVERA see Valek, Jiri

LA PASIONARIA see Boero, Felipe

LA PASSIONE DI MIA MADRE see Toschi, Pietro

LA PASSIONE DI NOSTRO SIGNORE GESU CRISTO see Scarlatti, Alessandro

LA PASTORA FEDELE see Sinigaglia, Leone

LA PASTORELLA see Schubert, Franz (Peter)

LA PASTORELLA DELLE ALPI (Rossini) solo,pno FORLIVESI 11932 s.p.   (L29)

LA PASTORELLA SUL PRIMO ALBORE see Vivaldi, Antonio

LA PAUVRE FLEUR DISAIT see Cui, Cesar Antonovitch

LA PAUVRE PIERRE see Schumann, Robert (Alexander)

LA PAUVRESSE DE BAZEILLES see Ronge, Jean-Baptiste

LA PAYSE A JEAN see Dupin, Paul

LA PECHE DES MOULES see La Musique, Douzieme Cahier

LA PECORELLA SMARRITA see Tortone, A.

LA PERLA see Bianchini, Guido

LA PERNETTE see Berger, Jean

LA PERRONNELLE see La Musique, Treizieme Cahier

LA PERRUCHE AU MIROIR see Defontaine, M.

LA PESCA DELL'ANELLO see Pizzetti, Ildebrando

LA PETITE DESOBEISSANTE see Lacome, Paul

LA PETITE EGLISE see Delmet, Paul

LA PETITE FEUILLE MORTE see Leroux, Xavier (Henry Napoleon)

LA PETITE PENDULE see Lacome, Paul

LA PETITE PRINCESSE see Schmitt, Florent

LA PETITE SERVANTE see Poulenc, Francis

LA PETROUILLE PERDUE see Petrov, A.

LA PIETA see Perissas, M.

LA PIETA D'AVIGNON see Rosenthal, Manuel

LA PIEUVRE see Georges, Alexandre

LA PIGEONNE see Bernicat, F.

LA PIMPANTE LIBELLULE see Schlosser, Paul

LA PINTADE see Ravel, Maurice

LA PISANELLA see Pizzetti, Ildebrando

LA PISON! (Carlo, Musi) solo,pno (Bolognese dialect) BONGIOVANI 2082 s.p. see from El Mi Canzunett   (L30)

LA PLAINE see Carolus-Duran, P.

LA PLAINTE see Paray, Paul

LA PLAINTE DU VENT see Rhene-Baton

LA PLUIE see Georges, Alexandre

LA PLUIE SUR LES ROSES see Mignan, Edouard-Charles-Octave

LA PLUS BELLE see Godard, Benjamin Louis Paul

LA PLUS JOLIE see Chaminade, Cecile

LA POSTE see Schubert, Franz (Peter), Die Post

LA POULE see Bloch, Augustyn

LA POULE BLANCHE see Arma, Paul

LA POUPEE see Lacome, Paul

LA POUPEE MECANIQUE see Absil, Jean

LA POURSUITE DU VENT ET DE L'AMOUR see Mignan, Edouard-Charles-Octave

LA POUSSIERE see Georges, Alexandre

LA PREMIER DENT see Indy, Vincent d'

LA PREMIERE ROSE see Lacombe, Paul

LA PREMIERE VIOLETTE see Mendelssohn-Bartholdy, Felix

LA PREPHETIE DE GWENC' HLAN see Favre, Georges, Diougan Gwenc' Hlan

LA PRESUMIDA see Vives, Amadeo

LA PRIERE AU DRAPEAU see Holmes, Alfred

LA PRIERE DU POETE see Desrez

LA PRIERE DU POETE see Rasse, Francois

LA PRIERE D'UN GUEUX see Buxeuil, R. de

LA PRIGIONIERA see Pizzetti, Ildebrando

LA PRIMAVERA see Albini, F.

LA PRIMERA PREGUNTA see Guastavino, Carlos

LA PRINCESSE see Holmes, Alfred

LA PRINCESSE DU PRINTEMPS see Defontaine, M.

LA PRINCESSE LOINTAINE see Mulder, Ernest W.

LA PROCESSION see Franck, Cesar

LA PROMENEUSE see Labey, Marcel

LA PROMESSA see Rossini, Gioacchino

LA PURTINARA (Carlo, Musi) solo,pno (Bolognese dialect) BONGIOVANI 2095 s.p. see from El Mi Canzunett Seconda Serie   (L31)

LA QUADREGLIA (Carlo, Musi) solo,pno (Bolognese dialect) BONGIOVANI 2053 s.p. see from El Mi Canzunett   (L32)

LA QUENOUILLE see Chapuis, Auguste-Paul-Jean-Baptiste

LA QUERELLE see Delabre, L.G.

LA QUESTION see Lonque, Georges

LA QUIETE DELLA NOTTE see Ghedini, Giorgio Federico

LA QUIETE MERIDIANA NELL'ALPE see Sinigaglia, Leone

LA RANA E IL ROSPO see Sinigaglia, Leone

LA RAPSODIE FORAINE ET LE PARDON DE SAINT-ANNE see Bondeville, Emmanuel de

LA REGATA VENEZIANA see Rossini, Gioacchino

LA REINE AU VERGER see Defontaine, M.

LA REINE DE MON COEUR see Chaminade, Cecile

LA REINE DE SABA see Gounod, Charles Francois

LA REINE FIAMMETTE see Vidal, Paul

LA REPASSEUSE see Brero, Cesare

LA REPETIERE see Dufresne, C.

LA RESURRECTION see Ronge, Jean-Baptiste

LA RETRAITE see Arrieu, Claude

LA REVANCHE see Delbruck, A.

LA REVOLUTION (PART 2) see Milhaud, Darius

LA RICORDANZA see Bellini, Vincenzo

LA RIVEDRA' NELL'ESTASI see Verdi, Giuseppe

LA RONDE see Caplet, Andre

LA RONDE see Sancan, P.

LA RONDINE IMPORTUNA see Sinigaglia, Leone

LA ROSA see Ariosti, Attilio

LA ROSA see Sammartino, Luis

LA ROSA ALS LLAVIS see Toldra, Eduardo

LA ROSA BLANCA see Lasala, Angel

LA ROSA Y EL SAUCE see Guastavino, Carlos

LA ROSE see Rabey, Rene

LA ROSE AU ROSIER BLANC see Cuvillier, Charles

LA ROSE ET LE RESEDA see Arrieu, Claude

LA ROSE ET LE RESEDA see Auric, Georges

LA ROSE ET LE ROSSIGNOL see Rimsky-Korsakov, Nikolai, Aimant La Rose, Le Rossignol

LA ROSE NOIRE see Delmet, Paul

LA ROSE ROUGE see Sonzogno, Giulio Cesare

LA ROSE SAUVAGE see Schubert, Franz (Peter)

LA ROTISSERIE DE LA REINE PEDAUQUE see Levade, Charles (Gaston)

LA ROUTE see Ropartz, Joseph Guy

LA ROUTE see Vuillemin, L.

LA RUCHE see Lacome, Paul

LA RUINA Y EL VIENTO see Boero, Felipe

LA SAGA DU BERSEKIR see Dupin, Paul

LA SAGESSE PARLE D'ELLE MEME see Mirandolle, Ludovicus

LA SAISON DES ROSES see Marcelles, P.

LA SAISON QUI DEVET LE BOIS see Beydts, L.

LA SALUTATION ANGELIQUE see Busser, Henri-Paul

LA SCHECCIA ANGOT! (Carlo, Musi) solo,pno (Bolognese dialect) BONGIOVANI 2088 s.p. see from El Mi Canzunett   (L33)

LA SCUFFIAREINA (Carlo, Musi) solo,pno (Bolognese dialect) BONGIOVANI 2080 s.p. see from El Mi Canzunett   (L34)

LA SEMAILLE see Carman, M.

LA SERA see Benvenuti, Giacomo

LA SERA see Respighi, Ottorino

LA SERA FIESOLANA see Casella, Alfredo

LA SERENADE see Migot, Georges

LA SERENATA see Braga, Gaetana

LA SERENATA see Cimara, Pietro, Dormi!

LA SERENATA see Metra, Jules Louis Olivier

LA SERENATA see Tosti, Francesco Paolo

LA SERENATA see Zandonai, Riccardo

LA SERVANTE see Leduc, Jacques, Aquah Laluh, Ghana

LA SERVANTE MAITRESSE see Pergolesi, Giovanni Battista

LA SEULE PENSEE see Lange-Muller, Peter Erasmus

LA SIESTE see Godard, Benjamin Louis Paul

LA SIESTE see Louis, E.

LA SIESTE INTERROMPUE see Devreese, Godefroid

LA SINGE ET LE LEOPARD see Thomson, Virgil

LA SIRENE see Holmes, Alfred

LA SIRENE see Voormolen, Alexander
Nicolas

LA SIRENE DE SCHEVENINGUE see Rivier,
Jean

LA SOLITAIRE see Saint-Saens, Camille

LA SOLITUDINE see Handel, George
Frideric

LA SOLTAIRE see Saint-Saens, Camille

LA SOMBRA. YARAVI see De Rogatis,
Pascual

LA SOMMEILLEUSE see Casadesus, Henri
Gustave

LA "SONAMBULA"
(Carlo, Musi) solo,pno (Bolognese
dialect) BONGIOVANI 2091 s.p. see
from El Mi Canzunett Seconda Serie
(L35)

LA SORCIERE ET LE PIRATE see Barraud,
Henry

LA SORELLINA DORME see Recli, Giulia

LA SORGENTE D'AMORE see Porrino, Ennio

LA SOURCE see Gallois, Ch.

LA SOURCE see Schubert, Franz (Peter)

LA SPERANZA E GIUNTA see Handel, George
Frideric

LA SPLENDEUR see Saint-Saens, Camille

LA SPLENDEUR VIDE see Saint-Saens,
Camille

LA SPOSA DI BELTRAMO see Sinigaglia,
Leone

LA STANZA DA GIUOCO see Tocchi, Gian-
Luca

LA STATUE DE BRONZE see Satie, Erik

LA STELLA BOARA see Pratella, Francesco
Balilla

LA STIRPE DI DAVIDE see Mannino, Franco

LA STRADA BIANCA see Pratella,
Francesco Balilla

LA STRADE NOTTURNE see Pratella,
Francesco Balilla

LA SUA MAN NON ANCOR OGGI LA MIA TOCCO
see Thomas, Ambroise

LA SULAMITE see Chabrier, Emmanuel

LA SULAMITE see Melan-Gueroult

LA SURPRISE AMOUREUSE (LA BELLE
ENDORMIE) see Migot, Georges

LA SUZON see Lantier, Pierre

LA TABAQUERITA see Espoile, Raoul H.

LA TAPERA see Jurafsky, Abraham

LA TARENTELLE see Casadesus, Robert
Marcel

LA TASSA SOUVRA AI TLON!
(Carlo, Musi) solo,pno (Bolognese
dialect) BONGIOVANI 2064 s.p. see
from El Mi Canzunett   (L36)

LA TCHEN see Vellones, P.

LA TELESITA see Gomez Carrillo, Manuel

LA TENTATION DE ST. ANTOINE see Egk,
Werner

LA TERRA NUDA see De Angelis, Ugalberto

LA TERRE, LES EAUX VA BUVANT see
Honegger, Arthur

LA TESSITRICE see Gandino, Adolfo

LA TIRANNA see Beethoven, Ludwig van

LA TISSEUSE CELESTE see Bantock,
Granville, Celestial Weaver

LA TOILETTE DE LA MARIEE see Michiels,
G.

LA TORTUE see Quinet, Marcel

LA TORTUE ET LE LIEVRE see Schmitt,
Florent

LA TOURTERELLE see Milhaud, Darius

LA TOUSSAINT see Lacome, Paul

LA TOUTE-PUISSANCE see Schubert, Franz
(Peter)

LA TRAGIQUE HISTOIRE DU PETIT RENE see
Poulenc, Francis

LA TRAVERSEE see Caby, R.

LA TREGUA see Massarani, E.

LA TREGUA see Sinigaglia, Leone

LA TRISTESSE see Doyen, Albert

LA TRISTESSE DES LEVRES see Delmet,
Paul

LA TRUITE see Migot, Georges

LA TRUITE see Schubert, Franz (Peter),
Die Forelle

LA TUA NON E LA MANO see Massenet,
Jules

LA TUNA see Lacome, Paul

LA ULTIMA ROSA DE VERANO see Flotow,
Friedrich von, Letzte Rose

LA VAGUE ET LA CLOCHE see Duparc, Henri

LA VALLEE see Bagge, G.

LA VALSE see Magne, Michel

LA VALSE see Schumann, Robert
(Alexander)

LA VALSE DE LA NEIGE see Geney, Michel

LA VALSE DE L'OURSON see Roget, H.

LA VALSE DES ROUSSES see Vieu, Jane

LA VALSE DU PRINCE see Caryll, Ivan

LA VASE BRISE see Franck, Cesar

LA VEILLE see Vermeulen, Matthijs

LA VENDEMMIA see Gandino, Adolfo

LA VENTANA ABIERTA see Aponte-Ledee,
Rafael

LA VERDURE DOREE see Ibert, Jacques

LA VERGINE DEGLI ANGELI see Verdi,
Giuseppe

LA VERITE see Legley, Victor

LA VERRE DE BOHEME see Lacome, Paul

LA VEUVE see Cannon, (Jack) Phillip

LA VICTOIRE DU PRINTEMPS see Blech, Leo

LA VIE D'UNE FEMME see Schumann, Robert
(Alexander), Frauenliebe Und Leben

LA VIE EST GRISE see Cuvillier, Charles

LA VIEILLE AU MANTEAU NOIR see Ponzio,
L.

LA VIEILLE DANSE see Denis, Didier

LA VIERGE see Fragerolle, G.

LA VIERGE see Marietti, G.

LA VIERGE A LA CRECHE see Franck, Cesar

LA VIERGE A LA CRECHE see Perilhou,
Albert

LA VIERGE A LA CRECHE see Renie

LA VIEUX DE LA PETITE see Berger, Rod.

LA VIOLETTA see Mozart, Wolfgang
Amadeus, Das Veilchen

LA VIRGIN VA CAMINANDO see Palau Boix,
M.

LA VISION DE DANTE see Ollone, Max d'

LA VISPA TERESA see Bizzelli, Annibale

LA VITA FUGGE E NON S'ARRESTA UN'ORA
see Pizzetti, Ildebrando

LA VIUDITA see Giacobbe, Juan Francisco

LA VOIX DE LA VIERGE ERIGONE see
Debussy, Claude

LA VOIX HUMAINE see Poulenc, Francis

LA VOYANTE see Sauguet, Henri

LA ZANZARA E LA MOSCA see Rocca,
Lodovico

LA ZEINTA DAZIARIA
(Carlo, Musi) solo,pno (Bolognese
dialect) BONGIOVANI 2042 s.p. see
from El Mi Canzunett   (L37)

LAAT DE LUIKEN GESLOTEN ZIJN see Colaco
Osorio-Swaab, Reine

LAAT DE LUIKEN GESLOTEN ZIJN see
Mulder, Herman

LAAT MIJ NIMMERMEER see Zagwijn, Henri

LAAT MIJ NIMMERMEER see Zweers,
[Bernard]

LAATOKKA see Merikanto, Oskar

LAATSTE WAGEN VAN LIJN ELF see Witte,
D.

L'ABANDON see Milhaud, Darius

L'ABEILLE see Ferroud, Pierre-Octave

L'ABEILLE see Godard, Benjamin Louis
Paul

L'ABENCE see Beethoven, Ludwig van

LABEUR see Schlosser, Paul

LABEY, MARCEL (1875-1968)
Contraste
solo,pno/inst DURAND s.p. see from
Trois Poemes D'Henri De Regnier
(L38)

La Danse Au Bord Du Lac
S solo,pno voc sc DURAND s.p. (L39)
S solo,pno,4strings sc DURAND s.p.
(L40)

La Promeneuse
solo,pno/inst DURAND s.p. see from
Trois Poemes D'Henri De Regnier
(L41)

Le Reveil
solo,pno/inst DURAND s.p. see from
Trois Poemes D'Henri De Regnier
(L42)

Trois Poemes D'Henri De Regnier *see
Contraste; La Promeneuse; Le
Reveil   (L43)

LABORECKY, JOZEF
Detske Radosti *CCU
boy solo/girl solo,pno
SLOV.HUD.FOND s.p.   (L44)

L'ABRI see Dupin, Paul

LABROCA, MARIO (1896-1973)
Tre Liriche *CC3U
solo,pno ZERBONI 3508 s.p.   (L45)

L'ABSENTE see Chaminade, Cecile

L'ACACIA BLANC see Bondeville, Emmanuel
de

L'ACCADEMIA DE "LA LIRA"
(Carlo, Musi) solo,pno (Bolognese
dialect) BONGIOVANI 2078 s.p. see
from El Mi Canzunett   (L46)

LACHAUME, A.
A L'Absente
see Deux Chansons D'exil

Au Pays D'exil
see Deux Chansons D'exil

Avril
solo,pno ENOCH s.p.   (L47)

Chanson Boheme
solo,pno ENOCH s.p.   (L48)

Chanson Fleurie
solo,pno ENOCH s.p.   (L49)

Chemineau
solo,pno ENOCH s.p.   (L50)

Cheu Nous On Est Comme Ca
solo,acap ENOCH s.p.   (L51)
solo,pno ENOCH s.p.   (L52)

Cocorico
solo,orch (available in 2 keys)
ENOCH s.p.   (L53)
solo,pno (available in 2 keys)
ENOCH s.p.   (L54)

Dans Votre Berceau
solo,pno ENOCH s.p.   (L55)

Deux Chansons D'exil
solo,pno cmplt ed ENOCH s.p.
available in 2 keys

LACHAUME, A. (cont'd.)

contains: A L'Absente; Au Pays
  D'exil   (L56)

Encore Un Soir
  solo,pno (available in 2 keys)
    ENOCH s.p.   (L57)

Folle Caresse
  solo,acap ENOCH s.p.   (L58)
  solo,pno ENOCH s.p.   (L59)

Jardin D'Amour
  solo,pno ENOCH s.p.   (L60)

Jean Loriot
  solo,pno ENOCH s.p.   (L61)

La Moisson Des Roses
  solo,pno ENOCH s.p.   (L62)

Le Vieux Francais
  solo,pno ENOCH s.p.   (L63)
  solo,acap ENOCH s.p.   (L64)

Les Fileuses
  solo,pno (available in 2 keys)
    ENOCH s.p.   (L65)

Les Pantins
  solo,pno ENOCH s.p.   (L66)

Les Vielles Lettres
  solo,pno (available in 2 keys)
    ENOCH s.p.   (L67)

Ma Vie
  solo,pno ENOCH s.p.   (L68)
  solo,acap ENOCH s.p.   (L69)

Madrigal Timide
  solo,pno ENOCH s.p.   (L70)

Musique Sur L'eau
  solo,pno ENOCH s.p.   (L71)

Serenade A L'Etoile
  solo,pno ENOCH s.p.   (L72)
  solo,acap ENOCH s.p.   (L73)

Un Baiser
  solo,pno ENOCH s.p.   (L74)

Vals D'Avril (from Madame Malbrough)
  S solo,pno ENOCH s.p.   (L75)
  Mez solo,pno ENOCH s.p. (L76)

Valse D'Avril
  solo,pno (available in 2 keys)
    ENOCH s.p.   (L77)
  solo,acap (available in 2 keys)
    ENOCH s.p.   (L78)

Viens Nous Aimer
  solo,pno (available in 2 keys)
    ENOCH s.p.   (L79)

Vitrail
  solo,pno ENOCH s.p.   (L80)

LACHENMANN, HELMUT (1935-   )
Tema
  solo,fl,vcl GERIG HG 737 s.p. (L81)

LACOMBE, LOUIS (TROUILLON) (1818-1884)
L'Ete, La Nuit, L'Amour
  solo,pno ENOCH s.p.   (L82)

Si Mes Vers Avaient Des Ailes
  solo,pno ENOCH s.p.   (L83)

Soixante Lieder, Vol. I *CC30L
  solo,pno ENOCH s.p.   (L84)

Soixante Lieder, Vol. II *CC30L
  solo,pno ENOCH s.p.   (L85)

LACOMBE, PAUL (1837-1927)
Baiser Sur Les Yeux
  solo,pno ENOCH s.p.   (L86)

Chanson Triste
  solo,pno ENOCH s.p.   (L87)

Comme L'eau
  solo,pno (available in 2 keys)
    ENOCH s.p.   (L88)

Dors, Ma Pensee Te Berce
  solo,pno ENOCH s.p.   (L89)

Fleur Meurtrie
  solo,pno ENOCH s.p.   (L90)

Il Pleut Des Petales De Fleurs
  solo,pno ENOCH s.p.   (L91)

Je Ne Sais Pas De Fleur
  solo,pno (available in 2 keys)
    ENOCH s.p.   (L92)

La Bonne Mante
  solo,pno ENOCH s.p.   (L93)

LACOMBE, PAUL (cont'd.)
La Premiere Rose
  solo,pno (available in 2 keys)
    ENOCH s.p.   (L94)

L'Exile
  solo,pno (available in 2 keys)
    ENOCH s.p.   (L95)

Ou Tu N'es Pas
  solo,pno (available in 2 keys)
    ENOCH s.p.   (L96)

Que Mon Ame Murmure
  solo,pno ENOCH s.p.   (L97)

Tendresse
  solo,pno ENOCH s.p.   (L98)

LACOME, PAUL (1838-1920)
A Celle Qui Part
  solo,pno (available in 2 keys)
    ENOCH s.p.   (L99)

A Une Fleur
  solo,pno (available in 2 keys)
    ENOCH see also Vingt Melodies,
      Vol. II   (L100)

Adieu
  solo,pno (available in 2 keys)
    ENOCH see also Vingt Melodies,
      Vol. I   (L101)

Adieu! C'est Dit (from Madame
  Boniface)
  solo,pno ENOCH s.p.   (L102)

Admirez Le Joli Vainqueur (from Le
  Beau Nicolas)
  solo,pno ENOCH s.p.   (L103)

Ainsi Que Vous J'ignore (from Paques
  Fleuries)
  solo,pno ENOCH s.p.   (L104)

Air A Boire
  solo,pno ENOCH see also Vingt
    Melodies, Vol. II   (L105)

Au Temps D'automne
  solo,pno (available in 2 keys)
    ENOCH see also Vingt Melodies,
      Vol. II   (L106)

Aubade Familiere
  solo,acap solo pt ENOCH s.p. (L107)
  solo,pno (available in 2 keys)
    ENOCH see also Vingt Melodies,
      Vol. II   (L108)

Avec Les Larmes De Mon Coeur
  solo,pno ENOCH s.p.   (L109)

Aveu
  solo,pno (available in 2 keys)
    ENOCH see also Vingt Melodies,
      Vol. II   (L110)

Balancelle
  solo,pno (available in 2 keys)
    ENOCH s.p.   (L111)

Barbe-Bleue
  solo,acap solo pt ENOCH s.p. (L112)
  solo,pno ENOCH s.p. see also Les
    Contes De Perrault   (L113)

Berceuse
  2 soli,pno ENOCH s.p. voc sc, solo
    pt   (L114)

Bonjour Suzon
  solo,acap solo pt ENOCH s.p. (L115)
  solo,pno (available in 2 keys)
    ENOCH see also Vingt Melodies,
      Vol. I   (L116)

Bonsoir Mignonne
  solo,pno (available in 2 keys)
    ENOCH see also Vingt Melodies,
      Vol. I   (L117)

Calino
  solo,pno ENOCH s.p.   (L118)
  solo,acap ENOCH s.p.   (L119)

Celle Que J'aime (from Le Beau
  Nicolas)
  solo,pno ENOCH s.p.   (L120)
  Bar solo,pno ENOCH s.p. (L121)

Cendrillon
  solo,acap solo pt ENOCH s.p. (L122)
  solo,pno ENOCH s.p. see also Les
    Contes De Perrault   (L123)

C'est La Fille A Jean-Pierre (from Le
  Beau Nicolas)
  solo,pno ENOCH s.p.   (L124)

Cette Ligne Est Un Signe (from Paques
  Fleuries)
  solo,pno ENOCH s.p.   (L125)

LACOME, PAUL (cont'd.)
Chanson (from Jeanne, Jeannette Et
  Jeanneton)
  solo,pno ENOCH s.p.   (L126)

Chanson Arabe
  solo,pno (available in 2 keys)
    ENOCH see also Vingt Melodies,
      Vol. II   (L127)

Chanson De La Marguerite
  solo,pno (available in 2 keys)
    ENOCH s.p.   (L128)
  solo,acap (available in 2 keys)
    ENOCH s.p.   (L129)

Chanson De Pierrot
  solo,pno (available in 2 keys)
    ENOCH s.p.   (L130)

Chanson De Printemps
  solo,pno (available in 2 keys)
    ENOCH see also Vingt Melodies,
      Vol. I   (L131)

Chanson D'Ete
  solo,acap solo pt ENOCH s.p. (L132)
  solo,pno (available in 2 keys)
    ENOCH see also Vingt Melodies,
      Vol. I   (L133)

Chanson D'Hiver
  solo,pno ENOCH see also Vingt
    Melodies, Vol. I   (L134)

Chanson Lorraine
  solo,acap solo pt ENOCH s.p. (L135)
  solo,pno (available in 2 keys)
    ENOCH see also Vingt Melodies,
      Vol. I   (L136)

Chaque Pays A Sa Maniere (from Paques
  Fleuries)
  solo,pno ENOCH s.p.   (L137)

Comme La Fleur (from Madame Boniface)
  solo,pno ENOCH s.p.   (L138)

Comme Un Navire Sans Boussole (from
  Le Beau Nicolas)
  solo,pno ENOCH s.p.   (L139)

Consolation
  solo,acap solo pt ENOCH s.p. (L140)
  solo,pno (available in 3 keys)
    ENOCH see also Vingt Melodies,
      Vol. I   (L141)

Croquemitaine
  solo,acap ENOCH s.p.   (L142)
  solo,pno ENOCH s.p.   (L143)

Czardas
  2 soli,pno ENOCH s.p. solo pt, voc
  sc   (L144)

Dans Ma Raison (from Madame Boniface)
  solo,pno ENOCH s.p.   (L145)

Deborah *Bibl
  2 soli,pno ENOCH s.p. voc sc, solo
  pt   (L146)

Depuis Longtemps (from Jeanne,
  Jeannette Et Jeanneton)
  solo,pno ENOCH s.p.   (L147)

Dieu! Quelle Faiblesse (from Jeanne,
  Jeannette Et Jeanneton)
  solo,pno ENOCH s.p.   (L148)

Don Quichotte
  solo,pno ENOCH s.p.   (L149)
  solo,acap ENOCH s.p.   (L150)

Dors, Cher Petit
  solo,pno (available in 2 keys)
    ENOCH s.p.   (L151)
  solo,acap (available in 2 keys)
    ENOCH s.p.   (L152)

En Galant Militaire (from Jeanne,
  Jeannette Et Jeanneton)
  solo,pno ENOCH s.p.   (L153)

Envoi
  solo,pno (available in 2 keys)
    ENOCH see also Vingt Melodies,
      Vol. II   (L154)

Estudiantina
  [It] 2 soli,pno (D maj) voc sc
    ENOCH s.p.   (L155)
  2 soli,pno (D maj) voc sc ENOCH
    s.p.   (L156)
  2 soli,pno (C maj) voc sc,solo pt
    ENOCH s.p.   (L157)
  SMez/TBar soli (D maj) voc sc,solo
    pt ENOCH s.p.   (L158)
  solo,acap solo pt ENOCH s.p. (L159)
  solo,pno (available in 2 keys)
    ENOCH see also Vingt Melodies,
      Vol. I   (L160)
  [It] solo,pno (available in 2 keys)
    ENOCH see also Vingt Melodies,

LACOME, PAUL (cont'd.)

Vol. I   (L161)

Farandole Printaniere
  solo,acap solo pt ENOCH s.p.   (L162)
  solo,pno (available in 2 keys)
  ENOCH see also Vingt Melodies,
  Vol. II   (L163)

Gavotte
  solo,pno (available in 2 keys)
  ENOCH see also Vingt Melodies,
  Vol. II   (L164)

Intermezzo Melancolique
  solo,pno (available in 2 keys)
  ENOCH see also Vingt Melodies,
  Vol. II   (L165)

J'ai Deux Amoureux (from Jeanne,
  Jeannette Et Jeanneton)
  solo,pno ENOCH s.p.   (L166)

J'ai Perdu Myrtille
  solo,pno (available in 2 keys)
  ENOCH s.p.   (L167)
  solo,acap (available in 2 keys)
  ENOCH s.p.   (L168)

J'aime Douloureusement
  solo,pno ENOCH s.p. see from Trois
  Poemes   (L169)

J'avais Reve (from La Nuit De Saint-
  Jean)
  solo,pno (available in 2 keys)
  ENOCH s.p.   (L170)

J'avais Une Amoureuse (from Le Beau
  Nicolas)
  solo,pno ENOCH s.p.   (L171)

Je Lui Dirai: Bon Chevalier (from
  Madame Boniface)
  solo,pno ENOCH s.p.   (L172)

Je Suis Femme Et Cabaretiere (from
  Jeanne, Jeannette Et Jeanneton)
  solo,pno ENOCH s.p.   (L173)

Je Suis Toujours Ouvriere (from
  Jeanne, Jeannette Et Jeanneton)
  solo,pno ENOCH s.p.   (L174)

La Belle Au Bois Dormant
  solo,acap solo pt ENOCH s.p.   (L175)
  solo,pno ENOCH s.p. see also Les
  Contes De Perrault   (L176)

La Belle Jeune Fille Du Midi
  solo,pno ENOCH s.p. see from Trois
  Poemes   (L177)

La Charmante Aventure (from Le Beau
  Nicolas)
  2 soli,pno ENOCH s.p.   (L178)

La Chronique Medisante (from Jeanne,
  Jeannette Et Jeanneton)
  solo,pno ENOCH s.p.   (L179)

La Danse Des Epees
  2 soli,pno ENOCH s.p. voc sc, solo
  pt   (L180)
  2 soli, piano 4 hands voc sc ENOCH
  s.p.   (L181)

La Famille Polichinelle
  solo,pno ENOCH s.p.   (L182)
  solo,acap ENOCH s.p.   (L183)

La Farandole
  2 soli,pno ENOCH s.p. voc sc, solo
  pt   (L184)

La Fille Au Sabotier (from Le Beau
  Nicolas)
  solo,pno ENOCH s.p.   (L185)

La Fille De Jephte *Bibl
  2-4 soli,pno ENOCH s.p. voc sc,
  solo pt   (L186)

La Petite Desobeissante
  solo,acap ENOCH s.p.   (L187)
  solo,pno ENOCH s.p.   (L188)

La Petite Pendule
  solo,acap ENOCH s.p.   (L189)
  solo,pno ENOCH s.p.   (L190)

La Poupee
  solo,acap ENOCH s.p.   (L191)
  solo,pno ENOCH s.p.   (L192)

La Ruche
  2 soli,pno ENOCH s.p. voc sc, solo
  pt   (L193)

La Toussaint
  solo,acap solo pt ENOCH s.p.   (L194)
  solo,pno (available in 3 keys)
  ENOCH see also Vingt Melodies,
  Vol. II   (L195)

LACOME, PAUL (cont'd.)

La Tuna
  solo,acap solo pt ENOCH s.p.   (L196)

La Verre De Boheme
  solo,pno ENOCH s.p.   (L197)
  solo,acap ENOCH s.p.   (L198)

L'Arc-En-Ciel *Bibl
  2 soli,pno ENOCH s.p. voc sc, solo
  pt   (L199)

Le Captivite De Babylone *Bibl
  2 soli,pno ENOCH s.p. voc sc, solo
  pt   (L200)

Le Chat Botte
  solo,acap solo pt ENOCH s.p.   (L201)
  solo,pno ENOCH s.p. see also Les
  Contes De Perrault   (L202)

Le Colombier
  2 soli,pno ENOCH s.p. voc sc, solo
  pt   (L203)

Le Coq Et Le Renard
  solo,acap ENOCH s.p.   (L204)
  solo,pno ENOCH s.p.   (L205)

Le Grillon
  2 soli,pno ENOCH s.p. voc sc, solo
  pt   (L206)

Le Maitre D'Ecole
  solo,pno ENOCH s.p.   (L207)
  solo,acap ENOCH s.p.   (L208)

Le Misanthrope
  solo,pno ENOCH s.p.   (L209)
  solo,acap ENOCH s.p.   (L210)

Le Pays De Cocagne
  solo,pno ENOCH s.p.   (L211)
  solo,acap ENOCH s.p.   (L212)

Le Pays Des Reves
  solo,pno (available in 2 keys)
  ENOCH see also Vingt Melodies,
  Vol. I   (L213)

Le Petit Chaperon Rouge
  solo,acap solo pt ENOCH s.p.   (L214)
  solo,pno ENOCH s.p. see also Les
  Contes De Perrault   (L215)

Le Petit Noel
  solo,pno ENOCH s.p.   (L216)
  solo,acap ENOCH s.p.   (L217)

Le Petit Poucet
  solo,acap solo pt ENOCH s.p.   (L218)
  solo,pno ENOCH s.p. see also Les
  Contes De Perrault   (L219)

Le Plus Doux Chemin
  solo,pno (available in 2 keys)
  ENOCH see also Vingt Melodies,
  Vol. II   (L220)

Le Prince Au Long Nez
  solo,pno ENOCH s.p.   (L221)
  solo,acap ENOCH s.p.   (L222)

Le Princesse Sucree
  solo,pno ENOCH s.p.   (L223)
  solo,acap ENOCH s.p.   (L224)

Le Ruisseau
  2 soli,pno ENOCH s.p. voc sc, solo
  pt   (L225)

Le Soldat De Carton
  solo,pno ENOCH s.p.   (L226)
  solo,acap ENOCH s.p.   (L227)

Le Suisse
  solo,pno ENOCH s.p.   (L228)
  solo,acap ENOCH s.p.   (L229)

Le Traineau
  2 soli,pno ENOCH s.p. voc sc, solo
  pt   (L230)

L'Entresol
  solo,pno ENOCH s.p.   (L231)

Les Contes De Perrault
  ENOCH s.p. solo,pno cmplt ed,voc
  sc; solo,acap cmplt ed,solo pt
  contains & see also: Barbe Bleue;
  Cendrillon; La Belle Au Bois
  Dormant; Le Chat Botte; Le
  Petit Chaperon Rouge; Le Petit
  Poucet; Les Fees; Les Souhaits
  Ridicules; Peau D'ane; Riquet A
  La Houppe   (L232)

Les Fees
  solo,acap solo pt ENOCH s.p.   (L233)
  solo,pno ENOCH s.p. see also Les
  Contes De Perrault   (L234)

Les Fetes Chretiennes: Les Rois *ora
  solo,pno ENOCH s.p.   (L235)

LACOME, PAUL (cont'd.)

Les Fetes Chretiennes: Les Saints
  Innocents *ora
  solo,pno ENOCH s.p.   (L236)

Les Fetes Chretiennes: Paques *ora
  solo,pno ENOCH s.p.   (L237)

Les Filles De Tosa
  solo,pno (available in 2 keys)
  ENOCH see also Vingt Melodies,
  Vol. II   (L238)

Les Fillettes Au Bois
  2 soli, piano 4 hands voc sc ENOCH
  s.p.   (L239)
  2 soli,pno ENOCH s.p. voc sc,
  solo pt   (L240)

Les Groseilles
  solo,pno ENOCH s.p.   (L241)

Les Hannetons
  solo,pno ENOCH s.p.   (L242)
  solo,acap ENOCH s.p.   (L243)
  solo,acap solo pt ENOCH s.p.   (L244)

Les Marguerites
  solo,pno ENOCH s.p.   (L245)

Les Mures
  solo,pno ENOCH s.p.   (L246)

Les Patineurs
  2 soli,pno voc sc,solo pt ENOCH
  s.p.   (L247)
  2 soli, piano 4 hands voc sc ENOCH
  s.p.   (L248)

Les Pecheurs De La Cote
  2 soli,pno ENOCH s.p. voc sc, solo
  pt   (L249)

Les Petits Oiseaux
  solo,pno ENOCH s.p.   (L250)
  solo,acap ENOCH s.p.   (L251)

Les Souhaits Ridicules
  solo,acap solo pt ENOCH s.p.   (L252)
  solo,pno ENOCH s.p. see also Les
  Contes De Perrault   (L253)

Les Voyages
  solo,pno ENOCH s.p.   (L254)

Lilas Blancs
  solo,pno (available in 2 keys)
  ENOCH s.p.   (L255)

Lyda
  solo,acap solo pt ENOCH s.p.   (L256)
  solo,pno (available in 2 keys)
  ENOCH see also Vingt Melodies,
  Vol. I   (L257)

Ma Belle Divine Repose
  solo,pno ENOCH s.p. see from Trois
  Poemes   (L258)

Mademoiselle Pompon
  solo,pno ENOCH s.p.   (L259)

Mademoiselle Tartine
  solo,pno ENOCH s.p.   (L260)
  solo,acap ENOCH s.p.   (L261)

Marquise
  solo,pno ENOCH s.p.   (L262)

Moi, Si J'etais Epoux (from Madame
  Boniface)
  solo,pno ENOCH s.p.   (L263)

Moise *Bibl
  2 soli,pno ENOCH s.p. voc sc, solo
  pt   (L264)

Monseigneur! (from Le Beau Nicolas)
  solo,pno ENOCH s.p.   (L265)

Monsieur De Crac
  solo,acap ENOCH s.p.   (L266)
  solo,pno ENOCH s.p.   (L267)
  solo,acap solo pt ENOCH s.p.   (L268)

Monsieur, Je Suis A Boniface (from
  Madame Boniface)
  male solo,pno ENOCH s.p.   (L269)

Nocturne
  2 soli,pno ENOCH s.p. voc sc, solo
  pt   (L270)

Nocturne Havanais
  2 soli,orch ENOCH rental   (L271)

Noel *sac
  2 soli,pno ENOCH s.p. voc sc, solo
  pt   (L272)
  solo,acap solo pt ENOCH s.p.   (L273)
  solo,pno (available in 2 keys)
  ENOCH see also Vingt Melodies,
  Vol. I   (L274)

LACOME, PAUL (cont'd.)

Obeissance A La Consigne (from
   Jeanne, Jeannette Et Jeanneton)
   solo,pno ENOCH s.p.   (L275)

On M'a Dit (from Paques Fleuries)
   solo,pno ENOCH s.p.   (L276)

Oui, Je Comprends (from Paques
   Fleuries)
   solo,pno ENOCH s.p.   (L277)

Ouistiti
   solo,pno ENOCH s.p.   (L278)
   solo,acap ENOCH s.p.   (L279)

Peau D'Ane
   solo,acap solo pt ENOCH s.p.   (L280)
   solo,pno ENOCH s.p. see also Les
      Contes De Perrault   (L281)

Philosophie
   solo,pno ENOCH s.p.   (L282)
   solo,acap ENOCH s.p.   (L283)

Pour Aller Vers Toi
   solo,pno ENOCH s.p.   (L284)
   solo,acap ENOCH s.p.   (L285)

Promenade Militaire
   solo,pno ENOCH s.p.   (L286)
   solo,acap ENOCH s.p.   (L287)

Puisqu'ici-bas Toute Ame
   solo,pno (available in 2 keys)
      ENOCH see also Vingt Melodies,
      Vol. I   (L288)

Que Dites-Vous Mignonne
   solo,pno (available in 2 keys)
      ENOCH see also Vingt Melodies,
      Vol. I   (L289)

Riquet A La Houppe
   solo,acap solo pt ENOCH s.p.   (L290)
   solo,pno ENOCH s.p. see also Les
      Contes De Perrault   (L291)

Rose Fleurie
   solo,acap solo pt ENOCH s.p.   (L292)
   solo,pno ENOCH see also Vingt
      Melodies, Vol. II   (L293)

Roses D'au Dela
   solo,pno (available in 2 keys)
      ENOCH s.p.   (L294)

Rosette
   solo,pno (available in 2 keys)
      ENOCH see also Vingt Melodies,
      Vol. I   (L295)

Ruth Et Noemie *Bibl
   2 soli,pno ENOCH s.p. voc sc, solo
      pt   (L296)

Segoviane
   2 soli,pno voc sc,solo pt ENOCH
      s.p.   (L297)
   2 soli, piano 4 hands voc sc ENOCH
                                    (L298)

Serenade A Ninon
   solo,acap solo pt ENOCH s.p.   (L299)
   solo,pno (available in 2 keys)
      ENOCH see also Vingt Melodies,
      Vol. I   (L300)

Serenade Melancolie
   solo,pno (available in 2 keys)
      ENOCH see also Vingt Melodies,
      Vol. II   (L301)

Si Vous Voulez
   solo,pno (available in 2 keys)
      ENOCH s.p.   (L302)

Sicilienne
   2 soli,pno voc sc,solo pt ENOCH
      s.p.   (L303)
   2 soli, piano 4 hands voc sc ENOCH
      s.p.   (L304)

Supplication
   solo,pno (available in 2 keys)
      ENOCH s.p.   (L305)

Te Deum
   solo,pno (available in 2 keys)
      ENOCH see also Vingt Melodies,
      Vol. II   (L306)

Trois Pigeons Aimaient (from La Dot
   Mal Placee)
   solo,pno ENOCH s.p.   (L307)

Trois Poemes *see J'aime
   Douloureusement; La Belle Jeune
   Fille Du Midi; Ma Belle Divine
   Repose   (L308)

Tu Vas M'ecouta (from Madame
   Boniface)
   solo,pno ENOCH s.p.   (L309)

LACOME, PAUL (cont'd.)

Un Bal D'etoiles
   solo,pno (available in 2 keys)
      ENOCH s.p.   (L310)

Un Bal D'oiseaux
   solo,acap solo pt ENOCH s.p.   (L311)
   solo,pno (available in 2 keys)
      ENOCH see also Vingt Melodies,
      Vol. I   (L312)

Un Peu De Vin (from Paques Fleuries)
   solo,pno ENOCH s.p.   (L313)

Valse D'Automne
   2 soli,pno ENOCH s.p. voc sc, solo
      pt   (L314)
   2 soli, piano 4 hands voc sc ENOCH
      s.p.   (L315)

Vielle Romance
   solo,pno ENOCH s.p.   (L316)

Vingt Melodies, Vol. I *CC20L
   solo,pno cmplt ed ENOCH available
      in 2 keys
      see also: Adieu; Bonjour Suzon;
      Bonsoir Mignonne; Chanson De
      Printemps; Chanson D'Ete;
      Chanson D'Hiver; Chanson
      Lorraine; Consolation;
      Estudiantina; Le Pays Des
      Reves; Lyda; Noel; Puisqu'ici-
      bas Toute Ame; Que Dites-Vous
      Mignonne; Rosette; Serenade A
      Ninon; Un Bal D'oiseaux   (L317)

Vingt Melodies, Vol. II *CC20L
   solo,pno cmplt ed ENOCH available
      in 2 keys
      see also: A Une Fleur; Air A
      Boire; Au Temps D'automne;
      Aubade Familiere; Aveu; Chanson
      Arabe; Envoi; Farandole
      Printaniere; Gavotte;
      Intermezzo Melancolique; La
      Toussaint; Le Plus Doux Chemin;
      Les Filles De Tosa; Rose
      Fleurie; Serenade Melancolique;
      Te Deum   (L318)

Vous Allez Comprendre (from Jeanne,
   Jeannette Et Jeanneton)
   solo,pno ENOCH s.p.   (L319)

Vous Avez, Madame (from La Dot Mal
   Placee)
   solo,pno ENOCH s.p.   (L320)

Vraiment On En Verrait (from Paques
   Fleuries)
   solo,pno ENOCH s.p.   (L321)

L'ACQUABBELLE see Albanese, Guido

L'ACQUEDOTT
   (Carlo, Musi) solo,pno (Bolognese
   dialect) BONGIOVANI 2079 s.p. see
   from El Mi Canzunett   (L322)

LACRIMA CHRISTI see Nordoff, Paul

LACRIMAE CHRISTI see Bohm, Carl

LACY, DELLA
   Teach Me To Know
      low solo,pno (D flat maj) WILLIS
      $.60   (L323)
      high solo,pno (F maj) WILLIS $.60
                                    (L324)

LACY, STEVE (1934-   )
   Examples
      solo,sax,trp,vibra,perc MODERN
      rental   (L325)

LAD VAAREN KOMME, MENS DEN VIL see
   Sjogren, Emil

LADDER OF GOLD, A see Scalerica De Oro

L'ADDIO see Baldacci, Giov. Bruna

L'ADDIO see Nielsen, Riccardo

L'ADDIO see Veneziani, Vittore

LADERMAN, EZRA (1924-   )
   Riddles, The
      S solo,pno (med) OXFORD 96.306
      $1.50 see also Songs For Eve
                                    (L326)
   Songs For Eve *CCU
      S solo,pno (med diff) cmplt ed
      OXFORD 96.305 s.p.
      see also: Riddles, The   (L327)

LADIES OF BATH, THE see Oliver, Herbert

LADIES' VOICES *sac,CC16UL
   (Stringfield, R. W.; Tench, Ethel) 4
   female soli,pno LILLENAS MB-100
   $1.25   (L328)

L'ADIEU see Aubert, Louis-Francois-
   Marie

L'ADIEU see Caby, R.

L'ADIEU see Chantrier, A.

L'ADIEU see Dufresne, C.

L'ADIEU see Honegger, Arthur

L'ADIEU see Leguerney, Jacques

L'ADIEU see Voormolen, Alexander
   Nicolas

L'ADIEU DU HUSSARD see Schumann, Robert
   (Alexander)

L'ADIEU DU MARIN see Fiorillo, V.

L'ADIEU EN BARQUE see Caplet, Andre

LADMIRAULT, PAUL (EMILE) (1877-1944)
   Dominical *CCU
      4 soli,pno sc JOBERT s.p.   (L329)

   Melodieux Automne
      high solo,pno sc JOBERT s.p. (L330)
      med solo,pno sc JOBERT s.p.   (L331)

LADOGA see Merikanto, Oskar, Laatokka

L'ADOLESCENCE CLEMENTINE see Francaix,
   Jean

L'ADOLESCENTE MALATO see Peragallo,
   Mario

L'ADORABLE AVENTURE see Mouton, H.

L'ADORABLE HANTISE see Rabey, Rene

L'ADORABLE SYMPHONIE see Cuvillier,
   Charles

L'ADORATA see Rocca, Lodovico

LADS IN THEIR HUNDREDS, THE see Orr,
   Charles Wilfred

LADY ANNE BOTHWELL'S LULLABY see
   Lawson, Malcolm

LADY MACBETH see Horovitz, Joseph

LADY MINE see Gilder, Eric

LADY MOON see Backer-Lunde, J.

LADY OF THE AMBER WHEAT see
   Dittenhaver, Sarah Louise

LADY SHALOTT see Tate, Phyllis

LADY! THOU QUEEN OF ISRAEL see Parry,
   Charles Hubert Hastings

LADY, WHEN I BEHOLD see Diack, John
   Michael

LADYE GREENSLEEVES
   (Geehl, Henry) low solo,pno (E min)
      ASHDOWN s.p.   (L332)
   (Geehl, Henry) high solo,pno (G min)
      ASHDOWN s.p.   (L333)

LAENGSEL see Kjerulf, [Halfdan]

LAENGSEL "JEG KUNDE SLET IKKE SOVE" see
   Kjerulf, [Halfdan]

LAENGSEL "VILDESTE FUGL I FLUGT see
   Kjerulf, [Halfdan]

LAER MIG, NATTENS STJAERNE see Nielsen,
   Carl

LAET SANG EN SPIEL, TAMBOUR EN FLUYT
   see Ruyneman, Daniel

LAET STAEN see Moulaert, Raymond

LAETATA SUM see Kayser, Leif

LAETATUS SUM see Klerk, Albert de

LAFFITTE, J.
   Marche Bourguignonne
      solo,acap ENOCH s.p. see from
      CHANSONS DE TROUPE   (L334)
      solo,pno ENOCH s.p.   (L335)
      solo,acap ENOCH s.p.   (L336)

LAFITE, C.
   Alt-Ottakring *CCU
      solo,pno DOBLINGER 08 604 s.p. (L337)

   Drei Mystische Gesange *sac,CC3U
      female solo,strings DOBLINGER s.p.
                                    (L338)

LAFORGE, FRANK (1879-1953)
   And There Were Shepherds Abiding In
      The Field *Xmas
      high solo,pno (G maj) FISCHER,C
      V 1367   (L339)

LAFORGE, FRANK (cont'd.)

low solo,pno (E flat maj) FISCHER,C
V 1368   (L340)

Before The Crucifix *sac
[Eng/It] med solo,pno (F min)
SCHIRM.G $.75   (L341)
low solo,pno (G maj) ALLANS s.p.
(L342)
[Eng/It] low solo,pno (E flat min)
SCHIRM.G $.75   (L343)
high solo,pno (E maj) ALLANS s.p.
(L344)
med solo,pno (F maj) ALLANS s.p.
(L345)

Come Unto These Yellow Sands
high solo,pno (G maj) SCHIRM.G $.75
(L346)

Hills
high solo,pno BELWIN $1.50   (L347)
low solo,pno BELWIN $1.50   (L348)

Retreat *see Schlupfwinkel

Schlupfwinkel
"Retreat" [Ger/Eng] low solo,pno (F
maj) SCHIRM.G $.60   (L349)

To A Violet
high solo,pno (G flat maj) SCHIRM.G
$.60   (L350)

Unrequited Love
med solo,pno PRESSER $.75   (L351)
high solo,pno PRESSER $.75   (L352)

LAGERCRANTZ, WILHELM
Anda
solo,pno LUNDQUIST s.p.   (L353)

Kallan
solo,pno LUNDQUIST s.p.   (L354)

Tonerna
solo,pno LUNDQUIST s.p.   (L355)

LAGERGREN
Alverden Skal Synge
solo,pno LUNDQUIST s.p. see from
Tre Sanger   (L356)

Nu Susar Kvallen
solo,pno LUNDQUIST s.p. see from
Tre Sanger   (L357)

Tre Sanger *see Alverden Skal Synge;
Nu Susar Kvallen; Varlat (L358)

Varlat
solo,pno LUNDQUIST s.p. see from
Tre Sanger   (L359)

LAGERHEIM-ROMARE, MARGIT
Annas Snackskrin
solo,pno,opt gtr GEHRMANS s.p.
(L360)

Barndomsjulen
solo,pno,opt gtr GEHRMANS s.p.
(L361)

Da Tar Jag Min Gitarr
solo,pno,opt gtr GEHRMANS s.p.
(L362)

Du Kan Aldrig Fanga Mej
solo,pno,opt gtr GEHRMANS s.p.
(L363)

Flickan I Marseille
see Fran Grander Och Glantor
solo,pno,opt gtr GEHRMANS s.p.
(L364)

Fran Grander Och Glantor
solo,pno,opt gtr GEHRMANS s.p.
contains: Flickan I Marseille;
Mote I Granden; Stilla
Septemberskog; Ti-Ri-Tu; Vackra
Smeden; Varens Kavaljerer
(L365)

Karlek Per Telefon
solo,pno,opt gtr GEHRMANS s.p.
(L366)

Lat Tystnaden Tala
solo,pno,opt gtr GEHRMANS s.p.
(L367)

Livets Forsta Dag
solo,pno,opt gtr GEHRMANS s.p.
(L368)

Mor, Du Ar Mig Nara
solo,pno,opt gtr GEHRMANS s.p.
(L369)

Mote I Granden
see Fran Grander Och Glantor
solo,pno,opt gtr GEHRMANS s.p.
(L370)

Rollita
solo,pno,opt gtr GEHRMANS s.p.
(L371)

Sensommar
high solo,pno GEHRMANS s.p.   (L372)
med solo,pno GEHRMANS s.p.   (L373)

Stilla Septemberskog
see Fran Grander Och Glantor

Ti-Ri-Tu
see Fran Grander Och Glantor
solo,pno,opt gtr GEHRMANS s.p.

LAGERHEIM-ROMARE, MARGIT (cont'd.)
(L374)
Vackra Smeden
see Fran Grander Och Glantor

Varens Kavaljerer
see Fran Grander Och Glantor

LAGG OMT DIN KIND INTILL MIN KIND see
Soderman, (Johan) August

LAGO, MARIO
Aftonsang
see NY SAMLING SANGDUETTER, HEFT 2

LAGOANERE, OSCAR DE (1853-1918)
Soirs D'amour
solo,pno ENOCH s.p.   (L375)
solo,acap ENOCH s.p.   (L376)

LAGRIME MESTI see Pisador, Diego

LAHDETTYAS see Kaski, Heino

LAHTO see Madetoja, Leevi

LAI see Gandino, Adolfo

LAI see Gerschefski, Edwin

LAI LOULI see Bloch, Augustyn

LAIRD O' COCKPEN, THE *folk,Scot
solo,pno (E min) PATERSON FS44 s.p.
(L377)

LAIRD OF COCKPEN, THE see Parry,
Charles Hubert Hastings

LAIRD, W.
Hundred Years Hence
solo,pno (B flat maj) BOOSEY $1.50
(L378)

LAISSER-COURRE see Baudrier, Yves

LAISSEZ GLANER see Goublier, G.

LAISSEZ JOUER, JEUNES GENS see Coppola,
Piero

LAISSEZ LA VERTE COULEUR see Le Roy, A.

LAISSEZ VENIR A MOI see Vuillemin, L.

LAITENEN, ARVO (1893-1966)
Die Neue Harfe *see Koske, Herra,
Kielihin

Die Tiefsten Wunden *see Syvimmat
Haavat

Ernste Gesange
solo,pno FAZER F3410 s.p.
contains: Koske, Herra, Kielihin,
"Die Neue Harfe", Op.22,No.3;
Syvimmat Haavat, "Die Tiefsten
Wunden", Op.22,No.1; Syvyyksia,
"Tiefen", Op.22,No.2 (L379)

Koske, Herra, Kielihin *Op.22,No.3
"Die Neue Harfe" see Ernste Gesange

Syvimmat Haavat *Op.22,No.1
"Die Tiefsten Wunden" see Ernste
Gesange

Syvyyksia *Op.22,No.2
"Tiefen" see Ernste Gesange

Tiefen *see Syvyyksia

LAJOVIC, ALEKSANDER (1920-   )
Misel Na Ljubico
"To My Dear Love" solo,pno DRUSTVO
DSS 15 rental   (L380)

Preproste Popevke *CCU
solo,pno DRUSTVO DSS 373 rental
(L381)

Stirje Samospevi *CC4U
solo,pno DRUSTVO DSS 202 rental
(L382)

To My Dear Love *see Misel Na
Ljubico

LAJOVIC, ANTON (1878-1960)
Album Samospevov *CCU
solo,pno SLOV.AKA. SAZU 8 rental
(L383)
From The Youth *see Iz Mladih Dni

Iz Mladih Dni *song cycle
"From The Youth" solo,pno DRZAVNA
rental   (L384)

Tri Pesmi *CC3U
high solo,pno SLOV.AKA. SAZU 1
rental   (L385)

LAJTHA, LASZLO (1891-1963)
Ballada
solo,pno/orch LEDUC s.p.   (L386)

Chant Des Recruteurs
Bar solo,pno/orch LEDUC s.p. (L387)

LAJTHA, LASZLO (cont'd.)
Motet *Op.8
[Fr/Hung/Ger] Mez/A/B solo,org/pno
LEDUC s.p.   (L388)

LAKE, THE see Birch, Robert Fairfax

LAKE ISLE OF INNISFREE, THE see
Herbert, Muriel

LAKES OF OULD IRELAND see Evans, Hal

LAKEUS see Kilpinen, Yrio

LAKEUS II see Kilpinen, Yrio

LAKEUS III see Kilpinen, Yrio

LAKEUS IV see Kilpinen, Yrio

LAKEUS V see Kilpinen, Yrio

L'ALBA D'AMORE see Friml, Rudolf

L'ALBA SEPARA DALLA LUCE L'OMBRA see
Tosti, Francesco Paolo

L'ALLEE D'EMERAUDE ET D'OR see
Chaminade, Cecile

L'ALLEE EST DESERTE see Arrieu, Claude

L'ALLEGRIA see Kox, Hans

L'ALLEGRIA see Veretti, Antonio

LALO, EDOUARD (1823-1892)
Aubade (from Le Roi D'ys)
[Fr] T solo,pno HEUGEL 5515 B s.p.
(L389)
high solo,pno (G maj) ALLANS s.p.
(L390)
low solo,pno (F maj) ALLANS s.p.
(L391)
"In Olden Spain" low solo,pno (G
maj) ASHDOWN   (L392)
"In Olden Spain" high solo,pno (A
maj) ASHDOWN   (L393)

In Olden Spain *see Aubade

L'ALOUETTE see Bagge, G.

L'ALOUETTE see Chailley, Jacques

L'ALOUETTE see Delage, Maurice

L'ALPHABET see Auric, Georges

L'ALTRA NOTTE IN FONDO AL MARE see
Boito, Arrigo

L'AMANT AU TOMBEAU DE SA MAITRESSE see
Delmet, Paul

L'AMANT MALHEUREUX see Saint-Saens,
Camille

LAMB, THE see Chandler, T.

LAMB, THE see Kubik, Gail

LAMB, THE see Morgan, Hilda

LAMB, THE see Pinkham, Daniel

LAMB, THE see Raphael, Mark

LAMB, THE see Stupp

LAMB, HENRY
Volunteer Organist
med solo,pno PAXTON P925 s.p.
(L394)

LAMB OF GOD see Bizet, Georges, Agnus
Dei

LAMB OF GOD! THOU SHALT REMAIN FOREVER
see Grimm, Johann D.

LAMBELET, VIVIEN
Memory
solo,pno CRAMER   (L395)

LAMBERT
En Gang Blir Allting Stilla
solo,pno LUNDQUIST s.p.   (L396)

Give A Man A Horse He Can Ride
low solo,pno (G min) CRAMER $.90
(L397)
high solo,pno (B min) CRAMER $.90
(L398)
med solo,pno (A min) CRAMER $1.15
(L399)

I Vantan Pa Far
solo,pno LUNDQUIST s.p.   (L400)

When I Step Off On That Beautiful
Shore *sac
solo,pno BENSON S8432-S $1.00
(L401)

LAMBERT, CONSTANT (1905-1951)
Intruder, The
see Three Poems Bi Li-Po

On The City Street
see Three Poems Bi Li-Po

Ruin Of The Ku-Su Palace, The
see Three Poems Bi Li-Po

Song Cycle On The Birth Of Jesus, A
*sac,Xmas,song cycle
[Eng] S solo,harp/pno CHESTER s.p.
(L402)

Three Poems Bi Li-Po
[Eng] high solo,kbd CHESTER s.p.
contains: Intruder, The; On The
City Street; Ruin Of The Ku-Su
Palace, The   (L403)

LAMBERT, FR.
Valse Caressante
solo,pno ENOCH s.p.   (L404)
solo,acap ENOCH s.p.   (L405)

LAMBERT, HELFRID
Det Var Dans Bort I Vagen
solo,pno,opt gtr GEHRMANS 665 s.p.
(L406)

En Skepparevisa
solo,pno GEHRMANS 666 s.p.   (L407)

LAMBILLOTTE, LOUIS (1796-1855)
O Salutaris *sac
BB soli,pno/org HEUGEL s.p.   (L408)
high solo,pno/org HEUGEL s.p.
(L409)

On This Day, O Beautiful Mother
*sac,Marriage
(Hammelle) 1-2 med soli,pno BELWIN
$1.50   (L410)

LAMBRECHTS, F.
De Torens Van Amsterdam
solo,pno BROEKMANS 765A s.p. (L411)

LAMBRECHTS-VOS, A.
Huwelijkszang
female solo,pno/org ALSBACH s.p.
(L412)

LAMB'S HOLY FEAST, THE see Azevedo, Lex
de

L'AME DE WALLONIE see Georges,
Alexandre

L'AME DES IRIS see Rhene-Baton

L'AME EN FLEUR see Rabey, Rene

L'AME ERRANTE see Aubert, Louis-
Francois-Marie

LAMENT see Ricketts, L.

LAMENT, A see Shaw, Martin

LAMENT FOR A CITY see Dvorak, Antonin

LAMENT FOR FIDELE see Keel, Frederick

LAMENT FOR MACLEAN OF ARDGOUR see
Lawson, Malcolm

LAMENT OF A WARRIOR'S WIFE see Kubik,
Ladislav

LAMENT OF ISIS see Bantock, Granville

LAMENT OF KILCASH see Sharpe, Evelyn

LAMENT OF MICHAL, THE see Rhodes,
Phillip

LAMENT OF SHAH JEHAN see Ronald, Sir
Landon

LAMENT OF THE BLIND see Strauss,
Richard, Blindenklage

LAMENT OF THE BORDER WIDOW see Lawson,
Malcolm

LAMENTATIO PRIMA see Fiocco, Joseph-
Hector

LAMENTATIO SECUNDA see Fiocco, Joseph-
Hector

LAMENTATIO TERTIA see Fiocco, Joseph-
Hector

LAMENTATION see Bach, Erik

LAMENTATION see Bernstein, Leonard

LAMENTATION see Birch, Robert Fairfax

LAMENTATION see Pisk, Paul Amadeus

LAMENTATION DE LA VIERGE AU PIED DE LA
CROIX see Anonymous

LAMENTATION OF DAVID see Fromm, Herbert

LAMENTATIONS see Beale, James

LAMENTI see Hovland, Egil.

LAMENTI see Szonyi, Erzsebet

LAMENTO see Caamano, Roberto

LAMENTO see Duparc, Henri

LAMENTO see Ganne, Louis Gaston

LAMENTO see Hartmann, Karl Amadeus

LAMENTO see Lopez-Buchardo, Carlos

LAMENTO see Viardot-Garcia, Pauline

LAMENTO D'ARIANNA see Monteverdi,
Claudio, Lasciatemi Morire

LAMENTO D'ARIANNA see Petrassi,
Goffredo

LAMENTO DI DANAE see Chailly, Luciano

LAMENTO DI FEDERICO see Cilea,
Francesco

LAMENTO D'U TRENU see Tomasi, H.

LAMENTO INDIO see Quaratino, Pascual

L'AMERO, SARO COSTANTE see Morley,
Thomas

L'AMERO SARO COSTANTE see Mozart,
Wolfgang Amadeus

L'AMI FIDELE see Petrov, A.

L'AMI PRINTEMPS see Hubans, Ch.

LAMMASPAIMEN see Sonninen, Ahti

LA MONTAINE, JOHN (1920-   )
Bird's Courting Song
med solo,pno GALAXY 1.2746.7 $1.25
(L413)
Lord Is My Shepherd, The *sac
med solo,pno BELWIN $1.50   (L414)

Songs Of The Nativity *sac,CCU,Xmas
med solo,org/bells BELWIN $3.00
(L415)

Songs Of The Rose Of Sharon *Op.6,
No.1-7, CC7L
S solo,pno, English text voc sc
BROUDE BR. $6.00; S solo,orch,
English or German text sc BROUDE
BR. $15.00; S solo,orch study sc
BROUDE BR. 24 s.p., ipr   (L416)

Stopping By Woods On A Snowy Evening
med solo,pno (G maj) GALAXY
1.2274.7 $1.00   (L417)

Three Poems Of Holly Beye *CC3U
med solo,pno GALAXY 1.2745.7 $1.50
(L418)

L'AMORE ARTIGIANO see Handel, George
Frideric

LAMOTE DE GRIGNON, RICARD (1899-1962)
Siete Cancioncillas En Estilo Popular
Y Serranilla *CC7U
[Span] med-high solo,pno UNION ESP.
$1.50   (L419)

L'AMOUR see Dalcroze, Jacques

L'AMOUR see Godard, Benjamin Louis Paul

L'AMOUR see Delden, Lex van

L'AMOUR BLESSE see Saint-Saens, Camille

L'AMOUR CACHE see d'Hardelot, Guy

L'AMOUR CAPTIF see Chaminade, Cecile

L'AMOUR, CE DIVIN MAITRE see Chabrier,
Emmanuel

L'AMOUR CHANTE see Milhaud, Darius

L'AMOUR DES GUEUX see Street, G.

L'AMOUR D'HELIODORA see Levade, Charles
(Gaston)

L'AMOUR D'HELIODORA see Levade, Charles
(Gaston)

L'AMOUR DIVIN see Saint-Saens, Camille

L'AMOUR DU PROCHAIN see Beethoven,
Ludwig van, Die Liebe Des Nachsten

L'AMOUR D'UNE FEMME see Schumann,
Robert (Alexander), Frauenliebe Und
Leben

L'AMOUR D'UNE ROSE see Desormes, L.

L'AMOUR ENCHANTEUR see Xilser, R.

L'AMOUR EST MON TRESOR see Delmet, Paul

L'AMOUR EST UN OISEAU REBELLE see
Bizet, Georges

L'AMOUR INVISIBLE see Chaminade, Cecile

L'AMOUR LOINTAIN see Gedalge, Andre

L'AMOUR MAITRE D'ARMES see Liouville,
F.

L'AMOUR MALHEUREUX see Mozart, Wolfgang
Amadeus

L'AMOUR MOUILLE see Fragerolle, G.

L'AMOUR OYSEAU see Saint-Saens, Camille

L'AMOUR QUAND MEME see Varney, Pierre
Joseph Alphonse

L'AMOUR QUI CHANTE see Holmes, Alfred

L'AMOUR QUI PASSE see Berger, Rod.

L'AMOUR QUI PASSE see Haring, Ch.

L'AMOUR SE PLAIT see Duni, R.

L'AMOUR S'EFFEUILLE see Zagwijn, Henri

L'AMOUREUSE see Cannon, (Jack) Phillip

LAMP UNTO MY FEET, A see Freudenthal,
Josef

L'AMPHORE see Bonifanti

LAMPIONS ETEINTS see Berger, Jean

LAMURAGLIA, NICOLAS
Figuras
[Span] solo,pno cmplt ed RICORDI-
ARG BA 7439 s.p.
contains: La Lechuza; Mi Madre
(L420)
La Lechuza
see Figuras

Mi Madre
see Figuras

L'AN MIL see Pierne, Gabriel

LANCAN VEI LA FOLHA see Ventadorn,
Bernart de

LANCEN
Printanieres *CC5U,vocalise
high solo,pno HINRICHSEN H299A
$3.50   (L421)

Trois Chansons Dans Un Style Francais
*CC3U
[Fr/Eng] med solo,pno HINRICHSEN
H369 $3.50   (L422)

L'ANCIEN REGIME (PART 1) see Milhaud,
Darius

L'ANCIENNE see Delmet, Paul

LANCOIS, JEAN
Huit Chansons *see Arma, Paul

Huit Chansons *see Arma, Paul

La Poule Blanche *see Arma, Paul

Le Petit Lapin *see Arma, Paul

Les Clochetons Du Muguet *see Arma,
Paul

Les Fleurs Butinees *see Arma, Paul

Les Moineaux *see Arma, Paul

Reveil Au Bois Dormant *see Arma,
Paul

Six Chansons *see Arma, Paul

LAND, THE see Flagello, Nicholas

LAND DIRGE, A see Holden, David

LAND IN THE OCEAN, THE see Attwood,
Thomas

LAND OF DREAMS see Morawetz, Oskar

LAND OF HEART'S DESIRE
(Kennedy-Fraser, M.; MacLeod, K.)
solo,pno (F maj) BOOSEY $1.75
(L423)

LAND OF HOPE AND GLORY see Elgar,
Edward

LAND OF MINE see Nutting, Godfrey

LAND OF THE ALMOND BLOSSOM see
Arundale, Claude

LAND OF THE LITTLE PEOPLE *Scot
solo,pno PATERSON s.p. see from
Hebridean Songs, Vol. IV (L424)

LAND OF WONDER WHY see Taylor, W.
Davenport

LAND WHERE DREAMS COME TRUE, THE see
Friml, Rudolf

LAND WITHOUT TEARS *sac
(Carmichael, Ralph) solo,pno WORD
S-113 (L425)

LANDE DOUBLE see Bernard, R.

LANDERS, BILL
Dove *sac,CC10L
solo,pno WORD 37615 $2.50 (L426)

There Is A Fountain *sac
med solo,pno CRESPUB CP-S5056 $1.00
(L427)

LANDGRAVE, PHILLIP
Love Is *sac
solo,pno HOPE 56 $.75 (L428)

Yes, God Is Real *sac
solo,pno HOPE 498 $.75 (L429)

LANDLICHE WEISEN see Westerman, G. von

LANDLICHES LIED see Schumann, Robert
(Alexander)

LANDOWSKI, M.
Trois Reverences A La Mort
[Fr] CHOUDENS C403 s.p. (L430)

LANDRE, GUILLAUME (1905-1968)
Groet Der Martelaren
Bar solo,3fl,2ob,2clar,2bsn,4horn,
2trp,3trom,tuba,timp,perc,strings
DONEMUS s.p. (L431)

LANDRE, WILLEM (1874-1948)
Drei Liebeslieder
high solo,pno ALSBACH s.p.
contains: Du; Fur Dich;
Sommernacht (L432)

Drei Lieder
med solo/high solo,pno ALSBACH s.p.
contains: Liebestriumph;
Sommernacht [2]; Traumbild
(L433)

Du
see Drei Liebeslieder

Fur Dich
see Drei Liebeslieder

Liebestriumph
see Drei Lieder

Sommernacht
see Drei Liebeslieder

Sommernacht [2]
see Drei Lieder

Traumbild
see Drei Lieder

LANDRY, AL.
Chansons Enfantines *see Le Petit
Ane Gris; Mechante Minette;
Petits Bebes, Petits Tourments
(L434)

Le Petit Ane Gris
solo,pno/inst DURAND s.p. see from
Chansons Enfantines (L435)

Mechante Minette
solo,pno/inst DURAND s.p. see from
Chansons Enfantines (L436)

Petits Bebes, Petits Tourments
solo,pno/inst DURAND s.p. see from
Chansons Enfantines (L437)

LANDSCAPE see Stout, Alan

LANDSCHAFT see Kilpinen, Yrio, Landskap

LANDSKAP see Kilpinen, Yrio

LANDWIRTSCHAFTLICHE MASCHINEN see
Milhaud, Darius

LANE
Touring That City *sac
solo,pno BENSON S8247-S $1.00
(L438)

LANE, GERALD M.
Berceuse De La Vie
solo,pno (available in 2 keys)
ENOCH s.p. (L439)
solo,acap (available in 2 keys)
ENOCH s.p. (L440)

LANE, GERALD M. (cont'd.)

Carmencita
low solo,pno (D maj) LEONARD-ENG
(L441)
high solo,pno (A maj) LEONARD-ENG
(L442)
med-high solo,pno (G maj) LEONARD-
ENG (L443)
med solo,pno (F maj) LEONARD-ENG
(L444)

Life's Lullaby
low solo,pno (F maj) ASHDOWN (L445)
med solo,pno (G maj) ASHDOWN (L446)
med-high solo,pno (A flat maj)
ASHDOWN (L447)
high solo,pno (B flat maj) ASHDOWN
(L448)

Tatters
low solo,pno (E flat maj) CRAMER
(L449)
med solo,pno (E maj) CRAMER (L450)
high solo,pno (F maj) CRAMER (L451)

LANE, LEWIS
In Silent Countryside
med solo,pno SEESAW $1.00 (L452)

L'ANE CADICHON see Schlosser, Paul

LANE O' THE THRUSHES see Harty, Sir
Hamilton

L'ANELLO see Spezzaferri, Giovanni

LANERI, ROBERTO
Esorcismi I
solo,clar,vla,trom,perc SEESAW
(L453)

LANE-WILSON, H.
Before You Came
2 soli,pno (C maj) CRAMER (L454)
high solo,pno (E flat maj) CRAMER
(L455)
med solo,pno (D maj) CRAMER (L456)
low solo,pno (B flat maj) CRAMER
(L457)
2 soli,pno (B flat maj) CRAMER
(L458)

Yokel
solo,pno CRAMER (L459)

LANG
Lord, Who Throughout These Forty Days
*sac
med-high solo,pno (F maj) BOSTON
$1.50 (L460)

Merry Roundelay
med-high solo,pno (G maj) BOSTON
$1.50 (L461)

Spring Rhapsody
med-high solo,pno (E flat maj)
BOSTON $1.50 (L462)

LANG' ERSEHNT ICH see Kilpinen, Yrio,
Viikon Vuottelin Kakea

LANG, IVANA (1919-)
By The Roadside
[Slav] solo,pno CROATICA s.p.
(L463)

Comfort Of Hair, The
[Slav] solo,pno CROATICA s.p.
(L464)

Five Istrian Songs *CC5U
[Slav] solo,pno CROATICA s.p.
(L465)

Flax
[Slav] solo,pno CROATICA s.p.
(L466)

Mulberry Tree, The
[Slav] solo,pno CROATICA s.p.
(L467)

To Lisinski
[Slav] solo,pno CROATICA s.p.
(L468)

LANG, MAX (1917-)
Liederheft Schwabischer Dichter
*CC15L
solo,pno TONOS 5421 s.p. (L469)

LANG PA ELVA see Braein, Edvard Fliflet

LANG SISTERS TRIOS NO. I see Mickelson,
Paul

LANG SISTERS TRIOS NO. II see
Mickelson, Paul

LANGAGE DES FLEURS see Lesur, Daniel

LANGDON, AL
Walk With Me *sac
solo,pno BENSON S8320-S $1.00
(L470)
solo,pno SINGSPIR 7086-SN $1.00
(L471)

LANGE
He's Only A Prayer Away *sac
solo,pno BENSON S5792-R $1.00
(L472)

I Asked The Lord (composed with
Duncan) *sac
solo,pno BENSON S5936-R $1.00

LANGE (cont'd.)
(L473)
I Found The Answer *sac
solo,pno BENSON S6012-R $1.00
(L474)
Somebody Bigger Than You And I
(composed with Heath; Burke)
*sac
solo,pno BENSON S7548-R $1.00
(L475)

L'ANGE see Gretchaninov, Alexander
Tikhonovitch

L'ANGE see Wagner, Richard, Der Engel

L'ANGE GARDEN see Franck, Cesar

L'ANGE GARDIEN see Gounod, Charles
Francois

LANGE-MULLER, PETER ERASMUS (1850-1926)
La Seule Pensee
solo,pno ENOCH s.p. see also CHANTS
DU NORD (L476)

L'ANGELO see Esposito, E.

L'ANGELO see Toschi, Pietro

L'ANGELUS see Chaminade, Cecile

L'ANGELUS D'AMOUR see Chantrier, A.

L'ANGELUS DE LA MER see Goublier, G.

LANGENBURG
Too Late Tomorrow
low solo,pno (F maj) ALLANS s.p.
(L477)
high solo,pno (G maj) ALLANS s.p.
(L478)

LANGER, HANS-KLAUS
Toujours L'amour
coloratura sop,2fl,ob,2clar,bsn,
4horn,2trp,2trom,timp,perc,harp,
cel,gtr,strings TONOS s.p. (L479)

LANGER, RICHARD (1907-)
Funf Lieder In Schweizer Mundart
*Op.31,No.1-5, CC5U
solo,pno HUG s.p. (L480)

LANGLEY FAIR see Martin, Easthope

L'ANGOUMOIS *Fr
(Canteloube, J.) solo,acap DURAND
s.p. see also Anthologie Des Chants
Populaires Francais Tome III (L481)

LANGSAMT SOM KVALLSKYN see Willebrand,
F.R. von

LANGT BORTOM RYMDEN VIDA *sac,CC9L
(Strandsjo, Gote) solo,pno GEHRMANS
s.p. (L482)

LANGTAN see Soderman

LANGTAN FRAN HAVET see Josephson, Jacob
Axel

LANGTAN HETER see Sibelius, Jean

LANGTAN HETER MIN ARVEDEL see Peterson-
Berger, (Olof) Wilhelm

LANGTAN "SER JAG STJARNORNA SPRIDA SITT
FLAMMANDE SKEN" see Soderman,
(Johan) August

LANGTAN STADSKE SOKER see Soinne,
Aatto, Tuonne, Tuonne Kaipaan

LANGUAGE OF FLOWERS see Sluka, Lubos

LANGUEDOC *Fr
(Canteloube, J.) solo,acap DURAND
s.p. see also Anthologie Des Chants
Populaires Francais Tome I (L483)

LANGUIR ME FAIS see Enesco, Georges

LANIER, GARY
I Believe In God *sac
MARK CP-M 005 $.35 (L484)
med solo,pno CRESPUB CP-S5020 $1.00
(L485)
In My Distress *sac
med solo,pno CRESPUB CP-S5021 $1.00
(L486)
In The Quietness Of My Life *sac
med solo,pno CRESPUB CP-S5022 $1.00
(L487)
My Life, My Love, I Give *sac
MARK CP-M 004 $.35 (L488)
Need The Love Of Jesus *sac
MARK CP-M 002 $.30 (L489)
Questions *sac
MARK CP-M 001 $.25 (L490)
Unclouded Day *sac
MARK CP-M 003 $.30 (L491)

L'ANIMA CHE DISPENSA see Bettinelli,
    Bruno

L'ANIMA HO STANCA see Cilea, Francesco

L'ANNEAU D'ARGENT see Chaminade, Cecile

L'ANNEAU DU SOLDAT see Chaminade,
    Cecile

L'ANNEE EN VAIN CHASSE L'ANNEE see
    Debussy, Claude

LANNOY, K.
    Voorjaarsbloemen En Bevrijdingslied
        solo,pno BROEKMANS 742 s.p. (L492)

LANTFLICKANS VISA see Satherberg

LANTIER, PIERRE
    La Suzon
        [Fr] solo,acap oct DURAND s.p.
                                        (L493)
        solo,pno/inst DURAND s.p.   (L494)

LAPARRA, RAOUL (1876-1943)
    A San Lorenzo
        solo,orch ENOCH rental   (L495)
        solo,pno ENOCH s.p.   (L496)

    Alyssa *cant
        solo,pno ENOCH s.p.   (L497)

    C'est La Brise Du Soir (from La
        Habanera)
        solo,pno ENOCH   (L498)

    Des Pas De Sabots
        solo,orch ENOCH rental   (L499)
        solo,pno ENOCH s.p.   (L500)

    Elle Se Nomme: Chair! (from La
        Habanera)
        solo,pno ENOCH   (L501)

    Et C'est A Moi Que L'on Dit (from La
        Habanera)
        solo,pno ENOCH   (L502)

    Et Quand Nous Serons Vieux, Chere Ame
        (from La Habanera)
        solo,pno ENOCH   (L503)

    Jamais On Ne Saura (from La Habanera)
        solo,pno ENOCH   (L504)

    Je Sais Que Je L'aime Plus Que La
        Terre (from La Habanera)
        solo,pno ENOCH   (L505)

    La Chasse Au Furet
        SMez/SA soli,pno voc sc,solo pt
        ENOCH s.p.   (L506)
        SBar/SB soli,pno voc sc,solo pt
        ENOCH s.p.   (L507)

    Le Sort M'a Designe (from La
        Habanera)
        solo,pno ENOCH   (L508)

    L'Eternel Est Dans Mon Tourment (from
        La Habanera)
        solo,pno ENOCH   (L509)

    Lettre A Une Espagnole
        solo,pno ENOCH rental   (L510)
        solo,orch ENOCH rental   (L511)

    Ma Main N'est Pas Blanche, Gare!
        (from La Habanera)
        solo,pno ENOCH   (L512)

    Nous Irons Lui Porter Des Fleurs
        (from La Habanera)
        solo,pno ENOCH   (L513)

L'APE E LA SERPE SPESSO... see Martini,
    Giambattista

LAPEYRE, THERESE
    Au Petit Luxembourg
        see Quatre Chansons

    Les Amis D'Enfance
        see Quatre Chansons

    Prenez Donc Le Train!
        see Quatre Chansons

    Quatre Chansons
        solo,pno cmplt ed TRANSAT. s.p.
        contains: Au Petit Luxembourg;
        Les Amis D'Enfance; Prenez Donc
        Le Train!; Sousceyrac   (L514)

    Sousceyrac
        see Quatre Chansons

LAPORTE, ANDRE (1931-)
    Le Morte Chitarre *cant
        T solo,fl,14strings TONOS 7242 s.p.
                                        (L515)
L'APPEL DU PRINTEMPS see Holmes, Alfred

L'APPELLO see Chailly, Luciano

LAPPER KRISPIJN see Clercq, R. de

LA PRESLE, JACQUES (PAUL GABRIEL) DE
    (1888-1969)
    Pere Eternal *prayer
        S solo,pno/inst LEDUC s.p.   (L516)

LAPS SUOMEN see Klemetti, Heikki

LAPSELLE see Merikanto, Oskar

LAPSI see Pesonen, Olavi (Samuel)

LAPUENTE, P.G.
    Decimas En Tono Menor
        [Span] med solo,pno UNION ESP.
        $1.25   (L517)

LAPUSTER see Janssen, Gunnar

LAQUELLE? see Scotto, Vincent

L'ARAIGNEE see Absil, Jean

L'ARAIGNEE see Arrieu, Claude

L'ARAIGNEE see Chadal, M.

LARBEY, V.
    A Isis
        solo,pno/inst DURAND s.p. see also
        Album De Timbres   (L518)

    Album De Timbres
        solo,pno/inst cmplt ed DURAND s.p.
        contains & see also: A Isis;
        Cendres; Danse; Hymenee; Le
        Square; Si L'on Gardait (L519)

    Cendres
        solo,pno/inst DURAND s.p. see also
        Album De Timbres   (L520)

    Danse
        solo,pno/inst DURAND s.p. see also
        Album De Timbres   (L521)

    Hymenee
        solo,pno/inst DURAND s.p. see also
        Album De Timbres   (L522)

    Le Square
        solo,pno/inst DURAND s.p. see also
        Album De Timbres   (L523)

    Si L'on Gardait
        solo,pno/inst DURAND s.p. see also
        Album De Timbres   (L524)

L'ARBRE see Saint-Saens, Camille

L'ARBRE DE NOEL see Grieg, Edvard
    Hagerup

L'ARC-EN-CIEL see Lacome, Paul

L'ARCHE DE NOE see Schmitt, Florent

L'ARCHET see Malipiero, Gian Francesco

LARGO see Dvorak, Antonin

LARGO see Handel, George Frideric,
    Ombra Mai Fu

LARGO see Mule, Giuseppe

LARGO AL FACTOTUM DELLA CITTA see
    Rossini, Gioacchino

L'ARIA DEL MOLINO see Sinigaglia, Leone

LARK see Clarke, Henry Leland

LARK, THE see Dvorak, Antonin, Die
    Lerche

LARK IN THE CLEAR AIR *Ir
    low solo,pno (F maj) ALLANS s.p.
                                        (L525)
    high solo,pno (A flat maj) ALLANS
        s.p.   (L526)
    (Geehl, H.) low solo,pno (F maj)
        ASHDOWN s.p.   (L527)
    (Geehl, H.) high solo,pno (A flat
        maj) ASHDOWN s.p.   (L528)

LARK IN THE CLEAR AIR see Tate, Phyllis

LARK IN THE CLEAR AIR, THE
    see Three Irish Folk Songs

LARKAN see Heland

LARK'S GRAVE, THE see Stanford, Charles
    Villiers

LARKSANG see Kilpinen, Yrio

LARMANJAT, J.
    Chanson A Boire
        solo,pno ENOCH s.p.   (L529)

LARMES see Dauly, G.

LARMES see Le Corbeiller

LARMES D'AUBE see Migot, Georges

LARMES EN SONGE see Ferrari, Gabriella

LARMES REFOULEES see Cuvillier, Charles

LA ROWE, JANE
    I Was In His Mind *sac
        solo,pno SINGSPIR 7107 $1.00   (L530)

L'ARRIVO see Campogalliani, E.

LARSSON, LARS-ERIK (1908-   )
    Atta Sanger *Op.52, CC8U
        solo,pno GEHRMANS s.p.   (L531)

    Nattens Ljus
        solo,pno,opt gtr GEHRMANS s.p.
                                        (L532)

    Nio Sanger *Op.35, CC9U
        solo,pno GEHRMANS s.p.   (L533)

    Norge I Rodt, Hvitt Og Blatt
        solo,pno MUSIKK s.p.   (L534)

    Tills Det Blir Sista Gang
        solo,pno GEHRMANS s.p.   (L535)

    Twelve Songs On Words By Emil
        Hagstrom *CC12U
        [Swed] solo,pno,opt gtr GEHRMANS
        s.p.   (L536)

L'ARTE MUSICALE IN ITALIA *sac/sec,
    CCU,It,14-18th cent
    (Torchi, Luigi) contains vocal, organ
    and instrumental works microfiche
    UNIV.MUS.ED. $55.00   (L537)

LAS CANCIONES DEL PUEBLO ESPANOL *CCU,
    Span
    (Aguila) [Span] med solo,pno UNION
    ESP. $5.00   (L538)

LAS CURRUTACAS MODESTAS see Granados,
    Enrique

LAS HIJAS DEL ZEBEDEO see Chapi, R.

LAS MURMURACIONES DEL PRADO see
    Laserna, Blas de

LAS MUSAS DE ANDALUCIA see Turina,
    Joaquin

LAS NUBES see Guastavino, Carlos

LAS ROPAS DESCENIDAS see Cinque

LAS SEIS CUERDAS see Cortes, Ramiro

LAS SEQUIDILLAS DEL APASIONADO see
    Valledor, J.

LASALA, ANGEL
    Angel
        see Poemas Nortenos

    Ay, Lunita!...
        see Canciones Argentinas

    Canciones Argentinas
        [Span] solo,pno cmplt ed RICORDI-
        ARG BA 10405 s.p.
        contains: Ay, Lunita!...; Dicen
        Que Andan Diciendo..; Tropilla
        De Estrellas   (L539)

    Cantares
        [Span] solo,pno cmplt ed RICORDI-
        ARG BA 10838 s.p.
        contains: Coplas; Cuyana; Estoy
        En Un Verde Prado; Serrana
                                        (L540)

    Coplas
        see Cantares

    Cuyana
        see Cantares

    Dicen Que Andan Diciendo..
        see Canciones Argentinas

    Estoy En Un Verde Prado
        see Cantares

    La Flecha Y La Cancion
        see Poemas Americanos

    La Rosa Blanca
        see Poemas Americanos

    Los Tres Reyes Magos
        see Poemas Americanos

    Misterio
        see Poemas Nortenos

    Nube
        see Poemas Nortenos

LASALA, ANGEL (cont'd.)

Poemas Americanos
[Span] solo,pno cmplt ed RICORDI-
ARG BA 10929 s.p.
contains: La Flecha Y La Cancion;
La Rosa Blanca; Los Tres Reyes
Magos (L541)

Poemas Nortenos
[Span] solo,pno,fl cmplt ed
RICORDI-ARG BA11021 s.p.
contains: Angel; Misterio; Nube
(L542)

Serrana
see Cantares

Tropilla De Estrellas
see Canciones Argentinas

L'ASCENSIONE see Tortone, A.

LASCERA L'AMATA SALMA see Wolf, Hugo

LASCIA CH'IO PIANGA see Handel, George
Frideric

LASCIA, DEH LASCIA see Scarlatti,
Alessandro

LASCIAMI CRUDO AMOR see Scarlatti,
Domenico

LASCIAMI PIANGERE see Scarlatti,
Domenico

LASCIATEMI MORIRE see Monteverdi,
Claudio

LASERNA, BLAS DE (1751-1816)
El Majo Y La Italiana Fingida
(Subira) [Span] ST soli,pno UNION
ESP. $4.25 (L543)

La Beata
(Subira) [Span] 2 soli,pno UNION
ESP. $4.00 (L544)

Las Murmuraciones Del Prado
(Subira) [Span] med solo,pno UNION
ESP. $3.25 (L545)

LASH'D TO THE HELM see Hook, James

LASKA see Foerster, Josef Bohuslav

LASKA see Karel, Rudolf

LASKA, BOZE, LASKA, SES. 1-2 see
Vycpalek, Ladislav

LASKA MA PRAVO see Jezek, Jaroslav

LASS DEN VORSATZ DIR NICHT TRUBEN see
Handel, George Frideric

LASS ER DOCH HOREN see Lortzing,
(Gustav) Albert

LASS ES EINMAL NUR GESCHEHEN see
Mozart, Wolfgang Amadeus, Deh, Per
Questo Istante Solo

LASS FAHREN see Kilpinen, Yrio, Lat
Vara

LASS FROM THE LOW-COUNTREE, THE see
Niles, John Jacob

LASS, KUTSCHER, DIE RAPPEN NUR GEH'N
*folk,Russ
[Ger/Russ] solo,pno ZIMMER. 1539 s.p.
(L546)

LASS MICH MIT TRANEN see Handel, George
Frideric, Lascia Ch'io Pianga

LASS MICH MIT TRANEN MEIN LOS BEKLAGEN
see Handel, George Frideric, Lascia
Ch'io Pianga

LASS MIR MEINEN STILLEN KUMMER see
Mozart, Wolfgang Amadeus, Per
Pieta, Non Ricercate

LASS O' GOWRIE, THE *folk,Scot
solo,pno (A maj/G maj) PATERSON FS45
s.p. (L547)
(Diack, J. M.) SB soli,pno PATERSON
s.p. (L548)

LASS O' PATIE'S MILL, THE *folk,Scot
solo,pno (B flat maj/C maj) PATERSON
FS46 s.p. (L549)

LASS OD DEE, THE see Arne, Michael

LASS OF MINE see Phillips, H. Lyall

LASS OF RICHMOND HILL, THE see Hook,
James

LASS SCHARREN DEINER ROSSE HUF see
Pfitzner, Hans

LASS WITH THE DELICATE AIR, THE see
Arne, Michael

LASSAILLY, E.
Nous Reprendrons Notre Belgique
solo,pno ENOCH s.p. (L550)

LASSE LITEN see Sibelius, Jean

LASSE LITEN see Sibelius, Jean, Lasse
Liten

LASSE LITTEN see Sibelius, Jean

LASSEN, EDUARD (1830-1904)
Allhelgonadag
low solo,pno GEHRMANS s.p. (L551)
high solo,pno GEHRMANS s.p. (L552)

Du Som I Rosig Fagrings Var
solo,pno GEHRMANS s.p. (L553)

Ich Hatte Einst Ein Schones Vaterland
solo,pno RIES s.p. (L554)

Jag Har I Drommen Gratit
solo,pno GEHRMANS s.p. (L555)

Min Hemlighet
low solo,pno GEHRMANS s.p. (L556)
high solo,pno GEHRMANS s.p. (L557)

Varen Och Karleken
2 soli,pno LUNDQUIST s.p. (L558)

When Thy Blue Eyes
low solo,pno (F maj) LEONARD-ENG
(L559)
med solo,pno (G maj) LEONARD-ENG
(L560)
high solo,pno (A maj) LEONARD-ENG
(L561)

L'ASSENTE see Rosi, Gino

LASSETER'S LAST RIDE see Dawson

LASSIE WI' THE LINT WHITE LOCKS *folk,
Scot
solo,pno (B flat maj/C maj) PATERSON
FS116 s.p. (L562)

LASSIE WI' THE YELLOW COATIE see
McLeod, Robert

LASSIME STAR see Bianchini, Guido

LASSITUDE see Chausson, Ernest

LASSITUDE see Delmet, Paul

L'ASSIUOLO see Zandonai, Riccardo

LASST UNS LOBEN see Quack, Erhard

LASST UNS SINGEN see Mendelssohn-
Bartholdy, Felix

LASSUS, ROLAND DE (ORLANDUS)
(1532-1594)
Collected Works *CCU
(Haberl, F.X.; Sandberger, Adolf)
contains works for a variety of
instruments and vocal
combinations microfiche
UNIV.MUS.ED. $100.00 reprints of
Breitkopf & Hartel Editions;
contains 21 volumes (L563)

Mon Coeur Se Recommande A Vous
(Wekerlin, J.-B.) med solo,pno/inst
DURAND s.p. (L564)

LAST HOPE, THE see Gottschalk

LAST MILE OF THE WAY, THE *sac,gospel
solo,pno ABER.GRP. $1.50 (L565)

LAST MILE OF THE WAY, THE see Oatman

LAST POEMS OF WALLACE STEVENS see
Rorem, Ned

LAST ROSE OF SUMMER *Ir
low solo,pno (C maj) CRAMER (L566)
high solo,pno (E maj) CRAMER (L567)
med solo,pno (F maj) ALLANS s.p.
(L568)
high solo,pno (G maj) ALLANS s.p.
(L569)
(Page, C.N.) med solo,pno PRESSER
$.75 (L570)
(Stubbs, Harry) solo,pno CRAMER
(L571)

LAST ROSE OF SUMMER, THE see Moore,
Thomas

LAST SONG, A see Barber, Samuel

LAST SONG, THE see Tosti, Francesco
Paolo, L'ultima Canzone

LAST SPRING see Grieg, Edvard Hagerup,
Letzter Fruhling

LAST SUNDAY, THE see Dartt

LAST WORDS OF DAVID, THE see
Freudenthal, Josef

LAST YEAR see Anderson, William H.

LASTEN LAULUJA see Nyberg, Mikael

LASTEN OMAT JOULULAULUT *CCU,Xmas
(Marvia) solo,pno FAZER F 3446 s.p.
(L572)

LASTU LAINEHILLA see Sibelius, Jean

LAT I SKOGEN see Fordell, Erik
(Fritiof)

LAT TYSTNADEN TALA see Lagerheim-
Romare, Margit

LAT VARA see Kilpinen, Yrio

LAT VID GUNGAN see Bergman, Erik

LATE EIGHTEENTH CENTURY SONGS see
Krumpholtz, Johann Baptist

LATE LARK see Delius, Frederick

LATE ZON see Bijvanck, Henk

LATER OM JANTER A FRIING see Froding

LATERNE see Kludas, Erich

LATERNE, LATERNE, SONNE, MOND UND
STERNE *CC23U,folk
(Dietrich, Fritz) solo,pno (easy)
BAREN. 1003 $3.50 (L573)

LATOMIE see Contilli, Gino

LATROBE, CHRISTIAN I.
How Shall A Mortal Song Aspire
solo,pno (A maj) BOOSEY $1.50
(L574)

LATT SOM EN FJADER see Grafstrom

L'ATTENTE see Chevillard, (Paul
Alexandre) Camille

L'ATTENTE see Diemer, Louis

L'ATTENTE see Godard, Benjamin Louis
Paul

L'ATTENTE see Saint-Saens, Camille

L'ATTENTE MYSTIQUE see Andriessen,
Hendrik

LATTES, M.
Elles Sont Venues
solo,pno (available in 2 keys)
ENOCH s.p. (L575)

Je Voudrais
solo,pno (available in 2 keys)
ENOCH s.p. (L576)

Louvain
solo,pno ENOCH s.p. (L577)

Mai
solo,pno ENOCH s.p. (L578)

Reims
solo,pno ENOCH s.p. (L579)

Reverie
solo,pno ENOCH s.p. (L580)

LATU see Kaski, Heino

LAUANTAI-ILTA see Marvia, Einari

LAUANTAI-ILTA see Merikanto, Oskar

LAUB UND GRAS, DIE TROCKEN ALLE see
Kilpinen, Yrio, Kuusen Juuret
Kuivettuvat

L'AUBE see Boisdeffre, Charles-Henri-
Rene de

L'AUBE SPIRITUELLE see Andriessen,
Hendrik

L'AUBEPINE DE SAINT-PATRICK see Holmes,
Alfred

LAUBIN, E.F.
Offering *sac
A solo,pno BELWIN $1.50 (L581)

LAUDA DELLA TRINITA see Napoli, Jacopo

LAUDA PER LA NATIVITA DEL SIGNORE see
Respighi, Ottorino

LAUDA SION SALVATOREM see Buxtehude,
Dietrich

LAUDAMUS see Owen

LAUDAMUS TE see Mozart, Wolfgang
Amadeus

LAUDATE DOMINUM see Buxtehude, Dietrich

LAUDATE PUERI see Perti, Giacomo
Antonio

LAUDATE PUERI see Vivaldi, Antonio

LAUDATE, PUERI, DOMINUM see Caldara,
Antonio

LAUDE see Siciliani, Francesco

LAUDES DE CRISTO REY see Espoile, Raoul
H.

LAUDI ALLA VERGINE see Mulder, Ernest
W.

LAUDI ALLA VERGINE MARIA see Verdi,
Giuseppe

LAUDS see Berkeley, Lennox

LAUFT, IHR HIRTEN
see Vier Kleine Weihnachtslieder

LAUFT, IHR HIRTEN, ALLZUGLEICH see
Haydn, (Johann) Michael

LAUGH, LITTLE RIVER see Newton, Ernest

LAUGHING SONG see Strauss, Johann, Mein
Herr Marquis

LAUGHLIN, PAUL
Remember Me *sac
med solo,pno CRESPUB CP-S5025 $1.00
(L582)

LAULA TYTTO see Jalkanen, Teppo

LAULA TYTTO see Merikanto, Oskar

LAULAKAA JUMALALLE see Sonninen, Ahti

LAULAKAAMME *CCU
1-3 soli,pno FAZER F 3122 s.p. (L583)

LAULAN ILMAN LAINEHILTA see Kilpinen,
Yrio

LAULAN LASTA NUKKUMAHAN see Kauppi,
Emil

LAULAN LASTA NUKKUMAHAN see Merikanto,
Oskar

LAULEMA see Fougstedt, Nils-Eric, Visa

LAULU see Luolajan-Mikkola, Vilho

LAULU HAMARISSA see Pylkkanen, Tauno
Kullervo

LAULU HELSINGILLE see Sonninen, Ahti

LAULU ONNESTA see Sonninen, Ahti

LAULU VIERAALLA MAALLA see Salonen,
Sulo, Visa I Frammande Land

LAULUJA KANTELETTAREN RUNOIHIN, VOL. I
see Kilpinen, Yrio

LAULUJA KANTELETTAREN RUNOIHIN, VOL. II
see Kilpinen, Yrio

LAULUJA KANTELETTAREN RUNOIHIN, VOL.
III see Kilpinen, Yrio

LAULUJA KANTELETTAREN RUNOIHIN, VOL. IV
see Kilpinen, Yrio

LAULUJA KANTELETTAREN RUNOIHIN, VOL. V
see Kilpinen, Yrio

LAULUJA KANTELETTAREN RUNOIHIN, VOL. VI
see Kilpinen, Yrio

LAULUJA KANTELETTAREN RUNOIHIN, VOL.
VII see Kilpinen, Yrio

LAULUJA KANTELETTAREN RUNOIHIN, VOL.
VIII see Kilpinen, Yrio

LAULULLE see Kilpinen, Yrio

LAUNDRY SONG, THE see Korte, Karl

LAUNIS, ARMAS (EMMANUEL) (1884-   )
Kullervon Kehtolaulu
solo,pno FAZER F 3423 s.p. (L584)

L'AUNIS ET LA SAINTONGE *Fr
(Canteloube, J.) solo,acap DURAND
s.p. see also Anthologie Des Chants
Populaires Francais Tome III (L585)

LAUREL, J.
Six Chansons Vendeennes *CC6U
solo,pno OUVRIERES s.p. (L586)

LAURETTE see Durand, Jacques

LAURIE, MALCOLM
Breathes The Man
low solo,pno (C min) CRAMER (L587)
high solo,pno (D min) CRAMER (L588)

O Were There An Island
low solo,pno (E maj) CRAMER $.95
(L589)
high solo,pno (G flat maj) CRAMER
$.90 (L590)

LAURIE'S SONG see Copland, Aaron

LAURI VOLPI, GIACOMO
Perche Non Torni?
[It] T solo,pno SONZOGNO 2905 s.p.
(L591)

L'AURORE see Cuvillier, Charles

LAUS DEO see Milford, Robin

LAUS MEA DOMINUS see Chaumont, Lambert

LAUTER WONNE, LAUTER FREUDE see
Telemann, Georg Philipp

L'AUTOMNE see Mendelssohn-Bartholdy,
Felix

L'AUTOMNE see Vellere, Lucie

L'AUTOMOBILE see Louis, A.

L'AUTRE JOUR EN VOULANT DANSER
see Chants De France Vol. II

L'AUTRE SOIR see Bouval, J.

L'AUTRE VOIX see Souris, Andre

LAVAL, D.
Hei, Gruass Die Gott Landle *sac
solo,pno BOHM s.p. (L592)

LAVALEE, C.
O Canada!
solo,pno THOMP.G (L593)

LAVATER
Break, Break
solo,pno ALLANS s.p. (L594)

Four Little Johnny Cakes
solo,pno ALLANS s.p. (L595)

Old Bark Hut
solo,pno ALLANS s.p. (L596)

L'AVE MARIA see Bossi, Renzo

LAVENDA, PINCUS
Die Drei Shwester *Jew
solo,pno KAMMEN 402 $1.00 see also
JEWISH THEATRE SONGS, VOL. 1
(L597)

L'AVEUGLE see Lilien, Ignace

LAVIGNAC, (ALEXANDRE JEAN) ALBERT
(1846-1916)
Paques Fleuries
solo,pno (available in 2 keys)
ENOCH s.p. (L598)

LAVILLA, F.
Cuarto Canciones *CC4U
[Span] med solo,pno UNION ESP.
$1.50 (L599)

Cuarto Canciones Espanolas *CC4U
[Span] med solo,pno UNION ESP.
$1.25 (L600)

Cuarto Canciones Vascas *CC4U
[Span] med solo,pno UNION ESP.
$1.25 (L601)

LAVRY, MARC (1903-1967)
Zichron Wine Song
solo,opt cor,pno ISRAELI 1003 $1.40
(L602)

LAWES
Hymn To The Holy Trinity *sac
Mez/Bar solo,cont OXFORD 62.733
$3.70 (L603)

LAWES, HENRY (1596-1662)
Dialogues For Two Voices And Continuo
*see Lawes, William

On A Kiss
see VIER DIALOGE

Shepherd And Nymph
see VIER DIALOGE

Trois Chansons *CC3U
cmplt ed,cloth,min sc OISEAU s.p.
(L604)

LAWES, WILLIAM (1602-1645)
Charon And Philomel
see VIER DIALOGE

LAWES, WILLIAM (cont'd.)

Daphne And Strephon
see VIER DIALOGE

Dialogues For Two Voices And Continuo
(composed with Lawes, Henry)
*CCU
(Jesson, Roy) ST/TB/SB soli,cont
PENN STATE PSMS 3 $3.00 (L605)

LAWN AS WHITE AS DRIVEN SNOW see
Castelnuovo-Tedesco, Mario

LAWSON, MALCOLM
Ae Fond Kiss
solo,pno CRAMER (L606)

As I Gaed Doun Glemoriston
solo,pno CRAMER (L607)

Aye Waulking O'
solo,pno CRAMER (L608)

Ayont Yon Hill
solo,pno CRAMER (L609)

Bessie Bell And Mary Gray
solo,pno CRAMER (L610)

Bonnie Banks Of Loch Lomond, The
low solo,pno (F maj) CRAMER (L611)
high solo,pno (A flat maj) CRAMER
(L612)

Bonnie Earl O'Moray, The
solo,pno CRAMER $.95 (L613)

Bonnie George Campbell
solo,pno CRAMER (L614)

Bonnie Strathyre
solo,pno CRAMER (L615)

Bonnie Wee Rose
solo,pno CRAMER (L616)

Brown Haired Maiden
solo,pno CRAMER (L617)

Bush Aboon Traquair
solo,pno CRAMER (L618)

Ca' The Yowes To The Knowes
solo,pno CRAMER (L619)

Colins Cattle
solo,pno CRAMER (L620)

Cooper O' Fife, The
solo,pno CRAMER (L621)

Earlie's Son
solo,pno CRAMER (L622)

Fair Young Mary
solo,pno CRAMER (L623)

Farewell Glenalbin
solo,pno CRAMER (L624)

Farewell To Fiunary
solo,pno CRAMER (L625)

Health And Joy Be With You
solo,pno CRAMER (L626)

Heiress
solo,pno CRAMER (L627)

Helen Of Kirkconnel
solo,pno CRAMER (L628)

Herding Song
low solo,pno (B maj) CRAMER (L629)
high solo,pno (D maj) CRAMER (L630)

Ho Ro My Nut Brown Maiden
solo,pno CRAMER (L631)

Jacobite Lament
solo,pno CRAMER (L632)

Lady Anne Bothwell's Lullaby
solo,pno CRAMER (L633)

Lament For Maclean Of Ardgour
solo,pno CRAMER (L634)

Lament Of The Border Widow
solo,pno CRAMER (L635)

Linten Lowrin
solo,pno CRAMER (L636)

Lord Reoch's Daughter
solo,pno CRAMER (L637)

Maiden Of Morven
solo,pno CRAMER (L638)

Morag
solo,pno CRAMER (L639)

My Faithful Fond One
solo,pno CRAMER (L640)

LAWSON, MALCOLM (cont'd.)

O Can Ye Sew Cushions?
solo,pno CRAMER   (L641)

O'er The Moor
high solo,pno (E flat maj) CRAMER
                                   (L642)
low solo,pno (F maj) CRAMER   (L643)

Praise Of Islay
solo,pno CRAMER   (L644)

Proud Maisie
solo,pno CRAMER   (L645)

Rest, My Ain Bairnie
solo,pno CRAMER   (L646)

Roderick Vich Alphine Dhu
solo,pno CRAMER   (L647)

Royal Rose
solo,pno CRAMER   (L648)

Sound The Pibroch
solo,pno CRAMER   (L649)

This Is No My Plaid
solo,pno CRAMER   (L650)

Thyme In My Garden
solo,pno CRAMER   (L651)

To Lucasta
solo,pno CRAMER   (L652)

Touch Not The Nettle
low solo,pno (A maj) CRAMER   (L653)
high solo,pno (C maj) CRAMER (L654)

Turn Ye To Me
high solo,pno (F maj) CRAMER $1.10
                                   (L655)
low solo,pno (E maj) CRAMER $.95
                                   (L656)

Twa Corbies
solo,pno CRAMER   (L657)

We Will Take The Good Old Way
solo,pno CRAMER   (L658)

Weaving Song
solo,pno CRAMER   (L659)

Willie's Gane To Melville Castle
solo,pno CRAMER   (L660)

Women Are A' Gane Wud
solo,pno CRAMER   (L661)

LAWYER see Vaughan Williams, Ralph

LAY A GARLAND ON MY HEARSE see Bush,
Geoffrey

LAY A GARLAND ON MY HEARSE see Stevens,
Halsey

LAYLA see Hovhaness, Alan

L'AZALEE see Milhaud, Darius

LAZAR, FILIP (1894-1936)
Deux Chansons D'amour Et Une Autre
Gaie *CC3U
[Fr] S/T solo,orch DURAND s.p.
                                   (L662)
Trois Pastorales *CC3U
solo,orch DURAND s.p., ipr   (L663)

LAZARUS, DANIEL (1898-   )
Epitaphe
A solo,pno/inst DURAND s.p.   (L664)

Mouettes
A solo,pno/inst DURAND s.p.   (L665)

Sonnet XVII
A solo,pno/inst DURAND s.p.   (L666)

Sonnet XXII
A solo,pno/inst DURAND s.p.   (L667)

LAZY ANDY ANT see Wolpe, Stefan

L'CHU V'NIVNEH see Chajes, Julius

L'DOR VODOR see Beimel, Jacob

LE BACHELIER DE SALAMANQUE see Ropartz,
Joseph Guy

LE BAISER QUI FUIT see Delmet, Paul

LE BAL DES FLEURS see Mendelssohn-
Bartholdy, Felix

LE BAL MASQUE see Poulenc, Francis

LE BALCON see Debussy, Claude

LE BALCON see Vermeulen, Matthijs

LE BAMBOLETTE see Ferrari-Trecate,
Luigi

LE BANC DE PIERRE see Godard, Benjamin
Louis Paul

LE BAPTEME DE MIARKA see Georges,
Alexandre

LE BAPTIEME DE MIARKA (HYMNE A LA
RIVIERE ET HYMNE AU SOLEIL) see
Georges, Alexandre

LE BEAU CHANTEUR see Chaminade, Cecile

LE BEDEAU DE SAINT-GILLES
(Fragerolle, G.) solo,pno ENOCH s.p.
see from Chansons Du Pays-Lorrain
                                   (L668)
(Fragerolle, G.) solo,acap ENOCH s.p.
see from Chansons Du Pays-Lorrain
                                   (L669)

LE BERCEAU see Cuvillier, Charles

LE BERGER COLLINET see Delvincourt,
Claude

LE BERGER FIDELE see Rameau, Jean-
Philippe

LE BESTIAIRE, OU CORTEGE D'ORPHEE see
Poulenc, Francis

LE BOA see Quinet, Marcel

LE BOIS DE PINS see Massenet, Jules

LE BON AU PORTEUR see Legay, Marcel

LE BON CHIEN DE GARDE see Schlosser,
Paul

LE BON DIEU DANS LA FORET see Abt,
Franz

LE BON GITE see Michiels, G.

LE BON PASTEUR see Hively, Wells

LE BON SENECHAL DE POITIERS see Saint-
Saens, Camille

LE BON VIEUX TEMPS
see La Musique, Deuxieme Cahier

LE BONHEUR see Mesritz Van Velthuysen,
Annie

LE BONHEUR see Roget, H.

LE BONHEUR D'ETRE VIEUX see Chautagne,
Marc

LE BONHEUR EST CHOSE LEGERE see Saint-
Saens, Camille

LE BONHEUR EST DANS LE PRE see Canal,
Marguerite

LE BONHEUR EST DANS LE PRE see Tomasi,
H.

LE BONHEUR PARFAIT see Schumann, Robert
(Alexander)

LE BONNE GARDE see Louis, E.

LE BOSTON DU PASSE see Bozi, Harold de

LE BOUC see Mussorgsky, Modest

LE BOUQUET see Schlosser, Paul

LE BOURGEOIS GENTILHOMME see Lully
(Lulli), Jean-Baptiste

LE BRICK PERDU see Dufresne, C.

LE BRICK, POEME DE RENE CHALUPT see
Milhaud, Darius

LE CAFE see Bernier, Nicolas

LE CAILLOU BLEU see Legley, Victor

LE CALVAIRE see Gounod, Charles
Francois

LE CAMPANE DI MALINES see Cimara,
Pietro

LE CANZONI DEL NIENTE see Pratella,
Francesco Balilla

LE CAPISTON MARCHAND see Fragerolle, G.

LE CAPITAINE CUPIDON see Wachs, F.

LE CAPITAINE ET LE SECOND see Arrieu,
Claude

LE CAPTIF see Gretchaninov, Alexander
Tikhonovitch

LE CAPTIVITE DE BABYLONE see Lacome,
Paul

LE CARABE see Quinet, Marcel

LE CARNAVAL DES TRANCHEES see Jongen,
Joseph-Marie-Alphonse-Nicholas

LE CATARIGOLE see Bianchini, Guido

LE CAUCHEMAR DU CHAUFFEUR DE TAXI see
Kosma, J.

LE CAVALIER ET LA BERGERE
(Fragerolle, G.) solo,pno ENOCH s.p.
see from Chansons Du Pays-Lorrain
                                   (L670)
(Fragerolle, G.) solo,acap ENOCH s.p.
see from Chansons Du Pays-Lorrain
                                   (L671)

LE CERCEAU see Schlosser, Paul

LE CERCLE DES HEURES see Samazeuilh,
Gustave

LE CERSIER see Schmitt, Florent

LE CHAMP DE BATAILLE see Paray, Paul

LE CHAMPAGNE EST UN VIN CHARMANT see
Levade, Charles (Gaston)

LE CHANSON DES PROMIS see Rabey, Rene

LE CHANSON DU SABOTIER see Rabey, Rene

LE CHANSONNIER D'ARRAS *CC72U,Fr,12-
13th cent
cloth JOHNSON 0-384-08465-6 $25.25
                                   (L672)
LE CHANSONNIER FRANCAIS DE SAINT-
GERMAIN-DES PRES *CCU,Fr,Mediev
JOHNSON cloth $32.25, pap $28.00
                                   (L673)

LE CHANT D'AUBE see Casanova, Andre

LE CHANT DE LA NOUVELLE ANNEE see
Bendix, Victor Emmanuel

LE CHANT DE LABOUR see Rabey, Rene

LE CHANT DE L'ALLIANCE see Missa,
Edmond Jean Louis

LE CHANT DE ZARATHOUSTRA see Doyen,
Albert

LE CHANT DES COMMUNIANTES see Stevens,
M.

LE CHANT DES FORETS see Shostakovich,
Dmitri

LE CHANT DES VEILLES MAISONS see
Lenormand, Rene

LE CHANT DU BERGER see Galos

LE CHANT DU DEPOSSEDE see Nigg, Serge

LE CHANT DU PATRE see Boisdeffre,
Charles-Henri-Rene de

LE CHANT DU STADE see Loucheur, R.

LE CHANT DU TOMBEAU see Rasse, Francois

LE CHANT DU VEILLEUR see Nin, Joaquin

LE CHANT DU WELFARE see Deblocq, G.

LE CHANTE DE MIGNON see Liszt, Franz,
Mignons Lied

LE CHANTEUR DES BOIS see Delmet, Paul

LE CHANTEUR FLORENTIN see Duprato,
Jules-Laurent

LE CHANVRE see Coquard, Arthur

LE CHAPEAU CHINOIS see Absil, Jean

LE CHAPELIER see Satie, Erik

LE CHAPLET D'AMOUR see Goublier, G.

LE CHARITE MA BELLE DAME see Saint-
Saens, Camille

LE CHARME D'AMOUR see Chaminade, Cecile

LE CHARME EST ROMPU see Gedalge, Andre

LE CHASSEUR DU BOIS D'ETE see Gade,
Niels Wilhelm

LE CHAT see Steenhuis, Francois

LE CHAT BOTTE see Fragerolle, G.

LE CHAT BOTTE see Lacome, Paul

LE CHAT I see Sauguet, Henri

LE CHAT II see Sauguet, Henri

LE CHATEAU D'O see Migot, Georges

LE CHAUSSEUR PERDU EN FORET see Honegger, Arthur

LE CHEMIN DE LA CROIX see Andriessen, Hendrik

LE CHEMIN DES ECOLIERES see Gedalge, Andre

LE CHEMIN DU CIEL see Holmes, Alfred

LE CHEMIN DU VISIBLE A L'INVISIBLE see Middeleer, Jean De

LE CHEMINEAU MAIGRE see Coppola, Piero

LE CHEVRIER see Paray, Paul

LE CHIC see Ratz, Ludo

LE CHIEN see Cuvillier, Charles

LE CHIEN QUI LACHE SA PROIE POUR L'OMBRE see Pascal, Andre

LE CHRIST AU JARDIN DES OLIVIERS see Serpette, Gaston

LE CIARAMELLE see Gandino, Adolfo

LE CIEL COMME UN LAC PALE see Mulot, M.

LE CIEL EN NUIT S'EST DEPLIE see Horst, Anton van der

LE CIEL EST BLEU see Chaminade, Cecile

LE CIEL EST GAI, C'EST JOLI MAI see Gaubert, Philippe

LE CIEL EST PAR-DESSES LE TOIT see Doyen, Albert

LE CLAIR DE LUNE see Delbruck, J.

LE CLAQUEMENT BREF DES SABOTS see Rhene-Baton

LE CLOCHER CHANGE see Barber, Samuel

LE CLOCHER CHANTE see Orthel, Leon

LE COCHER see Ganne, Louis Gaston

LE COEUR CONTENT see Bach, Johann Sebastian

LE COEUR DE L'EAU see Roger-Ducasse, Jean-Jules Aimable

LE COEUR DE LISON see Stanislas, Ad.

LE COEUR DU POETE see Delmet, Paul

LE COEUR FROID see Kelkel, Manfred

LE COLIBRI see Vuillemin, L.

LE COLLET BLEU see Vellones, P.

LE COLLIER see Messiaen, Oliver

LE COLLIER see Mignan, Edouard-Charles-Octave

LE COLOMBIER see Lacome, Paul

LE COLONEL see Stravinsky, Igor

LE COMBAT see Kersters, Willem, Het Gevecht

LE COMMISAIRE see Michiels, G.

LE COMPARTIMENT DES FUMEURS see Chassaigne, F.

LE COMPLIMENT DU PETIT JOST see Guiraud, Ernest

LE CONVOI D'UNE PAUVRE FILLE see Bijl, Theo van der

LE COQ see Schlosser, Paul

LE COQ DU CLOCHER see Cuvillier, Charles

LE COQ ET LE PERLE see Pascal, Andre

LE COQ ET LE RENARD see Francaix, Jean

LE COQ ET LE RENARD see Lacome, Paul

LE COQ WALLON.U VIERGES ET MERES see Georges, Alexandre

LE COR see Flegier, Ange

LE CORBEAU ET LE RENARD see Caplet, Andre

LE CORBEAU ET LE RENARD see Delage, Maurice

LE CORBEAU ET LE RENARD see Delbruck, J.

LE CORDIER see Vidal

LE CORTEGE D'AMPHITRITE see Richepin, T.

LE COSAQUE see Moniuszko, Stanislaw

LE COUCOU CHANTE see Bagge, G.

LE COUER INUTILE see Beydts, L.

LE COUPLE(T) see Knap, Rolf

LE CRAPAUD see Schlosser, Paul

LE CREDO DE LA VICTOIRE see Messager, Andre

LE CREPUSCULE see Beydts, L.

LE CRI DES EAUX see Campbell-Tipton, Louis

LE CRUCIFIX see Decruck, F.

LE CYGNE see Ravel, Maurice

LE CYGNE see Saint-Saens, Camille

LE DANGER PRESSE see Meyerbeer, Giacomo

LE DE see Schlosser, Paul

LE DELPHINIM see Honegger, Arthur

LE DEPART see Milhaud, Darius

LE DEPART DES PATRES see Beethoven, Ludwig van

LE DEPART DU MATELOT see Gaubert, Philippe

LE DEPOT EST OBLIGATOIRE see Jacob, Dom Clement

LE DESERT see Enesco, Georges

LE DESESPOIR see Boutnikoff, J.

LE DESIR see Vuillermoz, Emile

LE DESTIN see Aubert, Louis-Francois-Marie

LE DEUX MENETRIERS see Chaminade, Cecile

LE DIABLE DANS LA NUIT see Bosmans, Henriette

LE DIABLE DANS LA NUIT see Roget, H.

LE DIEU QUE J'AI PRIE see Mariotte, Antoine

LE DIMANCHE AU BORD DU RHIN see Schumann, Robert (Alexander)

LE DISPARU see Poulenc, Francis

LE DON SILENCIEUX see Grovlez, Gabriel (Marie)

LE DORMEUR DU VAL see Andriessen, Hendrik

LE DORMEUR DU VAL see Bergmann, R.

LE DORMEUR DU VAL see Orthel, Leon

LE DRAPEAU DES ECOLIERS FRANCAIS see Haring, Ch.

LE DROIT DU SEIGNEUR see Fragerolle, G.

LE DUVET DU PISSENLIT see Defontaine, M.

LE FAMEUX CHANTRE DE LA THRACE see Clerambault, Louis-Nicolas

LE FAUCHEUR see Street, G.

LE FAUNE see Debussy, Claude

LE FAUNE ET LA BERGERE see Stravinsky, Igor

LE FER see Delbruck, J.

LE FEU see Delbruck, J.

LE FIAMME SU L'ALTARE see Guerrini, Guido

LE FILS DE LA TEMPETE see Schumann, Robert (Alexander)

LE FILS DES MUSES see Schubert, Franz (Peter)

LE FLEUVE see Saint-Saens, Camille

LE FLOCON DE NEIGE see Stehman, Jacques

LE FORGERON see Brahms, Johannes

LE FOUR see Stravinsky, Igor

LE FOYER see Anjou, P. d'

LE FOYER see Doyen, Albert

LE FUSILLE see Caby, R.

LE GALANT RENDEZ-VOUS see Berger, Rod.

LE GALERIEN see Poll

LE GALLOP see Duparc, Henri

LE GALOP see Enesco, Georges

LE GARCON DE LIEGE see Poulenc, Francis

LE GAS DU MOUSTOIR see Fragerolle, G.

LE GERANIUM see Arrieu, Claude

LE GIBET see Eisma, Will

LE GODILLOTS see Cuvillier, Charles

LE GOELAND see Filipucci, Edm.

LE GRAND ENVOL see Migot, Georges

LE GRANDS JASMINS see Rhene-Baton

LE GRILLON see Lacome, Paul

LE GRILLON see Rameau, Jean-Philippe

LE GRILLON see Ravel, Maurice

LE GUE see Strong, George Templeton

LE GUE see Vellones, P.

LE HANAP DE L'ANCESTRE see Stenhammar, Wilhelm

LE HANNETON see Truillet-Soyer, M.

LE HERISSON see Absil, Jean

LE ILLUSIONI see Gubitosi, Emilia

LE JARDIN see Griffes, Charles Tomlinson

LE JARDIN CLOS see Faure, Gabriel-Urbain

LE JARDIN DE MA TANTE see Moulaert, Raymond

LE JARDIN DE NOTRE SOEUR CLAIRE see Chailley, Jacques

LE JARDIN DES CARESSES [1] see Boutnikoff, J.

LE JARDIN DES CARESSES [2] see Boutnikoff, J.

LE JARDIN MOUILLE see Gaubert, Philippe

LE JARDIN MOUILLE see Roussel, Albert

LE JET D'EAU see Bertouille, Gerard

LE JET D'EAU see Debussy, Claude

LE JEUNE HOMME AU BORD DE LA SOURCE see Schubert, Franz (Peter)

LE JEUNE PATRE BRETON see Berlioz, Hector

LE JOLI SONGE see Messager, Andre

LE JOUR see Magne, Michel

LE JOUR see Speaks, Oley

LE JOUR BRILLANT see Rimsky-Korsakov, Nikolai

LE JOUR DU SEIGNEUR see Goeyens, Fern.

LE JOUR ET LA NUIT see d'Hardelot, Guy

LE JOUR, SOUS LE SOLEIL BENI see Messager, Andre

LE JUIF ERRANT see Fragerolle, G.

LE KERIOKLEPTE see Roussel, Albert

LE LAC see Pandelides, S.

LE LAIT see Mesritz Van Velthuysen, Annie

LE LAPIN see Quinet, Marcel

LE LECON DE TAMBOUR see Baggers, J.

LE LEPREUX see Lilien, Ignace

LE LEVER DE LA LUNE see Saint-Saens, Camille

LE LEZARD see Leeuw, Ton de

LE LIEVRE ET LA TORTUE see Delbruck, J.

LE LIT LAQUE BLANC see Halffter, Ernesto

LE LITANIE D'AMORE see Cantu, M.

LE LIVRE DE LA FOI JUREE see Casanova, Andre

LE LONG DU CHEMIN see De Lara, Isadore

LE LOUP see Planquette, Robert

LE LOUP ET L'AGNEAU see Caplet, Andre

LE LUTH see Puget, Paul-Charles-Marie

LE MAI
see La Musique, Troisieme Cahier

LE MAI D'AMOUR see Delmet, Paul

LE MAIN DANS LA MAIN see Delmet, Paul

LE MAITRE D'ECOLE see Lacome, Paul

LE MALHEUR see Middeleer, Jean De

LE MANIOR see Ropartz, Joseph Guy

LE MANUSCRIT DE BAYEUX *CC103U,15th cent
(Gerold, Theodore) solo MINKOFF s.p.
(L674)

LE MARCHAND DE SABLE see Roget, H.

LE MARCHE DU POETE see Dufresne, C.

LE MARIAGE DES ROSES see Franck, Cesar

LE MARINIER JOLI see Richepin, T.

LE MARRIAGE DES ROSES see Franck, Cesar

LE MARTEAU SANS MAITRE see Boulez, Pierre

LE MARTIN-PECHEUR see Ravel, Maurice

LE MATIN see Bizet, Georges

LE MATIN see Saint-Saens, Camille

LE MAUDIT see Schubert, Franz (Peter)

LE MELE E IL BACIO see Rocca, Lodovico

LE MENETRIER see Godard, Benjamin Louis Paul

LE MENETRIER see Schubert, Franz (Peter)

LE MESSAGE see Blair Fairchild

LE MESSAGE see Busser, Henri-Paul

LE MIRAGE see Aubert, Louis-Francois-Marie

LE MISANTHROPE see Lacome, Paul

LE MISTRAL see Clerice, J.

LE MISTRAL see Dufresne, C.

LE MOINEAU EST ASSIS see Stravinsky, Igor

LE MOIS D'AVRIL S'EN EST ALLE
see La Musique, Neuvieme Cahier

LE MOIS DE MAI see Kucken, Friedrich Wilhelm

LE MORT MAUDIT see Street, G.

LE MORTE CHITARRE see Laporte, Andre

LE MORTE CHITARRE see Modugno, Domenico

LE MOULIN see Scotto, Vincent

LE MOULIN see Truillet-Soyer, M.

LE MOULIN D'AMOUR see Rabey, Rene

LE NEGRE-BOULANGER see Bourguignon, Francis de

LE NENUFAR see Absil, Jean

LE NEZ DE MARTIN see Aubert, Louis-Francois-Marie

LE NOEL DES OISEAUX see Chaminade, Cecile

LE NOEL DES PETITS ENFANTS see Lecocq, Charles

LE NOVE SON SUONATE see Gandino, Adolfo

LE NOYER see Schumann, Robert (Alexander)

LE NOZZE DELL'ALPIGIANO see Sinigaglia, Leone

LE NUAGE see Rasse, Francois

LE NUAGE A DIT UN JOUR see Rimsky-Korsakov, Nikolai

LE NUOVE MUSICHE see Caccini, Giulio

LE NUOVE MUSICHE see Caccini, Giulio

LE PAGE see Migot, Georges

LE PAGE LANCELOT see Fragerolle, G.

LE PAIN DE L'AMOUR see Delmet, Paul

LE PAIN DE SERPENT see Bondon, Jacques

LE PAIN DE SERPENT see Bondon, Jacques

LE PAON see Ravel, Maurice

LE PAPILLON see Falkenberg, G.

LE PAPILLON see Levade, Charles (Gaston)

LE PAPILLON see Paray, Paul

LE PAPILLON see Rabey, Rene

LE PAPPILLON see Gelli, E., La Farfalla

LE PARALYTIQUE see Lilien, Ignace

LE PARC D'AUTOMNE see Aubert, Louis-Francois-Marie

LE PARFUM see Wall, C. v.d.

LE PARFUM INPERISSABLE see Pesse, M.

LE PARISIEN N'AIME PAS see Messager, Andre

LE PARTERRE D'HYACINTHE see Kosma, J.

LE PAS D'ARMES DU ROI JEAN see Saint-Saens, Camille

LE PASSANT DE PASSY see Schmitt, Florent

LE PASSE QUI FILE see Cuvillier, Charles

LE PASSEUR see Wellings, M.

LE PAYS A L'ENVERS see Leduc, Jacques

LE PAYS ARROSE see Roos, Robert de

LE PAYS DE COCAGNE see Lacome, Paul

LE PAYS DE COCAGNE see Schumann, Robert (Alexander)

LE PAYS DES REVES see Lacome, Paul

LE PAYS NATAL see Schlosser, Paul

LE PECHEUR ET L'ONDINE see Chaminade, Cecile

LE PEINTRE AU VILLAGE see Michiels, G.

LE PELERIN D'ASSISE see Chailley, Jacques

LE PERCHERON see Quinet, Marcel

LE PETIT ANE BLANC see Ibert, Jacques

LE PETIT ANE GRIS see Landry, Al.

LE PETIT BOIS see Auric, Georges

LE PETIT CANARD see Dere, Jean

LE PETIT CHAPERON ROUGE see Lacome, Paul

LE PETIT COQ see Migot, Georges

LE PETIT ESCARGOT DE VIGNE see Schlosser, Paul

LE PETIT FANFARON see Perronnet, Amelie

LE PETIT GARCON MALADE see Absil, Jean

LE PETIT GARCON TROP BIEN PORTANT see Poulenc, Francis

LE PETIT GORET see Schlosser, Paul

LE PETIT LAPIN see Arma, Paul

LE PETIT NAVIRE see Delmet, Paul

LE PETIT NOEL see Lacome, Paul

LE PETIT OISEAU see Delbruck, J.

LE PETIT OISEAU TRISTE see Arensky, Anton Stepanovitch

LE PETIT PIGEON BLEU see Beydts, L.

LE PETIT PONEY see Schlosser, Paul

LE PETIT POUCET see Lacome, Paul

LE PETIT POULET see Truillet-Soyer, M.

LE PETIT SAVOYARD see Killmayer, Wilhelm

LE PETIT SERIN EN CAGE see Beydts, L.

LE PETIT SOLDAT see Perissas, M.

LE PETIT TAMBOUR see Baggers, J.

LE PETITE EGLISE see Delmet, Paul

LE PETITE MARIE see Delbruck, J.

LE PIC DU MINEUR see Ravize, A.

LE PINSON see Arensky, Anton Stepanovitch

LE PLUS DOUX CHEMIN see Lacome, Paul

LE POETE BLESSE see Tremisot, Ed.

LE POETE ET LA MUSE see Paray, Paul

LE POETE PORTE LE DEUIL DES JOIES PAS ENCORE NEES see Vuillemin, L.

LE POISSON GRIS see Brero, Cesare

LE POISSON VOLANT see Vellones, P.

LE POLONAIS EST TRISTE ET GRAVE see Chabrier, Emmanuel

LE PONT see Poulenc, Francis

LE PORTAIL DE GLACE see Martin, Frank

LE PORTRAIT see Godard, Benjamin Louis Paul

LE PORTRAIT see Mozart, Wolfgang Amadeus

LE PORTRAIT see Poulenc, Francis

LE PORTRAIT see Vuillemin, L.

LE PORTRAIT see Wall, C. v.d.

LE POULET see Steenhuis, Francois

LE POULET ET LE RENARD see Mercenier, P.

LE PRE D'AMOUR see Delmet, Paul

LE PREMIER JOUR OU JE VIS see Rhene-Baton

LE PRESAGE DE LA CROIX see Saint-Saens, Camille

LE PRESENT see Beydts, L.

LE PRINCE AU LONG NEZ see Lacome, Paul

LE PRINCESSE SUCREE see Lacome, Paul

LE PRINTEMPS see Cuvillier, Charles

LE PRINTEMPS see Koechlin, Charles

LE PRINTEMPS see Marty, (Eugene) Georges

LE PRINTEMPS see Schubert, Franz (Peter), Fruhlingsglaube

LE PRINTEMPS A PLEINS VERRES see Delmet, Paul

LE PRINTEMPS, C'EST TOI see Chretien, H.

LE PRINTEMPS DES GUEUX see Street, G.

LE PRINTEMPS, LE LONG DES BUISSONS...
  see Chevreuille, Raymond

LE PRISONNIER see Fells, G.

LE PROMENOIR DES DEUX AMANTS see
  Debussy, Claude

LE P'TIT QUINQUIN
  (Desrousseaux) solo,pno GRAS s.p.
                                    (L675)
LE RAMIER see Haring, Ch.

LE RANE see Bossi, Renzo

LE RELAIS DE BOISSIERE see Bernadac, L.

LE RELIQUAIRE see Delmet, Paul

LE RENARD ET LES RAISINS see Pascal,
  Andre

LE RENDEZ-VOUS see Chaminade, Cecile

LE RENDEZ-VOUS see Flegier, Ange

LE RENDEZ-VOUS see Honegger, Arthur

LE RENOUVEAU
  see La Musique, Premier Cahier

LE RENOUVEAU see Coquard, Arthur

LE RENOUVEAU see Delmet, Paul

LE RENOUVEAU see Koechlin, Charles

LE REPOS EN EGYPTE see Gaubert,
  Philippe

LE REPOS EN EGYPTE see Rhene-Baton

LE RETOUR
  (Fragerolle, G.) solo,pno ENOCH s.p.
    see from Chansons Du Pays-Lorrain
                                    (L676)
  (Fragerolle, G.) solo,acap ENOCH s.p.
    see from Chansons Du Pays-Lorrain
                                    (L677)
LE RETOUR see Bonnal, Ermend

LE RETOUR see Chantrier, A.

LE RETOUR DE LA CROISADE see
  Fragerolle, G.

LE RETOUR DES HIRONDELLES see Durand,
  E.

LE RETOUR DU PRINTEMPS see Cuvillier,
  Charles

LE RETOUR DU PRINTEMPS see Desrez

LE RETOUR DU PRINTEMPS see Godard,
  Benjamin Louis Paul

LE RETOUR DU ROSSIGNOL
  see La Musique, Troisieme Cahier

LE REVE see Arditi, Luigi, Il Bacio

LE REVE see Marechal, Henri-Charles

LE REVE see Moniuszko, Stanislaw

LE REVE DE DES GRIEUX see Massenet,
  Jules

LE REVE DE JOEL see Fragerolle, G.

LE REVEIL see Labey, Marcel

LE REVEIL see Tremisot, Ed.

LE REVEIL DE LA MARIEE see Ravel,
  Maurice

LE REVEIL DES FLEURS see Beethoven,
  Ludwig van

LE REVEILLON see Griffes, Charles
  Tomlinson

LE REVOIR see Rhene-Baton

LE RIDEAU DE MA VOISINE see Tesson, P.

LE ROI D'AMOUR EST MON PASTEUR see
  Gounod, Charles Francois

LE ROI DE THULE see Schubert, Franz
  (Peter), Erlkonig

LE ROI DES AULNES see Schubert, Franz
  (Peter), Erlkonig

LE ROI M'A DIT see Bernicat, F.

LE ROI MALGRE LUI see Chabrier,
  Emmanuel

LE ROI MARC see Tranchant, J.

LE ROI RENARD
  see Two French Folk Songs

LE ROMAN DE KAPITAGOLEI see Englert,
  Giuseppe Giorgio

LE ROMAN DE PIERROT see Berger, Rod.

LE ROMARIN see Fourdrain, Felix

LE ROMERAGE see Dufresne, C.

LE ROSSIGNOL see Bozza, Eugene

LE ROSSIGNOL see Delibes, Leo

LE ROSSIGNOL see Dere, Jean

LE ROSSIGNOL see Milhaud, Darius

LE ROSSIGNOL see Saint-Saens, Camille

LE ROSSIGNOL see Schlosser, Paul

LE ROSSIGNOL see Seiber, Matyas

LE ROSSIGNOL A PRIS SON VOL see Saint-
  Saens, Camille

LE ROSSIGNOL DE LA FORET see Bagge, G.

LE ROSSIGNOL ET LE PETIT SOLDAT see
  D'Hack, A.

LE ROUET see Vierne, Louis

LE RUISSEAU see Gastinel, Leon-Gustave-
  Cypien

LE RUISSEAU see Lacome, Paul

LE RUISSEAU see Schubert, Franz
  (Peter), Wohin

LE SABLE DU SABLIER see Arrieu, Claude

LE SACRE see Mulder, Ernest W.

LE SAPIN see Wagner, Richard

LE SAVOIR see Georges, Alexandre

LE SECRET see Colomb, A.

LE SECRET see Gaubert, Philippe

LE SECRET see Schubert, Franz (Peter),
  Geheimes

LE SEIGNEUR DE BONDY see Fragerolle, G.

LE SEMEUR see Malo, Ch.

LE SEMINARISTE see Mussorgsky, Modest

LE SENTIER see Gedalge, Andre

LE SENTIER see Godard, Benjamin Louis
  Paul

LE SERAPHIN DES SOIRS see Mulot, M.

LE SETTE ALLEGREZZE D'AMORE see
  Malipiero, Gian Francesco

LE SETTE STELLE see Pratella, Francesco
  Balilla

LE SIGNE A MAM'ZELLE BOUSQUET see
  Serpette, Gaston

LE SILENCE see Leeuw, Ton de

LE SILENCE see Levade, Charles (Gaston)

LE SINGE QUI MONTRE LA LANTERNE MAGIQUE
  see Mercenier, P.

LE SOIR AU LIDO see Scotto, Vincent

LE SOIR DESCEND SUR LA COLLINE see
  Saint-Saens, Camille

LE SOIR, QU'AMOUR see Schmitt, Florent

LE SOIR VIENT see Godard, Benjamin
  Louis Paul

LE SOLDAT DE CARTON see Lacome, Paul

LE SOLEIL NI LA MORT see Clarke, Henry
  Leland

LE SOLEIL RESTE see Carolus-Duran, P.

LE SOLEIL S'EST COUCHE DERRIERE LA
  MONTAGNE see Blanter, M.

LE SOMBRE MAI see Milhaud, Darius

LE SOMMEIL DE CANOPE see Samazeuilh,
  Gustave

LE SOMMEIL DE LEILAH see Tremisot, Ed.

LE SOMMEIL DE LEILAH see Wieniawski,
  Adam (Tadeusz)

LE SOMMEIL DE L'ENFANT JESUS see
  Buesser

LE SOMMEIL DES COLOMBES see Aubert,
  Louis-Francois-Marie

LE SOMMEIL DES FLEURS see Saint-Saens,
  Camille

LE SON DU COR S'AFFLIGE see Debussy,
  Claude

LE SORT M'A DESIGNE see Laparra, Raoul

LE SOURIRE see Messiaen, Oliver

LE SOUVENIR DE LA NEIGE see Orthel,
  Leon

LE SPHINX see Fragerolle, G.

LE SPHINX see Fragerolle, G.

LE SQUARE see Larbey, V.

LE STAGIONI ITALICHE see Malipiero,
  Gian Francesco

LE SUISSE see Lacome, Paul

LE SULTAN see Bosmans, Henriette

LE SUPPLICE DE CLAES see Vogel,
  Wladimir

LE TAMBOURIN see Rameau, Jean-Philippe

LE TEMP S'ENVOLE see Gounod, Charles
  Francois

LE TEMPS see Barbier, Rene

LE TEMPS A LAISSE SON MANTEAU see
  Millot, E.

LE TEMPS A LAISSIE SON MANTEAU see
  Debussy, Claude

LE TEMPS D'AIMER see Duteil d'Ozanne,
  A.

LE TEMPS DES AMOURS see Haring, Ch.

LE TEMPS DES LILAS see Chausson, Ernest

LE THE see Koechlin, Charles

LE THRENE DU VIEUX ROI see Chaminade,
  Cecile

LE TILLEUL see Schubert, Franz (Peter),
  Die Lindenbaum

LE TOMBE see Rocca, Lodovico

LE TOMBEAU D'ANTAR see Boutnikoff, J.

LE TOMBEAU DE KATHLEEN FERRIER see
  Hemel, Oscar van

LE TOMBEAU DE RONSARD see Rivier, Jean

LE TOMBEAU DE ZULEIKA see Chapuis,
  Auguste-Paul-Jean-Baptiste

LE TOMBEAU DES NAIADES see Debussy,
  Claude

LE TONNELIER see Fragerolle, G.

LE TORRENT see Letocart, H.

LE TOURNOI see Moulaert, Raymond

LE TRAINEAU see Lacome, Paul

LE TRAVAIL DU PEINTRE see Poulenc,
  Francis

LE VAINCU see Aubert, Louis-Francois-
  Marie

LE VAL HARMONIEUX see Gaubert, Philippe

LE VANNEUR see Grandjany, Marcel

LE VASE see Bonifanti, L'amphore

LE VASE BRISE see Franck, Cesar

LE VASE OU MEURT CETTE VERVEINE see
  Absil, Jean

LE VEILLEUR DE LA LUNE see Bondon,
  Jacques

LE VENDREDI see Cuvillier, Charles

LE VENT see Dalcroze, Jacques

LE VENT DANS LA PLAINE see Saint-Saens,
  Camille

LE VENT DE MAI see Rabey, Rene

LE VENT EST DOUX see Ropartz, Joseph Guy

LE VERGER see Massenet, Jules

LE VIEUX BANC see Delmet, Paul

LE VIEUX CHEMIN see Mariotte, Antoine

LE VIEUX COFFRET see Caplet, Andre

LE VIEUX DE LA PETITE see Berger, Rod.

LE VIEUX ET LE LIEVRE see Stravinsky, Igor

LE VIEUX FOSSOYEUR see Sureau-Bellet, J.

LE VIEUX FRANCAIS see Lachaume, A.

LE VIEUX MENDIANT see Delmet, Paul

LE VIEUX MENESTRIER (TRIAL) see Dupin, Paul

LE VIEUX PECHEUR see Bantock, Granville, Old Fisherman, The

LE VIEUX POMMIER see Bonnal, Ermend

LE VIGNERON
  see La Musique, Troisieme Cahier

LE VILLAGE see Chaminade, Cecile

LE VILLAGE see Gastinel, Leon-Gustave-Cypien

LE VIN see Schumann, Robert (Alexander)

LE VIN EST L'ELIXIR SACRE see Levade, Charles (Gaston)

LE VIN PERDU see Ferroud, Pierre-Octave

LE VIOLETTE see Scarlatti, Alessandro

LE VISAGE PENCHE see Aubert, Louis-Francois-Marie

LE VISITEUR see Leduc, Jacques

LE VITTRAIL see Dubois, Theodore

LE VIVIER see Rivier, Jean

LE VOILIER see Migot, Georges

LE VOLANT see Schlosser, Paul

LE VOULEZ-VOUS see Berger, Rod.

LE VOYAGE see Strong, George Templeton

LE VOYAGE DU ROI see Lesur, Daniel

LE VOYAGEUR see Godard, Benjamin Louis Paul

LE VOYAGEUR see Legley, Victor

LE ZODIAQUE see DuBois, Pierre Max

LEA RIG, THE   *folk,Scot
  solo,pno (B flat maj/G maj) PATERSON
  FS47 s.p.   (L678)

LEAD, KINDLY LIGHT see Bosmans, Henriette

LEAD KINDLY LIGHT see Dykes, John Bacchus

LEAD KINDLY LIGHT see Mana-Zucca, Mme., Duc Alma Lux

LEAD, KINDLY LIGHT see Pughe-Evans, D.

LEAD ME BACK TO CALVARY see Pace, Millie Lou

LEAD ME, GUIDE ME   *sac,gospel
  solo,pno ABER.GRP. $1.50   (L679)

LEAD ME, LORD see Wesley

LEAD ME TO THE ROCK THAT'S HIGHER THAN
  I   *sac,gospel
  solo,pno ABER.GRP. $1.50   (L680)

LEAD US, HEAVENLY FATHER see Rickard, Jeffrey

LEAD US, O FATHER see Galbraith, J.

LEADEN ECHO AND THE GOLDEN ECHO, THE
  see Parris, Robert

LEAFY LANES OF ENGLAND, THE see Harding, Phyllis

LEANIN' see Bennet, T.C.S.

LEAPING GALLEY   *Scot
  high solo,pno (D flat maj) PATERSON
    see from Hebridean Songs, Vol. IV
                                    (L681)
  low solo,pno (B flat maj) PATERSON
    see from Hebridean Songs, Vol. IV
                                    (L682)

LEARNING TO LIVE see DeSantis

L'EAU PASSE see Moulaert, Raymond

L'EAU QUI COURT see Georges, Alexandre

LEAVE A WELL IN THE VALLEY see Jensen, Gordon

LEAVE IT WITH HIM see Ellis

LEAVE ME see Handel, George Frideric

LEAVE, O LEAVE ME TO MY SORROWS see Flagello, Nicholas

LEAVE OFF, OH LEAVE OFF see Scarlatti, Alessandro, Lascia, Deh Lascia

LEAVE OUT MY NAME see Orgad, Ben-Zion

LEAVES' SECRET, THE see Franco, Johan

LEBE WOHL see Schubert, Franz (Peter)

LEBE WOHL, MEIN FLANDRISCH MADCHEN see Lortzing, (Gustav) Albert

LEBEN see Marvia, Einari, Elama

LEBEN IN LIEDERN   *CC60U,Ger,17-20th
  cent
  (Losse) [Ger] high solo,pno PETERS
    4299A $11.00; med solo,pno PETERS
    4299B $11.00; low solo,pno PETERS
    4299C $11.00   (L683)

LEBENDIG BEGRABEN see Schoeck, Othmar

LEBENSDANK see Bijvanck, Henk

LEBENSFESTE see Vycpalek, Ladislav

LEBEWOHL UND AUF WIEDERSEHN see
  Kilpinen, Yrio, Jaa Hyvasti Ja
  Nakemiin

LEBRUN, PAUL HENRI JOSEPH (1861-1920)
  A Toi
    [Fr] solo,acap oct DURAND s.p.
                                    (L684)
  A Toi, Idylle
    Mez/Bar solo,pno/inst DURAND s.p.
                                    (L685)
  Serenade
    Mez/Bar solo,pno/inst DURAND s.p.
                                    (L686)

L'ECHELONNEMENT DES HAIES see Debussy, Claude

LECHNER, KONRAD (1911-   )
  Cantica I
    Mez solo,chamb.grp. GERIG HG 550
    s.p.   (L687)

  Cantica II
    S solo,fl,vcl,perc,treb inst/
    cembalo GERIG HG 942 s.p.   (L688)

  Requiem
    [Lat] A solo,2ob,English horn,vla,
    vcl,bvl,cembalo/org study sc
    PETERS 5858 $4.00   (L689)

L'ECHO see Cui, Cesar Antonovitch

LECHTHALER, JOSEF (1891-1948)
  Freitagabend   *Op.18, sac,Gd.Fri.
    solo,strings BOHM rental   (L690)

  Geigerin   *Op.20, sac
    S solo,strings BOHM rental   (L691)

  Weihnachtsbuchlein   *Op.62, CCU,Xmas
    [Ger] med solo,inst/pno&rec cmplt
    ed OSTER $1.30   (L692)

L'ECLAT DE RIRE see Auber, Daniel-Francois-Esprit

L'ECLAT DE TANT DE GLOIRE see Lully (Lulli), Jean-Baptiste

L'ECO see Malipiero, Gian Francesco

LECOCQ, CHARLES (1832-1918)
  Ballade De Chambree
    solo,pno ENOCH s.p.   (L693)

  Ca Commencait Si Gentiment
    solo,acap ENOCH s.p.   (L694)
    solo,pno ENOCH s.p.   (L695)

  Chansons D'Amour   *CC20U
    [Fr] high solo,pno CHOUDENS C97
    s.p.   (L696)

LECOCQ, CHARLES (cont'd.)
  Couplets De La Rose Et Du Muguet
    (from Les Pres Saint-Gervais)
    solo,pno ENOCH s.p.   (L697)

  Dans La Ganterie (from Les Pres
    Saint-Gervais)
    solo,pno ENOCH s.p.   (L698)

  Dans Toute Circonstance (from Les
    Pres Saint-Gervais)
    solo,pno ENOCH s.p.   (L699)

  Faut De La Mefiance (from Les Pres
    Saint-Gervais)
    solo,pno ENOCH s.p.   (L700)

  Femme Sensible (from Les Pres Saint-
    Gervais)
    solo,pno ENOCH s.p.   (L701)

  Fleurs Parisiennes   *CC8U
    [Fr] high solo,pno CHOUDENS C96
    s.p.   (L702)

  Il Avait Cinq Pieds (from Les Pres
    Saint-Gervais)
    solo,pno ENOCH s.p.   (L703)

  Il Faut Vous Apprendre (from Les Pres
    Saint-Gervais)
    solo,pno ENOCH s.p.   (L704)

  Je Sens Dans Mon Coeur (from Les Pres
    Saint-Gervais)
    solo,pno ENOCH s.p.   (L705)

  La Noel Des Anges
    solo,pno ENOCH s.p.   (L706)

  La Noel Des Coucous
    solo,pno ENOCH s.p.   (L707)

  Le Noel Des Petits Enfants   *sac,Xmas
    3 soli,pno/org HEUGEL s.p.   (L708)

  Les Petits Enfants
    solo,pno ENOCH s.p.   (L709)
    solo,acap ENOCH s.p.   (L710)

  Lilas Blanc
    solo,pno ENOCH s.p.   (L711)

  Monsieur Je Crois (from Les Pres
    Saint-Gervais)
    2 soli,pno ENOCH s.p.   (L712)

  Ou Donc Courez-Vous (from Les Pres
    Saint-Gervais)
    solo,pno ENOCH s.p.   (L713)

  Que Cherchez-Vous (from Les Pres
    Saint-Gervais)
    solo,pno ENOCH s.p.   (L714)

  Two Birds
    SA soli,pno CRAMER   (L715)

  Vous Qui Savez Les Choses (from Les
    Pres Saint-Gervais)
    solo,pno ENOCH s.p.   (L716)

LECON D'HISTOIRE see Georges, Alexandre

LECONS DE TENEBRES see Couperin (le Grand), Francois

LECONS DE TENEBRES, PREMIERE LECON see
  Couperin (le Grand), Francois

LECONS DE TENEBRES, SECOND LECON see
  Couperin (le Grand), Francois

LECONS DE TENEBRES, TROISIEME LECON see
  Couperin (le Grand), Francois

LE CORBEILLER
  Au Jardin De L'Infante   *see Larmes
                                    (L717)
  Larmes
    SSA soli,pno DURAND s.p. see from
    Au Jardin De L'Infante   (L718)

LECOVED DEM HEILIGEN SCHABESS
  see Six Folk Songs

LECTIO LIBRI SAPIENTIAE see Ghedini, Giorgio Federico

L'ECUCREUIL see Migot, Georges

LECUONA, ERNESTO (1896-1963)
  Andalusia
    [It] solo,pno CURCI 5338 s.p.
                                    (L719)

  Malaguena
    [It] solo,pno CURCI 5357 s.p.
                                    (L720)

L'ECUREUIL see Quinet, Marcel

LED BY THE MASTER'S HAND see Lister, Mosie

L'EDEN, AUX BORD DU GANGE see
  Mendelssohn-Bartholdy, Felix

LEDERER, GEORGE
  Psalm 104 *sac,Psalm
    solo,pno PATERSON s.p.   (L721)

LEDOVA KRALOVNA see Risinger, Karel

LEDUC, JACQUES (1932-)
  A Verviers *Op.17,No.5
    see Aquarelles

  Abandon *see Birago Diop, Senegal

  Abioseh Nicol, Sierra Leone *Op.20,
    No.5
    "Au Plus Profond Des Terres" see
    Sortileges Africains

  Accords *see Birago Diog, Senegal

  Anvers *Op.17,No.2
    see Aquarelles

  Aquah Laluh, Ghana *Op.20,No.4
    "La Servante" see Sortileges
    Africains

  Aquarelles
    Mez solo,pno cmplt ed CBDM s.p.
    contains: A Verviers, Op.17,No.5;
    Anvers, Op.17,No.2; Crepuscule
    En Province, Op.17,No.6; Joli
    Mai, Op.17,No.3; Le Pays A
    L'envers, Op.17,No.4; Le
    Visiteur, Op.17,No.1   *(L722)

  Au Plus Profond Des Terres *see
    Abioseh Nicol, Sierra Leone

  Birago Diog, Senegal *Op.20,No.3
    "Accords" see Sortileges Africains

  Birago Diop, Senegal *Op.20,No.1
    "Abandon" see Sortileges Africains

  Cet Instant-La *see Dei Anang, Ghana

  Crepuscule En Province *Op.17,No.6
    see Aquarelles

  Dei Anang, Ghana *Op.20,No.2
    "Cet Instant-La" see Sortileges
    Africains

  Joli Mai *Op.17,No.3
    see Aquarelles

  La Servante *see Aquah Laluh, Ghana

  Le Pays A L'envers *Op.17,No.4
    see Aquarelles

  Le Visiteur *Op.17,No.1
    see Aquarelles

  Six Ballades De Paul Fort *Op.14,
    CC6U
    SMezBar soli,acap cmplt ed CBDM
    s.p.   (L723)

  Sortileges Africains
    med solo,al-sax,pno,perc cmplt ed
    CBDM s.p.
    contains: Abioseh Nicol, Sierra
    Leone, "Au Plus Profond Des
    Terres", Op.20,No.5; Aquah
    Laluh, Ghana, "La Servante",
    Op.20,No.4; Birago Diog,
    Senegal, "Accords", Op.20,No.3;
    Birago Diop, Senegal,
    "Abandon", Op.20,No.1; Dei
    Anang, Ghana, "Cet Instant-La",
    Op.20,No.2   (L724)

LEE, DON
  Calvary *sac
    solo,pno BENSON S5244-R $1.00
        (L725)
  Follow Jesus *sac
    solo,pno BENSON S5470-R $1.00
        (L726)
  Get In Touch With The Savior *sac
    solo,pno BENSON S5509-R $1.00
        (L727)
  God's Mighty Peace *sac
    solo,pno BENSON S5574-R $1.00
        (L728)
  I'm Looking For Jesus *sac
    solo,pno LILLENAS SM-917: SN $1.00
        (L729)
  Jesus, He Is The Son Of God *sac
    solo,pno BENSON S6707-R $1.00
        (L730)
  Keep Singin' That Love Song *sac
    solo,pno BENSON S6811-R $1.00
        (L731)
  Let Him In Today *sac
    solo,pno BENSON S6843-R $1.00
        (L732)
  Little Flowers *sac
    solo,pno BENSON S6873-R $1.00
        (L733)

LEE, DON (cont'd.)
  Our House *sac
    solo,pno BENSON S7330-R $1.00
        (L734)
  Someday *sac
    solo,pno BENSON S7537-R $1.00
        (L735)
  That's The Man I'm Looking For *sac
    solo,pno WORD S-432   (L736)
    solo,pno BENSON S7746-R $1.00
        (L737)

LEE, E. MARKHAM
  Dream Seller, The
    2 soli,pno ROBERTON 71559 s.p.
        (L738)
  Go, Lovely Rose
    2 soli,pno ROBERTON 71606 s.p.
        (L739)

LEE, LARRY
  Let Me Live At The Foot Of The Cross
    *sac
    solo,pno WORD S-357   (L740)

LEECH
  Hiding Place, The *sac
    solo,pno GENTRY $1.00   (L741)

LEES, BENJAMIN (1924-)
  Cyprian Songs *CCU
    Bar solo,pno BOOSEY $5.00   (L742)

  Six Songs Of The Night *CC6U
    S solo,pno/orch BOOSEY $3.00 (L743)

  Three Songs *CC3U
    A solo,pno BOOSEY $3.00   (L744)

LEEUW, TON DE (1926-)
  Aan Een Bode
    see Leeuw, Ton de, De Toverfluit

  Acht Europese Liederen
    med solo,pno DONEMUS s.p.   (L745)

  Aloette
    see Vier Liederen

  Als Een Droom
    solo,pno BROEKMANS 260 s.p. (L746)

  Als Ik Een Vogeltje Was
    see Leeuw, Ton de, De Toverfluit

  Berceuse Presque Negre
    med solo,pno DONEMUS s.p.   (L747)

  Brabant
    med solo,3fl,3ob,3clar,3bsn,4horn,
    3trp,3trom,tuba,timp,perc,cel,
    harp,strings DONEMUS s.p. (L748)

  Cloche
    see Vijf Liederen Van F.G. Lorca

  Danse
    see Vijf Liederen Van F.G. Lorca

  De Ontrouwe Liefste
    see Leeuw, Ton de, De Toverfluit

  De Toverfluit
    S solo,fl,vcl,pno DONEMUS s.p.
    contains also: De Ontrouwe
    Liefste; Als Ik Een Vogeltje Was;
    Onbeschrijfelijke Vreugde; Aan
    Een Bode   (L749)

  De Ueren Van De Bittere Passie Jesu
    Christi *sac
    med solo,pno DONEMUS s.p.   (L750)

  Diablerie
    S solo,pno DONEMUS s.p.   (L751)

  Die Weise Von Liebe Und Tod
    high solo,pno DONEMUS s.p.   (L752)

  Ghequetst Ben Ic Van Binnen
    see Vier Liederen

  Goden En Zangers
    S solo,pno DONEMUS s.p.   (L753)

  Haiku *CCU
    [Eng] S solo,pno DONEMUS D335 s.p.
        (L754)

  Haiku II *CCU
    S solo,5fl,5ob,4clar,4bsn,4horn,
    4trp,4trom,tuba,perc,strings
    DONEMUS s.p.   (L755)

  Le Lezard
    see Vijf Liederen Van F.G. Lorca

  Le Silence
    see Vijf Liederen Van F.G. Lorca

  Onbeschrijfelijke Vreugde
    see Leeuw, Ton de, De Toverfluit

  Prelude
    see Vijf Liederen Van F.G. Lorca

LEEUW, TON DE (cont'd.)
  Scherzando
    see Vier Liederen

  Trouvaille
    see Twee Liederen Van Gabriela
    Mistral

  Tu M'as
    see Twee Liederen Van Gabriela
    Mistral

  Twee Liederen Van Gabriela Mistral
    S solo,pno DONEMUS s.p.
    contains: Trouvaille; Tu M'as
        (L756)

  Twee Spreuken
    see Vier Liederen

  Vier Liederen
    med solo,3rec DONEMUS s.p.
    contains: Aloette; Ghequetst Ben
    Ic Van Binnen; Scherzando; Twee
    Spreuken   (L757)

  Vijf Liederen Van F.G. Lorca
    low solo,pno DONEMUS s.p.
    contains: Cloche; Danse; Le
    Lezard; Le Silence; Prelude
        (L758)

LEEUWERIK see Zagwijn, Henri

LEEUWERIK see Zweers, [Bernard]

LEEZIE LINDSAY *folk,Scot
  solo,pno (F maj) PATERSON FS48 s.p.
    (L759)

LEFANU, NICOLA (1947-)
  But Stars Remaining *scena
    female solo,acap NOVELLO 17.0287.04
    s.p.   (L760)

  Il Cantico Dei Cantici II *scena
    female solo,acap NOVELLO 17.0286.06
    s.p.   (L761)

LEFEBURE-WELY, LOUIS JAMES ALFRED
  (1817-1869)
  O Salutaris *sac
    solo,pno/org HEUGEL s.p. see from
    CHANTS RELIGIEUX   (L762)
    solo,pno/org (available in 2 keys)
    HEUGEL s.p.   (L763)
    solo,pno,vln (available in 2 keys)
    HEUGEL s.p.   (L764)

LEFEBVRE, CHANNING
  Aveu
    (Bordese, Stephen) solo,pno
    (available in 2 keys) ENOCH s.p.
    see also CHANSONS DE PAGE (L765)

  Bel Automne
    SATBar soli,pno DURAND s.p. (L766)

  Est-Ce Toi Dont Je Sens La Divine
    Presence (from Djelma)
    S solo,orch DURAND s.p., ipr (L767)
    Mez solo,orch DURAND s.p., ipr
        (L768)

  Harmonie
    2 soli,pno DURAND s.p.   (L769)

  Jour Fatal Ou Des Dieux Memes (from
    Djelma)
    S solo,pno/inst DURAND s.p. (L770)

  Les Libellules
    2 soli,pno DURAND s.p.   (L771)
    SB/MezB soli,pno DURAND s.p. (L772)

  Loin D'ici S'ouvre Un Vallon Sterile
    (from Djelma)
    Mez solo,pno/inst DURAND s.p.
        (L773)

  O Brahma, Maitre De La Vie (from
    Djelma)
    T solo,pno/inst DURAND s.p. (L774)
    Bar solo,pno/inst DURAND s.p.
        (L775)

  Souffle Des Bois
    SMezT/SMezBar soli,pno DURAND s.p.
        (L776)

  Tu Sais Trop Bien Lire En Mon Ame
    (from Djelma)
    Bar solo,pno/inst DURAND s.p.
        (L777)

LEFEVRE
  Without Him *sac
    solo,pno BENSON S8536-S $1.00
        (L778)

LE FLEM, PAUL (1881-)
  A Vous, Amants
    solo,pno/inst DURAND s.p. see from
    Cinq Chansons De Croisade (L779)

  Ahi, Amour
    solo,orch DURAND s.p., ipr see from
    Cinq Chansons De Croisade (L780)

  Cinq Chansons De Croisade *see A
    Vous, Amants; Ahi, Amour; Dame
    Ainsi Est; Li Departir De La
    Douce Contree; Seigneur, Sachez
        (L781)

LE FLEM, PAUL (cont'd.)

Dame Ainsi Est
    solo,pno/inst DURAND s.p. see from
        Cinq Chansons De Croisade (L782)

Li Departir De La Douce Contree
    solo,orch DURAND s.p., ipr see from
        Cinq Chansons De Croisade (L783)

Seigneur, Sachez
    solo,pno/inst DURAND s.p. see from
        Cinq Chansons De Croisade (L784)

LE FLEMING, CHRISTOPHER (KAYE)
    (1908-   )
    Quiet Company *Op.18, CCU
        solo,pno CRAMER   (L785)

    Three Sisters
        solo,pno CRAMER   (L786)

LEFORT, G.
    Demandez-Moi Pourquoi
        solo,acap ENOCH s.p.   (L787)
        solo,pno ENOCH s.p.   (L788)

    Hue! Ho! Tonnere!
        solo,acap ENOCH s.p.   (L789)
        solo,pno ENOCH s.p.   (L790)

LEG UW BEIDE BLANKE HANDJES see
    Dresden, Sem

LEG UW BEIDE BLANKE HANDJES see Oort,
    H.C.v.

LEG UW BEIDE BLANKE HANDJES see
    Zagwijn, Henri

LEGAY, MARCEL
    Ballade Du Desespere
        solo,pno ENOCH s.p.   (L791)
        solo,acap ENOCH s.p.   (L792)

    Berceuse
        solo,acap ENOCH s.p.   (L793)
        solo,pno ENOCH s.p.   (L794)

    Chanson De Floreal
        solo,orch ENOCH rental   (L795)

    Idylle Fanee
        solo,pno ENOCH s.p.   (L796)
        solo,acap ENOCH s.p.   (L797)

    La Chanson De Brumaire
        solo,pno ENOCH s.p. see from Les
            Chansons Du Peuple Deuxieme Serie
                                     (L798)

    La Chanson De Consolation
        solo,pno ENOCH s.p. see from Les
            Chansons Du Peuple Quatrieme
            Serie   (L799)

    La Chanson De Floreal
        solo,pno ENOCH s.p. see from LES
        CHANSONS DU PEUPLE PREMIERE SERIE
                                     (L800)

    La Chanson De Frimaire
        solo,pno ENOCH s.p. see from Les
            Chansons Du Peuple Quatrieme
            Serie   (L801)

    La Chanson De Fructidor
        solo,pno ENOCH s.p. see from Les
            Chansons Du Peuple Deuxieme Serie
                                     (L802)

    La Chanson De Germinal
        solo,pno ENOCH s.p. see from Les
            Chansons Du Peuple Deuxieme Serie
                                     (L803)

    La Chanson De La Fileuse
        solo,pno ENOCH s.p. see from Les
            Chansons Du Peuple Cinquieme
            Serie   (L804)

    La Chanson De La Muse
        solo,pno (available in 2 keys)
            ENOCH s.p. see from Les Chansons
            Du Peuple Cinquieme Serie (L805)

    La Chanson De La Paix
        solo,pno ENOCH s.p. see from Les
            Chansons Du Peuple Cinquieme
            Serie   (L806)

    La Chanson De La Rose Blanche
        solo,pno ENOCH s.p. see from Les
            Chansons Du Peuple Troisieme
            Serie   (L807)

    La Chanson De La Terre
        solo,pno ENOCH s.p. see from Les
            Chansons Du Peuple Troisieme
            Serie   (L808)

    La Chanson De La Voilette
        solo,pno ENOCH s.p. see from LES
        CHANSONS DU PEUPLE PREMIERE SERIE
                                     (L809)

    La Chanson De L'Hymenee
        solo,pno (available in 2 keys)
            ENOCH s.p. see from LES CHANSONS
            DU PEUPLE PREMIERE SERIE (L810)

LEGAY, MARCEL (cont'd.)

    La Chanson De Messidor
        solo,pno ENOCH s.p. see from Les
            Chansons Du Peuple Deuxieme Serie
                                     (L811)

    La Chanson De Mon Village
        solo,pno ENOCH s.p. see from Les
            Chansons Du Peuple Quatrieme
            Serie   (L812)

    La Chanson De Nivose
        solo,pno ENOCH s.p. see from Les
            Chansons Du Peuple Troisieme
            Serie   (L813)

    La Chanson De Pluvoise
        solo,pno ENOCH s.p. see from Les
            Chansons Du Peuple Troisieme
            Serie   (L814)

    La Chanson De Prairial
        solo,pno (available in 2 keys)
            ENOCH s.p. see from Les Chansons
            Du Peuple Deuxieme Serie (L815)

    La Chanson De Thermidor
        solo,pno (available in 2 keys)
            ENOCH s.p. see from Les Chansons
            Du Peuple Quatrieme Serie (L816)

    La Chanson De Vendemiaire
        solo,pno ENOCH s.p. see from LES
        CHANSONS DU PEUPLE PREMIERE SERIE
                                     (L817)

    La Chanson De Ventose
        solo,pno ENOCH s.p. see from Les
            Chansons Du Peuple Deuxieme Serie
                                     (L818)

    La Chanson Des Catherines
        solo,pno ENOCH s.p. see from Les
            Chansons Du Peuple Cinquieme
            Serie   (L819)

    La Chanson Des Coupes
        solo,pno ENOCH s.p. see from Les
            Chansons Du Peuple Cinquieme
            Serie   (L820)

    La Chanson Des Petites Daneuses
        solo,pno (available in 2 keys)
            ENOCH s.p. see from Les Chansons
            Du Peuple Troisieme Serie (L821)

    La Chanson Des Petits Mendiants
        solo,vln ENOCH s.p. see from LES
        CHANSONS DU PEUPLE PREMIERE SERIE
                                     (L822)

    La Chanson Des Pleurs
        solo,pno ENOCH s.p. see from Les
            Chansons Du Peuple Quatrieme
            Serie   (L823)

    La Chanson Du Chemin
        solo,pno ENOCH s.p. see from Les
            Chansons Du Peuple Cinquieme
            Serie   (L824)

    La Chanson Du Chrysantheme
        solo,pno ENOCH s.p. see from Les
            Chansons Du Peuple Troisieme
            Serie   (L825)

    La Chanson Du Coucou
        solo,pno ENOCH s.p. see from Les
            Chansons Du Peuple Quatrieme
            Serie   (L826)

    La Chanson Du Myosotis
        solo,pno ENOCH s.p. see from LES
        CHANSONS DU PEUPLE PREMIERE SERIE
                                     (L827)

    Le Bon Au Porteur
        solo,pno ENOCH s.p.   (L828)
        solo,acap ENOCH s.p.   (L829)

    Les Chansons Du Peuple Deuxieme Serie
        *see La Chanson De Brumaire; La
        Chanson De Fructidor; La Chanson
        De Germinal; La Chanson De
        Messidor; La Chanson De Prairial;
        La Chanson De Ventose   (L830)

    Les Chansons Du Peuple Troisieme
        Serie *see La Chanson De La Rose
        Blanche; La Chanson De La Terre;
        La Chanson De Nivose; La Chanson
        De Pluvoise; La Chanson Des
        Petites Daneuses; La Chanson Du
        Chrysantheme   (L831)

    Les Chansons Du Peuple Quatrieme
        Serie *see La Chanson De
        Consolation; La Chanson De
        Frimaire; La Chanson De Mon
        Village; La Chanson De Thermidor;
        La Chanson Des Pleurs; La Chanson
        Du Coucou   (L832)

    Les Chansons Du Peuple Cinquieme
        Serie *see La Chanson De La
        Fileuse; La Chanson De La Muse;
        La Chanson De La Paix; La Chanson
        Des Catherines; La Chanson Des
        Coupes; La Chanson Du Chemin
                                     (L833)

LEGAY, MARCEL (cont'd.)

    Les Cloches
        solo,pno ENOCH s.p.   (L834)
        solo,acap ENOCH s.p.   (L835)

    Mensonges
        solo,pno ENOCH s.p.   (L836)
        solo,acap ENOCH s.p.   (L837)

    Mepris
        solo,pno ENOCH s.p.   (L838)
        solo,acap ENOCH s.p.   (L839)

    Pourquoi Files-Tu?
        solo,pno ENOCH s.p.   (L840)
        solo,acap ENOCH s.p.   (L841)

    Salut Aux Alpes
        solo,pno ENOCH s.p.   (L842)
        solo,acap ENOCH s.p.   (L843)

    Soir De Mai
        solo,pno ENOCH s.p.   (L844)
        solo,acap ENOCH s.p.   (L845)

    Sujetion
        solo,acap ENOCH s.p.   (L846)
        solo,pno ENOCH s.p.   (L847)

    Tout Doux
        solo,pno ENOCH s.p.   (L848)
        solo,acap ENOCH s.p.   (L849)

    Venez Ma Mie
        solo,pno ENOCH s.p.   (L850)
        solo,acap ENOCH s.p.   (L851)

    Virelai D'Alsace
        solo,pno (available in 2 keys)
            ENOCH s.p.   (L852)
        solo,acap (available in 2 keys)
            ENOCH s.p.   (L853)

LEGE, GUNTER
    Ubi Caritas
        TBarB soli,fl,4vln (diff) study sc
            BOSSE BE 410 s.p., ipr   (L854)

LEGEND see Fromm, Herbert

LEGEND see Tchaikovsky, Piotr Ilyitch

LEGEND OF KLEINZACK see Offenbach,
    Jacques

LEGENDE see Beck, Reinhold, I.

LEGENDE see Bloch, Ernest

LEGENDE see Chabrier, Emmanuel

LEGENDE BRETONNE see Georges, Alexandre

LEGENDE DES ETOILES see Pierne, Gabriel

LEGENDE DES FLEURS see Fontenailles, H.
    de

LEGENDE DU PAPILLON see Delmet, Paul

LEGENDY see Blatny, Pavel

LEGEREMENT LE BAMBOU REMUAIT see
    Quinet, Marcel

LEGET EUCH DEM HEILAND UNTER see Bach,
    Johann Sebastian

LEGLEY, VICTOR (1915-   )
    Amalia Rodriguez *Op.47,No.3
        see Brieven Uit Portugal

    Barque D'or *Op.15,No.3
        see Cinq Melodies Francaises

    Brieven Uit Portugal
        med solo,pno cmplt ed CBDM s.p.
            contains: Amalia Rodriguez,
            Op.47,No.3; Torre De Belem,
            Op.47,No.2; Voor Degeraad,
            Op.47,No.1   (L855)

    Cinq Melodies Francaises
        A solo,pno cmplt ed CBDM s.p.
            contains: Barque D'or, Op.15,
            No.3; Faubourg Gitane, Op.15,
            No.4; La Mort, Op.15,No.2; Le
            Voyageur, Op.15,No.5; Odelette,
            Op.15,No.1   (L856)

    Een Lied Der Blijdschap *Op.50
        T solo,pno CBDM s.p.   (L857)

    Faubourg Gitane *Op.15,No.4
        see Cinq Melodies Francaises

    La Mort *Op.15,No.2
        see Cinq Melodies Francaises

    La Verite *Op.45,No.1
        see Migration Des Ames

    Le Caillou Bleu *Op.45,No.2
        see Migration Des Ames

LEGLEY, VICTOR (cont'd.)

Le Voyageur *Op.15,No.5
see Cinq Melodies Francaises

Migration Des Ames
S solo,pno cmplt ed CBDM s.p.
contains: La Verite, Op.45,No.1;
Le Caillou Bleu, Op.45,No.2;
Nous Rencontrerons-Nous?,
Op.45,No.4; Quand Finira Le
Sortilege, Op.45,No.3   (L858)

Nous Rencontrerons-Nous? *Op.45,No.4
see Migration Des Ames

Odelette *Op.15,No.1
see Cinq Melodies Francaises

Quand Finira Le Sortilege *Op.45,
No.3
see Migration Des Ames

Torre De Belem *Op.47,No.2
see Brieven Uit Portugal

Voor Degeraad *Op.47,No.1
see Brieven Uit Portugal

Zeng *Op.63,No.1-7, CC7L
S solo,pno/4strings cmplt ed CBDM
s.p.   (L859)

L'EGLISE DU VILLAGE see Cuvillier,
Charles

LEGRENZI, GIOVANNI (1626-1690)
Acclamazioni Divote A Voce Sola *CCU
solo,pno FORNI s.p.   (L860)

Cantatas And Canzonets For Solo Voice
*CCU
(Seay, Albert) [It] A/B/S/T solo,
inst A-R ED s.p.   (L861)

Tosto Dal Vicin Bosco (from Totila)
solo,trp,timp CARISH s.p. (L862)

LEGS, THE see Blank, Allan

LEGUERNEY, JACQUES (1906-   )
A Son Page
med solo,pno SALABERT-US $3.00 see
from Vingt Poemes De La Pleiade
(L863)

Au Sommeil
high solo,pno SALABERT-US $2.25 see
from Vingt Poemes De La Pleiade
(L864)

Bel Aubepin
high solo,pno SALABERT-US $3.75 see
from Vingt Poemes De La Pleiade
(L865)

Clotilde
see Deux Melodies

Deux Melodies
solo,pno/inst cmplt ed DURAND s.p.
contains: Clotilde; L'adieu
(L866)

Genievres Herisses
high solo,pno SALABERT-US $3.75 see
from Vingt Poemes De La Pleiade
(L867)

Je Me Lamente
high solo,pno SALABERT-US $3.75 see
from Vingt Poemes De La Pleiade
(L868)

Je Vous Envoie
high solo,pno SALABERT-US $3.75 see
from Vingt Poemes De La Pleiade
(L869)

L'adieu
see Deux Melodies

Ma Douce Jouvence Est Passee
med solo,pno SALABERT-US $1.50 see
from Vingt Poemes De La Pleiade
(L870)

Si Mille Oeillets
high solo,pno SALABERT-US $3.75 see
from Vingt Poemes De La Pleiade
(L871)

Vingt Poemes De La Pleiade *see A
Son Page; Au Sommeil; Bel
Aubepin; Genievres Herisses; Je
Me Lamente; Je Vous Envoie; Ma
Douce Jouvence Est Passee; Si
Mille Oeillets   (L872)

LEHAR, FRANZ (1870-1948)
Bimba Vuoi Trovar Un Bel Garzon (from
Frasquita)
[It] solo,pno BONGIOVANI 943 s.p.
(L873)

Bimbe Mie, A Vent'anni Mi Par Di
Tornar (from Frasquita)
[It] solo,pno BONGIOVANI 935 s.p.
(L874)

Cancion De Vilia (from Die Lustige
Witwe)
[Ger/Span] S solo,pno RICORDI-ARG
BA 10308 s.p.   (L875)

LEHAR, FRANZ (cont'd.)

Chissa Chi Amero Doman (from
Frasquita)
[It] solo,pno BONGIOVANI 937 s.p.
(L876)

Chiudi Gli Occhi (from Frasquita)
[It] solo,pno BONGIOVANI 945 s.p.
(L877)

Cuor D'amante Richiede Gran Cosa Lo
Sai (from Frasquita)
[It] solo,pno BONGIOVANI 934 s.p.
(L878)

Da Geh Ich Zu Maxim (from Die Lustige
Witwe)
solo,pno DOBLINGER 88 511 s.p.
(L879)

Dein Ist Mein Ganzes Herz (from El
Pais De Las Sonrisas)
"Tuyo Es Mi Corazon" [Ger/Span] T
solo,pno RICORDI-ARG BA 10046
s.p.   (L880)

Dell'alcova Nel Tepor (from
Frasquita)
[It] solo,pno BONGIOVANI 936 s.p.
(L881)

En Mi Cama Hay Un Dosel *see Hab'
Ein Blaues Himmelbett!

Fox-Trot De Las "Giglettes" (from La
Danza Della Libelule)
[Span] solo,pno RICORDI-ARG BA 8136
s.p.   (L882)

Gern Hab' Ich Die Frau'n Gekusst
(from Paganini)
"Siempre A Una Mujer Bese" [Ger/
Span] T solo,pno RICORDI-ARG
BA 10015 s.p.   (L883)

Hab' Ein Blaues Himmelbett! (from
Frasquita)
"En Mi Cama Hay Un Dosel" [Ger/
Span] T solo,pno RICORDI-ARG
BA 10016 s.p.   (L884)

Je Chante Pour Toi
solo,pno ENOCH s.p. see from LES
CHANSONS DU PEUPLE PREMIERE SERIE
(L885)
solo,acap ENOCH s.p. see from LES
CHANSONS DU PEUPLE PREMIERE SERIE
(L886)

Komm In Den Kleinen Pavillon (from
Die Lustige Witwe)
solo,pno DOBLINGER 88 512 s.p.
(L887)

Lippen Schweigen (from Die Lustige
Witwe)
solo,pno DOBLINGER 88 510 s.p.
(L888)

Quand'in Ciel Steso Un Vel (from
Frasquita)
[It] solo,pno BONGIOVANI 933 s.p.
(L889)

Siempre A Una Mujer Bese *see Gern
Hab' Ich Die Frau'n Gekusst

Tuyo Es Mi Corazon *see Dein Ist
Mein Ganzes Herz

Vilia (from Die Lustige Witwe)
med solo,pno (F maj) CENTURY 3350
(L890)

Vilja-Lied (from Die Lustige Witwe)
high solo,pno DOBLINGER 88 508 s.p.
(L891)
low solo,pno DOBLINGER 88 509 s.p.
(L892)

War Es Auch Nichts Als Ein Traum Vom
Gluck (from Eva)
solo,pno DOBLINGER 88 513 s.p.
(L893)

LEHDOKKI see Kilpinen, Yrio

LEHMAN
Love Of God, The *sac,gospel
solo,pno LILLENAS SM-607: RN $1.00
(L894)
solo,pno BENSON S7972-S $1.00
(L895)
solo,pno ABER.GRP. $1.50   (L896)

LEHMANN, HANS ULRICH (1937-   )
A La Recherche
solo,org GERIG HG 1128 s.p. (L897)

Bringen Um Zu Kommen
S solo,fl,clar,bass clar,vln,vcl
GERIG HG 1038 s.p.   (L898)

LEHMANN, LIZA (1862-1918)
Ah, Moon Of My Delight!
low solo,pno (F maj) CRAMER $.70
(L899)
high solo,pno (G maj) CRAMER $1.10
(L900)
med-high solo,pno (F maj) BOSTON
$1.50   (L901)
high solo,pno (G maj) BOSTON $1.50
(L902)
high solo,pno (G maj) ALLANS s.p.
(L903)
low solo,pno (F maj) ALLANS s.p.
(L904)

LEHMANN, LIZA (cont'd.)

Alas That Spring
solo,pno CRAMER   (L905)

Bird In The Sky
solo,pno CRAMER   (L906)

Cuckoo
solo,pno (C maj) BOOSEY $1.50
(L907)

If I Had But Two Little Wings
solo,pno CRAMER   (L908)

If No One Ever Marries Me
high solo,pno (D maj) BOOSEY $1.50
(L909)
low solo,pno (C maj) BOOSEY $1.50
(L910)

In A Persian Garden *song cycle
4 soli,pno SCHIRM.G $3.50 (L911)
solo,pno CRAMER   (L912)

Myself When Young
high solo,pno (F maj) CRAMER (L913)
low solo,pno (E flat maj) CRAMER
(L914)

When The Shadows Fall To-Night
solo,pno CRAMER   (L915)

Whene'er A Snowflake Leaves The Sky
low solo,pno CRAMER   (L916)
med solo,pno CRAMER   (L917)
high solo,pno CRAMER   (L918)

LEHNER, LEO (1900-   )
Frohsinn Im Ranzel
solo,inst DOBLINGER 08 810 s.p.
(L919)

Funf Wanderlieder *CC5U
solo,pno DOBLINGER s.p., ea. (L920)

Ganseblumchen Und Schmetterling
solo,pno DOBLINGER 08 621 s.p.
(L921)

Kindersang Schafft Frohe Herzen
*CC17U
solo,pno DOBLINGER 08 623 s.p.
(L922)

LEHNER, WALTER
Und Fried Den Menschen Auf Der Erd
*CC6U, Xmas
[Ger] med solo,2vln,vcl sc
DOBLINGER $1.50   (L923)

LEHNERT, JOSEF ROBERT (1891-1968)
Brousek Pro Tvuj Jazycek
"Schleisten Fur Deine Kleine Zunge"
[Czech/Ger] high solo,pno PANTON
s.p.   (L924)

Schleisten Fur Deine Kleine Zunge
*see Brousek Pro Tvuj Jazycek

LEICHTLING, ALAN
Canticle No. 1
S solo,fl sc SEESAW $5.00 (L925)

Eleven Songs From "A Shropshire Lad"
*CC11U
Bar solo,chamb.orch sc SEESAW
$50.00   (L926)

Psalm 37 *sac
A solo,harp,pno,4perc,4strings sc
SEESAW $24.00   (L927)

Rubaiyat Fragments
B solo,clar,horn,pno sc SEESAW
$15.00   (L928)

Songs In Winter
S solo,pno sc SEESAW $15.00 (L929)

Three Songs By E. Dickinson *CC3U
Bar solo,vcl sc SEESAW $3.00 (L930)

Trial And Death Of Socrates
B solo,clar,fl,harp sc SEESAW $6.00
(L931)

Two Proverbs *CC2U
A solo,3clar sc SEESAW $4.00 (L932)

LEID see Schmitt, Florent

LEIGH, F.
Only A Little Box Of Soldiers *see
Arnold, Malcolm

LEIH MIR VON DEINEM SAITENSPIEL see
Borris, Siegfried

LEIKITAANKO see Merikanto, Oskar

LEISE FLEHEN MEINE LIEDER see Schubert,
Franz (Peter), Standchen

LEISE, GANZ LEISE see Straus, Oscar

LEISE, LEISE, FROMM WEISE see Weber,
Carl Maria von

LEISE LIEDER see Strauss, Richard

LEISES LIED see Strauss, Richard

LEISRING, VOLKMAR (1588-1637)
Nouse, Ole Kirkas
"Res Dig, Var Ljus" solo,pno FAZER
F 3660 s.p. (L933)

Res Dig, Var Ljus *see Nouse, Ole
Kirkas

LEISTNER-MAYER, ROLAND
Stauung
female solo,perc,vcl,bvl,gtr study
sc ORLANDO s.p. (L934)

Wahrend Das Drama Der Zeit
S solo,drums,timp,bvl, bass trumpet
ORLANDO s.p. (L935)

LEIVISKA, HELVI (LEMMIKKI) (1902-   )
Liekki *Op.34,No.2
solo,pno FAZER F 5201 s.p. (L936)

Runolintuni *Op.34,No.1
solo,pno FAZER F 5202 s.p. (L937)

Sydan *Op.13,No.1
solo,pno FAZER F 5200 s.p. (L938)

LEIVONEN see Kilpinen, Yrio

LEIVONEN see Palmgren, Selim

LEJDSTROM
Ingalill
solo,pno LUNDQUIST s.p. (L939)

LE JEUNE, H.
Chanson
(Pujol) [Fr] med solo,gtr ESCHIG
E1320 $.90 (L940)

LEKBERG, SVEN (1899-   )
Ballad Of Trees And The Master
high solo,pno (G maj) GALAXY
1.1809.7 $1.00 (L941)

Come Let Us Sing Unto The Lord *sac
high solo/med solo,pno (C maj)
GALAXY 1.2285.7 $1.25 (L942)

O, Lord, Thou Hast Searched Me *sac
med-high solo,pno (C min) SCHIRM.G
$.85 (L943)

Road To Avrille, The
high solo,pno (G flat maj) SCHIRM.G
$.85 (L944)

Spring And The Fall, The
high solo,pno (F min) SCHIRM.G $.85
(L945)

LEKENDE BARN see Kjeldaas, Arnljot

LELANT see Piggott, Audrey

L'ELEVE DE SAINT-CYR see Ugalde, Mme

LELITA see Levidis, Dimitri

L'ELOGIO DELLA BOCCA see Panizza,
Ettore

L'ELUE see Fabre, G.

LEMAIRE
Marchioness, Your Dancing
low solo,pno (F maj) ALLANS s.p.
(L946)
high solo,pno (G maj) ALLANS s.p.
(L947)

LEMAIRE, F.
Berceuse
solo,pno (available in 2 keys)
ENOCH s.p. (L948)

Eveille-Toi
solo,pno (available in 2 keys)
ENOCH s.p. (L949)

Fleurs Fanees
solo,pno (available in 2 keys)
ENOCH s.p. (L950)

Serenade
solo,pno ENOCH s.p. (L951)

LEMARE
Andantino
low solo,pno (G maj) CENTURY 3627
(L952)

L'EMBARQUEMENT POUR L'IDEAL see Paray,
Paul

LEMBRANCAS DO CORACAO see Prado,
Almeida

LEMMENHENKI see Merikanto, Oskar

LEMON, L.G.
My Ain Folk
low solo,pno (D flat maj) BOOSEY
$1.50 (L953)
med solo,pno (E flat maj) BOOSEY
$1.50 (L954)
med-high solo,pno (F maj) BOOSEY

LEMON, L.G. (cont'd.)
$1.50 (L955)
high solo,pno (G maj) BOOSEY $1.50
(L956)

LEMONT, CEDRIC WILMOT (1879-1954)
No More Trouble For Me
med solo,pno PRESSER $.75 (L957)

L'EMPREINTE see Daniel-Lesur

LENAU-LIEDER see Philipp, Franz

LEND ME YOUR AID see Gounod, Charles
Francois, Inspirez Moi!

LENEL, LUDWIG
All Praise To Thee, Eternal God *sac
med solo,pno oct CONCORDIA 98-1402
$.25 (L958)

O Morning Star, So Pure, So Bright
*sac
med solo,pno oct CONCORDIA 98-1452
$.25 (L959)

Wachet Auf! Ruft Uns Die Stimme *sac
"Wake, Awake, For Night Is Flying"
med solo,pno oct CONCORDIA
98-1453 $.30 (L960)

Wake, Awake, For Night Is Flying
*see Wachet Auf! Ruft Uns Die
Stimme

L'ENFANCE see Kosma, J.

L'ENFANCE DE L'ART see Daniel-Lesur

L'ENFANT see Delage, Maurice

L'ENFANT AU PARADIS see Mesritz Van
Velthuysen, Annie

L'ENFANT DISAIT UN SOIR see Mesritz Van
Velthuysen, Annie

L'ENFANT ET LE PAPILLON see Arensky,
Anton Stepanovitch

L'ENLEVEMENT see Saint-Saens, Camille

L'ENLEVEMENT EN MER see Delvincourt,
Claude

LENNOX, L.
Songs And Jokes For Little Folks
*CCU
solo,pno LEONARD-ENG (L961)

LENORMAND, RENE (1846-1932)
A La Grand'Messe
solo,pno (available in 2 keys)
ENOCH s.p. (L962)

Dans La Brume
solo,pno (available in 2 keys)
ENOCH s.p. (L963)

Le Chant Des Veilles Maisons
solo,pno (available in 2 keys)
ENOCH s.p. (L964)

LENOT, JACQUES (1945-   )
Air De Concert
Mez solo,orch sc ZERBONI 7932 s.p.
(L965)
Cinq Sonnets De Louise Labe *CC5U
S solo,pic,fl,clar,pno,cel,marimba,
vibra,vcl,bvl,gtr AMPHION A 313
s.p. (L966)

Karl Exsultate
S solo,orch sc,quarto ZERBONI 7861
s.p. (L967)

LENSKI'S ARIA see Tchaikovsky, Piotr
Ilyitch, Lensky's Song

LENSKY'S ARIA see Tchaikovsky, Piotr
Ilyitch

LENSKY'S ARIA see Tchaikovsky, Piotr
Ilyitch, Lensky's Song

LENSKY'S SONG see Tchaikovsky, Piotr
Ilyitch

LENTE see Mulder, Ernest W.

LENTE see Rennes, Cath. v.

LENTE see Witte, D.

LENTE TRIOLETTEN see Faddegon-Keene, E.

LENTELEVEN see Rennes, Cath. v.

LENTEMENT, DOUCEMENT, TENDREMENT see
Hermite, M.

LENTEMENT, LENTEMENT see Filipucci,
Edm.

LENTEMENT TU ME PRENDS MA VIE see
Filipucci, Edm.

L'ENTRESOL see Lacome, Paul

LENZ see Lilien, Ignace

LENZ see Schafer, Dirk

LENZGESANG see Sibelius, Jean

LENZHOFFEN see Bijvanck, Henk

LENZPASSION see Trunk, Richard

LEO, LEONARDO (1694-1744)
Praebe, Virgo, Benignas Aures *sac,
mot
(Ewerhart, Rudolf) [Lat] solo,org
BIELER CS 15 s.p. (L968)

Salve Regina *sac,cant
(Ewerhart, Rudolf) [Lat] S solo,
2vln,cont sc BIELER DK 4 s.p.
ipa (L969)

LEONARD
I Heard A Robin Singing
solo,pno ALLANS s.p. (L970)

LEONCAVALLO, RUGGIERO (1858-1919)
Aubade *see Mattinata

E Destin! Debbo Andarmene (from La
Boheme)
[It/Ger] Mez solo,pno SONZOGNO 1008
s.p. (L971)

E Un Riso Gentil (from Zaza)
[It] T solo,pno SONZOGNO 1066 $1.25
(L972)

His Eyes With Fire Were Flaming *see
Qual Fiamma Avea Nel Guardo

Io Non Ho Che Una Povera Stanzetta
(from La Boheme)
[It/Ger] T solo,pno SONZOGNO 953
s.p. (L973)

Mattinata
[It] S/T solo,pno RICORDI-ARG
BA 6384 s.p. (L974)
high solo,pno LUNDQUIST s.p. (L975)
low solo,pno LUNDQUIST s.p. (L976)
"Aubade" [Fr/It] S/T solo,pno (sold
in France only) RICORDI-FR s.p.
(L977)
"'Tis The Day" low solo,pno BELWIN
$1.50 (L978)
"'Tis The Day" high solo,pno BELWIN
$1.50 (L979)
"Wake With The Dawn" [It/Eng] med
solo,pno (D flat maj) SCHIRM.G
$.85 (L980)

No! Pagliaccio Non Son (from
Pagliacci)
[It] T solo,pno SONZOGNO 718 $1.25
(L981)

O Colombina (from Pagliacci)
[It] T solo,pno SONZOGNO 717 $1.25
(L982)
[It/Eng] T solo,pno (A min)
SCHIRM.G $.60 (L983)

O Mio Piccolo Tavolo (from Zaza)
[It] T solo,pno SONZOGNO 1067 $1.25
(L984)

Pauvre Paillasse (from Pagliacci)
solo,orch HENN s.p. (L985)

Put On Your Smock *see Vesti La
Giubba

Qual Fiamma Avea Nel Guardo (from
Pagliacci)
[It] S solo,pno SONZOGNO 715 $1.25
(L986)
"His Eyes With Fire Were Flaming"
[It/Eng] S solo,pno SCHIRM.G $.85
(L987)

Serenade Francaise
[Fr] high solo,pno CHOUDENS C16
s.p. (L988)
[Fr] high solo,vln,pno CHOUDENS
C234 s.p. (L989)
[Fr] med solo,pno CHOUDENS C17 s.p.
(L990)

Serenade Napolitaine
[Fr] high solo,pno CHOUDENS C18
s.p. (L991)
[Fr] med solo,pno CHOUDENS C19 s.p.
(L992)

Serenata De Arlequin (from Pagliacci)
[It] T solo,pno RICORDI-ARG BA 9750
s.p. (L993)

Si Puo? (from I Pagliacci)
[It] Bar solo,pno RICORDI-ARG
BA 9748 s.p. (L994)
[It] Bar solo,pno SONZOGNO 714
$1.25 (L995)
[It/Eng] Bar solo,pno BELWIN
NY 1399 $1.00 (L996)

LEONCAVALLO, RUGGIERO (cont'd.)

Testa Adorata (from La Boheme)
[It/Ger] T solo,pno SONZOGNO 2360
s.p.   (L997)

'Tis The Day   *see Mattinata

Vesti La Giubba (from Pagliacci)
[It] T solo,pno SONZOGNO 716 $1.25
(L998)
"Put On Your Smock" [It/Eng] T
solo,pno (D min) SCHIRM.G $.85
(L999)
"Put On Your Smock" [It/Eng] T
solo,pno (E min) SCHIRM.G $.85
(L1000)
Wake With The Dawn *see Mattinata

Zaza, Piccola Zingara (from Zaza)
[It/Ger/Eng] Bar solo,pno SONZOGNO
1069 $1.25   (L1001)
[It/Eng] Bar solo,pno INTERNAT.
$1.00   (L1002)

LEONI, FRANCO
Little China Figure, A
high solo,pno (G maj) SCHIRM.G $.75
(L1003)
Stars
high solo,pno (F maj) CRAMER
(L1004)
low solo,pno (C maj) CRAMER (L1005)

Tally-Ho!
low solo,pno (D maj) SCHIRM.G $.85
(L1006)
low solo,pno (D maj) ALLANS s.p.
(L1007)
high solo,pno (F maj) ALLANS s.p.
(L1008)

LEONIDAS see Wissmer, Pierre

LEONORA'S ARIA see Godard, Benjamin
Louis Paul

LEONOREN LAULU see Pacius, Fredrik

LEONORES SANG see Pacius, Fredrik,
Leonoren Laulu

L'EPINGLE see Bernicat, F.

L'EPIPHANIE DES EXILES see Jongen,
Joseph-Marie-Alphonse-Nicholas

L'EPITAPHE VILLON see Booren, Jo VAN
DEN

L'EPOUSE see Messiaen, Oliver

L'ERA FASOL!
(Carlo, Musi) solo,pno (Bolognese
dialect) BONGIOVANI 2071 s.p. see
from El Mi Canzunett   (L1009)

LERCHENLIED see Smetana, Bedrich

LERKA see Beck, Thomas [Ludvigsen]

LERMA, P.
Dicen
[Span] med solo,pno UNION ESP.
$1.25   (L1010)

Duermete Ya
[Span] med solo,pno UNION ESP.
$1.10   (L1011)

LEROUX, XAVIER (HENRY NAPOLEON)
(1863-1919)
La Petite Feuille Morte
solo,pno ENOCH s.p.   (L1012)

Les Tendres Erreurs
solo,pno ENOCH s.p.   (L1013)

L'Infidele En Terre
solo,pno ENOCH s.p.   (L1014)

Par Les Chemins De France *CC10L
solo,pno cmplt ed ENOCH s.p.   (L1015)

LE ROY, A.
J'ai Le Rebours
(Pujol) [Fr] med solo,gtr ESCHIG
E1311 $.90   (L1016)

Je Ne Suis Moins Aimable
(Pujol) [Fr] med solo,gtr ESCHIG
E1312 $.90   (L1017)

Laissez La Verte Couleur
(Pujol) [Fr] med solo,gtr ESCHIG
E1313 $.90   (L1018)

Mes Peines Et Ennuis
(Pujol) [Fr] med solo,gtr ESCHIG
E1310 $1.00   (L1019)

LES ABEILLES DE GRAND-MERE see
Schlosser, Paul

LES ADIEUX see Ronald, Sir Landon

LES ADIEUX DE CLAES see Vogel, Wladimir

LES ADIEUX DE NEMOURS see Migot,
Georges

LES AILES DU REVE see Chretien, H.

LES AILES DU REVE see Mignan, Edouard-
Charles-Octave

LES AILES VICTORIEUSES see Amirian,
M.T.

LES ALPINS see Fragerolle, G.

LES AMANTS see Scotto, Vincent

LES AMANTS SEPARES see Lesur, Daniel

LES AMANTS TRAHIS see Rameau, Jean-
Philippe

LES AMAZONES see Chaminade, Cecile

LES AMIS D'ENFANCE see Lapeyre, Therese

LES AMOUREUSES see Berger, Rod.

LES AMOURS DU POETE see Schumann,
Robert (Alexander), Dichterliebe

LES AMOURS D'UN POETE see Schumann,
Robert (Alexander), Dichterliebe

LES ANGES see Satie, Erik

LES ANIMAUX ET LEURS HOMMES see
Sauguet, Henri

LES APOTHEOSES see Tremisot, Ed.

LES ARMES DU BARON
(Fragerolle, G.) solo,pno ENOCH s.p.
see from Chansons Du Pays-Lorrain
(L1020)
(Fragerolle, G.) solo,acap ENOCH s.p.
see from Chansons Du Pays-Lorrain
(L1021)

LES ATTRAITS see Viardot-Garcia,
Pauline

LES AVOCATS DE L'HIVER see Michiels, G.

LES BAINS DE MER see Collin, L.

LES BAISERS see Goublier, G.

LES BAISERS D'AUTREFOIS see Douay, G.

LES BAISERS SONT DES FLEURS see
Fontenailles, H. de

LES BAISERS SONT DES PAPILLONS see
Mignan, Edouard-Charles-Octave

LES BALADINS see Migot, Georges

LES BARQUES ETERNELLES see Hue,
[Georges-Adolphe]

LES BATELIERS see Georges, Alexandre

LES BETISES see Roger, Victor

LES BETISES QUE DIT NICOLAS see
Delbruck, J.

LES BIENS DONT VOUS ESTES LA DAME see
Roger-Ducasse, Jean-Jules Aimable

LES BLES see Mendelssohn-Bartholdy,
Felix

LES BLEUETS see Delmet, Paul

LES BLEUETS, LES MARGUERITES, LES
COQUELICOTS see Dere, Jean

LES BOEUFS see Albersenn

LES BOHEMIENS see Schumann, Robert
(Alexander), Zigeunerleben

LES BRETELLES see Chatau, H.

LES BRUITS DE LA NUIT see Kosma, J.

LES BULLETINS DE VOTE see Pourny, Ch.

LES CAILLOUX see Dere, Jean

LES CANARDS see Vellere, Lucie

LES CANARDS, LES CYGNES, LES OIES see
Stravinsky, Igor

LES CANCANS see Berger, Rod.

LES CANETONS see Schlosser, Paul

LES CAPRICES DE MARIANNE see Sauguet,
Henri

LES CHAGRINS ROSES see Delmet, Paul

LES CHANSONS COMPOSEES SUR LA POESIE
CHINOISE see Bazlik, Miro

LES CHANSONS D'AGNOUTINE see Bonnal,
Ermend

LES CHANSONS DE BILITIS see Debussy,
Claude

LES CHANSONS DE FRANCOISE SAGAN see
Magne, Michel

LES CHANSONS DE J. GRANIER see
Serpette, Gaston

LES CHANSONS DE MIARKA see Georges,
Alexandre

LES CHANSONS DE PARIS *CC34U,Fr
[Fr] med solo,pno FRANCE $1.25, ea.
in two volumes   (L1022)

LES CHANSONS DU PEUPLE PREMIERE SERIE
*see Legay, Marcel, La Chanson De
Floreal; Legay, Marcel, La Chanson
De La Voilette; Legay, Marcel, La
Chanson De L'Hymenee; Legay,
Marcel, La Chanson De Vendemiaire;
Legay, Marcel, La Chanson Des
Petits Mendiants; Legay, Marcel, La
Chanson Du Myosotis; Lehar, Franz,
Je Chante Pour Toi   (L1023)

LES CHANSONS DU PEUPLE DEUXIEME SERIE
see Legay, Marcel

LES CHANSONS DU PEUPLE TROISIEME SERIE
see Legay, Marcel

LES CHANSONS DU PEUPLE QUATRIEME SERIE
see Legay, Marcel

LES CHANSONS DU PEUPLE CINQUIEME SERIE
see Legay, Marcel

LES CHANTEFLEURS see Wiener, Jean

LES CHANTERIES DU JEUNE AGE see
Strimer, Joseph

LES CHANTS DE LA JEUNESSE, VOL. I
*CC20L
solo,pno DURAND s.p. contains works
by: Mozart; Saint-Saens;
Rothschild;Carpentier; Gluck and
others   (L1024)

LES CHANTS DE L'AMOUR see Maurat,
Edmond

LES CHARPENTIERS DU ROI see Aubert,
Louis-Francois-Marie

LES CHATS see Diepenbrock, Alphons

LES CHEMINS see Trabadelo, A. de

LES CHEMINS DE L'AMOUR see Poulenc,
Francis

LES CHEVALIERS DU CIEL see Holmes,
Alfred

LES CHEVAUX MARINS see Arrieu, Claude

LES CHEVEUX see Debussy, Claude

LES CHOSES VONT PARTOUT DE LA SORTE A
LA RONDE see Levade, Charles
(Gaston)

LES CHRYSANTHEMES see King, Harold C.

LES CHRYSANTHEMES D'OR see Migot,
Georges

LES CIGALES see Chabrier, Emmanuel

LES CINQ FILLES D'ORLAMONDE see Dukas,
Paul

LES CLOCHES see Carolus-Duran, P.

LES CLOCHES see Debussy, Claude

LES CLOCHES see Denza, Luigi

LES CLOCHES see Honegger, Arthur

LES CLOCHES see Legay, Marcel

LES CLOCHES DE LA MER see Saint-Saens,
Camille

LES CLOCHES DU SOIR see Franck, Cesar

LES CLOCHETONS DU MUGUET see Arma, Paul

LES COLOMBES see Delage, Maurice

LES COLOMBES see Falla, Manuel de

LES COLOMBES see Gui, Vittorio

LES COLUMBES see Pennequin, J.-G.

LES CONSTRUCTEURS see Durey, Louis

LES CONTES DE PERRAULT see Lacome, Paul

LES COQUELICOTS see Defontaine, M.

LES COUDES DANS L'HERBE see Barbier, Rene

LES CYGNES see Darcieux, F.

LES DAMES DE COEUR see Wachs, F.

LES DANSES DE LORMONT see Franck, Cesar

LES DEMOISELLES D'AVIGNON see Delage, Maurice

LES DENTELLES see Berger, Rod.

LES DEUX AMES see Gaubert, Philippe

LES DEUX BAISERS see Georges, Alexandre

LES DEUX BAISERS see Vieu, Jane

LES DEUX COEURS see Chaminade, Cecile

LES DEUX COEURS see Fontenailles, H. de

LES DEUX COLOMBES see Gastinel, Leon-Gustave-Cypien

LES DEUX CORTEGES see Wolff, A.

LES DEUX ENFANTS DE ROIS see Holmes, Alfred

LES DEUX FLUTES see Beekhuis, Hanna

LES DEUX GGRENADIERS see Schumann, Robert (Alexander), Die Beiden Grenadiere

LES DEUX GRENADIERS see Schumann, Robert (Alexander)

LES DEUX GRENOUILLES see Schlosser, Paul

LES DEUX GUERRIERS see Messiaen, Oliver

LES DEUX MENETRIERS see Chaminade, Cecile

LES DEUX SOEURS see Dupre, Marcel

LES DIAMANTS see Dukas, Paul

LES DIEUX QUE J'APPELAIS see Beydts, L.

LES DINDONS NOIRS see Schlosser, Paul

LES DINERS SE FONT EN COURANT see Schmitt, Florent

LES DIONYSIES see Vuillermoz, Emile

LES DOUZE see Woronoff, Wladmir

LES DUEX GRENADIERS see Wagner, Richard

LES ELFES see Badings, Henk

LES ELFES see Mendelssohn-Bartholdy, Felix

LES ELOIGNES see Dufresne, C.

LES EMBOITEURS see Perpignan, F.

LES ENFANTS see Georges, Alexandre

LES ENFANTS DE NOTRE BRETAGNE see Levade, Charles (Gaston)

LES ENFANTS ET LES AMOUREUX see Flegier, Ange

LES ENFANTS QUI S'AIMENT see Kosma, J.

LES ERRANTS see Bijl, Theo van der

LES ERREURS see DuBois, Pierre Max

LES ETOILES see Carolus-Duran, P.

LES ETOILES D'OR see Rabey, Rene

LES EXILES see Holmes, Alfred

LES FABLES DE LA FONTAINE see Pascal, Andre

LES FAUCHEURS see Berger, Jean

LES FAUNES see Coppola, Piero

LES FEES see Lacome, Paul

LES FEES see Saint-Saens, Camille

LES FEMMES see Campra, Andre

LES FEMMES DE FRANCE see Delmet, Paul

LES FEMMES SAVANTES see Varques, F.

LES FETES CHRETIENNES: LES ROIS see Lacome, Paul

LES FETES CHRETIENNES: LES SAINTS INNOCENTS see Lacome, Paul

LES FETES CHRETIENNES: PAQUES see Lacome, Paul

LES FETES ROUGES see Jongen, Joseph-Marie-Alphonse-Nicholas

LES FEUILLES MORTES see Kosma, J.

LES FEUX DU BIVOUAC see Caby, R.

LES FIANCES see Chaminade, Cecile

LES FILEUSES see Lachaume, A.

LES FILLES DE CADIX see Delibes, Leo

LES FILLES DE MAYFAIR see Arrieu, Claude

LES FILLES DE TOSA see Lacome, Paul

LES FILLES DES CADIX see Delibes, Leo

LES FILLETTES AU BOIS see Lacome, Paul

LES FLEURS see Bloch, Ernest

LES FLEURS see Satie, Erik

LES FLEURS BUTINEES see Arma, Paul

LES FLEURS NE MENTENT JAMAIS see Hermite, M.

LES FLOCONS DE NEIGE BLANCS see Bagge, G.

LES FONDATEURS DE L'OPERA-COMIQUE *CC24L
1-2 soli,pno cmplt ed ENOCH s.p.
contains works by: De La Halle;
Noverre; Dauvergne; Philidor;
Dalayrac and others (L1025)

LES FONDATEURS DE L'OPERA FRANCAIS *CC20L
solo,pno cmplt ed ENOCH s.p. contains
works by: Lulli; Campra; Destouches
(L1026)

LES FORETS see Gretchaninov, Alexander Tikhonovitch

LES FOURMIS see Schlosser, Paul

LES GARBES DOMEN AL CAMP see Toldra, Eduardo

LES GODILLOTS see Cuvillier, Charles

LES GRANDS PEUPLIERS see Richepin, T.

LES GRANDS VENTS VENUS D'OUTRE-MER see Ravel, Maurice

LES GROSEILLES see Lacome, Paul

LES GUEUSES see Scotto, Vincent

LES GUEUX AU PARADIS see Arrieu, Claude

LES HANNETONS see Lacome, Paul

LE'S HAVE A UNION see Johnson, Hall

LES HEURES see Chausson, Ernest

LES HEURES D'ETE see Rhene-Baton

LES HEURES PROPICES see Ropartz, Joseph Guy

LES HEUREUSES see Chaminade, Cecile

LES HIBOUX see Revel, Peter

LES HIRONDELLES see Cuvillier, Charles

LES HIRONDELLES DE MER see Flegier, Ange

LES ILLUMINATIONS see Bordewijk-Roepman, Johanna

LES ILLUMINATIONS DE RIMBAUD see Britten, Benjamin

LES INESTIMABLES CHRONIQUES DU BON GEANT GARGANTUA see Francaix, Jean

LES INGENUS see Debussy, Claude

LES JARDINS DE LA TOUR PENTHIEVRE see Pascal, Andre

LES JETS D'EAU see Roger-Ducasse, Jean-Jules Aimable

LES JEUX DE PARIS see Stehman, Jacques

LES JOURS PERDUS see Magne, Michel

LES LACS see Migot, Georges

LES LANGUAGES DE FEU see Jongen, Joseph-Marie-Alphonse-Nicholas

LES LAPINS see Tremisot, Ed.

LES LARMES see Andriessen, Hendrik

LES LARMES see Godard, Benjamin Louis Paul

LES LETTRES see Rabey, Rene

LES LEVRES see Delmet, Paul

LES LIBELLULES see Darcieux, F.

LES LIBELLULES see Lefebvre, Channing

LES LISERONS see Dere, Jean

LES LOUPS BLANCS see Cuvillier, Charles

LES LUNETTES see Mercenier, P.

LES LUPINS see Dere, Jean

LES LYS see Rhene-Baton

LES LYS BLEUS see Holmes, Alfred

LES MAGNANS see Dufresne, C.

LES MAITRES MUSICIENS DE LA RENAISSANCE FRANCAISE *CCUL,Renais
contains works for a variety of
instruments and vocal combinations
microfiche UNIV.MUS.ED. $70.00
reprint of A. Leduc Edition;
contains vocal works by:
Attaingnant, Pierre; Jannequin,
Clement; Mauduit, Jacques; Regnard,
Francois; Le Jeune, Claude and
others; contains 23 volumes plus
Vol. 3 & 8 of the Bibliographie
Thematique (L1027)

LES MAITRESSES see Delmet, Paul

LES MARGUERITES see Lacome, Paul

LES MARRONNIERS see Stehman, Jacques

LES MOINEAUX see Arma, Paul

LES MOINEAUX see Cadier, M.

LES MOIS see Privas, Xavier

LES MOTS QUE TU M'AS DITS see Pillois, Jacques

LES MOUETTES see Cuvillier, Charles

LES MOULINS see Georges, Alexandre

LES MOUTONS DES ANGES see Holmes, Alfred

LES MURES see Lacome, Paul

LES MURES DU CHEMIN CREUX see Stehman, Jacques

LES MUSES GALANTES see Baud-Bovy

LES MYOPES see Roger, Victor

LES MYRTES see Schumann, Robert (Alexander), Myrthen

LES NOCES DE LA MESSANGE see Dere, Jean

LES NOCES D'OR see Wellings, M.

LES NOCES DU CROCODILE see Beekhuis, Hanna

LES NOUNOUS VACHES see Dere, Jean

LES NUIT D'ETE see Berlioz, Hector

LES NUITS CONSOLENT see Fragerolle, G.

LES NUITS D'ETE see Berlioz, Hector

LES NUITS DU BOIS see Bozi, Harold de

LES OEILLETS INCARNADINS see Messager, Andre

LES OIES see Schlosser, Paul

LES OISEAUX D'ALENTOUR see Rameau, Jean-Philippe

LES OISEAUX DANS LA CHARMILLE see
  Offenbach, Jacques

LES OISEAUX ET LES BAISERS see
  Ferraris, P.

LES OISEAUX ET LES BAISERS see
  Letocart, H.

LES OISEAUX VOYAGEURS see Mendelssohn-
  Bartholdy, Felix

LES PALAIS NOMADES see Migot, Georges

LES PANTINS see Lachaume, A.

LES PAPILLONS see Chausson, Ernest

LES PAPILLONS see Gallois, Ch.

LES PAPILLONS see Godard, Benjamin
  Louis Paul

LES PAPILLONS see Thomas, Arthur Goring

LES PAROLES QUE TU M'AS DITES see
  Gaubert, Philippe

LES PARTISANS
  [Fr] solo,pno CHANT s.p.   (L1028)

LES PAS see Absil, Jean

LES PAS see Ferroud, Pierre-Octave

LES PASSEREAUX see Bernicat, F.

LES PATINEURS see Lacome, Paul

LES PAUVRES see Bordewijk-Roepman,
  Johanna

LES PAYSANS see Roques, J.

LES PECHEURS DE LA COTE see Lacome,
  Paul

LES PECHEUSES see Cuvillier, Charles

LES PECHEUSES DE CREVETTES see
  Dufresne, C.

LES PETIOTS see Biancheri, A.

LES PETITES BLANCHISSEUSES see Pradels,
  O.

LES PETITES BONNES D'HOTEL see Xanrof,
  Leon

LES PETITES CLOCHETTES BLEUES see
  Richepin, T.

LES PETITES MOMES see Alin, Pierre

LES PETITS CHAMPIGNONS see Dere, Jean

LES PETITS CHATS see Rasse, Francois

LES PETITS ELFES see Cuvillier, Charles

LES PETITS ENFANTS see Lecocq, Charles

LES PETITS GARS DE 1915 see Banes, A.

LES PETITS GARS DE 1918 see Banes, A.

LES PETITS MOUTONS see Schlosser, Paul

LES PETITS OISEAUX see Lacome, Paul

LES PEUPLES CHANTENT NOEL   *CC113U,Xmas
  (Arma, Paul) [Fr] solo,pno OUVRIERES
  s.p.   (L1029)

LES PICKPOCKETS see Allier, Gabriel

LES PIECES D'EAU see Roger-Ducasse,
  Jean-Jules Aimable

LES PIGEONS see Schlosser, Paul

LES PIGEONS DE PARIS see Stehman,
  Jacques

LES PLAINTES DE CHTCHAZA see Volkonsky,
  A.

LES PLAINTES DE LA JEUNE FILLE see
  Schubert, Franz (Peter)

LES PLAINTES DE SULEIKA see
  Mendelssohn-Bartholdy, Felix

LES PLUS BEAUX AIRS DE L'OPERA
  FRANCOIS: BARITONE AND BASS ALBUM
  *CC12L,17-18th cent
  (Grovlez, G.) [Fr/Eng] B/Bar solo,pno
  CHESTER s.p. contains works by:
  Lully; Campra; Monteclair;
  Destouches; Rameau; Philidor and
  others   (L1030)

LES PLUS BEAUX AIRS DE L'OPERA
  FRANCOIS: MEZZOSOPRANO AND
  CONTRALTO ALBUM *CC12L,17-18th

cent
  [Fr/Eng/It] Mez/A solo,kbd CHESTER
  s.p. contains works by: Lully;
  Campra; Charpentier; Colasse;
  Gossec; Mouret and others   (L1031)

LES PLUS BEAUX AIRS DE L'OPERA
  FRANCOIS: SOPRANO ALBUM *CC12L,17-
  18th cent
  (Grovlez, G.) [Fr/Eng] solo,kbd
  CHESTER s.p. contains works by:
  Lully; Campra; Desmarets; Rameau;
  Mondonville; Gretry and others
                                  (L1032)

LES PLUS BEAUX AIRS DE L'OPERA
  FRANCOIS: TENOR ALBUM *CC12L,17-
  18th cent
  (Grovlez, G.) [Fr/Eng] T solo,kbd
  CHESTER s.p. contains works by:
  Lully; Campra; Rameau; Gretry;
  Mehul and others   (L1033)

LES PLUS JOLIES CHANSONS, VOL. I see
  Delmet, Paul

LES PLUS JOLIES CHANSONS, VOL. II see
  Delmet, Paul

LES PLUS JOLIES CHANSONS, VOL. III see
  Delmet, Paul

LES PLUS JOLIES CHANSONS, VOL. IV see
  Delmet, Paul

LES PLUS PRESSES see Wachs, F.

LES POEMES DU BRUGNON see Migot,
  Georges

LES POEMES DU BRUGNON PREMIER RECUEIL
  see Migot, Georges

LES POEMES DU BRUGNON DEUXIEME RECUEIL
  see Migot, Georges

LES POEMES DU BRUGNON TROISIEME RECUEIL
  see Migot, Georges

LES POETES PRECIEUX see Moulaert,
  Raymond

LES PONTS DE VIGILANCE see Georges,
  Alexandre

LES "POURQUOI" DE SOLANGE see Dupin,
  Paul

LES POURQUOI D'EVE see Betove

LES POUSSINS see Schlosser, Paul

LES PREMIERS MOTS D'AMOUR see Ferrari,
  Gustave

LES PREMIERS PAS see Bonnal, Ermend

LES PRESAGES see Steenhuis, Francois

LES PRESENTS see Chaminade, Cecile

LES QUATRE PETITS LAPINS see Schlosser,
  Paul

LES RAMEAUX see Faure, Jean-Baptiste

LES RAMEAUX see Gretchaninov, Alexander
  Tikhonovitch

LES REVES see Araujo, Gino de

LES REVES see Chaminade, Cecile

LES REVES see Rabey, Rene

LES REVES see Vuillemin, L.

LES REVES SONT DES BULLES DE SAVON see
  Hermite, M.

LES ROIS MAGES see Dihau, Desire

LES ROSES see Fievet, P.

LES ROSES DE MON BALCON see Hermite, M.

LES ROSES DE NAZARETH see Boisdeffre,
  Charles-Henri-Rene de

LES ROSES DE SAADI see Delden, Lex van

LES ROSES DE SAADI see Huybrechts,
  Albert

LES ROSES EFFEUILLEES see Pandelides,
  S.

LES ROSIERS see Savino, D.

LES ROSIERS BLANCS
  (Fragerolle, G.) 2 soli,pno ENOCH
  s.p. see from Chansons Du Pays-
  Lorrain   (L1034)
  (Fragerolle, G.) 2 soli,acap ENOCH
  s.p. see from Chansons Du Pays-
  Lorrain   (L1035)

LES ROSIERS BLANCS see Fragerolle, G.

LES SAISONS see Casemajor, L.

LES SAPINS see Saint-Saens, Camille

LES SEPT IVRESSES see Holmes, Alfred

LES SEPT PECHES CAPITAUX see Gallois
  Montbrun

LES SIRENES see Waldteufel, Emil

LES SOIREES DE PETROGRADE see Milhaud,
  Darius

LES SOLDATS, CA MARCHE see Oberfeld, C.

LES SOLDATS DE BOIS see Fock, A.

LES SOUCIS see Brero, Cesare

LES SOUHAITS RIDICULES see Lacome, Paul

LES SOULIERS DE L'AVOCAT see Aubert,
  Louis-Francois-Marie

LES SOURCES see De Lara, Isadore

LES SYIPHES see Godard, Benjamin Louis
  Paul

LES TAMBOURS QUI PARLENT see Schmitt,
  Florent

LES TENDRES ERREURS see Leroux, Xavier
  (Henry Napoleon)

LES TRINGLES DES SISTRES TINTAIENT see
  Bizet, Georges

LES TRIOLETS DE LA MARQUISE see
  Cuvillier, Charles

LES TROIS AGES DE L'AMOUR see Delmet,
  Paul

LES TROIS BAISERS see Chaminade, Cecile

LES TROIS BAISERS see Levade, Charles
  (Gaston)

LES TROIS BRIGADIERS see Michiels, G.

LES TROIS COMPLAINTES DU SOLDAT see
  Jolivet, Andre

LES TROIS CORBEAUX
  see La Musique, Cinquieme Cahier

LES TROIS HEURES DE LA VIE see Ganne,
  Louis Gaston

LES TROIS PAGES see Holmes, Alfred

LES TROIS PETITS OISEAUX see Pierne,
  Gabriel

LES TROIS PLAIES see Georges, Alexandre

LES TROIS RUBANS
  see Five French Folk Songs

LES TROIS TZIGANES see Liszt, Franz,
  Die Drei Zigeuner

LES VENDANGES see Saint-Saens, Camille

LES VEPRES SONNENT see Ropartz, Joseph
  Guy

LES VIEILLES DE CHEZ NOUS see Levade,
  Charles (Gaston)

LES VIELLES LETTRES see Lachaume, A.

LES VIERGES DE VINGT ANS see Wolff, A.

LES VIERGES SAGES see Arrieu, Claude

LES VIEUX PAPILLONS see Fragerolle, G.

LES VILAINES PUCES see Dere, Jean

LES VOEUX see Goublier, G.

LES VOYAGES see Lacome, Paul

LES VOYAGES DE GULLIVER see Bois, Rob
  du

LES YEUX see Aubert, Louis-Francois-
  Marie

LES YEUX see Pennequin, J.-G.

LES YEUX see Tremisot, Ed.

LES YEUX BLEUS DE GRAND'MERE see
  Stehman, Jacques

LES YEUX COULEUR DU TEMPS see
  Malipiero, Gian Francesco

LESBOS see Southam

L'ESCALIER see Delmet, Paul

L'ESCAMOTEUR see Moulaert, Raymond

L'ESCARPOLETTE see Schmitt, Florent

LESKOVIC, BOGOMIR (1909-   )
  De Profundis *sac,CC5U
    S solo,pno DRUSTVO DSS 261 rental
                                    (L1036)

LESLIE, HENRY DAVID (1882-1896)
  Annabelle Lee
    low solo,pno (E maj) CRAMER (L1037)
    high solo,pno (G maj) CRAMER
                                    (L1038)
  Love Trio
    SAT soli,pno CRAMER   (L1039)
  Memory
    high solo,pno (F maj) CRAMER
                                    (L1040)
    low solo,pno (E flat maj) CRAMER
                                    (L1041)
  Memory Trio
    SAT soli,pno (F maj) CRAMER (L1042)
    SAT soli,pno (G flat maj) CRAMER
                                    (L1043)
  Speed On My Bark
    low solo,pno (E flat maj) CRAMER
                                    (L1044)
    high solo,pno (F maj) CRAMER
                                    (L1045)

LESLIE, R.
  Best Of All
    low solo,pno (E flat maj) BOOSEY
      $1.50   (L1046)
    high solo,pno (A flat maj) BOOSEY
      $1.50   (L1047)
    med solo,pno (F maj) BOOSEY $1.50
                                    (L1048)

LESLIE-SMITH, K.
  Canterbury Fair
    high solo,pno (F maj) BOOSEY $1.50
                                    (L1049)
    low solo,pno (E flat maj) BOOSEY
      $1.50   (L1050)

L'ESPACE DU DEDANS see Sauguet, Henri

L'ESPAGNOL DE MA RUE see Middeleer,
  Jean De

LESS OF ME see Campbell

LESS THAN THE DUST see Woodforde-
  Finden, Amy

LESSARD, JOHN AYRES (1920-   )
  Agenda
    low solo,pno AM.COMP.AL. $1.10
                                    (L1051)
    med solo,pno AM.COMP.AL. $1.10
                                    (L1052)
  Amarillis
    high solo,pno AM.COMP.AL. $1.37
                                    (L1053)
  Ariel's Song
    solo,pno GENERAL 258 $1.75 (L1054)
  Bag Of The Bee, The
    high solo,pno AM.COMP.AL. $.82
                                    (L1055)
  Doctor Fell
    see Mother Goose
  Don Quixote And The Sheep
    BarB soli,2fl,ob,2clar,2bsn,2horn,
    2trp,2trom,harp,perc,strings
    AM.COMP.AL. sc $33.00, voc sc
    $12.10   (L1056)
  Five Poems By Robert Herrick *CC5U
    Mez solo,vln,pno sc AM.COMP.AL.
    $8.25, ipa   (L1057)
  Four Songs About Love *CC4U
    med solo,pno AM.COMP.AL. $7.70
                                    (L1058)
  Full Fathom Five
    solo,pno GENERAL 257 $1.75 (L1059)
  Going To St. Ives
    see Mother Goose
  House Of The Dying, The
    med solo,pno AM.COMP.AL. $3.30
                                    (L1060)
  Interior
    med solo,pno AM.COMP.AL. $1.37
                                    (L1061)
  Lullaby
    high solo,pno AM.COMP.AL. $1.37
                                    (L1062)
  Man In The Moon, The
    see Mother Goose
  Morning Song
    solo,pno GENERAL 49 $1.50 (L1063)
  Mother Goose
    solo,pno PEER $1.00
      contains: Doctor Fell; Going To
      St. Ives; Man In The Moon, The;
      There Was An Old Woman; Three

LESSARD, JOHN AYRES (cont'd.)
    Wise Men Of Gotham; T'other
    Little Tune   (L1064)
  Orpheus
    low solo,pno MERCURY $.95   (L1065)
    med solo,pno GENERAL 748 $1.00
                                    (L1066)
  Recuerdo
    solo,pno GENERAL 56 $1.00   (L1067)
  Rose Cheek'd Laura
    solo,pno GENERAL 463 $1.50 (L1068)
  Sebastian
    solo,pno GENERAL 52 $1.00   (L1069)
  Siesta
    med solo,pno AM.COMP.AL. $1.37
                                    (L1070)
  Summer Wind
    med solo,pno AM.COMP.AL. $1.10
                                    (L1071)
  There Was An Old Woman
    see Mother Goose
  Three Songs About Larr *CC3U
    med solo,pno AM.COMP.AL. $3.85
                                    (L1072)
  Three Wise Men Of Gotham
    see Mother Goose
  T'other Little Tune
    see Mother Goose
  Whenas In Silks My Julia Goes
    solo,pno GENERAL 57 $1.50   (L1073)

LESSER, RENA S.
  God Bless This Day *sac,Marriage
    high solo,pno (E flat maj) SCHIRM.G
      $.85   (L1074)
    (E flat maj) SCHIRM.G $.85   (L1075)

LESSER, WOLFGANG (1923-   )
  Ein Tag In Unserer Stadt *song cycle
    med solo,pno DEUTSCHER 9033 s.p.
                                    (L1076)

LEST I FORGET see Good, Dwayne

LESTER, WILLIAM
  O Irish Hills
    high solo/low solo,pno FITZSIMONS
      $.60   (L1077)

LESUR, DANIEL (1908-   )
  Berceuses A Tenir Eveille
    solo,pno/inst DURAND s.p.   (L1078)
  Chansons Cambodgiennes
    solo,pno DURAND s.p.
      contains: Langage Des Fleurs; Le
      Voyage Du Roi; L'Etang Du Roi;
      Pirogues; Sangsar   (L1079)
  Langage Des Fleurs
    see Chansons Cambodgiennes
  Le Voyage Du Roi
    see Chansons Cambodgiennes
  Les Amants Separes
    SBar soli,pno DURAND s.p.   (L1080)
  L'Etang Du Roi
    see Chansons Cambodgiennes
  Pirogues
    see Chansons Cambodgiennes
  Quatre Lieder Avec Accompagnement
    *CC4U
    solo,orch/fl&harp&vln&vla&vcl
    DURAND s.p., ipa, ipr   (L1081)
  Sangsar
    see Chansons Cambodgiennes

LET ALL MY LIFE BE MUSIC see Spross,
  Charles Gilbert

LET ALL THE MULTITUDES OF LIGHT see
  Bach, Johann Sebastian

LET ALL THE WORLD IN EVERY CORNER SING
  see Willan, Healey

LET AN EMPTY FLATTERING SPIRIT see
  Shield, William

LET EV'RY DAY BE CHRISTMAS *sac,gospel
  solo,pno ABER.GRP. $1.50   (L1082)

LET HER BELIEVE see Puccini, Giacomo,
  Ch'ella Mi Creda Libero E Lontano

LET HIM GO see Vine, John

LET HIM IN TODAY see Lee, Don

LET IT BE FORGOTTEN see Kagen, Sergius

LET ME BE WORTHY *sac,gospel
  solo,pno ABER.GRP. $1.50   (L1083)

LET ME LIVE AT THE FOOT OF THE CROSS
  see Lee, Larry

LET ME LOSE MY LIFE AND FIND IT LORD IN
  THEE see Minkler, Ross

LET ME REST HERE ALONE see
  Rachmaninoff, Sergey Vassilievitch

LET ME TELL YOU 'BOUT A MAN see Moore,
  Gene

LET ME TOUCH HIM see Ellis

LET MINE EYES SEE THEE see Berkeley,
  Lennox

LET MY HEART BE A CHAPEL see Lister,
  Mosie

LET MY LIGHT SHINE see Holm

LET MY SONG FILL YOUR HEART see
  Charles, Ernest

LET NOT YOUR HEART BE TROUBLED see
  Haeussler, P.

LET NOT YOUR HEART BE TROUBLED see
  Reese, Dorothy

LET NOT YOUR HEART BE TROUBLED see
  Speaks, Oley

LET NOTHING DISTURB THEE see Diamond,
  David

LET SPRINGTIME COME see Delius,
  Frederick

LET THE BEAUTY OF THE LORD BE UPON US
  see Fischer, Irwin

LET THE BRIGHT SERAPHIM see Handel,
  George Frideric

LET THE COSMOS RING! see Winter, Sister
  Miriam Therese

LET THE NIGHT PERISH see Purcell, Henry

LET THE PEOPLE PRAISE THEE, O GOD see
  Hammerschmidt, Andreas

LET THE WORD OF CHRIST DWELL IN YOU
  RICHLY see Pinkham, Daniel

LET THIS MIND BE IN YOU see Humphreys,
  Don

LET THY MANTLE FALL ON ME see Hawkins

LET THY SONG BE LOVE see Hiller,
  Wilfred

LET US BREAK BREAD TOGETHER *spir
  (Burleigh, H. T.) high solo,pno
    BELWIN $1.50   (L1084)
  (Burleigh, H. T.) med solo,pno BELWIN
    $1.50   (L1085)
  (Burleigh, H. T.) low solo,pno BELWIN
    $1.50   (L1086)

LET US BREAK BREAD TOGETHER see Gounod,
  Charles Francois

LET US BREAK BREAD TOGETHER see Myers,
  Gordon

LET US CHEER THE WEARY TRAVELER *spir
  (Burleigh, H. T.) high solo,pno
    BELWIN $1.50   (L1087)
  (Burleigh, H. T.) low solo,pno BELWIN
    $1.50   (L1088)

LET US CLIMB THE HILL TOGETHER see
  Clark

LET US GARLANDS BRING see Finzi, Gerald

LET US GO TO THE DEEP BLUE RIVERS see
  Schouwman, Hans

LET US HASTE TO KELVIN GROVE see Rorem,
  Ned

LET US HAVE MUSIC FOR SINGING SONGS see
  Purcell, Henry

LET US SING FOR CYPRIA see Farkas,
  Ferenc

LET US SING UNTO THE LORD see
  Freudenthal, Josef

LET YOUR HEART DO THE WALKING see
  Derricks, Cleavant

LET YOUR SONG BE DELICATE see Aked,
  Lindsay

L'ETANG see Carolus-Duran, P.

L'ETANG see Delmet, Paul

L'ETANG see Schmitt, Florent

L'ETANG DU ROI see Lesur, Daniel

L'ETE see Koechlin, Charles

L'ETE DE LA SAINT-MARTIN see Cuvillier, Charles

L'ETE DE NUIT see Gagic, Bogdan

L'ETE, LA NUIT, L'AMOUR see Lacombe, Louis (Trouillon)

LETECKA see Strniste, Jiri

LETEM DETSKYM SVETEM see Sauer, Frantisek

L'ETERNEL EST DANS MON TOURMENT see Laparra, Raoul

L'ETERNELLE BERCEUSE see Dupin, Paul

L'ETERNELLE CHANSON see Barbirolli, A.

L'ETERNELLE CHANSON see Wolff, A.

LETHE see Pfitzner, Hans

LETME OKAMZIKY see Jindrich, Jindrich

LETMY HOST see Zich, Jaroslav

LETNI NALADY see Haba, Karel

LETOCART, H.
  Aveu
    solo,pno ENOCH s.p.   (L1089)

  En Avril
    solo,pno ENOCH s.p.   (L1090)

  Le Torrent
    solo,pno ENOCH s.p.   (L1091)

  Les Oiseaux Et Les Baisers
    solo,pno ENOCH s.p.   (L1092)

L'ETOILE see Godard, Benjamin Louis Paul

L'ETOILE see Saint-Saens, Camille

L'ETOILE D'AMOUR see Delmet, Paul

L'ETOILE DU BERGER see Delmet, Paul

L'ETOILE DU MATIN
  see La Musique, Treizieme Cahier

L'ETOILE FILANTE see Berners, Lord

LETS ALL BUILD AMERICA see Beter, P.D.

LET'S ALL GO DOWN TO THE RIVER see Montgomery

LET'S GO TO THE COUNTRY *CCU
  solo,pno GENERAL 158 $2.50 (L1093)

LET'S JUST PRAISE THE LORD see Gaither

LET'S PLAY MACCABEES see Haufrecht, Herbert

LET'S SING A SONG ABOUT JESUS see Wolfe, Lanny

LET'S SING DUETS NO. 1 *sac,CC32UL
  2 female soli/2 male soli,pno
  SINGSPIR 5080 $1.25   (L1094)

LET'S SING DUETS NO. 2 *sac,CC31UL
  2 female soli/2 male soli,pno
  SINGSPIR 5081 $1.25   (L1095)

LET'S SING DUETS NO. 3 *sac,CC28UL
  2 female soli/2 male soli,pno
  SINGSPIR 5082 $1.25   (L1096)

LET'S SING DUETS NO. 4 *sac,CC28UL
  2 female soli/2 male soli,pno
  SINGSPIR 5083 $1.25   (L1097)

LET'S SING DUETS NO. 5 *sac,CCUL
  2 female soli/2 male soli,pno
  SINGSPIR 5084 $1.25   (L1098)

LET'S TAKE A WALK see Thomson, Virgil

LET'S TALK ABOUT JESUS *sac,gospel
  solo,pno ABER.GRP. $1.50 (L1099)

LETTER, THE see Seeger, C.

LETTER FROM THE DRAFT BOARD see Heilner, Irwin

LETTER SCENE, THE see Tchaikovsky, Piotr Ilyitch, Letter Song, The

LETTER SONG see Offenbach, Jacques, Perichole's Letter

LETTER SONG, THE see Tchaikovsky, Piotr Ilyitch

LETTER TO FREDDY see Bowles, Paul Frederic

LETTERA ALLA MADRE see Ramous, Gianni

LETTERINA D'AMORE see Petralia

LETTERS see Srebotnjak, Alojz F., Pisma

LETTERS, THE see Massenet, Jules

LETTERS FOUND NEAR A SUICIDE see Kim, Andy

LETTERS FROM COMPOSERS see Argento, Dominick

LETTERS FROM MOROCCO see Glanville-Hicks, Peggy

LETTERS FROM SAINT PAUL see Pinkham, Daniel

LETTRE A LA MARQUISE see Dubreuilh, G.

LETTRE A MON MARI RESERVISTE see Planquette, Robert

LETTRE A NINON see Delmet, Paul

LETTRE A UNE ESPAGNOLE see Laparra, Raoul

LETTRE DE JERUSALEM see Prado, Almeida

LETTRE DE M. L'ABBE D'OLIVET A M. LE PRESIDENT BOUHIER see Mul, Jan

LETTRE D'UN AMI see Bernier, Nicolas

LETTRE D'UNE PENSIONNAIRE see Berger, Rod.

LETTRE VALSEE see Berger, Rod.

LETTRES AIMEES see Rabey, Rene

LETTRES D'AMOUR see Chaminade, Cecile

LETTRES DE LA RELIGEUSE PORTUGAISE see Bucchi, Valentino

LETZTE AHREN see Sialm, D.

LETZTE ROSE see Flotow, Friedrich von

LETZTER ABEND see Orthel, Leon

LETZTER FRUHLING see Grieg, Edvard Hagerup

LETZTES WIEGENLIED see Pylkkanen, Tauno Kullervo, Viimeinen Kehtolaulu

LEUCHTE, HELLER SPIEGEL MIR see Offenbach, Jacques

LEUCHTENDE NACHT see Brugk, Hans Melchoir

LEUCHTEST MIR ZUM LETZTEN MAL see Glinka, Mikhail Ivanovitch

LEVADE, CHARLES (GASTON) (1869-1948)
  Aubade D'Avril
    solo,pno ENOCH   (L1100)

  Aurore
    solo,pno (available in 2 keys)
    ENOCH   (L1101)

  Avril Fleuri
    solo,pno (available in 2 keys)
    ENOCH   (L1102)

  C'est Le Meme Qu'hier, Je Cherchais
    (from La Rotisserie De La Reine
    Pedauque)
    solo,pno (available in 2 keys)
    ENOCH s.p.   (L1103)

  C'est Un Vieux Vin De Malvoisie (from
    La Rotisserie De La Reine
    Pedauque)
    solo,pno (available in 2 keys)
    ENOCH s.p.   (L1104)

  Chanson
    solo,pno ENOCH   (L1105)

  Comme Les Lys
    solo,pno ENOCH   (L1106)

  Dans Ce Parc Peuple De Marbres (from
    La Rotisserie De La Reine
    Pedauque)
    solo,pno (available in 2 keys)
    ENOCH s.p.   (L1107)

  Dans La Nuit
    solo,pno (available in 2 keys)
    ENOCH   (L1108)

LEVADE, CHARLES (GASTON) (cont'd.)
  Delire
    solo,pno ENOCH   (L1109)

  Derniere Page
    solo,pno (available in 2 keys)
    ENOCH   (L1110)

  Desesperance
    solo,orch ENOCH rental   (L1111)
    solo,acap (available in 2 keys)
    ENOCH   (L1112)
    solo,pno (available in 2 keys)
    ENOCH   (L1113)

  Enlevement
    (Bordese, Stephen) solo,pno
    (available in 2 keys) ENOCH s.p.
    see also CHANSONS DE PAGE (L1114)

  Helas! Cette Nuit S'acheve, Et Mon
    Reve S'enfuit (from La Rotisserie
    De La Reine Pedauque)
    solo,pno (available in 2 keys)
    ENOCH s.p.   (L1115)

  Idylle Parisienne
    solo,pno (available in 2 keys)
    ENOCH   (L1116)

  Il Neige
    solo,pno (available in 2 keys)
    ENOCH   (L1117)

  Inquietude
    solo,pno (available in 2 keys)
    ENOCH   (L1118)

  Inviolata *sac
    [Lat] solo,pno/org ENOCH s.p.
        (L1119)

  Jane
    solo,orch ENOCH rental   (L1120)
    solo,pno (available in 2 keys)
    ENOCH   (L1121)

  La Bete Noire
    Mez solo,orch (A min) ENOCH rental
        (L1122)
    solo,pno (available in 2 keys)
    ENOCH   (L1123)

  La Claire Fonatine
    solo,acap ENOCH   (L1124)
    solo,pno ENOCH   (L1125)

  La Morte
    solo,acap ENOCH s.p. see from Poeme
    Pour La Morte   (L1126)
    solo,pno ENOCH s.p. see from Poeme
    Pour La Morte   (L1127)

  La Rotisserie De La Reine Pedauque
    solo,orch ENOCH rental   (L1128)

  L'Amour D'Heliodora *CC7L
    solo,pno cmplt ed ENOCH s.p.
        (L1129)

  L'Amour D'Heliodora
    solo,orch ENOCH rental   (L1130)

  Le Champagne Est Un Vin Charmant
    (from Sophie)
    solo,pno ENOCH s.p.   (L1131)

  Le Papillon
    solo,pno (available in 2 keys)
    ENOCH   (L1132)

  Le Silence
    solo,pno ENOCH s.p. see from Poeme
    Pour La Morte   (L1133)
    solo,acap ENOCH s.p. see from Poeme
    Pour La Morte   (L1134)

  Le Vin Est L'elixir Sacre (from La
    Rotisserie De La Reine Pedauque)
    solo,pno (available in 2 keys)
    ENOCH s.p.   (L1135)

  Les Choses Vont Partout De La Sorte A
    La Ronde (from La Rotisserie De
    La Reine Pedauque)
    solo,pno (available in 2 keys)
    ENOCH s.p.   (L1136)

  Les Enfants De Notre Bretagne
    Mez/Bar solo,pno RICORDI-FR s.p.
        (L1137)
    S/T solo,pno RICORDI-FR s.p.
        (L1138)

  Les Trois Baisers
    Mez/Bar solo,pno RICORDI-FR s.p.
        (L1139)
    S/T solo,pno RICORDI-FR s.p.
        (L1140)

  Les Vieilles De Chez Nous
    solo,gtr ENOCH s.p.   (L1141)
    solo,pno (available in 2 keys)
    ENOCH s.p.   (L1142)
    Mez solo,orch (G maj) ENOCH s.p.,
    ipa   (L1143)

LEVADE, CHARLES (GASTON) (cont'd.)

Madrigal De Ronsard
solo,pno (available in 2 keys)
ENOCH s.p. (L1144)
solo,acap (available in 2 keys)
ENOCH s.p. (L1145)
S solo,orch (D maj, available in 2
keys) ENOCH rental (L1146)

Mirage
solo,pno (available in 2 keys)
ENOCH (L1147)

Mon Bel Ami
solo,pno ENOCH (L1148)

Nous Nous Aimerons
solo,pno ENOCH (L1149)

O Salutaris! *sac
[Lat] solo,pno/org (available in 2
keys) ENOCH s.p. (L1150)

Oubli D'amour
solo,pno (available in 2 keys)
ENOCH (L1151)

Paradis D'Amour
solo,pno (available in 2 keys)
ENOCH (L1152)

Poeme Pour La Morte *see La Morte;
Le Silence; Pressentiment;
Solitude (L1153)

Polichinelle
solo,pno ENOCH (L1154)

Pour Dresser Un Jeune Courrier (from
La Rotisserie De La Reine
Pedauque)
solo,pno (available in 2 keys)
ENOCH s.p. (L1155)

Prends Cette Rose
solo,pno (available in 2 keys)
ENOCH (L1156)

Pressentiment
solo,acap ENOCH s.p. see from Poeme
Pour La Morte (L1157)
solo,pno ENOCH s.p. see from Poeme
Pour La Morte (L1158)

Quand Naissent Les Etoiles
solo,pno (available in 2 keys)
ENOCH (L1159)

Quand Un Aime, Vous A-t-on Ce Visage
Bleme? (from La Rotisserie De La
Reine Pedauque)
solo,pno (available in 2 keys)
ENOCH s.p. (L1160)

Que Fait-Tu Mechante Sophie? (from
Sophie)
solo,pno ENOCH s.p. (L1161)

Romances Fancees
solo,orch ENOCH rental (L1162)

Romances Fanees
solo,pno (available in 2 keys)
ENOCH (L1163)

Rossignol, Mon Mignon
solo,pno ENOCH (L1164)

Solitude
solo,pno ENOCH s.p. see from Poeme
Pour La Morte (L1165)
solo,acap ENOCH s.p. see from Poeme
Pour La Morte (L1166)

Son Charme
solo,pno ENOCH (L1167)

Sous Le Porche De Saint-Benoit (from
La Rotisserie De La Reine
Pedauque)
solo,pno (available in 2 keys)
ENOCH s.p. (L1168)

Ultime Amour
solo,pno ENOCH (L1169)

Vers Les Etoiles
solo,pno (available in 2 keys)
ENOCH (L1170)

Voici Comment, Sans Didactique (from
Sophie)
solo,pno ENOCH s.p. (L1171)

LEVAYSME AMOR D'AQUESTA TERRA see
Milan, Luis

LEVE-TOI see Durand, Jacques

LEVE-TOI see Duvernoy, Victor-Alphonse

LEVENSLES see Mengelberg, Rudolf

LEVENSLIED see Bonset, Jac.

LEVENSLOOP see Dijk, Jan van

L'EVENTAIL see Cuvillier, Charles

L'EVENTAIL see d'Hardelot, Guy

LEVER DE SOLEIL SUR LE NIL see Saint-
Saens, Camille

LEVER DU JOUR see Biancheri, A.

LEVER MIN DAG FOR DIG
solo,pno LUNDQUIST s.p. (L1172)

LEVEZ CES COUVRE-CHEFS PLUS HAUT see
Francaix, Jean

LEVIDIS, DIMITRI (1886-1951)
Lelita *Op.51
solo,orch DURAND s.p. (L1173)

Offrande *Op.48
low solo,orch DURAND s.p. (L1174)

Tes Yeux *Op.50
solo,orch DURAND s.p. (L1175)

L'EVIER SENT FORT see Absil, Jean

LEVOMMI IL MIO PENSIER IN PARTE OV'ERA
see Pizzetti, Ildebrando

LEVY, FRANK (1930-)
Specks Of Light
S solo,fl,horn,vln,vla,vcl,harp sc
SEESAW $8.00 (L1176)

LEVY, MARVIN DAVID (1932-)
One Person *song cycle
A solo,orch BOOSEY $3.50 (L1177)

LEWERTH
Dina Bla Ogon
2 soli,pno LUNDQUIST s.p. (L1178)
MezBar soli,pno LUNDQUIST s.p. (L1179)

LEWIE GORDON *folk,Scot
solo,pno (F maj) PATERSON FS133 s.p. (L1180)

LEWIS
How Long? *sac
solo,pno BENSON S5915-R $1.00 (L1181)

LEWIS BOAT SONG
(Roberton, Hugh S.) solo,pno (A maj)
ROBERTON 2784 s.p. (L1182)

LEWIS BRIDAL SONG
(Roberton, Hugh S.) solo,pno (G maj)
ROBERTON 2743 s.p. see also Songs
Of The Isles (L1183)

LEWIS, ERV
Such A Love *sac
solo,pno SINGSPIR 7121 $1.00 (L1184)

LEWIS, IDRIS
Love's Poem
low solo,pno (C maj) CRAMER (L1185)
high solo,pno (E flat maj) CRAMER (L1186)

LEWIS, PETER TOD
Five Japanese Songs *CC5U,Jap
ST soli,vln,vla,vcl sc AM.COMP.AL.
$6.60, ipa (L1187)

Song
S solo,3strings sc AM.COMP.AL.
$3.30 (L1188)

Tender Glow, A
Mez solo,pno AM.COMP.AL. $2.20 (L1189)

LEWIS, RAY
Old Ship Of Zion, The *sac
solo,pno WORD S-456 (L1190)

LEWKOVITCH, BERNHARD (1927-)
Cantata Sacra *sac,cant
[Lat] T solo,6inst cmplt ed HANSEN-
DEN s.p. (L1191)

Canzonetta
see Three Canzonets For Baritone

Der Er En Brond *Op.8,No.1
see Six Songs

Folkevise *Op.8,No.4
see Six Songs

Her Star De Gronne Stammer *Op.8,
No.5
see Six Songs

Ja, Det Er Forar *Op.8,No.6
see Six Songs

La Belta Presto Finisce
see Three Canzonets For Baritone

Manon *Op.8,No.3
see Six Songs

LEWKOVITCH, BERNHARD (cont'd.)

Six Songs
[Dan] Bar solo,kbd HANSEN-DEN s.p.
contains: Der Er En Brond, Op.8,
No.1; Folkevise, Op.8,No.4; Her
Star De Gronne Stammer, Op.8,
No.5; Ja, Det Er Forar, Op.8,
No.6; Manon, Op.8,No.3;
Walpurgisnat, Op.8,No.2 (L1192)

Three Canzonets For Baritone
[It] Bar solo,kbd HANSEN-DEN s.p.
contains: Canzonetta; La Belta
Presto Finisce; Un Bel Riso (L1193)

Tre Orationes *CC3U
[Lat] T solo,ob,bsn cmplt ed
HANSEN-DEN s.p. (L1194)

Un Bel Riso
see Three Canzonets For Baritone

Walpurgisnat *Op.8,No.2
see Six Songs

L'EXILE see Lacombe, Paul

LEZTE ROSE see Flotow, Friedrich von

L'HERITIER DE CROQUEMITAINE see
Michiels, G.

L'HEURE CAPTIVE see Aubert, Louis-
Francois-Marie

L'HEURE D'AIMER see Fontenailles, H. de

L'HEURE DELICIEUSE see Staub, V.

L'HEURE DU BERGER see Doyen, Albert

L'HEURE DU BERGER see Vierne, Louis

L'HEURE DU MYSTERE see Schumann, Robert
(Alexander)

L'HEURE EXQUISE see Hahn, Reynaldo

L'HEURE SILENCIEUSE see Staub, V.

L'HEUREUX BERGER see Godard, Benjamin
Louis Paul

L'HEUREUX VAGABOND see Bruneau

L'HIRONDELLE see Coquard, Arthur

L'HIRONDELLE see Kucken, Friedrich
Wilhelm

L'HISTOIRE DU SOLDAT see Stravinsky,
Igor

L'HOMME DE LA TERRE see Dupin, Paul

L'HOMME N'EST PAS SANS DEFAUT see
Saint-Saens, Camille

L'HORA GRISA see Mompou, Federico

L'HORIZON CHIMERIQUE see Faure,
Gabriel-Urbain

L'HORIZON S'ETEINT see Rimsky-Korsakov,
Nikolai

LHOTKA-KALINSKI, IVO (1913-)
Ballads Of Petrica Kerempuh, The
*CCU
[Slav] solo,pno CROATICA s.p. (L1195)

LI DEPARTIR DE LA DOUCE CONTREE see Le
Flem, Paul

LIADOV, ANATOL KONSTANTINOVITCH
(1855-1914)
Music Box, The *Op.32
[Russ/Fr/Eng] med solo,pno BELAIEFF
277 s.p. (L1196)

Musical Snuff-Box, The *see Une
Tabatiere A Musique

Une Tabatiere A Musique
(Aslanoff) "Musical Snuff-Box, The"
[Fr/Eng] high solo,pno (D maj)
SCHIRM.G $.60 (L1197)

Vier Lieder *Op.1,No.1-4, CC4U
[Russ/Fr/Eng] solo,pno BREITKOPF-W
57 03094 s.p. (L1198)

LIA'S RECITATIVE AND ARIA see Debussy,
Claude

LIBERA see Haydn, (Johann) Michael

LIBERTE see Delmet, Paul

LIBIAMO NE' LIETI CALICI see Verdi,
Giuseppe

LICHT see Bonset, Jac.

LICHTE WOLKE see Micheelsen, Hans-
Friedrich

LICHTEND ONTWAKEN see Zagwijn, Henri

LIDDELL, CLAIRE
Twelve Burns Songs *CC12L
high solo,pno ROBERTON 1505 s.p.
(L1199)

LIDDELL, R.
Cross Was Hewn From A Tree, A *sac
(Wild) solo,pno BERANDOL DC 5 $1.50
(L1200)

Dawn Of Creation *sac
(Wild) solo,pno BERANDOL DC 2 $1.50
(L1201)

It Costs So Little *sac
(Wild) solo,pno BERANDOL DC 7 $1.50
(L1202)

Life's Journey *sac
(Wild) solo,pno BERANDOL DC 1 $1.50
(L1203)

We Travel Together *sac
solo,pno BERANDOL DC 6 $1.50
(L1204)

LIDDLE, SAMUEL
Abide With Me
low solo,pno (C maj) BOOSEY $1.50
(L1205)
high solo,pno (E flat maj) BOOSEY
$1.50   (L1206)
med solo,pno (D flat maj) BOOSEY
$1.50   (L1207)

Farewell
solo,pno (B flat maj) BOOSEY $1.50
(L1208)

Garden Where The Praties Grow
med solo,pno STAINER 3.1305.7 $1.50
(L1209)

How Lovely Are Thy Dwellings (Psalm
84) sac
med solo,pno (C maj) BOOSEY $1.50
(L1210)
med-high solo,pno (D flat maj)
BOOSEY $1.50   (L1211)
low solo,pno (B flat maj) BOOSEY
$1.50   (L1212)
high solo,pno (E flat maj) BOOSEY
$1.50   (L1213)

Like As The Hart (Psalm 62) sac
solo,pno (D min) BOOSEY $1.50
(L1214)

Lord Is My Shepherd (Psalm 23) sac,
Psalm
solo,pno (available in 4 keys)
ASHLEY $.95   (L1215)
low solo,pno (C maj) BOOSEY $1.50
(L1216)
med solo,pno (D maj) BOOSEY $1.50
(L1217)
med-high solo,pno (E flat maj)
BOOSEY $1.50   (L1218)
high solo,pno (F maj) BOOSEY $1.50
(L1219)

Old French Carol
[Eng/Fr] low solo,pno (D flat maj)
BOOSEY $1.50   (L1220)
[Eng/Fr] high solo,pno (F maj)
BOOSEY $1.50   (L1221)

Psalm 23 *see Lord Is My Shepherd

Psalm 62 *see Like As The Hart

Psalm 84 *see How Lovely Are Thy
Dwellings

L'IDEAL see Chaminade, Cecile

L'IDEAL see Ruyneman, Daniel

LIDHOLM, INGVAR (1921-   )
Den Sista Kvallen
see Six Songs

For Vilsna Fotter Sjunger Graset
see Six Songs

Jungfrulin
see Six Songs

Madonnans Vaggvisa
see Six Songs

Rosetta's Song (from Leonce And Lena)
solo,pno NORDISKA 6510 s.p. (L1222)

Saga
see Six Songs

Six Songs
[Swed] med solo,kbd NORDISKA s.p.
contains: Den Sista Kvallen; For
Vilsna Fotter Sjunger Graset;
Jungfrulin; Madonnans Vaggvisa;
Saga; Vid Medelhavet   (L1223)

Vid Medelhavet
see Six Songs

L'IDIOT DU VILLAGE see Daniel-Lesur

LIDL, VACLAV (1922-   )
Pampelisky *CC6U
[Czech/Ger] S solo,harp,fl CZECH
s.p.   (L1224)

Tri Milostne Pisne *CC3U
S solo,fl,harp CZECH s.p.   (L1225)

LIDOVE BALADY see Macha, Otmar

LIDOVE PISNE *CC30U,folk
(Weis, K.) solo,pno SUPRAPHON s.p.
(L1226)

LIDOVE PISNE O ZVIRATECH *CCU,folk
(Nejedly, V.) Bar solo,pno SUPRAPHON
s.p.   (L1227)

LIDOVE PISNE Z TESINKA, SES. 1-2 *CCU,
folk
(Vogel, J.) solo,pno SUPRAPHON s.p.,
ea.   (L1228)

LIDOVE PISNICKY Z RAKOVNICKA A
KRIVOKLATSKA *CCU,folk
(Cmiral, A.) solo,pno SUPRAPHON s.p.
(L1229)

LIE, HARALD (1902-1942)
Ballade *Op.18,No.2
see Tvo Sangar

Mit Deinen Augen *Op.9,No.2
see Zwei Sonette Von Michelangelo

Nykelen *Op.18,No.1
see Tvo Sangar

O Nacht, Zwar Schwarze *Op.9,No.1
see Zwei Sonette Von Michelangelo

Skinnvengbrev *Op.6
solo,pno MUSIKK s.p.   (L1230)

Tvo Sangar
solo,pno MUSIKK s.p.
contains: Ballade, Op.18,No.2;
Nykelen, Op.18,No.1   (L1231)

Zwei Sonette Von Michelangelo
[Ger] solo,pno MUSIKK s.p.
contains: Mit Deinen Augen, Op.9,
No.2; O Nacht, Zwar Schwarze,
Op.9,No.1   (L1232)

LIEB NACHTIGALL
see Vier Kleine Weihnachtslieder

LIEB NACHTIGALL, WACH AUF see Metzger,
Hans-Arnold

LIEBE see Bijvanck, Henk

LIEBE see Strauss, Richard

LIEBE GEFINT SHOIN A WEG *Jew
solo,pno KAMMEN 468 $1.00   (L1233)

LIEBE HAT RECHT see Jezek, Jaroslav,
Laska Ma Pravo

LIEBE IM SCHNEE see Weingartner, (Paul)
Felix

LIEBE IST DUFT see Bijvanck, Henk

LIEBE, LIEBSTER IN DER FERNE see
Bijvanck, Henk

LIEBE, RUCKBLICKEND see Rietz, Johannes

LIEBEN BRUDER, SCHICKET EUCH IN DIE
ZEIT see Distler, Hugo

LIEBER GOTT ERBARME DICH see Baird,
Tadeusz, Bozemojzmituj Sie Nade Mna

LIEBER HERRE GOTT see Rosenmuller,
Johann

LIEBERMANN, ROLF (1910-   )
Capriccio
S solo,vln,pno UNIVER. 13018 $11.50
(L1234)

Chinesische Liebeslieder *CCU
[Ger/Eng] high solo,pno UNIVER.
12357 $3.25   (L1235)

Lieder Der Yvette Aus Leonore *CCU
[Fr] high solo,pno UNIVER. 12163
$3.25   (L1236)

LIEBES-LIEDER see Svedbom, Vilhelm

LIEBES-LIEDER see Weigl, Karl

LIEBES MANDEL, WO IS 'S BANDEL see
Mozart, Wolfgang Amadeus

LIEBES MANDEL, WO IST'S BANDEL see
Mozart, Wolfgang Amadeus

LIEBES SCHMERTZEN see Picon, Molly

LIEBESBETORUNG see King, Harold C.

LIEBESBLUMEN see Jirak, Karel Boleslav,
Milodejne Kviti

LIEBESBOTSCHAFT see Schubert, Franz
(Peter)

LIEBESFEIER see Weingartner, (Paul)
Felix

LIEBESGESCHENK see Strauss, Richard

LIEBESGESTANDNIS see Thome, Francis,
Simple Aveu

LIEBESGLUCK see Ehrenberg, Carl Emil
Theodor

LIEBESHYMNEN see Ehrenberg, Carl Emil
Theodor

LIEBESKLAGE see Diepenbrock, Alphons

LIEBESKLAGE see Lothar, Mark

LIEBESLIED see Haydn, (Franz) Joseph

LIEBESLIED see Schmalstich, Clemens

LIEBESLIED see Schumann, Robert
(Alexander)

LIEBESLIED see Weigl, Karl

LIEBESLIED see Weill, Kurt

LIEBESLIED see Zagwijn, Henri

LIEBESLIED see Zipp, Friedrich

LIEBESLIEDER see Krenek, Ernst

LIEBESLIEDER see Strauss, Johann

LIEBESLIEDER WALTZES, OP. 52, AND NEW
LIEBESLIEDER WALTZES, OP. 65 see
Brahms, Johannes

LIEBESLIEDER-WALZER see Brahms,
Johannes

LIEBESREIME see Peterson-Berger, (Olof)
Wilhelm

LIEBESREIME see Driessler, Johannes

LIEBESSUCHE see Kilpinen, Yrio

LIEBESTRAUM see Liszt, Franz

LIEBESTREU see Brahms, Johannes

LIEBESTRIUMPH see Landre, Willem

LIEBESTRUNKEN see Bosmans, Henriette

LIEBESWALZER see Strauss, Johann

LIEBESZAUBER see Stephan, R.

LIEBHABER IN ALLEN GESTALTEN see
Schubert, Franz (Peter)

LIEBLICH ROTEN SICH DIE WANGEN see
Lortzing, (Gustav) Albert

LIEBLICHE WALDER see Handel, George
Frideric

LIEBST DU UM SCHONHEIT see Mahler,
Gustav

LIEBSTER HERR JESU, WO BLEIBST DU SO
LANGE see Bach, Johann Sebastian

LIEBSTER JESU, DEINE LIEBE FINDET
IHRESGLEICHEN NICHT see Stolzel,
Gottfried Heinrich

LIEBSTER JESU, KEHRE WIEDER see
Telemann, Georg Philipp

LIEBSTER! NUR DICH SEH'N see Dresden,
Sem

LIEBSTER, SAGT IN SUSSEN SCHMERZEN see
Schutz, Heinrich

LIED see Chabrier, Emmanuel

LIED see Franck, Cesar

LIED see Geraedts, Jaap

LIED see Kersters, Willem

LIED see Marx, Joseph

LIED see Middeleer, Jean De, Chanson

LIED see Newlin, Dika

LIED see Schmitt, Florent

LIED see Schouwman, Hans

LIED see Schumann, Robert (Alexander)

LIED see Tremisot, Ed.

LIED see Vuillemin, L.

LIED AM HERDE see Distler, Hugo

LIED AN MEINEN SOHN see Strauss, Richard

LIED AUF DEM FLUSSE see Gilse, Jan van

LIED DER BRAUT [1] see Schumann, Robert (Alexander)

LIED DER BRAUT [2] see Schumann, Robert (Alexander)

LIED DER FRAUEN see Strauss, Richard

LIED DER HEILIGEN JUNGFRAU see Gilse, Jan van

LIED DER JUNGEN SCHWEIZER see Graf, M.

LIED DER LULU see Berg, Alban

LIED DER OUDSTRIJDERS see Zagwijn, Henri

LIED DER SCHENKWIRTIN see Mussorgsky, Modest

LIED DER SOLDATEN see Carriere, Paul

LIED DER SONNE see Lothar, Mark

LIED DER SPINNERIN see Diepenbrock, Alphons

LIED DER STARENSCHWARME see Wiemer, Wolfgang

LIED DER VERFOLGTEN IM TURM see Mahler, Gustav

LIED DER VLAAMSCHE HOGESCHOOL see Hullebroeck, Em.

LIED DER WALDTAUBE see Schoenberg, Arnold

LIED DER WALKURE see Eyken, Heinrich van

LIED DES BETRUNKENEN see Chrennikow, Tichon

LIED DES BRANDER see Busoni, Ferruccio Benvenuto

LIED DES LOPEZ see Milhaud, Darius

LIED DES MADCHENS AM FENSTER I & II see Linnala, Eino

LIED DES MEPHISTOPHELES see Busoni, Ferruccio Benvenuto

LIED DES MEPHISTOPHELES see Mussorgsky, Modest, Song Of The Flea

LIED DES MEPHISTOPHELES IN AUERBACHS KELLER see Mussorgsky, Modest, Song Of The Flea

LIED DES TAUMANNCHENS see Humperdinck, Engelbert

LIED DES TURMERS see Philipp, Franz

LIED DES UNMUTS see Busoni, Ferruccio Benvenuto

LIED DU SOIR see Ropartz, Joseph Guy

LIED EINES GEFANGENEN see Kaminski, Heinrich

LIED EINES MADCHENS see Marx, Joseph

LIED FUN A CHAVER see Freudenthal, Josef

LIED IN DER DAMMERUNG see Pylkkanen, Tauno Kullervo, Laulu Hamarissa

LIED NO. 14 see Espoile, Raoul H.

LIED OM DEN BLIJEN EN ONVOORZIENEN DOOD see Delden, Lex van

LIED TOT ALLE VERMOEIJDE ZIELEN see Badings, Henk

LIED UBER DEM KIND see Drejsl, Radim, Pisen Nad Ditetem

LIED UBER DEN FRIEDEN see Eisler, Hanns

LIED- UND GITARRENSPIEL, BAND I-II *CCU
(Bresgen; Zanoskar) solo,gtr SCHOTTS 5414-5415 s.p., ea.   (L1237)

LIED VAN DE ARBEID see Bijl, Theo van der

LIED VAN DEN HOP see Diepenbrock, Alphons

LIED VOM ALLTAG see Pahlen, Kurt

LIED VOM MEER see Zagwijn, Henri

LIED VON DER BELEBENDEN WIRKUNG DES GELDES see Eisler, Hanns

LIED VON DER BLEIBE see Kurzbach, Paul

LIED VON PRAG see Soukup, Vladimir, Pisen O Praze

LIEDCHEN AUF 2 SEITEN see Martinu, Bohuslav, Pisnicky Na 2 Stranky

LIEDCHEN DER ARBEITSRESERVEN see Gregor, Cestmir, Pisnicki Pracovnich Zaloh

LIEDCHEN UBER LIEBE see Salich, Milan, Pisnicky O Lasce

LIEDEKEN see Bunge, Sas

LIEDEKEN see Voormolen, Alexander Nicolas

LIEDER see Chaun, Frantisek, Pisne

LIEDER see Marx, Joseph

LIEDER see Strong, George Templeton

LIEDER see Haydn, (Franz) Joseph

LIEDER see Mozart, Wolfgang Amadeus

LIEDER see Mozart, Wolfgang Amadeus

LIEDER see Matthus, Siegfried

LIEDER see Wagner-Regeny, Rudolf

LIEDER see Schumann, Robert (Alexander)

LIEDER see Schoeck, Othmar

LIEDER see Schubert, Franz (Peter)

LIEDER see Beethoven, Ludwig van

LIEDER see Skolaude, Walter

LIEDER see Rosegger, Sepp

LIEDER see Mozart, Wolfgang Amadeus

LIEDER see Smetana, Bedrich

LIEDER-ALBUM see Niggli, Friedrich

LIEDER ALBUM *CC26L
(Schiotz, Aksel) [Ger] med solo,pno HANSEN-DEN s.p. contains works by: Mozart; Haydn; Beethoven; Schubert; Schumann   (L1238)

LIEDER ALBUM see Berners, Lord

LIEDER AM KLAVIER ZU SINGEN see Bornefeld, Helmut

LIEDER AN DEN KNABEN ELIS see Wildgans, Friedrich

LIEDER AUF DER FLUCHT see Semegen, Daria

LIEDER AUF EINE SEITE see Martinu, Bohuslav

LIEDER AUF WORTE VON ELISKA KRASNOHORSKA see Dvorak, Antonin

LIEDER AUF WORTE VON PFLEGER-MORAVSKY see Dvorak, Antonin

LIEDER AUF ZWEI SEITEN see Martinu, Bohuslav

LIEDER AUS ASIEN see Strategier, Herman

LIEDER AUS ASIEN III see Verhaar, Ary

LIEDER AUS DEM SCHNECKENHAUS see Baum, A.

LIEDER AUS DEM WESTOSTLICHEN DIWAN VON GOETHE see Schoeck, Othmar

LIEDER AUS DEM WUNDERHORN see Schollum, Robert

LIEDER AUS DER FREMDE see Wellesz, Egon

LIEDER AUS DER KONIGINHOFER HANDSCHRIFT see Dvorak, Antonin

LIEDER AUS DER OPER see Schultze, Norbert

LIEDER AUS WIEN see Wellesz, Egon

LIEDER-AUSWAHL see Brahms, Johannes

LIEDER-AUSWAHL see Schubert, Franz (Peter)

LIEDER-AUSWAHL see Schumann, Robert (Alexander)

LIEDER-AUSWAHL see Wolf, Hugo

LIEDER, BAND 6 see Schubert, Franz (Peter)

LIEDER, BAND 7 see Schubert, Franz (Peter)

LIEDER, BAND I, TEIL A see Schubert, Franz (Peter)

LIEDER, BAND I, TEIL A UND B see Schubert, Franz (Peter)

LIEDER, BAND I, TEIL B see Schubert, Franz (Peter)

LIEDER DER FRUHE see Wagner-Regeny, Rudolf

LIEDER DER HEIMAT see Soukup, Vladimir, Pisne Domova

LIEDER DER KINDHEIT HEFT I see Lothar, Mark

LIEDER DER KINDHEIT HEFT II see Lothar, Mark

LIEDER DER KINDHEIT (SELECTED WORKS FROM THE COLLECTION) see Lothar, Mark

LIEDER DER LIEBE see Woll

LIEDER DER LIEBE see Reutter, Hermann

LIEDER DER LIEBE see Schwickert, Gustav

LIEDER DER LIEBE see Heiss, Hermann

LIEDER DER LIEBE, LANDSCHAFT, GESELLIGKEIT see Schubert, Franz (Peter)

LIEDER DER REIFE UND ERNTE see Haas, Joseph

LIEDER DER SCHLESIER *CCU
(Strecke) solo,pno TONGER s.p.   (L1239)

LIEDER DER VOLKER, HEFT 1 *CC5U
(Behrend, Siegfried) med solo,gtr ZIMMER. 1398 $2.00   (L1240)

LIEDER DER VOLKER, HEFT 2 *CC4U
(Behrend, Siegfried) med solo,gtr ZIMMER. 1709 $2.00   (L1241)

LIEDER DER VOLKER, HEFT 3 *CC4U
(Behrend, Siegfried) med solo,gtr ZIMMER. 1745 $2.00   (L1242)

LIEDER DER VOLKER, HEFT 4 *CCU
(Behrend, Siegfried) med solo,gtr ZIMMER. 1784 s.p.   (L1243)

LIEDER DER VOLKER, HEFT 5 *CCU
(Behrend, Siegfried) med solo,gtr ZIMMER. 1785 s.p.   (L1244)

LIEDER DER VOLKER, HEFT 6 *CCU
(Behrend, Siegfried) med solo,gtr ZIMMER. 1786 s.p.   (L1245)

LIEDER DER WEIHNACHT *CC100U,Xmas
solo,pno,2treb inst sc BREITKOPF-L EB 5871A s.p.   (L1246)

LIEDER DER YVETTE AUS LEONORE see Liebermann, Rolf

LIEDER DES ABSCHIEDS see Zillig, Winfried

LIEDER DES ANGLERS see Wagner-Regeny, Rudolf

LIEDER DES GLUCKS see Haas, Joseph

LIEDER DES HERBSTES see Zillig, Winfried

LIEDER EINER MUTTER see Herrmann, Hugo

LIEDER EINES FAHRENDEN GESELLEN see Mahler, Gustav

LIEDER EINES FAHRENDEN GESELLEN see Mahler, Gustav

LIEDER EINES LUMPEN see Hessenberg, Kurt

LIEDER FUR BARITON see Mussorgsky, Modest

LIEDER FUR EINE SINGSTIMME UND KLAVIER *CCU
    solo,pno KRENN 1.7 s.p. contains works by: Kastner De Heusch, Margarethe and Ewers, Jurgen
                                        (L1247)

LIEDER FUR GESANG UND KLAVIER UND LIEDER FUR CHOR UND KLAVIER see Khachaturian, Karen

LIEDER FUR HOHE STIMME see Mozart, Wolfgang Amadeus

LIEDER FUR HOHE STIMME UND KLAVIER see Kvapil, Jaroslav

LIEDER FUR SINGSTIMME UND GITARRE see Mozart, Wolfgang Amadeus

LIEDER FUR SOPRAN see Hindemith, Paul

LIEDER FURS LEBEN *CC200U,folk,Ger [Ger] solo,inst cloth OSTER $3.00
                                        (L1248)

LIEDER (MORGENSTERN) see Schulthess, W.

LIEDER NACH DIALEKTGEDICHTEN see Vollenwyder, H.

LIEDER NACH DICHTUNGEN VON ST. GEORGE see Wellesz, Egon

LIEDER NACH GEDICHTEN VON B. BRECHT see Wagner-Regeny, Rudolf

LIEDER NACH GEDICHTEN VON E. MORIKE see Wolf, Hugo

LIEDER NACH GEDICHTEN VON EICHENDORFF see Wolf, Hugo

LIEDER NACH GEDICHTEN VON GOETHE see Schoeck, Othmar

LIEDER NACH GEDICHTEN VON HUUGO JALKANEN, OP. 15 see Kilpinen, Yrio

LIEDER NACH GEDICHTEN VON HUUGO JALKANEN, OP. 16 see Kilpinen, Yrio

LIEDER NACH GEDICHTEN VON HUUGO JALKANEN, OP. 17 see Kilpinen, Yrio

LIEDER NACH GEDICHTEN VON HUUGO JALKANEN, OP. 18 see Kilpinen, Yrio

LIEDER NACH GEDICHTEN VON INA SEIDEL see Warner, Theodor

LIEDER NACH GEDICHTEN VON LENAU, HEBBEL, DEHMEL UND SPITTELER see Schoeck, Othmar

LIEDER NACH GEDICHTEN VON SPITTELER, GAMPER, HESSE UND KELLER see Schoeck, Othmar

LIEDER NACH GEDICHTEN VON UHLAND UND EICHENDORFF see Schoeck, Othmar

LIEDER NACH R. CAPRI see Siegl, Otto

LIEDER NIEDEROSTERREICHISCHER KOMPONISTEN *CC9U,Aus (Pandion) [Ger] med solo,pno OSTER $1.25   (L1249)

LIEDER OF RICHARD STRAUSS, VOL. 1: OP. 10 TO OP. 41 see Strauss, Richard

LIEDER OF RICHARD STRAUSS, VOL. 2: OP. 43 TO OP. 68 see Strauss, Richard

LIEDER OF RICHARD STRAUSS, VOL. 3: OP. 69 TO OP. 88 see Strauss, Richard

LIEDER OF RICHARD STRAUSS, VOL. 4 see Strauss, Richard

LIEDER SALZBURGER KOMPONISTEN *CC14U, Ger (Reichert) [Ger] med solo,pno OSTER $2.25   (L1250)

LIEDER, SONGS, KANTATEN see Eisler, Hanns

LIEDER SOWETISCHER KOMPONISTEN HEFT I *CCU (Lehmann, D.) [Russ/Ger] solo,pno DEUTSCHER 9003 s.p. contains works by: Alexandrow; Arakischwili; Chatschturijan; Dunajewski; Katz; Lipatow and many more   (L1251)

LIEDER SOWETISCHER KOMPONISTEN HEFT II *CCU (Lehmann, D.) [Russ/Ger] solo,pno DEUTSCHER 9004 s.p. contains works by: Niss; Oganesjan; Prokofjew;

Salmanow; Satjan; Schebalin; Schostakowitsch and others (L1252)

LIEDER (STAMM) see Schulthess, W.

LIEDER STEIRISCHER KOMPONISTEN *CC14U (Siegl) [Ger] med solo,pno OSTER $2.00   (L1253)

LIEDER UM EINE KLEINE STADT see Kilpinen, Yrio

LIEDER UM OSTERN *CC8U,Easter (Schaller) [Ger] med solo,A rec/vln, vla/vln,vcl,gtr cmplt ed OSTER $2.00   (L1254)

LIEDER UM WEIHNACHT *CC8U,Xmas,folk (Schaller) [Ger] med solo,A rec/vln, pno/gtr cmplt ed OSTER $1.75
                                        (L1255)

LIEDER UND ARIEN see Telemann, Georg Philipp

LIEDER UND BALLADEN NACH GEDICHTEN VON F. GARCIA LORCA see Bialas, Gunther

LIEDER UND GESANGE see Meyer, Ernst Hermann

LIEDER UND GESANGE see Mozart, Wolfgang Amadeus

LIEDER UND GESANGE, BAND I see Mahler, Gustav

LIEDER UND GESANGE, BAND II see Mahler, Gustav

LIEDER UND GESANGE, BAND III see Mahler, Gustav

LIEDER UND KANTATEN BAND I see Eisler, Hanns

LIEDER UND KANTATEN BAND X see Eisler, Hanns

LIEDER UND KIRCHENMUSIKALISCHE WERKE see Pacher, Anton

LIEDER UND ROMANZEN see Chrennikow, Tichon

LIEDER UND TANZE DES TODES see Mussorgsky, Modest

LIEDER VOM LEBEN see Haas, Joseph

LIEDER VON BAUM UND WALD see Haas, Joseph

LIEDER ZUR GITARRE HEFT 1 UND 2 *CCU (Schwarz-Reiflingen, Erwin) solo,gtr SIKORSKI 210 A; 210 B s.p., ea.
                                        (L1256)

LIEDER ZUR WEIHNACHT see Wolf, Hugo

LIEDERALBUM see Sialm, D.

LIEDERALBUM, BAND 1-3 see Schoeck, Othmar

LIEDERBANDE I see Strauss, Richard

LIEDERBANDE II see Strauss, Richard

LIEDERBANDE III see Strauss, Richard

LIEDERBANDE IV see Strauss, Richard

LIEDERBUCH see Genzmer, Harald

LIEDERBUCH see Wolf, Hugo

LIEDERBUCH AUS BOHMEN see Komma, Karl Michael

LIEDERBUCH FUR HOCH STIMME see Brahms, Johannes

LIEDERBUCH FUR KINDER see Rheinberger, Josef

LIEDERBUCH FUR KLEINE KINDER *CCU [Russ] solo,pno SIKORSKI R 6359 s.p.
                                        (L1257)

LIEDERBUCH FUR MITTEL STIMME see Brahms, Johannes

LIEDERBUCH FUR TIEFE STIMME see Brahms, Johannes

LIEDERBUCH NACH GEDICHTEN VON PAUL GERHARDT see Pepping, Ernst

LIEDERBUCHLEIN see Wagner-Regeny, Rudolf

LIEDEREN see Beekhuis, Hanna

LIEDEREN see Oskam, Izaak J.

LIEDEREN see Mesritz Van Velthuysen, Annie

LIEDEREN IN VOLKSTOON, OP. 46, HEFT 1 see Spoel, A.

LIEDEREN MET EEN PRUIK OP see Mul, Jan

LIEDEREN, SERIE 1 see Cuypers, H.

LIEDEREN, SERIE 2: VAN 'T SPINSTERKE see Cuypers, H.

LIEDEREN, SERIE 3 see Cuypers, H.

LIEDEREN UIT DE TONEELMUZIEK BY "THE TEMPEST" see Pijper, Willem

LIEDEREN VAN DE NIJL see Sigtenhorst-Meyer, Bernhard van den

LIEDEREN VAN DEN DOOD see Badings, Henk

LIEDEREN VAN DOOD EN LEVEN see Badings, Henk

LIEDEREN VAN R. TAGORE "THE GARDENER" see Mengelberg, Karel

LIEDEREN VAN WALT WHITMAN see Wijdeveld, Wolfgang

LIEDEREN, VOL. 1 see Clercq, R. de

LIEDEREN, VOL. 2 see Clercq, R. de

LIEDEREN, VOL. 2 see Hullebroeck, Em.

LIEDEREN, VOL. 3 see Clercq, R. de

LIEDEREN, VOL. 3 see Hullebroeck, Em.

LIEDEREN, VOL. 4 see Clercq, R. de

LIEDEREN, VOL. 4 see Hullebroeck, Em.

LIEDEREN, VOL. 5 see Clercq, R. de

LIEDEREN, VOL. 6 see Clercq, R. de

LIEDEREN, VOL. 7 see Clercq, R. de

LIEDEREN, VOL. 7 see Hullebroeck, Em.

LIEDEREN, VOL. 8 see Hullebroeck, Em.

LIEDEREN, VOL. 10 see Hullebroeck, Em.

LIEDEREN, VOL. 11 see Hullebroeck, Em.

LIEDEREN, VOL. 12 see Hullebroeck, Em.

LIEDEREN, VOL. 13 see Hullebroeck, Em.

LIEDEREN, VOL. 14 see Hullebroeck, Em.

LIEDEREN, VOL. 15 see Hullebroeck, Em.

LIEDEREN, VOL. 16 see Hullebroeck, Em.

LIEDEREN, VOL. 17: DE LIEDEREN DER VLAAMSCHE MARTELING see Hullebroeck, Em.

LIEDEREN, VOL. 18 see Hullebroeck, Em.

LIEDEREN, VOL. 19 see Hullebroeck, Em.

LIEDERFOLGE see Kilpinen, Yrio

LIEDERHEFT FUR MARGOT UND H.H.S. *CC7U [Ger] med-high solo,pno BOTE $2.25 contains works by: Blacher; Klebe; Erbse and others   (L1258)

LIEDERHEFT, HEFT 1, 2 see Vollenwyder, H.

LIEDERHEFT SCHWABISCHER DICHTER see Lang, Max

LIEDERKREIS see Schumann, Robert (Alexander)

LIEDERZYKLUS VON DER LIEBE see Toman, Josef, Cyklus Pisni O Lasce Na Text J.V. Sladka

LIEDESLIEDER see Dvorak, Antonin

LIEDJE see Andriessen, K.

LIEDJE see Reynvaan, M.C.C.

LIEDJE see Schouwman, Hans

LIEDJE see Weegenhuise, Johan

LIEDJES EN VERSJES see Berger, B.

LIEF GA NIET HEEN ZONDER AFSCHEID see Mengelberg, Karel

LIEFDADIGHEIDSLIED see Hullebroeck, Em.

LIEJ, MIJN HART VERLANGT see Mengelberg, Karel

LIEKKI see Leiviska, Helvi (Lemmikki)

LIENERT, O.H.
Schlofliedli
solo,pno HUG s.p.   (L1259)

LIEPINS, A.
Five Romances To Lyrics By Sergei
Yesenin *CC5U
[Russ] solo,pno MEZ KNIGA 2.93 s.p.
(L1260)

LIER, BERTUS VAN (1906-   )
Atfile Fun A Ghettojid *see Gebed
Van Een Ghetto-Jood

De Dijk
narrator,2fl,2ob,2clar,2bsn,2horn,
3trp,2trom,tuba,timp,perc,harp,
pno,strings DONEMUS s.p.   (L1261)

Drie Oud-Perzische Kwatrijnen *CC3U
S solo,pno, oboe d'amore, alto
flute DONEMUS s.p.   (L1262)

Gebed Van Een Ghetto-Jood
"Atfile Fun A Ghettojid" low solo,
pno DONEMUS s.p.   (L1263)

Valerius Gedenckklank
solo,pno BROEKMANS 406 s.p.   (L1264)

LIETTUALUALAINEN LAULU see Hannikainen,
Ilmari

LIEURANCE, THURLOW (1878-1963)
Remembered
med solo,vln (E flat maj) WILLIS
$.60   (L1265)

LIEVE VROUW DER LAGE LANDEN see
Hullebroeck, Em.

LIEVELINGSKIND see Adriessen, Willem

LIEVELINGSLIED see Jonge, De.

LIFE see Curran, Pearl Gildersleeve

LIFE see Haufrecht, Herbert

LIFE see Schouwman, Hans

LIFE AND DEATH see Diamond, David

LIFE FOREVER see Gagliardi, George

LIFE HE ENDURED, THE see Sexton,
William

LIFE IN GHANA see Clarke, Henry Leland

LIFE IN JESUS see Stipe

LIFE IS A PASSING SHADOW see Kosakoff,
Reuven

LIFE NEVER CAME EASILY see Johnson, P.

LIFE REALLY BEGAN see Wilson, Al

LIFE THAT SINGS, A see Terrell, Beverly

LIFE WORTH LIVING, A *sac
(Carmichael, Ralph) solo,pno WORD
S-508   (L1266)

LIFE'S JOURNEY see Liddell, R.

LIFE'S LOVELY THINGS see Tamblyn,
Bertha

LIFE'S LULLABY see Lane, Gerald M.

LIFE'S RAILWAY TO HEAVEN *sac,gospel
solo,pno ABER.GRP. $1.50   (L1267)

LIFE'S ROSE see Mallinson, (James)
Albert

LIFE'S SHADOWS see Hope, H. Ashworth

LIFE'S STORY see Fraser, Dennise

LIFSHITZ, SHULAMIT
Songs For Rachel *CCU
solo,pno OR-TAV $.60   (L1268)

LIFT EVERY VOICE: THE SECOND PEOPLE'S
SONGBOOK *CC75U,folk
(Silber, Irwin) solo,pno/gtr OAK
000043 $2.95   (L1269)

LIFT EV'RY VOICE AND SING see Johnson

LIFT IT UP TO JESUS see Ellis

LIFT NOT THE PAINTED VEIL see Diamond,
David

LIFT THOU THE BURDENS, FATHER see
Hageman, Richard

LIFT UP A SONG see Armstrong, F.A.

LIFT UP YOUR VOICE *sac,CC32UL
(Stearns, M.B.) med solo,pno/org
COBURN $4.50 contains works by:
Bach; Handel; Mozart; Mendelssohn;
Dvorak; Schubert; Sullivan; Wolf;
Cornelius and others   (L1270)

LIGETI, GYORGY (1923-   )
Aventures
SABar soli,fl,horn,perc,pno,
cembalo,vcl,bvl sc PETERS 4838
$17.50   (L1271)

Nouvelles Aventures
SABar soli,fl,horn,perc,pno,
cembalo,vcl,bvl sc PETERS 5913
$17.50   (L1272)

LIGHT see Malipiero, Gian Francesco

LIGHT see Ropartz, Joseph Guy

LIGHT see Roussel, Albert

LIGHT A STAR FOR ME see Harwood-Jones,
H.F.

LIGHT BENSH'N *folk,Jew
med solo,pno HATIKVAH ED. 51 $.35
(L1273)

LIGHT IN DARKNESS see Cowen, Sir
Frederic Hymen

LIGHT MATTER see Finnessy, Michael

LIGHT, MY LIGHT see Carpenter, John
Alden

LIGHT OF HEAVEN, THE see Lister, Mosie

LIGHT OF THE SUNSET GLOW see Martin

LIGHT OF THE WORLD see St. Quentin,
Edward

LIGHT THAT IS FELT, THE see Ives,
Charles

LIGHT UP THE SKY see Lister, Mosie

LIGHTHOUSE, THE see Hinson, D.

LIGHTLY LIKE MUSIC RUNNING see Binkerd,
Gordon

LIGUORI, E.
Due Liriche
[It] solo,pno cmplt ed CURCI 9509
s.p.
contains: Inseguo La Notte; Ombre
(L1274)

Inseguo La Notte
see Due Liriche

Ombre
see Due Liriche

LIK EN GRONSKANDE FLADER see Brahms,
Johannes

LIKE A CLEAR, DEEP POOL see Kubik, Gail

LIKE A LAMB WHO NEEDS THE SHEPHERD
*sac
(Carmichael, Ralph) solo,pno WORD
S-509   (L1275)

LIKE A THIEF IN THE NIGHT see Fox,
Baynard

LIKE AS THE HART see Liddle, Samuel

LIKE AS THE HART DESIRETH see Allitsen,
Frances

LIKE AS THE HART DESIRETH THE
WATERBROOKS see Harker, F.
Flaxington

LIKE AS THE HART DESIRETH THE
WATERBROOKS see Willan, Healey

LIKE FROSTED SNOW THE SHEEP LAY THERE
see Worth, Amy

LIKNELSE see Merikanto, Oskar

LIKSOM DEN UNGA ZEPHYR see Peterson-
Berger, (Olof) Wilhelm

LILAC TREE see Gartlan

LILACS see Adolphus, Milton

LILACS see Kernochan, Marshall

LILACS see Rachmaninoff, Sergey
Vassilievitch

LILACS ARE IN BLOOM see Mann, Adolf

LILAS see Gedalge, Andre

LILAS BLANC see Lecocq, Charles

LILAS BLANCS see Lacome, Paul

L'ILE DE DELOS see Clerambault, Louis-
Nicolas

L'ILE DES BAISERS see Delmet, Paul

L'ILE HEUREUSE see Chabrier, Emmanuel

LILES, DAVID
Prayer Of Our Lord, The
high solo,pno WHITE HARV. VOS 751
$1.00   (L1276)

LILI see Cairone, Renato

LILIANE see Migot, Georges

LILIE DER AUEN see Genzmer, Harald

LILIEN, IGNACE (1897-1964)
Als Wij Later Elkaar Weerzien
see Drie Gedichten Van A. Donker

Am Laufenden Band
see Mietskaserne

Avendgeluiden
see Twee Gedichten Van P. Van
Ostayen
see Vier Liederen

Ballade Van Westerbork
T solo,pno DONEMUS s.p.
contains: De Kindertrein; Razzia
(L1277)

Berceuse
see Drie Oud-Vlaamsche Liederen En
Drie Kinderliedjes

Boerecharleston
see Twee Gedichten Van P. Van
Ostayen
see Vier Gedichten

Cancion De Luna Para Dormir A Un
Negrito
see Tres Poemas Negros

Canzonetta
see Vier Liederen

De Kindertrein
see Ballade Van Westerbork

De Muis, Die Knaagt
see Vier Gedichten

De Uitverkorene
see Vier Gedichten

Der Aussatzige
see Vier Lied Vom Gott Der Bettler

Der Blinde
see Vier Lied Vom Gott Der Bettler

Der Gelahmte
see Vier Lied Vom Gott Der Bettler

Desnudo Bajo La Iluvia
see Tres Poemas De Hilda Balbiani

Die Leierfrau
see Vier Lied Vom Gott Der Bettler

Die Nacht Des Zwiefels
see Sechs Gedichte Von R.M. Rilke

Die Nachtegaal
see Drie Oud-Vlaamsche Liederen En
Drie Kinderliedjes

Die Naherin
see Mietskaserne

Die Schmiede
see Mietskaserne

Drie Gedichten Van A. Donker
high solo,pno DONEMUS s.p.
contains: Als Wij Later Elkaar
Weerzien; Hoe Ver Ook Weg;
Montmartre   (L1278)

Drie Oud-Vlaamsche Liederen En Drie
Kinderliedjes
med solo,pno DONEMUS s.p.
contains: Berceuse; Die
Nachtegaal; Ghequetst Ben Ic
Van Binnen; Ik Zag Cecilia
Komen; Jan Broeder; Marc Groet
'S Morgens De Dingen   (L1279)

Elegie Sur La Mort D'une Princesse
Enchantee
high solo/med solo,pno ALSBACH s.p.
(L1280)

Funf Trunkene Lieder
Bar solo,pno ALSBACH s.p.
contains: Herz; Lenz; Nacht; Tod;
Weib   (L1281)

Galgen
see Veronica

LILIEN, IGNACE (cont'd.)

Ghequetst Ben Ic Van Binnen
    see Drie Oud-Vlaamsche Liederen En
    Drie Kinderliedjes

Herbst
    see Sechs Gedichte Von R.M. Rilke

Herz
    see Funf Trunkene Lieder

Het Geitenweitje
    see Vier Liederen

Hoe Ver Ook Weg
    see Drie Gedichten Van A. Donker

Ik Zag Cecilia Komen
    see Drie Oud-Vlaamsche Liederen En
    Drie Kinderliedjes

Im Weinblattdammer
    see Sechs Gedichte Von R.M. Rilke

Jan Broeder
    see Drie Oud-Vlaamsche Liederen En
    Drie Kinderliedjes

La Comparsa Del Farol
    see Tres Poemas Negros

La Femme A L'accordeon
    see Quatre Chansons Des Mendiants

La Guitarra De Los Negros
    see Tres Poemas Negros

L'aveugle
    see Quatre Chansons Des Mendiants

Le Lepreux
    see Quatre Chansons Des Mendiants

Le Paralytique
    see Quatre Chansons Des Mendiants

Lenz
    see Funf Trunkene Lieder

Lockung
    see Veronica

Madchen Am Fenster
    see Mietskaserne

Marc Groet 'S Morgens De Dingen
    see Drie Oud-Vlaamsche Liederen En
    Drie Kinderliedjes

Mietskaserne
    med solo,pno DONEMUS s.p.
    contains: Am Laufenden Band; Die
    Naherin; Die Schmiede; Madchen
    Am Fenster   (L1282)

Montmartre
    see Drie Gedichten Van A. Donker

Nacht
    see Funf Trunkene Lieder

Negen Liederen In Spaanschen Trant
    *CC9U
    high solo,pno DONEMUS s.p.   (L1283)

No Te Vayas Amor
    see Tres Poemas De Hilda Balbiani

O Wenn Mein Herz
    see Sechs Gedichte Von R.M. Rilke

Over Het Gras
    see Vier Gedichten

Pan
    see Vier Liederen

Quatre Chansons Des Mendiants
    med solo/high solo,pno ALSBACH s.p.
    contains: La Femme A L'accordeon;
    L'aveugle; Le Lepreux; Le
    Paralytique   (L1284)

Razzia
    see Ballade Van Westerbork

Sechs Gedichte Von R.M. Rilke
    med solo/low solo,pno DONEMUS s.p.
    contains: Die Nacht Des Zwiefels;
    Herbst; Im Weinblattdammer; O
    Wenn Mein Herz; Vor Lauter
    Lauschen; Wiener Walzer (L1285)

Seis Miniaturas *CC6UL
    [Eng] Mez solo,pno DONEMUS s.p.
                            (L1286)

Tarde Azul
    see Tres Poemas De Hilda Balbiani

Tod
    see Funf Trunkene Lieder

Tres Poemas De Hilda Balbiani
    high solo,pno DONEMUS s.p.
    contains: Desnudo Bajo La Iluvia;

LILIEN, IGNACE (cont'd.)

No Te Vayas Amor; Tarde Azul
                            (L1287)

Tres Poemas Negros
    high solo,pno DONEMUS s.p.
    contains: Cancion De Luna Para
    Dormir A Un Negrito; La
    Comparsa Del Farol; La Guitarra
    De Los Negros   (L1288)

Twee Gedichten Van P. Van Ostayen
    med solo,2fl,2ob,2clar,2bsn,4horn,
    trp,timp,perc,cel,harp,strings
    DONEMUS s.p.
    contains: Avendgeluiden;
    Boerecharleston   (L1289)

Veronica
    high solo/med solo,pno ALSBACH s.p.
    contains: Galgen; Lockung;
    Veronica Tanzt; Veronicas
    Todesgebet   (L1290)

Veronica Tanzt
    see Veronica

Veronicas Todesgebet
    see Veronica

Vier Gedichten
    high solo,pno DONEMUS s.p.
    contains: Boerecharleston; De
    Muis, Die Knaagt; De
    Uitverkorene; Over Het Gras
                            (L1291)

Vier Lied Vom Gott Der Bettler
    med solo,2fl,2ob,2clar,2bsn,4horn,
    2trp,3trom,tuba,timp,perc,cel,
    harp,pno,strings DONEMUS s.p.
    contains: Der Aussatzige; Der
    Blinde; Der Gelahmte; Die
    Leierfrau   (L1292)

Vier Liederen
    high solo/med solo,pno DONEMUS s.p.
    contains: Avendgeluiden;
    Canzonetta; Het Geitenweitje;
    Pan   (L1293)

Vor Lauter Lauschen
    see Sechs Gedichte Von R.M. Rilke

Weib
    see Funf Trunkene Lieder

Wiener Walzer
    see Sechs Gedichte Von R.M. Rilke

LILIES ARE WHITE see Fiske, R.

LILIOM (AIR DE LA ROUSSE) see Arrieu,
    Claude

LILJEFORS, RUBEN (1871-1936)
    Atervando Till Livet
    see Tre Sanger

Bleib' Bei Mir
    "Droj Hos Mig" solo,pno GEHRMANS
    s.p.   (L1294)

Blommornas Bok
    solo,pno GEHRMANS s.p.   (L1295)

Droj Hos Mig *see Bleib' Bei Mir

Fyra Dikter *CC4U
    solo,pno GEHRMANS s.p.   (L1296)

Fyra Sanger *CC4U
    solo,pno GEHRMANS s.p.   (L1297)

Himlens Bla
    solo,pno GEHRMANS s.p.   (L1298)

Hostens Var
    solo,pno GEHRMANS s.p.   (L1299)

Jungfru Maria *sac
    solo,pno GEHRMANS s.p.   (L1300)

Kung Liljekonvalje
    see Tva Sanger

Mote
    see Tre Sanger

Nar Det Lider Mot Jul
    solo,pno GEHRMANS s.p.   (L1301)

Sang
    see Tre Sanger

Sav, Sav Susa
    see Tva Sanger

Trad
    solo,pno GEHRMANS s.p.   (L1302)

Tre Sanger
    solo,pno GEHRMANS s.p.
    contains: Atervando Till Livet;
    Mote; Sang   (L1303)

LILJEFORS, RUBEN (cont'd.)

Troll- Och Tomtehistorier
    solo,pno GEHRMANS s.p.   (L1304)

Tva Sanger
    solo,pno GEHRMANS s.p.
    contains: Kung Liljekonvalje;
    Sav, Sav Susa   (L1305)

Upplandssangen
    solo,pno LUNDQUIST s.p.   (L1306)

Vi Ses Igen
    solo,pno GEHRMANS s.p.   (L1307)

LILLA ANNA see Sjogren, Emil

LILLA BLOMMA DU AR see Gounod, Charles
    Francois, Faites-Lui Mes Aveux

LILLA BLOMMA, HUR ENSAM DU AR see
    Kjellander

LILLEBARN see Nordqvist, Gustaf

LILLEMOR see Planck

LILLENAS, HALDOR
    Calvary Road, The *sac
    solo,pno LILLENAS SM-403: RN $1.00
                            (L1308)

This Same Jesus *sac
    solo,pno GOSPEL 05 TM 0446 $1.00
                            (L1309)

LILLIAN, ISADORE
    Die Sun Hot Far Mir Noch Kein Muhl
    Nit Gesheint *Jew
    solo,pno KAMMEN 241 $1.00 see also
    JEWISH THEATRE SONGS, VOL. 1
                            (L1310)

Dus Raidele Drait Sich *Jew
    solo,pno KAMMEN 64 $1.00 see also
    JEWISH THEATRE SONGS, VOL. 1
                            (L1311)

In A Klein Shtiebele *Jew
    solo,pno KAMMEN 18 $1.00 see also
    FAVORITE JEWISH SONGS, VOL. 2
                            (L1312)

Schwartze Karshelach *Jew
    solo,pno KAMMEN 450 $1.00 see also
    FAVORITE JEWISH SONGS, VOL. 2
                            (L1313)

LILLYGAY see Heseltine, Philip

LILY, THE see Geehl, Henry Ernest

LILY AND THE ROSE see Glover, Stephen

LILY OF THE VALLEY IS MY LORD, THE see
    Croft, Colbert

LILY PONS SONG ALBUM, BOOK 1 *CCU
    (La Forge) solo,pno FISCHER,C O 3213
                            (L1314)

LILY PONS SONG ALBUM, BOOK 2 *CCU
    (La Forge) solo,pno FISCHER,C O 3512
                            (L1315)

L'IMAGE see Busser, Henri-Paul

L'IMAGE see Canal, Marguerite

LIMANN
    Hymne De La Liberation
    solo,pno/inst DURAND s.p. (L1316)
    [Fr] solo,acap oct DURAND s.p.
                            (L1317)

LIMEHOUSE REACH see Head, Michael
    (Dewar)

LIMERICK POINT TO POINT RACE see
    Stanford, Charles Villiers

LIMOUSIN *Fr
    (Canteloube, J.) solo,acap DURAND
    s.p. see also Anthologie Des Chants
    Populaires Francais Tome III
                            (L1318)

L'IMPATIENCE see Rameau, Jean-Philippe

LIMPIDA FRESCA NOTTE see Davico,
    Vincenzo

LINA see Jarnefelt, Armas

LINCKE, PAUL (1866-1946)
    Froken Chic
    solo,pno GEHRMANS 468 s.p. (L1319)

LINCOLN'S GETTYSBURG ADDRESS see Wayne,
    Bernie

L'INCONNU see Arrieu, Claude

LINDAGULL, LINDAGULL LILLA see Alfven,
    Hugo

LINDAGULLS KRONA see Nordqvist, Gustaf

LINDBERG
    Make Me Willing *sac
    solo,pno BENSON S7004-R $1.00
                            (L1320)

LINDBERG, RUSS
    I'm Beginning To Understand *sac
        solo,pno WORD S-115   (L1321)

LINDBLAD, ADOLF FREDRIK (1801-1878)
    Den Gamle
        B solo,pno GEHRMANS s.p. see from
        SANGEN II   (L1322)

    En Sommardag
        solo,pno GEHRMANS 732 s.p.   (L1323)

    En Vardag
        solo,pno GEHRMANS 773-74 s.p.
                                     (L1324)
    Karin Mansdotters Vaggvisa For Erik
    XIV
        med solo,pno GEHRMANS 731 s.p.
                                     (L1325)
    Man Tro? Jo, Jo!
        solo,pno GEHRMANS 248 s.p.   (L1326)

    Sanger Och Visor, Vols. III, V, VI &
    IX *CCU
        solo,pno GEHRMANS s.p., ea. (L1327)

    Skjutsgossen Pa Hemvagen
        solo,pno GEHRMANS 730 s.p.   (L1328)

LINDBLAD, OTTO (1809-1864)
    Fyra Sanger *CC4U
        solo,pno GEHRMANS s.p.   (L1329)

    Livdrabanten Och Kung Erik
        T solo,pno GEHRMANS s.p.   (L1330)
        B solo,pno GEHRMANS s.p.   (L1331)

    Sex Romanser *CC6U
        solo,pno GEHRMANS s.p.   (L1332)

    Trolhattan
        B solo,pno HIRSCHS s.p. see from
        SANGEN II   (L1333)

    Trollhattan
        solo,pno GEHRMANS 733 s.p.   (L1334)
        Mez/Bar solo,pno HIRSCHS s.p. see
        from SANGEN I   (L1335)

LINDEN LEA see Vaughan Williams, Ralph

LINDEN, NICO VAN DER (1893-   )
    'T Was Lente
        S/T solo,pno ALSBACH s.p.   (L1336)

LINDEN TREE see Schubert, Franz
    (Peter), Der Lindenbaum

LINDEN TREE, THE see Schubert, Franz
    (Peter), Der Lindenbaum

L'INDIFFERENT see Ravel, Maurice

L'INDIFFERENTE see Badings, Henk

L'INDIFFERENTE see Hermans, Nico

LINDSAY, MISS
    Owl And Pussy Cat, The
        solo,pno CRAMER   (L1337)

LINDSAY, MRS.
    Owl And The Cockatoo
        solo,pno CRAMER   (L1338)

LINDSAY, M.
    Far Away
        2 soli,pno LEONARD-ENG   (L1339)

    Pulaski's Banner
        solo,pno CRAMER   (L1340)
        2 soli,pno LEONARD-ENG   (L1341)

    Tired *sac
        high solo,pno (D maj) LEONARD-ENG
                                     (L1342)
        low solo,pno (C maj) LEONARD-ENG
                                     (L1343)
        med solo,pno (D flat maj) LEONARD-
        ENG   (L1344)
        2 soli,pno LEONARD-ENG   (L1345)

    When Sparrows Build
        solo,pno (G maj) LEONARD-ENG
                                     (L1346)

LINE see Jarnefelt, Armas, Lina

LINES FOR THE FALLEN see Lybbert,
    Donald

L'INEVITABLE JOUR see Migot, Georges

L'INFIDELE see Absil, Jean

L'INFIDELE see Defossez, Rene

L'INFIDELE EN TERRE see Leroux, Xavier
    (Henry Napoleon)

L'INFINITO see Castelnuovo-Tedesco,
    Mario

L'INFINITO see Cimara, Pietro

L'INFINITO see Flagello, Nicholas

LINK OF LOVE, THE see Nichols, Ted

LINKE, NORBERT (1933-   )
    Benn-Epitaph
        A/Bar solo,clar,vln,vcl,pno GERIG
        HG 592 s.p.   (L1347)

    Lyrical Symphony
        high solo,fl,2ob,2bsn,2horn,3timp,
        perc,strings sc GERIG HG 575 s.p.
                                     (L1348)
    There Will Always Be Gardens (from
    Lyrical Symphony) CC3U
        high solo,orch GERIG s.p.   (L1349)

    Time Has Big Handles (from Lyrical
    Symphony)
        high solo,orch GERIG s.p.   (L1350)

LINKO, ERNST (FREDRIK) (1889-   )
    Augustinatt *see Elokuun Yo

    Dit Min Tanke Gar *see Sinne

    Ehtoo *Op.24,No.2
        "Kvall" solo,pno FAZER F 3521 s.p.
        see from Sex Sanger Till Dikter
        Av Aune Linko   (L1351)

    Elokuun Yo *Op.24,No.6
        "Augustinatt" solo,pno FAZER 3525
        s.p. see from Sex Sanger Till
        Dikter Av Aune Linko   (L1352)

    Kevatlauantai *Op.24,No.1
        "Lordagskvall Om Varen" solo,pno
        FAZER F 3520 s.p. see from Sex
        Sanger Till Dikter Av Aune Linko
                                     (L1353)
    Kvall *see Ehtoo

    Lordagskvall Om Varen *see
    Kevatlauantai

    Pa Angen Vid Rian *see Riihiniitylla

    Purolla *Op.24,No.4
        "Vid Backen" solo,pno FAZER F 3523
        s.p. see from Sex Sanger Till
        Dikter Av Aune Linko   (L1354)

    Riihiniitylla *Op.24,No.5
        "Pa Angen Vid Rian" solo,pno FAZER
        F 3524 s.p. see from Sex Sanger
        Till Dikter Av Aune Linko (L1355)

    Sex Sanger Till Dikter Av Aune Linko
        *see Ehtoo, "Kvall", Op.24,No.2;
        Elokuun Yo, "Augustinatt", Op.24,
        No.6; Kevatlauantai,
        "Lordagskvall Om Varen", Op.24,
        No.1; Purolla, "Vid Backen",
        Op.24,No.4; Riihiniitylla, "Pa
        Angen Vid Rian", Op.24,No.5;
        Sinne, "Dit Min Tanke Gar",
        Op.24,No.3   (L1356)

    Sinne *Op.24,No.3
        "Dit Min Tanke Gar" solo,pno FAZER
        F 3522 s.p. see from Sex Sanger
        Till Dikter Av Aune Linko (L1357)

    Vid Backen *see Purolla

LINKS GEHT DER FERDINAND see Petermann,
    Ernst

LINLEY, GEORGE (1798-1865)
    O Bid Your Faithful Ariel Fly (from
    Tempest, The)
        solo,pno CRAMER   (L1358)

LINNALA, EINO (1896-1973)
    Die Dreizehnjahrige *CCU
        solo,pno FAZER W 2411 s.p.   (L1359)

    Fromm
        "Hartaus" solo,pno FAZER W 2412
        s.p.   (L1360)
    Hartaus *see Fromm

    Jeesus Sana Elaman *sac
        "Jesus Livets Helga Ord" 2 soli,pno
        FAZER W 1913 s.p.   (L1361)

    Jesus Livets Helga Ord *see Jeesus
    Sana Elaman

    Kaksi Karjalaista Kansanlaulua *CC2U
        solo,pno FAZER W 1830 s.p.   (L1362)

    Kun Helmin Heijastaapi
        "Nar Himlens Faste Malar" 2 soli,
        pno FAZER W 1914 s.p.   (L1363)

    Lied Des Madchens Am Fenster I & II
    *CC2U
        solo,pno FAZER F 2626-27 s.p., ea.
                                     (L1364)
    Madrigal
        "Madrigali" solo,pno FAZER W 2413
        s.p.   (L1365)

LINNALA, EINO (cont'd.)
    Madrigali *see Madrigal

    Med Sina Skonaste Sanger
        solo,pno FAZER W 2414 s.p.   (L1366)

    Nar Himlens Faste Malar *see Kun
    Helmin Heijastaapi

LINNAVUORI, FRANZ
    Mina Laulan Sun Iltasi Tahtihin *CCU
        solo,pno FAZER W 621 s.p.   (L1367)

LINNETT, ANNE
    Sweet Thing *CCU
        solo,pno HANSEN-DEN 29230 s.p.
                                     (L1368)

L'INSAISISSABLE see Pesse, M.

LINSEN, GABRIEL
    Sylvias Visa: "Jag Gungar Pa Hogsta
    Grenen"
        solo,pno FAZER W 975 s.p.   (L1369)

L'INSENSIBLE
        solo,pno DURAND 228 s.p.   (L1370)

LINSTEAD MARKET see Benjamin, Arthur

LINTEN LOWRIN see Lawson, Malcolm

LINTU SININEN see Madetoja, Leevi

L'INUTILE SERMENT see Rabey, Rene

L'INVERNO see Ivanova, Lidia

L'INVITAION AU VOYAGE see Andriessen,
    Hendrik

L'INVITATION see Migot, Georges

L'INVITATION AU VOYAGE see Diepenbrock,
    Alphons

L'INVITATION AU VOYAGE see Lutoslawski,
    Witold

LION AND THE LAMB, THE see Kalmanoff,
    Martin

LIONCOURT, GUY DE (1885-   )
    Je N'ose
        solo,pno/inst DURAND s.p.   (L1371)

    Musique Sur L'eau
        solo,pno/inst DURAND s.p.   (L1372)

    Nocturne
        solo,pno/inst DURAND s.p.   (L1373)

LIONNET, A.
    Petit Pioupiou
        solo,pno ENOCH s.p.   (L1374)
        solo,acap ENOCH s.p.   (L1375)

LIONS AND CROCIDILES see Roberton, Hugh
    Stevenson

LIOUVILLE, F.
    L'Amour Maitre D'armes
        solo,pno ENOCH s.p.   (L1376)
        solo,acap ENOCH s.p.   (L1377)

    Madame Le Docteur
        solo,pno ENOCH s.p.   (L1378)
        solo,acap ENOCH s.p.   (L1379)

    Picards Et Normands
        solo,pno ENOCH s.p.   (L1380)
        solo,acap ENOCH s.p.   (L1381)

LIPOVSEK, MARIJAN (1910-   )
    Devet Samospevov *CC9U
        solo,pno DRZAVNA rental   (L1382)

    Sedem Samospevov *CC7U
        solo,pno DRUSTVO DSS 167 rental
                                     (L1383)
    Shine, Little Sun! *see Soncece,
    Sij!

    Sixteen Songs *CC16U
        high solo,pno DRUSTVO DSS 28 rental
        Yugoslavian text   (L1384)

    Soncece, Sij! *song cycle
        "Shine, Little Sun!" S solo,pno
        DRUSTVO DSS 86 rental   (L1385)

    Verzi *CC6U
        solo,pno DRUSTVO DSS 281 rental
                                     (L1386)

LIPPACHER, CL.
    Chanson De La Patrie
        solo,pno (available in 2 keys)
        ENOCH s.p. see from Noels
        D'Alsace   (L1387)

    Chanson D'hiver
        solo,pno ENOCH s.p. see from Noels
        D'Alsace   (L1388)

LIPPACHER, CL. (cont'd.)

Noels D'Alsace *see Chanson De La
Patrie; Chanson D'hiver   (L1389)

LIPPE
How Do I Love Thee
high solo,pno (E flat maj) BOSTON
$1.50
(L1390)
low solo,pno (D flat maj) BOSTON
$1.50
(L1391)

LIPPEN SCHWEIGEN see Lehar, Franz

LIPPINCOTT
Piper, The
med solo,pno SEESAW $2.00   (L1392)

LIQUIDITE see Roos, Robert de

LIRICHE see Orefice, Giacomo

LIRICHE DELLA RESISTENZA VIETNAMITA see
Chailly, Luciano

LIRICHE GIAPPONESI see Davico, Vincenzo

LIRICHE MISTICHE DAL POEMA DI GESU see
Tortone, A.

LIRICHE, VOL. I see Losavio, Giovanni

LIRICNI SPEVI see Ravnik, Janko

L'IRONIQUE SERENADE see Filipucci, Edm.

L'ISBA EN FLAMMES see Fourdrain, Felix

LISBON PSALMS, SET I see Ore, Charles
W.

LISBON PSALMS, SET II see Ore, Charles
W.

LISE see Godard, Benjamin Louis Paul

LISE see Rabey, Rene

LISINSKI, VATROSLAV (1819-1854)
Selected Works, Vol. I: Solo Songs
*CCU
[Slav] solo,pno CROATICA s.p.
(L1393)

L'ISOLA DEI SOGNI see Fuga, Sandro

LISSMANN, KURT (1902-   )
Neun Lieder *CC9U
low solo,pno TONGER s.p.   (L1394)

LISTEN see Schouwman, Hans

LISTEN see Skillings, Otis

LISTEN see Weigl, Vally

LISTEN, IF YOU PLEASE... see Borodin,
Alexander Porfirievitch

LISTEN! THE WIND see Dougherty, Celius

LISTENING see Thiman, Eric Harding

LISTER, HOVIE
As Time Goes By *sac
solo,pno LILLENAS SM-902: SN $1.00
(L1395)
When I Come To The End *sac
solo,pno LILLENAS SM-946: SN $1.00
(L1396)

LISTER, MOSIE
All Of Me *sac
solo,pno LILLENAS SM-633: RN $1.00
(L1397)
solo,pno LILLENAS SM-866: SN $1.00
(L1398)
At The Crossing *sac
solo,pno LILLENAS SM-701: SN $1.00
(L1399)
Behold, He Stands And Knocks *sac
solo,pno LILLENAS SM-497: SN $1.00
(L1400)
Come And See The Man *sac
solo,pno LILLENAS SM-867: SN $1.00
(L1401)
Coming Again *sac
solo,pno LILLENAS SM-882: SN $1.00
(L1402)
Day Of Miracles, The *sac
solo,pno LILLENAS SM-705: RN $1.00
(L1403)
solo,pno LILLENAS SM-856: SN $1.00
(L1404)
Desert Shall Bloom Like A Rose, The
*sac
solo,pno LILLENAS SM-877: SN $1.00
(L1405)
Freedom! *sac
solo,pno LILLENAS SM-863: SN $1.00
(L1406)
Gentle Stranger, The *sac
solo,pno LILLENAS SM-709: SN $1.00
(L1407)
Good-Bye, World, Good-Bye *sac
solo,pno LILLENAS SM-712: SN $1.00
(L1408)

LISTER, MOSIE (cont'd.)

Good Old Gospel Singing *sac
solo,pno LILLENAS SM-849: SN $1.00
(L1409)
Gospel According To Ole John, The
*sac
solo,pno LILLENAS SM-876: SN $1.00
(L1410)
He Knows Just What I Need *sac
solo,pno LILLENAS SM-715 $1.00
(L1411)
Heaven Has Already Begun *sac
solo,pno LILLENAS SM-825: SN $1.00
(L1412)
He's Coming Back--And Soon *sac
solo,pno LILLENAS SM-872: SN $1.00
(L1413)
He's Everything To Me *sac
solo,pno LILLENAS SM-717: SN $1.00
(L1414)
He's Only A Prayer Away *sac
solo,pno LILLENAS SM-718: SN $1.00
(L1415)
Highest Hill, The *sac
solo,pno LILLENAS SM-720 $1.00
(L1416)
His Grace Is Sufficient For Me *sac
solo,pno LILLENAS SM-721: SN $1.00
(L1417)
His Hand In Mine *sac
solo,pno LILLENAS SM-722: SN $1.00
(L1418)
How Long Has It Been? *sac
solo,pno LILLENAS SM-723: SN $1.00
(L1419)
solo,pno BENSON S5916 $1.00 (L1420)
I Reached Up *sac
solo,pno LILLENAS SM-878: SN $1.00
(L1421)
I Won't Turn Back *sac
solo,pno LILLENAS SM-728: SN $1.00
(L1422)
I'll Follow Jesus *sac
solo,pno LILLENAS SM-865: SN $1.00
(L1423)
I'm Bound For The Kingdom *sac
solo,pno LILLENAS SM-731: SN $1.00
(L1424)
I'm Climbing Up The Mountain *sac
solo,pno LILLENAS SM-732: SN $1.00
(L1425)
I'm Feeling Fine *sac
solo,pno LILLENAS SM-735: SN $1.00
(L1426)
In The Arms Of Sweet Deliverance
*sac
solo,pno LILLENAS SM-797: SN $1.00
(L1427)
In The Eyes Of The Lord *sac
solo,pno LILLENAS SM-837: SN $1.00
(L1428)
It's Alright Now *sac
solo,pno LILLENAS SM-744: SN $1.00
(L1429)
I've Been Changed *sac
solo,pno LILLENAS SM-738: SN $1.00
(L1430)
Joy Of Heaven Come Down, The *sac
solo,pno LILLENAS SM-852: SN $1.00
(L1431)
King And I, The *sac
solo,pno BENSON S7924-S $1.00
(L1432)
solo,pno LILLENAS SM-746: SN $1.00
(L1433)
Led By The Master's Hand *sac
solo,pno LILLENAS SM-747: SN $1.00
(L1434)
Let My Heart Be A Chapel *sac
solo,pno LILLENAS SM-806: SN $1.00
(L1435)
Light Of Heaven, The *sac
solo,pno LILLENAS SM-862: SN $1.00
(L1436)
Light Up The Sky *sac
solo,pno LILLENAS SM-879: SN $1.00
(L1437)
Lister Sung By Shea *sac,CC15UL
solo,pno LILLENAS MB-277 $2.50
(L1438)
Lister's Quartet Favorites No. I
*sac,CC19UL
4 soli,pno LILLENAS MB-135 $2.00
(L1439)
Lister's Quartet Favorites No. II
*sac,CC21UL
solo,pno LILLENAS MB-136 $2.00
(L1440)
Man On The Middle Cross, The *sac
solo,pno LILLENAS SM-751: SN $1.00
(L1441)
More And More *sac
solo,pno LILLENAS SM-869: SN $1.00
(L1442)
Mosie Lister's Song Folio *sac,
CC14UL
solo,pno LILLENAS MB-138 $2.00
(L1443)
Old-Time Faith, The *sac
solo,pno LILLENAS SM-838: SN $1.00
(L1444)
Restore My Soul *sac
solo,pno LILLENAS SM-873: SN $1.00
(L1445)

LISTER, MOSIE (cont'd.)

Showers Of Blessing *sac
solo,pno LILLENAS SM-850: SN $1.00
(L1446)
Sing Out The Glory *sac
solo,pno LILLENAS SM-886: SN $1.00
(L1447)
Talkin' 'Bout The Love Of God *sac
solo,pno LILLENAS SM-773: SN $1.00
(L1448)
Then I Met The Master *sac
solo,pno LILLENAS SM-774: SN $1.00
(L1449)
solo,pno BENSON S8096-S $1.00
(L1450)
Though Unworthy Am I *sac
solo,pno LILLENAS SM-885: SN $1.00
(L1451)
'Til The Storm Passes By *sac
solo,pno LILLENAS SM-779: SN $1.00
(L1452)
solo,pno LILLENAS SM-803: RN $1.00
(L1453)
solo,pno BENSON S8184-S $1.00
(L1454)
Touch Of His Hand, The *sac
solo,pno LILLENAS SM-781: SN $1.00
(L1455)
Touched By The Hand Of The Lord *sac
solo,pno LILLENAS SM-868: SN $1.00
(L1456)
Turn Me On! Light Me Up! *sac
solo,pno LILLENAS SM-857: SN $1.00
(L1457)
Way Of The Cross Led Me Home, The
*sac
solo,pno LILLENAS SM-864: SN $1.00
(L1458)
Where No One Stands Alone *sac
solo,pno LILLENAS SM-793: SN $1.00
(L1459)
While Ages Roll *sac
solo,pno LILLENAS SM-799: SN $1.00
(L1460)

LISTER SUNG BY SHEA see Lister, Mosie

LISTER'S QUARTET FAVORITES NO. I see
Lister, Mosie

LISTER'S QUARTET FAVORITES NO. II see
Lister, Mosie

LISTER'S QUARTET FAVORITES NO. III
*sac,CC19UL
solo,pno LILLENAS MB-137 $2.00
(L1461)

LISZT, FRANZ (1811-1886)
Aimez, Aimez, Pendant La Vie Entiere
*see Wie Entgehn

Amour Celeste *see Hohe Liebe

Bois Epais (from Amadis De Gaule)
Mez/Bar solo,pno/inst DURAND s.p.
(L1462)
Colected Works *CCUL
(d'Albert; Busoni; Raabe, Peter;
Stradal, August; da Motta, J.V.;
Kellermann, B.; Bartok, Bela;
Taubmann, Otto; Wolfrum, Philipp;
Stavenhagen, B.) contains works
for a variety of instruments and
vocal combinations microfiche
UNIV.MUS.ED. $150.00 reprints of
Breitkopf & Hartel Editions
(L1463)
'Comment' Disaient-Ils *see O Lieb,
So Lang Du Lieben Kannst

Der Du Von Dem Himmel Bist
[Ger] solo,orch KAHNT rental
(L1464)
Der Fischerknabe
[Ger] high solo,orch KAHNT rental
(L1465)
"Fischerknabe, Hirt Alpenjager"
[Ger] solo,orch KAHNT rental
(L1466)
Der Konig Von Thule
[Ger] med solo,orch KAHNT rental
(L1467)
Die Drei Zigeuner
[Ger] solo,orch KAHNT rental
(L1468)
"Les Trois Tziganes" solo,pno/inst
DURAND s.p.
(L1469)
Die Loreley
"La Loreley" solo,pno/inst DURAND
s.p.
(L1470)
Die Tote Nachtigall
[Ger] high solo,orch KAHNT rental
(L1471)
Die Vatergruft
[Ger] low solo,orch KAHNT rental
(L1472)
Dream Of Love *see Liebestraum

Drei Lieder Aus Schillers Wilhelm
Tell *CC3U
[Ger] high solo,orch KAHNT rental
(L1473)

LISZT, FRANZ (cont'd.)

Du Bist Wie Eine Blume
[Ger] high solo,orch KAHNT rental
(L1474)
"Du Liknar Skara Blomman" high
solo,pno GEHRMANS s.p.   (L1475)

Du Liknar Skara Blomman *see Du Bist
Wie Eine Blume

Ein Fichtenbaum Steht Einsam
[Ger] low solo,orch KAHNT rental
(L1476)

Es Muss Ein Wunderbares Sein
[Ger] med solo,orch KAHNT rental
(L1477)
[Ger] high solo,orch KAHNT rental
(L1478)
[Hung/Ger] solo,pno BUDAPEST 1895
s.p.   (L1479)
[Ger] low solo,orch KAHNT rental
(L1480)

Fischerknabe, Hirt Alpenjager *see
Der Fischerknabe

Five Songs *CC5U
[Hung] solo,pno BUDAPEST 3745 s.p.
(L1481)

Freudvoll Und Liedvoll
[Ger] low solo,pno KAHNT rental
(L1482)

Hohe Liebe
"Amour Celeste" solo,pno/inst
DURAND s.p.   (L1483)

Ich Liebe Dich
[Ger] solo,orch KAHNT rental
(L1484)

Ich Mochte Hingehn
[Ger] high solo,pno KAHNT rental
(L1485)

Ich Verlor Die Kraft Und Das Leben
[Ger] solo,orch KAHNT rental
(L1486)

Im Liebeslust
[Ger] high solo,orch KAHNT rental
(L1487)

Im Rhein, Im Schonen Strome
[Ger] high solo,orch KAHNT rental
(L1488)

Kling Leise, Mein Lied
[Ger] high solo,orch KAHNT rental
(L1489)

La Loreley *see Die Loreley

Le Chante De Mignon *see Mignons
Lied

Les Trois Tziganes *see Die Drei
Zigeuner

Liebestraum
low solo,pno (D maj) ALLANS s.p.
(L1490)
high solo,pno (F maj) ALLANS s.p.
(L1491)
"Dream Of Love" solo,pno (available
in 2 keys) ASHLEY $.95   (L1492)
"Love Dreams" low solo,pno (G maj)
CENTURY 3625   (L1493)

Loreley
[Ger] high solo,orch KAHNT rental
(L1494)
[Ger] med solo,orch KAHNT rental
(L1495)
[Ger] low solo,orch KAHNT rental
(L1496)
[Hung/Ger] solo,pno BUDAPEST 1894
s.p.   (L1497)
high solo,pno (G maj) ALLANS s.p.
(L1498)

Love Dreams *see Liebestraum

Mein Kind, War Ich Konig
[Ger] high solo,orch KAHNT rental
(L1499)

Mignon *see Mignons Lied

Mignons Lied
"Le Chante De Mignon" solo,pno/inst
DURAND s.p.   (L1500)
"Mignon" [Ger] med solo,orch KAHNT
rental   (L1501)

O, Komm Im Traum *see Oh! Quand Je
Dors

O Komm' In Traum
"Oh! Quand Je Dors" solo,pno/inst
DURAND s.p.   (L1502)

O Komm'in Traum *see Oh! Quand Je
Dors

O Lieb, So Lang Du Lieben Kannst
"'Comment' Disaient-Ils" solo,pno/
inst DURAND s.p.   (L1503)

Oh! Quand Je Dors
[Hung/Ger/Fr] solo,pno BUDAPEST
1896 s.p.   (L1504)
"O, Komm Im Traum" [Ger] high solo,
orch KAHNT rental   (L1505)
"O Komm'in Traum" solo,pno/inst

LISZT, FRANZ (cont'd.)

DURAND s.p.   (L1506)

Oh! Quand Je Dors *see O Komm' In
Traum

St. Cecilia
Mez solo,orch KAHNT $4.00   (L1507)

Serenade *see Standchen

Songs, Vol. 1 *CCU
S solo,pno BUDAPEST 3346 s.p. with
Hungarian and original texts
(L1508)
Songs, Vol. 2 *CCU
Mez solo,pno BUDAPEST 3347 s.p.
with Hungarian and original texts
(L1509)
Songs, Vol. 3 *CCU
A solo,pno BUDAPEST 3348 s.p. with
Hungarian and original texts
(L1510)
Songs, Vol. 4 *CCU
S solo,pno BUDAPEST 4005 s.p. with
Hungarian and original texts
(L1511)
Songs, Vol. 5 *CCU
Mez solo,pno BUDAPEST 4006 s.p.
with Hungarian and original texts
(L1512)
Songs, Vol. 6 *CCU
A solo,pno BUDAPEST 4007 s.p. with
Hungarian and original texts
(L1513)

Standchen
"Serenade" solo,pno/inst DURAND
s.p.   (L1514)

Suenos De Amor
(Pardo) [Span] solo,pno
(transcribed from: Nocturne no.
3) RICORDI-ARG BA 8725 s.p.
(L1515)

Trente Melodies *CC30L
[Fr/Ger] solo,pno DURAND 12.137
s.p.   (L1516)

Twelve Songs *CC12L
high solo,pno SCHIRM.G 1614 $2.50;
low solo,pno SCHIRM.G 1613 $2.50
(L1517)

Uber Allen Gipfeln Ist Ruh
[Ger] low solo,orch KAHNT rental
(L1518)

Wie Entgehn
"Aimez, Aimez, Pendant La Vie
Entiere" S solo,pno/inst DURAND
s.p.   (L1519)
"Aimez, Aimez, Pendant La Vie
Entiere" Mez solo,pno/inst DURAND
s.p.   (L1520)

Wieder Mocht Ich Dir Begegnen
[Ger] high solo,orch KAHNT rental
(L1521)

Wo Weilt Er?
[Ger] solo,orch KAHNT rental
(L1522)

L'ITALIA TORNA see Cinque, Vincenzo

LITANEI see Schoenberg, Arnold

LITANEI see Schubert, Franz (Peter)

LITANIE see Schubert, Franz (Peter),
Litanei

LITANIES PASSIONEES see Hue, [Georges-
Adolphe]

LITANY see Schubert, Franz (Peter),
Litanei

LITANY, A see Anderson, William H.

LITANY, A see Pinkham, Daniel

LITANY, THE see Harris, Russell G.

LITANY, FOR ALL SOULS DAY see Schubert,
Franz (Peter), Litanei

LITEN KARIN
solo,pno GEHRMANS 207 s.p. contains
also: Sa Odsligt Molnen Pa Fastet
Ga   (L1523)

LITEN KARINS VAGGVISA see Heijkorn

LITEN KARLEKSSANG see Tolonen, Jouko
(Paavo Kalervo), Pieni Rakkauslaulu

LITEN KNOPP, MODERS HOPP see Sjogren,
Emil

LITEN, MIN SJAL AR SJUK see Korling,
Felix

LITEN PRINS I VAGGAN see Sjogren, Emil

LITHANISK VISA see Chopin, Frederic

LITHENIUS, SOFIE
Tva Julvisor Mormors Tid *CC2U,Xmas
solo,pno FAZER W 3221 s.p.   (L1524)

LITLA BARN MEO LOKKINN BJARTA see
Stefansson, Fjolnir

LITTLE
Sorry, I Never Knew You *see Branch

LITTLE see Drynan, Margaret

LITTLE BELLS THROUGH DARK OF NIGHT see
Kountz, Richard

LITTLE BILLY BUTTERCUP see Darke,
Robert

LITTLE BIRD KEEPS CALLING, A see
Frauchiger, Ch., Ein Voglein Singt
So Susse

LITTLE BIRDLING IN A TREE see Keats,
Horace

LITTLE BIT OF HEAVEN, SURE THEY CALL IT
IRELAND see Ball, Ernest R.

LITTLE BLACK BOY see Cumming, R.

LITTLE BLACK BOY, THE see Cowell, Henry
Dixon

LITTLE BOXES AND OTHER HANDMADE SONGS
see Reynolds, Malvina

LITTLE BOY BLUE see Diack, John Michael

LITTLE BOY BLUE see Nevin, Ethelbert
Woodbridge

LITTLE BOY FROM THE CARPENTER SHOP, THE
see Friend

LITTLE BOY LOST see Stout, Alan

LITTLE BOY LOST see Wetherington

LITTLE BOY'S PRAYER, A see Moore, John
W.

LITTLE BROWN BROTHER see Batten, Mrs.
George

LITTLE BROWN COTTAGE see Dickson,
Stanley

LITTLE BROWN THING see Harrhy, Edith

LITTLE BUTTERCUP see Sullivan, Sir
Arthur Seymour

LITTLE CHINA FIGURE, A see Leoni,
Franco

LITTLE CLAY CART, THE see Avshalomov,
Jacob

LITTLE COLOURED COON see Hope, H.
Ashworth

LITTLE DAMOZEL see Novello, Ivor

LITTLE DAVID PLAY ON YOUR HARP *spir
(Burleigh, H. T.) low solo,pno BELWIN
$1.50   (L1525)
(Roberton, H.S.) 3 soli,pno ROBERTON
72101 s.p.   (L1526)
(Widdicombe) 2 soli,pno ROBERTON
72559 s.p.   (L1527)

LITTLE DEEDS see Younce, George

LITTLE DONKEY see Boswell, Eric

LITTLE DOOR OPENED IN HEAVEN see
Protheroe, Daniel

LITTLE DREAM SHOP see Baynon, Arthur

LITTLE DRUMMER BOY see Davis

LITTLE DRUMMER BOY see Davis, Katherine
K.

LITTLE DUSTMAN, THE see Brahms,
Johannes, Sandmannchen

LITTLE DUTCH TILES see Sharpe, Evelyn

LITTLE DUTCH TILES see Sharpe, Evelyn

LITTLE ELEGY see Duke, John Woods

LITTLE ELEGY see Strilko, Anthony

LITTLE FINNISH FOLK SONG
(Vehanen, Kosti) med solo,pno GALAXY
1.0791.7 $1.00   (L1528)

LITTLE FLOWERS see Lee, Don

LITTLE FOUR PAWS see Dougherty, Celius

LITTLE FRENCH CLOCK see Kountz, Richard

LITTLE GREEN FOREST, THE see Turner, Olive

LITTLE GREY FRIEND see Arundale, Claude

LITTLE HILLS, THE see Gleeson, Horace

LITTLE IRISH GIRL, THE see Lohr, Hermann

LITTLE ISLAND, THE see Rachmaninoff, Sergey Vassilievitch

LITTLE ISLAND, THE see Rachmaninoff, Sergey Vassilievitch, Little Island, The

LITTLE IVORY FIGURES PULLED WITH STRING see Gideon, Miriam

LITTLE JACK HORNER see Diack, John Michael

LITTLE JESUS see Rowley, Alec

LITTLE JESUS CAME TO TOWN see Anderson

LITTLE JESUS CAME TO TOWN see Anderson, William H.

LITTLE JESUS, SWEETLY SLEEP see Sowerby, Leo

LITTLE JOHN'S MORNING AFTER see Dekker, Dirk

LITTLE LAMB WHO MADE THEE? see Oldenburg, Bob

LITTLE LAMBKIN see Guastavino, Carlos, Corderito

LITTLE LASSE see Sibelius, Jean, Lasse Liten

LITTLE LORD JESUS see Slater

LITTLE LORD JESUS, THE see Protheroe, Daniel

LITTLE LOST BOY, THE see Youse, Glad Robinson

LITTLE LOVE-GOD, THE see Ketting, Otto

LITTLE MAID OF MINE see Canal, Marguerite, Ma Petit Fille Est Si Blonde

LITTLE MAN, THE see Humperdinck, Engelbert

LITTLE MARY CASSIDY see Somervell, Arthur

LITTLE MAY-TIME SONG see Dvorak, Antonin

LITTLE MOTHER OF MINE
    (Burleigh, H. T.) low solo,pno (D
    flat maj) BELWIN $1.50   (L1529)
    (Burleigh, H. T.) high solo,pno (F
    maj) BELWIN $1.50   (L1530)

LITTLE NUT-TREE, THE
    see Songs Of Wonder

LITTLE PEOPLE'S PRAYER see Cruickshank, R.

LITTLE PIGGY PORKER see Anderson, Marion

LITTLE POLLY FLINDERS see Diack, John Michael

LITTLE PRETTY NIGHTINGALE see Russell, Welford

LITTLE PRINCE see Howell, Dorothy

LITTLE PRINCESS, LOOK UP! see Faraday, Michael

LITTLE RED LARK see Willan, Healey

LITTLE ROAD TO BETHLEHEM see Dunhill, Thomas Frederick

LITTLE ROAD TO BETHLEHEM see Head, Michael (Dewar)

LITTLE SANDMAN, THE see Brahms, Johannes, Sandmannchen

LITTLE SHEPHERDESS see West, Monica

LITTLE SHEPHERD'S SONG, THE see Watts, Wintter

LITTLE SINGERS, THE see Weigl, Vally

LITTLE SONG see Shaw, C.

LITTLE SONG OF LIFE, A see Malotte, Albert Hay

LITTLE SONGS FOR LIBBY see Stutschevsky, Joachim

LITTLE STAR see Chabrier, Emmanuel

LITTLE STAR see Ponce, Manuel Maria, Estrellita

LITTLE TASTE OF HEAVEN, A see Wolfe, Lanny

LITTLE THINGS see Mourant, Walter

LITTLE THINGS THAT MATTER see Crabtree, Ralph

LITTLE TOWN IN THE OULD COUNTY DOWN see Sanders

LITTLE TOWN OF BETHLEHEM see Dunhill, Thomas Frederick

LITTLE TURTLE, THE see Sherman, H.

LITTLE WAVES OF BREFFNY, THE see Shaw, Martin

LITTLE WHITE HOUSE see Arundale, Claude

LITTLE WHITE HOUSE ON THE HILL see McGeoch, Daisy

LITTLE WINDING ROAD, A see Ronald, Sir Landon

LITTLE WORM, THE see Sachs

LITTMARCK
    Salig Farmor
        solo,pno LUNDQUIST s.p.   (L1531)

    Vackert Sa
        solo,pno LUNDQUIST s.p.   (L1532)

LIVDRABANTEN OCH KUNG ERIK see Lindblad, Otto

LIVE IN THE SUN see Hovhaness, Alan

LIVE IN THE SUNLIGHT see Androzzo, Alma Bazel

LIVE WITHOUT MY FAIR EURIDICE? see Gluck, Christoph Willibald Ritter von, Che Faro Senza Euridice?

LIVETS FORSTA DAG see Lagerheim-Romare, Margit

LIVIABELLA, LINO (1902-1964)
    Canzone Del Bimbo
        [It] solo,pno SANTIS 364 s.p.
                                     (L1533)
    La Gandola
        [It] solo,pno SANTIS 549 s.p.
                                     (L1534)
    La Madre *sac
        solo,chamb.orch (triptych) sc
        SANTIS L. 38 rental   (L1535)

    Ninna Nanna Al Bambino Gesu
        solo,pno ZERBONI 4490 s.p.   (L1536)

LIVING FOUNTAIN, THE see Naylor, Bernard

LIVING GOD, THE see O'Hara, Geoffrey

LIVINGSTON, BILL
    Lord Has Given Me A Song, The
        (composed with Wise, Jessie
        Moore) *sac
        high solo,pno (G maj) SCHIRM.G $.75
                                     (L1537)
        med-low solo,pno (B flat maj)
        SCHIRM.G $.75   (L1538)

LJAT HYRSKYJA PAIN see Madetoja, Leevi

LJUDANDE STRANG see Merikanto, Oskar, Soipa Kieli

LJUNG see Jalkanen, Teppo, Kanervan Kukka

LJUNGBY HORN see Frieberg, F.A.

LJUVA HEM see Bishop, Sir Henry Rowley, Home Sweet Home

LJUVT VAR DET DOCK! see Korling, Felix

LLANKIRAI see Espoile, Raoul H.

LLONGUERAS J.
    Buen Aire Y Bellas Canciones *CC6U
        [Span] med solo,pno UNION ESP.
        $2.00   (L1539)

LLONGUERAS J. (cont'd.)
    El Despertar De Las Flores
        [Span] med solo,pno UNION ESP. $.60
        see from Escenas Cantadas Y
        Danzadas   (L1540)

    Escenas Cantadas Y Danzadas *see El
        Despertar De Las Flores; La Madre
        Doncella; Pajarillos Del Aire
                                     (L1541)

    La Madre Doncella
        [Span] med solo,pno UNION ESP. $.60
        see from Escenas Cantadas Y
        Danzadas   (L1542)

    Pajarillos Del Aire
        [Span] med solo,pno UNION ESP. $.60
        see from Escenas Cantadas Y
        Danzadas   (L1543)

    Reir Y Cantar, Jugar Y Danzar *CC6U
        [Span] med solo,pno UNION ESP.
        $1.35   (L1544)

LLORA EL GAUCHO see Gianneo, Luis

LLORABA LA NINA see D'Esposito, Salve

LLUEVE SOBRE EL RIO see Mompou, Federico

LO see Jersild, Jorgen

LO, BEHOLD, WE COME TO ADORE HIM see Nivers, Guillaume Gabriel

LO CONOSCO A QUEGLI OCCHIETTI see Paisiello, Giovanni

LO, HERE THE GENTLE LARK see Bishop, Sir Henry Rowley

LO, HOW A ROSE E'ER BLOOMING see Erdlen, Hermann

LO, QUHAT IT IS TO LOVE see Innes, Gertrude

LO SPETTRO see Rocca, Lodovico

LO SPOSO THIO ALLA SUA ATTI see Rocca, Lodovico

LO SPOSO THIO ALLA SUA ATTI E LA RISPOSTA DELLA SPOSA see Rocca, Lodovico

LO! THE FACTOTUM see Rossini, Gioacchino, Largo Al Factotum Della Citta

LO-YANG see Heilner, Irwin

LOAM, ARTHUR S.
    Bird's Prayer
        low solo,pno (F maj) ALLANS s.p.
                                     (L1545)
        high solo,pno (G maj) ALLANS s.p.
                                     (L1546)
    Irish Fairies In June
        high solo,pno (D maj) ALLANS s.p.
                                     (L1547)
        low solo,pno (C maj) ALLANS s.p.
                                     (L1548)
    West Wind
        solo,pno ALLANS s.p.   (L1549)

LOB AUF DIE MUSIKA see Taubert, Karl Heinz

LOB DES FRUHLINGS see Marx, Joseph

LOB DES HOHEN VERSTANDS see Mahler, Gustav

LOB DES LEIDENS see Strauss, Richard

LOB DES SOMMERS see Finke, Fidelio Fritz

LOB DES SOMMERS see Finke, Fidelio Fritz

LOB UND EHRE ZOLLT DEM HERREN see Schutz, Heinrich, Jubilate Deo Omnis Terra

LOBE DEN HERREN see Vierdanck, Johann

LOBE DEN HERREN, MEINE SEELE see Hammerschmidt, Andreas

LOBE DEN HERRN, MEINE SEELE see Micheelsen, Hans-Friedrich

LOBE DEN HERRN, MEINE SEELE see Wiemer, Wolfgang

LOBET DEN HERREN, ALLE HEIDEN see Schutz, Heinrich

LOBET DEN HERREN, DER ZU ZION WOHNET see Schutz, Heinrich

LOBET DEN HERRN IN SEINEM HEILIGTUM see Schutz, Heinrich

LOBGESANG see Schutz, Heinrich, Lobet Den Herrn In Seinem Heiligtum

LOBT DEN HERRN see Schutz, Heinrich, Jubilate Deo

LOBT GOTT, IHR CHRISTEN, ALLZUGLEICH see In Dulci Jubilo

L'OCELL PROFETA see Granados, Enrique

LOCH TAY BOAT SONG
(McLeod, Robert) solo,pno CRAMER
(L1550)

LOCK
Thy Presence Lord *sac
solo,pno HOPE 161 $1.00 (L1551)

LOCK THE DOOR, LARISTON *folk,Scot
low solo,pno (G maj) PATERSON FS49
s.p. (L1552)
high solo,pno (A min) PATERSON FS49
s.p. (L1553)

LOCKE, MATTHEW (1630-1677)
Trois Chansons *CC3U
cmplt ed,cloth,min sc OISEAU s.p.
(L1554)

LOCKE NUR see Telemann, Georg Philipp

LOCKFAGELN see Korling

LOCKHEAD, A.
My Nancy
high solo,pno (E flat maj) PATERSON
s.p. (L1555)
low solo,pno (C maj) PATERSON s.p.
(L1556)

LOCKLAT see Peterson-Berger, (Olof) Wilhelm

LOCKSLEY HALL see Franco, Johan

LOCKUNG see Lilien, Ignace

LOCKUNG see Pfitzner, Hans

LOCKUNG see Schoenberg, Arnold

LOCKUNG see Sibelius, Jean

LOCKUNG see Sibelius, Jean, Lockung

LOCKWOOD, NORMAND (1906-)
Dialogue Of Abraham And Isaac, The
2 male soli,pno sc AM.COMP.AL.
$7.70 (L1557)

Golden Lady, The
med solo,pno BROUDE BR. $.95
(L1558)

I Know Starlight *spir
S solo,pno AM.COMP.AL. $.82 (L1559)
S solo,2fl,ob,clar,bsn,2horn,timp,
strings sc AM.COMP.AL. $3.30
(L1560)

Joseph, Dearest Joseph
med-high solo,pno AMP $.60 (L1561)

Mary, Who Stood In Sorrow
S solo,2fl,ob,clar,bsn,2horn,trp,
trom,timp,perc,harp,strings
AM.COMP.AL. (L1562)

Psalm 23
S solo,2fl,ob,2clar,bsn,2horn,2trp,
tuba,timp,strings AM.COMP.AL.
(L1563)

LODE AL CIEL see Paisiello, Giovanni

LODI DELLA MUSICA see Verovio, S.

LOEHR
Out Of The Deep
low solo,pno (A maj) CENTURY 83
(L1564)

L'OEILLET ROUGE see Berger, Rod.

LOES, HARRY DIXON (1892-1965)
Christmas Spirit, The (composed with
Schuler, George S.) *sac,CC14UL,
Xmas
1-2 soli,pno LILLENAS MC-201 $1.00
(L1565)

LOEWE, CARL
Archibald Douglas
Bar/Mez solo,3fl,4ob,4clar,3bsn,
6horn,3trp,3trom,tuba,timp,harp,
strings BREITKOPF-L rental
(L1566)

Die Uhr
high solo,pno HUG s.p. (L1567)
med solo,pno HUG s.p. (L1568)

Dreiunddreissig Balladen Und Lieder,
Band I & II *CCU
solo,pno SCHOTTS 604; 605 s.p., ea.
(L1569)

Herr Oluf
Bar/Mez solo,3fl,2ob,3clar,bsn,
4horn,2trp,3trom,tuba,harp,
strings BREITKOPF-L rental
(L1570)

LOEWE, CARL (cont'd.)
Odins Meeresritt
Bar/Mez solo,3fl,2ob,2clar,2bsn,
2horn,2trp,4trom,5tuba,timp,perc,
2harp,strings BREITKOPF-L
(L1571)

LOEWE, GILBERT
At Eventide
low solo,pno (E flat maj) LEONARD-
ENG (L1572)
high solo,pno (G maj) LEONARD-ENG
(L1573)
med solo,pno (F maj) LEONARD-ENG
(L1574)

Be Near Me
high solo,pno (G maj) LEONARD-ENG
(L1575)
med solo,pno (F maj) LEONARD-ENG
(L1576)
low solo,pno (E flat maj) LEONARD-
ENG (L1577)

Deep In Your Eyes
med solo,pno (E flat maj) LEONARD-
ENG (L1578)
low solo,pno (C maj) LEONARD-ENG
(L1579)
high solo,pno (F maj) LEONARD-ENG
(L1580)

Till Dawn
low solo,pno,opt vln (D flat maj)
LEONARD-ENG (L1581)
high solo,pno,opt vln (G maj)
LEONARD-ENG (L1582)
2 soli,pno LEONARD-ENG (L1583)
med solo,pno,opt vln (E flat maj)
LEONARD-ENG (L1584)
med-high solo,pno,opt vln (F maj)
LEONARD-ENG (L1585)

LOEWE, KARL GOTTFRIED (1796-1869)
Ballads And Songs, Vol. I *CC15UL
[Ger] med solo,pno PETERS 2960A
$8.00; low solo,pno PETERS 2961A
s.p. (L1586)

Ballads And Songs, Vol. II *CC20UL
[Ger] med solo,pno PETERS 2960B
$8.00; low solo,pno PETERS 2961B
$8.00 (L1587)

Carl Loewes Werke *CC446UL
[Ger] solo,pno microfiche
UNIV.MUS.ED. $65.00 reprints of
Breitkopf & Hartel Editions;
contains 17 volumes of music for
the voice (L1588)

LOF DER GODHEID see Zweers, [Bernard]

LOF VAN NEDERLAND, VOL. I see King,
Harold C.

LOF VAN NEDERLAND, VOL. II see King,
Harold C.

LOFFELSCHLIIFI see Horler, A.

L'OFFERTA DELLA ROSE see Piccioli, G.

L'OFFICIER EN BOURGEOIS see Michiels,
G.

L'OFFRANDE see Vuillermoz, Emile

LOFLIED see Schouwman, Hans

LOFSANG see Voormolen, Alexander
Nicolas

LOFTENA KUNNA EJ SVIKA
see Andliga Sanger, Heft 4

LOFZANGEN see Sigtenhorst-Meyer,
Bernhard van den

LOGAN WATER *folk,Scot
low solo,pno (E min) PATERSON FS51
s.p. (L1589)
high solo,pno (F sharp min) PATERSON
FS51 s.p. (L1590)

LOGATOME see Heiss, Hermann

LOGIE O' BUCHAN *folk,Scot
solo,pno (B flat maj) PATERSON FS50
s.p. (L1591)

LOHR, FREDERIC N.
Needles And Pins
low solo,pno (A maj) LEONARD-ENG
(L1592)
high solo,pno (E flat maj) LEONARD-
ENG (L1593)

Suffer Little Children
solo,pno CRAMER (L1594)

LOHR, HANNS
Five Songs *CC5U
solo,pno SCHAUR EE 2990 s.p.
(L1595)

Man Wunschte Sich
solo,pno SCHAUR EE 3090 s.p.
(L1596)

LOHR, HANNS (cont'd.)
Out On The Deep
high solo,pno (B flat maj) ASHDOWN
(L1597)
low solo,pno (G maj) ASHDOWN
(L1598)
med solo,pno (A maj) ASHDOWN
(L1599)

LOHR, HERMANN
Little Irish Girl, The
high solo,pno (D maj) WILLIS $.75
(L1600)
low solo,pno (B flat maj) WILLIS
$.75 (L1601)

To My First Love
see Two Little Irish Songs
see Two Little Irish Songs

Two Little Irish Songs *Ir
high solo,pno (E maj) WILLIS $.75
(L1602)

Two Little Irish Songs *Ir
low solo,pno (C maj) WILLIS $.75
contains: To My First Love; To My
First Love; You'd Better Ask
Me; You'd Better Ask Me (L1603)

You'd Better Ask Me
see Two Little Irish Songs
see Two Little Irish Songs

LOHR, INA (1903-)
Drei Psalmfragmente *sac,CC3U
med solo,treb inst,bass inst
LAUDINELLA LR 87 s.p. (L1604)

LOHSE, FRED (1908-)
Lyrisches Brevier *CCU
med solo,ob,vln BREITKOPF-L rental
(L1605)

LOIN DE MA MIE see Schule, B.

LOIN DE MA TOMBE OBSCURE see Beethoven,
Ludwig van, In Questa Tomba Oscura

LOIN D'ICI S'OUVRE UN VALLON STERILE
see Lefebvre, Channing

LOIN DU MONDE see Schlosser, Paul

LOIN DU PAYS see Berger, Rod.

L'OISEAU A VU TOUT CELA see Sauguet,
Henri

L'OISEAU BLEU see Beydts, L.

L'OISEAU BLEU see Glimes, J.de

L'OISEAU BLEU see Toutain-Grun, J.

L'OISEAU D'AMOUR see Grieg, Edvard
Hagerup

L'OISEAU INAUGURAL see Werner, Jean-
Jacques

L'OISEAU S'EST TU see Busser, Henri-
Paul

L'OISELEUR see Cuvillier, Charles

LOLA see Saint-Saens, Camille

LOLINI
Attorno Al Nome Lucia
S solo,pno RICORDI-ENG 132066 s.p.
(L1606)

LOLITA see Buzzi-Peccia, Arturo

L'OLMO see Ariosti, Attilio

LOMBARDO, ROBERT
Song For Morpheus
solo,pno BOOSEY $1.50 (L1607)

L'OMBRA MI ADUGGIA see Respighi,
Ottorino

LOMIR SICH IBERBETEN *Jew
solo,pno KAMMEN 70 $1.00 (L1608)

L'ONCLE ARMAND see Stravinsky, Igor

L'ONDINE DU LEMAN see Chaminade, Cecile

L'ONDINE ET LE PECHEUR see Schubert,
Franz (Peter)

LONDON see Kagen, Sergius

LONDON, EDWIN (1929-)
Bear's Song, The
solo,pno NEW VALLEY $2.25 (L1609)

Portraits Of Three Ladies
[Eng] narrator,Mez solo,fl,ob,clar,
bass clar,sax,horn,2trp,trom,
tuba,2perc,vln,vcl,bvl PETERS
66546 rental (L1610)

LONDON GIRL see Snodgrass, Louise

LONDON TOWN see German, Edward

LONDONDERRY AIR
  (Gould, Monk) low solo,pno (D flat
    maj) ASHDOWN s.p.   (L1611)
  (Gould, Monk) high solo,pno (E flat
    maj) ASHDOWN s.p.   (L1612)
  (Rolfe) low solo,pno (C maj) CENTURY
    3474   (L1613)

LONDONDERRY AIR see Stanford, Charles
  Villiers

LONE DOG see Head, Michael (Dewar)

LONE, WILD BIRD, THE *sac
  (Johnson, David N.) med solo,pno
    AUGSBURG 11-0726 $.65   (L1614)

LONELINESS see Van De Water, B.

LONELY BUGLE GRIEVES, THE see Verrall,
  John

LONELY CABIN, THE see Hier, Ethel Glenn

LONELY FARM ON THE HILL, THE
  see Three Bohemian Songs

LONELY GATE OF CRIMSON RUBIES, WALK ON
  see Respighi, Ottorino, Bella Porta
  Di Rubini

LONELY I CAN NEVER BE see Dunlop,
  Merrill

LONELY ISLE, THE see Birch, Robert
  Fairfax

LONELY OF HEART, THE see Nelson,
  Havelock

LONELY PEOPLE see Berger, Jean

LONELY STAR see Siegmeister, Elie

LONELY VOICES see Hanks

LONELY WOMAN see Lovec, Vladimir,
  Osamljena

LONESOME TUNES *CCU
  (Brockway, Howard) med solo,pno
    BELWIN $4.00   (L1615)

LONESOME VALLEY see Wilson

LONESOME WALLS see Wood, Joseph

LONG AGO IN BETHLEHEM
  see Three Moravian Carols

LONG AGO IN BETHLEHEM see De Vito,
  Albert

LONG BEAT HOME see Hope, H. Ashworth

LONG, H.
  How To Sing Naturally *CCU
    solo,pno LEONARD-ENG   (L1616)

LONG, LONG AGO see Weigl, Vally

LONG ROADS, THE see Heilner, Irwin

LONG SHIPS see McKellar, K.

LONG TIME AGO, A see Berkeley, Lennox

LONG TIME AGO, A see De Angelis,
  Ugalberto

LONG WAY FROM HOME, A see Allan, Lewis

LONG WHARF SONGS
  (Pitcher; McBradd) med solo,pno
    WILLIS $1.25
    contains: Cass County; Fable;
    Octobrian Mood; Passacablia
                               (L1617)

LONG YEARS AGO IN BETHLEHEM see
  Clayton, Norman

LONGAS
  My Heart Is Like A Singing Bird
    solo,pno ALLANS s.p.   (L1618)

LONGER I SERVE HIM, THE see Gaither

LONGING see Church, Harden

LONGING see Sibelius, Jean, Sehnsucht

LONGING see Stansell

LONGING FOR JESUS see Baker, Richard

LONGO, ACHILLE (1900-1954)
  Serenatella
    [It] solo,pno CURCI 477 s.p.
                               (L1619)
  Spingole Francesi
    [It] solo,pno CURCI 478 s.p.
                               (L1620)

LONGO, ACHILLE (cont'd.)
  Tiriti, Tiritombola
    [It] solo,pno CURCI 488 s.p.
                               (L1621)
  Vocca Addurosa
    [It] solo,pno CURCI 479 s.p.
                               (L1622)

LONGSHOREMAN, THE see Chesham, Edward
  M.

LONQUE, GEORGES (1900-1967)
  Au Gre Des Vents *Op.16
    S solo,pno CBDM s.p.   (L1623)
  Dernieres Feuilles *Op.18
    A/Bar solo,pno CBDM s.p.   (L1624)
  Faune *Op.21
    S solo,pno CBDM s.p.   (L1625)
  Je N'ai Pas Oublie *Op.2
    med solo,pno CBDM s.p.   (L1626)
  La Question *Op.46
    S solo,pno CBDM s.p.   (L1627)
  Portrait *Op.47
    S solo,pno CBDM s.p.   (L1628)
  Vos Yeux *Op.3
    S solo,pno CBDM s.p.   (L1629)

LONTANA see Persico, Mario

LONTANA see Zandonai, Riccardo

LONTANO, LONTANO see Boito, Arrigo

LOOFT GOD DEN HEER see Schouwman, Hans

LOOK, THE see Flothius, Marius

LOOK DOWN DEAR EYES see Fisher, Howard

LOOK DOWN FAIR MOON see Mollicone,
  Henry

LOOK DOWN, HARMONIUS SAINT see Handel,
  George Frideric

LOOK FOR ME AT JESUS' FEET see Parsons

LOOK, FRIEND, AT ME see Rovics, Howard

LOOK HOW THE FLOOR OF HEAVEN see
  Finney, Ross Lee

LOOK HOW THE FLOOR OF HEAVEN see
  Thomson, Virgil

LOOKING AT A BLACKBIRD see Glanville-
  Hicks, Peggy

LOOKING FOR A CITY *sac
  solo,pno STAMPS 7272 $1.00   (L1630)

LOOKING FOR THE MAN NAMED JESUS *sac
  (Carmichael, Ralph) solo,pno WORD
    S-511   (L1631)

LOOM, THE see Williams, Grace

LOOMHEID IS OP UW HART see Andriessen,
  Hendrik

LOOTS, PH.
  Aan Zee *Op.63,No.3
    solo,pno ALSBACH s.p.   (L1632)
  Bij Het Uitleiden Van St. Nicolaas
    see Vier Sinterklaasliedjes
  Een Lentekind
    solo,pno ALSBACH s.p.   (L1633)
  Gloria Jezuke, Gloria *Op.67,No.1
    see Twee Kerstliedjes
  Ik Heb Gezien *Op.64,No.2
    see Twee Gedichtjes
  Meiliedje *Op.63,No.1
    solo,pno ALSBACH s.p.   (L1634)
  Sinterklaas
    see Vier Sinterklaasliedjes
  Sinterklaas-Polka
    see Vier Sinterklaasliedjes
  Tranendichtjes *Op.29
    Bar solo,pno ALSBACH s.p. (L1635)
  Twee Gedichtjes
    solo,pno ALSBACH s.p.
    contains: Ik Heb Gezien, Op.64,
    No.2; Wil Je 'T Niet Zeggen?,
    Op.64,No.1   (L1636)
  Twee Kerstliedjes *sac
    solo,pno ALSBACH s.p.
    contains: Gloria Jezuke, Gloria,
    Op.67,No.1; Zij Hielden Er
    Wacht, Op.67,No.2   (L1637)

LOOTS, PH. (cont'd.)
  Vier Sinterklaasliedjes
    solo,pno ALSBACH s.p.
    contains: Bij Het Uitleiden Van
    St. Nicolaas; Sinterklaas;
    Sinterklaas-Polka; Welkom
                               (L1638)
  Welkom
    see Vier Sinterklaasliedjes
  Wil Je 'T Niet Zeggen? *Op.64,No.1
    see Twee Gedichtjes
  Zij Hielden Er Wacht *Op.67,No.2
    see Twee Kerstliedjes

LOPEZ-BUCHARDO, CARLOS (1881-1948)
  Cancion De Ausencia
    [Span] solo,pno RICORDI-ARG BA 8927
    s.p.   (L1639)
  Cancion De Perico
    [Span] solo,pno RICORDI-ARG BA 8928
    s.p.   (L1640)
  Cancion Del Carretero
    see Seis Canciones Al Estilo
    Popular
    [Span] S/T solo,pno (C min)
    RICORDI-ARG BA 6117 s.p.   (L1641)
  Cancion Del Nino Pequenito
    [Span] solo,pno RICORDI-ARG
    BA 10104 s.p.   (L1642)
  Canta Tu Canto, Ruisenor Y Vuela
    [Span] solo,pno RICORDI-ARG
    BA 10139 s.p.   (L1643)
  Cinco Canciones Argentinas Al Estilo
    Popular
    [Span] S/T solo,pno RICORDI-ARG
    BA 7207 s.p.
    contains: Frescas Sombras De
    Sauces; Malhaya La Suerte Mia!;
    Oye Mi Llanto; Prendiditos De
    La Mano; Si Lo Hallas..   (L1644)
  Copla Criolla
    [Span] solo,pno RICORDI-ARG BA 8929
    s.p.   (L1645)
  Desdichas De Mi Pasion
    see Seis Canciones Al Estilo
    Popular
  Frescas Sombras De Sauces
    see Cinco Canciones Argentinas Al
    Estilo Popular
  Jujena
    see Seis Canciones Al Estilo
    Popular
  Lamento
    [Span] solo,pno RICORDI-ARG BA 8930
    s.p.   (L1646)
  Los Punalitos
    see Seis Canciones Al Estilo
    Popular
  Malhaya La Suerte Mia!
    see Cinco Canciones Argentinas Al
    Estilo Popular
  Oye Mi Llanto
    see Cinco Canciones Argentinas Al
    Estilo Popular
  Pampeana
    [Span] solo,pno RICORDI-ARG
    BA 10138 s.p.   (L1647)
  Petite Ynga
    [Fr] solo,pno RICORDI-ARG BA 10140
    s.p.   (L1648)
  Pobres Jazmines Criollos! (from La
    Perichona)
    [Span] solo,pno RICORDI-ARG
    BA 10140 s.p.   (L1649)
  Portenita
    [Span] solo,pno RICORDI-ARG BA 7085
    s.p.   (L1650)
  Prendiditos De La Mano
    see Cinco Canciones Argentinas Al
    Estilo Popular
  Querendona
    [Span] solo,pno RICORDI-ARG BA 8931
    s.p.   (L1651)
  Seis Canciones Al Estilo Popular
    [Span] S/T solo,pno cmplt ed
    RICORDI-ARG BA 6020 s.p.
    contains: Cancion Del Carretero;
    Desdichas De Mi Pasion; Jujena;
    Los Punalitos; Vidala; Vidalita
                               (L1652)
  Si Lo Hallas..
    see Cinco Canciones Argentinas Al
    Estilo Popular

LOPEZ-BUCHARDO, CARLOS (cont'd.)

Vidala
see Seis Canciones Al Estilo
Popular
[Span] solo,pno (F sharp maj)
RICORDI-ARG BA 11097 s.p. (L1653)

Vidalita
see Seis Canciones Al Estilo
Popular

LOPEZ PEREYRA see Chazarreta

LOPEZ DE LA ROSA, HORATIO
Con Una Manzana Verde
see Tres Canciones Americanas, Op.
15

La Campana
see Tres Canciones Americanas, Op.
15

Tres Canciones Americanas, Op. 15
*So Am
[Span] solo,pno cmplt ed RICORDI-
ARG BA 11885 s.p.
contains: Con Una Manzana Verde;
La Campana; Villancico (L1654)

Villancico
see Tres Canciones Americanas, Op.
15

L'OR DI NOTTE see Gandino, Adolfo

LORA, ANTONIO
At Sunset Time
Mez solo,4strings AM.COMP.AL. sc
$3.85, ipa, voc sc $3.30 (L1655)

Desire
high solo,pno AM.COMP.AL. $1.10
(L1656)

Dream
med solo,pno AM.COMP.AL. $1.10
(L1657)

Elixir
low solo,pno AM.COMP.AL. $1.10
(L1658)
high solo,pno AM.COMP.AL. $1.10
(L1659)

Faerie Frolic
high solo,pno AM.COMP.AL. $3.30
(L1660)

Galatea
med solo,2fl,2ob,2clar,2bsn,4horn,
3trp,3trom/tuba,timp,triangle,
strings sc AM.COMP.AL. $6.60
(L1661)

Green Air
S solo,fl,ob,clar,bsn,horn,trp,
trom,timp,strings AM.COMP.AL. sc
$11.00, voc sc $3.85 (L1662)

Holy Hill, A
med solo,pno AM.COMP.AL. $1.37
(L1663)

I Saw The Rose
high solo,pno AM.COMP.AL. $1.10
(L1664)

If You Had Died
high solo,pno AM.COMP.AL. $2.75
(L1665)

In Love With Time
high solo,pno AM.COMP.AL. $1.10
(L1666)

Maiden
med solo,pno SEESAW $1.00 (L1667)
high solo,pno AM.COMP.AL. $1.10
(L1668)

Miletus
high solo,pno AM.COMP.AL. $1.10
(L1669)

Nostalgia
high solo,pno AM.COMP.AL. $1.10
(L1670)

Our Lady Of Sorrow
med solo,pno AM.COMP.AL. $1.10
(L1671)

Poet's Dream, The
high solo,pno AM.COMP.AL. $1.10
(L1672)

Release
med solo,pno AM.COMP.AL. $1.10
(L1673)

Sail Away
high solo,pno AM.COMP.AL. $1.10
(L1674)

Sea Song
low solo,pno AM.COMP.AL. $3.02
(L1675)
high solo,pno AM.COMP.AL. $3.02
(L1676)

She Walks In Beauty
high solo,pno AM.COMP.AL. $1.37
(L1677)

Silhouettes
high solo/med solo,pno SEESAW $1.00
(L1678)

Song Of The Waterfront
low solo,pno AM.COMP.AL. $1.37
(L1679)

Souvenir
high solo,pno AM.COMP.AL. $1.10
(L1680)

LORA, ANTONIO (cont'd.)

Three Songs *CC3U
high solo,pno AM.COMP.AL. $5.50
(L1681)

Through The Eyes Of A Babe
med solo,pno AM.COMP.AL. $1.37
(L1682)

Tryst
high solo,pno AM.COMP.AL. $1.10
(L1683)

Veil, The
high solo,pno AM.COMP.AL. $1.10
(L1684)

Wanderlust
high solo,pno AM.COMP.AL. $1.37
(L1685)

L'ORA CHE PARTE see Pratella, Francesco
Balilla

L'ORA, O TIRSI see Puccini, Giacomo

L'ORAGE S'EST CALME see Bizet, Georges

LORAND, ISTVAN
Four Songs *CC4U
[Hung/Ger] solo,pno BUDAPEST 4197
s.p. (L1686)

LORCA, F.G.
Canciones Espanolas Antiguas *CC13U,
Span
(Garcia Velasco) [Span] med solo,
gtr UNION ESP. $3.75 (L1687)

LORCA SONGS see Kazacsay, T.

LORD ABOVE, THE see Skillings, Otis

LORD ACCEPTED ME, THE see Wetherington

LORD ALL HOLY, ALL MERCIFUL see Bach,
Johann Sebastian

LORD ALMIGHTY GOD see Tchaikovsky,
Piotr Ilyitch

LORD BLESS YOU, THE see Bach, Johann
Sebastian

LORD BLESS YOU AND KEEP YOU, THE see
Lutkin, Peter Christian

**LORD BY WISDOM HATH FOUNDED THE EARTH,
THE** see Fischer, Irwin

LORD COMETH, THE see Franco, Johan

LORD, DAVIS
Wife Of Winter, The
[Eng] Mez solo,pno UNIVER. 15365
$4.75 (L1688)

LORD, DO THOU GUIDE ME see Binder,
Abraham Wolfe

LORD, DON'T LET ME FAIL see Jenkins,
Margaret Aikens

LORD, DON'T LET ME FAIL YOU see Davis

LORD, GIVE ME A SONG see Akers, Doris

LORD GOD OF ABRAHAM see Mendelssohn-
Bartholdy, Felix

LORD HAS A CHILD, THE see Schuman, W.

LORD HAS GIVEN ME A SONG, THE see
Livingston, Bill

LORD, I ADORE THEE *sac,gospel
solo,pno ABER.GRP. $1.50 (L1689)

LORD I WANT TO BE see Wille, Stewart

LORD, I WANT TO GO HOME see
Wetherington

LORD, I WANT TO GO TO HEAVEN see
Wetherington

LORD, I'M COMING HOME TODAY see Dalton,
Larry

LORD, IN THEE DO I TRUST see Buxtehude,
Dietrich

LORD IS A BUSY MAN, THE *sac,gospel
solo,pno ABER.GRP. $1.50 (L1690)

LORD IS EXALTED, THE see Edwards, Clara

LORD IS GOD see Davis, Katherine K.

LORD IS IN HIS HOLY TEMPLE see Peter,
Johann Friedrich

LORD IS MY CAPTAIN see Twohig

LORD IS MY LIGHT see Allitsen, Frances

LORD IS MY LIGHT, THE see Allitsen,
Frances

LORD IS MY LIGHT, THE see Buck, Dudley

LORD IS MY LIGHT, THE see Edwards,
Clara

LORD IS MY LIGHT, THE see Speaks, Oley

LORD IS MY SHEPHERD see Liddle, Samuel

LORD IS MY SHEPHERD see Wooler, A.

LORD IS MY SHEPHERD, THE see Binder,
Abraham Wolfe, Adonoy Ro-ee

LORD IS MY SHEPHERD, THE see Clarke,
Henry Leland

LORD IS MY SHEPHERD, THE see Davidson,
Charles

LORD IS MY SHEPHERD, THE see Fischer,
Irwin

LORD IS MY SHEPHERD, THE see
Freudenthal, Josef

LORD IS MY SHEPHERD, THE see Gilbert,
Norman

LORD IS MY SHEPHERD, THE see Grant,
David

LORD IS MY SHEPHERD, THE see Humphreys,
Don

LORD IS MY SHEPHERD, THE see La
Montaine, John

LORD IS MY SHEPHERD, THE see Matthews,
Thomas

LORD IS MY SHEPHERD, THE see O'Connor-
Morris, G.

LORD IS MY SHEPHERD, THE see Rosner,
Arnold

LORD IS MY SHEPHERD, THE see Sifler,
Paul J.

LORD IS MY SHEPHERD, THE see Smart,
Henry Thomas

LORD IS MY SHEPHERD, THE see Sowerby,
Leo

LORD IS MY SHEPHERD, THE see
Tchaikovsky, Piotr Ilyitch

LORD, IT BELONGS NOT TO MY CARE see
Fox, George

LORD JESUS CHRIST! see Barber, Samuel

LORD JESUS CHRIST, THOU PRINCE OF PEACE
see Bach, Johann Sebastian

LORD JESUS, THINK ON ME see Owens, Sam
Batt

LORD LET ME LIVE TODAY see Moore, F.C.

LORD, LISTEN TO YOUR CHILDREN PRAYING
see Medema, Ken

LORD, LORD, OPEN TO US see Bender, Jan

LORD, MAKE ME THINE INSTRUMENT see
York, Daniel Stanley

LORD MAY THEIR LIVES see Carroll, J.
Robert

LORD MAYOR'S TABLE, THE see Walton,
William

LORD, MY GOD, BE PRAISED, THE see Bach,
Johann Sebastian

LORD OF ALL see Wilson, John F.

LORD OF OUR LIFE see Bateman, Ronald

LORD RANDALL
(Scott) med solo,pno ELKIN 27.1572.04
s.p. (L1691)

LORD RENDAL
(Bantock, Granville) solo,pno CRAMER
$1.15 (L1692)

LORD REOCH'S DAUGHTER see Lawson,
Malcolm

LORD SEND ME see Watters, Bob

LORD, TAKE THE HAND OF THIS CHILD see
Croft, Colbert

LORD, TEACH ME THY STATUTES see
Fischer, Irwin

LORD THE GOOD SHEPHERD, THE see
Zavaglia, Francis L.

LORD, WHAT IS MAN see Purcell, Henry

LORD, WHAT IS MAN, LOST MAN see
    Purcell, Henry

LORD, WHO SHALL DWELL UPON THY HOLY
    HILL? see Marcello, Benedetto

LORD, WHO THROUGHOUT THESE FORTY DAYS
    see Lang

LORD WILL MAKE A WAY, THE *sac,gospel
    solo,pno ABER.GRP. $1.50   (L1693)

LORDAGSAFTON see Merikanto, Oskar,
    Lauantai-Ilta

LORDAGSKVALL OM VAREN see Linko, Ernst
    (Fredrik), Kevatlauantai

LORDLY HUDSON, THE see Rorem, Ned

LORD'S BLESSING, THE see Freudenthal,
    Josef

LORD'S CONTROVERSY WITH HIS PEOPLE, THE
    see Gerschefski, Edwin

LORD'S MY SHEPHERD (Psalm 23) sac,Scot
    (Mueller) med solo,pno (F maj)
    FISCHER,C V 2300   (L1694)

LORD'S PRAYER see Head, Michael (Dewar)

LORD'S PRAYER, THE *sac
    solo,pno STAMPS 7243 $1.00   (L1695)

LORD'S PRAYER, THE see Burton, Eldin

LORD'S PRAYER, THE see Cadzow, D.

LORD'S PRAYER, THE see Carey

LORD'S PRAYER, THE see Cory, George

LORD'S PRAYER, THE see Earls, Paul

LORD'S PRAYER, THE see Forsyth,
    Josephine

LORD'S PRAYER, THE see Franco, Johan

LORD'S PRAYER, THE see Heller, A.

LORD'S PRAYER, THE see Hoffmeister,
    Leon Abbott

LORD'S PRAYER, THE see Malotte, Albert
    Hay

LORD'S PRAYER, THE see Moore, J. Chris

LORD'S PRAYER, THE see Peeters, Flor,
    Pater Noster

LORD'S PRAYER, THE see Proulx, Richard

LORD'S PRAYER, THE see Robertson, E.

LORD'S PRAYER, THE see Rorem, Ned

LORD'S PRAYER, THE see Strals

LORD'S PRAYER, THE see Williamson

LORELEY see Liszt, Franz

LORELEY see Silcher

LORENZ, ELLEN JANE (1907-   )
    Three Songs For Sacred Occasions
    *sac,CC3U,Commun/Marriage
    med solo,pno ABINGDON APM-348 $1.00
    Baptism   (L1696)

LORENZINI, DANILO (1952-   )
    Il Viaggiatore
    solo,pno ZERBONI 8075 s.p.   (L1697)

    Tre Liriche Han *CC3U
    S solo,9inst voc sc ZERBONI 7258
    s.p.   (L1698)

LORENZO IL MAGNIFICO see Markevitch,
    Igor

L'ORGUE see Arrieu, Claude

L'ORGUE see Chaminade, Cecile

LORNA'S SONG see Ross, Colin

LORRAINE *Fr
    (Canteloube, J.) solo,acap DURAND
    s.p. see also Anthologie Des Chants
    Populaires Francais Tome III
                                 (L1699)

LORSQUE JE MOURRAI see Saint Jean Du
    Sacre Coeur, Soeur

LORSQUE JE PARTIS DE METRO-BAZAR see
    Cuvillier, Charles

LORSQUE J'ETAIS TANT AMOUREUSE
    see Chants De France Vol. II

LORSQUE NOUS AVIONS TRIOS DINDONS see
    Strimer, Joseph

LORSQUE TU DORS see Gallois Montbrun

LORTZING, (GUSTAV) ALBERT (1801-1851)
    A, B, C, D (from Der Wildschutz)
    SB soli,2fl,2ob,2bsn,2horn,2trp,
    timp,strings BREITKOPF-L rental
                                 (L1700)
    Auch Ich War Ein Jungling (from Der
    Waffenschmied)
    Bar/B solo,2fl,2clar,2bsn,2horn,
    timp,strings BREITKOPF-L rental
                                 (L1701)
    Auf Des Lebens Raschen Wogen (from
    Der Wildschutz)
    S solo,2fl,2ob,2clar,2bsn,2horn,
    2trp,timp,strings BREITKOPF-L
    rental   (L1702)
    Darf Eine Niedre Magd Es Wagen (from
    Zar Und Zimmermann)
    ST soli,2fl,2clar,2bsn,4horn,
    strings BREITKOPF-L rental
                                 (L1703)
    Die Eifersucht Ist Eine Plage (from
    Zar Und Zimmermann)
    S solo,2fl,2ob,2clar,2bsn,2horn,strings
    BREITKOPF-L rental   (L1704)
    Du Bist Ein Arbeitsamer Mensch (from
    Der Waffenschmied)
    TB soli,2fl,2clar,2bsn,2horn,
    strings BREITKOPF-L rental
                                 (L1705)
    Er Schlaft, Wir Alle Sind In Angst
    Und Not (from Der Waffenschmied)
    S solo,2fl,2ob,2clar,2bsn,4horn,
    trp,timp,strings BREITKOPF-L
    rental   (L1706)
    Funftausend Taler (from Der
    Wildschutz)
    B solo,2fl,2ob,2bsn,2horn,2trp,
    timp,strings BREITKOPF-L rental
                                 (L1707)
    Heiterkeit Und Frohlichkeit (from Der
    Wildschutz)
    Bar solo,2fl,2ob,2clar,2bsn,4horn,
    2trp,3trom,timp,strings
    BREITKOPF-L rental   (L1708)
    Ich War In Meinen Jungen Jahren (from
    Undine)
    B solo,fl,2ob,2bsn,strings
    BREITKOPF-L rental   (L1709)
    Ihr Wisst, Dass Er Euch Liebt (from
    Der Waffenschmied)
    SBar soli,2fl,2clar,2bsn,4horn,
    strings BREITKOPF-L rental
                                 (L1710)
    Lass Er Doch Horen (from Der
    Wildschutz)
    SB soli,2fl,2ob,2bsn,4horn,strings
    BREITKOPF-L rental   (L1711)
    Lebe Wohl, Mein Flandrisch Madchen
    (from Zar Und Zimmermann)
    T solo,2fl,2ob,2bsn,2horn,strings
    BREITKOPF-L rental   (L1712)
    Lieblich Roten Sich Die Wangen (from
    Zar Und Zimmermann)
    S solo,mix cor,2fl,2ob,2clar,2bsn,
    4horn,2trp,3trom,timp,perc,
    strings BREITKOPF-L rental
                                 (L1713)
    Man Wird Ja Einmal Nur Geboren (from
    Der Waffenschmied)
    T solo,2fl,2clar,2bsn,2horn,strings
    BREITKOPF-L rental   (L1714)
    Nun Ist's Vollbracht! Du Kehrst Zur
    Heimat Wieder (from Undine)
    Bar solo,cor,2fl,2ob,2clar,2bsn,
    4horn,2trp,3trom,timp,strings
    BREITKOPF-L rental   (L1715)
    O Sancta Justitia (from Zar Und
    Zimmermann)
    B solo,2fl,2ob,2clar,2bsn,2horn,
    2trp,timp,strings BREITKOPF-L
    rental   (L1716)
    So Wisse, Dass In Allen Elementen
    (from Undine)
    S solo,2fl,2clar,2bsn,2horn,timp,
    strings BREITKOPF-L rental
                                 (L1717)
    Sonst Spielt Ich Mit Zepter (from Zar
    Und Zimmermann)
    Bar solo,fl,2clar,2bsn,2horn,2trp,
    3trom,timp,strings BREITKOPF-L
    rental   (L1718)
    Vater, Mutter, Schwestern, Bruder
    (from Undine)
    T solo,fl,2clar,2bsn,strings
    BREITKOPF-L rental   (L1719)
    Was Seh Ich? (from Undine)
    TB soli,2fl,2clar,2bsn,2horn,
    strings BREITKOPF-L rental
                                 (L1720)

LORTZING, (GUSTAV) ALBERT (cont'd.)

    Welt, Du Kannst Mir Nicht Gefallen
    (from Der Waffenschmied)
    Mez/A solo,2fl,2ob,2bsn,2horn,
    strings BREITKOPF-L rental
                                 (L1721)
    Wir Armen, Armen Madchen (from Der
    Waffenschmied)
    S solo,2fl,2ob,2bsn,2horn,strings
    BREITKOPF-L rental   (L1722)

LOS ALAMOS BAJO LA LUNA see Grisolia,
    Pascual

LOS BARCOS PASAN TAN CERCA DE LA ORILLA
    see Ficher, Jacobo

LOS BILBILCOS
    (Neumann, Richard) "Nightingales,
    The" solo,pno/org (Ladino text)
    TRANSCON. WJ 405 $1.00   (L1723)

LOS DIAS PERDIDOS see Guastavino,
    Carlos

LOS PUEBLOS DEL MUNDO CANTAN ASI
    *CC74L
    (Pahlen) [Span] solo,pno RICORDI-ARG
    BA 10146 s.p.   (L1724)

LOS PUNALITOS see Lopez-Buchardo,
    Carlos

LOS TRES REYES MAGOS see Lasala, Angel

LOSAVIO, GIOVANNI (1872-1938)
    Liriche, Vol. I *CC5U
    [It] solo,pno BERBEN 1379 s.p.
                                 (L1725)

LOSSIUS, LUKAS (1508-1582)
    Holy, Holy, Holy *sac
    (Bunjes) med solo,pno oct CONCORDIA
    98-1102 $.18   (L1726)

LOSST MICH LEBEN see Behrend, Siegfried

LOST see Smith, Melville

LOST CHORD, THE see Sullivan, Sir
    Arthur Seymour

LOST IS MY QUIET see Purcell, Henry

LOST LAGOON see McIntyre, M.

LOST LANDS, THE see Hoskins, William

LOST LOVE see Handel, George Frideric,
    A Suoi Piedi

LOST ONE, THE see Bantock, Granville

LOST STAR, THE see Walton, Kenneth

LOSTOMIGE WIND see Mulder, Herman

LOTHAR, MARK
    Acht Lieder Nach Gedichten Von Chr.
    Morgenstern Heft I
    solo,pno RIES s.p.
    contains: Elbenreigen, Op.18,
    No.4; Fips, Op.18,No.3; Herr
    Loffel Und Frau Gabel, Op.18,
    No.2; Traumliedchen, Op.18,No.1
                                 (L1727)
    Acht Lieder Nach Gedichten Von Chr.
    Morgenstern Heft II
    solo,pno RIES s.p.
    contains: Das Weihnachtsbaumlein,
    Op.18,No.5; Die Drei Spatzen,
    Op.18,No.7; Lied Der Sonne,
    Op.18,No.8; Winternacht, Op.18,
    No.6   (L1728)

    Altdeutsche Lieder
    S solo,fl,pic,ob,2clar,bsn,
    contrabsn,2horn,timp,perc,harp,
    cel,strings RIES s.p.
    contains: Aussicht Auf Himmlische
    Freuden, Op.41a,No.2; Das
    Himmlische Menuett, Op.41a,
    No.5; Gruss, Op.41a,No.1;
    Liebesklage, Op.41a,No.3;
    Stelldichein, Op.41a,No.4
                                 (L1729)
    Arie Des Schafers *Op.14,No.1
    solo,pno RIES s.p. see from Vier
    Lieder   (L1730)

    Aussicht Auf Himmlische Freuden
    *Op.41a,No.2
    see Altdeutsche Lieder

    Das Himmlische Menuett *Op.41a,No.5
    see Altdeutsche Lieder
    solo,pno RIES s.p.   (L1731)

    Das Regenlied *Op.38,No.5
    see Lieder Der Kindheit Heft II

    Das Weihnachtsbaumlein *Op.18,No.5
    see Acht Lieder Nach Gedichten Von
    Chr. Morgenstern Heft II

LOTHAR, MARK (cont'd.)

Der Hahn *Op.14,No.4
    solo,pno RIES s.p. see from Vier
    Lieder   (L1732)

Der Mondfleck *Op.4,No.1
    solo,pno RIES s.p. see from Drei
    Heitere Lieder   (L1733)

Der Pavillon Aus Porzellan *Op.4,
    No.2
    solo,pno RIES s.p. see from Drei
    Heitere Lieder   (L1734)

Der Pirol *Op.38,No.7
    see Lieder Der Kindheit Heft II
    see Lieder Der Kindheit (Selected
    Works From The Collection)

Der Reiher Des Vergessens *Op.76,
    CC5U
    solo,pno RIES s.p.   (L1735)

Der Tanzbar *Op.38,No.6
    see Lieder Der Kindheit Heft II
    see Lieder Der Kindheit (Selected
    Works From The Collection)

Die Drei Spatzen *Op.18,No.7
    see Acht Lieder Nach Gedichten Von
    Chr. Morgenstern Heft II

Die Guten Gaben *Op.38,No.8
    see Lieder Der Kindheit Heft II

Die Kleine Stadt *Op.38a,No.1
    see Lieder Der Kindheit (Selected
    Works From The Collection)
    see Lieder Der Kindheit Heft I

Die Weidenflote *Op.38,No.2
    see Lieder Der Kindheit Heft I

Die Witwe Schickedanz *Op.38,No.4
    see Lieder Der Kindheit Heft I

Dorftanz *Op.4,No.3
    solo,pno RIES s.p. see from Drei
    Heitere Lieder   (L1736)

Drei Heitere Lieder *see Der
    Mondfleck, Op.4,No.1; Der
    Pavillon Aus Porzellan, Op.4,
    No.2; Dorftanz, Op.4,No.3 (L1737)

Drei Marienlieder *see Ora Pro
    Nobis, Op.7,No.1; Pieta, Op.7,
    No.3; Wiegenlied Einer Frommen
    Magd, Op.7,No.2   (L1738)

Elbenreigen *Op.18,No.4
    see Acht Lieder Nach Gedichten Von
    Chr. Morgenstern Heft I

Fips *Op.18,No.3
    see Acht Lieder Nach Gedichten Von
    Chr. Morgenstern Heft I

Gruss *Op.41a,No.1
    see Altdeutsche Lieder

Herr Loffel Und Frau Gabel *Op.18,
    No.2
    see Acht Lieder Nach Gedichten Von
    Chr. Morgenstern Heft I

Im Marzwind *Op.38a,No.3
    see Lieder Der Kindheit (Selected
    Works From The Collection)
    see Lieder Der Kindheit Heft I

Jahresringe Heft I: Bergengruen-
    Duette *Op.44, CCU
    SA soli,pno RIES s.p.   (L1739)

Jahresringe Heft II: Morgenstern-
    Duette *Op.45, CCU
    SA soli,pno RIES s.p.   (L1740)

Kleine Weihnachtsgeschichte *Op.51,
    song cycle
    solo,pno RIES s.p.   (L1741)

Liebesklage *Op.41a,No.3
    see Altdeutsche Lieder

Lied Der Sonne *Op.18,No.8
    see Acht Lieder Nach Gedichten Von
    Chr. Morgenstern Heft II

Lieder Der Kindheit Heft I
    solo,pno RIES s.p.
    contains: Die Kleine Stadt,
    Op.38,No.1; Die Weidenflote,
    Op.38,No.2; Die Witwe
    Schickedanz, Op.38,No.4; Im
    Marzwind, Op.38a,No.3   (L1742)

Lieder Der Kindheit Heft II
    solo,pno RIES s.p.
    contains: Das Regenlied, Op.38,
    No.5; Der Pirol, Op.38,No.7;
    Der Tanzbar, Op.38,No.6; Die
    Guten Gaben, Op.38,No.8 (L1743)

LOTHAR, MARK (cont'd.)

Lieder Der Kindheit (Selected Works
    From The Collection)
    med solo,fl,pic,2English horn,3bass
    clar,2contrabsn,4horn,3trp,3trom,
    tuba,timp,perc,harp,pno,cel,
    strings RIES s.p.
    contains: Der Pirol, Op.38a,No.7;
    Der Tanzbar, Op.38a,No.6; Die
    Kleine Stadt, Op.38a,No.1; Im
    Marzwind, Op.38a,No.3   (L1744)

Musik Des Einsamen *Op.69, song
    cycle
    med solo,7inst RIES s.p.   (L1745)

Nele's Lied *Op.12 (from Tyll)
    high solo,pic,2fl,2English horn,
    2bass clar,2contrabsn,4horn,3trp,
    3trom,tuba,timp,harp,strings RIES
    s.p.   (L1746)

Oboen-Lieder Nach Gedichten Von Georg
    Schwarz *Op.47, CCU
    solo,ob,pno RIES s.p.   (L1747)

Ora Pro Nobis *Op.7,No.1, sac
    solo,pno RIES s.p. see from Drei
    Marienlieder   (L1748)

Pieta *Op.7,No.3, sac
    solo,pno RIES s.p. see from Drei
    Marienlieder   (L1749)

Ringelnatz-Lieder *Op.46
    solo,pno RIES s.p.   (L1750)

Standchen *Op.14,No.3
    solo,pno RIES s.p. see from Vier
    Lieder   (L1751)

Stelldichein *Op.41a,No.4
    see Altdeutsche Lieder

Traumliedchen *Op.18,No.1
    see Acht Lieder Nach Gedichten Von
    Chr. Morgenstern Heft I

Vier Lieder *see Arie Des Schafers,
    Op.14,No.1; Der Hahn, Op.14,No.4;
    Standchen, Op.14,No.3; Wanderung
    Zur Nacht, Op.14,No.2   (L1752)

Wanderung Zur Nacht *Op.14,No.2
    solo,pno RIES s.p. see from Vier
    Lieder   (L1753)

Wiegenlied Einer Frommen Magd *Op.7,
    No.2, sac
    solo,pno RIES s.p. see from Drei
    Marienlieder   (L1754)

Winternacht *Op.18,No.6
    see Acht Lieder Nach Gedichten Von
    Chr. Morgenstern Heft II

LOTI, E.
    Premiere Rue A Gauche
    solo,pno ENOCH s.p.   (L1755)
    solo,acap ENOCH s.p.   (L1756)

LOTOS FLOWER see Frohlich, O.,
    Lotosblume

LOTOSBLATTER see Strauss, Richard

LOTOSBLUME see Frohlich, O.

LOTTI, ANTONIO (1667-1740)
    Pur Diceste I Bocca Bella
    solo,pno CRAMER   (L1757)

    Pur Dicesti Bocca Bella
    solo,pno FORLIVESI 10879 s.p.
                                      (L1758)

LOTUS, THE see Schumann, Robert
    (Alexander)

LOTUS BLOOM, THE see Niles, John Jacob

LOTUS FLOWER see Schumann, Robert
    (Alexander), Die Lotosblume

LOTUS FLOWER, THE see Schumann, Robert
    (Alexander), Die Lotosblume

LOTUS MYSTIQUE see Schumann, Robert
    (Alexander), Die Lotosblume

L'OUBLI see Migot, Georges

LOUCHEUR, R.
    Le Chant Du Stade
    [Fr] solo,acap oct DURAND s.p.
                                      (L1759)
    solo,pno/inst DURAND s.p.   (L1760)

LOUDON'S BONNIE WOODS AND BRAES *folk,
    Scot
    solo,pno (C maj) PATERSON FS52 s.p.
                                      (L1761)

LOUDOVA, IVANA (1941-   )
    Rozlef Se, Moje Pisnicko
    solo,pno SUPRAPHON s.p.   (L1762)

LOUGHAREEMA see Eisdell, Hubert

LOUGHBOROUGH, RAYMOND
    Darkness And Dawn
    low solo,pno (C maj) LEONARD-ENG
                                      (L1763)
    high solo,pno (E flat maj) LEONARD-
    ENG   (L1764)
    med solo,pno (D flat maj) LEONARD-
    ENG   (L1765)

    Homing Ship, The
    solo,orch (E flat maj) ASHDOWN
    s.p., ipr   (L1766)

    How Lovely Is The Hand Of God
    high solo,pno PRESSER $.95   (L1767)

    Ireland, Mother Ireland
    solo,pno (B flat maj) BOOSEY $1.50
                                      (L1768)

    Song In The Night
    solo,pno (E flat maj) BOOSEY $1.50
                                      (L1769)

LOUHEN HYVASTIJATTO TYTTARELLEEN see
    Merikanto, Oskar

LOUHIVUORI, HEMMO
    Avsked *see Ero

    Ero
    "Avsked" solo,pno FAZER F 3172 s.p.
                                      (L1770)

LOUIS, A.
    L'Automobile
    solo,acap ENOCH s.p.   (L1771)
    solo,pno ENOCH s.p.   (L1772)

LOUIS, E.
    Barcarolle
    solo,pno ENOCH s.p.   (L1773)

    La Sieste
    solo,pno ENOCH s.p.   (L1774)

    Le Bonne Garde
    solo,pno ENOCH s.p.   (L1775)
    solo,acap ENOCH s.p.   (L1776)

    Moise Mourant *sac,Bibl
    Bar solo,pno ENOCH s.p.   (L1777)

    O Salutaris! *sac
    [Lat] Bar/Mez solo,pno ENOCH s.p.
                                      (L1778)

LOULULAULUJA LAPSILLE see Kokkonen,
    Joonas

LOURDES see Fragerolle, G.

LOUS DOLHAIRES see Berger, Jean, Les
    Faucheurs

LOUVAIN see Lattes, M.

L'OUVERTURE DE LA CHASSE see
    Fragerolle, G.

LOVAD VARE HERREN *sac,Psalm
    (Olson, Daniel) solo,pno/org ERIKS
    K 112 s.p.   (L1779)

LOVE *sac
    (Carmichael, Ralph) solo,pno WORD
    S-235   (L1780)

LOVE see Birch, Robert Fairfax

LOVE see Boardman, Reginald

LOVE see Broones

LOVE see Butcher

LOVE see Fischer, Irwin

LOVE see Friml, Rudolf

LOVE see MacDermid

LOVE see Molchanov, K.

LOVE see Root

LOVE see Rorem, Ned

LOVE see Schouwman, Hans

LOVE see Van Dyke, May

LOVE AND ARITHMETIC see Thomas, Henry

LOVE AND BEAUTY see Puccini, Giacomo,
    Vissi D'arte

LOVE AND PITY see Orland, Henry

LOVE AND STRIFE see Flothius, Marius

LOVE AND TIME see Diamond, David

LOVE AT HOME *sac
  (King Family) solo,pno WORD S-31
                                  (L1781)
LOVE CAME STROLLING DOWN THE LANE see
  Sharpe, Evelyn

LOVE CAME TO ME see Day, Ruth E.

LOVE CAN BE DREAMED see Strauss, Johann

LOVE DIVINE see Oliver, Herbert

LOVE DIVINE, ALL LOVE EXCELLING see
  Stainer, John

LOVE DIVINE ALL LOVE'S EXCELLING see
  Stainer, John

LOVE DREAMS see Liszt, Franz,
  Liebestraum

LOVE ENTRAPPED ME see Dalway

LOVE FOR BEAUTY, LOVE, AND COMPASSION
  see Puccini, Giacomo, Vissi D'arte

LOVE HAS EYES see Bishop, Sir Henry
  Rowley

LOVE HATH EVER WROUGHT see Haubiel,
  Charles

LOVE, I COME TO YOU see Chenoweth,
  Wilbur

LOVE, I HAVE WON YOU see Ronald, Sir
  Landon

LOVE IN A LIFE see Rorem, Ned

LOVE IN A LITTLE CHILD see Wright,
  Reginald

LOVE IN MY BOSOM LIKE A BEE see
  Russell, Welford

LOVE IN THY YOUTH see Howard

LOVE IN THY YOUTH FAIR MAID see
  Russell, Welford

LOVE IS see Landgrave, Phillip

LOVE IS A BABEL see Parry, Charles
  Hubert Hastings

LOVE IS A MAN see Skillings, Otis

LOVE IS A RIDDLE see Scott, John
  Prindle

LOVE IS A SICKNESS see Innes, Gertrude

LOVE IS LIKE A FIREFLY see Friml,
  Rudolf

LOVE IS MINE see Gartner, Clarence

LOVE IS MORE see Diamond, David

LOVE IS OF GOD see Baumgartner, H.
  Leroy

LOVE IS OF GOD see Charles, Ernest

LOVE IS SURRENDER see Carmichael, Ralph

LOVE IS WHY see Ellis

LOVE-LAND see Friml, Rudolf

LOVE LIFTED ME see Rowe

LOVE ME see Mills, Charles

LOVE ME AND THE WORLD IS MINE see Ball,
  Ernest R.

LOVE ME NOT FOR COMELY GRACE see
  Joubert, John

LOVE ME OR NOT
  (Lehmann, Amelia) solo,pno (E maj)
  BOOSEY $1.50   (L1782)

LOVE ME OR NOT see Arne, Thomas
  Augustine

LOVE NEVER FAILETH see Blair, K.

LOVE NEVER FAILETH see Haskins, Vernon
  C.

LOVE NOTE, A see Rogers, James
  Hotchkiss

LOVE OF A MOTHER, THE see Rumsey, M.

LOVE OF GOD see Keedy

LOVE OF GOD, THE see Ellis

LOVE OF GOD, THE see Lehman

LOVE OF GOD IS REAL, THE see Ellis

LOVE OF MY HEART see Nutting, Godfrey

LOVE ON MY HEART see Milford, Robin

LOVE ONE ANOTHER see Fischer, Irwin

LOVE PIPES OF JUNE see Day, Maude
  Craske

LOVE REACHED DOWN see Croft, Colbert

LOVE REPAID see Dalway

LOVE SLEEPS IN A ROSE see Hall, L.W.

LOVE SONG see Benton, Daniel

LOVE SONG see Kilpinen, Yrio,
  Kussekraut

LOVE SONG see Thomson, Virgil

LOVE SONG, A see Edwards, Clara

LOVE SONG, A see Matthews

LOVE SONG MUSIC AND MEMORIES *sac,CCU
  solo,pno WORD 37728 $4.95   (L1783)

LOVE-SONG OF HAR DYAL see Batten, Mrs.
  George

LOVE SONG OF LIFE, THE see Russell,
  Kennedy

LOVE SONGS OF HAFIZ see Hovhaness, Alan

LOVE STARTS WITH YOU see Van Dyke,
  Vonda

LOVE THE VAGRANT see Bizet, Georges,
  Habanera

LOVE THEM NOW see Young, Carlton R.

LOVE THY MOTHER LITTLE ONE see Sharpe,
  Cedric

LOVE TRIO see Leslie, Henry David

LOVE TRIUMPHANT see Wheeler

LOVE UNDER THE REPUBLICANS see Reif,
  Paul

LOVE WAS A WANDERER see Chalk, C.

LOVE WAS WHEN see Walvoord, John

LOVE WAS WITH ME YESTERDAY see Golde,
  Walter

LOVE WENT A-RIDING see Bridge, Frank

LOVE WILL FIND A WAY see Fraser

LOVEC, VLADIMIR (1922-   )
  Lonely Woman *see Osamljena

  Osamljena
    "Lonely Woman" solo,pno DRUSTVO
    DSS 15 rental   (L1784)

  Trije Recitativi *CC3U
    rental solo,fl,ob,clar,bsn,horn,
    trp,perc,harp,strings sc DRUSTVO
    DSS 468; solo,pno voc sc DRUSTVO
    DSS 300   (L1785)

  Trije Samospevi *CC3U
    solo,pno DRUSTVO DSS 217 rental
                               (L1786)
LOVED ONES ARE WAITING see Hubbard, H.

LOVELACE, AUSTIN C. (1919-   )
  Jesus, Stand Beside Them *sac,
    Marriage
    low solo,pno ABINGDON APM-159 $.75
                               (L1787)
    high solo,pno ABINGDON APM-158 $.75
                               (L1788)
  My Beloved *Marriage
    med-high solo,pno (E flat maj)
    BOSTON $1.50   (L1789)
  O God Of Love To Thee We Bow Low
    *sac,Marriage
    solo,pno ABINGDON APM-161 $.75
                               (L1790)
    med solo,pno AUGSBURG 11-0734 $.85
                               (L1791)
  O Ye Who Taste That Love Is Sweet
    *sac,Marriage
    high solo&low solo,pno ABINGDON
    APM-157 $.75   (L1792)
  Our Father, By Whose Name *sac,
    Marriage
    low solo,pno ABINGDON APM-156 $.75
                               (L1793)
    high solo,pno ABINGDON APM-155 $.75
                               (L1794)

LOVELACE, AUSTIN C. (cont'd.)

  Our Lady Sat Within Her Bower *sac
    high solo,pno BELWIN $1.50   (L1795)

  Prayer For Communion
    med solo,pno PRESSER $.75   (L1796)

  Song Of The Wise Men
    med solo,pno GALAXY 1.1892.7 $1.00
                               (L1797)

  Star In The East
    low solo,pno GALAXY 1.1949.7 $1.00
                               (L1798)

  We Lift Our Hearts To Thee *sac
    med solo,pno (F maj) SCHIRM.G $.75
                               (L1799)

  Wedding Benediction, A *sac
    med solo,pno (E flat maj) SCHIRM.G
    $1.00   (L1800)
    SA soli,pno SCHIRM.G $1.00 (L1801)

  Wedding Music For The Church Organist
    And Soloist *sac,CCU,Marriage
    solo,org ABINGDON APM-164 $2.00
                               (L1802)

LOVELIEST IMMANUEL see Antes, John

LOVELIEST OF TREES see Butterworth,
  George Sainton Kaye

LOVELIEST OF TREES see Dougherty,
  Celius

LOVELIEST OF TREES see Duke, John Woods

LOVELIEST OF TREES see Dukelsky,
  Vladimir

LOVELIEST OF TREES see Moeran, Ernest
  J.

LOVELIEST OF TREES see Monet, J.

LOVELIEST OF TREES see Woodgate, Leslie

LOVELINESS MORE FAIR see Baxter, Maude
  Stewart

LOVELINESS OF OLD TIME THINGS see
  Sharpe, Evelyn

LOVELY ARMOY see Nelson, H.

LOVELY EVENING IN SUMMER see Grieg,
  Edvard Hagerup

LOVELY FLOWERS, WILL YE see Gounod,
  Charles Francois, Faites-Lui Mes
  Aveux

LOVELY GATE OF CRIMSON RUBIES see
  Respighi, Ottorino, Bella Porta Di
  Rubini

LOVELY LITTLE DREAM see Coleridge-
  Taylor, Samuel

LOVELY MAID IN THE MOONLIGHT see
  Puccini, Giacomo, O Soave Fanciulla

LOVELY MOLLY *folk,Scot
  low solo,pno (D flat maj) PATERSON
  FS118 s.p.   (L1803)
  high solo,pno (E flat maj) PATERSON
  FS118 s.p.   (L1804)

LOVELY ROSE, THE see Franz, Robert

LOVELY SONG MY HEART IS SINGING, THE
  see Goulding, Edmund

LOVER AND HIS LASS, THE see Moeran,
  Ernest J.

LOVER AND THE NIGHTINGALE see Granados,
  Enrique, La Maya Y Ruisenor

LOVER AS MIRROR, THE see Diamond, David

LOVERS see Mourant, Walter

LOVERS' PLEDGE, THE see Strauss,
  Richard, Heimliche Aufforderung

LOVER'S PROGRESS see Bush, Geoffrey

LOVERS SIGHS see Baxter, Maude Stewart

LOVE'S ADORATION see Mana-Zucca, Mme.,
  Priere D'Amour

LOVE'S CAUTION see Fox, G.

LOVE'S DAWN see Irving, W.W.S.

LOVE'S FAITH see Brahms, Johannes,
  Liebestreu

LOVE'S GARDEN see Chaminade, Cecile

LOVE'S GROWTH see Finney, Ross Lee

LOVE'S HOMAGE see Handel, George
  Frideric

LOVE'S LAMENT see Head, Michael (Dewar)

LOVE'S MESSAGE see Schubert, Franz (Peter), Liebesbotschaft

LOVE'S MESSENGER see Arditi, Luigi, Il Bacio

LOVE'S OLD SWEET SONG see Molloy, James Lyman

LOVE'S OWN KISS see Friml, Rudolf

LOVE'S OWN SWEET SONG see Kalman

LOVE'S PHILOSOPHY see Bell, H.

LOVE'S PHILOSOPHY see Delius, Frederick

LOVE'S PHILOSOPHY see Quilter, Roger

LOVE'S POEM see Lewis, Idris

LOVES REQUEST see Reichardt, R.

LOVE'S ROUNDELAY see Strauss, Johann

LOVE'S SECRET see Duke, John Woods

LOVE'S SECRET see Mourant, Walter

LOVE'S SECRET see Schirmer, Rudolph [E.]

LOVE'S SNARE see Hoag, Charles K.

LOVES TOMORROW see Hemery, Valentine

LOVESCAPES see Blumenfeld, Harold

LOVEST THOU ME see Gaither

LOVETT, MRS. GEORGE
About Little Girls I Know
solo,pno CRAMER   (L1805)

LOVING ME see Cain, Noble

LOVOFFER see Josephson, Jacob Axel

LOVSANG see Dahl

LOVSANG see Eklof, Einar

LOVSANG see Nordqvist, Gustaf

LOW BACKED CAR see Hughes, Herbert

LOW VOICE HYMNS OF COMFORT *sac,CC48UL
low solo,inst LILLENAS MB-108 $1.25
                                   (L1806)

LOW VOICE SERIES, NOS. 1-8 *CCUL
low solo,kbd SINGSPIR 5221-5228
$1.25, ea.   (L1807)

LOW VOICE SERIES, NOS. 9-15 *CCUL
low solo,kbd SINGSPIR 5229-5236
$1.25, ea.   (L1808)

LOW VOICE SOLOS *sac,CCU
(Boggs, Frank) low solo,pno WORD
10006 $1.00   (L1809)

LOW VOICE SOLOS *sac,CCUL
(Peterson, John W.) A/Bar solo,pno
SINGSPIR $2.95   (L1810)

LOW VOICE SOLOS NO. I *sac,CC30UL
A/Bar/B solo,pno LILLENAS MB-109
$1.25   (L1811)

LOW VOICE SOLOS NO. II *sac,CC30UL
A/Bar/B solo,pno LILLENAS MB-110
$1.25   (L1812)

LOW VOICE SOLOS NO. III *sac,CC30UL
A/Bar/B solo,pno LILLENAS MB-111
$1.25   (L1813)

LOW VOICE SOLOS NO. IV *sac,CC30UL
A/Bar/B solo,pno LILLENAS MB-112
$1.25   (L1814)

LOW VOICE SOLOS NO. V *sac,CC30UL
A/Bar/B solo,pno LILLENAS MB-113
$1.25   (L1815)

LOW VOICE SOLOS NO. VI *sac,CC30UL
A/Bar/B solo,pno LILLENAS MB-114
$1.25   (L1816)

LOW VOICE SOLOS NO. VII *sac,CC30UL
A/Bar/B solo,pno LILLENAS MB-115
$1.25   (L1817)

LOW VOICE SOLOS NO. VIII *sac,CC30UL
A/Bar/B solo,pno LILLENAS MB-116
$1.25   (L1818)

LOW VOICE SOLOS NO. IX *sac,CC30UL
A/Bar/B solo,pno LILLENAS MB-117
$1.25   (L1819)

LOW VOICE SOLOS NO. X *sac,CC30UL
A/Bar/B solo,pno LILLENAS MB-118
$1.25   (L1820)

LOW VOICE SOLOS NO. XI *sac,CC30UL
A/Bar/B solo,pno LILLENAS MB-119
$1.25   (L1821)

LOW VOICE SOLOS NO. XII *sac,CC30UL
A/Bar/B solo,pno LILLENAS MB-120
$1.25   (L1822)

LOW VOICE SOLOS NO. XIII *sac,CC30UL
A/Bar/B solo,pno LILLENAS MB-279
$1.25   (L1823)

LOW VOICE SOLOS NO. XIV *sac,CC30UL
A/Bar/B solo,pno LILLENAS MB-353
$1.25   (L1824)

LOW VOICE SPECIALS, VOL. 1 *sac,CCU
low solo,pno HOPE 511 $1.25 (L1825)

LOW VOICE SPECIALS, VOL. 2 *sac,CCU
low solo,pno HOPE 513 $1.25 (L1826)

LOWDOWN, LONESOME LOW
(Heenan, Ashley) solo,pno/orch (D
min) ROBERTON 2597 s.p.   (L1827)

LOWE, AUGUSTUS
Seek Ye The Lord
solo,pno CRAMER   (L1828)

LOWENWRITH, SAM
Dus Chupe Kleid *Jew
solo,pno KAMMEN 20 $1.00 see also
FAVORITE JEWISH SONGS, VOL. 2
                            (L1829)

LOWEST PLACE, THE see Ashley, Derick

LOWESTOFT BOAT, THE see Elgar, Edward

LOWTHIAN, CAROLINE
Bittersweet
2 soli,pno CRAMER   (L1830)

Reign Of The Roses, The
low solo,pno (C maj) CRAMER (L1831)
med solo,pno (D maj) CRAMER (L1832)
high solo,pno (F maj) CRAMER
                            (L1833)
2 soli,pno CRAMER   (L1834)

Venetia
solo,pno/inst DURAND s.p.   (L1835)
[Fr] solo,acap oct DURAND s.p.
                            (L1836)

LU PIANTE DE LE FOJJE see Albanese, Guido

LUBBOCK, MARK H.
Blackbird In The Apple Tree
high solo,pno (A flat maj) CRAMER
                            (L1837)
low solo,pno (G maj) CRAMER (L1838)

Lullaby River
solo,pno CRAMER   (L1839)

LUBECK, VINCENTIUS (1654-1740)
Willkommen, Susser Brautigam *sac,
cant
SS/SSB soli,2vln,cont sc HANSSLER
29.001 s.p., ipa, solo pt
HANSSLER s.p.   (L1840)

L'UBRIACONE see Peragallo, Mario

LUCANTONI, GIOVANNI (1825-1902)
Night In Venice
2 soli,pno (G flat maj) CRAMER
                            (L1841)
2 soli,pno (E flat maj) CRAMER
                            (L1842)

LUCAS
Christian Way, The *sac
solo,pno LILLENAS SM-937: SN $1.00
                            (L1843)

LUCAS, CLARENCE
When The Evening Shadows Fall
low solo,pno (E flat maj) ASHDOWN
                            (L1844)
high solo,pno (G maj) ASHDOWN
                            (L1845)

L'UCCELLINO DEL BOSCO see Sinigaglia, Leone

LUCE see Alfano, Franco

LUCI CARE, LUCI BELLE see Mozart, Wolfgang Amadeus

LUCIA see Torlind

LUCIA see Torlind, Tore

LUCIA, ETTORE (1882-1970)
A Papa Giovanni XXIII *cant
[It] solo,pno BONGIOVANI 2528 s.p.
                            (L1846)

LUCIER, ALVIN (1931-   )
Song For Soprano
S solo,acap BERANDOL BER 1133 $5.00
                            (L1847)

LUCIFER see Carissimi, Giacomo

LUCINDA MATLOCK see Raphling, Sam

LUCKE, K.
Since You Awakened Love
high solo/med solo,pno SEESAW $1.00
                            (L1848)

Song On The Wind, A
high solo,pno SEESAW $1.00   (L1849)

LUD GIDIA see Wladigeroff, P.

LUDIONS see Satie, Erik

L'UDIR TALVOLTA see Respighi, Ottorino

LUDLOW TOWN see Head, Michael (Dewar)

LUDT, FINN
Kaffegrut Og Fantasi
solo,pno MUSIKK s.p.   (L1850)

LUDUS AMERICANUS see Schmidt

LUGETE O VENERES CUPIDINESQUE see Cattini, U.

LUGN AR NATTEN see Sonninen, Ahti, Yo On Tyyni

LUGN VILAR SJON see Pfeil

LUIGINI, ALEXANDRE (1850-1906)
Neiges D'Avril
solo,pno ENOCH s.p.   (L1851)

LUISTEREN see Middeleer, Jean De, Obeir

LUKEY'S BOAT
see Six Regional Canadian Folksongs

LULLABY see Bissell, Keith W.

LULLABY see Brahms, Johannes, Wiegenlied

LULLABY see Drynan, Margaret

LULLABY see Godard, Benjamin Louis Paul

LULLABY see Gretchaninov, Alexander Tikhonovitch

LULLABY see Kalinenko, K.

LULLABY see Lessard, John Ayres

LULLABY see Menotti, Gian Carlo

LULLABY see Mozart, Wolfgang Amadeus, Wiegenlied

LULLABY see Rubel, Joseph

LULLABY see Schirmer, Rudolph [E.]

LULLABY see Scott, Cyril Meir

LULLABY see Stanford, Charles Villiers

LULLABY see Tesoriero, Gaetano, Buona Sera

LULLABY see Thompson, Randall

LULLABY see Van Dyke, May

LULLABY see Wigglesworth, Frank

LULLABY, A see Bax, Sir Arnold

LULLABY, A see Fischer, Irwin

LULLABY, A see Sampson, Godfrey

LULLABY FOR A MAN CHILD see Read, Gardner

LULLABY FOR A RELUCTANT SLEEPER see Clarke, Henry Leland

LULLABY FROM "NATIVE ISLAND" see Weigl, Vally

LULLABY OF THE LAKE see Hovhaness, Alan

LULLABY OF THE MADONNA see Williams, David McK.

LULLABY OF THE WOMAN OF THE MOUNTAIN see Rorem, Ned

LULLABY OF THE ZOO see Krasnow

LULLABY RIVER see Lubbock, Mark H.

LULLABY TO A DOLL see Davidson, M.T.

LULLABY TREES see Besly, Maurice

LULLY (LULLI), JEAN-BAPTISTE (1632-1740)
Air De Caron (from Alceste)
Mez/Bar solo,pno/inst DURAND s.p.
                            (L1852)
Bar solo,orch HENN s.p.   (L1853)

LULLY (LULLI), JEAN-BAPTISTE (cont'd.)

Air De Venus (from Thesee)
Mez/Bar solo,pno/inst DURAND s.p.
(L1854)

Airs *CCU
(Matthes) solo,pno HENN 196 s.p.
(L1855)

Amour Que Veux-Tu (from Amadis De
Gaule)
solo,orch HENN s.p. contains also:
L'eclat De Tant De Gloire (L1856)

Au Clair De La Lune
solo,pno/inst (available in 2 keys)
LEDUC s.p.   (L1857)

Au Clair De Lune
solo,pno/inst LEDUC s.p.   (L1858)

Blest Are They
(Davis) med solo,pno GALAXY
1.2067.7 $1.00   (L1859)

Bois Epais
"Woods So Dense" low solo,pno (E
flat maj) ALLANS s.p.   (L1860)
"Woods So Dense" med solo,pno (F
maj) ALLANS s.p.   (L1861)

Le Bourgeois Gentilhomme
solo,pno DURAND s.p.   (L1862)

L'eclat De Tant De Gloire (from
Amadis De Gaule)
see Lully (Lulli), Jean-Baptiste,
Amour Que Veux-Tu

Woods So Dense *see Bois Epais

L'ULTIMA CANZONE see Tosti, Francesco
Paolo

L'ULTIMO CARRO see Ferrari-Trecate,
Luigi

L'ULTIMO SOGNO see Gubitosi, Emilia

LUM HAT WANTIN' THE CROON, THE see
Rorie, David

LUMIERE DANS LA NUIT see Roos, Robert
de

LUMITUNNELMA see Hannikainen, Ilmari

LUMPKIN
No One To Welcome Me Home *sac
solo,pno LILLENAS SM-930: SN $1.00
(L1863)

LUNA see Pannain, Guido

LUNA D'ESTATE see Davico, Vincenzo

LUNA D'ESTATE STORNELLO see Tosti,
Francesco Paolo

LUNA, P.
Cancion Del Capitan (from Molinos De
Viento)
[Span/It] TBar soli,pno RICORDI-ARG
BA 7037 s.p.   (L1864)

El Nino Judio
(Azpiazu) [Span] high solo,gtr
UNION ESP. $.75   (L1865)

Quinteto De La Carta (from Molinos De
Viento)
[Span/It] 5 soli,pno RICORDI-ARG
BA 7038 s.p.   (L1866)

Vals Lento (from Molinos De Viento)
[Span/It] ST soli,pno RICORDI-ARG
BA 7026 s.p.   (L1867)

LUNA QUE RELUCES see Ferguson, Edwin
Earle

LUNDBORG, GOSTA (1903-   )
Fru Sommar
see Tre Sanger

Jag Ar En Gast Och Framling
solo,pno GEHRMANS s.p.   (L1868)

Till Smartan
see Tre Sanger

Tre Sanger
solo,pno GEHRMANS s.p.
contains: Fru Sommar; Till
Smartan; Visa I Juli   (L1869)

Visa I Juli
see Tre Sanger

LUNDEN, LENNART
Svensk Sang
solo,pno GEHRMANS s.p.   (L1870)

LUNDKVIST, PER
Bekransa Mig!
solo,pno LUNDQUIST s.p.   (L1871)

LUNDKVIST, PER (cont'd.)

Glom Mig Ej
solo,pno LUNDQUIST s.p.   (L1872)

Melodi
solo,pno LUNDQUIST s.p. contains
also: Serenad   (L1873)

Serenad
see Lundkvist, Per, Melodi

LUNDSTROM
Rich Man Am I, A *sac
solo,pno BENSON S5052-R $1.00
(L1874)

LUNDVIK, HILDOR
Margit
solo,pno GEHRMANS s.p.   (L1875)

LUNE DE CUIVRE see Rhene-Baton

LUNGI DAL CARO BENE see Sarti, Giuseppe

LUNGI LUNGI see Gandino, Adolfo

LUNOVIS see Badings, Henk

LUOLAJAN-MIKKOLA, VILHO
Brollopsdansen *see Haatanhu

En Ole Syotava Soria
solo,pno FAZER F 2689 s.p.   (L1876)

Haatanhu
"Brollopsdansen" solo,pno FAZER
W 2538 s.p.   (L1877)

Ilta
solo,pno FAZER F 2758 s.p.   (L1878)

Kiurun Tie
solo,pno FAZER F 2783 s.p.   (L1879)

Koiruoho, Ruusukukka
solo,pno FAZER W 3167 s.p.   (L1880)

Laulu *CCU
solo,pno FAZER F 2759 s.p.   (L1881)

LUONNOTAR see Sibelius, Jean

LUSKIN, SAMUEL
And Thou Shalt Love The Lord *see
Kaufman, H.H.

LUSTERN FLUSTERN DIE ZWEIGE see
Schumann, Georg

LUSTIG, J.W. (1709-1796)
Musikaels Tydverdryf, Vol. 1: July
*CCU
solo,pic,ob,vla,cembalo HEUWEKE.
250 s.p.   (L1882)

Musikaels Tydverdryf, Vol. 2:
Augustus *CCU
solo,pic,ob,vla,cembalo HEUWEKE.
251 s.p.   (L1883)

Musikaels Tydverdryf, Vol. 3:
September *CCU
solo,pic,ob,vla,cembalo HEUWEKE.
252 s.p.   (L1884)

LUTAT MOT GARDET see Stenhammar,
Wilhelm

LUTE, THE see Martino, Donald, Die
Laute

LUTE, THE see Waterman, Constance

LUTE CAROLL, A see Caldwell, Mary
Elizabeth

LUTE PLAYER see Peel, Graham

LUTE PLAYER, THE see Allitsen, Frances

LUTHOLD, E.
E Herzigs Meiteli
solo,pno HUG s.p.   (L1885)

LUTKIN, PETER CHRISTIAN (1858-1931)
Lord Bless You And Keep You, The
*sac
med-high solo,pno (C maj) BOSTON
$1.50   (L1886)

LUTOSLAWSKI, WITOLD (1858-1931)
Five Songs *CC5U
[Pol/Eng/Ger] female solo,pno/
30inst s.p. study sc MOECK 5007,
voc sc MOECK 5006   (L1887)

L'invitation Au Voyage
S,opt narrator,3clar,pno,perc MOECK
5134 rental   (L1888)

LUTYENS, ELIZABETH (1906-   )
O Saisons, O Chateaux! *Op.13
S solo,mand,gtr,harp,strings BELWIN
solo pt $3.00, sc rental   (L1889)

LUTZ, OSWALD (1908-   )
Funf Lieder Nach Gedichten Von
Christian Morgenstern *CC5U
solo,pno MODERN s.p.   (L1890)

LUULIT MA KATSELIN SUA see Madetoja,
Leevi

LUX AETERNA FOR FIVE MASKED MUSICIANS
see Crumb, George

LUX PURPURATA RADIIS. DILIGITE
JUSTICIAM see Jacopo Da Bologna

LUZZASCHI, LUZZASCO (1545-1607)
Madrigali Per Cantare E Sonare
*CC12U,madrigal
(Cavicchi, Adriano) S/SS/SSS soli,
cont (diff) BAREN. s.p.   (L1891)

LUZZATTI, ARTURO
Ansisdad
[Span] solo,pno RICORDI-ARG BA 9937
s.p.   (L1892)

Coplas
[Span] solo,pno RICORDI-ARG BA 9312
s.p.   (L1893)

LUZZI, LUIGI (1828-1876)
Ave Maria *sac
[It/Fr] Mez/Bar solo,pno RICORDI-
ENG 100971 s.p.   (L1894)
high solo,pno BELWIN $1.50   (L1895)
S/T solo,pno FORLIVESI 11934 s.p.
(L1896)
[It/Eng] high solo,pno (G flat maj)
SCHIRM.G $.60   (L1897)
[Lat] low solo,pno (E flat maj)
SCHIRM.G $.75   (L1898)
[Lat] high solo,pno (G flat maj)
SCHIRM.G $.75   (L1899)
low solo,pno BELWIN $1.50   (L1900)

LYANOVA, ADRIANA
Canti Popolari Russi *CCU
solo,pno ZERBONI 4149 s.p.   (L1901)

LYBBERT, DONALD
From Harmonium *song cycle
high solo,pno PRESSER $2.00 (L1902)

Lines For The Fallen
[Fr] S solo,2pno PETERS 66174 $3.50
(L1903)

LYBERG, MARGOT
Polska
see Tva Visor

Tva Visor
solo,pno GEHRMANS s.p.
contains: Polska; Vi Tva (L1904)

Vi Tva
see Tva Visor

LYCKA SKE LANDET see Nordqvist, Gustaf

LYDA see Lacome, Paul

LYDISCHE NACHT see Diepenbrock, Alphons

LYKKEN MELLEM TO MENNESKER see Alnaes,
Eyvind

LYMAN, ED.
All My Troubles *sac
solo,pno WORD S-123   (L1905)

I Have A Melody *sac
solo,pno WORD S-152   (L1906)

In A Silent World *sac
solo,pno WORD S-159   (L1907)

Man Of Steel *sac
solo,pno WORD S-166   (L1908)

Now Sound Of Ed Lyman, The *sac,
CC11UL
solo,pno BENSON BO840 $2.50 (L1909)

Poor Little Lost Lamb *sac
(Bock, Fred) solo,pno WORD S-50
(L1910)

LYONELIN ROMANSSI see Flotow, Friedrich
von, Ach! So Fromm

LYONNAIS *Fr
(Canteloube, J.) solo,acap DURAND
s.p. see also Anthologie Des Chants
Populaires Francais Tome III
(L1911)

LYRIC see Reuland, Jacques

LYRIC SONGS II see Schoenbach, D.

LYRICAL SUITE see Weigl, Vally

LYRICAL SYMPHONY see Linke, Norbert

LYRICKE ZPEVY see Matys, Jiri

LYRICS see Cossetto, Emil

LYRICS see Svarc, Alfred

LYRISCHE SUITE see Enthoven

LYRISCHER PROLOG see Herrmann, Hans

LYRISCHES BREVIER see Lohse, Fred

LYRISCHES INTERMEZZO see Jirak, Karel
Boleslav

L'YSER see Gallon, Noel

LYSS TILL GRANEN VID DIN MODERS HYDDA
see Runback, Albert

M

M-PIRIFORM see Connolly, Justin
[Riveagh]

MA BELLE DIVINE REPOSE see Lacome, Paul

MA BELLE M'A DIT see Cuvillier, Charles

MA BELLE SI TON AME see Coppola, Piero

MA BERGERE (LE PATRE DES MONTAGNES) see
Nivelet

MA BIEN-AIMEE see Delmet, Paul

MA BIEN-AIMEE see Gedalge, Andre

MA CHAMBRE see Schlosser, Paul

MA CHATTE DANSE see Strimer, Joseph

MA CHE VI FECE - SPERAI VICINO AL LIDO
see Mozart, Wolfgang Amadeus

MA CHEVRE BLANCHETTE see Schlosser,
Paul

MA CIGALE (1) see Vuillemin, L.

MA CIGALE (2) see Vuillemin, L.

MA COME POTREI see Respighi, Ottorino

MA CONFIANCE EN TOI S'EST BIEN MONTRE
see Wagner, Richard

MA DALL'ARIDO STELO DIVULSA see Verdi,
Giuseppe

MA DOUCE ANNETTE see Delmet, Paul

MA DOUCE JOUVENCE EST PASSEE see
Leguerney, Jacques

MA DOULEUR ET SA COMPAGNE see Milhaud,
Darius

MA DZIRI see Bozi, Harold de

MA ELAN see Merikanto, Oskar

MA GRISE CHAUMIERE see Bellecour,
Maurice

MA JOLIE see Delmet, Paul

MA LI'L BATTEAU see Strickland, Lily
Teresa

MA LISETTE see Indy, Vincent d'

MA LITTLE BANJO see Dichmont, William

MA LYKKAAN PURTENI LAINEILLEN see
Merikanto, Oskar

MA MAIN N'EST PAS BLANCHE, GARE! see
Laparra, Raoul

MA MAISON see Fourdrain, Felix

MA MERE ETAIT UNE PAYSANNE see Bonnal,
Ermend

MA MERE L'OYE see Absil, Jean

MA-OZ TSUR see Marcello, Benedetto

MA-OZTSUR   *Jew
solo,pno KAMMEN 497 $1.00   (M1)

MA PERCHE ARROSSIR see Hajos, Karl

MA PETIT FILLE EST SI BLONDE see Canal,
Marguerite

MA PETITE BERGERE see Petitjean, M.

MA POUPEE see Serpette, Gaston

MA POUPEE CHERIE see De Severac, Deodat

MA POUT' see Bartos, Jan Zdenek

MA PREMIERE LETTRE see Chaminade,
Cecile

MA PRIMIERE LETTRE see Chaminade,
Cecile

MA REINE see Bozi, Harold de

MA SE M'E FORZA PERDERTI see Verdi,
Giuseppe

MA TENDRE AMIE see Delmet, Paul

MA TETE see Secretan, G.

MA TOVU
(Helfman, Max) "O Lovely Valley"
[Heb] med solo,pno TRANSCON. IS 512
$.50   (M2)

MA VIE see Lachaume, A.

MA VIE EST UN COMBAT DOULOUREUX see
Tremisot, Ed.

MA VIGNE ET MA MIE see Cuvillier,
Charles

MAA BONNY LAD   *folk
(Moore, Gerald) high solo,pno UNIVER.
12315 $.75   (M3)
(Moore, Gerald) med solo,pno UNIVER.
12315 $.75   (M4)

MAALISKUUN LOPPU see Salonen, Sulo,
Marsslut

MAANLICHT see Badings, Henk

MAANLICHT see Sigtenhorst-Meyer,
Bernhard van den

MAANLIG see Mulder, Ernest W.

MAASALO, ARMAS (1885-1960)
Atta Julsanger   *Op.21,No.1-8, sac,
CC8L,Xmas
solo,pno FAZER W 537 s.p.   (M5)

Gebet   *see Rukous

Grabgesang   *see Hautalaulu

Hautalaulu   *Op.40,No.4
"Grabgesang" solo,pno FAZER F 2364
s.p.   (M6)

Kay Seimen Luo   *Op.40,No.2, Xmas
"Till Krubban Ga" solo,pno FAZER
F 2362 s.p.   (M7)

Kun Mun Kultani Tulisi   *Op.2,No.2
solo,pno FAZER F 940 s.p. contains
also: Rukous, "Gebet", Op.40,No.3
(M8)

Nun Lodert Dankgefullt Mein
Opferfeuer   *see Nyt Nousee
Kiitokseni Uhrisauhu

Nyt Nousee Kiitokseni Uhrisauhu
*Op.40,No.5
"Nun Lodert Dankgefullt Mein
Opferfeuer" solo,pno FAZER F 2365
s.p.   (M9)

Rukous   *Op.40,No.3
"Gebet" see Maasalo, Armas, Kun Mun
Kultani Tulisi

Till Krubban Ga   *see Kay Seimen Luo

MAASSA MARJANI MAKAVI see Kilpinen,
Yrio

MAASZ, GERHARD (1906-   )
Niederdeutsche Lieder Und Tanze   *CCU
solo,fl,ob,clar,rec,2horn,trp,perc,
pno,acord,3vln,vla,vcl,bvl sc
GERIG HG 274 s.p., ipa   (M10)

MACABRE REFLECTIONS see Calabro, Louis

MCAFEE
Near To The Heart Of God   *sac
low solo,pno (E flat maj) ALLANS
s.p.   (M11)
med solo,pno (F maj) ALLANS s.p.
(M12)
high solo,pno (G maj) ALLANS s.p.
(M13)

MCAFEE, DON
Contemporary Christmas Carols   *CCU,
Xmas,carol
solo,pno GENERAL 591 $2.50   (M14)

Psalm 139   *sac
low solo,pno ABINGDON APM-770 $1.25
(M15)
high solo,pno ABINGDON APM-769
$1.25   (M16)

Two Songs For Medium Voice   *sac,CC2U
med solo,pno ABINGDON APM-661 $1.25
(M17)

MC BRADD
In The Inn
high solo,pno SHAWNEE IA5024 $.85
(M18)

MACBRIDE, DAVID
Duo
SS soli,vla,bsn,pno,org,perc SEESAW
(M19)

MC BRIDE, ROBERT GUYN (1911-   )
Commentary
T solo,2trp,2trom,pno,bvl,drums,
synthesizer sc AM.COMP.AL. $6.60,
ipa   (M20)

MC BRIDE, ROBERT GUYN (cont'd.)

Nonsense Syllables *vocalise
S solo,fl AM.COMP.AL. $2.75   (M21)

Vocalise *vocalise
S solo,fl,pno sc AM.COMP.AL. $3.30,
ipa   (M22)

Vocalise No. 3 On Nonsense Syllables
*vocalise
T solo,pno,cembalo,drums sc
AM.COMP.AL. $3.57, ipa   (M23)

Wayfarin' Stranger
SS soli,gtr,hpsd sc AM.COMP.AL.
$2.47, ipa   (M24)

MCBURNEY
Persian Song Of Spring
solo,pno ALLANS s.p.   (M25)

MC CABE
Adieu, Farewell
see Five Elegies

Do Not Go Gentle
see Five Elegies

Eyes That Last I Saw In Tears
see Five Elegies

Five Elegies
S solo,chamb.orch OXFORD rental
contains: Adieu, Farewell; Do Not
Go Gentle; Eyes That Last I Saw
In Tears; Hag, The; Hourglass   (M26)

From The Psalms
Bar solo,pno OXFORD s.p. see from
Songs From Michelangelo   (M27)

Hag, The
see Five Elegies

Hourglass
see Five Elegies

Songs From Michelangelo *see From
The Psalms   (M28)

MC CABE, JOHN (1939-   )
Hush-A-Ba, Birdie, Croon, Croon
see Three Folk Songs

John Peel
see Three Folk Songs

Johnny Has Gone For A Soldier
see Three Folk Songs

Three Folk Songs
high solo,pno,opt clar NOVELLO
17.0250.05 s.p.
contains: Hush-A-Ba, Birdie,
Croon, Croon; John Peel; Johnny
Has Gone For A Soldier   (M29)

MCCANN, LELAND
Thy Will Be Done *sac
solo,pno SINGSPIR 7048 $1.00 (M30)

Why Should I Fear? *sac
solo,pno SINGSPIR 7049 $.35   (M31)

MCCLINTIC, GERRY
Carousel Of Life *sac
solo,pno WORD S-315   (M32)

MCCOY, HOBART
This Day Is Mine
med solo,pno (E flat maj) WILLIS
$.60   (M33)

MACCUNN, HAMISH (1868-1916)
In A Palace Garden
solo,pno CRAMER   (M34)

MACDERMID
Christ My Refuge
high solo,pno (D maj) FISCHER,C
V 1581   (M35)

Christmas Morn *sac,Xmas
high solo,pno (D maj) FISCHER,C
V 1585   (M36)
low solo,pno (B flat maj) FISCHER,C
V 1586   (M37)

Feed My Sheep *sac
high solo,pno (E flat maj) FISCHER,
C V 1593   (M38)
low solo,pno (C maj) FISCHER,C
V 1594   (M39)

Love
high solo,pno (F maj) FISCHER,C
V 1583   (M40)
low solo,pno (D maj) FISCHER,C
V 1584   (M41)

Mother's Evening Prayer
low solo,pno (B flat maj) FISCHER,C
V 1588   (M42)
high solo,pno (D maj) FISCHER,C
V 1587   (M43)

MACDERMID (cont'd.)

Satisfied
low solo,pno (G maj) FISCHER,C
V 1590   (M44)

Saw Ye My Saviour? *sac
high solo,pno (E flat maj) FISCHER,
C V 1591   (M45)

MCDILL
Didn't He Shine? *see Reynolds

MACDOWELL, EDWARD ALEXANDER (1861-1908)
Edward MacDowell Songs *CCU
solo,pno DA CAPO $9.50 contains Op.
40, 47, 56, 58, 60   (M46)

In The Woods *Op.47,No.6
[Eng/Ger] low solo,pno AMP $.60 (M47)

Sea, The *Op.47,No.7
[Eng/Ger] high solo,pno AMP $.50 (M48)
[Eng/Ger] low solo,pno AMP $.50 (M49)

Thy Beaming Eyes
high solo,pno (F maj) WILLIS $.75 (M50)
low solo,pno (E flat maj) WILLIS
$.75   (M51)

To A Wild Rose
high solo,pno ELKIN 27.1656.09 s.p.
                              (M52)
med solo,pno ELKIN 27.1655.00 s.p.
                              (M53)
low solo,pno ELKIN 27.1654.02 s.p.
                              (M54)

MCFADDEN, LARRY
One Thing I Know *sac
solo,pno oct MASTER CP-MM 2004
$1.25   (M55)

MACFADYEN, A.
Bow Down Thine Ear, O Lord
med solo,pno PRESSER $.75   (M56)

MCFALL
Thank God, I Am Free *sac
solo,pno BENSON S7704-S $1.00 (M57)

MACFARLANE, WILLIAM CHARLES (1870-1945)
Open Our Eyes *sac
low solo,pno (D flat maj) SCHIRM.G
$.60   (M58)

MCFEETERS, RAYMOND (1899-   )
Gentle Mary
solo,pno ALLANS s.p.   (M59)

MCGEOCH, DAISY
Chintz And Chippendale *CCU
solo,pno LEONARD-ENG   (M60)

I've Brought Some Songs *CCU
solo,pno LEONARD-ENG   (M61)

Kiddies *CCU
solo,pno LEONARD-ENG   (M62)

Little White House On The Hill
solo,pno LEONARD-ENG   (M63)

My Heart's A Shrine
low solo,pno (B flat maj) LEONARD-
ENG   (M64)
high solo,pno (D flat maj) LEONARD-
ENG   (M65)

My Little Exquisite Love
solo,pno (A flat maj) LEONARD-ENG
                              (M66)

My Love's Grey Eyes
low solo,pno (E flat maj) LEONARD-
ENG   (M67)
high solo,pno (F maj) LEONARD-ENG
                              (M68)

Noah's Ark *CCU
solo,pno LEONARD-ENG   (M69)

Once When My Heart
high solo,pno (E flat maj) LEONARD-
ENG   (M70)
low solo,pno (C maj) LEONARD-ENG
                              (M71)
med solo,pno (D maj) LEONARD-ENG
                              (M72)

Spring Flower And Summer Roses
solo,pno (F maj) CRAMER   (M73)

Two Eyes Of Grey
low solo,pno (B flat maj) LEONARD-
ENG   (M74)
med solo,pno (C maj) LEONARD-ENG
                              (M75)
high solo,pno (D maj) LEONARD-ENG
                              (M76)

MCGEORGE, MURIEL
Sunshine Garden
low solo,pno (G maj) CRAMER   (M77)
high solo,pno (A flat maj) CRAMER
                              (M78)

MCGILL, JOSEPHINE (1877-1919)
Duna
low solo,pno (B flat maj) BOOSEY
$1.50   (M79)
high solo,pno (C maj) BOOSEY $1.50
                              (M80)

MACGIMSEY, ROBERT (1938-   )
New Christmas Morning, Hallelujah
*Xmas
med solo,pno (D flat maj) FISCHER,C
V 1997   (M81)

Shadrack
high solo,pno (G min) FISCHER,C
V 1396   (M82)
low solo,pno (F min) FISCHER,C
V 1356   (M83)
med solo,pno (D min) FISCHER,C
V 1429   (M84)
solo,pno ALLANS s.p.   (M85)

Sweet Little Jesus Boy *Xmas
low solo,pno (D maj) PATERSON s.p.
                              (M86)
high solo,pno (F maj) PATERSON s.p.
                              (M87)
med solo,pno (F min) FISCHER,C
V 1233   (M88)
low solo,pno (D min) FISCHER,C
V 1234   (M89)

Think On These Things *Bib
high solo,pno (F maj) FISCHER,C
V 2026   (M90)
med solo,pno (D flat maj) FISCHER,C
V 1848   (M91)

Trouble
med solo,pno FISCHER,C V 1382 (M92)
low solo,pno FISCHER,C V 1207 (M93)

MCGLENNON
Sons Of The Sea
solo,pno ALLANS s.p.   (M94)

MACH MICH ZUM WACHTER see Schoenberg,
Arnold

MACHA, OTMAR (1922-   )
Arie Kaci (from Hratky S Certem)
see ARIE A ZPEVY ZE SOUCASNYCH
OPER: ALT

Ctyri Monology *CC4U
SBar soli,orch PANTON 1068 s.p.
                              (M95)

Janinka Zpiva *CCU
S solo,orch PANTON 1297 s.p. (M96)

Lidove Balady *CCU
solo,pno SUPRAPHON s.p.   (M97)

Maly Triptych *CC3U
S solo,fl,perc CZECH s.p.   (M98)

Materidouska
solo,pno SUPRAPHON s.p.   (M99)

MCHARDY, DONALD
Red Red Rose
solo,pno CRAMER   (M100)

MACHAVARIANI, A.
Vocal Works *CCU
[Russ] solo,pno MEZ KNIGA 2.96 s.p.
                              (M101)

MACHE DICH AUF, WERDE LICHT see Becker-
Foss, Jurgen

MACHET DIE TORE WEIT see Boxberg,
Christian Ludwig

MACHET DIE TORE WEIT see Grimm,
Heinrich

MACHMOED see Sigtenhorst-Meyer,
Bernhard van den

MACINTOSH'S LAMENT see Somervell,
Arthur

MCINTYRE, M.
Lost Lagoon
solo,pno BERANDOL BER 1322 $1.50
                              (M102)

MACK, HEBE
Tutankhamen
solo,pno CRAMER   (M103)

MCKELLAR, K.
Long Ships
solo,pno (E min) BOOSEY $1.50
                              (M104)

MAC KENZIE
You Should Have Come Sooner *sac
solo,pno BENSON S8582-R $1.00
                              (M105)

MACKENZIE, A.C.
Tell Me Where Is Fancy Bred
solo,pno CRAMER   (M106)

MCKINNEY, HOWARD D. (1890-   )
Holy Mother Sings *sac
med solo,pno BELWIN $1.50   (M107)
high solo,pno BELWIN $1.50   (M108)

MCKINNEY, HOWARD D. (cont'd.)

O Babe Divine *see Tu Scendi Dalle
Stelle

Tu Scendi Dalle Stelle *sac
(McKinney, Howard D.) "O Babe
Divine" high solo/med solo,pno
BELWIN $1.50   (M109)

MCLAIN, A.
My Choice
high solo,pno PRESSER $.75   (M110)

MCLEAN
Plenty Of Time *sac
solo,pno BENSON S7378-S $1.00
(M111)

MC LELLAN
Put Your Hand In The Hand *sac
solo,pno BENSON S7406-S $1.00
(M112)

solo,pno BENSON S7407-R $1.00
(M113)

MAC LEOD, A.C.
Skye Boat Song
low solo,pno (G maj) CRAMER (M114)
high solo,pno (B flat maj) CRAMER
(M115)
2 soli,pno (G maj) CRAMER (M116)
2 soli,pno (B flat maj) CRAMER
(M117)

MCLEOD, ROBERT
Highland Pastoral
low solo,pno (D min) CRAMER $.95
(M118)
high solo,pno (F min) CRAMER (M119)

Hungry For The Sea
solo,pno CRAMER   (M120)

Kirsty Forsyth
solo,pno CRAMER   (M121)

Lassie Wi' The Yellow Coatie
solo,pno CRAMER   (M122)

Oor Ain Glen
low solo,pno (F maj) CRAMER (M123)
med solo,pno (G maj) CRAMER (M124)
high solo,pno (A flat maj) CRAMER
(M125)

Over The River
solo,pno CRAMER   (M126)

Song Of The Passing Soul
solo,pno CRAMER   (M127)

Tarrin' O' The Yoll
solo,pno CRAMER   (M128)

MACLEOD'S GALLEY *Scot
solo,pno PATERSON s.p. see from
Hebridean Songs, Vol. IV   (M129)

MACMURROUGH, DERMOT
Fairy Ways
low solo,pno (D maj) ASHDOWN (M130)
high solo,pno (E flat maj) ASHDOWN
(M131)
Macushla
high solo,pno (B flat maj) BOOSEY
$1.75   (M132)
low solo,pno (F maj) BOOSEY $1.75
(M133)
med solo,pno (A flat maj) BOOSEY
(M134)
Shepherdess
low solo,pno (D maj) BOOSEY $1.50
(M135)
high solo,pno (F maj) BOOSEY $1.50
(M136)
Shepherdess, The
low solo,pno (D maj) ASHDOWN (M137)
high solo,pno (F maj) ASHDOWN
(M138)

MACNAMARA'S BAND see O'Connor, Shamus

MACNUTT, WALTER
Atque Vale
solo,pno BERANDOL BER 1320 $1.50
(M139)
May They In Thee Be One *sac
low solo,pno BERANDOL BER 1290
$1.50   (M140)
med solo,pno BERANDOL BER 1289
$1.50   (M141)

O Love, Be Deep
solo,pno (D flat maj) LESLIE 7033
$.80   (M142)

Two Songs Of William Blake *CC2U
solo,pno BERANDOL BER 1321 $2.00
(M143)

MAC PHAIL, FRANCES
My Master *sac,Gen/Lent
high solo,pno BELWIN $1.50   (M144)
low solo,pno BELWIN $1.50   (M145)

MACUDZINSKI, RUDOLF
Styri Piesne Vdaky *CC4U
Bar solo,pno SLOV.HUD.FOND s.p.
(M146)

MACUSHLA see Macmurrough, Dermot

MAD KNIGHT'S SONG, THE see Duke, John
Woods

MAD MAID'S SONG, THE see Diamond, David

MAD MAID'S SONG, THE see Hind, John

MAD SCENE see Parris, Robert

MAD SCENE, THE see Donizetti, Gaetano,
Ardon Gli'incensi

MADALENA GURE PATROINA see Bonnal,
Ermend

MADAM AND THE MINISTER see Roe, Betty

MADAM TO YOU see Siegmeister, Elie

MADAME, A VOS VERTUS see Rabey, Rene

MADAME EST SERVIE see Chantrier, A.

MADAME JE VOUDRAIS! see Delmet, Paul

MADAME JEANNETTE see Murray, Alan

MADAME LE DOCTEUR see Liouville, F.

MADAME MIM'S WORK SONG see Sims, Ezra

MADAMINA! IL CATALOGO E QUESTA see
Mozart, Wolfgang Amadeus

MADAMINA! IL CATALOGO E QUESTO see
Mozart, Wolfgang Amadeus

MADCHEN AM FENSTER see Koetsier, Jan

MADCHEN AM FENSTER see Lilien, Ignace

MADCHEN KAM VOM STELLDICHEIN see
Sibelius, Jean, Flickam Kom Ifran
Sin Alsklings Mote

MADCHEN KAM VOM STELLDICHEIN see
Sibelius, Jean, Flickan Kom Ifran
Sin Alsklings Mote

MADCHEN MIT DEM ROTEN MUNDCHEN see
Gall, Jan

MADCHEN, SO TREIBT IHR'S MIT ALLEN see
Mozart, Wolfgang Amadeus, Donne
Mie, La Fatte A Tanti

MADCHENLIED see Borris, Siegfried

MADCHENLIED see Schoenberg, Arnold

MADCHENLIEDER see Schumann, Georg

MADCHEN'S WUNSCH see Chopin, Frederic

MADDALENA ALLA CROCE see Frescobaldi,
Girolamo

MADDEN, CHARLES
Geococcyx Californianus
5 soli MEDIA 3104 $4.50   (M147)

MADE BY VILLON AT HIS MOTHER'S REQUEST
AS A PRAYER TO THE VIRGIN MARY see
Debussy, Claude, Ballade Que Feit
Villon A La Requeste De Sa Mere
Pour Prier Notre-Dame

MADELEINE see Chaminade, Cecile

MADELEINE see Saint-Saens, Camille

MADELIEFJE see Tetterode, L. Adr. von

MADELINETTE see Wachs, F.

MADELON see Mulder, Herman

MADEMOISELLE POMPON see Lacome, Paul

MADEMOISELLE TARTINE see Lacome, Paul

MADER, CLARENCE
Three Biblical Songs *CC3U,Bibl
med solo,org WESTERN WIM128 $5.00
(M148)

MADERNA, BRUNO (1920-1973)
Aria Da Hyperion
S solo,fl,orch sc,quarto ZERBONI
6327 s.p.   (M149)

Venetian Journal
T solo,orch,electronic tape sc
RICORDI-ENG 131987 s.p. (M150)

MADETOJA, LEEVI (1887-1947)
Du Trodde Mig Betrakta *see Luulit
Ma Katselin Sua

Dunkle Blatter *see Yrtit Tummat

Evigt Svallet Emot *see Ljat
Hyrskyja Pain

MADETOJA, LEEVI (cont'd.)

Fagel Bla *see Lintu Sininen

Finlands Vartrad *see Suomen Puu

God Natt *see Hyvaa Yota

Gunga, Gunga *see Heijaa, Heijaa

Heijaa, Heijaa *Op.60,No.1
"Gunga, Gunga" solo,pno FAZER W 532
s.p.   (M151)

Host *see Syksy

Hyvaa Yota *Op.68,No.4
"God Natt" solo,pno FAZER W 1662
s.p.   (M152)

Itkisit Joskus Illoin
"Vid Avfarden" solo,pno FAZER
F 1261 s.p.   (M153)

Lahto *Op.68,No.2
"Uppbrott" solo,pno FAZER W 1660
s.p.   (M154)

Lintu Sininen *Op.68,No.5
"Fagel Bla" solo,pno FAZER W 1663
s.p.   (M155)

Ljat Hyrskyja Pain *Op.68,No.6
"Evigt Svallet Emot" solo,pno FAZER
W 1664 s.p.   (M156)

Luulit Ma Katselin Sua *Op.68,No.3
"Du Trodde Mig Betrakta" solo,pno
FAZER W 1661 s.p.   (M157)

Romance Sans Paroles
"Sanaton Romanssi" solo,pno FAZER
F 972 s.p.   (M158)

Sanaton Romanssi *see Romance Sans
Paroles

Serenadi *Op.16,No.1
"Standchen" solo,pno FAZER F801
s.p.   (M159)

Standchen *see Serenadi

Suomen Puu *Op.49,No.2
"Finlands Vartrad" solo,pno FAZER
F 1260 s.p.   (M160)

Syksy *Op.68,No.1
"Host" solo,pno FAZER W 1659 s.p.
(M161)

Uppbrott *see Lahto

Vid Avfarden *see Itkisit Joskus
Illoin

Yiais Lied I & II *Op.58,No.1-2,
CC2U
solo,pno FAZER F 3085 s.p. (M162)

Yrtit Tummat *Op.9,No.1
"Dunkle Blatter" solo,pno FAZER
W 2272 s.p.   (M163)

MADONNA see Haubiel, Charles

MADONNA FIORENTINA see Billi

MADONNA MIA FA see Anonymous

MADONNA MIA FA see Pisador, Diego

MADONNA OF THE EVENING FLOWERS see
Dougherty, Celius

MADONNA SANCTA MARIA see Dallapiccola,
Luigi

MADONNA VAN MANTEGNA see Bijvanck, Henk

MADONNANS VAGGVISA see Lidholm, Ingvar

MADRE, PIETOSA VERGINE see Verdi,
Giuseppe

MADRE VIDALITAY see Calcagno, Elsa

MADRIGAL see Arizaga, Rodolfo

MADRIGAL see Chaminade, Cecile

MADRIGAL see Fontenla, Jorge

MADRIGAL see Holford, Franz

MADRIGAL see Linnala, Eino

MADRIGAL see Mendelssohn-Bartholdy,
Felix

MADRIGAL see Ruyneman, Daniel

MADRIGAL see Saenz, Pedro

MADRIGAL see Saint-Saens, Camille

MADRIGAL see Segond, Pierre

MADRIGAL see Strauss, Richard

MADRIGAL see Voormolen, Alexander
    Nicolas

MADRIGAL D'ANTAN see Delmet, Paul

MADRIGAL DE RONSARD see Levade, Charles
    (Gaston)

MADRIGAL II see Mather, Bruce

MADRIGAL TIMIDE see Lachaume, A.

MADRIGAL, TIRE DE LA PSYCHE, MOLIERE
    see Saint-Saens, Camille

MADRIGALE see D'Ambrosi, Dante

MADRIGALE DI PRIMAVERA see Petralia

MADRIGALE SPIRITUALE see Wuorinen,
    Charles

MADRIGALI see Linnala, Eino, Madrigal

MADRIGALI E CANZONETTE see Melli, D.

MADRIGALI PER CANTARE E SONARE see
    Luzzaschi, Luzzasco

MADRIGALS A 6, BOOK I (1581) see
    Marenzio, Luca

MADRIGALS, BOOK I see Crumb, George

MADRIGALS, BOOK II see Crumb, George

MADRIGALS, BOOK III see Crumb, George

MADRIGALS, BOOK IV see Crumb, George

MADSEN, AGE
    Voggesang For Ein Bytting
    solo,pno MUSIKK s.p.   (M164)

MADSEN, ELEANOR
    Bridal Vow, A *sac,Marriage
    solo,pno SINGSPIR 7110 $1.00 (M165)

    His And Hers *sac,Marriage
    solo,pno SINGSPIR 7111 $1.00 (M166)

MADSEN, ERIK
    Det Hendte I Den Gamle By
    solo,pno MUSIKK s.p.   (M167)

MAEDER
    La-Bas Sur La Mer
    solo,pno HENN 329 s.p.   (M168)

    Un Conte
    solo,pno HENN 330 s.p.   (M169)

MAEGAARD JAN (1926-   )
    Elegy Of Equinox *see
        Jaevndognselegi I

    Jaevndognselegi I
    "Elegy Of Equinox" [Dan/Eng] S
        solo,vcl,org sc FØG III, 196 s.p.
                                  (M170)
MAENDELYKS MUSIKAELS TYDVERDRYF, VOL.
    1: OCTOBER see Mahaut, Antonio

MAENDELYKS MUSIKAELS TYDVERDRYF, VOL.
    2: NOVEMBER see Mahaut, Antonio

MAENDELYKS MUSIKAELS TYDVERDRYF, VOL.
    3: DECEMBER see Mahaut, Antonio

MAENDELYKS MUSIKAELS TYDVERDRYF, VOL.
    4: JANUARI see Mahaut, Antonio

MAENDELYKS MUSIKAELS TYDVERDRYF, VOL.
    5: FEBRUARI see Mahaut, Antonio

MAENDELYKS MUSIKAELS TYDVERDRYF, VOL.
    6: MAERT see Mahaut, Antonio

MAENDELYKS MUSIKAELS TYDVERDRYF, VOL.
    7: APRIL see Mahaut, Antonio

MAENDELYKS MUSIKAELS TYDVERDRYF, VOL.
    8: MEY see Mahaut, Antonio

MAENDELYKS MUSIKAELS TYDVERDRYF, VOL.
    9: JUNY see Mahaut, Antonio

MAES, L.
    E Lieke
    solo,pno ALSBACH s.p.   (M171)

MAG see Kagen, Sergius

MAG see Raphling, Sam

MAG DAS SCHICKSAL DES EW'GEN RICHTERS
    see Purcell, Henry

MAGANINI, QUINTO (1897-1974)
    Bright Star
    solo,pno MUSICUS $1.00 see also
        Four Orchestral Songs   (M172)

    Cynara
    solo,pno MUSICUS $1.00 see also
        Four Orchestral Songs   (M173)

    Four Orchestral Songs
    solo,pno cmplt ed MUSICUS $3.75
        contains & see also: Bright Star;
        Cynara; Jealousy; Sonnet To
        Byron   (M174)

    Jealousy
    solo,pno MUSICUS $1.00 see also
        Four Orchestral Songs   (M175)

    Maria's Trinity *sac
    high solo,pno (E flat maj) MUSICUS
        $1.25   (M176)

    Prayer
    ST soli,pno (C maj) MUSICUS $1.50
                                   (M177)

    Song Of A Chinese Fisherman
    med solo,pno (D min) MUSICUS $1.25
                                   (M178)

    Sonnet To Byron
    solo,pno MUSICUS $1.00 see also
        Four Orchestral Songs   (M179)

    Three Lyrics *CC3U
    high solo,fl,drums MUSICUS $2.00
                                   (M180)

MAGDALENE see Warren

MAGDIC, JOSIP (1937-   )
    Tri Pesmi *CC3U
    Bar solo,pno DRUSTVO DSS 213 rental
                                   (M181)

MAGEN AVOT see Barkan, Emanuel

MAGGIE LAUDER *folk,Scot
    solo,pno (A maj) PATERSON FS54 s.p.
                                   (M182)

MAGGIE TEYTE ALBUM OF FRENCH SONGS
    *CC18L,Fr
    [Fr/Eng] solo,pno SCHIRM.G $3.50
        contains works by: Monsigny; Gluck;
        Offenbach; Debussy and others
                                   (M183)

MAGGIO see Salvatori, P. Salvatore

MAGGIOLATA see Cimara, Pietro

MAGGIOLI, PIETRO
    Soli
    S solo,pno SANTIS 611 s.p.   (M184)

MAGIC MOMENTS PASS A'WING see Harwood-
    Jones, H.F.

MAGIES see Miroglio, Francis

MAGNA RES EST AMOR see Andriessen,
    Hendrik

MAGNANI, FAUSTO
    Berceuse
    S solo,pno sc JOBERT s.p.   (M185)

MAGNANI, L.
    Barcarola
    solo,pno BONGIOVANI 2017 s.p.
                                   (M186)

MAGNE, MICHEL
    La Valse
    see Les Chansons De Francoise Sagan

    Le Jour
    see Les Chansons De Francoise Sagan

    Les Chansons De Francoise Sagan
    solo,pno cmplt ed TRANSAT. s.p.
        contains: La Valse; Le Jour; Les
        Jours Perdus; Pour Toi Et Moi;
        Sans Vous Aimer; Vous Mon Coeur
                                   (M187)

    Les Jours Perdus
    see Les Chansons De Francoise Sagan

    Pour Toi Et Moi
    see Les Chansons De Francoise Sagan

    Sans Vous Aimer
    see Les Chansons De Francoise Sagan

    Vous Mon Coeur
    see Les Chansons De Francoise Sagan

MAGNIFICAT see Arfken, Ernst

MAGNIFICAT see Braal, Andries de

MAGNIFICAT see Burkhard, Willy

MAGNIFICAT see Coral, Giampaolo

MAGNIFICAT see Gaslini, Giorgio

MAGNIFICAT see Hovland, Egil.

MAGNIFICAT see Kroll, Georg

MAGNIFICAT see Mengelberg, Rudolf

MAGNIFICAT see Reuland, Jacques

MAGNIFICAT see Telemann, Georg Philipp

MAGNIFICAT see Thorne, Francis

MAH LINDY LOU see Strickland, Lily
    Teresa

MAH NOMAR LEFONECHO see Adler, Hugo Ch.

MAH TOVU see Feuer, Joseph

MAH YAFIM see Chajes, Julius

MAHAUT, ANTONIO
    Maendelyks Musikaels Tydverdryf, Vol.
        1: October *CCU
    (Elzevier, K.) solo,pic,ob,vla,
        cembalo HEUWEKE. 241 s.p. (M188)

    Maendelyks Musikaels Tydverdryf, Vol.
        2: November *CCU
    (Elzevier, K.) solo,pic,ob,vla,
        cembalo HEUWEKE. 242 s.p. (M189)

    Maendelyks Musikaels Tydverdryf, Vol.
        3: December *CCU
    (Elzevier, K.) solo,pic,ob,vla,
        cembalo HEUWEKE. 243 s.p. (M190)

    Maendelyks Musikaels Tydverdryf, Vol.
        4: Januari *CCU
    (Elzevier, K.) solo,pic,ob,vla,
        cembalo HEUWEKE. 244 s.p. (M191)

    Maendelyks Musikaels Tydverdryf, Vol.
        5: Februari *CCU
    (Elzevier, K.) solo,pic,ob,vla,
        cembalo HEUWEKE. 245 s.p. (M192)

    Maendelyks Musikaels Tydverdryf, Vol.
        6: Maert *CCU
    (Elzevier, K.) solo,pic,ob,vla,
        cembalo HEUWEKE. 246 s.p. (M193)

    Maendelyks Musikaels Tydverdryf, Vol.
        7: April *CCU
    (Elzevier, K.) solo,pic,ob,vla,
        cembalo HEUWEKE. 247 s.p. (M194)

    Maendelyks Musikaels Tydverdryf, Vol.
        8: Mey *CCU
    (Elzevier, K.) solo,pic,ob,vla,
        cembalo HEUWEKE. 248 s.p. (M195)

    Maendelyks Musikaels Tydverdryf, Vol.
        9: Juny *CCU
    (Elzevier, K.) solo,pic,ob,vla,
        cembalo HEUWEKE. 249 s.p. (M196)

MAHLER, GUSTAV (1860-1911)
    Ablosung Im Sommer
    see Twenty-Four Songs, Vol. III

    Antonius Von Padua
    [Ger/Eng] low solo,pno UNIVER.
        3644B $2.75 see also Vierzehn
        Lieder Aus "Des Knaben
        Wunderhorn"   (M197)
    [Ger/Eng] high solo,pno UNIVER.
        3644A $2.75 see also Vierzehn
        Lieder Aus "Des Knaben
        Wunderhorn"   (M198)

    Aus! Aus!
    see Twenty-Four Songs, Vol. II

    Blicke Mir Nicht
    see Twenty-Four Songs, Vol. IV

    Blicke Mir Nicht In Der Lieder
        *Op.5,No.3
    high solo,pno sc KALMUS $4.00
                                   (M199)
    Das Irdische Leben
    see Twenty-Four Songs, Vol. II
    [Ger/Eng] low solo,pno UNIVER.
        3643B $2.75 see also Vierzehn
        Lieder Aus "Des Knaben
        Wunderhorn"   (M200)
    [Ger/Eng] high solo,pno UNIVER.
        3643A $2.75 see also Vierzehn
        Lieder Aus "Des Knaben
        Wunderhorn"   (M201)

    Der Schildwache Nachtlied
    [Ger/Eng] high solo,pno UNIVER.
        3639A $2.75 see also Vierzehn
        Lieder Aus "Des Knaben
        Wunderhorn"   (M202)
    [Ger/Eng] low solo,pno UNIVER.
        3639B $2.75 see also Vierzehn
        Lieder Aus "Des Knaben
        Wunderhorn"   (M203)

    Der Tamboursg'sell
    see Twenty-Four Songs, Vol. IV

    Erinnerung
    see Twenty-Four Songs, Vol. I

MAHLER, GUSTAV (cont'd.)

Es Sungen Drei Engel
[Ger/Eng] low solo,pno UNIVER.
3649B $2.75 see also Vierzehn
Lieder Aus "Des Knaben
Wunderhorn" (M204)
[Ger/Eng] high solo,pno UNIVER.
3649A $2.75 see also Vierzehn
Lieder Aus "Des Knaben
Wunderhorn" (M205)

Fruhlingsmorgen
see Twenty-Four Songs, Vol. I

Hans Und Grethe
see Twenty-Four Songs, Vol. I

Ich Atmet Einen Linden Duft
see Twenty-Four Songs, Vol. IV
[Ger/Eng] low solo,pno INTERNAT.
$1.00 (M206)
[Ger/Eng] high solo,pno INTERNAT.
$1.00 (M207)

Ich Bin Der Welt
see Twenty-Four Songs, Vol. IV

Ich Bin Der Welt Abhanden Gekommen
*Op.5,No.4
solo,pno sc KALMUS $3.00 (M208)

Ich Ging Mit Lust
see Twenty-Four Songs, Vol. II
high solo,pno SCHOTTS 1571 s.p.
(M209)

Kindertotenlieder *CCU
[Ger/Eng] INTERNAT. high solo,pno
$2.50; med solo,pno $2.50 (M210)

Kindertotenlieder *CCU
[Ger/Eng] s.p. high solo,pno KAHNT
FK12; low solo,pno KAHNT FK13
(M211)

Kindertotenlieder *CCU
solo,pno PETERS 9263 $10.00 (M212)

Kindertotenlieder *CC5U
solo,pno/orch study sc KALMUS 100
$3.00 (M213)

Liebst Du Um Schonheit
see Twenty-Four Songs, Vol. IV

Lied Der Verfolgten Im Turm
[Ger/Eng] high solo,pno UNIVER.
3646A $2.75 see also Vierzehn
Lieder Aus "Des Knaben
Wunderhorn" (M214)
[Ger/Eng] low solo,pno UNIVER.
3646B $2.75 see also Vierzehn
Lieder Aus "Des Knaben
Wunderhorn" (M215)

Lieder Eines Fahrenden Gesellen *CCU
[Ger/Eng] INTERNAT. high solo,pno
$2.50; med solo,pno $2.50 (M216)

Lieder Eines Fahrenden Gesellen *CCU
[Ger/Eng] AMP WBR high solo,pno
$2.75; low solo,pno $2.75 (M217)

Lieder Und Gesange, Band I *CCU
s.p. high solo,pno SCHOTTS 829; low
solo,pno SCHOTTS 830 (M218)

Lieder Und Gesange, Band II *CCU
s.p. high solo,pno SCHOTTS 831; low
solo,pno SCHOTTS 832 (M219)

Lieder Und Gesange, Band III *CCU
s.p. high solo,pno SCHOTTS 833; low
solo,pno SCHOTTS 834 (M220)

Lob Des Hohen Verstands
see Twenty-Four Songs, Vol. III
[Ger/Eng] high solo,pno UNIVER.
3648A $2.75 see also Vierzehn
Lieder Aus "Des Knaben
Wunderhorn" (M221)
[Ger/Eng] low solo,pno UNIVER.
3648B $2.75 see also Vierzehn
Lieder Aus "Des Knaben
Wunderhorn" (M222)

Nicht Wiedersehen!
see Twenty-Four Songs, Vol. III

O Mensch (from Symphony No. 3)
[Ger/Eng] A solo,pno UNIVER. 2943
$3.25 (M223)

Phantasie
see Twenty-Four Songs, Vol. I

Rheinlegendchen
[Ger/Eng] low solo,pno UNIVER.
3645B $2.75 see also Vierzehn
Lieder Aus "Des Knaben
Wunderhorn" (M224)
[Ger/Eng] high solo,pno UNIVER.
3645A $2.75 see also Vierzehn
Lieder Aus "Des Knaben
Wunderhorn" (M225)

MAHLER, GUSTAV (cont'd.)

Scheiden Und Meiden
see Twenty-Four Songs, Vol. III

Selbstgefuhl
see Twenty-Four Songs, Vol. III

Selected Songs *CCU
[Russ] solo,pno MEZ KNIGA 89 s.p.
(M226)

Serenade
see Twenty-Four Songs, Vol. I

Seven Songs From The Last Period
*CC7U
[Ger/Eng] med solo,pno KAHNT FK15
s.p. (M227)

Song Of The Wayfarer
solo,pno study sc KALMUS 111 $3.00
(M228)

Starke Einbildungskraft
see Twenty-Four Songs, Vol. II

Trost Im Ungluck
[Ger/Eng] high solo,pno UNIVER.
3641A $2.75 see also Vierzehn
Lieder Aus "Des Knaben
Wunderhorn" (M229)
[Ger/Eng] low solo,pno UNIVER.
3641B $2.75 see also Vierzehn
Lieder Aus "Des Knaben
Wunderhorn" (M230)

Twenty-Four Songs, Vol. I
[Ger/Eng] high solo/low solo,pno
INTERNAT. $2.50 available in high
or low edition
contains: Erinnerung;
Fruhlingsmorgen; Hans Und
Grethe; Phantasie; Serenade;
Wer Hat Dies Liedlein Erdacht?
(M231)

Twenty-Four Songs, Vol. II
[Ger/Eng] high solo/low solo,pno
INTERNAT. $2.50 available in high
or low edition
contains: Aus! Aus!; Das Irdische
Leben; Ich Ging Mit Lust;
Starke Einbildungskraft; Um
Schlimme Kinder; Wo Die Schonen
Trompeten (M232)

Twenty-Four Songs, Vol. III
[Ger/Eng] high solo/low solo,pno
INTERNAT. $2.50 available in high
or low edition
contains: Ablosung Im Sommer; Lob
Des Hohen Verstands; Nicht
Wiedersehen!; Scheiden Und
Meiden; Selbstgefuhl; Zu
Strassburg Auf Der Schanz
(M233)

Twenty-Four Songs, Vol. IV
[Ger/Eng] high solo/low solo,pno
INTERNAT. $2.50 available in high
or low edition
contains: Blicke Mir Nicht; Der
Tamboursg'sell; Ich Atmet Einen
Linden Duft; Ich Bin Der Welt;
Liebst Du Um Schonheit; Um
Mitternacht (M234)

Um Mitternacht *Op.5,No.5
see Twenty-Four Songs, Vol. IV
solo,pno sc KALMUS $4.00 (M235)

Um Schlimme Kinder
see Twenty-Four Songs, Vol. II

Urlicht (from Symphony No. 2)
[Ger/Eng] low solo,pno INTERNAT.
$1.00 (M236)
[Ger/Eng] high solo,pno UNIVER.
2938A $2.75 see also Vierzehn
Lieder Aus "Des Knaben
Wunderhorn" (M237)
[Ger/Eng] low solo,pno UNIVER.
2938B $2.75 see also Vierzehn
Lieder Aus "Des Knaben
Wunderhorn" (M238)

Verlorne Muh'l
[Ger/Eng] low solo,pno UNIVER.
3640B $2.75 see also Vierzehn
Lieder Aus "Des Knaben
Wunderhorn" (M239)
[Ger/Eng] high solo,pno UNIVER.
3640A $2.75 see also Vierzehn
Lieder Aus "Des Knaben
Wunderhorn" (M240)

Vierzehn Lieder Aus "Des Knaben
Wunderhorn" *CC14UL
[Ger/Eng] high solo,pno UNIVER.
14786A $8.00; low solo,pno
UNIVER. 14786B $8.00
see also: Antonius Von Padua; Das
Irdische Leben; Der Schildwache
Nachtlied; Es Sungen Drei
Engel; Lied Der Verfolgten Im
Turm; Lob Des Hohen Verstands;
Rheinlegendchen; Trost Im
Ungluck; Urlicht (from Symphony
No. 2); Verlorne Muh'l; Wer Hat

MAHLER, GUSTAV (cont'd.)

Dies Liedlein Erdacht?; Wo Die
Schonen Trompeten (M241)

Vierzehn Lieder Und Gesange Aus Der
Jugendzeit Band I *CCU
high solo,pno UNIVER. 3952 $3.00
(M242)

Vierzehn Lieder Und Gesange Aus Der
Jugendzeit, Band II *CCU
high solo,pno UNIVER. 3953A $3.00;
low solo,pno UNIVER. 3953B $3.00
(M243)

Vierzehn Lieder Und Gesange Aus Der
Jugendzeit, Band III *CCU
high solo,pno UNIVER. 3954A $3.00;
low solo,pno UNIVER. 3954B $3.00
(M244)

Wer Hat Dies Liedlein Erdacht?
see Twenty-Four Songs, Vol. I
[Ger/Eng] low solo,pno INTERNAT.
$1.00 (M245)
[Ger/Eng] high solo,pno INTERNAT.
$1.00 (M246)
[Ger/Eng] low solo,pno UNIVER.
3642B $2.75 see also Vierzehn
Lieder Aus "Des Knaben
Wunderhorn" (M247)
[Ger/Eng] high solo,pno UNIVER.
3642A $2.75 see also Vierzehn
Lieder Aus "Des Knaben
Wunderhorn" (M248)

Wir Geniessen Die Himmlischen Freuden
(from Symphony No. 4)
[Ger/Eng] S solo,pno UNIVER. 2946
$3.25 (M249)
S solo,orch/pno KALMUS 3689 $1.50
(M250)

Wo Die Schonen Trompeten
see Twenty-Four Songs, Vol. II
[Ger/Eng] low solo,pno UNIVER.
3647B $2.75 see also Vierzehn
Lieder Aus "Des Knaben
Wunderhorn" (M251)
[Ger/Eng] high solo,pno UNIVER.
3647A $2.75 see also Vierzehn
Lieder Aus "Des Knaben
Wunderhorn" (M252)

Wunderhorn Songs *CC14L
[Ger/Eng] SCHIRM.G high solo,pno
$5.00; low solo,pno $5.00 (M253)

Zu Strassburg Auf Der Schanz
see Twenty-Four Songs, Vol. III

MAHRISCHE BALLANDEN see Vycpalek,
Ladislav

MAHRISCHE VOLKSPOESIE IN LIEDERN see
Janacek, Leos

MAI see Lattes, M.

MAI see Ravize, A.

MAI see Saint-Saens, Camille

MAI! see Tirindelli, Pier Adolfo

MAI VIENT see Messager, Andre

MAID ME LOVED see Barab, Seymour

MAID OF BUNCLODY see Noble, H.

MAID OF GANGES see Mendelssohn-
Bartholdy, Felix, Auf Flugeln Des
Gesanges

MAID OF LODI, THE see Shield, William

MAIDEN see Lora, Antonio

MAIDEN AND THE BUTTERFLY, THE see
d'Albert, Eugene Francis Charles,
Das Madchen Und Der Schmetterling

MAIDEN OF MORVEN see Lawson, Malcolm

MAIDEN SNOW see Hundley, Richard

MAIDEN YONDER SINGS, A see Sibelius,
Jean, Im Feld Ein Madchen Singt

MAIDENBLOSSOMS see Strauss, Richard

MAIDEN'S PLAINT, THE see Schubert,
Franz (Peter), Des Madchen's Klage

MAIDEN'S SONG FROM "ST. WINEFRED'S
WELL" see Nowak, Lionel

MAIDEN'S WISH, THE see Chopin,
Frederic, Madchen's Wunsch

MAIDS OF CADIZ see Delibes, Leo, Les
Filles Des Cadix

MAIDS OF CADIZ, THE see Delibes, Leo,
Les Filles De Cadix

MAIENFAHRT *CCU,folk,Ger
   (Taubert, Karl Heinz) solo,treb inst,
   or piano 4 hands RIES s.p. sc, solo
   pt   (M254)

MAILIED see Schumann, Robert
   (Alexander)

MAILIED see Trapp, Max

MAIN DOMINEE PAR LE COEUR see Poulenc,
   Francis

MAINE *Fr
   (Canteloube, J.) solo,acap DURAND
   s.p. see also Anthologie Des Chants
   Populaires Francais Tome IV   (M255)

MAINI, MANLIO
   Inverno
      solo,pno SANTIS 721 s.p.   (M256)

   Un Sogno
      solo,pno SANTIS 720 s.p.   (M257)

   Vespro D'agosto
      solo,pno SANTIS 719 s.p.   (M258)

MAINTENANT, O MON DIEU see Bernard, R.

MAINTENANT QUE LE PERE DE PELLEAS EST
   SAUVE see Debussy, Claude

MAIS CE DIEU QUE PEUT-IL? see Gounod,
   Charles Francois

MAIS QUE JE PLEURE see Schlosser, Paul

MAISE FUN A PASTUCH'L see Fromm,
   Herbert

MAITIA NUN ZIRA *folk
   (Lavie) "Adieu Chere Vallee" [Fr/
   Span] med solo,gtr ESCHIG $1.00 see
   from Three Popular Songs   (M259)
   (Lavie, Ferandez) "Adieu Chere
   Vallee" [Span/Fr/It] solo,gtr
   SCHOTTS GA 195 s.p. see from Alte
   Und Neue Werke   (M260)

MAITLAND, JOHN ALEXANDER FULLER
   North Country Maid *Eng
      solo,pno CRAMER   (M261)

MAITRE! BON! APRES L'AMI see Saint-
   Saens, Camille

MAIWUNDER see Prohaska, Carl

MAIZEL, B.
   Romances To Lyrics By Garcia Lorca
   *CCU
      [Russ] med solo,pno MEZ KNIGA 2.94
      s.p.   (M262)

MAIZTEGUI, ISIDRO
   El Paraiso
      [Span] solo,pno RICORDI-ARG BA 9956
      s.p.   (M263)

   Nocturno En Los Muelles
      [Span] solo,pno RICORDI-ARG
      BA 10390 s.p.   (M264)

MAJ see Peterson-Berger, (Olof) Wilhelm

MAJ see Rangstrom, Ture

MAJ see Sibelius, Jean

MAJ I MUNGA see Peterson-Berger, (Olof)
   Wilhelm

MAJNATT see Hasse

MAJO, GIAN FRANCESCO DE
   Sicut Cerva, Quae Per Valles *sac
   (Ewerhart, Rudolf) S solo,org
   BIELER CS 36 s.p.   (M265)

MAJOVA LASKA see Urbanec, Bartolomej

MAJSANG see Hiller

MAKAAJA-ONNI see Kilpinen, Yrio

MAKAROVA, NINA VLADIMIROVNA (1908-   )
   Songs And Romances *CCU
      [Russ] solo,pno MEZ KNIGA 2.95 s.p.
                               (M266)

MAKE A JOYFUL NOISE TO THE LORD see
   Suben, Joel

MAKE A JOYFUL NOISE UNTO THE LORD see
   Fischer, Irwin

MAKE ME A NEW CREATURE see Holm

MAKE ME WILLING see Lindberg

MAKE MY SON A TREE see Ortlund, Anne

MAKE PRAYER YOUR PARTNER see Dungan,
   Olive

MALAGUENA see Caggiano, Roberto

MALAGUENA see Lecuona, Ernesto

MALAGUENA DE ANTEQUERA
   see Internationale Volkslieder, Vol.
   2

MALA'IB EL NUR *CCU
   (Tuvya, Ovadia) solo,pno
   ISR.MUS.INST. 2001 s.p. Arabic
   songs by various composers   (M267)

MALARNA FLADDRAR see Hallnas, Hilding

MALASHKIN, LEONID DIMITRIEVITCH
   (1842-1902)
   Could I But Feel My Sorrow
      high solo,pno (D min) ALLANS s.p.
                               (M268)
      low solo,pno (B min) ALLANS s.p.
                               (M269)
   Oh, Could I But Express In Song
      [Eng] low solo,kbd CHESTER s.p.
                               (M270)
      [Eng] high solo,kbd CHESTER s.p.
                               (M271)

MALATESTA, LUIGI (1900-   )
   Canti Della Montagna *CCU
      solo,pno ZERBONI 3726 s.p.   (M272)

MALAY TO HIS MASTER, THE see Bauer,
   Marion Eugenie

MALE QUARTET *sac,CC73UL
   (Gerig, Richard E.) 4 male soli,pno
   LILLENAS MB-121 $1.50   (M273)

MALE SMUTKY see Eben, Petr

MALEC, IVO (1925-   )
   Oral Fur Rezitator Und Grosses
   Orchester
      narrator,3pic,2English horn,2bass
      clar,2contrabsn,4horn,4trp,4trom,
      tuba,timp,perc,harp,cel,pno,
      strings sc,quarto GERIG HG 589
      s.p.   (M274)

MALEDETTO SIA L'ASPETTO see Monteverdi,
   Claudio

MALEDICTION see Sydeman, William

MALEISCHE LIEDEREN see Wall, C. v.d.

MALEISCHE LIEDEREN, BD.1 see
   Hullebroeck, Em.

MALEST CORNIFICI see Cattini, U.

MALGRE NOUS see Chaminade, Cecile

MALGRE VENTS ET TEMPETE see Wagner,
   Richard

MALHAYA LA SUERTE MIA! see Lopez-
   Buchardo, Carlos

MALIA see Tosti, Francesco Paolo

MALINCONIA see Siccardi, Honorio

MALIPIERO, GIAN FRANCESCO (1882-1973)
   Ariette
      see Five Songs

   Ballata
      see Tre Poesie Di Angelo Poliziano

   Bereaved Mother, The *see La Madre
      Folle

   Chanson Morave
      see Five Songs

   Cinque Favole *song cycle
      [It] solo,orch RICORDI-ENG PR 543
      s.p.   (M275)

   Dialogo Con Jacopone Da Todi
      solo,2pno RICORDI-ENG 129403 s.p.
                               (M276)

   Due Sonetti Del Berni *CC2U
      S solo,pno RICORDI-ENG 119002 s.p.
                               (M277)

   Five Songs
      [Fr] med solo,pno SALABERT-US $6.00
      contains: Ariette; Chanson
      Morave; L'Archet; Les Yeux
      Couleur Du Temps; Pegase (M278)

   Il Cantastorie (from Setti Canzoni)
      "Minstrel, The" Bar solo,kbd
      CHESTER s.p.   (M279)

   Inno A Maria Nostra Donna
      see Tre Poesie Di Angelo Poliziano

   Keepsake
      [Fr] high solo,kbd CHESTER s.p.
      contains: Light; Song; Stream
                               (M280)

   La Madre Folle
      "Bereaved Mother, The" S solo,kbd
      CHESTER s.p. see from Setti

MALIPIERO, GIAN FRANCESCO (cont'd.)

   Canzoni   (M281)

   La Morte Di Socrate
      [It] Bar solo,orch RICORDI-ENG
      PR 875 s.p. see from Otto
      Dialoghi   (M282)

   L'Archet
      see Five Songs

   Le Sette Allegrezze D'amore
      female solo,14inst voc sc ZERBONI
      4127 s.p.   (M283)

   Le Stagioni Italiche
      S solo,pno RICORDI-ENG 119650 s.p.
                               (M284)

   L'Eco
      see Tre Poesie Di Angelo Poliziano

   Les Yeux Couleur Du Temps
      see Five Songs

   Light
      see Keepsake

   Minstrel, The *see Il Cantastorie

   Mondi Celesti (from Mondi Celesti E
   Infernali)
      S solo,pno RICORDI-ENG 128067 s.p.
                               (M285)
      [It] solo,10inst RICORDI-ENG PR 390
      s.p.   (M286)

   Otto Dialoghi *see La Morte Di
      Socrate   (M287)

   Pegase
      see Five Songs

   Preludio E Morte Di Macbeth
      [It] Bar solo,orch RICORDI-ENG
      PR 909 s.p.   (M288)

   Quattro Sonetti Del Burchiello *CC4U
      solo,pno BONGIOVANI 1426 s.p.
                               (M289)

   Quattro Vecchie Canzoni *CC4U
      Bar solo,7inst min sc ZERBONI 3874
      s.p.   (M290)

   Serenade *see Serenata

   Serenata
      "Serenade" T solo,kbd CHESTER s.p.
      see from Setti Canzoni   (M291)

   Sette Canzonette Veneziane *CC7U
      [It] med solo,pno UNIVER. 12105
      $3.75   (M292)

   Setti Canzoni *see La Madre Folle,
      "Bereaved Mother, The"; Serenata,
      "Serenade"   (M293)

   Song
      see Keepsake

   Stream
      see Keepsake

   Three Songs From "Setti Canzoni"
   *CC3U
      Bar solo,pno CHESTER s.p.   (M294)

   Tre Poesie Di Angelo Poliziano
      [It] high solo,kbd CHESTER s.p.
      contains: Ballata; Inno A Maria
      Nostra Donna; L'Eco   (M295)

   Uno Dei Dieci
      solo,pno RICORDI-ENG 131868 s.p.
                               (M296)

MALIPIERO, RICCARDO (1914-   )
   Antico Sole
      solo,2fl,2ob,2clar,2bsn,2horn,2trp,
      perc,pno CARISH s.p.   (M297)

   Due Ballate *CC2U
      solo,gtr ZERBONI 6840 s.p. (M298)

   Go Placidly...
      Bar solo,orch voc sc ZERBONI 8017
      s.p.   (M299)

   In Time Of Daffodils
      SBar soli,7inst voc sc ZERBONI 6341
      s.p.   (M300)

   Monologo
      female solo,strings voc sc ZERBONI
      6876 s.p.   (M301)

   Motivi *CCU
      solo,pno ZERBONI 6231 s.p. (M302)

   Preludio, Adagio E Finale
      female solo,5perc voc sc ZERBONI
      6407 s.p.   (M303)

   Sei Poesie Di Dylan Thomas *CC6U
      S solo,10inst voc sc ZERBONI 5534
      s.p.   (M304)

MALIPIERO, RICCARDO (cont'd.)

Sette Variazioni Su "Les Roses"
*CC7U
solo,pno ZERBONI 4963 s.p.   (M305)

Sinfonia Cantata
Bar solo,orch sc ZERBONI 5323 s.p.
(M306)

MALJA see Marvia, Einari

MALLINSON, (JAMES) ALBERT (1870-1946)
Birds At Winter Nightfall
solo,pno CRAMER $.95   (M307)

Five Sonnets *CC5U
solo,pno CRAMER   (M308)

From The Unknown Island Of A Heart
solo,pno CRAMER   (M309)

Garden Is A Lovesome Thing, A
solo,pno CRAMER $.95   (M310)

In The Dusky Path Of A Dream
solo,pno CRAMER $.95   (M311)

Jenny And The Goldsmith
solo,pno CRAMER   (M312)

Life's Rose
solo,pno (D maj) LEONARD-ENG (M313)

My Heart, The Bird Of The Wilderness
solo,pno CRAMER $.95   (M314)

Night But Abides For A Span
solo,pno CRAMER $.95   (M315)

Old Bridge At Florence, The
solo,pno CRAMER $.95   (M316)

Shepherds Rise And Shake Off Sleep
solo,pno CRAMER   (M317)

Sicilian Lullaby
solo,pno CRAMER $.95   (M318)

MALMFURU see Olsen, Sparre

MALMSTROM
Fadernas Arv
solo,pno LUNDQUIST s.p.   (M319)

MALO, CH.
Le Semeur
solo,acap ENOCH s.p.   (M320)
solo,pno ENOCH s.p.   (M321)

Svunnen Lycka
solo,pno LUNDQUIST s.p.   (M322)

MALOTTE, ALBERT HAY (1895-1964)
Beatitudes, The *sac
high solo,pno (E min) SCHIRM.G $.85
(M323)
low solo,pno (C min) SCHIRM.G $.85
(M324)

Blow Me Eyes
solo,pno ALLANS s.p.   (M325)

Bridal Hymn *Marriage
(Gramlich) solo,pno FOX,S (M326)

David And Goliath
solo,pno ALLANS s.p.   (M327)

Holy Bible, The *sac
med solo,pno (F maj) SCHIRM.G $.75
(M328)

I Am Proud To Be An American
med solo,pno (F maj) SCHIRM.G $.75
(M329)

Little Song Of Life, A
high solo,pno (D maj) ALLANS s.p.
(M330)
low solo,pno (C maj) ALLANS s.p.
(M331)
med solo,pno (D maj) SCHIRM.G $.85
(M332)

Lord's Prayer, The *sac
high solo,pno/org (E flat maj)
SCHIRM.G $1.00   (M333)
low solo,pno/org (G maj) SCHIRM.G
$1.00   (M334)
low solo,pno/org (B flat maj)
SCHIRM.G $1.00   (M335)
med solo,pno/org (D flat maj)
SCHIRM.G $1.00   (M336)
med solo,pno/org (C maj) SCHIRM.G
$1.00   (M337)
high solo,pno (E flat maj) ALLANS
s.p.   (M338)
med solo,pno (D flat maj) ALLANS
s.p.   (M339)
low solo,pno (B flat maj) ALLANS
s.p.   (M340)
med solo,pno BENSON S7964 $1.25
(M341)
(Deis) ABar soli,pno SCHIRM.G $1.00
(M342)
(Deis) ST soli,pno SCHIRM.G $1.00
(M343)
(Deis) SA soli,pno SCHIRM.G $1.00
(M344)

MALOTTE, ALBERT HAY (cont'd.)

My Friend
high solo,pno (G maj) SCHIRM.G $.85
(M345)
med solo,pno (F maj) SCHIRM.G $.85
(M346)
low solo,pno (E flat maj) SCHIRM.G
$.85   (M347)

Pledge To The Flag
med-high solo,pno (F maj) SCHIRM.G
$.75   (M348)
low solo,pno (C maj) SCHIRM.G $.75
(M349)

Psalm 23 *sac
high solo,pno (G maj) SCHIRM.G $.85
(M350)
med solo,pno (F maj) SCHIRM.G $.85
(M351)
low solo,pno (E flat maj) SCHIRM.G
$.85   (M352)
low solo,pno (E flat maj) ALLANS
s.p.   (M353)
med solo,pno (F maj) ALLANS s.p.
(M354)
high solo,pno (G maj) ALLANS s.p.
(M355)

Sing A Song Of Sixpence
solo,pno ALLANS s.p.   (M356)

Understanding Heart, An
med solo,pno (B flat maj) SCHIRM.G
$.75   (M357)

MALY TRIPTYCH see Macha, Otmar

MAMAN, AVANT DE DIRE see Vogel, A.

MAMAN, JE ME RAPPELLE see Vogel, A.

MAMAN POUR TA FETE see Buxeuil, R. de

MAMANGAKIS, NIKOS (1929-   )
Kassandra
S solo,fl,horn,tuba,2perc,harp
MODERN rental   (M358)

Musik Fur Vier Protagonisten
SATB soli,fl,clar,bsn,2perc,pno,vln
MODERN rental   (M359)

MAMA'S TEACHING ANGELS HOW TO SING see
Rambo

MAMBLE see Blower, Maurice

MAMINKA see Podest, Ludvik

MAMLOCK, URSULA
Daybreak
S solo,pno AM.COMP.AL. $3.30 (M360)
Mez solo,pno AM.COMP.AL. $3.30
(M361)
Five Songs From "Stray Birds" *CC5U
S solo,fl,vcl sc AM.COMP.AL. $7.70
(M362)
Haiku Settings *CCU
S solo,fl AM.COMP.AL. $4.95 (M363)

MAMMA FAMMI LA PAPPA see Caggiano,
Roberto

MAMMA, IL GIOVANE PRINCIPE see Alfano,
Franco

MAMMA, IL TUO CUORE see Guarino, C.

MAMMA, QUEL VINO E GENEROSO see
Mascagni, Pietro

MAMMAS NYA VISOR see Schaar, Aina

MAMMAS VISOR see Schaar, Aina

MAMMY SINGS see Heilner, Irwin

MAMMY'S LIL' BABY
(Burleigh, H.T.) low solo,pno PRESSER
$.75   (M364)

MAMORSKY, MORRIS (1906-   )
Despedida
low solo,pno BROUDE BR. $.95 (M365)

I Find My Love
med solo,pno BROUDE BR. $.95 (M366)

MAMZELL ZIZI see Beekhuis, Hanna

MAMZE'LLE NITOUCHE see Herve

MAN see Humphreys

MAN, THE *sac
(Carmichael, Ralph) solo,pno WORD
S-51   (M367)

MAN AND WOMAN see Benjamin, Arthur

MAN FROM WAYOUT, THE see Poglietti,
Alessandro

MAN IN THE MOON, THE see Lessard, John
Ayres

MAN IN THE MOON, THE see Musgrave,
Thea, Man-In-The-Mune, The

MAN-IN-THE-MUNE, THE see Musgrave, Thea

MAN IS FOR THE WOMAN MADE see Purcell,
Henry

MAN MADE FROM SLEEP see Sallinen, Aulis

MAN OF STEEL see Lyman, Ed.

MAN ON THE MIDDLE CROSS, THE see
Lister, Mosie

MAN, THAT IS BORN OF A WOMAN see
Pinkham, Daniel

MAN TRO? JO, JO! see Lindblad, Adolf
Fredrik

MAN UPSTAIRS, THE *sac,gospel
solo,pno ABER.GRP. $1.50   (M368)

MAN WIRD JA EINMAL NUR GEBOREN see
Lortzing, (Gustav) Albert

MAN WUNSCHTE SICH see Lohr, Hanns

MANA-ZUCCA, MME. (1894-   )
Ahm Yisroel Chai
"Israel Lives" low solo/high solo,
pno CONGRESS $.60   (M369)

Big Brown Bear, The
med-high solo,pno (F maj) SCHIRM.G
$1.00   (M370)
low solo,pno (D maj) SCHIRM.G $1.00
(M371)

Call Of Love (from Queue Of Ki,Lu)
S solo,pno CONGRESS $.75   (M372)

Double The Trouble (from Queue Of Ki-
Lu, The)
B solo,pno CONGRESS $.75   (M373)

Doux Plaisir
"Sweet Pleasure" high solo,pno
CONGRESS $.60   (M374)

Duc Alma Lux
"Lead Kindly Light" med solo,pno
CONGRESS $.60   (M375)

Duet (from Queue Of Ki-Lu)
SBar soli,pno CONGRESS $.75 (M376)

Fairest Of All *see Piu Bello Del
Sole

Fantasy (from Queue Of Ki-Lu, The)
T solo,pno CONGRESS $.75   (M377)

First Love *see On Revient Toujours

For Us Two *see Im Lenz

Frage
"Question" low solo/high solo,pno
CONGRESS $.60   (M378)

God's Voice Has Softly Called *sac,
Gen
low solo,pno (B flat maj) WILLIS
$.50   (M379)
med solo,pno (C maj) WILLIS $.50
(M380)
high solo,pno (B flat maj) WILLIS
$.50   (M381)

Greetings *see Sholom Alechem

Holy Holy *see Kodosh-Kodosh

I Love Life
high solo,pno PRESSER $.95 (M382)
low solo,pno PRESSER $.95 (M383)
high solo,pno (F maj) ALLANS s.p.
(M384)
low solo,pno (D maj) ALLANS s.p.
(M385)
(Anka, Paul) med solo,pno PRESSER
$.95   (M386)

I Must Away (from Queue Of Ki-Lu,
The)
T solo,pno CONGRESS $.75   (M387)

I Would Fain Forget *see Je Voudrais
Oublier

Im Lenz
"For Us Two" high solo,pno CONGRESS
$.60   (M388)

Indian Lullaby *see Puva

Israel Lives *see Ahm Yisroel Chai

It Is Fate (from Queue Of Ki-Lu, The)
Bar solo,pno CONGRESS $.75 (M389)

Je Voudrais Oublier
"I Would Fain Forget" high solo,pno
CONGRESS $.60   (M390)

MANA-ZUCCA, MME. (cont'd.)

Kodosh-Kodosh
"Holy Holy" low solo/high solo,pno
CONGRESS $.60   (M391)

Lead Kindly Light *see Duc Alma Lux

Love's Adoration *see Priere D'Amour

Moon Of Kwang Tung (from Queue Of Ki-
Lu, The)
Bar solo,pno CONGRESS $.75   (M392)

Nichevo
"Nothing Matters" high solo/med
solo/low solo,pno CONGRESS $.60
                                 (M393)

Nothing Matters *see Nichevo

On Revient Toujours
"First Love" low solo/high solo,pno
CONGRESS $.60   (M394)

Ora Vorrei Partir
"Solace" high solo/low solo,pno
CONGRESS $.60   (M395)

Piu Bello Del Sole
"Fairest Of All" med solo/high
solo,pno CONGRESS $.60   (M396)

Priere D'Amour
"Love's Adoration" high solo,pno
CONGRESS $.75   (M397)

Puva
"Indian Lullaby" low solo/high
solo,pno CONGRESS $.60   (M398)

Quand Tu Es La
"When You Are Near" med solo,pno
CONGRESS $.60   (M399)

Question *see Frage

Sholom Alechem
"Greetings" low solo/high solo,pno
CONGRESS $.60   (M400)

Solace *see Ora Vorrei Partir

Sweet Pleasure *see Doux Plaisir

Was Ist Ein Kuss
"What Is A Kiss?" med solo,pno
CONGRESS $.60   (M401)

What Is A Kiss? *see Was Ist Ein
Kuss

When You Are Near *see Quand Tu Es
La

MANCHICOURT, PIERRE DE (1510-1586)
Twenty-Nine Chansons *CC29U
(Baird, Margery Anthea) solo,pno A-
R ED s.p.   (M402)

MANCHMAL GESCHIEHT ES IN TIEFER NACHT
see Voormolen, Alexander Nicolas

MANCINI, GIOVANNI
Soli Calanti
[It] solo,pno CURCI 7629 s.p.
                                 (M403)

MANCINI, VINCENZO
Ave Maria *sac
solo,pno SANTIS 1050 s.p.   (M404)

Dirigadur, Domine. Oratio Mea *sac
T solo,org SANTIS 925 s.p.   (M405)

Melodia Vesperale *sac
solo,pno SANTIS 1025 s.p.   (M406)

MANDINA AMABILE see Mozart, Wolfgang
Amadeus

MANDOLIN, THE see Gounod, Charles
Francois

MANDOLINE see Bourguignon, Francis de

MANDOLINE see Braga, Gaetana

MANDOLINE see Chaminade, Cecile

MANDOLINE see Chansarel, R.

MANDOLINE see Debussy, Claude

MANDOLINE see Diepenbrock, Alphons

MANDOLINE see Kowalski, Max

MANDOLINEN see Trunk, Richard

MANDOM MOD OCH MORSKE MAN
see Du Gamla Du Fria

MANDORLO FIORITO see Alaleone, Domenico

MANDY AND THE SPIDERS see Tombo,
Lorraine

MANELLA MIA see Giannini, Vittorio,
Dear Little Hand

MANEN, JOAN (1883-   )
Canciones Ibericas *see Flecha,
Op.26a   (M407)

Flecha *Op.26a
[Span/Fr] med solo,pno ESCHIG $1.00
see from Canciones Ibericas
                                 (M408)

Trois Chansons *Op.9a, CC3U
[Fr] med solo,pno ESCHIG $2.00
                                 (M409)

MANGERS see Holford, Franz

MANGONE, GIOACCHINO
Ave Maria *sac
[It] ST soli,org/harmonium CURCI
3865 s.p.   (M410)

MANHA MOLHADA see Prado, Almeida

MANHYMN VID LAMBERTSMASSEN see
Peterson-Berger, (Olof) Wilhelm

MANI D'AUTUNNO see Guarino, C.

MANN
I Know *see Burns

MANN, ADOLF
Lilacs Are In Bloom
low solo,pno (A flat maj) CRAMER
                                 (M411)
high solo,pno (C maj) CRAMER (M412)

MANNEKE, DANIEL (1939-   )
Five Songs On English Poems *CC5U
low solo,hpsd/pno/org DONEMUS s.p.
                                 (M413)

MANNER SUCHEN STETS ZU NASCHEN see
Mozart, Wolfgang Amadeus

MANNER, WENN DIE MADELN SCHMEICHELN see
Haibel, Jakob J.

MANNERTREU see Kilpinen, Yrio

MANNING, KATHLEEN LOCKHART
Shoes
med solo,pno (D maj) SCHIRM.G $.85
                                 (M414)
Winter Afternoon, A
med solo,pno (E flat maj) SCHIRM.G
$.60   (M415)

MANNING, RICHARD
Shenandoah
low solo,pno (E flat maj) GALAXY
1.1667.7 $1.00   (M416)

Wife Trouble
high solo,pno (A min) GALAXY
1.2111.7 $1.00   (M417)

MANNINO, FRANCO (1924-   )
Due Arie Per Soprano (from Viva) CC2U
[It] S solo,pno CURCI 9221 s.p.
                                 (M418)
Due Liriche Tedesche E Un Congedo Di
Giosue Carducci *Op.66, CC3U
s.p. S solo,orch sc,quarto RICORDI-
ENG 131785; S solo,pno voc sc
RICORDI-ENG 131787   (M419)

Ecco La Notte
Mez/Bar solo,pno RICORDI-ENG 131382
s.p.   (M420)

Il Quadro Delle Meraviglie *cant
[It] solo,pno voc sc CURCI 7881
s.p.   (M421)

La Stirpe Di Davide *sac
[It] solo,pno voc sc CURCI 7656
s.p.   (M422)

MANNISKANS HEM see Kilpinen, Yrio

MANOJICO see Mingote, A.

MANON see Lewkovitch, Bernhard

MANON see Svobodo, Jiri

MANOURY, P.
Puzzle
S/Mez solo,fl,ob,English horn,clar,
bass clar,horn,2trp,trom,harp,
Hamm,pno,cel,3perc,strings,
cimbalo RIDEAU rental   (M423)

MAN'S A MAN FOR A' THAT, A *folk,Scot
solo,pno (F maj/G maj) PATERSON FS3
s.p.   (M424)

MANSION OVER THE HILLTOP *sac,gospel
solo,pno ABER.GRP. $1.50   (M425)

MANSION OVER THE HILLTOP see Stanphill,
Ira F.

MANSKEN see Stenhammar, Wilhelm

MANSKENSNATT see Schumann, Robert
(Alexander), Mondnacht

MANSKENSVIT OCH MIDNATTSBLA see
Hallnas, Hilding

MANSTRALAR KLARA
solo,pno LUNDQUIST s.p.   (M426)

MANSTRLAR see Norman

MANTEAU DE FLEURS see Ravel, Maurice

MANTON, ROBERT WILLIAM (1894-   )
Three New England Lyrics *CC3U
high solo/med solo,pno SEESAW $1.50
                                 (M427)

MANUELA see Petralia

MANY A GIRL OF THE SOUTH IS WHITE AND
LUCENT see Bliss, Sir Arthur

MANY KINDS OF YES see Orr, Buxton

MANY THINGS HAVE I LOVED see Arlen,
Albert

MANYANAS LIEBESLIEDER see Beers,
Jacques

MAORI-LIEDER see Fruh

M'APPARI TUTT'AMOR see Flotow,
Friedrich von, Ach, So Fromm

MAQAMAT see Szekely, E.

MAR-RI-IA-A see Olive, Joseph

MARAVILLA, L.
Cuando Sali De Marbella (from
Malaguena)
[Span] med solo,gtr UNION ESP. $.75
                                 (M428)

Nana
[Span] med-high solo,pno UNION ESP.
$.60   (M429)

Vengo De Tierras De Oriente
[Span] med solo,pno UNION ESP. $.60
                                 (M430)

MARC GROET 'S MORGENS DE DINGEN see
Lilien, Ignace

MARC GROET 'S MORGENS DE SINGEN see
Beekhuis, Hanna

MARCELLES, P.
Dodinette
solo,pno ENOCH s.p.   (M431)

La Saison Des Roses
solo,pno ENOCH s.p.   (M432)

MARCELLO, BENEDETTO (1686-1739)
And With Songs I Will Celebrate *sac
SA/TB soli,pno oct CONCORDIA
98-1047 $.30   (M433)

Aria Sacra (Psalm 19) sac
(Adler, Charles) high solo,pno
TRANSCON. TV 488 $.75   (M434)
(Adler, Charles) med solo,pno
TRANSCON. TV 492 $.75   (M435)

B'rochos Shel Chanukoh
(Putterman; Kosakoff) solo,pno/org
TRANSCON. WJ 439 $1.00 contains
also: Marcello, Benedetto, Ma-Oz
Tsur; Mo-Oz Tsur   (M436)

Lord, Who Shall Dwell Upon Thy Holy
Hill? *sac
med solo,pno oct CONCORDIA 98-1551
$.20   (M437)

Ma-Oz Tsur
see Marcello, Benedetto, B'rochos
Shel Chanukoh

O Lord, Deliver Me *sac
SA/TB soli,pno oct CONCORDIA
98-1044 $.25   (M438)

O Lord, Our Governor *sac
med solo,pno oct CONCORDIA 98-1045
$.30   (M439)

Oh, Hold Thou Me Up *sac
SA/TB soli,pno oct CONCORDIA
98-1046 $.30   (M440)

Psalm 19 *see Aria Sacra

Thou Madest Man But Lower Than The
Angels *sac
med solo,pno oct CONCORDIA 98-1549
$.20   (M441)

Thou, O Lord, Art My Shepherd *sac
2 med soli,pno oct CONCORDIA
98-1851 $.25   (M442)

Voi Mi Piagaste, O Dio *sac
S solo,fl,harp,strings sc CARISH
21337 s.p., ipa   (M443)

MARCH 31, 1970 see Diemente, Edward

MARCHE *Fr
(Canteloube, J.) solo,acap DURAND
s.p. see also Anthologie Des Chants
Populaires Francais Tome III (M444)

MARCHE BASQUE see Trabadelo, A. de

MARCHE BOULEVARDIERE see Spencer, E.

MARCHE BOURGUIGNONNE see Laffitte, J.

MARCHE BRETONNE see Gauwin, Ad.

MARCHE COLONIAL see Szanto, Theodor

MARCHE D'AUVERGNE see Ganne, Louis
Gaston

MARCHE DE LA CITE GLORIEUSE see
Filipucci, Edm.

MARCHE DE PLUIE see Biancheri, A.

MARCHE DES AMOUREUX see Ganne, Louis
Gaston

MARCHE DES CADETS DE GASCOGNE see
Poujade, L.

MARCHE DES CONSCTRITS DANS LA MONTAGNE
see Indy, Vincent d'

MARCHE DES ENFANTS DE FRANCE see
Strimer, Joseph

MARCHE DES GAMINS DE PARIS see Berger,
Rod.

MARCHE DES GYMNASTES see Roques, L.

MARCHE DES PETITES BONNES see Duval, A.

MARCHE DES PETITS CABOTS see Berger,
Rod.

MARCHE DES PETITS PIOUPIOUS see Allier,
Gabriel

MARCHE DES P'TITS PIOUPIOUS see Allier,
Gabriel

MARCHE DU GAS LOUBET see Berger, Rod.

MARCHE FLAMANDE see Marie, Gabriel

MARCHE FRANC-COMTOISE see Ratez, Emile-
Pierre

MARCHE GRECQUE see Ganne, Louis Gaston

MARCHE LORRAINE see Ganne, Louis Gaston

MARCHE LYONNAISE see Allier, Gabriel

MARCHE RIANTE see Mouton, H.

MARCHE ROMANE see Georges, Alexandre

MARCHE RUSSE see Ganne, Louis Gaston

MARCHEN see Schilling, M. von

MARCHEN DER KINDHEIT see Bijvanck, Henk

MARCHEN VON DEM KROKODIL AUS BRUNN see
Krivinka, Gustav, Pohadka O
Brnenskem Krokodylovi

MARCHES D'AUVERGNE see Ganne, Louis
Gaston

MARCHES FRANC-COMTOISE see Ratez,
Emile-Pierre

MARCHES LYONNAISE see Allier, Gabriel

MARCHESI
La Folletta
Mez/Bar solo,pno RICORDI-ENG 48258
s.p. (M445)

MARCHETTI
Fascination
solo,pno ASHLEY $.95 (M446)

MARCHING ALONG see Harrison, Julius
Allen Greenway

MARCHING SONG see Franco, Johan

MARCHIONESS, YOUR DANCING see Lemaire

MARCOMIR, LE NOBLE EPOUX see Saint-
Saens, Camille

MARE JA HANEN POIKANSA see Pylkkanen,
Tauno Kullervo

MARE OCH HENNES SON see Pylkkanen,
Tauno Kullervo, Mare Ja Hanen
Poikansa

MARECHAL, HENRI-CHARLES (1842-1924)
Le Reve
(Bordese, Stephen) solo,pno
(available in 2 keys) ENOCH s.p.
see also CHANSONS DE PAGE (M447)

MARECHIARE see Tosti, Francesco Paolo

MARENZIO, LUCA (1553-1599)
Madrigals A 6, Book I (1581) *CCU,
madrigal
solo,pno BROUDE BR. (M448)

MAREZ OYENS, TERA DE (1932-   )
Der Chinesische Spiegel
T solo,2fl,2ob,2clar,2bsn,4horn,
2trp,3trom,timp,perc,cel,harp,
strings DONEMUS s.p. (M449)

Ryoanji Temple
A solo,ob,vln,vla,vcl DONEMUS s.p.
(M450)

MARGARET see Morgan, D.

MARGARET'S CRADLE SONG see Grieg,
Edvard Hagerup

MARGERY GREEN see Beresford, Arnold

MARGETSON, EDWARD J.
Tommy, Lad
low solo,pno (C maj) BOOSEY $1.50
(M451)
med solo,pno (D maj) BOOSEY $1.50
(M452)
high solo,pno (F maj) BOOSEY $1.50
(M453)

MARGIS, A.
La Chatelaine
solo,acap ENOCH s.p. (M454)
solo,pno ENOCH s.p. (M455)

MARGIT see Lundvik, Hildor

MARGOLA, FRANCO (1908-   )
Alle Termopili
see Tre Epigrammi Greci

Cammina, Cammina
solo,pno BONGIOVANI 2140 s.p.
(M456)

La Memoria E L'oblio
see Tre Epigrammi Greci

Poi Che 'L Cammin
solo,pno BONGIOVANI 2184 s.p.
(M457)

Possa Tu Giungere
S/T solo,pno RICORDI-ENG 129538
s.p. (M458)
Mez/Bar solo,pno RICORDI-ENG 129539
s.p. (M459)

Sulla Tomba Di Anacreonte
see Tre Epigrammi Greci

Tre Epigrammi Greci
[It] solo,pno cmplt ed BONGIOVANI
2471 s.p.; solo,horn,pno cmplt ed
BONGIOVANI 2507 s.p.
contains: Alle Termopili; La
Memoria E L'oblio; Sulla Tomba
Di Anacreonte (M460)

MARGOT, PRENDS GARDE! see Durand,
Jacques

MARGOTON VA-T-A-L'IAU *Fr
[Fr] solo,pno DURAND 79 s.p. (M461)

MARGRET'S GARDEN ARIA see Beeson, Jack
Hamilton

MARGUERITE see Schubert, Franz (Peter),
Gretchen Am Spinnrade

MARGUERITE AU ROUET see Schubert, Franz
(Peter), Gretchen Am Spinnrade

MARGUERITE, ELLE EST MALADE see Seiber,
Matyas

MARIA see Peeters, Flor

MARIA CATLINA see Sinigaglia, Leone

MARIA CONINGHINNE see Schouwman, Hans

MARIA DIE ZOUDE NAER BETHLEHEM GAAN see
Beekhuis, Hanna

MARIA KLAR see Krol, Bernhard

MARIA MEIN IM ROSENHAG see Kowalski,
Max

MARIA OCH RIZZIO see Campana

MARIA PAASLIED see Schouwman, Hans

MARIA SCHONE VROUWE see Andriessen,
Hendrik

MARIA WIEGENLIED see Reger, Max

MARIA ZART VON EDLER see Andriessen,
Hendrik

MARIA ZART VON EDLER ART see
Andriessen, Hendrik

MARIAE WIEGENLIED see Polzer, Odo

MARIAGE BLEU see Fragerolle, G.

MARIAGE D'AMES see Colomb, A.

MARIAN ANDERSON ALBUM OF SONGS AND
SPIRITUALS *sac/sec,CC20L,spir
solo,pno SCHIRM.G $3.95 contains
works by: Bach; Haydn; Franck;
Schubert and others (M462)

MARIAN KEHTOLAULU see Melartin, Erkki,
Marias Vaggsang

MARIANINA *It
solo,pno ALLANS s.p. (M463)

MARIANNA see Vive La Canadienne!

MARIANNS VISA see Wideen

MARIA'S TRINITY see Maganini, Quinto

MARIAS VAGGSANG see Melartin, Erkki

MARIAS VAGGSANG see Reger, Max, Maria
Wiegenlied

MARIE see Godard, Benjamin Louis Paul

MARIE see Rossellini, Renzo

MARIE, GABRIEL (1852-1928)
Marche Flamande
solo,acap ENOCH s.p. see from
CHANSONS DE TROUPE (M464)
solo,pno ENOCH s.p. (M465)

MARIEKE see Hullebroeck, Em.

MARIEN-KONZERT see Girnatis, Walter

MARIENKANTATE see Borris, Siegfried

MARIENKLAGE see Monteverdi, Claudio

MARIENLEGENDE see Jochum, Otto

MARIENLIED see Marx, Joseph

MARIENLIED see Rinaldini, Dr. Joseph

MARIENLIED see Roselius, Ludwig

MARIENLIEDER see Peeters, Flor

MARIENLIEDER see Zilcher, Hermann

MARIENSTROPHE see Bijvanck, Henk

MARIER
Christmas Is Here *sac,Xmas
(Champagne) solo,pno HARRIS $.90
(M466)

MARIETAN, PIERRE (1935-   )
Recit Suivi De Legende
S solo,fl,English horn,clar,horn,
pno,harp,vla sc JOBERT s.p.
(M467)

Scene I (from Sur-Sis)
S solo,fl,2clar,bsn,horn,trp,trom,
perc,harp,pno,vln,vcl AMPHION
A 285 s.p. (M468)

MARIETTAS LIED ZUM LAUTE see Korngold,
Erich Wolfgang

MARIETTI, G.
La Vierge
solo,acap ENOCH s.p. (M469)
solo,pno ENOCH s.p. (M470)

MARIGOLD GARDEN see Rowley, Alec

MARIN, J.
Dos Pasacalles *CC2U
(Tarrago) [Span] med-high solo,pno
UNION ESP. $.75 (M471)

MARINE see Durand, Jacques

MARINE see Massenet, Jules

MARINERO EN TIERRA, OP. 27 see
Halffter, Rodolfo

MARINETTE see Delmet, Paul

MARINIER, P.
Dormeuse
solo,pno ENOCH s.p. (M472)
solo,acap ENOCH s.p. (M473)

Il A Neige
solo,pno ENOCH s.p. (M474)
solo,acap ENOCH s.p. (M475)

MARINS D'ISLANDE see Tremisot, Ed.

MARIO, E.A.
　Santa Lucia, Lebe Wohl
　　solo,pno SCHAUR EE 3557 s.p. (M476)

MARION COUNTY TRADITION *sac,CCU
　(Cantrell; Terry; Pairamore) solo,pno
　　WORD S-433 (M477)

MARIONETTENLIED see Hullebroeck, Em.

MARIOTTE, ANTOINE (1875-1944)
　Berceuse
　　solo,pno ENOCH see also Intimites
　　　　(M478)
　Dieu D'Israel (from Esther)
　　solo,pno ENOCH s.p. (M479)
　Ils M'ont Dit, Pour Parer Ton Corps
　　(from Esther)
　　solo,pno ENOCH s.p. (M480)
　Intimites
　　ENOCH solo,pno cmplt ed s.p.; solo,
　　orch cmplt ed rental
　　contains & see also: Berceuse;
　　　Menuet; Si Je T'aime (M481)
　Israel En Bataille (from Esther)
　　solo,pno ENOCH s.p. (M482)
　Le Dieu Que J'ai Prie (from Esther)
　　solo,pno ENOCH s.p. (M483)
　Le Vieux Chemin
　　solo,pno ENOCH s.p. (M484)
　　solo,orch ENOCH rental (M485)
　Menuet
　　solo,pno ENOCH s.p. see also
　　　Intimites (M486)
　O Mon Dieu! Toi Qui Seul Conduis
　　(from Esther)
　　solo,pno ENOCH s.p. (M487)
　Poeme De Pitie
　　solo,pno ENOCH s.p. (M488)
　　solo,orch ENOCH rental (M489)
　Si Je T'aime
　　solo,pno ENOCH s.p. see also
　　　Intimites (M490)

MARITS VISOR see Peterson-Berger,
　(Olof) Wilhelm

MARJORIE JONES SONGBOOK, VOL. 1 see
　Jones, Marjorie

MARK THE PERFECT MAN see Barker

MARKEVITCH, IGOR (1912-)
　Lorenzo Il Magnifico
　　S solo,orch voc sc ZERBONI 3905
　　s.p. (M491)

MARKOVIC, ADALBERT (1925-)
　Three Songs From "Free Nights" *CC3U
　　[Slav] solo,pno CROATICA s.p.
　　　　(M492)

MARKS
　Last Mile Of The Way, The *see
　　Oatman

MARKS, J.C.
　Now The Day Is Over
　　low solo,pno (E flat maj) ASHDOWN
　　　　(M493)
　　high solo,pno (F maj) ASHDOWN
　　　　(M494)
　Out Of The Deep *sac
　　low solo,pno BELWIN $1.50 (M495)

MARLEENTJE see Hullebroeck, Em.

MAROS, MIKLOS
　Descort
　　S solo,fl,bvl NORDISKA 10232 s.p.
　　　　(M496)

MARQUISE see Dupre, Marcel

MARQUISE see Lacome, Paul

MARSCHLIED see Franken, Wim

MARSCHNER, HEINRICH (AUGUST)
　(1795-1861)
　An Jenem Tag (from Hans Heiling)
　　Bar solo,2fl,2ob,2clar,2bsn,4horn,
　　　strings BREITKOPF-L rental (M497)

MARSH
　I Want Jesus More Than Anything *sac
　　solo,pno BENSON S6141-R $1.00
　　　　(M498)

MARSH, ROGER (1949-)
　PS
　　female solo,trom,bvl NOVELLO rental
　　　　(M499)
　Streim
　　S solo,fl,clar,trp,bvl NOVELLO
　　　rental (M500)

MARSHALL, C.
　I Hear You Calling Me
　　low solo,pno (A flat maj) BOOSEY
　　$1.50 (M501)
　　high solo,pno (C maj) BOOSEY $1.50
　　　　(M502)
　　med solo,pno (B flat maj) BOOSEY
　　$1.50 (M503)

MARSHALL, L.
　Would You Know?
　　med solo,pno SEESAW $1.00 (M504)

MARSHALL, VIRGINIA
　God Is So Wonderful *sac
　　solo,pno WORD S-227 (M505)

MARSICK, M.-P.
　Fugit Amor
　　solo,vln ENOCH (M506)

MARSIK, EMANUEL (1875-1936)
　Du Bist Wieder Gekommen *see Ty's
　　Prisel Zase
　Kdyz Kvetly Stromy Nejkrasneji (from
　　Cerny Leknin)
　　"Wenn Die Baume Am Schonsten
　　　Bluhten" Bar solo,pno CZECH s.p.
　　　　(M507)
　Me Vlny, Vlny Bile (from Cerny
　　Leknin)
　　"Meine Wellen, Weisse Wellen" T
　　　solo,pno CZECH s.p. (M508)
　Meine Wellen, Weisse Wellen *see Me
　　Vlny, Vlny Bile
　Mina's Lied *see Zpev Miny
　Pisne 1-2 Pro Sopran *CCU
　　S solo,pno CZECH s.p. (M509)
　Ty's Prisel Zase (from Cerny Leknin)
　　"Du Bist Wieder Gekommen" S solo,
　　　pno CZECH s.p. (M510)
　Wenn Die Baume Am Schonsten Bluhten
　　*see Kdyz Kvetly Stromy
　　Nejkrasneji
　Zpev Miny (from Studentska Laska)
　　"Mina's Lied" S solo,pno CZECH s.p.
　　　　(M511)

MARSMAN-CYCLUS see Masseus, Jan

MARSSLUT see Salonen, Sulo

MARTERN ALLER ARTEN see Mozart,
　Wolfgang Amadeus

MARTHA'S DIVINATION see Mussorgsky,
　Modest

MARTHE ET MARIE see Chaminade, Cecile

MARTI, ESTEBAN
　M'en Etais Alle
　　solo,pno ENOCH (M512)
　　solo,acap ENOCH (M513)

MARTIN
　Broken Pieces (composed with Kitchen)
　　*sac
　　solo,pno BENSON S5232-S $1.00
　　　　(M514)
　Eastern Gate, The *sac
　　(Mercer) solo,pno BENSON S7827-S
　　$1.00 (M515)
　Light Of The Sunset Glow
　　med solo,pno (E flat maj) ALLANS
　　　s.p. (M516)
　　low solo,pno (C maj) ALLANS s.p.
　　　　(M517)
　　high solo,pno (F maj) ALLANS s.p.
　　　　(M518)

MARTIN, EASTHOPE
　Absence
　　low solo,pno (G min) ASHDOWN (M519)
　　med solo,pno (A min) ASHDOWN (M520)
　　high solo,pno (B min) ASHDOWN
　　　　(M521)
　All For You
　　low solo,pno (B flat maj) BOOSEY
　　$1.50 (M522)
　　high solo,pno (E flat maj) BOOSEY
　　$1.50 (M523)
　All In A Lily-White Gown
　　low solo,pno (B flat maj) BOOSEY
　　$1.50 (M524)
　　high solo,pno (D maj) BOOSEY $1.50
　　　　(M525)
　　med solo,pno (C maj) BOOSEY $1.50
　　　　(M526)
　All The Fun Of The Fair
　　med solo,orch (G maj) ASHDOWN s.p.,
　　　ipr (M527)
　　low solo,orch (F maj) ASHDOWN s.p.,
　　　ipr (M528)
　　high solo,orch (B flat maj) ASHDOWN
　　　s.p., ipr (M529)

MARTIN, EASTHOPE (cont'd.)
　Ballad Monger, The
　　low solo,pno (D maj) ASHDOWN (M530)
　　high solo&low solo,pno ASHDOWN s.p.
　　　　(M531)
　　high solo,pno (E maj) ASHDOWN
　　　　(M532)
　Break, Break, Break
　　solo,pno (D flat maj) ASHDOWN
　　　　(M533)
　Bridal Dawn
　　low solo,orch (F maj) ASHDOWN
　　$1.50 (M534)
　　high solo,orch (B flat maj) ASHDOWN
　　$1.50, ipr (M535)
　　med solo,orch (A flat maj) ASHDOWN
　　$1.50, ipr (M536)
　Brightest Day, The
　　high solo,orch (D flat maj) ASHDOWN
　　　s.p., ipr (M537)
　　med-high solo,orch (C maj) ASHDOWN
　　　s.p., ipr (M538)
　　med solo,orch (B flat maj) ASHDOWN
　　　s.p., ipr (M539)
　　low solo,orch (A flat maj) ASHDOWN
　　　s.p., ipr (M540)
　Come To The Fair
　　high solo,orch (C maj) ASHDOWN
　　$1.50, ipr (M541)
　　med-high solo,orch (B flat maj)
　　　ASHDOWN $1.50, ipr (M542)
　　med solo,orch (A maj) ASHDOWN
　　$1.50, ipr (M543)
　　low solo,orch (G maj) ASHDOWN
　　$1.50, ipr (M544)
　　med solo&med solo,pno ASHDOWN $1.75
　　　　(M545)
　　high solo&med solo,pno ASHDOWN
　　$1.75 (M546)
　Crown Of The Year, The
　　med solo,orch (B flat maj) ASHDOWN
　　$1.50, ipr (M547)
　　low solo,orch (A flat maj) ASHDOWN
　　$1.50, ipr (M548)
　　high solo,orch (C maj) ASHDOWN
　　$1.50, ipr (M549)
　Day At The Fair, A *CC4U
　　ASHDOWN low solo,pno s.p.; med
　　　solo,pno s.p.; high solo,pno s.p.
　　　　(M550)
　De Profundis
　　"Out Of The Deep I Call" low solo,
　　　orch (C maj) ASHDOWN $1.50, ipr
　　　　(M551)
　　"Out Of The Deep I Call" med solo,
　　　orch (D maj) ASHDOWN $1.50, ipr
　　　　(M552)
　　"Out Of The Deep I Call" high solo,
　　　orch (E flat maj) ASHDOWN $1.50,
　　　ipr (M553)
　Dusk Of Dreams
　　solo,pno (F maj) BOOSEY $1.50
　　　　(M554)
　Everywhere I Go
　　low solo,orch (B flat maj) ASHDOWN
　　$1.50, ipr (M555)
　　high solo,orch (E flat maj) ASHDOWN
　　$1.50, ipr (M556)
　　med-high solo,orch (D maj) ASHDOWN
　　$1.50, ipr (M557)
　　med solo,orch (C maj) ASHDOWN
　　$1.50, ipr (M558)
　Fairings
　　low solo,orch (A maj) ASHDOWN s.p.,
　　　ipr (M559)
　　high solo&low solo,pno ASHDOWN s.p.
　　　　(M560)
　　high solo,orch (C maj) ASHDOWN
　　　s.p., ipr (M561)
　　med solo,orch (B flat maj) ASHDOWN
　　　s.p., ipr (M562)
　Harp Of The Woodland
　　low solo,orch (G maj) ASHDOWN s.p.,
　　　ipr (M563)
　　high solo,orch (C maj) ASHDOWN
　　　s.p., ipr (M564)
　　med solo,orch (A maj) ASHDOWN s.p.,
　　　ipr (M565)
　Hatfield Bells
　　med solo,orch (A flat maj) ASHDOWN
　　　s.p., ipr (M566)
　　low solo,orch (F maj) ASHDOWN s.p.,
　　　ipr (M567)
　　high solo,orch (B flat maj) ASHDOWN
　　　s.p., ipr (M568)
　Holy Child, The
　　low solo,orch (A flat maj) ASHDOWN
　　$1.50, ipr (M569)
　　high solo,orch (C maj) ASHDOWN
　　$1.50, ipr (M570)
　　med solo,orch (B flat maj) ASHDOWN
　　$1.50, ipr (M571)
　　high solo&med solo,pno ASHDOWN
　　$1.75 (M572)

MARTIN, EASTHOPE (cont'd.)

Langley Fair
  low solo,orch (E flat maj) ASHDOWN
    s.p., ipr   (M573)
  high solo&low solo,pno ASHDOWN s.p.
                                     (M574)
  high solo,orch (F maj) ASHDOWN
    s.p., ipr   (M575)

Minstrel, The
  low solo,orch (F maj) ASHDOWN s.p.,
    ipr   (M576)
  high solo,orch (A flat maj) ASHDOWN
    s.p., ipr   (M577)

Mountebanks, The *song cycle
  4 soli,orch ASHDOWN s.p., ipr   (M578)

Out Of The Deep I Call *see De
  Profundis

Philosopher And The Lady, The *song
  cycle
  4 soli,pno ASHDOWN s.p.   (M579)

Red-Letter Days *CC4U
  ASHDOWN low solo,pno s.p.; high
    solo,pno s.p.   (M580)

St. Nicholas Day In The Morning
  low solo,orch (C maj) ASHDOWN
    $1.50, ipr   (M581)
  med solo,orch (D maj) ASHDOWN
    $1.50, ipr   (M582)
  high solo,orch (E flat maj) ASHDOWN
    $1.50, ipr   (M583)

Shall I Complain?
  high solo,pno (A flat maj) CRAMER
                                     (M584)
  low solo,pno (F maj) CRAMER   (M585)

Songs Of Open Country *CC3U
  ASHDOWN low solo,pno s.p.; med
    solo,pno s.p.; high solo,pno s.p.
                                     (M586)
Starlight And Lovelight
  low solo,orch (E flat maj) ASHDOWN
    s.p., ipr   (M587)
  high solo,orch (F maj) ASHDOWN
    s.p., ipr   (M588)

Three More Songs Of The Fair *CC3U
  ASHDOWN low solo,pno s.p.; med
    solo,pno s.p.; high solo,pno s.p.
                                     (M589)
Wayfarer's Night Song
  low solo,orch (D maj) ASHDOWN
    $1.50, ipr   (M590)
  med solo,orch (E flat maj) ASHDOWN
    $1.50, ipr   (M591)
  high solo,orch (F maj) ASHDOWN
    $1.50, ipr   (M592)

Who Goes A-Walking
  high solo&low solo,pno ASHDOWN s.p.
                                     (M593)
MARTIN, F.
Quatre Sonnets *CC4U
  Mez solo,fl,vla,vcl HUG sc s.p.,
    ipa, voc sc s.p.   (M594)

MARTIN, FRANK (1890-1974)
Drei Weihnachtslieder *CC3U,Xmas
  [Fr/Ger/Eng] high solo,fl,pno
    UNIVER. 13486 $5.75   (M595)

Drey Minnelieder *CCU
  [Ger/Eng] S solo,pno UNIVER. 13831
    $34.50   (M596)

Le Portail De Glace
  solo,orch HENN s.p.   (M597)

Quatre Sonnets A Cassandre (from
  Amours De Ronsard) CC4U
  [Fr] Mez solo,pno/pno&fl&vla&vcl
    voc sc HUG A41 s.p., sc HUG A40
    s.p.   (M598)

Sechs Monologe Aus "Jedermann" *CC6U
  [Ger] med solo,pno UNIVER. 12105
    $7.50   (M599)

Trois Poemes Paiens *CC3U
  solo,orch HENN s.p.   (M600)

MARTIN, GILBERT M.
No Golden Carriage, No Bright Toy
  *sac
  med solo,pno LORENZ $1.00   (M601)

MARTINA see Pratella, Francesco Balilla

MARTINI, GIAMBATTISTA (1706-1784)
Ah Ritorna Eta Dell'oro
  (Pedron, Carlo) [It] SB soli,pno
    BONGIOVANI 1163 s.p. see from
    Dodici Duetti Da Camera   (M602)

Basta Cosi T'intendi
  (Pedron, Carlo) [It] SS soli,pno
    BONGIOVANI 1165 s.p. see from
    Dodici Duetti Da Camera   (M603)

MARTINI, GIAMBATTISTA (cont'd.)
Che Serena Che Placida Calma..
  (Pedron, Carlo) [It] SS soli,pno
    BONGIOVANI 1155 s.p. see from
    Dodici Duetti Da Camera   (M604)

Dell' Aria Amica
  (Pedron, Carlo) [It] SA soli,pno
    BONGIOVANI 1158 s.p. see from
    Dodici Duetti Da Camera   (M605)

Dodici Duetti Da Camera *see Ah
  Ritorna Eta Dell'oro; Basta Cosi
  T'intendi; Che Serena Che Placida
  Calma..; Dell' Aria Amica; Entra
  L'uomo Allor Che Nasce; Gonfio Tu
  Vedi Il Fiume; Io Non Pretendo O
  Stelle; L'ape E La Serpe
  Spesso...; O Come Spesso Il
  Mondo...; Quell'onda Che Rovina;
  Quercia Annosa Sull'erte Pendici;
  Tutto Cangia E Il Di' Che Viene   (M606)

Entra L'uomo Allor Che Nasce
  (Pedron, Carlo) [It] ST soli,pno
    BONGIOVANI 1162 s.p. see from
    Dodici Duetti Da Camera   (M607)

Gonfio Tu Vedi Il Fiume
  (Pedron, Carlo) [It] ST soli,pno
    BONGIOVANI 1159 s.p. see from
    Dodici Duetti Da Camera   (M608)

Io Non Pretendo O Stelle
  (Pedron, Carlo) [It] SS soli,pno
    BONGIOVANI 1161 s.p. see from
    Dodici Duetti Da Camera   (M609)

L'ape E La Serpe Spesso...
  (Pedron, Carlo) [It] SA soli,pno
    BONGIOVANI 1156 s.p. see from
    Dodici Duetti Da Camera   (M610)

O Come Spesso Il Mondo...
  (Pedron, Carlo) [It] SA soli,pno
    BONGIOVANI 1154 s.p. see from
    Dodici Duetti Da Camera   (M611)

Quell'onda Che Rovina
  (Pedron, Carlo) [It] SA soli,pno
    BONGIOVANI 1157 s.p. see from
    Dodici Duetti Da Camera   (M612)

Quercia Annosa Sull'erte Pendici
  (Pedron, Carlo) [It] TB soli,pno
    BONGIOVANI 1164 s.p. see from
    Dodici Duetti Da Camera   (M613)

Tutto Cangia E Il Di' Che Viene
  (Pedron, Carlo) [It] SB soli,pno
    BONGIOVANI 1160 s.p. see from
    Dodici Duetti Da Camera   (M614)

MARTINI, GIOVANNI
see MARTINI, JEAN PAUL EGIDE

MARTINI, JEAN PAUL EGIDE (1741-1816)
Bergerette
  2 soli,pno DURAND s.p.   (M615)

Joys Of Love, The *see Plaisir
  D'Amour

Piacer D'amor
  solo,pno FORLIVESI 11926 s.p.
                                     (M616)
Piacer D'amor *see Plaisir D'amour

Plaisir D'amour
  Mez/Bar solo,orch DURAND s.p., ipr
                                     (M617)
  high solo,pno/inst DURAND s.p.
                                     (M618)
  ENOCH   (M619)
  med solo,pno (F maj) ALLANS s.p.
                                     (M620)
  high solo,pno (G maj) ALLANS s.p.
                                     (M621)
  med solo,pno (F maj) CENTURY 3432
                                     (M622)
  low solo,orch (F maj) ASHDOWN s.p.,
    ipr   (M623)
  high solo,orch (A flat maj) ASHDOWN
    s.p., ipr   (M624)
  low solo,pno (E flat maj) ALLANS
    s.p.   (M625)
  (Deis) "Joys Of Love, The" [Fr/Eng]
    med solo,pno (F maj) SCHIRM.G
    $1.00   (M626)
  (Parisotti) [Fr/It] S/T solo,pno
    RICORDI-ARG BA 8163 s.p.   (M627)
  (Parisotti) "Piacer D'amor" [It/Fr]
    S/T solo,pno RICORDI-ENG 121041
    s.p.   (M628)
  (Parisotti) "Piacer D'amor" [It/Fr]
    Mez/Bar solo,pno RICORDI-ENG
    51953 s.p.   (M629)

MARTINO, DONALD (1931-   )
Alone
  see Three Songs

Aus Einer Sturmnacht VIII
  "On A Stormy Night VIII" see Two
  Rilke Songs

MARTINO, DONALD (cont'd.)
Die Laute
  "Lute, The" see Two Rilke Songs

Lute, The *see Die Laute

Memory Of The Players In A Mirror At
  Midnight, A
  see Three Songs

On A Stormy Night VIII *see Aus
  Einer Sturmnacht VIII

Three Songs
  144A S/T solo,pno SCHIRM.EC 144A
    s.p.; B solo,pno SCHIRM.EC 144B
    s.p.
  contains: Alone; Memory Of The
    Players In A Mirror At
    Midnight, A; Tutto E Sciolto
                                     (M630)
Tutto E Sciolto
  see Three Songs

Two Rilke Songs
  Mez solo,pno SCHIRM.EC 145 s.p.
  contains: Aus Einer Sturmnacht
    VIII, "On A Stormy Night VIII";
    Die Laute, "Lute, The"   (M631)

MARTINU, BOHUSLAV (1890-1959)
Balada Letni
  "Sommerballade" see Tri Chansony

Bar
  "Die Bar" see Tri Chansony

Bergmannslied *see Havirska

Die Bar *see Bar

Havirska
  "Bergmannslied" see Tri Chansony

Koleda Milostna *CC2U
  (Kapralova) solo,pno SUPRAPHON (M632)

Liedchen Auf 2 Seiten *see Pisnicky
  Na 2 Stranky

Lieder Auf Eine Seite *CCU
  [Czech/Eng] solo,pno SUPRAPHON s.p.
                                     (M633)
Lieder Auf Zwei Seiten *CCU
  [Czech/Eng] solo,pno SUPRAPHON s.p.
                                     (M634)
Nove Slovenske Pisne *CCU
  solo,pno PANTON 769 s.p.   (M635)

Petrklic *CC12U
  [Czech/Eng/Ger] SA soli,pno,inst
    PANTON 044 s.p.   (M636)

Pisnicky Na 2 Stranky *song cycle
  "Liedchen Auf 2 Seiten" [Czech/Eng]
    med solo,pno SUPRAPHON s.p.   (M637)

Sommerballade *see Balada Letni

Songs On Two Pages *CCU
  [Czech/Eng] solo,pno ARTIA $2.75
                                     (M638)
Tri Chansony
  med solo,pno CZECH s.p.
  contains: Balada Letni,
    "Sommerballade"; Bar, "Die
    Bar"; Havirska, "Bergmannslied"
                                     (M639)

MARTIN VAN LENNEP, H.
Burmese Maid
  solo,pno LEONARD-ENG   (M640)

MARTIRANO, S.
Chansons Innocentes *CCU
  [Eng] solo,pno SCHOTTS 10903 s.p.
                                     (M641)

MARTTINEN, TAUNO (1912-   )
Andante Religioso *sac
  solo,pno FAZER W 3515 s.p.   (M642)

Eskon Haalaulu
  see Viisi Laulua

Ikavyys
  see Viisi Laulua

Miksi Kay Aatokseni Piiri Niin
  Himmeaksi
  see Viisi Laulua

Pidot *CC7L
  solo,pno FAZER W 3603 s.p.   (M643)

Timon Laulu
  see Viisi Laulua

Tuonen Kehtolaulu
  see Viisi Laulua

Viisi Laulua
  solo,pno FAZER W 3514 s.p.
  contains: Eskon Haalaulu;
    Ikavyys; Miksi Kay Aatokseni
    Piiri Niin Himmeaksi; Timon
    Laulu; Tuonen Kehtolaulu (M644)

MARTUCCI, GIUSEPPE (1856-1909)
La Canzone Dei Ricordi
Mez/Bar solo,pno RICORDI-ENG 60202
s.p.   (M645)

MARTY, (EUGENE) GEORGES (1860-1908)
Au Matin
solo,pno (available in 2 keys)
ENOCH s.p.   (M646)
Mez solo,orch (B flat maj) ENOCH
rental   (M647)

Fou D'Amour
solo,pno (available in 2 keys)
ENOCH s.p.   (M648)

Le Printemps
SSS soli,orch ENOCH rental   (M649)

Ou Donc Es-Tu Partie?
solo,pno (available in 2 keys)
ENOCH s.p.   (M650)

Reverie
solo,pno ENOCH s.p.   (M651)

Si Tu Savais Comme Je T'aime
solo,pno (available in 2 keys)
ENOCH s.p.   (M652)

Sonnet A Ophelie
solo,pno ENOCH s.p.   (M653)
solo,orch ENOCH rental   (M654)
solo,vln ENOCH s.p.   (M655)

MARVIA, EINARI (1915-   )
Aamu *Op.3,No.1
"Morgen" solo,pno FAZER F 2667 s.p.
                                    (M656)
April *see Huhtikuu

Armahan Kulku *Op.1,No.3
"Min Karas Vag" solo,pno FAZER
F 2549 s.p.   (M657)

Becher *see Malja

Der Mass Des Mannes *Op.7,No.5
solo,pno FAZER s.p.   (M658)

Der Stierkampfer *Op.27, song cycle
solo,pno FAZER s.p.   (M659)

Die Seerose *Op.25,No.4
solo,pno FAZER s.p.   (M660)

Die Weissen Morgen *see Valkeat
Aamut

Dodsfornimmelsen *see Kuoleman Tantu

Elama *Op.30,No.5
"Leben" see Sechs Lieder Nach
Gedichten Von Katri Vala

En Sang For Varje Arstid
solo,pno FAZER F 4917 s.p.
contains: Huhtikuu, "April";
Mittumaari, "Midsommar";
Syyspaiva, "Hostdag"; Talviyo,
"Vinternatt"   (M661)

Fahrt Zum Aufgebot *see
Kuulutusmatka

Fruhling *see Kevat

Gayatri *Op.29
solo,pno FAZER s.p.   (M662)

Glomkans Land *see Unhon Maa

Hostdag *see Syyspaiva

Huhtikuu
"April" see En Sang For Varje
Arstid

Kevat *Op.30,No.2
"Fruhling" see Sechs Lieder Nach
Gedichten Von Katri Vala

Kun Mina Mokoman Saisin *Op.1,No.4
solo,pno FAZER F 2550 s.p.   (M663)

Kuoleman Tantu *Op.6,No.1
"Dodsfornimmelsen" 2 soli,pno FAZER
F 2888 s.p.   (M664)

Kuulutusmatka *Op.3,No.3
"Fahrt Zum Aufgebot" solo,pno FAZER
F 2669 s.p.   (M665)

Lauantai-Ilta *Op.3,No.2
"Samstagsabend" solo,pno FAZER
F 2668 s.p.   (M666)

Leben *see Elama

Malja *Op.30,No.1
"Becher" see Sechs Lieder Nach
Gedichten Von Katri Vala

Midsommar *see Mittumaari

MARVIA, EINARI (cont'd.)

Min Karas Vag *see Armahan Kulku

Mittumaari
"Midsommar" see En Sang For Varje
Arstid

Morgen *see Aamu

Myrsky *Op.30,No.6
"Sturm" see Sechs Lieder Nach
Gedichten Von Katri Vala

Saima Harmaja *Op.15, song cycle
solo,pno FAZER s.p.   (M667)

Samstagsabend *see Lauantai-Ilta

Sechs Lieder Nach Gedichten Von Katri
Vala
solo,pno FAZER s.p.
contains: Elama, "Leben", Op.30,
No.5; Kevat, "Fruhling", Op.30,
No.2; Malja, "Becher", Op.30,
No.1; Myrsky, "Sturm", Op.30,
No.6; Taj Mahal, "Tadsch
Mahal", Op.30,No.4; Valkeat
Aamut, "Die Weissen Morgen",
Op.30,No.3   (M668)

Serenata *Op.9,No.4
solo,pno FAZER s.p.   (M669)

Sturm *see Myrsky

Syyspaiva
"Hostdag" see En Sang For Varje
Arstid

Tadsch Mahal *see Taj Mahal

Taj Mahal *Op.30,No.4
"Tadsch Mahal" see Sechs Lieder
Nach Gedichten Von Katri Vala

Talviyo
"Vinternatt" see En Sang For Varje
Arstid

Unhon Maa *Op.5, song cycle
"Glomkans Land" solo,pno FAZER
W 2419 s.p.   (M670)

Valkeat Aamut *Op.30,No.3
"Die Weissen Morgen" see Sechs
Lieder Nach Gedichten Von Katri
Vala

Vinternatt *see Talviyo

MARVIN
This Day Is Yours *see Gollohan

MARX, JOSEPH (1882-1964)
Abends
[Ger] med solo,pno UNIVER. 5220
$2.75   (M671)

Abschied
[Ger] med solo,pno UNIVER. 10690
$3.25 see from Das Verklarte Jahr
                                    (M672)
Auf Der Campagna
[Ger] med solo,pno UNIVER. 10694
$3.25 see from Das Verklarte Jahr
                                    (M673)
Das Verklarte Jahr *see Abschied;
Auf Der Campagna; Dezember; In
Meiner Traume Heimat; Lieder
                                    (M674)
Dem Genius Des Augenblicks
[Ger/Eng] med solo,pno UNIVER. 5153
$2.75   (M675)

Der Dichter
[Ger] med solo,pno UNIVER. 5217
s.p.   (M676)

Der Gast
[Ger/Eng] med solo,pno UNIVER. 5194
$2.75   (M677)

Der Rauch
[Ger/Eng] med solo,pno UNIVER. 5184
s.p.   (M678)

Der Ton
[Ger/Eng] med solo,pno UNIVER. 5186
$2.75   (M679)

Dezember
[Ger] med solo,pno UNIVER. 10691
$3.25 see from Das Verklarte Jahr
                                    (M680)
Ein Fichtenbaum
[Ger] med solo,pno UNIVER. 5195
$2.75   (M681)

Erinnerung
[Ger/Eng] med solo,pno UNIVER. 5180
s.p.   (M682)

Frage Und Antwort
[Ger/Eng] high solo,pno UNIVER.
5158 s.p.   (M683)

MARX, JOSEPH (cont'd.)

Gesang Des Lebens
[Ger] med solo,pno UNIVER. 5201
$2.75   (M684)

Herbstzeitlose
[Ger] med solo,pno UNIVER. 5198
$2.75   (M685)

Hochsommernacht
[Ger] high solo,pno UNIVER. 5161
$2.75   (M686)

In Maien
[Ger] high solo,pno UNIVER. 5197
$2.75   (M687)

In Meiner Traume Heimat
[Ger] med solo,pno UNIVER. 10693
$3.25 see from Das Verklarte Jahr
                                    (M688)
Japan *see Regenlied

Kolumbine
[Ger/Eng] high solo,pno UNIVER.
5187 $2.75   (M689)

Lied
[Ger] high solo,pno UNIVER. 5163
$2.75   (M690)

Lied Eines Madchens
[Ger/Eng] high solo,pno UNIVER.
5182 $2.75   (M691)

Lieder
[Ger] med solo,pno UNIVER. 10692
$3.25 see from Das Verklarte Jahr
                                    (M692)
Lob Des Fruhlings
[Ger] high solo,pno UNIVER. 5164
$2.75   (M693)

Marienlied
[Ger/Eng] high solo,pno UNIVER.
5166 $2.75   (M694)

Nachtgebet
[Ger] high solo,pno UNIVER. 5204
$2.75   (M695)

Neugriechische Madchenlied
[Ger] high solo,pno UNIVER. 5168
$2.75   (M696)

Nimm Dir Ein Schones Weib
[Ger] med solo,pno UNIVER. 5229
$2.75   (M697)

Pierrot Dandy
[Ger] high solo,pno UNIVER. 5170
$2.75   (M698)

Regen
[Ger/Eng] med solo,pno UNIVER. 5185
$2.75   (M699)

Regenlied
"Japan" [Ger/Eng/Fr] high solo,pno
UNIVER. 5162A $2.75   (M700)

Schliesse Mir Die Augen
[Ger/Eng] med solo,pno UNIVER. 5598
s.p.   (M701)

September-Morgen
[Ger/Eng] high solo,pno UNIVER. 5171
$2.75   (M702)

Sonnenland
[Ger] med solo,pno UNIVER. 5173
$2.75   (M703)

Traumgekront
[Ger] high solo,pno UNIVER. 5203
$2.75   (M704)

Und Gestern Hat Er Mir Rosen Gebracht
[Ger/Eng/Fr] high solo,pno UNIVER.
5174 $2.75   (M705)

Venezianisches Wiegenlied
[Ger/Eng/Fr] med solo,pno UNIVER.
5231A $2.75   (M706)

Windrader
[Ger/Eng] med solo,pno UNIVER. 5178
$3.25   (M707)

MARX, KARL (1897-   )
Abschiedslied *Op.42a,No.1
see Drei Liebeslieder

Bist Du Auch Meere Weit *Op.42a,No.3
see Drei Liebeslieder

Botschaft *Op.41, cant
S solo,2S rec,pno (med diff) BAREN.
1642 $4.75   (M708)
S solo,2S rec,5strings (med diff)
BAREN. 1816 rental   (M709)

Da Christus Geboren War *sac,Xmas
A solo,fl,vln,vcl,cembalo (med
diff) BAREN. 2522 $10.50   (M710)

MARX, KARL (cont'd.)

Das Karussell Und Andere Rilke-
Gedichte *Op.50,No.2, CCU
high solo,pno (med) BAREN. 2423
$5.50   (M711)

Deingedenken *Op.42a,No.2
see Drei Liebeslieder

Der Panther Und Andere Rilke-Gedichte
*Op.50,No.1, CCU
low solo,pno (med) BAREN. 2422
$5.00   (M712)

Drei Liebeslieder
S solo,4strings cmplt ed BAREN.
1729 $11.25
contains: Abschiedslied, Op.42a,
No.1; Bist Du Auch Meere Weit,
Op.42a,No.3; Deingedenken,
Op.42a,No.2   (M713)

Fruhlingstau, In Deinen Augen
*Op.38, cant
A solo,S rec/fl/ob,pno (med) BAREN.
1454 $5.50   (M714)

Jede Norgen Geht Die Sonne Auf
solo,inst (easy) BAREN. 1468 s.p.
                               (M715)

Neue Lieder *Op.29, CCU
high solo,pno (med) BAREN. 1116
$4.25   (M716)

Reifende Frucht *Op.23, CC3U
SA soli,pno (med diff) BAREN. 1826
$4.75   (M717)

Rilke-Lieder *Op.45, CC5U
S solo,pno (med) BAREN. 2090 s.p.
                               (M718)

Vier Gesange Vom Tage *Op.25, CC4U
B solo,5strings/orch (med diff)
BAREN. 1039 rental   (M719)

Vierzehn Lieder *Op.26, CC14U
S solo,pno (med) BAREN. 1038 $5.75
                               (M720)

Zwolf Lieder Und Spruche *Op.49,
CC12U
high solo,pno (med) BAREN. 2421
$5.75   (M721)

MARY see Richardson, T.

MARY AND THE KITTEN see Bryn, Gordon

MARY AT THE CRADLE see Franck, Cesar,
La Vierge A La Creche

MARY HYNES see Mourant, Walter

MARY JAMIESON see Somervell, Arthur

MARY MORISON *folk,Scot
solo,pno (B min/D min) PATERSON FS108
s.p.   (M722)

MARY OF ARGYLE
solo,pno CRAMER   (M723)

MARY OF ARGYLE see Nelson, S.

MARY O'MORE see Ashworth-Hope, H.

MARY RUANE see Mourant, Walter

MARY, WHAT DO YOU SEE IN THE SKY? see
Franco, Johan

MARY, WHO STOOD IN SORROW see Lockwood,
Normand

MARY'S GIFT see Bales, Richard

MARY'S LITTLE BOY JESUS see Hairston

MARY'S LULLABY see Brown, Myrtle Hare

MARY'S LULLABY see Pasfield, W.R.

MARY'S SOLILOQUY see Effinger, Cecil

MARZIALS, THEO
Friendship
2 soli,pno CRAMER   (M724)

Of You I Dream
2 soli,pno CRAMER   (M725)

Sing Lullaby For The Year
2 soli,pno CRAMER   (M726)

Such Merry Folk Are We
solo,pno CRAMER   (M727)

MARZIALS, THOMAS
Eight Vocal Duets *CC8U
2 soli,pno CRAMER   (M728)

MARZLIED see Borris, Siegfried

MARZLIED see Trunk, Richard

MARZO see Tocchi, Gian-Luca

MARZSCHNEE see Sibelius, Jean

MARZSCHNEE see Sibelius, Jean,
Marzschnee

MAS CERCA see Armando, J.

MASCAGNI, PIETRO (1863-1945)
Addio Alla Madre (from Cavalleria
Rusticana)
[It/Ger] T solo,pno BOTE $.90
                               (M729)

Ah! Ritrovarla Nella Sua Capanna
(from Lodoletta)
[It] T solo,pno SONZOGNO 2041 $1.25
                               (M730)

Air De Santuzza (from Cavalleria
Rusticana)
solo,orch HENN s.p.   (M731)

Apri La Tua Finestra (from Iris)
T solo,pno RICORDI-ENG 102333 s.p.
                               (M732)

Ave Maria (from Cavaliera Rusticana)
sac
solo,pno/org HEUGEL s.p. see from
CHANTS RELIGIEUX   (M733)
Mez solo,org/pno (available in 2
keys) HEUGEL s.p.   (M734)
med solo,pno (E flat maj) CENTURY
592 $.40   (M735)
[It/Eng] low solo,pno (C maj)
SCHIRM.G $.60   (M736)
[It/Eng] med solo,pno (E flat maj)
SCHIRM.G $.60   (M737)
Mez solo,harmonium,vln,vcl
(available in 2 keys) HEUGEL s.p.
                               (M738)

Bimba Non Piangere (from Lodoletta)
[It] T solo,pno SONZOGNO 2040 $1.25
                               (M739)

Cuore, Come Un Fiore (from Zanetto)
[It] Mez solo,pno SONZOGNO 1312
$1.25   (M740)

Ed Anche Beppe Amo (from L'Amico
Fritz)
T solo,pno SONZOGNO 555 $1.25
                               (M741)

Fem Sanger *CC5U
high solo,pno GEHRMANS s.p.   (M742)

Fior Di Giaggiolo (from Cavalleria
Rusticana)
[It] Mez solo,pno SONZOGNO 608
$1.25   (M743)

Flammen Perdonami (from Lodoletta)
[It] S solo,pno SONZOGNO $1.25
                               (M744)

Flammen Pieta (from Lodoletta)
[It] S solo,pno SONZOGNO 2043 $1.25
                               (M745)

Mamma, Quel Vino E Generoso (from
Cavalleria Rusticana)
[It] T solo,pno SONZOGNO 1872 $1.25
                               (M746)

Non Mi Resta Che Il Pianto Ed Il
Dolore (from L'Amico Fritz)
S solo,pno SONZOGNO 552 $1.25
                               (M747)

O Lola Ch'ai Di Latti (from
Cavalleria Rusticana)
[It] T solo,pno SONZOGNO 506 $1.25
                               (M748)

O Pallida, Che Un Giorno Mi Guardasti
(from L'Amico Fritz)
Mez solo,pno SONZOGNO 551 $1.25
                               (M749)

O Popolo Di Vili (from Isabeau)
T solo,pno SONZOGNO 1636 $1.25
                               (M750)

Oh! Il Signore Vi Manda (from
Cavalleria Rusticana)
[It] SBar soli,pno SONZOGNO 1871
$1.25   (M751)

Per Averti Vicina (from Le Maschere)
[It] ST soli,pno SONZOGNO 1935
$1.25   (M752)

Piu Presso Il Ciel (from Amica)
Bar solo,pno CHOUDENS 4412 s.p.
                               (M753)

Questo Mio Bianco Manto (from
Isabeau)
S solo,pno SONZOGNO 1635 $1.25
                               (M754)

S'e Spento Il Sol (from Silvano)
[It] T solo,pno SONZOGNO 919 $1.25
                               (M755)

Se Tu Amasti Me (from Amica)
Bar solo,pno CHOUDENS 4414 s.p.
                               (M756)

Sicilliana (from Cavalleria
Rusticana)
[It/Ger] high solo,pno BOTE $1.25
                               (M757)

Son Pochi Fiori (from L'Amico Fritz)
[It] S solo,pno RICORDI-ARG BA 9758
s.p.   (M758)
[It/Eng] S solo,pno SONZOGNO 554
$1.25   (M759)
[It/Eng] S solo,pno INTERNAT. $.90

MASCAGNI, PIETRO (cont'd.)
                               (M760)
Stornello Di Lola (from Cavalleria
Rusticana)
[It/Ger] Mez solo,pno BOTE $.75
                               (M761)

Suzel, Buon Di (from L'Amico Fritz)
ST soli,pno SONZOGNO 553 $1.25
                               (M762)

Tu Ch'odi Lo Mio Grido (from Isabeau)
T solo,pno SONZOGNO 1647 $1.25
                               (M763)

Tu Qui Santuzza (from Cavalleria
Rusticana)
[It] ST soli,pno SONZOGNO 1870
$1.25   (M764)

Venne Una Vecchierella Alla Mia Corte
(from Isabeau)
S solo,pno SONZOGNO 1648 $1.25
                               (M765)

Viva Il Vion Spumeggiante (from
Cavalleria Rusticana)
[It] T solo,pno SONZOGNO 510 $1.25
                               (M766)

Voi Lo Sapete (from Cavalleria
Rusticana)
[It] S solo,pno RICORDI-ARG BA 9755
s.p.   (M767)
[It] S solo,pno SONZOGNO 508 $1.25
                               (M768)
"Well Do You Know" [It/Eng] S solo,
pno (E min) SCHIRM.G $.85   (M769)

Well Do You Know *see Voi Lo Sapete

MASCARADE see Renie

MASCHERONI, ANGELO
For All Eternity
[Fr/Ger] high solo,pno,opt vln (E
flat maj) LEONARD-ENG   (M770)
2 soli,pno LEONARD-ENG   (M771)
[Eng/It] high solo,pno,opt vln (E
flat maj) LEONARD-ENG   (M772)
[Eng/It] med-high solo,pno,opt vln
(D maj) LEONARD-ENG   (M773)
[Eng/It] med solo,pno,opt vln (C
maj) LEONARD-ENG   (M774)
[Eng/It] low solo,pno,opt vln (B
flat maj) LEONARD-ENG   (M775)
[Fr/Ger] med solo,pno,opt vln (D
maj) LEONARD-ENG   (M776)
[Fr/Ger] low solo,pno,opt vln (C
maj) LEONARD-ENG   (M777)
"I Evighet" solo,pno LUNDQUIST s.p.
                               (M778)

I Evighet *see For All Eternity

Songs We Used To Sing
[Eng/It] high solo,pno,opt vln (F
maj) CRAMER   (M779)
[Eng/It] low solo,pno,opt vln (C
maj) CRAMER   (M780)
[Eng/It] med solo,pno,opt vln (D
maj) CRAMER   (M781)

Woodland Serenade
low solo,pno (A maj) LEONARD-ENG
                               (M782)
high solo,pno (G maj) LEONARD-ENG
                               (M783)

MASKENBALL IM HOCHGEBIRGE see Jelinek,
Hanns

MASKROSORNAS VISA see Korling, Felix

MASQUES see Damase, Jean-Michel

MASS see Beerman, Burton

MASS FOR SOLO VOICE (OR UNISON CHOIR)
see Thomson, Virgil

MASS OF A PILGRIM PEOPLE see Winter,
Sister Miriam Therese

MASSA
La Maderecita *sac
[It] solo,pno RICORDI-ARG BA 6147
s.p.   (M784)

MASSAGE see Hazzard, Peter

MASSARANI, E.
Canzonetta
solo,pno BONGIOVANI 1384 s.p. see
from Sette Liriche   (M785)

Dialogo Di Marionette
solo,pno BONGIOVANI 1379 s.p. see
from Sette Liriche   (M786)

La Contrada Senza Sole
solo,pno BONGIOVANI 1382 s.p. see
from Sette Liriche   (M787)

La Tregua
solo,pno BONGIOVANI 1385 s.p. see
from Sette Liriche   (M788)

Per Farti Addormentare
solo,pno BONGIOVANI 1380 s.p. see
from Sette Liriche   (M789)

MASSARANI, E. (cont'd.)

Qu'as Tu Fait?
  solo,pno BONGIOVANI 1381 s.p. see
    from Sette Liriche   (M790)

Quattro Ragazze Nella Mia Stanza
  solo,pno BONGIOVANI 1383 s.p. see
    from Sette Liriche   (M791)

Sette Liriche *see Canzonetta;
  Dialogo Di Marionette; La
  Contrada Senza Sole; La Tregua;
  Per Farti Addormentare; Qu'as Tu
  Fait?; Quattro Ragazze Nella Mia
  Stanza   (M792)

MASSARANI, RENZO (1898-1975)
Bescignad Annegnila
  solo,pno SANTIS 288 s.p.   (M793)

MASSE
Aria Del Ruisenor (from Les Noces De
  Jeannette)
  [It] S solo,pno,fl RICORDI-ARG
    BA 9846 s.p.   (M794)

MASSENET, JULES (1842-1912)
Addio, O Nostro Picciol Desco *see
  Adieu, Notre Petite Table

Adieu De Manon *see Je Ne Suis Que
  Faiblesse

Adieu, Notre Petite Table (from
  Manon)
  [Fr/Eng] S solo,pno INTERNAT. $1.00
                                (M795)
  "Addio, O Nostro Picciol Desco"
    [It] S solo,pno HEUGEL 4469 s.p.
                                (M796)
  "Addio, O Nostro Picciol Desco"
    [Fr] S solo,pno HEUGEL 4469 B
      s.p.   (M797)

Ah! Dispar Vision (from Manon)
  [Fr] T solo,pno HEUGEL 4470 B s.p.
                                (M798)
  [It] T solo,pno HEUGEL 4470 s.p.
                                (M799)

Ah! Fuyez, Douce Image! (from Manon)
  [Fr/It] T solo,pno RICORDI-ARG
    BA 8537 s.p.   (M800)

Ah, Non Mi Ridestar! (from Werther)
  [It] T solo,pno HEUGEL 4444 s.p.
                                (M801)
  [Fr] T solo,pno HEUGEL 4444 B s.p.
                                (M802)

Ancor Son Io Tutt'attonita (from
  Manon)
  [It] S solo,pno HEUGEL 4466 s.p.
                                (M803)
  [Fr] S solo,pno HEUGEL 4466 B s.p.
                                (M804)

Autumn Thought, An
  low solo,pno (E flat maj) ASHDOWN
                                (M805)
  med-high solo,pno (G maj) ASHDOWN
                                (M806)
  med solo,pno (F maj) ASHDOWN (M807)
  high solo,pno (A maj) ASHDOWN
                                (M808)

Ave Maria *sac
  solo,pno/org HEUGEL s.p. see from
    CHANTS RELIGIEUX   (M809)
  solo,pno/org (available in 2 keys)
    HEUGEL s.p.   (M810)
  [Lat/Eng] high solo,pno MARKS $1.50
                                (M811)
  solo,pno,vln (available in 2 keys)
    HEUGEL s.p.   (M812)

Bonne Nuit
  [Fr] solo,acap oct DURAND s.p.
                                (M813)
  Mez/Bar solo,pno/inst DURAND s.p.
    see also Trois Melodies, Deux
    Duos Et Un Trio   (M814)

Chiudo Gli Occhi (from Manon)
  [Fr] T solo,pno HEUGEL 4442 B s.p.
                                (M815)
  [It] T solo,pno HEUGEL 4442 s.p.
                                (M816)

Dismoi Que Je Suis Belle (from Thais)
  [Fr/Eng] solo,pno INTERNAT. $1.25
                                (M817)

Dividerci Dobbiam (from Werther)
  [It] ST soli,pno HEUGEL 4482 s.p.
                                (M818)

Duetto Dell'Oasi (from Thais)
  [Fr] SBar soli,pno HEUGEL 5488 B
    s.p.   (M819)

Ecco Dunque L'orribil Citta (from
  Thais)
  [Fr] Bar solo,pno HEUGEL 5486 B
    s.p.   (M820)

Elegia *see Elegie

Elegia, No. 2
  [Fr/Span] S/T solo,pno RICORDI-ARG
    BA 10309 s.p.   (M821)

MASSENET, JULES (cont'd.)

Elegie
  high solo,pno (G min) ASHDOWN
                                (M822)
  med-high solo,pno (F min) ASHDOWN
                                (M823)
  med solo,pno (E min) ASHDOWN (M824)
  low solo,pno (D min) ASHDOWN (M825)
  high solo,vcl (G min) ASHDOWN
                                (M826)
  med solo,vcl (F min) ASHDOWN (M827)
  low solo,vcl (E min) ASHDOWN (M828)
  "Elegia" [Fr] S solo,pno/vln&vcl&
    pno HEUGEL 10683-2 s.p., ipa
                                (M829)
  "Elegia" [Fr] Mez solo,pno/vln&vcl&
    pno HEUGEL 10683-1 s.p., ipa
                                (M830)
  "Elegia" [Fr] T solo,pno/vln&vcl&
    pno HEUGEL 10683-3 s.p., ipa
                                (M831)

Herode, Ne Me Refuse Pas (from
  Herodiade)
  [Fr/Eng] Mez solo,pno INTERNAT.
    $1.00   (M832)

Il Nome Vostro Io So (from Manon)
  [Fr] ST soli,pno HEUGEL 4468 B s.p.
                                (M833)
  [It] ST soli,pno HEUGEL 4468 s.p.
                                (M834)

Il Pianto Che Si Vuol Frenare (from
  Werther)
  [It] Mez solo,pno HEUGEL 4489 s.p.
                                (M835)

Je Ne Suis Que Faiblesse (from Manon)
  "Adieu De Manon" [Fr/It] S solo,pno
    RICORDI-ARG BA 8526 s.p.   (M836)

Joie
  [Fr/Ger] 2 soli,pno (available in 2
    keys) DURAND s.p. see also Trois
    Melodies, Deux Duos Et Un Trio
                                (M837)

La Melodie Des Baisers
  solo,pno (available in 2 keys;
    available in 3 keys) ENOCH s.p.
                                (M838)

La Tua Non E La Mano (from Manon)
  [Fr] S solo,pno HEUGEL 4472 B s.p.
                                (M839)
  [It] S solo,pno HEUGEL 4472 s.p.
                                (M840)

Le Bois De Pins
  [Fr] solo,acap oct DURAND s.p.
                                (M841)
  S/T solo,pno/inst DURAND s.p. see
    also Trois Melodies, Deux Duos Et
    Un Trio   (M842)
  S/T solo,pno/inst DURAND s.p. see
    also Trois Melodies, Deux Duos Et
    Un Trio   (M843)

Le Reve De Des Grieux (from Manon)
  [Fr/It] T solo,pno RICORDI-ARG
    BA 2028 s.p.   (M844)

Le Verger
  Mez/Bar solo,pno/inst DURAND s.p.
    see also Trois Melodies, Deux
    Duos Et Un Trio   (M845)

Letters, The (from Werther)
  [Fr/Eng] Mez solo,pno INTERNAT.
    $1.25   (M846)

Marine
  [Fr/Ger] 2 soli,pno DURAND s.p. see
    also Trois Melodies, Deux Duos Et
    Un Trio   (M847)

Matinee D'ete
  SSA soli,pno DURAND s.p. see also
    Trois Melodies, Deux Duos Et Un
    Trio   (M848)

Meditation From Thais *sac
  low solo,pno (F maj) ALLANS s.p.
                                (M849)
  high solo,pno (A flat maj) ALLANS
    s.p.   (M850)

M'ha Scritto Che M'ama (from Werther)
  [It] Mez solo,pno HEUGEL 4491 s.p.
                                (M851)
  [Fr] Mez solo,pno HEUGEL 4491 B
    s.p.   (M852)

O Natura Di Grazia Piena *see O
  Nature

O Nature (from Werther)
  [Fr/Eng] T solo,pno INTERNAT. $1.25
                                (M853)
  "O Natura Di Grazia Piena" [Fr] T
    solo,pno HEUGEL 4481 B s.p. (M854)
  "O Natura Di Grazia Piena" [It] T
    solo,pno HEUGEL 4481 s.p.   (M855)

O Salutaris *sac
  S solo,opt cor,org,harmonium
    (available in 2 keys) HEUGEL s.p.
                                (M856)

MASSENET, JULES (cont'd.)

Obbediamo Del Core Alla Voce (from
  Manon)
  [It] S solo,pno HEUGEL 4480 s.p.
                                (M857)
  [Fr] S solo,pno HEUGEL 4480 B s.p.
                                (M858)

Open Thy Blue Eyes *see Ouvre Tes
  Yeux Bleus

Or Via Manon (from Manon)
  [Fr] S solo,pno HEUGEL 4467 B s.p.
                                (M859)

Ouvre Tes Yeux Bleus
  [Fr/It] S/T solo,pno RICORDI-ARG
    BA 1879 s.p.   (M860)
  "Open Thy Blue Eyes" low solo,pno
    (D maj) ASHDOWN   (M861)
  "Open Thy Blue Eyes" med-low solo,
    pno (E flat maj) ASHDOWN   (M862)
  "Open Thy Blue Eyes" med solo,pno
    (E maj) ASHDOWN   (M863)
  "Open Thy Blue Eyes" med-high solo,
    pno (F maj) ASHDOWN   (M864)
  "Open Thy Blue Eyes" high solo,pno
    (G maj) ASHDOWN   (M865)

Perdona A Me (from Manon)
  [Fr] ST soli,pno HEUGEL 4471 s.p.
                                (M866)

Piangete Miei Occhi (from Il Cid)
  [Fr] solo,pno HEUGEL 4290 BIS s.p.
                                (M867)

Pourquoi Me Reveiller (from Werther)
  [Fr/Eng] T solo,pno INTERNAT. $1.25
                                (M868)

Preghiera (from Il Cid)
  T solo,pno HEUGEL 4289 BIS s.p.
                                (M869)

Serenade De Zanetto
  [Fr/Ger] Mez solo,pno RICORDI-ARG
    BA 1877 s.p.   (M870)

Sevillana (from Don Cesar De Bazan)
  [Fr/It] solo,pno RICORDI-ARG
    BA 1876 s.p.   (M871)
  [Fr/Eng] high solo,pno (D maj)
    SCHIRM.G $.85   (M872)

Souvenez-Vous Vierge Marie *sac
  solo,pno/org HEUGEL s.p. see from
    CHANTS RELIGIEUX   (M873)
  solo,pno/org (available in 2 keys)
    HEUGEL s.p.   (M874)
  S solo,vln,org HEUGEL s.p.   (M875)
  STB soli,pno/org HEUGEL s.p. (M876)

Tears, The (from Werther)
  [Fr/Eng] Mez solo,pno INTERNAT.
    $1.00   (M877)

Tristesse Du Soir
  [Fr/Eng] solo,pno,opt vln/vcl
    (available in 3 keys) sc JOBERT
    s.p.   (M878)

Trois Melodies, Deux Duos Et Un Trio
  DURAND s.p.
    contains: Bonne Nuit (solo,pno/
      inst); Joie (2 soli,pno/inst);
      Le Bois De Pins (solo,pno/
      inst); Le Verger (solo,pno/
      inst); Marine (2 soli,pno/
      inst); Matinee D'ete (3 soli,
      pno/inst)
    see also: Bonne Nuit; Joie; Le
      Bois De Pins; Le Verger;
      Marine; Matinee D'ete   (M879)

Twilight
  low solo,pno (G maj) ASHDOWN (M880)
  high solo,pno (A maj) ASHDOWN
                                (M881)

Vision Fuggitiva (from Erodiade)
  [Fr] Bar solo,pno HEUGEL 5511 BIS
    s.p.   (M882)

MASSEUS, JAN (1913-   )
Aanhef
  see Masseus, Jan, Ars Poetica

Ars Poetica
  S solo,pno DONEMUS s.p. contains
    also: De Akelei; Aanhef;
    Herinnering; In Memoriam   (M883)

De Akelei
  see Masseus, Jan, Ars Poetica

Gazelle Liederen *Op.26
  SA soli,perc, piano 4-hands DONEMUS
    s.p.   (M884)

Herinnering
  see Masseus, Jan, Ars Poetica

In Memoriam
  see Masseus, Jan, Ars Poetica

Marsman-Cyclus *Op.20, song cycle
  A solo,pno DONEMUS s.p.   (M885)

My Kingdom *Op.47, CC5U
  med solo,pno DONEMUS s.p.   (M886)

MASSEUS, JAN (cont'd.)

Seven Tile Tableaux, The *Op.44
Bar solo,brass,perc,bvl DONEMUS
s.p.   (M887)

MASSLO, AVI
Sameach T'samach *CCU
solo,pno OR-TAV $.60   (M888)

MASTER DESIGNER see Kaiser, Kurt

MASTER, WE TOILED ALL NIGHT see Krapf,
Gerhard

MASTERPIECES OF SACRED SONG, VOLUME I
*sac,CCU
(Haywood) high solo,pno MARKS $2.50
(M889)

MASTERS
God's Love *sac
solo,pno BENSON S5573-R $1.00
(M890)

Soul Down *sac
solo,pno BENSON S7575-R $1.00
(M891)

MASTERS OF SONG, VOL. 1 *CCU
(Adam, J.) [Hung] solo,pno BUDAPEST
1751 also contains original text
(M892)

MASTERS OF SONG, VOL. 2 *CCU
(Adam, J.) [Hung] solo,pno BUDAPEST
2110 also contains original text
(M893)

MASTERS OF SONG, VOL. 3 *CCU
(Adam, J.) [Hung] solo,pno BUDAPEST
2262 also contains original text
(M894)

MASTERS OF SONG, VOL. 4 *CCU
(Adam, J.) [Hung] solo,pno BUDAPEST
2909 also contains original text
(M895)

MASTERS OF SONG, VOL. 5 *CCU
(Adam, J.) [Hung] solo,pno BUDAPEST
3118 also contains original text
(M896)

MASTERS OF SONG, VOL. 6 *CCU
(Adam, J.) [Hung] solo,pno BUDAPEST
3602 also contains original text
(M897)

MASTERS OF SONG, VOL. 7: BOOKS A-C
*CCU
(Adam, J.) [Hung] solo,pno BUDAPEST
4470-4472 also contains original
text   (M898)

MATAI see Glantz, Yehuda Leib

MATAI YAVO HA-MASHIACH
(Helfman, Max) "When Will The
Redeemer Come?" [Heb] med solo,pno
TRANSCON. IS 513 $.40   (M899)

MATEJ, JOZKA (1922-   )
Der Stachlige Himmel *see Ostnate
Nebe

Ostnate Nebe *song cycle
"Der Stachlige Himmel" [Czech/Ger]
high solo,pno CZECH s.p.   (M900)

Ukolebavka
solo,pno SUPRAPHON s.p.   (M901)

MATER CASTISSIMA see Kubizek,
Augustinian

MATERIDOUSKA see Macha, Otmar

MATESKY, T.
Behold How Good And How Pleasant
(Psalm 133)
med solo,pno PRESSER $.95   (M902)

Four American Songs *CC4U
med solo,pno MERCURY $1.00   (M903)

I Will Praise Thee With My Whole
Heart (Psalm 138)
med solo,pno MERCURY $.95   (M904)

Mother
med solo,pno MERCURY $.95   (M905)
low solo,pno MERCURY $.95   (M906)

Psalm 133 *see Behold How Good And
How Pleasant

Psalm 138 *see I Will Praise Thee
With My Whole Heart

With This Ring
med solo,pno MERCURY $.95   (M907)

MATHER, BRUCE (1939-   )
Madrigal II
SMez soli,fl,harp,vln,vla,vcl sc
JOBERT s.p., ipr   (M908)

MATHESON, H.
Someone Is Waiting For Me
solo,pno (D flat maj) CRAMER (M909)

MATHIAS, WILLIAM (1934-   )
Vision Of Time And Eternity, A
solo,pno OXFORD s.p.   (M910)

MATHIL
De Tout Mon Coeur, Cahier 1 & 2 *CCU
solo,pno HENN 455-6 s.p.   (M911)

Miniatures *CCU
solo,pno HENN 457 s.p.   (M912)

MATHISEN, HALVAAN
Det Store Gledesbud *Xmas
solo,pno MUSIKK s.p.   (M913)

MATI see Srebotnjak, Alojz F.

MATI MOJA see Figus-Bystry, Villiam

MATICCE see Zich, Otakor

MATIERE see Trow, Karel

MATIN DE MAI see Gedalge, Andre

MATIN DE PAQUES see Aubert, Louis-
Francois-Marie

MATIN PASTORAL see Dalcroze, Jacques

MATINEE D'ETE see Massenet, Jules

MATKA see Devaty, Antonin

MATKAMIEHEN VIRSI see Hannikainen,
Ilmari

MATKANI MUISTOT see Backman, Hjalmar

MATOS, RODRIQUEZ
La Comparsita
solo,pno AMPHION R 1122 s.p. (M914)

MATOUSEK, LUKAS (1943-   )
Kantat II *cant
S solo,clar,bsn,trom CZECH s.p.
(M915)

MATRON CAT'S SONG see Head, Michael
(Dewar)

MATROSEN-SONG see Weill, Kurt

MATSUDAIRA, YORI AKKI (1931-   )
Substitution
S solo,pno ZERBONI 7587 s.p. (M916)

What's Next?
S solo,perc ZERBONI 7401 s.p.
(M917)

MATSUDAIRA, YORITSUNE (1907-   )
Katsura
solo,fl,harp,perc,gtr ONGAKU s.p.
(M918)

Koromogae
S solo,19inst sc ZERBONI 5435 s.p.
(M919)

Metamorfosi Sinfoniche
S solo,18inst sc ZERBONI 5178 s.p.
(M920)

Roei "Jisei"
female solo,11inst sc,quarto
ZERBONI 7146 s.p.   (M921)

MATSUMURA, T.
Achime
S solo,11inst ONGAKU s.p.   (M922)

MATSUSHITA, S.
Musique Pour Soprano Et Ensemble De
Chambre
S solo,chamb.orch ONGAKU s.p.
(M923)

MATTHEW, MARK, LUKE AND JOHN see Shaw,
Martin

MATTHEW TWENTY-FOUR *sac,Bibl
(Brown, Aaron) solo,pno WORD S-381
(M924)

MATTHEWS
Believing *sac
solo,pno LILLENAS SM-874: SN $1.00
(M925)

Can't Wait 'Til He's Here *sac
solo,pno LILLENAS SM-883: SN $1.00
(M926)

He Comforts Me *sac
solo,pno LILLENAS SM-909: SN $1.00
(M927)

He Won't Let You Down *sac
solo,pno LILLENAS SM-881:SN $1.00
(M928)

I'm Gonna Tell The World *sac
solo,pno LILLENAS SM-641: RN $1.00
(M929)

It's A Long, Lonesome Road *sac
solo,pno LILLENAS SM-922: SN $1.00
(M930)

Love Song, A *sac
solo,pno LILLENAS SM-880: SN $1.00
(M931)

MATTHEWS, DAVID
I Ask None Else Of Thee *sac
solo,pno WORD S-306   (M932)

MATTHEWS, HARVEY ALEXANDER (1879-   )
Harvest Is Abundant, The *sac
high solo,pno BELWIN $1.50   (M933)
low solo,pno BELWIN $1.50   (M934)

My Heav'nly Father *sac
high solo,pno (F maj) SCHIRM.G $.60
(M935)
low solo,pno (E flat maj) SCHIRM.G
$.60   (M936)

O Love That Casts Our Fear *sac
high solo,pno BELWIN $1.50   (M937)

O Love That Will Not Let Me Go *sac
high solo,pno BELWIN $1.50   (M938)

Voices Of The Sky (from Story Of
Christmas, The) sac
high solo,pno (E flat maj) SCHIRM.G
$.75   (M939)

MATTHEWS, RANDY
Didn't He *sac
solo,pno WORD S-402   (M940)

Hallelujah, Brother! *sac
solo,pno WORD S-341   (M941)

I Guess That I've Changed *sac
solo,pno WORD S-339   (M942)

Plastic Clown *sac
solo,pno WORD S-340   (M943)

Sunday Morning *sac
solo,pno WORD S-342   (M944)

MATTHEWS, THOMAS
Lord Is My Shepherd, The *sac
high solo,pno FITZSIMONS $.75
(M945)

MATTHUS, SIEGFRIED (1934-   )
Alles, Was Wahr Ist, Kann Leise Sein
A solo,3pt wom cor,fl,clar,perc,
harp,cel,strings sc DEUTSCHER
1351 s.p., ipr   (M946)

Galilei
solo,fl,trom,pno,marimba,vcl
DEUTSCHER rental   (M947)

Lieder *CCU
high solo,pno DEUTSCHER 9037 s.p.
(M948)

MATTINATA see Albanese, Guido

MATTINATA see Cimara, Pietro

MATTINATA see Ivanova, Lidia

MATTINATA see Leoncavallo, Ruggiero

MATTINATA see Morelli, A.

MATTINATA see Pratella, Francesco
Balilla

MATTINATA see Respighi, Ottorino

MATTINATA see Rosseau, Norbert

MATTINATA DI MAGGIO see Denza, Luigi

MATTINATA, NO. 1 see Tosti, Francesco
Paolo

MATTINATA, NO. 2 see Tosti, Francesco
Paolo

MATTINATA VENEZIANA see Cinque

MATTINO D'APRILE NEL BOSCO see Porrino,
Ennio

MATTINO DI LUCE see Respighi, Ottorino

MATTOIDENS SANGER see Bach, Erik

MATUTIN see Bloch, Waldemar

MATUTINA see Fleury, H.

MATYS, JIRI (1927-   )
Lyricke Zpevy *CCU
Bar solo,strings CZECH s.p. (M949)

MAUDITE A JAMAIS SOIT LA RACE see
Saint-Saens, Camille

MAUERSBERGER, ERHARD
We Saw His Glory *sac
med solo,pno oct CONCORDIA 98-1914
$.25   (M950)

MAURAT, EDMOND
C'en Est Fait, Ce Coeur Brule *Op.7,
No.2
[Fr] S/T solo,pno ESCHIG $3.75 see
from Les Chants De L'Amour (M951)

Deux Implorations Sacrees *CC2U
[Fr] med-high solo,pno ESCHIG $2.75
(M952)

MAURAT, EDMOND (cont'd.)

    Les Chants De L'Amour *see C'en Est
    Fait, Ce Coeur Brule, Op.7,No.2;
    Mon Couer, Un Clair Matin, Op.7,
    No.1; Quel Fier, Troublant Et
    Noble Port, Op.7,No.3   (M953)

    Mon Couer, Un Clair Matin *Op.7,No.1
    [Fr] S/T solo,pno ESCHIG $1.75 see
    from Les Chants De L'Amour (M954)

    Quel Fier, Troublant Et Noble Port
    *Op.7,No.3
    [Fr] S/T solo,pno ESCHIG $3.00 see
    from Les Chants De L'Amour (M955)

    Six Vocal Rhapsodies, Vol. I *CC6U
    med-high solo,pno ESCHIG $3.75
                                    (M956)
    Six Vocal Rhapsodies, Vol. II *CC6U
    med-high solo,pno ESCHIG $4.50
                                    (M957)
    Six Vocal Rhapsodies, Vol. III *CC6U
    med-high solo,pno ESCHIG $5.00
                                    (M958)

    Strophes A L'amitie *Op.13
    [Fr] med solo,pno ESCHIG $3.50
                                    (M959)

    Un Reve *Op.35
    [Fr] B solo,pno ESCHIG $3.25 (M960)

MAUREEN see Roberton, Hugh Stevenson

MAURICE, PIERRE (1868-1936)
    Gorm Grym
    solo,orch HENN s.p.   (M961)

    La Fille De Jepthe *sac
    solo,pno ENOCH s.p.   (M962)

    Vierges Mortes
    solo,orch HENN s.p.   (M963)

MAURY, LOWNDES (1911-   )
    Some Girls Are Prettier
    med-low solo,pno PRESSER $.75
                                    (M964)

MAW, NICHOLAS
    Scenes And Arias *CCU
    S/Mez/A solo,orch BOOSEY $10.00
                                    (M965)
    Voice Of Love *song cycle
    Mez solo,pno BOOSEY $7.00   (M966)

MAXWELL
    Dear Friends And Gentle Hearts
    (composed with Wirges)
    solo,pno SHAWNEE IA 28 $.40 (M967)

    Peace I Leave With You (composed with
    Wirges)
    low solo,pno SHAWNEE IA5047 $.85
                                    (M968)
    Singer, The
    low solo,pno (E flat maj) ALLANS
    s.p.   (M969)
    high solo,pno (G maj) ALLANS s.p.
                                    (M970)

MAY see Aked, Lindsay

MAY see Kennedy, John Brodbin

MAY see Sibelius, Jean, Maj

MAY DAY CAROL
    (Taylor, Deems) high solo,pno BELWIN
    $1.50   (M971)
    (Taylor, Deems) med solo,pno BELWIN
    $1.50   (M972)
    (Taylor, Deems) low solo,pno BELWIN
    $1.50   (M973)

MAY-DAY MORN see Slater, David D.

MAY DEW see Bennett, Sir William
    Sterndale

MAY-DEW see Bennett, W.E.

MAY, ED.
    Ich Weiss Ein Fass In Einem Tiefen
    Keller
    solo,pno SCHAUR EE 3549 s.p. (M974)

MAY I INTRODUCE YOU TO A FRIEND? see
    Owens, Jamie

MAY I NEVER LOSE THE WONDER see Zilch,
    Margot

MAY LAURELS CROWN THY BROW see Verdi,
    Giuseppe, Ritorna Vincitor

MAY LILIES see O'Neill, Norman

MAY MAGNIFICAT, A see Mellers, Wilfrid
    Howard

MAY NIGHT, THE see Brahms, Johannes,
    Die Mainacht

MAY THE LORD WATCH OVER THIS HOUSE see
    Powell, Robert J.

MAY THE WORDS see Grieb, Herbert [C.]

MAY THE WORDS see Helfman, Max

MAY THE WORDS see Wyner, Yehudi

MAY THEY IN THEE BE ONE see MacNutt,
    Walter

MAY TIME see Geehl, Henry Ernest

MAY WE KNOW PEACE see Roe, Gloria [Ann]

MAY WE LIE DOWN see Gottlieb, Jack

MAYBE see Kagen, Sergius

MAYER
    Barbara, What Have You Done?
    SA soli,pno FISCHER,C O 4773 (M975)

MAYER, B.
    Weihnachten *Xmas
    solo,pno DOBLINGER 08 624 s.p.
                                    (M976)

MAYER, M.
    Das Weihnachtsevangelium
    (Koschinsky) [Ger] SA soli,2vln,S
    rec,A rec,org cmplt ed NAGELS
    $1.50   (M977)

MAYER, MILAN (1895-1967)
    Five Songs *CC5U
    [Slav] solo,pno CROATICA s.p.
                                    (M978)
    Four Songs *CC4U
    [Slav] solo,pno CROATICA s.p.
                                    (M979)

MAYERL, B.
    These Precious Things
    solo,pno (D flat maj) BOOSEY $1.50
                                    (M980)

MAYFIELD, LARRY
    I Want You To Know *sac
    solo,pno SINGSPIR 7113 $1.00 (M981)

MAYIM L'DAVID *sac
    solo,pno OR-TAV $.50   (M982)

M'AYMEREZ-VOUS BIEN? see Beekhuis,
    Hanna

MAYO LOVE SONG see Harty, Sir Hamilton

MAYTIDE IN MY GARDEN see Cowen, Sir
    Frederic Hymen

MAYUZUMI, TOSHIRO (1929-   )
    Sphenogrammes *CCU
    A solo,fl,al-sax,marimba,vln,vcl,
    piano 4-hands PETERS 6327 rental
                                    (M983)

MAZELDIGER MOISHELE *Jew
    solo,pno KAMMEN 465 $1.00   (M984)

MAZURCA see Chueca, Federico

MAZURCA DE LA PERDIZ see Chueca,
    Federico

MAZURCA DE LA SOMBRILLA see Moreno
    Torroba, Federico

MAZURCA DE LOS PARAGUAS see Chueca,
    Federico

MAZZAFERRATA, G.B.
    Canzonette E Cantate A Due Voci *CCU
    2 soli,pno FORNI s.p.   (M985)

ME AND YOU see Bennett, Sir William
    Sterndale

ME SUIS MISE EN DANCE
    see Five French Folk Songs

ME TAIRE? NON. J'AI TROP SOUFFERT see
    Wolff, A.

ME VLNY, VLNY BILE see Marsik, Emanuel

ME VOICI DANS SON BOUDOIR see Thomas,
    Ambroise

ME VOILA SEULE DANS LA NUIT see Bizet,
    Georges

MEADOW-SAFFRONS see Pisk, Paul Amadeus

MEADOWSWEET see Brahe, May H.

MECHANTE MINETTE see Landry, Al.

MECHEM, KIRKE (1925-   )
    Farewell, A
    see Four Songs For Baritone

    Four Songs For Baritone
    Bar solo,pno SCHIRM.EC 146 s.p.
    contains: Farewell, A; Green-
    Blooded Fish, The; Inferiority
    Complex; July Rain   (M986)

    Green-Blooded Fish, The
    see Four Songs For Baritone

MECHEM, KIRKE (cont'd.)

    Inferiority Complex
    see Four Songs For Baritone

    July Rain
    see Four Songs For Baritone

MECIENDO see Guastavino, Carlos

MECO ALL'ALTAR DI VENERE see Bellini,
    Vincenzo

MED EN PRIMULA VERIS see Grieg, Edvard
    Hagerup

MED EN VANDLILJE see Grieg, Edvard
    Hagerup

MED ROZAMI see Scek, Breda

MED SINA SKONASTE SANGER see Linnala,
    Eino

MEDAN NATTEN GAR see Hedar, Josef

MEDBORGARSANG see Stenhammar, Wilhelm

MEDEA see Regt, Hendrik de

MEDEMA, KEN
    Lord, Listen To Your Children Praying
    *sac
    med solo,pno CRESPUB CP-S5046 $1.25
                                    (M987)
    Treasures *sac,CC9L
    solo,pno WORD 37644 $2.50   (M988)

MEDICINA E MUSICA see Vecchi, G.

MEDICUS, V. (1896-   )
    Ultime Rose
    solo,fl,ob,clar,bsn,2horn CARISH
    s.p.   (M989)

MEDIEVAL CAROL see Hoddinott, Alun

MEDIEVAL DIPTYCH see Rawsthorne

MEDIEVAL FRENCH SONGS see Crosse

MEDITACE see Hurnik, Ilja

MEDITACE see Mikoda, Borivoj

MEDITATION see Bach, Johann Sebastian,
    Ave Maria

MEDITATION see Jirak, Karel Boleslav

MEDITATION see Mikoda, Borivoj,
    Meditace

MEDITATION see Schuller, Gunther

MEDITATION FROM THAIS see Massenet,
    Jules

MEDITATIVE SONGS see Burns, William K.

MEDITAZIONE SULLA MASCHERA DI
    MODIGLIANI see Vogel, Wladimir

MEDJE see Gounod, Charles Francois

MEDTNER, NIKOLAI KARLOVITCH (1880-1951)
    Captive, The *Op.52,No.7
    [Ger/Eng] med solo,pno ZIMMER. 1072
    s.p. see from Sieben Gedichte Von
    Puschkin   (M990)

    Elegy *Op.52,No.3
    [Ger/Eng] med solo,pno ZIMMER. 1068
    see from Sieben Gedichte Von
    Puschkin   (M991)
    [Ger/Eng] high solo,pno ZIMMER.
    1083 s.p. see from Vier Lieder
    Nach Puschkin Und Tjutschew
                                    (M992)
    Fountain, The *Op.46,No.6
    [Ger/Eng] med solo/low solo,pno
    ZIMMER. 1064 s.p. see from Sieben
    Gedichte Von Goethe, Eichendorff,
    Chamisso   (M993)

    Gaily Singing *Op.46,No.7
    [Ger/Eng] high solo,pno ZIMMER.
    1065 s.p. see from Sieben
    Gedichte Von Goethe, Eichendorff,
    Chamisso   (M994)

    In The Forest *Op.46,No.4
    [Ger/Eng] med solo,pno ZIMMER. 1062
    s.p. see from Sieben Gedichte Von
    Goethe, Eichendorff, Chamisso
                                    (M995)
    Omens *Op.52,No.4
    [Ger/Eng] med solo,pno ZIMMER. 1069
    s.p. see from Sieben Gedichte Von
    Puschkin   (M996)

    Praeludium *Op.46,No.1
    [Ger/Eng] high solo,pno ZIMMER.
    1059 s.p. see from Sieben
    Gedichte Von Goethe, Eichendorff,
    Chamisso   (M997)

MEDTNER, NIKOLAI KARLOVITCH (cont'd.)

Raven, The *Op.52,No.2
[Ger/Eng] med solo,pno ZIMMER. 1067
s.p. see from Sieben Gedichte Von
Puschkin   (M998)

Sacred Grove, The *Op.46,No.2
[Ger/Eng] med solo,pno ZIMMER. 1060
s.p. see from Sieben Gedichte Von
Goethe, Eichendorff, Chamisso
(M999)

Sechs Gedichte Von Puschkin *Op.36,
No.1-6, CC6U
solo,pno ZIMMER. 1438 s.p.   (M1000)

Serenade *Op.46,No.3
[Ger/Eng] high solo,pno ZIMMER.
1061 s.p. see from Sieben
Gedichte Von Goethe, Eichendorff,
Chamisso   (M1001)

Serenade [2] *Op.52,No.6
[Ger/Eng] med solo,pno ZIMMER. 1071
s.p. see from Sieben Gedichte Von
Puschkin   (M1002)

Seven Posthumous Songs *Op.61,No.1-
7, CC7U
[Ger/Eng/Russ] solo,pno BELAIEFF
278 s.p.   (M1003)

Sieben Gedichte Von Goethe,
Eichendorff, Chamisso *see
Fountain, The, Op.46,No.6; Gaily
Singing, Op.46,No.7; In The
Forest, Op.46,No.4; Praeludium,
Op.46,No.1; Sacred Grove, The,
Op.46,No.2; Serenade, Op.46,No.3;
Winter Night, Op.46,No.5 (M1004)

Sieben Gedichte Von Puschkin *see
Captive, The, Op.52,No.7; Elegy,
Op.52,No.3; Omens, Op.52,No.4;
Raven, The, Op.52,No.2; Serenade
[2], Op.52,No.6; Spanish Romance,
Op.52,No.5; Window, The, Op.52,
No.1   (M1005)

Sonate Vocalise *Op.41,No.1,
vocalise
high solo/med solo,pno ZIMMER. 1267
$2.50   (M1006)

Spanish Romance *Op.52,No.5
[Ger/Eng] med solo,pno ZIMMER. 1070
s.p. see from Sieben Gedichte Von
Puschkin   (M1007)

Suite Vocalise *Op.41,No.2, vocalise
high solo/med solo,pno ZIMMER. 1051
$2.00   (M1008)

Vier Lieder Nach Puschkin Und
Tjutschew *Op.45,No.2-4, CC3U
solo,pno ZIMMER. 1084-1085-1086
s.p., ea.   (M1009)

Vier Lieder Nach Puschkin Und
Tjutschew *see Elegy, Op.45,No.1
(M1010)

Window, The *Op.52,No.1
[Ger/Eng] med solo,pno ZIMMER. 1066
s.p. see from Sieben Gedichte Von
Puschkin   (M1011)

Winter Night *Op.46,No.5
[Ger/Eng] high solo,pno ZIMMER.
1063 s.p. see from Sieben
Gedichte Von Goethe, Eichendorff,
Chamisso   (M1012)

MEEK, KENNETH
There Is No Rose Of Such Virtue *sac
solo,pno BERANDOL BER 1291 $1.50
(M1013)
MEETING see Strauss, Richard, Begegnung

MEETING AT NIGHT, PARTING AT MORNING
see Gerschefski, Edwin

MEETING IN THE WOODS see Schumann,
Robert (Alexander), Waldesgesprach

MEETING OF SIGHS, THE see Sutherland,
Margaret

MEETING OF THE WATERS see Hughes,
Herbert

MEETINGS see Kozina, Marijan, Srecanja

MEG AKARLAK TARTANTI see Frid, Geza

MEGRELIAN SONGS see Taktakishvili, Otar

MEHA see Capoul, V.

MEHAS, JANET COOPER
Trust In The Lord With All Thine
Heart *Gen,funeral
med solo,pno WHITE HARV. VOS 755
$.75   (M1014)

MEHLER, FRIEDRICH
Forgaves Uppa Stigen
see Fyra Gotlandska Visor

Fyra Gotlandska Visor
solo,pno GEHRMANS s.p.
contains: Forgaves Uppa Stigen;
Nu Kommer Den Forsta Friarn;
Och Alla Gotlands Gossar;
Vaggsang   (M1015)

Nu Kommer Den Forsta Friarn
see Fyra Gotlandska Visor

Och Alla Gotlands Gossar
see Fyra Gotlandska Visor

Vaggsang
see Fyra Gotlandska Visor

MEHRSTIMMIGE GESANGE see Mozart,
Wolfgang Amadeus

MEHUL, ETIENNE-NICOLAS (1763-1817)
A Peine Au Sortir De L'enfance (from
Joseph)
[Fr] T solo,pno CHOUDENS C269 s.p.
(M1016)
Champs Paternels (from Joseph)
[Fr] T solo,pno CHOUDENS C355 s.p.
(M1017)
MEHUL, H.
Joseph
see LA MUSIQUE, QUATRIEME CAHIER

Romance (from Joseph)
see LA MUSIQUE, HUITIEME CAHIER

MEI see Zweers, [Bernard]

MEIBLOEMKEN see Mengelberg, Rudolf

MEIDLACH, WEIBLACH see Rumshinsky, Jos.
M.

MEIDOORN see Tussenbroek, H. von

MEIER, JAROSLAV
Mojim Det'om
boy solo/girl solo,pno
SLOV.HUD.FOND s.p.   (M1018)

Nocne Piesne *song cycle
Mez solo,pno SLOV.HUD.FOND s.p.
(M1019)
Slohy Lasky *song cycle
Bar solo,pno SLOV.HUD.FOND s.p.
(M1020)
MEIHOVEKE see Tussenbroek, H. von

MEILIED see Tetterode, L. Adr. von

MEILIEDJE see Loots, Ph.

MEIN BLAUES KLAVIER see Nadelmann, L.

MEIN ERSHTER VALSE *Jew
solo,pno KAMMEN 476 $1.00   (M1021)

MEIN GANZES LEBEN LIEBE see Glombig, E.

MEIN GELIEBTER SCHLAFT IM SARGE see
Kilpinen, Yrio, Armar Arkussa Ajavi

MEIN GLAS IST LEER *folk,Russ
[Ger/Russ] solo,pno ZIMMER. 1525 s.p.
(M1022)
MEIN GLAUBIGES HERZE see Bach, Johann
Sebastian

MEIN GOLDELE see Rumshinsky, Jos. M.

MEIN GOTT UND HERR see Capricornus,
Samuel

MEIN GREENER KOSIN MOTKE FON SLOBODKE
*Jew
solo,pno KAMMEN 36 $1.00   (M1023)

MEIN HEIMATLAND *CCU
1-2 soli,gtr SCHOTTS 5000 s.p.
(M1024)
MEIN HERR MARQUIS see Strauss, Johann

MEIN HERZ IN STETEN TREUEN see
Schoenberg, Arnold

MEIN HERZ IST BEREIT see Bruhns,
Nicholaus

MEIN HERZ IST BEREIT see Buxtehude,
Dietrich

MEIN HERZ IST BEREIT see Schutz,
Heinrich

MEIN HERZ IST BEREIT see Vierdanck,
Johann

MEIN HERZ IST DIR GEWOGEN see Muller-
Medek, Tilo

MEIN HERZ IST GERUSTET see Schutz,
Heinrich, Paratum Cor Meum, Deus

MEIN HERZ IST MIR GEMENGET see
Schoenberg, Arnold

MEIN HERZ IST WIE DIE DUNKLE NACHT see
Svedbom, Vilhelm

MEIN HERZ SCHMUCKT SICH MIT DIR see
Bijvanck, Henk

MEIN HERZE SCHWIMMT IM BLUT see Bach,
Johann Sebastian

MEIN KIND, WAR ICH KONIG see Liszt,
Franz

MEIN LEID UND ALLE QUALEN see Purcell,
Henry

MEIN LIEBER SCHWAN see Wagner, Richard

MEIN LIEBLING, DU SOLLST HIER VERWEILEN
see Ippolitov-Ivanov, Mikhail
Mikhailovitch

MEIN LIEDERBUCH see Kranz, Albert

MEIN MADEL HAT ZWEI AUGLEIN BRAUN see
Schmalstich, Clemens

MEIN MAME'S LEIDELE *Jew
solo,pno KAMMEN 49 $1.00   (M1025)

MEIN MARCHENLAND see Kilpinen, Yrio,
Mitt Sagoland

MEIN SCHATZELEIN see Reger, Max

MEIN SHIKSAL *Jew
solo,pno KAMMEN 82 $1.00   (M1026)

MEIN SHTETLE BELZ *Jew
solo,pno KAMMEN 419 $1.00   (M1027)

MEIN STERNLEIN see Reinhardt, L.

MEIN TRAUM see Trunk, Richard

MEIN VOLK see Colaco Osorio-Swaab,
Reine

MEIN WEG GEHT JETZT WORUBER see Newlin,
Dika

MEIN WEIB SHLEPT SICH MIT *Jew
solo,pno KAMMEN 19 $1.00   (M1028)

MEIN WEISSE BLOOM *Jew
solo,pno KAMMEN 412 $1.00   (M1029)

MEIN YIDDISHE MEIDELE see Shorr, Anshel

MEINACHT see Adriessen, Willem

MEINE DUNKELN HANDE see Reutter,
Hermann

MEINE KLEINEN LIEDER see Dimmler, L.

MEINE LIEBE IST GRUN see Brahms,
Johannes

MEINE LIEBLICHE PLATANE - SO SCHATT'GEN
RAUM see Handel, George Frideric

MEINE LIEDER, MEINE SANGE see Weber,
Carl Maria von

MEINE MUTTER HAT'S GEWOLLT see Trunk,
Richard

MEINE ROSEN see Peterson-Berger, (Olof)
Wilhelm

MEINE SEELE ERHEBT DEN HERREN see
Schutz, Heinrich

MEINE SEELE ERHEBT DEN HERREN see
Schutz, Heinrich, Das Magnificat

MEINE SEELE ERHEBT DEN HERRN see
Weyrauch, Johannes

MEINE SEELE HARRET AUF GOTT see
Rosenmuller, Johann

MEINE SEELE HORT IM SEHEN see Handel,
George Frideric

MEINE SEELE IST STILL ZU GOTT see
Reger, Max

MEINE SEELE RUHMT UND PREIST see Bach,
Johann Sebastian

MEINE SEELE RUHMT UND PREIST see
Hoffmann, Georg Melchoir

MEINE SEHNSUCHT see Bijvanck, Henk

MEINE WELLEN, WEISSE WELLEN see Marsik,
Emanuel, Me Vlny, Vlny Bile

MEINEM KINDE see Strauss, Richard

MEINER ALLERLIEBSTEN SCHONEN see Bach,
    Johann Christian

MEISCHEMER see Orthel, Leon

MEISJE see Tussenbroek, H. von

MEISTER, C.
    Myr Zweui
        solo,pno HUG s.p.   (M1030)

MEISTER, WIR HABEN DIE GANZE NACHT
    GEARBEITET see Schutz, Heinrich

MELANCHOLIA see Aubert, Louis-Francois-
    Marie

MELANCHOLICKE SERENADY O LASCE see
    Chlubna, Oswald

MELANCHOLISCHE LIEDER UBER DIE LIEBE
    see Novak, V.

MELANCHOLISCHE SERENADEN UBER LIEBE see
    Chlubna, Oswald, Melancholicke
    Serenady O Lasce

MELANCHOLY see Goosens, Eugene

MELANCHOLY SONG, A see Hopkins, Anthony

MELANCOLIA see Siccardi, Honorio,
    Malinconia

MELANCOLIE see Cuvillier, Charles

MELANCOLIE see Delmet, Paul

MELANCOLIE see Toutain-Grun, J.

MELAN-GUEROULT
    La Sulamite
        solo,pno (available in 2 keys)
        ENOCH s.p.   (M1031)

MELARTIN, ERKKI (1875-1937)
    Aamulaulu "Korkeasta Veisusta"
        *Op.3,No.2
        "Morgonsang Ur "Hoga Visan"" see
        Melartin, Erkki, Marias Vaggsang

    Ainon Aaria Koivulle (from Aino)
        "Ainos Aria Till Bjorken" solo,pno
        FAZER F3000 s.p.   (M1032)

    Ainos Aria Till Bjorken *see Ainon
        Aaria Koivulle

    Bittra Tarar *see Silloin Mina Itkin

    Den Langtande *see Kaipaava

    Det Ar En Ros Utsprungen
        solo,pno LUNDQUIST s.p.   (M1033)

    Dina Ogon Och Mina Ogon *see Sinun
        Silmas Ja Minun Silmat

    Fader Var *see Isa Meidan

    Finska Folkvisor *see Jeva, Op.148,
        No.2; Silloin Mina Itkin, "Bittra
        Tarar", Op.148,No.3   (M1034)

    Gib Mir Dein Herze *Op.73,No.1
        "Suo Mulle Syommes" solo,pno FAZER
        F 776 s.p.   (M1035)

    Heilini Soitteli *Op.130,No.2
        "Minns Du Pa Mar Knadsdansen I
        Staden" solo,pno FAZER W 1483
        s.p. see from Nya Folkvisor (M1036)

    Indisches Lied *Op.19,No.1
        "Indisk Sang" solo,pno FAZER F 450
        s.p.   (M1037)

    Indisk Sang *see Indisches Lied

    Isa Meidan *Op.151,No.4
        "Fader Var" solo,pno FAZER W 1573
        s.p.   (M1038)

    Jeva *Op.148,No.2
        solo,pno FAZER F 2255 s.p. see from
        Finska Folkvisor   (M1039)

    Kaipaava *Op.130,No.1
        "Den Langtande" solo,pno FAZER
        W 1482 s.p. see from Nya
        Folkvisor   (M1040)

    Kansanlauluja Kakisalmelta I-III
        *CCU
        solo,pno FAZER W 789-791 s.p., ea.
                                    (M1041)

    La Lune Blanche *Op.19,No.2
        "Sang" solo,pno FAZER F 451 s.p.
                                    (M1042)

    Marian Kehtolaulu *see Marias
        Vaggsang

    Marias Vaggsang *Op.3,No.1
        "Marian Kehtolaulu" solo,pno FAZER
        F 237 s.p. contains also:
        Aamulaulu "Korkeasta Veisusta",

MELARTIN, ERKKI (cont'd.)
    "Morgonsang Ur "Hoga Visan"",
    Op.3,No.2   (M1043)

    Min Lyckoo *see Onneni Saari

    Minns Du Pa Mar Knadsdansen I Staden
        *see Heilini Soitteli

    Morgonsang Ur "Hoga Visan" *see
        Aamulaulu "Korkeasta Veisusta"

    Nya Folkvisor *see Heilini Soitteli,
        "Minns Du Pa Mar Knadsdansen I
        Staden", Op.130,No.2; Kaipaava,
        "Den Langtande", Op.130,No.1;
        Sinun Silmas Ja Minun Silmat,
        "Dina Ogon Och Mina Ogon",
        Op.130,No.3   (M1044)

    O, Herre - -
        solo,pno LUNDQUIST s.p.   (M1045)

    Onneni Saari *Op.32,No.3
        "Min Lyckoo" solo,pno FAZER F883
        s.p.   (M1046)

    Paluu *see Ritorno

    Ritorno *Op.24,No.1
        "Paluu" solo,pno FAZER W 1000 s.p.
                                    (M1047)

    Rosa Rorans Bonitatem *Op.32,No.1
        solo,pno FAZER F 491 s.p.   (M1048)

    Sang *see La Lune Blanche

    Silloin Mina Itkin *Op.148,No.3
        "Bittra Tarar" solo,pno FAZER
        F 2256 s.p. see from Finska
        Folkvisor   (M1049)

    Sinun Silmas Ja Minun Silmat
        *Op.130,No.3
        "Dina Ogon Och Mina Ogon" solo,pno
        FAZER W 1484 s.p. see from Nya
        Folkvisor   (M1050)

    Spelmansvisa *see Spielmannslied

    Spielmannslied *Op.116,No.4
        "Spelmansvisa" solo,pno FAZER
        F 1116 s.p.   (M1051)

    Suo Mulle Syommes *see Gib Mir Dein
        Herze

    Tili, Tili Tengan Loysin *Op.128,
        No.1
        solo,pno FAZER F 1981 s.p. (M1052)

    Vandringar *Op.166,No.1
        solo,pno FAZER F 1113 s.p. (M1053)

    Viisi Kansanlaulusovitusta *Op.164,
        CCU
        solo,pno FAZER F 2501 s.p. (M1054)

MELBY, JOHN
    Due Canti Di Leopardi *CC2U
        S/T solo,horn,pno sc AM.COMP.AL.
        $3.85   (M1055)

    Two Norwegian Songs *CC2U,Norw
        S/T solo,pno sc AM.COMP.AL. $3.85
                                    (M1056)

    Valedictory
        S solo, computer sc AM.COMP.AL.
        $9.35   (M1057)

MELECCI
    Candle, The *sac,Xmas
        high solo,pno HARRIS $.75   (M1058)
        low solo,pno HARRIS $.75   (M1059)

MELICHAR
    Alma Mia *see Wann Kommt Die Stunde?

    Dormi, Dormi
        see Melichar, Mil Querubines En
        Coro

    Mil Querubines En Coro
        [It/Span] solo,pno (on a theme by
        Schubert) RICORDI-ARG BA 7300
        s.p. contains also: Dormi, Dormi
                                    (M1060)

    Wann Kommt Die Stunde?
        "Alma Mia" [Ger/Span] solo,pno
        RICORDI-ARG BA 7359 s.p.   (M1061)

MELIEDJE see Pijper, Willem

MELLAN BROARNA see Stenhammar, Wilhelm

MELLANDER, OSKAR
    Intet Ar Forgaves
        solo,pno GEHRMANS s.p.   (M1062)

MELLERS, WILFRID HOWARD (1914-   )
    May Magnificant, A
        Mez solo,fl,ob,clar,bsn,horn,trp,
        perc,vibra/cel,harp,strings
        NOVELLO rental   (M1063)

MELLERS, WILFRID HOWARD (cont'd.)
    Rose Of May
        narrator&S solo,fl,clar,4strings
        NOVELLO s.p.
        narrator&S solo,fl,clar,2vln,vla,
        vcl NOVELLO rental   (M1064)
                                    (M1065)

    Ship Of Death *cant
        ST soli,2clar,2vln,vla,vcl NOVELLO
        rental   (M1066)

MELLI, D.
    Madrigali E Canzonette *CCU
        solo,hpsd BONGIOVANI 2417 s.p.
                                    (M1067)

MELODI see Lundkvist, Per

MELODI see Nordqvist, Gustaf

MELODI see Peterson-Berger, (Olof)
    Wilhelm

MELODIA see Alfano, Franco

MELODIA VESPERALE see Mancini, Vincenzo

MELODIE, DIE ICH VERLOREN HATTE see
    Kunad, Rainer

MELODIES see Chabrier, Emmanuel

MELODIES see Franck, Cesar

MELODIES see Messager, Andre

MELODIES CHOISES see Schumann, Robert
    (Alexander)

MELODIES ET AIRS CHOISIS see Bach,
    Johann Sebastian

MELODIES FROM THE EAST see Ben-Haim,
    Paul

MELODIES PASSAGERES see Barber, Samuel

MELODIES PERSANES OP. 26 see Saint-
    Saens, Camille

MELODIES TEXTES FRANCAIS, ANGLAIS ET
    ALLEMAND VOL. I see Brahms,
    Johannes

MELODIES TEXTES FRANCAIS, ANGLAIS ET
    ALLEMAND VOL. II see Brahms,
    Johannes

MELODIES TEXTES FRANCAIS, ANGLAIS ET
    ALLEMAND VOL. III see Brahms,
    Johannes

MELODIES TEXTES FRANCAIS, ANGLAIS ET
    ALLEMAND VOL. IV see Brahms,
    Johannes

MELODIES YOU SING, THE see Shaw, Martin

MELODIEUX AUTOMNE see Ladmirault, Paul
    (Emile)

MELODY-AIRE SOLOS AND DUETS, NO. 1
    *sac,CCUL
    1-2 soli,pno SINGSPIR 5906 $1.00
                                    (M1068)

MELODY-AIRES NO. 2 *sac,CCUL
    (Peterson, John W.) 3 soli,pno
    SINGSPIR 5909 $1.00   (M1069)

MELODY IN F see Rubinstein, Anton

MELONS, COUPONS! see Bizet, Georges

MELOPEE see Delden, Lex van

MELPOMENE see Turina, Joaquin

MELTON, CAROL
    From This Day On *sac,CCU
        solo,pno HOPE 113 $2.95   (M1070)

MEMENTO MORI see Bornefeld, Helmut

MEMNON see Schubert, Franz (Peter)

MEMNONIN LAULU see Kilpinen, Yrio

MEMORARE see Bijl, Theo van der

MEMORARE see Diepenbrock, Alphons

MEMORARE, THE see Kreutz, Robert E.

MEMORIAL PRAYER see Brenner, Walter

MEMORIES OF HUNGARY *CCU,Hung
    [Hung/Eng] solo,pno MARKS $2.00
                                    (M1071)

MEMORIES OF ITALY *CCU,It
    [It/Eng] solo,pno MARKS $2.50 (M1072)

MEMORIES OF JOHANN STRAUSS see Strauss,
    Johann

MEMORIES OF LATIN-AMERICA *CCU
  (Recuerdo) [Span/Eng] solo,pno MARKS
  $2.00 Latin-American   (M1073)

MEMORIES OF MEXICO *CCU,Mex
  [Span/Eng] solo,pno MARKS $2.00
                                (M1074)

MEMORIES OF MORNING: NIGHT see Crosse

MEMORIES OF SPAIN *CCU,Span
  [Span/Eng] solo,pno MARKS $2.50
                                (M1075)

MEMORIES OF STEPHEN FOSTER see Foster,
  Stephen Collins

MEMORIES OF SWEDEN *CCU,Swed
  [Swed/Eng] solo,pno MARKS $2.00
                                (M1076)

MEMORIES WITH THE DUSK RETURN see
  Bantock, Granville

MEMORY see Lambelet, Vivien

MEMORY see Leslie, Henry David

MEMORY see Roberton, Hugh Stevenson

MEMORY see Rorem, Ned

MEMORY, A see Anderson, William H.

MEMORY, A see Barry, Katherine

MEMORY, A see Fairchild

MEMORY, A see Ganz, Rudolph

MEMORY, COME HITHER see Birch, Robert
  Fairfax

MEMORY, HITHER COME see Cumming, R.

MEMORY, HITHER COME see Kagen, Sergius

MEMORY OF THE PLAYERS IN A MIRROR AT
  MIDNIGHT, A see Martino, Donald

MEMORY OF YOUR SONG see Dearing,
  Dorothy

MEMORY TRIO see Leslie, Henry David

M'EN ETAIS ALLE see Marti, Esteban

MEN JAG HORDE EN SANG see Nordqvist,
  Gustaf

MEN KON LEBEN NOR MEN LOST NIT see
  Goldstein, Gus

MEN KUNDE VI BARA FA VIND IGEN see
  Soderlundh, Lille Bror

MEN MIN FAGEL MARKS DOCK ICKE see
  Sibelius, Jean, Men Nin Fagel Marks
  Dock Inte

MEN MIN FAGEL MARKS DOCK INTE see
  Sibelius, Jean, Men Nin Fagel Marks
  Dock Inte

MEN NIN FAGEL MARKS DOCK INTE see
  Sibelius, Jean

MEN OF EUREKA AND OTHER SONGS *CCU
  (Jones) solo,pno ALLANS s.p. (M1077)

MEN SEGHET, DIE SWANE see Strategier,
  Herman

MENASCE, JACQUES DE (1905-1960)
  Ballade
    see Quatre Chansons Pour Tenor Et
    Orchestre A Cordes

  Chanson
    see Quatre Chansons Pour Tenor Et
    Orchestre A Cordes

  Deux Lettres D'enfants *CC2U
    solo,pno/inst DURAND s.p.   (M1078)

  Epigramme De Soy Meme
    see Quatre Chansons Pour Tenor Et
    Orchestre A Cordes

  Outrenuit *song cycle
    solo,pno DURAND s.p.   (M1079)

  Quatre Chansons Pour Tenor Et
    Orchestre A Cordes
    T solo,strings DURAND cmplt ed
    s.p., ipa, solo pt,sc
    contains: Ballade; Chanson;
      Epigramme De Soy Meme; Qui La
      Regarde De Mes Yeux   (M1080)

  Qui La Regarde De Mes Yeux
    see Quatre Chansons Pour Tenor Et
    Orchestre A Cordes

MENDELSSOHN-ALBUM PISNI see
  Mendelssohn-Bartholdy, Felix

MENDELSSOHN-BARTHOLDY, FELIX
  (1809-1847)
  Adieu Gentilles Hirondelles
    2 soli,pno ENOCH s.p. voc sc, solo
    pt   (M1081)

  Amour Cache
    solo,pno ENOCH   (M1082)

  Ange Ou Femme
    solo,pno (available in 2 keys)
    ENOCH   (M1083)

  Aubade
    solo,pno (available in 2 keys)
    ENOCH   (M1084)

  Auf Flugeln Des Gesanges *Op.34,No.2
    "En Alas De Mi Canto" [Span] T
    solo,pno RICORDI-ARG BA 8566 s.p.
                                (M1085)
    "Maid Of Ganges" [Ger/Eng] med
    solo,pno (A flat maj) SCHIRM.G
    $1.25   (M1086)
    "On Wings Of Song" high solo,pno (A
    flat maj) ASHDOWN   (M1087)
    "On Wings Of Song" low solo,pno (F
    maj) FISCHER,C S 4669   (M1088)
    "On Wings Of Song" low solo,pno (F
    maj) CENTURY 3427   (M1089)
    "On Wings Of Song" high solo,pno (A
    flat maj) FISCHER,C S 4668
                                (M1090)
    "On Wings Of Song" [Ger/Eng] solo,
    pno CRAMER   (M1091)
    "On Wings Of Song" med solo,pno (G
    maj) ALLANS s.p.   (M1092)
    "On Wings Of Song" high solo,pno (A
    flat maj) ALLANS s.p.   (M1093)
    "On Wings Of Song" low solo,pno (F
    maj) ASHDOWN   (M1094)
    (Northcote) "On Wings Of Song" high
    solo,pno ELKIN 27.3669.01 s.p.
                                (M1095)
    (Northcote) "On Wings Of Song" low
    solo,pno ELKIN 27.3668.04 s.p.
                                (M1096)

  Ave Maria (from Loreley)
    solo,cor,pno DURAND s.p.   (M1097)

  Ballade Printaniere
    solo,pno (available in 2 keys)
    ENOCH   (M1098)

  Barcarolle
    2 soli,pno ENOCH s.p. voc sc, solo
    pt   (M1099)

  Barcarolle Ventienne
    solo,pno (available in 2 keys)
    ENOCH   (M1100)

  Belle Jeunesse *Op.67,No.3
    (Devrivis, Louis) SMezTB soli,pno
    (words adapted by Paul Collin)
    voc sc,solo pt ENOCH see from
    Romances Sans Paroles   (M1101)

  Bonjour Hirondelles
    solo,pno (available in 2 keys)
    ENOCH   (M1102)

  Brise De Mai
    solo,pno (available in 2 keys)
    ENOCH   (M1103)

  But The Lord Is Mindful Of His Own
    (from St. Paul) sac
    A solo,pno (G maj) SCHIRM.G $.85
                                (M1104)

  Canto De Primavera *see
    Fruhlingslied

  Chanson De Printemps *see
    Fruhlingslied

  Collected Edition *CCU
    (Rietz, Julius) contains works for
    a variety of instruments and
    vocal combinations microfiche
    UNIV.MUS.ED. $175.00 reprints of
    Breitkopf & Hartel Editions;
    contains series 1-19   (M1105)

  Comme Ils Ont Fui
    2 soli,pno ENOCH s.p. voc sc, solo
    pt   (M1106)

  Complete Songs Of Mendelssohn, Vols.
    1-4 *CCU
    solo,pno study sc KALMUS 1212-1215
    $1.50, ea.   (M1107)

  Confidences De Fleurs
    solo,pno (available in 2 keys)
    ENOCH   (M1108)

  Det Vare Nog! *see Es Ist Genug

  Douze Duos *CC12L
    [Fr/Ger] SMez soli,pno/inst DURAND
    1077 s.p.   (M1109)

  Duodici Canti A Due Voci *CC12U
    2 soli,pno RICORDI-ENG 45626 s.p.
                                (M1110)

MENDELSSOHN-BARTHOLDY, FELIX (cont'd.)
  Eighteen Duets *CC18L
    [Ger/Dan] SMez soli,pno HANSEN-DEN
    s.p.   (M1111)

  En Alas De Mi Canto *see Auf Flugeln
    Des Gesanges

  Engelterzett (from Elias) sac
    SSA soli,pno (D maj) LIENAU HOS 194
    s.p.   (M1112)

  Es Ist Genug (from Elias) sac
    Bar solo,pno (F sharp min) LIENAU
    HOS 95 s.p.   (M1113)
    "Det Vare Nog!" Bar solo,pno
    GEHRMANS 560 s.p.   (M1114)
    "It Is Enough" B solo,pno NOVELLO
    17.0082.00 s.p.   (M1115)
    "It Is Enough" B solo,pno (F sharp
    maj) SCHIRM.G $1.00   (M1116)

  Est-Il Vrai?
    solo,pno (available in 2 keys)
    ENOCH   (M1117)

  Fleurs De Mai
    2 soli,pno ENOCH s.p. voc sc, solo
    pt   (M1118)

  Fruhlingslied *Op.62,No.6
    "Spring Song" solo,orch (G maj)
    ASHDOWN s.p., ipr   (M1119)
    "Spring Song" med solo,pno (F maj)
    CENTURY 1227   (M1120)
    "Varsang" solo,pno GEHRMANS s.p.
                                (M1121)
    (Devrivis, Louis) "Chanson De
    Printemps" ST soli,opt eq voices,
    pno (words adapted by Paul
    Collin) voc sc,solo pt ENOCH see
    from Romances Sans Paroles
                                (M1122)
    (Pardo) "Canto De Primavera" [Span]
    solo,pno (G maj) RICORDI-ARG
    BA 8572 s.p.   (M1123)
    (Vilbac) "Canto De Primavera"
    [Span] solo,pno (F maj) RICORDI-
    ARG BA 6598 s.p.   (M1124)

  Garland, The
    solo,pno ASHDOWN s.p.   (M1125)

  Hear My Prayer
    solo,pno CRAMER   (M1126)

  Hear Ye, Israel *see Hore Israel

  Hore Israel (from Elias) sac
    S/T solo,pno (B min) LIENAU HOS 96
    s.p.   (M1127)
    A/Bar solo,pno (G min) LIENAU
    HOS 97 s.p.   (M1128)
    "Hear Ye, Israel" S solo,pno
    NOVELLO 17.0066.09 s.p.   (M1129)
    "Hear Ye, Israel" S solo,pno (B
    min) SCHIRM.G $1.00   (M1130)

  Hostsang
    see NY SAMLING SANGDUETTER, HEFT 1

  I Am A Roamer
    solo,pno (D maj) ASHDOWN   (M1131)

  I Waited For The Lord *see Ich
    Harrette Des Herrn

  Ich Harrette Des Herrn (from Hymn Of
    Praise) sac
    "I Waited For The Lord" SA soli,pno
    WATERLOO $.65   (M1132)
    "I Waited For The Lord" med-high
    solo,pno (C maj) BOSTON $1.50
                                (M1133)
    "I Waited For The Lord" high solo,
    pno (E flat maj) BOSTON $1.50
                                (M1134)
    "I Waited For The Lord" [Ger/Eng]
    SMez soli,pno SCHIRM.G $.85
                                (M1135)

  If With All Your Hearts *see So Ihr
    Mich Von Ganzen Herzen

  In Heavenly Love Abiding *sac
    (Deis) med-high solo,pno (A flat
    maj) SCHIRM.G $.60   (M1136)

  Is Not His Word Like A Fire (from
    Elias) sac
    B solo,pno NOVELLO 17.0081.02 s.p.
                                (M1137)

  It Is Enough *see Es Ist Genug

  Jag Tackar Dig, Herre Gud (from
    Elias)
    solo,pno GEHRMANS 561 s.p. (M1138)

  Jerusalem! (from Paulus) sac
    A solo,pno (G maj) LIENAU HOS 110
    s.p.   (M1139)
    S solo,pno (B flat maj) LIENAU
    HOS 109 s.p.   (M1140)

MENDELSSOHN-BARTHOLDY, FELIX (cont'd.)

La Premiere Violette
  solo,pno (available in 2 keys)
  ENOCH   (M1141)

Lasst Uns Singen (from Paulus) sac
  S solo,pno (F maj) LIENAU HOS 111
  s.p.   (M1142)

L'automne
  2 soli,pno DURAND s.p. see from
  DOUZE DOUS   (M1143)

Le Bal Des Fleurs
  2 soli,pno DURAND s.p. see from
  DOUZE DOUS   (M1144)

L'Eden, Aux Bord Du Gange
  Mez/Bar solo,pno/inst DURAND s.p.
                                   (M1145)

Les Bles
  2 soli,pno DURAND s.p. see from
  DOUZE DOUS   (M1146)

Les Elfes
  solo,pno/inst DURAND s.p.   (M1147)
  [Fr] solo,acap oct DURAND s.p.
                                   (M1148)

Les Oiseaux Voyageurs
  2 soli,pno DURAND s.p. see from
  DOUZE DOUS   (M1149)

Les Plaintes De Suleika
  solo,pno/inst DURAND s.p.   (M1150)

Lord God Of Abraham (from Elijah) sac
  B solo,pno (E flat maj) SCHIRM.G
  $.85   (M1151)
  B solo,pno NOVELLO 17.0099.05 s.p.
                                   (M1152)

Madrigal
  2 soli,pno ENOCH s.p. voc sc, solo
  pt   (M1153)

Maid Of Ganges *see Auf Flugeln Des
  Gesanges

Mendelssohn-Album Pisni *CCU
  solo,pno SUPRAPHON s.p.   (M1154)

Nineteen Duets *CC19U
  (Friedlander) [Ger] 2 high soli/
  high solo&med solo,pno PETERS
  1747 $5.50   (M1155)

O For The Wings Of A Dove *sac
  S solo,pno NOVELLO 17.0133.09 s.p.
                                   (M1156)
  solo,pno CRAMER   (M1157)
  low solo,pno (E flat maj) ASHDOWN
                                   (M1158)
  med solo,pno (F maj) ASHDOWN
                                   (M1159)
  high solo,pno (G maj) ASHDOWN
                                   (M1160)
  med solo,pno (F maj) ALLANS s.p.
                                   (M1161)
  high solo,pno (G maj) ALLANS s.p.
                                   (M1162)

O God, Have Mercy (from St. Paul) sac
  B solo,pno (B min) SCHIRM.G $.85
                                   (M1163)

O, Lugna Din Sjal (from Elias)
  solo,pno LUNDQUIST s.p.   (M1164)

O Nuit Tranquille *Op.80,No.9
  (Devrivis, Louis) SATB soli,pno
  (words adapted by Paul Collin)
  voc sc,solo pt ENOCH see from
  Romances Sans Paroles   (M1165)

O Rest In The Lord (from Elias) sac
  A solo,pno NOVELLO 17.0138.10 s.p.
                                   (M1166)
  high solo,pno (E flat maj) CRAMER
                                   (M1167)
  low solo,pno (C maj) CRAMER   (M1168)
  A solo,pno (C maj) SCHIRM.G $1.25
                                   (M1169)
  low solo,pno (C maj) ASHDOWN
                                   (M1170)
  high solo,pno (E maj) ASHDOWN
                                   (M1171)
  med solo,pno (D maj) ASHDOWN
                                   (M1172)
  med-high solo,pno (E flat maj)
  ASHDOWN   (M1173)

Om Av Allt Ert Hjarta I Mig Soken
  *see Sei Stille Dem Herrn

On Wings Of Faith *sac
  med solo,pno (A flat maj) SCHIRM.G
  $.75   (M1174)

On Wings Of Song *see Auf Flugeln
  Des Gesanges

Open The Gates Of The Temple *sac
  high solo,pno (G maj) FISCHER,C
  V 1948   (M1175)
  med-high solo,pno (F maj) FISCHER,C
  V 1949   (M1176)
  med solo,pno (E maj) FISCHER,C
  V 1950   (M1177)

MENDELSSOHN-BARTHOLDY, FELIX (cont'd.)

  med-low solo,pno (E flat maj)
  FISCHER,C V 1951   (M1178)
  low solo,pno (D maj) FISCHER,C
  V 1952   (M1179)
  B solo,pno (C maj) FISCHER,C V 1953
                                   (M1180)

Ou S'en Vont Mes Reves
  see LA MUSIQUE, HUITIEME CAHIER
  solo,pno/inst DURAND s.p.   (M1181)

Pres De Toi
  2 soli,pno ENOCH s.p. voc sc, solo
  pt   (M1182)

Reveil Du Coeur
  solo,pno (available in 2 keys)
  ENOCH   (M1183)

Romances Sans Paroles *see Belle
  Jeunesse, Op.67,No.3; Chanson De
  Printemps, Op.62,No.6; O Nuit
  Tranquille, Op.80,No.9; Sur Les
  Ailes Des Songes, Op.67,No.5   (M1184)

Roses Fanees
  solo,pno (available in 2 keys)
  ENOCH   (M1185)

Sei Getreu (from Paulus) sac
  T solo,pno (C maj) LIENAU HOS 113
  s.p.   (M1186)
  Mez solo,pno (B flat maj) LIENAU
  HOS 113A s.p.   (M1187)
  Bar solo,pno (A maj) LIENAU HOS 114
  s.p.   (M1188)

Sei Stille Dem Herrn (from Elias) sac
  S solo,pno (G maj) LIENAU HOS 98
  s.p.   (M1189)
  A solo,pno (C maj) LIENAU HOS 99
  s.p.   (M1190)
  "Om Av Allt Ert Hjarta I Mig Soken"
  Bar solo,pno (B maj) GEHRMANS
  s.p.   (M1191)
  "Om Av Allt Ert Hjarta I Mig Soken"
  T solo,pno (D flat maj) GEHRMANS
  s.p.   (M1192)

Sixteen Two-Part Songs *CC16L
  [Ger/Eng] 2 soli,pno SCHIRM.G 377
  $3.00   (M1193)

So Ihr Mich Von Ganzen Herzen (from
  Elias) sac
  T solo,pno (E flat maj) LIENAU
  HOS 100 s.p.   (M1194)
  Bar solo,pno (C maj) LIENAU HOS 101
  s.p.   (M1195)
  "If With All Your Hearts" T solo,
  pno NOVELLO 17.0071.05 s.p.   (M1196)
  "If With All Your Hearts" T solo,
  pno (C maj) SCHIRM.G $1.00   (M1197)
  "If With All Your Heats" T solo,
  pno (E flat maj) SCHIRM.G $1.00 (M1198)

Sontagsmorgen
  "Sunnuntaiaamu" 2 soli,pno FAZER
  F 2818 s.p.   (M1199)

Spring Song *see Fruhlingslied

Sunnuntaiaamu *see Sontagsmorgen

Sur Les Ailes Des Songes *Op.67,No.5
  (Devrivis, Louis) SATB soli,pno
  (words adapted by Paul Collin)
  voc sc,solo pt ENOCH see from
  Romances Sans Paroles   (M1200)

Sur Les Ailes Du Reve
  solo,pno (available in 2 keys)
  ENOCH   (M1201)

Twenty Selected Songs *CC20U
  [Ger] high solo,pno PETERS 4570A
  $4.75; med solo,pno PETERS 4570B
  $4.75   (M1202)

Varsang *see Fruhlingslied

Ve Dem Att Fran Mig De Vika (from
  Elias) sac
  A solo,pno GEHRMANS s.p.   (M1203)

Villanelle
  see LA MUSIQUE, SIXIEME CAHIER
  solo,pno/inst DURAND s.p.   (M1204)

Vogue, Leger Zephir
  2 soli,pno DURAND s.p. see from
  DOUZE DOUS   (M1205)

MENDELSSOHN JA RUBINSTEININ DUETTOJA
  *CC16U
  2 soli,pno FAZER F 3589 s.p. contains
  works by: Mendelssohn, Felix;
  Rubinstein, Anton   (M1206)

MENDIANTS see Rhene-Baton

MENELAUS see Vaughan Williams, Ralph

MENEUT ROSE see Ganne, Louis Gaston

MENGELBERG, KAREL (1902-   )
  Ah M'abbandoni - In Questa Selva
  Oscura
  B solo,vla,cembalo, viola da gamba
  DONEMUS s.p.   (M1207)

  Dag Aan Dag Komt Hij En Gaat
  see Liederen Van R. Tagore "The
  Gardener"

  Liederen Van R. Tagore "The Gardener"
  [Fr/Dut/Eng] S solo,2fl,2ob,2clar,
  2bsn,4horn,3trp,3trom,tuba,timp,
  perc,cel,2harp,strings, carillon
  DONEMUS s.p.
  contains: Dag Aan Dag Komt Hij En
  Gaat; Lief Ga Niet Heen Zonder
  Afscheid; Liej, Mijn Hart
  Verlangt   (M1208)

  Lief Ga Niet Heen Zonder Afscheid
  see Liederen Van R. Tagore "The
  Gardener"

  Liej, Mijn Hart Verlangt
  see Liederen Van R. Tagore "The
  Gardener"

MENGELBERG, RUDOLF (1892-1959)
  Adore Te Devote *sac
  solo,pno BROEKMANS 221 s.p.   (M1209)

  Adoro Te
  A solo,2fl,3ob,3clar,3bsn,3horn,
  2trp,strings DONEMUS s.p.   (M1210)

  Afscheid
  see Vijf Liederen Op Oud-
  Nederlandsche Teksten

  Ballade Van Den Boer
  narrator,2fl,3ob,3clar,2bsn,4horn,
  2trp,3trom,tuba,timp,cel,harp,
  strings DONEMUS s.p.   (M1211)

  Chamber Music *song cycle
  [Eng] Mez solo,pno BROEKMANS 715
  s.p.   (M1212)

  Die Stem Van Suid-Africa
  med solo,pno EIGEN UITGAVE s.p.
                                   (M1213)

  Drie Liederen
  A solo,pno DONEMUS s.p.
  contains: Kind; Moeder; Toekomst
                                   (M1214)

  Drinklied
  see Vijf Liederen Op Oud-
  Nederlandsche Teksten

  Eichendorff Lieder I *CCU
  solo,pno BROEKMANS 301 s.p.   (M1215)

  Haec Dies *sac
  high solo,pno EIGEN UITGAVE s.p.
                                   (M1216)

  Hart Van Vlaanderen
  solo,pno BROEKMANS 283 s.p.   (M1217)

  Kind
  see Drie Liederen

  Levensles
  see Vijf Liederen Op Oud-
  Nederlandsche Teksten

  Magnificat
  A solo,2fl,2ob,3clar,2bsn,3horn,
  trp,2trom,timp,strings DONEMUS
  s.p.   (M1218)

  Meibloemken
  see Vijf Liederen Op Oud-
  Nederlandsche Teksten

  Minneklacht
  see Vijf Liederen Op Oud-
  Nederlandsche Teksten

  Moeder
  see Drie Liederen

  Salve Regina *sac
  S solo,pno BROEKMANS 230 s.p.
                                   (M1219)

  Sleep Little Baby
  solo,pno BROEKMANS 340 s.p.   (M1220)

  Toekomst
  see Drie Liederen

  Twee Geestelijke Liederen *CC2U
  S solo,org BROEKMANS 401 s.p.
                                   (M1221)

  Valse De Poupee
  med solo,pno ROSSUM s.p.   (M1222)

  Vijf Liederen Op Oud-Nederlandsche
  Teksten
  med solo,pno MUNSTER s.p.
  contains: Afscheid; Drinklied;
  Levensles; Meibloemken;

MENGELBERG, RUDOLF (cont'd.)

    Minneklacht   (M1223)

MENIER, G.
  Pourquoi Je M'en Vais
    solo,pno ENOCH   (M1224)

MENNYT PAIVA see Ranta, Sulho

MENOTTI, GIAN CARLO (1911-   )
  Black Swan, The (from Medium, The)
    [Fr/Eng] Mez solo,pno (G min)
    SCHIRM.G $.85   (M1225)

  Canti Della Lontananza *CCU
    [It] solo,pno SCHIRM.G $2.50
                                        (M1226)

  Canti Della Lontananza (Dedicati A
    Elisabeth Schwarzkopf) *CCU
    solo,pno RICORDI-ENG 131417 s.p.
                                        (M1227)

  Che Gli Dirai Quel Giorno (from Last
    Savage, The)
    "How Can My Lips Deny It?" solo,pno
    BELWIN $1.50   (M1228)

  Empty-Handed Traveler, The (from
    Consul, The)
    med-low solo,pno SCHIRM.G $.60
                                        (M1229)

  Hero, The
    med solo,pno SCHIRM.G $.75   (M1230)

  How Can My Lips Deny It? *see Che
    Gli Dirai Quel Giorno

  Lullaby (from Consul, The)
    low solo,pno (F maj) SCHIRM.G $.85
                                        (M1231)

  Steal Me, Sweet Thief (from Old Maid
    And The Thief, The)
    S solo,pno BELWIN NY 1703 $1.00
                                        (M1232)

    solo,pno BELWIN $1.50   (M1233)

  Till The Sandman Comes
    high solo,pno BELWIN $1.50   (M1234)

  To This We've Come (from Consul, The)
    high solo,pno SCHIRM.G $1.50 (M1235)

  Vola Intanto L'ora Insonne (from
    Amelia Al Ballo)
    "While I Waste These Precious
    Hours" S solo,pno BELWIN $1.25
                                        (M1236)

  While I Waste These Precious Hours
    *see Vola Intanto L'ora Insonne

MENS JEG LEVER see Gronneberg, Hanna

MEN'S VOICES NO. I *sac,CC62UL
  4 male soli,pno LILLENAS MB-125 $1.50
                                        (M1237)

MEN'S VOICES NO. II *sac,CC46UL
  4 male soli,pno LILLENAS MB-126 $1.50
                                        (M1238)

MEN'S VOICES NO. III *sac,CC47UL
  4 male soli,pno LILLENAS MB-127 $1.50
                                        (M1239)

MENSAGEM see Homberg, Johannes

MENSCH, DURF TE LEVEN see Witte, D.

MENSONGES see Legay, Marcel

MENTA I FARIGOLA see Toldra, Eduardo

MENTIR, MENTIR see Guiraud, Ernest

MENTON see Mouton, H.

MENTRE CADE LA NEVE see Cimara, Pietro

MENTRE FRA MILLE FIORI see Petz (Pez),
  Johann Christoph

MENTRE TI LASCIO, O FIGLIA see Mozart,
  Wolfgang Amadeus

MENUET see Chaminade, Cecile

MENUET see Exaudet

MENUET see Mariotte, Antoine

MENUET CHANTE see Rameau, Jean-Philippe

MENUET DE LA PRINCESSE see Vieu, Jane

MENUETS DE VADE see Cuvillier, Charles

MENUETT see Trunk, Richard

MEPRIS see Legay, Marcel

MER HAHN EN NEUE OBERKEET see Bach,
  Johann Sebastian

MER, SOLEIL ET ROSE see Schumann,
  Robert (Alexander)

MERCADANTE, G. SAVERIO (1795-1870)
  Salve Regina *sac
    Mez/Bar solo,pno FORLIVESI 11267
    s.p.   (M1240)

MERCE', DILETTE AMICHE see Verdi,
  Giuseppe

MERCE DILETTE AMICHI see Donizetti,
  Gaetano

MERCENIER, P.
  Le Poulet Et Le Renard
    solo,pno/inst DURAND s.p.   (M1241)

  Le Singe Qui Montre La Lanterne
    Magique
    solo,pno/inst DURAND s.p.   (M1242)

  Les Lunettes
    solo,pno/inst DURAND s.p.   (M1243)

MERCER
  Each Step I Take *sac
    solo,pno BENSON S5408-R $1.00
                                        (M1244)

  I Found It All In Jesus *sac
    solo,pno BENSON S6014-R $1.00
                                        (M1245)

  If I Could Sing A Thousand Melodies
    *sac
    solo,pno BENSON S6468-RS $1.00
                                        (M1246)

  Nailing My Sins To His Cross *sac
    solo,pno BENSON S7128-S $1.00
                                        (M1247)

  Song Was Born, A *sac
    solo,pno BENSON S5060-R $1.00
                                        (M1248)

  Through An Empty Tomb *sac
    solo,pno BENSON S8181-S $1.00
                                        (M1249)

  Way That He Loves, The *sac
    solo,pno BENSON S8080-RS $1.00
                                        (M1250)

MERCER, W. ELMO
  Recorded Gospel Hits *sac,CC12L
    solo,pno BENSON B0870 $2.50 (M1251)

MERCI CHER PEUPLE see Wagner, Richard

MERCILESS BEAUTY see Vaughan Williams,
  Ralph

MERCURE, PIERRE (1927-   )
  Colloque
    solo,pno BERANDOL BER 1323 $1.50
                                        (M1252)

MERCY, LORD *sac,gospel
    solo,pno ABER.GRP. $1.50   (M1253)

MERCY, PITY, PEACE, AND LOVE see
  Clarke, Henry Leland

MERE see Rasse, Francois

MERE see Schoemaker, Maurice

MERE see Peeters, Flor

MERE SOIS MES AMOURS see Delbruck, J.

MEREL see Koetsier, Jan

MERELLA see Merikanto, Oskar

MERENKUNINKAAN TYTAR see Sonninen, Ahti

MERENRANTAKUISTILLA see Sibelius, Jean,
  Pa Verandan Vid Havet

MERIKANTO, AARRE (1893-1958)
  Roster I Morkret *Op.7,No.2
    solo,pno FAZER F 881 s.p.   (M1254)

  Tretton Ar *Op.7,No.1
    solo,pno FAZER F 880 s.p.   (M1255)

MERIKANTO, OSKAR (1868-1924)
  Ainut Hetki *see Den Enda Stunden

  Aiti Ja Kulkuripoika
    "Modern Och Tiggargossen" 2 soli,
    pno FAZER F 534 s.p. see from
    Fyra Duetter   (M1256)

  An I Minnet Jag Atervander *see
    Vallinkorvan Laulu

  Appelblommor *see Omenankukat

  Auf Dem Meer *see Merella

  Barnet *see Lapselle

  Bygatan Utfor *Op.32,No.4
    see Fyra Sanger

  Dar Bjorkarna Susa
    solo,pno/org ERIKS K 281   (M1257)

  De Vackraste Solosanger, Vol. 1
    *CC24L
    solo,pno F 5547 s.p.   (M1258)

MERIKANTO, OSKAR (cont'd.)

  De Vackraste Solosanger, Vol. 2
    *CC20L
    solo,pno FAZER F 5548 s.p.   (M1259)

  Den Enda Stunden *Op.36,No.1
    "Ainut Hetki" see Tre Sanger II

  Du Mitt Klara Hjartegull *see Kullan
    Murunen

  Ein Kindermarchen Am Kaminfeuer *see
    En Barnsaga Vid Brasen

  En Barnsaga Vid Brasan
    solo,pno GEHRMANS s.p.   (M1260)

  En Barnsaga Vid Brasen *Op.82,No.3
    "Ein Kindermarchen Am Kaminfeuer"
    solo,pno FAZER 41 s.p.   (M1261)

  Erloschene Glut *see Kuin Hiipuva
    Hiillos Tummentuu

  Fairy Story By The Fire
    med solo,pno BELWIN $1.50   (M1262)
    high solo,pno BELWIN $1.50   (M1263)
    low solo,pno BELWIN $1.50   (M1264)

  Fairy Story By The Fire, A
    [Eng/Fr] med solo,kbd CHESTER s.p.
                                        (M1265)

  Finska Sangkompositioner II
    solo,pno FAZER W 1011 s.p.
    contains: Kevatlinnuile Etelassa,
    "Till Flyttfaglarna I Sodern",
    Op.11,No.1; Muistellessa,
    "Kanjag Val Glomma", Op.11,
    No.2; Yolla, "I Natten", Op.11,
    No.3   (M1266)

  Finska Sangkompositioner IV
    solo,pno FAZER W 1016 s.p.
    contains: Laula Tytto, Op.30,
    No.2; Laulan Lasta Nukkumahan,
    Op.30,No.1; Myrskylintu, Op.30,
    No.4; Tule, Op.30,No.3   (M1267)

  Finska Sangkompositioner V
    solo,pno FAZER W 1023 s.p.
    contains: Oi, Minne Emon Lintunen
    Lensi, "O, Vart Flog Moderns
    Gyllene Fagel", Op.52,No.2;
    Omenankukat, "Appelblommor",
    Op.52,No.1   (M1268)

  Finska Sangkompositioner VII *see
    Kevatlaulu, "Varsang", Op.58,
    No.4; Lapselle, "Barnet", Op.58,
    No.2   (M1269)

  Folksang *Op.90,No.1
    solo,pno FAZER F 960 s.p.   (M1270)

  Folkvisa *see Kansanlaulu

  Fyra Duetter *see Aiti Ja
    Kulkuripoika, "Modern Och
    Tiggargossen"; Leikitaanko,
    "Ska'vi Leka"; Oi Kiitos, Sa
    Luojani Armollinen, "Pris Ske
    Dig, Allsmaktige Skapare God";
    Soipa Kieli, "Ljudande Strang"
                                        (M1271)

  Fyra Sanger
    solo,pno FAZER W 1017 s.p.
    contains: Bygatan Utfor, Op.32,
    No.4; Han Kulkevi Kuin Yli
    Kukkien, Op.32,No.3; Ma Lykkaan
    Purteni Laineillen, Op.32,No.1;
    Se Kvisten Skvaller, Op.32,No.2
                                        (M1272)

  God Natt *see Hyvaa Yota

  Han Kulkevi Kuin Yli Kukkien *Op.32,
    No.3
    see Fyra Sanger

  Hyvaa Yota *Op.75,No.1
    "God Natt" see Tre Sanger III

  I Natten *see Yolla

  Ikavissa
    see Tukkijoella I

  Jag Lever *see Ma Elan

  Juhannustulilla *CC9L
    solo,pno FAZER F 239 s.p.   (M1273)

  Kanjag Val Glomma *see Muistellessa

  Kansanlaulu *Op.90,No.1
    "Folkvisa" 2 soli,pno FAZER F 1460
    s.p.   (M1274)

  Kevatlaulu *Op.58,No.4
    "Varsang" solo,pno FAZER 1025D s.p.
    see from Finska Sangkompositioner
    VII   (M1275)

  Kevatlinnuile Etelassa *Op.11,No.1
    "Till Flyttfaglarna I Sodern" see
    Finska Sangkompositioner II

MERIKANTO, OSKAR (cont'd.)

Klagen *see Soi Vienosti Murheeni
    Soitto

Kom Med Mig *see Tule Kanssani

Kottarainen *Op.36,No.2
    "Staren" see Tre Sanger II

Kuin Hiipuva Hiillos Tummentuu
    *Op.47,No.2
    "Erloschene Glut" solo,pno FAZER
    W 1020B s.p.   (M1276)

Kullan Murunen *Op.20,No.1
    "Du Mitt Klara Hjartegull" see Tre
    Sanger I

Kun Nukahdan Katsoen Tahtiin *see
    Somnar Jag Med Blicken Fast

Kun Paiva Paistaa *Op.24,No.1
    "Nar Solen Lyser" solo,pno FAZER
    W 1015 s.p. contains also:
    Vallinkorvan Laulu, "An I Minnet
    Jag Atervander", Op.24,No.2
                                     (M1277)

Kun Vaan Laulaa Saan
    solo,pno FAZER F 117 s.p.   (M1278)

Kuolema Kannelta Loi
    solo,pno FAZER F 118 s.p.   (M1279)

Laatokka *Op.83,No.1
    "Ladoga" solo,pno FAZER W 1169 s.p.
                                     (M1280)

Ladoga *see Laatokka

Lapselle *Op.58,No.2
    "Barnet" solo,pno FAZER W 1025B
    s.p. see from Finska
    Sangkompositioner VII   (M1281)

Lauantai-Ilta *Op.75,No.2
    "Lordagsafton" see Tre Sanger III

Laula Tytto *Op.30,No.2
    see Finska Sangkompositioner IV

Laulan Lasta Nukkumahan *Op.30,No.1
    see Finska Sangkompositioner IV

Leikitaanko
    "Ska'vi Leka" 2 soli,pno FAZER
    F 535 s.p. see from Fyra Duetter
                                     (M1282)

Lemmenhenki
    see Tukkijoella I

Liknelse *Op.20,No.3
    "Vertaus" see Tre Sanger I

Ljudande Strang *see Soipa Kieli

Lordagsafton *see Lauantai-Ilta

Louhen Hyvastijatto Tyttarelleen
    solo,pno FAZER F 604 s.p.   (M1283)

Ma Elan *Op.71,No.1
    "Jag Lever" solo,pno FAZER F 670
    s.p.   (M1284)

Ma Lykkaan Purteni Laineillen
    *Op.32,No.1
    see Fyra Sanger

Merella *Op.47,No.4
    "Auf Dem Meer" solo,pno FAZER
    W 1658 s.p.   (M1285)

Miksi Laulan *Op.20,No.2
    "Varfor Sjunger Jag" see Tre Sanger
    I

Modern Och Tiggargossen *see Aiti Ja
    Kulkuripoika

Muistellessa *Op.11,No.2
    "Kanjag Val Glomma" see Finska
    Sangkompositioner II

Mustalainen *Op.22,No.1
    solo,pno FAZER W 883 s.p.   (M1286)

Myrskylintu *Op.30,No.4
    see Finska Sangkompositioner IV

Nar Solen Lyser *see Kun Paiva
    Paistaa

Niin Sinua Katsoin, Neiti *Op.81,
    No.3
    solo,pno FAZER F 873 s.p.   (M1287)

O, Vart Flog Moderns Gyllene Fagel
    *see Oi, Minne Emon Lintunen
    Lensi

Oi Kiitos, Sa Luojani Armollinen
    "Pris Ske Dig, Allsmaktige Skapare
    God" 2 soli,pno FAZER F 533 s.p.
    see from Fyra Duetter   (M1288)

MERIKANTO, OSKAR (cont'd.)

Oi, Minne Emon Lintunen Lensi
    *Op.52,No.2
    "O, Vart Flog Moderns Gyllene
    Fagel" see Finska
    Sangkompositioner V

Omenankukat *Op.52,No.1
    "Appelblommor" see Finska
    Sangkompositioner V

Onnelliset *CC2U
    2 soli,pno FAZER F 199 s.p. (M1289)

Onneton *Op.2,No.3
    see Suomalaisia Laulusavellyksia

Pai, Pai Paitaressu *Op.2,No.1
    "Schlaf, Schlaf Herzensliebling"
    see Suomalaisia Laulusavellyksia

Pris Ske Dig, Allsmaktige Skapare God
    *see Oi Kiitos, Sa Luojani
    Armollinen

Rakkaus
    see Tukkijoella I

Schlaf, Schlaf Herzensliebling *see
    Pai, Pai Paitaressu

Se Kvisten Skvaller *Op.32,No.2
    see Fyra Sanger

Ska'vi Leka *see Leikitaanko

Soi Vienosti Murheeni Soitto *Op.36,
    No.3
    "Klagen" see Tre Sanger II

Soipa Kieli
    "Ljudande Strang" 2 soli,pno FAZER
    F 532 s.p. see from Fyra Duetter
                                     (M1290)

Somnar Jag Med Blicken Fast *Op.54
    "Kun Nukahdan Katsoen Tahtiin"
    solo,pno FAZER W 1024 s.p.
                                     (M1291)

Staren *see Kottarainen

Suomalaisia Laulusavellyksia
    solo,pno FAZER W 1009 s.p.
    contains: Onneton, Op.2,No.3;
    Pai, Pai Paitaressu, "Schlaf,
    Schlaf Herzensliebling", Op.2,
    No.1; Vanha Mummo, Op.2,No.2
                                     (M1292)

Till Flyttfaglarna I Sodern *see
    Kevatlinnuile Etelassa

Tre Sanger I
    solo,pno FAZER W 1014 s.p.
    contains: Kullan Murunen, "Du
    Mitt Klara Hjartegull", Op.20,
    No.1; Liknelse, "Vertaus",
    Op.20,No.3; Miksi Laulan,
    "Varfor Sjunger Jag", Op.20,
    No.2   (M1293)

Tre Sanger II
    solo,pno FAZER W 1018 s.p.
    contains: Den Enda Stunden,
    "Ainut Hetki", Op.36,No.1;
    Kottarainen, "Staren", Op.36,
    No.2; Soi Vienosti Murheeni
    Soitto, "Klagen", Op.36,No.3
                                     (M1294)

Tre Sanger III
    solo,pno FAZER F 756 s.p.
    contains: Hyvaa Yota, "God Natt",
    Op.75,No.1; Lauantai-Ilta,
    "Lordagsafton", Op.75,No.2;
    Tule Kanssani, "Kom Med Mig",
    Op.75,No.3   (M1295)

Tukkijoella I
    solo,pno FAZER F 249 s.p.
    contains: Ikavissa; Lemmenhenki;
    Rakkaus; Tuulan Tei;
    Tuulenhenki; Voi Minun Nuorta
    Sydantani   (M1296)

Tule *Op.30,No.3
    see Finska Sangkompositioner IV

Tule Kanssani *Op.75,No.3
    "Kom Med Mig" see Tre Sanger III

Tuulan Tei
    see Tukkijoella I
    solo,pno GEHRMANS s.p.   (M1297)

Tuulenhenki
    see Tukkijoella I

Vallinkorvan Laulu *Op.24,No.2
    "An I Minnet Jag Atervander" see
    Merikanto, Oskar, Kun Paiva
    Paistaa

Vanha Mummo *Op.2,No.2
    see Suomalaisia Laulusavellyksia

MERIKANTO, OSKAR (cont'd.)

Varfor Sjunger Jag *see Miksi Laulan

Varsang *see Kevatlaulu

Venezianska Visor *CCU
    solo,pno FAZER F 377-379 s.p., ea.
                                     (M1298)

Vertaus *see Liknelse

Voi Minun Nuorta Sydantani
    see Tukkijoella I

Yolla *Op.11,No.3
    "I Natten" see Finska
    Sangkompositioner II

MERKU, PAVLE (1927-   )
    Divertimento I *Op.42, song cycle
    T solo,fl,ob,clar,bsn,horn,trp,
    trom,perc,harp,pno,strings rental
    sc DRUSTVO DSS 209, voc sc
    DRUSTVO DSS 220   (M1299)

Kind Death *see Prijazna Smrt

Midday Psalm *see Opoldanski Psalm

Opoldanski Psalm *sac
    "Midday Psalm" solo,pno DRUSTVO
    DSS 15 rental   (M1300)

Oui O Altrove
    Bar solo,orch ZERBONI 7701 s.p.
                                     (M1301)

Prijazna Smrt *Op.34, song cycle
    "Kind Death" B solo,pno DRUSTVO
    DSS 260 rental   (M1302)

MERMAID REMEMBERED see Binkerd, Gordon

MERMAID'S SONG see Scott, Cyril Meir

MERMAIDS SONG, THE see Haydn, (Franz)
    Joseph, Die Seejungfer

MERRIWEATHER, ROY
    Christians Tribulation *see Hubbard,
    H.

Great Joy *sac,gospel
    solo,pno SAUL AVE   (M1303)

He Said He Would Deliver Me *see
    Redd, G.C.

I Am Thine *see Hubbard, H.

I'm Sheltered In His Arms *see
    Hubbard, H.

New Way Of Life, A *see Hubbard, H.

They Shall Be Mine *see Hubbard, H.

MERRY MAY, THE see Hively, Wells

MERRY MONTH OF MAY see Keel, Frederick

MERRY MONTH OF MAY, THE see Stanford,
    Charles Villiers

MERRY PIPE see Sharpe, Evelyn

MERRY ROUNDELAY see Lang

MERRY WANDERER see Shaw, Martin

MERRY WIFE, THE see Cannon, (Jack)
    Phillip, La Bien Mariee

MERSON, OLIVER
    Dans Le Parc
    see ALBUM MODERNE

MES AMIS ECOUTEZ L'HISTOIRE see Adam,
    Adolphe-Charles

MES EXERCISES see Perier, Jean

MES PEINES ET ENNUIS see Le Roy, A.

MES PENSERS see Hartmann, Johan Peder
    Emilius

MESANGE see Orthel, Leon

MESRITZ VAN VELTHUYSEN, ANNIE
    (1897-1965)
    Adieu
    see Liederen

Barque D'or
    see Liederen

Deux Poems *CC2U
    solo,pno BROEKMANS 161 s.p. (M1304)

Die Alte Kirche
    A solo,pno DONEMUS s.p.   (M1305)

Drie Liederen Van M. Luka
    Mez solo,fl,vcl,pno DONEMUS s.p.
    contains: Le Lait; L'enfant Au
    Paradis; L'enfant Disait Un

MESRITZ VAN VELTHUYSEN, ANNIE (cont'd.)

Soir   (M1306)

Le Bonheur
see Liederen

Le Lait
see Drie Liederen Van M. Luka

L'enfant Au Paradis
see Drie Liederen Van M. Luka

L'enfant Disait Un Soir
see Drie Liederen Van M. Luka

Liederen
S solo,2fl,2ob,2clar,bsn,2horn,
2trp,cel,harp,strings DONEMUS
s.p.
contains: Adieu; Barque D'or; Le
Bonheur   (M1307)

Riwajak Kampong
T/A solo,ob,pno,2vln,vla,vcl
DONEMUS s.p.   (M1308)

Trois Chansons *CC3U
solo,pno BROEKMANS 200 s.p. (M1309)

Twee Liederen *CC2U
solo,pno BROEKMANS 187 s.p. (M1310)

Two Songs *CC2U
solo,pno BROEKMANS 253 s.p. (M1311)

MESSAGE see Brahms, Johannes, Botschaft

MESSAGE D'AMOUR see Holmes, Alfred

MESSAGE TO DENMARK HILL see Wuorinen,
Charles

MESSAGER, ANDRE (1853-1929)

A La Tasse, Au Verre (from Francois
Les Bas-Bleus)
solo,pno ENOCH s.p.   (M1312)

A Toi J'avais Donne Ma Vie (from
Francois Les Bas-Bleus)
solo,pno ENOCH s.p.   (M1313)

A Une Fiance
[Fr] high solo,pno CHOUDENS C21
s.p.   (M1314)
[Fr] med solo,pno CHOUDENS C23 s.p.
(M1315)
[Fr] med solo,pno CHOUDENS C22 s.p.
(M1316)

Adieu, Ma Fanchon (from Francois Les
Bas-Bleus)
solo,pno ENOCH s.p.   (M1317)

Amis, Le Grand Jour Est Venu (from La
Fauvette Du Temple)
solo,pno ENOCH s.p.   (M1318)

Amour, Amour, Quel Est Donc Ton
Pouvoir (from Les Dragons De
L'Imperatrice)
solo,pno ENOCH s.p.   (M1319)
S solo,pno ENOCH s.p.   (M1320)

Arioso
solo,orch ENOCH rental see from
Melodies   (M1321)
solo,pno ENOCH s.p. see also Quinze
Melodies   (M1322)

Astique Ton Fourniment (from Francois
Les Bas-Bleus)
solo,pno ENOCH s.p.   (M1323)

Au Bruit De L'eau Qui Coule (from
Isoline)
solo,pno ENOCH s.p.   (M1324)

Avec Soin, Formez Chaque Lettre (from
Francois Les Bas-Bleus)
2 soli,pno ENOCH s.p.   (M1325)

Beau Cent-Garde, Votre Cuirasse (from
Les Dragons De L'Imperatrice)
solo,pno ENOCH s.p.   (M1326)

C'est Du Vin De Gascogne (from La
Bernaise)
solo,pno ENOCH s.p.   (M1327)

C'est Francois Les Bas-Bleus (from
Francois Les Bas-Bleus)
T solo,pno ENOCH s.p.   (M1328)
Bar solo,pno ENOCH s.p.   (M1329)

C'est Toi Que Je Revois (from
Francois Les Bas-Bleus)
solo,pno ENOCH s.p.   (M1330)

Chacun, Madame, A Son Aspect (from La
Bernaise)
solo,pno ENOCH s.p.   (M1331)

Chanson De La Musique Militaire (from
La Fauvette Du Temple)
solo,pno ENOCH s.p.   (M1332)

MESSAGER, ANDRE (cont'd.)

Chanson De Ma Mie
solo,pno ENOCH s.p. see also Quinze
Melodies   (M1333)

Chanson Des Loups (Le Petit Poucet)
solo,pno ENOCH   (M1334)

Chanson Melancolique
solo,pno (available in 2 keys)
ENOCH s.p. see also Quinze
Melodies   (M1335)

Chant D'amour
Mez/A solo,pno sc JOBERT s.p.
(M1336)

Charme, Reve, Image (from Isoline)
T solo,pno ENOCH s.p.   (M1337)
solo,pno ENOCH s.p.   (M1338)
solo,orch ENOCH rental   (M1339)

Couplets De Jacquet (from La
Bernaise)
solo,pno ENOCH s.p.   (M1340)

Couplets De La Casquette (from La
Fauvette Du Temple)
solo,pno ENOCH s.p.   (M1341)

Couplets Dialogues (from La Fauvette
Du Temple)
solo,pno ENOCH s.p.   (M1342)

Dans Le Royaume Du Cancan (from Les
Dragons De L'Imperatrice)
Mez solo,pno ENOCH s.p.   (M1343)
solo,pno ENOCH s.p.   (M1344)

Dans Les Arbres Blancs De Givre
solo,pno ENOCH s.p. see also
Nouveau Printemps   (M1345)

Dans Un Champ De Bles D'or (from La
Fauvette Du Temple)
solo,pno ENOCH s.p.   (M1346)

De Ci, De La, Cahin, Caha (from
Veronique)
[Fr] SBar soli,pno CHOUDENS C81
s.p.   (M1347)

Douce Chanson
high solo,pno sc JOBERT s.p.
(M1348)

Duo Des Chameliers (from La Fauvette
Du Temple)
2 soli,pno ENOCH s.p.   (M1349)

Duo Du Mariage (from La Fauvette Du
Temple)
2 soli,pno ENOCH s.p.   (M1350)

Eh Bien! Monsieur, Ne Serait-Ce Pas
Charmant (from Les Dragons De
L'Imperatrice)
solo,pno ENOCH s.p.   (M1351)

Eh Bien! Parlez, Monsieur (from Les
Dragons De L'Imperatrice)
2 soli,pno ENOCH s.p.   (M1352)

Esperance En D'heureux Jours (from
Francois Les Bas-Bleus)
T solo,pno ENOCH s.p.   (M1353)
Bar solo,pno ENOCH s.p.   (M1354)

Est-Ce Le Prestige Du Casque (from
Les Dragons De L'Imperatrice)
solo,pno ENOCH s.p.   (M1355)

Fais Nono (from La Bernaise)
solo,pno ENOCH s.p.   (M1356)

Helas, Je Ne Dois Plus Entendre (from
La Fauvette Du Temple)
solo,pno ENOCH s.p.   (M1357)

Il Est Brillant Comme L'aurore (from
Les Dragons De L'Imperatrice)
Mez solo,pno ENOCH s.p.   (M1358)
solo,pno ENOCH s.p.   (M1359)

Il Etait Un Joli Dragon (from Les
Dragons De L'Imperatrice)
solo,pno ENOCH s.p.   (M1360)

Il M'aime, J'en Suis Bien Certaine
(from Les Dragons De
L'Imperatrice)
solo,pno ENOCH s.p.   (M1361)
Mez solo,pno ENOCH s.p.   (M1362)

J'ai De La Figure (from Francois Les
Bas-Bleus)
solo,pno ENOCH s.p.   (M1363)

J'ai Des Refrains (from Francois Les
Bas-Bleus)
solo,pno ENOCH s.p.   (M1364)

J'aimais Mon Cousin (from Les Dragons
De L'Imperatrice)
solo,pno ENOCH s.p.   (M1365)
Mez solo,pno ENOCH s.p.   (M1366)

MESSAGER, ANDRE (cont'd.)

J'aime La Femme (from Francois Les
Bas-Bleus)
solo,pno ENOCH s.p.   (M1367)

Je Suis Une Pauvre Fille (from La
Bernaise)
solo,pno ENOCH s.p.   (M1368)

Je Viens D'etre Compromise (from La
Bernaise)
solo,pno ENOCH s.p.   (M1369)

Je Voudrais Etre Voltigeur (from La
Fauvette Du Temple)
solo,pno ENOCH s.p.   (M1370)

Joli Seigneur (from Isoline)
solo,pno ENOCH s.p.   (M1371)

La Chanson Des Cerises
solo,orch ENOCH rental see from
Melodies   (M1372)
solo,pno (available in 2 keys)
ENOCH s.p. see also Quinze
Melodies   (M1373)

La Lune Egrene En Perles Blondes
solo,pno ENOCH s.p. see also
Nouveau Printemps   (M1374)

Le Credo De La Victoire
2 soli,pno ENOCH voc sc, solo pt
(M1375)
solo,acap ENOCH s.p.   (M1376)
solo,pno ENOCH s.p.   (M1377)
solo,orch ENOCH rental   (M1378)

Le Joli Songe (from La Fauvette Du
Temple)
2 soli,pno ENOCH s.p.   (M1379)

Le Jour, Sous Le Soleil Beni (from
Madame Chrysantheme)
[Fr] high solo,pno CHOUDENS C78
s.p.   (M1380)
[Fr] low solo,pno CHOUDENS C80 s.p.
(M1381)
[Fr] med solo,pno CHOUDENS C79 s.p.
(M1382)

Le Parisien N'aime Pas (from La
Fauvette Du Temple)
solo,pno ENOCH s.p.   (M1383)

Les Oeillets Incarnadins (from
Isoline)
S/T solo,pno ENOCH s.p.   (M1384)
2 soli,pno ENOCH s.p.   (M1385)
Mez/Bar solo,pno ENOCH s.p.   (M1386)

Mai Vient
solo,pno ENOCH s.p. see also
Nouveau Printemps   (M1387)

Melodies *see Arioso; La Chanson Des
Cerises; Mimosa   (M1388)

Mimosa
solo,orch ENOCH rental see from
Melodies   (M1389)
solo,pno ENOCH s.p. see also Quinze
Melodies   (M1390)

Mon Colonel, J'ai Fait Mes Preuves
(from Les Dragons De
L'Imperatrice)
solo,pno ENOCH s.p.   (M1391)

Monsieur Le Marquis (from Francois
Les Bas-Bleus)
solo,pno ENOCH s.p.   (M1392)

Ne Vous Emballez Pas (from Les
Dragons De L'Imperatrice)
solo,pno ENOCH s.p.   (M1393)

Neige Rose
solo,pno (available in 2 keys)
ENOCH s.p. see also Quinze
Melodies   (M1394)

Nouveau Printemps
solo,pno cmplt ed ENOCH s.p.
contains & see also: Dans Les
Arbres Blancs De Givre; La Lune
Egrene En Perles Blondes; Mai
Vient; Se Peut-Il Qu'une Larme;
Un Reseau D'ombre Emprisonne
(M1395)

On Dit Le Parisien (from Francois Les
Bas-Bleus)
solo,pno ENOCH s.p.   (M1396)

Parmi Les Blancheurs De Neige (from
Isoline)
solo,pno ENOCH s.p.   (M1397)

Peuple Francais (from Francois Les
Bas-Bleus)
solo,pno ENOCH s.p.   (M1398)

Pour Un Detail, Une Nuance (from La
Bernaise)
solo,pno ENOCH s.p.   (M1399)

MESSAGER, ANDRE (cont'd.)

Priere Est Sauve (from La Fauvette Du Temple)
solo,pno ENOCH s.p.   (M1400)

Prologue Et Reve (from Isoline)
solo,orch ENOCH rental   (M1401)

Quand Vous Souriez (from Isoline)
2 soli,orch ENOCH rental   (M1402)

Quand Vous Tournez Vers Moi Les Yeux (from Isoline)
2 soli,pno ENOCH s.p.   (M1403)

Quinze Melodies *CC15L
solo,pno cmplt ed ENOCH s.p.
see also: Arioso; Chanson De Ma Mie; Chanson Melancolique; La Chanson Des Cerises; Mimosa; Neige Rose; Regret D'Avril   (M1404)

Regret D'Avril
solo,pno ENOCH s.p. see also Quinze Melodies   (M1405)

Rondeau De Saint-Angenor (from La Fauvette Du Temple)
solo,pno ENOCH s.p.   (M1406)

Se Peut-Il Qu'une Larme
solo,pno ENOCH s.p. see also Nouveau Printemps   (M1407)

Si J'avais Vos Ailes
[Fr] S solo,pno CHOUDENS C14 s.p.   (M1408)
[Fr] Mez solo,pno CHOUDENS C15 s.p.   (M1409)

Songe A Quels Dangers (from Les Dragons De L'Imperatrice)
2 soli,pno ENOCH s.p.   (M1410)

Sous Ton Balcon (from La Bernaise)
solo,pno ENOCH s.p.   (M1411)

Souvent A La Devanture (from La Bernaise)
solo,pno ENOCH s.p.   (M1412)

Un Reseau D'ombre Emprisonne
solo,pno ENOCH s.p. see also Nouveau Printemps   (M1413)

Une Gentille Fauvette (from La Fauvette Du Temple)
solo,pno ENOCH s.p.   (M1414)
Mez solo,pno ENOCH s.p.   (M1415)

Valse Du Miroir (from Isoline)
solo,pno ENOCH s.p.   (M1416)
solo,orch (E flat maj) ENOCH rental   (M1417)

Votre Femme M'a Dit Je T'aime (from Francois Les Bas-Bleus)
solo,pno ENOCH s.p.   (M1418)

Votre Nez, Mon Cher Capitaine (from Les Dragons De L'Imperatrice)
solo,pno ENOCH s.p.   (M1419)

Y Avait Un Petit Mat'lot (from Francois Les Bas-Bleus)
solo,pno ENOCH s.p.   (M1420)

MESSAGES see Schumann, Robert (Alexander), Auftrage

MESSAGGIO see Alfano, Franco

MESSE DE BERCEUSE see Westering, P. Chr. v.

MESSE MODALE EN SEPTUOR see Alain, Jehan

MESSE ZU EHREN DES HEILIGE ULRICH see Bauer, Josef

MESSIAEN, OLIVER (1908-   )
Action
see Poemes Pour Mi, Premier Livre

Antienne Du Silence
see Chants De Terre Et De Ciel

Arc-En-Ciel D'innocence
see Chants De Terre Et De Ciel

Bail Avec Mi
see Chants De Terre Et De Ciel

Chants De Terre Et De Ciel
solo,orch DURAND s.p.
contains: Antienne Du Silence; Arc-En-Ciel D'innocence; Bail Avec Mi; Danse Du Bebe-Pilule; Minuit Pile Et Face; Resurrection   (M1421)

Danse Du Bebe-Pilule
see Chants De Terre Et De Ciel

MESSIAEN, OLIVER (cont'd.)

Epouvante
see Poemes Pour Mi, Premier Livre

Harawi *CC12L
solo,orch cmplt ed LEDUC s.p.
deluxe edition also available in limited quantities   (M1422)

La Fiancee Perdue
see Trois Melodies

La Maison
see Poemes Pour Mi, Premier Livre

La Mort Du Nombre
ST soli,pno,vln DURAND $3.00   (M1423)

Le Collier
see Poemes Pour Mi, Deuxieme Livre

Le Sourire
see Trois Melodies

L'Epouse
see Poemes Pour Mi, Deuxieme Livre

Les Deux Guerriers
see Poemes Pour Mi, Deuxieme Livre

Minuit Pile Et Face
see Chants De Terre Et De Ciel

Paysage
see Poemes Pour Mi, Premier Livre

Poemes Pour Mi, Premier Livre
solo,pno DURAND s.p.
contains: Action; Epouvante; La Maison; Paysage   (M1424)

Poemes Pour Mi, Deuxieme Livre
solo,pno DURAND s.p.
contains: Le Collier; L'Epouse; Les Deux Guerriers; Priere Exaucee; Ta Voix   (M1425)

Pourquoi
see Trois Melodies

Priere Exaucee
see Poemes Pour Mi, Deuxieme Livre

Resurrection
see Chants De Terre Et De Ciel

Ta Voix
see Poemes Pour Mi, Deuxieme Livre

Trois Melodies
S solo,pno/inst cmplt ed DURAND s.p.
contains: La Fiancee Perdue; Le Sourire; Pourquoi   (M1426)

MESSIDORO see De Crescenzo

MESSMATES see Statham, Heathcote (Dicken)

MESSNER, JOSEPH (1893-   )
Erfullung *Op.64, sac
S solo,strings sc BOHM s.p., ipa   (M1427)

Stabat Mater *Op.74, sac
S solo,org/orch sc BOHM s.p., ipr   (M1428)

MESTRES-QUADRENY, JOSEP MARIA (1929-   )
Invencions Movils II
S solo,trp, electric guitar sc SEESAW $5.00   (M1429)

Musica Per A Anna
S solo,4strings sc MOECK 5066 s.p.   (M1430)

Poemma
S solo,pno sc SEESAW $3.00   (M1431)

MET EEN ZOET, ZOET LIEDJE see Clercq, R. de

MET EENEN DROEVEN SANGHE see Ruyneman, Daniel

METAMORFOSI SINFONICHE see Matsudaira, Yoritsune

METAMORPHOSE D'ECHO see Prey, Claude

METAMORPHOSES see Poulenc, Francis

METCALF, JOHN W.
Absent
high solo,pno (A maj) WILLIS $.60   (M1432)
low solo,pno (F maj) WILLIS $.60   (M1433)
med solo,pno (G maj) WILLIS $.60   (M1434)

Blessed Are The Pure Of Heart
solo,pno SHAWNEE IA 45 $.50   (M1435)

METCALFE, WILLIAM
D'ye Ken John Peel
solo,pno CRAMER   (M1436)

METHOLD, DIANA
Down By The Sally Gardens
solo,pno CRAMER $.95   (M1437)

Pipe
solo,pno CRAMER   (M1438)

Why Have You Stolen My Delight?
solo,pno CRAMER $.95   (M1439)

METHUSELAH see Sacco, John [Charles]

METHVEN
When You Look In The Heart Of A Rose
solo,pno ALLANS s.p.   (M1440)

METNER, N.R. (1880-1951)
Song Of The Elves *Op.6,No.3
[Eng/Fr] med solo,kbd CHESTER s.p.   (M1441)

METRA, JULES LOUIS OLIVIER (1830-1889)
Baynes, Sidney *see La Serenata

La Serenata
"Baynes, Sidney" solo,pno CRAMER   (M1442)

METRAL, PIERRE (1936-   )
Villes
narrator,SMez soli,cembalo,perc, 12inst TONOS s.p.   (M1443)

METTEZ LA MAIN AU CORBEILLON see La Musique, Onzieme Cahier

METZGER, HANS-ARNOLD (1913-   )
Den Die Hirten Lobeten Sehre
solo,inst SCHUL 299 s.p. contains also: Kommet Ihr Hirten (solo, inst); Lieb Nachtigall, Wach Auf (2 soli, inst); Vom Himmel Hoch, O Englein Kommt (solo,inst) (M1444)

Kommet Ihr Hirten
see Metzger, Hans-Arnold, Den Die Hirten Lobeten Sehre

Lieb Nachtigall, Wach Auf
see Metzger, Hans-Arnold, Den Die Hirten Lobeten Sehre

Vom Himmel Hoch, O Englein Kommt
see Metzger, Hans-Arnold, Den Die Hirten Lobeten Sehre

METZLER, FRIEDRICH (1910-   )
Kinderreime *CCU
solo,pno RIES s.p.   (M1445)

METZLER'S MASTERPIECES VOL. 1: SCHUBERT LIEDER FOR SOPRANO see Schubert, Franz (Peter)

METZLER'S MASTERPIECES VOL. 2: SCHUBERT LIEDER FOR CONTRALTO OR MEZZO-SOPRANO see Schubert, Franz (Peter)

METZLER'S MASTERPIECES VOL. 3: SCHUBERT LIEDER FOR TENOR see Schubert, Franz (Peter)

METZLER'S MASTERPIECES VOL. 4: SCHUBERT LIEDER FOR BARITONE OR BASS see Schubert, Franz (Peter)

METZLER'S MASTERPIECES VOL. 5: SCHUMANN LIEDER FOR SOPRANO see Schumann, Robert (Alexander)

METZLER'S MASTERPIECES VOL. 6: SCHUMANN LIEDER FOR CONTRALTO OR MEZZO-SOPRANO see Schumann, Robert (Alexander)

METZLER'S MASTERPIECES VOL. 7: SCHUMANN LIEDER FOR TENOR see Schumann, Robert (Alexander)

METZLER'S MASTERPIECES VOL. 8: SCHUMANN LIEDER FOR BARITONE OR BASS see Schumann, Robert (Alexander)

METZLER'S MASTERPIECES VOL. 9: BRAHMS LIEDER FOR SOPRANO see Brahms, Johannes

METZLER'S MASTERPIECES VOL. 10: BRAHMS LIEDER FOR CONTRALTO OR MEZZO-SOPRANO see Brahms, Johannes

METZLER'S MASTERPIECES VOL. 11: BRAHMS LIEDER FOR TENOR see Brahms, Johannes

METZLER'S MASTERPIECES VOL. 12: BRAHMS LIEDER FOR BARITONE OR BASS see Brahms, Johannes

METZLER'S MASTERPIECES VOL. 13: SIX SONGS FOR SOPRANO
(Klein, Herman; Kreuz, Emil) S solo, pno CRAMER s.p.
contains: Brahms, Johannes, Die

Mainacht, "Night In May";
Schubert, Franz (Peter), Die
Allmacht, "Almighty, The";
Schubert, Franz (Peter), Die
Junge Nonne, "Young Nun, The";
Schubert, Franz (Peter), Du Ring
An Meinem Finger, "Dear Ring Upon
My Finger"; Schumann, Robert
(Alexander), Er, Der Herrlichste
Von Allen, "He Of All True Men
The Noblest"; Schumann, Robert
(Alexander), Mondnacht,
"Moonlight"   (M1446)

METZLER'S MASTERPIECES VOL. 14: SIX
   SONGS FOR MEZZO-SOPRANO OR
   CONTRALTO
   (Klein, Herman; Kreuz, Emil) Mez/A
   solo,pno CRAMER s.p.
   contains: Brahms, Johannes, Die
   Mainacht, "Night In May";
   Schubert, Franz (Peter), Du Bist
   Die Ruh, "With Thee Is Peace";
   Schubert, Franz (Peter), Gretchen
   Am Spinnrade, "Gretchen At The
   Spinning Wheel"; Schumann, Robert
   (Alexander), Dein Angesicht, "Thy
   Face"; Schumann, Robert
   (Alexander), Volksliedchen, "When
   At Morn"; Schumann, Robert
   (Alexander), Widmung, "Greeting"
                                    (M1447)

METZLER'S MASTERPIECES VOL. 15: SIX
   SONGS FOR TENOR
   (Klein, Herman; Kreuz, Emil) T solo,
   pno CRAMER s.p.
   contains: Brahms, Johannes, Von
   Ewiger Liebe, "Enduring Love";
   Schubert, Franz (Peter), Litanei,
   "Litany, For All Souls Day";
   Schubert, Franz (Peter), Wohin?,
   "Whither?"; Schumann, Robert
   (Alexander), Abendlied,
   "Evensong"; Schumann, Robert
   (Alexander), Intermezzo,
   "Intermezzo"; Schumann, Robert
   (Alexander), Wanderlied,
   "Farewell Toast, A"   (M1448)

METZLER'S MASTERPIECES VOL. 16: SIX
   SONGS FOR BARITONE OR BASS
   (Klein, Herman; Kreuz, Emil) Bar/B
   solo,pno CRAMER s.p.
   contains: Brahms, Johannes, Von
   Ewiger Liebe, "Enduring Love";
   Schubert, Franz (Peter), Das
   Fischermadchen, "Fischer-Maiden,
   The"; Schubert, Franz (Peter),
   Ungeduld, "Impatience"; Schumann,
   Robert (Alexander), Du Bist Wie
   Eine Blume, "Thou Art So Like A
   Flower"; Schumann, Robert
   (Alexander), Im Wunderschonen
   Monat Mai, "Wond'rous Month Of
   May, The"; Schumann, Robert
   (Alexander), Wenn Ich In Deine
   Augen Seh, "While Gazing Into Thy
   Dear Eyes"   (M1449)

MEXICAN FIESTA ALBUM *CCU,Mex
   [Span/Eng] solo,pno MARKS $2.00
                                    (M1450)
MEYER, ERNST HERMANN (1905-   )
   Lieder Und Gesange *CC60L
   solo,pno BREITKOPF-L EB 4033 s.p.
                                    (M1451)
   Now, Voyager
   Bar/Mez solo,4strings CRAMER
                                    (M1452)
MEYER-HELMUND, ERIK (1861-1932)
   Ballroom Whispers
   solo,pno SCHAUR EE 3550 s.p.
                                    (M1453)
   Das Zauberlied
   low solo,pno RIES s.p.   (M1454)
   med solo,pno RIES s.p.   (M1455)
   high solo,pno RIES s.p.   (M1456)

   Du Standigt Fragar
   high solo,pno GEHRMANS s.p.   (M1457)
   low solo,pno GEHRMANS s.p.   (M1458)

   Rococo-Serenad
   high solo,pno GEHRMANS s.p.   (M1459)
   low solo,pno GEHRMANS s.p.   (M1460)

MEYERBEER, GIACOMO (1791-1864)
   Ach Mein Sohn (from Der Prophet)
   A solo,3fl,2ob,2clar,2bsn,2horn,
   strings BREITKOPF-L rental
                                    (M1461)
   Beaute Divine Enchanteresse (from Les
   Huguenots)
   TS soli,pno SALABERT-US $4.50
                                    (M1462)
   Bianca Al Par Di Neve Alpina (from
   Les Huguenots)
   T solo,pno RICORDI-ENG 130868 s.p.
                                    (M1463)
   Dans La Nuit Ou Seul Je Veille (from
   Les Huguenots)
   BarS soli,pno SALABERT-US $4.50
                                    (M1464)
   Le Danger Presse (from Les Huguenots)
   TS soli,pno SALABERT-US $4.50
                                    (M1465)

MEYERBEER, GIACOMO (cont'd.)
   O Beau Pays De La Touraine (from Les
   Huguenots)
   S&SSA soli,pno SALABERT-US $4.50
                                    (M1466)
   O Gebt (from Der Prophet)
   Mez/A solo,2fl,2ob,2clar,4bsn,
   2horn,strings BREITKOPF-L rental
                                    (M1467)
   O Paradis Sorti De L'Onde (from
   L'Africaine)
   [Fr/It/Eng] T solo,pno (G flat maj)
   SCHIRM.G $.60   (M1468)
   "O Paradiso Dall'onda Uscito" [It]
   T solo,pno RICORDI-ARG BA 8530
   s.p.   (M1469)
   "O Paradiso Dall'onda Uscito" T
   solo,pno RICORDI-ENG 96280 s.p.
                                    (M1470)
   O Paradiso Dall'onda Uscito *see O
   Paradis Sorti De L'Onde

   Ombra Leggera *see Ombre Legere

   Ombre Legere (from Dinorah)
   "Ombra Leggera" [It] S solo,pno
   RICORDI-ARG BA 11784 s.p. (M1471)
   (Liebling) "Shadow Song" [Fr/It/
   Eng] S solo,pno (D flat maj)
   SCHIRM.G $1.00   (M1472)

   Quand Je Quittais La Normandie (from
   Robert Le Diable)
   S solo,pno SALABERT-US $4.50
                                    (M1473)
   Robert, Toi Que J'aime (from Robert
   Le Diable)
   ST soli,pno SALABERT-US $4.50
                                    (M1474)
   Robert, Toi Que J'amie
   [Fr/Eng] low solo,pno (D min)
   CRAMER   (M1475)
   [Fr/Eng] high solo,pno (F min)
   CRAMER   (M1476)

   Shadow Song *see Ombre Legere

   Triomphe Que J'aime (from Robert Le
   Diable)
   SBar soli,pno SALABERT-US $4.50
                                    (M1477)
   Va! Dit-Elle (from Robert Le Diable)
   S solo,pno SALABERT-US $4.50
                                    (M1478)

MEYEROWITZ, DAVID
   A Mamme's Trehren *Jew
   solo,pno KAMMEN 31 $1.00 see also
   FAVORITE JEWISH SONGS, VOL. 2
                                    (M1479)
   Aheim, Aheim, Briederlach Aheim *Jew
   solo,pno KAMMEN 484 $1.00 see also
   JEWISH THEATRE SONGS, VOL. 1
                                    (M1480)
   Gam'se L'Toivoh *Jew
   solo,pno KAMMEN 32 $1.00 see also
   FAVORITE JEWISH SONGS, VOL. 2
                                    (M1481)
   Oisgeshpielt *Jew
   solo,pno KAMMEN 63 $1.00 see also
   JEWISH THEATRE SONGS, VOL. 1
                                    (M1482)
   Wen Es Fehlt Uns A Mame's Gebet *Jew
   solo,pno KAMMEN 16 $1.00 see also
   JEWISH THEATRE SONGS, VOL. 1
                                    (M1483)
   Wu Nemt Men Parnusse *Jew
   solo,pno KAMMEN 420 $1.00 see also
   JEWISH THEATRE SONGS, VOL. 1
                                    (M1484)
   Wu Sannen Meine Sieben Gute Yohr
   *Jew
   solo,pno KAMMEN 61 $1.00 see also
   JEWISH THEATRE SONGS, VOL. 1
                                    (M1485)
   Zion's Liedele *Jew
   solo,pno KAMMEN 39 $1.00 see also
   JEWISH THEATRE SONGS, VOL. 1
                                    (M1486)
MEYEROWITZ, JAN (1913-   )
   Ave Maria *sac
   [Eng] med solo,pno BROUDE BR. $.95
                                    (M1487)
   Bright Star
   S solo,pno EMI s.p.   (M1488)
   Gentle Dove
   high solo,pno BROUDE BR. $.95
                                    (M1489)
   On The Land And On The Sea
   med solo,pno BROUDE BR. $.95
                                    (M1490)
MEYERS
   He's On His Way (composed with
   Dietschmann) *sac
   solo,pno BENSON S5789-R $1.00
                                    (M1491)
MEYLIED see Schouwman, Hans

MEYLIED I see Schouwman, Hans

MEYLIED II see Schouwman, Hans

MEZIDON see Berger, Rod.

M'HA SCRITTO CHE M'AMA see Massenet,
   Jules

MI CANCION see Napolitano, Emilio

MI CHIAMANO MIMI see Puccini, Giacomo

MI-CLOSES see Delmet, Paul

MI DOMANDANO see Benvenuti, Giacomo

MI GARGANTA see Guastavino, Carlos

MI LAGNERO TACENDO see Mozart, Wolfgang
   Amadeus

MI MADRE see Lamuraglia, Nicolas

MI PAR D'UDIR ANCORA see Bizet,
   Georges, Je Crois Entendre Encore

MI TRADI see Mozart, Wolfgang Amadeus

MI VIDA ES DICHA Y AMOR see Strauss,
   Josef

MI YODEA see Reinhardt, Bruno

MIA CLIMENE ADORATA see Heinichen,
   Johann David

MIA SPERANZA ADORATA see Mozart,
   Wolfgang Amadeus

MIA SPERANZA ADORATA - AH, NON SAI see
   Mozart, Wolfgang Amadeus

MIARKA S'EN VA see Georges, Alexandre

MICAELAS ARIA see Bizet, Georges

MICE see Weigl, Vally

MICH RUFT DEIN BILD see Edler, Robert

MICH RUFT ZUWEILEN EINE STILLE see
   Niel, Matty

MICH ZU TRENNEN VON DIR see Mozart,
   Wolfgang Amadeus, Ch'io Mi Scordi
   Di Te

MICHAEL, EDWARD
   Kamaal
   narrator,orch min sc TRANSAT. s.p.
                                    (M1492)
MICHAELA'S SONG see Bizet, Georges

MICHEELSEN, HANS-FRIEDRICH (1902-1973)
   Drei Lieder Auf Gedichte Von Emil
   Hecker *CC3U
   S solo,pno (med) BAREN. 2148 $4.25
                                    (M1493)
   Drei Lieder On Poems By E. Hecker
   S solo,pno BAREN. 2148 $4.25
   contains: Im Strom; Lichte Wolke;
   Wunderbares Herz   (M1494)

   Herr, Wie Sind Deine Werke
   see Solokantaten

   Ich Weiss, Dass Mein Erloser Lebt
   see Solokantaten

   Im Strom
   see Drei Lieder On Poems By E.
   Hecker

   Lichte Wolke
   see Drei Lieder On Poems By E.
   Hecker

   Lobe Den Herrn, Meine Seele
   see Solokantaten

   Singet Dem Herrn *sac,cant
   S solo,fl,org (med diff) BAREN.
   2950 $4.25   (M1495)

   Solokantaten *sac,cant
   med solo,org,opt vln (med) cmplt ed
   BAREN. 1319 $4.00
   contains: Herr, Wie Sind Deine
   Werke; Ich Weiss, Dass Mein
   Erloser Lebt; Lobe Den Herrn,
   Meine Seele   (M1496)

   Was Betrubst Du Dich, Meine Seele
   (from Symphonia Sacra Von Der
   Schopfung) sac
   A/B solo,vln,org (med diff) BAREN.
   1756 $3.25   (M1497)

   Wenn Ich Mit Menschen- Und Mit
   Engelszungen Redete *sac,cant
   low solo,vln,org BAREN. 2146 $4.25
                                    (M1498)
   Wunderbares Herz
   see Drei Lieder On Poems By E.
   Hecker

MICHEL, CH.-H.
   Annie
   solo,pno ENOCH   (M1499)

MICHEL, CH.-H. (cont'd.)

La Chanson Du Rouet
  solo,pno (available in 2 keys)
  ENOCH   (M1500)

MICHEL, PAUL-BAUDOUIN (1930-   )
  Trajectoires Interieures
  med solo,pno CBDM s.p.   (M1501)

MICHELANGELO-LIEDER see Wolf, Hugo

MICHELANGELO SONGS see Wolf, Hugo

MICHIELS, G.
  Histoire D'une Pomme
    solo,pno ENOCH s.p.   (M1502)
    solo,acap ENOCH s.p.   (M1503)

  La Greve Des Baisers
    solo,pno ENOCH s.p.   (M1504)
    solo,acap ENOCH s.p.   (M1505)

  La Toilette De La Mariee
    solo,pno ENOCH s.p.   (M1506)
    solo,acap ENOCH s.p.   (M1507)

  Le Bon Gite
    solo,pno ENOCH s.p.   (M1508)
    solo,acap ENOCH s.p.   (M1509)

  Le Commisaire
    solo,pno ENOCH s.p.   (M1510)
    solo,acap ENOCH s.p.   (M1511)

  Le Peintre Au Village
    solo,pno ENOCH s.p.   (M1512)
    solo,acap ENOCH s.p.   (M1513)

  Les Avocats De L'hiver
    solo,pno ENOCH s.p.   (M1514)
    solo,acap ENOCH s.p.   (M1515)

  Les Trois Brigadiers
    solo,pno ENOCH s.p.   (M1516)
    solo,acap ENOCH s.p.   (M1517)

  L'Heritier De Croquemitaine
    solo,pno ENOCH s.p.   (M1518)
    solo,acap ENOCH s.p.   (M1519)

  L'Officier En Bourgeois
    solo,acap ENOCH s.p.   (M1520)
    solo,pno ENOCH s.p.   (M1521)

  Mon Chapeau Des Dimanches
    solo,pno ENOCH s.p.   (M1522)
    solo,acap ENOCH s.p.   (M1523)

MICHIELSEN, A.
  De Spin
    solo,pno BROEKMANS 690 s.p. (M1524)
    SA soli,pno BROEKMANS 690 s.p.
                                            (M1525)
  Rim Ram Rare
    solo,pno BROEKMANS 464 s.p. (M1526)

MICHTOM L'DOVID see Nowakowsky, David

MICKELSON, PAUL
  Lang Sisters Trios No. I *sac,CC12UL
    3 female soli,pno LILLENAS MB-101
    $1.50   (M1527)

  Lang Sisters Trios No. II *sac,
    CC10UL
    3 female soli,pno LILLENAS MB-102
    $1.50   (M1528)

MICROBE, THE see Persichetti, Vincent

MICROFORMOBILES II see Antunes, Jorge

MICROSONGS see Srebotnjak, Alojz F.

MIDDAY PSALM see Merku, Pavle,
  Opoldanski Psalm

MIDDELEER, JEAN DE (1908-   )
  A Mon Frere
    "Aan Mijn Broeder" see Le Chemin Du
    Visible A L'invisible

  Aan Mijn Broeder *see A Mon Frere

  Alleen *see Seule

  Anonyme
    "Naamloos" see Le Chemin Du Visible
    A L'invisible

  Chanson
    "Lied" see Plaies Vives

  Cinq Petites Filles
    "Vilf Kleine Meisjes" see Poemes
    D'Epinal

  Een Hand *see Une Main

  Emotion
    "Ontroering" see Plaies Vives

  En Flots Tumultueux *see Op 'T Wilde
    Golven

MIDDELEER, JEAN DE (cont'd.)

  Frisson D'eau Vive
    med solo,pno CBDM s.p.   (M1529)

  Het Ongeluk *see Le Malheur

  Het Uurwerk *see La Montre

  Ik Ben Treurig *see Je Suis Triste

  Ik Voel Mijn Leven
    "Inexorable" see Onmachstranen

  Ils Partent Tous
    Mez/Bar solo,pno CBDM s.p. (M1530)

  Inexorable *see Ik Voel Mijn Leven

  Je Suis Triste
    "Ik Ben Treurig" see Poemes
    D'Epinal

  J'entends Mon Coeur *see Mijn Hart
    Klopt Hoorbaar

  La Goutte De Pluie
    med solo,pno CBDM s.p.   (M1531)

  La Montre
    "Het Uurwerk" see Poemes D'Epinal

  Le Chemin Du Visible A L'invisible
    [Fr/Dan] med solo,pno cmplt ed CBDM
    s.p.
      contains: A Mon Frere, "Aan Mijn
      Broeder"; Anonyme, "Naamloos";
      Une Main, "Een Hand"   (M1532)

  Le Malheur
    "Het Ongeluk" see Poemes D'Epinal

  L'Espagnol De Ma Rue
    med solo,pno CBDM s.p.   (M1533)

  Lied *see Chanson

  Luisteren *see Obeir

  Mijn Hart Klopt Hoorbaar
    "J'entends Mon Coeur" see
    Onmachstranen

  Naamloos *see Anonyme

  O Froid Funebre *see O Klamme Koude

  O Klamme Koude
    "O Froid Funebre" see Onmachstranen

  Obeir
    "Luisteren" see Poemes D'Epinal

  Onmachstranen
    [Dan/Fr] B/A solo,pno cmplt ed CBDM
    s.p.
      contains: Ik Voel Mijn Leven,
      "Inexorable"; Mijn Hart Klopt
      Hoorbaar, "J'entends Mon
      Coeur"; O Klamme Koude, "O
      Froid Funebre"; Op 'T Wilde
      Golven, "En Flots Tumultueux"
                                  (M1534)

  Ontroering *see Emotion

  Op 'T Wilde Golven
    "En Flots Tumultueux" see
    Onmachstranen

  Place Poelaert
    med solo,pno CBDM s.p.   (M1535)

  Plaies Vives
    [Fr/Dan] med solo,pno cmplt ed CBDM
    s.p.
      contains: Chanson, "Lied";
      Emotion, "Ontroering"; Rails,
      "Rails"; Seule, "Alleen"
                                  (M1536)

  Poemes D'Epinal
    [Fr/Dan] med solo,pno cmplt ed CBDM
    s.p.
      contains: Cinq Petites Filles,
      "Vilf Kleine Meisjes"; Je Suis
      Triste, "Ik Ben Treurig"; La
      Montre, "Het Uurwerk"; Le
      Malheur, "Het Ongeluk"; Obeir,
      "Luisteren"   (M1537)

  Rails
    "Rails" see Plaies Vives

  Rails *see Rails

  Seule
    "Alleen" see Plaies Vives

  Une Main
    "Een Hand" see Le Chemin Du Visible
    A L'invisible

  Valse Avec Une Etoile
    S/T solo,pno CBDM s.p.   (M1538)

MIDDELEER, JEAN DE (cont'd.)

  Vilf Kleine Meisjes *see Cinq
    Petites Filles

MIDDELEEUWS KERSTLIEDJE see Beekhuis,
  Hanna

MIDI EN CAMPINE ET CREPUSCULE EN
  CAMPINE see Moulaert, Raymond

MIDNIGHT see Gibbs, Cecil Armstrong

MIDNIGHT see Wolf, Artur, Chatzos

MIDNIGHT MEDITATION, THE see Diamond,
  David

MIDNIGHT SUN, THE see Rorem, Ned

MIDSOMMAR see Dahl

MIDSOMMAR see Marvia, Einari,
  Mittumaari

MIDSOMMARNATT II see Sonninen, Ahti

MIDSUMMER see Worth

MIDSUMMER NIGHTS see Rachmaninoff,
  Sergey Vassilievitch

MIEIR
  His Name Is Wonderful *sac
    solo,pno BENSON S5860-R $1.00
                                  (M1539)

MIEL see De Rogatis, Pascual

MIETSKASERNE see Lilien, Ignace

MIGHTY BUILDER, THE see Day, Maude
  Craske

MIGHTY FORTRESS IS OUR GOD, A see
  Schein, Johann Hermann

MIGHTY HE HATH DETHRONED, THE see Bach,
  Johann Sebastian

MIGHTY LAK' A ROSE see Nevin, Ethelbert
  Woodbridge

MIGHTY LORD AND KING ALL GLORIOUS see
  Bach, Johann Sebastian

MIGNAN, EDOUARD-CHARLES-OCTAVE
  (1884-1969)
  Bercement
    see Trois Chants Arabes

  Hymne National A Jehanne D'Arc
    solo,pno ENOCH s.p.   (M1540)
    solo,acap ENOCH s.p.   (M1541)

  Kranaos
    see Trois Chants Arabes

  La Pluie Sur Les Roses
    ENOCH s.p.   (M1542)

  La Poursuite Du Vent Et De L'amour
    see Trois Chants Arabes

  Le Collier
    ENOCH s.p.   (M1543)

  Les Ailes Du Reve
    ENOCH s.p.   (M1544)

  Les Baisers Sont Des Papillons
    ENOCH s.p.   (M1545)

  Trois Chants Arabes
    solo,pno cmplt ed ENOCH s.p.
      contains: Bercement; Kranaos; La
      Poursuite Du Vent Et De L'amour
                                  (M1546)

MIGNON see Beethoven, Ludwig van

MIGNON see Diepenbrock, Alphons

MIGNON see Gounod, Charles Francois

MIGNON see Liszt, Franz, Mignons Lied

MIGNON see Schumann, Robert
  (Alexander), Kennst Du Das Land?

MIGNON see Wolf, Hugo

MIGNON [2] see Wolf, Hugo

MIGNONETTE see Fisher, Howard

MIGNONNE see Holmes, Alfred

MIGNONNE see Viardot-Garcia, Pauline

MIGNONNE see Wagner, Richard

MIGNONS LIED see Liszt, Franz

MIGOT, GEORGES (1891-   )
Au Jardin Joli
see Trois Monodies

Ballade Du Roulier
see Trois Monodies

C'est Le Soir
see Trois Chants Suivis D'un Air A
Vocalises

Chanson
see Quatre Melodies

Chanson De Boheme
see Hommage A Thibaut De Champagne

Chanson Funebre
see Les Poemes Du Brugnon Premier
Recueil

Comme J'allais Couvert De La
Poussiere Du Voyage
see Trois Chants

Cygne Blanc
see Trois Chansons De Margot

Dans Le Calme, La Barque Se Balance
see Trois Chants

Dans Un Village D'Aveyron
see Les Poemes Du Brugnon Deuxieme
Recueil

Derniere Danse
see Les Poemes Du Brugnon Troisieme
Recueil

Deux Chants
solo,orch LEDUC s.p.
contains: Il Me L'a Dit Qu'a La
Moisson; Si Quelquefois Tu
Pleures   (M1547)

Deux Melodies
solo,pno/inst LEDUC s.p.
contains: Le Grand Envol; Notre-
Dame De Bonne Humeur   (M1548)

Deux Melodies *see Fees; Roses
D'automne   (M1549)

Deux Steles De Victor Segalen
solo,harp,cel,drums,bvl,cym sc
LEDUC B.L.684 s.p.
contains: Les Lacs; Ordre Au
Soleil   (M1550)

Douceur
see Trois Chansons De Margot

Elegie A Clymene
solo,orch LEDUC s.p.   (M1551)

Fauvette Et Ronde De La Chauve-Souris
see Trois Chants Suivis D'un Air A
Vocalises

Fees
solo,pno/inst LEDUC s.p. see from
Deux Melodies   (M1552)

Hirondelle Qui Part Aux Indes
see Les Poemes Du Brugnon Deuxieme
Recueil

Hommage A Thibaut De Champagne
solo,acap LEDUC s.p.
contains: Chanson De Boheme; La
Serenade; Le Page; Liliane;
Sabbot   (M1553)

Il Me L'a Dit Qu'a La Moisson
see Deux Chants

Images III
see Quatre Melodies

La Balancelle
see Les Poemes Du Brugnon Premier
Recueil

La Serenade
see Hommage A Thibaut De Champagne

La Surprise Amoureuse (La Belle
Endormie)
solo,pno/inst LEDUC s.p.   (M1554)

La Truite
see Les Poemes Du Brugnon Premier
Recueil

Larmes D'aube
see Trois Poemes De Gilles Normand

Le Chateau D'O
see Les Poemes Du Brugnon Premier
Recueil

Le Grand Envol
see Deux Melodies

MIGOT, GEORGES (cont'd.)

Le Page
see Hommage A Thibaut De Champagne

Le Petit Coq
see Trois Poemes De Gilles Normand

Le Voilier
solo,pno/inst LEDUC s.p. see also
Les Poemes Du Brugnon Deuxieme
Recueil   (M1555)

L'Ecucreuil
see Les Poemes Du Brugnon Troisieme
Recueil

Les Adieux De Nemours
see Les Poemes Du Brugnon Troisieme
Recueil

Les Baladins
see Trois Monodies

Les Chrysanthemes D'or
solo,pno/inst LEDUC s.p.   (M1556)

Les Lacs
see Deux Steles De Victor Segalen

Les Palais Nomades
see Quatre Melodies

Les Poemes Du Brugnon *CC17L
solo,orch cmplt ed LEDUC s.p.
                               (M1557)
Les Poemes Du Brugnon Premier Recueil
solo,orch/pno LEDUC B.L.689 s.p.
contains: Chanson Funebre; La
Balancelle; La Truite; Le
Chateau D'O; Poeme Du Brugnon;
Quand Tout Ceci Ne Sera Plus
see also: L'Oubli; Quand Tout
Ceci Ne Sera Plus   (M1558)

Les Poemes Du Brugnon Deuxieme
Recueil
solo,orch/pno LEDUC B.L.690 s.p.
contains: Dans Un Village
D'Aveyron; Hirondelle Qui Part
Aux Indes; Le Voilier;
L'Inevitable Jour;
L'Invitation; L'Oubli
see also: Le Voilier;
L'Invitation   (M1559)

Les Poemes Du Brugnon Troisieme
Recueil
solo,orch/pno LEDUC B.L.691 s.p.
contains: Derniere Danse;
L'Ecucreuil; Les Adieux De
Nemours; Poeme De La Rose;
Venez Me Faire Danser   (M1560)

Liliane
see Hommage A Thibaut De Champagne

L'Inevitable Jour
see Les Poemes Du Brugnon Deuxieme
Recueil

L'Invitation
solo,pno/inst LEDUC s.p. see also
Les Poemes Du Brugnon Deuxieme
Recueil   (M1561)

L'Oubli
see Les Poemes Du Brugnon Deuxieme
Recueil
solo,orch LEDUC s.p. see also Les
Poemes Du Brugnon Premier Recueil
                               (M1562)

Ne Damandons A L'avenir
see Trois Chants Pour Trois Poetes

Nenni-Da
see Trois Chansons De Margot

Notre-Dame De Bonne Humeur
see Deux Melodies

Nous Nous Taisions
see Trois Chants

Nuit
see Trois Chants Suivis D'un Air A
Vocalises

Nuit Sur La Lande
see Quatre Melodies

Ordre Au Soleil
see Deux Steles De Victor Segalen

Poeme De La Rose
see Les Poemes Du Brugnon Troisieme
Recueil

Poeme Du Brugnon
see Les Poemes Du Brugnon Premier
Recueil

Printemps
see Trois Chants Pour Trois Poetes

MIGOT, GEORGES (cont'd.)

Printemps Maussade
see Trois Poemes De Gilles Normand

Quand Tout Ceci Ne Sera Plus
solo,orch LEDUC s.p. see also Les
Poemes Du Brugnon Premier Recueil
                               (M1563)
Quatre Melodies
solo,orch LEDUC s.p.
contains: Chanson; Images III;
Les Palais Nomades; Nuit Sur La
Lande   (M1564)

Renouveau
see Trois Chants Pour Trois Poetes

Reposoir Grave, Noble Et Pur...
solo,fl,harp,opt pno LEDUC s.p.
                               (M1565)

Roses D'automne
solo,pno/inst LEDUC s.p. see from
Deux Melodies   (M1566)

Sabbot
see Hommage A Thibaut De Champagne

Sept Petites Images Du Japon *song
cycle
solo,orch LEDUC s.p.   (M1567)

Si Quelquefois Tu Pleures
see Deux Chants

Trois Berceuses Chantees *CC3U
solo,orch LEDUC s.p.   (M1568)

Trois Chansons De Margot
SMez soli,pno/inst LEDUC s.p.
contains: Cygne Blanc; Douceur;
Nenni-Da   (M1569)

Trois Chants
solo,orch LEDUC s.p.
contains: Comme J'allais Couvert
De La Poussiere Du Voyage; Dans
Le Calme, La Barque Se Balance;
Nous Nous Taisions   (M1570)

Trois Chants Pour Trois Poetes
LEDUC s.p.
contains: Ne Damandons A L'avenir
(solo,orch); Printemps (solo,
orch); Renouveau (solo,pno/
inst)   (M1571)

Trois Chants Suivis D'un Air A
Vocalises
solo,orch LEDUC s.p.
contains: C'est Le Soir; Fauvette
Et Ronde De La Chauve-Souris;
Nuit   (M1572)

Trois Monodies
solo,acap LEDUC s.p.
contains: Au Jardin Joli; Ballade
Du Roulier; Les Baladins
                               (M1573)
Trois Poemes De Gilles Normand
solo,pno/inst LEDUC s.p.
contains: Larmes D'aube; Le Petit
Coq; Printemps Maussade (M1574)

Venez Me Faire Danser
see Les Poemes Du Brugnon Troisieme
Recueil

MIGRANT, THE see Kilpinen, Yrio,
Muuttilintu

MIGRATION DES AMES see Legley, Victor

MIHALOVICI, MARCEL (1898-   )
Abendgesang *Op.75, song cycle
solo,pno SCHOTTS 5083 s.p.   (M1575)

MIHALY, ANDRAS (1917-   )
Psalms Of Piety *CCU,Psalm
[Hung/Ger] solo,pno BUDAPEST 5829
s.p.   (M1576)

Six Songs *CC6U
[Hung/Ger] solo,pno BUDAPEST 4258
s.p.   (M1577)

Six Songs For High Voice *CC6U
high solo,pno ZENEM. 573Z $4.00
                               (M1578)
Three Apocrypha *CC3U
[Hung/Ger] 3 female soli,clar,perc
BUDAPEST 4667 s.p.   (M1579)

MIJN EERSTE see Zweers, [Bernard]

MIJN FIENTJE see Hullebroeck, Em.

MIJN HART KLOPT HOORBAAR see Middeleer,
Jean De

MIJN KLEEN DOCHTERKEN see Clercq, R. de

MIJN KLEEN KLEEN DOCHTERKE see
Hullebroeck, Em.

MIJN KLEEN, KLEEN SOCHTERKE see
    Andriessen, K.

MIJN LAND see Hulst, G. v.d.

MIJN LANT WIL NIET MEER TREUREN see
    Horst, Anton van der

MIJN LIEVEKEN OPEN JE DEURKEN see
    Mortelmans, Lodewijk

MIJN LIEVEKEN OPEN JE DEURKEN EN LACH
    see Ruyneman, Daniel

MIJN PARADIJSJE see Hullebroeck, Em.

MIJN TROOST see Adriessen, Willem

MIJN VENTJE SLAAPT see Andriessen, K.

MIJN VRIENDEN see Dresden, Sem

MIJNE MOEDERTAAL see Brandts-Buys, L.F.

MIKAEL see Nordqvist, Gustaf

MIKAS ON POIKANA ELEA see Kilpinen,
    Yrio

MIKODA, BORIVOJ (1904-1970)
    Ctyri Pisne *Op.9, CC4U
        low solo,pno CZECH s.p.   (M1580)

    Das Antlitz *see Tvar

    Deine Stimme *see Tvuj Hlas

    Der Fruhling *see Jaro

    Die Gegenden *see Krajiny

    Fliehende Hindinnen *see Prchajici
        Lane

    Jaro *Op.16
        "Der Fruhling" med solo,pno CZECH
        s.p.   (M1581)

    Krajiny *Op.18, song cycle
        "Die Gegenden" med solo,pno CZECH
        s.p.   (M1582)

    Meditace *song cycle
        "Meditation" T/Bar solo,pno CZECH
        s.p.   (M1583)

    Meditation *see Meditace

    Nahrdelnik *Op.10, CC5U
        med solo,pno CZECH s.p.   (M1584)

    Prchajici Lane *Op.25, song cycle
        "Fliehende Hindinnen" med solo,pno
        CZECH s.p.   (M1585)

    Sonata
        S solo,fl,pno CZECH s.p.   (M1586)

    Tri Pisne *Op.38, CC3U
        med solo,pno CZECH s.p.   (M1587)

    Tvar *Op.13, song cycle
        "Das Antlitz" med solo,pno CZECH
        s.p.   (M1588)

    Tvuj Hlas *Op.6
        "Deine Stimme" med solo,pno CZECH
        s.p.   (M1589)

MIKSI EN VASYISI see Kilpinen, Yrio

MIKSI KAY AATOKSENI PIIRI NIIN
    HIMMEAKSI see Marttinen, Tauno

MIKSI LAULAN see Merikanto, Oskar

MIKULA, ZDENKO (1916-   )
    Dnes
        med solo,pno SLOV.HUD.FOND s.p.
                                    (M1590)
    To Bude Rano
        T solo,pno SLOV.HUD.FOND s.p.
                                    (M1591)

MIL QUERUBINES EN CORO see Melichar

MILAGRO see Dublanc, Emilio

MILAN
    Toda Mi Vida Os Ame
        solo,gtr RICORDI-ENG BA 11757 s.p.
                                    (M1592)

MILAN, LUIS (ca. 1500-ca. 1564)
    El Maestro
        solo,gtr ZERBONI 6405 s.p. (M1593)

    Levaysme Amor D'aquesta Terra
        (Azpiazu) [Span] med solo,gtr UNION
        ESP. $1.10   (M1594)

    Pavanen, Fantasien, Romanzen Und
        Vilancicos *CCU
        (Behrend, Siegfried) solo,gtr
        SIKORSKI 200 s.p.   (M1595)

MILAN, LUIS (cont'd.)
    Toda Mi Vida Os Ame
        (Lavie) [Span/Fr] med solo,gtr
        ESCHIG $1.25   (M1596)
        (Lavie, Ferandez) "Toute Ma Vie Je
        Vous Ai Aimee" [Span/Fr/It] solo,
        gtr SCHOTTS GA 193 s.p. see from
        ALTE UND NEUE WERKE   (M1597)

    Toute Ma Vie Je Vous Ai Aimee *see
        Toda Mi Vida Os Ame

MILANESE
    Ave Maria
        S solo,org RICORDI-ARG BA 11497
        s.p.   (M1598)

MILANO, R.
    Ninna Nanna
        solo,pno PRESSER $.95   (M1599)

MILANS, TOMAS
    Drei Motetten *sac,CC3U,mot
        (Ewerhart, Rudolf) [Lat] S/T/B
        solo,cont BIELER CS 12 s.p.
                                    (M1600)

MILD MOTHER, THE see Rorem, Ned

MILD UND LEISE, WIE ER LACHELT see
    Wagner, Richard

MILENCI see Haba, Alois

MILENCI see Kohout, J.

MILETUS see Lora, Antonio

MILFORD, ROBIN (1903-1959)
    Elegy
        high solo,pno NOVELLO 17.0044.08
        s.p.   (M1601)

    Laus Deo *sac
        low solo,pno NOVELLO 17.0091.10
        s.p.   (M1602)

    Love On My Heart
        low solo,pno NOVELLO 17.0109.06
        s.p.   (M1603)

    So Sweet Love Seemed
        high solo,pno NOVELLO 17.0180.00
        s.p.   (M1604)

MILHAM, RICHARD
    He Is Near (from Searcher, The) sac
        (Burroughs, Bob) solo,pno BROADMAN
        4590-38 $1.00   (M1605)

MILHAUD, DARIUS (1892-1974)
    Abandonnee
        see Chansons De Negresse

    Adieu
        solo,fl,vla,harp ELKAN-V $4.00
                                    (M1606)
    Canti Popolari Ebraici *CC6U,Heb
        [Fr] solo,pno HEUGEL 10696 s.p.
                                    (M1607)
    Chanson D'automne
        see Quatre Poemes De Paul Claudel

    Chanson De L'aveugle
        solo,orch ENOCH rental   (M1608)

    Chanson Du Printemps
        solo,orch ENOCH rental   (M1609)

    Chansons Bas *CCU
        [Fr] med solo,pno ESCHIG $4.00
                                    (M1610)
    Chansons De Negresse
        med solo,pno SALABERT-US $3.75
        contains: Abandonnee; Mon
        Histoire; Sans Feu Ni Lieu (M1611)
    Chansons De Ronsard *CCU
        [Eng/Fr] S solo,orch BOOSEY $7.50
                                    (M1612)
    Chansons Du Carnaval De Londres (from
        Beggar's Opera, The) CCU
        [Eng/Fr] med solo,orch/pno voc sc
        SALABERT-US $13.50   (M1613)

    Cinq Prieres *sac,CC5U
        med solo,pno/org HEUGEL s.p.
                                    (M1614)
    Deux Chansons Du Film: Madame Bovary
        *CC2U
        ENOCH s.p.   (M1615)

    Deux Petits Airs *CC2U
        [Fr] med solo,pno ESCHIG $2.75
                                    (M1616)
    Deux Poemes
        SATB soli,acap cmplt ed DURAND s.p.
        contains: Eloge, Poeme De St-
        Leger-Leger; Le Brick, Poeme De
        Rene Chalupt   (M1617)

    Due Poemi Di Coventry Patmore
        [Fr/Eng] solo,pno HEUGEL 10910 s.p.
        contains: L'azalee; Le Depart
                                    (M1618)

MILHAUD, DARIUS (cont'd.)
    Eloge, Poeme De St-Leger-Leger
        see Deux Poemes

    Israel Lebt
        [Ger] solo,pno UNIVER. 8483
        $2.75   (M1619)

    La Revolution (Part 2)
        see Les Soirees De Petrograde

    La Tourterelle
        see Quatre Poemes De Leo Latil

    L'abandon
        see Quatre Poemes De Leo Latil

    L'Amour Chante *CC9U
        [Eng/Fr] S solo,pno PRESSER $3.00
                                    (M1620)
    L'ancien Regime (Part 1)
        see Les Soirees De Petrograde

    Landwirtschaftliche Maschinen *song
        cycle
        [Ger/Fr] med solo,7inst sc,oct
        UNIVER. 8142 $7.00   (M1621)

    L'azalee
        see Due Poemi Di Coventry Patmore

    Le Brick, Poeme De Rene Chalupt
        see Deux Poemes

    Le Depart
        see Due Poemi Di Coventry Patmore

    Le Rossignol
        see Quatre Poemes De Leo Latil

    Le Sombre Mai
        see Quatre Poemes De Paul Claudel

    Les Soirees De Petrograde
        solo,pno DURAND s.p.
        contains: La Revolution (Part 2);
        L'ancien Regime (Part 1)   (M1622)
    Lied Des Lopez (from Maximilian)
        [Ger/Fr] solo,pno UNIVER. 10583
        $2.75   (M1623)

    Ma Douleur Et Sa Compagne
        see Quatre Poemes De Leo Latil

    Mon Histoire
        see Chansons De Negresse

    Nuptial Cantata *Marriage,cant
        [Eng/Fr] S solo,pno SALABERT-US
        $7.50   (M1624)

    Obsession
        see Quatre Poemes De Paul Claudel

    Poemes Juifs *CCU
        [Fr] med solo,pno ESCHIG $7.75
                                    (M1625)
    Poemes Juifs *CCU
        [Fr] solo,pno SCHOTTS 2037 s.p.
                                    (M1626)
    Psalm 129 *sac
        [Ger/Fr] Bar solo,2pno (two copies
        needed for performance) UNIVER.
        11713 $3.25   (M1627)

    Quatre Poemes De Leo Latil
        solo,pno DURAND s.p.
        contains: La Tourterelle;
        L'abandon; Le Rossignol; Ma
        Douleur Et Sa Compagne   (M1628)

    Quatre Poemes De Paul Claudel
        Bar solo,pno/inst DURAND s.p.
        contains: Chanson D'automne; Le
        Sombre Mai; Obsession; Tenebres
                                    (M1629)
    Recreation *CC4U
        [Fr] solo,pno HEUGEL 10917 s.p.
                                    (M1630)
    Sans Feu Ni Lieu
        see Chansons De Negresse

    Selected Vocal Works *CCU
        [Russ] solo,pno MEZ KNIGA 90 s.p.
                                    (M1631)
    Seven Poems Of Paul Claudel *CC7L
        med solo,pno SALABERT-US $15.00
                                    (M1632)
    Tenebres
        see Quatre Poemes De Paul Claudel

    Three Troubador Songs *CC3U
        [Fr] high solo,pno SALABERT-US
        $3.00   (M1633)

    Tristesses *CCU
        [Fr/Eng] Bar solo,pno HEUGEL 10927
        s.p.   (M1634)

    Trois Poemes *CC3U
        [Fr] med solo,pno ESCHIG $4.00
                                    (M1635)

MILKEY, E.T.
  I Must Go Forth Into The Morning
    solo,pno (B flat maj) BOOSEY $1.50
                                          (M1636)
  'Tis Weary Waiting
    solo,pno (F maj) BOOSEY $1.50
                                          (M1637)

MILKMAIDS see Edmund, J.

MILKMAIDS see Heseltine, Philip

MILL, THE see Pergament, Moses, Kvarnen

MILL IN THE VALLEY see In Einem Kuhlen
  Grunde

MILL WHEEL see Davis, Katherine K.

MILL WHEEL, THE see Sibelius, Jean,
  Kvarnhjulet

MILLA MAKSAN MAAMMON MAION see
  Kilpinen, Yrio

MILLARD, HARRISON (1829-1895)
  Ave Maria *sac
    med solo,pno (E flat maj) CENTURY
      1368 $.40   (M1638)
    high solo,pno (F maj) CENTURY 1367
      $.40   (M1639)
  Pilot Brave
    solo,pno CRAMER   (M1640)
    2 soli,pno CRAMER   (M1641)
  Such Merry Maids Are We
    2 soli,pno CRAMER   (M1642)
  Trip, Trip, Trip *canon
    2 soli,pno (C maj) CRAMER   (M1643)
    2 soli,pno (E flat maj) CRAMER
                                          (M1644)

MILLAY
  Songs For Soprano And Cello (composed
    with Mullins) *CCU
    S solo,vcl WESTERN BMP67 $1.00
                                          (M1645)

MILLE FILI DI PIOGGIA see De Grandis,
  Renato

MILLE REGRETZ *CCU
  (Azpiazu) [Fr/Span] med solo,pno/org/
    hpsd,gtr BOTE $1.10 contains works
    by: Des Prez; Narvaez   (M1646)

MILLENNIUM, THE see Diamond, David

MILLER
  Boats Of Mine
    med solo,pno SHAWNEE IA5002 $.60
                                          (M1647)
    high solo,pno SHAWNEE IA5006 $.60
                                          (M1648)
  Create In Me A Clean Heart O God
    *sac
    high solo,pno (G maj) FISCHER,C
      RS 123   (M1649)
    low solo,pno (E flat maj) FISCHER,C
      RS 124   (M1650)
  I'd Rather Have Jesus (composed with
    Shea, George Beverly) *sac
    solo,pno BENSON S6224-R $1.00
                                          (M1651)
  Think On These Things *Bibl
    high solo,pno (E flat maj) FISCHER,
      C RS 65   (M1652)
    low solo,pno (D flat maj) FISCHER,C
      RS 66   (M1653)

MILLER, EDWARD
  Mists And Waters
    S solo,vln,clar,pno,perc sc
    AM.COMP.AL. $8.80   (M1654)

MILLER, FRANZ R.
  Schwabische Liebeslieder *sac,song
    cycle
    S/Bar solo,brass/pno BOHM sc s.p.,
    ipr, solo pt s.p.   (M1655)

MILLER, HERB
  We Hear You, Israel
    [Eng] solo,org/pno TRANSCON. SP 30
    $.95   (M1656)

MILLER, JAMES
  Daniel
    low solo,pno GALAXY 1.1681.7 $1.00
                                          (M1657)
  I Am Seeking For A City
    high solo,pno (E flat maj) GALAXY
      1.1556.7 $1.00   (M1658)
  Jim Miller Sings *sac,CCU
    solo,pno HOPE 123 $2.95   (M1659)
  You Gonna Reap
    med solo/low solo,pno (E flat maj)
      GALAXY 1.1424.7 $1.00   (M1660)

MILLER OF WINCHELSEA see Dix, J. Airlie

MILLER'S DAUGHTER, THE see Vauclain,
  Constant

MILLOCKER, KARL (1842-1899)
  Ack, Jag Gav Henne Blott Uppa
    Skuldran En Kyss (from
    Tiggatstudenten)
    solo,pno LUNDQUIST s.p.   (M1661)
  Det Tacka Konet Jag Studerat (from
    Tiggatstudenten)
    solo,pno LUNDQUIST s.p.   (M1662)
  Durch Diesen Kuss (from Der
    Bettelstudent)
    2 soli,pno DOBLINGER 88 506 s.p.
                                          (M1663)
  Nu Ar Jag Pank Och Fagelfri (from
    Tiggatstudenten)
    solo,pno LUNDQUIST s.p.   (M1664)
  Soll Ich Reden, Darf Ich Schweigen
    (from Der Bettelstudent)
    2 soli,pno DOBLINGER 88 507 s.p.
                                          (M1665)

MILLOM ROSOR see Grieg, Edvard Hagerup

MILLOT, E.
  Dieu! Qu'il La Fait Bon Regarder
    solo,pno/inst DURAND s.p.   (M1666)
  Je Me Mets En Votre Merci
    Mez/Bar solo,pno/inst DURAND s.p.
                                          (M1667)
    S/T solo,pno/inst DURAND s.p.
                                          (M1668)
  Le Temps A Laisse Son Manteau
    med solo,pno/inst DURAND s.p.
                                          (M1669)
  Villanelle
    solo,pno/inst DURAND s.p.   (M1670)

MILLS
  Holy Spirit, Flow Through Me *sac
    solo,pno BENSON S5877-R $1.00
                                          (M1671)
  One Day I Will (composed with
    Stallings) *sac
    solo,pno BENSON S7286-S $1.00
                                          (M1672)

MILLS, CHARLES (1914-   )
  Butterfly Caught In The Wind, A
    Mez solo,pno AM.COMP.AL. $.82
                                          (M1673)
  Canticle Of The Sun, The
    high solo,pno AM.COMP.AL. $3.30
                                          (M1674)
  Christ Child, The *sac
    med solo,pno AM.COMP.AL. $.55
                                          (M1675)
  Everlasting Contenders, The
    Mez solo,pno AM.COMP.AL. $.82
                                          (M1676)
  Expiration, The
    med solo,pno AM.COMP.AL. $1.37
                                          (M1677)
  Flo
    med solo,pno AM.COMP.AL. $1.37
                                          (M1678)
  Folk Song From The Greek *Op.72,
    No.1, folk,Greek
    med solo,pno AM.COMP.AL. $1.37
                                          (M1679)
  Four Songs *Op.80, CC4U
    med solo,pno AM.COMP.AL. $5.50
                                          (M1680)
  How Do I Love Thee
    Mez solo,pno AM.COMP.AL. $1.37
                                          (M1681)
  I Fell In Love With A Dragon
    med solo,pno AM.COMP.AL. $.82
                                          (M1682)
  Imaginary Islands
    A solo,pno AM.COMP.AL. $1.37
                                          (M1683)
  Joy
    S solo,pno AM.COMP.AL. $1.37
                                          (M1684)
  Love Me
    med solo,pno AM.COMP.AL. $.82
                                          (M1685)
  Miracle
    med solo,pno AM.COMP.AL. $1.37
                                          (M1686)
  Pastorale
    med solo,pno AM.COMP.AL. $1.37
                                          (M1687)
  Piece For Miss Peggy Lee
    med solo,pno AM.COMP.AL. $.55
                                          (M1688)
  Sacred Canticle *sac
    med solo,pno AM.COMP.AL. $.82
                                          (M1689)
  Song Without Words
    A solo,pno AM.COMP.AL. $1.37
                                          (M1690)
  Swamp Dance *Op.72,No.2
    med solo,pno AM.COMP.AL. $.82
                                          (M1691)
  There Is Nothing False In Thee
    med solo,pno AM.COMP.AL. $1.37
                                          (M1692)
  True Beauty, The *madrigal
    5 soli,pno sc AM.COMP.AL. $1.37
                                          (M1693)
  Voyage, The
    med solo,pno AM.COMP.AL. $1.37
                                          (M1694)

MILLS, CHARLES (cont'd.)
  Wail For Our Dead Guitarist
    med solo,pno AM.COMP.AL. $3.30
                                          (M1695)
  Wintersong
    med solo,pno AM.COMP.AL. $.55
                                          (M1696)

MILNER, ANTHONY (1925-   )
  Dawn
    high solo,pno NOVELLO 17.0038.03
    s.p.   (M1697)
  Our Lady's Hours *song cycle
    high solo,pno NOVELLO 17.0151.07
    s.p.   (M1698)
  Song Of Akhenaten, The
    S solo,chamb.orch NOVELLO
      17.0273.04 s.p.   (M1699)
    S solo,fl,ob,clar,bsn,horn,trp,
      strings NOVELLO rental   (M1700)

MILODEJNE KVITI see Jirak, Karel
  Boleslav

MILODEJNE KVITI see Kapral, Vaclav

MILONGA see Sammartino, Luis

MILOSTNE PISNE see Kapr, Jan

MILOSTNE PISNE see Kricka, Jaroslav

MILOSTNE PISNE NA SLOVA STARE CINSKE
  POESIE see Palkovsky, Oldrich

MILTON see King, Harold C.

MILVEDEN, INGEMAR
  Fyra Visor *CC4U
    solo,pno GEHRMANS s.p.   (M1701)
  Ingenting Far Stora Var Stund Med
    Varandra
    see Tre Sanger
  Karlekens Visa
    see Tre Sanger
  Klart
    see Tva Kammarsanger Till Dikter Av
      Nils Ferlin
  Misterioso
    see Tva Kammarsanger Till Dikter Av
      Nils Ferlin
  Som Ett Blommande Mandeltrad
    see Tre Sanger
  Tre Sanger
    solo,pno GEHRMANS s.p.
    contains: Ingenting Far Stora Var
      Stund Med Varandra; Karlekens
      Visa; Som Ett Blommande
      Mandeltrad   (M1702)
  Tva Kammarsanger Till Dikter Av Nils
    Ferlin
    solo,pno GEHRMANS s.p.
    contains: Klart; Misterioso
                                          (M1703)

MILWID, ANTONI
  Sub Tuum Praesidium *sac,cant
    SB soli,fl,2vln,vcl,cont sc FMA
    FMA 3 s.p.   (M1704)

MIMAAMAKIM see Weiner, Lazar

MIMAAMAQUIM see Honegger, Arthur

MIMAROGLU, ILHAN KAMALEDDIN (1926-   )
  Epicedium
    Mez solo,clar,vln,vcl,pno sc SEESAW
    $5.00   (M1705)

MIMI'S FAREWELL see Puccini, Giacomo,
  Donde Lieta Usci

MIMOSA see Messager, Andre

MIN ELSKTE, JEG ER BUNDEN see Kjerulf,
  [Halfdan]

MIN GUD OG MIN FRELSER see Westergaard,
  Richard

MIN HE'AFAR see Orgad, Ben-Zion

MIN HEMLIGHET see Lassen, Eduard

MIN KARAS VAG see Marvia, Einari,
  Armahan Kulku

MIN KRUSLOCKIGA BABY see Clutsam,
  George H., My Curly Headed Baby

MIN LILLA VRA BLAND BERGEN see
  Sandstrom, Sven-David

MIN LYCKOO see Melartin, Erkki, Onneni
  Saari

MIN ROS see Wennerberg, Gunnar

MIN SANG see Hallstrom, Ivar

MIN SANG see Norlen, Hakan

MIN SKAT see Kjerulf, [Halfdan]

MIN TANKE ER ET MAEGTIGT FJELD see
   Grieg, Edvard Hagerup

MIN TANKES DUVA see Grafstrom

MIN TOS see Hultner

MINA LAULAN SUN ILTASI TAHTIHIN see
   Linnavuori, Franz

MINA LEVNADSTIMMAR STUPA see Froding

MINAMI, HIROAKI (1934-   )
   Banka
      S solo,orch sc ZERBONI 7003 s.p.
                                    (M1706)
   Tanabata
      S solo,orch sc,quarto ZERBONI 7195
         s.p.   (M1707)
      S solo,orch (revised version) sc,
         quarto ZERBONI 7690 s.p.   (M1708)

MINA'S LIED see Marsik, Emanuel, Zpev
   Miny

MINDFULNESS OF BREATHING see Parsons,
   Michael

MINE
   Ave Maria *sac
      solo,pno/org (available in 2 keys)
      HEUGEL s.p.   (M1709)

MINE ALONE see Strauss, Johann

MINGOTE, A.
   Doce Canciones Infantiles *CC12U
      [Span] med solo,pno UNION ESP.
      $1.85   (M1710)
   Manojico
      [Span] med-high solo,pno UNION ESP.
      $1.75   (M1711)
   Navidades
      [Span] med solo,pno UNION ESP. $.50
                                    (M1712)

MINGULAY BOAT SONG
   (Roberton, Hugh S.) solo,pno (E maj)
   ROBERTON 2749 s.p. see also Songs
   Of The Isles   (M1713)

MINIATURAS MEDIEVALES see Munoz
   Molleda, J.

MINIATURE CYCLE OF SIX LITTLE SONGS see
   Nutting, Godfrey

MINIATURES see Mathil

MINKLER, ROSS
   In The Shady Green Pastures
      solo,pno GENTRY $1.00   (M1714)
   Let Me Lose My Life And Find It Lord
      In Thee *sac
      solo,pno SINGSPIR 7025 $1.00
      contains also: Peterson, John W.,
      God Did A Wonderful Thing For Me;
      Moore, John W., Why?   (M1715)
   You're Not Your Own
      solo,pno GENTRY $1.00   (M1716)

MINNE EN DOOD see Zagwijn, Henri

MINNEDEUNTJES see Ketting, Otto

MINNEKLACHT see Mengelberg, Rudolf

MINNELIED see Brahms, Johannes

MINNELIED see Klerk, Albert de

MINNELIED see Kramer, A. Walter

MINNELIED see Kuhn, Siegfried

MINNELIED, A
   low solo,pno (F maj) ALLANS s.p.
                                    (M1717)

MINNELIEDER, LOVE SONGS FROM THE
   MEDIEVAL GERMAN see Schafer, M.

MINNESANG *CCU
   [Czech/Ger] solo,pno SUPRAPHON s.p.
   with original texts   (M1718)

MINNESANGARN I SVERIGE see Peterson-
   Berger, (Olof) Wilhelm

MINNESPIEL see Herrmann, Hugo

MINNS DU PA MAR KNADSDANSEN I STADEN
   see Melartin, Erkki, Heilini
   Soitteli

MINOR BIRD, A see Ames, W.T.

MINOR BIRD, A see Dougherty, Celius

MINSTREL, THE see Malipiero, Gian
   Francesco, Il Cantastorie

MINSTREL, THE see Martin, Easthope

MINSTREL BOY see Sauerbrey

MINSTREL SHOW SONGS see Foster, Stephen
   Collins

MINSTREL'S SONG see Grieg, Edvard
   Hagerup, Spillemaend

MINUET see Schouwman, Hans

MINUET FROM BERENICE see Handel, George
   Frideric

MINUETTO see Gandino, Adolfo

MINUETTO CANTATO see Traetta, Tommaso
   (Michele Francesco Saverio)

MINUIT PILE ET FACE see Messiaen,
   Oliver

MINUN SYDAMENI ON VALMIS, JUMALA see
   Sonninen, Ahti

MIO DIO see Benvenuti, Giacomo

MIO PADRE E TRA I FORZATI see Giordano,
   Umberto

MIORITA see Fussl, K.H.

MIR BIST DU TOT see Pfitzner, Hans

MIR GLANZEN DIE AUGEN see Trunk,
   Richard

MIR IST SO WUNDERBAR see Beethoven,
   Ludwig van

MIR TRAUMTE VON EINEM KONIGSKIND see
   Trunk, Richard

MIR TRAUMTE VON EINEM SCHONEN KIND see
   Weegenhuise, Johan

MIRA NERO DE TARPEYA see Bermudo, Fray
   Juan

MIRACLE see Mills, Charles

MIRACLE, THE see Bush, Geoffrey

MIRACLE OF FAITH, THE *sac
   (Carmichael, Ralph) solo,pno WORD
   S-368   (M1719)

MIRACLE OF GRACE see Wilson, Al

MIRACLE OF GRACE, THE *sac
   (Carmichael, Ralph) solo,pno WORD
   S-110   (M1720)

MIRACULOUS see Roe, Gloria [Ann]

MIRAGE see Chaminade, Cecile

MIRAGE see Levade, Charles (Gaston)

MIRAGE see Schumann, Robert (Alexander)

MIRAGE, THE see Rachmaninoff, Sergey
   Vassilievtch

MIRAGES see Faure, Gabriel-Urbain

MIRAGES see Wolff, A.

MIRANDA see Gandino, Adolfo

MIRANDA see Hageman, Richard

MIRANDOLLE, LUDOVICUS
   Deux Chants Spirituels *sac
      B solo,org BROEKMANS s.p.
      contains: Hymne; Mort Et
         Resurrection   (M1721)
   Die Kindlein Wissen's
      see Drei Lieder Fur Hohe Stimme
   Drei Lieder Fur Hohe Stimme
      high solo,pno BROEKMANS s.p.
      contains: Die Kindlein Wissen's;
         Gaukle, Gaukle, Madchenfalter;
         Nachtl, Regung   (M1722)
   Gaukle, Gaukle, Madchenfalter
      see Drei Lieder Fur Hohe Stimme
   Hymne
      see Deux Chants Spirituels
   La Sagesse Parle D'elle Meme
      solo,org BROEKMANS s.p.   (M1723)

MIRANDOLLE, LUDOVICUS (cont'd.)
   Mort Et Resurrection
      see Deux Chants Spirituels
   Nachtl, Regung
      see Drei Lieder Fur Hohe Stimme

MIRELE *Jew
   solo,pno KAMMEN 487 $1.00   (M1724)

MIRJAMIN LAULU see Sonninen, Ahti

MIRK, VASILIJ (1884-1962)
   Dva Samospeva *CC2U
      solo,pno DRUSTVO DSS 92 rental
                                    (M1725)
   Pesmi Iz Sanj *song cycle
      "Songs From Dreams" med solo,pno
      DRUSTVO DSS 442 rental   (M1726)
   Songs From Dreams *see Pesmi Iz Sanj
   Stiri Pesmi *CC4U
      solo,pno DRUSTVO DSS 369 rental
                                    (M1727)

MIRLITON see Huybrechts, Albert

MIROGLIO, FRANCIS (1924-   )
   Magies
      S solo,10inst sc ZERBONI 6177 s.p.
                                    (M1728)

MIROIR see Bernier, Rene

MIROIR DE PEINE see Andriessen, Hendrik

MIROIR DE VOTRE FAUST see Pousseur,
   Henri

MIROIRS BRULANTS see Poulenc, Francis

MIROLOGIO PER UN BAMBINO see Pizzetti,
   Ildebrando

MIRROR, THE see Ferrari, Gustave

MIRROR FROM VENICE, THE see Andriessen,
   Hendrik, De Spiegel Uit Venetie

MIRROR OF LIFE see Peeters, Flor,
   Spiegel Des Lebens

MIRROR SONG see Offenbach, Jacques

MIRRORED LOVE see Bohun, Lyle de

MIS OJOS TIENEN LA CULPA see Gomez
   Carrillo, Manuel

MISEL NA LJUBICO see Lajovic,
   Aleksander

MISER CATULLE see Huzella, E.

MISERA, DOVE SON! see Mozart, Wolfgang
   Amadeus

MISERA, DOVE SON! - AH! NON SON IO see
   Mozart, Wolfgang Amadeus

MISEREMINI MEI see Steenman, J.

MISERERE see Scheidt, Samuel

MISERERE see Skold

MISERERE see Verdi, Giuseppe

MISERERE A DUE CANTI SOLI see Jommelli,
   Niccolo

MISERERE A-MOLL see Mozart, Wolfgang
   Amadeus

MISERERE, CHRISTE, MEI see Ebart,
   Samuel

MISERERE MEI see Rabaud, Henri

MISERI NOI, MISERA PATRIA see Haydn,
   (Franz) Joseph

MISERICORDISSIME JESU see Schutz,
   Heinrich

MISERO ME - MISERO PARGOLETTO see
   Mozart, Wolfgang Amadeus

MISERO! O SOGNO - AURA, CHE INTORNO
   SPIRI see Mozart, Wolfgang Amadeus

MISON, LUIS (? -1766)
   Una Mesonera Y Un Arriero
      (Subira) [Span] 2 soli,pno UNION
      ESP. $4.00   (M1729)

MISS BREVIS see Reutter, Hermann

MISS FLIRT see Berger, Rod.

MISS T see Kagen, Sergius

MISSA see Dijk, Jan van

MISSA ARMAHIN see Kilpinen, Yrio

MISSA, EDMOND JEAN LOUIS (1861-1910)
Bebe Chante *CC12L
solo,pno cmplt ed ENOCH s.p.
(M1730)

Le Chant De L'Alliance
solo,pno ENOCH s.p.   (M1731)
solo,acap ENOCH s.p.   (M1732)

Vierge Sainte
high solo,pno,pno/pno&vln/
harmonium&vln sc JOBERT s.p.
(M1733)
med solo,pno,pno/pno&vln/harmonium&
vln sc JOBERT s.p.   (M1734)

MISSA IN NATIVITATE DOMINI see
Platamone, Stefano

MISSA MINIMA see Wildgans, Friedrich

MISSA QUATOUR VOCUM see Scarlatti,
Domenico

MISSA UNISONA see Kraft, Karl

MISSIROLI, BINDO
Serenata
[It] solo,pno SONZOGNO 2753 s.p.
(M1735)

MIST ON THE RIVER see Burrows, Rex

MISTA SINNE TIE MENEVI see Kilpinen,
Yrio

MISTAH SHAKESPEAH see Cadman, Charles
Wakefield

MISTER BANJO see Nickerson, Camille

MISTER WESTCOTT'S ONE MILLION DOLLAR
INHERITANCE see Wigglesworth, Frank

MISTERIO see Lasala, Angel

MISTERIOSO see Milveden, Ingemar

MISTERO see Cremesini, M.

MISTERO see Zandonai, Riccardo

MISTICA see Zandonai, Riccardo

MISTLETOE, THE see Berkeley, Lennox

MISTRAL CANTATA see Genzmer, Harald

MISTRESS MINE see Handel, George
Frideric

MISTS see Respighi, Ottorino, Nebbie

MISTS AND WATERS see Miller, Edward

MISTS RISE OVER THE STILL POOLS, THE
see Sydeman, William

MIT DEINEN AUGEN see Lie, Harald

MIT DEINEN BLAUEN AUGEN see Strauss,
Richard

MIT DIR see Bergman, Erik

MIT EINEM GEMALTEN BAND see Beethoven,
Ludwig van

MIT FRIED UND FREUD ICH FAHR DAHIN see
Buxtehude, Dietrich

MIT HJERTE OG MIN LYRE see Kjerulf,
[Halfdan]

MIT MADELN SICH VERTRAGEN see
Beethoven, Ludwig van

MIT MYRTEN UND ROSEN see Schumann,
Robert (Alexander)

MIT WECHSELNDEM SCHLUSSEL see Baur,
Jurg

MIT WURD UND HOHEIT ANGETAN see Haydn,
(Franz) Joseph

MITA TUOSTA, JOS MA LAULAN see
Kilpinen, Yrio

MITAPA SUREN SANOISTA see Kilpinen,
Yrio

MITCHELL
He Giveth More Grace *sac
solo,pno LILLENAS SM-409: RN $1.00
(M1736)

MITCHELL, RAYMOND [EARLE] (1895-   )
Sing No Sad Songs For Me
high solo/med solo,pno FITZSIMONS
$.60   (M1737)

West Wind, The
high solo,pno (F maj) WILLIS $.60
(M1738)
med solo,pno (D maj) WILLIS $.60
(M1739)

MITCHELL, RAYMOND [EARLE] (cont'd.)

low solo,pno (C maj) WILLIS $.60
(M1740)

MITHER HEART, THE see Stickles, William

MITT ALSKADE LILLA SOCKERSKRIN see
Soderman, (Johan) August

MITT HJARTA BEHOVER ETT LITET BARN see
Alvin, Erik

MITT LAND see Rangstrom, Ture

MITT SAGOLAND see Kilpinen, Yrio

MITT TROLLSLOTT see Peterson-Berger,
(Olof) Wilhelm

MITTAGSWELT see Kallausch, Kurt

MITTE DES LEBENS see Fortner, Wolfgang

MITTEN IN DER NACHT see Edler, Robert

MITTERGRADNEGGER, GUNTHER (1923-   )
Heiteres Herbarium
med solo,gtr DOBLINGER GKM 78 $4.00
(M1741)

MITTERHOFER, ALFRED (1940-   )
Drei Geistliche Lieder *sac,CC3U
Bar solo,org DOBLINGER 08 859 s.p.
(M1742)

MITTUMAARI see Marvia, Einari

MIXA, FRANZ
Drei Lieder *CC3U
high solo,pno KRENN 1.42 s.p.
(M1743)

Drei Lieder *CC3U
Bar solo,pno KRENN 1.44 s.p.
(M1744)

Sechs Lieder Im Volkston *CC6U
[Ger] med-high solo,pno OSTER $.50,
ea. in two volumes   (M1745)

Theodor-Storm-Lieder, Folge I *CCU
high solo,pno KRENN 1.46 s.p.
(M1746)
Theodor-Storm-Lieder, Folge II *CCU
B solo,pno KRENN 1.47 s.p.   (M1747)
Theodor-Storm-Lieder, Folge III *CCU
med solo,pno KRENN 1.48 s.p.
(M1748)
Theodor-Storm-Lieder, Folge IV *CCU
Bar solo,pno KRENN 1.49 s.p.
(M1749)
Theodor-Storm-Lieder, Folge V *CCU
T solo,pno KRENN 1.50 s.p.   (M1750)

Vier Lieder *CC4U
med solo,pno KRENN 1.43 s.p.
(M1751)

Vier Lieder *CC4U
low solo,pno KRENN 1.45 s.p.
(M1752)

MIXCO see Gideon, Miriam

MIXTURES see Beerman, Burton

MIYOSHI, AKIRA (1933-   )
En Blanc *CC4U
solo,pno ONGAKU s.p.   (M1753)

MIZMOR-CHIR see Benhamou, Maurice

MIZMOR L'DAVID see Weiner, Lazar

MIZUNO, S.
Autonomy Of Voice
solo,pno ONGAKU s.p.   (M1754)

MJUKA SMA HANDER see Sjogren, Emil

MLADOST see Holoubek, Ladislav

M'N EERSTE see Witte, D.

MNEMOSYNE I see Pousseur, Henri

MO CHE, PICKMANN?!
(Carlo, Musi) solo,pno (Bolognese
dialect) BONGIOVANI 2076 s.p. see
from El Mi Canzunett   (M1755)

MO MARIA see Jillett, David

MO MARIA YOU ARE NEAR see Jillett,
David, Mo Maria

MO-OZ TSUR
see Marcello, Benedetto, B'rochos
Shel Chanukoh

MOBILE FOR SHAKESPEARE see Haubenstock-
Ramati, Roman

MOCHTE SINGEN see Kilpinen, Yrio, Ei
Runo Rahatta Laula

MOCKING BIRD, THE see Bishop, Sir Henry
Rowley

MOCKING FAIRY see Keel, Frederick

MODER SVERIGE see Nordqvist, Gustaf

MODEREN see Nielsen, Carl

MODERENS SANG see Juel-Frederiksen,
Emil

MODERN see Kilpinen, Yrio

MODERN FRENCH SONGS, VOL. I: BEMBERG TO
FRANCK *CCU
(Hale, P.) [Eng/Fr] PRESSER $5.00
high solo,pno; low solo,pno (M1756)

MODERN FRENCH SONGS, VOL. II: GEORGES
TO WIDOR *CCU
(Hale, P.) [Eng/Fr] PRESSER $5.00
high solo,pno; low solo,pno (M1757)

MODERN OCH TIGGARGOSSEN see Merikanto,
Oskar, Aiti Ja Kulkuripoika

MODERN RUSSIAN SONGS, VOL. I: ALPHERAKY
TO MOUSSORGSKY *CCU
(Newman, E.) [Eng] PRESSER $5.00 high
solo,pno; low solo,pno   (M1758)

MODERN RUSSIAN SONGS, VOL. II:
MOUSSORGSKY TO WIHTOL *CCU
(Newman, E.) [Eng] PRESSER $5.00 high
solo,pno; low solo,pno   (M1759)

MODERN SCANDINAVIAN SONGS, VOL. II:
LANGE-MULLER TO WINGE *CCU
(Warrenrath, R.) [Eng/Norw] PRESSER
$5.00 high solo,pno; low solo,pno
(M1760)

MODERN SOPRANO OPERATIC ALBUM, THE
*CCU
S solo,pno BELWIN $6.00   (M1761)

MODERN TENOR OPERATIC ALBUM, THE *CCU
T solo,pno BELWIN $6.00   (M1762)

MODERNE NEDERLANDSE LIED
solo,pno cmplt ed HEUWEKE. 418 s.p.
contains: Beekhuis, Hanna,
Cupidotje; Hartsuiker, Andries,
Sancta Caecilia; Rontgen,
Johannes, Diablerie   (M1763)

MODEST LOVE, A see Sydeman, William

MODINHA see Nobre, Marlos

MODINHAS Y CANCOES, VOL. I see Villa-
Lobos, Heitor

MODINHAS Y CANCOES, VOL. II see Villa-
Lobos, Heitor

MODLITBA see Fibich, Zdenko

MODUGNO, DOMENICO (1928-   )
Le Morte Chitarre
[It] solo,pno CURCI 7096 s.p.
(M1764)

MOE, DANIEL
Greatest Of These Is Love, The *sac
med-low solo,pno AUGSBURG 11-0703
$.75   (M1765)
med-high solo,pno AUGSBURG 11-0702
$.75   (M1766)

MOEDER see Mengelberg, Rudolf

MOEDERDAGLIEDJE see Vladeracken, G. von

MOEDERKE ALLEEN see Clercq, R. de

MOEDERKE ALLEEN see Hullebroeck, Em.

MOEDERS LIEDJE see Bijl, Theo van der

MOEDERTJE see Zweers, [Bernard]

MOEGERLE
Alleluia *sac
solo,pno BENSON S5111-R $1.00
(M1767)

MOERAN
Seven Poems By James Joyce *CC7L
Bar solo,pno OXFORD 62.002 $3.00
(M1768)

MOERAN, ERNEST J. (1894-1950)
Bean Flower, The
see Two Songs

Day Of Palms, The
solo,pno CRAMER $.95   (M1769)

Four Shakespeare Songs
med-high solo,pno NOVELLO
17.0251.03 s.p.
contains: Lover And His Lass,
The; When Daisies Pied; When
Icicles Hang By The Wall; Where
The Bee Sucks   (M1770)

Impromptu In March
see Two Songs

MOERAN, ERNEST J. (cont'd.)

Invitation In Autumn
high solo,pno NOVELLO 17.0080.04
s.p.   (M1771)

Loveliest Of Trees
solo,pno (E maj) ROBERTON 2525 s.p.
                              (M1772)

Lover And His Lass, The
see Four Shakespeare Songs

Nocturne
Bar solo,2fl,3ob,2clar,2bsn,4horn,
3trom,timp,cym,cel,harp,strings
NOVELLO rental   (M1773)

Rosaline
solo,pno (G maj) BOOSEY $1.50
                              (M1774)

Six Suffolk Folk Songs *CC6U,folk,
Eng
med solo,pno FABER C02979 s.p.
                              (M1775)

Two Songs
[Eng] high solo,kbd CHESTER s.p.
contains: Bean Flower, The;
Impromptu In March   (M1776)

When Daisies Pied
see Four Shakespeare Songs

When Icicles Hang By The Wall
see Four Shakespeare Songs

Where The Bee Sucks
see Four Shakespeare Songs

MOESCHINGER, ALBERT (1897-   )
Kantate *Op.24
S solo,vln,pno SCHOTTS 2248 s.p.
                              (M1777)

MOEVS, ROBERT W. (1921-   )
Youthful Songs *CCU
low solo,pno ESCHIG $1.95   (M1778)

MOGLICHKEITEN EINER FAHRT see Schibler,
Armin

MOHAMMEDAANSCH GEBED see Wall, C. v.d.

MOHLER, PHILIPP (1908-   )
Cantata Domestica *cant
solo,2vln,vcl GERIG HG 410 s.p.,
ipa   (M1779)

Vagabundenlieder *Op.36,No.1-3, CC3U
med solo,pno SIKORSKI 143 s.p.
                              (M1780)

MOHNBLUMEN see Strauss, Richard

MOHORI see Ung, Chinary

MOI, J'AI PAS D'CHANCE see Pelemans,
Willem

MOI, JE N'AI PAS UNE AME see Chabrier,
Emmanuel

MOI, SI J'ETAIS EPOUX see Lacome, Paul

MOIN DESCENN' SAINT-PIE see Passani,
Emile

MOIR, F.L.
Down The Vale
low solo,pno (C maj) BOOSEY $1.50
                              (M1781)
high solo,pno (G maj) BOOSEY $1.50
                              (M1782)
med-high solo,pno (F maj) BOOSEY
$1.50   (M1783)
med solo,pno (E flat maj) BOOSEY
$1.50   (M1784)

When Celia Sings
high solo,pno (F maj) CRAMER
                              (M1785)
low solo,pno (E flat maj) CRAMER
                              (M1786)

MOIROLGI see Becker, G.

MOISE see Fragerolle, G.

MOISE see Lacome, Paul

MOISE MOURANT see Louis, E.

MOISHE, MACH ES NOCH AMUHL see Kammen,
Joseph

MOJIM DET'OM see Meier, Jaroslav

MOKOCE CE-MAKA see Villa-Lobos, Heitor

MOLCHANOV, K.
Love *song cycle
[Russ] Bar solo,pno MEZ KNIGA 2.97
s.p.   (M1787)

MOLENAARS DOCHTERKE see Clercq, R. de

MOLINBURSKY PESNICKY see Kunc, Jan

MOLITOR, J.B.
Ode Genethliaque
solo,orch HENN s.p.   (M1788)

MOLLER, SVEND-OVE (1903-1949)
To Og Tyve Sange *Op.18, CC22U
[Dan] FOG III, 160 s.p.   (M1789)

MOLLICONE, HENRY
Ave Maria *sac
S solo,org AM.COMP.AL. $1.10
                              (M1790)

Cleopatra's Dream
S solo,pno AM.COMP.AL. $3.85
                              (M1791)

Come Away, Come Sweet Love
S solo,pno AM.COMP.AL. $2.75
                              (M1792)

Eurydice To Orpheus
S solo,pno AM.COMP.AL. $1.10
                              (M1793)

Geometry
S solo,pno AM.COMP.AL. $1.37
                              (M1794)

God Makes Ducks *song cycle
(Lewis, R.) S solo,pno AM.COMP.AL.
$5.50   (M1795)

Kyrie Eleison
S solo,trom AM.COMP.AL. $2.75
                              (M1796)

Look Down Fair Moon
S solo,pno AM.COMP.AL. $2.75
                              (M1797)

Murali
Mez solo,harp,English horn,2perc sc
AM.COMP.AL. $15.40   (M1798)

Two Love Songs *CC2U
T solo,vla AM.COMP.AL. $2.75
                              (M1799)

MOLLOY, JAMES LYMAN (1837-1909)
Bantry Bay
solo,pno (C maj) BOOSEY $1.50
                              (M1800)

Clang Of The Wooden Spoon, The
low solo,pno (C maj) CRAMER (M1801)
high solo,pno (G maj) CRAMER
                              (M1802)
med-high solo,pno (E maj) CRAMER
                              (M1803)
med solo,pno (D maj) CRAMER (M1804)

Kerry Dance
high solo,pno (F maj) BOOSEY $1.50
                              (M1805)
low solo,pno (E flat maj) BOOSEY
$1.50   (M1806)
med solo,pno PRESSER $.75 (M1807)
2 soli,pno (F maj) BOOSEY $2.00
                              (M1808)

Love's Old Sweet Song
med solo,pno (F maj) BOOSEY $1.50
                              (M1809)
low solo,pno (E flat maj) BOOSEY
$1.50   (M1810)
2 soli,pno (G maj) BOOSEY $1.75
                              (M1811)
high solo,pno (G maj) BOOSEY $1.50
                              (M1812)

Two Little Wooden Shoes
solo,pno CRAMER   (M1813)

MOLLY see Holford, Franz

MOMENT, THE see Nystedt, Knut

MOMENT OF TRUTH, THE see Kaiser, Kurt

MOMENTO see Tirindelli, Pier Adolfo

MOMENTO D'AMORE A UNA COROLLA see
Cairone, Renato

MOMMERS, H.G.
Die Heiligen Drei Konige
[Ger] A solo,chamb.orch BOTE $3.75
                              (M1814)

MOMPELLO, FEDERICO (1908-   )
Fiaba
[It] solo,pno CURCI 485 s.p.
                              (M1815)

Il Paese
[It] solo,pno CURCI 487 s.p.
                              (M1816)

Il Pettirosso
[It] solo,pno CURCI 486 s.p.
                              (M1817)

MOMPOU, FEDERICO (1893-   )
Aquesta Nit Un Mateix Vent
see Combat Del Somni

Aureana Do Sil
[Span] med solo,pno SALABERT-US
$2.25   (M1818)

Canco De La Fira
[Span/Fr] med solo,pno SALABERT-US
$2.25   (M1819)

Cantar Del Alma
med solo,pno SALABERT-US $2.25
                              (M1820)

Combat Del Somni
med solo,pno SALABERT-US $2.25
Catalan, French And Spanish Texts

MOMPOU, FEDERICO (cont'd.)

contains: Aquesta Nit Un Mateix
Vent; Damunt De Tu Nomes Les
Flors; Jo Et Pressentia Com La
Mar   (M1821)

Comptines, Book I *CCU
med solo,pno SALABERT-US $3.00
Catalan And French Texts   (M1822)

Comptines, Book II *CCU
med solo,pno SALABERT-US $3.00
Catalan, French And Spanish Texts
                              (M1823)

Cortina De Fullatge
see Four Songs

Damunt De Tu Nomes Les Flors
see Combat Del Somni

Four Songs
med solo,pno SALABERT-US $4.50
Catalan And French Texts
contains: Cortina De Fullatge;
Incertitud; Neu; Rosa Del Cami
                              (M1824)

Incertitud
see Four Songs

Jo Et Pressentia Com La Mar
see Combat Del Somni

L'Hora Grisa
[Span] med solo,pno UNION ESP. $.90
                              (M1825)

Llueve Sobre El Rio
see Two Songs

Neu
see Four Songs

Pastoral
see Two Songs

Rosa Del Cami
see Four Songs

Two Songs
[Span] med solo,pno SALABERT-US
$3.00
contains: Llueve Sobre El Rio;
Pastoral   (M1826)

MON AME CROYANTE TRESSAILLE ET CHANTE
see Bach, Johann Sebastian, Mein
Glaubiges Herze

MON AMI see Godard, Benjamin Louis Paul

MON AMOUR FLEURIT see Brahms, Johannes,
Meine Liebe Ist Grun

MON ARABELLE see Scotto, Vincent

MON BEL AMI see Levade, Charles
(Gaston)

MON CADAVRE EST DOUX COMME UN GANT see
Poulenc, Francis

MON CAPRICE see Richepin, T.

MON CHAPEAU DES DIMANCHES see Michiels,
G.

MON COEUR A REVE see Delmet, Paul

MON COEUR BALANCE see Frid, Geza

MON COEUR CHANTE see Chaminade, Cecile

MON COEUR DORT see Gedalge, Andre

MON COEUR EST CONTENT see Bonnal,
Ermend

MON COEUR EST LOURD see Bondeville,
Emmanuel de

MON COEUR EST SOUS LA PIERRE see Saint-
Saens, Camille

MON COEUR NE PEUT CHANGER! see Gounod,
Charles Francois

MON COEUR SE RECOMMANDE A VOUS see
Lassus, Roland de (Orlandus)

MON COEUR SOUPIRE see Mozart, Wolfgang
Amadeus

MON COEUR S'OUVRE A TA VOIX see Saint-
Saens, Camille

MON COEUR VEUT S'ENDORMIR see
Fontenailles, H. de

MON COLONEL, J'AI FAIT MES PREUVES see
Messager, Andre

MON COUER, UN CLAIR MATIN see Maurat,
Edmond

MON CYGNE AIME see Wagner, Richard, Mein Lieber Schwan

MON DESIR see Gaubert, Philippe

MON DIEU VOUS M'AVEZ APPELE PARMI LES HOMMES see Honegger, Arthur

MON DOUX JESUS SERA L'ARMURE see Bach, Johann Sebastian

MON ENFANT see Goeyens, Fern.

MON EPOUSEE, MA SOEUR see Canal, Marguerite

MON GRAND-PERE AVAIT TROIS CHATS see Schlosser, Paul

MON HISTOIRE see Milhaud, Darius

MON JARDIN see Fourdrain, Felix

MON JESUS ETAIT MORT see Bach, Johann Sebastian

MON JESUS, TA PATIENCE see Bach, Johann Sebastian

MON LIED see Barbirolli, A.

MON LO DIRO COL LABBRO see Handel, George Frideric

MON MOULIN see Delmet, Paul

MON PARADIS see Rhene-Baton

MON PAYS! see Gretchaninov, Alexander Tikhonovitch

MON PERE A FAIT BATIR MAISON "Down In The Meadow" see Crystal Fountain, The

MON PERE M'A DONNE UN MARI see Inghelbrecht, Desire Emile

MON PETIT CHAT see Vellere, Lucie

MON REVE FAMILIER see Bosmans, Henriette

MON REVE FAMILIER see Czernik, W.

MON REVE FAMILIER see Panizza, Ettore

MON VILLAGE see Trabadelo, A. de

MONA see Adams, Stephen

MONADNOCK CADENZAS AND VARIATIONS see Koch, Frederick

MONARCHS IN MELODY see Wreford, Reynold

MOND UND SONNE see Kuusisto, Ilkka

MONDANITE see Berger, Rod.

MONDI CELESTI see Malipiero, Gian Francesco

MONDLICHT see Wolpert

MONDNACHT see Schumann, Robert (Alexander)

MONDSCHEIN see Kowalski, Max

MONDSCHEIN see Trexler, Georg

MONDSCHEIN see Trunk, Richard

MONDSCHEIN-ODE see Kilpinen, Yrio

MONDSEC see Kleiner, S.

MONDWACHE see Bergman, Erik

MONET, J.
Loveliest Of Trees
med solo,pno PRESSER $.75 (M1827)

MONFERRATO, NATALE
Alma Redemptoris Mater *sac
(Ewerhart, Rudolf) S/T solo,cont
BIELER CS 49 s.p. (M1828)

MONITO see Mozart, Wolfgang Amadeus

MONIUSZKO, STANISLAW (1819-1872)
Cracoviak
solo,pno/inst DURAND s.p. (M1829)
2 soli,pno DURAND 105 s.p. (M1830)

Le Cosaque
solo,pno/inst DURAND s.p. (M1831)
solo,pno DURAND 99 s.p. (M1832)

Le Reve
solo,vln/vcl DURAND s.p. (M1833)
solo,vcl/vln DURAND s.p. (M1834)

MONK, WILLIAM HENRY (1823-1889)
Abide With Me *sac
low solo,pno (C maj) CENTURY 3619
$.40 (M1835)

MONKEYS see Wyner, Yehudi

MONKEY'S CAROL see Stanford, Charles Villiers

MONKS AND RAISINS see Barber, Samuel

MONMOUTH see Busoni, Ferruccio Benvenuto

MONN, GEORG MATTHIAS
Zwei Deutsche Marienlieder *CC2U
(Moder, R.) A solo,org,vln,bvl
DOBLINGER 08 803 sc s.p., ipa,
solo pt s.p. (M1836)

MONNIKENDAM, MARIUS (1896-   )
Invocation
S solo,org DONEMUS s.p. (M1837)

Tre Cantici *CC3U
S solo,org/vcl&pno DONEMUS s.p.
(M1838)

MONODRAMA I see Becker, John J.

MONODY see Diamond, David

MONODY FOR CORPUS CHRISTI see Birtwistle, Harrison

MONOLOG DER STELLA see Krenek, Ernst

MONOLOG DES BLINDEN see Jelinek, Hanns

MONOLOG EINER ALTERNDEN FRAU see Haupt, Walter

MONOLOGEN AUS JEREMIAS VON STEFAN ZWEIG see Roos, Robert de

MONOLOGO see Malipiero, Riccardo

MONOLOGO DI DOSITEO see Mussorgsky, Modest

MONOLOGO DI VITTORE see Neglia, Francesco Paolo

MONOLOGUE OF BORIS see Mussorgsky, Modest

MONOLOGUE OF THE PRINCESS see Strauss, Richard

MONOLOGY see Benes, Juraj

MONSEIGNEUR! see Lacome, Paul

MONSIEUR BOUDE see Clerice, J.

MONSIEUR DE CRAC see Lacome, Paul

MONSIEUR JE CROIS see Lecocq, Charles

MONSIEUR, JE SUIS A BONIFACE see Lacome, Paul

MONSIEUR LE MARQUIS see Messager, Andre

MONSIEUR NOEL see Vieu, Jane

MONSIEUR PEPINET see DuBois, Pierre Max

MONSIEUR PRINTEMPS see Galland, E.

MONSIGNY, PIERRE-ALEXANDRE (1729-1817)
Il Etait Un Oiseau Gris (from Rose Et Colas)
solo,pno DURAND 192 s.p. (M1839)
solo,pno DURAND s.p. (M1840)

O Ma Tendre Musette
solo,pno/inst DURAND s.p. (M1841)

Pour Vous Mon Coeur (from Le Maitre En Droit)
(Flothius, Marius) S solo,ob,pno
BROEKMANS 395-14 s.p. (M1842)

MONT' ON MULLA MORSIANTA see Kilpinen, Yrio

MONTANAS DE CANIGO see Pahissa, Jaime

MONTE CIRCEO see Porrino, Ennio

MONTECLAIR, MICHEL PIGNOLET DE (ca. 1667-1737)
Cantatas For One And Two Voices, Book III *CC9U,cant
(Anthony, James R.; Akmajian, Diran) 1-2 soli,inst A-R ED s.p.
(M1843)

MONTEVERDI, CLAUDIO (ca. 1567-1643)
A Voce Sola
(Malipiero) solo,cont/cembalo cmplt ed RICORDI-ENG 128500 s.p.
contains: Eri Gia Tutta Mia; La Mia Turca; Lasciatemi Morire, "Lamento D'Arianna"; Maledetto Sia L'aspetto; Ohime Ch'io

MONTEVERDI, CLAUDIO (cont'd.)

Cado; Se I Languidi Miei Sguardi; Si Dolce E 'L Tormento
(M1844)

Arioso D'Euridice (from La Favola D' Orfeo)
see Quattro Canti

Arnalta's Lullaby (from L'Incoronazione Di Poppea)
[It/Eng] A solo,kbd FABER F0138 s.p. (M1845)

Canzonetten Heft I *CC10U
(Trede, Hilmar) [Ger/It] SSA soli, pno (med) BAREN. 1562 $4.25 (M1846)

Canzonetten Heft II *CC11U
(Trede, Hilmar) [Ger/It] SSA soli, pno (med) BAREN. 1754 $5.25 (M1847)

Chioma D'Oro
(Manning) "Golden Tresses" high solo,pno ELKIN 27.2442.01 s.p. (M1848)

Combattimento Di Tancredi E Clorinda *cant
(Malipiero, G.F.) [It/Eng] STBar soli,strings,cont sc CHESTER s.p. (M1849)
(Mortari, V.) 2 soli,strings, cembalo sc CARISH 20322 s.p., ipa (M1850)
(Toni, A.) 2 soli,narrator,strings CARISH s.p. (M1851)
(Toni, A.) 2 soli,narrator,2clar, 2bsn,4horn,3trp,4trom,tuba,timp, harp,cembalo (free elaboration)
voc sc CARISH 18740 s.p. (M1852)

Dreistimmige Canzonetten, Heft I *CC7U
solo,S rec,A rec,T rec UNIVER. 12607 $2.25 (M1853)

Dreistimmige Canzonetten, Heft II *CC7U
solo,2S rec,A rec UNIVER. 12608 $2.00 (M1854)

Dreistimmige Canzonetten, Heft III *CC7U
solo,S rec,A rec,T rec UNIVER. 12609 $2.00 (M1855)

Drinking Song (from L'Incoronazione Di Poppea)
[It/Eng] TT soli,kbd FABER F0141 s.p. (M1856)

Duetto Finale (from L'Incoronazione Di Poppea)
"Final Love Duet" [It/Eng] ST soli, kbd FABER F0139 s.p. (M1857)
(Goehr) [It/Ger] 2 soli,pno UNIVER. 13109 $2.75 (M1858)

Duodici Composizioni Vocali Profane E Sacre *sac/sec,CC12L
(Osthoff, W.) solo,pno/cont RICORDI-ENG 129631 s.p. (M1859)

Ecco Di Dolci Raggi
see Scherzi Musicali

Ed E Pur Dungue Vero
(Flothius, Marius) [It] S solo,fl& ob&pno/vla&pno BROEKMANS 395-3 s.p. (M1860)

Eri Gia Tutta Mia
see A Voce Sola
see Scherzi Musicali

Exulta Filia *mot
[Lat/Eng/Ger] high solo,pno SCHOTTS 10549 s.p. (M1861)

Final Love Duet *see Duetto Finale

Five Songs *CC5U
(Hunter, G.; Palisca, C.) [Eng/It] PRESSER $3.00 (M1862)

Golden Tresses *see Chioma D'Oro

Hor Che'l Ciel E La Terra *madrigal
(Stevens, Denis) SSATTB soli,2vln, cont (med) sc PENN STATE PSM 7 s.p., ipa (M1863)

Io Ch'armato Sin Hor
see Scherzi Musicali

Jam Moriar, Mi Fili *sac
(Ewerhart, Rudolf) S solo,cont BIELER CS 58 s.p. (M1864)

Klage Der Ariadne *see Lasciatemi Morire

La Mia Turca
see A Voce Sola
see Scherzi Musicali

MONTEVERDI, CLAUDIO (cont'd.)

Lamento D'Arianna *see Lasciatemi
    Morire

Lasciatemi Morire (from L'Arianna)
  see DREI ARIEN AUS DEM SEIBZEHNTEN
    JAHRHUNDERT
  "Lamento D'Arianna" see A Voce Sola
  "Lamento D'Arianna" see Quattro
    Canti
  solo,pno FORLIVESI 10880 s.p.
                                       (M1865)
  (Mingardo, R.) "Lamento D'Arianna"
    [It] solo,pno CURCI 9235 s.p.
                                       (M1866)
  (Orff, Carl) "Klage Der Ariadne"
    [Ger] A solo,orch voc sc SCHOTTS
    2874 s.p., ipa   (M1867)
  (Orff, Carl) "Lamento D'Arianna"
    [It] A solo,orch voc sc SCHOTTS
    4311 s.p.   (M1868)
  (Parisotti) [It/Fr] Mez/Bar solo,
    pno RICORDI-ARG BA 11800 s.p.
                                       (M1869)

Maledetto Sia L'aspetto
  see A Voce Sola
  see Scherzi Musicali

Marienklage *sac
  (Bornefeld, Helmut) [Lat/Ger] A
    solo,org (med diff) BAREN. 2447
    $8.50   (M1870)

Ohime Ch'io Cado
  see A Voce Sola

Ottavia's Farewell (from
    L'Incoronazione Di Poppea)
  [It/Eng] S solo,kbd FABER F0137
    s.p.   (M1871)

Ottavia's Lament (from
    L'Incoronazione Di Poppea)
  [It/Eng] S solo,kbd FABER F0136
    s.p.   (M1872)

Partenza Amorosa
  (Mingardo, R,) [It] solo,pno CURCI
    9234 s.p.   (M1873)

Quattro Canti
  (Flothius, Marius) [It] A solo,pno
    BROEKMANS B18 s.p.
    contains: Arioso D'Euridice (from
      La Favola D' Orfeo); Lamento
      D'Arianna (from L'Arianna);
      Recitativo Della Speranza (from
      La Favola D' Orfeo); Recitativo
      Ed Aria D'Arnalta (from
      L'incoranazione Di Poppea)
                                       (M1874)

Quel Sguardo
  see Scherzi Musicali

Recitativo Della Speranza (from La
    Favola D' Orfeo)
  see Quattro Canti

Recitativo Ed Aria D'Arnalta (from
    L'incoronazione Di Poppea)
  see Quattro Canti

Renaissance-Lieder *CCU,Renais
  (Gamble, Edwin) T solo,vln,vla,vcl
    (med) PENN STATE PSM 4 s.p., ipa
    contains works by: Finck;
    Lapicida; Stolzer   (M1875)

Salve, O Regina *sac
  (Ewerhart, Rudolf) [Lat] S/T solo,
    cont BIELER CS 7 s.p.   (M1876)

Scene Buffa (from L'Incoronazione Di
    Poppea)
  [It/Eng] ST soli,kbd FABER F0140
    s.p.   (M1877)

Scherzi Musicali
  (Flothius, Marius) [It] S solo,pno
    BROEKMANS B713 s.p.
    contains: Ecco Di Dolci Raggi;
      Eri Gia Tutta Mia; Io Ch'armato
      Sin Hor; La Mia Turca;
      Maledetto Sia L'aspetto; Quel
      Sguardo   (M1878)

Scherzi Musicali *CCU
  (Behrend, Siegfried) solo,gtr
    SIKORSKI 672 s.p.   (M1879)

Scherzi Musicali, Heft I *CCU
  (Trede, Hilmar) SSB soli,2vln,vcl,
    cont (med) BAREN. 1563 $4.00
                                       (M1880)

Scherzi Musicali, Heft II *CCU
  (Trede, Hilmar) SSB soli,2vln,vcl,
    cont (med) BAREN. 1755-6466 $5.75
                                       (M1881)

Se I Languidi Miei Sguardi
  see A Voce Sola
  (Mingardo, R.) [It] solo,pno CURCI
    9015 s.p.   (M1882)

MONTEVERDI, CLAUDIO (cont'd.)

Si Dolce E 'L Tormento
  see A Voce Sola

Six Chamber Duets *CC6U
  (Landshoff) [Ger/It] SS/TT soli,pno
    PETERS 3824A $4.75   (M1883)

Tempro La Cetra
  solo,strings,cembalo sc CARISH
    21404 s.p., ipa   (M1884)

Tre Madrigali *CC3U,madrigal
  (Behrend, Siegfried) solo,gtr
    SIKORSKI 574 s.p.   (M1885)

Zwei Motetten *sac,CC2U,mot
  (Ewerhart, Rudolf) B solo,cont
    BIELER CS 65 s.p.   (M1886)

MONTGOMERY
  Let's All Go Down To The River
    (composed with Richards) *sac
    solo,pno BENSON S6859-S $1.00
                                       (M1887)

MONTGOMERY, BRUCE (1921-   )
  Come Away, Death
    see Four Shakespeare Songs Set 1

  Fair Helen
    high solo,pno NOVELLO 17.0056.01
      s.p.   (M1888)

  Four Shakespeare Songs Set 1
    med solo,pno NOVELLO 17.0252.01
      s.p.
      contains: Come Away, Death; Full
        Fathom Five; O Mistress Mine;
        Tell Me, Where Is Fancy Bred?
                                       (M1889)

  Four Shakespeare Songs Set 2
    med solo,pno NOVELLO 17.0253.01
      s.p.
      contains: Take, O Take Those Lips
        Away; Under The Greenwood Tree;
        When Icicles Hang By The Wall;
        Who Is Sylvia?   (M1890)

  Full Fathom Five
    see Four Shakespeare Songs Set 1

  My True Love Hath My Heart
    med solo,pno NOVELLO 17.0126.06
      s.p.   (M1891)

  O Mistress Mine
    see Four Shakespeare Songs Set 1

  Take, O Take Those Lips Away
    see Four Shakespeare Songs Set 2

  Tell Me, Where Is Fancy Bred?
    see Four Shakespeare Songs Set 1

  Under The Greenwood Tree
    see Four Shakespeare Songs Set 2

  When Icicles Hang By The Wall
    see Four Shakespeare Songs Set 2

  Who Is Sylvia?
    see Four Shakespeare Songs Set 2

  Willie Drowned In Yarrow
    med solo,pno NOVELLO 17.0222.10
      s.p.   (M1892)

MONTMARTRE see Lilien, Ignace

MONTMARTRE see Mulder, Ernest W.

MONTOYA, G.
  Serenade Jalouse
    solo,pno ENOCH s.p.   (M1893)
    solo,acap ENOCH s.p.   (M1894)

MONTPARNASSE see Poulenc, Francis

MONTSALVATGE, XAVIER (1912-   )
  Canciones Para Ninos *CCU
    [Span] med-high solo,pno UNION ESP.
      $3.25   (M1895)

  Canco Amorosa
    [Span] high solo,pno UNION ESP.
      $1.50   (M1896)

  Deschecha De Romance Que Cantaron Los
    Seraphines
    [Span] med solo,pno UNION ESP. $.75
                                       (M1897)

  Oracao
    [Port] med solo,pno UNION ESP. $.75
                                       (M1898)

MONUMENT see Osorio Swaab, R.

MOODY, JAMES
  Con Amore
    solo,pno CRAMER   (M1899)

MOON, THE see Cooke, S.C.

MOON, THE see Hindemith, Paul

MOON AT THE FULL see Ronald, Sir Landon

MOON COMPLAINING see Bury, Winifred

MOON HAS A FACE, THE see Hovhaness,
    Alan

MOON HAS GONE, THE see Alette, C.

MOON I WAIT, THE see Nystroem, Gosta,
    Jag Vantar Manen

MOON MAGIC see Parke, Dorothy

MOON MAGIC see Smoldon, W.L.

MOON OF KWANG TUNG see Mana-Zucca, Mme.

MOON VIGIL see Bergman, Erik, Mondwache

MOON WITH THY LOVELINESS BEAMING see
    Ferguson, Edwin Earle, Luna Que
    Reluces

MOON, YOUR GOD, AND YOU, THE *sac,
    gospel
    solo,pno ABER.GRP. $1.50   (M1900)

MOONBEAMS see Herbert, Victor

MOONLIGHT see Hengeveld, G.

MOONLIGHT see Moss, Katie

MOONLIGHT see Schumann, Robert
    (Alexander), Mondnacht

MOONLIGHT PALLID see Stravinsky, Igor

MOONLIT APPLES see Holford, Franz

MOORE
  In All I Do Today
    med-high solo,pno (F maj) BOSTON
      $1.50   (M1901)

MOORE, DONALD LEE
  For My Sake Thou Hast Died *sac
    med solo,pno PRESSER $.75   (M1902)

  God's Hallowed Place *sac,Gen
    low solo,pno (C maj) WILLIS $.60
                                       (M1903)
    high solo,pno (E flat maj) WILLIS
      $.60   (M1904)

  Help Me To Be Kind
    low solo,pno PRESSER $.75   (M1905)

  I Come Before Thy Throne
    med solo,pno PRESSER $.75   (M1906)

  If I But Touch His Garment's Hem
    *sac,Gen
    med solo,pno (G maj) WILLIS $.60
                                       (M1907)

  Peace I Leave With You *sac
    high solo,pno (A flat maj) SCHIRM.G
      $.85   (M1908)
    low solo,pno (C maj) SCHIRM.G $.85
                                       (M1909)

MOORE, DOROTHY RUDD
  From The Dark Tower
    Mez solo,2fl,3ob,3clar,2bsn,4horn,
      3trp,3trom,tuba,cel,timp,strings
      sc AM.COMP.AL. $13.75   (M1910)
    Mez solo,vcl,pno sc AM.COMP.AL.
      $12.10   (M1911)

  Songs *CCU
    Mez solo,ob sc AM.COMP.AL. $4.95
                                       (M1912)

  Weary Blues
    Bar solo,vcl,pno sc AM.COMP.AL.
      $3.30   (M1913)

MOORE, DOUGLAS STUART (1893-1969)
  Adam Was My Grandfather
    med solo,pno GALAXY 1.0897.7 $1.00
                                       (M1914)

  Ballad Of William Sycamore
    B solo,fl,trom,pno GALAXY 1.2554.7
      $3.75   (M1915)

  Dear Dark Head
    high solo,pno (A maj) GALAXY
      1.2293.7 $1.00   (M1916)

  Dove Song, The (from Wings Of The
    Dove, The)
    S solo,pno (G maj) SCHIRM.G $.75
                                       (M1917)

  I Lie Awake And Listen
    Mez solo,pno GALAXY 1.2483.7 $1.00
                                       (M1918)

  I've Got A Ram (from Devil And Daniel
    Webster, The)
    Bar solo,pno BOOSEY $1.50   (M1919)

  Now May There Be A Blessing (from
    Devil And Daniel Webster, The)
    S solo,pno BOOSEY $1.50   (M1920)

MOORE, F.C.
Lord Let Me Live Today
med solo,pno PRESSER $.75   (M1921)

MOORE, GARY
Bethlehem, Tiny Town *sac,Xmas
solo,pno STAMPS 7265-SN $1.00
(M1922)

MOORE, GENE
Fill Your Life With Love *sac
solo,pno WORD S-313   (M1923)

God's Newest Angel *sac
solo,pno WORD S-350   (M1924)

Let Me Tell You 'Bout A Man *sac
solo,pno WORD S-367   (M1925)

MOORE, J. CHRIS
Lord's Prayer, The
solo,pno CHANTRY VOS 736 s.p.
(M1926)

Two Songs From Pilgrim's Progress
*CC2U
solo,pno CHANTRY VOS 737 s.p.
(M1927)

MOORE, JOHN W.
Burdens Are Lifted At Calvary *sac
[Eng/Swed] solo,pno SINGSPIR 7033
$1.00   (M1928)

Little Boy's Prayer, A *sac
solo,pno SINGSPIR 7014 $.50 (M1929)

Why?
see Minkler, Ross, Let Me Lose My
Life And Find It Lord In Thee

MOORE, JUDY
Keep America Free *sac
med solo,pno CRESPUB CP-S5015 $1.25
(M1930)

MOORE, THOMAS (1779-1852)
Last Rose Of Summer, The
low solo,pno (D maj) ASHDOWN
(M1931)
high solo,pno (F maj) ASHDOWN
(M1932)
med solo,pno (E maj) ASHDOWN
(M1933)

MOORISH MAID, THE see Parker, Henry

MOORLAND LILT *Scot
solo,pno PATERSON s.p. see from
Hebridean Songs, Vol. IV   (M1934)

MOORTEL, ARIE VAN DE (1918-   )
Que Dieu M'accueille Avec Les Oiseaux
*Op.51
solo,pno CBDM s.p.   (M1935)

MOPOKE see Hill

MOR see Palmgren

MOR BRITTA see Peterson-Berger, (Olof)
Wilhelm

MOR, DU AR MIG NARA see Lagerheim-
Romare, Margit

MORAG see Lawson, Malcolm

MORAG'S CRADLE SONG *folk,Scot
(Roberton, Hugh S.) 3 soli,pno
ROBERTON 72072 s.p.   (M1936)

MORALIST, THE see Birch, Robert Fairfax

MORAWETZ, OSKAR (1917-   )
I Love The Jocund Dance
solo,pno THOMP.G   (M1937)

Land Of Dreams
solo,pno THOMP.G   (M1938)

Piping Down The Valleys Wild
solo,pno THOMP.G   (M1939)

MORE AND MORE see Lister, Mosie

MORE OF JESUS AND LESS OF ME *sac,
gospel
solo,pno ABER.GRP. $1.50   (M1940)

MORE PRECIOUS THAN JEWELS *sac,gospel
solo,pno ABER.GRP. $1.50   (M1941)

MORE, SO MUCH MORE see Oldenburg, Bob

MORE THAN LIFE see Redman, Reginald

MORE THAN YOU'LL EVER KNOW see Johnson,
P.

MORE THINGS ARE WROUGHT BY PRAYER see
Warren, Elinor Remick

MOREAU, H.
Pour Bercer Le Coeur
solo,pno ENOCH s.p.   (M1942)

MORELLI, A.
Disperata
[It] solo,pno CURCI 193 s.p.
(M1943)

Il Regno Mio
[It] solo,pno CURCI 195 s.p.
(M1944)

Mattinata
[It] solo,pno CURCI 190 s.p.
(M1945)

Passa La Nave Mia
[It] solo,pno CURCI 192 s.p.
(M1946)

MORENO TORROBA, FEDERICO
Ay Madrilena! (from La Chulapona)
[Span] solo,pno RICORDI-ARG
BA 10031 s.p.   (M1947)

Ay, Mi Morena (from Luisa Fernanda)
[Span] solo,pno RICORDI-ARG BA 7490
s.p.   (M1948)

Mazurca De La Sombrilla (from Luisa
Fernanda)
[Span] solo,pno RICORDI-ARG BA 7488
s.p.   (M1949)

Petenera (from La Marchenera)
[Span] solo,pno RICORDI-ARG
BA 10030 s.p.   (M1950)

MORERA DE MI TIERRA see Gil, Jose

MORERA, ENRIQUE (1865-1942)
Canciones Callejeras *CCU
[Span] high solo,pno,opt gtr UNION
ESP. $2.50   (M1951)

MORGAN, D.
Margaret
solo,pno BERANDOL BER 1324 $1.50
(M1952)

MORGAN, FRANK
Ave Maria
solo,pno CRAMER   (M1953)

MORGAN, HILDA
Lamb, The *sac
solo,pno (G maj) LESLIE 7054
(M1954)

MORGAN LE FAY see Bantock, Granville

MORGAN, ORLANDO
At Christmastide
med solo,pno (E maj) ASHDOWN $1.50
(M1955)
low solo,pno (D flat maj) ASHDOWN
$1.50   (M1956)
high solo,pno (F maj) ASHDOWN $1.50
(M1957)

Clorinda
low solo,orch (F min) ASHDOWN
$1.50, ipr   (M1958)
high solo,orch (A min) ASHDOWN
$1.50, ipr   (M1959)

Fair Rosalind
high solo,pno (F maj) CRAMER $.95
(M1960)
low solo,pno (D maj) CRAMER $.95
(M1961)

My Gentle White Dove
high solo,pno (F maj) CRAMER
(M1962)
low solo,pno (C maj) CRAMER
(M1963)

Vale Of Mont-Marie, The
low solo,pno (E min) ASHDOWN
(M1964)
high solo,pno (G min) ASHDOWN
(M1965)

MORGAN THAU see Grieg, Edvard Hagerup,
Morgendug

MORGEN see Badings, Henk

MORGEN see Bergman, Erik

MORGEN see Kilpinen, Yrio, Aamu

MORGEN see Marvia, Einari, Aamu

MORGEN see Strauss, Richard

MORGEN I NAPOLI see Schierbeck, Poul

MORGEN IN DEN TENGER see Sigtenhorst-
Meyer, Bernhard van den

MORGENDAMMERUNG see Knab, Armin

MORGENDUG see Grieg, Edvard Hagerup

MORGENHYMNE see Henschel, Isadore
George

MORGENLIED see Kilpinen, Yrio

MORGENROOD see Hullebroeck, Em.

MORGENSANG see Nordqvist, Gustaf

MORGENSTERN, L.
Four Ancient Songs Of Solomon *sac,
CC4U
[Heb/Eng] low solo/med solo/cantor,
pno TRANSCON. WJ 424 $1.50
(M1966)

MORGENSTIMMUNG see Bijvanck, Henk

MORGENSTOND see Koetsier, Jan

MORGENZANG see Mulder, Herman

MORGENZANG see Zagwijn, Henri

MORGON see Eklof, Einar

MORGON - DAG - KVELD see Olsen, Sparre

MORGONEN see Sibelius, Jean

MORGONSANG see Abt, Franz

MORGONSANG see Wohlfart, Karl

MORGONSANG UR "HOGA VISAN" see
Melartin, Erkki, Aamulaulu
"Korkeasta Veisusta"

MORGONSTUND see Nystedt, Knut

MORGUE see Thomass, Eugen C.

MORIKE-LIEDER see Wolf, Hugo

MORIKE SONGS, VOL. I: NOS. 1-12 see
Wolf, Hugo

MORIKE SONGS, VOL. II: NOS. 13-24 see
Wolf, Hugo

MORIKE SONGS, VOL. III: NOS. 25-39 see
Wolf, Hugo

MORIKE SONGS, VOL. IV: NOS. 40-44 see
Wolf, Hugo

MORIKE SONGS, VOL. IV: NOS. 40-53 see
Wolf, Hugo

MORIKE SONGS, VOL. IV: NOS. 45-51, 53
see Wolf, Hugo

MORIN, JEAN BAPTISTE
Ad Mensam Coelitus Paratam *sac
(Ewerhart, Rudolf) S/T solo,cont
BIELER CS 45 s.p.   (M1967)

Venite, Exsultemus Domino *sac
(Ewerhart, Rudolf) S/T solo,cont
BIELER CS 50 s.p.   (M1968)

MORIR! SI PURA E BELLA see Verdi,
Giuseppe

MORIRE see Pratella, Francesco Balilla

MORITAT VOM MACKIE MESSER see Weill,
Kurt

MORITAT VOM VERLASSENEN MARIECHEN see
Rasch, Kurt

MORITZ, EDVARD (1891-   )
Fire And Ice
med solo,pno PRESSER $.75   (M1969)

I Feel Me Near To Some High Thing
med solo,pno PRESSER $.75   (M1970)

Improvisation
med-high solo,pno PRESSER $.75
(M1971)

MORLACCHI, FRANCESCO (1784-1841)
Sei Ariette Per Soprano
Coll'accompagnamento Del
Pianoforte *CC6U
S solo,pno FORNI s.p.   (M1972)

MORLEY, THOMAS (1557-1602)
En Varvisa
solo,pno,opt gtr GEHRMANS s.p.
(M1973)

Faithful Heart Enraptured *see
L'Amero, Saro Costante

First Book Of Ayres *CCU
STAINER 3.1336.7 $5.50   (M1974)

It Was A Lover And His Lass
see AS YOU LIKE IT
high solo,pno (F maj) SCHIRM.G $.50
(M1975)

L'Amero, Saro Costante (from Il Re
Pastore)
(Deis) "Faithful Heart Enraptured"
[It/Eng] high solo,vln/fl,pno (E
flat maj) SCHIRM.G $1.25 (M1976)

Two-Part Canzonets For Voices And
Recorders (Viols) *CC13U
(Boalch) SS/ST/AT/SA/TT soli,pno/
strings HINRICHSEN H1998 $2.75
(M1977)

MORMORIO DI FOGLIE see Davico, Vincenzo

MORNEMENT, INA
  Speckled Thrush
    solo,pno ALLANS s.p.   (M1978)

MORNING see Bergman, Erik, Morgen

MORNING see Rachmaninoff, Sergey
  Vassilievitch

MORNING see Sharpe, Evelyn

MORNING see Speaks, Oley, Le Jour

MORNING, THE see Arne, Thomas Augustine

MORNING DEW, THE
  see Five Canadian Folk Songs

MORNING GLORY see Shepherd, Arthur

MORNING HYMN see Henschel, Isadore
  George, Morgenhymne

MORNING PRAYER see Krapf, Gerhard

MORNING SONG see Lessard, John Ayres

MORNING SONG see Thiman, Eric Harding

MORNING STAR see Delius, Frederick

MORNING SUN, THE see Henley, Peter J.

MORRIS, C.H.
  Stranger Of Galilee, The *sac
    high solo,pno (G maj) BOSTON $1.50
                                  (M1979)
    med-high solo,pno (F maj) BOSTON
      $1.50   (M1980)
    low solo,pno (E flat maj) BOSTON
      $1.50   (M1981)
    SA soli,pno BOSTON $1.75   (M1982)
    solo,pno ALLANS s.p.   (M1983)

MORRO, MA PRIMA IN GRAZIA see Verdi,
  Giuseppe

MORS OGON see Hannikainen, Ilmari,
  Aidin Silmat

MORSE, CHARLES HENRY (1853-1927)
  God Is Love *sac
    2 soli,pno BELWIN $1.50   (M1984)

MORT D'ISOLDE see Wagner, Richard

MORT ET RESURRECTION see Mirandolle,
  Ludovicus

MORTAL STORM see Owens, Robert

MORTARI, VIRGILIO (1902-   )
  Alfabeto A Sorpresa
    [It] 3 soli,2pno CURCI 7281 s.p.
                                  (M1985)
  Canzone-Vocalizzo *CCU
    S solo,fl SANTIS 682 s.p.   (M1986)

  De Campassione Matris Ad Filium
    see Due Laude

  De Compassione Matrem Tempora
    Passonis Sue
    see Due Laude

  Due Laude *sac
    solo,2fl,ob,2clar,2bsn,2horn,trp,
    pno sc CARISH 21693 s.p., ipa
    contains: De Compassione Matris
      Ad Filium; De Compassione
      Matrem Tempora Passonis Sue
                                  (M1987)
  Due Liriche *see Secchi E Sberlechi
                                  (M1988)
  Giro Giro Tondo *CC7L
    solo,pno FORLIVESI 11329 s.p.
                                  (M1989)
  Il Mio Uccelo Nel Deserto
    see Tre Liriche Di R. Tagore

  Parlami Amor Mio
    see Tre Liriche Di R. Tagore

  Secchi E Sberlechi
    Mez/Bar solo,pno RICORDI-ENG 120109
    s.p. see from Due Liriche (M1990)

  Sopra Le Verdi E Gialle Risaie
    see Tre Liriche Di R. Tagore

  Tre Liriche Di R. Tagore
    solo,pno cmplt ed BONGIOVANI 789
    s.p.
    contains: Il Mio Uccelo Nel
      Deserto; Parlami Amor Mio;
      Sopra Le Verdi E Gialle Risaie
                                  (M1991)
MORTE DI BORIS see Mussorgsky, Modest,
  Death Of Boris, The

MORTELLE SOUFFRANCE see Guiraud, Ernest

MORTELMANS, LODEWIJK (1868-1952)
  De Vlaamsche Tale *No.4
    solo,pno ALSBACH s.p.   (M1992)

  Doornroosje *No.18
    solo,pno ALSBACH s.p.   (M1993)

  Gebed Van Stella
    S solo,pno CBDM s.p.   (M1994)

  Hansje *No.15
    solo,pno ALSBACH s.p.   (M1995)

  Heil U, Moeder *No.11
    solo,pno ALSBACH s.p.   (M1996)

  Het Jonge Jaar *No.7
    solo,pno ALSBACH s.p.   (M1997)

  Het Strooien Dak *No.5
    solo,pno ALSBACH s.p.   (M1998)

  Hoe Schoon De Morgendauw *No.3
    solo,pno ALSBACH s.p.   (M1999)

  In 'T Avondduister Dwaal Ik *No.19
    solo,pno ALSBACH s.p.   (M2000)

  'K Hoore Tuitend' Hoornen *No.12
    solo,pno ALSBACH s.p.   (M2001)

  Kindje Wat Ben Je Toch Zacht *No.16
    solo,pno ALSBACH s.p.   (M2002)

  Klokkenzang *No.13
    solo,pno ALSBACH s.p.   (M2003)

  Mijn Lieveken Open Je Deurken *No.17
    solo,pno ALSBACH s.p.   (M2004)

  Pardoent *No.1
    solo,pno ALSBACH s.p.   (M2005)

  'T Avondt *No.8
    solo,pno ALSBACH s.p.   (M2006)

  'T Groeit Een Blomken *No.9
    solo,pno ALSBACH s.p.   (M2007)

  'T Is De Mandel *No.2
    solo,pno ALSBACH s.p.   (M2008)

  'T Meezeken *No.10
    solo,pno ALSBACH s.p.   (M2009)

  Treurzang *No.20
    solo,pno ALSBACH s.p.   (M2010)

  Wiegeliedje *No.14
    solo,pno ALSBACH s.p.   (M2011)

  Wierook *No.6
    solo,pno ALSBACH s.p.   (M2012)

MORTES LES FLEURS see Paray, Paul

MORTI see Caggiano, Roberto

MORTICINO see D'Ambrosi, Dante

MORTIMER, C.G.
  Three Songs Of The Birds *CC3U
    solo,pno LEONARD-ENG   (M2013)

MORTO see Gandino, Adolfo

MORTON, DAVID
  Tears, Idle Tears
    S solo,ob,harp sc HARP PUB $3.75
                                  (M2014)
MORVA see Newton, Ernest

MORYL, RICHARD
  Corridors
    med solo,perc AM.COMP.AL. $1.65
                                  (M2015)
MOSCHEO
  Worry, Who, I? *sac
    solo,pno LILLENAS SM-947: SN $1.00
                                  (M2016)
MOSENTHAL, JOSEPH (1834-1896)
  I Will Magnify Thee, O God *sac
    S&high solo,pno SCHIRM.G $1.00
                                  (M2017)
MOSER, RUDOLF
  Sieben Lieder *Op.14,No.1-7, CC7U
    solo,pno HUG s.p.   (M2018)

MOSIE LISTER'S SONG FOLIO see Lister,
  Mosie

MOSKAUER NACHTE
  see Internationale Volkslieder, Vol.
  2

MOSS, KATIE
  Moonlight
    low solo,pno (C maj) LEONARD-ENG
                                  (M2019)
    high solo,pno (E flat maj) LEONARD-
    ENG   (M2020)

  Out Of The Silence
    high solo,pno (G maj) CRAMER
                                  (M2021)
    low solo,pno (F maj) CRAMER (M2022)

MOSS, LAWRENCE
  Three Rilke Songs *CC3U
    A solo,pno sc SEESAW $6.00   (M2023)

MOSTLY ABOUT LOVE see Thomson, Virgil

MOSZKOWSKI, MORITZ (1854-1925)
  Pres Du Berceau
    solo,pno ENOCH s.p.   (M2024)
    solo,acap ENOCH s.p.   (M2025)

MOT DET HOGA! see Chrisander, Nils

MOT KVALL see Berg, Gottfrid

MOT NORD see Bergman, Erik

MOTE see Liljefors, Ruben

MOTE I GRANDEN see Lagerheim-Romare,
  Margit

MOTET see Lajtha, Laszlo

MOTET AND MADRIGAL see Pleskow, Raoul

MOTETS A JOUER SUR LE PIPEAU see
  Anonymous

MOTETS DU TREIZIEME SIECLE see
  Anonymous

MOTETTI A CANTO SOLO CON STROMENTI see
  Vivaldi, Antonio

MOTETTI A VOCE SOLA see Cazzati,
  Maurizio

MOTH, THE see Berkeley, Lennox

MOTHER see Matesky, T.

MOTHER see Srebotnjak, Alojz F., Mati

MOTHER see Thordarson, Sigurdur

MOTHER, THE see Nielsen, Carl, Moderen

MOTHER AT THY FEET IS KNEELING see
  Saint Jean Du Sacre Coeur, Soeur

MOTHER COMFORT see Britten, Benjamin

MOTHER GOOSE see Lessard, John Ayres

MOTHER GOOSE SONGS see Haubiel, Charles

MOTHER I WILL HAVE A HUSBAND see Jacob,
  Gordon

MOTHER MACHREE see Ball, Ernest R.

MOTHER NIGHT see Sharpe, Evelyn

MOTHER ON THIS BLESSED DAY see Wilber,
  Lawrence

MOTHER TO BABE see Ashley, Derick

MOTHER TO SON see Buric, Marijan

MOTHER WRITES A PRAYER see Smith,
  Herbert Arnold

MOTHER'S DAY see Weigl, Vally

MOTHER'S DAY HYMN, A see Barnes, Edward
  Shippen

MOTHER'S EVENING PRAYER see Brown

MOTHER'S EVENING PRAYER see Butcher

MOTHER'S EVENING PRAYER see Fischer,
  Irwin

MOTHER'S EVENING PRAYER see MacDermid

MOTION AND STILLNESS see Vaughan
  Williams, Ralph

MOTIVI see Malipiero, Riccardo

MOTKE FON SLOBODKE *Jew
  solo,pno KAMMEN 36 $1.00   (M2026)

MOTO-GIRL see Berger, Rod.

MOTS D'AMOUR see Chaminade, Cecile

MOTSATSER see Hallstrom, Ivar

MOTT, JOYCE LOCK
  John McKay Sings Joyce Mott *sac,
    CCUL
    solo,kbd SINGSPIR 5018 $1.00
                                  (M2027)
  Thank You, Jesus *sac
    solo,pno oct MASTER CP-MM 2001
    $1.25   (M2028)

MOTTE, DIETHER DE LA (1928-   )
  Drei Gesange Nach Gedichten Von
    Andreas Gryphius *CC3U
    Bar solo,org (diff) BAREN. 4117
    $9.75   (M2029)

MOTTE LA CROIX, A.F.
A Bethleem
[Fr] med solo,pno ESCHIG $1.10 see
from Noels (M2030)

Au Soir De Noel
[Fr] med solo,pno ESCHIG $.60 see
from Noels (M2031)

La Creche
[Fr] med solo,pno ESCHIG $.60 see
from Noels (M2032)

Noels *see A Bethleem; Au Soir De
Noel; La Creche (M2033)

MOUE, QUAND J'ETAIS CHEZ MON PERE
see Chants De France Vol. II

MOUETTES see Lazarus, Daniel

MOULAERT, RAYMOND (1875-1962)
Alle Sotten En Draghen Gheen Bellen
see Zes Oud-Nederlandse Gedichten

Blanche Com Lys...
see Poemes De La Vieille France,
Deuxieme Recueil

Die Minne Bidde Ic
see Zes Oud-Nederlandse Gedichten

Ghequetst Ben Ic Van Binnen
see Zes Oud-Nederlandse Liederen

Het Daghet In Den Oosten
see Zes Oud-Nederlandse Liederen

Het Waren Twee Coninckinderen
see Zes Oud-Nederlandse Liederen

Hoe Gariel Maria Vond
see Zes Oud-Nederlandse Gedichten

Ick Seg Adieu
see Zes Oud-Nederlandse Liederen

Laet Staen
see Zes Oud-Nederlandse Gedichten

Le Jardin De Ma Tante
see Quatre Poemes De Tristan
Klingsor

Le Tournoi
see Poemes De La Vieille France,
Deuxieme Recueil

L'eau Passe *CC10L
med solo cmplt ed CBDM s.p. (M2034)

Les Poetes Precieux
see Poemes De La Vieille France,
Deuxieme Recueil

L'escamoteur
see Quatre Poemes De Tristan
Klingsor

Midi En Campine Et Crepuscule En
Campine
Mez/Bar solo,pno/org CBDM s.p.
(M2035)

Naer Oostland
see Zes Oud-Nederlandse Liederen

O Oogen
see Zes Oud-Nederlandse Gedichten

Passacaille Sur En Theme De Jean-
Sebastien Bach *vocalise
S solo,pno CBDM s.p. (M2036)

Petit Mercier
see Poemes De La Vieille France,
Deuxieme Recueil

Poemes De La Vieille France, Deuxieme
Recueil
med solo,pno cmplt ed CBDM s.p.
contains: Blanche Com Lys...; Le
Tournoi; Les Poetes Precieux;
Petit Mercier (M2037)

Poemes De La Vieille France,
Quatrieme Recueil *CC7L
med solo cmplt ed CBDM s.p. (M2038)

Quatre Poemes De Tristan Klingsor
cmplt ed CBDM s.p.
contains: Le Jardin De Ma Tante
(Mez solo,pno) (song cycle,
contains: Chanson De La
Citrouille; Chanson De
L'oignon; Chanson De
L'artichaut); L'escamoteur
(Mez/Bar solo,pno) (M2039)

Sij Heeft Met Mij Den Zot Gescheert
see Zes Oud-Nederlandse Gedichten

Slaap, Kindeken, Slaap
see Zes Oud-Nederlandse Liederen

MOULAERT, RAYMOND (cont'd.)
Zes Oud-Nederlandse Gedichten
med solo,pno cmplt ed CBDM s.p.
contains: Alle Sotten En Draghen
Gheen Bellen; Die Minne Bidde
Ic; Hoe Gariel Maria Vond; Laet
Staen; O Oogen; Sij Heeft Met
Mij Den Zot Gescheert (M2040)

Zes Oud-Nederlandse Liederen
med solo,pno cmplt ed CBDM s.p.
contains: Ghequetst Ben Ic Van
Binnen; Het Daghet In Den
Oosten; Het Waren Twee
Coninckinderen; Ick Seg Adieu;
Naer Oostland; Slaap, Kindeken,
Slaap (M2041)

MOUMOUTTE see Perronnet, Amelie

MOUNTAIN BREEZES see Williams, Meirion

MOUNTAIN BROOK see Kountz, Richard

MOUNTAIN BROOK, THE see Kilpinen, Yrio,
Tunturilahde

MOUNTAIN GLORY SONGS *sac,CC11UL
solo,pno,gtr LILLENAS MB-341 $1.95
music by "Mountain Glory" Group
(M2042)

MOUNTAIN LOVERS see Squire, W.H.

MOUNTAIN MAID, THE see Grieg, Edvard
Hagerup, Haugtussa

MOUNTAINS see Rasbach, Oscar

MOUNTAINS ARE DANCING, THE see Duke

MOUNTAINS OF ALLAH, THE see Geehl,
Henry Ernest

MOUNTAINS OF ALLAH, THE see Geehl,
Henry Ernest

MOUNTEBANKS, THE see Martin, Easthope

MOUNTEBANK'S SONG see Wishart

MOURANT, WALTER
Anthony O'Daly
med solo,pno AM.COMP.AL. $.55
(M2043)

Arpeggio
med solo,pno AM.COMP.AL. $.55
(M2044)

Barbarians
med solo,pno AM.COMP.AL. $1.10
(M2045)

Bessie Bobtail
A solo,pno AM.COMP.AL. $1.10
(M2046)

Bird Sings Now, A
med solo,pno AM.COMP.AL. $.55
(M2047)

Breakfast Time
med solo,pno AM.COMP.AL. $.55
(M2048)

Buds, The
med solo,pno AM.COMP.AL. $1.10
(M2049)

Check
med solo,pno AM.COMP.AL. $1.10
(M2050)

Chill Of The Eve
med solo,pno AM.COMP.AL. $1.10
(M2051)

Coolin, The
med solo,pno AM.COMP.AL. $1.10
(M2052)

Daisies, The
med solo,pno AM.COMP.AL. $1.10
(M2053)

Egan O'Rahilly
med solo,pno AM.COMP.AL. $1.10
(M2054)

Evening Falls, An
med solo,pno AM.COMP.AL. $1.10
(M2055)

Everything That I Can Spy
med solo,pno AM.COMP.AL. $1.10
(M2056)

Goat Paths, The
med solo,pno AM.COMP.AL. $2.75
(M2057)

Hour Cometh, The *Bibl
low solo,pno AM.COMP.AL. $1.10
(M2058)

Indian Serenade, The
med solo,pno AM.COMP.AL. $2.20
(M2059)

Katty Gollagher
med solo,pno AM.COMP.AL. $.55
(M2060)

Little Things
med solo,pno AM.COMP.AL. $1.10
(M2061)

Lovers
S solo,pno AM.COMP.AL. $1.10
(M2062)

Love's Secret
med solo,pno AM.COMP.AL. $1.10
(M2063)

MOURANT, WALTER (cont'd.)
Mary Hynes
med solo,pno AM.COMP.AL. $.55
(M2064)

Mary Ruane
med solo,pno AM.COMP.AL. $.55
(M2065)

Nancy Walsh
med solo,pno AM.COMP.AL. $.55
(M2066)

Nothing At All
med solo,pno AM.COMP.AL. $2.75
(M2067)

On The Eve Of His Execution
Bar solo,pno sc AM.COMP.AL. $2.20
(M2068)

Paps Of Dana, The
med solo,pno AM.COMP.AL. $1.10
(M2069)

Peggy Mitchell
med solo,pno AM.COMP.AL. $.55
(M2070)

Rivals, The
med solo,pno AM.COMP.AL. $1.10
(M2071)

Rose On The Wind, The
med solo,pno AM.COMP.AL. $1.10
(M2072)

Secret, The
A solo,pno AM.COMP.AL. $.55 (M2073)

Shell, The
med solo,pno AM.COMP.AL. $2.75
(M2074)

Tale Of Mad Brigid, The
med solo,pno AM.COMP.AL. $2.75
(M2075)

To Helen
med solo,pno AM.COMP.AL. $1.10
(M2076)

Tryst
low solo,pno AM.COMP.AL. $1.10
(M2077)

Voice Of God, The
med solo,pno AM.COMP.AL. $1.10
(M2078)

Washed In Silver
med solo,pno AM.COMP.AL. $.55
(M2079)

Weep You No More
med solo,pno AM.COMP.AL. $1.10
(M2080)

When You Are Old
med solo,pno AM.COMP.AL. $1.10
(M2081)

When You Walk
med solo,pno AM.COMP.AL. $.27
(M2082)

White Fields
med solo,pno AM.COMP.AL. $.55
(M2083)

White Window, The
A solo,pno AM.COMP.AL. $1.65
(M2084)

Woman Is A Branchy Tree, A
med solo,pno AM.COMP.AL. $.55
(M2085)

MOURN! MOURN! see Weber

MOURNING SCENE FROM SAMUEL see Rorem,
Ned

MOUTET
Pacifico
solo,pno AMPHION s.p. solo pt, voc
sc (M2086)

MOUTON, H.
Automne
solo,pno/inst DURAND s.p. (M2087)

Enchainement
solo,pno/inst DURAND s.p. (M2088)

Je Ne Sais
med solo,pno/inst DURAND s.p.
(M2089)

Je T'aime
[Fr] solo,acap oct DURAND s.p.
(M2090)
solo,pno/inst DURAND s.p. (M2091)

L'Adorable Aventure
[Fr] solo,acap oct DURAND s.p.
(M2092)
solo,pno/inst DURAND s.p. (M2093)

Marche Riante
[Fr] solo,acap oct DURAND s.p.
(M2094)
solo,pno/inst DURAND s.p. (M2095)

Menton
[Fr] solo,acap oct DURAND s.p.
(M2096)
solo,pno/inst DURAND s.p. (M2097)

Nuit D'Ete
solo,pno/inst DURAND s.p. (M2098)

Quand L'amour Veille
med solo,pno/inst DURAND s.p.
(M2099)

MOUTON, H. (cont'd.)

Recueillement
solo,pno/inst DURAND s.p.   (M2100)
[Fr] solo,acap oct DURAND s.p.
                         (M2101)

Soir Sur L'eau
solo,pno/inst DURAND s.p.   (M2102)

Sur Le Chemin D'amour
solo,pno/inst DURAND s.p.   (M2103)
[Fr] solo,acap oct DURAND s.p.
                         (M2104)

Venez, Prince Charmant
solo,pno/inst DURAND s.p.   (M2105)
[Fr] solo,acap oct DURAND s.p.
                         (M2106)

MOVING PULSES see Ezaki, K.

MOY, PAUVRE FILLE see Besard, Jean-
Baptiste

MOYZES, ALEXANDER (1906-)
Cesta
S solo,orch/pno SLOV.HUD.FOND s.p.
                         (M2107)

Detske Pesnicky *CCU
high solo,pno SUPRAPHON s.p.
                         (M2108)

Piesne *CCU
solo,pno SLOV.HUD.FOND s.p. (M2109)

Ranna Rosa *song cycle
Mez solo,pno SLOV.HUD.FOND s.p.
                         (M2110)

Slovenske Ludove Piesne *CCU
solo,pno SLOV.HUD.FOND s.p. (M2111)

Tri Dvojspevy *CC3U
boy solo/girl solo,pno
SLOV.HUD.FOND s.p.   (M2112)

V Jeseni
Mez solo,pno SLOV.HUD.FOND s.p.
                         (M2113)

MOZART-ALBUM see Mozart, Wolfgang
Amadeus

MOZART IN PRAG see Pokorny, Antonin,
Mozart V Praze

MOZART, LEOPOLD (1719-1787)
Du Wahrer Mensch Und Gott *sac
S solo,org,vln sc BOHM s.p. (M2114)

MOZART V PRAZE see Pokorny, Antonin

MOZART, WOLFGANG AMADEUS (1756-1791)
A Berenice E Vologeso - Sol Nascente
*K.70
S solo,2ob,2horn,strings BREITKOPF-
L rental   (M2115)

A Cloe *see An Chloe

A Questo Seno Deh Vieni, Idolo Mio -
Or Che Il Cielo A Me Ti Rende
*K.374
"Komm An Mein Herz, O Liebling
Meiner Seele - All Des Lebens
Selikeiten" see Mozart, Wolfgang
Amadeus, Ah, Lo Previdi
[It/Eng] S solo,pno INTERNAT. $1.00
                         (M2116)
"Komm An Mein Herz, O Liebling
Meiner Seele - All Des Lebens
Seligkeiten" S solo,2ob,2horn,
strings BREITKOPF-L rental
                         (M2117)

Abendempfindung *K.523
(Mottl, F.) S solo,fl,ob,clar,bsn,
2horn,strings BREITKOPF-L rental
                         (M2118)

Ach, Ich Fuhls (from Die Zauberflote)
S solo,pno/orch KALMUS $3.00
                         (M2119)
S solo,fl,ob,bsn,strings voc sc
BREITKOPF-W EB 208 s.p. contains
also: Der Vogelfanger Bin Ich Ja
(B solo,2clar,2bsn,2horn,
strings); Dies Bildnis Ist
Bezauberned Schon (T solo,fl,2clar,
2bsn,2horn,strings); Ein Madchen
Oder Weibchen Wunscht Papageno
Sich (B solo,fl,2ob,2bsn,2horn,
cel,strings); In Diesen Heil'gen
Hallen (B solo,2fl,2bsn,2horn,
strings); O Isis Und Osiris,
Schenket Der Weisheit Geist (B
solo,2bsn,3trom,strings, 2
bassethorns); O Zittre Nicht,
Mein Lieber Sohn - Zum Leider Bin
Ich Ausekoren (S solo,2ob,2bsn,
2horn,strings)
S solo,fl,ob,bsn,strings BREITKOPF-
L rental   (M2121)
(Deis) [Ger/It/Eng] S solo,pno (G
min) SCHIRM.G $.85   (M2122)

Ach Meine Ahnung *see Ah, Lo Previdi

Ach, Meine Ahnung - Ha! Entflieh Aus
Meinen Augen *see Ah Lo Previdi
- Ah! T'invola Agl'occhi Miei

Ach Offnet Aug' Und Ohren *see
Aprite Un Po' Quegl' Occhi

Ach, Sie Stirbt, Meine Hoffnung *see
Mia Speranza Adorata - Ah, Non
Sai

Ach, Sie Stirbt, Meine Hoffnung -
Ach, Sie Schwanden, Meine Freuden
*see Mia Speranza Adorata - Ah,
Non Sai

Ach, Was Verbrach Ihr Sterne - Schon
Hoff Ich Das Ufer *see Ma Che Vi
Fece - Sperai Vicino Al Lido

Agnus Dei (from Kronungsmesse) sac
S solo,pno (F maj) LIENAU HOS 117
s.p.   (M2123)
Mez solo,pno (E flat maj) LIENAU
HOS 118 s.p.   (M2124)

Ah, Lo Previdi *K.272
see Concert Arias
"Ach Meine Ahnung" S solo,2ob,
2horn,strings voc sc BREITKOPF-W
EB 6851 s.p. contains also: A
Questo Seno Deh Vieni, Idolo Mio
- Or Che Il Cielo A Me Ti Rende,
"Komm An Mein Herz, O Liebling
Meiner Seele - All Des Lebens
Selikeiten", K.374 (S solo,2ob,
2horn,strings); Bella Mia Fiamma
- Resta O Cara, "Teuerstes
Madchen, Ich Scheide", K.528 (S
solo,fl,2ob,2bsn,2horn,strings);
Ma Che Vi Fece - Sperai Vicino Al
Lido, "Ach, Was Verbrach Ihr
Sterne - Schon Hoff Ich Das
Ufer", K.368 (S solo,2fl,2bsn,
2horn,strings); Mia Speranza
Adorata - Ah, Non Sai, "Ach, Sie
Stirbt, Meine Hoffnung", K.416 (S
solo,2ob,2bsn,2horn,strings);
Misero! O Sogno - Aura, Che
Intorno Spiri, "Wehe Mir! Ist's
Wahrheit - Eilet, Mitleid'ge
Lufte", K.431 (T solo,2fl,2bsn,
2horn,strings)   (M2125)

Ah Lo Previdi - Ah! T'invola
Agl'occhi Miei *K.272, scena
"Ach, Meine Ahnung - Ha! Entflieh
Aus Meinen Augen" S solo,2ob,
2horn,strings BREITKOPF-L rental
                         (M2126)

Ah, Lo So, Piu Non M'avanza (from Die
Zauberflote)
[It] S solo,pno RICORDI-ARG BA 8657
s.p.   (M2127)

Ah, Quand Je Suis Loin D'elle (from
Don Giovanni)
T solo,pno/inst DURAND s.p. (M2128)

Ah, Se In Ciel, Benigne Stelle
*K.538
S solo,2ob,2bsn,2horn,strings voc
sc BREITKOPF-W s.p.   (M2129)
S solo,2ob,2bsn,2horn,strings
BREITKOPF-L rental   (M2130)

Ah, Vous Dirai-Je Maman
(Adam) [It] S solo,pno,fl
(variations on the theme)
RICORDI-ARG s.p.   (M2131)

Air De Despina (from Cosi Fan Tutte)
S solo,orch HENN s.p.   (M2132)

Air De Suzanne (from Le Nozze Di
Figaro)
solo,orch HENN s.p.   (M2133)

Al Desio Di Chi T'adora (from Le
Nozze Di Figaro)
see Songs From Figaro, Book 1:
Soprano (The Countess)

Alcandro, Lo Confesso *K.294
[It/Eng] B solo,pno INTERNAT. s.p.,
ipr   (M2134)
(Stuber) [It/Ger] S solo,2fl,2clar,
2bsn,2horn,strings sc MUSIKWISS.
BR50 s.p.   (M2135)

Alcandro, Lo Confesso [Kv 512]
*K.512
B solo,fl,2ob,2bsn,2horn,strings
voc sc BREITKOPF-W EB 6450 s.p.
contains also: Cosi Dunque
Tradisci, K.432 (B solo,2fl,2ob,
2bsn,2horn,strings); Mentre Ti
Lascio, O Figlia, K.513 (B solo,
fl,2clar,2bsn,2horn,strings); Per
Questa Bella Mano, K.612 (B solo,
fl,2ob,2bsn,2horn,strings);
Rivolgete A Lui Lo Sguardo, K.584
(B solo,2ob,2bsn,2trp,timp,
strings); Un Bacio Di Mano, K.541
(B solo,fl,2ob,2bsn,2horn,
strings)   (M2136)

MOZART, WOLFGANG AMADEUS (cont'd.)

Alcandro, Lo Confesso - Non So D'onde
Viene *K.294
S solo,2fl,2clar,2bsn,2horn,strings
voc BREITKOPF-W s.p.   (M2137)
S solo,2fl,2clar,2bsn,2horn,strings
BREITKOPF-L rental   (M2138)
S solo,2fl,2clar,2bsn,2horn,strings
KALMUS $3.00   (M2139)
"O Freund, Was Mich Ergriffen -
Woher Dieses Bangen" Bar/B solo,
fl,2ob,2bsn,2horn,strings
BREITKOPF-L rental   (M2140)
(Stueber, Carl) [It/Ger] S solo,pno
(med diff) voc sc ALKOR AE 259A
s.p.   (M2141)

Alleluia (from Exsultate Jubilate)
sac,Easter
[Lat] med solo,pno MARKS $1.50
                         (M2142)
[Lat] high solo,pno MARKS $1.50
                         (M2143)
med solo,pno (E flat maj) WATERLOO
$.65   (M2144)
S solo,pno NOVELLO 17.0001.04 s.p.
                         (M2145)
low solo,pno (C maj) FISCHER,C
S 5727   (M2146)
med solo,pno (E flat maj) FISCHER,C
S 5726   (M2147)
high solo,pno (F maj) FISCHER,C
S 5721   (M2148)
low solo,pno (C maj) SCHIRM.G $.85
                         (M2149)
med solo,pno (E flat maj) SCHIRM.G
$.85   (M2150)
high solo,pno (F maj) SCHIRM.G $.85
                         (M2151)
[Lat] med solo,pno/org SCHOTT-FRER
SCH121 s.p.   (M2152)
[Lat] high solo,pno/org SCHOTT-FRER
SCH120 s.p.   (M2153)
high solo,pno (F maj) ALLANS s.p.
                         (M2154)
med solo,pno (E flat maj) ALLANS
s.p.   (M2155)
S solo,org sc BOHM s.p.   (M2156)
high solo,pno (F maj) ASHDOWN
                         (M2157)
low solo,pno (E flat maj) ASHDOWN
                         (M2158)
(Becker) [Lat] high solo,pno
RICORDI-ENG 128021 s.p.   (M2159)

Allelujah (from Exultate, Jubilate)
(Lehmann) [Lat] med solo,pno BOTE
$1.50   (M2160)
(Lehmann) [Lat] high solo,pno BOTE
$1.50   (M2161)

Alles Ist Richtig - Ach, Offnet Eure
Augen *see Aprite Un Po' Quegl'
Occhi

Alma Grande E Nobil Core *K.578
S solo,2ob,2bsn,2trp,strings
BREITKOPF-L rental   (M2162)

Amour, Approche Et Prends Mon Ame
(from Le Nozze Di Figaro)
female solo,pno/inst DURAND s.p.
                         (M2163)

An Chloe
"A Cloe" see Sei Melodie
[Fr/It] Mez/Bar solo,pno/inst
DURAND s.p.   (M2164)
(Howe) "To Chloe" T solo,pno PAXTON
P40612 s.p.   (M2165)

Aprite Un Po' Quegl' Occhi (from Le
Nozze Di Figaro)
see Songs From Figaro, Book 3:
Baritone (Figaro)
"Ach Offnet Aug' Und Ohren" B solo,
2clar,2bsn,2horn,strings voc sc
BREITKOPF-W EB 1716 s.p. contains
also: Giunse Alfin Il Momento -
Non Tardar Amato Bene, "Endlich
Naht Sich Die Stunde - O Saume
Langer Nicht" (S solo,fl,ob,bsn,
strings); Porgi Amor, "Hor' Amor
Flehn, O Gott Der Liebe" (S solo,
2clar,2bsn,2horn,strings); Non So
Piu Sosa Son, "Ich Weiss Nicht,
Wo Ich Bin", "Nun Vergiss, Leises
Flehn", "Euch Holde Frauen" (S
solo,2clar,2bsn,2horn,strings) (B
solo,2fl,2ob,2bsn,2horn,2trp,
timp,strings) (S solo,fl,ob,clar,
bsn,2horn,strings) (M2166)
"Alles Ist Richtig - Ach, Offnet
Eure Augen" B solo,2clar,2bsn,
2horn,strings BREITKOPF-L rental
                         (M2167)

Arias From Operas For Bass *CC10L
(Kagen, Sergius) B solo,pno
INTERNAT. $3.00   (M2168)

Arias From Operas For Bass Or
Baritone, Vol. I *CC10L
(Kagen, Sergius) Bar/B solo,pno
INTERNAT. $3.00   (M2169)

MOZART, WOLFGANG AMADEUS (cont'd.)

Arias From Operas For Bass Or
   Baritone, Vol. II *CC10L
   (Kagen, Sergius) Bar/B solo,pno
   INTERNAT. $3.00   (M2170)

Arias From Operas For Coloratura
   Soprano *CC10L
   (Kagen, Sergius) coloratura sop,pno
   INTERNAT. $3.00   (M2171)

Arias From Operas For Contralto
   *CC10L
   (Kagen, Sergius) A solo,pno
   INTERNAT. $3.00   (M2172)

Arias From Operas For Mezzo-Soprano
   *CC10L
   (Kagen, Sergius) Mez solo,pno
   INTERNAT. $3.00   (M2173)

Arias From Operas For Soprano, Vol. I
   *CC10L
   (Kagen, Sergius) S solo,pno
   INTERNAT. $3.00   (M2174)

Arias From Operas For Soprano, Vol.
   II *CC10L
   (Kagen, Sergius) S solo,pno
   INTERNAT. $3.00   (M2175)

Arias From Operas For Soprano, Vol.
   III *CC10L
   (Kagen, Sergius) S solo,pno
   INTERNAT. $3.00   (M2176)

Arias From Operas For Soprano, Vol.
   IV *CC10L
   (Kagen, Sergius) S solo,pno
   INTERNAT. $3.00   (M2177)

Arias From Operas For Tenor *CC10L
   (Kagen, Sergius) T solo,pno
   INTERNAT. $3.00   (M2178)

Arie Scelte (Dalle Opera), Vol. I:
   Soprano Leggero *CC19L
   (Becker) [It/Ger] S solo,pno
   RICORDI-ENG ER 2288 s.p.   (M2179)

Arie Scelte (Dalle Opera), Vol. II:
   Soprano *CC20L
   (Becker) [It/Ger] S/Mez solo,pno
   RICORDI-ENG ER 2289 s.p.   (M2180)

Arie Scelte (Dalle Opera), Vol. III:
   Tenore *CC18L
   (Becker) [It/Ger] T solo,pno
   RICORDI-ENG 2290 s.p.   (M2181)

Arie Scelte (Dalle Opera), Vol. IV:
   Baritono E Basso *CC22L
   (Becker) [It/Ger] Bar/B solo,pno
   RICORDI-ENG ER 2291 s.p.   (M2182)

Arien, Vol. I *CCU
   [It] solo,pno cmplt ed,cloth BAREN.
   4548 $70.00 New Mozart Edition
                              (M2183)

Arien, Vol. II *CCU
   [It] solo,pno cmplt ed,cloth BAREN.
   4551 $70.00 New Mozart Edition
                              (M2184)

Arien, Vol. III *CCU
   [It/Ger] solo,pno cmplt ed,cloth
   BAREN. 4559 $70.00 New Mozart
   Edition   (M2185)

Arien, Vol. IV *CCU
   [It/Ger] solo,pno cmplt ed,cloth
   BAREN. 4560 $52.50 New Mozart
   Edition   (M2186)

Auf Denn Zum Feste (from Don
   Giovanni)
   Bar solo,2fl,2ob,2clar,2bsn,2horn,
   strings BREITKOPF-L rental
                              (M2187)

Ave, Verum Coprus *sac
   [Lat] S solo,pno RICORDI-ENG 127671
   s.p.   (M2188)

Ave, Verum Corpus *K.618, sac,mot
   low solo,pno HUG s.p.   (M2189)
   high solo,pno HUG s.p.   (M2190)
   [Lat/Ger] med-low solo,pno SCHOTTS
   09631 s.p.   (M2191)
   [Lat/Ger] high solo,pno SCHOTTS
   09630 s.p.   (M2192)
   [Lat] med solo,pno/vln/vcl LIENAU
   R88 s.p.   (M2193)
   [Lat] high solo,pno,vln/vcl LIENAU
   R88 R87 s.p.   (M2194)
   S/T solo,pno FORLIVESI 11268 s.p.
                              (M2195)
   solo,org,4strings BREITKOPF-W
   EB 3705 $.90   (M2196)
   S/T solo,pno (F maj) LIENAU HOS 115
   s.p.   (M2197)
   A/Bar solo,pno (D maj) LIENAU
   HOS 116 s.p.   (M2198)

Away With Philandering (from Le Nozze
   Di Figaro)
   low solo,pno (G maj) ALLANS s.p.

MOZART, WOLFGANG AMADEUS (cont'd.)

                              (M2199)
Bald Muss Ich Dich Verlassen *see Io
   Ti Lascio, O Figlia

Bandel-Terzett (from Der
   Schauspeildirektor)
   3 soli,2fl,2ob,2bsn,2horn,strings
   BREITKOPF-W s.p.   (M2200)

Basta, Vincesti - Ah Non Lasciarmi
   S solo,2fl,2bsn,2horn,strings
   BREITKOPF-L rental   (M2201)

Batti, Batti O Bel Masetto (from Don
   Giovanni)
   [It] S solo,pno RICORDI-ARG
   BA 11701 s.p. see also Doce Arias
   De Operas   (M2202)
   [It] S solo,pno RICORDI-ENG 54346
   s.p.   (M2203)
   S solo,pno/orch sc KALMUS $3.00
                              (M2204)
   "Frappe, Frappe Une Innocente" S
   solo,pno/inst DURAND s.p. (M2205)
   "Schmale, Tobe, Lieber Junge" S
   solo,fl,ob,bsn,2horn,strings
   BREITKOPF-L rental   (M2206)
   (Deis) [It/Eng] S solo,pno (F maj)
   SCHIRM.G $.85   (M2207)

Bei Mannern, Welche Liebe Fuhlen
   (from Die Zauberflote)
   SBar soli,2clar,2bsn,2horn,strings
   BREITKOPF-L rental   (M2208)
   SBar soli,2clar,2bsn,2horn,strings
   BREITKOPF-W s.p.   (M2209)

Bella Mia Fiamma, Addio *K.528
   see Concert Arias

Bella Mia Fiamma - Resta O Cara
   *K.528
   "Teurstes Madchen, Ich Scheide"
   see Mozart, Wolfgang Amadeus, Ah,
   Lo Previdi
   [Czech/It] solo,pno SUPRAPHON s.p.
                              (M2210)
   "Teurstes Madchen, Ich Scheide -
   Weib Mein Alles?" S solo,fl,2ob,
   2bsn,2horn,strings BREITKOPF-L
   rental   (M2211)

Berceuse *see Wiegenlied

Bester Jungling! Mit Entzucken (from
   Der Schauspieldirektor)
   S solo,2clar,2bsn,2horn,strings
   BREITKOPF-L rental   (M2212)
   [Ger/Eng] S solo,pno INTERNAT.
   $1.00   (M2213)

Betracht Dies Herz (from Grabmusik)
   sac,Psntd
   S solo,org,vln sc BOHM s.p. (M2214)

Cancion De Cuna *see Wiegenlied

Cara, Se Le Mie Pene
   (Plath, Wolfgang) S solo,2horn,vln,
   vla,bvl (med) BAREN. 4758 $12.50,
   ipr   (M2215)

C'est Elle (from Le Nozze Di Figaro)
   SMez soli,pno DURAND s.p. see from
   DOUZE DOUS   (M2216)

Chere Dame *see Madamina! Il
   Catalogo E Questo

Chi Sa, Chi Sa, Qual Sia *K.582
   S solo,2clar,2bsn,2horn,strings
   BREITKOPF-L rental   (M2217)

Ch'io Mi Scordi Di Te *K.505, scena
   see Concert Arias
   S solo,clar,2bsn,2horn,strings,opt
   pno sc KALMUS $3.50   (M2218)
   "Mich Zu Trennen Von Dir?" S solo,
   2clar,2bsn,2horn,strings,pno
   BREITKOPF-L rental contains also:
   Non Temer, Amato Bene, "Zage
   Nicht"   (M2219)
   "Mich Zu Trennen Von Dir" S solo,
   2clar,2bsn,2horn,strings,pno voc
   sc BREITKOPF-W EB 6852 s.p.
   contains also: Misera, Dove Son!
   - Ah! Non Son Io, "Wehe Mir, Ach
   - Leben Soll Ich", K.369 (S solo,
   2fl,2horn,strings); Non Piu,
   Tutto Ascoltai - Non Temer, Amato
   Bene, "Genug, Ich Bin
   Entschlossen - Lass, O Freund,
   Uns Standhaft Scheiden 2clar,
   2bsn, 2horn, Str"; Per Pieta, Non
   Ricercate, "Lass Mir Meinen
   Stillen Kummer", K.420 (T solo,
   2clar,2bsn,2horn,strings) (M2220)

Coloratura Arias
   (Lehmann, Lilli) [It/Ger/Lat]
   coloratura sop,pno PETERS 3552B
   $4.50
   contains: Et Incarnatus Est (from
   Mass In C Minor, K. 427) (sac);

MOZART, WOLFGANG AMADEUS (cont'd.)

   Laudamus Te (from Mass In C
   Minor, K. 427) (sac); Mia
   Speranza Adorata, K.416; No,
   No, Che No Sei Capace, K.419;
   Popoli Di Tessaglia, K.316
                              (M2221)

Complete Edition *CCU
   (Brahms, J.; Espagne, F.;
   Goldschmidt, O.; Joachim, J.;
   Ritter von Koechel, Ludwig;
   Nottebohm, G.; Reinecke, C.;
   Rudorff, E.; Spitta, P.; Wilder,
   V.; Wuellner, F.; Waldersee, P.)
   contains works for a variety of
   instruments and vocal
   combinations microfiche
   UNIV.MUS.ED. reprints of
   Breitkopf & Hartel Editions;
   contains series 1-24; $290.00
                              (M2222)

Complete Songs Of Mozart, Vol. 5
   *CCU
   solo/soli,pno study sc KALMUS $1.50
                              (M2223)

Complete Songs Of Mozart, Vols. 1-4
   *CCU
   solo,pno study sc KALMUS 943-956
   $1.50, ea.   (M2224)

Con Ossequio, Con Rispetto *K.210
   T solo,2ob,2horn,strings BREITKOPF-
   L rental   (M2225)

Concert Arias
   (Lehmann, Lilli) [It/Ger] S solo,
   pno PETERS 3552A $4.50
   contains: Ah, Lo Previdi, K.272;
   Bella Mia Fiamma, Addio, K.528;
   Ch'io Mi Scordi Di Te, K.505
                              (M2226)

Conservati Fedele *K.23
   S solo,strings BREITKOPF-L rental
                              (M2227)

Cosi Dunque Tradisci *K.432
   see Mozart, Wolfgang Amadeus,
   Alcandro, Lo Confesso [Kv 512]
   [It/Eng] B solo,pno INTERNAT. $1.50
                              (M2228)

Cosi Dunque Tradisci - Aspiri Rimorsi
   Atroci *K.432
   Bar/B solo,2fl,2ob,2bsn,2horn,
   strings BREITKOPF-L rental
                              (M2229)

Cradle Song
   high solo,pno (F maj) ALLANS s.p.
                              (M2230)
   med solo,pno (E flat maj) ALLANS
   s.p.   (M2231)

Crudele? Ah No, Mio Bene (from Don
   Giovanni)
   "Cruelle? Suis-Je Cruelle?" female
   solo,pno/inst DURAND s.p. (M2232)

Cruelle? Suis-Je Cruelle? *see
   Crudele? Ah No, Mio Bene

Da Schlagt Die Abschiedsstunde (from
   Impresario, The)
   [Ger/Eng] S solo,pno INTERNAT.
   $1.00   (M2233)

Dalla Sua Pace (from Don Giovanni)
   see Songs From Don Giovanni, Book
   3: Tenor (Don Ottavio)

Dalla Sua Pace La Mia Dipende (from
   Don Giovanni)
   [It] T solo,pno RICORDI-ENG 109964
   s.p.   (M2234)

Dans Quels Parjures (from Don
   Giovanni)
   female solo,pno/inst DURAND s.p.
                              (M2235)

Das Bandel *see Liebes Mandel, Wo Is
   'S Bandel

Das Veilchen
   "La Violetta" see Sei Melodie
   med solo,pno SCHOTTS 01227 1-2 s.p.
                              (M2236)
   high solo,pno SCHOTTS 01226 1-2
   s.p.   (M2237)
   "Violet, The" solo,pno ASHDOWN s.p.
                              (M2238)
   "Violet, The" [Ger/Eng] solo,pno
   CRAMER   (M2239)
   (Randegger) "Violet, The" low solo,
   pno ELKIN 27.9397.00 s.p. (M2240)

Deh, Per Questo Istante Solo (from La
   Clemenza Di Tito)
   "Lass Es Einmal Nur Geschehen" Mez
   solo,fl,2ob,2bsn,2horn,strings
   BREITKOPF-L rental   (M2241)

Deh, Vieni Alla Finestra! (from Don
   Giovanni)
   [It] Bar solo,pno RICORDI-ARG
   BA 11700 s.p.   (M2242)
   [It] Bar solo,pno RICORDI-ENG 54449
   s.p.   (M2243)
   "Feinsliebchen, Komm Ans Fenster"

MOZART, WOLFGANG AMADEUS (cont'd.)

Bar solo,strings,mand BREITKOPF-L
rental   (M2244)
"Parais A Ta Fenetre" B solo,pno/
inst DURAND s.p.   (M2245)

Deh Vieni, Non Tardar (from Le Nozze
Di Figaro)
see Songs From Figaro, Book 2:
Soprano (Susanna & Cherubino)
[It] S solo,pno RICORDI-ENG 109842
s.p.   (M2246)
[It] S solo,pno RICORDI-ARG BA 8519
s.p.   (M2247)

Dein Bin Ich   *see L'amero Saro
Costante

Den Busen Bewegt Mir   *see Un Moto Di
Gioia

Der Holle Rache Kockt In Meinem
Herzen (from Die Zauberflote)
S solo,2fl,2ob,2bsn,2horn,2trp,
timp,strings BREITKOPF-L rental (M2248)
Der Holle Rachen Kocht In Meinem
Herzen (from Die Zauberflote)
solo,pno/orch KALMUS $3.00   (M2249)

Der Odem Der Liebe   *see Un' Aura
Amorosa

Der Prozess Schon Gewonnen - Ich Soll
Ein Gluck Entbehren (from Le
Nozze Di Figaro)
Bar solo,2fl,2ob,2bsn,2horn,2trp,
timp,strings BREITKOPF-L rental
                              (M2250)

Der Sylphe Des Friedens   *see Ridente
La Calma

Der Vogelfanger Bin Ich Ja (from Die
Zauberflote)
see Mozart, Wolfgang Amadeus, Ach,
Ich Fuhl's
Bar/B solo,2ob,2bsn,2horn,strings
BREITKOPF-L rental   (M2251)

Die Ihr Des Unermesslichen Weltalls
Schopfer Ehrt *K.619, cant
(Liebeskind, J.) T solo,2fl,2ob,
2clar,2bsn,2horn,2trp,strings,
timp voc sc BREITKOPF-L EB 5901
s.p., ipr   (M2252)
(Liebeskind, J.) S solo,2fl,2ob,
2clar,2bsn,2horn,2trp,timp,
strings voc sc BREITKOPF-L
EB 5901 $1.10, ipr   (M2253)

Dies Bildnis Ist Bezaubernd Schon
(from Die Zauberflote)
see Mozart, Wolfgang Amadeus, Ach,
Ich Fuhl's
T solo,2clar,2bsn,2horn,strings
BREITKOPF-L rental   (M2254)
solo,pno/orch KALMUS $3.00   (M2255)
[Eng/Ger] T solo,pno BOOSEY $1.50
                              (M2256)

Dite Almeno, In Che Maniera *K.479
"Sagt, Was Hab' Ich Denn" STBB
soli,2ob,2clar,2bsn,2horn,strings
BREITKOPF-W s.p.   (M2257)
"Sagt, Was Hab Ich Denn
Verbrochen?" STBB soli,2ob,2clar,
2bsn,2horn,strings BREITKOPF-L
rental   (M2258)

Doce Arias De Operas *CC12L
S solo,pno RICORDI-ARG s.p. most
texts in Italian, some are in
Italian and German
see also: Batti, Batti O Bel
Masetto (from Don Giovanni)
                              (M2259)
Donne Mie, La Fatte A Tanti (from
Cosi Fan Tutte)
"Madchen, So Treibt Ihr's Mit
Allen" Bar solo,2fl,2ob,2bsn,
2horn,2trp,timp,strings
BREITKOPF-L rental   (M2260)

Dove Sono (from Le Nozze Di Figaro)
see Songs From Figaro, Book 1:
Soprano (The Countess)
high solo,pno (C maj) ALLANS s.p.
                              (M2261)
(Spicker) "Where Now" [It/Eng] S
solo,pno (C maj) SCHIRM.G $.85
                              (M2262)
Dreizehn Arien Aus Mozarts Messen,
Vespern, Motetten Und Kantaten
*sac,CC13U
(Berberich) [Lat] high solo,pno
UNIVER. 9303 $10.50   (M2263)

Drink To Me Only With Thine Eyes
low solo,pno (C maj) CENTURY 3473
                              (M2264)
Due Pupille Amabili   *K.439
see Six Nocturnes

Durch Zartlichkeit Und Schmeicheln
(from Die Entfuhrung Aus Dem
Serail)

MOZART, WOLFGANG AMADEUS (cont'd.)

S solo,strings BREITKOPF-L rental
                              (M2265)
Ecco Il Punto - Non, Piu Di Fiori
(from La Clemenza Di Tito)
"Jetzt, Vitellia! Schlagt Die
Stunde - Nie Soll Mit Rosen" Mez/
A solo,fl,2ob,clar,2bsn,2horn,
strings BREITKOPF-L rental   (M2266)
Ecco Quel Fiero Istante *K.436
see Six Nocturnes
SSB soli, 3 bassett horns
BREITKOPF-W s.p.   (M2267)

Ein Madchen Oder Weibchen Wunscht
Papageno Sich (from Die
Zauberflote)
see Mozart, Wolfgang Amadeus, Ach,
Ich Fuhl's
Bar/B solo,fl,2ob,2bsn,2horn,glock,
strings BREITKOPF-L rental   (M2268)
Endlich Naht Sich Die Stunde   *see
Giunse Alfin Il Momento - Non
Tardar Amato Bene

Endlich Naht Sich Die Stunde - O
Saume Langer Nicht   *see Giunse
Alfin Il Momento - Non Tardar
Amato Bene

Ergo Interest - Quaere Superna
*K.143
S solo,strings,org BREITKOPF-L
rental   (M2269)

Et Incarnatus Est (from Mass In C
Minor, K. 427)
see Coloratura Arias
[Lat/Eng] S solo,pno INTERNAT.
$1.00   (M2270)

Euch Holde Frauen   *see Non So Piu
Sosa Son

Euch, Ihr Einsamen Schatten -
Zephiretten Leicht Gefiedert
(from Idomeneo, Re Di Creta)
S solo,2fl,2clar,2bsn,2horn,strings
BREITKOPF-L rental   (M2271)

Exsultate Jubilate *K.165, sac,mot
S solo,orch voc sc KALMUS 6332
$1.00   (M2272)
S solo,2ob,2horn,strings,org study
sc BREITKOPF-L PB 4451 s.p., ipr
                              (M2273)
(Kagen, Sergius) [Lat/Eng] solo,pno
INTERNAT. $2.00   (M2274)
(Klengel, P.) S solo,pno voc sc
BREITKOPF-L EB 5232 $1.50   (M2275)

Feinsliebchen, Komm Ans Fenster   *see
Deh Vieni Alla Finestra

Femmes Si Belles, Repondez-Moi (from
Le Nozze Di Figaro)
male solo,pno/inst DURAND s.p.
                              (M2276)
Frappe, Frappe Une Innocente   *see
Batti, Batti, O Bel Masetto

Funfzig Ausgewahlte Lieder *CC50U
(Moser) $10.00 high solo,pno PETERS
4699A; low solo,pno PETERS 4699B
                              (M2277)
Genug, Ich Bin Entschlossen - Lass, O
Freund, Uns Standhaft Scheiden
*see Non Piu! Tutto Ascoltai -
Non, Temer, Amato Bene

Genug, Ich Bin Entschlossen - Lass, O
Freund, Uns Standhaft Scheiden
2clar, 2bsn, 2horn, Str *see Non
Piu, Tutto Ascoltai - Non Temer,
Amato Bene

Gesellige Gesange *CC10L
3 soli,pno (med) BAREN. 1767 $5.75
                              (M2278)
Giunse Alfin Il Momento (from Le
Nozze Di Figaro)
solo,pno/orch sc KALMUS $3.00
                              (M2279)
"Yes, At Length 'Tis The Moment"
[It/Eng] S solo,pno (C maj)
SCHIRM.G $.85   (M2280)

Giunse Alfin Il Momento - Non Tardar
Amato Bene (from Le Nozze Di
Figaro)
"Endlich Naht Sich Die Stunde - O
Saume Langer Nicht" see Mozart,
Wolfgang Amadeus, Aprite Un Po'
Quegl' Occhi
"Endlich Naht Sich Die Stunde" S
solo,fl,ob,bsn,strings BREITKOPF-
L rental   (M2281)

Gli Angui D'inferno (from Die
Zauberflote)
[It] S solo,pno RICORDI-ARG BA 8663
s.p.   (M2282)

MOZART, WOLFGANG AMADEUS (cont'd.)

Her I'll Love
high solo,pno,opt vln PRESSER $.90
                              (M2283)
Hor' Amor Flehn, O Gott Der Liebe
*see Porgi Amor

Hor Mein Flehn, O Gott Der Liebe
(from Le Nozze Di Figaro)
S solo,2clar,2bsn,2horn,strings
BREITKOPF-L rental   (M2284)

I Don't Know   *see Non So Piu Cosa
Son

I Seek Some Comely Maiden (from Die
Zauberflote)
med solo,pno (F maj) ALLANS s.p.
                              (M2285)
Ich Erwahle Mir Den Braunen   *see
Prendero Quel Brunnettio

Ich Weiss Nicht, Wo Ich Bin   *see Non
So Piu Cosa Son

Ihr Machtigen (from Zaide)
"You Who Are Powerful" [Ger/Eng] B
solo,pno INTERNAT. $1.25, ipr
                              (M2286)
Il Mio Tesoro Intanto (from Don
Giovanni)
see Songs From Don Giovanni, Book
3: Tenor (Don Ottavio)
high solo,pno (B flat maj) ALLANS
s.p.   (M2287)
T solo,pno/orch sc KALMUS $3.00
                              (M2288)
[It] T solo,pno RICORDI-ENG 126000
s.p.   (M2289)
[It] T solo,pno RICORDI-ARG BA 8894
s.p.   (M2290)
"To My Beloved, O Hasten" [It/Eng]
T solo,pno (B flat maj) SCHIRM.G
$.75   (M2291)

In Blessed Contentment   *see Ridente
La Calma

In Diesen Heil'gen Hallen (from Die
Zauberflote)
see Mozart, Wolfgang Amadeus, Ach,
Ich Fuhl's
B solo,2fl,2bsn,2horn,strings
BREITKOPF-L rental   (M2292)
KALMUS $3.00   (M2293)
"To Scenes Of Peace Retiring" [Ger/
It/Eng] B solo,pno (E maj)
SCHIRM.G $.85   (M2294)
"Within These Holy Portals" low
solo,pno (E maj) ALLANS s.p.   (M2295)
In Te Spero, O Sposo Amato *K.440
(Reichert, Ernst) S solo,2ob,2horn,
strings sc BREITKOPF-W PB 3754
s.p., ipa, voc sc BREITKOPF-W
EB 6204 $2.00   (M2296)

Io Ti Lascio *K.245
[It/Eng] B/A solo,pno INTERNAT.
$1.00, ipr   (M2297)

Io Ti Lascio, O Figlia *K.513
B solo,fl,2clar,2bsn,2horn,strings
KALMUS $3.00   (M2298)
[It/Eng] B solo,pno INTERNAT.
$1.50, ipr   (M2299)
"Bald Muss Ich Dich Verlassen" Bar/
B solo,fl,2clar,2bsn,2horn,
strings BREITKOPF-L rental
                              (M2300)
Jetzt, Vitellia! Schlagt Die Stunde -
Nie Soll Mit Rosen   *see Ecco Il
Punto - Non, Piu Di Fiori

Jeunes Filles, Vos Songes Heureux
(from Don Giovanni)
2 soli,cor,pno/inst DURAND s.p.
                              (M2301)
Komm An Mein Herz, O Liebling Meiner
Seele - All Des Lebens
Seligkeiten   *see A Questo Seno
Deh Vieni, Idolo Mio - Or Che Il
Cielo A Me Ti Rende

Komm An Mein Herz, O Liebling Meiner
Seele - All Des Lebens Seligkeiten
*see A Questo Seno Deh Vieni,
Idolo Mio - Or Che Il Cielo A Me
Ti Rende

Kommet Her, Ihr Frechen Sunder
*K.146
S solo,strings,org BREITKOPF-L
rental   (M2302)
Konzert-Arien Fur Bass *CCU
(Haverkampf) [It] B solo,orch
BREITKOPF-W EB 6450 $8.75 (M2303)

Konzert-Arien Fur Hohe Stimme Band I
*CCU
[It/Ger] high solo,orch BREITKOPF-W
EB 6851 $6.75   (M2304)

MOZART, WOLFGANG AMADEUS (cont'd.)

Konzert-Arien Fur Hohe Stimme Band II
  *CCU
  [It/Ger] high solo,orch BREITKOPF-W
  EB 6852 $6.75   (M2305)

La Ci Darem (from Don Giovanni)
  2 soli,pno ALLANS s.p.   (M2306)

La Ci Darem La Mano (from Don
  Giovanni)
  [It] SBar soli,pno RICORDI-ENG
  110282 s.p.   (M2307)
  [It] SBar soli,pno RICORDI-ARG
  BA 11702 s.p.   (M2308)
  SBar soli,pno/orch sc KALMUS $3.00
                                   (M2309)
  "Nay, Bid Me Not Resign, Love" [It/
  Eng] SBar soli,pno SCHIRM.G $.85
                                   (M2310)
  "Nay, Bid Me Not Resign, Love" high
  solo&med solo,pno (A maj)
  FISCHER,C S 5934   (M2311)

La Jeune Fille Et La Violette
  S/T solo,pno/inst DURAND s.p.
                                   (M2312)

La Violetta *see Das Veilchen

L'amero Saro Costante (from Il Re
  Pastore)
  [It/Ger] T solo,pno,vln LIENAU R86
  s.p.   (M2313)
  high solo,pno (B flat maj) ALLANS
  s.p.   (M2314)
  "Dein Bin Ich" [Ger/It] S solo,2fl,
  2English horn,2bsn,2horn,strings
  sc BREITKOPF-W PB 4874 s.p., ipa,
  voc sc BREITKOPF-W EB 5473 $1.50
                                   (M2315)
  (Stuber) [It/Ger] S solo,2fl,2ob,
  2English horn,2bsn,2horn,strings
  voc sc MUSIKWISS. BR51 s.p.
                                   (M2316)
  (Stueber, Carl) [It/Ger] S solo,pno
  (med diff) voc sc ALKOR 262 s.p.
                                   (M2317)

L'amour Malheureux
  solo,pno/inst DURAND s.p.   (M2318)

Lass Es Einmal Nur Geschehen *see
  Deh, Per Questo Istante Solo

Lass Mir Meinen Stillen Kummer *see
  Per Pieta, Non Ricercate

Laudamus Te (from Mass In C Minor, K.
  427)
  see Coloratura Arias

Le Portrait (from Cosi Fan Tutte)
  2 soli,pno DURAND s.p. see from
  DOUZE DOUS   (M2319)

Liebes Mandel, Wo Is 'S Bandel
  *K.441
  (Burkhart, F.) "Das Bandel" STB
  soli,pno voc sc DOBLINGER 08 560
  s.p., solo pt DOBLINGER s.p.
                                   (M2320)

Liebes Mandel, Wo Ist's Bandel (from
  Der Schauspieldirektor)
  (Seidelmann, H.) STB soli,2fl,2ob,
  2bsn,2horn,strings BREITKOPF-L
  rental   (M2321)

Lieder *CC7L
  (Leuchter) solo,pno cmplt ed
  RICORDI-ARG BA 11376 s.p.
  original and Spanish texts
                                   (M2322)

Lieder *CC30U
  (Ballin, Ernst August) solo,pno
  (med diff) BAREN. 4534 cmplt ed,
  pap $14.00, cmplt ed,cloth $19.50
                                   (M2323)

Lieder *CCU
  [Czech] solo,pno SUPRAPHON s.p.
                                   (M2324)

Lieder Fur Hohe Stimme *CC30U
  high solo,pno BREITKOPF-W EB 103
  $3.00 original editions   (M2325)

Lieder Fur Singstimme Und Gitarre
  *CCU
  (Behrend, Siegfried) solo,gtr
  SIKORSKI 573 s.p.   (M2326)

Lieder Und Gesange *CCU
  (Reichert) S solo,pno OSTER $3.50
  in 2 volumes; original and German
  texts   (M2327)

Luci Care, Luci Belle *K.346
  see Six Nocturnes

Lullaby *see Wiegenlied

Ma Che Vi Fece - Sperai Vicino Al
  Lido *K.368
  "Ach, Was Verbrach Ihr Sterne -
  Schon Hoff Ich Das Ufer" see
  Mozart, Wolfgang Amadeus, Ah, Lo
  Previdi
  "Ach, Was Verbrach Ihr Sterne -

MOZART, WOLFGANG AMADEUS (cont'd.)

  Schon Hoff Ich Das Ufer" S solo,
  2fl,2bsn,2horn,strings BREITKOPF-
  L rental   (M2328)

Madamina! Il Catalogo E Questa (from
  Don Giovanni)
  "Schone Donna! Dieses Kleine
  Register" B solo,2fl,2ob,2bsn,
  2horn,strings voc sc BREITKOPF-L
  EB 2180 s.p., ipr   (M2329)

Madamina! Il Catalogo E Questo (from
  Don Giovanni)
  [It] B solo,pno RICORDI-ENG 54473
  s.p.   (M2330)
  "Chere Dame" B solo,pno/inst DURAND
  s.p.   (M2331)

Madchen, So Treibt Ihr's Mit Allen
  *see Donne Mie, La Fatte A Tanti

Mandina Amabile *K.480
  STB soli,2fl,2ob,2clar,2bsn,2horn,
  strings BREITKOPF-W s.p. (M2332)
  "Willst Du Mein Liebchen Sein" STB
  soli,2fl,2ob,2clar,2bsn,2horn,
  strings BREITKOPF-L rental
                                   (M2333)

Manner Suchen Stets Zu Naschen
  *K.433 (from Der
  Schauspieldirektor)
  S solo,2ob,2horn,strings BREITKOPF-
  L rental   (M2334)
  (Moser, Rudolf) B solo,2ob,2horn,
  strings voc sc BREITKOPF-W s.p.
                                   (M2335)

Martern Aller Arten (from Die
  Entfuhrung Aus Dem Serail)
  S solo,fl,ob,2clar,2bsn,2horn,2trp,
  timp,perc BREITKOPF-L rental
                                   (M2336)
  high solo,pno (C maj) ALLANS s.p.
                                   (M2337)

Mehrstimmige Gesange *CCU
  [Eng/Ger/It] soli,pno cmplt ed,
  cloth BAREN. 4557 $28.00 (M2338)

Mentre Ti Lascio, O Figlia *K.513
  see Mozart, Wolfgang Amadeus,
  Alcandro, Lo Confesso [Kv 512]

Mi Lagnero Tacendo *K.437
  see Six Nocturnes
  SSB soli,2clar, bassett horn
  BREITKOPF-W s.p.   (M2339)

Mi Tradi (from Don Giovanni)
  see Songs From Don Giovanni, Book
  1: Soprano (Donna Anna & Donna
  Elvira)

Mia Speranza Adorata *K.416
  see Coloratura Arias

Mia Speranza Adorata - Ah, Non Sai
  *K.416
  "Ach, Sie Stirbt, Meine Hoffnung"
  see Mozart, Wolfgang Amadeus, Ah,
  Lo Previdi
  S solo,2ob,2bsn,2horn,strings sc
  KALMUS $3.00   (M2340)
  "Ach, Sie Stirbt, Meine Hoffnung -
  Ach, Sie Schwanden, Meine
  Freuden" S solo,2ob,2bsn,2horn,
  strings BREITKOPF-L rental
                                   (M2341)

Mich Zu Trennen Von Dir? *see Ch'io
  Mi Scordi Di Te

Misera, Dove Son!
  [It/Eng] S solo,pno INTERNAT. $1.50
                                   (M2342)

Misera, Dove Son! - Ah! Non Son Io
  *K.369
  "Wehe Mir, Ach - Leben Soll Ich"
  see Mozart, Wolfgang Amadeus,
  Ch'io Mi Scordi Di Te
  "Wehe Mir, Ach - Leben Soll Ich" S
  solo,2fl,2horn,strings BREITKOPF-
  L rental   (M2343)

Miserere A-Moll *K.85
  (Federhofer, Hellmut) ATB soli,org
  (med) BAREN. 4759 $5.00   (M2344)

Misero Me - Misero Pargoletto *K.77
  S solo,2ob,2bsn,2horn,strings
  BREITKOPF-L rental   (M2345)

Misero! O Sogno - Aura, Che Intorno
  Spiri *K.431
  "Wehe Mir! Ist's Wahrheit - Eilet,
  Mitleid'ge Lufte" see Mozart,
  Wolfgang Amadeus, Ah, Lo Previdi
  "Wehe Mir! Ist's Wahrheit - Eilet,
  Mitleid'ge Lufte" T solo,2fl,
  2bsn,2horn,strings BREITKOPF-L
  rental   (M2346)

Mon Coeur Soupire (from Le Nozze Di
  Figaro)
  Mez solo,pno/inst DURAND s.p.
                                   (M2347)
  S solo,pno/inst DURAND s.p. (M2348)

MOZART, WOLFGANG AMADEUS (cont'd.)

Monito
  see Sei Melodie

Mozart-Album *CC29UL
  (Friedlander) [Ger] $4.25 high
  solo,pno PETERS 299A; med solo/
  low solo,pno PETERS 299B (M2349)

Musst' Ich Auch Durch Tausend Drachen
  T solo,fl,ob,clar,2bsn,2horn,2trp,
  timp,strings sc DOBLINGER DM 400
  s.p., ipa, voc sc DOBLINGER
  DM 400A s.p.   (M2350)

Nay, Bid Me Not Resign, Love *see La
  Ci Darem La Mano

Nehmt Meinen Dank, Ihr Holden Gonner
  *K.383
  (Zilcher, H.) S solo,fl,ob,bsn,
  strings sc BREITKOPF-L PB 815A
  s.p., ipr, voc sc BREITKOPF-L
  EB 5316 s.p.   (M2351)

Ninna Nanna *see Wiegenlied

No, No, Che No Sei Capace *K.419
  see Coloratura Arias

No, No, Che Non Sei Capace *K.419
  S solo,2ob,2horn,2trp,timp,strings
  BREITKOPF-L rental   (M2352)
  S solo,2ob,2horn,2trp,drums,strings
  sc KALMUS $3.00   (M2353)

Non Mi Dir (from Don Giovanni)
  see Songs From Don Giovanni, Book
  1: Soprano (Donna Anna & Donna
  Elvira)
  S solo,pno/orch sc KALMUS $3.00
                                   (M2354)

Non Piu Andrai (from Le Nozze Di
  Figaro)
  see Songs From Figaro, Book 3:
  Baritone (Figaro)
  [It] B solo,pno RICORDI-ENG 110088
  s.p.   (M2355)
  "Now Your Days Of Philandering Are
  Over" [It/Eng] B solo,pno (C maj)
  SCHIRM.G $1.00   (M2356)

Non Piu, Tutto Ascoltai - Non Temer,
  Amato Bene *K.490
  "Genug, Ich Bin Entschlossen -
  Lass, O Freund, Uns Standhaft
  Scheiden 2clar, 2bsn, 2horn, Str"
  see Mozart, Wolfgang Amadeus,
  Ch'io Mi Scordi Di Te
  "Genug, Ich Bin Entschlossen -
  Lass, O Freund, Uns Standhaft
  Scheiden" S solo,2clar,2bsn,
  2horn,vla,strings BREITKOPF-L
  rental   (M2357)
  (Flothius, Marius) S solo,vla,pno
  BROEKMANS s.p.   (M2358)

Non Pui Andrai Farfallone Amoroso
  (from Le Nozze Di Figaro)
  [It] B solo,pno RICORDI-ARG
  BA 11776 s.p.   (M2359)

Non So Piu Cosa Son (from Le Nozze Di
  Figaro)
  see Songs From Figaro, Book 2:
  Soprano (Susanna & Cherubino)
  [It] S solo,pno RICORDI-ARG BA 8740
  s.p.   (M2360)
  [It] Mez solo,pno RICORDI-ENG
  109841 s.p.   (M2361)
  Mez/S solo,pno sc KALMUS $3.00
                                   (M2362)
  "I Don't Know" [It/Eng] S solo,pno
  (E maj) SCHIRM.G $.85   (M2363)
  "Ich Weiss Nicht, Wo Ich Bin" S
  solo,2clar,2bsn,2horn,strings
  BREITKOPF-L rental   (M2364)

Non So Piu Sosa Son (from Le Nozze Di
  Figaro)
  "Euch Holde Frauen" see Mozart,
  Wolfgang Amadeus, Aprite Un Po'
  Quegl' Occhi
  "Euch Holde Frauen" S solo,fl,ob,
  clar,bsn,2horn,strings BREITKOPF-
  L rental   (M2365)

Non Temer, Amato Bene
  "Zage Nicht" see Mozart, Wolfgang
  Amadeus, Ch'io Mi Scordi Di Te

Now Your Days Of Philandering Are
  Over *see Non Piu Andrai

Nun Vergiss Leises Flehn (from Le
  Nozze Di Figaro)
  Bar/B solo,2fl,2ob,2bsn,2horn,2trp,
  timp BREITKOPF-L rental   (M2366)

O Freund, Was Mich Ergriffen - Woher
  Dieses Bangen *see Alcandro Lo
  Confesso - Non So D'onde Viene

MOZART, WOLFGANG AMADEUS (cont'd.)

O Isis And Osiris *see O Isis Und
   Osiris, Schenket Der Weisheit
   Geist

O Isis Und Osiris, Schenket Der
   Weisheit Geist (from Die
   Zauberflote)
   see Mozart, Wolfgang Amadeus, Ach,
   Ich Fuhl's
   solo,pno/orch KALMUS $3.00 (M2367)
   B solo,men cor,2bsn,3trom,2vla,vcl
   BREITKOPF-L rental   (M2368)
   "O Isis And Osiris" [Ger/It/Eng] B
   solo,pno (F maj) SCHIRM.G $.85
                                (M2369)

O, Wie Will Ich Triumphieren (from
   Die Entfuhrung Aus Dem Serail)
   B solo,fl,2ob,2clar,2bsn,2horn,
   strings BREITKOPF-L rental
                                (M2370)

O Zittre Nicht (from Die
   Zauberflote)
   [Eng/Ger] S solo,pno BOOSEY $1.50
                                (M2371)

O Zittre Nicht, Mein Lieber Sohn -
   Zum Leiden Bin Ich Auserkoren
   (from Die Zauberflote)
   S solo,2ob,2bsn,2horn,strings
   BREITKOPF-L rental   (M2372)

O Zittre Nicht, Mein Lieber Sohn -
   Zum Leider Bin Ich Ausekoren
   (from Die Zauberflote)
   see Mozart, Wolfgang Amadeus, Ach,
   Ich Fuhl's

Oh, Believe *see Porgi, Amor,
   Qualche Ristoro

Ombra Felice *K.255
   (Kneusslin) [It] A solo,2ob,2horn,
   strings sc KNUS K11 $6.50, ipa
                                (M2373)

Ombra Felice - Io Ti Lascio *K.255,
   sec
   A solo,ob,2horn,strings sc KNUS
   EKN 13 s.p., ipa   (M2374)
   Mez/A solo,2ob,2horn,strings
   BREITKOPF-L rental   (M2375)
   [It/Eng] A solo,pno INTERNAT.
   $2.00, ipr   (M2376)

Or Che Il Dover - Tali E Cotanti Sono
   *K.36
   T solo,2ob,2bsn,2horn,2trp,timp,
   strings BREITKOPF-L rental
                                (M2377)

Ou Sont-Elles, Ces Heures Douces
   (from Le Nozze Di Figaro)
   female solo,pno/inst DURAND s.p.
                                (M2378)

Pa-Pa-Pa (from Die Zauberflote)
   SBar soli,2fl,2ob,2bsn,2horn,
   strings BREITKOPF-W s.p.   (M2379)

Papagena, Papageno (from Die
   Zauberflote)
   SB soli,2fl,2ob,2bsn,2horn,strings
   BREITKOPF-L rental   (M2380)
   solo,pno/orch KALMUS $3.00 (M2381)

Parais A Ta Fenetre *see Deh Vieni
   Alla Finestra

Parto! Ma Tu Ben Mio (from Titus)
   [It/Eng] S solo,pno,opt clar
   INTERNAT. $2.00   (M2382)

Parto, Parto (from Le Clemenza Di
   Tito)
   (Flothius, Marius) [It] S solo,
   clar,pno BROEKMANS 395-5 s.p.
                                (M2383)

Parto, Parto, Ma Tu Ben Mio (from La
   Clemenza Di Tito)
   "Wohl Denn, Doch Dann Geliebte"
   [It/Ger] S solo,2ob,clar,2bsn,
   2horn,strings voc sc BREITKOPF-L
   EB 4066 $2.50, ipr   (M2384)

Passionlied *K.146
   see Tre Arie

Passionslied *K.146, sac
   S solo,org sc BOHM s.p.   (M2385)

Pauvre Mazetto Veux-Tu Connaitre
   (from Don Giovanni)
   S solo,pno/inst DURAND s.p. (M2386)

Per Pieta, Bell' Idol Mio *K.78
   S solo,2ob,2horn,strings BREITKOPF-
   L rental   (M2387)

Per Pieta, Non Ricercate *K.420
   see Tre Arie
   "Lass Mir Meinen Stillen Kummer"
   see Mozart, Wolfgang Amadeus,
   Ch'io Mi Scordi Di Te
   "Lass Mir Meinen Stillen Kummer" T
   solo,2clar,2bsn,2horn,strings
   BREITKOPF-L rental   (M2388)

MOZART, WOLFGANG AMADEUS (cont'd.)

Per Questa Bella Mano *K.612
   see Mozart, Wolfgang Amadeus,
   Alcandro, Lo Confesso [Kv 512]
   [It/Eng] B solo,pno,opt bvl/vcl
   INTERNAT. $2.00, ipr   (M2389)
   [It] B solo,bvl/pno DOBLINGER
   DM 257A $3.25   (M2390)
   Bar/B solo,fl,2ob,2bsn,2horn,
   strings BREITKOPF-L rental
                                (M2391)
   (Malaric, R.) B solo,fl,2ob,2bsn,
   2horn,strings sc DOBLINGER DM 257
   s.p., ipa, voc sc DOBLINGER
   DM 257A s.p.   (M2392)

Piu Non Si Trovano *K.549
   see Six Nocturnes
   SSB soli, 3 bassett horns
   BREITKOPF-W s.p.   (M2393)

Poir Cette Fete (from Don Giovanni)
   B solo,pno/inst DURAND s.p. (M2394)

Popoli Di Tessaglia *K.316
   see Coloratura Arias

Popoli Di Tessaglia - Io Non Chiedo,
   Eterni *K.316
   S solo,ob,bsn,2horn,strings
   BREITKOPF-L rental   (M2395)

Porgi Amor (from Le Nozze Di Figaro)
   "Hor' Amor Flehn, O Gott Der Liebe"
   see Mozart, Wolfgang Amadeus,
   Aprite Un Po' Quegl' Occhi

Porgi, Amor, Qualche Ristoro (from Le
   Nozze Di Figaro)
   see Songs From Figaro, Book 1:
   Soprano (The Countess)
   [It] S solo,pno RICORDI-ARG BA 8838
   s.p.   (M2396)
   [It] S solo,pno RICORDI-ENG 109869
   s.p.   (M2397)
   S solo,pno/orch sc KALMUS $3.00
   s.p.   (M2398)
   high solo,pno (E flat maj) ALLANS
   s.p.   (M2399)
   "Oh, Believe" [Eng/It] high solo,
   pno PRESSER $.75   (M2400)
   "Pour, O Love, Sweet Consolation"
   [It/Eng] S solo,pno (E flat maj)
   SCHIRM.G $.75   (M2401)

Pour, O Love, Sweet Consolation *see
   Porgi, Amor, Qualche Ristoro

Prayer Of Thanksgiving *sac
   (Hamlin) high solo,pno (F maj)
   BOSTON $1.50   (M2402)

Prendero Quel Brunnettio (from Cosi
   Fan Tutte)
   "Ich Erwahle Mir Den Braunen" see
   Mozart, Wolfgang Amadeus, Un'
   Aura Amorosa

Quaere Superna *K.143, sac
   S solo,org,vln sc BOHM s.p. (M2403)

Que L'Amour Fasse Lui-Meme (from Le
   Nozze Di Figaro)
   female solo,pno/inst DURAND s.p.
                                (M2404)

Queen Of The Night
   high solo,pno (C min) ALLANS s.p.
                                (M2405)

Recit Et Air D'Idomenee (from
   Idomeneo, Re Di Creta)
   female solo,pno/inst DURAND s.p.
                                (M2406)

Recit Et Rondo (from Cosi Fan Tutte)
   solo,orch HENN s.p.   (M2407)

Recitatif Et Air De Vitelia (from La
   Clemenza Di Tito)
   female solo,pno/inst DURAND s.p.
                                (M2408)

Reich Mir Die Hand, Mein Leben (from
   Don Giovanni)
   SBar soli,fl,2ob,2bsn,2horn,strings
   BREITKOPF-L rental   (M2409)

Ridente La Calma *K.152
   see Sei Melodie
   (Jacobson) "In Blessed Contentment"
   [It/Eng] solo,pno (D maj)
   ROBERTON 2598 s.p.   (M2410)
   (Mottl, F.) "Der Sylphe Des
   Friedens" S solo,ob,2clar,2bsn,
   2horn,strings BREITKOPF-L rental
                                (M2411)
   (Northcote) [Eng/It] solo,pno (F
   maj) BOOSEY $1.50   (M2412)

Rivolgete A Lui Lo Sguardo *K.584
   see Mozart, Wolfgang Amadeus,
   Alcandro, Lo Confesso [Kv 512]
   Bar/B solo,2ob,2bsn,2trp,timp,
   strings BREITKOPF-L rental
                                (M2413)
   [It/Eng] B solo,pno INTERNAT.
   $1.75, ipr   (M2414)

MOZART, WOLFGANG AMADEUS (cont'd.)

Ruhe Sanft Mein Holdes Leben (from
   Zaide)
   S solo,ob,bsn,strings BREITKOPF-L
   rental   (M2415)

Sag Farval Lilla Fjaril (from Le
   Nozze Di Figaro)
   solo,pno LUNDQUIST s.p.   (M2416)

Sagt, Was Hab' Ich Denn *see Dite
   Almeno, In Che Maniera

Sagt, Was Hab Ich Denn Verbrochen?
   *see Dite Almeno, In Che Maniera

Scatalogical Songs And Canons Of
   Wolfgang Amadeus Mozart *sac,CCU
   (Shepard, Thomas) solo,pno voc sc
   WALTON M 111 $1.50   (M2417)

Schmale, Tobe, Lieber Junge *see
   Batti, Batti, O Bel Masetto

Schon Ein Madchen Von Funfzehn Jahren
   (from Cosi Fan Tutte)
   S solo,fl,bsn,2horn,strings
   BREITKOPF-L rental   (M2418)

Schon Lacht Der Holde Fruhling
   *K.580
   (Leibholz) [Ger/Eng] S solo,vln,pno
   voc sc BREITKOPF-L EB 5885 $2.75
                                (M2419)
   (Seidelmann, H.) S solo,2clar,2bsn,
   2horn,strings sc BREITKOPF-L
   PB 4010 s.p., ipa   (M2420)

Schone Donna! Dieses Kleine Register
   *see Madamina! Il Catalogo E
   Questa

Se Lontan, Ben Mio, Tu Sei *K.438
   see Six Nocturnes

Se Tu Di Me Fai Dono (from Il Re
   Pastore)
   [It/Eng] S solo,pno INTERNAT. $1.00
                                (M2421)

Se Vuol Ballare (from Le Nozze Di
   Figaro)
   see Songs From Figaro, Book 3:
   Baritone (Figaro)

Sei Melodie
   solo,pno cmplt ed FORLIVESI 12075 B
   s.p.
   contains: An Chloe, "A Cloe"; Das
   Veilchen, "La Violetta";
   Monito; Ridente La Calma; Un
   Moto Di Gioia; Wiegenlied,
   "Ninna Nanna"   (M2422)

Si Mostra La Sorte *K.209
   T solo,2fl,2horn,strings BREITKOPF-
   L rental   (M2423)

Six Nocturnes
   sc PETERS 4522 $3.75, ipa
   contains: Due Pupille Amabili,
   K.439 (SSB soli,pno/2vln&vcl);
   Ecco Quel Fiero Istante, K.436
   (SSB soli,pno/2vln&vcl); Luci
   Care, Luci Belle, K.346 (3
   soli,pno/2vln&vcl); Mi Lagnero
   Tacendo, K.437 (SSB soli,pno/
   2vln&vcl); Piu Non Si Trovano
   (22B,pno/2vln&vcl); Se Lontan,
   Ben Mio, Tu Sei, K.438 (3 soli,
   pno/2vln&vcl)   (M2424)

So Al Labbro Mio Non Credi *K.295
   T solo,2fl,2ob,2bsn,2horn,strings
   BREITKOPF-L rental   (M2425)

So Lang Hab Ich Geschmachtet (from Le
   Nozze Di Figaro)
   SBar soli,2fl,2bsn,2horn,strings
   BREITKOPF-L rental   (M2426)

Solosanger Och Duetter Med Piano
   (from Le Nozze Di Figaro) CCU
   solo/2 soli,pno GEHRMANS s.p.
                                (M2427)

Songs *CCU
   solo,pno KALMUS 6322 $3.00 original
   keys   (M2428)

Songs From Don Giovanni, Book 1:
   Soprano (Donna Anna & Donna
   Elvira) (from Don Giovanni)
   S solo,pno NOVELLO 17.0258.00 s.p.
   contains: Mi Tradi; Non Mi Dir
                                (M2429)

Songs From Don Giovanni, Book 3:
   Tenor (Don Ottavio) (from Don
   Giovanni)
   T solo,pno NOVELLO 17.0259.09 s.p.
   contains: Dalla Sua Pace; Il Mio
   Tesoro Intanto   (M2430)

Songs From Figaro, Book 1: Soprano
   (The Countess) (from Le Nozze Di
   Figaro)
   S solo,pno NOVELLO 17.0254.08 s.p.

MOZART, WOLFGANG AMADEUS (cont'd.)

contains: Al Desio Di Chi
T'adora; Dove Sono; Porgi,
Amor, Qualche Ristoro   (M2431)

Songs From Figaro, Book 2: Soprano
(Susanna & Cherubino) (from Le
Nozze Di Figaro)
S solo,pno NOVELLO 17.0255.06 s.p.
contains: Deh Vieni, Non Tardar;
Non So Piu Cosa Son; Un Moto Di
Gioja; Voi, Che Sapete   (M2432)

Songs From Figaro, Book 3: Baritone
(Figaro) (from Le Nozze Di
Figaro)
Bar solo,pno NOVELLO 17.0256.04
s.p.
contains: Aprite Un Po' Quegl'
Occhi; Non Piu Andrai; Se Vuol
Ballare   (M2433)

Sono In Amore (from La Finta
Semplice)
S solo,2fl,strings BREITKOPF-L
rental   (M2434)

Sub Tuum Praesidium *K.198, sac
ST soli,strings sc BOHM s.p.
(M2435)

Sull' Aria (from Le Nozze Di Figaro)
solo,pno/orch sc KALMUS $3.00
(M2436)

"Sweet Zephyr" [It/Eng] SS soli,pno
SCHIRM.G $1.00   (M2437)

Susse Rache, Ja Susse Rache (from Le
Nozze Di Figaro)
B solo,2fl,2ob,2bsn,2horn,2trp,
timp,strings BREITKOPF-L rental
(M2438)

Sweet Zephyr *see Sull' Aria

Tell Me, Fair Ladies *see Voi Che
Sapete

Teuerstes Madchen, Ich Scheide *see
Bella Mia Fiamma - Resta O Cara

Teuerstes Madchen, Ich Scheide - Weib
Mein Alles? *see Bella Mia
Fiamma - Resta, O Cara

Tiger! Wetze Nur Die Klauen (from
Zaide)
[Ger/Eng] S solo,pno INTERNAT.
$1.25   (M2439)

To Chloe *see An Chloe

To My Beloved, O Hasten *see Il Mio
Tesoro Intanto

To Scenes Of Peace Retiring *see In
Diesen Heil'gen Hallen

Tout Mon Coeur Est Nouveau (from Le
Nozze Di Figaro)
male solo,pno/inst DURAND s.p.
(M2440)

Tre Arie
(Cantu, M.) S solo,fl,clar,ob,bsn,
2horn cmplt ed CARISH s.p.
contains: Passionlied, K.146; Per
Pieta, Non Ricercate, K.420;
Vado, Ma Dove? - Oh Dei!, K.583
(M2441)

Tu Sais Quel Infame (from Don
Giovanni)
female solo,pno/inst DURAND s.p.
(M2442)

Tu Virginum Corona (from Exultate
Jubilate)
solo,pno ASHDOWN   (M2443)

Twenty-One Concert Arias For Soprano,
Vol. I *CC10L
S solo,pno SCHIRM.G 1751 $3.50
(M2444)

Twenty-One Concert Arias For Soprano,
Vol. II *CC11L
S solo,pno SCHIRM.G 1752 $4.50
(M2445)

Un' Aura Amorosa (from Cosi Fan
Tutte)
"Der Odem Der Liebe" T solo,2clar,
2bsn,2horn,strings BREITKOPF-L
rental   (M2446)
"Der Odem Der Liebe" T solo,2clar,
2bsn,2horn,strings voc sc
BREITKOPF-W EB 1666 s.p. contains
also: Prendero Quel Brunnettio,
"Ich Erwahle Mir Den Braunen" (SS
soli,2ob,2bsn,2horn,strings)
(M2447)

Un Bacio Di Mano *K.541
see Mozart, Wolfgang Amadeus,
Alcandro, Lo Confesso [Kv 512]
[It/Eng] B solo,pno INTERNAT.
$1.25, ipr   (M2448)
B solo,fl,2ob,2bsn,2horn,strings sc
KALMUS $3.00   (M2449)
Bar/B solo,fl,2ob,2bsn,2horn,
strings BREITKOPF-L rental
(M2450)

MOZART, WOLFGANG AMADEUS (cont'd.)

Un Moto Di Gioia *K.579
see Sei Melodie
"Den Busen Bewegt Mir" S solo,fl,
ob,bsn,2horn,strings voc sc
BREITKOPF-W s.p.   (M2451)

Un Moto Di Gioja (from Le Nozze Di
Figaro)
see Songs From Figaro, Book 2:
Soprano (Susanna & Cherubino)

Un'aura Amorosa (from Cosi Fan Tutte)
[It] T solo,pno RICORDI-ARG
BA 11699 s.p.   (M2452)

Va, Dal Furor Portata *K.21
T solo,2ob,2bsn,2horn,strings
BREITKOPF-L rental   (M2453)

Vado, Ma Dove? - Oh Dei! *K.583
see Tre Arie
S solo,2clar,2bsn,2horn,strings
BREITKOPF-L rental   (M2454)

Vedrai, Carino, Se Sei Buonimo (from
Don Giovanni)
[Eng/It] S solo,pno BOOSEY $1.50
(M2455)

Vedrai, Carino, Se Sei Buonino (from
Don Giovanni)
[It] S solo,pno RICORDI-ENG 54347
s.p.   (M2456)
S solo,pno/orch sc KALMUS $3.00
(M2457)

Venti, Fulgura, Procellae *mot
[Lat] S solo,2fl,2ob,2horn,strings
sc DOBLINGER DM 567 s.p., ipa,
voc sc DOBLINGER DM 567A $6.25
(M2458)

Vieni, Vieni O Mia Ninetta (from La
Finta Semplice)
[It/Eng] B solo,pno INTERNAT.
$1.25, ipr   (M2459)

Viens Une Voix T'appelle (from Don
Giovanni)
BB soli,pno/inst DURAND s.p.
(M2460)

Violet, The *see Das Veilchen

Voi Avete Un Cor Fedele *K.217
S solo,2ob,2horn,strings BREITKOPF-
L rental   (M2461)

Voi, Che Sapete (from Le Nozze Di
Figaro)
see Songs From Figaro, Book 2:
Soprano (Susanna & Cherubino)
[It] S solo,pno RICORDI-ARG BA 8239
s.p.   (M2462)
[It] S solo,pno RICORDI-ENG 54349
s.p.   (M2463)
[It] low solo,pno (G maj) CRAMER
(M2464)
[It] high solo,pno (B flat maj)
CRAMER   (M2465)
high solo,pno (B flat maj) FISCHER,
C S 4910   (M2466)
low solo,pno (A flat maj) FISCHER,C
S 4911   (M2467)
Mez solo,pno/orch sc KALMUS $3.00
(M2468)
med solo,pno (A maj) ALLANS s.p.
(M2469)
high solo,pno (B flat maj) ALLANS
s.p.   (M2470)
"Tell Me, Fair Ladies" [It/Fr/Ger/
Eng] A solo,pno (A flat maj)
SCHIRM.G $.85   (M2471)
"Tell Me, Fair Ladies" [It/Fr/Ger/
Eng] S solo,pno (B flat maj)
SCHIRM.G $.85   (M2472)

Vorrei Spiegarvi, Oh Dio *K.418
S solo,2ob,2bsn,2horn,strings
BREITKOPF-L rental   (M2473)

Vous Souvient-Il?
solo,pno/inst DURAND s.p.   (M2474)

Warnung
high solo,pno SCHOTTS 09634 1-2
s.p.   (M2475)
med solo,pno SCHOTTS 09571 1-2 s.p.
(M2476)

Wehe Mir, Ach - Leben Soll Ich *see
Misera, Dove Son! - Ah! Non Son
Io

Wehe Mir! Ist's Wahrheit - Eilet,
Mitleid'ge Lufte *see Misero! O
Sogno - Aura, Che Intorno Spiri

Wenn Die Sanften Abendwinde (from Le
Nozze Di Figaro)
SS soli,ob,bsn,strings BREITKOPF-L
rental   (M2477)

Wenn Du Fein Fromm Bist (from Don
Giovanni)
S solo,2fl,2ob,2bsn,2horn,strings
BREITKOPF-L rental   (M2478)

MOZART, WOLFGANG AMADEUS (cont'd.)

When A Maiden Takes Your Fancy (from
Die Entfuhrung Aus Dem Serial)
[Eng/Ger] B solo,pno BOOSEY $1.50
(M2479)

When You Find A Maiden Charming (from
Il Seraglio)
low solo,pno (G min) ALLANS s.p.
(M2480)

Where Now *see Dove Sono

Wiegenlied
"Ninna Nanna" see Sei Melodie
"Berceuse" [Fr] solo,acap oct
DURAND s.p.   (M2481)
"Berceuse" Mez/Bar solo,pno/inst
DURAND s.p.   (M2482)
"Cancion De Cuna" [Ger/Span] solo,
pno RICORDI-ARG BA 8915 s.p.
(M2483)
"Lullaby" [Ger/Eng] high solo,pno
(F maj) SCHIRM.G $.80   (M2484)
"Ninna Nanna" solo,pno FORLIVESI
12075 s.p.   (M2485)

Will Der Herr Graf Ein Tanzchen Nun
Wagen (from Le Nozze Di Figaro)
Bar/B solo,2ob,2bsn,2horn,strings
BREITKOPF-L rental   (M2486)

Willst Du Mein Liebchen Sein *see
Mandina Amabile

Within These Holy Portals *see In
Diesen Heil'gen Hallen

Wohin Flohen Die Wonnestunden (from
Le Nozze Di Figaro)
S solo,2ob,2bsn,2horn,strings
BREITKOPF-L rental   (M2487)

Wohl Denn, Doch Dann Geliebte *see
Parto, Parto, Ma Tu Ben Mio

Yes, At Length 'Tis The Moment *see
Giunse Alfin Il Momento

You Who Are Powerful *see Ihr
Machtigen

Zage Nicht *see Non Temer, Amato
Bene

Zeffiretti, Lusinghieri (from
Idomeneo)
[It/Eng] S solo,pno INTERNAT. $1.00
(M2488)
solo,pno (E maj) ASHDOWN   (M2489)

MUDAI see Koellreutter, Hans-Joachim

MUDARRA, ALONSO DE (ca. 1506-1580)
Isabel, Perdiste La Tu Faxa
(Azpiazu) [Span] med solo,gtr UNION
ESP. $.90   (M2490)

Tres Libros De Musica En Cifra Para
Vihuela *CC3U
(Tarrago) med solo,gtr UNION ESP.
$15.00   (M2491)

Triste Estaba El Rey David
(Azpiazu) [Span] med solo,gtr UNION
ESP. $1.10   (M2492)
(Pujol) med solo,gtr ESCHIG E1302
$.90   (M2493)

MUELLER, CARL F. (1892-   )
Create In Me A Clean Heart, O God
(Psalm 100) sac
low solo,pno (C min) SCHIRM.G $.85
(M2494)
high solo,pno (E min) SCHIRM.G $.85
(M2495)
solo,pno SHAWNEE IA5049 $.85
(M2496)
Psalm 100 *see Create In Me A Clean
Heart, O God

MUERTE DE ELENA see Sciammarella, Valdo

MUERTE DEL SENOR DON GATO see
Sciammarella, Valdo

MUHLER, P. ZUR
Allemaal Vriendjes
solo,acap BROEKMANS 696 s.p.
(M2497)

MUINAINEN KAKENI see Kilpinen, Yrio

MUIR
Four Scenes For Soprano And Brass
Quintet *see Plog

MUISTELLESSA see Merikanto, Oskar

MUISTO see Kilpinen, Yrio

MUL, JAN (1911-   )
Afspraak
see Galant Kwartet

Coplas *CCU
solo,pno BROEKMANS 249 s.p. (M2498)

MUL, JAN (cont'd.)

De Bescheiden Herder
see Galant Kwartet

Deux Poems De J. Passerat *CCU
solo,pno BROEKMANS 64 s.p.   (M2499)

Drie Latijnse Minneliederen
S solo,fl,clar,perc,strings DONEMUS
s.p.
contains: Floret Silva; Stetit
Puella; Veni, Veni Venias
  (M2500)
Drie Latijnse Minneliederen *CC3U
solo,pno BROEKMANS 3 s.p.   (M2501)

Floret Silva
see Drie Latijnse Minneliederen

Galant Kwartet
DONEMUS S solo,fl,vcl,pno s.p.; S
solo,fl,ob,clar,bsn,perc,strings
rental
contains: Afspraak; De Bescheiden
Herder; Geven En Nemen; Triolet
  (M2502)

Geven En Nemen
see Galant Kwartet

'K Zal Mij Van Te Dichten Zwichten
med solo,pno DONEMUS s.p.   (M2503)

Lettre De M. L'Abbe D'Olivet A M. Le
President Bouhier
Bar solo,2fl,2ob,2clar,2bsn,2horn,
2trp,2trom,timp,perc,harp,strings
DONEMUS s.p.   (M2504)

Liederen Met Een Pruik Op *CCU
solo,pno BROEKMANS 14 s.p.   (M2505)

Old Familiar Faces, The
B solo,fl,clar,perc,strings DONEMUS
s.p.   (M2506)

Rondeel Der Herders
solo,pno BROEKMANS 76 s.p.   (M2507)

Stetit Puella
see Drie Latijnse Minneliederen

Triolet
see Galant Kwartet

Van Langendonck Liederen
A solo,pno BROEKMANS 721 s.p.
  (M2508)

Veni, Veni Venias
see Drie Latijnse Minneliederen

Vier Coplas *CC4U
high solo,2fl,2ob,2clar,2bsn,2horn,
timp,strings DONEMUS s.p. (M2509)

MULBERRY TREE, THE see Lang, Ivana

MULDER, ERNEST W. (1898-1959)

Amsterdam
solo,pno BROEKMANS 504 s.p. (M2510)

An Die Geliebte
see Vier Liederen

Aus Den Gesangen Ossian's
see Vier Liederen

Ave Maris Stella
see Vijf Geestslijke Motetten

Blomme
see Vier Liederen Op Afrikaanse
Teksten

Cantus Mysticus
see Twee Liederen Van R.J. Spitz

Cleopatre I
see Trois Chansons

Cleopatre II
see Trois Chansons

Crepuscule Pluvieux
see Trois Chansons

De Bruid
high solo,pno DONEMUS s.p. (M2511)

Die Erste Nag
see Symphonietta

Die Kleine Vlam In Het Duister
see Vier Liederen

Die Windjie
see Vier Liederen Op Afrikaanse
Teksten

Diep Rivier
see Symphonietta

Gedenkt Mij In Uw Gebeden
see Vier Liederen

MULDER, ERNEST W. (cont'd.)

Green
see Trois Chansons

Herfstmorgen
see Vijf Liederen Van Chr. V.D.
Weye

Hoe Lank Nog, Herr
see Vier Liederen Op Afrikaanse
Teksten

Holland *hymn
med solo,pno PARIS s.p.   (M2512)

Hymn
see Vijf Geestslijke Motetten

In Duisternis
see Vier Liederen

Je Ne Veux Plus Aimer Que Ma Mere
Marie
see Vijf Geestslijke Motetten

Katjies
see Symphonietta

La Bonne Chanson *CC7L
high solo,pno DONEMUS s.p.   (M2513)

La Princesse Lointaine
see Twee Liederen Van R.J. Spitz

Laudi Alla Vergine
see Vijf Geestslijke Motetten

Le Sacre
see Vier Liederen

Lente
see Symphonietta

Maanlig
see Vier Liederen Op Afrikaanse
Teksten

Montmartre
see Vijf Liederen Van Chr. V.D.
Weye

O Diepe Baai En Altijd Open Haven
see Vier Liederen

Parle Moi Que Ta Voix Me Touche
see Trois Chansons

Sancta Maria
see Vijf Geestslijke Motetten

Slaapliedje Uit Den Oorlogstijd
see Vijf Liederen Van Chr. V.D.
Weye

Soir
see Trois Chansons
see Vier Liederen

Symphonietta
med solo,2fl,2ob,2clar,2bsn,2horn,
2trp,timp,perc,harp,strings
DONEMUS s.p.
contains: Die Erste Nag; Diep
Rivier; Katjies; Lente   (M2514)

Trois Chansons
Mez/A solo,pno DONEMUS s.p.
contains: Crepuscule Pluvieux;
Green; Parle Moi Que Ta Voix Me
Touche   (M2515)

Trois Chansons
S solo,fl,ob,clar,bsn,horn,timp,
pno,strings DONEMUS s.p.
contains: Cleopatre I; Cleopatre
II; Soir   (M2516)

Twee Liederen Van R.J. Spitz
Mez solo,pno DONEMUS s.p.
contains: Cantus Mysticus; La
Princesse Lointaine   (M2517)

Verlossing
see Vijf Liederen Van Chr. V.D.
Weye

Vier Liederen
med solo,pno DONEMUS s.p.
contains: An Die Geliebte; Aus
Den Gesangen Ossian's; Le
Sacre; Soir   (M2518)

Vier Liederen
low solo,org DONEMUS s.p.
contains: Die Kleine Vlam In Het
Duister; Gedenkt Mij In Uw
Gebeden; In Duisternis; O Diepe
Baai En Altijd Open Haven
  (M2519)

Vier Liederen Op Afrikaanse Teksten
med solo,pno DONEMUS s.p.
contains: Blomme; Die Windjie;
Hoe Lank Nog, Herr; Maanlig
  (M2520)

MULDER, ERNEST W. (cont'd.)

Vijf Geestslijke Motetten *sac,mot
S solo,inst DONEMUS s.p.
contains: Ave Maris Stella; Hymn;
Je Ne Veux Plus Aimer Que Ma
Mere Marie; Laudi Alla Vergine;
Sancta Maria   (M2521)

Vijf Liederen Van Chr. V.D. Weye
med solo,pno DONEMUS s.p.
contains: Herfstmorgen;
Montmartre; Slaapliedje Uit Den
Oorlogstijd; Verlossing;
Voorjaarslied   (M2522)

Voer Mij Waar Uw Vrede Wenkt
med solo,org DONEMUS s.p.   (M2523)

Voorjaarslied
see Vijf Liederen Van Chr. V.D.
Weye

MULDER, HERMAN (1894-   )

Acht Liederen Naar Gedichten Van Jan
Engelman *CC8L
solo,pno DONEMUS s.p.   (M2524)

Afscheid *Op.86,No.3
see Vier Liederen Van H. Marsman

Antwoord Op Een Brief
high solo,pno DONEMUS s.p.   (M2525)

Branding
see Vijf Liederen

Cyclamen
see Twee Liederen

Dat Jaar
see Twee Liederen Van F. Bastiaanse

De Liefdegift
see Twee Liederen Van A. Verwey

De Oude Viool
see Drie Liederen Van J. Schurmann

De Strijder
see Vier Liederen Van M. Vos

De Winden Lachen Zacht
see Vier Liederen Van M. Vos

De Zon
see Twee Liederen Van J. Prins

Die Kleine Vlam In Het Duister
see Vier Liederen

Dorschen
see Drie Liederen Van J. Schurmann

Dreamland
Bar/A solo,3fl,3ob,4clar,4horn,
timp,perc,xylo,harp,strings
DONEMUS s.p.   (M2526)
Bar/A solo,pno DONEMUS s.p. (M2527)

Drie Liederen
med solo,fl,pno DONEMUS s.p.
contains: Goede Dood; In Fijne
Vingertoppen; O Dood, Geheime
Nachtegaal   (M2528)

Drie Liederen Van J. Schurmann
low solo,pno DONEMUS s.p.
contains: De Oude Viool;
Dorschen; Wanneer Niet Meer
  (M2529)

Drie Nachtliederen Van F. Bastiaanse
*CC3U
low solo,pno DONEMUS s.p.   (M2530)

Droomland
Bar/A solo,pno DONEMUS s.p. (M2531)

Duisternis
see Vier Liederen Van M. Vos

Een Dissonant
med solo,pno DONEMUS s.p.   (M2532)

Gedenkt Mij In Uw Gebeden
see Vier Liederen

Gedicht
see Vijf Liederen

Goede Dood
see Drie Liederen

Heel Mijn Leven
high solo/med solo,pno DONEMUS s.p.
  (M2533)

Het Ezeltje
see Twee Liederen Van J. Prins

Het Lied Dat Fluistert
Mez/A solo,pno DONEMUS s.p. (M2534)

Het Lied Van De Regen
low solo,pno DONEMUS s.p.   (M2535)

MULDER, HERMAN (cont'd.)

Ik Hoor De Nacht
   see Vijf Liederen

In Duisternis
   see Vier Liederen

In Fijne Vingertoppen
   see Drie Liederen

In Gedempten Toon *Op.110, song
   cycle
   Mez solo,pno DONEMUS s.p.   (M2536)

Laat De Luiken Gesloten Zijn
   see Vijf Liederen

Lostomige Wind
   see Vier Liederen Van M. Vos

Madelon *Op.111, song cycle
   Mez solo,pno DONEMUS s.p.   (M2537)

Morgenzang
   see Twee Liederen

Neen Laat Mij
   med solo,pno DONEMUS s.p. contains
   also: Verloren   (M2538)

Nevel
   A/Bar solo,pno DONEMUS s.p. (M2539)

O Diepe Baai En Altijd Open Haven
   see Vier Liederen

O Dood, Geheime Nachtegaal
   see Drie Liederen

Ontwaken *Op.86,No.2
   see Vier Liederen Van H. Marsman

Opnieuw De Nacht
   see Vijf Liederen

Oud Lied
   low solo,pno DONEMUS s.p.   (M2540)

Paradise Regained *Op.86,No.1
   see Vier Liederen Van H. Marsman

Rozen
   see Twee Liederen Van A. Verwey

Sneeuwstorm *Op.86,No.4
   see Vier Liederen Van H. Marsman

Sonnettenkring *Op.130-130a, CC8U
   A/Bar solo,pno DONEMUS s.p. (M2541)

Sonnettenkring *CC8U
   low solo,2fl,2ob,3clar,2bsn,2horn,
   harp,strings DONEMUS s.p.   (M2542)

Twaalf Liederen, Bds. I & II *Op.90,
   CC12U
   high solo,pno DONEMUS s.p., ea.
                                (M2543)

Twee Liederen
   low solo,pno DONEMUS s.p.
   contains: Cyclamen; Morgenzang
                                (M2544)

Twee Liederen Van A. Verwey
   low solo,pno DONEMUS s.p.
   contains: De Liefdegift; Rozen
                                (M2545)

Twee Liederen Van F. Bastiaanse
   low solo,pno DONEMUS s.p.
   contains: Dat Jaar; Zomernacht
                                (M2546)

Twee Liederen Van J. Prins
   med solo,pno DONEMUS s.p.
   contains: De Zon; Het Ezeltje
                                (M2547)

Verloren
   see Mulder, Herman, Neen Laat Mij

Vier Liederen
   low solo,pno DONEMUS s.p.
   contains: Die Kleine Vlam In Het
   Duister; Gedenkt Mij In Uw
   Gebeden; In Duisternis; O Diepe
   Baai En Altijd Open Haven
                                (M2548)

Vier Liederen Van H. Marsman
   high solo,pno DONEMUS s.p.
   contains: Afscheid, Op.86,No.3;
   Ontwaken, Op.86,No.2; Paradise
   Regained, Op.86,No.1;
   Sneeuwstorm, Op.86,No.4 (M2549)

Vier Liederen Van M. Vos
   Bar solo,fl,ob,clar,bsn,horn,trp,
   trom,timp,perc,harp,strings
   DONEMUS s.p.
   contains: De Strijder; De Winden
   Lachen Zacht; Duisternis;
   Lostomige Wind   (M2550)

Vijf Liederen
   med solo,pno DONEMUS s.p.
   contains: Branding; Gedicht; Ik
   Hoor De Nacht; Laat De Luiken
   Gesloten Zijn; Opnieuw De Nacht
                                (M2551)

MULDER, HERMAN (cont'd.)

Voer Mij Waar Uw Vrede Wenkt
   med solo,pno DONEMUS s.p.   (M2552)

Wanneer Niet Meer
   see Drie Liederen Van J. Schurmann

Zeven Liederen Van I.M. Gerhardt
   *CC7L
   high solo,pno DONEMUS s.p.   (M2553)

Zomernacht
   see Twee Liederen Van F. Bastiaanse

MULE, GIUSEPPE (1885-1951)
A Lei
   S/T solo,pno BONGIOVANI 217 s.p.
                                (M2554)
   S/T solo,pno,vln/vcl BONGIOVANI 231
   s.p.   (M2555)

Largo (from La Dentro Il Mister)
   solo,pno BONGIOVANI 2148 s.p.
                                (M2556)

Pianto Antico
   solo,pno BONGIOVANI 289 s.p.
                                (M2557)

MULL' ON KULTAA KOLMETOISTA see
   Sonninen, Ahti

MULLEN
   Afterwards
   low solo,pno (G maj) CENTURY 3
                                (M2558)

MULLEN, F.
   Naggletons, The
   2 soli,pno CRAMER   (M2559)

MULLER, A.
   Die Welt Steht Auf Kein Fall Mehr
   Lang
   solo,pno DOBLINGER 08 561 s.p.
                                (M2560)

MULLER, P.
   Psalm 91
   high solo,org HUG s.p.   (M2561)
   med solo,org HUG s.p.   (M2562)

Schweizer Hymne
   solo,pno HUG s.p.   (M2563)

MULLER, RUDOLF
   Dort, Wo Die Klaren Bachlein
   solo,2vln,vla,vcl,bvl GERIG HG 450
   s.p., ipa contains also: S'ist
   Alles Dunkel   (M2564)

Rheinische Serenade Und Spielmusik
   solo,2vln,vla,vcl,bvl sc GERIG
   HG 271 s.p., ipa   (M2565)

S'ist Alles Dunkel
   see Muller, Rudolf, Dort, Wo Die
   Klaren Bachlein

MULLER-MEDEK, TILO (1940-   )
   Altagyptische Liebeslieder *CCU
   2 soli,fl,clar,bsn,trp,trom,perc,
   harp,pno,strings DEUTSCHER rental
                                (M2566)

Mein Herz Ist Dir Gewogen
   med-high solo,pno DEUTSCHER 9006
   s.p.   (M2567)

MULLINS
   Songs For Soprano And Cello *see
   Millay

MULOT, M.
   Calmes Aux Quais Deserts *Op.17,No.1
   solo,pno/inst DURAND s.p. see from
   Soirs   (M2568)

Le Ciel Comme Un Lac Pale *Op.17,
   No.3
   solo,pno/inst DURAND s.p. see from
   Soirs   (M2569)

Le Seraphin Des Soirs *Op.17,No.2
   solo,pno/inst DURAND s.p. see from
   Soirs   (M2570)

Soirs *see Calmes Aux Quais Deserts,
   Op.17,No.1; Le Ciel Comme Un Lac
   Pale, Op.17,No.3; Le Seraphin Des
   Soirs, Op.17,No.2   (M2571)

Visions *Op.16, CC3U
   solo,pno/inst DURAND s.p.   (M2572)

MUMLA, TUMLA, HUMLA see Peterson-
   Berger, (Olof) Wilhelm

MUMSIE O' MINE see Richley, Tom

MUNKIKSI JOUTUVA see Sonninen, Ahti

MUNKTELL
   Jul
   solo,pno LUNDQUIST s.p.   (M2573)

Sov, Sov
   solo,pno LUNDQUIST s.p.   (M2574)

MUNOZ MOLLEDA, J.
   Miniaturas Medievales *CCU
   [Span] med-high solo,pno UNION ESP.
   $1.00   (M2575)

MUNSEY
   Here Comes The Bride *sac
   solo,pno BENSON S5834-S $1.00
                                (M2576)

MURA RIVER FLOWING, THE see Odak, Krsto

MURAI, TSUGUJI (1934-   )
   Ha-Ru-No Yo-Ni
   see Three Lyric Poems

Se-I-Re-I-Ni-Yo-Su
   see Three Lyric Poems

Ta-Ga-I-Ni Ho-Re-Te
   see Three Lyric Poems

Three Lyric Poems
   solo,pno JAPAN 7406 s.p.
   contains: Ha-Ru-No Yo-Ni; Se-I-
   Re-I-Ni-Yo-Su; Ta-Ga-I-Ni Ho-
   Re-Te   (M2577)

MURALI see Mollicone, Henry

MURHEEN KELLOT see Kilpinen, Yrio

MURRAY
   How Come
   high solo/low solo,pno oct SCHMITT
   2137 $.40   (M2578)

In The Cross Of Christ I Glory *sac
   (Bowring) high solo,pno GENTRY
   $1.00   (M2579)

MURRAY, ALAN
   Breath Of Home, A
   low solo,pno (F maj) PATERSON s.p.
                                (M2580)
   high solo,pno (A flat maj) PATERSON
   s.p.   (M2581)

Constant Flame
   high solo,pno (G maj) PATERSON s.p.
                                (M2582)
   low solo,pno (E flat maj) PATERSON
   s.p.   (M2583)

God Bless The Hills
   med solo,pno (C maj) CRAMER (M2584)
   low solo,pno (B flat maj) CRAMER
                                (M2585)
   high solo,pno (D flat maj) CRAMER
                                (M2586)

Goodnight Mister Moon
   solo,pno CRAMER   (M2587)

Madame Jeannette
   solo,pno PATERSON s.p.   (M2588)

One Morning In May
   low solo,pno (F maj) PATERSON s.p.
                                (M2589)
   high solo,pno (A flat maj) PATERSON
   s.p.   (M2590)

Songs Of The 'Forty-Five *CCU
   solo,pno CRAMER available in 2 keys
                                (M2591)

Wandering Player, The
   low solo,pno (A flat maj) PATERSON
   s.p.   (M2592)
   high solo,pno (G maj) PATERSON s.p.
                                (M2593)

When Mother Says "Goodnight"
   low solo,pno (F maj) PATERSON s.p.
                                (M2594)
   high solo,pno (A flat maj) PATERSON
   s.p.   (M2595)

MURRAY, LYN (1909-   )
   Peace Comes To Me
   solo,pno BOOSEY $1.50   (M2596)

MURRILL, HERBERT (HENRY JOHN)
   (1909-1952)
   Humpty Dumpty
   high solo,pno (G maj) PATERSON s.p.
                                (M2597)
   low solo,pno (E flat maj) PATERSON
   s.p.   (M2598)

MUSA JOCOSA MIHI see Elliott, Kenneth

MUSE OF LOVE see Dalby, Martin

MUSE OF PARKER STREET, THE see
   Reynolds, Malvina

MUSETTA'S WALTZ see Puccini, Giacomo,
   Quando M'en Vo Soletta

MUSETTA'S WALTZ SONG see Puccini,
   Giacomo, Quando M'en Vo Soletta

MUSETTE see Badings, Henk

MUSETTE see O'Neill, Norman

MUSGRAVE, CARTER
  Red River Valley
    solo,pno (E flat maj) CRAMER
                                    (M2599)
MUSGRAVE, DOROTHY
  Black Swans
    solo,pno ALBERT AE218 s.p. (M2600)
MUSGRAVE, THEA (1928-   )
  Bairn's Prayer At Night, A
    "Child's Prayer At Night, A" see
      Suite Of Bairnsangs, A

  Cherry Tree, The *see Gean, The

  Child's Prayer At Night, A *see
    Bairn's Prayer At Night, A

  Daffins
    "Daffodils" see Suite Of
      Bairnsangs, A

  Daffodils *see Daffins

  Except I Love
    see Five Love Songs

  Five Love Songs
    (Jessett, Michael) [Eng] S solo,gtr
      CHESTER s.p.
      contains: Except I Love; O Love,
        How Strangely Sweet; Poor Is
        The Life; Spring Of Joy Is Dry,
        The; Weep Eyes, Break Heart
                                    (M2601)
  Gean, The
    "Cherry Tree, The" see Suite Of
      Bairnsangs, A

  Man In The Moon, The *see Man-In-
    The-Mune, The

  Man-In-The-Mune, The
    "Man In The Moon, The" see Suite Of
      Bairnsangs, A

  O Love, How Strangely Sweet
    see Five Love Songs

  Poor Is The Life
    see Five Love Songs

  Song For Christmas, A
    [Eng] high solo,kbd CHESTER s.p.
                                    (M2602)
  Spring Of Joy Is Dry, The
    see Five Love Songs

  Suite Of Bairnsangs, A
    [Scot/Eng] high solo,kbd CHESTER
      s.p.
      contains: Bairn's Prayer At
        Night, A, "Child's Prayer At
        Night, A"; Daffins,
        "Daffodils"; Gean, The, "Cherry
        Tree, The"; Man-In-The-Mune,
        The, "Man In The Moon, The";
        Willie Wabster, "Willie
        Webster"   (M2603)

  Weep Eyes, Break Heart
    see Five Love Songs

  Willie Wabster
    "Willie Webster" see Suite Of
      Bairnsangs, A

  Willie Webster *see Willie Wabster

MUSIC see Franco, Johan

MUSIC see Admoni, I.

MUSIC see Franco, Johan

MUSIC see Riegger, Wallingford

MUSIC see Vis, Lucas

MUSIC see Werther, R.T.

MUSIC AND HER SISTER SONG see Glover,
  Stephen

MUSIC BOX see Turner, J.G.

MUSIC BOX, THE see Liadov, Anatol
  Konstantinovitch

MUSIC FOR ALBION MOONLIGHT see Bedford,
  David

MUSIC FOR AWHILE see Purcell, Henry

MUSIC FOR "LOVE'S LABOUR'S LOST" see
  Finzi, Gerald

MUSIC FOR SINGER see Childs, Barney

MUSIC FOR SOPRANO AND ORCHESTRA see
  Barber, Samuel

MUSIC FOR SOPRANO AND ORCHESTRA see
  Beale, James

MUSIC FOR SOPRANO SOLO AND ACAPPELLA
  CHORUS see Bialosky, Marshall

MUSIC FOR TEN INSTRUMENTS AND SOPRANO
  see Kahn, Erich Itor

MUSIC FOR THE CHRISTIAN WEDDING
  *CC25UL,Marriage
    solo,pno/org (med easy) LILLENAS
      MB-139 $2.95 vocal and instrumental
      numbers   (M2604)
MUSIC FOR THE JEWISH WEDDING *sac,CCU,
  Marriage,Heb
    solo,pno BELWIN $5.00   (M2605)
MUSIC FOR THE MARRIAGE SERVICE see
  Stevens, Halsey

MUSIC FOR THE MORNING OF THE WORLD see
  Schafer, M.

MUSIC I HEARD WITH YOU see Cory, George

MUSIC I HEARD WITH YOU see Hageman,
  Richard

MUSIC I HEARD WITH YOU see Nordoff,
  Paul

MUSIC IN CERVANTES WORKS *CCU
  (Querol) [Span] med solo,pno UNION
    ESP. $7.00   (M2606)
MUSIC IN HEAVEN see Birch, Robert
  Fairfax

MUSIC IN MY HEART see Tauber, Richard

MUSIC IS BEAUTY see Kendricks, Virginia

MUSIC OF HAWAII *sac,CCU
  (Henderson) solo,pno BOSTON $3.00
                                    (M2607)
MUSIC OF THE MORAVIANS IN AMERICA
  *sac,CC10U,concerto
    (David) [Eng/Ger] S solo,org,opt
      strings PETERS 6084 $4.50, ipa
                                    (M2608)
MUSIC OF THE TREES see Day, Maude
  Craske

MUSIC PER FLAUTO [2] see Regt, Hendrik
  de

MUSIC THAT HER ECHO IS, THE see
  Bedford, David

MUSIC, THOU SOUL OF HEAVEN see Pinkham,
  Daniel

MUSIC TO HEAR see Hogenhaven, Knud

MUSIC TO HEAR see Ketting, Otto

MUSIC TO LIVE BY see Braun, Gene

MUSIC TO THE SOUL see Birch, Robert
  Fairfax

MUSIC WHEN SOFT VOICES DIE see Diamond,
  David

MUSIC, WHEN SOFT VOICES DIE see Gold,
  Ernest

MUSIC WHEN SOFT VOICES DIE see Holford,
  Franz

MUSIC WHEN SOFT VOICES DIE see Hurst,
  G.

MUSIC WHEN SOFT VOICES DIE see Keel,
  Frederick

MUSIC WHEN SOFT VOICES DIE see Porter,
  Quincy

MUSIC, WHEN SOFT VOICES DIE see
  Quilter, Roger

MUSICA BOLIVIANA see Torrez, S.P.

MUSICA IN HORTO see Respighi, Ottorino

MUSICA PER A ANNA see Mestres-Quadreny,
  Josep Maria

MUSICA PER FLAUTO, PERCUSSIONE E VOCE
  see Regt, Hendrik de

MUSICA PROIBITA see Gastaldon,
  Stanislas

MUSICAL ALPHABET, THE see Hardt,
  Richard

MUSICAL BANQUET, A (1610) see Dowland,
  Robert

MUSICAL ENTERTAINER, THE, VOLS. I & II
  see Bickham, George

MUSICAL SNUFF-BOX, THE see Liadov,
  Anatol Konstantinovitch, Une
  Tabatiere A Musique

MUSICAL ZOO see Dukelsky, Vladimir

MUSICHE PER LA "TWELFTH NIGHT" DI
  SHAKESPEARE see Parodi, Renato

MUSIK see Korling, Sven

MUSIK AUS WIEN
  [Ger] solo,gtr DOBLINGER 05 924 s.p.;
    solo,pno DOBLINGER 89 000 $4.50
                                    (M2609)
MUSIK BEWEGT MICH see Peterson-Berger,
  (Olof) Wilhelm

MUSIK DER TRAUER see Jacob

MUSIK DES EINSAMEN see Lothar, Mark

MUSIK FUR HEISSENBUTTEL see Kelemen,
  Milko

MUSIK FUR VIER PROTAGONISTEN see
  Mamangakis, Nikos

MUSIK IM HAUSLICHEN LEBEN see Crappius,
  Andreas

MUSIK, MUSIK AR DU see Grafstrom

MUSIKAELS TYDVERDRYF, VOL. 1: JULY see
  Lustig, J.W.

MUSIKAELS TYDVERDRYF, VOL. 2: AUGUSTUS
  see Lustig, J.W.

MUSIKAELS TYDVERDRYF, VOL. 3: SEPTEMBER
  see Lustig, J.W.

MUSIKALISCHES TAGEBUCH NO. I see Suter,
  Robert

MUSIKALISCHES TAGEBUCH NO. II see
  Suter, Robert

MUSIKANTEN, DIE KOMMEN see Pudelko,
  Walter

MUSIKDEL see Wennerburg, [Gunnar]

MUSIQUE D'ANTAN see Cuvillier, Charles

MUSIQUE "IN-HORTO" see Coppola, Piero

MUSIQUE POUR L'HOMME see Straesser,
  Joep

MUSIQUE POUR SOPRANO ET ENSEMBLE DE
  CHAMBRE see Matsushita, S.

MUSIQUE SUR L'EAU see Jongen, Leon

MUSIQUE SUR L'EAU see Lachaume, A.

MUSIQUE SUR L'EAU see Lioncourt, Guy de

MUSIQUE SUR L'EAU see Schmitt, Florent

MUSKAT see Jurovsky, Simon

MUSKATLI *CC97U,folk,Hung
  (Deak; Bardos) solo,pno BUDAPEST 1734
    s.p.   (M2610)
MUSS NICHT DER MENSCH AUF DIESER ERDEN
  see Bruhns, Nicholaus

MUSSORGSKY, MODEST (1839-1881)
  Ah, Poor Marina! (from Boris
    Godounov)
    "Aria Di Marina" [It/Span] Mez/S
      solo,pno BESSEL 4765 s.p. (M2611)
    "Arie Der Marina" [Russ/Fr] S solo,
      orch voc sc BREITKOPF-W 57 03051
      s.p.   (M2612)

  Aria Di Chaklovitz (from
    Khovanshchina)
    [Fr/Eng] Bar solo,pno BESSEL 4770 B
      s.p.   (M2613)

  Aria Di Marina *see Ah, Poor Marina!

  Arie Der Marina *see Ah, Poor
    Marina!

  Arie Des Pimen *see Pimen's Tale

  Auf Dem Dnjepr
    see Sechs Nachgelassene Lieder

  Aux Champignons
    [Russ/Fr] med solo,pno BELAIEFF 291
      s.p. see also Seven Romances And
      Chansons   (M2614)

  Berceuse
    solo,orch HENN s.p.   (M2615)

  Boris' Monologue (from Boris Godunov)
    [Russ/Eng] solo,pno INTERNAT. $1.25
                                    (M2616)
  By The Forts Of Kazan *see Varlamm's
    Song

MUSSORGSKY, MODEST (cont'd.)

Canzone Di Marta (from Khovanshchina)
[Fr/Eng] Mez solo,pno BESSEL 4768
s.p. (M2617)

Canzone Di Parassia (from Sorochintsy
Fair)
[Russ/Fr] S solo,pno BESSEL 4772 B
s.p. (M2618)

Canzone Di Varlaam (from Boris
Godounov)
[Fr/Russ] B solo,pno BESSEL
4764 BIS s.p. (M2619)

Chanson De La Puce
"Song Of The Flea, The" [Russ/Fr/
Eng] Bar solo,pno (B min)
SCHIRM.G $.75 (M2620)

Chant Juif
[Russ/Fr] med solo,pno BELAIEFF 290
s.p. see also Seven Romances And
Chansons (M2621)

Chants Et Danses De La Mort *see
Song And Dances Of Death

Death Of Boris, The (from Boris
Godunov)
[Russ/Eng/Fr] Bar solo,kbd CHESTER
s.p. (M2622)
"Death Of Tsar Boris, The" [Ger/
Eng] Bar solo,pno BESSEL $1.50
(M2623)
"Morte Di Boris" [Fr/Russ] Bar
solo,pno BESSEL 4766 BIS s.p.
(M2624)
"Tod Des Zaren Boris" [Ger/Eng] Bar
solo,3fl,2ob,2bass clar,2bsn,
4horn,2trp,timp,harp,strings
BREITKOPF-W 57 03054 s.p. (M2625)

Death Of Tsar Boris, The *see Death
Of Boris, The

Der Feldherr
(Rimsky-Korsakov; Ljabunow;
Labinsky) [Russ/Ger/Eng] A/Bar
solo,orch voc sc BREITKOPF-W
57 03065 s.p. see from Lieder Und
Tanze Des Todes (M2626)
(Rimsky-Korsakov; Ljabunow;
Labinsky) [Russ/Ger/Eng] A solo,
orch voc sc BREITKOPF-W 57 03064
s.p. see from Lieder Und Tanze
Des Todes (M2627)
(Rimsky-Korsakov; Ljabunow;
Labinsky) [Russ/Fr/Ger/Eng] S/T
solo,orch voc sc BREITKOPF-W
57 03063 s.p. see from Lieder Und
Tanze Des Todes (M2628)

Der Spottvogel
see Sechs Nachgelassene Lieder

Die Hochste Macht Ist Mein (from
Boris Godunov)
B solo,3fl,2ob,3clar,2bsn,4horn,
3trp,3trom,tuba,timp,strings
BREITKOPF-L rental (M2629)
[Eng/Ger] Bar solo,orch voc sc
BREITKOPF-W 57 03050 s.p. (M2630)

Die Hupfende Elster
see Sechs Nachgelassene Lieder

Die Nacht
see Sechs Nachgelassene Lieder

Die Prophezeiung Der Marfa *see
Martha's Divination

Dimitri's Monolog (from Boris
Godunov)
[Russ/Fr] T solo,orch voc sc
BREITKOPF-W 57 03052 s.p. (M2631)

Dis-Moi, Pourquoi
[Russ/Fr] med solo,pno BELAIEFF 287
s.p. see also Seven Romances And
Chansons (M2632)

Divination De Marthe *see Martha's
Divination

Duett Marina - Dimitri (from Boris
Godunov)
[Ger/Eng] ST soli,pno BREITKOPF-W
57 03077 s.p. (M2633)

Enfantines *CC7L
[Eng/Fr] med solo,kbd CHESTER s.p.
(M2634)

Gestattet Ihr, Dem Unscheinbaren
Knechte Gottes (from Boris
Godunov)
MezBar soli,3fl,2ob,3clar,2bsn,
4horn,3trp,3trom,tuba,timp,2harp,
strings BREITKOPF-L rental
(M2635)

Gopak (from Shevchenko)
solo,2pic,2ob,2clar,2bsn,4horn,
2trp,3trom,tuba,timp,perc,strings
BREITKOPF-W s.p. (M2636)

MUSSORGSKY, MODEST (cont'd.)

Hopak
see Twenty-Eight Songs, Vol. I
low solo,pno (E min) ALLANS s.p.
(M2637)
med solo,pno (F sharp min) ALLANS
s.p. (M2638)
[Russ/Fr] med solo,pno BELAIEFF 289
s.p. see also Seven Romances And
Chansons (M2639)

Horet Mich An, Geheime Machte (from
Khovanshchina)
(Rimsky-Korsakov, N.) Mez/A solo,
3fl,2ob,2clar,2bsn,4horn,2trp,
3trom,timp,harp,strings
BREITKOPF-L rental (M2640)

Hort, Was Einst In Der Stadt Kasan
Geschehen (from Boris Godunov)
B solo,3fl,2ob,3clar,2bsn,4horn,
2trom,3trom,tuba,timp,perc,strings
BREITKOPF-L rental (M2641)

J'ai Le Pouvoir Supreme *see My
Pow'r Is Now Supreme

Kinderstube (from Kinderleben)
[Ger/Russ/Eng] Mez solo,pno
BREITKOPF-W 57 03056 s.p. (M2642)

Kinderstube *CCU
[Czech/Russ] solo,pno SUPRAPHON
s.p. (M2643)

Klatschhandchenspiel (from Boris
Godunov)
[Ger/Eng] MezMez soli,pno
BREITKOPF-W 57 03076 s.p. (M2644)

Le Bouc
[Russ/Fr] med solo,pno BELAIEFF 293
s.p. see also Seven Romances And
Chansons (M2645)

Le Seminariste
[Russ/Fr] low solo,pno BELAIEFF 294
s.p. (M2646)

Lied Der Schenkwirtin (from Boris
Godunov)
[Russ/Fr] Mez solo,orch voc sc
BREITKOPF-W 57 03048 s.p. (M2647)

Lied Des Mephistopheles *see Song Of
The Flea

Lied Des Mephistopheles In Auerbachs
Keller *see Song Of The Flea

Lieder Fur Bariton *CCU
[Ger] Bar solo,pno SIKORSKI 2161
s.p. (M2648)

Lieder Und Tanze Des Todes *see Der
Feldherr; Standchen; Trepak;
Wiegenlied (M2649)

Martha's Divination (from
Khovanshchina)
"Die Prophezeiung Der Marfa" [Russ/
Fr/Ger/Eng] Mez solo,pno
BREITKOPF-W 57 03055 s.p. (M2650)
"Divination De Marthe" [Russ/Fr/
Eng/Ger] Mez solo,pno BESSEL
4769 B s.p. (M2651)

Monologo Di Dositeo (from
Khovanshchina)
[Fr/Eng] B solo,pno BESSEL 4771 B
s.p. (M2652)

Monologue Of Boris (from Boris
Godunov)
[Russ/Eng/Fr] B solo,kbd CHESTER
s.p. (M2653)

Morte Di Boris *see Death Of Boris,
The

My Pow'r Is Now Supreme (from Boris
Godunov)
[Ger/Eng] Bar solo,pno BESSEL $1.50
(M2654)
"J'ai Le Pouvoir Supreme" [Fr/Russ]
Bar solo,pno BESSEL 5262 BIS s.p.
contains also: Oh! J'etouffais
(M2655)

Non Pianger (from Boris Godunov)
[It/Fr] B solo,pno BESSEL 4762 s.p.
(M2656)

Nursery, The *song cycle
see Twenty-Eight Songs, Vol. I
(Kagen, Sergius) [Russ/Eng] solo,
pno INTERNAT. $2.50 (M2657)

Oh! J'etouffais (from Boris Godounov)
see Mussorgsky, Modest, My Pow'r Is
Now Supreme

Ohne Sonne *see Sunless

Pimen's Erzahlung *see Pimen's Tale

MUSSORGSKY, MODEST (cont'd.)

Pimen's Monolog (from Boris Godunov)
[Fr/It] B solo,orch voc sc
BREITKOPF-W 57 03046 s.p. (M2658)

Pimen's Tale (from Boris Godounov)
[Ger/Eng] B solo,pno BESSEL $1.50
(M2659)
"Arie Des Pimen" [Fr/It] B solo,
orch voc sc BREITKOPF-W 57 03047
s.p. (M2660)
"Pimen's Erzahlung" [Ger/Eng] B
solo,orch s.p. sc BREITKOPF-W
57 03053, voc sc BREITKOPF-W
61 03129 (M2661)
"Pimen's Erzahlung" [Fr/It] B solo,
2fl,2ob,2clar,2bsn,4horn,2trp,
3trom,tuba,strings voc sc
BREITKOPF-W s.p. (M2662)

Pirouchka
[Russ/Fr] med solo,pno BELAIEFF 292
s.p. see also Seven Romances And
Chansons (M2663)

Pour Terminer (from Boris Godounov)
[Fr/Russ] B solo,pno BESSEL 5261
s.p. (M2664)

Romances And Songs, Vol. I *CCU
[Russ] solo,pno MEZ KNIGA 60 s.p.
(M2665)

Savichna, Ma Lumiere
[Russ/Fr] med solo,pno BELAIEFF 288
s.p. see also Seven Romances And
Chansons (M2666)

Schlummre Leis Und Lind, Du
Bauernkind
see Sechs Nachgelassene Lieder

Schone Chiwria (from Der Jahrmarkt
Von Sorotschinzi)
Mez solo,2fl,2ob,2clar,2bsn,4horn,
2trp,3trom,perc,strings
BREITKOPF-L rental (M2667)

Sechs Nachgelassene Lieder
(Markewitsch, Igor) [Fr/Ger/Eng]
voc sc BREITKOPF-W s.p. orch.
mat. (it.-russ.)
contains: Auf Dem Dnjepr (S solo,
2fl,2ob,2clar,2bsn,rec,4horn,
2trp,2trom,tuba,timp,perc,harp,
strings); Der Spottvogel (S
solo,2fl,2English horn,2rec,
2bsn,4horn,2trp,2trom,tuba,
timp,perc); Die Hupfende Elster
(S solo,2fl,2English horn,2rec,
2bsn,3horn,trp,trom,timp,perc,
strings); Die Nacht (S solo,
2fl,2rec,3horn,timp,harp,cel,
strings); Schlummre Leis Und
Lind, Du Bauernkind (S solo,
2fl,2English horn,2rec,2bsn,
4horn,trp,timp,harp,strings);
Sternlein, Sag' Mir An (S solo,
2fl,2rec,2bsn,harp,strings)
(M2668)

Sei Melodie *CC3U
S solo,orch sc ZERBONI 4244 s.p.
(M2669)

Serenade
solo,orch HENN s.p. (M2670)

Seven Romances And Chansons
[Russ] med solo,pno BELAIEFF 286
s.p.
contains & see also: Aux
Champignons; Chant Juif; Dis-
Moi, Pourquoi; Hopak; Le Bouc;
Pirouchka; Savichna, Ma Lumiere
(M2671)

Sogno Del Giovane Paesano (from
Sorochintsy Fair)
[Russ/Fr] T solo,pno BESSEL 4773 B
s.p. (M2672)

Song And Dances Of Death *song cycle
(Rimsky-Korsakov) "Chants Et Danses
De La Mort" [Fr/Russ/It] solo,pno
BREITKOPF-W 57 03066 s.p. (M2673)

Song Of The Flea
low solo,pno (A min) ALLANS s.p.
(M2674)
med solo,pno (B min) ALLANS s.p.
(M2675)
"Lied Des Mephistopheles" Bar/B
solo,pno BREITKOPF-L DLV 5932
s.p. (M2676)
(Howe) Bar solo,pno PAXTON P40603
s.p. (M2677)
(Rimsky-Korsakov; Stravinsky) "Lied
Des Mephistopheles In Auerbachs
Keller" [Fr/Ger/Eng] Bar solo,
3fl,2ob,2clar,2bsn,4horn,2trp,
3trom,timp,harp,strings voc
sc BREITKOPF-W 57 03057 $1.75
(M2678)

Song Of The Flea, The
[Russ/Eng/Fr] solo,kbd CHESTER s.p.
(M2679)

MUSSORGSKY, MODEST (cont'd.)

Song Of The Flea, The *see Chanson De La Puce

Songs And Dances Of Death *song cycle
see Twenty-Eight Songs, Vol. I.
[Russ/Eng] med solo,pno INTERNAT.
$2.50   (M2680)
[Russ/Eng] low solo,pno INTERNAT.
$2.50   (M2681)
[Russ/Eng] high solo,pno INTERNAT.
$2.50   (M2682)

Standchen
(Rimsky-Korsakov; Ljabunow;
Labinsky) [Russ/Ger/Eng] A/Bar
solo,orch voc sc BREITKOPF-W
57 03062 s.p. see from Lieder Und
Tanze Des Todes   (M2683)
(Rimsky-Korsakov; Ljabunow;
Labinsky) [Russ/Fr/Ger/Eng] S/T
solo,orch voc sc BREITKOPF-W
57 03061 s.p. see from Lieder Und
Tanze Des Todes   (M2684)

Sternlein, Sag' Mir An
see Sechs Nachgelassene Lieder

Sunless *song cycle
"Ohne Sonne" [Ger] med solo,pno
PETERS 3791 $4.00   (M2685)
(Rimsky-Korsakov) [Eng/Fr] Mez/Bar
solo,kbd CHESTER s.p.   (M2686)

Tod Des Zaren Boris *see Death Of Boris, The

Trepak
solo,orch HENN s.p.   (M2687)
(Rimsky-Korsakov; Ljabunow;
Labinsky) [Russ/Fr/Ger/Eng] S/T
solo,orch voc sc BREITKOPF-W
57 03058 s.p. see from Lieder Und
Tanze Des Todes   (M2688)
(Rimsky-Korsakov; Ljabunow;
Labinsky) [Russ/Ger/Eng] A/Bar
solo,orch voc sc BREITKOPF-W
57 03059 s.p. see from Lieder Und
Tanze Des Todes   (M2689)

Twenty-Eight Songs, Vol. I
[Ger] PETERS 3394A $4.75
contains: Hopak (med solo,pno);
Nursery, The (high solo,pno)
(song cycle); Songs And Dances
Of Death (med solo,pno) (song
cycle)   (M2690)

Twenty-Eight Songs, Vol. II *CC7UL
[Ger] med solo,pno PETERS 3394B
$4.75   (M2691)

Twenty-Eight Songs, Vol. III *CC7UL
[Ger] med solo/low solo,pno PETERS
3394C $4.75   (M2692)

Un Galletto (from Boris Godounov)
[It/Span] Mez solo,pno BESSEL 4763
s.p.   (M2693)

Un Humble Moine (from Boris Godounov)
[Fr/Russ] B solo,pno BESSEL
5264 BIS s.p.   (M2694)

Varlam's Ballad (from Boris Godounuv)
[Russ/Fr/Eng] B solo,kbd CHESTER
s.p.   (M2695)

Varlamm's Song (from Boris Godounov)
"By The Forts Of Kazan" [Ger/Eng] B
solo,pno BESSEL $1.50   (M2696)

Warlaam's Lied (from Boris Godunov)
[Ger/Eng] B solo,2fl,2ob,3clar,
2bsn,4horn,2trp,3trom,tuba,timp,
perc BREITKOPF-W 57 03049 s.p.
                         (M2697)

Was Soll Dein Weinen, Liebster? (from
Der Jahrmarkt Von Sorotschinzi)
S solo,3fl,2ob,2clar,2bsn,4horn,
3trp,trom,tuba,perc,harp,strings
BREITKOPF-L rental   (M2698)

Wiegenlied
(Rimsky-Korsakov; Ljabunow;
Labinsky) [Russ/Fr/Ger/Eng] S/T
solo,orch voc sc BREITKOPF-W
57 03060 s.p. see from Lieder Und
Tanze Des Todes   (M2699)
(Rimsky-Korsakov; Ljabunow;
Labinsky) [Russ/Fr/Ger/Eng] A/Bar
solo,orch voc sc BREITKOPF-W s.p.
see from Lieder Und Tanze Des
Todes   (M2700)

Without Sun *song cycle
[Russ/Eng] solo,pno INTERNAT. $2.50
                         (M2701)
MUSST' ICH AUCH DURCH TAUSEND DRACHEN
see Mozart, Wolfgang Amadeus

MUST JESUS BEAR ANOTHER CROSS? see
O'Hara, Geoffrey

MUST JESUS BEAR THE CROSS? see
Schroeder, John

MUST THE WINTER COME SO SOON see
Barber, Samuel

MUSTAA VAI VALKOISTA see Snare, Sigurd,
Svart Eller Vitt

MUSTALAINEN see Merikanto, Oskar

MUSTALAISLAULUJA see Brahms, Johannes

MUSTAT RUUSUT see Sibelius, Jean,
Svarta Rosor

MUTABILITY see Fine, Irving

MUTTER UND KIND see Stoll, B.

MUTTERTANDELEI see Strauss, Richard

MUUT KUULI KIRKONKELLON see Kilpinen,
Yrio

MUUTTILINTU see Kilpinen, Yrio

MUUTTOLINNUT see Kaski, Heino

MUZIEK see Franco, Johan

MUZIEK TER BRUILOFT see Paap, Wouter

MUZIKANTI K TANCI HRALI see Sauer,
Frantisek

MY AHMED HAS GONE TO GIVE BATTLE see
Fuleihan, Anis

MY AIN FOLK see Lemon, L.G.

MY BELOVED see Lovelace, Austin C.

MY BELOVED AND I see Kosakoff, Reuven

MY BETROTHED see Castelnuovo-Tedesco,
Mario

MY BOY *Bar mitzvah,Jew
solo,pno KAMMEN 1001 $1.00   (M2702)

MY BOY TAMMIE *folk,Scot
solo,pno (C min/D min) PATERSON FS57
s.p.   (M2703)

MY BRAVE BOY see Stanford, Charles
Villiers

MY BROTHER'S BROTHER see Reynolds,
William Jensen

MY CANADIAN BRIDE
see Five Canadian Folk Songs

MY CATHEDRAL see Roff, Joseph

MY CHOICE see McLain, A.

MY CHRISTMAS PRAYER see Carleton

MY COTTAGE-O see Redden, Finvola

MY COUNTRY LOVE see Glass, Dudley

MY CROW PLUTO see Thomson, Virgil

MY CURLY HEADED BABBY see Clutsam,
George H.

MY CURLY HEADED BABY see Clutsam,
George H.

MY DANCING DAY see Aston, Peter G.

MY DARK HANDS see Raphael, Gunther

MY DEAR BRETHREN, MEET THE DEMANDS OF
THIS TIME see Distler, Hugo

MY DEAR HIELAND LADDIE *folk,Scot
solo,pno (E flat maj/F maj) PATERSON
FS56 s.p.   (M2704)

MY DEAR OLD TOWN see Brahe, May H.

MY DEAR SOUL see Sanderson, Wilfred

MY DESIGN, FOR A DREAM see Coles, Jack

MY DESIRE see Dorsey

MY DEVOTION see Novello, Ivor

MY DOVE see Sveinbjornsson, Sveinbjorn

MY EARLY HOME see Blower, Maurice

MY FAIRY BOAT see Wales

MY FAITH LOOKS UP TO THEE see Bassford,
William Kipp

MY FAITH STILL HOLDS see Gaither

MY FAITHFUL FAIR ONE *folk,Scot
low solo,pno (E flat maj) PATERSON
FS65 s.p.   (M2705)
high solo,pno (F maj) PATERSON FS65
s.p.   (M2706)

MY FAITHFUL FOND ONE see Lawson,
Malcolm

MY FATHER HAS SOME VERY FINE SHEEP see
Hughes, Herbert

MY FATHER'S FAVORITE SONGS *sac,CC11UL
(Carmichael, Ralph) solo,pno WORD
30033 $1.95   (M2707)

MY FATHER'S TABLE *sac
(Carmichael, Ralph) solo,pno WORD
S-268   (M2708)

MY FAVORITE SCRAPBOOK SOLOS *sac,CC58U
(McKay, John) solo,pno WORD 37509
$1.95   (M2709)

MY FLOCK see Salas, Juan Orrego, El
Ganadico

MY FRIEND *sac,gospel
solo,pno ABER.GRP. $1.50   (M2710)

MY FRIEND see Malotte, Albert Hay

MY GENTLE WHITE DOVE see Morgan,
Orlando

MY GIFT see Ramsay, Harold

MY GOD CAN DO ANYTHING see Ellis

MY GOD HATH SENT HIS ANGEL see Davis,
Katherine K.

MY GOD IS REAL *sac,gospel
solo,pno ABER.GRP. $1.50   (M2711)

MY GOD WON'T EVER LET ME DOWN see
Sumner

MY GRACE IS SUFFICIENT FOR YOU see Roe,
Gloria [Ann]

MY GRANDFATHER'S CLOCK see Work, Henry
Clay

MY HAPPY GARDEN see Barry, Katherine

MY HAVEN OF DREAMS see Barry, Katherine

MY HEART AND I see Tauber, Richard

MY HEART AT THY SWEET VOICE see Saint-
Saens, Camille, Mon Coeur S'ouvre A
Ta Voix

MY HEART EVER FAITHFUL see Bach, Johann
Sebastian, Mein Glaubiges Herze

MY HEART HATH A MIND see Gaines, Samuel
Richards

MY HEART IS A RIVER see Schirmer,
Rudolph [E.]

MY HEART IS A SILENT VIOLIN see Fox,
Oscar

MY HEART IS EV'RY BEAUTY'S PREY see
Croft, William

MY HEART IS LIKE A SINGING BIRD see
Longas

MY HEART IS LIKE A SINGING BIRD see
Parry, Charles Hubert Hastings

MY HEART IS READY, O GOD see Ferris,
William

MY HEART IS SAIR FOR SOMEBODY *folk,
Scot
solo,pno (G maj) PATERSON FS58 s.p.
                         (M2712)

MY HEART IS YOURS see Friml, Rudolf

MY HEART REJOICETH see Bach, Johann
Sebastian

MY HEART REMEMBERS see Wragg, Russell

MY HEART SINGS see Willard, James

MY HEART SINGS see Wilson, Al

MY HEART, THE BIRD OF THE WILDERNESS
see Mallinson, (James) Albert

MY HEART'S A SHRINE see McGeoch, Daisy

MY HEART'S IN THE HIGHLANDS *folk,Scot
solo,pno (F maj) PATERSON FS139 s.p.
                         (M2713)

MY HEAV'NLY FATHER see Matthews, Harvey
Alexander

MY HERO see Straus, Oscar

MY HOME, AMERICA see Wyrtzen, Don

MY HOMELAND, TENNESSEE see Smith, Roy Lamont

MY JESUS I LOVE THEE see Smith, Tedd

MY JESUS IS MY LASTING JOY see Buxtehude, Dietrich

MY JO, JANET *folk,Scot
solo,pno (C maj/D maj) PATERSON FS61
s.p.   (M2714)

MY JOHANN see Grieg, Edvard Hagerup

MY JOHNNY WAS A SHOEMAKER see Broadwood, Lucy E.

MY JOURNEY'S END see Foster, Fay

MY JOURNEY'S END see Foster, Stephen Collins

MY KINGDOM see Goldman, Richard Franko

MY KINGDOM see Masseus, Jan

MY LADY DEBONAIR see Paderewski, Ignace Jan

MY LADY GREENSLEEVES see Quilter, Roger

MY LADY WALKS IN LOVELINESS see Charles, Ernest

MY LADYE'S GLOVE see Dainty, E.

MY LAGAN LOVE see Harty, Sir Hamilton

MY LEMAN IS SO TRUE see Holst, Gustav

MY LIFE IS YOURS see Craven, Louise

MY LIFE, MY LOVE, I GIVE see Lanier, Gary

MY LIFE'S COMPANION see Bowden, Alfreda

MY LITTLE EXQUISITE LOVE see McGeoch, Daisy

MY LITTLE FEATHERED FRIEND see Gleeson, Horace

MY LITTLE MOTHER see Diamond, David

MY LITTLE NUT TREE see Diack, John Michael

MY LITTLE SISTER see Thordarson, Sigurdur

MY LITTLE SON see Heilner, Irwin

MY LITTLE STAR see Ponce, Manuel Maria, Estrellita

MY LITTLE SWEETHEART see Reger, Max, Mein Schatzelein

MY LITTLE WORLD *sac,CC10UL
solo,pno WORD 37522 $2.50   (M2715)

MY LITTLE WORLD *sac
(Carmichael, Ralph) solo,pno WORD
S-252   (M2716)

MY LIZARD see Barber, Samuel

MY LODGING IT IS ON THE COLD GROUND see Somervell, Arthur

MY LORD see Younce, George

MY LORD AND MY GOD see Guion, David Wendall Fentress

MY LORD WHAT A MORNING *sac,spir
(Burleigh, H. T.) high solo,pno
BELWIN $1.50   (M2717)
(Burleigh, H. T.) low solo,pno BELWIN
$1.50   (M2718)
(Dawson, William L.) high solo/low
solo,pno FITZSIMONS $.60   (M2719)

MY LOVE IN HER ATTIRE see Joubert, John

MY LOVE IS A FLOWER see Franz, Robert, Ich Lieb' Eine Blume

MY LOVE IS AS THE DAWN see Henderson, W.G.

MY LOVE IS IN A LIGHT ATTIRE see Sterne, Colin

MY LOVE IS LIKE A RED, RED ROSE *folk, Scot
solo,pno (B flat maj) PATERSON FS117
s.p.   (M2720)

MY LOVE SHE'S BUT A LASSIE YET *folk, Scot
solo,pno (B flat maj) PATERSON FS59
s.p.   (M2721)

MY LOVE SONG TO A TREE see Walters, Oscar W.

MY LOVELY CELIA
(Wilson, H.L.) low solo,pno (E maj)
BOOSEY $1.50   (M2722)
(Wilson, H.L.) high solo,pno (G maj)
BOOSEY $1.50   (M2723)

MY LOVELY MAIDEN, SING NO MORE see Rachmaninoff, Sergey Vassilievitch, Oh, Never Sing To Me Again

MY LOVER IS A FISHERMAN see Strickland, Lily Teresa

MY LOVE'S AN ARBUTUS see Stanford, Charles Villiers

MY LOVE'S GREY EYES see McGeoch, Daisy

MY LOVE'S IN GERMANIE
(McVicar, G.C.) [Eng] med solo,kbd
CHESTER s.p.   (M2724)

MY LUTE, AWAKE! see Russell, W.

MY LUVE'S IN GERMANY *folk,Scot
solo,pno (G min) PATERSON FS60 s.p.
                                  (M2725)

MY LYTELL PRETTY ONE see Dolmetsch, Arnold

MY MASTER *sac
(Carmichael, Ralph) solo,pno WORD
S-92   (M2726)

MY MASTER see Mac Phail, Frances

MY MASTER HATH A GARDEN see Thiman, Eric Harding

MY MASTER HATH A GARDEN see Thompson, Randall

MY MASTER HATH A GARDEN see Thomson, Virgil

MY MIND IS LIKE A MOUNTAIN STEEP see Grieg, Edvard Hagerup, Min Tanke Er Et Maegtigt Fjeld

MY MOTHER BIDS ME BIND see Haydn, (Franz) Joseph, Bind' Auf Dein Haar

MY MOTHER BIDS ME BIND MY HAIR see Haydn, (Franz) Joseph, Bind' Auf Dein Haar

MY NANCY see Lockhead, A.

MY NANNIE'S AWA' *folk,Scot
solo,pno (A maj) PATERSON FS62 s.p.
                                  (M2727)

MY NEW DAY IS DAWNING see Franco, Johan

MY OLD BLACK BILLY AND OTHER SONGS see Jeffries

MY OWN COUNTRY see Heseltine, Philip

MY OWN DEAR LOVE see Carroll, Peter

MY OWN PRETTY BOY
(Pearson, William) solo,pno (D min)
ROBERTON 2611 s.p.   (M2728)
(Pearson, William) solo,pno (G min)
ROBERTON 2611 s.p.   (M2729)

MY PAPA'S WALTZ see Diamond, David

MY PAPA'S WALTZ see Rorem, Ned

MY PARTY FROCK see Hope, H. Ashworth

MY PEOPLE see Sternberg, Erich Walter

MY POW'R IS NOW SUPREME see Mussorgsky, Modest

MY PRAYER see Bradley

MY PRAYER see Hill, Eugene

MY PRAYER see Huerter, Charles

MY PRAYER see Humphreys, Don

MY PRAYER see Roe, Gloria [Ann]

MY PRAYER see Squire, W.H.

MY PRAYER FOR YOU see Brahe, May H.

MY PRETTY DOVE see Offenbach, Jacques

MY QUEEN see Blumenthal, Jacob (Jacques)

MY REDEEMER AND MY LORD see Buck, Dudley

MY SAVIOUR AND MY GUIDE see Ellis

MY SHELTER see Schubert, Franz (Peter), Aufenthalt

MY SHEPHERD OF GALILEE see Jones, James Edmund

MY SHEPHERD WILL SUPPLY MY NEED *sac, folk
(Thomson, Virgil) high solo/med solo,
pno BELWIN $1.50   (M2730)

MY SINS ARE GONE *sac,gospel
solo,pno ABER.GRP. $1.50   (M2731)

MY SON, WHEREFORE HAST THOU DONE THIS TO US? see Schutz, Heinrich

MY SONG IS OF THE STURDY NORTH see German, Edward

MY SONG OF SONGS see Hallett, John C.

MY SOUL DOTH MAGNIFY see Sandresky, M.V.

MY SOUL DOTH MAGNIFY THE LORD see Bouman, Paul

MY SOUL DOTH MAGNIFY THE LORD see Saxton, Stanley E.

MY SOUL DOTH MAGNIFY THE LORD see Thompson, Randall

MY SOUL DOTH MAGNIFY THE LORD see Wilson, John F.

MY SOUL HAS BEEN SET FREE see Derricks, Cleavant

MY SOUL HAS NOUGHT BUT FIRE AND ICE see Holst, Gustav

MY SOUL IS AN ENCHANTED BOAT see Duke, John Woods

MY SOUL IS ATHIRST FOR GOD see Stickles, William

MY SOUL IS ON MY LIPS see Birch, Robert Fairfax

MY SOUL IS SET AMONG THE STARS see Sharpe, Evelyn

MY SOUL, NOW BLESS THY MAKER see Hammerschmidt, Andreas

MY SOUL, NOW BLESS THY MAKER see Schein, Johann Hermann

MY SOUL SHALL BE JOYFUL see Keegan, Patrick

MY SPIRIT WILL NOT HAUNT THE MOUND see Diamond, David

MY SUNSHINE see Di Capua, [Eduardo], O Sole Mio

MY SWEET BAMBINA see Friml, Rudolf

MY TALENTS NOT FOR MEDITATION see Tchaikovsky, Piotr Ilyitch, Olga's Song

MY TASK see Ashford, E.L.

MY TREASURE see Trevalsa, Joan

MY TRIBUTE see Crouch, Andrae

MY TRIBUTE *sac,CC10L
(Dino) solo,pno WORD 37724 $2.95
                                  (M2732)

MY TRUE LOVE HATH MY HEART
(Baker, Scott) solo,pno CRAMER
                                  (M2733)
(Duncan, Stuart) solo,pno CRAMER
                                  (M2734)

MY TRUE LOVE HATH MY HEART see Montgomery, Bruce

MY TRUE LOVE HATH MY HEART see Parry, Charles Hubert Hastings

MY TRUE LOVE HATH MY HEART see Plumstead, Mary

MY TRUE LOVE HATH MY HEART see Russell, W.

MY WAY'S CLOUDY *spir
(Burleigh, H. T.) med solo,pno BELWIN
$1.50   (M2735)

MY WIFE'S A WINSOME WEE THING *folk, Scot
solo,pno (C maj) PATERSON FS64 s.p.
                                  (M2736)

MY WILD IRISH ROSE see Olcott

MY WORLD *sac,Marriage
  med solo,pno ASHLEY $1.00   (M2737)
  low solo,pno ASHLEY $1.00   (M2738)
  high solo,pno ASHLEY $1.00   (M2739)

MY WORLD see Geehl, Henry Ernest

MY YIDDISHE MOMME *folk,Jew
  solo,pno OR-TAV $.50   (M2740)

MYERS, GORDON
  Let Us Break Bread Together *sac,
    Commun
    med solo,pno ABINGDON APM-680 $1.00
                                 (M2741)

MYLE CHARAINE see Somervell, Arthur

MYR ZWEUI see Meister, C.

MYRBERG, AUGUST M.
  Aftonklockan
    see NY SAMLING SANGDUETTER, HEFT 1
    2 soli,pno LUNDQUIST s.p.   (M2742)

  Aftonstamning
    2 soli,pno LUNDQUIST s.p.   (M2743)

  Aftonstjarnan
    2 soli,pno LUNDQUIST s.p.   (M2744)

  Den Heliga Julnatten *sac
    solo,pno LUNDQUIST s.p.   (M2745)

  Det Klappar Sa Sakta
    solo,pno LUNDQUIST s.p.   (M2746)

  Fagelsang
    2 soli,pno LUNDQUIST s.p.   (M2747)

  Fem Sanger For Tvenne Roster *CC5U
    2 soli,pno LUNDQUIST s.p.   (M2748)

  Fjarran Toner
    2 soli,pno LUNDQUIST s.p.   (M2749)

  For Lange Se'n
    solo,pno LUNDQUIST s.p.   (M2750)

  Hostvisa
    2 soli,pno LUNDQUIST s.p.   (M2751)

  Nar Jag Fran Dig Far
    2 soli,pno LUNDQUIST s.p.   (M2752)

  Nattetid Vid Stranden
    see NY SAMLING SANGDUETTER, HEFT 2

  Nattliga Drommar
    see NY SAMLING SANGDUETTER, HEFT 2

  Pa Lagunen
    2 soli,pno LUNDQUIST s.p.   (M2753)

  Serenad
    high solo,pno GEHRMANS s.p. (M2754)
    med solo,pno GEHRMANS 668 s.p.
                                 (M2755)

  Sjokonungen
    solo,pno LUNDQUIST s.p.   (M2756)

  Spansk Serenad
    solo,pno GEHRMANS s.p.   (M2757)

  Vad Viskade Du?
    2 soli,pno LUNDQUIST s.p.   (M2758)

  Vallgossens Visa
    solo,pno GEHRMANS s.p.   (M2759)

  Varbacken
    see NY SAMLING SANGDUETTER, HEFT 1

  Vinden Somnat I Den Stilla Kvall
    2 soli,pno LUNDQUIST s.p.   (M2760)

MYRSKY see Marvia, Einari

MYRSKYLINTU see Merikanto, Oskar

MYRTEN UND ROSEN, BAND I *CC77U
  (Vogel; Dost) solo,pno HUG s.p.
                                 (M2761)
MYRTEN UND ROSEN, BAND II *CC21U
  2 soli,pno HUG s.p.   (M2762)

MYRTHEN see Schumann, Robert
  (Alexander)

MYRTLE BLOSSOMS FROM EDEN see Ben-Haim,
  Paul

MYRTLE SHADE, THE see Purcell, Henry

MYSELF WHEN YOUNG see Lehmann, Liza

MYSELL, BELLA
  Glick - Du Bist Gekummen Tzu Shpait
    *Jew
    solo,pno KAMMEN 443 $1.00 see also
    FAVORITE JEWISH SONGS, VOL. 2
                                 (M2763)

MYSELS
  One Little Candle (composed with
    Roach)
    med solo,pno SHAWNEE IA5040 $.85
                                 (M2764)

MYSTERIOUS RESEMBLANCE see Puccini,
  Giacomo, Recondita Armonia

MYSTERY see Floyd, Carlisle

MYSTERY OF LOVE see Ohnaka, Megumi

MYSTICA see Pratella, Francesco Balilla

MYSTICITE see Cimara, Pietro

MYSTISCHES TRIPTYCHON see Tittel, Ernst

MYTHOLOGIE see Chapuis, Auguste-Paul-
  Jean-Baptiste

MYTHOS see Vlijmen, Jan van

N

'N LIED VAN DE VRIJHEID see Vredenburg,
  Max

NA JAREN see Felderhof, Jan

NA ROZLOUCENOU see Vycpalek, Ladislav

NA STASTNOU CESTU see Seidel, Jan

NAAMLOOS see Middeleer, Jean De,
  Anonyme

NAAR DROOMELAND TOE see Zagwijn, Henri

NAAR GEEN ANDER see Clercq, R. de

NAAR SCHERPENHEUVEL see Hullebroeck,
  Em.

NABOKOV, NICOLAS (1903-   )
  Quatre Poemes De Pasternak *CC4U
    solo,pno AMPHION R 2006-15 s.p.
                                 (N1)

  Rasputin's End
    solo,pno AMPHION s.p. solo pt, voc
    sc   (N2)

  Return Of Pushkin, The
    [Russ/Eng/Ger] high solo,pno
    BELAIEFF 295 s.p.   (N3)

  Symboli Chrestiani
    Bar solo,2fl,2bsn,2horn,2trp,timp,
    perc,pno,cel,harp,strings AMPHION
    R 1471 s.p., ipr   (N4)

NACAMULI, GUIDO
  Dantesca
    see Seis Cantos Espirtuales

  Intermezzo
    see Seis Cantos Espirtuales

  Orazione Di S. Bernardo A Maria
    see Seis Cantos Espirtuales

  Padre Nostro
    see Seis Cantos Espirtuales

  Preghiera
    see Seis Cantos Espirtuales

  Seis Cantos Espirtuales *sac
    [It] solo,pno cmplt ed RICORDI-ARG
    BA 12101 s.p.
    contains: Dantesca; Intermezzo;
      Orazione Di S. Bernardo A
      Maria; Padre Nostro; Preghiera;
      Ultimo Canto   (N5)

  Ultimo Canto
    see Seis Cantos Espirtuales

NACH HAUSE GEHN WIR NICHT see Reckmann,
  J.

NACHGELASSENE LIEDER, HEFT 1 see Knab,
  Armin

NACHGELASSENE LIEDER, HEFT 2 see Knab,
  Armin

NACHGELASSENE LIEDER II see Wolf, Hugo

NACHHALL see Schoeck, Othmar

NACHHAUSEWEG see Kuiler, Cor.

NACHKLANGE see Erbse, Heimo

NACHLESE see Strauss, Richard

NACHT see Edler, Robert

NACHT see Gretchaninov, Alexander
  Tikhonovitch

NACHT see Hermans, Nico

NACHT see Knab, Armin

NACHT see Koetsier, Jan

NACHT see Lilien, Ignace

NACHT see Schmalstich, Clemens

NACHT [2] see Gretchaninov, Alexander
  Tikhonovitch

NACHT DER FARBEN see Griesbach, Karl-
  Rudi

NACHT, O BRICH DOCH SCHNELL EIN (from
  Prince Igor)
  [Russ/Fr/Ger] A solo,pno BELAIEFF 249
  s.p.   (N6)

NACHT-STILTE see Dijk, Jan van

NACHT- UND SPUKGESANGE see Graener,
   Paul

NACHT UND TRAUME see Schubert, Franz
   (Peter)

NACHTELEGIEN see Geissler, Fritz

NACHTGANG see Haas, Joseph

NACHTGEBET see Marx, Joseph

NACHTGERAUSCHE see Zagwijn, Henri

NACHTGESANG see Trapp, Max

NACHTGESANGE see Beekhuis, Hanna

NACHTIGALLENARIE see Handel, George
   Frideric

NACHTL, REGUNG see Mirandolle,
   Ludovicus

NACHTLICHE HEERSHAU "DES NACHTS UM DIE
   ZWOLFTE STUNDE" see Glinka, Mikhail
   Ivanovitch

NACHTLICHE SCHEU see Prohaska, Carl

NACHTLICHER GANG see Strauss, Richard

NACHTLIED see Clercq, R. de

NACHTLIED see Frederich, Otto

NACHTLIED see Schumann, Robert
   (Alexander)

NACHTLIEDER see Flury, Richard

NACHTLIEDJE see Pijper, Willem

NACHTLIEDJE see Witte, D.

NACHTLIEGJE see Franco Mendes, H.

NACHTLOSE NACHTE see Pylkkanen, Tauno
   Kullervo, Yoton Yo

NACHTMUZIKANTEN see Henkemans, Hans

NACHTS see Knab, Armin

NACHTS see Reger, Max

NACHTSTILTE see Bijvanck, Henk

NACHTSTILTE see Hermans, Nico

NACHTSTUCK see Reimann, Aribert

NACHTVIOLE see Kilpinen, Yrio, Lehdokki

NACHTVIOLEN see Schubert, Franz (Peter)

NACHTWACHE see Zillig, Winfried

NACHTWACHTERLIED see Holler, Karl

NACHTWANDERER see Pfitzner, Hans

NACHTWANDLER see Kuhn, Siegfried

NACHTWANDLER see Schoenberg, Arnold

NACKEN see Sibelius, Jean

NACKENS POLSKA
   solo,pno GEHRMANS 202 s.p.   (N7)

NACQUI ALL'AFFANNO E AL PIANTO see
   Rossini, Gioacchino

NADELMANN, L.
   Mein Blaues Klavier
   S solo,pno UNIVER. 14795 $4.25 (N8)

NADIR, SPRICH see Bizet, Georges

NADIRS ROMANS see Bizet, Georges

NAER OESTERLANT see Beuningen, W.v.

NAER OOSTLAND see Moulaert, Raymond

NAGELI, JOHANN (HANS) GEORG (1773-1836)
   Alemannische Gedichte *CCU
   1-2 soli,pno HUG s.p.   (N9)

NAGGLETONS, THE see Mullen, F.

NAGINSKI, CHARLES (1909-1940)
   Pasture, The
   med solo,pno (E flat min) SCHIRM.G
   $.85   (N10)

NAHANDOVE see Ravel, Maurice

NAHE DES GELIEBTEN see Trapp, Max

NAHELIEDERBUCH see Desch, Rudolf

NAHONDOVE see Ravel, Maurice

NAHRDELNIK see Mikoda, Borivoj

NAIADS see Dvorak, Antonin

NAIDES see Ugarte, Floro M.

NAILING MY SINS TO HIS CROSS see Mercer

NAISSANCES see Arrieu, Claude

NAISSANVE DE BOUDDHA see Delage,
   Maurice

NAKADA, YOSHINAO (1923-   )
   Akogare
   see Elegant Songs To Confess Love

   Elegant Songs To Confess Love
   A solo,pno JAPAN 7014 s.p.
   contains: Akogare; Habataki;
   Otazure; Samayoi; Tokimeki;
   Yobigoe   (N11)

   Habataki
   see Elegant Songs To Confess Love

   Otazure
   see Elegant Songs To Confess Love

   Samayoi
   see Elegant Songs To Confess Love

   Six Chansons Enfantines *CC6U
   solo,pno ONGAKU s.p.   (N12)

   Song Album *CCU
   solo,pno ONGAKU s.p.   (N13)

   Songs Of Japanese Toys *CCU
   solo,pno ONGAKU s.p.   (N14)

   Tokimeki
   see Elegant Songs To Confess Love

   Wooden Spoon, A *song cycle
   solo,pno ONGAKU s.p.   (N15)

   Yobigoe
   see Elegant Songs To Confess Love

NAKTERGALEN see Volkmann, Robert

NAME GOTTES see Bijvanck, Henk

NAME OF JOY, A see Hustad, Donald P.

NANA see Falla, Manuel de

NANA see Grau, Eduardo

NANA see Maravilla, L.

NANA see Romero, A.

NANCY HANKS see Davis, Katherine K.

NANCY WALSH see Mourant, Walter

NANCY'S HAIR IS YELLOW LIKE GOWD see
   Kennedy-Fraser, Marjory

NANNA see Tomasi, H.

NAO POSSO MAIS ESCONDER QUE TE AMO see
   Camargo Guarnieri

NAO SEI see Camargo Guarnieri

NAPOLI, JACOPO (1911-   )
   Grida Di Venditori Napoletani *CC7L
   [It] solo,pno CURCI 8861 s.p. (N16)

   Lauda Della Trinita *sac
   SMez soli,orch quarto RICORDI-ENG
   131485 s.p.   (N17)
   [It] SMez soli,orch voc sc RICORDI-
   ENG 131487 s.p.   (N18)

NAPOLITANO, EMILIO
   Cancion De Cuna *Op.2,No.1
   [Span] solo,pno RICORDI-ARG BA 7632
   s.p.   (N19)

   Flor De Cardon *Op.2,No.3
   [Span] solo,pno RICORDI-ARG BA 8254
   s.p.   (N20)

   La Cancion Del Saldan *Op.2,No.2
   [Span] solo,pno RICORDI-ARG BA 9337
   s.p.   (N21)

   La Cenicienta *Op.6,No.2
   [Span] solo,pno RICORDI-ARG BA 9108
   s.p.   (N22)

   La Mariposa *Op.6,No.1
   [Span] solo,pno RICORDI-ARG BA 8920
   s.p.   (N23)

   Mi Cancion *Op.7
   [Span] solo,pno RICORDI-ARG BA 9810
   s.p.   (N24)

NAPOLITANO, EMILIO (cont'd.)
   Picaflor *Op.2,No.4
   [Span] solo,pno RICORDI-ARG BA 8252
   s.p.   (N25)

   Serenata *Op.2,No.5
   [Span] solo,pno RICORDI-ARG BA 9651
   s.p.   (N26)

NAR ALLA FAGLAR TIGA see Kjellander

NAR DAGEN LYKTAT HAR SIN GANG
   see Blott En Dag Ett Ogonblick I
   Sander

NAR DET LIDER MOT JUL see Liljefors,
   Ruben

NAR DU SLUTER MINA OGON see Damm,
   Svenerik

NAR HAN KOMMER
   see Andliga Sanger, Heft 1

NAR HIMLENS FASTE MALAR see Linnala,
   Eino, Kun Helmin Heijastaapi

NAR JAG BLEV SJUTTON AR
   solo,pno GEHRMANS 167 s.p.   (N27)

NAR JAG BLIR GAMMAL see Boberg

NAR JAG DROMMER see Sibelius, Jean

NAR JAG FOR MIG SJALV I MORKA SKOGEN
   GAR see Peterson-Berger, (Olof)
   Wilhelm

NAR JAG FRAN DIG FAR see Myrberg,
   August M.

NAR JAG I TRON MIN JESUS SER
   see Andliga Sanger, Heft 1

NAR JAG VAR PRINS UTAV ARKADIEN see
   Offenbach, Jacques

NAR JULDAGSMORGON GLIMMAR see Wikander,
   David

NAR LOVEN FALLA see Runback, Albert

NAR SOLEN LYSER see Merikanto, Oskar,
   Kun Paiva Paistaa

NAR SOM MAJVINDAR SUSA see Runback,
   Albert

NAR STJARNEHAREN BLANKER see Korling,
   August

NAR TILL HEMMET SVALAN FAR see Abt,
   Franz

NAR VAREN STAR I BLOM see Korling,
   August

NAR VI BLI GAMLA see Holmquist, Nils-
   Gustaf

NARAMORE, ARCH
   Jayhawk Song, The
   med solo,pno (F maj) WILLIS $.60
                                   (N28)

NARCISS see Sibelius, Jean

NARDI, NACHUM
   Chanuka Songs *CCU,Hanakkah
   solo,pno OR-TAV $.60   (N29)

   Passover Songs *CCU,Passover
   solo,pno OR-TAV $.60   (N30)

   Purim Songs *CCU,Purim
   solo,pno OR-TAV $.60   (N31)

   Sabbath Songs *CCU,Sab-Eve/Sab-Morn
   solo,pno OR-TAV $.60   (N32)

   Selection Of Israeli Songs *CCU
   solo,pno OR-TAV $1.00   (N33)

   Shavuot Songs *CCU,Shovuot
   solo,pno OR-TAV $.60   (N34)

   Tu-Bi'Shvat Songs *CCU
   solo,pno OR-TAV $.60   (N35)

NARODNI PISNE Z HORICKA see Simek,
   Miroslav

NARRAZIONE TRAGICA see Platamone,
   Stefano

NARVAEZ, LUIS DE
   Con Que La Lavare
   (Azpiazu) [Span] med solo,gtr UNION
   ESP. $1.10   (N36)

NARZISSE see Sibelius, Jean, Narciss

NAS BARYK see Kricka, Jaroslav

NASCERE, NASCERE, DIVE PUELLULE see
    Bassani, Giovanni Battista

NASE PANI BOZENA NEMCOVA see Kricka,
    Jaroslav

NASH, S.
    Sonnet No. 104
        solo,pno (E maj) BOOSEY $1.50 (N37)

NASIJARVEN RANNALLA see Simila, Arpo

NATALE DEL BIMBO GOLOSO see Tocchi,
    Gian-Luca

NATHALIE see Arrieu, Claude

NATIONAL ANTHEMS OF THE UNITED NATIONS
    AND THEIR ALLIES *sac,CCU
    solo,pno BOSTON $3.00   (N38)

NATIVITA see Bossi, Renzo

NATIVITY CAROLS *CCU,Xmas,carol
    (Cassler, G. Winston) solo,pno
    AUGSBURG 11-9296 $2.50   (N39)

NATT see Dorumsgaard, Arne

NATT see Kuula, Toivo, Yo

NATTENS LJUS see Larsson, Lars-Erik

NATTETID VID STRANDEN see Myrberg,
    August M.

NATTHIMMELN see Geijer, Erik Gustaf

NATTIG SKIDFARD VUORELA see Sonninen,
    Ahti, Talviyon Hiihtaja

NATTLIGA DROMMAR see Myrberg, August M.

NATTRYMDEN SKYMMER see Pylkkanen, Tauno
    Kullervo, Yon Piiri

NATTVANDRARENS SANG see Rubinstein,
    Anton

NATUR see Schoenberg, Arnold

NATUR - LIEBE - TOD see Egk, Werner

NATURAL HIGH *sac
    (Carmichael, Ralph) solo,pno WORD
    S-257   (N40)

NATURE AUGUSTE ET DOUCE see Rimsky-
    Korsakov, Nikolai

NATURE MOODS see Weigl, Vally

NATURE, THE GENTLEST MOTHER see
    Copland, Aaron

NATURE'S PLAYMATES see Canning, Thomas

NATURE'S SONG see Swanson, Joan

NATURFREIHEIT see Pfitzner, Hans

NATUS EST JESUS see Boddecker, Philipp
    Friedrich

NAUMANN
    Sangaren Pa Vandring *CCU
        high solo,pno LUNDQUIST s.p. (N41)

NAUSICAA see Tremisot, Ed.

NAUTI see Kotilainen, Otto

NAVIDADES see Mingote, A.

NAVZDY see Kapralova, Viteslaza

NAY, BID ME NOT RESIGN, LOVE see
    Mozart, Wolfgang Amadeus, La Ci
    Darem La Mano

NAYLOR, BERNARD (1907-   )
    Dreams Of The Sea
        solo,pno (C maj) LESLIE 7032 $1.20
                                   (N42)
    Ecstatic, The
        low solo,pno LESLIE 7008   (N43)
        high solo,pno LESLIE 7008 (N44)
    Fallen Poplar, The
        solo,pno (F min) LESLIE 7036 (N45)
    Gentle Sleep
        solo,pno (C maj) ROBERTON 1002 s.p.
                                   (N46)
    House Of Clay, The *cant
        Bar solo,fl,clar,bsn,vln,vla,vcl
        NOVELLO rental   (N47)
    Living Fountain, The *cant
        high solo,strings NOVELLO rental
                                   (N48)
        high solo,strings NOVELLO
        17.0095.02 s.p.   (N49)

NAYLOR, BERNARD (cont'd.)
    Not So Far As The Forest
        S solo,2vln,vla,vcl NOVELLO rental
                                   (N50)
    Rose Berries
        solo,pno (E min) LESLIE 7037 (N51)
    Sing O My Love *cant
        Bar solo,strings NOVELLO rental
                                   (N52)
    Speaking From The Snow *song cycle
        high solo,pno ROBERTON 1501 s.p.
                                   (N53)

NAZARETH see Gounod, Charles Francois

NE... see Doyen, Albert

NE DAMANDONS A L'AVENIR see Migot,
    Georges

NE DERANGEZ PAS LE MONDE see DuBois,
    Pierre Max

NE JOUE PAS AVEC MON COEUR see Faraut,
    B.

NE L'OUBLIEZ PAS see Saint-Saens,
    Camille

NE MEN CON L'OMBRE see Handel, George
    Frideric

NE PLEURE PAS QUAND JE MOURRAI see
    Brun, G.

NE RIEZ PAS see Chabrier, Emmanuel

NE SUIS-JE PAS see Guiraud, Ernest

NE VOUS EMBALLEZ PAS see Messager,
    Andre

NEAR TO THE HEART OF GOD see McAfee

NEARER, MY GOD, TO THEE see Carey,
    Lewis

NEARING JORDAN'S CROSSING *sac
    solo,pno STAMPS 7247 $1.00   (N54)

'NEATH THE STARS see Thomas, Arthur
    Goring, Sous Les Etoiles

NEBBIA see Alaleone, Domenico

NEBBIA see Setaccioli, Giacomo

NEBBIE see Respighi, Ottorino

NEBEL see Respighi, Ottorino, Nebbie

NEBEL AM WATTENMEER UND GEHT LEISE see
    Winter, R.

NEBEL HANGT see Edler, Robert

N'ECRIS PAS see Schlosser, Paul

NEDBAL, MANFRED J.M. (1902-   )
    Drei Liebeslieder *Op.8,No.1-3, CC3U
        S/T solo,pno DOBLINGER 08 620 $2.00
                                   (N55)

NEDERLANDSE STEDEN see Schouwman, Hans

NEED THE LOVE OF JESUS see Lanier, Gary

NEEDHAM, ALICIA ADELAIDE
    Four Ducks On A Pond
        high solo,pno (F maj) CRAMER $1.00
                                   (N56)
        low solo,pno (D flat maj) CRAMER
        s.p.   (N57)
    On The Tide-Top
        solo,pno CRAMER   (N58)
    There's No Land Like Ireland
        solo,pno CRAMER   (N59)
    Yest' Reen
        solo,pno CRAMER   (N60)

NEEDLES AND PINS see Lohr, Frederic N.

NEEN LAAT MIJ see Mulder, Herman

NEERGEBRAND see Gilse, Jan van

NEES, G.
    De Zonne Zegent De Wereld
        solo,pno ALSBACH s.p.   (N61)

NEGEN LIEDEREN IN SPAANSCHEN TRANT see
    Lilien, Ignace

NEGLIA, FRANCESCO PAOLO (1874-1932)
    Ave Maria *Op.10
        [It] Mez solo,opt vln BERBEN 1441
        s.p.   (N62)
    Elegia Di Marco (from Zelia)
        [It] T solo,pno BERBEN 1414 (N63)

NEGLIA, FRANCESCO PAOLO (cont'd.)
    Il Saluto Di Beatrice *Op.25
        [It] Mez solo,pno BERBEN 1413 s.p.
                                   (N64)
    Monologo Di Vittore (from Zelia)
        [It] Bar solo,pno BERBEN 1415 (N65)
    Quartetto Vocale Del Primo Atto (from
    Zelia)
        STBarB soli,pno BERBEN 1416 (N66)
    Scena Della Seduzione (from Zelia)
        scena
        S solo,pno BERBEN 1417   (N67)

NEGRI, GINO
    Uno Stabat, Comunque
        SBar soli,2fl,bsn,2horn,2trp,perc,
        pno,2cembalo,strings SONZOGNO
        rental   (N68)

NEGRO LAMENT see Flothius, Marius

NEGRO SONGS FROM ALABAMA *CC75U
    (Courlander, Harold) solo,pno OAK
    000084 $3.95   (N69)

NEGRO SPIRITUALS *CCU,spir
    (Johnson, J. Rosamond) med solo,pno
    MARKS $2.00   (N70)

NEGRO SPIRITUALS *CCU,spir
    (Johnson, J. Rosamond) solo,pno MARKS
    $2.00   (N71)

NEGRO SPIRITUALS *CCU,spir
    solo,1-2gtr GERIG HG 439 s.p. (N72)

NEGRO SPIRITUALS, VOL. I *CC10L
    (Burleigh) [Eng] solo,pno RICORDI-ENG
    120875 s.p.   (N73)

NEGRO SPIRITUALS, VOL. II *CC10L
    (Burleigh) [Eng] solo,pno RICORDI-ENG
    122335 s.p.   (N74)

NEHMT MEINEN DANK, IHR HOLDEN GONNER
    see Mozart, Wolfgang Amadeus

NEHMT WAHR DAS LICHT see Haller, Hans
    Christoph

NEI CIELI see Novikoff, Sergio

NEI GIORNI TUOI FELICI see Beethoven,
    Ludwig van

NEI MERIGGI see Clausetti, P.

NEIDLINGER, WILLIAM HAROLD (1863-1924)
    Birthday Of A King *sac,Xmas
        med solo,pno (A flat maj) SCHIRM.G
        $.85   (N75)
        high solo,pno (B flat maj) SCHIRM.G
        $.85   (N76)
        solo,pno HARRIS $.85   (N77)
        med solo,pno (B flat maj) WATERLOO
        $.65   (N78)
        med solo,pno LORENZ $1.00 (N79)
        solo,pno (available in 3 keys)
        ASHLEY $.95   (N80)
        low solo,pno (A flat maj) FISCHER,C
        S 7667   (N81)
        med solo,pno (B flat maj) FISCHER,C
        S 7666   (N82)
        high solo,pno (C maj) FISCHER,C
        S 7668   (N83)
        low solo,pno (F maj) SCHIRM.G $.85
                                   (N84)
    Birthday Of A King, The *sac,Xmas
        SA soli,pno SCHIRM.G $1.00 (N85)
    Spirit Of God
        high solo,pno PRESSER $.95 (N86)
        med solo,pno PRESSER $.95 (N87)
        low solo,pno PRESSER $.95 (N88)

NEIGE see Damase, Jean-Michel

NEIGE see Daniel-Lesur

NEIGE see Delannoy, Marcel

NEIGE ROSE see Messager, Andre

NEIGE TOMBE see Strimer, Joseph

NEIGES D'AVRIL see Luigini, Alexandre

NEIGHBORS OF BETHLEHEM, THE see
    Puccini, Giacomo

NEIN, ICH KANN NICHT see Kilpinen,
    Yrio, Ei Minusta Lienekana

NEIN, LANGER TRAG ICH NICHT DIE QUALEN
    see Weber, Carl Maria von

NEIRINCKX, G.
    Avond
        solo,pno ALSBACH s.p.   (N89)

NEITHER DO I CONDEMN THEE *sac
    (Snow) solo,pno BENSON S7140-S $1.00
                                   (N90)

NEITHER NOR see Back, Sven-Erick

NEJEDLY, VIT (1912-1945)
  Vitezstvi Bude Nase
    solo,pno SUPRAPHON s.p.   (N91)

NEL CHIUSO CENTRO see Pergolesi,
  Giovanni Battista

NEL COR PIU NON ME SENTO (VARIACIONES
  SOBRE EL TEMA) see Paisiello,
  Giovanni

NEL COR PIU NON MI SENTO see Paisiello,
  Giovanni

NEL GIARDIN DEL BELLO see Verdi,
  Giuseppe

NEL GIARDINO see Bettarini, Luciano

NEL GIARDINO see Respighi, Ottorino

NEL RIDESTARMI see Cilea, Francesco

NELE'S LIED see Lothar, Mark

NELHYBEL, VACLAV (1919-   )
  Trois Poemes De A. Rimbaud *CC3U
    high solo,pno KERBY 7250 $4.50
                                     (N92)

NELJA SUOMALAISTA KANSANLAULUDUETTOA
  see Haapalainen, Vaino

NELL, G.
  Un Voyage Extraordinaire
    solo,pno/inst DURAND s.p.   (N93)

NELLA NEVE see Venticinque, R.S.

NELLA NOTTE see Paczolay, I., Koesiutaz
  E' Jesakaban

NELLA NOTTE D'APRIL see Tosti,
  Francesco Paolo

NELLA NOTTURNA SELVA see Wolf-Ferrari,
  Ermanno

NELLA SERA see Bettinelli, Bruno

NELL'ORTO see Veneziani, Vittore, Dans
  Le Potager

NELSON
  Consolation *sac
    solo,pno LILLENAS SM-626: RN $1.00
                                     (N94)
  Contentment *sac
    solo,pno LILLENAS SM-637: RN $1.00
                                     (N95)
  He Met Me There *sac
    solo,pno LILLENAS SM-473: RN $1.00
                                     (N96)
  It All Depends *sac
    solo,pno LILLENAS SM-471: RN $1.00
                                     (N97)
  Unchained *sac
    solo,pno LILLENAS SM-628: RN $1.00
                                     (N98)

NELSON, H.
  Lovely Armoy
    solo,pno (F min) BOOSEY $1.50 (N99)

  Town Tree
    solo,pno (F maj) BOOSEY $1.50
                                     (N100)

NELSON, HAVELOCK
  Lonely Of Heart, The
    3 soli,pno ROBERTON 72658 s.p.
                                     (N101)

NELSON, S.
  Mary Of Argyle
    solo,pno (A maj) BOOSEY $1.50
                                     (N102)
  Pilot
    solo,pno CRAMER   (N103)

NEMETH-SAMORINSKY, STEFAN (1896-   )
  Zahoracke Pesnicky *CCU
    solo,pno SLOV.HUD.FOND s.p.   (N104)

NEMICO DELLA PATRIA see Giordano,
  Umberto

NENIA see Recli, Giulia

NENIA see Veneziani, Vittore

NENIA EROICA see Vignati, Milos

NENNI-DA see Migot, Georges

NEOPOLITAN SONGS *CCU
  [It/Eng] solo,pno,opt vln,acord,gtr,
    ukelele and banjo MUSIC 0200023
    $4.95   (N105)

NEPISES see Urbanec, Bartolomej

NERA NERELLA see Gubitosi, Emilia

NESSLER, ROBERT (1919-   )
  Sonnengesang Des Heiligen Franziskus
    S solo,2fl,2ob,2clar,2bsn,4horn,
    2trp,2trom,tuba,pno,perc,strings
    MODERN rental   (N106)

NESSUN DORMA see Puccini, Giacomo

NESSUNO see Caggiano, Roberto

N'EST-CE-PAS? see Chaminade, Cecile

NET OF FIREFLIES, A see Persichetti,
  Vincent

NEU see Mompou, Federico

NEUE GALGENLIEDER VON CHRISTIAN
  MORGENSTERN see Graener, Paul

NEUE GEISTLICHE LIEDER see Beers,
  Jacques

NEUE GLEICHNISSE see Steffens, Walter

NEUE KINDERLIEDER see Handel, George
  Frideric

NEUE LIEBE see Wolf, Hugo

NEUE LIEBE, NEUES LEBEN see Beethoven,
  Ludwig van

NEUE LIEBESLIEDER-WALZER see Brahms,
  Johannes

NEUE LIEDER see Marx, Karl

NEUE SAMMLUNG RUSSISCHER VOLKSLIEDER
  *CCU,folk,Russ
  (Ignatieff, Michail; Ignatieff,
    Nadia) solo,pno SIKORSKI 746 s.p.
                                     (N107)

NEUE WEIHNACHTSLIEDER *CC34U,Xmas
  solo,pno (easy) voc sc BAREN. 1371
    $4.25, solo pt BAREN. 1345 $2.75
                                     (N108)

NEUENDORF, E.
  Rattenfangerlied
    solo,pno SCHAUR EE 3552 s.p. (N109)

NEUER FRUHLING see Adriessen, Willem

NEUES FEDERSPIEL see Braunfels, Walter

NEUES VOLKSLIEDERHEFT see Beethoven,
  Ludwig van

NEUF MELODIES see Orthel, Leon

NEUF TANKAS see Komatsu, Kiyoshi

NEUGRIECHISCHE MADCHENLIED see Marx,
  Joseph

NEUMANN, RICHARD J.
  Hob Ich Mir A Mantl
    med solo,pno (Yiddish text)
    TRANSCON. WJ 409 $.75   (N110)

NEUMEYER, FRITZ (1900-   )
  Dreiunddreissig Volkslieder *CC33U,
    folk
    med solo,pno (med easy) BAREN. 1900
    $7.00   (N111)

NEUN ALTE WEIHNACHTSGESANGE *CC9U,Xmas
  (Johner) solo,pno HUG s.p.   (N112)

NEUN DEUTSCHE ARIEN see Handel, George
  Frideric

NEUN GEDICHTE AUS "SANGE EINES
  FAHRENDEN SPIELMANNS" see Frommel,
  Gerhard

NEUN LIEDER see Burkhard, Willy

NEUN LIEDER see Reutter, Hermann

NEUN LIEDER see Lissmann, Kurt

NEUN LIEDER (AUS OP. 9, 15, 19) see
  Krenek, Ernst

NEUN LIEDER NACH GEDICHTEN VON R. HUCH
  see Reutter, Hermann

9 X 11 NEUE KINDERLIEDER ZUR BIBEL
  *sac,CC99U,Bibl
  (Watkinson, G.) solo,org CHRIS 50570
    s.p.   (N113)

NEUNUNDSECHZIG GESANGE ZU SCHEMELLIS
  MUSICALISCHEM GESANGBUCH 1736: BWV
  439-507 see Bach, Johann Sebastian

NEUNUNDZWANZIG LIEDER see Flury,
  Richard

NEVEL see Mulder, Herman

NEVER A MAN LIKE HIM see Baker, Richard

NEVER DID I BEHOLD SO FAIR A MAIDEN see
  Puccini, Giacomo, Donna Non Vidi
  Mai

NEVER MIND THE WHY AND WHERE-FORE see
  Sullivan, Sir Arthur Seymour

NEVER THE SAME AGAIN see Baker, Richard

NEVER WEATHER-BEATEN SAIL see Bunge,
  Sas

NEVER WEATHER-BEATEN SAIL see Davies,
  Henry Walford

NEVICATA see Respighi, Ottorino

NEVIN, ETHELBERT WOODBRIDGE (1862-1901)
  Holy Hour, The *sac
    low solo,pno (B flat maj) BOSTON
      $1.50   (N114)
    high solo,pno (E flat maj) BOSTON
      $1.50   (N115)

  Into The Woods My Master Went *sac
    high solo,pno (G maj) ALLANS
                                   (N116)
    low solo,pno (E flat maj) ALLANS
      s.p.   (N117)

  Little Boy Blue
    solo,pno ALLANS s.p.   (N118)
    med-high solo,pno (A flat maj)
      BOSTON $1.50   (N119)
    high solo,pno (B flat maj) BOSTON
      $1.50   (N120)

  Mighty Lak' A Rose
    high solo,pno (A maj) BOSTON $1.50
                                   (N121)
    med solo,pno PRESSER $.75   (N122)
    low solo,pno (E flat maj) BOSTON
      $1.50   (N123)
    med-low solo,pno (F maj) BOSTON
      $1.50   (N124)
    med-high solo,pno (G maj) BOSTON
      $1.50   (N125)
    med-low solo,pno PRESSER $.75
                                   (N126)

  Oh That We Two Were Maying
    low solo,pno (E flat maj) ASHDOWN
                                   (N127)
    med solo,pno (F maj) ASHDOWN (N128)
    med-high solo,pno (G maj) ASHDOWN
                                   (N129)
    high solo,pno (A flat maj) ASHDOWN
                                   (N130)

  Rosary, The *sac
    ST soli,pno BOSTON $1.75   (N131)
    high solo,pno (F maj) BOSTON $1.50
                                   (N132)
    med-high solo,pno (E flat maj)
      BOSTON $1.50   (N133)
    med-high solo,pno (D flat maj)
      BOSTON $1.50   (N134)
    med-low solo,pno (C maj) BOSTON
      $1.50   (N135)
    med-low solo,pno (B maj) BOSTON
      $1.50   (N136)
    low solo,pno (B flat maj) BOSTON
      $1.50   (N137)
    solo,pno (available in 4 keys)
      ASHLEY $.95   (N138)
    solo,pno,vln,gtr,acord,sax (D maj)
      ALLANS s.p.   (N139)
    low solo,pno (E flat maj) ALLANS
      s.p.   (N140)
    med-low solo,pno (D flat maj)
      ALLANS s.p.   (N141)
    med solo,pno (C maj) ALLANS s.p.
                                   (N142)
    med solo,pno (B maj) ALLANS s.p.
                                   (N143)
    med-high solo,pno (B flat maj)
      ALLANS s.p.   (N144)
    high solo,pno (F maj) ALLANS s.p.
                                   (N145)
    2 low soli,pno (C maj) ALLANS s.p.
                                   (N146)
    2 high soli,pno (E flat maj) ALLANS
      s.p.   (N147)

NEW ANTHOLOGY OF AMERICAN SONG, A
  *CC25L,US
  SCHIRM.G high solo,pno $4.00; low
    solo,pno $4.00 contains works by:
    Barder; Carpenter; Deis; Hadley and
    others   (N148)

NEW BORN see Dello Joio, Norman

NEW BORN KING, THE see L'Espoir

NEW CHRISTMAS MORNING, HALLELUJAH see
  MacGimsey, Robert

NEW DAY see Bush

NEW ENGLAND PASTORAL see Dougherty,
  Celius

NEW ENGLISH BROADSIDES *CC75U,folk,Eng
  (Joseph, Nathan; Winter, Eric) solo,
    pno OAK 000085 $3.95   (N149)

NEW GHOST, THE see Vaughan Williams, Ralph

NEW GOSPEL SONGS *sac,CCUL,gospel
  solo,pno STAMPS 4815-SN $1.00 (N150)

NEW HAMPSHIRE see Thomas, A.

NEW IMPERIAL EDITION OF SONGS, VOL. 1
  *CCU
  (Northcote) S solo,pno BOOSEY $7.50
                                      (N151)

NEW IMPERIAL EDITION OF SONGS, VOL. 2
  *CCU
  (Northcote) Mez solo,pno BOOSEY $7.50
                                      (N152)

NEW IMPERIAL EDITION OF SONGS, VOL. 3
  *CCU
  (Northcote) A solo,pno BOOSEY $7.50
                                      (N153)

NEW IMPERIAL EDITION OF SONGS, VOL. 4
  *CCU
  (Northcote) T solo,pno BOOSEY $7.50
                                      (N154)

NEW IMPERIAL EDITION OF SONGS, VOL. 5
  *CCU
  (Northcote) Bar solo,pno BOOSEY $7.50
                                      (N155)

NEW IMPERIAL EDITION OF SONGS, VOL. 6
  *CCU
  (Northcote) B solo,pno BOOSEY $7.50
                                      (N156)

NEW KIND OF HAPPINESS see Van Dyke, Vonda

NEW LIFE, A see Kirk

NEW LOST CITY RAMBLERS SONG BOOK, THE
  *CC125U,folk
  (Cohen, John; Seeger, Mike; Wood,
  Hally) solo,pno OAK 000046 $4.95
                                      (N157)

NEW LOVE, NEW LIFE see Beethoven,
  Ludwig van, Neue Liebe, Neues Leben

NEW LOVE NEW LIFE see Taylor, H.
  Stanley

NEW MIND, A *sac
  (Carmichael, Ralph) solo,pno WORD
  S-98   (N158)

NEW NATIONAL SONG BOOK *CCU
  (Northcote; Wiseman) BOOSEY pap
  $6.00, cloth $8.00   (N159)

NEW POEMS FOR VOICE AND VIBRAPHONE see
  Steiner, Gitta

NEW SACRED SOLOS AND DUETS *sac,
  CC150UL
  (Lillenas, Haldor) 1-2 soli,pno
  LILLENAS MB-140 $1.50   (N160)

NEW SONGS FOR ALL GOD'S CHILDREN *sac,
  CC100UL
  solo,pno,gtr LILLENAS MB-372 $5.95
                                      (N161)

NEW SONGS FROM NORMAN CLAYTON see
  Clayton, Norman

NEW SONGS OF OLD MOTHER GOOSE see Koch,
  Johannes H.E.

NEW SONGS ON FOUR ROMANTIC POEMS see
  Raphling, Sam

NEW TESTAMENT SONGS *sac,CCU,Bibl
  solo,pno HOPE 501 $2.50 contains
  works by: Rogers; McAfee; Burroughs
                                      (N162)

NEW TUNES TO NEW RHYMES see Rowley,
  Alec

NEW TWENTY-THIRD, THE (Psalm 23) sac
  (Carmichael, Ralph) solo,pno WORD
  S-207   (N163)

NEW VISTAS IN SONG *CCU
  high solo,pno MARKS $3.00   (N164)

NEW WAY OF LIFE, A see Hubbard, H.

NEW WINE *sac
  (Carmichael, Ralph) solo,pno WORD
  S-501   (N165)

NEW WORLD, A see Huff, Ronn

NEW WORLD, A see Boyer, Dave

NEW YORK TIMES: AUGUST 30, 1964, THE
  see Farberman, Harold

NEWLIN, DIKA (1923-   )
  Der Du Von Dem Himmel Bist
    med solo,pno AM.COMP.AL. $.55
                                      (N166)

  Haus In Bonn
    med solo,pno AM.COMP.AL. $.55
                                      (N167)

  I Saw In Louisiana A Live Oak Growing
    med solo,pno AM.COMP.AL. $2.75
                                      (N168)

NEWLIN, DIKA (cont'd.)
  Lied
    med solo,pno AM.COMP.AL. $.27
                                      (N169)

  Mein Weg Geht Jetzt Woruber
    med solo,pno AM.COMP.AL. $1.10
                                      (N170)

  Psalm 100 *sac
    med solo,pno AM.COMP.AL. $1.10
                                      (N171)

  Psalm 150 *sac
    med solo,pno AM.COMP.AL. $1.10
                                      (N172)

  Quidditie, The
    (Herbert, G.; Summers, Joseph) med
    solo,pno AM.COMP.AL. $1.10 (N173)

  To Mrs. Anna Flaxman
    med solo,pno AM.COMP.AL. $.55
                                      (N174)

NEWMAN, ANTHONY
  Barricades
    med solo,gtr/kbd SCHIRM.G $1.50 (N175)

NEWMAN, ROY
  Sicilian Lullaby
    med solo,pno (F maj) WILLIS $.60
                                      (N176)

NEWTON, ERNEST
  Bill And Jack
    2 soli,pno (G maj) LEONARD-ENG
                                      (N177)

  Down The Flowing Stream
    2 soli,pno CRAMER   (N178)

  Extra Special Constables
    solo,pno LEONARD-ENG   (N179)

  First Christmas Morn, The
    med solo,pno (C maj) LEONARD-ENG
                                      (N180)
    low solo,pno (B flat maj) LEONARD-
    ENG   (N181)
    high solo,pno (E flat maj) LEONARD-
    ENG   (N182)

  Girl And The Duck, The
    2 soli,pno LEONARD-ENG   (N183)

  God Who Madest Earth And Heaven
    low solo,pno (E flat maj) LEONARD-
    ENG   (N184)
    high solo,pno (G maj) LEONARD-ENG
                                      (N185)
    med solo,pno (F maj) LEONARD-ENG
                                      (N186)

  Going To Kildare
    solo,pno CRAMER   (N187)

  Irish Slumber Song
    high solo,pno (F maj) LEONARD-ENG
                                      (N188)
    low solo,pno (E flat maj) LEONARD-
    ENG   (N189)
    2 soli,pno LEONARD-ENG   (N190)

  Laugh, Little River
    2 soli,pno LEONARD-ENG   (N191)

  Morva
    low solo,pno (C maj) LEONARD-ENG
                                      (N192)
    high solo,pno (E flat maj) LEONARD-
    ENG   (N193)
    med solo,pno (D maj) LEONARD-ENG
                                      (N194)

  Nita Gitana
    low solo,pno (G maj) LEONARD-ENG
                                      (N195)
    med solo,pno (A maj) LEONARD-ENG
                                      (N196)
    high solo,pno (C maj) LEONARD-ENG
                                      (N197)

  Piper Spring, The
    solo,pno (B flat maj) ASHDOWN
                                      (N198)

  Polly Has Her Eye On Me
    low solo,pno (F maj) CRAMER   (N199)
    high solo,pno (G maj) CRAMER   (N200)

  Scent Of The Clover
    low solo,pno (G maj) CRAMER   (N201)
    high solo,pno (A maj) CRAMER   (N202)

  Shoemaker Ned
    solo,pno CRAMER   (N203)

  Six Popular Vocal Duets, Book I
    *CC6U
    SA soli,pno LEONARD-ENG   (N204)

  Vale Of Llanherne
    low solo,pno (C maj) CRAMER   (N205)
    med solo,pno (D maj) CRAMER   (N206)
    high solo,pno (E flat maj) CRAMER
                                      (N207)

  Violet Girl
    high solo,pno (C maj) CRAMER   (N208)
    low solo,pno (B flat maj) CRAMER
                                      (N209)

  Way A Man Should Go
    high solo,pno (C maj) CRAMER   (N210)
    low solo,pno (B flat maj) CRAMER
                                      (N211)

NEWTON, ERNEST (cont'd.)
  When Love Was Young
    2 soli,pno CRAMER   (N212)

  Where The Chestnuts Bloom
    high solo,pno (A maj) LEONARD-ENG
                                      (N213)
    low solo,pno (F maj) LEONARD-ENG
                                      (N214)
    med solo,pno (G maj) LEONARD-ENG
                                      (N215)
    2 soli,pno LEONARD-ENG   (N216)

NEWTON, JOHN
  Amazing Grace, How Can It Be?
    (Fox, B.) solo,pno FOX $1.00   (N217)

  Amazing Grace - Unbounded Grace
    (composed with Wyrtzen, Don)
    *sac
    solo,pno SINGSPIR 7093 $1.00 (N218)

NEXT STEP, THE see Campbell

NEXT, WINTER COMES SLOWLY see Purcell,
  Henry

NICE LA BELLE see Chaminade, Cecile

NICHEVO see Mana-Zucca, Mme.

NICHOCHEY CHATZIR 1974 *CCU
  solo,pno OR-TAV $1.00 Kibbutz songs
                                      (N219)

NICHOCHEY CHATZIR 1975 *CCU
  solo,pno OR-TAV $1.50 Kibbutz songs
                                      (N220)

NICHOL, H. ERNEST
  I Dunno
    solo,pno (D flat maj) BOOSEY $1.50
                                      (N221)

NICHOLS, TED
  Link Of Love, The *sac
    solo,pno SINGSPIR 7109 $1.00 (N222)

NICHT EIN WOLKCHEN AM HORIZONT see
  Valek, Jiri, Ani Mracku Na Obzoru

NICHT MEHR ZU DIR GEHEN see Beethoven,
  Ludwig van

NICHT MIT ENGELN see Bijvanck, Henk

NICHT RAST, NICHT RUHE see Borodin,
  Alexander Porfirievitch

NICHT UNS, NUR DIR ALLEIN see Telemann,
  Georg Philipp

NICHT WIEDERSEHEN! see Mahler, Gustav

NICK, EDMUND
  Uber Der Oder
    solo,pno SIKORSKI 146 s.p.   (N223)

NICK SPENCE see Peel, Graham

NICKERSON, CAMILLE
  Mister Banjo
    solo,pno ALLANS s.p.   (N224)

NICKLASS-KEMPNER, S.
  Czardas
    solo,pno SCHAUR EE 3553 s.p. (N225)

NICODE, JEAN LOUIS (1853-1919)
  Erbarmen *Op.33, hymn
    solo,pno BREITKOPF-W s.p.   (N226)

NICOLAI
  Visa Ur Muntra Fruarna
    solo,pno LUNDQUIST s.p.   (N227)

NICOLAI, OTTO (1810-1849)
  Als Bublein Klein (from Die Lustigen
    Weiber Von Windsor)
    B solo,2fl,2ob,2clar,2bsn,4horn,
    2trp,3trom,timp,perc,strings
    BREITKOPF-L rental   (N228)

  Drinking Song (from Die Lustigen
    Weiber Von Windsor)
    low solo,pno (E maj) ALLANS s.p.
                                      (N229)

  Nun Eilt Herbei (from Die Lustigen
    Weiber Von Windsor)
    S solo,2fl,2ob,2clar,2bsn,2horn,
    2trp,timp,strings BREITKOPF-L
    rental   (N230)

  Salve Regina *sac
    S solo,org,vln sc BOHM s.p.   (N231)

NICOLETTE see Hively, Wells

NICOLETTE see Ravel, Maurice

NIDS D'OISEAUX see Tremisot, Ed.

NIDS ET BERCEAUX see Wangermez, Ed.

NIE SOLL DES SCHIFFES STEUERMANN DEM
  STILLEN MEER VERTRAUEN see Handel,
  George Frideric

NIE WARD ICH see Schoenberg, Arnold

NIEDERDEUTSCHE LIEDER UND TANZE see
Maasz, Gerhard

NIEDERMEYER, LOUIS (1802-1861)
Pater Noster *sac
solo,pno/org HEUGEL s.p. see from
CHANTS RELIGIEUX   (N232)

NIEL, MATTY (1918-   )
Drie Liederen
low solo,pno DONEMUS s.p.
contains: Mich Ruft Zuweilen Eine
Stille; O Nacht; Wenn Nachts
Die Brunnen Rauschen   (N233)

Mich Ruft Zuweilen Eine Stille
see Drie Liederen

O Nacht
see Drie Liederen

Wenn Nachts Die Brunnen Rauschen
see Drie Liederen

NIELAND, H.
Cradle Song
solo,pno BROEKMANS 220 s.p. (N234)

De Poedelman
solo,acap BROEKMANS 760 s.p. (N235)

De Wim-Wam Reus
solo,pno BROEKMANS 744A s.p. (N236)

De Zon Schijnt In Mijn Ziel
solo,pno BROEKMANS 796 s.p. (N237)

Drie Werkjes
2 soli,pno ALSBACH s.p.
contains: Het Looze
Moolenarinnetje; Sneewklokjes;
Zondagmorgen   (N238)

Gij Bad Op Enen Berg
solo,pno BROEKMANS 192 s.p. (N239)

Het Looze Moolenarinnetje
see Drie Werkjes

Het Onze Vader
S solo,org ALSBACH s.p.   (N240)

Schlaf Wohl Du Himmelsknaben
solo,pno BROEKMANS 194 s.p. (N241)

Sneewklokjes
see Drie Werkjes

Timmeren *CCU
solo,pno BROEKMANS 346 s.p. (N242)

Zondagmorgen
see Drie Werkjes

NIELAND, JAN
Die Winter Is Verganghen
see Twee Liederen Op Oud-
Nederlandsche Teksten

Jesu Allerliefst Kind
see Twee Liederen

Twee Liederen
solo,pno ALSBACH s.p.
contains: Jesu Allerliefst Kind;
Wiegeliedje   (N243)

Twee Liederen Op Oud-Nederlandsche
Teksten
solo,pno ALSBACH s.p.
contains: Die Winter Is
Verganghen; Waar Staat Jouw
Vaders Huis En Hof   (N244)

Waar Staat Jouw Vaders Huis En Hof
see Twee Liederen Op Oud-
Nederlandsche Teksten

Wiegeliedje
see Twee Liederen

NIELSEN, CARL (1865-1931)
Aebleblomst *Op.10,No.1
"Apfelbluthen" see Six Songs

Aladdin
[Dan] med solo,kbd HANSEN-DEN s.p.
contains: Alt Maanen Oprejst
Star, Op.34,No.3; Cithar, Lad
Min Bon Dig Nore, Op.34,No.1;
Visselulle Nu, Barnlil!, Op.34,
No.2   (N245)

Album Of Nine Songs *CC9L
[Dan/Eng] med solo,kbd HANSEN-DEN
s.p.   (N246)

Alt Maanen Oprejst Star *Op.34,No.3
see Aladdin

An Erinnerungsee's Strand *see
Erindringens So

NIELSEN, CARL (cont'd.)

Apfelbluthen *see Aebleblomst

Ariel's Song
[Dan] med solo,kbd HANSEN-DEN s.p.
(N247)

Balladen Om Bjornen *Op.47
[Dan] med-high solo,kbd HANSEN-DEN
s.p.   (N248)

Cithar, Lad Min Bon Dig Nore *Op.34,
No.1
see Aladdin

Danservise (from Herr Oluf Han Rider)
[Dan] med solo,kbd HANSEN-DEN s.p.
(N249)

De Unges Sang
[Dan] med solo,kbd HANSEN-DEN s.p.
(N250)

Den Forste Laerke *Op.21,No.5
"Die Erste Lerche" see Strophic
Songs, Vol. 2

Der Adler *see Hogen

Der Alte Steinklopfer *see Jens
Vejmand

Det Bodes Der For *Op.6,No.4
see Five Songs

Die Erste Lerche *see Den Forste
Laerke

En Snes Danske Viser, Vol. 2 *CC22U,
folk,Dan
(Nielsen, C.; Laub, T.) [Dan] med
solo,kbd HANSEN-DEN s.p.   (N251)

Erindringens So *Op.10,No.2
"An Erinnerungsee's Strand" see Six
Songs

Fire Folkelige Melodier
[Dan] med solo,kbd HANSEN-DEN s.p.
contains: Hvad Synger Du Om; Laer
Mig, Nattens Stjaerne; Nu Skal
Det Abenbares; Sangen Har
Lysning   (N252)

Five Songs
[Dan] med solo,kbd HANSEN-DEN s.p.
contains: Har Dagen Sanket Al Sin
Sorg, Op.4,No.5; I Seraillets
Have, Op.4,No.2; Irmelin Rose,
Op.4,No.4; Solnedgang, Op.4,
No.1; Til Asali, Op.4,No.3   (N253)

Five Songs
[Dan] med solo,kbd HANSEN-DEN s.p.
contains: Det Bodes Der For,
Op.6,No.4; Genrebillede, Op.6,
No.1; Seraferne, Op.6,No.2;
Silkesko Over Gylden Laest!,
Op.6,No.3; Vise, Op.6,No.5   (N254)

Fredlys Din Jord, Du Danske Mand
[Dan] med solo,kbd HANSEN-DEN s.p.
(N255)

Gebet Obdach! *see Husvild

Genrebillede *Op.6,No.1
see Five Songs

Godnat *Op.21,No.7
"Gute Nacht" see Strophic Songs,
Vol. 2

Gramle Anders Rogsters Sang
see Two Songs From Ulvens-Son

Gruss *see Hilsen

Gry
[Dan] med solo,kbd HANSEN-DEN s.p.
(N256)

Gute Nacht *see Godnat

Har Dagen Sanket Al Sin Sorg *Op.4,
No.5
see Five Songs

Hellidens Sang (from Herr Oluf Han
Rider)
[Dan] med solo,kbd HANSEN-DEN s.p.
(N257)

Herr Olufs Sang (from Herr Oluf Han
Rider)
[Dan] med solo,kbd HANSEN-DEN s.p.
(N258)

Heut Abend *see I Aften

Hilsen *Op.10,No.6
"Gruss" see Six Songs

Hogen *Op.21,No.2
"Der Adler" see Strophic Songs,
Vol. 1

Husvild *Op.21,No.6
"Gebet Obdach!" see Strophic Songs,
Vol. 2

NIELSEN, CARL (cont'd.)

Hvad Synger Du Om
see Fire Folkelige Melodier

I Aften *Op.10,No.5
"Heut Abend" see Six Songs

I Seraillets Have *Op.4,No.2
see Five Songs

Irmelin Rose *Op.4,No.4
see Five Songs

Jens Vejmand *Op.21,No.3
"Der Alte Steinklopfer" see
Strophic Songs, Vol. 1
[Dan] med-low solo,kbd HANSEN-DEN
s.p.   (N259)

Julesang
[Dan] med solo,kbd HANSEN-DEN s.p.
(N260)

Kobmands-Vise
[Dan] med solo,kbd HANSEN-DEN s.p.
(N261)

Kommer I Snart, I Husmaend
see Two Songs From Ulvens-Son

Laer Mig, Nattens Stjaerne
see Fire Folkelige Melodier

Moderen *Op.41
"Mother, The" [Dan] MezMez soli,
orch HANSEN-DEN s.p.   (N262)

Mother, The *see Moderen

Nu Skal Det Abenbares
see Fire Folkelige Melodier

Paske-Liljen
[Dan] med solo,kbd HANSEN-DEN s.p.
(N263)

Saenk Kun Dit Hoved, Du Blomst
*Op.21,No.4
"Senke Dein Kopfchen" see Strophic
Songs, Vol. 2

Sang Bag Ploven *Op.10,No.4
"Sang Hinterm Pflug" see Six Songs

Sang Hinterm Pflug *see Sang Bag
Ploven

Sangen Har Lysning
see Fire Folkelige Melodier

Senke Dein Kopfchen *see Saenk Kun
Dit Hoved, Du Blomst

Seraferne *Op.6,No.2
see Five Songs

Silkesko Over Gylden Laest! *Op.6,
No.3
see Five Songs

Six Songs
[Dan/Ger] med solo,kbd HANSEN-DEN
s.p.
contains: Aebleblomst,
"Apfelbluthen", Op.10,No.1;
Erindringens So, "An
Erinnerungsee's Strand", Op.10,
No.2; Hilsen, "Gruss", Op.10,
No.6; I Aften, "Heut Abend",
Op.10,No.5; Sang Bag Ploven,
"Sang Hinterm Pflug", Op.10,
No.4; Sommersang, "Sommerlied",
Op.10,No.3   (N264)

Skal Blomsterne Da Visne? *Op.21,
No.1
"Soll Denn Die Blumen Welken?" see
Strophic Songs, Vol. 1

Soll Denn Die Blumen Welken? *see
Skal Blomsterne Da Visne?

Solnedgang *Op.4,No.1
see Five Songs

Sommerlied *see Sommersang

Sommersang *Op.10,No.3
"Sommerlied" see Six Songs

Strophic Songs, Vol. 1
[Dan/Ger] med solo,kbd HANSEN-DEN
s.p.
contains: Hogen, "Der Adler",
Op.21,No.2; Jens Vejmand, "Der
Alte Steinklopfer", Op.21,No.3;
Skal Blomsterne Da Visne?,
"Soll Denn Die Blumen Welken?",
Op.21,No.1   (N265)

Strophic Songs, Vol. 2
[Dan/Ger] med solo,kbd HANSEN-DEN
s.p.
contains: Den Forste Laerke, "Die
Erste Lerche", Op.21,No.5;
Godnat, "Gute Nacht", Op.21,
No.7; Husvild, "Gebet Obdach!",
Op.21,No.6; Saenk Kun Dit

NIELSEN, CARL (cont'd.)

    Hoved, Du Blomst, "Senke Dein
      Kopfchen", Op.21,No.4   (N266)

    Studie Efter Naturen
    [Dan] med solo,kbd HANSEN-DEN s.p.
                             (N267)

    Til Asali   *Op.4,No.3
    see Five Songs

    Two Songs From Ulvens-Son
    [Dan] med solo,kbd HANSEN-DEN s.p.
      contains: Gramle Anders Rogsters
      Sang; Kommer I Snart, I
      Husmaend   (N268)

    Vise   *Op.6,No.5
    see Five Songs

    Visselulle Nu, Barnlil! *Op.34,No.2
    see Aladdin

NIELSEN, RICCARDO (1908-   )
    Ancora Due Poesie Di Apollinaire
    [It] solo,pno cmplt ed BONGIOVANI
    2516 2516 s.p.
      contains: Io Non So Piu; Se N'e
      Andata Via   (N269)

    Due Poesie Di Apollinaire
    (Zoli, Udo) [It] solo,pno cmplt ed
    BONGIOVANI 2505 s.p.
      contains: L'addio; Ora Noi (N270)

    Ganymed
    [It] S solo,clar,vcl,pno BONGIOVANI
    2458 s.p.   (N271)

    Io Non So Piu
    see Ancora Due Poesie Di
      Apollinaire

    L'addio
    see Due Poesie Di Apollinaire

    Ora Noi
    see Due Poesie Di Apollinaire

    Se N'e Andata Via
    see Ancora Due Poesie Di
      Apollinaire

    Vier Goethe Lieder   *CC4U
    [It] solo,pno BONGIOVANI 2459 s.p.
                             (N272)

NIELSEN, SVEND (1937-   )
    Duetter 1964 *CCU
    [Dan/Ger] SA soli,fl,perc,vcl sc
    HANSEN-DEN s.p.   (N273)

NIELTJE IN HET AQUARIUM see Beekhuis,
    Hanna

NIEMANDSLAND see Rietz, Johannes

NIEUW KERSTLIED see Schouwman, Hans

NIEUWE LENTELIEDEREN see Tierie, J.F.

NIGG, SERGE (1924-   )
    Le Chant Du Depossede *CCU
    Bar&narrator,3fl,3ob,2clar,3bsn,
    4horn,3trp,3trom,tuba,perc,2timp,
    pno,cel,harp,strings JOBERT s.p.
    sc, voc sc   (N274)

NIGGELING, WILLI (1900-   )
    Ein Fruhlingslied
    see Vier Lieder

    Johanni
    see Vier Lieder

    Sommerglück
    see Vier Lieder

    Vier Lieder
    high solo,pno cmplt ed BREITKOPF-L
    EB 5720 s.p.
      contains: Ein Fruhlingslied;
      Johanni; Sommerglück;
      Vorfruhling   (N275)

    Vorfruhling
    see Vier Lieder

NIGGLI, FRIEDRICH
    Lieder-Album *CCU
    solo,pno HUG s.p.   (N276)

NIGHT see Broutman, E.

NIGHT see Rimsky-Korsakov, Nikolai, La
    Nuit

NIGHT see Thompson, A.

NIGHT AND THE CURTAINS DRAWN see
    Ferrata, Giuseppe

NIGHT BEFORE EASTER, THE see Friend

NIGHT BUT ABIDES FOR A SPAN see
    Mallinson, (James) Albert

NIGHT CROW see Rorem, Ned

NIGHT HAS A THOUSAND EYES see Hageman,
    Richard

NIGHT HAS A THOUSAND EYES, THE see
    Barry, Katherine

NIGHT HAS A THOUSAND EYES, THE see
    Paulsen, P. Marinus

NIGHT IN MAY see Brahms, Johannes, Die
    Mainacht

NIGHT IN SPRING see Schumann, Robert
    (Alexander), Fruhlingnacht

NIGHT IN VENICE see Lucantoni, Giovanni

NIGHT IS MOURNFUL see Rachmaninoff,
    Sergey Vassilievitch

NIGHT NURSERY see Arundale, Claude

NIGHT OF NIGHTS see Van De Water, B.

NIGHT OF STARS AND NIGHT OF LOVE see
    Offenbach, Jacques, Belle Nuit, O
    Nuit D'amour

NIGHT OF STARS, NIGHT OF LOVE see
    Offenbach, Jacques, Belle Nuit, O
    Nuit D'amour

NIGHT OF THE FOUR MOONS see Crumb,
    George

NIGHT OF THE FULL MOON, THE see Franco,
    Johan

NIGHT ON THE MOUNTAIN see Bantock,
    Granville

NIGHT PIECE see Dyson, George

NIGHT SONG see Swanson, Howard

NIGHT SONG see Williams, W.S.Gwynn

NIGHT VIOLETS see Schubert, Franz
    (Peter), Nachtviolen

NIGHT WILL NEVER STAY, THE see Weigl,
    Vally

NIGHTINGALE see Alabiev, Alexander
    Nicholaevich

NIGHTINGALE see Curry, W. Lawrence

NIGHTINGALE see Delius, Frederick

NIGHTINGALE see Grieg, Edvard Hagerup

NIGHTINGALE see Rorem, Ned

NIGHTINGALE see Shaw, C.

NIGHTINGALE, THE see Rinker, Alton

NIGHTINGALE AND THE ROSE see Glover,
    Stephen

NIGHTINGALE AND THE ROSE, THE see
    Thompson, Jack

NIGHTINGALES, THE see Los Bilbilcos

NIGHTINGALES OF LINCOLN'S INN see
    Oliver, Herbert

NIGHTMARE see Holm, Mogens Winkel

NIGHTMARE? AN EVIL DREAM?, A see Verdi,
    Giuseppe, E Sogno? O Realta?

NIGHTMUSIC see Josephs, Wilfred

NIGHTS, NIGHTS see Noches, Noches

NIGHT'S POETS see Sohal, Naresh

NIGHTS REMEMBER, THE see Beaudrie, M.

NIGUNIM - FOR THE WHOLE YEAR ROUND see
    Stutschevsky, Joachim

NIHON NO HANA see Hirai, Kozaburo

NIIN ON MEITA PIIKASIA see Kilpinen,
    Yrio

NIIN SINUA KATSOIN, NEITI see
    Merikanto, Oskar

NIINKUIN KUKKIVA MANTELIPUU see
    Fordell, Erik (Fritiof), Som Ett
    Blommande Mandeltrad

NILES
    Black Oak Tree
    high solo,pno FISCHER,C V 2046
                           (N277)
    med solo,pno FISCHER,C V 2094
                           (N278)

NILES (cont'd.)
    He's Goin' Away
    high solo,pno FISCHER,C V 2240
                           (N279)
    low solo,pno FISCHER,C V 2251
                           (N280)

    Silent Stars *Xmas
    med solo,pno (G maj) FISCHER,C
    V 2025   (N281)

NILES, JOHN JACOB (1892-   )
    Ballad Book Of John Jacob Niles, The
    *CC110U
    (Mandyczewski, E.) solo,pno,opt gtr
    pap 22716-2 $3.50   (N282)

    Black Dress, The
    med solo,pno (E maj) SCHIRM.G $.85
                           (N283)

    Black Is The Color Of My True Love's
    Hair
    high solo,pno (B flat maj) SCHIRM.G
    $1.00   (N284)
    low solo,pno (G flat maj) SCHIRM.G
    $1.00   (N285)
    med solo,pno (A flat maj) SCHIRM.G
    $1.00   (N286)

    Calm Is The Night
    med solo,pno (B maj) SCHIRM.G $.60
                           (N287)

    Carol Of The Birds, The *sac
    high solo,pno (F maj) SCHIRM.G $.75
                           (N288)
    low solo,pno (D maj) SCHIRM.G $.75
                           (N289)

    Come Gentle Dark
    solo,pno HINSHAW HMV 101 $1.00
                           (N290)

    Evening
    med solo,pno (C maj) SCHIRM.G $.85
                           (N291)

    Five Gambling Songs *see Gambler,
    Don't You Lose Your Place;
    Gambler's Lament, The; Gambler's
    Wife, The; Rovin' Gambler, The
                           (N292)

    Gambler, Don't You Lose Your Place
    med-high solo,pno (F maj) SCHIRM.G
    $.85 see from Five Gambling Songs
                           (N293)

    Gambler's Lament, The
    low solo,pno (E min) SCHIRM.G $.85
    see from Five Gambling Songs
                           (N294)

    Gambler's Wife, The
    high solo,pno (G flat maj) SCHIRM.G
    $.85 see from Five Gambling Songs
                           (N295)

    Go 'Way From My Window
    med-high solo,pno (E flat maj)
    SCHIRM.G $1.00   (N296)
    low solo,pno (C maj) SCHIRM.G $1.00
                           (N297)

    I Wonder As I Wander *sac,Xmas
    low solo,pno HARRIS $.85 (N298)
    solo,pno (C min) ALLANS s.p. (N299)
    low solo,pno (G min) SCHIRM.G $1.25
                           (N300)
    high solo,pno (C min) SCHIRM.G
    $1.25   (N301)
    high solo,pno HARRIS $.85 (N302)

    Jesus, Jesus, Rest Your Head *sac
    low solo,pno (D maj) SCHIRM.G $1.25
                           (N303)
    high solo,pno (G maj) SCHIRM.G
    $1.25   (N304)

    Lass From The Low-Countree, The
    med-low solo,pno (B min) SCHIRM.G
    $.85   (N305)

    Lotus Bloom, The
    high solo,pno (D min) SCHIRM.G $.60
                           (N306)

    Rovin' Gambler, The
    high solo,pno (G flat maj) SCHIRM.G
    $1.00 see from Five Gambling
    Songs   (N307)
    low solo,pno (E flat maj) SCHIRM.G
    $1.00 see from Five Gambling
    Songs   (N308)

    Softly Blew The East Wind *sac,Xmas
    med solo,kbd HINSHAW HMV102 $1.00
                           (N309)

    Symbol *Marriage,prayer
    med solo/low solo,kbd FOSTER MF 753
    $1.25   (N310)

    Wayfaring Stranger
    med solo,pno (E min) SCHIRM.G $1.00
                           (N311)

    What Songs Were Sung *sac,Xmas
    med solo,pno (D min) SCHIRM.G $.75
                           (N312)

NILSSON
    Sjungande Sjofolk Och Landkrabbor
    *CCU
    solo,pno,gtr LUNDQUIST s.p. (N313)

NILSSON, BO (1937-   )
Quartets *CCU
SATB soli, 8 instrumental quartets
using a wide variety of wind
instruments PETERS 66209 rental
(N314)

Stunde Eines Blocks
[Swed] S solo,6inst sc NORDISKA
s.p.   (N315)

NILSSON, TORSTEN (1920-   )
Communiomusik *sac,Commun
solo,org NORDISKA 6390 s.p.   (N316)

Consolamini, Consolamini, Popule Meus
*sac,concerto
high solo,org (diff) BAREN. 4460
$12.00   (N317)

NIMM DIR EIN SCHONES WEIB see Marx,
Joseph

N'IMPLOREZ PLUS see Bernier, Nicolas

NIN, JOAQUIN (1879-1949)
Le Chant Du Veilleur
[Fr/Dut] Mez solo,vln,pno cmplt ed
ESCHIG $2.50   (N318)

NIN-CULMELL, JOAQUIN (1908-   )
Cuarto Canciones Populares De
Andalucia *CC4U,Span
[Span] med solo,pno ESCHIG $4.50
(N319)
Cuarto Canciones Populares De
Catalana *CC4U,Span
[Span] med solo,pno ESCHIG $4.75
(N320)
Cuarto Populares De Salamanca *CC4U,
Span
[Span] med solo,pno ESCHIG $4.00
(N321)
Dos Poemas De Jorge Manrique *CC2U
[Span] S solo,4strings cmplt ed
ESCHIG $8.75   (N322)
Three Poems Of Gil Vicente *CC3U
[Span] med solo,pno ESCHIG $5.25
(N323)
Twelve Catalan Songs, First Series
*CC12U,Span
[Span] med solo,pno ESCHIG $5.00
(N324)
Twelve Popular Catalan Songs, Second
Series *CC12U,Span
[Span] med solo,pno ESCHIG $8.25
(N325)

NINA see Pergolesi, Giovanni Battista,
Tre Giorni Son Che Nina

NINA BOBO see Hullebroeck, Em.

NINA, EN MI CIELO see Grau, Eduardo

NINA NANA DE LA BONA MARE see Sadero,
G.

NINA SE'L ZIELO see Tocchi, Gian-Luca

NINANDO see Gnattali, Radames

NINE ART SONGS see Stutschevsky,
Joachim

NINE ENGLISH SONGS see Hindemith, Paul

NINE HUNDRED MILES: THE BALLADS, BLUES,
AND FOLKSONGS OF CISCO HOUSTON
*CC70U,folk
solo,pno OAK 000047 $2.95   (N326)

NINE SONGS see Bijvanck, Henk

NINE SONGS see Ives, Charles

NINE SONGS see Hahn, Reynaldo

NINE SONGS see Toch, Ernst

NINE SONGS see Ahuvia, Haim

NINE TRADITIONAL SONGS *CC9L,Eng/Fr/
Ger/Span
(Jessett, M.) med solo,gtr CHESTER
s.p. original texts   (N327)

NINETEEN DUETS see Mendelssohn-
Bartholdy, Felix

NINETEEN SONGS see Ives, Charles

1924 see Solodukho, J.

NINETTE see Durand, Jacques

NINETY AND NINE, THE see Campion,
Edward

NINETY SONGS see Schumann, Robert
(Alexander)

NINNA NANNA see Albanese, Guido

NINNA NANNA see Aprea, T.

NINNA-NANNA see Brahms, Johannes,
Wiegenlied

NINNA NANNA see Casagrande, A.

NINNA NANNA see Castelnuovo-Tedesco,
Mario

NINNA NANNA see De Ninno, Alfredo

NINNA NANNA see Gandino, Adolfo

NINNA-NANNA see Giuranna, Barbara

NINNA NANNA see Milano, R.

NINNA NANNA see Mozart, Wolfgang
Amadeus, Wiegenlied

NINNA-NANNA see Pilati, Mario

NINNA-NANNA see Pizzetti, Ildebrando

NINNA NANNA see Schubert, Franz
(Peter), Wiegenlied

NINNA NANNA A SERA see Toschi, Pietro

NINNA NANNA ABRUZZESE see Davico,
Vincenzo

NINNA NANNA AL BAMBINO GESU see
Liviabella, Lino

NINNA NANNA, CORBELLINA see Casella,
Alfredo

NINNA-NANNA COSACCA see Gubitosi,
Emilia

NINNA NANNA DI GESU BAMBINO see
Sinigaglia, Leone

NINNA-NANNA STRAPAESANA see Ferro, P.

NINNA-NINNA DI MEZZANOTTE see Alfano,
Franco

NINON see Tosti, Francesco Paolo

NINON OUVRE TA PORTE see Raynal, F.

NIO DANSKA SANGER, HAFTE 1-2 see
Svedbom, Vilhelm

NIO SANGER see Larsson, Lars-Erik

NIO SMA SANGER see Schonberg, Stig
Gustav

NIRVANA see Adams, Stephen

NIRVANA see Torjussen, Trygve

NISI DOMINUS see Vivaldi, Antonio

NISI DOMINUS AEDIFICAVERIT DOMUM see
Biber, Heinrich Ignaz Franz von

NISI DOMINUS AEDIFICAVERIT DOMUM see
Heinichen, Johann David

NITA see Kratz, Ray

NITA GITANA see Newton, Ernest

NIUN MI TEMA see Verdi, Giuseppe

NIVELET
Ma Bergere (Le Patre Des Montagnes)
solo,orch (A maj) LEDUC s.p. (N328)
solo,acap LEDUC s.p.   (N329)

NIVERNAIS *Fr
(Canteloube, J.) solo,acap DURAND
s.p. see also Anthologie Des Chants
Populaires Francais Tome III (N330)

NIVERS, GUILLAUME GABRIEL (1617-1714)
Drei Marienmotetten *sac,CC3U,mot
(Ewerhart, Rudolf) S/T solo,cont
BIELER CS 59 s.p.   (N331)

Lo, Behold, We Come To Adore Him
*sac
SA soli,cont oct CONCORDIA 98-1841
$.20   (N332)

Vier Motetten *sac,CC4U,mot
(Ewerhart, Rudolf) S/T solo,cont
BIELER CS 68 s.p.   (N333)

NJUT see Kotilainen, Otto, Nauti

NO see Shaw, Martin

NO ANDO PORQUE TE QUIERO see Gianneo,
Luis

NO ESCAPE see Dvorak, Antonin

NO EXIT see Damase, Jean-Michel

NO GOLDEN CARRIAGE, NO BRIGHT TOY see
Martin, Gilbert M.

NO GREATER LOVE *sac
(Carmichael, Ralph) solo,pno WORD
S-116   (N334)

NO GREATER LOVE see Gaither

NO GREATER LOVE see Westover

NO KOMA GUDS ENGLAR see Beck, Thomas
[Ludvigsen]

NO LULLABY NEED MARY SING see Clokey,
Joseph Waddell

NO MA JULEN SKUNDE SEG see Davik,
Ingebrigt

NO-MAN'S-LAND see Sharpe, Evelyn

NO MEASURE OF TIME see Ballard, Ann

NO MORE DAMS I'LL MAKE see Castelnuovo-
Tedesco, Mario

NO MORE DEATH see Peterson, John W.

NO MORE I WILL THY LOVE IMPORTUNE see
Weisgall, Hugo

NO MORE TROUBLE FOR ME see Lemont,
Cedric Wilmot

NO NA JULEN SKUNDE SEG see Davik,
Ingebrigt

NO NIGHT THERE
low solo,pno (A maj) BOOSEY $1.50
(N335)
high solo,pno (C maj) BOOSEY $1.50
(N336)

NO, NO, CHE NO SEI CAPACE see Mozart,
Wolfgang Amadeus

NO, NO, CHE NON SEI CAPACE see Mozart,
Wolfgang Amadeus

NO, NON E MORTO IL FIGLIO TUO see
Respighi, Ottorino

NO, NON TURBATI! see Beethoven, Ludwig
van

NO ONE BUT JESUS KNOWS *sac,gospel
solo,pno ABER.GRP. $1.50   (N337)

NO ONE KNOWS THIS ROAD LIKE JESUS see
Wyrtzen, Don

NO ONE TO WELCOME ME HOME see Lumpkin

NO ONE UNDERSTANDS LIKE JESUS see
Peterson, John W.

NO OTHER NAME see Kranendonk

NO OTHER SONG see Peterson, John W.

NO! PAGLIACCIO NON SON see Leoncavallo,
Ruggiero

NO PROPHET see Rachmaninoff, Sergey
Vassilievitch

NO QUIERO TUS AVELLANAS see Guridi,
Jesus

NO-RAI see Polin, Claire

NO SE EMENDERA JAMAS see Handel, George
Frideric

NO SHADE SO RARE see Handel, George
Frideric, Ombra Mai Fu

NO TE VAYAS AMOR see Lilien, Ignace

NO WAY IS HARD see Hovhaness, Alan

NOA-NOA see Tomasi, H.

NOAH'S ARK see McGeoch, Daisy

NOBLE DAME POUR VOUS PLAIRE see Saint-
Saens, Camille

NOBLE, FELIX DE (1907-   )
Huwelijkslied
solo,pno BROEKMANS 267 s.p.   (N338)

Irish Lullaby
[Eng] med solo/low solo,pno
BROEKMANS 347 s.p.   (N339)

Kerstliederen *CCU
solo,pno BROEKMANS 47 s.p.   (N340)

NOBLE, H.
Arran Homing Song
solo,pno (D maj) BOOSEY $1.50
(N341)
Maid Of Bunclody
solo,pno (E flat maj) BOOSEY $1.50
(N342)

NOBLE, THOMAS TERTIUS (1867-1953)
    Grieve Not The Holy Spirit *sac
        high solo,pno BELWIN $1.50   (N343)

NOBODY CARED see Hayford

NOBODY KNOWS see Hope, H. Ashworth

NOBODY KNOWS DE TROUBLE I SEE *spir
    (Johnson, J. Rosamond) solo,pno (E
        flat maj) ROBERTON 2730 s.p. (N344)
    (Roberton, Hugh S.) 3 soli,pno
        ROBERTON 72113 s.p.   (N345)

NOBODY KNOWS DE TROUBLE I'VE SEEN
    *spir
    (Burleigh, H. T.) high solo,pno
        BELWIN $1.50   (N346)
    (Burleigh, H. T.) low solo,pno BELWIN
        $1.50   (N347)

NOBODY KNOWS THE TROUBLE I'VE SEEN
    *spir
    (Furey) low solo,pno MARKS $1.50
                                      (N348)

NOBRE, MARLOS
    Beiramar
        solo,pno TONOS s.p.   (N349)

    Dia De Graca
        solo,gtr TONOS s.p.   (N350)

    Modinha
        solo,fl,gtr TONOS s.p.   (N351)

    O Canto Multiplicado
        solo,strings study sc TONOS 10208
        s.p.   (N352)

    Poemas De Negra *CCU
        solo,pno TONOS s.p.   (N353)

    Praianas
        solo,pno TONOS s.p.   (N354)

    Tres Cancoes *CC3U
        solo,pno TONOS s.p.   (N355)

    Tres Trovas *CC3U
        solo,pno TONOS s.p.   (N356)

NOC see Albrecht, Alexander

NOCES D'OR see Delmet, Paul

NOCH EIN TANTZ *Jew
    solo,pno KAMMEN 475 $1.00   (N357)

NOCH LAGERT DAMMERUNG see Bruch, Max

NOCH SINGT MEIN MUND see Roelli, H.

NOCHE DE ENSUENOS see Chopin, Frederic

NOCHE DE SAN JUAN see Azpiazu, Jose de

NOCHES, NOCHES
    (Neumann, Richard) "Nights, Nights"
        solo,pno/org (Ladino text)
        TRANSCON. WJ 406 $1.00   (N358)

NOCI see Drazan, Josef

NOCI see Schreiber, Josef

NOCNE PIESNE see Meier, Jaroslav

NOCTURN I see Koetsier, Jan

NOCTURN II see Koetsier, Jan

NOCTURNA ROSA see Chavez, Carlos

NOCTURNAL ROSE see Chavez, Carlos,
    Nocturna Rosa

NOCTURNE
    see Three Poems Of Walt Whitman

NOCTURNE see Aubert, Louis-Francois-
    Marie

NOCTURNE see Bantock, Granville

NOCTURNE see Barber, Samuel

NOCTURNE see Barbier, Rene

NOCTURNE see Beekhuis, Hanna

NOCTURNE see Bergman, Erik

NOCTURNE see Britten, Benjamin

NOCTURNE see Coquard, Arthur

NOCTURNE see Curran, Pearl Gildersleeve

NOCTURNE see Cuvillier, Charles

NOCTURNE see Daniel-Lesur

NOCTURNE see Durand, Jacques

NOCTURNE see Fischer, Irwin

NOCTURNE see Franck, Cesar

NOCTURNE see Franck, Cesar, O Fraiche
    Nuit

NOCTURNE see Holmes, Alfred

NOCTURNE see Keel, Frederick

NOCTURNE see Kilpinen, Yrio

NOCTURNE see Lacome, Paul

NOCTURNE see Lioncourt, Guy de

NOCTURNE see Moeran, Ernest J.

NOCTURNE see Nystroem, Gosta

NOCTURNE see Rabey, Rene

NOCTURNE see Rhene-Baton

NOCTURNE see Roos, Robert de

NOCTURNE see Saint-Saens, Camille

NOCTURNE see Taube, Evert

NOCTURNE see Verhaar, Ary

NOCTURNE see Witte, D.

NOCTURNE A DEUX VOIX see Fournier, P.

NOCTURNE FOR FOUR VOICES see Tate,
    Phyllis

NOCTURNE HAVANAIS see Lacome, Paul

NOCTURNE PYRENEEN see Chaminade, Cecile

NOCTURNEN see Andriessen, Louis

NOCTURNES see Cooke, S.C.

NOCTURNES see Rinaldini, Dr. Joseph

NOCTURNES see Borris, Siegfried

NOCTURNES FOR VOICE AND PIANO see
    Thorne, Francis

NOCTURNO see Grisolia, Pascual

NOCTURNO see Stout, Alan

NOCTURNO EN LOS MUELLES see Maiztegui,
    Isidro

NOCTURNOS see Tuxen-Bang, Carlos

NOD see Gibbs, Cecil Armstrong

NOD see Tobin, John

NOE, J.T.
    Everlasting Arms *sac
        low solo,pno (E flat maj) ALLANS
        s.p.   (N359)
        high solo,pno (G maj) ALLANS s.p.
                                      (N360)
    In An Eastern Alley
        low solo,pno (E flat maj) ALLANS
        s.p.   (N361)
        high solo,pno (G maj) ALLANS s.p.
                                      (N362)
    Thou Light Of Life
        low solo,pno (D maj) ALLANS s.p.
                                      (N363)
        high solo,pno (G maj) ALLANS s.p.
                                      (N364)

NOEL see Bachelet, Alfred

NOEL see Bondeville, Emmanuel de

NOEL see Emmanuel, Maurice

NOEL see Fevrier, Henri

NOEL see Georges, Alexandre

NOEL see Gounod, Charles Francois

NOEL see Hahn, Reynaldo

NOEL see Lacome, Paul

NOEL see Roff, Joseph

NOEL see Ronge, Jean-Baptiste

NOEL see Samuel-Rosseau, Marcel

NOEL see Schloss, M.

NOEL see Weber, Carl Maria von

NOEL see Weckerlin, Jean-Baptiste-
    Theodore

NOEL ALSACIEN see Tiersot, (Jean
    Baptiste Elisee) Julien

NOEL ANCIEN (NO. 1) see Respighi,
    Ottorino

NOEL ANCIEN (NO. 2) see Respighi,
    Ottorino

NOEL ARDENNAIS
    (Fragerolle, G.) solo,pno ENOCH s.p.
        see from Vieux Noels De France
                                      (N365)
    (Fragerolle, G.) solo,acap ENOCH s.p.
        see from Vieux Noels De France
                                      (N366)

NOEL, CHANTONS NOEL *CC151U,Xmas,Fr
    (Arma, Paul) solo,pno OUVRIERES s.p.
                                      (N367)

NOEL DE BATZ *CCU
    (Leleu, H.) med solo,opt inst HEUGEL
        406 s.p.   (N368)

NOEL DE CHALONS
    (Fragerolle, G.) solo,acap ENOCH s.p.
        see from Vieux Noels De France
                                      (N369)
    (Fragerolle, G.) solo,pno ENOCH s.p.
        see from Vieux Noels De France
                                      (N370)

NOEL DE FRANCE see Dupre, Marcel

NOEL DE STENAY
    (Fragerolle, G.) solo,acap ENOCH s.p.
        see from Vieux Noels De France
                                      (N371)
    (Fragerolle, G.) solo,pno ENOCH s.p.
        see from Vieux Noels De France
                                      (N372)

NOEL DE TROYES
    (Fragerolle, G.) solo,pno ENOCH s.p.
        see from Vieux Noels De France
                                      (N373)
    (Fragerolle, G.) solo,acap ENOCH s.p.
        see from Vieux Noels De France
                                      (N374)

NOEL! DEJA see Guiraud, Ernest

NOEL DES ENFANTS QUI N'ONT PLUS DE
    MAISONS see Debussy, Claude

NOEL DES ISLETTES
    (Fragerolle, G.) solo,pno ENOCH s.p.
        see from Vieux Noels De France
                                      (N375)
    (Fragerolle, G.) solo,acap ENOCH s.p.
        see from Vieux Noels De France
                                      (N376)

NOEL DES JOUETS see Ravel, Maurice

NOEL DES ROSES see Roger-Ducasse, Jean-
    Jules Aimable

NOEL DU BON PETIT BERGER see Schule, B.

NOEL DU DOYENNE
    (Fragerolle, G.) solo,pno ENOCH s.p.
        see from Vieux Noels De France
                                      (N377)
    (Fragerolle, G.) solo,acap ENOCH s.p.
        see from Vieux Noels De France
                                      (N378)

NOEL DU GUEUX see Privas, Xavier

NOEL DU PATRE see Versepuy, Marius

NOEL-NOEL *CC18U,Xmas
    (Kirby, Walter) solo,pno SCHIRM.G
        $1.25   (N379)

NOEL, NOEL, BELLS ARE RINGING see
    Chenoweth, Wilbur

NOEL PROVENCAL II see Tiersot, (Jean
    Baptiste Elisee) Julien

NOEL SUR LE LAC DE COME see Galos

NOELS see Motte La Croix, A.F.

NOELS D'ALSACE see Lippacher, Cl.

NOELS D'AUTREFOIS *CC4U,Xmas
    (Brueggen) [Fr] BROEKMANS B240 s.p.
                                      (N380)

NOELS DE FRANCE see Pijper, Willem

NOETEL, KONRAD FRIEDRICH (1903-1947)
    Sechs Lieder *CC6U
        med solo,pno (diff) BAREN. 1837
        $4.75   (N381)

NOG MINNS JAG HUR DET VAR, NAR SOM
    LILLA VANNEN FOR see Soderman,
    (Johan) August

NOG VET JAG EN MO see Wideen

NOHAR, Y.
    Sur Une Vieille Lettre D'amoure
        [Fr] med solo,pno ESCHIG $.85
                                      (N382)

NOIN SANOI MINUN EMONI see Kilpinen,
    Yrio

NOISE OF WATERS see Persichetti,
    Vincent

NOKKEN "JEG LAGDE MIT ORE TIL KILDENS BRED see Kjerulf, [Halfdan]

NOMAD, THE see Hamblen, Bernard

NON see Cuvillier, Charles

NON AL SUO AMANTE see Jacopo Da Bologna

NON CONOSCI IL BEL SUOL? see Thomas, Ambroise

NON E LA VITA see Giordano, Umberto

NON HAI UDITO I SUOI PASSI see Alfano, Franco

NON LA SOSPIRI LA NOSTRA CASETTA see Puccini, Giacomo

NON LOIN DU PAYS DE GASCOGNE see Offenbach, Jacques

NON M'AMATE PIU see Tosti, Francesco Paolo

NON MI DIR see Mozart, Wolfgang Amadeus

NON MI RESTA CHE IL PIANTO ED IL DOLORE see Mascagni, Pietro

NON NOBIS, DOMINE see Quilter, Roger

NON PARTIRE, AMOR MIO.. see Benvenuti, Giacomo

NON PIANGER see Mussorgsky, Modest

NON PIANGERE, LIU see Puccini, Giacomo

NON PIU see Cimara, Pietro

NON PIU ANDRAI see Mozart, Wolfgang Amadeus

NON PIU, TUTTO ASCOLTAI - NON TEMER, AMATO BENE see Mozart, Wolfgang Amadeus

NON PUI ANDRAI FARFALLONE AMOROSO see Mozart, Wolfgang Amadeus

NON SA CHE SIA DOLORE see Bach, Johann Sebastian

NON SO... see Alfano, Franco

NON SO PIU COSA SON see Mozart, Wolfgang Amadeus

NON SO PIU SOSA SON see Mozart, Wolfgang Amadeus

NON T'AMO PIU see Denza, Luigi

NON T'AMO PIU see Tosti, Francesco Paolo

NON TEMER, AMATO BENE see Mozart, Wolfgang Amadeus

NON, TU NE M'AIMES PAS, BRUNETTE see Durand, Jacques

NON VOS RELINQUAM ORPHANOS see Pinkham, Daniel

NON VUO PREGARE see Vecchi, H.

NONE BUT THE LONELY HEART see Tchaikovsky, Piotr Ilyitch, Nur, Wer Die Sehnsucht Kennt

NONE BUT THE LONGING HEART see Tchaikovsky, Piotr Ilyitch, Nur, Wer Die Sehnsucht Kennt

NONE HE LOVES BUT ME see Eckert, Karl Anton Florian, Er Liebt Nur Mich Allein

NONE SHALL SLEEP TONIGHT! see Puccini, Giacomo, Nessun Dorma!

NONE-SO-PRETTY see Brahe, May H.

NONE SO SWEET
  (Roberton, Hugh S.) solo,pno (A flat maj) ROBERTON 2754 s.p.   (N383)

NONNA RACCONTA see Rosa, M.

NONNA, SORRIDI? see Tosti, Francesco Paolo

NONNENKLAGE see Orthel, Leon

NONSENSE SYLLABLES see Mc Bride, Robert Guyn

NORBERG
  Til Mor
    solo,pno LUNDQUIST s.p.   (N384)

NORDEEN, LAJUANA
  Walkin' In This World (composed with Nordeen, Lynn) *sac,CC10L
    solo,pno/gtr WORD 20024 $1.95
          (N385)

NORDEEN, LYNN
  Walkin' In This World *see Nordeen, LaJuana

NORDEN *Op.90,No.1
  "Der Norden" [Swed/Ger] med-high
    solo,kbd HANSEN-DEN s.p. see from
    Six Songs   (N386)

NORDEN see Sibelius, Jean

NORDHOLM, H.
  Farval!
    solo,pno GEHRMANS s.p.   (N387)

NORDIO, C. (1891-   )
  Elegia Romantica
    solo,2fl,2ob,2clar,2bsn,4horn,3trp,
    3trom,timp,harp,pno CARISH s.p.
          (N388)

NORDKVIST, MARTIN
  Ett Fang Av Roda Rosor
    solo,pno,opt gtr GEHRMANS s.p.
          (N389)

  Vad Skiljer Oss At
    solo,pno,opt gtr GEHRMANS s.p.
          (N390)

NORDLANDS TROMPET see Johansen, David Monrad

NORDOFF, PAUL (1909-   )
  Can Life Be A Blessing
    high solo,pno BELWIN $2.00   (N391)

  Fair Annette's Song
    med solo,pno BELWIN $2.00   (N392)

  Lacrima Christi
    med solo,pno MERCURY $.95   (N393)

  Music I Heard With You
    med solo,pno BELWIN $1.50   (N394)

  Serenade
    med solo,pno BELWIN $1.50   (N395)

  Tell Me, Thyrsis
    high solo,pno BELWIN $2.00   (N396)

  There Shall Be More Joy
    med solo,pno BELWIN $1.50   (N397)

  This Is The Shape Of The Leaf
    med solo,pno BELWIN $1.50   (N398)

  Time, I Dare Thee To Discover
    high solo,pno BELWIN $1.50   (N399)

NORDQVIST, GUSTAF
  Ack Hjalp Mig, Du, Som Hjalpen Ar *sac
    solo,pno LUNDQUIST s.p. see from
    Tva Andliga Sanger   (N400)

  Akallan *sac
    solo,pno LUNDQUIST s.p. see from
    Tva Andliga Sanger   (N401)

  Av Rosor, Rosor Roda
    see Sanger Och Visor, Heft 2

  Bon
    solo,pno LUNDQUIST s.p.   (N402)

  Bon I Ofredstid
    solo,pno LUNDQUIST s.p.   (N403)

  Dagar Komma, Dagar Ser Jag Lykta
    solo,pno LUNDQUIST s.p. see from
    Himfys Karlekssanger   (N404)

  Dalbolat
    solo,pno LUNDQUIST s.p.   (N405)

  Den Gyllene Stunden
    solo,pno LUNDQUIST s.p.   (N406)

  Det Borde Varit Stjarnor
    see Tre Froding-Dikter

  Det Stiger, Det Stiger En Bolja
    see Fyra Dikter

  Det Var En Gang
    solo,pno LUNDQUIST s.p. see from
    Fem Visor   (N407)

  Drivsno
    solo,pno LUNDQUIST s.p.   (N408)

  En Gladje Jag Gick Att Mota
    see Fyra Dikter

  En Runa
    solo,pno LUNDQUIST s.p.   (N409)

  En Sommarmelodi
    solo,pno LUNDQUIST s.p.   (N410)

NORDQVIST, GUSTAF (cont'd.)

  En Vintervisa
    see Tre Froding-Dikter

  Fem Visor *see Det Var En Gang; Over Granarnas Kronor Star Himmelen Bla; Varfor; Varvisa; Vinden Blaser   (N411)

  Fosterlandshymn
    solo,pno LUNDQUIST s.p.   (N412)

  Fyra Dikter
    solo,pno LUNDQUIST s.p.
    contains: Det Stiger, Det Stiger En Bolja; En Gladje Jag Gick Att Mota; Junidagen Lekte; Vida, Vilande Midnatt   (N413)

  Fyra Sanger *see Jag Hor En Stamma Sa Kand Och Kar; Lillebarn; Sa Kom Du; Vid Dammen   (N414)

  Gammal Bonde
    solo,pno LUNDQUIST s.p.   (N415)

  Gammal Sorg
    solo,pno LUNDQUIST s.p.   (N416)

  Glans Over Sjo Och Strand *see Julsang

  Hav Tack
    see Sanger Och Visor, Heft 1
    solo,pno LUNDQUIST s.p.   (N417)

  Hennes Ljuva Rost Mig Rorde
    solo,pno LUNDQUIST s.p. see from
    Himfys Karlekssanger   (N418)

  Herre, Jag Takker Dig! *sac
    solo,pno LUNDQUIST s.p. see from
    Tre Andliga Sanger   (N419)

  Himfys Karlekssanger *see Dagar Komma, Dagar Ser Jag Lykta; Hennes Ljuva Rost Mig Rorde; Sasom Hjorten Nadd Av Pilen; Svalan Flyktar, Loven Falla
          (N420)

  Hjartat
    [Ger/Swed] solo,pno LUNDQUIST s.p.
    see from Hjartat Sjunger   (N421)

  Hjartat Sjunger *see Hjartat; Hjartats Sommar; Kvall I Skogen; Sjung Mitt Hjarta   (N422)

  Hjartats Sommar
    [Ger/Swed] solo,pno LUNDQUIST s.p.
    see from Hjartat Sjunger   (N423)

  I Aften
    solo,pno LUNDQUIST s.p. see from
    Tre Dikter Av L. Holstein   (N424)

  Ingalill
    see Tre Froding-Dikter

  Ingrid Sjunger I Klostret
    solo,pno LUNDQUIST s.p.   (N425)

  Innan Det Skymmer
    solo,pno LUNDQUIST s.p. see from
    Tva Visor I Folkton   (N426)

  Jag Hor En Stamma Sa Kand Och Kar
    solo,pno LUNDQUIST s.p. see from
    Fyra Sanger   (N427)

  Jag Horde Din Rost
    see Tre Bo Bergman-Dikter

  Jordens Onskan
    see Tre Bo Bergman-Dikter

  Jul, Jul, Stralande Jul
    solo,pno LUNDQUIST s.p.   (N428)

  Julsang *Xmas
    "Glans Over Sjo Och Strand" solo,
    pno LUNDQUIST s.p.   (N429)

  Junidagen Lekte
    see Fyra Dikter

  Kanske Finge Du Ro
    see Tva Religiosa Sanger

  Karleken Ar En Rosenlund
    see Tre Bo Bergman-Dikter

  Kommen Till En Fader Ater
    solo,pno LUNDQUIST s.p.   (N430)

  Kunde Jag Dikta En Visa
    see Sanger Och Visor, Heft 1

  Kvall I Skogen
    [Ger/Swed] solo,pno LUNDQUIST s.p.
    see from Hjartat Sjunger   (N431)

  Kyss Mej Paa Ojnene, Sol
    solo,pno LUNDQUIST s.p. see from
    Tre Dikter Av L. Holstein   (N432)

NORDQVIST, GUSTAF (cont'd.)

Lillebarn
solo,pno LUNDQUIST s.p. see from
Fyra Sanger   (N433)

Lindagulls Krona
solo,pno LUNDQUIST s.p.   (N434)

Lovsang *sac
solo,pno LUNDQUIST s.p. see from
Tre Andliga Sanger   (N435)

Lycka Ske Landet
low solo,pno LUNDQUIST s.p.   (N436)
high solo,pno LUNDQUIST s.p.   (N437)

Melodi
solo,pno LUNDQUIST s.p.   (N438)

Men Jag Horde En Sang
solo,pno GEHRMANS s.p.   (N439)

Mikael
solo,pno LUNDQUIST s.p.   (N440)

Moder Sverige
solo,pno LUNDQUIST s.p.   (N441)

Morgensang
solo,pno LUNDQUIST s.p. see from
Tre Dikter Av L. Holstein   (N442)

Norrland
solo,pno LUNDQUIST s.p.   (N443)

Ny Dag
solo,pno LUNDQUIST s.p.   (N444)

Nya Stjarnor
see Sanger Och Visor, Heft 2

Odesvisan
solo,pno LUNDQUIST s.p.   (N445)

Om Sommaren
solo,pno LUNDQUIST s.p. see from
Tva Visor I Folkton   (N446)

Om Varen
solo,pno LUNDQUIST s.p.   (N447)

Over Granarnas Kronor Star Himmelen
Bla
solo,pno LUNDQUIST s.p. see from
Fem Visor   (N448)

Paradisets Blomma
see Psalm Och Sang

Prinsessan
solo,pno LUNDQUIST s.p.   (N449)

Psalm 23
see Psalm Och Sang

Psalm Och Sang *sac
solo,pno LUNDQUIST s.p.
contains: Paradisets Blomma;
Psalm 23; Ro, Ro; Vi Vanta Val
Alla   (N450)

Ro, Ro
see Psalm Och Sang

Rodaste Guld
solo,pno LUNDQUIST s.p.   (N451)

Sa Kom Du
solo,pno LUNDQUIST s.p. see from
Fyra Sanger   (N452)

Sang Till Stockholm
solo,pno LUNDQUIST s.p.   (N453)

Sang Till Sverige
solo,pno LUNDQUIST s.p.   (N454)

Sangen Om Dalsland
solo,pno LUNDQUIST s.p.   (N455)

Sanger Och Visor, Heft 1
solo,pno LUNDQUIST s.p.
contains: Hav Tack; Kunde Jag
Dikta En Visa; Visa   (N456)

Sanger Och Visor, Heft 2
solo,pno LUNDQUIST s.p.
contains: Av Rosor, Rosor Roda;
Nya Stjarnor; Slattervisa   (N457)

Sasom Hjorten Nadd Av Pilen
solo,pno LUNDQUIST s.p. see from
Himfys Karlekssanger   (N458)

Serenad
solo,pno LUNDQUIST s.p.   (N459)

Sjomanssang
solo,pno LUNDQUIST s.p.   (N460)

Sjung Mitt Hjarta
[Ger/Swed] solo,pno LUNDQUIST s.p.
see from Hjartat Sjunger   (N461)

NORDQVIST, GUSTAF (cont'd.)

Slattervisa
see Sanger Och Visor, Heft 2

Sol Over Sverige
solo,pno LUNDQUIST s.p.   (N462)

Solblind Jag Andas
solo,pno LUNDQUIST s.p.   (N463)

Som Hjorten Pa Den Torra Hed
see Tva Religiosa Sanger

Sov
solo,pno GEHRMANS s.p.   (N464)

Spinnerskan
solo,pno LUNDQUIST s.p.   (N465)

Stlots Gullevi
solo,pno LUNDQUIST s.p.   (N466)

Svalan Flyktar, Loven Falla
solo,pno LUNDQUIST s.p. see from
Himfys Karlekssanger   (N467)

Tre Andliga Sanger *see Herre, Jag
Takker Dig!; Lovsang; Vart An Det
Bar   (N468)

Tre Bo Bergman-Dikter
solo,pno GEHRMANS s.p.
contains: Jag Horde Din Rost;
Jordens Onskan; Karleken Ar En
Rosenlund   (N469)

Tre Dikter Av L. Holstein *see I
Aften; Kyss Mej Paa Ojnene, Sol;
Morgensang   (N470)

Tre Froding-Dikter
solo,pno LUNDQUIST s.p.
contains: Det Borde Varit
Stjarnor; En Vintervisa;
Ingalill   (N471)

Tva Andliga Sanger *see Ack Hjalp
Mig, Du, Som Hjalpen Ar; Akallan   (N472)

Tva Hostdikter *CC2U
solo,pno LUNDQUIST s.p.   (N473)

Tva Religiosa Sanger *sac
solo,pno LUNDQUIST s.p.
contains: Kanske Finge Du Ro; Som
Hjorten Pa Den Torra Hed   (N474)

Tva Visor I Folkton *see Innan Det
Skymmer; Om Sommaren   (N475)

Varfor
solo,pno LUNDQUIST s.p. see from
Fem Visor   (N476)

Vart An Det Bar *sac
solo,pno LUNDQUIST s.p. see from
Tre Andliga Sanger   (N477)

Varvisa
solo,pno LUNDQUIST s.p. see from
Fem Visor   (N478)

Vi Aro Landet
solo,pno LUNDQUIST s.p.   (N479)

Vi Vanta Val Alla
see Psalm Och Sang

Vid Dammen
solo,pno LUNDQUIST s.p. see from
Fyra Sanger   (N480)

Vida, Vilande Midnatt
see Fyra Dikter

Vinden Blaser
solo,pno LUNDQUIST s.p. see from
Fem Visor   (N481)

Visa
see Sanger Och Visor, Heft 1

Visa I Folkton
solo,pno LUNDQUIST s.p.   (N482)

NORDSJO, EGIL
Utvalgte Norske Sange Og Romanser
*CCU
solo,pno NORSK 8762 s.p.   (N483)

NOREN
I Varlden Ar Jag Blott En Gast
*Psalm
solo,pno LUNDQUIST s.p.   (N484)

Konungars Konung (Psalm 118)
high solo,pno LUNDQUIST s.p.   (N485)
low solo,pno LUNDQUIST s.p.   (N486)
med solo,pno LUNDQUIST s.p.   (N487)

Psalm 118 *see Konungars Konung

**NORFOLK AVAIT DIT VRAI see Saint-Saens,
Camille**

**NORGE I RODT, HVITT OG BLATT see
Larsson, Lars-Erik**

NORHOLM, IB
Tavole Per Orfeo *Op.42
Mez solo,gtr HANSEN-DEN 29139 s.p.
(N488)

NORLANDER, EMIL
Kanner Ni Fia Jansson (from Forgyllda
Lergoken)
see Norlander, Emil, Kovan Kommer,
Kovan Gar

Kovan Kommer, Kovan Gar (from
Forgyllda Lergoken)
solo,pno GEHRMANS 573 s.p. contains
also: Kanner Ni Fia Jansson
(N489)

NORLEN, HAKAN
Min Sang
solo,pno LUNDQUIST s.p.   (N490)

Vandringssang
solo,pno LUNDQUIST s.p.   (N491)

NORMAN
Manstrlar *Op.49,No.2
solo,pno LUNDQUIST s.p.   (N492)

NORMAN, LARRY
I Wish We'd All Been Ready *sac
solo,pno WORD S-308   (N493)
solo,pno BENSON S6181-R $1.00
(N494)
Sweet, Sweet Song Of Salvation *sac
solo,pno BENSON S7635-R $1.00
(N495)

NORMAN, LORNA
He That Loves A Rosy Cheek
low solo,pno (D maj) ASHDOWN (N496)
high solo,pno (G maj) ASHDOWN
(N497)
Pan Among The Daffodils
low solo,pno (C maj) ASHDOWN (N498)
med solo,pno (D flat maj) ASHDOWN
(N499)
high solo,pno (E flat maj) ASHDOWN
(N500)
Song Of The Morning-O
low solo,pno (F maj) ASHDOWN (N501)
high solo,pno (A flat maj) ASHDOWN
(N502)
Thrush At Dawn, A
low solo,pno (C maj) ASHDOWN (N503)
med solo,pno (D maj) ASHDOWN (N504)
high solo,pno (E flat maj) ASHDOWN
(N505)
When My Lady Goes A-Shopping
low solo,pno (D maj) ASHDOWN (N506)
high solo,pno (F maj) ASHDOWN
(N507)

NORMAN, LUCILLE
I Wish We'd All Been Ready
med solo,pno GENTRY $1.00   (N508)

NORMAN, LUDVIG
Blomstring *Op.37,No.3
see Sanger Och Visor

Flickans Langtan *Op.37,No.1
see Sanger Och Visor

Karlek *Op.37,No.5
see Sanger Och Visor

Sanger Och Visor
solo,pno GEHRMANS s.p.
contains: Blomstring, Op.37,No.3;
Flickans Langtan, Op.37,No.1;
Karlek, Op.37,No.5; Sjalens
Frid, Op.37,No.2; Varsparven,
Op.37,No.4; Vi Ses Igen, Op.37,
No.6   (N509)

Signes Visa (from Humleplockningen)
solo,pno GEHRMANS s.p.   (N510)

Sjalens Frid *Op.37,No.2
see Sanger Och Visor

Varsparven *Op.37,No.4
see Sanger Och Visor

Vi Ses Igen *Op.37,No.6
see Sanger Och Visor

NORMAN, PIERRE
If I Forget To Pray
solo,pno PEER $.85   (N511)

NORMANDIE *Fr
(Canteloube, J.) solo,acap DURAND
s.p. see also Anthologie Des Chants
Populaires Francais Tome IV (N512)

NORRIS, HARRY
Hear My Prayer, O Lord *sac
solo,pno (C maj) LESLIE 7022 (N513)

There Is Sweet Music
solo,pno (D flat maj) LESLIE 7034
(N514)

NORRLAND see Hallen, Andreas

NORRLAND see Nordqvist, Gustaf

NORRLANNINGENS HEMLANGTAN see Brooman

NORRMAN, JOHN
  Guds Lov *sac
    solo,pno GEHRMANS s.p.   (N515)

  Hemmets Sanger *CC10U
    solo,pno GEHRMANS s.p.   (N516)

NORSKE FOLKETONER TIL NORSKE FOLKEVISER
  OG ARNULF OVERLANDS "OM KVELDEN"
  see Groven, Eivind

NORTH COUNTRY MAID see Maitland, John
  Alexander Fuller

NORTH, MICHAEL
  Evening
    solo,pno (E flat maj) BOOSEY $1.50
                       (N517)
  If You Are There
    solo,pno (F maj) BOOSEY $1.50
                       (N518)
  Sound Of Your Name
    solo,pno (D flat maj) BOOSEY $1.50
                       (N519)
  Such Lovely Things
    low solo,pno (F maj) BOOSEY $1.75
                       (N520)
    med solo,pno (A flat maj) BOOSEY
      $1.75   (N521)
    high solo,pno (B flat maj) BOOSEY
      $1.75   (N522)
    2 soli,pno (B flat maj) BOOSEY
      $1.75   (N523)

NORTON
  Cobblers' Song
    solo,pno ALLANS s.p.   (N524)

NORWAY SINGS *CC43U,folk,Norw
  [Norw] med solo,kbd NORSK s.p. (N525)

NORWEGIAN FOLKSONGS *CC19U,folk,Norw
  (Olsen) [Norw/Eng] med solo,pno NORSK
  $1.50   (N526)

NORWEGIAN SONG, A see Aspinall, George

NOS AMIS DE LA FERME ET DES CHAMPS VOL.
  I see Schlosser, Paul

NOS AMIS DE LA FERME ET DES CHAMPS VOL.
  II see Schlosser, Paul

NOS LANCES SONT DES AIGUILLES see
  Chabrier, Emmanuel

NOS PETITS MATELOTS see Ganne, Louis
  Gaston

NOSEGAY, THE see Dvorak, Antonin, Das
  Strausschen

NOSKE, W.
  Dix Romances Francaises *CC10U
    solo,pno BROEKMANS 65 s.p. (N527)

NOSTALGIA see Cimara, Pietro

NOSTALGIA see Jurafsky, Abraham

NOSTALGIA see Lora, Antonio

NOSTALGIA see Veneziani, Vittore

NOSTALGIA INDIGENA see Gomez Carrillo,
  Manuel

NOSTALGIES see Escher, Rudolf George

NOT AS THE SONG OF OTHER LANDS see
  Brumby, Colin

NOT MY WILL see Smith

NOT SO FAR AS THE FOREST see Naylor,
  Bernard

NOT SOMEDAY, BUT NOW see Cates, Bill

NOT WITH A SWORD *sac
  (Carmichael, Ralph) solo,pno WORD
  S-261   (N528)

NOTA VE QUESTA DEA see Frederick II of
  Prussia

NOTE DEL REDENTOR see Bianchini, Guido

NOTE LEFT ON A DOORSTEP see Dello Joio,
  Norman

NOTES PRISES A NEW YORK see Werner,
  Jean-Jacques

NOTHING AT ALL see Mourant, Walter

NOTHING BUT AMAZING see Kaiser, Kurt

NOTHING MATTERS see Mana-Zucca, Mme.,
  Nichevo

NOTRE AMOUR EST UN SECRET see Bozza,
  Eugene

NOTRE CHAUMIERE EN YVELINE see Caplet,
  Andre

NOTRE-DAME DE BONNE HUMEUR see Migot,
  Georges

NOTRE-DAME DE FRANCE see Gounod,
  Charles Francois

NOTRE GENEVE see Dalcroze, Jacques

NOTRE HEURE see Rhene-Baton

NOTRE MEUNIER see Dalayrac, [Nicolas]

NOTRE PAYS CHANTE *CCU
  [Russ] solo,pno cmplt ed CHANT s.p.
                       (N529)

NOTRE PERE see Faure, Jean-Baptiste

NOTRE PERE see Yung, Alfred

NOTTE see Cremesini, M.

NOTTE see Gandino, Adolfo

NOTTE see Respighi, Ottorino

NOTTE see Siciliani, Francesco

NOTTE see Vene, Ruggero

NOTTE, CHINATO IL VOLTO see Davico,
  Vincenzo

NOTTE D'AGOSTO see Cantu, M.

NOTTE D'AMORE see De Crescenzo

NOTTE D'ESTATE see Cimara, Pietro

NOTTE DI NEVE see Albanese, Guido

NOTTE DI NEVE see Persico, Mario

NOTTE DI NEVE see Zandonai, Riccardo

NOTTE DI VENTO see Scuderi, Gaspare

NOTTE, DIVINA NOTTE see Donati, Pino

NOTTE DOLOROSA see Persico, Mario

NOTTE 'E LUNA see Giazotto, Remo

NOTTE MARINA see Bossi, Renzo

NOTTURNI DI BEVOITORI BERGAMASCHI see
  Gavazzeni, Gianandrea

NOTTURNINO see Farina, Guido

NOTTURNINO see Venticinque, R.S.

NOTTURNO see Bendl, Karel

NOTTURNO see Cantu, M.

NOTTURNO see Donati

NOTTURNO see Gandino, Adolfo

NOTTURNO see Kilpinen, Yrio

NOTTURNO see Schoeck, Othmar

NOTTURNO see Steffen, Wolfgang

NOTTURNO see Strauss, Richard

NOTTURNO see Veneziani, Vittore

NOTTURNO D'AMORE see Drigo, Riccardo

NOTTURNO DELLA LUNA see Toni, Alceo

NOTTURNO SCORDATO see Jensch, Lothar

NOTTURNO UIT "SAPFO" see Schouwman,
  Hans

NOUGUES, JEAN (1875-1932)
  C'etait A L'aube Derniere (from Qou
    Vadis?)
    solo,pno ENOCH s.p.   (N530)

  Des Fleurs De Ce Jardin (from Qou
    Vadis?)
    female solo,vln ENOCH s.p. (N531)

  Errer A Travers Les Mers (from Qou
    Vadis?)
    solo,pno ENOCH s.p.   (N532)

  Rara-Hu
    solo,pno ENOCH s.p.   (N533)

  Viens Pres De Moi... Effeuillez Les
    Roses (from Qou Vadis?)
    2 soli,pno ENOCH s.p.   (N534)

NOUGUES, JEAN (cont'd.)

  Vois! Phoebe Elle-Meme (from Qou
    Vadis?)
    solo,pno ENOCH s.p.   (N535)

NOUNOU see Fragerolle, G.

NOUS ATTENDIONS DES HEROINES see
  Segond, Pierre

NOUS AVONS FRAPPE DES EPEES see
  Chabrier, Emmanuel

NOUS AVONS UN NOUVEAU GOUVERNEUR see
  Bach, Johann Sebastian, Mer Hahn En
  Neue Oberkeet

NOUS ELEVONS NOS FILS see Tremisot, Ed.

NOUS ENTRERONS DANS CE JOLI MOIS see
  Indy, Vincent d'

NOUS IRONS LUI PORTER DES FLEURS see
  Laparra, Raoul

NOUS NE CONNAISSIONS JUSQU'ICI see
  Cuvillier, Charles

NOUS NE VOUS CHANTONS PAS (ELUARD) see
  Auric, Georges

NOUS N'HABITERONS PAS AU BORD DE LA
  GRAND'ROUTE see Ropartz, Joseph Guy

NOUS NOUS AIMERONS see Levade, Charles
  (Gaston)

NOUS NOUS AIMIONS see Chaminade, Cecile

NOUS NOUS TAISIONS see Migot, Georges

NOUS RENCONTRERONS-NOUS? see Legley,
  Victor

NOUS REPRENDRONS NOTRE BELGIQUE see
  Lassailly, E.

NOUS SOMMES TOUS VENUS
  see La Musique, Quatrieme Cahier

NOUS SOMMESSEULS see Wagner, Richard

NOUS VOULONS UNE PETITE SOEUR see
  Poulenc, Francis

NOUSE, OLE KIRKAS see Leisring, Volkmar

NOUVE LIRICHE TAGORIANE see Alfano,
  Franco

NOUVEAU PRINTEMPS see Messager, Andre

NOUVEL EVANGILE see Delmet, Paul

NOUVELLES AVENTURES see Ligeti, Gyorgy

NOVA JAR see Freso, Tibor

NOVA PIESEN ZNIE see Francisci, Ondrej

NOVAK, JAN (1921-)
  Joci Vernales
    B solo,4perc,harp,pno, electric
    band MODERN rental   (N536)

  Passer Catulli *CCU
    B solo,fl,ob,clar,bsn,horn,vln,vla,
    vcl,bvl MODERN s.p.   (N537)

NOVAK, MILAN (1927-)
  Den Clivo Dohara
    S solo,pno SLOV.HUD.FOND s.p.
                       (N538)

  Do Kolecka, Dokola
    boy solo/girl solo,pno
    SLOV.HUD.FOND s.p.   (N539)

  Dumka O Nalepkovi
    solo,pno SLOV.HUD.FOND s.p. (N540)

  Hory A Srdce
    Bar solo,pno/orch SLOV.HUD.FOND
    s.p.   (N541)

  Hrame Sa Hrame
    boy solo/girl solo,pno
    SLOV.HUD.FOND s.p.   (N542)

  Keby Vsetky Deti
    boy solo/girl solo,pno
    SLOV.HUD.FOND s.p.   (N543)

  Vdaka, Ujo Partizan
    boy solo/girl solo,pno,perc
    SLOV.HUD.FOND s.p.   (N544)

NOVAK, V.
  Annchens Lieder *CCU
    [Czech/Ger] solo,pno SUPRAPHON s.p.
                       (N545)
  Balada O Dusi J. Nerudy
    B solo,pno SUPRAPHON s.p. (N546)

NOVAK, V. (cont'd.)

Ctyri Ukolebavky *CC4U
solo,pno SUPRAPHON s.p.   (N547)

In Memoriam
[Czech/Ger] solo,pno SUPRAPHON s.p.
                                 (N548)

Jihoceske *CCU
solo,pno SUPRAPHON s.p.   (N549)

Melancholische Lieder Uber Die Liebe
*CCU
[Czech/Ger] high solo,pno SUPRAPHON
s.p.   (N550)

Pisnicky Na Slova Lidove Poezie
Moravske, Rada I-V *CCU
solo,pno SUPRAPHON s.p. contains
respectively: Op.16, Op. 17, Op.
21, Op. 74, Op. 75   (N551)

Slowakische Gesange *CCU
[Czech] solo,pno SUPRAPHON s.p.
                                 (N552)

NOVAK, VITEZSLAV (1870-1949)
Gipsy Melodies *Op.14, CCU
solo,pno SCHAUR EE 3388 s.p. (N553)

NOVARA LA BELLA see Sinigaglia, Leone

NOVE CESKOSLOVENSKO see Kapr, Jan

NOVE SLOVENSKE PISNE see Martinu,
Bohuslav

NOVELLO, IVOR
Little Damozel
high solo,pno (G maj) BOOSEY $1.50
                                 (N554)
med solo,pno (F maj) BOOSEY $1.50
                                 (N555)
low solo,pno (E flat maj) BOOSEY
$1.50   (N556)

My Devotion
low solo,orch (D maj) ASHDOWN s.p.,
ipr   (N557)
high solo,orch (G maj) ASHDOWN
s.p., ipr   (N558)
med solo,orch (F maj) ASHDOWN s.p.,
ipr   (N559)

Page's Road Song, A
low solo,pno (D maj) ASHDOWN $1.50
                                 (N560)
med solo,pno (E maj) ASHDOWN $1.50
                                 (N561)
high solo,pno (F maj) ASHDOWN $1.50
                                 (N562)

NOVEMBER see Boedijn, Gerard H.

NOVEMBER see Freed, Isadore

NOVEMBER THRUSH see Cook, A.

NOVEMBERVISA see Runback, Albert

NOVEMBRE see Davico, Vincenzo

NOVEMBRE see Tremisot, Ed.

NOVIA Y HERMANA see Espoile, Raoul H.

NOVIKOFF, SERGIO
Il Fiorellino Bucaneve
solo,pno SANTIS 212 s.p.   (N563)

Nei Cieli
solo,pno SANTIS 295 s.p.   (N564)

Nubi
solo,pno SANTIS 338 s.p.   (N565)

Tu E Voi
solo,pno SANTIS 348 s.p.   (N566)

NOVOTNY, J.
Balladen Von Der Seele *Op.4, CCU
[Czech/Ger] solo,pno SUPRAPHON s.p.
                                 (N567)
Ze Srdce *song cycle
med solo,pno SUPRAPHON s.p.   (N568)

NOVOTNY, VACLAV JUDA (1849-1922)
Recicke Pisne *CCU
solo,pno SUPRAPHON s.p.   (N569)

NOVY DEN see Gollwell, John

NOW ALL THE FINGERS OF THIS TREE see
Werle, Lars-Johan

NOW ARE WE THE SONS OF GOD see
O'Connor-Morris, G.

NOW DREARY DAWNS THE EASTERN LIGHT see
Heilner, Irwin

NOW FROM YOUR EYES NO LONGER SHINES THE
STARLIGHT see Chavez, Carlos, Hoy
No Lucio La Estrella De Tus Ojos

NOW HOLLOW FIRES see Dukelsky, Vladimir

NOW I HAVE EVERYTHING see Ingles

NOW I ONLY KNOW IN PART *sac
(Carmichael, Ralph) solo,pno WORD
S-18   (N570)

NOW IS THE TIME see Alcorn, Jeannie Vee

NOW MAY THERE BE A BLESSING see Moore,
Douglas Stuart

NOW MEN - SING! *sac,CC32UL
(Lister, Mosie) 4 male soli,pno
LILLENAS MB-141 $1.50   (N571)

NOW, MY TONGUE, THE MYSTERY TELLING see
Charpentier, Marc-Antoine

NOW ON LAND AND SEA DESCENDING see
Butterworth, Arthur

NOW ONCE I DID COURT
see Schirmer's American Folk-Song
Series, Set XXI (American-English
Folk-Songs From The Southern
Appalachian Mountains)

NOW SLEEPS THE CRIMSON PETAL see
Quilter, Roger

NOW SOUND OF ED LYMAN, THE see Lyman,
Ed.

NOW THAT TIME HAS GATHERED TO ITSELF
see Pinkham, Daniel

NOW THE BIRDS ARE GONE TO REST see
Verdi, Giuseppe

NOW THE DAY IS OVER see Holler, John

NOW THE DAY IS OVER see Marks, J.C.

NOW THE DAY IS OVER see Speaks, Oley

NOW THE LUSTY SPRING see Bush, Geoffrey

NOW THE SHEEP SECURE ARE GRAZING see
Bach, Johann Sebastian, Schafe
Konnen Sicher Weiden

NOW THE TRUMPET SUMMONS US AGAIN see
Pinkham, Daniel

NOW THRO' NIGHT'S CARESSING GRIP see
Britten, Benjamin

NOW, VOYAGER see Meyer, Ernst Hermann

NOW WALK WITH GOD see Skillings, Otis

NOW WILL I PRAISE THE LORD see
Dietterich, Philip R.

NOW WILL I PRAISE THE LORD WITH ALL MY
HEART see Schutz, Heinrich, Ich
Will Den Herren Loben Allezeit

NOW WILL I SING TO GOD see Kellie,
Lawrence

NOW YOUR DAYS OF PHILANDERING ARE OVER
see Mozart, Wolfgang Amadeus, Non
Piu Andrai

NOWAK, LIONEL (1911-   )
Five Songs *CC5U
Mez solo,vcl,pno sc AM.COMP.AL.
$3.85   (N572)

Maiden's Song From "St. Winefred's
Well"
S solo,pno,vln,clar sc AM.COMP.AL.
$9.90, ipa   (N573)

Zwei Lieder Nach Goethe *CC2U
med solo,pno AM.COMP.AL. $1.37
                                 (N574)

NOWAKOWSKY, DAVID (1848-1921)
Hashkivenu *sac,Jew
solo,pno/org SAC.MUS.PR. 409 (N575)

Michtom L'Dovid (Psalm 16) sac,Jew
solo,pno/org SAC.MUS.PR. 404 (N576)

Psalm 16 *see Michtom L'Dovid

NOX AERIS TEMPORIS see Rouse,
Christopher

NOX...AMOR see Holmes, Alfred

NOX ET SOLITUDO see Suchon, Eugen

NOX...SILENTIUM see Holmes, Alfred

NOZANI-HA see Villa-Lobos, Heitor

NOZEMAN, JACOB (1693-1745)
Drie Liederen Uit P. Merkmans
Gezangen *CC3U
solo,pno HEUWEKE. 556 s.p.   (N577)

NU AR DET JUL IGEN *CC79U
(Marvia) solo,pno FAZER F 5211 s.p.
                                 (N578)

NU AR DIN SEGERTIMMA see Svedlund,
Karl-Erik

NU AR JAG PANK OCH FAGELFRI see
Millocker, Karl

NU DIKTAR KVALLEN SIN SAGA see Palm,
Hermann

NU KLAR SIG VAREN IGEN SA GRON see
Soderman, (Johan) August

NU KOMMER DEN FORSTA FRIARN see Mehler,
Friedrich

NU LAET ONS ALLEN GODE LOVEN see Horst,
Anton van der

NU LAET ONS ALLEN GODE LOVEN see
Schouwman, Hans

NU LICHT VERGETEN see Vredenburg, Max

NU LOSER SOLEN SITT BLONDA HAR see
Olson, Daniel

NU SA KOMMER JULEN see Sibelius, Jean

NU SIJT WELLEKOME see Dijk, Jan van

NU SKAL DET ABENBARES see Nielsen, Carl

NU STAR JUL VID SNOIG PORT see
Sibelius, Jean

NU SUSAR KVALLEN see Lagergren

NUAGES see Barbier, Rene

NUAGES see Georges, Alexandre

NUAGES D'AMOUR see Dufresne, C.

NUAGES ROSES see Berger, Rod.

NUBE see Lasala, Angel

NUBI see Novikoff, Sergio

NUEVE CANCIONES POPULARES CATALANAS
*CC9U, Span
(Toldra) med solo,pno UNION ESP.
$2.00   (N579)

NUIT see Doyen, Albert

NUIT see Halphen, F.

NUIT see Migot, Georges

NUIT see Wissmer, Pierre

NUIT BLANCHE see Rhene-Baton

NUIT D'AUTOMNE see Caplet, Andre

NUIT D'AUTREFOIS see Rhene-Baton

NUIT D'AZUR see Beethoven, Ludwig van

NUIT DE PRINTEMPS see Schumann, Robert
(Alexander), Fruhlingsnacht

NUIT D'ETE see Chaminade, Cecile

NUIT D'ETE see Mouton, H.

NUIT D'ETE see Tremisot, Ed.

NUIT D'ETIOLES see Debussy, Claude

NUIT D'ISAPHAN see Cuvillier, Charles

NUIT D'ISPAHAN see Cuvillier, Charles

NUIT ET SONGES see Schubert, Franz
(Peter)

NUIT ETOILEE see Chaminade, Cecile

NUIT ETOILEE see Duvernoy, Victor-
Alphonse

NUIT ETOILEE see Kleiner, S., Mondsec

NUIT MAURESQUE see Aubert, Louis-
Francois-Marie

NUIT MERIDIONALE see Rimsky-Korsakov,
Nikolai

NUIT SEREINE see Durand, Jacques

NUIT SEREINE see Rodney, Paul

NUIT SUR LA LANDE see Migot, Georges

NUL NE PEUT VAINCRE LA MORT see Bach,
Johann Sebastian

NUMBER SONGS see Rusette, L. de

NUMBERS SONG, THE *sac
(Carmichael, Ralph) solo,pno WORD
S-33   (N580)

NUN BEUT DIE FLUR see Haydn, (Franz) Joseph

NUN BIST DU HIN see Hengeveld, G.

NUN BITTEN WIR DEN HEILIGEN GEIST see Hellmann, Diethard

NUN DA SO WARM DER SONNENSCHEIN see Pfitzner, Hans

NUN DIE SCHATTEN DUNKELN see Zillig, Winfried

NUN EILT HERBEI see Nicolai, Otto

NUN FREUT EUCH, IHR FROMMEN MIT MIR see Buxtehude, Dietrich

NUN IST DER HIMMEL AUFGETAN see Wenzel, Eberhard

NUN IST'S VOLLBRACHT! DU KEHRST ZUR HEIMAT WIEDER see Lortzing, (Gustav) Albert

NUN JAUCHZET ALL, IHR FROMMEN see Cruger, Johann

NUN JUBLE LAUT, ALL KREATUR see Koch, Johannes H.E.

NUN KOMM, DER HEIDEN HEILAND see Schutz, Heinrich

NUN LASST UNS GEHN UND TRETEN see Cruger, Johann

NUN LODERT DANKGEFULLT MEIN OPFERFEUER see Maasalo, Armas, Nyt Nousee Kiitokseni Uhrisauhu

NUN RUHEN ALLE WALDER see Karg-Elert, Sigfrid

NUN SAG' ICH DIR see Schoenberg, Arnold

NUN SCHEINT IN VOLLEM GLANZE see Haydn, (Franz) Joseph

NUN SCHWEIGET WINDE see Handel, George Frideric, Silete Venti

NUN SEI BEDANKT, MEIN LIEBER SCHWAN see Wagner, Richard, Mein Lieber Schwan

NUN TAKES THE VEIL, A see Barber, Samuel

NUN VERGISS LEISES FLEHN see Mozart, Wolfgang Amadeus

NUNC DIMITTIS see Thorne, Francis

NUORI METSAMIES see Sibelius, Jean, Jagargossen

NUOVE MUSICHE E NUOVA MANIERA DI SCRIVERLE see Caccini, Giulio

NUPTIAE FACTAE SUNT see Hindemith, Paul

NUPTIAL BLESSING see Proulx, Richard

NUPTIAL CANTATA see Milhaud, Darius

NUPTIAL SONG see Weisgall, Hugo

NUR DER STEHT FEST see Bijvanck, Henk

NUR EINE KLEINE GEIGE see Haas, Joseph

NUR EINS ERBITTE ICH see Handel, George Frideric

NUR MUT! see Strauss, Richard

NUR, WER DIE SEHNSUCHT KENNT see Tchaikovsky, Piotr Ilyitch

NURNY SONG, THE see Owens

NURSERY, THE see Mussorgsky, Modest

NURSERY ODE, A see Binkerd, Gordon

NURSERY RHYMES see Curran, Pearl Gildersleeve

NURSERY RHYMES *CCU,folk,Hung (Kerenyi) solo,pno BUDAPEST 2336 s.p. (N581)

NURSE'S SONG see Dukelsky, Vladimir

NUT, THE see Kozina, Marijan, Oreh

NUTTING, GODFREY
Garden I Love
high solo,pno,opt vln (F maj)
LEONARD-ENG (N582)
med-high solo,pno,opt vln (E flat maj) LEONARD-ENG (N583)
med solo,pno,opt vln (D flat maj) LEONARD-ENG (N584)
low solo,pno,opt vln (C maj) LEONARD-ENG (N585)

NUTTING, GODFREY (cont'd.)

God Lit His Stars
high solo,pno (C maj) LEONARD-ENG (N586)
low solo,pno (B flat maj) LEONARD-ENG (N587)

Land Of Mine
solo,pno (F maj) LEONARD-ENG (N588)

Love Of My Heart
low solo,pno (C maj) LEONARD-ENG (N589)
high solo,pno (E flat maj) LEONARD-ENG (N590)
med solo,pno (D flat maj) LEONARD-ENG (N591)

Miniature Cycle Of Six Little Songs *CC6U
solo,pno LEONARD-ENG (N592)

Sing! Sing! Bird On The Wing
high solo,pno (E flat maj) BOSTON $1.50 (N593)
med-high solo,pno (D maj) BOSTON $1.50 (N594)
low solo,pno (C maj) BOSTON $1.50 (N595)

NUVOLETTA see Barber, Samuel

NY DAG see Nordqvist, Gustaf

NY MUSIK ATT SJUNGA OCH SPELA, HAFTE I (GLADA SANGER) - HAFTE II (ALLVARLIGA SANGER) (Franzen, Bengt) solo,pno GEHRMANS s.p., ea. (N596)

NY SAMLING SANGDUETTER, HEFT 1 (Uppling) 2 soli,pno LUNDQUIST s.p. contains: Anjou, P. d', Tindrande; Mendelssohn-Bartholdy, Felix, Hostsang; Myrberg, August M., Aftonklockan; Myrberg, August M., Varbacken; Palm, Hermann, Under Ronn Och Syren (N597)

NY SAMLING SANGDUETTER, HEFT 2 (Uppling) 2 soli,pno LUNDQUIST s.p. contains: Adam, Adolphe-Charles, Julsang; Bengzon, Varjubel; Haggbom, Afton I Skogen; Lago, Mario, Aftonsang; Myrberg, August M., Nattetid Vid Stranden; Myrberg, August M., Nattliga Drommar (N598)

NYA FOLKVISOR see Melartin, Erkki

NYA STJARNOR see Nordqvist, Gustaf

NYBERG, MIKAEL
Hehkuva Henki
2 soli,pno FAZER F 1871 s.p. (N599)

Lasten Lauluja
solo,pno FAZER W 3475 s.p. (N600)

NYBLOM, C.G.
Grinpojken
Mez/Bar solo,pno GEHRMANS s.p. see from SANGEN I (N601)

Vaggvisa
solo,pno GEHRMANS s.p. (N602)

Visor
solo,pno LUNDQUIST s.p. (N603)

NYKELEN see Lie, Harald

NYMPHS AND SHEPHERDS see Purcell, Henry

NYSTEDT, KNUT (1915-)
Before Him *sac
med solo,pno oct CONCORDIA 98-1804 $.25 (N604)

Fire Orheimsongar
solo,pno MUSIKK s.p. contains: Heimlengsla, Op.11, No.4; I Ungdoms Ar, Op.11,No.3; Morgonstund, Op.11,No.1; Valet, Op.11,No.2 (N605)

Heimlengsla *Op.11,No.4
see Fire Orheimsongar

I Ungdoms Ar *Op.11,No.3
see Fire Orheimsongar

Moment, The *Op.52
S solo,cel,perc sc AMP $2.00 (N606)

Morgonstund *Op.11,No.1
see Fire Orheimsongar

O Perfect Love *sac
med solo,pno AUGSBURG 11-0735 $.60 (N607)

Til Deg, Herre, Set Eg Mi Lit *sac, mot
[Norw] solo,org/pno LYCHE LY562 s.p. (N608)

NYSTEDT, KNUT (cont'd.)

Tre Religiose Folketoner *Op.34, sac,CC3U
[Norw] high solo/med solo,org/pno LYCHE LY259 s.p. (N609)

Valet *Op.11,No.2
see Fire Orheimsongar

NYSTROEM, GOSTA (1890-1966)
Day Will Find Us, A *see Ute I Skaren

Det Enda (from Sinfonia Del Mare)
"To The Sea" [Swed/Eng/Fr/Ger/It] high solo,kbd NORDISKA s.p. (N610)

Havets Visa
"Sea's Music, The" [Swed/Eng] med solo,kbd NORDISKA s.p. (N611)

I Built A Home Near Wide Seas *see Jag Har Ett Hem Vid Havet

Jag Har Ett Hem Vid Havet
"I Built A Home Near Wide Seas" [Swed/Eng] med solo,kbd NORDISKA s.p. (N612)

Jag Vantar Manen
"Moon I Wait, The" [Swed/Eng] med solo,kbd NORDISKA s.p. (N613)

Moon I Wait, The *see Jag Vantar Manen

Nocturne
[Swed/Eng] med solo,kbd NORDISKA s.p. (N614)

Sea's Music, The *see Havets Visa

To The Sea *see Det Enda

Ute I Skaren
"Day Will Find Us, A" [Swed/Eng] med solo,kbd NORDISKA s.p. (N615)

NYT HERRAN KANSA LAULA see Elovaara, Toivo

NYT NOUSEE KIITOKSENI UHRISAUHU see Maasalo, Armas

NYT ON KAIKKI KALLISTUNNA see Kilpinen, Yrio

O

O, ALS IK DOOD ZAL ZIJN see Badings, Henk

O ALS IK DOOD ZAL ZIJN see Flothius, Marius

O! ALS IK JE EENS MOCHT ZEGGEN see Oort, H.C.v.

O AMANTISSIME SPONSE JESU see Ritter, Christian

O AMOR, DU TYRANN see Handel, George Frideric, Crudel Tiranno, Amor

O ANGENIETJE see Rontgen, [Julius]

O BABE DIVINE see McKinney, Howard D., Tu Scendi Dalle Stelle

O BAJADERA see Kalman, Emerich

O BE JOYFUL see Harding, Harvey

O BE JOYFUL see Sowerby, Leo

O BEAU PAYS DE LA TOURAINE see Meyerbeer, Giacomo

O BEAUTY OF BEAUTY see Birch, Robert Fairfax

O BEAUTY, PASSING BEAUTY see Golde, Walter

O BEAUX REVES EVANOUIS see Saint-Saens, Camille

O BELLA see Toni, Alceo

O! BELLE ET DOUCE NUIT see Schlosser, Paul

O BELLE NUIT see Ronald, Sir Landon, O Lovely Night!

O BEWAHRET UND BEFEUERT see Handel, George Frideric, Conservate, Raddoppiate

O BID YOUR FAITHFUL ARIEL FLY see Linley, George

O BIEN AIME(E) LORSQUE TES PAS T'ENTRAINENT LOIN DE MOI see Pillois, Jacques

O BLESS OUR GOD see Peri, Jacopo

O BON VIN, OU AS-TU CRU? see Roussel, Albert

O BONE JESU see Tommasini, Vincenzo

O BRAHMA, MAITRE DE LA VIE see Lefebvre, Channing

O BROTHER MAN see Banks, Harry

O BY THE BY see Dougherty, Celius

O CAN YE SEW CUSHIONS? *folk,Scot solo,pno (E flat maj) PATERSON FS111 s.p.   (O1)
(Moore, Gerald) high solo,pno UNIVER. 12317 $.75   (O2)
(Moore, Gerald) med solo,pno UNIVER. 12317 $.75   (O3)

O CAN YE SEW CUSHIONS? see Lawson, Malcolm

O CAN YOU SEW CUSHIONS see Taylor

O CANADA! see Lavalee, C.

O CANTO MULTIPLICADO see Nobre, Marlos

O CAPTAIN, MY CAPTAIN see Wolpe, Stefan

O CES AUTELS see Orthel, Leon

O CESSATE DI PIAGARMI see Scarlatti, Alessandro

O CESSEZ DE ME PLAINDRE see Scarlatti, Alessandro, O Cessate Di Piagarmi

O CHE NUOVO STUPOR see Caccini, Francesca

O CHILD DIVINE see Frederickson, Carl

O CIEL, EXAUCE MA PIERE see Wagner, Richard

O CIELI AZZURRI see Verdi, Giuseppe

O CLAP YOUR HANDS see Couperin (le Grand), Francois

O CLEMENS, O MITIS, O COELESTIS PATER see Buxtehude, Dietrich

O COLOMBINA see Leoncavallo, Ruggiero

O, COME CHIARE E BELLE see Handel, George Frideric

O COME, CREATOR SPIRIT, COME see Charpentier, Marc-Antoine

O COME, SOFT REST OF CARES see Joubert, John

O COME SPESSO IL MONDO... see Martini, Giambattista

O COME TO MY HEART, LORD JESUS see Ambrose, [Paul]

O CONFORTANTE VOCE see Cairone, Renato

O COR AMORIS see Heidet, le R. P.

O COUNTRY BRIGHT AND FAIR see Parker, Horatio William

O CRUAUTE DES DIEUX see Saint-Saens, Camille

O CRUEL AND INIMICAL ABSENCE! see Clerambault, Louis-Nicolas, La Musette

O CUBA see Sanchez de Fuentes, Eduardo

O DAFFODILS see Browne

O DAISIES see Quilter, Roger

O DAUGHTERS OF JERUSALEM see Tz'ena Ur'ena

O DAY DIVINE see Oliver, Herbert

O DEAR, O FRIENDLY, O KIND AND GENTLE SAVIOR see Schutz, Heinrich

O DEATH, HOW BITTER ART THOU see Brahms, Johannes, O Tod, Wie Bitter Bist Du

O DEATH, ROCK ME ASLEEP see Edmunds, John

O DEATH, WHERE IS THY STING? see Trombly, Preston

O DEL MIO AMATO BEN see Donaudy, Stefano

O DEL MIO DOLCE ARDOR see Gluck, Christoph Willibald Ritter von

O DETECH see Burian, Emil Frantisek

O DIEPE BAAI EN ALTIJD OPEN HAVEN see Mulder, Ernest W.

O DIEPE BAAI EN ALTIJD OPEN HAVEN see Mulder, Herman

O DIEPSTE LIEFDE see Sigtenhorst-Meyer, Bernhard van den

O DIEU BRAHMAL see Bizet, Georges

O DIEU DE QUELLE IVRESSE see Offenbach, Jacques

O DIEU, DONNE-MOI DELIVRANCE DE CET HOMME PERNICIEUX see Honegger, Arthur

O DIVINE REDEEMER see Gounod, Charles Francois, Repentir

O DOLCE CONCENTO see Drouet, L.F.Ph.

O DOLCE NOTTE see Cimara, Pietro

O DOLCI MANI see Puccini, Giacomo

O DOMOVINA see Kozina, Marijan

O DON FATALE see Verdi, Giuseppe

O DOOD, GEHEIME NACHTEGAAL see Mulder, Herman

O DOUCE ETOILE see Wagner, Richard

O DOUCE NUIT D'AMOUR! see Gounod, Charles Francois

O DOUX SOMMEIL see Handel, George Frideric

O DREAM, O DREAMING see Hornung

O DU ANGENEHMER SCHATZ see Bach, Johann Sebastian

O DU, DIE MIR DAS LEBEN GAB see Gluck, Christoph Willibald Ritter von, O Toi, Qui Prolongaes Mes Jours

O DU MEIN HOLDER ABENDSTERN see Wagner, Richard

O DU MEIN TROST see Frank, J.W.

O DU SALIGA see En Liten Julhalsning

O DU WOGENDES FELD see Rachmaninoff, Sergey Vassilievitch, Harvest Of Sorrow, The

O DULCIS AMOR see Campra, Andre

O, FADERSHEM, MOT DIG JAR SER see Dannstrom, Isidor

O FAIR ART THOU see Grandi, Alessandro

O FALCE DI LUNA see Gandino, Adolfo

O FALCE DI LUNA see Respighi, Ottorino

O, FALMOUTH IS A FINE TOWN see Shaw, Martin

O FATHER, ALL CREATING see Fetler, David

O FATHER, O FATHER see Flagello, Nicholas

O FLEUR VERMEILLE see Schumann, Robert (Alexander)

O FOR A BOOK see Birch, Robert Fairfax

O FOR A CLOSER WALK see Thiman, Eric Harding

O FOR THE WINGS OF A DOVE see Mendelssohn-Bartholdy, Felix

O FRAGE NICHT see Reger, Max

O FRAICHE NUIT see Franck, Cesar

O FREUDE UBER FREUDE see Burkhart, Franz

O FREUND, WAS MICH ERGRIFFEN - WOHER DIESES BANGEN see Mozart, Wolfgang Amadeus, Alcandro Lo Confesso - Non So D'onde Viene

O FRIEDE, DER NUN ALLES FULLET see Bijvanck, Henk

O FROHLICH STUNDEN see Buxtehude, Dietrich

O FROID FUNEBRE see Middeleer, Jean De, O Klamme Koude

O, FUHRT MICH IN DIE STILLE GRUFT see Purcell, Henry

O, FUNNE JAG DEN VAG IGEN see Brahms, Johannes

O GEBT see Meyerbeer, Giacomo

O, GEH NICHT FORT, VERLASS MICH NICHT *folk,Russ [Ger/Russ] solo,pno ZIMMER. 1511 s.p.   (O4)

O GENTIL MENZOGNA see Delibes, Leo

O GENTLE PRESENCE see Boardman, Reginald

O GIJ MIJN TROOST, MIJN ZOET VERLANGEN see Zwart, Jan

O GIN MY LOVE WERE YON RED ROSE *folk, Scot
low solo,pno (B maj/C maj) PATERSON FS120 s.p.   (O5)
high solo,pno (D flat maj/E flat maj) PATERSON FS120 s.p.   (O6)

O GIVE ME A SOAPBOX see Wyrtzen, Don

O GLAD DIG, MITT HJARTA see Bach, Johann Sebastian

O GLAUBIG HERZ, GEBENEDEI see Bornefeld, Helmut

O GLOIRE QUI M'ALARME see Clerambault, Louis-Nicolas

O GLORIOSA DOMINA see Head, Michael (Dewar)

O GLORIOSA VERGINE MARIA see Thybo, Leif

O GOD, HAVE MERCY see Mendelssohn-Bartholdy, Felix

O GOD, I WILL PRAISE THEE see Schutz, Heinrich, Ich Danke Dem Herrn Von Ganzem Herzen

O GOD, MY HEART IS READY see Schutz, Heinrich, Paratum Cor Meum, Deus

O GOD OF LIGHT see Sowerby, Leo

O GOD OF LOVE see Gretchaninov, Alexander Tikhonovitch

O GOD OF LOVE see Trued, S. Clarence

O GOD OF LOVE see Wood, Dale

O GOD OF LOVE TO THEE WE BOW LOW see Lovelace, Austin C.

O GODDESS OF THE SEA see Hovhaness, Alan

O GOTTES STADT see Buxtehude, Dietrich

O GRACIOUS LORD GOD, MAY WE BE VIGILANT see Schutz, Heinrich

O GRANDI OCCHI LUCENTI DI FEDE see Giordano, Umberto

O HATT' ICH JUBALS HARF see Handel, George Frideric

O, HAUL THE WATER see Kramer, A. Walter

O HEIRI, MACH MER JO KEI SCHAND see Horler, A.

O HERR, HILF, O HERR, LASS WOHLGELINGEN see Schutz, Heinrich

O HERR, HILF, O HERR, LASS WOHLGELINGEN [2] see Schutz, Heinrich

O, HERRE - - see Melartin, Erkki

O HILF, CHRISTE, GOTTES SOHN see Raphael, Gunther

O HILF, CHRISTE, GOTTES SOHN see Schutz, Heinrich

O HIMMEL! WAS HORT MEIN SINN? see Blow, John, Ah Heav'n! What Is't I Hear?

O HOLDER TAG, ERWUNSCHTE ZEIT see Bach, Johann Sebastian

O HOLY NIGHT see Adam, Adolphe-Charles, Cantique De Noel

O, HONEYED SONG see Tornquist, F., O, Milda Sang

O, HUR UNDERSKON AR EJ VARENS TID see Abt, Franz

O IHR ZARTLICHEN see Rautavaara, Einojuhani

O IRISH HILLS see Lester, William

O ISIS AND OSIRIS see Mozart, Wolfgang Amadeus, O Isis Und Osiris, Schenket Der Weisheit Geist

O ISIS UND OSIRIS, SCHENKET DER WEISHEIT GEIST see Mozart, Wolfgang Amadeus

O JESU CHRIST, DEIN KRIPPLEIN IST see Cruger, Johann

O JESU CHRISTE, GOTTES SOHN see Buxtehude, Dietrich

O JESU CHRISTE, GOTTES SOHN see Schein, Johann Hermann

O JESU EGO AMO TE see Diepenbrock, Alphons

O JESU, NAME MOST LOVELY see Schutz, Heinrich, O Jesu, Nomen Dulce

O JESU, NOMEN DULCE see Schutz, Heinrich

O JESU VOL GENADEN see Weegenhuise, Johan

O JESULEIN SUSS see In Dulci Jubilo

O JESULEIN SUSS see Bach, Johann Sebastian

O JESULEIN ZART see In Dulci Jubilo

O JESUS, I HAVE PROMISED see Casner, Myron D.

O JESUS, LORD see Sowerby, Leo

O JOUEUSE DE FLUTE see Wieniawski, Adam (Tadeusz)

O JOUEUSE DE TAMBOURIN see Wieniawski, Adam (Tadeusz)

O JOUR AFFREUX see Rameau, Jean-Philippe

O JUBEL MIJN HART see Kuiler, Cor.

O KATHERINE, DEAREST see Smit, Leo

O KENMURE'S ON AND AWA' *folk,Scot solo,pno (E flat maj) PATERSON FS67 s.p. (O7)

O KING OF KINGS see Handel, George Frideric

O KLAMME KOUDE see Middeleer, Jean De

O, KOM MED MIG I STJARNEGLANS! see Sjogren, Emil

O, KOMM IM TRAUM see Liszt, Franz, Oh! Quand Je Dors

O KOMM' IN TRAUM see Liszt, Franz

O KOMM'IN TRAUM see Liszt, Franz, Oh! Quand Je Dors

O KONNT NUR EINMAL MEIN MUDES HAUPT see Schumann, Georg

O KONNTEST DU EINMAL VERGESSEN see Ippolitov-Ivanov, Mikhail Mikhailovitch

O LA LA see Felderhof, Jan

O LACRIMOSA see Krenek, Ernst

O LADY MOON see Hovhaness, Alan

O LAMB OF GOD, MOST HOLY see Schein, Johann Hermann

O LAMM GOTTES, UNSCHULDIG see Raphael, Gunther

O LAND OF HOPE, AMERICA! see Wright, D.

O LAY THY LOOF IN MINE, LASS *folk, Scot solo,pno (B min/G min) PATERSON FS130 s.p. (O8)

O LEAVE YOUR SHEEP *sac,carol,Fr (Grimes, Travis) med solo,fl,org,vcl oct CONCORDIA 98-3004 $.40 (O9)

O LEAVE YOUR SHEEP see Hazelhurst, Cecil, Quittez Pasteurs

O LEBEN, LEBEN see Welter, Friedrich

O LEGERE HIRONDELLE see Gounod, Charles Francois

O LET US TURN TO BETHLEHEM see O'Hara, Geoffrey

O LIEB, SO LANG DU LIEBEN KANNST see Liszt, Franz

O LIEBE! MEINEM HASS STEH'ZUR see Saint-Saens, Camille, Amour! Viens Aider

O LIEBER HERRE GOTT, WECKE UNS AUF see Schutz, Heinrich

O LIEBES JESULEIN see Holler, Karl

O, LIED see Beekhuis, Hanna

O, LIKENESS, DIM AND FADED see Donaudy, Stefano, Vaghissima Sembianza

O LIL LAMB see Frierson

O LI'L LAMB! see Haufrecht, Herbert

O LINGER YET see Jensen, Ludwig Irgens

O LITTLE ONE SLEEP see Coleman, Henry

O LITTLE TOWN OF BETHLEHEM *sac,Xmas (Lane) solo,pno HARRIS $.75 (O10) (Miller) med solo,pno (G maj) WATERLOO $.65 (O11)

O, LIV, JAG SAG DIG see Peterson-Berger, (Olof) Wilhelm

O LOLA CH'AI DI LATTI see Mascagni, Pietro

O LORD, BE MERCIFUL see Bartlett, Homer Newton

O LORD CORRECT ME see Handel, George Frideric, Lascia Ch'io Pianga

O LORD, DELIVER ME see Marcello, Benedetto

O LORD, HOW MANIFOLD ARE THY WORKS see Fischer, Irwin

O LORD, I WILL PRAISE THEE see Krapf, Gerhard

O LORD, LOOK DOWN FROM HEAVEN see Schein, Johann Hermann

O LORD MOST HOLY see Franck, Cesar, Panis Angelicus

O LORD, OUR GOVERNOR see Marcello, Benedetto

O LORD, OUR LORD, HOW EXCELLENT IS THY NAME see Swack, Erwin

O, LORD, THOU HAST SEARCHED ME see Lekberg, Sven

O LORD, WE PRAY FOR DAILY GRACE see Handel, George Frideric

O LORD WHOSE MERCIES NUMBERLESS see Handel, George Frideric

O LOVE, BE DEEP see MacNutt, Walter

O LOVE DIVINE see Brace

O LOVE, HOW STRANGELY SWEET see Musgrave, Thea

O LOVE, HOW THOU ART TIRED OUT WITH RHYME! see Donovan, Richard [Frank]

O LOVE ME NOT see Haubiel, Charles

O LOVE THAT CASTS OUR FEAR see Matthews, Harvey Alexander

O LOVE THAT GUIDES OUR WAY see Branscombe, Gena

O LOVE THAT WILL NOT LET ME GO see Matthews, Harvey Alexander

O LOVE THAT WILT NOT LET ME GO see Harker, F. Flaxington

O LOVE WILL VENTURE IN *folk,Scot solo,pno (A min/C min) PATERSON FS68 s.p. (O12)

O LOVELY NIGHT see Offenbach, Jacques, Belle Nuit, O Nuit D'amour

O LOVELY NIGHT! see Ronald, Sir Landon

O LOVELY VALLEY see Ma Tovu

O LOVELY WORLD see Charles, Ernest

O LUANDE-LUA see Prado, Almeida

O LUCE DI QUEST'ANIMA see Donizetti, Gaetano

O, LUGNA DIN SJAL see Mendelssohn-Bartholdy, Felix

O LUNA, CHE CON FALCE AMPIA D'ARGENTO see Pratella, Francesco Balilla

O LUNA CHE FAI LUME see Davico, Vincenzo

O LURCHER-LOVING COLLIER see Berkeley, Lennox

O LUX BEATA TRINITAS see Kraft, Walter

O MA BELLE REBELLE see Gounod, Charles Francois

O MA CHERE MAISON see Pesse, M.

O MA JOLIE, O MA CALINE see Absil, Jean

O MA LYRE IMMORTELLE see Gounod, Charles Francois

O MA PHRYNE, C'EST TROP PEU QUE JE T'AIME see Saint-Saens, Camille

O MA TENDRE MUSETTE see Monsigny, Pierre-Alexandre

O MAGNIFY THE LORD see Handel, George Frideric

O MALHEUREUSE IPHIGENIE see Gluck, Christoph Willibald Ritter von

O MAMI OUAMA see Fraggi, H.

O MAMICKE see Cikker, Jan

O MAN VAN SMARTE see Adriessen, Willem

O MARY, GO CALL THE CATTLE HOME see Briggs, C.S.

O MEN FROM THE FIELDS see Thorp

O MENSCH see Mahler, Gustav

O MEREL see Dresden, Sem

O MES SOEURS see Roussel, Albert

O MIA CASETTA see Ferrari-Trecate, Luigi

O MIA CUNA FIORITA see Cilea, Francesco

O, MILDA SANG see Tornquist, F.

O MIMI, TU PIU NON TORNI see Puccini, Giacomo

O MIO BABBINO CARO see Puccini, Giacomo

O MIO FERNANDO see Donizetti, Gaetano

O MIO PICCOLO TAVOLO see Leoncavallo, Ruggiero

O MISERICORDISSIME JESU see Schutz, Heinrich

O MISTRESS MINE see Chanler, Theodore Ward

O MISTRESS MINE see Cook, John

O MISTRESS MINE see Dale, Benjamin J.

O MISTRESS MINE see Davies, Henry Walford

O MISTRESS MINE see Finzi, Gerald

O MISTRESS MINE see Montgomery, Bruce

O MISTRESS MINE see Quilter, Roger

O MISTRESS MINE see Sullivan, Sir Arthur Seymour

O MISTRESS MINE see Sutherland, Margaret

O MON DIEU! TOI QUI SEUL CONDUIS see Mariotte, Antoine

O, MON DOUX JESUS see Bach, Johann Sebastian

O MON FILS QUE J'ADORE see Duvernoy, Victor-Alphonse

O MON MAITRE ET SEIGNEUR see Saint-Saens, Camille

O MON PERE, SI TU VOULAIS see Handel, George Frideric

O MON ROI, BIEN QU'ETANT PAR VOUS DELAISSEE see Saint-Saens, Camille

O MONEY see Head, Michael (Dewar)

O MORNING STAR, SO PURE, SO BRIGHT see Lenel, Ludwig

O MOST KIND AND MOST MERCIFUL JESU see Schutz, Heinrich, Misericordissime Jesu

O MOTHER, TELL ME HOW TO DIE see Smit, Leo

O MOUNT AND GO   *folk,Scot
low solo,pno (B flat maj) PATERSON FS74 s.p.   (O13)
high solo,pno (C maj) PATERSON FS74 s.p.   (O14)

O MUSE DONT LES PAS DANSENT see Bernier, Nicolas

O MUTO ASIL DEL PIANTO see Rossini, Gioacchino

O MY BELOVED DADDY see Puccini, Giacomo, O Mio Babbino Caro

O MY KITTEN A KITTEN see Fiske, R.

O NACHT... see Flothius, Marius

O NACHT see Niel, Matty

O NACHT see Zagwijn, Henri

O NACHT, ZWAR SCHWARZE see Lie, Harald

O NATURA DI GRAZIA PIENA see Massenet, Jules, O Nature

O NATURE see Massenet, Jules

O NEVER, NEVER BOW WE DOWN see Handel, George Frideric

O NIGHTINGALE see Damase, Jean-Michel

O NO LONGER SEEK TO PAIN ME see Scarlatti, Alessandro, O Cessate Di Piagarmi

O NOBLE EPOUX see Saint-Saens, Camille

O NUIT TRANQUILLE see Mendelssohn-Bartholdy, Felix

O OOGEN see Moulaert, Raymond

O' PALIDA MADONA see Villa-Lobos, Heitor

O PALLIDA, CHE UN GIORNO MI GUARDASTI see Mascagni, Pietro

O PARADIS SORTI DE L'ONDE see Meyerbeer, Giacomo

O PARADISO DALL'ONDA USCITO see Meyerbeer, Giacomo, O Paradis Sorti De L'Onde

O PATRIA MIA see Verdi, Giuseppe

O PEACE, THOU FAIREST CHILD OF HEAVEN see Arne, Thomas Augustine

O PERFECT LOVE see Barnby, Sir Joseph

O PERFECT LOVE see Burleigh, Henry Thacker

O PERFECT LOVE see Clough-Leighter, Henry

O PERFECT LOVE see Harker, F. Flaxington

O PERFECT LOVE see Nystedt, Knut

O PERFECT LOVE see Sowerby, Leo

O PERFECT LOVE see Stevens, Halsey

O PICCOL BEL CAVALIER see Kalman, Emerich

O PLENUS IRARUM DIES see Brossard, Sebastien de

O POPOLO DI VILI see Mascagni, Pietro

O PRAISE THE LORD see Ford

O PREHISTORIC RAIMENT see Puccini, Giacomo, Vecchia Zimarra, Senti

O PRIMAVERA see Kelemen, Milko

O PRIMAVERA! see Tirindelli, Pier Adolfo

O PUIRTITH CAULD   *folk,Scot
solo,pno (E flat maj) PATERSON FS66 s.p.   (O15)

O PURE EXTASE see Saint-Saens, Camille

O PURE WHITE ROSE see Quayle, Eileen

O QUALIS DE COELO SONUS see Handel, George Frideric

O QUAM FULGIDO SPLENDORE see Foggia, Antonio

O QUAM PULCHRA ES see Carissimi, Giacomo

O QUAM TU PULCHRA ES see Schutz, Heinrich

O QUI COELI TERRAEQUE SERENITAS see Vivaldi, Antonio

O RATTLIN', ROARIN' WILLIE   *folk,Scot
solo,pno (D maj/E maj) PATERSON FS69 s.p.   (O16)

O RAVISHING DELIGHT see Arne, Thomas Augustine

O REJOICE IN THE LORD AT ALL TIMES see Distler, Hugo

O REST IN THE LORD see Mendelssohn-Bartholdy, Felix

O RIANTE NATURE! see Gounod, Charles Francois

O RICORDO CHE SOLO MI RIMANI see Pizzetti, Ildebrando

O RIJKE HEILIGE NACHT see Tierie, J.F.

O ROCKS DON'T FALL ON ME   *spir
(Burleigh, H. T.) high solo,pno
BELWIN $1.50   (O17)

(Burleigh, H. T.) low solo,pno BELWIN
$1.50   (O18)

O ROUGES FLAMBOYANTS see Romanette, I.

O SACRED HEAD, NOW WOUNDED see Bach, Johann Sebastian

O SACRED ORACLES OF TRUTH see Handel, George Frideric

O SACRUM CONVIVIUM see Andriessen, Hendrik

O SAISONS, O CHATEAUX! see Lutyens, Elizabeth

O SALUTARIS see Boulay, J.

O SALUTARIS see Cherubini, Luigi

O SALUTARIS! see Delmet, Paul

O SALUTARIS see Dubois, Theodore

O SALUTARIS see Faure, Jean-Baptiste

O SALUTARIS see Hahn, Reynaldo

O SALUTARIS see Honegger, Arthur

O SALUTARIS see Lambillotte, Louis

O SALUTARIS see Lefebure-Wely, Louis James Alfred

O SALUTARIS! see Levade, Charles (Gaston)

O SALUTARIS! see Louis, E.

O SALUTARIS see Massenet, Jules

O SALUTARIS! see Ordinaire, R.

O SALUTARIS see Perilhou, Albert

O SALUTARIS see Samuel-Rosseau, Marcel

O SALUTARIS! see Vieu, Jane

O SALVADOR MUNDI see Tommasini, Vincenzo

O SANCTA JUSTITIA see Lortzing, (Gustav) Albert

O SANCTISSIMA   *CC10U,Xmas,Eur
(Ragossnig, K.) med solo,gtr ZIMMER.
1719 $1.50   (O19)

O SANCTISSIMA see Dvorak, Antonin

O SAVIOUR, HEAR ME see Gluck, Christoph Willibald Ritter von

O, SCHAU, HOCH OBEN see Rimsky-Korsakov, Nikolai

O SCHMACH, O WUT - O ROSIG WIE DIE PFIRSICHE see Handel, George Frideric

O SCHONE JUGENDTAGE see Kienzl, Wilhelm

O SEELEN-PARADIES see Bach, Johann Sebastian

O SI CHERE see Gui, Vittorio

O SING NO MORE see Rachmaninoff, Sergey Vassilievitch, Oh, Never Sing To Me Again

O SING UNTO THE LORD see Whikehart, Lewis W.

O SING UNTO THE LORD A NEW SONG see Gore, Richard T.

O SLEEP, WHY DOST THOU LEAVE ME? see Handel, George Frideric

O SLOBODE see Kowalski, Julius

O SOAVE FANCIULLA see Puccini, Giacomo

O SOFT WAS THE SONG see Elgar, Edward

O SOLE MIO see Di Capua, [Eduardo]

O SOMMEIL, DOUX SOMMEIL! see Handel, George Frideric, O Sleep, Why Dost Thou Leave Me?

O SONG DIVINE see Temple, Gordon

O SPIRITUS ANGELICI see Brevi, Giovanni Battista

O SPRICH, WAS WILLST DU DICH SCHAMEN see Svedbom, Vilhelm

O STAR OF EVE see Wagner, Richard, O Du Mein Holder Abendstern

O STAY, MY LOVE, FORSAKE ME NOT see
     Rachmaninoff, Sergey Vassilievitch

O, STODE DU I KYLIG BLAST see Alfven,
     Hugo

O SUSSER JESU CHRIST see Kittel,
     Christoph

O SUSSER JESU CHRIST see Schutz,
     Heinrich

O SUSSER, O FREUNDLICHER see Schutz,
     Heinrich

O SWASTIKA see Hullebroeck, Em.

O SWEET SPONTANEOUS EARTH see Taub,
     Bruce J.H.

O, 'T RUISCHEN VAN HET RANKE RIET see
     Rontgen, Johannes

O TAG! see Arlberg, Fritz

O TARDI VENUTO see Toni, Alceo

O TASTE AND SEE see Bach, Johann
     Sebastian

O TENDER, O BOUNTIFUL see Schutz,
     Heinrich, O Susser, O Freundlicher

O TENDRE REVE see Wagner, Richard

O THAT I KNEW WHERE I MIGHT FIND HIM
     see Rowley, Alec

O THAT WE TWO WERE MAYING see Gatty, A.
     Scott

O THE BONNY FISHER LAD see Tate,
     Phyllis

O THIS IS NO MY AIN LASSIE *folk,Scot
     low solo,pno (A flat maj) PATERSON
     FS70 s.p.   (O20)
     high solo,pno (B flat maj) PATERSON
     FS70 s.p.   (O21)

O THOU BELOV'D see Gluck, Christoph
     Willibald Ritter von, O Del Mio
     Dolce Ardor

O THY BEAUTY, ISRAEL see Orgad, Ben-
     Zion, Hatzvi Israel

O TO BE IN ENGLAND see Head, Michael
     (Dewar)

O TOD, WIE BITTER BIST DU see Brahms,
     Johannes

O TOI QUI POUR AVOIR BU DU VIN see
     Blair Fairchild

O TOI QUI PROLOGEAS MES JOURS see
     Gluck, Christoph Willibald Ritter
     von

O TOI, QUI PROLONGAES MES JOURS see
     Gluck, Christoph Willibald Ritter
     von

O TOI QUI PROLONGEAS MES JOURS see
     Gluck, Christoph Willibald Ritter
     von

O TOI QUI SAIS AIMER see Favre, Georges

O TRISTE ETAIT MON AME see Vierne,
     Louis

O TROUBLED HEART BE STILL see Hamblen

O TU CHE IN SENO AGLI ANGELI see Verdi,
     Giuseppe

O, TU, PALERMO, TERRA ADORATA see
     Verdi, Giuseppe

O VAGABONDA STELLA D'ORIENTE see Cilea,
     Francesco

O, VANISHED LONELINESS see Donaudy,
     Stefano, O Del Mio Amato Ben

O, VART FLOG MODERNS GYLLENE FAGEL see
     Merikanto, Oskar, Oi, Minne Emon
     Lintunen Lensi

O VENUS, YOU AND YOUR SON see Smit, Leo

O, VIDSTE DU BARE! see Kjerulf,
     [Halfdan]

O VIERGE SAINTE see Wagner, Richard,
     Dich Theure Halle

O VIN DISCACCIA LA TRISTEZZA see
     Thomas, Ambroise

O VOR' JAG ETT MINNE see Soderman,
     (Johan) August

O VOS OMNES see Dubois, Theodore

O, VRBA! see Scek, Breda

O VULNERA DOLORIS see Carissimi,
     Giacomo

O WALY WALY see Boatwright, Howard

O WALY, WALY, UP THE BANK *folk
     solo,pno (B flat maj/C maj) PATERSON
     FS71 s.p.   (O22)

O WALY, WALY UP THE BANK see Russell,
     Welford

O WAR ICH SCHON MIT DIR VEREINT see
     Beethoven, Ludwig van

O WELCH' EIN LEBEN! EIN GANZES MEER see
     Beethoven, Ludwig van

O WENN MEIN HERZ see Lilien, Ignace

O WERE THERE AN ISLAND see Laurie,
     Malcolm

O, WERT THOU HERE: THE ROSES BLOSSOM
     see Sibelius, Jean, Aus Banger
     Brust

O WERT THOU IN THE COULD BLAST *folk,
     Scot
     solo,pno (B flat maj/D flat maj)
     PATERSON FS112 s.p.   (O23)

O WESTERN WIND! see Brahe, May H.

O WHA'S AT THE WINDOW *folk,Scot
     solo,pno (A flat maj) PATERSON FS76
     s.p.   (O24)

O WHAT LOVE IS HERE DISPLAYED see
     Grimm, Johann D.

O WHISTLE AND I'LL COME TO YOU *folk,
     Scot
     low solo,pno (A maj) PATERSON FS72
     s.p.   (O25)
     high solo,pno (B flat maj) PATERSON
     FS72 s.p.   (O26)

O WHY LEFT I MY HOME *folk,Scot
     solo,pno (E flat maj/G maj) PATERSON
     FS73 s.p.   (O27)

O WIE BERUCKEND see Schutz, Heinrich, O
     Quam Tu Pulchra Es

O WIE BITTER EIN KNECHT ZU SEIN see
     Kilpinen, Yrio, Pah' On Orjana Elea

O WIE SCHON IST DEINE WELT see
     Schubert, Franz (Peter), Im
     Abendrot

O, WIE WILL ICH TRIUMPHIEREN see
     Mozart, Wolfgang Amadeus

O WIEN, MEIN LIEBES WIEN see Ziehrer,
     Carl Michael

O WILL HE YET DRAW NEAR AGAIN see Hines

O WORLD see Hovhaness, Alan

O WUNDER, WAS WILL DAS BEDEUTEN *CCU,
     Adv
     (Draths) 2 soli,opt gtr SCHOTTS 5750
     s.p.   (O28)

O WURDE CELIA MICH VERSTEH'N see Blow,
     John

O YE WHO SEEK THE LORD see Cadman,
     Charles Wakefield

O YE WHO TASTE THAT LOVE IS SWEET see
     Lovelace, Austin C.

O YES, JUST SO see Bach, Johann
     Sebastian

O YOU WHOM I OFTEN see Reif, Paul

O YOU WHOM I OFTEN AND SILENTLY COME
     see Rorem, Ned

O ZITTERE NICHT see Mozart, Wolfgang
     Amadeus

O ZITTRE NICHT, MEIN LIEBER SOHN - ZUM
     LEIDEN BIN ICH AUSERKOREN see
     Mozart, Wolfgang Amadeus

O ZITTERE NICHT, MEIN LIEBER SOHN - ZUM
     LEIDER BIN ICH AUSEKOREN see
     Mozart, Wolfgang Amadeus

OAK TREE BOUGH, THE see Bairstow,
     Edward Cuthbert

OASEN see Schouwman, Hans

OATMAN
     Last Mile Of The Way, The (composed
          with Marks) *sac
          solo,pno BENSON S7936-RS $1.00
                                       (O29)

OB EIN GOTT SEI? see Beethoven, Ludwig
     van, An Die Hoffnung

OB ICH MICH WEHRE see Haas, Joseph

OBBEDIAMO DEL CORE ALLA VOCE see
     Massenet, Jules

OBCY see Baird, Tadeusz

OBEIR see Middeleer, Jean De

OBEISSANCE A LA CONSIGNE see Lacome,
     Paul

OBERFELD, C.
     J'arrose Mes Galons
          solo,acap solo pt ENOCH s.p. (O30)

     Les Soldats, Ca Marche
          solo,acap solo pt ENOCH s.p. (O31)

OBEY THE SPIRIT OF THE LORD see Croft,
     Colbert

OBLIO! see Tosti, Francesco Paolo

OBOE SOMMERSO see Parac, Franco

OBOEN-LIEDER NACH GEDICHTEN VON GEORG
     SCHWARZ see Lothar, Mark

OBOENLIEDER see Steffens, Walter

OBOUSSIER, ROBERT (1900-1957)
     Drei Arien Auf Texte Von Friedrich G.
          Klopstock *CC3U
          coloratura sop,ob,cembalo (diff)
          BAREN. 2471 rental   (O32)

     Drei Lieder Nach Eichendorff Und
          Hebbel *CC3U
          Bar solo,pno (diff) BAREN. 2472
          rental   (O33)

     Gesange Der Ferne *CCU
          coloratura sop,pno (diff) BAREN.
          2473 rental   (O34)

     Vie Et Mort *CC12U
          [Fr/Ger] A solo,pno (diff) BAREN.
          2464 $10.50   (O35)

OBRADORS, FERNANDO
     Classical Spanish Songs *CC7L,Span
          [Span/Eng] solo,pno INTERNAT. $2.50
                                        (O36)
     La Casada Infiel *CCU
          (Lorca) [Span] med-high solo,pno
          UNION ESP. $1.00   (O37)

O'BRIEN, BILL
     Disciple's Prayer, A (from
          Namegivers, The) (composed with
          Sellers, Rob) sac
          (Willcoxon, Larry) solo,pno
          BROADMAN 4590-40 $1.00   (O38)

O'BRIEN, VINCENT
     Fairy Tree, The
          [Eng] med solo,kbd CHESTER s.p. (O39)

O'BRYON, JIM
     Portrait Of A Man *sac
          solo,pno SINGSPIR 7116 $1.00 (O40)

OBSERVATOIRE see Ferroud, Pierre-Octave

OBSESSION see Bertouille, Gerard

OBSESSION see Milhaud, Darius

OBSESSION see Rabey, Rene

OBSESSION see Voormolen, Alexander
     Nicolas

OBSTINATION see Fontenailles, H. de

OBYEDOV, YU.
     Vernal Triptych *CC3U
          [Russ] S solo,pno MEZ KNIGA 2.98
          s.p.   (O41)

OCCHI see Spezzaferri, Giovanni

OCCHI DI FATA see Denza, Luigi

OCCHI FONDI NERI see Kalman, Emerich

OCCHI SOAVI see Zandonai, Riccardo

OCENAS, ANDREJ (1911-   )
     Ako Hviezdy Padaju *song cycle
          high solo,pno SLOV.HUD.FOND s.p.
                                        (O42)

OCH ALLA GOTLANDS GOSSAR see Mehler,
     Friedrich

OCH FAST DU SVIKIT DIN FLICKAS TRO see
Soderman, (Johan) August

OCH FINNS DET EN TANKE see Sibelius,
Jean

OCH FINS DET AN TANKE see Sibelius,
Jean

OCH HAR AR DUNGEN DAR GOKEN GOL see
Wideen, Ivar

OCH HAVETS UNGA TARNA see Pacius,
Fredrik

OCH HOR DU UNGA DORA
see Jag Tror Jag Far Borja Overge Att
Sorja

OCH INTE VILL JAG SORJA
solo,pno GEHRMANS 217 s.p. contains
also: Varvindar Friska   (O43)

OCH INTE VILL JAG SORJA, MEN SORJER
ANDA see Sjogren, Emil

OCH JUNGFRUN GICK AT KILLAN
solo,pno GEHRMANS 216 s.p. contains
also: Och Minns Du Vad Du Lovade
                                (O44)

OCH LIGDY NU EN SLAEPT see Weegenhuise,
Johan

OCH LINDEN BLOMMAR see Olsson, Otto
Emmanuel

OCH MINNS DU VAD DU LOVADE
see Och Jungfrun Gick At Killan

OCH RIDDAREN DROG UTI OSTERLAND see
Peterson-Berger, (Olof) Wilhelm

OCH STOD DU I DEN KALLA BLAST see
Kilpinen, Yrio

OCH VOOR DEN DOOT see Horst, Anton van
der

OCHO CANCIONES HEBREAS MODERNAS see
Klotzman, D.

OCHO CANCIONES SALTENAS see Palma,
Athos

OCHO CANCIONES VASCAS see Arambarri, J.

OCHTENDBEDE see Zagwijn, Henri

O'CONNER, FREDERICK
Old House, The
high solo,pno (A flat maj) CRAMER
$.90   (O45)
low solo,pno (F maj) CRAMER s.p.
                                (O46)
Quietude
solo,pno CRAMER   (O47)

O'CONNOLLY
Sevillane
(Montoya, G.) solo,pno ENOCH s.p.
                                (O48)
(Montoya, G.) solo,acap ENOCH s.p.
                                (O49)
Votre Ame
(Montoya, G.) solo,pno ENOCH s.p.
                                (O50)

O'CONNOR, SHAMUS
Macnamara's Band
solo,orch (G maj) ASHDOWN s.p., ipr
                                (O51)

O'CONNOR-MORRIS, G.
Alleluia
high solo,pno (E flat maj) BOOSEY
$1.50   (O52)
low solo,pno (D maj) BOOSEY $1.50
                                (O53)
Communion *sac
solo,pno PATERSON s.p.   (O54)

Father-Mother *sac
solo,pno PATERSON s.p.   (O55)

Fill Thou My Life, O Lord *sac
solo,pno PATERSON s.p.   (O56)

Fulfilment *sac
solo,pno PATERSON s.p.   (O57)

Lord Is My Shepherd, The *sac
solo,pno PATERSON s.p.   (O58)

Now Are We The Sons Of God *sac
solo,pno PATERSON s.p.   (O59)

Praise *sac
solo,pno PATERSON s.p.   (O60)

Psalm 91 *sac
solo,pno PATERSON s.p.   (O61)

OCTOBRE see Rhene-Baton

OCTOBRIAN MOOD
see Long Wharf Songs

OCTROI see Schmitt, Florent

OD PRAGA DO PRAGA see Sivic, Pavle

OD STMIVANI DO USVITU see Tucapsky,
Antonin

OD UNORA 1948 see Haba, Alois

ODA NA MLADOST' see Kafenda, Frico

ODA SAFICA see Brahms, Johannes,
Sapphische Ode

ODAK, KRSTO (1888-1965)
Mura River Flowing, The
[Slav] solo,pno CROATICA s.p. (O62)

ODAS SANG see Carlson, Bengt (Ivar)

ODDONE, E.
Autunno
solo,pno BONGIOVANI 929 s.p.   (O63)

Ben Arrivata
2 soli,pno BONGIOVANI 902 s.p. see
also Rispetti E Stornelli Della
Lucchesia   (O64)

Che C-Cosa E Stato?
2 soli,pno BONGIOVANI 901 s.p. see
also Rispetti E Stornelli Della
Lucchesia   (O65)

Epistola Di Pulcinella A Columbina
solo,pno BONGIOVANI 930 s.p.   (O66)

I Canti Dei Campi
2 soli,pno BONGIOVANI 1079 s.p.
                                (O67)
Rispetti E Stornelli Della Lucchesia
2 soli,pno cmplt ed BONGIOVANI 899
s.p.
contains & see also: Ben
Arrivata; Che C-Cosa E Stato?;
Sento Un Fischietto Venire Di
Lontano; Si Da Principio A
Questa Serenata; Stornelli;
Vedo Un Cavallin   (O68)

Sento Un Fischietto Venire Di Lontano
2 soli,pno BONGIOVANI 900 s.p. see
also Rispetti E Stornelli Della
Lucchesia   (O69)

Sera
solo,pno BONGIOVANI 928 s.p.   (O70)

Si Da Principio A Questa Serenata
2 soli,pno BONGIOVANI 904 s.p. see
also Rispetti E Stornelli Della
Lucchesia   (O71)

Stornelli
2 soli,pno BONGIOVANI 905 s.p. see
also Rispetti E Stornelli Della
Lucchesia   (O72)

Vedo Un Cavallin
2 soli,pno BONGIOVANI 903 s.p. see
also Rispetti E Stornelli Della
Lucchesia   (O73)

Versi Per Lei
solo,pno BONGIOVANI 931 s.p.   (O74)

ODE see Diamond, David

ODE see Goossen, Frederic

ODE see Zagwijn, Henri

ODE A DIANE ET A APOLLON see Binet,
Jean

ODE A LA MUSIQUE see Rasse, Francois

ODE DU PREMIER JOUR DE MAI see
Berkeley, Lennox

ODE GENETHLIAQUE see Molitor, J.B.

ODE SAPHIQUE see Brahms, Johannes,
Sapphische Ode

ODE TO FREEDOM see Jacobi, Frederick

ODE TO GREAT MEN see Scott, Cyril Meir

ODE TO JOY see Beethoven, Ludwig van

ODE TO LOVE see Goemanne, Noel

ODE TO THE MUSE, PROSODION see
Ruyneman, Daniel

ODE TO THE WEST WIND see Arnell,
Richard

ODELETTE see Aubert, Louis-Francois-
Marie

ODELETTE see Legley, Victor

ODELETTE see Voormolen, Alexander
Nicolas

ODELETTE see Vredenburg, Max

ODELETTE X see Witkowski, Georges
Martin

ODELETTTE VIII see Witkowski, Georges
Martin

ODES ANACREONTIQUES see Roussel, Albert

ODESVISAN see Nordqvist, Gustaf

ODEVISAN see Peterson-Berger, (Olof)
Wilhelm

ODILE see Ferroud, Pierre-Octave

ODINS MEERESRITT see Loewe, Carl

ODSEVI HAJAMOVIH STIHOV see Jirim,
Frantisek

ODYSSEUS AND NAUSIKAA see Flothius,
Marius

OEDIPUS' CRADLE SONG see Avshalomov,
Jacob

OEILLETS see Tremisot, Ed.

O'ER THE MOOR see Lawson, Malcolm

O'ER WAITING HARP STRINGS OF THE MIND
see Boardman, E.

OERANIA see Zagwijn, Henri

OF ALL THE BIRDS see Jacob

OF FLOWERS THE FAIREST see Bach, Johann
Sebastian

OF HIJ ZAL KOMEN see Cuypers, H.

OF HIS GREAT LOVE see Ware, Broadman

OF LOVE see Berger, Jean

OF LOVE I SING see Peterson, John W.

OF NIGHT AND THE SEA see Palmer, Robert

OF WEEPING see Finney, Ross Lee

OF YOU I DREAM see Marzials, Theo

OFF TO THE GREENWOOD see Brahe, May H.

OFFENBACH, ISAAC
Brotherhood *sac
(Binder, A.W.) high solo,pno
TRANSCON. TV 486 $.60   (O75)
(Binder, A.W.) med solo,pno
TRANSCON. TV 487 $.60   (O76)

OFFENBACH, JACQUES (1819-1880)
All The Birds Above A-Winging *see
Les Oiseaux Dans La Charmille

Barcarolla *see Barcarolle

Barcarolle (from Les Contes
D'Hoffmann)
low solo,pno (C maj) CENTURY 3623
                                (O77)
med solo,pno (D maj) CENTURY 1690
                                (O78)
"Barcarolla" [Fr/Span] S solo,pno
RICORDI-ARG BA 8738 s.p.   (O79)

Belle Nuit, O Nuit D'amour (from Les
Contes D'Hoffmann)
[Fr] TBar soli,pno CHOUDENS C89
s.p.   (O80)
[Fr] 2 soli,pno (D maj) CRAMER
                                (O81)
[Fr] solo,pno CRAMER   (O82)
[Fr] 2 soli,pno (F maj) CRAMER
                                (O83)
"Night Of Stars And Night Of Love"
low solo,pno (C maj) CRAMER (O84)
"Night Of Stars And Night Of Love"
med solo,pno (D maj) CRAMER (O85)
"Night Of Stars And Night Of Love"
high solo,pno (F maj) CRAMER
                                (O86)
"Night Of Stars And Night Of Love"
2 soli,pno (F maj) CRAMER   (O87)
"Night Of Stars And Night Of Love"
2 soli,pno (D maj) CRAMER   (O88)
"Night Of Stars, Night Of Love" 2
high soli,pno (F maj) ALLANS s.p.
                                (O89)
"Night Of Stars, Night Of Love" 2
low soli,pno (D maj) ALLANS s.p.
                                (O90)
"Night Of Stars, Night Of Love" med
solo,pno (D maj) ALLANS s.p.
                                (O91)
"Night Of Stars, Night Of Love" low
solo,pno (C maj) ALLANS s.p.
                                (O92)
"Night Of Stars, Night Of Love"

OFFENBACH, JACQUES (cont'd.)

    high solo,pno (F maj) ALLANS s.p.
                   (O93)
    "O Lovely Night" [Fr/Eng] S solo,
    pno (F maj) SCHIRM.G $.75 (O94)
    "O Lovely Night" [Fr/Eng] SA/MezA
    soli,pno SCHIRM.G $1.00 (O95)

C'est L'Espagne
    solo,pno CRAMER   (O96)

C'est Une Chanson D'amour (from Les
    Contes D'Hoffmann)
    [Fr] ST soli,pno CHOUDENS C278 s.p.
                   (O97)
    [Fr] Mez/Bar solo,pno CHOUDENS C276
    s.p.   (O98)
    [Fr] MezBar soli,pno CHOUDENS C275
    s.p.   (O99)

Doll's Song
    low solo,pno (F maj) CRAMER (O100)
    high solo,pno (A flat maj) CRAMER
                 (O101)

Elle A Fui (from Les Contes
    D'Hoffmann)
    [Fr] S solo,pno CHOUDENS C88 s.p.
                 (O102)

Enfant Aux Airs D'Imperatrice
    [Fr] Bar solo,pno CHOUDENS C84 s.p.
                 (O103)

Gendarmes *sac
    2 med soli,pno (D maj) ALLANS s.p.
                 (O104)
    2 med soli,pno (D maj) ALLANS s.p.
                 (O105)
    2 high soli,pno (F maj) ALLANS s.p.
                 (O106)
    2 high soli,pno (F maj) ALLANS s.p.
                 (O107)
    "Gendarmes' Duet" 2 low soli,pno (D
    maj) BOOSEY $2.00   (O108)
    "Gendarmes' Duet" 2 high soli,pno
    (F maj) BOOSEY $2.00 (O109)

Gendarmes' Duet *see Gendarmes

I En Skog Pa Berget Ida
    solo,pno LUNDQUIST s.p. (O110)

Il Etait Une Fois (from Les Contes
    D'Hoffmann)
    [Fr] T solo,pno CHOUDENS C86 s.p.
                 (O111)

Je Ne Sais Vraiment Madame Comment
    Vous Dire (from Les Brigands)
    [Fr] med solo,pno CHOUDENS C83 s.p.
                 (O112)

Legend Of Kleinzack (from Tales Of
    Hoffmann)
    solo,pno CRAMER   (O113)

Les Oiseaux Dans La Charmille (from
    Les Contes D'Hoffmann)
    [Fr] S solo,pno CHOUDENS C87 s.p.
                 (O114)
    "All The Birds Above A-Winging"
    [Fr/Eng] S solo,pno (A flat maj)
    SCHIRM.G $.75   (O115)

Letter Song *see Perichole's Letter

Leuchte, Heller Spiegel Mir (from Les
    Contes D'Hoffmann)
    solo,pno DOBLINGER 08 562 s.p.
                 (O116)

Mirror Song (from Les Contes
    D'Hoffmann)
    solo,pno CRAMER   (O117)

My Pretty Dove (from Tales Of
    Hoffmann)
    solo,pno CRAMER   (O118)

Nar Jag Var Prins Utav Arkadien
    solo,pno LUNDQUIST s.p. (O119)

Night Of Stars And Night Of Love
    *see Belle Nuit, O Nuit D'amour

Night Of Stars, Night Of Love *see
    Belle Nuit, O Nuit D'amour

Non Loin Du Pays De Gascogne
    [Fr] med solo,pno CHOUDENS C82 s.p.
                 (O120)

O Dieu De Quelle Ivresse (from Les
    Contes D'Hoffmann)
    [Fr] T solo,pno CHOUDENS C280 s.p.
                 (O121)

O Lovely Night *see Belle Nuit, O
    Nuit D'amour

Orfeus V Podsveti
    solo,pno SUPRAPHON s.p. (O122)

Perichole's Letter (from La
    Perichole)
    [Fr/Eng] med solo,pno (E flat maj)
    SCHIRM.G $.85   (O123)
    "Letter Song" S solo,pno BOOSEY
    $1.50   (O124)
    "Letter Song" solo,pno (E flat maj)
    ALLANS s.p.   (O125)

OFFENBACH, JACQUES (cont'd.)

    Perichole's Tipsy Song (from La
    Perichole)
    [Fr/Eng] med solo,pno (E flat maj)
    SCHIRM.G $.60   (O126)

    Scintille Diamant (from Les Contes
    D'Hoffmann)
    [Fr] Bar solo,pno CHOUDENS C90 s.p.
                 (O127)

    Spaniard Knows (from La Perichole)
    solo,pno BOOSEY $1.50 (O128)

    Une Poupee Aux Yeux D'email (from Les
    Contes D'Hoffmann)
    [Fr] S solo,pno CHOUDENS C271 s.p.
                 (O129)

OFFENE ARME UND POCHENDE BRUST see
    Sjogren, Emil

OFFENES HAUS see Felix, Vaclav,
    Otevreny Dum

OFFERANDE see Boedijn, Gerard H.

OFFERGAVE see Devreese, Godefroid,
    Offrande

OFFERING see Laubin, E.F.

OFFERTA see Cimara, Pietro

OFFERTA MUSICALE see Contilli, Gino

OFFRANDE see Boussion, E.

OFFRANDE see Devreese, Godefroid

OFFRANDE see Levidis, Dimitri

OFFRANDE see Davico, Vincenzo

OFFRANDES see Varese, Edgar

OFFRANDES see Varese, Edgar

OFT DECKEN WOLKEN see Handel, George
    Frideric, Cuopre Tal Volta Il Cielo

OFT IN THE STILLY NIGHT see Hughes,
    Herbert

OG ALLE MINE VISER see Beck, Thomas
    [Ludvigsen]

OG JEG VIL DRAGE FRA SYDENS BLOMMER see
    Sjogren, Emil

OG JEG VIL HA MEG EN HJERTENSKJAER see
    Grieg, Edvard Hagerup

OG KAN MIN HU DU EJ FORSTAAE see
    Sjogren, Emil

OGGI see Ferritto, John

OGGI HO VISTO UNA ROSA see Toni, Alceo

OGIER LE DANOIS see Holmes, Alfred

OGIHARA, TOSHITSUGU (1910-   )
    Six Poemes Of Eiko Sadamatsu
    S solo,clar,vcl,pno JAPAN 7402 s.p.
                 (O130)

OGNI PENA CCHIU SPIETATA see Pergolesi,
    Giovanni Battista

OGNI SABATO AVRETE IL LUME ACCESO see
    Gordigiani, Luigi

OH, BELIEVE see Mozart, Wolfgang
    Amadeus, Porgi, Amor, Qualche
    Ristoro

OH, BEWARE see Strauss, Johann, Oh
    Habet Acht

OH BOAT, COME BACK TO ME see Beekhuis,
    Hanna

OH, BY AN' BY *spir
    (Roberton, Hugh S.) 3 soli,pno
    ROBERTON 72102 s.p. (O131)

OH! CH'AL SCUSA!
    (Carlo, Musi) solo,pno (Bolognese
    dialect) BONGIOVANI 2077 s.p. see
    from El Mi Canzunett (O132)

OH! CHE MIRAQUEL!
    (Carlo, Musi) solo,pno (Bolognese
    dialect) BONGIOVANI 2065 s.p. see
    from El Mi Canzunett (O133)

OH! CHE ZUCCA
    (Carlo, Musi) solo,pno (Bolognese
    dialect) BONGIOVANI 2081 s.p. see
    from El Mi Canzunett (O134)

OH, COULD I BUT EXPRESS IN SONG see
    Malashkin, Leonid Dimitrievitch

OH! DE' VERD'ANNI MIEI see Verdi,
    Giuseppe

OH DEAR! OH DEAR! OH DEAR!!!
    (Newton, Ernest) 2 soli,pno CRAMER
                 (O135)

OH DEAR! WHAT CAN THE MATTER BE? see
    Bax, Sir Arnold

OH DIDN'T IT RAIN *spir
    (Burleigh, H. T.) high solo,pno
    BELWIN $1.50   (O136)

OH FAIR TO SEE see Finzi, Gerald

OH FATAL GIFT see Verdi, Giuseppe, O
    Don Fatale

OH! FIE, SHEPHERD, FIE see Poston,
    Elizabeth

OH! FOR A CLOSER WALK WITH GOD see
    Foster, Myles Birket

OH FOR A MARCH WIND see Head, Michael
    (Dewar)

OH GREAT GOD *sac
    (Carmichael, Ralph) solo,pno WORD
    S-270   (O137)

OH GREAT GOD *sac,CC10L
    (Carmichael, Ralph) solo,pno WORD
    37539 $2.50   (O138)

OH HABET ACHT see Strauss, Johann

OH! HAD I JUBAL'S LYRE see Handel,
    George Frideric

OH, HOLD THOU ME UP see Marcello,
    Benedetto

OH HOLY NIGHT see Adam, Adolphe-Charles

OH, HOW BLESSED see Buxtehude, Dietrich

OH HOW HE LOVES YOU AND ME see Kaiser,
    Kurt

OH, HOW OFTEN see Steffani, Agostino,
    Quanto, Quanto

OH, I NEED HIM see Crouch, Andrae

OH! IL SIGNORE VI MANDA see Mascagni,
    Pietro

OH! J'ETOUFFAIS see Mussorgsky, Modest

OH! LA PITOYABLE AVENTURE see Ravel,
    Maurice

OH! LA TROUBLANTE VOLUPTE see
    Cuvillier, Charles

OH, LORD IS IT I *sac,gospel
    solo,pno ABER.GRP. $1.50 (O139)

OH LORD SPREAD THY WINGS O'ER ME see
    Webber, Lloyd

OH, LORD, WHAT THEN *sac,spir
    (Rivenburg) med solo,pno (C maj)
    BOSTON $1.50   (O140)

OH, LOVE! see Fulton, F.

OH! MA NINI, MA NINETTE see Bozi,
    Harold de

OH! MES AMOURS see Arrieu, Claude

OH MISTRESS MINE see Castelnuovo-
    Tedesco, Mario

OH MO'NAH see Washburn, C.

OH! MY BELOVED DADDY! see Puccini,
    Giacomo, O Mio Babbino Caro

OH, MY NATIVE COUNTRY see Kozina,
    Marijan, O Domovina

OH MY WILD ROSE see Haddock, B.

OH, NEVER SING TO ME AGAIN see
    Rachmaninoff, Sergey Vassilievitch

OH! OH! QU'EST-CE QUE C'EST see
    Debussy, Claude

OH! OPEN THE DOOR *folk,Scot
    solo,pno (C maj/E flat maj) PATERSON
    FS75 s.p.   (O141)

OH, PETER, GO RING DEM BELLS *spir
    (Roberton, Hugh S.) 3 soli,pno
    ROBERTON 72095 s.p. (O142)

OH! PETITE ETOILE see Chabrier,
    Emmanuel

OH, PRAY FOR PEACE see Brahe, May H.

OH, PROMISE ME see De Koven, Henry
    Louis Reginald

OH! QUAND JE DORS see Liszt, Franz

OH! QUAND JE DORS see Liszt, Franz, O Komm' In Traum

OH! QUANTE VOLTE see Bellini, Vincenzo

OH QUERER QUE ME TIENDES LAS ALAS see Espoile, Raoul H.

OH, SAVIOR see Crouch, Andrae

OH SEE HOW THICK THE GOLDCUP FLOWERS see Orr, Charles Wilfred

OH THAT WE TWO WERE MAYING see Nevin, Ethelbert Woodbridge

OH, THE COMFORT OF A GARDEN see Arundale, Claude

OH, THE SUMMER see Coleridge-Taylor, Samuel

OH, THE SWEET DELIGHTS OF LOVE see Purcell, Henry

OH THOU MINE OWN DEAR EVENING STAR see Wagner, Richard, O Du Mein Holder Abendstern

OH, THOU WAVING FIELD OF GOLDEN GRAIN see Rachmaninoff, Sergey Vassilievitch, Harvest Of Sorrow, The

OH, WHAT A BEAUTIFUL CITY! *sac,spir
(Boatner) high solo,pno (B flat maj) SCHIRM.G $.75   (O143)
(Boatner) med-low solo,pno (G maj) SCHIRM.G $.75   (O144)

OH WHAT A COUNTRY FOR PEOPLE TO MARRY see Shield, William

OH, WHAT A DAY *sac,gospel
solo,pno ABER.GRP. $1.50   (O145)

OH, WHAT A SUNRISE see Ballard, Ann

OH WHAT LOVE see Rich, Fred

OH, WHEN I WAS IN LOVE see Dukelsky, Vladimir

OH WHERE DO I CROSS THESE RANGES? see Salas, Juan Orrego, Por Do Pasare Esta Sierra?

OH, WOULD I WERE THAT SWEET LINNET see Beethoven, Ludwig van

OH, YOICKS! TALLY HO! see Irving, W.W.S.

O'HARA, GEOFFREY (1882-1867)
Art Thou The Christ?
high solo,pno (C min) SCHIRM.G $.85   (O146)
Come To The Stable With Jesus *sac, Xmas
high solo,pno HARRIS $.85   (O147)
low solo,pno HARRIS $.85   (O148)
med solo,pno HARRIS $.85   (O149)
low solo,pno (F maj) SCHIRM.G $.85   (O150)
med solo,pno (A flat maj) SCHIRM.G $.85   (O151)
high solo,pno (C maj) SCHIRM.G $.85   (O152)
Could I Have Held His Nail-Pierced Hands *sac
med-high solo,pno (D maj) SCHIRM.G $.85   (O153)
Count Your Blessings *sac
low solo,pno (D flat maj) SCHIRM.G $.85   (O154)
Father
high solo,pno (E flat maj) WILLIS $.60   (O155)
low solo,pno (C maj) WILLIS $.60   (O156)
Give A Man A Horse He Can Ride
low solo,pno (G maj) WILLIS $.60   (O157)
high solo,pno (D maj) ALLANS s.p.   (O158)
med solo,pno (B flat maj) ALLANS s.p.   (O159)
low solo,pno (G maj) ALLANS s.p.   (O160)
med solo,pno (B flat maj) WILLIS $.60   (O161)
high solo,pno (D maj) WILLIS $.60   (O162)
God Lives In My Heart *sac
low solo,pno (A maj) SCHIRM.G $.75   (O163)
He Smiled On Me *sac
med-low solo,pno (G maj) SCHIRM.G $1.25   (O164)
high solo,pno (B flat maj) SCHIRM.G $1.25   (O165)

O'HARA, GEOFFREY (cont'd.)
Hour Of Calvary, The *sac
med solo,pno BELWIN $1.50   (O166)
high solo,pno BELWIN $1.50   (O167)
I Carried Both Lord And King *sac
low solo,pno (E flat maj) SCHIRM.G $.60   (O168)
high solo,pno (G maj) SCHIRM.G $.60   (O169)
I Love A Little Cottage
(Stott) high solo&low solo,pno FOX, S   (O170)
(Stott) solo,pno FOX,S   (O171)
(Stott) med solo&low solo,pno FOX,S   (O172)
(Stott) ST soli,pno FOX,S   (O173)
I Walked Today Where Jesus Walked *sac
ABar soli,pno SCHIRM.G $1.00 (O174)
ST soli,pno SCHIRM.G $1.00 (O175)
SA soli,pno SCHIRM.G $1.00 (O176)
low solo,pno (E maj) SCHIRM.G $1.25   (O177)
med solo,pno (G maj) SCHIRM.G $1.25   (O178)
high solo,pno (B flat maj) SCHIRM.G $1.25   (O179)
I Walked Today Where Jesus Walked *see Twoig
I Was The Tree *sac,Gen
med solo,pno (F maj) WILLIS $.75   (O180)
high solo,pno (A maj) WILLIS $.75   (O181)
low solo,pno (D maj) WILLIS $.75   (O182)
If Christ Came Back
med solo,pno PRESSER $.75   (O183)
Living God, The *sac,Gen
med solo,pno (F min) WILLIS $.75   (O184)
high solo,pno (G min) WILLIS $.75   (O185)
med solo,pno (A flat maj) ALLANS s.p.   (O186)
low solo,pno (F maj) ALLANS s.p.   (O187)
high solo,pno (B flat maj) ALLANS s.p.   (O188)
low solo,pno (D min) WILLIS $.75   (O189)
Lord Is My Captain *see Twohig
Must Jesus Bear Another Cross? *sac
low solo,pno (C maj) SCHIRM.G $.85   (O190)
med solo,pno (E flat maj) SCHIRM.G $.85   (O191)
high solo,pno (G maj) SCHIRM.G $.85   (O192)
O Let Us Turn To Bethlehem *sac
low solo,pno (C maj) SCHIRM.G $.75   (O193)
Our Flag
high solo,pno (D maj) WILLIS $.60   (O194)
low solo,pno (C maj) WILLIS $.60   (O195)
Prayer Of Thanksgiving *sac,Dut
(Downing, K.) med-high solo,pno (E flat maj) SCHIRM.G $.85   (O196)
(Downing, K.) low solo,pno (C maj) SCHIRM.G $.85   (O197)
Soft Were Your Hands, Dear Jesus *sac,Gen
high solo,pno (E flat maj) WILLIS $.75   (O198)
med solo,pno (F flat maj) WILLIS $.75   (O199)
low solo,pno (B flat maj) WILLIS $.75   (O200)
Star Road, The *sac
med-low solo,pno (C maj) SCHIRM.G $.75   (O201)
Still Small Voice, The *sac
med solo,pno (E flat maj) SCHIRM.G $.75   (O202)
Take My Life O Lord
solo,pno BRODT $.75   (O203)
Thanks *sac
med solo,pno (C maj) SCHIRM.G $.75   (O204)
low solo,pno (A maj) SCHIRM.G $.75   (O205)
This Is God's Love *sac
med-high solo,pno (C maj) SCHIRM.G $.85   (O206)
low solo,pno (A maj) SCHIRM.G $.85   (O207)
This Is The Story Of Jesus *sac
low solo,pno (C maj) BOSTON $1.50   (O208)

O'HARA, GEOFFREY (cont'd.)
Waters Of Thy Love, The *sac,Gen
high solo,pno (D maj) WILLIS $.60   (O209)
low solo,pno (B flat maj) WILLIS $.60   (O210)

O'HARA SONGS, THE see Feldman, Morton

OHDAKE see Salonen, Sulo, Tistel

OHE! LES AMOUREUX see Delmet, Paul

OHEL SCHA'H see Schlionsky, Verdina

OHIE MENECHE see Giannini, Vittorio

OHIME CH'IO CADO see Monteverdi, Claudio

OHNAKA, MEGUMI (1924-   )
Mystery Of Love *song cycle
S solo,pno JAPAN 7210 s.p.   (O211)

OHNE SONNE see Mussorgsky, Modest, Sunless

OHNIVE LETO see Soukup, Vladimir

OHOH KULLAISTA KOTIA see Kilpinen, Yrio

OHR DER FRUHE see Gerhard

OI AVREMEL *Jew
solo,pno KAMMEN 84 $1.00   (O212)

OI HERRA, IHMISEN SYDAN see Fordell, Erik (Fritiof), Ack, Herre, Ett Manniskohjarta

OI KALLIS SUOMENMAA see Klemetti, Heikki

OI KIITOS, SA LUOJANI ARMOLLINEN see Merikanto, Oskar

OI MAMME! BIN ICH FARLIEBT!! see Ellstein, Abe

OI, MINNE EMON LINTUNEN LENSI see Merikanto, Oskar

OI, OI, ICH HOB DICH *Jew
solo,pno KAMMEN 435 $1.00   (O213)

OI SA RIEMUISA
see Pieni Joulutervehdyts

OI UKKO, YLINEN HERRA see Kilpinen, Yrio

OI VEI IS TZU MIR *Jew
solo,pno KAMMEN 450 $1.00   (O214)

OI WET MIR DER REBE SHMEISEN *Jew
solo,pno KAMMEN 56 $1.00   (O215)

OIF'N PRIPETCHOK *folk,Jew
solo,pno KAMMEN 6 $1.00 see also Favorite Jewish Songs, Vol. 2   (O216)

OISGESHPIELT see Meyerowitz, David

OISI MULLA VALLAN MIEKKA see Kilpinen, Yrio

OJOS CLAROS, SERENOS see Farga, O.

OJOS GARCOS HA LA NINA see Salas, Juan Orrego

OKOLOWICZ, E.
J'ai Passe Par La
solo,pno ENOCH s.p.   (O217)
solo,acap ENOCH s.p.   (O218)

OLAF, IL VECCHIO RE see Gandino, Adolfo

OLAZABAL, ZIRSO DE
Cancion
see Dos Canciones Castellanas De Garcilaso De La Vega

Dos Canciones Castellanas De Garcilaso De La Vega
solo,pno cmplt ed RICORDI-ARG BA 11626 s.p.
contains: Cancion; Villancico   (O219)

Villancico
see Dos Canciones Castellanas De Garcilaso De La Vega

OLCOTT
My Wild Irish Rose
solo,pno ALLANS s.p.   (O220)
solo,pno (available in 3 keys) ASHLEY $.95   (O221)

OLD ABRAM BROWN
see Songs Of Wonder

OLD AGE AND NIGHT see Wijdeveld, Wolfgang

OLD AMERICAN SONGS, VOL. 1 see Copland, Aaron

OLD AMERICAN SONGS, VOL. 2 see Copland, Aaron

OLD AUSTRALIAN BUSH BALADS see Sutherland

OLD BARK HUT see Lavater

OLD BLACK JOE see Foster, Stephen Collins

OLD BRIDGE AT FLORENCE, THE see Mallinson, (James) Albert

OLD CAROL see Quilter, Roger

OLD CLOTHES AND FINE CLOTHES see Shaw, Martin

OLD ENGLISH MELODIES *CCU,Eng
(Wilson, H. Lane) solo,pno BOOSEY
$5.00   (O222)

OLD ENGLISH SONG CYCLE, AN
(Coleman, Henry) PATERSON high solo,
pno s.p.; low solo,pno s.p.
contains: Arne, Thomas Augustine,
Love Me Or Not; Handel, George
Frideric, Pack Clouds Away;
Howard, Love In Thy Youth (O223)

OLD FAMILIAR FACES, THE see Mul, Jan

OLD FASHIONED REVIVAL HOUR SONGS, VOL.
1 *sac,CC129U
(Fuller; Green; Macdougall) solo,pno
WORD 20032 $1.95   (O224)

OLD FASHIONED REVIVAL HOUR SONGS, VOL.
2 *sac,CCU
(Fuller; Green) solo,pno WORD 20033
$1.50   (O225)

OLD FISHERMAN, THE see Bantock, Granville

OLD FLAGGED PATH see Arundale, Claude

OLD FOLKS AT HOME *CC40U
(Bohlander) [Eng] solo,gtr SCHOTTS
5041 s.p.   (O226)

OLD FOLKS AT HOME see Foster, Stephen Collins

OLD FRENCH CAROL see Liddle, Samuel

OLD FURNITURE see Arundale, Claude

OLD HARP, THE see Heilner, Irwin

OLD HOUSE, THE see Geehl, Henry Ernest

OLD HOUSE, THE see O'Conner, Frederick

OLD JERUSALEM see Chajes, Julius, Hineh Bar'chu

OLD KING, THE see Duke, John Woods

OLD LAD, THE see Bilotti, Anton

OLD MAN AT THE CROSSING see Pugh

OLD MASTERS OF THE GERMAN LIED *CC46U,
17-18th cent
[Ger] med solo,pno PETERS 3495 $6.00
                               (O227)

OLD MOTHER HUBBARD see Hely-Hutchinson,
(Christian) Victor

OLD MOTHER HUBBARD see Hutchinson

OLD MOTHER SEA see Arundale, Claude

OLD PAINT see Sanders, Robert L.

OLD POEM see Copland, Aaron

OLD REFRAIN, THE see Kreisler

OLD RUGGED CROSS, THE see Bennard, George

OLD RUGGED CROSS MADE THE DIFFERENCE,
THE see Gaither

OLD RUSSIAN ROMANCES *CCU
[Russ] solo,pno MEZ KNIGA 62 s.p.
                               (O228)

OLD SEA DOG see Hilliam, B.C.

OLD SHEPHERD'S PRAYER, THE see
Anderson, William H.

OLD SHIP OF ZION, THE see Lewis, Ray

OLD SIR FAULK see Walton, William

OLD SONG RE-SUNG, AN see Griffes,
Charles Tomlinson

OLD SPINET see Arundale, Claude

OLD-TIME FAITH, THE see Lister, Mosie

OLD TIME POPULAR SONGS, BOOK I *CCU
solo,pno PAXTON P15358 s.p.   (O229)

OLD TIME POPULAR SONGS, BOOK IV *CCU
solo,pno PAXTON P33105 s.p.   (O230)

OLD TIME WAY, THE see Cole, Elmer

OLD TOWLER see Shield, William

OLD TOWLER see Somervell, Arthur

OLD VIOLIN see Fisher, H.

OLD WOMAN, THE see Birch, Robert
Fairfax

OLD WOMAN, THE see Haufrecht, Herbert

OLD WOMAN, THE see Roberton, Hugh
Stevenson

OLDENBURG, BOB
Little Lamb Who Made Thee?
med solo,pno SEESAW $1.00   (O231)

More, So Much More *sac
med solo,pno CRESPUB CP-R 654 $1.00
                               (O232)
high solo,pno CRESPUB CP-R 656
$1.00   (O233)

OLDHAM, ARTHUR (1926-   )
Fishing
see Five Chinese Lyrics

Five Chinese Lyrics
high solo,pno NOVELLO 17.0261.00
s.p.
contains: Fishing; Gentle Wind,
A; Herd Boy's Song, The; Pedlar
Of Spells, The; Under The
Pondweed   (O234)

Gentle Wind, A
see Five Chinese Lyrics

Herd Boy's Song, The
see Five Chinese Lyrics

Pedlar Of Spells, The
see Five Chinese Lyrics

Under The Pondweed
see Five Chinese Lyrics

OLDHAM, DOUG
For Such A Time As This *sac,CC13UL
solo,pno BENSON BO860 $2.50 (O235)

Have You Heard...God Loves You *sac,
CC12UL
solo,pno BENSON BO465 $2.50 (O236)

Redemption Draweth Nigh *sac,CC13L
solo,pno BENSON BO467 $2.50 (O237)

OLDHAM SINGS GAITHER, VOL. I see
Gaither

OLDHAM SINGS GAITHER, VOL. II see
Gaither

OLE LUONANI SILLOIN see Tuuri, Jaako

OLGA'S SCENE AND ARIA see Tchaikovsky,
Piotr Ilyitch, Olga's Song

OLGA'S SONG see Tchaikovsky, Piotr
Ilyitch

OLI LEIVOSEN HELKETTA HAASSA see
Fougstedt, Nils-Eric, Det Var
Larksang Och Glans Over Liden

OLIT TUSKASTA VARISTEN HERANNYT SYON
see Kilpinen, Yrio

OLIVE, JOSEPH
Mar-Ri-Ia-A
S solo,fl,clar,horn,vln,vcl,2perc,
electronic tape sc AM.COMP.AL.
$13.20, ipa   (O238)

OLIVE TREE, THE
see By The Sea

OLIVER
What's The Time, Blackbird
low solo,pno (C maj) ALLANS s.p.
                               (O239)
high solo,pno (E flat maj) ALLANS
s.p.   (O240)

OLIVER, HERBERT
Buy My Strawberries
med solo,pno (G maj) ASHDOWN (O241)
low solo,pno (F maj) ASHDOWN (O242)
high solo,pno (B flat maj) ASHDOWN
                               (O243)

OLIVER, HERBERT (cont'd.)
Call, The
low solo,pno (G maj) ASHDOWN (O244)
med-high solo,pno (B flat maj)
ASHDOWN   (O245)
med solo,pno (A flat maj) ASHDOWN
                               (O246)
high solo,pno (D flat maj) ASHDOWN
                               (O247)

Dance While The World Is Young
low solo,pno (B flat maj) ASHDOWN
                               (O248)
high solo,pno (D maj) ASHDOWN
                               (O249)
med solo,pno (C maj) ASHDOWN (O250)

Dancing Lesson, The
high solo,orch (B flat maj) ASHDOWN
s.p., ipr   (O251)
med solo,orch (A maj) ASHDOWN s.p.,
ipr   (O252)
low solo,orch (G maj) ASHDOWN s.p.,
ipr   (O253)

Down Vauxhall Way
low solo,orch (C maj) ASHDOWN s.p.,
ipr   (O254)
high solo&low solo,pno ASHDOWN s.p.
                               (O255)
high solo,orch (E maj) ASHDOWN
s.p., ipr   (O256)
med-high solo,orch (E flat maj)
ASHDOWN s.p., ipr   (O257)
med solo,orch (D maj) ASHDOWN s.p.,
ipr   (O258)

Elopers, The
high solo&low solo,orch ASHDOWN
s.p., ipr   (O259)

Gipsy Spring
low solo,pno (D maj) ASHDOWN (O260)
high solo,pno (G maj) ASHDOWN
                               (O261)
med solo,pno (F maj) ASHDOWN (O262)

God Bless The Morning
high solo,pno (F maj) ASHDOWN
                               (O263)
med-high solo,pno (E flat maj)
ASHDOWN   (O264)
med solo,pno (D flat maj) ASHDOWN
                               (O265)
low solo,pno (C maj) ASHDOWN (O266)

Ladies Of Bath, The
high solo,pno (F maj) ASHDOWN
                               (O267)
med solo,pno (E flat maj) ASHDOWN
                               (O268)
low solo,pno (C maj) ASHDOWN (O269)

Love Divine
low solo,orch (C maj) ASHDOWN s.p.,
ipr   (O270)
high solo,orch (F maj) ASHDOWN
s.p., ipr   (O271)
med-high solo,orch (E flat maj)
ASHDOWN s.p., ipr   (O272)
med solo,orch (D flat maj) ASHDOWN
s.p., ipr   (O273)

Nightingales Of Lincoln's Inn
low solo,orch (D maj) ASHDOWN s.p.,
ipr   (O274)
high solo,orch (F maj) ASHDOWN
s.p., ipr   (O275)
med solo,orch (E flat maj) ASHDOWN
s.p., ipr   (O276)

O Day Divine
med solo,orch (D flat maj) ASHDOWN
s.p., ipr   (O277)
low solo,orch (C maj) ASHDOWN s.p.,
ipr   (O278)
high solo,orch (F maj) ASHDOWN
s.p., ipr   (O279)
med-high solo,orch (E flat maj)
ASHDOWN s.p., ipr   (O280)

Passing Show, The *song cycle
4 soli,pno ASHDOWN s.p.   (O281)

Songs Of Old London *CCU
ASHDOWN low solo,pno s.p.; med
solo,pno s.p.; high solo,pno s.p.
                               (O282)

Spreading The News
low solo,orch (G maj) ASHDOWN s.p.,
ipr   (O283)
med solo,orch (B flat maj) ASHDOWN
s.p., ipr   (O284)
high solo,orch (C maj) ASHDOWN
s.p., ipr   (O285)

When Throstles Sing
low solo,pno (C maj) CRAMER (O286)
high solo,pno (E flat maj) CRAMER
                               (O287)

OLL NATTURAN FER ENN AO DEYJA
see Fimm Numer I Islenzkum
Pjoobuningum

OLLONE, MAX D' (1875-1959)
Adieu
solo,pno (available in 2 keys)
ENOCH s.p. (O288)

Ave Maria *sac
[Lat] solo,org ENOCH s.p. (O289)
[Lat] solo,pno/harmonium ENOCH s.p.
(O290)

Fredegonde *cant
solo,pno ENOCH s.p. (O291)

Jeanne D'Arc A Domremy *ora
solo,pno ENOCH s.p. (O292)

La Vision De Dante
solo,pno ENOCH s.p. (O293)

Oublier
solo,pno (available in 2 keys)
ENOCH s.p. (O294)

Paques Fleuries
solo,pno (available in 2 keys)
ENOCH s.p. (O295)

Reve
solo,pno (available in 2 keys)
ENOCH s.p. (O296)

OLLOS HUOLETON, POIKAS VALVEILL' ON
*CC20U
(Turunen) solo,pno FAZER F 2622 s.p.
(O297)

OLMSTEAD, CLARENCE
So Is My Beloved
med solo,pno (A maj) SCHIRM.G $.75
(O298)

Thy Sweet Singing
high solo,pno (D flat maj) SCHIRM.G
$.75 (O299)

OLSEN, POUL ROVSING (1922-   )
A L'Inconnu *Op.48
solo,harp,5vln,3vla,2vcl,bvl,gtr sc
MOECK 5022 s.p. (O300)

OLSEN, SPARRE (1903-   )
A Seille
see Fem Sanger Fra Op. 52

Arefrykt For Livet
see Fem Sanger Fra Op. 52

Banvise *Op.26,No.2
see Tre Sanger

Fem Sanger Fra Op. 52
solo,pno MUSIKK s.p.
contains: A Seille; Arefrykt For
Livet; Pa Langferd; Vart Liv;
Vuggevise (O301)

Gluck Auf', Guds Fred
solo,pno MUSIKK s.p. (O302)

God Natt *Op.26,No.1
see Tre Sanger

Hymne, Aere Det Evige Forar I Livet
solo,pno MUSIKK s.p. (O303)

Kvi Tralar Det Ikkje Lenger I Skogen
see Tvo Songar

Malmfuru
solo,pno MUSIKK s.p. (O304)

Morgon - Dag - Kveld *Op.32,No.1-9
solo,pno MUSIKK s.p. (O305)

Pa Langferd
see Fem Sanger Fra Op. 52

Sju Krokann-Songar *Op.28,No.1-7,
CC7L
solo,pno MUSIKK s.p. (O306)

Til Min Gyldenlak *Op.26,No.3
see Tre Sanger

Tre Sanger
solo,pno MUSIKK s.p.
contains: Banvise, Op.26,No.2;
God Natt, Op.26,No.1; Til Min
Gyldenlak, Op.26,No.3 (O307)

Tvo Songar
solo,pno MUSIKK s.p.
contains: Kvi Tralar Det Ikkje
Lenger I Skogen; Voggsong
(O308)

Vart Liv
see Fem Sanger Fra Op. 52

Voggsong
see Tvo Songar

Vuggevise
see Fem Sanger Fra Op. 52

OLSHANETSKY, ALEX
Ich Benk Noch Der East Side Fin Amuhl
*Jew
solo,pno KAMMEN 460 $1.00 see also
JEWISH THEATRE SONGS, VOL. 1

OLSHANETSKY, ALEX (cont'd.)
(O309)

OLSON
Paradisets Timma
solo,pno LUNDQUIST s.p. (O310)

OLSON, DANIEL (1898-   )
Fest Pa Skansen
solo,pno GEHRMANS s.p. (O311)

Nu Loser Solen Sitt Blonda Har
see Tva Duetter

Psalmodikon
see Tva Duetter

Se Jag Star For Dorren Och Klapper
S/T solo,pno/org*vln GEHRMANS s.p.
(O312)

Stilla Komme, Och Valkomna
solo,org,opt vln GEHRMANS s.p.
(O313)

Tva Duetter
2 soli,pno GEHRMANS s.p.
contains: Nu Loser Solen Sitt
Blonda Har; Psalmodikon (O314)

OLSSON
Tre Lustiga Riddare *CC3U
solo,pno LUNDQUIST s.p. (O315)

OLSSON, OTTO EMMANUEL (1879-1964)
Dalvisa
solo,pno GEHRMANS 669 s.p. (O316)

Jan Hinnerk
solo,pno GEHRMANS 670 s.p. (O317)

Och Linden Blommar
solo,pno GEHRMANS s.p. (O318)

Septemberafton
solo,pno GEHRMANS s.p. (O319)

OLUF'S BALLADE see Gade, Niels Wilhelm

OM AV ALLT ERT HJARTA I MIG SOKEN see
Mendelssohn-Bartholdy, Felix, Sei
Stille Dem Herrn

OM DAGEN VID MITT ARBETE
solo,pno GEHRMANS 210 s.p. contains
also: Kristallen Den Fina (O320)

OM DE STILTE see Beyerman-Walraven,
Jeanne

OM GUD SA VILL
solo,pno LUNDQUIST s.p. (O321)

OM HET EEUWIGE see Schouwman, Hans

OM SOMMAREN see Nordqvist, Gustaf

OM SOMMAREN SKONA
solo,pno GEHRMANS 205 s.p. (O322)

OM TILL DIN BADD see Wiren, Dag Ivar

OM VAREN see Nordqvist, Gustaf

OMARTIAN
Jesus Made Me Higher *sac
solo,pno BENSON S6730-RS $1.25
(O323)

OMAT ON VIRRET OPPIMIANI see Kilpinen,
Yrio

OMBR DES BOIS see Handel, George
Frideric, Ombra Mai Fu

OMBRA CARA see Handel, George Frideric

OMBRA FELICE see Mozart, Wolfgang
Amadeus

OMBRA FELICE - IO TI LASCIO see Mozart,
Wolfgang Amadeus

OMBRA LEGGERA see Meyerbeer, Giacomo,
Ombre Legere

OMBRA MAI FU see Handel, George
Frideric

OMBRE see Bernard, R.

OMBRE see Liguori, E.

OMBRE DES BOIS see Rabey, Rene

OMBRE D'HAMLET see Berger, Jean

OMBRE ECLATEE see Bancquart, Alain

OMBRE ET LUEUR see Fischhof, R.

OMBRE ET LUMIERE see Wellings, M.

OMBRE LEGERE see Meyerbeer, Giacomo

OMBRES ADOREE see Duringer

OMBRES DES ARBRES DANS L'EAU see
Casterede, Jacques

OMENANKUKAT see Merikanto, Oskar

OMENS see Medtner, Nikolai Karlovitch

OMMEREN, A. V.
Zeven Liederen *CC7U
solo,pno ALSBACH s.p. (O324)

OMNIA TEMPUS HABENT see Zimmermann

OMNIPOTENCE see Schubert, Franz
(Peter), Die Allmacht

OMRIM YESHNA ERETZ see Engel, Joel

ON A DAY, ALACK THE DAY! see Ruyneman,
Daniel

ON A FLY DRINKING OUT OF HIS CUP see
Hindemith, Paul

ON A GREY DAY see O'Neill, Norman

ON A HOLIDAY see Gass, Irene

ON A KISS see Lawes, Henry

ON A ROSEBUD SENT TO HER LOVER see
Stevens, Halsey

ON A RUGGED HILL *sac,gospel
solo,pno ABER.GRP. $1.50 (O325)

ON A STORMY NIGHT VIII see Martino,
Donald, Aus Einer Sturmnacht VIII

ON BELIEF see Walvoord, John

ON CHERCHE QUI VOUS A NUI see Chabrier,
Emmanuel

ON CHRISTMAS DAY see Surdin, M.

ON DEATH see Diamond, David

ON DIST QUE see Schmitt, Florent

ON DIT LE PARISIEN see Messager, Andre

ON FRAPPE see Bosmans, Henriette

ON HEARING 'THE LAST ROSE OF SUMMER'
see Hindemith, Paul

ON HIGH RAISE YOUR GLASSES see Verdi,
Giuseppe, Libiamo Ne' Lieti Calici

ON HIS BLINDNESS see Gerschefski, Edwin

ON HIS BLINDNESS see Thybo, Leif

ON HUNDRED SONGS OF ENGLAND *CC100U
(Bantock, G.) low solo,pno PRESSER
$5.00 (O326)

ON IKKUNASSA LIEKKA see Snare, Sigurd,
I Fonstret Star Ett Ljus

ON JACOB'S PILLOW see Plumstead, Mary

ON JE VSE see Tucapsky, Antonin

ON KAIKKI SYKSYN TAHDET SYTTYNEET see
Kilpinen, Yrio

ON KUMPIAKI see Kilpinen, Yrio

ON LIFE'S HIGHWAY see Brown, Bertrand

ON M'A DIT see Lacome, Paul

ON MA JOURNEY *spir
(Boatner, Edward) high solo,pno
BELWIN $1.50 (O327)
(Boatner, Edward) low solo,pno BELWIN
$1.50 (O328)

ON MAY MORNING see Finney, Ross Lee

ON MIGHTY PENS see Haydn, (Franz)
Joseph

ON MY SHEPHERD I RELY see Bach, Johann
Sebastian

ON NEWLYN HILL see Rowley, Alec

ON RACONTE QU'UN ARCHONTE see Saint-
Saens, Camille

ON REVIENT TOUJOURS see Mana-Zucca,
Mme.

ON THE BEACH AT FONTANA see Sessions,
Roger

ON THE BIRTH OF HIS SON see Heilner,
Irwin

ON THE BLUE DANUBE see Strauss, Johann,
An Der Schonen Blauen Donau

ON THE CITY STREET see Lambert, Constant

ON THE DAY WHEN DEATH WILL KNOCK AT THY DOOR see Carpenter, John Alden

ON THE EVE OF HIS EXECUTION see Mourant, Walter

ON THE JERICHO ROAD *sac,gospel
solo,pno ABER.GRP. $1.50   (O329)

ON THE LAND AND ON THE SEA see Meyerowitz, Jan

ON THE LIFE OF MAN see Finney, Ross Lee

ON THE RAFT see Wuorinen, Charles

ON THE RIVER see Haussermann, R.

ON THE RIVER see Schubert, Franz (Peter), Auf Dem Strom

ON THE ROAD TO MANDALAY see Speaks, Oley

ON THE SEASHORE OF ENDLESS WORLDS see Carpenter, John Alden

ON THE SLEEP OF PLANTS see Jacobi, Frederick

ON THE TIDE-TOP see Needham, Alicia Adelaide

ON THE T'UNG T'ING LAKE see Avshalomov, Jacob

ON THE WAY HOME see Robinson

ON THE WAY HOME see Robinson, Betty Jean

ON THE WAY TO YOU see Wood, Daniel

ON THE WINGS OF THE WIND see Head, Michael (Dewar)

ON THIS DAY, O BEAUTIFUL MOTHER *sac
med solo,org (E flat maj) ASHLEY $1.00   (O330)

ON THIS DAY, O BEAUTIFUL MOTHER see Lambillotte, Louis

ON THIS DAY, O BEAUTIFUL MOTHER see Van Hulse, Camil

ON THIS ISLAND see Britten, Benjamin

ON TIME see Wellesz, Egon

ON WENLOCK EDGE see Vaughan Williams, Ralph

ON WINGS OF FAITH see Mendelssohn-Bartholdy, Felix

ON WINGS OF SONG see Mendelssohn-Bartholdy, Felix, Auf Flugeln Des Gesanges

ONAWAY, AWAKE, BELOVED see Cowen, Sir Frederic Hymen

ONBESCHRIJFELIJKE VREUGDE see Henkemans, Hans

ONBESCHRIJFELIJKE VREUGDE see Leeuw, Ton de

ONCE FELL A MAID ASLEEP see Dvorak, Antonin

ONCE I HEARD A SONG see Paisley, Artur

ONCE I LOVED A MAIDEN FAIR see Somervell, Arthur

ONCE ON A BOUGH see Tennent, H.M.

ONCE WHEN MY HEART see McGeoch, Daisy

ONDEE PRINTANIERE see King, Harold C.

ONDER JONGE BLOEMEN see Zweers, [Bernard]

ONE DAY AT A TIME see Wilkin, Marijohn

ONE DAY CLOSER see Wolfe, Lanny

ONE DAY I WILL see Mills

ONE DAY TOO LATE see Wolfe, Lanny

ONE FINE DAY see Puccini, Giacomo, Un Bel Di Vedremo

ONE FOOT IN EDEN see Binkerd, Gordon

ONE GIFT see Dodson, Carolyn

ONE HOUR OF LOVE see Baxter, Maude Stewart

ONE HUNDRED FAVORITE SONGS OF INSPIRATION *sac,CC100UL
solo,pno WORD 37756 $5.95   (O331)

ONE HUNDRED-ONE CHASSIDIC SONGS AND DANCES *CC101U
(Haydu, Andre; Mazur, Yakov) solo,pno OR-TAV $4.00   (O332)

ONE HUNDRED SONGS BY TEN MASTERS, VOL. II *CCU
low solo,pno PRESSER $5.00 contains works by: Brahms; Grieg; Strauss; Tchaikovsky; Wolf   (O333)

ONE HUNDRED SONGS YOU LOVE TO SING *sac,CC100UL
(Carmichael, Ralph) solo,pno WORD 37720 $5.95   (O334)

ONE HUNDRED TWELVE FAMILIAR HYMNS AND GOSPEL SONGS *CC112U
solo,pno WORD 075003 $.75   (O335)

ONE HUNDRED TWENTY-FOUR SONGS see Stougie

ONE IN HEART AND ONE IN MIND see Bach, Johann Sebastian

ONE KISS see Burrows, Rex

ONE LEFT BEHIND, THE see Wolfe, Lanny

ONE LITTLE CANDLE see Mysels

ONE LITTLE HOUR see Sharpe, Evelyn

ONE MASTER see Davidson, Mark

ONE MORE SKY, ONE MORE SEA see Birch, Robert Fairfax

ONE MORE VALLEY see Rambo

ONE MORNING IN MAY see Boatwright, Howard

ONE MORNING IN MAY see Murray, Alan

ONE MORNING, OH! SO EARLY see Diack, John Michael

ONE OF THESE DAYS see Adams

ONE PERFECT HOUR WITH YOU see Sawyer, Yvonne

ONE PERFECT LIFE see Blanchard, Richard

ONE PERSON see Levy, Marvin David

ONE SOLITARY LIFE see Bock, Fred

ONE SWEETLY SOLEMN THOUGHT see Ambrose, R.S.

ONE THING HAVE I DESIRED see Schutz, Heinrich

ONE THING I KNOW see McFadden, Larry

ONE TOUCH see Plunkett, Bonnie

ONE WAY see Hughes

ONE WORD IS TOO OFTEN PROFANED see Quilter, Roger

ONE WORD ONE SMILE see Tarrant, F.W.

ONEGIN'S SCENE AND ARIA see Tchaikovsky, Piotr Ilyitch, Onegin's Song

ONEGIN'S SONG see Tchaikovsky, Piotr Ilyitch

O'NEILL, CHARLES
When I Survey The Wondrous Cross *sac
low solo,pno (F maj) WATERLOO $.75   (O336)

O'NEILL, NORMAN (1875-1934)
Bird Songs *CCU
solo,pno CRAMER   (O337)

Five Rondels *CC5U
solo,pno CRAMER   (O338)

Golden Hour Of Noon, The
solo,pno CRAMER $.95   (O339)

Home Of Mine
solo,pno CRAMER   (O340)

I Have A Flaunting Air
solo,pno CRAMER   (O341)

May Lilies
solo,pno CRAMER $.95   (O342)

O'NEILL, NORMAN (cont'd.)

Musette
solo,pno CRAMER   (O343)

On A Grey Day
high solo,pno (F maj) CRAMER (O344)
low solo,pno (D flat maj) CRAMER   (O345)

When May Walks By
solo,pno CRAMER   (O346)

ONEYNDIG GOED see Sigtenhorst-Meyer, Bernhard van den

ONLY see Hubbard, H.

ONLY A LITTLE BOX OF SOLDIERS see Arnold, Malcolm

ONLY BE STILL see Bach, Johann Sebastian

ONLY BELIEVE see Rader

ONLY I see Smith

ONLY JESUS CAN SATISFY YOUR SOUL see Wolfe, Lanny

ONLY JESUS CAN SATISFY YOUR SOUL see Wolfe, Lanny

ONLY ONE LIFE see Wolfe, Lanny

ONLY SON FROM HEAVEN, THE see Bach, Johann Sebastian

ONMACHSTRANEN see Middeleer, Jean De

ONNELLISET see Kilpinen, Yrio

ONNELLISET see Merikanto, Oskar

ONNENI SAARI see Melartin, Erkki

ONNETON see Merikanto, Oskar

ONPA TIETTY TIETYSSANI see Kilpinen, Yrio

ONS LIED see Spoel, A.

ONS LIED see Tussenbroek, H. von

ONS PRINSESJE see Spoel, A.

ONTROERING see Middeleer, Jean De, Emotion

ONTWAKEN see Mulder, Herman

ONWARD CHRISTIAN SOLDIERS see Sullivan, Sir Arthur Seymour

ONWARD FOR GOD AND MY COUNTRY see Dolph

ONWARD, YE PEOPLES see Sibelius, Jean

ONZE CHANTS HEBRAIQUES see Shostakovich, Dmitri

ONZE VADER see Bonset, Jac.

ONZE VLAG see Wall, C. v.d.

OOGST see Schouwman, Hans

OOR AIN GLEN see McLeod, Robert

OORSPRONKELIJKE MELODIE see Wilhelmus van Nassouwe

OORT, H.C.V.
Abendlied *Op.21,No.1
see Vier Lieder

Avond *Op.20,No.1
see Twee Liederen

Avondstilte *Op.20,No.2
see Twee Liederen

Daar Stond Een Ster Te Gloren *Op.9b,No.1
see Twee Kerstliederen

De Herdertjes Lagen Bij Nachte *Op.9b,No.2
see Twee Kerstliederen

Es Muss Ein Wunderbares Sein *Op.10, No.1
see Vier Lieder

Friede *Op.21,No.4
see Vier Lieder

Geen Overpad *Op.12,No.2
solo,pno ALSBACH s.p.   (O347)

Hohenflug *Op.21,No.2
see Vier Lieder

OORT, H.C.V. (cont'd.)

Ich Frage Nicht Wie Soll Es Enden
*Op.9,No.2
med solo,pno ALSBACH s.p.   (0348)

Leg Uw Beide Blanke Handjes *Op.8,
No.1
med solo,pno ALSBACH s.p.   (0349)

O! Als Ik Je Eens Mocht Zeggen
*Op.17,No.1
solo,pno ALSBACH s.p.   (0350)

Schliesse Mir Die Augen Beide
*Op.10,No.2
see Vier Lieder

Schwere Nachte *Op.9,No.1
low solo,pno ALSBACH s.p.   (0351)

Sie Liebten Sich Beide *Op.10,No.3
see Vier Lieder

Tote Tage *Op.21,No.3
see Vier Lieder

Trauungsgesang *Op.10,No.5, sac
solo,pno/org ALSBACH s.p.   (0352)
2 soli,pno/org ALSBACH s.p.   (0353)

Twee Kerstliederen
solo,pno ALSBACH s.p.
contains: Daar Stond Een Ster Te
Gloren, Op.9b,No.1; De
Herdertjes Lagen Bij Nachte,
Op.9b,No.2   (0354)

Twee Kerstliederen *Op.9c, CC2U
2 soli,pno/org ALSBACH s.p.   (0355)

Twee Liederen
solo,pno ALSBACH s.p.
contains: Avond, Op.20,No.1;
Avondstilte, Op.20,No.2 (0356)

Vier Lieder
solo,pno ALSBACH s.p.
contains: Abendlied, Op.21,No.1;
Friede, Op.21,No.4; Hohenflug,
Op.21,No.2; Tote Tage, Op.21,
No.3   (0357)

Vier Lieder
solo,pno ALSBACH s.p.
contains: Es Muss Ein Wunderbares
Sein, Op.10,No.1; Schliesse Mir
Die Augen Beide, Op.10,No.2;
Sie Liebten Sich Beide, Op.10,
No.3; Zuweilen Dunkt Es Mich,
Op.10,No.4   (0358)

Waar Gij Zult Henengaan *Op.23
solo,pno/org ALSBACH s.p.   (0359)

Zuweilen Dunkt Es Mich *Op.10,No.4
see Vier Lieder

OP DEN WEEFSTOEL see Cuypers, H.

OP EENEN MORGENSTONT see Beekhuis,
Hanna

OP FANNY GOODWIN see Reynvaan, M.C.C.

OP HET MUSYCK-BOECK VAN MEESTER
CORNELIS SCHUYT VAN LEYDEN see
Paap, Wouter

OP HET STUK see Clercq, R. de

OP JONGHVROUW ISABEL LE BLON see Paap,
Wouter

OP KERSTDAG see Hullebroeck, Em.

OP LICHTE VLEUGELEN see Tussenbroek, H.
von

OP! SCHROOMLIJKE REUS see Zagwijn,
Henri

OP 'T WILDE GOLVEN see Middeleer, Jean
De

OPAL see Carse, Adam von Ahn

OPEN OUR EYES see Macfarlane, William
Charles

OPEN ROAD, OPEN SKY see Strauss, Johann

OPEN SECRET, AN see Woodman, Raymond
Huntington

OPEN THE DOOR SOFTLY see Hughes,
Herbert

OPEN THE DOOR TO SPRING see Sharpe,
Evelyn

OPEN THE GATES OF THE TEMPLE see Knapp,
(Mrs.) Joseph F.

OPEN THE GATES OF THE TEMPLE see
Mendelssohn-Bartholdy, Felix

OPEN THOU MY LIPS *sac,gospel
solo,pno ABER.GRP. $1.50   (0360)

OPEN THY BLUE EYES see Massenet, Jules,
Ouvre Tes Yeux Bleus

OPEN THY MERCIFUL ARMS *sac,gospel
solo,pno ABER.GRP. $1.50   (0361)

OPEN TO ME GATES OF JUSTICE see
Buxtehude, Dietrich, Aperite Mihi
Portas Justitiae

OPEN UP THE PEARLY GATES *sac,gospel
solo,pno ABER.GRP. $1.50   (0362)

OPENING OF THE KEY see Somervell,
Arthur

OPERA AIRS *CC2U
med solo,pno CHESTER s.p.   (0363)

OPERA AIRS FOR BOYS' CLASSES *CC16L
[Eng] solo,kbd CHESTER s.p. contains
works by: Arne; Berlioz; Gounod;
Handel; Mozart and others   (0364)

OPERA AIRS FOR GIRLS' CLASSES *CC17L
(Easson, J.; Merchant, D.) [Eng]
solo,kbd CHESTER s.p. contains
works by: Arne; Bizet; Cimarosa;
Bizet; Delibes; Glinka; Handel;
Mozart and others   (0365)

OPERA ARIAS FOR ALTO *CC34U
A/Mez solo,pno PETERS 4232 $7.50 in
original language with German
translation; contains works by:
Adam; Bizet; Gluck; Handel;
Nicolai; Rossini; Schubert and
others   (0366)

OPERA ARIAS FOR BARITONE *CC30U
Bar solo,pno PETERS 4234 $9.50 in
original language with German
translation; contains works by:
D'Albert; Beethoven; Bizet;
Donizetti; Gounod; Handel;
Lortzing; Mozart and others   (0367)

OPERA ARIAS FOR BASS *CC34U
B solo,pno PETERS 4235 $9.50 in
original language with German
translation; contains works by:
Adam; Auber; Beethoven; Cherubini;
Cornelius; Flotow; Handel; Mozart
and others   (0368)

OPERA ARIAS FOR SOPRANO, VOL. I *CC36U
S solo,pno PETERS 4231A $10.00 in
original language with German
translation; contains works by:
Beethoven; Gluck; Handel; Mozart;
Pergolesi   (0369)

OPERA ARIAS FOR SOPRANO, VOL. II
*CC44U
S solo,pno PETERS 4231B $12.50 in
original language with German
translation; contains works by:
D'Albert; Auber; Bellini; Bizet;
Donizetti; Flotow; Gounod and
others   (0370)

OPERA ARIAS FOR TENOR *CC47U
T solo,pno PETERS 4233 $11.00 in
original language with German
translation; contains works by:
Adam; Auber; Beethoven; Bizet;
Cornelius; Donizetti; Flotow;
Gluck; Weber; Smetana and others
(0371)

OPERA REPERTOIRE FOR SOPRANO *CCU
(Castleton, G.) S solo,pno PRESSER
$5.00   (0372)

OPERA REPERTOIRE FOR TENOR *CCU
(Castleton, G.) T solo,pno PRESSER
$4.00   (0373)

OPERATIC ANTHOLOGY, VOL. I *CC44L
(Adler) S solo,pno SCHIRM.G $6.00
contains works by: Verdi; Bizet;
Gounod; Puccini and others   (0374)

OPERATIC ANTHOLOGY, VOL. II *CC40L
(Adler) Mez/A solo,pno SCHIRM.G $6.00
contains works by: Verdi;
Mussorgsky; Gluck; Handel and
others   (0375)

OPERATIC ANTHOLOGY, VOL. III *CC43L
(Adler) T solo,pno SCHIRM.G $6.00
contains works by: Gounod; Verdi;
Wagner; Puccini and others   (0376)

OPERATIC ANTHOLOGY, VOL. IV *CC37L
(Adler) Bar solo,pno SCHIRM.G $6.00
contains works by: Verdi;
Offenbach; Tchaikovsky; Mozart and
others   (0377)

OPERATIC ANTHOLOGY, VOL. V *CC41L
(Adler) Bar solo,pno SCHIRM.G $6.00
contains works by: Rossini; Verdi;
Wagner; Mozart and others   (0378)

OPERETTA SERIES: ARIAS AND SONGS FROM
CLASSICAL FRENCH OPERETTAS *CCU
[Russ] male solo,pno MEZ KNIGA 110
s.p.   (0379)

OPERETTA SERIES: ARIAS AND SONGS FROM
OPERETTAS BY SOVIET COMPOSERS *CCU
[Russ] S solo,pno MEZ KNIGA 109 s.p.
(0380)

OPERETTAS SERIES: ARIAS, SONGS AND
DUETS FROM OPERETTAS see Slonov,
Yu.

OPGANG see Witte, D.

OPHELIA see Strilko, Anthony

OPHELIA'S MAD SCENE see Saguer, Louis

OPHELIE see Cuvillier, Charles

OPIENSKI, HENRYK (1870-1942)
Chansons Populaires Polonaises *CCU
solo,pno HENN 604 s.p.   (0381)

OPNIEUW DE NACHT see Mulder, Herman

OPOLDANSKI PSALM see Merku, Pavle

OPPNA HJARTATS DORR
see Andliga Sanger, Heft 3

OPUS SCIR see Sinopoli, Giuseppe

OPUSTENA see Foerster, Josef Bohuslav

OR CHE IL DOVER - TALI E COTANTI SONO
see Mozart, Wolfgang Amadeus

OR SON SEI MESI see Puccini, Giacomo

OR SUS VOUS DORMES TROP see Anonymous

OR VIA MANON see Massenet, Jules

ORA NOI see Nielsen, Riccardo

ORA PRO NOBIS see Lothar, Mark

ORA PRO NOBIS see Piccolomini, Marietta

ORA VORREI PARTIR see Mana-Zucca, Mme.

ORACAO see Montsalvatge, Xavier

ORACLE see Joubert, John

ORAGE see Absil, Jean

ORAIN NA CLARSAICH see Campbell, Hilda
M.

ORAISON see Chausson, Ernest

ORAISON DOMINICALE see Wangermez, Ed.

ORAL FUR REZITATOR UND GROSSES
ORCHESTER see Malec, Ivo

ORAN-A-CHREE see Roberton, Hugh
Stevenson

ORANGE see Srebotnjak, Alojz F., Oranza

ORANJE GLORIE see Bonset, Jac.

ORANJE MAY LIED see Bordewijk-Roepman,
Johanna

ORANZA see Srebotnjak, Alojz F.

ORATIO see Horst, Anton van der

ORAZIONE DI S. BERNARDO A MARIA see
Nacamuli, Guido

ORCHESTERSTUCK NO. 1 see Zechlin, Ruth

ORCHIDS see Hinson, D.

ORDINAIRE, R.
O Salutaris! *sac
[Lat] Bar/Mez solo,vln,pno/org
ENOCH s.p.   (0382)

ORDRE AU SOLEIL see Migot, Georges

ORE, CHARLES W.
Lisbon Psalms, Set I *sac
solo,pno CONCORDIA 97-5299 $5.25
contains: Psalm 1; Psalm 4; Psalm
23; Psalm 25   (0383)

Lisbon Psalms, Set II *sac,CCU
solo,org CONCORDIA 97-5300 $3.75
(0384)

Psalm 1
see Lisbon Psalms, Set I

ORE, CHARLES W. (cont'd.)

Psalm 4
see Lisbon Psalms, Set I

Psalm 23
see Lisbon Psalms, Set I

Psalm 25
see Lisbon Psalms, Set I

ORE DOLCI E DIVINE see Puccini, Giacomo

ORE TRISTI E SERENE see Rossellini, Renzo

OREFICE, GIACOMO (1865-1922)
Fuga Di Barnabo Visconti
[It] solo,pno RICORDI-ENG 128298
s.p.   (O385)

Liriche *CCU
[It] solo,pno RICORDI-ENG 128293
s.p.   (O386)

Sette Canti, Vol. I *CCU
[It] solo,pno RICORDI-ENG 128290
s.p.   (O387)

Sette Canti, Vol. II *CCU
[It] solo,pno RICORDI-ENG 128291
s.p.   (O388)

Tanke Giapponesi *CC5U
[It] solo,pno RICORDI-ENG 128297
s.p.   (O389)

OREH see Kozina, Marijan

O'REILLY
How'd You Like To Be A Baby Girl
solo,pno ALLANS s.p.   (O390)

ORENTES D'ABRIL see Vives, Amadeo

ORFANO see Gandino, Adolfo

ORFANO see Pagliuca, C.

ORFANO see Persico, Mario

ORFANO see Salvatori, P. Salvatore

ORFEO see Finnessy, Michael

ORFEO see Pergolesi, Giovanni Battista,
Nel Chiuso Centro

ORFEUS V PODSVETI see Offenbach,
Jacques

ORGAD, BEN-ZION
Hatzvi Israel
"O Thy Beauty, Israel" Bar solo,
orch (symphony in 2 movements)
study sc ISR.MUS.INST. 030 s.p.
(O391)

Leave Out My Name *song cycle
[Heb] Mez solo,fl,pno PRESSER $1.80
(O392)

Min He'afar
"Out Of The Dust" Mez/A solo,fl,
bsn,vla,vcl study sc
ISR.MUS.INST. 002 s.p.   (O393)

O Thy Beauty, Israel *see Hatzvi
Israel

Out Of The Dust *see Min He'afar

ORGANA DOMESTICA see Keller

ORGANUM JERONIMUS, BOOK I (LETTER J-E-
R) see Arrigo, Girolamo

ORGELCHORALSATZE HEFT I: ADVENT BIS
DREIEINIGKEIT see Bornefeld, Helmut

ORGELCHORALSATZE HEFT II: (GENERAL
USAGE) see Bornefeld, Helmut

ORGELCHORALSATZE HEFT III: LOB UND
DANK, GLAUBE, TAGESZEITEN see
Bornefeld, Helmut

ORIENTAL MINIATURES see Carr

ORISON & THINGS ETERNAL see Birch,
Robert Fairfax

ORLAND, HENRY
Begegnung
med solo,pno sc SEESAW $5.00 (O394)

Colloque Sentimental
A solo,pno sc SEESAW $2.00   (O395)

Drei Lieder By Politzer *CC3U
med solo,pno sc SEESAW $5.00 (O396)

Elegie
high solo,pno sc SEESAW $3.00
(O397)

Love And Pity
S solo,clar,vla sc SEESAW $2.00
(O398)

ORLAND, HENRY (cont'd.)

Reve
med solo,pno sc SEESAW $2.00 (O399)

Serenade
high solo,pno sc SEESAW $2.00
(O400)

Six Occasional Songs *CC6U
med solo,pno sc SEESAW $5.00 (O401)

Songs Of The Shepherd
T solo,pno sc SEESAW $6.00   (O402)

Two Ballads By Goethe *CC2U
low solo,pno sc SEESAW $8.00 (O403)

ORLEANAIS *Fr
(Canteloube, J.) solo,acap DURAND
s.p. see also Anthologie Des Chants
Populaires Francais Tome IV (O404)

ORPHEE see Clerambault, Louis-Nicolas

ORPHEE see Rameau, Jean-Philippe

ORPHEE, ORPHELIN see Hively, Wells

ORPHEUS see Hart

ORPHEUS see Lessard, John Ayres

ORPHEUS see Weismann, Julius

ORPHEUS BRITANNICUS see Purcell, Henry

ORPHEUS WITH HIS LUTE see Bunge, Sas

ORPHEUS WITH HIS LUTE see Castelnuovo-
Tedesco, Mario

ORPHEUS WITH HIS LUTE see Davies, Henry
Walford

ORPHEUS WITH HIS LUTE see German,
Edward

ORPHEUS WITH HIS LUTE see Schumann,
William Howard

ORPHEUS WITH HIS LUTE see Sullivan, Sir
Arthur Seymour

ORPHEUS WITH HIS LUTE: NO. 1 see
Vaughan Williams, Ralph

ORPHEUS WITH HIS LUTE: NO. 2 see
Vaughan Williams, Ralph

ORR, BUXTON
Ballad Of Mr. And Mrs. Discobbolos
T solo,pno EULENBURG GM 213 s.p.
(O405)

Many Kinds Of Yes *song cycle
SA soli,pno EULENBURG GM 214 s.p.
(O406)

ORR, CHARLES WILFRED (1893-   )
Carpenter's Son, The
[Eng] high solo,kbd CHESTER s.p.
(O407)

Earl Of Bristol's Farewell, The
see Two Seventeenth Century Poems

Hymn Before Sleep
solo,pno (G maj) LESLIE 7048 $.80
(O408)

In Valleys Green And Still
solo,pno (E flat maj) LESLIE 7050
$1.00   (O409)

Into My Heart An Air That Kills
see Three Songs From A Shropshire
Lad

Isle Of Portland, The
[Eng] Bar solo,kbd CHESTER s.p.
(O410)

Lads In Their Hundreds, The
solo,pno (F maj) ROBERTON 1006 s.p.
(O411)

Oh See How Thick The Goldcup Flowers
see Three Songs From A Shropshire
Lad

Plucking The Rushes
[Eng] med solo,kbd CHESTER s.p.
(O412)

Soldier From The Wars Returning
solo,pno (D maj) ROBERTON 1008 s.p.
(O413)

Three Songs From A Shropshire Lad
[Eng] T solo,kbd CHESTER s.p.
contains: Into My Heart An Air
That Kills; Oh See How Thick
The Goldcup Flowers; Westward
On The High-Hilled Plains
(O414)

Tryste Noel
solo,pno (C min) ROBERTON 1009 s.p.
(O415)

Two Seventeenth Century Poems
solo,pno (E maj) ROBERTON 1007 s.p.
contains: Earl Of Bristol's
Farewell, The; Whenas I Wake
(O416)

ORR, CHARLES WILFRED (cont'd.)

Westward On The High-Hilled Plains
see Three Songs From A Shropshire
Lad

When I Was One And Twenty
[Eng] solo,kbd CHESTER s.p.   (O417)

When The Lad For Longing Sighs
[Eng] high solo,kbd CHESTER s.p.
(O418)

Whenas I Wake
see Two Seventeenth Century Poems

While Summer On Is Stealing
solo,pno (D maj) LESLIE 7049 $1.20
(O419)

ORR, J.
Captain Sam
low solo,pno PRESSER $.75   (O420)

ORREGO SALAS, JUAN (1919-   )
Psalms *Op.51, CCU
narrator,4fl,pic,4ob,English horn,
4clar,bass clar,4bsn,contrabsn,
6horn,4trp,4trom,tuba,timp,4perc,
harp,bvl PETERS 6523 rental
(O421)

ORTHEL, LEON (1905-   )
A Une Mendiante Rousse *Op.72,No.1
see Deux Melodies

Apres Une Journee De Vent *Op.63,
No.4
see Six Quatrains Valaisans

Auferstehung *Op.74,No.3
see Three Songs

Chemin Qui Tourne *Op.63,No.6
see Six Quatrains Valaisans

Comme Aux Saintes Maries *Op.62,No.4
see Quatre Esquisses Valaisannes

Dame Vor Dem Spiegel
see Twee Liederen Van Rainer Maria
Rilke

Der Tod Des Geliebten
see Twee Liederen Van Rainer Maria
Rilke

Deux Melodies
high solo,pno DONEMUS s.p.
contains: A Une Mendiante Rousse,
Op.72,No.1; La Musique, Op.72,
No.2   (O422)

Die Entfuhrung *Op.16,No.2
see Twee Liederen Van Rainer Maria
Rilke

Die Kurtisane *Op.51,No.2
see Drie Liederen Van Rainer Maria
Rilke

Die Laute *Op.26,No.2
see Drie Liederen Van Rainer Maria
Rilke

Drie Liederen Van E.L. Smelik
S solo,pno DONEMUS s.p.
contains: Het Hert, Op.49,No.1;
Meischemer, Op.49,No.3; Oude
Kerk, Op.49,No.2   (O423)

Drie Liederen Van Rainer Maria Rilke
high solo,pno ALSBACH s.p.
contains: Die Laute, Op.26,No.2;
Eva, Op.26,No.3; Schlaflied,
Op.26,No.1   (O424)

Drie Liederen Van Rainer Maria Rilke
[Ger] S solo,pno DONEMUS D35 s.p.
contains: Die Kurtisane, Op.51,
No.2; Eine Welke, Op.51,No.1;
Letzter Abend, Op.51,No.3   (O425)

Ein Frauenschicksal
see Twee Liederen Van Rainer Maria
Rilke

Eine Welke *Op.51,No.1
see Drie Liederen Van Rainer Maria
Rilke

Ernste Stunde *Op.74,No.1
see Three Songs

Eva *Op.26,No.3
see Drie Liederen Van Rainer Maria
Rilke

Four Songs *Op.64, CC4U
S/T solo,clar&pno DONEMUS s.p.
(O426)

Het Hert *Op.49,No.1
see Drie Liederen Van E.L. Smelik

Ist Ein Schloss
see Twee Liederen Van Rainer Maria
Rilke

ORTHEL, LEON (cont'd.)

Kindheit *Op.74,No.2
see Three Songs

La Musique *Op.72,No.2
see Deux Melodies

Le Clocher Chante *Op.63,No.1
see Six Quatrains Valaisans

Le Dormeur Du Val *Op.58,No.1
see Trois Chasonnettes

Le Souvenir De La Neige *Op.62,No.1
see Quatre Esquisses Valaisannes

Letzter Abend *Op.51,No.3
see Drie Liederen Van Rainer Maria
Rilke

Meischemer *Op.49,No.3
see Drie Liederen Van E.L. Smelik

Mesange *Op.62,No.2
see Quatre Esquisses Valaisannes

Neuf Melodies *Op.65,CC9U
S solo,pno DONEMUS s.p.   (O427)

Nonnenklage *Op.25
S solo,pno DONEMUS s.p.   (O428)
S solo,2fl,3clar,2horn,harp,strings
DONEMUS s.p.   (O429)

O Ces Autels *Op.63,No.3
see Six Quatrains Valaisans

Oude Kerk *Op.49,No.2
see Drie Liederen Van E.L. Smelik

Pays Silencieux *Op.63,No.5
see Six Quatrains Valaisans

Petite Cascade *Op.63,No.2
see Six Quatrains Valaisans

Premiere Soiree *Op.58,No.3
see Trois Chasonnettes

Quatre Esquisses Valaisannes
S solo,pno DONEMUS s.p.
contains: Comme Aux Saintes
Maries, Op.62,No.4; Le Souvenir
De La Neige, Op.62,No.1;
Mesange, Op.62,No.2; Rossignol,
Op.62,No.3   (O430)

Reve Pour L'hiver *Op.58,No.2
see Trois Chasonnettes

Rossignol *Op.62,No.3
see Quatre Esquisses Valaisannes

Schlaflied *Op.26,No.1
see Drie Liederen Van Rainer Maria
Rilke

Sept Melodies De R.M. Rilke *Op.61,
No.1-7, CC7L
S solo,pno DONEMUS s.p.   (O431)

Six Quatrains Valaisans
S solo,pno DONEMUS s.p.
contains: Apres Une Journee De
Vent, Op.63,No.4; Chemin Qui
Tourne, Op.63,No.6; Le Clocher
Chante, Op.63,No.1; O Ces
Autels, Op.63,No.3; Pays
Silencieux, Op.63,No.5; Petite
Cascade, Op.63,No.2   (O432)

Three Songs
S solo,pno DONEMUS s.p.
contains: Auferstehung, Op.74,
No.3; Ernste Stunde, Op.74,
No.1; Kindheit, Op.74,No.2
(O433)

Three Songs On A Text By R.M. Rilke
*Op.55, CC3U
med solo,pno DONEMUS s.p.   (O434)

Trois Chasonnettes
high solo,pno DONEMUS s.p.
contains: Le Dormeur Du Val,
Op.58,No.1; Premiere Soiree,
Op.58,No.3; Reve Pour L'hiver,
Op.58,No.2   (O435)

Twee Liederen Van Rainer Maria Rilke
S solo,pno DONEMUS s.p.
contains: Dame Vor Dem Spiegel;
Ein Frauenschicksal   (O436)

Twee Liederen Van Rainer Maria Rilke
S solo,pno ALBERSEN s.p.
contains: Die Entfuhring, Op.16,
No.2; Ubung Am Klavier, Op.16,
No.1   (O437)

Twee Liederen Van Rainer Maria Rilke
S solo,pno DONEMUS s.p.
contains: Der Tod Des Geliebten;
Ist Ein Schloss   (O438)

ORTHEL, LEON (cont'd.)

Two Songs *Op.54, CC2U
Bar solo,pno DONEMUS s.p.   (O439)

Two Songs On A Text By R.M. Rilke
*Op.56, CC2U
B/Bar solo,pno DONEMUS s.p.   (O440)

Ubung Am Klavier *Op.16,No.1
see Twee Liederen Van Rainer Maria
Rilke

ORTIZ DE GUINEA
Ave Maria
[Lat] solo,pno RICORDI-ARG BA 8926
s.p.   (O441)

ORTLUND, ANNE
Make My Son A Tree *sac
solo,pno LILLENAS SM-627: RN $1.00
(O442)

ORTON, IRV
Just One Day At A Time *sac
SA soli,pno SCHIRM.G $1.00   (O443)
SBar soli,pno SCHIRM.G $1.00   (O444)
ST soli,pno SCHIRM.G $1.00   (O445)

OSAMLJENA see Lovec, Vladimir

OSBORNE, T.L. JR.
Searching *sac
solo,pno SINGSPIR 7016 $1.00 (O446)

OSCARSON, GUN
Vaarbrud
solo,pno LUNDQUIST s.p.   (O447)

OSCURO E IL CIEL... see Pizzetti,
Ildebrando

O'SE SHALOM *sac
solo,pno OR-TAV $.50   (O448)

OSEM NARODNIH PESMI *CC8U,folk
(Tomc, Matija) solo,pno DRUSTVO
DSS 357 rental   (O449)

OSEM OTROSKIH PESMI see Koporc, Srecko

OSEM SAMOSPEVOV see Pregelj, Ciril

OSIRELO DITE see Ostrcil, Otakor

OSKAM, IZAAK J. (1897-1962)
Chant D'Avril
see Liederen

De Waterlelie
see Liederen

Liederen
med solo,pno DONEMUS s.p.
contains: Chant D'Avril; De
Waterlelie; Winterwald   (O450)

Winterwald
see Liederen

OSM PISNI see Risinger, Karel

OSORIO SWAAB, R.
Monument
solo,pno BROEKMANS 33 s.p.   (O451)

OSTATNIA PIESN see Baird, Tadeusz

OSTENDORF, JENS-PETER
Absurde Betrachtungen
SS soli, microphone SIKORSKI 820
s.p.   (O452)

OSTERC, SLAVKO (1895-1941)
Samospevi *CCU
solo,pno PROSVETNI rental   (O453)

Vier Gradnik-Lieder *CC4U
Mez solo,4strings sc GERIG HG 1108
s.p.   (O454)

OSTERGLOCKEN see Zagwijn, Henri

OSTLING
Huru Dyrbar Ar Ej Din Nad
solo,pno LUNDQUIST s.p.   (O455)

OSTNATE NEBE see Matej, Jozka

OSTPREUSENLAND! see Borschel, Erich

OSTRCIL, OTAKOR (1879-1935)
Der Fremde Gast *Op.16
[Czech/Ger] T solo,pno SUPRAPHON
s.p.   (O456)

Dev Pisne *CC2U
SUPRAPHON s.p. high solo,pno; low
solo,pno; med solo,pno   (O457)

Dve Pisne Pro Sopran *CC2U
S solo,pno SUPRAPHON s.p.   (O458)

Dve Pisne Pro Tenor *CC2U
T solo,pno SUPRAPHON s.p.   (O459)

OSTRCIL, OTAKOR (cont'd.)

Osirelo Dite
Mez solo,pno SUPRAPHON s.p.   (O460)

OSTROVSKI, A.
Du Soleil Pour Tout Le Monde
(Drejac, J.) solo,pno CHANT s.p.
(O461)

OTAZURE see Nakada, Yoshinao

OTEO
Eres Tu
(Meyers) "Without You" [Eng/Span]
low solo,pno (D flat maj) WILLIS
$.50   (O462)
(Meyers) "Without You" [Eng/Span]
high solo,pno (G maj) WILLIS $.50
(O463)

Without You *see Eres Tu

OTETTIIN MINUSTA OUTO see Kilpinen,
Yrio

OTEVRENY DUM see Felix, Vaclav

OTHEGRAVEN, AUGUST J. VON (1864-1946)
Gesange
med-low solo,pno LEUCKART s.p.
contains: Heimkehr, Op.19,No.3;
Sehnsucht, Op.19,No.1; Warum,
Op.19,No.2   (O464)

Heimkehr *Op.19,No.3
see Gesange

Sehnsucht *Op.19,No.1
see Gesange

Warum *Op.19,No.2
see Gesange

OTHER AMERICAS *CCU,So Am
(Cugat) [Span/Eng] solo,pno MARKS
$1.50   (O465)

OTHMAYR, KASPAR (1515-1553)
Geistliche Zwiegesange *sac,CC32U
(Lipphardt, Walther) 2 soli,org
(med) BAREN. 1933 s.p.   (O466)

OTSA, H.
Five Epic Songs From The Island Of
Hijumaa *CC5U
[Russ] solo,pno MEZ KNIGA 2.99 s.p.
(O467)

OTT, J.
Have You Tried The Lord Today? *sac
solo,pno LILLENAS SM-908: SN $1.00
(O468)

I've Found A New Way *sac
solo,pno LILLENAS SM-918: SN $1.00
(O469)

Wait For Me *sac
solo,pno LILLENAS SM-944: SN $1.00
(O470)

OTTAVIA'S FAREWELL see Monteverdi,
Claudio

OTTAVIA'S LAMENT see Monteverdi,
Claudio

OTTEN, LUDWIG (1924-   )
Divertimento
S solo,fl,English horn,vla,vcl
DONEMUS s.p.   (O471)

Kwintet
S solo,4strings DONEMUS s.p. (O472)

Quadro
S solo,fl,vla,pno DONEMUS s.p.
(O473)

OTTO CANTILENE SU TESTI D'ORIENTE [1]
see Rocca, Lodovico

OTTO CANTILENE SU TESTI D'ORIENTE [2]
see Rocca, Lodovico

OTTO DIALOGHI see Malipiero, Gian
Francesco

OTTO, E.
Forsythis
med solo,pno PARAGON $.85   (O474)

OU ALLER see Schubert, Franz (Peter)

OU DONC? see Godard, Benjamin Louis
Paul

OU DONC COUREZ-VOUS see Lecocq, Charles

OU DONC ES-TU PARTIE? see Marty,
(Eugene) Georges

OU IRAI-JE ME PLAINDRE
see Chants De France Vol. I

OU LE COQ A-T-IL LA PLUME? see Absil,
Jean

OU NOUS AVONS AIME see Saint-Saens,
Camille

OU QUE TU SOIS, JUNON see Saint-Saens, Camille

OU S'EN VONT MES REVES see Brahms, Johannes

OU S'EN VONT MES REVES see Mendelssohn-Bartholdy, Felix

OU SONT-ELLES, CES HEURES DOUCES see Mozart, Wolfgang Amadeus

OU TU N'ES PAS see Lacombe, Paul

OU VA LA JEUNE INDOUE see Delibes, Leo

OUBLI see Flegier, Ange

OUBLI see Gui, Vittorio

OUBLI see Revel, Peter

OUBLI D'AMOUR see Levade, Charles (Gaston)

OUBLIER see Ollone, Max d'

OUCHTERLONY, DAVID
Cradle Carol *sac,Xmas
solo,pno HARRIS $.90   (O475)

OUD-DRIEKONIGENLIED see Breman, W.F.

OUD LIED see Mulder, Herman

OUD LIEDEKEN see Adriessen, Willem

OUD LIEDJE see Baeyens, August-L.

OUD-NEDERLANDSCHE LIEDEREN see Beuningen, W.v.

OUD-NEDERLANDSCHE LIEDEREN, VOL. 1 see Schouwman, Hans

OUD-NEDERLANDSCHE LIEDEREN, VOL. 2 see Schouwman, Hans

OUD-NEDERLANDSE KINDERLIEDEREN *CCU
(Michielsen, A.) solo,pno BROEKMANS
52 s.p.   (O476)

OUD-NEDERLANDSE LIEDEREN NAAR VALERIUS see Rontgen, [Julius]

OUD-NEDERLANDSE VOLKSLIEDEREN, VOL. 3-4 see Rontgen, [Julius]

OUD SPINET see Dresden, Sem

OUDE KERK see Orthel, Leon

OUDE KOPPEL see Clercq, R. de

OUDEJAARSAVOND see Witte, D.

OUI, C'EST L'AMOUR see Cuvillier, Charles

OUI, JE COMPRENDS see Lacome, Paul

OUI O ALTROVE see Merku, Pavle

OUISTITI see Lacome, Paul

OULD JOHN BRADDLEUM see Johnston, Lyell

OULD LAMMAS FAIR, THE see Vine, John

OULD PLAID SHAWL, THE see Haynes, Walter Battison

OULD SIDE CAR, THE see Dix, J. Airlie

OUR BLEST REDEEMER see Williams, David H.

OUR DAILY BREAD *sac,gospel
solo,pno ABER.GRP. $1.50   (O477)

OUR DEBTS WILL BE PAID see Wetherington

OUR FATHER see Peeters, Flor, Pater Noster

OUR FATHER see Watson, G.

OUR FATHER, BY WHOSE NAME see Lovelace, Austin C.

OUR FATHER CARES see Dunlap, Fern Glasgow

OUR FLAG see O'Hara, Geoffrey

OUR FRONT PORCH *CCU
(Carmichael, Ralph) solo,pno WORD
37520 $1.95   (O478)

OUR GARDEN see Howard, L.

OUR GOD IS GREAT *sac,Swed
AB soli,pno LORENZ $1.00   (O479)
SA soli,pno LORENZ $1.00   (O480)
med solo,pno LORENZ $1.00   (O481)

OUR HEART SHALL REJOICE IN THE LORD see Powell, Robert J.

OUR HOUSE see Lee, Don

OUR HOUSE IS FULL OF FAIRIES see Cooke, Herbert L.

OUR HUNTING FATHERS see Britten, Benjamin

OUR JOY see Cardew, Cornelius

OUR LADY OF SORROW see Lora, Antonio

OUR LADY SAT WITHIN HER BOWER see Lovelace, Austin C.

OUR LADY'S BEDSTRAW see Baxter, Maude Stewart

OUR LADY'S HOURS see Milner, Anthony

OUR LIMPED STREAMS WITH FREEDOM FLOW see Handel, George Frideric

OUR LORD AND OUR LADY see Gover, Gerald

OUR LORD'S PRAYER see Van Dyke, Vonda

OUR MOUNTAIN HOME see Parker, Henry

OUR NATIONAL SONGS see Somervell, Arthur

OUR PASCHAL JOY see Yon, Pietro Alessandro

OUR SACRED HONOR see Yahres, Samuel C.

OUR TWO SOULS see Surinach, Carlos

OUT IN THE FIELDS see Dawson

OUT OF EGYPT INTO CANAAN *sac
solo,pno STAMPS 7245 $1.00   (O482)

OUT OF THE CRIMSON WEST see Gartner, Clarence

OUT OF THE DEEP see Loehr

OUT OF THE DEEP see Marks, J.C.

OUT OF THE DEEP I CALL see Martin, Easthope, De Profundis

OUT OF THE DEPTHS *sac,gospel
solo,pno ABER.GRP. $1.50   (O483)

OUT OF THE DEPTHS see Bantock, Granville

OUT OF THE DEPTHS see Honegger, Arthur, Mimaamaquim

OUT OF THE DEPTHS see Hovhaness, Alan

OUT OF THE DEPTHS see Scott, John Prindle

OUT OF THE DEPTHS see Weiner, Lazar, Mimaamakim

OUT OF THE DUST see Orgad, Ben-Zion, Min He'afar

OUT OF THE MORNING see Persichetti, Vincent

OUT OF THE SILENCE see Moss, Katie

OUT OF THE SKY ON HIGH see Puccini, Giacomo, Donna Non Vidi Mai

OUT ON THE DEEP see Lohr, Hanns

OUTRENUIT see Menasce, Jacques de

OUTWARDS see Escher, Rudolf George

OUVRE TA FENETRE see Goeyens, Fern.

OUVRE TES YEUX BLEUS see Massenet, Jules

OUVRE TON COEUR see Bizet, Georges

OUVREZ AUX ENFANTS see Cuvillier, Charles

OVE FUGGO see Cimarosa, Domenico

OVER ALL THE TREETOPS see Ives, Charles, Ilmenau

OVER ALLE DAKEN see Zagwijn, Henri

OVER AND OVER see Jensen, Gordon

OVER AND OVER AND OVER AGAIN see Harris, Ron

OVER DE HOJE FJELDE see Kjerulf, [Halfdan]

OVER DINA HANDER LUTAD see Berggreen, Andreas Peter

OVER GRANARNAS KRONOR STAR HIMMELEN BLA see Nordqvist, Gustaf

OVER HET GRAS see Lilien, Ignace

OVER IN BETHLEHEM *sac
(Carmichael, Ralph) solo,pno WORD
S-231   (O484)

OVER THE LAND IS APRIL see Charles, Ernest

OVER THE LAND IS APRIL see Quilter, Roger

OVER THE MOUNTAINS see Quilter, Roger

OVER THE NEXT HILL WE'LL BE HOME *sac
(Cash, Johnny) solo,pno WORD S-417
(O485)

OVER THE RIM OF THE MOON see Head, Michael (Dewar)

OVER THE RIVER see McLeod, Robert

OVER THE SEA see Bury, Winifred

OVER THE STEPPE see Gretchaninov, Alexander Tikhonovitch, Triste Est La Steppe

OVER THE SUNSET MOUNTAINS see Peterson, John W.

OVER THE SUNSET TRAIL *sac,gospel
solo,pno ABER.GRP. $1.50   (O486)

OVERBY, ROLF PETER (1936-1959)
Come My Beloved *sac
med solo,pno AUGSBURG 11-0723 $.75
(O487)

OVERHALT
Hallelujah Square *sac
solo,pno BENSON S5614-S $1.00
(O488)

OVERHEAD see Clarke, Henry Leland

OVERHEARD ON A SALT MARSH see Bissell, Keith W.

OVERHOLT, R.
Ten Thousand Angels *sac
solo,pno LILLENAS SM-419 $1.00
(O489)
solo,pno BENSON S7688-RS $1.00
(O490)

OVERLANDSSANGER see Dorumsgaard, Arne

OVERSHADOWED *sac,gospel
solo,pno ABER.GRP. $1.50   (O491)

OVERTON, HALL (1920-   )
Patrico's Song
med solo,pno AM.COMP.AL. $1.10
(O492)

Slow, Slow, Fresh Fount
high solo,pno AM.COMP.AL. $1.10
(O493)

Toast, A
high solo,pno AM.COMP.AL. $2.75
(O494)

OWEN
Laudamus *sac
"Unto Thee All Praise Be Given" low
solo,pno (G maj) BOSTON $1.50
(O495)

Unto Thee All Praise Be Given *see
Laudamus

OWEN, RICHARD
I Saw A Man Pursuing The Horizon
solo,pno GENERAL 302 $1.00   (O496)

Impulse, The
solo,pno GENERAL 301 $1.25   (O497)

Patterns
med solo,pno GENERAL 797 $3.00
(O498)

There Were Many Who Went In Huddled Procession
solo,pno GENERAL 303 $1.00   (O499)

Till We Watch The Last Low Star
solo,pno GENERAL 304 $1.00   (O500)

OWENS
Discovery *sac
solo,pno LILLENAS SM-618: RN $1.00
(O501)

Earth Will Sing, The *sac
(Hauge) solo,pno LILLENAS
SM-617: RN $1.00   (O502)

He Died For Us *sac
solo,pno LILLENAS SM-625: RN $1.00
(O503)

Is It Any Wonder? *sac
solo,pno LILLENAS SM-619: RN $1.00
(O504)

Nurny Song, The
(Reid) solo,pno PRESSER $1.00
(O505)

OWENS, JAMIE
   May I Introduce You To A Friend?
      *sac
      solo,pno WORD S-423   (O506)

OWENS, JIMMY
   Holy, Holy *sac
      solo,pno WORD S-500   (O507)

   If My People Will Pray *sac
      solo,pno WORD S-420   (O508)

   Jimmy Owens Songs *sac,CC10L
      solo,pno WORD 37554 $2.50 (O509)

   True Love Comes From God
      see THERE'S GOING TO BE A WEDDING

OWENS, PATRICIA
   Reach Out And Touch Jesus *sac
      med solo,pno CRESPUB CP-S5018 $1.00
                                 (O510)

   Saga Of A Star, The *sac
      med solo,pno CRESPUB CP-S5028 $1.25
                                 (O511)

OWENS, ROBERT
   Border Line *song cycle
      Bar solo,pno ORLANDO s.p. (O512)

   Desire *song cycle
      T solo,pno ORLANDO s.p.   (O513)

   Four Motivations For Voice *CC4U
      solo,pno ORLANDO s.p.   (O514)

   Heart On The Wall *CC5U
      S solo,pno ORLANDO s.p.   (O515)

   Mortal Storm *CC5U
      Bar solo,pno ORLANDO s.p. (O516)

   Silver Rain *song cycle
      T solo,pno ORLANDO s.p.   (O517)

   Stanzas For Music *CC4U
      T solo,pno ORLANDO s.p.   (O518)

   Tearless *CC8U
      low solo,pno ORLANDO s.p. (O519)

   Three Songs *CC3U
      high solo,pno ORLANDO s.p. (O520)

OWENS, RON
   You Don't Have To Go Far *sac
      med solo,pno CRESPUB CP-S5029 $1.00
                                 (O521)

OWENS, SAM BATT
   Lord Jesus, Think On Me *sac
      high solo,pno ABINGDON APM-772
      $1.50   (O522)

OWL see Cooke, S.C.

OWL, THE see Keel, Frederick

OWL AND PUSSY CAT, THE see Lindsay,
   Miss

OWL AND THE COCKATOO see Lindsay, Mrs.

OWL AND THE PUSSY-CAT see Stravinsky,
   Igor

OWL AND THE PUSSY CAT, THE see Birch,
   Robert Fairfax

OWL AND THE PUSSY CAT, THE see Hely-
   Hutchinson, (Christian) Victor

OWL AND THE PUSSY-CAT, THE see Seiber,
   Matyas

OXDRAGARSANG see Taube, Evert

OXEN, THE see Thompson, A.

OYE MI LLANTO see Lopez-Buchardo,
   Carlos

OZEAN, DU UNGEHEUER see Weber, Carl
   Maria von

OZVENY Z POVSTALECKYCH HOR see
   Andrasovan, Tibor

OZYMANDIAS see Bales, Richard

P

PA ANGEN VID RIAN see Linko, Ernst
   (Fredrik), Riihiniitylla

PA DIN TAERSKEL see Colding-Jorgensen,
   Henrik

PA FASTET STIGER MANEN see Bergman,
   Erik

PA FLODEN see Wiklund, Adolf

PA HIMALAYAS see Bergman, Erik,
   Nocturne

PA LAGUNEN see Myrberg, August M.

PA LANGFERD see Olsen, Sparre

PA NYARSDAGEN see Geijer, Erik Gustaf

PA-PA-PA see Mozart, Wolfgang Amadeus

PA ROINES STRAND see Collan, Karl

PA SANGENS JUBLANDE VINGAR see Wibergh,
   Olof

PA VAGEN UPPAT
   see Andliga Sanger, Heft 2

PA VARDSHUSET see Peterson-Berger,
   (Olof) Wilhelm

PA VERANDAN VID HAVET see Sibelius,
   Jean

PA'AMAYIM KI TOV
   solo,pno OR-TAV $.50   (P1)

PAAP, WOUTER (1908-   )
   Aen Constantinus Huygens
      see Vijf Liederen Rond De
      Muiderkring

   Aen Den Heere Duarte
      see Vijf Liederen Rond De
      Muiderkring

   Aen Joffre Francisca Duarte
      see Vijf Liederen Rond De
      Muiderkring

   De Drukkunst
      narrator,2fl,2ob,2clar,bsn,2horn,
      trp,timp,harp,strings DONEMUS
      s.p.   (P2)

   Muziek Ter Bruiloft
      T solo,2fl,2ob,2clar,2bsn,2horn,
      timp,perc,harp,strings DONEMUS
      s.p.   (P3)

   Op Het Musyck-Boeck Van Meester
      Cornelis Schuyt Van Leyden
      see Vijf Liederen Rond De
      Muiderkring

   Op Jonghvrouw Isabel Le Blon
      see Vijf Liederen Rond De
      Muiderkring

   Vijf Liederen Rond De Muiderkring
      high solo,fl,ob,clar,bsn,2horn,trp,
      timp,harp,strings DONEMUS s.p.
      contains: Aen Constantinus
         Huygens; Aen Den Heere Duarte;
         Aen Joffre Francisca Duarte; Op
         Het Musyck-Boeck Van Meester
         Cornelis Schuyt Van Leyden; Op
         Jonghvrouw Isabel Le Blon (P4)

   Vijf Minneliederen Op Middeleeuwse
      Teksten *CC5U
      high solo,pno WAGENAAR s.p. (P5)

PAARLENDE WEBBEN see Felderhof, Jan

PAASLIED see Bonset, Jac.

PABLO, LUIS DE (1930-   )
   Comentarios
      S solo,pic,vibra,bvl MODERN rental
                                  (P6)
   Ein Wort
      solo,clar,pno,vln TONOS 7205 s.p.
                                  (P7)
   Glosa
      solo,2horn,vibra,pno TONOS 7203
      s.p.   (P8)

PACCAGNINI, A.
   Brevi Canti *CCU
      Mez solo,pno UNIVER. 13735 $4.25
                                  (P9)

PACE, MILLIE LOU
   Happy Jubilee, The *sac
      solo,pno LILLENAS SM-499: SN $1.00
                                 (P10)

   Jesus, The Master *sac
      solo,pno BENSON S6748-RS $1.00
                                 (P11)

   Lead Me Back To Calvary *sac
      solo,pno GOSPEL 05 TM 0121 $1.00
                                 (P12)

   Savior Came In Search Of Me, The
      *sac
      solo,pno WORD S-48   (P13)

   Serve Him With All Your Heart *sac
      solo,pno GOSPEL 05 TM 0122 $1.00
                                 (P14)

PACE, PACE MIO DIO see Verdi, Giuseppe

PACE VESPERTINA see Bossi, Renzo

PACHELBEL, JOHANN (1653-1706)
   What God Ordains Is Always Good *sac
      med solo,pno oct CONCORDIA 98-1560
      $.30   (P15)

PACHER, ANTON
   Lieder Und Kirchenmusikalische Werke
      *sac/sec,CCU
      solo,pno KRENN 1.23 s.p.   (P16)

PACIFICO see Moutet

PACIUS, FREDRIK (1809-1891)
   Ballad *see Balladi

   Balladi
      "Ballad" solo,pno FAZER F 2692 s.p.
                                 (P17)
   Hubertin Laulu
      "Huberts Sang" see Tva Sanger

   Huberts Sang *see Hubertin Laulu

   Leonoren Laulu
      "Leonores Sang" see Tva Sanger

   Leonores Sang *see Leonoren Laulu

   Och Havets Unga Tarna
      Mez/Bar solo,pno GEHRMANS s.p. see
      from SANGEN I   (P18)

   Skamt Och Allvar *CC7L
      solo,pno FAZER F 2039 s.p. (P19)

   Soldatgossen
      high solo,pno GEHRMANS 168 s.p.
                                 (P20)
      low solo,pno GEHRMANS 566 s.p.
                                 (P21)
      solo,pno LUNDQUIST s.p.   (P22)

   Solosanger *CCU
      solo,pno FAZER F 3802 s.p. (P23)

   Suomis Sang
      solo,pno GEHRMANS 169 s.p. (P24)
      solo,pno LUNDQUIST s.p.   (P25)

   Tva Sanger
      solo,pno FAZER F 2053 s.p.
         contains: Hubertin Laulu,
         "Huberts Sang"; Leonoren Laulu,
         "Leonores Sang"   (P26)

   Vart Land
      solo,pno GEHRMANS 170 s.p. (P27)

PACK CLOUDS AWAY see Handel, George
   Frideric

PACZOLAY, I.
   Add Nekem A Szmeidet
      "Dammi I Tuoi Occhi" [It/Czech]
      solo,pno SANTIS 546 s.p.   (P28)

   Dammi I Tuoi Occhi *see Add Nekem A
      Szmeidet

   Koesiutaz E' Jesakaban
      "Nella Notte" [It/Czech] solo,pno
      SANTIS 543 s.p.   (P29)

   Nella Notte *see Koesiutaz E'
      Jesakaban

PADDY FLYNNS WEDDING see Warren, Cyril

PADDY'S PERPLEXITY see Kenward, Maurice

PADDY'S WEDDING see Grant, Douglas

PADEREWSKI, IGNACE JAN (1860-1941)
   My Lady Debonair
      solo,pno (F maj) ASHDOWN s.p. (P30)

PADILLA
   Princesita
      high solo,pno (A maj) ALLANS s.p.
                                 (P31)
      low solo,pno (G maj) ALLANS s.p.
                                 (P32)

PADRE NOSTRO see Nacamuli, Guido

PADRE NOSTRO see Santucci, Pellegrino

PADVINDERS VOORUIT see Hullebroeck, Em.

PAESAGGIO see Cimara, Pietro

PAGAN SAINT see Hovhaness, Alan

PAGANINI see Poulenc, Francis

PAGEANT OF SUMMER, A see Brahe, May H.

PAGES FROM A SUMMER JOURNAL see
    Steiner, Gitta

PAGE'S ROAD SONG, A see Novello, Ivor

PAGLIUCA, C.
    Di Luglio
        [It] S solo,pno CURCI 9373 s.p.
                                            (P33)
    Orfano
        [It] S solo,pno CURCI 9372 s.p.
                                            (P34)

PAH' ON ORJANA ELEA see Kilpinen, Yrio

PAHISSA, JAIME (1880-1969)
    Anoranzas
        see Seis Canciones

    Cancion De Estudiante
        see Seis Canciones

    Cancion De La Pepa Galana
        see Canciones Populares Catalanes

    Cancion De Vendimia
        see Seis Canciones

    Cancion Del Panuelo
        see Seis Canciones

    Canciones Populares Catalanes
        solo,pno cmplt ed RICORDI-ARG
        BA 10065 s.p. Catalan and Spanish
        texts
            contains: Cancion De La Pepa
            Galana; El Adios De Las Hadas;
            El Canto De Los Pajaros; El Noi
            De La Mare; Montanas De Canigo;
            Tunc-Catantunc   (P35)

    El Adios De Las Hadas
        see Canciones Populares Catalanes

    El Canto De Los Pajaros
        see Canciones Populares Catalanes

    El Noi De La Mare
        see Canciones Populares Catalanes

    La Calesita
        see Seis Canciones

    Montanas De Canigo
        see Canciones Populares Catalanes

    Seis Canciones
        solo,pno cmplt ed RICORDI-ARG
        BA 9648 s.p. Catalan and Spanish
        texts
            contains: Anoranzas; Cancion De
            Estudiante; Cancion De
            Vendimia; Cancion Del Panuelo;
            La Calesita; Un Abanico   (P36)

    Tunc-Catantunc
        see Canciones Populares Catalanes

    Un Abanico
        see Seis Canciones

PAHLEN, KURT (1907-   )
    Lied Vom Alltag *CC6U
        solo,pno DOBLINGER s.p.   (P37)

PAI, PAI PAITARESSU see Merikanto,
    Oskar

PAIMENLAULU see Kilpinen, Yrio

PAIMENTYTON KEHTOLAULU see Tuuri, Jaako

PAIMENTYTON SUNNUNTAI see Bull, Ole
    Bornemann

PAISAJE see Guastavino, Carlos

PAISIELLO, GIOVANNI (1740-1816)
    Chi Vuol La Zingarella? (from Gli
        Zingari In Fiera)
        solo,pno FORLIVESI 12078 s.p. (P38)
        (Parisotti) [It/Fr] Mez solo,pno
        RICORDI-ENG 113476 s.p.   (P39)

    Donne Vaghe (from La Serva Padrona)
        [It] S solo,pno RICORDI-ENG 119625
        s.p.   (P40)
        solo,pno FORLIVESI 12081 s.p. (P41)
        (Gubitosi, E.) solo,2ob,2bsn,2horn
        CARISH s.p.   (P42)

    Il Mio Ben Quando Verra (from Nina
        Pazza Per Amore)
        solo,pno FORLIVESI 10882 s.p. (P43)
        (Parisotti) [It] Mez solo,pno

PAISIELLO, GIOVANNI (cont'd.)

        RICORDI-ENG 51952 s.p.   (P44)

    Je Suis Lindor (from Barbier De
        Seville)
        solo,pno DURAND 229 s.p.   (P45)

    Lo Conosco A Quegli Occhietti (from
        La Serva Padrona)
        (Gubitosi, E.) solo,2ob,2horn
        CARISH s.p.   (P46)

    Lode Al Ciel (from Il Barbiere Di
        Siviglia)
        (Flothius, Marius) [It] S solo,fl,
        pno BROEKMANS 395-15 s.p.   (P47)

    Nel Cor Piu Non Me Sento (Variaciones
        Sobre El Tema)
        (Ricci) [It] S solo,pno RICORDI-ARG
        BA 9848 s.p.   (P48)

    Nel Cor Piu Non Mi Sento (from La
        Molinara)
        solo,pno FORLIVESI 10881 s.p. (P49)
        (Parisotti) [It] Mez/Bar solo,pno
        RICORDI-ARG BA 7582 s.p.   (P50)
        (Parisotti) [It/Fr] Mez solo,pno
        RICORDI-ENG 113475 s.p.   (P51)

    Rachelina - Notaro (from La Bella
        Molinara)
        (Gubitosi; Napolitano) 2 soli,2ob,
        2horn sc CARISH 21770 s.p., ipa,
        voc sc CARISH 21772 s.p.   (P52)

    Rossine's Aria (from Il Barbieri Di
        Siviglia)
        (Behrend) [Fr] S solo,S rec/mand,
        gtr BOTE $1.25   (P53)

PAISLEY, ARTUR
    Once I Heard A Song
        med solo,pno (E flat maj) WILLIS
        $.60   (P54)
        high solo,pno (G maj) WILLIS $.60
                                        (P55)

PAISLEY, WILLIAM M.
    How Do I Know
        med solo,pno (A flat maj) WILLIS
        $.50   (P56)

PAISTA PAIVANEN JUMALA see Kilpinen,
    Yrio

PAIVA KALLISTUU JO ILTAAN see Snare,
    Sigurd, Dagen Svalnar

PAJARILLOS DEL AIRE see Llongueras J.

PAJARITOS CRIOLLOS see Giacobbe, Juan
    Francisco

PAJARO MUERTO see Guastavino, Carlos

PALABRAS A MAMA see Ficher, Jacobo

PALACIO
    Chants D'Espagne *CC6U
        [Fr] solo,pno cmplt ed CHANT s.p.
                                        (P57)

PALADILHE, EMILE (1844-1926)
    Pauvre Martyr Obscur (from Patrie)
        [Fr] Bar solo,pno CHOUDENS C272
        s.p.   (P58)

PALATINE'S DAUGHTER, THE see Hughes,
    Herbert

PALAU BOIX, M.
    Arroyuelo Del Molino
        [Span] med-high solo,pno UNION ESP.
        $.75   (P59)

    Del Oriente Lejano
        [Span] med solo,pno UNION ESP.
        $1.50   (P60)

    La Palerma
        [Span] med solo,pno UNION ESP.
        $1.25   (P61)

    La Virgin Va Caminando
        [Span] med solo,pno UNION ESP. $.75
                                        (P62)

    Partida
        [Span] Mez solo,pno UNION ESP. $.40
                                        (P63)

    Que Sentis, Coracon Mio
        [Span] low solo,pno UNION ESP.
        $1.25   (P64)

PALENICEK, JOSEF (1914-   )
    Ctyri Pisne *CC4U
        Bar solo,pno CZECH s.p.   (P65)

    Zpevy Stare Ciny *CC4U
        S solo,pno CZECH s.p.   (P66)

PALESTER, ROMAN (1907-   )
    Tre Sonetti A Orfeo *CC3U
        S solo,orch ZERBONI 5580 rental
                                        (P67)

PALESTINEAN FOLK SONGS, BOOK I *CCU,
    folk
    (Binder, A.W.) [Heb] solo,pno
    TRANSCON. SP 21 $1.50   (P68)

PALESTINIAN NIGHTS see Chajes, Julius,
    Mah Yafim

PALESTRINA, GIOVANNI (1525-1594)
    First Critical Edition Of The Works
        Of Palestrina *CCU
        (Witt, Theodor de; Rauch,
        J.N.;Espagne, Fr.;Commer, Fr.;
        Haberl, Fr.X.) contains works for
        a variety of instruments and
        vocal combinations microfiche
        UNIV.MUS.ED. reprints of
        Breitkopf & Hartel Editions;
        contains 33 volumes $240.00 (P69)

PALIMPSEST see Hespos, Hans-Joachim

PALKOVSKY, OLDRICH (1907-   )
    Milostne Pisne Na Slova Stare Cinske
        Poesie *CCU
        high solo,pno CZECH s.p.   (P70)

PALLAS-ATHENE see Saint-Saens, Camille

PALLIDO IL SOLE see Hasse, Johann
    Adolph

PALLOLEIKKI TRAINONISSA see Sibelius,
    Jean, Bollspelet Vid Trainon

PALM, HERMANN
    En Faders Bon
        solo,pno LUNDQUIST s.p.   (P71)

    Nu Diktar Kvallen Sin Saga
        solo,pno LUNDQUIST s.p.   (P72)

    Tvenne Reigiosa Dikter *sac,CC2U
        SB soli,pno LUNDQUIST s.p.   (P73)

    Under Ronn Och Syren
        see NY SAMLING SANGDUETTER, HEFT 1
        solo,pno GEHRMANS s.p.   (P74)

    Vaggvisa
        solo,pno LUNDQUIST s.p.   (P75)

PALM SUNDAY see Gretchaninov, Alexander
    Tikhonovitch, Les Rameaux

PALM SUNDAY see Kountz, Richard

PALMA, ATHOS (1891-1951)
    Ocho Canciones Saltenas *CC8L
        solo,pno cmplt ed RICORDI-ARG
        BA 6002 s.p.   (P76)

PALMER, ROBERT (1915-   )
    Of Night And The Sea
        SATBar soli,11inst PEER rental
                                        (P77)

PALMGREN
    Mor
        solo,pno LUNDQUIST s.p.   (P78)

PALMGREN, SELIM (1878-1951)
    Aamun Autereessa *Op.106,No.2
        "Klarnad Morgon" solo,pno FAZER
        W 2384 s.p.   (P79)

    Anna-Mi
        solo,pno GEHRMANS s.p.   (P80)

    Asparnas Susning
        solo,pno GEHRMANS s.p.   (P81)

    Die Lerche *see Leivonen

    Eine Winterweise *see En Vintervisa

    En Vintervisa *Op.20,No.1
        "Eine Winterweise" solo,pno FAZER
        F 946 s.p.   (P82)

    Hur Mangen Gang
        solo,pno GEHRMANS s.p.   (P83)

    I Vassen
        "Ruohikossa" solo,pno FAZER F 423
        s.p.   (P84)

    Klarnad Morgon *see Aamun Autereessa

    Leivonen *Op.94,No.1
        "Die Lerche" solo,pno FAZER F 2506
        s.p.   (P85)

    Ruohikossa *see I Vassen

    Sjofararen Vid Milan
        solo,pno GEHRMANS s.p.   (P86)

    Tonen
        solo,pno GEHRMANS s.p.   (P87)

    Vid Min Lutas Silvertoner
        solo,pno GEHRMANS s.p.   (P88)

    Vineta
        solo,pno FAZER F 1933 s.p.   (P89)

PALMS, THE see Faure, Jean-Baptiste, Les Rameaux

PALMSTROM SINGT see Graener, Paul

PALMSTROM-SONATE see Raphael, Gunther

PALOMA DESEPERADA see Ficher, Jacobo

PALOMINO, J.
El Canape
(Subira) [Span] high solo,pno UNION ESP. $2.25   (P90)

PALUDE see Pannain, Guido

PALUDE see Porrino, Ennio

PALUU see Melartin, Erkki, Ritorno

PAMATCE NERUDOVE see Jindrich, Jindrich

PAMIATKE JIRIHO WOLKRA see Zimmer, Jan

PAMPEANA see Lopez-Buchardo, Carlos

PAMPEANA see Quaratino, Pascual

PAMPEANAS see Gianneo, Luis

PAMPELISKY see Lidl, Vaclav

PAN see Lilien, Ignace

PAN AIMAIT EKHO see Roussel, Albert

PAN AMONG THE DAFFODILS see Norman, Lorna

PAN IS MASTER OF US ALL see Bach, Johann Sebastian

PAN-PAN see Perronnet, Amelie

PANDELIDES, S.
Coucher De Soleil
see Quatre Melodies

Le Lac
see Quatre Melodies

Les Roses Effeuillees
see Quatre Melodies

Quatre Melodies
solo,pno cmplt ed TRANSAT. s.p.
contains: Coucher De Soleil; Le Lac; Les Roses Effeuillees; Souvenir   (P91)

Souvenir
see Quatre Melodies

PANDER, O. V.
Sinfonie Des Frauenlebens *sac
A solo,strings,pno BOHM rental   (P92)

PANETTI, JOAN
I Assure You
see Three Songs

I Think
see Three Songs

Three Songs
solo,pno NEW VALLEY $2.50
contains: I Assure You; I Think; What Are Words   (P93)

What Are Words
see Three Songs

PANGE LINGUA see Reale, Paul

PANIS ANGELICUS see Dubois, Theodore

PANIS ANGELICUS see Fauchey, Paul

PANIS ANGELICUS see Franck, Cesar

PANIS ANGELICUS see Pardo

PANIS ANGELICUS see Samuel-Rosseau, Marcel

PANIS ANGELICUS see Sjogren, Emil

PANIZZA, ETTORE (1875-1967)
A Clymene
[Fr] solo,pno RICORDI-ARG BA 11193 s.p.   (P94)

Ariettes Oubliees *see Cancion De La Bandera   (P95)

Ariettes Oubliees *CCU
[Fr] solo,pno RICORDI-ARG BA 11221 s.p.   (P96)

Cancion De La Bandera
[Span] solo,pno RICORDI-ARG BA 6278 s.p. see also Ariettes Oubliees   (P97)

Chanson D'automne
[Fr] solo,pno RICORDI-ARG BA 8634 s.p.   (P98)

PANIZZA, ETTORE (cont'd.)

Chanson Galante
[Fr] solo,pno RICORDI-ARG BA 7677 s.p.   (P99)

Colloque Sentimental
[Fr] solo,pno RICORDI-ARG BA 11222 s.p.   (P100)

En Sourdine
[Fr] solo,pno RICORDI-ARG BA 8635 s.p.   (P101)

Green
[Fr] solo,pno RICORDI-ARG BA 11223 s.p.   (P102)

L'elogio Della Bocca (from Medio Evo Latino)
[It] T solo,pno RICORDI-ARG BA 7680 s.p.   (P103)

Mon Reve Familier
[Fr] solo,pno RICORDI-ARG BA 8636 s.p.   (P104)

Sagesse
[Fr] solo,pno RICORDI-ARG BA 8637 s.p.   (P105)

Serenade
[Fr] solo,pno RICORDI-ARG BA 11224 s.p.   (P106)

PANNAIN, GUIDO (1891-)
Luna
see Pannain, Guido, Palude

Palude
[It] solo,pno CURCI 6495 s.p.
contains also: Luna; Sogno (P107)

Sogno
see Pannain, Guido, Palude

PANNI, MARCELLO (1940-)
Empedokles Lied
[Ger] Bar solo,2fl,2English horn, 3clar,2bsn,4horn,2trp,3trom,tuba, timp,perc,harp,pno,gtr,strings HINRICHSEN rental   (P108)

Quattro Melodie *CC4U
S solo,3inst ZERBONI 7009 rental   (P109)

Tre Arie E Quattro Danze *CC7U
Mez solo,7inst sc ZERBONI 7010 s.p.   (P110)

PANTOMIME see Durand, Jacques

PANTOMIME see Kowalski, Max

PANTOMIME see Pijper, Willem

PANTOMINA see Veretti, Antonio

PANTOMINE see Debussy, Claude

PANTOUM NEGLIGE see Busser, Henri-Paul

PAPAE CURUMIASSU see Villa-Lobos, Heitor

PAPAGENA, PAPAGENO see Mozart, Wolfgang Amadeus

PAPER SLIPS see Bozay, Attila

PAPERTE, F.
Universal Prayer Of Peace
med solo,pno PRESSER $.75   (P111)

PAPIERENE KINDER *Jew
solo,pno KAMMEN 401 $1.00   (P112)

PAPILLON BLANC see Cuvillier, Charles

PAPILLON INCONSTANT see Rameau, Jean-Philippe

PAPILLONS see Saint-Saens, Camille

PAPILLONS, VOLEZ! see Schlosser, Paul

PAPIROSSEN *Jew
"Cigarettes" solo,pno KAMMEN 411 $1.00   (P113)

PAPPA LUPAS see Haapalainen, Vaino

PAPS OF DANA, THE see Mourant, Walter

PAQUES FLEURIES see Cuvillier, Charles

PAQUES FLEURIES see Lavignac, (Alexandre Jean) Albert

PAQUES FLEURIES see Ollone, Max d'

PAQUITA see Cros, Charles

PAR CET ETOIT SENTIER see Bizet, Georges

PAR LES CHEMINS DE FRANCE see Leroux, Xavier (Henry Napoleon)

PAR LES PORTES D'ORKENISE see Caby, R.

PAR LES PRES see Delmet, Paul

PAR LES SOIRS see Respighi, Ottorino

PAR L'ETREINTE see Respighi, Ottorino

PAR MIN DIRTI see Wolf, Hugo

PAR SAINT-JACQUES see Fragerolle, G.

PAR UN SOIR D'HIVER see Rhene-Baton

PARA ACORDAR TEU CORACAO see Camargo Guarnieri

PARAAT EN CORDAAT see Bijl, Theo van der

PARABOLISCH see Schwaen, Kurt

PARAC, FRANCO (1948-)
Oboe Sommerso
Mez solo,ob,fl,pic,clar,bass clar, bsn,2perc,vla,vcl,gtr MUSIC INFO rental   (P114)

PARADIES DER HEIMAT see Doubrava, Jaroslav, Raj Domova

PARADIS D'AMOUR see Levade, Charles (Gaston)

PARADISE ISLAND *sac,gospel
solo,pno ABER.GRP. $1.50   (P115)

PARADISE REGAINED see Albeniz, Isaac

PARADISE REGAINED see Mulder, Herman

PARADISETS BLOMMA see Nordqvist, Gustaf

PARADISETS TIMMA see Olson

PARAIS A TA FENETRE see Guiraud, Ernest

PARAIS A TA FENETRE see Mozart, Wolfgang Amadeus, Deh Vieni Alla Finestra

PARANJOTI
Song Of Radha, The
[Eng] high solo,pno HINRICHSEN H671 $2.50   (P116)

PARANZELLE see Cimara, Pietro

PARANZELLE see Persico, Mario

PARAPHRASE FOR ALTO VOICE AND 11 PLAYERS see Raxach, Enrique

PARATUM COR MEUM see Bruhns, Nicholaus

PARATUM COR MEUM, DEUS see Schutz, Heinrich

PARAULES DE CADA DIA see Benguerel, Xavier

PARAY, PAUL (1886-)
Chanson Napolitaine
high solo,pno sc JOBERT s.p. (P117)

Chanson Violette
med solo,pno sc JOBERT s.p. (P118)
high solo,pno sc JOBERT s.p. (P119)

Il Est D'etranges Soirs
high solo,pno sc JOBERT s.p. (P120)

La Plainte
high solo,pno sc JOBERT s.p. (P121)

Le Champ De Bataille
high solo,pno sc JOBERT s.p. (P122)
med solo,pno sc JOBERT s.p. (P123)

Le Chevrier
med solo,pno sc JOBERT s.p. (P124)
high solo,pno sc JOBERT s.p. (P125)

Le Papillon
high solo,pno sc JOBERT s.p. (P126)
med solo,pno sc JOBERT s.p. (P127)

Le Poete Et La Muse
med solo,pno sc JOBERT s.p. (P128)

L'embarquement Pour L'ideal
high solo,pno sc JOBERT s.p. (P129)

Mortes Les Fleurs
high solo,pno sc JOBERT s.p. (P130)

Quatre Poemes De Jean Lahor *CC4U
solo,pno sc JOBERT s.p. (P131)

Sur La Route
high solo,pno sc JOBERT s.p. (P132)

PARAY, PAUL (cont'd.)

Trois Melodies *CC3U
high solo,pno sc JOBERT s.p. (P133)

Villanelle
high solo,pno sc JOBERT s.p. (P134)

Viole
high solo,pno sc JOBERT s.p. (P135)
med solo,pno sc JOBERT s.p. (P136)

PARCHMAN, GEN
Concerto For Soprano And Orchestra
*concerto
S solo,orch sc SEESAW $24.00 (P137)

Cycle Of Novelties *song cycle
S solo,pno sc SEESAW $4.00 (P138)

PARDO
A La Ronda Del Corral
see Dos Liricas

Agnus Dei
see Triptico Sacro

Ave Maria
see Triptico Sacro

Chistt
see Dos Liricas

Dos Liricas
[Span] solo,pno cmplt ed RICORDI-
ARG BA 8414 s.p.
contains: A La Ronda Del Corral;
Chistt (P139)

Panis Angelicus
see Triptico Sacro

Tejedora!
[Span] solo,pno RICORDI-ARG BA 9403
s.p. (P140)

Triptico Sacro *sac
[Lat] solo,pno cmplt ed RICORDI-ARG
BA 9174 s.p.
contains: Agnus Dei; Ave Maria;
Panis Angelicus (P141)

PARDOENT see Mortelmans, Lodewijk

PARDON, GODDESS OF THE NIGHT see
Castelnuovo-Tedesco, Mario

PARDON, GODDESS OF THE NIGHT see
Thomson, Virgil

PARDON US, GRACIOUS LORD see Bach,
Johann Sebastian

PARDONNE, OUBLIE see Wellings, M.

PARDONNEZ-MOI, MADEMOISELLE see Saint-
Saens, Camille

PAREMPI OLISI OLLUT see Klemetti,
Heikki

PAREMPI SYNTYMATTA see Kilpinen, Yrio

PARES, PH.
Hymne De A Legion D'honneur
[Fr] solo,acap oct DURAND s.p.
(P142)

Hymne De La Legion D'Honneur
solo,pno/inst DURAND s.p. (P143)

PARFUM see Gaubert, Philippe

PARFUM EXOTIQUE see Biancheri, A.

PARI SIAMO! see Verdi, Giuseppe

PARIGI, O CARA see Verdi, Giuseppe

PARIS
Glory Of Calvary's Cross, The *sac
solo,pno LILLENAS SM-858: SN $1.00
(P144)

Had Sin In My Life *sac
solo,pno LILLENAS SM-861: SN $1.00
(P145)

I'm So Happy *sac
solo,pno LILLENAS SM-860: SN $1.00
(P146)

Will You Receive The Lord? *sac
solo,pno LILLENAS SM-859: SN $1.00
(P147)

PARIS NEW-YORK see Alger

PARIS, VOILA PARIS see Guiraud, Ernest

PARISIANA see Poulenc, Francis

PARKE, DOROTHY
Kilkeel
solo,pno PATERSON s.p. (P148)

Moon Magic
med solo,pno PAXTON P40531 s.p.
(P149)

PARKE, DOROTHY (cont'd.)

Saint Columbia's Poem
solo,pno CRAMER (P150)

PARKER, CLIFTON (1905-   )
Blessed Is The People *sac
solo,pno PATERSON s.p. (P151)

I Will Lift Up Mine Eyes Unto The
Hills *sac
solo,pno PATERSON s.p. (P152)

If Thou Prepare Thine Heart *sac
solo,pno PATERSON s.p. (P153)

PARKER, GEORGE
Spiritual Songs, Book One *CCU
solo,pno CRAMER (P154)

Spiritual Songs, Book Two *CCU
solo,pno CRAMER (P155)

PARKER, HENRY
At My Window
low solo,pno (A flat maj) CRAMER
(P156)
high solo,pno (B flat maj) CRAMER
(P157)

Hark To The Mandoline
2 soli,pno (D maj) CRAMER (P158)
2 soli,pno (C maj) CRAMER (P159)

In The Dusk Of The Twilight
2 soli,pno (F maj) CRAMER (P160)
2 soli,pno (G sharp maj) CRAMER
(P161)

Jerusalem *sac
low solo,pno (E flat maj) CRAMER
(P162)
low solo,pno (E flat maj) CENTURY
53 $.40 (P163)
low solo,pno (E flat maj) SCHIRM.G
$.85 (P164)
med solo,pno (F maj) SCHIRM.G $.85
(P165)
high solo,pno (G maj) SCHIRM.G $.85
(P166)
high solo,pno (G maj) CRAMER (P167)
med solo,pno (F maj) CRAMER (P168)

Moorish Maid, The
med solo,pno (D maj) CRAMER (P169)
low solo,pno (C maj) CRAMER (P170)
high solo,pno (E maj) CRAMER (P171)

Our Mountain Home
2 soli,pno (F maj) CRAMER (P172)
2 soli,pno (G maj) CRAMER (P173)

Sea Maidens
2 soli,pno (C maj) CRAMER (P174)
2 soli,pno (D maj) CRAMER (P175)

Spirit Of The Wood
2 soli,pno CRAMER (P176)

Vicar Of Bray
high solo,pno (C maj) CRAMER (P177)
low solo,pno (D maj) CRAMER (P178)

PARKER, HORATIO WILLIAM (1863-1919)
Jerusalem
solo,pno LUNDQUIST s.p. (P179)

O Country Bright And Fair *sac
S solo,pno BELWIN $1.50 (P180)

Pearl, The
med-high solo,pno GALAXY 1.0932.7
$1.25 (P181)

South Wind
high solo,pno GALAXY 1.0933.7 $1.25
(P182)
low solo,pno GALAXY 1.0936.7 $1.25
(P183)

PARKER, KITTY
To A Seagull
low solo,pno (D maj) CRAMER (P184)
high solo,pno (E maj) CRAMER (P185)

PARKS, JOE E.
Song Was Born, A *sac,Xmas,cant/
gospel
soli,pno STAMPS 4816-SN $1.95
(P186)

PARKYNS, B.
Posy Of Proverbs, A *CCU
solo,pno LEONARD-ENG (P187)

PARLA see Arditi, Luigi

PARLA see Tirindelli, Pier Adolfo

PARLA! see Tosti, Francesco Paolo

PARLAMI AMOR MIO see Mortari, Virgilio

PARLE-MOI D'AUTRE CHOSE see Delettre,
J.

PARLE-MOI DE LA MERE see Bizet, Georges

PARLE-MOI DOUCEMENT see Schlosser, Paul

PARLE MOI QUE TA VOIX ME TOUCHE see
Mulder, Ernest W.

PARME see Viardot-Garcia, Pauline

PARMI LES BLANCHEURS DE NEIGE see
Messager, Andre

PARMI VEDER LE LAGRIME see Verdi,
Giuseppe

PARNUSSE *Jew
solo,pno KAMMEN 420 $1.00 (P188)

PARODI, RENATO (1900-   )
Musiche Per La "Twelfth Night" Di
Shakespeare
[It] T solo,2fl,pic,2ob,2clar,2bsn,
4horn,2trp,3trom,tuba,timp,perc,
glock,xylo,harp,cel,org,strings
sc CURCI 8485 rental (P189)

PAROLE ALLA MAMMA see Ficher, Jacobo,
Palabras A Mama

PAROLE DI SALMI see Platamone, Stefano

PAROLE DI SAN PAOLO see Dallapiccola,
Luigi

PAROLE E FATTI see Espoile, Raoul H.

PAROLES A L'ABSENTE see Grovlez,
Gabriel (Marie)

PAROLES A L'ABSENTE see Boussion, E.

PARRIS, ROBERT (1924-   )
Leaden Echo And The Golden Echo, The
Bar solo,pic,3fl,2ob,2clar,2bsn,
2horn,2trp,2trom,timp,strings
AM.COMP.AL. sc $14.30, voc sc
$8.25 (P190)

Mad Scene
SBarBar soli,fl,ob,clar,bsn,horn,
trp,perc,4strings AM.COMP.AL. sc
$14.30, voc sc $7.70 (P191)

Three Love Lyrics *CC3U
T solo,pno AM.COMP.AL. $3.30 (P192)

PARRY, CHARLES HUBERT HASTINGS
(1848-1918)
Armida's Garden
T solo,pno NOVELLO 17.0005.07 s.p.
(P193)

Crabbed Age And Youth
S solo,pno NOVELLO 17.0115.00 s.p.
(P194)

Dirge In Woods
A solo,pno NOVELLO 17.0040.05 s.p.
(P195)

Dream Pedlary
high solo,pno NOVELLO 17.0041.03
s.p. (P196)

English Lyrics, First Set
solo,pno NOVELLO 17.0262.09 s.p.
contains: Good-Night; My True
Love Hath My Heart; Where Shall
The Lover Rest; Willow, Willow,
Willow (P197)

God Breaketh The Battle (from Judith)
sac
T solo,pno NOVELLO 17.0061.08 s.p.
(P198)

Good-Night
see English Lyrics, First Set

Jerusalem
solo,pno/orch (D maj) ROBERTON
902009 s.p. (P199)
(Howe) med solo,pno PAXTON P40620
s.p. (P200)

Lady! Thou Queen Of Israel (from
Judith)
S solo,pno NOVELLO 17.0088.10 s.p.
(P201)

Laird Of Cockpen, The
low solo,pno NOVELLO 17.0089.08
s.p. (P202)

Love Is A Babel
Bar solo,pno NOVELLO 17.0106.01
s.p. (P203)

My Heart Is Like A Singing Bird
Mez solo,pno NOVELLO 17.0121.05
s.p. (P204)

My True Love Hath My Heart
see English Lyrics, First Set

Poet's Song, The
low solo,pno (D maj) ASHDOWN s.p.
(P205)
med solo,pno (E maj) ASHDOWN s.p.
(P206)
high solo,pno (F maj) ASHDOWN s.p.
(P207)

PARRY, CHARLES HUBERT HASTINGS
    (cont'd.)

  Sleep
    med solo,pno NOVELLO 17.0173.08
    s.p.   (P208)

  Stray Nympth Of Dian, A
    S solo,pno NOVELLO 17.0188.06 s.p.
                                      (P209)

  Three Aspects
    high solo,pno NOVELLO 17.0194.00
    s.p.   (P210)

  Through The Ivory Gate
    Bar solo,pno NOVELLO 17.0196.07
    s.p.   (P211)

  To Althea, From Prison
    Bar solo,pno NOVELLO 17.0197.05
    s.p.   (P212)

  When Lovers Meet Again
    high solo,pno NOVELLO 17.0214.09
    s.p.   (P213)

  Whence
    low solo,pno NOVELLO 17.0217.03
    s.p.   (P214)

  Where Shall The Lover Rest
    see English Lyrics, First Set

  Willow, Willow, Willow
    see English Lyrics, First Set

PARSON AND ME see Arundale, Claude

PARSONS
  Look For Me At Jesus' Feet *sac
    solo,pno BENSON S6901 $1.00 (P215)

PARSONS, MICHAEL
  Mindfulness Of Breathing
    low male solo,inst EXPERIMENTAL
    s.p.   (P216)

PART-TIME CHRISTIAN see Smith

PARTED see Tosti, Francesco Paolo

PARTENZA AMOROSA see Monteverdi,
  Claudio

PARTIDA see Palau Boix, M.

PARTING see Gold, Ernest

PARTING PRAYER see Brahe, May H.

PARTITA see Fiorda, Giuseppe Nuccio

PARTNERS WITH GOD see Waters

PARTO! MA TU BEN MIO see Mozart,
  Wolfgang Amadeus

PARTO, PARTO see Mozart, Wolfgang
  Amadeus

PARTO, PARTO, MA TU BEN MIO see Mozart,
  Wolfgang Amadeus

PARTONS, JOLI COEUR see Busser, Henri-
  Paul

PARTOUT! see Chaminade, Cecile

PARTY GAMES OR FROLICS see Wreford,
  Reynold

PAS D'ARME DU ROI JEAN see Saint-Saens,
  Camille

PAS LA PEINE D'EN FAIRE UN ROMAN see
  Buxeuil, R. de

PASACALLE DE LAS ESCALERAS see Guerrero

PASATIERI, THOMAS (1945-   )
  Heloise And Abelard
    SBar soli,pno BELWIN $4.00 (P217)

  Rites De Passage *song cycle
    med solo,chamb.orch/4strings BELWIN
    $6.00, ipr   (P218)

  Selected Songs *CC8L
    solo,pno PEER $5.00   (P219)

  Three Poems Of James Agee *CC3U
    med solo,pno BELWIN $3.00   (P220)

PASCAL
  Botany Bay
    solo,pno ALLANS s.p.   (P221)

PASCAL, ANDRE
  Le Chien Qui Lache Sa Proie Pour
    L'ombre
    see Les Fables De La Fontaine

  Le Coq Et Le Perle
    see Les Fables De La Fontaine

PASCAL, ANDRE (cont'd.)
  Le Renard Et Les Raisins
    see Les Fables De La Fontaine

  Les Fables De La Fontaine
    solo,pno/inst cmplt ed DURAND s.p.
    contains: Le Chien Qui Lache Sa
      Proie Pour L'ombre; Le Coq Et
      Le Perle; Le Renard Et Les
      Raisins   (P222)

  Les Jardins De La Tour Penthievre
    solo,pno TRANSAT. s.p.   (P223)

  Qu'il Est Beau Mon Pays
    solo,pno TRANSAT. s.p.   (P224)

  Sonnet
    solo,pno/inst DURAND s.p.   (P225)

PASCHEN see Hullebroeck, Em.

PASFIELD, W.R.
  Mary's Lullaby
    high solo,pno ELKIN 27.2375.01 s.p.
                                    (P226)

PASIFLORA see Foerster, Josef Bohuslav

PASKE-LILJEN see Nielsen, Carl

PASQUINI, BERNARDO (1637-1710)
  Giran Pure In Ciel Le Sfere
    solo,pno FORLIVESI 11528 s.p.
                                    (P227)

PASS IT ON see Kaiser, Kurt

PASSA LA NAVE MIA see Caltabiano, S.

PASSA LA NAVE MIA see Morelli, A.

PASSA LA NAVE MIA see Terni, Enrico

PASSACABLIA
  see Long Wharf Songs

PASSACAILLE SUR EN THEME DE JEAN-
  SEBASTIEN BACH see Moulaert,
  Raymond

PASSAGE-BIRDS' FAREWELL see Hildach,
  Eugen, Abschied Der Vogel

PASSAGE D'UNE NURSE see Rivier, Jean

PASSANI, EMILE
  Adie Foula!
    see Chansons Martiniquaises

  Amour Et Grammaire *CC6U
    S solo,3fl,2ob,2clar,2bsn,2horn,
    2trp,3trom,harp,cel,glock,xylo,
    chimes,timp,perc,strings JOBERT
    sc rental, voc sc s.p.   (P228)

  Chansons Martiniquaises
    solo,pno AMPHION A 113 $2.25
    contains: Adie Foula!; Colby;
      Moin Descenn' Saint-Pie; Ya-Ya
                                    (P229)

  Colby
    see Chansons Martiniquaises

  Moin Descenn' Saint-Pie
    see Chansons Martiniquaises

  Trois Conseils *CC3U
    high solo,pno sc JOBERT s.p. (P230)

  Ya-Ya
    see Chansons Martiniquaises

PASSE-TEMPS see Baeyens, August-L.

PASSEGGIATA see Pizzetti, Ildebrando

PASSEGGIATA FRANCESCANA see Rosa, M.

PASSENGER, THE see Thompson, Randall

PASSEPIED see Delibes, Leo

PASSER CATULLI see Novak, Jan

PASSER DELICIAE MEAE PUELLAE see
  Cattini, U.

PASSEZ-MOI L'MADERE see Gangloff, L.

PASSING BY see Purcell, Edward C.

PASSING SHOW, THE see Oliver, Herbert

PASSIO IESU CHRISTI see Soler, Josep

PASSION, THE see Warren, Raymond

PASSIONATE SHEPHERD, THE see Heseltine,
  Philip

PASSIONATE SHEPHERD, THE see Reif, Paul

PASSIONATE SHEPHERD, THE see Van Etten,
  Jane

PASSIONATE SHEPHERD TO HIS LOVE, THE
  see Grayson, Richard

PASSIONATE SHEPHERD TO HIS LOVE, THE
  see Taylor, H. Stanley

PASSIONE see Davico, Vincenzo

PASSIONLIED see Mozart, Wolfgang
  Amadeus

PASSIONSLIED see Mozart, Wolfgang
  Amadeus

PASSOVER SONGS see Nardi, Nachum

PASTECHL
  see Internationale Volslieder, Vol 1

PASTICHEN see Rangstrom, Ture

PASTORAALI see Pylkkanen, Tauno
  Kullervo

PASTORAL
  (Lehmann, Amelia) solo,pno (F maj)
    BOOSEY $1.50   (P231)

PASTORAL see Mompou, Federico

PASTORAL, A see Veracini, Francesco
  Maria

PASTORAL MUSIC see Bach, Johann
  Sebastian

PASTORALE see Badings, Henk

PASTORALE see Donati, Pino

PASTORALE see Mills, Charles

PASTORALE see Pylkkanen, Tauno
  Kullervo, Pastoraali

PASTORALE see Roos, Robert de

PASTORALE see Saint-Saens, Camille

PASTORALE see Schlionsky, Verdina

PASTORALE see Stravinsky, Igor

PASTORALE see Verhaar, Ary

PASTORALE DES COCHONS ROSES see
  Chabrier, Emmanuel

PASTORALE POUR JEANNETTE see Badings,
  Henk

PASTORALE RELIGIOSO see Herrmann, Hugo

PASTORALI see Farkas, Ferenc

PASTORELLA, VAGHA BELLA see Handel,
  George Frideric

PASTORES see Hively, Wells

PASTORES, DUM CUSTODISTIS see Gratiani,
  Bonifatio

PASTORES LOQUEBANTUR see Hindemith,
  Paul

PASTOURELLE see Barraine, Elsa

PASTOURELLES *CC20U,18th cent
  (Weckerlin, Jean Baptiste) [Fr] solo,
    pno HEUGEL 10530 s.p.   (P232)

PASTURE, THE see Cowell

PASTURE, THE see Naginski, Charles

PAT BOONE FAMILY, THE *CC8L
  solo,pno WORD 37609 $2.50   (P233)

PAT LUDOVYCH PIESNI see Cikker, Jan

PAT TERRY GROUP SONGBOOK see Terry, Pat

PATCH OF OLD SNOW, A see Ames, W.T.

PATCHES OF SUNLIGHT see Van Dyke, Vonda

PATENZA see Handel, George Frideric

PATER see Durand, (Marie-)Auguste

PATER NOSTER see Bonifanti

PATER NOSTER see Bonset, Jac.

PATER NOSTER see Cordara

PATER NOSTER see Heiller, Anton

PATER NOSTER see Holler, Karl

PATER NOSTER see Niedermeyer, Louis

PATER NOSTER see Peeters, Flor

PATER NOSTER see Samuel-Rosseau, Marcel

PATER NOSTER see Widor, Charles-Marie

PATERO ZPEVU see Fibich, Zdenko

PATERSON IRISH SONG BOOK, THE *CCU
(Redmond Friel) solo,pno PATERSON voc
sc s.p., solo pt s.p. (P234)

PATET VIA see Schouwman, Hans

PATHOGENESIS see Weddington, Maurice

PATHWAYS OF SONG, VOL. 1 *CCU
(LaForge, Frank; Earhart, Will) $2.95
low solo,pno WARNER VF0132; high
solo,pno WARNER VF2002 (P235)

PATHWAYS OF SONG, VOL. 2 *CCU
(LaForge, Frank; Earhart, Will) $2.95
low solo,pno WARNER VF0133; high
solo,pno WARNER VF2003 (P236)

PATHWAYS OF SONG, VOL. 3 *CCU
(LaForge, Frank; Earhart, Will) $2.95
low solo,pno WARNER VF0134; high
solo,pno WARNER VF2004 (P237)

PATHWAYS OF SONG, VOL. 4 *CCU
(LaForge, Frank; Earhart, Will) $2.95
low solo,pno WARNER VF0135; high
solo,pno WARNER VF2005 (P238)

PATRIA EN EL MAR see Espoile, Raoul H.

PATRICO'S SONG see Overton, Hall

PATRIE see Abt, Franz

PATRIOTIC MEMORIES see St. Quentin,
Edward

PATTERNS see Bottje, Will Gay

PATTERNS see Owen, Richard

PATTERSON
Christmas Calypso *Xmas
high solo/low solo,pno oct SCHMITT
8073 $.40 (P239)

PATTI *CC9L
(Dalton, Larry) solo,pno WORD 37621
$2.50 (P240)

PATTI WALTZ SONG see Pattison, John
Nelson

PATTISON, JOHN NELSON (1845-1905)
Patti Waltz Song
solo,pno CRAMER (P241)

PATUELLI, G.
I Bi Temp D-La Purtinara
solo,pno (Bolognese dialect)
BONGIOVANI 2115 s.p. (P242)

PAUCITATEM DIERUM see Rossler, Ernst
Karl

PAUER, JIRI (1919-)
Bajky *CC6U
[Czech/Eng/Ger] solo,pno PANTON 217
s.p. (P243)

Canto Triste
solo,inst PANTON 1487 s.p. (P244)

Detske Ukolebavky *CCU
boy solo/girl solo,pno SUPRAPHON
s.p. (P245)

Kaleidoskop *CCU
[Czech/Ger] med solo,pno PANTON 772
s.p. (P246)

Ukolebavka *CCU
solo,pno SUPRAPHON s.p. (P247)

PAUL ET VIRGINIE see Poulenc, Francis

PAULINE'S ROMANCE see Tchaikovsky,
Piotr Ilyitch

PAULSEN, P. MARINUS
Night Has A Thousand Eyes, The
high solo/low solo,pno FITZSIMONS
$.40 (P248)

PAUV' PITI' see Beekhuis, Hanna

PAUVRE AVEUGLE see Biancheri, A.

PAUVRE JACQUES
[Fr] solo,pno DURAND 16 s.p. (P249)

PAUVRE JACQUES see de Travenet

PAUVRE JEAN see Arrieu, Claude

PAUVRE MARTYR OBSCUR see Paladilhe,
Emile

PAUVRE MAZETTO VEUX-TU CONNAITRE see
Mozart, Wolfgang Amadeus

PAUVRE PAILLASSE see Leoncavallo,
Ruggiero

PAUVRES AMANTS see Berger, Rod.

PAVANE DE LA PETITE MARQUISE see
Strimer, Joseph

PAVANEN, FANTASIEN, ROMANZEN UND
VILANCICOS see Milan, Luis

PAVILION OF ABOUNDING JOY, THE see
Bantock, Granville

PAX HOMINIBUS see Weigl, Vally

PAX VOBISCUM see Schubert, Franz
(Peter)

PAXSON, THEODORE
He Was Alone *sac
low solo,pno (E min) SCHIRM.G $.75
(P250)

PAYNTER, JOHN P.
Shine Out Fair Sun
solo,pno OXFORD 63.065 $1.80 (P251)

PAYS SANS NOM see Aubert, Louis-
Francois-Marie

PAYS SILENCIEUX see Orthel, Leon

PAYSAGE see Duteil d'Ozanne, A.

PAYSAGE see Gaubert, Philippe

PAYSAGE see Hahn, Reynaldo

PAYSAGE see Messiaen, Oliver

PAYSAGE MAUVAIS see Baudrier, Yves

PAYSAGE SENTIMENTAL see Debussy, Claude

PAZZO SON, GUARDATE see Puccini,
Giacomo

PEACE see Binkerd, Gordon

PEACE see Gold, Ernest

PEACE COMES TO ME see Murray, Lyn

PEACE I LEAVE WITH YOU see Dichmont,
William

PEACE I LEAVE WITH YOU see Maxwell

PEACE I LEAVE WITH YOU see Moore,
Donald Lee

PEACE IN THE VALLEY *sac,gospel
solo,pno ABER.GRP. $1.50 (P252)

PEACE IS A LOVELY WORD see Heilner,
Irwin

PEACE, JOY AND LOVE see Holm

PEACE OF MIND see Cory, George

PEACE WAITS AMONG THE HILLS see Davies,
Henry Walford

PEACEFUL SLUMB'RING ON THE OCEAN see
Storace, Stephen

PEARL, THE see Parker, Horatio William

PEARL OF GREAT PRICE *sac
(Carmichael, Ralph) solo,pno WORD
S-414 (P253)

PEARLY, ELY
Songs *CCU
solo,pno OR-TAV $1.00 (P254)

PEARSON, ALBIE
Fear Thou Not (composed with Roe,
Gloria [Ann]) *sac
solo,pno WORD S-134 (P255)

Yes, I Love Him *sac
(Roe, Gloria) solo,pno WORD S-202
(P256)

PEARSON, EDITH
These Are The Lovely Things
solo,pno (E flat maj) ASHDOWN s.p.
(P257)

PEASLEE, RICHARD
Songs From The Chinese *CCU
solo,pno BOONIN MM1 $4.00 (P258)

PEAU D'ANE see Absil, Jean

PEAU D'ANE see Lacome, Paul

PEAU D'ANE see Voormolen, Alexander
Nicolas

PEDIDO see Camargo Guarnieri

PEDLAR OF SPELLS, THE see Oldham,
Arthur

PEDLAR'S BASKET see Baynon, Arthur

PEDRELL, F.
Canciones Arabescas *CCU
[Span] med solo,pno UNION ESP.
$2.25 (P259)

Cuarto Canciones Argentinas *CC4U,So
Am
[Span/Fr] med solo,pno ESCHIG $3.25
(P260)

Quatre Chansons *CC4U
[Fr/Span] high solo,pno ESCHIG
$2.75 (P261)

Tres Pastorales *CC3U
[Span/Fr] high solo,pno ESCHIG
$3.00 (P262)

PEE-WEE THE PICCOLO see Kleinsinger,
George

PEEL, GRAHAM
Ettrick
solo,pno CRAMER $.95 (P263)

Ferry Me Across The Water
high solo,pno (D maj) CRAMER $.70
(P264)
low solo,pno (C maj) CRAMER s.p.
(P265)

Go Down To Kew In Lilac Time
high solo,pno (G maj) CRAMER (P266)
low solo,pno (F maj) CRAMER (P267)

Lute Player
high solo,pno (G maj) CRAMER $1.15
(P268)
med solo,pno (E maj) CRAMER $.95
(P269)
low solo,pno (D maj) CRAMER s.p.
(P270)

Nick Spence
solo,pno CRAMER $.95 (P271)

Piper O' Dundee, The
solo,pno CRAMER $1.15 (P272)

Tartary
solo,pno CRAMER $.95 (P273)

Wild Swan, The
low solo,pno (B flat maj) CRAMER
s.p. (P274)
high solo,pno (E flat maj) CRAMER
$.95 (P275)

PEER GYNT see Grieg, Edvard Hagerup

PEER GYNT'S SERENADE see Grieg, Edvard
Hagerup

PEERY, ROBERT ROY (1903-)
There Is Comfort In Jesus *sac
med solo,pno (D flat maj) BOSTON
$1.50 (P276)

PEETERS, FLOR (1903-)
Ave Maria *Op.104a, sac
"Hail Mary" [Lat/Eng] high solo,
org/pno PETERS 6345A $1.25 (P277)
"Hail Mary" [Lat/Eng] med solo,org/
pno PETERS 6345B $1.25 (P278)
"Hail Mary" [Lat/Eng] SA/TB soli,
org/pno PETERS 6343 $.30 (P279)
"Hail Mary" [Lat/Eng] low solo,pno
PETERS 6345C $1.25 (P280)

Blessed, The
see Marienlieder

Bride And Mother
see Marienlieder

Elected, The
see Marienlieder

Hail Mary *see Ave Maria

Hidden Wonder
see Marienlieder

Ivory Tower
see Marienlieder

Lord's Prayer, The *see Pater Noster

Maria
see Marienlieder

Marienlieder *sac
solo,pno PETERS 6147 $3.50 English-
Flemish Texts
contains: Blessed, The; Bride And
Mother; Elected, The; Hidden
Wonder; Ivory Tower; Maria
(P281)

Mere *CC6U
low solo,pno HEUWEKE. 266 s.p.
(P282)

Mirror Of Life *see Spiegel Des
Lebens

PEETERS, FLOR (cont'd.)

Our Father *see Pater Noster

Pater Noster *Op.102b, sac
  "Lord's Prayer, The" [Eng] med
    solo,pno/org 6201B $1.25   (P283)
  "Lord's Prayer, The" [Eng] low
    solo,pno/org 6201C $1.25   (P284)
  "Lord's Prayer, The" [Eng] SA/TB
    soli,org/pno 6202 $.40   (P285)
  "Lord's Prayer, The" [Eng] high
    solo,pno/org 6201A $1.25   (P286)
  "Our Father" [Lat/Eng] high solo,
    org/pno 6342A $1.25   (P287)
  "Our Father" [Lat/Eng] med solo,
    org/pno 6342B $1.25   (P288)
  "Our Father" [Lat/Eng] low solo,
    org/pno 6342C $1.25   (P289)
  "Our Father" [Lat/Eng] SA/TB soli,
    org/pno 6341 $.30   (P290)

Six Love Songs *Op.50, CC6U
  [Eng/Ger] solo,pno 6146 $3.50   (P291)

Spiegel Des Lebens *Op.36
  "Mirror Of Life" [Eng/Ger] solo,
    org/pno 6053 $3.75   (P292)

Whither Thou Goest *see Wo Du
  Hingehst

Wo Du Hingehst *Op.103b, Marriage
  "Whither Thou Goest" [Eng/Ger] med
    solo,org/pno 6244B $1.50   (P293)
  "Whither Thou Goest" [Eng/Ger] low
    solo,org/pno 6244C $1.50   (P294)
  "Whither Thou Goest" [Eng/Ger] high
    solo,org/pno 6244A $1.50   (P295)

PEETJE'S BRIEF see Hullebroeck, Em.

PEG AWAY see Bevan, Frederick

PEGASE see Malipiero, Gian Francesco

PEGGY MALONE see Trotere, Henry

PEGGY MITCHELL see Duke, John Woods

PEGGY MITCHELL see Mourant, Walter

PEGGY'S LITTLE WAY see Arundale, Claude

PEINE D'AMOUR see Haring, Ch.

PELEMANS, WILLEM (1901-   )
  Clochard
    see Clochards

  Clochards
    med solo,pno cmplt ed CBDM s.p.
      contains: Clochard; J'aime Pas La
      Lune; Moi, J'ai Pas D'chance
        (P296)

  J'aime Pas La Lune
    see Clochards

  Moi, J'ai Pas D'chance
    see Clochards

PELISSIER, H.G.
  Awake
    low solo,pno (E flat maj) LEONARD-
      ENG   (P297)
    high solo,pno (G maj) LEONARD-ENG
      (P298)
    med solo,pno (F maj) LEONARD-ENG
      (P299)
    2 soli,pno (F maj) LEONARD-ENG
      (P300)
    2 soli,pno (G maj) LEONARD-ENG
      (P301)

PELLE, STACKERS GOSSE see Korling

PELLEGRINI, DOMENICO
  Dicite, Mortales *sac
    (Ewerhart, Rudolf) S/T solo,cont
      BIELER CS 54 s.p.   (P302)

PELLIOT, A.
  Berceuse
    solo,pno ENOCH s.p.   (P303)

PELOQUIN, C. ALEXANDER
  I Believe That My Redeemer Lives
    *sac,funeral
    solo,org (med easy) GIA G-1636
      $1.00   (P304)

PELT, R.A. VAN
  Feest In Huis *CCU
    solo,pno BROEKMANS 722 s.p.   (P305)

PELZ, WALTER L. (1926-   )
  Wedding Blessing *sac
    high solo,pno AUGSBURG 11-0736
      $1.00   (P306)
    med solo,pno AUGSBURG 11-0737 $1.00
      (P307)

PENA TIRANNA see Handel, George
  Frideric

PENAS see Wagner, Richard, Schmerzen

PENDANT QUE LA PLUIE AUX CARREAUX see
  Chevreuille, Raymond

PENDANT QUE VOUS DORMEZ see Rhene-Baton

PENELOPE, EIN GEWAND WIRKEND see Bruch,
  Max

PENELOPE'S TRAUER see Bruch, Max

PENGUIN BOOK OF ACCOMPANIED SONGS *CCU
  (Harewood; Duncan) solo,pno PENGUIN
    Q39 $2.85   (P308)

PENGUIN BOOK OF AMERICAN FOLK SONGS
  *CCU,folk,US
  (Lomax) solo,pno PENGUIN Q19 $3.95
    (P309)

PENGUIN BOOK OF CANADIAN FOLK SONGS
  *CCU,folk
  (Fowke) solo,pno PENGUIN Q42 $2.95
    (P310)

PENITENT see Van De Water, B.

PENITENT, THE see Van De Water, B.

PENN
  Smilin' Through
    low solo,pno (C maj) ALLANS s.p.
      (P311)
    med solo,pno (D maj) ALLANS s.p.
      (P312)
    med-high solo,pno (E flat maj)
      ALLANS s.p.   (P313)
    high solo,pno (F maj) ALLANS s.p.
      (P314)

PENN, ARTHUR A. (1875-1941)
  Stars Are Memories, The
    low solo,pno (C maj) WILLIS $.50
      (P315)
    high solo,pno (E flat maj) WILLIS
      $.50   (P316)

PENNEQUIN, J.-G.
  Calme Nocturne
    solo,pno ENOCH s.p.   (P317)

  Fileuse
    solo,pno ENOCH s.p.   (P318)

  Les Columbes
    solo,pno ENOCH s.p.   (P319)

  Les Yeux
    solo,pno ENOCH s.p.   (P320)

PENNINGTON, CHESTER
  Come Along And Dance
    low solo,pno (B flat maj) ALLANS
      s.p.   (P321)
    high solo,pno (D maj) ALLANS s.p.
      (P322)
    med solo,pno (C maj) ALLANS s.p.
      (P323)

PENNISI, FRANCESCO (1934-   )
  Cantata On Melancholy, A
    S solo,orch sc,quarto ZERBONI 6840
      s.p.   (P324)

  Fossile
    male solo,8inst sc,quarto ZERBONI
      6824 s.p.   (P325)

  Sylvia Simplex *scena
    S solo,orch sc ZERBONI 7546 s.p.
      (P326)

PENNIWIT, THE ARTIST see Raphling, Sam

PENNYCANDYSTORE BEHIND THE EL-S AND
  BAN, THE see Blank, Allan

PENSEE D'AUTREFOIS see Fontenailles, H.
  de

PENSEE D'HIVER see Delmet, Paul

PENSIERI NOTTURNI DI FILLI: NEL DOLCE
  DELL' OBLIO see Handel, George
  Frideric

PENSIERI NOTTURNI DI FILLI: NEL DOLCE
  DELL'OBLIO see Handel, George
  Frideric

PENSO!... see Tosti, Francesco Paolo

PEOPLE GOT TO BE FREE see Brigati

PEOPLE THAT WALKED IN DARKNESS see
  Handel, George Frideric

PEOPLE TO PEOPLE see Reynolds, William
  Jensen

PEOPLE'S MARCH see Wolpe, Stefan

PEOPLE'S SONGBOOK, THE *CC100U,folk
  (Hille, Waldemar) solo,pno,gtr OAK
    000050 $2.95   (P327)

PEPPING, ERNST (1901-   )
  As Ik Hier Dit Jaar Wer *song cycle
    high solo,pno (med diff) BAREN.
      2253 $9.75   (P328)

PEPPING, ERNST (cont'd.)

  Bicinien Heft I *sac,CC34U,chorale
    SA soli,org (med) BAREN. 2759 s.p.
      (P329)

  Bicinien Heft II *CC12U,Psalm
    SA soli,org (med) BAREN. 2746 s.p.
      (P330)

  Bicinien Heft III *sac,CC9U
    SA soli,org (med) BAREN. 3217 s.p.
      (P331)

  Funf Lieder Aus Dem Paul-Gerhardt-
    Liederbuch *CC5U
    (Beyer, Frank Michael) med solo,org
      (diff) BAREN. 4112 $14.00   (P332)

  Haus- Und Trostbuch Teil I *CCU
    S solo,pno (med diff) BAREN. 2251A
      $7.00   (P333)

  Haus- Und Trostbuch Teil II *CCU
    S solo,pno (med diff) BAREN. 2251B
      $7.00   (P334)

  Haus- Und Trostbuch Teil III *CCU
    S solo,pno (med diff) BAREN. 2251C
      $5.75   (P335)

  Haus- Und Trostbuch Teil IV *CCU
    S solo,pno (med diff) BAREN. 2251D
      $5.75   (P336)

  Haus- Und Trostbuch Teil I-IV *CC42U
    S solo,pno (med diff) cmplt ed
      BAREN. 2251 $26.75   (P337)

  Liederbuch Nach Gedichten Von Paul
    Gerhardt *sac,CC12U
    med solo,pno (med diff) BAREN. 2250
      $24.50   (P338)

  Vaterland *song cycle
    T solo,pno (med diff) BAREN. 2252
      $9.75   (P339)

PEPUSCH, JOHN CHRISTOPHER (1667-1752)
  Corydon *cant
    S solo,A rec,cont UNIVER. 12562
      $1.75   (P340)
    (Wailes) [Eng/Ger] S solo,fl,pno,
      opt vcl SCHOTTS 10543 s.p.   (P341)

  Cupid, Cupid Bend Thy Bow
    (Bevan) A solo,pno ELKIN 27.2593.02
      s.p.   (P342)

PEPYS, SAMUEL (1633-1703)
  Trois Chansons De Son Choix *CC3U
    cmplt ed,cloth,min sc OISEAU s.p.
      (P343)

PEQUENO ALBUM DE MUSICA ANTIGUA *CC11L
  (Parisotti) [It] T solo,pno RICORDI-
    ARG BA 11103 s.p. contains works
    by: Bencini; Caccini, F.; Cavalli;
    Falconieri; Frescobaldi; Manfroce;
    Stradella and others   (P344)

PER AVERTI VICINA see Mascagni, Pietro

PER CREDERE see Scarlatti, Domenico

PER FARTI ADDORMENTARE see Massarani,
  E.

PER LA TOMBA DI TRE FANCIULLE MILESIE
  see Rocca, Lodovico

PER LA VIA see Veneziani, Vittore, Dans
  La Rue

PER ME GIUNTO E IL DI SUPREMO see
  Verdi, Giuseppe

PER PIETA, BELL' IDOL MIO see Mozart,
  Wolfgang Amadeus

PER PIETA, NON RICERCATE see Mozart,
  Wolfgang Amadeus

PER QUESTA BELLA MANO see Mozart,
  Wolfgang Amadeus

PER SVINAHERDE *folk
  high solo,pno GEHRMANS 215 s.p.
    (P345)
  low solo,pno GEHRMANS 567 s.p.   (P346)

PERAGALLO, MARIO (1910-   )
  Contadino (from La Collina)
    [It/Ger] B solo,2pno (two copies
      needed for performance) UNIVER.
      12000B $2.75   (P347)

  Il Giudice Somers (from La Collina)
    [It/Ger] Bar solo,2pno (two copies
      needed for performance) UNIVER.
      12000F $2.75   (P348)

  Il Suicida (from La Collina)
    [It/Ger] T solo,2pno (two copies
      needed for performance) UNIVER.
      12000G $3.75   (P349)

  La Longeva (from La Collina)
    [It/Ger] S solo,2pno (two copies
      needed for performance) UNIVER.

PERAGALLO, MARIO (cont'd.)

12000H $7.50 (P350)

L'Adolescente Malato (from La
Collina)
[It/Ger] T solo,2pno (two copies
needed for performance) UNIVER.
12000D $2.75 (P351)

L'Ubriacone (from La Collina)
[It/Ger] B solo,2pno (two copies
needed for performance) UNIVER.
12000E $2.75 (P352)

Soldato (from La Collina)
[It/Ger] Bar solo,2pno (two copies
needed for performance) UNIVER.
12000C $3.75 (P353)

PERAKORVAN JUKKA see Simila, Arpo

PERCEVAL, JULIO (1903-1963)
Triste Me Voy A Los Campos
solo,pno BARRY-ARG BC 2001 s.p.
(P354)

[Span] solo,pno (F sharp min)
BARRY-ARG $1.50 (P355)

PERCHE? see Veneziani, Vittore

PERCHE ALLO SPUNTAR DEL GIORNO see
Alfano, Franco

PERCHE LO SGUARDO VOLGI AL SUOL see
Thomas, Ambroise

PERCHE NON TORNI? see Lauri Volpi,
Giacomo

PERCHE SIEDI LA see Alfano, Franco

PERDONA A ME see Massenet, Jules

PERDONATE, SIGNOR MIO see Cimarosa,
Domenico

PERDRAI-JE MA PEINE
(Fragerolle, G.) solo,pno ENOCH s.p.
see from Chansons Du Pays-Lorrain
(P356)
(Fragerolle, G.) solo,acap ENOCH s.p.
see from Chansons Du Pays-Lorrain
(P357)

PERE ETERNAL see La Presle, Jacques
(Paul Gabriel) de

PERERA, RONALD (1941-)
Dove Sta Amore
S solo,electronic tape sc SCHIRM.EC
149 s.p. (P358)

PEREZ
Ay, Ay, Ay
solo,pno SUPRAPHON s.p. (P359)

PERFECT DAY, A see Bond, Carrie Jacobs

PERFECT PRAYER see Day, Maude Craske

PERGAMENT, MOSES (1893-)
Barnet Og Faaret
see Tva Sanger

Blomsterflickan
"Flower Girl, The" [Swed/Eng] med
solo,kbd NORDISKA s.p. (P360)

Flower Girl, The *see
Blomsterflickan

I Natt Skall Jag Do
"Tonight I Must Die" [Swed/Eng] med
solo,kbd NORDISKA s.p. (P361)

Impromptu
[Swed/Eng] med solo,kbd NORDISKA
s.p. (P362)

Kvall I Skogen
see Tva Sanger

Kvarnen
"Mill, The" [Swed/Eng] med solo,kbd
NORDISKA s.p. (P363)

Mill, The *see Kvarnen

Ror Ikke Ved Mitt Hjerte Idag
solo,pno/org ERIKS K 138 s.p.
(P364)

Tonight I Must Die *see I Natt Skall
Jag Do

Tragisk Ballad I Ystad
solo,pno GEHRMANS s.p. (P365)

Tva Sanger
solo,pno GEHRMANS s.p.
contains: Barnet Og Faaret; Kvall
I Skogen (P366)

Vem Speler I Natten
"Who Plays In The Night-Time"
[Swed/Eng] med solo,opt fl
NORDISKA s.p. (P367)

PERGAMENT, MOSES (cont'd.)

Who Plays In The Night-Time *see Vem
Speler I Natten

PERGOLESI, GIOVANNI BATTISTA
(1710-1736)
Ave Verum *sac
(Gubitosi, E.) [It] solo,strings sc
CURCI 8107 rental, voc sc CURCI
8108 rental (P368)

Cantatas *CCU
[Russ] solo,pno MEZ KNIGA 91 s.p.
(P369)

Celebre Siciliana
solo,pno FORLIVESI 10104 s.p.
(P370)

Chi Disse Che La Femmena (from Lo
Frate 'Nnamorato)
(Gubitosi, E.) solo,strings CARISH
s.p. (P371)

Chi Non Ode E Chi Non Vede *cant
(Mortari, V.) S solo,strings sc
CARISH 20798 s.p., ipa, voc sc
CARISH 20799 s.p. (P372)

Die Sieben Worte Des Erlosers Am
Kreuz *see Septum Verba

Gnora Creditemi (from Lo Frate
'Nnamorato)
(Gubitosi, E.) solo,strings CARISH
s.p. (P373)

If Thou Lov'st Me *see Se Tu M'Ami

La Servante Maitresse
see LA MUSIQUE, PREMIER CAHIER

Nel Chiuso Centro *cant
"Orfeo" S solo,orch HENN s.p.
(P374)
"Orfeo" [It] S solo,strings,cembalo
sc PETERS 8015 $7.50, ipa (P375)
"To This Dark Dungeon" S solo,2vln,
vla,cont sc GERIG AV 126 s.p.,
ipa (P376)

Nina *see Tre Giorni Son Che Nina

Ogni Pena Cchiu Spietata (from Lo
Frate 'Nnamorato)
(Gubitosi, E.) solo,strings CARISH
s.p. (P377)

Orfeo *see Nel Chiuso Centro

Psalm 51 *see Stabat Mater

Salve Regina *sac
(Falk) S solo,pno PRESSER $1.50
(P378)
(Gerelli, E.) [Lat] S solo,org,
strings rental sc CURCI 7183, voc
sc CURCI 7335 (P379)

Se Tu M'ami
solo,pno FORLIVESI 10883 s.p.
(P380)
"If Thou Lov'st Me" [It/Eng] high
solo,pno (G min) SCHIRM.G $.85
(P381)
(Parisotti) [It/Fr] S/T solo,pno
RICORDI-ARG BA 8147 s.p. (P382)
(Parisotti) [It/Fr] Mez/Bar solo,
pno RICORDI-ENG 113470 s.p.
(P383)
(Parisotti) [It/Fr] S/T solo,pno
RICORDI-ENG 121043 s.p. (P384)

Septum Verba *sac,Easter,ora
"Die Sieben Worte Des Erlosers Am
Kreuz" 4 soli,orch voc sc ARS
VIVA AV 22 s.p. (P385)

Siste, Superbe Fragor *sac,mot
(Gerelli, E.) [Lat] low solo,org,
strings rental sc CURCI 7251, voc
sc CURCI 7336 (P386)

Stabat Mater (Psalm 51) sac
[Lat] SA soli,strings,org voc sc
RICORDI-ENG 123718 s.p. (P387)
(Bach, Johann Sebastian) "Tilge,
Hochster, Meine Sunde" [Ger] SA
soli,2vln,vla,cont sc HANSSLER
10.151 s.p., ipa, voc sc HANSSLER
s.p. (P388)

Stizzoso Mio Stizzoso
solo,pno FORLIVESI 12079 s.p.
(P389)
(Parisotti) [It] Mez/Bar solo,pno
RICORDI-ARG BA 11854 s.p. (P390)
(Parisotti) [It] Mez solo,pno
RICORDI-ENG 51944 s.p. (P391)

Sun Above Me
(Lehmann) low solo,pno ELKIN
27.1096.10 s.p. (P392)

Tilge, Hochster, Meine Sunde *see
Stabat Mater

PERGOLESI, GIOVANNI BATTISTA (cont'd.)

To This Dark Dungeon *see Nel Chiuso
Centro

Tre Giorni Son Che Nina
[It] solo,pno DURAND 154 s.p.
(P393)
[It] solo,pno RICORDI-ARG BA 9168
s.p. (P394)
[It] S/T solo,pno RICORDI-ENG
128076 s.p. (P395)
[It] Mez/Bar solo,pno RICORDI-ENG
36235 s.p. (P396)
"Nina" [It/Eng] low solo,pno (D
min) SCHIRM.G $.85 (P397)
"Nina" med solo,pno (E min) ALLANS
s.p. (P398)
"Nina" high solo,pno PRESSER $.75
(P399)

PERI, JACOPO (1561-1633)
O Bless Our God *sac
solo,pno PATERSON s.p. (P400)

PERICHOLE'S LETTER see Offenbach,
Jacques

PERICHOLE'S TIPSY SONG see Offenbach,
Jacques

PERIER, JEAN (1869-1954)
Mes Exercises *vocalise
solo,pno SALABERT-US $7.50 (P401)

PERILHOU, ALBERT
Ave Maria *sac
solo,pno/org HEUGEL s.p. (P402)

Complainte De St. Nicolas *sac
med solo,pno/org HEUGEL s.p. (P403)

La Vierge A La Creche *sac
med solo,pno/org HEUGEL s.p. (P404)

O Salutaris *sac
solo,pno/org HEUGEL s.p. (P405)

PERILOUS WAYS see Shaw, Martin

PERISSAS, M.
Complainte De L'oiseau *CCU
solo,pno OUVRIERES s.p. (P406)

D'un Livre D'images *CC8L
solo,pno quarto OUVRIERES s.p.
(P407)

Il Faut Te Faire Soldat
see Le Petit Soldat

La Fontaine
see Le Petit Soldat

La Pieta
see Le Petit Soldat

Le Petit Soldat
solo,pno quarto OUVRIERES s.p.
contains: Il Faut Te Faire
Soldat; La Fontaine; La Pieta;
Retour; Vocero (P408)

Retour
see Le Petit Soldat

Reve A Deux
solo,pno OUVRIERES s.p. (P409)
solo,acap OUVRIERES s.p. (P410)

Vocero
see Le Petit Soldat

PERLAS BLANCAS see Espoile, Raoul H.

PERLAS NEGRAS see Espoile, Raoul H.

PERLEN..VOR DIE SAUE see Finkbeiner,
Reinhold

PERLES see Sinding, Christian

PERLTAU SCHON FUNKELT see Sibelius,
Jean, Lockung

PERLY SLEZSKE see Kubin, Rudolf

PERMETTEZ, ASTRE DU JOUR see Rameau,
Jean-Philippe

PERPIGNAN, F.
Duo Turc
2 soli,pno ENOCH voc sc, solo pt
(P411)

Les Emboiteurs
2 soli,pno ENOCH voc sc, solo pt
(P412)

Sur Le Bateau Mouche
2 soli,pno ENOCH voc sc, solo pt
(P413)

PERRONNET, AMELIE
Chanson D'Ecolier
solo,pno ENOCH s.p. see from
Chansons De Grand'mere (P414)

Chansons De Grand'mere *see Chanson
D'Ecolier; Je Flane; Le Petit
Fanfaron; Moumoutte; Pan-Pan;

PERRONNET, AMELIE (cont'd.)

    Trotte, Trotte; Ui-I Puitt!
    Puitt!; Un Tresor   (P415)

    Je Flane
    solo,pno ENOCH s.p. see from
      Chansons De Grand'mere   (P416)

    Le Petit Fanfaron
    solo,pno ENOCH s.p. see from
      Chansons De Grand'mere   (P417)

    Moumoutte
    solo,pno ENOCH s.p. see from
      Chansons De Grand'mere   (P418)

    Pan-Pan
    solo,pno ENOCH s.p. see from
      Chansons De Grand'mere   (P419)

    Trotte, Trotte
    solo,pno ENOCH s.p. see from
      Chansons De Grand'mere   (P420)

    Ui-I Puitt! Puitt!
    solo,pno ENOCH s.p. see from
      Chansons De Grand'mere   (P421)

    Un Tresor
    solo,pno ENOCH s.p. see from
      Chansons De Grand'mere   (P422)

PERROT-HURET
    Chants De Joie *CC4U
    solo,pno OUVRIERES s.p.   (P423)

    Chants De Paix *CC4U
    solo,pno OUVRIERES s.p.   (P424)

PERRY, JULIA
    How Beautiful Are The Feet
    med solo,pno GALAXY 1.1978.7 $1.00
                         (P425)

    I'm A Poor Lil Orphan In This World
    med solo,pno GALAXY 1.1874.7 $1.00
                         (P426)

    Stabat Mater *sac
    [Lat/Eng] A solo,strings voc sc
      PEER $2.00   (P427)

PERSEPHONE see Hovhaness, Alan

PERSIAN SONG OF SPRING see McBurney

PERSIAN SONGS see Vincze, I.

PERSICHETTI, VINCENT (1915-   )
    Four Emily Dickinson Songs *see
      Grass, The; I'm Nobody; Out Of
      The Morning; When The Hills Do
                         (P428)

    Grass, The
    solo,pno ELKAN-V $.95 see from Four
      Emily Dickinson Songs   (P429)

    Harmonium *song cycle
    S solo,pno ELKAN-V $6.00   (P430)

    I'm Nobody
    solo,pno ELKAN-V $.95 see from Four
      Emily Dickinson Songs   (P431)

    James Joyce Songs *see Noise Of
      Waters; Unquiet Heart   (P432)

    Microbe, The
    see Two Belloc Songs

    Net Of Fireflies, A *song cycle
    solo,pno ELKAN-V $3.00   (P433)

    Noise Of Waters
    solo,pno ELKAN-V $.95 see from
      James Joyce Songs   (P434)

    Out Of The Morning
    solo,pno ELKAN-V $.95 see from Four
      Emily Dickinson Songs   (P435)

    Thou Child So Wise
    see Two Belloc Songs

    Two Belloc Songs
    solo,pno ELKAN-V $.95
      contains: Microbe, The; Thou
      Child So Wise   (P436)

    Unquiet Heart
    solo,pno ELKAN-V $.95 see from
      James Joyce Songs   (P437)

    When The Hills Do
    solo,pno ELKAN-V $.95 see from Four
      Emily Dickinson Songs   (P438)

PERSICO, MARIO (1892-   )
    Assenza
    [It] solo,pno CURCI 164 s.p. see
      from Sette Piccole Liriche, Vol.
      I   (P439)

    Con Gli Angioli
    [It] solo,pno CURCI 169 s.p. see
      from Sette Piccole Liriche, Vol.
      II   (P440)

PERSICO, MARIO (cont'd.)

    Fides
    [It] solo,pno CURCI 436 s.p. (P441)

    Lontana
    [It] solo,pno CURCI 435 s.p. (P442)

    Notte Di Neve
    [It] solo,pno CURCI 168 s.p. see
      from Sette Piccole Liriche, Vol.
      II   (P443)

    Notte Dolorosa
    [It] solo,pno CURCI 166 s.p. see
      from Sette Piccole Liriche, Vol.
      I   (P444)

    Orfano
    [It] solo,pno CURCI 165 s.p. see
      from Sette Piccole Liriche, Vol.
      I   (P445)

    Paranzelle
    [It] solo,pno CURCI 163 s.p. see
      from Sette Piccole Liriche, Vol.
      I   (P446)

    Rosemonde
    [It] solo,pno CURCI 1896 s.p.
                          (P447)

    Sette Piccole Liriche, Vol. I *see
      Assenza; Notte Dolorosa; Orfano;
      Paranzelle   (P448)

    Sette Piccole Liriche, Vol. II *see
      Con Gli Angioli; Notte Di Neve;
      Ultimo Canto   (P449)

    Ultimo Canto
    [It] solo,pno CURCI 167 s.p. see
      from Sette Piccole Liriche, Vol.
      II   (P450)

PERSONNE see Schumann, Robert
  (Alexander)

PERSONNE NE SAURA JAMAIS see Ibert,
  Jacques

PERTI, GIACOMO ANTONIO (1661-1756)
    Il Mose *sac,cant
    5 soli,strings FORNI s.p. (P451)

    La Notte Illuminata *sac,Xmas,cant
    B solo,strings FORNI s.p. (P452)

    Laudate Pueri *sac,cant
    (Berger, Jean) med solo,vln,vla,
      vcl,bvl (med diff) PENN STATE
      PSM 10 s.p.   (P453)
    (Berger, Jean) S/A/T/B solo,vln,
      vla,cont PENN STATE PSMS 10 $3.75
                         (P454)

    Tre Cantate Morali E Storiche Per
      Voce E Archi *CC3U,cant
      solo,strings FORNI s.p. (P455)

PERUSIO, MATHEUS DE
    Gloria In Excelsis *sac,mot
    3 soli OISEAU s.p.   (P456)

PESEM OD LEPE VIDE see Kozina, Marijan

PESKO, ZOLTAN (1937-   )
    Icone Di Una Grande Citta
    S solo,orch voc sc ZERBONI 6431
      s.p.   (P457)

PESMI IZ SANJ see Mirk, Vasilij

PESMI ZA DAN ZENA, VOL. I see Rozanc,
  Mihael

PESMI ZA DAN ZENA, VOL. II see Rozanc,
  Mihael

PESONEN, OLAVI (SAMUEL) (1909-   )
    Aftonsky *see Iltapilvi

    Barnet *see Lapsi

    Gott! Wirf Mich Nicht Zu Deinen
      Steinen *Op.26, song cycle
    solo,pno FAZER W 3348 s.p. (P458)

    Iltapilvi *Op.1,No.1
    "Aftonsky" solo,pno FAZER F 2514
      s.p.   (P459)

    Kesan Onni *Op.20,No.1
    "Sommarens Lycka" solo,pno FAZER
      F 2853 s.p.   (P460)

    Kulkurin Kosinta *Op.1,No.4
    "Vandrarens Frieri" solo,pno FAZER
      F 2517 s.p.   (P461)

    Lapsi *Op.1,No.3
    "Barnet" solo,pno FAZER F 2516 s.p.
                         (P462)

    Pienella Huilulla Huutelen *Op.1,
      No.2
    "Spela Jag Vill Pa Min Lilla Flojt"
      solo,pno FAZER F 2515 s.p. (P463)

PESONEN, OLAVI (SAMUEL) (cont'd.)

    Sommarens Lycka *see Kesan Onni

    Spela Jag Vill Pa Min Lilla Flojt
      *see Pienella Huilulla Huutelen

    Vandrarens Frieri *see Kulkurin
      Kosinta

    Varens Och Hostens Sanger *Op.21,
      No.1-12, CC12L
    solo,pno FAZER F 2919 s.p. (P464)

PESSE, M.
    Le Parfum Inperissable
    solo,pno (available in 2 keys)
      ENOCH s.p.   (P465)

    L'Insaisissable
    Mez/Bar solo,pno/inst DURAND s.p.
                         (P466)
    [Fr] solo,acap oct DURAND s.p.
                         (P467)

    O Ma Chere Maison
    solo,pno/inst DURAND s.p. (P468)

    Un Nom
    solo,pno (available in 2 keys)
      ENOCH s.p.   (P469)

PESTALOZZA, HEINRICH (1873-1949)
    Ciribiribin
    med solo,pno (F maj) CENTURY 1511
                         (P470)
    low solo,pno (F maj) ALLANS
      s.p.   (P471)
    high solo,pno (A maj) ALLANS s.p.
                         (P472)
    med solo,pno (G maj) ALLANS s.p.
                         (P473)
    (Wallis) med-high solo,pno (F maj)
      BOSTON $1.50   (P474)

PESTALOZZI, HEINRICH (1878-1940)
    Zauberspruch
    solo,pno HUG s.p.   (P475)

PESTER CSARDAS see Strauss, Johann

PET LIDOVYCH PISNI see Plavec, Josef

PET MILOSTNYCH PISNI LIDOVYCH Z MORAVY
  see Haba, Alois

PET NARODNI PESMI see Krek, Uros

PET OTROSKIH PESMI see Unger, Makso

PET PESMI see Sivic, Pavle

PET PESMI see Sivic, Pavle

PET PISNI see Huth, Gustav

PET PISNI NA TEXTY J.A. KOMENSKEHO see
  Krejci, Isa

PET VARIACI NA TEMA "VERITAS" see
  Valek, Jiri

PETALES see Devreese, Godefroid

PETCET CSARDAS *CC50U,Hung
  (Farkas, F.) solo,pno BUDAPEST 2132
  s.p.   (P476)

PETENERA see Moreno Torroba, Federico

PETENERA DE LA MARCHENERA see Torroba,
  F.M.

PETER
    Here In These Words
    (Brooks) solo,pno BRODT $.75 (P477)

    When I Was One And Twenty
    (Brooks) solo,pno BRODT $.75 (P478)

PETER CORNELIUS MUSICAL WORKS see
  Cornelius, Peter

PETER, JOHANN FRIEDRICH (1746-1813)
    Lord Is In His Holy Temple *sac
    solo,pno (B flat maj) BOOSEY $1.50
                         (P479)

PETER, L.
    Jennie Kissed Me
    solo,pno BRODT $.60   (P480)

PETER, MIEG
    Quatre Poemes Algimantas Narakas
      *CC4U
    solo,pno HENN 928 s.p.   (P481)

PETER QUINCE AT THE CLAVIER see
  Tanenbaum, Elias

PETERISMS SET 1 see Heseltine, Philip

PETERKIN
    By A Bank I Lay
    SS soli,4strings (med) OXFORD
      rental   (P482)

PETERKIN (cont'd.)

I Heard A Piper Piping
  Mez solo,chamb.orch (easy) voc sc
  OXFORD 63.748 $1.15   (P483)

PETERMANN, ERNST
  Links Geht Der Ferdinand
  solo,pno SCHAUR s.p.   (P484)

PETERS
  Rhenvinets Lov
  solo,pno LUNDQUIST s.p.   (P485)

PETERS, W.F.
  Keep Me Faithful (composed with
    Gerald, Thomas J.) *sac
    low solo,pno CHAPLET $.85   (P486)
    high solo,pno CHAPLET $.85   (P487)

PETERSEN, WILHELM (1890-1957)
  Der Alte Garten *Op.44,No.1-9, CC9U
    low solo,pno (diff) MULLER 1363
    s.p.   (P488)

  Drei Barock-Lieder *Op.26,No.1-3,
    CC3U
    med solo,pno (diff) MULLER 1059
    s.p.   (P489)

  Funf Gesange Nach Friedrich Holderlin
    Und Stefan George *Op.20,No.1-5,
    CC5U
    med solo,pno (diff) MULLER 1060
    s.p.   (P490)

  Goethe-Lieder *Op.40,No.1-9, CC9U
    high solo,pno (diff) MULLER 1061
    s.p.   (P491)

  Wunderhorn-Lieder Heft I (Op. 12)
    *CCU
    med solo,pno (diff) MULLER 1354-I
    s.p.   (P492)

  Wunderhorn-Lieder Heft II (OP.12)
    *CCU
    med solo,pno (diff) MULLER 1354-II
    s.p.   (P493)

  Wunderhorn-Lieder Heft III (OP. 12)
    *CCU
    med solo,pno (diff) MULLER 1354-III
    s.p.   (P494)

PETERSON, JOHN W.
  Above Every Name *sac
    solo,pno SINGSPIR 7286 $1.00 (P495)

  Am I In Love? (from Worlds Apart) sac
    solo,pno SINGSPIR 7037 $.35 (P496)

  Chariot Of Clouds *sac
    solo,pno SINGSPIR 7117-SN $1.00
                                 (P497)

  Christmas Is For Children *sac
    solo,pno SINGSPIR 7120 $1.00 (P498)

  Come, Holy Spirit *sac
    solo,pno SINGSPIR 7103 $1.00 (P499)

  Do You Know The Christ Of Christmas
    *sac
    solo,pno WORD S-130   (P500)

  Five Rows Back *sac
    solo,pno SINGSPIR 7285 $1.00 (P501)

  God Did A Wonderful Thing For Me
    see Minkler, Ross, Let Me Lose My
    Life And Find It Lord In Thee

  He Walked That Lonesome Road *sac
    solo,pno SINGSPIR 7018 $1.00 (P502)

  Heaven Came Down And Glory Filled My
    Soul *sac
    solo,pno SINGSPIR 7031-SN $1.00
                                 (P503)
    solo,pno SINGSPIR 7051 $1.00 (P504)

  Here's To A Soldier Hero (from Worlds
    Apart) sac
    solo,pno SINGSPIR 7035 $.35 (P505)

  He's Filling Up Heaven With Sinners
    *sac
    solo,pno SINGSPIR 7099 $1.00 (P506)

  Higher Hands *sac
    solo,pno SINGSPIR 7040 $.75 (P507)

  I Believe In Miracles *sac
    solo,pno SINGSPIR 7023 $1.00 (P508)

  I Love America *sac
    solo,pno SINGSPIR 7282 $1.00 (P509)

  I'm Just A Flag Waving American *sac
    solo,pno SINGSPIR 7283 $1.00 (P510)

  In The Image Of God *sac
    solo,pno SINGSPIR 7034 $1.00 (P511)

PETERSON, JOHN W. (cont'd.)

  It's Not An Easy Road *sac
    solo,pno SINGSPIR 7022 $1.00 (P512)
    solo,pno SINGSPIR 7045-SN $.35
                                 (P513)

  It's Time To Pray *sac
    solo,pno SINGSPIR 7281 $1.00 (P514)

  Jesus Is Coming *sac
    solo,pno SINGSPIR 7112 $1.00 (P515)

  Jesus Is Coming Again *sac
    solo,pno SINGSPIR 7002 $1.00 (P516)

  Jesus Is Still Wonderful *sac
    solo,pno SINGSPIR 7030-SN $1.00
                                 (P517)
    solo,pno SINGSPIR 7127 $1.00 (P518)

  John Peterson's Folio Of Favorites
    *sac,CC15UL
    solo,kbd SINGSPIR 5035 $1.95 (P519)

  John W. Peterson's Song Favorites
    *sac,CCUL
    med solo,pno SINGSPIR $1.95 (P520)

  Katarina (from Worlds Apart) sac
    solo,pno SINGSPIR 7038 $.35 (P521)

  Kids Of The Street (from Worlds
    Apart) sac
    solo,pno SINGSPIR 7039 $.35 (P522)

  No More Death *sac
    solo,pno SINGSPIR 7105 $1.00 (P523)

  No One Understands Like Jesus *sac
    solo,pno WORD S-172   (P524)

  No Other Song *sac
    solo,pno SINGSPIR 7017 $1.00 (P525)

  Of Love I Sing *sac
    solo,pno SINGSPIR 7041 $.35 (P526)

  Over The Sunset Mountains *sac
    solo,pno SINGSPIR 7008 $1.00 (P527)

  Red, White And Blue, The (composed
    with Wyrtzen, Don) *sac
    solo,pno SINGSPIR 7284 $1.00 (P528)

  Shepherd Of Love *sac
    solo,pno SINGSPIR 7043 $.75 (P529)

  So Send I You *sac
    solo,pno SINGSPIR 7007 $1.00 (P530)

  Solos For Christmas From John W.
    Peterson Cantatas, Series Nos. 1-
    2 *sac,CCUL,Xmas
    low solo,kbd SINGSPIR $1.50, ea.
    available for medium and low
    voice   (P531)

  Solos For Easter From John W.
    Peterson Cantatas *sac,CCUL
    med solo,pno SINGSPIR 5937 $1.50;
    low solo,pno SINGSPIR 5938 $1.50
                                 (P532)

  Springs Of Living Water *sac
    solo,pno SINGSPIR 7047-SN $.35
                                 (P533)

  Surely Goodness And Mercy *sac
    solo,pno SINGSPIR 7032-SN $1.00
                                 (P534)
    solo,pno SINGSPIR 7050 $1.00 (P535)

  That's What It's Like In The Army
    (from Worlds Apart) sac
    solo,pno SINGSPIR 7036 $.35 (P536)

  There Is No Greater Love *sac
    solo,pno SINGSPIR 7015 $1.00 (P537)

  Together *sac
    solo,pno SINGSPIR 7044 $.35 (P538)

  Wonder Of Wonders *sac
    solo,pno SINGSPIR 7100 $1.00 (P539)

  Worlds Apart (from Worlds Apart) sac
    solo,pno SINGSPIR 7042 $.35 (P540)

PETERSON-BERGER, (OLOF) WILHELM
  (1867-1942)
  Aftonstamning
    solo,pno LUNDQUIST s.p.   (P541)

  An Korpens Vinge Min Tanke Ta'r
    see Tva Dikter

  Appelgarden
    see Minnesangarn I Sverige

  Arnljot
    Bar solo,pno LUNDQUIST s.p.
      contains: Arnljot Halsar
      Jamtland; Arnljots Karlekssang;
      Tormods Kvad
      see also: Arnljot Halsar Jamtland
                                 (P542)

PETERSON-BERGER, (OLOF) WILHELM
  (cont'd.)

  Arnljot Halsar Jamtland
    Bar solo,pno LUNDQUIST s.p. see
    also Arnljot   (P543)

  Arnljots Karlekssang
    see Arnljot

  Aspakerspolska
    see Svensk Lyrik, Series 2, Heft 2:
    Ur Fridolins Lustgard
    low solo,pno LUNDQUIST s.p. (P544)
    high solo,pno LUNDQUIST s.p. (P545)

  Aterkomst
    see Svensk Lyrik, Series 3, Heft 2:
    Offerkransar

  Bevaringsvisa
    see Svensk Lyrik, Series 2, Heft 5:
    Fyra Muntra Visor
    Bar solo,pno LUNDQUIST s.p. (P546)

  Bland Skogens Hogo Furustammar
    *Op.5,No.4
    see Fyra Visor I Svensk Folkton

  Boljebyvals
    see Svensk Lyrik, Series 2, Heft 2:
    Ur Fridolins Lustgard
    high solo,pno LUNDQUIST s.p. (P547)
    low solo,pno LUNDQUIST s.p. (P548)

  Dag, Som Jag Levat!
    see Dikter Av F. Nietzsche, Heft 2

  Dagen Flyr
    see Ur En Karlekssaga, Hafte I

  Dalmarsch
    high solo,pno LUNDQUIST s.p. (P549)
    low solo,pno LUNDQUIST s.p. (P550)

  Dar Hjortronen Blomma
    see Tva Dikter

  Det Blir Ej Till Stoft
    see Svensk Lyrik, Series 3, Heft 2:
    Offerkransar

  Die Letzte Nacht
    see Fyra Dikter

  Dikter Av F. Nietzsche, Heft 1
    solo,pno LUNDQUIST s.p.
      contains: Ecce Homo; Meine Rosen;
      Venedig; Zarathustras
      Rundgesang   (P551)

  Dikter Av F. Nietzsche, Heft 2
    solo,pno LUNDQUIST s.p.
      contains: Dag, Som Jag Levat!;
      Dionysos; Dithyramb Ej Langre
      Torsta Du Skall; Glattighet,
      Gyllene, Kom!   (P552)

  Dina Ogon Aro Eldar
    see Svensk Lyrik, Series 2, Heft 2:
    Ur Fridolins Lustgard

  Dionysos
    see Dikter Av F. Nietzsche, Heft 2

  Dithyramb Ej Langre Torsta Du Skall
    see Dikter Av F. Nietzsche, Heft 2

  Ditt Namm Jag Hade Skrivit *Op.5,
    No.2
    see Fyra Visor I Svensk Folkton

  Dromd Lycka
    see Svensk Lyrik, Series 2, Heft 4:
    Ur Vildmarks- Och Karleksvisor
    solo,pno LUNDQUIST s.p.   (P553)

  Du Ler
    see Svensk Lyrik, Series 2, Heft 1:
    Ur Fridolins Visor

  Ecce Homo
    see Dikter Av F. Nietzsche, Heft 1

  En Gammal Dansrytm
    see Svensk Lyrik, Series 3, Heft 4:
    Tredikter

  En Madrigal
    see Svensk Lyrik, Series 2, Heft 3:
    Ur Fridolins Lustgard

  En Spelmansvisa
    see Svensk Lyrik, Series 2, Heft 4:
    Ur Vildmarks- Och Karleksvisor
    solo,pno LUNDQUIST s.p.   (P554)

  En Vintervisa
    solo,pno LUNDQUIST s.p.   (P555)

  En Visa Om Karlek
    solo,pno LUNDQUIST s.p.   (P556)

  Fanjunkar Berg
    see Svensk Lyrik, Series 2, Heft 5:
    Fyra Muntra Visor

PETERSON-BERGER, (OLOF) WILHELM
(cont'd.)

solo,pno LUNDQUIST s.p.   (P557)

Fjallvandring
see Jamtlandsminnen

Frukttid
solo,pno LUNDQUIST s.p.   (P558)

Fyra Dikter
solo,pno LUNDQUIST s.p.
contains: Die Letzte Nacht;
Liebesreime; Musik Bewegt Mich;
Vorfruhling   (P559)

Fyra Visor I Svensk Folkton
solo,pno LUNDQUIST s.p.
contains: Bland Skogens Hogo
Furustammar, Op.5,No.4; Ditt
Namm Jag Hade Skrivit, Op.5,
No.2; Nar Jag For Mig Sjalv I
Morka Skogen Gar, Op.5,No.1;
Som Stjarnorna Pa Himmelen,
Op.5,No.3   (P560)

Gammal Ramsa
see Hosthorn

Glattighet, Gyllene, Kom!
see Dikter Av F. Nietzsche, Heft 2

Gratulation
solo,pno LUNDQUIST s.p.   (P561)

Hemlangtan *Op.9,No.1
see Tva Sanger

Herr Ollondal
see Svensk Lyrik, Series 2, Heft 3:
Ur Fridolins Lustgard

Hesperis
see Svensk Lyrik, Series 3, Heft 2:
Offerkransar

Hogt Pa Fallets Ormbunkssnar
see Svensk Lyrik, Heft 5:
Gullebarns Vaggsanger

Hosthorn
solo,pno LUNDQUIST s.p.
contains: Gammal Ramsa; Humlor;
Vandring   (P562)

Humlevisa
see Svensk Lyrik, Series 2, Heft 1:
Ur Fridolins Visor

Humlor
see Hosthorn

Ibland Myrten Och Jasminer
solo,pno GEHRMANS s.p.   (P563)

Intet Ar Som Vantans Tider
see Svensk Lyrik, Series 2, Heft 1:
Ur Fridolins Visor
high solo,pno LUNDQUIST s.p.   (P564)
low solo,pno LUNDQUIST s.p.   (P565)

Irmelin Rose
high solo,pno LUNDQUIST s.p.   (P566)
low solo,pno LUNDQUIST s.p.   (P567)

Jamtlandsminnen
solo,pno LUNDQUIST s.p.
contains: Fjallvandring; Locklat
                               (P568)

Jorum
see Svensk Lyrik, Series 2, Heft 1:
Ur Fridolins Visor

Jungfrun Under Lind
high solo,pno LUNDQUIST s.p.   (P569)
low solo,pno LUNDQUIST s.p.   (P570)

Kopparflojeln
see Svensk Lyrik, Series 2, Heft 3:
Ur Fridolins Lustgard

Langtan Heter Min Arvedel
see Svensk Lyrik, Series 2, Heft 2:
Ur Fridolins Lustgard

Liebesreime
see Fyra Dikter

Liksom Den Unga Zephyr
see Ur En Karlekssaga, Hafte I

Locklat
see Jamtlandsminnen

Maj
see Svensk Lyrik, Heft 1

Maj I Munga
see Svensk Lyrik, Series 2, Heft 2:
Ur Fridolins Lustgard

Manhymn Vid Lambertsmassen
see Svensk Lyrik, Series 2, Heft 1:
Ur Fridolins Visor

PETERSON-BERGER, (OLOF) WILHELM
(cont'd.)

Marits Visor *CCU
solo,pno LUNDQUIST s.p.   (P571)

Meine Rosen
see Dikter Av F. Nietzsche, Heft 1

Melodi
see Svensk Lyrik, Series 3, Heft 3:
Tva Dikter

Minnesangarn I Sverige
solo,pno LUNDQUIST s.p.
contains: Appelgarden; Sorg
                               (P572)

Mitt Trollslott
see Svensk Lyrik, Series 3, Heft 1:
Fyra Dikter

Mor Britta
solo,pno LUNDQUIST s.p.   (P573)

Mumla, Tumla, Humla
see Svensk Lyrik, Heft 5:
Gullebarns Vaggsanger

Musik Bewegt Mich
see Fyra Dikter

Nar Jag For Mig Sjalv I Morka Skogen
Gar *Op.5,No.1
see Fyra Visor I Svensk Folkton

O, Liv, Jag Sag Dig
see Svensk Lyrik, Series 3, Heft 2:
Offerkransar

Och Riddaren Drog Uti Osterland
solo,pno GEHRMANS s.p.   (P574)

Odevisan
see Svensk Lyrik, Series 3, Heft 3:
Tva Dikter

Pa Vardshuset
see Svensk Lyrik, Series 2, Heft 3:
Ur Fridolins Lustgard

Positivvisa
see Tva Romantiska Visor

Sag Ostan, Sag Vastan?
see Svensk Lyrik, Heft 5:
Gullebarns Vaggsanger

Sagan Om Rosalind
see Svensk Lyrik, Series 2, Heft 4:
Ur Vildmarks- Och Karleksvisor

Sang Efter Skordeanden
see Svensk Lyrik, Series 2, Heft 5:
Fyra Muntra Visor
solo,pno LUNDQUIST s.p.   (P575)

Selinda Och Leander
see Svensk Lyrik, Series 2, Heft 5:
Fyra Muntra Visor
solo,pno LUNDQUIST s.p.   (P576)

Semele
see Svensk Lyrik, Series 3, Heft 1:
Fyra Dikter

Serenad
see Svensk Lyrik, Series 2, Heft 4:
Ur Vildmarks- Och Karleksvisor

Serenata *Op.9,No.2
see Tva Sanger

Sikta, Sikta, Gullkorn
see Svensk Lyrik, Heft 5:
Gullebarns Vaggsanger

Sju Rosor Och Sju Eldar
see Svensk Lyrik, Series 3, Heft 1:
Fyra Dikter

Som Stjarnorna Pa Himmelen *Op.5,
No.3
see Fyra Visor I Svensk Folkton

Sommarsang
solo,pno LUNDQUIST s.p.   (P577)

Sorg
see Minnesangarn I Sverige

Sporj Ostan, Sporj Vastan!
see Svensk Lyrik, Heft 5:
Gullebarns Vaggsanger

Svensk Lyrik, Heft 1
solo,pno LUNDQUIST s.p.
contains: Maj; Till Bruden;
Titania   (P578)

Svensk Lyrik, Heft 2: Florez Och
Blazeflor *CCU
solo,pno LUNDQUIST s.p.   (P579)

Svensk Lyrik, Heft 3: Hostsang *CCU
Bar solo,pno LUNDQUIST s.p.   (P580)

PETERSON-BERGER, (OLOF) WILHELM
(cont'd.)

Svensk Lyrik, Heft 4: Alven Till
Flickan *CCU
solo,pno LUNDQUIST s.p.   (P581)

Svensk Lyrik, Heft 5: Gullebarns
Vaggsanger
solo,pno LUNDQUIST s.p.
contains: Hogt Pa Fallets
Ormbunkssnar; Mumla, Tumla,
Humla; Sag Ostan, Sag Vastan?;
Sikta, Sikta, Gullkorn; Sporj
Ostan, Sporj Vastan!   (P582)

Svensk Lyrik, Series 2, Heft 1: Ur
Fridolins Visor
solo,pno LUNDQUIST s.p.
contains: Du Ler; Humlevisa;
Intet Ar Som Vantans Tider;
Jorum; Manhymn Vid
Lambertsmassen   (P583)

Svensk Lyrik, Series 2, Heft 2: Ur
Fridolins Lustgard
solo,pno LUNDQUIST s.p.
contains: Aspakerspolska;
Boljebyvals; Dina Ogon Aro
Eldar; Langtan Heter Min
Arvedel; Maj I Munga   (P584)

Svensk Lyrik, Series 2, Heft 3: Ur
Fridolins Lustgard
solo,pno LUNDQUIST s.p.
contains: En Madrigal; Herr
Ollondal; Kopparflojeln; Pa
Vardshuset   (P585)

Svensk Lyrik, Series 2, Heft 4: Ur
Vildmarks- Och Karleksvisor
solo,pno LUNDQUIST s.p.
contains: Dromd Lycka; En
Spelmansvisa; Sagan Om
Rosalind; Serenad   (P586)

Svensk Lyrik, Series 2, Heft 5: Fyra
Muntra Visor
solo,pno LUNDQUIST s.p.
contains: Bevaringsvisa;
Fanjunkar Berg; Sang Efter
Skordeanden; Selinda Och
Leander   (P587)

Svensk Lyrik, Series 2, Heft 6:
Loskekarlarnes Sang *CCU
solo,pno LUNDQUIST s.p.   (P588)

Svensk Lyrik, Series 3, Heft 1: Fyra
Dikter
solo,pno LUNDQUIST s.p.
contains: Mitt Trollslott;
Semele; Sju Rosor Och Sju
Eldar; Villemo   (P589)

Svensk Lyrik, Series 3, Heft 2:
Offerkransar
solo,pno LUNDQUIST s.p.
contains: Aterkomst; Det Blir Ej
Till Stoft; Hesperis; O, Liv,
Jag Sag Dig   (P590)

Svensk Lyrik, Series 3, Heft 3: Tva
Dikter
solo,pno LUNDQUIST s.p.
contains: Melodi; Odevisan   (P591)

Svensk Lyrik, Series 3, Heft 4:
Tredikter
solo,pno LUNDQUIST s.p.
contains: En Gammal Dansrytm;
Under Vintergatan; Vid Assjorna
                               (P592)

Svensk Medborgarsang *CCU
solo,pno LUNDQUIST s.p.   (P593)

Til Maidag
solo,pno LUNDQUIST s.p.   (P594)

Till Bruden
see Svensk Lyrik, Heft 1

Till Rosorna
solo,pno LUNDQUIST s.p.   (P595)

Titania
see Svensk Lyrik, Heft 1

Tormods Kvad
see Arnljot

Tva Dikter
solo,pno LUNDQUIST s.p.
contains: An Korpens Vinge Min
Tanke Ta'r; Dar Hjortronen
Blomma   (P596)

Tva Klara Stjarnor Har Himlen Mist
see Ur En Karlekssaga, Hafte I

Tva Romantiska Visor
solo,pno LUNDQUIST s.p.
contains: Positivvisa;
Zigeunerlied   (P597)

PETERSON-BERGER, (OLOF) WILHELM
(cont'd.)

Tva Sanger
solo,pno LUNDQUIST s.p.
contains: Hemlangtan, Op.9,No.1;
Serenata, Op.9,No.2   (P598)

Under Vintergatan
see Svensk Lyrik, Series 3, Heft 4:
Tredikter

Ur En Karlekssaga, Hafte I
solo,pno GEHRMANS s.p.
contains: Dagen Flyr; Liksom Den
Unga Zephyr; Tva Klara Stjarnor
Har Himlen Mist; Vackra Barn
Dar Vid Ditt Fonster   (P599)

Vackra Barn Dar Vid Ditt Fonster
see Ur En Karlekssaga, Hafte I

Vainos Sanger
S solo,pno LUNDQUIST s.p.   (P600)
solo,pno LUNDQUIST s.p.   (P601)

Vandring
see Hosthorn

Varsang
solo,pno LUNDQUIST s.p.   (P602)

Venedig
see Dikter Av F. Nietzsche, Heft 1

Vid Assjorna
see Svensk Lyrik, Series 3, Heft 4:
Tredikter

Vid Froso Kyrka
solo,pno LUNDQUIST s.p.   (P603)

Villemo
see Svensk Lyrik, Series 3, Heft 1:
Fyra Dikter

Vorfruhling
see Fyra Dikter

Zarathustras Rundgesang
see Dikter Av F. Nietzsche, Heft 1

Zigeunerlied
see Tva Romantiska Visor

PETIT, A.
Cadet-Coquelin
solo,acap solo pt ENOCH s.p. (P604)

PETIT CONCERT see Trimble, Lester

PETIT COURS DE MORALE see Honegger,
Arthur

PETIT JEAN see Delbruck, J.

PETIT MARI see Delmet, Paul

PETIT MATIN see Daniel-Lesur

PETIT MERCIER see Moulaert, Raymond

PETIT, P.
Il Neige De La Joie
solo,pno/inst LEDUC s.p.   (P605)

Il Neige Des Secrets
solo,pno/inst LEDUC s.p.   (P606)

PETIT PIOUPIOU see Lionnet, A.

PETIT TOUT PETIT see Cuvillier, Charles

PETITE AMERICAINE see Berger, Rod.

PETITE ANNONCE see Berger, Rod.

PETITE BERCEUSE see Arensky, Anton
Stepanovitch

PETITE CASCADE see Orthel, Leon

PETITE FLAMME see Fourdrain, Felix

PETITE MESSE SOLUNNELLE see Rossini,
Gioacchino

PETITE SAINTE see Ryelandt, Joseph

PETITE YNGA see Lopez-Buchardo, Carlos

PETITES HISTOIRES MISES EN MUSIQUE see
Ravize, A.

PETITES LITANIES DE JESUS see Ruyneman,
Daniel

PETITJEAN, M.
Ma Petite Bergere
(Montoya, G.) solo,pno ENOCH s.p.
(P607)
(Montoya, G.) solo,acap ENOCH s.p.
(P608)
Pour Les Femmes
(Montoya, G.) solo,pno ENOCH s.p.
(P609)

PETITJEAN, M. (cont'd.)

(Montoya, G.) solo,acap ENOCH s.p.
(P610)
Tu Mettras Dans Tes Cheveux
(Montoya, G.) solo,acap ENOCH s.p.
(P611)
(Montoya, G.) solo,pno ENOCH s.p.
(P612)

PETITS BEBES, PETITS TOURMENTS see
Landry, Al.

PETITS COEURS see Chaminade, Cecile

PETITS FRERES see Bondon, Jacques

PETITS POTINS see Berger, Rod.

PETOFI SONGS see Farkas, Ferenc

PETRALIA
Arrivederci... Addio
solo,pno FORLIVESI 11609 s.p.
(P613)
Disturna Di Rispetti Toscani
solo,pno FORLIVESI 11852 s.p.
(P614)
Dormi Fanciulla Cara
solo,pno FORLIVESI 12072 s.p.
(P615)
I Tetti
solo,pno FORLIVESI 11562 s.p.
(P616)
In Riva All'Arno
solo,pno FORLIVESI 11704 s.p.
(P617)
Letterina D'amore
solo,pno FORLIVESI 11868 s.p.
(P618)
Madrigale Di Primavera
solo,pno FORLIVESI 11450 s.p.
(P619)
Manuela
solo,pno FORLIVESI 11549 s.p.
(P620)
Vendemmia
solo,pno FORLIVESI 11431 s.p.
(P621)

PETRASSI, GOFFREDO (1904-   )
Beatitudines
Bar/B solo,5inst min sc ZERBONI
6879 s.p.   (P622)
Colori Del Tempo
[It] S/T solo,pno RICORDI-ENG
122952 s.p.   (P623)
Due Liriche Di Saffo *CC2U
S solo,inst voc sc ZERBONI 3925
s.p.   (P624)
Lamento D'Arianna
[It] S/T solo,pno RICORDI-ENG
123793 s.p.   (P625)
Propos D'Alain
Bar solo,12inst voc sc ZERBONI 5792
s.p.   (P626)
Quattro Inni Sacri *sac,CC4U,hymn
TBar soli,org/orch voc sc ZERBONI
4172 s.p.   (P627)
Tre Liriche *CC3U
solo,pno ZERBONI 4187 s.p.   (P628)
Vocalizzo Per Soprano
S solo,fl,ob,clar,bsn,trp,harp,
strings CARISH s.p.   (P629)

PETRI, H.
Slumra Nu, Liten Min
low solo,pno GEHRMANS s.p.   (P630)
high solo,pno GEHRMANS s.p.   (P631)

PETRIE, H.W.
Seemannslos
med solo,pno SCHAUR EE 3554 s.p.
(P632)

PETRKLIC see Martinu, Bohuslav

PETROLINI
Er Sor Capanna
solo,pno FORLIVESI 10340 s.p.
(P633)

PETROV, A.
Je M'balade Dans Moscau
(Bonifay, F.) solo,pno CHANT s.p.
(P634)
La Petrouille Perdue
(Bonifay, F.) solo,pno CHANT s.p.
(P635)
L'ami Fidele
(Philippe-Gerard) solo,pno CHANT
s.p.   (P636)

PETRUCCI, F. LEE
By My Side *sac
solo,pno WORD S-441   (P637)

It Is Almost Time *sac
solo,pno WORD S-450   (P638)

PETRUCCI, OTTAVIANO (1466-1539)
Harmonice Musices Odhecaton A *CCU
solo,pno BROUDE BR. $32.50   (P639)

PETRZELKA, VILEM (1889-1967)
Der Weg *Op.14, song cycle
T solo,pno SUPRAPHON s.p.   (P640)

Einsamkeiten Der Seele *Op.10
high solo,pno SUPRAPHON s.p.   (P641)

PETTICOAT LANE see Haufrecht, Herbert

PETZ (PEZ), JOHANN CHRISTOPH
(1664-1716)
Guter Geber, Lob Und Preis Sei Dir
*sac
med solo,2S rec,cont HANSSLER 5.059
s.p. see also GESANGE ZUM
KIRCHENJAHR   (P642)

Mentre Fra Mille Fiori *cant
(Winter) S solo,fl,cont SIKORSKI
649 s.p.   (P643)

PETZOLD, RUDOLF (1908-   )
Drei Lieder *Op.10, CC3U
S solo,pno GERIG HG 556 s.p. (P644)

Vier Lieder *Op.29, CC4U
med solo,pno GERIG HG 557 s.p.
(P645)

PEUPLE DU CHRIST see Honegger, Arthur

PEUPLE FRANCAIS see Messager, Andre

PEUT-ETRE see Ferrari, Gustave

PEUT-ETRE see Saint-Saens, Camille

PEUT-IL SE REPOSER see Poulenc, Francis

PEYRETTI, ALBERTO
Canciones *CCU
SONZOGNO 2885 S/T solo,pno voc sc
s.p.; S/T solo,fl,ob,clar,2bsn,
2horn,timp,perc,xylo,strings
rental   (P646)

Tre Liriche *CC3U
B solo,pno voc sc SONZOGNO 2886
s.p.; B solo,2fl,3ob,2clar,2bsn,
2horn,timp,strings SONZOGNO
rental   (P647)

PEYROT
Chantez, Jouez *CC10U
solo,pno HENN 847 s.p.   (P648)

Cinq Quatrains Portugais *CC5U
solo,pno HENN 827 s.p.   (P649)

Trois Poemes *CC3U
solo,pno HENN 938 s.p.   (P650)

PEZZATI, ROMANO (1939-   )
Correspondances
S solo,7inst sc ZERBONI 7683 s.p.
(P651)
Und Wenig Wissen
S solo,orch sc ZERBONI 7180 s.p.
(P652)

PFALZISCHE VOLKSLIEDER *CCU
(Muller-Blattau, Joseph) solo,pno
SCHOTTS 5300 s.p.   (P653)

PFANNER, ADOLF
Drei Lieder *Op.42, sac,CC3U
S solo,strings BOHM rental   (P654)

PFARRER VON CLEVERSULZBACH see Korn,
Peter Jona

PFAUTSCH, LLOYD (1921-   )
I Wonder Why *sac
solo,pno HOPE 51 $1.00   (P655)

PFEIL
Lugn Vilar Sjon
2 soli,pno LUNDQUIST s.p.   (P656)
solo,pno LUNDQUIST s.p.   (P657)

PFITZNER, HANS (1869-1949)
Abbitte *Op.29,No.1
med solo,pno FURST s.p. see from
Vier Lieder   (P658)

Abendlied
see Sechs Jugendlieder

Alte Weisen Nach G. Keller, Op. 33,
Heft I *CCU
high solo,pno FURST   (P659)

Alte Weisen Nach G. Keller, Op. 33,
Heft II *CCU
high solo,pno FURST   (P660)

Das Verlassene Magdelein
see Sechs Jugendlieder

Das Verlassene Magdlein *Op.30,No.2
high solo,pno FURST s.p. see from
Vier Lieder   (P661)

PFITZNER, HANS (cont'd.)

Denk Es, Oh Seele *Op.30,No.3
  high solo,pno FURST s.p. see from
  Vier Lieder   (P662)

Der Arbeitsmann *Op.30,No.4
  med solo,pno FURST s.p. see from
  Vier Lieder   (P663)

Der Bote *Op.5,No.3
  S solo,pno FURST s.p. see from Drei
  Lieder   (P664)

Die Baume Wurden Gelb *Op.6,No.5
  Bar solo,pno FURST s.p. see from
  Sechs Lieder   (P665)

Die Stille Stadt *Op.29,No.4
  med solo,pno FURST s.p. see from
  Vier Lieder   (P666)

Drei Lieder *see Der Bote, Op.5,
  No.3; Frieden, Op.5,No.1;
  Wiegenlied, Op.5,No.2   (P667)

Eingelegte Ruder *Op.32,No.3
  Bar/B solo,pno FURST s.p. see from
  Vier Lieder Nach C.F. Meyer
                                 (P668)

Frieden *Op.5,No.1
  S solo,pno FURST s.p. see from Drei
  Lieder   (P669)
  low solo,pno FURST s.p.   (P670)

Funf Lieder *see Hast Du Von Den
  Fischerkindern, Op.7,No.1;
  Lockung, Op.7,No.4;
  Nachtwanderer, Op.7,No.2; Uber
  Ein Stundlein, Op.7,No.3; Wie
  Fruhlinsahnung, Op.7,No.5   (P671)

Hast Du Von Den Fischerkindern
  *Op.7,No.1
  low solo,pno RIES s.p. see from
  Funf Lieder   (P672)
  high solo,pno RIES s.p. see from
  Funf Lieder   (P673)

Herbsthauch *Op.29,No.2
  med solo,pno FURST s.p. see from
  Vier Lieder   (P674)

Hussens Kerker *Op.32,No.1
  Bar/B solo,pno FURST s.p. see from
  Vier Lieder Nach C.F. Meyer
                                 (P675)

Ich Will Mich Im Grunen Wlad *Op.6,
  No.2
  Bar solo,pno FURST s.p. see from
  Sechs Lieder   (P676)

Kuriose Geschichte
  see Sechs Jugendlieder

Lass Scharren Deiner Rosse Huf
  *Op.32,No.4
  Bar/B solo,pno FURST s.p. see from
  Vier Lieder Nach C.F. Meyer
                                 (P677)

Lethe *Op.37
  Bar solo,orch voc sc FURST s.p.
                                 (P678)

Lockung *Op.7,No.4
  med solo,pno RIES s.p. see from
  Funf Lieder   (P679)

Mir Bist Du Tot
  see Sechs Jugendlieder

Nachtwanderer *Op.7,No.2
  med solo,pno RIES s.p. see from
  Funf Lieder   (P680)

Naturfreiheit
  see Sechs Jugendlieder

Nun Da So Warm Der Sonnenschein
  see Sechs Jugendlieder

Saerspruch *Op.32,No.2
  Bar/B solo,pno FURST s.p. see from
  Vier Lieder Nach C.F. Meyer
                                 (P681)

Sechs Jugendlieder
  solo,pno RIES s.p.
    contains: Abendlied; Das
    Verlassene Magdelein; Kuriose
    Geschichte; Mir Bist Du Tot;
    Naturfreiheit; Nun Da So Warm
    Der Sonnenschein   (P682)

Sechs Liebeslieder, Op. 35, Heft I
  *CCU
  FURST high female solo,pno; low
    female solo,pno   (P683)

Sechs Liebeslieder, Op. 35, Heft II
  *CCU
  low female solo,pno FURST   (P684)

Sechs Lieder *see Die Baume Wurden
  Gelb, Op.6,No.5; Ich Will Mich Im
  Grunen Wlad, Op.6,No.2;
  Wasserfahrt, Op.6,No.6; Widmung,
  Op.6,No.4; Zugvogel, Op.6,No.3;

PFITZNER, HANS (cont'd.)

Zweifelnde Liebe, Op.6,No.1
                                 (P685)

Sehnsucht Nach Vergessen *Op.30,No.1
  high solo,pno FURST s.p. see from
  Vier Lieder   (P686)

Six Songs, Vol. I: Op. 40, Nos. 1-3
  *CC3U
  [Ger] med solo,pno PETERS 4293A
  $4.75   (P687)

Six Songs, Vol.II: Op. 40, Nos. 4-6
  *CC3U
  [Ger] med solo,pno PETERS 4293B
  $4.75   (P688)

Three Sonnets *Op.41,No.1-3, CC3U
  [Ger] Bar/B solo,pno PETERS 4295
  $7.50   (P689)

Uber Ein Stundlein *Op.7,No.3
  med solo,pno RIES s.p. see from
  Funf Lieder   (P690)
  low solo,fl,2ob,2clar,2bsn,horn,
  timp,harp,strings RIES s.p.
                                 (P691)

Vier Lieder *see Abbitte, Op.29,
  No.1; Die Stille Stadt, Op.29,
  No.4; Herbsthauch, Op.29,No.2;
  Willkommen Und Abschied, Op.29,
  No.3   (P692)

Vier Lieder *see Das Verlassene
  Magdlein, Op.30,No.2; Denk Es, Oh
  Seele, Op.30,No.3; Der
  Arbeitsmann, Op.30,No.4;
  Sehnsucht Nach Vergessen, Op.30,
  No.1   (P693)

Vier Lieder Nach C.F. Meyer *see
  Eingelegte Ruder, Op.32,No.3;
  Hussens Kerker, Op.32,No.1; Lass
  Scharren Deiner Rosse Huf, Op.32,
  No.4; Saerspruch, Op.32,No.2
                                 (P694)

Wasserfahrt *Op.6,No.6
  Bar solo,pno FURST s.p. see from
  Sechs Lieder   (P695)

Widmung *Op.6,No.4
  Bar solo,pno FURST s.p. see from
  Sechs Lieder   (P696)

Wie Fruhlinsahnung *Op.7,No.5
  high solo,pno RIES s.p. see from
  Funf Lieder   (P697)
  low solo,pno RIES s.p. see from
  Funf Lieder   (P698)

Wiegenlied *Op.5,No.2
  S solo,pno FURST s.p. see from Drei
  Lieder   (P699)

Willkommen Und Abschied *Op.29,No.3
  med solo,pno FURST s.p. see from
  Vier Lieder   (P700)

Zugvogel *Op.6,No.3
  Bar solo,pno FURST s.p. see from
  Sechs Lieder   (P701)

Zweifelnde Liebe *Op.6,No.1
  Bar solo,pno FURST s.p. see from
  Sechs Lieder   (P702)

PFLUEGER, CARL
  How Long Wilt Thou Forget Me? *sac,
  Gen
  low solo,pno (D flat maj) WILLIS
  $.75   (P703)
  med solo,pno (E flat maj) WILLIS
  $.75   (P704)
  high solo,pno (G maj) WILLIS $.75
                                 (P705)

PFLUGER
  Vier Lieder Nach Texten Von Friedrich
  Nietzsche *CC4U
  solo,pno BREITKOPF-W EB 6628 s.p.
                                 (P706)

PFOHL, J.C.
  A Trilogy Of Southern Lyrics
  solo,pno BRODT $1.25   (P707)

PHACELIA see Gubaidulina, S.

PHANOMEN see Brahms, Johannes

PHANTASIE see Mahler, Gustav

PHANTASIES OF A PRISONER, THE see
  Tanenbaum, Elias

PHARES see Bernard, R.

PHASEN see Kayn, Roland

PHELPS, DAVID
  If I Knew Then *see Brown, Aaron

  Sure Of It All *sac
  solo,pno WORD S-449   (P708)

PHELPS, DAVID (cont'd.)

'Til He Appears *sac
  solo,pno WORD S-388   (P709)

PHELPS, ELLSWORTH (1827-1913)
  Heart That Warm'd My Guileless
  Breast, The
  solo,pno/hpsd HEUWEKE. 126 s.p.
                                 (P710)

PHEOBE see Bennett, Sir William
  Sterndale

PHIEFFER, DON
  It's A Happy Day
  (Bock, F.) solo,pno GENTRY $1.00
                                 (P711)

PHILIDOR, ANNE (1681-1728)
  Quand On Aime Bien (from Le Marechal
  Ferrant)
  (Flothius, Marius) [Fr] S solo,ob,
  pno BROEKMANS 395-12 s.p.   (P712)

PHILIDOR, FRANCOIS ANDRE DANICAN
  (1729-1795)
  Je Vais Seulette (from Sancho Panca)
  (Flothius, Marius) [Fr] S solo,ob,
  pno BROEKMANS 395-11 s.p.   (P713)

PHILIPP, FRANZ (1890-   )
  Aus Dem Kinderland *sac,CC18U
  solo,pno BOHM s.p. sc, solo pt
                                 (P714)
  Drei Duette *Op.51, sac,CC3U
  ST soli,pno BOHM rental   (P715)
  Lenau-Lieder *Op.1, sac,CCU
  A solo,clar,bsn,strings BOHM rental
                                 (P716)
  Lied Des Turmers *Op.75, sac
  T solo,pno sc BOHM s.p.   (P717)
  Bar solo,pno sc BOHM s.p.   (P718)

PHILIPPART-GONZALEZ, RENEE
  Dors Mon Soleil
  solo,pno/harp DURAND s.p.   (P719)

  Serenade
  see Venise

  Venise
  T/Mez solo,pno/inst DURAND s.p.
    contains: Serenade; Venise La
    Rouge   (P720)

  Venise La Rouge
  see Venise

PHILLIPS
  Bush Lyrics *song cycle
  low solo,pno ALLANS s.p.   (P721)
  high solo,pno ALLANS s.p.   (P722)

  Saw Ye My Saviour? *sac
  low solo,pno (D maj) FISCHER,C
  V 1641   (P723)

PHILLIPS, H. LYALL
  Lass Of Mine
  solo,pno CRAMER   (P724)

PHILOCTETE DEMEURE! see Saint-Saens,
  Camille

PHILOMEL see Goosens, Eugene

PHILOSOPHER AND THE LADY, THE see
  Martin, Easthope

PHILOSOPHIE see Delmet, Paul

PHILOSOPHIE see Lacome, Paul

PHILOSOPHIST, THE see Birch, Robert
  Fairfax

PHILOSOPHY see Emmel

PHOENIX see Andriessen, Juriaan

PHONEMES POUR CATHY see Pousseur, Henri

PHRASES I see Garant, S.

PHYLLIS UND THIRSIS see Bach, Karl
  Philipp Emanuel

PIACER D'AMOR see Martini, Jean Paul
  Egide

PIACER D'AMOR see Martini, Jean Paul
  Egide, Plaisir D'amour

PIANEFFORTE 'E NOTTE see Giazotto, Remo

PIANGETE MIEI OCCHI see Massenet, Jules

PIANGETE OCCHI see Campogalliani, E.

PIANGETE, OHIME, PIANGETE see
  Carissimi, Giacomo

PIANGI, SI, PIANGI see Alfano, Franco

PIANGO, GEMO, SOSPIRO see Verdi, Giuseppe

PIANGO GEMO SOSPIRO see Vivaldi, Antonio

PIANISSIMO see Dougherty, Celius

PIANTO see Gandino, Adolfo

PIANTO ANTICO see Caltabiano, S.

PIANTO ANTICO see Mule, Giuseppe

PIANTO NELL'OMBRA see Brogi

PIAZZA, GAETANO
Tonat Coelum Cum Furore *sac
(Ewerhart, Rudolf) S solo,org
BIELER CS 42 s.p. (P725)

PIBERNIK, ZLATKO (1926-)
Yellow Lily, The
[Slav] Mez solo,fl,harp CROATICA
s.p. (P726)

PIBROCH, THE see Stanford, Charles Villiers

PIBROCH O' DONUIL DHU *folk,Scot
solo,pno (E flat maj) PATERSON FS138
s.p. (P727)

PICAFLOR see Napolitano, Emilio

PICARDIE *Fr
(Canteloube, J.) solo,acap DURAND
s.p. see also Anthologie Des Chants
Populaires Francais Tome IV (P728)

PICARDS ET NORMANDS see Liouville, F.

PICASSO-MUSIK see Heider, Werner

PICCANINNY MINE see Trotere, Henry

PICCINELLI, NINO
Berceuse
solo,pno SANTIS 885 s.p. (P729)

Cancion Moresca
[Span/It] solo,pno SANTIS 805 s.p.
(P730)

I'sta Canzona Nun'a Saccio Fa
solo,pno SANTIS 890 s.p. (P731)

PICCINNI, NICCOLO (1728-1800)
Spiega L'ali Dolce Sonno
(Gubitosi, E.) solo,2fl,2horn
CARISH s.p. (P732)

PICCIOLI, G. (1905-1961)
Berceuse
solo,pno BONGIOVANI 2413 s.p.
(P733)

La Madre Piange
[It/Ger] solo,pno BONGIOVANI 1766
s.p. (P734)

L'Offerta Della Rose
solo,3fl,3ob,2clar,2bsn,4horn,3trp,
3trom,tuba,timp,perc,cembalo,
harp,pno sc CARISH 18736 s.p.
(P735)

PICCOLA BIANCA MANO see Respighi, Ottorino

PICCOLO MAGNIFICAT see Bach, Johann Sebastian

PICCOLO PICCOLO see Straus, Oscar

PICCOLOMINI, MARIETTA (1834-1899)
Ora Pro Nobis
solo,pno LUNDQUIST s.p. (P736)

Toilers, The
low solo,pno (B flat maj) ASHDOWN
s.p. (P737)
med solo,pno (C maj) ASHDOWN s.p.
(P738)
med-high solo,pno (D maj) ASHDOWN
s.p. (P739)
high solo,pno (E flat maj) ASHDOWN
s.p. (P740)

PICHA, FRANTISEK (1893-1946)
Die Stimme Des Vaterlands *see Rodne
Hroudy Hlas

Hlasy Noci *Op.3, CCU
solo,pno SUPRAPHON s.p. (P741)

Po Letech *Op.1, CC6U
high solo,pno SUPRAPHON s.p. (P742)

Rodne Hroudy Hlas
"Die Stimme Des Vaterlands" med
solo,pno CZECH s.p. (P743)

Rodne Hroudy Hlas I *CCU
Bar/B solo,pno SUPRAPHON s.p.
(P744)

Rodne Hroudy Hlas II *CCU
Mez solo,pno SUPRAPHON s.p. (P745)

PICHA, FRANTISEK (cont'd.)

Samoty Duse *song cycle
high solo,pno SUPRAPHON s.p. (P746)

PICK-MANGIAGALLI, RICCARDO (1882-1949)
Ecco Settembre
solo,2fl,3ob,2clar,2bsn,4horn,
strings CARISH s.p. (P747)

Fiorile
solo,2fl,2ob,2clar,2bsn,2horn,
strings CARISH s.p. (P748)

PICKPOCKETS see Allier, Gabriel

PICON, MOLLY
Liebes Schmertzen *Jew
solo,pno KAMMEN 52 $1.00 see also
FAVORITE JEWISH SONGS, VOL. 2
(P749)

PICTURES see Farr, Ian

PICTURES FROM THE TALE OF ALADDIN see
Rogers, Bernard

PIDOT see Marttinen, Tauno

PIE JESU see Faure, Gabriel-Urbain

PIE JESU see Faure, Jean-Baptiste

PIECE FOR MISS PEGGY LEE see Mills, Charles

PIECECITOS see Guastavino, Carlos

PIECES DE CHAIR II see Bussotti, Sylvano

PIENELLA HUILULLA HUUTELEN see Pesonen, Olavi (Samuel)

PIENI JOULUTERVEHDYTS
solo,pno FAZER F 3727 s.p.
contains: Arkihuolesi Kaikki Heita;
Enkeli Taivaan; Hei Tonttu-Ukot
Hyppikaa; Kilisee Kulkunen; Oi Sa
Riemuisa (P750)

PIENI RAKKAUSLAULU see Tolonen, Jouko
(Paavo Kalervo)

PIERINA see Taube, Evert

PIERNE, GABRIEL (1863-1937)
Aubade (from Izeyl)
T solo,pno/inst DURAND s.p. (P751)
solo,pno/inst DURAND s.p. (P752)

Boutique Japonaise
solo,pno ENOCH s.p. (P753)

Chanson De Prisca
S solo,pno sc JOBERT s.p. (P754)

Chanson De Yanthis
solo,pno (available in 2 keys) sc
JOBERT s.p. (P755)

L'An Mil
solo,cor,orch ENOCH rental (P756)

Legende Des Etoiles (from La Croisade
Des Enfants) sac
solo,pno/org (available in 2 keys)
HEUGEL s.p. (P757)

Les Trois Petits Oiseaux
solo,pno/inst LEDUC s.p. (P758)

Serenade
solo,orch (available in 2 keys)
LEDUC s.p. (P759)

Vingt Melodies Vol. 1 *CCUL
low solo,pno/inst LEDUC B.L.188
s.p. (P760)

Vingt Melodies Vol. 2 *CCUL
high solo,pno/inst LEDUC B.L.189
s.p. (P761)

PIERRET, P.
Carnaval
solo,pno ENOCH s.p. (P762)

PIERROT see Debussy, Claude

PIERROT see Hutchison, William M.

PIERROT see Read, Gardner

PIERROT see Swanson, Howard

PIERROT DANDY see Marx, Joseph

PIERROT PENDU see Bijvanck, Henk

PIESENZO ZALMU ZEME PODKARPATSKEJ see
Suchon, Eugen

PIESNE see Bella, Jan Levoslav

PIESNE see Moyzes, Alexander

PIESNE O HORACH see Urbanec, Bartolomej

PIESNE O JARI see Zimmer, Jan

PIESNE O LASKE see Kardos, Dezider

PIESNE O VEL'KOM PRIATELSTVE see
Urbanec, Bartolomej

PIETA see Del Corona, Rodolfo

PIETA see Lothar, Mark

PIETA DI ME see Haydn, (Franz) Joseph

PIETA, RISPETTO, AMORE see Verdi, Giuseppe

PIETA, SIGNORE see Stradella, Alessandro

PIETA TI PRENDA MIO DIO see Bach, Johann Sebastian

PIETRI, GIUSEPPE (1886-1946)
Io Conosco Un Giardino
T solo,orch voc sc ZERBONI 5398
s.p. (P763)

PIGEN SYNGER
see Det Var En Lordagsaften

PIGGOTT, AUDREY
Lelant
solo,pno (D maj) LESLIE 7055 (P764)

PIGNON, PAUL (1939-)
Five Movements For Chamber Group And
Tenor
T solo,chamb.grp. MUSIC INFO rental
(P765)

PIJACKA see Soukup, Vladimir

PIJACKE PISNE see Drejsl, Radim

PIJPER, WILLEM (1894-1947)
Acht Oud-Hollandsche Liederen
med solo,pno WAGENAAR s.p. (P766)

Allerseelen
see Pijper, Willem, Douwdeuntje

Cortege
see Fetes Galantes

Douwdeuntje
med solo,pno DONEMUS s.p. contains
also: Allerseelen (P767)

Fetes Galantes
DONEMUS Mez solo,pno s.p.; Mez
solo,3fl,2ob,3clar,bsn,2horn,trp,
timp,perc,harp,strings rental
contains: Cortege; Pantomime; Sur
L'herbe (P768)

Hymne
B/Bar solo,2fl,3ob,3clar,3bsn,
4horn,3trp,3trom,tuba,timp,perc,
harp,strings DONEMUS s.p. (P769)

Liederen Uit De Toneelmuziek By "The
Tempest" *CCU
med solo,fl,clar,horn,pno,perc,
strings DONEMUS s.p. (P770)

Meliedje
see Vier Liederen Van Bertha De
Bruyn

Nachtliedje
see Vier Liederen Van Bertha De
Bruyn

Noels De France *CCU
med solo,pno WAGENAAR s.p. (P771)

Pantomime
see Fetes Galantes

Romance Sans Paroles
Mez solo,3fl,2ob,3clar,bsn,3horn,
3trp,perc,cel,2harp,pno,xylo,
strings,gtr,2mand DONEMUS s.p.
(P772)

Sneeuwklokjes
see Vier Liederen Van Bertha De
Bruyn

Sur L'herbe
see Fetes Galantes

Vieilles Chansons De France
med solo,pno WAGENAAR s.p. (P773)

Vier Liederen Van Bertha De Bruyn
med solo/high solo,pno DONEMUS s.p.
contains: Meliedje; Nachtliedje;
Sneeuwklokjes; Vlinderliedje
(P774)

Vlinderliedje
see Vier Liederen Van Bertha De
Bruyn

PIKET, FREDERICK (1903-1974)
    Ahavas Olom *sac
        [Heb] med solo/cantor,pno TRANSCON.
        WJ 436 $.85   (P775)
        [Heb] high solo/cantor,pno
        TRANSCON. WJ 435 $.85   (P776)

    Eso Enai *sac,Jew
        solo,pno/org SAC.MUS.PR. 402
        contains also: V'ohavto   (P777)

    Sim Sholom *sac
        [Heb] med solo,pno TRANSCON. WJ 437
        $.75   (P778)

    Three Biblical Songs *sac,CC3U,Bibl
        med solo,pno TRANSCON. TV 580
        $1.75; high solo,pno TRANSCON.
        TV 581 $1.75   (P779)

    V'ohavto
        see Piket, Frederick, Eso Enai

PIKKU LASSE see Sibelius, Jean, Lasse
    Liten

PILATI, MARIO (1903-1938)
    Ninna-Nanna
        [It] solo,pno CURCI 413 s.p. (P780)

PILEUR
    Chant De Marriage *Marriage
        solo,pno HENN 388 s.p.   (P781)

PILGERSPRUCH see Haas, Joseph

PILGRIM OF LOVE see Bishop, Sir Henry
    Rowley

PILGRIMAGE see Floyd, Carlisle

PILGRIMES SOLACE AND THREE SONGS FROM A
    MUSICALL BANQUET see Dowland, John

PILGRIM'S CHORUS see Wagner, Richard

PILGRIM'S PSALM (from Pilgrim's
    Progress) sac,Bibl
    Bar solo,pno (med) OXFORD 62.204
    $1.50   (P782)

PILGRIMS SONG see Tchaikovsky, Piotr
    Ilyitch, To The Forest

PILKINGTON, FRANCIS (ca. 1562-1638)
    First Book Of Songs *CCU
        solo,pno STAINER 3.1339.7 $5.50
                                       (P783)

PILLOIS, JACQUES (1877-1935)
    Chanson
        solo,pno/inst DURAND s.p. see from
        Trois Poemes Feminins   (P784)

    Ecouter Et Ne Rien Entendre
        see Six Proses Lyriques

    Il N'y A Pas De Mots Assez Profonds
        see Six Proses Lyriques

    Jardin Pres De La Mer
        solo,pno/inst DURAND s.p. see from
        Trois Poemes Feminins   (P785)

    La Ou Tu Respires, Bien Aime(E)
        see Six Proses Lyriques

    Les Mots Que Tu M'as Dits
        see Six Proses Lyriques

    O Bien Aime(e) Lorsque Tes Pas
        T'entrainent Loin De Moi
        see Six Proses Lyriques

    Poeme
        solo,pno/inst DURAND s.p. see from
        Trois Poemes Feminins   (P786)

    Que Mon Ame Murmure
        see Six Proses Lyriques

    Six Proses Lyriques
        solo,pno cmplt ed DURAND s.p.
        contains: Ecouter Et Ne Rien
            Entendre; Il N'y A Pas De Mots
            Assez Profonds; La Ou Tu
            Respires, Bien Aime(E); Les
            Mots Que Tu M'as Dits; O Bien
            Aime(e) Lorsque Tes Pas
            T'entrainent Loin De Moi; Que
            Mon Ame Murmure   (P787)

    Trois Poemes Feminins *see Chanson;
        Jardin Pres De La Mer; Poeme
                                       (P788)

PILOT see Nelson, S.

PILOT, THE see Protheroe, Daniel

PILOT BRAVE see Millard, Harrison

PIMEA ISOTON PIRTTI see Kilpinen, Yrio

PIMEN'S ERZAHLUNG see Mussorgsky,
    Modest, Pimen's Tale

PIMEN'S MONOLOG see Mussorgsky, Modest

PIMEN'S TALE see Mussorgsky, Modest

PIMPINELLA see Tchaikovsky, Piotr
    Ilyitch

PINE TREE TOWERS LONELY, A see Heller,
    A.

PINE-TREES see Scek, Breda, Bori

PINKHAM, DANIEL (1923-   )
    Ave Regina Coelorum
        [Lat] T solo,pno AM.COMP.AL. $1.10
                                       (P789)
        [Lat] S solo,pno AM.COMP.AL. $1.10
                                       (P790)
    But Of The Times And The Seasons
        see Letters From Saint Paul

    Eight Poems Of Gerard Manley Hopkins
        *CC8L
        Bar/T solo,vla SCHIRM.EC 132 s.p.
                                       (P791)
    Go Thy Way, Eat Thy Bread With Joy
        see Three Songs From Ecclesiastes

    Hour Glass, The
        high solo,pno SCHIRM.EC 127 s.p.
                                       (P792)
    I Will Not Leave You Comfortless
        *see Non Vos Relinquam Orphanos

    In Youth Is Pleasure
        med solo,gtr/pno SCHIRM.EC 2814
        s.p.   (P793)

    Lamb, The
        high solo,gtr/pno SCHIRM.EC 2594
        s.p.   (P794)

    Let The Word Of Christ Dwell In You
        Richly
        see Letters From Saint Paul

    Letters From Saint Paul *sac,Bibl
        high solo,org/pno/8strings/strings
        SCHIRM.EC 142 s.p.
        contains: But Of The Times And
            The Seasons; Let The Word Of
            Christ Dwell In You Richly;
            Rejoice In The Lord Alway;
            Wherefore Seeing We Are Also
            Compassed About; Who Shall
            Separate Us From The Love Of
            Christ?   (P795)

    Litany, A
        SS soli,pno/org AMP A483 $.25
                                       (P796)
    Man, That Is Born Of A Woman *sac
        Mez solo,gtr SCHIRM.EC 143A s.p.
                                       (P797)
    Music, Thou Soul Of Heaven
        high solo,pno AM.COMP.AL. $.82
                                       (P798)
    Non Vos Relinquam Orphanos
        "I Will Not Leave You Comfortless"
        see Two Motets

    Now That Time Has Gathered To Itself
        med solo,pno (elegy) SCHIRM.EC 126
        s.p.   (P799)

    Now The Trumpet Summons Us Again
        high solo,3fl,3ob,3clar,2bsn,4horn
        3trp,3trom,tuba,timp,perc,harp,
        strings PETERS 6874B rental
                                       (P800)
        high solo,pno PETERS 6874 $2.00
                                       (P801)
    Psalm 79
        T solo,pno AM.COMP.AL. $.82   (P802)

    Rejoice In The Lord Alway
        see Letters From Saint Paul

    Safe In Their Alabaster Chambers
        Mez solo,electronic tape sc
        SCHIRM.EC 150 s.p.   (P803)

    Sea Ritual, The
        low solo,pno AM.COMP.AL. $.82
                                       (P804)
    Signs Of The Zodiac
        narrator,3fl,3ob,3clar,3bsn,4horn,
        3trp,3trom,tuba,timp,2perc,harp,
        pno,cel,strings study sc PETERS
        6899 $7.50   (P805)

    Slow, Slow, Fresh Fount
        high solo,pno PETERS 6452A $1.25
                                       (P806)
        med solo,pno PETERS 6452B $1.25
                                       (P807)
        low solo,pno PETERS 6452C $1.25
                                       (P808)
    Te Lucis Ante Terminum
        "To Thee, Before The Close Of Day"
        see Two Motets

    Three Songs From Ecclesiastes *sac,
        Bibl
        high solo,pno/4strings/strings
        SCHIRM.EC 128 s.p.

PINKHAM, DANIEL (cont'd.)
        contains: Go Thy Way, Eat Thy
            Bread With Joy; To Every Thing
            There Is A Season; Vanity Of
            Vanities   (P809)

    To Every Thing There Is A Season
        see Three Songs From Ecclesiastes

    To Thee, Before The Close Of Day
        *see Te Lucis Ante Terminum

    Two Motets *sac,mot
        S/T solo,fl,gtr SCHIRM.EC 131 s.p.
        contains: Non Vos Relinquam
            Orphanos, "I Will Not Leave You
            Comfortless"; Te Lucis Ante
            Terminum, "To Thee, Before The
            Close Of Day"   (P810)

    Vanity Of Vanities
        see Three Songs From Ecclesiastes

    Wedding Song (from Wedding Cantata)
        Marriage
        high solo,org PETERS 66565   (P811)

    Wherefore Seeing We Are Also
        Compassed About
        see Letters From Saint Paul

    Who Shall Separate Us From The Love
        Of Christ?
        see Letters From Saint Paul

PINKSTERLIED see Bonset, Jac.

PINOS-SIMANDEL, ALOIS (1925-   )
    Dicta Antiquorum
        [Lat] narrator/B solo CZECH s.p.
                                       (P812)
PINSUTI, CIRO (1829-1888)
    A Rivederci!
        4 soli,pno CRAMER   (P813)

    Bedouin Love Song, The
        low solo,pno (B maj) ASHDOWN s.p.
                                       (P814)
        high solo,pno (B maj) ASHDOWN s.p.
                                       (P815)
        med-high solo,pno (C maj) ASHDOWN
        s.p.   (P816)
        med solo,pno (D maj) ASHDOWN s.p.
                                       (P817)
    I Fear No Foe
        high solo,pno (E flat maj) CRAMER
                                       (P818)
        low solo,pno (C maj) CRAMER (P819)

    'Tis I
        low solo,pno (G maj) CRAMER (P820)
        high solo,pno (B flat maj) CRAMER
                                       (P821)
    Touch Of A Vanished Hand
        solo,pno CRAMER   (P822)

PIOGGIA see Davico, Vincenzo

PIOGGIA see Respighi, Ottorino

PIONEER SONGS OF ISRAEL *CCU,Isr
    (Binder) [Heb/Eng] solo,pno MARKS
    $2.00   (P823)

PIOUS ORGIES see Handel, George
    Frideric

PIOUS SELINDA see Clark

PIPE see Methold, Diana

PIPER see Head, Michael (Dewar)

PIPER, THE see Adler, Samuel

PIPER, THE see Lippincott

PIPER FROM OVER THE WAY see Brahe, May
    H.

PIPER O' DUNDEE see Seton

PIPER O' DUNDEE, THE *folk,Scot
    solo,pno (G min) PATERSON FS77 s.p.
                                       (P824)
PIPER O' DUNDEE, THE see Peel, Graham

PIPER SPRING, THE see Newton, Ernest

PIPING DOWN THE VALLEYS WILD see Cooke,
    S.C.

PIPING DOWN THE VALLEYS WILD see
    Morawetz, Oskar

PIPING DOWN THE VALLEYS WILD see Read,
    Gardner

PIPPA'S SONG see Rorem, Ned

PIPPA'S SONG see Weigl, Vally

PIPPELOENTJE UIT LOGEREN see Hengeveld,
    G.

PIRATE, THE see Turner-Maley, Florence

PIRATE GOLD see French, G.

PIRATENLIED see Girnatis, Walter

PIROGUES see Lesur, Daniel

PIRON EL FURNAR
(Carlo, Musi) solo,pno (Bolognese
dialect) BONGIOVANI 2059 s.p. see
from El Mi Canzunett   (P825)

PIROUCHKA see Mussorgsky, Modest

PIRTISSANI PIMENEE see Ikonen, Lauri

PISADOR, DIEGO (ca. 1508-1557)
En La Fuente Del Rosel *see Vasquez,
Juan

Guarte, Guarte El Rey Don Sancho
(Azpiazu) [Span] med solo,gtr UNION
ESP. $.90   (P826)
(Tarrago) [Span] med solo,gtr UNION
ESP. $1.10   (P827)

La Manana De San Juan
(Azpiazu) [Span] med solo,gtr UNION
ESP. $.50   (P828)

Lagrime Mesti
[Span] solo,gtr BROEKMANS 817 s.p.
                              (P829)

Madonna Mia Fa
[Span] solo,gtr BROEKMANS 507 s.p.
                              (P830)

Quien Tu Viese Tal Poder
[Span] solo,gtr BROEKMANS 487 s.p.
                              (P831)

Si La Noche Hace Oscura
[Span] solo,gtr BROEKMANS 489 s.p.
                              (P832)

Si Te Vas A Banar Juanica
(Pujol) [Span] med solo,gtr ESCHIG
E1306 $.90   (P833)

PISEN NAD DITETEM see Drejsl, Radim

PISEN O PRAZE see Soukup, Vladimir

PISEN O VIKTORCE see Zahradnik, Zdenek

PISEN SASKOVA see Foerster, Josef
Bohuslav

PISEN SESTRY see Hanus, Jan

PISK, PAUL AMADEUS (1893-   )
Five Folk Songs *CC5U,folk
med solo,fl,ob,2clar,2bsn,2horn,
perc,strings AM.COMP.AL.   (P834)

Four Sacred Songs *see Lamentation,
Op.97,No.1; Salomon's Prayer,
Op.97,No.2; Spirit Of God, The,
Op.97,No.3; Two Wisdoms, Op.97,
No.4   (P835)

Lamentation *Op.97,No.1, sac
med solo,pno/org AM.COMP.AL. $1.37
see from Four Sacred Songs (P836)

Meadow-Saffrons
A solo,clar,bass clar sc PRESSER
$1.00   (P837)

Salomon's Prayer *Op.97,No.2, sac
med solo,pno/org AM.COMP.AL. $3.30
see from Four Sacred Songs (P838)

Spirit Of God, The *Op.97,No.3, sac
med solo,pno/org AM.COMP.AL. $3.30
see from Four Sacred Songs (P839)
high solo&med solo,pno/org sc
AM.COMP.AL. $2.75   (P840)

Three Psalms *Op.21, CC3U,Psalm
Bar solo,2fl,2ob,2clar,2bsn,2horn,
2trp,perc,strings AM.COMP.AL.
                              (P841)

Two Goethe Songs *CC2U
med solo,pno sc AM.COMP.AL. $1.10
                              (P842)

Two Wisdoms *Op.97,No.4, sac,Bibl
med solo,pno/org AM.COMP.AL. $1.37
see from Four Sacred Songs (P843)
high solo&med solo,pno sc
AM.COMP.AL. $2.75   (P844)

Waning Moon, The *Op.23b
solo,vln,vcl,pno sc AM.COMP.AL.
$3.85   (P845)

PISMA see Srebotnjak, Alojz F.

PISNE see Dolansky, L.

PISNE see Chaun, Frantisek

PISNE 1-2 PRO SOPRAN see Marsik,
Emanuel

PISNE see Jeremias, Otakar

PISNE A TANCE Z TESINSKA see Schulhoff,
Erwin

PISNE CERNOVYCH DNU see Foerster, Josef
Bohuslav

PISNE DOMOVA see Soukup, Vladimir

PISNE HEYDUKOVY see Jindrich, Jindrich

PISNE KRASNOHORSKE see Jindrich,
Jindrich

PISNE LETNI NOCI see Vomacka, Boleslav

PISNE MADLENKY see Borkovec, Pavel

PISNE MILOSTNE see Vignati, Milos

PISNE MILOSTNE PRO TENOR A KLAVIR see
Blazek, Zdenek

PISNE MLADYCH TEXTILAKU see Bartos, Jan
Zdenek

PISNE NA SLOVA RAINERA MARII RILKA see
Chaun, Frantisek

PISNE NA STARE MOTIVY see Podest,
Ludvik

PISNE NA TEXTY S. JESEJINA see
Stanislav, Josef

PISNE NARODU SSSR *CCU
(Urban; Hronek) solo,pno PANTON 527
s.p.   (P846)

PISNE NELASKAVE see Eben, Petr

PISNE NELASKAVE see Eben, Petr

PISNE NOVEHO WERTHERA see Berg, Josef

PISNE PANA JENIKA Z BRATRIC see
Vycpalek, Ladislav

PISNE POTULNEHO PEVCE see Goldbach,
Stanislav

PISNE PRO SOPRAN see Hruska, J.

PISNE PRO VYSSI HLAS see Jeremias,
Otakar

PISNE PRO VYSSI HLAS NA TEXTY S.
JESESNINA see Stanislav, Josef

PISNE, SES. 1-2 see Jindrich, Jindrich

PISNE SOUMRAKU see Foerster, Josef
Bohuslav

PISNE Z VOJNY see Zitek, Otakar

PISNICKI PRACOVNICH ZALOH see Gregor,
Cestmir

PISNICKY see Kovaricek, Frantisek

PISNICKY A BALADY see Satra, Antonin

PISNICKY NA SLOVA LIDOVE POESIE see
Blatny, Pavel

PISNICKY NA SLOVA LIDOVE POEZIE
MORAVSKE, RADA I-V see Novak, V.

PISNICKY NA 2 STRANKY see Martinu,
Bohuslav

PISNICKY O LASCE see Zouhar, Zdenek

PISNICKY O LASCE see Salich, Milan

PISNICKY PRO NIZSI HLAS see Kupka,
Karel

PIT, THE see Cossetto, Emil

PITCHER see Davis, Katherine K.

PITFIELD, THOMAS BARON (1903-   )
By The Dee At Night
solo,pno CRAMER $1.15   (P847)

Carrion Crow
solo,pno CRAMER   (P848)

Christmas Lullaby
solo,pno CRAMER   (P849)

Cuckoo And Chestnut Time
solo,pno CRAMER   (P850)

Desdemona's Song
solo,pno CRAMER   (P851)

Donkey Riding
solo,pno CRAMER $.95   (P852)

In The Moonlight
solo,pno CRAMER   (P853)

PITFIELD, THOMAS BARON (cont'd.)
Policeman, The
solo,pno CRAMER   (P854)

September Lovers
solo,pno CRAMER   (P855)

Wagon Of Life
solo,pno CRAMER   (P856)

PITIE see Schumann, Robert (Alexander)

PIT'OM ACHSHAV, PIT'OM HAYOM
solo,pno OR-TAV $.50   (P857)

PITTALUGA, GUSTAVO (1906-   )
Canciones Del Teatro De Federico
Garcia Lorca *CCU
[Span] solo,inst UNION ESP. $5.50
                              (P858)

Romance De Solita From "The Cuckold's
Fair"
(Garcia Lorca) [Span] med solo,pno
UNION ESP. $.75   (P859)

PITY THE MAN see Hemphill

PIU BELLO DEL SOLE see Mana-Zucca, Mme.

PIU NON SI TROVANO see Mozart, Wolfgang
Amadeus

PIU PRESSO IL CIEL see Mascagni, Pietro

PIXIE PIPER MAM see Elliott

PIXIES PICNIC, THE see Day, Maude
Craske

PIZENSKE PISNE see Bradac, J.

PIZMONIM BE'TSAMERET *CCU
solo,pno OR-TAV $3.50   (P860)

PIZZETTI, ILDEBRANDO (1880-1968)
Altre Cinque Liriche *see Oscuro E
Il Ciel...   (P861)

Angelica
solo,pno FORLIVESI 10741 s.p. see
from Due Liriche Napoletane
                              (P862)

Assunta
solo,pno FORLIVESI 10740 s.p. see
from Due Liriche Napoletane
                              (P863)

Augurio
see Tre Canti Greci

Bebro E Il Suo Cavallo
see Tre Liriche Drammatiche

Canzone Per Ballo
see Tre Canti Greci

Cinque Liriche *see I Pastori; Il
Clefta Prigione; La Madre Al
Figlio Lontano; Passeggiata; San
Basilio   (P864)

Donna Lombarda
see Tre Canzoni
[It] S solo,pno RICORDI-ENG 120236
s.p. see from Tre Canzoni (P865)

Due Liriche Napoletane *see
Angelica; Assunta   (P866)

E Il Mio Dolore Io Canto
solo,pno FORLIVESI 11961 s.p. see
from Tre Canti D'amore   (P867)

Erotica
[It] solo,pno BONGIOVANI 1299 s.p.
                              (P868)

I Pastori
solo,pno FORLIVESI 10614 s.p. see
from Cinque Liriche   (P869)

Il Clefta Prigione
solo,pno FORLIVESI 10617 s.p. see
from Cinque Liriche   (P870)

In Questa Notte Carica Di Stelle
see Tre Liriche Drammatiche

La Madre Al Figlio Lontano
solo,pno FORLIVESI 10615 s.p. see
from Cinque Liriche   (P871)

La Pesca Dell'anello
see Tre Canzoni

La Pisanella
solo,pno FORLIVESI 11044 s.p. see
from Tre Canti D'amore   (P872)

La Prigioniera
see Tre Canzoni
[It] solo,pno RICORDI-ENG 120237
s.p. see from Tre Canzoni (P873)

La Vita Fugge E Non S'arresta Un'ora
[It] Mez/Bar solo,pno RICORDI-ENG
119228 s.p. see from Tre Sonetti

PIZZETTI, ILDEBRANDO (cont'd.)

  Del Petrarca   (P874)

  Levommi Il Mio Pensier In Parte
    Ov'era
    [It] S/T solo,pno RICORDI-ENG
    119230 s.p. see from Tre Sonetti
    Del Petrarca   (P875)

  Mirologio Per Un Bambino
    see Tre Canti Greci

  Ninna-Nanna
    S solo,2fl,2ob,horn,pno voc sc
    CARISH 17254 s.p. see from Santa
    Uliva   (P876)

  O Ricordo Che Solo Mi Rimani (from
    Clitenniestra)
    [It] S solo,pno RICORDI-ENG 131367
    s.p.   (P877)

  Oscuro E Il Ciel...
    [It] Mez/Bar solo,pno RICORDI-ENG
    122836 s.p. see from Altre Cinque
    Liriche   (P878)

  Passeggiata
    solo,pno FORLIVESI 10618 s.p. see
    from Cinque Liriche   (P879)

  Quel Rosignuol Che Si Soave Piange
    [It] S/T solo,pno RICORDI-ENG
    119229 s.p. see from Tre Sonetti
    Del Petrarca   (P880)

  San Basilio
    solo,pno FORLIVESI 10616 s.p. see
    from Cinque Liriche   (P881)

  Santa Uliva *see Ninna-Nanna   (P882)

  Scuote Amore Il Mio Cuore
    solo,pno FORLIVESI 12351 s.p. see
    from Tre Canti D'amore   (P883)

  Tre Canti D'amore *see E Il Mio
    Dolore Io Canto; La Pisanella;
    Scuote Amore Il Mio Cuore   (P884)

  Tre Canti Greci
    [It] RICORDI-ENG s.p.
    contains: Augurio (Mez/Bar solo,
      pno); Canzone Per Ballo (S/T
      solo,pno); Mirologio Per Un
      Bambino (Mez/Bar solo,pno)
                                        (P885)

  Tre Canzoni *see Donna Lombarda; La
    Prigioniera   (P886)

  Tre Canzoni
    solo,4strings cmplt ed RICORDI-ENG
    PR 669 s.p.
    contains: Donna Lombarda; La
      Pesca Dell'anello; La
      Prigioniera   (P887)

  Tre Liriche Drammatiche
    solo,pno cmplt ed FORLIVESI s.p.
    contains: Bebro E Il Suo Cavallo;
      In Questa Notte Carica Di
      Stelle; Vorrei Voler, Signor
      Quel Ch'io Non Voglio   (P888)

  Tre Sonetti Del Petrarca *see La
    Vita Fugge E Non S'arresta
    Un'ora; Levommi Il Mio Pensier In
    Parte Ov'era; Quel Rosignuol Che
    Si Soave Piange   (P889)

  Un Vecchio Padre (from Orseolo)
    [It] B solo,pno RICORDI-ENG 131366
    s.p.   (P890)

  Vocalizzo *vocalise
    [It] Mez solo,orch sc CURCI 7080
    s.p.   (P891)

  Vorrei Voler, Signor Quel Ch'io Non
    Voglio
    see Tre Liriche Drammatiche

PLA, M.
  El Soldado
    (Subira) [Span] 2 soli,pno UNION
    ESP. $4.00   (P892)

PLA, R.
  Cuarto Canciones Sefardies *CC4U,Jew
    [Span] med solo,pno,opt gtr UNION
    ESP. $1.00   (P893)

PLACE AU FEU, PLACE A LA CHANDELLE see
  Vasseur, Leon (-Felix-Augustin-
  Joseph)

PLACE OF PEACE, A see Slaughter, Henry

PLACE POELAERT see Middeleer, Jean De

PLACET FUTILE see Debussy, Claude

PLACET FUTILE see Ravel, Maurice

PLAGE see Daniel-Lesur

PLAGUE OF LOVE see Head, Michael
  (Dewar)

PLAIES VIVES see Middeleer, Jean De

PLAINT, THE see Purcell, Henry

PLAINTE see Saint-Saens, Camille

PLAINTES D'AMOUR see Chaminade, Cecile

PLAINTES SUR LA MORT DE SYLVIE see
  Cuvillier, Charles

PLAISIR D'AMOUR see Martini, Jean Paul
  Egide

PLANA RUZE see Tomasek, V.J.

PLANCK
  Lillemor *CC7U
    solo,pno LUNDQUIST s.p.   (P894)

PLANGE SION see Vladeracken, G. von

PLANQUETTE, ROBERT
  Couplets De La Gourmande (from La
    Grace De Dieu)
    solo,pno ENOCH s.p.   (P895)

  Il Pleuvait
    solo,acap ENOCH s.p.   (P896)
    solo,pno ENOCH s.p.   (P897)

  Infidelibus
    solo,acap ENOCH s.p.   (P898)
    solo,pno ENOCH s.p.   (P899)

  La Journee D'une Danseuse (from La
    Grace De Dieu)
    solo,pno ENOCH s.p.   (P900)

  Le Loup
    solo,pno ENOCH s.p.   (P901)
    solo,acap ENOCH s.p.   (P902)

  Lettre A Mon Mari Reserviste
    solo,acap ENOCH s.p.   (P903)
    solo,pno ENOCH s.p.   (P904)

  Reponse Du Reservist
    solo,pno ENOCH s.p.   (P905)
    solo,acap ENOCH s.p.   (P906)

  Victor Le Mauvais Sujet
    solo,pno ENOCH s.p.   (P907)
    solo,acap ENOCH s.p.   (P908)

PLANTEN, R.
  When You Walk In A Field
    med solo,pno SEESAW $1.00   (P909)

PLANTS CANNOT TRAVEL see Flanagan,
  William

PLANYAVSKY, PETER (1947-   )
  Zwei Geistliche Gesange *sac,CC2U
    [Lat] S solo,org DOBLINGER 08 856
    $5.25   (P910)

  Zwei Psalmen *sac,CC2U,Psalm
    Mez solo,org DOBLINGER 08 857 s.p.
                                        (P911)

PLASTIC CLOWN see Matthews, Randy

PLATAMONE, STEFANO
  Ave Maria *sac
    solo,pno SANTIS 685 s.p.   (P912)

  Due Canti Di Kabir *CC2U
    solo,pno SANTIS 503 s.p.   (P913)

  Due Liriche
    solo,pno cmplt ed SANTIS 635 s.p.
    contains: Il Vaggio Definitivo;
      Inverno   (P914)

  Il Vaggio Definitivo
    see Due Liriche

  Il Viggiatore Chimerico
    solo,pno cmplt ed SANTIS 625 s.p.
    contains: Signora; Sperduto; Una
      Grande Tristezza   (P915)

  Inverno
    see Due Liriche

  Missa In Nativitate Domini *sac
    solo,org,strings voc sc SANTIS 683
    s.p., sc SANTIS rental   (P916)

  Narrazione Tragica
    S solo,orch voc sc SANTIS 689 s.p.
                                        (P917)

  Parole Di Salmi *sac,CCU,Psalm
    solo,orch voc sc SANTIS 684 s.p.
                                        (P918)

  Rondel
    solo,pno SANTIS 741 s.p.   (P919)

  Signora
    see Il Viggiatore Chimerico

PLATAMONE, STEFANO (cont'd.)

  Sperduto
    see Il Viggiatore Chimerico

  Terzo Canto Di Kabir *CC30U
    solo,pno SANTIS 512 s.p.   (P920)

  Tre Liriche Giapponesi *CC3U
    solo,pno SANTIS 690 s.p.   (P921)

  Tre Liriche Spagnole *CC3U
    solo,pno SANTIS 975 s.p.   (P922)

  Un Canto Della Nostalgia Indiana
    solo,pno SANTIS 527 s.p.   (P923)

  Una Grande Tristezza
    see Il Viggiatore Chimerico

PLATTITUDES EN OCCASION see Alcalay,
  Luna

PLAVEC, JOSEF (1905-   )
  Dva Zpevy *CC2U
    high solo,harp,4strings CZECH s.p.
                                        (P924)

  Jen V Nas Je Jaro *song cycle
    low solo,pno SUPRAPHON s.p.   (P925)

  Pet Lidovych Pisni *CC5U
    solo,pno SUPRAPHON s.p.   (P926)

  Tri Pisne Pro Stredni Hlas *CC3U
    med solo,pno SUPRAPHON s.p.   (P927)

PLAVEIERS see Clercq, R. de

PLE, SIMONE
  Angelus *sac
    3 soli,pno/org HEUGEL s.p.   (P928)

  Ave Maria *sac
    3 soli,pno/org HEUGEL s.p.   (P929)

PLEADING see Elgar, Edward

PLEADING see Kramer, A. Walter

PLEASE DO NOT PASS ME BY see Deane, Uel

PLEASING TALES IN DEAR ROMANCES see
  Arne, Thomas Augustine

PLEASURES OF MERELY CIRCULATING, THE
  see Blank, Allan

PLEDGE TO THE FLAG see Malotte, Albert
  Hay

PLEGARIA see Schwartz, Francis

PLEGARIA DEL CERRO see Quaratino,
  Pascual

PLEINE EAU see Biancheri, A.

PLENILUNIO ESTIVO see Davico, Vincenzo

PLENTY OF ROOM IN THE FAMILY see
  Gaither

PLENTY OF TIME see McLean

PLESKOW, RAOUL
  Due Bicinia *CC2U
    [Lat] SS soli,fl,clar,vcl sc
    AM.COMP.AL. $5.50, ipa   (P930)

  For Five Players And Baritone
    Bar solo,fl,clar,vln,vcl,pno sc
    AM.COMP.AL. $8.80, ipa   (P931)

  Motet And Madrigal *Bibl
    TS soli,fl,clar,vln,vcl,pno sc
    AM.COMP.AL. $7.70, ipa   (P932)

  Three Songs *CC3U
    T solo,vln,vla,vcl,clar,bass clar,
    pno sc AM.COMP.AL. $8.25   (P933)

  Two Songs On Latin Fragments *CC2U
    S solo,pno AM.COMP.AL. $3.85   (P934)

PLESSIS, HUBERT DU (1922-   )
  Care-Charming Sleep
    see Five Invocations

  Dirge
    see Five Invocations

  Five Invocations
    T solo,pno NOVELLO 17.0240.08 s.p.
    contains: Care-Charming Sleep;
      Dirge; God Lyaeus; Hark, Now
      Everything Is Still; River-
      God's Song, The   (P935)

  God Lyaeus
    see Five Invocations

  Hark, Now Everything Is Still
    see Five Invocations

PLESSIS, HUBERT DU (cont'd.)

River-God's Song, The
  see Five Invocations

PLETKA, J.
Polske Revolucni Pisne *CCU
  PANTON 1531 s.p.   (P936)

PLEUREZ MES YEUX see Berger, Rod.

PLEUREZ! PRIEZ! see Georges, Alexandre

PLOG
Four Scenes For Soprano And Brass
  Quintet (composed with Muir)
  *CC4U
  S solo,5brass WESTERN BMP66 (P937)

Two Scenes For Soprano, Trumpet And
  Organ *CC2U
  S solo,trp,org WESTERN BMP77 (P938)

PLOUGH BOY see Britten, Benjamin

PLOUGHBOY see Shield, William

PLOUGHMAN, THE see Rowley, Alec

PLOUGHMANS LIFE, THE see Reuland,
  Jacques

PLUCK THIS LITTLE FLOWER see Ronald,
  Sir Landon

PLUCKING THE RUSHES see Heilner, Irwin

PLUCKING THE RUSHES see Orr, Charles
  Wilfred

PLUIE AU MATIN see Koechlin, Charles

PLUIE D'ETE see Desrez

PLUIES see Vellones, P.

PLUISTER, SIMON (1913-   )
De Dans Der Goden
  see Drie Chineesche Liederen
  see Drie Liederen Van H. Swarth

De Lenteregen
  see Drie Chineesche Liederen
  see Drie Liederen Van H. Swarth

Drie Chineesche Liederen
  A solo,2fl,2ob,2clar,2bsn,3horn,
  perc,cel,2harp,strings DONEMUS
  s.p.
  contains: De Dans Der Goden; De
  Lenteregen; Een Jonge Dichter
  Denkt Aan De Geliefde   (P939)

Drie Liederen Van H. Swarth
  low solo,pno DONEMUS s.p.
  contains: De Dans Der Goden; De
  Lenteregen; Een Jonge Dichter
  Denkt Aan De Geliefde   (P940)

Een Jonge Dichter Denkt Aan De
  Geliefde
  see Drie Chineesche Liederen
  see Drie Liederen Van H. Swarth

Slaapliederen Voor Grote Mensen
  S solo,2fl,2ob,2clar,2bsn,2horn,
  2trp,perc,harp,strings DONEMUS
  s.p.   (P941)

PLUME D'EAU CLAIRE see Poulenc, Francis

PLUMES OF TIME, THE see Hamilton,
  Alisdair

PLUMSTEAD, MARY
Close Thine Eyes
  high solo,pno ELKIN 27.4028.01 s.p.
                            (P942)
  low solo,pno ELKIN 27.2028.00 s.p.
                            (P943)
  med solo,pno ELKIN 27.2727.07 s.p.
                            (P944)
Ha'nacker Mill
  solo,pno (C min) ROBERTON 1005 s.p.
                            (P945)
My True Love Hath My Heart
  A solo,pno ELKIN 27.2029.09 s.p.
                            (P946)
On Jacob's Pillow *sac
  low solo,pno ELKIN 27.2346.08 s.p.
                            (P947)
Sigh No More, Ladies
  solo,pno (B flat maj) ROBERTON 2589
  s.p.   (P948)
Song Of The Cross, The
  solo,pno (E min) ROBERTON 2613 s.p.
                            (P949)
  solo,pno (G min) ROBERTON 2613 s.p.
                            (P950)
Where Are You Going To, My Pretty
  Maid
  solo,pno (B flat maj) BOOSEY $1.50
                            (P951)

PLUNKETT, BONNIE
One Touch *sac
  solo,pno GOSPEL 05 TM 0442 $1.00
                            (P952)

PLUS D'AMOUR, PLUS DE ROSES see Gustave
  de Suede, (Prince)

PLUS DE PEINES, PLUS DE LARMES see
  Bach, Johann Sebastian

PLUS...UN CROISSANT see Barbier, Rene

PLUTON SURPRIS D'ENTENDRE see
  Clerambault, Louis-Nicolas

PO CESKU see Kricka, Jaroslav

PO LETECH see Picha, Frantisek

PO' LI'L LAM' see Harding, Harvey

PO MONER GOT A HOME AT LAS' see
  Johnson, Hall

POBRE MI NEGRA see Gomez Carrillo,
  Manuel

POBRES JAZMINES CRIOLLOS! see Lopez-
  Buchardo, Carlos

PODEST, LUDVIK (1921-1968)
Maminka *song cycle
  med solo,pno SUPRAPHON s.p. (P953)

Pisne Na Stare Motivy *CCU
  solo,pno SUPRAPHON s.p.   (P954)

Tesknice *CCU
  low solo,vla,vcl,fl,pno CZECH s.p.
                            (P955)
PODESVA, JAROMIR (1927-   )
Blizky Hlas *CCU
  solo,pno SUPRAPHON s.p.   (P956)

Der Fragebogen Des Herzens *see
  Dotaznik Srdce

Dotaznik Srdce *cant
  "Der Fragebogen Des Herzens" Bar
  solo,fl,trp,perc,chimes,harp,pno,
  vln,vla,vcl CZECH s.p.   (P957)

PODZIEL SIE ZE MNA see Baird, Tadeusz

PODZIMNI NALADY see Haba, Karel

PODZIMNI TOULKY see Kricka, Jaroslav

POEM see Fibich

POEM FOR SOPRANO AND FOUR INSTRUMENTS
  see Hellermann, Herbert

POEMA DA CRIANCA E SUA MAMA see Villa-
  Lobos, Heitor

POEMA EN FORMA DE CANCIONES see Turina,
  Joaquin

POEMA EROTICO see Grieg, Edvard Hagerup

POEMA PARA UNA MUERTA VOZ see Jurafsky,
  Abraham

POEMAS AMERICANOS see Lasala, Angel

POEMAS DE NEGRA see Nobre, Marlos

POEMAS NORTENOS see Lasala, Angel

POEME see Pillois, Jacques

POEME DE LA ROSE see Migot, Georges

POEME DE L'AMOUR ET DE LA MER see
  Chausson, Ernest

POEME DE LOUISE DE VILMORIN see Arrieu,
  Claude

POEME DE PITIE see Mariotte, Antoine

POEME DISCONTINU see Regteren Altena,
  Lucas van

POEME D'ITABIRA see Villa-Lobos, Heitor

POEME DU BRUGNON see Migot, Georges

POEME D'UN JOUR see Faure, Gabriel-
  Urbain

POEME D'UN JOUR see Faure, Gabriel-
  Urbain

POEME FUNEBRE see Chaix

POEME HEBRAIQUE see Schlionsky, Verdina

POEME LYRIQUE see Doyen, Albert

POEME POUR LA MORTE see Levade, Charles
  (Gaston)

POEMES see Caby, R.

POEMES D'AUTOMNE see Gaubert, Philippe

POEMES DE GUERRE see Ancelin, Pierre

POEMES DE LA VIEILLE FRANCE, DEUXIEME
  RECUEIL see Moulaert, Raymond

POEMES DE LA VIEILLE FRANCE, QUATRIEME
  RECUEIL see Moulaert, Raymond

POEMES DE TRISTAN CORBIERE see
  Baudrier, Yves

POEMES D'EPINAL see Middeleer, Jean De

POEMES D'ORIENT see Vuataz

POEMES INTIMES see Jolivet, Andre

POEMES INTIMES DE COLETTE see Wolff, A.

POEMES JUIFS see Milhaud, Darius

POEMES JUIFS see Milhaud, Darius

POEMES MARINS see Favre, Georges

POEMES POUR LA PAIX see Rorem, Ned

POEMES POUR MI, PREMIER LIVRE see
  Messiaen, Oliver

POEMES POUR MI, DEUXIEME LIVRE see
  Messiaen, Oliver

POEMES SALOMNIQUES see Desrez

POEMETTO TRAGICO see Spezzaferri, L.

POEMMA see Mestres-Quadreny, Josep
  Maria

POEMS BY EMILY DICKINSON see Vries
  Robbe, Willem de

POEMS OF LOVE AND THE RAIN see Rorem,
  Ned

POEMS OF THE HEART see Yakhnina, Ye.

POEMS OF THE SEA see Kaburagi, Mitsugu

POESIES DU SOIR see Walters

POET AND THE NIGHTINGALE see Granados,
  Enrique

POET SINGS, THE see Watts, Wintter

POETRY OF DRESS - THREE SONGS see
  Blyton, Carey

POET'S DREAM, THE see Lora, Antonio

POET'S ECHO, THE see Britten, Benjamin

POET'S HYMN, A see Dyson, George

POET'S LOVE see Schumann, Robert
  (Alexander), Dichterliebe

POET'S LOVE, A see Hartmann, Thomas
  Alexandrovich de

POET'S SONG see Copland, Aaron

POET'S SONG, THE see Parry, Charles
  Hubert Hastings

POGLED NARAVE see Jez, Jakob

POGLIETTI, ALESSANDRO (1661-1683)
His Grace Will See Us Through *sac
  solo,pno BRIDGE Z 0624 s.p. (P958)

Man From Wayout, The *sac
  solo,pno BRIDGE Z 0625 s.p. (P959)

Reach Out For Life *sac
  solo,pno BRIDGE Z0605 s.p.   (P960)

Turn Your Life Over To Jesus *sac
  solo,pno BRIDGE Z0585 s.p.   (P961)

POHADKA O BRNENSKEM KROKODYLOVI see
  Krivinka, Gustav

POHJOLAAN see Bergman, Erik, Mot Nord

POHLE, DAVID (1624-1695)
Psalm 42 *see Wie Der Hirsch
  Schreyet

Wie Der Hirsch Schreyet (Psalm 42)
  sac,concerto
  (Winter) T solo,2vln,bsn,cont sc
  SIKORSKI 650-P s.p., ipa   (P962)

Zwolf Liebesgesange *CC12U
  (Gurlitt, Wilibald) 2 female soli,
  2vln,cont (med) BAREN. 1245 $8.50
                            (P963)

POI CHE 'L CAMMIN see Margola, Franco

POINT CHARLES see Strilko, Anthony

POINT OF RETURN, THE see Schibler, Armin

POIR CETTE FETE see Mozart, Wolfgang Amadeus

POISE, (JEAN ALEXANDRE) FERDINAND (1828-1892)
  A La Fenetre Demiclose (from L'Amour Medecin)
    T solo,orch DURAND s.p., ipa (P964)
    Bar/Mez solo,orch DURAND s.p., ipa (P965)
  Ah! Ah! Ah! La Belle Affaire (from L'Amour Medecin)
    SBar soli,pno/inst DURAND s.p. (P966)
  Ah! Quel Malheur (from L'Amour Medecin)
    S solo,pno/inst DURAND s.p. (P967)
  Ainsi Qu'au Pays Des Aimees (from L'Amour Medecin)
    T solo,pno/inst DURAND s.p. (P968)
  Aubade (from L'Amour Medecin)
    [Fr] solo,acap oct DURAND s.p. (P969)
  Chanson De Colombine (from Surprise De L'Amour)
    [Fr] solo,acap oct DURAND s.p. (P970)
  Dis-Moi De Ton Coeur (from L'Amour Medecin)
    Bar/Mez solo,pno/inst DURAND s.p. (P971)
  Elle Est Sans Facon, Lisette (from L'Amour Medecin)
    S solo,pno/inst DURAND s.p. (P972)
    Mez solo,pno/inst DURAND s.p. (P973)
  Pour Nous Deux L'avenir (from L'Amour Medecin)
    Mez solo,pno/inst DURAND s.p. (P974)
  Si Tu Savais, Ma Catherine (from L'Amour Medecin)
    Bar solo,pno/inst DURAND s.p. (P975)

POITOU *Fr
  (Canteloube, J.) solo,acap DURAND s.p. see also Anthologie Des Chants Populaires Francais Tome III (P976)

POKAL see Strauss, Richard

POKORNY, ANTONIN (1890-   )
  Mozart In Prag *see Mozart V Praze

  Mozart V Praze *song cycle
    "Mozart In Prag" med solo,pno CZECH s.p. (P977)

POLDOWSKI, LADY DEAN PAUL (1880-1932)
  Bruxelles
    Mez solo,pno/inst DURAND s.p. (P978)
  Dimanche D'Avril
    Mez solo,pno/inst DURAND s.p. (P979)

POLICEMAN, THE see Pitfield, Thomas Baron

POLICHINELLE see Barbier, Rene

POLICHINELLE see Levade, Charles (Gaston)

POLICKI, (?)
  Benedictus *sac
    low solo,2vln,cont sc FMA FMA 23 s.p. (P980)

POLIN, CLAIRE
  Infinito
    S,narrator,mix cor,sax sc SEESAW $6.00 (P981)
  No-Rai
    S solo,fl,bvl SEESAW (P982)
  Rosa Mundi
    countertenor,TB soli,pno SEESAW (P983)

POLISH SONGS see Chopin, Frederic

POLK, VIDET
  Give Me A Double Portion *sac
    solo,pno STAMPS 7266-SN $1.00 (P984)

POLKA VOCALISE see Gretchaninov, Alexander Tikhonovitch

POLKU PIENI see Ikonen, Lauri

POLL
  Le Galerien
    solo,pno AMPHION E-2-N s.p. (P985)

POLLACK, BERNARD
  Tri Pisne *CC3U
    S solo,pno CZECH s.p. (P986)
  Tri Pisne *CC3U
    B solo,pno CZECH s.p. (P987)

POLLY HAS HER EYE ON ME see Newton, Ernest

POLLY PILLICOTE
  see Songs Of Wonder

POLLY WILLIS see Arne, Thomas Augustine

POLMAN, TH.H.
  Verjaardagliedje
    solo,pno ALSBACH s.p. (P988)

POLO see Falla, Manuel de

POLO GITANO O FLAMENCO see Tarrago, G.

POLOLANIK, ZDENEK (1935-   )
  Cantus Psalmorum
    [Lat] med solo,harp,org,perc CZECH s.p. (P989)
  Tiche Svetlo *CC4U
    Bar solo,org CZECH s.p. (P990)

POLONAISE see Delden, Lex van

POLOVINKIN, LEONID (1894-1949)
  Selected Romances *CCU
    [Russ] solo,pno MEZ KNIGA 72 s.p. (P991)

POLSKA see Lyberg, Margot

POLSKE REVOLUCNI PISNE see Pletka, J.

POLZER, ODO
  Ave Maria *sac
    S/T solo,org,vln sc BOHM s.p. (P992)
  Mariae Wiegenlied *sac
    solo,vln/fl,org,sc BOHM s.p. (P993)

POM-POM see Betove

POMLADNE PESMI see Tomc, Matija

POMOZEME SLAVIKOVI see Kardos, Dezider

POMPADOR see Vieu, Jane

POMPER, A.
  Draag Nu Den Olijftak Aan
    solo,org ALSBACH s.p. (P994)
  Een Kruis Met Rozen
    solo,org ALSBACH s.p. (P995)
  Het Gebed Des Heeren
    med solo,vla,org/pno ALSBACH s.p. (P996)

PONCE, MANUEL MARIA (1882-1948)
  Estrellita
    high solo,pno (F maj) CENTURY 3630 (P997)
    "Little Star" solo,pno ASHLEY $.95 (P998)
    "Little Star" [Eng/Span] high solo,pno PRESSER $.75 (P999)
    "My Little Star" low solo,pno (D flat maj) FISCHER,C S 5707 (P1000)
    "My Little Star" high solo,pno (F maj) FISCHER,C S 5706 (P1001)
    (LaForge) "Little Star" low solo,pno BELWIN $1.50 (P1002)

  Little Star *see Estrellita

  My Little Star *see Estrellita

PONCHIELLI, AMILCARE (1834-1886)
  Cielo E Mar (from La Giocondo)
    [It] T solo,pno RICORDI-ARG BA 8837 s.p. (P1003)
    [It] T solo,pno RICORDI-ENG 109989 s.p. (P1004)
  Stella Del Marinar (from La Gioconda)
    [It] Mez solo,pno RICORDI-ENG 109904 s.p. (P1005)
  Suicidio! (from La Gioconda)
    [It] S solo,pno RICORDI-ENG 109871 s.p. (P1006)
  Voce Di Donna O D'angelo (from La Gioconda)
    [It] A solo,pno RICORDI-ENG 109923 s.p. (P1007)

PONSE, LUCTOR (1914-   )
  Appareillage
    see Trois Chants
  Guepe
    see Trois Chants
  Reflets
    see Trois Chants

PONSE, LUCTOR (cont'd.)
  Trois Chants
    DONEMUS med solo/high solo,2fl,2ob, 2clar,2bsn,3horn,timp,perc,harp, pno,strings s.p.; S/Mez solo,pno s.p.
    contains: Appareillage; Guepe; Reflets (P1008)

PONT BLEU see Revel, Peter

PONT SUPERIEUR see Ferroud, Pierre-Octave

PONTET, HENRY
  Broken Pitcher, The
    low solo,pno (A flat maj) LEONARD-ENG (P1009)
    high solo,pno (C maj) LEONARD-ENG (P1010)
    2 soli,pno LEONARD-ENG (P1011)
    med solo,pno (B flat maj) LEONARD-ENG (P1012)
  Dolly's Revenge
    high solo,pno (E flat maj) LEONARD-ENG (P1013)
    low solo,pno (D maj) LEONARD-ENG (P1014)
  Tit For Tat
    low solo,pno (C maj) ASHDOWN s.p. (P1015)
    high solo,pno (E flat maj) ASHDOWN s.p. (P1016)

PONZIO, L.
  La Vieille Au Manteau Noir
    solo,pno ENOCH s.p. (P1017)

POOR FLY see Blyton, Carey

POOR HENRY see Berkeley, Lennox

POOR IS THE LIFE see Musgrave, Thea

POOR LITTLE LOST LAMB see Lyman, Ed.

POOR MAN'S GARDEN see Rorem, Ned

POOR OLD ADAM *sac,gospel
  solo,pno ABER.GRP. $1.50 (P1018)

POOR PANTALOON see Arundale, Claude

POOR SOUL SAT SIGHING, THE see Castelnuovo-Tedesco, Mario

POOS, HEINRICH (1928-   )
  Herr Christ, Der Einig Gotts Sohn *sac,cant
    S solo,rec,org sc HANSSLER 10.121 s.p., ipa, solo pt HANSSLER s.p. (P1019)

POOT, MARCEL (1901-   )
  Chanson A Boire
    T solo,pno CBDM s.p. (P1020)

POPE, H. LEFEVRE
  Sleep
    solo,pno (D flat maj) ASHDOWN s.p. (P1021)

POPOLI DI TESSAGLIA see Mozart, Wolfgang Amadeus

POPOLI DI TESSAGLIA - IO NON CHIEDO, ETERNI see Mozart, Wolfgang Amadeus

POPULAR FRENCH AND CANADIAN SONGS *CC7L
  (Vuillermoz, Emile) med solo,pno SALABERT-US $13.00 (P1022)

POPULAR SONGS see Schulz, Joh. Abraham Peter

POPULAR SONGS OF THE NINETEENTH CENTURY AMERICA *CC64L
  (Jackson, Richard) solo,pno pap DOVER 23270-0 $5.95 (P1023)

POR DO PASARE ESTA SIERRA? see Salas, Juan Orrego

POR EL HUMO SE SABE DONDE ESTA EL FUEGO see Vives, Amadeo

POR LOS CAMPOS VERDES see Guastavino, Carlos

POR MAYO, ERA POR MAYO see Rodrigo, Joaquin

PORCELAIN AND POTTERY see Arundale, Claude

PORENA, BORIS (1927-   )
  La Mort De Pierrot
    A solo,6inst sc ZERBONI 6836 s.p. (P1024)
  Vier Kanonische Lieder *CC4U
    solo,pno ZERBONI 6883 s.p. (P1025)
  Vier Lieder Aus Dem Barock *CC4U
    S solo,2inst ZERBONI 7016 rental (P1026)

PORGI AMOR see Mozart, Wolfgang Amadeus

PORGI, AMOR, QUALCHE RISTORO see Mozart, Wolfgang Amadeus

PORPORA, NICOLA ANTONIO (1686-1768)
Chieggio Al Lido
see ANONIMI VARI DEI SECOLI XVII E XVIII, PART II

Ecco, Ecco, L'infausto Lido *cant
solo,pno BONGIOVANI 2334 s.p.
(P1027)

Vigilate, Oculi Mei *sac
(Ewerhart, Rudolf) [Lat] S/T solo,
cont BIELER CS 20 s.p. (P1028)

PORRINO, ENNIO (1910-1959)
Afa
see Canti Di Stagione

Autunnale
see Canti Di Stagione

Canti Di Stagione
S solo,2fl,ob,clar,2bsn,2horn,trp,
trom,tuba,perc,harp,pno voc sc
CARISH 18773 s.p.
contains: Afa; Autunnale; Mattino
D'aprile Nel Bosco; Una Notte
D'inverno (P1029)

Due Pagine D'Album
solo,strings,pno voc sc CARISH
20875 s.p.
contains: Palude; Un Mot (P1030)

I Canti Dell'Esilio *CC13L
solo,orch CARISH s.p. (P1031)

Io Per L'antico Diritto (from Gli Orazi)
[It/Ger] B solo,pno SONZOGNO 2856
$1.25 (P1032)

La Sorgente D'amore
solo,pno SANTIS 308 s.p. (P1033)

Mattino D'aprile Nel Bosco
see Canti Di Stagione

Monte Circeo
[It] T solo,pno SONZOGNO 2866 s.p.
(P1034)

Palude
see Due Pagine D'Album

Tre Canti Regionali *CC3U
S solo,fl,ob,clar,bsn,2horn,trp,
trom,timp,perc,harp,pno CARISH
s.p. (P1035)

Un Mot
see Due Pagine D'Album

Una Notte D'inverno
see Canti Di Stagione

PORTAMI IL GIRASOLE see Bettinelli, Bruno

PORTAMI VIA see Zandonai, Riccardo

PORTENITA see Lopez-Buchardo, Carlos

PORTER, QUINCY (1867-)
Desolate City, The
Bar solo,3fl,2ob,2clar,2bsn,4horn,
3trp,3trom,tuba,timp,perc,strings
AM.COMP.AL. sc $6.87, voc sc
$5.50 (P1036)

Music When Soft Voices Die
med-low solo,pno PRESSER $.75
(P1037)
Twelve Songs For Helen And One For Bill *CC13U
S solo,fl,ob,clar,bsn,perc,strings
sc AM.COMP.AL. $13.20 nursery
rhymes (P1038)

PORTER-BROWN, R.
When All The World Was Gay
solo,orch (F maj) ASHDOWN s.p., ipr
(P1039)
PORTNOJ
Skylark Sings
solo,pno ALLANS s.p. (P1040)

PORTRAIT see Chaminade, Cecile

PORTRAIT see Kernochan, Marshall

PORTRAIT see Lonque, Georges

PORTRAIT, A see Diamond, David

PORTRAIT DE NADIA BOULANGER see Prado, Almeida

PORTRAIT INTERIEUR see Binkerd, Gordon

PORTRAIT OF A MAN see O'Bryon, Jim

PORTRAIT OF F. B. see Thomson, Virgil

PORTRAIT SANS MODELE see Delmet, Paul

PORTRAITS IN VOICE *sac,CC13UL
(Fasig, Bill) 1-2 soli,pno LILLENAS
MB-278 $1.50 (P1041)

PORTRAITS OF THREE LADIES see London, Edwin

POSAMANICK, BEATRICE
Croon For The Christ Child
med solo,pno GALAXY 1.0742.7 $1.00
(P1042)

POSCH, ISAAC (ca. 1623?)
Auf Dich, Herr, Steht Mein Vertrauen *sac
med solo,cont HANSSLER 5.124 s.p.
(P1043)
Early Music Series, Vol. 1: Harmonia Concertans, Part I *CCU
(Geiringer, Karl) soli,inst PRESSER
$6.00 (P1044)

Early Music Series, Vol. 4: Harmonia Concertans, Part II *CCU
(Geiringer, Karl) soli,inst PRESSER
$6.00 (P1045)

Early Music Series, Vol. 6: Harmonia Concertans, Part III *CCU
(Geiringer, Karl) soli,inst PRESSER
$6.00 (P1046)

POSER, HANS (1917-1970)
Astronomisches Bilderbuch *Op.22, CCU
med solo,pno SIKORSKI 245 s.p.
(P1047)
Damon Und Daphne *Op.33, concerto
SBar soli,pno SIKORSKI 247 s.p.
(P1048)
Das Traurige Herz *Op.27, CC6U
Bar solo,pno SIKORSKI 246 s.p.
(P1049)
Fourteen Christmas Songs For Soprano, Recorder, And Other Instruments *CC14U,Xmas
S solo,rec,inst SCHAUR EE 3054 s.p.
(P1050)
Kritik Des Herzens *Op.26,No.1-6, CC6U
med solo,pno SIKORSKI 180 s.p.
(P1051)

POSITIVVISA see Peterson-Berger, (Olof) Wilhelm

POSLEDNI PISNE F.X. SVOBODY see Foerster, Josef Bohuslav

POSLEDNJI SPEVI see Kogoj, Marij

POSPISIL, JURAJ
Styri Piesne *CC5U
solo,pno SLOV.HUD.FOND s.p. (P1052)

POSSA TU GIUNGERE see Margola, Franco

POSSESSION see Doyen, Albert

POSSESSION FRANCAISE see Escher, Rudolf George

POST-CARD see Damase, Jean-Michel

POST, PIET (1919-)
Drie Liederen *CC3U
solo,pno BROEKMANS 189 s.p. (P1053)

POSTCARD FROM SPAIN see Hundley, Richard

POSTE RESTANTE see Berger, Rod.

POSTON, ELIZABETH (1905-)
Oh! Live, Shepherd, Fie
(Defesch) solo,pno (D maj) ROBERTON
2593 s.p. (P1054)

Sheepfolds *sac
low solo,pno ELKIN 27.2520.07 s.p.
(P1055)
Sweet Suffolk Owl
solo,pno (A flat maj) BOOSEY $1.50
(P1056)
POSY OF PROVERBS, A see Parkyns, B.

POTATO LIFTIN' *Scot
solo,pno PATERSON s.p. see from
Hebridean Songs, Vol. IV (P1057)

POUGET, LEO
Aupres De Feu
solo,pno ENOCH s.p. (P1058)
solo,acap ENOCH s.p. (P1059)

Aveu
solo,pno ENOCH s.p. (P1060)
solo,acap ENOCH s.p. (P1061)

Crainte
solo,pno (available in 2 keys)
ENOCH s.p. (P1062)
solo,acap (available in 2 keys)
ENOCH s.p. (P1063)

POUGET, LEO (cont'd.)
Dernier Rayon
solo,pno ENOCH s.p. (P1064)
solo,acap ENOCH s.p. (P1065)

En Passant
solo,pno ENOCH s.p. (P1066)
solo,acap ENOCH s.p. (P1067)

Envoi De Roses
solo,pno ENOCH s.p. (P1068)
solo,acap ENOCH s.p. (P1069)

Et Vous Ne Verez Pas Nos Larmes
solo,pno ENOCH s.p. (P1070)

Evocation
solo,acap ENOCH s.p. (P1071)
solo,pno ENOCH s.p. (P1072)

Invocation A La Vierge *sac
solo,acap ENOCH s.p. (P1073)
solo,pno ENOCH s.p. (P1074)
[Fr] solo,pno/org ENOCH (P1075)

POUHE, JOSEPH FRANK (1939-)
Amorous Line, The *song cycle
med-high solo,pno KERBY 1250 $4.50
(P1076)

POUJADE, L.
Marche Des Cadets De Gascogne
solo,acap ENOCH s.p. (P1077)
solo,pno ENOCH s.p. (P1078)

Rever, Aimer, Pleurer
(Montoya, G.) solo,acap ENOCH s.p.
(P1079)
(Montoya, G.) solo,pno ENOCH s.p.
(P1080)

POULENC, FRANCIS (1899-1963)
A Sa Guitare
solo,pno/inst DURAND s.p. (P1081)

Air Champetre
see Airs Chantes
[Eng/Fr/Ger] S solo,pno/orch
SALABERT-US $2.25 see from Airs
Chantes 1898c., The.. (P1082)

Air Grave
see Airs Chantes
[Eng/Fr/Ger] S solo,pno/orch
SALABERT-US $2.25 see from Airs
Chantes 1898c., The.. (P1083)

Air Romantique
see Airs Chantes
[Eng/Fr/Ger] S solo,pno/orch
SALABERT-US $2.25 see from Airs
Chantes 1898c., The.. (P1084)

Air Vif
see Airs Chantes
[Eng/Fr/Ger] S solo,pno/orch
SALABERT-US $3.75 see from Airs
Chantes 1898c., The.. (P1085)

Airs Chantes
[Eng/Fr/Ger] S solo,pno SALABERT-US
$7.75
contains: Air Champetre; Air
Grave; Air Romantique; Air Vif
(P1086)
Airs Chantes 1898c., The.. *see Air
Champetre; Air Grave; Air
Romantique; Air Vif (P1087)

Allons Plus Vite
med solo,pno SALABERT-US $2.25
(P1088)

Amoureuses
see Cinq Poemes De Paul Eluard

Au-Dela
solo,pno/inst DURAND s.p. see from
Trois Poemes De Louise De
Vilmorin (P1089)

Aux Officiers De La Garde Lanche
solo,pno/inst DURAND s.p. see from
Trois Poemes De Louise De
Vilmorin (P1090)

Avant Le Cinema
med solo,pno SALABERT-US $2.25
(P1091)

Banalites *CCU
[Fr] med solo,pno ESCHIG $9.75
(P1092)

Berceuse
see Five Poems Of Max Jacob

Bleuet
solo,pno/inst DURAND s.p. (P1093)

Calligrammes *CC7U
[Fr] solo,pno HEUGEL 10932 s.p.
(P1094)

Ce Doux Petit Visage
med solo,pno SALABERT-US $2.25
(P1095)

C'est Ainsi Que Tu Est
see Metamorphoses

POULENC, FRANCIS (cont'd.)

Chanson
   see Five Poems Of Max Jacob

Chansons Villageoises *CCU
   [Fr] med solo,orch ESCHIG $9.75
                                    (P1096)

Cimitiere
   see Five Poems Of Max Jacob

Cinq Poemes De Paul Eluard *see
   Rodeuse Au Front De Verre (P1097)

Cinq Poemes De Paul Eluard
   solo,pno DURAND s.p.
      contains: Amoureuses; Il La Prend
      Dans Ses Bras; Peut-Il Se
      Reposer; Plume D'eau Claire;
      Rondeuse Au Front De Verre
                                    (P1098)

Cocardes *CCU
   [Fr] high solo,pno ESCHIG $3.50
                                    (P1099)

Dans Le Jardin D'Anna
   med solo,pno SALABERT-US $3.00
                                    (P1100)

Dans L'herbe
   see Fiancailles Pour Rire

Dernier Poeme
   [Fr] med solo,pno ESCHIG $8.00
                                    (P1101)

Deux Melodies *CC2U
   [Fr] med solo,pno ESCHIG $5.50
                                    (P1102)

Dialogues Des Carmelites
   solo,pno AMPHION s.p. solo pt, voc
   sc   (P1103)

Douze Chants Pour Voix Moyennes
   *CC12L
   med solo,pno/inst DURAND s.p.
                                    (P1104)

Douze Poemes *CC12U
   [Fr/Eng/Ger] med solo,pno ESCHIG
   $9.50   (P1105)

Epitaphe
   [Fr] Bar/Mez solo,pno SALABERT-US
   $2.25   (P1106)

Fiancailles Pour Rire
   high solo,pno cmplt ed SALABERT-US
   $7.00
      contains: Dans L'herbe; Il Vole;
      La Dame D'Andre; Mon Cadavre
      Est Doux Comme Un Gant; Violon
      Fleurs
      see also: Il Vole   (P1107)

Five Poems Of Max Jacob
   [Fr] high solo,pno SALABERT-US
   $5.50
      contains: Berceuse; Chanson;
      Cimitiere; La Petite Servante;
      Souric Et Mouric   (P1108)

Four Poems Of Guillaume Apollinaire
   *CC4UL
   Bar/Mez solo,pno SALABERT-US $5.50
                                    (P1109)

Hier
   [Eng/Fr/Ger] high solo,pno
   SALABERT-US $2.25   (P1110)

Huit Chansons Polonaises *CC8L
   [Pol/Fr] med solo,pno SALABERT-US
   $7.50   (P1111)

Hyde Park
   see Two Songs

Hymn From The Roman Breviary *see
   Sombre Nuit, Aveugles Tenebres

Il Fait Tout Lui-Meme Monsieur Sans
   Souci
   solo,pno ENOCH s.p.   (P1112)
   solo,acap ENOCH s.p.   (P1113)
   solo,orch ENOCH rental   (P1114)

Il La Prend Dans Ses Bras
   see Cinq Poemes De Paul Eluard

Il Vole
   high solo,pno SALABERT-US $2.25 see
      also Fiancailles Pour Rire
                                    (P1115)

Je Nommerai Ton Front
   see Miroirs Brulants

Joueur Du Bugle
   see Parisiana

La Courte Paille *CC7U
   [Fr] med solo,pno ESCHIG $8.75
                                    (P1116)

La Dame D'Andre
   see Fiancailles Pour Rire

La Dame De Montecarlo
   S solo,2fl,2ob,2clar,2bsn,2horn,
   2trp,timp,perc,harp,strings
   AMPHION R 2160 s.p., ipr (P1117)
   [Fr] ST soli,orch voc sc RICORDI-

POULENC, FRANCIS (cont'd.)

   ENG R 2160 s.p.   (P1118)

La Fraicheur Et Le Feu
   [Fr] med solo,pno ESCHIG $8.50
                                    (P1119)

La Grenouillere
   med solo,pno SALABERT-US $1.50
                                    (P1120)

La Petite Servante
   see Five Poems Of Max Jacob

La Tragique Histoire Du Petit Rene
   solo,pno ENOCH s.p.   (P1121)
   solo,orch ENOCH rental   (P1122)
   solo,acap ENOCH s.p.   (P1123)

La Voix Humaine
   solo,pno AMPHION s.p. solo pt, voc
   sc   (P1124)

Le Bal Masque *sec,cant
   Bar/Mez solo,chamb.orch voc sc
   SALABERT-US $14.50, ipr   (P1125)

Le Bestiaire, Ou Cortege D'Orphee
   *CCU
   [Fr/Ger/Eng] med solo,fl,clar,bsn,
   4strings ESCHIG $3.50   (P1126)

Le Disparu
   med solo,pno SALABERT-US $2.25
                                    (P1127)

Le Garcon De Liege
   solo,pno/inst DURAND s.p. see from
   Trois Poemes De Louise De
   Vilmorin   (P1128)

Le Petit Garcon Trop Bien Portant
   solo,acap ENOCH s.p.   (P1129)
   solo,orch ENOCH rental   (P1130)
   solo,pno ENOCH s.p.   (P1131)

Le Pont
   see Two Songs

Le Portrait
   med solo,pno SALABERT-US $2.25
                                    (P1132)

Le Travail Du Peintre
   [Fr] med solo,pno ESCHIG $9.00
                                    (P1133)

Les Chemins De L'Amour
   [Fr] med solo,pno ESCHIG $1.75
                                    (P1134)

Main Dominee Par Le Coeur
   med solo,pno SALABERT-US $2.25
                                    (P1135)

Metamorphoses
   med solo,pno SALABERT-US $4.50
      contains: C'est Ainsi Que Tu Est;
      Paganini; Reine Des Mouettes
                                    (P1136)

Miroirs Brulants
   med solo,pno SALABERT-US $4.50
      contains: Je Nommerai Ton Front;
      Tu Vois Le Feu Du Soir (P1137)

Mon Cadavre Est Doux Comme Un Gant
   see Fiancailles Pour Rire

Montparnasse
   see Two Songs

Nous Voulons Une Petite Soeur
   solo,pno ENOCH s.p.   (P1138)
   solo,acap ENOCH s.p.   (P1139)
   solo,orch ENOCH rental   (P1140)

Paganini
   see Metamorphoses

Parisiana
   med solo,pno SALABERT-US $3.75
      contains: Joueur Du Bugle; Vous
      N'ecrivez Plus?   (P1141)

Paul Et Virginie
   [Fr] med solo,pno ESCHIG $2.75
                                    (P1142)

Peut-Il Se Reposer
   see Cinq Poemes De Paul Eluard

Plume D'eau Claire
   see Cinq Poemes De Paul Eluard

Priez Pour Paix
   med solo/low solo,pno SALABERT-US
   $2.25   (P1143)

Reine Des Mouettes
   see Metamorphoses

Rodeuse Au Front De Verre
   solo,pno/inst DURAND s.p. see from
   Cinq Poemes De Paul Eluard
                                    (P1144)

Rondeuse Au Front De Verre
   see Cinq Poemes De Paul Eluard

Rosemonde
   [Fr] med solo,pno ESCHIG $5.75
                                    (P1145)

POULENC, FRANCIS (cont'd.)

Six Melodies *CC6U
   [Fr] med solo,pno ESCHIG $6.00
                                    (P1146)

Sombre Nuit, Aveugles Tenebres
   "Hymn From The Roman Breviary" Bar
   solo,pno SALABERT-US $2.25
                                    (P1147)

Souric Et Mouric
   see Five Poems Of Max Jacob

Tel Jour, Telle Nuit *song cycle
   solo,pno DURAND s.p.   (P1148)

Trois Poemes De Louise De Vilmorin
   *see Au-Dela; Aux Officiers De La
   Garde Lanche; Le Garcon De Liege
                                    (P1149)

Tu Vois Le Feu Du Soir
   see Miroirs Brulants

Twelve Songs, Volume I *CC12L
   high solo,pno SALABERT-US $13.50
                                    (P1150)

Twelve Songs, Volume II *CC12L
   med solo,pno SALABERT-US $13.50
                                    (P1151)

Two Poems Of Louis Aragon *CC2UL
   [Fr] high solo,pno SALABERT-US
   $3.75   (P1152)

Two Songs
   [Fr] med-high solo,pno ESCHIG $3.50
      contains: Le Pont; Un Poeme
                                    (P1153)

Two Songs
   [Fr] med solo,pno ESCHIG $4.00
      contains: Hyde Park; Montparnasse
                                    (P1154)

Un Poeme
   see Two Songs

Une Herbe Pauvre (from Tel Jour Telle
   Nuit)
   solo,pno/inst DURAND s.p.   (P1155)

Violon Fleurs
   see Fiancailles Pour Rire

Vous N'ecrivez Plus?
   see Parisiana

POUR ALLER VERS TOI see Lacome, Paul

POUR BERCER LE COEUR see Moreau, H.

POUR CE QUE PLAISANCE EST MORTE see
   Debussy, Claude

POUR CELLES QUI RESTENT see Rhene-Baton

POUR DRESSER UN JEUNE COURRIER see
   Levade, Charles (Gaston)

POUR ENDORMIR L'ENFANT see Canal,
   Marguerite

POUR FAIRE CHANTER LA POLONAISE see
   Bois, Rob du

POUR FAIRE LE PORTRAIT D'UN OISEAU see
   Kruyf, Ton de

POUR LA FETE DES MERES see Schlosser,
   Paul

POUR LA LIBERTE see Arrieu, Claude

POUR L'ABSENTE see Gaubert, Philippe

POUR LE LYS see Rhene-Baton

POUR LES FEMMES see Petitjean, M.

POUR LES MAUVAIS JOURS see DuBois,
   Pierre Max

POUR LES PETITS ET POUR LES GRANDS see
   Truillet-Soyer, M.

POUR MA MIGNONNE see Gedalge, Andre

POUR MON COEUR see Rhene-Baton

POUR NINON DE LENCLOS see Blanchard,
   Roger

POUR NOEL see Stevens, Halsey

POUR NOUS DEUX L'AVENIR see Poise,
   (Jean Alexandre) Ferdinand

POUR, O LOVE, SWEET CONSOLATION see
   Mozart, Wolfgang Amadeus, Porgi,
   Amor, Qualche Ristoro

POUR PORTER LE LAIT see Serpette,
   Gaston

POUR QUE LA NUIT SOIT DOUCE see Busser,
   Henri-Paul

POUR TERMINER see Mussorgsky, Modest

POUR TOI ET MOI see Magne, Michel

POUR UN DETAIL, UNE NUANCE see
Messager, Andre

POUR UN SOURIRE see Delmet, Paul

POUR UNE AMIE PERDUE see Dupre, Marcel

POUR VIVRE LONGUEMENT see Ropartz,
Joseph Guy

POUR VOS SEIZE ANS see Delmet, Paul

POUR VOTRE FETE see Delmet, Paul

POUR VOUS DE PEINE see Schmitt, Florent

POUR VOUS MON COEUR see Monsigny,
Pierre-Alexandre

POUR VOUS MON COEUR FUT SANS MERCI see
Saint-Saens, Camille

POURNY, CH.
Les Bulletins De Vote
solo,acap ENOCH s.p. (P1156)
solo,pno ENOCH s.p. (P1157)

POURQUOI? see Chaminade, Cecile

POURQUOI see Gedalge, Andre

POURQUOI see Godard, Benjamin Louis
Paul

POURQUOI see Messiaen, Oliver

POURQUOI see Widor, Charles-Marie

POURQUOI FILES-TU? see Legay, Marcel

POURQUOI JE M'EN VAIS see Menier, G.

POURQUOI ME REVEILLER see Massenet,
Jules

POURQUOI RESTER SEULETTE see Saint-
Saens, Camille

POURQUOI SE FANENT TES FEUILLES? see
Gretchaninov, Alexander
Tikhonovitch

POURQUOI SUIS-JE VENUE see Saint-Saens,
Camille

POURQUOI TARDER see Filipucci, Edm.

POURTANT J'AI GARDE DANS MON COEUR see
Vasseur, Leon (-Felix-Augustin-
Joseph)

POURVU QUE L'ON TRAVAILLE see Delbruck,
J.

POUSSEUR, HENRI (1929-   )
Crosses Of Crossed Colors
female solo,2-5pno,6inst sc,quarto
ZERBONI 7300 s.p. (P1158)

Echos II De Votre Faust
Mez solo,fl,vcl,pno UNIVER. 15104
$12.00 (P1159)

Miroir De Votre Faust
S solo,pno UNIVER. 14254 $21.75
(P1160)

Mnemosyne I
solo ZERBONI 7017 s.p. (P1161)

Phonemes Pour Cathy
solo ZERBONI 7399 s.p. (P1162)

Trois Chants Sacres *sac,CC3U
S solo,3inst ZERBONI 6069 rental
(P1163)

POUSSIVITE see DuBois, Pierre Max

POVERE GGIRASOLE see Albanese, Guido

POVERI FIORI see Cilea, Francesco

POVERO COR see Respighi, Ottorino

POWELL
Bless That Wonderful Name *sac
solo,pno BENSON S5199-R $1.00
(P1164)
He Did It All For Me *see Allen

POWELL, M.
Haiku Settings *CCU
solo,pno SCHIRM.G $2.00 (P1165)

POWELL, ROBERT J.
Blessed Are Those Who Fear The Lord
see Three Wedding Songs

May The Lord Watch Over This House
see Three Wedding Songs

Our Heart Shall Rejoice In The Lord
see Three Wedding Songs

POWELL, ROBERT J. (cont'd.)
Three Wedding Songs *sac
solo,pno CONCORDIA 97-5278 $1.50
contains: Blessed Are Those Who
Fear The Lord; May The Lord
Watch Over This House; Our
Heart Shall Rejoice In The Lord
(P1166)

POWER TO BE see Cotton, Gene

POWER TO CHOOSE, THE see Skillings,
Otis

POWERS
Taking Leave Of A Friend
med solo,pno (F sharp maj) MUSICUS
$1.25 (P1167)

POWERS, GEORGE
Create In Me *sac
high solo,pno ABINGDON APM-539 $.50
(P1168)
low solo,pno ABINGDON APM-536 $.50
(P1169)

POWROT see Baird, Tadeusz

POZEHNANI LETA see Blazek, Zdenek

POZNY BTASK see Baird, Tadeusz

PR' UN LAVATIV!
(Carlo, Musi) solo,pno (Bolognese
dialect) BONGIOVANI 2049 s.p. see
from El Mi Canzunett (P1170)

PRAAG, HENRI C. VAN (1894-   )
Egidius
A solo,pno DONEMUS s.p. (P1171)

Koekoek
Mez/A solo,pno DONEMUS s.p. (P1172)

PRACTICAL LIBRARY OF SACRED SONGS, BOOK
1 *sac,CCU
(Row) high solo,pno FISCHER,C RB 47;
low solo,pno FISCHER,C RB 48
(P1173)
PRACTICAL LIBRARY OF SACRED SONGS, BOOK
2 *sac,CCU
(Row) high solo,pno FISCHER,C RB 73;
low solo,pno FISCHER,C RB 74
(P1174)

PRADAS, JOSEP
Cantata
(Nin-Culmell) [Span] Mez solo,hpsd/
org ESCHIG $10.50 (P1175)

El Amor *cant
S solo,2vln,cont sc GERIG AV 125
s.p., ipa (P1176)

PRADELS, O.
Les Petites Blanchisseuses
solo,acap ENOCH s.p. (P1177)
solo,pno ENOCH s.p. (P1178)

PRADO, ALMEIDA
Bem-Vinda
see Zwei Lieder

Lembrancas Do Coracao *CC3U
solo,pno TONOS 10313 s.p. (P1179)

Lettre De Jerusalem
S,narrator,pno,perc TONOS 10309
s.p. (P1180)

Manha Molhada
solo,pno TONOS 10314 s.p. (P1181)

O Luande-Lua
see Zwei Lieder

Portrait De Nadia Boulanger
solo,pno TONOS 10305 s.p. (P1182)

Zwei Lieder
solo,pno TONOS 10307 s.p.
contains: Bem-Vinda; O Luande-Lua
(P1183)

PRAEBE, VIRGO, BENIGNAS AURES see Leo,
Leonardo

PRAELUDIUM see Medtner, Nikolai
Karlovitch

PRAETORIUS, MICHAEL (1571-1621)
Herr, Kehre Dich Wieder Zu Uns *sac,
concerto
S solo,cont HANSSLER 5.125 s.p.
(P1184)
Zwiegesange Heft I: Der Jahreskreis
*sac,CC21U
(Schwarz, Gerhard) 2 soli,org (med
easy) BAREN. 1929 s.p. (P1185)
Zwiegesange Heft II: Der Tageskreis
*sac,CC28U
(Schwarz, Gerhard) 2 soli,org (med
easy) BAREN. 1930 s.p. (P1186)

PRAG MEIN EINZIGES see Dobias, Vaclav

PRAHO JEDINA see Dobias, Vaclav

PRAIANAS see Nobre, Marlos

PRAIRIE BOY, PRAIRIE BOY see Surdin, M.

PRAISE see O'Connor-Morris, G.

PRAISE BOOK, A see Hazzard, Peter

PRAISE OF ISLAY see Lawson, Malcolm

PRAISE THE LORD see Adams, John T.

PRAISE THE LORD see White, Louie L.,
Gloria In Excelsis Deo

PRAISE THE LORD, HE NEVER CHANGES see
Harris, Ron

PRAISE THE LORD HIS GLORIES SHOW see
Weaver, Powell

PRAISE THE LORD WITH A CHEERFUL NOISE
see Handel, George Frideric

PRAISE THE LORD WITH CHEERFUL NOISE see
Handel, George Frideric

PRAISE THE LORD YE HEAVENS ADORE HIM
see Weber

PRAISE WE THE LORD see Edmunds

PRAISE YE THE LORD see Bantock,
Granville

PRAISE YE THE LORD see Fischer, Irwin

PRAISE YE THE LORD see Grieg, Edvard
Hagerup

PRAISE YE THE LORD see Humphreys, Don

PRAISES see Crouch, Andrae

PRAISES AND PRAYERS see Thomson, Virgil

PRANDI, A.
Canta La Sponda
[It] solo,pno CURCI 5731 s.p.
(P1187)

PRATELLA, FRANCESCO BALILLA (1880-1955)
Astro D'amore *Op.7,No.2
solo,pno BONGIOVANI 739 s.p. see
from Quattro Liriche (P1188)

Ballata Antica *Op.42
S/T solo,pno BONGIOVANI 630 s.p.
(P1189)

Cantilene A Colombina *Op.45
solo,pno BONGIOVANI 1311 s.p.
(P1190)

Deh! Lascia O Fanciulla *Op.9,No.4
solo,pno BONGIOVANI 747 s.p. see
from Storia D'amore (P1191)

Deh! Non Giurare.. *Op.7,No.4
solo,pno BONGIOVANI 741 s.p. see
from Quattro Liriche (P1192)

Desiderare *Op.26,No.1
solo,pno BONGIOVANI 732 s.p. see
from Impressioni (P1193)

Donetta *Op.36,No.1
solo,pno BONGIOVANI 834 s.p. see
also Le Canzoni Del Niente
(P1194)

Due Liriche *see Mystica, Op.8,No.2;
Romanza D'autunno, Op.8,No.1
(P1195)

Fantasticare *Op.26,No.4
solo,pno BONGIOVANI 735 s.p. see
from Impressioni (P1196)

Felicta-Giovinezza *Op.27,No.1
solo,pno BONGIOVANI 736 s.p. see
from Stati D'anima (P1197)

Gelsa *Op.36,No.4
solo,pno BONGIOVANI 837 s.p. see
also Le Canzoni Del Niente
(P1198)

Il Pastore *Op.36,No.5
solo,pno BONGIOVANI 1198 s.p. see
from La Strade Notturne (P1199)
solo,pno BONGIOVANI 838 s.p. see
also Le Canzoni Del Niente
(P1200)

Il Viandante
solo,pno BONGIOVANI 1199 s.p. see
from La Strade Notturne (P1201)

Impressioni *see Desiderare, Op.26,
No.1; Fantasticare, Op.26,No.4;
Inebbriarsi, Op.26,No.2; Morire,
Op.26,No.3 (P1202)

In Mezzo Al Mare *Op.9,No.1
solo,pno BONGIOVANI 744 s.p. see
from Storia D'amore (P1203)

Inebbriarsi *Op.26,No.2
solo,pno BONGIOVANI 733 s.p. see
from Impressioni (P1204)

PRATELLA, FRANCESCO BALILLA (cont'd.)

La Gaggia *Op.7,No.3
solo,pno BONGIOVANI 741 s.p. see
from Quattro Liriche   (P1205)

La Morte Di Anita *Op.11
solo,pno BONGIOVANI 748 s.p.
(P1206)

La Stella Boara *Op.36,No.9
solo,pno BONGIOVANI 842 s.p. see
also Le Canzoni Del Niente
(P1207)

La Strada Bianca *Op.36,No.2
solo,pno BONGIOVANI 835 s.p. see
also Le Canzoni Del Niente
(P1208)

"White Road, The" [It/Eng] S/Mez
solo,pno BONGIOVANI 1630 s.p. see
also Le Canzoni Del Niente
(P1209)

La Strade Notturne *see Il Pastore;
Il Viandante; Reginetta   (P1210)

Le Canzoni Del Niente *Op.36,No.1-
10, CC10L
solo,pno cmplt ed BONGIOVANI 844
s.p.
see also: Donetta, Op.36,No.1;
Gelsa, Op.36,No.4; Il Pastore,
Op.36,No.5; La Stella Boara,
Op.36,No.9; La Strada Bianca,
"White Road, The", Op.36,No.2;
Le Sette Stelle, Op.36,No.3;
L'ora Che Parte, Op.36,No.7;
Martina, Op.36,No.10; Siepi
D'autunno, Op.36,No.6;
Un'allodola, Op.36,No.8 (P1211)

Le Sette Stelle *Op.36,No.3
solo,pno BONGIOVANI 836 s.p. see
also Le Canzoni Del Niente
(P1212)

L'ora Che Parte *Op.36,No.7
solo,pno BONGIOVANI 840 s.p. see
also Le Canzoni Del Niente
(P1213)

Martina *Op.36,No.10
solo,pno BONGIOVANI 843 s.p. see
also Le Canzoni Del Niente
(P1214)

Mattinata *Op.7,No.1
solo,pno BONGIOVANI 738 s.p. see
from Quattro Liriche   (P1215)

Morire *Op.26,No.3
solo,pno BONGIOVANI 734 s.p. see
from Impressioni   (P1216)

Mystica *Op.8,No.2
solo,pno BONGIOVANI 743 s.p. see
from Due Liriche   (P1217)

O Luna, Che Con Falce Ampia D'argento
*Op.9,No.3
solo,pno BONGIOVANI 746 s.p. see
from Storia D'amore   (P1218)

Quattro Liriche *see Astro D'amore,
Op.7,No.2; Deh! Non Giurare..,
Op.7,No.4; La Gaggia, Op.7,No.3;
Mattinata, Op.7,No.1   (P1219)

Raccolta Di Musiche Monodiche E
Melodiche Poco Divulgate *CCU
solo,pno BONGIOVANI 1981 s.p.
(P1220)

Reginetta
solo,pno BONGIOVANI 1197 s.p. see
from La Strade Notturne   (P1221)

Romanza D'autunno *Op.8,No.1
solo,pno BONGIOVANI 742 s.p. see
from Due Liriche   (P1222)

Siepi D'autunno *Op.36,No.6
solo,pno BONGIOVANI 839 s.p. see
also Le Canzoni Del Niente
(P1223)

Stati D'anima *see Felicta-
Giovinezza, Op.27,No.1;
Tristezza-Solitudine, Op.7,No.2
(P1224)

Stava Il Sol Nel Firmamento *Op.9,
No.2
solo,pno BONGIOVANI 745 s.p. see
from Storia D'amore   (P1225)

Storia D'amore *see Deh! Lascia O
Fanciulla, Op.9,No.4; In Mezzo Al
Mare, Op.9,No.1; O Luna, Che Con
Falce Ampia D'argento, Op.9,No.3;
Stava Il Sol Nel Firmamento,
Op.9,No.2   (P1226)

Tristezza-Solitudine *Op.7,No.2
solo,pno BONGIOVANI 737 s.p. see
from Stati D'anima   (P1227)

Un'allodola *Op.36,No.8
solo,pno BONGIOVANI 841 s.p. see
also Le Canzoni Del Niente
(P1228)

White Road, The *see La Strada
Bianca

PRATERS see Witte, D.

PRAYER see Curran, Pearl Gildersleeve

PRAYER see Diamond, David

PRAYER see Guion, David Wendall
Fentress

PRAYER see Harrhy, Edith

PRAYER see Hiller, Ferdinand, Herr, Den
Ich Tief Im Herzen Trage

PRAYER see Maganini, Quinto

PRAYER see Schouwman, Hans

PRAYER, A see Saint-Saens, Camille

PRAYER AND SUPPLICATION see Binder,
Abraham Wolfe

PRAYER AT THE PORTAL see Franco, Johan

PRAYER FOR COMMUNION see Lovelace,
Austin C.

PRAYER FOR EASTER DAY see Thompson, A.

PRAYER FOR EVENING, A see Sifler, Paul
J.

PRAYER FOR GRACE see Grieg, Edvard
Hagerup

PRAYER FOR HANUKKAH, A see Binder,
Abraham Wolfe

PRAYER FOR MOTHER'S DAY, A see Grimm,
Carl Hugo

PRAYER FOR PEACE see Hains, S.B.

PRAYER FOR PEACE see Kingsley, Gershon

PRAYER FOR REALIZATION, A see Franco,
Johan

PRAYER FOR THE DAY OF JUDGMENT, A see
Silver, Mark

PRAYER FOR THIS HOUSE see Young, Gordon

PRAYER FOR THOSE AT HOME see Tuthill,
Burnet Corwin

PRAYER IN ABSENCE, A see Brahe, May H.

PRAYER OF OUR LORD, THE see Liles,
David

PRAYER OF ST. FRANCIS see Banks, Harry

PRAYER OF ST. FRANCIS OF ASISSI see
Woollen, Russell

PRAYER OF THANKSGIVING see Mozart,
Wolfgang Amadeus

PRAYER OF THANKSGIVING see O'Hara,
Geoffrey

PRAYER OF THANKSGIVING *Dut
(Downing, K.) med-high solo,pno (E
flat maj) SCHIRM.G $.85   (P1229)
(Downing, K.) low solo,pno (C maj)
SCHIRM.G $.85   (P1230)

PRAYER OF THE NORWEGIAN CHILD see
Kountz, Richard

PRAYER PERFECT, THE see Speaks, Oley

PRAYER PERFECT, THE see Stenson, E.J.

PRAYER TO JESUS see Birch, Robert
Fairfax

PRAYER TO PERSEPHONE see Ricketts, L.

PRAYER TO SAINT CATHERINE, A see
Thomson, Virgil

PRAYER TO THE TRINITY see Eichhorn,
Hermene Warlick

PRAYERS see Arundale, Claude

PRAYERS see Surinach, Carlos

PRAYERS OF STEEL see Weigl, Vally

PRAYING HANDS see Acuff-Rose

PRAYING HANDS see Gray

PRCHAJICI LANE see Mikoda, Borivoj

PRECEPTS OF MICAH, THE see Freudenthal,
Josef

PRECIOSILLA see Thomson, Virgil

PRECIOUS MEMORIES *sac,gospel
solo,pno ABER.GRP. $1.50   (P1231)

PREGELJ, CIRIL (1887-1966)
Osem Samospevov *CC8U
solo,pno DRUSTVO DSS 264 rental
(P1232)

PREGHIERA see Massenet, Jules

PREGHIERA see Nacamuli, Guido

PREGHIERA A SAN SERGIO see Donati

PREGHIERA ALLA MADONNA see Alfano,
Franco

PREGHIERA ALLA MADONNA see Diepenbrock,
Alphons

PREGHIERA DELL'ALBA see Caltabiano, S.

PREGHIERA D'UN CLEFTA see Caltabiano,
S.

PREGHIERE see Dallapiccola, Luigi

PREIS DER TONKUNST see Handel, George
Frideric, Look Down, Harmonius
Saint

PREISEN WILL ICH ALLEZEIT see Schutz,
Heinrich, Benedicam Dominum

PREISUNGEN see Bialas, Gunther

PREKRASNE ZEMI see Seidel, Jan

PRELOVEC, ZORKO (1887-1939)
Sest Samospevov *CC6U
solo,pno DRZAVNA rental   (P1233)

PRELUDE see Aubert, Louis-Francois-
Marie

PRELUDE see Leeuw, Ton de

PRELUDE see Ronald, Sir Landon

PRELUDE see Verhaar, Ary

PRELUDE: HYMNE AU SOLEIL see Desrez

PRELUDES see Caplet, Andre

PRELUDES E RONDEAUX see Togni, Camillo

PRELUDIO, ADAGIO E FINALE see
Malipiero, Riccardo

PRELUDIO E MORTE DI MACBETH see
Malipiero, Gian Francesco

PREMIER AIR DE L'ARCHANGE see Franck,
Cesar

PREMIER CHAGRIN see Ferroud, Pierre-
Octave

PREMIER RECEUEIL DE CHANSONS see Kosma,
J.

PREMIERE see Aubert, Louis-Francois-
Marie

PREMIERE RUE A GAUCHE see Loti, E.

PREMIERE SOIREE see Orthel, Leon

PRENDERO QUEL BRUNNETTIO see Mozart,
Wolfgang Amadeus

PRENDI, L'ANEL TI DONO see Bellini,
Vincenzo

PRENDIDITOS DE LA MANO see Lopez-
Buchardo, Carlos

PRENDS CETTE ROSE see Levade, Charles
(Gaston)

PRENDS CETTE ROSE see Terrier-Vicini,
L.

PRENDS MON COEUR see Fontenailles, H.
de

PRENEZ DONC LE TRAIN! see Lapeyre,
Therese

PREPARE TO MEET JESUS see Bigelow

PREPARE YE THE WAY OF THE LORD see
Thorne, Francis

PREPROSTE POPEVKE see Lajovic,
Aleksander

PRES DE SYLVIE see Blanchard, Roger

PRES DE TOI see Mendelssohn-Bartholdy,
Felix

PRES DES RAMPARTS DE SEVILLE see Bizet,
Georges

PRES DES REMPARTS DE SEVILLE see Bizet, Georges

PRES DU BERCEAU see Moszkowski, Moritz

PRES DU LIT OU TU CHANTES see Charpentier, Jean Jacques Beauvarlet

PRES D'UN BERCEAU see Renie

PRES D'UN ETANG see Widor, Charles-Marie

PRESCRIPTION FOR SALVATION see Derricks, Cleavant

PRESENCE, THE see Brooke, Harry

PRESENCE, THE see Schoenfeld, William C.

PRESENCE OF CHRIST, THE see Cates, Bill

PRESENT DE COULEUR BLANCHE see Enesco, Georges

PRESENT FOR CHANUKA, A see Weiner-Sela, Yehudit

PRESENTS see Vuillemin, L.

PRESENTS FROM HEAVEN see Farjeon, Harry

PRESLE, DE LA
see LA PRESLE, JACQUES (PAUL GABRIEL) DE

PRESSENTIMENT see Levade, Charles (Gaston)

PRESSER, WILLIAM
Bye Baby Bunting
see Four Nursery Rhymes

Epitaph Upon A Child That Died
see Three Epitaphs

Epitaph Upon A Maid
see Three Epitaphs

Epitaph Upon A Virgin
see Three Epitaphs

Four Nursery Rhymes
med solo,pno TRI-TEN $1.20
contains: Bye Baby Bunting; Het
Diddle Diddle; Humpty Dumpty;
Pussy Cat   (P1234)

Het Diddle Diddle
see Four Nursery Rhymes

Humpty Dumpty
see Four Nursery Rhymes

Hymne To God The Father, A *sac
high solo,pno,vln/vcl TRI-TEN $2.50
(P1235)
Pussy Cat
see Four Nursery Rhymes

Three Epitaphs
high solo,pno TRI-TEN $1.20
contains: Epitaph Upon A Child
That Died; Epitaph Upon A Maid;
Epitaph Upon A Virgin   (P1236)

PRESSO UNA FONTANA see Cimara, Pietro

PRETTY BETTY see Rowley, Alec

PRETTY POLLY OLIVER see Somervell, Arthur

PREY, CLAUDE (1925-   )
Metamorphose D'Echo
Mez solo,strings AMPHION s.p.
(P1237)
PRIBAOUTKI see Stravinsky, Igor

PRICE, ADDISON
Sicilian Serenade
low solo,pno CRAMER   (P1238)
high solo,pno CRAMER   (P1239)

Swift Fly The Hours Of Love
solo,pno CRAMER   (P1240)

PRICE, FLORENCE B. (1888-1953)
Back Home *sac
solo,pno WORD S-366   (P1241)

Bright New World *sac
solo,pno WORD S-234   (P1242)

Gonna Wake Up Singin' *sac
solo,pno WORD S-57   (P1243)

He's Listening *sac
solo,pno WORD S-422   (P1244)

Trusting Is Believing *sac
solo,pno WORD S-506   (P1245)

PRICE, JACK
Jack Price Songbook, Vol. I *sac,
CC11UL
solo,pno BENSON BO995 $2.50 (P1246)

Jack Price Songbook, Vol. II *sac,
CC11UL
solo,pno BENSON BO996 $2.50 (P1247)

PRIERE see Beethoven, Ludwig van, Bitten

PRIERE see Delbruck, J.

PRIERE see Gounod, Charles Francois

PRIERE see Rabaud, Henri

PRIERE see Rhene-Baton

PRIERE D'AMOUR see Mana-Zucca, Mme.

PRIERE DE L'AURORE see Boutnikoff, J.

PRIERE DE L'AVANT MATIN see Boutnikoff, J.

PRIERE DE MIDI see Barraud, Henry

PRIERE DE PADMAVATI see Roussel, Albert

PRIERE: DIEU QUI DEROULEZ see Wolff, A.

PRIERE DU COUCHER DU SOLEIL see Boutnikoff, J.

PRIERE DU MATIN see Ropartz, Joseph Guy

PRIERE DU MIDI see Boutnikoff, J.

PRIERE DU SOIR see Backer-Grondahl, Agathe Ursula

PRIERE DU SOIR see Barraud, Henry

PRIERE DU SOIR see Francaix, Jean

PRIERE EST SAUVE see Messager, Andre

PRIERE EXAUCEE see Messiaen, Oliver

PRIERE NORMANDE see Caplet, Andre

PRIERE NUPTIALE see Bonay

PRIERE POUR AVOIR UNE FEMME SIMPLE see Huybrechts, Albert

PRIERE POUR DEMANDER PARDON see Chailley, Jacques

PRIERE POUR DORMIR HEUREUX see Arrieu, Claude

PRIERE POUR NOUS AUTRES CHARNELS see Alain, Jehan

PRIESTERMORGEN see Bijl, Theo van der

PRIESTERWIJDING see Verhoeven, A.

PRIEZ POUR PAIX see Poulenc, Francis

PRIJAZNA SMRT see Merku, Pavle

PRIMA DONNA'S ALBUM, THE *CC42L
solo,pno SCHIRM.G $6.00 contains
works by: Rossini; Mozart;
Donizetti; Verdi and others (P1248)

PRIMAVERA see Cimara, Pietro

PRIMAVERA see Dougherty, Celius

PRIMAVERA see Faccenda, O.

PRIMAVERA see Kuusisto, Ilkka

PRIMAVERA see Saint-Saens, Camille, Printemps Qui Commence

PRIMAVERA D'AMORE see Ivanova, Lidia

PRIMAVERA GARIBALDINA see Carosio, N.

PRIMEVAL see Baxter, Maude Stewart

PRIMEVERE see Cuvillier, Charles

PRIMEVERE see Delbos, Cl.

PRIMO AMORE PIACER DEL CIEL see Beethoven, Ludwig van

PRIMROSE see Klein, Ivy Frances

PRIN, YVES (1933-   )
Au Souffle D'une Voix
SB soli,pno,cel,org,4horn,4trp,
3trom,bass trom,tuba,perc,
electronic tape,strings sc RIDEAU
rental, min sc RIDEAU 083 s.p.
(P1249)
PRINCE ET BERGERE see Schmitt, Florent

PRINCE GALITZKY'S ARIA see Borodin, Alexander Porfirievitch

PRINCE IGOR'S ARIA see Borodin, Alexander Porfirievitch

PRINCE'S ARIA see Tchaikovsky, Piotr Ilyitch

PRINCESITA see Padilla

PRINCESS see Grieg, Edvard Hagerup, Prinsessen

PRINE'S ARIA see Tchaikovsky, Piotr Ilyitch

PRINSEBARNA see Hauger, Kristian

PRINSEESA JA TRUBADUURI see Ranta, Sulho

PRINSESSAN see Hinrichs, F.

PRINSESSAN see Nordqvist, Gustaf

PRINSESSAN OCH TRUBADUREN see Ranta, Sulho, Prinseesa Ja Trubaduuri

PRINSESSEN see Grieg, Edvard Hagerup

PRINSESSEN see Sjogren, Emil

PRINSESSEN see Soderman, (Johan) August

PRINSESSEN SAD HOJT I SIT JOMFRUBUR see Kjerulf, [Halfdan]

PRINTANIERES see Lancen

PRINTEMPS see Auric, Georges

PRINTEMPS see Godard, Benjamin Louis Paul

PRINTEMPS see Migot, Georges

PRINTEMPS see Quinet, Marcel

PRINTEMPS see Schlosser, Paul

PRINTEMPS see Steenhuis, Francois

PRINTEMPS ANNAMITE see Tcherepnin, Alexander

PRINTEMPS BRETON see Favre, Georges

PRINTEMPS D'ANJOU
(Emmerechts; Joulain, Emile) solo,pno
GRAS s.p.   (P1250)

PRINTEMPS MAUSSADE see Migot, Georges

PRINTEMPS QUI COMMENCE see Saint-Saens, Camille

PRIS SKE DIG, ALLSMAKTIGE SKAPARE GOD
see Merikanto, Oskar, Oi Kiitos, Sa
Luojani Armollinen

PRISE AUX RESEAUX D'OR see Schmitt, Florent

PRISON SCENE see Cavalli, (Pietro) Francesco

PRISONER OF LOVE see Rambo

PRISTER, BRUNO (1909-   )
Gypsy Variations *CCU
[Slav] solo,pno CROATICA s.p.
(P1251)
Two Songs *CC2U
[Slav] solo,pno CROATICA s.p.
(P1252)

PRITCHETT, J.
Stay, Summer, Stay
solo,pno (B flat maj) BOOSEY $1.50
(P1253)

PRITSKER, D.
Tale Of The Silly Little Mouse
[Russ] high solo,pno MEZ KNIGA
2.100 s.p.   (P1254)

PRIVAS, XAVIER
Chanson Pour Ma Mie
solo,acap ENOCH s.p.   (P1255)
solo,pno ENOCH s.p.   (P1256)

Fumee
solo,acap ENOCH s.p.   (P1257)
solo,pno ENOCH s.p.   (P1258)

Juin: Roses, Cerises, Parfums
(composed with Stanislas, Ad.)
solo,pno ENOCH s.p. see also Les
Mois   (P1259)

Les Mois (composed with Stanislas,
Ad.) *CC12L
solo,pno cmplt ed ENOCH s.p.
see also: Juin: Roses, Cerises,
Parfums   (P1260)

PRIVAS, XAVIER (cont'd.)

Noel Du Gueux
  solo,acap ENOCH s.p.   (P1261)
  solo,pno ENOCH s.p.   (P1262)

PRIVILEGES see Schmitt, Florent

PRO MEMORIA see Kazacsay, T.

PROCACCINI, T. (1934-   )
  Dannazione E Preghiera (from
    Sentimento Nel Tempo)
    (Ungaretti, G.) Mez solo,strings
     CARISH s.p.   (P1263)

PROCESSION see Franck, Cesar

PROCH, HEINRICH (1809-1878)
  Beaux Jours Passes
    solo,pno/inst DURAND s.p.   (P1264)

  Deh! Torna Mio Bene *see Woher
    Dieses Sehnen

  Woher Dieses Sehnen *Op.164
    "Deh! Torna Mio Bene" [Ger/It] S
    solo,pno (theme and variation)
    RICORDI-ARG BA 8495 s.p. (P1265)

PROCHE see Bancquart, Alain

PROCRIS see Vaughan Williams, Ralph

PROFES, A.
  Quand Les Roses
    solo,pno ENOCH s.p.   (P1266)
    solo,acap ENOCH s.p.   (P1267)

PROFESSIONAL TOAST see Franco, Johan

PROFILES FROM CHINA see Glanville-
  Hicks, Peggy

PROFUMI ORIENTALI see Bellenghi, G.

PROFUMO see Caltabiano, S.

PROFUMO see D'Ambrosi, Dante

PROHASKA, CARL (1869-1927)
  Maiwunder *Op.21,No.1
    see Zwei Gedichte Von Richard
    Dehmel

  Nachtliche Scheu
    solo,4strings BREITKOPF-W s.p.
                    (P1268)
  Vier Orchesterlieder *Op.24,No.1-4,
    CC4U
    solo,pno/orch voc sc DOBLINGER
    s.p., ea., ipr   (P1269)

  Wiegenlied *Op.21,No.2
    see Zwei Gedichte Von Richard
    Dehmel

  Zwei Gedichte Von Richard Dehmel
    S solo,4strings BREITKOPF-W s.p.
    contains: Maiwunder, Op.21,No.1;
    Wiegenlied, Op.21,No.2 (P1270)

PROKOFIEV, SERGE (1891-1953)
  Kinderlieder *Op.68, CCU
    [Eng/Russ] solo,pno SIKORSKI R 6177
    s.p.   (P1271)

  Ugly Duckling, The *song cycle
    [Eng/Fr/Ger] Mez solo,orch BOOSEY
    $4.50   (P1272)

  Vocal Works, Vol. II *CCU
    [Russ] 1-2 soli,pno MEZ KNIGA 73
    s.p.   (P1273)

  Zwolf Lieder Fur Mittlere Stimme, Op.
    104; Zwei Duette Fur Tenor Und
    Bass, Op. 106 *CC12U
    [Russ] med solo/TB soli,pno
    SIKORSKI R 6178 s.p.   (P1274)

PROLOGUE ET REVE see Messager, Andre

PROMENADE see Revel, Peter

PROMENADE MILITAIRE see Lacome, Paul

PROMENADES see Jacob, Dom Clement

PROMESA see Camargo Guarnieri

PROMESSE ETERNELLE see Glombig, E.,
  Mein Ganzes Leben Lang

PROMETHEUS see Rontgen, [Julius]

PROMETHEUS see Wolf, Hugo

PROMISES see Rambo

PROOF IS CALVARY, THE see Chennault,
  Judy

PROPERTY IN HEAVEN see Johnson, Wendy

PROPHECY FROM "LOCKSLEY HALL" see
  Franco, Johan

PROPHETIE see Cuvillier, Charles

PROPOS CHINOIS SUR LES ANIMAUX see
  Sussman, Ettel

PROPOS D'ALAIN see Petrassi, Goffredo

PROSE see Bossi, Renzo

PROSES LYRIQUES see Debussy, Claude

PROSES LYRIQUES see Debussy, Claude

PROSEV, TOMA (1931-   )
  Boje
    "Colours" SATB,2 narrators,fl,ob,
    clar,bsn,horn,trp,trom,perc,pno,
    5strings MUSIC INFO rental
                    (P1275)

  Colours *see Boje

  Diametria *see Dijametrija

  Dijametrija
    "Diametria" solo,fl,ob,clar,bsn,
    horn,trp,trom,perc,5strings MUSIC
    INFO rental   (P1276)

PROSPERI, CARLO (1921-   )
  Cinque Strofe Dal Greco *CC5U
    S solo,orch voc sc ZERBONI 7219
    s.p.   (P1277)

  Cinque Strofe Dal Greco *CC5U
    S solo,orch voc sc ZERBONI 7219
    s.p.   (P1278)

  Tre Frammenti Di Saffo *CC3U
    solo,pno ZERBONI 7436 s.p. (P1279)

PROSTE MOTIVY see Jindrich, Jindrich

PROTHEROE, DANIEL (1866-1934)
  Ah! Love But A Day
    high solo,pno (A flat maj) ALLANS
    s.p.   (P1280)

  Backslidin'
    med solo,pno FITZSIMONS $.50
                    (P1281)

  Dey Can't Cotch Me To Bury Me
    med solo,pno FITZSIMONS $.50
                    (P1282)

  Ginger Cat, The
    med solo,pno FITZSIMONS $.40
                    (P1283)

  Little Door Opened In Heaven
    med solo,pno FITZSIMONS $.50
                    (P1284)

  Little Lord Jesus, The *sac,Xmas
    med solo,pno FITZSIMONS $.40
                    (P1285)

  Pilot, The
    high solo,pno PRESSER $.75 (P1286)

  Springtime Is Calling
    high solo,pno FITZSIMONS $.40
                    (P1287)

PROTI TME ZIVOTA see Sauer, Frantisek

PROUD MAISIE see Lawson, Malcolm

PROUD MAISIE see Vauclain, Constant

PROULX, RICHARD
  Beloved Let Us Love *sac
    med solo,pno AUGSBURG 11-0715 $1.00
                    (P1288)
  Lord's Prayer, The *sac,folk/hymn
    med solo,pno/org (easy) GIA G-1705
    $1.00   (P1289)

  Nuptial Blessing *sac
    med solo,pno AUGSBURG 11-0731 $.75
                    (P1290)

PROVENCE *Fr
  (Canteloube, J.) solo,acap DURAND
  s.p. see also Anthologie Des Chants
  Populaires Francais Tome I (P1291)

PROVENZALE, FRANCESCO (1627-1704)
  Deh, Rendetemi Ombre Care (from
    Stellidaure Vendicata)
    (Gubitosi, E.) solo,strings CARISH
    s.p.   (P1292)

PROVERBS see Hancocks, B.J.

PROVERBS see Beale, James

PROVINCIALES see Jongen, Leon

PROVOST, HEINZ
  Intermezzo (A Love Story)
    solo,pno ALLANS s.p.   (P1293)
    solo,pno GEHRMANS s.p.   (P1294)

PROVOST, W.
  Cinderella
    solo,pno PRESSER $1.00   (P1295)

PRUFUNG DES KUSSENS see Beethoven,
  Ludwig van

PRVNI TOUHY, SES. 1-2 see Kricka,
  Jaroslav

PRYTZ, HOLGER
  Arkadisk Fabel
    A solo,clar,vcl,pno FOG s.p.
                    (P1296)

PS see Marsh, Roger

PSALM see Dijk, Jan van

PSALM 1 see Bone, First Psalm

PSALM 1 see Ore, Charles W.

PSALM 4 see Ore, Charles W.

PSALM 5 see Beekhuis, Hanna

PSALM 6 see Telemann, Georg Philipp,
  Ach Herr, Strafe Mich Nicht

PSALM 8 see Cortese, Luigi, Salmo VIII

PSALM 8 see Freed, Isadore

PSALM 8 see Swack, Erwin, O Lord, Our
  Lord, How Excellent Is Thy Name

PSALM 8 see Wright, Norman Soreng

PSALM 14 see Braal, Andries de

PSALM 16 see Nowakowsky, David, Michtom
  L'Dovid

PSALM 19 see Marcello, Benedetto, Aria
  Sacra

PSALM 22 see Bloch, Ernest

PSALM 23 see Archer, Violet, Twenty-
  Third Psalm

PSALM 23 see Beekhuis, Hanna

PSALM 23 see Ben-Haim, Paul

PSALM 23 see Berlinski, Herman

PSALM 23 see Brown, R.J.

PSALM 23 see Carey

PSALM 23 see Clarke, Henry Leland, Lord
  Is My Shepherd, The

PSALM 23 see Creston, Paul

PSALM 23 see Davidson, Charles, Lord Is
  My Shepherd, The

PSALM 23 see Drischner, Max, Der Herr
  Ist Mein Hirte

PSALM 23 see Dvorak, Antonin

PSALM 23 see Eville, V., I Will Dwell
  In The House Of The Lord

PSALM 23 see Fischer, Irwin, Lord Is My
  Shepherd, The

PSALM 23 see Freudenthal, Josef, Lord
  Is My Shepherd, The

PSALM 23 see Garlick, Anthony

PSALM 23 see Grant, Crimond

PSALM 23 see Heilmann, Harald

PSALM 23 see Kohs, Ellis B.

PSALM 23 see Kosakoff, Reuven

PSALM 23 see Liddle, Samuel, Lord Is My
  Shepherd

PSALM 23 see Lockwood, Normand

PSALM 23 see Malotte, Albert Hay

PSALM 23 see Nordqvist, Gustaf

PSALM 23 see Ore, Charles W.

PSALM 23 see Rosner, Arnold, Lord Is My
  Shepherd, The

PSALM 23 see Smart, Henry Thomas, Lord
  Is My Shepherd, The

PSALM 24 see Freudenthal, Josef, Earth
  Is The Lord's, The

PSALM 25 see Ore, Charles W.

PSALM 27 see Allitsen, Frances, Lord Is
  My Light

PSALM 27 see Allitsen, Frances, Lord Is My Light, The

PSALM 27 see Charles, Ernest, Psalm Of Exultation

PSALM 27 see Edwards, Clara, Lord Is My Light, The

PSALM 29 see Weiner, Lazar, Mizmor L'David

PSALM 33 see Beekhuis, Hanna

PSALM 34 see Honegger, Arthur, Jamais Ne Cesserai De Magnifier Le Seigneur

PSALM 37 see Leichtling, Alan

PSALM 42 see Barbe, Helmut

PSALM 42 see Pohle, David, Wie Der Hirsch Schreyet

PSALM 42 see Schutz, Heinrich, Was Betrubst Du Dich, Meine Seele

PSALM 51 see Pergolesi, Giovanni Battista, Stabat Mater

PSALM 58 see Stout, Alan, Aria

PSALM 62 see Allitsen, Frances, Like As The Hart Desireth

PSALM 62 see Liddle, Samuel, Like As The Hart

PSALM 62 see Reger, Max, Meine Seele Ist Still Zu Gott

PSALM 66 see Wyner, Yehudi, Halleluya

PSALM 67 see Freudenthal, Josef, Lord's Blessing, The

PSALM 68 see Rogers, Bernard

PSALM 70 see Sutermeister, Heinrich

PSALM 71 see Schoof, Armin, Herr, Ich Traue Auf Dich

PSALM 76 see Brod, Max

PSALM 79 see Pinkham, Daniel

PSALM 84 see Liddle, Samuel, How Lovely Are Thy Dwellings

PSALM 84 see Strandqvist, Alfred

PSALM 85 see Hofmann, Wolfgang, Herr, Neig' Dein Ohr Zu Mir

PSALM 86 see Kingsley, Gershon, Teach Me, O Lord

PSALM 86 see Sutermeister, Heinrich

PSALM 88 see Honegger, Arthur, Il Faut Que De Tous Mes Esprits J'exalte

PSALM 90 see Bialas, Gunther

PSALM 90 see Drischner, Max, Herr Gott, Du Bist Unsere Zuflucht

PSALM 91 see Muller, P.

PSALM 91 see O'Connor-Morris, G.

PSALM 93 see Blazek, Vilem, Zalmy 93

PSALM 95 see Freudenthal, Josef, Let Us Sing Unto The Lord

PSALM 98 see Kayser, Leif, Dominus Regnat

PSALM 100 see Blazek, Vilem, Zalmy 100

PSALM 100 see Bruhns, Nicholaus, Jauchzet Dem Herrn Alle Welt

PSALM 100 see Mueller, Carl F., Create In Me A Clean Heart, O God

PSALM 100 see Newlin, Dika

PSALM 100 see Rorem, Ned, Psalm Of Praise, A

PSALM 100 see Schauss-Flake, Magdalene, Jauchzet Dem Herrn, Alle Welt

PSALM 103 see Stephenson, Richard T.

PSALM 103 see Wiemer, Wolfgang, Lobe Den Herrn, Meine Seele

PSALM 104 see Lederer, George

PSALM 108 see Bialas, Gunther

PSALM 108 see Fordell, Erik (Fritiof)

PSALM 112 see Caldara, Antonio, Laudate, Pueri, Dominum

PSALM 112 see Vivaldi, Antonio, Laudate Pueri

PSALM 114 see Bloch, Ernest

PSALM 115 see Bialas, Gunther

PSALM 118 see Buxtehude, Dietrich, Aperite Mihi Portas Justitiae

PSALM 118 see Noren, Konungars Konung

PSALM 118 see Strategier, Herman

PSALM 119 see Freudenthal, Josef, Lamp Unto My Feet, A

PSALM 120 see Rorem, Ned, Song Of David, A

PSALM 121 see Eville, V., I Will Lift Up Mine Eyes

PSALM 121 see Gober, Belle Baird, I Will Lift Up Mine Eyes

PSALM 121 see Horst, Anton van der

PSALM 121 see Kayden, M.

PSALM 121 see Kayser, Leif, Laetata Sum

PSALM 121 see Kendrick, Virginia, I Will Lift Up Mine Eyes Unto The Hills

PSALM 121 see Klerk, Albert de, Laetatus Sum

PSALM 121 see Kosakoff, Reuven

PSALM 123 see Hambraeus, Bengt

PSALM 126 see Glantz, Yehuda Leib, B'shuv Adonoy

PSALM 126 see Herrmann, Hans

PSALM 126 see Vivaldi, Antonio, Nisi Dominus

PSALM 127 see Biber, Heinrich Ignaz Franz von, Nisi Dominus Aedificaverit Domum

PSALM 127 see Ferris, William, Behold, Thus Is The Man Blessed

PSALM 127 see Heinichen, Johann David, Nisi Dominus Aedificaverit Domum

PSALM 128 see Bender, Jan, Wedding Song

PSALM 128 see Fordell, Erik (Fritiof)

PSALM 128 see Sinzheimer, Max, Blessed Are Those Who Fear The Lord

PSALM 128 see Wetzler, Robert Paul

PSALM 129 see Boulanger, Lili, Ils M'ont Assez Opprime Des Ma Jeunesse

PSALM 129 see Kayser, Leif, De Profundis Clamavi

PSALM 129 see Milhaud, Darius

PSALM 130 see Drischner, Max, Aus Der Tiefe Rufe Ich, Herr, Zu Dir

PSALM 130 see Honegger, Arthur, Mimaamaquim

PSALM 130 see Kosakoff, Reuven

PSALM 132 see Braal, Andries de

PSALM 133 see Blazek, Vilem, Zalmy 133

PSALM 133 see Fordell, Erik (Fritiof)

PSALM 133 see Klerk, Albert de, Ecce Nunc

PSALM 133 see Matesky, T., Behold How Good And How Pleasant

PSALM 134 see Blazek, Vilem, Zalmy 134

PSALM 134 see Fordell, Erik (Fritiof)

PSALM 134 see Rosenmuller, Johann, Auf, Nun Lobet Gott

PSALM 137 see Berens, Hermann, Vid Alvarna I Babylon

PSALM 137 see Chajes, Julius, By The Rivers Of Babylon

PSALM 137 see Dijk, Jan van, By The Rivers Of Babylon

PSALM 137 see Richards, Stephen, By The Waters Of Babylon

PSALM 137 see Seeger, C.

PSALM 138 see Matesky, T., I Will Praise Thee With My Whole Heart

PSALM 139 see Drischner, Max, Herr, Du Erforschest Mich

PSALM 139 see McAfee, Don

PSALM 140 see Sessions, Roger

PSALM 142 see Sowerby, Leo

PSALM 143 see Clark, Henry A., Hear My Prayer, O Lord

PSALM 150 see Appledoorn, Dina, Harpzang Van David

PSALM 150 see Newlin, Dika

PSALM 150 see Schilling, Psalm 150 In Form Einer Ciacona

PSALM 160 see Honegger, Arthur, O Dieu, Donne-Moi Delivrance De Cet Homme Pernicieux

PSALM CYCLE, A see Hartley, Walter S.

PSALM I UNGDOMEN see Wikmark, Torbjorn

PSALM OCH SANG see Nordqvist, Gustaf

PSALM OF CHRIST see Huber, Klaus

PSALM OF EXULTATION see Charles, Ernest

PSALM OF PRAISE see Fischer, Irwin

PSALM OF PRAISE, A see Rorem, Ned

PSALM 150 IN FORM EINER CIACONA see Schilling

PSALMEN see Dvorak, Antonin

PSALMI see Baumann, Max

PSALMODIKON see Olson, Daniel

PSALMS see Orrego Salas, Juan

PSALMS AND EARLY SONGS see Wyner, Yehudi

PSALMS OF LOVE see Becker, John J.

PSALMS OF LOVE see Chlaidze, G.

PSALMS OF PIETY see Mihaly, Andras

PSAUME DE LA DANSE see Schmit, Camille

PSAUME DE LA NUIT see Schmit, Camille

PSAUME DU TORRENT see Schmit, Camille

PSAUTIER see Schmit, Camille

PST! PST! PST!
(Carlo, Musi) solo,pno (Bolognese dialect) BONGIOVANI 2086 s.p. see from El Mi Canzunett (P1297)

PTACI SVATBY see Kalabis, Viktor

PTACI ZNELKY see Urks, I.J.

P'TIT FI! see Varney, Pierre Joseph Alphonse

PU VEIST EI NEITT see Sveinsson, Gunnar Reynir

PUBLICAN, THE see Van De Water, B.

PUCCINI, GIACOMO (1858-1924)
Addio Fiorito Asil (from Madama Butterfly)
[It] T solo,pno RICORDI-ENG 127454 s.p. see from It-Eng (P1298)
[It/Eng] T solo,pno RICORDI-ARG BA 10573 s.p. (P1299)

And The Stars Shone Brightly *see E Lucevan Le Stelle

Avete Torto! (from Gianni Schicchi)
[It] T solo,pno (B flat maj) RICORDI-ENG 117793 s.p. (P1300)

Bimba Dagli Occhi Pieni Di Malia (from Madama Butterfly)
[It] ST soli,pno RICORDI-ENG 126420 s.p. (P1301)

PUCCINI, GIACOMO (cont'd.)

Che Gelida Manina (from La Boheme)
T solo,pno/orch sc KALMUS $3.00
(P1302)
[It] T solo,pno (D flat maj)
RICORDI-ENG 99341 (P1303)
[It] T solo,pno RICORDI-ARG BA 8324
s.p. (P1304)
"How Cold Your Little Hand Is" [It/
Eng] T solo,pno SCHIRM.G $.85
(P1305)
"I'll Hold Your Hand" [It/Eng] T
solo,pno (C maj) BELWIN NY 1722
$1.00 (P1306)
"I'll Hold Your Hand" [It/Eng] T
solo,pno (D flat maj) BELWIN
NY 1721 $1.00 (P1307)
"I'll Hold Your Hand" [It/Eng] T
solo,pno (B flat maj) BELWIN
NY 1723 $1.00 (P1308)
"I'll Hold Your Hand In My Hand"
high solo,pno (D flat maj) BELWIN
$.75 (P1309)
"Your Tiny Hand Is Frozen" T solo,
pno INTERNAT. $1.00 (P1310)

Che Tua Madre Dovra (from Madama
Butterfly)
[It] S solo,pno RICORDI-ENG 11012
s.p. (P1311)

Ch'ella Mi Creda Libero E Lontano
(from La Fanciulla Del West)
[It] T solo,pno RICORDI-ARG
BA 10592 s.p. (P1312)
[It] T solo,pno (G flat maj)
RICORDI-ENG 115326 s.p. (P1313)
"Let Her Believe" [It/Eng] T solo,
pno BELWIN NY 1638 $1.00 (P1314)

Chi Il Bel Sogno (from La Rondine)
[It] S solo,pno SONZOGNO 2033 s.p. (P1315)

Day After Day *see Quando M'en Vo
Soletta

Donde Lieta Usci (from La Boheme)
[It] S solo,pno RICORDI-ARG BA 8327
s.p. (P1316)
"It's The End Of My Life" [It/Eng]
S solo,pno BELWIN NY 1689 $1.00
(P1317)
"Mimi's Farewell" S solo,pno
INTERNAT. $1.00 (P1318)

Donna Non Vidi Mai (from Manon
Lescaut)
[It] T solo,pno RICORDI-ARG
BA 10593 s.p. (P1319)
[It] T solo,pno RICORDI-ENG 96426
s.p. (P1320)
[It/Eng] T solo,pno INTERNAT. $1.00 (P1321)
"Never Did I Behold So Fair A
Maiden" solo,pno BELWIN $.75
(P1322)
(Ducloux) "Out Of The Sky On High"
[It/Eng] S solo,pno SCHIRM.G $.75
(P1323)

E L'uccellino
[It] Mez/Bar solo,pno RICORDI-ENG
102625 (P1324)

E Lucevan Le Stelle (from Tosca)
[It] T solo,pno RICORDI-ARG BA 8521
s.p. (P1325)
[It/Eng] T solo,pno INTERNAT. $1.00 (P1326)
T solo,pno RICORDI-ENG 103315 s.p. (P1327)
T solo,pno/orch sc KALMUS $3.00
(P1328)
"And The Stars Shone Brightly" [It/
Eng] T solo,pno (A min) BELWIN
NY 1904 $1.00 (P1329)
"And The Stars Shone Brightly" [It/
Eng] T solo,pno (B min) BELWIN
NY 1903 $1.00 (P1330)

Every Flower *see Tutti I Fiori

Fanciulla, Sbocciato E L'amore (from
La Rondine)
[It] S solo,pno SONZOGNO 2034 s.p. (P1331)

Figlio Del Cielo (from Turandot)
S solo,pno RICORDI-ENG 120204 s.p. (P1332)

Forty Songs, Vol. I *CC10L
INTERNAT. $2.50 available in high
or low edition (P1333)

Forty Songs, Vol. II *CC10L
INTERNAT. $2.50 available in high
or low edition (P1334)

Forty Songs, Vol. III *CC10L
INTERNAT. $2.50 available in high
or low edition (P1335)

Forty Songs, Vol. IV *CC10L
INTERNAT. $2.50 available in high
or low edition (P1336)

PUCCINI, GIACOMO (cont'd.)

Guardate, Pazzo Io Son (from Manon
Lescaut)
[It] T solo,pno RICORDI-ENG 125880
s.p. (P1337)

Here In This Silken World Of Mine
*see In Quelle Trine Morbide

How Cold Your Little Hand Is *see
Che Gelida Manina

I Go My Way *see Quando Me'n Vo
Soletta

I'll Hold Your Hand *see Che Gelida
Manina

I'll Hold Your Hand In My Hand *see
Che Gelida Manina

I'm Always Called Mimi *see Mi
Chiamano Mimi

In Quelle Trine Morbide (from Manon
Lescaut)
[It] S solo,pno RICORDI-ARG BA 8840
s.p. (P1338)
[It/Eng] S solo,pno INTERNAT. $1.00
(P1339)
[It] S solo,pno RICORDI-ENG 96427
s.p. (P1340)
"In These Soft Silken Curtains"
[It/Eng] S solo,pno BELWIN
NY 1577 $1.00 (P1341)
(Ducloux) "Here In This Silken
World Of Mine" [It/Eng] S solo,
pno SCHIRM.G $.85 (P1342)

In Questa Reggia (from Turandot)
S solo,pno RICORDI-ENG 120203 s.p. (P1343)
In Strange Mysterious Fashion *see
Recondita Armonia

In These Soft Silken Curtains *see
In Quelle Trine Morbide

Inno A Roma
[It] solo,pno SONZOGNO 2238 s.p. (P1344)
It-Eng *see Addio Fiorito Asil (from
Madama Butterfly) (P1345)

It's The End Of My Life *see Donde
Lieta Usci

La Canzone Di Doretta (from La
Rondine)
[It/Eng] high solo,pno UNIVER.
14929 $2.75 (P1346)

Let Her Believe *see Ch'ella Mi
Creda Libero E Lontano

L'ora, O Tirsi (from Manon Lescaut)
[It] S solo,pno RICORDI-ENG 96429
s.p. (P1347)

Love And Beauty *see Vissi D'arte

Love For Beauty, Love, And Compassion
*see Vissi D'arte

Lovely Maid In The Moonlight *see O
Soave Fanciulla

Mi Chiamano Mimi (from La Boheme)
[It] S solo,pno (D maj) RICORDI-ENG
99343 (P1348)
S solo,pno INTERNAT. $1.00 (P1349)
"I'm Always Called Mimi" [It/Eng] S
solo,pno (D maj) SCHIRM.G $.85
(P1350)
Mimi's Farewell *see Donde Lieta
Usci

Musetta's Waltz *see Quando M'en Vo
Soletta

Musetta's Waltz Song *see Quando
M'en Vo Soletta

Mysterious Resemblance *see
Recondita Armonia

Neighbors Of Bethlehem, The *sac
(Dickinson, C.) solo,pno BELWIN
$1.50 (P1351)

Nessun Dorma (from Turandot)
[It] T solo,pno RICORDI-ARG
BA 10594 s.p. (P1352)
[It/Eng] solo,pno BELWIN NY 2286
$1.00 (P1353)
T solo,pno RICORDI-ENG 120205 s.p. (P1354)
"None Shall Sleep Tonight!" solo,
pno BELWIN $1.50 (P1355)

Never Did I Behold So Fair A Maiden
*see Donna Non Vidi Mai

PUCCINI, GIACOMO (cont'd.)

Non La Sospiri La Nostra Casetta
(from Tosca)
S solo,pno RICORDI-ENG 103312 s.p. (P1356)
Non Piangere, Liu (from Turandot)
[It] T solo,pno RICORDI-ARG
BA 11770 s.p. (P1357)
T solo,pno RICORDI-ENG 120202 s.p. (P1358)

None Shall Sleep Tonight! *see
Nessun Dorma!

O Dolci Mani (from Tosca)
T solo,pno RICORDI-ENG 125892 s.p. (P1359)

O Mimi, Tu Piu Non Torni (from La
Boheme)
"Though Your Love Is Gone" [It/Eng]
TBar soli,pno BELWIN NY 1704
$1.00 (P1360)

O Mio Babbino Caro (from Gianni
Schicchi)
[It] S solo,pno RICORDI-ENG 117666
s.p. (P1361)
[It] S solo,pno RICORDI-ARG BA 8164
s.p. (P1362)
[It/Eng] S solo,pno (F maj) BELWIN
NY 2294 $1.00 (P1363)
"O My Beloved Daddy" [It/Eng] S
solo,pno (F maj) BELWIN NY 2291
$1.00 (P1364)
"Oh! My Beloved Daddy!" low solo,
pno BELWIN $1.50 (P1365)
"Oh! My Beloved Daddy!" high solo,
pno BELWIN $1.50 (P1366)

O My Beloved Daddy *see O Mio
Babbino Caro

O Prehistoric Raiment *see Vecchia
Zimarra, Senti

O Soave Fanciulla (from La Boheme)
[It/Eng] ST soli,pno RICORDI-ENG
120660 (P1367)
ST soli,pno/orch sc KALMUS $3.00
(P1368)
"Lovely Maid In The Moonlight" [It/
Eng] ST soli,pno RICORDI-ARG
BA 11753 s.p. (P1369)
"Lovely Maid In The Moonlight"
solo,pno BELWIN $1.50 (P1370)

Oh! My Beloved Daddy! *see O Mio
Babbino Caro

One Fine Day *see Un Bel Di Vedremo

Or Son Sei Mesi (from La Fanciulla
Del West)
[It] T solo,pno RICORDI-ENG 115789
s.p. (P1371)

Ore Dolci E Divine (from La Rondine)
[It/Eng] high solo,pno UNIVER.
14928 $3.25 (P1372)

Out Of The Sky On High *see Donna
Non Vidi Mai

Pazzo Son, Guardate (from Manon
Lescaut)
[It/Eng] T solo,pno INTERNAT. $1.00
(P1373)

Quando Me'n Vo Soletta (from La
Boheme)
[It] S solo,pno RICORDI-ARG BA 8326
s.p. (P1374)
[It] S solo,pno RICORDI-ENG
99345 (P1375)
"Day After Day" [It/Eng] S solo,pno
(E maj) SCHIRM.G $1.00 (P1376)
"I Go My Way" [It/Eng] S solo,pno
(E flat maj) BELWIN NY 1686 $1.00
(P1377)
"I Go My Way" [It/Eng] S solo,pno
(E maj) BELWIN NY 1685 $1.00
(P1378)
"I Go My Way" [It/Eng] S solo,pno
(D maj) BELWIN NY 1687 $1.00 (P1379)
"Musetta's Waltz" solo,pno/orch sc
KALMUS $3.00 (P1380)
"Musetta's Waltz Song" S solo,pno
INTERNAT. $1.00 (P1381)

Recondita Armonia (from Tosca)
[It] T solo,pno RICORDI-ARG BA 8520
s.p. (P1382)
T solo,pno (F maj) RICORDI-ENG
103310 s.p. (P1383)
[It/Eng] T solo,pno INTERNAT. $1.00
(P1384)
"Mysterious Resemblance" [It/Eng] T
solo,pno BELWIN NY 1846 $1.00
(P1385)
(Gutman) "In Strange Mysterious
Fashion" [It/Eng] T solo,pno
SCHIRM.G $.75 (P1386)

Se La Giurata Fede (from Tosca)
Bar solo,pno RICORDI-ENG 103313
s.p. (P1387)

PUCCINI, GIACOMO (cont'd.)

Senza Mamma, O Bimbo, Tu Sei Morto!
(from Suor Angelica)
[It] S solo,pno RICORDI-ARG
BA 11703 s.p. (P1388)
[It] S solo,pno RICORDI-ENG 117663
s.p. (P1389)

Si, Mi Chiamano Mimi (from La Boheme)
[It] S solo,pno RICORDI-ARG BA 8325
s.p. (P1390)
"They Call Me Mimi" [It/Eng] S
solo,pno (D maj) BELWIN NY 1671
$1.00 (P1391)
"They Call Me Mimi" [It/Eng] S
solo,pno (C maj) BELWIN NY 1672
$1.00 (P1392)

Signore, Ascolta! (from Turandot)
S solo,pno RICORDI-ENG 120201 s.p.
(P1393)

Sola, Perduta, Abbandonata (from
Manon Lescaut)
[It] S solo,pno RICORDI-ENG 126075
s.p. (P1394)
[It/Eng] S solo,pno INTERNAT. $1.00
(P1395)

Soon We'll See At Daybreak *see Un
Bel Di Vedremo

Spira Sul Mare (from Madama
Butterfly)
[It] S solo,pno RICORDI-ENG 126069
s.p. (P1396)

Tanto Amore Segreto (from Turandot)
[It] S solo,pno RICORDI-ARG
BA 10596 s.p. (P1397)
S solo,pno RICORDI-ENG 120206 s.p.
(P1398)

They Call Me Mimi *see Si, Mi
Chiamano Mimi

Though Your Love Is Gone *see O
Mimi, Tu Piu Non Torni

Torna Ai Felici Di (from Le Villi)
T solo,pno RICORDI-ENG 125898 s.p.
(P1399)

Tu Che Di Gel Sei Cinta (from
Turandot)
[It] S solo,pno RICORDI-ARG BA 8425
s.p. (P1400)
S solo,pno RICORDI-ENG 120207 s.p.
(P1401)

Tu, Tu Piccolo Iddio (from Madama
Butterfly)
[It] S solo,pno RICORDI-ENG 126072
s.p. (P1402)

Tutti I Fiori (from Madama Butterfly)
[It/Ger] SMez soli,pno RICORDI-ENG
127454 s.p. (P1403)
"Every Flower" SMez soli,pno BELWIN
$1.50 (P1404)

Un Bel Di Vedremo (from Madama
Butterfly)
[It] S solo,pno RICORDI-ARG BA 8313
s.p. (P1405)
[It] S solo,pno RICORDI-ENG 110011
s.p. (P1406)
[It/Eng] S solo,pno (F maj) BELWIN
NY 66 $1.00 (P1407)
[It/Eng] S solo,pno INTERNAT. $1.25
(P1408)
"One Fine Day" high solo,pno (G
flat maj) BELWIN $1.50 (P1409)
"One Fine Day" low solo,pno (E flat
maj) BELWIN $1.50 (P1410)
"One Fine Day" med solo,pno (F maj)
BELWIN $1.50 (P1411)
"One Fine Day" solo,pno (available
in 3 keys) ASHLEY $.95 (P1412)
"Soon We'll See At Daybreak" [It/
Eng] high solo,pno (G flat maj)
SCHIRM.G $1.00 (P1413)
"Soon We'll See At Daybreak" [It/
Eng] med solo,pno (F maj)
SCHIRM.G $1.00 (P1414)
"Soon We'll See At Daybreak" [It/
Eng] low solo,pno (E flat maj)
SCHIRM.G $1.00 (P1415)

Vecchia Zimarra, Senti (from La
Boheme)
[It] B solo,pno RICORDI-ENG 99349
(P1416)
"O Prehistoric Raiment" B solo,pno
BELWIN NY 1673 $1.00 (P1417)

Vissi D'arte (from Tosca)
[It] S solo,pno RICORDI-ARG BA 8148
s.p. (P1418)
S solo,pno RICORDI-ENG 103314 s.p.
(P1419)
[It/Eng] S solo,pno INTERNAT. $1.00
(P1420)
S solo,pno/orch sc KALMUS $2.00
(P1421)
"Love And Beauty" [It/Eng] S solo,
pno (E flat maj) BELWIN NY 1906
$1.50 (P1422)
"Love And Beauty" [It/Eng] S solo,
pno (D maj) BELWIN NY 1907 $1.50

PUCCINI, GIACOMO (cont'd.)

(P1423)
"Love For Beauty, Love, And
Compassion" [It/Eng] S solo,pno
(E flat maj) SCHIRM.G $.85
(P1424)

Vogliatemi Bene (from Madama
Butterfly)
[It] ST soli,pno (E flat maj)
RICORDI-ENG 125538 s.p. (P1425)

Your Tiny Hand Is Frozen *see Che
Gelida Manina

PUDELKO, WALTER
Funfundzwanzig Kinderlieder *see
Musikanten, Die Kommen (P1426)

Musikanten, Die Kommen
(Knab, Armin) solo,pno (easy)
BAREN. 1720 $3.50 see from
Funfundzwanzig Kinderlieder
(P1427)

PUEBLITO, MI PUEBLO see Guastavino,
Carlos

PUEBLO *CC59U,folk
(Benedito) [Span] med solo,pno UNION
ESP. $15.00 (P1428)

PUEBLO, VOL. IX *CC6U,folk
(Benedito) [Span] med solo,pno UNION
ESP. $1.00 (P1429)

PUEBLO, VOL. V *CC5U,folk
(Benedito) [Span] med solo,pno UNION
ESP. $1.00 (P1430)

PUEBLO, VOL. VII *CC6U,folk
(Benedito) [Span] med solo,pno UNION
ESP. $1.00 (P1431)

PUEBLO, VOL. VIII *CC6U,folk
(Benedito) [Span] med solo,pno UNION
ESP. $1.00 (P1432)

PUEBLO, VOL. X *CC6U,folk
(Benedito) [Span] med solo,pno UNION
ESP. $.95 (P1433)

PUER NATUS EST see Felderhof, Jan

PUER NATUS EST NOBIS see Dubois,
Theodore

PUER NOBIS NASCITUR see Badings, Henk

PUERTO RICO SINGS *CCU
[Span/Eng] solo,pno MARKS $2.00
Puerto Rican (P1434)

PUES BIEN...IRE LEJANA see Catalani,
Alfredo

PUGET, PAUL-CHARLES-MARIE (1848-1917)
Le Luth
(Bordese, Stephen) solo,pno
(available in 2 keys) ENOCH s.p.
see also CHANSONS DE PAGE (P1435)

PUGET SOUND CINQUAIN see Clarke, Henry
Leland

PUGH
Old Man At The Crossing
[Eng] med solo,pno HINRICHSEN H485
$1.75 (P1436)

PUGHE-EVANS, D.
Lead, Kindly Light *sac
low solo,pno NOVELLO 17.0093.06
s.p. (P1437)

PUIS-JE CROIRE QUE C'EST BIEN VRAI see
Saint-Saens, Camille

PUISQUE L'AUBE GRANDIT see Diepenbrock,
Alphons

PUISQUE TOUT PASSE see Barber, Samuel

PUISQUE VOICI LES SOIRS EMBRUMES DE
L'HIVER see Ropartz, Joseph Guy

PUISQU'ICI-BAS TOUTE AME see Lacome,
Paul

PUISSANCE DE DIEU see Beethoven, Ludwig
van, Gottes Macht Und Vorsehung

PULASKI'S BANNER see Lindsay, M.

PULL, EDWIN
Christ Child *sac,Xmas
med solo,pno (D maj) WATERLOO $.75
(P1438)
Come Unto Me And Rest *sac
(Park, Dorothy Allan; Bissell,
Keith W.) low solo,pno (D maj)
WATERLOO $.90 (P1439)

Gate Of The Year (New Year's) *sac,
Xmas
med solo,pno (F maj) WATERLOO $.75
(P1440)

PULL, EDWIN (cont'd.)

It Is I, Be Not Afraid *sac
low solo,pno (E flat maj) WATERLOO
$.75 (P1441)

PULL ON THE OARS
see Six Regional Canadian Folksongs

PUPILLETTE see Falconieri, Andrea

PUR DICESTE I BOCCA BELLA see Lotti,
Antonio

PUR DICESTI BOCCA BELLA see Lotti,
Antonio

PUR DOLENTE SON IO see Cilea, Francesco

PUR NEL SONNO AL MEN TAL'ORA see
Scarlatti, Domenico

PURA SICCOME UN ANGELO see Verdi,
Giuseppe

PURCELL, EDWARD C.
Passing By
med solo,pno (G maj) SCHIRM.G $.85
(P1442)
high solo,pno (A maj) SCHIRM.G $.85
(P1443)
low solo,pno (F maj) BOOSEY $1.50
(P1444)
low solo,pno (F maj) FISCHER,C
S 5449 (P1445)
high solo,pno (A maj) FISCHER,C
S 5448 (P1446)
low solo,pno (E flat maj) SCHIRM.G
$.85 (P1447)
med-high solo,orch (A maj) ASHDOWN
s.p., ipr (P1448)
med solo,orch (A flat maj) ASHDOWN
s.p., ipr (P1449)
med-low solo,orch (G maj) ASHDOWN
s.p., ipr (P1450)
low solo,orch (F maj) ASHDOWN s.p.,
ipr (P1451)
high solo,pno (B flat maj) BOOSEY
$1.50 (P1452)
med-high solo,pno (A maj) BOOSEY
$1.50 (P1453)
med solo,pno (A flat maj) BOOSEY
$1.50 (P1454)
med-low solo,pno (G maj) BOOSEY
$1.50 (P1455)
high solo&low solo,pno ASHDOWN s.p.
(P1456)
high solo,orch (B flat maj) ASHDOWN
s.p., ipr (P1457)

PURCELL, HENRY (ca. 1659-1695)
Abendhymne *see Evening Hymn

Ach, Wie Suss Zu Lieben Ist *see Ah!
How Sweet It Is To Love

Ah! How Sweet It Is To Love
"Ach, Wie Suss Zu Lieben Ist" [Eng/
Ger] low solo,pno SCHOTTS VK 16
s.p. (P1458)
"Ach, Wie Suss Zu Lieben Ist" [Eng/
Ger] high solo,pno SCHOTTS VK 16
s.p. (P1459)

Album Fur Sopran *CCU
[Eng/Ger] S solo,pno/cembalo
SCHOTTS 4349 s.p. (P1460)

Anacreon's Defeat
see Six Songs For Bass

Arise, Ye Subterranean Winds
see Six Songs For Bass

Bashful Thames, The
(Marting, Elizabeth) T solo,2A rec,
B rec,cont SCHIRM.EC 2045 s.p.
(P1461)
Blessed Virgin's Expostulation (from
Harmonia Sacra) sac
see Four Sacred Songs
(Britten; Pears) solo,pno (C maj)
BOOSEY $5.00 (P1462)

Dido's Lament *see When I Am Laid In
Earth

Die Nacht *CC3U
(Just, Herbert) high solo,5strings
(med) sc BAREN. HM 141 s.p.
(P1463)

Die Stunde Naht
[Eng/Ger] high solo,pno SCHOTTS
VK 18 s.p. (P1464)
[Eng/Ger] low solo,pno SCHOTTS
VK 18 s.p. (P1465)

Earth Trembled, The
see Six Sacred Songs

Elegie *see Queen's Epicedium, The

Evening Hymn (from Harmonia Sacra)
see Four Sacred Songs
med solo,pno NOVELLO 17.0051.00
s.p. (P1466)

PURCELL, HENRY (cont'd.)

med solo,pno (F maj) ALLANS s.p.
(P1467)

low solo,pno NOVELLO 17.0052.09
s.p.
(P1468)

(Darrow, Carl) "Abendhymne" solo,
strings sc BREITKOPF-W PB 4819
s.p., ipa
(P1469)

(Shaw, Martin) high solo,pno (G
maj) CRAMER
(P1470)

(Shaw, Martin) low solo,pno (E flat
maj) CRAMER
(P1471)

(Vaughn Williams) solo,5strings
OXFORD
(P1472)

Fifteen Songs And Airs, Set 1 *CC15L
s.p. high solo,pno NOVELLO
17.0263.07; low solo,pno NOVELLO
17.0264.05
(P1473)

Fifteen Songs And Airs, Set 2 *CC15L
s.p. high solo,pno NOVELLO
17.0265.03; low solo,pno NOVELLO
17.0266.01
(P1474)

Five Songs (from Orpheus Britannicus)
CC5U
(Britten; Pears) med solo,pno
BOOSEY $5.00
(P1475)

Four Sacred Songs (from Harmonia
Sacra) sac
(Kagen, Sergius) INTERNAT. high
solo,pno $2.50; low solo,pno
$2.50
contains: Blessed Virgin's
Expostulation; Evening Hymn;
Lord, What Is Man; We Sing To
Him
(P1476)

Hark! The Echoing Air (from Fairy
Queen, The)
(Brown, F. E.) solo,pno CRAMER
$1.10
(P1477)

Hence With Your Trifling Deity
see Six Songs For Bass

Here Let My Life (from If Ever I More
Riches Did Desire)
(Flothius, Marius) [Eng] T solo,
vla,pno BROEKMANS 395-10 s.p.
(P1478)

How Long, Great God
see Six Sacred Songs

How Pleasant Is This Flowery Plain
And Ground *cant
(Just, Herbert) "Wie Wonnig Ist's
Auf Blumigem Gefild" ST soli,2S
rec,cont (med) sc BAREN. HM 164
$5.00
(P1479)

I Attempt From Love's Sickness To Fly
low solo,pno INTERNAT. $.75 (P1480)
high solo,pno INTERNAT. $.75
(P1481)
med-high solo,pno (G maj) SCHIRM.G
$.85
(P1482)
(Howe) high solo,pno PAXTON P40617
s.p.
(P1483)

If Music Be The Food Of Love
(Howe) T solo,pno PAXTON P40502
s.p.
(P1484)

I'll Sail Upon The Dog-Star
high solo,pno INTERNAT. $.75
(P1485)
low solo,pno INTERNAT. $.75 (P1486)

In The Black, Dismal Dungeon Of
Despair
see Six Sacred Songs

Job's Curse *sac
(Britten; Pears) solo,pno (C maj)
BOOSEY $3.00
(P1487)

Let The Night Perish
see Six Sacred Songs

Let Us Have Music For Singing Songs
*CCU
high solo,pno FISCHER,C RB 55; low
solo,pno FISCHER,C RB 56 (P1488)

Lord, What Is Man (from Harmonia
Sacra)
see Four Sacred Songs

Lord, What Is Man, Lost Man
see Six Sacred Songs

Lost Is My Quiet
SB soli,pno SCHOTTS VK 31 s.p.
(P1489)
(Stubbs, H.) 2 soli,pno CRAMER
(P1490)

Mag Das Schicksal Des Ew'gen Richters
[Eng/Ger] Bar solo,pno SCHOTTS
VK 28 s.p.
(P1491)

PURCELL, HENRY (cont'd.)

Man Is For The Woman Made
(Britten; Pears) solo,pno (B flat
maj) BOOSEY $1.50
(P1492)
(Pinkham) low solo,pno FISCHER,C
RS 104
(P1493)
(Pinkham) high solo,pno FISCHER,C
RS 103
(P1494)

Mein Leid Und Alle Qualen
[Eng/Ger] low solo,pno SCHOTTS
VK 19 s.p.
(P1495)
[Eng/Ger] high solo,pno SCHOTTS
VK 19 s.p.
(P1496)

Music For Awhile
low solo,pno INTERNAT. $.75 (P1497)
high solo,pno INTERNAT. $.75
(P1498)
solo,pno (B flat maj) ASHDOWN
s.p.
(P1499)
(Howe) med solo,pno PAXTON P40485
s.p.
(P1500)

Myrtle Shade, The
(Dunhill) low solo,pno (G maj)
ROBERTON 2522L s.p.
(P1501)
(Dunhill) high solo,pno (B flat
maj) ROBERTON 2522H s.p.
(P1502)

Next, Winter Comes Slowly
see Six Songs For Bass

Nymphs And Shepherds
high solo,pno INTERNAT. $.75
(P1503)
high solo,pno (G maj) LEONARD-ENG
(P1504)
med solo,pno (F maj) LEONARD-ENG
(P1505)
low solo,pno (D maj) LEONARD-ENG
(P1506)
high solo,pno (G maj) ALLANS
s.p.
(P1507)
med solo,pno (F maj) ALLANS s.p.
(P1508)
high solo,pno (F maj) ASHDOWN
s.p.
(P1509)
low solo,pno (E flat maj) ASHDOWN
s.p.
(P1510)
high solo,pno (G maj) SCHIRM.G $.85
(P1511)
low solo,pno INTERNAT. $.75 (P1512)

O, Fuhrt Mich In Die Stille Gruft
[Eng/Ger] low solo,pno SCHOTTS
VK 22 s.p.
(P1513)
[Eng/Ger] high solo,pno SCHOTTS
VK 22 s.p.
(P1514)

Oh, The Sweet Delights Of Love (from
Prophetess, The)
(Flothius, Marius) SS soli,pno
BROEKMANS 395-19 s.p.
(P1515)

Orpheus Britannicus *CCU
1-3 soli,pno BROUDE BR. $30.00
(P1516)

Plaint, The (from Fairy Queen, The)
(Flothius, Marius) [Eng] S solo,
vla,pno BROEKMANS 395-2 s.p.
(P1517)

Queen Dido's Lament
solo,pno CRAMER
(P1518)

Queen's Epicedium, The
"Elegie" [Lat] SS soli,pno/cembalo
SCHOTTS VK 3 s.p.
(P1519)
(Britten; Pears) [Lat] solo,pno (C
min) BOOSEY $4.50
(P1520)

Saul And The Witch At Endor (from
Harmonia Sacra) song cycle
(Britten; Pears) STB soli,pno
BOOSEY $3.75
(P1521)

Secrecy's Song (from Fairy Queen,
The)
(Flothius, Marius) [Eng] A solo,
2fl,pno BROEKMANS 395-9 s.p.
(P1522)

Seven Songs (from Orpheus
Britannicus) CC7U
(Britten; Pears) high solo/med
solo,pno BOOSEY $6.50
(P1523)

Six Duets *CC6U
(Britten; Pears) high solo&low
solo,pno BOOSEY $7.50
(P1524)

Six Sacred Songs *sac
S/Mez/T/Bar solo,pno NOVELLO
17.0267.10 s.p.
contains: Earth Trembled, The;
How Long, Great God; In The
Black, Dismal Dungeon Of
Despair; Let The Night Perish;
Lord, What Is Man, Lost Man;
With Sick And Famish'd Eyes
(P1525)

Six Songs (from Orpheus Britannicus)
CC6U
(Britten; Pears) high solo/med
solo,pno BOOSEY $7.50 (P1526)

PURCELL, HENRY (cont'd.)

Six Songs For Bass
(Kagen, Sergius) B solo,pno
INTERNAT. $2.50
contains: Anacreon's Defeat;
Arise, Ye Subterranean Winds;
Hence With Your Trifling Deity;
Next, Winter Comes Slowly;
Wondrous Machine; Ye Twice Ten
Hundred Deities
(P1527)

Six Vocal Duets *CC6U
2 soli,pno GALLIARD 2.4129.7 $2.00
(P1528)

Stimmt Die Saiten
[Eng/Ger] high solo,pno SCHOTTS
VK 20 s.p.
(P1529)
[Eng/Ger] low solo,pno SCHOTTS
VK 20 s.p.
(P1530)

Suite Of Songs (from Orpheus
Britannicus) CCU
(Britten; Pears) high solo,orch
BOOSEY $6.00
(P1531)

There's Not A Swain On The Plain
med solo,pno (F maj) ALLANS s.p.
(P1532)
high solo,pno (G maj) ALLANS
s.p.
(P1533)

Thert Is Ne'er Was So Wretches A
Lover
SB soli,pno SCHOTTS VK 32 s.p.
(P1534)

Three Divine Hymns (from Harmonia
Sacra) CC3U
(Britten; Pears) med solo,pno
BOOSEY $5.00
(P1535)

Thy Hand, Belinda (from Dido And
Aeneas)
solo,pno BELWIN $1.50 contains
also: When I Am Laid In Earth
(P1536)

Twenty Favourite Songs *CC20U
solo,pno GALLIARD 2.8942.7 $5.75
(P1537)

Two Divine Hymns And Alleluia (from
Harmonia Sacra) CC3U
(Britten; Pears) solo,pno BOOSEY
$3.50
(P1538)

Vom Rosenbett
[Eng/Ger] high solo,pno SCHOTTS
VK 23 s.p.
(P1539)
[Eng/Ger] low solo,pno SCHOTTS
VK 23 s.p.
(P1540)

Was Kann Ich Tun
[Eng/Ger] high solo,pno SCHOTTS
VK 21 s.p.
(P1541)
[Eng/Ger] low solo,pno SCHOTTS
VK 21 s.p.
(P1542)

We Sing To Him (from Harmonia Sacra)
see Four Sacred Songs

What Can We Poor Females Do?
(Franklin) Mez solo,pno ELKIN
27.2538.10 s.p.
(P1543)

What Shall I Do To Show How Much I
Love Her
(Howe) Bar solo,pno PAXTON P40484
s.p.
(P1544)

When I Am Laid In Earth (from Dido
And Aeneas)
see Purcell, Henry, Thy Hand,
Belinda
high solo,pno NOVELLO 17.0213.00
s.p.
(P1545)
high solo,pno INTERNAT. $.75
(P1546)
low solo,pno INTERNAT. $.75 (P1547)
"Dido's Lament" med solo,pno BELWIN
$1.50
(P1548)
(Howe) S solo,pno PAXTON P40482
s.p.
(P1549)

Wie Wonnig Ist's Auf Blumigem Gefild
*see How Pleasant Is This Flowery
Plain And Ground

With Sick And Famish'd Eyes
see Six Sacred Songs

Wondrous Machine
see Six Songs For Bass

Ye Twice Ten Hundred Deities
see Six Songs For Bass

You Say 'Tis Love
SB soli,SB,cont sc SCHIRM.EC 130
s.p., ipa
(P1550)

PURETE see Roos, Robert de

PURIM SONGS see Nardi, Nachum

PUROLLA see Linko, Ernst (Fredrik)

PUSH ME, LORD see Cates, Bill

PUSSY CAT see Presser, William

PUT A ROSEBUD ON HER LIPS see Roberts, Mervyn

PUT JESUS FIRST IN YOUR LIFE see Harris, Ron

PUT ON YOUR SMOCK see Leoncavallo, Ruggiero, Vesti La Giubba

PUT OUT MY EYES see Birch, Robert Fairfax

PUT YOUR HAND IN HIS NAILSCARRED HAND
*sac,gospel
solo,pno ABER.GRP. $1.50   (P1551)

PUT YOUR HAND IN THE HAND see Mc Lellan

PUTZMAMSELLCHEN see Trunk, Richard

PUVA see Mana-Zucca, Mme.

PUZZLE see Manoury, P.

PYHAIN MIESTEN PAIVANA see Kilpinen, Yrio

PYLKKANEN, TAUNO KULLERVO (1918-   )
Das Kreuz Im Schnee *see Risti Lumessa

Den Vita Hustruns Sang *see Valkean Vaimon Laulu

Der Schwan Des Todes *see Joutsenlaulu, "Schwanengesang", Op.21,No.5; Kuoleman Jousten, "Der Schwan Des Todes", Op.21, No.1; Pastoraali, "Pastorale", Op.21,No.2; Taivainen Rekiretki, "Himmlische Schlittenfahrt", Op.21,No.4; Viimeinen Kehtolaulu, "Letztes Wiegenlied", Op.21,No.3
(P1552)
Der Schwan Des Todes *see Kuoleman Jousten

Die Mondbrucke *see Kuun Silta, "Die Mondbrucke", Op.55,No.3; Laulu Hamarissa, "Lied In Der Dammerung", Op.55,No.1; Risti Lumessa, "Das Kreuz Im Schnee", Op.55,No.2; Vaulluslaulu, "Wanderlied", Op.55,No.4 (P1553)

Die Mondbrucke *see Kuun Silta

Die Nachtigall *see Satakieli

En Skugga *see Varjo

En Tieda, Muistatko Mua
"Jag Vet Ej Om Du Mig Minnes" solo, pno FAZER F 2949 s.p.   (P1554)

Himmlische Schlittenfahrt *see Taivainen Rekiretki

Im Boot *see Venheessa

Jag Vet Ej Om Du Mig Minnes *see En Tieda, Muistatko Mua

Joutsenlaulu *Op.21,No.5
"Schwanengesang" solo,pno FAZER F 2678 s.p. see from Der Schwan Des Todes   (P1555)

Kuoleman Jousten *Op.21,No.1
"Der Schwan Des Todes" solo,pno FAZER F 2674 s.p. see from Der Schwan Des Todes   (P1556)

Kuun Silta *Op.55,No.3
"Die Mondbrucke" solo,pno (contains also: Vaelluslaulu) FAZER W 2857 s.p. see from Die Mondbrucke   (P1557)

Laulu Hamarissa *Op.55,No.1
"Lied In Der Dammerung" solo,pno (contains also: Risti Lumessa) FAZER W 2856 s.p. see from Die Mondbrucke   (P1558)

Letztes Wiegenlied *see Viimeinen Kehtolaulu

Lied In Der Dammerung *see Laulu Hamarissa

Mare Ja Hanen Poikansa
"Mare Och Hennes Son" solo,pno FAZER W 2597 s.p.   (P1559)

Mare Och Hennes Son *see Mare Ja Hanen Poikansa

Nachtlose Nachte *see Yoton Yo

Nattrymden Skymmer *see Yon Piiri

PYLKKANEN, TAUNO KULLERVO (cont'd.)
Pastoraali *Op.21,No.2
"Pastorale" solo,pno FAZER F 2675 s.p. see from Der Schwan Des Todes   (P1560)

Pastorale *see Pastoraali

Risti Lumessa *Op.55,No.2
"Das Kreuz Im Schnee" solo,pno (contains also: Laulu Hamarissa) FAZER W 2856 s.p. see from Die Mondbrucke   (P1561)

Satakieli *Op.68,No.1
"Die Nachtigall" solo,pno FAZER W 3700 s.p. contains also: Venheessa, "Im Boot", Op.68,No.2   (P1562)
Schwanengesang *see Joutsenlaulu

Taivainen Rekiretki *Op.21,No.4
"Himmlische Schlittenfahrt" solo, pno FAZER F 2677 s.p. see from Der Schwan Des Todes   (P1563)

Valkean Vaimon Laulu (from Simo Hurtta)
"Den Vita Hustruns Sang" solo,pno FAZER F 3036 s.p.   (P1564)

Varjo
"En Skugga" solo,pno FAZER F 3419 s.p.   (P1565)

Vaulluslaulu *Op.55,No.4
"Wanderlied" solo,pno (contains also: Kuun Silta) FAZER W 2857 s.p. see from Die Mondbrucke   (P1566)

Venheessa *Op.68,No.2
"Im Boot" see Pylkkanen, Tauno Kullervo, Satakieli

Viimeinen Kehtolaulu *Op.21,No.3
"Letztes Wiegenlied" solo,pno FAZER F 2676 s.p. see from Der Schwan Des Todes   (P1567)

Wanderlied *see Vaulluslaulu

Yon Piiri
"Nattrymden Skymmer" solo,pno FAZER F 2950 s.p.   (P1568)

Yoton Yo *Op.74, song cycle
"Nachtlose Nachte" solo,pno FAZER F 5155 s.p.   (P1569)

Q

QUA-SIE see Dittrich, Paul-Heinz

QUACK, ERHARD (1904-   )
Lasst Uns Loben *sac
solo,org CHRIS 50535-36 s.p.   (Q1)

QUADERNI PASCOLIANI see Bettarini, Luciano

QUADRO see Otten, Ludwig

QUAERE SUPERNA see Mozart, Wolfgang Amadeus

QUAL FARFALLETTA AMANTE see Scarlatti, Domenico

QUAL FIAMMA AVEA NEL GUARDO see Leoncavallo, Ruggiero

QUALEN OHNE ENDE see Handel, George Frideric, Pena Tiranna

QUALITY OF MERCY, THE see Clarke, Henry Leland

QUAM CANDIDUS ES see Casola, Francesco

QUAM DULCE EST, INHAERERE TIBI see Campra, Andre

QUAND, A TES GENOUX see Aubert, Louis-Francois-Marie

QUAND FINIRA LE SORTILEGE see Legley, Victor

QUAND' IN CIELO BRILLAN LE STELLE see Kalman, Emerich

QUAND J'AI OUY LE TABOURIN see Debussy, Claude

QUAND JE QUITTAIS LA NORMANDIE see Meyerbeer, Giacomo

QUAND J'ETAIS CHEZ MON PERE
see La Musique, Quatrieme Cahier

QUAND LA FLAMME see Bizet, Georges

QUAND LA HACHE TOMBE see Gretchaninov, Alexander Tikhonovitch

QUAND LA MARIE S'EN VA-T'A L'IAU
see Chants De France Vol. II

QUAND L'AMOUR VEILLE see Mouton, H.

QUAND L'AQUILON FOUGUEUX see Rameau, Jean-Philippe

QUAND LE BIEN-AIME REVIENDRA see Dalayrac, [Nicolas]

QUAND LE REVE A TOI see Beechgaard, Julius

QUAND LE ROI PART AUX COMBATS see Koeneman, T.

QUAND LES PINS CHANTERONT see Bonnal, Ermend

QUAND LES ROSES see Profes, A.

QUAND MON MARI SE FACHERA
see Five French Folk Songs

QUAND NAISSENT LES ETOILES see Levade, Charles (Gaston)

QUAND NOUS SERONS VIEUX! see Delmet, Paul

QUAND ON AIME see Chabrier, Emmanuel

QUAND ON AIME BIEN see Philidor, Anne

QUAND ON EST DANS LA PUREE see Tranchant, J.

QUAND ON EST UN GRAND ARTISTE see Serpette, Gaston

QUAND ON MARIE LES FILLES
(Fragerolle, G.) solo,pno ENOCH s.p. see from Chansons Du Pays-Lorrain
(Q2)
(Fragerolle, G.) solo,acap ENOCH s.p. see from Chansons Du Pays-Lorrain
(Q3)
QUAND ON S'REVOIT see Scotto, Vincent

QUAND REVERRAI-JE, HELAS see Caplet, Andre

QUAND SUR L'EAU CHANGEANTE see Chapuis,
Auguste-Paul-Jean-Baptiste

QUAND TON SOURIRE ME SURPRIT see
Andriessen, Hendrik

QUAND TOUT CECI NE SERA PLUS see Migot,
Georges

QUAND TU DORS see Kjerulf, [Halfdan]

QUAND TU ES LA see Mana-Zucca, Mme.

QUAND TU LA VERRAS see Trabadelo, A. de

QUAND TU M'APPELLES see Scotto, Vincent

QUAND TU VIENDRA see Rhene-Baton

QUAND UN AIME, VOUS A-T-ON CE VISAGE
BLEME? see Levade, Charles (Gaston)

QUAND VERRAI-JE ILES? see Arrieu,
Claude

QUAND VIENT LE SOIR... see Rasse,
Francois

QUAND VOUS PASSEZ see Deutsch de la
Meurthe, H.

QUAND VOUS RIEZ see Wolff, A.

QUAND VOUS SOURIEZ see Messager, Andre

QUAND VOUS TOURNEZ VERS MOI LES YEUX
see Messager, Andre

QUAND VOUS VOUDREZ FAIRE UNE AMIE see
Coppola, Piero

QUAND VOUS VOUDREZ FAIRE UNE AMYE see
Delvincourt, Claude

QUAND'IN CIEL STESO UN VEL see Lehar,
Franz

QUANDO EMBALADA see Guarnieri, Camargo
Mozart

QUANDO IN NOTTE see Scarlatti, Domenico

QUANDO LE SERE AL PLACIDO see Verdi,
Giuseppe

QUANDO ME'N VO SOLETTA see Puccini,
Giacomo

QUANDO NASCESTE VOI see Respighi,
Ottorino

QUANN'A FEMMENA VO! see De Crescenzo

QUANTO E BELLA, QUANTO E CARA see
Donizetti, Gaetano

QUANTO MAI FELICI SIETE see
Dittersdorf, Karl Ditters von

QUANTO, QUANTO see Steffani, Agostino

QUARANTA, FELICE
San Gabriel
solo,inst quarto RICORDI-ENG 131322
s.p.   (Q4)

QUARANTE MELODIES CHOISIES see
Schubert, Franz (Peter)

QUARATINO, PASCUAL
Caja Chayera
[Span] solo,pno RICORDI-ARG
BA 11377 s.p.   (Q5)

Cancion Para El Nino En La Cuna
[Span] solo,pno RICORDI-ARG BA 8876
s.p.   (Q6)

Cerro, Luna Y Aire
[Span] solo,pno RICORDI-ARG
BA 11378 s.p.   (Q7)

El Flechazo
[Span] solo,pno RICORDI-ARG BA 6902
s.p.   (Q8)

Guadiana
[It] solo,pno RICORDI-ARG BA 6317
s.p.   (Q9)

Lamento Indio
[Span] solo,pno RICORDI-ARG BA 7466
s.p.   (Q10)

Pampeana
[Span] solo,pno RICORDI-ARG BA 6873
s.p.   (Q11)

Plegaria Del Cerro
[Span] solo,pno RICORDI-ARG
BA 10523 s.p.   (Q12)

Ronda Del Sol
[Span] solo,pno RICORDI-ARG BA 9894
s.p.   (Q13)

QUARATINO, PASCUAL (cont'd.)

Siesta
[Span] solo,pno RICORDI-ARG BA 6340
s.p.   (Q14)

QUARTET see Karlins, M. William

QUARTET NO. 6 see Kapr, Jan

QUARTETS see Nilsson, Bo

QUARTETS, VOL. I see Brahms, Johannes

QUARTETS, VOL. III GYPSY SONGS see
Brahms, Johannes

QUARTETTO VOCALE DEL PRIMO ATTO see
Neglia, Francesco Paolo

QUARTORZE AIRS ANCIENS   *CC14U,Span,
17th cent/18th cent
(Nin) [Fr/Span] med solo,pno ESCHIG
$13.25 in two volumes   (Q15)

QU'AS TU FAIT? see Massarani, E.

QUATORZE MELODIES see Abt, Franz

QUATRAIN see Barraud, Henry

QUATRE BALADES FRANCAISES DE PAUL FORT
see Gaubert, Philippe

QUATRE BALLADES FRANCAISES DE PAUL
FORET see Roget, H.

QUATRE CHANSONS see Enrichi

QUATRE CHANSONS see Pedrell, F.

QUATRE CHANSONS see Lapeyre, Therese

QUATRE CHANSONS AVEC TEXTES HONGROIS
see Frid, Geza

QUATRE CHANSONS DE CLEMENT MAROT see
Delvincourt, Claude

QUATRE CHANSONS DE JEUNESSE see
Debussy, Claude

QUATRE CHANSONS DE RAMUZ see Binet,
Jean

QUATRE CHANSONS DES MENDIANTS see
Lilien, Ignace

QUATRE CHANSONS FRANCAISES see
Casadesus, Henri Gustave

QUATRE CHANSONS POPULAIRES see Holmes,
Alfred

QUATRE CHANSONS POPULAIRES DU CANADA
see Stevens, Halsey

QUATRE CHANSONS POPULAIRES FRANCAISES
see Inghelbrecht, Desire Emile

QUATRE CHANSONS POUR TENOR ET ORCHESTRE
A CORDES see Menasce, Jacques de

QUATRE CHANTS see David, Karl Heinrich

QUATRE CHANTS RUSSES see Stravinsky,
Igor

QUATRE ESQUISSES VALAISANNES see
Orthel, Leon

QUATRE HAI-KAI see Quinet, Marcel

QUATRE LIEDER AVEC ACCOMPAGNEMENT see
Lesur, Daniel

QUATRE MELODIES see Migot, Georges

QUATRE MELODIES see Chapuis, Auguste-
Paul-Jean-Baptiste

QUATRE MELODIES *see Dupre, Marcel,
Pour Une Amie Perdue   (Q16)

QUATRE MELODIES see Dupre, Marcel

QUATRE MELODIES see Franck, Cesar

QUATRE MELODIES see Pandelides, S.

QUATRE MELODIES SUR DES TEXTES D'ANDRE
GIDE see Gabus, Monique

QUATRE MONOCANTES see Schmitt, Florent

QUATRE ODELETTES DE H. REGNIER see
Ropartz, Joseph Guy

QUATRE ODES DE RONSARD see Cortese,
Luigi

QUATRE PETITES MELODIES see Satie, Erik

QUATRE POEMES see Caplet, Andre

QUATRE POEMES see Honegger, Arthur

QUATRE POEMES ALGIMANTAS NARAKAS see
Peter, Mieg

QUATRE POEMES DE GEORGES GABORY see
Auric, Georges

QUATRE POEMES DE JEAN LAHOR see Paray,
Paul

QUATRE POEMES DE LANZA DEL VASTRO see
Barraud, Henry

QUATRE POEMES DE LEO LATIL see Milhaud,
Darius

QUATRE POEMES DE MAETERLINCK see Absil,
Jean

QUATRE POEMES DE PASTERNAK see Nabokov,
Nicolas

QUATRE POEMES DE PAUL CLAUDEL see
Milhaud, Darius

QUATRE POEMES DE ROBERT DESNOS see
Casterede, Jacques

QUATRE POEMES DE RONSARD see Schmitt,
Florent

QUATRE POEMES DE TRISTAN KLINGSOR see
Moulaert, Raymond

QUATRE POEMES HINDOUS see Delage,
Maurice

QUATRE PROPHETIES DE NOSTRADAMUS:
"1999" see Bon, Willem Frederik

QUATRE PSAUMES DE TOUKARAM see
Charpentier, Jean Jacques
Beauvarlet

QUATRE REGRETS DE JOACHIM DU BELLAY see
Delannoy, Marcel

QUATRE ROMANCES see Jaubert, Maurice

QUATRE SONNETS see Martin, F.

QUATRE SONNETS A CASSANDRE see Martin,
Frank

QUATRE VERSETS D'UN MOTET see Couperin
(le Grand), Francois

QUATRE-VINGT DICTEES MUSICALES see
Dandelot, [Georges]

QUATRO CANTATE see Scarlatti,
Alessandro

QUATRO CANTIGAS see Camargo Guarnieri

QUATRO CANZONI DE AMARANTA see Tosti,
Francesco Paolo

QUATRO LIRICHE see Respighi, Ottorino

QUATRO LIRICHE see Rossellini, Renzo

QUATRO PEZZI SACRI see Verdi, Giuseppe

QUATTER MINIATURES RUMANTSCHAS see
Flothius, Marius

QUATTRO ARIE PER SOPRANO see Vivaldi,
Antonio

QUATTRO CANTI see Monteverdi, Claudio

QUATTRO CANTI DELLA MORTE see Gui,
Vittorio

QUATTRO CANTI NAPOLETANI see Ghedini,
Giorgio Federico

QUATTRO CANZONI see Egk, Werner

QUATTRO DUETTI SU TESTI SACRI see
Ghedini, Giorgio Federico

QUATTRO FIORI see Gandino, Adolfo

QUATTRO INNI SACRI see Petrassi,
Goffredo

QUATTRO LIRICHE see Pratella, Francesco
Balilla

QUATTRO LIRICHE see Respighi, Ottorino

QUATTRO LIRICHE see Ferrari-Trecate,
Luigi

QUATTRO LIRICHE see Agosti, Guido

QUATTRO LIRICHE see Bucchi, Valentino

QUATTRO LIRICHE DI MACHADO see
Dallapiccola, Luigi

QUATTRO LIRICHE DI ST. MALLARME see
Gui, Vittorio

QUATTRO LIRICHE FROM "MATTINO
DOMENICALE" see Taylor, Clifford

QUATTRO LIRICHE ITALIANE see Rieti,
Vittorio

QUATTRO LIRICHE PER I VERSI DI
LEOPARDI, SHAKESPEARE, GOETHE E
MALARME see Colonna, Luigi

QUATTRO LIRICHE ROMANTICHE see Toni,
Alceo

QUATTRO MELODIE see Panni, Marcello

QUATTRO MELOPEE SU EPIGRAMMI SEPOLCRALI
GRECI [1] see Rocca, Lodovico

QUATTRO MELOPEE SU EPIGRAMMI SEPOLCRALI
GRECI [2] see Rocca, Lodovico

QUATTRO PAESAGGI ABRUZZESI see Gandino,
Adolfo

QUATTRO PEZZI see Kounadis, Arghyris

QUATTRO POESIE DI VIGOLO see Veretti,
Antonio

QUATTRO RAGAZZE NELLA MIA STANZA see
Massarani, E.

QUATTRO RISPETTI see Wolf-Ferrari,
Ermanno

QUATTRO RISPETTI see Wolf-Ferrari,
Ermanno

QUATTRO RISPETTI TOSCANI see Respighi,
Ottorino

QUATTRO SONETTI DEL BURCHIELLO see
Malipiero, Gian Francesco

QUATTRO STRAMBOTTI DI GIUSTINIANI see
Ghedini, Giorgio Federico

QUATTRO VECCHIE CANZONI see Malipiero,
Gian Francesco

QU'AVEZ-VOUS FAIT see Delmet, Paul

QUAYLE, EILEEN
O Pure White Rose
med solo,pno (D flat maj) CRAMER
(Q17)
low solo,pno (C maj) CRAMER (Q18)
high solo,pno (F maj) CRAMER (Q19)
med-high solo,pno (E flat maj)
CRAMER (Q20)

QUE ALTOS LOS BALCONES see Halffter,
Rodolfo

QUE BIEN CANTA UN RUISENOR see Garcia
Morillo, Roberto

QUE CES LIEUX see Anonymous

QUE CHERCHEZ-VOUS see Lecocq, Charles

QUE CRAIGNEZ-VOUS see Rameau, Jean-
Philippe

QUE D'AVENTURES see Guiraud, Ernest

QUE DIEU M'ACCUEILLE AVEC LES OISEAUX
see Moortel, Arie van de

QUE DITES-VOUS MIGNONNE see Lacome,
Paul

QUE FAIT-TU MECHANTE SOPHIE? see
Levade, Charles (Gaston)

QUE JAMAIS MES YEUX see Charpentier,
Jean Jacques Beauvarlet

QUE JOYEUX PARAIT LE TEMPS see Bach,
Johann Sebastian

QUE L'AMOUR FASSE LUI-MEME see Mozart,
Wolfgang Amadeus

QUE LE CIEL EST TRISTE... see Quinet,
Marcel

QUE LE JOUR ME DURE see Rousseau, Jean-
Jacques

QUE LINDA SOIS! see Gomez Carrillo,
Manuel

QUE ME FAIT TOUTE LA TERRE? see De
Lara, Isadore

QUE ME FAIT TOUTE LA TERRE see Ropartz,
Joseph Guy

QUE ME HAS HECHO, QUE ME HAS HECHO! see
Jurafsky, Abraham

QUE MON AME MURMURE see Lacombe, Paul

QUE MON AME MURMURE see Pillois,
Jacques

QUE NE PUIS-JE COMME ELLEVIOU? see
Cuvillier, Charles

QUE NE SUIS-JE PLUTOT see Caryll, Ivan

QUE NE VEUX-TU? see Delmet, Paul

QUE SENTIS, CORACON MIO see Palau Boix,
M.

QUE VOIS-JE? UN PAVRE VOYEUR see
Debussy, Claude

QUEEN DIDO'S LAMENT see Purcell, Henry

QUEEN OF THE NIGHT see Mozart, Wolfgang
Amadeus

QUEEN OF THE ROSARY see Bangert, Em.

QUEEN'S EPICEDIUM, THE see Purcell,
Henry

QUEEN'S MARIES, THE *folk,Scot
solo,pno (D maj/E flat maj) PATERSON
FS128 s.p. (Q21)

QUEEN'S MARYS, THE *folk,Scot
(Roberton, Hugh S.) 3 soli,pno
ROBERTON 72087 s.p. (Q22)

QUEGLI ORCHIETTI see Dittersdorf, Karl
Ditters von

QUEL CONTINO E UN PO FURBETTO see
Dittersdorf, Karl Ditters von

QUEL FIER, TROUBLANT ET NOBLE PORT see
Maurat, Edmond

QUEL GALANT! see Ravel, Maurice

QUEL ROSIGNUOL CHE SI SOAVE PIANGE see
Pizzetti, Ildebrando

QUEL SGUARDO see Monteverdi, Claudio

QUELL' USIGNUOLO see Caldara, Antonio

QUELL'AMOR see Handel, George Frideric

QUELLE MAIN FAIT MOUVOIR MON CORPS see
Charpentier, Jean Jacques
Beauvarlet

QUELLE PLAINTE EN CES LIEUX M'APPELLE?
see Rameau, Jean-Philippe

QUELL'ONDA CHE ROVINA see Martini,
Giambattista

QUELQUES ENFANTS QUELQUES SOLDATS see
Ruyneman, Daniel

QUELQUES QUATRAINS EXTRAITS DU
CHANSONNIER DES GRACES DE 1828 see
Durand, Jacques

QUELS BIENS, JE FREMIS see Rameau,
Jean-Philippe

QUEM ME ESSE DICITIS see Schouwman,
Hans

QUEMADMODUM DESIDERAT see Schutz,
Heinrich

QUEMADMODUM DESIDERAT CERVUS see
Brossard, Sebastien de

QUEMADMODUM DESIDERAT CERVUS see
Campra, Andre

QUERCIA ANNOSA SULL'ERTE PENDICI see
Martini, Giambattista

QUERENDONA see Lopez-Buchardo, Carlos

QUERFELDEIN *CCU
(Zschiesche) 1-2 soli,gtr SCHOTTS
3587 s.p. (Q23)

QUEST see Smith, Eleanor

QUEST FOR GOD see Allen

QUESTA O QUELLA PER ME PARI SONO see
Verdi, Giuseppe

QUESTION see Mana-Zucca, Mme., Frage

QUESTIONER, THE see Schubert, Franz
(Peter), Der Neugierige

QUESTIONS see Lanier, Gary

QUESTIONS OF NATURE see Gideon, Miriam

QUESTO MIO BIANCO MANTO see Mascagni,
Pietro

QUESTO SIMBOLO DI FIOR see Hajos, Karl

QUESTS OF ODYSSEUS see Bottje, Will Gay

QUI COELI TERRAEQUE see Vivaldi,
Antonio

QUI DONC COMMANDE QUAND IL AIME see
Saint-Saens, Camille

QUI DONC ELEVE ICI LA VOIX see Saint-
Saens, Camille

QUI DONC VOUS A DONNE VOS YEUX? see
Godard, Benjamin Louis Paul

QUI DOVE AL GERMOGLIAR see Scarlatti,
Alessandro

QUI EST HOMO see Rossini, Gioacchino

QUI LA REGARDE DE MES YEUX see Menasce,
Jacques de

QUI LA VOCE SUA SOAVE see Bellini,
Vincenzo

QUI SOLA VERGIN ROSA see Flotow,
Friedrich von, Lezte Rose

QUICKEN ME, O LORD see Fischer, Irwin

QUID EST, CATULLE see Cattini, U.

QUIDDITIE, THE see Newlin, Dika

QUIEN TU VIESE TAL PODER see Pisador,
Diego

QUIERO DORMIR Y NO PUEDO see Ferguson,
Edwin Earle

QUIET see Sanderson, Wilfred

QUIET AIRS
med solo,pno PRESSER $2.00 (Q24)

QUIET AIRS see Bacon

QUIET COMPANY see Le Fleming,
Christopher (Kaye)

QUIET NIGHT, THE see Dunhill, Thomas
Frederick

QUIET OF THE WOODS see Reger, Max,
Waldeinsamkeit

QUIET PLACE, A *CC12L
(Carmichael, Ralph) solo,pno WORD
37550 $2.50 (Q25)

QUIET PLACE, A see Carmichael, Ralph

QUIETE see Tocchi, Gian-Luca

QUIETLY AS ROSEBUDS see Sutherland,
Margaret

QUIETUDE see O'Conner, Frederick

QU'IL EST BEAU MON PAYS see Pascal,
Andre

QU'IL EST EXQUIS TON AMOUR see Canal,
Marguerite

QUILTER, ROGER (1877-1953)
Arnold Book Of Old Songs *CCU
(Britten; Pears) solo,pno BOOSEY
$3.50 (Q26)

Ash Grove
solo,pno (A flat maj) BOOSEY $1.50
(Q27)

Barbara Allen
solo,pno (D maj) BOOSEY $1.50 (Q28)

Believe Me, If All Those Endearing
Young Charms
solo,pno (E flat maj) BOOSEY $1.50
(Q29)

Blow, Blow, Thou Winter Wind
high solo,pno (E maj) BOOSEY $1.50
(Q30)
low solo,pno (C maj) BOOSEY $1.50
(Q31)

Cradle In Bethlehem, The
2 soli,pno/orch ROBERTON 72221 s.p.
(Q32)

Dream Valley
high solo,pno (D maj) BOOSEY $1.50
(Q33)
high solo,pno (F maj) BOOSEY $1.50
(Q34)

Drink To Me Only With Thine Eyes
low solo,pno (E flat maj) BOOSEY
$1.50 (Q35)
high solo,pno (G flat maj) BOOSEY
$1.50 (Q36)
med solo,pno (F maj) BOOSEY $1.50
(Q37)

Fair House Of Joy
high solo,pno (D flat maj) BOOSEY
$1.50 (Q38)
med solo,pno (B flat maj) BOOSEY

QUILTER, ROGER (cont'd.)

$1.50   (Q39)
low solo,pno (A flat maj) BOOSEY
$1.50   (Q40)

Five Shakespeare Songs *CC5U
(Britten; Pears) high solo/low
solo,pno BOOSEY $3.75   (Q41)

Fuchsia Tree
low solo,pno (A min) BOOSEY $1.75
(Q42)
high solo,pno (C sharp min) BOOSEY
$1.75   (Q43)
med solo,pno (B min) BOOSEY $1.75
(Q44)

Hark! Hark! The Lark
solo,pno (F maj) BOOSEY $1.50 (Q45)

I Arise From Dreams Of Thee
solo,pno (C min) BOOSEY $1.50 (Q46)

I Will Go With My Father A-Ploughing
low solo,pno ELKIN 27.1425.06 s.p.
(Q47)

Jealous Lover
solo,pno (C maj) BOOSEY $1.50 (Q48)

Jocund Dance, The
T solo,pno ELKIN 27.0791.08 s.p.
(Q49)

June
low solo,pno (D maj) BOOSEY $1.50
(Q50)
high solo,pno (F maj) BOOSEY $1.50
(Q51)
med solo,pno (E maj) BOOSEY $1.50
(Q52)

Love's Philosophy
med solo,pno (D maj) BOOSEY $1.50
(Q53)
low solo,pno (C maj) BOOSEY $1.50
(Q54)
high solo,pno (F maj) BOOSEY $1.50
(Q55)

Music, When Soft Voices Die
solo,pno (A flat maj) BOOSEY $1.50
(Q56)

My Lady Greensleeves
solo,pno (F min) BOOSEY $1.50 (Q57)

Non Nobis, Domine
solo,pno (C maj) BOOSEY $1.50 (Q58)

Now Sleeps The Crimson Petal
high solo,pno (G flat maj) BOOSEY
(Q59)
med-high solo,pno (F maj) BOOSEY
$1.25   (Q60)
med solo,pno (E flat maj) BOOSEY
$1.25   (Q61)
low solo,pno (D maj) BOOSEY $1.25
(Q62)
low solo,pno (E flat maj) WILLIS
$.75   (Q63)
high solo,pno (F maj) WILLIS $.75
(Q64)

O Daisies
high solo,pno (D flat maj) BOOSEY
$1.50   (Q65)
low solo,pno (B flat maj) BOOSEY
$1.50   (Q66)

O Mistress Mine
high solo,pno (G maj) BOOSEY $1.50
(Q67)
low solo,pno (E flat maj) BOOSEY
$1.50   (Q68)

Old Carol
high solo,pno (G flat maj) BOOSEY
$1.50   (Q69)
low solo,pno (D maj) BOOSEY $1.50
(Q70)

One Word Is Too Often Profaned
solo,pno (G maj) ROBERTON 2562 s.p.
(Q71)

Over The Land Is April
med solo,pno ELKIN 27.1310.01 s.p.
(Q72)

Over The Mountains
high solo,pno (A maj) BOOSEY $1.50
(Q73)
low solo,pno (G maj) BOOSEY $1.50
(Q74)

Seven Elizabethan Lyrics *CC7U
high solo/low solo,pno BOOSEY $4.00
(Q75)

Spring Is At The Door
med solo,pno ELKIN 27.0813.02 s.p.
(Q76)
low solo,pno ELKIN 27.0812.04 s.p.
(Q77)

Three Shakespeare Songs *CC3U
high solo/low solo,pno BOOSEY $3.75
(Q78)

QU'IMPORTE! see Delmet, Paul

QUINCE CANCIONES DE LAS PROVINCIAS DE
FRANCIA *CC15L,Fr
(Thiriet) [Fr/Span] solo,pno RICORDI-
ARG BA 10817 s.p.   (Q79)

QUINDICI COMPOSIZIONI DA CAMERA see
Bellini, Vincenzo

QUINDICI POESIE T'ANG see Abbado,
Marcello

QUINET, MARCEL (1915-   )
Arche De Noe
med solo,pno cmplt ed CBDM s.p.
contains: La Tortue; Le Boa; Le
Carabe; Le Lapin; Le Percheron;
L'ecureuil   (Q80)

Automne
see Chanson De Quatre Saisons

Chanson De Quatre Saisons
S/A/Bar solo,pno cmplt ed CBDM s.p.
contains: Automne; Ete; Hiver;
Printemps   (Q81)

Dans Les Herbes...
see Quatre Hai-Kai

Ete
see Chanson De Quatre Saisons

Hiver
see Chanson De Quatre Saisons

La Lune Etait Tres Haute...
see Quatre Hai-Kai

La Tortue
see Arche De Noe

Le Boa
see Arche De Noe

Le Carabe
see Arche De Noe

Le Lapin
see Arche De Noe

Le Percheron
see Arche De Noe

L'ecureuil
see Arche De Noe

Legerement Le Bambou Remuait
see Quatre Hai-Kai

Printemps
see Chanson De Quatre Saisons

Quatre Hai-Kai
Mez solo,pno cmplt ed CBDM s.p.
contains: Dans Les Herbes...; La
Lune Etait Tres Haute...;
Legerement Le Bambou Remuait;
Que Le Ciel Est Triste... (Q82)

Que Le Ciel Est Triste...
see Quatre Hai-Kai

QUINTETO DE LA CARTA see Luna, P.

QUINZE CHANSONS DE BILITIS, VOL. I see
Dandelot, [Georges]

QUINZE CHANSONS DE BILITIS, VOL. II see
Dandelot, [Georges]

QUINZE CHANSONS DE BILITIS, VOL. III
see Dandelot, [Georges]

QUINZE CHANSONS, VOL. I see Delmet,
Paul

QUINZE CHANSONS, VOL. II see Delmet,
Paul

QUINZE CHANSONS, VOLS. I & II see
Delmet, Paul

QUINZE LIEDER, CAHIER I see Wolf, Hugo

QUINZE LIEDER, CAHIER II see Wolf, Hugo

QUINZE MELODIES see Messager, Andre

QUITTEZ PASTEURS see Hazelhurst, Cecil

QUODLIBET see Bach, Johann Sebastian

QUOI! VOUS PARTEZ SI TOT see Saint-
Saens, Camille

R

RAAB
Bjorkens Visa
solo,pno LUNDQUIST s.p.   (R1)

RABAUD, HENRI (1873-1949)
Chanson
solo,pno (available in 2 keys)
ENOCH s.p.   (R2)

Crepuscule
solo,pno ENOCH s.p.   (R3)

Miserere Mei *sac
[Lat] solo,pno/org/vln&harp/vcl&
harp (available in 2 keys) ENOCH
s.p.   (R4)

Priere
solo,pno ENOCH s.p.   (R5)

Tu M'as Dit
solo,pno ENOCH s.p.   (R6)

RABBI AKIBA see Feldman, Morton

RABBI AKIBA see Werner, E.

RABBI SHIMON see Werner, E.

RABBI TARPHON see Werner, E.

RABEY, RENE
A Ceux De La-Bas
solo,pno/inst DURAND s.p.   (R7)

Adoration
solo,pno/inst DURAND s.p.   (R8)

Apaisement
high solo,pno/inst DURAND s.p. (R9)

Au Fond Des Forets Endormies
med solo,vln/vcl DURAND s.p.   (R10)
med solo,pno/inst DURAND s.p. (R11)

Au Matin Clair
Mez/Bar solo,pno/inst (in 2 keys)
DURAND s.p.   (R12)

Au Pays Du Reve
S/T solo,pno/inst DURAND s.p. (R13)
Mez/Bar solo,pno/inst DURAND s.p.
(R14)

Au Trot
solo,pno/inst DURAND s.p.   (R15)

Automne
Mez solo,pno/inst DURAND s.p. (R16)

Berceuse De L'Oubli
A solo,pno/inst DURAND s.p.   (R17)

Ce Que J'aimais Le Mieux En Toi
solo,pno/inst DURAND s.p.   (R18)

Chanson Breve
solo,pno/inst DURAND s.p.   (R19)

Chanson D'Avril
med solo,vln/vcl DURAND s.p.   (R20)
med solo,pno/inst DURAND s.p. (R21)

Chanson Naive
med solo,pno/inst DURAND s.p. (R22)

Dors, Ma Poupee
solo,pno/inst DURAND s.p.   (R23)

En Un Joli Voyage
med solo,pno/inst DURAND s.p. (R24)

Idylle Legere
med solo,pno/inst DURAND s.p. (R25)

J'aurais Tant De Choses A Dire
med solo,pno/inst DURAND s.p. (R26)

Je Fis Un Reve
solo,pno/inst DURAND s.p. see from
L'Ame En Fleur   (R27)

La Derniere Flamme
med solo,pno/inst DURAND s.p. (R28)

La Minute Heureuse
solo,pno/inst DURAND s.p. see from
L'Ame En Fleur   (R29)

La Rose
med solo,pno/inst DURAND s.p. (R30)

L'Adorable Hantise
Mez/Bar solo,pno/inst DURAND s.p.
(R31)
S/T solo,pno/inst DURAND s.p. (R32)

RABEY, RENE (cont'd.)

L'Ame En Fleur *see Je Fis Un Reve;
La Minute Heureuse; Lettres
Aimees (R33)

Le Chanson Des Promis
solo,pno/inst DURAND s.p. (R34)

Le Chanson Du Sabotier
solo,pno/inst DURAND s.p. (R35)

Le Chant De Labour
med solo,pno/inst DURAND s.p. (R36)

Le Moulin D'amour
solo,pno/inst DURAND s.p. (R37)

Le Papillon
solo,opt vln DURAND s.p. (R38)

Le Vent De Mai
med solo,pno/inst DURAND s.p. (R39)

Les Etoiles D'Or
med solo,pno/inst DURAND s.p. (R40)

Les Lettres
solo,pno/inst DURAND s.p. (R41)

Les Reves
med solo,pno/inst DURAND s.p. (R42)

Lettres Aimees
solo,pno/inst DURAND s.p. see from
L'Ame En Fleur (R43)

L'inutile Serment
med solo,pno/inst DURAND s.p. (R44)

Lise
med solo,pno/inst DURAND s.p. (R45)

Madame, A Vos Vertus
med solo,pno/inst DURAND s.p. (R46)

Nocturne
med solo,pno,vln,vcl DURAND s.p.
(R47)

Obsession
med solo,pno/inst DURAND s.p. (R48)

Ombre Des Bois
med solo,pno/inst DURAND s.p. (R49)

Resignation
med solo,pno/inst DURAND s.p. (R50)

Reves Du Soir
med solo,pno/inst DURAND s.p. (R51)

Rondel Melancholique
Mez/Bar solo,pno/inst DURAND s.p.
(R52)

Serenade
Mez solo,pno/inst DURAND s.p. (R53)

Si Je Ne Dois Jamais
T solo,pno/inst DURAND s.p. (R54)

Si Je Ne T'aimais Pas
solo,pno/inst DURAND s.p. (R55)

Si Matin, D'ou Viens-Tu
med solo,pno/inst DURAND s.p. (R56)

Si Tu Le Veux
Mez/Bar solo,pno/inst DURAND s.p.
(R57)

Ta Bouche
solo,pno/inst DURAND s.p. (R58)

Tes Yeux
high solo,opt vln/orch DURAND s.p.,
ipr (R59)
med solo,pno/inst DURAND s.p. (R60)
[Fr] solo,acap oct DURAND s.p.
(R61)

Toi
high solo,pno/inst DURAND s.p.
(R62)

Voeux
S/T solo,pno/inst DURAND s.p. (R63)
Mez/Bar solo,pno/inst DURAND s.p.
(R64)

Votre Sourire
solo,pno/inst DURAND s.p. (R65)

Vous M'aimiez, Je Vous Aimais
med solo,pno/inst DURAND s.p. (R66)

Voyage
solo,pno ENOCH s.p. (R67)

Yanina
solo,pno (available in 2 keys)
ENOCH s.p. (R68)
solo,acap (available in 2 keys)
ENOCH s.p. (R69)

RABOTAI, HA'HISTORIA CHOZERET *CCU
solo,pno OR-TAV $3.50 (R70)

RACCOLTA DI CANTI ITALIANI *CC6U
solo,perc,pno BERBEN 1624 s.p. (R71)

RACCOLTA DI MUSICHE MONODICHE E
MELODICHE POCO DIVULGATE see
Pratella, Francesco Balilla

RACE, THE see Wolfe, Lanny

RACHEL see Berkeley, Lennox

RACHEL, QUAND DU SEIGNEUR LA GRACE
TUTELAIRE see Halevy, [Jacques-
Francois-Fromental-Elie]

RACHELINA - NOTARO see Paisiello,
Giovanni

RACHETY COO! see Friml, Rudolf

RACHMANINOFF, SERGEY VASSILIEVITCH
(1873-1943)
Album Of Four Songs
[Swed/Eng] med solo,kbd CHESTER
s.p.
contains: Harvest Of Sorrow, The,
Op.4,No.5; In The Silent Night,
Op.4,No.3; Soldier's Wife, The,
Op.8,No.4; Spring Waters,
Op.14,No.11 (R72)

Album Of Songs *sac,CCU
BOSTON high solo,pno $2.50; low
solo,pno $2.50 (R73)

Alder Tree, The
high solo,pno BELWIN $1.50 (R74)

All Once I Gladly Owned
[Eng/Fr/Russ/Ger] solo,pno (F sharp
min) BOOSEY $1.75 (R75)

All Things Depart *Op.26,No.15
[Eng/Fr/Russ/Ger] high solo,pno (F
min) BOOSEY $1.75 (R76)
[Eng/Fr/Russ/Ger] low solo,pno (E
flat min) BOOSEY $1.75 (R77)

Answer, The *Op.14,No.9
[Eng/Fr/Russ/Ger] high solo,pno (D
flat maj) BOOSEY $1.75 (R78)
[Eng/Fr/Russ/Ger] low solo,pno (B
flat maj) BOOSEY $1.75 (R79)

As Fair As Day In Blaze Of Noon
[Eng/Fr/Russ/Ger] solo,pno (E flat
maj) BOOSEY $1.75 (R80)

At Night
med solo,pno (D maj) ALLANS s.p.
(R81)
high solo,pno (A maj) ALLANS s.p.
(R82)

Before The Image *Op.21,No.10
[Eng/Fr/Russ/Ger] low solo,pno (E
flat min) BOOSEY $1.75 (R83)
[Eng/Fr/Russ/Ger] high solo,pno (F
sharp min) BOOSEY $1.75 (R84)

Beloved, Let Us Fly *Op.26,No.5
[Eng/Fr/Russ/Ger] low solo,pno (F
maj) BOOSEY $1.75 (R85)
[Eng/Fr/Russ/Ger] high solo,pno (A
flat maj) BOOSEY $1.75 (R86)

Christ Is Risen *Op.26,No.6, sac
"Christ Is Risen" low solo,pno
GALAXY 1.1286.7 $1.00 (R87)
"Christ Is Risen" high solo/med
solo,pno GALAXY 1.1287.7 $1.25
(R88)
"Christ Is Risen" [Eng/Fr/Russ/Ger]
low solo,pno (F min) BOOSEY $1.75
(R89)
"Christ Is Risen" [Eng/Fr/Russ/Ger]
high solo,pno (G min) BOOSEY
$1.75 (R90)
"Der Herr Erstand" Mez solo,pno
BREITKOPF-L DLV 5924 s.p. (R91)

Christ Is Risen *see Christ Is Risen

Das Inselchen *see Little Island,
The

Der Herr Erstand *see Christ Is
Risen

Dream, The
high solo,pno BELWIN $1.50 (R92)

Floods Of Spring *see Spring Waters

Fountain, The
(Farrar) high solo,pno BELWIN $1.50
(R93)

Fruhlingsfluten *see Spring Waters

Glorious Forever *sac
low solo,pno (E flat maj) BOSTON
$1.50 (R94)

Harvest Of Sorrow, The *Op.4,No.5
"Harvest Of Sorrow, The" see Album
Of Four Songs
"O Du Wogendes Feld" S/T solo,pno
BREITKOPF-L DLV 5921 s.p. (R95)
"Oh, Thou Waving Field Of Golden
Grain" high solo,pno BELWIN $1.50

RACHMANINOFF, SERGEY VASSILIEVITCH
(cont'd.)
(R96)
Harvest Of Sorrow, The *see Harvest
Of Sorrow, The

Heart's Secret
[Eng/Fr/Russ/Ger] solo,pno (D flat
maj) BOOSEY $1.75 (R97)

Here Beauty Dwells
[Russ/Eng] high solo,pno BELWIN
$1.50 (R98)

How Fair This Spot
[Eng/Fr/Russ/Ger] solo,pno (F maj)
BOOSEY $1.75 (R99)

In The Silent Night *Op.4,No.3
see Album Of Four Songs
[Eng/Fr/Russ/Ger] low solo,pno (D
maj) BOOSEY $1.75 (R100)
high solo,pno (F maj) SCHIRM.G $.85
(R101)
[Eng/Fr/Russ/Ger] high solo,pno (F
maj) BOOSEY $1.75 (R102)

Let Me Rest Here Alone *Op.26,No.9
[Eng/Fr/Russ/Ger] solo,pno (C min)
BOOSEY $1.75 (R103)

Lilacs *Op.21,No.5
low solo,pno (E maj) BOSTON $1.50
(R104)
high solo,pno (A flat maj) BOSTON
$1.50 (R105)
[Eng/Fr/Russ/Ger] high solo,pno (A
flat maj) BOOSEY $1.75 (R106)
[Eng/Fr/Russ/Ger] low solo,pno (E
flat maj) BOOSEY $1.75 (R107)

Little Island, The *Op.14,No.2
"Das Inselchen" S/T solo,pno
BREITKOPF-L DLV 5922 s.p. (R108)
"Little Island, The" [Eng/Fr/Russ/
Ger] high solo,pno (G maj) BOOSEY
$1.75 (R109)
"Little Island, The" [Eng/Fr/Russ/
Ger] low solo,pno (E maj) BOOSEY
$1.75 (R110)

Little Island, The *see Little
Island, The

Midsummer Nights *Op.4,No.2
[Eng/Fr/Russ/Ger] solo,pno (C maj)
BOOSEY $1.75 (R111)

Mirage, The
med solo,pno BELWIN $1.50 (R112)

Morning *Op.4,No.2
high solo,pno BELWIN $1.50 (R113)
low solo,pno BELWIN $1.50 (R114)
med solo,pno BELWIN $1.50 (R115)

My Lovely Maiden, Sing No More *see
Oh, Never Sing To Me Again

Night Is Mournful *Op.26,No.12
[Eng/Fr/Russ/Ger] solo,pno (A min)
BOOSEY $1.75 (R116)

No Prophet
[Eng/Fr/Russ/Ger] high solo,pno (E
flat maj) BOOSEY $1.75 (R117)
[Eng/Fr/Russ/Ger] low solo,pno (D
flat maj) BOOSEY $1.75 (R118)

O Du Wogendes Feld *see Harvest Of
Sorrow, The

O Sing No More *see Oh, Never Sing
To Me Again

O Stay, My Love, Forsake Me Not
*Op.4,No.1
[Eng/Fr/Russ/Ger] low solo,pno (D
min) BOOSEY $1.75 (R119)
[Eng/Fr/Russ/Ger] high solo,pno (E
min) BOOSEY $1.75 (R120)

Oh, Never Sing To Me Again *Op.4,
No.4
[Eng/Fr/Russ/Ger] high solo,pno (A
min) BOOSEY $1.75 (R121)
[Eng/Fr/Russ/Ger] low solo,pno (F
sharp min) BOOSEY $1.75 (R122)
"My Lovely Maiden, Sing No More"
[Eng/Russ] S/T solo,kbd CHESTER
s.p. (R123)
"O Sing No More" high solo,pno (G
min) ALLANS s.p. (R124)
"O Sing No More" low solo,pno (E
min) ALLANS s.p. (R125)

Oh, Thou Waving Field Of Golden Grain
*see Harvest Of Sorrow, The

Reverie
high solo,pno BELWIN $1.50 (R126)

So Many Hours, So Many Fancies
[Eng/Fr/Russ/Ger] low solo,pno (E
maj) BOOSEY $1.75 (R127)

RACHMANINOFF, SERGEY VASSILIEVITCH
(cont'd.)

  [Eng/Fr/Russ/Ger] high solo,pno (G
    maj) BOOSEY $1.75   (R128)

Soldier's Wife, The *Op.8,No.4
  see Album Of Four Songs
  [Eng/Fr/Russ/Ger] high solo,pno (A
    min) BOOSEY $1.75   (R129)
  [Eng/Fr/Russ/Ger] low solo,pno (G
    min) BOOSEY $1.75   (R130)

Songs Of Sergei Rachmaninoff, Vol. 1:
  Op. 4 To Op. 21 *CCU
  solo,pno BOOSEY $12.00 with
    original, Russian and English
    texts   (R131)

Songs Of Sergei Rachmaninoff, Vol. 2:
  Op. 26 To Op. 38 *CCU
  solo,pno BOOSEY $12.00 with
    original, Russian and English
    texts   (R132)

Songs Vol. 1: Op. 4, 8, 14, 21 *CCU
  solo,pno BOOSEY $12.00   (R133)

Songs, Vol. 2: Op. 26, 34, 38 *CCU
  solo,pno BOOSEY $12.00   (R134)

Spring Waters *Op.14,No.11
  "Spring Waters" see Album Of Four
    Songs
  "Floods Of Spring" high solo,pno (E
    flat maj) SCHIRM.G $.85   (R135)
  "Floods Of Spring" [Eng/Ger] low
    solo,pno PRESSER $.75   (R136)
  "Fruhlingsfluten" S/T solo,pno
    BREITKOPF-L DLV 5923 s.p. (R137)
  "Spring Waters" [Eng/Fr/Russ/Ger]
    high solo,pno (E flat maj) BOOSEY
    $1.75   (R138)
  "Spring Waters" [Eng/Fr/Russ/Ger]
    low solo,pno (D flat maj) BOOSEY
    $1.75   (R139)

Spring Waters *see Spring Waters

Spring's Return
  low solo,pno (B flat maj) ALLANS
    s.p.   (R140)
  high solo,pno (D flat maj) ALLANS
    s.p.   (R141)

Three Russian Folk Songs *CC3U
  solo,pno BELWIN $1.50   (R142)

Thy Pity I Implore *Op.26,No.8
  [Eng/Fr/Russ/Ger] low solo,pno (F
    sharp min) BOOSEY $1.75   (R143)
  [Eng/Fr/Russ/Ger] high solo,pno (A
    min) BOOSEY $1.75   (R144)

To The Children *Op.26,No.7
  [Eng/Fr/Russ/Ger] low solo,pno (F
    maj) BOOSEY $1.75   (R145)
  [Eng/Fr/Russ/Ger] high solo,pno (G
    maj) BOOSEY $1.75   (R146)

Tryst, The
  high solo,pno BELWIN $1.50   (R147)

Twelve Selected Songs, Op. 4, 14, 21,
  26, 34 *CCU
  [Eng/Fr/Russ/Ger] high solo/med
    solo,pno BOOSEY $4.25   (R148)

Vocalise *Op.34,No.14
  S/T solo,pno BREITKOPF-L DLV 5925
    s.p.   (R149)
  high solo,pno (C sharp min)
    SCHIRM.G $.85   (R150)
  med-low solo,pno (A min) SCHIRM.G
    $.85   (R151)
  [Eng/Fr/Russ/Ger] low solo,pno (A
    min) BOOSEY $1.75   (R152)
  [Eng/Fr/Russ/Ger] high solo,pno (C
    sharp min) BOOSEY $1.75   (R153)

RADAUER, IRMFRIED (1928-   )
  Siau-Tschu
    S,narrator,pic,fl,English horn,sax,
    3perc,harp,cel,vln,bvl,gtr study
    sc PETERS 5810 $6.00   (R154)

RADCLIFFE, PHILIP (FITZHUGH)
  (1905-   )
  Shepherd Boy's Song, The
    solo,pno CRAMER $1.15   (R155)

RADER
  Only Believe *sac
    (Presley, Elvis) solo,pno WORD
    S-307   (R156)
    (Roe, Gloria) solo,pno WORD S-176
                               (R157)

RADIC, DUSAN (1929-   )
  Index *see Spisak

  Spisak
    "Index" SMez soli,3ob,3sax,bass
    clar,harp,2perc,bvl MUSIC INFO
    rental   (R158)

RAE, KENNETH
  Crown, The
    low solo,pno (F maj) ASHDOWN s.p.
                               (R159)
    high solo,pno (B flat maj) ASHDOWN
      s.p.   (R160)
    med-high solo,pno (A flat maj)
      ASHDOWN s.p.   (R161)
    med solo,pno (G maj) ASHDOWN s.p.
                               (R162)

RAEBECK
  Elizabethan Song Bag, An *CCU
    soli,rec,gtr,Orff inst. MARKS $3.00
                               (R163)

RAEBEL, M.
  Harpolekarens Karlekssang
    solo,pno GEHRMANS s.p.   (R164)

  Jul *Xmas
    solo,pno GEHRMANS s.p.   (R165)

RAFF, JOSEPH JOACHIM (1822-1882)
  Ingen Vag Ar For Lang
    high solo,pno GEHRMANS s.p. (R166)
    low solo,pno GEHRMANS s.p. (R167)

  Serenade
    [Eng/Ger] low solo,pno (F maj)
      CRAMER   (R168)
    [Eng/Ger] high solo,pno (A flat
      maj) CRAMER   (R169)

RAGAMALIKA see Delage, Maurice

RAGMAN, THE see Buchanan, George

RAGNA see Grieg, Edvard Hagerup

RAGTIME PIPE OF PAN, THE see Romberg,
  Sigmund

RAGTIME SONGBOOK, THE *CC50U
  (Charters, Ann) solo,pno/gtr OAK
    000086 $3.95 contains works by:
    Joplin, Scott; Cannon, Hughie;
    Harney, Ben; Marion, Will; Rogers,
    Alex and others   (R170)

RAGWORT, THE see Bliss, Sir Arthur

RAICHL, MIROSLAV (1930-   )
  Tri Pisne Na Slova N. Guillena *CC3U
    Bar solo,fl,clar,pno,perc,gtr,bvl
    CZECH s.p.   (R171)

RAIL NO MORE, YE LEARNED ASSES see
  Boyce, William

RAILS see Middeleer, Jean De

RAILS see Middeleer, Jean De, Rails

RAIN see Curran, Pearl Gildersleeve

RAIN! see Russell, Kennedy

RAIN AT NIGHT see Weigl, Vally,
  Regennacht

RAIN COMES DOWN see Fink, Michael

RAIN FAIRY see Arundale, Claude

RAIN HAS FALLEN see Barber, Samuel

RAIN HAS FALLEN ALL THE DAY see Ward,
  Robert

RAIN IN SPRING see Rorem, Ned

RAIN IN SUMMER see Weigl, Vally

RAIN OF PEACE see Red, Buryl

RAINBOW, THE see Thiman, Eric Harding

RAINDROPS see Bantock, Granville

RAINDROPS see Kelly, Robert

RAISING OF LAZARUS, THE see Barker

RAJ DOMOVA see Doubrava, Jaroslav

RAJA- JA ITAKARJALAISIA KANSANLAULUJA
  *CCU
  (Hannikaninen) solo,pno FAZER W 3399
    s.p.   (R172)

RAK HA-YAREACH
  solo,pno OR-TAV $.50   (R173)

RAKASTAN KAUNEUTTA see Kilpinen, Yrio

RAKKAUS see Merikanto, Oskar

RAKOW, NIKOLAJ
  Estnische Lieder *CCU
    solo,pno SIKORSKI R 6314 s.p.
                               (R174)

RALF, EINAR
  Bohemia
    solo,pno GEHRMANS s.p.   (R175)

RALSTON, BOB
  Rising Of The Sun, The *sac
    solo,pno WORD S-415   (R176)

RAMASASIRI see Straesser, Joep

RAMBLIN' BOY AND OTHER SONGS *CC40U,
  folk
  (Paxton, Tom) solo,pno/gtr OAK 000007
    $2.95   (R177)

RAMBO
  Build My Mansion *sac
    solo,pno BENSON S5234-S $1.00
                               (R178)

  Don't Take My Cross Away *sac
    solo,pno BENSON S5384-S $1.00
                               (R179)

  He Restoreth My Soul *sac
    solo,pno BENSON S5710-S $1.00
                               (R180)

  I Just Came To Talk With You, Lord
    *sac
    solo,pno BENSON S6052-S $1.00
                               (R181)

  If That Isn't Love *sac
    solo,pno BENSON S6488-S $1.00
                               (R182)

  It's Me Again, Lord *sac
    solo,pno BENSON S6668-S $1.00
                               (R183)

  Mama's Teaching Angels How To Sing
    *sac
    solo,pno BENSON S7012-S $1.00
                               (R184)

  One More Valley (composed with Davis)
    *sac
    solo,pno BENSON S7296-S $1.00
                               (R185)

  Prisoner Of Love *sac
    solo,pno BENSON S7404-S $1.00
                               (R186)

  Promises *sac
    solo,pno BENSON S7405-S $1.00
                               (R187)

  Remind Me, Dear Lord *sac
    solo,pno BENSON S7420-S $1.00
                               (R188)

  Sacred Treasures *sac
    solo,pno BENSON S7443-S $1.00
                               (R189)

  Sheltered In The Arms Of God
    (composed with Davis) *sac
    solo,pno BENSON S7476-S $1.00
                               (R190)

  Tears Will Never Stain The Streets Of
    That City *sac
    solo,pno BENSON S7685-S $1.00
                               (R191)

  Thank You For The Valley *sac
    solo,pno BENSON S7708-S $1.00
                               (R192)

RAMBO, DOTTIE
  Dottie Rambo-Songbook *sac,CC11UL
    solo,pno BENSON BO820 $2.50 (R193)

  If That Isn't Love *sac,CC15L
    solo,pno BENSON BO823 $2.50 (R194)

RAMBO, REBA
  Resurrection *sac,CC12L
    solo,pno BENSON BO825 $2.95 (R195)

RAMEAU, JEAN-PHILIPPE (1683-1764)
  A L'amour, Rendez Les Armes (from
    Hippolyte Et Aricie)
    [Fr] solo,acap oct DURAND s.p.
                               (R196)

  Ah! Que Me Faites-Vous Entendre (from
    Les Indes Galantes)
    Bar solo,pno/inst DURAND s.p.
                               (R197)

  Air De Pollux (from Castor Et Pollux)
    solo,orch HENN s.p.   (R198)

  Air Du Rossignol (from Hippolyte Et
    Aricie)
    Mez solo,orch DURAND s.p., ipr
                               (R199)

  Airs Extraits Des Oeuvres Completes
    Vol. I *CCU
    med solo,pno/inst oct DURAND s.p.
                               (R200)

  Airs Extraits Des Oeuvres Completes
    Vol. II *CCU
    high solo,pno/inst oct DURAND s.p.
                               (R201)

  Amour, Quand Tu Veux Nous Surprendre
    (from Dardanus)
    see Arien Aus Opern, Arien Fur
    Tenor Band I

  Apres Ces Discours Menacants (from
    Aquilon Et Orithie)
    Bar solo,cont DURAND s.p. (R202)

  Aquilon Et Orithie *cant
    Bar solo,cont DURAND s.p. (R203)

  Arien Aus Opern, Arien Fur Sopran
    Band I *sec,CC7L
    cmplt ed MUS. RARA MR 1221 s.p.
                               (R204)

  Arien Aus Opern, Arien Fur Tenor Band
    I *sec
    cmplt ed MUS. RARA MR 1259 s.p.

RAMEAU, JEAN-PHILIPPE (cont'd.)

contains: Amour, Quand Tu Veux
Nous Surprendre (from
Dardanus); Dans Nos Jeux (from
Zais); Fatal Amour (from
Pygmalion); Que Craignez-Vous
(from Zephyre); Regne Amour
(from Pygmalion)   (R205)

Aux Langueurs D'Apollon (from
Plantee)
S solo,pno/inst DURAND s.p. (R206)

Complete Works *CCU
(Saint-Saens, Camille; Malherbe,
Ch.; Emmanuel, M.; Teneo, M.)
contains works for a variety of
instruments and vocal
combinations microfiche
UNIV.MUS.ED. reprints of
Breitkopf & Hartel Editions;
contains 18 volumes; $220.00
(R207)

Cruelle Mere Des Amours (from
Hippolyte Et Aricie)
S solo,pno/inst DURAND s.p. (R208)

Dans Nos Jeux (from Zais)
see Arien Aus Opern, Arien Fur
Tenor Band I

Der Treue Schafer *see Le Berger
Fidele

Diane Et Acteon *cant
S solo,cont DURAND s.p.   (R209)

Dieu! Pourquoi Separer Deux Coeurs
(from Hippolyte Et Aricie)
S solo,pno/inst DURAND s.p. (R210)

Du Dieu Amour (from Les Amans Trahis)
solo,pno/inst DURAND s.p.   (R211)

Fatal Amour (from Pygmalion)
see Arien Aus Opern, Arien Fur
Tenor Band I

Forets Paisibles (from Les Indes
Galantes)
ST soli,pno/inst DURAND s.p. (R212)

Gavotte Chantee, A L'Amour Rendez Les
Armes (from Hippolyte Et Aricie)
Mez solo,pno/inst DURAND s.p.
(R213)

Invocation Et Hymne Au Soleil (from
Les Indes Galantes)
B solo,pno/inst DURAND s.p. (R214)

La Musette *cant
Bar solo,cont DURAND s.p.   (R215)

Le Berger Fidele *cant
S solo,cont DURAND s.p.   (R216)
(Bernstein) "Der Treue Schafer"
[Fr/Ger] high solo,2vln,cont sc
DEUTSCHER 9506 s.p., ipa   (R217)

Le Grillon
see LA MUSIQUE, SIXIEME CAHIER

Le Tambourin
(Pagans, L.) solo,pno/inst DURAND
s.p.   (R218)

Les Amants Trahis *cant
TBar soli,vcl DURAND s.p., ipa see
from DOUZE DOUS   (R219)

Les Oiseaux D'alentour (from
L'Impatience)
T solo,cont DURAND s.p.   (R220)

L'Impatience *cant
T solo,cont DURAND s.p.   (R221)

Menuet Chante (from Castor Et Pollux)
T solo,cor,pno/inst DURAND cmplt ed
s.p., cor pts s.p.   (R222)

O Jour Affreux (from Dardanus)
S solo,pno/inst DURAND s.p. (R223)

Orphee *cant
S solo,cont DURAND s.p.   (R224)

Papillon Inconstant (from Les Indes
Galantes)
S solo,pno/inst DURAND s.p. (R225)

Permettez, Astre Du Jour (from Les
Indes Galantes)
B solo,pno/inst DURAND s.p. (R226)

Quand L'aquilon Fougueux (from
Dardanus)
S solo,pno/inst DURAND s.p. (R227)

Que Craignez-Vous (from Zephyre)
see Arien Aus Opern, Arien Fur
Tenor Band I

RAMEAU, JEAN-PHILIPPE (cont'd.)

Quelle Plainte En Ces Lieux
M'appelle? (from Hippolyte Et
Aricie)
S solo,pno/inst DURAND s.p. (R228)

Quels Biens, Je Fremis (from
Hippolyte Et Aricie)
B solo,pno/inst DURAND s.p. (R229)
Bar solo,pno/inst DURAND s.p.
(R230)

Regne Amour (from Pygmalion)
see Arien Aus Opern, Arien Fur
Tenor Band I

Regnez, Plaisirs Et Jeux (from Les
Indes Galantes)
Mez solo,pno/inst DURAND s.p.
(R231)

Sejour De L'eternelle Paix (from
Castor Et Pollux)
Bar solo,pno/inst DURAND s.p.
(R232)
T solo,pno/inst DURAND s.p. (R233)

Tambourin
(Truillet-Soyer, M.) 2 soli,pno
DURAND s.p. see from DOUZE DOUS
(R234)

Temple Sacre (from Hippolyte Et
Aricie)
Mez solo,pno/inst DURAND s.p.
(R235)

Thetis *cant
Bar solo,cont DURAND s.p.   (R236)

Trio Des Parques (from Hippolyte Et
Aricie)
ATB soli,pno/inst DURAND s.p.
(R237)

Tristes Apprets (from Castor Et
Pollux)
Mez solo,orch (without recitative)
DURAND s.p.   (R238)
Mez solo,orch DURAND s.p.   (R239)

Voici Les Tristes Lieux (from
Dardanus)
Bar solo,pno/inst DURAND s.p.
(R240)

RAMOUS, GIANNI (1939-   )
Lettera Alla Madre
Bar solo,orch sc ZERBONI 6060 s.p.
(R241)

RAMSAY, HAROLD
My Gift
solo,pno PATERSON s.p.   (R242)

Sanctuary
solo,pno PATERSON s.p.   (R243)

RAMSEY
I Won't Have To Cross Jordon Alone
(composed with Durham) *sac
solo,pno BENSON S6192-RS $1.00
(R244)

RAMSHORST, J.D. VON
Wij Zijn Jong *CC12L
1-3 soli,pno ALSBACH s.p.   (R245)

RANDALL, J.K.
Improvisation On A Poem By E.E.
Cummings
S/A solo,clar,al-sax,trp,gtr,pno sc
AM.COMP.AL. $7.70, ipa   (R246)

RANDEGGER, ALBERTO (1832-1911)
Save Me, O God
low solo,pno (G maj) CRAMER (R247)
high solo,pno (B flat maj) CRAMER
(R248)

RANDEL, ANDREAS
Varmlanningarne *CCU
solo,pno GEHRMANS s.p.   (R249)

RANENU HA'CHASSIDIM see Benet, Haim

RANGSTROM, TURE (1884-1947)
Ater
solo,pno GEHRMANS s.p.   (R250)

Dromvisa
see Stilla Visor

En Bat Med Blommor
solo,pno GEHRMANS s.p.   (R251)

En Gammal Nyarsvisa
solo,pno GEHRMANS s.p.   (R252)

Hor Du Augusti Sommarregn
solo,pno GEHRMANS s.p.   (R253)

Hymne "De Brente Vare Garder
solo,pno GEHRMANS s.p.   (R254)

I Drommande Nattens Stillhet
solo,pno LUNDQUIST s.p.   (R255)

Jag Har Dromt
see Vildmark

Junkerns Serenad
solo,pno GEHRMANS s.p.   (R256)

RANGSTROM, TURE (cont'd.)

Kejsar Karls Visa
solo,pno GEHRMANS s.p.   (R257)

Kvall I Skogen
solo,pno GEHRMANS s.p.   (R258)

Kvallsvisa
see Stilla Visor

Maj
solo,pno GEHRMANS s.p.   (R259)

Mitt Land
solo,pno LUNDQUIST s.p.   (R260)

Pastichen *CC5U
solo,pno LUNDQUIST s.p.   (R261)

Soluppgang
see Tva Sommarvisor

Sommar
see Tva Sommarvisor

Stilla Visor
solo,pno LUNDQUIST s.p.
contains: Dromvisa; Kvallsvisa;
Vaggvisa   (R262)

Stjarnoga
solo,pno LUNDQUIST s.p.   (R263)

Tva Ballader *CC2U
solo,pno LUNDQUIST s.p.   (R264)

Tva Sommarvisor
solo,pno LUNDQUIST s.p.
contains: Soluppgang; Sommar
(R265)

Twenty-Two Songs *CC22U
[Swed/Ger] solo,kbd NORDISKA s.p.
(R266)

Vaggvisa
see Stilla Visor

Varkanning
see Vildmark

Vildmark
solo,pno LUNDQUIST s.p.
contains: Jag Har Dromt;
Varkanning   (R267)

Vita Liljorna Dofta
solo,pno LUNDQUIST s.p.   (R268)

Zwei Minnelieder, Heft 1-2 *CCU
solo,pno LUNDQUIST s.p., ea. (R269)

RANKEN, RUTH
Guitarre
solo,pno CRAMER   (R270)

RANKI, GYORGY (1907-   )
Fekete Szolo *CCU,folk,Hung
[Hung] solo,pno BUDAPEST 2838 s.p.
(R271)

Six Songs *CC6U
solo,pno BUDAPEST 5646 s.p. (R272)

RANKL
Four Scottish Songs *CC4U
solo,orch OXFORD rental   (R273)

RANNA ROSA see Moyzes, Alexander

RANNALTA I see Kilpinen, Yrio

RANNALTA II see Kilpinen, Yrio

RANNOCH, BY GLENCOE see Thomas, A.

RANSAK MEG see Tonnessen, Peder

RANSKALAISIA PAIMENLAULUJA *CC18U
(Weckerlin) solo,pno FAZER W 2542
s.p.   (R274)

RANSOMED OF THE LORD, THE see
Humphreys, Don

RANTA-ASTERI see Salonen, Sulo,
Strandaster

RANTA, SULHO (1901-1960)
Chanson Monotone *Op.27,No.2
solo,pno FAZER F 2525 s.p. see from
Junge Lyrik   (R275)

Die Goldfische *see Kultakalat

Junge Lyrik *see Chanson Monotone,
Op.27,No.2; Kultakalat, "Die
Goldfische", Op.27,No.1   (R276)

Kesaaamu *Op.63,No.3
"Sommarmorgon" solo,pno FAZER
F 2611 s.p.   (R277)

Kevatlintu *Op.63,No.2
"Varens Fagel" solo,pno FAZER
F 2609 s.p.   (R278)

RANTA, SULHO (cont'd.)

Kultakalat *Op.27,No.1
"Die Goldfische" solo,pno FAZER
F 2524 s.p. see from Junge Lyrik
(R279)

Mennyt Paiva *Op.7,No.1
solo,pno FAZER F 2484 s.p.   (R280)

Prinseesa Ja Trubaduuri *Op.3a,No.3
"Prinsessan Och Trubaduren" solo,
pno FAZER W 1366 s.p.   (R281)

Prinsessan Och Trubaduren *see
Prinseesa Ja Trubaduuri

Rarahu *Op.3a,No.1
solo,pno FAZER W 1346 s.p.   (R282)

Sommarmorgon *see Kesaaamu

Tsheremissilainen Laulu *Op.7,No.2
solo,pno FAZER W 2485 s.p.   (R283)

Vaeltajan Joulurukous *Op.23,No.1,
Xmas
solo,pno FAZER F 2487 s.p.   (R284)
solo,pno FAZER F 2487 s.p.   (R285)

Varens Fagel *see Kevatlintu

RANTUM TANTUM see Heseltine, Philip

RAPHAEL, GUNTHER (1903-1960)
Acht Gedichte Von Hermann Hesse
*Op.72,No.1-8, CC8U
S/T solo,2fl,2ob,2clar,2bsn,2horn,
2trp,3trom,strings,harp,cel,pno,
strings sc BREITKOPF-L rental,
voc sc BREITKOPF-L EB 6838 s.p.
(R286)

Advent- Und Weihnachtslieder *sac,
CCU,Adv/Xmas
solo,pno MULLER 2325 s.p.   (R287)

Der Du, Herr Jesu, Ruh Und Rast
see Drei Geistliche Gesange

Drei Geistliche Gesange *Op.31,No.1-
3, CC3U
A solo,pno BREITKOPF-L EB 5553 s.p.
(R288)

Drei Geistliche Gesange *sac
solo,pno BREITKOPF-W EB 5966 s.p.
contains: Der Du, Herr Jesu, Ruh
Und Rast; O Hilf, Christe,
Gottes Sohn; O Lamm Gottes,
Unschuldig   (R289)

Drei Geistliche Gesange (1931)
*Op.31,No.1-3, CC3U
A solo,org BREITKOPF-W $1.20 (R290)

Gesang Der Erzengel *Op.79
SABar soli,pno/brass voc sc
BREITKOPF-W EB 6208 s.p., ipa
(R291)

Herr Christ, Hilf Uns *sac
SA soli,org HANSSLER 5.029 s.p. see
also GESANGE ZUM KIRCHENJAHR
(R292)

In Dem Herren Freuet Euch *sac
SA soli,2S rec,cont HANSSLER 5.039
s.p. see also GESANGE ZUM
KIRCHENJAHR   (R293)

My Dark Hands *Op.86, CC5U
Bar solo,pno,bvl,drums voc sc GERIG
HG 408 s.p.   (R294)

O Hilf, Christe, Gottes Sohn
see Drei Geistliche Gesange

O Lamm Gottes, Unschuldig
see Drei Geistliche Gesange

Palmstrom-Sonate *Op.69
T solo,clar,vln,drums,perc,pno s.p.
sc BREITKOPF-W EB 6992, voc sc
BREITKOPF-W EB 6993, study sc
BREITKOPF-W PB 3828   (R295)

Schmucket Das Fest *sac
SA soli,2S rec,cont HANSSLER 5.055
s.p. see also GESANGE ZUM
KIRCHENJAHR   (R296)

RAPHAEL, MARK
Lamb, The
solo,pno (F sharp min) ROBERTON
1003 s.p.   (R297)

Weep No More
med solo,pno ELKIN 27.2652.01 s.p.
(R298)

RAPHLING, SAM (1910-   )
Anne Rutledge
med solo,pno MERCURY $.75 see from
Spoon River Anthology   (R299)

Autograph Album
solo,pno GENERAL 284 $2.00   (R300)

Beat! Beat! Drums
solo,pno GENERAL 284 $1.50   (R301)

RAPHLING, SAM (cont'd.)

Cool Tombs
med solo,pno PRESSER $.95 see from
Songs On Poems By Carl Sandburg
(R302)

Fog
low solo,pno PRESSER $.95 see from
Songs On Poems By Carl Sandburg
(R303)

Fugue On Money
low solo,pno MERCURY $.95   (R304)
high solo,pno MERCURY $.95   (R305)

Gone
med solo,pno PRESSER $.95 see from
Songs On Poems By Carl Sandburg
(R306)

John James Audubon
med solo,pno PRESSER $.75   (R307)

Lucinda Matlock
med solo,pno MERCURY $.75 see from
Spoon River Anthology   (R308)

Mag
low solo,pno PRESSER $.95 see from
Songs On Poems By Carl Sandburg
(R309)

New Songs On Four Romantic Poems
*CC4U
solo,pno GENERAL 285 $2.00   (R310)

Penniwit, The Artist
low solo,pno MERCURY $.75 see from
Spoon River Anthology   (R311)
med solo,pno MERCURY $.75 see from
Spoon River Anthology   (R312)

Shadows In The Sun *CC11U
solo,pno GENERAL 624 $5.00   (R313)

Shine, Great Sun
Bar solo,pno MERCURY $.95   (R314)

Songs On Poems By Carl Sandburg *see
Cool Tombs; Fog; Gone; Mag;
Washington Monument By Night
(R315)

Spoon River Anthology *see Anne
Rutledge; Lucinda Matlock;
Penniwit, The Artist   (R316)

Washington Monument By Night
med solo,pno PRESSER $.95 see from
Songs On Poems By Carl Sandburg
(R317)

RAPIDA CERVA, FUGE see Galuppi,
Baldassare

RAPPAPORT, EDA
Drinking Song
med solo,pno TRANSCON. TV 462 $.50
(R318)

Harhorey Laila
(Helfman, Max) "Thoughts In The
Night" [Heb] high solo,pno
TRANSCON. WJ 422 $.50   (R319)

River, The
high solo/med solo,pno TRANSCON.
TV 458 $.40   (R320)

Sleep, Little Baby
high solo/med solo,pno TRANSCON.
TV 459 $.35   (R321)

Thoughts In The Night *see Harhorey
Laila

To A Cactus
high solo/med solo,pno TRANSCON.
TV 461 $.50   (R322)

Vacation
med solo,pno TRANSCON. TV 460 $.50
(R323)

RAPPAPORT, MOSHE
Adam Ki Yamut *sac
"Valley Of Jezreel" [Heb/Eng] med
solo,pno TRANSCON. SP 8 $.60
(R324)

Hora
[Heb] med solo,pno TRANSCON. SP 7
$.60   (R325)

Valley Of Jezreel *see Adam Ki Yamut

RAPSODIA see Brahms, Johannes, Alto
Rhapsody

RAPSODIA see Turchi, Guido

RAPTURE *sac,CC7L
(Mickelson, Paul) solo,kbd SINGSPIR
$2.95   (R326)

RAPUNZEL see Duke, John Woods

RARA-HU see Nougues, Jean

RARAHU see Ranta, Sulho

RASBACH, OSCAR (1888-1975)
Mountains
high solo,pno (D flat maj) SCHIRM.G
$.75   (R327)

Trees
high solo,pno (E maj) SCHIRM.G
$1.25   (R328)
[Fr/Span/Ger/It] med solo,pno (D
maj) SCHIRM.G $1.25   (R329)
med solo,pno (D maj) SCHIRM.G $1.25
(R330)
med solo,pno (D flat maj) SCHIRM.G
$1.25   (R331)
low solo,pno (C maj) SCHIRM.G $1.25
(R332)
low solo,pno (B flat maj) SCHIRM.G
$1.25   (R333)
(Deis) SA soli,pno SCHIRM.G $.85
(R334)

RASCH, HUGO
Zehn Lieder Im Volkston Nach
Gedichten Von Emil Grimm *CC10U
solo,pno RIES s.p.   (R335)

RASCH, KURT
Moritat Vom Verlassenen Mariechen
T solo,acord,strings sc BREITKOPF-W
CMN 22   (R336)

RASKA FOTTER SPRINGA
see En Liten Julhalsning

RASLEY, JOHN M. (1913-   )
Beholding Thee, Lord Jesus *see
Christiansen, L.

RASPUTIN'S END see Nabokov, Nicolas

RASSE, FRANCOIS (1873-1955)
Bonheur
Bar solo,pno CBDM s.p.   (R337)

Chanson Boheme
Mez/Bar solo,pno CBDM s.p.   (R338)

Chanson Pour Maria Chapdelaine
S solo,pno CBDM s.p.   (R339)

Dans Un Parfum De Roses Blanches
see La Chanson D'Eve

Deux Poemes De Maurice Careme
S/T solo,pno cmplt ed CBDM s.p.
contains: Evasion; La Priere Du
Poete   (R340)

En Foret
S/T solo,pno CBDM s.p.   (R341)

Evasion
see Deux Poemes De Maurice Careme

Je Vis
T solo,pno CBDM s.p.   (R342)

La Chanson D'Eve
S/T solo,pno cmplt ed CBDM s.p.
contains: Dans Un Parfum De Roses
Blanches; Quand Vient Le
Soir...   (R343)

La Priere Du Poete
see Deux Poemes De Maurice Careme

Le Chant Du Tombeau
A/Mez solo,pno CBDM s.p.   (R344)

Le Nuage
S/T solo,pno CBDM s.p.   (R345)

Les Petits Chats
S/T solo,pno CBDM s.p.   (R346)

Mere
A/B solo,pno CBDM s.p.   (R347)

Ode A La Musique
S/T solo,pno CBDM s.p.   (R348)

Quand Vient Le Soir...
see La Chanson D'Eve

RASTLOSE LIEBE see Trapp, Max

RATCLIFFE, DESMOND
Bee, The
high solo,pno NOVELLO 17.0010.03
s.p.   (R349)

RATEZ, EMILE-PIERRE (1851-1934)
Marche Franc-Comtoise
solo,acap ENOCH s.p.   (R350)
solo,pno ENOCH s.p.   (R351)

Marches Franc-Comtoise
solo,acap ENOCH s.p. see from
CHANSONS DE TROUPE   (R352)

RATHAUS, KAROL (1895-1954)
Song Of Israel
solo,pno ISRAELI 1001 $1.40   (R353)

Three English Songs *CC3U
med solo,pno AMP $4.00   (R354)

RATHBUN, F.G.
    I Heard The Voice Of Jesus Say *sac
        high solo,pno PRESSER $.75   (R355)
        ST soli,pno PRESSER $.75   (R356)
        low solo,pno PRESSER $.75   (R357)
        ABar soli,pno PRESSER $.75   (R358)

RATSUMIES see Kuusisto, Taneli

RATTENFANGERLIED see Neuendorf, E.

RATZ, LUDO
    Effleurement
        solo,pno ENOCH s.p.   (R359)
        solo,acap ENOCH s.p.   (R360)

    Le Chic
        solo,pno ENOCH s.p.   (R361)
        solo,acap ENOCH s.p.   (R362)

    Sur La Promenade
        solo,pno ENOCH s.p.   (R363)
        solo,acap ENOCH s.p.   (R364)

RAUMSPIEL TEIL 1 see Dimov, Bojidar

RAUMSPIEL TEIL 2 see Dimov, Bojidar

RAUSCHENDER BLATTER HOLD GEFLUSTER see
    Ippolitov-Ivanov, Mikhail
    Mikhailovitch

RAUTAVAARA, EINOJUHANI (1928-   )
    Da Stieg Ein Baum *Op.9,No.1
        see Funf Sonette An Oprheus

    Ein Gott Vermags *Op.9,No.3
        see Funf Sonette An Oprheus

    Errichtet Keinen Denkstein *Op.9,
        No.5
        see Funf Sonette An Oprheus

    Funf Sonette An Oprheus
        solo,pno FAZER F 5015 s.p.
        contains: Da Stieg Ein Baum,
            Op.9,No.1; Ein Gott Vermags,
            Op.9,No.3; Errichtet Keinen
            Denkstein, Op.9,No.5; O Ihr
            Zartlichen, Op.9,No.4; Und Fast
            Ein Madchen Wars, Op.9,No.2
                                      (R365)
    Fyra Andliga Sanger *CC4U
        solo,pno FAZER F 5310 s.p.   (R366)

    O Ihr Zartlichen *Op.9,No.4
        see Funf Sonette An Oprheus

    Three Sonnets Of Shakespeasre
        *Op.14,No.1-3, CC3U
        solo,pno FAZER F 5374 s.p.   (R367)

    Und Fast Ein Madchen Wars *Op.9,No.2
        see Funf Sonette An Oprheus

RAVANA see Chaminade, Cecile

RAVEL, MAURICE (1875-1937)
    Adieu Cellule, Adieu Donjon (from
        L'Heure Espagnole)
        T solo,orch DURAND s.p., ipr (R368)

    Air De L'Enfant (from L'Enfant Et Les
        Sortileges)
        S solo,pno/inst DURAND s.p. (R369)

    Air De L'Horloge (from L'Enfant Et
        Les Sortileges)
        Mez/Bar solo,pno/inst DURAND s.p.
                                      (R370)
    Air Du Feu (from L'Enfant Et Les
        Sortileges)
        S solo,pno,inst/orch DURAND s.p.,
        ipr   (R371)

    Aoua
        see Chansons Madecasses (Edition
        Originale)
        solo,pno/inst DURAND s.p. see also
        Chansons Madecasses   (R372)

    Asie
        [Fr/Eng] S solo,pno DURAND s.p. see
        also Sheherazade   (R373)

    Chanson A Boire
        high solo&med solo&Bar solo,pno
        DURAND s.p. see from Don
        Quichotte A Dulcinee   (R374)

    Chanson Des Cueilleuses De Lentisques
        [Greek/Fr] solo,pno/orch DURAND
        s.p., ipr see also Cinq Melodies
        Populaires Grecques   (R375)

    Chanson Epique
        high solo&med solo&Bar solo,pno
        DURAND s.p. see from Don
        Quichotte A Dulcinee   (R376)

    Chanson Espagnole
        solo,pno/inst DURAND s.p. see from
        Chants Populaires   (R377)

RAVEL, MAURICE (cont'd.)
    Chanson Francaise
        solo,pno/inst DURAND s.p. see from
        Chants Populaires   (R378)

    Chanson Hebraique
        solo,pno/inst DURAND s.p. see from
        Chants Populaires   (R379)
        solo,orch DURAND s.p., ipa see from
        CHANTS POPULAIRES   (R380)

    Chanson Italienne
        solo,pno/inst DURAND s.p. see from
        Chants Populaires   (R381)

    Chanson Romanesque
        high solo&med solo&Bar solo,pno
        DURAND s.p. see from Don
        Quichotte A Dulcinee   (R382)

    Chansons Madecasses
        solo,pno/inst cmplt ed DURAND s.p.
        contains & see also: Aoua; Il Est
            Doux De Se Coucher; Nahandove
                                      (R383)
    Chansons Madecasses (Edition
        Originale)
        solo,fl,vcl,pno cmplt ed DURAND
        s.p.
        contains: Aoua; Il Est Doux De Se
            Coucher; Nahondove   (R384)

    Chants Populaires *see Chanson
        Espagnole; Chanson Francaise;
        Chanson Hebraique; Chanson
        Italienne   (R385)

    Choeur Des Patres (from L'Enfant Et
        Les Sortileges)
        SA soli,pno/inst DURAND s.p. (R386)

    Cinq Melodies Populaires Grecques
        [Fr/Eng] solo,orch cmplt ed DURAND
        s.p.
        contains & see also: Chanson Des
            Cueilleuses De Lentisques; La-
            Bas Vers L'eglise; Le Reveil De
            La Mariee; Quel Galant!; Tout
            Gai!   (R387)

    D'Anne Jouant De L'Espinette
        see Three Songs
        [Fr] med solo,pno ESCHIG $3.25 see
        from Two Epigrammes Of Marot
                                      (R388)
    D'Anne Que Me Jecta De La Neige
        [Fr] med solo,pno ESCHIG $3.25 see
        from Two Epigrammes Of Marot
                                      (R389)
    D'Anne Qui Me Jecta De La Neige
        see Three Songs

    Das Zauberwort
        [Ger] solo,pno DURAND s.p.   (R390)

    Deux Melodies Hebraiques
        med solo,pno/harp/orch DURAND s.p.,
        ipa
        contains: Enigme Eternelle
            (Hebrew and French texts);
            Kaddisch (Hebrew text)   (R391)

    Don Quichotte A Dulcinee *see
        Chanson A Boire; Chanson Epique;
        Chanson Romanesque   (R392)

    Douze Chants *CC12L
        [Fr/Eng] DURAND med solo,pno/inst
        s.p.; high solo,pno/inst s.p.
                                      (R393)
    Duo De La Theiere Et De La Tasse
        (from L'Enfant Et Les Sortileges)
        MezT soli,pno/inst DURAND s.p.
                                      (R394)
    Enigme Eternelle
        see Deux Melodies Hebraiques

    Five Greek Folk Songs *CC5U
        [Greek/Fr/Eng] solo,pno INTERNAT.
        $2.50   (R395)

    Four Folk Songs *CC4U,Fr/Heb/It/Span
        [Fr/Eng] solo,pno INTERNAT. $2.00
                                      (R396)
    Histoires Naturelles
        solo,pno/inst cmplt ed DURAND s.p.
        contains & see also: La Pintade;
            Le Cygne; Le Grillon; Le
            Martin-Pecheur; Le Paon (R397)

    Il Est Doux De Se Coucher
        see Chansons Madecasses (Edition
        Originale)
        solo,pno/inst DURAND s.p. see also
        Chansons Madecasses   (R398)

    Il Etait Temps, Voici Gonzalve (from
        L'Heure Espagnole)
        TS soli,pno/inst DURAND s.p. (R399)

    Kaddisch
        see Deux Melodies Hebraiques

RAVEL, MAURICE (cont'd.)
    La-Bas Vers L'eglise
        [Greek/Fr] solo,pno/orch DURAND
        s.p., ipr see also Cinq Melodies
        Populaires Grecques   (R400)

    La Flute Enchantee (from Sheherazade)
        [Fr/Eng] INTERNAT. $.75   (R401)
        [Fr/Eng] Mez solo,fl&pno/pno DURAND
        s.p. see also Sheherazade   (R402)

    La Pintade
        solo,pno/inst DURAND s.p. see also
        Histoires Naturelles   (R403)

    Le Cygne
        solo,pno/inst DURAND s.p. see also
        Histoires Naturelles   (R404)

    Le Grillon
        solo,pno/inst DURAND s.p. see also
        Histoires Naturelles   (R405)

    Le Martin-Pecheur
        solo,pno/inst DURAND s.p. see also
        Histoires Naturelles   (R406)

    Le Paon
        solo,pno/inst DURAND s.p. see also
        Histoires Naturelles   (R407)

    Le Reveil De La Mariee
        [Greek/Fr] solo,pno/orch DURAND
        s.p., ipr see also Cinq Melodies
        Populaires Grecques   (R408)

    Les Grands Vents Venus D'Outre-Mer
        Mez/Bar solo,pno/inst DURAND s.p.
                                      (R409)
    L'Indifferent
        [Fr/Eng] Mez solo,pno DURAND s.p.
        see also Sheherazade   (R410)

    Manteau De Fleurs
        see Three Songs

    Nahandove
        solo,pno/inst DURAND s.p. see also
        Chansons Madecasses   (R411)

    Nahondove
        see Chansons Madecasses (Edition
        Originale)

    Nicolette
        solo,pno/inst DURAND s.p. see from
        Trois Chansons   (R412)

    Noel Des Jouets
        med solo,pno SALABERT-US $3.75, ipr
                                      (R413)
    Oh! La Pitoyable Aventure (from
        L'Heure Espagnole)
        S solo,orch DURAND s.p., ipr (R414)

    Placet Futile
        see Trois Poemes De Stephane
        Mellarme

    Quel Galant!
        [Greek/Fr] solo,pno/orch DURAND
        s.p., ipr see also Cinq Melodies
        Populaires Grecques   (R415)

    Reves
        solo,pno/inst DURAND s.p.   (R416)

    Ronde
        solo,pno/inst DURAND s.p. see from
        Trois Chansons   (R417)

    Ronsard A Son Ame
        solo,orch DURAND s.p., ipr   (R418)

    Sainte
        Mez/Bar solo,pno/inst DURAND s.p.
                                      (R419)
    Sheherazade *song cycle
        [Fr/Eng] INTERNAT. $2.50   (R420)

    Sheherazade
        [Fr/Eng] S/Mez solo,orch cmplt ed,
        voc sc DURAND s.p., rental
        contains & see also: Asie; La
            Flute Enchantee; L'Indifferent
                                      (R421)
    Soupir
        see Trois Poemes De Stephane
        Mellarme

    Sur L'herbe
        solo,pno/inst DURAND s.p.   (R422)

    Surgi De La Croupe Et Du Bond
        see Trois Poemes De Stephane
        Mellarme

    Three Songs
        [Fr/Eng] high solo,pno INTERNAT.
        $1.50
        contains: D'Anne Jouant De
            L'Espinette; D'Anne Qui Me
            Jecta De La Neige; Manteau De
            Fleurs   (R423)

RAVEL, MAURICE (cont'd.)

Tout Gai!
[Greek/Fr] solo,pno/orch DURAND
s.p., ipr see also Cinq Melodies
Populaires Grecques   (R424)

Trois Beaux Oiseaux De Paradis
solo,pno/inst DURAND s.p. see from
Trois Chansons   (R425)

Trois Chansons *see Nicolette;
Ronde; Trois Beaux Oiseaux De
Paradis   (R426)

Trois Poemes De Stephane Mellarme
[Fr] med solo,orch cmplt ed DURAND
s.p., ipa
contains: Placet Futile; Soupir;
Surgi De La Croupe Et Du Bond
                             (R427)

Two Epigrammes Of Marot *see D'Anne
Jouant De L'espinette; D'Anne Que
Me Jecta De La Neige   (R428)

Un Financier Et Un Poete (from
L'Heure Espagnole)
SATBarB soli,pno/inst DURAND s.p.
                             (R429)

Un Grand Sommeil Noir
solo,pno/inst DURAND s.p.   (R430)

RAVEN, THE see Medtner, Nikolai
Karlovitch

RAVEN, THE see Schubert, Franz (Peter),
Die Krahe

RAVEN RIVER see Hovhaness, Alan

RAVIZE, A.
Balbi-Balba
solo,pno/inst DURAND s.p. see also
Dix Chansons D'Enfants   (R431)

Berceuse
solo,pno/inst DURAND s.p. see also
Dix Chansons D'Enfants   (R432)

Chanson
solo,pno/inst DURAND s.p. see also
Dix Chansons D'Enfants   (R433)

Chant De Facheur
solo,pno/inst DURAND s.p. see also
Dix Chansons D'Enfants   (R434)

Chant De Labour
solo,pno/inst DURAND s.p. see also
Dix Chansons D'Enfants   (R435)

Complainte De Petite Lumiere Et De
L'Ourse
solo,pno/inst DURAND s.p. see also
Dix Chansons D'Enfants   (R436)

Divertissements Et Airs A Danser
*CCU
solo,fl,perc cmplt ed DURAND s.p.
                             (R437)

Dix Chansons D'Enfants
solo,pno/inst cmplt ed DURAND s.p.
contains & see also: Balbi-Balba;
Berceuse; Chanson; Chant De
Facheur; Chant De Labour;
Complainte De Petite Lumiere Et
De L'Ourse; Le Pic Du Mineur;
Mai; Ronde Flamande; Vers Le
Bal   (R438)

Dix Chansons Populaires *CC10U
solo,fl,perc cmplt ed DURAND s.p.
see also: Savez-Vous Planter Les
Choux   (R439)

Le Pic Du Mineur
solo,pno/inst DURAND s.p. see also
Dix Chansons D'Enfants   (R440)

Mai
solo,pno/inst DURAND s.p. see also
Dix Chansons D'Enfants   (R441)

Petites Histoires Mises En Musique
*CC12L
solo,pno/inst cmplt ed DURAND s.p.
                             (R442)

Ronde Flamande
solo,pno/inst DURAND s.p. see also
Dix Chansons D'Enfants   (R443)

Savez-Vous Planter Les Choux
solo,fl,perc DURAND s.p. see also
Dix Chansons Populaires   (R444)

Vers Le Bal
solo,pno/inst DURAND s.p. see also
Dix Chansons D'Enfants   (R445)

RAVNIK, JANKO (1891-   )
Liricni Spevi *CCU
solo,pno DRUSTVO DSS 41 rental
                             (R446)

Slovenske Narodne *CCU,folk,Slav
solo,pno DRZAVNA rental   (R447)

RAWLS, R. MAINES
God Gave Me Love *sac
solo,pno BROADMAN 4590-31 $1.00
                             (R448)

RAWSTHORNE
Medieval Diptych
Bar solo,orch OXFORD rental (R449)

Symphony II
S solo,orch (diff) sc OXFORD 77.957
$4.75   (R450)

Tankas Of The Four Seasons *CCU
T solo,ob,clar,bsn,vln,vcl (med
diff) OXFORD 63.062 $3.50   (R451)

RAWSTHORNE, ALAN (1905-1971)
Carol
solo,pno OXFORD 62.623 $1.50 (R452)

Two Fish
solo,pno OXFORD $1.60   (R453)

RAXACH, ENRIQUE (1932-   )
Fragmento II
S solo,3inst DONEMUS s.p.   (R454)

Paraphrase For Alto Voice And 11
Players
A solo,fl,bass clar,bsn,horn,trp,
2perc,harp,vln,vla,vcl sc PETERS
7137 $9.00   (R455)

Sine Nomine
S solo,2fl,2ob,2clar,2bsn,al-sax,
2horn,2trp,2trom,2perc,harp,org,
cembalo,strings,gtr,mand,opt pno&
synthesizer DONEMUS s.p.   (R456)

RAYNAL, F.
A Nos Levres
solo,acap ENOCH s.p.   (R457)
solo,pno ENOCH s.p.   (R458)

Berceuse D'Amants
solo,acap ENOCH s.p.   (R459)
solo,pno ENOCH s.p.   (R460)

Ninon Ouvre Ta Porte
solo,acap ENOCH s.p.   (R461)
solo,pno ENOCH s.p.   (R462)

Voulez-Vous Ma Toute Belle!
solo,pno ENOCH s.p.   (R463)
solo,acap ENOCH s.p.   (R464)

RAYOS DE LUNA see De Rogatis, Pascual

RAZA *CCU,Span
(Benedito) [Span] med solo,pno UNION
ESP. $1.00, ea. in two volumes
                             (R465)
RAZZI, FAUSTO (1932-   )
Improvvisazione III
SSB soli,5inst sc,quarto ZERBONI
6760 s.p.   (R466)

RAZZIA see Lilien, Ignace

RAZZOLAN, SOPRA A L'AJA, LE GALLINE see
Respighi, Ottorino

RDECI OBLAKI see Sivic, Pavle

RE DELL'ABISSO, AFFRETTATI see Verdi,
Giuseppe

REACH OUT AND TOUCH see Brown, Charles
F.

REACH OUT AND TOUCH see Skillings, Otis

REACH OUT AND TOUCH JESUS see Owens,
Patricia

REACH OUT FOR LIFE see Poglietti,
Alessandro

REACH OUT, TAKE THE HAND see Dirkson,
Dan

REACH OUT TO JESUS see Carmichael,
Ralph

REACH UP see Van Dyke, Vonda

REACH UP *CC8L
solo,pno WORD 37600 $1.95 contains
works by: Van Dyke, Vonda;
Hildebrand, Ray   (R467)

REACH YOUR HAND see Kaiser, Kurt

READ, GARDNER (1913-   )
All Day I Hear
solo,pno BOOSEY $1.50   (R468)

At Bedtime
solo,pno PEER $.85   (R469)

From A Lute Of Jade
med solo,pno SEESAW $3.00   (R470)

It Is Pretty In The City
solo,pno PEER $.85   (R471)

READ, GARDNER (cont'd.)

Lullaby For A Man Child
med solo,pno GALAXY 1.2128.7 $1.00
                             (R472)

Pierrot
high solo/med solo,pno GALAXY
1.1385.7 $1.00   (R473)

Piping Down The Valleys Wild
med solo/low solo,pno GALAXY
1.1808.7 $1.00   (R474)

READY TO LEAVE see Hemphill

REALE, PAUL
Pange Lingua *sac
Bar solo,2ob,clar,vcl,2English horn
sc AM.COMP.AL. $5.50   (R475)

Three Songs From The Chinese *CC3U,
Chin
Mez solo,xylo,ob/English horn,timp
sc AM.COMP.AL. $3.57   (R476)

Traveller, The
T solo,fl,pno AM.COMP.AL.   (R477)

REAPER, THE see Chavez, Carlos, Segador

REAPERS, THE see Ha-Kotzrim

REASONS WHY see Young, Gordon

REAVEN, THE see Gerstel, Oswald

REBEL, THE see Wallace, William

REBEL, MIJN HART see Flothius, Marius

RECESSIONAL see De Koven, Henry Louis
Reginald

RECHENEXEMPEL
see Bruder Liederlich

RECICKE PISNE see Novotny, Vaclav Juda

RECIT DE L'EMERAUDE see Indy, Vincent
d'

RECIT DE L'ETRANGER see Indy, Vincent
d'

RECIT ET AIR see Bach, Johann Sebastian

RECIT ET AIR D'AZAEL see Debussy,
Claude

RECIT ET AIR DE LIA see Debussy, Claude

RECIT ET AIR D'IDOMENEE see Mozart,
Wolfgang Amadeus

RECIT ET RONDO see Mozart, Wolfgang
Amadeus

RECIT SUIVI DE LEGENDE see Marietan,
Pierre

RECITAR CANTANDO *CCU,18-19th cent
(Mingardo) Bar/B solo,pno ZERBONI
8024 s.p.   (R478)

RECITATIF ET AIR DE VITELIA see Mozart,
Wolfgang Amadeus

RECITATIV UND ARIE see Handel, George
Frideric

RECITATIVARIE see Kagel, Mauricio

RECITATIVE AND ARIA OF ARSINDA see
Bach, Johann Christian

RECITATIVO DELLA SPERANZA see
Monteverdi, Claudio

RECITATIVO ED ARIA D'ARNALTA see
Monteverdi, Claudio

RECKMANN, J.
Nach Hause Gehn Wir Nicht
solo,pno SCHAUR s.p.   (R479)

RECLI, GIULIA
Campanella
[It] solo,pno CURCI 8205 s.p.
                             (R480)

Crepuscolo
[It] S/T solo,pno BONGIOVANI 805
s.p.   (R481)
[It] Mez/Bar solo,pno BONGIOVANI
806 s.p.   (R482)

Fra Le Spiche
[It] S/T solo,pno BONGIOVANI 807
s.p.   (R483)
[It] Mez/Bar solo,pno BONGIOVANI
808 s.p.   (R484)

Frammento Di Ballata
[It] solo,pno BONGIOVANI 2469 s.p.
                             (R485)

RECLI, GIULIA (cont'd.)

La Barca
[It] solo,pno CURCI 8206 s.p.
(R486)

La Sorellina Dorme
SA soli,pno BONGIOVANI 809 s.p.
(R487)

Nenia
[It] S/T solo,pno BONGIOVANI 803
s.p.
(R488)
[It] Mez/Bar solo,pno BONGIOVANI
804 s.p.
(R489)

Voce Di Laguna
[It] Mez/Bar solo,pno BONGIOVANI
802 s.p.
(R490)
[It] S/T solo,pno BONGIOVANI 801
s.p.
(R491)

RECOLHI NO MEU CORACAO A TUA VOZ see
Camargo Guarnieri

RECOLLECTIONS OF A SUMMER PAST see
Rhodes, Phillip

RECONDITA ARMONIA see Puccini, Giacomo

RECORDED GOSPEL HITS see Mercer, W.
Elmo

RECREATION see Milhaud, Darius

RECUEIL DE CHANSONS ET RONDES
POPULAIRES see Bozi, Harold de

RECUEIL MODERNE VOL. I *CC20L
solo,acap oct DURAND s.p. contains
works by: Arditi; Debussy; Godard;
Mozart; Saint-Saens and others
(R492)

RECUEIL MODERNE VOL. II *CC17L
solo,acap oct DURAND s.p. conatins
works by: Bellenghi; Diemer;
Durand, J.; Gelli; Lebrun; Wagner
and others
(R493)

RECUEILLE see Diepenbrock, Alphons

RECUEILLEMENT see Baaren, Kees van

RECUEILLEMENT see Debussy, Claude

RECUEILLEMENT see Erlanger, Camille

RECUEILLEMENT see Hopkins, Anthony

RECUEILLEMENT see Mouton, H.

RECUEILLEMENT see Tincler, G.

RECUERDATE DE MI VIDA see Salas, Juan
Orrego

RECUERDO see Azpiazu, Jose de

RECUERDO see Lessard, John Ayres

RED BIRD see Youse, Glad Robinson

RED, BURYL
God's Grace Is Ehough For Me
BROADMAN 4590-42 $1.00
(R494)

His Gentle Look (from Hello, World!)
solo,pno BROADMAN 4590-26 $1.00
(R495)

I Quietly Turned To You (from
Celebrate Life)
solo,pno BROADMAN 4525-06 $1.00
(R496)

Isolated Moment (from Hello, World!)
solo,pno BROADMAN 4590-20 $1.00
(R497)

Rain Of Peace *sac
solo,pno WORD S-343
(R498)

Would You *sac
solo,pno WORD S-333
(R499)

RED CLOUDS see Sivic, Pavle, Rdeci
Oblaki

RED COCKATOO, THE see Heilner, Irwin

RED HAWTHORN see Bjerno, Erling D.

RED-LETTER DAYS see Martin, Easthope

RED RED ROSE see McHardy, Donald

RED, RED ROSE, A see Gold, Ernest

RED RIVER VALLEY see Musgrave, Carter

RED ROAD, THE see Black

RED ROOFS see Brahe, May H.

RED ROOFS OF BENDON, THE see Elliott,
Percy

RED ROSE see Bacon, Ernst

RED ROSES see Strauss, Richard, Rote
Rosen

RED, WHITE AND BLUE, THE see Peterson,
John W.

REDA, SIEGFRIED (1916-1968)
Evangelienmusik *sac,CCU
S solo,org (diff) BAREN. 435 $5.75
(R500)

Ich Ruf Zu Dir, Herr Jesu Christ
*sac
high solo,org (med diff) BAREN. 167
$.50
(R501)

Verkundigung Der Geburt Unseres
Heilandes
solo,S rec,A rec,2vln (med) sc
BAREN. 2159 $4.25
(R502)

Zehn Weihnachtslieder *CC10U,Xmas
med solo,pno (easy) BAREN. 2082
$2.75
(R503)

REDD, G.C.
Christians Tribulation *see Hubbard,
H.

Everything Will Be All Right *see
Hubbard, H.

He Said He Would Deliver Me (composed
with Merriweather, Roy) *sac,
gospel
solo,pno SAUL AVE
(R504)

Heaven Will Be My Home *see Hubbard,
H.

I Am Thine *see Hubbard, H.

I Wish That I Had Been There *see
Hubbard, H.

I'm Sheltered In His Arms *see
Hubbard, H.

Jesus Died *see Hubbard, H.

Jesus Will Move Every *see Hubbard,
H.

Loved Ones Are Waiting *see Hubbard,
H.

New Way Of Life, A *see Hubbard, H.

There's Nothing Like The Holy Ghost
*see Hubbard, H.

Think Of The Goodness Of God *see
Hubbard, H.

Walk On The Pathway *see Hubbard, H.

Where Were You Going *see Hubbard,
H.

Yes I'll Know Him *see Hubbard, H.

REDDEN, FINVOLA
Boat Song *sec
(Johnston) high solo,pno (A flat
maj) WATERLOO $.75
(R505)
(Johnston) low solo,pno (F maj)
WATERLOO $.75
(R506)

My Cottage-O *sec
(Peacock, Kenneth) med solo,pno (B
flat maj) WATERLOO $.90
(R507)

REDEL, MARTIN CHRISTOPH
Epilog
[Ger] B solo,gtr, alto flute BOTE
$11.50
(R508)

REDEMPTION DRAWETH NIGH see Oldham,
Doug

REDEMPTION DRAWETH NIGH see Jensen,
Gordon

REDENTOR IN FAMEGIA see Bianchini,
Guido

REDL, F.
Die Alten Strassen Noch
med solo,pno SCHAUR EE 3555A s.p.
(R509)
low solo,pno SCHAUR EE 3555B s.p.
(R510)

REDMAN, REGINALD (1892-   )
Credo
low solo,pno (C maj) ASHDOWN s.p.
(R511)
high solo,pno (E flat maj) ASHDOWN
s.p.
(R512)

Five Chinese Miniatures *song cycle
S solo,2fl,pic,ob,2clar,bsn,vibra,
glock,cel,harp,strings NOVELLO
rental
(R513)

I Feel So Good About It *sac
solo,pno BENSON S6004-S $1.00
(R514)

REDMAN, REGINALD (cont'd.)

More Than Life *sac
solo,pno BENSON S7050-R $1.00
(R515)

Silver
solo,pno (A min) ROBERTON 2614 s.p.
(R516)
solo,pno (F min) ROBERTON 2614 s.p.
(R517)

Three Kings Of Somerset
solo,pno CRAMER
(R518)

Waters Of Severn, The
solo,pno CRAMER $.95
(R519)

You Won't Believe The Difference
*sac
solo,pno BENSON S8583-S $1.00
(R520)

REED, PHYLLIS LUIDENS
I Have A Dream
med solo,pno GALAXY 1.2550.7 $1.00
(R521)

REESE, DOROTHY
Let Not Your Heart Be Troubled *sac
high solo,pno FITZSIMONS $.50
(R522)

REEVE
Friar Of Orders Grey
solo,pno CRAMER
(R523)

REFLECTIONS ON HAIAM POETRY see Jirim,
Frantisek, Odsevi Hajamovih Stihov

REFLEKSIJA BR. 6 see Kiraly, Erno

REFLETS see Bernier, Rene

REFLETS see Ponse, Luctor

REFLETS DANS L'EAU see Faure, Gabriel-
Urbain

REFLETS DU JAPON see Beekhuis, Hanna

REFLEXA see Hibbard, William

REFLEXION NO. VI see Kiraly, Erno,
Refleksija Br. 6

REFLEXIONS I see Ruyneman, Daniel

REFORMATIONSARIA see Andren, Adolf

REFRAIN D'AMOUR see Bemberg, Herman

REFRAIN DE NOVEMBRE see Chaminade,
Cecile

REFRAIN PRINTANIER see Trabadelo, A. de

REFRAIN THY VOICE FROM WEEPING see
Sullivan, Sir Arthur Seymour

REFUGEE, THE see Weigl, Karl

REGAIN D'INNOCENCE see Varney, Pierre
Joseph Alphonse

REGARDEZ PASSER LA PATRIE see Trepard,
E.

REGARDS see Ruyneman, Daniel

REGARDS SUR L'INFINI see Dupre, Marcel

REGEN see Marx, Joseph

REGEN see Trunk, Richard

REGENDROPPELS see Clercq, R. de

RE'GENERATION *sac,CC12L
solo,pno BENSON BO468 $2.50
(R524)

REGENLIED see Marx, Joseph

REGENNACHT see Weigl, Vally

REGER, MAX (1873-1916)
Abendlied *Op.14,No.2
see Funf Duette Fur Sopran Und Alt

Acht Lieder *Op.79c,No.1-8, CC8U
solo,pno cmplt ed SIKORSKI 453 s.p.
(R525)

Am Dorfsee *Op.48,No.6
med solo,pno UNIVER. 1229 $2.75
(R526)

An Die Hoffnung *Op.124
[Ger] A solo,2fl,2ob,2clar,2bsn,
4horn,2trp,timp,strings voc sc
PETERS 3287 rental, PETERS 3379
$3.50
(R527)

Aus Den Himmelsaugen *Op.98,No.1
[Ger] solo,2fl,2ob,2clar,2bsn,
4horn,timp,strings PETERS rental
(R528)

Cancion De Cuna De La Virgen *see
Maria Wiegenlied

Children's Prayer, The *see Des
Kindes Gebet

REGER, MAX (cont'd.)

Der Alte *Op.55,No.15
  med solo,pno UNIVER. 1267 $2.75
                                    (R529)

Der Himmel Hat *Op.35,No.2
  med solo,pno UNIVER. 1194 $2.75
                                    (R530)

Der Mond Gluht *Op.51,No.1
  high solo,pno UNIVER. 1235 $2.75
                                    (R531)

Des Kindes Gebet *Op.76,No.22
  "Children's Prayer, The" [Ger/Eng]
  med solo,pno BOTE $.75   (R532)
  "Children's Prayer, The" [Ger/Eng]
  low solo,pno BOTE $.75   (R533)
  "Children's Prayer, The" [Ger/Eng]
  high solo,pno BOTE $.75   (R534)

Ehre Sei Gott In Der Hohe! *sac,Xmas
  solo,harmonium/org BREITKOPF-W
  EB 6745 s.p.   (R535)
  solo,pno/harmonium/org BREITKOPF-W
  EB 6745 s.p.   (R536)

Fruhlingsmorgen *Op.51,No.11
  med solo,pno UNIVER. 1245 $2.75
                                    (R537)

Funf Duette Fur Sopran Und Alt
  SA soli,pno SCHOTTS 309 s.p.
  contains: Abendlied, Op.14,No.2;
  Gab's Ein Einzig Brunnelein,
  Op.14,No.4; Nachts, Op.14,No.1;
  O Frage Nicht, Op.14,No.5;
  Sommernacht, Op.14,No.3   (R538)

Gab's Ein Einzig Brunnelein *Op.14,
  No.4
  see Funf Duette Fur Sopran Und Alt

Golden Bird, The *see Zum Schlafen

Gute Nacht *Op.55,No.13
  med solo,pno UNIVER. 1265 $2.75
                                    (R539)

Helle Nacht *Op.37,No.1
  med solo,pno UNIVER. 1201 $2.75
                                    (R540)

Hymnus Der Liebe *Op.136
  [Ger] A/Bar solo,2fl,2ob,2clar,
  2bsn,4horn,2trp,timp,harp,strings
  sc PETERS 3982 rental, sc PETERS
  3983 $4.75   (R541)

Ich Glaub *Op.31,No.2
  med solo,pno UNIVER. 1183 $2.75
                                    (R542)

Ich Hab *Op.31,No.4
  med solo,pno UNIVER. 1185 $2.75
                                    (R543)

Ich Sehe Dich In Tausend Bildern
  *Op.105,No.1
  see Zwei Geistliche Lieder

Maria Wiegenlied *Op.76,No.62, sac
  [Ger] med solo,org,opt vln/vcl BOTE
  $2.25   (R544)
  "Cancion De Cuna De La Virgen"
  [Ger/Span] solo,pno (E flat maj)
  RICORDI-ARG BA 9400 s.p.   (R545)
  "Cancion De Cuna De La Virgen"
  [Ger/Span] solo,pno (G maj)
  RICORDI-ARG BA 9399 s.p.   (R546)
  "Marias Vaggsang" [Swed] solo,pno/
  org ERIKS K 275 s.p.   (R547)
  "Virgin's Slumber Song" [Ger/Eng]
  med solo,pno (E flat maj) AMP
  $1.75   (R548)
  "Virgin's Slumber Song" [Ger/Eng]
  low solo,pno (D flat maj) AMP
  $1.75   (R549)
  "Virgin's Slumber Song" high solo,
  pno (A flat maj) ALLANS s.p. (R550)
  "Virgin's Slumber Song" low solo,
  pno (F maj) ALLANS s.p.   (R551)
  "Virgin's Slumber Song" [Ger/Eng]
  med-high solo,pno (F maj) AMP
  $1.75   (R552)
  "Virgin's Slumber Song" [Ger/Eng]
  SS soli,pno BOTE $.60   (R553)
  "Virgin's Slumber Song" [Ger/Eng]
  high solo,pno (G maj) AMP $1.75
                                    (R554)
  "Virgin's Slumber Song" [Ger/Eng]
  high solo,pno (A flat maj) AMP
  $1.75   (R555)

Marias Vaggsang *see Maria
  Wiegenlied

Mein Schatzelein *Op.76,No.14
  "My Little Sweetheart" [Ger/Eng]
  med solo,pno BOTE $.75   (R556)
  "My Little Sweetheart" [Ger/Eng]
  low solo,pno BOTE $.75   (R557)
  "My Little Sweetheart" [Ger/Eng]
  high solo,pno BOTE $.75   (R558)

Meine Seele Ist Still Zu Gott (Psalm
  62) Op.105,No.2
  see Zwei Geistliche Lieder

My Little Sweetheart *see Mein
  Schatzelein

REGER, MAX (cont'd.)

Nachts *Op.14,No.1
  see Funf Duette Fur Sopran Und Alt

O Frage Nicht *Op.14,No.5
  see Funf Duette Fur Sopran Und Alt

Psalm 62 *see Meine Seele Ist Still
  Zu Gott

Quiet Of The Woods *see
  Waldeinsamkeit

Schlichte Weisen, Book I *Op.76,
  No.1-15, CCU
  [Ger/Eng] BOTE high solo,pno $6.75;
  med solo,pno $6.75   (R559)

Schlichte Weisen, Book II *Op.76,
  No.16-30, CCU
  [Ger/Eng] BOTE high solo,pno $8.50;
  med solo,pno $8.50   (R560)

Schlichte Weisen, Book III *Op.76,
  No.31-36, CCU
  [Ger/Eng] BOTE high solo,pno $3.50;
  med solo,pno $3.50   (R561)

Schlichte Weisen, Book IV *Op.76,
  No.37-43, CCU
  [Ger/Eng] BOTE high solo,pno $5.00;
  med solo,pno $5.00   (R562)

Schlichte Weisen, Book V *Op.76,
  No.44-51, CCU
  [Ger/Eng] med solo,pno BOTE $5.00
                                    (R563)

Schlichte Weisen, Book VI *Op.76,
  No.52-60, CCU
  [Ger/Eng] BOTE high solo,pno $3.00;
  med solo,pno $3.00   (R564)

Schlummerlied
  solo,pno SIKORSKI 697 s.p.   (R565)

Sommernacht *Op.14,No.3
  see Funf Duette Fur Sopran Und Alt

Traume Du *Op.51,No.3
  high solo,pno UNIVER. 1237 $2.75
                                    (R566)

Unvergessen *Op.48,No.7
  med solo,pno UNIVER. 1230 $2.75
                                    (R567)

Virgin's Slumber Song *see Maria
  Wiegenlied

Vom Kussen *Op.23,No.4
  med solo,pno UNIVER. 1179 $2.75
                                    (R568)

Waldeinsamkeit *Op.76,No.3
  "Quiet Of The Woods" [Ger/Eng] low
  solo,pno BOTE $.75   (R569)
  "Quiet Of The Woods" [Ger/Eng] med
  solo,pno BOTE $.75   (R570)
  "Quiet Of The Woods" [Ger/Eng] high
  solo,pno BOTE $.75   (R571)

Wiegenlied *Op.43
  med solo,pno UNIVER. 9821 $2.75
                                    (R572)
  med solo,pno PETERS 3272 $2.00
                                    (R573)

Zum Schlafen *Op.76,No.59
  "Golden Bird, The" [Ger/Eng] high
  solo,pno BOTE $.75   (R574)
  "Golden Bird, The" [Ger/Eng] low
  solo,pno BOTE $.75   (R575)
  "Golden Bird, The" [Ger/Eng] med
  solo,pno BOTE $.75   (R576)

Zwei Geistliche Lieder
  [Ger/Eng] med solo,pno/org LEUCKART
  s.p.
  contains: Ich Sehe Dich In
  Tausend Bildern, Op.105,No.1;
  Meine Seele Ist Still Zu Gott
  (Psalm 62) Op.105,No.2   (R577)

Zwolf Geistliche Gesange *Op.137,
  No.1-12, sac,CC12L
  [Ger] med solo,pno/org cmplt ed
  PETERS 6832-ENG $3.00, cmplt ed
  PETERS 3452-GER $4.75   (R578)

REGI AUTEM see Rossler, Ernst Karl

REGINA BELLA D'AMORE see Botti, C.

REGINETTA see Pratella, Francesco
  Balilla

REGNAVA NEL SILENZIO see Donizetti,
  Gaetano

REGNAVIT DOMINUS see Dommange, L.

REGNE AMOUR see Rameau, Jean-Philippe

REGNET SLAR OCH SLAR see Hallnas,
  Hilding

REGNET SLAR OCH SLAR OCH SLAR ETT LITET
  HUS see Hedar, Josef

REGNEY, NOEL
  Do You Hear What I Hear? *sac,Xmas
  solo,pno HARRIS $1.10   (R579)

REGNEZ, PLAISIRS ET JEUX see Rameau,
  Jean-Philippe

REGNUM DEI see Ahrens, Joseph

REGRET see Heilner, Irwin

REGRET see Schubert, Franz (Peter)

REGRET D'AVRIL see Messager, Andre

REGRETS see Dufresne, C.

REGRETS POUR ELLE see Delmet, Paul

REGT, HENDRIK DE (1950-   )
  Canzoni E Scherzi *Op.30, CCU
  S solo,fl,harp DONEMUS s.p.   (R580)

  Medea
  S solo,ob,cembalo DONEMUS s.p.
                                    (R581)
  Music Per Flauto [2] *Op.19
  narrator,perc DONEMUS s.p.   (R582)

  Musica Per Flauto, Percussione E Voce
  solo,fl,perc DONEMUS s.p.   (R583)

REGTEREN ALTENA, LUCAS VAN (1924-   )
  Poeme Discontinu
  S solo,fl,vln,pno DONEMUS s.p.
                                    (R584)

REICH MIR DIE HAND, MEIN LEBEN see
  Mozart, Wolfgang Amadeus

REICHARD, JOHANN GEORG
  Weihnachts-Weissagung *Xmas
  (Steude) [Ger/Eng] med solo,2vln,
  vla,cont sc DEUTSCHER 9515 s.p.,
  ipa   (R585)

REICHARDT, JOHANN FRIEDRICH (1752-1814)
  Das Erbe Deutscher Musik, Band 58:
  Goethes Lieder, Oden, Balladen
  Und Romanzen Mit Musik Teil I
  *CCU
  solo,pno cloth HENLE s.p.   (R586)

  Goethes Lieder, Oden, Balladen Und
  Romanzen *CCU
  solo,pno BREITKOPF-L SD 162 s.p.
                                    (R587)
  Rosens Bild
  solo,pno GEHRMANS 171 s.p.   (R588)

REICHARDT, LUISE (1779-1826)
  Hoffnung
  "When The Roses Bloom" [Ger/Eng]
  high solo,pno (G maj) SCHIRM.G
  $.50   (R589)

  When The Roses Bloom *see Hoffnung

REICHARDT, R.
  Loves Request
  high solo,pno (F maj) LEONARD-ENG
                                    (R590)
  low solo,pno (C maj) LEONARD-ENG
                                    (R591)

REICHERT, E.
  Sechs Gesange *CC6U
  [Ger] high solo,pno OSTER $1.25
                                    (R592)

REICHNER, BICKLEY
  If You Know The Lord
  solo,pno FOX,S   (R593)

REIF, PAUL (1910-   )
  ...And Be My Love
  solo,pno GENERAL 309 $2.50
  contains: Love Under The
  Republicans; Passionate
  Shepherd, The   (R594)

  Artist, The
  AB soli,fl,clar,bsn,horn,trp,perc,
  vln sc SEESAW $15.00   (R595)

  Birches *song cycle
  high solo,orch BOOSEY $1.75   (R596)

  Campaign
  TB soli,opt mix cor,ob,horn,trp,
  trom,gtr,bvl,3perc, rock singer
  sc SEESAW $26.00   (R597)

  Circus, The
  S solo,pno sc SEESAW $11.00   (R598)

  Fishes And The Poet's Hands, The
  S solo,pno sc SEESAW $7.00   (R599)

  Five Finger Exercises *CCU
  solo,pno GENERAL 204 $3.00   (R600)

  German For Americans
  solo,pno sc SEESAW $8.00   (R601)

  Love Under The Republicans
  see ...And Be My Love

REIF, PAUL (cont'd.)

O You Whom I Often
S solo,pno sc SEESAW $2.00 (R602)

Passionate Shepherd, The
see ...And Be My Love

Richard Cory
S solo,pno sc SEESAW $2.00 (R603)

White Roses
S solo,pno sc SEESAW $2.00 (R604)

REIFEN EINST see Kilpinen, Yrio,
Kummalstako Kuuleminen

REIFENDE FRUCHT see Marx, Karl

REIGN OF THE ROSES, THE see Lowthian,
Caroline

REIMANN, ARIBERT (1936-)
Drei Lieder *CC3U
[Ger] med-high solo,pno BOTE $3.75
(R605)

Drei Sonette Von W. Shakespeare
*CC3U
[Eng] Bar solo,pno ARS VIVA AV 13
s.p. (R606)

Drei Spanische Lieder *CC3U,Span
[Span/Ger] S solo,fl,harp,vcl BOTE
$2.00 (R607)

Ein Totentanz *CCU
Bar solo,chamb.orch voc sc ARS VIVA
AV 7 s.p., ipr (R608)

Engfuhrung
[Ger] T solo,pno ARS VIVA AV 34
s.p. (R609)

Epitaph
[Eng] T solo,7inst ARS VIVA AV s.p.
(R610)

Funf Gedichte Von Paul Celan *CC5U
Bar solo,pno ARS VIVA AV 35 s.p.
(R611)

Nachtstuck
[Eng/Ger] Bar solo,pno ARS VIVA
AV 26 s.p. (R612)

REIMANN, HEINRICH (1850-1906)
Alte Deutsche Weihnachtsgesange *CCU
[Ger] solo,pno SCHAUR EE 1037 s.p.
(R613)

Wiegenlied Der Hirten *Xmas
med solo,pno SCHAUR EE 1038 $.60
(R614)

REIME, REIGEN *sac/sec,CC36U
(Lemb, R.) solo,pno SCHOTTS 6352 s.p.
(R615)

REIMERS, IVAR
Dags Visor
solo,pno GEHRMANS s.p. (R616)

Fem Visor I Folkton *CC5U
solo,pno GEHRMANS s.p. (R617)

REIMS see Lattes, M.

REINAGLE, ALEXANDER ROBERT (1799-1877)
America, Commerce And Freedom
med solo,pno PRESSER $.75 (R618)

REINE BLONDE see Delmet, Paul

REINE DES MOUETTES see Poulenc, Francis

REINE! JE SERAI REINE see Saint-Saens,
Camille

REINECKE, CARL (1824-1910)
Achtunddreissig Kinderlieder
*Op.135, CC38U
solo,pno BREITKOPF-L EB 1092 $1.75
(R619)

Die Hindumadchen *Op.151
A/Mez solo,2fl,2ob,2clar,2bsn,
2horn,2trp,timp,strings sc
BREITKOPF-W (R620)

Kinderlieder I *CCU
solo,pno BREITKOPF-W EB 1040 s.p.
(R621)

Kinderlieder II *CCU
solo,pno BREITKOPF-W EB 1092 s.p.
(R622)

REINER, KAREL (1910-)
Drei Lieder Auf Gedichte Von F.Th.
Csokora *CC3U
[Czech/Ger] B solo,pno DOBLINGER
$3.00 (R623)

Ej, Uhorny, Ej, Lany
med solo,pno SUPRAPHON s.p. (R624)

REINHARDT, BRUNO
Mi Yodea
Bar solo,pno OR-TAV $.60 (R625)

REINHARDT, L.
Mein Sternlein
solo,pno HUG s.p. (R626)

REINHART, W.
Geistliche Lieder Mit Orgelbegleitung
*sac,CCU
solo,org HUG s.p. (R627)

REIR Y CANTAR, JUGAR Y DANZAR see
Llongueras J.

REISEBUCH AUS DEN OSTERREICHISCHEN
ALPEN, OP 62, BOOKS I-IV see
Krenek, Ernst

REISELIED see Schoeck, Othmar

REISSIGER
Doux Foyer, Sois Beni
[Ger] solo,pno DURAND 57 s.p.
(R628)

REJECTED LOVER, THE
see Schirmer's American Folk-Song
Series, Set XXI (American-English
Folk-Songs From The Southern
Appalachian Mountains)

REJOICE GREATLY, O DAUGHTER OF ZION!
see Handel, George Frideric

REJOICE GREATLY, O DAUGHTER OF ZION see
Willan, Healey

REJOICE IN THE LORD see Humphreys, Don

REJOICE IN THE LORD ALWAY see Pinkham,
Daniel

REJOICE O JUDAH see Handel, George
Frideric

REJOICE WITH ME, FOR I HAVE FOUND MY
SHEEP see Krapf, Gerhard

REJOICE, YOU'RE A CHILD OF THE KING see
Gaither

RELEASE see Lora, Antonio

RELIQUARY OF ENGLISH SONG, VOL. I
(1250- 1700) *CC51L
(Potter) solo,pno SCHIRM.G $4.00
contains works by: Purcell; Lawes;
Morley; Dowland and others (R629)

REMBRANDT'S "SAUL EN DAVID" see
Dresden, Sem

REMEMBER see Ruyneman, Daniel

REMEMBER ADAM'S FALL see Thomson,
Virgil

REMEMBER, LADY DISDAINFUL! see Salas,
Juan Orrego, Recuerdate De Mi Vida

REMEMBER ME see Laughlin, Paul

REMEMBER ME DEAR FRIEND see Sharpe,
Evelyn

REMEMBER THEE! REMEMBER THEE! see
Schirmer, Rudolph [E.]

REMEMBERED see Lieurance, Thurlow

REMEMBRANCE see Damase, Jean-Michel

REMEMBRANCE see Davenport, Gladys

REMEMBRANCE see Duke, John Woods

REMEMBRANCE see Keel, Frederick

REMIND ME, DEAR LORD see Rambo

RENAISSANCE-LIEDER see Monteverdi,
Claudio

RENAISSANCE LIEDER *CCU,Renais
(Gamble, James) T solo,vln,vla,vcl
PENN STATE PSMS 4 $3.00 contains
works by: Finck, Heinrich;
Lapicida, Erasmus; Stolzer, Thomas
(R630)

RENAISSANCE SUITE see Whear, Paul
William

RENAUD, A.
Au Bord De La Mer
2 soli,pno DURAND s.p. see from
DOUZE DOUS (R631)

Habenera
2 soli,pno DURAND s.p. see from
DOUZE DOUS (R632)

RENCESVALS see Dallapiccola, Luigi

RENCONTRE see Faure, Gabriel-Urbain

RENDAHL
Sangen Om Mor
solo,pno LUNDQUIST s.p. (R633)

RENGAINE A PLEURER see DuBois, Pierre
Max

RENGAINE POUR PIANO MECANIQUE see
DuBois, Pierre Max

RENIE
Cloches De Paques
see Fetes Enfantines

Fetes Enfantines
solo,harp/pno LEDUC s.p.
contains: Cloches De Paques; La
Vierge A La Creche; Mascarade
(R634)

La Vierge A La Creche
see Fetes Enfantines

Mascarade
see Fetes Enfantines

Pres D'un Berceau
solo,harp,pno LEDUC s.p. (R635)

RENNES, CATH. V.
Avondrust
see Lenteleven

Goeden Nacht
see Lenteleven

Het Angelus
see Lenteleven

Het Angelus Klept In De Verte
solo,pno/org/harmonium ALSBACH s.p.
(R636)
2 soli,pno ALSBACH s.p. (R637)

Lente
see Lenteleven

Lenteleven
solo,org ALSBACH s.p.
contains: Avondrust; Goeden
Nacht; Het Angelus; Lente; 'T
Viooltje (R638)

'T Viooltje
see Lenteleven

RENONCEMENT see Schlosser, Paul

RENOUVEAU see Delmet, Paul

RENOUVEAU see Flegier, Ange

RENOUVEAU see Gui, Vittorio

RENOUVEAU see Migot, Georges

RENOUVEAU see Sauguet, Henri

REPENT YE see Scott, John Prindle

REPENTIR see Gounod, Charles Francois

REPERTOIRE OF BEGINNER SINGER *CCU
[Russ] Mez solo,pno MEZ KNIGA 100
s.p. (R639)

REPIT see Wolff, A.

REPONSE A AMOUREUSE see Berger, Rod.

REPONSE AU SONNET D'ARVERS see
Casalonga, M.

REPONSE DU RESERVIST see Planquette,
Robert

REPONSE D'UNE EPOUSE SAGE see Ropartz,
Joseph Guy

REPONSE D'UNE EPOUSE SAGE see Roussel,
Albert

REPOS see Schubert, Franz (Peter), Du
Bist Die Ruh

REPOS EN EGYPTE see Respighi, Ottorino

REPOSE see Birch, Robert Fairfax

REPOSE ENFANT see Delbruck, J.

REPOSOIR GRAVE, NOBLE ET PUR... see
Migot, Georges

REPP, RAY
Hear Them Cryin' *sac,CC10L
solo,pno WORD 37610 $2.50 (R640)

REPPER, CHARLES
Candle Lights Of Christmas *Xmas
solo,pno BRANDEN $.40 (R641)

Carmencita
solo,pno BRANDEN $.50 (R642)

REPPER, CHARLES (cont'd.)

Circle Of The Keys, The
   solo,pno BRANDEN $.50   (R643)

Desert Stars
   solo,pno BRANDEN $.75   (R644)

Dixie Night
   low solo,pno (C maj) BRANDEN $.50
                                  (R645)
   high solo,pno (E flat maj) BRANDEN
   $.50   (R646)

Dusk
   low solo,pno (D flat maj) BRANDEN
   $.50   (R647)
   med solo,pno (E maj) BRANDEN $.50
                                  (R648)

Far Away Isles
   solo,pno BRANDEN $.50   (R649)

Gardens By The Sea
   solo,pno BRANDEN $.50   (R650)

In The Garden Of The World
   low solo,pno (E flat maj) BRANDEN
   $.50   (R651)
   med solo,pno (F maj) BRANDEN $.50
                                  (R652)

Song Is So Old
   high solo,pno (E maj) BRANDEN $.50
                                  (R653)
   med solo,pno (D flat maj) BRANDEN
   $.50   (R654)

To A Madonna
   solo,pno BRANDEN $.50   (R655)

Where Lilacs Blow
   solo,pno BRANDEN $.50   (R656)

REPRINTS FROM SING OUT!, VOL. 1
   *CC50U,folk,US
   solo,pno OAK 000201 $1.50   (R657)

REPRINTS FROM SING OUT!, VOL. 2
   *CC50U,folk,US
   solo,pno OAK 000202 $1.50   (R658)

REPRINTS FROM SING OUT!, VOL. 3
   *CC50U,folk,US
   solo,pno OAK 000203 $1.50   (R659)

REPRINTS FROM SING OUT!, VOL. 4
   *CC50U,folk,US
   solo,pno OAK 000204 $1.50   (R660)

REPRINTS FROM SING OUT!, VOL. 5
   *CC50U,folk,US
   solo,pno OAK 000205 $1.50   (R661)

REPRINTS FROM SING OUT!, VOL. 6
   *CC50U,folk,US
   solo,pno OAK 000206 $1.50   (R662)

REPRINTS FROM SING OUT!, VOL. 7
   *CC50U,folk,US
   solo,pno OAK 000207 $1.50   (R663)

REPRINTS FROM SING OUT!, VOL. 8
   *CC50U,folk,US
   solo,pno OAK 000208 $1.50   (R664)

REPRINTS FROM SING OUT!, VOL. 9
   *CC50U,folk,US
   solo,pno OAK 000209 $1.50   (R665)

REPRINTS FROM SING OUT!, VOL. 10
   *CC50U,folk,US
   solo,pno OAK 000210 $1.50   (R666)

REPRINTS FROM SING OUT!, VOL. 11
   *CC50U,folk,US
   solo,pno OAK 000211 $1.50   (R667)

REPRINTS FROM SING OUT!, VOL. 12
   *CC50U,folk,US
   solo,pno OAK 000212 $2.45   (R668)

REPRINTS FROM THE PEOPLE'S SONGS
   BULLETIN (1946-1949) *CCU,folk,US
   (Silber, Irwin) solo,pno OAK 000051
   $2.45   (R669)

REPROCHES see Schumann, Robert
   (Alexander)

REPUBLIQUE ARGENTINE see Escher, Rudolf
   George

REQUEST, A see Woodforde-Finden, Amy

REQUIEM see Gilse, Jan van

REQUIEM see Haller, Hans Christoph

REQUIEM see Heiss, Hermann

REQUIEM see Homer

REQUIEM see Lechner, Konrad

REQUIEM see Rorem, Ned

REQUIEM see Schmid, Reinhold

REQUIEM see Trunk, Richard

REQUIEM 1965 see Barbe, Helmut

REQUIEM FOR ALLISON see Weigl, Vally

REQUIEM FUR EINEN UNBEKANNTEN see
   Hochmann, Klaus

REQUIEM PRO VIVENTIBUS see Zelenka,
   Istvan

REQUIEMS FOR THE PARTY GIRL see
   Schafer, M.

REQUIESCAT see Sharpe, Evelyn

REQUIESCAT see Young, Gordon

RES DIG, VAR LJUS see Leisring,
   Volkmar, Nouse, Ole Kirkas

RESIGNATION see Rabey, Rene

RESONET IN LAUDIBUS see Strutius,
   Thomas

RESPIGHI, OTTORINO (1879-1936)
   Abbandono
      [It] solo,pno BONGIOVANI 382 s.p.
      see from Sei Melodie   (R670)

   Acqua
      see Deita Silvane

   Au Milieu Du Jardin
      [Fr] solo,pno BONGIOVANI 483 s.p.
      see from Sei Liriche (Prima
      Serie)   (R671)

   Ballade *see Ballata

   Ballata
      [It] solo,pno BONGIOVANI 389 s.p.
      see from Cinque Canti All'antica
                               (R672)
      "Ballade" [It] Mez solo,pno
      BONGIOVANI 597 s.p. see from
      Cinque Canti All'antica   (R673)

   Bella Porta Di Rubini
      [It] Mez solo,pno BONGIOVANI 390
      s.p. see from Cinque Canti
      All'antica   (R674)
      [It] S solo,pno BONGIOVANI 549 s.p.
      see from Cinque Canti All'antica
                               (R675)
      "Lonely Gate Of Crimson Rubies,
      Walk On" [It/Eng] Mez solo,pno
      BONGIOVANI s.p. see from Cinque
      Canti All'antica   (R676)
      "Lovely Gate Of Crimson Rubies"
      [Eng] Mez solo,pno BONGIOVANI
      s.p.   (R677)

   Brouillards *see Nebbie

   Canto Funebre
      see Cinque Liriche

   Canzone Di Re Enzo
      [It] T solo,pno BONGIOVANI 391 s.p.
      see from Cinque Canti All'antica
                               (R678)

   Cinque Canti All'antica *see
      Ballata; Bella Porta Di Rubini;
      Canzone Di Re Enzo; L'udir
      Talvolta; Ma Come Potrei (R679)

   Cinque Liriche
      Mez/Bar solo,pno cmplt ed RICORDI-
      ENG 117196 s.p.
         contains: Canto Funebre; I Tempi,
         Assai Lontani; La Fine; Par Les
         Soirs; Par L'etreinte   (R680)

   Constrasto
      [It] Mez solo,pno BONGIOVANI 253
      s.p.   (R681)

   Crepuscolo
      see Deita Silvane

   Deita Silvane
      solo,pno cmplt ed RICORDI-ENG
      117086 s.p.
         contains: Acqua; Crepuscolo;
         Egle; I Fauni; Musica In Horto
                               (R682)

   E Se Un Giorno Tornasse...
      Mez solo,pno RICORDI-ENG 117459
      s.p.   (R683)

   Egle
      see Deita Silvane

   I Fauni
      see Deita Silvane

   I Tempi, Assai Lontani
      see Cinque Liriche

RESPIGHI, OTTORINO (cont'd.)
   Il Sogno Che T'innamora (from La
      Fiamma)
      S solo,pno RICORDI-ENG 131369 s.p.
                               (R684)

   Il Tramonto
      [It] Mez solo,4strings sc RICORDI-
      ENG 117087 s.p., ipa, voc sc
      RICORDI-ENG 117089 s.p.   (R685)
      female solo,2vln,vla,vcl quarto
      RICORDI-ENG 117087 s.p.   (R686)
      Mez solo,pno RICORDI-ENG 117089
      s.p.   (R687)

   In Alto Mare
      [It] solo,pno BONGIOVANI 381 s.p.
      see from Sei Melodie   (R688)

   Invito Alla Danza
      [It] Bar solo,pno BONGIOVANI 254
      s.p.   (R689)
      [It] T solo,pno BONGIOVANI 288 s.p.
                               (R690)

   Io Sono La Madre
      A solo,pno RICORDI-ENG 118786 s.p.
      see from Quatro Liriche   (R691)

   La Fine
      see Cinque Liriche

   La Mamma E Come Il Pane Caldo
      A/B solo,pno RICORDI-ENG 118785
      s.p. see from Quatro Liriche
                               (R692)

   La Najade
      [It] solo,pno BONGIOVANI 1273 s.p.
      see from Quattro Liriche (R693)

   La Sera
      [It] solo,pno BONGIOVANI 1274 s.p.
      see from Quattro Liriche (R694)

   Lauda Per La Nativita Del Signore
      *sac,Xmas
      solo,pno RICORDI-ENG 121983 s.p.
                               (R695)

   L'ombra Mi Aduggia (from Il Fiamma)
      S solo,pno RICORDI-ENG 131368 s.p.
                               (R696)

   Lonely Gate Of Crimson Rubies, Walk
      On *see Bella Porta Di Rubini

   Lovely Gate Of Crimson Rubies *see
      Bella Porta Di Rubini

   L'udir Talvolta
      [It] solo,pno BONGIOVANI 387 s.p.
      see from Cinque Canti All'antica
                               (R697)

   Ma Come Potrei
      [It] solo,pno BONGIOVANI 388 s.p.
      see from Cinque Canti All'antica
                               (R698)

   Mattinata
      [Eng] solo,pno BONGIOVANI 1636 s.p.
      see from Sei Melodie   (R699)
      [It] solo,pno BONGIOVANI 383 s.p.
      see from Sei Melodie   (R700)

   Mattino Di Luce
      A/B solo,pno RICORDI-ENG 118787
      s.p. see from Quatro Liriche
                               (R701)

   Mists *see Nebbie

   Musica In Horto
      see Deita Silvane

   Nebbie
      [It] S/T solo,pno BONGIOVANI 255
      s.p.   (R702)
      [It] Mez/Bar solo,pno BONGIOVANI
      251 s.p.   (R703)
      [It] A solo,pno BONGIOVANI 550 s.p.
                               (R704)
      "Brouillards" [It/Fr] Mez solo,pno
      BONGIOVANI 590 s.p.   (R705)
      "Mists" [It/Eng] Mez solo,pno
      BONGIOVANI 592 s.p.   (R706)
      "Mists" [It/Eng] S/T solo,pno
      BONGIOVANI 1335 s.p.   (R707)
      "Mists" [It/Eng] A solo,pno
      BONGIOVANI 1336 s.p.   (R708)
      "Nebel" [It/Ger] Mez solo,pno
      BONGIOVANI 591 s.p.   (R709)

   Nebel *see Nebbie

   Nel Giardino
      [It] Mez solo,pno BONGIOVANI 526
      s.p. see from Sei Liriche
      (Seconda Serie)   (R710)

   Nevicata
      [It] Mez/Bar solo,pno BONGIOVANI
      252 s.p.   (R711)
      [It/Eng] Mez solo,pno BONGIOVANI
      885 s.p.   (R712)
      [It] S/T solo,pno BONGIOVANI 256
      s.p.   (R713)
      [It/Eng] S solo,pno BONGIOVANI 886
      s.p.   (R714)

RESPIGHI, OTTORINO (cont'd.)

No, Non E Morto Il Figlio Tuo
A/B solo,pno RICORDI-ENG 118784
s.p. see from Quatro Liriche
(R715)

Noel Ancien (No. 1)
[Fr] solo,pno BONGIOVANI 484 s.p.
see from Sei Liriche (Prima
Serie)   (R716)

Noel Ancien (No. 2)
[It] Mez solo,pno BONGIOVANI 524
s.p. see from Sei Liriche
(Seconda Serie)   (R717)

Notte
[It/Eng] Mez solo,pno BONGIOVANI
595 s.p. see from Sei Liriche
(Seconda Serie)   (R718)
[It] S solo,pno BONGIOVANI 521A
s.p. see from Sei Liriche
(Seconda Serie)   (R719)
[It] Mez solo,pno BONGIOVANI 521
s.p. see from Sei Liriche
(Seconda Serie)   (R720)
[Eng] S solo,pno BONGIOVANI 1694
s.p. see from Sei Liriche
(Seconda Serie)   (R721)

O Falce Di Luna
Mez solo,pno BONGIOVANI 481 s.p.
see from Sei Liriche (Prima
Serie)   (R722)
S solo,pno BONGIOVANI 481A s.p. see
from Sei Liriche (Prima Serie)
(R723)

Par Les Soirs
see Cinque Liriche

Par L'etreinte
see Cinque Liriche

Piccola Bianca Mano
[It] Mez solo,pno BONGIOVANI 525
s.p. see from Sei Liriche
(Seconda Serie)   (R724)

Pioggia
Mez solo,pno BONGIOVANI 486 s.p.
see from Sei Liriche (Prima
Serie)   (R725)
S solo,pno BONGIOVANI 486A s.p. see
from Sei Liriche (Prima Serie)
(R726)

Povero Cor
[It] solo,pno BONGIOVANI 384 s.p.
see from Sei Melodie   (R727)

Quando Nasceste Voi
[It] S solo,pno BONGIOVANI 586 s.p.
see from Quattro Rispetti Toscani
(R728)

Quatro Liriche *see Io Sono La
Madre; La Mamma E Come Il Pane
Caldo; Mattino Di Luce; No, Non E
Morto Il Figlio Tuo   (R729)

Quattro Liriche *see La Najade; La
Sera; Sopra Un'aria Antica; Un
Sogno   (R730)

Quattro Rispetti Toscani *see Quando
Nasceste Voi; Razzolan, Sopra A
L'aja, Le Galline; Venitelo A
Vedere 'I Mi' Piccino; Vieni Di
La, Lontan Lontano...   (R731)

Razzolan, Sopra A L'aja, Le Galline
[It] S solo,pno BONGIOVANI 589 s.p.
see from Quattro Rispetti Toscani
(R732)

Repos En Egypte
[Fr] Mez solo,pno BONGIOVANI 523
s.p. see from Sei Liriche
(Seconda Serie)   (R733)

Scherzo
[It] S/Mez solo,pno BONGIOVANI 238
s.p.   (R734)

Sei Liriche (Prima Serie) *see Au
Milieu Du Jardin; Noel Ancien
(No. 1); O Falce Di Luna;
Pioggia; Serenata Indiana; Van Li
Effluvi De Le Rose   (R735)

Sei Liriche (Seconda Serie) *see Nel
Giardino; Noel Ancien (No. 2);
Notte; Piccola Bianca Mano; Repos
En Egypte; Su Una Violetta Morta
(R736)

Sei Melodie *see Abbandono; In Alto
Mare; Mattinata; Povero Cor; Si
Tu Veux; Soupir   (R737)

Serenata Indiana
[It] solo,pno BONGIOVANI 485 s.p.
see from Sei Liriche (Prima
Serie)   (R738)

Si Tu Veux
[Fr] solo,pno BONGIOVANI 385 s.p.
see from Sei Melodie   (R739)

RESPIGHI, OTTORINO (cont'd.)

Sopra Un'aria Antica
[It] solo,pno BONGIOVANI 1275 s.p.
see from Quattro Liriche   (R740)

Soupir
[Fr] solo,pno BONGIOVANI 386 s.p.
see from Sei Melodie   (R741)

Stornellatrice
[It] S/T solo,pno BONGIOVANI 267
s.p.   (R742)
[It] Mez/Bar solo,pno BONGIOVANI
268 s.p.   (R743)
[Eng] S/T solo,pno BONGIOVANI 1693
s.p.   (R744)
[It/Eng] Mez/Bar solo,pno
BONGIOVANI 593 s.p.   (R745)

Stornello (from Re Enzo)
[It] 1-2 soli,pno BONGIOVANI 236
s.p.   (R746)
2 soli,pno BONGIOVANI 236 s.p.
(R747)

Su Una Violetta Morta
[It] Mez solo,pno BONGIOVANI 522
s.p. see from Sei Liriche
(Seconda Serie)   (R748)

Un Sogno
[It] solo,pno BONGIOVANI 1272 s.p.
see from Quattro Liriche   (R749)

Van Li Effluvi De Le Rose
solo,pno BONGIOVANI 482 s.p. see
from Sei Liriche (Prima Serie)
(R750)

Venitelo A Vedere 'I Mi' Piccino
[It] S solo,pno BONGIOVANI 587 s.p.
see from Quattro Rispetti Toscani
(R751)
[It] Mez solo,pno BONGIOVANI 587A
s.p.   (R752)

Vieni Di La, Lontan Lontano...
[It] S solo,pno BONGIOVANI 588 s.p.
see from Quattro Rispetti Toscani
(R753)

RESPONSE see Walker, George

RESSEMBLANCE see Chaminade, Cecile

REST see Glanville-Hicks, Peggy

REST see Handel, George Frideric, Ombra
Mai Fu

REST IN THE LORD see Stickles, William

REST, MY AIN BAIRNIE see Lawson,
Malcolm

REST, O MY DEAR ONE see Brahms,
Johannes, Ruhe Sussliebchen Im
Schatten

RESTA... E TI RIPOSA see Charpentier,
Gustave

RESTA IMMOBILE see Rossini, Gioacchino

RESTA IN PACE IDOLO MIO see Cimarosa,
Domenico

RESTE! see Chaminade, Cecile

RESTLESS AUTUMN see Szollosy, A.

RESTLESS ONES, THE (THEME SONG) *sac
(Carmichael, Ralph) solo,pno WORD
S-32   (R754)

RESTORE MY SOUL see Lister, Mosie

RESURRECTION see Rambo, Reba

RESURRECTION see Messiaen, Oliver

RESURRECTION, THE see Curran, Pearl
Gildersleeve

RESURRECTION, THE see Rorem, Ned

RESURRECTION MORN, THE see Rodney, Paul

RETOUR see Perissas, M.

RETOUR see Vuillemin, L.

RETOUR A LA TERRE see Schmitt, Florent

RETOURNONS DANS LES BOIS see Casadesus,
Henri Gustave

RETREAT see LaForge, Frank,
Schlupfwinkel

RETREAT, THE see Albeniz, Isaac

RETURN *sac
(Carmichael, Ralph) solo,pno WORD
S-424   (R755)

RETURN, THE see DiBiase, E.

RETURN, THE see Hier, Ethel Glenn

RETURN OF PUSHKIN, THE see Nabokov,
Nicolas

RETURN OH GOD see Handel, George
Frideric

RETURNING, WE HEAR THE LARKS see Cooke,
S.C.

REULAND, JACQUES (1918-   )
Five Lyrics *CC5U
Mez solo,pno DONEMUS s.p.   (R756)

Handsome Nell
see Songs By Robert Burns

Here's To The Health
see Songs By Robert Burns

Lyric
solo,2fl,ob,2clar,2horn,2trp,
strings DONEMUS s.p.   (R757)

Magnificat
solo,fl,pno DONEMUS s.p.   (R758)

Ploughmans Life, The
see Songs By Robert Burns

Songs By Robert Burns
high solo,pno DONEMUS s.p.
contains: Handsome Nell; Here's
To The Health; Ploughmans Life,
The   (R759)

REUNION IN HEAVEN see Alcorn, Jerry

REUTER, FRITZ (1896-1963)
Der Hase Und Der Igel
narrator,2fl,2ob,2clar,2bsn,4horn,
2trp,trom,timp,perc,strings,pno
voc sc BREITKOPF-L EB 4049 $4.00,
ipr   (R760)

REUTTER, HERMANN (1900-   )
Acht Russische Lieder *Op.21, CC8U
high solo,pno SCHOTTS 2042 s.p.
(R761)

Alte Weihnachtslieder *CCU,Xmas
(Ruhrmann) solo,pno,1inst SCHOTTS
3932 s.p.   (R762)

Andalusiana
S solo,orch voc sc SCHOTTS 5286
s.p., ipa   (R763)

Bogenschutzen *song cycle/vocalise
high solo,pno SCHOTTS 6496 s.p.
(R764)

Chamber Music By James Joyce *song
cycle
B solo,pno SCHOTTS 6494 s.p. (R765)

Die Jahreszeiten *CC4U
med solo,pno SCHOTTS 4799 s.p.
(R766)

Die Weise Von Liebe Und Tod *Op.31
solo,pno SCHOTTS 3852 s.p. (R767)

Drei Altagyptische Gedichte *CC3U
B solo,pno SCHOTTS 5287 s.p. (R768)

Drei Gesange *Op.56, CC3U
low solo,pno SCHOTTS 3738 s.p.
(R769)

Drei Lieder *Op.61, CC3U
high solo,pno SCHOTTS 3871 s.p.
(R770)

Drei Lieder *Op.67, CC3U
high solo,pno SCHOTTS 3851 s.p.
(R771)

Drei Lieder *Op.60, CC3U
high solo,pno SCHOTTS 3872 s.p.
(R772)

Drei Monologe Des Empedokles *CC3U
Bar solo,pno/orch voc sc SCHOTTS
6264 s.p.   (R773)

Drei Zigeunerromanzen *CC3U
med solo,pno SCHOTTS 4943 s.p.
(R774)

Ein Fullen Ward Geboren
med solo,pno SCHOTTS 5299 s.p.
(R775)

Ein Kleines Requiem *sac
B solo,vcl,pno SCHOTTS 5190 s.p.
(R776)

Epitaph Fur Einen Dichter
high solo,pno SCHOTTS 5289 s.p.
(R777)

Funf Antike Oden *Op.57, CC5U
med female solo,vla,pno SCHOTTS
3674 s.p.   (R778)

Funf Fragmente Nach Fr. Holderlin
*CC5U
T solo,pno SCHOTTS 5532 s.p. (R779)

Funf Lieder *Op.58, CC5U
low solo,pno SCHOTTS 3675 s.p.
(R780)

REUTTER, HERMANN (cont'd.)

Funf Lieder Nach Gedichten Von M.L.
   Kaschnitz *song cycle
   med solo,pno SCHOTTS 6495 s.p.
                                        (R781)

Gesicht Und Antlitz *Op.64, CC7U
   B solo,pno SCHOTTS 3666 s.p. (R782)

Gesicht Und Antlitz *Op.65, CC12U
   high solo,pno SCHOTTS 3667 s.p.
                                        (R783)

Hymne An Deutschland
   solo,pno SCHOTTS s.p.   (R784)

Kleine Ballade Von Den Drei Flussen
   solo,pno/orch voc sc SCHOTTS 5169
   s.p., ipa   (R785)

Kleines Geitliches Konzert *sac,
   concerto
   A solo,vla SCHOTTS 4486 s.p. (R786)

Lieder Der Liebe
   S solo,pno SCHOTTS 4298 s.p. (R787)

Meine Dunkeln Hande
   Bar solo,pno SCHOTTS 4761 s.p.
                                        (R788)

Miss Brevis *Op.22, sac
   A solo,vln,vcl SCHOTTS 3153 s.p.
                                        (R789)

Neun Lieder *Op.59, CC9U
   high solo,pno SCHOTTS 3668 s.p.
                                        (R790)

Neun Lieder Nach Gedichten Von R.
   Huch *song cycle
   female solo/male solo,pno SCHOTTS
   6492 s.p.   (R791)

Sechs Gedichte Aus Goethes
   Westostlichem Diwan *Op.73, CC6U
   SBar soli,pno SCHOTTS 4118 s.p.
                                        (R792)

Sechs Russische Lieder *Op.23, CC6U
   high solo,pno SCHOTTS 2139 s.p.
                                        (R793)

Sechs Spate Gedichte *CC6U
   med solo,pno SCHOTTS 4798 s.p.
                                        (R794)

Sieben Russische Gesange *Op.68,
   CC7U
   med-high solo,pno SCHOTTS 3297 s.p.
                                        (R795)

Solo-Kantate *Op.45, cant
   A solo,pno,vla SCHOTTS 3853 s.p.
                                        (R796)

Spanischen Totentanz *CCU
   2 med soli,orch/pno voc sc SCHOTTS
   5756 s.p., ipa   (R797)

Szene Und Monolog Der Marfa (from
   Demetrius)
   S solo,orch voc sc SCHOTTS 5923
   s.p.   (R798)

Triptychon "Sankt Sebastian
   Bar solo,pno SCHOTTS 6112 s.p.
                                        (R799)

Vier Lieder Nach Gedichten Von N.
   Sachs *song cycle
   med solo,pno SCHOTTS 6493 s.p.
                                        (R800)

Weihnachtskantilene *Xmas
   med solo,pno SCHOTTS 4487 s.p.
                                        (R801)

REVE see Carolus-Duran, P.

REVE see Goublier, G.

REVE see Ollone, Max d'

REVE see Orland, Henry

REVE A DEUX see Perissas, M.

REVE D'AMANT see Delmet, Paul

REVE D'AMOUR see Sieulle, J.

REVE DE NOEL see Absil, Jean

REVE DE TROTIN see Berger, Rod.

REVE D'UN SOIR see Chaminade, Cecile

REVE FANTASQUE see Absil, Jean

REVE NOIR see Absil, Jean

REVE POUR L'HIVER see Orthel, Leon

REVE SUR LE SABLE see Ropartz, Joseph
   Guy

REVEIL see Barbier, Rene

REVEIL AU BOIS DORMANT see Arma, Paul

REVEIL DU COEUR see Mendelssohn-
   Bartholdy, Felix

REVEILLEZ-VOUS
   see Chants De France Vol. I

REVEILLEZ-VOUS see Seiber, Matyas

REVEILLEZ-VOUS BERGERE JOLIE see
   Schule, B.

REVEL, PETER
   Autrefois
      solo,pno/inst DURAND s.p. (R802)

   Confession, The
      solo,pno (E flat maj) ASHDOWN s.p.
                                        (R803)

   Dance Of The Crystal Fairy
      solo,pno (B flat maj) ASHDOWN
      s.p.   (R804)

   Les Hiboux
      solo,pno/inst DURAND s.p. (R805)

   Oubli
      solo,pno/inst DURAND s.p. (R806)

   Pont Bleu
      solo,pno/inst DURAND s.p. (R807)

   Promenade
      solo,pno/inst DURAND s.p. (R808)

   Serenade To A Beautiful Day
      low solo,orch (E flat maj) ASHDOWN
      s.p., ipr   (R809)
      high solo,orch (F maj) ASHDOWN
      s.p., ipr   (R810)

   Spring Comes To Stay
      solo,orch (E flat maj) ASHDOWN
      s.p., ipr   (R811)

   Summer Evening
      solo,orch (G maj) ASHDOWN s.p., ipr
                                        (R812)

   Un Jour Ailleurs
      solo,pno/inst DURAND s.p. (R813)

REVELACION see Ugarte, Floro M.

REVER, AIMER, PLEURER see Poujade, L.

REVERIE see Hahn, Reynaldo

REVERIE see Lattes, M.

REVERIE see Marty, (Eugene) Georges

REVERIE see Rachmaninoff, Sergey
   Vassilievitch

REVERIE see Rhene-Baton

REVERIE see Saint-Saens, Camille

REVERIE see Shepherd, Arthur

REVERIE see Williams, Alice Crane

REVERIE-BARCAROLLE see Jacopo Da
   Bologna

REVERIE OF A SOLDIER see Thompson, A.

REVES see Gedalge, Andre

REVES see Ravel, Maurice

REVES see Wagner, Richard, Traume

REVES see Absil, Jean

REVES DE MERE see Schumann, Robert
   (Alexander)

REVES DEFUNTS see Chaminade, Cecile

REVES DU SOIR see Rabey, Rene

REVES TROMPEUR see Schumann, Robert
   (Alexander)

REVEUSE see Depecker, Rose

REVEUSE DEMOISELLE see Delmet, Paul

REVEYRON, JOSEPH
   Sh'ma Yisrael
      high solo,pno ISRAELI 222H $2.10
                                        (R814)
      low solo,pno ISRAELI 222L $2.10
                                        (R815)

REVIENS NYSA see Clerice, J.

REVIVE OUR SPIRIT, O LORD see Tompkins

REVOLTE see Busser, Henri-Paul

REVOLUTION COME THE SPRING see Illo,
   Maria

REYNOLDS
   Didn't He Shine? (composed with
   McDill) *sac
   solo,pno BENSON S5346-R $1.00
                                        (R816)

REYNOLDS, ALFRED
   Ah! How Delightful The Morning
   Mez solo,pno ELKIN 27.1550.03 s.p.
                                        (R817)

REYNOLDS, MALVINA
   Little Boxes And Other Handmade Songs
   *CC50U
   solo,pno OAK 000044 $2.95   (R818)

   Muse Of Parker Street, The *CC56U
   solo,pno OAK 000045 $2.95   (R819)

REYNOLDS, ROGER (1934-   )
   Again
   SS soli,2fl,2trom,2perc,2bvl,
   electronic tape PETERS 66249 s.p.
                                        (R820)

   Emperor Of Ice Cream, The
   8 soli,perc,pno,bvl sc PETERS 6616
   $5.50   (R821)

REYNOLDS, WILLIAM JENSEN (1920-   )
   Give The Lord A Chance (from Reaching
   People)
   solo,pno BROADMAN 4590-32 $1.00
                                        (R822)

   I Believe *sac
   solo,pno BROADMAN 4590-35 $1.00
                                        (R823)

   My Brother's Brother *sac
   solo,pno BROADMAN 4590-18 $.75
                                        (R824)

   People To People
   high solo,pno BROADMAN 4590-25
   $1.00   (R825)
   solo,pno BROADMAN 4590-19 $.75
                                        (R826)

   Share His Love (from Reaching People)
   solo,pno BROADMAN 4590-34 $1.00
                                        (R827)

   We Have To Find A Way *sac
   solo,pno BROADMAN 4590-16 $.75
                                        (R828)

REYNVAAN, M.C.C.
   Aan...
   see Shelly Lieder

   Aan Mary Shelly
   see Shelly Lieder

   Dehmel Lieder *CC7L
   solo,pno ALSBACH s.p.   (R829)

   Een Klaagzang
   see Shelly Lieder

   Liedje
   see Shelly Lieder

   Op Fanny Goodwin
   see Shelly Lieder

   Shelly Lieder
   solo,pno ALSBACH s.p.
      contains: Aan...; Aan Mary
      Shelly; Een Klaagzang; Liedje;
      Op Fanny Goodwin   (R830)

   Zeven Liederen *CC7L
   solo,pno ALSBACH s.p.   (R831)

REZAC, IVAN (1924-   )
   Ctyri Pisne *CC4U
   low solo,pno CZECH s.p.   (R832)

   Kainar Beim Wasser *see Kainar U
   Vody

   Kainar U Vody *song cycle
   "Kainar Beim Wasser" B solo,pno
   CZECH s.p.   (R833)

REZEDA *CC95U,folk,Hung
   (Domokos) solo,pno BUDAPEST 1501 s.p.
                                        (R834)

REZITATIVE UND ARIEN AUS KANTATEN HEFT
   I see Bach, Johann Sebastian

REZITATIVE UND ARIEN AUS KANTATEN HEFT
   II see Bach, Johann Sebastian

REZNICEK, EMIL NIKOLAUS VON (1860-1945)
   Der Traurige Garten
   voc sc BIRNBACH s.p. see also Drei
   Deutsche Volkslieder Aus "Des
   Knaben Wunderhorn"   (R835)

   Drei Deutsche Volkslieder Aus "Des
   Knaben Wunderhorn"
   BIRNBACH solo,2fl,2ob,2clar,2bsn,
   2horn,2trp,timp,perc,strings sc
   s.p.; rental
      contains & see also: Der Traurige
      Garten; Gedankenstille; Schwimm
      Hin, Ringlein   (R836)

   Gedankenstille
   voc sc BIRNBACH s.p. see also Drei
   Deutsche Volkslieder Aus "Des
   Knaben Wunderhorn"   (R837)

   Schwimm Hin, Ringlein
   voc sc BIRNBACH s.p. see also Drei
   Deutsche Volkslieder Aus "Des
   Knaben Wunderhorn"   (R838)

REZNICK, HYMAN
Seal Upon Thy Heart, A *see Simeni
Chachosom

Simeni Chachosom *sac,Marriage
"Seal Upon Thy Heart, A" [Heb/Eng]
high solo/med solo,pno TRANSCON.
TV 485 $.85   (R839)

RHAPSODIE see Birch, Robert Fairfax

RHAU, JOHANNES (1520-1600)
Deutsche Zwiegesange *sec,CC12U
(Ameln, Konrad) TB/TT/ST soli,org
(med) BAREN. 68 s.p.   (R840)

RHEINBERGER, JOSEF (1839-1901)
Ave Maria *Op.171,No.1
[Lat/Eng] A/Bar solo,pno LEUCKART
$1.25   (R841)
[Lat/Eng] S/T solo,pno LEUCKART
$1.25   (R842)

Holy Night *sac
high solo,pno BELWIN $1.50   (R843)

Kleiner Und Leichter Messgesang
*Op.62, sac,Mass
S solo,org/harmonium LEUCKART s.p.
                              (R844)
Liederbuch Fur Kinder *Op.152, CC30U
solo,pno LEUCKART s.p.   (R845)

RHEINISCHE LIEDER UND TANZE see
Schmidt, Hugo Wolfram

RHEINISCHE SERENADE UND SPIELMUSIK see
Muller, Rudolf

RHEINLEGENDCHEN see Mahler, Gustav

RHENE-BATON (1879-1940)
Apaisement *Op.29,No.4
see Au Coin De L'atre

Apporte Les Cristaux Dores *Op.14,
No.1
low solo,pno/inst DURAND s.p. see
also Les Heures D'ete   (R846)

Au Coin De L'atre
solo,pno/inst cmplt ed DURAND s.p.
contains: Apaisement, Op.29,No.4;
Fumees, Op.29,No.3; La Flamme
Chante, Op.29,No.1; Par Un Soir
D'hiver, Op.29,No.2   (R847)

Au Desert *Op.16,No.3
med solo,pno/inst DURAND s.p. see
also Cinq Melodies Sur Des
Poesies De Jean Lahor   (R848)

Berceuse *Op.7,No.7
[Fr/Eng] Mez/Bar solo,pno/inst
DURAND s.p. see also Chansons
Douces   (R849)
[Fr/Eng] S/T solo,pno/inst DURAND
s.p. see also Chansons Douces (R850)

Bretonnes
Bar/Mez solo,pno/inst DURAND s.p.
                              (R851)

Ce Que J'aime *Op.7,No.8
[Fr/Eng] Mez solo,pno/inst DURAND
s.p. see also Chansons Douces (R852)

Chansons Bretonnes
med solo,pno/inst cmplt ed DURAND
s.p.
contains & see also: La Chanson
De La Fleur Rouge; La Chanson
De La Maison Triste; La Chanson
De L'Exile; La Chanson De Noel;
La Chanson Des Fleurs
Nouvelles; La Chanson Du Bois
D'Amour; La Chanson Du Bouquet
D'anjoncs; La Chanson Du Verger
Fleuri   (R853)

Chansons Douces *Op.7,No.1-12
[Fr/Eng] Mez solo,pno/inst cmplt ed
DURAND s.p.
contains & see also: Berceuse,
Op.7,No.7; Ce Que J'aime, Op.7,
No.8; Crepuscule, Op.7,No.9; Je
Ne Me Souviens Plus, Op.7,No.3;
Je Veux, Op.7,No.5; La Plainte
Du Vent, Op.7,No.10; Le Revoir,
Op.7,No.11; Reverie, Op.7,
No.12; Silence, Op.7,No.6; Soir
D'hiver, Op.7,No.4; Soyons
Unis, Op.7,No.1; Un Bruit De
Rames, Op.7,No.2   (R854)

Chansons Pour Marycinthe
solo,orch DURAND s.p., ipr
contains: Douceur Du Soir Dans Le
Village, Op.50,No.3; Le
Claquement Bref Des Sabots,
Op.50,No.2; Le Premier Jour Ou
Je Vis, Op.50,No.1; Pendant Que
Vous Dormez, Op.50,No.4; Vous
Aurez Une Maison Blanche,
Op.50,No.6; Vous Ne Pourriez
Savior, Op.50,No.5
see also: Douceur Du Soir Dans Le

RHENE-BATON (cont'd.)

Village, Op.50,No.3   (R855)

Cinq Melodies Sur Des Poesies De Jean
Lahor *Op.16,No.1-5
med solo,pno/inst cmplt ed DURAND
s.p.
contains & see also: Au Desert,
Op.16,No.3; Nocturne, Op.16,
No.2; Nuit D'autrefois, Op.16,
No.1; Serenade Melancolique,
Op.16,No.4; Tendresse, Op.16,
No.5   (R856)

Crepuscule *Op.7,No.9
[Fr/Eng] Mez solo,pno/inst DURAND
s.p. see also Chansons Douces (R857)

Dans Un Coin De Violettes
med solo,orch cmplt ed DURAND s.p.,
ipr
contains & see also: Pour Le Lys;
Pour Mon Coeur; Priere;
Sanctuaire D'Asie; Sous La
Protection Des Violettes;
Veillee Heureuse   (R858)

Deux Melodies *see Le Repos En
Egypte, Op.18,No.2; Nuit Blanche,
Op.18,No.1   (R859)

Deux Melodies Sur Des Poesies De
Renee Vivien *see Mon Paradis,
Op.47,No.2; Notre Heure, Op.47,
No.1   (R860)

Douceur Du Soir Dans Le Village
*Op.50,No.3
solo,orch DURAND s.p., ipr see also
Chansons Pour Marycinthe   (R861)

Espoir En Dieu *Op.15,No.2
Mez solo,pno/inst DURAND s.p. see
from Trois Melodies   (R862)

Fleurs D'ajonc *Op.52,No.5
solo,pno/inst DURAND s.p. see from
Pour Celles Qui Restent   (R863)

Frele Comme Un Harmonica *Op.14,No.2
low solo,pno/inst (in 2 keys)
DURAND s.p. see also Les Heures
D'ete   (R864)

Fumees *Op.29,No.3
see Au Coin De L'atre

Il Pleut Des Petales De Fleurs
*Op.14,No.6
low solo,pno/inst DURAND s.p. see
also Les Heures D'ete   (R865)

Je Ne Me Souviens Plus *Op.7,No.3
[Fr/Eng] Mez solo,pno/inst DURAND
s.p. see also Chansons Douces (R866)

Je Veux *Op.7,No.5
[Fr/Eng] Mez solo,pno/inst DURAND
s.p. see also Chansons Douces (R867)

La Chanson De Celles Qui Restent
*Op.52,No.7
solo,pno/inst DURAND s.p. see from
Pour Celles Qui Restent   (R868)

La Chanson De La Fleur Rouge
med solo,pno/inst DURAND s.p. see
also Chansons Bretonnes   (R869)

La Chanson De La Maison Triste
med solo,pno/inst DURAND s.p. see
also Chansons Bretonnes   (R870)

La Chanson De L'Exile
med solo,pno/inst DURAND s.p. see
also Chansons Bretonnes   (R871)

La Chanson De Noel
med solo,pno/inst DURAND s.p. see
also Chansons Bretonnes   (R872)

La Chanson Des Fleurs Nouvelles
med solo,pno/inst DURAND s.p. see
also Chansons Bretonnes   (R873)

La Chanson Du Bois D'Amour
med solo,pno/inst DURAND s.p. see
also Chansons Bretonnes   (R874)

La Chanson Du Bouquet D'anjoncs
med solo,pno/inst DURAND s.p. see
also Chansons Bretonnes   (R875)

La Chanson Du Verger Fleuri
med solo,pno/inst DURAND s.p. see
also Chansons Bretonnes   (R876)

La Derniere Berceuse *Op.52,No.3
solo,pno/inst DURAND s.p. see from
Pour Celles Qui Restent   (R877)

La Flamme Chante *Op.29,No.1
see Au Coin De L'atre

RHENE-BATON (cont'd.)

La Plainte Du Vent *Op.7,No.10
[Fr/Eng] Mez solo,pno/inst DURAND
s.p. see also Chansons Douces
                              (R878)

L'Ame Des Iris *Op.15,No.1
S/T solo,pno/inst DURAND s.p. see
from Trois Melodies   (R879)
Mez/Bar solo,pno/inst DURAND s.p.
see from Trois Melodies   (R880)

Le Claquement Bref Des Sabots
*Op.50,No.2
see Chansons Pour Marycinthe

Le Grands Jasmins *Op.14,No.4
low solo,pno/inst DURAND s.p. see
also Les Heures D'ete   (R881)

Le Premier Jour Ou Je Vis *Op.50,
No.1
see Chansons Pour Marycinthe

Le Repos En Egypte *Op.18,No.2
low solo,pno/inst DURAND s.p. see
from Deux Melodies   (R882)

Le Revoir *Op.7,No.11
[Fr/Eng] Mez solo,pno/inst DURAND
s.p. see also Chansons Douces (R883)

Les Heures D'ete *Op.14,No.1-6
low solo,pno/inst cmplt ed DURAND
s.p.
contains & see also: Apporte Les
Cristaux Dores, Op.14,No.1;
Frele Comme Un Harmonica,
Op.14,No.2; Il Pleut Des
Petales De Fleurs, Op.14,No.6;
Le Grands Jasmins, Op.14,No.4;
Lune De Cuivre, Op.14,No.3; Ton
Menton Pose Dans Ta Main,
Op.14,No.5   (R884)

Les Lys *Op.52,No.6
solo,pno/inst DURAND s.p. see from
Pour Celles Qui Restent   (R885)

Lune De Cuivre *Op.14,No.3
low solo,pno/inst (in 2 keys)
DURAND s.p. see also Les Heures
D'ete   (R886)

Mendiants *Op.52,No.2
solo,pno/inst DURAND s.p. see from
Pour Celles Qui Restent   (R887)

Mon Paradis *Op.47,No.2
solo,pno/inst DURAND s.p. see from
Deux Melodies Sur Des Poesies De
Renee Vivien   (R888)

Nocturne *Op.16,No.2
med solo,pno/inst DURAND s.p. see
also Cinq Melodies Sur Des
Poesies De Jean Lahor   (R889)

Notre Heure *Op.47,No.1
solo,pno/inst DURAND s.p. see from
Deux Melodies Sur Des Poesies De
Renee Vivien   (R890)

Nuit Blanche *Op.18,No.1
med solo,pno/inst DURAND s.p. see
from Deux Melodies   (R891)

Nuit D'autrefois *Op.16,No.1
med solo,pno/inst DURAND s.p. see
also Cinq Melodies Sur Des
Poesies De Jean Lahor   (R892)

Octobre *Op.52,No.4
solo,pno/inst DURAND s.p. see from
Pour Celles Qui Restent   (R893)

Par Un Soir D'hiver *Op.29,No.2
see Au Coin De L'atre

Pendant Que Vous Dormez *Op.50,No.4
see Chansons Pour Marycinthe

Pour Celles Qui Restent *see Fleurs
D'ajonc, Op.52,No.5; La Chanson
De Celles Qui Restent, Op.52,
No.7; La Derniere Berceuse,
Op.52,No.3; Les Lys, Op.52,No.6;
Mendiants, Op.52,No.2; Octobre,
Op.52,No.4; Quand Tu Viendra,
Op.52,No.1   (R894)

Pour Le Lys
med solo,orch DURAND s.p., ipr see
also Dans Un Coin De Violettes
                              (R895)

Pour Mon Coeur
med solo,orch DURAND s.p. see
also Dans Un Coin De Violettes
                              (R896)
Priere
med solo,orch DURAND s.p., ipr see
also Dans Un Coin De Violettes
                              (R897)

Quand Tu Viendra *Op.52,No.1
solo,pno/inst DURAND s.p. see from
Pour Celles Qui Restent   (R898)

RHENE-BATON (cont'd.)

Reverie *Op.7,No.12
[Fr/Eng] Mez solo,pno/inst DURAND
s.p. see also Chansons Douces
(R899)

Sanctuaire D'Asie
med solo,orch DURAND s.p., ipr see
also Dans Un Coin De Violettes
(R900)

Serenade Melancolique *Op.16,No.4
med solo,pno/inst DURAND s.p. see
also Cinq Melodies Sur Des
Poesies De Jean Lahor   (R901)

Silence *Op.7,No.6
[Fr/Eng] Mez solo,pno/inst DURAND
s.p. see also Chansons Douces
(R902)

Soir D'hiver *Op.7,No.4
[Fr/Eng] Mez solo,pno/inst DURAND
s.p. see also Chansons Douces
(R903)

Sous La Protection Des Violettes
med solo,orch DURAND s.p., ipr see
also Dans Un Coin De Violettes
(R904)

Soyons Unis *Op.7,No.1
[Fr/Eng] Mez solo,pno/inst DURAND
s.p. see also Chansons Douces
(R905)

Tendresse *Op.16,No.5
med solo,pno/inst DURAND s.p. see
also Cinq Melodies Sur Des
Poesies De Jean Lahor   (R906)

Ton Menton Pose Dans Ta Main *Op.14,
No.5
low solo,pno/inst DURAND s.p. see
also Les Heures D'ete   (R907)

Trois Melodies *see Espoir En Dieu,
Op.15,No.2; L'Ame Des Iris,
Op.15,No.1; Ultima Verba, Op.15,
No.3   (R908)

Ultima Verba *Op.15,No.3
DURAND s.p. see from Trois Melodies
(R909)

Un Bruit De Rames *Op.7,No.2
[Fr/Eng] Mez solo,pno/inst DURAND
s.p. see also Chansons Douces
(R910)

Veillee Heureuse
med solo,orch DURAND s.p., ipr see
also Dans Un Coin De Violettes
(R911)

Vous Aurez Une Maison Blanche
*Op.50,No.6
see Chansons Pour Marycinthe

Vous Ne Pourriez Savior *Op.50,No.5
see Chansons Pour Marycinthe

RHENVINETS LOV see Peters

RHODES, PHILLIP (1940-   )
Autumn Setting
S solo,4strings sc PETERS 66472
$5.50, ipa   (R912)

Lament Of Michal, The
S solo,3fl,ob,English horn,2clar,
2bsn,4horn,2trp,3trom,tuba,timp,
4perc,harp,strings PETERS 66358
$1.25   (R913)

Recollections Of A Summer Past *CCU
AM.COMP.AL. T solo,pno $4.40; S
solo,pno $4.40   (R914)

RHOSYN YR HAF. see Williams, Meirion

RHYME see Walton, William

RHYMES FROM THE HILL see Gideon, Miriam

RIADIS, EMILE (1890-1935)
Thirteen Short Greek Songs, Book II
*CC7L
[Greek/Fr] high solo,pno SALABERT-
US $7.75   (R915)

RIBA, P.R. DE LA
Espines
[Span] med solo,pno UNION ESP. $.75
(R916)

RIBARI, ANTAL
Three Songs To Poems Of Shelley
*CC3U
solo,pno GENERAL 678 $3.00   (R917)

Two Songs To Poems Of Michelangelo
*CC2U
solo,pno GENERAL 680 $3.00   (R918)

RICCIO, GIOVANNI BATTISTA
Jubilent Omnes *sac,concerto
(Adrio, Adam) high solo,fl/vln,cont
(med) NAGELS NMA 75 $6.25   (R919)

RICCIOLINA TROTTA TROTTA see Farina,
Guido

RICCIUS, AUGUST FERDINAND (1819-1886)
Julottesang
2 soli,pno LUNDQUIST s.p.   (R920)

RICE, RUTH
Christmas Time Is A Happiness Time
*sac
solo,pno WORD S-236   (R921)

RICE, THOMAS
Fully Clothed In Armor, With Her
Shield And Spear, Athena Emerged
From The Forehead Of Zeus
SBar soli,pno sc SEESAW $6.00
(R922)

La Corona
T&narrator,chamb.orch SEESAW (R923)

RICE, TIM
Any Dream Will Do *see Webber,
Andrew Lloyd

Close Every Door *see Webber, Andrew
Lloyd

RICH, FRED
Oh What Love *sac
solo,pno WORD S-285   (R924)

RICH, GLADYS
American Lullaby
med-high solo,pno (F maj) SCHIRM.G
$.85   (R925)

Beneath A Southern Sky
high solo,pno BELWIN $1.50   (R926)

RICH MAN see Hageman, Richard

RICH MAN AM I, A see Lundstrom

RICHARD CORY see Reif, Paul

RICHARD II QUARANTE see Arrieu, Claude

RICHARD II QUARANTE see Auric, Georges

RICHARD, LEONE
Shepherd's Song, The (composed with
Hager, Joan) *sac
solo,pno SINGSPIR 7052 $1.00 (R927)

RICHARDS
Let's All Go Down To The River *see
Montgomery

RICHARDS, DAVID
Cymru Fach
low solo,pno (B flat maj) ASHDOWN
s.p.   (R928)
high solo,pno (E flat maj) ASHDOWN
s.p.   (R929)
med solo,pno (C maj) ASHDOWN s.p.
(R930)

RICHARDS, SHANE
Jesus Cares For Me *see Brown, Aaron

RICHARDS, STEPHEN
By The Waters Of Babylon (Psalm 137)
[Eng] high solo,pno/org TRANSCON.
TV 578 $1.00   (R931)

Psalm 137 *see By The Waters Of
Babylon

RICHARDSON, BETSY
Just Take Him At His Word *sac
solo,pno SINGSPIR 7108 $1.00 (R932)

RICHARDSON, T.
Mary
low solo,pno (E flat maj) PATERSON
s.p.   (R933)
med-high solo,pno (G maj) PATERSON
s.p.   (R934)
med solo,pno (F maj) PATERSON s.p.
(R935)
high solo,pno (A flat maj) PATERSON
s.p.   (R936)

RICHEPIN, T.
Fin Du Jour
solo,pno ENOCH s.p.   (R937)

Joli Joker
solo,pno AMPHION s.p. solo pt, voc
sc   (R938)

Le Cortege D'Amphitrite
solo,pno (available in 2 keys)
ENOCH s.p.   (R939)

Le Marinier Joli
solo,pno (available in 2 keys)
ENOCH s.p.   (R940)

Les Grands Peupliers
solo,vln ENOCH s.p.   (R941)

Les Petites Clochettes Bleues
solo,orch ENOCH rental   (R942)
solo,pno ENOCH s.p.   (R943)

Mon Caprice
solo,orch ENOCH rental   (R944)
solo,pno (available in 2 keys)

RICHEPIN, T. (cont'd.)

ENOCH s.p.   (R945)

RICHLEY, TOM
Mumsie O' Mine
low solo,pno (D flat maj) WILLIS
$.60   (R946)
med solo,pno (F maj) WILLIS $.60
(R947)
high solo,pno (A flat maj) WILLIS
$.60   (R948)

RICHNAU
Tess Lordan
solo,pno LUNDQUIST s.p.   (R949)

RICHTER, [ADA] (1944-   )
Today It Came
high solo,pno PRESSER $.75   (R950)

RICHTER, NICO (1915-1945)
Song For Voice And Piano
solo,pno DONEMUS s.p.   (R951)

RICKARD, JEFFREY
Lead Us, Heavenly Father
see FIVE WEDDING SONGS

RICKETTS, L.
Chorus
high solo/med solo,pno SEESAW $1.00
(R952)
Lament
high solo/med solo,pno SEESAW $1.00
(R953)

Prayer To Persephone
high solo/med solo,pno SEESAW $1.00
(R954)

RICORDI DI CELEBRI ARIE DI OPERE, VOL.
I: SOPRANO LEGGERO *CC12L
[It] S solo,pno cmplt ed RICORDI-ENG
127532 s.p. contains works by:
Bellini; Donizetti; Mayerbeer;
Rossini; Verdi   (R955)

RICORDI DI CELEBRI ARIE DI OPERE, VOL.
II: SOPRANO *CC12L
[It] S solo,pno cmplt ed RICORDI-ENG
127533 s.p. contains works by:
Boito; Puccini; Catalani; Mozart;
Ponchinelli; Rossini; Verdi (R956)

RICORDI DI CELEBRI ARIE DI OPERE, VOL.
III: MEZZOSOPRANO E CONTRALTO
*CC12L
[It] Mez/A solo,pno cmplt ed RICORDI-
ENG 127534 s.p. contains works by:
Bellini; Donizetti; Flotow; Gluck;
Ponchielli; Rossini; Verdi   (R957)

RICORDI DI CELEBRI ARIE DI OPERE, VOL.
IV: TENOR *CC12L
[It] T solo,pno cmplt ed RICORDI-ENG
127535 s.p. contains works by:
Boito; Donizetti; Flotow;
Ponchielli; Puccini; Verdi   (R958)

RICORDI DI CELEBRI ARIE DI OPERE, VOL.
V: BARITONO *CC12L
[It] Bar solo,pno cmplt ed RICORDI-
ENG 127536 s.p. contains works by:
Donizetti; Mozart; Puccini;
Rossini; Verdi; Wagner   (R959)

RICORDI DI CELEBRI ARIE DI OPERE, VOL.
VI: BASSO *CC12L
[It] B solo,pno cmplt ed RICORDI-ENG
127537 s.p. contains works by:
Bellini; Boito; Gomes; Gounod;
Mozart; L'Ebrea; Rossini; Puccini;
Verdi   (R960)

RIDA RANKA see Ekenberg

RIDDER, C. DE
De Sterrezienster
solo,pno ALSBACH s.p.   (R961)

RIDDLE OF THE GUITAR, THE see Cortes,
Ramiro, Adivinanza De La Guitarra

RIDDLE SONG, THE
see Schirmer's American Folk-Song
Series, Set XXI (American-English
Folk-Songs From The Southern
Appalachian Mountains)

RIDDLES, THE see Laderman, Ezra

RIDE see Britten, Benjamin

RIDE ON KING JESUS *spir
(Burleigh, H. T.) med solo,pno BELWIN
$1.50   (R962)

RIDE ON, KING JESUS see Johnson

RIDE ON! RIDE ON! see Scott

RIDE STRAIGHT see Dunhill, Thomas
Frederick

RIDENTE LA CALMA see Mozart, Wolfgang
Amadeus

RIDER, DALE G. (1948-   )
Baptism Of Jesus, The
high solo,pno (Baptism) WHITE HARV.
VOS 747 $1.25   (R963)

Establish A House *Gen/Marriage
low solo,pno WHITE HARV. VOS 724
$.75   (R964)
high solo,pno WHITE HARV. VOS 734
$.75   (R965)
high solo,pno CHANTRY VOS 734H $.75
(R966)
low solo,pno CHANTRY VOS 724L $.75
(R967)

Every Good And Perfect Gift Is From
Above *Fest/Gen
high solo/med solo,pno WHITE HARV.
VOS CH $.75   (R968)

See My Chosen One
see Two Solos For Guitar And Voice

Two Solos For Guitar And Voice
med solo/low solo,pno WHITE HARV.
VOS 752 $1.00, ipa
contains: See My Chosen One;
Wondrous Love   (R969)

Vision Of Love
high solo/med solo,pno WHITE HARV.
VOS 745 $.75   (R970)

Wondrous Love
see Two Solos For Guitar And Voice

RIDOUT, GODFREY (1918-   )
What Star Is This? *sac,Xmas
Mez/Bar solo,pno (very easy) OXFORD
62.918 $.60   (R971)

RIEDE, E.
Song Album *CC16U
[Ger] S solo,pno BOTE $9.00   (R972)

RIEGGER, WALLINGFORD (1885-   )
Dying Of The Light, The *Op.59
(Thomas, D.) med-high solo,pno AMP
$.60   (R973)

Music *Op.23, vocalise
high solo,fl/ob BOMART $1.25   (R974)

Somber Pine, The
high solo,pno AMP $.60   (R975)

Two Bergerette *CC2U
[Fr] solo,pno PEER $.95   (R976)

Ye Banks And Braes O' Bonnie Doon
solo,pno PEER $1.00   (R977)

RIEN N'EFFACERA NOS CARESSES see
Berger, Rod.

RIENTONI see Klemetti, Heikki

RIES, FRANZ (1846-1932)
Am Rhein, Am Deutschen Rhein *Op.35
solo,2fl,ob,2clar,bsn,2horn,2trp,
3trom,timp,glock,strings RIES
s.p.   (R978)
med solo,pno RIES s.p.   (R979)
high solo,pno RIES s.p.   (R980)

Wiegenlied *Op.33,No.4
solo,2fl,2ob,2clar,2bsn,2horn,timp,
strings RIES s.p.   (R981)
high solo,pno RIES s.p.   (R982)
low solo,pno RIES s.p.   (R983)

Wo Du Hingehst *Op.40,No.2
high solo,pno RIES s.p.   (R984)

RIETI, VITTORIO (1898-   )
Five Elizabethan Songs *CC5U
solo,pno GENERAL 490 $3.50   (R985)

Four D.H. Lawrence Songs *CC4U
solo,pno GENERAL 7 $2.50   (R986)

Quattro Liriche Italiane *CC4U
solo,pno GENERAL 336 $2.50   (R987)

Two Songs Between Waltzes *CC2U
solo,pno GENERAL 22 $2.50   (R988)

RIETZ, JOHANNES (1905-   )
Die Treppe
see Turkische Lieder

Eh Vergilbt Dein Hag
see Turkische Lieder

Liebe, Ruckblickend
see Vier Lieder Fur Eine Dunkle
Frauenstimme Und Klavier

Niemandsland
see Vier Lieder Fur Eine Dunkle
Frauenstimme Und Klavier

Turkische Lieder
[Ger] S solo,pno TONOS 5409 s.p.
contains: Die Treppe; Eh Vergilbt
Dein Hag; Warum?   (R989)

RIETZ, JOHANNES (cont'd.)
Uber Dem Hafen Von Lindos
see Vier Lieder Fur Eine Dunkle
Frauenstimme Und Klavier

Vier Lieder Fur Eine Dunkle
Frauenstimme Und Klavier
Mez/A solo,pno TONOS 5410 s.p.
contains: Liebe, Ruckblickend;
Niemandsland; Uber Dem Hafen
Von Lindos; Vorgefuhl   (R990)

Vorgefuhl
see Vier Lieder Fur Eine Dunkle
Frauenstimme Und Klavier

Warum?
see Turkische Lieder

RIFLESSI DI SOLE see Bossi, Renzo

RIGHT BY MY SIDE see Hensen, Gloria

RIGHT NOW *CCUL
(Carmichael, Ralph) solo,pno WORD
37524 $2.50   (R991)

RIGOLO see Becker, Gunther

RIIHINIITYLLA see Linko, Ernst
(Fredrik)

RIJMPJE see Zweers, [Bernard]

RIJP, A.W.
Hervormingslied
solo,org ALSBACH s.p.   (R992)
solo,org ALSBACH s.p.   (R993)

RIKUD HA-GOREN
(Helfman, Max) "Barn Dance" [Heb] med
solo,pno TRANSCON. IS 515 $.45
(R994)

RILEY, DENNIS (1943-   )
Cantata I
Mez solo,sax,vibra,vcl,pno PETERS
66432 $1.25   (R995)

Five Songs On Japanese Haiku *CC5U
S solo,vln,vcl, clarinet in A
PETERS 66137 $3.00   (R996)

RILKE-LIEDER see Marx, Karl

RIM RAM RARE see Michielsen, A.

RIMBAUD SONGS see Farr, Ian

RIMES ENFANTINES see Stehman, Jacques

RIMES FRANCOISES ET ITALIENNES see
Sweelinck, Jan Pieterszoon

RIMES TENDRES see Aubert, Louis-
Francois-Marie

RIMOS Y ABROJOS see Espoile, Raoul H.

RIMPIANTO see Cantu, M.

RIMPIANTO see Veneziani, Vittore

RIMPROVERO see Caltabiano, S.

RIMSKY-KORSAKOV, NIKOLAI (1844-1908)
A Che Mai Nell'ombra (from La
Pskovitana)
[Russ/Fr/Eng] T solo,pno BESSEL
4786 s.p.   (R997)

A L'heure Dite (from Snegourotchka)
[Fr/Ger] Bar solo,pno BESSEL 4774 B
s.p.   (R998)

A Me Rispondi Astro D'or (from Golden
Cockerel, The)
[Fr/Eng] S solo,pno,opt vln/fl/ob
FORBERG 5482 B s.p.   (R999)

Ah! Que J'ai Mal (from Snegourotchka)
[Fr/Ger] S solo,pno BESSEL 4778 B
s.p.   (R1000)

Ahime Che Far? (from La Pskovitana)
[Russ/Fr/Eng] S solo,pno BESSEL
4788 B s.p.   (R1001)

Aimant La Rose, Le Rossignol *Op.2,
No.2
"Rose Enslaves The Nightingale,
The" see Four Songs
"La Rose Et Le Rossignol" [Ger/Fr]
solo,pno RICORDI-ARG BA 8334 s.p.
(R1002)
"Rose Enslaves The Nightingale,
The" high solo,pno (F min) BOSTON
$1.50   (R1003)
"Rose Enslaves The Nightingale,
The" low solo,pno (D min) BOSTON
$1.50   (R1004)

Al Pianto Mio (from La Pskovitana)
[It/Eng] S solo,pno BESSEL 4790
s.p.   (R1005)

RIMSKY-KORSAKOV, NIKOLAI (cont'd.)
Allez Au Bois (from Snegourotchka)
[Fr] S solo,pno BESSEL 4775 B
s.p.   (R1006)

Am Felsenufer Toben Ungestuem Die
Wellen (from Sadko)
[Russ/Fr/Ger] B solo,pno BELAIEFF
307 s.p.   (R1007)

Aria Di Kachtcheevna (from Kashchey
The Immortal)
[Fr/Russ/Ger/Eng] Mez solo,pno
BESSEL 4784 B s.p.   (R1008)

Attends, Snegourotchka (from
Snegourotchka)
[Fr/Ger] SBar soli,pno BESSEL
4783 B s.p.   (R1009)

Au Royaume Du Vin Et Des Roses
"Come To The Realm Of Roses And
Wine" see Four Songs

Berceuse *Op.2,No.3
"Cradle Song" see Four Songs

Berceuse Della Principessa (from
Kashchey The Immortal)
[Fr/Russ/Ger/Eng] S solo,pno BESSEL
4785 B s.p.   (R1010)

Cancion Hindu (from Sadko)
[Fr/Span] S/T solo,pno RICORDI-ARG
BA 8465 s.p.   (R1011)

Chanson De Zuleika *Op.26,No.4
[Russ/Fr] solo,pno BELAIEFF 300
s.p.   (R1012)

Chanson Hindoue (from Sadko)
"Hindu Song" [Eng/Fr/Ger] low solo,
pno BELAIEFF 306B s.p.   (R1013)
"Hindu Song" [Eng/Fr/Ger] high
solo,pno BELAIEFF 306A s.p.
(R1014)
"Song Of India" med solo,pno (F
maj) CENTURY 2460   (R1015)
"Song Of India" med solo,pno (A
maj) CENTURY 3626   (R1016)
"Song Of India, A" [Fr/Eng] high
solo,pno (G maj) SCHIRM.G $.75
(R1017)
"Song Of India, A" [Fr/Eng] low
solo,pno (E flat maj) SCHIRM.G
$.75   (R1018)

Chanson Indoue
med solo,pno (F maj) CENTURY 2460
(R1019)
Come To The Realm Of Roses And Wine
*see Au Royaume Du Vin Et Des
Roses

Comment, Cher Lel, As Tu Le Coeur...
(from Snegourotchka)
[Fr/Ger] S solo,pno BESSEL 4782 B
s.p.   (R1020)

Confessa Dunque (from La Pskovitana)
[Russ/Fr/Eng] B solo,pno BESSEL
4791 B s.p.   (R1021)

Cradle Song *see Berceuse

Deutlich Liegt Vor Mir (from Tsar's
Bride, The)
[Russ/Fr/Ger] S solo,pno BELAIEFF
309 s.p.   (R1022)

Durch Den Wald Ein Rauschen Zieht
(from Schneeflockchen)
T solo,2fl,2ob,2clar,2bsn,4horn,
strings BREITKOPF-L rental
(R1023)

Enfin Les Noirs Nuages *Op.42,No.3
[Russ/Fr] solo,pno BELAIEFF 302
s.p.   (R1024)

Four Songs
[Eng/Fr] med solo,kbd CHESTER s.p.
contains: Aimant La Rose, Le
Rossignol, "Rose Enslaves The
Nightingale, The", Op.2,No.2;
Au Royaume Du Vin Et Des Roses,
"Come To The Realm Of Roses And
Wine"; Berceuse, "Cradle Song",
Op.2,No.3; La Nuit, "Night",
Op.8,No.2   (R1025)

Hindu Song *see Chanson Hindoue

Hundert Russische Volkslieder, Op.
24, Band I *CCU
[Russ/Ger/Fr/Eng] solo,pno
BREITKOPF-W 57 03067 s.p.   (R1026)

Hundert Russische Volkslieder, Op.
24, Band II *CCU
[Russ/Ger/Fr/Eng] solo,pno
BREITKOPF-W 57 03068 s.p.   (R1027)

Hundert Russische Volkslieder, Op.
24, Band III *CCU
[Russ/Ger/Fr/Eng] solo,pno

RIMSKY-KORSAKOV, NIKOLAI (cont'd.)

BREITKOPF-W 57 03069 s.p. (R1028)

Hymn To The Sun (from Le Coq D'or)
S solo,pno BOOSEY $1.50   (R1029)

J'ai Attendu (from Sadko)
[Russ/Fr] Mez solo,pno BELAIEFF 308
s.p.   (R1030)

Je Connais Ma Mere (from
Snegourotchka)
[Fr/Eng] S solo,pno BESSEL 4776 B
s.p.   (R1031)

La Nuit *Op.8,No.2
"Night" see Four Songs

La Rose Et Le Rossignol *see Aimant
La Rose, Le Rossignol

Le Jour Brillant (from Snegourotchka)
[Fr/Ger] T solo,pno BESSEL 4780 B
s.p.   (R1032)

Le Nuage A Dit Un Jour (from
Snegourotchka)
[Fr/Eng] Mez solo,pno BESSEL 4781 B
s.p.   (R1033)

L'Horizon S'eteint *Op.39,No.2
[Russ/Fr] solo,pno BELAIEFF 301
s.p.   (R1034)

Nature Auguste Et Douce (from
Snegourotchka)
[Russ/Ger] T solo,pno BESSEL 4779 B
s.p.   (R1035)

Night *see La Nuit

Nuit Meridionale *Op.3,No.2
[Russ/Fr] solo,pno BELAIEFF 296
s.p.   (R1036)

O, Schau, Hoch Oben (from Tsar's
Bride, The)
[Russ/Fr/Ger] S solo,pno BELAIEFF
310 s.p.   (R1037)

Rose Enslaves The Nightingale, The
*see Aimant La Rose, Le Rossignol

Rose Has Charmed The Nightingale
med solo,pno (E min) ALLANS s.p.
                            (R1038)
high solo,pno (F sharp min) ALLANS
s.p.   (R1039)

Rossignols, Moucherons, Tout Se Tait
*Op.4,No.3
[Russ/Fr] solo,pno BELAIEFF 298
s.p.   (R1040)

Selected Arias From Operas *CCU
[Russ] Mez solo,pno MEZ KNIGA 61
                            (R1041)

Si Ho Graziato Pskov (from La
Pskovitana)
[It/Eng] B solo,pno BESSEL 4789
s.p.   (R1042)

Silent Night, The
solo,pno (D maj) ASHDOWN s.p.
                            (R1043)

Snegourotchka Je Suis Heureuse! (from
Snegourotchka)
[Fr/Ger] S solo,pno BESSEL 4777 B
s.p.   (R1044)

Song Of India *see Chanson Hindoue

Song Of India, A *see Chanson
Hindoue

Springs Awakening
solo,pno ASHDOWN s.p.   (R1045)

Sur La Rive Errait Le Reve (from
Sadko)
[Russ/Fr] S solo,pno BELAIEFF 305
s.p.   (R1046)

Sur Les Collines De Georgie *Op.3,
No.4
[Russ/Fr] solo,pno BELAIEFF 297
s.p.   (R1047)

Von Heissem Wahrheitsdrang Verzehrt
*Op.49,No.2
[Russ/Fr/Ger] low solo,pno BELAIEFF
303 s.p.   (R1048)

Wohl Weiss Ich Es *Op.56,No.1
[Russ/Fr/Ger] high solo,pno
BELAIEFF 304 s.p.   (R1049)

Zu Dem Donner Eine Wolke Sprach (from
Schneeflockchen)
T solo,clar,bsn,3horn,timp,tamb,
harp,strings BREITKOPF-L rental
                            (R1050)

RINALDINI, DR. JOSEPH (1893-   )
Barcarole
solo,pno DOBLINGER s.p.   (R1051)

Das Grune Blatt
solo,pno DOBLINGER s.p.   (R1052)

Drei Lieder *CC3U
solo,pno DOBLINGER s.p.   (R1053)

Im Schnee
solo,pno DOBLINGER s.p.   (R1054)

Marienlied
solo,pno DOBLINGER s.p. contains
also: Schone Nacht   (R1055)

Nocturnes *CC7U
B/Bar solo,pno DOBLINGER 08 638
$2.75   (R1056)

Schone Nacht
see Rinaldini, Dr. Joseph,
Marienlied

Sechs Lieder *CC6U
solo,pno DOBLINGER s.p.   (R1057)

RING A DUMB CARILLON see Birtwistle,
Harrison

RING, BELLS RING see Day, Maude Craske

RING-KING see Hullebroeck, Em.

RING-KING see Zagwijn, Henri

RING OF GRASS see Dvoracek, Jiri

RING ON SWEET ANGELUS see Gounod,
Charles Francois

RING OUT, WILD BELLS see Gounod,
Charles Francois

RING-RING see Clercq, R. de

RING THE BELLS see Bollbach, Harry

RINGELNATZ-LIEDER see Lothar, Mark

RINGGER, ROLF URS (1935-   )
Vier Lieder Auf Chinesische Texte
*CC4U
S solo,fl,bass clar,trom,harp,cel,
vln,vcl,bvl MODERN rental (R1058)

Vier Lieder Auf Japanische Lyrik
*CC4U
S solo,clar,horn,harp,vln,vla,bvl
MODERN s.p.   (R1059)

RINKER, ALTON (1907-   )
Nightingale, The
med solo,pno BROUDE BR. $.95
                            (R1060)

RINUNCIA see Bossi, Renzo

RIO GRANDE see Dougherty, Celius

RIO GRANDE, THE see Berkeley, Lennox

RIPPLING RIVER see Beney, Theresa

RIQUET A LA HOUPPE see Lacome, Paul

RIQUEZA see Guastavino, Carlos

RIS, VENT D'ETE, SUR LA GIROUETTE...
see Chevreuille, Raymond

RISE AND FOLLOW LOVE
(Roberton, Hugh S.) solo,pno (G maj)
ROBERTON 2746 s.p.   (R1061)

RISE, MY SOUL, AND PRAISE GOD'S
KINDNESS see Albert, Heinrich

RISING OF THE LARK, THE *folk,Welsh
(Roberton, Hugh S.) 3 soli,pno
ROBERTON 72189 s.p.   (R1062)

RISING OF THE SUN, THE see Ralston, Bob

RISINGER, KAREL (1920-   )
Die Eiskonigin *see Ledova Kralovna

Ledova Kralovna
"Die Eiskonigin" A solo,pno CZECH
s.p.   (R1063)

Osm Pisni *CC8U
S solo,pno CZECH s.p.   (R1064)

Tri Zenske Dvojzpevy *CC3U
SA soli,pno CZECH s.p.   (R1065)

RISPETTI see Stam, Henk

RISPETTI E STORNELLI DELLA LUCCHESIA
see Oddone, E.

RISPETTO see Agosti, Guido

RISPETTO TOSCANO see Del Corona,
Rodolfo

RISTI LUMESSA see Pylkkanen, Tauno
Kullervo

RITES DE PASSAGE see Pasatieri, Thomas

R'ITIHA
(Waghalter, Ignatz) "Arabian Love
Song" [Heb/Eng] med solo,pno
TRANSCON. SP 10 $.50   (R1066)

RITORNA VINCITOR see Verdi, Giuseppe

RITORNO see Melartin, Erkki

RITOURNELLE see Caby, R.

RITOURNELLE see Chaminade, Cecile

RITOURNELLE see Delmet, Paul

RITT DURCHS LEBEN see Bijvanck, Henk

RITTER, CHRISTIAN (ca. 1640-ca. 1720)
O Amantissime Sponse Jesu *cant
Mez/A solo,strings,org,cembalo
BREITKOPF-L rental   (R1067)

RIVALS see Arundale, Claude

RIVALS, THE see Barab, Seymour

RIVALS, THE see Mourant, Walter

RIVEDRAI LE FORESTE IMBALSAMATE see
Verdi, Giuseppe

RIVER, THE see Birch, Robert Fairfax

RIVER, THE see Rappaport, Eda

RIVER DREAM, A see Thomas, Arthur
Goring

RIVER-GOD'S SONG, THE see Plessis,
Hubert du

RIVER NIGHT see Koch, Frederick

RIVER OF JORDAN, THE see Houser

RIVER ROSES see Cooke, S.C.

RIVIER, JEAN (1896-   )
"A Traduire En Esthonien"
see Four Poems Of Rene Chalupt

Bel Aubepin
see Four Poems Of Ronsard And Marot

Cartomancie
see Four Poems Of Rene Chalupt

Dedans Paris, Ville Jolie
see Four Poems Of Ronsard And Marot

Four Poems Of Rene Chalupt
med solo,pno SALABERT-US $3.75
contains: "A Traduire En
Esthonien"; Cartomancie;
Hommage A Valery-Larbaud; Le
Vivier   (R1068)

Four Poems Of Ronsard And Marot
med solo,pno SALABERT-US $5.50
contains: Bel Aubepin; Dedans
Paris, Ville Jolie; Le Tombeau
De Ronsard; Rossignol   (R1069)

Hommage A Valery-Larbaud
see Four Poems Of Rene Chalupt

La Fable Du Village
see Three Poems Of Paul Gilson

La Sirene De Scheveningue
see Three Poems Of Paul Gilson

Le Tombeau De Ronsard
see Four Poems Of Ronsard And Marot

Le Vivier
see Four Poems Of Rene Chalupt

Passage D'une Nurse
see Three Poems Of Paul Gilson

Rossignol
see Four Poems Of Ronsard And Marot

Three Poems Of Paul Gilson
Bar/Mez solo,pno SALABERT-US $5.50
contains: La Fable Du Village; La
Sirene De Scheveningue; Passage
D'une Nurse   (R1070)

RIVOLGETE A LUI LO SGUARDO see Mozart,
Wolfgang Amadeus

RIVULET see Shaw, Martin

RIWAJAK KAMPONG see Mesritz Van
Velthuysen, Annie

RIZZI, ALBA
  Every Star Is A Dream
    solo,pno CRAMER   (R1071)

  Stonecracker, The
    solo,pno CRAMER $1.15   (R1072)

RO, RO see Nordqvist, Gustaf

RO, RO OGONSTEN see Sjogren, Emil

ROACH
  One Little Candle *see Mysels

ROAD, A see Kaburagi, Mitsugu

ROAD THAT LEADS TO YOU, THE see Geehl,
  Henry Ernest

ROAD THRO' THE VALLEY see Hope, H.
  Ashworth

ROAD TO AVRILLE, THE see Lekberg, Sven

ROAD TO PARADISE, THE see Romberg,
  Sigmund

ROAD TO THE ISLES
  (Kennedy-Fraser, M.; MacLeod, K.) low
    solo,pno (G maj) BOOSEY $1.50
                                       (R1073)
  (Kennedy-Fraser, M.; MacLeod, K.)
    high solo,pno (A maj) BOOSEY $1.50
                                       (R1074)

ROADSIDE FIRE see Vaughan Williams,
  Ralph

ROBE OF CALVARY *sac,gospel
  solo,pno ABER.GRP. $1.50   (R1075)

ROBERT BURNS SONG BOOK, THE see Burns,
  Robert

ROBERT, PIERRE
  Deux Motets Pour La Chapelle Du Roy
    *sac,CC2U,mot
    solo,orch HEUGEL s.p., ipr   (R1076)

ROBERT, TOI QUE J'AIME see Meyerbeer,
  Giacomo

ROBERT, TOI QUE J'AMIE see Meyerbeer,
  Giacomo

ROBERTON, HUGH STEVENSON (1874-1952)
  All In The April Evening *see Yno Yn
    Hwyrddydd Ebrill

  Aubade
    3 soli,pno ROBERTON 72088 s.p.
                                       (R1077)
  Birds Are Singing
    3 soli,pno ROBERTON 71452 s.p.
                                       (R1078)
  Blake's Cradle Song
    3 soli,pno ROBERTON 72108 s.p.
                                       (R1079)
    solo,pno (A flat maj) ROBERTON 2536
    s.p.   (R1080)

  Cherry Ripe
    (Horn) 3 soli,pno ROBERTON 71523
    s.p.   (R1081)

  Lions And Crocidiles *CCU
    solo,pno PATERSON s.p.   (R1082)

  Maureen
    low solo,pno (C maj) PATERSON s.p.
                                       (R1083)
    high solo,pno (F maj) PATERSON s.p.
                                       (R1084)
    med solo,pno (E flat maj) PATERSON
    s.p.   (R1085)

  Memory
    3 soli,pno ROBERTON 71541 s.p.   (R1086)
  Old Woman, The
    low solo,pno (F maj) PATERSON s.p.
                                       (R1087)
    high solo,pno (A flat maj) PATERSON
    s.p.   (R1088)

  Oran-A-Chree
    (Bell) 2 soli,pno ROBERTON 72180
    s.p.   (R1089)

  Shepherdess, The
    3 soli,pno ROBERTON 71500 s.p.
                                       (R1090)
  Wee Toun Clerk
    solo,pno PATERSON s.p.   (R1091)

  White Waves On The Water
    2 soli,pno ROBERTON 72174 s.p.
                                       (R1092)
  Whither Away?
    3 soli,pno ROBERTON 72075 s.p.
                                       (R1093)

  Yno Yn Hwyrddydd Ebrill *sac
    "All In The April Evening" 2 soli,
      pno ROBERTON 72044 s.p. (R1094)
    "All In The April Evening" 3 soli,
      pno ROBERTON 72120 s.p. (R1095)
    "All In The April Evening" solo,pno

ROBERTON, HUGH STEVENSON (cont'd.)
    (E maj, with English and Welsh
      texts) ROBERTON 2555 s.p. (R1096)
    "All In The April Evening" med
      solo,pno (E maj) SCHIRM.G $.85
                                       (R1097)
    "All In The April Evening" [Welsh]
      2 soli,pno ROBERTON 72044 s.p.
                                       (R1098)
ROBERTS
  All Ye Who Seek For Sure Relief *sac
    low solo,pno (E flat maj) CENTURY 5
    $.40   (R1099)

  God Bless You; Go With God *sac
    solo,pno LILLENAS SM-906: SN $1.00
                                       (R1100)
ROBERTS, GEORGE
  Sandman Is Calling You
    high solo,pno BELWIN $1.50 (R1101)
    low solo,pno BELWIN $1.50   (R1102)
ROBERTS, J. VARLEY
  Seek Ye The Lord *sac
    (Deis) med-high solo,pno (A flat
      maj) SCHIRM.G $.85   (R1103)
    (Deis) low solo,pno (F maj)
      SCHIRM.G $.85   (R1104)
ROBERTS, MERVYN (1906-   )
  Christmas Day
    med solo,pno NOVELLO 17.0023.05
    s.p.   (R1105)

  Elsewhere
    med solo,pno NOVELLO 17.0049.09
    s.p.   (R1106)

  Put A Rosebud On Her Lips
    med solo,pno NOVELLO 17.0155.10
    s.p.   (R1107)

  Saint Govan
    med solo,pno NOVELLO 17.0161.04
    s.p.   (R1108)

  Sentry, The
    med solo,pno NOVELLO 17.1065.07
    s.p.   (R1109)

ROBERT'S ROMANCE see Tchaikovsky, Piotr
  Ilyitch

ROBERTSON, E.
  Lord's Prayer, The *sac
    solo,pno BERANDOL BER 1081 $1.50
                                       (R1110)
ROBERTSON, R. RITCHIE
  Jolly Roger, The
    med-low solo,pno (F maj) SCHIRM.G
    $.85   (R1111)

ROBIN, THE see Arensky, Anton
  Stepanovitch, Le Pinson

ROBIN-A-THRUSH see Broadwood, Lucy E.

ROBIN ADAIR *Scot
  solo,pno CRAMER   (R1112)

ROBIN ANSWERS, THE see Clarke, Henry
  Leland

ROBIN DES BOIS see Busser, Henri-Paul

ROBINS see Russell, Kennedy

ROBIN'S CAROL see Head, Michael (Dewar)

ROBIN'S SONG see White

ROBINSON
  On The Way Home *sac
    solo,pno BENSON S7281-S $1.00
                                       (R1113)
ROBINSON, A.
  Water Boy
    solo,pno (G maj) BOOSEY $1.50
                                       (R1114)
ROBINSON, BETTY JEAN
  On The Way Home *sac
    solo,pno WORD S-462   (R1115)
ROBRECHT, C.
  Fruhling Am Bergeshang
    [Ger] high solo,pno BOTE $1.75
                                       (R1116)
ROBYN
  Heart That's Free
    low solo,pno (D maj) ALLANS s.p.
                                       (R1117)
    high solo,pno (E flat maj) ALLANS
    s.p.   (R1118)
ROCCA, LODOVICO (1895-   )
  Biribu Occhi Di Rana
    med solo,pno,4strings sc CARISH 18876
    s.p., ipa, voc sc CARISH 18829
    s.p.   (R1119)

  Il Bimbo
    [It] solo,pno BONGIOVANI 1045 s.p.
      see also Otto Cantilene Su Testi
      D'oriente [1]   (R1120)
    [It/Ger/Fr/Eng] solo,pno BONGIOVANI

ROCCA, LODOVICO (cont'd.)
    1475 s.p. see also Otto Cantilene
      Su Testi D'oriente [2]   (R1121)

  Il Viaggio Della Luna
    [It/Ger/Fr/Eng] solo,pno BONGIOVANI
      1573 s.p. see also Otto Cantilene
      Su Testi D'oriente [2]   (R1122)
    [It] solo,pno BONGIOVANI 1043 s.p.
      see also Otto Cantilene Su Testi
      D'oriente [1]   (R1123)

  La Fine Della Volpe
    [It/Ger/Fr/Eng] solo,pno BONGIOVANI
      1474 s.p. see also Otto Cantilene
      Su Testi D'oriente [2]   (R1124)
    [It] solo,pno BONGIOVANI 1044 s.p.
      see also Otto Cantilene Su Testi
      D'oriente [1]   (R1125)

  La Zanzara E La Mosca
    [It] solo,pno BONGIOVANI 1046 s.p.
      see also Otto Cantilene Su Testi
      D'oriente [1]   (R1126)
    [It/Ger/Fr/Eng] solo,pno BONGIOVANI
      1476 s.p. see also Otto Cantilene
      Su Testi D'oriente [2]   (R1127)

  L'adorata
    [It/Ger/Fr/Eng] solo,pno BONGIOVANI
      1478 s.p. see also Quattro
      Melopee Su Epigrammi Sepolcrali
      Greci [2]   (R1128)
    [It] solo,pno BONGIOVANI 1035 s.p.
      see also Quattro Melopee Su
      Epigrammi Sepolcrali Greci [1]
                                       (R1129)

  Le Mele E Il Bacio
    [It] solo,pno BONGIOVANI 1040 s.p.
      see also Otto Cantilene Su Testi
      D'oriente [1]   (R1130)
    [It/Ger/Fr/Eng] solo,pno BONGIOVANI
      1470 s.p. see also Otto Cantilene
      Su Testi D'oriente [2]   (R1131)

  Le Tombe
    [It] solo,pno BONGIOVANI 1041 s.p.
      see also Otto Cantilene Su Testi
      D'oriente [1]   (R1132)
    [It/Ger/Fr/Eng] solo,pno BONGIOVANI
      1472 s.p. see also Otto Cantilene
      Su Testi D'oriente [2]   (R1133)

  Lo Spettro
    [It] solo,pno BONGIOVANI 1039 s.p.
      see also Otto Cantilene Su Testi
      D'oriente [1]   (R1134)
    [It/Ger/Fr/Eng] solo,pno BONGIOVANI
      1469 s.p. see also Otto Cantilene
      Su Testi D'oriente [2]   (R1135)

  Lo Sposo Thio Alla Sua Atti
    [It] solo,pno BONGIOVANI 1037 s.p.
      see also Quattro Melopee Su
      Epigrammi Sepolcrali Greci [1]
                                       (R1136)
    [It/Ger/Ger/Eng] solo,pno BONGIOVANI
      1480 s.p. see also Quattro
      Melopee Su Epigrammi Sepolcrali
      Greci [2]   (R1137)

  Lo Sposo Thio Alla Sua Atti E La
    Risposta Della Sposa
    [It/Eng/Ger/Fr] 2 soli,pno
      BONGIOVANI 1482 s.p.   (R1138)
    [It] 2 soli,pno BONGIOVANI 1034
    s.p.   (R1139)

  Otto Cantilene Su Testi D'oriente [1]
    [It] solo,pno cmplt ed BONGIOVANI
      1047 s.p.
      contains & see also: Il Bimbo; Il
        Viaggio Della Luna; La Fine
        Della Volpe; La Zanzara E La
        Mosca; Le Mele E Il Bacio; Le
        Tombe; Lo Spettro; Spesa
        Inutile   (R1140)

  Otto Cantilene Su Testi D'oriente [2]
    [It/Ger/Fr/Eng] solo,pno cmplt ed
      BONGIOVANI 1468 s.p.
      contains & see also: Il Bimbo; Il
        Viaggio Della Luna; La Fine
        Della Volpe; La Zanzara E La
        Mosca; Le Mele E Il Bacio; Le
        Tombe; Lo Spettro; Spesa
        Inutile   (R1141)

  Per La Tomba Di Tre Fanciulle Milesie
    [It/Ger/Fr/Eng] solo,pno BONGIOVANI
      1479 s.p. see also Quattro
      Melopee Su Epigrammi Sepolcrali
      Greci [2]   (R1142)
    [It] solo,pno BONGIOVANI 1036 s.p.
      see also Quattro Melopee Su
      Epigrammi Sepolcrali Greci [1]
                                       (R1143)

  Quattro Melopee Su Epigrammi
    Sepolcrali Greci [1]
    [It] solo,pno cmplt ed BONGIOVANI
      1048 s.p.
      contains: L'adorata; Lo Sposo
        Thio Alla Sua Atti; Per La
        Tomba Di Tre Fanciulle Milesie;
        Sulla Tomba Di Un Vecchio

ROCCA, LODOVICO (cont'd.)

see also: L'adorata; Lo Sposo
Thio Alla Sua Atti; Per La
Tomba Di Tre Fanciulle Milesie
(R1144)

Quattro Melopee Su Epigrammi
Sepolcrali Greci [2]
[It/Ger/Fr/Eng] solo,pno cmplt ed
BONGIOVANI 1477 s.p.
contains & see also: L'adorata;
Lo Sposo Thio Alla Sua Atti;
Per La Tomba Di Tre Fanciulle
Milesie; Sulla Tomba Di Un
Vecchio   (R1145)

Spesa Inutile
[It] solo,pno BONGIOVANI 1042 s.p.
see also Otto Cantilene Su Testi
D'oriente [1]   (R1146)
[It/Ger/Fr/Eng] solo,pno BONGIOVANI
1472 s.p. see also Otto Cantilene
Su Testi D'oriente [2]   (R1147)

Sulla Tomba Di Un Vecchio
see Quattro Melopee Su Epigrammi
Sepolcrali Greci [1]
[It/Ger/Fr/Eng] solo,pno BONGIOVANI
1481 s.p. see also Quattro
Melopee Su Epigrammi Sepolcrali
Greci [2]   (R1148)

ROCHBERG, GEORGE (1918-   )
Eleven Songs *CC11U
Mez solo,pno PRESSER $5.00 (R1149)

Two Songs From " Tableaux" *CC2U
solo,pno PRESSER $1.25   (R1150)

ROCIO see Guastavino, Carlos

ROCK, A see Kaburagi, Mitsugu

ROCK-A-BY see Guastavino, Carlos,
Meciendo

ROCK-A-BY LADY, THE see Weigl, Vally

ROCK-A-BYE TRAIN see Akers, Maddalena
H.

ROCK-'N-ROLL SESSION see Heilner, Irwin

ROCK OF AGES see Cole

ROCKED IN THE CRADLE OF THE DEEP see
Knight

ROCOCO-SERENAD see Meyer-Helmund, Erik

ROD LYSER STUGAN see Wideen

RODASTE GULD see Nordqvist, Gustaf

RODEHEAVER
Collection Of Sacred Songs *sac,CCU
solo,pno COLE $3.00   (R1151)

RODEHEAVER GOSPEL SOLOS AND DUETS, VOL.
4 *sac,CCUL
1-2 soli,pno WORD 30041 $1.95 (R1152)

RODEHEAVER LOW VOICE COLLECTION, VOL. 1
*sac,CCUL
A/Bar/B solo,pno WORD 10038 $1.00
(R1153)
RODEHEAVER LOW VOICE COLLECTION, VOL. 2
*sac,CCUL
A/Bar/B solo,pno WORD 10039 $1.00
(R1154)
RODEHEAVER LOW VOICE COLLECTION, VOL. 3
*sac,CCUL
A/Bar/B solo,pno WORD 10040 $1.00
(R1155)
RODEHEAVER LOW VOICE COLLECTION, VOL. 4
*sac,CCUL
A/Bar/B solo,pno WORD 10041 $1.00
(R1156)
RODEHEAVER LOW VOICE COLLECTION, VOL. 5
*sac,CCUL
A/Bar/B solo,pno WORD 10042 $1.00
(R1157)
RODEHEAVER LOW VOICE COLLECTION, VOL. 6
*sac,CCUL
A/Bar/B solo,pno WORD 10043 $1.00
(R1158)

RODERICK VICH ALPHINE DHU see Lawson,
Malcolm

RODEUSE AU FRONT DE VERRE see Poulenc,
Francis

RODGERS, JOHN (1917-   )
All Mothers Everywhere *sac
high solo,pno (Mother's Day) BELWIN
$1.50   (R1159)

RODHARIG AR MIN HJARTANS KAR see
Steinbach, E.

RODIN-KANTATE see Krebs, H.

RODNE HROUDY HLAS see Picha, Frantisek

RODNE HROUDY HLAS I see Picha,
Frantisek

RODNE HROUDY HLAS II see Picha,
Frantisek

RODNEY, PAUL
Calvary *sac,Easter/Gd.Fri.
high solo,pno (E min) SCHIRM.G $.85
(R1160)
high solo,pno (D maj) ASHDOWN s.p.
(R1161)
med solo,pno (C maj) ASHDOWN s.p.
(R1162)
low solo,pno (A maj) ASHDOWN s.p.
(R1163)
low solo,pno (A min) SCHIRM.G $.85
(R1164)
high solo,pno LORENZ $1.00 (R1165)
low solo,pno LORENZ $1.00   (R1166)
ST soli,pno LORENZ $1.00   (R1167)
med solo,pno LORENZ $1.00   (R1168)

Je Reve A Toi
solo,pno (available in 2 keys)
ENOCH s.p.   (R1169)

Nuit Sereine
solo,pno (available in 2 keys)
ENOCH s.p.   (R1170)

Resurrection Morn, The
med solo,pno (B flat maj) ASHDOWN
$1.75   (R1171)
low solo,pno (A flat maj) ASHDOWN
$1.75   (R1172)
high solo,pno (C maj) ASHDOWN $1.75
(R1173)

RODRIGO, JOAQUIN (1902-   )
Cancion Del Grumete
[Span] med solo,pno UNION ESP.
$1.50   (R1174)

Canco Del Teuladi
[Port] med solo,pno UNION ESP. $.75
(R1175)

Cantos De Amor Y De Guerra *CCU
(Ascencio-Kamhi) [Span] med solo,
pno UNION ESP. $2.50   (R1176)

Con Antonio Machado
[Span] med-low solo,pno UNION ESP.
$6.75   (R1177)

Con Que La Lavare?
"With What Then May I Bathe" see
Cuatro Madrigales Amatorios

Cuarto Madrigales Amatorios *CC4U
[Span] UNION ESP. high solo,pno
$3.75; med solo,pno $3.75 (R1178)

Cuatro Madrigales Amatorios
[Span/Eng] med solo/high solo,kbd
CHESTER s.p.
contains: Con Que La Lavare?,
"With What Then May I Bathe";
De Donde Venis, Amore?, "From
Where Have You Come Beloved?";
De Los Alamos Vengo, Madre, "I
Have Been By The Poplars"; Vos
Me Matasteis, "You Have
Destroyed Me"   (R1179)

De Donde Venis, Amore?
"From Where Have You Come Beloved?"
see Cuatro Madrigales Amatorios

De Los Alamos Vengo, Madre
"I Have Been By The Poplars" see
Cuatro Madrigales Amatorios

Dos Canciones Para Cantar A Los Ninos
*CC2U
[Span] med-low solo,pno UNION ESP.
$2.50   (R1180)

Dos Poemas *CC2U
[Span] med solo,pno/fl UNION ESP.
$1.50   (R1181)

From Where Have You Come Beloved?
*see De Donde Venis, Amore?

I Have Been By The Poplars *see De
Los Alamos Vengo, Madre

Por Mayo, Era Por Mayo
[Span] med-high solo,pno UNION ESP.
$1.25   (R1182)

Romance Del Comendador De Ocana
[Span] high solo,pno UNION ESP.
$1.25   (R1183)

Three Spanish Songs *CC3U
[Eng/Span] solo,gtr SCHOTTS 10601
s.p.   (R1184)

Villancicos
[Span] med solo,pno UNION ESP.
$2.00   (R1185)

Vos Me Matasteis
"You Have Destroyed Me" see Cuatro
Madrigales Amatorios

RODRIGO, JOAQUIN (cont'd.)

With What Then May I Bathe *see Con
Que La Lavare?

You Have Destroyed Me *see Vos Me
Matasteis

RODRIGUEZ, AUGUSTO (1904-   )
La Cumparsita
solo,pno ASHLEY $.95   (R1186)

RODRIGUEZ ALBERT, R.
Cuarto Canciones *CC4U
[Span] med-high solo,gtr UNION ESP.
$1.50   (R1187)

ROE, BETTY (1930-   )
Euphonium Dance
see Jazz Songs For Soprano And
Double Bass

Jazz Songs *CCU
S solo,bvl YORKE 8.0024.7 $2.00
(R1188)
Jazz Songs For Soprano And Double
Bass
S solo,bvl (easy) YORKE YE 0024
s.p.
contains: Euphonium Dance; Madam
And The Minister   (R1189)

Madam And The Minister
see Jazz Songs For Soprano And
Double Bass

ROE, GLORIA [ANN] (1935-   )
Abiding Love *sac
solo,pno WORD S-119   (R1190)

Fear Thou Not *see Pearson, Albie

Greatest Of These Is Love, The *sac
solo,pno WORD S-142   (R1191)

He Is The One *sac
solo,pno WORD S-148   (R1192)

May We Know Peace *sac
solo,pno WORD S-165   (R1193)

Miraculous *sac
solo,pno WORD S-168   (R1194)

My Grace Is Sufficient For You *sac
solo,pno WORD S-169   (R1195)

My Prayer *sac
solo,pno WORD S-543   (R1196)

See The Light *sac
solo,pno WORD S-180   (R1197)

So Great Salvation *sac
solo,pno WORD S-182   (R1198)

That's What He Did For Me *sac
solo,pno WORD S-186   (R1199)

There's Something Special *sac
solo,pno WORD S-542   (R1200)

To Know Him *sac
solo,pno WORD S-190   (R1201)

Unworthy *sac
solo,pno WORD S-301   (R1202)

Young Heart *sac
solo,pno WORD S-203   (R1203)

ROECKEL, J.L.
Bird In Hand, A
high solo,pno (C maj) ASHDOWN s.p.
(R1204)
low solo,pno (B flat maj) ASHDOWN
s.p.   (R1205)

Green Isle Of Erin
med solo,orch (E flat maj) ASHDOWN
s.p., ipr   (R1206)
low solo,orch (D maj) ASHDOWN s.p.,
ipr   (R1207)
high solo,orch (G maj) ASHDOWN
s.p., ipr   (R1208)
med-high solo,orch (F maj) ASHDOWN
s.p., ipr   (R1209)

I Couldn't Could I?
med solo,pno (E flat maj) ASHDOWN
s.p.   (R1210)
low solo,pno (C maj) ASHDOWN s.p.
(R1211)
high solo,pno (F maj) ASHDOWN s.p.
(R1212)

ROEI "JISEI" see Matsudaira, Yoritsune

ROELLI, H.
Bimbeli Bambeli
solo,pno HUG s.p.   (R1213)

Noch Singt Mein Mund *CC25U
solo,pno HUG s.p.   (R1214)

ROESCH
  Christ, The Living Way
    solo,pno SHAWNEE IA5051 $.85
                                    (R1215)

ROESSEL, LOUIS
  Trauungsgesang, Op. 25 *see Wenn Ich
    Mit Menschen- Und Mit
    Engelszungen Redete   (R1216)

  Wenn Ich Mit Menschen- Und Mit
    Engelszungen Redete *sac
    Mez solo,pno (F maj) LIENAU HOS 125
    s.p. see from Trauungsgesang, Op.
    25   (R1217)
    A/Bar solo,pno (D maj) LIENAU
    HOS 126 s.p. see from
    Trauungsgesang, Op. 25   (R1218)
    S/T solo,pno (G maj) LIENAU HOS 124
    s.p. see from Trauungsgesang, Op.
    25   (R1219)

ROETSCHER, KONRAD
  Four Sonnets Of Louize Labe *Op.24,
    CC4U
    [Ger] S solo,pno BOTE $2.50 (R1220)

  Sechs Lieder Nach Schottischen Texten
    *CC6U
    S solo,4fl sc BOTE $3.00   (R1221)

  Vier Lieder Der Braut *Op.17, CC4U
    [Ger] high solo,pno BOTE $1.50
                                    (R1222)

ROFF, JOSEPH
  Bless, O Lord, These Rings *sac,
    Marriage
    1-2 soli,org (easy) GIA G-1609
    $1.00   (R1223)

  Elegy *sec
    med solo,pno (C maj) WATERLOO $.90
                                    (R1224)

  God Bless Canada *sec
    med solo,pno (F maj) WATERLOO $.60
                                    (R1225)

  Greatest Gift, The
    solo,pno BERANDOL BER 1325 $1.50
                                    (R1226)

  My Cathedral
    high solo/med solo,pno BELWIN $1.50
                                    (R1227)

  Noel *sac,Xmas
    med solo,pno (B flat maj) WATERLOO
    $.90   (R1228)

ROGER-DUCASSE, JEAN-JULES AIMABLE
    (1873-1954)
  Adieu, Vous Dy La Larme A L'oeil
    solo,pno/inst DURAND s.p. see from
    Deux Rondels   (R1229)

  Deux Rondels *see Adieu, Vous Dy La
    Larme A L'oeil; Les Biens Dont
    Vous Estes La Dame   (R1230)

  Le Coeur De L'eau
    Mez/Bar solo,orch DURAND s.p., ipr
                                    (R1231)

  Les Biens Dont Vous Estes La Dame
    solo,pno/inst DURAND s.p. see from
    Deux Rondels   (R1232)

  Les Jets D'eau
    med solo,pno/inst DURAND s.p.
                                    (R1233)

  Les Pieces D'eau
    solo,orch DURAND s.p., ipr (R1234)

  Noel Des Roses
    solo,pno ENOCH s.p.   (R1235)

  Rondel
    see ALBUM MODERNE

ROGER, VICTOR (1854-1903)
  Les Betises
    solo,pno ENOCH s.p.   (R1236)
    solo,acap ENOCH s.p.   (R1237)

  Les Myopes
    solo,pno ENOCH s.p.   (R1238)
    solo,acap ENOCH s.p.   (R1239)

ROGERS
  Shepherds In Judea *sac
    med solo,pno PRESSER $.95   (R1240)

  Sing Your Praises *Xmas/Easter
    high solo/low solo,opt tamb&
    maracas&bvl oct SCHMITT 360 $.40
                                    (R1241)

ROGERS, BERNARD (1893-1968)
  Pictures From The Tale Of Aladdin
    narrator,2fl,pic,2ob,English horn,
    2clar,bass clar,2bsn,contrabsn,
    4horn,3trp,3trom,tuba,timp,5perc,
    harp,pno,cel PETERS 66057 s.p.
                                    (R1242)

  Psalm 68 *sac
    Bar solo,3fl,2ob,2clar,2bsn,4horn,
    3trp,3trom,tuba,timp,perc,strings
    PEER sc rental, voc sc $1.50
                                    (R1243)

ROGERS, JAMES HOTCHKISS (1857-1940)
  At Parting
    low solo,pno (D maj) SCHIRM.G $.75
                                    (R1244)

  Cloud-Shadows
    med solo,pno (F min) SCHIRM.G $.75
                                    (R1245)

  Great Peace Have They Which Love Thy
    Law *sac
    high solo,pno (D flat maj) SCHIRM.G
    $1.00   (R1246)
    low solo,pno (G maj) SCHIRM.G $1.00
                                    (R1247)
    med solo,pno (B flat maj) SCHIRM.G
    $1.00   (R1248)

  Love Note, A
    low solo,pno (E flat min) SCHIRM.G
    $.60   (R1249)

  Star, The
    high solo,pno (D flat maj) SCHIRM.G
    $.75   (R1250)
    low solo,pno (B flat maj) SCHIRM.G
    $.75   (R1251)
    high solo,pno (D flat maj) ALLANS
    s.p.   (R1252)
    low solo,pno (A flat maj) ALLANS
    s.p.   (R1253)
    med solo,pno (B flat maj) ALLANS
    s.p.   (R1254)

ROGET, H.
  Chanson De L'or
    see Trois Ballades Francaises De
    Paul Foret

  Il Faut Nous Aimer Sur Terre
    see Quatre Ballades Francaises De
    Paul Foret

  La Chanson Du Marin
    see Trois Ballades Francaises De
    Paul Foret

  La Chanson Fatale
    see Trois Ballades Francaises De
    Paul Foret

  La Valse De L'Ourson
    solo,pno/inst LEDUC s.p.   (R1255)

  Le Bonheur
    see Quatre Ballades Francaises De
    Paul Foret

  Le Diable Dans La Nuit
    see Quatre Ballades Francaises De
    Paul Foret

  Le Marchand De Sable
    solo,pno/inst LEDUC s.p.   (R1256)

  Quatre Ballades Francaises De Paul
    Foret
    solo,pno/inst LEDUC s.p.
    contains: Il Faut Nous Aimer Sur
    Terre; Le Bonheur; Le Diable
    Dans La Nuit; Si Le Bon Dieu
    L'avait Voulu   (R1257)

  Si Le Bon Dieu L'avait Voulu
    see Quatre Ballades Francaises De
    Paul Foret

  Trois Ballades Francaises De Paul
    Foret
    solo,orch LEDUC s.p.
    contains: Chanson De L'or; La
    Chanson Du Marin; La Chanson
    Fatale   (R1258)

ROHR, H.
  Funfzig Gesange Zu Messfeier Und
    Wortgottesdienst Mit Kindern
    *sac,CC50U
    solo,inst CHRIS 50581-83 s.p.
                                    (R1259)

ROISTER DOISTER see Ferrers, Herbert

ROITE BLETLECH see Gelbart, M.

ROITMAN, DAVID
  Selected Recitatives *sac,CCU,Jew
    solo,acap SAC.MUS.PR. 410   (R1260)

ROK see Jirak, Karel Boleslav

ROK V REZAVEM LESE see Jirasek, Ivo

ROKOKO see Scholz, Erwin Christian

ROKOKO-SUITE see Zilcher, Hermann

ROLAND-MANUEL, ALEXIS (1891-1966)
  Delie Object De Plus Haulte Vertu
    *CC3U
    solo,pno/inst DURAND s.p.   (R1261)

  Deux Rondels De Peronnelle
    D'Armentieres *CC2U
    solo,orch DURAND s.p., ipr (R1262)

  Farizade Au Sourire De Rose *CC7L
    med solo,pno/inst DURAND s.p.
                                    (R1263)

ROLL ME OVER *CCU,folk,US
  (Babad, Harry) solo,pno OAK 000067
  $3.95   (R1264)

ROLLICKING, ROLLING STONE, A see
  Fisher, Howard

ROLLICUM-RORUM see Finzi, Gerald

ROLLING DOWN TO RIO see German

ROLLING DOWN TO RIO see German, Edward

ROLLITA see Lagerheim-Romare, Margit

ROMAINE
  Within *sac
    solo,pno LILLENAS SM-623: RN $1.00
                                    (R1265)

ROMAINS, RELEVEZ-VOUS see Saint-Saens,
  Camille

ROMAN, JOHAN HELMICH (1694-1758)
  Aria (from Svenska Massan)
    solo,pno/org ERIKS K 232 s.p.
                                    (R1266)

  Sa Ar Nu Intet Fordomligt (from
    Husandakt)
    (Bjarnegard) solo,pno/org ERIKS
    K 241 s.p.   (R1267)

  Vieni Prode Federico (from Per Il
    Giorno Natale Della S.M. Il Re)
    sac,Xmas
    (Rosenberg) solo,pno GEHRMANS s.p.
                                    (R1268)

ROMANCE see Albeniz, Isaac

ROMANCE see Berners, Lord

ROMANCE see Bizet, Georges

ROMANCE see Debussy, Claude

ROMANCE see Friml, Rudolf

ROMANCE see Gretry, Andre Ernest
  Modeste

ROMANCE see Mehul, H.

ROMANCE see Rubinstein, Anton

ROMANCE see Shaw, C.

ROMANCE see Tchaikovsky, Piotr Ilyitch

ROMANCE see Vuillemin, L.

ROMANCE A FRANCINETTE see Chadal, M.

ROMANCE DE LA CONQUISTA DE ALHAMA see
  Grau, Eduardo

ROMANCE DE LA LUNA, LUNA see Hively,
  Wells

ROMANCE DE LA MUERTE TEMPRANA see
  Jurafsky, Abraham

ROMANCE DE L'ETOILE see Wagner, Richard

ROMANCE DE NADIR see Bizet, Georges

ROMANCE DE SOLITA FROM "THE CUCKOLD'S
  FAIR" see Pittaluga, Gustavo

ROMANCE DEL COMENDADOR DE OCANA see
  Rodrigo, Joaquin

ROMANCE DEL DUERO see Gombau, G.

ROMANCE DU FOU see Dufresne, C.

ROMANCE DU SOIR see Saint-Saens,
  Camille

ROMANCE ET AIR D'ANNETTE see Weber,
  Carl Maria von, Einst Traumte
  Meiner Sel'gen Base

ROMANCE FANEE see Delmet, Paul

ROMANCE NAPOLITAINE see Sauguet, Henri

ROMANCE OF NINA see Glazounov,
  Alexander Konstantinovitch

ROMANCE, ORACION Y SAETA see Surinach,
  Carlos

ROMANCE ORIENTALE see Glazounov,
  Alexander Konstantinovitch

ROMANCE SANS PAROLES see Madetoja,
  Leevi

ROMANCE SANS PAROLES see Pijper, Willem

ROMANCE, WHO LOVES TO NOD AND SING see
  Hoskins, William

ROMANCES see Arapov, B.

ROMANCES see Boiko, R.

ROMANCES *CCU
  [Russ] solo,pno MEZ KNIGA 2.90 s.p.
    contains works by: Gabarayev, I.;
    Khalmamedov, N.; Kuzhamyarov, K.
                                      (R1269)
ROMANCES see Saliman-Vladimirov, D.

ROMANCES AND SONGS see Bortniansky,
  Dimitri Stepanovitch

ROMANCES AND SONGS BY GEORGIAN
  COMPOSERS *CCU
  [Russ] solo,pno MEZ KNIGA 74 s.p.
                                      (R1270)
ROMANCES AND SONGS BY KIRGHIZIAN
  COMPOSERS *CCU
  [Russ] solo,pno MEZ KNIGA 75 s.p.
                                      (R1271)
ROMANCES AND SONGS BY SOVIET COMPOSERS
  *CCU
  [Russ] solo,pno MEZ KNIGA 76 s.p.
                                      (R1272)
ROMANCES AND SONGS, VOL. I see
  Mussorgsky, Modest

ROMANCES AND SONGS, VOL. III see
  Alabiev, Alexander Nicholaevich

ROMANCES AND SONGS, VOL. IV see
  Varlamov, A.

ROMANCES BY SOVIET COMPOSERS *CCU
  [Russ] S solo,pno MEZ KNIGA 101 s.p.
                                      (R1273)
ROMANCES BY SOVIET COMPOSERS TO
  PUSHKIN'S LYRICS *CCU
  [Russ] solo,pno MEZ KNIGA 77 s.p.
                                      (R1274)
ROMANCES BY SOVIET COMPOSERS, VOL. 4
  *CCU
  [Russ] s.p. high solo,pno MEZ KNIGA
    2.102; med solo,pno MEZ KNIGA 2.103
                                      (R1275)
ROMANCES BY SOVIET COMPOSERS, VOL. 5
  *CCU
  [Russ] Bar/B solo,pno MEZ KNIGA 2.101
    s.p.   (R1276)
ROMANCES DEL AMOR Y LA MUERTE see
  Garcia Morillo, Roberto

ROMANCES FANCEES see Levade, Charles
  (Gaston)

ROMANCES FANEES see Levade, Charles
  (Gaston)

ROMANCES FOR TWO VOICES see Glinka,
  Mikhail Ivanovitch

ROMANCES SANS PAROLES see Mendelssohn-
  Bartholdy, Felix

ROMANCES TO LYRICS BY ENGLISH POETS see
  Bunin, R.

ROMANCES TO LYRICS BY GARCIA LORCA see
  Maizel, B.

ROMANCILLO DE VERONICA see Romero, A.

ROMANCILLOS DE LA COLONIA see
  Sciammarella, Valdo

ROMANETTE, I.
  O Rouges Flamboyants
  [Fr] low solo,pno ESCHIG $.60
                                      (R1277)
ROMANETTE, JEAN
  Serenade
  [Fr] med solo,pno ESCHIG $1.00
                                      (R1278)
ROMANS see Sjogren, Emil

ROMANSSI ELOKUVASTA see Fougstedt,
  Nils-Eric

ROMANZA D'AUTUNNO see Pratella,
  Francesco Balilla

ROMANZA DE ENRIQUE see Espoile, Raoul
  H., Novia Y Hermana

ROMANZA DE LA ESTRELLA see Wagner,
  Richard

ROMANZA DEL PRISONERO see Andriessen,
  Juriaan

ROMANZE see Schubert, Franz (Peter)

ROMANZE see Sibelius, Jean

ROMANZE PAULINENS see Tchaikovsky,
  Piotr Ilyitch

ROMANZEN see Aljabjew, Alexander A.

ROMANZEN-SUITE see Shostakovich, Dmitri

ROMANZEN UND LIEDER see Borodin,
  Alexander Porfirievitch

ROMANZEN UND LIEDER, BAND 1 see
  Tchaikovsky, Piotr Ilyitch

ROMANZEN UND LIEDER, BAND 2 see
  Tchaikovsky, Piotr Ilyitch

ROMANZEN UND LIEDER, BAND 2 see Glinka,
  Mikhail Ivanovitch

ROMANZEN UND LIEDER, BAND 3 see
  Tchaikovsky, Piotr Ilyitch

ROMANZEN UND LIEDER, BAND 4 see
  Tchaikovsky, Piotr Ilyitch

ROMANZEN UND LIEDER, BAND I see
  Schaporin, Jurij

ROMANZEN UND LIEDER, BAND II see
  Schaporin, Jurij

ROMBERG, SIGMUND (1887-1951)
  Auf Wiedersehn (from Blue Paradise,
    The)
    med solo, ukulele (F maj) SCHIRM.G
      $.75   (R1279)
    high solo, ukulele (A flat maj)
      SCHIRM.G $.75   (R1280)

  Dancing Will Keep You Young (from
    Maytime)
    high solo,pno (E maj) SCHIRM.G $.60
                                      (R1281)
  Gypsy Song (from Maytime)
    high solo,pno (D min) SCHIRM.G $.60
                                      (R1282)
    low solo,pno (A min) SCHIRM.G $.60
                                      (R1283)
  Jump, Jim Crow (from Maytime)
    med-high solo,pno (A maj) SCHIRM.G
      $.60   (R1284)
  Ragtime Pipe Of Pan, The (from World
    Of Pleasure, A)
    low solo,pno (B flat min) SCHIRM.G
      $.60   (R1285)
    med-high solo,pno (D min) SCHIRM.G
      $.60   (R1286)
  Road To Paradise, The (from Maytime)
    ABar soli,pno SCHIRM.G $.60   (R1287)
    ST soli,pno SCHIRM.G $.60   (R1288)
    med solo,pno (F maj) SCHIRM.G $.60
                                      (R1289)
  Will You Remember (from Maytime)
    med solo,pno (C maj) SCHIRM.G $.85
                                      (R1290)
    SA/SBar soli,pno SCHIRM.G $1.00   (R1291)

ROMEO see Sibelius, Jean

ROMEO see Sibelius, Jean, Romeo

ROMEO IN GEORGIA see Scott, John
  Prindle

ROMERICO see Encina, Juan Del

ROMERO, A.
  En Las Fuentes De Aranjuez
    [Span] med solo,pno UNION ESP. $.65
                                      (R1292)
  La Nina De La Reja
    [Span] high solo,pno UNION ESP.
      $.65   (R1293)
  Nana
    [Span] med solo,pno UNION ESP. $.50
                                      (R1294)
  Romancillo De Veronica
    [Span] high solo,pno UNION ESP.
      $.60   (R1295)
  Tres Canciones *CC3U
    [Span] high solo,pno UNION ESP.
      $.75   (R1296)
  Tristeza De Hilo Blanco
    [Span] high solo,pno UNION ESP.
      $.60   (R1297)

ROMERO, M.
  Cantando Van Los Pastores (composed
    with Romero, V.)
    [Span] med solo,pno UNION ESP. $.40
                                      (R1298)
ROMERO, V.
  Cantando Van Los Pastores *see
    Romero, M.

ROMISCHE ELEGIEN see Klebe, Giselher

RON SALSBURY AND THE J.C. POWER OUTLET
  *sac,CC10L
  solo,pno WORD 37646 $2.50 contains
    works by: Slasbury, Ron; Crouch,
    Andrae   (R1299)

RONALD, SIR LANDON (1873-1938)
  Adonais
    S solo,orch (D maj) ASHDOWN s.p.,
      ipr   (R1300)

  All A Merry May-Time
    low solo,pno (B flat maj) BOOSEY
      $1.50   (R1301)

RONALD, SIR LANDON (cont'd.)

    high solo,pno (E flat maj) BOOSEY
      $1.50   (R1302)

  Away On The Hill
    low solo,orch (D maj) ASHDOWN s.p.,
      ipr contains also: Little Winding
      Road, A   (R1303)
    high solo,orch (E maj) ASHDOWN
      $1.50, ipr contains also: Little
      Winding Road, A   (R1304)
    med solo,orch (E maj) ASHDOWN
      $1.50, ipr contains also: Little
      Winding Road, A   (R1305)

  Believe Me, If All Those Endearing
    Young Charms
    med-high solo,pno (G maj) ASHDOWN
      $1.50   (R1306)
    med solo,pno (F maj) ASHDOWN $1.50
                                      (R1307)
    med-low solo,pno (E maj) ASHDOWN
      $1.50   (R1308)
    low solo,pno (E flat maj) ASHDOWN
      $1.50   (R1309)
    high solo,pno (A flat maj) ASHDOWN
      $1.50   (R1310)

  Birthday Morn, The
    low solo,pno (C maj) LEONARD-ENG
                                      (R1311)
    2 soli,pno (E flat maj) LEONARD-ENG
                                      (R1312)
    high solo,pno (E flat maj) LEONARD-
      ENG   (R1313)
    2 soli,pno (D flat maj) LEONARD-ENG
                                      (R1314)

  C'etait En Avril
    solo,pno ENOCH s.p.   (R1315)

  Cycle Of Life, A *CC5U
    ASHDOWN low solo,pno $2.00; med
      solo,pno $2.00; high solo,pno
      $2.00   (R1316)

  Dove, The
    low solo,pno (F maj) ASHDOWN s.p.
      contains also: 'Tis June   (R1317)
    high solo,pno (A flat maj) ASHDOWN
      s.p. contains also: 'Tis June
                                      (R1318)

  Down In The Forest
    high solo&high solo,pno ASHDOWN
      $1.75   (R1319)
    low solo&low solo,pno ASHDOWN $1.75
                                      (R1320)
    high solo,orch (E maj) ASHDOWN
      $1.50, ipr   (R1321)
    med-high solo,orch (E flat maj)
      ASHDOWN $1.50, ipr   (R1322)
    med solo,orch (D maj) ASHDOWN
      $1.50, ipr   (R1323)
    med-low solo,orch (C maj) ASHDOWN
      $1.50, ipr   (R1324)
    low solo,orch (B flat maj) ASHDOWN
      $1.50, ipr   (R1325)

  Five Canzonets *CC5U
    ASHDOWN low solo,pno s.p.; med
      solo,pno s.p.; high solo,pno s.p.
                                      (R1326)
  Four Songs Of The Hill *CC4U
    ASHDOWN low solo,pno s.p.; high
      solo,pno s.p.   (R1327)

  If I Might Love You
    low solo,pno (C maj) BOOSEY $1.50
                                      (R1328)
    high solo,pno (E flat maj) BOOSEY
      $1.50   (R1329)

  Lament Of Shah Jehan
    Bar solo,orch ASHDOWN s.p., ipr
                                      (R1330)

  Les Adieux
    solo,pno (available in 2 keys)
      ENOCH s.p.   (R1331)

  Little Winding Road, A
    see Ronald, Sir Landon, Away On The
      Hill
    see Ronald, Sir Landon, Away On The
      Hill
    see Ronald, Sir Landon, Away On The
      Hill

  Love, I Have Won You
    low solo,pno (E flat maj) BOOSEY
      $1.50   (R1332)
    high solo,pno (A flat maj) BOOSEY
      $1.50   (R1333)
    med solo,pno (F maj) BOOSEY $1.50
                                      (R1334)

  Moon At The Full
    med solo,pno (E maj) BOOSEY $1.50
                                      (R1335)
    low solo,pno (D maj) BOOSEY $1.50
                                      (R1336)
    high solo,pno (G maj) BOOSEY $1.50
                                      (R1337)

  O Belle Nuit *see O Lovely Night!

  O Lovely Night!
    low solo,orch (B flat maj) ASHDOWN
      $1.50, ipr   (R1338)

RONALD, SIR LANDON (cont'd.)

med solo,orch (D flat maj) ASHDOWN
$1.50, ipr   (R1339)
med-low solo,orch (C maj) ASHDOWN
$1.50, ipr   (R1340)
high solo&high solo,pno ASHDOWN
$1.75   (R1341)
low solo&low solo,pno ASHDOWN $1.75
                              (R1342)
high solo&low solo,pno ASHDOWN
$7.15   (R1343)
high solo,orch (E flat maj) ASHDOWN
$1.50, ipr   (R1344)
"O Belle Nuit" solo,vln (available
in 2 keys) ENOCH s.p.   (R1345)

Pluck This Little Flower
med solo,orch (G maj) ASHDOWN s.p.,
ipr   (R1346)
low solo,orch (F maj) ASHDOWN s.p.,
ipr   (R1347)
high solo,orch (A flat maj) ASHDOWN
s.p., ipr   (R1348)

Prelude
low solo,pno (F maj) ASHDOWN $1.75
                              (R1349)
high solo,pno (A flat maj) ASHDOWN
$1.75   (R1350)
med solo,pno (G maj) ASHDOWN $1.75
                              (R1351)

Serenade Espagnole
solo,pno (available in 2 keys)
ENOCH s.p.   (R1352)

Sheepfold Song
low solo,pno (E min) BOOSEY $1.50
                              (R1353)
med solo,pno (G min) BOOSEY $1.50
                              (R1354)
high solo,pno (A min) BOOSEY $1.50
                              (R1355)

Songs Of Springtime *CC5U
ASHDOWN low solo,pno s.p.; med
solo,pno s.p.; high solo,pno s.p.
                              (R1356)

Summertime *CC4U
ASHDOWN low solo,pno $3.00; med
solo,pno $3.00; high solo,pno
$3.00   (R1357)

Sunbeams
low solo,pno (C maj) ASHDOWN $1.50
                              (R1358)
med solo,pno (D maj) ASHDOWN $1.50
                              (R1359)
high solo,pno (E flat maj) ASHDOWN
$1.50   (R1360)
"Vive Le Soleil" solo,pno
(available in 2 keys) ENOCH s.p.
                              (R1361)

Sylvan
low solo,pno (C maj) ASHDOWN s.p.
                              (R1362)
med solo,pno (E flat maj) ASHDOWN
s.p.   (R1363)
high solo,pno (F maj) ASHDOWN s.p.
                              (R1364)
low solo&low solo,pno ASHDOWN s.p.
                              (R1365)
high solo&high solo,pno ASHDOWN
s.p.   (R1366)

'Tis June
see Ronald, Sir Landon, Dove, The
see Ronald, Sir Landon, Dove, The

To Live For You
high solo,pno (D maj) CRAMER
                              (R1367)
low solo,pno (B flat maj) CRAMER
                              (R1368)
med solo,pno (C maj) CRAMER (R1369)

Vive Le Soleil *see Sunbeams

Wander-Thirst
high solo,pno (F maj) BOOSEY $1.50
                              (R1370)
low solo,pno (C maj) BOOSEY $1.50
                              (R1371)
med solo,pno (E flat maj) BOOSEY
$1.50   (R1372)

RONDA DEL SOL see Quaratino, Pascual

RONDE see Biancheri, A.

RONDE see Bloch, Ernest

RONDE see Dalcroze, Jacques

RONDE see Dela, M.

RONDE see Geraedts, Jaap

RONDE see Godard, Benjamin Louis Paul

RONDE see Ravel, Maurice

RONDE see Vellere, Lucie

RONDE D'AMOUR see Chaminade, Cecile

RONDE DU BOIS DORE see Cuvillier,
Charles

RONDE DU VIN DOUX
(Emmereshts; Beldent) solo,pno GRAS
s.p.   (R1373)

RONDE FLAMANDE see Ravize, A.

RONDE POITEVINE see Indy, Vincent d'

RONDEAU see Badings, Henk

RONDEAU see Cuvillier, Charles

RONDEAU see Godard, Benjamin Louis Paul

RONDEAU D'ADAM see Betove

RONDEAU DE SAINT-ANGENOR see Messager,
Andre

RONDEAU REDOUBLE see Clarke, Henry
Leland

RONDEAUX see Vries Robbe, Willem de

RONDEAUX AMOUREUX see Boer, Jan den

RONDEAUX PER 10 see Togni, Camillo

RONDEEL DER HERDERS see Mul, Jan

RONDEL see Espoile, Raoul H.

RONDEL see Flothius, Marius

RONDEL see Gui, Vittorio

RONDEL see Platamone, Stefano

RONDEL see Roger-Ducasse, Jean-Jules
Aimable

RONDEL see Toutain-Grun, J.

RONDEL DE L'ADIEU see De Lara, Isadore

RONDEL GALANT see Filipucci, Edm.

RONDEL MELANCHOLIQUE see Rabey, Rene

RONDEL OF SPRING see Bibb

RONDEL SUR UNE JOUEUSE DE FLUTE see
Vuillemin, L.

RONDELAY see Rorem, Ned

RONDELL see Straesser, Joep

RONDELS see Koechlin, Charles

RONDELS MELANCOLIQUES see Vuillemin, L.

RONDES ET CHANSONETTES ENFANTINES see
Delbruck, J.

RONDEUSE AU FRONT DE VERRE see Poulenc,
Francis

RONDINE AL NIDO see De Crescenzo

RONDO see Cairone, Renato

RONDO see Gandino, Adolfo

RONDO see Veneziani, Vittore

RONDO DU VEAU D'OR see Gounod, Charles
Francois

RONDO VOM GOLDENEN KALB see Gounod,
Charles Francois, Rondo Du Veau
D'or

RONGE, JEAN-BAPTISTE (1825-1882)
La Pauvresse De Bazeilles
solo,acap ENOCH s.p.   (R1374)
solo,pno ENOCH s.p.   (R1375)

La Resurrection *sac
[Lat/Fr] solo,pno ENOCH   (R1376)

Noel *sac,Xmas
[Fr/Lat] solo,pno/org (available in
2 keys) ENOCH s.p.   (R1377)
[Fr/Lat] solo,acap (available in 2
keys) ENOCH s.p.   (R1378)

RONGER, FLORIMOND
see HERVE

RONNEFELD, PETER (1935-1965)
Funf Lieder Im Herbst *CC5U
high solo,pno MODERN s.p.   (R1379)

Vier Wiegenlieder *CC4U
S solo,fl MODERN rental   (R1380)

Zwei Lieder Zur Pauke *CC2U
A solo,fl,4timp MODERN rental
                              (R1381)
RONSARD A SON AME see Ravel, Maurice

RONTGEN, JOHANNES (1898-   )
Beruhignung
see Funf Lieder

Das Lied Von Ferne
see Funf Lieder

Das Madchen Am Teiche Singt
see Funf Lieder

Das Mitleidige Madel
see Drei Lieder

Das Nest
see Drei Lieder

De Graafbuiksspreker
see Drie Redolze Duetten

Diablerie
see MODERNE NEDERLANDSE LIED

Die Fruhen Kranze
see Zwei Lieder Von Stefan Zweig

Drei Lieder
S solo,pno ALSBACH s.p.
contains: Das Mitleidige Madel;
Das Nest; Jeannette   (R1382)

Drie Redolze Duetten
SA soli,fl,clar,pno DONEMUS s.p.
contains: De Graafbuiksspreker;
Een Maharadja In Malakka;
Garnalenwals   (R1383)

Een Maharadja In Malakka
see Drie Redolze Duetten

Elf Dierkundige Dictoefeningen Van
Trijnte Fop *CC11U
DONEMUS Bar solo,pno s.p.; Mez/A
solo,pno s.p.   (R1384)

Funf Lieder
S solo,pno ALSBACH s.p.
contains: Beruhignung; Das Lied
Von Ferne; Das Madchen Am
Teiche Singt; Hinter Einer
Grunen Weide; Sommer   (R1385)

Garnalenwals
see Drie Redolze Duetten

Graues Land
see Zwei Lieder Von Stefan Zweig

Het Lied Van De Jeugd
solo,pno HEUWEKE. 559 s.p. (R1386)

Hinter Einer Grunen Weide
see Funf Lieder

Jeannette
see Drei Lieder

O, 'T Ruischen Van Het Ranke Riet
Mez solo,clar,pno DONEMUS s.p.
                              (R1387)
Sommer
see Funf Lieder

Zwei Lieder Von Stefan Zweig
S solo,fl,vla ALSBACH s.p.
contains: Die Fruhen Kranze;
Graues Land   (R1388)

RONTGEN, [JULIUS] (1855-1932)
Bede Voor Het Vaderland
see Oud-Nederlandse Liederen Naar
Valerius

Dankgebed
see Oud-Nederlandse Liederen Naar
Valerius

De Hollander En De Zeeuw
see Oud-Nederlandse Liederen Naar
Valerius

Een Liedje Van De Zee
see Oud-Nederlandse Liederen Naar
Valerius

O Angenietje
see Oud-Nederlandse Liederen Naar
Valerius

Oud-Nederlandse Liederen Naar
Valerius
solo,pno ALSBACH s.p.
contains: Bede Voor Het
Vaderland; Dankgebed; De
Hollander En De Zeeuw; Een
Liedje Van De Zee; O
Angenietje; Wilhelmus Van
Nassouwe   (R1389)

Oud-Nederlandse Volksliederen, Vol.
3-4 *CCU
solo,pno ALSBACH s.p., ea. (R1390)

Prometheus *Op.99
solo,pno ALSBACH s.p.   (R1391)

RONTGEN, [JULIUS] (cont'd.)

  Wilhelmus Van Nassouwe
    see Oud-Nederlandse Liederen Naar
    Valerius

ROOD PIOENEKE see Clercq, R. de

ROOM AT THE CROSS see Stanphill, Ira F.

ROOM AT THE CROSS FOR YOU *sac,gospel
  solo,pno ABER.GRP. $1.50   (R1392)

ROOS, ROBERT DE (1907-   )
  Adam In Ballingschap
    2 narrators,2fl,2horn,strings
    DONEMUS s.p.   (R1393)

  Au Temp Des Foins
    see Cinq Quatrians Von Fr. Jammes,
    Series II

  Chaleur
    see Cinq Quatrains Von Fr, Jammes,
    Series I

  Cinq Quatrains Von Fr, Jammes, Series
    I
    high solo,pno DONEMUS s.p.
      contains: Chaleur; Liquidite;
      Lumiere Dans La Nuit; Nocturne;
      Pastorale   (R1394)

  Cinq Quatrians Von Fr. Jammes, Series
    II
    high solo,pno DONEMUS s.p.
      contains: Au Temp Des Foins;
      Depouillement; Estang; Le Pays
      Arrose; Purete   (R1395)

  Depouillement
    see Cinq Quatrians Von Fr. Jammes,
    Series II

  Der Ewige Weg
    see Monologen Aus Jeremias Von
    Stefan Zweig

  Die Letzte Not
    see Monologen Aus Jeremias Von
    Stefan Zweig

  Die Umkehr
    see Monologen Aus Jeremias Von
    Stefan Zweig

  Erhebe Die Hande
    A solo,vcl DONEMUS s.p.   (R1396)

  Estang
    see Cinq Quatrians Von Fr. Jammes,
    Series II

  Le Pays Arrose
    see Cinq Quatrians Von Fr. Jammes,
    Series II

  Liquidite
    see Cinq Quatrians Von Fr. Jammes,
    Series I

  Lumiere Dans La Nuit
    see Cinq Quatrians Von Fr. Jammes,
    Series I

  Monologen Aus Jeremias Von Stefan
    Zweig
    male solo,pno DONEMUS s.p.
      contains: Der Ewige Weg; Die
      Letzte Not; Die Umkehr (R1397)

  Nocturne
    see Cinq Quatrians Von Fr. Jammes,
    Series I

  Pastorale
    see Cinq Quatrians Von Fr. Jammes,
    Series I

  Purete
    see Cinq Quatrians Von Fr. Jammes,
    Series II

  Zeven Kerstliederen *sac,CC7L
    S solo,pno DONEMUS s.p.   (R1398)

  Zwei Lieder *CC2U
    Bar solo,fl,ob,clar,cel,pno,1-4vla,
    1-4vcl DONEMUS s.p.   (R1399)

ROOT
  Christ My Refuge
    high solo,pno (A flat maj) FISCHER,
      C V 2145   (R1400)
    low solo,pno (F maj) FISCHER,C
      V 2146   (R1401)

  Christmas Morn *sac,Xmas
    high solo,pno (E flat maj) FISCHER,
      C V 2147   (R1402)
    low solo,pno (C maj) FISCHER,C
      V 2148   (R1403)

  Love
    high solo,pno (F maj) FISCHER,C
      V 2149   (R1404)

ROOT (cont'd.)

    low solo,pno (D maj) FISCHER,C
      V 2150   (R1405)

  Saw Ye My Saviour? *sac
    high solo,pno (F maj) FISCHER,C
      V 2153   (R1406)

ROOT CELLAR see Rorem, Ned

ROPARTZ, JOSEPH GUY (1864-1955)
  Ah! S'en Aller
    see Reve Sur Le Sable

  Ce Coeur Plaintif
    see Two Songs

  Chante Si Doucement
    see Quatre Odelettes De H. Regnier

  Des Fleurs Font Une Broderie
    see Six Melodies

  Deux Poemes *see Le Manior; Lied Du
    Soir   (R1407)

  Jazz Dans La Nuit
    see Six Melodies

  Je N'ai Rien Que Trois Feuilles D'or
    see Quatre Odelettes De H. Regnier

  La Naissance De La Lyre
    solo,pno DURAND s.p.   (R1408)

  La Route
    med solo,pno/inst DURAND s.p.
                             (R1409)

  Le Bachelier De Salamanque
    see Six Melodies

  Le Manior
    med solo,orch DURAND s.p. see from
      Deux Poemes   (R1410)

  Le Vent Est Doux
    see Reve Sur Le Sable

  Les Heures Propices *see Nous
    N'habiterons Pas Au Bord De La
    Grand'route; Pour Vivre
    Longuement; Puisque Voici Les
    Soirs Embrumes De L'hiver (R1411)

  Les Vepres Sonnent
    3 female soli,orch DURAND s.p., ipr
                             (R1412)

  Lied Du Soir
    med solo,orch DURAND s.p. see from
      Deux Poemes   (R1413)

  Light
    see Six Melodies

  Nous N'habiterons Pas Au Bord De La
    Grand'route
    solo,pno/inst DURAND s.p. see from
      Les Heures Propices   (R1414)

  Pour Vivre Longuement
    solo,pno/inst DURAND s.p. see from
      Les Heures Propices   (R1415)

  Priere Du Matin
    see Reve Sur Le Sable

  Puisque Voici Les Soirs Embrumes De
    L'hiver
    solo,pno/inst DURAND s.p. see from
      Les Heures Propices   (R1416)

  Quatre Odelettes De H. Regnier
    solo,orch cmplt ed DURAND s.p., ipr
      contains: Chante Si Doucement; Je
      N'ai Rien Que Trois Feuilles
      D'or; Si Tu Disais; Un Petit
      Roseau M'a Suffi   (R1417)

  Que Me Fait Toute La Terre
    see Two Songs

  Reponse D'une Epouse Sage
    see Six Melodies

  Reve Sur Le Sable
    med solo,orch cmplt ed DURAND s.p.,
    ipr
      contains: Ah! S'en Aller; Le Vent
      Est Doux; Priere Du Matin; Soir
      D'adieu; Ton Image   (R1418)

  Sarabande
    see Six Melodies

  Si Tu Disais
    see Quatre Odelettes De H. Regnier

  Six Melodies
    solo,pno DURAND s.p.
      contains: Des Fleurs Font Une
      Broderie; Jazz Dans La Nuit; Le
      Bachelier De Salamanque; Light;
      Reponse D'une Epouse Sage;
      Sarabande   (R1419)

ROPARTZ, JOSEPH GUY (cont'd.)

  Soir D'adieu
    see Reve Sur Le Sable

  Ton Image
    see Reve Sur Le Sable

  Two Songs
    high solo,pno SALABERT-US $3.75
      contains: Ce Coeur Plaintif; Que
      Me Fait Toute La Terre (R1420)

  Un Petit Roseau M'a Suffi
    see Quatre Odelettes De H. Regnier

  Voeu
    solo,pno/inst DURAND s.p. (R1421)

ROPULJ PAVA see Jardanyi, [Pal]

ROQUES, J.
  La Chanson Du Soleil
    solo,pno ENOCH s.p.   (R1422)
    solo,acap ENOCH s.p.   (R1423)

  Les Paysans
    solo,pno (available in 2 keys)
      ENOCH s.p.   (R1424)
    solo,acap (available in 2 keys)
      ENOCH s.p.   (R1425)

ROQUES, L.
  Marche Des Gymnastes
    med solo,pno/inst DURAND s.p.
                             (R1426)
    [Fr] solo,acap oct DURAND s.p.
                             (R1427)

ROR IKKE VED MITT HJERTE IDAG see
  Pergament, Moses

RORATE COELI DESUPER see Schutz,
  Heinrich

ROREM, NED (1923-   )
  Absalom
    solo,pno BOOSEY $1.50   (R1428)

  An Angel Speaks To The Shepherds
    *Xmas
    solo,pno PEER $.95   (R1429)

  Ariel *CC5U
    S solo,clar,pno BOOSEY $9.50
                             (R1430)

  As Adam Early In The Morning
    med solo,pno PETERS 6269 $1.25
                             (R1431)

  Catullus: On The Burial Of His
    Brother
    solo,pno BOOSEY $1.50   (R1432)

  Conversation
    solo,pno BOOSEY $1.50   (R1433)

  Cradle Song
    coloratura sop,pno PETERS 6373B
      $1.25 see also Six Songs For High
      Voice   (R1434)

  Cycle Of Holy Songs *sac,song cycle
    solo,pno PEER $2.00   (R1435)

  Early In The Morning
    med-low solo,pno PETERS 6370 $1.25
                             (R1436)

  Echo's Song
    solo,pno (G flat maj) BOOSEY $1.50
                             (R1437)

  Five Poems Of Walt Whitman *CC5U
    solo,pno BOOSEY $2.75   (R1438)

  Flight For Heaven *song cycle
    B solo,pno PRESSER $2.00   (R1439)
    B solo,pno PRESSER $2.00   (R1440)

  For Poulenc
    med-high solo,pno SCHIRM.EC 138
      s.p.   (R1441)

  Four Dialogues *CC4U
    2 soli,2pno BOOSEY $7.50   (R1442)

  Four Poems Of Tennyson *CC4U
    solo,pno BOOSEY $4.00   (R1443)

  From An Unknown Past
    solo,pno PEER $2.00   (R1444)

  Gloria *song cycle
    SMez soli,pno BOOSEY $2.50 (R1445)

  Hearing *song cycle
    med-low solo,pno BOOSEY $3.50
                             (R1446)

  I Am Rose
    med solo,pno PETERS 6625 $1.25
                             (R1447)

  In A Gondola
    coloratura sop,pno PETERS 6373E
      $1.25 see also Six Songs For High
      Voice   (R1448)

  Jack L'Eventreur
    solo,pno BOOSEY $1.50   (R1449)

ROREM, NED (cont'd.)

King Midas *song cycle
    solo/2 soli/4 soli,pno BOOSEY $4.00
                                    (R1450)

Last Poems Of Wallace Stevens *CCU
    solo,vcl,pno BOOSEY $6.00 (R1451)

Let Us Haste To Kelvin Grove
    solo,pno PEER $.85   (R1452)

Lordly Hudson, The
    med solo,pno MERCURY $.95 (R1453)

Lord's Prayer, The *sac
    med solo,pno/org PETERS 6371 $1.25
                                    (R1454)

Love
    solo,pno (E maj) BOOSEY $1.50
                                    (R1455)

Love In A Life
    solo,pno BOOSEY $1.50   (R1456)

Lullaby Of The Woman Of The Mountain
    solo,pno (C sharp min) BOOSEY $1.50
                                    (R1457)

Memory
    med solo,pno PETERS 6285 $1.25
                                    (R1458)

Midnight Sun, The
    med-high solo,pno SCHIRM.EC 139
    s.p.   (R1459)

Mild Mother, The
    med-high solo,pno SCHIRM.EC 140
    s.p.   (R1460)

Mourning Scene From Samuel
    [Eng] T solo,4strings/strings sc
    PETERS 6374 $6.00   (R1461)

My Papa's Waltz
    med solo,pno PETERS 6626 $1.50
                                    (R1462)

Night Crow
    med solo,pno PETERS 6627 $1.25
                                    (R1463)

Nightingale
    solo,pno (F sharp min) BOOSEY $1.50
                                    (R1464)

O You Whom I Often And Silently Come
    med solo,pno PETERS 6284 $1.25
                                    (R1465)

Pippa's Song
    coloratura sop,pno PETERS 6373A
    $1.25 see also Six Songs For High
    Voice   (R1466)

Poemes Pour La Paix *CCU
    Mez solo,pno/strings BOOSEY $3.50
                                    (R1467)

Poems Of Love And The Rain *CCU
    Mez solo,pno BOOSEY $3.50 (R1468)

Poor Man's Garden
    high solo,pno (D flat maj) BOOSEY
    $1.50   (R1469)
    low solo,pno (C maj) BOOSEY $1.50
                                    (R1470)

Psalm 100 *see Psalm Of Praise, A

Psalm 120 *see Song Of David, A

Psalm Of Praise, A (Psalm 100)
    med solo,pno AMP $.75   (R1471)

Rain In Spring
    solo,pno (D maj) BOOSEY $1.50
                                    (R1472)

Requiem
    solo,pno PEER $.95   (R1473)

Resurrection, The
    solo,pno PEER $2.00   (R1474)

Rondelay
    coloratura sop,pno PETERS 6373D
    $1.25 see also Six Songs For High
    Voice   (R1475)

Root Cellar
    med solo,pno PETERS 6628 $1.25
                                    (R1476)

Sally's Smile
    high solo,pno PETERS 6367 $1.25
                                    (R1477)

See How They Love Me
    med-high solo,pno PETERS 6368 $1.25
                                    (R1478)

Serpent, The
    solo,pno BOOSEY $1.50   (R1479)

Silver Swan, The
    solo,pno PEER $1.25   (R1480)

Six Irish Poems *CC6U
    med solo,orch PEER sc $7.00, ipr,
    voc sc $2.00   (R1481)

Six Songs For High Voice
    coloratura sop,2fl,2ob,2clar,2bsn,
    2horn,trp,trom,pno,harp,strings
    sc PETERS 6373 $4.00, ipr
    contains & see also: Cradle Song;
    In A Gondola; Pippa's Song;
    Rondelay; Song For A Girl; Song

ROREM, NED (cont'd.)

    To A Fair Young Lady   (R1482)

Snake
    med solo,pno PETERS 6629 $1.25
                                    (R1483)

Some Trees *song cycle
    3 soli,pno BOOSEY $3.50 (R1484)

Song For A Girl
    coloratura sop,pno PETERS 6373C
    $1.25 see also Six Songs For High
    Voice   (R1485)

Song Of David, A (Psalm 120)
    med solo,pno AMP $.60   (R1486)

Song To A Fair Young Lady
    coloratura sop,pno PETERS 6373F
    $1.50 see also Six Songs For High
    Voice   (R1487)

Spring
    solo,pno BOOSEY $1.50   (R1488)

Spring And Fall
    med solo,pno MERCURY $.95 (R1489)

Such Beauty As Hurts To Behold
    med solo,pno PETERS 6321 $1.50
                                    (R1490)

Sun *song cycle
    S solo,orch BOOSEY $4.00 (R1491)

Three Poems Of Demetrios Capetanakis
    *CC3U
    solo,pno BOOSEY $1.75   (R1492)

Three Poems Of Paul Goodman *CC3U
    solo,pno BOOSEY $1.75   (R1493)

Tulip Tree, The
    med-high solo,pno SCHIRM.EC 141
    s.p.   (R1494)

Two Poems Of Theodore Roethke *CC2U
    solo,pno BOOSEY $1.50   (R1495)

Visits To St. Elizabeth's
    solo,pno (E min) BOOSEY $1.50
                                    (R1496)

Waking, The
    med solo,pno PETERS 6320 $1.50
                                    (R1497)

War Scenes *song cycle
    med-low solo,pno BOOSEY $4.50
                                    (R1498)

Youth, Day, Old Age And Night
    med solo,pno PETERS 6369 $1.25
                                    (R1499)

RORIE, DAVID
    Lum Hat Wantin' The Croon, The
    solo,pno PATERSON s.p.   (R1500)

RORY O'MORE see Hughes, Herbert

ROSA
    Star Vicino
    med solo,pno (A flat maj) ALLANS
    s.p.   (R1501)

ROSA see Denza, Luigi

ROSA DEL CAMI see Mompou, Federico

ROSA LILL' see Kilpinen, Yrio

ROSA, M.
    Due Poemetti
    [It] solo,pno BONGIOVANI 965 s.p.
    contains: Nonna Racconta;
             Passeggiata Francescana (R1502)

    Nonna Racconta
    see Due Poemetti

    Passeggiata Francescana
    see Due Poemetti

ROSA MUNDI see Polin, Claire

ROSA MYSTICA see Einem, Gottfried von

ROSA MYSTICA see Andriessen, K.

ROSA RORANS BONITATEM see Melartin,
    Erkki

ROSA, S.
    Star Vicino
    "To Be Near The Fair Idol" [Eng/It]
    med solo,pno PRESSER $.75 (R1503)

    To Be Near The Fair Idol *see Star
    Vicino

ROSALIND'S MADRIGAL
    high solo,pno (D flat maj) CRAMER
                                    (R1504)
    low solo,pno (B flat maj) CRAMER
                                    (R1505)
    med solo,pno (C maj) CRAMER (R1506)

ROSALINE see Moeran, Ernest J.

ROSARY, THE see Hannikainen, Ilmari,
    Rukousnauha

ROSARY, THE see King

ROSARY, THE see Nevin, Ethelbert
    Woodbridge

ROSAS DEL SUR see Strauss, Johann,
    Rosen Aus Dem Suden

ROSCHEN BISS DEN APFEL AN see Trunk,
    Richard

ROSE, THE see Dvorak, Antonin, Die Rose

ROSE AND THE WILLOW, THE see
    Guastavino, Carlos, La Rosa Y El
    Sauce

ROSE BERRIES see Naylor, Bernard

ROSE BLANCHE see Wall, C. v.d.

ROSE CHEEK'D LAURA see Lessard, John
    Ayres

ROSE D'AMOUR see Cuvillier, Charles

ROSE D'AMOUR see Delmet, Paul

ROSE DE GRENADE see Bos, Jane

ROSE DES BRUYERES see Schubert, Franz
    (Peter), Heidenroslein

ROSE ENSLAVES THE NIGHTINGALE, THE see
    Rimsky-Korsakov, Nikolai, Aimant La
    Rose, Le Rossignol

ROSE ET CADICHON
    (Gras, M.-B.; Beldent) solo,pno GRAS
    s.p.   (R1507)

ROSE FAMILY, THE see Carter, E.

ROSE FLEURIE see Lacome, Paul

ROSE HAS CHARMED THE NIGHTINGALE see
    Rimsky-Korsakov, Nikolai

ROSE, HUGH DUNCAN
    Sing Me The Songs Of Yesterday
    low solo,pno (B flat maj) WILLIS
    $.50   (R1508)

ROSE IN MY GARDEN DREAMING see
    Kinnersley, Elizabeth

ROSE MARIE see Collan, Karl

ROSE MESSAGERE see Barbirolli, A.

ROSE, MICHAEL (1916-   )
    Coming Home To You
    high solo,pno (F maj) LEONARD-ENG
                                    (R1509)
    low solo,pno (E flat maj) LEONARD-
    ENG   (R1510)

ROSE NOIRE see Delmet, Paul

ROSE OF ERIN see Schertzinger, V.

ROSE OF ISPAHAN see Geehl, Henry Ernest

ROSE OF KILLARNEY see Stanford, Charles
    Villiers

ROSE OF MAY see Mellers, Wilfrid Howard

ROSE OF THE WORLD, THE see Verrall,
    John

ROSE OF TRALEE, THE
    (Kane) med solo,pno PAXTON P2206 s.p.
                                    (R1511)

ROSE OF TRALEE, THE see Glover, Charles
    W.

ROSE, ON AN AUTUMN DAY see Irving,
    W.W.S.

ROSE ON THE WIND, THE see Mourant,
    Walter

ROSE SOFTLY BLOOMING see Spohr, Ludwig
    (Louis)

ROSE SONG, THE see Birch, Robert
    Fairfax

ROSE UND TOD see Grant, W. Parks

ROSE WILL BLOW, THE see King, Wilton

ROSEBUD BY MY EARLY WALK, A *folk,Scot
    solo,pno (C maj/D maj) PATERSON FS6
    s.p.   (R1512)

ROSEBUD ON THE HILL-SIDE see Schubert,
    Franz (Peter), Heidenroslein

ROSEE AMERE see Abt, Franz

ROSEES see Busser, Henri-Paul

ROSEGGER, SEPP
Lieder *CCU
solo,pno KRENN 1.28 s.p.   (R1513)

ROSELEIN see Kilpinen, Yrio, Rosa Lill'

ROSELIUS, LUDWIG (1902-   )
Acht Lieder Im Volkston *Op.21,CC8U
[Ger] BOTE $2.00   (R1514)

Das Heckenlied *Op.14,No.1
[Ger] high solo,pno BOTE $.75 see
from Drei Heitere Lieder   (R1515)

Das Reh *Op.13,No.2
[Ger] high solo,pno BOTE $.75 see
from Drei Lieder   (R1516)
[Ger] low solo,pno BOTE $.75 see
from Drei Lieder   (R1517)

Der Hutejunge *Op.13,No.3
[Ger] high solo,pno BOTE $.75 see
from Drei Lieder   (R1518)
[Ger] low solo,pno BOTE $.75 see
from Drei Lieder   (R1519)

Der Kuckuck *Op.14,No.3
[Ger] high solo,pno BOTE $.75 see
from Drei Heitere Lieder   (R1520)

Die Junge Hexe *Op.19,No.2
[Ger] high solo,pno BOTE $1.25 see
from Two Ballads   (R1521)
[Ger] low solo,pno BOTE $1.25 see
from Two Ballads   (R1522)

Die Katze *Op.14,No.2
[Ger] high solo,pno BOTE $.75 see
from Drei Heitere Lieder   (R1523)

Drei Heitere Lieder *see Das
Heckenlied, Op.14,No.1; Der
Kuckuck, Op.14,No.3; Die Katze,
Op.14,No.2   (R1524)

Drei Lieder *see Das Reh, Op.13,
No.2; Der Hutejunge, Op.13,No.3;
Marienlied, Op.13,No.1   (R1525)

Drei Lieder Aus Lilofee *Op.17,CC3U
[Ger] BOTE $1.00   (R1526)

Drei Lieder Der Andacht *Op.15,CC3U
[Ger] low solo,pno BOTE $1.00
                                  (R1527)

Herr Glomme *Op.19,No.1
[Ger] low solo,pno BOTE $1.25 see
from Two Ballads   (R1528)
[Ger] high solo,pno BOTE $1.25 see
from Two Ballads   (R1529)

Marienlied *Op.13,No.1
[Ger] high solo,pno BOTE $.75 see
from Drei Lieder   (R1530)
[Ger] low solo,pno BOTE $.75 see
from Drei Lieder   (R1531)

Stunden Einer Liebe *Op.20,CCU
[Ger] SBar soli,pno BOTE $2.50
                                  (R1532)

Two Ballads *see Die Junge Hexe,
Op.19,No.2; Herr Glomme, Op.19,
No.1   (R1533)

Zwei Geistliche Gesange *Op.11,No.1-
2, CC2U
low solo,vla,pno RIES s.p. (R1534)

ROSEMARIN, SAMSON
Dirge
med-low solo,pno TRANSCON. TV 467
$.40   (R1535)

ROSEMONDE see Honegger, Arthur

ROSEMONDE see Persico, Mario

ROSEMONDE see Poulenc, Francis

ROSEN AUS DEM ROSENGARTEN, BAND II see
Frey, Martin

ROSEN AUS DEM SUDEN see Strauss, Johann

ROSEN, JEROME (1921-   )
Scenes From "Calisto And Melibea"
3 soli,fl,ob,clar,bsn,horn,trp,
trom,pno,perc,2vln,vla,2vcl sc
AM.COMP.AL. $42.90   (R1536)

ROSENBUSCHE see Kilpinen, Yrio

ROSENLIED see Sibelius, Jean

ROSENLIEDER see Eulenberg, P.

ROSENMULLER, JOHANN (ca. 1620-1684)
Andere Kernspruche *see Ich Bin Das
Brot Des Lebens; Siehe, Des
Herren Auge Siehet Auf Die, So
Ihn Furchten; Weil Wir Wissen,
Dass Der Mensch Durch Des

ROSENMULLER, JOHANN (cont'd.)

Gesetzes Werke   (R1537)

Auf, Nun Lobet Gott (Psalm 134) sac
(Hamel, Fred) med solo/low solo,
2vln,cont (med) NAGELS NMA 81
s.p.   (R1538)

Danket Dem Herrn Und Prediget Seinen
Namen *sac,cant
AT soli,2vln,cont sc HANSSLER
10.041 s.p., ipa, solo pt
HANSSLER s.p. see from
Kernspruchen   (R1539)

Das Ist Ein Kostlich Ding *sac,cant
ST soli,strings,cont sc HANSSLER
10.044 s.p., ipa, solo pt
HANSSLER s.p. see from
Kernspruchen   (R1540)

Das Ist Meine Freude *sac,cant
S solo,2vln,cont sc HANSSLER 5.048
s.p., ipa   (R1541)

Dream Of Olwen, The
(Williams) solo,pno BELWIN $1.50
                                  (R1542)

Ecstasy Of Spring
high solo,pno BELWIN $1.50 (R1543)

Hebet Eure Augen Auf Gen Himmel
*sac,cant
ST soli,2vln,cont sc HANSSLER
10.038 s.p., ipa, solo pt
HANSSLER s.p. see from
Kernspruchen   (R1544)

Herr, Wenn Ich Nur Dich Habe *sac,
cant
S solo,strings,cont sc HANSSLER
5.069 s.p., ipa   (R1545)

Ich Bin Das Brot Des Lebens *sac,
cant
ATB soli,2vln,cont sc HANSSLER
10.163 s.p., ipa, solo pt
HANSSLER s.p. see from Andere
Kernspruche   (R1546)

Ist Gott Fur Uns *sac,cant
S solo,strings,cont sc HANSSLER
5.070 s.p., ipa   (R1547)

Kernspruche *see Meine Seele Harret
Auf Gott   (R1548)

Kernspruchen *see Danket Dem Herrn
Und Prediget Seinen Namen; Das
Ist Ein Kostlich Ding; Hebet Eure
Augen Auf Gen Himmel   (R1549)

Lieber Herre Gott *sac,Adv,cant
(Langin, Folkmar) S solo,2vln,cont
(med) BAREN. 2891 $3.50   (R1550)

Meine Seele Harret Auf Gott *sac,
cant
ATB soli,2vln,cont sc HANSSLER
10.040 s.p., ipa, solo pt
HANSSLER s.p. see from
Kernspruche   (R1551)

Psalm 134 *see Auf, Nun Lobet Gott

Siehe, Des Herren Auge Siehet Auf
Die, So Ihn Furchten *sac,cant
STB soli,2vln,cont sc HANSSLER
10.162 s.p., ipa, solo pt
HANSSLER s.p. see from Andere
Kernspruche   (R1552)

Since This World Is Only Passing
*sac
med solo,pno oct CONCORDIA 98-1820
$.25   (R1553)

Von Den Himmlischen Freuden *sac,
cant
(Hamel, Fred) B solo,cont (med)
BAREN. 451 $3.25   (R1554)

Weil Wir Wissen, Dass Der Mensch
Durch Des Gesetzes Werke *sac,
cant
ATB soli,2vln,cont sc HANSSLER
10.161 s.p., ipa, solo pt
HANSSLER s.p. see from Andere
Kernspruche   (R1555)

ROSENS BILD see Reichardt, Johann
Friedrich

ROSENSTENGEL, ALBRECHT
Westfalische Lieder Und Tanze *CCU
solo,fl,ob,clar,horn,trp,timp,
triangle,tamb,glock,A rec,2vln,
vcl/bvl sc GERIG HG 263 s.p., ipa
                                  (R1556)

ROSENTHAL, MANUEL (1904-   )
Chansons Du Monsieur Bleu *CC12U
Mez solo,fl,ob,clar,bsn,horn,sax,
harp,timp,perc,harmonium,strings
JOBERT sc s.p., voc sc s.p., voc
sc,solo pt s.p., ea.   (R1557)

ROSENTHAL, MANUEL (cont'd.)

Deux Prieres Pour Les Temps
Malheureux *CC2U
Bar solo,2fl,2ob,2clar,2bsn,2horn,
2trp,trom,perc,strings JOBERT sc
s.p., voc sc s.p.   (R1558)

Deux Sonnets De Jean Cassou *CC2U
S solo,fl,ob,clar,bsn,horn,harp,
timp,strings JOBERT s.p. sc, voc
sc   (R1559)

La Pieta D'Avignon *CC6U,prayer
4 soli,trp,strings JOBERT s.p. sc,
voc sc   (R1560)

Trois Chansons D'Amour *CC3U
S solo,2fl,ob,2clar,bsn,horn,trp,
perc,strings JOBERT s.p. sc, voc
sc   (R1561)

Trois Chants De Femmes Berberes
*CC3U
SA soli,pno voc sc JOBERT s.p.
                                  (R1562)

Trois Melodies *CC3U
Mez/T solo,2fl,2ob,2clar,2bsn,
2horn,harp,timp,perc,strings
JOBERT s.p. sc, voc sc   (R1563)

Trois Precieuses *CC3U
S solo,2fl,ob,2clar,bsn,horn,trp,
perc,strings JOBERT s.p. sc, voc
sc   (R1564)

ROSES see Kilpinen, Yrio, Rosenbusche

ROSES AND YOU see Walker, Edwin

FOSES ARE HERE AGAIN see Trotere, Henry

ROSES DANS LA NUIT see Dupre, Marcel

ROSES D'AU DELA see Lacome, Paul

ROSES D'AUTOMNE see Migot, Georges

ROSES DE MAI see Durand, Jacques

ROSES D'OCTOBRE see Delage, Maurice

ROSES DU SOIR see Aubert, Louis-
Francois-Marie

ROSES ET PAPILLONS see Desrez

ROSES ET PAPILLONS see Franck, Cesar

ROSES FANEES see Mendelssohn-Bartholdy,
Felix

ROSES OF THE SOUTH see Strauss, Johann,
Rosen Aus Dem Suden

ROSETTA'S SONG see Lidholm, Ingvar

ROSETTE see Lacome, Paul

ROSETTI, FRANCESCO ANTIONIO (1746-1792)
Ad Festa, Fideles *sac
(Ewerhart, Rudolf) [Lat] B solo,
cont BIELER CS 31 s.p.   (R1565)

ROSEWIG, A.H.
Ave Maria *sac
low solo,pno BELWIN $1.50   (R1566)
high solo,pno BELWIN $1.50   (R1567)

ROSHENKIS MIT MANDLIN *Jew
sclo,pno KAMMEN 404 $1.00   (R1568)

ROSI, GINO
Canzone A Ballo Del Poliziano
solo,pno SANTIS 122 s.p.   (R1569)

I Campani
solo,pno SANTIS 072 s.p.   (R1570)

L'assente
solo,pno SANTIS 071 s.p.   (R1571)

ROSINE see Delmet, Paul

ROSING, J.
Home
solo,pno (D maj) BOOSEY $1.50
                                  (R1572)

ROSMARIN see Dvorak, Antonin, Rozmaryna

ROSNER, ARNOLD
Lord Is My Shepherd, The (Psalm 23)
sac
solo,pno CHAPLET $.85   (R1573)

Psalm 23 *see Lord Is My Shepherd,
The

ROSOR TIL MOR see Stigen, Fredrik

ROSORNA FORGAR see Bjornstrand, Gunnar

ROSS
Enough To Know
high solo,pno SHAWNEE IA5029 $.60
(R1574)
med solo,pno SHAWNEE IA5012 $.60
(R1575)

ROSS, COLIN
Cherry Hung With Snow, The
solo,pno (B flat min) ROBERTON 2606
s.p. (R1576)

Lorna's Song
solo,pno CRAMER $.70 (R1577)

ROSSEAU, NORBERT (1907-)
Mattinata *Op.16
T solo,pno CBDM s.p. (R1578)

Vingt-Quatre Vocalises
Dodecaphoniques *Op.55, CC25U,
vocalise
med solo,pno cmplt ed CBDM s.p.
(R1579)

ROSSELLINI, RENZO (1908-)
Canti Di Rilke *CCU
[It] RICORDI-ENG 125753 s.p.
(R1580)

Chanson De Barberine
solo,pno SANTIS 266 s.p. (R1581)

La Canzone Di Cherubino
[It] A/B solo,pno RICORDI-ENG
127455 s.p. (R1582)

La Canzone Di Fortunio
[It] Mez/Bar solo,pno RICORDI-ENG
127447 s.p. (R1583)

La Chambre Vide
solo,pno SANTIS 265 s.p. (R1584)

Marie
solo,pno SANTIS 267 s.p. (R1585)

Ore Tristi E Serene
[It] solo,strings RICORDI-ENG
131892 s.p. (R1586)

Quatro Liriche *CC4U
[It] B/Bar solo, piano left hand
only RICORDI-ENG 131449 s.p.
(R1587)

ROSSETER, PHILIP (ca. 1568-1623)
Book Of Ayres *CCU
solo,pno STAINER 3.1338.7 $6.25
(R1588)

ROSSI, SALOMONE (ca. 1570-ca. 1630)
Il Primo Libro Delle Canzonette A Tre
Voci Di S. Rossi *CC19U
(Avenary, Hanoch) [It/Heb] 3 soli,
pno ISR.MUS.INST. 1013 s.p.
(R1589)

ROSSIGNOL see Encina, Juan Del,
Romerico

ROSSIGNOL see Orthel, Leon

ROSSIGNOL see Rivier, Jean

ROSSIGNOL ET RSSOGNOLET see Viardot-
Garcia, Pauline

ROSSIGNOL, MON MIGNON see Levade,
Charles (Gaston)

ROSSIGNOL MON MIGNON see Roussel,
Albert

ROSSIGNOLET DU BOIS see Indy, Vincent
d'

ROSSIGNOLS, MOUCHERONS, TOUT SE TAIT
see Rimsky-Korsakov, Nikolai

ROSSINE'S ARIA see Paisiello, Giovanni

ROSSINI, CARLO
Christ The Victor *sac
high solo,pno BELWIN $1.50 (R1590)
med solo,pno BELWIN $1.50 (R1591)

ROSSINI, GIOACCHINO (1792-1868)
A Un Dottor Della Mia Sorte (from Il
Barbiere Di Siviglia)
[It] B solo,pno RICORDI-ENG 125922
s.p. (R1592)

Bel Raggio Lusinghier (from
Semiramide)
[It] S solo,pno RICORDI-ENG 54359
s.p. (R1593)

Cavatine (from Il Barbiere Di
Siviglia)
solo,orch HENN s.p. (R1594)
"Kavatine Des Figaro" [Czech/Ger/
It] solo,pno SUPRAPHON s.p.
(R1595)

Comic Duet For Two Cats *see Duetto
Buffo Di Due Gatti

Cuius Animam (from Stabat Mater) sac
[Lat] T solo,pno RICORDI-ENG 13782
s.p. (R1596)

ROSSINI, GIOACCHINO (cont'd.)
Dal Tuo Stellato Soglio (from Mose)
[It] SMezTB soli,pno RICORDI-ENG
27304 s.p. (R1597)

Dance, The *see La Danza

Di Piacer Mi Balza Il Cor (from La
Gazza Ladra)
[It] S solo,pno RICORDI-ENG 96265
s.p. (R1598)

Die Verleumdung, Sie Ist Ein Luftchen
(from Il Barbiere Di Siviglia)
B solo,fl,2ob,2clar,2bsn,2horn,
2trp,perc,strings BREITKOPF-L
rental (R1599)

Duetto Buffo Di Due Gatti
2 soli,pno PETERS 7145 $2.50
(R1600)
"Comic Duet For Two Cats" 2 female
soli,pno SCHAUR EE 3361 $3.00
(R1601)
(Ludwig, Chr.; Berry, W.; Werba,
E.) "Katzen-Duett" 2 soli,pno
DÖBLINGER 08 550 $4.00 (R1602)
(Stueber, Carl) 2 soli,pno RICORDI-
ENG 131699 s.p. (R1603)

Ecco, Ridente In Cielo (from Il
Barbiere Di Siviglia)
[It] T solo,pno RICORDI-ENG 54427
s.p. (R1604)

Frag Ich Mein Beklommen Herz (from Il
Barbiere Di Siviglia)
S solo,fl,ob,2clar,2bsn,2horn,2trp,
strings BREITKOPF-L rental
(R1605)

Gluck Und Huld, Mein Herr, Zum Grusse
(from Il Barbieri Di Siviglia)
TB soli,2clar,2bsn,2horn,strings
BREITKOPF-L rental (R1606)

Ich Bin Das Faktotum *see Largo Al
Factotum Della Citta

Katzen-Duett *see Duetto Buffo Di
Due Gatti

Kavatine Des Figaro *see Cavatine

La Calunnia E Un Venticello (from Il
Barbiere Di Siviglia)
[It] B solo,pno RICORDI-ARG
BA 11842 s.p. (R1607)
[It] B solo,pno RICORDI-ENG 54474
s.p. (R1608)

La Danza
[It] S/T solo,pno RICORDI-ENG 32364
s.p. (R1609)
high solo,pno (A min) ALLANS s.p.
(R1610)
med solo,pno (G min) ALLANS s.p.
(R1611)
[Ger/It/Fr] solo,pno/orch voc sc
SCHOTTS s.p., ipa (R1612)
[It] Mez/Bar solo,pno RICORDI-ENG
15331 s.p. (R1613)
"Dance, The" [It/Eng] high solo,pno
(A min) SCHIRM.G $.85 (R1614)

La Promessa
[It/Eng] S/T solo,pno RICORDI-ENG
LD 370 s.p. (R1615)

La Regata Veneziana *CC3U
S/T solo,pno RICORDI-ENG ER 2558
s.p. (R1616)

Largo Al Factotum Della Citta (from
Il Barbiere Di Siviglia)
[It] Bar solo,pno RICORDI-ARG
BA 8538 s.p. (R1617)
[Eng/It] Bar solo,pno PRESSER $.75
(R1618)
[It] Bar solo,pno RICORDI-ENG 54451
s.p. (R1619)
"Ich Bin Das Faktotum" Bar solo,
2fl,2clar,2bsn,2horn,2trp,strings
BREITKOPF-L rental (R1620)
"Lo! The Factotum" solo,pno (B flat
maj) ASHDOWN s.p. (R1621)

Lo! The Factotum *see Largo Al
Factotum Della Citta

Nacqui All'affanno E Al Pianto (from
La Cenerentola)
[It] A solo,pno RICORDI-ENG 54400
s.p. (R1622)

O Muto Asil Del Pianto (from Gugliemo
Tell)
[It] T solo,pno RICORDI-ENG 109974
s.p. (R1623)

Petite Messe Solunnelle *sac
(Tomelleri, Luciano) SATB soli,pno,
harmonium TRANSAT. s.p. (R1624)

ROSSINI, GIOACCHINO (cont'd.)
Qui Est Homo (from Stabat Mater)
"Where's The Cold Heart So
Unfeeling" [Lat/Eng] SA soli,pno
PRESSER $.60 (R1625)

Resta Immobile (from Gugliemo Tell)
[It] Bar solo,pno RICORDI-ENG
125904 s.p. (R1626)

Se Il Mio Nome Saper Voi Bramate
(from Il Barbiere Di Siviglia)
[It] T solo,pno RICORDI-ARG BA 8755
s.p. (R1627)
[It] T solo,pno RICORDI-ENG 96281
s.p. (R1628)

Selva Opaca, Desrta Brughiera (from
Gugliemo Tell)
[It] S solo,pno RICORDI-ENG 54357
s.p. (R1629)

Serate Musicali, Vol. I *CC8U
[It/Fr] S/T solo,pno RICORDI-ENG
ER 2413 s.p. (R1630)

Serate Musicali, Vol. II *CC4U
[It/Fr] 2 soli,pno RICORDI-ENG
ER 2414 s.p. (R1631)

Soirees Musicales, Vol. I *CC8L
[It/Fr] S/T solo,pno cmplt ed
RICORDI-ARG BA 9205 s.p. (R1632)

There's A Voice That I Enshrine *see
Una Voce Poco Fa

Una Voce Poco Fa (from Il Barbiere Di
Siviglia)
[It] S solo,pno (E maj) RICORDI-ARG
BA 8742 s.p. (R1633)
[It] A solo,pno RICORDI-ENG 54355
s.p. (R1634)
[It] solo,pno (F maj) voc sc
BONGIOVANI 2213 s.p. (R1635)
low solo,pno (E maj) ASHDOWN s.p.
(R1636)
high solo,pno (F maj) ASHDOWN s.p.
(R1637)
A solo,pno/orch sc KALMUS $3.00
(R1638)
med solo,pno (E maj) ALLANS s.p.
(R1639)
high solo,pno (F maj) ALLANS s.p.
(R1640)
(Liebling) "There's A Voice That I
Enshrine" [It/Eng] S solo,pno (F
maj) SCHIRM.G $.85 (R1641)
(Liebling) "There's A Voice That I
Enshrine" [It/Eng] Mez solo,pno
(E maj) SCHIRM.G $.85 (R1642)
(Marengo) [It] S solo,pno (F maj)
RICORDI-ARG BA 10311 s.p. (R1643)

Varianten Zur Cavatine Der Rosina
"Una Voce Poco Fa" (from Il
Barbieri Di Siviglia)
(Beyer) solo,pno EULENBURG GM 108
s.p. (R1644)

Where's The Cold Heart So Unfeeling
*see Qui Est Homo

ROSSLER, ERNST KARL
Jamunder Cantional *see Paucitatem
Dierum; Regi Autem (R1645)

Paucitatem Dierum *sac
S solo,org (diff) BAREN. 3528 $4.25
see from Jamunder Cantional
(R1646)

Regi Autem *sac
S solo,org (diff) BAREN. 3521 $4.25
see from Jamunder Cantional
(R1647)

ROSTER I MORKRET see Merikanto, Aarre

ROTE ROSEN see Strauss, Richard

ROTENBERG, M.
Songs And Tunes For Sabbath And
Holidays *sac,CCU
solo,pno OR-TAV $3.00 (R1648)

ROTHSCHILD, MME W. DE
Ah! Que Son Jeune Coeur
solo,pno (available in 2 keys)
ENOCH s.p. (R1649)

Viens Avec Moi
solo,pno (available in 2 keys)
ENOCH s.p. (R1650)

ROTHSCHUH, FRITZ (1921-)
Goldne Wiegen
solo,pno TONOS 5413 s.p. (R1651)

ROTOLI
I Walked Today Where Jesus Walked
*sac
high solo,pno (G maj) ALLANS s.p.
(R1652)
med solo,pno (F maj) ALLANS s.p.
(R1653)
low solo,pno (E maj) ALLANS s.p.

ROTOLI (cont'd.)
                                   (R1654)
   Jesus Only *sac
     high solo,pno (D flat maj) BOSTON
     $1.50   (R1655)
     low solo,pno (B flat maj) BOSTON
     $1.50   (R1656)
     med solo,pno (C maj) ALLANS
                                 (R1657)
     low solo,pno (B flat maj) ALLANS
     s.p.   (R1658)
     high solo,pno (D flat maj) ALLANS
     s.p.   (R1659)

ROTTERDAM see Schouwman, Hans

ROTTURA, JOSEPH JAMES (1929-   )
   Come, Touch My Hand
     solo,pno ALLOWAY A-111   (R1660)

ROUGE see Jongen, Joseph-Marie-
      Alphonse-Nicholas

ROUGET DE L'ISLE, CLAUDE JOSEPH
     (1760-1836)
   La Marseillaise
     [Fr] solo,acap oct DURAND s.p.
                                 (R1661)
     solo,pno/inst DURAND s.p.   (R1662)
     solo,pno ASHLEY $.95   (R1663)

ROUGIER, A.
   Trois Melodies *CC3U
     solo,pno sc JOBERT s.p.   (R1664)

ROULIS DES GREVES see Chaminade, Cecile

ROUND see Hamm, Charles

ROUND POND, THE see Sharpe, Evelyn

ROUNDELAY see Birch, Robert Fairfax

ROUSE, CHRISTOPHER
   Chandni Chitakna
     pno/perc, soprano or percussion sc
     AM.COMP.AL. $4.95   (R1665)

   Ecstasis Mane Eburnei
     2A rec/cel,vla/perc,2perc, piano or
     vibraslap, offstage soprano sc
     AM.COMP.AL. $9.35, ipa   (R1666)

   I Know *see Burns

   Insani
     ob, actor or percussion sc
     AM.COMP.AL. $7.15   (R1667)

   Kiss, The
     Bar solo,bass clar,harp,pno,cel,
     perc sc AM.COMP.AL. $5.50 (R1668)

   Nox Aeris Temporis
     ob,2pno,perc, offstage: soprano, 3
     violins, and cello sc AM.COMP.AL.
     $8.25, ipa   (R1669)

   Subjectives V
     A solo,perc sc AM.COMP.AL. $3.57
                                 (R1670)

   Three Songs After Edgar Allan Poe
     *CC3U
     S solo,pno sc AM.COMP.AL. $3.57
                                 (R1671)

ROUSSEAU, JEAN-JACQUES (1712-1778)
   Dans La Verte Ramure
     2 soli,pno ENOCH voc sc, solo pt
                                 (R1672)

   Que Le Jour Me Dure
     solo,pno/inst DURAND s.p.   (R1673)

ROUSSEL, ALBERT (1869-1937)
   Amoureux Separes
     [Eng/Fr] med solo,pno SALABERT-US
     $3.75   (R1674)

   Bachelier De Salamanque *Op.20,No.1
     med solo,orch DURAND s.p., ipr
                                 (R1675)

   Chant De Nakamti (from Padmavati)
     Mez solo,pno/inst DURAND s.p.
                                 (R1676)

   Chant Du Brahmane (from Padmavati)
     T solo,pno/inst DURAND s.p. (R1677)

   Ciel Oer Et Vens
     see Deux Poemes De Ronsard

   Coeur En Peril *Op.50,No.2
     solo,pno/inst DURAND s.p.   (R1678)

   Des Fleurs Font Une Broderie *Op.35,
     No.1
     solo,pno/inst DURAND s.p.   (R1679)

   Deux Idylles
     solo,pno/inst cmplt ed DURAND s.p.
     contains: Le Kerioklepte; Pan
       Aimait Ekho   (R1680)

   Deux Poemes Chinois, Op. 47
     solo,pno/inst cmplt ed DURAND s.p.
     contains: Favorite Abandonnee;
       Vois De Belles Filles   (R1681)

ROUSSEL, ALBERT (cont'd.)
   Deux Poemes De Ronsard
     solo,fl cmplt ed DURAND s.p.
     contains: Ciel Oer Et Vens;
       Rossignol Mon Mignon   (R1682)

   Elpenor *Op.59
     solo,pno/inst DURAND s.p.   (R1683)

   Farewell
     [Fr/Eng] med solo,pno/inst DURAND
     s.p.   (R1684)

   Favorite Abandonnee
     see Deux Poemes Chinois, Op. 47

   Heure Du Retour *Op.50,No.1
     solo,pno/inst DURAND s.p.   (R1685)

   Jazz Dans La Nuit *Op.38
     solo,orch DURAND s.p., ipr   (R1686)

   Le Jardin Mouille
     [Eng/Fr] med solo,pno SALABERT-US
     $3.75   (R1687)

   Le Kerioklepte
     see Deux Idylles

   Light *Op.19,No.1
     [Fr/Eng] med solo,pno/inst DURAND
     s.p.   (R1688)

   O Bon Vin, Ou As-Tu Cru?
     solo,pno/inst DURAND s.p.   (R1689)

   O Mes Soeurs (from Padmavati)
     A solo,pno/inst DURAND s.p. (R1690)

   Odes Anacreontiques *Op.31-32, CCU
     solo,pno/inst DURAND s.p.   (R1691)

   Pan Aimait Ekho
     see Deux Idylles

   Priere De Padmavati (from Padmavati)
     A solo,pno/inst DURAND s.p. (R1692)

   Reponse D'une Epouse Sage *Op.35,
     No.2
     solo,orch DURAND s.p., ipr   (R1693)

   Rossignol Mon Mignon
     see Deux Poemes De Ronsard

   Sarabande *Op.20,No.2
     med solo,orch DURAND s.p., ipr
                                 (R1694)

   Une Fleur Donnee A Ma Fille
     [Fr/Eng] solo,pno/inst DURAND s.p.
                                 (R1695)

   Vieilles Cartes, Vieilles Mains
     *Op.55
     solo,pno/inst DURAND s.p.   (R1696)

   Vois De Belles Filles
     see Deux Poemes Chinois, Op. 47

ROUSSILLON *Fr
   (Canteloube, J.) solo,acap DURAND
     s.p. see also Anthologie Des Chants
     Populaires Francais Tome I   (R1697)

ROUSSOTTE, LA BONNE LAITIERE see
     Schlosser, Paul

ROUX, E.
   Dernier Souhait
     see ALBUM MODERNE

ROVICS, HOWARD
   Broken Doll, The
     A solo,pno AM.COMP.AL. $1.37
                                 (R1698)

   Echo
     solo,fl,pno sc AM.COMP.AL. $3.85
                                 (R1699)

   Haunted Objects (In Memorium Stefan
     Wolpe)
     S narrator,ob,English horn,bsn,
     electronic tape, hecklephone sc
     AM.COMP.AL. $11.00   (R1700)

   Hunter, The
     S solo,vla sc AM.COMP.AL. $3.57
                                 (R1701)

   Look, Friend, At Me
     S solo,pno AM.COMP.AL. $3.57
                                 (R1702)

   What Grandma Knew
     S solo,pno AM.COMP.AL. $2.75
                                 (R1703)

ROVIN' GAMBLER, THE see Niles, John
     Jacob

ROVSING OLSEN, PAUL (1922-   )
   Am Abend *Op.28,No.4
     see Schicksalslieder Von Holderlin

   An Die Parzen *Op.28,No.3
     see Schicksalslieder Von Holderlin

   Halfte Des Lebens *Op.28,No.1
     see Schicksalslieder Von Holderlin

ROVSING OLSEN, PAUL (cont'd.)
   Hyperions Schicksalslied *Op.28,No.2
     see Schicksalslieder Von Holderlin

   Schicksalslieder Von Holderlin
     high solo,fl,clar,vln,vla,vcl,bvl
     sc FOG s.p.
     contains: Am Abend, Op.28,No.4;
       An Die Parzen, Op.28,No.3;
       Halfte Des Lebens, Op.28,No.1;
       Hyperions Schicksalslied,
       Op.28,No.2   (R1704)

ROW WEEL, MY BOATIE, ROW WEEL *folk,
     Scot
     solo,pno (F maj) PATERSON FS79 s.p.
                                 (R1705)

ROWAN TREE, THE *folk,Scot
     solo,pno (D maj/F maj) PATERSON FS78
     s.p.   (R1706)

ROWE
   If I Could Hear My Mother Pray Again
     *see Gerald

   Love Lifted Me (composed with Smith)
     *sac
     (Stevens, Ray) solo,pno BENSON
     S6978-R $1.00   (R1707)

ROWLEY, ALEC (1892-1958)
   Birds, The
     high solo,pno (G min) ASHDOWN s.p.
                                 (R1708)
     low solo,pno (E min) ASHDOWN
     s.p.   (R1709)

   Blue Water
     solo,pno ASHDOWN s.p.   (R1710)

   Cherry Tree, The
     solo,pno (E flat maj) LESLIE 7045
                                 (R1711)

   Counting Sheep
     high solo,pno (F maj) ASHDOWN s.p.
                                 (R1712)
     low solo,pno (D maj) ASHDOWN s.p.
                                 (R1713)

   Dream Village
     high solo,pno (F maj) CRAMER $1.00
                                 (R1714)
     low solo,pno (D maj) CRAMER $1.15
                                 (R1715)

   Fairy Path, The
     solo,pno CRAMER   (R1716)

   Fairy Pedlar, The
     low solo,pno (E flat maj) CRAMER
     $1.00   (R1717)
     high solo,pno (G maj) CRAMER $.90
                                 (R1718)

   Here, Lord, We Meet *Marriage
     solo,pno (E flat maj) LESLIE 7047
     $1.00   (R1719)

   If I Had Twenty Cherries
     solo,pno (E flat maj) LESLIE 7044
                                 (R1720)

   If Wishes Were Horses
     solo,pno CRAMER   (R1721)

   Jenny Wren
     solo,pno CRAMER   (R1722)

   Johnny Shall Have A New Bonnet
     solo,pno (E flat maj) BOOSEY $1.50
                                 (R1723)

   Little Jesus
     solo,pno CRAMER   (R1724)

   Marigold Garden *CCU
     solo,pno CRAMER   (R1725)

   New Tunes To New Rhymes *CCU
     solo,pno LEONARD-ENG   (R1726)

   O That I Knew Where I Might Find Him
     *sac
     solo,pno (G maj) BOOSEY $1.50
                                 (R1727)

   On Newlyn Hill
     solo,pno ASHDOWN s.p.   (R1728)

   Ploughman, The
     low solo,pno (B min) ASHDOWN s.p.
                                 (R1729)
     high solo,pno (D min) ASHDOWN s.p.
                                 (R1730)

   Pretty Betty
     Bar solo,pno (med diff) OXFORD
     61.150 $1.00   (R1731)

   Sheep
     solo,pno CRAMER   (R1732)

   Spring Joy
     (Howe) high solo,pno PAXTON P40532
     s.p.   (R1733)

   Sweet Nelly, My Heart's Delight
     low solo,orch (F maj) ASHDOWN s.p.
                                 (R1734)
     high solo,orch (A maj) ASHDOWN s.p.
                                 (R1735)

ROWLEY, ALEC (cont'd.)

Three Mystical Songs *CC3U
high solo,pno BOOSEY $2.00 (R1736)

Woodland Message, A
solo,pno (E flat maj) LESLIE 7018
(R1737)

ROXBURGH, EDWIN
How Pleasant To Know Mr. Lear *song
cycle
narrator,fl,ob,clar,bsn,horn,cel,
perc,strings sc UNITED MUS s.p.
(R1738)

ROYAL FAMILY, THE see Ballard, Ann

ROYAL MOUNTED see Kent, Mrs. Ada Twohy

ROYAL ROSE see Lawson, Malcolm

ROYLE, F.
Grace Of Heaven
low solo,pno (D maj) BOOSEY $1.50
(R1739)

med solo,pno (E flat maj) BOOSEY
$1.50 (R1740)

high solo,pno (F maj) BOOSEY $1.50
(R1741)

ROY'S WIFE O' ALDIVALLOCH *folk,Scot
solo,pno (B flat maj/C maj) PATERSON
FS137 s.p. (R1742)

ROZANC, MIHAEL (1885-1971)
Pesmi Za Dan Zena, Vol. I *CCU
solo,pno DRUSTVO DSS 271 rental
Mother's day (R1743)

Pesmi Za Dan Zena, Vol. II *CCU
solo,pno DRUSTVO DSS 305 rental
Mother's day (R1744)

ROZCINAM POMARANCZE BOLN see Baird,
Tadeusz

ROZEN see Mulder, Herman

ROZIN, ALBERT
Cause Us, O Lord, Our God *sac
high solo/med solo,pno TRANSCON.
TV 572 $.75 (R1745)

ROZINKES MIT MANDLEN *folk,Jew
med solo,pno HATIKVAH ED. 33 $.35
(R1746)

ROZLEF SE, MOJE PISNICKO see Loudova,
Ivana

ROZMARING *CC91U,folk,Hung
(Kiss) solo,pno BUDAPEST 871 s.p.
(R1747)

ROZMARNE see Borkovec, Pavel

ROZMARNE PISNE see Foerster, Josef
Bohuslav

ROZMARYNA see Dvorak, Antonin

ROZPRAVKA see Urbanec, Bartolomej

ROZSA *CC94U,folk,Hung
(Peczely) solo,pno BUDAPEST 1310 s.p.
(R1748)

ROZSTANIE JEST PTAKIEM see Baird,
Tadeusz

R'TZE see Helfman, Max

R'TZEH see Ancis, Solomon

RUBAYIAT FRAGMENTS see Leichtling, Alan

RUBBEN, HERMANNJOSEF (1928-   )
Ausschliesslich Heiter *CCU
med solo,pno BREITKOPF-W EB 6477
$3.25 (R1749)

RUBEL, JOSEPH
Lullaby
high solo/med solo,pno TRANSCON.
TV 452 $.35 (R1750)

Sharecroppers
med solo,pno TRANSCON. TV 452 $.35
(R1751)

RUBENS, PAUL ALFRED (1875-1917)
I Love You, Ma Cherie
low solo,pno (F maj) CRAMER (R1752)
high solo,pno (G maj) CRAMER
(R1753)

Sea And Sky
solo,pno CRAMER (R1754)

When The Stars Were Young
solo,pno CRAMER (R1755)

RUBEZAHL see Weingartner, (Paul) Felix

RUBIAYAT, ZYKLUS 1 see Eisenmann, W.

RUBIAYAT, ZYKLUS 2 see Eisenmann, W.

RUBIN, MARCEL (1905-   )
Dorfbilder *CC6U
med solo,pno DOBLINGER 08 637 $2.50
(R1756)

RUBIN, MARCEL (cont'd.)

Sechs Lieder Nach Gedichten Von
Goethe *CC6U
high solo,pno BREITKOPF-L EN 4015
$1.50 (R1757)

RUBIN, W.
So Zwoi Wie Wir Zwoi
solo,pno HUG s.p. (R1758)

RUBINSTEIN, ANTON (1829-1894)
Dream Of Delight
(Jacobsen) solo,pno CRAMER (R1759)

Eighteen Duets *CC18U
(Friedlander) [Ger] SA soli,pno
PETERS 3787 $9.00 contains Op. 48
& 67 (R1760)

Melody In F
med solo,pno (G maj) CENTURY 997
(R1761)

Nattvandrarens Sang
2 soli,pno FAZER F 2821 s.p.
(R1762)

Romance
low solo,pno (D flat maj) ALLANS
s.p. (R1763)
high solo,pno (E flat maj) ALLANS
s.p. (R1764)

Since First I Met Thee
med solo,pno (D flat maj) SCHIRM.G
$.60 (R1765)

Slaven
Bar solo,pno GEHRMANS 671 s.p.
(R1766)
high solo,pno GEHRMANS s.p. (R1767)

Thou Art Like A Flower
low solo,pno (F maj) CRAMER (R1768)
high solo,pno (E flat maj) CRAMER
(R1769)

True Romance
(Burrows) solo,pno CRAMER (R1770)

Twelve Duets *Op.48, CC12L
[Ger/Dan] SA soli,pno HANSEN-DEN
s.p. (R1771)

Vid Nattetid
2 soli,pno LUNDQUIST s.p. (R1772)

Voices Of The Woods
low solo,pno (F maj) ASHDOWN s.p.
(R1773)
med solo,pno (G maj) ASHDOWN s.p.
(R1774)
high solo,pno (B flat maj) ASHDOWN
s.p. (R1775)

RUCHE DE REVES see Arma, Paul

RUCKKEHR see Baird, Tadeusz, Powrot

RUCKKEHR IN DIE HEIMAT see Strauss,
Richard

RUCKKEHR VOM SCHLACHTFELD see Vomacka,
Boleslav

RUCKLEBEN see Strauss, Richard

RUDHYAR, DANE (1895-   )
Three Invocations *CC3U
med solo,pno AM.COMP.AL. $2.20
(R1776)

RUDLOFF, P.
Kleine Ursula
[Ger] BOTE $.90 (R1777)

RUDOLPE, M.
Ich Kusse Deine Lippen *Op.89
solo,pno SCHAUR EE 3556 s.p.
(R1778)

RUE FRANCOIS PREMIER see Kelly, Earl

RUGIADA see Baldacci, Giov. Bruna

RUGIADA see Eisma, Will

RUHE see Trunk, Richard

RUHE, MEINE SEELE see Strauss, Richard

RUHE SANFT IN GOTTES FRIEDEN see
Schumann, Robert (Alexander)

RUHE SANFT MEIN HOLDES LEBEN see
Mozart, Wolfgang Amadeus

RUHE SUSSLIEBCHEN IM SCHATTEN see
Brahms, Johannes

RUIN OF THE KU-SU PALACE, THE see
Lambert, Constant

RUINES DU COEUR see Wolff, A.

RUIZ PIPO', ANTONIO
Cantos A La Noche *CCU
[Span] solo,gtr BERBEN 1519 s.p.
(R1779)

RUKKILAULU see Tolonen, Jouko (Paavo
Kalervo)

RUKOUS see Maasalo, Armas

RUKOUSNAUHA see Hannikainen, Ilmari

RULE BRITANNIA see Arne, Thomas
Augustine

RUM BIDI BUM see Haas, Joseph

RUMMEL, WALTER MORSE (1887-1953)
Ecstasy
high solo,pno (D flat maj) SCHIRM.G
$.75 (R1780)

RUMMELPLATZ see Kludas, Erich

RUMSEY, M.
Love Of A Mother, The
med solo,pno PRESSER $.75 (R1781)

RUMSHINSKY, JOS. M.
Der Morgen Shtern *Jew
solo,pno KAMMEN 17 $1.00 see also
FAVORITE JEWISH SONGS, VOL. 2
(R1782)

Die Roumanishe Kretchme *Jew
solo,pno KAMMEN 480 $1.00 see also
JEWISH THEATRE SONGS, VOL. 1
(R1783)

Dir A Nickel, Mir A Nickel *Jew
solo,pno KAMMEN 482 $1.00 see also
JEWISH THEATRE SONGS, VOL. 1
(R1784)

Meidlach, Weiblach *Jew
solo,pno KAMMEN 21 $1.00 see also
JEWISH THEATRE SONGS, VOL. 1
(R1785)

Mein Goldele *Jew
solo,pno KAMMEN 50 $1.00 see also
JEWISH THEATRE SONGS, VOL. 1
(R1786)

RUN, YE SHEPHERDS, TO THE LIGHT see
Haydn, (Johann) Michael, Lauft, Ihr
Hirten, Allzugleich

RUNBACK, ALBERT
Aftonklockan
see Runback, Albert, Lyss Till
Granen Vid Din Moders Hydda

En Blomma
solo,pno/org ERIKS K 250 s.p.
(R1787)

Ensamhet
see Runback, Albert, Lyss Till
Granen Vid Din Moders Hydda

Fran Var Till Host
solo,pno/org ERIKS s.p.
contains: Nar Loven Falla; Nar
Som Majvindar Susa;
Novembervisa; Sommarkvall; Var
(R1788)

Frid *Xmas
female solo,pno/org ERIKS K181 s.p.
(R1789)

Gudstjanstringning
see Runback, Albert, Lyss Till
Granen Vid Din Moders Hydda

Lyss Till Granen Vid Din Moders Hydda
solo,pno/org ERIKS s.p. contains
also: Gudstjanstringning;
Ensamhet; Vaggvisa; Stilla Mitt
Hjarta; Aftonklockan (R1790)

Nar Loven Falla
see Fran Var Till Host

Nar Som Majvindar Susa
see Fran Var Till Host

Novembervisa
see Fran Var Till Host

Sommarkvall
see Fran Var Till Host

Stilla Mitt Hjarta
see Runback, Albert, Lyss Till
Granen Vid Din Moders Hydda

Vaggvisa
see Runback, Albert, Lyss Till
Granen Vid Din Moders Hydda

Var
see Fran Var Till Host

RUND, MORRIS
Dus Ken Ich Nit *Jew
solo,pno KAMMEN 440 $1.00 see also
FAVORITE JEWISH SONGS, VOL. 2
(R1791)

RUNES see Ferrari, Gabriella

RUNNING SUN, THE see Helps, Robert

RUNOLINTUNI see Leiviska, Helvi
(Lemmikki)

RUNYAN
Great Is Thy Faithfulness *sac
solo,pno HOPE 493 $.75   (R1792)

RUOHIKOSSA see Palmgren, Selim, I
Vassen

RUPPE, C.F. (1753-1826)
Twaalf Stukjes *CC12U
solo,pno HEUWEKE. s.p.   (R1793)

Twaalf Stukjes *CC12U
solo,pno HEUWEKE. 152 s.p.   (R1794)

RUPPEL, PAUL ERNST (1913-   )
Der Herr Ist Mein Licht Und Mein Heil
*sac,concerto
SA soli,fl,org HANSSLER 12.222 s.p.
(R1795)

RUPTURE see Borel-Clerc, Charles

RUPTURE D'AUTOMNE see Delmet, Paul

RUSALKAS LIED AN DEN MOND see Dvorak,
Antonin

RUSALKA'S SONG TO THE MOON see Dvorak,
Antonin, Rusalkas Lied An Den Mond

RUSETTE, L. DE
Number Songs *CCU
solo,pno CRAMER   (R1796)

RUSH, LOREN (1935-   )
Dans Le Sable
SAAAA&narrator,fl,English horn,bsn,
horn,flugel,trom,vibra,harp,pno,
strings,gtr JOBERT voc sc s.p.,
sc rental   (R1797)

RUSHFORD
Jesus Is Coming Back Again *sac
solo,pno LILLENAS SM-624: RN $1.00
(R1798)

What Love! *sac
solo,pno LILLENAS SM-638: RN $1.00
(R1799)

RUSSELL, ARMAND
Ballad With Epitaphs
2 soli,perc sc SEESAW $5.00 (R1800)

RUSSELL, F.
Because He Came *sac,Xmas
solo,pno HARRIS $.75   (R1801)

RUSSELL, KENNEDY
Angelus, The
low solo,pno (C maj) ASHDOWN s.p.
(R1802)
med-high solo,pno (E flat maj)
ASHDOWN s.p.   (R1803)
med solo,pno (D flat maj) ASHDOWN
s.p.   (R1804)
high solo,pno (F maj) ASHDOWN s.p.
(R1805)
As You Pass By
solo,pno (E flat maj) BOOSEY $1.50
(R1806)
Cara Mia
high solo,pno (C maj) BOOSEY $1.50
(R1807)
low solo,pno (B flat maj) BOOSEY
$1.50   (R1808)
Children Of Men
low solo,pno (A flat maj) ALLANS
s.p.   (R1809)
high solo,pno (B flat maj) ALLANS
s.p.   (R1810)
Children's Corner
high solo,pno (G maj) ASHDOWN s.p.
(R1811)
low solo,pno (F maj) ASHDOWN s.p.
(R1812)
Dear Little Jammy Face
solo,pno ALLANS s.p.   (R1813)
Gypsy River
solo,pno PATERSON s.p.   (R1814)
Hush Me To Dreams
med solo,pno,opt vln (B flat maj)
LEONARD-ENG   (R1815)
low solo,pno,opt vln (A flat maj)
LEONARD-ENG   (R1816)
high solo,pno,opt vln (C maj)
LEONARD-ENG   (R1817)
I Love My Ladye
low solo,pno (G maj) ASHDOWN s.p.
(R1818)
high solo,pno (C maj) ASHDOWN s.p.
(R1819)
med solo,pno (B flat maj) ASHDOWN
s.p.   (R1820)
I Shall Pass This Way Again
high solo,pno (F maj) ASHDOWN s.p.
(R1821)
low solo,pno (E flat maj) ASHDOWN
s.p.   (R1822)
I'll Set My Love To Music
low solo,pno (E flat maj) ASHDOWN
s.p.   (R1823)

RUSSELL, KENNEDY (cont'd.)

high solo,pno (F maj) ASHDOWN s.p.
(R1824)
Jane's Big Umbrella
high solo,orch (F maj) ASHDOWN s.p.
(R1825)
med solo,orch (E flat maj) ASHDOWN
s.p.   (R1826)
low solo,orch (D maj) ASHDOWN s.p.
(R1827)
Just Because The Violets
low solo,pno (C maj) ASHDOWN s.p.
(R1828)
high solo,pno (E flat maj) ASHDOWN
s.p.   (R1829)
med solo,pno (D maj) ASHDOWN s.p.
(R1830)
Love Song Of Life, The
high solo,pno (A maj) ASHDOWN s.p.
(R1831)
low solo,pno (G maj) ASHDOWN s.p.
(R1832)
Rain!
high solo,pno (C maj) ASHDOWN s.p.
(R1833)
med-high solo,pno (B flat maj)
ASHDOWN s.p.   (R1834)
med solo,pno (G maj) ASHDOWN s.p.
(R1835)
low solo,pno (F maj) ASHDOWN s.p.
(R1836)
Robins
solo,pno PATERSON s.p.   (R1837)
Sacred Farewell
low solo,pno (F maj) BOOSEY $1.50
(R1838)
high solo,pno (B flat maj) BOOSEY
$1.50   (R1839)
Saint Christopher
low solo,pno (C maj) ASHDOWN s.p.
(R1840)
high solo,pno (E flat maj) ASHDOWN
s.p.   (R1841)
Stars Through The Trees
solo,pno PATERSON s.p.   (R1842)
Tear Kerchief, The
low solo,pno (B flat maj) ASHDOWN
s.p.   (R1843)
high solo,pno (C maj) ASHDOWN s.p.
(R1844)
Vale
low solo,orch (F maj) ASHDOWN
$1.50, ipr   (R1845)
med solo,orch (G maj) ASHDOWN
$1.50, ipr   (R1846)
med-high solo,orch (A flat maj)
ASHDOWN $1.50, ipr (R1847)
high solo,orch (B flat maj) ASHDOWN
$1.50, ipr   (R1848)
high solo&med solo,pno ASHDOWN s.p.
(R1849)
Via Sacra
low solo,pno (C maj) ASHDOWN s.p.
(R1850)
med solo,pno (E flat maj) ASHDOWN
s.p.   (R1851)
high solo,pno (F maj) ASHDOWN s.p.
(R1852)

RUSSELL, W.
Ah, What Is Love?
solo,pno BERANDOL BER 1326 $1.50
(R1853)
Blow, Blow Thou Winter Wind
solo,pno BERANDOL BER 1327 $1.50
(R1854)
Come Away, Come Away Death
solo,pno BERANDOL BER 1328 $1.50
(R1855)
Have You Seen But A Bright Lily Grow?
solo,pno BERANDOL BER 1329 $1.50
(R1856)
I Gave Her Cakes And I Gave Her Ale
solo,pno BERANDOL BER 1330 $1.50
(R1857)
My Lute, Awake!
solo,pno BERANDOL BER 1331 $1.50
(R1858)
My True Love Hath My Heart
solo,pno BERANDOL BER 1332 $1.50
(R1859)

RUSSELL, WELFORD
Come Hither, You That Love *sec
low solo,pno (F maj) WATERLOO $.90
(R1860)
Come Live With Me And Be My Love
*sec
low solo,pno (F maj) WATERLOO $.90
(R1861)
Fair Is The Rose *sec
med solo,pno (F maj) WATERLOO $.75
(R1862)
Give Me My Scallop Shell Of Quiet
*sec
low solo,pno (D maj) WATERLOO $.90
(R1863)
If I Freely May Discover *sec
high solo,pno (G maj) WATERLOO $.75
(R1864)
Little Pretty Nightingale *sec
med solo,pno (G maj) WATERLOO $.75
(R1865)

RUSSELL, WELFORD (cont'd.)

Love In My Bosom Like A Bee *sec
med solo,pno (G maj) WATERLOO $.75
(R1866)
Love In Thy Youth Fair Maid *sec
low solo,pno (D maj) WATERLOO $.75
(R1867)
O Waly, Waly Up The Bank *sec
low solo,pno (E maj) WATERLOO $.75
(R1868)
Shall I Come Sweet Love To Thee *sec
med solo,pno (G maj) WATERLOO $.75
(R1869)
Sleep Wayward Thoughts *sec
low solo,pno (E flat maj) WATERLOO
$.75   (R1870)
Under The Greenwood Tree *sec
low solo,pno (F maj) WATERLOO $.75
(R1871)

RUSSIAN FOLK SONGS *CCU,folk,Russ
(Sorokin, K.) [Russ] solo,pno MEZ
KNIGA 2.106 s.p.   (R1872)

RUSSIAN MAIDEN'S SONG see Stravinsky,
Igor

RUSSIAN PICNIC see Enders, Harvey

THE RUSSIAN SONG BOOKS, VOL. 1: BASS
*CC7L,Russ,19-20th cent
[Fr/Eng] B solo,pno CHESTER s.p.
contains works by: Bleichmann;
Arensky; Koeneman; Tcherepnin;
Sokolov   (R1873)

THE RUSSIAN SONG BOOKS, VOL. 1: SOPRANO
*CC7L,Russ,19-20th cent
[Fr/Eng] S solo,pno CHESTER s.p.
contains works by: Borodin; Glinka;
Arensky; Metner and others   (R1874)

THE RUSSIAN SONG BOOKS, VOL. 2: SOPRANO
*CC7L,Russ,19-20th cent
[Fr/Eng] S solo,pno CHESTER s.p.
contains works by: Cui; Borodin;
Rimsky-Korsakov; Tsherepnin;
Arensky and others   (R1875)

RUSSIAN SONGS *CC40U,Russ
(Silverman, Jerry) [Russ/Eng] solo,
pno OAK 000087 $3.95   (R1876)

RUSSIAN SPIRITUAL, A see Stravinsky,
Igor

RUSSISCHE LIEDER see Dvorak, Antonin

RUSSISCHE VOLKSLIEDER
solo,acord DOBLINGER 08 563 s.p.
contains: Abendlauten; Schwarze
Augen; Zwei Gitarren   (R1877)

RUSSISCHE VOLKSLIEDER *CCU,folk,Russ
(Axman, E.) [Czech/Russ] solo,pno
SUPRAPHON s.p.   (R1878)

RUSSISCHE VOLKSLIEDER *CCU,folk,Russ
(Michailow, A.) [Russ] solo,pno
SIKORSKI R 6315 s.p.   (R1879)

RUST MIJN ZIEL UW GOD IS KONING see
Eyken, Jan Albert van

RUSTHOI, ESTHER KERR
When We See Christ *sac
solo,pno SINGSPIR 7024 $1.00
(R1880)

RUSTIC SONG see Ferrari-Trecate, Luigi,
Strambotto In Serenata

RUSTICANELLA see Cortopassi, D.

RUTH see Faisst, Clara

RUTH see Weiner, Lazar

RUTH ET NOEMIE see Lacome, Paul

RUTTER, IDA
I've, Been Roaming
low solo,pno (C maj) ASHDOWN s.p.
(R1881)
high solo,pno (F maj) ASHDOWN s.p.
(R1882)
med solo,pno (D flat maj) ASHDOWN
s.p.   (R1883)

RUTTER, JOHN
Shepherds Pipe Carol
solo,pno OXFORD $1.00   (R1884)

RUTTERKIN see Bush, Geoffrey

RUTTERKIN see Heseltine, Philip

RUYNEMAN, DANIEL (1886-1963)
Adieu
see Trois Chansons Des Maquisards
Condamnes

Aloette, Voghel Clein
S solo,pno DONEMUS s.p.   (R1885)

RUYNEMAN, DANIEL (cont'd.)

Ancient Greek Songs
    low solo/med solo,pno DONEMUS s.p.
    contains: Fragment Of Orestes;
        Ode To The Muse, Prosodion;
        Tekmessa   (R1886)

April
    see Seven Melodies, Vol. 2

Bonheur
    see Cinq Melodies

Chanson
    see Cinq Melodies

Chineesche Liederen
    med solo/high solo,pno ALSBACH s.p.
    contains: De Verstooten Vriendin
        Van Den Keizer; De Wonderfluit;
        Een Jonge Dichter Denkt Aan
        Zijn Geliefde   (R1887)

Cinq Melodies
    med solo,pno DONEMUS s.p.
    contains: Bonheur; Chanson;
        Madrigal; Petites Litanies De
        Jesus; Regards   (R1888)

De Deerne
    solo,pno ALSBACH s.p.   (R1889)

De Verstooten Vriendin Van Den Keizer
    see Chineesche Liederen

De Wonderfluit
    see Chineesche Liederen

Die Weise Von Liebe Und Tod Des
    Kornets Christoph Rilke
    narrator,3fl,3ob,4clar,3bsn,3horn,
    2trp,3trom,tuba,timp,perc,cel,
    harp,xylo,strings DONEMUS s.p.
                                    (R1890)
    narrator,pno DONEMUS s.p.   (R1891)

Die Winter Is Vergangen
    see Vier Oud-Nederlandsche Liederen

Drei Persische Lieder *CC3U
    high solo,pno DONEMUS s.p.   (R1892)

Een Jonge Dichter Denkt Aan Zijn
    Geliefde
    see Chineesche Liederen

Everlasting Voices, The
    see Seven Melodies, Vol. 2

Fragment Of Orestes
    see Ancient Greek Songs

Het Viel Een Hemels Douwe
    see Vier Oud-Nederlandsche Liederen

Ik Ben Genoodigd Tot Het Feest Dezer
    Wereld
    med solo,pno ALSBACH s.p. see also
    Twee Wijzangen   (R1893)

Ik Weet Niet Van Uit Welken Verren
    Tijd
    med solo,pno ALSBACH s.p. see also
    Twee Wijzangen   (R1894)

Il Pleut Doucement Sur La Ville
    med solo,pno ALSBACH s.p. see also
    Trois Melodies   (R1895)

In Claghen
    see Vier Liederen Van J.H. Leopold

Krontjong Liedjes
    solo,pno ALSBACH s.p.   (R1896)

La Lune Blanche
    med solo,pno ALSBACH s.p. see also
    Trois Melodies   (R1897)

Laet Sang En Spiel, Tambour En Fluyt
    see Vier Oud-Nederlandsche Liederen

L'ideal
    med solo,pno ALSBACH s.p. see also
    Trois Melodies   (R1898)

Madrigal
    see Cinq Melodies

Met Eenen Droeven Sanghe
    see Vier Oud-Nederlandsche Liederen

Mijn Lieveken Open Je Deurken En Lach
    S/T solo,pno ALSBACH s.p.   (R1899)

Ode To The Muse, Prosodion
    see Ancient Greek Songs

On A Day, Alack The Day!
    see Seven Melodies, Vol. 2

Petites Litanies De Jesus
    see Cinq Melodies

RUYNEMAN, DANIEL (cont'd.)

Quelques Enfants Quelques Soldats
    see Trois Chansons Des Maquisards
    Condamnes

Reflexions I *CCU
    S solo,fl,vibra,xylo,perc,vla,gtr
    DONEMUS s.p.   (R1900)

Regards
    see Cinq Melodies

Remember
    see Seven Melodies, Vol. 2

Seven Melodies, Vol. 1
    med solo,pno DONEMUS s.p.
    contains: Sonnet: On Hearing The
        Dies Irae Sung In The Sistine
        Chapel; To A Child Dancing In
        The Wind; Why Is My Verse
                                    (R1901)

Seven Melodies, Vol. 2
    med solo,pno DONEMUS s.p.
    contains: April; Everlasting
        Voices, The; On A Day, Alack
        The Day!; Remember   (R1902)

Soefisch
    see Vier Liederen Van J.H. Leopold

Sonnet: On Hearing The Dies Irae Sung
    In The Sistine Chapel
    see Seven Melodies, Vol. 1

Sous Le Ciel Immobile J'ai Compte
    Jusqu'a Mille
    see Trois Chansons Des Maquisards
    Condamnes

Sous Le Pont Mirabeau
    SA soli,fl,2vln,vla,vcl,harp
    DONEMUS s.p.   (R1903)

Symphonia
    see Vier Liederen Van J.H. Leopold

Tekmessa
    see Ancient Greek Songs

To A Child Dancing In The Wind
    see Seven Melodies, Vol. 1

Trois Chansons Des Maquisards
    Condamnes
    DONEMUS A/Bar solo,pno s.p.; A/Bar
    solo,2fl,3ob,3clar,2bsn,2horn,
    2trp,2trom,timp,perc,harp,strings
    s.p.
    contains: Adieu; Quelques Enfants
        Quelques Soldats; Sous Le Ciel
        Immobile J'ai Compte Jusqu'a
        Mille   (R1904)

Trois Melodies
    med solo,pno ALSBACH s.p.
    contains & see also: Il Pleut
        Doucement Sur La Ville; La Lune
        Blanche; L'ideal   (R1905)

Twee Wijzangen
    med solo,pno ALSBACH s.p.
    contains & see also: Ik Ben
        Genoodigd Tot Het Feest Dezer
        Wereld; Ik Weet Niet Van Uit
        Welken Verren Tijd   (R1906)

Uit "Omar Khayam"
    see Vier Liederen Van J.H. Leopold

Vier Liederen *CC4UL
    high solo,pno ALSBACH s.p.   (R1907)

Vier Liederen Van J.H. Leopold
    T solo,2fl,2ob,2clar,bsn,2horn,
    timp,perc,cel,harp,strings
    DONEMUS s.p.
    contains: In Claghen; Soefisch;
        Symphonia; Uit "Omar Khayam"
                                    (R1908)
Vier Oud-Nederlandsche Liederen
    med solo/high solo,pno ALSBACH s.p.
    contains: Die Winter Is
        Vergangen; Het Viel Een Hemels
        Douwe; Laet Sang En Spiel,
        Tambour En Fluyt; Met Eenen
        Droeven Sanghe   (R1909)

Why Is My Verse
    see Seven Melodies, Vol. 1

Wiegenlied
    solo,pno ALSBACH s.p.   (R1910)

Winterabend
    med solo,pno ALSBACH s.p.   (R1911)

Zoet Jesusken Schudt Er Zijn Beddeken
    Uit *sac
    med solo,pno ALSBACH s.p.   (R1912)

RUZDJAK, MARKO (1946-   )
    Trois Chansons De Geste *CC3U
    Bar solo,2fl/2pic,2ob,2clar,2bsn,
    horn,trp,trom,4perc,strings MUSIC
    INFO rental   (R1913)

RUZICKA, PETER
    Esta Noche
    A solo,fl,English horn,vla,vcl
    SIKORSKI 811 s.p.   (R1914)

RYCHLIK, JAN (1916-1964)
    Jihoceske Pisne A Pisnicky *CC18U
    female solo/male solo,pno SUPRAPHON
                                    (R1915)

RYDEN
    Trad
    solo,pno LUNDQUIST s.p.   (R1916)

RYELANDT, JOSEPH
    Dame Therese *Op.121,No.3
    see Trois Invocations

    Petite Sainte *Op.121,No.2
    see Trois Invocations

    Soeur Claire *Op.121,No.1
    see Trois Invocations

    Trois Invocations
    S solo,pno cmplt ed CBDM s.p.
    contains: Dame Therese, Op.121,
        No.3; Petite Sainte, Op.121,
        No.2; Soeur Claire, Op.121,No.1
                                    (R1917)

RYOANJI TEMPLE see Marez Oyens, Tera de

RYTTAREN see Kuusisto, Taneli,
    Ratsumies

S

S PISNIKOU U KLAVIRU *CCU
(Prusova; Janzurova) solo,pno
SUPRAPHON   (S1)

SA AR NU INTET FORDOMLIGT see Roman,
Johan Helmich

SA DANSA see Kilpinen, Yrio

SA DRYGE BERG see Beck, Thomas
[Ludvigsen]

SA KOM DU see Nordqvist, Gustaf

SA MENIT see Kilpinen, Yrio

SA MYKKA MATKALAINEN MAAN see Kilpinen,
Yrio

SA ODSLIGT MOLNEN PA FASTET GA
see Liten Karin

SAA SOD VAR SOMMERNATTENS BLUND see
Sjogren, Emil

SAA STANDSED OG DER DEN BLODETS STROM
see Sjogren, Emil

SAA TAG MIT HJERTE see Alfven, Hugo

SAAVUTHAN, YO see Sibelius, Jean, Kom
Nu Hit, Dod

SABBATH JOY see Fromm, Herbert

SABBATH QUEEN see Fromm, Herbert

SABBATH SONGS see Nardi, Nachum

SABBOT see Migot, Georges

SABINO, A. (1898-1946)
Il Flaso Pellegrino
solo,2fl,2ob,2clar,2bsn,2horn,2trp,
timp,perc CARISH s.p.   (S2)

Il Ragno Saltimbanco
solo,2fl,2ob,2clar,2bsn,2horn,2trp,
timp,perc,pno CARISH s.p.   (S3)

SABOR DE ESPANA see Fuste, E.

SABRE EN MAIN see Saint-Saens, Camille

SACCHINI, ANTONIO (MARIA GASPARO
GIOACCHINO) (1730-1786)
Furie D'Averno (from Edipo A Colono)
(Gubitosi, E.) 2 soli,2ob,2bsn,
2horn,2trp,timp CARISH s.p.   (S4)

SACCO
Highland Song
high solo,pno (G maj) BOSTON $1.50
                                       (S5)

SACCO, JOHN [CHARLES] (1905-   )
Methuselah
med solo,pno (D min) SCHIRM.G $.75
                                       (S6)
Strictly Germ-Proof
med solo,pno (D min) SCHIRM.G $.80
                                       (S7)

SACHEZ DEFENDRE TOUS VOS DROITS see
Wagner, Richard

SACHS
Grandma
high solo,pno SHAWNEE IA5014 $.60
                                       (S8)
Little Worm, The
low solo,pno SHAWNEE IA5020 $.60
                                       (S9)

SACHT WIE VOM ABENDROT see Sibelius,
Jean

SACRAE SYMPHONIAE I see Gabrieli,
Giovanni

SACRED AND SECULAR SONGS FOR THREE
VOICES see Turnhout, Gerard de

SACRED ARIAS AND SONGS *sac,CC23U
high solo,org/pno PETERS 2451 $6.50
contains works by: Bach; Beethoven;
Franck; Handel; Haydn; Krebs;
Mozart; Reger; Stradella; Wolf
                                       (S10)

SACRED CANTICLE see Mills, Charles

SACRED DUET MASTERPIECES *sac,CCU
(Fredrickson) high solo&low solo,pno
FISCHER,C RB 58; med solo&low solo,
pno FISCHER,C RB 59; 2 high soli,
pno FISCHER,C RB 60   (S11)

SACRED DUETS *sac,CCU
(Shakespeare, W.) [Ger] PRESSER 2
high soli,pno $5.00; high solo&low
solo,pno $5.00   (S12)

SACRED DUETS FOR ALL VOICES *sac,CCU
[Ger] 2 soli,pno PRESSER $5.00 (S13)

SACRED DUETS FOR EQUAL VOICES *sac,CCU
(Cassler, G. Winston) 2 soli,pno
AUGSBURG 11-9372 $3.25   (S14)

SACRED DUETS NO. I *sac,CCUL
2 soli,pno LILLENAS MB-166 $1.25
                                       (S15)

SACRED DUETS NO. II *sac,CCUL
2 soli,pno LILLENAS MB-167 $1.25
                                       (S16)

SACRED DUETS NO. III *sac,CCUL
2 soli,pno LILLENAS MB-168 $1.25
                                       (S17)

SACRED FAREWELL see Russell, Kennedy

SACRED GROVE, THE see Medtner, Nikolai
Karlovitch

SACRED HOUR OF SONG *sac,CCU
(Harrell) high solo,pno FISCHER,C
O 2933; med solo,pno FISCHER,C
O 2893   (S18)

SACRED SELECTIONS FOR LOW VOICE *sac,
CC16UL
(Carle, Bill; Boersma, James) low
solo,pno WORD 30043 $1.95   (S19)

SACRED SONG MASTERPIECES, BOOK 1 *sac,
CCU
(Fredrickson) high solo,pno FISCHER,C
RB 49; low solo,pno FISCHER,C RB 50
                                       (S20)

SACRED SONG MASTERPIECES, BOOK 2 *sac,
CCU
(Fredrickson) high solo,pno FISCHER,C
RB 75; low solo,pno FISCHER,C RB 76
                                       (S21)

SACRED SONGS see Ives, Charles

SACRED SONGS see Bach, Karl Philipp
Emanuel

SACRED SONGS *sac,CCU
(Henderson, W.J.) T/B solo,pno
PRESSER $4.50   (S22)

SACRED SONGS *sac,CC50U
solo,pno MUSIC 0200036 $3.95 contains
works by: Bach; Gounod;
Mendelssohn; Sullivan; Handel and
others   (S23)

SACRED SONGS AND ARIAS, THE see Bach,
Johann Sebastian

SACRED SONGS FOR ALL OCCASIONS *sac,
CCU
(Fredrickson) high solo,pno FISCHER,C
RB 61; low solo,pno FISCHER,C RB 62
                                       (S24)

SACRED SONGS FOR GENERAL USE *sac,
CC12U,Gen
BOSTON high solo,pno $2.50; low solo,
pno $2.50 contains works by: Nevin;
Lang; Franck; Galbraith; Hamblen
and others   (S25)

SACRED SONGS FOR PANTHEISTS see Ward,
Robert

SACRED SONGS FROM SCHEMELLI'S
GESANGBUCH see Bach, Johann
Sebastian

SACRED TREASURES see Rambo

SACRED TRIOS FOR SOPRANOS AND ALTOS,
VOL. 2 *sac,CCUL
3 female soli,pno WORD 10057 $1.00
contains works by: Mendelssohn;
Gaul; Rossini and others   (S26)

SACRED TRUST see Kreutz, Robert E.

SACRILEGE OF ALAN KENT, THE see
Hutchison, Warner

SAD LITTLE BIRD, THE see Arensky, Anton
Stepanovitch, Le Petit Oiseau
Triste

SAD SONG, A see Heseltine, Philip

SADANT AR LIVET see Sjogren, Emil

SADERO, G.
Fa La Nana Bambin
low solo,pno (D maj) ALLANS s.p.
                                       (S27)
high solo,pno (G maj) ALLANS s.p.
                                       (S28)
Nina Nana De La Bona Mare
[It] solo,pno BONGIOVANI 2028 s.p.
                                       (S29)

SADLY RUSTLE THE LEAVES see Kodaly,
Zoltan

SADOT SHE-BA-EMEK
(Helfman, Max) "Fields Of The Emek"
[Heb] high solo,pno TRANSCON.
IS 519 $.50   (S30)

SAELE JOLEKVELD see Beck, Thomas
[Ludvigsen]

SAENK KUN DIT HOVED, DU BLOMST see
Nielsen, Carl

SAENZ, PEDRO
Esa Cancion
see Tres Canciones

Idilio
see Tres Canciones

Madrigal
see Tres Canciones

Tres Canciones
[Span] solo,pno cmplt ed RICORDI-
ARG BA 11749 s.p.
contains: Esa Cancion; Idilio;
Madrigal   (S31)

SAERSPRUCH see Pfitzner, Hans

SAETA, EN FORMA DE SALVE see Turina,
Joaquin

SAEVERUD, HARALD (1897-   )
Tre Peer Gynt Salmer *Op.28, CC3U
solo,pno/org MUSIKK s.p.   (S32)

SAFE IN THEIR ALABASTER CHAMBERS see
Pinkham, Daniel

SAFFEL, J. DE
Zing Een Lieken
solo,pno ALSBACH s.p.   (S33)

SAG' AN, WIRD SICH DEIN LIEBEN see
Haydn, (Franz) Joseph

SAG FARVAL LILLA FJARIL see Mozart,
Wolfgang Amadeus

SAG' MIR NUR EINMAL JA see Herrmann,
Georg

SAG OM ALL NATUREN HAR SIN FAGRING MIST
see Sjogren, Emil

SAG OSTAN, SAG VASTAN? see Peterson-
Berger, (Olof) Wilhelm

SAG', WO WEILST DU, MEIN LIEB? see
Kilpinen, Yrio

SAGA see Lidholm, Ingvar

SAGA OF A STAR, THE see Owens, Patricia

SAGAN OM ROSALIND see Peterson-Berger,
(Olof) Wilhelm

SAGAN OM ROSALIND see Wideen

SAGESSE see Panizza, Ettore

SAGT, WAS HAB' ICH DENN see Mozart,
Wolfgang Amadeus, Dite Almeno, In
Che Maniera

SAGT, WAS HAB ICH DENN VERBROCHEN? see
Mozart, Wolfgang Amadeus, Dite
Almeno, In Che Maniera

SAGUER, LOUIS
Ophelia's Mad Scene
S solo,2fl,2ob,2clar,2bsn,2horn,
2trp,perc,glock,cel,harp,strings
JOBERT s.p. sc, voc sc   (S34)

Trois Poemes De Louis Parrot *CC3U
med solo,pno JOBERT s.p.   (S35)

SAIL AWAY see Lora, Antonio

SAILORMEN see Wolfe, Jacques

SAILOR'S GRAVE see Sullivan, Sir Arthur
Seymour

SAILOR'S LAST VOYAGE, THE see Alnaes,
Eyvind

SAILOR'S LIFE, A see Hilliam, B.C.

SAILORS SONG see Haydn, (Franz) Joseph

SAILOR'S SONGS OR CHANTEYS *CCU
solo,pno PAXTON P15285 s.p.   (S36)

SAIMA HARMAJA see Marvia, Einari

SAINT AGNES MORN see Shaw, Geoffrey
[Turton]

ST. AGNES MORNING see Cowell

SAINT ANTOINE ET SAINT NICOLAS see
Arrieu, Claude

ST. CECILIA see Liszt, Franz

SAINT CHRISTOPHER see Russell, Kennedy

SAINT COLUMBIA'S POEM see Parke,
Dorothy

ST. FRANCIS' PRAYER see Beveridge,
Thomas G.

SAINT FRANCIS PRAYER see Schreiber,
L.P.

SAINT GOVAN see Roberts, Mervyn

SAINT JEAN DU SACRE COEUR, SOEUR
Lorsque Je Mourrai
solo,pno BERANDOL BER 1333 $1.50
(S37)
Mother At Thy Feet Is Kneeling *sac
solo,pno ASHLEY $.95   (S38)

ST. JOSEPH, SISTER OF
Star Of Hope *sac
med solo,pno (D maj) CENTURY 1456
$.40   (S39)

ST. MARTINS-LIEDER *CCU
(Draths) 2 soli,opt gtr SCHOTTS 5944
s.p.   (S40)

ST. NICHOLAS DAY IN THE MORNING see
Martin, Easthope

ST. QUENTIN, EDWARD
Light Of The World
solo,pno (A flat maj) LEONARD-ENG
(S41)
Patriotic Memories *CCU
solo,pno CRAMER   (S42)

SAINT-REQUIER, LEON (1872-1964)
Chante, Rossignol!
med solo,opt cor,pno/inst DURAND
s.p. see from Deux Melodies
Populaires Francaises   (S43)
Deux Melodies Populaires Francaises
*see Chante, Rossignol!;
J'entends Le Moulin   (S44)
J'entends Le Moulin
med solo,opt cor,pno/inst DURAND
s.p. see from Deux Melodies
Populaires Francaises   (S45)

SAINT-SAENS, CAMILLE (1835-1921)
A L'ombre Des Noires Tours (from
Ascanio)
Bar solo,pno/inst DURAND s.p. (S46)
T solo,pno/inst DURAND s.p.   (S47)
A Sainte-Blaise
T solo,pno/inst DURAND s.p.   (S48)
Adieu, Beaute, Ma Mie (from Ascanio)
Mez/Bar solo,pno/inst DURAND s.p.
(S49)
Ah! Le Destin Va-T-Il Realiser Mon
Reve (from Ascanio)
Bar solo,pno/inst DURAND s.p. (S50)
Aime! Eros (from La Lyre Et La Harpe)
SA soli,pno/inst DURAND s.p. (S51)
Aimons-Nous
Mez/Bar solo,pno/inst DURAND s.p.
(S52)
S/T solo,pno/inst DURAND s.p. (S53)
T solo,orch DURAND s.p., ipr (S54)
Air De Dalila (from Samson Et Dalila)
Mez solo,orch HENN s.p.   (S55)
Air Du Rossignol (from Parysatis)
S solo,orch DURAND s.p., ipr (S56)
Allez, O Vous Que J'aime (from
Proserpine)
STBar soli,pno/inst DURAND s.p.
(S57)
Allez Pourtant, Mes Chers Enfants
(from Ascanio)
Bar solo,pno/inst DURAND s.p. (S58)
Altes Trinlied *see Chanson A Boire
Du Vieux Temps
Amour Viens Aider (from Samson Et
Dalila)
solo,pno/orch sc KALMUS $3.00 (S59)
"O Liebe! Meinem Hass Steh'zur"
[Fr/Ger] Mez solo,pno/inst DURAND
s.p., ipa   (S60)
"O Liebe! Meinem Hass Steh'zur"
[Fr/Ger] S solo,pno/inst DURAND
s.p., ipa   (S61)
Amour Viril
S/T solo,pno/inst DURAND s.p. (S62)
Mez solo,pno/inst DURAND s.p. (S63)
Bar solo,pno/inst DURAND s.p. (S64)
Amour Vrai, Source Pure (from
Proserpine)
Mez solo,pno/inst DURAND s.p. (S65)
Angelus
T solo,orch DURAND s.p., ipr (S66)

SAINT-SAENS, CAMILLE (cont'd.)
Anne, Ma Bien-Aimee (from Henry VIII)
T solo,pno/inst DURAND s.p.   (S67)
Bar solo,pno/inst DURAND s.p. (S68)
[Fr] solo,acap oct DURAND s.p.
(S69)
Au Cimetiere
see Melodies Persanes Op. 26
Au Cimitiere
S/T solo,pno/inst DURAND s.p. (S70)
Mez/Bar solo,pno/inst DURAND s.p.
(S71)
Aux Conquerants De L'Air
2 soli,pno DURAND s.p. see from
DOUZE DOUS   (S72)
Avril
S/T solo,pno/inst DURAND s.p. (S73)
Ballade De Colombe (from Ascanio)
solo,acap DURAND s.p.   (S74)
Car Je Ne Suis Qu'une Etrangere (from
Henry VIII)
S solo,pno/inst DURAND s.p.   (S75)
Mez solo,pno/inst DURAND s.p. (S76)
Ce N'est Pas Comme Vous (from
Dejanire)
S solo,pno/inst DURAND s.p.   (S77)
Ce Soir On Me Dedaigne (from Etienne
Marcel)
Bar solo,pno/inst DURAND s.p. (S78)
Cendre Rouge (La) *CC10L
med solo,pno/inst DURAND s.p. (S79)
C'est A Moi De Margarita (from
L'Ancetre)
S solo,pno/inst DURAND s.p.   (S80)
C'est Bien Fini, Je Dois Compte A
Dieu (from Etienne Marcel)
SMezBar soli,pno/inst DURAND s.p.
(S81)
C'est Elle (from Etienne Marcel)
SMezTBar soli,pno/inst DURAND s.p.
(S82)
C'est Ici Qu'habite Phryne (from
Phryne)
S solo,pno/inst DURAND s.p.   (S83)
Mez solo,pno/inst DURAND s.p. (S84)
Chanson A Boire Du Vieux Temps
"Altes Trinlied" Bar/T solo,pno/
inst DURAND s.p.   (S85)
Chanson De Scozzone (from Ascanio)
[Fr] solo,acap oct DURAND s.p.
(S86)
Chanson Du Senechal (from Etienne
Marcel)
[Fr] solo,acap oct DURAND s.p.
(S87)
Chanson Triste
Mez/S solo,pno/inst DURAND s.p.
(S88)
A solo,pno/inst DURAND s.p.   (S89)
Chant De Margarita (from L'Ancetre)
S solo,pno/inst DURAND s.p.   (S90)
Chere Ame (from Proserpine)
SMezT soli,pno/inst DURAND s.p.
(S91)
Chere Anne Que J'adore (from Henry
VIII)
MezBar soli,pno/inst DURAND s.p.
(S92)
Clair De Lune
Mez/Bar solo,pno/inst DURAND s.p.
(S93)
S/T solo,pno/inst DURAND s.p. (S94)
Comment Dire Bien (from Proserpine)
T solo,pno/inst DURAND s.p.   (S95)
Bar solo,pno/inst DURAND s.p. (S96)
Dans Les Coins Bleus
Mez/Bar solo,pno/inst DURAND s.p.
(S97)
Danse Macabre
[Fr] solo,acap oct DURAND s.p.
(S98)
Mez/Bar solo,pno/inst DURAND s.p.
(S99)
Das Turnier *see Le Pas D'armes Du
Roi Jean
De Ton Regard La Douceur Me Penetre
(from Henry VIII)
Bar solo,pno/inst DURAND s.p.
(S100)
T solo,pno/inst DURAND s.p.   (S101)
De Ton Regard La Doucheur Me Penetre
(from Henry VIII)
[Fr] solo,acap oct DURAND s.p.
(S102)
Des Pas Dans L'allee *madrigal
SATB soli,acap DURAND s.p.   (S103)

SAINT-SAENS, CAMILLE (cont'd.)
Desir D'amour
Mez solo,pno DURAND s.p.   (S104)
Bar solo,pno DURAND s.p.   (S105)
Desir De L'Orient
Mez/Bar solo,pno/inst DURAND s.p.
(S106)
S/T solo,pno/inst DURAND s.p.
(S107)
Die Entfuhrung *see L'Enlevement
Die Ertwartung *see L'Attente
Die Glocke *see La Cloche
Die Meerfahrt *see Soiree En Mer
Die Sonne Sie Lachte *see Printemps
Qui Commence
Douze Chants *CC12L
DURAND high solo,pno/inst s.p.; med
solo,pno/inst s.p.   (S108)
Duo De Margarita Et Tebaldo (from
L'Ancetre)
ST soli,pno/inst DURAND s.p. (S109)
Duo D'Helene Et De Paris (from
Helene)
ST soli,pno/inst DURAND s.p. (S110)
Ecoutez, Tout Se Tait (from Les
Barbares)
ST soli,pno/inst DURAND s.p. (S111)
El Desdichado
SA soli,orch DURAND s.p., ipr see
from DOUZE DOUS   (S112)
El Ruisenor (from Parysatis)
[Span] S solo,pno RICORDI-ARG
BA 8820 s.p.   (S113)
Elle
Bar solo,pno/inst DURAND s.p.
(S114)
Mez solo,pno/inst DURAND s.p.
(S115)
En Un Sourire De Clemence (from
L'Ancetre)
solo,pno/inst DURAND s.p.   (S116)
Enfant, Je Te Donne L'exemple (from
Phryne)
TBar soli,pno/inst DURAND s.p.
(S117)
Enfants, Je Ne Vous En Veux Pas (from
Ascanio)
Mez solo,orch DURAND s.p.   (S118)
Bar solo,orch DURAND s.p., ipa
(S119)
S/T solo,orch DURAND s.p.   (S120)
[Fr] solo,acap oct DURAND s.p.
(S121)
Epithalame
S/T solo,pno/inst DURAND s.p.
(S122)
Mez/Bar solo,pno/inst DURAND s.p.
(S123)
Etoile Du Matin
see LA MUSIQUE, DIXIEME CAHIER
Mez/Bar solo,pno/inst DURAND s.p.
(S124)
Exaucant Ta Priere (from Helene)
A solo,pno/inst/orch DURAND s.p.,
ipr   (S125)
Extase
A/Bar solo,orch DURAND s.p., ipr
(S126)
Mez/Bar solo,orch DURAND s.p., ipr
(S127)
Fiere Beaute
B solo,pno/inst DURAND s.p. (S128)
Bar solo,pno/inst DURAND s.p.
(S129)
Fiorentinelle! Ah! Qui M'apelle?
(from Ascanio)
S solo,pno/inst DURAND s.p. (S130)
A solo,pno/inst/orch DURAND s.p.
(S131)
Mez solo,pno/inst DURAND s.p.
(S132)
Fluch Euch! Ew'ger Fluch Eurem Stamme
*see Maudite A Jamais Soit La
Race
Freia, La Blonde Aux Yeux D'azur
(from Les Barbares)
ST soli,pno/inst DURAND s.p. (S133)
Grasselette Et Maigrelette
Bar solo,pno/inst DURAND s.p.
(S134)
Guitares Et Mandoline
Mez/Bar solo,orch DURAND s.p., ipr
(S135)
S/T solo,orch DURAND s.p., ipr
(S136)
Honneur A L'Amerique
[Fr] solo,acap oct DURAND s.p.
(S137)
med solo,orch DURAND s.p., ipr

SAINT-SAENS, CAMILLE (cont'd.)

(S138)
Hymne A Eros (from Antigone)
    Bar solo,pno/inst DURAND s.p.
                                              (S139)
Hymne A La Paix
    S/T solo,orch DURAND s.p., ipr
                                              (S140)
    [Fr] solo,acap oct DURAND s.p.
                                              (S141)
Ich Erklomm Diese Felsen *see J'ai
    Gravi La Montagne

Il Est Deux Nobles Coeurs Que J'aime
    (from Ascanio)
    Bar solo,pno/inst DURAND s.p.
                                              (S142)
Inclinez-Vous, Mon Lis! (from
    Ascanio)
    SMezTBar soli,pno/inst DURAND s.p.
                                              (S143)
Israel! Romps Ta Chaine (from Samson
    Et Dalila)
    "Israel! Werde Frei" [Fr/Ger] T
    solo,pno/inst DURAND s.p. (S144)
Israel! Werde Frei *see Israel!
    Romps Ta Chaine

J'ai Gravi La Montagne (from Samson
    Et Dalila)
    "Ich Erklomm Diese Felsen" [Fr/Ger]
    MezBar soli,pno/inst DURAND s.p.
                                              (S145)
J'aime, Dans Son Lointain Mystere
    (from La Princesse Jaune)
    T solo,pno/inst DURAND s.p. (S146)
Je Crois, J'attends, J'espere (from
    Etienne Marcel)
    T solo,pno/inst/orch DURAND s.p.,
    ipr   (S147)
Je Faisais Un Reve Insense (from La
    Princesse Jaune)
    S solo,pno/inst DURAND s.p. (S148)
Je Marchais Au Milieu Des Fleurs
    (from Lola)
    S solo,pno/inst DURAND s.p. (S149)
Je Ne Te Reverrai Jamais (from Henry
    VIII)
    S solo,orch DURAND s.p., ipr (S150)
    Mez solo,pno/inst DURAND s.p.
                                              (S151)
Je Suis Votre Feal (from Ascanio)
    SBar soli,pno/inst DURAND s.p.
                                              (S152)
Jouis! C'est Au Fleuve (from La Lyre
    Et La Harpe)
    Bar solo,orch DURAND s.p., ipa
                                              (S153)
Jour De Pluie
    A solo,pno/inst DURAND s.p. (S154)
La-Bas
    Mez/Bar solo,pno/inst DURAND s.p.
                                              (S155)
    S/T solo,pno/inst DURAND s.p.
                                              (S156)
La Beaute Que Je Sers Est Telle (from
    Henry VIII)
    Mez/Bar solo,pno/inst DURAND s.p.
                                              (S157)
    T solo,pno/inst DURAND s.p. (S158)
La Brise
    see Melodies Persanes Op. 26
    2 soli,orch DURAND s.p., ipr see
    from DOUZE DOUS   (S159)
    Mez/Bar solo,orch DURAND s.p., ipr
                                              (S160)
La Cloche
    [Fr] solo,acap oct DURAND s.p.
                                              (S161)
    "Die Glocke" [Fr/Ger] S/T solo,pno/
    inst DURAND   (S162)
    "Die Glocke" [Fr/Ger] Mez/Bar solo,
    orch DURAND s.p., ipr   (S163)
La Coccinelle
    S/T solo,pno/inst DURAND s.p.
                                              (S164)
La Columbe Descend (from La Lyre Et
    La Harpe)
    S solo,orch DURAND s.p., ipa (S165)
La Feuille De Peuplier
    Mez/Bar solo,orch DURAND s.p., ipr
                                              (S166)
    [Fr] solo,acap oct DURAND s.p.
                                              (S167)
La Feuille Du Peuplier
    see LA MUSIQUE, DOUZIEME CAHIER

La Fiancee Du Timbalier
    [Ger/Fr] Mez/Bar solo,orch DURAND
    solo pt s.p., sc s.p., ipa (S168)

La Libellule
    S solo,pno/inst DURAND s.p. (S169)

SAINT-SAENS, CAMILLE (cont'd.)

La Mort D'Ophelie
    Mez/Bar solo,pno/inst DURAND s.p.
                                              (S170)
La Solitaire
    (Argent) Mez/Bar solo,orch DURAND
    s.p., ipr   (S171)
La Soltaire
    see Melodies Persanes Op. 26

La Splendeur
    Mez solo,pno/orch DURAND s.p., ipa
                                              (S172)
La Splendeur Vide
    see Melodies Persanes Op. 26

L'Amant Malheureux
    T solo,pno/inst DURAND s.p. (S173)
L'Amour Blesse
    S solo,pno/inst DURAND s.p. (S174)
L'amour Divin (from La Lyre Et La
    Harpe)
    AT soli,pno/inst DURAND s.p. (S175)
L'Amour Oyseau
    Mez/Bar solo,pno/inst DURAND s.p.
                                              (S176)
L'Arbre
    Bar solo,pno/inst DURAND s.p.
                                              (S177)
L'Attente
    "Die Ertwartung" [Ger/Fr] S/T solo,
    orch DURAND s.p.   (S178)
    "Die Ertwartung" [Ger/Fr] Mez/Bar
    solo,orch DURAND s.p., ipr (S179)
Le Bon Senechal De Poitiers (from
    Etienne Marcel)
    Bar solo,pno/inst DURAND s.p.
                                              (S180)
Le Bonheur Est Chose Legere
    [Fr] high solo,pno CHOUDENS C11
    s.p.   (S181)
    [Fr] med solo,pno CHOUDENS C12 s.p.
                                              (S182)
    [Fr] high solo,vln,pno CHOUDENS C13
    s.p.   (S183)
Le Charite Ma Belle Dame (from
    Ascanio)
    STBar soli,pno/inst DURAND s.p.
                                              (S184)
Le Cygne
    med solo,pno/inst DURAND s.p.
                                              (S185)
Le Fleuve
    T solo,pno/inst DURAND s.p. (S186)
Le Lever De La Lune
    Mez/Bar solo,pno/inst DURAND s.p.
                                              (S187)
Le Matin
    [Fr] solo,acap oct DURAND s.p.
                                              (S188)
    Mez/Bar solo,pno/inst DURAND s.p.
                                              (S189)
Le Pas D'armes Du Roi Jean
    "Das Turnier" [Fr/Ger] S/T solo,
    orch DURAND s.p., ipa   (S190)
    "Das Turnier" [Fr/Ger] B solo,orch
    DURAND s.p., ipa   (S191)
    "Das Turnier" [Fr/Ger] Mez/Bar
    solo,orch DURAND s.p., ipa (S192)
Le Presage De La Croix
    S/T solo,pno/inst DURAND s.p.
                                              (S193)
Le Rossignol
    Mez/Bar solo,pno/inst DURAND s.p.
                                              (S194)
    S/T solo,pno/inst DURAND s.p.
                                              (S195)
Le Rossignol A Pris Son Vol (from
    Lola)
    S solo,pno/inst DURAND s.p. (S196)
Le Soir Descend Sur La Colline
    AT soli,pno DURAND s.p.   (S197)
Le Sommeil Des Fleurs
    Mez/Bar solo,pno/inst DURAND s.p.
                                              (S198)
Le Vent Dans La Plaine
    med solo,pno/inst DURAND s.p.
                                              (S199)
L'Enlevement
    "Die Entfuhrung" A solo,orch DURAND
    s.p., ipa   (S200)
    "Die Entfuhrung" Mez/Bar solo,orch
    DURAND s.p., ipa   (S201)
    "Die Entfuhrung" S/T solo,orch
    DURAND s.p., ipa   (S202)
Les Cloches De La Mer
    A solo,orch DURAND s.p.   (S203)
Les Fees
    Mez/Bar solo,pno/orch DURAND s.p.,
    ipr   (S204)
    Mez/Bar solo,2pno/orch DURAND s.p.,
    ipr   (S205)

SAINT-SAENS, CAMILLE (cont'd.)

Les Sapins
    A solo,pno/inst DURAND s.p. (S206)
Les Vendanges
    S/T solo,orch DURAND s.p., ipr
                                              (S207)
L'Etoile
    T solo,pno/inst DURAND s.p. (S208)
Lever De Soleil Sur Le Nil
    Mez/Bar solo,orch DURAND s.p., ipr
                                              (S209)
L'homme N'est Pas Sans Defaut (from
    Phryne)
    Bar solo,pno/inst DURAND s.p.
                                              (S210)
    B solo,pno/inst DURAND s.p. (S211)
Lola *Op.116, scena
    S solo,acap DURAND s.p.   (S212)
Madeleine
    Mez/Bar solo,pno/inst DURAND s.p.
                                              (S213)
    S/T solo,pno/inst DURAND s.p.
                                              (S214)
Madrigal (from Proserpine)
    SS soli,pno/inst DURAND s.p. (S215)
    TB soli,pno/inst DURAND s.p. (S216)
Madrigal, Tire De La Psyche, Moliere
    T solo,men cor,pno/inst DURAND s.p.
                                              (S217)
Mai
    Mez solo,pno/inst DURAND s.p.
                                              (S218)
Maitre! Bon! Apres L'ami (from
    Ascanio)
    MezBar soli,pno/inst DURAND s.p.
                                              (S219)
Marcomir, Le Noble Epoux (from Les
    Barbares)
    S solo,pno/inst DURAND s.p. (S220)
    Mez solo,pno/inst DURAND s.p.
                                              (S221)
Maudite A Jamais Soit La Race (from
    Samson Et Dalila)
    "Fluch Euch! Ew'ger Fluch Eurem
    Stamme" [Fr/Ger] Bar solo,pno/
    inst DURAND s.p.   (S222)
Melodies Persanes Op. 26
    [Ger/Eng] solo,pno DURAND s.p.
    contains: Au Cimetiere; La Brise;
    La Soltaire; La Splendeur Vide;
    Sabre En Main; Tournoiement (S223)
Mon Coeur Est Sous La Pierre (from
    Ascanio)
    S solo,pno/inst DURAND s.p. voc sc,
    solo pt   (S224)
Mon Coeur S'ouvre A Ta Voix (from
    Samson Et Dalila) sac
    [Fr] solo,acap oct DURAND s.p.
                                              (S225)
    [Fr] A solo,pno/inst (C maj) DURAND
    s.p., ipa   (S226)
    "My Heart At Thy Sweet Voice" [Fr/
    Eng] A solo,pno (C maj) SCHIRM.G
    $.85   (S227)
    "My Heart At Thy Sweet Voice" [Fr/
    Eng] Mez solo,pno (D flat maj)
    SCHIRM.G $.85   (S228)
    "My Heart At Thy Sweet Voice" high
    solo,pno (E flat maj) FISCHER,C
    S 5332   (S229)
    "My Heart At Thy Sweet Voice" low
    solo,pno (C maj) FISCHER,C S 5334
                                              (S230)
    "My Heart At Thy Sweet Voice" med
    solo,pno (D flat maj) FISCHER,C
    S 5333   (S231)
    "My Heart At Thy Sweet Voice" med
    solo,pno (C maj) CENTURY 3705
                                              (S232)
    "My Heart At Thy Sweet Voice" solo,
    pno (available in 2 keys) ASHLEY
    $.95   (S233)
    "My Heart At Thy Sweet Voice" solo,
    pno/orch sc KALMUS $3.00   (S234)
    "Sieh' Mein Herz Erschliesset Sich"
    [Fr/Ger] S solo,pno/inst (E maj)
    DURAND s.p., ipa   (S235)
    "Sieh' Mein Herz Erschliesset Sich"
    [Fr/Ger] Mez solo,pno/inst (D
    flat maj) DURAND s.p., ipa (S236)
My Heart At Thy Sweet Voice *see Mon
    Coeur S'ouvre A Ta Voix

Ne L'oubliez Pas
    A solo,pno/inst DURAND s.p. (S237)
Noble Dame Pour Vous Plaire (from
    Henry VIII)
    solo,wom cor,pno/inst DURAND cmplt
    ed s.p., solo pt s.p.   (S238)
Nocturne
    S/T solo,pno/inst DURAND s.p.
                                              (S239)
    Mez/Bar solo,pno/inst DURAND s.p.
                                              (S240)

SAINT-SAENS, CAMILLE (cont'd.)

Norfolk Avait Dit Vrai (from Henry VIII)
Bar solo,pno/inst DURAND s.p. (S241)

T solo,pno/inst DURAND s.p. (S242)

O Beaux Reves Evanouis (from Etienne Marcel)
S solo,orch DURAND s.p., ipr (S243)
[Fr] solo,acap oct DURAND s.p. (S244)

Mez solo,pno/inst DURAND s.p. (S245)

O Cruaute Des Dieux (from Dejanire)
Bar solo,pno/inst DURAND s.p. (S246)

O Liebe! Meinem Hass Steh'zur *see Amour! Viens Aider

O Ma Phryne, C'est Trop Peu Que Je T'aime (from Phryne)
Bar solo,pno/inst DURAND s.p. (S247)

T solo,pno/inst DURAND s.p. (S248)

O Mon Maitre Et Seigneur (from Henry VIII)
SBar soli,pno/inst DURAND s.p. (S249)

O Mon Roi, Bien Qu'etant Par Vous Delaissee (from Henry VIII)
T solo,pno/inst DURAND s.p. (S250)
Bar solo,pno/inst DURAND s.p. (S251)

O Noble Epoux (from Les Barbares)
S solo,pno/inst DURAND s.p. (S252)
Mez solo,pno/inst DURAND s.p. (S253)

O Pure Extase (from Etienne Marcel)
ST soli,pno/inst DURAND s.p. (S254)

On Raconte Qu'un Archonte (from Phryne)
Bar/Mez solo,pno/inst DURAND s.p. (S255)
2 soli,pno/inst DURAND s.p. (S256)

Ou Nous Avons Aime
T solo,orch DURAND s.p., ipr (S257)

Ou Que Tu Sois, Junon (from Dejanire)
S solo,pno/inst DURAND s.p. (S258)

Pallas-Athene
Mez/Bar solo,orch DURAND s.p., ipr (S259)
S/T solo,orch DURAND s.p., ipr (S260)

Papillons
S solo,orch DURAND s.p., ipr (S261)

Pardonnez-Moi, Mademoiselle (from Ascanio)
ST soli,pno/inst DURAND s.p. (S262)

Pas D'arme Du Roi Jean
Bar solo,orch HENN s.p. (S263)

Pastorale
[Ger/Fr] SB soli,pno DURAND s.p.
see from DOUZE DOUS (S264)
SBar soli,pno DURAND s.p. (S265)

Peut-Etre
Mez/Bar solo,pno/inst DURAND s.p. (S266)
S/T solo,pno/inst DURAND s.p. (S267)

Philoctete Demeure! (from Dejanire)
S solo,pno/inst DURAND s.p. (S268)

Plainte
S/T solo,orch DURAND s.p., ipr (S269)

Pour Vous Mon Coeur Fut Sans Merci (from Henry VIII)
SMezTBar soli,orch DURAND s.p., ipa (S270)

Pourquoi Rester Seulette
S/T solo,pno/inst DURAND s.p. (S271)
Mez/Bar solo,pno/inst DURAND s.p. (S272)

Pourquoi Suis-Je Venue (from Proserpine)
Mez solo,pno/inst DURAND s.p. (S273)

Prayer, A *sac
(Dickinson) med solo,opt vln BELWIN $1.50 (S274)

Primavera *see Printemps Qui Commence

Printemps Qui Commence (from Samson Et Dalila)
[Fr] S/med-low female solo,pno/inst DURAND s.p. (S275)
[Fr] solo,acap oct DURAND s.p. (S276)

"Die Sonne Sie Lachte" [Fr/Ger] S solo,pno/inst DURAND s.p. (S277)
"Die Sonne Sie Lachte" [Fr/Ger] Mez solo,pno/inst DURAND s.p. (S278)

SAINT-SAENS, CAMILLE (cont'd.)

"Primavera" T solo,pno/inst (B flat maj) DURAND s.p. (S279)
"Primavera" S solo,pno/inst (A flat maj) DURAND s.p. (S280)
"Primavera" Mez/Bar solo,pno/inst (G maj) DURAND s.p. (S281)

Puis-Je Croire Que C'est Bien Vrai (from Proserpine)
Bar solo,pno/inst DURAND s.p. (S282)

T solo,pno/inst DURAND s.p. (S283)

Qui Donc Commande Quand Il Aime (from Henry VIII)
Bar solo,orch DURAND s.p. (S284)
T solo,orch DURAND s.p. (S285)

Qui Donc Eleve Ici La Voix (from Samson Et Dalila)
"Wer Ist's, Von Dem Der Ruf Ertont?" [Fr/Ger] Bar solo,pno/inst DURAND s.p. (S286)

Quoi! Vous Partez Si Tot (from Phryne)
ST soli,pno/inst DURAND s.p. (S287)

Reine! Je Serai Reine (from Henry VIII)
Mez solo,pno/inst DURAND s.p. (S288)

Reverie
[Fr] solo,acap oct DURAND s.p. (S289)
Mez/Bar solo,orch DURAND s.p., ipa (S290)

Romains, Relevez-Vous (from Les Barbares)
T solo,pno/inst DURAND s.p. (S291)

Romance Du Soir
SATB soli,acap DURAND s.p. (S292)

Sabre En Main
see Melodies Persanes Op. 26
T solo,orch DURAND s.p., ipr (S293)

Scene De Venus Avec Le Choeur Des Nymphes (from Helene)
S solo,pno/inst DURAND s.p. (S294)

Serenite
Mez/Bar solo,pno/inst DURAND s.p. (S295)
S/T solo,pno/inst DURAND s.p. (S296)

Si Je L'osais
Mez/Bar solo,pno/inst DURAND s.p. (S297)

Si Le Front Couronne De Lierre (from Phryne)
Mez solo,pno/inst DURAND s.p. (S298)
S solo,pno/inst DURAND s.p. (S299)

Si Loin Et Si Haut Dans L'espace (from Ascanio)
Bar solo,pno/inst DURAND s.p. (S300)

T solo,pno/inst DURAND s.p. (S301)

Si Vous N'avez Rien A Me Dire
Mez/Bar solo,pno/inst DURAND s.p. (S302)

Sieh' Mein Herz Erschliesset Sich *see Mon Coeur S'ouvre A Ta Voix

Siehe Mein Elend, Herr Sieh' Meine Qualen *see Vois Ma Misere, Helas!

S'il Est Un Charmant Gazon
S solo,pno/inst DURAND s.p. (S303)

Soeur Anne
S/T solo,pno/inst DURAND s.p. (S304)

Softly Awakes My Heart
high solo,pno (D flat maj) ALLANS s.p. (S305)
low solo,pno (B flat maj) ALLANS s.p. (S306)
med solo,pno (C maj) ALLANS s.p. (S307)

Soir Romantique
Mez/Bar solo,pno/inst DURAND s.p. (S308)

Soiree En Mer
"Die Meerfahrt" Mez solo,pno/inst DURAND s.p. (S309)
"Die Meerfahrt" A solo,pno/inst DURAND s.p. (S310)

Sommeil Des Fleurs
see LA MUSIQUE, NEUVIEME CAHIER

Sonnet
Mez solo,pno/inst DURAND s.p. (S311)

Souvenances
S solo,orch DURAND s.p., ipr (S312)

SAINT-SAENS, CAMILLE (cont'd.)

Sur L'eau Claire Et Sans Ride (from La Princesse Jaune)
S solo,pno/inst DURAND s.p. (S313)

Suzette Et Suzon
S/T solo,pno/inst DURAND s.p. (S314)
Mez/Bar solo,pno/inst DURAND s.p. (S315)

Temps Nouveau
S/T solo,pno/inst DURAND s.p. (S316)

Theme Varie
S solo,orch DURAND s.p., ipa (S317)

Tournoiement
see Melodies Persanes Op. 26
T solo,pno/inst DURAND s.p. (S318)

Tout Dort Dans La Nuit Lourde (from Les Barbares)
SMez soli,pno/inst DURAND s.p. (S319)

Trinquons
SATB soli,acap DURAND s.p. (S320)

Triomphant De Multiples Epreuves (from Dejanire)
S solo,pno/inst DURAND s.p. (S321)

Tristesse
Mez/Bar solo,pno/inst DURAND s.p. (S322)

Tu Vas Le Coeur Plein D'allegresse (from Etienne Marcel)
A solo,pno/inst DURAND s.p. (S323)
S solo,pno/inst DURAND s.p. (S324)

Un Message Du Roi (from Ascanio)
TBar soli,orch DURAND s.p., ipr (S325)

Un Siecle Avant Le Christ (from Les Barbares)
Bar solo,pno/inst DURAND s.p. (S326)

Un Soir, J'errais Sur Le Rivage (from Phryne)
solo&opt SST soli,pno/inst DURAND s.p. (S327)

Une Flute Invisible
Mez/Bar solo,pno&fl/vln DURAND s.p. (S328)

Venus
TBar soli,pno DURAND s.p. see from DOUZE DOUS (S329)

Venus Qui Peut Briser (from Les Barbares)
Mez solo,pno/inst DURAND s.p. (S330)

S solo,pno/inst DURAND s.p. (S331)

Victoire
med solo,pno/inst DURAND s.p. (S332)

Viens
SBar soli,pno DURAND s.p. (S333)

Viens, O Toi Dont Le Clair Visage (from Dejanire)
T solo,pno/inst DURAND s.p. (S334)
Bar solo,pno/inst DURAND s.p. (S335)

Villanelle
Mez/Bar solo,pno/inst DURAND s.p. (S336)

Vin Qui Rougis Ma Trogne (from Proserpine)
T solo,pno/inst DURAND s.p. (S337)
Bar solo,pno/inst DURAND s.p. (S338)

Vingt Melodies Et Dous, Vol. I *CC20L
1-2 soli,pno/inst DURAND s.p. (S339)

Vingt Melodies Et Dous, Vol. II *CC20L
1-2 soli,pno/inst DURAND s.p. (S340)

Violons Dans Le Soir
Mez/Bar solo,vln DURAND s.p. (S341)

Vive La France
med solo,pno/orch DURAND s.p., ipr (S342)
[Fr] solo,acap oct DURAND s.p. (S343)

Vogue, Vogue La Galere
Mez/Bar solo,opt org DURAND s.p. (S344)

Vois Ma Misere, Helas! (from Samson Et Dalila)
"Siehe Mein Elend, Herr Sieh' Meine Qualen" [Fr/Ger] T solo,pno/inst DURAND s.p. (S345)

Wer Ist's, Von Dem Der Ruf Ertont?
*see Qui Donc Eleve Ici La Voix

Zehn Lieder Und Duette *CC10L
[Ger/Fr] 1-2 soli,pno cmplt ed DURAND s.p. (S346)

SAINTE see Ravel, Maurice

SAINTE-MARIE see Gillet, Ernest

SAIRAS SOITTAJA see Kauppi, Emil

SAISINKO KAELTA KIELEN see Kilpinen, Yrio

SAISON D'AMOUR see Duteil d'Ozanne, A.

SAISONS see Bringuet-Idiartborde, A.

SAKAC, BRANIMIR (1918-   )
Ballade De Rats Et De Souris *see Barasou

Barasou
"Ballade De Rats Et De Souris"
solo,4-10inst MUSIC INFO rental
(S347)

Bellatrix-Alleluia
solo,trom,cel/org,pno/cembalo,
2perc,bass clar,strings MUSIC
INFO rental   (S348)

SAKONTALA see Valen, Fartein

SALADIN, O.
Das Rosenband
solo,pno ZIMMER. 1439 s.p. see from
Drei Lieder   (S349)

Die Fruhnen Graber
solo,pno ZIMMER. 1441 s.p. see from
Drei Lieder   (S350)

Die Sommernacht
solo,pno ZIMMER. 1440 s.p. see from
Drei Lieder   (S351)

Drei Lieder *see Das Rosenband; Die
Fruhnen Graber; Die Sommernacht
(S352)

SALAS, JUAN ORREGO (1919-   )
Canciones Castellanas
[Swed/Eng] high solo,chamb.grp. sc,
voc sc CHESTER s.p.
contains: Dicen Que Me Case Yo,
"They'd Have Me Get Married,
Oh!"; El Ganadico, "My Flock";
Ojos Garcos Ha La Nina, "What
Blue Eyes Adorn This Maiden";
Por Do Pasare Esta Sierra?, "Oh
Where Do I Cross These
Ranges?"; Recuerdate De Mi
Vida, "Remember, Lady
Disdainful!"   (S353)

Dicen Que Me Case Yo
"They'd Have Me Get Married, Oh!"
see Canciones Castellanas

El Ganadico
"My Flock" see Canciones
Castellanas

My Flock *see El Ganadico

Oh Where Do I Cross These Ranges?
*see Por Do Pasare Esta Sierra?

Ojos Garcos Ha La Nina
"What Blue Eyes Adorn This Maiden"
see Canciones Castellanas

Por Do Pasare Esta Sierra?
"Oh Where Do I Cross These Ranges?"
see Canciones Castellanas

Recuerdate De Mi Vida
"Remember, Lady Disdainful!" see
Canciones Castellanas

Remember, Lady Disdainful! *see
Recuerdate De Mi Vida

They'd Have Me Get Married, Oh! *see
Dicen Que Me Case Yo

What Blue Eyes Adorn This Maiden
*see Ojos Garcos Ha La Nina

SALBERT, DIETER
Schwarz-Wie Die Teppiche Salomos
high female solo,vibra ZIMMER. 1881
s.p.   (S354)

SALCE, SALCE see Verdi, Giuseppe

SALEM ALEIKUM see Cornelius, Peter

SALICH, MILAN (1927-   )
Liedchen Uber Liebe *see Pisnicky O
Lasce

Pisnicky O Lasce
"Liedchen Uber Liebe" S solo,pno
CZECH s.p.   (S355)

Schlesische Volkslieder *see Slezske
Lidove Pisne

Slezske Lidove Pisne
"Schlesische Volkslieder" S solo,
pno CZECH s.p.   (S356)

SALIERI, ANTONIO (1750-1825)
Die Wage Des Glucks
see Zwei Kanons

Steter Tropfen
see Zwei Kanons

Zwei Kanons *canon
(Cadow, Paul) TTBar soli,pno
BREITKOPF-W s.p.
contains: Die Wage Des Glucks;
Steter Tropfen   (S357)

SALIG FARMOR see Littmarck

SALIGA VANTAN see Hallnas, Hilding

SALIMAN-VLADIMIROV, D.
Romances *CCU
[Russ] solo,pno MEZ KNIGA 2.104
s.p.   (S358)

SALLHETEN see Ahlstrom

SALLINEN, AULIS (1935-   )
Cradle Song For A Dead Horseman
see Four Dream Songs

Four Dream Songs
S solo,pno FAZER s.p.
contains: Cradle Song For A Dead
Horseman; Man Made From Sleep;
There Is No Stream; Three
Dreams Each Within Each   (S359)

Man Made From Sleep
see Four Dream Songs

There Is No Stream
see Four Dream Songs

Three Dreams Each Within Each
see Four Dream Songs

SALLY IN OUR ALLEY
(Levey, W. C.) solo,pno CRAMER (S360)

SALLY IN OUR ALLEY see Carey, Henry

SALLY'S SMILE see Rorem, Ned

SALMHOFER, FRANZ (1900-   )
Heiteres Herbarium
high solo,pno DOBLINGER 08 650
$4.50   (S361)
med solo,pno DOBLINGER 08 651 $4.50
(S362)
Vier Lieder *Op.5, CC4U
med solo,pno UNIVER. 7476 $3.25
(S363)

SALMO DI DAVID see Salviucci, Giovanni

SALMO GIOIOSO see Bloch, Augustyn

SALMO VIII see Cortese, Luigi

SALOME see Kersters, Willem

SALOME'S SOLO SCENE see Strauss,
Richard, Ah! Du Wolltest Mich Nicht

SALOMO see Herrmann, Hans

SALOMON, KAREL (? -1974)
Doth Not Wisdom Cry *cant
low solo,pno ISRAELI 332 $4.20
(S364)
Elegy And Dance
S solo,2fl/vln sc ISRAELI 216 $4.20
(S365)
Two Songs Of Faith *CC2U
high solo,pno ISRAELI 201 $2.80
(S366)
SALOMON'S PRAYER see Pisk, Paul Amadeus

SALONEN, SULO (1899-   )
En Varvisa *Op.17,No.5
"Kevatlaulu" see Fem Sanger

Fem Sanger
solo,pno FAZER F 4693 s.p.
contains: En Varvisa,
"Kevatlaulu", Op.17,No.5;
Marsslut, "Maaliskuun Loppu",
Op.17,No.1; Strandaster,
"Ranta-Asteri", Op.17,No.4;
Tistel, "Ohdake", Op.17,No.3;
Visa I Frammande Land, "Laulu
Vieraalla Maalla", Op.17,No.2
(S367)

Kevatlaulu *see En Varvisa

Laulu Vieraalla Maalla *see Visa I
Frammande Land

Maaliskuun Loppu *see Marsslut

Marsslut *Op.17,No.1
"Maaliskuun Loppu" see Fem Sanger

Ohdake *see Tistel

Ranta-Asteri *see Strandaster

SALONEN, SULO (cont'd.)

Strandaster *Op.17,No.4
"Ranta-Asteri" see Fem Sanger

Tistel *Op.17,No.3
"Ohdake" see Fem Sanger

Visa I Frammande Land *Op.17,No.2
"Laulu Vieraalla Maalla" see Fem
Sanger

SALSBURY, SONNY
Father Loves You, The *sac
solo,pno WORD S-298   (S368)

God Speaking To You *sac
solo,pno WORD S-228   (S369)

SALTERIO POPOLARE I: SETTE POESIE
POPOLARI - DUE CANTATE see De
Grandis, Renato

SALTERIO POPOLARE II: NOVE POESIE
POPOLARI - EL KALENDARIO DEL POPOLO
see De Grandis, Renato

SALTIMBANQUES see Honegger, Arthur

SALUT A TOI, A NOBLE DEMEURE see
Wagner, Richard, Elisabeth's Arie

SALUT A TOI, O BEAU CIEL, O PATRIE see
Wagner, Richard

SALUT AU DRAPEAU see Gillet, Ernest

SALUT AUX ALPES see Legay, Marcel

SALUT D'AMOUR see Elgar, Edward

SALUTATIO see Heiss, Hermann

SALUTATION OF THE DAWN, THE see Weigl,
Vally

SALVADOR, M.
Canciones De Nana Y Desvelo *CCU
[Span/Fr] med-high solo,pno UNION
ESP. $2.00   (S370)

SALVATION NOW TO US HAS COME see
Schein, Johann Hermann

SALVATION'S PLAN see Sexton, William

SALVATORI, P. SALVATORE
Alla Mamma
[It] solo,pno BONGIOVANI 2036 s.p.
(S371)
Maggio
[It] solo,pno BONGIOVANI 2037 s.p.
(S372)
Orfano
[It] solo,pno BONGIOVANI 2035 s.p.
(S373)

SALVE, DIMORA CASTA E PURA see Gounod,
Charles Francois

SALVE, JESU see Buxtehude, Dietrich

SALVE, O REGINA see Monteverdi, Claudio

SALVE REGINA see Bantock, Granville

SALVE REGINA see Bormioli, Cesare

SALVE REGINA see Doppelbauer, Josef
Friedrich

SALVE REGINA see Gletle, Johann
Melchoir

SALVE, REGINA see Gratiani, Bonifatio

SALVE REGINA see Handel, George
Frideric

SALVE REGINA see Leo, Leonardo

SALVE REGINA see Mengelberg, Rudolf

SALVE REGINA see Mercadante, G. Saverio

SALVE REGINA see Nicolai, Otto

SALVE REGINA see Pergolesi, Giovanni
Battista

SALVE REGINA see Scarlatti, Domenico

SALVE REGINA see Schubert, Franz
(Peter)

SALVE, REGINA see Terziani, Pietro

SALVE REGINA see Vivaldi, Antonio

SALVE, REGINA see Werner, Gregor Joseph

SALVE REGINA (B-DUR) see Schubert,
Franz (Peter)

SALVE, SALVE, PUELLULE see Carissimi,
Giacomo

SALVIUCCI, GIOVANNI (1907-1937)
Salmo Di David *sac,Psalm
S solo,fl,ob,clar,bsn,horn,trp,
trom,pno min sc CARISH 17145 s.p.
(S374)

SALVUM ME FAC see Killmayer, Wilhelm

SALZBURGER WEIHNACHTSLIED "SCHLAF, MEIN
LIEBES KINDLEIN"
see In Dulci Jubilo

SAMAMA
Wedding Cantata *Marriage,cant
T solo,org WESTERN WIM118 $2.50
(S375)

SAMAYOI see Nakada, Yoshinao

SAMAZEUILH, GUSTAVE (1877-1967)
Chasses Lasses
see Deux Poemes Chantes

Dans La Brume Argentee
Mez solo,orch DURAND s.p., ipr
(S376)

Deux Poemes Chantes
solo,orch cmplt ed DURAND s.p., ipr
contains: Chasses Lasses; La
Barque   (S377)

Feuillage Du Coeur
high solo,pno/inst DURAND s.p.
(S378)

Japonnerie
med solo,orch DURAND s.p., ipr
(S379)

La Barque
see Deux Poemes Chantes

Le Cercle Des Heures *song cycle
[Ger/Fr] solo,pno DURAND s.p.
(S380)

Le Sommeil De Canope
solo,orch DURAND s.p., ipr (S381)

Tendresse
high solo,pno/inst DURAND s.p.
(S382)

SAMBA-CLASSICO see Villa-Lobos, Heitor

SAMBURSKY, D.
Hora Telem
solo,pno ISRAELI 1002 $1.40 (S383)

SAMEACH T'SAMACH see Masslo, Avi

SAMENKLANK - MODERNE NEDERLANDSE
LIEDEREN, VOL. I *CCU
solo,pno BROEKMANS 418 s.p. (S384)

SAMENKLANK - MODERNE NEDERLANDSE
LIEDEREN, VOL. II *CCU
solo,pno BROEKMANS 419 s.p. (S385)

SAMINSKY, LAZARE (1882-1959)
Eili Eili
med solo,pno FISCHER,C V 1677
(S386)

Green Stillness *Op.35,No.2
see Two Songs Of Sueskind Von
Timberg

Thought And Paean, A *Op.35,No.1
see Two Songs Of Sueskind Von
Timberg

Two Songs Of Sueskind Von Timberg
high solo,pno PRESSER $.75
contains: Green Stillness, Op.35,
No.2; Thought And Paean, A,
Op.35,No.1   (S387)

SAMIT UND SEID see Gilrod, Louis

SAMLADE SANGER II see Sjogren, Emil

SAMLADE SANGER III-IV see Sjogren, Emil

SAMMARTINO, LUIS
De Mi Patria
[Span] solo,pno cmplt ed RICORDI-
ARG BA 9390 s.p.
contains: Gato; Milonga; Triste
(S388)

Gato
see De Mi Patria

La Rosa
[Span] solo,pno RICORDI-ARG RF 6688
s.p.   (S389)

Milonga
see De Mi Patria

Sendas De Nostalgia
[Span] solo,pno RICORDI-ARG
BA 10516 s.p.   (S390)

Triste
see De Mi Patria

SAMMUNUT see Sibelius, Jean, Erloschen

SAMONOV, A.
From Pushkin's Times *CC7U
[Russ] med solo,pno MEZ KNIGA 2.105
s.p.   (S391)

SAMOSPEVI I see Skerjanc, Lucijan
Marija

SAMOSPEVI II see Skerjanc, Lucijan
Marija

SAMOSPEVI III see Skerjanc, Lucijan
Marija

SAMOSPEVI IV see Skerjanc, Lucijan
Marija

SAMOSPEVI V see Skerjanc, Lucijan
Marija

SAMOSPEVI VI see Skerjanc, Lucijan
Marija

SAMOSPEVI VII see Skerjanc, Lucijan
Marija

SAMOSPEVI VIII see Skerjanc, Lucijan
Marija

SAMOSPEVI IX see Skerjanc, Lucijan
Marija

SAMOSPEVI see Kogoj, Marij

SAMOSPEVI see Osterc, Slavko

SAMOSPEVI see Zigon, Marko

SAMOSPEVI ZVEZEK 1 see Grbec, Ivan

SAMOSPEVI ZVEZEK 2 see Grbec, Ivan

SAMOTY DUSE see Picha, Frantisek

SAMPSON, GODFREY (1902-   )
Constant Lover, The
low solo,pno NOVELLO 17.0036.07
s.p.   (S392)
high solo,pno NOVELLO 17.0035.09
s.p.   (S393)

Lullaby, A
med solo,pno NOVELLO 17.0113.04
s.p.   (S394)

Willie Drowned In Yarrow
med solo,pno NOVELLO 17.0221.01
s.p.   (S395)

SAMSON see Wetherington

SAMSTAGSABEND see Marvia, Einari,
Lauantai-Ilta

SAMTLICHE LIEDER see Beethoven, Ludwig
van

SAMUEL-HOLEMAN, EUGENE (1863-1942)
Berceuse
med solo,pno CBDM s.p.   (S396)

SAMUEL-ROSSEAU, MARCEL
Ave Maria *sac
solo,pno/org (available in 2 keys)
HEUGEL s.p.   (S397)

Ave Verum *sac
solo,pno/org (available in 2 keys)
HEUGEL s.p.   (S398)

Ecce Panis *sac
2 soli,pno/org HEUGEL s.p. (S399)

Noel *sac,Xmas
solo,opt cor,harmonium (available
in 2 keys) HEUGEL s.p.   (S400)

O Salutaris *sac
solo,pno/org (available in 2 keys)
HEUGEL s.p.   (S401)

Panis Angelicus *sac
Mez/B solo,pno/org (D flat maj)
HEUGEL s.p.   (S402)
solo,pno/org (available in 2 keys)
HEUGEL s.p.   (S403)
BB soli,opt cor,vln,bvl,harmonium
(D flat maj) HEUGEL s.p. (S404)

Pater Noster *sac
2 soli,pno/org HEUGEL s.p. (S405)

SAN BASILIO see Pizzetti, Ildebrando

SAN FRANCISCO NIGHT see Damase, Jean-
Michel

SAN GABRIEL see Quaranta, Felice

SAN MARTEIN
(Carlo, Musi) solo,pno (Bolognese
dialect) BONGIOVANI 2103 s.p. see
from El Mi Canzunett Seconda Serie
(S406)

SAN VINCENZO see Gandino, Adolfo

SANATON ROMANSSI see Madetoja, Leevi,
Romance Sans Paroles

SANCAN, P.
C'est La Pluie Douce
see Trois Impressions

Entends Contre Le Vieux Peuplier
see Trois Impressions

La Ronde
see Trois Impressions

Trois Impressions
solo,pno/inst cmplt ed DURAND s.p.
contains: C'est La Pluie Douce;
Entends Contre Le Vieux
Peuplier; La Ronde   (S407)

SANCHEZ, B.
Al Pie De La Cruz Del Roque
[Span/Fr] med solo,pno/gtr ESCHIG
$.90   (S408)

Arrorro
[Span/Fr] med solo,gtr ESCHIG $1.75
(S409)

Ingenio
[Span] med-high solo,pno ESCHIG
$1.75   (S410)

SANCHEZ DE FUENTES, EDUARDO (1874-1944)
Espera
solo,pno ALLANS s.p.   (S411)

O Cuba
[Span/Eng] high solo,pno PRESSER
$.75   (S412)

SANCTA CAECILIA see Hartsuiker, Andries

SANCTA ET IMMACULATA VIRGINITAS see
Head, Michael (Dewar)

SANCTA LUCIA
solo,pno LUNDQUIST s.p.   (S413)

SANCTA MARIA see Faure, Jean-Baptiste

SANCTA MARIA see Mulder, Ernest W.

SANCTUAIRE D'ASIE see Rhene-Baton

SANCTUARY see Ramsay, Harold

SANCTUS see Hemel, Oscar van

SANCTUS FOR ST. CECELIA'S DAY see
Clarke, Henry Leland

SANDALS see Hively, Wells

SANDALS see Walvoord, John

SANDE
Faith Unlocks The Door *see Scott

SANDERS
Little Town In The Ould County Down
low solo,pno (D maj) ALLANS s.p.
(S414)
med solo,pno (E flat maj) ALLANS
s.p.   (S415)
high solo,pno (A flat maj) ALLANS
s.p.   (S416)
med-high solo,pno (F maj) ALLANS
s.p.   (S417)

SANDERS, PAUL F. (1891-   )
Drie Liederen *CC3U
solo,pno BROEKMANS 251 s.p. (S418)

SANDERS, ROBERT L. (1906-1974)
Old Paint
B solo,pno (F maj) GALAXY 1.0895.7
$1.00   (S419)

SANDERSON, G.
Chanson Persane
solo,pno (available in 2 keys)
ENOCH s.p.   (S420)

SANDERSON, WILFRED
Break O' Day
low solo,pno (B flat maj) BOOSEY
$1.50   (S421)
high solo,pno (C maj) BOOSEY $1.50
(S422)

Captain Mac'
solo,pno (C maj) BOOSEY $1.50
(S423)

Four Songs *CC4U
solo,pno LEONARD-ENG   (S424)

Friend O' Mine
low solo,pno (F maj) BOOSEY $1.50
(S425)
high solo,pno (C maj) BOOSEY $1.50
(S426)
med-high solo,pno (B flat maj)
BOOSEY $1.50   (S427)
med solo,pno (A flat maj) BOOSEY
$1.50   (S428)

SANDERSON, WILFRED (cont'd.)

Gather Ye Rosebuds
high solo,pno (B flat maj) LEONARD-
ENG   (S429)
med-high solo,pno (A maj) LEONARD-
ENG   (S430)
med solo,pno (G maj) LEONARD-ENG
(S431)
low solo,pno (F maj) LEONARD-ENG
(S432)

Green Pastures
low solo,pno (E flat maj) BOOSEY
$1.50   (S433)
high solo,pno (G maj) BOOSEY $1.50
(S434)

Hills Of Donegal
low solo,pno (A maj) BOOSEY $1.75
(S435)
high solo,pno (B flat maj) BOOSEY
$1.75   (S436)

In All The Lovely Gardens
low solo,pno (F maj) LEONARD-ENG
(S437)
high solo,pno (B flat maj) LEONARD-
ENG   (S438)
med solo,pno (G maj) LEONARD-ENG
(S439)

Indian Serenade
high solo,pno (F min) LEONARD-ENG
(S440)
low solo,pno (D min) LEONARD-ENG
(S441)

My Dear Soul
solo,pno (B flat maj) BOOSEY $1.50
(S442)

Quiet
solo,pno (D flat maj) BOOSEY $1.50
(S443)

Shipmates O' Mine
solo,pno (F maj) BOOSEY $1.50
(S444)

Spring's Awakening
solo,pno (G maj) BOOSEY $1.50
(S445)

Storm Lullaby
low solo,pno (D maj) BOOSEY $1.50
(S446)
high solo,pno (E flat maj) BOOSEY
$1.50   (S447)

There Is A Green Hill
high solo,pno (F maj) CRAMER (S448)
low solo,pno (D flat maj) CRAMER
(S449)
med solo,pno (E flat maj) CRAMER
(S450)

Until
low solo,pno (D flat maj) BOOSEY
$1.50   (S451)
med solo,pno (E flat maj) BOOSEY
$1.50   (S452)
high solo,pno (F maj) BOOSEY $1.50
(S453)
2 low soli,pno (E flat maj) BOOSEY
$1.75   (S454)
2 high soli,pno (F maj) BOOSEY
$1.75   (S455)

Up From Somerset
low solo,pno (B flat maj) BOOSEY
$1.50   (S456)
high solo,pno (C maj) BOOSEY $1.50
(S457)

Valley Of Laughter
low solo,pno (E flat maj) BOOSEY
$1.50   (S458)
high solo,pno (F maj) BOOSEY $1.50
(S459)

SANDMAN see Brahms, Johannes,
Sandmannchen

SANDMAN IS CALLING YOU see Roberts,
George

SANDMANNCHEN see Brahms, Johannes

SANDRESKY, M.V.
My Soul Doth Magnify *sac
high solo,pno BELWIN $1.50   (S460)

SANDSTROM, SVEN-DAVID
Just A Bit
S solo,bsn,harp,vln sc NORDISKA
6469 s.p.   (S461)

Min Lilla Vra Bland Bergen
solo,pno LUNDQUIST s.p.   (S462)

SANFT WIE DU LEBTEST see Beethoven,
Ludwig van

SANG see Hallnas, Hilding

SANG see Liljefors, Ruben

SANG see Melartin, Erkki, La Lune
Blanche

SANG BAG PLOVEN see Nielsen, Carl

SANG EFTER SKORDEANDEN see Peterson-
Berger, (Olof) Wilhelm

SANG HINTERM PFLUG see Nielsen, Carl,
Sang Bag Ploven

SANG TILL STOCKHOLM see Nordqvist,
Gustaf

SANG TILL SVERIGE see Nordqvist, Gustaf

SANGAREN PA VANDRING see Naumann

SANGARKONST see Korling, August

SANGE EINES FAHRENDEN SPIELMANNS see
Colaco Osorio-Swaab, Reine

SANGEN see Hallstrom, Ivar

SANGEN HAR LYSNING see Nielsen, Carl

SANGEN I *see Arlberg, Fritz, O Tag!;
Backer-Grondahl, Agathe Ursula;
Bjorken Berattar; Beethoven, Ludwig
van, Vakteln; Hallstrom, Ivar, Visa
"Nar Vikingen For Vida"; Lindblad,
Otto, Trollhattan; Nyblom, C.G.,
Grinpojken; Pacius, Fredrik, Och
Havets Unga Tarna; Soderman,
(Johan) August, Soldatvisa   (S463)

SANGEN II *see Lindblad, Adolf
Fredrik, Den Gamle; Lindblad, Otto,
Trolhattan; Wennerburg, [Gunnar],
Jatten   (S464)

SANGEN OM DALSLAND see Nordqvist,
Gustaf

SANGEN OM KORSSPINDELN see Sibelius,
Jean

SANGEN OM LYCKAN see Sonninen, Ahti,
Laulu Onnesta

SANGEN OM MOR see Rendahl

SANGENS MASTARE I *CC33U
solo,pno GEHRMANS s.p. contains works
by: Brahms and Beethoven   (S465)

SANGENS MASTARE II see Schubert, Franz
(Peter)

SANGER see Grafstrom

SANGER, HEFT 1 see Geijer

SANGER, HEFT 2 see Geijer

SANGER MED PIANO see Heland

SANGER OCH VISOR see Korling, Sven

SANGER OCH VISOR see Norman, Ludvig

SANGER OCH VISOR, HEFT 1 see Nordqvist,
Gustaf

SANGER OCH VISOR, HEFT 2 see Nordqvist,
Gustaf

SANGER OCH VISOR HEFT II & III see
Casserman, Hjalmar

SANGER OCH VISOR II-III see Kjerulf,
[Halfdan]

SANGER OCH VISOR, VOLS. III, V, VI & IX
see Lindblad, Adolf Fredrik

SANGER OM BLOMMOR OCH FJARILAR see
Eriksson, Josef

SANGER OM DODEN see Grafstrom

SANGER TILL DIG see Grafstrom

SANGER UR EGNA TORVAN see Korling

SANGIORGIO, A.
Dialogo Di Marionette
[It] solo,pno CURCI 493 s.p. (S466)

SANGPARLOR II *CC15U
solo,pno FAZER F 2563 s.p.   (S467)

SANGRE VIENESA see Strauss, Johann,
Wienerblut Muss Was Eigenes Sein

SANGSAR see Lesur, Daniel

SANKT GEORG see King, Harold C.

SANNER
Bon
solo,pno LUNDQUIST s.p.   (S468)

SANOISSA KULUVA see Kilpinen, Yrio

SANS AMOUR see Chaminade, Cecile

SANS AVOIR L'AIR see Betove

SANS FEU NI LIEU see Milhaud, Darius

SANS-SOUCI
When Song Is Sweet
low solo,pno (D flat maj) ALLANS
s.p.   (S469)
med solo,pno (E flat maj) ALLANS
s.p.   (S470)
high solo,pno (G maj) ALLANS s.p.
(S471)

SANS VOUS AIMER see Magne, Michel

SANTA LUCIA *folk,It
solo,pno (D flat maj) ALLANS s.p.
(S472)
[It] S/T solo,pno RICORDI-ENG 53850
s.p.   (S473)
[It] Mez/Bar solo,pno RICORDI-ENG
53851 s.p.   (S474)
low solo,pno (C maj) ASHDOWN s.p.
(S475)
high solo,pno (E flat maj) ASHDOWN
s.p.   (S476)

SANTA LUCIA see Cottrau, Teodoro

SANTA LUCIA, LEBE WOHL see Mario, E.A.

SANTA ORAZIONE ALLA VERGINE MARIA see
Jachino, Carlo

SANTA ULIVA see Pizzetti, Ildebrando

SANTE NOTTE see Gruber, Franz Xaver,
Stille Nacht Heil'ge Nacht

SANTESTEBAN, J. DE
Heure Blanche
solo,pno ENOCH s.p.   (S477)

SANTIS see Gilse, Jan van

SANTOLIQUIDO, FRANCESCO (1883-   )
Je Sais La Source...
solo,pno CURCI 6605 s.p.   (S478)

Tre Poesie Persiane, Vol. I-III
*CC3U
solo,pno FORLIVESI 10803-10805
s.p., ea.   (S479)

SANTONJA, O.
Dormidito Le Vi Yo
[Span] BOTE $.50   (S480)

SANTUCCI, PELLEGRINO (1921-   )
Padre Nostro *sac
solo,org BERBEN 1279 s.p.   (S481)

SAPER VORREI SE M'AMI see Haydn,
(Franz) Joseph

SAPER VORRESTE see Verdi, Giuseppe

SAPP
There Is A River *sac
solo,pno BENSON S8107-S $1.00 (S482)

SAPP, GARY
Shimo
S solo,fl,pno sc SEESAW $3.00
(S483)

SAPPHIC ODE see Brahms, Johannes,
Sapphische Ode

SAPPHISCHE ODE see Brahms, Johannes

SAPPHO see Bantock, Granville

SARABANDE see Ropartz, Joseph Guy

SARABANDE see Roussel, Albert

SARAI, TIBOR
Diagnosis '69
T solo,orch BUDAPEST 10137 s.p.
(S484)

SARASTUS see Bergman, Erik

SARJEANT, J.
Blow, Blow, Thou Winter Wind
B solo,pno PRESSER $.75   (S485)

Watchman! What Of The Night
2 low soli,pno (F maj) BOOSEY $2.00
(S486)
2 high soli,pno (G maj) BOOSEY
$2.00   (S487)

SARLOTTEKEN see Cuypers, H.

SARTI, GIUSEPPE (1729-1802)
Far From My Love I Languish *see
Lungi Dal Caro Bene

Lungi Dal Caro Bene
S/T solo,pno FORLIVESI 11909 s.p.
(S488)
Mez/Bar solo,pno FORLIVESI 10884
s.p.   (S489)
(Huhn) "Far From My Love I
Languish" [It/Eng] low solo,pno
(F maj) SCHIRM.G $.75   (S490)

SAS, ANDRES (1900-1967)
Alas De Oro
see Seis Cantos Indio Del Peru

Amor Se Paga
see Seis Cantos Indio Del Peru

El Pajonal
see Seis Cantos Indio Del Peru

La Cuzquenita
see Seis Cantos Indio Del Peru

La Parihuana
see Seis Cantos Indio Del Peru

Seis Cantos Indio Del Peru
[Span] solo,pno cmplt ed RICORDI-
ARG BA 11533 s.p.
contains: Alas De Oro; Amor Se
Paga; El Pajonal; La
Cuzquenita; La Parihuana; Suray
Surita   (S491)

Suray Surita
see Seis Cantos Indio Del Peru

SASOM HJORTEN NADD AV PILEN see
Nordqvist, Gustaf

SATA TIETA see Sibelius, Jean, Hundra
Vagar

SATAKIELI see Pylkkanen, Tauno Kullervo

SATEREN, LELAND BERNHARD (1913-   )
God Of Earth And Heaven
see FIVE WEDDING SONGS

In His Care *sac
med solo,pno AUGSBURG 11-0733 $.75
                                 (S492)

To Know Thou Art *sac
high solo,pno AUGSBURG 11-0738 $.85
                                 (S493)
med solo,pno AUGSBURG 11-0739 $.85
                                 (S494)

We Three Are One *sac
med solo,pno AUGSBURG 11-0730 $.60
                                 (S495)

SATHERBERG
Lantflickans Visa
solo,pno LUNDQUIST s.p.   (S496)

SATIE, ERIK (1866-1925)
Air Du Poete
see Ludions

Air Du Rat
see Ludions

Chanson
see Three Other Songs

Chanson Du Chat
see Ludions

Chanson Medievale
see Three Other Songs

Dapheneo
med solo,pno/orch SALABERT-US
$3.00, ipr see from Three Songs
                                 (S497)

Eight Poems Of Guillaume Apollinaire
*CC8L
high solo,pno SALABERT-US $7.75
                                 (S498)

Elegie
see Three Songs (1886)

Hymne
med solo,pno SALABERT-US $2.25
                                 (S499)

Je Te Veux
T solo,pno/orch SALABERT-US $4.50,
ipr   (S500)

La Diva De "L'Empire"
med solo,pno SALABERT-US $3.00   (S501)

La Grenouille Americaine
see Ludions

La Statue De Bronze
med solo,pno/orch SALABERT-US
$3.75, ipr see from Three Songs
                                 (S502)

Le Chapelier
med solo,pno/orch SALABERT-US
$3.75, ipr see from Three Songs
                                 (S503)

Les Anges
see Three Songs (1886)

Les Fleurs
see Three Other Songs

Ludions
med solo,pno SALABERT-US $5.50
contains: Air Du Poete; Air Du
Rat; Chanson Du Chat; La
Grenouille Americaine; Spleen
                                 (S504)

SATIE, ERIK (cont'd.)

Quatre Petites Melodies *CC4U
[Ger] ESCHIG $3.50   (S505)

Spleen
see Ludions

Sylvie
see Three Songs (1886)

Tendrement
med solo,pno/orch SALABERT-US
$3.75, ipr   (S506)

Three Other Songs
high solo,pno SALABERT-US $4.50
contains: Chanson; Chanson
Medievale; Les Fleurs   (S507)

Three Songs *see Dapheneo; La Statue
De Bronze; Le Chapelier   (S508)

Three Songs (1886)
high solo,pno SALABERT-US $4.50
contains: Elegie; Les Anges;
Sylvie   (S509)

Trois Poemes D'amour *CC3U
med solo,pno SALABERT-US $3.75
                                 (S510)

SATIRES OF CIRCUMSTANCE see Shifrin,
Seymour J.

SATISFIED see Boardman, Reginald

SATISFIED see Broones

SATISFIED see Brown

SATISFIED see Fischer, Irwin

SATISFIED see MacDermid

SATRA, ANTONIN (1901-   )
Canzonette E Ballate *song cycle
T solo,pno PANTON s.p.   (S511)

Pisnicky A Balady *song cycle
solo,pno PANTON 450 s.p.   (S512)

SATURN see Hovhaness, Alan

SAUDADES see Heseltine, Philip

SAUER, FRANTISEK (1938-   )
Detsky Koutek *CCU
boy solo/girl solo,pno SUPRAPHON
s.p.   (S513)

Letem Detskym Svetem *CCU
solo,pno SUPRAPHON s.p.   (S514)

Muzikanti K Tanci Hrali *CCU
solo,pno SUPRAPHON s.p.   (S515)

Proti Tme Zivota *CC4U
med solo,pno PANTON 1344 s.p.
                                 (S516)

Zpivejte S Misou
solo,pno SUPRAPHON s.p.   (S517)

SAUERBREY
Minstrel Boy
high solo,pno (F maj) CRAMER (S518)
low solo,pno (D maj) CRAMER (S519)

SAUGUET, HENRI (1901-   )
Berceuse Creole
med solo,pno SALABERT-US $1.25
                                 (S520)

Clair De Lune De Novembre
see Six Melodies Sur Des Poemes
Symbolistes

Crepuscule De Mi-Juillet
see Six Melodies Sur Des Poemes
Symbolistes

Deux Poemes De Shakespeare *CC2U
med solo,pno sc JOBERT s.p. (S521)

La Voyante *scena
solo,orch sc OISEAU rental   (S522)

Le Chat I
see Six Melodies Sur Des Poemes
Symbolistes

Le Chat II
see Six Melodies Sur Des Poemes
Symbolistes

Les Animaux Et Leurs Hommes
med solo,pno sc JOBERT s.p. (S523)

Les Caprices De Marianne
solo,pno AMPHION s.p. solo pt, voc
sc   (S524)

L'Espace Du Dedans
(Michaux) [Fr] B solo,acap ESCHIG
$2.25   (S525)

SAUGUET, HENRI (cont'd.)

L'oiseau A Vu Tout Cela
[Fr] Bar solo,pno/strings voc sc
HEUGEL 10465 s.p.   (S526)

Renouveau
see Six Melodies Sur Des Poemes
Symbolistes

Romance Napolitaine
solo,pno AMPHION R 1600 s.p. (S527)

Six Melodies Sur Des Poemes
Symbolistes
solo,pno AMPHION A 115 $2.50
contains: Clair De Lune De
Novembre; Crepuscule De Mi-
Juillet; Le Chat I; Le Chat II;
Renouveau; Tristesse D'ete
                             (S528)

Tristesse D'ete
see Six Melodies Sur Des Poemes
Symbolistes

SAUL AND THE WITCH AT ENDOR see
Purcell, Henry

SAUL, GEORGE BRANDON
As The Violets Came
see Four Songs

Four Songs
solo,pno BRANDEN $1.00
contains: As The Violets Came;
Invitation To Late Love; Song:
Dream The Nightingale; Song:
For Eileen   (S529)

Invitation To Late Love
see Four Songs

Song: Dream The Nightingale
see Four Songs

Song: For Eileen
see Four Songs

SAUNAKAMARI, LAULUSARJA see Kuusisto,
Taneli

SAUNDERS, MERVYN
There Lived A Snail
solo,pno CRAMER   (S530)

SAUSLE, LIEBE MYRTHE see Strauss,
Richard

SAUTE, SAUTERELLE! see Schlosser, Paul

SAUVAGEOT, M.
Et Moi Aussi *CCU
solo,pno OUVRIERES s.p.   (S531)

SAV, SAV SUSA see Liljefors, Ruben

SAV, SAV, SUSA see Sibelius, Jean

SAVE ME, O GOD see Charles, Ernest

SAVE ME, O GOD see Randegger, Alberto

SAVE ME, O LORD see Williams, D.S.

SAVE OUR BLEST AMERICA see Derricks,
Cleavant

SAVED FROM THE STORM see Barri, Occardo

SAVELET see Fordell, Erik (Fritiof),
Toner

SAVEZ-VOUS PLANTER LES CHOUX see
Ravize, A.

SAVICHNA, MA LUMIERE see Mussorgsky,
Modest

SAVINO, D.
Les Rosiers
solo,pno ENOCH s.p.   (S532)

SAVIONI, MARIO
Early Music Series, Vol. 3: Six
Cantatas *CC6U,cant
(Geiringer, Karl) 1-3 soli,inst
PRESSER $6.00   (S533)

SAVIOR CAME IN SEARCH OF ME, THE see
Pace, Millie Lou

SAVIOR IS WAITING, THE *sac
(Carmichael, Ralph) solo,pno WORD S-3
                             (S534)

SAVIOR KNOWS, THE see Good, Dwayne

SAVIOR OF THE WORLD see Stevens, Sammy

SAVIOUR, MAKE ME ALL THINE OWN see
Bach, Johann Sebastian

SAVOIE *Fr
(Canteloube, J.) solo,acap DURAND
s.p. see also Anthologie Des Chants
Populaires Francais Tome III (S535)

SAVOLAISIA KANSANLAULUJA II see
Kuusisto, Taneli

SAW A GRAVE UPON A HILL see Swanson,
Howard

SAW YE JOHNNIE COMIN'? *folk,Scot
solo,pno (F maj) PATERSON FS80 s.p.
(S536)

SAW YE MY SAVIOUR? see MacDermid

SAW YE MY SAVIOUR? see Phillips

SAW YE MY SAVIOUR? see Root

SAW YE MY SAVIOUR? see Steward

SAWYER, YVONNE
Falling Blossom
solo,pno CRAMER   (S537)

One Perfect Hour With You
low solo,pno (E flat maj) CRAMER
(S538)
high solo,pno (G maj) CRAMER (S539)

Tramp
low solo,pno (C maj) CRAMER (S540)
high solo,pno (D flat maj) CRAMER
(S541)

SAXE, SERGE
Andonais
solo,pno PEER $1.00   (S542)

Sonnet
solo,pno PEER $.95   (S543)

Wedded Souls
S solo,2fl,2ob,2clar,2bsn,4horn,
2trp,3trom,tuba,timp,perc,harp,
strings PEER sc rental, voc sc
$.95   (S544)

Why Did I Laugh To-Night?
Bar solo,pno PEER $.95   (S545)

SAXTON, STANLEY E. (1904-   )
My Soul Doth Magnify The Lord *sac
high solo,pno GALAXY 1.1641.7 $1.00
(S546)
low solo,pno GALAXY 1.1642.7 $1.00
(S547)

SAY A LITTLE PRAYER FOR ME *sac,gospel
solo,pno ABER.GRP. $1.50   (S548)

SAY I DO see Hildebrand, Ray

SAYINGS OF THE WORD see Franco, Johan

SBOHEM A SATECEK see Kapralova,
Viteslaza

SCALERICA DE ORO
(Neumann, Richard) "Ladder Of Gold,
A" solo,pno/org (Ladino text)
TRANSCON. WJ 402 $1.00   (S549)

SCARLATTI, ALESSANDRO (1660-1725)
Agar Et Ismaele Esiliati *ora
(Bianchi, Lino) soli,strings,cont
SANTIS OS 11:1039 s.p.   (S550)

Air De Laodice (from Miridate
Eupatore)
[Fr/It] S solo,pno/inst DURAND s.p.
(S551)
Arianna *cant
(Meylan) [It] S solo,strings,
cembalo PETERS 8011 $7.50, ipa (S552)
Ariette
high solo,2vln,cont SCHIRM.EC s.p.
(S553)
Caldo Sangue (from Sedecia, Re Di
Gerusalemme)
(Gubitosi, E.) solo,strings CARISH
s.p.   (S554)

Christmas Cantata *sac,Xmas
S solo,hpsd,4strings (med) voc sc
OXFORD 63.305 $1.25, sc OXFORD
$3.85, ipa   (S555)

Correa Nel Seno Amato
[It/Ger] S solo,2vln,cont BAREN.
6459 $21.00   (S556)
S solo,strings,cont sc ZERBONI 7787
s.p.   (S557)

Elitropio D'amor
see Quatro Cantate

Fermate Omai Fermate
see Quatro Cantate

Gia Il Sole Del Gange
(Parisotti) [It] Mez/Bar solo,pno
RICORDI-ENG 53999 s.p.   (S558)

Il Giardino Di Amore
(Seidel, M.; Drechler, O.) [It] SA
soli,strings,cont voc sc WILHELM.
s.p.   (S559)

SCARLATTI, ALESSANDRO (cont'd.)

Infirmata Vulnerata *sac,cant
(Ewerhart, Rudolf) [Lat] A solo,
2vln,cont sc BIELER DK 5 s.p.,
ipa   (S560)

Io Morirei Contento
see Quatro Cantate

La Passione Di Nostro Signore Gesu
Cristo *sac,Easter,ora
(Bianchi, Lino) soli,strings,cont
sc SANTIS OS VI 1   (S561)

Lascia, Deh Lascia *cant
"Leave Off, Oh Leave Off" S solo,
cont GERIG AV 124 s.p.   (S562)

Le Violette
[It] S/T solo,pno RICORDI-ARG
BA 8821 s.p.   (S563)
S/T solo,pno FORLIVESI 11929 s.p.
(S564)
Mez/Bar solo,pno FORLIVESI 11930
s.p.   (S565)
(Parisotti) [It] S/T solo,pno
RICORDI-ENG 123728 s.p.   (S566)

Leave Off, Oh Leave Off *see Lascia,
Deh Lascia

O Cessate Di Piagarmi
solo,pno FORLIVESI 10885 s.p.
(S567)
"O No Longer Seek To Pain Me" [It/
Eng] low solo,pno (E min)
SCHIRM.G $.60   (S568)
(Lavie) [Fr/It] med solo,gtr ESCHIG
$1.50   (S569)
(Lavie, Ferandez) "O Cessez De Me
Plaindre" [Span/Fr/It] solo,gtr
SCHOTTS GA 192 s.p. see from ALTE
UND NEUE WERKE   (S570)
(Parisotti) [It/Fr] Mez/Bar solo,
pno RICORDI-ARG BA 11855 s.p.
(S571)
(Parisotti) [It/Fr] S/T solo,pno
RICORDI-ENG 113457 s.p.   (S572)
(Parisotti) [It/Fr] Mez/Bar solo,
pno RICORDI-ENG 121044 s.p.
(S573)

O Cessez De Me Plaindre *see O
Cessate Di Piagarmi

O No Longer Seek To Pain Me *see O
Cessate Di Piagarmi

Quatro Cantate
(Tintori) [It/Eng] solo,pno cmplt
ed RICORDI-ENG 129554 s.p.
contains: Elitropio D'amor;
Fermate Omai Fermate; Io
Morirei Contento; Speranze Mie
(S574)
Qui Dove Al Germogliar
(Meylan) [It] S solo,strings,
cembalo PETERS 8012 $7.50, ipa (S575)

Se Delitto E L'adorarti
see Tres Arias

Se Florindo E Fedele
solo,pno FORLIVESI 10886 s.p.
(S576)
(Parisotti) [It/Fr] Mez/Bar solo,
pno RICORDI-ARG BA 11856 s.p.
(S577)
(Parisotti) [It/Fr] S/T solo,pno
RICORDI-ENG 121045 s.p.   (S578)

Sento Nel Core *sec
(Abloniz) solo,gtr RICORDI-ENG
129352 s.p.   (S579)
(Johnston; Vinci) low solo,pno (F
maj) WATERLOO $.75   (S580)
(Johnston; Vinci) med solo,pno (A
flat maj) WATERLOO $.75   (S581)
(Johnston; Vinci) high solo,pno (B
flat maj) WATERLOO $.75   (S582)
(Parisotti) [It] Mez/Bar solo,pno
RICORDI-ENG 53997 s.p.   (S583)

So Venite A Consiglio *sec
(Johnston; Vinci) low solo,pno (E
maj) WATERLOO $.75   (S584)
(Johnston; Vinci) high solo,pno (A
maj) WATERLOO $.75   (S585)

Solitude, Ah, How Welcome! *see
Solitudine Avvenne

Solitudine Avvenne *cant
"Solitude, Ah, How Welcome!" [It/
Eng/Ger] S solo,fl,pno ZIMMER
1028 s.p.   (S586)

Speranze Mie
see Quatro Cantate

Su Le Sponde Del Tebro *cant
(Paumgartner) [It] S solo,trp,2vln,
vcl,cembalo MULLER WM3 s.p.,
ipa   (S587)

SCARLATTI, ALESSANDRO (cont'd.)

Ten Arias For High Voice *CC10L
solo,pno SCHIRM.G 1853 $2.50 (S588)

Toglietemi La Vita Ancor
see Tres Arias
solo,pno FORLIVESI 10887 s.p.
(S589)

Tres Arias
(Parisotti) [It] solo,pno cmplt ed
RICORDI-ARG BA 11952 s.p.
contains: Se Delitto E
L'adorarti; Toglietemi La Vita
Ancor; Tu Lo Sai   (S590)

Tu Lo Sai
see Tres Arias

Vengo, Vengo A Stringerti (from Il
Ciearco In Negroponte)
T solo,fl,ob,bsn CARISH s.p. (S591)

SCARLATTI, DOMENICO (1685-1757)
Acht Arien Der Thetis (from Tetide In
Sciro) sec,CC8L
S solo,inst,cont sc FMA FMA 6 s.p.,
ipa   (S592)
Ainsi Qu'un Papillon Leger *see Qual
Farfalletta Amante

Amando Tacendo (from Tetide In Sciro)
see Scarlatti, Domenico, Vorebbe
Dal Tuo Cor

Amenissimi Prati *cant
B solo,cont GERIG AV 121 s.p.
(S593)
Care Luci Ben Mio
med solo,4strings,cont BROEKMANS
1084 s.p.   (S594)

Cosi Orgogliosa (from Tetide In
Sciro)
see Funf Arien Der Antiope

Credimi O Core (from Tetide In Sciro)
see Drei Arien Der Deidamia

Drei Arien Der Deidamia (from Tetide
In Sciro) sec
Mez solo,1-3vln,cont sc FMA FMA 8
s.p.
contains: Credimi O Core; Io
Credea; Per Credere   (S595)

Five Songs *CC5U
high solo,pno FISCHER,C RB 44; med
solo,pno FISCHER,C RB 57   (S596)

Funf Arien Der Antiope (from Tetide
In Sciro) sec
S solo,inst,cont sc FMA FMA 7 s.p.,
ipa
contains: Cosi Orgogliosa;
Lasciami Crudo Amor; Quando In
Notte; Se Da Un Empio; Sento
L'aura   (S597)

Impara A Compatir L'altrui Martir
(from Tetide In Sciro)
see Zwei Arien Des Lykomedes

Io Credea (from Tetide In Sciro)
see Drei Arien Der Deidamia

Lasciami Crudo Amor (from Tetide In
Sciro)
see Funf Arien Der Antiope

Lasciami Piangere (from Tetide In
Sciro)
see Scarlatti, Domenico, Vorebbe
Dal Tuo Cor

Missa Quatour Vocum *sac,Mass
(Bianchi, Lino) solo,orch sc SANTIS
1023 s.p.   (S598)

Per Credere (from Tetide In Sciro)
see Drei Arien Der Deidamia

Pur Nel Sonno Al Men Tal'ora *cant
(Bianchi, Lino) S solo,2vln,cont sc
SANTIS 1028 s.p.   (S599)

Qual Farfalletta Amante
"Ainsi Qu'un Papillon Leger" [Fr/
It] S solo,pno/inst DURAND s.p.
(S600)
Quando In Notte (from Tetide In
Sciro)
see Funf Arien Der Antiope

Salve Regina *sac,cant
S solo,2vln,vla,cont sc GERIG
AV 135 s.p., ipa   (S601)
SA soli,cont BAREN. 012-6451 $5.25
(S602)
Se Da Un Empio (from Tetide In Sciro)
see Funf Arien Der Antiope

Se Non Vedo Quei Bei Lumi (from
Tetide In Sciro)
see Zwei Arien Des Lykomedes

SCARLATTI, DOMENICO (cont'd.)

Se Vuoi D'alloro Cinger La Chioma
(from Tetide In Sciro)
see Zwei Arien Des Lykomedes

Sento L'aura (from Tetide In Sciro)
see Funf Arien Der Antiope

Sieben Arien Des Achilles (from
Tetide In Sciro) sec,CC7L
T solo,inst,cont sc FMA FMA 9 s.p.
(S603)

Vorebbe Dal Tuo Cor (from Tetide In
Sciro) sec
SSMez soli,cont FMA FMA 5 s.p.
contains also: Amando Tacendo
(SSMez soli,cont); Lasciami
Piangere (ST soli,cont)   (S604)

Zwei Arien Des Lykomedes (from Tetide
In Sciro) sec
Bar solo,vln,vla,cont sc FMA FMA 10
s.p.
contains: Impara A Compatir
L'altrui Martir; Se Non Vedo
Quei Bei Lumi; Se Vuoi D'alloro
Cinger La Chioma   (S605)

SCARS IN THE HANDS OF JESUS, THE see
Wilkin, Marijohn

SCAT see Stock, David

SCATALOGICAL SONGS AND CANONS OF
WOLFGANG AMADEUS MOZART see Mozart,
Wolfgang Amadeus

SCEK, BREDA (1893-1968)
Among The Flowers *see Med Rozami

Bori *song cycle
"Pine-Trees" solo,pno DRUSTVO
DSS 325 rental   (S606)

Hostages *see Talci

Med Rozami *song cycle
"Among The Flowers" solo,pno
DRUSTVO DSS 13 rental   (S607)

O, Vrba! *song cycle
solo,pno DRUSTVO DSS 319 rental
(S608)

Pine-Trees *see Bori

Talci *song cycle
"Hostages" solo,pno DRUSTVO DSS 339
rental   (S609)

SCEK, IVAN (1925-   )
Deset Otroskih Saljivk *CC10U
boy solo/girl solo,pno DRUSTVO
DSS 282 rental   (S610)

Tri Pesmi *CC3U
solo,pno DRUSTVO DSS 163 rental
(S611)

SCELSI, GIACINTO (1905-   )
Tre Canti *CC3U
solo,pno SANTIS 733 s.p.   (S612)

SCENA DELLA SEDUZIONE see Neglia,
Francesco Paolo

SCENA DI BERENICE see Haydn, (Franz)
Joseph

SCENA DI ELETTRA see Strauss, Richard

SCENDESTI DAL TUO TRONO see Alfano,
Franco

SCENE AND HABANERA see Bizet, Georges

SCENE BUFFA see Monteverdi, Claudio

SCENE DE L'ARRIVEE DU PRINCE see
Caryll, Ivan

SCENE DE VENUS AVEC LE CHOEUR DES
NYMPHES see Saint-Saens, Camille

SCENE ET LEGENDE see Chabrier, Emmanuel

SCENE FROM "VESTAS FEUER" see
Beethoven, Ludwig van

SCENE (HELLE ET GAUTIER) see Duvernoy,
Victor-Alphonse

SCENE I see Marietan, Pierre

SCENE OF BERENICE see Haydn, (Franz)
Joseph

SCENES AND ARIAS see Maw, Nicholas

SCENES FROM "CALISTO AND MELIBEA" see
Rosen, Jerome

SCENT OF THE CLOVER see Newton, Ernest

SCHAAP OF LEEUW see Hullebroeck, Em.

SCHAAR, AINA
Mammas Nya Visor *CCU
solo,pno GEHRMANS s.p.   (S613)

Mammas Visor *CCU
solo,pno GEHRMANS s.p.   (S614)

Sigvards Visor *CCU
solo,pno GEHRMANS s.p.   (S615)

SCHAATSENRIJDERS see Schouwman, Hans

SCHACHTENLIEFDE see Hullebroeck, Em.

SCHAFE KONNEN SICHER WEIDEN see Bach,
Johann Sebastian

SCHAFER, DIRK (1873-1931)
Lenz *Op.16,No.3
solo,pno ALSBACH s.p.   (S616)

Wenn Ich Abschied Nehme *Op.16,No.4
solo,pno ALSBACH s.p.   (S617)

Zomernacht *Op.16,No.2
solo,pno ALSBACH s.p.   (S618)

SCHAFER, M.
Five Studies On Texts By Prudentius
*CC5U
S solo,4fl BERANDOL BER 1091 $5.00
(S619)

Kinderlieder *CCU
solo,pno BERANDOL BER 1647 $5.00
(S620)

Minnelieder, Love Songs From The
Medieval German *CCU
Mez solo,5winds sc BERANDOL $10.00,
ipa   (S621)

Music For The Morning Of The World
*CCU
S solo,electronic tape BERANDOL
UE 15550 $6.00   (S622)

Requiems For The Party Girl
Mez solo,9inst BERANDOL BER 1093
$10.00   (S623)

Three Contemporaries *CC3U
solo,pno BERANDOL BER 1650 $3.50
(S624)

SCHAFERLIED see Kilpinen, Yrio

SCHAFERS SONNTAGSLIED see Weingartner,
(Paul) Felix

SCHAFFE IM MIR, GOTT, EIN REIN HERZ see
Buxtehude, Dietrich

SCHAFFE IN MIR, GOTT, EIN REIN HERZ see
Buxtehude, Dietrich

SCHAFFE IN MIR, GOTT, EIN REINES HERZ
see Schutz, Heinrich

SCHAFFEN SIE WAS GUT'S, IHR GNADEN see
Haibel, Jakob J.

SCHAFMEISTER
Three Songs *CC3U
med solo,pno SEESAW $2.00   (S625)

We Are Together
high solo,pno SEESAW $1.50   (S626)

SCHALK UND SCHERZ see Dockhorn, Lotte

SCHALKHAFT SPIELT MIT SCHLAUEN BLICKEN
see Handel, George Frideric

SCHAPORIN, JURIJ
Romanzen Und Lieder, Band I *CCU
[Russ/Fr/Eng] solo,pno SIKORSKI
R 6316 s.p.   (S627)

Romanzen Und Lieder, Band II *CCU
[Russ/Fr/Eng] solo,pno SIKORSKI
R 6339 s.p.   (S628)

SCHARESLIEP see Clercq, R. de

SCHAT, PETER (1935-   )
Canto General
Mez solo,vln,pno DONEMUS s.p.
(S629)

Cryptogamen
Bar solo,3fl,2ob,4clar,3bsn,4horn,
3trp,2trom,tuba,timp,perc,cel,
harp,strings DONEMUS s.p. (S630)

Entelechie II *CCU
Mez solo,fl,clar,trp,cel,harp,pno,
perc,vibra,vln,vla,vcl DONEMUS
s.p.   (S631)

Improvisaties Uit Het Labyrint *CCU
ATB soli,bass clar,perc,pno,bvl
DONEMUS s.p.   (S632)

Stemmen Uit Het Labyrint
ATB soli,3fl,3ob,2clar,3bsn,4horn,
3trp,3trom,2tuba,timp,perc,harp,
pno,strings, sarrusaphone DONEMUS
s.p.   (S633)

SCHAT, PETER (cont'd.)

To You
solo,kbd,gtr, electronics DONEMUS
s.p.   (S634)

SCHATTENLAND STROME see Kunad, Rainer

SCHATTIGE RUH (LARGO) see Handel,
George Frideric

SCHAUE, MALE, SINGE see Hartlieb

SCHAUSS-FLAKE, MAGDALENE (1921-   )
Jauchzet Dem Herrn, Alle Welt (Psalm
100) sac
B solo,ob,org sc HANSSLER 7.159
s.p., ipa   (S635)

Psalm 100 *see Jauchzet Dem Herrn,
Alle Welt

SCHEEL, J.G. (1879-1946)
Dormi Jesu *Op.59
solo,opt ob/vln,pno HUG s.p. (S636)

SCHEIDEN BEIDEN see Clercq, R. de

SCHEIDEN UND MEIDEN see Mahler, Gustav

SCHEIDT, SAMUEL (1587-1654)
Canzone XXVI
solo,orch HENN s.p.   (S637)

Miserere *sac
STB soli,orch sc ZERBONI 7312 s.p.
(S638)

SCHEIN, JOHANN HERMANN (1586-1630)
Christe, Der Du Bist Tag Und Licht
see Sechs Choralkonzerte

Collected Works *CCU
(Pruefer, Arthur) contains works
for a variety of instruments and
vocal combinations microfiche
UNIV.MUS.ED. $65.00 reprints of
Breitkopf & Hartel Editions;
contains 7 volumes   (S639)

Dear Christians, One And All Rejoice
*sac
high solo&low solo,pno oct
CONCORDIA 98-1863 $.25   (S640)

Drei Choralkonzerte *CC3U
(Doormann, Ludwig) SSTB soli,cont
(med easy) BAREN. 1117-6465 s.p.
(S641)

Eight Chorale Settings (from Opella
Nova) sac,CC8L
(Lenel, Ludwig) SS/TT soli,pno
CONCORDIA 97-4713 $2.25   (S642)

Ein Feste Burg
see Sechs Choralkonzerte

Erschienen Ist Der Herrlich Tag
see Sechs Choralkonzerte

From Depths Of Woe I Cry To Thee
*sac
high solo&low solo,pno oct
CONCORDIA 98-1866 $.25   (S643)

Furwahr, Er Trug Unsere Krankheit
*sac,concerto
T solo,vln,vcl,cont sc HANSSLER
5.022 s.p., ipa   (S644)

Gott Der Vater Wohn Uns Bei
see Sechs Choralkonzerte

Herr, Nun Lasst Du Deinen Diener
*sac,concerto
B solo,ob/2vln,opt inst,cont sc
HANSSLER 5.134 s.p., ipa   (S645)

Herr, Nun Lasst Du Deinen Diener Im
Frieden Fahren *sac,concerto
B solo,2vln,vcl,cont sc HANSSLER
5.134 s.p.   (S646)

Holy Redeemer *sac
high solo,vln CHANTRY VOS 662 $.75
(S647)

Ich Ruf Zu Dir
see Sechs Choralkonzerte

Mighty Fortress Is Our God, A *sac
high solo&low solo,pno oct
CONCORDIA 98-1859 $.25   (S648)

My Soul, Now Bless Thy Maker *sac
high solo&low solo,pno oct
CONCORDIA 98-1865 $.25   (S649)

O Jesu Christe, Gottes Sohn *sac,
concerto
S solo,vln,cont HANSSLER 5.097 s.p.
(S650)

O Lamb Of God, Most Holy *sac
high solo&low solo,pno oct
CONCORDIA 98-1864 $.25   (S651)

SCHEIN, JOHANN HERMANN (cont'd.)

O Lord, Look Down From Heaven *sac
high solo&low solo,pno oct
CONCORDIA 98-1860 $.25   (S652)

Salvation Now To Us Has Come *sac
high solo&low solo,pno oct
CONCORDIA 98-1861 $.25   (S653)

Sechs Choralkonzerte *sac,concerto
(Doormann, Ludwig) 2 med soli,cont
(med) BAREN. 1115 $7.00
contains: Christe, Der Du Bist
Tag Und Licht; Ein Feste Burg;
Erschienen Ist Der Herrlich
Tag; Gott Der Vater Wohn Uns
Bei; Ich Ruf Zu Dir; Vater
Unser Im Himmelreich   (S654)

Uns Ist Ein Kind Geboren *sac,Xmas,
concerto
T solo,bsn,trom,vln,cont sc
HANSSLER 5.129 s.p.   (S655)
(Trotschel, Heinrich R.) T solo,
2vln,vla,vcl,cont (med easy) sc
MULLER 2476 s.p.   (S656)

Vater Unser Im Himmelreich
see Sechs Choralkonzerte

SCHEIN UND SEIN see Sipila, Eero

SCHEIN UND SEIN see Finke, Fidelio
Fritz

SCHEINDELE *Jew
solo,pno KAMMEN 422 $1.00   (S657)

SCHEINE HELL, O SONNE see Kilpinen,
Yrio, Paista Paivanen Jumala

SCHELLE, JOHANN HERMANN (1648-1701)
Ach, Mein Herzliebes Jesulein
(Schering, A.) 2 high soli,cont voc
sc BREITKOPF-L rental   (S658)

SCHELLEKENS, G.
Herinnering
SA/TBar soli,pno ALSBACH s.p.
(S659)

SCHELLENGELAUT *folk,Russ
[Ger/Russ] solo,pno ZIMMER. 1891 s.p.
(S660)

SCHELM, HALT FEST see Weber, Carl Maria
von

SCHEMELLI SONG BOOK see Bach, Johann
Sebastian

SCHEMELLI SONG BOOK see Bach, Johann
Sebastian

SCHENELL, PER
Delsbovalsen
solo,pno,opt gtr GEHRMANS s.p.
(S661)

SCHENK MIR DEINEN GOLDNEN KAMM see
Schoenberg, Arnold

SCHERTZINGER, V.
Rose Of Erin
high solo,pno PRESSER $.75   (S662)

SCHERZANDO see Leeuw, Ton de

SCHERZI MUSICALI see Monteverdi,
Claudio

SCHERZI MUSICALI see Monteverdi,
Claudio

SCHERZI MUSICALI, HEFT I see
Monteverdi, Claudio

SCHERZI MUSICALI, HEFT II see
Monteverdi, Claudio

SCHERZO see Cimara, Pietro

SCHERZO see Respighi, Ottorino

SCHIBLER, ARMIN (1920-   )
Antworten, Bitte *Op.97
solo,2orch EULENBURG EES 466 s.p.
(S663)

Der Tod Enkidus
narrator&solo,orch EULENBURG GM 84
s.p.   (S664)

Moglichkeiten Einer Fahrt *Op.89
[Ger/Eng] narrator,pno EULENBURG
GM 39 s.p.   (S665)

Point Of Return, The
narrator&solo,inst voc sc EULENBURG
GM 63 s.p.   (S666)

SCHICKSALSLIEDER VON HOLDERLIN see
Rovsing Olsen, Paul

SCHIERBECK, POUL
Galm *Op.28,No.2
see Tre Italienske Duetter

SCHIERBECK, POUL (cont'd.)

Haxa *Op.48
[Dan/Eng] S solo,2fl,4horn,2trp,
3trom,tuba,timp,perc,cym,drums,
cel,harp,org,5strings FOG
III, 148 s.p.   (S667)

Morgen I Napoli *Op.28,No.1
see Tre Italienske Duetter

Solnedgang *Op.28,No.3
see Tre Italienske Duetter

Tre Italienske Duetter
[Dan] 2 soli,pno FOG III, 55 s.p.
contains: Galm, Op.28,No.2;
Morgen I Napoli, Op.28,No.1;
Solnedgang, Op.28,No.3   (S668)

SCHIFFERLIED see Trunk, Richard

SCHILDT, MELCHIOR (ca. 1592-1667)
Ach Mein Herzliebes Jesulein *sac,
Xmas,cant
(Breig, Werner) S solo,2vln,bsn,
cont (diff) BAREN. 2892 $5.50
(S669)

SCHILFROHR, SAUS'LE see Sibelius, Jean,
Sav, Sav Susa

SCHILLING
Psalm 150 *see Psalm 150 In Form
Einer Ciacona

Psalm 150 In Form Einer Ciacona
(Psalm 150)
S/T solo,org BREITKOPF-W EB 6445
$3.50   (S670)

SCHILLING, HANS LUDWIG (1927-   )
Singet, Preiset Gott Mit Freuden
*sac
med solo,org HANSSLER 25.003 s.p.
(S671)

SCHILLING, M. VON
Das Mitleidige Madel *Op.13,No.1
[Ger] high solo,pno BOTE $1.25
(S672)

Freude Soll In Deinen Werken Sein
*Op.16,No.1
[Ger] high solo,pno BOTE $1.25
(S673)

Julinacht *Op.2,No.2
[Ger/Fr] BOTE $1.25   (S674)

Marchen *Op.13,No.2
[Ger] high solo,pno BOTE $1.50
(S675)

Wie Wundersam *Op.2,No.3
[Ger/Fr] BOTE $1.00   (S676)

SCHILLING, OTTO-ERICH (1910-1967)
Uberall Ist Wunderland *cant
2 soli,chamb.orch/inst TONOS 7051
s.p.   (S677)

SCHIMMENSPEL see Wall, C. v.d.

SCHINDLER, GERHARD
Archaischer Totenhain
[Ger] med solo,pno SCHAUR EE 3295
$2.25   (S678)

SCHINELLI, ACHILLE (1882-   )
Canzoniere Dei Fanciulli, Vol. I:
Canti Religiosi *sac,CCU
[It] solo,pno RICORDI-ENG 120177
s.p.   (S679)

Canzoniere Dei Fanciulli, Vol. II:
Canti Patriottici *CCU
[It] solo,pno RICORDI-ENG 120172
s.p.   (S680)

Canzoniere Dei Fanciulli, Vol. III:
Canti Di Argomento Diverso *CCU
[It] solo,pno RICORDI-ENG 120173
s.p.   (S681)

Canzoniere Dei Fanciulli, Vol. IV:
Brani Di Opere Teatrali *CCU
[It] solo,pno RICORDI-ENG 120175
s.p.   (S682)

Trentacinque Canti Popolari Italiani
*CC35U
solo,pno ZERBONI 4745 s.p.   (S683)

SCHINHAN, J.P.
Fruhlingstag
solo,pno BRODT $.75   (S684)

Whither Shall I Go From Thy Spirit
solo,pno BRODT $.75   (S685)

SCHIPPER, DIRK (1912-   )
Five Songs *CC5U
high solo,pno DONEMUS s.p.   (S686)

SCHIRMER, RUDOLPH [E.] (1919-   )
Bluebird
med-high solo,pno (G maj) SCHIRM.G
$.75   (S687)

SCHIRMER, RUDOLPH [E.] (cont'd.)

Form Of Wooing
med-low solo,pno (A maj) SCHIRM.G
$.75   (S688)

Gift Of Christmas, The *sac,Xmas
med solo,pno (A flat maj) SCHIRM.G
$.75   (S689)

Honey Shun
med-low solo,pno (F maj) SCHIRM.G
$.75   (S690)

Ianthe
med-low solo,pno (A flat maj)
SCHIRM.G $.75   (S691)

Love's Secret
high solo,pno (C maj) SCHIRM.G $.60
(S692)

Lullaby
low solo,pno (A flat maj) SCHIRM.G
$.75   (S693)

My Heart Is A River
low solo,pno (C maj) SCHIRM.G $.75
(S694)

Remember Thee! Remember Thee!
med solo,pno (C maj) SCHIRM.G $.60
(S695)

So We'll Go No More A-Roving
high solo,pno (C maj) SCHIRM.G $.60   (S696)

Sound Of Laughter
med-low solo,pno (G min) SCHIRM.G
$.75   (S697)

Wanderlust
med-low solo,pno (F maj) SCHIRM.G
$.75   (S698)

SCHIRMER'S AMERICAN FOLK-SONG SERIES,
SET II (12 FOLK-SONGS FROM
LOUISIANA) *CC12L,folk,US
(Monroe, Mina) solo,pno SCHIRM.G
$2.50   (S699)

SCHIRMER'S AMERICAN FOLK-SONG SERIES,
SET XII (36 SOUTH CAROLINA
SPIRITUALS) *sac,CC36L,folk/spir,
US
(Diton, Carl) solo,pno SCHIRM.G $1.00
(S700)

SCHIRMER'S AMERICAN FOLK-SONG SERIES,
SET XIV (SONGS OF THE HILL-FOLK)
*CC12L,folk,US
(Niles, John J.) solo,pno SCHIRM.G
$1.35   (S701)

SCHIRMER'S AMERICAN FOLK-SONG SERIES,
SET XVI (TEN CHRISTMAS CAROLS FROM
THE SOUTHERN APPALACHIAN MOUNTAINS
*sac,CC10L,Xmas,carol/folk,US
(Niles, John J.) solo,pno SCHIRM.G
$1.35   (S702)

SCHIRMER'S AMERICAN FOLK-SONG SERIES,
SET XVIII (BALLADS, CAROLS, AND
TRAGIC LEGENDS FROM THE SOUTHERN
APPALACHIAN MOUNTAINS) *CC10L,
folk,US
(Niles, John J.) solo,pno SCHIRM.G
$1.25   (S703)

SCHIRMER'S AMERICAN FOLK-SONG SERIES,
SET XX (BALLADS, LOVE-SONGS AND
TRAGIC LEGENDS FROM THE SOUTHERN
APPALACHIAN MOUNTAINS) *CC10L,
folk,US
(Niles, John J.) solo,pno SCHIRM.G
$1.00   (S704)

SCHIRMER'S AMERICAN FOLK-SONG SERIES,
SET XXI (AMERICAN-ENGLISH FOLK-
SONGS FROM THE SOUTHERN APPALACHIAN
MOUNTAINS) *folk,US
(Sharp, Cecil J.) solo,pno SCHIRM.G
$1.50
contains: Come All Ye Fair And
Tender Ladies; Dear Companion,
The; False Young Man, The; Now
Once I Did Court; Rejected Lover,
The; Riddle Song, The   (S705)

SCHIRMER'S AMERICAN FOLK-SONG SERIES,
SET XXII (AMERICAN-ENGLISH FOLK-
BALLADS FROM THE SOUTHERN
APPALACHIAN MOUNTAINS) *folk,Eng/
US
(Sharp, Cecil J.) solo,pno SCHIRM.G
$1.25
contains: Cruel Brother, The;
Edward; False Knight Upon The
Road, The; Two Brothers, The;
Wife Wrapt In Wether's Skin, The;
Young Hunting   (S706)

SCHIRMER'S AMERICAN FOLK-SONG SERIES,
SET XXV (AMERICAN FOLK-SONGS FOR
YOUNG SINGERS) *CC49L,folk,US
(Matteson, Maurice) 1-3 soli,pno
(easy) SCHIRM.G $2.00   (S707)

SCHIRMER'S FAVORITE SACRED DUETS FOR
  VARIOUS VOICES *sac,CC15L
  2 soli,pno SCHIRM.G $3.00 contains
  works by: Faure; Gounod; Shelley;
  Adam and others   (S708)

SCHIRMER'S FAVORITE SECULAR DUETS FOR
  VARIOUS VOICES *CC15L
  2 soli,pno SCHIRM.G $2.50 contains
  works by: Grieg; Mozart; Offenbach;
  Schubert and others   (S709)

SCHIRRMANN, CHARLES
  Sing My Soul *sac
  high solo,pno BELWIN $1.50   (S710)
  med solo,pno BELWIN $1.50   (S711)

SCHISA, M.
  Ti Comprendo
  [It] solo,pno BONGIOVANI 2488 s.p.
                                   (S712)

SCHISKE, KARL (1916-   )
  Drei Lieder *Op.19,No.1-3, CC3U
  high solo,pno DOBLINGER 08 640 s.p.
                                   (S713)
  Zwei Lieder *Op.12,No.1-2, CC2U
  DOBLINGER 08 639 s.p. high solo,
  pno; med solo,pno   (S714)

SCHIZZO see De Angelis, Ruggero

SCHLAF EIN "MEIN BLEICHER LIEBLING SOLL
  GIESSEN" see Sibelius, Jean

SCHLAF, NUR SCHLAF see Kilpinen, Yrio,
  Tuuti, Tuuti Tummaistani

SCHLAF, SCHLAF HERZENSLIEBLING see
  Merikanto, Oskar, Pai, Pai
  Paitaressu

SCHLAF WOHL DU HIMMELSKNABEN see
  Nieland, H.

SCHLAFE, HOLDER SUSSER KNABE see
  Schubert, Franz (Peter), Wiegenlied

SCHLAFE MEIN PRINZCHEN see Flies, J.
  Bernhard

SCHLAFEN, SCHLAFEN see Trunk, Richard

SCHLAFENDES JESUSKIND see Wolf, Hugo

SCHLAFLIED see Orthel, Leon

SCHLAFLIED FUR MIRJAM see Breman, W.F.

SCHLAGE DOCH, GEWUNSCHTE STUNDE see
  Bach, Johann Sebastian

SCHLAGE DOCH, GEWUNSCHTE STUNDE see
  Hoffmann, Georg Melchoir

SCHLAGENDE HERZEN see Strauss, Richard

SCHLECHTER TROST see Busoni, Ferruccio
  Benvenuto

SCHLECHTES WETTER see Strauss, Richard

SCHLEHENBLUT' UND WILDE ROSE see
  Schumann, Georg

SCHLEISTEN FUR DEINE KLEINE ZUNGE see
  Lehnert, Josef Robert, Brousek Pro
  Tvuj Jazycek

SCHLENKER, MANFRED (1926-   )
  Wer Unter Dem Schirm Des Hochsten Ist
  *sac
  med solo,2vln/S rec,cont HANSSLER
  5.123 s.p.   (S715)

SCHLESISCHE LIEDER see Jirasek, Ivo,
  Slezske Pisne

SCHLESISCHE PERLEN see Kubin, Rudolf,
  Perly Slezske

SCHLESISCHE VOLKSLIEDER see Salich,
  Milan, Slezske Lidove Pisne

SCHLICHTE WEISEN see Strauss, Richard

SCHLICHTE WEISEN, BOOK I see Reger, Max

SCHLICHTE WEISEN, BOOK II see Reger,
  Max

SCHLICHTE WEISEN, BOOK III see Reger,
  Max

SCHLICHTE WEISEN, BOOK IV see Reger,
  Max

SCHLICHTE WEISEN, BOOK V see Reger, Max

SCHLICHTE WEISEN, BOOK VI see Reger,
  Max

SCHLICTE WEISEN see Strauss, Richard

SCHLIESSE MIR DIE AUGEN see Marx,
  Joseph

SCHLIESSE MIR DIE AUGEN BEIDE see
  Carriere, Paul

SCHLIESSE MIR DIE AUGEN BEIDE see
  Ehrenberg, Carl Emil Theodor

SCHLIESSE MIR DIE AUGEN BEIDE see Oort,
  H.C.v.

SCHLIONSKY, VERDINA
  Images Palestiniennes, Vol. II
  [Heb/Fr] med solo,pno SALABERT-US
  $3.00
  contains: Ohel Scha'h; Pastorale;
  Poeme Hebraique   (S716)

  Ohel Scha'h
  see Images Palestiniennes, Vol. II

  Pastorale
  see Images Palestiniennes, Vol. II

  Poeme Hebraique
  see Images Palestiniennes, Vol. II

SCHLITTENFAHRT see Trunk, Richard

SCHLOFLIEDLI see Lienert, O.H.

SCHLOSS, M.
  Noel *sac,Xmas
  [Lat] solo,vln,pno/org (available
  in 2 keys) ENOCH s.p.   (S717)
  [Lat] solo,acap (available in 2
  keys) ENOCH s.p.   (S718)

SCHLOSSER, PAUL
  Chant De Noel *CCU,Xmas
  solo,pno/inst cmplt ed DURAND s.p.
                                   (S719)

  Chant De Noel
  2 soli,pno DURAND s.p.   (S720)

  Crois-Moi
  solo,pno/inst DURAND s.p. see from
  Huit Poemes De M. Desbordes-
  Valmore   (S721)

  Dix Chants Pour La Jeunesse
  solo,pno/inst cmplt ed DURAND s.p.
  contains & see also: Grand-Pere;
  Labeur; Le Bouquet; Le Cerceau;
  Le De; Le Pays Natal; Le
  Rossignol; Le Volant; O! Belle
  Et Douce Nuit; Printemps (S722)

  Fierte, Pardonne-Moi
  solo,pno/inst DURAND s.p. see from
  Huit Poemes De M. Desbordes-
  Valmore   (S723)

  Grand-Pere
  solo,pno/inst solo pt DURAND s.p.
  see also Dix Chants Pour La
  Jeunesse   (S724)

  Grisonne, La Bonne Jument
  solo,pno solo pt DURAND s.p. see
  also Nos Amis De La Ferme Et Des
  Champs Vol. II   (S725)

  Huit Poemes De M. Desbordes-Valmore
  *see Crois-Moi; Fierte, Pardonne-
  Moi; Loin Du Monde; Ma Chambre;
  Mais Que Je Pleure; N'ecris Pas;
  Parle-Moi Doucement; Renoncement
                                   (S726)

  La Pimpante Libellule
  solo,pno solo pt DURAND s.p. see
  also Nos Amis De La Ferme Et Des
  Champs Vol. II   (S727)

  Labeur
  solo,pno/inst solo pt DURAND s.p.
  see also Dix Chants Pour La
  Jeunesse   (S728)

  L'ane Cadichon
  solo,pno/inst solo pt DURAND s.p.
  see also Nos Amis De La Ferme Et
  Des Champs Vol. I   (S729)

  Le Bon Chien De Garde
  solo,pno/inst solo pt DURAND s.p.
  see also Nos Amis De La Ferme Et
  Des Champs Vol. I   (S730)

  Le Bouquet
  solo,pno/inst solo pt DURAND s.p.
  see also Dix Chants Pour La
  Jeunesse   (S731)

  Le Cerceau
  solo,pno/inst solo pt DURAND s.p.
  see also Dix Chants Pour La
  Jeunesse   (S732)

  Le Coq
  solo,pno/inst solo pt DURAND s.p.
  see also Nos Amis De La Ferme Et
  Des Champs Vol. I   (S733)

  Le Crapaud
  solo,pno solo pt DURAND s.p. see
  also Nos Amis De La Ferme Et Des
  Champs Vol. II   (S734)

SCHLOSSER, PAUL (cont'd.)
  Le De
  solo,pno/inst solo pt DURAND s.p.
  see also Dix Chants Pour La
  Jeunesse   (S735)

  Le Pays Natal
  solo,pno/inst solo pt DURAND s.p.
  see also Dix Chants Pour La
  Jeunesse   (S736)

  Le Petit Escargot De Vigne
  solo,pno/inst solo pt DURAND s.p.
  see also Nos Amis De La Ferme Et
  Des Champs Vol. I   (S737)

  Le Petit Goret
  solo,pno solo pt DURAND s.p. see
  also Nos Amis De La Ferme Et Des
  Champs Vol. II   (S738)

  Le Petit Poney
  solo,pno/inst solo pt DURAND s.p.
  see also Nos Amis De La Ferme Et
  Des Champs Vol. I   (S739)

  Le Rossignol
  solo,pno/inst solo pt DURAND s.p.
  see also Dix Chants Pour La
  Jeunesse   (S740)

  Le Volant
  solo,pno/inst solo pt DURAND s.p.
  see also Dix Chants Pour La
  Jeunesse   (S741)

  Les Abeilles De Grand-Mere
  solo,pno/inst solo pt DURAND s.p.
  see also Nos Amis De La Ferme Et
  Des Champs Vol. I   (S742)

  Les Canetons
  solo,pno/inst solo pt DURAND s.p.
  see also Nos Amis De La Ferme Et
  Des Champs Vol. I   (S743)

  Les Deux Grenouilles
  solo,pno/inst solo pt DURAND s.p.
  see also Nos Amis De La Ferme Et
  Des Champs Vol. I   (S744)

  Les Dindons Noirs
  solo,pno solo pt DURAND s.p. see
  also Nos Amis De La Ferme Et Des
  Champs Vol. II   (S745)

  Les Fourmis
  solo,pno/inst solo pt DURAND s.p.
  see also Nos Amis De La Ferme Et
  Des Champs Vol. I   (S746)

  Les Oies
  solo,pno solo pt DURAND s.p. see
  also Nos Amis De La Ferme Et Des
  Champs Vol. II   (S747)

  Les Petits Moutons
  solo,pno solo pt DURAND s.p. see
  also Nos Amis De La Ferme Et Des
  Champs Vol. II   (S748)

  Les Pigeons
  solo,pno solo pt DURAND s.p. see
  also Nos Amis De La Ferme Et Des
  Champs Vol. II   (S749)

  Les Poussins
  solo,pno/inst solo pt DURAND s.p.
  see also Nos Amis De La Ferme Et
  Des Champs Vol. I   (S750)

  Les Quatre Petits Lapins
  solo,pno/inst solo pt DURAND s.p.
  see also Nos Amis De La Ferme Et
  Des Champs Vol. I   (S751)

  Loin Du Monde
  solo,pno/inst DURAND s.p. see from
  Huit Poemes De M. Desbordes-
  Valmore   (S752)

  Ma Chambre
  solo,pno/inst DURAND s.p. see from
  Huit Poemes De M. Desbordes-
  Valmore   (S753)

  Ma Chevre Blanchette
  solo,pno solo pt DURAND s.p. see
  also Nos Amis De La Ferme Et Des
  Champs Vol. II   (S754)

  Mais Que Je Pleure
  solo,pno/inst DURAND s.p. see from
  Huit Poemes De M. Desbordes-
  Valmore   (S755)

  Mon Grand-Pere Avait Trois Chats
  solo,pno/inst solo pt DURAND s.p.
  see also Nos Amis De La Ferme Et
  Des Champs Vol. I   (S756)

  N'ecris Pas
  solo,pno/inst DURAND s.p. see from
  Huit Poemes De M. Desbordes-
  Valmore   (S757)

SCHLOSSER, PAUL (cont'd.)

Nos Amis De La Ferme Et Des Champs
Vol. I
solo,pno/inst cmplt ed DURAND s.p.
contains & see also: L'ane
Cadichon; Le Bon Chien De
Garde; Le Coq; Le Petit
Escargot De Vigne; Le Petit
Poney; Les Abeilles De Grand-
Mere; Les Canetons; Les Deux
Grenouilles; Les Fourmis; Les
Poussins; Les Quatre Petits
Lapins; Mon Grand-Pere Avait
Trois Chats   (S758)

Nos Amis De La Ferme Et Des Champs
Vol. II
solo,pno cmplt ed DURAND s.p.
contains & see also: Grisonne, La
Bonne Jument; La Pimpante
Libellule; Le Crapaud; Le Petit
Goret; Les Dindons Noirs; Les
Oies; Les Petits Moutons; Les
Pigeons; Ma Chevre Blanchette;
Papillons, Volez!; Roussotte,
La Bonne Laitiere; Saute,
Sauterelle!   (S759)

O! Belle Et Douce Nuit
solo,pno/inst solo pt DURAND s.p.
see also Dix Chants Pour La
Jeunesse   (S760)

Papillons, Volez!
solo,pno solo pt DURAND s.p. see
also Nos Amis De La Ferme Et Des
Champs Vol. II   (S761)

Parle-Moi Doucement
solo,pno/inst DURAND s.p. see from
Huit Poemes De M. Desbordes-
Valmore   (S762)

Pour La Fete Des Meres
solo,pno/inst DURAND s.p.   (S763)

Printemps
solo,pno/inst solo pt DURAND s.p.
see also Dix Chants Pour La
Jeunesse   (S764)

Renoncement
solo,pno/inst DURAND s.p. see from
Huit Poemes De M. Desbordes-
Valmore   (S765)

Roussotte, La Bonne Laitiere
solo,pno solo pt DURAND s.p. see
also Nos Amis De La Ferme Et Des
Champs Vol. II   (S766)

Saute, Sauterelle!
solo,pno solo pt DURAND s.p. see
also Nos Amis De La Ferme Et Des
Champs Vol. II   (S767)

SCHLOTTMANN, LOUIS (1826-1905)
Skon Gertrud
high solo,pno GEHRMANS s.p.   (S768)
low solo,pno GEHRMANS s.p.   (S769)

SCHLUMMERLIED see Hengeveld, G.

SCHLUMMERLIED see Kuhn, Siegfried

SCHLUMMERLIED see Reger, Max

SCHLUMMRE LEIS UND LIND, DU BAUERNKIND
see Mussorgsky, Modest

SCHLUPFWINKEL see LaForge, Frank

SCHLUSZSTUCK see Koetsier, Jan

SCHMALE, TOBE, LIEBER JUNGE see Mozart,
Wolfgang Amadeus, Batti, Batti, O
Bel Masetto

SCHMALER MOND see Borris, Siegfried

SCHMALSTICH, CLEMENS
Abschied *Op.88,No.1
see Der Liebesgarten

An Die Sonne *Op.46,No.2
med solo,2fl,2ob,2clar,2bsn,4horn,
2trp,2trom,tuba,timp,perc,harp,
strings BIRNBACH sc rental, voc
sc s.p.   (S770)

Das Pfand *Op.88,No.4
see Der Liebesgarten

Der Liebesgarten
solo,2fl,ob,2clar,bsn,2horn,harp,
strings BIRNBACH sc rental, voc
sc s.p.
contains: Abschied, Op.88,No.1;
Das Pfand, Op.88,No.4;
Liebeslied, Op.88,No.2; Mein
Madel Hat Zwei Auglein Braun,
Op.88,No.3; Was Ich Hab',
Op.88,No.6; Wenn Ich Dich
Frag', Op.88,No.5   (S771)

SCHMALSTICH, CLEMENS (cont'd.)

Dorine *Op.84,No.2
coloratura sop,fl,harp,perc,strings
BIRNBACH sc rental, voc sc s.p.
                               (S772)

Du Gibst Die Liebe Hin *Op.36,No.2
solo,2fl,2ob,2clar,2bsn,4horn,2trp,
trom,timp,perc,harp,strings
BIRNBACH sc rental, voc sc s.p.
                               (S773)

Gedenken *Op.30,No.2
high solo,2fl,ob,2clar,bsn,2horn,
2trp,trom,timp,perc,harp,strings
BIRNBACH sc rental, voc sc s.p.
                               (S774)

Liebeslied *Op.88,No.2
see Der Liebesgarten

Mein Madel Hat Zwei Auglein Braun
*Op.88,No.3
see Der Liebesgarten

Nacht *Op.46,No.1
solo,2fl,2ob,2clar,2bsn,4horn,2trp,
timp,harp,strings BIRNBACH sc
rental, voc sc s.p.   (S775)

Spielmannsart *Op.73,No.3
solo,2fl,ob,2clar,2bsn,2horn,2trp,
trom,timp,perc,harp,strings
BIRNBACH sc rental, voc sc s.p.
                               (S776)

Trinkspruch *Op.17,No.1
high solo/low solo,2fl,ob,2clar,
bsn,4horn,2trp,3trom,timp,perc,
harp,strings BIRNBACH sc rental,
voc sc s.p.   (S777)

Was Ich Hab' *Op.88,No.6
see Der Liebesgarten

Wenn Ich Dich Frag' *Op.88,No.5
see Der Liebesgarten

SCHMALZ, PAUL (1904-   )
Berner Mundartliedli *CCU
solo,pno HUG s.p.   (S778)

Buzzelis Liedlein *CCU
solo,pno HUG s.p.   (S779)

Der Kleine Mozart
solo,pno HUG s.p.   (S780)

SCHMENDRIK IS A KNIAKER *Jew
solo,pno KAMMEN 65 $1.00   (S781)

SCHMERZEN see Wagner, Richard

SCHMID, REINHOLD (1902-   )
Die Zehn Neuen Fiedellieder, Heft 1
*song cycle
Bar solo,pno DOBLINGER 08 607 $1.50
                               (S782)
Die Zehn Neuen Fiedellieder, Heft 2
*song cycle
Bar solo,pno DOBLINGER 08 608 $1.50
                               (S783)
Die Zehn Neuen Fiedellieder, Heft 3
*song cycle
Bar solo,pno DOBLINGER 08 609 $1.50
                               (S784)

Requiem *song cycle
A/Bar solo,pno DOBLINGER 08 610
s.p.   (S785)

Zehn Madchenlieder Nach Ukrainischen
Volksweisen *CC10U
S solo,ob,pno DOBLINGER 08 813 s.p.
                               (S786)

SCHMIDT
Beast, The
narrator,pno WESTERN AV186 $3.00
                               (S787)

Ludus Americanus *song cycle
narrator,perc WESTERN AV182 $2.50
                               (S788)

SCHMIDT, HUGO WOLFRAM (1903-   )
Rheinische Lieder Und Tanze *CCU
solo,fl,ob,clar,S rec,A rec,horn,
2trp,trom,glock/xylo,triangle/
tamb,drums,acord/gtr,2vln,vcl,bvl
sc GERIG HG 266 s.p., ipa   (S789)

SCHMIED SCHMERZ see Bordewijk-Roepman,
Johanna

SCHMIED SCHMERZ see Bosmans, Henriette

SCHMIER, J.
Tantum Ergo Genitori *sac
solo,org ALSBACH s.p.   (S790)

SCHMILZ, O HARTER SINN see Handel,
George Frideric

SCHMIT, CAMILLE (1908-   )
La Halte Des Heures *cant
A/Bar solo,pno CBDM s.p.   (S791)

Psaume De La Danse
see Psautier
med solo,pno CBDM s.p.   (S792)

SCHMIT, CAMILLE (cont'd.)

Psaume De La Nuit
see Psautier

Psaume Du Torrent
see Psautier

Psautier
cmplt ed CBDM s.p.
contains: Psaume De La Danse (med
solo,pno); Psaume De La Nuit
(med solo,ob/English horn,pno);
Psaume Du Torrent (med solo,
clar,bsn,pno)   (S793)

SCHMITT, FLORENT (1870-1958)
A Contre-Voix
SATB soli,acap cmplt ed DURAND s.p.
contains: Bonnet Vole; L'Arche De
Noe; Pour Vous De Peine; Retour
A La Terre; Si Mes Poches;
Trois Goelettes   (S794)

Antennes *Op.115,No.3
see Quatre Monocantes

Ballade Pour La Paix *Op.136,No.2
see Trois Duos

Bonnet Vole
see A Contre-Voix

C'est L'heure *Op.118,No.3
see Trois Poemes De R. Ganzo

Chanson De La Nourrice (from Le Petit
Elfe Ferme L'oeil)
solo,pno/inst DURAND s.p.   (S795)

De Pleurs S'egrene *Op.118,No.1
see Trois Poemes De R. Ganzo

D'un Mille-Pattes Amoureux
SMezA soli,orch solo pt DURAND s.p.
see also Trois Trios   (S796)

Elle Etait Venne *Op.98,No.1
solo,pno/inst DURAND s.p. see from
Trois Chants   (S797)

Eloge Des Chapons *Op.136,No.3
see Trois Duos

En Bonnes Voix
3 soli/3 female soli/3 male soli,
acap cmplt ed DURAND s.p.
contains: La Mode Commode, Op.91,
No.6; La Mort Du Rossignol,
Op.91,No.5; Le Passant De
Passy, Op.91,No.3; On Dist Que,
Op.91,No.1; Prince Et Bergere,
Op.91,No.2; Tournez S'il Vous
Plait, Op.91,No.4   (S798)

Fils De La Vierge *Op.4,No.3
"Virgin's Threads, The" see Trois
Melodies
Mez/Bar solo,pno/inst DURAND s.p.
                               (S799)

Il Pleure Dans Mon Coeur *Op.4,No.2
"Tears Falling In My Heart" see
Trois Melodies
Mez/Bar solo,pno/inst DURAND s.p.
                               (S800)

Invocation Pour Le Fete D'Aristote
*Op.71,No.1
Bar solo,orch DURAND s.p., ipr see
from Trois Chants En L'honneur
D'Auguste Comte   (S801)

Kerob-Shal *see Octroi, Op.67,No.1;
Star, Op.67,No.2; Vendredi XIII,
Op.67,No.3   (S802)

La Citerne Des Mille Colonnes
*Op.98,No.2
solo,pno/inst DURAND s.p. see from
Trois Chants   (S803)

La Mode Commode *Op.91,No.6
see En Bonnes Voix

La Mort Du Rossignol *Op.91,No.5
see En Bonnes Voix

La Petite Princesse *Op.115,No.2
see Quatre Monocantes

La Tortue Et Le Lievre *Op.98,No.3
solo,pno/inst DURAND s.p. see from
Trois Chants   (S804)

L'Arche De Noe
see A Contre-Voix

Le Cersier *Op.115,No.4
see Quatre Monocantes

Le Passant De Passy *Op.91,No.3
see En Bonnes Voix

Le Soir, Qu'Amour
solo,pno/inst DURAND s.p. see from
Quatre Poemes De Ronsard   (S805)

SCHMITT, FLORENT (cont'd.)

Leid
Mez/Bar solo,pno/inst DURAND s.p.
(S806)

Les Diners Se Font En Courant
*Op.118,No.2
see Trois Poemes De R. Ganzo

Les Tambours Qui Parlent
SMezA soli,orch solo pt DURAND s.p.
see also Trois Trios (S807)

L'escarpolette *Op.136,No.1
see Trois Duos

L'etang
SMezA soli,orch solo pt DURAND s.p.
see also Trois Trios (S808)

Lied *Op.4,No.1
see Trois Melodies

Musique Sur L'eau
med solo,pno/orch SALABERT-US
$4.00, ipr (S809)

Octroi *Op.67,No.1
solo,orch DURAND s.p., ipr see from
Kerob-Shal (S810)

On Dist Que *Op.91,No.1
see En Bonnes Voix

Pour Vous De Peine
see A Contre-Voix

Prince Et Bergere *Op.91,No.2
see En Bonnes Voix

Prise Aux Reseaux D'Or *Op.115,No.1
see Quatre Monocantes

Privileges
solo,pno/inst DURAND s.p. see from
Quatre Poemes De Ronsard (S811)

Quatre Monocantes
solo,pno/inst cmplt ed DURAND s.p.
contains: Antennes, Op.115,No.3;
La Petite Princesse, Op.115,
No.2; Le Cersier, Op.115,No.4;
Prise Aux Reseaux D'Or, Op.115,
No.1 (S812)

Quatre Poemes De Ronsard *see Le
Soir, Qu'Amour; Privileges; Ses
Deux Yeux; Si (S813)

Retour A La Terre
see A Contre-Voix

Ses Deux Yeux
solo,pno/inst DURAND s.p. see from
Quatre Poemes De Ronsard (S814)

Si
solo,pno/inst DURAND s.p. see from
Quatre Poemes De Ronsard (S815)

Si Mes Poches
see A Contre-Voix

Star *Op.67,No.2
solo,orch DURAND s.p., ipr see from
Kerob-Shal (S816)

Tears Falling In My Heart *see Il
Pleure Dans Mon Coeur

Tournez S'il Vous Plait *Op.91,No.4
see En Bonnes Voix

Trois Chants *see Elle Etait Venne,
Op.98,No.1; La Citerne Des Mille
Colonnes, Op.98,No.2; La Tortue
Et Le Lievre, Op.98,No.3 (S817)

Trois Chants En L'honneur D'Auguste
Comte *see Invocation Pour Le
Fete D'Aristote, Op.71,No.1
(S818)

Trois Duos
cmplt ed DURAND s.p.
contains: Ballade Pour La Paix,
Op.136,No.2; Eloge Des Chapons,
Op.136,No.3; L'escarpolette,
Op.136,No.1 (S819)

Trois Goelettes
see A Contre-Voix

Trois Melodies
[Fr/Eng] solo,pno/inst cmplt ed
DURAND s.p.
contains: Fils De La Vierge,
"Virgin's Threads, The", Op.4,
No.3; Il Pleure Dans Mon Coeur,
"Tears Falling In My Heart",
Op.4,No.2; Lied, Op.4,No.1
(S820)

Trois Poemes De R. Ganzo
solo,pno/inst cmplt ed DURAND s.p.
contains: C'est L'heure, Op.118,
No.3; De Pleurs S'egrene,
Op.118,No.1; Les Diners Se Font

SCHMITT, FLORENT (cont'd.)

En Courant, Op.118,No.2 (S821)

Trois Trios
SMezA soli,orch cmplt ed DURAND
s.p., ipr
contains & see also: D'un Mille-
Pattes Amoureux; Les Tambours
Qui Parlent; L'etang (S822)

Vendredi XIII *Op.67,No.3
solo,orch DURAND s.p., ipr see from
Kerob-Shal (S823)

Virgin's Threads, The *see Fils De
La Vierge

SCHMUCKET DAS FEST see Raphael, Gunther

SCHNEEFLOCKCHEN see Gretchaninov,
Alexander Tikhonovitch

SCHNEEGESTOBER *folk,Russ
[Ger/Russ] solo,pno ZIMMER. 1886 s.p.
(S824)

SCHNEEWALZER see Schriebl, Karl

SCHNEEWEISS, JAN (1904-)
Dvanact Lidovych Pisni Z Holesovska
*CCU
solo,pno PANTON 1304 s.p. (S825)

SCHNEEWITTCHEN see Kuiler, Cor.

SCHNEEWITTCHEN UND ANDERE KINDERLIEDER
see Haegi, A.

SCHNEIDER-TRNAVSKY, MIKULAS (1881-1958)
Drobne Kvety
solo,pno SLOV.HUD.FOND s.p. (S826)

Slovenske Narodne Piesne I-V *CCU
solo,pno SLOV.HUD.FOND s.p., ea.
(S827)

Slzy A Usemevy
solo,pno SLOV.HUD.FOND s.p. (S828)

Wiegenlied
[Ger/Slav] solo,pno SUPRAPHON s.p.
(S829)

Zo Srdca
solo,pno SLOV.HUD.FOND s.p. (S830)

SCHNITTERLIED see Gilse, Jan van

SCHNITTERLIED see Trunk, Richard

SCHNYDER VON WARTENSEE, XAVER
(1797-1843)
Sechs Lieder Nach Gedichten Von L.
Uhland *CC6U
solo,pno HUG s.p. (S831)

SCHOECK, OTHMAR (1886-1957)
Ausgewahlte Lieder Und Gesange Band I
*CC9L
[Ger/Fr/Eng] $3.50 high solo,pno
BREITKOPF-L EB 5291A; med solo,
pno BREITKOPF-L EB 5291B; low
solo,pno BREITKOPF-L EB 5291C
(S832)
Ausgewahlte Lieder Und Gesange Band
II *CC10L
[Ger/Fr/Eng] $3.50 high solo,pno
BREITKOPF-L EB 5292A; med solo,
pno BREITKOPF-L EB 5292B; low
solo,pno BREITKOPF-L EB 5292C
(S833)
Ausgewahlte Lieder Und Gesange Band
III *CC9L
[Ger/Fr/Eng] $3.50 high solo,pno
BREITKOPF-L EB 5293A; med solo,
pno BREITKOPF-L EB 5293B; low
solo,pno BREITKOPF-L EB 5293C
(S834)
Befreite Sehnsucht *Op.66
solo,pno HUG s.p. (S835)

Das Holde Bescheiden, Op. 62, Part I
*song cycle
solo,pno UNIVER. 12381 $10.00
(S836)
Das Holde Bescheiden, Op. 62, Part II
*song cycle
solo,pno UNIVER. 12382 $10.00
(S837)
Das Stille Leuchten *Op.60, song
cycle
med solo,pno UNIVER. 11834 $6.75
(S838)
Das Wandsbeker Liederbuch *Op.52,
song cycle
med solo,pno UNIVER. 10981 $7.50
(S839)
Der Gott Und Die Bajadere *Op.34
(from Boris Godunov)
(David, K.H.) Bar/B solo,3fl,3ob,
3clar,3bsn,4horn,3trp,3trom,tuba,
perc,timp,harp,cel,org,strings
voc sc BREITKOPF-L EB 5203 $5.00,
ipr (S840)

Der Sanger, Op. 57, Part I *song
cycle
high solo,pno UNIVER. 11832 $6.75

SCHOECK, OTHMAR (cont'd.)

(S841)
Der Sanger, Op. 57, Part II *song
cycle
high solo,pno UNIVER. 11833 $6.75
(S842)
Drei Lieder *CC3U
1-2 soli,pno HUG s.p. (S843)

Elegie (from Boris Godunov) CC24L
[Ger/Fr] Bar/B solo,fl,ob,2clar,
horn,timp,perc,pno,strings study
sc BREITKOPF-L PB 2658 s.p., ipr,
voc sc BREITKOPF-L EB 5247 $8.00
(S844)
Gaselen *Op.38 (from Boris Godunov)
CCU
Bar solo,fl,ob,bass clar,trp,perc,
pno voc sc BREITKOPF-L 5264
$5.25, sc BREITKOPF-L rental
(S845)
Im Nebel
solo,pno BREITKOPF-W EB 6503 s.p.
(S846)
Lebendig Begraben *Op.40, CC14U
Mez/Bar solo,2fl,2ob,3clar,3bsn,
4horn,2trp,3trom,tuba,timp,perc,
xylo,cel,harp,strings,org,pno voc
sc BREITKOPF-L EB 5428 $7.50, ipr
(S847)
Lieder *Op.14b, CCU
[Ger] solo,pno BREITKOPF-L EB 5027
rental (S848)
Lieder Aus Dem Westostlichen Diwan
Von Goethe *Op.19b, CCU
solo,pno BREITKOPF-W EB 6866 $3.25
(S849)
Lieder Nach Gedichten Von Goethe
*Op.19a, CCU
solo,pno BREITKOPF-W EB 6865 s.p.
(S850)
Lieder Nach Gedichten Von Lenau,
Hebbel, Dehmel Und Spitteler
*CCU
med-high solo,pno BREITKOPF-W
EB 6867 $3.00 (S851)
Lieder Nach Gedichten Von Spitteler,
Gamper, Hesse Und Keller *CCU
high solo,pno BREITKOPF-W EB 6868
$5.25 (S852)
Lieder Nach Gedichten Von Uhland Und
Eichendorff *CC14U
med solo,pno BREITKOPF-W EB 5026
$4.50 (S853)
Liederalbum, Band 1-3 *CCU
solo,pno HUG s.p. (S854)

Nachhall
med solo,pno UNIVER. 12525 $6.75
(S855)
Notturno *Op.47
Bar solo,4strings voc sc UNIVER.
13841 $11.00 (S856)
Bar solo,4strings sc UNIVER. 10575
$6.25, ipa (S857)
Reiselied *Op.12,No.1
med solo,pno HUG s.p. (S858)
high solo,pno HUG s.p. (S859)

Spielmannsweisen *song cycle
high solo,harp/pno UNIVER. 11693
$4.75 (S860)
Unter Sternen, Op. 54, Part I *CCU
med solo,pno UNIVER. 11498 $6.75
(S861)
Unter Sternen, Op. 54, Part II *CCU
med solo,pno UNIVER. 11499 $6.75
(S862)
Vom Fischer Un Syner Fru *Op.43,
cant
STB soli,2fl,2ob,2clar,3bsn,3horn,
trp,trom,timp,perc,strings,pno sc
BREITKOPF-L PB 3460 s.p. (S863)
Wanderspruche *Op.42, CCU
S/T solo,clar,horn,perc,pno voc sc
BREITKOPF-L EB 6882 $5.75, ipr
(S864)
Wanderung Im Gebirge *Op.45
solo,pno HUG s.p. (S865)

Zehn Lieder Nach Gedichten Von
Hermann Hesse *CC10U
solo,pno BREITKOPF-W EB 5509 s.p.
(S866)
Zwolf Eichendorff-Lieder *Op.30,
CC12U
low solo,pno BREITKOPF-W EB 5201
$3.00 (S867)
Zwolf Hafis-Lieder *Op.33, CC12U
med solo,pno BREITKOPF-W EB 5024
$4.50 (S868)

SCHOEMAKER, MAURICE (1890-1964)
Bonheur Impossible
med solo,pno CBDM s.p. (S869)

SCHOEMAKER, MAURICE (cont'd.)

Mere *CC7L
  med solo,pno cmplt ed CBDM s.p.
                                    (S870)

Suite Sylvestre *CC7L
  med solo,pno cmplt ed CBDM s.p.
                                    (S871)

SCHOENBACH, D.
  Canticum Psalmi Resurrectionis
  S solo,6inst,perc sc,oct UNIVER.
  13061 $5.25   (S872)

  Lyric Songs II *CCU
  [Ger] Mez solo,2pno PETERS 5974
  $12.00   (S873)

SCHOENBERG, ARNOLD (1874-1951)
  Abschied *Op.1,No.2
  Bar solo,pno UNIVER. 3651 $3.00 see
    from Zwei Lieder   (S874)
  solo,pno voc sc BIRNBACH s.p. see
    from Zwei Gesange   (S875)

  Acht Lieder *see Alles, Op.6,No.2;
    Am Wegrand, Op.6,No.6; Der
    Wanderer, Op.6,No.8; Ghasel,
    Op.6,No.5; Lockung, Op.6,No.7;
    Madchenlied, Op.6,No.3;
    Traumleben, Op.6,No.1; Verlassen,
    Op.6,No.4   (S876)

  Acht Lieder *see Alles, Op.6,No.2;
    Am Wegrand, Op.6,No.6; Der
    Wanderer, Op.6,No.8; Ghasel,
    Op.6,No.5; Lockung, Op.6,No.7;
    Madchenlied, Op.6,No.3;
    Traumleben, Op.6,No.1; Verlassen,
    Op.6,No.4   (S877)

  Alles *Op.6,No.2
  solo,pno voc sc BIRNBACH s.p. see
    from Acht Lieder   (S878)
  high solo,pno UNIVER. 3613 $2.75
    see from Acht Lieder   (S879)

  Am Wegrand *Op.6,No.6
  high solo,pno UNIVER. 3617 $2.75
    see from Acht Lieder   (S880)
  solo,pno voc sc BIRNBACH s.p. see
    from Acht Lieder   (S881)

  Dank *Op.1,No.1
  solo,pno voc sc BIRNBACH s.p. see
    from Zwei Gesange   (S882)
  Bar solo,pno UNIVER. 3650 $3.00 see
    from Zwei Lieder   (S883)

  Das Wappenschild *Op.8,No.2
  high solo,orch UNIVER. 3042 $3.50
    see also Sechs Orchesterlieder
                                    (S884)

  Der Mai Tritt Ein Mit Freuden
  see Four German Folk Songs

  Der Verlorene Haufen *Op.12,No.2
  Bar solo,pno UNIVER. 6208 $3.75 see
    from Zwei Balladen   (S885)

  Der Wanderer *Op.6,No.8
  solo,pno voc sc BIRNBACH s.p. see
    from Acht Lieder   (S886)
  high solo,pno UNIVER. 3619 $2.75
    see from Acht Lieder   (S887)

  Die Aufgeregten *Op.3,No.2
  med solo,pno UNIVER. 3657 $3.00 see
    from Sechs Lieder   (S888)
  solo,pno voc sc BIRNBACH s.p. see
    from Sechs Lieder   (S889)

  Du Wunderschone Tove
  med solo,pno UNIVER. 5332 $3.75 see
    from Gurrelieder   (S890)

  Entruckung (from String Quartet, No
    2, Op. 10)
  S solo,4strings UNIVER. 6863 $3.25
                                    (S891)

  Erhebung *Op.2,No.3
  solo,pno voc sc BIRNBACH s.p. see
    from Vier Lieder   (S892)

  Erwartung *Op.2,No.1
  solo,pno voc sc BIRNBACH s.p. see
    from Vier Lieder   (S893)

  Es Gingen Zwei Gespielen Gut
  see Four German Folk Songs

  Four German Folk Songs
  [Ger] solo,pno PETERS 4826 $3.25
    contains: Der Mai Tritt Ein Mit
    Freuden; Es Gingen Zwei
    Gespielen Gut; Mein Herz In
    Steten Treuen; Mein Herz Ist
    Mir Gemenget   (S894)

  Freihold *Op.3,No.6
  med solo,pno UNIVER. 3661 $3.00 see
    from Sechs Lieder   (S895)
  solo,pno voc sc BIRNBACH s.p. see
    from Sechs Lieder   (S896)

SCHOENBERG, ARNOLD (cont'd.)

  Funfzehn Gedichte Aus "Buch Der
    Hangenden Garten" *Op.15,No.1-
    15, CC15U
  [Ger/Fr] high solo,pno UNIVER. 5338
  $8.00   (S897)

  Geubtes Herz *Op.3,No.5
  med solo,pno UNIVER. 3660 $3.00 see
    from Sechs Lieder   (S898)
  solo,pno voc sc BIRNBACH s.p. see
    from Sechs Lieder   (S899)

  Ghasel *Op.6,No.5
  high solo,pno UNIVER. 3616 $2.75
    see from Acht Lieder   (S900)
  solo,pno voc sc BIRNBACH s.p. see
    from Acht Lieder   (S901)

  Gurrelieder *see Du Wunderschone
    Tove; Lied Der Waldtaube; Nun
    Sag' Ich Dir; So Tanzen Die Engel
                                    (S902)

  Herzgewachse *Op.20
  S solo,cel,harmonium,harp UNIVER.
  7927 $3.25   (S903)
  S solo,cel,harmonium,harp sc
  UNIVER. 6209 $5.25, voc sc
  UNIVER. 7927 $3.25   (S904)

  Hochzeitslied *Op.3,No.4
  med solo,pno UNIVER. 3659 $3.00 see
    from Sechs Lieder   (S905)
  solo,pno voc sc BIRNBACH s.p. see
    from Sechs Lieder   (S906)

  Ich Darf Nicht *Op.14,No.1
  med solo,pno UNIVER. 6205 $3.75 see
    from Zwei Lieder   (S907)

  In Diesen Wintertagen *Op.14,No.2
  high solo,pno UNIVER. 6206 $3.75
    see from Zwei Lieder   (S908)

  Jane Grey *Op.12,No.1
  high solo,pno UNIVER. 6207 $3.75
    see from Zwei Balladen   (S909)

  Lied Der Waldtaube
  med solo,pno UNIVER. 5333 $3.75 see
    from Gurrelieder   (S910)

  Litanei (from String Quartet, No. 2,
    Op. 10)
  S solo,4strings UNIVER. 6862 $3.25
                                    (S911)

  Lockung *Op.6,No.7
  solo,pno voc sc BIRNBACH s.p. see
    from Acht Lieder   (S912)
  high solo,pno UNIVER. 3618 $2.75
    see from Acht Lieder   (S913)

  Mach Mich Zum Wachter *Op.22,No.3
  see Vier Orchesterlieder

  Madchenlied *Op.6,No.3
  high solo,pno UNIVER. 3614 $2.75
    see from Acht Lieder   (S914)
  solo,pno voc sc BIRNBACH s.p. see
    from Acht Lieder   (S915)

  Mein Herz In Steten Treuen
  see Four German Folk Songs

  Mein Herz Ist Mir Gemenget
  see Four German Folk Songs

  Nachtwandler
  S solo,pic,trp,pno UNIVER. 15167
  $35.50   (S916)

  Natur *Op.8,No.1
  med solo,orch UNIVER. 3041 $3.50
    see also Sechs Orchesterlieder
                                    (S917)

  Nie Ward Ich *Op.8,No.4
  high solo,orch UNIVER. 3044 $3.50
    see also Sechs Orchesterlieder
                                    (S918)

  Nun Sag' Ich Dir
  med solo,pno UNIVER. 5331 $3.75 see
    from Gurrelieder   (S919)

  Schenk Mir Deinen Goldnen Kamm
    *Op.2,No.2
  solo,pno voc sc BIRNBACH s.p. see
    from Vier Lieder   (S920)

  Sechs Lieder *see Die Aufgeregten,
    Op.3,No.2; Freihold, Op.3,No.6;
    Geubtes Herz, Op.3,No.5;
    Hochzeitslied, Op.3,No.4;
    Warnung, Op.3,No.3; Wunderhorn,
    Op.3,No.1   (S921)

  Sechs Lieder *see Die Aufgeregten,
    Op.3,No.2; Freihold, Op.3,No.6;
    Geubtes Herz, Op.3,No.5;
    Hochzeitslied, Op.3,No.4;
    Warnung, Op.3,No.3; Wie Georg Von
    Frundsberg Von Sich Selber Sang,
    Op.3,No.1   (S922)

SCHOENBERG, ARNOLD (cont'd.)

  Sechs Orchesterlieder *Op.8,No.1-6
  cmplt ed UNIVER. 13540 $7.75
    contains & see also: Das
    Wappenschild, Op.8,No.2; Natur,
    Op.8,No.1; Nie Ward Ich, Op.8,
    No.4; Sehnsucht, Op.8,No.3;
    Voll Jener Susse, Op.8,No.5;
    Wenn Voglein Klagen, Op.8,No.6
                                    (S923)

  Sehnsucht *Op.8,No.3
  high solo,orch UNIVER. 3043 $3.50
    see also Sechs Orchesterlieder
                                    (S924)

  Seraphita *Op.22,No.1
  see Vier Orchesterlieder

  So Tanzen Die Engel
  med solo,pno UNIVER. 5330 $3.75 see
    from Gurrelieder   (S925)

  Three Songs *Op.48, CC3U
  [Ger] low solo,pno BOMART $3.00
                                    (S926)

  Traumleben *Op.6,No.1
  solo,pno voc sc BIRNBACH s.p. see
    from Acht Lieder   (S927)
  med solo,pno UNIVER. 3612 $2.75 see
    from Acht Lieder   (S928)

  Verlassen *Op.6,No.4
  med solo,pno UNIVER. 3615 $2.75 see
    from Acht Lieder   (S929)
  solo,pno voc sc BIRNBACH s.p. see
    from Acht Lieder   (S930)

  Vier Lieder *see Erhebung, Op.2,
    No.3; Erwartung, Op.2,No.1;
    Schenk Mir Deinen Goldnen Kamm,
    Op.2,No.2; Waldsonne, Op.2,No.4
                                    (S931)

  Vier Orchesterlieder
  solo,orch cmplt ed UNIVER. 12058
  $6.25
    contains: Mach Mich Zum Wachter,
    Op.22,No.3; Seraphita, Op.22,
    No.1; Vorgefuhl, Op.22,No.4;
    Welche Dich Suchen, Op.22,No.2
                                    (S932)

  Voll Jener Susse *Op.8,No.5
  med solo,pno UNIVER. 3045 $3.50 see
    also Sechs Orchesterlieder (S933)

  Vorgefuhl *Op.22,No.4
  see Vier Orchesterlieder

  Waldsonne *Op.2,No.4
  solo,pno voc sc BIRNBACH s.p. see
    from Vier Lieder   (S934)

  Warnung *Op.3,No.3
  med solo,pno UNIVER. 3658 $3.00 see
    from Sechs Lieder   (S935)
  solo,pno voc sc BIRNBACH s.p. see
    from Sechs Lieder   (S936)

  Welche Dich Suchen *Op.22,No.2
  see Vier Orchesterlieder

  Wenn Voglein Klagen *Op.8,No.6
  high solo,orch UNIVER. 3046 $3.50
    see also Sechs Orchesterlieder
                                    (S937)

  Wie Georg Von Frundsberg Von Sich
    Selber Sang *Op.3,No.1
  solo,pno voc sc BIRNBACH s.p. see
    from Sechs Lieder   (S938)

  Wunderhorn *Op.3,No.1
  med solo,pno UNIVER. 3656 $3.00 see
    from Sechs Lieder   (S939)

  Zwei Balladen *see Der Verlorene
    Haufen, Op.12,No.2; Jane Grey,
    Op.12,No.1   (S940)

  Zwei Gesange *see Abschied, Op.1,
    No.2; Dank, Op.1,No.1   (S941)

  Zwei Lieder *see Abschied, Op.1,
    No.2; Dank, Op.1,No.1   (S942)

  Zwei Lieder *see Ich Darf Nicht,
    Op.14,No.1; In Diesen
    Wintertagen, Op.14,No.2   (S943)

SCHOENFELD, WILLIAM C. (1893-   )
  Presence, The *sac
  high solo,pno ABINGDON APM-300 $.75
                                    (S944)

  low solo,pno ABINGDON APM-365 $.75
                                    (S945)

SCHOLANDER, TORKEL
  En Borde Inte Sova
  solo,pno MUSIKK s.p.   (S946)

SCHOLAR IN THE NARROW STREET, THE see
  Heilner, Irwin

SCHOLLUM, ROBERT (1913-   )
  Alltag Der Augen *Op.37,No.1-7, CC7U
  med solo,pno DOBLINGER 08 647 $3.00
                                    (S947)

SCHOLLUM, ROBERT (cont'd.)

Drei Weihnachtsgesange *CC3U,Xmas
med female solo,3strings DOBLINGER
08 819 s.p.   (S948)

Ein Jeder Von Dem Seinen *Op.49,
No.1-2, CC2U
S solo,vln,pno DOBLINGER s.p.
(S949)

Lieder Aus Dem Wunderhorn *Op.12,
CCU
high solo,pno DOBLINGER 08 646
$3.50   (S950)

Zwei Hymnen *Op.53, CC2U
[Ger] A solo,pno OSTER $1.25 (S951)

SCHOLTEN, J.
Ave Maria *sac
solo,pno BROEKMANS 186 s.p. (S952)

SCHOLTZ, S.
Haha, Du Stolta Janta
high solo,pno GEHRMANS s.p. (S953)
low solo,pno GEHRMANS s.p. (S954)

SCHOLZ, ERWIN CHRISTIAN (1910-   )
Als Ware Meine Seele Eine Flote
solo,pno DOBLINGER 08 613 s.p.
contains also: Ich Weiss Den Tag
Noch   (S955)

Am Abend
solo,pno DOBLINGER 08 612 s.p.
contains also: Chanson Triste
(S956)

Chanson Triste
see Scholz, Erwin Christian, Am
Abend

Ich Weiss Den Tag Noch
see Scholz, Erwin Christian, Als
Ware Meine Seele Eine Flote

Im Volkston
see Scholz, Erwin Christian, Welke
Blumen

Kinderreime *Op.64
S solo,pno DOBLINGER 08 648 $2.25
(S957)

Rokoko
solo,pno DOBLINGER 08 611 s.p.
(S958)

Welke Blumen
solo,pno DOBLINGER 08 614 s.p.
contains also: Im Volkston (S959)

SCHOLZE, J.
Advents- En Kerstliederen *sac,CCU
solo,pno BROEKMANS 662 s.p. (S960)

Toverfluit Knabes Wunderhorn, Vol. I
*CCU
solo,pno BROEKMANS 642 s.p. (S961)

Toverfluit Knabes Wunderhorn, Vol. II
*CCU
solo,pno BROEKMANS 643 s.p. (S962)

SCHON EILET FROH DER ACKERSMANN see
Haydn, (Franz) Joseph

SCHON EIN MADCHEN VON FUNFZEHN JAHREN
see Mozart, Wolfgang Amadeus

SCHON GRETLEIN see Fielitz, Alexander
von

SCHON HEDWIG see Schumann, Robert
(Alexander)

SCHON IST ES ZU STERBEN IM KAMPFE see
Kilpinen, Yrio, Soria Sotahan
Kuolla

SCHON LACHT DER HOLDE FRUHLING see
Mozart, Wolfgang Amadeus

SCHONBERG, STIG GUSTAV
Nio Sma Sanger *CC9L
solo,pno/org ERIKS K 257   (S963)

SCHONE CHIWRIA see Mussorgsky, Modest

SCHONE DONNA! DIESES KLEINE REGISTER
see Mozart, Wolfgang Amadeus,
Madamina! Il Catalogo E Questa

SCHONE NACHT see Rinaldini, Dr. Joseph

SCHONSTER JESU, LIEBSTES LEBEN see
Buxtehude, Dietrich

SCHOOF, ARMIN (1940-   )
Herr, Ich Traue Auf Dich (Psalm 71)
sac
S solo,rec,vla,org sc HANSSLER
10.305 s.p., ipa   (S964)

Psalm 71 *see Herr, Ich Traue Auf
Dich

SCHOONE LELIE see Appledoorn, Dina

SCHOONHEID see Schouwman, Hans

SCHOP, JOHANN (? -1665)
Vom Himmel Hoch, Da Komm Ich Her
*sac,concerto
(Strube, Adolf) STB soli,cont
(easy) NAGELS NMA 69 $5.50 (S965)

SCHOPENHAUER CANTATE see Frid, Geza

SCHOUWMAN, HANS (1902-1967)
Aan De Maan *Op.17,No.2
see Drie Romantische Miniaturen Van
Staring

Aan Fillis
see Drie Danswijzen

Adeline Verbeid *Op.17,No.3
see Drie Romantische Miniaturen Van
Staring

Amsteldam *Op.28,No.1
see Nederlandse Steden

Arnhem *Op.28,No.4
see Nederlandse Steden

Ballet *Op.18,No.1
see Drie Danswijzen Op Oud-
Nederlandse Gedichten

Clematis *Op.5,No.3
see Vier Gedichten Uit
"Experimenten"

Dans Der Maegdekens *Op.14b,No.2
see Oud-Nederlandsche Liederen,
Vol. 2

De Boeren *Op.14a,No.1
see Oud-Nederlandsche Liederen,
Vol. 1

De Minnebode *Op.14b,No.1
see Oud-Nederlandsche Liederen,
Vol. 2

De Oude Wijsheid *Op.46,No.2
see Schouwman, Hans, In Duisternis

De Ziel Spreekt *Op.32,No.1
see Drie Gedichten Van P.C. Boutens

Deuntje *Op.19,No.2
see Twee Gedichten Van Joost Van
Den Vondel

Diogenes *Op.19,No.1
see Twee Gedichten Van Joost Van
Den Vondel

Drie Danswijzen
S/T solo,2fl,perc,strings min sc
WAGENAAR s.p.
contains: Aan Fillis; Eens Meien
Morgens Vroege; Het Gebrek In
Chloris   (S966)

Drie Danswijzen Op Oud-Nederlandse
Gedichten
high solo,pno WAGENAAR s.p.
contains: Ballet, Op.18,No.1;
Gavotte, Op.18,No.3; Minuet,
Op.18,No.2   (S967)

Drie Gedichten Van P.C. Boutens
S solo,fl,ob,clar,bsn,horn voc sc
DONEMUS s.p.
contains: De Ziel Spreekt, Op.32,
No.1; Patet Via, Op.32,No.2;
Sterrenhemel, Op.32,No.3 (S968)

Drie Liedjes Uit "De Laatste Reis Van
Don Andrees" *CC3U
low solo/med solo,pno DONEMUS s.p.
(S969)

Drie Romantische Miniaturen Van
Staring
high solo/med solo,pno WAGENAAR
s.p.
contains: Aan De Maan, Op.17,
No.2; Adeline Verbeid, Op.17,
No.3; Zefir En Chloris, Op.17,
No.1   (S970)

Een Ding Heb Ik Begeerd *Op.5,No.1
see Vier Gedichten Uit
"Experimenten"

Een Goed Lyedeken *Op.72b
med solo,fl,org/pno DONEMUS s.p.
(S971)

Eens Meien Morgens Vroege
see Drie Danswijzen

Envoi [1] (From "I Promise")
*Op.48a,No.2
see Songs Of The Master

Envoi [2] (From "What We Shall
Teach") *Op.48a,No.3
see Songs Of The Master

SCHOUWMAN, HANS (cont'd.)

Flower, A *Op.48a,No.1
see Songs Of The Master

Friesland *Op.44,No.1
low solo,2fl,2ob,2clar,2bsn,horn,
perc,harp,strings DONEMUS s.p.
contains also: Schaatsenrijders,
Op.44,No.2; Heerenveen, Op.44,
No.3; Herfst In Friesland, Op.44,
No.4   (S972)
low solo,pno DONEMUS s.p. contains
also: Schaatsenrijders, Op.44,
No.2; Heerenveen, Op.44,No.3;
Herfst In Friesland, Op.44,No.4
(S973)

Gavotte *Op.18,No.3
see Drie Danswijzen Op Oud-
Nederlandse Gedichten

Gezicht *Op.47,No.3
see Om Het Eeuwige

God's Thought Of Himself *Op.56,No.1
see Two Poems By A. Besant

Groningen *Op.28,No.3
see Nederlandse Steden

Heerenveen *Op.44,No.3
see Schouwman, Hans, Friesland
see Schouwman, Hans, Friesland

Heidestemmingen *Op.26, CCU
high solo,pno WAGENAAR s.p. (S974)

Herfst In Friesland *Op.44,No.4
see Schouwman, Hans, Friesland
see Schouwman, Hans, Friesland

Het Gebrek In Chloris
see Drie Danswijzen

Het Hemelsch Jerusalem *Op.14a,No.3
see Oud-Nederlandsche Liederen,
Vol. 1

Het Verwaend Kwezeltje *Op.15b,No.4
see Vier Samenzangen

Het Wuf Die Spon *Op.14a,No.4
see Oud-Nederlandsche Liederen,
Vol. 1

In Duisternis *Op.46,No.1
low solo,org DONEMUS s.p. contains
also: De Oude Wijsheid, Op.46,
No.2   (S975)

Let Us Go To The Deep Blue Rivers
*Op.62,No.1
see Vier Liederen Van Josselin De
Jong

Lied *Op.5,No.2
see Vier Gedichten Uit
"Experimenten"

Liedje *Op.62,No.3
see Vier Liederen Van Josselin De
Jong

Life *Op.58b,No.1
see Two Poems By C. Jinarajadasa

Listen *Op.62,No.2
see Vier Liederen Van Josselin De
Jong

Loflied *Op.15b,No.3
see Vier Samenzangen

Looft God Den Heer *sac
high solo,ob,pno/org DONEMUS s.p.
(S976)

Love *Op.58b,No.2
see Two Poems By C. Jinarajadasa

Maria Coninghinne *Op.15b,No.2
see Vier Samenzangen

Maria Paaslied *Op.62,No.4
see Vier Liederen Van Josselin De
Jong

Meylied *Op.15b,No.1
see Vier Samenzangen

Meylied I *Op.14b,No.3
see Oud-Nederlandsche Liederen,
Vol. 2

Meylied II *Op.14b,No.4
see Oud-Nederlandsche Liederen,
Vol. 2

Minuet *Op.18,No.2
see Drie Danswijzen Op Oud-
Nederlandse Gedichten

Nederlandse Steden
low solo,pno DONEMUS s.p. s.p.
contains: Amsteldam, Op.28,No.1;
Arnhem, Op.28,No.4; Groningen,
Op.28,No.3; Rotterdam, Op.28,

SCHOUWMAN, HANS (cont'd.)

No.5; Veere, Op.28,No.2 (S977)

Nieuw Kerstlied *Op.71b, sac,CCU
SA soli,pno DONEMUS s.p.
(S978)

Notturno Uit "Sapfo" *Op.59
Mez solo,vcl,pno DONEMUS s.p.
(S979)

Nu Laet Ons Allen Gode Loven
med solo,fl,pno/harp DONEMUS s.p.
(S980)

Oasen *Op.73, song cycle
A solo,ob,pno DONEMUS s.p. (S981)

Om Het Eeuwige
A solo,pno DONEMUS s.p.
contains: Gezicht, Op.47,No.3;
Schoonheid, Op.47,No.2;
Zondagochtend, Op.47,No.1
(S982)

Oogst *Op.48a,No.4
see Songs Of The Master

Oud-Nederlandsche Liederen, Vol. 1
low solo/med solo,pno WAGENAAR s.p.
contains: De Boeren, Op.14a,No.1;
Het Hemelsch Jerusalem, Op.14a,
No.3; Het Wuf Die Spon, Op.14a,
No.4; 'T Godsdeel Of Den
Rommelpot, Op.14a,No.2 (S983)

Oud-Nederlandsche Liederen, Vol. 2
high solo,pno WAGENAAR s.p.
contains: Dans Der Maegdekens,
Op.14b,No.2; De Minnebode,
Op.14b,No.1; Meylied I, Op.14b,
No.3; Meylied II, Op.14b,No.4
(S984)

Patet Via *Op.32,No.2
see Drie Gedichten Van P.C. Boutens

Prayer *Op.56,No.2
see Two Poems By A. Besant

Quem Me Esse Dicitis *Op.5,No.4
see Vier Gedichten Uit
"Experimenten"

Rotterdam *Op.28,No.5
see Nederlandse Steden

Schaatsenrijders *Op.44,No.2
see Schouwman, Hans, Friesland
see Schouwman, Hans, Friesland

Schoonheid *Op.47,No.2
see Om Het Eeuwige

Songs Of The Master *sac
med solo,pno DONEMUS s.p.
contains: Envoi [1] (From "I
Promise"), Op.48a,No.2; Envoi
[2] (From "What We Shall
Teach"), Op.48a,No.3; Flower,
A, Op.48a,No.1; Oogst, Op.48a,
No.4 (S985)

Sterrenhemel *Op.32,No.3
see Drie Gedichten Van P.C. Boutens

'T Godsdeel Of Den Rommelpot
*Op.14a,No.2
see Oud-Nederlandsche Liederen,
Vol. 1

Three Dialogues From "The Gardener"
*Op.8, CC3U
solo,pno DONEMUS s.p. (S986)

Twee Gedichten Van Joost Van Den
Vondel
med solo,pno WAGENAAR s.p.
contains: Deuntje, Op.19,No.2;
Diogenes, Op.19,No.1 (S987)

Twee Liederen Voor Een Huwelijksfeest
*Op.50, sac,CC2U,Holywk
med solo,pno WAGENAAR s.p. (S988)

Two Poems By A. Besant
med solo/low solo,pno DONEMUS s.p.
contains: God's Thought Of
Himself, Op.56,No.1; Prayer,
Op.56,No.2 (S989)

Two Poems By C. Jinarajadasa
Mez solo,pno DONEMUS s.p.
contains: Life, Op.58b,No.1;
Love, Op.58b,No.2 (S990)

Veere *Op.28,No.2
see Nederlandse Steden

Vier Gedichten Uit "Experimenten"
high solo,pno WAGENAAR s.p.
contains: Clematis, Op.5,No.3;
Een Ding Heb Ik Begeerd, Op.5,
No.1; Lied, Op.5,No.2; Quem Me
Esse Dicitis, Op.5,No.4 (S991)

Vier Gedichten Uit "Fluisteringen Van
Den Avondwind" *Op.1, CC4U
med solo,pno ALSBACH s.p. (S992)

SCHOUWMAN, HANS (cont'd.)

Vier Liederen Van Josselin De Jong
A/Mez solo,pno DONEMUS s.p.
contains: Let Us Go To The Deep
Blue Rivers, Op.62,No.1;
Liedje, Op.62,No.3; Listen,
Op.62,No.2; Maria Paaslied,
Op.62,No.4 (S993)

Vier Samenzangen
SA soli,pno WAGENAAR s.p.
contains: Het Verwaend Kwezeltje,
Op.15b,No.4; Loflied, Op.15b,
No.3; Maria Coninghinne,
Op.15b,No.2; Meylied, Op.15b,
No.1 (S994)

Zefir En Chloris *Op.17,No.1
see Drie Romantische Miniaturen Van
Staring

Zondagochtend *Op.47,No.1
see Om Het Eeuwige

SCHRAMM, HAROLD
Song Of Tayumanavar
S solo,fl PRESSER $1.25 (S995)

SCHREIBER, JOSEF (1900-   )
Die Nachte *see Noci

Noci
"Die Nachte" high solo,fl,pno CZECH
s.p. (S996)

SCHREIBER, L.P.
Saint Francis Prayer
high solo,pno PRESSER $.75 (S997)

SCHREKER, FRANZ (1878-1934)
Acht Lieder, Heft I *CCU
med solo,pno UNIVER. 3868 $3.25
(S998)

Acht Lieder, Heft II *CCU
med solo,pno UNIVER. 3869 $2.75
(S999)

Funf Lieder *Op.4,No.1-5, CC5U
high solo,pno UNIVER. 3872 $3.25
(S1000)

Sommerfaden *Op.2,No.1
med solo,pno UNIVER. $2.75 (S1001)

Stimmen Des Tages *Op.2,No.2
med solo,pno UNIVER. $2.75 (S1002)

Tod Eines Kindes *Op.5,No.1-2, CC2U
med solo,pno UNIVER. 3873 $2.75
(S1003)

SCHRIEBL, KARL
Schneewalzer
(Bauer, R.) solo,pno/acord LEUCKART
s.p. (S1004)

SCHRIJVERS, JEAN
Venite Adoremus *sac,CC25U
solo,pno HEUWEKE. s.p. (S1005)

SCHROEDER, F.
Wenn Ich Wieder Komm
[Ger] BOTE $.90 (S1006)

SCHROEDER, HERMANN (1904-   )
Drei Weihnachtslieder *CC3U,Xmas
solo,pno SCHOTTS 3880 s.p. (S1007)

Sechs Weihnachtslieder *CC6U,Xmas
2 med soli/2 female soli,pno/org
voc sc SCHOTTS 3887 s.p., solo pt
SCHOTTS s.p. (S1008)

SCHROEDER, JOHN
Must Jesus Bear The Cross? *sac
high solo,pno BELWIN $1.50 (S1009)

SCHUBEL, MAX
To The Beloved
high solo,pno SEESAW $1.50 (S1010)

SCHUBERT, FRANZ (PETER) (1797-1828)
Ach Um Deine Feuchten Schwingen *see
Suleikas Zweiter Gesang

Ach Was Soll Ich Beginnen *see
Delphine

Adieu *see Lebe Wohl

Almighty, The *see Die Allmacht

Am Meer
"By The Sea" [Ger/Fr/Eng] high
solo,pno (C maj) SCHIRM.G $.50
(S1011)

An Die Musik *Op.88,No.4
see Sechs Lieder
"To Music" [Ger/Eng] med solo,pno
(D maj) SCHIRM.G $1.00 (S1012)
"To Music" high solo,pno PRESSER
$.95 (S1013)
"To Music" high solo,pno (D maj)
ALLANS s.p. (S1014)
(Reger, Max) S/T solo,fl,ob,clar,
bsn,2horn,timp,strings sc
BREITKOPF-L PB 2392 s.p., ipr
(S1015)

SCHUBERT, FRANZ (PETER) (cont'd.)

Auf Dem Strom *Op.119
solo,horn,pno BREITKOPF-W EB 5892
$2.75 (S1016)
solo,horn,pno KALMUS 6426 $3.00
(S1017)
S solo,horn,pno PETERS 9409 s.p.
(S1018)
"On The River" [Ger/Eng] solo,pno,
opt horn INTERNAT. (S1019)

Auf Dem Wasser Zu Singen
"Water Song" see Metzler's
Masterpieces Vol. 1: Schubert
Lieder For Soprano

Aufenthalt
"My Shelter" see Metzler's
Masterpieces Vol. 2: Schubert
Lieder For Contralto Or Mezzo-
Soprano

Ausgewahlte Lieder *CCU
(Durr, Walther) solo,pno (diff)
BAREN. 19 301 $4.00 (S1020)

Ave Maria *Op.52,No.6, sac
see Bach, Johann Sebastian, Ave
Maria
see Bach, Johann Sebastian, Ave
Maria
see Bach, Johann Sebastian, Ave
Maria
see Bach, Johann Sebastian, Ave
Maria
"Ave Maria" see Metzler's
Masterpieces Vol. 1: Schubert
Lieder For Soprano
S/T solo,pno (B flat maj) LIENAU
HOS 129 s.p. (S1021)
A/Bar solo,pno (G maj) LIENAU
HOS 131 s.p. (S1022)
Mez solo,pno (A flat maj) LIENAU
HOS 130 s.p. (S1023)
[Ger/Fr] solo,pno (in 3 keys)
DURAND s.p. (S1024)
[Lat] S/T solo,pno BILLAUDOT s.p.
(S1025)
[Lat] Bar/A solo,pno BILLAUDOT s.p.
(S1026)
[Fr] Bar/A solo,pno BILLAUDOT s.p.
(S1027)
[Ger/Fr/It/Lat] Mez/Bar solo,pno (A
flat maj) RICORDI-ARG BA 8540
s.p. (S1028)
Mez/Bar solo,pno CURCI 4278 s.p.
(S1029)
[It/Ger] S/T solo,pno RICORDI-ENG
12870 s.p. (S1030)
[It/Fr] Mez/Bar solo,pno RICORDI-
ENG 93443 s.p. (S1031)
[Ger/Fr/It/Lat] S/T solo,pno (B
flat maj) RICORDI-ARG BA 6644
s.p. (S1032)
[Fr] T solo,pno (C maj) BILLAUDOT
s.p. (S1033)
[Fr] S solo,pno BILLAUDOT s.p.
(S1034)
[Lat] high solo,pno/org SCHOTT-FRER
SCH122 s.p. (S1035)
[Ger] high solo,pno/org,opt vln
LIENAU R89 s.p. (S1036)
[Lat] med solo,pno/org SCHOTT-FRER
SCH123 s.p. (S1037)
[Lat/Ger/Fr] med solo,pno MARKS
$1.50 (S1038)
Mez/Bar solo,pno FORLIVESI 11980
s.p. (S1039)
S/T solo,pno FORLIVESI 11270 s.p.
(S1040)
S/T solo,pno CURCI 5951 s.p.
(S1041)
high solo,pno (B flat maj) FISCHER,
C S 4954 (S1042)
high solo,pno (B flat maj) BOSTON
$1.50 (S1043)
solo,pno (available in 3 keys)
ASHLEY $.95 (S1044)
med solo,pno (A flat maj) CENTURY
3246 $.40 (S1045)
low solo,pno (G maj) FISCHER,C
S 7631 (S1046)
low solo,pno (A flat maj) FISCHER,C
S 4955 (S1047)
high solo,pno (B flat maj) ALLANS
s.p. (S1048)
med solo,pno (A flat maj) ALLANS
s.p. (S1049)
low solo,pno (G maj) ALLANS s.p.
(S1050)
low solo,pno LUNDQUIST s.p. (S1051)
high solo,pno LUNDQUIST s.p.
(S1052)
solo,pno FAZER F 2912 s.p. (S1053)
"Ave Maria" [Lat/Ger/Eng] low solo,
vln,fl/vcl,pno (G maj) SCHIRM.G
$.85 (S1054)
"Ave Maria" solo,pno CRAMER (S1055)
"Ave Maria" [Lat/Eng/Ger] high
solo,pno (B flat maj) SCHIRM.G
$.85 (S1056)
"Ave Maria" [Lat/Eng/Ger] med solo,
pno (A flat maj) SCHIRM.G $.85
(S1057)
'Ave Maria" [Lat/Eng/Ger] low solo,

SCHUBERT, FRANZ (PETER) (cont'd.)

pno (G maj) SCHIRM.G $1.00
(S1058)

"Ave Maria" [Lat/Eng/Ger] low solo,
pno (G maj) SCHIRM.G $.85 (S1059)

"Ave Maria" [Lat/Ger/Eng] high
solo,vln,fl/vcl (B flat maj)
SCHIRM.G $.85 (S1060)

(Scott) solo,pno (B flat maj)
PAXTON P40559 s.p. (S1061)

(Scott) med solo,pno PAXTON P2167
s.p. (S1062)

Ave Maria *see Ave Maria

Barcarolle
[Fr] solo,pno BILLAUDOT s.p.
(S1063)

Bonne Nuit
[Fr] solo,pno BILLAUDOT s.p.
(S1064)

By The Sea *see Am Meer

Chant Du Cynge *see Swannengesang

Cinquante Melodies Choisies *CC50U
[Fr] cmplt ed BILLAUDOT s.p. high
solo,pno; low solo,pno (S1065)

Complete Song Cycles
(Mandyczewski, E.) [Ger/Eng] solo,
pno pap 22649-2 $4.00 reprints
from the: Breitkopf & Hartel
Critical Edition Of 1884-97,
Series 20
contains: Die Schone Mullern;
Die Winterreise; Schwanengesang
(S1066)

Complete Songs Of Schubert, The *CCU
[Ger] solo,pno min sc KALMUS $1.50,
ea. published in 28 volumes
(S1067)

Complete Works *CCU
(Brahms, J.; Bruell, I.; Door, A.;
Fuchs, J.N.; Gaensbacher, J.;
Epstein J.; Hellmesberger, J.;
Mandyczewski, E.) contains works
for a variety of instruments and
vocal combinations microfiche
UNIV.MUS.ED. $185.00 contains 21
volumes (S1068)

The Complete Works Of Franz Schubert,
Vol. 14 (Pts. III, IV): LIEDER:
AUGUST 1815 THROUGH 1816 *CCU
(Mandyczewski, E.) solo,pno cloth
213336-6 $7.50 reprints from the:
Breitkopf & Hartel Critical
Edition Of 1884-97, Series 20
(S1069)

The Complete Works Of Franz Schubert,
Vol. 15 (Pts. V, VI): Lieder:
1817 To 1821 *CCU
(Mandyczewski, E.) solo,pno cloth
213337-4 $7.50 reprints from the:
Breitkopf & Hartel Critical
Edition Of 1884-97, Series 20
(S1070)

The Complete Works Of Franz Schubert,
Vol. 16 (Pts. VII, VIII): Lieder:
1822 To "Die Winterreise", 1827
*CCU
(Mandyczewski, E.) solo,pno cloth
21338-2 $7.50 reprints from the:
Breitkopf & Hartel Critical
Edition Of 1884-97, Series 20
(S1071)

The Complete Works Of Franz Schubert,
Vol. 17 (Pts. IX, X): Lieder:
From "Die Winterreise" To
"Schwanengsang", 1828 *CCU
(Mandyczewski, E.) solo,pno cloth
21339-0 $7.50 reprints from the:
Breitkopf & Hartel Critical
Edition Of 1884-97, Series 20
(S1072)

Cradle Song *see Wiegenlied

Das Fischermadchen
"Fischer-Maiden, The" see METZLER'S
MASTERPIECES VOL. 16: SIX SONGS
FOR BARITONE OR BASS
"Fisher-Maiden, The" see Metzler's
Masterpieces Vol. 3: Schubert
Lieder For Tenor
"La Fille Du Pecheur" [Fr] solo,pno
BILLAUDOT s.p. (S1073)

Dear Ring Upon My Finger *see Du
Ring An Meinem Finger

Death And The Maiden *see Der Tod
Und Das Madchen

Degel
[Fr] solo,pno BILLAUDOT s.p.
(S1074)

Delphine *Op.124,No.2
(Mottl, F.) "Ach Was Soll Ich
Beginnen" S solo,2fl,2ob,2clar,
2bsn,4horn,3trom,timp,strings
BREITKOPF-L rental (S1075)

SCHUBERT, FRANZ (PETER) (cont'd.)

Dem Unendlichen
(Reger, Max) "Wie Erhebet Sich Das
Herz" A/B solo,3fl,2ob,2clar,
2bsn,4horn,2trp,3trom,tuba,timp,
2harp,strings BREITKOPF-L rental
(S1076)

Den Tag Hindurch Nur Einmal Mag Ich
Sprechen *see Memnon

Der Doppelganger
"Double, The" see Metzler's
Masterpieces Vol. 4: Schubert
Lieder For Baritone Or Bass
"La Double (Le Sosie)" [Ger/Fr]
solo,pno (in 3 keys) DURAND s.p.
(S1077)

Der Hirt Auf Dem Felsen *Op.129
solo,clar,pno sc BREITKOPF-W
EB 6479 s.p., voc sc BREITKOPF-W
EB 4188 $2.50 (S1078)
"Shepherd On The Rock, The" solo,
pno GALLIARD 2.8959.7 $2.50
(S1079)
"Shepherd On The Rocks, The" [Ger/
Eng] solo,pno,opt.clar INTERNAT.
$2.00 (S1080)
(Deis) "Shepherd On The Rock, The"
[Eng/Ger] high solo,clar/vln/fl,
pno (B flat maj) SCHIRM.G $1.50
(S1081)

Der Hochzeitsbraten *Op.104
STB soli,pno BREITKOPF-L EB 4071
s.p. (S1082)
STB soli,pno voc sc BREITKOPF-W
EB 6454 $2.75, sc BREITKOPF-W
EB 4071 s.p. (S1083)

Der Lindenbaum
"Linden Tree, The" see Metzler's
Masterpieces Vol. 4: Schubert
Lieder For Baritone Or Bass
"Linden Tree" med solo,pno (E min)
ALLANS s.p. (S1084)

Der Neugierige
"Questioner, The" see Metzler's
Masterpieces Vol. 3: Schubert
Lieder For Tenor

Der Tod Und Das Madchen *Op.7,No.3
"Death And The Maiden" see
Metzler's Masterpieces Vol. 2:
Schubert Lieder For Contralto Or
Mezzo-Soprano
(Mottl, F.) Mez/A solo,ob,2clar,
2bsn,horn,timp,strings BREITKOPF-
L rental (S1085)

Der Vollmond Strahlt Auf Bergeshohn
(from Rosamunde)
T solo,2ob,2clar,2bsn,2horn,vla,vcl
BREITKOPF-L rental (S1086)

Der Wanderer
"Wanderer, The" see Metzler's
Masterpieces Vol. 4: Schubert
Lieder For Baritone Or Bass
"Wanderer, The" [Ger/Eng] low solo,
pno (D maj) SCHIRM.G $.75 (S1087)
"Wanderer, The" med solo,pno (C
sharp min) ALLANS s.p. (S1088)
"Wanderer, The" low solo,pno (B
min) ALLANS s.p. (S1089)
"Wanderer, The" [Ger/Eng] solo,pno
CRAMER (S1090)

Des Madchen's Klage
"Maiden's Plaint, The" see
Metzler's Masterpieces Vol. 2:
Schubert Lieder For Contralto Or
Mezzo-Soprano

Die Allmacht *Op.79,No.2, sac
"Almighty, The" see Metzler's
Masterpieces Vol. 2: Schubert
Lieder For Contralto Or Mezzo-
Soprano
"Almighty, The" see METZLER'S
MASTERPIECES VOL. 13: SIX SONGS
FOR SOPRANO
A/Bar solo,pno (A maj) LIENAU
HOS 134 s.p. (S1091)
Mez solo,pno (B flat maj) LIENAU
HOS 133A s.p. (S1092)
S/T solo,pno (C maj) LIENAU HOS 133
s.p. (S1093)
(Deis) "Omnipotence" [Ger/Eng] med
solo,pno (A maj) SCHIRM.G $.85
(S1094)
(Deis) "Omnipotence" [Ger/Eng] low
solo,pno (G maj) SCHIRM.G $.85
(S1095)
(Deis) "Omnipotence" [Ger/Eng] high
solo,pno (C maj) SCHIRM.G $.85
(S1096)
(Deis) "Omnipotence" [Ger/Eng] med
solo,pno (A maj) SCHIRM.G $.85
(S1097)
(Deis) "Omnipotence" [Ger/Eng] low
solo,pno (G maj) SCHIRM.G $.85
(S1098)
(Deis) "Omnipotence" [Ger/Eng] high
solo,pno (C maj) SCHIRM.G $.85
(S1099)

SCHUBERT, FRANZ (PETER) (cont'd.)

(Mottl, F.) "Gross Ist Jehova" S
solo,2fl,2ob,2clar,2bsn,4horn,
3trp,3trom,tuba,timp,harp,strings
BREITKOPF-L rental (S1100)

Die Erde
see Schubert, Franz (Peter),
Vollendung

Die Forelle
"La Truite" see LA MUSIQUE,
DEUXIEME CAHIER
"La Truite" [Ger/Fr] solo,pno (in 3
keys) DURAND s.p. (S1101)
"La Truite" [Fr] solo,pno BILLAUDOT
s.p. (S1102)
"Trout, The" [Ger/Eng] high solo,
pno (D flat maj) SCHIRM.G $.85
(S1103)
"Trout, The" [Ger/Eng] med solo,pno
(B maj) SCHIRM.G $.85 (S1104)
(Howe) "Trout, The" med solo,pno
PAXTON P40619 s.p. (S1105)

Die Junge Nonne *Op.43,No.1
see Sechs Lieder
"Young Nun, The" see Metzler's
Masterpieces Vol. 2: Schubert
Lieder For Contralto Or Mezzo-
Soprano
"Young Nun, The" see METZLER'S
MASTERPIECES VOL. 13: SIX SONGS
FOR SOPRANO

Die Krahe
"Raven, The" see Metzler's
Masterpieces Vol. 3: Schubert
Lieder For Tenor

Die Lindenbaum
"Le Tilleul" [Ger/Fr] A/B solo,pno
DURAND s.p. (S1106)
"Le Tilleul" [Ger/Fr] Mez/Bar solo,
pno DURAND s.p. (S1107)
"Le Tilleul" [Fr] solo,pno
BILLAUDOT s.p. (S1108)

Die Post
"La Poste" [Fr] solo,pno BILLAUDOT
s.p. (S1109)
"La Poste" [Ger/Fr] S/T solo,pno
DURAND s.p. (S1110)

Die Rose *Op.73
(Mottl, F.) "Es Lockte Schone
Warme" S solo,2fl,2ob,2clar,2bsn,
2horn,strings BREITKOPF-L rental
(S1111)

Die Schone Mullerin *song cycle
see Complete Song Cycles
[Eng/Ger] high solo,pno SCHIRM.G
$4.00 (S1112)
solo,pno KALMUS 6427 $2.50 (S1113)
[Eng/Ger] low solo,pno SCHIRM.G
$4.00 (S1114)
(Kagen, Sergius) [Ger/Eng] med
solo,pno INTERNAT. $2.50 (S1115)
(Kagen, Sergius) [Ger/Eng] high
solo,pno INTERNAT. $2.50 (S1116)
(Kagen, Sergius) [Ger/Eng] low
solo,pno INTERNAT. $2.50 (S1117)

Die Winterreise *song cycle
see Complete Song Cycles
(Kagen, Sergius) [Ger/Eng] low
solo,pno INTERNAT. $2.50 (S1118)
(Kagen, Sergius) [Ger/Eng] med
solo,pno INTERNAT. $2.50 (S1119)
(Kagen, Sergius) [Ger/Eng] high
solo,pno INTERNAT. $2.50 (S1120)

Double, The *see Der Doppelganger

Du Bist Die Ruh *Op.59,No.3
see Sechs Lieder
"With Thee Is Peace" see Metzler's
Masterpieces Vol. 1: Schubert
Lieder For Soprano
"With Thee Is Peace" see METZLER'S
MASTERPIECES VOL. 14: SIX SONGS
FOR MEZZO-SOPRANO OR CONTRALTO
"Repos" [Ger/Fr] solo,pno (in 3
keys) DURAND s.p. (S1121)
"Thou Are Repose" [Ger/Eng] high
solo,pno (E flat maj) SCHIRM.G
$.85 (S1122)
"Thou Are Repose" [Ger/Eng] med
solo,pno (C maj) SCHIRM.G $.85
(S1123)
(Reger, Max) [Ger/Eng] S solo,2fl,
ob,2clar,2bsn,2horn,timp,strings
BREITKOPF-L rental (S1124)

Du Ring An Meinem Finger
"Dear Ring Upon My Finger" see
METZLER'S MASTERPIECES VOL. 13:
SIX SONGS FOR SOPRANO

Erkling, The *see Erlkonig

Erl King *see Erlkonig

SCHUBERT, FRANZ (PETER) (cont'd.)

Erlking, The *see Erlkonig

Erlkonig *Op.1
    see Sechs Lieder
    "Erkling, The" see Metzler's
        Masterpieces Vol. 4: Schubert
        Lieder For Baritone Or Bass
    "Erl King" [Ger/Eng] high solo,pno
        (G maj) CRAMER s.p.   (S1125)
    "Erl King" med solo,pno (F min)
        ALLANS s.p.   (S1126)
    "Erl King" low solo,pno (E min)
        ALLANS s.p.   (S1127)
    "Erl King" [Ger/Eng] low solo,pno
        (E maj) CRAMER s.p.   (S1128)
    "Erlking, The" [Ger/Eng] low solo,
        pno (E min) SCHIRM.G $.85 (S1129)
    "Le Roi De Thule" [Fr] solo,pno
        BILLAUDOT s.p.   (S1130)
    "Le Roi Des Aulnes" [Ger/Fr] solo,
        pno (in 3 keys) DURAND s.p.
                                 (S1131)
    "Le Roi Des Aulnes" [Fr] Bar/B
        solo,pno BILLAUDOT s.p. (S1132)
    "Le Roi Des Aulnes" [Fr] T solo,pno
        BILLAUDOT s.p.   (S1133)

Erstes Offertorium *Op.46
    S solo,2fl,clar,2horn,org,strings
    BREITKOPF-W s.p.   (S1134)

Es Lockte Schone Warme *see Die Rose

Evig Vila
    solo,pno LUNDQUIST s.p.   (S1135)

Faith In Spring *see Fruhlingsglaube

Fifty Additional Songs *CC50U
    [Eng/Ger] PRESSER $5.00 high solo,
    pno; low solo,pno   (S1136)

Fifty Songs *CC50U
    [Eng/Ger] high solo,pno PRESSER
    $5.00   (S1137)

Fifty-Two Selected Songs *CC52U
    [Ger] A/B solo,pno PETERS 3505
    $9.00   (S1138)

First Vocal Album *CC81L
    [Ger/Eng] high solo,pno SCHIRM.G
    342 $7.50; low solo,pno SCHIRM.G
    343 $7.50 in four parts
    including: Die Shone Mullerin;
    Winterreise; Schwanengesang;
    Twenty-Four Favorite Songs
                                 (S1139)

Fischer-Maiden, The *see Das
    Fischermadchen

Fisher-Maiden, The *see Das
    Fischermadchen

Fruhlingsglaube
    "Faith In Spring" see Metzler's
        Masterpieces Vol. 1: Schubert
        Lieder For Soprano
    "Faith In Spring" [Ger/Eng] high
        solo,pno (A flat maj) SCHIRM.G
        $.50   (S1140)
    "Le Printemps" [Fr] solo,pno
        BILLAUDOT s.p.   (S1141)

Funfzehn Lieder *CC15L
    (Leuchter, Kurzmann) [Ger/Span] med
    solo,pno RICORDI-ARG BA 8714 s.p.
                                 (S1142)

Ganymed *Op.19,No.3
    see Sechs Lieder

Geheimes
    "Le Secret" [Ger/Fr] solo,pno (in 3
        keys) DURAND s.p.   (S1143)
    "Le Secret" [Fr] T solo,pno
        BILLAUDOT s.p.   (S1144)
    "Le Secret" [Fr] Bar solo,pno
        BILLAUDOT s.p.   (S1145)

Geistliche Arien, Teil I *sac,CCU
    (Pfannhauser, K.) high solo,pno
    DOBLINGER 08 566 s.p.   (S1146)

Geistliche Arien, Teil II *sac,CCU
    (Pfannhauser, K.) high solo,pno
    DOBLINGER 08 567 s.p.   (S1147)

Gentle The Night Winds
    low solo,pno (C min) ASHDOWN s.p.
                                 (S1148)
    high solo,pno (D min) ASHDOWN s.p.
                                 (S1149)

Goethe Songs *CCU
    high solo,pno BAREN. 012-19 305
                                 (S1150)

Greisengesang *Op.60,No.1
    (Reger, Max) [Ger/Eng] B solo,fl,
    2ob,2clar,bsn,2horn,timp,strings
    BREITKOPF-W s.p.   (S1151)

Gretchen Am Spinnrade
    "Gretchen At The Spinning Wheel"
        see Metzler's Masterpieces Vol.
        1: Schubert Lieder For Soprano

"Gretchen At The Spinning Wheel"
    see METZLER'S MASTERPIECES VOL.
    14: SIX SONGS FOR MEZZO-SOPRANO
    OR CONTRALTO
    "Marguerite" [Fr] solo,pno
        BILLAUDOT s.p.   (S1152)
    "Marguerite Au Rouet" [Ger/Fr]
        solo,pno (in 3 keys) DURAND s.p.
                                 (S1153)

Gretchen At The Spinning Wheel *see
    Gretchen Am Spinnrade

Gross Ist Jehova *see Die Allmacht

Happiness
    med solo,pno (C maj) ALLANS s.p.
                                 (S1154)
    high solo,pno (E maj) ALLANS s.p.
                                 (S1155)

Hark! Hark! The Lark
    med solo,pno (B flat maj) ALLANS
        s.p.   (S1156)
    high solo,pno (C maj) ALLANS s.p.
                                 (S1157)
    "Serenade De Shakespeare" [Fr]
        solo,pno BILLAUDOT s.p. (S1158)
    (Howe) S solo,pno PAXTON P40487
        s.p.   (S1159)

Heather Rose *see Heidenroslein

Hedge-Roses *see Heidenroslein

Heidenroslein
    "Rosebud On The Hill-Side" see
        Metzler's Masterpieces Vol. 1:
        Schubert Lieder For Soprano
        solo,pno HIRSCHS s.p.   (S1160)
    "Heather Rose" med solo,pno (E maj)
        ALLANS s.p.   (S1161)
    "Hedge-Roses" [Ger/Eng] low solo,
        pno (D maj) SCHIRM.G $.85 (S1162)
    "Hedge-Roses" [Ger/Eng] high solo,
        pno (G maj) SCHIRM.G $.85 (S1163)
    "Hedge Roses" med solo,pno PRESSER
        $.75   (S1164)
    "Rose Des Bruyeres" [Ger/Fr] solo,
        pno (in 3 keys) DURAND s.p.
                                 (S1165)

Heilge Nacht, Du Sinkest Nieder *see
    Nacht Und Traume

Ich Schleiche Bang Und Still Herum
    (from Die Verschworenen)
    (Flothius, Marius) [Ger] S solo,
    clar,pno BROEKMANS 395-6 s.p.
                                 (S1166)

Im Abendrot
    (Reger, Max) [Ger/Eng] T solo,fl,
    ob,2clar,2bsn,2horn,timp,strings
    BREITKOPF-W s.p.   (S1167)
    (Reger, Max) "O Wie Schon Ist Deine
    Welt" Mez/A solo,fl,ob,2clar,
    2bsn,2horn,timp,perc BREITKOPF-L
    rental   (S1168)

Im Abendroth
    (Howe) "Sunset Glow" med solo,pno
    PAXTON P40618 s.p.   (S1169)

Impatience *see Ungeduld

La-Bas
    [Fr] solo,pno BILLAUDOT s.p.
                                 (S1170)

La Belle Meuniere *CCU
    [Fr] solo,pno cmplt ed BILLAUDOT
    s.p.   (S1171)

La Berceuse *see Wiegenlied

La Calme Plat
    [Fr] solo,pno BILLAUDOT s.p.
                                 (S1172)

La Double (Le Sosie) *see Der
    Doppelganger

La Fee
    [Ger/Fr] solo,pno DURAND s.p.
                                 (S1173)

La Fille Du Pecheur *see Das
    Fischermadchen

La Jeune Fille Et La Mort
    [Fr] solo,pno BILLAUDOT s.p.
                                 (S1174)

La Jeune Mere
    [Fr] solo,pno BILLAUDOT s.p.
                                 (S1175)

La Jeune Religeuse
    [Fr] solo,pno BILLAUDOT s.p.
                                 (S1176)

La Joueur De Vielle
    [Fr] solo,pno BILLAUDOT s.p.
                                 (S1177)

La Pastorella
    [It] med-high solo,pno DOBLINGER
    08 565 $2.00   (S1178)

La Poste *see Die Post

La Rose Sauvage
    [Fr] solo,pno BILLAUDOT s.p.
                                 (S1179)

SCHUBERT, FRANZ (PETER) (cont'd.)

La Source
    see LA MUSIQUE, CINQUIEME CAHIER
    solo,acap DURAND s.p.   (S1180)

La Toute-Puissance
    Bar solo,orch HENN s.p.   (S1181)

La Truite *see Die Forelle

Le Fils Des Muses
    [Fr] solo,pno BILLAUDOT s.p.
                                 (S1182)

Le Jeune Homme Au Bord De La Source
    [Fr] solo,pno BILLAUDOT s.p.
                                 (S1183)

Le Maudit
    [Ger/Fr] solo,pno DURAND s.p.
                                 (S1184)

Le Menetrier
    [Fr] solo,pno BILLAUDOT s.p.
                                 (S1185)

Le Printemps *see Fruhlingsglaube

Le Roi De Thule *see Erlkonig

Le Roi Des Aulnes *see Erlkonig

Le Ruisseau *see Wohin

Le Secret *see Geheimes

Le Tilleul *see Die Lindenbaum

Lebe Wohl
    "Adieu" [Fr] Bar solo,pno BILLAUDOT
        s.p.   (S1186)
    "Adieu" [Fr] T solo,pno BILLAUDOT
        s.p.   (S1187)

Leise Flehen Meine Lieder *see
    Standchen

Les Plaintes De La Jeune Fille
    [Fr] solo,pno BILLAUDOT s.p.
                                 (S1188)

Liebesbotschaft
    "Love's Message" see Metzler's
        Masterpieces Vol. 3: Schubert
        Lieder For Tenor

Liebhaber In Allen Gestalten
    solo,pno DOBLINGER 08 564 s.p.
    contains also: Seligkeit   (S1189)

Lieder *CCU
    (Domandl) [Ger] med solo,gtr SCHAUR
    EE 3072 $2.25   (S1190)

Lieder-Auswahl *CCU
    s.p. high solo,pno SCHOTTS 5932;
    low solo,pno SCHOTTS 5933   (S1191)

Lieder, Band 6 *CCU
    (Durr, Walther) med solo,pno (diff)
    cmplt ed,cloth BAREN. 5503 $33.00
                                 (S1192)

Lieder, Band 7 *CCU
    (Durr, Walther) med solo,pno (diff)
    cmplt ed,cloth BAREN. 5502 $34.00
                                 (S1193)

Lieder, Band I, Teil A *CCU
    (Durr, Walther) solo,pno (diff)
    cmplt ed,cloth BAREN. 5506A s.p.
                                 (S1194)

Lieder, Band I, Teil A Und B *CCU
    (Durr, Walther) solo,pno (diff)
    cmplt ed BAREN. $60.00   (S1195)

Lieder, Band I, Teil B *CCU
    (Durr, Walther) solo,pno (diff)
    cmplt ed,cloth BAREN. 5506B s.p.
                                 (S1196)

Lieder Der Liebe, Landschaft,
    Gesellligkeit *CCU
    (Werbe) [Ger] OSTER $1.25   (S1197)

Linden Tree *see Der Lindenbaum

Linden Tree, The *see Der Lindenbaum

Litanei *sac
    "Litany" see Metzler's Masterpieces
        Vol. 4: Schubert Lieder For
        Baritone Or Bass
    "Litany, For All Souls Day" see
        METZLER'S MASTERPIECES VOL. 15:
        SIX SONGS FOR TENOR
    S/T solo,pno (F maj) LIENAU HOS 136
        s.p.   (S1198)
    Mez solo,pno (E flat maj) LIENAU
        HOS 137 s.p.   (S1199)
    A/Bar solo,pno (D flat maj) LIENAU
        HOS 138 s.p.   (S1200)
    "Litanie" [Fr] solo,pno BILLAUDOT
        s.p.   (S1201)
    "Litany For All Souls' Day" [Ger/
        Eng] med solo,pno (E flat maj)
        SCHIRM.G $.50   (S1202)
    (Reger, Max) [Ger/Eng] Mez/A solo,
        fl,ob,2clar,2horn,timp,strings
        BREITKOPF-L rental   (S1203)

SCHUBERT, FRANZ (PETER) (cont'd.)

Litanie *see Litanei

Litany *see Litanei

Litany, For All Souls Day *see Litanei

L'Ondine Et Le Pecheur
[Ger/Fr] solo,pno DURAND s.p.
(S1204)

Love's Message *see Liebesbotschaft

Maiden's Plaint, The *see Des Madchen's Klage

Marguerite *see Gretchen Am Spinnrade

Marguerite Au Rouet *see Gretchen Am Spinnrade

Memnon *Op.6,No.1
(Reger, Max) "Den Tag Hindurch Nur Einmal Mag Ich Sprechen" [Ger/Eng] Mez/A solo,2fl,2clar,2bsn,2horn,timp,strings BREITKOPF-L rental
(S1205)

Metzler's Masterpieces Vol. 1: Schubert Lieder For Soprano
(Klein, Herman; Kreuz, Emil) S solo,pno CRAMER s.p.
contains: Auf Dem Wasser Zu Singen, "Water Song"; Ave Maria, "Ave Maria"; Du Bist Die Ruh, "With Thee Is Peace"; Fruhlingsglaube, "Faith In Spring"; Gretchen Am Spinnrade, "Gretchen At The Spinning Wheel"; Heidenroslein, "Rosebud On The Hill-Side"
(S1206)

Metzler's Masterpieces Vol. 2: Schubert Lieder For Contralto Or Mezzo-Soprano
(Klein, Herman; Kreuz, Emil) A/Mez solo,pno CRAMER s.p.
contains: Aufenthalt, "My Shelter"; Der Tod Und Das Madchen, "Death And The Maiden"; Des Madchen's Klage, "Maiden's Plaint, The"; Die Allmacht, "Almighty, The"; Die Junge Nonne, "Young Nun, The"; Wiegenlied, "Cradle Song"
(S1207)

Metzler's Masterpieces Vol. 3: Schubert Lieder For Tenor
(Klein, Herman; Kreuz, Emil) T solo,pno CRAMER s.p.
contains: Das Fischermadchen, "Fisher-Maiden, The"; Der Neugierige, "Questioner, The"; Die Krahe, "Raven, The"; Liebesbotschaft, "Love's Message"; Standchen, "Serenade"; Ungeduld, "Impatience"
(S1208)

Metzler's Masterpieces Vol. 4: Schubert Lieder For Baritone Or Bass
(Klein, Herman; Kreuz, Emil) Bar/B solo,pno CRAMER s.p.
contains: Der Doppelganger, "Double, The"; Der Lindenbaum, "Linden Tree, The"; Der Wanderer, "Wanderer, The"; Erlkonig, "Erkling, The", Op.91; Litanei, "Litany"; Wohin?, "Whither?"
(S1209)

My Shelter *see Aufenthalt

Nacht Und Traume *Op.43,No.2
(Reger, Max) "Heilge Nacht, Du Sinkest Nieder" Mez/A solo,fl,clar,3horn,timp,strings BREITKOPF-L rental
(S1210)

Nachtviolen
"Night Violets" [Ger/Eng] solo,pno CRAMER
(S1211)

Night Violets *see Nachtviolen

Ninna Nanna *see Wiegenlied

Nuit Et Songes
[Fr] solo,pno BILLAUDOT s.p.
(S1212)

O Wie Schon Ist Deine Welt *see Im Abendrot

Omnipotence *see Die Allmacht

On The River *see Auf Dem Strom

Ou Aller
[Fr] solo,pno BILLAUDOT s.p.
(S1213)

Pax Vobiscum *sac
S/T solo,pno (A flat maj) LIENAU HOS 139 s.p.
(S1214)

SCHUBERT, FRANZ (PETER) (cont'd.)

A/Bar solo,pno (E flat maj) LIENAU HOS 141 s.p.   (S1215)
Mez solo,pno (F maj) LIENAU HOS 140 s.p.   (S1216)

Quarante Melodies Choisies *CC40U
[Fr] solo,pno cmplt ed BILLAUDOT s.p.   (S1217)

Questioner, The *see Der Neugierige

Raven, The *see Die Krahe

Regret
solo,pno CRAMER   (S1218)

Repos *see Du Bist Die Ruh

Romanze (from Die Verschworenen)
(Spiegl) S solo,clar,pno (med easy) OXFORD 63.048 $1.25   (S1219)

Rose Des Bruyeres *see Heidenroslein

Rosebud On The Hill-Side *see Heidenroslein

Salve Regina *Op.153, sac
S solo,strings sc KNUS EKN 10 s.p., ipa   (S1220)
[Lat] S solo,strings KNUS K14 s.p., ipa   (S1221)
S solo,strings BREITKOPF-L rental   (S1222)

Salve Regina (B-Dur)
S solo,2ob,2bsn,2horn,org,strings BREITKOPF-W s.p.   (S1223)

Sangens Mastare II *CC33U
solo,pno GEHRMANS s.p.   (S1224)

Schlafe, Holder Susser Knabe *see Wiegenlied

Schubert Album *CCU
(Adam) [Hung/Ger] solo,pno BUDAPEST 4473 s.p.   (S1225)

Schubert-Album I *CC92UL
(Friedlander) [Ger] high solo,pno PETERS 20A $7.50; med solo,pno PETERS 20B $7.50; low solo,pno PETERS 20C $7.50, low solo,pno, very low edition, contains 80 songs PETERS 20D $11.00   (S1226)

Schubert-Album II *CC75U
(Friedlander) [Ger] high solo,pno PETERS 178A $7.00; med solo,pno PETERS 178B $7.00; low solo,pno PETERS 178C $9.00   (S1227)

Schubert-Album III *CC45U
(Friedlander) [Ger] high solo,pno PETERS 790A $7.00; low solo,pno PETERS 790B $10.50; low solo,pno PETERS 790C $10.50   (S1228)

Schubert-Album IV *CC62U
(Friedlander) [Ger] PETERS 791 $7.50 original keys   (S1229)

Schubert-Album V *CC52U
(Friedlander) [Ger] PETERS 792 $7.50 original keys   (S1230)

Schubert-Album VI *CC69U
(Friedlander) [Ger] PETERS 793 $7.50 original keys   (S1231)

Schubert-Album VII *CC51U
(Friedlander) [Ger] PETERS 2270 $6.00 original keys   (S1232)

Schubert Lieder Band I *CCU
(Ruckauf) high solo,pno UNIVER. 316 $7.00; med solo,pno UNIVER. 317 $7.00 contains three song cycles and 34 selected lieder   (S1233)

Schwanengesang
see Complete Song Cycles

Sechs Lieder
cmplt ed BREITKOPF-W s.p.
contains: An Die Musik, Op.88, No.4 (A/Bar solo,fl,ob,2clar,2bsn,timp,harp,strings); Die Junge Nonne, Op.43,No.1 (A/Bar solo,fl,ob,2clar,2bsn,3horn,trom,timp,perc,harp,strings); Du Bist Die Ruh, Op.59,No.3 (A/Bar solo,fl,ob,2clar,2bsn,4horn,timp,harp,strings); Erlkonig, Op.1 (A/Bar solo,fl,ob,2clar,2bsn,4horn,2trp,2trom,perc,timp,harp,strings); Ganymed, Op.19,No.3 (A/Bar solo,fl,ob,2clar,2bsn,4horn,timp,harp,strings); Wehmut, Op.22,No.2 (A/Bar solo,fl,ob,2clar,2bsn,4horn,timp,harp,strings)   (S1234)

SCHUBERT, FRANZ (PETER) (cont'd.)

Sechs Lieder *CC6U
[Czech/Ger] solo,pno SUPRAPHON s.p.   (S1235)

Sejour
[Fr] solo,pno BILLAUDOT s.p.   (S1236)

Selected Songs *CCUL
(Friedlander, Max) [Ger/Eng] high solo,pno PETERS 8250A $12.50; med solo,pno PETERS 8250B $12.50; low solo,pno PETERS 8250C $12.50   (S1237)

Selected Songs, Vol. II: Songs To Words By Schiller And Mayrhofer *CCU
(Khokhlov, Yu.) [Russ] solo,pno MEZ KNIGA 95 s.p.   (S1238)

Seligkeit
see Schubert, Franz (Peter), Liebhaber In Allen Gestalten

Serenad *see Standchen

Serenade *see Standchen

Serenade De Shakespeare *see Hark, Hark, The Lark

Serenata *see Standchen

Sest Pisni *CC6U
solo,pno SUPRAPHON s.p.   (S1239)

Shepherd On The Rock, The *see Der Hirt Auf Dem Felsen

Shepherd On The Rocks, The *see Der Hirt Auf Dem Felsen

Songs By Schubert *CC9U
(Duarte, J.W.) [Eng] solo,gtr BERBEN 1819 s.p.   (S1240)

Standchen (from Schwanengesang)
"Serenade" see Metzler's Masterpieces Vol. 3: Schubert Lieder For Tenor
"Serenad" solo,pno HIRSCHS s.p.   (S1241)
"Serenad" solo,pno GEHRMANS 172 s.p.   (S1242)
"Serenad" solo,pno LUNDQUIST s.p.   (S1243)
"Serenade" [Ger/Fr] solo,pno (in 3 keys) DURAND s.p.   (S1244)
"Serenade" [Ger/Eng] low solo,pno (B min) SCHIRM.G $.85   (S1245)
"Serenade" [Ger/Eng] med solo,pno (C min) SCHIRM.G $.85   (S1246)
"Serenade" high solo,pno (D min) CENTURY 510   (S1247)
"Serenade" [Russ] high solo,pno MEZ KNIGA 116 s.p.   (S1248)
"Serenade" med solo,pno (C min) ALLANS s.p.   (S1249)
"Serenade" high solo,pno (D min) ALLANS s.p.   (S1250)
"Serenade" [Fr] B/A solo,pno BILLAUDOT s.p.   (S1251)
"Serenade" [Fr] T solo,pno BILLAUDOT s.p.   (S1252)
"Serenade" [Fr] Bar/Mez solo,pno BILLAUDOT s.p.   (S1253)
"Serenade" solo,pno (available in 2 keys) ASHLEY $.95   (S1254)
"Serenade" [Eng/Ger/It] SA soli,pno PRESSER $.60   (S1255)
"Serenade" low solo,pno (B min) ALLANS s.p.   (S1256)
"Serenata" [It] S/T solo,pno CURCI 5952 s.p.   (S1257)
"Serenata" [It] Mez/Bar solo,pno CURCI 5953 s.p.   (S1258)
"Serenata" [Ger/Span/Fr/It] Mez/Bar solo,pno (C min) RICORDI-ARG BA 6653 s.p.   (S1259)
"Serenata" [Ger/Span/Fr/It] S/T solo,pno (D min) RICORDI-ARG BA 6645 s.p.   (S1260)
"Serenata" [It/Ger] S/T solo,pno RICORDI-ENG 128271 s.p.   (S1261)
(Mottl, F.) "Leise Flehen Meine Lieder" T solo,2fl,ob,2clar,2horn,harp,strings sc BREITKOPF-L PB 1626 s.p., ipr   (S1262)

Suleika *see Suleikas Erster Gesang

Suleikas Erster Gesang *Op.14,No.1
"Suleika" [Ger/Fr] solo,pno (A min) DURAND s.p.   (S1263)
"Suleika" [Ger/Fr] solo,pno (B min) DURAND s.p.   (S1264)
(Mottl, F.) "Was Bedeutet Die Bewegung" S solo,2fl,2ob,2clar,2bsn,2horn,strings BREITKOPF-L rental   (S1265)

Suleikas Zweiter Gesang *Op.31
(Mottl, F.) "Ach Um Deine Feuchten Schwingen" S solo,2fl,2ob,2clar,2bsn,2horn,strings BREITKOPF-L rental   (S1266)

SCHUBERT, FRANZ (PETER) (cont'd.)

Sunset Glow *see Im Abendroth

Swannengesang *song cycle
  "Chant Du Cynge" [Fr] solo,pno
  cmplt ed BILLAUDOT s.p.   (S1267)

Thekla, Eine Geisterstimme *Op.88,
  No.2
  (Mottl, F.) "Wo Ich Sei Und Wo Mich
  Hingewendet" S solo,2fl,2ob,
  2clar,2bsn,2horn,harp,strings
  BREITKOPF-L rental   (S1268)

Thou Are Repose *see Du Bist Die
  Ruh'

Time Lightly Hath Flown Over Me
  solo,pno CRAMER   (S1269)

To Music *see An Die Musik

Trente Melodies *CC30L
  [Ger/Fr] solo,pno DURAND s.p.
  published in three volumes
                              (S1270)

Trockne Blumen
  "Weary Flowers" [Ger/Eng] low solo,
  pno (B flat min) CRAMER   (S1271)
  "Weary Flowers" [Ger/Eng] high
  solo,pno (D min) CRAMER   (S1272)

Trout, The *see Die Forelle

Tu Es Le Repos
  [Fr] solo,pno BILLAUDOT s.p.
                              (S1273)

Twenty-Five Selected Songs *CC25U
  [Ger] Bar/B solo,pno PETERS 3963
  $7.50   (S1274)

Twenty-Four Favorite Songs *CC24L
  high solo,pno SCHIRM.G 350 $2.70;
  low solo,pno SCHIRM.G 351 $3.00
                              (S1275)

Two Hundred Songs, Vol. I (Contains
  All The Cycles Plus 42 Selected
  Songs) *CC100U
  (Kagen, Sergius) [Ger] INTERNAT.
  $9.00 available in high or low
  edition   (S1276)

Two Hundred Songs, Vol. II *CC50L
  (Kagen, Sergius) [Ger] INTERNAT.
  $7.50 available in high or low
  edition   (S1277)

Two Hundred Songs, Vol. III *CC50L
  (Kagen, Sergius) [Ger] INTERNAT.
  $7.50 available in high or low
  edition   (S1278)

Ungeduld
  "Impatience" see Metzler's
  Masterpieces Vol. 3: Schubert
  Lieder For Tenor
  "Impatience" see METZLER'S
  MASTERPIECES VOL. 16: SIX SONGS
  FOR BARITONE OR BASS
  "Impatience" med solo,pno (F maj)
  ALLANS s.p.   (S1279)
  "Impatience" [Ger/Eng] solo,pno
  CRAMER   (S1280)

Valse Printaniere
  solo,pno/inst LEDUC s.p.   (S1281)

Vollendung
  high solo,pno BAREN. 012-19 303
  contains also: Die Erde   (S1282)

Voyage D'hiver Rscycl *see
  Winterreise

Voyages
  see LA MUSIQUE, TROISIEME CAHIER

Wanderer, The *see Der Wanderer

Was Bedeutet Die Bewegung *see
  Suleikas Erster Gesang

Was Ist Sylvia? *see Who Is Sylvia?

Water Song *see Auf Dem Wasser Zu
  Singen

Weary Flowers *see Trockne Blumen

Weep Not For Friends Departed
  solo,pno CRAMER   (S1283)

Wehmut *Op.22,No.2
  see Sechs Lieder

Whither? *see Wohin?

Who Is Sylvia? *Op.106,No.4
  solo,pno CRAMER   (S1284)
  low solo,pno (G maj) ASHDOWN s.p.
                              (S1285)
  high solo,pno (A maj) ASHDOWN
  s.p.   (S1286)
  med solo,pno (G maj) ALLANS s.p.
                              (S1287)

SCHUBERT, FRANZ (PETER) (cont'd.)

  high solo,pno (A maj) ALLANS s.p.
                              (S1288)
  "Was Ist Sylvia?" [Ger/Eng] med
  solo,pno (G maj) SCHIRM.G $.85
                              (S1289)

Wie Erhebet Sich Das Herz *see Dem
  Unendlichen

Wiegenlied *Op.98,No.2
  "Cradle Song" see Metzler's
  Masterpieces Vol. 2: Schubert
  Lieder For Contralto Or Mezzo-
  Soprano
  "Cradle Song" med solo,pno (G maj)
  ALLANS s.p.   (S1290)
  "Cradle-Song" [Ger/Fr/Eng] high
  solo,pno (A flat maj) SCHIRM.G
  $.60   (S1291)
  "La Berceuse" [Fr] solo,pno
  BILLAUDOT s.p.   (S1292)
  "Ninna Nanna" ST soli,pno FORLIVESI
  11933 s.p.   (S1293)
  "Schlafe, Holder Susser Knabe" S
  solo,fl,clar,strings BREITKOPF-L
  rental   (S1294)

Winterreise *song cycle
  high solo,pno SCHIRM.G 346 $2.50
                              (S1295)
  low solo,pno SCHIRM.G 347 $2.50
                              (S1296)
  high solo,pno KALMUS 6428 $2.75
                              (S1297)
  low solo,pno KALMUS 6429 $2.75
                              (S1298)
  "Voyage D'hiver Rscycl" [Fr] solo,
  pno cmplt ed BILLAUDOT s.p. (S1299)

With Thee Is Peace *see Du Bist Die
  Ruh

Wo Ich Sei Und Wo Mich Hingewendet
  *see Thekla, Eine Geisterstimme

Wohin?
  "Whither?" see Metzler's
  Masterpieces Vol. 4: Schubert
  Lieder For Baritone Or Bass
  "Whither?" see METZLER'S
  MASTERPIECES VOL. 15: SIX SONGS
  FOR TENOR
  "Le Ruisseau" [Ger/Fr] solo,pno (in
  3 keys) DURAND s.p.   (S1300)
  "Whither" [Ger/Eng] solo,pno CRAMER
                              (S1301)

Young Nun, The *see Die Junge Nonne

Zastavenicko
  solo,pno SUPRAPHON s.p.   (S1302)

SCHUBERT, HEINZ
  Hymnisches Konzert *concerto
  ST soli,fl,ob,bsn,3trp,org,strings
  RIES s.p.   (S1303)

  Vom Unendlichen
  S solo,strings RIES s.p.   (S1304)

SCHUBERT ALBUM see Schubert, Franz
  (Peter)

SCHUBERT-ALBUM I see Schubert, Franz
  (Peter)

SCHUBERT-ALBUM II see Schubert, Franz
  (Peter)

SCHUBERT-ALBUM III see Schubert, Franz
  (Peter)

SCHUBERT-ALBUM IV see Schubert, Franz
  (Peter)

SCHUBERT-ALBUM V see Schubert, Franz
  (Peter)

SCHUBERT-ALBUM VI see Schubert, Franz
  (Peter)

SCHUBERT-ALBUM VII see Schubert, Franz
  (Peter)

SCHUBERT LIEDER BAND I see Schubert,
  Franz (Peter)

SCHULE, B.
  Ballade Des Pauvres Gueux
  see Cinq Chansons Dans Le Style
  Populaire

  Chanson A Bercer
  see Cinq Chansons Dans Le Style
  Populaire

  Cinq Chansons Dans Le Style Populaire
  solo,pno quarto OUVRIERES s.p.
  contains: Ballade Des Pauvres
  Gueux; Chanson A Bercer; Loin
  De Ma Mie; Noel Du Bon Petit
  Berger; Reveillez-Vous Bergere
  Jolie   (S1305)

SCHULE, B. (cont'd.)

  Loin De Ma Mie
  see Cinq Chansons Dans Le Style
  Populaire

  Noel Du Bon Petit Berger
  see Cinq Chansons Dans Le Style
  Populaire

  Reveillez-Vous Bergere Jolie
  see Cinq Chansons Dans Le Style
  Populaire

SCHULER, GEORGE S.
  Christmas Spirit, The *see Loes,
  Harry Dixon

SCHULHOFF, ERWIN (1894-1942)
  Pisne A Tance Z Tesinska *CCU
  [Czech/Ger/Eng] solo,pno PANTON 081
  s.p.   (S1306)

SCHULLER, GUNTHER (1925-   )
  Meditation
  high solo,pno EMI s.p.   (S1307)

SCHULTHESS, W.
  Lieder (Morgenstern) *CCU
  solo,pno SCHOTTS 5838 s.p. (S1308)

  Lieder (Stamm) *CCU
  solo,pno SCHOTTS 5837 s.p. (S1309)

SCHULTZ
  I'll Live For Jesus *sac
  solo,pno STAMPS 7258-SN $1.00
                              (S1310)

SCHULTZE, NORBERT (1911-   )
  Lieder Aus Der Oper (from Schwarzer
  Peter) CCU
  solo,pno SIKORSKI 130 s.p. (S1311)

SCHULZ, JOH. ABRAHAM PETER (1747-1800)
  Der Mond Ist Aufgegangen *sac
  A/Bar solo,pno (F maj) LIENAU
  HOS 183 s.p.   (S1312)
  S/T solo,pno (A maj) LIENAU HOS 182
  s.p.   (S1313)

  Popular Songs *CC18U
  solo,pno,opt gtr TONGER T18 s.p.
                              (S1314)

  Stille Welt
  (Erdlen, Hermann) 3 soli,strings/
  4strings sc SIKORSKI 408-P s.p.,
  ipa, solo pt SIKORSKI 408-P s.p.,
                              (S1315)

SCHUMAN, W.
  Lord Has A Child, The *sac
  med solo,pno PRESSER $.95   (S1316)
  high solo,pno PRESSER $.95 (S1317)

SCHUMANN, GEORG (1886-1952)
  An Den Ufern Des Jordan *Op.17,No.2
  see Drei Lieder

  Dich Wollt Ich Vergessen *Op.17,No.3
  see Drei Lieder

  Drei Lieder
  med solo,pno LEUCKART s.p.
  contains: Jetzt Rede Du, Op.14,
  No.1; Kindesgebet, Op.14,No.2;
  Zu Dem Silberhellen Bache,
  Op.14,No.3   (S1318)

  Drei Lieder
  med solo,pno LEUCKART s.p.
  contains: Lustern Flustern Die
  Zweige, Op.16,No.2; O Konnt Nur
  Einmal Mein Mudes Haupt, Op.16,
  No.1; Wiegenlied, Op.16,No.3
                              (S1319)

  Drei Lieder
  med solo,pno LEUCKART s.p.
  contains: An Den Ufern Des
  Jordan, Op.17,No.2; Dich Wollt
  Ich Vergessen, Op.17,No.3;
  Wundersam Rauschte Der Wind,
  Op.17,No.1   (S1320)

  Ein Grauses Dunkel *Op.10,No.4
  see Vier Lieder

  Es Duftet Lind Die Fruhlingsnacht
  *Op.10,No.3
  see Vier Lieder

  Ich Habe Nur Einen Gedanken *Op.10,
  No.1
  see Vier Lieder

  Jetzt Rede Du *Op.14,No.1
  see Drei Lieder

  Kindesgebet *Op.14,No.2
  see Drei Lieder

  Lustern Flustern Die Zweige *Op.16,
  No.2
  see Drei Lieder

  Macchenlieder *Op.35,No.1-8, CC8L
  high solo,pno LEUCKART s.p. (S1321)

SCHUMANN, GEORG (cont'd.)

O Konnt Nur Einmal Mein Mudes Haupt
    *Op.16,No.1
    see Drei Lieder

Schlehenblut' Und Wilde Rose *Op.10,
    No.2
    see Vier Lieder

Vier Lieder
    med-high solo,pno LEUCKART s.p.
    contains: Ein Grauses Dunkel,
    Op.10,No.4; Es Duftet Lind Die
    Fruhlingsnacht, Op.10,No.3; Ich
    Habe Nur Einen Gedanken, Op.10,
    No.1; Schlehenblut' Und Wilde
    Rose, Op.10,No.2   (S1322)

Wiegenlied *Op.16,No.3
    see Drei Lieder

Wundersam Rauschte Der Wind *Op.17,
    No.1
    see Drei Lieder

Zu Dem Silberhellen Bache *Op.14,
    No.3
    see Drei Lieder

SCHUMANN, ROBERT (ALEXANDER)
    (1810-1856)
    A L'etoile Du Soir *see An Den
    Abendstern

A Ma Fiancee
    S/T solo,pno DURAND s.p.   (S1323)

Abendlied
    "Evensong" see METZLER'S
    MASTERPIECES VOL. 15: SIX SONGS
    FOR TENOR
    "Evensong" see Metzler's
    Masterpieces Vol. 8: Schumann
    Lieder For Baritone Or Bass

Amour Pour Amour
    solo,pno DURAND s.p.   (S1324)

An Den Abendstern *Op.103,No.4
    "A L'etoile Du Soir" 2 soli,pno
    DURAND s.p. see from Douze Duos
                               (S1325)

An Den Sonnenschein
    "To Sunshine" see Metzler's
    Masterpieces Vol. 7: Schumann
    Lieder For Tenor

An Die Nachtigall *Op.103,No.3
    "Au Rossignol" 2 soli,pno DURAND
    s.p. see from Douze Duos (S1326)

Au Loin
    Mez/Bar solo,pno DURAND s.p.
                               (S1327)

Au Rossignol *see An Die Nachtigall

Auftrage
    "Messages" see Metzler's
    Masterpieces Vol. 7: Schumann
    Lieder For Tenor

Auswahl Der Lieder *CCU
    [Czech/Ger] solo,pno SUPRAPHON s.p.
                               (S1328)

Berceuse
    see LA MUSIQUE, SIXIEME CAHIER
    solo,pno DURAND s.p.   (S1329)
    ST/MezT soli,pno DURAND s.p.
                               (S1330)

Beside The Rhine's Noble Waters *see
    Im Rheim, Heiligen Strome

C'est La Que Nous Aimons
    solo,pno DURAND s.p.   (S1331)

Chagrin
    solo,pno DURAND s.p.   (S1332)

Chanson D'Avril *see Fruhlingslied

Chanson De Mai *see Mailied

Chanson Du Matin
    solo,pno DURAND s.p.   (S1333)

Chansons Espagnoles
    solo,pno cmplt ed DURAND s.p. Op.
    74, Op. 138   (S1334)

Chansons Et Reveries
    solo,pno DURAND s.p.   (S1335)

Chant D'amour *see Liebeslied

Chant De La Fiancee (I) *see Lied
    Der Braut [1]

Chant De La Fiancee (II) *see Lied
    Der Braut [2]

Chant Du Soir *see Nachtlied

Charme De Printemps
    solo,pno DURAND s.p.   (S1336)

SCHUMANN, ROBERT (ALEXANDER) (cont'd.)

Cinq Melodies *Op.125, CC5U
    solo,pno DURAND s.p.   (S1337)

Cinquante Melodies, Choisies *CC50L
    [Ger/Fr] solo,pno DURAND 632 s.p.
                               (S1338)

Clos Ta Paupiere
    solo,pno DURAND s.p.   (S1339)

Complete Songs Of Schumann, Vols. 1-8
    *CCU
    solo,pno KALMUS $2.50. ea. (S1340)

Complete Works *CCU
    (Schumann, Clara; Brahms, Johannes)
    contains works for a variety of
    instruments and vocal
    combinations microfiche
    UNIV.MUS.ED. $135.00 reprints of
    Breitkopf & Hartel Editions;
    contains series 1-14   (S1341)

Dans La Foret *see Waldesgesprach

De Bagge Grenadjarerna *see Die
    Beiden Grenadiere

Dear Ring Upon My Finger *see Du
    Ring An Meinem Finger

Declaration
    solo,pno DURAND s.p.   (S1342)

Dedication *see Widmung

Dein Angesicht
    "Thy Face" see Metzler's
    Masterpieces Vol. 5: Schumann
    Lieder For Soprano
    "Thy Face" see METZLER'S
    MASTERPIECES VOL. 14: SIX SONGS
    FOR MEZZO-SOPRANO OR CONTRALTO
    "Thy Face" solo,pno CRAMER (S1343)

Der Nussbaum
    "Walnut-Tree, The" see Metzler's
    Masterpieces Vol. 5: Schumann
    Lieder For Soprano
    "Walnut Tree, The" see Six Songs
    For Medium Voice
    "Walnut Tree" high solo,pno (G maj)
    ALLANS s.p.   (S1344)

Des Flutes Sur La Pelouse
    Mez/Bar solo,pno DURAND s.p.
                               (S1345)

Dichterliebe *Op.48, song cycle
    [Eng] solo,pno ELKIN 27.0689.10
    s.p.   (S1346)
    [Ger/Fr] solo,pno DURAND s.p.
                               (S1347)
    "Les Amours Du Poete" [Fr/Ger]
    solo,pno DURAND 632B s.p. (S1348)
    "Les Amours D'un Poete" HEUGEL 248
    s.p.   (S1349)
    "Poet's Love" solo,pno FISCHER,C
    O 480   (S1350)
    (Kagen, Sergius) [Ger/Eng] high
    solo,pno INTERNAT. $2.25 (S1351)
    (Kagen, Sergius) [Ger/Eng] low
    solo,pno INTERNAT. $2.25 (S1352)
    (Kagen, Sergius) [Ger/Eng] med
    solo,pno INTERNAT. $2.25 (S1353)

Die Beiden Grenadiere
    "Two Grenadiers, The" see Metzler's
    Masterpieces Vol. 8: Schumann
    Lieder For Baritone Or Bass
    "Two Grenadiers, The" see Six Songs
    For Medium Voice
    "De Bagge Grenadjarerna" solo,pno
    LUNDQVIST s.p.   (S1354)
    "I Due Granatieri" Mez/Bar solo,pno
    FORLIVESI 12139 s.p.   (S1355)
    "Les Deux Ggrenadiers" Mez/Bar
    solo,orch DURAND s.p., ipr
                               (S1356)
    "Two Grenadiers, The" [Ger/Eng] med
    solo,pno (A min) SCHIRM.G $.85
                               (S1357)
    "Two Grenadiers, The" [Ger/Eng] low
    solo,pno (G min) SCHIRM.G $.85
                               (S1358)
    "Two Grenadiers, The" med solo,pno
    (A maj) ALLANS s.p.   (S1359)
    "Two Grenadiers, The" low solo,pno
    (G maj) ALLANS s.p.   (S1360)

Die Lotosblume *Op.25,No.7
    "Lotus Flower, The" see Metzler's
    Masterpieces Vol. 6: Schumann
    Lieder For Contralto Or Mezzo-
    Soprano
    "Lotus Flower" solo,pno (D maj)
    LEONARD-ENG   (S1361)
    "Lotus Flower" med solo,pno (E flat
    maj) ALLANS s.p.   (S1362)
    "Lotus-Flower, The" [Ger/Eng] high
    solo,pno (F maj) SCHIRM.G $.85
                               (S1363)
    "Lotus Mystique" S/T solo,pno
    DURAND s.p.   (S1364)
    "Lotus Mystique" solo,pno DURAND
    134 s.p.   (S1365)

SCHUMANN, ROBERT (ALEXANDER) (cont'd.)

Dieu Gouverne L'Orient
    solo,pno DURAND s.p.   (S1366)

Dis-Moi Pauvre Hirondelle
    see LA MUSIQUE, ONZIEME CAHIER

Douze Dous *CC12L
    2 soli,pno/inst DURAND 2944 s.p.
                               (S1367)

Douze Duos *see An Den Abendstern,
    "A L'etoile Du Soir", Op.103,
    No.4; An Die Nachtigall, "Au
    Rossignol", Op.103,No.3;
    Fruhlingslied, "Chanson D'Avril",
    Op.103,No.2; Landliches Lied,
    "Villanelle", Op.29,No.1;
    Mailied, "Chanson De Mai",
    Op.103,No.1; Spinnelied, "La
    Fortune", Op.79,No.24;
    Zigeunerleben, "Les Bohemiens",
    Op.29,No.3   (S1368)

Dreissig Ausgewahlte Lieder *CC30U
    (Friedlander) high solo,pno PETERS
    8160A $7.00; med solo,pno PETERS
    8160B $7.00; low solo,pno PETERS
    8160C $7.00   (S1369)

Du Bist Wie Eine Blume
    "Thou Art So Like A Flower" see
    Metzler's Masterpieces Vol. 7:
    Schumann Lieder For Tenor
    "Thou Art So Like A Flower" see
    METZLER'S MASTERPIECES VOL. 16:
    SIX SONGS FOR BARITONE OR BASS
    "Thou Art Like A Tender Flower" med
    solo,pno (F maj) ALLANS s.p.
                               (S1370)
    "Thou Art Like A Tender Flower"
    high solo,pno (A flat maj) ALLANS
    s.p.   (S1371)
    "Thou Art So Like A Flower" [Ger/
    Eng] high solo,pno (A flat maj)
    SCHIRM.G $.75   (S1372)

Du Ring An Meinem Finger
    "Dear Ring Upon My Finger" see
    Metzler's Masterpieces Vol. 6:
    Schumann Lieder For Contralto Or
    Mezzo-Soprano

Duos *CC17L
    [Ger/Span] 2 soli,pno cmplt ed
    RICORDI-ARG BA 11777 s.p. works
    from: Op. 103; Op. 79; Op. 138;
    Op. 43   (S1373)

Eighty-Five Songs *CC85U
    (Kagen, Sergius) [Ger/Eng] high
    solo,pno INTERNAT. $7.50 (S1374)

Elle Est A Toi
    S/T solo,pno DURAND s.p.   (S1375)
    Mez/Bar solo,pno DURAND s.p.
                               (S1376)

Elle Et Lui
    ST/MezT soli,pno DURAND s.p.
                               (S1377)

En Avant!
    see LA MUSIQUE, DEUXIEME CAHIER
    solo,pno DURAND s.p.   (S1378)

Ensueno *see Traumerei

Er, Der Herrlichste Von Allen
    "He Of All True Men The Noblest"
    see Metzler's Masterpieces Vol.
    6: Schumann Lieder For Contralto
    Or Mezzo-Soprano
    "He Of All True Men The Noblest"
    see METZLER'S MASTERPIECES VOL.
    13: SIX SONGS FOR SOPRANO

Ett Karlekslofte
    2 soli,pno FAZER F 2819 s.p.
                               (S1379)

Evensong *see Abendlied

Fanfare
    solo,pno DURAND s.p.   (S1380)

Farewell Toast, A *see Wanderlied

Fifty Songs *CC50U
    [Eng/Ger] PRESSER $5.00 high solo,
    pno; low solo,pno   (S1381)

Flamme Eternelle
    solo,pno DURAND s.p.   (S1382)

Frauenliebe Und Leben *Op.42, song
    cycle
    [Ger/Fr] solo,pno DURAND s.p.
                               (S1383)
    "La Vie D'une Femme" HEUGEL 247
    s.p.   (S1384)
    "L'Amour D'une Femme" [Ger/Fr]
    solo,pno DURAND 632 s.p. (S1385)
    "Woman's Life" high solo,pno KALMUS
    6446 $1.50   (S1386)
    "Woman's Life" low solo,pno KALMUS
    6447 $1.50   (S1387)
    "Woman's Life And Love" [Ger/Eng]
    low solo,pno SCHIRM.G 1357 $1.50

SCHUMANN, ROBERT (ALEXANDER) (cont'd.)

(S1388)
"Woman's Life And Love" [Ger/Eng]
high solo,pno SCHIRM.G 1356 $1.50
(S1389)
(Kagen, Sergius) [Ger/Eng] high
solo,pno INTERNAT. $2.25   (S1390)
(Kagen, Sergius) [Ger/Eng] low
solo,pno INTERNAT. $2.25   (S1391)

Fruhlingnacht
"Night In Spring" see Metzler's
Masterpieces Vol. 5: Schumann
Lieder For Soprano

Fruhlingslied *Op.103,No.2
"Chanson D'Avril" 2 soli,pno DURAND
s.p. see from Douze Duos (S1392)

Fruhlingsnacht
"Nuit De Printemps" S/T solo,pno
DURAND s.p.   (S1393)
"Nuit De Printemps" Mez/Bar solo,
pno DURAND s.p.   (S1394)

Funf Heitere Gesange *Op.125, CC5U
solo,pno quarto,cmplt ed DURAND
s.p.   (S1395)

Greeting *see Widmung

He Of All True Men The Noblest *see
Er, Der Herrlichste Von Allen

Heinrich-Heine-Lieder *CCU
solo,pno PETERS 4695 $9.50 (S1396)

I Due Granatieri *see Die Beiden
Grenadiere

I Judge Thee Not *see Ich Grolle
Nicht

I Murmur Not *see Ich Grolle Nicht

Ich Grolle Nicht
"I Murmur Not" see Metzler's
Masterpieces Vol. 8: Schumann
Lieder For Baritone Or Bass
"I Judge Thee Not" [Ger/Eng] med-
high solo,pno (C maj) SCHIRM.G
$.60   (S1397)

Im Rheim, Heiligen Strome
"Beside The Rhine's Noble Waters"
see Metzler's Masterpieces Vol.
8: Schumann Lieder For Baritone
Or Bass

Im Wunderschonen Monat Mai
"Wond'rous Month Of May, The" see
Metzler's Masterpieces Vol. 7:
Schumann Lieder For Tenor
"Wond'rous Month Of May, The" see
METZLER'S MASTERPIECES VOL. 16:
SIX SONGS FOR BARITONE OR BASS

Impatience
solo,pno DURAND s.p.   (S1398)

In May
see Six Songs For Medium Voice

Intermezzo
"Intermezzo" see METZLER'S
MASTERPIECES VOL. 15: SIX SONGS
FOR TENOR
"Intermezzo" see Metzler's
Masterpieces Vol. 8: Schumann
Lieder For Baritone Or Bass

Intermezzo *see Intermezzo

J'ai Pardonne
Mez/Bar solo,orch DURAND s.p., ipr
(S1399)
[Fr] solo,acap oct DURAND s.p.
(S1400)

Je Pense A Toi
ST/MezT soli,pno DURAND s.p.
(S1401)

Kennst Du Das Land?
"Mignon" see Metzler's Masterpieces
Vol. 5: Schumann Lieder For
Soprano

La Chanson Du Jeune Archer
see LA MUSIQUE, CINQUIEME CAHIER

La Coccinelle
see LA MUSIQUE, QUATRIEME CAHIER
solo,acap DURAND s.p.   (S1402)

La Fauvette
solo,pno DURAND s.p.   (S1403)

La Femme Du Chef
solo,pno DURAND s.p.   (S1404)

La Fortune *see Spinnelied

La Guerison Du Poete
solo,pno DURAND s.p.   (S1405)

SCHUMANN, ROBERT (ALEXANDER) (cont'd.)

La Pauvre Pierre
solo,pno (available in 2 keys)
ENOCH s.p.   (S1406)

La Valse
ST/MezT soli,pno DURAND s.p.
(S1407)

La Vie D'une Femme *see Frauenliebe
Und Leben

L'Adieu Du Hussard
solo,pno DURAND s.p.   (S1408)

L'Amour D'une Femme *see Frauenliebe
Und Leben

Landliches Lied *Op.29,No.1
"Villanelle" 2 soli,pno DURAND s.p.
see from Douze Duos   (S1409)

Le Bonheur Parfait
solo,pno DURAND s.p.   (S1410)

Le Dimanche Au Bord Du Rhin
solo,pno DURAND s.p.   (S1411)

Le Fils De La Tempete
solo,pno DURAND s.p.   (S1412)

Le Noyer
Mez/Bar solo,pno DURAND s.p.
(S1413)

Le Pays De Cocagne
see LA MUSIQUE, PREMIER CAHIER

Le Vin
solo,pno DURAND s.p.   (S1414)

Les Amours Du Poete *see
Dichterliebe

Les Amours D'un Poete *see
Dichterliebe

Les Bohemiens *see Zigeunerleben

Les Deux Ggrenadiers *see Die Beiden
Grenadiere

Les Deux Grenadiers
[Fr] solo,acap oct DURAND s.p.
(S1415)

Les Myrtes *see Myrthen

L'Heure Du Mystere
Mez/Bar solo,pno DURAND s.p.
(S1416)

Liebeslied *Op.51,No.5
"Chant D'amour" solo,pno DURAND
s.p.   (S1417)

Lied
3 soli,pno DURAND s.p.   (S1418)

Lied Der Braut [1] *Op.25,No.11
"Chant De La Fiancee (I)" solo,pno
DURAND s.p.   (S1419)

Lied Der Braut [2] *Op.25,No.12
"Chant De La Fiancee (II)" solo,pno
DURAND s.p.   (S1420)

Lieder *CCU
[Ger/Fr] solo,pno BREITKOPF-L
EB 1719 s.p. includes Op. 37, 39,
40, 42, 45, 48, 49, 51, 53
(S1421)

Lieder-Auswahl *CCU
s.p. high solo,pno SCHOTTS 5586;
low solo,pno SCHOTTS 5587 (S1422)

Liederkreis *Op.39,No.1-12, song
cycle
(Kagen, Sergius) [Ger/Eng] high
solo,pno INTERNAT. $2.25 (S1423)
(Kagen, Sergius) [Ger/Eng] low
solo,pno INTERNAT. $2.25 (S1424)

Lotus,
see Six Songs For Medium Voice

Lotus Flower *see Die Lotosblume

Lotus Flower, The *see Die
Lotosblume

Lotus Mystique *see Die Lotosblume

Mailied *Op.103,No.1
"Chanson De Mai" 2 soli,pno DURAND
s.p. see from Douze Duos (S1425)

Manskensnatt *see Mondnacht

Meeting In The Woods *see
Waldesgesprach

Melodies Choises *CCU
HEUGEL 305 s.p.   (S1426)

Mer, Soleil Et Rose
solo,pno DURAND s.p.   (S1427)

SCHUMANN, ROBERT (ALEXANDER) (cont'd.)

Messages *see Auftrage

Metzler's Masterpieces Vol. 5:
Schumann Lieder For Soprano
(Klein, Herman; Kreuz, Emil) S
solo,pno CRAMER s.p.
contains: Dein Angesicht, "Thy
Face"; Der Nussbaum, "Walnut-
Tree, The"; Fruhlingnacht,
"Night In Spring"; Kennst Du
Das Land?, "Mignon";
Volksliedchen, "When At Morn";
Widmung, "Greeting"   (S1428)

Metzler's Masterpieces Vol. 6:
Schumann Lieder For Contralto Or
Mezzo-Soprano
(Klein, Herman; Kreuz, Emil) A/Mez
solo,pno CRAMER s.p.
contains: Die Lotosblume, "Lotus
Flower, The"; Du Ring An Meinem
Finger, "Dear Ring Upon My
Finger"; Er, Der Herrlichste
Von Allen, "He Of All True Men
The Noblest"; Mondnacht,
"Moonlight"; Waldesgesprach,
"Meeting In The Woods"; Was
Will Die Einsame Thrane, "What
Means This Lonely Tear?" (S1429)

Metzler's Masterpieces Vol. 7:
Schumann Lieder For Tenor
(Klein, Herman; Kreuz, Emil) T
solo,pno CRAMER s.p.
contains: An Den Sonnenschein,
"To Sunshine"; Auftrage,
"Messages"; Du Bist Wie Eine
Blume, "Thou Art So Like A
Flower"; Im Wunderschonen Monat
Mai, "Wond'rous Month Of May,
The"; Mit Myrten Und Rosen,
"With Myrtle And Roses"; Wenn
Ich In Deine Augen Seh, "Whilst
Gazing Into Thy Dear Eyes"
(S1430)

Metzler's Masterpieces Vol. 8:
Schumann Lieder For Baritone Or
Bass
(Klein, Herman; Kreuz, Emil) Bar/B
solo,pno CRAMER s.p.
contains: Abendlied, "Evensong";
Die Beiden Grenadiere, "Two
Grenadiers, The"; Ich Grolle
Nicht, "I Murmur Not"; Im
Rheim, Heiligen Strome, "Beside
The Rhine's Noble Waters";
Intermezzo, "Intermezzo";
Wanderlied, "Farewell Toast, A"
(S1431)

Mignon *see Kennst Du Das Land?

Mirage
solo,pno DURAND s.p.   (S1432)

Mit Myrten Und Rosen
"With Myrtle And Roses" see
Metzler's Masterpieces Vol. 7:
Schumann Lieder For Tenor

Mondnacht
"Moonlight" see Metzler's
Masterpieces Vol. 6: Schumann
Lieder For Contralto Or Mezzo-
Soprano
"Moonlight" see METZLER'S
MASTERPIECES VOL. 13: SIX SONGS
FOR SOPRANO
"Manskensnatt" solo,pno GEHRMANS
s.p.   (S1433)

Moonlight *see Mondnacht

Myrthen *Op.25, song cycle
"Les Myrtes" [Ger] solo,pno DURAND
2083 s.p.   (S1434)

Nachtlied *Op.96,No.1
"Chant Du Soir" solo,pno DURAND
s.p.   (S1435)

Night In Spring *see Fruhlingnacht

Ninety Songs *CC90L
(Kagen, Sergius) [Ger/Eng] low
solo,pno INTERNAT. $7.50 (S1436)

Nuit De Printemps *see
Fruhlingsnacht

O Fleur Vermeille
solo,pno DURAND s.p.   (S1437)

Personne
see LA MUSIQUE, SEPTIEME CAHIER
solo,pno DURAND s.p.   (S1438)

Pitie
solo,org,vcl/vln DURAND 32 s.p.
(S1439)

Poet's Love *see Dichterliebe

Reproches
solo,pno DURAND s.p.   (S1440)

SCHUMANN, ROBERT (ALEXANDER) (cont'd.)

Reves De Mere
 solo,pno DURAND s.p. (S1441)

Reves Trompeur
 solo,pno DURAND s.p. (S1442)

Ruhe Sanft In Gottes Frieden *Op.25,
 No.26, sac
 Mez solo,pno (A flat maj) LIENAU
 HOS 142 s.p. (S1443)
 A/Bar solo,pno (F maj) LIENAU
 HOS 142A s.p. (S1444)

Schon Hedwig *Op.106
 narrator,pno HEUWEKE. 075 s.p.
 (S1445)

Schumann-Album I *CC77UL
 (Friedlander) [Ger] $6.50 high
 solo,pno PETERS 2383A; med solo,
 pno PETERS 2383B; low solo,pno
 PETERS 2383C (S1446)

Schumann-Album II *CC87U
 (Friedlander) [Ger] high solo,pno
 PETERS 2384A $7.50; med solo,pno
 PETERS 2384B $9.50 (S1447)

Schumann-Album III *CC82UL
 (Friedlander) [Ger] high solo,pno,
 opt harp PETERS 2385A $9.50; med
 solo,pno,opt harp PETERS 2385B
 $9.50 (S1448)

Secret
 solo,pno DURAND s.p. (S1449)

Separation
 solo,pno DURAND s.p. (S1450)

Serenade
 med solo,pno (F maj) ALLANS s.p.
 (S1451)

Serenade Venitienne
 solo,pno DURAND s.p. (S1452)

Since I First Beheld Him
 (Howe) Mez solo,pno PAXTON P40610
 s.p. (S1453)

Six Songs For Medium Voice
 med solo,pno NOVELLO 19.0009.09
 s.p.
 contains: Dedication; In May;
 Lotus, The; Thou'rt Like Unto A
 Flower; Two Grenadiers, The;
 Walnut Tree, The (S1454)

Slumber Song
 low solo,pno (C maj) ALLANS s.p.
 (S1455)
 high solo,pno (D maj) ALLANS s.p.
 (S1456)

Solitude
 solo,pno DURAND s.p. (S1457)

Son Amour Me Reste
 solo,pno DURAND s.p. (S1458)

Souvenirs De L'Ebre
 solo,pno DURAND s.p. (S1459)

Spanisches Liederspiel *Op.74, CC12U
 [Ger] S/T/Bar/SA/ST/SATB/TB soli,
 pno PETERS 2394 $5.50 (S1460)

Spinnelied *Op.79,No.24
 "La Fortune" 2 soli,pno DURAND s.p.
 see from Douze Duos (S1461)

Star-Spangled Banner, The
 (Smith, John S.; Damrosch) med
 solo,pno (B flat maj) SCHIRM.G
 $.60 (S1462)

Ta Beaute
 solo,pno DURAND s.p. (S1463)

Ten Songs *CC10U
 [Hung/Ger] solo,pno BUDAPEST 3493
 s.p. (S1464)

Thirty-Four Duets *CC34U
 (Friedlander) [Ger] SS/SA/ST/SBar/
 AB/TB soli,pno PETERS 2392 $7.50
 (S1465)

Thou Art Like A Tender Flower *see
 Du Bist Wie Eine Blume

Thou Art So Like A Flower *see Du
 Bist Wie Eine Blume

Thou'rt Like Unto A Flower
 see Six Songs For Medium Voice

Thy Face *see Dein Angesicht

Tillagnan *see Widmung

To Sunshine *see An Den Sonnenschein

Ton Image
 solo,pno DURAND s.p. (S1466)

SCHUMANN, ROBERT (ALEXANDER) (cont'd.)

Ton Visage
 solo,pno DURAND s.p. (S1467)

Toujours Dureront Nos Amours
 solo,pno DURAND s.p. (S1468)

Traumerei *Op.15,No.7
 solo,pno SCHAUR EE 3387 s.p.
 (S1469)
 (Pardo) "Ensueno" [Span] solo,pno
 RICORDI-ARG BA 8573 s.p. (S1470)

Two Grenadiers, The *see Die Beiden
 Grenadiere

Une Goutte D'eau
 solo,pno DURAND s.p. (S1471)

Vent-Cinq Melodies Choisies *CC25U
 solo,pno cmplt ed DURAND s.p.
 (S1472)

Villanelle *see Landliches Lied

Vingt-Cinq Melodies Celebres *CC25L
 [Ger] solo,pno DURAND 3798 s.p.
 (S1473)

Violettes De Mars
 solo,pno DURAND s.p. (S1474)

Vocal Album *CC55L
 [Ger/Eng] high solo,pno SCHIRM.G
 120 $4.00; low solo,pno SCHIRM.G
 $1.21 $4.00 (S1475)

Volksliedchen
 "When At Morn" see METZLER'S
 MASTERPIECES VOL. 14: SIX SONGS
 FOR MEZZO-SOPRANO OR CONTRALTO
 "When At Morn" see Metzler's
 Masterpieces Vol. 5: Schumann
 Lieder For Soprano

Waldesgesprach *Op.39,No.3
 "Meeting In The Woods" see
 Metzler's Masterpieces Vol. 6:
 Schumann Lieder For Contralto Or
 Mezzo-Soprano
 "Dans La Foret" solo,pno DURAND
 s.p. (S1476)

Walnut Tree *see Der Nussbaum

Walnut-Tree, The *see Der Nussbaum

Wanderlied
 "Farewell Toast, A" see Metzler's
 Masterpieces Vol. 8: Schumann
 Lieder For Baritone Or Bass
 "Farewell Toast, A" see METZLER'S
 MASTERPIECES VOL. 15: SIX SONGS
 FOR TENOR

Was Will Die Einsame Thrane
 "What Means This Lonely Tear?" see
 Metzler's Masterpieces Vol. 6:
 Schumann Lieder For Contralto Or
 Mezzo-Soprano

Wenn Ich In Deine Augen Seh
 "While Gazing Into Thy Dear Eyes"
 see METZLER'S MASTERPIECES VOL.
 16: SIX SONGS FOR BARITONE OR
 BASS
 "Whilst Gazing Into Thy Dear Eyes"
 see Metzler's Masterpieces Vol.
 7: Schumann Lieder For Tenor

What Means This Lonely Tear? *see
 Was Will Die Einsame Thrane

When At Morn *see Volksliedchen

While Gazing Into Thy Dear Eyes *see
 Wenn Ich In Deine Augen Seh

Whilst Gazing Into Thy Dear Eyes
 *see Wenn Ich In Deine Augen Seh

Widmung
 "Dedication" see Six Songs For
 Medium Voice
 "Greeting" see Metzler's
 Masterpieces Vol. 5: Schumann
 Lieder For Soprano
 "Greeting" see METZLER'S
 MASTERPIECES VOL. 14: SIX SONGS
 FOR MEZZO-SOPRANO OR CONTRALTO
 "Dedication" [Ger/Eng] low solo,pno
 (F maj) SCHIRM.G $.85 (S1477)
 "Dedication" low solo,pno (F maj)
 ALLANS s.p. (S1478)
 "Dedication" med solo,pno (G maj)
 ALLANS s.p. (S1479)
 "Dedication" high solo,pno (A flat
 maj) ALLANS s.p. (S1480)
 "Dedication" [Ger/Eng] high solo,
 pno (A flat maj) SCHIRM.G $.85
 (S1481)
 "Tillagnan" solo,pno GEHRMANS s.p.
 (S1482)

With Myrtle And Roses *see Mit
 Myrten Und Rosen

SCHUMANN, ROBERT (ALEXANDER) (cont'd.)

Woman's Life *see Frauenliebe Und
 Leben

Woman's Life And Love *see
 Frauenliebe Und Leben

Wond'rous Month Of May, The *see Im
 Wunderschonen Monat Mai

Zigeunerleben *Op.29,No.3
 "Les Bohemiens" 2 soli,pno DURAND
 s.p. see from Douze Duos (S1483)

Zwolf Lieder *CC12L
 (Leuchter, Kurzmann) [Ger/Span] med
 solo,pno cmplt ed RICORDI-ARG
 BA 8563 s.p. (S1484)

SCHUMANN, WILLIAM HOWARD (1910-)
Orpheus With His Lute
 med solo,pno (D min) SCHIRM.G $.85
 (S1485)

SCHUMANN-ALBUM I see Schumann, Robert
 (Alexander)

SCHUMANN-ALBUM II see Schumann, Robert
 (Alexander)

SCHUMANN-ALBUM III see Schumann, Robert
 (Alexander)

SCHUR, DODI!
 see Six Folk Songs

SCHURMANN, GERARD (1928-)
Chuench'i *song cycle
 S solo,pno NOVELLO 75.0005.10 s.p.
 (S1486)
 high solo,3fl,2pic,2ob,English
 horn,2clar,2bsn,4horn,2trp,3trom,
 timp,perc,xylo,vibra,glock,harp,
 cel,strings NOVELLO rental
 (S1487)

SCHUSTER, GIORA
Two Dialogues And Recitative *CCU
 solo,fl/ob,pno ISR.MUS.INST. 101
 s.p. (S1488)

SCHUTTERSLIED see Fouquet, V.

SCHUTZ, HEINRICH (1585-1672)
Ach, Mein Sohn Absalon *see Fili Mi,
 Absalon

Ach, Meine Seele *see Anima Mea
 Liquefacta Est

Adjuro Vos, Filiae Jerusalem *SWV
 264, sac
 (Gerber, Rudolf) "Ich Flehe Euch
 An" [Lat/Ger] TT soli,2English
 horn/rec/vln,cont (contains also:
 Anima Mea Liquefacta Est) BAREN.
 34 $5.25 see also Symphoniae
 Sacrae I, Heft I (S1489)

Allein Gott In Der Hoh Sei Ehr *SWV
 327
 see Kleine Geistliche Konzerte Heft
 IX

Als Ich Gott Den Herrn Gesucht *see
 Exquisivi Dominum

Anima Mea Liquefacta Est *SWV 263,
 sac
 (Gerber, Rudolf) "Ach, Meine Seele"
 [Lat/Ger] TT soli,2English horn/
 rec/vln,cont (contains also:
 Adjuro Vos, Filiae Jerusalem)
 BAREN. 34 $5.25 see also
 Symphoniae Sacrae I, Heft I
 (S1490)

Attendite, Popule Meus Legem Meam
 *SWV 270 (from Symphoniae Sacrae)
 sac,concerto
 B solo,4trom,cont sc MUS. RARA
 MR 1063 s.p. (S1491)
 [Lat] B solo,4trom,pno BROEKMANS
 920 s.p. (S1492)
 (Kirchner, Gerhard) "So Hore Doch,
 Meine Gemeinde" [Lat/Ger] B solo,
 4trom,cont sc BAREN. 37 $5.25,
 ipa see also Symphoniae Sacrae I,
 Heft II (S1493)

Auf Dem Gebirge Hat Man Ein Geschrei
 Gehoret *SWV 396, sac
 AA soli,strings BAREN. 528 s.p. see
 from Geistliche Chormusik 1648
 (S1494)

Auf Und Blaset Am Fest Des Neumonds
 Die Tuba *see Buccinate In
 Neomenia Tuba

Aufer Immensam *SWV 337
 see Kleine Geistliche Konzerte Heft
 XIX

Ave Maria, Gratia Plena *SWV 334,
 sac,concerto
 SA soli,5inst,cont sc HANSSLER
 20.334 s.p., ipa see from Kleine
 Geistliche Konzerte (S1495)

SCHUTZ, HEINRICH (cont'd.)

Benedicam Dominum *SWV 267, sac
  (Kirchner, Gerhard) "Preisen Will
  Ich Allezeit" [Lat/Ger] STB soli,
  vln,cont (contains also:
  Exquisivi Dominum) sc BAREN. 36
  $7.75, ipa see also Symphoniae
  Sacrae I, Heft II   (S1496)

Blessed Is He Who Walks Not In The
  Path Of The Wicked *sac
  SA soli,cont oct CONCORDIA 98-1920
  $.25   (S1497)

Bone Jesu, Verbum Patris *SWV 313
  see Kleine Geistliche Konzerte Heft
  XV

Bring To Jehovah *see Bringt Her Dem
  Herren

Bring To The Lord God *see Bringt
  Her Dem Herren

Bringt Her Dem Herren *SWV 283
  see Kleine Geistliche Konzerte Heft
  II
  see Kleine Geistliche Konzerte Heft
  I
  "Bring To Jehovah" see Five Sacred
  Songs
  "Bring To The Lord God" see Five
  Short Sacred Concertos (English
  Version)

Buccinate In Neomenia Tuba *SWV 275,
  sac
  (Gerber, Rudolf) "Auf Und Blaset Am
  Fest Des Neumonds Die Tuba" [Lat/
  Ger] TTB soli,2brass,bsn,cont
  (contains also: Jubilate Deo)
  BAREN. 42 $7.75 see also
  Symphoniae Sacrae I, Heft II
                               (S1498)
Cantabo Domino *SWV 260, sac
  (Gerber, Rudolf) "Ich Singe Dem
  Herrn" [Lat/Ger] T solo,2vln,cont
  BAREN. 31 $4.25 see also
  Symphoniae Sacrae I, Heft I
                               (S1499)
Collected Works *CCU
  (Spitta, Philipp; Schering, Arnold)
  [Ger/Lat/It] solo,inst, contains
  also choral works both secular and
  secular microfiche UNIV.MUS.ED.
  $90.00 reprints of Breitkopf &
  Hartel Editions; contains 18
  volumes   (S1500)

Das Blut Jesu Christi Machet Uns Rein
  *SWV 298, sac,concerto
  see Kleine Geistliche Konzerte Heft
  XII
  SSB soli,cont HANSSLER 20.298 s.p.
  see from Kleine Geistliche
  Konzerte   (S1501)

Das Magnificat
  (Lutge) "Meine Seele Erhebt Den
  Herren" [Ger] Mez solo,2vln,org,
  opt 2trp cmplt ed AMP $3.00
                               (S1502)
Der Herr Ist Gross *SWV 286
  see Kleine Geistliche Konzerte Heft
  IV

Der Herr Ist Mein Licht *SWV 359,
  sac
  (Bittenger, Werner) TT soli,2vln,
  cont sc BAREN. 5904 $4.75, ipa
  see also Symphoniae Sacrae II,
  Heft II   (S1503)

Der Herr Ist Meine Starke *SWV 345,
  sac,concerto
  S solo,2vln,cont sc HANSSLER 5.007
  s.p., ipa see from Symphoniae
  Sacrae II   (S1504)
  (Gerber, Rudolf) S/T solo,2vln,cont
  BAREN. 499 $4.25 see also
  Symphoniae Sacrae II, Heft I
                               (S1505)
Der Herr Schauet Vom Himmel *SWV
  292, sac,concerto
  see Kleine Geistliche Konzerte Heft
  XII
  SB soli,bvl,cont HANSSLER 5.003
  s.p. see from Kleine Geistliche
  Konzerte   (S1506)

Des Nachts Auf Meinem Lager *see In
  Lectulo Per Noctes

Die Furcht Des Herren Ist Der
  Weisheit Anfang *SWV 318, sac,
  concerto
  see Kleine Geistliche Konzerte Heft
  XI
  2 high soli,cont HANSSLER 20.318
  s.p. see from Kleine Geistliche
  Konzerte   (S1507)

Die Gottseligkeit Ist Zu Allen Dingen
  Nutze *SWV 299, sac,concerto
  see Kleine Geistliche Konzerte Heft

SCHUTZ, HEINRICH (cont'd.)

XII
SSB soli,cont HANSSLER 20.299 s.p.
  see from Kleine Geistliche
  Konzerte   (S1508)

Die Seele Christi Heilige Mich *SWV
  325
  see Kleine Geistliche Konzerte Heft
  IX

Die Sieben Worte Jesu Christi Am
  Kreuz *SWV 478
  SATTB soli,opt SATTB,2English horn,
  3bsn,strings sc HANSSLER 20.478
  s.p., ipa   (S1509)

Die So Ihr Den Herren Furchtet *SWV
  364, sac
  (Bittinger, Werner) ATB soli,2vln,
  cont sc BAREN. 5909 s.p., ipa see
  also Symphoniae Sacrae II, Heft
  III   (S1510)

Die Stimm Des Herren *SWV 331
  see Kleine Geistliche Konzerte Heft
  VIII

Dir, O Herr, Gilt All Mein Hoffen
  *see In Te, Domine, Speravi

Domine, Labia Mea Aperies *SWV 271,
  sac
  (Kirchner, Gerhard) [Lat] ST soli,
  ob,vln,trom,bsn,cont sc BAREN. 38
  $5.50, ipa see also Symphoniae
  Sacrae I, Heft II   (S1511)

Drei Schone Dinge Seind *SWV 365,
  sac
  (Bittinger, Werner) TTB soli,2vln,
  cont sc BAREN. 5910 s.p., ipa see
  also Symphoniae Sacrae II, Heft
  III   (S1512)
Du Schalksknecht *SWV 397, sac
  T solo,strings BAREN. 529 s.p. see
  from Geistliche Chormusik 1648
                               (S1513)
Eile, Mich, Gott, Zu Erretten *SWV
  282
  see Kleine Geistliche Konzerte Heft
  I
  "Haste Thee, Lord God, Haste To
  Save Me" see Five Sacred Songs

Ein Kind Ist Uns Geboren *SWV 302,
  sac,concerto
  see Kleine Geistliche Konzerte Heft
  III
  SATB soli,cont HANSSLER 20.302 sc
  s.p., ipa, solo pt s.p. see from
  Kleine Geistliche Konzerte
                               (S1514)
Eins Bitte Ich Vom Herren *SWV 294
  see Kleine Geistliche Konzerte Heft
  V

Erbarm Dich Mein, O Herre Gott *SWV
  447, sac,concerto
  S/med solo,4inst,cont sc HANSSLER
  20.447 s.p., ipa   (S1515)

Erhore Mich, Wenn Ich Rufe *SWV 289
  see Kleine Geistliche Konzerte Heft
  IV

Es Steh Gott Auf *SWV 356, sac
  (Bittenger, Werner) SS/TT soli,
  2vln,cont sc BAREN. 5903 $5.00,
  ipa see also Symphoniae Sacrae
  II, Heft II   (S1516)

Exquisivi Dominum *SWV 268, sac
  (Kirchner, Gerhard) "Als Ich Gott
  Den Herrn Gesucht" [Lat/Ger] STB
  soli,vln,cont (contains also:
  Benedicam Dominum) sc BAREN. 36
  $7.75, ipa see also Symphoniae
  Sacrae I, Heft II   (S1517)

Exultavit Cor Meum *SWV 258, sac
  (Gerber, Rudolf) "Freude Und Gluck"
  [Lat/Ger] S/T solo,2vln,cont
  BAREN. 29 $4.25 see also
  Symphoniae Sacrae I, Heft I
                               (S1518)
Father Abraham, Have Mercy On Me
  *sac
  [Ger/Eng] SSATB soli,2vln,2fl,cont
  sc CONCORDIA 97-9348 $3.00, ipa
                               (S1519)
Fear The Almighty *sac
  2 med soli,cont oct CONCORDIA
  98-1854 $.25   (S1520)

Fili Mi, Absalon *SWV 269 (from
  Symphoniae Sacrae I) sac
  (Gerber, Rudolf) "Ach, Mein Sohn
  Absalon" [Lat/Ger] B solo,4trom,
  cont BAREN. 40 $4.75 see also
  Symphoniae Sacrae I, Heft II
                               (S1521)
  (Shoemaker, John R.) B solo,4trom/
  strings/org&vcl CRESCENDO $6.50

SCHUTZ, HEINRICH (cont'd.)

                               (S1522)
Five Sacred Songs *sac
  [Eng/Ger] CONCORDIA 98-1370 $2.25
  contains: Bringt Her Dem Herren,
  "Bring To Jehovah"; Eile, Mich,
  Gott, Zu Erretten, "Haste Thee,
  Lord God, Haste To Save Me";
  Ich Danke Dem Herrn Von Ganzem
  Herzen, "O God, I Will Praise
  Thee"; Ich Will Den Herren
  Loben Allezeit, "Now Will I
  Praise The Lord With All My
  Heart"; Was Hast Du Verwirket?,
  "How Hast Thou Offended?"
                               (S1523)
Five Short Sacred Concertos (English
  Version) *sac,concerto
  PETERS 6894 $3.00
  contains: Bringt Her Dem Herren,
  "Bring To The Lord God";
  Hasten, O Lord, To Redeem Me; I
  Sing To The Lord; I Will Give
  Thanks To God Eternally; O
  Susser, O Freundlicher, "O
  Tender, O Bountiful"   (S1524)

Five Short Sacred Concertos (German
  Version) *sac,concerto
  PETERS 4174 $3.25   (S1525)

Freude Und Gluck *see Exultavit Cor
  Meum

Freuet Euch Des Herren, Ihr Gerechten
  *SWV 367, sac
  (Birtner, Herbert) AT soli,2vln,
  cont sc BAREN. 631 $5.75 see also
  Symphoniae Sacrae II, Heft III
                               (S1526)
Frohlocket Mit Handen *SWV 349, sac
  (Hoffmann, Hans) Bar/B solo,2vln,
  cont (contains also: Hutet Euch)
  BAREN. 1088 $5.50 see also
  Symphoniae Sacrae II, Heft I
                               (S1527)
From God Shall Naught Divide Me (from
  Symphoniae Sacrae II) sac
  [Eng/Ger] SSB soli,2vln,cont sc
  CONCORDIA 97-9330 $2.50, ipa
                               (S1528)
Furchte Dich Nicht *SWV 296
  see Kleine Geistliche Konzerte Heft
  VII

Geistliche Chormusik 1648 *see Auf
  Dem Gebirge Hat Man Ein Geschrei
  Gehoret, SWV 396; Du
  Schalksknecht, SWV 397; Sehet An
  Den Feigenbaum, SWV 394; Was Mein
  Gott Will, Das Gescheh Allzeit,
  SWV 392   (S1529)

Gib Unsern Fursten *SWV 355, sac
  (Bittenger, Werner) SS/TT soli,
  2vln,cont (contains also: Verleih
  Uns Frieden) BAREN. 4338 $5.50
  see also Symphoniae Sacrae II,
  Heft II   (S1530)

Habe Deine Lust An Dem Herrn *SWV
  311
  see Kleine Geistliche Konzerte Heft
  IV

Haste Thee, Lord God, Haste To Save
  Me *see Eile, Mich, Gott, Zu
  Erretten

Hasten, O Lord, To Redeem Me
  see Five Short Sacred Concertos
  (English Version)

Herr, Ich Hoffe Darauf *SWV 312
  see Kleine Geistliche Konzerte Heft
  VI

Herr, Neige Deine Himmel *SWV 361,
  sac
  (Bittenger, Werner) BB soli,2vln,
  cont sc BAREN. 5906 $4.75, ipa
  see also Symphoniae Sacrae II,
  Heft II   (S1531)

Herr, Nun Lassest Du Deinen Diener Im
  Friede Fahren *SWV 352, sac
  (Birtner, Herbert) B solo,2vln,cont
  BAREN. 630 $4.25 see also
  Symphoniae Sacrae II, Heft I
                               (S1532)
Herr, Unser Herrscher *SWV 343, sac
  (Birtner, Herbert) S/T solo,2vln,
  cont BAREN. 629 $5.25 see also
  Symphoniae Sacrae II, Heft I
                               (S1533)
Herr, Wann Ich Nur Dich Habe *SWV
  321
  see Kleine Geistliche Konzerte Heft
  XI

Herzlich Lieb Hab Ich Dich, O Herr
  *SWV 348, sac
  (Bittinger, Werner) A solo,2vln,
  cont BAREN. 1724 $4.00 see also
  Symphoniae Sacrae II, Heft I

SCHUTZ, HEINRICH (cont'd.)

(S1534)
Heute Ist Christus, Der Herr, Geboren
*SWV 439, sac,Xmas,concerto
SSS soli,opt inst,cont sc HANSSLER
20.439 s.p., ipa
(S1535)
"Jesus, Our Savior, For Us Was
Born" [Ger/Eng] SSA soli,cont oct
CONCORDIA 98-1570 $.40 (S1536)
(Bittinger, Werner) SSA soli,cont
(med diff) BAREN. 3445 $3.50
(S1537)

Himmel Und Erde Vergehen *SWV 300
see Kleine Geistliche Konzerte Heft
VII

Hodie Christus Natus Est *SWV 315
see Kleine Geistliche Konzerte Heft
XVII

How Hast Thou Offended? *see Was
Hast Du Verwirket?

Hutet Euch *SWV 351, sac
(Hoffmann, Hans) Bar/B solo,2vln,
cont (contains also: Frohlocket
Mit Handen) BAREN. 1088 $5.50 see
also Symphoniae Sacrae II, Heft I
(S1538)

I Sing To The Lord
see Five Short Sacred Concertos
(English Version)

I Will Give Thanks To God Eternally
see Five Short Sacred Concertos
(English Version)

Ich Beuge Meine Knie *SWV 319
see Kleine Geistliche Konzerte Heft
VII

Ich Bin Die Auferstehung *SWV 324
see Kleine Geistliche Konzerte Heft
XI

Ich Bin Die Auferstehung Und Das
Leben *SWV 324, sac,concerto
SSB soli,cont HANSSLER 20.324 s.p.
see from Kleine Geistliche
Konzerte (S1539)

Ich Bin Jung Gewesen *SWV 320
see Kleine Geistliche Konzerte Heft
VII

Ich Danke Dem Herrn *SWV 284
see Kleine Geistliche Konzerte Heft
II

Ich Danke Dem Herrn Von Ganzem Herzen
*SWV 284, sac,concerto
"O God, I Will Praise Thee" see
Five Sacred Songs
high solo,cont HANSSLER 5.033 s.p.
(S1540)

Ich Danke Dir, Herr *SWV 347, sac,
concerto
high solo,2vln,cont sc HANSSLER
5.018 s.p., ipa see from
Symphoniae Sacrae II (S1541)
(Bittinger, Werner) S/T solo,2vln,
cont (contains also: Ich Werde
Nicht Sterben) BAREN. 446 $5.25
see also Symphoniae Sacrae II,
Heft I (S1542)

Ich Flehe Euch An *see Adjuro Vos,
Filiae Jerusalem

Ich Hab Mein Sach Gott Heimgestellt
*SWV 305 (from Vitae Fugacitate)
sac,concerto
(Ehmann, Wilhelm) "Kleine
Geistliche Konzerte Heft X "
SSATB soli,cont (med) sc BAREN.
1708 $5.50 (S1543)
(Engelbrecht, Christiane) SSATB
soli,cont (med diff) sc BAREN.
3532 $9.00, ipa (S1544)

Ich Heb Mein Augen Sehnlich Auf *sac
Mez solo,pno (E min) LIENAU HOS 184
s.p. (S1545)
A/Bar solo,pno (D min) LIENAU
HOS 185 s.p. (S1546)

Ich Liege Und Schlafe *SWV 310, sac,
concerto
see Kleine Geistliche Konzerte Heft
VII
T solo,cont HANSSLER 5.015 s.p.
(S1547)

Ich Ruf Zu Dir, Herr Jesu Christ
*SWV 326, sac,concerto
see Kleine Geistliche Konzerte Heft
IX
SSSB soli,cont HANSSLER 20.326 s.p.
see from Kleine Geistliche
Konzerte (S1548)

Ich Singe Dem Herrn *see Cantabo
Domino

SCHUTZ, HEINRICH (cont'd.)

Ich Werde Nicht Sterben, Sondern
Leben *SWV 346, sac,concerto
high solo,2vln,cont sc HANSSLER
5.019 s.p., ipa see from
Symphoniae Sacrae II (S1549)
(Bittinger, Werner) S/T solo,2vln,
cont (contains also: Ich Danke
Dir, Herr) BAREN. 446 $5.25 see
also Symphoniae Sacrae II, Heft I
(S1550)

Ich Will Den Herren Loben Allezeit
*SWV 306
see Kleine Geistliche Konzerte Heft
I
"Now Will I Praise The Lord With
All My Heart" see Five Sacred
Songs

Ich Will Den Herrn Loben Allezeit
*SWV 306, sac,concerto
high solo,cont HANSSLER 5.027 s.p.
(S1551)

Ihr Heiligen, Lobsinget Dem Herrn
*SWV 288, sac,concerto
see Kleine Geistliche Konzerte Heft
VI
SA soli,cont HANSSLER 5.004 s.p.
see from Kleine Geistliche
Konzerte (S1552)

In Lectulo Per Noctes *SWV 272, sac
(Kirchner, Gerhard) "Des Nachts Auf
Meinem Lager" [Lat/Ger] SA soli,
3bsn,cont (contains also:
Invenerunt Me Custodes Civitatis)
sc BAREN. 39 $7.75, ipa see also
Symphoniae Sacrae I, Heft II
(S1553)

In Te, Domine, Speravi *SWV 259, sac
(Gerber, Rudolf) "Dir, O Herr, Gilt
All Mein Hoffen" [Lat/Ger] A
solo,vln,bsn/trom,cont BAREN. 30
$5.25 see also Symphoniae Sacrae
I, Heft I (S1554)

Invenerunt Me Custodes *SWV 273, sac
(Kirchner, Gerhard) "Und Es Trafen
Mich Dort" [Lat/Ger] SA soli,
3bsn,cont (contains also: In
Lectulo Per Noctes) sc BAREN. 39
$7.75, ipa see also Symphoniae
Sacrae I, Heft II (S1555)

Iss Dein Brot Mit Freuden *SWV 358,
sac
(Bittenger, Werner) SB soli,2vln,
cont BAREN. 1087 $4.00 see also
Symphoniae Sacrae II, Heft II
(S1556)

Ist Gott Fur Uns, Wer Mag Wider Uns
Sein? *SWV 329, sac,concerto
see Kleine Geistliche Konzerte Heft
VIII
SATB soli,cont HANSSLER 20.329 s.p.
see from Kleine Geistliche
Konzerte (S1557)

Itzt Blicken Durch Des Himmels Saal
*SWV 460, madrigal
(Kraft, Walter) SSATB soli,2vln,
cont (med) BAREN. 565 s.p.
(S1558)

Jesus, Our Savior, For Us Was Born
*see Heute Ist Christus, Der
Herr, Geboren

Joseph, Du Sohn David *SWV 323, sac,
concerto
see Kleine Geistliche Konzerte Heft
XII
SSB soli,cont HANSSLER 20.323 s.p.
see from Kleine Geistliche
Konzerte (S1559)

Jubilate Deo *SWV 332, sac,concerto
(Ehmann, Wilhelm) "Kleine
Geistliche Konzerte Heft XVIII "
SATB soli,cont (med) cmplt ed
BAREN. 3438 $5.00 (S1560)
(Gerber, Rudolf) "Lobt Den Herrn"
[Lat/Ger] TTB soli,bsn,2brass,
cont (contains also: Buccinate In
Neomenia Tuba) BAREN. 42 $7.75
see also Symphoniae Sacrae I,
Heft II (S1561)

Jubilate Deo Omnis Terra *SWV 262,
sac
(Gerber, Rudolf) "Lob Und Ehre
Zollt Dem Herren" [Lat/Ger] B
solo,2A rec,cont BAREN. 33 $4.25
see also Symphoniae Sacrae I,
Heft I (S1562)

Kleine Geistliche Konzerte *see Ave
Maria, Gratia Plena, SWV 334; Das
Blut Jesu Christi Machet Uns
Rein, SWV 298; Der Herr Schauet
Vom Himmel, SWV 292; Die Furcht
Des Herren Ist Der Weisheit
Anfang, SWV 318; Die
Gottseligkeit Ist Zu Allen Dingen
Nutze, SWV 299; Ein Kind Ist Uns
Geboren, SWV 302; Ich Bin Die

SCHUTZ, HEINRICH (cont'd.)

Auferstehung Und Das Leben, SWV
324; Ich Ruf Zu Dir, Herr Jesu
Christ, SWV 326; Ihr Heiligen,
Lobsinget Dem Herrn, SWV 288; Ist
Gott Fur Uns, Wer Mag Wider Uns
Sein?, SWV 329; Joseph, Du Sohn
David, SWV 323; Meister, Wir
Haben Die Ganze Nacht Gearbeitet,
SWV 317; Nun Komm, Der Heiden
Heiland, SWV 301; O Herr, Hilf, O
Herr, Lass Wohlgelingen, SWV 297;
O Lieber Herre Gott, Wecke Uns
Auf, SWV 287; Schaffe In Mir,
Gott, Ein Reines Herz, SWV 291;
Sei Gegrusset, Maria, SWV 333;
Siehe, Mein Fursprecher Ist Im
Himmel, SWV 304; Wann Unsre Augen
Schlafen Ein, SWV 316; Wer Will
Uns Scheiden Von Der Liebe
Gottes?, SWV 330 (S1563)

Kleine Geistliche Konzerte Heft I
*sac,concerto
(Hoffmann, Hans) S solo,cont (med)
cmplt ed BAREN. 1701 $4.75
contains: Bringt Her Dem Herren,
SWV 283; Eile, Mich, Gott, Zu
Erretten, SWV 282; Ich Will Den
Herren Loben Allezeit, SWV 306;
O Susser, O Freundlicher, SWV
285 (S1564)

Kleine Geistliche Konzerte Heft II
*sac,concerto
(Hoffmann, Hans) A solo,cont (med)
cmplt ed BAREN. 1702 $4.75
contains: Bringt Her Dem Herren,
SWV 283; Ich Danke Dem Herrn,
SWV 284; Was Hast Du Verwirket,
SWV 307 (S1565)

Kleine Geistliche Konzerte Heft III
*sac,concerto
(Hoffmann, Hans) SATB soli,cont
(med) cmplt ed BAREN. 1703 $4.75
contains: Ein Kind Ist Uns
Geboren, SWV 302; Siehe, Mein
Fursprecher Ist Im Himmel, SWV
304; Wir Glauben All An Einen
Gott, SWV 303 (S1566)

Kleine Geistliche Konzerte Heft IV
*sac,concerto
(Hoffmann, Hans) 2 med soli,cont
(med) cmplt ed BAREN. 1138 $5.25
contains: Der Herr Ist Gross, SWV
286; Erhore Mich, Wenn Ich
Rufe, SWV 289; Habe Deine Lust
An Dem Herrn, SWV 311; O Lieber
Herre Gott, Wecke Uns Auf, SWV
287 (S1567)

Kleine Geistliche Konzerte Heft V
*sac,concerto
(Hoffmann, Hans) 2 male soli,cont
(med) cmplt ed BAREN. 1089 $3.50
contains: Eins Bitte Ich Vom
Herren, SWV 294; Meister, Wir
Haben Die Ganze Nacht
Gearbeitet, SWV 317; O Hilf,
Christe, Gottes Sohn, SWV 295
(S1568)

Kleine Geistliche Konzerte Heft VI
*sac,concerto
(Ehmann, Wilhelm) (med) cmplt ed
BAREN. 1704 $4.75
contains: Herr, Ich Hoffe Darauf,
SWV 312 (SS soli,cont); Ihr
Heiligen, Lobsinget Dem Herrn,
SWV 288 (SA soli,cont); Lobet
Den Herren, Der Zu Zion Wohnet,
SWV 293 (AA soli,cont) (S1569)

Kleine Geistliche Konzerte Heft VII
*sac,concerto
(Ehmann, Wilhelm) (med) cmplt ed
BAREN. 1705 s.p.
contains: Furchte Dich Nicht, SWV
296 (BB soli,cont); Himmel Und
Erde Vergehen, SWV 300 (BBB
soli,cont); Ich Beuge Meine
Knie, SWV 319 (BB soli,cont);
Ich Bin Jung Gewesen, SWV 320
(BB soli,cont); Ich Liege Und
Schlafe, SWV 310 (B solo,cont)
(S1570)

Kleine Geistliche Konzerte Heft VIII
*sac,concerto
(Ehmann, Wilhelm) (med) cmplt ed
BAREN. 1706 $5.50
contains: Die Stimm Des Herren,
SWV 331 (SATB soli,cont); Ist
Gott Fur Uns, Wer Mag Wider Uns
Sein?, SWV 329 (SATB soli,
cont); Was Betrubst Du Dich,
SWV 335 (SSATB soli,cont); Wer
Will Uns Scheiden, SWV 330
(SATB soli,cont) (S1571)

Kleine Geistliche Konzerte Heft IX
*sac,concerto
(Ehmann, Wilhelm) (med) cmplt ed
BAREN. 1707 $5.50
contains: Allein Gott In Der Hoh

SCHUTZ, HEINRICH (cont'd.)

Sei Ehr, SWV 327 (SSTT soli,
cont); Die Seele Christi
Heilige Mich, SWV 325 (ATB
soli,cont); Ich Ruf Zu Dir,
Herr Jesu Christ, SWV 326 (SSSB
soli,cont); Nun Komm, Der
Heiden Heiland, SWV 301 (SSBB
soli,cont); Schaffe In Mir,
Gott, Ein Reines Herz, SWV 291
(ST soli,cont)   (S1572)

Kleine Geistliche Konzerte Heft X
*see Ich Hab Mein Sach Gott
Heimgestellt

Kleine Geistliche Konzerte Heft XI
*sac,concerto
(Ehmann, Wilhelm) (med) cmplt ed
BAREN. 3431 $5.00
contains: Die Furcht Des Herren
Ist Der Weisheit Anfang, SWV
318 (TTB soli,cont); Herr, Wann
Ich Nur Dich Habe, SWV 321 (SST
soli,cont); Ich Bin Die
Auferstehung, SWV 324 (TTB
soli,cont); O Herr, Hilf, O
Herr, Lass Wohlgelingen, SWV
297 (SST soli,cont)   (S1573)

Kleine Geistliche Konzerte Heft XII
*sac,concerto
(Ehmann, Wilhelm) (med) cmplt ed
BAREN. 3432 $4.00
contains: Das Blut Jesu Christi
Machet Uns Rein, SWV 298 (SSB
soli,cont); Der Herr Schauet
Vom Himmel, SWV 292 (SB soli,
cont); Die Gottseligkeit Ist Zu
Allen Dingen Nutze, SWV 299
(SSB soli,cont); Joseph, Du
Sohn David, SWV 323 (SSB soli,
cont); Wann Unsre Augen
Schlafen Ein, SWV 316 (SB soli,
cont)   (S1574)

Kleine Geistliche Konzerte Heft XIV
*sac,concerto
(Ehmann, Wilhelm) T/S solo,cont
(med) cmplt ed BAREN. 3434 $3.50
contains: O Jesu, Nomen Dulce,
SWV 308; O Misericordissime
Jesu, SWV 309   (S1575)

Kleine Geistliche Konzerte Heft XV
*sac,concerto
(Ehmann, Wilhelm) SS/TT soli,cont
(med) cmplt ed BAREN. 3435 $4.25
contains: Bone Jesu, Verbum
Patris, SWV 313; Verbum Caro
Factum Est, SWV 314   (S1576)

Kleine Geistliche Konzerte Heft XVII
*sac,concerto
(Ehmann, Wilhelm) (med) cmplt ed
BAREN. 3437 $5.50
contains: Hodie Christus Natus
Est, SWV 315 (ST soli,cont);
Rorate Coeli Desuper, SWV 322
(SSB soli,cont); Veni Sancte
Spiritus, SWV 328 (SSTT soli,
cont)   (S1577)

Kleine Geistliche Konzerte Heft XVIII
*see Jubilate Deo

Kleine Geistliche Konzerte Heft XIX
*sac,concerto
(Ehmann, Wilhelm) SATB soli,cont
(med) cmplt ed BAREN. 3439 $9.75
contains: Aufer Immensam, SWV
337; Quemadmodum Desiderat, SWV
336   (S1578)

Kleine Geistliche Konzerte Heft XX
*see Wohl Dem, Der Nicht Wandelt
Im Rate Der Gottlosen

Komm Doch, Geliebter Mein *see Veni,
Dilecte Mi

Kommt Alle Zu Mir *see Venite Ad Me

Liebster, Sagt In Sussen Schmerzen
*sac
SS soli,2vln,cont sc CONCORDIA
97-4266 $4.00   (S1579)

Lob Und Ehre Zollt Dem Herren *see
Jubilate Deo Omnis Terra

Lobet Den Herren, Alle Heiden *SWV
363, sac
(Bittinger, Werner) AT soli,2vln,
cont sc BAREN. 5908 s.p., ipa see
also Symphoniae Sacrae II, Heft
III   (S1580)

Lobet Den Herren, Der Zu Zion Wohnet
*SWV 293
see Kleine Geistliche Konzerte Heft
VI

SCHUTZ, HEINRICH (cont'd.)

Lobet Den Herrn In Seinem Heiligtum
*SWV 350, sac
(Bittinger, Werner) T solo,2vln,
cont BAREN. 4336 $5.00 see also
Symphoniae Sacrae II, Heft I
                            (S1581)
(Walter, Georg) "Lobgesang" S/T
solo,2fl,org,strings,opt 2trp&
timp BREITKOPF-L rental   (S1582)

Lobgesang *see Lobet Den Herrn In
Seinem Heiligtum

Lobt Den Herrn *see Jubilate Deo

Mein Herz Ist Bereit *SWV 341, sac
(Bittinger, Werner) S/T solo,2vln,
cont BAREN. 3448 $4.25 see also
Symphoniae Sacrae II, Heft I
                            (S1583)

Mein Herz Ist Gerustet *see Paratum
Cor Meum, Deus

Meine Seele Erhebt Den Herren *SWV
344, sac
(Bittinger, Werner) S solo,2A rec,
2trp,trom,2vln,cont BAREN. 4335
$5.50 see also Symphoniae Sacrae
II, Heft I   (S1584)

Meine Seele Erhebt Den Herren *see
Das Magnificat

Meister, Wir Haben Die Ganze Nacht
Gearbeitet *SWV 317, sac,
concerto
see Kleine Geistliche Konzerte Heft
V
TT soli,cont HANSSLER 5.032 s.p.
see from Kleine Geistliche
Konzerte   (S1585)

Misericordissime Jesu
"O Most Kind And Most Merciful
Jesu" see Three Sacred Concertos
(English Version)

My Son, Wherefore Hast Thou Done This
To Us? (from Symphoniae Sacrae
III) sac,Bibl
[Ger/Eng] AB soli,mix cor,strings,
cont sc CONCORDIA 97-9347 $2.50,
ipa   (S1586)

Now Will I Praise The Lord With All
My Heart *see Ich Will Den
Herren Loben Allezeit

Nun Komm, Der Heiden Heiland *SWV
301, sac,concerto
see Kleine Geistliche Konzerte Heft
IX
SSBB soli,cont HANSSLER 20.301 s.p.
see from Kleine Geistliche
Konzerte   (S1587)

O Dear, O Friendly, O Kind And Gentle
Savior *sac
[Ger/Eng] T/S solo,cont oct
CONCORDIA 98-1585 $.25   (S1588)

O God, I Will Praise Thee *see Ich
Danke Dem Herrn Von Ganzem Herzen

O God, My Heart Is Ready *see
Paratum Cor Meum, Deus

O Gracious Lord God, May We Be
Vigilant *sac
[Ger/Eng] SS soli,cont oct
CONCORDIA 98-1558 $.25   (S1589)

O Herr, Hilf, O Herr, Lass
Wohlgelingen *SWV 297, sac,
concerto
see Kleine Geistliche Konzerte Heft
XI
SST soli,cont sc HANSSLER 20.297
s.p., ipa see from Kleine
Geistliche Konzerte   (S1590)

O Herr, Hilf, O Herr, Lass
Wohlgelingen [2] *SWV 402, sac,
concerto
SSB soli,2vln,cont sc HANSSLER
20.402 s.p. see from Symphoniae
Sacrae III   (S1591)

O Hilf, Christe, Gottes Sohn *SWV
295
see Kleine Geistliche Konzerte Heft
V

O Jesu, Name Most Lovely *see O
Jesu, Nomen Dulce

O Jesu, Nomen Dulce *SWV 308
see Kleine Geistliche Konzerte Heft
XIV
see Zwei Geistliche Gesange
"O Jesu, Name Most Lovely" see
Three Sacred Concertos (English
Version)

SCHUTZ, HEINRICH (cont'd.)

O Lieber Herre Gott, Wecke Uns Auf
*SWV 287, sac,concerto
see Kleine Geistliche Konzerte Heft
IV
SS soli,cont HANSSLER 20.287 s.p.
see from Kleine Geistliche
Konzerte   (S1592)

O Misericordissime Jesu *SWV 309
see Kleine Geistliche Konzerte Heft
XIV
see Zwei Geistliche Gesange

O Most Kind And Most Merciful Jesu
*see Misericordissime Jesu

O Quam Tu Pulchra Es *SWV 265, sac
(Gerber, Rudolf) "O Wie Beruckend"
[Lat/Ger] TBar soli,2vln,cont
(contains also: Veni De Libano)
BAREN. 35 $5.25 see also
Symphoniae Sacrae I, Heft I
                            (S1593)

O Susser Jesu Christ *SWV 427, sac
(Kittel) high solo,2vln,cont sc
HANSSLER 20.604 s.p., ipa see
from Zwolf Geistliche Gesangen
                            (S1594)

O Susser, O Freundlicher *SWV 285,
sac,concerto
see Kleine Geistliche Konzerte Heft
I
"O Tender, O Bountiful" see Five
Short Sacred Concertos (English
Version)
high solo,cont HANSSLER 5.026 s.p.
                            (S1595)

O Tender, O Bountiful *see O Susser,
O Freundlicher

O Wie Beruckend *see O Quam Tu
Pulchra Es

One Thing Have I Desired *sac
[Ger/Eng] SS/2 boy soli/2 med male
soli,pno oct CONCORDIA 98-1369
$.25   (S1596)

Paratum Cor Meum, Deus *SWV 257, sac
"O God, My Heart Is Ready" [Eng/
Lat] high solo/med solo,2vln,kbd
HINRICHSEN H181 $4.50   (S1597)
(Gerber, Rudolf) "Mein Herz Ist
Gerustet" [Lat/Ger] S/T solo,
2vln,cont BAREN. 28 $4.25 see
also Symphoniae Sacrae I, Heft I
                            (S1598)

Preisen Will Ich Allezeit *see
Benedicam Dominum

Psalm 42 *see Was Betrubst Du Dich,
Meine Seele

Quemadmodum Desiderat *SWV 336
see Kleine Geistliche Konzerte Heft
XIX

Rorate Coeli Desuper *SWV 322
see Kleine Geistliche Konzerte Heft
XVII

Schaffe In Mir, Gott, Ein Reines Herz
*SWV 291, sac,concerto
see Kleine Geistliche Konzerte Heft
IX
ST soli,cont HANSSLER 5.013 s.p.
see from Kleine Geistliche
Konzerte   (S1599)

Sehet An Den Feigenbaum *SWV 394,
sac
ST soli,strings BAREN. 526 s.p. see
from Geistliche Chormusik 1648
                            (S1600)

Sei Gegrusset, Maria *SWV 333, sac,
concerto
2 soli,cont sc HANSSLER 20.333 s.p.
see from Kleine Geistliche
Konzerte   (S1601)

Siehe, Mein Fursprecher Ist Im Himmel
*SWV 304, sac,concerto
see Kleine Geistliche Konzerte Heft
III
SSTB soli,cont HANSSLER 20.304 s.p.
see from Kleine Geistliche
Konzerte   (S1602)

Sing, O Ye Saints *sac
[Ger/Eng] SA/TB soli,pno oct
CONCORDIA 98-1414 $.25   (S1603)

Singet Dem Herrn Ein Neues Lied *SWV
342, sac
(Bittinger, Werner) S/T solo,2vln,
cont BAREN. 3447 $4.75 see also
Symphoniae Sacrae II, Heft I
                            (S1604)

So Hore Doch, Meine Gemeinde *see
Attendite Popule Meus Legem Meam

Steige Herab Von Den Bergen *see
Veni De Libano

SCHUTZ, HEINRICH (cont'd.)

Symphoniae Sacrae I, Heft I *sac
(Gerber, Rudolf) [Lat/Ger] solo/
soli,strings,cont cmplt ed BAREN.
3661 $29.50
contains & see also: Adjuro Vos,
Filiae Jerusalem, "Ich Flehe
Euch An", SWV 264; Anima Mea
Liquefacta Est, "Ach, Meine
Seele", SWV 263; Cantabo
Domino, "Ich Singe Dem Herrn",
SWV 260; Exultavit Cor Meum,
"Freude Und Gluck", SWV 258; In
Te, Domine, Speravi, "Dir, O
Herr, Gilt All Mein Hoffen",
SWV 259; Jubilate Deo Omnis
Terra, "Lob Und Ehre Zollt Dem
Herren", SWV 262; O Quam Tu
Pulchra Es, "O Wie Beruckend",
SWV 265; Paratum Cor Meum,
Deus, "Mein Herz Ist Gerustet",
SWV 257; Veni De Libano,
"Steige Herab Von Den Bergen",
SWV 266; Venite Ad Me, "Kommt
Alle Zu Mir", SWV 261   (S1605)

Symphoniae Sacrae I, Heft II *sac
(Gerber, Rudolf; Kircher, Gerhard)
[Lat/Ger] cmplt ed BAREN. 3667
$40.50
contains & see also: Attendite
Popule Meus Legem Meam, "So
Hore Doch, Meine Gemeinde", SWV
270; Benedicam Dominum,
"Preisen Will Ich Allezeit",
SWV 267; Buccinate In Neomenia
Tuba, "Auf Und Blaset Am Fest
Des Neumonds Die Tuba", SWV
275; Domine, Labia Mea Aperies,
SWV 271; Exquisivi Dominum,
"Als Ich Gott Den Herrn
Gesucht", SWV 268; Fili Mi,
Absalon, "Ach, Mein Sohn
Absalon", SWV 269; In Lectulo
Per Noctes, "Des Nachts Auf
Meinem Lager", SWV 272;
Invenerunt Me Custodes, "Und Es
Trafen Mich Dort", SWV 273;
Jubilate Deo, "Lobt Den Herrn",
SWV 276; Veni, Dilecte Mi,
"Komm Doch, Geliebter Mein",
SWV 274   (S1606)

Symphoniae Sacrae II *see Der Herr
Ist Meine Starke, SWV 345; Ich
Danke Dir, Herr, SWV 347; Ich
Werde Nicht Sterben, Sondern
Leben, SWV 346   (S1607)

Symphoniae Sacrae II, Heft I *sac
(Bittinger, Werner) cmplt ed,cloth
BAREN. 3669 $42.00
contains & see also: Der Herr Ist
Meine Starke, SWV 345;
Frohlocket Mit Handen, SWV 349;
Herr, Nun Lassest Du Deinen
Diener Im Friede Fahren, SWV
352; Herr, Unser Herrscher, SWV
343; Herzlich Lieb Hab Ich
Dich, O Herr, SWV 348; Hutet
Euch, SWV 351; Ich Danke Dir,
Herr, SWV 347; Ich Werde Nicht
Sterben, Sondern Leben, SWV
346; Lobet Den Herrn In Seinem
Heiligtum, SWV 350; Mein Herz
Ist Bereit, SWV 341; Meine
Seele Erhebt Den Herren, SWV
344; Singet Dem Herrn Ein Neues
Lied, SWV 342   (S1608)

Symphoniae Sacrae II, Heft II *sac
(Bittenger, Werner) S/T solo,2vln,
cont cmplt ed,cloth BAREN. 3670
$35.00
contains & see also: Der Herr Ist
Mein Licht, SWV 359; Es Steh
Gott Auf, SWV 356; Gib Unsern
Fursten, SWV 355; Herr, Neige
Deine Himmel, SWV 361; Iss Dein
Brot Mit Freuden, SWV 358;
Verleih Uns Frieden, SWV 354;
Vom Aufgang Der Sonnen, SWV
362; Was Betrubst Du Dich, SWV
353; Wie Ein Rubin In Feinem
Golde Leuchtet, SWV 357;
Zweierlei Bitte Ich, Herr, Von
Dir, SWV 360   (S1609)

Symphoniae Sacrae II, Heft III *sac
(Bittinger, Werner) soli,2vln,cont
cmplt ed,cloth BAREN. 4470 $35.00
contains & see also: Die So Ihr
Den Herren Furchtet, SWV 364;
Drei Schone Dinge Seind, SWV
365; Freuet Euch Des Herren,
Ihr Gerechten, SWV 367; Lobet
Den Herren, Alle Heiden, SWV
363; Von Gott Will Ich Nicht
Lassen, SWV 366   (S1610)

Symphoniae Sacrae III *see O Herr,
Hilf, O Herr, Lass Wohlgelingen
[2], SWV 402   (S1611)

SCHUTZ, HEINRICH (cont'd.)

Three Sacred Concertos (English
Version) *sac,concerto
PETERS 66030 $3.00
contains: How Hast Thou Offended;
Misericordissime Jesu, "O Most
Kind And Most Merciful Jesu"; O
Jesu, Nomen Dulce, "O Jesu,
Name Most Lovely"   (S1612)

Three Sacred Concertos (German
Version) *sac,CC3U,concerto
PETERS 3785 $3.25   (S1613)

To Us A Child Is Born *sac
SATB soli,cont oct CONCORDIA
98-1494 $.25   (S1614)

Two Madrigals *sac,CC2U
[Ger/It] SSATB soli,pno CONCORDIA
97-4265 $2.50   (S1615)

Two Men Betook Themselves To Pray In
The Temple *sac
[Ger/Eng] SATB soli,cont oct
CONCORDIA 98-1569 $.40   (S1616)

Und Es Trafen Mich Dort *see
Invenerunt Me Custodes

Vater Abraham, Erbarme Dich Mein
*SWV 477
SSATB soli,2vln,2fl,cont sc
HANSSLER 20.477 s.p., ipa (S1617)

Veni De Libano *SWV 266, sac
(Gerber, Rudolf) "Steige Herab Von
Den Bergen" [Lat/Ger] TBar soli,
2vln,cont (contains also: O Quam
Tu Pulchra Es) BAREN. 35 $5.25
see also Symphoniae Sacrae I,
Heft I   (S1618)

Veni, Dilecte Mi *SWV 274, sac
(Kircher, Gerhard) "Komm Doch,
Geliebter Mein" [Lat/Ger] SST
soli,3trom,cont sc BAREN. 41
$5.50, ipa see also Symphoniae
Sacrae I, Heft II   (S1619)

Veni Sancte Spiritus *SWV 328
see Kleine Geistliche Konzerte Heft
XVII

Venite Ad Me *SWV 261, sac
(Gerber, Rudolf) "Kommt Alle Zu
Mir" [Lat/Ger] T solo,vln,cont
BAREN. 32 $4.75 see also
Symphoniae Sacrae I, Heft I
(S1620)

Verbum Caro Factum Est *SWV 314
see Kleine Geistliche Konzerte Heft
XV

Verleih Uns Frieden *SWV 354, sac
(Bittenger, Werner) SS/TT soli,
2vln,cont (contains also: Gib
Unsern Fursten) BAREN. 4338 $5.50
see also Symphoniae Sacrae II,
Heft II   (S1621)

Vier Hirtinnen *CC4U,madrigal
(Hoffmann) SSAT soli,cont BAREN.
1271 $3.50   (S1622)

Vier Hirtinnen *sac,CC4U
(Hoffmann, Hans) SSAT soli,cont
(med diff) cmplt ed BAREN. 1271
$3.50   (S1623)

Vom Aufgang Der Sonnen *SWV 362, sac
(Bittenger, Werner) BB soli,2vln,
cont sc BAREN. 5907 $4.75, ipa
see also Symphoniae Sacrae II,
Heft II   (S1624)

Von Gott Will Ich Nicht Lassen *SWV
366, sac
(Bittenger, Werner) SSB soli,2vln,
cont sc BAREN. 4337 $7.00 see
also Symphoniae Sacrae II, Heft
III   (S1625)

Wann Unsre Augen Schlafen Ein *SWV
316, sac,concerto
see Kleine Geistliche Konzerte Heft
XII
SB soli,cont HANSSLER 5.030 s.p.
see from Kleine Geistliche
Konzerte   (S1626)

Was Betrubst Du Dich *SWV 335, sac
see Kleine Geistliche Konzerte Heft
VIII
(Henking, Bernhard) S/T solo,2vln,
cont BAREN. 457 $4.75 see also
Symphoniae Sacrae II, Heft II
(S1627)

Was Betrubst Du Dich, Meine Seele
(Psalm 42) sac
(Hohmann, Edmund) SS/TT solo,pno,
2vln,opt vcl BREITKOPF-W s.p.
(S1628)

SCHUTZ, HEINRICH (cont'd.)

Was Hast Du Verwirket *SWV 307, sac,
concerto
see Kleine Geistliche Konzerte Heft
II
"How Hast Thou Offended?" see Five
Sacred Songs
"How Hast Thou Offended" see Three
Sacred Concertos (English
Version)
high solo,cont HANSSLER 5.034 s.p.
(S1629)

Was Mein Gott Will, Das Gescheh
Allzeit *SWV 392, sac
AT soli,strings BAREN. 524 s.p. see
from Geistliche Chormusik 1648
(S1630)

Wedding Song *sac,Marriage,Bibl
high solo,pno CHANTRY VOS 511H $.75
(S1631)
low solo,pno CHANTRY VOS 511L $.75
(S1632)

Wer Will Uns Scheiden *SWV 330
see Kleine Geistliche Konzerte Heft
VIII

Wer Will Uns Scheiden Von Der Liebe
Gottes? *SWV 330, sac,concerto
SATB soli,cont HANSSLER 20.330 s.p.
see from Kleine Geistliche
Konzerte   (S1633)

Wie Ein Rubin In Feinem Golde
Leuchtet *SWV 357, sac,concerto
(Gerber, Rudolf) SAB soli,2vln,cont
BAREN. 1086 $4.00 see also
Symphoniae Sacrae II, Heft II
(S1634)
(Kruger, Dietrich) SA soli,2vln,
cont voc sc BREITKOPF-W PB 4739
s.p., ipa   (S1635)

Wir Glauben All An Einen Gott *SWV
303
see Kleine Geistliche Konzerte Heft
III

Wo Gott Der Herr Nicht Bei Uns Halt
*SWV 467, sac,concerto
(Breig, Werner) SSS soli,cont (med
diff) cmplt ed BAREN. 5916 s.p.
(S1636)

Wohl Dem, Der Nicht Wandelt Im Rate
Der Gottlosen *SWV 290, sac,
concerto
(Hoffmann, Hans) "Kleine Geistliche
Konzerte Heft XX " SA soli,cont
(med) cmplt ed BAREN. 1270 $2.75
(S1637)

Woman, Why Weepest Thou? *sac,Easter
[Ger/Eng] SAB soli,cor,cont
CONCORDIA 97-6369 $1.00   (S1638)

Zwei Geistliche Gesange *sac
(Ragossnig, K.) [Lat] T/S solo,gtr
ZIMMER. 1718 $1.50
contains: O Jesu, Nomen Dulce; O
Misericordissime Jesu   (S1639)

Zweierlei Bitte Ich, Herr, Von Dir
*SWV 360, sac
(Bittenger, Werner) TT soli,2vln,
cont sc BAREN. 5905 $4.75, ipa
see also Symphoniae Sacrae II,
Heft II   (S1640)

Zwolf Geistliche Gesangen *see O
Susser Jesu Christ, SWV 427
(S1641)

SCHUURMAN, JR.M.
Twee Liederen *CC2U
solo,pno BROEKMANS 140 s.p. (S1642)

SCHUYT, NICO (1922-   )
Appelboompjes
see Drie Liederen Van M. Vasalis
Uit "De Vogel Phoenix"

Arkadia
med solo,pno DONEMUS s.p.   (S1643)
Mez solo,vla,vcl DONEMUS s.p.
(S1644)

Diep Van Mijzelf
see Drie Liederen Van M. Vasalis
Uit "De Vogel Phoenix"

Drie Liederen Van M. Vasalis Uit "De
Vogel Phoenix"
A/Bar solo,pno DONEMUS s.p.
contains: Appelboompjes; Diep Van
Mijzelf; Sprookje   (S1645)

Sprookje
see Drie Liederen Van M. Vasalis
Uit "De Vogel Phoenix"

SCHVEITZER, M.
Cinco Coplas Andalouses *CC5U,Span
[Span/Fr] high solo,pno ESCHIG
$3.75   (S1646)

SCHWABISCHE LIEBESLIEDER see Miller,
Franz R.

SCHWAEN, KURT (1909-   )
    Parabolisch *CC4U
        high solo,pno DEUTSCHER 9007 s.p.
                                        (S1647)

SCHWALBEN IM ABEND see Borris,
    Siegfried

SCHWANDA, H.
    Ski-Heil
        solo,inst DOBLINGER 08 809 s.p.
                                        (S1648)

SCHWANENGESANG see Pylkkanen, Tauno
    Kullervo, Joutsenlaulu

SCHWANENGESANG see Schubert, Franz
    (Peter)

SCHWANTNER, JOSEPH
    Shadows II
        Bar solo,fl,clar,bass clar,mand,
        gtr,vln,vla,vcl,perc,electronic
        tape sc AM.COMP.AL. $6.05 (S1649)

SCHWARTZ, ABE
    Die Shaine Yugend *Jew
        solo,pno KAMMEN 24 $1.00 see also
        JEWISH THEATRE SONGS, VOL. 1
                                        (S1650)

SCHWARTZ, FRANCIS
    Plegaria
        solo,orch PEER rental   (S1651)

    Suicida Y Requiescit
        S solo,chamb.orch PEER rental
                                        (S1652)

SCHWARTZ, GERHARD VON (1902-   )
    Ich Vermahne Euch Aber *Bibl/
        concerto
        S solo,org/pno/cembalo (med) BAREN.
        2157 $4.25   (S1653)

    Ihr Habt Nicht Einen Knechtischen
        Geist *concerto
        S solo,org/pno/cembalo (med) BAREN.
        2136 $4.25   (S1654)

SCHWARTZE KARSHELACH see Lillian,
    Isadore

SCHWARZ-SCHILLING, REINHARD (1904-   )
    Der Wandernde Musikant *song cycle
        Bar solo,pno (diff) BAREN. 2145
        $4.25   (S1655)

    Drei Geistliche Lieder *sac,CC3U
        med solo,org/3strings (med) BAREN.
        2428 $14.75, ipa   (S1656)

    Drei Lieder Nach Gedichten Von
        Eichendorff *CC3U
        Bar/A solo,pno (med) BAREN. 2144
        $4.25   (S1657)

SCHWARZ-WIE DIE TEPPICHE SALOMOS see
    Salbert, Dieter

SCHWARZE AUGEN
    see Funf Beruhmte Russische Lieder
    see Russische Volkslieder

SCHWARZE ROSEN see Sibelius, Jean,
    Svarta Rosor

SCHWEIG, DAMIT DICH NIEMAND WARNT see
    Weber, Carl Maria von

SCHWEIG, MEIN HARTZ *Jew
    solo,pno KAMMEN 430 $1.00 (S1658)

SCHWEIGEN see Ehrenberg, Carl Emil
    Theodor

SCHWEIGT STILLE, PLAUDERT NICHT see
    Anonymous

SCHWEIGT STILLE, PLAUDERT NICHT see
    Bach, Johann Sebastian

SCHWEIZER HYMNE see Muller, P.

SCHWEIZER NATIONALHYMNE
    (Niggli) solo,pno HUG s.p. contains
        also: Schweizer Psalm   (S1659)

SCHWEIZER PSALM
    see Schweizer Nationalhymne

SCHWEIZERSCHUTZENLIED see Angerer,
    Gottfried

SCHWER IST DAS HERZ MIR *folk,Russ
    [Ger/Russ] solo,pno ZIMMER. 1518 s.p.
                                        (S1660)

SCHWERE NACHTE see Oort, H.C.v.

SCHWERE TAGE see Bijvanck, Henk

SCHWICKERT, GUSTAV
    Funf Lieder *Op.14a,No.1-5, CC5U
        med solo,fl,ob,2clar,bsn,horn,
        strings RIES s.p.   (S1661)

    Lieder Der Liebe *Op.6a
        high solo,2fl,ob,2clar,2bsn,2horn,
        strings RIES s.p.   (S1662)

SCHWICKERT, GUSTAV (cont'd.)

    Sechs Lieder Nach Gedichten Von Emil
        Gott *CC6U
        solo,pno RIES s.p.   (S1663)

    Sturmnacht *Op.12, cant
        med solo,fl,pic,ob,2clar,bsn,2horn,
        trp,trom,timp,strings RIES s.p.
                                        (S1664)

SCHWIMM HIN, RINGLEIN see Reznicek,
    Emil Nikolaus von

SCHWINGT FREUDIG EUCH EMPOR see Bach,
    Johann Sebastian

SCHWUNG see Strauss, Richard

SCIAMMARELLA, VALDO
    Cantigas De Amigo *CCU
        [Span/Fr] solo,pno BOOSEY $3.00
                                        (S1665)

    Delgadina
        see Romancillos De La Colonia

    El Galan Y La Calavera
        see Romancillos De La Colonia

    Escogiendo Novia
        see Romancillos De La Colonia

    Muerte De Elena
        see Romancillos De La Colonia

    Muerte Del Senor Don Gato
        see Romancillos De La Colonia

    Romancillos De La Colonia
        [Span] med solo,pno cmplt ed
        RICORDI-ARG BA 11617 s.p.
        contains: Delgadina; El Galan Y
        La Calavera; Escogiendo Novia;
        Muerte De Elena; Muerte Del
        Senor Don Gato   (S1666)

SCILINGUAGNOLO see Tocchi, Gian-Luca

SCINTILLE DIAMANT see Offenbach,
    Jacques

SCOTS GIRL see Green, Philip

SCOTS WHA HAE *folk,Scot
    solo,pno (A flat maj/B flat maj)
    PATERSON FS81 s.p.   (S1667)

SCOTT
    Faith Unlocks The Door (composed with
        Sande) *sac
        solo,pno BENSON S5440-S $1.25
                                        (S1668)

    Ride On! Ride On!
        med solo,pno SHAWNEE IA5016 $.75
                                        (S1669)
        low solo,pno SHAWNEE IA5017 $.75
                                        (S1670)

SCOTT, ALICIA ANN
    see SCOTT, LADY JOHN

SCOTT, CYRIL MEIR (1879-1970)
    Arietta
        high solo,pno ELKIN 27.0585.00 s.p.
                                        (S1671)

    Blackbird's Song
        med solo,pno ELKIN 27.4357.04 s.p.
                                        (S1672)
        high solo,pno ELKIN 27.0358.00 s.p.
                                        (S1673)
        low solo,pno ELKIN 27.0357.02 s.p.
                                        (S1674)

    Don't Come In Sir, Please!
        Mez solo,pno ELKIN 27.0297.05 s.p.
                                        (S1675)

    D'Outremer *see From Afar

    From Afar
        "D'Outremer" high solo,pno ELKIN
        27.1344.06 s.p.   (S1676)

    Lullaby
        low solo,pno ELKIN 27.0431.05 s.p.
                                        (S1677)
        med solo,pno ELKIN 27.4431.07 s.p.
                                        (S1678)
        high solo,pno ELKIN 27.0432.03 s.p.
                                        (S1679)

    Mermaid's Song
        med solo,pno ELKIN 27.1757.03 s.p.
                                        (S1680)

    Ode To Great Men
        T/narrator,AAA,3fl,3ob,3clar,3bsn,
        4horn,3trp,3trom,tuba,perc,pno,
        cel,harp,org,strings NOVELLO
        rental   (S1681)

    Spring Ditty, A
        high solo,pno ELKIN 27.0572.09 s.p.
                                        (S1682)

    Unforeseen, The
        high solo,pno ELKIN 27.4611.05 s.p.
                                        (S1683)
        med solo,pno ELKIN 27.0611.03 s.p.
                                        (S1684)

SCOTT, LADY JOHN (1810-1900)
    Think On Me *sac
        low solo,pno (E flat maj) PATERSON
        s.p.   (S1685)
        med solo,pno (F maj) PATERSON s.p.
                                        (S1686)
        high solo,pno (G maj) PATERSON s.p.
                                        (S1687)
        solo,pno PATERSON s.p.   (S1688)
        high solo,pno (G maj) WILLIS $.75
                                        (S1689)
        low solo,pno (E flat maj) WILLIS
        $.75   (S1690)
        low solo,pno (E flat maj) ASHDOWN
        $1.50   (S1691)
        high solo,pno (G maj) ASHDOWN $1.50
                                        (S1692)
        (Perrenot) low solo,pno GALAXY
        1.0874.7 $1.00   (S1693)
        (Perrenot) high solo,pno GALAXY
        1.0873.7 $1.00   (S1694)
        (Perrenot) med solo,pno GALAXY
        1.1318.7 $1.00   (S1695)

SCOTT, JOHN PRINDLE
    April Time
        high solo,pno (E flat maj) WILLIS
        $.50   (S1696)

    Come, Ye Blessed *sac
        low solo,pno (E flat maj) SCHIRM.G
        $.85   (S1697)
        med solo,pno (F maj) SCHIRM.G $.85
                                        (S1698)
        high solo,pno (A flat maj) SCHIRM.G
        $.85   (S1699)

    Consider The Lilies *sac
        high solo,pno (D flat maj) SCHIRM.G
        $.85   (S1700)
        low solo,pno (B flat maj) SCHIRM.G
        $.85   (S1701)

    False Prophet
        low solo,pno (F maj) ALLANS s.p.
                                        (S1702)
        high solo,pno (A flat maj) ALLANS
        s.p.   (S1703)

    False Prophet, The
        high solo,pno (A flat maj) WILLIS
        $.60   (S1704)
        low solo,pno (F maj) WILLIS $.60
                                        (S1705)

    First Easter Morn, The *sac
        low solo,pno (D maj) SCHIRM.G $.75
                                        (S1706)

    Good Luck, Mr. Fisherman
        med solo,pno (E flat maj) WILLIS
        $.60   (S1707)

    He Shall Give His Angels Charge
        *sac,Gen
        low solo,pno (G maj) WILLIS $.60
                                        (S1708)
        high solo,pno (B flat maj) WILLIS
        $.60   (S1709)

    Love Is A Riddle
        med solo,pno (B flat maj) WILLIS
        $.60   (S1710)

    Out Of The Depths *sac,Gen
        high solo,pno (C min) WILLIS $.60
                                        (S1711)
        low solo,pno (C min) WILLIS $.60
                                        (S1712)

    Repent Ye *sac
        med solo,pno (E min) SCHIRM.G $.85
                                        (S1713)

    Romeo In Georgia
        high solo,pno (G maj) WILLIS $.60
                                        (S1714)
        low solo,pno (E flat maj) WILLIS
        $.60   (S1715)

    Trust Ye In The Lord *sac,Gen
        high solo,pno (F maj) WILLIS $.60
                                        (S1716)
        low solo,pno (D flat maj) WILLIS
        $.60   (S1717)

    Voice In The Wilderness, The *sac,
        Gen
        high solo,pno (A flat maj) WILLIS
        $.75   (S1718)
        low solo,pno (F maj) WILLIS $.75
                                        (S1719)

    When I Consider The Heavens *sac,Gen
        high solo,pno (B flat maj) WILLIS
        $.60   (S1720)
        low solo,pno (G maj) WILLIS $.60
                                        (S1721)

    Winds In The South, The
        med solo,pno (D flat maj) WILLIS
        $.60   (S1722)
        high solo,pno (E flat maj) WILLIS
        $.60   (S1723)

SCOTT, TOM (1912-1961)
    Gallows Tree, The
        med solo,pno PRESSER $.75 (S1724)

SCOTT-GATTY, ALFRED (1847-1918)
Ae Fond Kiss
solo,pno (G maj) BOOSEY $1.50
(S1725)

Bendemeer's Stream
low solo,pno (F maj) BOOSEY $1.50
(S1726)
high solo,pno (C maj) BOOSEY $1.50
(S1727)
med solo,pno (A flat maj) BOOSEY
$1.50 (S1728)

SCOTT-HUGHES, J.
Your Voice
2 soli,pno LEONARD-ENG (S1729)

SCOTTISH GIFT BOOK, THE *Scot
solo,pno PATERSON s.p. (S1730)

SCOTTISH ORPHEUS, VOL. I, THE *CCU
(Diack, J. Michael) solo,pno PATERSON
s.p., ea. with tartan or cloth
covers (S1731)

SCOTTISH ORPHEUS, VOL. II, THE *CCU
(Diack, J. Michael) solo,pno PATERSON
pap s.p., cloth s.p. (S1732)

SCOTTISH ORPHEUS, VOL. III, THE *CCU
(Diack, J. Michael) solo,pno PATERSON
pap s.p., cloth s.p. (S1733)

SCOTTISH SONG ALBUMS
(Diack, J. Michael) PATERSON S solo,
pno s.p.; A solo,pno s.p.; T solo,
pno s.p.; Bar solo,pno s.p.
selected from "The Scottish
Orpheus" (S1734)

SCOTTO, VINCENT
Alaska
solo,pno ENOCH s.p. (S1735)

Bout De Chou
solo,acap ENOCH s.p. see also Bout
De Chou (S1736)

Bout De Chou
solo,pno/acap cmplt ed ENOCH s.p.
contains & see also: Bout De
Chou; J'adore Les Femmes; Quand
On S'revoit (S1737)

Ce Sont Nos Petits Soldats
solo,acap ENOCH s.p. (S1738)
solo,pno ENOCH s.p. (S1739)

Dans Les Rues De Paris
solo,acap ENOCH s.p. (S1740)
solo,pno ENOCH s.p. (S1741)

Debout La-Dedans
solo,pno/acap cmplt ed ENOCH s.p.
contains & see also: Et Toc Et
Toc Pan Pan; Le Moulin; Quand
Tu M'appelles (S1742)

Dis-Moi Pourquoi
solo,acap ENOCH s.p. (S1743)
solo,pno ENOCH s.p. (S1744)

Et Toc Et Toc Pan Pan
solo,acap ENOCH s.p. see also
Debout La-Dedans (S1745)

Fiorella-Mia
solo,acap ENOCH s.p. (S1746)
solo,pno ENOCH s.p. (S1747)

J'adore Les Femmes
solo,acap ENOCH s.p. see also Bout
De Chou (S1748)

Laquelle?
solo,acap ENOCH s.p. (S1749)
solo,pno ENOCH s.p. (S1750)

Le Moulin
solo,acap ENOCH s.p. see also
Debout La-Dedans (S1751)

Le Soir Au Lido
solo,acap ENOCH s.p. (S1752)
solo,pno ENOCH s.p. (S1753)

Les Amants
solo,acap ENOCH s.p. (S1754)
solo,pno ENOCH s.p. (S1755)

Les Gueuses
solo,pno ENOCH s.p. (S1756)
solo,acap ENOCH s.p. (S1757)

Mon Arabelle
solo,acap ENOCH s.p. (S1758)
solo,pno ENOCH s.p. (S1759)

Quand On S'revoit
solo,acap ENOCH s.p. see also Bout
De Chou (S1760)

Quand Tu M'appelles
solo,acap ENOCH s.p. see also
Debout La-Dedans (S1761)

SCOTTO, VINCENT (cont'd.)
Si Vous Aimez Les Fleurs
solo,pno ENOCH s.p. (S1762)
solo,acap ENOCH s.p. (S1763)

SCUDERI, GASPARE (1889-1962)
A Nanna
see Sei Liriche

Il Brivido
see Sei Liriche

Il Nunzio
see Sei Liriche

La Felicita
see Sei Liriche

Notte Di Vento
see Sei Liriche

Sei Liriche
[It] solo,pno cmplt ed BONGIOVANI
1507 s.p.
contains: A Nanna; Il Brivido; Il
Nunzio; La Felicita; Notte Di
Vento; Vana Attesa (S1764)

Vana Attesa
see Sei Liriche

SCULPTURES see Huggler, John

SCUOTE AMORE IL MIO CUORE see Pizzetti,
Ildebrando

SCYTHE SONG see Chalk, C.

SE... see Denza, Luigi

SE, ALLENA HAR JAG VANDRAT see
Berggreen, Andreas Peter

SE CASA EL BOYERO see Jurafsky, Abraham

SE DA UN EMPIO see Scarlatti, Domenico

SE DELITTO E L'ADORARTI see Scarlatti,
Alessandro

SE EQUIVOCO LA PALOMA see Guastavino,
Carlos

SE FEDEL VUOCI CH'IO TI CREDA see
Handel, George Frideric

SE FLORINDO E FEDELE see Scarlatti,
Alessandro

SE GLAD UT see Josephson, Jacob Axel

SE GLASET LJUSETS BANA AR see Sjogren,
Emil

SE I LANGUIDI MIEI SGUARDI see
Monteverdi, Claudio

SE-I-RE-I-NI-YO-SU see Murai, Tsuguji

SE IL MIO NOME SAPER VOI BRAMATE see
Rossini, Gioacchino

SE IL TIMORE see Handel, George
Frideric

SE JAG STAR FOR DORREN OCH KLAPPER see
Olson, Daniel

SE KVISTEN SKVALLER see Merikanto,
Oskar

SE LA GIURATA FEDE see Puccini, Giacomo

SE LONTAN, BEN MIO, TU SEI see Mozart,
Wolfgang Amadeus

SE, NATTEN FLYR FOR DAGENS FROJD see
Finnborg

SE N'E ANDATA VIA see Nielsen, Riccardo

SE NON VEDO QUEI BEI LUMI see
Scarlatti, Domenico

SE PEUT-IL QU'UNE LARME see Messager,
Andre

SE POTESTE SOL PENSARE see Kalman,
Emerich

S'E SPENTO IL SOL see Mascagni, Pietro

SE TACI... see Alfano, Franco

SE TU AMASTI ME see Mascagni, Pietro

SE TU DI ME FAI DONO see Mozart,
Wolfgang Amadeus

SE TU M'AMI! see Pergolesi, Giovanni
Battista

SE, VI GA UPP TILL JERUSALEM see
Forsberg, Roland

SE VUOI D'ALLORO CINGER LA CHIOMA see
Scarlatti, Domenico

SE VUOL BALLARE see Mozart, Wolfgang
Amadeus

SEA, THE see Griffes, Charles
Tomlinson, La Mer

SEA, THE see MacDowell, Edward
Alexander

SEA AND SKY see Rubens, Paul Alfred

SEA BURTHEN, A see Keel, Frederick

SEA CHARM see Harris, Edward

SEA DREAM see Giannini, Vittorio

SEA FEAST *Scot
solo,pno PATERSON s.p. see from
Hebridean Songs, Vol. IV (S1765)

SEA FEVER see Andrews, Mark

SEA FEVER see De Vito, Albert

SEA FEVER see Enos, J.

SEA FEVER see Ireland, John

SEA GULLS see Haubiel, Charles

SEA HATH ITS PEARLS, THE see Cowen, Sir
Frederic Hymen

SEA LOVE see Bliss, Sir Arthur

SEA MAIDENS see Parker, Henry

SEA MOODS see Tyson, Mildred Lund

SEA MUSIC see Dyson, George

SEA PICTURES see Elgar, Edward

SEA RITUAL, THE see Pinkham, Daniel

SEA SLUMBER SONG see Elgar, Edward

SEA SONG see Lora, Antonio

SEA SONG, A see Benbow, Edwin

SEA THOUGHTS see Bohun, Lyle de

SEA WIND see Haubiel, Charles

SEABIRD, FLYING HITHER *Scot
solo,pno (contains also: Silent
Crane) PATERSON s.p. see from
Hebridean Songs, Vol. IV (S1766)

SEAGARD, JOHN
Epiphany Adoration *sac
solo,pno AUGSBURG 11-0741 $1.00
(S1767)

SEAGULL, THE see Shapiro, Norman

SEAL MY HEART see Castelnuovo-Tedesco,
Mario

SEAL UPON THY HEART, A see Reznick,
Hyman, Simeni Chachosom

SEAL WOMAN, THE see Flothius, Marius

SEAMARKS, COLIN
Six Mehitabel Magpies *CC6U
S solo,bvl (med diff) YORKE YE 0033
s.p. (S1768)

SEARCH, THE see Kilpinen, Yrio,
Liebessuche

SEARCH see Campbell, David

SEARCHING see Osborne, T.L. Jr.

SEARCHING FOR LAMBS
(Goosens, E.) [Eng] med solo,kbd
CHESTER s.p. (S1769)

SEARCHING FOR LAMBS see Vaughan
Williams, Ralph

SEARCHING QUESTIONS *sac
(Carmichael, Ralph) solo,pno WORD
S-250 (S1770)

SEARCHING QUESTIONS *sac,CC7L
(Carmichael, Ralph) solo,pno WORD
30072 $1.95 (S1771)

SEARLE, HUMPHREY (1915-   )
Counting The Beats *Op.40
high solo,pno FABER F0057 $1.25
(S1772)

Three Songs Of Jocelyn Brooke
*Op.25, CC3U
high solo,pno FABER FO163 $2.00
(S1773)

SEA'S MUSIC, THE see Nystroem, Gosta,
Havets Visa

SEASCAPE see Goosens, Eugene

SEASON FOR SINGING, THE *CCU,Xmas,
    carol
    (Langstaff, John) solo,pno DOUBLDAY
    ISBN: 0-385-06564-7 $5.95   (S1774)

SEASON OF STAR-SONG see Fischer, Irwin

SEASON OF THE LONG RAINS *sac
    (Carmichael, Ralph) solo,pno WORD
    S-377   (S1775)

SEASON OF THE YEAR, THE *CC58U,Xmas
    (Silber, Irwin) solo,pno OAK 000122
    $2.95   (S1776)

SEASONS see Thomas, F.W.G.

SEASONS, THE see Bantock, Granville

SEASONS see Winter, Sister Miriam
    Therese

SEAVER
    Just For Today
    (Partridge) high solo,pno FOX,S
                                     (S1777)
    (Partridge) med solo,pno FOX,S
                                     (S1778)
    (Partridge) ST soli,pno FOX,S
                                     (S1779)
    (Partridge) low solo,pno FOX,S
                                     (S1780)
    (Partridge) high solo&low solo,pno
    FOX,S   (S1781)
    (Partridge) med solo&low solo,pno
    FOX,S   (S1782)

SEBASTIAN see Lessard, John Ayres

SEBBEN, CRUDELE see Caldara, Antonio

SEBBEN SENTE see Wolf, Hugo

SECCHI E SBERLECHI see Mortari,
    Virgilio

SECHS ALTE MINNELIEDER see Zipp,
    Friedrich

SECHS ALTNIEDERLANDISCHE VOLKSLIEDER
    see Kremser, Edward

SECHS ARIEN AUS DEM HARMONISCHEN
    GOTTESDIENST see Telemann, Georg
    Philipp

SECHS AUSGEWAHLTE LIEDER see Strauss,
    Richard

SECHS CHORALKONZERTE see Schein, Johann
    Hermann

SECHS DEUTSCHE LIEDER see Spohr, Ludwig
    (Louis)

SECHS GEDICHTE see Haas, Joseph

SECHS GEDICHTE AUS GOETHES
    WESTOSTLICHEM DIWAN see Reutter,
    Hermann

SECHS GEDICHTE VON PAUL VERLAINE see
    Kowalski, Max

SECHS GEDICHTE VON PUSCHKIN see
    Medtner, Nikolai Karlovitch

SECHS GEDICHTE VON R.M. RILKE see
    Lilien, Ignace

SECHS GEISTLICHE LIEDER see Beethoven,
    Ludwig van

SECHS GESANGE see Reichert, E.

SECHS GESANGE see Westerman, G. von

SECHS HOLDERLIN FRAGMENTE see Britten,
    Benjamin

SECHS ITALIENISCHE DUETTINEN see Bach,
    Johann Christian

SECHS JUGENDLIEDER see Pfitzner, Hans

SECHS KINDERLIEDER NACH GEDICHTEN VON
    CHRISTIAN MORGENSTERN see Knorr,
    Ernst Lother von

SECHS LIEBESLIEDER, OP. 35, HEFT I see
    Pfitzner, Hans

SECHS LIEBESLIEDER, OP. 35, HEFT II see
    Pfitzner, Hans

SECHS LIEDER see Schoenberg, Arnold

SECHS LIEDER see Strauss, Richard

SECHS LIEDER see Uray, Ernst Ludwig

SECHS LIEDER see Webern, Anton von

SECHS LIEDER see Noetel, Konrad
    Friedrich

SECHS LIEDER see Eisler, Hanns

SECHS LIEDER see Eben, Petr

SECHS LIEDER see Kornauth, Egon

SECHS LIEDER see Kornauth, Egon

SECHS LIEDER see Rinaldini, Dr. Joseph

SECHS LIEDER see Bordewijk-Roepman,
    Johanna

SECHS LIEDER see Weismann, Wilhelm

SECHS LIEDER see Kilpinen, Yrio

SECHS LIEDER see Pfitzner, Hans

SECHS LIEDER see Beethoven, Ludwig van

SECHS LIEDER see Schubert, Franz
    (Peter)

SECHS LIEDER see Carriere, Paul

SECHS LIEDER see Trunk, Richard

SECHS LIEDER see Kunz, Ernst

SECHS LIEDER see Schubert, Franz
    (Peter)

SECHS LIEDER see Jentsch, Walter

SECHS LIEDER see Schoenberg, Arnold

SECHS LIEDER, BOOK I: LIEDER DER
    OPHEILIA see Strauss, Richard

SECHS LIEDER, BOOK II: LIEDER DEN
    BUCHERN DES UNMUTS DES RENDSCH
    NAMEH see Strauss, Richard

SECHS LIEDER (EICHENDORFF) see
    Kornauth, Egon

SECHS LIEDER (HESSE) see Kornauth, Egon

SECHS LIEDER IM VOLKSTON see Mixa,
    Franz

SECHS LIEDER NACH GEDICHTEN VON EMIL
    GOTT see Schwickert, Gustav

SECHS LIEDER NACH GEDICHTEN VON
    FRIEDRICH HOLDERLIN see Hindemith,
    Paul

SECHS LIEDER NACH GEDICHTEN VON GOETHE
    see Rubin, Marcel

SECHS LIEDER NACH GEDICHTEN VON
    GOTTFRIED KELLER see Trunk, Richard

SECHS LIEDER NACH GEDICHTEN VON KATRI
    VALA see Marvia, Einari

SECHS LIEDER NACH GEDICHTEN VON L.
    UHLAND see Schnyder von Wartensee,
    Xaver

SECHS LIEDER NACH GEDICHTEN VON OTHMAR
    LECHLER see Badings, Henk

SECHS LIEDER NACH SCHOTTISCHEN TEXTEN
    see Roetscher, Konrad

SECHS LIEDER NACH TEXTEN VON FR. M.
    FRANZEN UND J.L. RUNEBERG *see
    Sibelius, Jean, Die Anemone, Op.88,
    No.1; Sibelius, Jean, Die Beiden
    Rosen, Op.88,No.2; Sibelius, Jean,
    Die Blume, Op.88,No.6; Sibelius,
    Jean, Die Primel, Op.88,No.4;
    Sibelius, Jean, Die Sternblume,
    Op.88,No.3; Sibelius, Jean, Tornet,
    "Der Dornbusch", Op.88,No.5 (S1783)

SECHS LIEDER NACH TEXTEN VON J.L.
    RUNEBERG *see Be Still, My Soul
    (from Finlandia); Der Morgen,
    Op.90,No.3; Der Norden, Op.90,No.1;
    Der Vogelsteller, Op.90,No.4; Die
    Sommernacht, Op.90,No.5; Heimat,
    Sieh Des Morgens Helle Schwingen
    (from Finlandia); Ihre Botschaft,
    Op.90,No.2; Wer Hat Dich
    Hergefuhrt, Op.90,No.6   (S1784)

SECHS LIEDER UM DEN TOD see Kilpinen,
    Yrio

SECHS LIEDER ZUM SINGEN MIT GITARRE see
    Hiller

SECHS LYRISCHE LIEDER see Wladigeroff,
    P.

SECHS MINNELIEDER see Eben, Petr

SECHS MONOLOGE AUS "JEDERMANN" see
    Martin, Frank

SECHS NACHGELASSENE LIEDER see
    Mussorgsky, Modest

SECHS ORCHESTERLIEDER see Schoenberg,
    Arnold

SECHS ROMANZEN see Shostakovich, Dmitri

SECHS RUSSISCHE LIEDER see Reutter,
    Hermann

SECHS SOMMERSEGEN see Kilpinen, Yrio

SECHS SPATE GEDICHTE see Reutter,
    Hermann

SECHS STIMMUNGSBILDER see Westerman, G.
    von

SECHS WEIHNACHTSLIEDER see Schroeder,
    Hermann

SECHS WEIHNACHTSLIEDER see Cornelius,
    Peter

SECHSE, SIEBEN ODER ACHT see Brull,
    Ignaz

SECHSUNDZWANZIG VOLKSBALLADEN see
    Janacek, Leos

SECHZEHN FRUHE LIEDER see Tiessen,
    Heinz

SECHZEHN KINDERLIEDER see Tchaikovsky,
    Piotr Ilyitch

SECHZEHN LIEDER see Babadjanjan, Arno

SECHZEHN LIEDER see Sendt, Willy

SECHZEHN LIEDER HEFT I see Wolf, Hugo

SECHZEHN LIEDER HEFT II see Wolf, Hugo

SECOND BOOK OF AYRES see Dowland, John

SECOND BOOK OF FOLK SONGS *CC24U
    (Lund, Engel; Rauter, Ferdinand)
    solo,pno OXFORD 68.702 $2.50
                                     (S1785)

SECOND BOOK OF SONGS see Heseltine,
    Philip

SECOND CHAPTER OF ACTS SONG BOOK *sac,
    CCUL,Bibl
    solo,pno WORD 37748 $3.95   (S1786)

SECOND MINUET see Besly, Maurice

SECRECY see Wolf, Hugo, Verborgenheit

SECRECY'S SONG see Purcell, Henry

SECRET see Schumann, Robert (Alexander)

SECRET see Wardale, Joseph

SECRET, THE see Mourant, Walter

SECRET, THE see Sena, Tony

SECRET, THE see Strauss, Richard, Das
    Geheimnis

SECRET AVEU see Aubert, Louis-Francois-
    Marie

SECRET ROOM, THE see Hatch

SECRETAN, G.
    Ma Tete
    solo,pno ENOCH s.p.   (S1787)
    solo,acap ENOCH s.p.   (S1788)

SECULAR SOLOS FOR BASS see Handel,
    George Frideric

SECULAR SPANISH SONGS OF THE
    SEVENTEENTH CENTURY, VOL. I *sec,
    CCU,Span,17th cent
    (Pujol) [Span] med solo,gtr ESCHIG
    E1321A $4.50   (S1789)

SECULAR SPANISH SONGS OF THE
    SEVENTEENTH CENTURY, VOL. II *sec,
    CCU,Span,17th cent
    (Pujol) [Span] med solo,gtr ESCHIG
    E1321B $4.50   (S1790)

SECULAR VOCAL MUSIC see Dering, Richard

SECUNDA, SHOLOM (1894-1974)
    Shabes Tzu Nacht *Jew
    solo,pno KAMMEN 37 $1.00 see also
    JEWISH THEATRE SONGS, VOL. 1
                                     (S1791)

SEDEM NARODNIH PESMI see Tomc, Matija

SEDEM SAMOSPEVOV see Lipovsek, Marijan

SEDM BAJEK PODLE EZOPA see Valek, Jiri

SEDM PISNI see Burian, Emil Frantisek

SEDM PISNI PRO SOPRAN see Borkovec, Pavel

SEDM RONDEAUX NA BASNE J. SEIFERT see Vomacka, Boleslav

SEDUCTION see Vieu, Jane

SEE HOW THEY LOVE ME see Flanagan, William

SEE HOW THEY LOVE ME see Rorem, Ned

SEE MY CHOSEN ONE see Rider, Dale G.

SEE THE LIGHT see Roe, Gloria [Ann]

SEED AND THE SOWER, THE *sac
   (Carmichael, Ralph) solo,pno WORD
   S-106   (S1792)

SEEGER, C.
   Letter, The
      solo,pno PRESSER $1.75 contains
         also: Psalm 137 (narrator,pno)
                                     (S1793)
   Psalm 137
      see Seeger, C., Letter, The

SEEK NOT THERE see Birch, Robert Fairfax

SEEK THE LORD TODAY see Horne, Roger

SEEK YE FIRST THE KINGDOM OF GOD see Fisher, William Arms

SEEK YE THE LORD see Humphreys, Don

SEEK YE THE LORD see Lowe, Augustus

SEEK YE THE LORD see Roberts, J. Varley

SEEKING YOU see Weigl, Vally

SEELE, LERNE DICH ERKENNEN see Telemann, Georg Philipp

SEEMANNSLIEDER ZUR GITARRE, HEFT 2
   *CCU
   (Stoppa) solo,gtr SIKORSKI 209B s.p.
                                     (S1794)

SEEMANNSLIEDER ZUR GITARRE, HEFT I
   *CCU
   (Schwarz-Reiflingen, Erwin) solo,gtr
   SIKORSKI 209A s.p.   (S1795)

SEEMANNSLOS see Petrie, H.W.

SEERAUBER-JENNY see Weill, Kurt

SEGADOR see Chavez, Carlos

SEGELFAHRT see Bijvanck, Henk

SEGERSTAM, LEIF (1944-   )
   Sieben Rote Augenblicke *CC7L
      [Finn/Ger] solo,pno FAZER F 5447
      s.p.   (S1796)

   Three Leaves Of Grass *CC3U
      high solo,pno WEINBERGER $2.00
                                     (S1797)

SEGOND, PIERRE (1913-   )
   Berceuse
      see Trois Melodies

   Madrigal
      see Trois Melodies

   Nous Attendions Des Heroines
      see Trois Melodies

   Trois Melodies
      solo,pno cmplt ed DURAND s.p.
         contains: Berceuse; Madrigal;
         Nous Attendions Des Heroines
                                     (S1798)

SEGOVIANE see Lacome, Paul

SEGRETO see Tosti, Francesco Paolo

SEGUEDILLE see Bizet, Georges, Pres Des Remparts De Seville

SEGUIDILLA see Bizet, Georges, Pres Des Ramparts De Seville

SEGUIDILLA AND DUET see Bizet, Georges, Pres Des Ramparts De Seville

SEGUIDILLA MURCIANA see Falla, Manuel de

SEGUIDILLA MURICIANA see Falla, Manuel de

SEGUIDILLAS
   see La Musique, Septieme Cahier

SEGUIDILLAS MURCIANAS see Carol, M.

SEGUIDILLE see Falla, Manuel de

SEHET AN DEN FEIGENBAUM see Schutz, Heinrich

SEHLSTEDT *CC8L
   solo,pno,opt gtr LUNDQUIST s.p.
                                     (S1799)

SEHNSUCHT see Borup-Jorgensen, Axel

SEHNSUCHT see Cuypers, H.

SEHNSUCHT see Othegraven, August J. von

SEHNSUCHT see Schoenberg, Arnold

SEHNSUCHT see Sibelius, Jean

SEHNSUCHT NACH DER HEIMAT see Genzmer, Harald

SEHNSUCHT NACH VERGESSEN see Pfitzner, Hans

SEI ARIE see Donizetti, Gaetano

SEI ARIE see Vivaldi, Antonio

SEI ARIETTE PER SOPRANO
   COLL'ACCOMPAGNAMENTO DEL PIANOFORTE
   see Morlacchi, Francesco

SEI BALADAS see Albeniz, Isaac

SEI BEREIT! see Edler, Robert

SEI CANTI INFANTILI see Barbera, G.

SEI CANTI SACRI see Beethoven, Ludwig van

SEI CANZONI NAPOLETANE DA CAMERA [2]
   see Giazotto, Remo

SEI CANZONI NAPOLETANE DA CAMERA see Giazotto, Remo

SEI GEGRUSSET, MARIA see Schutz, Heinrich

SEI GEPRIESEN, DU LAUSCHIGE NACHT see Ziehrer, Carl Michael

SEI GETREU see Mendelssohn-Bartholdy, Felix

SEI GETROST see Bordewijk-Roepman, Johanna

SEI LIRICHE see Scuderi, Gaspare

SEI LIRICHE see Zandonai, Riccardo

SEI LIRICHE (PRIMA SERIE) see Respighi, Ottorino

SEI LIRICHE (SECONDA SERIE) see Respighi, Ottorino

SEI MELODIE see Zandonai, Riccardo

SEI MELODIE see Respighi, Ottorino

SEI MELODIE see Mussorgsky, Modest

SEI MELODIE see Mozart, Wolfgang Amadeus

SEI MIA GIOIA see Handel, George Frideric

SEI NOTTURNI see Togni, Camillo

SEI PICCOLE LIRICHE see Cairone, Renato

SEI POESIE DI DYLAN THOMAS see Malipiero, Riccardo

SEI STILLE DEM HERRN see Mendelssohn-Bartholdy, Felix

SEI STORNELLI see Veretti, Antonio

SEI TU... AMORE see Tirindelli, Pier Adolfo

SEI VOCALIZZI DA CONCERTO see Jesi, Ada

SEI WILLKOMMEN, LIEBER THOMAS see Kilpinen, Yrio, Tule Meille, Tuomas-Kulta

SEIBENUNDZWANZIG LIEDER NACH GEDICHTEN VON ERIK BLOMBERG, VOL. I see Kilpinen, Yrio

SEIBER, MATYAS (1905-1960)
   Drei Morgensternlieder *CC3U
      high solo,clar UNIVER. 12430 $3.75
                                     (S1800)
   Four Greek Folksongs *CC4U
      S/T solo,pno/strings BOOSEY $4.50
                                     (S1801)

SEIBER, MATYAS (cont'd.)

   Four Old French Songs *CC4U,Fr
      [Fr/Eng] med solo,gtr FABER C02989
      s.p.   (S1802)

   J'ai Descendu
      see Vier Franzosische Volkslieder

   Le Rossignol
      see Vier Franzosische Volkslieder

   Marguerite, Elle Est Malade
      see Vier Franzosische Volkslieder

   Owl And The Pussy-Cat, The
      [Eng] high solo,pno SCHOTTS 10689
      s.p.   (S1803)

   Reveillez-Vous
      see Vier Franzosische Volkslieder

   Vier Franzosische Volkslieder
      [Fr] S solo,pno/strings voc sc
      SCHOTTS 4630 s.p., ipr
      contains: J'ai Descendu; Le
         Rossignol; Marguerite, Elle Est
         Malade; Reveillez-Vous   (S1804)

SEIDEL, JAN (1908-   )
   Kdyz Se Dva Setkaji
      "Wenn Ihnen Zwei Begegnen" med
      solo,pno CZECH s.p.   (S1805)

   Na Stastnou Cestu *CCU
      solo,pno SUPRAPHON s.p.   (S1806)

   Prekrasne Zemi *CC10U
      solo,pno SUPRAPHON s.p.   (S1807)

   Vonicka *song cycle
      solo,pno SUPRAPHON s.p.   (S1808)

   Wenn Ihnen Zwei Begegnen *see Kdyz
      Se Dva Setkaji

SEIGNEUR, SACHEZ see Le Flem, Paul

SEIMEN AARELLA *CCU,Xmas
   (Tenkku) solo,pno FAZER F 3709 s.p.
                                     (S1809)

SEIS CANCIONES see Pahissa, Jaime

SEIS CANCIONES see Garcia Leoz, J.

SEIS CANCIONES see Toldra, Eduardo

SEIS CANCIONES AL ESTILO POPULAR see Lopez-Buchardo, Carlos

SEIS CANCIONES ANTIGUAS *CC6U,Carib,
   16th cent
   (Tarrago) [Span] med solo,gtr UNION
   ESP. $2.50   (S1810)

SEIS CANCIONES CASTELLANAS see Guridi, Jesus

SEIS CANCIONES DE CUNA DE GABRIELA MISTRAL see Guastavino, Carlos

SEIS CANCIONES DE FEDERICO GARCIA LORCA see Apivor, Denis

SEIS CANCIONES DEL PARANA, OP. 77 see Ficher, Jacobo

SEIS CANCIONES ESPANOLAS *CC6U,Span
   (Lehmberg) [Span] med solo,pno UNION
   ESP. $2.75   (S1811)

SEIS CANCIONES INFANTILES see Guridi, Jesus

SEIS CANTOS ESPIRTUALES see Nacamuli, Guido

SEIS CANTOS INDIO DEL PERU see Sas, Andres

SEIS HABANERAS TRADICIONALES *CC6U
   (Aguila) high solo,pno UNION ESP.
   $1.25   (S1812)

SEIS MINIATURAS see Lilien, Ignace

SEIS VILLANCICOS RUSTICOS ESPANOLES
   *CC6U
   (Benedito) [Span] med solo,pno UNION
   ESP. $1.00   (S1813)

SEIT DU MIR FERNE BIST see Bijvanck, Henk

SEIT ICH DIE HEIMAT MUSSTE LASSEN see Hannikainen, Ilmari

SEIT LANGER ZEIT (from Prince Igor)
   [Russ/Fr/Ger] S solo,pno BELAIEFF 248
   s.p.   (S1814)

SEITDEM DEIN AUG'IN MEINES SCHAUTE see Strauss, Richard

SEIZE ANS see Cuvillier, Charles

SEJOUR see Schubert, Franz (Peter)

SEJOUR DE L'ETERNELLE PAIX see Rameau,
   Jean-Philippe

SEKS SANGER see Bergman, Erik

SEKSTENDE ARHUNDREDE MARIALIED *CCU,
   16th cent
   (Pijper, W.) solo,pno BROEKMANS 218
   s.p.   (S1815)

SELBST GELERNT HAB' ICH MEINE LIEDER
   see Kilpinen, Yrio, Omat On Virret
   Oppimiani

SELBSTBILDNIS DES MARC AUREL see
   Jelinek, Hanns

SELBSTGEFUHL see Mahler, Gustav

SELECT COLLECTION OF THE MOST ADMIRED
   SONGS FROM OPERAS AND FROM OTHER
   WORKS, A *CCU
   [It/Fr/Eng] 2 soli,pno FORNI s.p.
   contains works by various composers
                                       (S1816)
SELECT ENGLISH SONGS AND DIALOGUES OF
   THE SIXTEENTH AND SEVENTEENTH
   CENTURIES *CCU,Eng,16-17th cent
   (Dolmetsch, A.) high solo,pno BOOSEY
   $5.00, ea. available in two volumes
                                       (S1817)
SELECT FRENCH SONGS FROM THE TWELFTH TO
   THE EIGHTEENTH CENTURIES *CCU,Fr,
   12-18th cent
   (Dolmetsch, A.) solo,kbd BOOSEY $5.00
                                       (S1818)
SELECT VOCAL SOLOS FOR THE CHURCH
   MUSICIAN, VOLUME I *sac,CCU
   (Kugel, William F.) low solo,pno
   ABINGDON APM-312 $2.50; high solo,
   pno ABINGDON APM-308 $2.50 (S1819)

SELECTED ARIAS see Bach, Johann
   Sebastian

SELECTED ARIAS FROM OPERAS see Rimsky-
   Korsakov, Nikolai

SELECTED DUETS see Cornelius, Peter

SELECTED FRENCH ART SONGS *CCU,Fr
   [Fr/Eng] solo,pno MARKS $1.75 (S1820)

SELECTED GOETHE SONGS see Wolf, Hugo

SELECTED POEMS OF CHINESE POETESSES
   FROM THE HAN TO QING DYNASTIES see
   Kashiwagi, Toshio

SELECTED RECITATIVES see Roitman, David

SELECTED ROMANCES see Tchaikovsky,
   Piotr Ilyitch

SELECTED ROMANCES see Polovinkin,
   Leonid

SELECTED ROMANCES see Shaporin, Yuri
   Alexandrovitch

SELECTED ROMANCES see Debussy, Claude

SELECTED ROMANCES AND SONGS see
   Dargomyzhsky, [Alexander
   Sergeyevitch]

SELECTED SONGS see Pasatieri, Thomas

SELECTED SONGS see Grieg, Edvard
   Hagerup

SELECTED SONGS see Tchaikovsky, Piotr
   Ilyitch

SELECTED SONGS see Weber

SELECTED SONGS see Schubert, Franz
   (Peter)

SELECTED SONGS *CCU
   solo,pno MUSIC 020045 $3.95 (S1821)

SELECTED SONGS see Grieg, Edvard
   Hagerup

SELECTED SONGS see Grieg, Edvard
   Hagerup

SELECTED SONGS see Copland, Aaron

SELECTED SONGS see Mahler, Gustav

SELECTED SONGS see Hatze, Josip

SELECTED SONGS see Farkas, Ferenc

SELECTED SONGS see Kosa, Gyorgy

SELECTED SONGS FROM ITALIAN LYRICS see
   Wolf, Hugo

SELECTED SONGS FROM SPANISH LYRICS
   (SECULAR) see Wolf, Hugo

SELECTED SONGS, VOL. 1 *CCU
   (Wolfes, Felix) [Ger] high solo,pno
   PRESSER $3.00   (S1822)

SELECTED SONGS, VOL. 2 *CCU
   (Wolfes, Felix) [Ger] high solo,pno
   PRESSER $3.00   (S1823)

SELECTED SONGS, VOL. 3 *CCU
   (Wolfes, Felix) [Ger] med solo,pno
   PRESSER $3.00   (S1824)

SELECTED SONGS, VOL. 4 *CCU
   (Wolfes, Felix) [Ger] med solo,pno
   PRESSER $3.00   (S1825)

SELECTED SONGS, VOL. 5 *CCU
   (Wolfes, Felix) [Ger] low solo,pno
   PRESSER $3.00   (S1826)

SELECTED SONGS, VOL. I see Brahms,
   Johannes

SELECTED SONGS, VOL. II see Brahms,
   Johannes

SELECTED SONGS, VOL. II: SONGS TO WORDS
   BY SCHILLER AND MAYRHOFER see
   Schubert, Franz (Peter)

SELECTED VOCAL WORKS see Milhaud,
   Darius

SELECTED WORKS, VOL. I: SOLO SONGS see
   Lisinski, Vatroslav

SELECTION OF ISRAELI SONGS see Nardi,
   Nachum

SELECTIONS FROM "REISEBUCH AUS DEN
   OSTERREICHISCHEN ALPEN" see Krenek,
   Ernst

SELF BANISHED, THE see Blow, John

SELIG SIND, DIE VERFOLGUNG LEIDEN see
   Kienzl, Wilhelm

SELIGKEIT see Borris, Siegfried

SELIGKEIT see Schubert, Franz (Peter)

SELINDA OCH LEANDER see Peterson-
   Berger, (Olof) Wilhelm

SELLE, THOMAS (1599-1663)
   Domine, Exaudi Orationem Meam *sac,
      concerto
      B solo,4trom,cont sc HANSSLER 5.091
      s.p., ipa   (S1827)

   Erstanden Ist Der Herre Christ *sac,
      concerto
      high solo,2trom,cont,vln sc
      HANSSLER 5.086 s.p., ipa (S1828)

SELLERS, ROB
   Disciple's Prayer, A *see O'Brien,
      Bill

SELSKE PISNE see Spilka, Frantisek

SELVA E MARE see Gandino, Adolfo

SELVA OPACA, DESRTA BRUGHIERA see
   Rossini, Gioacchino

SEMEGEN, DARIA
   Lieder Auf Der Flucht *CCU
      S solo,fl,clar,horn,2perc,vln,vcl,
      pno sc AM.COMP.AL. $9.35 (S1829)

SEMELE see Peterson-Berger, (Olof)
   Wilhelm

SEMINI, CARLO FLORINDO
   Tre Poemi Di Hermann Hesse *CC3U
      solo,7inst sc CURCI 9164 rental,
      voc sc CURCI 9163 s.p.   (S1830)

SEMMLER, R.
   Funf Lieder *Op.1,No.1-5, CC5U
      solo,pno HUG s.p.   (S1831)

SEMPRE DOLCI, ED AMOROSE see Handel,
   George Frideric

SEN HAR JAG EJ FRAGAT MERA see Korling,
   Felix

SE'N HAR JAG EJ FRAGAT MERA see
   Sibelius, Jean

SEN NOCI SVATOJANSKE see Trojan, Vaclav

SENA, TONY
   Secret, The *sac
      solo,pno BENSON S8034-R $1.00
                                       (S1832)
      solo,pno GENTRY $1.00   (S1833)

SEND HOME MY LONG STRAYED EYES see
   Flanagan, William

SENDAS DE NOSTALGIA see Sammartino,
   Luis

SENDT, WILLY (1907-1952)
   Sechzehn Lieder *CC16U
      high solo,pno TONGER s.p.   (S1834)

SENGER, DE
   Souvenir De Patrie
      S solo,orch HENN s.p.   (S1835)

SENKE DEIN KOPFCHEN see Nielsen, Carl,
   Saenk Kun Dit Hoved, Du Blomst

SENN, KARL (1878-   )
   Ave, Du Wonne Der Frauen *sac
      low solo,org LEUCKART s.p. (S1836)

SENNES, H.
   Ave Maria *sac
      SA soli,org/pno sc BOHM s.p.
                                       (S1837)

SENNIS ALP see Knellwolf, J.

SENSATION see Andriessen, Hendrik

SENSOMMAR see Lagerheim-Romare, Margit

SENTI, SENTI see Bossi, Renzo

SENTO CHE T'AMO see Vene, Ruggero

SENTO CON QUEL DILETTO see Wolf, Hugo

SENTO L'AURA see Scarlatti, Domenico

SENTO NEL CORE see Scarlatti,
   Alessandro

SENTO UN FISCHIETTO VENIRE DI LONTANO
   see Oddone, E.

SENTRY, THE see Roberts, Mervyn

SENZA MAMMA, O BIMBO, TU SEI MORTO! see
   Puccini, Giacomo

SEPARATION see Schumann, Robert
   (Alexander)

SEPARONS-NOUS see Delmet, Paul

SEPHARDIC KIDDUSH see Weiner, Lazar

SEPT CHANSONS DE CLEMENT MAROT see
   Enesco, Georges

SEPT CHANSONS DE ROBERT BURNS see
   Gedalge, Andre

SEPT CHANSONS POUR LES MOINS DE 10 ANS
   see Bianchini, V.

SEPT COMPLAINTES see Bourgeois, H.

SEPT HAI-KAIS see Delage, Maurice

SEPT MELODIES see Handman, Dorel

SEPT MELODIES DE R.M. RILKE see Orthel,
   Leon

SEPT MELODIES POUR CHANT, PIANO, VIOLON
   ET VIOLONCELLE see Shostakovich,
   Dmitri

SEPT PAIRS DE SOULIERS see Delannoy,
   Marcel

SEPT PETITES IMAGES DU JAPON see Migot,
   Georges

SEPT RUBAIJAT DES OMAR KHAJJAM see
   Cerha, Friedrich

SEPT VERSETS D'UN MOTET (1704) see
   Couperin (le Grand), Francois

SEPTEM CANTICA see Strategier, Herman

SEPTEMBER LOVERS see Pitfield, Thomas
   Baron

SEPTEMBER-MORGEN see Marx, Joseph

SEPTEMBER SERENADE see Chaminade,
   Cecile, Automne

SEPTEMBERAFTON see Olsson, Otto
   Emmanuel

SEPTEMBERSONETT see Kilpinen, Yrio,
   Syyskuun Sonetti

SEPTET see Dijk, Jan van

SEPTUM VERBA see Pergolesi, Giovanni
   Battista

SER DU see Hallnas, Hilding

SERA see Castelnuovo-Tedesco, Mario

SERA see Oddone, E.

SERA DI FESTA DOPO IL RITORNO DALLA GUERRA see Toschi, Pietro

SERA FESTIVA see Gandino, Adolfo

SERA SUI MONTI see Fuga, Sandro

SERAFERNE see Nielsen, Carl

SERAPHITA see Schoenberg, Arnold

SERATE D'OPERE DI ESZTERHAZA, VOL. 1 *CCU
(Vecsey; Somfai) [It] S/Mez solo,pno BUDAPEST 3383 $4.25 (S1838)

SERATE D'OPERE DI ESZTERHAZA, VOL. 2 *CCU
(Vecsey; Somfai) [It] T solo,pno BUDAPEST 3384 $4.25 (S1839)

SERATE D'OPERE DI ESZTERHAZA, VOL. 3 *CCU
(Vecsey; Somfai) [It] Bar/B solo,pno BUDAPEST 3385 $4.25 (S1840)

SERATE MUSICALI, VOL. I see Rossini, Gioacchino

SERATE MUSICALI, VOL. II see Rossini, Gioacchino

SERENAD see Bruch, Max

SERENAD see Korling, Felix

SERENAD see Lundkvist, Per

SERENAD see Myrberg, August M.

SERENAD see Nordqvist, Gustaf

SERENAD see Peterson-Berger, (Olof) Wilhelm

SERENAD see Schubert, Franz (Peter), Standchen

SERENAD see Sjogren, Emil

SERENAD "TALLARNAS BARR" see Wideen, Ivar

SERENADE see Andriessen, Juriaan

SERENADE see Aubert, Louis-Francois-Marie

SERENADE see Beethoven, Ludwig van

SERENADE see Bergman, Erik

SERENADE see Biber, Heinrich Ignaz Franz von

SERENADE see Bilotti, Anton

SERENADE see Bondeville, Emmanuel de

SERENADE see Braga, Gaetana, La Serenata

SERENADE see Britten, Benjamin

SERENADE see Campolieti

SERENADE see Chansarel, R.

SERENADE see Chapuis, Auguste-Paul-Jean-Baptiste

SERENADE see Clerice, J.

SERENADE see Drigo, Riccardo

SERENADE see Gedalge, Andre

SERENADE see Gillet, Ernest

SERENADE see Gounod, Charles Francois

SERENADE see Gretry, Andre Ernest Modeste

SERENADE see Grovlez, Gabriel (Marie)

SERENADE see Kowalski, Max

SERENADE see Lebrun, Paul Henri Joseph

SERENADE see Lemaire, F.

SERENADE see Liszt, Franz, Standchen

SERENADE see Mahler, Gustav

SERENADE see Malipiero, Gian Francesco, Serenata

SERENADE see Medtner, Nikolai Karlovitch

SERENADE see Mussorgsky, Modest

SERENADE see Nordoff, Paul

SERENADE see Orland, Henry

SERENADE see Panizza, Ettore

SERENADE see Philippart-Gonzalez, Renee

SERENADE see Pierne, Gabriel

SERENADE see Rabey, Rene

SERENADE see Raff, Joseph Joachim

SERENADE see Romanette, Jean

SERENADE see Schubert, Franz (Peter), Standchen

SERENADE see Schumann, Robert (Alexander)

SERENADE see Serpette, Gaston

SERENADE see Shepherd, Arthur

SERENADE see Sibelius, Jean, Sernad

SERENADE see Strauss, Johann

SERENADE see Strauss, Richard, Standchen

SERENADE see Toselli, Enrico, Serenata

SERENADE see Tosti, Francesco Paolo, La Serenata

SERENADE see Trunk, Richard

SERENADE see Villa-Lobos, Heitor

SERENADE see Werther, Rudolf

SERENADE, A see Creston, Paul

SERENADE [2] see Medtner, Nikolai Karlovitch

SERENADE A L'ETOILE see Lachaume, A.

SERENADE A NINON see Lacome, Paul

SERENADE "AV MANESTRALER NATTEN VAEVER" see Kjerulf, [Halfdan]

SERENADE COMPLAINTE see Tomasi, H.

SERENADE D'ALADIN see Vieu, Jane

SERENADE DE SHAKESPEARE see Schubert, Franz (Peter), Hark, Hark, The Lark

SERENADE DE ZANETTO see Massenet, Jules

SERENADE DU BOURGEOIS GENTILHOMME see Faure, Gabriel-Urbain

SERENADE ESPAGNOLE see Ronald, Sir Landon

SERENADE FLORENTINE see Duparc, Henri

SERENADE FLORENTINE see Hirschmann, H.

SERENADE FRANCAISE see Leoncavallo, Ruggiero

SERENADE INUTILE see Brahms, Johannes, Vergebliches Standchen

SERENADE JALOUSE see Montoya, G.

SERENADE JAPONAISE see Vieu, Jane

SERENADE LANGOUREUSE see Durand, Jacques

SERENADE MELANCOLIQUE see Aubert, Louis-Francois-Marie

SERENADE MELANCOLIQUE see Lacome, Paul

SERENADE MELANCOLIQUE see Rhene-Baton

SERENADE NAPOLITAINE see Leoncavallo, Ruggiero

SERENADE "NATTEN ER SA STILLE see Kjerulf, [Halfdan]

SERENADE NO. 5 see Susa, Conrad

SERENADE PAIENNE see Ganne, Louis Gaston

SERENADE PARISIENNE see Chantrier, A.

SERENADE PRINTANIERE see Filipucci, Edm.

SERENADE TO A BEAUTIFUL DAY see Revel, Peter

SERENADE VED STRANBREDDEN "HYTTEN ER LUKKET" see Kjerulf, [Halfdan]

SERENADE VED STRANDBREDDEN see Kjerulf, [Halfdan]

SERENADE VENITIENNE see Schumann, Robert (Alexander)

SERENADES see Beekhuis, Hanna

SERENADI see Madetoja, Leevi

SERENATA see Bracco

SERENATA see Chaminade, Cecile

SERENATA see De Angelis, Ruggero

SERENATA see Donatoni, Franco

SERENATA see Gandino, Adolfo

SERENATA see Malipiero, Gian Francesco

SERENATA see Marvia, Einari

SERENATA see Missiroli, Bindo

SERENATA see Napolitano, Emilio

SERENATA see Peterson-Berger, (Olof) Wilhelm

SERENATA see Schubert, Franz (Peter), Standchen

SERENATA see Sinigaglia, Leone

SERENATA see Toselli, Enrico

SERENATA CAMPERA see Aguirre, Julian

SERENATA DE ARLEQUIN see Leoncavallo, Ruggiero

SERENATA DELLE RONDINI see Billi

SERENATA INDIANA see Respighi, Ottorino

SERENATA INUTIL see Brahms, Johannes, Vergebliches Standchen

SERENATA PER VOCE DA DONNA see Tsouyopoulos, Georges S.

SERENATA PRIMA see De Grandis, Renato

SERENATELLA see Longo, Achille

SERENITE see Saint-Saens, Camille

SERENITY see Buck, Vera

SERENITY see Ives, Charles

SERESTAS see Villa-Lobos, Heitor

SERGEANT OF HORSE see Dix, J. Airlie

SERGEANT'S SONG see Holst, Gustav

SERGEANT'S SONG, THE see Keel, Frederick

SERLY, TIBOR (1900-)
Flight Of The Lark, The solo,pno PEER $.85 (S1841)

SERMENT D'AMANT see Delmet, Paul

SERMENT LA VITA see Indy, Vincent d'

SERMISY, CLAUDE DE (ca. 1490-1562)
Tant Que Vivrai *see Attaignant, Pierre

SERMON see Binet, Jean

SERMON ON THE MOUNT see Besly, Maurice

SERNAD see Sibelius, Jean

SEROCKI, KAZIMIERZ (1922-)
Augen Der Luft
[Pol/Eng/Ger] S solo,orch/pno s.p. study sc MOECK 5009, voc sc MOECK 50009 (S1842)

Gleichnisse *CC4U
[Pol/Ger] S solo,chamb.orch s.p. study sc MOECK 5078, solo pt MOECK coedition with PWM Krakow (S1843)

Herz Der Nacht *song cycle
[Pol/Eng/Ger] Bar solo,orch/pno (coedition with PWM Krakow) s.p. sc MOECK 50003, voc sc MOECK 50002 (S1844)

SERPENT, THE see Kubik, Gail

SERPENT, THE see Rorem, Ned

SERPETTE, GASTON (1846-1904)
Devant Satan, Suivant L'usage (from
Madame Le Diable)
solo,pno ENOCH s.p.   (S1845)

J'ai Bu De Cette Boisson (from Madame
Le Diable)
solo,pno ENOCH s.p.   (S1846)

Je Suis Sergent Instructeur (from
Madame Le Diable)
male solo,pno ENOCH s.p.   (S1847)

Je Te Jure, O Mon Amour (from Madame
Le Diable)
solo,pno ENOCH s.p.   (S1848)

La Chanson Du Capitaine
solo,pno ENOCH s.p.   (S1849)
solo,acap ENOCH s.p.   (S1850)

Le Christ Au Jardin Des Oliviers
*sac
solo,pno ENOCH s.p.   (S1851)
[Fr] solo,pno ENOCH   (S1852)

Le Signe A Mam'zelle Bousquet
solo,pno ENOCH s.p.   (S1853)
solo,acap ENOCH s.p.   (S1854)

Les Chansons De J. Granier *CCU
solo,pno cmplt ed ENOCH s.p.
(S1855)

Ma Poupee
solo,pno ENOCH s.p.   (S1856)
solo,acap ENOCH s.p.   (S1857)

Pour Porter Le Lait (from Madame Le
Diable)
solo,pno ENOCH s.p.   (S1858)

Quand On Est Un Grand Artiste (from
Madame Le Diable)
solo,pno ENOCH s.p.   (S1859)

Serenade
solo,pno ENOCH s.p.   (S1860)

Tout Doucement (from Madame Le
Diable)
solo,pno ENOCH s.p.   (S1861)

SERRADELL, NARCISCO
La Golondrina
solo,pno ALLANS s.p.   (S1862)

SERRANA see Lasala, Angel

SERRE CHAUDE see Chausson, Ernest

SERRE D'ENNUI see Chausson, Ernest

SERRES CHAUDES see Chausson, Ernest

SERVE HIM WITH ALL YOUR HEART see Pace,
Millie Lou

SES DEUX YEUX see Schmitt, Florent

SES YEUX see Chaminade, Cecile

SES YEUX see Filipucci, Edm.

SESINI, U.
Canzoni Trobadoriche *CCU
[It] solo,pno BONGIOVANI 2278 s.p.
(S1863)

SESSIONS, ROGER (1896-   )
On The Beach At Fontana
T solo,pno EMI s.p.   (S1864)

Psalm 140 *sac
high solo,pno MARKS $1.50   (S1865)

SEST KAJUHOVIH PESMI see Bravnicar,
Matija

SEST LIDOVYCH PISNI see Jindrich,
Jindrich

SEST MLADINSKIH PESMI see Skerjanc,
Lucijan Marija

SEST MONOLOGU O LASCE see Valek, Jiri

SEST PESMI see Vremsak, Samo

SEST PISNE NA SLOVA CESKYCH BASNIKU see
Foerster, Josef Bohuslav

SEST PISNI see Schubert, Franz (Peter)

SEST PISNI NA SLOVA A.S. PUSKINA see
Foerster, Josef Bohuslav

SEST PISNI PRO ZPEV NA TEXTY JEANA
COCTEAU, NEZVALA A SEIFERTA see
Jezek, Jaroslav

SEST SAMOSPEVOV see Prelovec, Zorko

SESTERO PIESNI MILOSTNYCH see Eben,
Petr

SESTERO PISNI PRO STREDNI HLAS see
Fibich, Zdenko

SESTINA see Krenek, Ernst

SET ME AS A SEAL see Clokey, Joseph
Waddell

SET ME AS A SEAL UPON THY HEART see
Helfman, Max, Simeni Chachotam

SETACCIOLI, GIACOMO (1868-1925)
Implorazione
solo,pno SANTIS 113 s.p.   (S1866)

La Campana
solo,pno SANTIS 110 s.p.   (S1867)

Nebbia
solo,pno SANTIS 111 s.p.   (S1868)

SETON
Piper O' Dundee
solo,pno OXFORD s.p.   (S1869)

SETTE BREVI CANZONI ROMANTICHE see
Ferrari-Trecate, Luigi

SETTE CANTI DALL'ANTOLOGIA MANYOSHU see
Toda, Kunio

SETTE CANTI, VOL. I see Orefice,
Giacomo

SETTE CANTI, VOL. II see Orefice,
Giacomo

SETTE CANZONETTE VENEZIANE see
Malipiero, Gian Francesco

SETTE LIRICHE see Massarani, E.

SETTE LIRICHE see Alfano, Franco

SETTE PICCOLE LIRICHE, VOL. I see
Persico, Mario

SETTE PICCOLE LIRICHE, VOL. II see
Persico, Mario

SETTE VARIAZIONI SU "LES ROSES" see
Malipiero, Riccardo

SETTI CANZONI see Malipiero, Gian
Francesco

SEUFZER, TRANEN, KUMMER, NOT see Bach,
Johann Sebastian

SEUIL DE LA VRAIE JEUNESSE see Gabus,
Monique

SEUL see Stehman, Jacques

SEULE see Middeleer, Jean De

SEULE DANS MA MISERE see Wagner,
Richard

SEVEN, THE see Bertelsen, Michael

SEVEN AMERICAN POEMS see Bliss, Sir
Arthur

SEVEN CHESHIRE FOLK SONGS *CC7U,folk,
Eng
(Dearnley; Frisbee) solo,pno OXFORD
58.635 $1.80   (S1870)

SEVEN DEVOTIONAL SONGS see Hokanson,
Margrethe

SEVEN ELIZABETHAN LYRICS see Quilter,
Roger

SEVEN EPIGRAMS see Childs, Barney

SEVEN GOETHE SONGS see Howe, Mary

SEVEN GREEK FOLK SONGS *CC7U,folk,
Greek
(Cafagna, Maria Pia) [Fr] med solo,
pno SALABERT-US $7.50   (S1871)

SEVEN HAIKU see Gerhard, Roberto

SEVEN MELODIES, VOL. 1 see Ruyneman,
Daniel

SEVEN MELODIES, VOL. 2 see Ruyneman,
Daniel

SEVEN PETOFI SONGS see Kadosa, [Paul]

SEVEN POEMS BY JAMES JOYCE see Moeran

SEVEN POEMS FROM ENSAMHETENS TANKAR see
Stenhammar, Wilhelm

SEVEN POEMS OF PAUL CLAUDEL see
Milhaud, Darius

SEVEN POEMS OF ROBERT GRAVES see
Hattey, P.

SEVEN POEMS OF STURISS see Holloway,
Robin

SEVEN POEMS OF T'ANG DYNASTY see Chou,
Wen-Chung

SEVEN POEMS UNDER A TREE see Franco,
Johan

SEVEN POSTHUMOUS SONGS see Medtner,
Nikolai Karlovitch

SEVEN PRAYERS see Fromm, Herbert

SEVEN PSALMS see Childs, David

SEVEN ROMANCES AND CHANSONS see
Mussorgsky, Modest

SEVEN SACRED SOLOS see Goode, Jack C.

SEVEN SEAS SHANTY BOOK *CCU
(Sampson; Harris) solo,pno BOOSEY
$5.00   (S1872)

SEVEN SONGS see Shepherd, Arthur

SEVEN SONGS see Huggler, John

SEVEN SONGS see Diamond, David

SEVEN SONGS see Ives, Charles

SEVEN SONGS see Weiner, Lazar

SEVEN SONGS see Weigl, Vally

SEVEN SONGS see Strauss, Richard

SEVEN SONGS see Purcell, Henry

SEVEN SONGS see Kadosa, [Paul]

SEVEN SONGS see Thordarson, Sigurdur

SEVEN SONGS see Sveinbjornsson,
Sveinbjorn

SEVEN SONGS FROM THE LAST PERIOD see
Mahler, Gustav

SEVEN SONGS ON CHINESE POEMS see
Tcherepnin, Alexander

SEVEN SONGS, OP. 6 see Kodaly, Zoltan

SEVEN SONGS, VOL. I see Backer-
Grondahl, Agathe Ursula

SEVEN SONGS, VOL. II see Backer-
Grondahl, Agathe Ursula

SEVEN SONNETS OF MICHELANGELO see
Britten, Benjamin

SEVEN TILE TABLEAUX, THE see Masseus,
Jan

SEVENTEEN SACRED SONGS *sac,CC17L
(Kirby, Walter) SCHIRM.G high solo,
pno $2.50; low solo,pno $2.50
contains works by: Gounod; Handel;
Mendelssohn; Gaul and others,
suitable for Christian Science
Services   (S1873)

SEVENTEENTH CENTURY ENGLISH SONGS
*CCU,Eng,17th cent
(Williams, John) solo,gtr STAINER
3.5540.7 $2.50   (S1874)

SEVENTY SONGS see Brahms, Johannes

SEVERA VILLAFANE see Guastavino, Carlos

SEVILLANA see Massenet, Jules

SEVILLANE see O'Connolly

SEX ANDLIGA SANGER see Dannstrom,
Isidor

SEX CARMINA ALCAEI see Dallapiccola,
Luigi

SEX DIKTER see Ekberg

SEX DUETTER *CC6U
(Korling, Felix) 2 soli,pno GEHRMANS
s.p.   (S1875)

SEX POLSKOR see Dannstrom, Isidor

SEX ROMANSER see Lindblad, Otto

SEX SANGER I see Sibelius, Jean

SEX SANGER II see Sibelius, Jean

SEX SANGER III see Sibelius, Jean

SEX SANGER TILL DIKTER AV AUNE LINKO
see Linko, Ernst (Fredrik)

SEX SANGER TILL DIKTER AV RUNEBERG see
Sibelius, Jean

SEX SUOMALAISTA KANSANLAULUA see
Simila, Arpo

SEXTON
I Want To See Jesus *sac
solo,pno BENSON S6146-S $1.00
(S1876)

SEXTON, WILLIAM
Life He Endured, The *sac
solo,pno WORD S-437   (S1877)

Salvation's Plan *sac
solo,pno WORD S-465   (S1878)

SEYFRIT, MICHAEL
Winter's Warmth
B solo,clar,bsn,harp,vln,vla,vcl sc
AM.COMP.AL. $6.60, ipa (S1879)

"SH" see Drynan, Margaret

SHABBATH see Stutschevsky, Joachim

SHABES TZU NACHT see Secunda, Sholom

SHADE
Show Me Thy Ways, O Lord *sac
solo,pno LILLENAS SM-934: SN $1.00
(S1880)

SHADOW OF THE CROSS see Dirkson, Dan

SHADOW OF THE PLUM see Birch, Robert
Fairfax

SHADOW OF THY WINGS, THE see Andrews,
Mark

SHADOW SONG see Meyerbeer, Giacomo,
Ombre Legere

SHADOW WOOD see Benson, Warren

SHADOWS II see Schwantner, Joseph

SHADOWS IN THE SUN see Raphling, Sam

SHADOWS OF A FLOATING LIFE see
Hutcheson, Jere

SHADOWS OF NIGHT see Somervell, Arthur

SHADRACK see MacGimsey, Robert

SHAFER, SANGER
Baptism Of Jess Taylor, The *see
Frazier, Dallas

SHAFTS OF CUPID, THE see Fletcher,
Percy Eastman

SHAKESPEARE SONGS see Thomson, Virgil

SHAKESPEARE-SONGS see Fortner, Wolfgang

SHAKESPEARE SONGS FOR BARITONE, SET 1
see Castelnuovo-Tedesco, Mario

SHAKESPEARE SONGS FOR BARITONE, SET 2
see Castelnuovo-Tedesco, Mario

SHAKESPEARE SONGS FOR CONTRALTO OR
BARITONE, SET 1 see Castelnuovo-
Tedesco, Mario

SHAKESPEARE SONGS FOR CONTRALTO OR
BARITONE, SET 2 see Castelnuovo-
Tedesco, Mario

SHAKESPEARE SONGS FOR SOPRANO see
Castelnuovo-Tedesco, Mario

SHAKESPEARE SONGS FOR TENOR, SET 1 see
Castelnuovo-Tedesco, Mario

SHAKESPEARE SONGS FOR TENOR, SET 2 see
Castelnuovo-Tedesco, Mario

SHAKESPEARE'S WINTERAVONDSPROOKJE see
Ketting, Otto

SHALL I COME SWEET LOVE TO THEE see
Russell, Welford

SHALL I COMPARE THEE see Gold, Ernest

SHALL I COMPARE THEE TO A SUMMER'S DAY?
see Andrews, David

SHALL I COMPARE THEE TO A SUMMER'S DAY?
see Sifler, Paul J.

SHALL I COMPLAIN? see Martin, Easthope

SHALL I IN MAMRE'S FERTILE PLAIN see
Handel, George Frideric

SHAPIRO, NORMAN
Fish, The
S solo,pno SCHIRM.EC 120 s.p.
(S1881)
Seagull, The
S solo,pno SCHIRM.EC 121 s.p.
(S1882)

SHAPIRO, NORMAN (cont'd.)

Termite, The
S solo,pno SCHIRM.EC 122 s.p.
(S1883)

SHAPORIN, YURI ALEXANDROVITCH
(1887-1966)
Selected Romances *CCU
[Russ] solo,pno MEZ KNIGA 80 s.p.
(S1884)

SHARE HIS LOVE see Reynolds, William
Jensen

SHARE THE BLESSINGS see Dodd, Ruth

SHARECROPPERS see Rubel, Joseph

SHARPE, CEDRIC (1891-   )
It Was The Time Of Roses
solo,pno CRAMER   (S1885)

Love Thy Mother Little One
solo,pno CRAMER   (S1886)

SHARPE, EVELYN
Apology, An
low solo,pno (D maj) LEONARD-ENG
(S1887)
high solo,pno (F maj) LEONARD-ENG
(S1888)
med solo,pno (E flat maj) LEONARD-
ENG   (S1889)

Behold The Sea
high solo,pno (D min) CRAMER
(S1890)
low solo,pno (C min) CRAMER (S1891)

Bird Of Morn
low solo,pno (F maj) CRAMER (S1892)
high solo,pno (A maj) CRAMER
(S1893)
med solo,pno (G maj) CRAMER (S1894)

Blossom Time
low solo,pno (D flat maj) CRAMER
(S1895)
high solo,pno (F maj) CRAMER
(S1896)

Brave New World
low solo,pno (G maj) LEONARD-ENG
(S1897)
high solo,pno (A flat maj) LEONARD-
ENG   (S1898)

Bubble Song
solo,pno CRAMER $.95   (S1899)

Day Will Come, The
high solo,pno (G maj) CRAMER $.95
(S1900)
low solo,pno (E flat maj) CRAMER
s.p.   (S1901)

Dedication And Four Songs *CC5U
solo,pno CRAMER   (S1902)

Elf And The Chestnut Tree, The
solo,pno CRAMER $.95   (S1903)

Faithful Of Allah
high solo,pno (D maj) CRAMER
(S1904)
med solo,pno (C maj) CRAMER (S1905)
low solo,pno (B flat maj) CRAMER
(S1906)

Fate The Fiddler
solo,pno CRAMER   (S1907)

Fionnphort Ferry
solo,pno CRAMER $1.15 (S1908)

Ghost, The
solo,pno CRAMER   (S1909)

Holy Week At Genoa
solo,pno LEONARD-ENG   (S1910)

Husheen Husho
solo,pno CRAMER $.95   (S1911)

Lament Of Kilcash
low solo,pno (F maj) CRAMER (S1912)
high solo,pno (G maj) CRAMER
(S1913)

Little Dutch Tiles *CCU
solo,pno CRAMER available in two
keys   (S1914)

Little Dutch Tiles
low solo,pno CRAMER   (S1915)
high solo,pno CRAMER   (S1916)

Love Came Strolling Down The Lane
low solo,pno (G maj) CRAMER (S1917)
high solo,pno (A flat maj) CRAMER
(S1918)

Loveliness Of Old Time Things
solo,pno (G maj) LEONARD-ENG
(S1919)

Merry Pipe
high solo,pno (G maj) CRAMER
(S1920)
low solo,pno (F maj) CRAMER (S1921)

SHARPE, EVELYN (cont'd.)

Morning
high solo,pno (A flat maj) CRAMER
(S1922)
low solo,pno (F maj) CRAMER (S1923)

Mother Night
high solo,pno (F maj) LEONARD-ENG
(S1924)
low solo,pno (E flat maj) LEONARD-
ENG   (S1925)

My Soul Is Set Among The Stars
solo,pno CRAMER   (S1926)

No-Man's-Land
low solo,pno (A flat maj) CRAMER
(S1927)
high solo,pno (C maj) CRAMER
(S1928)
med solo,pno (B flat maj) CRAMER
(S1929)

One Little Hour
high solo,pno (E flat maj) CRAMER
(S1930)
med solo,pno (D maj) CRAMER (S1931)
2 soli,pno CRAMER   (S1932)
low solo,pno (B flat maj) CRAMER
(S1933)

Open The Door To Spring
high solo,pno (B flat maj) CRAMER
$.90   (S1934)
med solo,pno (A flat maj) CRAMER
$.95   (S1935)
low solo,pno (G maj) CRAMER $.90
(S1936)

Remember Me Dear Friend
low solo,pno (D maj) CRAMER (S1937)
high solo,pno (E flat maj) CRAMER
(S1938)

Requiescat
solo,pno CRAMER $1.15 (S1939)

Round Pond, The
low solo,pno (F maj) CRAMER $.95
(S1940)
high solo,pno (G maj) CRAMER $.95
(S1941)

Silent Pool, The
solo,pno CRAMER $.70   (S1942)

Sleep Voyage, The
solo,pno CRAMER $1.15 (S1943)

Song For March, A
solo,pno CRAMER $.95   (S1944)

South Wind
solo,pno CRAMER   (S1945)

Stars All Dotted Over The Sky
low solo,pno (D min) CRAMER $1.15
(S1946)
high solo,pno (F sharp min) CRAMER
$.90   (S1947)

Sunset
solo,pno CRAMER $.95   (S1948)

Tent In The Desert *CCU
solo,pno CRAMER available in 3 keys
(S1949)

Three Candlelight Songs *CC3U
solo,pno CRAMER available in 3 keys
(S1950)

To A Nightingale
solo,pno CRAMER   (S1951)

Water Meadows
solo,pno CRAMER $.95   (S1952)

Wayside Cross
low solo,pno (C maj) CRAMER (S1953)
high solo,pno (F maj) CRAMER
(S1954)

When The Great Red Dawn Is Shining
low solo,pno (G maj) CRAMER (S1955)
med solo,pno (A flat maj) CRAMER
(S1956)
high solo,pno (B flat maj) CRAMER
(S1957)

Where The Milestones End
low solo,pno (F maj) CRAMER (S1958)
med solo,pno (G maj) CRAMER (S1959)
high solo,pno (A flat maj) CRAMER
(S1960)

Whit-Monday Morning
low solo,pno (C maj) LEONARD-ENG
(S1961)
high solo,pno (D maj) LEONARD-ENG
(S1962)

Winter Wakeneth All My Care
solo,pno CRAMER $1.15 (S1963)

SHAVUOT SONGS see Nardi, Nachum

SHAW
Columbia, The Gem Of The Ocean
med solo,pno (A flat maj) CENTURY
1292   (S1964)

SHAW, C.
  If There Be Ecstasy
    med solo,pno PRESSER $.75   (S1965)

  Little Song
    med solo,pno PRESSER $.75 . (S1966)

  Nightingale
    med solo,pno PRESSER $.95   (S1967)

  Romance
    high solo,pno PRESSER $.75   (S1968)

SHAW, CLIFFORD
  To You
    solo,pno PEER $.85   (S1969)

SHAW, GEOFFREY [TURTON] (1879-1943)
  Cold's The Wind
    solo,pno (E min) LEONARD-ENG
                                 (S1970)
  Saint Agnes Morn
    med solo,pno (B flat maj) CRAMER
                                 (S1971)
    low solo,pno (A flat maj) CRAMER
                                 (S1972)
    high solo,pno (C maj) CRAMER
                                 (S1973)

SHAW, MARTIN (1875-1958)
  Accursed Wood, The
    solo,pno CRAMER $.95   (S1974)

  Airmen, The
    solo,pno CRAMER $.90   (S1975)

  Annabel Lee
    low solo,pno (C maj) CRAMER s.p.
                                 (S1976)
    high solo,pno (F maj) CRAMER $1.15
                                 (S1977)
  At Columbine's Grave
    solo,pno CRAMER $.95   (S1978)

  Avona
    high solo,pno (F maj) CRAMER $.95
                                 (S1979)
    low solo,pno (C maj) CRAMER $.95
                                 (S1980)
  Banks Of Allan Water
    high solo,pno (C maj) CRAMER $1.10
                                 (S1981)
    med solo,pno (B flat maj) CRAMER
    $1.10   (S1982)
    low solo,pno (A flat maj) CRAMER
    $1.10   (S1983)
  Bells Of Christmas, The
    low solo,pno (A min) CRAMER $.90
                                 (S1984)
    high solo,pno (D min) CRAMER $1.15
                                 (S1985)
    med solo,pno (B min) CRAMER $.95
                                 (S1986)
  Caravan, The
    high solo,pno (A maj) CRAMER $.70
                                 (S1987)
    low solo,pno (F maj) CRAMER $1.15
                                 (S1988)
  Cargoes
    solo,pno CRAMER $1.15   (S1989)

  Conjuration, The
    high solo,pno (B maj) CRAMER $.95
                                 (S1990)
    low solo,pno (A maj) CRAMER $.95
                                 (S1991)
  Easter Carol
    solo,pno (C maj) ROBERTON 2121 s.p.
                                 (S1992)
  Full Fathom Five
    solo,pno CRAMER   (S1993)

  Glad Hearts Adventuring
    solo,pno CRAMER $.95   (S1994)

  Heffle Cuckoo Fair
    solo,pno (A maj) ROBERTON 2130 s.p.
                                 (S1995)
  I Know A Bank
    low solo,pno (F maj) CRAMER $.90
                                 (S1996)
    2 soli,pno (G maj) CRAMER $1.15
                                 (S1997)
    2 soli,pno (F maj) CRAMER $.90
                                 (S1998)
    high solo,pno (B flat maj) CRAMER
    $.90   (S1999)
    med solo,pno (G maj) CRAMER $1.15
                                 (S2000)
  Jack Overdue
    solo,pno CRAMER $.95   (S2001)

  Knight's Song, A
    low solo,orch (A flat maj) ASHDOWN
    s.p., ipr   (S2002)
    high solo,orch (C maj) ASHDOWN
    s.p., ipr   (S2003)
    med solo,orch (B flat maj) ASHDOWN
    s.p., ipr   (S2004)
  Lament, A
    solo,pno CRAMER $.90   (S2005)

  Little Waves Of Breffny, The
    solo,pno CRAMER $.95   (S2006)

SHAW, MARTIN (cont'd.)
  Matthew, Mark, Luke And John
    2 soli,pno ROBERTON 72128 s.p.
                                 (S2007)
  Melodies You Sing, The
    solo,pno CRAMER $1.15   (S2008)

  Merry Wanderer
    solo,pno CRAMER $.70   (S2009)

  No
    solo,pno CRAMER $1.15   (S2010)

  O, Falmouth Is A Fine Town
    solo,pno (A maj) ROBERTON 2165 s.p.
                                 (S2011)
  Old Clothes And Fine Clothes
    low solo,pno (B flat maj) CRAMER
    $.70   (S2012)
    high solo,pno (C maj) CRAMER $.95
                                 (S2013)
  Perilous Ways
    solo,pno CRAMER $.70   (S2014)

  Rivulet
    high solo,pno (A maj) CRAMER
                                 (S2015)
    low solo,pno (G maj) CRAMER (S2016)

  Ships Of Yule
    high solo,pno (A maj) CRAMER $.95
                                 (S2017)
    low solo,pno (F maj) CRAMER s.p.
                                 (S2018)
    med solo,pno (G maj) CRAMER s.p.
                                 (S2019)
  Song Of The Palaquin Bearers, The
    high solo,pno/orch (E maj) ROBERTON
    2124H s.p.   (S2020)
    low solo,pno/orch (B flat maj)
    ROBERTON 2124L s.p.   (S2021)

  Summer
    solo,pno (E min) ROBERTON 2125 s.p.
                                 (S2022)
  Sursum Corda
    T solo,3fl,3ob,2clar,2bsn,2horn,
    2trp,3trom,timp,perc,harp,strings
    NOVELLO rental   (S2023)

  Tides
    solo,pno CRAMER $1.15   (S2024)

  To Sea!
    solo,pno CRAMER $1.15   (S2025)

  Trees
    med solo,pno (G maj) CRAMER $.95
                                 (S2026)
    high solo,pno (B maj) CRAMER $.70
                                 (S2027)
    low solo,pno (F maj) CRAMER $.70
                                 (S2028)
  Two Songs *CC2U
    solo,pno CRAMER $.95   (S2029)

  Ungentle Guest *song cycle
    solo,4strings,harp CRAMER   (S2030)

  Water Folk *song cycle
    solo,4strings,pno CRAMER   (S2031)

  Wind And The Sea, The
    solo,pno CRAMER $.95   (S2032)

  Wood Magic
    low solo,pno (C min) CRAMER $.90
                                 (S2033)
    high solo,pno (E min) CRAMER $1.15
                                 (S2034)
  World's Delight, The
    solo,pno CRAMER   (S2035)

  Ye Banks And Braes
    low solo,pno (F maj) CRAMER (S2036)
    high solo,pno (A maj) CRAMER
                                 (S2037)

SHE, A TUNGYANG GIRL see Bliss, Sir
  Arthur

SHE ALONE CHARMETH MY SADNESS see
  Gounod, Charles Francois, La Reine
  De Saba

SHE DWELT AMONG THE UNTRODDEN WAYS see
  Kellie, Lawrence

SHE HATH AN ART see Daubney, Brian

SHE IS A SOUTHERN GIRL see Bliss, Sir
  Arthur

SHE IS A WINSOME WEE THING see Van
  Grove, Isaac

SHE IS ASLEEP I see Cage, John

SHE IS ASLEEP II see Cage, John

SHE IS FAR FROM THE LAND see Hughes,
  Herbert

SHE IS GATHERING LOTUS BUDS see Bliss,
  Sir Arthur

SHE IS NOT FAIR see Diack, John Michael

SHE MOVED THRO' THE FAIR see Hughes,
  Herbert

SHE NEVER TOLD HER LOVE see Haydn,
  (Franz) Joseph

SHE WALKS IN BEAUTY see Lora, Antonio

SHE WANDERED DOWN THE MOUNTAIN SIDE see
  Clay, Frederic

SHE WEEPS OVER RAHOON see Fine, Vivian

SHE WEEPS OVER RAHOON see Strickland,
  William

SHE WHO IS DEAR TO ME see Holst, Gustav

SHE WHO WAS ALL PIETY see Kubik, Gail

SHE WILL TEND HIM see Sullivan, Sir
  Arthur Seymour

SHEA, GEORGE BEVERLY
  I'd Rather Have Jesus *see Miller

  Wonder Of It, The *sac
    solo,pno BENSON S8088-R $1.00
                                 (S2038)
SHEA SINGS *sac,CC17UL
  (Smith, Tedd) Bar/A solo,pno LILLENAS
  MB-183 $1.95   (S2039)

SHEA'S ALBUM OF SACRED SONGS *sac,
  CC16UL
  solo,pno,gtr LILLENAS MB-184 $1.95
                                 (S2040)
SHED NO TEAR see Huss, Henry Holden

SHEEHAN, R.
  Watcher
    solo,pno (D maj) BOOSEY $1.50
                                 (S2041)
SHEEP see Rowley, Alec

SHEEP AND LAMBS see Homer, Sidney

SHEEP MAY SAFELY GRAZE see Bach, Johann
  Sebastian, Schafe Konnen Sicher
  Weiden

SHEEPFOLD SONG see Ronald, Sir Landon

SHEEPFOLDS see Poston, Elizabeth

SHEHERAZADE see Ravel, Maurice

SHEHERAZADE see Ravel, Maurice

SHEIKEWITZ, WOLF
  Elegie *Jew
    [Eng/Heb/Jew] solo,pno KAMMEN 5
    $1.00 see also FAVORITE JEWISH
    SONGS, VOL. 2   (S2042)

SHEINKMAN, M.
  Funf Lieder *CC5U
    [Ger] BOTE $3.50   (S2043)

SHELL, THE see Mourant, Walter

SHELLEY, HARRY ROWE (1858-1947)
  God Is Love *sac
    high solo&low solo,pno SCHIRM.G
    $.85   (S2044)
  Hark! Hark, My Soul *sac
    SA soli,pno SCHIRM.G $.80   (S2045)

  King Of Love My Shepherd Is, The
    *sac
    high solo&low solo,pno SCHIRM.G
    $.85   (S2046)
    med solo,pno (D flat maj) SCHIRM.G
    $.85   (S2047)

SHELLING PEAS see Duke, John Woods

SHELLY LIEDER see Reynvaan, M.C.C.

SHELTERED IN THE ARMS OF GOD see Rambo

SHEMER, NAOMI
  All My Songs *CCU
    solo,pno OR-TAV $3.50   (S2048)

SHENANDOAH
  (Terry, R.R.) solo,pno/orch (E flat
  maj) ROBERTON 2707 s.p.   (S2049)

SHENANDOAH see Dougherty, Celius

SHENANDOAH see Manning, Richard

SHENK MIR DEIN HARTZ *Jew
  solo,pno KAMMEN 423 $1.00   (S2050)

SHEPHERD, THE see Cooke, S.C.

SHEPHERD AND NYMPH see Lawes, Henry

SHEPHERD, ARTHUR (1880-1958)
  Fiddlers, The
    solo,pno NEW VALLEY $1.25   (S2051)

  Golden Stockings
    solo,pno NEW VALLEY $1.25 see also
      Seven Songs   (S2052)

  Morning Glory
    solo,pno NEW VALLEY $1.25 see also
      Seven Songs   (S2053)

  Reverie
    solo,pno NEW VALLEY $1.25 see also
      Seven Songs   (S2054)

  Serenade
    solo,opt vla NEW VALLEY $1.75 see
      also Seven Songs   (S2055)

  Seven Songs
    cmplt ed NEW VALLEY $8.00
    contains & see also: Golden
      Stockings; Morning Glory;
      Reverie; Serenade; Softly Along
      The Road Of Evening; To A
      Trout; Virgil   (S2056)

  Softly Along The Road Of Evening
    solo,pno NEW VALLEY $1.25 see also
      Seven Songs   (S2057)

  Starling Lake
    solo,pno NEW VALLEY $1.25   (S2058)

  To A Trout
    solo,pno NEW VALLEY $1.25 see also
      Seven Songs   (S2059)

  Tryptych For High Voice And String
    Quartet *CCU
    sc PRESSER $7.00   (S2060)

  Virgil
    solo,pno NEW VALLEY $1.25 see also
      Seven Songs   (S2061)

SHEPHERD BOY SINGS IN THE VALLEY OF
  HUMILIATION see Diamond, David

SHEPHERD BOY'S SONG, THE
  see Three Songs Of Old Quebec

SHEPHERD BOY'S SONG, THE see Radcliffe,
  Philip (FitzHugh)

SHEPHERD OF LOVE see Gaddy, Carol

SHEPHERD OF LOVE see Peterson, John W.

SHEPHERD ON THE ROCK, THE see Schubert,
  Franz (Peter), Der Hirt Auf Dem
  Felsen

SHEPHERD ON THE ROCKS, THE see
  Schubert, Franz (Peter), Der Hirt
  Auf Dem Felsen

SHEPHERD, SHEPHERD HARK THAT CALLING!
  see Berkeley, Lennox

SHEPHERD, THY DEMEANOR VARY
  (Wilson, H.L.) solo,pno (F maj)
    BOOSEY $1.50   (S2062)

SHEPHERDESS see Macmurrough, Dermot

SHEPHERDESS, THE see Bruce, M. Campbell

SHEPHERDESS, THE see Friedell, Harold
  W.

SHEPHERDESS, THE see Macmurrough,
  Dermot

SHEPHERDESS, THE see Roberton, Hugh
  Stevenson

SHEPHERDS AND THE INN see Gaul

SHEPHERD'S CAROL see Hamerton, Ann

SHEPHERD'S CRADLE SONG see Somervell,
  Arthur

SHEPHERDS IN JUDEA see Rogers

SHEPHERDS LAMENT, THE
  (Lehmann, Amelia) low solo,pno (E
    min) ASHDOWN   (S2063)
  (Lehmann, Amelia) high solo,pno (G
    min) ASHDOWN   (S2064)

SHEPHERDS OF SOULS see Jones, Edward

SHEPHERDS PIPE CAROL see Rutter, John

SHEPHERDS RISE AND SHAKE OFF SLEEP see
  Mallinson, (James) Albert

SHEPHERDS SING, THE see Young, Stuart

SHEPHERD'S SONG see Edel, Yitzchak,
  Achalei Bachalili

SHEPHERD'S SONG see Kilpinen, Yrio,
  Schaferlied

SHEPHERD'S SONG, THE see Richard, Leone

SHEPHERD'S STORY see Fromm, Herbert,
  Maise Fun A Pastuch'l

SHEPHERDS' STORY, THE see Dickinson,
  Clarence

SHERIFF, NOAM
  Ashrei
    "Blessed Is The Man" A solo,fl,
      drums,2harp study sc
      ISR.MUS.INST. 016 s.p.   (S2065)

  Blessed Is The Man *see Ashrei

SHERMAN, H.
  Bubble Fairy, The
    med solo,pno SEESAW $1.00   (S2066)

  Little Turtle, The
    med solo,pno SEESAW $1.00   (S2067)

  To A Tree In Bloom
    med solo,pno SEESAW $1.00   (S2068)

  Wash Day And Rainy Day
    med solo,pno SEESAW $1.00   (S2069)

SHERRILL, BILLY
  I Wonder How John Felt *see Wilson

SHERRINGTON, LOUIS F.
  Sweet Early Violets
    low solo,pno (B flat maj) CRAMER
                                 (S2070)
    med solo,pno (C maj) CRAMER (S2071)
    med-high solo,pno (D maj) CRAMER
                                 (S2072)
    high solo,pno (E flat maj) CRAMER
                                 (S2073)

SHE'S FAIR AND FAUSE *folk,Scot
  solo,pno (E min) PATERSON FS82 s.p.
                                 (S2074)

SHE'S GONE see Handel, George Frideric

SHE'S LIKE THE SWALLOW
  see Folk Songs Of Eastern Canada

SHIBATA, MINAO (1916-
  La Bonne Chanson *CC4U
    solo,pno ONGAKU s.p.   (S2075)

SHICHELACH *Jew
  solo,pno KAMMEN 403 $1.00   (S2076)

SHIELD OF ACHILLES see Kelly, Bryan

SHIELD OF ACHILLES, THE see Kelly,
  Bryan

SHIELD, WILLIAM (1748-1829)
  Ere Bright Rosina Met My Eyes
    (Bush) T solo,pno ELKIN 27.2472.03
      s.p.   (S2077)

  Heaving Of The Lead, The
    solo,pno HEUWEKE. 133 s.p.   (S2078)

  I've Kissed And I've Prattled (from
    Rosina)
    solo,pno HEUWEKE. 127 s.p.   (S2079)

  Let An Empty Flattering Spirit
    female solo,2horn,2clar,2vln,bvl
      HEUWEKE. 128 s.p.   (S2080)

  Maid Of Lodi, The
    solo,harp/pno HEUWEKE. 134 s.p.
                                 (S2081)
  Oh What A Country For People To Marry
    solo,pno HEUWEKE. 129 s.p.   (S2082)

  Old Towler
    solo,pno HEUWEKE. 130 s.p.   (S2083)

  Ploughboy
    med solo,pno (G maj) ALLANS s.p.
                                 (S2084)
  Still Let Thy Plaintive Numbers Flow
    solo,pno HEUWEKE. 131 s.p.   (S2085)

  Sweet Mary Come To Me
    solo,pno HEUWEKE. 132 s.p.   (S2086)

  This Lock Of Dear Selina's Hair
    solo,pno HEUWEKE. 135 s.p.   (S2087)

  Thorn
    solo,pno CRAMER   (S2088)

SHIELDS, ALICE
  Wildcat Songs *CCU
    S solo,pic AM.COMP.AL. $5.50
                                 (S2089)

SHIFRIN, SEYMOUR J. (1926-   )
  Satires Of Circumstance
    S solo,fl,clar,pno,vln,vcl,bvl sc
      PETERS 66475 $25.00, ipa (S2090)

SHIKER IS A GOY *folk,Jew
  low solo,pno HATIKVAH ED. 59 $.30
                                 (S2091)

SHILOH *sac,CC12L
  solo,pno WORD 37613 $1.95 contains
    works by: Baker, David; Bolin,
    David; English, Tina   (S2092)

SHIMO see Sapp, Gary

SHINE, GREAT SUN see Raphling, Sam

SHINE, LITTLE SUN! see Lipovsek,
  Marijan, Soncece, Sij!

SHINE OUT FAIR SUN see Paynter, John P.

SHINE OUT O STARS see Day, Maude Craske

SHIP OF DEATH see Mellers, Wilfrid
  Howard

SHIP OF RIO see Britten, Benjamin

SHIP OF RIO see Keel, Frederick

SHIPMATES O' MINE see Sanderson,
  Wilfred

SHIPS OF ARCADY see Head, Michael
  (Dewar)

SHIPS OF YULE see Shaw, Martin

SHIPWRECK AND LOVE SCENE see Thomson,
  Virgil

SHIR HA-ADAMAH *folk,Jew
  (Low, Leo) "Dos Lid Vun Der Erd"
    solo,pno HATIKVAH HCL 28 $.50 (S2093)

SHIR HA-AVODA
  (Helfman, Max) "Joyful Hymn Of Toil"
    [Heb] med solo,pno TRANSCON. IS 520
    $.45   (S2094)

SHIR HA-EMEK
  (Helfman, Max) "Song Of The Emek"
    [Heb] med solo,pno TRANSCON. IS 521
    $.45   (S2095)

SHIR HA-MERED
  (Helfman, Max) "Song Of Revolt" [Heb]
    med solo,pno TRANSCON. IS 522 $.50
                                 (S2096)

SHIR LA-MOLEDAT
  (Helfman, Max) "Hymn Of Liberation"
    [Heb] med solo,pno TRANSCON. IS 523
    $.50   (S2097)

SHIR L'EREV HA'CHAG
  solo,pno OR-TAV .50   (S2098)

SHIR V'NIVNEH see Chajes, Julius

SHIRLEY, P.
  Hail To Maine
    [Ger] AMP $.75   (S2099)

SH'MA KOLEYNU see Helfman, Max

SH'MA YISRAEL see Reveyron, Joseph

SHMENDRIK IN YEDEN LAND *Jew
  solo,pno KAMMEN 66 $1.00   (S2100)

SHMENDRIK'S KALLE see Gilrod, Louis

SHOCKHEADED PETER see Hughes, Herbert

SHOEMAKER, THE see Heseltine, Philip

SHOEMAKER NED see Newton, Ernest

SHOES see Manning, Kathleen Lockhart

SHOLOM ALECHEM see Mana-Zucca, Mme.

SHOLOM ROV see Adler, Samuel

SHON MARIA, MEINE BEERE see Kilpinen,
  Yrio, Kukkalatva Kuusi

SHORE LEAVE see Hurd, Michael

SHORN LAMB see Wansborough

SHORR, ANSHEL
  Mein Yiddishe Meidele *Jew
    solo,pno KAMMEN 479 $1.00 see also
      FAVORITE JEWISH SONGS, VOL. 2
                                 (S2101)

SHORT
  He Loves You (composed with Aldridge)
    *sac
    solo,pno BENSON S5699-R $1.00
                                 (S2102)

SHORT PSALM, A see Jenni, Donald

SHORT STORY see Siebert, F., Kleine
  Geschicte

SHORTNIN' BREAD see Wolfe, Jacques

SHOSTAKOVICH, DMITRI (1906-1975)
  Au Devant De La Vie
    (Porret, J.) [Fr] solo,pno CHANT
      s.p. solo pt, sc, voc sc   (S2103)

SHOSTAKOVICH, DMITRI (cont'd.)

Cinq Romances
[Fr] B solo,pno cmplt ed CHANT s.p.
contains: Jour De Joie, Op.98,
No.4; Jour De Reconnaissance,
Op.98,No.1; Jour De Rencontre,
Op.98,No.2; Jour De Souvenir,
Op.98,No.5; Jour D'offense,
Op.98,No.3   (S2104)

Four Romances, Op. 46; Four
Monologues, Op. 91 *CC8U
(Friedlander) [Ger/Russ] low solo,
pno PETERS 4793 $11.00   (S2105)

Jour De Joie *Op.98,No.4
see Cinq Romances

Jour De Reconnaissance *Op.98,No.1
see Cinq Romances

Jour De Rencontre *Op.98,No.2
see Cinq Romances

Jour De Souvenir *Op.98,No.5
see Cinq Romances

Jour D'offense *Op.98,No.3
see Cinq Romances

Le Chant Des Forets *ora
[Fr] solo,pno CHANT s.p.   (S2106)

Onze Chants Hebraiques *Op.79, CC11U
[Fr] SAT soli,pno CHANT s.p.
(S2107)

Romanzen-Suite *Op.127, CCU
(Koerth) [Russ/Ger] S solo,vln,vcl,
pno sc DEUTSCHER 9401 s.p., ipa
(S2108)

Sechs Romanzen *Op.62,No.1-6, CC6U
(Hellmundt) [Russ/Ger/Eng] B solo,
pno DEUTSCHER 9012 s.p.   (S2109)

Sept Melodies Pour Chant, Piano,
Violon Et Violoncelle *CC7U
[Fr] solo,pno,vln,vcl CHANT s.p.
(S2110)

Songs After Jewish Folk Poems
*Op.79,No.1-11, CC11U
[Ger] S/A/T/SA/ST/AT/SAT soli,pno
PETERS 4727 $11.00   (S2111)

Vocal Works (Third Edition, Enlarged)
*CCU
[Russ] solo,pno MEZ KNIGA 81 s.p.
(S2112)

Vokalwerke *CCU
[Russ] solo,pno SIKORSKI R 6231
s.p. contains Op. 46, 62, 79, 91,
98, 100, 109   (S2113)

SHOT'NS see Weiner, Lazar

SHOULD HE UPBRAID see Bishop, Sir Henry
Rowley

SHOULD YOU EVER FIND HER COMPLYING see
Arne, Thomas Augustine

SHOUT FREEDOM! see Stringfield, Lamar

SHOW ME THE WAY see Brown, Aaron

SHOW ME THY HANDS, BLESSED JESUS see
Armes, Sybil L.

SHOW ME THY WAYS, O LORD see Shade

SHOWERS OF BLESSING see Lister, Mosie

SHPIEL, KLEZMER SHPIEL *Jew
solo,pno KAMMEN 472 $1.00   (S2114)

SHRADER, JOHN L.
I'll Go Over Jordan Some Day *sac
solo,pno STAMPS 7264-SN $1.00
(S2115)

SHTILE LICHT see Weiner, Lazar

SHTILE TENER see Weiner, Lazar

SHTUMER PROTEST see Vigoda, Samuel

SHULE AGRA see Somervell, Arthur

SHUSTER, HALT SICH BEIN DEIN DRATWE
*Jew
solo,pno KAMMEN 44 $1.00   (S2116)

SHUT OUT THAT MOON see Binkerd, Gordon

SI see Schmitt, Florent

SI ADDENSANO LE NUBI see Alfano, Franco

SI AL RETIRO ME LLEVAS see Granados,
Enrique

SI CHINA IL GIORNO see Caggiano,
Roberto

SI DA PRINCIPIO A QUESTA SERENATA see
Oddone, E.

SI DE MON PREMIER REVE see Aubert,
Louis-Francois-Marie

SI DOLCE E 'L TORMENTO see Monteverdi,
Claudio

SI, FUI SOLDATO see Giordano, Umberto

SI HO GRAZIATO PSKOV see Rimsky-
Korsakov, Nikolai

SI J'AI PARLE DE MON AMOUR see Chapuis,
Auguste-Paul-Jean-Baptiste

SI J'AVAIS SU! see Berger, Rod.

SI J'AVAIS VOS AILES see Messager,
Andre

SI JE L'OSAIS see Saint-Saens, Camille

SI JE NE DOIS JAMAIS see Rabey, Rene

SI JE NE T'AIMAIS PAS see Rabey, Rene

SI JE POUVAIS MOURIR see Barbirolli, A.

SI JE T'AIME see Mariotte, Antoine

SI J'ETAIS CHARLES D'ORLEANS see
Berthomieu, Marc

SI J'ETAIS DIEU see Desrez

SI J'ETAIS DIEU see Fontenailles, H. de

SI J'ETAIS JARDINIER see Chaminade,
Cecile

SI J'ETAIS ROI see Thomas, Arthur
Goring

SI J'ETAIS RONSARD see Berthomieu, Marc

SI LA MORT EST LE BUT see Desrez

SI LA NOCHE HACE OSCURA see Pisador,
Diego

SI LA RIGUEUR ET LA VENGEANCE see
Halevy, [Jacques-Francois-
Fromental-Elie]

SI LA STANCHEZZA see Verdi, Giuseppe,
Ai Nostri Monti

SI LE BON DIEU L'AVAIT VOULU see Roget,
H.

SI LE FRONT COURONNE DE LIERRE see
Saint-Saens, Camille

SI LO HALLAS.. see Lopez-Buchardo,
Carlos

SI LOIN ET SI HAUT DANS L'ESPACE see
Saint-Saens, Camille

SI L'ON GARDAIT see Larbey, V.

SI L'ON TE DISAIT see Galeotti, Cesare

SI LOS DELFINES see Andriessen, Juriaan

SI MATIN, D'OU VIENS-TU see Rabey, Rene

SI MES POCHES see Schmitt, Florent

SI MES VERS AVAIENT DES AILES see
Chapuis, Auguste-Paul-Jean-Baptiste

SI MES VERS AVAIENT DES AILES! see
Hahn, Reynaldo

SI MES VERS AVAIENT DES AILES see
Lacombe, Louis (Trouillon)

SI, MI CHIAMANO MIMI see Puccini,
Giacomo

SI MILLE OEILLETS see Leguerney,
Jacques

SI MOSTRA LA SORTE see Mozart, Wolfgang
Amadeus

SI PUO? see Leoncavallo, Ruggiero

SI QUELQUEFOIS TU PLEURES see Migot,
Georges

SI QUIERES QUE YO TE DIGA see Espoile,
Raoul H.

SI TE VAS A BANAR JUANICA see Pisador,
Diego

SI TON COEUR S'ABONDONNE see Bach,
Johann Sebastian

SI TON ESPRIT see Delage, Maurice

SI TU DISAIS see Ropartz, Joseph Guy

SI TU LE VEUX see Koechlin, Charles

SI TU LE VEUX see Rabey, Rene

SI TU M'AIMAIS see Denza, Luigi

SI TU SAVAIS COMME JE T'AIME see Marty,
(Eugene) Georges

SI TU SAVAIS, MA CATHERINE see Poise,
(Jean Alexandre) Ferdinand

SI TU VAS A PARIS see Trenet, Charles

SI TU VEUX see Cuvillier, Charles

SI TU VEUX see Respighi, Ottorino

SI TU VOULAIS see Filipucci, Edm.

SI UN BEAU JOUR... see Absil, Jean

SI VOUS AIMEZ LES FLEURS see Scotto,
Vincent

SI VOUS N'AVEZ RIEN A ME DIRE see
Saint-Saens, Camille

SI VOUS N'AVEZ RIEN ME DIRE see Desrez

SI VOUS PENSEZ see Delage, Maurice

SI VOUS VOULEZ see Lacome, Paul

SI VOUS VOULIEZ see De Lara, Isadore

SIA BENEDETTA see Cimara, Pietro

SIALM, D.
Ada *song cycle
solo,pno HUG s.p.   (S2117)

Davosas Spigias
solo,pno HUG s.p. contains also:
Letzte Ahren   (S2118)

Letzte Ahren
see Sialm, D., Davosas Spigias

Liederalbum *CCU
solo,pno HUG s.p.   (S2119)

SIAMO PROSSIMI AL RISVEGLIO see
Gentilucci, A.

SIASONS MOROSES see Cuvillier, Charles

SIAU-TSCHU see Radauer, Irmfried

SIBELIUS, JEAN (1865-1957)
Aller Augen Warten Auf Dich
see Drei Hymnische Gesange

Alvan Och Snigeln *Op.57,No.1
"Snail, The" [Eng/Ger] high solo,
pno LIENAU R150 s.p. see from
Eight Songs   (S2120)
"Snail, The" [Eng/Ger] low solo,pno
LIENAU R151 s.p. see from Eight
Songs   (S2121)

An Den Abend *see Illalle

An Frigga *see Till Frigga

Arioso *Op.3
solo,pno FAZER W 2295 s.p.   (S2122)
"Ging An Einem Wintermorgen" [Ger/
Finn/Swed] solo,pno BREITKOPF-W
57 05017 s.p.   (S2123)

Atenarnes Sang *Op.31,No.3
"Atenarnes Sang" solo,pno MUSIKK
s.p.   (S2124)
"Gesang Der Athener" [Ger] solo,pno
BREITKOPF-W DLV 5177 s.p.   (S2125)
"War Song Of Tyrtaeus" [Eng/Fr]
solo,pno BREITKOPF-W DLV 3479
s.p.   (S2126)

Atenarnes Sang *see Atenarnes Sang

Auf Dem Soller Am Meer *see Pa
Verandan Vid Havet

Auringonnousu *see Soluppgang

Aus Banger Brust *Op.50,No.4
"O, Wert Thou Here: The Roses
Blossom" [Eng/Ger] low solo,pno
LIENAU R145 s.p. see from Six
Songs   (S2127)
"O, Wert Thou Here: The Roses
Blossom" [Eng/Ger] high solo,pno
LIENAU R144 s.p. see from Six
Songs   (S2128)

Ballspiel In Trianon *see Bollspelet
Vid Trainon

Ballspiel In Trianon *see Bollspelet
Vid Trianon

Baron Magnus *see Hertig Magnus

SIBELIUS, JEAN (cont'd.)

Blasippan *Op.88,No.1
"Die Anemone" [Swed/Finn/Ger] solo,
pno BREITKOPF-W 57 05045 s.p. see
from SECHS LIEDER NACH TEXTEN VON
FR. M. FRANZEN UND J.L. RUNEBERG
(S2129)
"Die Anemone" solo,pno FAZER W 482
s.p.
(S2130)

Blommans Ode *Op.88,No.6
"Die Blume" see Six Songs [2]
"Die Blume" [Swed/Finn/Ger] solo,
pno BREITKOPF-W 57 05050 s.p. see
from SECHS LIEDER NACH TEXTEN VON
FR. M. FRANZEN UND J.L. RUNEBERG
(S2131)
"Die Blumme" solo,pno FAZER W 487
s.p.
(S2132)

Bollspelet Vid Trainon *Op.36,No.3
"Ballspiel In Trianon" [Swed/Ger/
Eng] med-high solo,pno BREITKOPF-
W $1.50 see also Drei Lieder
(S2133)
"Palloleikki Trainonissa" solo,pno
FAZER F 3213 see from Sex Sanger
I
(S2134)

Bollspelet Vid Trainon *Op.36,No.3
solo,pno MUSIKK s.p.
(S2135)
"Tennis At Trianon" [Eng/Fr] solo,
pno BREITKOPF-W 57 05028 s.p.
(S2136)
(Pingoud, Ernest) "Ballspiel In
Trianon" [Finn/Ger] S solo,2fl,
ob,2clar,2contrabsn,2horn,timp,
perc,harp,strings BREITKOPF-W
rental
(S2137)

Bonn
solo,pno MUSIKK s.p.
(S2138)

Das Lied Von Der Kreuzspinne *Op.27,
No.4
[Swed/Ger] A solo,pno BREITKOPF-W
EB 4747 s.p.
(S2139)
[Swed/Ger] A solo,perc,harp,strings
BREITKOPF-W rental
(S2140)

De Bagge Rosorna *Op.88,No.2
"Die Biden Rosen" see Six Songs [2]
"Die Beiden Rosen" [Swed/Finn/Ger]
solo,pno BREITKOPF-W 57 05046
s.p. see from SECHS LIEDER NACH
TEXTEN VON FR. M. FRANZEN UND
J.L. RUNEBERG
(S2141)
"Die Beiden Rosen" solo,pno FAZER
W 483 s.p.
(S2142)

Demanten Pa Marssnon *Op.36,No.6
solo,pno MUSIKK s.p.
(S2143)
"Der Diamant Auf Dem Marzschnee"
[Finn/Swed/Ger] A solo,2fl,ob,
2clar,bsn,2horn,harp,strings
BREITKOPF-W rental
(S2144)
"Der Diamant Auf Dem Marzschnee"
[Swed/Ger] med solo,pno
BREITKOPF-W DLV 5286 $1.50
(S2145)
"Timantti Hangella" solo,pno FAZER
W 956 see from Sex Sanger I
(S2146)
(Wecksell) "Der Diamant Auf Dem
Marzschnee" [Finn/Swed/Ger] A
solo,2fl,2clar,harp,strings
BREITKOPF-W rental
(S2147)

Den Forsta Kyssen *Op.37,No.1
solo,pno MUSIKK s.p.
(S2148)
"Der Erste Kuss" [Eng/Fr/Ger] S
solo,pno BREITKOPF-W EB 5937
$2.25
(S2149)
"Der Erste Kuss" [Swed/Finn] S
solo,pno BREITKOPF-W 57 05034
s.p.
(S2150)
"Ensi Suudelma" solo,pno FAZER
F 3215 see from Fem Sanger I
(S2151)
(Fougstedt, Nils Erik) "Der Erste
Kuss" [Swed/Ger] S solo,2fl,2ob,
2clar,2bsn,4horn,harp,strings
BREITKOPF-W rental
(S2152)
(Hellmann, Ivar) "Der Erste Kuss"
[Eng/Fr/Ger] S solo,2fl,2ob,
2clar,2bsn,4horn,2trp,3trom,tuba,
harp,strings BREITKOPF-W rental
(S2153)

Der Diamant Auf Dem Marzschnee *see
Demanten Pa Marssnon

Der Dornbusch *see Tornet

Der Erste Kuss *see Den Forsta
Kyssen

Der Harfenspieler Und Sein Sohn *see
Harpolekaren Och Hans Son

Der Jagerknabe *see Jagargossen

Der Kuss *see Kyssen

SIBELIUS, JEAN (cont'd.)

Der Morgen *see Morgonen

Der Norden *see Norden

Der Span Auf Den Wellen *see Lastu
Lainehilla

Der Traum *see Drommen

Der Vogelstaller *see Fagelfangaren

Der Wanderer Und Der Bach *Op.72,
No.5
[Ger] med solo,pno BREITKOPF-W
DLV 5460 $1.50
(S2154)
"Vandraren Och Backen" solo,pno
FAZER F 4509 s.p. see from Sex
Sanger II
(S2155)

Des Fahrmanns Braute *see
Koskenlaskian Morsiamet

Des Herzens Morgen *see Hjartats
Morgon

Die Anemone *see Blasippan

Die Beiden Rosen *see De Bagge
Rosorna

Die Biden Rosen *see De Bagge
Rosorna

Die Blume *see Blommans Ode

Die Blume *see Blommans Ode

Die Blume *see Blommans Ode

Die Blumme *see Blommans Ode

Die Echonymphe *see Kaiutar

Die Libelle "Schone Libelle,
Schwirrtest Mir Herein" *Op.17,
No.5
[Swed/Ger] S solo,pno BREITKOPF-W
DLV 5195 $1.50
(S2156)
(Borg, Kim) [Swed/Ger] S solo,orch
BREITKOPF-W rental
(S2157)
(Jalas, Jussi) [Swed/Ger] S solo,
2fl,2clar,2bsn,timp,perc,strings
BREITKOPF-W rental
(S2158)

Die Primel *see Sippan

Die Sommernacht *see Sommarnatten

Die Sternblume *see Vit Sippan

Die Sternblume *see Vit Sippan

Die Sternblume *see Vit Sippan

Die Sternblume *see Vitsippan

Die Stilla Stadt *Op.50,No.5
"Silent Town, The" [Eng/Ger] low
solo,pno LIENAU R147 s.p. see
from Six Songs
(S2159)
"Silent Town, The" [Eng/Ger] high
solo,pno LIENAU R146 s.p. see
from Six Songs
(S2160)

Doch Mein Vogel Kehrt Nicht Wieder
*see Men Nin Fagel Marks Dock
Inte

Dolce Far Niente *Op.61,No.6
[Ger/Eng/Swed] high solo,pno
BREITKOPF-W DLV 5412 $1.50
(S2161)

Dold Forening *Op.86,No.3
see Six Songs

Dream, The *see Drommen

Drei Hymnische Gesange
[Ger] LIENAU R90 s.p.
contains: Aller Augen Warten Auf
Dich (med solo,vcl);
Gluckseligkeits-Ode (med solo,
harp/pno); Herr, Wohin Sollen
Wir Gehen? (med solo,org)
(S2162)

Drei Lieder
[Swed/Ger/Eng] BREITKOPF-W DLV 4775
s.p.
contains & see also: Bollspelet
Vid Trainon, "Ballspiel In
Trianon", Op.36,No.3; Doch Mein
Vogel Kehrt Nicht Wieder,
Op.36,No.2; Svarta Rosor,
"Schwarze Rosen", Op.36,No.1
(S2163)

Drommen *Op.13,No.5
"Der Traum" [Swed/Ger] low solo,pno
BREITKOPF-W DLV 5588 s.p. (S2164)
"Der Traum" [Swed/Ger] high solo,
pno BREITKOPF-W DLV 3948 s.p.
(S2165)
"Dream, The" [Eng/Fr] high solo,pno
BREITKOPF-W 57 05021 s.p. (S2166)
"Uni" solo,pno FAZER F 4500 s.p.

SIBELIUS, JEAN (cont'd.)

see from Sju Sanger Till Dikter
Av Runeberg
(S2167)

Eight Songs *see Alvan Och Snigeln,
"Snail, The", Op.57,No.1; En
Blomma Stad Vid Vagen, "Wild
Flower, The", Op.57,No.2; Hertig
Magnus, "Baron Magnus", Op.57,
No.6; Kvarnhjulet, "Mill Wheel,
The", Op.57,No.3; Maj, "May",
Op.57,No.4; Nacken, "Elfking,
The", Op.57,No.8; Tree, The,
Op.57,No.5; Vanskapens Blomma,
"Friendship", Op.57,No.7 (S2168)

Eitle Wunsche *Op.61,No.7
[Ger/Eng/Swed] high solo,pno
BREITKOPF-W DLV 5413-14 $3.00
(S2169)

Ekonymfen *see Kaiutar

Eksyksissa *see Vilse

Elfking, The *see Nacken

En Blomma Stad Vid Vagen *Op.57,No.2
"Wild Flower, The" [Eng/Ger] low
solo,pno LIENAU R153 s.p. see
from Eight Songs
(S2170)
"Wild Flower, The" [Eng/Ger] high
solo,pno LIENAU R152 s.p. see
from Eight Songs
(S2171)

Ensi Suudelma *see Den Forsta Kyssen

Erloschen
"Sammunut" solo,pno FAZER s.p.
(S2172)

Fagelfangaren
"Der Vogelstaller" solo,pno FAZER
W 239 s.p. see from Sex Sanger
Till Dikter Av Runeberg (S2173)

Fem Sanger I *see Den Forsta Kyssen,
"Ensi Suudelma", Op.37,No.1;
Flickan Kom Ifran Sin Alsklings
Mote, "Tuli Tytto Luota
Armahansa", Op.37,No.5; Lasse
Liten, "Pikku Lasse", Op.37,No.2;
Soluppgang, "Auringonnousu",
Op.37,No.3; Var Det En Drom?,
"Untako Vain", Op.37,No.4 (S2174)

Fem Sanger Till Dikter Av Rydberg
*see Harpolekaren Och Hans Son,
"Harpunsoittaja Ja Hanen
Poikansa", Op.38,No.4; Hostkvall,
"Syysilta", Op.38,No.1; I Natten,
"Yossa", Op.38,No.3; Pa Verandan
Vid Havet, "Merenrantakuistilla",
Op.38,No.2
(S2175)

Finlandia-Hymn *see Finlandia-Hymnen

Finlandia-Hymnen *Op.26,No.7, Finn
solo,pno FAZER F 3210 s.p. (S2176)
"Finlandia-Hymn" [Swed/Ger/Finn]
BREITKOPF-W $1.25
(S2177)
"Finlandiahymnen" solo,pno MUSIKK
s.p.
(S2178)

Finlandiahymnen *see Finlandia-
Hymnen

Flickam Kom Ifran Sin Alsklings Mote
*Op.37,No.5
"Madchen Kam Vom Stelldichein"
[Swed/Ger] S solo,pno BREITKOPF-W
DLV 3473 $1.50
(S2179)
"Tryst, The" [Eng/Fr] S solo,pno
BREITKOPF-W DLV 3488 $1.50
(S2180)

Flickan Kom Ifran Sin Alsklings Mote
*Op.37,No.5
solo,pno MUSIKK s.p.
(S2181)
"Madchen Kam Vom Stelldichein"
[Eng/Ger] S solo,pno BREITKOPF-W
EB 5905 s.p.
(S2182)
"Tuli Tytto Luota Armahansa" solo,
pno FAZER F 3218 see from Fem
Sanger I
(S2183)
(Pingoud, Ernest) "Madchen Kam Vom
Stelldichein" [Swed/Ger] S solo,
fl,ob,2clar,2bsn,2horn,3trom,
timp,harp,strings BREITKOPF-W
rental
(S2184)

Friendship *see Vanskapens Blomma

Fruhling Schwindet Eilig *see Varen
Flyktar Hastigt

Fruhlingszauber *see Vartagen

Funfzehn Ausgewahlte Lieder *CC15L
[Ger/Eng/Swed] high solo,pno
BREITKOPF-W EB 6943 $7.50; low
solo,pno BREITKOPF-W EB 6944
$7.50
(S2185)

Gesang Der Athener *see Atenarnes
Sang

SIBELIUS, JEAN (cont'd.)

Ging An Einem Wintermorgen *see
  Arioso

Gluckseligkeits-Ode
  see Drei Hymnische Gesange

Hallila, Uti Storm Och Regn *Op.60,
  No.2
  "Hei Ja Hoi, Miten Myrsky Se Soi"
    solo,pno FAZER F 4507 s.p. see
    from Two Songs From "Twelfth
    Night"   (S2186)
  (Borg, Kim) "Heissa, Hopsa, Bei
    Regen Und Wind" [Swed/Ger] B
    solo,harp,strings BREITKOPF-W
    rental   (S2187)

Harpolekaren Och Hans Son *Op.38,
  No.4
  "Der Harfenspieler Und Sein Sohn"
    [Swed/Ger] med solo,pno
    BREITKOPF-W DLV 3477 $1.75
                                    (S2188)
  "Harpunsoittaja Ja Hanen Poikansa"
    solo,pno FAZER F 4505 s.p. see
    from Fem Sanger Till Dikter Av
    Rydberg   (S2189)

Harpunsoittaja Ja Hanen Poikansa
  *see Harpolekaren Och Hans Son

Hei Ja Hoi, Miten Myrsky Se Soi *see
  Hallila, Uti Storm Och Regn

Heissa, Hopsa, Bei Regen Und Wind
  *Op.60,No.2
  [Ger/Swed] B solo,pno BREITKOPF-W
    DLV 5256 $1.50   (S2190)

Heissa, Hopsa, Bei Regen Und Wind
  *see Hallila, Uti Storm Och Regn

Hennes Budskap *Op.90,No.2
  "Ihre Botschaft" solo,pno FAZER
    W 237 s.p. see from Sex Sanger
    Till Dikter Av Runeberg   (S2191)

Herbstabend *see Hostkvall

Herr, Wohin Sollen Wir Gehen?
  see Drei Hymnische Gesange

Hertig Magnus *Op.57,No.6
  "Baron Magnus" [Eng/Ger] high solo,
    pno LIENAU R159 s.p. see from
    Eight Songs   (S2192)
  "Baron Magnus" [Eng/Ger] low solo,
    pno LIENAU R160 s.p. see from
    Eight Songs   (S2193)

Hjartats Morgon *Op.13,No.3
  "Des Herzens Morgen" [Swed/Ger]
    solo,pno BREITKOPF-W DLV 5586
    s.p.   (S2194)

Hostkvall *Op.38,No.1
  solo,pno MUSIKK s.p.   (S2195)
  "Herbstabend" [Swed/Ger] S solo,pno
    voc sc BREITKOPF-L DLV 3474 s.p.
                                    (S2196)
  "Herbstabend" S solo,2ob,3clar,
    3bsn,4horn,3trom,tamb,harp,
    strings sc BREITKOPF-L rental
                                    (S2197)
  "Herbstabend" S solo,
    2ob,2bass clar,2contrabsn,4horn,
    3trom,perc,harp,strings
    BREITKOPF-W rental   (S2198)
  "Syysilta" solo,pno FAZER F 3219
    s.p. see from Fem Sanger Till
    Dikter Av Rydberg   (S2199)

Hundert Wege *see Hundra Vagar

Hundra Vagar *Op.72,No.6
  "Hundert Wege" [Ger/Eng/Swed] S
    solo,pno BREITKOPF-W DLV 5461
    $1.50   (S2200)
  "Sata Tieta" solo,pno FAZER F 4510
    s.p. see from Sex Sanger II   (S2201)
  (Jalas, Jussi) "Hundert Wege"
    [Swed/Ger] S solo,harp,strings
    BREITKOPF-W rental   (S2202)
  (Sandberg, Sven) "Hundert Wege"
    [Swed/Ger] S solo,2fl,2ob,2clar,
    2bsn,3horn,2trp,strings
    BREITKOPF-W rental   (S2203)

Hymn To Thais
  "Hymni Thais'lle" solo,pno FAZER
    F 4094 s.p.   (S2204)

Hymni Thais'lle *see Hymn To Thais

I Natten *Op.38,No.3
  "Yossa" solo,pno FAZER F 4504 s.p.
    see from Fem Sanger Till Dikter
    Av Rydberg   (S2205)

I Systrar, I Broder, I Alskande Par
  *Op.86,No.6
  see Six Songs
  solo,pno FAZER W 1210 s.p. see from

SIBELIUS, JEAN (cont'd.)

Sex Sanger III   (S2206)

Ich Mochte, Ich Ware Im Indierland
  *Op.38,No.5
  [Swed/Ger] med solo,pno BREITKOPF-W
    DLV 3478 $1.75   (S2207)

Ihre Botschaft *see Hennes Budskap

Illalle *Op.17,No.6
  "An Den Abend" [Finn/Ger] high
    solo,pno BREITKOPF-W DLV 5196
    s.p.   (S2208)
  "An Den Abend" [Finn/Ger] A solo,
    pno BREITKOPF-W DLV 5510 s.p.   (S2209)
  "Till Kvalen" solo,pno FAZER F 3208
    s.p. see from Sju Sanger   (S2210)
  "Till Kvallen" solo,pno MUSIKK s.p.
                                    (S2211)
  (Hellmann, Ivar) "An Den Abend"
    [Finn/Ger] A solo,10winds,strings
    BREITKOPF-W rental   (S2212)
  (Jalas, Jussi) "An Den Abend"
    [Finn/Ger] A solo,2fl,2ob,2clar,
    bsn,strings BREITKOPF-W rental (S2213)

Im Feld Ein Madchen Singt *Op.50,
  No.3
  "Maiden Yonder Sings, A" [Eng/Ger]
    low solo,pno LIENAU R143 s.p. see
    from Six Songs   (S2214)
  "Maiden Yonder Sings, A" [Eng/Ger]
    high solo,pno LIENAU R142 s.p.
    see from Six Songs   (S2215)

In Der Nacht *Op.38,No.3
  A solo,bass clar,2bsn,4horn,timp,
    strings BREITKOPF-W rental
                                    (S2216)
  [Swed/Ger] A solo,pno BREITKOPF-W
    DLV 3476 $1.50   (S2217)

Jagargossen *Op.13,No.7
  "Der Jagerknabe" [Swed/Ger] high
    solo,pno BREITKOPF-W DLV 3950
    s.p.   (S2218)
  "Der Jagerknabe" [Swed/Ger] low
    solo,pno BREITKOPF-W DLV 5590
    s.p.   (S2219)
  "Nuori Metsamies" solo,pno FAZER
    F 4501 s.p. see from Sju Sanger
    Till Dikter Av Runeberg   (S2220)
  "Young Sportsman, The" [Eng/Fr]
    high solo,pno BREITKOPF-W
    57 05023 s.p.   (S2221)

Jo On Joulu Taalla *see Nu Sa Kommer
  Julen

Joulupukki Kolkuttaa *see Nu Star
  Jul Vid Snoig Port

Joulupukki Koltuttaa *see Nu Star
  Jul Vid Snoig Port

Jouluvirsi *Op.1,No.4, Xmas
  "Weihnachtsweise" solo,pno FAZER
    W 2470 s.p.   (S2222)

Jubal *Op.35,No.1
  (Pingoud, Ernest) S solo,2fl,ob,
    2clar,2bsn,2horn,perc,harp,
    strings BREITKOPF-W rental
                                    (S2223)

Kaiutar *Op.72,No.4
  "Ekonymfen" solo,pno FAZER F4508
    s.p. see from Sex Sanger II   (S2224)
  (Borg, Kim) "Die Echonymphe" [Finn/
    Ger] S solo,3fl,English horn,
    2bass clar,perc,harp,strings
    BREITKOPF-W rental   (S2225)
  (Jalas, Jussi) "Die Echonymphe"
    [Ger/Finn] S solo,2fl,English
    horn,2clar,2bsn,perc,harp,strings
    sc BREITKOPF-W DLV 5458-59 $2.50
                                    (S2226)

Kerkein Kevat Rientaa *see Varen
  Flyktar Hastigt

Kleiner Lasse *see Lasse Liten

Kleiner Lasse *see Lasse Litten

Kom Nu Hit, Dod *Op.60,No.1
  "Komm Herbei, Tod" [Ger/Swed/Eng/
    Fr] A solo,pno BREITKOPF-W
    DLV 5253 s.p.   (S2227)
  "Komm Herbei, Tod" [Swed/Ger] A
    solo,pno BREITKOPF-W 08 00369
    $1.50   (S2228)
  "Komm Herbei, Tod!" [Swed/Ger] A
    solo,harp,strings BREITKOPF-W
    rental   (S2229)
  "Saavuthan, Yo" solo,pno FAZER
    F 4506 s.p. see from Two Songs
    From "Twelfth Night"   (S2230)

Komm Herbei, Tod! *see Kom Nu Hit,
  Dod

SIBELIUS, JEAN (cont'd.)

Koskenlaskian Morsiamet *Op.33
  A/Bar solo,2fl,2ob,2clar,2bsn,
    4horn,2trp,3trom,timp,perc,
    strings BREITKOPF-W rental
                                    (S2231)
  "Des Fahrmanns Braute" Bar solo,
    2fl,2ob,2clar,2bsn,4horn,2trp,
    3trom,timp,perc,strings
    BREITKOPF-L rental   (S2232)

Kulervo Valitus *Op.7
  "Kullervos Klage" [Ger/Finn/Swed]
    low solo,pno BREITKOPF-W 57 05019
    s.p.   (S2233)
  "Kullervos Klage" [Ger/Finn/Swed]
    high solo,pno BREITKOPF-W
    57 05018 s.p.   (S2234)

Kullervon Valitus *Op.7
  "Kullervos Klagan" solo,cor,orch
    FAZER F 4617 s.p.   (S2235)

Kullervos Klagan *see Kullervon
  Valitus

Kullervos Klage *see Kulervon
  Valitus

Kusses Hoffnung *see Kyssens Hopp

Kvarnhjulet *Op.57,No.3
  "Mill Wheel, The" [Eng/Ger] med
    solo,pno LIENAU R154 s.p. see
    from Eight Songs   (S2236)

Kyssen *Op.72,No.3
  "Der Kuss" [Ger/Swed] med-high
    solo,pno BREITKOPF-W DLV 5456-57
    $1.75   (S2237)

Kyssens Hopp *Op.13,No.2
  "Kusses Hoffnung" [Swed/Ger] low
    solo,pno BREITKOPF-W DLV 5585
    s.p.   (S2238)
  "Kusses Hoffnung" [Swed/Ger] solo,
    pno BREITKOPF-W DLV 3945 s.p.   (S2239)

Langtan Heter *Op.86,No.2
  see Six Songs

Lasse Liten *Op.37,No.2
  "Kleiner Lasse" [Swed/Ger] med
    solo,pno BREITKOPF-W DLV 5511
    $1.50   (S2240)
  "Lasse Liten" solo,pno MUSIKK s.p.
                                    (S2241)
  "Little Lasse" [Eng/Fr] med solo,
    pno BREITKOPF-W DLV 3480 $1.50 (S2242)
  "Pikku Lasse" solo,pno FAZER F 3216
    see from Fem Sanger I   (S2243)

Lasse Liten *see Lasse Liten

Lasse Litten
  "Kleiner Lasse" [Swed/Finn] med
    solo,pno BREITKOPF-W 57 05035
    $1.50   (S2244)

Lastu Lainehilla *Op.17,No.7
  "Der Span Auf Den Wellen" [Finn/
    Ger] A solo,pno BREITKOPF-W
    DLV 5136 s.p.   (S2245)
  "Der Span Auf Den Wellen" [Finn/
    Ger] S solo,pno BREITKOPF-W
    DLV 5197 s.p.   (S2246)
  "Spanet Pa Vattnet" solo,pno MUSIKK
    s.p.   (S2247)
  "Spanet Pa Vattnet" solo,pno FAZER
    F 3209 s.p. see from Sju Sanger
                                    (S2248)
  (Borg, Kim) "Der Span Auf Den
    Wellen" [Finn/Ger] B solo,fl,
    clar,2horn,strings BREITKOPF-W
    rental   (S2249)
  (Jalas, Jussi) "Der Span Auf Den
    Wellen" [Finn/Ger] S solo,2fl,
    2ob,2clar,2bsn,2horn,timp,perc,
    strings BREITKOPF-W rental
                                    (S2250)
  (Pingoud, Ernest) "Der Span Auf Den
    Wellen" [Finn/Ger] A solo,ob,
    2clar,2bsn,horn,harp,strings
    BREITKOPF-W rental   (S2251)

Lenzgesang *Op.50,No.1
  "Song Of Spring, A" [Eng/Ger] high
    solo,pno LIENAU R138 s.p. see
    from Six Songs   (S2252)

Little Lasse *see Lasse Liten

Lockung *Op.17,No.3
  "Perltau Schon Funkelt" [Swed/Ger]
    S solo,pno BREITKOPF-W DLV 3498
    s.p.   (S2253)
  (Borg, Kim) "Lockung" [Swed/Ger] B
    solo,2fl,ob,clar,horn,harp,cel,
    strings BREITKOPF-W rental
                                    (S2254)
  (Pingoud, Ernest) "Lockung" [Swed/
    Ger] S solo,fl,horn,perc,strings,
    harp/pno BREITKOPF-W rental
                                    (S2255)

SIBELIUS, JEAN (cont'd.)

Lockung *see Lockung

Longing *see Sehnsucht

Luonnotar *Op.70
[Swed/Ger] S solo,2fl,2ob,2bass
clar,2bsn,4horn,2trp,3trom,timp,
2harp,strings BREITKOPF-W rental
(S2256)

Madchen Kam Vom Stelldichein *see
Flickam Kom Ifran Sin Alsklings
Mote

Madchen Kam Vom Stelldichein *see
Flickan Kom Ifran Sin Alsklings
Mote

Maiden Yonder Sings, A *see Im Feld
Ein Madchen Singt

Maj *Op.57,No.4
"May" [Eng/Ger] high solo,pno
LIENAU R155 s.p. see from Eight
Songs   (S2257)
"May" [Eng/Ger] low solo,pno LIENAU
R156 s.p. see from Eight Songs
(S2258)

Marzschnee *Op.36,No.5
[Swed/Ger] A solo,pno BREITKOPF-W
DLV 5285 $1.50   (S2259)
(Jalas, Jussi) "Marzschnee" [Swed/
Ger] A solo,2fl,2clar,2bsn,timp,
strings BREITKOPF-W rental
(S2260)

Marzschnee *see Marzschnee

May *see Maj

Men Min Fagel Marks Dock Icke *see
Men Nin Fagel Marks Dock Inte

Men Min Fagel Marks Dock Inte *see
Men Nin Fagel Marks Dock Inte

Men Nin Fagel Marks Dock Inte
*Op.36,No.2
"Doch Mein Vogel Kehrt Nicht
Wieder" [Swed/Ger/Eng] med solo,
pno BREITKOPF-W $1.50 see also
Drei Lieder   (S2261)
"Men Min Fagel Marks Dock Icke"
[Swed/Finn] S solo,pno BREITKOPF-
W DLV 5027 s.p.   (S2262)
"Men Min Fagel Marks Dock Inte"
solo,pno MUSIKK s.p.   (S2263)
"Vaan Mun Lintuain Ei Kuulu" solo,
pno FAZER F 3212 see from Sex
Sanger I   (S2264)
(Pingoud, Ernest) "Doch Mein Vogel
Kehrt Nicht Wieder" [Swed/Finn] S
solo,2fl,2English horn,2clar,
2bsn,2horn,2trp,3trom,tuba,harp,
strings BREITKOPF-W rental
(S2265)

Merenrantakuistilla *see Pa Verandan
Vid Havet

Mill Wheel, The *see Kvarnhjulet

Morgonen *Op.90,No.3
"Der Morgen" solo,pno FAZER W 238
s.p. see from Sex Sanger Till
Dikter Av Runeberg   (S2266)

Mustat Ruusut *see Svarta Rosor

Nacken *Op.57,No.8
"Elfking, The" [Eng/Ger] high solo,
pno LIENAU R163 s.p. see from
Eight Songs   (S2267)
"Elfking, The" [Eng/Ger] low solo,
pno LIENAU R164 s.p. see from
Eight Songs   (S2268)

Nar Jag Drommer *Op.61,No.3
"Wenn Ich Traume" [Ger/Eng/Swed]
med-high solo,pno BREITKOPF-W
DLV 5298 $1.50   (S2269)

Narciss
"Narzisse" solo,pno FAZER W 1828
s.p.   (S2270)

Narzisse *see Narciss

Norden *Op.90,No.1
"Der Norden" solo,pno FAZER W 236
s.p. see from Sex Sanger Till
Dikter Av Runeberg   (S2271)

Nu Sa Kommer Julen *Op.1,No.2
"Jo On Joulu Taalla" see Tva
Julvisor
"Jo On Joulu Taalla" see Tva
Julsanger

Nu Star Jul Vid Snoig Port *Op.1,
No.1
"Joulupukki Kolkuttaa" see Tva
Julsanger
"Joulupukki Koltuttaa" see Tva
Julvisor

SIBELIUS, JEAN (cont'd.)

Nuori Metsamies *see Jagargossen

O, Wert Thou Here: The Roses Blossom
*see Aus Banger Brust

Och Finns Det En Tanke *Op.86,No.4
solo,pno FAZER W 1208 s.p. see from
Sex Sanger III   (S2272)

Och Fins Det An Tanke *Op.86,No.4
see Six Songs

Onward, Ye Peoples
high solo,pno (G maj) GALAXY
1.1207.7 $1.00   (S2273)
med solo/low solo,pno GALAXY
1.1233.7 $1.00   (S2274)

Pa Verandan Vid Havet *Op.38,No.2
[Swed/Finn] A solo,pno BREITKOPF-W
DLV 3475 $1.50   (S2275)
solo,pno MUSIKK s.p.   (S2276)
"Merenrantakuistilla" solo,pno
FAZER F 3220 s.p. see from Fem
Sanger Till Dikter Av Rydberg
(S2277)
(Rydberg) "Auf Dem Soller Am Meer"
[Swed/Ger] A solo,2ob,2clar,2bsn,
4horn,timp,strings BREITKOPF-W
rental   (S2278)

Palloleikki Trainonissa *see
Bollspelet Vid Trainon

Perltau Schon Funkelt *see Lockung

Pikku Lasse *see Lasse Liten

Romanze *Op.61,No.5
[Ger/Eng/Swed] med solo,pno
BREITKOPF-W DLV 5300 $1.50
(S2279)

Romeo *Op.61,No.4
[Ger/Eng/Swed] high solo,pno
BREITKOPF-W DLV 5299 $1.50
(S2280)
(Jalas, Jussi) "Romeo" [Swed/Ger] S
solo,2fl,2clar,2bsn,timp,perc,
strings BREITKOPF-W rental
(S2281)

Romeo *see Romeo

Rosenlied *Op.50,No.6
"Song Of Roses, The" [Eng/Ger] high
solo,pno LIENAU R148 s.p. see
from Six Songs   (S2282)
"Song Of Roses, The" [Eng/Ger] low
solo,pno LIENAU R149 s.p. see
from Six Songs   (S2283)

Saavuthan, Yo *see Kom Nu Hit, Dod

Sacht Wie Vom Abendrot *Op.61,No.1
[Ger/Eng/Swed] S solo,pno
BREITKOPF-W DLV 5295 $1.50
(S2284)
(Funtek, Leo) [Swed/Ger] S solo,fl,
ob,2clar,horn,perc,harp,strings
BREITKOPF-W rental   (S2285)

Sammunut *see Erloschen

Sangen Om Korsspindeln *Op.27,No.4
solo,pno MUSIKK s.p.   (S2286)

Sata Tieta *see Hundra Vagar

Sav, Sav Susa *Op.36,No.4
solo,pno MUSIKK s.p.   (S2287)
"Schilfrohr, Saus'le" [Swed/Ger]
med solo,pno BREITKOPF-W DLV 5198
s.p.   (S2288)
"Schilfrohr, Saus'le" [Swed/Ger] A
solo,pno BREITKOPF-W DLV 3468
$1.50   (S2289)
"Soi, Soi, Kaisla" solo,pno FAZER
F 3214 see from Sex Sanger I
(S2290)
(Hellmann, Ivar) "Schilfrohr,
Saus'le" [Swed/Ger] A solo,2fl,
2ob,2clar,2bsn,2trp,2horn,trom,
harp,pno,strings BREITKOPF-W
rental   (S2291)
(Hellmann, Ivar) "Schilfrohr,
Saus'le" [Swed/Ger] A solo,2fl,
2ob,2clar,2bsn,4horn,2trp,3trom,
tuba,harp,pno,strings BREITKOPF-W
rental   (S2292)

Schilfrohr, Saus'le *see Sav, Sav
Susa

Schlaf Ein "Mein Bleicher Liebling
Soll Giessen" *Op.17,No.2
[Swed/Ger] A solo,pno BREITKOPF-W
DLV 3497 s.p.   (S2293)
(Pingoud, Ernest) [Swed/Ger] A
solo,2fl,2clar,2bsn,horn,strings
BREITKOPF-W rental   (S2294)

Schwarze Rosen *see Svarta Rosor

SIBELIUS, JEAN (cont'd.)

Schwarze Rosen *see Svarta Rosor

Schwarze Rosen *see Svarta Rosor

Sehnsucht *Op.50,No.2
"Longing" [Eng/Ger] low solo,pno
LIENAU R141 s.p. see from Six
Songs   (S2295)
"Longing" [Eng/Ger] high solo,pno
LIENAU R140 s.p. see from Six
Songs   (S2296)

Se'n Har Jag Ej Fragat Mera *Op.17,
No.1
"Und Ich Fragte Dann Nicht Wieder"
[Swed/Ger] A solo,pno BREITKOPF-W
DLV 3496 $1.50   (S2297)
"Und Ich Fragte Dann Nicht Wieder"
[Swed/Ger] A solo,2fl,2ob,bass
clar,2bsn,4horn,perc,strings
BREITKOPF-W rental   (S2298)

Serenade *see Sernad

Sernad
"Serenade" solo,pno FAZER F 4216
s.p.   (S2299)

Sex Sanger I *see Bollspelet Vid
Trainon, "Palloleikki
Trainonissa", Op.36,No.3;
Demanten Pa Marssnon, "Timantti
Hangella", Op.36,No.6; Men Nin
Fagel Marks Dock Inte, "Vaan Mun
Lintuain Ei Kuulu", Op.36,No.2;
Sav, Sav, Susa, "Soi, Soi,
Kaisla", Op.36,No.4; Svarta
Rosor, "Mustat Ruusut", Op.36,
No.1   (S2300)

Sex Sanger II *see Der Wanderer Und
Der Bach, "Vandraren Och Backen",
Op.72,No.5; Hundra Vagar, "Sata
Tieta", Op.72,No.6; Kaiutar,
"Ekonymfen", Op.72,No.4 (S2301)

Sex Sanger III *see I Systrar, I
Broder, I Alskande Par, Op.86,
No.6; Och Finns Det En Tanke,
Op.86,No.4   (S2302)

Sex Sanger Till Dikter Av Runeberg
*see Fagelfangaren, "Der
Vogelstaller"; Hennes Budskap,
"Ihre Botschaft", Op.90,No.2;
Morgonen, "Der Morgen", Op.90,
No.3; Norden, "Der Norden",
Op.90,No.1; Sommarnatten, "Die
Sommernacht", Op.90,No.5; Vem
Styrde Hit Din Vag?, "Wer Hat
Dich Hergefuhrt", Op.90,No.6
(S2303)

Silent Town, The *see Die Stilla
Stadt

Simma, And Fran Blaa Fjardar *see
Souda, Souda Sinisorsa

Sippan *Op.88,No.4
"Die Primel" see Six Songs [2]
"Die Primel" [Swed/Finn/Ger] solo,
pno BREITKOPF-W 57 05048 s.p. see
from SECHS LIEDER NACH TEXTEN VON
FR. M. FRANZEN UND J.L. RUNEBERG
(S2304)
"Die Primel" solo,pno FAZER W 485
s.p.   (S2305)

Six Songs [2]
[Swed/Ger] med-high solo,kbd
HANSEN-DEN s.p.
contains: Blommans Ode, "Die
Blume", Op.88,No.6; De Bagge
Rosorna, "Die Biden Rosen",
Op.88,No.2; Sippan, "Die
Primel", Op.88,No.4; Vit
Sippan, "Die Sternblume",
Op.88,No.3   (S2306)

Six Songs *see Aus Banger Brust, "O,
Wert Thou Here: The Roses
Blossom", Op.50,No.4; Die Stilla
Stadt, "Silent Town, The", Op.50,
No.5; Im Feld Ein Madchen Singt,
"Maiden Yonder Sings, A", Op.50,
No.3; Lenzgesang, "Song Of
Spring, A", Op.50,No.1; Die
Rosenlied, "Song Of Roses, The",
Op.50,No.6; Sehnsucht, "Longing",
Op.50,No.2   (S2307)

Six Songs
[Swed] med-high solo,kbd HANSEN-DEN
s.p.
contains: Dold Forening, Op.86,
No.3; I Systrar, I Broder, I
Alskande Par, Op.86,No.6;
Langtan Heter, Op.86,No.2; Och
Fins Det An Tanke, Op.86,No.4;
Var Fornimmelser, Op.86,No.1
(S2308)

Sju Sanger *see Illalle, "Till
Kvalen", Op.17,No.6; Lastu
Lainehilla, "Spanet Pa Vattnet",

SIBELIUS, JEAN (cont'd.)

Op.17,No.7; Vilse, "Eksyksissa",
   Op.17,No.4   (S2309)

Sju Sanger Till Dikter Av Runeberg
   *see Drommen, "Uni", Op.13,No.5;
   Jagargossen, "Nuori Metsamies",
   Op.13,No.7; Varen Flykter
   Hastigt, "Kerkein Kevat Rientaa",
   Op.13,No.4   (S2310)

Snail, The   *see Alvan Och Snigeln

Soi, Soi, Kaisla   *see Sav, Sav, Susa

Soluppgang   *Op.37,No.3
   "Auringonnousu" solo,pno FAZER
   F 4503 see from Fem Sanger I
                                 (S2311)
   "Sonnenaufgang" [Swed/Ger] S solo,
   pno BREITKOPF-W DLV 3471 $1.50
                                 (S2312)
   "Sonnenaufgang" [Swed/Ger] S solo,
   2fl,2clar,2bsn,4horn,strings
   BREITKOPF-W rental   (S2313)

Sommarnatten   *Op.90,No.5
   "Die Sommernacht" solo,pno FAZER
   W 240 s.p. see from Sex Sanger
   Till Dikter Av Runeberg   (S2314)

Song Of Roses, The   *see Rosenlied

Song Of Spring, A   *Op.50,No.1
   [Eng/Ger] low solo,pno LIENAU R139
   s.p. see from Six Songs   (S2315)

Song Of Spring, A   *see Lenzgesang

Sonnenaufgang   *see Soluppgang

Souda, Souda Sinisorsa
   "Simma, And Fran Blaa Fjardar"
   solo,pno FAZER F 2564 s.p.
                                 (S2316)

Spanet Pa Vattnet   *see Lastu
   Lainehilla

Spring Is Flying   *see Varen Flyktar
   Hastigt

Svarta Rosor   *Op.36,No.1
   [Swed/Finn] solo,pno BREITKOPF-W
   57 05026 s.p.   (S2317)
   "Mustat Ruusut" solo,pno FAZER
   F 3211 see from Sex Sanger I
                                 (S2318)
   "Schwarze Rosen" [Swed/Ger/Eng] S
   solo,pno BREITKOPF-W $1.50 see
   also Drei Lieder   (S2319)
   "Schwarze Rosen" [Ger/Eng/Swed] S
   solo,pno BREITKOPF-W EB 5906 s.p.
                                 (S2320)
   "Schwarze Rosen" [Swed/Ger] high
   solo,pno BREITKOPF-W DLV 5607
   s.p.   (S2321)
   "Schwarze Rosen" [Eng/Swed] med
   solo,pno AMP $.75 see from SIX
   SONGS   (S2322)
   "Schwarze Rosen" [Eng/Swed] low
   solo,pno AMP $.75 see from SIX
   SONGS   (S2323)
   "Svarta Rosor" solo,pno MUSIKK s.p.
                                 (S2324)
   (Hellmann, Ivar) "Schwarze Rosen"
   [Swed/Ger] S solo,2fl,2ob,2clar,
   2bsn,4horn,2trp,3trom,tuba,harp,
   strings BREITKOPF-W rental
                                 (S2325)

Svarta Rosor   *see Svarta Rosor

Syysilta   *see Hostkvall

Tennis At Trianon   *see Bollspelet
   Vid Trianon

Theodora   *Op.35,No.2
   [Ger/Eng/Swed] med solo,pno
   BREITKOPF-W DLV 5233-34 $2.50
                                 (S2326)

There Comes Another Morrow
   low solo,pno (F maj) WILLIS $.60
                                 (S2327)
   high solo,pno (A flat maj) WILLIS
   $.60   (S2328)

Three Blind Sisters, The   *Op.46,No.4
   (from Pelleas And Melisande)
   [Eng/Ger] med solo,pno LIENAU R165
   s.p.   (S2329)

Till Frigga   *Op.13,No.6
   "An Frigga" [Swed/Ger] solo,pno
   BREITKOPF-W DLV 3949 $1.50
                                 (S2330)

Till Kvalen   *see Illalle

Till Kvallen   *see Illalle

Timantti Hangella   *see Demanten Pa
   Marssnon

Tornet   *Op.88,No.5
   "Der Dornbusch" [Swed/Finn/Ger]
   solo,pno BREITKOPF-W 57 05049

SIBELIUS, JEAN (cont'd.)

s.p. see from SECHS LIEDER NACH
TEXTEN VON FR. M. FRANZEN UND
J.L. RUNEBERG   (S2331)
   "Der Dornbusch" solo,pno FAZER
   W 486 s.p.   (S2332)

Tree, The   *Op.57,No.5
   [Eng/Ger] high solo,pno LIENAU R157
   s.p. see from Eight Songs   (S2333)
   [Eng/Ger] low solo,pno LIENAU R158
   s.p. see from Eight Songs   (S2334)

Trust   *sac
   (Stickles) high solo,pno/org (G
   maj) SCHIRM.G $.60   (S2335)
   (Stickles) low solo,pno/org (E flat
   maj) SCHIRM.G $.60   (S2336)

Tryst, The   *see Flickam Kom Ifran
   Sin Alsklings Mote

Tuli Tytto Luota Armahansa   *see
   Flickan Kom Ifran Sin Alsklings
   Mote

Tva Julsanger   *Xmas
   solo,pno FAZER W 1211 s.p.
   contains: Nu Sa Kommer Julen, "Jo
   On Joulu Taalla", Op.1,No.2; Nu
   Star Jul Vid Snoig Port,
   "Joulupukki Kolkuttaa", Op.1,
   No.1   (S2337)

Tva Julvisor   *Xmas
   [Swed/Finn] solo,pno BREITKOPF-W
   57 05016 s.p.
   contains: Nu Sa Kommer Julen, "Jo
   On Joulu Taalla", Op.1,No.2; Nu
   Star Jul Vid Snoig Port,
   "Joulupukki Koltuttaa", Op.1,
   No.1   (S2338)

Two Songs From "Twelfth Night"   *see
   Hallila, Uti Storm Och Regn, "Hei
   Ja Hoi, Miten Myrsky Se Soi",
   Op.60,No.2; Kom Nu Hit, Dod,
   "Saavuthan, Yo", Op.60,No.1
                                 (S2339)

Und Ich Fragte Dann Nicht Wieder
   *see Se'n Har Jag Ej Fragat Mera

Under Strandens Graver   *Op.13,No.1
   "Unter Ufertannen Spielt' Der
   Knabe" [Swed/Ger] A solo,pno
   BREITKOPF-W DLV 5584 s.p.   (S2340)
   (Jalas, Jussi) "Unter Ufertannen
   Spielt' Der Knabe" [Swed/Ger] A
   solo,2fl,2ob,2bass clar,2bsn,
   4horn,timp,perc,strings
   BREITKOPF-W rental   (S2341)

Uni   *see Drommen

Untako Vain   *see Var Det En Drom?

Unter Ufertannen Spielt' Der Knabe
   *see Under Strandens Graver

Vaan Mun Lintuain Ei Kuulu   *see Men
   Nin Fagel Marks Dock Inte

Vandraren Och Backen   *see Der
   Wanderer Und Der Bach

Vanskapens Blomma   *Op.57,No.7
   "Friendship" [Eng/Ger] high solo,
   pno LIENAU R161 s.p. see from
   Eight Songs   (S2342)
   "Friendship" [Eng/Ger] low solo,pno
   LIENAU R162 s.p. see from Eight
   Songs   (S2343)

Var Det En Drom?   *Op.37,No.4
   solo,pno MUSIKK s.p.   (S2344)
   "Untako Vain" solo,pno FAZER F 3217
   see from Fem Sanger I   (S2345)
   "War Es Ein Traum?" [Swed/Ger] A
   solo,pno BREITKOPF-W DLV 3472
   $3.50   (S2346)
   "Was It A Dream?" [Eng/Fr] A solo,
   pno BREITKOPF-W DLV 3481 $2.25
                                 (S2347)
   (Jalas, Jussi) "War Es Ein Traum"
   [Swed/Ger] A solo,2fl,2ob,2clar,
   2bsn,4horn,timp,strings
   BREITKOPF-W rental   (S2348)

Var Fornimmelser   *Op.86,No.1
   see Six Songs

Varen Flyktar Hastigt   *Op.13,No.4
   "Fruhling Schwindet Eilig" [Finn/
   Ger] S solo,2fl,4horn,perc,
   strings BREITKOPF-W rental
                                 (S2349)
   "Fruhling Schwindet Eilig" [Swed/
   Ger] med solo,pno BREITKOPF-W
   DLV 5587 s.p.   (S2350)
   "Fruhling Schwindet Eilig" [Swed/
   Ger] S solo,pno BREITKOPF-W
   DLV 3947 s.p.   (S2351)
   "Kerkein Kevat Rientaa" solo,pno
   FAZER F 3207 s.p. see from Sju
   Sanger Till Dikter Av Runeberg

SIBELIUS, JEAN (cont'd.)

                                 (S2352)
   "Spring Is Flying" [Eng/Fr] S solo,
   pno BREITKOPF-W 57 05020 s.p.
                                 (S2353)
   "Varen Flykter Hastigt" solo,pno
   MUSIKK s.p.   (S2354)

Varen Flykter Hastigt   *see Varen
   Flyktar Hastigt

Vartagen   *Op.61,No.8
   "Fruhlingszauber" [Ger/Eng/Swed]
   high solo,pno BREITKOPF-W EB 5928
   $1.50   (S2355)

Vem Styrde Hit Din Vag?   *Op.90,No.6
   "Wer Hat Dich Hergefuhrt" solo,pno
   FAZER W 246 s.p. see from Sex
   Sanger Till Dikter Av Runeberg
                                 (S2356)

Verirrt "Wir Liefen Wohl Irre Den
   Andern Voran"   *see Vilse

Vilse   *Op.17,No.4
   "Eksyksissa" solo,pno FAZER F 4502
   s.p. see from Sju Sanger   (S2357)
   "Verirrt "Wir Liefen Wohl Irre Den
   Andern Voran"" [Swed/Ger] high
   solo,pno BREITKOPF-W DLV 3467
   s.p.   (S2358)
   "Verirrt "Wir Liefen Wohl Irre Den
   Andern Voran"" [Swed/Ger] low
   solo,pno BREITKOPF-W DLV 5591
   s.p.   (S2359)

Vit Sippan   *Op.88,No.3
   "Die Sternblume" see Six Songs [2]
   "Die Sternblume" [Swed/Finn/Ger]
   solo,pno BREITKOPF-W 57 05047
   s.p. see from SECHS LIEDER NACH
   TEXTEN VON FR. M. FRANZEN UND
   J.L. RUNEBERG   (S2360)

Vitsippan   *Op.88,No.3
   "Die Sternblume" solo,pno FAZER
   W 484 s.p.   (S2361)

War Es Ein Traum   *see Var Det En
   Drom?

War Song Of Tyrtaeus   *see Atenarnes
   Sang

Was It A Dream?   *see Var Det En
   Drom?

Weihnachtsweise   *see Jouluvirsi

Wellenflustern   *Op.61,No.2
   [Ger/Eng/Swed] med solo,pno
   BREITKOPF-W DLV 5296-97 $2.50
                                 (S2362)

Wenn Ich Traume   *see Nar Jag Drommer

Wer Hat Dich Hergefuhrt   *see Vem
   Styrde Hit Din Vag?

Wild Flower, The   *see En Blomma Stad
   Vid Vagen

Yossa   *see I Natten

Young Sportsman, The   *see
   Jagargossen

SIBELLA, GABRIELLE
   La Girometta
   [It/Eng] high solo,pno (G maj)
   SCHIRM.G $.85   (S2363)
   low solo,pno (D maj) ALLANS s.p.
                                 (S2364)
   high solo,pno (G maj) ALLANS s.p.
                                 (S2365)
   med solo,pno (F maj) ALLANS s.p.
                                 (S2366)

SIBILLAR GLI ANGUI D'ALETTO see Handel,
   George Frideric

SIC ET NON see Stedron, Milos

SICCARDI, HONORIO (1897-   )
   Desolacion   *see Desolazione

   Desolazione
   "Desolacion" see Dos Piezas

   Dos Piezas
   [Span/It] solo,pno cmplt ed
   RICORDI-ARG BA 7371 s.p.
   contains: Desolazione,
   "Desolacion"; Malinconia,
   "Melancolia"   (S2367)

   Malinconia
   "Melancolia" see Dos Piezas

   Melancolia   *see Malinconia

SICILIAN LULLABY see Mallinson, (James)
   Albert

SICILIAN LULLABY see Newman, Roy

SICILIAN SERENADE see Price, Addison

SICILIANI, FRANCESCO
Canto Notturno Del Viandante
[It] solo,pno SANTIS 470 s.p.
(S2368)
Laude
[It] solo,pno SANTIS 471 s.p.
(S2369)
Notte
[It] solo,pno SANTIS 472 s.p.
(S2370)

SICILIENNE see Lacome, Paul

SICILLIANA see Mascagni, Pietro

SICUT CERVA, QUAE PER VALLES see Majo,
Gian Francesco de

SICUT MODO GENITI INFANTES see
Buxtehude, Dietrich

SICUT MOSES see Buxtehude, Dietrich

SICUT UMBRA see Dallapiccola, Luigi

SIDE BY SIDE see Wood, Jeff

SIDE BY SIDE TO THE BETTER LAND see
Hutchison, William M.

SIDE CAR see Fisher, Howard

SIE HABEN LEID see Verhaar, Ary

SIE LIEBTEN SICH BEIDE see Oort, H.C.v.

SIE SIND SO STILL see Verhaar, Ary

SIE WAR DEIN EIGEN see Gretchaninov,
Alexander Tikhonovitch, Jadis Tu
M'as Aime

SIE WERDEN LEBEN see Verhaar, Ary

SIE WISSEN'S NICHT see Strauss, Richard

SIE WOLL'N MICH HEIRATEN see Strauss,
Richard

SIEBEN ARIEN DES ACHILLES see
Scarlatti, Domenico

SIEBEN CHINESISCHE VOLKSLIEDER see
Tcherepnin, Alexander

SIEBEN DEUTSCHE LIEDER see Heller,
Stephen

SIEBEN DIVERSE LIEDER see Bartok, Bela

SIEBEN DREISTIMMIGE SENTENZEN NACH
WORTEN VON GUNTHER MICHEL see
Heiss, Hermann

SIEBEN EICHENDORFF-LIEDER see Trunk,
Richard

SIEBEN FRUHE LIEDER see Berg, Alban

SIEBEN GEDICHTE VON GOETHE,
EICHENDORFF, CHAMISSO see Medtner,
Nikolai Karlovitch

SIEBEN GEDICHTE VON PUSCHKIN see
Medtner, Nikolai Karlovitch

SIEBEN GEISTLICHE LIEDER see
Castelberg, M.

SIEBEN GOETHE-LIEDER see Groot, Cor
(Cornelius Wilhelmus) de

SIEBEN HAIKU see Dohl, Friedhelm

SIEBEN JAPANISCHE LIEDER see Kishi,
Koichi

SIEBEN KAMMERLIEDER see
Frischenschlager, Friedrich

SIEBEN KLEINE MEISEN see Zipp,
Friedrich

SIEBEN LEBEN MOCHT ICH HABEN see
Hessenberg, Kurt

SIEBEN LIEDER see Driessler, Johannes

SIEBEN LIEDER see Zechlin, Ruth

SIEBEN LIEDER see Kienzl, Wilhelm

SIEBEN LIEDER see Einem, Gottfried von

SIEBEN LIEDER see Kilpinen, Yrio

SIEBEN LIEDER see Trunk, Richard

SIEBEN LIEDER see Moser, Rudolf

SIEBEN LIEDER AUS DER LAUTENTABULATUR
see Dowland, John

SIEBEN MOTETTEN see Charpentier, Marc-
Antoine

SIEBEN ROTE AUGENBLICKE see Segerstam,
Leif

SIEBEN RUSSISCHE GESANGE see Reutter,
Hermann

SIEBEN SIEGEL see Strauss, Richard

SIEBEN SONETTE VON EICHENDORFF see
Zillig, Winfried

SIEBEN SPENCER LIEDER see Sims, Ezra

SIEBEN WEIHNACHTSLIEDER see Trunk,
Richard

SIEBENUNDDREISSIG LIEDER NACH GEDICHTEN
VON V.A. KOSKENNIEMI, VOL. I see
Kilpinen, Yrio

SIEBENUNDDREISSIG LIEDER NACH GEDICHTEN
VON V.A.KOSKENNIEMI, VOL. II see
Kilpinen, Yrio

SIEBENUNDDREISSIG LIEDER NACH GEDICHTEN
VON V.A. KOSKENNIEMI, VOL. III see
Kilpinen, Yrio

SIEBENUNDDREISSIG LIEDER NACH GEDICHTEN
VON V.A. KOSKENNIEMI, VOL. IV see
Kilpinen, Yrio

SIEBENUNDDREISSIG LIEDER NACH GEDICHTEN
VON V.A. KOSKENNIEMI, VOL. V see
Kilpinen, Yrio

SIEBENUNDDREISSIG LIEDER NACH GEDICHTEN
VON V.A. KOSKENNIEMI, VOL. VI see
Kilpinen, Yrio

SIEBENUNDDREISSIG LIEDER NACH GEDICHTEN
VON V.A. KOSKENNIEMI, VOL. VII see
Kilpinen, Yrio

SIEBENUNDZWANZIG LIEDER AUS DEM
"DREISTROPHENKALENDER" HEFT I
*CC9U
SBar soli,pno DEUTSCHER 9008 s.p.
(S2371)

SIEBENUNDZWANZIG LIEDER AUS DEM
"DREISTROPHENKALENDER" HEFT II
*CC8U
SB soli,pno DEUTSCHER 9009 s.p.
(S2372)

SIEBENUNDZWANZIG LIEDER AUS DEM
"DREISTROPHENKALENDER" HEFT III
*CC9U
AT soli,pno DEUTSCHER 9010 s.p.
(S2373)

SIEBENUNDZWANZIG LIEDER NACH GEDICHTEN
VON ERIK BLOMBERG, VOL. II see
Kilpinen, Yrio

SIEBENUNDZWANZIG LIEDER NACH GEDICHTEN
VON ERIK BLOMBERG, VOL. III see
Kilpinen, Yrio

SIEBENUNDZWANZIG LIEDER NACH GEDICHTEN
VON ERIK BLOMBERG, VOL. IV see
Kilpinen, Yrio

SIEBENUNDZWANZIG LIEDER NACH GEDICHTEN
VON ERIK BLOMBERG, VOL. V see
Kilpinen, Yrio

SIEBENUNDZWANZIG SOLOGESANGE UND
GESANGSVARIATIONEN see Silcher,
Friedrich

SIEBERT, F.
Kleine Geschichte
S solo,orch voc sc EULENBURG
EES 440 s.p.   (S2374)

Kleine Geschicte
"Short Story" [Eng/Ger] S solo,pno
ZIMMER. Z440 s.p.   (S2375)

Short Story *see Kleine Geschicte

SIEBZEHN LIEDER see Flury, Richard

SIEBZEHN LIEDER NACH GEDICHTEN VON
SOPHIE HAEMMERLI-MARTI see Wehrli,
Werner

SIEGL, OTTO (1896-   )
Ausgewahlte Lieder *sac,CC6U
high solo,pno sc BOHM s.p.   (S2376)

Die Schenke Am See
S solo,4strings cmplt ed DOBLINGER
08 811 s.p., sc DOBLINGER 08 812
s.p.   (S2377)

Gesange Nach P. Sturmbusch *Op.10,
CCU
solo,pno DOBLINGER 08 601 s.p.
(S2378)
Lieder Nach R. Capri *Op.40, CCU
solo,pno DOBLINGER 08 602 s.p.
(S2379)

SIEGL, OTTO (cont'd.)

Vier Lieder *CC4U
med-high solo,pno DOBLINGER 08 603
$1.75   (S2380)

Wald-Sonate *Op.123, sac,sonata
S solo,strings BOHM rental (S2381)

Zwei Gesange *CC2U
solo,pno KRENN 1.58 s.p.   (S2382)

SIEGMEISTER, ELIE (1909-   )
Lonely Star
solo,pno PEER $.85   (S2383)

Madam To You
solo,pno PETERS 66512 s.p. (S2384)

Strange Funeral In Braddock, The
med solo,pno PRESSER $1.25 (S2385)

SIEH' MEIN HERZ ERSCHLIESSET SICH see
Saint-Saens, Camille, Mon Coeur
S'ouvre A Ta Voix

SIEHE, DES HERREN AUGE SIEHET AUF DIE,
SO IHN FURCHTEN see Rosenmuller,
Johann

SIEHE MEIN ELEND, HERR SIEH' MEINE
QUALEN see Saint-Saens, Camille,
Vois Ma Misere, Helas!

SIEHE, MEIN FURSPRECHER IST IM HIMMEL
see Schutz, Heinrich

SIEHE, WIE FEIN UND LIEBLICH IST ES see
Bach, Johann Christoph

SIEHE, WIE FEIN UND LIEBLICH IST'S see
Vierdanck, Johann

SIEHE, WIE HERRLICH! see Tucapsky,
Antonin, Hele, Jak Nadherne

SIELUT see Kuula, Toivo

SIEMPRE A UNA MUJER BESE see Lehar,
Franz, Gern Hab' Ich Die Frau'n
Gekusst

SIEMPRE QUE SUENO LAS PLAYAS see
Halffter, Rodolfo

SIEPI D'AUTUNNO see Pratella, Francesco
Balilla

SIEPRAWSKI, PAWEL
Justus Germinavit *sac,CCU,mot
S solo,vln,cont sc HANSSLER s.p.
(S2386)

SIESTA see Guastavino, Carlos

SIESTA see Lessard, John Ayres

SIESTA see Quaratino, Pascual

SIESTE see Honegger, Arthur

SIETE CANCIONCILLAS EN ESTILO POPULAR Y
SERRANILLA see Lamote de Grignon,
Ricard

SIETE CANCIONES ESPANOLES see Tal,
Marjo

SIETE CANCIONES POPULARES ESPANOLAS see
Falla, Manuel de

SIETE CANCIONES POPULARES ESPANOLAS see
Falla, Manuel de

SIETE PIU BELLA see Cimara, Pietro

SIEULLE, J.
Reve D'amour
high solo,pno/inst DURAND s.p.
(S2387)
Veillee De Noel
S solo,pno DURAND s.p.   (S2388)
[Fr] solo,acap oct DURAND s.p.
(S2389)

SIFFLEZ, MERLES, SIFFLEZ see
Bourguignon, Francis de

SIFLER, PAUL J.
Birds' Courting Song
med solo,pno GALAXY   (S2390)

Black Is The Color Of My True Love's
Hair
solo,pno FREDONIA $2.00   (S2391)

Child's Prayer, A
med solo,pno/org GRAY   (S2392)

De Profundis *sac
Bar/B solo,pno BELWIN $1.50 (S2393)

Four Songs For Soprano *Op.2, CC4U
S solo,pno,fl/vln sc,cmplt ed
FREDONIA $6.00   (S2394)

SIFLER, PAUL J. (cont'd.)

Fragments From The Song Of Songs
*Op.29, CCU, Bibl
S solo, orch FREDONIA voc sc $4.50,
sc $40.00, ipr   (S2395)

Invocation *Op.4
med solo, pno FREDONIA $2.50 (S2396)

Lord Is My Shepherd, The
high solo, pno/org GRAY   (S2397)
med solo, pno/org GRAY   (S2398)

Prayer For Evening, A
med solo, pno/org FREDONIA $2.00
(S2399)

Shall I Compare Thee To A Summer's
Day?
high solo, pno FREDONIA $2.00
(S2400)

Songs Of The Nativity *Op.13a, CCU,
Xmas
med solo, org, perc GRAY   (S2401)

Songs Of The Rose Of Sharon *Op.6,
CCU, Bibl/song cycle
S solo, pno/orch BOTE   (S2402)

Sonnets Of Shakespeare *Op.12, CCU
FREDONIA high solo, pno/orch voc sc
$6.50, ipr; med solo, pno voc sc
$6.50   (S2403)

Stopping By Woods
med solo, pno GALAXY   (S2404)

Three Poems Of Holly Beye *Op.15,
CC3U
med solo, pno GALAXY   (S2405)

Wilderness Journal *Op.41
Bar/B solo, org, orch FREDONIA voc sc
$17.00, study sc $7.50, ipr
(S2406)

SIGH see Finzi, Gerald

SIGH NO MORE LADIES see Adrian, Walter

SIGH NO MORE, LADIES see Bush, Geoffrey

SIGH NO MORE, LADIES see Castelnuovo-
Tedesco, Mario

SIGH NO MORE, LADIES see Plumstead,
Mary

SIGH NO MORE, LADIES see Thomson,
Virgil

SIGNES VISA see Norman, Ludvig

SIGNOR NE PRINCIPE IO LO VORREI see
Verdi, Giuseppe

SIGNORA see Platamone, Stefano

SIGNORE, ASCOLTA! see Puccini, Giacomo

SIGNORINA VUOL see Kalman, Emerich

SIGNS OF THE ZODIAC see Pinkham, Daniel

SIGTENHORST-MEYER, BERNHARD VAN DEN
(1888-1953)
Ach! Eenig Eeuwig Een *Op.21, No.4
see Vijf Geestelijke Liederen Van
Jan Luyken

Ach Neen, Ach Neen *Op.21, No.1
see Vijf Geestelijke Liederen Van
Jan Luyken

Bij Den Tempel
high solo, pno ALSBACH s.p.
contains: De Beelden En De
Gamelan, Op.3, No.1; De Boro-
Boedoer, Op.3, No.3; 'T
Jongetje, Op.3, No.2   (S2407)

Claere *Op.15, No.5
see Veltdeuntjes

De Beelden En De Gamelan *Op.3, No.1
see Bij Den Tempel

De Boro-Boedoer *Op.3, No.3
see Bij Den Tempel

De Nare Schaduw *Op.21, No.5
see Vijf Geestelijke Liederen Van
Jan Luyken

De Pisangblaren *Op.6, No.3
see Stemmingen

Den Hoogen Hemel *Op.37, No.2
see Vier Geestelijke Liederen Uit
Jezus En De Ziel

Doode Steden
high solo, pno ALSBACH s.p.
contains: Harderwijk, Op.10, No.2;
Hoorn, Op.10, No.1   (S2408)

SIGTENHORST-MEYER, BERNHARD VAN DEN
(cont'd.)

Eerrijckjen *Op.15, No.4
see Veltdeuntjes

Fluisteringen *Op.5, CC3U
med solo, pno ALSBACH s.p.   (S2409)

Gelijk Een Waterdrop *Op.37, No.3
see Vier Geestelijke Liederen Uit
Jezus En De Ziel

Haesjen *Op.15, No.1
see Veltdeuntjes

Harderwijk *Op.10, No.2
see Doode Steden

Het Naardermeer
high solo/med solo, pno ALSBACH s.p.
(S2410)

Hoorn *Op.10, No.1
see Doode Steden

Ick Meende Oock De Gotheyt Woonde
Verre *Op.21, No.2
see Vijf Geestelijke Liederen Van
Jan Luyken

Ick Sagh De Schoonheyt *Op.37, No.1
see Vier Geestelijke Liederen Uit
Jezus En De Ziel

Liederen Van De Nijl
S solo, fl/ob ALSBACH s.p.
contains: Machmoed, Op.44, No.2;
'T Bijbeluur, Op.44, No.3;
Zonneweelde, Op.44, No.1 (S2411)

Lofzangen *Op.35, sac, CC4U
[Dut/Eng] S solo, pno/org ALSBACH
s.p.   (S2412)

Maanlicht *Op.6, No.2
see Stemmingen

Machmoed *Op.44, No.2
see Liederen Van De Nijl

Morgen In Den Tenger *Op.6, No.1
see Stemmingen

O Diepste Liefde *Op.37, No.4
see Vier Geestelijke Liederen Uit
Jezus En De Ziel

Oneyndig Goed *Op.21, No.3
see Vijf Geestelijke Liederen Van
Jan Luyken

Stemmingen
med solo, pno ALSBACH s.p.
contains: De Pisangblaren, Op.6,
No.3; Maanlicht, Op.6, No.2;
Morgen In Den Tenger, Op.6, No.1
(S2413)

Swaentjen *Op.15, No.3
see Veltdeuntjes

'T Bijbeluur *Op.44, No.3
see Liederen Van De Nijl

'T Jongetje *Op.3, No.2
see Bij Den Tempel

Valckenoochje *Op.15, No.2
see Veltdeuntjes

Veltdeuntjes
med solo, pno ALSBACH s.p.
contains: Claere, Op.15, No.5;
Eerrijckjen, Op.15, No.4;
Haesjen, Op.15, No.1; Swaentjen,
Op.15, No.3; Valckenoochje,
Op.15, No.2   (S2414)

Vier Geestelijke Liederen Uit Jezus
En De Ziel *sac
high solo, pno ALSBACH s.p.
contains: Den Hoogen Hemel,
Op.37, No.2; Gelijk Een
Waterdrop, Op.37, No.3; Ick Sagh
De Schoonheyt, Op.37, No.1; O
Diepste Liefde, Op.37, No.4
(S2415)

Vijf Geestelijke Liederen Van Jan
Luyken *sac
[Dut/Eng] high solo, pno/org ALSBACH
s.p.
contains: Ach! Eenig Eeuwig Een,
Op.21, No.4; Ach Neen, Ach Neen,
Op.21, No.1; De Nare Schaduw,
Op.21, No.5; Ick Meende Oock De
Gotheyt Woonde Verre, Op.21,
No.2; Oneyndig Goed, Op.21, No.3
(S2416)

Zonneweelde *Op.44, No.1
see Liederen Van De Nijl

SIGVARDS VISOR see Schaar, Aina

SIINTAA METSA see Sonninen, Ahti

SIJ HEEFT MET MIJ DEN ZOT GESCHEERT see
Moulaert, Raymond

SIKTA, SIKTA, GULLKORN see Peterson-
Berger, (Olof) Wilhelm

S'IL AVAIT SU see Durand, Jacques

S'IL EST UN CHARMANT GAZON see Franck,
Cesar

S'IL EST UN CHARMANT GAZON see Saint-
Saens, Camille

SILBEN see Clementi, Aldo

SILCHER
Loreley
low solo, pno (C maj) ALLANS s.p.
(S2417)
high solo, pno (D maj) ALLANS s.p.
(S2418)

SILCHER, FRIEDRICH (1789-1860)
Siebenundzwanzig Sologesange Und
Gesangsvariationen *CC27U
(Dahmen, Hermann Josef) solo, pno
(med) NAGELS EN 1218 s.p. (S2419)

SILENCE see Aubert, Louis-Francois-
Marie

SILENCE see Rhene-Baton

SILENCE INEFFABLE DE L'HEURE see Widor,
Charles-Marie

SILENCES see Ultan, Lloyd

SILENT COURTSHIP see Bennett, Sir
William Sterndale

SILENT CRANE *Scot
solo, pno (contains also: Seabird,
Flying Hither) PATERSON s.p. see
from Hebridean Songs, Vol. IV
(S2420)

SILENT DEVOTION see Wyner, Yehudi

SILENT MOON see Warren, Elinor Remick

SILENT MUSIC see Turner, J.G.

SILENT NIGHT
high solo&low solo, pno ASHDOWN s.p.
(S2421)
(Palmer) med solo, pno PAXTON P2250
s.p.   (S2422)

SILENT NIGHT see Gruber, Franz Xaver,
Stille Nacht, Heil'ge Nacht

SILENT NIGHT, THE see Rimsky-Korsakov,
Nikolai

SILENT NIGHT, HOLY NIGHT see Gruber,
Franz Xaver, Stille Nacht, Heil'ge
Nacht

SILENT NOON see Cone, Edward T.

SILENT NOON see Vaughan Williams, Ralph

SILENT O'MOYLE see Hughes, Herbert

SILENT, O'MOYLE! BE THE ROAR OF THY
WATER *Ir
(Moore) med solo, pno (G min) WILLIS
$.50   (S2423)

SILENT PARTNER *sac, gospel
solo, pno ABER.GRP. $1.50   (S2424)

SILENT POOL, THE see Sharpe, Evelyn

SILENT STARS see Niles

SILENT STRINGS see Bantock, Granville

SILENT TOWN, THE see Sibelius, Jean,
Die Stilla Stadt

SILENT WORSHIP see Handel, George
Frideric, Mon Lo Diro Col Labbro

SILENZIO see Baldacci, Giov. Bruna

SILENZIO! ZITTI LA! see Bach, Johann
Sebastian, Schweigt Stille,
Plaudert Nicht

SILETE VENTI see Handel, George
Frideric

SILHOUETTE see Bernstein, Leonard

SILHOUETTE see Wissmer, Pierre

SILHOUETTE ANGLAISE see Berger, Rod.

SILHOUETTES see Lora, Antonio

SILKESKO OVER GYLDEN LAEST! see
Nielsen, Carl

SILLOIN LAULAN see Kilpinen, Yrio

SILLOIN MINA ITKIN see Melartin, Erkki

S'ILS GAGNENT BATAILLE see Gaubert, Philippe

SILVA
Beside Still Waters *sac
solo,pno STAMPS 7257-SN $1.00
(S2425)

SILVER see Berkeley, Lennox

SILVER see Gibbs, Cecil Armstrong

SILVER see Greenhill, Harold

SILVER see Koch, Johannes H.E.

SILVER see Redman, Reginald

SILVER see Weigl, Vally

SILVER BIRCH, THE see Thiman, Eric Harding

SILVER, MARK (1892-1965)
Prayer For The Day Of Judgment, A
*sac,Jew
[Heb/Eng] solo,org/orch SAC.MUS.PR.
406 (S2426)

SILVER RAIN see Owens, Robert

SILVER RHINE see Hutchison, William M.

SILVER RING, THE see Chaminade, Cecile

SILVER SWAN, THE see Rorem, Ned

SILVER SWAN, THE see Thiman, Eric Harding

SILVER TON'D TRUMPET, THE see Arne, Michael

SILVERMAN, FAYE-ELLEN
In Shadow
S solo,clar,gtr sc SEESAW $3.00
(S2427)

SILVESTER, FREDERICK C.
Jesu, The Very Thought
ABar soli,pno (D maj) LESLIE 7901
(S2428)
Spirit Of God
solo,pno (E flat maj) LESLIE 7041
$1.00 (S2429)

SIM SHOLOM see Piket, Frederick

SIMCUS, BRIAN
Ave Maria *sac
[Lat] solo,pno RICORDI-ARG BA 7367
s.p. (S2430)

SIMEK, MIROSLAV (1891-1967)
Narodni Pisne Z Horicka *CCU
med solo,pno CZECH s.p. (S2431)

SIMENI CHACHOSOM see Reznick, Hyman

SIMENI CHACHOTAM see Helfman, Max

SIMEON see Cornelius, Peter

SIMEONE
Grandma's Thanksgiving
solo,pno SHAWNEE IA 31 $1.00
(S2432)

SIMILA, ARPO
Kakonen Se Kukkuu
see Sex Suomalaista Kansanlauluua

Kannel
see Sex Suomalaista Kansanlauluua

Kotimaani Ompi Suomi
see Sex Suomalaista Kansanlauluua

Nasijarven Rannalla
see Sex Suomalaista Kansanlauluua

Perakorvan Jukka
see Sex Suomalaista Kansanlauluua

Sex Suomalaista Kansanlauluua
solo,pno FAZER W 1852 s.p.
contains: Kakonen Se Kukkuu;
Kannel; Kotimaani Ompi Suomi;
Nasijarven Rannalla; Perakorvan
Jukka; Tuku Tuku Lampaitani
(S2433)

Tuku Tuku Lampaitani
see Sex Suomalaista Kansanlauluua

SIMILITUDE see Weigl, Karl, Ein Gleiches

SIMILITUDINE see Gandino, Adolfo

SIMMA, AND FRAN BLAA FJARDAR see
Sibelius, Jean, Souda, Souda Sinisorsa

SIMON
Three Goethe Songs *CC3U
[Ger] Bar solo,horn,harp,timp sc
LIENAU R54 s.p., ipa (S2434)

SIMON FRAN CYRENE see Stenlund, Bertil O.

SIMON, HERMANN
Herr, Den Ich Tief Im Herzen Trage
*sac
S/T solo,pno (D min) LIENAU HOS 186
s.p. (S2435)
A/Bar solo,pno (A min) LIENAU
HOS 188 s.p. (S2436)
Mez solo,pno (C min) LIENAU HOS 187
s.p. (S2437)

SIMON, J.
Zes Liederen *CC6U
solo,pno BROEKMANS 219 s.p. (S2438)

SIMONIS, JEAN-MARIE (1931-)
Trois Lagu Dolanan *Op.20,No.1, CC3U
S solo,perc CBDM s.p. (S2439)

SIMONS, NETTY
Diverse Settings
solo,fl,ob,clar,bsn,perc,vibra,
2vln,vla,vcl,bvl sc AM.COMP.AL.
$12.10, ipa (S2440)

Three Songs *CC3U
Mez solo,pno AM.COMP.AL. $4.95
(S2441)
Trialogue No. 1
ABar soli,vla sc AM.COMP.AL. $4.40
(S2442)
Trialogue No. 2: Myselves Grieve
ABar soli,vla sc AM.COMP.AL. $5.50
(S2443)
Trialogue No. 3: Now, Say Nay
MezBar soli,vla sc AM.COMP.AL.
$3.85 (S2444)

SIMPLE AVEU see Thome, Francis

SIMPLE DAY, A see Blank, Allan

SIMPLE GIFTS see Copland, Aaron

SIMPLE ROMANCE see Filipucci, Edm.

SIMPLE SONG, A see Bernstein, Leonard

SIMPLESSE see Strimer, Joseph

SIMPSON, DONALD
Blows The Wind
solo,pno CRAMER (S2445)

SIMPSON, NELLIE
Beat Of The Drum
low solo,pno (F maj) CRAMER (S2446)
high solo,pno (G maj) CRAMER
(S2447)
Your England And Mine
low solo,pno (C maj) ASHDOWN s.p.
(S2448)
med solo,pno (D maj) ASHDOWN s.p.
(S2449)
med-high solo,pno (E flat maj)
ASHDOWN s.p. (S2450)
high solo,pno (F maj) ASHDOWN s.p.
(S2451)

SIMS
He's Already Done *sac
(Martin) solo,pno LILLENAS
SM-912: SN $1.00 (S2452)

Unseen Hand, The *sac
solo,pno BENSON S8074-S $1.00
(S2453)

SIMS, EZRA (1928-)
Cantata Three, 1961 *cant
Mez solo,castanets sc AM.COMP.AL.
$22.00 (S2454)

Chanson D'Aventure *Eng
T solo,hpsd/pno sc AM.COMP.AL.
$3.57 (S2455)

Charles Guiteau
Bar solo,pno AM.COMP.AL. $3.30
(S2456)

In Memoriam Alice Hawthorne
narrator&TBar soli,4clar,2marimba,
horn sc AM.COMP.AL. $27.50
(S2457)

Madame Mim's Work Song
med solo,pno sc AM.COMP.AL. $1.00
(S2458)

Sieben Spencer Lieder *CC7U
high solo,pno AM.COMP.AL. $3.85
(S2459)

Streets Of Laredo, The
Bar solo,pno AM.COMP.AL. $.27
(S2460)

Three Songs (from Cantata 1960) CC3U
T solo,2fl,2ob,2clar,2bsn,2horn,
2trp,glock,vibra,pno,strings sc
AM.COMP.AL. $20.35 (S2461)

SIN PODER CON ESTA LENGUA see Jurafsky, Abraham

SINA see Jarnefelt, Armas, Du

SINCE FIRST I MET THEE see Rubinstein, Anton

SINCE FIRST I MET THEE see Watson, Michael

SINCE I FIRST BEHELD HIM see Schumann, Robert (Alexander)

SINCE I LEFT YOU see Ketting, Otto

SINCE JESUS PASSED BY see Gaither

SINCE THAT FAIR DAY see Charpentier, Gustave, Depuis Le Jour

SINCE THE MOMENT I MET JESUS see Baker, Richard

SINCE THIS WORLD IS ONLY PASSING see Rosenmuller, Johann

SINCE YOU AWAKENED LOVE see Lucke, K.

SINCERITY see Clarke, Emile

SINCLAIR, J.
Johnny Sands
solo,pno LEONARD-ENG (S2462)

SIND ALLE HERBSTES STERNE AUFGEGLUHT
see Kilpinen, Yrio, On Kaikki
Syksyn Tahdet Syttyneet

SINDING, CHRISTIAN (1856-1941)
Cradle Song, A *Op.126,No.1
AMP $.50 (S2463)

Perles
solo,pno ENOCH s.p. see also CHANTS
DU NORD (S2464)

So Many Dreams Are Over *see Viel
Traume

Viel Traume
"So Many Dreams Are Over" [Eng/Ger/
Fr] med solo,pno FORBERG F31 s.p.
(S2465)

SINE NOMINE see Raxach, Enrique

SINFONIA CANTATA see Malipiero, Riccardo

SINFONIA NO. 1 see Castiglioni, Niccolo

SINFONIA NO. I CON LIRICA SUL POEMA DI
T.S. ELIOT "EYES THAT LAST I SAW IN
TEARS" see Christou, Jani

SINFONIE DES FRAUENLEBENS see Pander, O. v.

SING *sac,gospel
solo,pno ABER.GRP. $1.50 (S2466)

SING A NEW SONG *sac,CCU
solo,kbd SINGSPIR $1.95 (S2467)

SING A SONG OF PURPLE HEATHER see
Braun, Charles

SING A SONG OF SIXPENCE see Malotte,
Albert Hay

SING A SONGS OF WONDERS *CC14U
(Leroy; Livingston) solo,pno GENERAL
415 $2.50 (S2468)

SING AGAIN see Gounod, Charles Francois

SING AND WORSHIP *sac,CC20L
(Stickles, William) BOSTON high solo,
pno/org $3.50; low solo,pno/org
$3.50 contains works by: Sullivan;
Neidlinger; Mendelssohn; Gounod;
Handel; Franck; Allitsen and others
(S2469)

SING AT THE WHEEL
(Roberton, Hugh S.) solo,pno (F min)
ROBERTON 2755 s.p. see also Songs
Of The Isles (S2470)

SING LITTLE BIRD see Thompson

SING LULLABY FOR THE YEAR see Marzials,
Theo

SING ME A CHANTEY WITH A YO-HEAVE-HO
see Wellesley, Grant

SING ME THE SONGS OF YESTERDAY see
Rose, Hugh Duncan

SING ME TO SLEEP see Greene

SING MEIN HERZE see Kilpinen, Yrio,
Sjung Mitt Hjarta

SING MIR, MORENA! *CCU,folk,Fr/Span
(Zsciesche) solo,gtr SCHOTTS 4841
s.p. (S2471)

SING MY SOUL see Schirrmann, Charles

SING NO SAD SONGS FOR ME see Mitchell, Raymond [Earle]

SING O MY LOVE see Naylor, Bernard

SING, O YE SAINTS see Schutz, Heinrich

SING ON, GOD'S CHILDREN, SING ON *sac, gospel
  solo,pno ABER.GRP. $1.50   (S2472)

SING ON THERE IN THE SWAMP see Hindemith, Paul

SING OUT THE GLORY see Lister, Mosie

SING! SING! BIRD ON THE WING see Nutting, Godfrey

SING, SING, EV'RYONE SING! see Wild, Eric

SING, SMILE, SLUMBER see Gounod, Charles Francois, Serenade

SING SONG FOLKSONGS *CCU,folk
  (Andersen, Sven Jorn) solo,pno
  HANSEN-DEN 29190 s.p.   (S2473)

SING SONGS OF PRAISE see Handel, George Frideric

SING, SOUL OF MINE see Allen, Robert E.

SING SWEET BIRD see Ganz, Wilhelm

SING TO GOD THE LORD see Buxtehude, Dietrich, Cantate Domino Canticum Novum

SING TO THE LORD A NEW SONG see Buxtehude, Dietrich

SING TRIOS, VOL. 1 *sac,CCUL
  3 soli,pno WORD 10050 $1.00   (S2474)

SING TRIOS, VOL. 2 *sac,CCUL
  3 soli,pno WORD 10051 $1.00   (S2475)

SING UNTO THE LORD *sac,CCU
  (Agay, Denes) solo,pno MUSIC 040022
  $3.95   (S2476)

SING UNTO THE LORD A NEW SONG see Couperin (le Grand), Francois

SING UNTO THE LORD, ALL THE EARTH see Herbert, Muriel

SING UNTO THE LORD, VOL. 1 *sac,CCU
  (Davis; Loring) solo,pno FISCHER,C
  O 3634   (S2477)

SING UNTO THE LORD, VOL. 2 *sac,CCU
  (Davis; Loring) solo,pno FISCHER,C
  O 3635   (S2478)

SING YOUR PRAISES see Rogers

SINGABLE SONGS *CCU
  (Mason, M.) PRESSER high solo,pno
  $3.00; med solo,pno $4.95   (S2479)

SINGAROUND FOLKSONGS, BK. 1 *CCU
  (Hyman, Joy; Rice, Jennifer) solo,gtr
  GALLIARD 2.2028.7 $2.75   (S2480)

SINGAROUND FOLKSONGS, BK. 2 *CCU
  (Hyman, Joy; Rice, Jennifer) solo,gtr
  GALAXY 2.2029.7 $2.75   (S2481)

SINGE, CHRISTENHEIT! *sac,CCU
  (Rothenberg, F.S.; Thurmair, G.)
  solo,org CHRIS 50579 s.p.   (S2482)

SINGE, MEIN SCHONES MADCHEN see Kilpinen, Yrio, Soitapas

SINGE-, SPIEL- UND GENERALBASSUBUNGEN see Telemann, Georg Philipp

SINGENDES, KLINGENDES OSTERREICH *CCU
  (Hammerschmied, G.) solo,gtr
  DOBLINGER 05 923 s.p.   (S2483)

SINGER see Head, Michael (Dewar)

SINGER, THE see Maxwell

SINGER AND THE ACCOMPANIST, THE *CCU
  [Russ] solo,pno MEZ KNIGA 113 s.p.
  arias and scenes from operas
                              (S2484)

SINGER IN THE WOOD, THE see Bantock, Granville

SINGER, W.
  He Ain't Coming Here To Die No More
  solo,pno (B flat maj) BOOSEY $1.50
                              (S2485)

SINGET DEM HERRN see Buxtehude, Dietrich

SINGET DEM HERRN see Micheelsen, Hans-Friedrich

SINGET DEM HERRN EIN NEUES LIED see Becker-Foss, Jurgen

SINGET DEM HERRN EIN NEUES LIED see Schutz, Heinrich

SINGET, PREISET GOTT MIT FREUDEN see Schilling, Hans Ludwig

SINGING BABY TO SLEEP see Weinberg, M.

SINGING FAMILY OF THE CUMBERLANDS
  *CC40U,folk,US
  (Ritchie, Jean) solo,pno OAK 000088
  $3.95   (S2486)

SINGING ISRAEL, THE see Freudenthal, Josef

SINGING JOHN MATHEWS FAMILY, THE *sac,
  CC10UL
  solo,pno LILLENAS MB-318 $1.95 (S2487)

SINGING LESSON see Squire, W.H.

SINGING ROAD, VOL. 1 *CCU
  (Ward) med-high solo,pno FISCHER,C
  O 2794; med-low solo,pno FISCHER,C
  O 2793   (S2488)

SINGING ROAD, VOL. 2 *CCU
  (Ward) med-high solo,pno FISCHER,C
  O 3516; med-low solo,pno FISCHER,C
  O 3517   (S2489)

SINGING ROAD, VOL. 3 *CCU
  (Ward) med-high solo,pno FISCHER,C
  O 3652; med-low solo,pno FISCHER,C
  O 3653   (S2490)

SINGSANG see Wimberger, Gerhard

SINGT MEIN SCHATZ WIE EIN FINK see Jentsch, Walter

SINIGAGLIA, LEONE (1868-1944)
  Canto Dell'ospite *Op.37,No.1
  solo,2fl,3ob,2clar,2bsn,4horn,2trp,
  timp,strings CARISH s.p.   (S2491)

  Cecilia *Op.40,No.6
  solo,2fl,2ob,2clar,2bsn,2horn,2trp,
  timp,triangle CARISH s.p.   (S2492)

  Donna Bianca *Op.40,No.31
  solo,2fl,2ob,2clar,2bsn,3horn,2trp,
  timp CARISH s.p.   (S2493)

  I Falciatori *Op.40,No.13
  solo,2fl,ob,2clar,2bsn,2horn CARISH
  s.p.   (S2494)

  Il Cacciatore Del Bosco *Op.40,No.2
  2 soli,orch CARISH s.p.   (S2495)

  Il Figlio Del Re *Op.40,No.35
  solo,2fl,2ob,2clar,2bsn,2horn,2trp,
  timp,strings CARISH s.p.   (S2496)

  Il Grillo E La Formica *Op.40,No.5
  solo,2fl,ob,2clar,2bsn,horn,timp,
  perc CARISH s.p.   (S2497)

  Il Maritino *Op.40,No.3
  2 female soli,2fl,ob,2clar,2bsn,
  2horn,trp,timp,triangle,4strings
  CARISH s.p.   (S2498)

  Il Pellegrino Di S. Giacomo *Op.40,
  No.30
  solo,fl,ob,clar,bsn,horn,triangle
  CARISH s.p.   (S2499)

  Il Rifugio *Op.37,No.3
  solo,2fl,2ob,2clar,2bsn,2horn,
  strings CARISH s.p.   (S2500)

  Invito Respinto *Op.40,No.27
  solo,strings CARISH s.p.   (S2501)
  SA soli,ob,clar,bsn,horn CARISH
  s.p.   (S2502)

  La Pastora Fedele *Op.40,No.1, sac
  2 female soli,2fl,ob,2clar,2horn,
  timp,triangle,4strings CARISH
  s.p.   (S2503)

  La Quiete Meridiana Nell'Alpe
  *Op.37,No.2
  solo,2fl,3ob,2clar,2bsn,2horn,harp,
  triangle CARISH s.p.   (S2504)

  La Rana E Il Rospo *Op.40,No.16
  solo,strings CARISH s.p.   (S2505)

  La Rondine Importuna *Op.40,No.15
  solo,fl,ob,2clar,bsn,harp,triangle
  CARISH s.p.   (S2506)

  La Sposa Di Beltramo *Op.40,No.33
  solo,2fl,2ob,2clar,2bsn,4horn,2trp,
  timp,perc CARISH s.p.   (S2507)

SINIGAGLIA, LEONE (cont'd.)

  La Tregua *Op.23,No.3
  solo,2fl,3ob,2clar,2bsn,4horn,2trp,
  timp,harp,pno CARISH s.p.   (S2508)

  L'Aria Del Molino *Op.40,No.10
  2 female soli,2fl,ob,2clar,2bsn,
  2horn,timp,4strings CARISH s.p.
                              (S2509)

  Le Nozze Dell'alpigiano *Op.40,No.28
  solo,2fl,2ob,2clar,2bsn,2horn,timp,
  triangle CARISH s.p.   (S2510)

  L'Uccellino Del Bosco *Op.40,No.19
  solo,strings CARISH s.p.   (S2511)

  Maria Catlina *Op.40,No.11
  solo,2fl,2ob,2clar,2bsn,2horn,2trp,
  timp,strings CARISH s.p.   (S2512)

  Ninna Nanna Di Gesu Bambino *Op.40,
  No.32, sac
  SSS soli,2fl,2clar,horn,harp,
  triangle CARISH s.p.   (S2513)

  Novara La Bella *Op.40,No.36
  solo,2fl,2ob,2clar,2bsn,2horn,2trp,
  timp,perc CARISH s.p.   (S2514)

  Serenata *Op.23,No.2
  solo,2fl,ob,2clar,2bsn,timp,
  triangle CARISH s.p.   (S2515)

  Triste Sera *Op.23,No.1
  solo,fl,2ob,2clar,2bsn,4horn,timp
  CARISH s.p.   (S2516)

  Ventiquatro Vecchie Canzoni Populari
  Del Piemonte *Op.40,No.2a, CC24U
  (Rognoni) [It] S/T solo,pno
  RICORDI-ENG 129037 s.p.   (S2517)

SINK SONG see Blyton, Carey

SINNE see Linko, Ernst (Fredrik)

SINNER MAN see Boatwright, Howard

SINNER PLEASE DOAN LET DIS HARVES' PASS
  *spir
  (Burleigh, H. T.) med solo,pno BELWIN
  $1.50   (S2518)

SINOPOLI, GIUSEPPE (1946-   )
  Opus Scir
  Mez solo,15inst sc ZERBONI 7367
  s.p.   (S2519)

  Sunyata
  S solo,5strings ZERBONI 7194 rental
                              (S2520)

SINTERKLAAS see Loots, Ph.

SINTERKLAAS-POLKA see Loots, Ph.

SINUN SILMAS JA MINUN SILMAT see Melartin, Erkki

SINUS see Beurle, Jurgen

SINZHEIMER, MAX (1894-   )
  Blessed Are Those Who Fear The Lord
  (Psalm 128) sac,Marriage
  CONCORDIA 97-4893 $1.25   (S2521)

  Psalm 128 *see Blessed Are Those Who
  Fear The Lord

S'IO TI VEDESSI see Toni, Alceo

SIOHAN, ROBERT (1894-   )
  Chemin De Ronde
  solo,pno DURAND s.p.   (S2522)

  Sur La Devise "Non Ce Que Je Pense"
  solo,pno DURAND s.p.   (S2523)

SIONA see Bornefeld, Helmut

SIPILA, EERO (1918-1972)
  Schein Und Sein *song cycle
  "Ulkokuori Ja Todellisuus" solo,pno
  FAZER W 3784 s.p.   (S2524)

  Ulkokuori Ja Todellisuus *see Schein
  Und Sein

SIPKOVA RUZE see Kricka, Jaroslav

SIPPAN see Sibelius, Jean

SIR, COME DOWN BEFORE MY CHILD DIES see Bender, Jan

SIRMIONE see Trunk, Richard

SIROTEK see Dvorak, Antonin

SIRS TO YOUR TOAST see Bizet, Georges

S'IST ALLES DUNKEL see Muller, Rudolf

SISTE, SUPERBE FRAGOR see Pergolesi, Giovanni Battista

SISTER AWAKE! see Innes, Gertrude

SISTER JANE see Diamond, David

SISU ET YERUSHALAIM
solo,pno OR-TAV $.50 (S2525)

SITTIN' IN THE CORNFIELDS see Harding,
Phyllis

SITTIN' THINKIN' see Fisher, H.

SITTING BY THE WINDOW see Desmond,
Charles

SIVIC, PAVLE (1908-)
Concentricities *see Sosredja

Incantations *see Zaklinjanja

Iveri
"Splinters" solo,pno DRUSTVO
DSS 237 rental (S2526)

Od Praga Do Praga *song cycle
"Von Schwelle Zu Schwelle" Mez
solo,strings sc DRUSTVO DSS 488
rental (S2527)

Pet Pesmi *CC5U
Mez solo,pno DRUSTVO DSS 154 rental
(S2528)

Pet Pesmi *CC5U
S solo,pno DRUSTVO DSS 152 rental
(S2529)

Rdeci Oblaki *song cycle
"Red Clouds" SB soli,2fl,2ob,2clar,
bsn,contrabsn,4horn,3trp,3trom,
tuba,timp,perc,harp,strings
rental sc DRUSTVO DSS 484, voc sc
DRUSTVO DSS 83 (S2530)

Red Clouds *see Rdeci Oblaki

Sosredja
"Concentricities" solo,narrator,
2fl,pic,2ob,2clar,2bsn,4horn,
3trp,3trom,tuba,timp,perc,harp,
strings sc DRUSTVO DSS 486 rental
(S2531)

Splinters *see Iveri

Stiri Pesmi *CC4U
B solo,pno DRUSTVO DSS 156 rental
(S2532)

Stiri Pesmi Na Liriko Mateja Bora
*CC4U
solo,pno DRUSTVO DSS 153 rental
(S2533)

Tri Pesmi *CC3U
Bar solo,pno DRUSTVO DSS 155 rental
(S2534)

Tri Zenske Pesmi *CC3U
S solo,pno DRUSTVO DSS 157 rental
(S2535)

Von Schwelle Zu Praga *see Od
Praga Do Praga

Zaklinjanja
"Incantations" med solo,2fl,pic,
2ob,clar,bass clar,bsn,contrabsn,
4horn,2trp,3trom,tuba,timp,perc,
vibra,pno/cel,strings sc DRUSTVO
DSS 485 rental (S2536)

SIVRY, CH. DE
Chanson Mignarde
solo,acap ENOCH s.p. (S2537)
solo,pno ENOCH s.p. (S2538)

SIX BALLADES DE PAUL FORT see Leduc,
Jacques

SIX BLAKE SONGS see Butterley, Nigel

SIX CANTUS FIRMUS SETTINGS see Katz, E.

SIX CANZONETS see Graeff, J.G.

SIX CHAMBER DUETS see Monteverdi,
Claudio

SIX CHANSONS see DuBois, Pierre Max

SIX CHANSONS see Arma, Paul

SIX CHANSONS DE SAINTE THERESE D'AVILA
see Jacob, Dom Clement

SIX CHANSONS ENFANTINES see Nakada,
Yoshinao

SIX CHANSONS ET DIX CHANSONS, POEMES DE
JEAN CUTTAT see Binet, Jean

SIX CHANSONS, POEMES DE JEAN CUTTAT see
Binet, Jean

SIX CHANSONS POUR ENFANTS see
Defontaine, M.

SIX CHANSONS PROVENCALES see Dufresne,
C.

SIX CHANSONS VENDEENNES see Laurel, J.

SIX CHANTS EXOTIQUES see Gailhard,
Andre

SIX CHANTS POPULAIRES SLAVES see Bagge,
G.

SIX CHILDREN'S SONGS see Weigl, Karl

SIX CHILDREN'S SONGS see Arensky, Anton
Stepanovitch

SIX DESIGNS see Tanenbaum, Elias

SIX DUETS see Purcell, Henry

SIX DUOS see Franck, Cesar

SIX EARLY AMERICAN SPIRITUALS *CC6U,
spir,US
(Cowell, S. R.) med solo,3rec sc AMP
$.60 (S2539)

SIX ELIZABETHAN SONGS see Argento,
Dominick

SIX ENGLISH LYRICS see Williamson,
Malcolm

SIX FOLK SONGS *folk
(Algazi, L.) [Heb/Fr] med solo,pno
SALABERT-US $6.00 several with
Yiddish texts
contains: Efent, Rebetsin!; Hinne
Ma Tov!; Ismah'h Hatan Becala;
Lecoved Dem Heiligen Schabess;
Schur, Dodi!; Yome, Yome (S2540)

SIX FRENCH FOLKSONGS see Kolinski, M.

SIX HAIKU see Yttrehus, Rolv

SIX IRISH POEMS see Rorem, Ned

SIX ITALIAN ARIAS, VOL. I see Handel,
George Frideric

SIX ITALIAN ARIAS, VOL. II see Handel,
George Frideric

SIX ITALIAN CHAMBER DUETS see Handel,
George Frideric

SIX KOREAN FOLKSONGS see Bavicchi, John

SIX LIGHT HUMOROUS SONGS *CC6U
solo,pno CRAMER (S2541)

SIX LITTLE SONGS FOR SOMEBODY see
Howard, L.

SIX LOVE SONGS see Peeters, Flor

SIX MARITIME FOLKSONGS, SET 1 see
Bissell, Keith W.

SIX MARITIME FOLKSONGS, SET 2 see
Bissell, Keith W.

SIX MEHITABEL MAGPIES see Seamarks,
Colin

SIX MELODIES see Ropartz, Joseph Guy

SIX MELODIES see Gaubert, Philippe

SIX MELODIES see Tcherepnin, Alexander

SIX MELODIES see Duteil d'Ozanne, A.

SIX MELODIES see Poulenc, Francis

SIX MELODIES see Bosmans, Henriette

SIX MELODIES RELIGIEUSES see Beethoven,
Ludwig van

SIX MELODIES SUR DES POEMES SYMBOLISTES
see Sauguet, Henri

SIX NOCTURNES see Mozart, Wolfgang
Amadeus

SIX NURSERY TUNES see Fiske, R.

SIX OCCASIONAL SONGS see Orland, Henry

SIX PIECES FOR SOLO VOICE see Arma,
Paul

SIX POEMES ARABES see Aubert, Louis-
Francois-Marie

SIX POEMES DE JEAN COCTEAU see Jacob,
Dom Clement

SIX POEMES OF EIKO SADAMATSU see
Ogihara, Toshitsugu

SIX POEMS OF APOLLINAIRE see Honegger,
Arthur

SIX POEMS OF EMILY BRONTE, OP.63 see
Joubert, John

SIX POLISH CHRISTMAS CAROLS *sac,Xmas,
carol/folk,Pol
(Rebe, Louise C.) solo,pno SCHIRM.G
$.60
contains: Baby Jesus In A Manger;
Christ Is Born; Hear! Bethlehem;
In The Silence Of The Night;
Sleep, Little Jesus; Tell Us,
Wise Men (S2542)

SIX POPULAR VOCAL DUETS, BOOK I see
Newton, Ernest

SIX PROSES LYRIQUES see Pillois,
Jacques

SIX QUATRAINS VALAISANS see Orthel,
Leon

SIX REGIONAL CANADIAN FOLKSONGS *folk
(Blyton, Carey) solo,pno ROBERTON
72623 s.p.
contains: An Eskimo Lullaby;
Auction Block; Donkey Riding;
Kelligrews Soirree; Lukey's Boat;
Pull On The Oars (S2543)

SIX ROLAND HOLST-SONGS see Broekman,
Hans

SIX ROMANCES see Grieg, Edvard Hagerup

SIX RONDEAUX see Berger, Jean

SIX RUBAYYAT OF OMAR KHAYYAM see
Broder, T.

SIX SACRED SONGS see Purcell, Henry

SIX SELECT SONGS FROM THE JEWISH
FOLKLORE *CC6U,folk
(Kosakoff, Reuven) med solo/high
solo,pno TRANSCON. WJ 419 $2.00
Hebrew and Yiddish texts (S2544)

SIX SIGNIFICANT LANDSCAPES see Blank,
Allan

SIX SLAUERHOFF SONGS see Franken, Wim

SIX SOLO CANTATAS see Carissimi,
Giacomo

SIX SONGS [2] see Sibelius, Jean

SIX SONGS see Sibelius, Jean

SIX SONGS see Bacon, Ernst

SIX SONGS *see Sibelius, Jean,
Schwarze Rosen (S2545)

SIX SONGS see Tansman, Alexander

SIX SONGS see Beethoven, Ludwig van

SIX SONGS see Weigl, Karl

SIX SONGS see Franck, Cesar

SIX SONGS see Purcell, Henry

SIX SONGS see Grieg, Edvard Hagerup

SIX SONGS see Kilpinen, Yrio

SIX SONGS see Lewkovitch, Bernhard

SIX SONGS see Nielsen, Carl

SIX SONGS see Sibelius, Jean

SIX SONGS see Lidholm, Ingvar

SIX SONGS *see Fogelfangaren, "Der
Vogelsteller", Op.90,No.4; Hennes
Budskap, "Ihre Botschaft", Op.90,
No.2; Hvem Styrde Hit Din Vag?,
"Wer Hat Dich Hergefuhrt?", Op.90,
No.6; Norden, "Der Norden", Op.90,
No.1; Sommernatten, "Die
Sommernacht", Op.90,No.5 (S2546)

SIX SONGS see Jemnitz, S.

SIX SONGS see Mihaly, Andras

SIX SONGS see Ranki, Gyorgy

SIX SONGS see Sveinbjornsson,
Sveinbjorn

SIX SONGS (A.E.HOUSMAN) see Dukelsky,
Vladimir

SIX SONGS AFTER POEMS BY CLEMENS
BRENTANO see Strauss, Richard

SIX SONGS FOR BASS see Purcell, Henry

SIX SONGS FOR HIGH VOICE see Rorem, Ned

SIX SONGS FOR HIGH VOICE see Strauss,
Richard

SIX SONGS FOR HIGH VOICE see Mihaly,
Andras

SIX SONGS FOR MEDIUM VOICE see
Schumann, Robert (Alexander)

SIX SONGS FROM A SHROPSHIRE LAD see
Butterworth, George Sainton Kaye

SIX SONGS IN PROVENCAL see Ventadorn,
Bernart de

SIX SONGS OF THE NIGHT see Lees,
Benjamin

SIX SONGS ON POEMS BY O. J. BIERBAUM
see Weigl, Karl

SIX SONGS, VOL. I: OP. 40, NOS. 1-3 see
Pfitzner, Hans

SIX SONGS, VOL.II: OP. 40, NOS. 4-6 see
Pfitzner, Hans

SIX SONNETS DE MICHEL-ANGE see Jacob,
Dom Clement

SIX STANDARD ENGLISH SONGS *CC6U,Eng
(Newton, Ernest) ASHDOWN T&Bar/T&B
soli,pno s.p.; S&Mez/S&A soli,pno
s.p.   (S2547)

SIX STRINGS, THE see Cortes, Ramiro,
Las Seis Cuerdas

SIX SUFFOLK FOLK SONGS see Moeran,
Ernest J.

SIX VILLANELLES see Godard, Benjamin
Louis Paul

SIX VOCAL DUETS see Purcell, Henry

SIX VOCAL RHAPSODIES, VOL. I see
Maurat, Edmond

SIX VOCAL RHAPSODIES, VOL. II see
Maurat, Edmond

SIX VOCAL RHAPSODIES, VOL. III see
Maurat, Edmond

SIX YIDDISH ART SONGS see Weiner, Lazar

SIXT, JOHANN ABRAHAM (1757-1797)
Zwolf Lieder *CC12U
(Fischer) [Ger] BOTE $1.75 (S2548)

SIXTEEN SILLY SONGS FOR KIDS see Dale,
Mervyn

SIXTEEN SONGS see Lipovsek, Marijan

SIXTEEN TWO-PART SONGS see Mendelssohn-
Bartholdy, Felix

SIXTEENTH-CENTURY BICINIA: A COMPLETE
EDITION OF MUNICH, BAYERISCHE
STAATSBIBLIOTHEK, MUS. MS. 260
*CCU,16th cent
(Bellingham, Bruce; Evans, Edward G.,
Jr.) 2 soli,opt 2inst A-R ED s.p.
                             (S2549)

SIXTY-FIVE SONGS see Wolf, Hugo

SIXTY PATROITIC SONGS OF ALL NATIONS
*CCU
(Bantock, G.) med solo,pno PRESSER
$5.00   (S2550)

SIXTY-SEVEN SONGS see Beethoven, Ludwig
van

SIXTY-TWO MESOSTICS RE MERCE CUNNINGHAM
see Cage, John

SIXTY-TWO OUTRAGEOUS SONGS *CC62U,
folk,US
(Silverman, Jerry) solo,pno OAK
000049 $3.95   (S2551)

SIXTY-TWO SOUTHLAND SPIRITUALS *sac,
CC62U,spir
solo,pno WORD 15042 $1.25   (S2552)

SIZ NITO KAIN NECHTN see Wyner, Yehudi

SJALARNA see Kuula, Toivo, Sielut

SJALENS FRID see Norman, Ludvig

SJALENS LANGTAN
see Andliga Sanger, Heft 3

SJIRE KODESJ see Gokkes, S.

SJOBERG
Visions *see Balogh

SJOBERG, BIRGER
Den Forsta Gang Jag Sa Dig
solo,pno MUSIKK s.p.   (S2553)

SJOBERG, C.L.
Tonerna
high solo,pno GEHRMANS 761 s.p.
                             (S2554)
low solo,pno GEHRMANS 762 s.p.
                             (S2555)

SJOFARAREN VID MILAN see Wohlfart, Karl

SJOFARAREN VID MILAN see Palmgren,
Selim

SJOGREN, EMIL (1853-1918)
Aftonstjarnan
solo,pno LUNDQUIST s.p.   (S2556)

Bergmanden *Op.2,No.1
see Tre Sanger

Contrabandieren
low solo,pno GEHRMANS s.p. (S2557)

De Vare Elleve Svende
solo,pno GEHRMANS s.p.   (S2558)

Der Driver En Dug
high solo,pno GEHRMANS s.p. (S2559)
low solo,pno GEHRMANS s.p. (S2560)

Det Forste Mode
solo,pno LUNDQUIST s.p.   (S2561)

Din Rost
solo,pno LUNDQUIST s.p.   (S2562)

Dors, Chere Prunelle
solo,pno ENOCH s.p. see also CHANTS
DU NORD   (S2563)

Dryckesvisa
solo,pno LUNDQUIST s.p.   (S2564)

Du Schaust Mich An Mit Stummen Fragen
"Du Ser Pa Mig Med Hemlig Fraga"
low solo,pno LUNDQUIST s.p.
                             (S2565)
"Du Ser Pa Mig Med Hemlig Fraga"
high solo,pno LUNDQUIST s.p.
                             (S2566)
Du Ser Pa Mig Med Hemlig Fraga *see
Du Schaust Mich An Mit Stummen
Fragen

Du Sidder I Baaden Som Svommer
high solo,pno GEHRMANS s.p. (S2567)
med solo,pno GEHRMANS s.p. (S2568)

Elegie *Op.62
solo,pno LUNDQUIST s.p.   (S2569)

En Varvintervisa
solo,pno GEHRMANS s.p.   (S2570)

Ett Dromackord
solo,pno GEHRMANS s.p.   (S2571)

Falks Sang Ur Karlekens Komedi
low solo,pno GEHRMANS s.p. (S2572)
high solo,pno GEHRMANS s.p. (S2573)

Fyra Nya Sanger
solo,pno LUNDQUIST s.p.
contains: I Dodens Tysta
Tempelgardar; Och Inte Vill Jag
Sorja, Men Sorjer Anda; Saa
Standsed Og Der Den Blodets
Strom; Visa   (S2574)

Holder Du Av Mig
low solo,pno GEHRMANS s.p. (S2575)
high solo,pno GEHRMANS s.p. (S2576)

Hvil Over Verden, Du Dybe Fred
low solo,pno GEHRMANS s.p. (S2577)

I De Sidste Oijeblikke
solo,pno LUNDQUIST s.p.   (S2578)

I Dodens Tysta Tempelgardar
see Fyra Nya Sanger

I Dodens Tysta Templgardar
low solo,pno LUNDQUIST s.p. (S2579)
high solo,pno LUNDQUIST s.p.
                             (S2580)

I Drommen Du Ar Mig Nara
low solo,pno GEHRMANS s.p. (S2581)
med solo,pno GEHRMANS s.p. (S2582)
high solo,pno GEHRMANS s.p. (S2583)

I Seraljens Lustgard *Op.22,No.1
solo,pno LUNDQUIST s.p.   (S2584)

Ich Mochte Schweben
low solo,pno LUNDQUIST s.p. (S2585)

Jahrlang Mocht' Ich So Dich Halten
high solo,pno LUNDQUIST s.p.
                             (S2586)
low solo,pno LUNDQUIST s.p. (S2587)

Jeg Giver Mit Digt Til Vaaren
solo,pno LUNDQUIST s.p.   (S2588)

Jeg Ser For Mit Oje Som Det Fineste
Spind
med solo,pno GEHRMANS s.p. (S2589)

SJOGREN, EMIL (cont'd.)
Julens Alla Vackra Klockor Ringen
high solo,pno GEHRMANS s.p. (S2590)

Lad Vaaren Komme, Mens Den Vil
solo,pno GEHRMANS s.p.   (S2591)

Lilla Anna
solo,pno LUNDQUIST s.p.   (S2592)

Liten Knopp, Moders Hopp
solo,pno LUNDQUIST s.p.   (S2593)

Liten Prins I Vaggan
solo,pno GEHRMANS s.p.   (S2594)

Mjuka Sma Hander
solo,pno LUNDQUIST s.p.   (S2595)

O, Kom Med Mig I Stjarneglans!
2 soli,pno LUNDQUIST s.p.   (S2596)

Och Inte Vill Jag Sorja, Men Sorjer
Anda
see Fyra Nya Sanger

Offene Arme Und Pochende Brust
solo,pno LUNDQUIST s.p.   (S2597)

Og Jeg Vil Drage Fra Sydens Blommer
med solo,pno GEHRMANS s.p. (S2598)
high solo,pno GEHRMANS s.p. (S2599)

Og Kan Min Hu Du Ej Forstaae
high solo,pno GEHRMANS s.p. (S2600)

Panis Angelicus
solo,pno GEHRMANS s.p.   (S2601)

Prinsessen
solo,pno GEHRMANS s.p.   (S2602)

Ro, Ro Ogonsten
solo,pno LUNDQUIST s.p.   (S2603)

Romans *Op.2,No.2
see Tre Sanger

Saa Sod Var Sommernattens Blund
high solo,pno GEHRMANS s.p. (S2604)
low solo,pno GEHRMANS s.p. (S2605)

Saa Standsed Og Der Den Blodets Strom
see Fyra Nya Sanger

Sadant Ar Livet
solo,pno GEHRMANS s.p.   (S2606)

Sag Om All Naturen Har Sin Fagring
Mist
solo,pno LUNDQUIST s.p.   (S2607)

Samlade Sanger II *CCU
solo,pno GEHRMANS s.p. pap, cloth
                             (S2608)

Samlade Sanger III-IV *CCU
solo,pno GEHRMANS pap s.p., ea.,
cloth s.p., ea.   (S2609)

Se Glaset Ljusets Bana Ar
solo,pno GEHRMANS s.p.   (S2610)

Serenad *Op.2,No.3
see Tre Sanger

Sommarens Sista Ros "Se Blommande
Allena"
solo,pno LUNDQUIST s.p.   (S2611)

Sommaridyll
solo,pno LUNDQUIST s.p.   (S2612)

Sover Du Min Sjael
med solo,pno GEHRMANS s.p. (S2613)

Tag Emod Kransen
solo,pno LUNDQUIST s.p.   (S2614)

Tand Stjarnor
med solo,pno GEHRMANS s.p. (S2615)

Tonerna
high solo,pno LUNDQUIST s.p.
                             (S2616)
low solo,pno LUNDQUIST s.p. (S2617)

Tre Efterlamnade Sanger *CC3U
solo,pno LUNDQUIST s.p.   (S2618)

Tre Sanger
B solo,pno LUNDQUIST s.p.
contains: Bergmanden, Op.2,No.1;
Romans, Op.2,No.2; Serenad,
Op.2,No.3   (S2619)

Vedt Kredser Du, Min Vilde Fugl
med solo,pno GEHRMANS s.p. (S2620)

Visa
see Fyra Nya Sanger

Vor Meinem Auge
high solo,pno LUNDQUIST s.p.
                             (S2621)
low solo,pno LUNDQUIST s.p. (S2622)

SJOGREN, EMIL (cont'd.)

Wie Soll Ich's Bergen
high solo,pno LUNDQUIST s.p.
(S2623)

low solo,pno LUNDQUIST s.p. (S2624)

SJOKONUNGEN see Myrberg, August M.

SJOMANSFLICKAN see Korling, August

SJOMANSSANG see Nordqvist, Gustaf

SJU DIKTER see Alfven, Hugo

SJU KROKANN-SONGAR see Olsen, Sparre

SJU LAULUA UNKARILAISIIN KANSANRUNOIHIN
I see Sonninen, Ahti

SJU LAULUA UNKARILAISIIN KANSANRUNOIHIN
II see Sonninen, Ahti

SJU ROSOR OCH SJU ELDAR see Peterson-
Berger, (Olof) Wilhelm

SJU SANGER see Sibelius, Jean

SJU SANGER TILL DIKTER AV RUNEBERG see
Sibelius, Jean

SJU SVENSKA FOLKVISOR, HEFT 1-2 *CC14L
(Torlind) solo,pno LUNDQUIST s.p.,
ea. (S2625)

SJU VISOR see Hallnass, Gun

SJUNG FOR MIG! see Soderman, (Johan)
August

SJUNG MIG EN SANG see Thompson

SJUNG MITT HJARTA see Kilpinen, Yrio

SJUNG MITT HJARTA see Nordqvist, Gustaf

SJUNG OM STUDENTENS LYCKLIGA DAG see
Gustave de Suede, (Prince)

SJUNG, SJUNG! see Soderman, (Johan)
August

SJUNG, SJUNG, DET AR SOMMARDAG
(Korling, Felix) solo,pno GEHRMANS
s.p. (S2626)

SJUNG, SJUNG DU UNDERDARA SANG see
Josephson, Jacob Axel

SJUNGANDE SJOFOLK OCH LANDKRABBOR see
Nilsson

SKADA, SKADA HUR DET VARAS see Skold

SKAL BLOMSTERNE DA VISNE? see Nielsen,
Carl

SKAMT OCH ALLVAR see Pacius, Fredrik

SKA'VI LEKA see Merikanto, Oskar,
Leikitaanko

SKEPPARVISA see Korling

SKERJANC, LUCIJAN MARIJA (1900-   )
Samospevi I *CCU
solo,pno DRUSTVO DSS 306 rental
(S2627)

Samospevi II *CCU
solo,pno DRUSTVO DSS 314 rental
(S2628)

Samospevi III *CCU
solo,pno DRUSTVO DSS 368 rental
(S2629)

Samospevi IV *CCU
solo,pno DRUSTVO DSS 71 rental
(S2630)

Samospevi V *CCU
solo,pno DRUSTVO DSS 72 rental
(S2631)

Samospevi VI *CCU
solo,pno DRUSTVO DSS 119 rental
(S2632)

Samospevi VII *CCU
solo,pno DRUSTVO DSS 233 rental
(S2633)

Samospevi VIII *CCU
solo,pno DRUSTVO DSS 240 rental
(S2634)

Samospevi IX *CCU
solo,pno DRUSTVO DSS 257 rental
(S2635)

Sest Mladinskih Pesmi *CC6U
1-2 soli,pno DRZAVNA rental (S2636)

SKETCH see Smith, Melville

SKI-HEIL see Schwanda, H.

SKILLINGS, OTIS
Bond Of Love, The *sac
solo,pno LILLENAS SM-631: RN $1.00
(S2637)

Born Again *sac
solo,pno LILLENAS SM-483: RN $1.00
(S2638)

SKILLINGS, OTIS (cont'd.)

Come Along With Me *sac
solo,pno LILLENAS SM-468: RN $1.00
(S2639)

Great To Be Alive *sac
solo,pno LILLENAS SM-603: RN $1.00
(S2640)

He Is The Way, He Is The Truth, He Is
The Life *sac
solo,pno LILLENAS SM-836: SN $1.00
(S2641)

solo,pno LILLENAS SM-487: RN $1.00
(S2642)

I've Got A Reason To Sing *sac
solo,pno LILLENAS SM-605: RN $1.00
(S2643)

solo,pno LILLENAS SM-493: SN $1.00
(S2644)

Listen *sac
solo,pno LILLENAS SM-479: SN $1.00
(S2645)

Lord Above, The *sac
solo,pno LILLENAS SM-481: RN $1.00
(S2646)

Love Is A Man *sac
solo,pno LILLENAS SM-629: RN $1.00
(S2647)

Now Walk With God *sac
solo,pno LILLENAS SM-469: RN $1.00
(S2648)

Power To Choose, The *sac
solo,pno LILLENAS SM-606: RN $1.00
(S2649)

Reach Out And Touch *sac
solo,pno LILLENAS SM-630: RN $1.00
(S2650)

You Can Experience *sac
solo,pno LILLENAS SM-601: RN $1.00
(S2651)

SKINNVENGBREV see Lie, Harald

SKIPPER, THE see Jude, William Herbert

SKJAERAASENSANGER see Braein, Edvard
Fliflet

SKJUTSGOSSEN PA HEMVAGEN see Lindblad,
Adolf Fredrik

SKOGEN BLANAR see Sonninen, Ahti,
Siintaa Metsa

SKOGEN SOVER see Alfven, Hugo

SKOGEN SOVER see Valentin, Karl

SKOLAUDE, WALTER
Lieder *CCU
solo,pno KRENN 1.20 s.p. (S2652)

SKOLD
Aftonbon
solo,pno LUNDQUIST s.p. (S2653)

Dodspolka
solo,pno LUNDQUIST s.p. see from
Fyra Dikter (S2654)

Fyra Dikter *see Dodspolka; Jag Vill
Ge Min Hjartans Lille Broder;
Miserere; Skada, Skada Hur Det
Varas (S2655)

Jag Vill Ge Min Hjartans Lille Broder
solo,pno LUNDQUIST s.p. see from
Fyra Dikter (S2656)

Kom, Jul, Med Klara, Vita Ljus
solo,pno LUNDQUIST s.p. (S2657)

Miserere
solo,pno LUNDQUIST s.p. see from
Fyra Dikter (S2658)

Skada, Skada Hur Det Varas
solo,pno LUNDQUIST s.p. see from
Fyra Dikter (S2659)

Tre Visor *CC3U
solo,pno,lute LUNDQUIST s.p.
(S2660)

SKOLD, SVEN
Inte Ar Jad Ensam
high solo,pno GEHRMANS s.p. (S2661)

Tuna Ting
low solo,pno GEHRMANS s.p. (S2662)

SKON GERTRUD see Schlottmann, Louis

SKONSTA ROS FORDROJ DITT FALL see
Soderman, (Johan) August

SKORZENY, FRITZ (1900-1965)
Drei Lieder *CC3U
solo,pno DOBLINGER 08 615 s.p.
(S2663)

Kinderlieder Nach Texten Von Chr.
Morgenstern *CCU
med-high solo,pno DOBLINGER 08 616
$3.50 (S2664)

Sopran-Album *CC16U
S solo,pno DOBLINGER 08 501 $5.00
contains works by: Bach;

SKORZENY, FRITZ (cont'd.)

Beethoven; Gounod; Haydn; Mozart;
Weber; Verdi (S2665)

Tenor-Album *CC16U
T solo,pno DOBLINGER 08 502 $6.75
contains works by: Adam;
Beethoven; Donizetti; Flotow;
Verdi; Wagner and others (S2666)

Vier Lieder I *CC4U
med-low solo,pno DOBLINGER 08 617
$2.00 (S2667)

Vier Lieder II *CC4U
med-high solo,pno DOBLINGER 08 618
$4.25 (S2668)

Vier Lieder (Lenau) *CC4U
med solo,pno DOBLINGER 08 619 $2.75
(S2669)

Weihnachten *Xmas
solo,pno DOBLINGER 08 606 s.p.
(S2670)

SKREDDARSVEINEN see Dorumsgaard, Arne

SKULL, THE see Burt, [Francis]

SKY see Hayashi, H.

SKY ABOVE THE ROOF see Vaughan
Williams, Ralph

SKY ROSES see Holland, Kenneth

SKYE BOAT SONG see Mac Leod, A.C.

SKYLARK SINGS see Portnoj

SKYMNING see Jarnefelt, Armas

SLAAP, KINDEKEN, SLAAP see Moulaert,
Raymond

SLAAPLIEDEREN VOOR GROTE MENSEN see
Pluister, Simon

SLAAPLIEDJE UIT DEN OORLOGSTIJD see
Mulder, Ernest W.

SLADKOVY PISNE, SES. 1-2 see Jindrich,
Jindrich

SLATER
For I Am His *sac
SB soli,pno BOSTON $1.75 (S2671)

Little Lord Jesus *sac,Xmas
solo,pno HARRIS $.75 (S2672)

SLATER, ARTHUR
It's In My Heart *sac
solo,pno GOSPEL 05 TM 0426 $1.00
(S2673)

SLATER, DAVID D.
Echoes In The Orchard
low solo,pno (B flat maj) ASHDOWN
s.p. (S2674)
high solo,pno (D maj) ASHDOWN s.p.
(S2675)
med solo,pno (C maj) ASHDOWN s.p.
(S2676)

I Wonder If Ever The Rose
high solo,pno (E maj) ASHDOWN s.p.
(S2677)
med solo,pno (D maj) ASHDOWN s.p.
(S2678)
low solo,pno (C maj) ASHDOWN s.p.
(S2679)

May-Day Morn
low solo,orch (C maj) ASHDOWN s.p.,
ipr (S2680)
med-high solo,orch (E flat maj)
ASHDOWN s.p., ipr (S2681)
med solo,orch (D maj) ASHDOWN s.p.,
ipr (S2682)
high solo,orch (F maj) ASHDOWN
s.p., ipr (S2683)

SLATTERVISA see Nordqvist, Gustaf

SLAUGHTER, HAZEL
Henry And Hazel Slaughter-Songbook
(composed with Slaughter, Henry)
*sac,CC12UL
solo,pno BENSON BO470 $2.50 (S2684)

Henry And Hazel Slaughter-Songbook,
Vol. II (composed with Slaughter,
Henry) *sac,CCUL
solo,pno BENSON BO471 $2.50 (S2685)

SLAUGHTER, HENRY
Faith And Prayer *sac
solo,pno SINGSPIR 7074 $1.00
(S2686)

God Is The Answer *sac
solo,pno SINGSPIR 7073 $1.00
(S2687)

Henry And Hazel Slaughter-Songbook
*see Slaughter, Hazel

Henry And Hazel Slaughter-Songbook,
Vol. II *see Slaughter, Hazel

SLAUGHTER, HENRY (cont'd.)

If The Lord Isn't Walking By My Side
*sac
solo,pno SINGSPIR 7085-SN $1.00
(S2688)

Keep On Holding To Those Nail-Scarred
Hands *sac
solo,pno SINGSPIR 7081-SN $1.00
(S2689)

Place Of Peace, A *sac
solo,pno SINGSPIR 7076 $.25 (S2690)

SLAUGHTER, WALTER A. (1860-1908)
Dear Home-Land, The
high solo,pno (G maj) CRAMER
(S2691)

med-high solo,pno (F maj) CRAMER
(S2692)

med solo,pno (D maj) CRAMER (S2693)
low solo,pno (C maj) CRAMER (S2694)

SLAVE SONGS OF THE UNITED STATES
*CC136U,folk,US
(Schlein, Irving) solo,pno/gtr OAK
000089 $5.95   (S2695)

SLAVEN see Rubinstein, Anton

SLAVICKY, KLEMENT (1910-   )
Ej, Srdenko Moje I *CCU
solo,pno SUPRAPHON s.p.   (S2696)

Vonicka *song cycle
high solo,pno SUPRAPHON s.p.
(S2697)

Zpev Rodne Zeme *CCU
solo,pno SUPRAPHON s.p.   (S2698)

SLAVNE SOVETSKE HISTORICKE A VEZENSKE A
REVOLUCNI PISNE *CCU
(Urban, J.; Hronek, M.) solo,pno
PANTON 1511 s.p.   (S2699)

SLAVNI PEVCI *CCU
[Czech/Ger] T solo,pno SUPRAPHON s.p.
(S2700)

SLEEP see Gurney, Ivor

SLEEP see Heseltine, Philip

SLEEP see Joubert, John

SLEEP see Parry, Charles Hubert
Hastings

SLEEP see Pope, H. Lefevre

SLEEP see Stravinsky, Igor

SLEEP see Walton

SLEEP AND THE ROSES see Tate, Arthur

SLEEP DEAR LOVE see Debussy, Claude,
Aimons-Nous Et Dormons

SLEEP LITTLE BABY see Mengelberg,
Rudolf

SLEEP, LITTLE BABY see Rappaport, Eda

SLEEP, LITTLE JESUS
see Six Polish Christmas Carols

SLEEP LITTLE JESUS see Anderson,
William H.

SLEEP MY CHILD see Somervell, Arthur

SLEEP, MY LADDIE SLEEP see Browning, M.

SLEEP NOW, DREAM NOW see Fontrier,
Gabriel

SLEEP OF THE INFANT JESUS, THE *sac,
carol,Fr
(Grimes, Travis) med solo,fl,org,vcl
oct CONCORDIA 98-3005 $.25 (S2701)

SLEEP SOFTLY HERE see Baiss, E.

SLEEP THAT FLITS ON BABY'S EYES, THE
see Carpenter, John Alden

SLEEP VOYAGE, THE see Sharpe, Evelyn

SLEEP WAYWARD THOUGHTS see Russell,
Welford

SLEEP, YAH-TOE-CHEE, LITTLE ONE
(O'Hara) med solo,pno (E flat maj,
American Indian) WILLIS $.60
(S2702)

SLEEPING BEAUTY, THE see Thomson,
Virgil, La Belle En Dormant

SLEEPWALKING SCENE see Verdi, Giuseppe

SLEETH, NATALIE
Christmas Is A Feeling *Xmas
solo,kbd,opt fl/vln HINSHAW HMV100
$1.00   (S2703)

SLEIGH, THE see Kountz, Richard

SLENDER BOY see Somervell, Arthur

SLEZAK, PAVEL (1941-   )
Tri Pisne *CC3U
high female solo&low female solo,
pno,cym,sax,bvl CZECH s.p.
(S2704)

SLEZSKE LIDOVE PISNE see Salich, Milan

SLEZSKE PISNE see Hurnik, Ilja

SLEZSKE PISNE see Jirasek, Ivo

SLEZSKE PISNE NA SLOVA P. BEZRUCE see
Cernik, Josef

SLOCKNAD STJARNAS SKEN NAR HIT see
Hallnas, Hilding

SLOGEDAL, BJARNE
How Glorious Is Thy Name *see Hvor
Herlig Klinger Ditt Navn

Hvor Herlig Klinger Ditt Navn
"How Glorious Is Thy Name" solo,
pno/org NORSK 8747 s.p.   (S2705)

SLOHY LASKY see Meier, Jaroslav

SLONOV, YU.
Operettas Series: Arias, Songs And
Duets From Operettas *CCU
[Russ] 1-2 soli,pno MEZ KNIGA 112
s.p.   (S2706)

SLOTH, THE see Kubik, Gail

SLOVACKA PISEN see Kovarovic, Karel

SLOVENSKE LUDOVE PIESNE see Moyzes,
Alexander

SLOVENSKE NARODNE see Ravnik, Janko

SLOVENSKE NARODNE PIESNE I-V see
Schneider-Trnavsky, Mikulas

SLOVENSKE SPEVY see Jiranek, A.

SLOW, SLOW, FRESH FOUNT see Bassett,
Leslie

SLOW, SLOW, FRESH FOUNT see Overton,
Hall

SLOW, SLOW, FRESH FOUNT see Pinkham,
Daniel

SLOWAKISCHE GESANGE see Novak, V.

SLUIMERLIEDJE see Zagwijn, Henri

SLUKA, LUBOS (1928-   )
Language Of Flowers *song cycle
Mez/Bar solo,pno PANTON s.p.
(S2707)

SLUMBER see Birch, Robert Fairfax

SLUMBER, O HOLY JESU see Wood, Dale

SLUMBER ON see Bach, Johann Sebastian

SLUMBER SONG see Bohun, Lyle de

SLUMBER SONG see Britten, Benjamin

SLUMBER SONG see Gretchaninov,
Alexander Tikhonovitch

SLUMBER SONG see Schumann, Robert
(Alexander)

SLUMBER SONG see Williams, Meirion

SLUMBER SONG OF THE CHILD JESUS see
Buesser, Le Sommeil De L'enfant
Jesus

SLUMBER SONG OF THE MADONNA see Head,
Michael (Dewar)

SLUMBER SONGS see d'Albert, Eugene
Francis Charles

SLUMRA, BOLJA BLA see Korling, August

SLUMRA NU, LITEN MIN see Petri, H.

SLUNECKA, SES. 1-2 see Konvalinka,
Milos

SLZY A USEMEVY see Schneider-Trnavsky,
Mikulas

SMALL CHRISTMAS TREE see Head, Michael
(Dewar)

SMALL, SOLOMON
Zion, Zion Heilige, Bleibst Shoin
*Jew
solo,pno KAMMEN 483 $1.00 see also
JEWISH THEATRE SONGS, VOL. 1
(S2708)

SMART see Berger, Rod.

SMART, HENRY THOMAS (1813-1879)
Hark! The Goat Bells Ringing
2 soli,pno LEONARD-ENG   (S2709)

Lord Is My Shepherd, The (Psalm 23)
sac
SA soli,pno SCHIRM.G $1.00 (S2710)
high solo&low solo,pno (A flat maj)
FISCHER,C V 2202   (S2711)

Psalm 23 *see Lord Is My Shepherd,
The

SMASH AND GRAB WORLD see Smith, Tedd

SMEDEN see Alnaes, Eyvind

SMEDERSLIED see Hullebroeck, Em.

SMETANA, BEDRICH (1824-1884)
Abendlieder
[Czech/Ger/Eng] solo,pno SUPRAPHON
s.p.   (S2712)

Arie Des Blazenka (from Das
Geheimnis)
[Czech/Ger] solo,pno SUPRAPHON s.p.
(S2713)
[Czech/Eng] solo,pno SUPRAPHON s.p.
(S2714)

Arie Des Dalibor
[Czech/Ger] solo,pno SUPRAPHON s.p.
(S2715)
[Czech/Eng] solo,pno SUPRAPHON s.p.
(S2716)

Lerchenlied (from Der Kuss)
[Czech/Eng] solo,pno SUPRAPHON s.p.
(S2717)
[Czech/Ger] solo,pno SUPRAPHON s.p.
(S2718)

Lieder *CCU
[Czech/Ger] solo,pno SUPRAPHON s.p.
(S2719)

Wiegenlieder (from Der Kuss)
[Czech/Eng] solo,pno SUPRAPHON s.p.
(S2720)
[Czech/Ger] solo,pno SUPRAPHON s.p.
(S2721)

SMIDJE-SMEE see Zagwijn, Henri

SMILE OF SPRING, THE see Fletcher,
Percy Eastman

SMILIN' KITTY O'DAY see Torrence, E.

SMILIN' THROUGH see Penn

SMILING AGAIN see Spitalny, H.L.

SMILING HOURS, THE see Handel, George
Frideric

SMIT, H.J.
Doe Je Mee *CCU
solo,acap BROEKMANS 697 s.p.
(S2722)

Zing Maar Blij *CCU
solo,acap BROEKMANS 784 s.p.
(S2723)

SMIT, LEO (1921-   )
Four Motets *mot
med solo,2fl&vln/2S rec&T rec study
sc BROUDE BR. 20 $2.00
contains: O Katherine, Dearest; O
Mother, Tell Me How To Die; O
Venus, You And Your Son; Wake
Up, My Love   (S2724)

Kleine Prelude Van Ravel
A solo,pno DONEMUS s.p.   (S2725)

La Mort
SA soli,pno DONEMUS s.p.
contains: La Mort Des Amants; La
Mort Des Artistes; La Mort Des
Pauvres   (S2726)

La Mort Des Amants
see La Mort

La Mort Des Artistes
see La Mort

La Mort Des Pauvres
see La Mort

O Katherine, Dearest
see Four Motets

O Mother, Tell Me How To Die
see Four Motets

O Venus, You And Your Son
see Four Motets

Wake Up, My Love
see Four Motets

SMIT SIBINGA, TH. H. (1899-1958)
Aan De Sneeuw
S solo,pno DONEMUS s.p.   (S2727)

SMIT SIBINGA, TH. H. (cont'd.)

Enfants-Poetes *CCU
S/Mez solo,pno DONEMUS s.p. (S2728)

Grootmoeders Rust
S solo,pno DONEMUS s.p. (S2729)

SMITH
And Still I Smile *see Gerald

Happy Side Of Life, The *sac
solo,pno LILLENAS SM-486: RN $1.00
(S2730)

I Never Knew Love *sac
solo,pno BENSON S6091-S $1.00 (S2731)

I Saw A Man *sac
solo,pno BENSON S6108-S $1.00 (S2732)

I Want The World To Know *sac
solo,pno LILLENAS SM-622: RN $1.00 (S2733)

Love Lifted Me *see Rowe

Not My Will *sac
solo,pno BENSON S7196-S $1.00 (S2734)

Only I (composed with Spear)
solo,pno CHAPLET $.85 (S2735)

Part-Time Christian *sac
med solo,pno LORENZ $1.00 (S2736)

To Love Is To Give *sac
med solo,pno LORENZ $1.00 (S2737)

When I Need Him *sac
solo,pno LILLENAS SM-482: RN $1.00
(S2738)

You Laughed Me Out Of Your Heart
*see Gerald

SMITH, ALFRED B.
Think *sac
solo,pno WORD S-309 (S2739)

SMITH, ALFRED M.
Surely Goodness And Mercy *see
Peterson, John W.

SMITH, C. STEPHEN
What A Difference Jesus Makes *sac
solo,pno WORD S-401 (S2740)

What A Morning That Will Be *sac
solo,pno WORD S-400 (S2741)

SMITH, ELEANOR
Quest
low solo,pno (A flat maj) WILLIS
$.50 (S2742)

SMITH, F.S. BREVILLE
Harlequin's Rose
solo,pno (B flat maj) LEONARD-ENG
(S2743)

SMITH, HALE
Beyond The Rim Of Day
high solo,pno MARKS $1.50 (S2744)

Valley Wind, The *song cycle
med solo,pno MARKS $2.00 (S2745)

SMITH, HERBERT ARNOLD (1887-   )
Come Lovely Sleep
solo,pno CRAMER $.95 (S2746)

For All Of These (We Thank Thee,
Lord)
solo,pno CRAMER $.95 (S2747)

Mother Writes A Prayer
solo,pno CRAMER (S2748)

To An Old Cottage
solo,pno CRAMER $.70 (S2749)

SMITH, J.
Vocal Selections From "Daisy" *see
Harding, B.

SMITH, LELAND (1925-   )
Three Pacifist Songs *CC3U
med solo,pno AM.COMP.AL. $4.40
(S2750)

SMITH, MELVILLE
Lost
see Three Songs

Sketch
see Three Songs

Teamster's Farewell, A
see Three Songs

Three Songs
solo,pno NEW VALLEY $2.50
contains: Lost; Sketch;
Teamster's Farewell, A (S2751)

SMITH, ROY LAMONT
My Homeland, Tennessee
med solo,pno (D maj) WILLIS $.40
(S2752)

SMITH, TAB
I Believe Jesus *sac
solo,pno WORD S-418 (S2753)

I Never Knew Love *sac
solo,pno WORD S-399 (S2754)

SMITH, TEDD
My Jesus I Love Thee *sac
solo,pno HOPE 483 $.75 (S2755)

Smash And Grab World *sac,CCU
solo,pno WORD 37506 $2.95 (S2756)

Where's Christmas *sac,Xmas
solo,pno WORD S-260 (S2757)

SMITH, THE see Brahms, Johannes, Der
Schmeid

SMITH-BRINDLE, REGINALD (1917-   )
Genesis Dream
[Eng] med-low female solo,fl,2clar,
trp,3perc,pno PETERS 7103 rental
(S2758)

SMOKING ROOM see Arundale, Claude

SMOLANOFF, MICHAEL
Day Of Calm Sea
S solo,fl,clar,bsn,harp,vln,vla,
vcl,perc sc SEESAW $5.00 (S2759)

Four Haiku Songs *CC4U
S solo,pno sc SEESAW $1.00 (S2760)

From The Orient
S solo,fl,harp,electronic tape
SEESAW (S2761)

Hear O Israel *sac
B solo,SATB,strings/pno sc SEESAW
$4.00 (S2762)

Heralds Of Green Youth, The
A solo,4fl,English horn,harp,timp,
2perc sc SEESAW $7.00 (S2763)

World Today Is Wild, The
B solo,fl,ob,clar,bsn,2horn,2trp,
trom,tuba,3perc sc SEESAW $10.00
(S2764)

SMOLDON, W.L.
Irish Love-Song, An
solo,pno (G maj) ASHDOWN s.p.
(S2765)

Moon Magic
solo,pno ASHDOWN s.p. (S2766)

SMRT MAJKE JUGOVICA see Komadina, Vojin

SMUGGLERS SONGS see Kernochan, Marshall

SMUTKY see Kunc, Jan

SNAIL, THE see Sibelius, Jean, Alvan
Och Snigeln

SNAIL SONG see Whitehead, Percy A.

SNAKE see Rorem, Ned

SNARE, SIGURD
Dagen Svalnar
"Paiva Kallistuu Jo Iltaan" see Fem
Sanger

En Onskan
"Toivomus" see Fem Sanger

En Strimma Hav
"Vain Kaista Merta" see Fem Sanger

Fem Sanger
solo,pno FAZER W 3294 s.p.
contains: Dagen Svalnar, "Paiva
Kallistuu Jo Iltaan"; En
Onskan, "Toivomus"; En Strimma
Hav, "Vain Kaista Merta"; I
Fonstret Star Ett Ljus, "On
Ikkunassa Liekka"; Svart Eller
Vitt, "Mustaa Vai Valkoista"
(S2767)

I Fonstret Star Ett Ljus
"On Ikkunassa Liekka" see Fem
Sanger

Mustaa Vai Valkoista *see Svart
Eller Vitt

On Ikkunassa Liekka *see I Fonstret
Star Ett Ljus

Paiva Kallistuu Jo Iltaan *see Dagen
Svalnar

Svart Eller Vitt
"Mustaa Vai Valkoista" see Fem
Sanger

Toivomus *see En Onskan

Vain Kaista Merta *see En Strimma
Hav

SNART SYNKER SOLEN see Korling, August

SNEEUW see Bijvanck, Henk

SNEEUWKLOKJES see Pijper, Willem

SNEEUWKLOKJES LUIEN DEN WINTER UIT see
Adriessen, Willem

SNEEUWSTORM see Mulder, Herman

SNEEUWVLOKJES see Clercq, R. de

SNEEWKLOKJES see Nieland, H.

SNEGOUROTCHKA JE SUIS HEUREUSE! see
Rimsky-Korsakov, Nikolai

SNEHAH see Kopelent, Marek

SNIDER
I've Got The Corners Turned Down
*sac
solo,pno LILLENAS SM-919: SN $1.00
(S2768)

SNJOTITTLINGUR see Stefansson, Fjolnir

SNOBLOMMOR see Kilpinen, Yrio

SNODGRASS, LOUISE
London Girl
solo,pno CRAMER (S2769)

When Peter Jackson Preached
high solo,pno (E min) WILLIS $.60
(S2770)
med solo,pno (D min) WILLIS $.60
(S2771)

SNOW, THE see Edwards, Clara

SNOW IS FALLING, THE see Cimara,
Pietro, Fiocca La Neve

SNOW MAN, THE see Hekster, Walter

SNOW TOWARD EVENING see Jenni, Donald

SNOWDROP, THE see Craxton, Harold

SNOWDUNES see Swanson, Howard

SNOWFALL see Birch, Robert Fairfax

SNOWFLAKES AT MY WINDOW see Cadman,
Charles Wakefield

SNOWIE THE SNOWMAN see Dale, Mervyn

SNOWY-BREASTED PEARL, THE see
Somervell, Arthur

SNY I, II, III see Figus-Bystry,
Villiam

SO! see Tirindelli, Pier Adolfo

SO AHNLICH WIE see Hamel, Peter Michael

SO AL LABBRO MIO NON CREDI see Mozart,
Wolfgang Amadeus

SO ANCH'IO LA VIRTU MAGICA see
Donizetti, Gaetano

SO APPEARS THY NATAL DAY see Bach,
Johann Sebastian

SO DEEP TO ME see Butcher, Orval

SO GREAT SALVATION see Roe, Gloria
[Ann]

SO HORE DOCH, MEINE GEMEINDE see
Schutz, Heinrich, Attendite Popule
Meus Legem Meam

SO IHR MICH VON GANZEN HERZEN see
Mendelssohn-Bartholdy, Felix

SO IS MY BELOVED see Olmstead, Clarence

SO LANG HAB ICH GESCHMACHTET see
Mozart, Wolfgang Amadeus

SO LEB' ICH NOCH see Cornelius, Peter

SO LONG MARY see Cohan, George Michael

SO MANY DREAMS ARE OVER see Sinding,
Christian, Viel Traume

SO MANY HOURS, SO MANY FANCIES see
Rachmaninoff, Sergey Vassilievitch

SO NACKT SIND DEINE AUGEN see Bergman,
Erik

SO NIMM DENN MEINE HANDE *sac
Mez solo,pno (E flat maj) LIENAU
HOS 159 s.p. (S2772)

SO RUHIG GEH' ICH MEINEN PFAD see Uhl,
Alfred

SO SEI'S - HERZ, DER LIEBE SUSSER BORN
see Handel, George Frideric

SO SEND I YOU see Peterson, John W.

SO SINGT MAN IN WIEN! *CC32U
(Steinbrecher) solo,pno UNIVER. 10940
$4.75   (S2773)

SO SWEET LOVE SEEMED see Milford, Robin

SO TANZE see Kilpinen, Yrio, Sa Dansa

SO TANZEN DIE ENGEL see Schoenberg,
Arnold

SO TEACH US, LORD see Bach, Johann
Sebastian

SO VENITE A CONSIGLIO see Scarlatti,
Alessandro

SO WAHR DIE SONNE SCHEINET see Jansen,
F. Gustav

SO WE'LL GO NO MORE A-ROVING see Cory,
George

SO WE'LL GO NO MORE A-ROVING see
Schirmer, Rudolph [E.]

SO WE'LL GO NO MORE A-ROVING see
Walker, George

SO WHITE, SO SOFT, SO SWEET IS SHE see
Delius, Frederick

SO WIE DIE TAUBE see Handel, George
Frideric

SO WISSE, DASS IN ALLEN ELEMENTEN see
Lortzing, (Gustav) Albert

SO YOU WANT PEACE see Swanson, Joan

SO ZWOI WIE WIR ZWOI see Rubin, W.

SOBOKU-NA-KOTO see Kumaki, Mamoru

SOBRE LAS OLAS see Delage, Maurice

SODERBERG
Valkullans Visa
(Svennung, G.) solo,pno LUNDQUIST
s.p.   (S2774)

SODERLUNDH, LILLE BROR
Flickan Fran Drommarans By
solo,pno,opt gtr GEHRMANS s.p.
                                  (S2775)
Men Kunde Vi Bara Fa Vind Igen
solo,pno,opt gtr GEHRMANS s.p.
                                  (S2776)

SODERMAN
Brollopsmarsch
2 soli,pno LUNDQUIST s.p.   (S2777)

Heidenroslein
solo,pno LUNDQUIST s.p.   (S2778)

I Sommarnatt
solo,pno LUNDQUIST s.p.   (S2779)

Im Wunderschonen Monat Mai
solo,pno LUNDQUIST s.p.   (S2780)

Langtan
solo,pno LUNDQUIST s.p.   (S2781)

Solveigs Vuggevise
solo,pno LUNDQUIST s.p.   (S2782)

Varningen
solo,pno LUNDQUIST s.p.   (S2783)

SODERMAN, (JOHAN) AUGUST (1832-1876)
Dans Ropte Felen
solo,pno GEHRMANS 680 s.p. (S2784)

Den Hvide, Rode Rose
solo,pno GEHRMANS 683 s.p. (S2785)

Digte Och Sange
solo,pno GEHRMANS s.p.   (S2786)

En Varnatt Frosten Foll
solo,pno GEHRMANS 693 s.p. (S2787)

Finge An En Gang
solo,pno GEHRMANS 692 s.p. contains
also: I Varens Underskona Maj
                                  (S2788)
Fjarran Ovan Stjarnor Alla *sac
SMez soli,pno GEHRMANS s.p. (S2789)

Flicka Med Den Roda Munnen
solo,pno GEHRMANS s.p.   (S2790)

Hymn "Fjarran, Ack Fjarran"
solo,pno GEHRMANS 699 s.p. (S2791)

I Varens Underskona Maj
see Soderman, (Johan) August, Finge
An En Gang

SODERMAN, (JOHAN) AUGUST (cont'd.)

Ingas Visa (from Brollopet Pa Ulfasa)
solo,pno GEHRMANS 690 s.p. (S2792)

Ingerid I Rosengard
solo,pno GEHRMANS 698 s.p. (S2793)

Killebukken
solo,pno GEHRMANS 676 s.p. (S2794)

Kung Heimer Och Aslog
Bar solo,pno GEHRMANS 700 s.p.
                                  (S2795)
B solo,pno GEHRMANS 787-8 s.p.
                                  (S2796)
T solo,pno GEHRMANS 779-80 s.p.
                                  (S2797)

Lagg Omt Din Kind Intill Min Kind
solo,pno GEHRMANS 694 s.p. (S2798)

Langtan "Ser Jag Stjarnorna Sprida
Sitt Flammande Sken"
solo,pno GEHRMANS 684 s.p. (S2799)

Mitt Alskade Lilla Sockerskrin
solo,pno GEHRMANS 697 s.p. contains
also: Nu Klar Sig Varen Igen Sa
Gron   (S2800)

Nog Minns Jag Hur Det Var, Nar Som
Lilla Vannen For
solo,pno GEHRMANS 688 s.p. (S2801)

Nu Klar Sig Varen Igen Sa Gron
see Soderman, (Johan) August, Mitt
Alskade Lilla Sockerskrin

O Vor' Jag Ett Minne
solo,pno GEHRMANS 686 s.p. (S2802)

Och Fast Du Svikit Din Flickas Tro
solo,pno GEHRMANS 687 s.p. (S2803)

Prinsessen
solo,pno GEHRMANS 681 s.p. (S2804)

Sjung For Mig!
solo,pno GEHRMANS 193 s.p. (S2805)

Sjung, Sjung!
solo,pno GEHRMANS 685 s.p. (S2806)

Skonsta Ros Fordroj Ditt Fall
solo,pno GEHRMANS 696 s.p. (S2807)

Soldatvisa
Mez/Bar solo,pno GEHRMANS s.p. see
from SANGEN I   (S2808)

Soldatvisa Ur Regina Von Emmeritz
solo,pno GEHRMANS 689 s.p. (S2809)

Solveigs Vuggevise
solo,pno GEHRMANS 691 s.p. (S2810)

Synden, Doden
solo,pno GEHRMANS 679 s.p. (S2811)

Tag Imod Kransen
solo,pno GEHRMANS 678 s.p. (S2812)

Traeet
solo,pno GEHRMANS 677 s.p. (S2813)

SODERSTROM, NILS
Dina Ogon Aro Eldar
solo,pno,opt gtr GEHRMANS s.p.
                                  (S2814)
Tag Ditt Glas Och Drick Ur, Sangvals
solo,pno GEHRMANS s.p.   (S2815)

SODGER'S RETURN, THE *folk,Scot
low solo,pno (F maj) PATERSON FS83
s.p.   (S2816)
high solo,pno (G maj) PATERSON FS83
s.p.   (S2817)

SODOMKA, K.
Jablicko S Poselstvim
SA soli,pno PANTON 1485 s.p.
                                  (S2818)

SOEFISCH see Ruyneman, Daniel

SOEUR ANNE see Saint-Saens, Camille

SOEUR CLAIRE see Ryelandt, Joseph

SOFT ARE YOUR ARMS see Klemm, Gustav

SOFT DAY see Stanford, Charles Villiers

SOFT INVADER OF MY SOUL see Howard,
John Tasker

SOFT WERE YOUR HANDS, DEAR JESUS see
O'Hara, Geoffrey

SOFTLY ALONG THE ROAD see Davies, Henry
Walford

SOFTLY ALONG THE ROAD OF EVENING see
Shepherd, Arthur

SOFTLY AND TENDERLY *sac,gospel
solo,pno ABER.GRP. $1.50   (S2819)

SOFTLY AWAKES MY HEART see Saint-Saens,
Camille

SOFTLY BLEW THE EAST WIND see Niles,
John Jacob

SOFTLY LULLING, SWEETLY THRILLING see
Hook, James

SOFTLY REST
(Howe) S solo,pno PAXTON P40512 s.p.
                                  (S2820)

SOFTLY SIGHS THE VOICE OF EVENING see
Weber, Carl Maria von, Leise,
Leise, Fromm Weise

SOFTLY THE SUMMER see Hundley, Richard

SOGNI see Ferritto, John

SOGNO see Pannain, Guido

SOGNO see Tosti, Francesco Paolo

SOGNO DEL GIOVANE PAESANO see
Mussorgsky, Modest

SOHAL, NARESH (1939-   )
Kavita 1
S solo,fl,ob,clar,bsn,trom,perc,
pno,vln,vcl NOVELLO rental
                                  (S2821)
Kavita 2
S solo,fl,pno NOVELLO rental
                                  (S2822)
Kavita 3
S solo, electric double-bass
NOVELLO rental   (S2823)

Night's Poets
S solo,2clar,vibra,pno NOVELLO
rental   (S2824)

SOI, SOI, KAISLA see Sibelius, Jean,
Sav, Sav, Susa

SOI VIENOSTI MURHEENI SOITTO see
Merikanto, Oskar

SOINNE, AATTO
Langtan Stadske Soker *see Tuonne,
Tuonne Kaipaan

Tuonne, Tuonne Kaipaan
"Langtan Stadske Soker" solo,pno
FAZER F 5290 s.p.   (S2825)

SOIPA KIELI see Merikanto, Oskar

SOIR see Brahms, Johannes

SOIR see Cras, Jean (Emile Paul)

SOIR see Mulder, Ernest W.

SOIR see Tranchant, J.

SOIR see Wolff, A.

SOIR D'ADIEU see Ropartz, Joseph Guy

SOIR D'AMERTUNE see De Lara, Isadore

SOIR DE MAI see Legay, Marcel

SOIR D'HIVER see Caron-Legris, A.

SOIR D'HIVER see Rhene-Baton

SOIR D'IDUMEE see Vellones, P.

SOIR EMPOURPRE see Gaubert, Philippe

SOIR PAIEN see Gaubert, Philippe

SOIR PAIEN see Hue, [Georges-Adolphe]

SOIR ROMANTIQUE see Saint-Saens,
Camille

SOIR SUR L'EAU see Mouton, H.

SOIREE EN MER see Saint-Saens, Camille

SOIREES MUSICALES, VOL. I see Rossini,
Gioacchino

SOIRS see Mulot, M.

SOIRS D'AMOUR see Lagoanere, Oscar de

SOIRS D'ETE see Widor, Charles-Marie

SOIRS D'HIVER see Desrez

SOITAPAS see Kilpinen, Yrio

SOIXANTE LIEDER, VOL. I see Lacombe,
Louis (Trouillon)

SOIXANTE LIEDER, VOL. II see Lacombe,
Louis (Trouillon)

SOKOLA, MILOS (1913-)
Ukolebavka *CCU
solo,pno SUPRAPHON s.p. (S2826)

SOKRATES see Graun, Karl Heinrich

SOL OVER SVERIGE see Nordqvist, Gustaf

SOL, SOL! see Kilpinen, Yrio

SOL TROPICAL see Gutierrez-Ponce, M.

SOLA, PERDUTA, ABBANDONATA see Puccini,
Giacomo

SOLACE see Mana-Zucca, Mme., Ora Vorrei
Partir

SOLBLIND JAG ANDAS see Nordqvist,
Gustaf

SOLCHES HORT' ICH see Kilpinen, Yrio,
Sopivaisia

SOLDARITATSLIED see Eisler, Hanns

SOLDATENLIEDJE IN VOLKSTOON see
Zagwijn, Henri

SOLDATGOSSEN see Pacius, Fredrik

SOLDATO see Peragallo, Mario

SOLDATVISA see Soderman, (Johan) August

SOLDATVISA UR REGINA VON EMMERITZ see
Soderman, (Johan) August

SOLDIER, THE see Davis, Katherine K.

SOLDIER FROM THE WARS RETURNING see
Orr, Charles Wilfred

SOLDIER JIM see Chesham, Edward M.

SOLDIER SONGS see Weisgall, Hugo

SOLDIER SONGS AND HOME-FRONT BALLADS OF
THE CIVIL WAR *CC50U,folk,US
(Silber, Irwin) solo,pno/gtr OAK
000052 $2.95 (S2827)

SOLDIER'S CHORUS see Gounod, Charles
Francois

SOLDIERS OF FORTUNE see Hemery,
Valentine

SOLDIERS OF THE CROSS, ARISE see Hope,
H. Ashworth

SOLDIERS OF THE PEACE see Weinberg,
Jacob, Chayaley Ha-Shalom

SOLDIER'S WIFE, THE see Rachmaninoff,
Sergey Vassilievitch

SOLE E CANTO *CCU
(Fasullo) solo,pno FORLIVESI 12296
s.p. (S2828)

SOLEIL see Franck, Cesar

SOLENNE IN QUEST'ORA see Verdi,
Giuseppe

SOLER, JOSEP (1935-)
Passio Iesu Christi *sac,Easter
SBar soli,vla,vcl,cembalo,org sc
MOECK 5064 s.p. (S2829)

SOLI see Maggioli, Pietro

SOLI CALANTI see Mancini, Giovanni

SOLIG MORGON see Taube, Evert

SOLILOQUE see Bernier, Rene

SOLILOQUY, THE see Clarke, Henry Leland

SOLITA SU ALMA see Ginastera, Alberto

SOLITARY HOTEL see Barber, Samuel

SOLITUDE see Ferroud, Pierre-Octave

SOLITUDE see Kodaly, Zoltan

SOLITUDE see Levade, Charles (Gaston)

SOLITUDE see Schumann, Robert
(Alexander)

SOLITUDE, AH, HOW WELCOME! see
Scarlatti, Alessandro, Solitudine
Avvenne

SOLITUDE CHAMPETRE see Brahms,
Johannes, Feldeinsamkeit

SOLITUDINE see Wolf, Hugo,
Verborgenheit

SOLITUDINE AVVENNE see Scarlatti,
Alessandro

SOLL DENN DIE BLUMEN WELKEN? see
Nielsen, Carl, Skal Blomsterne Da
Visne?

SOLL EIN SCHUH NICHT DRUCKEN see
Beethoven, Ludwig van

SOLL ICH REDEN, DARF ICH SCHWEIGEN see
Millocker, Karl

SOLLEN DIESEN WEG NUN GEHEN see
Kilpinen, Yrio, Mista Sinne Tie
Menevi

SOLLICITUDE see Ferroud, Pierre-Octave

SOLLT' AUCH ICH NICHT ERMUDEN see
Kilpinen, Yrio, Miksi En Vasyisi

SOLLT ICH MEINEM GOTT NICHT SINGEN
*CC44U
(Fritsch; Mohr) [Ger] med solo,inst
BREITKOPF-W $1.00 (S2830)

SOLMAN
Bells Of The Sea
(Lamb) Bar solo,pno FOX,S (S2831)
(Lamb) B solo,pno FOX,S (S2832)

SOLNEDGANG see Nielsen, Carl

SOLNEDGANG see Schierbeck, Poul

SOLO see D'Ambrosi, Dante

SOLO AND DUET SPECIALS, VOL. 1 *sac,
CCU
1-2 soli,pno HOPE 506 $1.25 (S2833)

SOLO AND DUET SPECIALS, VOL. 2 *sac,
CCU
1-2 soli,pno HOPE 508 $1.25 (S2834)

SOLO EL QUE SABA AMAR see Tchaikovsky,
Piotr Ilyitch, Nur Wer Die
Sehnsucht Kennt

SOLO FOR VOICE 1 see Cage, John

SOLO FOR VOICE 2 see Cage, John

SOLO-KANTATE see Reutter, Hermann

SOLO PER VOCE FUR CLAUDIA see Behrend,
Siegfried

SOLO PSALMIST, THE *sac,CCU,Psalm
med solo,pno SACRED $3.50 contains
works by: Butler, Eugene; Powell,
Robert J.; McAfee, Don (S2835)

SOLO SINGER, VOL. 1 *CCU
(Wilson) med-high solo,pno FISCHER,C
O 3015; med-low solo,pno FISCHER,C
O 3016 (S2836)

SOLO SONG, THE *CCU
(MacClintock) solo,pno PRESSER $2.50
(S2837)

SOLOCANTATA see Szekely, E.

SOLODUKHO, J.
1924
Bar solo,mix cor,orch MEZ KNIGA
2.47 s.p. (S2838)

Soul's Mirror, The *song cycle
[Russ] Bar solo,pno MEZ KNIGA 78
s.p. (S2839)

SOLOKANTATEN see Micheelsen, Hans-
Friedrich

SOLOMON, EDWARD
Glee Maiden
solo,pno CRAMER (S2840)

SOLOS FOR CHRISTMAS FROM JOHN W.
PETERSON CANTATAS, SERIES NOS. 1-2
see Peterson, John W.

SOLOS FOR EASTER FROM JOHN W. PETERSON
CANTATAS see Peterson, John W.

SOLOS FOR THE CHURCH SOLOIST *sac,
CC15L
(Pfautsch, Lloyd) LAWSON high solo,
pno $2.50; low solo,pno $3.00
contains works by: Bach; Franck;
Handel; Mozart and others (S2841)

SOLOS FOR THE CHURCH YEAR *sac,CC20L
(Pfautsch, Lloyd) SCHIRM.G high solo,
pno $2.50; low solo,pno $2.50
contains works by: Bach; Brahms;
Beethoven; Schumann and others
(S2842)

SOLOS FROM THE GREAT ORATORIOS *sac,
CC36L
S solo,pno SCHIRM.G $4.00 contains
works by: Bach; Brahms; Elgar;
Handel and others (S2843)

SOLOS FROM THE GREAT ORATORIOS *sac,
CC39L
Bar/B solo,pno SCHIRM.G $4.00
contains works by: Bach; Elgar;
Franck; Handel and others (S2844)

SOLOSANGER see Pacius, Fredrik

SOLOSANGER OCH DUETTER MED PIANO see
Mozart, Wolfgang Amadeus

SOLSTRALEN see Kilpinen, Yrio

SOLUPPGANG see Rangstrom, Ture

SOLUPPGANG see Sibelius, Jean

SOLVEIG'S LULLABY see Grieg, Edvard
Hagerup, Solveigs Vuggevise

SOLVEIGS SANG see Grieg, Edvard Hagerup

SOLVEIG'S SONG see Grieg, Edvard
Hagerup, Solveigs Sang

SOLVEIGS VUGGEVISE see Grieg, Edvard
Hagerup

SOLVEIGS VUGGEVISE see Soderman

SOLVEIGS VUGGEVISE see Soderman,
(Johan) August

SOLVEJGS LIED see Grieg, Edvard Hagerup

SOLVEJZINA PISEN see Grieg, Edvard
Hagerup

SOLVIRKNING "TIL FJELDS UNDER
GRANELIEN" see Kjerulf, [Halfdan]

SOM ETT BLOMMANDE MANDELTRAD see
Fordell, Erik (Fritiof)

SOM ETT BLOMMANDE MANDELTRAD see
Milveden, Ingemar

SOM ETT BLOMMANDE MANDELTRAD see
Wohlfart, Karl

SOM HJORTEN PA DEN TORRA HED see
Nordqvist, Gustaf

SOM I UNGDOMENS AR see Durand

SOM MANDELBLOM see Wiklund, Adolf

SOM STJARNORNA PA HIMMELEN see
Peterson-Berger, (Olof) Wilhelm

SOMBER PINE, THE see Riegger,
Wallingford

SOMBRE NUIT, AVEUGLES TENEBRES see
Poulenc, Francis

SOME FACES OF LOVE see Diemente, Edward

SOME GIRLS ARE PRETTIER see Maury,
Lowndes

SOME RIVAL HAS STOLEN MY TRUE LOVE AWAY
see Broadwood, Lucy E.

SOME TIME see Friml, Rudolf

SOME TREES see Rorem, Ned

SOMEBODY BIGGER THAN YOU AND I see
Lange

SOMEBODY FETCH MY FLUTE
(Cockshott, Gerald) med solo,pno
NOVELLO 17.0182.07 s.p. (S2845)

SOMEBODY'S CALLING MY NAME see
Goodrich, Thelma

SOMEDAY see Davis

SOMEDAY see Lee, Don

SOMEDAY I'LL WALK ON GOLD see Wolfe,
Lanny

SOMEDAY, SOMEWHERE see Hayakawa,
Masaaki

SOMEDAY THERE'LL BE NO TOMORROW *sac,
gospel
solo,pno ABER.GRP. $1.50 (S2846)

SOMEONE IS WAITING FOR ME see Matheson,
H.

SOMEONE WHO CAN see Harris, Ron

SOMERAN-GODFREY, M. VAN
Birthright
low solo,pno ELKIN 27.1467.01 s.p.
(S2847)

SOMERS, HARRY STEWART (1925-)
Bunch Of Rowan, A
solo,pno BERANDOL BER 1334 $1.50
(S2848)

SOMERS, HARRY STEWART (cont'd.)

Conversation Piece
  solo,pno BERANDOL BER 1335 $1.50
                                    (S2849)

Evocations *CCU
  solo,pno BERANDOL BER 1140 $2.50
                                    (S2850)

Five Songs For Dark Voice *CC5U
  solo,pno BERANDOL BER 1147 $3.50
                                    (S2851)

Kuyas *CCU
  solo,fl,perc BERANDOL BER 1142
  $2.50   (S2852)

Twelve Miniatures *CC12U
  solo,3inst BERANDOL BER 1143 $5.00
                                    (S2853)

SOMERSET BACHELOR see Hope, H. Ashworth

SOMERSET FARMER see Wilson, H. Lane

SOMERSET, LORD HENRY
  Still Present
    low solo,pno (E flat maj) CRAMER
                                    (S2854)
    high solo,pno (G maj) CRAMER
                                    (S2855)

SOMERVELL, ARTHUR (1863-1937)
  All Through The Night
    low solo,pno (A flat maj) CRAMER
    s.p.   (S2856)
    high solo,pno (F maj) CRAMER s.p.
                                    (S2857)

  At The Mid Hour Of Night
    solo,pno CRAMER $1.15   (S2858)

  Barney Brallaghan
    solo,pno CRAMER   (S2859)

  Castle Of Dromore
    solo,pno CRAMER   (S2860)

  Cupids Garden
    solo,pno CRAMER   (S2861)

  Dimpled Cheek
    solo,pno CRAMER   (S2862)

  Doun In Yon Bank
    solo,pno CRAMER   (S2863)

  Floodes Of Tears
    solo,pno CRAMER   (S2864)

  Gathering Daffodils
    high solo,pno (A flat maj) CRAMER
    $1.15   (S2865)
    low solo,pno (G maj) CRAMER $.90
                                    (S2866)

  Gentle Maiden
    high solo,pno (F maj) CRAMER $1.15
                                    (S2867)
    low solo,pno (E flat maj) CRAMER
    $1.15   (S2868)

  Go From My Window, Go
    med solo,pno (A flat maj) CRAMER
    $1.15   (S2869)
    low solo,pno (G maj) CRAMER $.70
                                    (S2870)
    high solo,pno (B flat maj) CRAMER
    $1.10   (S2871)

  Isle Of The Heather
    solo,pno CRAMER   (S2872)

  Jenny's Mantle
    solo,pno CRAMER   (S2873)

  Kathleen Ni Hoolhaun
    solo,pno CRAMER   (S2874)

  Kingdom By The Sea
    solo,pno (E maj) BOOSEY $1.50
                                    (S2875)

  Kitty Magee
    solo,pno CRAMER   (S2876)

  Little Mary Cassidy
    solo,pno CRAMER   (S2877)

  Macintosh's Lament
    solo,pno CRAMER   (S2878)

  Mary Jamieson
    solo,pno CRAMER   (S2879)

  My Lodging It Is On The Cold Ground
    solo,pno CRAMER   (S2880)

  Myle Charaine
    solo,pno CRAMER   (S2881)

  Old Towler
    solo,pno CRAMER   (S2882)

  Once I Loved A Maiden Fair
    solo,pno CRAMER   (S2883)

  Opening Of The Key
    solo,pno CRAMER   (S2884)

  Our National Songs *CCU
    solo,pno CRAMER s.p., ea. published
    in 4 books   (S2885)

SOMERVELL, ARTHUR (cont'd.)

  Pretty Polly Oliver
    low solo,pno (C maj) CRAMER (S2886)
    high solo,pno (E flat maj) CRAMER
                                    (S2887)

  Shadows Of Night
    solo,pno CRAMER   (S2888)

  Shepherd's Cradle Song *sac,Xmas
    low solo,pno (E flat maj) HARRIS
    $1.00   (S2889)
    med solo,pno (G maj) HARRIS $1.00
                                    (S2890)
    med solo,pno (F maj) HARRIS $1.00
                                    (S2891)
    high solo,pno (A maj) ASHDOWN $1.50
                                    (S2892)
    med-high solo,pno (G maj) ASHDOWN
    $1.50   (S2893)
    med solo,pno (F maj) ASHDOWN $1.50
                                    (S2894)
    low solo,pno (E flat maj) ASHDOWN
    $1.50   (S2895)
    high solo,pno (A maj) HARRIS $1.00
                                    (S2896)

  Shule Agra
    solo,pno CRAMER   (S2897)

  Sleep My Child
    med solo,pno (G maj) ASHDOWN s.p.
                                    (S2898)
    low solo,pno (F maj) ASHDOWN s.p.
                                    (S2899)
    high solo,pno (A flat maj) ASHDOWN
    s.p.   (S2900)

  Slender Boy
    solo,pno CRAMER   (S2901)

  Snowy-Breasted Pearl, The
    solo,pno CRAMER   (S2902)

  Thou Wilt Not Go And Leave Me Here
    solo,pno CRAMER   (S2903)

  Three Ravens
    solo,pno CRAMER   (S2904)

  Tree In The Wood, The
    solo,pno CRAMER   (S2905)

  When I Am Dead My Dearest
    solo,pno (F min) ASHDOWN s.p.
                                    (S2906)

  When The King Enjoys His Own Again
    solo,pno CRAMER   (S2907)

  Where Be Going?
    solo,pno CRAMER   (S2908)

  Will Ye No Come Back Again
    solo,pno CRAMER   (S2909)

  Yellow Boreen, The
    solo,pno CRAMER   (S2910)

  Young Love Lies Sleeping
    solo,pno (A flat maj) BOOSEY $1.50
                                    (S2911)

SOMERVILLE, REGINALD
  Song Of Kent
    solo,pno CRAMER   (S2912)

SOMETHING BEAUTIFUL see Gaither

SOMETHING GOOD IS GOING TO HAPPEN TO
  YOU *sac,CC10UL
  (Carmichael, Ralph) solo,pno WORD
  30066 $1.95   (S2913)

SOMETHING GOOD IS GOING TO HAPPEN TO
  YOU *sac
  (Carmichael, Ralph) solo,pno WORD
  S-204   (S2914)

SOMETHING GOOD IS GOING TO HAPPEN TO
  YOU see Carmichael, Ralph

SOMETHING HAS HAPPENED TO ME *sac,
  gospel
  solo,pno ABER.GRP. $1.50   (S2915)

SOMETHING I CAN FEEL see Cole

SOMETHING I CAN FEEL see Cole, Elmer

SOMETHING SEEMS TINGLE-INGLEING see
  Friml, Rudolf

SOMETHING SPECIAL see Croft, Colbert

SOMETHING TO HOLD ON TO see Hamill, Jim

SOMETHING TO SING *CCU
  (Baltzell, W.J.) med solo,pno PRESSER
  $3.50   (S2916)

SOMETHING WORTH LIVING FOR see Gaither

SOMETIMES I FEEL LIKE A MOTHERLESS
  CHILD *spir
  (Burleigh, H. T.) high solo,pno
  BELWIN $1.50   (S2917)
  (Burleigh, H. T.) med solo,pno BELWIN
  $1.50   (S2918)

  (Burleigh, H. T.) low solo,pno BELWIN
  $1.50   (S2919)

SOMEWHERE see Diamond, David

SOMEWHERE A VOICE IS CALLING see Tate,
  Arthur

SOMEWHERE I HAVE NEVER TRAVELLED see
  Binkerd, Gordon

SOMEWHERE I HAVE NEVER TRAVELLED see
  Blank, Allan

SOMEWHERE, SOMEDAY, SOMETIME *sac,
  gospel
  solo,pno ABER.GRP. $1.50   (S2920)

SOMMAR see Rangstrom, Ture

SOMMAREN see Dannstrom, Isidor

SOMMARENS LYCKA see Pesonen, Olavi
  (Samuel), Kesan Onni

SOMMARENS SISTA ROS "SE BLOMMANDE
  ALLENA" see Sjogren, Emil

SOMMARIDYLL see Sjogren, Emil

SOMMARKVALL see Runback, Albert

SOMMARMORGON see Ranta, Sulho, Kesaaamu

SOMMARMORGON see Wennerberg, Gunnar

SOMMARNATT PA STRANDEN see Jarnefelt,
  Armas

SOMMARNATT PA STRANDEN see Jarnefelt,
  Armas, Suvirannalla

SOMMARNATTEN see Sibelius, Jean

SOMMARSANG see Peterson-Berger, (Olof)
  Wilhelm

SOMMEIL see Wolff, A.

SOMMEIL D'ENFANT see Chaminade, Cecile

SOMMEIL DES FLEURS see Saint-Saens,
  Camille

SOMMER see Rontgen, Johannes

SOMMER, VLADIMIR (1921-   )
  Je Nam Dobre Na Zemi
    solo,pno SUPRAPHON s.p.   (S2921)

SOMMERBALLADE see Martinu, Bohuslav,
  Balada Letni

SOMMERFADEN see Schreker, Franz

SOMMERGLUCK see Niggeling, Willi

SOMMERLIED see Nielsen, Carl,
  Sommersang

SOMMERLIV see Backer-Grondahl, Agathe
  Ursula

SOMMERNACHT see Kilpinen, Yrio, Kesayo

SOMMERNACHT see Landre, Willem

SOMMERNACHT see Reger, Max

SOMMERNACHT [2] see Landre, Willem

SOMMERNACHT AUF EINEM FRIEDHOF see
  Kuula, Toivo, Kesayo Kirkkomaalla

SOMMERNACHTE see Berlioz, Hector, Les
  Nuit D'Ete

SOMMERNATTEN *Op.90,No.5
  "Die Sommernacht" [Swed/Ger] med-high
  solo,kbd HANSEN-DEN s.p. see from
  Six Songs   (S2922)

SOMMERNEIGE see Bijvanck, Henk

SOMMERPOESIE - WINTERPOESIE see
  Kahowez, Gunter

SOMMERSANG see Nielsen, Carl

SOMNA LJUVT LIKSOM VAGEN VID STRAND see
  Abt, Franz

SOMNAR JAG MED BLICKEN FAST see
  Merikanto, Oskar

SON AMOUR ME RESTE see Schumann, Robert
  (Alexander)

SON CHARME see Levade, Charles (Gaston)

SON COME FARFALLETTA see Anonymous

SON IO SPIRITO CHE NEGA see Boito,
  Arrigo

SON LA VECCHIA MADELON see Giordano, Umberto

SON NOM see Chaminade, Cecile

SON OF MARY see Diack, John Michael

SON OF MINE see Wallace, William

SON PIETOSA, SON BONINA see Haydn, (Franz) Joseph

SON POCHI FIORI see Mascagni, Pietro

SON VERGIN VEZZOSA see Bellini, Vincenzo

SON, WHY HAVE YOU TREATED US SO? see Bender, Jan

SONATA see Mikoda, Borivoj

SONATA FUR FRAUENSTIMME, FLOTE UND SCHLAGZEUG see Harrex, P.

SONATA IN D see Vycpalek, Ladislav

SONATE VOCALISE see Medtner, Nikolai Karlovitch

SONATINA see Dougherty, Celius

SONCECE, SIJ! see Lipovsek, Marijan

SONDAGSMORGON see Backman, Hjalmar, Sunnuntaiaamuna

SONETO A CORDOBA see Falla, Manuel de

SONETO A LA ARMONIA see Guastavino, Carlos

SONETO LXXI see Arizaga, Rodolfo

SONETT AUF DEN MARCHENVOGEL see Kilpinen, Yrio, Sonetti Sadun Linnusta

SONETT FUR WIEN see Korngold, Erich Wolfgang

SONETTE AUF TEXTEN VON DICHTERN DER RENAISSANCE see Hanus, Jan

SONETTI ROMANI see Gretchaninov, Alexander Tikhonovitch

SONETTI SADUN LINNUSTA see Kilpinen, Yrio

SONETTO see Stevens, Halsey

SONETTO D'OTTOBRE see Cantu, M.

SONETTO E BALLATA see De Angelis, Ruggero

SONETTO SPIRTUALE IN STILE RECITATIVO see Frescobaldi, Girolamo

SONETY see Hanus, Jan

SONG see Lewis, Peter Tod

SONG see Malipiero, Gian Francesco

SONG see Wigglesworth, Frank

SONG, A see Ballou, Esther W.

SONG 1 see Hobbs, Christopher

SONG 2 see Hobbs, Christopher

SONG see Honegger, Arthur

SONG ABOUT LEPA VIDA, THE see Kozina, Marijan, Pesem Od Lepe Vide

SONG ALBUM see Nakada, Yoshinao

SONG ALBUM see Riede, E.

SONG ALBUM see Foster, Stephen Collins

SONG ALBUM see Strauss, Richard

SONG ALBUM see Heseltine, Philip

SONG AND DANCES OF DEATH see Mussorgsky, Modest

SONG AT EVENING see Thiman, Eric Harding

SONG BOOK *CCU
(Arthur, Dave; Arthur, Toni) solo,pno GALLIARD 2.2025.7 $1.75 (S2923)

SONG BOOKS, VOL. 1: SOLOS FOR VOICE 3-58 see Cage, John

SONG BOOKS, VOL. II: SOLOS FOR VOICE 59-92 see Cage, John

SONG CLASSICS *CCU
(Parker, H.) T solo,pno PRESSER $3.00 (S2924)

SONG CYCLE see Kelly, Robert

SONG CYCLE see Weiner, Lazar

SONG CYCLE ON THE BIRTH OF JESUS, A see Lambert, Constant

SONG: DREAM THE NIGHTINGALE see Saul, George Brandon

SONG FOR A DANCE see Donovan, Richard [Frank]

SONG FOR A GIRL see Rorem, Ned

SONG FOR A WANDERER see Foss, Lukas, Wanders Gemutsruhe

SONG FOR A WINTER CHILD see Flanagan, William

SONG FOR AUTUMN see Dougherty, Celius

SONG FOR CHRISTMAS, A see Krogstad, Bob

SONG FOR CHRISTMAS, A see Musgrave, Thea

SONG: FOR EILEEN see Saul, George Brandon

SONG FOR LOVE, A see Van Etten, Jane

SONG FOR MARCH, A see Sharpe, Evelyn

SONG FOR MORPHEUS see Lombardo, Robert

SONG FOR SOPRANO see Karlins, M. William

SONG FOR SOPRANO see Lucier, Alvin

SONG FOR SUNRISE see Teed, Roy

SONG FOR THE LORD MAYOR'S TABLE, A see Walton, William

SONG FOR VOICE AND PIANO see Richter, Nico

SONG FROM "DEIRDRE" see Kauder, Hugo

SONG HOLY ANGELS CANNOT SING, A see Jensen, Gordon

SONG IN THE NIGHT see Loughborough, Raymond

SONG IS SO OLD see Repper, Charles

SONG OF A CHINESE FISHERMAN see Maganini, Quinto

SONG OF AHEZ THE PALE, THE see Buzzi-Peccia, Arturo

SONG OF AICHE see Johnson, Noel

SONG OF AKHENATEN, THE see Milner, Anthony

SONG OF APRIL see Godard, Benjamin Louis Paul, Chanson D'avril

SONG OF CHIEMSEE see Fielitz, Alexander von, Eliland

SONG OF CHRISTMAS, A see Dickinson, Clarence

SONG OF COMRADESHIP see Freudenthal, Josef, Lied Fun A Chaver

SONG OF CONSECRATION see Kennedy, Dion W.

SONG OF DAVID, A see Rorem, Ned

SONG OF DEVON see Hope, H. Ashworth

SONG OF DEVOTION see Beck, John Ness

SONG OF EXALTATION see Humphreys

SONG OF GEORGIA see Balakirev, Mily Alexeyevitch

SONG OF HOMECOMING see Ford, Donald

SONG OF HOPE see Hatikvah

SONG OF HUITZILOPOCHTLI see Blank, Allan

SONG OF HYBRIAS THE CRETAN see Elliott, J.W.

SONG OF INDIA see Rimsky-Korsakov, Nikolai, Chanson Hindoue

SONG OF INDIA, A see Rimsky-Korsakov, Nikolai, Chanson Hindoue

SONG OF INNOCENCE, A see Hall

SONG OF ISRAEL see Rathaus, Karol

SONG OF JOY see Beck, John Ness

SONG OF JOY see West, Monica

SONG OF JOY, A see Warren, Beverly

SONG OF JOYS, A see Creston, Paul

SONG OF KENT see Somerville, Reginald

SONG OF LIBERATION see Weinberg, Jacob, Haganah

SONG OF LIBERTY see Dougherty, Celius

SONG OF LIFE, THE see Franco, Johan

SONG OF LOVE see Chajes, Julius, Shir V'nivneh

SONG OF MARY see Anderson, William H.

SONG OF MOMUS TO MARS, THE see Boyce, William

SONG OF MOTHERS see Voris, W.R.

SONG OF PAN see Bach, Johann Sebastian

SONG OF PENITENCE *sac
[Eng/Ger] low solo,pno ASHLEY $1.00 (S2925)
[Eng/Ger] high solo,pno ASHLEY $1.00 (S2926)

SONG OF PRAISE AND PRAYER see Binkerd, Gordon

SONG OF RADHA, THE see Paranjoti

SONG OF REVOLT see Shir Ha-Mered

SONG OF ROSES, THE see Sibelius, Jean, Rosenlied

SONG OF RUTH see Goldman, Maurice

SONG OF SHADOWS see Fischer, Irwin

SONG OF SIXPENCE, A see Burge, D.

SONG OF SOLDIERS, THE see Hely-Hutchinson, (Christian) Victor

SONG OF SONGS see Helfman, Max, Ana Dodi

SONG OF SPRING see Stickles, William

SONG OF SPRING, A see Sibelius, Jean

SONG OF SPRING, A see Sibelius, Jean, Lenzgesang

SONG OF SUNSHINE see Thomas, Arthur Goring

SONG OF TAYUMANAVAR see Schramm, Harold

SONG OF THANKSGIVING, A see Allitsen, Frances

SONG OF THANKSGIVING, A see Harling, William Franke

SONG OF THE ANGELS see Dickinson, Clarence

SONG OF THE BANANA CARRIERS see Benjamin, Arthur

SONG OF THE BLACKMORE VALE see Hope, H. Ashworth

SONG OF THE BOW see Stanford, Charles Villiers

SONG OF THE BUTTON, THE see Fisher, Howard

SONG OF THE CAMEL DRIVER see Chajes, Julius, Gamal, G'mali

SONG OF THE CHASE see Kahn, Percy B. (Percival Benedict)

SONG OF THE CROSS, THE see Plumstead, Mary

SONG OF THE DEW see Stravinsky, Igor

SONG OF THE ELVES see Metner, N.R.

SONG OF THE EMEK see Shir Ha-Emek

SONG OF THE FELLS see Kilpinen, Yrio, Tunturilaulu

SONG OF THE FLEA see Mussorgsky, Modest

SONG OF THE FLEA, THE see Mussorgsky, Modest

SONG OF THE FLEA, THE see Mussorgsky,
Modest, Chanson De La Puce

SONG OF THE JASMINE see Dougherty,
Celius

SONG OF THE LEAVES OF LIFE (from
Pilgrim's Progress) sac,Bibl
S/2 soli,pno (med easy) OXFORD 62.206
$1.50   (S2927)

SONG OF THE LEAVES OF LIFE AND THE
WATERS OF LIFE see Vaughan
Williams, Ralph

SONG OF THE LOTUS-LILY see Woodforde-
Finden, Amy

SONG OF THE MORNING-O see Norman, Lorna

SONG OF THE NIGHTINGALE see Zeller

SONG OF THE NORTH WIND see Head, H.

SONG OF THE OPEN ROAD see Wijdeveld,
Wolfgang

SONG OF THE PALAQUIN BEARERS, THE see
Shaw, Martin

SONG OF THE PASSING SOUL see McLeod,
Robert

SONG OF THE PILGRIMS (from Pilgrim's
Progress)
Bar solo,pno (easy) OXFORD 62.203
$1.50   (S2928)

SONG OF THE RAINCHANT see Hively, Wells

SONG OF THE ROAD see Stanton, Geoffrey

SONG OF THE SOLDIERS, THE see Berkeley,
Lennox

SONG OF THE SUBMARINES see Bell,
Margaret

SONG OF THE THRUSH see Keel, Frederick

SONG OF THE TOREADOR see Bizet,
Georges, Votre Toast, Je Peux Le
Rendre

SONG OF THE VOLGA BOATMEN *Russ
solo,pno CRAMER   (S2929)

SONG OF THE VOLGA BOATMEN, THE see
Koeneman, T., Chant Des Bateliers
Du Volga

SONG OF THE WANDERER see Barrie, Stuart

SONG OF THE WATER GNOME see Dvorak,
Antonin

SONG OF THE WATERFRONT see Lora,
Antonio

SONG OF THE WAYFARER see Mahler, Gustav

SONG OF THE WILLOW BRANCHES see
Fischer, Irwin

SONG OF THE WISE MEN see Lovelace,
Austin C.

SONG OF TRUST see Zoeckler, Dorothy A.

SONG OF VANITY FAIR (from Pilgrim's
Progress)
Mez/Bar solo,pno (med diff) OXFORD
62.207 $1.50   (S2930)

SONG ON A MAY MORNING see Hively, Wells

SONG ON THE WIND, A see Lucke, K.

SONG PICTURES see Brahe, May H.

SONG: THE OWL see Weigl, Vally

SONG-THRUSH, THE see Thiman, Eric
Harding

SONG TIL NORDMORE see Braein, Edvard

SONG TO A FAIR YOUNG LADY see Rorem,
Ned

SONG TO A YOUNG PIANIST see Clarke,
Henry Leland

SONG TO BE SUNG IN A JUNE TWILIGHT see
Franco, Johan

SONG TO CELIA see Bunge, Sas

SONG TO THE LUTE IN MUSICK, A see
Wuorinen, Charles

SONG TO THE MOON see Dvorak, Antonin

SONG TO THE SEALS see Bantock,
Granville

SONG TO THE WITCH OF THE CLOISTERS see
Corigliano, John

SONG TREASURY OF OLD ISRAEL, A *CCU
(Saminsky, L.) [Heb] solo,pno PRESSER
$3.00   (S2931)

SONG WAS BORN, A see Mercer

SONG WAS BORN, A see Parks, Joe E.

SONG WITHOUT WORDS see Mills, Charles

SONGE see Caplet, Andre

SONGE A QUELS DANGERS see Messager,
Andre

SONGE D'UNE NUIT D'ETE see Caplet,
Andre

SONGES see Almquist, Carl Jonas Love

SONGS see Duparc, Henri

SONGS see Moore, Dorothy Rudd

SONGS see Campbell, Alex

SONGS see Pearly, Ely

SONGS (SECOND EDITION) see Karlowicz,
Mieczyslaw

SONGS see Glantz, Yehuda Leib

SONGS see Beethoven, Ludwig van

SONGS see Mozart, Wolfgang Amadeus

SONGS see Chopin, Frederic

SONGS see Vandor, S.

SONGS see Jonsson, Thorarinn

SONGS ABOUT WOMEN see Kubik, Gail

SONGS AFTER JEWISH FOLK POEMS see
Shostakovich, Dmitri

SONGS AND ARIAS WITH PIANO, VOLS. 1-2
see Beethoven, Ludwig van

SONGS AND BALLADS, VOL. I *CCU,folk,
Dan
(Kampp, Ejnar; Bro Rasmussen,
Henning) solo,pno HANSEN-DEN 29242
s.p.   (S2932)

SONGS AND DANCES OF DEATH see
Mussorgsky, Modest

SONGS AND EPILOGUES see Davis, Roy

SONGS AND JOKES FOR LITTLE FOLKS see
Lennox, L.

SONGS AND PROVERBS OF WILLIAM BLAKE see
Britten, Benjamin

SONGS AND ROMANCES see Makarova, Nina
Vladimirovna

SONGS AND STORY OF LAMB, THE *sac,
CC17L
solo,pno,gtr WORD 37750 $3.95 (S2933)

SONGS AND TUNES FOR SABBATH AND
HOLIDAYS see Rotenberg, M.

SONGS BY BETTY BRYAN see Bryan, Betty

SONGS BY COMPOSERS OF THE DEMOCRATIC
REPUBLIC OF VIETNAM *CCU
[Russ] solo,pno MEZ KNIGA 92 s.p.
                                    (S2934)

SONGS BY E.E. CUMMINGS see Dougherty,
Celius

SONGS BY MIGUEL DE CERVANTES AND OTHERS
FOR GUITAR AND VOICE see Behrend,
Siegfried

SONGS BY ROBERT BURNS see Reuland,
Jacques

SONGS BY SCHUBERT see Schubert, Franz
(Peter)

SONGS BY TOM WARING see Waring, Tom

SONGS BY TWENTY-TWO AMERICANS *CC27L
(Taylor) SCHIRM.G high solo,pno
$5.00; low solo,pno $5.00 contains
works by: Barber; Edwards; Malotte;
Thomson and others   (S2935)

SONGS, DRONES AND REFRAINS OF DEATH see
Crumb, George

SONGS EVERYBODY SINGS *sac,CCU
(Bond) solo,pno BOSTON $3.50 (S2936)

SONGS FOR A CHILD see Weigl, Vally

SONGS FOR A CHOSEN GENERATION *sac,
CC9UL
(Uphaus, Dwight) 1-2 soli,pno,gtr
LILLENAS MB-356 $2.50 contains
works by: Skillings; Butler;
Eugene; Johnson, Paul and others
                                    (S2937)

SONGS FOR A LITTLE SON see Hively,
Wells

SONGS FOR ARIEL see Tippett, Michael

SONGS FOR CHRISTIAN SCIENCE SERVICES
*sac,CCU
(Humphreys) high solo,pno FISCHER,C
RB 53; low solo,pno FISCHER,C RB 54
                                    (S2938)

SONGS FOR CHRISTMAS *sac,CCU,Xmas
(Hjertaas, Ella) solo,pno AUGSBURG
11-9433 $2.00   (S2939)

SONGS FOR EVE see Laderman, Ezra

SONGS FOR GIRLS *CCU
solo,pno PRESSER $2.50   (S2940)

SONGS FOR JUDITH see Drynan, Margaret

SONGS FOR MY CHILDREN see Baily, Mrs.
J.S.

SONGS FOR PATRICIA see Swanson, Howard

SONGS FOR PEACE *CC95U,folk,US
solo,pno OAK 000053 $3.95   (S2941)

SONGS FOR R P B see Eaton

SONGS FOR RACHEL see Lifshitz, Shulamit

SONGS FOR SOPRANO AND CELLO see Millay

SONGS FOR SPECIAL DAYS *sac,CCUL
1-4 soli,pno SINGSPIR 5428 $1.50
                                    (S2942)

SONGS FOR THE LUTE, VIOL AND VOICE see
Danyel, John

SONGS FOR WORSHIP *sac,CCU
(Brown) solo,pno FISCHER,C 0 3314
                                    (S2943)

SONGS FOR YOU AND ME see Howard, L.

SONGS FOR YOUNG SONGBIRDS see Davidson,
M.T.

SONGS FROM DON GIOVANNI, BOOK 1:
SOPRANO (DONNA ANNA & DONNA ELVIRA)
see Mozart, Wolfgang Amadeus

SONGS FROM DON GIOVANNI, BOOK 3: TENOR
(DON OTTAVIO) see Mozart, Wolfgang
Amadeus

SONGS FROM DREAMS see Mirk, Vasilij,
Pesmi Iz Sanj

SONGS FROM FIGARO, BOOK 1: SOPRANO (THE
COUNTESS) see Mozart, Wolfgang
Amadeus

SONGS FROM FIGARO, BOOK 2: SOPRANO
(SUSANNA & CHERUBINO) see Mozart,
Wolfgang Amadeus

SONGS FROM FIGARO, BOOK 3: BARITONE
(FIGARO) see Mozart, Wolfgang
Amadeus

SONGS FROM "MARKINGS" see Strilko,
Anthony

SONGS FROM MICHELANGELO see Mc Cabe

SONGS FROM "NATIVE ISLAND" see Weigl,
Vally

SONGS FROM "NO BOUNDARY" see Weigl,
Vally

SONGS FROM POEM OF DYUKICHI YAGI see
Kumaki, Mamoru

SONGS FROM PRINTED SOURCES *CC20U
solo,pno STAINER 3.1344.7 $8.50
contains works by: Alison; Campian;
Morley; Giles; Hume and others
                                    (S2944)

SONGS FROM ROSSETER'S BOOK OF AYRES
(1601) see Campian, Thomas

SONGS FROM SHAKESPEARE see Chausson,
Ernest

SONGS FROM SHAKESPEARE'S PLAYS AND
POPULAR SONGS OF SHAKESPEARE'S TIME
*CC60U,Eng,16th cent
(Kines, Tom) solo,gtr OAK 000068
$3.95   (S2945)

SONGS FROM SING OUT! *CCU,folk,US
(Silber, Irwin; Silverman, Jerry)
solo,pno OAK 000143 $1.95 contains
works by: Guthrie, Woody; Houston,

Cisco; Leadbelly; Seeger, Pete;
Dyer-Bennett, Richard and others
(S2946)

SONGS FROM SOUTH OF THE BORDER *CCU,
Cen Am/So Am
(Andre, Julie) [Span/Eng] solo,pno
MARKS $2.00   (S2947)

SONGS FROM THE BIBLE see Kosakoff,
Reuven

SONGS FROM THE CHINESE see Britten,
Benjamin

SONGS FROM THE CHINESE see Peaslee,
Richard

SONGS FROM THE HAVEN OF REST *sac,
CC128UL
solo,pno,gtr LILLENAS MB-248 $2.95
(S2948)

SONGS FROM THE ORATORIOS FOR BARITONE
OR BASS see Handel, George Frideric

SONGS FROM THE ORATORIOS FOR CONTRALTO
see Handel, George Frideric

SONGS FROM THE ORATORIOS FOR SOPRANO
see Handel, George Frideric

SONGS FROM THE ORATORIOS FOR TENOR see
Handel, George Frideric

SONGS FROM THE PLAYS OF SHAKESPEARE see
Hyman, Richard R.

SONGS FROM THE VELD *CC14L,folk,Afr
(Marais, Josef) solo,pno SCHIRM.G
$1.50 in Afrikaans and English
texts   (S2949)

SONGS FROM TRINIDAD *CC45U,folk
(Connor, Edric) solo/soli,gtr,drums,
bvl OXFORD 68.711 $2.75   (S2950)

SONGS I CAN SING MYSELF see Howard, L.

SONGS I SING IN SUNDAY SCHOOL *sac,CCU
(Bock, F.) solo,pno PRESSER $1.25
(S2951)

SONGS IN ENGLISH *CCU
(Taylor) high solo,pno FISCHER,C
O 4791; low solo,pno FISCHER,C
O 4792   (S2952)

SONGS IN WINTER see Leichtling, Alan

SONGS MY MOTHER TAUGHT ME see Dvorak,
Antonin, Als Die Alte Mutter

SONGS MY TRUE LOVE SINGS *CCU
(Landeck, Beatrice) solo,pno/gtr
MARKS $1.50   (S2953)

SONGS, ODES AND ARIAS see Gluck,
Christoph Willibald Ritter von

SONGS OF ACADIA *CCU,Nor Am
(Gaudet) [Eng/Fr] med solo,pno BMI
$1.00   (S2954)

SONGS OF AUSTRALIA see Elliott, Malcolm

SONGS OF AUVERGNE *see Bailero (S2955)

SONGS OF CHARM *CCU
high solo,pno PRESSER $2.00 (S2956)

SONGS OF ENGLAND, BOOK I *CCU
(Bantock) solo,pno PAXTON P15588 s.p.
contains illustrations   (S2957)

SONGS OF ENGLAND, BOOK II *CCU
(Bantock) solo,pno PAXTON P15619 s.p.
(S2958)

SONGS OF ENGLAND, VOL. 3 *CCU
(Hatton; Fanning) solo,pno BOOSEY
$6.00   (S2959)

SONGS OF ESTRANGEMENT see Bohun, Lyle
de

SONGS OF GERMANY *CC81U,folk,Ger
(Spicker, Max) [Ger/Eng] solo,pno
SCHIRM.G $3.50   (S2960)

SONGS OF INNOCENCE see Bois, Rob du

SONGS OF INNOCENCE see Bezanson, Philip

SONGS OF ITALY *CC65U,folk,It
(Marzo, Eduardo) [It/Eng] solo,pno
SCHIRM.G $3.50   (S2961)

SONGS OF JAPANESE TOYS see Nakada,
Yoshinao

SONGS OF JOE HILL *CCU,folk,US
(Stavis, Barrie; Harmon, Frank) solo,
pno OAK 000055 $2.95   (S2962)

SONGS OF LEE FISHER, THE see Fisher,
Lee

SONGS OF LIVING FAITH see Ashton, Bob

SONGS OF LIVING HOPE see Ashton, Bob

SONGS OF LOVE AND PARTING see Gold,
Ernest

SONGS OF MARJORIE JONES, VOL. 1 see
Jones, Marjorie

SONGS OF MARJORIE JONES, VOL. 2 see
Jones, Marjorie

SONGS OF MARY see Dodson

SONGS OF MICKEY HOLIDAY, THE *sac,
CC14UL
solo,kbd SINGSPIR 4340 $2.95 (S2963)

SONGS OF MY SPANISH SOIL *sac,CCU
(Osma) solo,pno BOSTON $3.25 (S2964)

SONGS OF OLD AGE see Warren, Raymond

SONGS OF OLD LONDON see Oliver, Herbert

SONGS OF OPEN COUNTRY see Martin,
Easthope

SONGS OF PERFECT PROPRIETY see Barab,
Seymour

SONGS OF PRAYER see Gerovitsch, Eliezer

SONGS OF ROCHEL see Daus, A.

SONGS OF SERGEI RACHMANINOFF, VOL. 1:
OP. 4 TO OP. 21 see Rachmaninoff,
Sergey Vassilievitch

SONGS OF SERGEI RACHMANINOFF, VOL. 2:
OP. 26 TO OP. 38 see Rachmaninoff,
Sergey Vassilievitch

SONGS OF SPRINGTIME see Ronald, Sir
Landon

SONGS OF THE AMERICAN WEST *CCU
(Lingenfelter, Richard E.; Dwyer,
Richard A.) solo,pno UNIV.CAL
$20.00   (S2965)

SONGS OF THE CHILD WORLD, VOL. 2 *CCU
(Gaynor; Riley) solo,pno PRESSER
$1.75   (S2966)

SONGS OF THE CONFEDERACY *CC38U,US,
19th cent
(Harwell) med solo,pno cloth BMI
$3.95   (S2967)

SONGS OF THE 'FORTY-FIVE see Murray,
Alan

SONGS OF THE GAY NINETIES *CC80U
solo,pno/gtr MUSIC 020055 $3.95
(S2968)

SONGS OF THE GREAT SOUTH BAY see
Thorne, Francis

SONGS OF THE HALF-LIGHT see Berkeley,
Lennox

SONGS OF THE HARP see Campbell, Hilda
M., Orain Na Clarsaich

SONGS OF THE HEBRIDES, VOLS. 1-3 *CCU
(Kennedy-Fraser, M.; MacLeod, K.)
solo,pno BOOSEY $21.00, ea. (S2969)

SONGS OF THE ISLES *CC20L
(Roberton, Hugh S.) [Eng] solo,pno,
opt gtr cmplt ed ROBERTON 6375 s.p.
see also: Fidgety Bairn, The;
Highland Cradle Song; Ho-Ree, Ho-
Ro, My Little Wee Girl!; Island
Spinning Song; Joy Of My Heart;
Lewis Bridal Song; Mingulay Boat
Song; Sing At The Wheel; Uist
Tramping Song; Westering Home
(S2970)

SONGS OF THE MASTER see Schouwman, Hans

SONGS OF THE NATIVITY see La Montaine,
John

SONGS OF THE NATIVITY see Sifler, Paul
J.

SONGS OF THE NORTH see Arundale, Claude

SONGS OF THE ROSE OF SHARON see La
Montaine, John

SONGS OF THE ROSE OF SHARON see Sifler,
Paul J.

SONGS OF THE SEASON see Harrhy, Edith

SONGS OF THE SEASONS see Custer, Arthur

SONGS OF THE SHEPHERD see Orland, Henry

SONGS OF THE SPIRIT see Franco, Johan

SONGS OF THE WAYFARER see Ireland, John

SONGS OF THOMAS D'URFEY see Urfey,
Thomas d'

SONGS OF TRAVEL see Vaughan Williams,
Ralph

SONGS OF VOYAGE see Gideon, Miriam

SONGS OF WALES *CCU
(Northcote; Davies) solo,pno BOOSEY
$7.00   (S2971)

SONGS OF WEN I-TO see Korte, Karl

SONGS OF WONDER
high solo,pno ELKIN 27.2629.07 s.p.
contains: Here Comes A Lusty Wooer;
Little Nut-Tree, The; Old Abram
Brown; Polly Pillicote; Wonder Of
Wonders, The   (S2972)

SONGS OF WONDER see Bush, Geoffrey

SONGS OF WORK AND PROTEST *CC100UL
(Fowke, Edith; Glazer, Joe) solo,pno,
opt gtr pap 22899-1 $3.50   (S2973)

SONGS OF YALE *CC108L
(Bartholomew) SCHIRM.G pap $4.00,
cloth $7.00   (S2974)

SONGS ON BUDAPEST see Hajdu, Mihaly

SONGS ON CHINESE POEMS see Horusitzky,
Z.

SONGS ON POEMS BY CARL SANDBURG see
Raphling, Sam

SONGS ON TWO PAGES see Martinu,
Bohuslav

SONGS, SUNG BY NOAM KANIEL *CCU
solo,pno OR-TAV $1.00   (S2975)

SONGS TO JEWISH POETRY see Hacken,
Emanuel

SONGS TO POEMS BY ARLO BATES see
Chadwick, George Whitefield

SONGS TO THE PLAYS OF SHAKESPEARE, VOL.
I *CCU
(Arne, T.) solo,pno PRESSER $1.50
(S2976)

SONGS, VOL. 1 see Liszt, Franz

SONGS VOL. 1: OP. 4, 8, 14, 21 see
Rachmaninoff, Sergey Vassilievitch

SONGS, VOL. 2 see Liszt, Franz

SONGS, VOL. 2: OP. 26, 34, 38 see
Rachmaninoff, Sergey Vassilievitch

SONGS, VOL. 3 see Liszt, Franz

SONGS, VOL. 4 see Liszt, Franz

SONGS, VOL. 5 see Liszt, Franz

SONGS, VOL. 6 see Liszt, Franz

SONGS WE USED TO SING see Mascheroni,
Angelo

SONGS WITH IMPROVISATION see Fennelley,
Brian

SONGS WITH PIANO, VIOLIN AND CELLO see
Beethoven, Ludwig van

SONGS WITH PIANO, VIOLIN AND CELLO,
VOLS. 2-4 see Beethoven, Ludwig van

SONGSTER'S AWAKENING see Fletcher,
Percy Eastman

SONITUS ARMORUM see Brossard, Sebastien
de

SONN', SONN! see Kilpinen, Yrio, Sol,
Sol!

SONNE CLAIRON see Chaminade, Cecile

SONNE DER INKAS see Denisov, Edison
Vasilievitch

SONNEDAAL see Hullebroeck, Em.

SONNENAUFGANG see Kilpinen, Yrio,
Auringon Nousu

SONNENAUFGANG see Sibelius, Jean,
Soluppgang

SONNENFINSTERNIS see Beck, Conrad

SONNENGESANG DES HEILIGEN FRANZISKUS
see Nessler, Robert

SONNENLAND see Marx, Joseph

SONNENSTRAHLEN see Kilpinen, Yrio, Solstralen

SONNET see Beekhuis, Hanna

SONNET see Birch, Robert Fairfax

SONNET see Borris, Siegfried

SONNET see Bunge, Sas

SONNET see Fearing, John

SONNET see Flothius, Marius

SONNET see Franco, Johan

SONNET see Pascal, Andre

SONNET see Saint-Saens, Camille

SONNET see Saxe, Serge

SONNET see Voormolen, Alexander Nicolas

SONNET A LA VIERGE MARIE see Boisdeffre, Charles-Henri-Rene de

SONNET A OPHELIE see Marty, (Eugene) Georges

SONNET DE JOACHIM DU BELLAY see Cuvillier, Charles

SONNET DE RONSARD see Dukas, Paul

SONNET IX see Bunge, Sas

SONNET IX see Delden, Lex van

SONNET NO. 104 see Nash, S.

SONNET NUMBER ONE TO JEAN RETI see Gerschefski, Edwin

SONNET: ON HEARING THE DIES IRAE SUNG IN THE SISTINE CHAPEL see Ruyneman, Daniel

SONNET POUR HELENE see Bunge, Sas

SONNET TO BYRON see Maganini, Quinto

SONNET WAERMEDE DEN LANDTMAN... see Baeyens, August-L.

SONNET XIV see Bunge, Sas

SONNET XVII see Lazarus, Daniel

SONNET XXII see Lazarus, Daniel

SONNET XXIV see Bunge, Sas

SONNET XXIV see Delden, Lex van

SONNETS AFTER ELIZABETH BARRETT BROWNING see Balazs, Frederic

SONNETS FROM FATAL INTERVIEW see Gideon, Miriam

SONNETS FROM SHAKESPEARE see Gideon, Miriam

SONNETS FROM SHAKESPEARE see Whear, Paul William

SONNETS OF SHAKESPEARE see Sifler, Paul J.

SONNETTE AN EAD see Bijvanck, Henk

SONNETTENKRING see Mulder, Herman

SONNETTENKRING see Mulder, Herman

SONNEZ, MUSETTES see Delmet, Paul

SONNINEN, AHTI (1914-   )
    Ala Kutsu Kukkaseksi
        "Ej En Blomma Ma Jag Kallas" see
        Sju Laulua Unkarilaisiin
        Kansanrunoihin II

    Anna, Armas, Sirpin Olla
        "Kara, Lat Du Skaran Vara" see Sju
        Laulua Unkarilaisiin
        Kansanrunoihin II

    Dansen *see Tanssit

    Ehatyssavu
        "Kallelserok" see Midsommarnatt II

    Ej En Blomma Ma Jag Kallas *see Ala
        Kutsu Kukkaseksi

    Faraherden *see Lammaspaimen

    Havskungens Dotter *see
        Merenkuninkaan Tytar

SONNINEN, AHTI (cont'd.)

    Herra On Minun Paimeneni
        see Viisi Laulua Raamatun Sanoihin

    Herra, Sinun Armosi Ulottuu
        Taivaisiin
        see Viisi Laulua Raamatun Sanoihin

    Kallelserok *see Ehatyssavu

    Kara, Lat Du Skaran Vara *see Anna,
        Armas, Sirpin Olla

    Karestor Tretton Nyss Jag Agde *see
        Mull' On Kultaa Kolmetoista

    Koska Valaissee Kointahtonen
        solo,pno FAZER F 4171 s.p. (S2977)

    Lammaspaimen
        "Faraherden" see Sju Laulua
        Unkarilaisiin Kansanrunoihin I

    Laulakaa Jumalalle
        see Viisi Laulua Raamatun Sanoihin

    Laulu Helsingille
        solo,pno FAZER F 3034 s.p. (S2978)

    Laulu Onnesta
        "Sangen Om Lyckan" solo,pno FAZER
        W 2730 s.p.   (S2979)

    Lugn Ar Natten *see Yo On Tyyni

    Merenkuninkaan Tytar
        "Havskungens Dotter" solo,pno FAZER
        F 3062 s.p.   (S2980)

    Midsommarnatt II *Op.21,No.2
        solo,pno FAZER F 2814 s.p.
            contains: Ehatyssavu,
            "Kallelserok"; Tanssit,
            "Dansen"   (S2981)

    Minun Sydameni On Valmis, Jumala
        see Viisi Laulua Raamatun Sanoihin

    Mirjamin Laulu
        see Viisi Laulua Raamatun Sanoihin

    Mull' On Kultaa Kolmetoista
        "Karestor Tretton Nyss Jag Agde"
        see Sju Laulua Unkarilaisiin
        Kansanrunoihin II

    Munkiksi Joutuva
        "Vilken Nytta Ar Av Mannen" see Sju
        Laulua Unkarilaisiin
        Kansanrunoihin II

    Nattig Skidfard Vuorela *see
        Talviyon Hiihtaja

    Sangen Om Lyckan *see Laulu Onnesta

    Siintaa Metsa
        "Skogen Blanar" see Sju Laulua
        Unkarilaisiin Kansanrunoihin I

    Sju Laulua Unkarilaisiin
        Kansanrunoihin I
        solo,pno FAZER W 2535 s.p.
            contains: Lammaspaimen,
            "Faraherden"; Siintaa Metsa,
            "Skogen Blanar"; Yo On Tyyni,
            "Lugn Ar Natten"   (S2982)

    Sju Laulua Unkarilaisiin
        Kansanrunoihin II
        solo,pno FAZER W 2536 s.p.
            contains: Ala Kutsu Kukkaseksi,
            "Ej En Blomma Ma Jag Kallas";
            Anna, Armas, Sirpin Olla,
            "Kara, Lat Du Skaran Vara";
            Mull' On Kultaa Kolmetoista,
            "Karestor Tretton Nyss Jag
            Agde"; Munkiksi Joutuva,
            "Vilken Nytta Ar Av Mannen"
                                    (S2983)

    Skogen Blanar *see Siintaa Metsa

    Talviyon Hiihtaja *Op.17,No.3
        "Nattig Skidfard Vuorela" solo,pno
        FAZER F 2851 s.p.   (S2984)

    Tanssit
        "Dansen" see Midsommarnatt II

    Unohtumaton Ehtoo
        solo,pno FAZER F 3427 s.p. (S2985)

    Viisi Laulua Raamatun Sanoihin
        solo,pno FAZER F 3966 s.p.
            contains: Herra On Minun
            Paimeneni; Herra, Sinun Armosi
            Ulottuu Taivaisiin; Laulakaa
            Jumalalle; Minun Sydameni On
            Valmis, Jumala; Mirjamin Laulu
                                    (S2986)

    Vilken Nytta Ar Av Mannen *see
        Munkiksi Joutuva

SONNINEN, AHTI (cont'd.)

    Yo On Tyyni
        "Lugn Ar Natten" see Sju Laulua
        Unkarilaisiin Kansanrunoihin I

SONNO see Davico, Vincenzo

SONNTAG see Brahms, Johannes

SONNTAG see Jarnefelt, Armas,
    Sunnuntaina

SONNTAG IST'S see Breu, S.

SONO IN AMORE see Mozart, Wolfgang
    Amadeus

SONS AND DAUGHTERS OF AUSTRALIA see
    Brumby, Colin

SONS DE CLOCHES see Versepuy, Marius

SONS OF THE SEA see McGlennon

SONST SPIELT ICH MIT ZEPTER see
    Lortzing, (Gustav) Albert

SONT TROIS JEUNES GARCONS
    see La Musique, Huitieme Cahier

SONT TROIS JEUNES GARCONS, TOUS TROIS
    ALLANT EN GUERRE see Indy, Vincent
    d'

SONTAGSMORGEN see Mendelssohn-
    Bartholdy, Felix

SONZOGNO, GIULIO CESARE (1906-   )
    La Luna E L'usignolo
        S solo,orch ZERBONI 3169 rental
                                    (S2987)
    La Rose Rouge
        S solo,orch ZERBONI 3168 rental
                                    (S2988)

SOON see Cardew, Cornelius

SOON I WILL BE DONE *spir
    (Boatner) high solo/med solo,pno
    BELWIN $1.50   (S2989)

SOON WE'LL SEE AT DAYBREAK see Puccini,
    Giacomo, Un Bel Di Vedremo

SOPHIE see Strauss, Richard

SOPIVAISIA see Kilpinen, Yrio

SOPRA LE VERDI E GIALLE RISAIE see
    Mortari, Virgilio

SOPRA UN'ARIA ANTICA see Respighi,
    Ottorino

SOPRAN-ALBUM see Skorzeny, Fritz

SOPRANO ARIAS FROM THE OPERAS see
    Strauss, Richard

SORCERERS SONG see Sullivan, Sir Arthur
    Seymour

SORG see Peterson-Berger, (Olof)
    Wilhelm

SORIA SOTAHAN KUOLLA see Kilpinen, Yrio

SOROR DOLOROSA see Gui, Vittorio

SORRENTINE, SORRENTE, SORRENTE see
    Guiraud, Ernest

SORRISI see Veneziani, Vittore,
    Sourires

SORRISI E BACI see Barbirolli, A.

SORRY, I NEVER KNEW YOU *sac
    (Little; Steele) solo,pno LILLENAS
    SM-935: SN $1.00   (S2990)

SORRY, I NEVER KNEW YOU see Branch

SORRY OF MYDATH see Ward, Robert

SORTIE MATINALE see Berger, Rod.

SORTILEGES AFRICAINS see Leduc, Jacques

SORTUNUT see Kotilainen, Otto

SOSPIRI AL VENTO see Brogi

SOSREDJA see Sivic, Pavle

SOTTO IL CIELO see Zandonai, Riccardo

SOUCI, G.S.
    Where Blossoms Grow
        med solo,pno PRESSER $.75 (S2991)

SOUDA, SOUDA SINISORSA see Sibelius,
    Jean

SOUERS, MILDRED (1894-   )
Feed My Sheep *sac
   med solo,pno (E flat maj) FISCHER,C
   V 2336   (S2992)

SOUFFLE DES BOIS see Lefebvre, Channing

SOUFFRANCE D'AIMER see Delmet, Paul

SOUHAIT see Chaminade, Cecile

SOUHAIT see Wissmer, Pierre

SOUKUP, VLADIMIR (1930-   )
Eroticke Pisne *CCU
   A solo,fl,pno CZECH s.p.   (S2993)

Lied Von Prag *see Pisen O Praze

Lieder Der Heimat *see Pisne Domova

Ohnive Leto *CCU
   [Czech/Ger] Bar solo,pno CZECH s.p.
                                  (S2994)
Pijacka
   "Trinklied" med solo,pno CZECH s.p.
                                  (S2995)
Pisen O Praze
   "Lied Von Prag" med solo,pno CZECH
   s.p.   (S2996)

Pisne Domova
   "Lieder Der Heimat" T solo,pno
   CZECH s.p.   (S2997)

Trinklied *see Pijacka

SOUL DOWN see Masters

SOUL OF THE MOOR see Baxter, Maude
   Stewart

SOULS, LORD see Katter, Vivian

SOUL'S MIRROR, THE see Solodukho, J.

SOULS OF THE RIGHTEOUS, THE see Foster,
   Myles Birket

SOUND AN ALARM see Handel, George
   Frideric

SOUND OF LAUGHTER see Schirmer, Rudolph
   [E.]

SOUND OF SPRING, THE see Hjorleifsson,
   Sigguringi E.

SOUND OF YOUR NAME see North, Michael

SOUND THE FLUTE see Dougherty, Celius

SOUND THE PIBROCH see Lawson, Malcolm

SOUNDS AND WORDS see Babbit, Milton

SOUNDS OF HIS COMING, THE see Wolfe,
   Lanny

SOUPIR see Busser, H.

SOUPIR see Debussy, Claude

SOUPIR see Duparc, Henri

SOUPIR see Enesco, Georges

SOUPIR see Ravel, Maurice

SOUPIR see Respighi, Ottorino

SOURIC ET MOURIC see Poulenc, Francis

SOURIRES see Veneziani, Vittore

SOURIRES ET BAISERS see Barbirolli, A.,
   Sorrisi E Baci

SOURIS, ANDRE (1899-1970)
Comptines Pour Enfants Sinistres
   SMez soli,3inst ZERBONI 4403 rental
                                  (S2998)
L'autre Voix
   S solo,fl,clar,vla,vcl,pno CBDM
   s.p.   (S2999)

SOUS BOIS see Ferrari, Gabriella

SOUS LA FEUILLEE see Thome, Francis

SOUS LA PLUIE see Dupre, Marcel

SOUS LA PROTECTION DES VIOLETTES see
   Rhene-Baton

SOUS LA RAMURE see Cuvillier, Charles

SOUS LA TONNELLE see Erlanger, Camille

SOUS LE CIEL GRIS see Barachin, P.

SOUS LE CIEL IMMOBILE J'AI COMPTE
   JUSQU'A MILLE see Ruyneman, Daniel

SOUS LE CIEL PALE DU SOIR see Favre,
   Georges

SOUS LE DOME DU CIEL see Bagge, G.

SOUS LE PONT MIRABEAU see Ruyneman,
   Daniel

SOUS LE PORCHE DE SAINT-BENOIT see
   Levade, Charles (Gaston)

SOUS L'EPAIS SYCOMORE see Chansarel, R.

SOUS LES ARBRES see Godard, Benjamin
   Louis Paul

SOUS LES ARCADES see Brero, Cesare

SOUS LES ETOILES see Hutchison, W.

SOUS LES ETOILES see Thomas, Arthur
   Goring

SOUS TON BALCON see Messager, Andre

SOUSCEYRAC see Lapeyre, Therese

SOUTAA PILVET VALKEAT see Kaski, Heino

SOUTH
Walk A Mile In My Shoes *sac
   solo,pno BENSON S8312-S $1.00
                                  (S3000)
SOUTH WIND see Parker, Horatio William

SOUTH WIND see Sharpe, Evelyn

SOUTHAM
Have You Seen But A White Lily
   solo,pno OXFORD $1.40   (S3001)

Lesbos
   A/Bar solo,pno (med) OXFORD 61.901
   $1.30   (S3002)

SOUVENANCES see Saint-Saens, Camille

SOUVENEZ-VOUS see Wangermez, Ed.

SOUVENEZ-VOUS VIERGE MARIE see
   Massenet, Jules

SOUVENIR see Gallois Montbrun

SOUVENIR see Lora, Antonio

SOUVENIR see Pandelides, S.

SOUVENIR DE PATRIE see Senger, de

SOUVENIR DE SYLVIE see Blanchard, Roger

SOUVENIR D'UN SOIR see Carolus-Duran,
   P.

SOUVENIRS DE L'EBRE see Schumann,
   Robert (Alexander)

SOUVENT A LA DEVANTURE see Messager,
   Andre

SOUVENT DE NOS BIENS, LE MEILLEUR see
   Aubert, Louis-Francois-Marie

SOUVENT J'AI DIT A MON MARI see
   Diamond, David

SOV see Nordqvist, Gustaf

SOV OCH DROM see Kjerulf, [Halfdan],
   Quand Tu Dors

SOV, OROLIGA HJARTA see Wiklund, Adolf

SOV, SOV see Munktell

SOV, SOV HJARTEBARN see Anjou, P. d'

SOVER DU MIN SJAEL see Sjogren, Emil

SOVETSKE PISNE OBRANY A PRACE *CCU
   (Pletka; Rysavy; Urban) solo,pno
   PANTON 1334 s.p.   (S3003)

SOVETSKE PISNE PRO MLADEZ *CCU
   (Urban; Hronek) boy solo/girl solo,
   pno PANTON 1535 s.p.   (S3004)

SOVIEL STERN AM HIMMEL STEHEN see
   Bijvanck, Henk

SOVNEN see Dorumsgaard, Arne

SOVNEN "DA BARNET SOV IND" see Kjerulf,
   [Halfdan]

SOVOVY PISNE see Jindrich, Jindrich

SOWERBY, LEO (1895-   )
Edge Of Dreams *song cycle
   med solo,pno BELWIN $1.50   (S3005)

Hear My Cry *sac
   low solo,pno BELWIN $1.50   (S3006)

SOWERBY, LEO (cont'd.)

How Long Wilt Thou? *sac
   low solo,pno BELWIN $1.50   (S3007)

I Will Lift Up *sac
   low solo,pno BELWIN $1.50   (S3008)

Little Jesus, Sweetly Sleep *sac
   med solo,pno FITZSIMONS $.60
                                  (S3009)
Lord Is My Shepherd, The *sac
   low solo,pno BELWIN $1.50   (S3010)

O Be Joyful *sac
   low solo,pno BELWIN $1.50   (S3011)

O God Of Light *sac
   high solo,pno BELWIN $1.50   (S3012)

O Jesus, Lord *sac
   high solo,pno BELWIN $1.50   (S3013)

O Perfect Love *sac
   high solo,pno BELWIN $1.50   (S3014)
   low solo,pno BELWIN $1.50   (S3015)

Psalm 142 *sac
   S/T solo,pno BELWIN $1.50   (S3016)

Thou Art My Strength *sac
   high solo,pno BELWIN $1.50   (S3017)

Who So Dwelleth *sac
   low solo,pno BELWIN $1.50   (S3018)

SOWER'S SONG see Stanford, Charles
   Villiers

SOYONS REPUBLICAINS see Chautagne, Marc

SOYONS UNIS see Rhene-Baton

SPACE-OUT see Wilson, Donald M.

SPACIOUS FIRMAMENT, THE see Handel,
   George Frideric

SPADARO
Firenze
   solo,pno FORLIVESI 11544 s.p.
                                  (S3019)
SPAGNOLATA see De Lucia, Nadir

SPALICEK see Trojan, Vaclav

SPANELSKY KRUH see Kalas, Julius

SPANET PA VATTNET see Sibelius, Jean,
   Lastu Lainehilla

SPANIARD KNOWS see Offenbach, Jacques

SPANISCHEN TOTENTANZ see Reutter,
   Hermann

SPANISCHES LIEDERBUCH see Wolf, Hugo

SPANISCHES LIEDERBUCH see Wolf, Hugo

SPANISCHES LIEDERSPIEL see Schumann,
   Robert (Alexander)

SPANISH CANTATA see Handel, George
   Frideric

SPANISH CAROL see Brown

SPANISH LADY see Hughes, Herbert

SPANISH LYRICS, VOL. I: NOS. 3, 4, 6, 9
   see Wolf, Hugo

SPANISH LYRICS, VOL. I: SACRED SONGS
   see Wolf, Hugo

SPANISH LYRICS, VOL. II: SECULAR SONGS
   NOS. 1-11 see Wolf, Hugo

SPANISH LYRICS, VOL. III: SECULAR SONGS
   NOS. 12-22 see Wolf, Hugo

SPANISH LYRICS, VOL. IV: SECULAR SONGS
   NOS. 23-34 see Wolf, Hugo

SPANISH ROMANCE see Medtner, Nikolai
   Karlovitch

SPANSK SERENAD see Myrberg, August M.

SPARKFORD HARRIERS see Hope, H.
   Ashworth

SPARROWS see Borgulya, A.

SPATE GEDANKEN EINER BACCHANTIN see
   Jentsch, Walter

SPATER GLANZ see Baird, Tadeusz, Pozny
   Btask

SPATSOMMER see Thomas, Kurt

SPATSOMMERNACHT see Bijvanck, Henk

SPEAK! see Arditi, Luigi, Parla!

SPEAK SOFTLY see Blickhan, Tim

SPEAKING FROM THE SNOW see Naylor,
Bernard

SPEAKS, OLEY (1874-1948)
Album Of Songs *CC12L
solo,pno SCHIRM.G $3.95   (S3020)

By The Waters Of Babylon *sac
low solo,pno (D min) SCHIRM.G $.75
(S3021)

Come, Spirit Of The Living God *sac
high solo,pno (B flat maj) SCHIRM.G
$.75   (S3022)

I Lay My Sins On Jesus *sac
high solo,pno PRESSER $.75 (S3023)

In The End Of The Sabbath *sac
high solo,pno (C min) SCHIRM.G $.85
(S3024)
(Stickles) high solo&low solo,pno/
org SCHIRM.G $.80   (S3025)

It Came Upon The Midnight Clear *sac
low solo,pno (A maj) SCHIRM.G $.75
(S3026)
high solo,pno (C maj) SCHIRM.G $.75
(S3027)

King Of Love My Shepherd Is, The
*sac
low solo,pno (B flat maj) SCHIRM.G
$.60   (S3028)

Le Jour
"Morning" [Fr/Eng] high solo,pno (D
min) SCHIRM.G $.85   (S3029)
"Morning" [Fr/Eng] med solo,pno (C
min) SCHIRM.G $.85   (S3030)
"Morning" high solo,pno (D maj)
ALLANS s.p.   (S3031)
"Morning" med solo,pno (C maj)
ALLANS s.p.   (S3032)
"Morning" low solo,pno (B flat maj)
ALLANS s.p.   (S3033)

Let Not Your Heart Be Troubled *sac
high solo,pno (D maj) SCHIRM.G $.85
(S3034)
med solo,pno (C maj) SCHIRM.G $.85
(S3035)
low solo,pno (A maj) SCHIRM.G $.85
(S3036)

Lord Is My Light, The *sac
low solo,pno (A flat maj) SCHIRM.G
$.85   (S3037)

Morning *see Le Jour

Now The Day Is Over *sac
med solo,pno (F maj) SCHIRM.G $.60
(S3038)

On The Road To Mandalay
med solo,pno (C maj) SCHIRM.G $.75
(S3039)
high solo,pno (E flat maj) SCHIRM.G
$.75   (S3040)
high solo,pno (E flat maj) ALLANS
s.p.   (S3041)
med solo,pno (C maj) ALLANS s.p.
(S3042)
low solo,pno (B flat maj) ALLANS
s.p.   (S3043)

Prayer Perfect, The *sac
med solo,pno (F maj) SCHIRM.G $.85
(S3044)
high solo,pno (G maj) ALLANS s.p.
(S3045)
med solo,pno (F maj) ALLANS s.p.
(S3046)
low solo,pno (E flat maj) ALLANS
s.p.   (S3047)
2 soli,pno ALLANS s.p.   (S3048)
low solo,pno (E flat maj) SCHIRM.G
$.85   (S3049)
(Deis) SBar/SA soli,pno SCHIRM.G
$1.00   (S3050)

Sylvia
high solo,pno (G maj) SCHIRM.G $.85
(S3051)
med solo,pno (F maj) SCHIRM.G $.85
(S3052)
med solo,pno (E flat maj) SCHIRM.G
$.85   (S3053)
low solo,pno (D flat maj) ALLANS
s.p.   (S3054)
high solo,pno (G maj) ALLANS s.p.
(S3055)
med solo,pno (E flat maj) ALLANS
s.p.   (S3056)
med-high solo,pno (F maj) ALLANS
s.p.   (S3057)
(Deis) ABar soli,pno SCHIRM.G $.75
(S3058)

There's A Song In The Air *sac
med solo,pno (F maj) SCHIRM.G $.85
(S3059)

Thou Wilt Keep Him In Perfect Peace
*sac
high solo,pno (A min) SCHIRM.G $.85
(S3060)

SPEAKS, OLEY (cont'd.)

med solo,pno (G min) SCHIRM.G $.85
(S3061)
low solo,pno (E min) SCHIRM.G $.85
(S3062)

To You
high solo,pno (G maj) SCHIRM.G $.75
(S3063)
med solo,pno (F maj) SCHIRM.G $.75
(S3064)
low solo,pno (E flat maj) SCHIRM.G
$.75   (S3065)

Twelve Sacred Songs *sac,CC12L
low solo,pno SCHIRM.G $2.00 (S3066)

SPEAR
Only I *see Smith

SPECIAL TRIO ARRANGEMENTS SERIES, NOS.
1-3 *sac,CCUL
(DeCou, Harold) 3 female soli,pno
SINGSPIR $1.25, ea.   (S3067)

SPECIAL VOICES NO. I *sac,CCUL
solo,pno LILLENAS MB-196 $1.50
(S3068)

SPECIAL VOICES NO. II *sac,CCUL
solo,pno LILLENAS MB-197 $1.50
(S3069)

SPECIAL VOICES NO. III *sac,CCUL
2 soli,pno LILLENAS MB-198 $1.50
(S3070)

SPECIAL VOICES NO. IV *sac,CCUL
solo,pno LILLENAS MB-199 $1.50
(S3071)

SPECIAL VOICES NO. V *sac,CCUL
solo,pno LILLENAS MB-200 $1.50
(S3072)

SPECIAL VOICES NO. VI *sac,CCUL
solo,pno LILLENAS MB-201 $1.50
(S3073)

SPECIAL VOICES NO. VII *sac,CCUL
solo,pno LILLENAS MB-355 $1.50
(S3074)

SPECKLED THRUSH see Mornement, Ina

SPECKS OF LIGHT see Levy, Frank

SPECTOGRAM see Hambraeus, Bengt

SPEED ON MY BARK see Leslie, Henry
David

SPEER FAMILY-SONGBOOK, THE *sac,CC11UL
solo,pno BENSON BO475 $2.50 (S3075)

SPEER, G.T.
He Is Mine And I Am His *sac
solo,pno STAMPS 7268-SN $1.00
(S3076)

SPEIDERSANG see Hauger, Kristian

SPEKTRUM 69, HEFT I *CCU
(Kirmsse, H.) solo,pno DEUTSCHER 9031
s.p. contains works by: Beez;
Butting; Dessau; Draeger; Eisler;
Graap; Reinhold; Schubert; Spies;
Wagner-Regeny and others   (S3077)

SPEKTRUM 69, HEFT II *CCU
(Kirmsse, H.) solo,pno DEUTSCHER 9032
s.p. contains works by: Asriel;
Cilensek; Collum; Finke; Geissler;
Kochan; Kohler; Kunad; Lohse; Meyer
and others   (S3078)

SPELA JAG VILL PA MIN LILLA FLOJT see
Pesonen, Olavi (Samuel), Pienella
Huilulla Huutelen

SPELDE WERKSTERLIED see Hullebroeck,
Em.

SPELDEWERKSTERSLIED see Hullebroeck,
Em.

SPELMANSVISA see Melartin, Erkki,
Spielmannslied

SPELMANSVISA see Wideen, Ivar

SPELMANSVISA see Wohlfart, Karl

SPENCER, E.
Marche Boulevardiere
solo,pno ENOCH s.p.   (S3079)

SPENCER, J.
Bread And Music
high solo/med solo,pno SEESAW $1.00
(S3080)
Fragment Of Heaven, A
med solo,pno SEESAW $1.00 (S3081)

SPENCER, MARQUERITA
June Magic
solo,pno THOMP.G   (S3082)

SPENDTHRIFT see Charles, Ernest

SPERANZE MIE see Scarlatti, Alessandro

SPERATE, O FIGLI see Verdi, Giuseppe

SPERDUTO see Platamone, Stefano

SPES ULTIMA DEA see Davico, Vincenzo

SPES, ULTIMA DEA see Gandino, Adolfo

SPESA INUTILE see Rocca, Lodovico

SPEVY JESENE see Holoubek, Ladislav

SPEVY Z VYCHODNEHO SLOVENSKA see
Kardos, Dezider

SPEZZAFERRI, GIOVANNI
Buona Gente, Parlate!
[It] solo,pno BONGIOVANI 1356 s.p.
see from Canti Drammatici Dal
Russo   (S3083)

Canti Drammatici Dal Russo *see
Buona Gente, Parlate!; L'anello;
Occhi; Tu Non Cantare, Usignolo!;
Tu Non Stormire, O Segala!
(S3084)

L'anello
[It] solo,pno BONGIOVANI 1357 s.p.
see from Canti Drammatici Dal
Russo   (S3085)

Occhi
[It] solo,pno BONGIOVANI 1360 s.p.
see from Canti Drammatici Dal
Russo   (S3086)

Tu Non Cantare, Usignolo!
[It] solo,pno BONGIOVANI 1358 s.p.
see from Canti Drammatici Dal
Russo   (S3087)

Tu Non Stormire, O Segala!
[It] solo,pno BONGIOVANI 1359 s.p.
see from Canti Drammatici Dal
Russo   (S3088)

SPEZZAFERRI, L.
Poemetto Tragico
[It] solo,pno BONGIOVANI 2328 s.p.
(S3089)

SPHARENKLANGE see Strauss, Josef

SPHENOGRAMMES see Mayuzumi, Toshiro

SPIAGGE AMATE see Gluck, Christoph
Willibald Ritter von

SPIANDO AI VETRI see Cimara, Pietro

SPIDER, A see Sydeman, William

SPIEGA L'ALI DOLCE SONNO see Piccinni,
Niccolo

SPIEGEL DES LEBENS see Peeters, Flor

SPIEGEL-SUITE see Wolkonskij, Andrej

SPIELMANNS-LIEDER see Kilpinen, Yrjo

SPIELMANNSART see Schmalstich, Clemens

SPIELMANNSLIED see Melartin, Erkki

SPIELMANNSWEISEN see Schoeck, Othmar

SPIELMUSIK see Bruhl, Heinrich

SPIERS, P.
He's The Lord Of Glory *sac
solo,pno GOSPEL 05 TM 0479 $1.00
(S3090)

SPIEVANA ABECEDA see Ferenczy, Oto

SPIJTIG see Voormolen, Alexander
Nicolas

SPIJTIG KLAARTJE see Voormolen,
Alexander Nicolas

SPILKA, FRANTISEK (1877-1960)
Selske Pisne *CCU
B solo,pno CZECH s.p.   (S3091)

SPILLEMAEND see Grieg, Edvard Hagerup

SPINDELVAV see Berggreen, Andreas Peter

SPINDRIFT see Fogg, Eric

SPINGOLE FRANCESI see Longo, Achille

SPINN! SPINN!
solo,pno LUNDQUIST s.p.   (S3092)

SPINNARIA see Hallstrom, Ivar

SPINNELIED see Schumann, Robert
(Alexander)

SPINNER, LEOPOLD
Funf Lieder *Op.8, CC5U
[Ger] S solo,pno BOOSEY $2.50
(S3093)

SPINNERSKAN see Nordqvist, Gustaf

SPINNING WHEEL see Waller, Murphy

SPINNING WHEEL, THE *folk,Scot
  low solo,pno (F maj) PATERSON FS102
  s.p.
                                    (S3094)
  high solo,pno (G maj) PATERSON FS102
  s.p.
                                    (S3095)

SPINNING WHEEL SONG see Arundale,
  Claude

SPINNROCKSSANG see Tolonen, Jouko
  (Paavo Kalervo), Rukkilaulu

SPIRA SUL MARE see Puccini, Giacomo

SPIRATE PUR, SPIRATE see Donaudy,
  Stefano

SPIRIT FILLED SONGS *sac,CCU
  solo,pno MEL BAY MB93317 $1.95
                                    (S3096)

SPIRIT FLOWER see Campbell-Tipton,
  Louis

SPIRIT FLOWER, A see Campbell-Tipton,
  Louis

SPIRIT OF DELIGHT see Clarke, Henry
  Leland

SPIRIT OF GOD see Neidlinger, William
  Harold

SPIRIT OF GOD see Silvester, Frederick
  C.

SPIRIT OF GOD, THE see Pisk, Paul
  Amadeus

SPIRIT OF JESUS IS IN THIS PLACE, THE
  see Gaither

SPIRIT OF THE WOOD see Parker, Henry

SPIRIT QUICKENETH, THE see Franco,
  Johan

SPIRIT'S SONG, THE see Haydn, (Franz)
  Joseph

SPIRITUAL MADRIGALS see Gideon, Miriam

SPIRITUAL SONGS, BOOK ONE see Parker,
  George

SPIRITUAL SONGS, BOOK TWO see Parker,
  George

SPIRITUALS *sac,CCU
  (Dett, R.N.) solo,pno BELWIN $1.00
                                    (S3097)

SPIRITUALS AND FOLKSONGS *CCU
  (Buhe) [Eng] solo,gtr SCHOTTS 4829
  s.p.   (S3098)

SPIRITUALS (FIVE NEGRO SONGS) *CC5U,
  spir
  (Brown, Lawrence) med solo,pno BELWIN
  $2.25   (S3099)

SPIRTO GENTIL see Donizetti, Gaetano

SPISAK see Radic, Dusan

SPITALNY, H.L.
  Smiling Again
    low solo,pno (A min) BOOSEY $1.50
                                    (S3100)
    high solo,pno (C min) BOOSEY $1.50
                                    (S3101)

SPLEEN see Dela, M.

SPLEEN see Haring, Ch.

SPLEEN see Satie, Erik

SPLENDE IL SOLE see Gandino, Adolfo

SPLENDOR AHEAD see Youse, Glad Robinson

SPLINTERS see Sivic, Pavle, Iveri

SPOEL, A.
  De Vlaggen Uit
    see Liederen In Volkstoon, Op. 46,
    Heft 1

  Hoe Jong-Hendrik Uit Vrijen Ging
    see Liederen In Volkstoon, Op. 46,
    Heft 1

  Liederen In Volkstoon, Op. 46, Heft 1
    solo,pno ALSBACH s.p.
      contains: De Vlaggen Uit; Hoe
      Jong-Hendrik Uit Vrijen Ging;
      Ons Prinsesje   (S3102)

  Ons Lied *Op.50a
    solo,pno ALSBACH s.p.   (S3103)

  Ons Prinsesje
    see Liederen In Volkstoon, Op. 46,
    Heft 1

SPOHR, LUDWIG (LOUIS) (1784-1859)
  Rose Softly Blooming
    high solo,pno (A maj) ASHDOWN s.p.
                                    (S3104)
    low solo,pno (G maj) ASHDOWN s.p.
                                    (S3105)
    high solo,pno (A maj) CRAMER
                                    (S3106)
    low solo,pno (G maj) CRAMER (S3107)
    high solo,pno (A maj) ALLANS
                                    (S3108)
    med solo,pno (G maj) ALLANS s.p.
                                    (S3109)

  Sechs Deutsche Lieder *Op.103,No.1-
    6, CC6U
    high solo,clar,pno BAREN. 19306
    $5.00   (S3110)

SPOMIENKA NA MOSKVU see Andrasovan,
  Tibor

SPOMIN see Jez, Jakob

SPOON RIVER ANTHOLOGY see Raphling, Sam

SPORJ OSTAN, SPORJ VASTAN! see
  Peterson-Berger, (Olof) Wilhelm

SPORJER DU BRODER see Hallnas, Hilding

SPRAY SELBDRITT' see Hanisch, Eduard

SPREADING THE NEWS see Oliver, Herbert

SPRICH, WO BIST DU? (from Prince Igor)
  [Russ/Fr/Ger] T solo,pno BELAIEFF 252
  s.p.   (S3111)

SPRIG OF BORONIA see Hull, Molly

SPRIG OF THYME
  (Collinson) med solo,pno PAXTON
  P40616 s.p.   (S3112)

SPRING see Fortner, Jack

SPRING see Bliss, Sir Arthur

SPRING see Grieg, Edvard Hagerup, Varen

SPRING see Handel, George Frideric, La
  Speranza E Giunta

SPRING see Harty, Sir Hamilton

SPRING see Hundley, Richard

SPRING see Rorem, Ned

SPRING see Stravinsky, Igor

SPRING see Sveinbjornsson, Sveinbjorn

SPRING AND FALL see Rorem, Ned

SPRING AND THE FALL, THE see Lekberg,
  Sven

SPRING COMES SINGING see Cowell, Henry
  Dixon

SPRING COMES TO STAY see Revel, Peter

SPRING DITTY, A see Scott, Cyril Meir

SPRING FLOWER AND SUMMER ROSES see
  McGeoch, Daisy

SPRING IS AT THE DOOR see Quilter,
  Roger

SPRING IS FLYING see Sibelius, Jean,
  Varen Flyktar Hastigt

SPRING JOY see Rowley, Alec

SPRING MAGIC see Anderson, William H.

SPRING OF JOY IS DRY, THE see Musgrave,
  Thea

SPRING RHAPSODY see Lang

SPRING SONG see Berkeley, Lennox

SPRING SONG see Farrand, Noel

SPRING SONG see Mendelssohn-Bartholdy,
  Felix, Fruhlingslied

SPRING SONGS see Tomc, Matija, Pomladne
  Pesmi

SPRING SORROW see Ireland, John

SPRING TAPPED AT MY WINDOW see Day,
  Maude Craske

SPRING THE FIDDLER see Ashworth-Hope,
  H.

SPRING, THE SWEET SPRING see Delius,
  Frederick

SPRING THE TRAVELLING MAN see Waters,
  Leslie

SPRING-TIME see Tirindelli, Pier
  Adolfo, O Primavera!

SPRING WATERS see Rachmaninoff, Sergey
  Vassilievitch

SPRING WATERS see Rachmaninoff, Sergey
  Vassilievitch, Spring Waters

SPRING'S A DANCER see Day, Maude Craske

SPRING'S A LOVABLE LADY see Elliott

SPRINGS AWAKENING see Rimsky-Korsakov,
  Nikolai

SPRING'S AWAKENING see Sanderson,
  Wilfred

SPRINGS OF LIVING WATER see Peterson,
  John W.

SPRING'S RETURN see Rachmaninoff,
  Sergey Vassilievitch

SPRINGTIME see Borris, Siegfried

SPRINGTIME see Weigl, Vally, Fruhling

SPRINGTIME IN SOMERSET see Ashworth-
  Hope, H.

SPRINGTIME IS CALLING see Protheroe,
  Daniel

SPRINKHANENCONCERT see Hengeveld, G.

SPROOKJE see Schuyt, Nico

SPROOKJESWEELDE see Hullebroeck, Em.

SPROSS, CHARLES GILBERT (1874-1961)
  Blessings
    high solo,pno PRESSER $.75 (S3113)

  Let All My Life Be Music
    high solo,pno PRESSER $.95 (S3114)
    low solo,pno PRESSER $.95   (S3115)

  Will-O-The Wisp
    high solo,pno PRESSER $.95 (S3116)

SPRUCH see Carriere, Paul

SPURR, THURLOW
  First Place *sac
    solo,pno WORD S-136   (S3117)

SQUIRE, FRED
  I'll Believe Forevermore *sac
    solo,pno GOSPEL 05 TM 0224 $1.00
                                    (S3118)

SQUIRE, W.H.
  Here Is My Song
    solo,pno (E flat maj) BOOSEY $1.50
                                    (S3119)

  If I Might Come To You
    low solo,pno (A flat maj) BOOSEY
    $1.50   (S3120)
    high solo,pno (C maj) BOOSEY $1.50
                                    (S3121)
    med solo,pno (B flat maj) BOOSEY
    $1.50   (S3122)

  In An Old-Fashioned Town
    solo,pno (E flat maj) BOOSEY $1.50
                                    (S3123)

  Mountain Lovers
    low solo,pno (C maj) BOOSEY $1.50
                                    (S3124)
    2 soli,pno (E flat maj) BOOSEY
    $1.75   (S3125)
    high solo,pno (E flat maj) BOOSEY
    $1.50   (S3126)

  My Prayer
    high solo,pno (F maj) BOOSEY $1.50
                                    (S3127)
    low solo,pno (E flat maj) BOOSEY
    $1.50   (S3128)

  Singing Lesson
    2 soli,pno (F maj) BOOSEY $1.75
                                    (S3129)

  When You Come Home
    low solo,pno (E flat maj) BOOSEY
    $1.50   (S3130)
    med solo,pno (F maj) BOOSEY $1.50
                                    (S3131)
    high solo,pno (G maj) BOOSEY $1.50
                                    (S3132)

SREBOTNJAK, ALOJZ F. (1931-   )
  Letters *see Pisma

  Mati *song cycle
    "Mother" solo,strings DRUSTVO
    DSS 74 rental   (S3133)

  Microsongs
    solo,fl,ob,clar/bass clar,bsn,horn,
    trp,perc,harp,strings DRUSTVO
    DSS 285 rental   (S3134)

SREBOTNJAK, ALOJZ F. (cont'd.)

Mother *see Mati

Orange *see Oranza

Oranza
    "Orange" solo,pno DRUSTVO DSS 15
    rental   (S3135)

Pisma *song cycle
    "Letters" S solo,harp DRUSTVO
    DSS 27 rental   (S3136)

Vojne Slike
    "War Pictures" A solo,perc,pno
    DRUSTVO DSS 96 rental   (S3137)

War Pictures *see Vojne Slike

SRECANJA see Kozina, Marijan

SRNKA, JIRI (1907-   )
    Tri Pisne Na Slova K.H. Machy *CC3U
    med solo,pno CZECH s.p.   (S3138)

STAAKE, P. V.D.
    Three Quatrains Of Omar Khayam *CC3U
    [Eng] solo,gtr BROEKMANS 237 s.p.
                                  (S3139)

STABAT MATER see Berkeley, Lennox

STABAT MATER see Haydn, (Franz) Joseph

STABAT MATER see Messner, Joseph

STABAT MATER see Pergolesi, Giovanni
    Battista

STABAT MATER see Perry, Julia

STABAT MATER see Thomson, Virgil

STABAT MATER see Verdi, Giuseppe

STABAT MATER see Vivaldi, Antonio

STAEMPFLI, EDWARD (1908-   )
    Tagebuch Aus Israel
    A solo,vln,vcl,clar sc ISRAELI 224
    $6.30, ipr   (S3140)

STAEPS, HANS ULRICH (1909-   )
    Amnis Aevi Omnipotens *sac,hymn
    [Lat] med solo,S rec,pno DOBLINGER
    FL 11 $3.75, ipa   (S3141)

    Das Lied Tont Fort
    [Ger] S solo,S rec&A rec&T rec/
    2vln&vla DOBLINGER $3.25   (S3142)

    Krippenlied
    med-high solo,treb inst,pno
    DOBLINGER 08 826 $2.00   (S3143)

STAFFANSVISAN
    solo,pno LUNDQUIST s.p.   (S3144)

STAFFELI, ATTILIO
    Ballata
    [It] solo,pno CURCI 502 s.p. (S3145)

STAFFORD, C.V.
    Fairy Lures
    solo,pno CRAMER $.95   (S3146)

STAHULJAK, DUBRAVKO (1920-   )
    Gogo *song cycle
    [Slav] solo,pno CROATICA s.p.
                                  (S3147)

STAINER, JOHN (1840-1901)
    God So Loved The World (from
    Crucifixion, The) sac
    high solo,pno (D flat maj) SCHIRM.G
    $.85   (S3148)
    low solo,pno (B flat maj) SCHIRM.G
    $.85   (S3149)

    Love Divine, All Love Excelling (from
    Daughter Of Jairus) sac,Marriage
    ST soli,pno SCHIRM.G $1.00   (S3150)
    ST soli,pno NOVELLO 17.0104.05 s.p.
                                  (S3151)
    med solo,pno (E flat maj) ALLANS
    s.p.   (S3152)
    low solo,pno (G maj) ALLANS s.p.
                                  (S3153)
    2 soli,pno (G maj) FISCHER,C S 5931
    s.p.   (S3154)
    ABar/AT soli,pno SCHIRM.G $1.00
                                  (S3155)
    Love Divine All Love's Excelling
    *sac
    high solo,pno (G maj) ALLANS s.p.
                                  (S3156)
    low solo,pno (F maj) ALLANS s.p.
                                  (S3157)

STAJARNOGA see Stenhammar, Wilhelm

STALL FLAGGAN SA JAG SER DEN see
    Alfven, Hugo

STALLINGS
    Everything's Under Control *sac
    solo,pno BENSON S5428-R $1.00
                                  (S3158)

    One Day I Will *see Mills

    Touching Jesus *sac
    solo,pno BENSON S8246-S $1.00
                                  (S3159)

    You're All Invited To My Mansion
    *sac
    solo,pno BENSON S8590-S $1.00
                                  (S3160)

STALLS
    Stepping On The Clouds *sac
    solo,pno BENSON S7591-S $1.00
                                  (S3161)

STALVEY, DORRANCE
    A Un Jeune Gentilhomme
    [Eng/Fr] med solo,pno SALABERT-US
    $3.75, ipr   (S3162)

STAM, HENK (1922-   )
    Rispetti
    Bar solo,strings DONEMUS s.p.
                                  (S3163)

STAMEGNA, NICOLO
    Et Cur Non Te Amo *sac
    (Ewerhart, Rudolf) S/T solo,cont
    BIELER CS 67 s.p.   (S3164)

STAMNINGSVISA see Kilpinen, Yrio

ST'AMORE see Guerrini, Guido

STAMPS-BAXTER FAVORITE GOSPEL SONGS
    *sac,CCUL,gospel
    solo,pno STAMPS 4825-SN $1.95; solo,
    pno STAMPS 4826-RN $1.95   (S3165)

STAMPS-BAXTER'S BOOK OF BRUMLEY
    FAVORITES *sac,CC112UL,folk/
    gospel/hymn
    4 soli,pno STAMPS 4847-SN $1.00
                                  (S3166)

STAMPS-BAXTER'S BOOK OF BRUMLEY'S
    FAVORITE SACRED SONGS *sac,CC97UL,
    gospel
    solo,pno STAMPS 4846-SN $1.00 (S3167)

STAN' STILL JORDAN *spir
    (Burleigh, H. T.) high solo,pno
    BELWIN $1.50   (S3168)
    (Burleigh, H. T.) med solo,pno BELWIN
    $1.50   (S3169)

STANCES A LEA see Sureau-Bellet, J.

STANCES A MANON see Delmet, Paul

STANCES A VICTOR-HUGO see Deutsch de la
    Meurthe, H.

STANCES D'AMOUR ET DE REVE see Vierne,
    Louis

STAND THOU STILL! see Wagner, Richard,
    Stehe Still!

STAND UP FOR JESUS *sac,gospel
    solo,pno ABER.GRP. $1.50   (S3170)

STANDARD ON THE BRAES O' MAR, THE
    *folk,Scot
    solo,pno (G maj) PATERSON FS84 s.p.
                                  (S3171)

STANDARD VOCAL REPERTOIRE, BOOK 1 *CCU
    high solo,pno FISCHER,C RB 45; low
    solo,pno FISCHER,C RB 46   (S3172)

STANDARD VOCAL REPERTOIRE, BOOK 2 *CCU
    high solo,pno FISCHER,C RB 71; low
    solo,pno FISCHER,C RB 72   (S3173)

STANDCHEN see Liszt, Franz

STANDCHEN see Lothar, Mark

STANDCHEN see Madetoja, Leevi, Serenadi

STANDCHEN see Mussorgsky, Modest

STANDCHEN see Schubert, Franz (Peter)

STANDCHEN see Strauss, Richard

STANDCHEN see Wolf, Hugo

STANDCHEN "DER MOND STEHT" see
    Beethoven, Ludwig van

STANDING HERE WONDERING WHICH WAY TO GO
    *sac,gospel
    solo,pno ABER.GRP. $1.50   (S3174)

STANFORD, CHARLES VILLIERS (1852-1924)
    Belle Dame Sans Merci
    solo,pno (F min) GALLIARD 2.1770.7
    $1.50   (S3175)

    Drake's Drum
    high solo,pno (D maj) BOOSEY $1.50
                                  (S3176)
    low solo,pno (C maj) BOOSEY $1.50
                                  (S3177)

STANFORD, CHARLES VILLIERS (cont'd.)

    Drop Me A Flower
    solo,pno CRAMER $1.10   (S3178)

    Fairy Lough
    solo,pno (D maj) BOOSEY $1.50 (S3179)

    Father O'Flynn
    solo,pno (A flat maj) BOOSEY $1.50
                                  (S3180)

    Irish Idyll In Six Miniatures *CC6U
    low solo,pno BOOSEY $5.00   (S3181)

    Irish Lover
    solo,pno CRAMER   (S3182)

    Japanese Lullaby
    med solo,pno (D flat maj) CRAMER
                                  (S3183)
    low solo,pno (B flat maj) CRAMER
    $.95   (S3184)
    high solo,pno (E flat maj) CRAMER
    $1.10   (S3185)

    Johneen
    solo,pno (D flat maj) BOOSEY $1.50
                                  (S3186)

    Lark's Grave, The
    2 soli,pno/orch ROBERTON 71037 s.p.
                                  (S3187)

    Limerick Point To Point Race
    solo,pno CRAMER   (S3188)

    Londonderry Air
    low solo,pno (C maj) CRAMER   (S3189)
    high solo,pno (E flat maj) CRAMER
                                  (S3190)
    med solo,pno (D maj) CRAMER   (S3191)

    Lullaby
    solo,pno CRAMER $.95   (S3192)

    Merry Month Of May, The
    solo,pno CRAMER $.95   (S3193)

    Monkey's Carol
    high solo,pno (D min) CRAMER $1.00
                                  (S3194)
    low solo,pno (B min) CRAMER $1.00
                                  (S3195)

    My Brave Boy
    solo,pno CRAMER   (S3196)

    My Love's An Arbutus
    high solo,pno (A flat maj) BOOSEY
    $1.50   (S3197)
    low solo,pno (G maj) BOOSEY $1.50
                                  (S3198)

    Pibroch, The
    med solo,pno (C sharp min) ASHDOWN
    $1.50   (S3199)
    low solo,pno (B min) ASHDOWN $1.50
                                  (S3200)
    high solo,pno (E min) ASHDOWN $1.50
                                  (S3201)

    Rose Of Killarney
    solo,pno CRAMER   (S3202)

    Soft Day
    high solo,pno (F maj) GALAXY
    3.1303.7 $1.25   (S3203)
    low solo,pno (D flat maj) GALAXY
    3.1304.7 $1.25   (S3204)

    Song Of The Bow
    high solo,pno (E flat maj) CRAMER
                                  (S3205)
    low solo,pno (G maj) CRAMER   (S3206)

    Sower's Song
    solo,pno CRAMER $.70   (S3207)

    Trottin' To The Fair
    solo,pno (D maj) BOOSEY $1.50
                                  (S3208)

    Unknown Sea
    solo,pno CRAMER   (S3209)

    Winds Of Bethlehem
    solo,pno CRAMER   (S3210)

    With The Dublin Fusiliers
    solo,pno CRAMER   (S3211)

STANGE, MAX (1856-1932)
    Karlek
    high solo,pno GEHRMANS s.p.   (S3212)
    low solo,pno GEHRMANS s.p.   (S3213)

STANISLAS, AD.
    Juin: Roses, Cerises, Parfums *see
    Privas, Xavier

    Le Coeur De Lison
    solo,pno ENOCH s.p.   (S3214)
    solo,acap ENOCH s.p.   (S3215)

    Les Mois *see Privas, Xavier

STANISLAV, JOSEF (1897-1971)
    Pisne Na Texty S. Jesejina *CCU
    high solo,pno PANTON s.p.   (S3216)

STANISLAV, JOSEF (cont'd.)

Pisne Pro Vyssi Hlas Na Texty S.
Jesesnina *Op.8, CCU
[Czech/Ger] solo,pno PANTON 1213
s.p.   (S3217)

Svetla Na Vychode *CCU
[Czech/Russ/Eng/Fr] S/T solo,pno
CZECH s.p.   (S3218)

Svetla Na Vychode *song cycle
solo,pno PANTON s.p.   (S3219)

STANLEY, JOHN (1713-1786)
Ave Maria *sac
[Lat/Eng] S/T solo,pno RICORDI-ENG
50499 s.p.   (S3220)

Be Pleasant, Be Airy
(Bevan) high solo,pno ELKIN
27.2486.03 s.p.   (S3221)

Cupid's Power I Despise
(Bevan) high solo,pno ELKIN
27.2608.04 s.p.   (S3222)

Sweet Pretty Bird
(Bevan) S solo,pno ELKIN 27.2245.03
s.p.   (S3223)

Welcome Death (from Teraminta)
[Eng] B solo,pno,opt 2vln&vcl&bvl
HINRICHSEN H279 $3.00   (S3224)

STANPHILL, IRA F.
Follow Me *sac,gospel
solo,pno ABER.GRP. $1.50   (S3225)
solo,pno SINGSPIR 7055-SN $1.00
                              (S3226)

Happiness Is The Lord *sac
solo,pno SINGSPIR 7092 $1.00
                              (S3227)

He Washed My Eyes With Tears *sac
solo,pno SINGSPIR 7056-SN $1.00
                              (S3228)

I Walk With His Hand In Mine *sac
solo,pno SINGSPIR 7070 $1.00
                              (S3229)

If I've Forgotten *sac
solo,pno SINGSPIR 7102 $1.00
                              (S3230)

I'm Gonna Make It Through Somehow
*sac
solo,pno SINGSPIR 7095 $1.00
                              (S3231)

Mansion Over The Hilltop *sac
solo,pno SINGSPIR 7059-SN $1.00
                              (S3232)

Room At The Cross *sac
solo,pno SINGSPIR 7057-SN $1.00
                              (S3233)

Suppertime *sac
solo,pno SINGSPIR 7060-SN $1.00
                              (S3234)

Thirty Pieces Of Silver *sac
solo,pno SINGSPIR 7063-SN $1.00
                              (S3235)

Unworthy *sac
solo,pno SINGSPIR 7058-SN $1.00
                              (S3236)

We'll Talk It Over *sac
solo,pno STAMPS 7269-SN $1.00
                              (S3237)

Workin' Man's Prayer *sac
solo,pno SINGSPIR 7097 $1.00
                              (S3238)

World Famous Songs *sac,CC12UL
solo,pno BENSON BO800 $2.50   (S3239)

Yesterday's Gone *sac
solo,pno SINGSPIR 7096 $1.00
                              (S3240)

STANSELL
Longing
med solo,pno SHAWNEE IA5004 $.60
                              (S3241)

STANTJE EN WANTJE see Hullebroeck, Em.

STANTON, GEOFFREY
Song Of The Road
low solo,pno (D maj) CRAMER (S3242)
high solo,pno (E flat maj) CRAMER
                              (S3243)

STANTON, LOUIS
World Will Laugh Again, The
med solo,pno (E flat maj) WILLIS
$.60   (S3244)

STANZAS FOR MUSIC see Owens, Robert

STANZAS OF CHARLES II see Voormolen,
Alexander Nicolas

STAR see Schmitt, Florent

STAR, THE see Rogers, James Hotchkiss

STAR, THE see Stevens, Sammy

STAR AT CHRISTMAS see Davis, Katherine
K.

STAR CANDLES see Head, Michael (Dewar)

STAR CLUSTERS, NEBULAE AND PLACES IN
DEVON see Bedford, David

STAR FELL DOWN, A see Ben-Haim, Paul,
Kochav Nafal

STAR IN THE EAST see Lovelace, Austin
C.

STAR OF BETHLEHEM see Adams, Stephen

STAR OF HOPE see St. Joseph, Sister Of

STAR OF THE COUNTY DOWN see Hughes,
Herbert

STAR OF THE EAST see Kennedy

STAR ROAD, THE see O'Hara, Geoffrey

STAR SPANGLED BANNER, THE
solo,pno (available in 3 keys) ASHLEY
$.95   (S3245)
(Key, Francis Scott; Smith, Stafford)
[Eng] solo,pno RICORDI-ARG BA 7257
s.p.   (S3246)
(Smith) med-high solo,pno (B flat
maj) BOSTON $1.50   (S3247)
(Smith) high solo,pno (A flat maj)
FISCHER,C V 1533   (S3248)
(Smith) high solo,pno (C maj) CENTURY
1299   (S3249)
(Smith, J.S.) med solo,pno PRESSER
$.95   (S3250)
(Smith, John S.; Diller, Angela) med
solo,pno (B flat maj) SCHIRM.G $.85
                              (S3251)
(Smith, John S.; Diller, Angela) low
solo,pno (A flat maj) SCHIRM.G $.85
                              (S3252)
(Smith, John S.; Diller, Angela) low
solo,pno (G maj,easy) SCHIRM.G $.60
                              (S3253)

STAR-SPANGLED BANNER, THE see Schumann,
Robert (Alexander)

STAR VICINO see Rosa

STAR VICINO see Rosa, S.

STAR WAS HIS CANDLE, A see Del Riego

STAREN see Merikanto, Oskar,
Kottarainen

STARER, ROBERT (1924-   )
Cantamus
SBar soli,vln,pno ISRAELI 206A
$10.00   (S3254)

Two Sacred Songs *sac,CC2U
solo,pno/inst PEER $1.50, ipr
                              (S3255)

STARKE EINBILDUNGSKRAFT see Mahler,
Gustav

STARKS, HOWARD
Through Love *sac
med solo,pno CRESPUB CP-S5019 $1.00
                              (S3256)

STARLIGHT AND LOVELIGHT see Martin,
Easthope

STARLIGHT OF NOON see Hovhaness, Alan

STARLING LAKE see Shepherd, Arthur

STARLINGS ON THE ROOF see Heilner,
Irwin

STAROMIEYSKI, J.
Drei Arien *CC3UL
S/A/B solo,vln,cont sc FMA FMA 26
s.p.   (S3257)

Fidelia Omnia
see Zwei Fragmente

Suscepit Israel
see Zwei Fragmente

Zwei Fragmente *sac,concerto
cmplt ed FMA FMA 16 s.p.
contains: Fidelia Omnia (S solo,
vln,vcl,cembalo); Suscepit
Israel (S solo,2vln)   (S3258)

STARS see Leoni, Franco

STARS ALL DOTTED OVER THE SKY see
Sharpe, Evelyn

STARS ARE LITTLE CHILDREN see Bland,
Helena M.

STARS ARE MEMORIES, THE see Penn,
Arthur A.

STARS HAVE NOT DEALT ME THE WORST THEY
COULD DO, THE see Heilner, Irwin

STARS THROUGH THE TREES see Russell,
Kennedy

STATHAM, HEATHCOTE (DICKEN) (1889-   )
Messmates
solo,pno CRAMER   (S3259)

STATI D'ANIMA see Pratella, Francesco
Balilla

STATUE OF LIBERTY, THE see Enloe, Neil

STAUB, V.
Je N'ose Pas
S solo,pno DURAND s.p.   (S3260)

L'heure Delicieuse
S solo,pno DURAND s.p.   (S3261)

L'heure Silencieuse
S solo,pno DURAND s.p.   (S3262)

STAUUNG see Leistner-Mayer, Roland

STAVA IL SOL NEL FIRMAMENTO see
Pratella, Francesco Balilla

STAY AWHILE AND LISTEN TO MY SONG see
Braden, Edwin

STAY, O SWEET, AND DO NOT RISE see
Joubert, John

STAY, SUMMER, STAY see Pritchett, J.

STEAL AWAY *sac,gospel/spir
solo,pno ABER.GRP. $1.50   (S3263)
(Burleigh, H. T.) high solo,pno
BELWIN $1.50   (S3264)
(Burleigh, H. T.) low solo,pno BELWIN
$1.50   (S3265)
(Waring) solo,pno SHAWNEE IA 9 $.60
                              (S3266)

STEAL AWAY TO JESUS *spir
(Roberton, Hugh S.) 3 soli,pno
ROBERTON 72104 s.p.   (S3267)

STEAL ME, SWEET THIEF see Menotti, Gian
Carlo

STEAM, STEAM, STEAM *Jew
solo,pno KAMMEN 92 $1.00   (S3268)

STEANE, BRUCE
I Heard The Voice Of Jesus Say
solo,pno CRAMER   (S3269)

STEARMAN
He Turned The Water Into Wine *sac
solo,pno LILLENAS SM-636: RN $1.00
                              (S3270)

STEARNS, PETER PINDAR
Five Lyrics From "The Prophet" *CC5U
S solo,fl,vla sc AM.COMP.AL. $3.57
                              (S3271)

Three Love Songs *CC3U
S solo,clar,bass clar,trp,trom,
harp,vln,vla,vcl sc AM.COMP.AL.
$8.25, ipa   (S3272)

Three Sacred Songs *sac,CC3U,Bibl
S solo,ob,horn,vcl sc AM.COMP.AL.
$3.30   (S3273)

Whitman Cycle IV *song cycle
S solo,pno AM.COMP.AL. $5.50
                              (S3274)

STEDRON, MILOS (1942-   )
Sic Et Non *cant
TB soli,pic,ob,trom,tuba CZECH s.p.
                              (S3275)

STEELE
Closer To Thee *sac
(Chapman; Little) solo,pno LILLENAS
SM-904: SN $1.00   (S3276)

STEEN, G. V.D.
Ariel's Songs *CCU
solo,pno BROEKMANS 398 s.p. (S3277)

STEENHUIS, FRANCOIS (1918-1956)
Amor
Mez solo,2fl,ob,2clar,2bsn,2horn,
strings DONEMUS s.p.
contains: Derniere Promenade,
Op.1,No.3; Les Presages, Op.1,
No.2; Printemps, Op.1,No.1
                              (S3278)

Derniere Promenade *Op.1,No.3
see Amor

La Carpe *Op.6,No.3
see Trois Melodies De Fr. Toussaint

Le Chat *Op.6,No.2
see Trois Melodies De Fr. Toussaint

Le Poulet *Op.6,No.1
see Trois Melodies De Fr. Toussaint

Les Presages *Op.1,No.2
see Amor

Printemps *Op.1,No.1
see Amor

Trois Melodies De Fr. Toussaint
med solo,pno DONEMUS s.p.
contains: La Carpe, Op.6,No.3; Le

STEENHUIS, FRANCOIS (cont'd.)

Chat, Op.6,No.2; Le Poulet,
Op.6,No.1   (S3279)

STEENMAN, J.
Miseremini Mei *sac
solo,opt STBB,pno/org (available in
2 keys) HEUGEL s.p.   (S3280)

STEEPLE-CHASE see Heland

STEERE, WILLIAM C.
Dear Lord And Father
med solo,pno PRESSER $.75   (S3281)

STEFANSSON, FJOLNIR (1930-   )
Kvoldvisa
see Three Songs

Litla Barn Meo Lokkinn Bjarta
see Three Songs

Snjotittlingur
see Three Songs

Three Songs *CC3U
S solo,pno ICELAND s.p.   (S3282)

Three Songs
S solo,pno ICELAND s.p.
contains: Kvoldvisa; Litla Barn
Meo Lokkinn Bjarta;
Snjotittlingur   (S3283)

STEFFANI, AGOSTINO (1654-1728)
Come My Dear One *see Vieni O Cara,
Amata Sposa

Come, Ye Children, And Hearken To Me
*sac
2 med-high soli,pno oct CONCORDIA
98-1593 $.25   (S3284)

Oh, How Often *see Quanto, Quanto

Quanto, Quanto (from Niobe)
(Wasner) "Oh, How Often" [It/Eng] T
solo,2A rec,vcl,hpsd/pno (F maj)
SCHIRM.G $.85   (S3285)

Vieni O Cara, Amata Sposa (from
Briseide)
(Wasner) "Come My Dear One" [It/
Eng] S solo,A rec/fl,ob/T rec,
vcl,hpsd/pno (G min) SCHIRM.G
$.85   (S3286)

STEFFE, WILLIAM
Battle Hymn Of The Republic
(Howe; Simon) med solo,pno FISCHER,
C V 2321   (S3287)

STEFFEN, WOLFGANG (1923-   )
Drei Lieder Fur Bariton
Bar solo,pno SIRIUS s.p.
contains: Fruhstuck; Inselgeburt;
Notturno   (S3288)

Fruhstuck
see Drei Lieder Fur Bariton

Inselgeburt
see Drei Lieder Fur Bariton

Notturno
see Drei Lieder Fur Bariton

Vier Sonette An Orpheus *Op.26, CC4U
[Ger] BOTE $7.25   (S3289)

STEFFENS, WALTER (1934-   )
Epitaph Auf Rimbaud *Op.2c
A solo,fl,clar,trp,pno,opt 2harp,
strings voc sc BREITKOPF-W s.p.
                           (S3290)

Neue Gleichnisse *Op.3b
S solo,fl,clar,vla BREITKOPF-W
EB 6591 $4.00   (S3291)

Oboenlieder *Op.9, CCU
A/B/Bar solo,ob BREITKOPF-W EB 6519
$5.75   (S3292)

STEHE STILL! see Wagner, Richard

STEHMAN, JACQUES (1912-1975)
Le Flocon De Neige
see Rimes Enfantines

Les Jeux De Paris
see Rimes Enfantines

Les Marronniers
see Rimes Enfantines

Les Mures Du Chemin Creux
see Rimes Enfantines

Les Pigeons De Paris
see Rimes Enfantines

Les Yeux Bleus De Grand'mere
see Rimes Enfantines

STEHMAN, JACQUES (cont'd.)

Rimes Enfantines
T solo,pno cmplt ed CBDM s.p.
contains: Le Flocon De Neige; Les
Jeux De Paris; Les Marronniers;
Les Mures Du Chemin Creux; Les
Pigeons De Paris; Les Yeux
Bleus De Grand'mere   (S3293)

Seul
Mez/T solo,pno CBDM s.p.   (S3294)

STEIGE HERAB VON DEN BERGEN see Schutz,
Heinrich, Veni De Libano

STEIN, LEON
Kaddish
Bar solo,pno sc AM.COMP.AL. $2.75
                           (S3295)
T solo,pno sc AM.COMP.AL. $2.75
                           (S3296)
String Quartet No. Five - Ekloge
S solo,4strings AM.COMP.AL. sc
$18.70, ipa, voc sc $3.85 (S3297)

STEIN SONG see Fenstad

STEINBACH, E.
Rodharig Ar Min Hjartans Kar
high solo,pno GEHRMANS s.p. (S3298)
low solo,pno GEHRMANS s.p. (S3299)

STEINBERG, BEN
Vay'chulu
[Heb] solo,pno/org TRANSCON. WJ 407
$1.00   (S3300)

STEINER, GITTA
Concert Piece For Seven, No. 2
S solo,fl,pno,bvl,2perc sc SEESAW
$11.00   (S3301)

Concert Piece For Seven, No. I
S solo,fl,pno,vcl,2perc sc SEESAW
$8.00   (S3302)

Dream Dialogue For Soprano And
Percussion
S solo,perc sc SEESAW $5.00 (S3303)

Four Songs For Medium Voice And
Vibraphone *CC4U
med solo,vibra sc SEESAW $6.00
                           (S3304)

Interludes For Voice And Vibraphone
*CCU
solo,vibra sc SEESAW $4.00 (S3305)

New Poems For Voice And Vibraphone
solo,vibra sc SEESAW $3.00 (S3306)

Pages From A Summer Journal
med solo,pno sc SEESAW $2.00
                           (S3307)

Three Poems For Voice And Two
Percussionists *CC3U
solo,2perc sc SEESAW $5.00 (S3308)

Three Songs For Voice And Piano
*CC3U
solo,pno sc SEESAW $4.00   (S3309)

Trio For Voice, Piano And Percussion
solo,pno,perc sc SEESAW $5.00
                           (S3310)

Two Songs For Soprano And Piano
*CC2U
S solo,pno sc SEESAW $3.00 (S3311)

STEINKE, GREG
Three Sonnets *CC3U
S solo,fl,strings sc SEESAW $4.00
                           (S3312)

STELE POUR SEI SHONAGON see Froidebise,
Pierre

STELLA see Faure, Jean-Baptiste

STELLA DEL MARINAR see Ponchielli,
Amilcare

STELLDICHEIN see Lothar, Mark

STELLE CHIARE see Cimara, Pietro

STEMMEN UIT HET LABYRINT see Schat,
Peter

STEMMING see Zagwijn, Henri

STEMMINGEN see Sigtenhorst-Meyer,
Bernhard van den

STEN STURE see Svedbom, Vilhelm

STENBOCKS KURIR see Hallen, Andreas

STENHAMMER
Denne Ar Min Kare Son
low solo,pno LUNDQUIST s.p. (S3313)
med solo,pno LUNDQUIST s.p. (S3314)
high solo,pno LUNDQUIST s.p.
                           (S3315)

STENHAMMAR, PER ULRIK (1829-1875)
Det Ar Min Vans Rost *sac
Mez solo,pno GEHRMANS s.p. (S3316)

Fyra Sanger Vid Piano *CC4U
[Ger/Swed] solo,pno GEHRMANS s.p.
                           (S3317)

Huru Lange Vill Du Sorja (from David
Och Saul) sac
B solo,pno GEHRMANS s.p.   (S3318)

STENHAMMAR, WILHELM (1871-1927)
Adagio *Op.20,No.5
solo,pno/org ERIKS K 130 see from
Fem Sanger   (S3319)
(Malmfors, A.) solo,2clar,strings
ERIKS rental   (S3320)
(Pergament, M.) high solo/low solo,
2clar,2bsn,2horn,strings ERIKS
rental, ea.   (S3321)

Ballad
low solo,pno GEHRMANS s.p. (S3322)

Behagen *Op.8,No.5
solo,pno/org ERIKS K 135 see from
Fem Visor   (S3323)

Den Tidiga Sorgen *Op.8,No.3
solo,pno/org ERIKS K 133 see from
Fem Visor   (S3324)

Dottern Sade *Op.8,No.2
solo,pno/org ERIKS K 132 see from
Fem Visor   (S3325)

Efterskord *CC5U
solo,pno GEHRMANS s.p.   (S3326)

En Positivvisa *Op.38,No.4
see Four Stockholm Poems

Fem Sanger *see Adagio, Op.20,No.5;
Gammal Nederlandare, Op.20,No.3;
Mansken, Op.20,No.4; Stjarnoga,
Op.20,No.1; Vid Fonstret, Op.20,
No.2   (S3327)

Fem Visor *see Behagen, Op.8,No.5;
Den Tidiga Sorgen, Op.8,No.3;
Dottern Sade, Op.8,No.2; Lutat
Mot Gardet, Op.8,No.1; Till En
Ros, Op.8,No.4   (S3328)

Flickan Knyter I Johannenatten
*Op.4b,No.2
see Stenhammar, Wilhelm, Flickan
Kom Ifran Sin Alsklings Mote
solo,pno/org ERIKS K 123   (S3329)

Flickan Kom Ifran Sin Alsklings Mote
*Op.4b,No.1
solo,2fl,2ob,2clar,2bsn,2horn,
strings ERIKS rental contains
also: Flickan Knyter I
Johannenatten, Op.4b,No.2 (S3330)
solo,pno/org ERIKS K 122   (S3331)

Four Stockholm Poems
[Swed] high solo,kbd NORDISKA s.p.
contains: En Positivvisa, Op.38,
No.4; I En Skogsbacke, Op.38,
No.2; Kvall I Klara, Op.38,
No.1; Mellan Broarna, Op.38,
No.3   (S3332)

Gammal Nederlandare *Op.20,No.3
solo,pno/org ERIKS K 128 see from
Fem Sanger   (S3333)
(Eckerberg, S.) solo,2fl,2ob,2clar,
2bsn,2horn,trp,strings ERIKS
rental   (S3334)

Hemmarschen, Ganglat
solo,pno GEHRMANS s.p.   (S3335)

I En Skogsbacke *Op.38,No.2
see Four Stockholm Poems

I Skogen
med solo,pno GEHRMANS s.p. (S3336)

Kvall I Klara *Op.38,No.1
see Four Stockholm Poems

Le Hanap De L'Ancestre
solo,pno ENOCH s.p. see also CHANTS
DU NORD   (S3337)

Lutat Mot Gardet *Op.8,No.1
solo,pno/org ERIKS K 131 see from
Fem Visor   (S3338)

Mansken *Op.20,No.4
solo,pno/org ERIKS K 129 see from
Fem Sanger   (S3339)
(Malmfors, A.) solo,fl,ob,2bsn,bsn,
strings ERIKS rental   (S3340)

Medborgarsang
solo,pno GEHRMANS s.p.   (S3341)

Mellan Broarna *Op.38,No.3
see Four Stockholm Poems

STENHAMMAR, WILHELM (cont'd.)

Seven Poems From Ensamhetens Tankar
    *Op.7, CC7L
    [Swed] med solo,kbd NORDISKA s.p.
                                    (S3342)
Stajarnoga
    (Malmfors, A.) solo,ob,2clar,
    strings ERIKS rental   (S3343)
    (Rybrant, S.) solo,2fl,ob,2clar,
    bsn,2horn,strings ERIKS rental
                                    (S3344)
Stjarnoga *Op.20,No.1
    solo,pno/org ERIKS K 126 see from
    Fem Sanger   (S3345)
Sverige
    high solo,pno GEHRMANS s.p. (S3346)
    med solo,pno GEHRMANS s.p. (S3347)
    low solo,pno GEHRMANS s.p. (S3348)
Till En Ros *Op.8,No.4
    solo,pno/org ERIKS K 134 see from
    Fem Visor   (S3349)
Vid Fonstret *Op.20,No.2
    solo,pno/org ERIKS K 127 see from
    Fem Sanger   (S3350)

STENKA RASIN *folk,Russ
    [Ger/Russ] solo,pno ZIMMER. 1551 s.p.
                                    (S3351)

STENLUND, BERTIL O.
Simon Fran Cyrene
    solo,pno/org ERIKS K 182 (S3352)

STENSON, E.J.
Prayer Perfect, The
    (Riley) high solo,pno FOX,S (S3353)
    (Riley) high solo&low solo,pno FOX,
    S   (S3354)
    (Riley) low solo,pno FOX,S (S3355)
    (Riley) med-low solo,pno FOX,S
                                    (S3356)
    (Riley) med-high solo,pno FOX,S
                                    (S3357)
    (Riley) med solo&low solo,pno FOX,S
                                    (S3358)
    (Riley) ST soli,pno FOX,S   (S3359)

STEPAN, V.
April Samt Mai *Op.7
    low solo,pno SUPRAPHON s.p. (S3360)

STEPANEK, JIRI (1917-)
Tri Vokalisy *CC3U,vocalise
    T/S solo,pno CZECH s.p.   (S3361)

STEPHAN, R.
Liebeszauber
    Bar solo,pno/orch voc sc SCHOTTS
    3057 s.p., ipa   (S3362)

STEPHEN-BURNETT COLLECTION OF SCOTS
    FOLK SONGS: SOPRANO ALBUM *CC26U,
    folk,Scot
    (Stephen-Burnett) S solo,pno PATERSON
    s.p.   (S3363)

STEPHEN FOSTER SONG BOOK see Foster,
    Stephen Collins

STEPHENS, WARD
Teach Me To Forgive *sac,Gen
    high solo,pno (E flat maj) WILLIS
    $.60   (S3364)
    low solo,pno (D flat maj) WILLIS
    $.60   (S3365)

STEPHENSON, RICHARD T.
Psalm 103 *sac,Psalm
    solo,pno PATERSON s.p.   (S3366)

STEPPING ON THE CLOUDS see Stalls

STERB ICH, SO HULLT IN BLUMEN MEINE
    GLIEDER see Wolf, Hugo

STERN see Strauss, Richard

STERN, HERMANN (1912-)
Hinunter Ist Der Sonnen Schein *sac
    SA soli,2S rec,cont HANSSLER 5.061
    s.p. see also GESANGE ZUM
    KIRCHENJAHR   (S3367)

STERNBERG, ERICH WALTER (1898-1974)
Distant Flute, The *CC3U
    [Heb/Ger] A/Bar/S solo,fl
    ISR.MUS.INST. 025 $5.00   (S3368)
Ferry, The
    med solo,pno ISRAELI 20.506 $1.40
                                    (S3369)
My People *CC5U
    [Heb/Eng/Ger] S/T solo,orch study
    sc ISR.MUS.INST. 024 $10.00, solo
    pt,voc sc ISR.MUS.INST. 024B
    $5.00   (S3370)
String Quartet No. 1
    Mez solo,4strings study sc ISRAELI
    506 $4.20, ipr   (S3371)

STERNDALE-BENNETT
Give And Take
    low solo,pno (E flat maj) ASHDOWN
    s.p.   (S3372)
    high solo,pno (F maj) ASHDOWN s.p.
                                    (S3373)

STERNE see Bijvanck, Henk

STERNE, COLIN
Dear Heart
    solo,pno PEER $.85   (S3374)
Gentle Lady
    solo,pno PEER $.85   (S3375)
My Love Is In A Light Attire
    solo,pno PEER $.85   (S3376)

STERNLEIN, SAG' MIR AN see Mussorgsky,
    Modest

STERNSEHERIN LIEDER see Knab, Armin

STERREN EN HEIDELIED see Zweers,
    [Bernard]

STERRENHEMEL see Schouwman, Hans

STERRENKIND see Godron, Hugo

STERVEND LICHT see Zagwijn, Henri

STETER TROPFEN see Salieri, Antonio

STETIT PUELLA see Mul, Jan

STEUERMANN, EDWARD (1892-)
Three Songs For Low Voice To Poems By
    Bert Brecht
    low solo,pno NEW VALLEY $2.50
                                    (S3377)

STEVENS
For Those Tears I Died *sac
    solo,pno BENSON S5483-R $1.00
                                    (S3378)

STEVENS, HALSEY (1908-)
Lay A Garland On My Hearse
    Mez solo,pno AM.COMP.AL. $.82
                                    (S3379)
Music For The Marriage Service
    *Marriage
    med solo,org/pno FOSTER $2.00
    contains: O Perfect Love; Wedding
    Prayer, A   (S3380)
O Perfect Love
    see Music For The Marriage Service
On A Rosebud Sent To Her Lover
    high solo,pno AM.COMP.AL. $.82
                                    (S3381)
Pour Noel
    med solo,pno AM.COMP.AL. $.82
                                    (S3382)
Quatre Chansons Populaires Du Canada
    *CC4U,Nor Am
    med solo,pno AM.COMP.AL. $7.70
                                    (S3383)
Sonetto
    low solo,pno AM.COMP.AL. $1.37
                                    (S3384)
Three Japanese Folksongs *CC3U,folk,
    Jap
    med solo,vln,vcl,pno sc AM.COMP.AL.
    $4.40, ipa   (S3385)
Three Songs From Mother Goose *CC3U
    med solo,pno AM.COMP.AL. $2.75
                                    (S3386)
Troubadour Songs *CCU
    med solo,pno AM.COMP.AL. $3.30
                                    (S3387)
Two English Folksongs *CC2U,Eng
    med solo,pno AM.COMP.AL. $3.85
                                    (S3388)
Two Shakespeare Songs *CC2U
    Mez solo,fl,clar sc AM.COMP.AL.
    $3.85, ipa   (S3389)
Wedding Prayer, A
    see Music For The Marriage Service

STEVENS, L.
Ask Me No More
    high solo,pno (D flat maj) BOOSEY
    $1.50   (S3390)
    low solo,pno (B flat maj) BOOSEY
    $1.50   (S3391)

STEVENS, M.
Chant Des Communiantes
    solo,pno (available in 2 keys)
    ENOCH s.p.   (S3392)
Le Chant Des Communiantes *sac
    [Fr] solo,pno (available in 2 keys)
    ENOCH   (S3393)

STEVENS, SAMMY
I Done Got Over *see Hubbard, H.
I Dreamed I Went To Heaven *see
    Hubbard, H.

STEVENS, SAMMY (cont'd.)

Only *see Hubbard, H.
Savior Of The World *sac,gospel
    solo,pno SAUL AVE   (S3394)
Star, The *sac,gospel
    solo,pno SAUL AVE   (S3395)

STEVENSON see Heilner, Irwin

STEWARD
Saw Ye My Saviour? *sac
    low solo,pno (E flat maj) FISCHER,C
    V 1609   (S3396)
    high solo,pno (G maj) FISCHER,C
    V 1608   (S3397)

STEWART
Give Me Your Hand
    solo,pno ALLANS s.p.   (S3398)

STEWART, BROMLEY
Just Across The Street
    solo,pno CRAMER   (S3399)

STEWART, ROBERT [PRESCOTT] (1825-1894)
La Lettre D'Amour
    solo,acap ENOCH s.p.   (S3400)
    solo,pno ENOCH s.p.   (S3401)

STIASNY
Forest Wind
    [Eng] high solo,pno HINRICHSEN
    H464A $2.50   (S3402)
Inscription For An Old Tomb
    [Eng] high solo/med solo,pno
    HINRICHSEN H464B $2.50   (S3403)

STICKLES, WILLIAM
Four And Twenty Snowflakes
    med solo,pno (E flat maj) WILLIS
    $.50   (S3404)
Grant Me, Dear Lord, Deep Peace Of
    Mind *sac,Gen
    high solo,pno (E flat maj) WILLIS
    $.60   (S3405)
    low solo,pno (C maj) WILLIS $.60
                                    (S3406)
Greensleeves
    med solo,pno (F min) SCHIRM.G $.75
                                    (S3407)
Mither Heart, The
    low solo,pno (D flat maj) WILLIS
    $.60   (S3408)
    med solo,pno (E flat maj) WILLIS
    $.60   (S3409)
    high solo,pno (F maj) WILLIS $.60
                                    (S3410)
My Soul Is Athirst For God
    high solo,pno AMP $.60   (S3411)
    low solo,pno AMP $.60   (S3412)
    med solo,pno AMP $.60   (S3413)
Rest In The Lord
    low solo,pno AMP $.50   (S3414)
    med solo,pno AMP $.50   (S3415)
Song Of Spring
    high solo,pno (E flat maj) WILLIS
    $.60   (S3416)
To Come, O Lord, To Thee *sac
    med-high solo,pno (A flat maj)
    SCHIRM.G $.60   (S3417)
    low solo,pno (F maj) SCHIRM.G $.60
                                    (S3418)
Who Knows
    low solo,pno (F maj) WILLIS $.60
                                    (S3419)
    high solo,pno (A flat maj) WILLIS
    $.60   (S3420)

STIEVENARD, M.
Chant Du Berceau
    solo,pno ENOCH s.p.   (S3421)

STIFFLER, GEORGIA
Healer Of Broken Hearts
    (Kerr) solo,pno GENTRY $1.00
                                    (S3422)

STIGELLI, GIORGIO (1815-1868)
Un Rayon De Tes Yeux
    [Ger] solo,pno DURAND s.p. (S3423)
    [Ger] solo,vln/vcl DURAND s.p.
                                    (S3424)

STIGEN, FREDRIK
Rosor Til Mor
    solo,pno MUSIKK s.p.   (S3425)
To Sanger *Op.1
    solo,pno MUSIKK s.p.   (S3426)

STILL AS THE NIGHT see Bohm, Carl,
    Still Wie Die Nacht

STILL IS THE NIGHT see Abt, Franz,
    Erinnerung

STILL LET THY PLAINTIVE NUMBERS FLOW
    see Shield, William

STILL LIFE see Swanson, Howard

STILL PRESENT see Somerset, Lord Henry

STILL SMALL VOICE, THE see O'Hara,
   Geoffrey

STILL SONGS see Kadosa, [Paul]

STILL THERE IS BETHLEHEM see Dickinson,
   Clarence

STILL THERE IS BETHLEHEM see Fischer,
   Irwin

STILL TO BE NEAT see Bunge, Sas

STILL WIE DIE NACHT see Bohm, Carl

STILL, WILLIAM GRANT (1895-   )
   Ev'ry Time I Feel The Spirit
      med solo,pno GALAXY 1.1724.7 $1.00
                                    (S3427)

STILLA KOMME, OCH VALKOMNA see Olson,
   Daniel

STILLA MITT HJARTA see Runback, Albert

STILLA SEPTEMBERSKOG see Lagerheim-
   Romare, Margit

STILLA VISOR see Rangstrom, Ture

STILLE NACHT, HEIL'GE NACHT see Gruber,
   Franz Xaver

STILLE NACHT, HEILIGE NACHT see Bonset,
   Jac.

STILLE NACHT, HEILIGE NACHT see Vogel,
   Hans

STILLE NACHT, HEILIGE NACHT *CC26U,
   Xmas
      solo,pno TONOS s.p.   (S3428)

STILLE WELT see Schulz, Joh. Abraham
   Peter

STILLES LIEBEN see Bedrich, Jan, Tiche
   Milovani

STIMMEN DER NACHT see Gretchaninov,
   Alexander Tikhonovitch, Voix
   Nocturnes

STIMMEN DES TAGES see Schreker, Franz

STIMMT DIE SAITEN see Purcell, Henry

STIMMUNG DER ABWESENHEIT see Antoniou,
   Theodor

STIMMUNGSLIED see Kilpinen, Yrio,
   Stamningsvisa

STINOHRA see Kricka, Jaroslav

STIPE
   Life In Jesus *sac
      solo,pno BENSON S6866-R $1.00
                                    (S3429)

STIRI KITAJSKE MINIATURE see Kozina,
   Marijan

STIRI PESMI see Svara, Danilo

STIRI PESMI see Mirk, Vasilij

STIRI PESMI see Sivic, Pavle

STIRI PESMI see Svara, Danilo

STIRI PESMI NA LIRIKO MATEJA BORA see
   Sivic, Pavle

STIRJE SAMOSPEVI see Lajovic,
   Aleksander

STIZZOSO MIO STIZZOSO see Pergolesi,
   Giovanni Battista

STJARNKLART see Josephson, Jacob Axel

STJARNOGA see Rangstrom, Ture

STJARNOGA see Stenhammar, Wilhelm

STJARNORNA ARO SA STILLA see Kilpinen,
   Yrio

STLOTS GULLEVI see Nordqvist, Gustaf

STMIVA SE see Aim, Vojtech Borivoj

STOCK, DAVID
   Scat
      S solo,fl,bass clar,vln,vcl sc
      AM.COMP.AL. $8.80   (S3430)

STOCK, FREDERICK
   To A Firefly
      med solo,pno FITZSIMONS $.75
                                    (S3431)

STOCKHAUSEN, KARLHEINZ (1928-   )
   Aus Den Sieben Tagen
      [Ger] solo,pno UNIVER. 14790 $5.75
                                    (S3432)
      [Fr] solo,pno UNIVER. 14790F $5.75
                                    (S3433)
      [Eng] solo,pno UNIVER. 14790E $5.75
                                    (S3434)

STOCKHOLM see Ek, Gunnar

STOCKMAYER, ERICH
   Acht Lieder Nach Verschiedenen
      Dichtern *CC8U
      med solo,pno TONOS 5405 s.p. (S3435)

STOLBA
   And Jesus Came *sac
      solo,pno LILLENAS SM-639: RN $1.00
                                    (S3436)

STOLL, B.
   Mutter Und Kind
      solo,pno HUG s.p.   (S3437)

   Vater Und Kind
      solo,pno HUG s.p.   (S3438)

STOLL, HELENE MARIANNE (1911-   )
   Der Morgenstern Ist Aufgedrungen
      *sac,cant
      ST soli,ob/vln,org sc HANSSLER
      10.104 s.p., ipa, solo pt
      HANSSLER s.p.   (S3439)

STOLZ, ROBERT (1880-1975)
   Swiss Fairyland
      solo,pno CRAMER   (S3440)

STOLZEL, GOTTFRIED HEINRICH (1690-1749)
   Liebster Jesu, Deine Liebe Findet
      Ihresgleichen Nicht *sac
      (Bachmair, J.) Mez/A solo,strings,
      cont BREITKOPF-L rental   (S3441)

STONE
   Come On Down *see Hayford

STONE WAS ROLLED AWAY, THE *sac,gospel
      solo,pno ABER.GRP. $1.50   (S3442)

STONECRACKER, THE see Rizzi, Alba

STOP, LOOK AND LISTEN FOR THE LORD
      *sac,gospel
      solo,pno ABER.GRP. $1.50   (S3443)

STOP, YOU SCOUNDRELS! see Falla, Manuel
   de, Deteneos

STOPPING BY WOODS see Sifler, Paul J.

STOPPING BY WOODS ON A SNOWY EVENING
   see Diers, Ann Mac Donald

STOPPING BY WOODS ON A SNOWY EVENING
   see Hoskins, William

STOPPING BY WOODS ON A SNOWY EVENING
   see La Montaine, John

STORA BARNET, MITT HJARTEGULL see
   Wideen

STORACE, J.
   Coquettes Song
      (Graves) med solo,pno ELKIN
      27.2610.06 s.p.   (S3444)

STORACE, STEPHEN (1763-1796)
   Peaceful Slumb'ring On The Ocean
      (Graves) 2 soli,pno ROBERTON 72258
      s.p.   (S3445)

STORIA D'AMORE see Pratella, Francesco
   Balilla

STORIA QUOTIDIANA see Alaleone,
   Domenico

STORIES OF A DAY see Komori, Akihiro

STORK, THE see Blyton, Carey

STORKE, THE see Clokey, Joseph Waddell

STORM see Joubert, John

STORM CHILD see Surdin, M.

STORM LULLABY see Sanderson, Wilfred

STORMY SCENES OF WINTER, THE
   see Five Canadian Folk Songs

STORNELLATRICE see Respighi, Ottorino

STORNELLI see Guarino, C.

STORNELLI see Oddone, E.

STORNELLI NELLO STILE POPOLARE see
   Ferrari-Trecate, Luigi

STORNELLO see Botti, C.

STORNELLO see Cimara, Pietro

STORNELLO see Giuranna, Barbara

STORNELLO see Respighi, Ottorino

STORNELLO DI LOLA see Mascagni, Pietro

STORY OF THE SPARROWS see Green, Philip

STOUGIE (1908-   )
   One Hundred Twenty-Four Songs
      *CC124U
      med solo,pno DONEMUS s.p.   (S3446)

STOUT, ALAN (1932-   )
   Allegory: Pride, An *Op.73,No.3
      S solo,clar,perc,pno,vcl sc
      AM.COMP.AL. $3.30, ipa   (S3447)

   Aria (Psalm 58) *sac
      Bar solo,pno AM.COMP.AL. $3.85
                                    (S3448)

   Autumn Day *see Syyspaiva

   Canticum Canticorum
      [Lat] S solo,fl,ob,clar,bsn,horn,
      perc,harp,cel,vla PETERS 6882
      s.p.   (S3449)

   Caritas
      see Two Hymns For Tenor And
         Orchestra

   Christmas Antiphon *Op.37, Xmas
      S/T solo,vcl,org, 4 tom-toms sc
      AM.COMP.AL. $2.75, ipa   (S3450)

   Commentary On T'ung Jen *Op.14
      S/T solo,ob,pno,opt drums sc
      AM.COMP.AL. $5.50, ipa   (S3451)

   Cradle Song
      high solo,pno AM.COMP.AL. $3.30
                                    (S3452)

   Crux Fidelis *Op.68,No.11
      Mez solo,2fl,English horn,2clar,
      2bsn,4horn,harp/2harp,cel/org,2-
      4perc,strings sc AM.COMP.AL.
      $4.95   (S3453)

   Eight Poems From The Japanese *CC8U,
      Jap
      high solo,pno AM.COMP.AL. $3.85
                                    (S3454)

   Fides
      see Two Hymns For Tenor And
         Orchestra

   George Lieder *CCU
      [Ger] Bar solo,fl,pic,ob,English
      horn,clar,bass clar,bsn,
      contrabsn,horn,2trp,trom,3perc,
      harp,pno,cel,strings PETERS 66545
      s.p.   (S3455)

   Landscape *Op.36
      Mez solo,fl,English horn,harp, tam-
      tam sc AM.COMP.AL. $3.30, ipa
                                    (S3456)

   Little Boy Lost
      Bar solo,pno AM.COMP.AL. $3.30
                                    (S3457)

   Nocturno
      see Two Finnish Songs

   Psalm 58 *see Aria

   Syyspaiva
      "Autumn Day" see Two Finnish Songs

   Three Whitman Songs *CC3U
      Bar solo,pno AM.COMP.AL. $2.75
                                    (S3458)

   Two Finnish Songs *Op.53, Finn
      S solo,3fl,2ob,3clar,2bsn,4horn,
      3trp,3trom,tuba,timp,2harp,perc,
      strings AM.COMP.AL. sc $12.10,
      voc sc $1.37
      contains: Nocturno; Syyspaiva,
      "Autumn Day"   (S3459)

   Two Hymns For Tenor And Orchestra
      *sac,hymn
      T solo,2fl,2ob,2clar,bsn,horn,trp,
      trom,timp,perc,harp,pno,strings
      sc AM.COMP.AL. $9.35
      contains: Caritas; Fides   (S3460)

   Who Is Sylvia
      high solo,pno AM.COMP.AL. $2.75
                                    (S3461)
      med solo,pno AM.COMP.AL. $2.75
                                    (S3462)
      low solo,pno AM.COMP.AL. $2.75
                                    (S3463)

STRACHEY, J.
   Don't Let The Sun Go Down
      solo,pno (F maj) BOOSEY $1.50
                                    (S3464)

STRADELLA, ALESSANDRO (1645-1682)
   Air D'Eglise *see Aria Di Chiesa

   Aria Di Chiesa *sac
      [It] S/T solo,pno RICORDI-ENG 16184
      s.p.   (S3465)

STRADELLA, ALESSANDRO (cont'd.)

S/T solo,pno FORLIVESI 11272 s.p.
(S3466)
[It] Mez/Bar solo,pno RICORDI-ENG
45638 s.p. (S3467)
"Air D'Eglise" solo,pno/org (F maj)
HEUGEL s.p. see from CHANTS
RELIGIEUX (S3468)
"Air D'Eglise" solo,pno/org
(available in 2 keys) HEUGEL s.p. (S3469)

Exultate In Deo Fideles *sac,mot
Bar/B solo,2vln,cont BROEKMANS 1083
s.p. (S3470)
B/Bar solo,2vln,cont BROEKMANS 1083
s.p. (S3471)

Hoga Madonna *sac
Mez/Bar solo,pno GEHRMANS s.p. (S3472)

Il Barcheggio
(Gentili Verona, G.) soli,trp,trom,
cembalo,strings CARISH s.p. (S3473)

Pieta Signore *sac
[It] S/T solo,pno RICORDI-ARG
BA 10941 s.p. (S3474)
[Fr/It] solo,pno DURAND 153 s.p. (S3475)

STRAESSER, JOEP (1934-   )
Die Fledermaus
see Eichenstadt Und Abenstern

Die Unterhose
see Eichenstadt Und Abenstern

Eichenstadt Und Abenstern
S solo,pno DONEMUS s.p.
contains: Die Fledermaus; Die
Unterhose; Geburtsakt Der
Philosophie; Rondell; Trauriger
Wind; Zwischendurch (S3476)

Geburtsakt Der Philosophie
see Eichenstadt Und Abenstern

Musique Pour L'homme
SATB soli,4fl,4ob,4clar,4bsn,4horn,
4trp,4trom,tuba,perc,strings
DONEMUS s.p. (S3477)

Ramasasiri
Mez solo,fl,pno,hpsd,perc DONEMUS
s.p. (S3478)

Rondell
see Eichenstadt Und Abenstern

Trauriger Wind
see Eichenstadt Und Abenstern

22 Pages
TBarB soli,4fl,4ob,4clar,4bsn,
4horn,4trp,4trom,tuba,perc,cel,
harp,pno,vibra,xylo,8bvl DONEMUS
s.p. (S3479)

Zwischendurch
see Eichenstadt Und Abenstern

STRAHLE, L.J.G.
Kansan Virsi Kansan Suussa *CC25U
solo,pno FAZER W 3168 s.p. (S3480)

STRALS
Lord's Prayer, The *sac
solo,pno BENSON S7963-R $1.25 (S3481)

STRAMBOTTO see Farina, Guido

STRAMBOTTO IN SERENATA see Ferrari-
Trecate, Luigi

STRAMPELCHEN MACHT GROSSE AUGEN see
Trunk, Richard

STRANDASTER see Salonen, Sulo

STRANDQVIST, ALFRED
Psalm 84 *Op.30
[Dan] S solo,vln,org voc sc FOG
III, 35 s.p. (S3482)

STRANDSJO, GOTE
Jag Ser Guds Spar
see FYRA SANGER I FOLKTON

Vid Jesu Hjarta
see Svedlund, Karl-Erik, De Sokte
Sitt

STRANDSJO, OLIVEBRING
Child Returns Home, A *sac
solo,pno WORD S-240 (S3483)

STRANGE, ALLEN
Vanity Faire
narrator,electronic tape, 3 music
boxes MEDIA 1805 $3.75 (S3484)

STRANGE FUNERAL IN BRADDOCK, THE see
Siegmeister, Elie

STRANGE LULLABY see Haufrecht, Herbert

STRANGE MEETING see Escher, Rudolf
George

STRANGE MEETING, A see Webber, Lloyd

STRANGER, THE see Dougherty, Celius

STRANGER, THE see James, Philip

STRANGER OF GALILEE see Sturgis

STRANGER OF GALILEE, THE see Morris,
C.H.

STRANO, ALFREDO
Sulla Via Maestra
[It] solo,pno voc sc CURCI 8949
s.p. (S3485)

STRATEGIER, HERMAN (1912-   )
Al Wie Ter Minne Is Zo Vroed
see Vijf Kleine Veldeken Liederen
see Vijf Minneliederen Uit "Henric
Van Veldeken"

Chinesische Lieder *Op.11,No.3
see Lieder Aus Asien

Der Feueranbeter *Op.11,No.2
see Lieder Aus Asien

Een Lied Van Den Wijn
see Vier Drinkliederen

Geisha Lieder *Op.11,No.1
see Lieder Aus Asien

Godvruchtig Drinklied
see Vier Drinkliederen

Henric Van Veldeke
Bar&narrator,2fl,2ob,2clar,2bsn,
4horn,3trp,3trom,timp,perc,cel,
harp,strings DONEMUS s.p. (S3486)

In Deez' Dagen Van Den Jare
see Vijf Kleine Veldeken Liederen
see Vijf Minneliederen Uit "Henric
Van Veldeken"

In Die Tijd Dat Binnen, Buiten
see Vijf Kleine Veldeken Liederen
see Vijf Minneliederen Uit "Henric
Van Veldeken"

Lieder Aus Asien
[Ger] A/T/S/B solo,pno DONEMUS s.p.
contains: Chinesische Lieder,
Op.11,No.3; Der Feueranbeter,
Op.11,No.2; Geisha Lieder,
Op.11,No.1; Vaganten Lieder,
Op.11,No.4 (S3487)

Men Seghet, Die Swane
see Vijf Kleine Veldeken Liederen
see Vijf Minneliederen Uit "Henric
Van Veldeken"

Psalm 118 *sac
Bar/Mez solo,2fl,2ob,2clar,2bsn,
3horn,3trp,3trom,timp,perc,cel,
harp,strings DONEMUS s.p. (S3488)

Septem Cantica *sac,CC7L
BANK Mez solo,fl,ob,clar,bsn,
strings s.p.; Mez solo,pno s.p.
(S3489)

'T Bloemke "Nimmermeerverdriet"
see Vijf Kleine Veldeken Liederen
see Vijf Minneliederen Uit "Henric
Van Veldeken"

Vaganten Lieder *Op.11,No.4
see Lieder Aus Asien

Vier Drinkliederen
BANK Bar solo,2fl,2ob,2clar,2bsn,
2horn,timp,perc,strings s.p.; Bar
solo,pno s.p.
contains: Een Lied Van Den Wijn;
Godvruchtig Drinklied; Wijnken,
Gij Zijt Groene; Zeit Die
Schone Vogt Eens Gloeien (S3490)

Vier Maria-Antiphonen *sac,CC4U
med solo,org BANK s.p. (S3491)

Vijf Kleine Veldeken Liederen
DONEMUS med solo,pno s.p.; med
solo,fl,strings s.p.
contains: Al Wie Ter Minne Is Zo
Vroed; In Deez' Dagen Van Den
Jare; In Die Tijd Dat Binnen,
Buiten; Men Seghet, Die Swane;
'T Bloemke "Nimmermeerverdriet"
(S3492)

Vijf Minneliederen Uit "Henric Van
Veldeken"
med solo,fl,4strings voc sc DONEMUS
s.p.
contains: Al Wie Ter Minne Is Zo
Vroed; In Deez' Dagen Van Den
Jare; In Die Tijd Dat Binnen,
Buiten; Men Seghet, Die Swane;

STRATEGIER, HERMAN (cont'd.)

'T Bloemke "Nimmermeerverdriet"
(S3493)
Wijnken, Gij Zijt Groene
see Vier Drinkliederen

Zeit Die Schone Vogt Eens Gloeien
see Vier Drinkliederen

THE STRATFORD SERIES OF SHAKESPEARE
SONGS, VOLUME I see Bridgewater,
Ernest Leslie

THE STRATFORD SERIES OF SHAKESPEARE
SONGS, VOLUME II see Bridgewater,
Ernest Leslie

THE STRATFORD SERIES OF SHAKESPEARE
SONGS, VOLUME III see Bridgewater,
Ernest Leslie

THE STRATFORD SERIES OF SHAKESPEARE
SONGS, VOLUME IV see Bridgewater,
Ernest Leslie

STRAUS, OSCAR (1870-1954)
Ein Schwipserl (from Rund Um Die
Liebe)
solo,pno DOBLINGER 88 519 s.p. (S3494)

Es Gibt Dingt, Die Muss Man Vergessen
(from Rund Um Die Liebe)
[Ger] ST soli,pno DOBLINGER $1.00 (S3495)

Komm, Komm, Held Meiner Traume (from
Der Tapfere Soldat)
high solo,pno DOBLINGER 88 520 s.p. (S3496)
low solo,pno DOBLINGER 88 521 s.p. (S3497)

Leise, Ganz Leise (from Ein
Walzertraum)
high solo,pno DOBLINGER 88 517 s.p. (S3498)
low solo,pno DOBLINGER 88 518 s.p. (S3499)

My Hero (from Chocolate Soldier, The)
2 soli,pno WARNER VD0009 $1.95 (S3500)
solo,pno WARNER VS0339 $1.95 (S3501)

Piccolo Piccolo
solo,pno CRAMER (S3502)

STRAUSS, JOHANN (1825-1899)
A Orillas Del Hermoso Danubio Azul
*see An Der Schonen Blauen Donau

Ach, Wie So Herrlich Zu Schau'n (from
Eine Nacht In Venedig)
solo,pno DOBLINGER 88 504 s.p. (S3503)

Adele's Laughing Song (from Die
Fledermaus)
S solo,pno (G maj) SCHIRM.G $.85 (S3504)

An Der Schonen Blauen Donau *Op.314
"Beautiful Blue Danube" low solo,
pno (C maj) CENTURY 3622 (S3505)
"Blue Danube" solo,pno (C maj,
simplified) ALLANS s.p. (S3506)
"Blue Danube" high solo,pno (D maj)
ALLANS s.p. (S3507)
"Blue Danube" low solo,pno (C maj)
ALLANS s.p. (S3508)
"On The Blue Danube" solo,pno (D
flat maj) ASHDOWN s.p. (S3509)
(Dumas) "A Orillas Del Hermoso
Danubio Azul" [Span] solo,pno
(transcribed from the waltzes)
RICORDI-ARG BA 7777 s.p. (S3510)
(Liebling) "Blue Danube, The" high
solo,pno (D maj) SCHIRM.G $1.00 (S3511)

Beautiful Blue Danube *see An Der
Schonen Blauen Donau

Blue Danube *see An Der Schonen
Blauen Donau

Blue Danube, The *see An Der Schonen
Blauen Donau

Bruderlein Und Schwesterlein (from
Die Fledermaus)
"Du Und Du" solo,pno/orch sc KALMUS
$5.00 (S3512)

Csardas *see Klange Der Heimat

Cuentos Del Bosque De Viena *see
G'schichten Aus Dem Wienerwald

Du Und Du *see Bruderlein Und
Schwesterlein

Emperor Waltz
solo,pno ALLANS s.p. (S3513)

Flirtation Intermezzo (from Gypsy
Baron, The)
high solo,pno SCHIRM.G $.60 (S3514)

STRAUSS, JOHANN (cont'd.)

Fruhlingsstimmen *Op.410
  "Voces De Primavera" [Span/It]
  solo,pno (transcribed from the
  waltzes) RICORDI-ARG BA 3343 s.p.
                                    (S3515)
Frulingsstimmen
  "Voices Of Spring" solo,pno (G maj)
  ALLANS s.p.   (S3516)

Girl With Yellow Hair (from Die
  Fledermaus)
  [Eng/Ger] S solo,pno BOOSEY $1.50
                                    (S3517)
G'schichten Aus Dem Wienerwald
  *Op.325
  coloratura sop,pno/orch DOBLINGER
  08 571 s.p., ipr   (S3518)
  (Martini) "Cuentos Del Bosque De
  Viena" [Span] solo,pno
  (transcribed from the waltzes)
  RICORDI-ARG BA 7959 s.p.   (S3519)

G'schicten Aus Dem Wienerwald
  "Tales From The Vienna Woods" solo,
  pno (F maj) CRAMER   (S3520)
  "Tales From The Vienna Woods" med
  solo,pno (G maj) CENTURY 3703
                                    (S3521)
  "Tales From The Vienna Woods" solo,
  pno ASHLEY $.95   (S3522)
  "Tales From The Vienna Woods" solo,
  pno ALLANS s.p.   (S3523)
  (Korngold) "Whisp'rings Of The
  Vienna Woods, The" med-high solo,
  pno BOTE $1.00   (S3524)

Heiligenstadter Rendezvous *Op.78
  coloratura sop,pno/orch voc sc
  KRENN s.p., ipr   (S3525)

Ja, So Singt Und Tanzt Man Nur In
  Wien (from Indigo Und Die Vierzig
  Rauber)
  coloratura sop,pno/orch voc sc
  KRENN s.p., ipr   (S3526)

Kaiserwalzer *Op.437
  (Schmid, R.) coloratura sop,pno
  DOBLINGER 08 572 s.p.   (S3527)

Klange Der Heimat (from Die
  Fledermaus)
  "Csardas" solo,pno/orch sc KALMUS
  $3.50   (S3528)

Kunsterleben *Op.316
  (Redl) "Vida De Artista" [Span]
  solo,pno (transcribed from the
  waltzes) RICORDI-ARG BA 9655 s.p.
                                    (S3529)
Kunstlerleben
  coloratura sop,pno/orch voc sc
  SCHOTTS s.p., ipa   (S3530)

Laughing Song *see Mein Herr Marquis

Liebeslieder *Op.114
  coloratura sop,pno/orch voc sc
  KRENN s.p., ipr   (S3531)

Liebeswalzer
  (Blech) [Ger] high solo,pno BOTE
  $1.00   (S3532)

Love Can Be Dreamed (from Gypsy
  Baron, The)
  med-high solo,pno (B flat maj)
  SCHIRM.G $.60   (S3533)
  solo,pno ALLANS s.p.   (S3534)

Love's Roundelay (from Waltz Dream)
  high solo,pno MARKS $1.50 (S3535)
  med solo,pno MARKS $1.50   (S3536)

Mein Herr Marquis (from Die
  Fledermaus)
  "Laughing Song" low solo,pno (F
  maj) ALLANS s.p.   (S3537)
  "Laughing Song" high solo,pno (G
  maj) ALLANS s.p.   (S3538)
  (Bantock) "Laughing Song" high
  solo,pno PAXTON P40542 s.p.
                                    (S3539)
Memories Of Johann Strauss *CCU
  [Ger/Eng] solo,pno MARKS $2.00
                                    (S3540)
Mine Alone
  solo,pno (C maj) ALLANS s.p.
                                    (S3541)
Oh, Beware *see Oh Habet Acht

Oh Habet Acht (from Gypsy Baron, The)
  "Oh, Beware" [Ger/Eng] solo,pno
  MARKS $1.50   (S3542)

On The Blue Danube *see An Der
  Schonen Blauen Donau

Open Road, Open Sky (from Gypsy
  Baron, The)
  med-high solo,pno SCHIRM.G $.75
                                    (S3543)
  solo,pno (D maj) ALLANS s.p.
                                    (S3544)

STRAUSS, JOHANN (cont'd.)

Pester Csardas *Op.23
  coloratura sop,pno/orch voc sc
  KRENN s.p., ipr   (S3545)

Rosas Del Sur *see Rosen Aus Dem
  Suden

Rosen Aus Dem Suden *Op.388
  "Roses Of The South" solo,pno
  ALLANS s.p.   (S3546)
  (Pahlen) "Rosas Del Sur" [Span]
  solo,pno (transcribed from the
  waltzes) RICORDI-ARG BA 9393 s.p.
                                    (S3547)
Roses Of The South *see Rosen Aus
  Dem Suden

Sangre Vienesa *see Wienerblut Muss
  Was Eigenes Sein

Serenade
  high solo,pno (F sharp maj) ALLANS
  s.p.   (S3548)
  med-high solo,pno (F maj) ALLANS
  s.p.   (S3549)
  med solo,pno (E maj) ALLANS s.p.
                                    (S3550)
  low solo,pno (D maj) ALLANS s.p.
                                    (S3551)
Strauss Vocal Waltzes *CCU
  (Bantock) solo,pno PAXTON P15582
                                    (S3552)
Tales From The Vienna Woods *see
  G'schicten Aus Dem Wienerwald

Vergessenes Lied
  S/T solo,pno/orch voc sc KRENN
  s.p., ipr   (S3553)

Vida De Artista *see Kunsterleben

Village Swallows In Austria
  solo,pno ALLANS s.p.   (S3554)

Vino, Mujer Y Canto *see Wein, Weib
  Und Gesang

Voces De Primavera *see
  Fruhlingsstimmen

Voices Of Spring *see
  Frulingsstimmen

Wein, Weib Und Gesang *Op.333
  (Pahlen) "Vino, Mujer Y Canto"
  [Span] solo,pno (transcribed from
  the waltzes) RICORDI-ARG BA 9389
  s.p.   (S3555)
Whisp'rings Of The Vienna Woods, The
  *see G'schicten Aus Dem
  Wienerwald

Wienerblut Muss Was Eigenes Sein
  *Op.354
  S/T solo,pno/orch voc sc KRENN
  s.p., ipr   (S3556)
  (Pardo) "Sangre Vienesa" [Span]
  solo,pno (transcribed from the
  waltzes) RICORDI-ARG BA 8574 s.p.
                                    (S3557)
Wienerwald Lerchen *Op.29
  coloratura sop,pno/orch voc sc
  KRENN s.p., ipr   (S3558)

Wo Die Citronen Bluh'n
  coloratura sop,pno/orch voc sc
  KRENN s.p., ipr   (S3559)

Your Eyes Shine In My Own (from Gypsy
  Baron, The)
  ST soli,pno SCHIRM.G $.60 (S3560)

STRAUSS, JOSEF (1827-1840)
Die Kleine Muhle *Op.57
  coloratura sop,pno/orch voc sc
  KRENN s.p., ipr   (S3561)

Dorfschwalben Aus Osterreich *Op.164
  (Lehnert, J.) coloratura sop,pno
  voc sc DOBLINGER 08 570 s.p., ipr
                                    (S3562)
Ewige Walzermelodie *Op.184
  coloratura sop,pno/orch voc sc
  KRENN s.p., ipr   (S3563)

Irgendwo Spielt Musik *Op.270
  S/T solo,pno/orch (published with
  Max. Muller Verlag) voc sc KRENN
  s.p., ipr   (S3564)

Mi Vida Es Dicha Y Amor
  [Span] solo,pno (transcribed from
  the waltzes) RICORDI-ARG BA 9386
  s.p.   (S3565)

Spharenklange *Op.235
  coloratura sop,pno/orch voc sc
  KRENN s.p., ipr   (S3566)

Wiener Kinder Singen Gern *Op.61
  S/T solo,pno/orch voc sc KRENN
  s.p., ipr   (S3567)

STRAUSS, RICHARD (1864-1949)
Ach Lieb', Ich Muss Scheiden *Op.21,
  No.3
  med solo,pno UNIVER. 5436B $2.75
  see from Schlicte Weisen   (S3568)

Ach Was Kummer, Qual Und Schmerzen
  *Op.49,No.7
  [Eng/Ger] solo,pno (D min) BOOSEY
  $2.25 see from Seven Songs
                                    (S3569)
Ach, Weh' Mir *Op.21,No.4
  low solo,pno UNIVER. 5437C $2.75
  see from Schlichte Weisen (S3570)

Acht Lieder *see Allerseelen, Op.10,
  No.8; Die Nacht, Op.10,No.3;
  Zueignung, Op.10,No.1   (S3571)

Ah! Du Wolltest Mich Nicht (from
  Salome) scena
  "Ah! Tu Non Hai Voluto" [It/Fr] S
  solo,pno FURST 5008* $2.75 (S3572)
  "Salome's Solo Scene" [Eng/Ger] S
  solo,pno BOOSEY $6.00   (S3573)

Ah! Tu Non Hai Voluto *see Ah! Du
  Wolltest Mich Nicht

All' Meine Gedanken *Op.21,No.1
  med solo,pno UNIVER. 5434B $2.75
  see from Schlichte Weisen (S3574)
  low solo,pno UNIVER. 5434C $2.75
  see from Schlichte Weisen (S3575)
  high solo,pno UNIVER. 5434A $2.75
  see from Schlichte Weisen (S3576)

All Meine Gedanken, Mein Herz Und
  Mein Sinn *Op.21,No.1
  high solo,pno BREITKOPF-L EB 3441
  s.p.   (S3577)

Allerseelen *Op.10,No.8
  med solo,pno UNIVER. 5427B $2.75
  see from Acht Lieder   (S3578)
  low solo,pno UNIVER. 5427C $2.75
  see from Acht Lieder   (S3579)
  high solo,pno UNIVER. 5427A $2.75
  see from Acht Lieder   (S3580)

Als Mir Dein Lied Erklang *Op.68,
  No.4
  [Ger] solo,pno (F sharp maj) BOOSEY
  $2.25 see from Six Songs After
  Poems By Clemens Brentano (S3581)

Am Ufer *Op.41,No.3
  [Ger/Eng] high solo,pno LEUCKART
  $3.00 see also Funf Lieder
                                    (S3582)
  [Ger/Eng] low solo,pno LEUCKART
  $3.00 see also Funf Lieder
                                    (S3583)
Amor *Op.68,No.5
  [Ger] solo,pno (G maj) BOOSEY $2.25
  see from Six Songs After Poems By
  Clemens Brentano   (S3584)

An Die Nacht *Op.68,No.1
  [Ger] solo,pno (E flat maj) BOOSEY
  $2.25 see from Six Songs After
  Poems By Clemens Brentano (S3585)

Auf Ein Kind *Op.47,No.1
  [Eng/Ger] solo,pno (C maj) BOOSEY
  $2.25 see from Four Songs (S3586)

Aus Den Liedern Der Trauer *Op.15,
  No.4
  "From The Songs Of Sorrow" see Five
  Songs For Medium Voice

Aus Den Liedern Der Trauer [II]
  *Op.17,No.4
  "From The Songs Of Sorrow [II]" see
  Six Songs For High Voice

Awakened Rose, The *see Die Erwachte
  Rose

Barcarole *Op.17,No.6
  see Six Songs For High Voice

Befreit *Op.39,No.4
  [Ger/Eng/Fr] med solo/low solo,pno
  FORBERG F12B s.p. see from Five
  Songs   (S3587)
  "Death The Releaser" [Ger/Eng] high
  solo,pno FORBERG F12A s.p. see
  from Five Songs   (S3588)
  "Death The Releaser" [Ger/Eng] high
  solo/med-low solo,2fl,2ob,2clar,
  2bsn,4horn,trp,perc,harp,strings
  voc sc FORBERG s.p.   (S3589)

Begegnung
  "Meeting" [Eng/Ger] med solo,pno
  PETERS 6150C $2.50 see from Three
  Love Songs   (S3590)

Blauer Sommer *Op.31,No.1
  [Eng/Ger] solo,pno (B maj) BOOSEY
  $2.25 see from Three Songs
                                    (S3591)

STRAUSS, RICHARD (cont'd.)

Blindenklage *Op.56,No.2
"Lament Of The Blind" [Ger/Eng] S
solo,pno BOTE $2.75   (S3592)

Breit Uber Mein Haupt *Op.19,No.2
med solo,pno UNIVER. 5429B $2.75
see from Lotosblatter   (S3593)
high solo,pno UNIVER. 5429A $2.75
see from Lotosblatter   (S3594)

Bruder Liederlich *Op.41,No.4
[Ger/Eng] high solo,pno LEUCKART
$3.00 see also Funf Lieder
(S3595)
[Ger/Eng] low solo,pno LEUCKART
$3.00 see also Funf Lieder
(S3596)

Cacilie *Op.27,No.2
low solo,pno UNIVER. 5442C $2.75
see from Vier Lieder   (S3597)
high solo,pno UNIVER. 5442A $2.75
see from Vier Lieder   (S3598)
med solo,pno UNIVER. 5442B $2.75
see from Vier Lieder   (S3599)
"Cecily" [Ger/Eng] med solo,pno
BOTE $.45   (S3600)

Cecily *see Cacilie

Closing Duet (from Der Rosenkavalier)
[Eng/Ger] SMez soli,pno BOOSEY
$2.50   (S3601)

Das Bachlein
S solo,pno UNIVER. 11611 $2.75
(S3602)

Das Geheimnis *Op.17,No.3
"Secret, The" see Six Songs For
High Voice

Das War Sehr Gut! (from Arabella)
2 soli,pno SCHOTTS s.p.   (S3603)

Death The Releaser *see Befreit

Der Arbeitsmann *Op.39,No.3
[Ger] low solo,pno FORBERG F85 s.p.
see from Five Songs   (S3604)

Di Rigori Armato Il Seno (from Der
Rosenkavalier)
T solo,pno FURST s.p.   (S3605)
[It] T solo,pno FURST 5032 s.p.
(S3606)

Dichters Abendgang *Op.47,No.2
[Eng/Ger] solo,pno (D flat maj)
BOOSEY $2.25 see from Four Songs
(S3607)

Die Allmachtige *Op.77,No.4
[Ger/Eng/Fr] T solo,pno LEUCKART
s.p. see from Gesange Des Orients
(S3608)
[Ger/Eng/Fr] med solo,pno LEUCKART
s.p. see from Gesange Des Orients
(S3609)

Die Erwachte Rose
"Awakened Rose, The" [Eng/Ger] med
solo,pno PETERS 6150B $2.50 see
from Three Love Songs   (S3610)

Die Heiligen Drei Konige *Op.56,No.6
"Three Holy Kings, The" [Ger/Eng] S
solo,pno BOTE $2.25   (S3611)

Die Nacht *Op.10,No.3
low solo,pno UNIVER. 5422A $2.75
see from Acht Lieder   (S3612)
high solo,pno UNIVER. 5422B $2.75
see from Acht Lieder   (S3613)
med solo,pno UNIVER. 5422C $2.75
see from Acht Lieder   (S3614)

Drei Lieder *see Traum Durch Die
Dammerung, Op.29,No.1   (S3615)

E'er Since Thine Eye Towards Mine Was
Wended *see Seitdem Dein Aug'in
Meines Schaute

Einsame *Op.51,No.2
[Eng/Ger] B solo,pno (D flat maj)
BOOSEY $2.50 see from Two Bass
Songs   (S3616)

Enoch Arden *Op.38
[Eng/Ger] narrator,pno FORBERG F59
s.p.   (S3617)

Epheu *Op.22,No.3
[Eng/Ger] solo,pno (E flat maj)
BOOSEY $2.25 see from
Maidenblossoms   (S3618)

Er Ist Der Richtige Nicht Fur Mich
(from Arabella)
2 soli,pno SCHOTTS s.p.   (S3619)

Festival Of Spring *see
Fruhlingsfeier

Five Songs *see Befreit, "Death The
Releaser", Op.39,No.4; Der
Arbeitsmann, Op.39,No.3; Jung
Hexenlied, Op.39,No.2; Leises

Lied, Op.39,No.1; Lied An Meinen
Sohn, Op.39,No.5   (S3620)

Five Songs *see Freundliche Vision,
Op.48,No.1; Ich Schwebe, Op.48,
No.2; Kling, Op.48,No.3;
Winterliebe, Op.48,No.5;
Winterweihe, Op.48,No.4   (S3621)

Five Songs For Medium Voice
[Ger/Eng] med solo,pno SCHAUR
EE 384 $3.50
contains: Aus Den Liedern Der
Trauer, "From The Songs Of
Sorrow", Op.15,No.4; Heimkehr,
"Homeward", Op.15,No.5; Lob Des
Leidens, "In Praise Of Sorrow",
Op.15,No.3; Madrigal, Op.15,
No.1; Winternacht, "Winter
Night", Op.15,No.2   (S3622)

Forty Songs *CC40U
[Eng/Ger] low solo,pno PRESSER
$5.00   (S3623)

Found *see Gefunden

Four Last Songs *CC4U
[Eng/Ger] high solo,orch BOOSEY
$5.50   (S3624)

Four Little Songs *see Pokal, Op.69,
No.2; Schlechtes Wetter, Op.69,
No.4; Stern, Op.69,No.1;
Waldesfahrt, Op.69,No.3   (S3625)

Four Songs *see Auf Ein Kind, Op.47,
No.1; Dichters Abendgang, Op.47,
No.2; Ruckleben, Op.47,No.3; Von
Den Sieben Zechbrudern, Op.47,
No.4   (S3626)

Freundliche Vision *Op.48,No.1
[Eng/Ger] solo,pno (C maj) BOOSEY
$2.25 see from Five Songs (S3627)
[Ger/Eng] high solo,pno FURST s.p.
see from Funf Lieder   (S3628)
[Ger/Eng] low solo,pno FURST s.p.
see from Funf Lieder   (S3629)
[Eng/Ger] solo,pno (D maj) BOOSEY
$2.25   (S3630)

From The Songs Of Sorrow *see Aus
Den Liedern Der Trauer

From The Songs Of Sorrow [II] *see
Aus Den Liedern Der Trauer [II]

Fruhlingsfeier *Op.56,No.5
"Festival Of Spring" [Ger/Eng] S
solo,pno BOTE $2.50   (S3631)

Funf Lieder *see Fur Funfzehn
Pfennig, Op.32,No.2; Hat Gesagt,
Op.32,No.3; Ich Trage Meine
Minne, Op.32,No.1   (S3632)

Funf Lieder *see Freundliche Vision,
Op.48,No.1; Ich Schwebe, Op.48,
No.2; Kling!, Op.48,No.3;
Winterliebe, Op.48,No.5;
Winterweihe, Op.48,No.4   (S3633)

Funf Lieder
[Ger/Eng] LEUCKART high solo,pno
cmplt ed $13.00; low solo,pno
cmplt ed $13.00
contains & see also: Am Ufer,
Op.41,No.3; Bruder Liederlich,
Op.41,No.4; In Der Campagna,
Op.41,No.2; Leise Lieder,
Op.41,No.5; Wiegenlied, Op.41,
No.1   (S3634)

Fur Funfzehn Pfennig *Op.32,No.2
low solo,pno UNIVER. 5454C $2.75
see also Funf Lieder   (S3635)

Gefunden *Op.56,No.1
"Found" [Ger/Eng] S solo,pno BOTE
$2.25   (S3636)

Gesange Des Orients *see Die
Allmachtige, Op.77,No.4;
Huldigung, Op.77,No.5; Ihre
Augen, Op.77,No.1;
Liebesgeschenk, Op.77,No.3;
Schwung, Op.77,No.2   (S3637)

Gesange (Ruckert), Op. 87 *CCU
B solo,pno UNIVER. 13910 $4.75
(S3638)

Gestern War Ich Atlas *Op.46,No.1
[Eng/Ger] solo,pno (A maj) BOOSEY
$2.25 see from Three Songs (S3639)

Gluckes Genug *Op.37,No.1
high solo,pno UNIVER. 5457A s.p.
see from Sechs Lieder   (S3640)

Hat Gesagt *Op.32,No.3
med solo,pno UNIVER. 5455B $2.75
see also Funf Lieder   (S3641)

STRAUSS, RICHARD (cont'd.)

Heimkehr *Op.15,No.5
"Homeward" see Five Songs For
Medium Voice
[Ger/Eng] high solo,pno SCHAUR
EE 385A $1.75   (S3642)
[Ger/Eng] med solo,pno SCHAUR
EE 385B $1.75   (S3643)

Heimliche Aufforderung *Op.27,No.3
low solo,pno UNIVER. 5443C $2.75
see from Vier Lieder   (S3644)
med solo,pno UNIVER. 5443B $2.75
see from Vier Lieder   (S3645)
high solo,pno UNIVER. 5443A $2.75
see from Vier Lieder   (S3646)
"Lovers' Pledge, The" [Ger/Eng]
high solo,pno BREITKOPF-W $.75
(S3647)

Herzens Kronelein *Op.21,No.2
med solo,pno UNIVER. 5435B $2.75
see from Schlicte Weisen   (S3648)
high solo,pno UNIVER. 5435A $2.75
see from Schlicte Weisen   (S3649)
low solo,pno UNIVER. 5435C $2.75
see from Schlicte Weisen   (S3650)

Hochzeitlich Lied *Op.37,No.6
med solo,pno UNIVER. 5462B $2.75
see from Sechs Lieder   (S3651)

Homeward *see Heimkehr

Hope On! *see Nur Mut!

Huldigung *Op.77,No.5
[Ger/Eng/Fr] T solo,pno LEUCKART
s.p. see from Gesange Des Orients
(S3652)
[Ger/Eng/Fr] med solo,pno LEUCKART
s.p. see from Gesange Des Orients
(S3653)
[Ger/Eng/Fr] S solo,pno LEUCKART
s.p. see from Gesange Des Orients
(S3654)

Hymne An Die Liebe *Op.71,No.1
[Ger] solo,pno (F maj) BOOSEY $3.50
see from Three Hymns By Friedrich
Holderlin   (S3655)

Ich Liebe Dich *Op.37,No.2
high solo,pno UNIVER. 5458A $2.75
see from Sechs Lieder   (S3656)

Ich Schwebe *Op.48,No.2
[Eng/Ger] solo,pno (A maj) BOOSEY
$2.25 see from Five Songs (S3657)
[Ger/Eng] low solo,pno FURST s.p.
see from Funf Lieder   (S3658)
[Ger/Eng] high solo,pno FURST s.p.
see from Funf Lieder   (S3659)

Ich Sehe Wie In Einem Spiegel
*Op.46,No.3
[Eng/Ger] solo,pno (A maj) BOOSEY
$2.25 see from Three Songs (S3660)

Ich Trage Meine Minne *Op.32,No.1
med solo,pno UNIVER. 5448B $2.75
see also Funf Lieder   (S3661)
low solo,pno UNIVER. 5448C $2.75
see also Funf Lieder   (S3662)
high solo,pno UNIVER. 5448A $2.75
see also Funf Lieder   (S3663)

Ich Wollt' Ein Strausslein Binden
*Op.68,No.2
[Ger] solo,pno (F maj) BOOSEY $2.25
see from Six Songs After Poems By
Clemens Brentano   (S3664)

Ihre Augen *Op.77,No.1
[Ger/Eng/Fr] S solo,pno LEUCKART
s.p. see from Gesange Des Orients
(S3665)
[Ger/Eng/Fr] T solo,pno LEUCKART
s.p. see from Gesange Des Orients
(S3666)
[Ger/Eng/Fr] med solo,pno LEUCKART
s.p. see from Gesange Des Orients
(S3667)

Im Spatboot *Op.56,No.3
"In The Late Boat" [Ger/Eng] B
solo,pno BOTE $1.50   (S3668)

In Der Campagna *Op.41,No.2
[Ger/Eng] high solo,pno LEUCKART
$3.00 see also Funf Lieder
(S3669)

In Goldener Fulle *Op.49,No.2
[Eng/Ger] solo,pno (A flat maj)
BOOSEY $2.25 see from Seven Songs
(S3670)

In Praise Of Sorrow *see Lob Des
Leidens

In The Late Boat *see Im Spatboot

Jung Hexenlied *Op.39,No.2
[Ger] low solo,pno FORBERG F84 s.p.
see from Five Songs   (S3671)

Junggesellenschwur *Op.49,No.5
[Eng/Ger] solo,pno (F min) BOOSEY
$2.25 see from Seven Songs

STRAUSS, RICHARD (cont'd.)

Kann Mich Auch An Ein Madel Erinnern
(from Der Rosenkavalier)
S solo,pno FURST s.p.   (S3673)

Kling *Op.48,No.3
[Eng/Ger] solo,pno (C maj) BOOSEY
$2.25 see from Five Songs   (S3674)
[Ger/Eng] high solo,pno FURST s.p.
see from Funf Lieder   (S3675)
[Ger/Eng] low solo,pno FURST s.p.
see from Funf Lieder   (S3676)

Kornblumen *Op.22,No.1
[Eng/Ger] solo,pno (D flat maj)
BOOSEY $2.25 see from
Maidenblossoms   (S3677)

Kramerspiegel *CCU
solo,pno BOOSEY $9.00   (S3678)

Lament Of The Blind *see
Blindenklage

Leise Lieder *Op.41,No.5
[Ger/Eng] low solo,pno LEUCKART
$3.00 see also Funf Lieder
(S3679)

Leises Lied *Op.39,No.1
[Ger] low solo,pno FORBERG F83 s.p.
see from Five Songs   (S3680)

Liebe *Op.71,No.3
[Ger] solo,pno (E maj) BOOSEY $3.50
see from Three Hymns By Friedrich
Holderlin   (S3681)

Liebesgeschenk *Op.77,No.3
[Ger/Eng/Fr] T solo,pno LEUCKART
s.p. see from Gesange Des Orients
(S3682)
[Ger/Eng/Fr] med solo,pno LEUCKART
s.p. see from Gesange Des Orients
(S3683)

Lied An Meinen Sohn *Op.39,No.5
[Ger] low solo,pno FORBERG F86 s.p.
see from Five Songs   (S3684)

Lied Der Frauen *Op.68,No.6
[Ger] solo,pno (C maj) BOOSEY $2.25
see from Six Songs After Poems By
Clemens Brentano   (S3685)

Lieder Of Richard Strauss, Vol. 1:
Op. 10 To Op. 41 *CCU
(Trenner, Franz) solo,pno BOOSEY
$40.00   (S3686)

Lieder Of Richard Strauss, Vol. 2:
Op. 43 To Op. 68 *CCU
(Trenner, Franz) solo,pno BOOSEY
$40.00   (S3687)

Lieder Of Richard Strauss, Vol. 3:
Op. 69 To Op. 88 *CCU
(Trenner, Franz) solo,pno BOOSEY
$40.00   (S3688)

Lieder Of Richard Strauss, Vol. 4
*CCU
(Trenner, Franz) solo,orch sc
BOOSEY $50.00   (S3689)

Liederbande I *CC11L
high solo,pno UNIVER. 5463A $4.50;
med solo,pno UNIVER. 5463B $4.50;
low solo,pno UNIVER. 5463C $4.50
(S3690)

Liederbande II *CC10L
high solo,pno UNIVER. 5464A $4.50;
med solo,pno UNIVER. 5464B $4.50;
low solo,pno UNIVER. 5464C $4.50
(S3691)

Liederbande III *CC10L
high solo,pno UNIVER. 5465A $4.50;
med solo,pno UNIVER. 5465B $4.50;
low solo,pno UNIVER. 5465C $4.50
(S3692)

Liederbande IV *CC12L
high solo,pno UNIVER. 5466A $4.50;
med solo,pno UNIVER. 5466B $4.50;
low solo,pno UNIVER. 5466C $4.50
(S3693)

Lob Des Leidens *Op.15,No.3
"In Praise Of Sorrow" see Five
Songs For Medium Voice

Lotosblatter *see Breit Uber Mein
Haupt, Op.19,No.2   (S3694)

Lovers' Pledge, The *see Heimliche
Aufforderung

Madrigal *Op.15,No.1
see Five Songs For Medium Voice

Maidenblossoms *see Epheu, Op.22,
No.3; Kornblumen, Op.22,No.1;
Mohnblumen, Op.22,No.2;
Wasserrose, Op.22,No.4   (S3695)

Meeting *see Begegnung

STRAUSS, RICHARD (cont'd.)

Meinem Kinde *Op.37,No.3
high solo,pno UNIVER. 5459A $2.75
see from Sechs Lieder   (S3696)

Mit Deinen Blauen Augen *Op.56,No.4
"When With Thine Eyes" [Ger/Eng] S
solo,pno BOTE $2.25   (S3697)
"When With Thine Eyes" [Ger/Eng] A
solo,pno BOTE $2.25   (S3698)

Mohnblumen *Op.22,No.2
[Eng/Ger] solo,pno (G maj) BOOSEY
$2.25 see from Maidenblossoms
(S3699)

Monologue Of The Princess (from Der
Rosenkavalier)
[Eng/Ger] S solo,pno BOOSEY $2.00
(S3700)

Morgen *Op.27,No.4
high solo,pno UNIVER. 5444A $2.75
see from Vier Lieder   (S3701)
med solo,pno UNIVER. 5444B $2.75
see from Vier Lieder   (S3702)
low solo,pno UNIVER. 5444C $2.75
see from Vier Lieder   (S3703)
"Tomorrow" [Ger/Eng] med solo,pno
(F maj) SCHIRM.G $.60   (S3704)
"Tomorrow" [Ger/Eng] low solo,pno
(D maj) SCHIRM.G $.60   (S3705)
"Tomorrow" high solo,pno (G maj)
BOSTON $1.50   (S3706)

Muttertandelei *Op.43,No.2
Mez solo,2fl,2ob,2clar,2bsn,2horn,
perc,strings BIRNBACH sc rental,
voc sc s.p.   (S3707)

Nachlese *CCU
[Ger] solo,pno BOOSEY $18.00
(S3708)

Nachtlicher Gang *Op.44,No.2
[Ger] low solo,pno FORBERG F88 s.p.
see from Two Songs   (S3709)

Notturno *Op.44,No.1
[Ger] low solo,pno,vln FORBERG F87
s.p. see from Two Songs (S3710)

Nur Mut! *Op.17,No.5
"Hope On!" see Six Songs For High
Voice

Pokal *Op.69,No.2
[Ger] solo,pno (G flat maj) BOOSEY
$2.25 see from Four Little Songs
(S3711)

Red Roses *see Rote Rosen

Rote Rosen
"Red Roses" [Eng/Ger] med solo,pno
PETERS 6150A $2.50 see from Three
Love Songs   (S3712)

Ruckkehr In Die Heimat *Op.71,No.2
[Ger] solo,pno (F sharp maj) BOOSEY
$3.50 see from Three Hymns By
Friedrich Holderlin   (S3713)

Ruckleben *Op.47,No.3
[Eng/Ger] solo,pno (B flat min)
BOOSEY $2.25 see from Four Songs
(S3714)

Ruhe, Meine Seele *Op.27,No.1
low solo,pno UNIVER. 5441C $2.75
see from Vier Lieder   (S3715)
high solo,pno UNIVER. 5441A $2.75
see from Vier Lieder   (S3716)
med solo,pno UNIVER. 5441B $2.75
see from Vier Lieder   (S3717)

Salome's Solo Scene *see Ah! Du
Wolltest Mich Nicht

Sausle, Liebe Myrthe *Op.68,No.3
[Ger] solo,pno (G maj) BOOSEY $2.25
see from Six Songs After Poems By
Clemens Brentano   (S3718)

Scena Di Elettra (from Elektra) scena
[It/Fr] S solo,pno FURST 5106 s.p.
(S3719)

Schlagende Herzen *Op.29,No.2
low solo,pno BREITKOPF-L EB 3457
s.p.   (S3720)

Schlechtes Wetter *Op.69,No.4
[Eng/Ger] low solo,pno (C maj)
BOOSEY $2.25 see from Four Little
Songs   (S3721)
[Eng/Ger] high solo,pno (F maj)
BOOSEY $2.25 see from Four Little
Songs   (S3722)

Schlichte Weisen *see Ach, Weh' Mir,
Op.21,No.4   (S3723)

Schlicte Weisen *see Ach Lieb', Ich
Muss Scheiden, Op.21,No.3; All'
Meine Gedanken, Op.21,No.1;
Herzens Kronelein, Op.21,No.2
(S3724)

Schwung *Op.77,No.2
[Ger/Eng/Fr] med solo,pno LEUCKART
s.p. see from Gesange Des Orients

STRAUSS, RICHARD (cont'd.)

(S3725)
[Ger/Eng/Fr] T solo,pno LEUCKART
s.p. see from Gesange Des Orients
(S3726)

Sechs Ausgewahlte Lieder *CC6U
solo,pno UNIVER. 10244 $3.00
(S3727)

Sechs Lieder *see Gluckes Genug,
Op.37,No.1; Hochzeitlich Lied,
Op.37,No.6; Ich Liebe Dich,
Op.37,No.2; Meinem Kinde, Op.37,
No.3   (S3728)

Sechs Lieder, Book I: Lieder Der
Opheilia *Op.67,No.1-3, CC3U
[Ger] high solo,pno BOTE $4.50
(S3729)

Sechs Lieder, Book II: Lieder Den
Buchern Des Unmuts Des Rendsch
Nameh *Op.67,No.4-6, CC3U
[Ger] high solo,pno BOTE $5.50
(S3730)

Secret, The *see Das Geheimnis

Seitdem Dein Aug'in Meines Schaute
*Op.17,No.1
"E'er Since Thine Eye Towards Mine
Was Wended" see Six Songs For
High Voice

Serenade *see Standchen

Seven Songs *see Ach Was Kummer,
Qual Und Schmerzen, Op.49,No.7;
In Goldener Fulle, Op.49,No.2;
Junggesellenschwur, Op.49,No.5;
Sie Wissen's Nicht, Op.49,No.4;
Waldeseligkeit, Op.49,No.1; Wer
Lieben Will, Muss Leiden, Op.49,
No.6; Wiegenliedchen, Op.49,No.3
(S3731)

Sie Wissen's Nicht *Op.49,No.4
[Eng/Ger] solo,pno (E maj) BOOSEY
$2.25 see from Seven Songs   (S3732)

Sie Woll'n Mich Heiraten (from
Arabella)
2 soli,pno SCHOTTS s.p.   (S3733)

Sieben Siegel *Op.46,No.2
[Eng/Ger] solo,pno (G maj) BOOSEY
$2.25 see from Three Songs   (S3734)

Six Songs After Poems By Clemens
Brentano *see Als Mir Dein Lied
Erklang, Op.68,No.4; Amor, Op.68,
No.5; An Die Nacht, Op.68,No.1;
Ich Wollt' Ein Strausslein
Binden, Op.68,No.2; Lied Der
Frauen, Op.68,No.6; Sausle, Liebe
Myrthe, Op.68,No.3   (S3735)

Six Songs For High Voice
[Ger/Eng] high solo,pno SCHAUR
EE 386 s.p.
contains: Aus Den Liedern Der
Trauer [II], "From The Songs Of
Sorrow [II]", Op.17,No.4;
Barcarole, Op.17,No.6; Das
Geheimnis, "Secret, The",
Op.17,No.3; Nur Mut!, "Hope
On!", Op.17,No.5; Seitdem Dein
Aug'in Meines Schaute, "E'er
Since Thine Eye Towards Mine
Was Wended", Op.17,No.1;
Standchen, "Serenade", Op.17,
No.2   (S3736)

Song Album *CCU
[Ger/Eng] high solo,pno BOOSEY
$8.00   (S3737)

Sophie (from Der Rosenkavalier)
[Eng/Ger] SMez soli,pno BOOSEY
$2.50   (S3738)

Soprano Arias From The Operas *CCU
[Eng/Ger] S solo,orch BOOSEY $6.00
(S3739)

Standchen *Op.17,No.2
"Serenade" see Six Songs For High
Voice
"Serenade" [Ger/Eng] high solo,pno
(F sharp maj) SCHIRM.G $.60
(S3740)
"Serenade" [Ger/Eng] med-high solo,
pno SCHAUR EE 387B $1.25, ea.
(S3741)
"Serenade" [Ger/Eng] med solo,pno
SCHAUR EE 387C $1.25, ea.   (S3742)
"Serenade" [Ger/Eng] high solo,pno
SCHAUR EE 387A $1.25, ea.   (S3743)
"Serenade" [Ger/Eng] low solo,pno
SCHAUR EE 387D $1.25, ea.   (S3744)
"Serenade" [Ger/Eng] low solo,pno
opt vln/vcl PRESSER $.75   (S3745)

Stern *Op.69,No.1
[Ger] solo,pno (F maj) BOOSEY $2.25
see from Four Little Songs
(S3746)

Tenor Aria (from Der Rosenkavalier)
[Eng/Ger] T solo,pno BOOSEY $2.50
(S3747)

STRAUSS, RICHARD (cont'd.)

Thal *Op.51,No.1
[Eng/Ger] B solo,pno (B flat maj)
BOOSEY $2.50 see from Two Bass
Songs   (S3748)

Thirty Songs *CC30L
(Kagen, Sergius) [Ger/Eng]
INTERNAT. high solo,pno $5.00;
med solo,pno $5.00; low solo,pno
$5.00   (S3749)

Three Holy Kings, The *see Die
Heiligen Drei Konige

Three Hymns By Friedrich Holderlin
*see Hymne An Die Liebe, Op.71,
No.1; Liebe, Op.71,No.3; Ruckkehr
In Die Heimat, Op.71,No.2 (S3750)

Three Love Songs *see Begegnung,
"Meeting"; Die Erwachte Rose,
"Awakened Rose, The"; Rote Rosen,
"Red Roses"   (S3751)

Three Songs *see Blauer Sommer,
Op.31,No.1; Weisser Jasmin,
Op.31,No.3; Wenn, Op.31,No.2
                                  (S3752)

Three Songs *see Gestern War Ich
Atlas, Op.46,No.1; Ich Sehe Wie
In Einem Spiegel, Op.46,No.3;
Sieben Siegel, Op.46,No.2 (S3753)

Tomorrow *see Morgen

Traum Durch Die Dammerung *Op.29,
No.1
med solo,pno UNIVER. 5445B $2.75
see from Drei Lieder   (S3754)
high solo,pno UNIVER. 5445A $2.75
see from Drei Lieder   (S3755)
low solo,pno UNIVER. 5445C $2.75
see from Drei Lieder   (S3756)

Trio (from Der Rosenkavalier)
[Eng/Ger] SSMez soli,pno BOOSEY
$2.50   (S3757)

Two Bass Songs *see Einsame, Op.51,
No.2; Thal, Op.51,No.1   (S3758)

Two Poems And Three Japanese Lyrics
*CC5U
[Russ/Fr/Eng/Ger] high solo,pno/
chamb.orch BOOSEY $10.00 (S3759)

Two Songs *see Nachtlicher Gang,
Op.44,No.2; Notturno, Op.44,No.1
                                  (S3760)

Vier Lieder *see Cacilie, Op.27,
No.2; Heimliche Aufforderung,
Op.27,No.3; Morgen, Op.27,No.4;
Ruhe, Meine Seele, Op.27,No.1
                                  (S3761)

Von Den Sieben Zechbrudern *Op.47,
No.4
[Eng/Ger] solo,pno (E min) BOOSEY
$2.25 see from Four Songs (S3762)

Waldeseligkeit *Op.49,No.1
[Eng/Ger] solo,pno (G flat maj)
BOOSEY $2.25 see from Seven Songs
                                  (S3763)

Waldesfahrt *Op.69,No.3
solo,pno (F sharp maj) BOOSEY $2.25
see from Four Little Songs
                                  (S3764)

Wasserrose *Op.22,No.4
[Eng/Ger] solo,pno (F sharp maj)
BOOSEY $2.25 see from
Maidenblossoms   (S3765)

Weisser Jasmin *Op.31,No.3
[Eng/Ger] solo,pno (C sharp min)
BOOSEY $2.25 see from Three Songs
                                  (S3766)

Wenn *Op.31,No.2
[Eng/Ger] solo,pno (E maj) BOOSEY
$2.25 see from Three Songs
                                  (S3767)

Wer Lieben Will, Muss Leiden *Op.49,
No.6
[Eng/Ger] solo,pno (F sharp min)
BOOSEY $2.25 see from Seven Songs
                                  (S3768)

When With Thine Eyes *see Mit Deinen
Blauen Augen

Wiegenlied *Op.41,No.1
[Ger/Eng] high solo,2fl,3ob,2clar,
2bsn,2horn,2harp,3vln,2vla,2vcl,
5strings LEUCKART rental see also
Funf Lieder   (S3769)
[Ger/Eng] high solo,pno LEUCKART
$3.00 see also Funf Lieder
                                  (S3770)
[Ger/Eng] low solo,pno LEUCKART
$3.00 see also Funf Lieder
                                  (S3771)

Wiegenliedchen *Op.49,No.3
[Eng/Ger] solo,pno (F sharp maj)
BOOSEY $2.25 see from Seven Songs
                                  (S3772)

STRAUSS, RICHARD (cont'd.)

Winter Night *see Winternacht

Winterliebe *Op.48,No.5
[Eng/Ger] solo,pno (B maj) BOOSEY
$2.25 see from Five Songs (S3773)
[Ger/Eng] T solo,pno FURST s.p. see
from Funf Lieder   (S3774)
[Eng/Ger] solo,pno (E maj) BOOSEY
$2.25   (S3775)

Winternacht *Op.15,No.2
"Winter Night" see Five Songs For
Medium Voice

Winterweihe *Op.48,No.4
[Eng/Ger] solo,pno (E flat maj)
BOOSEY $2.25 see from Five Songs
                                  (S3776)
[Ger/Eng] low solo,pno FURST s.p.
see from Funf Lieder   (S3777)
[Ger/Eng] high solo,pno FURST s.p.
see from Funf Lieder   (S3778)

Zerbinetta's Recitative And Aria
(from Ariadne Auf Naxos)
[Eng/Ger] S solo,pno BOOSEY $4.00
                                  (S3779)

Zueignung *Op.10,No.1
med solo,pno UNIVER. 5420B $2.75
see from Acht Lieder   (S3780)
high solo,pno UNIVER. 5420A $2.75
see from Acht Lieder   (S3781)
low solo,pno UNIVER. 5420C $2.75
see from Acht Lieder   (S3782)

STRAUSS VOCAL WALTZES see Strauss,
Johann

STRAVINSKY, IGOR (1882-1972)
Abraham And Isaac *song cycle
[Heb/Eng] Bar solo,chamb.orch
BOOSEY $6.00   (S3783)

Berceuses Du Chat
[Russ/Fr] med-low solo,kbd CHESTER
s.p.
contains: Ce Qu'il A Le Chat;
Dodo; Interieur; Sur Le Poele
                                  (S3784)

Canard
see Quatre Chants Russes

Ce Qu'il A Le Chat
see Berceuses Du Chat

Chanson Dissident
see Quatre Chants Russes

Chanson Pour Compter
see Quatre Chants Russes

Chansons De L'Ours
see Trois Histoires Pour Enfants

Dodo
see Berceuses Du Chat

Drake, The
see Four Songs

Elegy For J.F.K. *song cycle
Mez/Bar solo,3clar BOOSEY $3.00,
ipa   (S3785)

Four Songs
[Eng/Russ] high solo,fl,harp,gtr sc
CHESTER s.p.
contains: Drake, The; Geese And
Swans; Russian Spiritual, A;
Tilim-Bom   (S3786)

Geese And Swans
see Four Songs

In Memoriam Dylan Thomas *song cycle
T solo,4strings,4trom BOOSEY $4.00
                                  (S3787)

Interieur
see Berceuses Du Chat

Le Colonel
see Pribaoutki

Le Faune Et La Bergere *Op.2
[Fr/Ger] high solo,3fl,2ob,2clar,
2bsn,4horn,2trp,3trom,tuba,timp,
perc,strings sc BELAIEFF BEL336
s.p., study sc BELAIEFF BEL336A
s.p., voc sc BELAIEFF BEL311 s.p.
                                  (S3788)

Le Four
see Pribaoutki

Le Moineau Est Assis
see Quatre Chants Russes

Le Vieux Et Le Lievre
see Pribaoutki

Les Canards, Les Cygnes, Les Oies
see Trois Histoires Pour Enfants

STRAVINSKY, IGOR (cont'd.)

L'histoire Du Soldat
narrator,chamb.grp. study sc KALMUS
260 $3.00, sc KALMUS $15.00
                                  (S3789)

L'Oncle Armand
see Pribaoutki

Moonlight Pallid
see Two Songs

Owl And The Pussy-Cat
solo,pno BOOSEY $2.00   (S3790)

Pastorale
solo,4winds/pno voc sc SCHOTTS 2295
s.p., ipa   (S3791)
S solo,ob,English horn,clar,bsn
(without words) study sc SCHOTTS
3399 s.p., voc sc SCHOTTS 2295
s.p., ipa   (S3792)

Pribaoutki
[Russ/Fr] med solo,kbd CHESTER s.p.
contains: Le Colonel; Le Four; Le
Vieux Et Le Lievre; L'Oncle
Armand   (S3793)

Quatre Chants Russes
[Russ/Fr] high solo,kbd CHESTER
s.p.
contains: Canard; Chanson
Dissident; Chanson Pour
Compter; Le Moineau Est Assis
                                  (S3794)

Russian Maiden's Song
[Russ/Eng] solo,pno (B flat min)
BOOSEY $1.75   (S3795)

Russian Spiritual, A
see Four Songs

Sleep
see Two Songs

Song Of The Dew *Op.6,No.2
[Eng/Fr] solo,pno (B min) BOOSEY
$2.50 see from Two Songs (S3796)

Spring *Op.6,No.1
[Eng/Fr] solo,pno (G maj) BOOSEY
$2.50 see from Two Songs (S3797)

Sur Le Poele
see Berceuses Du Chat

Three Songs From William Shakespeare
*CC3U
Mez solo,fl,clar,vla BOOSEY $3.25,
ipa   (S3798)

Tilim-Bom
see Four Songs
[Russ/Fr] med solo,kbd CHESTER s.p.
see also Trois Histoires Pour
Enfants   (S3799)

Trois Histoires Pour Enfants
[Russ/Fr] med solo,kbd CHESTER s.p.
contains: Chansons De L'Ours; Les
Canards, Les Cygnes, Les Oies;
Tilim-Bom
see also: Tilim-Bom   (S3800)

Trois Petites Chansons-Souvenir De
Mon Enfance *CC3U
[Russ/Fr] solo,pno/orch BOOSEY
$2.00   (S3801)

Two Songs *see Song Of The Dew,
Op.6,No.2; Spring, Op.6,No.1
                                  (S3802)

Two Songs
[Eng/Fr/Ger] solo,pno BOOSEY $1.50
contains: Moonlight Pallid (B
flat min); Sleep (B flat min)
                                  (S3803)

STRAVINSKY, SOULIMA (1910-   )
Chantefables *CC10U
[Fr] solo,pno PETERS 66548 s.p.
                                  (S3804)

STRAW CAROL, THE see Friesen, Dick

STRAWBERRIES, THE see Dvorak, Antonin,
Die Erdbeeren

STRAY NYMPTH OF DIAN, A see Parry,
Charles Hubert Hastings

STREAM see Malipiero, Gian Francesco

STREET, A.
Birdies' Ball
solo,pno (D maj) LEONARD-ENG
                                  (S3805)

STREET, G.
Chanson A Boire
solo,pno ENOCH s.p.   (S3806)
solo,acap ENOCH s.p.   (S3807)

Envoi
solo,pno ENOCH s.p.   (S3808)
solo,acap ENOCH s.p.   (S3809)

STREET, G. (cont'd.)

La Chanson Du Battoir
solo,pno ENOCH s.p.   (S3810)
solo,acap ENOCH s.p.   (S3811)

L'Amour Des Gueux
solo,pno ENOCH s.p.   (S3812)
solo,acap ENOCH s.p.   (S3813)

Le Faucheur
solo,pno ENOCH s.p.   (S3814)
solo,acap ENOCH s.p.   (S3815)

Le Mort Maudit
solo,pno ENOCH s.p.   (S3816)
solo,acap ENOCH s.p.   (S3817)

Le Printemps Des Gueux
solo,pno ENOCH s.p.   (S3818)
solo,acap ENOCH s.p.   (S3819)

STREET, JAMES
Even As I First Loved You *sac
solo,pno WORD S-397   (S3820)

STREET SCENES see Ballou, Esther W.

STREETS OF LAREDO, THE see Sims, Ezra

STREIM see Marsh, Roger

STRELEZKI, ANTON (1859-1907)
Dreams
solo,pno (D maj) LEONARD-ENG
                             (S3821)

STRICKLAND, LILY TERESA (1887-1958)
At Eve I Heard A Flute
med solo,pno PRESSER $.75   (S3822)

Den Jag Alskar Ar En Fiskare *see My
Lover Is A Fisherman

Incline Your Ear *sac
high solo,pno (C maj) SCHIRM.G $.60
                             (S3823)
low solo,pno (A maj) SCHIRM.G $.60
                             (S3824)

Ma Li'l Batteau
high solo,pno BELWIN $1.50   (S3825)
low solo,pno BELWIN $1.50   (S3826)

Mah Lindy Lou
low solo,pno (C maj) SCHIRM.G $.75
                             (S3827)

My Lover Is A Fisherman
low solo,pno PRESSER $.95   (S3828)
high solo,pno PRESSER $.95   (S3829)
"Den Jag Alskar Ar En Fiskare"
[Swed/Eng] solo,pno GEHRMANS s.p.
                             (S3830)
"Den Jag Alskar Ar En Fiskare"
[Swed] low solo,pno GEHRMANS s.p.
                             (S3831)
"Den Jag Alskar Ar En Fiskare"
[Swed] high solo,pno GEHRMANS
s.p.   (S3832)

They Shall Not Hunger Nor Thirst
*sac
high solo,pno (A flat maj) SCHIRM.G
$.60   (S3833)
low solo,pno (F maj) SCHIRM.G $.60
                             (S3834)

With My Heart I Follow You
low solo,pno PRESSER $.75   (S3835)

STRICKLAND, WILLIAM (1914-   )
Flower Given To My Daughter
med solo,pno (B flat maj) GALAXY
1.2176.7 $1.00   (S3836)

Ione, Dead The Long Year
high solo,pno GALAXY 1.2175.7 $1.00
                             (S3837)

She Weeps Over Rahoon
solo,pno (E min) GALAXY 1.2177.7
$1.00   (S3838)

STRICTLY GERM-PROOF see Sacco, John
[Charles]

STRIDE LA VAMPA see Verdi, Giuseppe

STRIKE, THOU HOUR SO LONG EXPECTED see
Bach, Johann Sebastian

STRILKO, ANTHONY (1931-   )
Canal Bank, The
med solo,pno MERCURY $.95   (S3839)

Canticle To Apollo
med solo,pno MERCURY $.95   (S3840)

David's Harp *sac
med solo,pno MERCURY $.95   (S3841)

Fiddler's Coin, The
med solo,pno MERCURY $.95   (S3842)

From Autumn's Thrilling Tomb
high solo,pno MERCURY $1.00 (S3843)

Little Elegy
med solo,pno MERCURY $.95   (S3844)

STRILKO, ANTHONY (cont'd.)

Ophelia
high solo,pno MERCURY $.95   (S3845)
med solo,pno MERCURY $.95   (S3846)

Point Charles
high solo,pno MERCURY $.95   (S3847)
med solo,pno MERCURY $.95   (S3848)

Songs From "Markings" *CCU
MERCURY high solo,pno $1.00; med
solo,pno $1.00   (S3849)

STRIMER, JOSEPH (1881-   )
Au Gre Du Vent
solo,pno JOBERT s.p. see also Les
Chanteries Du Jeune Age   (S3850)

Berceuse Pour Le Petit Ours
solo,pno JOBERT s.p. see also Les
Chanteries Du Jeune Age   (S3851)

Chante L'alouette
solo,pno JOBERT s.p. see also Les
Chanteries Du Jeune Age   (S3852)

Dors Mon Petit Ange
solo,pno JOBERT s.p. see also Les
Chanteries Du Jeune Age   (S3853)

Humble Priere
solo,org/harmonium,vln/vcl DURAND
s.p.   (S3854)

Jeanneton Qui N'a Pas De Maman
solo,pno JOBERT s.p. see also Les
Chanteries Du Jeune Age   (S3855)

La Complainte Du Petit Ane
solo,pno JOBERT s.p. see also Les
Chanteries Du Jeune Age   (S3856)

Les Chanteries Du Jeune Age
solo,pno cmplt ed JOBERT s.p.
contains & see also: Au Gre Du
Vent; Berceuse Pour Le Petit
Ours; Chante L'alouette; Dors
Mon Petit Ange; Jeanneton Qui
N'a Pas De Maman; La Complainte
Du Petit Ane; Ma Chatte Danse;
Marche Des Enfants De France;
Neige Tombe; Pavane De La
Petite Marquise   (S3857)

Lorsque Nous Avions Trios Dindons
1-2 soli,pno DURAND s.p.   (S3858)

Ma Chatte Danse
solo,pno JOBERT s.p. see also Les
Chanteries Du Jeune Age   (S3859)

Marche Des Enfants De France
solo,pno JOBERT s.p. see also Les
Chanteries Du Jeune Age   (S3860)

Neige Tombe
solo,pno JOBERT s.p. see also Les
Chanteries Du Jeune Age   (S3861)

Pavane De La Petite Marquise
solo,pno JOBERT s.p. see also Les
Chanteries Du Jeune Age   (S3862)

Simplesse
solo,pno DURAND s.p.   (S3863)

STRING QUARTET NO. 1 see Sternberg,
Erich Walter

STRING QUARTET NO. 2 see Koch,
Frederick

STRING QUARTET NO. FIVE - EKLOGE see
Stein, Leon

STRINGFIELD, LAMAR (1897-1959)
Daniel Boone
solo,pno BRODT $.50   (S3864)

Shout Freedom!
solo,pno BRODT $.40   (S3865)

STRIPSODY see Berberian, Kathy

STRNISTE, JIRI (1914-   )
Fliegerlied *see Letecka

Letecka
"Fliegerlied" med solo,pno CZECH
s.p.   (S3866)

STROHBACH, SIEGFRIED (1929-   )
Halunkensongs *CCU
Bar solo,trp,vln,bvl,acord,perc sc
BREITKOPF-W PB 3776 s.p., voc sc
BREITKOPF-W EB 6229 $3.00, ipa
                             (S3867)
STROLLING PLAYER see Trotere, Henry

STRONG, GEORGE TEMPLETON (1856-1948)
Le Gue
solo,orch HENN s.p.   (S3868)

STRONG, GEORGE TEMPLETON (cont'd.)

Le Voyage
solo,orch HENN s.p.   (S3869)

Lieder
solo,orch HENN s.p.   (S3870)

STRONG IS YOUR LOVE see Jillett, David,
E Hehu Kerito

STROPHES see De Lara, Isadore

STROPHES A L'AMITIE see Maurat, Edmond

STROPHES ET INTERLUDES see De Lara,
Isadore

STROPHIC SONGS, VOL. 1 see Nielsen,
Carl

STROPHIC SONGS, VOL. 2 see Nielsen,
Carl

STRUTIUS, THOMAS (1621-1678)
Resonet In Laudibus *sac,concerto
(Grusnick, Bruno) [Lat/Ger] SSB
soli,2vln,cont (med easy) sc
BAREN. 3519 $5.75, ipa   (S3871)

STUART
Partners With God *see Waters

STUBBS DU PERRON, ED.
Chant D'amour Inca
solo,pno DURAND s.p.   (S3872)
[Fr] solo,acap oct DURAND s.p.
                             (S3873)

STUCHKOFF, N.
Warshe *Jew
solo,pno KAMMEN 488 $1.00 see also
FAVORITE JEWISH SONGS, VOL. 2
                             (S3874)

STUDENTENLIED see Hullebroeck, Em.

STUDENTSANG see Froding

STUDIE EFTER NATUREN see Nielsen, Carl

STUDY OF TWO PEARS, A see Warfield,
Gerald

STULTS, R.
Sweetest Story Ever Told, The *sac
med solo,pno (E flat maj) CENTURY
4080   (S3875)
solo,pno (available in 3 keys)
ASHLEY $.95   (S3876)

STULTZ, R.M.
Sweetest Story Ever Told
low solo,pno PRESSER $.95   (S3877)

STUM KARLEK see Wolf, Hugo

STUMBLING BLOCKS TO STEPPING STONES see
Wilson, Al

STUNDE DER ERFULLUNG see Bijvanck, Henk

STUNDE EINES BLOCKS see Nilsson, Bo

STUNDEN EINER LIEBE see Roselius,
Ludwig

STUPNICA PIESNI see Freso, Tibor

STUPP
Lamb, The
high solo,pno SHAWNEE IA5041 $.85
                             (S3878)

STURGIS
Stranger Of Galilee *sac,Easter
high solo,pno (G maj) WATERLOO $.65
                             (S3879)
med solo,pno (F maj) WATERLOO $.65
                             (S3880)
low solo,pno (E flat maj) WATERLOO
$.65   (S3881)

STURM see Marvia, Einari, Myrsky

STURMNACHT see Schwickert, Gustav

STUTSCHEVSKY, JOACHIM (1891-   )
Festivals And Holy Days
see Hassidic Tunes

Hassidic Tunes
ISR.MUS.INST. s.p.
contains: Festivals And Holy
Days; Nigunim - For The Whole
Year Round; Shabbath   (S3882)

Little Songs For Libby *CCU
solo,pno OR-TAV $.75   (S3883)

Nigunim - For The Whole Year Round
see Hassidic Tunes

Nine Art Songs *CC9U
solo,pno OR-TAV $1.75, ea. sold
separately   (S3884)

STUTSCHEVSKY, JOACHIM (cont'd.)

Shabbath
see Hassidic Tunes

Two Sephardic Prayers *CC2U
solo,pno OR-TAV $1.00   (S3885)

STYRI DVOJSPEVY see Urbanec, Bartolomej

STYRI LUDOVE PIESNE see Suchon, Eugen

STYRI PIESNE see Kafenda, Frico

STYRI PIESNE see Kresanek, Jozef

STYRI PIESNE see Pospisil, Juraj

STYRI PIESNE VDAKY see Macudzinski, Rudolf

SU LE SPONDE DEL TEBRO see Scarlatti, Alessandro

SU QUESTA SANTA CROCE see Giordano, Umberto

SU UNA VIOLETTA MORTA see Respighi, Ottorino

SUB TUUM PRAESIDIUM see Heiller, Anton

SUB TUUM PRAESIDIUM see Milwid, Antoni

SUB TUUM PRAESIDIUM see Mozart, Wolfgang Amadeus

SUBEN, JOEL
Make A Joyful Noise To The Lord *sac
high solo,pno BELWIN $1.50 (S3886)

SUBIRA *CC12L,Span
[Span/Eng] solo,pno INTERNAT. $3.00
contains works by: Castel; Esteve;
Ferandiere; Bustos and others
(S3887)

SUBJECTIVES V see Rouse, Christopher

SUBLIMATION see Avshalomov, Aaron

SUBMARINES see Elgar, Edward

SUBSTITUTION see Matsudaira, Yori Akki

SUCH A LIVELY MORNING see Casseus

SUCH A LOVE see Lewis, Erv

SUCH BEAUTY AS HURTS TO BEHOLD see Rorem, Ned

SUCH LOVELY THINGS see North, Michael

SUCH MERRY FOLK ARE WE see Marzials, Theo

SUCH MERRY MAIDS ARE WE see Millard, Harrison

SUCHON, EUGEN (1908-   )
Ad Astra
S solo,pno SLOV.HUD.FOND s.p.
(S3888)

Bacovske Piesne *CCU
Bar solo,pno SLOV.HUD.FOND s.p.
(S3889)

Nox Et Solitudo
Mez solo,pno SLOV.HUD.FOND s.p.
(S3890)

Piesenzo Zalmu Zeme Podkarpatskej
*sac,CCU,Psalm
T solo,pno SLOV.HUD.FOND s.p.
(S3891)

Styri Ludove Piesne *CC4U
solo,pno SLOV.HUD.FOND s.p. (S3892)

SUDDENLY THERE'S A VALLEY *sac,gospel
solo,pno ABER.GRP. $1.50   (S3893)

SUENOS DE AMOR see Liszt, Franz

SUFFER LITTLE CHILDREN see Lohr, Frederic N.

SUFFER THE CHILDREN TO COME UNTO ME see Fischer, Irwin

SUFFOLK OWL see Elwell, Herbert

SUFFOLK OWL, THE see Dunhill, Thomas Frederick

SUGAR, REZSO (1919-   )
Heroic Song *ora
solo,pno BUDAPEST 2133 s.p. (S3894)

SUGARSTICKS *sac,CC10L
(Perkins, Phil) solo,pno WORD 32036
$1.95   (S3895)

SUGGS
Is My Lord Satisfied With Me? *sac
solo,pno LILLENAS SM-920: SN $1.00
(S3896)

SUICIDA Y REQUIESCIT see Schwartz, Francis

SUICIDIO! see Ponchielli, Amilcare

SUID-AFRIKAANSE LIEDEREN *CCU,folk,Afr
(Mengelberg, R.) solo,pno BROEKMANS
279 s.p.   (S3897)

SUIS-TU LE MOUVEMENT see Guiraud, Ernest

SUITE A CHANTER see Delannoy, Marcel

SUITE AGRESTE see Ferro, Stefano

SUITE AUX TROUBADOURS see Bond, Victoria

SUITE FOR HIGH VOICE see Woollen, Russell

SUITE LITURIQUE see Jolivet, Andre

SUITE NEGRE *CCU,spir
(Zagwijn, Henri) Mez/Bar solo,fl,ob,
clar,bsn,horn,pno voc sc DONEMUS
s.p.   (S3898)

SUITE OF BAIRNSANGS, A see Musgrave, Thea

SUITE OF SONGS see Purcell, Henry

SUITE ON POLISH FOLK MELODIES see Behrend, Siegfried

SUITE SUR DES AIRS DE LA VIEILLE FRANCE see Fuleihan, Anis

SUITE SYLVESTRE see Schoemaker, Maurice

SUITE VOCALISE see Medtner, Nikolai Karlovitch

SUJETION see Legay, Marcel

SUK, JOSEF (1874-1935)
Tri Pisne *CC3U
solo,pno SUPRAPHON s.p.   (S3899)

SUKY, YOU SHALL BE MY WIFE see Fiske, R.

SUL FIL D'UN SOFFIO ETESIO see Verdi, Giuseppe

SUL MURO GRAFITO see Bettinelli, Bruno

SULAMIT see Hurnik, Ilja

SULEIKA see Schubert, Franz (Peter), Suleikas Erster Gesang

SULEIKA see Trunk, Richard

SULEIKA see Valen, Fartein

SULEIKAS ERSTER GESANG see Schubert, Franz (Peter)

SULEIKAS ZWEITER GESANG see Schubert, Franz (Peter)

SULFANEIN E LUSTER!
(Carlo, Musi) solo,pno (Bolognese
dialect) BONGIOVANI 2072 s.p. see
from El Mi Canzunett   (S3900)

SULIKO *folk,Russ
[Ger/Russ] solo,pno ZIMMER. 1553 s.p.
(S3901)

SULIRAM
see Internationale Volslieder, Vol 1

SULL' ARIA see Mozart, Wolfgang Amadeus

SULLA TOMBA DI ANACREONTE see Margola, Franco

SULLA TOMBA DI UN VECCHIO see Rocca, Lodovico

SULLA VIA MAESTRA see Strano, Alfredo

SULLE PIU BELLE PIANTE see Frederick II of Prussia

SULLIVAN, ALBERT
God Shall Wipe Away All Tears
high solo,pno (G maj) CRAMER
(S3902)
low solo,pno (E maj) CRAMER (S3903)

SULLIVAN, SIR ARTHUR SEYMOUR
(1842-1900)
Absent Minded Beggar, The
low solo,pno (C maj) ASHDOWN s.p.
(S3904)
high solo,pno (E maj) ASHDOWN s.p.
(S3905)
med solo,pno (D maj) ASHDOWN s.p.
(S3906)
Aimons-Nous
solo,pno ENOCH s.p.   (S3907)

SULLIVAN, SIR ARTHUR SEYMOUR (cont'd.)
Chorister, The
solo,pno CRAMER   (S3908)

Edward Gray
high solo,pno (G maj) CRAMER
(S3909)
low solo,pno (E maj) CRAMER (S3910)

Gilbert And Sullivan (composed with
Gilbert, William Schwenck) *CCU
solo,pno MUSIC 0200016 $3.95
(S3911)
Gilbert And Sullivan At Home *CCU
(Wier) med solo,pno BMI $1.75
(S3912)

Gwenllian
solo,pno CRAMER   (S3913)

Gwilym And Ellen
solo,pno CRAMER   (S3914)

Happy Young Heart (from Sorcerer, The)
2 soli,pno CRAMER   (S3915)
solo,pno CRAMER   (S3916)

He Is An Englishman (from H. M. S. Pinafore)
solo,pno CRAMER   (S3917)

I Am The Captain Of The Pinafore
(from H.M.S. Pinafore)
solo,pno CRAMER   (S3918)

I Am The Ruler Of The Queen's Navee
(from H.M.S. Pinafore)
solo,pno CRAMER   (S3919)

Josephine's Song (from H.M.S. Pinafore)
solo,pno CRAMER   (S3920)

King Henry's Song
high solo,pno (F maj) CRAMER
(S3921)
low solo,pno (E flat maj) CRAMER
(S3922)

Little Buttercup (from H.M.S. Pinafore)
solo,pno CRAMER   (S3923)

Lost Chord, The *sac
med solo,pno (G maj) CENTURY 64
$.40   (S3924)
high solo,pno (G maj) BOOSEY $1.50
(S3925)
med solo,pno (F maj) BOOSEY $1.50
(S3926)
low solo,pno (E flat maj) BOOSEY
$1.50   (S3927)
low solo,pno (F maj) CENTURY 65
$.40   (S3928)

Never Mind The Why And Where-Fore
(from H.M.S. Pinafore)
3 soli,pno CRAMER   (S3929)

O Mistress Mine
high solo,pno (G maj) CRAMER
(S3930)
low solo,pno (F maj) CRAMER (S3931)

Onward Christian Soldiers *sac
low solo,pno (C maj) CENTURY 3618
$.40   (S3932)

Orpheus With His Lute
high solo,pno (B flat maj) ASHDOWN
s.p.   (S3933)
med solo,pno (A maj) ASHDOWN s.p.
(S3934)
low solo,pno (G maj) ASHDOWN s.p.
(S3935)
high solo,pno (B flat maj) CRAMER
$1.15   (S3936)
med solo,pno (A maj) CRAMER $1.15
(S3937)
low solo,pno (G maj) CRAMER $1.15
(S3938)

Refrain Thy Voice From Weeping
high solo,pno (A flat maj) CRAMER
(S3939)
low solo,pno (C maj) CRAMER (S3940)

Sailor's Grave
med-high solo,pno (E flat maj)
ASHDOWN s.p.   (S3941)
med solo,pno (D maj) ASHDOWN s.p.
(S3942)
low solo,pno (C maj) ASHDOWN s.p.
(S3943)
high solo,pno (F maj) ASHDOWN s.p.
(S3944)

She Will Tend Him (from Sorcerer, The)
5 soli,pno CRAMER   (S3945)

Sorcerers Song (from Sorcerer, The)
solo,pno CRAMER   (S3946)

Sweet Dreamer
solo,pno CRAMER   (S3947)

SULLIVAN, SIR ARTHUR SEYMOUR (cont'd.)

Tit Willow (from Mikado, The)
   low solo,pno (G maj) CENTURY 3706
                                    (S3948)
Vicar's Song (from Sorcerer, The)
   solo,pno CRAMER   (S3949)

Willow Song
   low solo,pno (E maj) CRAMER (S3950)
   high solo,pno (G maj) CRAMER
                                    (S3951)

SUMMER see Bliss, Sir Arthur

SUMMER see Shaw, Martin

SUMMER BREEZE see Thiman, Eric Harding

SUMMER EVENING
   (Davis, K. K.) high solo,pno BELWIN
   $1.50   (S3952)

SUMMER EVENING see Revel, Peter

SUMMER LANDSCAPE see Delius, Frederick

SUMMER MEADOWS see Brahms, Johannes

SUMMER NIGHT, A see Thomas, Arthur
   Goring, Une Nuit De Mai

SUMMER NIGHTS see Thomas, Arthur
   Goring, Une Nuit De Mai

SUMMER NIGHTS, THE see Berlioz, Hector,
   Les Nuits D'Ete

SUMMER REVERIE see Birch, Robert
   Fairfax

SUMMER SCHEMES see Ireland, John

SUMMER SONG see Kilpinen, Yrio,
   Suvilaulu

SUMMER WIND see Lessard, John Ayres

SUMMER'S END see Weigl, Vally

SUMMERTIME see Ronald, Sir Landon

SUMNER
   My God Won't Ever Let Me Down *sac
   solo,pno LILLENAS SM-928: SN $1.00
                                    (S3953)
   Night Before Easter, The *see Friend

SUN see Rorem, Ned

SUN ABOVE ME see Pergolesi, Giovanni
   Battista

SUN AND LIFE see Svarc, Alfred

SUN ETEHENS LAPSI BETLEHEMIN see
   Kuusisto, Taneli

SUN RETURNS see Tchaikovsky, Piotr
   Ilyitch, Lensky's Song

SUN RISTIS JUUREHEN see Kuusisto,
   Taneli

SUN TUSKIN HUOMASIN see Kilpinen, Yrio

SUNBEAMS see Ronald, Sir Landon

SUNDAY see Brahms, Johannes, Sonntag

SUNDAY MORNIN' see Kaiser, Kurt

SUNDAY MORNING see Matthews, Randy

SUNDAY SOLO: EIGHTEEN SACRED SONGS FROM
   THE CLASSICS, THE *sac,CC18L
   (Tingley, Gertrude) SCHIRM.G high
   solo,pno $3.00; low solo,pno $2.00
   contains works by: Handel; Haydn;
   Purcell; Vivaldi and others (S3954)

SUNG BY THE SHEPHERDS see Thomson,
   Virgil

SUNLESS see Mussorgsky, Modest

SUNNESCHY UND RAGEWETTER *CCU
   (Muller, P.; Muller, H.) solo,pno HUG
   s.p.   (S3955)

SUNNSCHIEN OP'N WEG see Janssen, Gunnar

SUNNUNTAI see Turunen, Martti
   (Johannes)

SUNNUNTAIAAMU see Mendelssohn-
   Bartholdy, Felix, Sontagsmorgen

SUNNUNTAIAAMUNA see Backman, Hjalmar

SUNNUNTAINA see Jarnefelt, Armas

SUNNY LAND see Bennett, Sir William
   Sterndale

SUNRISE *sac,gospel
   solo,pno ABER.GRP. $1.50   (S3956)

SUNRISE see Ives, Charles

SUNRISE see Jensen, Gordon

SUNSET see Hayakawa, Masaaki

SUNSET see Sharpe, Evelyn

SUNSET see Thomas, Arthur Goring

SUNSET GLOW see Schubert, Franz
   (Peter), Im Abendroth

SUNSET POEM see Ellis, O.

SUNSHINE GARDEN see McGeorge, Muriel

SUNSHINE SONG see Grieg, Edvard
   Hagerup, Solveigs Sang

SUNYATA see Sinopoli, Giuseppe

SUO EI KASVA KIVIA see Haapalainen,
   Vaino

SUO-GAN
   (Williams, W.S. Gwynn) [Eng/Welsh] 2
   soli,pno ROBERTON 71997 s.p.
                                    (S3957)
SUO MULLE SYOMMES see Melartin, Erkki,
   Gib Mir Dein Herze

SUOMALAINEN RUKOUS see Kuusisto, Taneli

SUOMALAISIA KANSANLAULUDUETTOJA, VOLS.
   I-II see Kauppi, Emil

SUOMALAISIA LAULUSAVELLYKSIA see
   Merikanto, Oskar

SUOMEN PUU see Madetoja, Leevi

SUOMIS SANG see Pacius, Fredrik

SUONI ESTREMI see Eichenwald, Philipp

SUPPE, FRANZ VON (1819-1895)
   Florenz Hat Schone Frauen (from
   Boccaccio)
   2 soli,pno DOBLINGER 88 505 s.p.
                                    (S3958)
SUPPER TIME *sac,gospel
   solo,pno ABER.GRP. $1.50   (S3959)

SUPPERTIME see Stanphill, Ira F.

SUPPLICATION see Handel, George
   Frideric

SUPPLICATION see Lacome, Paul

SUPREME AVEU see Delmet, Paul

SUR DES POEMES D'ANDRE SPIRE see Doyen,
   Albert

SUR LA DEVISE "NON CE QUE JE PENSE" see
   Siohan, Robert

SUR LA FALAISE see Durand, Jacques

SUR LA MER, AU PALE SOLEIL see Gaubert,
   Philippe

SUR LA PLAGE see Chaminade, Cecile

SUR LA PROMENADE see Ratz, Ludo

SUR LA RIVE ERRAIT LE REVE see Rimsky-
   Korsakov, Nikolai

SUR LA ROUTE see Paray, Paul

SUR LE BASALTE see Honegger, Arthur

SUR LE BATEAU MOUCHE see Perpignan, F.

SUR LE CHEMIN D'AMOUR see Mouton, H.

SUR LE CHEMIN DU MOULIN see Bozza,
   Eugene

SUR LE FLOT BLEU NOUS GLISSIONS EN
   REVANT see Chabrier, Emmanuel

SUR LE MEME TROTTOIR see Tranchant, J.

SUR LE POELE see Stravinsky, Igor

SUR LE PONT DE BAMBOU see Vieu, Jane

SUR L'EAU see Absil, Jean

SUR L'EAU CLAIRE ET SANS RIDE see
   Saint-Saens, Camille

SUR LES AILES DES SONGES see
   Mendelssohn-Bartholdy, Felix

SUR LES AILES DU REVE see Mendelssohn-
   Bartholdy, Felix

SUR LES BORDS DU JO-YEH see Badings,
   Henk

SUR LES CLOCHERS see Bonnal, Ermend

SUR LES COLLINES DE GEORGIE see Rimsky-
   Korsakov, Nikolai

SUR LES MONTS see Berlioz, Hector

SUR L'HERBE see Pijper, Willem

SUR L'HERBE see Ravel, Maurice

SUR L'HERBE FOLLETTE see Delmet, Paul

SUR MON AME see Guiraud, Ernest

SUR UN NUAGE see Galeotti, Cesare

SUR UNE VIEILLE LETTRE D'AMOURE see
   Nohar, Y.

SURABAYA-JONNY see Weill, Kurt

SURAY SURITA see Sas, Andres

SURDIN, M.
   On Christmas Day
   solo,pno (A min) BOOSEY $1.50
                                    (S3960)
   Prairie Boy, Prairie Boy
   solo,pno (F maj) BOOSEY $1.50
                                    (S3961)
   Storm Child
   low solo,pno (E min) BOOSEY $1.50
                                    (S3962)
   high solo,pno (D min) BOOSEY $1.50
                                    (S3963)
   med solo,pno (A min) BOOSEY $1.50
                                    (S3964)

SURE OF IT ALL see Phelps, David

SURE ON THIS SHINING NIGHT see Barber,
   Samuel

SUREAU-BELLET, J.
   Amours Libres
   solo,pno ENOCH s.p.   (S3965)
   solo,acap ENOCH s.p.   (S3966)

   Haine D'Amour
   solo,pno ENOCH s.p.   (S3967)
   solo,acap ENOCH s.p.   (S3968)

   J'ai Scelle Mon Coeur
   solo,acap ENOCH s.p.   (S3969)
   solo,pno ENOCH s.p.   (S3970)

   Le Vieux Fossoyeur
   solo,acap ENOCH s.p.   (S3971)
   solo,pno ENOCH s.p.   (S3972)

   Stances A Lea
   solo,pno ENOCH s.p.   (S3973)
   solo,acap ENOCH s.p.   (S3974)

   Toute Une Histoire
   solo,pno ENOCH s.p.   (S3975)
   solo,acap ENOCH s.p.   (S3976)

SURELY GOODNESS AND MERCY see Peterson,
   John W.

SURELY, I WILL LORD *sac,gospel
   solo,pno ABER.GRP. $1.50   (S3977)

SURGI DE LA CROUPE ET DU BOND see
   Ravel, Maurice

SURINACH, CARLOS (1915-   )
   Flamenco Meditations *see How Do I
   Love Thee?; If Thou Must Love Me;
   Our Two Souls; With Thee Anear;
   Yet, Love Is Beautiful Indeed
                                    (S3978)
   How Do I Love Thee?
   high solo,pno AMP $.75 see from
   Flamenco Meditations   (S3979)

   If Thou Must Love Me
   high solo,pno AMP $.75 see from
   Flamenco Meditations   (S3980)

   Our Two Souls
   high solo,pno AMP $.75 see from
   Flamenco Meditations   (S3981)

   Prayers
   med solo,gtr AMP $1.50   (S3982)

   Romance, Oracion Y Saeta
   solo,pno BELWIN $3.00   (S3983)

   Tres Cantares *song cycle
   solo,pno BELWIN $2.50   (S3984)

   With Thee Anear
   high solo,pno AMP $.75 see from
   Flamenco Meditations   (S3985)

   Yet, Love Is Beautiful Indeed
   high solo,pno AMP $.75 see from
   Flamenco Meditations   (S3986)

SURSUM CORDA see Shaw, Martin

SUSA, CONRAD (1935-   )
Serenade No. 5
TT soli,ob,vcl,perc SCHIRM.EC 2324
s.p., ipr   (S3987)

SUSCEPIT ISRAEL see Staromieyski, J.

SUSE, LIEBE SUSE see Humperdinck,
Engelbert

SUSSE HOFFNUNG, WENN ICH FRAGE see
Telemann, Georg Philipp

SUSSE RACHE, JA SUSSE RACHE see Mozart,
Wolfgang Amadeus

SUSSE STILLE, SANFTE QUELLE see Handel,
George Frideric

SUSSEZZA, CUDGHEIN E ZAMPON
(Carlo, Musi) solo,pno (Bolognese
dialect) BONGIOVANI 2058 s.p. see
from El Mi Canzunett   (S3988)

SUSSMAN, ETTEL
Propos Chinois Sur Les Animaux
high solo,pno ISRAELI 218 $4.90
                                    (S3989)

SUSY LITTLE SUSY see Humperdinck,
Engelbert, Suse, Liebe Suse

SUTER, ROBERT (1919-   )
Musikalisches Tagebuch No. I *CCU
A solo,ob,bsn,vla,vln,vcl,bvl
MODERN rental   (S3990)

Musikalisches Tagebuch No. II *CCU
Bar solo,fl,clar,bass clar,horn,
vln,vla,vcl MODERN rental (S3991)

SUTERMEISTER, HEINRICH (1910-   )
Psalm 70
low solo,org SCHOTTS 4049 s.p.
contains also: Psalm 86   (S3992)

Psalm 86
see Sutermeister, Heinrich, Psalm
70

Vier Lieder Nach Schubart, Klopstock,
Weise Und Gunther *CC4U
high solo,pno SCHOTTS 4017 s.p.
                                    (S3993)

Vier Lieder Nach Texten
Schweizeriescher Minnesanger
*CC4U
Bar solo,pno voc sc SCHOTTS 6119
s.p.   (S3994)

Vier Lieder Nach Texten
Schweizerischer Minnesanger
*CC4U
Bar solo,fl,ob,bsn,cembalo,vln sc
SCHOTTS 5968 s.p.   (S3995)

SUTHERLAND
Old Australian Bush Balads *CCU,
Austral
solo,pno ALLANS s.p.   (S3996)

SUTHERLAND, MARGARET
Arab Love Song
solo,pno ALBERT AHL221 rental
                                    (S3997)

Break Of Day
SS soli,pno OISEAU s.p.   (S3998)

Cradle Song
solo,clar ALBERT AHL222 rental
                                    (S3999)

Four Blake Songs *CC4U
solo,pno ALBERT AHL223 rental
                                    (S4000)

Gentle Water-Bird, The
solo,vln,pno ALBERT AHL224 rental
                                    (S4001)

Green Singer, The
2 soli,pno OISEAU s.p.   (S4002)

I Strove With None
solo,pno ALBERT AHL225 rental
                                    (S4003)

Jenny Kissed Me
solo,pno ALBERT AHL226 rental
                                    (S4004)

Meeting Of Sighs, The
solo,pno OISEAU s.p.   (S4005)

O Mistress Mine
solo,pno ALBERT AHL227 rental
                                    (S4006)

Quietly As Rosebuds
SSA soli OISEAU s.p.   (S4007)

They Called Her Fair
solo,pno OISEAU s.p.   (S4008)

SUUTELO see Kuula, Toivo

SUVILAULU see Kilpinen, Yrio

SUVIRANNALLA see Jarnefelt, Armas

SUZEL, BUON DI see Mascagni, Pietro

SUZETTE see Delmet, Paul

SUZETTE ET SUZON see Saint-Saens,
Camille

SVADBA see Urbanec, Bartolomej

SVALAN FLYKTAR, LOVEN FALLA see
Nordqvist, Gustaf

SVANEN see Andree, Elfrida

SVANESANG see Hartmann, Luigi

SVARA, DANILO (1902-   )
Deset Narodnih, Vol. I *CCU
1-2 soli,pno DRZAVNA rental (S4009)

Deset Narodnih, Vol. II *CCU
1-2 soli,pno DRZAVNA rental (S4010)

Intima *CC5U
T solo,pno DRUSTVO DSS 45 rental
                                    (S4011)

Stiri Pesmi *CC4U
med solo,pno DRUSTVO DSS 358 rental
                                    (S4012)

Stiri Pesmi *CC4U
high solo,pno DRUSTVO DSS 81 rental
                                    (S4013)

Trije Spevi (from Preseren) CC3U
T solo,pno DRUSTVO DSS 361 rental
                                    (S4014)

SVARC, ALFRED (1907-   )
Lyrics *song cycle
[Slav] solo,pno CROATICA s.p.
                                    (S4015)

Sun And Life *song cycle
[Slav] solo,pno CROATICA s.p.
                                    (S4016)

SVARMERI see Arlberg, Fritz

SVART ELLER VITT see Snare, Sigurd

SVARTA ROSOR see Sibelius, Jean

SVARTA ROSOR see Sibelius, Jean, Svarta
Rosor

SVARTA SVANOR see Hallstrom, Ivar

SVEDBOM, VILHELM
Ave Maria *sac
solo,pno GEHRMANS s.p.   (S4017)

Des Waldes Wipfel Rauschen
see Liebes-Lieder

En Glad Visa
solo,pno GEHRMANS s.p.   (S4018)

Fyra Sma Visor *CC4U
solo,pno GEHRMANS s.p.   (S4019)

Goldne Brucken Seien Alle Lieder Mir
see Liebes-Lieder

Kallan
Mez solo,pno GEHRMANS s.p. (S4020)
S solo,pno GEHRMANS s.p.   (S4021)
A solo,pno GEHRMANS s.p.   (S4022)

Karneval
solo,pno GEHRMANS s.p.   (S4023)

Liebes-Lieder
solo,pno GEHRMANS s.p.
contains: Des Waldes Wipfel
Rauschen; Goldne Brucken Seien
Alle Lieder Mir; Mein Herz Ist
Wie Die Dunkle Nacht; O Sprich,
Was Willst Du Dich Schamen; Wie
Fluchtig Rinnt Die Stunde
                                    (S4024)

Mein Herz Ist Wie Die Dunkle Nacht
see Liebes-Lieder

Nio Danska Sanger, Hafte 1-2 *CCU
solo,pno GEHRMANS s.p., ea. (S4025)

O Sprich, Was Willst Du Dich Schamen
see Liebes-Lieder

Sten Sture
Bar solo,pno GEHRMANS s.p. (S4026)
T solo,pno GEHRMANS s.p.   (S4027)
B solo,pno GEHRMANS s.p.   (S4028)

Svennens Sang
Bar solo,pno GEHRMANS s.p. (S4029)
B solo,pno GEHRMANS s.p.   (S4030)

Wie Fluchtig Rinnt Die Stunde
see Liebes-Lieder

SVEDLUND, KARL-ERIK
De Sokte Sitt
solo,pno GEHRMANS s.p. contains
also: Svedlund, Karl-Erik, Under
Stjarnorna; Strandsjo, Gote, Vid
Jesu Hjarta   (S4031)

SVEDLUND, KARL-ERIK (cont'd.)

Han Klappar Pa
see FYRA SANGER I FOLKTON

I Himmelen, I Himmelen
see FYRA SANGER I FOLKTON

Nu Ar Din Segertimma
see FYRA SANGER I FOLKTON

Under Stjarnorna
see Svedlund, Karl-Erik, De Sokte
Sitt

SVEINBJORNSSON, SVEINBJORN
Daisy's Song
see Six Songs

I Love This Land
see Six Songs

My Dove
see Six Songs

Seven Songs *CC7L
solo,pno ICELAND s.p.   (S4032)

Six Songs
solo,pno ICELAND s.p.
contains: Daisy's Song; I Love
This Land; My Dove; Spring; To
The Nightingale; White Heather
                                    (S4033)

Spring
see Six Songs

To The Nightingale
see Six Songs

White Heather
see Six Songs

SVEINSSON, GUNNAR REYNIR (1933-   )
Brefio
see Sveinsson, Gunnar Reynir, Pu
Veist Ei Neitt

Hve Einfalt Er Bitt Fyrirheit
see Sveinsson, Gunnar Reynir, Pu
Veist Ei Neitt

Kletturinn
see Sveinsson, Gunnar Reynir, Pu
Veist Ei Neitt

Pu Veist Ei Neitt
solo,pno ICELAND s.p. contains
also: Hve Einfalt Er Bitt
Fyrirheit; Kletturinn; Brefio
                                    (S4034)
Ur Saungbok Garoars Holm *CC7L
solo,pno ICELAND s.p.   (S4035)

SVENNENS SANG see Svedbom, Vilhelm

SVENSK LYRIK, HEFT 1 see Peterson-
Berger, (Olof) Wilhelm

SVENSK LYRIK, HEFT 2: FLOREZ OCH
BLAZEFLOR see Peterson-Berger,
(Olof) Wilhelm

SVENSK LYRIK, HEFT 3: HOSTSANG see
Peterson-Berger, (Olof) Wilhelm

SVENSK LYRIK, HEFT 4: ALVEN TILL
FLICKAN see Peterson-Berger, (Olof)
Wilhelm

SVENSK LYRIK, HEFT 5: GULLEBARNS
VAGGSANGER see Peterson-Berger,
(Olof) Wilhelm

SVENSK LYRIK, SERIES 2, HEFT 1: UR
FRIDOLINS VISOR see Peterson-
Berger, (Olof) Wilhelm

SVENSK LYRIK, SERIES 2, HEFT 2: UR
FRIDOLINS LUSTGARD see Peterson-
Berger, (Olof) Wilhelm

SVENSK LYRIK, SERIES 2, HEFT 3: UR
FRIDOLINS LUSTGARD see Peterson-
Berger, (Olof) Wilhelm

SVENSK LYRIK, SERIES 2, HEFT 4: UR
VILDMARKS- OCH KARLEKSVISOR see
Peterson-Berger, (Olof) Wilhelm

SVENSK LYRIK, SERIES 2, HEFT 5: FYRA
MUNTRA VISOR see Peterson-Berger,
(Olof) Wilhelm

SVENSK LYRIK, SERIES 2, HEFT 6:
LOSKEKARLARNES SANG see Peterson-
Berger, (Olof) Wilhelm

SVENSK LYRIK, SERIES 3, HEFT 1: FYRA
DIKTER see Peterson-Berger, (Olof)
Wilhelm

SVENSK LYRIK, SERIES 3, HEFT 2:
OFFERKRANSAR see Peterson-Berger,
(Olof) Wilhelm

SVENSK LYRIK, SERIES 3, HEFT 3: TVA DIKTER see Peterson-Berger, (Olof) Wilhelm

SVENSK LYRIK, SERIES 3, HEFT 4: TREDIKTER see Peterson-Berger, (Olof) Wilhelm

SVENSK MEDBORGARSANG see Peterson-Berger, (Olof) Wilhelm

SVENSK SANG see Lunden, Lennart

SVERIGE see Stenhammar, Wilhelm

SVERIGES FARGER see Wernlund

SVERIGES FLAGGA see Alfven, Hugo

SVERIGES SKONASTE FOLKVISOR see Berens, J.R.

SVET PATRI NAM see Jezek, Jaroslav

SVETEL, HERIBERT (1895-1962)
  Tri Pesmi *CC3U
    rental female solo,pno DRUSTVO
    DSS 140; male solo,pno DRUSTVO
    DSS 141   (S4036)

SVETLA NA VYCHODE see Stanislav, Josef

SVETLA NA VYCHODE see Stanislav, Josef

SVETLO see Hanus, Jan

SVITANI PRO VYSSI HLAS see Kovarovic, Karel

SVOBODO, JIRI (1897-1973)
  Blues Des Bettelkindes *see Blues
    Zebraveho Ditete

  Blues Zebraveho Ditete
    "Blues Des Bettelkindes" T solo,pno
    CZECH s.p.   (S4037)

  Manon *Op.21
    Mez solo,pno PANTON 775 s.p.   (S4038)
    [Czech/Ger] Mez solo,pno PANTON
    s.p.   (S4039)

SVUNNEN LYCKA see Malo, Ch.

SWACK, ERWIN
  O Lord, Our Lord, How Excellent Is
    Thy Name (Psalm 8) sac
    high solo,clar/trp CHAPLET $1.50
                                    (S4040)
  Psalm 8 *see O Lord, Our Lord, How
    Excellent Is Thy Name

SWAENTJEN see Sigtenhorst-Meyer, Bernhard van den

SWAGGART, JIMMY
  Jimmy Swaggart-Songbook *sac,CC11L
    solo,pno BENSON BO782 $2.50 (S4041)

SWALLOW, THE see La Golondrina

SWALLOWS see Cowen, Sir Frederic Hymen

SWAMP DANCE see Mills, Charles

SWAN, A see Grieg, Edvard Hagerup, En Svane

SWAN, THE see Grieg, Edvard Hagerup, En Svane

SWANEE-RIVER-SONG see Krenek, Ernst

SWANNENGESANG see Schubert, Franz (Peter)

SWANSON, HOWARD (1909-   )
  Cahoots
    solo,pno WEINTRB $1.50   (S4042)

  Four Preludes *CC4U
    solo,pno WEINTRB $3.00   (S4043)

  Ghosts In Love
    solo,pno WEINTRB $1.50   (S4044)

  I Will Lie Down In Autumn
    solo,pno WEINTRB $1.50   (S4045)

  In Time Of Silver Rain
    solo,pno WEINTRB $1.50   (S4046)

  Junkman, The
    solo,pno WEINTRB $1.50   (S4047)

  Night Song
    solo,pno WEINTRB $1.50   (S4048)

  Pierrot
    solo,pno WEINTRB $1.50   (S4049)

  Saw A Grave Upon A Hill
    solo,pno WEINTRB $1.50   (S4050)

SWANSON, HOWARD (cont'd.)

  Snowdunes
    solo,pno WEINTRB $1.50   (S4051)

  Songs For Patricia *song cycle
    S solo,strings WEINTRB rental
                                    (S4052)
    S solo,pno WEINTRB $3.00   (S4053)

  Still Life
    solo,pno WEINTRB $1.50   (S4054)

  To Be Or Not To Be
    solo,pno WEINTRB $1.50   (S4055)

SWANSON, JOAN
  Nature's Song *sac
    solo,pno SINGSPIR 7013 $.50   (S4056)

  So You Want Peace *sac
    solo,pno SINGSPIR 7012 $.50   (S4057)

SWAT A LIFE see Blyton, Carey

SWEDEN SINGS *CC54U,folk,Swed
  [Swed/Eng] solo,kbd NORDISKA s.p.
                                    (S4058)

SWEELINCK, JAN PIETERSZOON (1562-1621)
  Collected Works *CCU
    (Gehrmann, Hermann) 2-8 soli,acap/
    inst, also contains works for
    organ or keyboard microfiche
    UNIV.MUS.ED. $60.00 reprints of
    Breitkopf & Hartel Editions;
    contains 10 volumes   (S4059)

  Rimes Francoises Et Italiennes *CCU
    (Hinnenthal, Johann Philipp) SA
    soli,org (med) BAREN. HM 75 $5.00
                                    (S4060)

SWEEPER see Henty, Dick

SWEEPERS, THE see Elgar, Edward

SWEET AFTON see Anderson, William H.

SWEET AND KIND see Diack, John Michael

SWEET-AND-TWENTY see Heseltine, Philip

SWEET ARE THE MOONBEAMS see Birch, Robert Fairfax

SWEET, BE NOT PROUD see Dyson, George

SWEET BIRD see Handel, George Frideric

SWEET CHANCE THAT LED MY STEPS see Head, Michael (Dewar)

SWEET DREAMER see Sullivan, Sir Arthur Seymour

SWEET DREAMS see Friml, Rudolf

SWEET EARLY VIOLETS see Sherrington, Louis F.

SWEET FORGETTING see Handel, George Frideric, Pensieri Notturni Di Filli: Nel Dolce Dell' Oblio

SWEET HOLY CHILD see Caldwell, Mary Elizabeth

SWEET JESUS see Goodwin, Paul

SWEET JULY see Dunhill, Thomas Frederick

SWEET, LET ME GO see Walker, George

SWEET LITTLE JESUS BOY *sac,Xmas
  low solo,pno (D maj) HARRIS $.85
                                    (S4061)
  med solo,pno (F maj) HARRIS $.85
                                    (S4062)

SWEET LITTLE JESUS BOY see MacGimsey, Robert

SWEET LOVE OF JESUS, THE see Crouch, Andrae

SWEET MARY COME TO ME see Shield, William

SWEET NELLY, MY HEART'S DELIGHT see Rowley, Alec

SWEET NIGHTINGALE *folk,Eng
  (Roberton, Hugh S.) 3 soli,pno
  ROBERTON 72100 s.p.   (S4063)

SWEET NIGHTINGALE see Bury, Winifred

SWEET O' THE YEAR, THE see Heseltine, Philip

SWEET ONE AND TWENTY see Handel, George Frideric

SWEET PLEASURE see Mana-Zucca, Mme., Doux Plaisir

SWEET PRETTY BIRD see Stanley, John

SWEET ROBINETTE see Hook, James

SWEET SALLY GRAY see Broadwood, Lucy E.

SWEET SONG OF LONG AGO see Charles, Ernest

SWEET SPRING IS YOUR TIME see Dougherty, Celius

SWEET, STAY AWHILE see Bush, Geoffrey

SWEET SUFFOLK OWL see Poston, Elizabeth

SWEET, SWEET SONG OF SALVATION see Norman, Larry

SWEET, SWEET SPIRIT see Akers, Doris

SWEET THING see Linnett, Anne

SWEET TO ME see Dale, Mervyn

SWEET WAS THE SONG see Taylor, H. Stanley

SWEET WAS THE SONG THE VIRGIN SANG
  *sac
  (Johnson, David N.) high solo,pno
  AUGSBURG 11-0732 $.75   (S4064)

SWEET ZEPHYR see Mozart, Wolfgang Amadeus, Sull' Aria

SWEETER FOR THE WAIT, THE see Gossler, G.

SWEETEST LOVE see Kelly, Bryan

SWEETEST MUSIC THIS SIDE OF HEAVEN see Derricks, Cleavant

SWEETEST STORY EVER TOLD see Stultz, R.M.

SWEETEST STORY EVER TOLD, THE see Stults, R.

SWEETHEARTS see Herbert, Victor

SWEETHEARTS AND WIVES see Head, Michael (Dewar)

SWEETLY SHE SLEEPS MY ALICE FAIR see Foster, Stephen Collins

SWIFT FLY THE HOURS OF LOVE see Price, Addison

SWIFTLY ALONG FLOWS THE RIVER see Weigl, Vally

SWING DAT HAMMER see Johnson, Hall

SWING LOW *CCU
  [Eng/Ger] SCHOTTS 4820 s.p.   (S4065)

SWING LOW, SWEET CHARIOT *sac,spir
  low solo,pno (F maj) CENTURY 3620
  $.40   (S4066)
  (Burleigh, H. T.) high solo,pno
  BELWIN $1.50   (S4067)
  (Burleigh, H. T.) low solo,pno BELWIN
  $1.50   (S4068)
  (Roberton, Hugh S.) 3 soli,pno
  ROBERTON 72103 s.p.   (S4069)
  (Widdicombe) 2 soli,pno ROBERTON
  72493 s.p.   (S4070)

SWISS ECHO SONG see Eckert, Karl Anton Florian

SWISS FAIRYLAND see Stolz, Robert

SYDAN see Leiviska, Helvi (Lemmikki)

SYDEMAN, WILLIAM (1928-   )
  Elegy
    see Three Songs On Elizabethan Texts

  Fly, The
    see Three Songs On Elizabethan Texts

  Four Japanese Songs
    S solo,2vln SCHIRM.EC 118 s.p.
    contains: I Passed By The Beach
      At Tago; In A Gust Of Wind;
      Mists Rise Over The Still
      Pools, The; When I Went Out In
      The Spring Meadows   (S4071)

  Full Circle
    SAB soli,clar,vcl,trom,perc,pno/org
    sc SEESAW $28.00   (S4072)

  Hope Is A Thing With Feathers
    see Three Songs After Emily Dickinson

  I Heard A Fly Buzz When I Died
    see Three Songs After Emily Dickinson

SYDEMAN, WILLIAM (cont'd.)

I Passed By The Beach At Tago
see Four Japanese Songs

I Taste A Liquor Never Brewed
see Three Songs After Emily
Dickinson

In A Gust Of Wind
see Four Japanese Songs

Jabberwocky
S/T solo,fl,vcl SCHIRM.EC 137 s.p.
(S4073)

Malediction
T solo,4strings,electronic tape sc
SEESAW $20.00   (S4074)

Mists Rise Over The Still Pools, The
see Four Japanese Songs

Modest Love, A
see Three Songs On Elizabethan
Texts

Spider, A
Bar solo,pno SCHIRM.EC 133 s.p.
(S4075)

Three Songs After Emily Dickinson
S/T solo,vcl SCHIRM.EC 136 s.p.
contains: Hope Is A Thing With
Feathers; I Heard A Fly Buzz
When I Died; I Taste A Liquor
Never Brewed   (S4076)

Three Songs On Elizabethan Texts
S/T solo,fl SCHIRM.EC 135 s.p.
contains: Elegy; Fly, The; Modest
Love, A   (S4077)

Upon Julia's Clothes
Bar solo,pno SCHIRM.EC 134 s.p.
(S4078)
When I Went Out In The Spring Meadows
see Four Japanese Songs

SYKSY see Madetoja, Leevi

SYLVAN see Ronald, Sir Landon

SYLVIA see Speaks, Oley

SYLVIA SIMPLEX see Pennisi, Francesco

SYLVIAN JOULULAULU see Collan, Karl

SYLVIAS JULVISA see Collan, Karl,
Sylvian Joululaulu

SYLVIAS VISA: "JAG GUNGAR PA HOGSTA
GRENEN" see Linsen, Gabriel

SYLVIE see Satie, Erik

SYMBOL see Niles, John Jacob

SYMBOLA see Corghi, Azio

SYMBOLI CHRESTIANI see Nabokov, Nicolas

SYMBOLS AND TOKENS *sac
(Carmichael, Ralph) solo,pno WORD
S-514   (S4079)

SYMIANE, MAGDELEINE
Joli Mai
solo,pno ENOCH s.p.   (S4080)
solo,acap ENOCH s.p.   (S4081)

SYMONDS, NORMAN (1920-   )
Deep Ground, Long Waters
med solo,pno KERBY 2250 $2.25
(S4082)
solo,fl,pno (original version)
KERBY $4.00   (S4083)

SYMPATHY see Friml, Rudolf

SYMPATI OCH PASSION see Areschoug,
Antonie

SYMPHONIA see Ruyneman, Daniel

SYMPHONIAE SACRAE I, HEFT I see Schutz,
Heinrich

SYMPHONIAE SACRAE I, HEFT II see
Schutz, Heinrich

SYMPHONIAE SACRAE II see Schutz,
Heinrich

SYMPHONIAE SACRAE II, HEFT I see
Schutz, Heinrich

SYMPHONIAE SACRAE II, HEFT II see
Schutz, Heinrich

SYMPHONIAE SACRAE II, HEFT III see
Schutz, Heinrich

SYMPHONIAE SACRAE III see Schutz,
Heinrich

SYMPHONIETTA see Mulder, Ernest W.

SYMPHONY see Weber, Ben

SYMPHONY II see Rawsthorne

SYMPHONY IN YELLOW see Griffes, Charles
Tomlinson

SYMPHONY NO. 4 see Franco, Johan

SYMPNONY NO. 1 see Hartmann, Karl
Amadeus, Erste Symphonie

SYNDEN, DODEN see Soderman, (Johan)
August

SYNNOVES SANG see Kjerulf, [Halfdan]

SYNTETISCH GEDICHT see Boogaard,
Bernard van den

SYNTHETIC POEME see Boogaard, Bernard
van den, Syntetisch Gedicht

SYT VROLYC GROOT EN KLEYNE see Klerk,
Albert de

SYV LAULUA EILA KIVIKK'AHON RUNOIHIN
see Kilpinen, Yrio

SYV LAULUA KIVIJARVEN LAULUNAYTELMASTA
TALKOOTANSSIT see Hannikainen,
Ilmari

SYV SANGER see Johansen, David Monrad

SYV SANGER see Kvandal, Johan

SYVAN AANETTOMYYDEN SYLIIN see Tolonen,
Jouko (Paavo Kalervo)

SYVIMMAT HAAVAT see Laitenen, Arvo

SYVVYKSIA see Laitenen, Arvo

SYYSILTA see Sibelius, Jean, Hostkvall

SYYSKUUN SONETTI see Kilpinen, Yrio

SYYSPAIVA see Marvia, Einari

SYYSPAIVA see Stout, Alan

SYYSSONETTI see Kilpinen, Yrio

SYYSTUNNELMA see Kuula, Toivo

SZABO, [FERENC] (1902-1969)
Three Songs *CC3U
[Hung/Ger] solo,pno BUDAPEST 5341
s.p.   (S4084)

SZANTO, THEODOR (1877-1934)
Marche Colonial
solo,pno ENOCH s.p.   (S4085)
solo,acap ENOCH s.p.   (S4086)

SZAZSZORSZEP *CC100U,folk,Hung
(Bardos) solo,pno BUDAPEST 2587 s.p.
(S4087)
SZEKELY, E.
Maqamat
S solo,inst BUDAPEST 10151 s.p.
(S4088)

Solocantata *cant
S solo,chamb.grp. BUDAPEST 10177
s.p.   (S4089)

SZENE UND MONOLOG DER MARFA see
Reutter, Hermann

SZERVANSZKY, ENDRE (1912-   )
Eight Petofi Songs *CC8U
solo,pno BUDAPEST 1256 s.p. (S4090)

Three Songs *CC3U
solo,pno BUDAPEST 5119 s.p. (S4091)

SZOL A NOTA, VOL. 1-10 (COLLECTIONS OF
HUNGARIAN SONGS) *CCU
solo,pno BUDAPEST s.p., ea. (S4092)

SZOL A NOTA, VOL. 11-12 *CCU
solo,pno BUDAPEST s.p., ea. (S4093)

SZOLLOSY, A.
Restless Autumn
[Hung] solo,pno BUDAPEST 2855 s.p.
(S4094)
SZONYI, ERZSEBET
Lamenti
A solo,fl,vla, dulcimer BUDAPEST
6034 s.p.   (S4095)

S'ZUSCHAUN see Bohm, Carl

SZYMANOWSKI, KAROL (1882-1937)
Bunte Lieder *Op.22,No.1-5, CC5U
[Ger/Pol] high solo,pno cmplt ed
UNIVER. 3865 s.p.   (S4096)

Das Grab Des Hafis
[Ger/Fr/Pol] high solo,pno UNIVER.
10947 $3.25   (S4097)

SZYMANOWSKI, KAROL (cont'd.)

Des Hafis Liebeslieder, Set I
*Op.24,No.1-6, CC6U
[Ger/Pol] S solo,pno UNIVER. 3867
$5.25   (S4098)

Trois Berceuses *Op.48,No.1-3, CC3U
[Ger/Pol/Fr] solo,pno UNIVER. 8597
$3.25   (S4099)

T

'T AVONDT see Mortelmans, Lodewijk

'T BEGIJNHOFSKLOKSKE see Dijk, Jan van

'T BIJBELUUR see Sigtenhorst-Meyer, Bernhard van den

'T BLOEMKE "NIMMERMEERVERDRIET see Strategier, Herman

'T DUTJE see Devreese, Godefroid, La Sieste Interrompue

'T GODSDEEL OF DEN ROMMELPOT see Schouwman, Hans

'T GROEIT EEN BLOMKEN see Mortelmans, Lodewijk

'T IS DE MANDEL see Mortelmans, Lodewijk

'T IS FEEST IN HUIS see Ammers, P. van

'T IS STILLE see Dijk, Jan van

'T IS VOORBIJ see Dijk, Jan van

'T JONGETJE see Sigtenhorst-Meyer, Bernhard van den

'T KINDEKE SLAAPT see Hullebroeck, Em.

'T MEEZEKEN see Mortelmans, Lodewijk

'T PORTRETJE see Witte, D.

'T VIOOLTJE see Rennes, Cath. v.

'T WAS LENTE see Linden, Nico van der

TA BEAUTE see Schumann, Robert (Alexander)

TA BOUCHE see Rabey, Rene

TA DENT DU FOND see Berger, Rod.

TA-GA-I-NI HO-RE-TE see Murai, Tsuguji

TA-TA
   (Carlo, Musi) solo,pno (Bolognese dialect) BONGIOVANI 2051 s.p. see from El Mi Canzunett   (T1)

TA VOIX see Messiaen, Oliver

TABLE AND THE CHAIR, THE see Hely-Hutchinson, (Christian) Victor

TABUYO, I.
   La Del Panuelo Rojo
   (Azpiazu) [Span] high solo,gtr
   UNION ESP. $.50   (T2)

TACEA LA NOTTE PLACIDA see Verdi, Giuseppe

TACTUS see Corghi, Azio

TADSCH MAHAL see Marvia, Einari, Taj Mahal

TAG DITT GLAS OCH DRICK UR, SANGVALS see Soderstrom, Nils

TAG EMOD KRANSEN see Sjogren, Emil

TAG FUR TAG see Alfano, Franco, Giorno Per Giorno

TAG IMOD KRANSEN see Soderman, (Johan) August

TAGEBUCH see Eisler, Hanns

TAGEBUCH AUS ISRAEL see Staempfli, Edward

TAGORE
   Trois Melodies   *CC3U
   solo,pno AMPHION R 2152-4 s.p. (T3)

TAGZEITEN see Krol, Bernhard

TAHMEELA see El-Dabh, Halim

TAHTILAULU see Kuusisto, Taneli

TAIVAINEN REKIRETKI see Pylkkanen, Tauno Kullervo

TAJ MAHAL see Marvia, Einari

TAKATA, SABURO (1913-   )
   Fifty Songs   *CC50U
   solo,pno ONGAKU s.p.   (T4)

TAKE A LOOK AT CALVARY see Jensen, Gordon

TAKE IT ALL see Jensen, Gordon

TAKE JOY HOME see Bassett, Karolyn Wells

TAKE ME BACK see Crouch, Andrae

TAKE ME BACK see Crouch, Andrae

TAKE ME HAND, PRECIOUS LORD   *sac, gospel
   solo,pno ABER.GRP. $1.50   (T5)

TAKE ME HOME see DeSylva

TAKE MNOU ZIJE AMERIKA! see Dvoracek, Jiri

TAKE MY LIFE O LORD see O'Hara, Geoffrey

TAKE, O TAKE THOSE LIPS AWAY see Castelnuovo-Tedesco, Mario

TAKE, O TAKE THOSE LIPS AWAY see Heseltine, Philip

TAKE, O TAKE THOSE LIPS AWAY see Montgomery, Bruce

TAKE, O TAKE THOSE LIPS AWAY see Thomson, Virgil

TAKE THEM WITH THEE see Bellini, Vincenzo, Deh! Con Te, Con Te Li Prendi

TAKE TIME FOR JESUS see Baker, Richard

TAKE TIME TO PRAY   *sac,gospel
   solo,pno ABER.GRP. $1.50   (T6)

TAKE UP THY CROSS see Grant, Cecil

TAKING LEAVE OF A FRIEND see Powers

TAKING THE VEIL see Blyton, Carey

TAKTAKISHVILI, OTAR (1924-   )
   Megrelian Songs
   T solo,men cor,chamb.orch (suite)
   MEZ KNIGA 2.48 s.p.   (T7)

TAL see Alter, I.

TAL, MARJO (1915-   )
   Eight Engelman-Songs   *CC8U
   med solo,pno DONEMUS s.p.   (T8)

   Siete Canciones Espanoles   *CC7U
   med solo,pno DONEMUS s.p.   (T9)

TALCI see Scek, Breda

TALE OF A FAIRY see Evans

TALE OF GREEN REED AND GENTIAN see Ishii, Kan

TALE OF MAD BRIGID, THE see Mourant, Walter

TALE OF THE SILLY LITTLE MOUSE see Pritsker, D.

TALES FROM THE VIENNA WOODS see Strauss, Johann, G'schicten Aus Dem Wienerwald

TALIESIN see Wijdeveld, Wolfgang

TALK ABOUT A CHILD THAT DO LOVE JESUS   *sac,spir
   (Dawson, William L.) high solo/low solo,pno FITZSIMONS $.60   (T10)

TALKIN' 'BOUT THE LOVE OF GOD see Lister, Mosie

TALL WIND see Ung, Chinary

TALLY-HO! see Leoni, Franco

TALTRASTEN see Alfven, Hugo

TALVIAAMU see Kaski, Heino

TALVIYO see Marvia, Einari

TALVIYON HIIHTAJA see Sonninen, Ahti

TAM GLEN   *folk,Scot
   low solo,pno (E maj) PATERSON FS122 s.p.   (T11)
   high solo,pno (D min) PATERSON FS122 s.p.   (T12)

TAM I' THE KIRK see Bury, Winifred

TAMBA, A.
   Ennea
   female solo,fl,clar,pno,5strings
   RIDEAU rental   (T13)

TAMBLYN, BERTHA
   Life's Lovely Things   *sec
   med solo,pno (G maj) WATERLOO $.90
                                         (T14)

TAMBOURIN see Badings, Henk

TAMBOURIN see Rameau, Jean-Philippe

TAME CAT see Koch, Johannes H.E.

TAMMY   *folk,Scot
   solo,pno (C maj) PATERSON FS141 s.p.
                                         (T15)

TANABATA see Minami, Hiroaki

TANAKA, H.
   Three Songs On The Poem By Shinpei Kusano   *CC3U
   solo,pno ONGAKU s.p.   (T16)

TANAKA, T.
   Isle Of Legend, The
   solo,pno ONGAKU s.p.   (T17)

TAND STJARNOR see Sjogren, Emil

TANDIS QUE TOUT SOMMEILLE see Gretry, Andre Ernest Modeste

TANENBAUM, ELIAS
   Cygnology   *CC3U
   S solo,fl,clar,pno,strings sc
   AM.COMP.AL. $16.50   (T18)

   Images
   female solo,pno,perc,electronic tape sc AM.COMP.AL. $8.25   (T19)

   Peter Quince At The Clavier
   S solo,fl/pic,clar,gtr,vla,bass trom sc AM.COMP.AL. $9.35, ipa
                                         (T20)

   Phantasies Of A Prisoner, The   *CCU
   Bar solo,fl,clar,trp,bass trom, harp,perc,vln,vcl sc AM.COMP.AL. $15.90   (T21)

   Six Designs   *CC6U
   S solo,2fl,2ob,3clar,3bsn,4horn, 3trp,3trom,tuba,harp,perc,strings AM.COMP.AL. $40.70   (T22)

TANGO see Albeniz, Isaac

TANGO-MILONGA see Guerrero

TANGO-MILONGA see Guerrero

TANGO SERPENTIN see Betove

TANK, NAR EN GANG DIMMAN AR FORSVUNNEN see Blott En Dag Ett Ogonblick I Sander

TANKAS OF THE FOUR SEASONS see Rawsthorne

TANKE GIAPPONESI see Orefice, Giacomo

TANKER DU ATT JAG FORLORADER AR see Ack, Varmeland Du Skona

TANNENBAUMCHEN UND VOGLEIN see Kilpinen, Yrio, Kuusi Ja Lintunen

TANSMAN, ALEXANDER (1897-   )
   Cinq Melodies   *CC5U
   [Fr] ESCHIG $3.50   (T23)

   Huit Melodies Japonaise   *CC8U
   [Fr/Pol] med-high solo,pno ESCHIG $2.50   (T24)

   Six Songs   *CC6U
   high solo,pno ESCHIG $4.75   (T25)

TANSSI see Kilpinen, Yrio

TANSSIT see Sonninen, Ahti

TANT QUE VIVRAI see Attaignant, Pierre

TANTO AMORE SEGRETO see Puccini, Giacomo

TANTUM ERGO see Dubois, Theodore

TANTUM ERGO GENITORI see Schmier, J.

TANZLIED see Trunk, Richard

TANZLIED DES PIERROT see Korngold, Erich Wolfgang

TANZLIED I see Hannikainen, Ilmari

TANZLIED II see Hannikainen, Ilmari

TAPS see Weinberg, Jacob

TARANTELLA see Belloc, Hilaire

TARANTELLE see Bizet, Georges

TARDE see Jurafsky, Abraham

TARDE AZUL see Lilien, Ignace

TARNER
Wedding Prayer *sac,gospel
solo,pno ABER.GRP. $1.50   (T26)

TARRAGO, G.
Canciones Populares Espanolas *CCU,
Span
[Span] med solo,pno,gtr UNION ESP.
$3.25   (T27)

Dos Villancicos Navidenos *CC2U
[Span] med solo,gtr UNION ESP. $.75
(T28)

Polo Gitano O Flamenco
[Span] med solo,gtr UNION ESP. $.90
(T29)

TARRANT, F.W.
One Word One Smile
low solo,pno (B flat maj) CRAMER
(T30)
high solo,pno (E flat maj) CRAMER
(T31)
med solo,pno (C maj) CRAMER   (T32)

TARRASCH
Early One Morning
med solo,pno FISCHER,C V 2185 (T33)

TARRIN' O' THE YOLL see McLeod, Robert

TAR'S LASS see Jude, William Herbert

TARTARY see Peel, Graham

TASTE AND SEE THAT THE LORD IS GOOD see
Fischer, Irwin

TATE, ARTHUR
Sleep And The Roses
low solo,pno (E flat maj) ASHDOWN
s.p.   (T34)
high solo,pno (B flat maj) ASHDOWN
s.p.   (T35)
med-high solo,pno (A flat maj)
ASHDOWN s.p.   (T36)
med solo,pno (G maj) ASHDOWN s.p.
(T37)
med-low solo,pno (F maj) ASHDOWN
s.p.   (T38)

Somewhere A Voice Is Calling
high solo,orch (G maj) ASHDOWN
s.p., ipr   (T39)
med-high solo,orch (F maj) ASHDOWN
s.p., ipr   (T40)
med solo,orch (E flat maj) ASHDOWN
s.p., ipr   (T41)
low solo,orch (D maj) ASHDOWN s.p.,
ipr   (T42)

TATE, PHYLLIS (1912-   )
Apparitions *CCU
solo,pno OXFORD 63.067 $14.40 (T43)

Billy Boy
solo,pno OXFORD $1.60   (T44)

Lady Shalott
solo,pno OXFORD rental   (T45)

Lark In The Clear Air
T solo,pno (easy) OXFORD 62.088
$1.00   (T46)
Bar solo,pno (easy) OXFORD 61.176
$.80   (T47)

Nocturne For Four Voices *cant
STBarB soli,acap (diff) OXFORD
rental   (T48)

O The Bonny Fisher Lad
solo,pno OXFORD $1.60   (T49)

Trois Chansons Tristes *CC3U
solo,pno OXFORD s.p.   (T50)

Victorian Garland
2 soli,pno/inst/orch OXFORD $9.50
(T51)

Water Of Tyne
solo,pno OXFORD $1.60   (T52)

TATENIU, MAMENIU *Jew
solo,pno KAMMEN 55 $1.00   (T53)

TATIANA SHMYGA SINGS *CCU
[Russ] solo,pno MEZ KNIGA 111 s.p.
(T54)

TATJANA'S LETTER SCENE see Tchaikovsky,
Piotr Ilyitch, Letter Song, The

TATTARE-EMMA see Jeremias I Trostlosa

TATTERS see Lane, Gerald M.

TAUB, BRUCE J.H.
O Sweet Spontaneous Earth
S solo,fl sc AM.COMP.AL. $5.50
(T55)

TAUBE, EVERT
Balladen
solo,pno,opt gtr GEHRMANS s.p.
(T56)

Diktaren Och Tiden
solo,pno,opt gtr GEHRMANS s.p.
(T57)

En Valsmelodi
solo,pno,opt gtr GEHRMANS s.p.
(T58)

Har Ar Den Skona Sommar
solo,pno,opt gtr GEHRMANS s.p.
(T59)

Huldas Karin
solo,pno,opt gtr GEHRMANS s.p.
(T60)

Nocturne
solo,pno,opt gtr GEHRMANS s.p.
(T61)

Oxdragarsang
solo,pno,opt gtr GEHRMANS s.p.
(T62)

Pierina
solo,pno,opt gtr GEHRMANS s.p.
(T63)

Solig Morgon
solo,pno,opt gtr GEHRMANS s.p.
(T64)

Vidalita
solo,pno,opt gtr GEHRMANS s.p.
(T65)

Vit Man Och Kinaman
solo,pno,opt gtr GEHRMANS s.p.
(T66)

TAUBER, RICHARD (1892-1948)
Music In My Heart
low solo,pno (F maj) ALLANS s.p.
(T67)
high solo,pno (A flat maj) ALLANS
s.p.   (T68)
med solo,pno (G maj) ALLANS s.p.
(T69)

My Heart And I
high solo,pno (D maj) ALLANS s.p.
(T70)
med solo,pno (C maj) ALLANS s.p.
(T71)
low solo,pno (B flat maj) ALLANS
s.p.   (T72)

TAUBERT, KARL HEINZ
Altdeutsches Liebeslied
med solo,pno/org&vcl/org&vln sc
RIES s.p., ipa   (T73)
med solo,pno voc sc RIES s.p. (T74)

Das Himmlische Menuett *Xmas
solo,pno SCHAUR EE 3386 s.p.   (T75)

Drei Eichendorff-Lieder *CC3U
solo,pno RIES s.p.   (T76)

Hausspruch
solo,fl,pno,opt gtr RIES s.p. (T77)

Knecht Ruprecht-Volkslieder *CCU,
Xmas/Gen
solo,pno/treb inst RIES s.p.   (T78)

Lob Auf Die Musika *CCU
solo,vcl,kbd RIES s.p. sc, solo pt
(T79)
Vom Baum Des Lebens *CC4U
med solo,pno SCHAUR EE 3209 $2.00
(T80)

Wiegenlied *CC3U
(Behrend, Siegfried) solo,pno,opt
gtr RIES s.p.   (T81)

Zwei Lieder Zur Jahreswende *CC2U
solo,pno RIES s.p.   (T82)

TAUET, HIMMEL, DEN GERECHTEN see
Cruger, Johann

TAUFKANTATE see Brunner, Adolf

TAUSINGER, JAN (1921-   )
Am Himmel Skizzierte Lieder *see
Cmaranice Po Nebi

Ave Maria *sac
S&narrator,orch PANTON 1269 s.p.
(T83)

Cmaranice Po Nebi *song cycle
"Am Himmel Skizzierte Lieder" S
solo,fl,bass clar,vibra,perc,pno
SUPRAPHON s.p.   (T84)

Konstelace Cyklus *see
Konstellationen Zyklus

Konstellationen Zyklus *song cycle
"Konstelace Cyklus" S solo,pno,inst
CZECH s.p.   (T85)

TAUTENHAHN, GUNTHER
Each Man
T solo,vln SEESAW   (T86)

TAVARES, HEKEL
Funeral Of A Nago King
low solo,pno GALAXY 1.1254.7 $1.00
(T87)

TAVERNER, JOHN (1944-   )
In Alium
[Fr/Lat] S solo,orch,electronic
tape sc CHESTER s.p.   (T88)

Three Surrealist Songs *CC3U
[Eng] Mez solo,pno,electronic tape,
bongos CHESTER s.p.   (T89)

TAVOLE PER ORFEO see Norholm, Ib

TAYLOR
I Wonder How John Felt *see Wilson

O Can You Sew Cushions
S solo,pno (very easy) OXFORD
63.601 $1.25   (T90)

TAYLOR, CHARLES H.
Holy Land *sac
solo,pno PATERSON s.p.   (T91)

TAYLOR, CLIFFORD
Collected Songs 1950-1954 *CCU
AM.COMP.AL. S solo,pno $8.25; T
solo,pno $8.25   (T92)

Quattro Liriche From "Mattino
Domenicale" *sac,CC4U
med solo,al-sax,pno sc AM.COMP.AL.
$9.90, ipa   (T93)

Two Songs *Op.5, CC2U
S/T solo,clar,pno sc AM.COMP.AL.
$5.50, ipa   (T94)

TAYLOR, D.
Foolish Questions
narrator,pno PRESSER $.75   (T95)

Time Enough
med solo,pno PRESSER $.75   (T96)

TAYLOR, DEEMS (JOSEPH) (1885-1966)
Eating Song
med solo,pno BELWIN $1.50   (T97)

TAYLOR, H. STANLEY
Daisy's Song
low solo,pno (G maj) CRAMER   (T98)
high solo,pno (B flat maj) CRAMER
(T99)
Die Sprode
high solo,pno (E flat maj) CRAMER
$.95   (T100)
low solo,pno (C maj) CRAMER s.p.
(T101)
Die Vatergruft
solo,pno CRAMER   (T102)

New Love New Life
low solo,pno (B flat maj) CRAMER
$.95   (T103)
high solo,pno (A flat maj) CRAMER
$.95   (T104)

Passionate Shepherd To His Love, The
low solo,pno (E maj) CRAMER s.p.
(T105)
high solo,pno (A flat maj) CRAMER
$1.10   (T106)

Sweet Was The Song
solo,pno (F min) ROBERTON 2596 s.p.
(T107)
Tramp, The
low solo,pno (G min) CRAMER $.95
(T108)
high solo,pno (A min) CRAMER (T109)

TAYLOR, JEREMY
Jeremy Taylor, Book 1 *CCU
solo,pno GALLIARD 2.0440.7 $2.25
(T110)

Jeremy Taylor, Book 2 *CCU
solo,pno GALLIARD 2.0401.7 $2.25
(T111)

TAYLOR, L.
Don't Go Away Without Jesus *sac
solo,pno GENTRY $1.00   (T112)

TAYLOR, W. DAVENPORT
Land Of Wonder Why *CCU
solo,pno CRAMER pap s.p., cloth
s.p.   (T113)

TCHAIKOVSKY, PIOTR ILYITCH (1840-1893)
Adieu Forets (from Jeanne D'Arc)
med solo,pno (B min) ALLANS s.p.
(T114)
high solo,pno (D min) ALLANS s.p.
(T115)
"Farewell, Ye Mountains" [Fr/Eng]
high solo,pno (D min) SCHIRM.G
$.85   (T116)

Arie Der Lisa (from Pique Dame)
[Russ/Fr/Ger/Eng] S solo,pno
BREITKOPF-W 61 03074 s.p.   (T117)

TCHAIKOVSKY, PIOTR ILYITCH (cont'd.)

Arie Des Fursten Gremin *see
   Prince's Aria

Arie Des Gremin *see Prince's Aria

Arie Des Lensky *see Lensky's Aria

Arie Lenskis *see Lensky's Song

Arioso Des Eugen Onegin (from Eugen
   Onegin)
   [Ger] solo,pno BREITKOPF-W 61 03095
   s.p.   (T118)

At Every Age (from Eugene Onegin)
   solo,pno LEONARD-ENG   (T119)

Bei Rauschendem Feste
   [Russ/Fr/Ger/Eng] Bar solo,pno
   BREITKOPF-W 61 03123 s.p.   (T120)

Can This Be Tatiana? *see Onegin's
   Song

Das Leben Gleicht Dem Spiel (from
   Pique Dame)
   [Ger] solo,pno SCHAUR EE 3385 s.p.
                                 (T121)

Es Geht Auf Mitternacht (from Pique
   Dame)
   [Ger] solo,pno SCHAUR EE 3384 s.p.
                                 (T122)

Farewell, Ye Mountains *see Adieu,
   Forets

Fifinella *see Pimpinella

Final Scene From "Eugene Onegin"
   [Russ] SBar soli,pno MEZ KNIGA 108
   s.p.   (T123)

Forty Songs *CC40U
   [Eng/Ger/Fr] PRESSER $5.00 high
   solo,pno; low solo,pno   (T124)

Gremin's Aria *see Prine's Aria

I Adore Thee (from Eugene Onegin)
   solo,pno LEONARD-ENG   (T125)
   "Ja Ich Lieb Sie" solo,pno SCHAUR
   EE 3375 s.p.   (T126)

Ja Ich Lieb Sie *see I Adore Thee

Johanna's Aria (from Jungfrau Von
   Orleans)
   [Ger/Fr] solo,pno SCHAUR EE 3381
   s.p.   (T127)

King Rebe's Aria (from Iolanta)
   [Russ] low solo,pno MEZ KNIGA 122
   s.p.   (T128)

King Rene's Aria (from Iolante)
   [Russ] low solo,pno MEZ KNIGA 122
   s.p.   (T129)

Legend *Op.54,No.5, sac,Xmas
   solo,pno SCHAUR EE 147A s.p. (T130)
   solo,pno HARRIS $.75   (T131)
   med solo,pno (E min) ALLANS s.p.
                                 (T132)
   [Eng/Fr] med solo,kbd CHESTER s.p.
                                 (T133)
   high solo,pno (E min) ASHDOWN $1.75
                                 (T134)
   low solo,pno (D min) ASHDOWN $1.75
                                 (T135)

Lenski's Aria *see Lensky's Song

Lensky's Aria (from Eugen Onegin)
   "Arie Des Lensky" [Russ/Fr/Ger/Eng]
   T solo,pno BREITKOPF-W 61 03125
   s.p.   (T136)

Lensky's Aria *see Lensky's Song

Lensky's Song (from Eugen Onegin)
   "Arie Lenskis" [Czech/Russ] solo,
   pno SUPRAPHON s.p.   (T137)
   "Lenski's Aria" [Ger] solo,pno
   SCHAUR EE 3378 s.p.   (T138)
   "Lenski's Aria" [Russ/Eng] T solo,
   pno INTERNAT. $1.25   (T139)
   "Lenski's Aria" [Eng/Russ] solo,pno
   SCHAUR EE 3378A s.p.   (T140)
   "Lensky's Aria" [Eng] T solo,pno
   BROUDE,A $2.50   (T141)
   "Sun Returns" solo,pno CRAMER
                                 (T142)

Letter Scene, The *see Letter Song,
   The

Letter Song, The (from Eugene Onegin)
   solo,pno ASHDOWN s.p.   (T143)
   "Letter Scene, The" [Eng] S solo,
   pno BROUDE,A $3.75   (T144)
   "Tatjana's Letter Scene" [Eng/Russ]
   solo,pno SCHAUR EE 3376A s.p.
                                 (T145)
   "Tatjana's Letter Scene" [Ger]
   solo,pno SCHAUR EE 3376 s.p.
                                 (T146)
   "You Wrote To Me" [Russ] med solo,

TCHAIKOVSKY, PIOTR ILYITCH (cont'd.)

   pno MEZ KNIGA 119 s.p.   (T147)

Lord Almighty God
   high solo/med solo,pno GALAXY
   1.1321.7 $1.00   (T148)

Lord Is My Shepherd, The *sac
   (Maxwell, R.; Feibel, F.) low solo,
   pno (F maj) SCHIRM.G $.75   (T149)

My Talents Not For Meditation *see
   Olga's Song

None But The Lonely Heart *see Nur,
   Wer Die Sehnsucht Kennt

None But The Longing Heart *see Nur,
   Wer Die Sehnsucht Kennt

Nur, Wer Die Sehnsucht Kennt *Op.6,
   No.6
   "None But The Lonely Heart" [Ger/
   Eng] med solo,pno (D flat maj)
   SCHIRM.G $1.00   (T150)
   "None But The Lonely Heart" [Ger/
   Eng] low solo,pno (C maj)
   SCHIRM.G $1.00   (T151)
   "None But The Lonely Heart" med
   solo,pno (C maj) CENTURY 3245
                                 (T152)
   "None But The Lonely Heart" low
   solo,pno (C maj) ALLANS s.p.
                                 (T153)
   "None But The Lonely Heart" med
   solo,pno (D maj) ALLANS s.p.
                                 (T154)
   "None But The Longing Heart" low
   solo,pno (C maj) ASHDOWN s.p.
                                 (T155)
   "None But The Longing Heart" med
   solo,pno (D flat maj) ASHDOWN
   s.p.   (T156)
   "None But The Longing Heart" med-
   high solo,pno (D maj) ASHDOWN
   s.p.   (T157)
   "None But The Longing Heart" high
   solo,pno (E flat maj) ASHDOWN
   s.p.   (T158)
   "Solo El Que Saba Amar" [Ger/Span]
   solo,pno RICORDI-ARG BA 8827 s.p.
                                 (T159)
   "Yearning" solo,pno ASHDOWN s.p.
                                 (T160)

Olga's Scene And Aria *see Olga's
   Song

Olga's Song (from Eugene Onegin)
   "My Talents Not For Meditation"
   solo,pno LEONARD-ENG   (T161)
   "Olga's Scene And Aria" [Ger] solo,
   pno SCHAUR EE 3374 s.p.   (T162)

Onegin's Scene And Aria *see
   Onegin's Song

Onegin's Song (from Eugene Onegin)
   "Can This Be Tatiana?" solo,pno
   LEONARD-ENG   (T163)
   "Onegin's Scene And Aria" [Ger]
   solo,pno SCHAUR EE 3377 s.p. (T164)

Pauline's Romance (from Pique Dame)
   [Ger] A solo,pno SCHAUR EE 3382
   s.p.   (T165)

Pilgrims Song *see To The Forest

Pimpinella *Op.38,No.6
   "Fifinella" med solo,pno (G maj)
   ALLANS s.p.   (T166)

Prince's Aria (from Eugen Onegin)
   "Arie Des Fursten Gremin" [Czech/
   Russ] solo,pno SUPRAPHON s.p.
                                 (T167)
   "Arie Des Gremin" [Russ/Fr/Ger/Eng]
   Bar solo,pno BREITKOPF-W 61 03126
   s.p.   (T168)

Prine's Aria (from Eugene Onegin)
   "Gremin's Aria" [Eng] B solo,pno
   BROUDE,A $2.50   (T169)
   "Gremin's Aria" [Ger] solo,pno
   SCHAUR EE 3379A s.p.   (T170)
   "Gremin's Aria" [Ger] solo,pno
   (easy) SCHAUR EE 3379B s.p.
                                 (T171)
   "Gremin's Aria" [Eng/Russ] solo,pno
   SCHAUR EE 3379C s.p.   (T172)

Robert's Romance (from Jolanthe)
   solo,pno SCHAUR EE 3380 s.p. (T173)

Romance *Op.5
   (Rufold, Eduard) solo,pno MUSIKK
   s.p.   (T174)

Romanze Paulinens (from Pique Dame)
   [Russ/Fr/Ger/Eng] Mez solo,pno
   BREITKOPF-W 61 03075 s.p.   (T175)

Romanzen Und Lieder, Band 1 *CCU
   solo,pno SIKORSKI R 6342 s.p.
                                 (T176)

TCHAIKOVSKY, PIOTR ILYITCH (cont'd.)

Romanzen Und Lieder, Band 2 *CCU
   solo,pno SIKORSKI R 6343 s.p.
                                 (T177)
Romanzen Und Lieder, Band 3 *CCU
   solo,pno SIKORSKI R 6348 s.p.
                                 (T178)
Romanzen Und Lieder, Band 4 *CCU
   solo,pno SIKORSKI R 6397 s.p.
                                 (T179)
Sechzehn Kinderlieder *Op.54, CC16U
   solo,pno SCHAUR EE 147 s.p.   (T180)

Selected Romances *CCU
   [Russ] high solo,pno MEZ KNIGA 64
   s.p.   (T181)

Selected Songs *CC20U
   [Russ/Ger] high solo,pno PETERS
   4651A $11.00; med solo,pno PETERS
   4651B $11.00; low solo,pno PETERS
   4651C $11.00   (T182)

Solo El Que Saba Amar *see Nur Wer
   Die Sehnsucht Kennt

Sun Returns *see Lensky's Song

Tatjana's Letter Scene *see Letter
   Song, The

To The Forest *Op.47,No.5
   solo,pno (F maj) BOOSEY $1.50
                                 (T183)
   "Pilgrims Song" low solo,orch (D
   maj) ASHDOWN s.p., ipr   (T184)
   "Pilgrims Song" high solo,orch (F
   maj) ASHDOWN s.p., ipr   (T185)
   "Pilgrims Song" med solo,orch (E
   maj) ASHDOWN s.p., ipr   (T186)

Vergonne Mir Ein Paar Minuten (from
   Pique Dame)
   Bar solo,pno SCHAUR EE 3383 s.p.
                                 (T187)

Vierundzwanzig Lieder Und Romanzen
   *CC24U
   [Czech] solo,pno SUPRAPHON s.p.
                                 (T188)

War Ich Nicht Ein Frisches Graslein
   [Russ/Fr/Ger/Eng] solo,pno
   BREITKOPF-W 61 03124 s.p.   (T189)

Warum? *Op.6,No.5
   "Why?" med solo,pno (B flat maj)
   ALLANS s.p.   (T190)
   "Why?" high solo,pno (D maj) ALLANS
   s.p.   (T191)
   "Why So Pale The Roses?" low solo,
   pno (B flat maj) ASHDOWN s.p.
                                 (T192)
   "Why So Pale The Roses?" high solo,
   pno (D maj) ASHDOWN s.p.   (T193)

Why? *see Warum?

Why So Pale The Roses? *see Warum?

Yearning *see Nur, Wer Die Sehnsucht
   Kennt

You Wrote To Me *see Letter Song,
   The

TCHEREPNIN, ALEXANDER (1899-   )
   Deux Melodies
   solo,pno cmplt ed DURAND s.p.
      contains: Je Vous Aime; Printemps
      Annamite   (T194)

Intoxication
   see Two Songs

Je Vous Aime
   see Deux Melodies

Printemps Annamite
   see Deux Melodies

Seven Songs On Chinese Poems *Op.71,
   CC7U
   [Chin/Eng/Russ] solo,pno BELAIEFF
   312 s.p.   (T195)

Sieben Chinesische Volkslieder
   *Op.95, CC7U
   low solo,pno GERIG HG 606 s.p.
                                 (T196)

Six Melodies *CC6U
   solo,pno cmplt ed DURAND s.p.
                                 (T197)

There Are Times, My Love
   see Two Songs

Two Songs
   [Eng] high solo,kbd CHESTER s.p.
      contains: Intoxication; There Are
      Times, My Love   (T198)

Vom Spass Und Ernst *cant
   med solo,strings/pno s.p. voc sc
   GERIG HG 524A, sc GERIG HG 524
                                 (T199)

TE AMO YA see Grieg, Edvard Hagerup,
Ich Liebe Dich

TE DEUM see Hure, Jean

TE DEUM see Lacome, Paul

TE DEUM see Verdi, Giuseppe

TE ERGO see Bruckner, Anton

TE LO VOGLIO DIRE see Albanese, Guido

TE LUCIS ANTE TERMINUM see Pinkham,
Daniel

TE SOUVIENS-TU see Godard, Benjamin
Louis Paul

TE SOUVIENT-IL DU JOUR see Wagner,
Richard

TEA SHOP, THE see Koch, Johannes H.E.

TEACH ME, O LORD see Kingsley, Gershon

TEACH ME THE WAY see Wijdeveld,
Wolfgang

TEACH ME TO FORGIVE see Davies,
[William] Henry

TEACH ME TO FORGIVE see Stephens, Ward

TEACH ME TO KNOW see Lacy, Della

TEACH ME TO PRAY see Jewett

TEAMSTER'S FAREWELL, A see Smith,
Melville

TEAR KERCHIEF, THE see Russell, Kennedy

TEARLESS see Owens, Robert

TEARS see Wagner, Richard, Schmerzen

TEARS see Wijdeveld, Wolfgang

TEARS, THE see Massenet, Jules

TEARS ARE A LANGUAGE see Jensen, Gordon

TEARS FALLING IN MY HEART see Schmitt,
Florent, Il Pleure Dans Mon Coeur

TEARS, IDLE TEARS see Morton, David

TEARS OF SHAME see Atwood, Tommy

TEARS THAT CHILDREN SHED see Arundale,
Claude

TEARS WILL NEVER STAIN THE STREETS OF
THAT CITY see Rambo

TEDFORD, JOHN
Touch Hands
solo,pno GENERAL 21 $1.00   (T200)

TEED, ROY (1928-   )
April Morning
see Two Songs

Holy Thursday
[Eng] high solo,kbd CHESTER s.p.
(T201)

Song For Sunrise
see Two Songs

Three Jolly Huntsmen
[Eng] med solo,kbd CHESTER s.p.
(T202)

Two Songs
[Eng] med solo,kbd CHESTER s.p.
contains: April Morning; Song For
Sunrise   (T203)

TEILE MIT MIR DAS TAGLICHE BROT see
Baird, Tadeusz, Podziel Sie Ze Mna

TEJEDORA! see Pardo

TEKMESSA see Ruyneman, Daniel

TEL JOUR, TELLE NUIT see Poulenc,
Francis

TELEMANN, GEORG PHILIPP (1681-1767)
Ach Herr, Strafe Mich Nicht (Psalm 6)
*sac
(Steude) [Ger/Eng] A solo,2vln,cont
sc DEUTSCHER 9501 s.p., ipa
(T204)

Auf Ehernen Mauern
see Sechs Arien Aus Dem
Harmonischen Gottesdienst

Ausgewahlte Lieder *sac,CCU
solo,kbd,opt vcl CONCORDIA 97-4264
$3.00   (T205)

Ausgewahlte Lieder *CCU
solo,cont KISTNER cmplt ed s.p., sc
s.p., ipa   (T206)

TELEMANN, GEORG PHILIPP (cont'd.)

Deine Toten Werden Leben
see Sechs Arien Aus Dem
Harmonischen Gottesdienst

Der Harmonische Teil I, Neujahr-
Reminiscere *sac,CCUL
(Fock, Gustav; Seiffert, Max) med
solo/high solo,vln&cont/fl&ob&A
rec&cont (med) sc,cloth BAREN.
2952 $35.00, ipa
see also: Ein Jeder Lauft, Der In
Den Schranken Lauft; Hemmet Den
Eifer, Verbannet Die Rache; Ihr
Volker Hort   (T207)

Der Harmonische Teil II, Oculi-
Pfingsten *sac,CCUL
(Fock, Gustav; Seiffert, Max) med
solo/high solo,vln&cont/fl&ob&A
rec&cont (med) sc,cloth BAREN.
2953 $35.00, ipa
see also: Ew'ge Quelle, Milder
Strom; Gott Will Mensch Und
Sterblich Werden; Jauchzt, Ihr
Christen, Seid Vergnugt (T208)

Der Harmonische Teil III, Trinitatis
*sac,CCU,Trin
(Fock, Gustav) med solo/high solo,
vln&cont/fl&ob&A rec&cont (med)
sc,cloth BAREN. 2954 $35.00, ipa
(T209)

Der Harmonische Teil IV, Sonntag Nach
Trinitatis - Weihnachten *sac,
CCU
(Fock, Gustav) med solo/high solo,
vln&cont/fl&ob&A rec&cont (med)
sc,cloth BAREN. 2955 $35.00, ipa
(T210)

Der Weiberorden *cant
[Ger/Eng] S solo,2vln,cont sc
DEUTSCHER 9502 s.p., ipa   (T211)

Die Hoffnung Ist Mein Leben *sac,
cant
(Menke, Werner) B solo,vln,cont
(med) BAREN. 768 $4.25   (T212)

Ein Jeder Lauft, Der In Den Schranken
Lauft *sac,Septua
(Fock, Gustav; Seiffert, Max) S/T
solo,ob/vln,cont (med) BAREN.
3627 $5.75 see also Der
Harmonische Teil I, Neujahr-
Reminiscere   (T213)

Erquicktes Herz *sac,cant
low solo,vln,cont sc HANSSLER
10.043 s.p., ipa   (T214)

Ew'ge Quelle, Milder Strom *sac,cant
(Fock, Gustav; Seiffert, Max) med
solo,fl/vln,cont (med) BAREN.
3629 $6.50 see also Der
Harmonische Teil II, Oculi-
Pfingsten   (T215)

Frohlocket, Ihr Seligen Kinder Der
Freien
see Sechs Arien Aus Dem
Harmonischen Gottesdienst

Gesegnet Ist Die Zuversicht *sac,
cant
(Durr, Alfred) TB/SB soli,2S rec,
2vln,cont (med) BAREN. 1978
$10.50   (T216)

Gott Will Mensch Und Sterblich Werden
*sac
(Fock, Gustav; Seiffert, Max) S/T
solo,vln,cont (med) BAREN. 718
$7.00 see also Der Harmonische
Teil II, Oculi-Pfingsten (T217)

Ha, Ha! Wo Will Wi Hut Noch Danzen
*cant
(Hobohm; Bernstein) [Ger/Eng] S
solo,vln,cont sc DEUTSCHER 9507
s.p.   (T218)

Harmonischen Gottesdienst *see
Lauter Wonne, Lauter Freude
(T219)

Hemmet Den Eifer, Verbannet Die Rache
*sac,Epiph
(Fock, Gustav; Seiffert, Max) S/T
solo,A rec,cont (med) BAREN. 3628
$5.75 see also Der Harmonische
Teil I, Neujahr-Reminiscere
(T220)

Herr Der Gnade, Gott Des Lichts
see Sechs Arien Aus Dem
Harmonischen Gottesdienst

Ich Weiss, Dass Mein Erloser Lebt
*sac,Easter,cant
(Schroder, O.) [Ger/Eng] T solo,
bsn,strings,cembalo (formerly
attributed to J.S. Bach - BWV
160) voc sc BREITKOPF-L EB 7160
s.p., ipr   (T221)

TELEMANN, GEORG PHILIPP (cont'd.)

Ihr Volker Hort *sac,Xmas
(Fock, Gustav; Seiffert, Max) S/T
solo,fl,cont (med) BAREN. 387
$7.00 see also Der Harmonische
Teil I, Neujahr-Reminiscere
(T222)

Ino *cant
Mez solo,2fl,2ob,bsn,2horn,cembalo,
strings sc BREITKOPF-W DDT BD. 28
s.p.   (T223)
(Straube, K.) Mez solo,2fl,bsn,
2horn,strings,cembalo BREITKOPF-L
rental   (T224)

Jauchzet, Frohlocket *sac,Xmas,cant
med solo,vln,cont sc VIEWEG 6121
$3.50, ipa   (T225)

Jauchzt, Ihr Christen, Seid Vergnugt
*sac
(Fock, Gustav; Seiffert, Max) S/T
solo,vln,cont (med) BAREN. 720
$7.00 see also Der Harmonische
Teil II, Oculi-Pfingsten (T226)

Kanarienvogel-Kantate *sac,cant
(Menke, Werner) med solo,2vln,vla,
cont (med) BAREN. 1788 $5.50
(T227)

Kleine Kantate Von Wald Und Au *cant
(Ermeler, Rolf) S/T solo,fl,cont
(med) BAREN. 1787 $5.50   (T228)

Lauter Wonne, Lauter Freude *sac,
Adv,cant
S solo,S rec,cont sc HANSSLER
10.184 s.p., ipa see from
Harmonischen Gottesdienst (T229)
S solo,A rec,cont sc VIEWEG 6135
$3.50, ipa   (T230)

Liebster Jesu, Kehre Wieder *sac,
Xmas
S solo,2rec,2vln,vla,vcl/bvl,kbd
voc sc VIEWEG 6113 $3.50, ipa
(T231)

Lieder Und Arien *CCU
(Degen, Helmut) high solo,pno (med)
BAREN. HM 12 $8.50   (T232)

Locke Nur *cant
(Bergmann) [Ger/Eng] S solo,fl,pno
SCHOTTS 10373 s.p.   (T233)

Magnificat *sac,cant
S solo,fl,strings,cont sc HANSSLER
10.139 s.p., ipa   (T234)

Nicht Uns, Nur Dir Allein
see Sechs Arien Aus Dem
Harmonischen Gottesdienst

Psalm 6 *see Ach Herr, Strafe Mich
Nicht

Sechs Arien Aus Dem Harmonischen
Gottesdienst
high solo,S rec,cont sc HANSSLER
10.308 s.p., ipa
contains: Auf Ehernen Mauern;
Deine Toten Werden Leben;
Frohlocket, Ihr Seligen Kinder
Der Freien; Herr Der Gnade,
Gott Des Lichts; Nicht Uns, Nur
Dir Allein; Seele, Lerne Dich
Erkennen   (T235)

Seele, Lerne Dich Erkennen
see Sechs Arien Aus Dem
Harmonischen Gottesdienst

Singe-, Spiel- Und Generalbassubungen
*CCU
(Seiffert, Max) solo,cont (med)
BAREN. 887 $6.25   (T236)

Susse Hoffnung, Wenn Ich Frage
(Menke, Werner) T solo,2vln,vla,
2bsn,cont (med) BAREN. 769 $5.50
(T237)

Tod Und Moder Dringt Herein
(Ermeler, Rolf) A solo,fl,pno,opt
vcl/bsn ZIMMER. 1132 s.p. (T238)

Vor Des Lichten Tages Schein *sac,
Adv,cant
med solo,fl,cont sc VIEWEG 6122
$3.50, ipa   (T239)

Weiche, Lust Und Frohlichkeit *sac,
cant
S solo,vln,vla,ob,cont sc HANSSLER
10.280 s.p., ipa   (T240)

Zerreiss Das Herz *sac,cant
S solo,S rec,strings,cont sc
HANSSLER 10.258 s.p., ipa (T241)

TELL IT ALL TO JESUS see Jenkins,
Margaret Aikens

TELL IT LIKE IS IS *sac
(Carmichael, Ralph) solo,pno WORD
S-93   (T242)

TELL ME, FAIR LADIES see Mozart,
Wolfgang Amadeus, Voi Che Sapete

TELL ME GIPSY see Day, Maude Craske

TELL ME LOVELY SHEPHERD see Boyce,
William

TELL ME MARY HOW TO WOO THEE see
Hodson, J.A.

TELL ME MISTRESS THIS I PRAY see Hope,
H. Ashworth

TELL ME MY HEART see Bishop, Sir Henry
Rowley

TELL ME NOT OF A LOVELY LASS see
Forsyth, Cecil

TELL ME, OH BLUE, BLUE SKY see
Giannini, Vittorio

TELL ME, THYRSIS see Nordoff, Paul

TELL ME WHERE IS FANCY BRED see Carter,
E.

TELL ME WHERE IS FANCY BRED see
Castelnuovo-Tedesco, Mario

TELL ME WHERE IS FANCY BRED see
Mackenzie, A.C.

TELL ME, WHERE IS FANCY BRED? see
Montgomery, Bruce

TELL ME WHERE IS FANCY BRED see
Thomson, Virgil

TELL ME, WHERE IS FANCY BRED see
Williams, R.H.

TELL THEM see Crouch, Andrae

TELL US OH TELL US WHERE SHALL WE FIND
see Glover, Stephen

TELL US, WISE MEN
see Six Polish Christmas Carols

TELOS NOMOU see Jacob, Werner

TEMA see Lachenmann, Helmut

TEMPEST, THE see Franco, Johan

TEMPLE, GORDON
O Song Divine
high solo,pno (G maj) ASHDOWN s.p.
(T243)
med-low solo,pno (D maj) ASHDOWN
s.p.   (T244)
low solo,pno (C maj) ASHDOWN s.p.
(T245)
med-high solo,pno (F maj) ASHDOWN
s.p.   (T246)
med solo,pno (E flat maj) ASHDOWN
s.p.   (T247)

TEMPLE, HOPE
Au Bord Des Flots
solo,pno (available in 2 keys)
ENOCH s.p.   (T248)

TEMPLE SACRE see Rameau, Jean-Philippe

TEMPRO LA CETRA see Monteverdi, Claudio

TEMPS NOUVEAU see Saint-Saens, Camille

TEN AIRS FROM MUSICKE OF SUNDRIE KINDES
see Ford, Thomas

TEN ARIAS FOR HIGH VOICE see Scarlatti,
Alessandro

TEN BLAKE SONGS see Vaughan Williams,
Ralph

TEN CHRISTMAS CAROLS FROM THE SOUTHERN
APPALACHIAN MOUNTAINS *sac,CC10L,
Xmas,US
(Niles, John Jacob) solo,pno (easy)
SCHIRM.G $1.35   (T249)

TEN CLASSICAL SONGS *CC10L
(Gavall, John) solo,gtr ELKIN
27.2543.06 s.p. contains works by:
Dowland; Bach; Handel; Mozart;
Liszt; Verdi and Grieg   (T250)

TEN FOLK SONGS OF CANADA *CC10U,folk
(Bissell, Keith) med solo,pno
WATERLOO $3.00   (T251)

TEN MELODIES see Bosmans, Henriette

TEN NORWEGIAN FOLK SONGS see Kjellsby,
Erling

TEN OPERATIC MASTERPIECES *CC10U
(Marker) [Eng] solo,inst cloth BMI
$10.00   (T252)

TEN SACRED SONGS FOR BARITONE *sac,
CC10U
(Hill, Howard) Bar solo,pno WATERLOO
$1.50   (T253)

TEN SACRED SONGS FOR CONTRALTO *sac,
CC10U
(Hill, Howard) A solo,pno WATERLOO
$1.50   (T254)

TEN SACRED SONGS FOR SOPRANO *sac,
CC10U
(Hill, Howard) S solo,pno WATERLOO
$1.50   (T255)

TEN SACRED SONGS FOR TENOR *sac,CC10U
(Hill, Howard) T solo,pno WATERLOO
$1.50   (T256)

TEN SELECTIONS FROM THE VARIOUS BEL
CANTO ALBUMS *CC10U
(Landshoff) [It] A/Mez solo,pno,opt
vln/vcl PETERS 3348B $6.50 contains
works by: Aldovrandini; Caccini;
Caldara; Carissimi; Gabrieli and
others   (T257)

TEN SONGS *CC10U
(Willan, Healey) solo,pno WATERLOO
$2.50   (T258)

TEN SONGS see Ives, Charles

TEN SONGS see Handel, George Frideric

TEN SONGS see Delius, Frederick

TEN SONGS see Zahavi, David

TEN SONGS see Schumann, Robert
(Alexander)

TEN SONGS FOR CHILDREN see Koerbler,
Milivoj

TEN SONGS FROM THE OPERETTA "BEWITCHED"
see Thordarson, Sigurdur

TEN THOUSAND ANGELS see Overholt, R.

TEN THOUSAND YEARS see Cole

TENDER GLOW, A see Lewis, Peter Tod

TENDERLY see Wetherington

TENDERLY HE WATCHES see Wiseman

TENDREMENT see Satie, Erik

TENDRESSE see Aubert, Louis-Francois-
Marie

TENDRESSE see Lacombe, Paul

TENDRESSE see Rhene-Baton

TENDRESSE see Samazeuilh, Gustave

TENEBRES see Milhaud, Darius

TENNENT, H.M.
Once On A Bough
low solo,pno (D flat maj) CRAMER
(T259)
high solo,pno (E flat maj) CRAMER
(T260)

TENNIS AT TRIANON see Sibelius, Jean,
Bollspelet Vid Trianon

TENOR-ALBUM see Skorzeny, Fritz

TENOR ARIA see Strauss, Richard

TENOR ARIA see Van Etten, Jane

TENOR SONGS (RADIO CITY ALBUM) *CCU
T solo,pno MARKS $1.50   (T261)

TENT IN THE DESERT see Sharpe, Evelyn

TERMITE, THE see Shapiro, Norman

TERNI, ENRICO
Due Liriche
S/T solo,pno cmplt ed SANTIS 822
s.p.
contains: Je Suis La Source;
Passa La Nave Mia   (T262)

Je Suis La Source
see Due Liriche

Passa La Nave Mia
see Due Liriche

Tre Liriche *CC3U
[It] solo,pno SANTIS 824 s.p.
(T263)

TERRA ADORATA DE' PADRI MIEI see
Donizetti, Gaetano

TERRELL, BEVERLY
Every Day Is A Better Day *see
Bartlett, Gene

Give Me A Vision *sac
solo,pno BROADMAN 4590-11 $.60
(T264)

Have A Good Day (composed with
Bartlett, Gene) *sac
solo,pno BROADMAN 4590-28 $1.00
(T265)

Life That Sings, A
med solo,pno CRESPUB CP-S5009 $1.00
(T266)

TERRIBLE NUIT see Indy, Vincent d'

TERRIER-VICINI, L.
Prends Cette Rose
solo,pno ENOCH s.p.   (T267)

TERROR see Eisenstein

TERRY
Answer
low solo,pno (A maj) ALLANS s.p.
(T268)
high solo,pno (D flat maj) ALLANS
s.p.   (T269)

TERRY, MY SON see Haubiel, Charles

TERRY, PAT
Pat Terry Group Songbook *CC24UL
solo,pno WORD 37749 $2.95   (T270)

TERUGBLICK, DEEL I, II, III & IV see
Bosmans, Henriette

TERZAKIS, DIMITRI (1938-   )
Achos
solo,gtr,perc SCHAUR EE 2705 s.p.
(T271)

Ethos B'
A/Bar solo,2treb inst GERIG HG 1006
s.p.   (T272)

Ethos Gamma
solo GERIG HG 1185 s.p.   (T273)

"X"
Bar solo,3pt mix cor,treb inst,
chamb.grp. GERIG HG 877 s.p.
(T274)

TERZETTO ADALINDA - LELIO - D. MERCURIO
see Guglielmi, Pietro Alessandro

TERZIANI, PIETRO
Salve, Regina *sac
(Ewerhart, Rudolf) S solo,org
BIELER CS 47 s.p.   (T275)

TERZINEN see Fortner, Wolfgang

TERZO CANTO DI KABIR see Platamone,
Stefano

TES YEUX see Delarue-Mardrus, Lucie

TES YEUX see Levidis, Dimitri

TES YEUX see Rabey, Rene

TESKNICE see Podest, Ludvik

TESORIERO, GAETANO
Ave Maria *sac
med solo,pno/org EMI s.p.   (T276)
solo,pno/org ALBERT AE 20 s.p.
(T277)

Bird In The Cherry Tree
solo,pno ALBERT AE153 s.p.   (T278)

Buona Sera
"Lullaby" solo,pno ALBERT AE 33
s.p.   (T279)
"Lullaby" med solo,pno EMI s.p.
(T280)

Lullaby *see Buona Sera

Wedding Song *Marriage
high solo,org/pno EMI s.p.   (T281)
solo,pno ALBERT AE 44 s.p.   (T282)

Welcome Holy Father *sac
solo,pno ALBERT AE185 s.p.   (T283)

TESORO MIO see Becucci

TESS LORDAN see Richnau

TESSON, P.
D'une Fontaine
solo,pno ENOCH rental   (T284)
solo,orch ENOCH rental   (T285)

La Chanson Des Chansons
solo,orch ENOCH rental   (T286)
solo,pno ENOCH s.p.   (T287)

Le Rideau De Ma Voisine
solo,pno ENOCH s.p.   (T288)
solo,orch ENOCH rental   (T289)

Tu Me Demandes Rieuse
solo,pno ENOCH s.p.   (T290)
solo,orch ENOCH rental   (T291)

TEST OF KISSING, THE see Beethoven, Ludwig van, Die Prufung Des Kussens

TESTA ADORATA see Leoncavallo, Ruggiero

TESTAMENT see Duparc, Henri

TESTAMENT VAN EEN STUDENT see Hullebroeck, Em.

TESTI, FLAVIO (1923-)
Cantata Seconda *Op.24
T solo,clar,trp,trom,pno,vln sc
RICORDI-ENG 132057 s.p.   (T292)

TETE DE FAUNE see Andriessen, Hendrik

TETRAPTIEK see Weegenhuise, Johan

TETTERODE, L. ADR. VON
Avond
see Zes Tweestemmige Kinderliederen

Een Hollandsch Lied
see Zes Tweestemmige Kinderliederen

Madeliefje
see Zes Tweestemmige Kinderliederen

Meilied
see Zes Tweestemmige Kinderliederen

Vogelnestje
see Zes Tweestemmige Kinderliederen

Zes Tweestemmige Kinderliederen
solo,org ALSBACH s.p.
contains: Avond; Een Hollandsch
Lied; Madeliefje; Meilied;
Vogelnestje; Zomerochtendliedje
(T293)
Zomerochtendliedje
see Zes Tweestemmige Kinderliederen

TEUERSTES MADCHEN, ICH SCHEIDE see Mozart, Wolfgang Amadeus, Bella Mia Fiamma - Resta O Cara

TEUERSTES MADCHEN, ICH SCHEIDE - WEIB MEIN ALLES? see Mozart, Wolfgang Amadeus, Bella Mia Fiamma - Resta, O Cara

TEWSON, WILLIAM
Canticle For Brothers Apart *sac
solo,pno WORD S-370   (T294)

TEXTDEL *CCU
2 soli,pno GEHRMANS s.p.   (T295)

THACKER
Walls Came Tumbling Down, The *sac
solo,pno BENSON S8078-S $1.00
(T296)

THAL see Strauss, Richard

THANATOS' AVONDLIED see Baeyens, August-L.

THANK GOD, I AM FREE see McFall

THANK YOU FOR THE VALLEY see Rambo

THANK YOU, JESUS see Mott, Joyce Lock

THANK YOU, LORD *sac,gospel
solo,pno ABER.GRP. $1.50   (T297)

THANK YOU, LORD see Burgess, Dan

THANKS see O'Hara, Geoffrey

THANKS see Weigl, Vally

THANKS BE TO GOD see Dickson, Stanley

THANKS BE TO THEE see Handel, George Frideric, Dank Sei Dir, Herr

THANKS FOR SUNSHINE see Gaither

THANKS TO CALVARY see Gaither

THANKS TO YOU see Ford, Donald

THANKSGIVING see Ireland, John

THARICHEN, W.
Concerto *Op.38
[Ger] high solo,orch BOTE $7.50
(T298)

THAT DAY IS ALMOST HERE see Tripp, LaVerne

THAT GOD IS GREAT see Handel, George Frideric

THAT IS WHY see Krahmer, Herbert

THAT NAME IS JESUS see Cox, Allan

THAT NIGHT IN MAY see Brahms, Johannes

THAT ROSE - YOUR LOVE see Harling, William Franke

THAT SOOTHIN' SONG see Carpenter, John Alden

THAT TIME MAY CEASE AND MIDNIGHT NEVER COME see Bezanson, Philip

THAT WHITE AND RADIANT LEGEND see Bedford, David

THAT'S ALL see Brahe, May H.

THAT'S FOR ME see Kaiser, Kurt

THAT'S HAPPY HOME see Hope, H. Ashworth

THAT'S THE MAN I'M LOOKING FOR see Lee, Don

THAT'S THE WAY IT IS see Kaiser, Kurt

THAT'S WHAT HE DID FOR ME see Roe, Gloria [Ann]

THAT'S WHAT IT'S LIKE IN THE ARMY see Peterson, John W.

THAT'S WHAT LOVE WILL DO TO YOU see Beni, J.

THAT'S WORTH EVERYTHING see Gaither

THEEROVY PISNE, SES. 1-2 see Jindrich, Jindrich

THEKLA, EINE GEISTERSTIMME see Schubert, Franz (Peter)

THEMA WEIHNACHTEN see Blarr, Oskar Gottlieb

THEME VARIE see Saint-Saens, Camille

THEN FALLS THE MIRACLE OF SNOW see Birch, Robert Fairfax

THEN I FLY TO MEET MY LOVE see Hook, James

THEN I FOUND JESUS see Younce, George

THEN I MET THE MASTER see Lister, Mosie

THEN SAY MY SWEET GIRL CAN YOU LOVE ME see Hook, James

THEN WHY THE TEARS? see Wolfe, Lanny

THEN WILL I JEHOVAH'S PRAISE see Handel, George Frideric

THEN YOU'LL REMEMBER ME see Balfe, Michael William

THEO see Ferroud, Pierre-Octave

THEODOR-STORM-LIEDER, FOLGE I see Mixa, Franz

THEODOR-STORM-LIEDER, FOLGE II see Mixa, Franz

THEODOR-STORM-LIEDER, FOLGE III see Mixa, Franz

THEODOR-STORM-LIEDER, FOLGE IV see Mixa, Franz

THEODOR-STORM-LIEDER, FOLGE V see Mixa, Franz

THEODORA see Sibelius, Jean

THEODORE see Berkeley, Lennox

THERE ARE FAIRIES IN THE GARDEN see Forbes-Smith, Netta

THERE ARE TIMES, MY LOVE see Tcherepnin, Alexander

THERE ARE TWA BONNIE MAIDENS *folk, Scot
solo,pno (D maj) PATERSON FS87 s.p.
(T299)

THERE COMES ANOTHER MORROW see Sibelius, Jean

THERE GROWS A BONNIE BRIER BUSH *folk, Scot
solo,pno (F maj) PATERSON FS131 s.p.
(T300)

THERE HAS FALLEN A SPLENDID TEAR see Hannikainen, Ilmari, Kayskelen Kukkatarhassain

THERE I SAW HER see Fromm, Herbert

THERE IS A BALM IN GILEAD see Dawson

THERE IS A FOUNTAIN see Landers, Bill

THERE IS A GARDEN IN HER FACE see Bush, Geoffrey

THERE IS A GREEN HILL see Gounod, Charles Francois, Le Calvaire

THERE IS A GREEN HILL see Sanderson, Wilfred

THERE IS A GREEN HILL FAR AWAY see Gounod, Charles Francois, Le Calvaire

THERE IS A LADY SWEET AND KIND see Dello Joio, Norman

THERE IS A LADYE see Bury

THERE IS A LADYE see Bury, Winifred

THERE IS A LAND see Engel, Joel, Omrim Yeshna Eretz

THERE IS A LAND see Johnson

THERE IS A LIGHT see Johnson, P.

THERE IS A RIVER see Sapp

THERE IS A TIME FOR EVERYTHING see Wild, Eric

THERE IS COMFORT IN JESUS see Peery, Robert Roy

THERE IS JUST NO PLACE LIKE HOME see Wolfe, Lanny

THERE IS MORE TO LIFE *sac
(Carmichael, Ralph) solo,pno WORD
S-111   (T301)

THERE IS MY DWELLING see Hustad, Donald P.

THERE IS NO GREATER LOVE see Peterson, John W.

THERE IS NO ROSE OF SUCH VIRTUE see Meek, Kenneth

THERE IS NO STREAM see Sallinen, Aulis

THERE IS NO TIME see Fischer, Irwin

THERE IS NOTHING FALSE IN THEE see Mills, Charles

THERE IS SO MUCH TO TELL YOU see Guarnieri, Camargo Mozart

THERE IS SOMEONE *sac
solo,pno (work by The Hawaiians)
LILLENAS SM-635: RN $1.00   (T302)

THERE IS SWEET MUSIC see Birch, Robert Fairfax

THERE IS SWEET MUSIC see Norris, Harry

THERE LIVED A SNAIL see Saunders, Mervyn

THERE SHALL BE MORE JOY see Nordoff, Paul

THERE SITS A BIRD ON YONDER TREE see Keel, Frederick

THERE STANDS A LITTLE MAN see Humperdinck, Engelbert

THERE WAS A WIND THAT BLEW see Kilpinen, Yrio, Mannertreu

THERE WAS AN OLD WOMAN see Lessard, John Ayres

THERE WERE MANY WHO WENT IN HUDDLED PROCESSION see Owen, Richard

THERE WHERE WHITE RINGDOVES FLUTTER see Kilpinen, Yrio, Der Schonste Platz

THERE WILL ALWAYS BE GARDENS see Linke, Norbert

THERE WILL BE OTHER SUMMERS see Young, Gordon

THERE'S A BONNIE HOUSE IN AYR see West, Monica

THERE'S A FJORD see Dorumsgaard, Arne

THERE'S A GARDEN IN ANTRIM IS LONELY TONIGHT see Franco, Johan

THERE'S A LAND see Allitsen, Frances

THERE'S A NEW NAME WRITTEN DOWN see Younce, George

THERE'S A SONG IN THE AIR see Speaks, Oley

THERE'S A VOICE THAT I ENSHRINE see Rossini, Gioacchino, Una Voce Poco Fa

THERE'S AN AWFUL LOT OF GLORY see
Wilson, Al

THERE'S ENOUGH OF GOD'S LOVE see
Jensen, Gordon

THERE'S GOING TO BE A WEDDING *sac,
Marriage
solo,pno/org WORD 37525 $2.50
contains: All My Life (Carmichael,
Ralph); It Seems I've Always
Loved You (Carmichael, Ralph);
Coleman, Jack, Your Tender Love;
Owens, Jimmy, True Love Comes
From God   (T303)

THERE'S GONNA BE SHOUTIN' see Ballard,
Ann

THERE'S MANY WILL LOVE A MAID see Head,
Michael (Dewar)

THERE'S NAE A THRUSH
see Three Irish Folk Songs

THERE'S NAE LUCK ABOUT THE HOUSE
*folk,Scot
low solo,pno (D maj) PATERSON FS85
s.p.   (T304)
high solo,pno (E maj) PATERSON FS85
s.p.   (T305)

THERE'S NO LAND LIKE IRELAND see
Needham, Alicia Adelaide

THERE'S NOT A SWAIN ON THE PLAIN see
Purcell, Henry

THERE'S NOTHING LIKE THE HOLY GHOST see
Hubbard, H.

THERE'S SOMEONE IN THE ORCHARD see
Austin, Harry

THERE'S SOMETHING ABOUT THAT NAME see
Gaither

THERE'S SOMETHING IN THE AIR see Wolfe,
Lanny

THERE'S SOMETHING SPECIAL see Roe,
Gloria [Ann]

THERT IS NE'ER WAS SO WRETCHES A LOVER
see Purcell, Henry

THESAURUS OF CANTORIAL LITURGY (PART I)
*sac,CCU,Jew
(Katchko, A.) cantor SAC.MUS.PR.
                                  (T306)

THESE ARE THE LOVELY THINGS see
Pearson, Edith

THESE ARE THE TIMES see Clarke, Henry
Leland

THESE DANCING DAYS ARE GONE see Harris,
Bryn

THESE OL' BONES *sac,gospel
solo,pno ABER.GRP. $1.50   (T307)

THESE PRECIOUS THINGS see Mayerl, B.

THETIS see Rameau, Jean-Philippe

THEY CALL HIM JESUS see Yon, Pietro
Alessandro

THEY CALL HIS NAME JESUS see Davis

THEY CALL ME MIMI see Puccini, Giacomo,
Si, Mi Chiamano Mimi

THEY CALLED HER FAIR see Sutherland,
Margaret

THEY LED MY LORD AWAY *spir
(Dorsey) low solo,pno (E flat maj)
SCHIRM.G $.60   (T308)

THEY SHALL BE MINE see Crouch, Andrae

THEY SHALL BE MINE see Hubbard, H.

THEY SHALL NOT HUNGER NOR THIRST see
Strickland, Lily Teresa

THEY THAT HAVE POWER see Butt

THEY THAT SOW IN TEARS see Gaither

THEY TORE THE OLD COUNTRY CHURCH DOWN
see Fralix

THEY'D HAVE ME GET MARRIED, OH! see
Salas, Juan Orrego, Dicen Que Me
Case Yo

THEY'RE TAXING ALE AGAIN see Webber,
Lloyd

THIELE, SIEGFRIED (1934-   )
Als Unser Herr Am Kreuzesstamm *sac
S solo,2S rec,org HANSSLER 5.050
s.p. see also GESANGE ZUM
KIRCHENJAHR   (T309)

Brich Herein, Susser Schein *sac
S solo,2S rec,org HANSSLER 5.060
s.p. see also GESANGE ZUM
KIRCHENJAHR   (T310)

Dieweil Auch Heuer Nach Advent *sac
SA soli,2S rec,cont HANSSLER 5.045
s.p. see also GESANGE ZUM
KIRCHENJAHR   (T311)

Gott Ist Liebe *sac
med solo,org HANSSLER 5.083 s.p.
contains also: Herr, Du Hast
Worte Des Ewigen Lebens   (T312)

Herr, Du Hast Worte Des Ewigen Lebens
see Thiele, Siegfried, Gott Ist
Liebe

THIERFELDER
Fortrostan
2 soli,pno LUNDQUIST s.p.   (T313)

Vaxelsang
2 soli,pno LUNDQUIST s.p.   (T314)

THIMAN, ERIC HARDING (1900-   )
Apple Blossom
3 soli,pno ROBERTON 72308 s.p.
                                  (T315)

Birds, The
high solo,pno NOVELLO 17.0012.10
s.p.   (T316)
med solo,pno NOVELLO 17.0011.01
s.p.   (T317)

Carol Of The Birds
solo,pno (E flat maj) BOOSEY $1.50
                                  (T318)

Easter Prayer, An
solo,pno CRAMER $1.15   (T319)

Evening In Lilac Time
med solo,pno NOVELLO 17.0054.05
s.p.   (T320)

Fain Would I Change That Note
3 soli,pno ROBERTON 72083 s.p.   (T321)

Flower Of Heaven, The
high solo,pno ELKIN 27.2200.03 s.p.
                                  (T322)

God Of Love My Shepherd Is, The
low solo,pno NOVELLO 17.0062.06
s.p.   (T323)
med solo,pno NOVELLO 17.0063.04
s.p.   (T324)

Happy Is The Man *sac
med solo,pno NOVELLO 17.0064.02
s.p.   (T325)

I Love All Graceful Things
solo,pno (A flat maj) ROBERTON 2580
s.p.   (T326)

In The Bleak Midwinter *sac
low solo,pno NOVELLO 17.0076.06
s.p.   (T327)
med solo,pno NOVELLO 17.0075.08
s.p.   (T328)

Jesus, The Very Thought Of Thee *sac
low solo,pno NOVELLO 17.0087.01
s.p.   (T329)
med solo,pno NOVELLO 17.0086.03
s.p.   (T330)

Listening
3 soli,pno ROBERTON 72692 s.p.
                                  (T331)

Morning Song
2 soli,pno ROBERTON 72673 s.p.
                                  (T332)

My Master Hath A Garden *sac
med solo,pno NOVELLO 17.0124.10
s.p.   (T333)
high solo,pno NOVELLO 17.0123.01
s.p.   (T334)

O For A Closer Walk *sac
low solo,pno BELWIN $1.50   (T335)
high solo,pno BELWIN $1.50   (T336)

Rainbow, The
low solo,pno NOVELLO 17.0157.06
s.p.   (T337)

Silver Birch, The
solo,pno (C maj) ROBERTON 2602 s.p.
                                  (T338)
solo,pno (F maj) ROBERTON 2602 s.p.
                                  (T339)

Silver Swan, The
high solo,pno NOVELLO 17.0171.01
s.p.   (T340)
low solo,pno NOVELLO 17.0172.10
s.p.   (T341)

THIMAN, ERIC HARDING (cont'd.)

Song At Evening
2 soli,pno ROBERTON 72683 s.p.
                                  (T342)

Song-Thrush, The
solo,pno (D maj) ROBERTON 2585 s.p.
                                  (T343)

Summer Breeze
3 soli,pno ROBERTON 72546 s.p.
                                  (T344)

Thou Wilt Keep Him *sac
high solo,pno BELWIN $1.50   (T345)
low solo,pno BELWIN $1.50   (T346)

Wee Road From Cushendall, The
2 soli,pno ROBERTON 72465 s.p.
                                  (T347)

Winter Nativity
3 soli,pno ROBERTON 72682 s.p.
                                  (T348)

THINE see Hemery, Valentine

THINE ALONE
2 soli,pno WARNER VD2008 $1.50   (T349)

THINE OWN HEART MAKES THE WORLD see
Clarke, Henry Leland

THING CALLED LOVE, A see Hubbard

THINGS ARE NOT THE SAME see Croft,
Colbert

THINGS SO DEAR TO MY HEART see Desmond,
Charles

THINK see Smith, Alfred B.

THINK NO MORE, LAD see Baksa, Robert

THINK OF THE GOODNESS OF GOD see
Hubbard, H.

THINK ON ME see Scott, Lady John

THINK ON THESE THINGS see Kirlin, June
C.

THINK ON THESE THINGS see MacGimsey,
Robert

THINK ON THESE THINGS see Miller

THIRD BOOK OF AYRES (C1617) see
Campian, Thomas

THIRD BOOK OF SONGS see Dowland, John

THIRD MORNING STAR CHOIR BOOK, A *sac,
CC16L
(Thomas, Paul) solo,pno CONCORDIA
97-4972 $2.00, ipa contains works
by: Bach; Dvorak; Nystedt; Schein
and others   (T350)

THIRIET, A.
Delice Du Vivant
solo,pno DURAND s.p.   (T351)

THIRTEEN SHORT GREEK SONGS, BOOK II see
Riadis, Emile

THIRTEEN SONGS see Ives, Charles

THIRTEEN SONGS see Duparc, Henri

THIRTEEN SONGS see Heseltine, Philip

THIRTEEN WAYS see Glanville-Hicks,
Peggy

THIRTEEN WAYS OF LOOKING AT A BLACKBIRD
see Blacher, Boris

THIRTY ARIAS FOR A FEMALE VOICE see
Handel, George Frideric

THIRTY CHANSONS FOR THREE AND FOUR
VOICES FROM ATTAINGNANT'S
COLLECTIONS *CC30U,16th cent
(Seay, Albert) A-R ED $8.95   (T352)

THIRTY-FIVE CANZONETTAS AND SONGS see
Haydn, (Franz) Joseph

THIRTY-FOUR DUETS see Schumann, Robert
(Alexander)

THIRTY-FOUR SONGS see Ives, Charles

THIRTY ITALIAN SONGS OF THE SEVENTEENTH
AND EIGHTEENTH CENTURIES, VOLUME II
*CC15L
(Dallapiccola, Luigi) [It] INTERNAT.
high solo,pno $3.00; med solo,pno
$3.00; low solo,pno $3.00 contains
works by: Caccini; Scarlatti;
Frescobaldi; Monteverdi and others
                                  (T353)
THIRTY ITALIAN SONGS OF THE SEVENTEENTH
AND EIGHTEENTH CENTURIES, VOLUME I
*CC15L
(Dallapiccola, Luigi) INTERNAT. high
solo,pno $3.00; med solo,pno $3.00;
low solo,pno $3.00 contains works

by: Monteverdi; Scarlatti;
Falconieri; Giordani and others
(T354)

THIRTY NEGRO SPIRITUALS *sac,CC30L,
folk/spir
(Johnson, Hall) solo,pno SCHIRM.G
$3.00   (T355)

THIRTY PIECES OF SILVER *sac,gospel
solo,pno ABER.GRP. $1.50   (T356)

THIRTY PIECES OF SILVER see Stanphill,
Ira F.

THIRTY SELECTED SONGS see Beethoven,
Ludwig van

THIRTY SONGS see Faure, Gabriel-Urbain

THIRTY SONGS see Strauss, Richard

THIRTY SONGS see Debussy, Claude

THIS COULD BE THE DAWNING OF THAT DAY
see Gaither

THIS DAY IS MINE see McCoy, Hobart

THIS DAY IS MINE see Ware

THIS DAY IS YOURS see Gollohan

THIS ENGLAND see Ewing, Porteous

THIS FAIRY COUNTRY see Veitch, William

THIS FROG HE WOULD A-WOOING RIDE see
Flagello, Nicholas

THIS GREAT LOVE OF JESUS *sac
(Taylor) solo,pno LILLENAS SM-940: SN
$1.00   (T357)

THIS IS GOD'S LOVE see O'Hara, Geoffrey

THIS IS JUST WHAT HEAVEN MEANS TO ME
*sac
(Mercer) solo,pno BENSON S8159-S
$1.00   (T358)

THIS IS JUST WHAT I'VE BEEN LOOKING FOR
see Johnson, P.

THIS IS MY PRAYER see Buck, Vera

THIS IS NO' MY PLAID *folk,Scot
solo,pno (G min) PATERSON FS86 s.p.
(T359)

THIS IS NO MY PLAID see Lawson, Malcolm

THIS IS OUR LAND see Zot Artzenu

THIS IS THE SHAPE OF THE LEAF see
Nordoff, Paul

THIS IS THE STORY OF JESUS see O'Hara,
Geoffrey

THIS IS THE TRUTH SENT FROM ABOVE see
Cugley, Ian

THIS LITTLE LIGHT O MINE see Work, John
[Wesley]

THIS LOCK OF DEAR SELINA'S HAIR see
Shield, William

THIS MODERN RELIGION *sac,gospel
solo,pno ABER.GRP. $1.50   (T360)

THIS QUIET HOUR *sac,CCUL,Marriage
solo,pno WORD 37688 $2.50 contains
works by: Matthews, Randy; Clark,
Lynn; Billman, Mark; Medema, Ken
and others   (T361)

THIS QUIET NIGHT see Wood

THIS SAME JESUS see Lillenas, Haldor

THIS SON SO YOUNG see White, Louie L.

THIS WAS ALMOST MINE see Wetherington

THIS WORLD IS NOT MY HOME *sac,gospel
solo,pno ABER.GRP. $1.50   (T362)

THIS WORLD IS NOT MY HOME see Diamond,
David

THIS WORLD OUTSIDE see Walvoord, John

THIS WORLDES JOIE *sac
(Bennett, Richard Rodney) S solo,pno
BELWIN $1.50   (T363)

THO' CLOUDS BY TEMPESTS see Weber, Carl
Maria von

THOMAS, A.
Cape Ann
high solo,pno PRESSER $.75   (T364)

New Hampshire
high solo,pno PRESSER $.75   (T365)

THOMAS, A. (cont'd.)

Rannoch, By Glencoe
high solo,pno PRESSER $.75   (T366)

Usk
high solo,pno PRESSER $.75   (T367)

Virginia
high solo,pno PRESSER $.75   (T368)

THOMAS, A. GORE
see THOMAS, ARTHUR GORING

THOMAS, AMBROISE (1811-1896)
Addio, Mignon, Fa Core! (from Mignon)
[Fr] T solo,pno HEUGEL 4307 B s.p.
(T369)
[It] T solo,pno HEUGEL 4307 s.p.
(T370)
Ah! Non Credevi Tu! (from Mignon)
[Fr] T solo,pno HEUGEL 4311 B s.p.
(T371)
Ai Vostri Giuochi Anch'io Prender
Parte Vorrei (from Amleto)
[Fr] S solo,pno HEUGEL 4318 BIS
s.p.   (T372)
Come Un Romito Fior (from Amleto)
[Fr] Bar solo,pno HEUGEL 4324 BIS
s.p.   (T373)
Connais-Tu Le Pays (from Mignon)
"Dost Thou Know That Fair Land?"
[Eng/Fr] low solo,pno PRESSER
$.75   (T374)
"Kanner Du Val Det Land" solo,pno
LUNDQUIST s.p.   (T375)
"Know'st Thou Not That Fair Land?"
[Fr/It/Eng] A solo,pno (C maj)
SCHIRM.G $.85   (T376)
"Know'st Thou Not That Fair Land?"
[Fr/It/Eng] Mez solo,pno (D flat
maj) SCHIRM.G $.85   (T377)
Dost Thou Know That Fair Land? *see
Connais-Tu Le Pays

Io Son Titania La Bionda *see Je
Suis Titania

Je Suis Titania (from Mignon)
"Io Son Titania La Bionda" [Fr] S
solo,pno HEUGEL 4308 B s.p.
(T378)
"Io Son Titania La Bionda" [It] S
solo,pno HEUGEL 4308 s.p.   (T379)
Kanner Du Val Det Land *see Connais-
Tu Le Pays

Know'st Thou Not That Fair Land?
*see Connais Tu Le Pays?

La Sua Man Non Ancor Oggi La Mia
Tocco (from Amleto)
[Fr] S solo,pno HEUGEL 4322 s.p.
(T380)
Me Voici Dans Son Boudoir (from
Mignon)
[Fr/It/Eng] Mez solo,pno (E flat
maj) SCHIRM.G $.60   (T381)
Non Conosci Il Bel Suol (from Mignon)
[It] Mez solo,pno HEUGEL 4303 s.p.
(T382)
[It] S solo,pno RICORDI-ARG BA 6282
s.p.   (T383)
[Fr] T solo,pno HEUGEL 4303 B s.p.
(T384)
O Vin Discaccia La Tristezza (from
Amleto)
[Fr] Bar solo,pno HEUGEL 4323 BIS
s.p.   (T385)
Perche Lo Sguardo Volgi Al Suol (from
Amleto)
[Fr] S/Bar solo,pno HEUGEL 4316 BIS
s.p.   (T386)

THOMAS, ARTHUR GORING (1850-1892)
Doubting Or Dreaming
solo,pno CRAMER   (T387)

Les Papillons
solo,pno CRAMER   (T388)

'Neath The Stars *see Sous Les
Etoiles

River Dream, A
low solo,pno (D maj) CRAMER   (T389)
high solo,pno (F maj) CRAMER   (T390)

Si J'Etais Roi
"Were I A King" high solo,pno (A
maj) CRAMER   (T391)
"Were I A King" low solo,pno (F
maj) CRAMER   (T392)

Song Of Sunshine
low solo,pno (C maj) CRAMER   (T393)
high solo,pno (E flat maj) CRAMER (T394)

THOMAS, ARTHUR GORING (cont'd.)

Sous Les Etoiles
2 soli,pno CRAMER   (T395)
"'Neath The Stars" [Fr/Eng] ST
soli,pno SCHIRM.G $.75   (T396)

Summer Night, A *see Une Nuit De Mai

Summer Nights *see Une Nuit De Mai

Sunset
2 soli,pno CRAMER   (T397)

Time's Garden
low solo,pno (F maj) CRAMER   (T398)
med solo,pno (G flat maj) CRAMER
(T399)
high solo,pno (A flat maj) CRAMER
(T400)

Twelve Lyrics *CC12U
solo,pno CRAMER   (T401)

Twelve New Lyrics *CC12U
solo,pno CRAMER   (T402)

Under Thy Window
low solo,pno (F maj) CRAMER   (T403)
high solo,pno (A flat maj) CRAMER
(T404)

Une Nuit De Mai
"Summer Night, A" low solo,pno (C
maj) CRAMER   (T405)
"Summer Night, A" med solo,pno (D
flat maj) CRAMER   (T406)
"Summer Night, A" high solo,pno (D
maj) CRAMER   (T407)
"Summer Night, A" 2 soli,pno (C
maj) CRAMER   (T408)
"Summer Night, A" 2 soli,pno (D
flat maj) CRAMER   (T409)
"Summer Nights" low solo,pno (C
maj) ALLANS s.p.   (T410)
"Summer Nights" high solo,pno (D
flat maj) ALLANS s.p.   (T411)

Viking's Daughter, The
high solo,pno (A min) CRAMER (T412)
low solo,pno (F min) CRAMER (T413)

Voices Of Spring
low solo,pno (C maj) CRAMER   (T414)
high solo,pno (F maj) CRAMER   (T415)

Were I A King *see Si J'Etais Roi

Willow, The
low solo,pno (F maj) CRAMER   (T416)
high solo,pno (A maj) CRAMER   (T417)

THOMAS, ED
Bells Of Christmas, The *sac
solo,pno WORD S-59   (T418)

THOMAS, F.W.G.
Seasons
solo,pno CRAMER   (T419)

Three Aspects
solo,pno CRAMER   (T420)

THOMAS, HENRY
Love And Arithmetic
med solo,pno FITZSIMONS $.50 (T421)

THOMAS, J.M.
Cuarto Canciones Populares
Mallorquinas *CC4U
[Span] med solo,gtr UNION ESP.
$1.00   (T422)

THOMAS, KURT (1904-1973)
Ablauf Der Zeit *Op.41,No.2
see Drei Abendlieder Nach Worten
Von Wolfram Brockmeier

Anruf
see Funf Lieder Nach Gedichten Aus
Wolfram Brockmeier

Drei Abendlieder Nach Worten Von
Wolfram Brockmeier
[Ger] solo,pno BREITKOPF-W EB 5714
s.p.
contains: Ablauf Der Zeit, Op.41,
No.2; Kurzer Tag, Op.41,No.1;
Winterlicher Mond, Op.41,No.3
(T423)
Flamme Bei Nacht
see Funf Lieder Nach Gedichten Aus
Wolfram Brockmeier

Friedliche Nacht
see Funf Lieder Nach Gedichten Aus
Wolfram Brockmeier

Funf Lieder Nach Gedichten Aus
Wolfram Brockmeier
A solo,kbd/strings sc,voc sc
BREITKOPF-W EB 6981, EB 5538A
s.p.
contains: Anruf; Flamme Bei
Nacht; Friedliche Nacht;
Glucklicher Tag; Spatsommer
(T424)

THOMAS, KURT (cont'd.)

Glucklicher Tag
   see Funf Lieder Nach Gedichten Aus
   Wolfram Brockmeier

Kurzer Tag *Op.41,No.1
   see Drei Abendlieder Nach Worten
   Von Wolfram Brockmeier

Spatsommer
   see Funf Lieder Nach Gedichten Aus
   Wolfram Brockmeier

Winterlicher Mond *Op.41,No.3
   see Drei Abendlieder Nach Worten
   Von Wolfram Brockmeier

THOMAS LUDOVICI VICTORIA ABULENSIS
OPERA OMNIA (COMPLETE WORKS) see
   Victoria, Tomas Luis de

THOMAS, M.

Buds In Spring
   solo,pno (D flat maj) BOOSEY $1.50
                                   (T425)

THOMASS, EUGEN C. (1927-   )

Klingsor-Lieder *CCU
   Bar solo,pno MODERN s.p.   (T426)

Morgue
   B solo,pno,perc MODERN rental
                                   (T427)

THOME, FRANCIS (1850-1909)

L'iebesgestandnis *see Simple Aveu

Simple Aveu
   [Fr] solo,acap oct DURAND s.p.
                                   (T428)
   "Liebesgestandnis" [Ger/Fr/Eng]
      Mez/Bar solo,pno/vln/vcl DURAND
      s.p.   (T429)
   "Liebesgestandnis" [Ger/Fr/Eng] S/T
      solo,pno/vln/vcl DURAND s.p.
                                   (T430)

Sous La Feuillee
   [Fr] solo,acap oct DURAND s.p.
                                   (T431)
   Mez/Bar solo,pno/inst DURAND s.p.
                                   (T432)

THOMPSON

Sing Little Bird
   solo,pno ALLANS s.p.   (T433)

Sjung Mig En Sang
   solo,pno LUNDQUIST s.p.   (T434)

THOMPSON, A.

Night
   solo,pno BERANDOL BER 1336 $1.50
                                   (T435)

Oxen, The *sac
   solo,pno BERANDOL BER 1292 $1.50
                                   (T436)

Prayer For Easter Day *sac
   solo,pno BERANDOL BER 1293 $1.50
                                   (T437)

Reverie Of A Soldier
   solo,pno BERANDOL BER 1337 $1.50
                                   (T438)

Where He Sleeps
   solo,pno BERANDOL BER 1338 $1.50
                                   (T439)

THOMPSON, ANN HARDING

Julian's Garden *CCU
   solo,pno CRAMER   (T440)

THOMPSON, DAVID CLEGHORN

Epitaph
   solo,pno CRAMER   (T441)

Knight Of Bethlehem, The *sac
   med solo,pno NOVELLO s.p.   (T442)
   high solo,pno NOVELLO s.p.   (T443)

THOMPSON, GORDON V.

Have Faith In God *sac
   solo,pno THOMP.G   (T444)

THOMPSON, JACK

Come Sing To Me
   low solo,orch (D maj) ASHDOWN
      $1.50, ipr   (T445)
   high solo&med solo,pno ASHDOWN s.p.
                                   (T446)
   med solo&low solo,pno ASHDOWN s.p.
                                   (T447)
   high solo,orch (G maj) ASHDOWN
      $1.50, ipr   (T448)
   med-high solo,orch (F maj) ASHDOWN
      $1.50, ipr   (T449)
   med solo,orch (E flat maj) ASHDOWN
      $1.50, ipr   (T450)

Emblem, An
   low solo,orch (B flat maj) ASHDOWN
      s.p., ipr   (T451)
   med-high solo,orch (D maj) ASHDOWN
      s.p., ipr   (T452)
   med solo,orch (C maj) ASHDOWN s.p.,
      ipr   (T453)
   high solo,orch (E flat maj) ASHDOWN
      s.p., ipr   (T454)

THOMPSON, JACK (cont'd.)

I'll Sing To You
   low solo,orch (C maj) ASHDOWN s.p.,
      ipr   (T455)
   high solo,orch (F maj) ASHDOWN
      s.p., ipr   (T456)
   med solo,orch (E flat maj) ASHDOWN
      s.p., ipr   (T457)

Nightingale And The Rose, The
   med solo,orch (F maj) ASHDOWN s.p.,
      ipr   (T458)
   low solo,orch (E flat maj) ASHDOWN
      s.p., ipr   (T459)
   high solo,orch (G maj) ASHDOWN
      s.p., ipr   (T460)

THOMPSON, RANDALL (1899-   )

Lullaby *sac,Xmas,Bibl
   S solo,opt SATB,pno SCHIRM.EC 125
      s.p.   (T461)

My Master Hath A Garden *sac
   med solo,pno SCHIRM.EC 113 s.p.
                                   (T462)

My Soul Doth Magnify The Lord *sac,
   Xmas,Bibl
   S solo,opt SATB,pno SCHIRM.EC 124
      s.p.   (T463)

Passenger, The
   Bar solo,pno SCHIRM.EC 119 s.p.
                                   (T464)

Velvet Shoes
   med solo,pno SCHIRM.EC 114 s.p.
                                   (T465)

THOMPSON, S.

Few Words About Jesus, A *see Haney,
   J.

THOMSON, VIRGIL (1896-   )

Air De Phedre
   S solo,pno PEER $2.50   (T466)

At The Spring
   med solo,pno BELWIN $1.50   (T467)

Before Sleeping *sac
   med solo,pno (F maj) SCHIRM.G $.85
      see from Praises And Prayers
                                   (T468)

Bell Doth Toll, The
   solo,pno PEER $.95   (T469)

Consider, Lord
   solo,pno PEER $.95   (T470)

Dirge
   med solo,pno (D min) SCHIRM.G $.60
                                   (T471)

Down At The Docks
   med-high solo,pno (D maj) SCHIRM.G
      $.75 see from Mostly About Love
                                   (T472)

English Usage
   med-high solo,pno SCHIRM.G $.75 see
      from Two By Marianne Moore (T473)

Five Songs From William Blake *CC5U
   solo,orch/pno PEER sc rental, voc
      sc $4.00   (T474)

Four Songs To The Poems Of Thomas
   Campion *CC4U
   Mez solo,clar&vla&harp/pno PEER voc
      sc $5.00, sc $10.00   (T475)

From The Canticle Of The Sun *sac
   med solo,pno (E maj) SCHIRM.G $.75
      see from Praises And Prayers
                                   (T476)

Hot Day At The Seashore, A *see Jour
   De Chaleur Aux Bains De Mer

If Thou A Reason Dost Desire To Know
   solo,pno PEER $.95   (T477)

Jerusalem, My Happy Home *sac
   med solo,pno (D maj) SCHIRM.G $.85
      see from Praises And Prayers
                                   (T478)

John Peel
   Bar solo,pno PEER $1.00   (T479)

Jour De Chaleur Aux Bains De Mer
   "Hot Day At The Seashore, A" solo,
      pno (C maj) BOOSEY $1.50   (T480)

La Belle En Dormant
   "Sleeping Beauty, The" [Fr/Eng] med
      solo,pno BOOSEY $2.50   (T481)

La Singe Et Le Leopard
   med solo,pno PEER $3.00   (T482)

Let's Take A Walk
   med-high solo,pno (F maj) SCHIRM.G
      $.75 see from Mostly About Love
                                   (T483)

Look How The Floor Of Heaven
   high solo,pno BELWIN $1.50   (T484)

Love Song
   med-high solo,pno (C maj) SCHIRM.G
      $.75 see from Mostly About Love

THOMSON, VIRGIL (cont'd.)

                                   (T485)
Mass For Solo Voice (Or Unison Choir)
   *sac
   med solo,pno SCHIRM.G $.60   (T486)

Mostly About Love *see Down At The
   Docks; Let's Take A Walk; Love
   Song; Prayer To Saint Catherine,
   A   (T487)

My Crow Pluto
   med-high solo,pno SCHIRM.G $.75 see
      from Two By Marianne Moore (T488)

My Master Hath A Garden *sac
   med solo,pno (E flat maj) SCHIRM.G
      $.85 see from Praises And Prayers
                                   (T489)

Pardon, Goddess Of The Night
   solo,pno PEER see from Shakespeare
      Songs   (T490)

Portrait Of F. B.
   high solo,pno (D maj) SCHIRM.G
      $1.25   (T491)

Praises And Prayers *see Before
   Sleeping; From The Canticle Of
   The Sun; Jerusalem; My Master
   Hath A Garden; My Happy
   Home; My Master Hath A Garden;
   Sung By The Shepherds   (T492)

Prayer To Saint Catherine, A
   med-high solo,pno (E flat maj)
      SCHIRM.G $.75 see from Mostly
      About Love   (T493)

Preciosilla
   high solo,pno SCHIRM.G $.75   (T494)

Remember Adam's Fall *sac
   med solo/low solo,pno BELWIN $1.50
                                   (T495)
   high solo,pno BELWIN $1.50   (T496)

Shakespeare Songs *see Pardon,
   Goddess Of The Night; Sigh No
   More, Ladies; Take, O Take Those
   Lips Away; Tell Me Where Is Fancy
   Bred; Was This Fair Face The
   Cause?   (T497)

Shipwreck And Love Scene
   T solo,orch PEER rental   (T498)

Sigh No More, Ladies
   solo,pno PEER $.95 see from
      Shakespeare Songs   (T499)

Sleeping Beauty, The *see La Belle
   En Dormant

Stabat Mater *sac
   [Fr/Eng] S solo,4strings BOOSEY
      $1.75, ipa   (T500)

Sung By The Shepherds *sac
   med-high solo,pno SCHIRM.G $.75 see
      from Praises And Prayers   (T501)

Take, O Take Those Lips Away
   solo,pno PEER $.95 see from
      Shakespeare Songs   (T502)

Tell Me Where Is Fancy Bred
   solo,pno PEER $.95 see from
      Shakespeare Songs   (T503)

Tiger, The
   med solo,pno SCHIRM.G $.75   (T504)

Tres Estampas De Ninez *CC3U
   [Span/Eng] solo,pno PEER $1.50
                                   (T505)

Two By Marianne Moore *see English
   Usage; My Crow Pluto   (T506)

Was This Fair Face The Cause?
   solo,pno PEER $.95 see from
      Shakespeare Songs   (T507)

THORA see Adams, Stephen

THORDARSON, SIGURDUR (1895-1969)

Cradle Song *Op.4,No.3
   see Five Songs

Days Pass On, The *Op.4,No.1
   see Five Songs

Elegy *Op.4,No.5
   see Five Songs

Five Songs
   solo,pno ICELAND s.p.
      contains: Cradle Song, Op.4,No.3;
      Days Pass On, The, Op.4,No.1;
      Elegy, Op.4,No.5; Mother, Op.4,
      No.2; My Little Sister, Op.4,
      No.4   (T508)

Mother *Op.4,No.2
   see Five Songs

THORDARSON, SIGURDUR (cont'd.)

My Little Sister   *Op.4,No.4
see Five Songs

Seven Songs   *CC7L
solo,pno ICELAND s.p.   (T509)

Ten Songs From The Operetta
"Bewitched"   *CC10U
solo,pno ICELAND s.p.   (T510)

Three Songs   *Op.1, CC3U
solo,pno ICELAND s.p.   (T511)

THORN see Shield, William

THORNE, FRANCIS (1922-   )
Magnificat
solo,pno GENERAL 693   (T512)

Nocturnes For Voice And Piano   *CCU
solo,pno GENERAL 688 $3.50   (T513)

Nunc Dimittis   *sac
solo,pno GENERAL 692   (T514)

Prepare Ye The Way Of The Lord   *sac
solo,pno GENERAL 691 s.p.   (T515)

Songs Of The Great South Bay   *CCU
S solo,pno,2triangle sc AM.COMP.AL.
$6.60   (T516)

THORNEHILL, BRUCE
What A Wonderful Time Up There   *sac
solo,pno WORD S-455   (T517)

THORP
O Men From The Fields
solo,pno SHAWNEE IA 8 $.60   (T518)

THOSE DANCING DAYS ARE GONE see Aston,
Peter G.

THOSE DANCING DAYS ARE GONE see
Watkins, Michael Blake

THOSE GREEN TRESSES OF SADNESS see
Chalayev, S.

THOSE LITTLE HANDS see Webb, Milton

THOU ARE REPOSE see Schubert, Franz
(Peter), Du Bist Die Ruh'

THOU ART LIKE A FLOWER see Rubinstein,
Anton

THOU ART LIKE A TENDER FLOWER see
Schumann, Robert (Alexander), Du
Bist Wie Eine Blume

THOU ART MY JOY see Bach, Johann
Sebastian, Bist Du Bei Mir

THOU ART MY STRENGTH see Sowerby, Leo

THOU ART SO LIKE A FLOWER see Schumann,
Robert (Alexander), Du Bist Wie
Eine Blume

THOU ART THE CREATOR see Chajes,
Julius, Atoh Hu Yotzrom

THOU CHILD SO WISE see Persichetti,
Vincent

THOU DIDST BLOW WITH THE WIND see
Handel, George Frideric

THOU HAST LEFT ME EVER, JAMIE   *folk,
Scot
solo,pno (D maj/F maj) PATERSON FS113
s.p.   (T519)

THOU LIGHT OF LIFE see Noe, J.T.

THOU MADEST MAN BUT LOWER THAN THE
ANGELS see Marcello, Benedetto

THOU, O LORD, ART MY SHEPHERD see
Marcello, Benedetto

THOU REMAINEST see Zilch, Margot

THOU SHALT BRING THEM IN see Handel,
George Frideric

THOU VISITEST THE EARTH see Greene,
Maurice

THOU, WHO HAST LOVED THE LITTLE CHILD
see Baumgartner, H. Leroy

THOU WILT KEEP HIM see Thiman, Eric
Harding

THOU WILT KEEP HIM see Wesley

THOU WILT KEEP HIM IN PERFECT PEACE see
Speaks, Oley

THOU WILT LIGHT MY CANDLE see Blair, K.

THOU WILT LIGHT MY CANDLE see Youse,
Glad Robinson

THOU WILT NOT GO AND LEAVE ME HERE see
Somervell, Arthur

THOUGH I TAKE THE WINGS see Beach, Mrs.
H.H.A.

THOUGH I'M MY FATHER'S ONLY CHILD
see Three Songs Of Old Quebec

THOUGH MEN CALL US FREE see Davis

THOUGH UNWORTHY AM I see Lister, Mosie

THOUGH WICKED MEN see Bach, Johann
Sebastian

THOUGH WITH THE TONGUES OF MEN AND HOLY
ANGELS see Brahms, Johannes, Wenn
Ich Mit Menschen-Und Mit
Engelszungen

THOUGH YOUR LOVE IS GONE see Puccini,
Giacomo, O Mimi, Tu Piu Non Torni

THOUGHT AND PAEAN, A see Saminsky,
Lazare

THOUGHTS see Fisher, Howard

THOUGHTS ABOUT GRASSHOPPERS see Weigl,
Vally

THOUGHTS IN THE NIGHT see Rappaport,
Eda, Harhorey Laila

THOU'RT LIKE UNTO A FLOWER see
Schumann, Robert (Alexander)

THOUSAND TIMES, A   *sac,gospel
solo,pno ABER.GRP. $1.50   (T520)

THREE ACHTERBERG-SONGS see Broekman,
Hans

THREE ADY SONGS see Hajdu, Mihaly

THREE AIRS FOR FRANK O'HARA'S ANGEL see
Foss, Lukas

THREE APOCRYPHA see Mihaly, Andras

THREE ASPECTS see Parry, Charles Hubert
Hastings

THREE ASPECTS see Thomas, F.W.G.

THREE BIBLICAL SONGS see Piket,
Frederick

THREE BIBLICAL SONGS see Mader,
Clarence

THREE BIRD SONGS see Blyton, Carey

THREE BLIND SISTERS, THE see Sibelius,
Jean

THREE BOHEMIAN SONGS   *folk
(Tate, Phyllis) solo,pno OXFORD
55.173 $.70
contains: I Had A Darling Dove;
Lonely Farm On The Hill, The; Up
The River, Down The River   (T521)

THREE BOURGEOIS SONGS see Cardew,
Cornelius

THREE CANDLELIGHT SONGS see Sharpe,
Evelyn

THREE CANZONETS FOR BARITONE see
Lewkovitch, Bernhard

THREE CAVATINAS see Hawkins, J.

THREE CONTEMPORARIES see Schafer, M.

THREE DIALOGUES FROM "THE GARDENER" see
Schouwman, Hans

THREE DIVINE HYMNS see Purcell, Henry

THREE DREAMS EACH WITHIN EACH see
Sallinen, Aulis

THREE DUETS see Brahms, Johannes

THREE EICHENDORFF SONGS see Erbse,
Heimo

THREE ELEGAIC AIRS see Kohs, Ellis B.

THREE ELEGIES see Gretchaninov,
Alexander Tikhonovitch

THREE ELIZABETHAN SONGS see Bush,
Geoffrey

THREE ENGLISH SONGS see Rathaus, Karol

THREE EPITAPHS see Presser, William

THREE EULAU SONGS see Farkas, Ferenc

THREE FINE SHIPS see Dunhill, Thomas
Frederick

THREE FOLK SONGS see Mc Cabe, John

THREE FOLK SONGS see Zonn, Paul

THREE FOLK SONGS   *CC3U,folk
(Koebler) [Slav] solo,pno CROATICA
s.p.   (T522)

THREE FOOD SONGS see Blyton, Carey

THREE FRENCH SONGS see Gerber, Steven

THREE GEORGIAN SONGS see Holloway,
Robin

THREE GERMAN FOLK SONGS see Butterworth

THREE GOETHE SONGS see Simon

THREE GOTHIC BALLADS see Duke, John
Woods

THREE GREEK SONGS see Berkeley, Lennox

THREE GUILLEVIC SONGS see Farkas,
Ferenc

THREE HOKKU see Howe, Mary

THREE HOLY KINGS, THE see Strauss,
Richard, Die Heiligen Drei Konige

THREE HOPKINS SONGS see Edwards, George

THREE HUSBANDS see Chanler, Theodore
Ward

THREE HYMNS BY FRIEDRICH HOLDERLIN see
Strauss, Richard

THREE HYMNS OF THE CHURCH see
Charpentier, Marc-Antoine

THREE IBSEN SONGS see Delius, Frederick

THREE IDYLLS see Bantock, Granville

THREE INSECT SONGS see Blyton, Carey

THREE INVOCATIONS see Rudhyar, Dane

THREE IRISH AIRS see Dalway

THREE IRISH FOLK SONGS
(Dawn, Muriel; Dawn, Douglas) solo,
pno NOVELLO 17.0239.04 s.p.
contains: Good Roarin' Fire, A;
Lark In The Clear Air, The;
There's Nae A Thrush   (T523)

THREE ITALIAN SONGS see Brumby, Colin

THREE JAPANESE FOLKSONGS see Stevens,
Halsey

THREE JOLLY HUNTSMEN see Teed, Roy

THREE JOLLY LIGHTBOBS see Trotere,
Henry

THREE KINGS OF SOMERSET see Redman,
Reginald

THREE LEAVES OF GRASS see Segerstam,
Leif

THREE LITTLE BIRDS see Clarke, Emile

THREE LOVE LETTERS see Argentson, R.

THREE LOVE LYRICS see Parris, Robert

THREE LOVE SONGS see Haubiel, Charles

THREE LOVE SONGS see Finney, Ross Lee

THREE LOVE SONGS see Strauss, Richard

THREE LOVE SONGS see Stearns, Peter
Pindar

THREE LOVELY THINGS THERE BE see
Buxtehude, Dietrich

THREE LUCEBERT SONGS see Voorn, Joop

THREE LYRIC POEMS see Murai, Tsuguji

THREE LYRIC SONGS see Holford, Franz

THREE LYRICS see Maganini, Quinto

THREE MINIATURES see Kasemets, U.

THREE MINIATURN see Weiner, Lazar

THREE MOODS see Haussermann, R.

THREE MOODS see Davis

THREE MOON SONGS see Hay, G.

THREE MORAVIAN CAROLS *sac,carol/folk
(Tate, Phyllis) solo,pno OXFORD
45.064 $.50
    contains: Andrew Mine, Jasper Mine;
    By The Wayside; Long Ago In
    Bethlehem   (T524)

THREE MORE SONGS OF THE FAIR see
Martin, Easthope

THREE MORIKE SONGS see Erbse, Heimo

THREE MUMMERS see Head, Michael (Dewar)

THREE MYSTICAL SONGS see Rowley, Alec

THREE NAILS, THE see Harrah

THREE NATURE SONGS see Haubiel, Charles

THREE NEW ENGLAND LYRICS see Manton,
Robert William

THREE NORTHERN COUNTY FOLK SONGS see
Johnston, Lyell

THREE ODES OF SOLOMON see Hovhaness,
Alan

THREE OF EDWARD LEAR'S NONSENSE SONGS
see Hely-Hutchinson, (Christian)
Victor

THREE OLD DUTCH SONGS see Badings, Henk

THREE OLD SONGS RESUNG see Abramson,
Robert

THREE OTHER SONGS see Satie, Erik

THREE PACIFIST SONGS see Smith, Leland

THREE PALESTINE POEMS see Fromm,
Herbert

THREE-PART SONGS see Haydn, (Franz)
Joseph

THREE PHILOSPHICAL SONGS see Haubiel,
Charles

THREE POEMS see Vinter, Gilbert

THREE POEMS BI LI-PO see Lambert,
Constant

THREE POEMS BIJ H.W. LONGFELLOW see
King, Harold C.

THREE POEMS BY G. TABIDZE see
Diakvnishvili, M.

THREE POEMS BY HAMILTON WILLIAMS see
Franco, Johan

THREE POEMS BY RILKE see Chance, Nancy

THREE POEMS BY S. GORODETSKY see
Golubev, E.

THREE POEMS FOR TENOR see Borris,
Siegfried

THREE POEMS FOR VOICE AND TWO
PERCUSSIONISTS see Steiner, Gitta

THREE POEMS OF BEN JONSON see Bunge,
Sas

THREE POEMS OF CLAUDEL see Honegger,
Arthur

THREE POEMS OF DEMETRIOS CAPETANAKIS
see Rorem, Ned

THREE POEMS OF EZRA POUND see Gerber,
Steven

THREE POEMS OF GIL VICENTE see Nin-
Culmell, Joaquin

THREE POEMS OF HOLLY BEYE see La
Montaine, John

THREE POEMS OF HOLLY BEYE see Sifler,
Paul J.

THREE POEMS OF JAMES AGEE see
Pasatieri, Thomas

THREE POEMS OF PAUL FORT see Honegger,
Arthur

THREE POEMS OF PAUL GILSON see Rivier,
Jean

THREE POEMS OF PAUL GOODMAN see Rorem,
Ned

THREE POEMS OF ROBERT LIDDELL LOWE see
Elwell, Herbert

THREE POEMS OF WALT WHITMAN
Bar solo,pno (med) OXFORD 60.301
$1.80
    contains: Clear Midnight, A; Joy,
    Shipmate, Joy; Nocturne   (T525)

THREE POEMS OF YEATS see Berger, A.

THREE POPULAR SONGS *see Maitia Nun
Zira, "Adieu Chere Vallee";
Vidalita; Vive Henry IV   (T526)

THREE PSALMS see Honegger, Arthur

THREE PSALMS see Pisk, Paul Amadeus

THREE QUATRAINS OF OMAR KHAYAM see
Staake, P. v.d.

THREE RADNOTI SONGS see Kadosa, [Paul]

THREE RAVENS see Somervell, Arthur

THREE RILKE SONGS see Moss, Lawrence

THREE ROMANTIC SONGS see Andriessen,
Hendrik

THREE RUSSIAN FOLK SONGS see
Rachmaninoff, Sergey Vassilievitch

THREE SACRED CONCERTOS see Distler,
Hugo

THREE SACRED CONCERTOS (ENGLISH
VERSION) see Schutz, Heinrich

THREE SACRED CONCERTOS (GERMAN VERSION)
see Schutz, Heinrich

THREE SACRED SOLOS FOR MEDIUM VOICE see
Wells, Dana F.

THREE SACRED SONGS see Kingsley,
Gershon

THREE SACRED SONGS see Stearns, Peter
Pindar

THREE SACRED SONGS FOR SOPRANO *sac,
CC3U
(Johnson; McCorkle) S solo,pno BOOSEY
$1.50   (T527)

THREE SALT WATER BALLADS see Keel,
Frederick

THREE SATIRES see Kagen, Sergius

THREE SECULAR CANTATAS see Verdi,
Giuseppe

THREE SECULAR SONGS see Alette, C.

THREE SEPHARDIC SONGS see Castelnuovo-
Tedesco, Mario

THREE SEVENTEENTH CENTURY LYRICS see
Finney, Ross Lee

THREE SHAKESPEARE SONGS see Hively,
Wells

THREE SHAKESPEARE SONGS see Quilter,
Roger

THREE SHAKESPEARE SONGS see Williamson,
Malcolm

THREE SHAKESPEARE SONNETS see
Horusitzky, Z.

THREE SISTERS see Le Fleming,
Christopher (Kaye)

THREE SLOVAK SONGS *folk,Slav
(Tate, Phyllis) solo,pno OXFORD
55.172 $.50
    contains: Cuckoo, The; Janko,
    Janko, Better Beware!; Through
    Our Town The Danube Flows (T528)

THREE SONGS see Schafmeister

THREE SONGS see Smith, Melville

THREE SONGS see Panetti, Joan

THREE SONGS see Hoag, Charles K.

THREE SONGS see Jacobi, Frederick

THREE SONGS see Johansson, Bengt

THREE SONGS see Falla, Manuel de

THREE SONGS see Ravel, Maurice

THREE SONGS see Bialas, Gunther

THREE SONGS see Orthel, Leon

THREE SONGS see Knab, Armin

THREE SONGS see Hovhaness, Alan

THREE SONGS see Falla, Manuel de

THREE SONGS see Honegger, Arthur

THREE SONGS see Satie, Erik

THREE SONGS see Martino, Donald

THREE SONGS see Backer-Grondahl, Agathe
Ursula

THREE SONGS see Hartig, Heinz Friedrich

THREE SONGS see Schoenberg, Arnold

THREE SONGS see Ives, Charles

THREE SONGS see Weigl, Karl

THREE SONGS see Simons, Netty

THREE SONGS see Lora, Antonio

THREE SONGS see Weigl, Karl

THREE SONGS see Beale, James

THREE SONGS see Pleskow, Raoul

THREE SONGS see Weigl, Karl

THREE SONGS see Yannatos, James

THREE SONGS see Sims, Ezra

THREE SONGS see Walton, William

THREE SONGS see Jacob

THREE SONGS see Owens, Robert

THREE SONGS see Strauss, Richard

THREE SONGS see Binkerd, Gordon

THREE SONGS see Galindo, Blas

THREE SONGS see Kodaly, Zoltan

THREE SONGS see Lees, Benjamin

THREE SONGS see Strauss, Richard

THREE SONGS see Berkeley, Lennox

THREE SONGS see Goosens, Eugene

THREE SONGS see Hannikainen, Ilmari

THREE SONGS see Valen, Fartein

THREE SONGS see Jersild, Jorgen

THREE SONGS see Horusitzky, Z.

THREE SONGS see Kadosa, [Paul]

THREE SONGS see Szabo, [Ferenc]

THREE SONGS see Szervanszky, Endre

THREE SONGS see Karlins, M. William

THREE SONGS see Stefansson, Fjolnir

THREE SONGS see Thordarson, Sigurdur

THREE SONGS see Stefansson, Fjolnir

THREE SONGS see Backer-Grondahl, Agathe
Ursula

THREE SONGS (1886) see Satie, Erik

THREE SONGS ABOUT LARR see Lessard,
John Ayres

THREE SONGS AFTER EDGAR ALLAN POE see
Rouse, Christopher

THREE SONGS AFTER EMILY DICKINSON see
Sydeman, William

THREE SONGS BY E. DICKINSON see
Leichtling, Alan

THREE SONGS FOR AMERICA see Amram,
David Werner

THREE SONGS FOR HIGH VOICE see Bush,
Geoffrey

THREE SONGS FOR LOW VOICE TO POEMS BY
BERT BRECHT see Steuermann, Edward

THREE SONGS FOR SACRED OCCASIONS see
Lorenz, Ellen Jane

THREE SONGS FOR SOPRANO AND CLARINET
see Bialosky, Marshall

THREE SONGS FOR SOPRANO AND FLUTE see
Turok, Paul

THREE SONGS FOR VOICE AND PIANO see
Steiner, Gitta

THREE SONGS FROM A SHROPSHIRE LAD see
Orr, Charles Wilfred

THREE SONGS FROM ECCLESIASTES see
Pinkham, Daniel

THREE SONGS FROM "FREE NIGHTS" see
Markovic, Adalbert

THREE SONGS FROM MEDEA see Kurtz,
Eugene

THREE SONGS FROM MOTHER GOOSE see
Stevens, Halsey

THREE SONGS FROM OMAR KHAYYAM see
Camilleri, Charles

THREE SONGS FROM SANCTUARY see
Converse, Frederick Shepherd

THREE SONGS FROM "SETTI CANZONI" see
Malipiero, Gian Francesco

THREE SONGS FROM SIXTEENTH AND
SEVENTEENTH CENTURY POEMS see
Karlins, M. William

THREE SONGS FROM THE BALLAD OPERAS see
Bush, Geoffrey

THREE SONGS FROM THE CHINESE see Reale,
Paul

THREE SONGS FROM THE HEBRIDES see Wood,
Joseph

THREE SONGS FROM WILLIAM SHAKESPEARE
see Stravinsky, Igor

THREE SONGS OF ADIEU see Dello Joio,
Norman

THREE SONGS OF CONTEMPLATION see Holt,
P.

THREE SONGS OF ELEGY see Horvit,
Michael M.

THREE SONGS OF INNOCENCE see Cooke,
S.C.

THREE SONGS OF JOCELYN BROOKE see
Searle, Humphrey

THREE SONGS OF OLD QUEBEC *folk
(Tate, Phyllis) solo,pno OXFORD
55.174 $.90
contains: Go To The Market,
Daughter Fair; Shepherd Boy's
Song, The; Though I'm My Father's
Only Child   (T529)

THREE SONGS OF PERSIA see Baynon,
Arthur

THREE SONGS OF THE BIRDS see Mortimer,
C.G.

THREE SONGS OF THE HEATHER see Braun,
Charles

THREE SONGS ON A TEXT BY R.M. RILKE see
Orthel, Leon

THREE SONGS ON BRITISH VERSE see
Voormolen, Alexander Nicolas

THREE SONGS ON ELIZABETHAN TEXTS see
Sydeman, William

THREE SONGS ON LATIN PSALM TEXTS see
Ahrens, Sieglinde

THREE SONGS ON LYRICS BY MICHELANGELO
see Wolf, Hugo

THREE SONGS ON THE POEM BY SHINPEI
KUSANO see Tanaka, H.

THREE SONGS TO JULIA see Dyson, George

THREE SONGS TO POEMS BY ALBERT
EHRISMANN see Dahl, Ingolf

THREE SONGS TO POEMS OF SHELLEY see
Ribari, Antal

THREE SONGS WITHOUT WORDS see Ben-Haim,
Paul

THREE SONNETS see Steinke, Greg

THREE SONNETS see Pfitzner, Hans

THREE SONNETS BY W. SHAKESPEARE see
Ketting, Otto

THREE SONNETS FROM SHAKESPEARE see
Ulehla Ludmila

THREE SONNETS OF DUBELLAY see Woollen,
Russell

THREE SONNETS OF SHAKESPEASRE see
Rautavaara, Einojuhani

THREE SPANISH SONGS see Cortes, Ramiro

THREE SPANISH SONGS see Rodrigo,
Joaquin

THREE SURREALIST SONGS see Taverner,
John

THREE SYMPHONIC CHORALES see Karg-
Elert, Sigfrid

THREE THINGS see Aston, Peter G.

THREE TROUBADOR SONGS see Milhaud,
Darius

THREE VILLAGE SONGS see Egon, Rodrigo

THREE VOCALISES see Vaughan Williams,
Ralph

THREE VROMAN SONGS see Voorn, Joop

THREE WEDDING SOLOS *sac,CC3U,Marriage
(Cassler, G. Winston) $1.60 med solo,
pno AUGSBURG 11-9498; high solo,pno
AUGSBURG 11-9499   (T530)

THREE WEDDING SONGS see Powell, Robert
J.

THREE WHITMAN SONGS see Stout, Alan

THREE WISE MEN OF GOTHAM see Lessard,
John Ayres

THRESHOLD see Goosens, Eugene

THRO' COPSE AND VALE see Johnston,
Lyell

THROSTLE ON THE HAWTHORN see Austin,
Harry

THROUGH AN EMPTY TOMB see Mercer

THROUGH GILDED TRELISES see Walton,
William

THROUGH IT ALL see Crouch, Andrae

THROUGH LOVE see Starks, Howard

THROUGH OUR TOWN THE DANUBE FLOWS
see Three Slovak Songs

THROUGH PEACE TO LIGHT see Buck, Dudley

THROUGH THE EYES OF A BABE see Lora,
Antonio

THROUGH THE IVORY GATE see Parry,
Charles Hubert Hastings

THROUGH THE LOOKING GLASS see Veyvoda,
Gerald

THROUGH THE NIGHT see Wolf, Hugo

THROUGH THE SILVER MIST see Josten,
Werner

THROUGH THE YEARS see Allison

THRU THE EMERALD MEADOWS see
Guastavino, Carlos, Por Los Campos
Verdes

THRUSH, THE see Harrhy, Edith

THRUSH AT DAWN, A see Norman, Lorna

THUNMAN-ERICSON
Vi Ga Over Daggstankta Berg
solo,pno LUNDQUIST s.p.   (T531)

THUS SPAKE JESUS see Head, Michael
(Dewar)

THY BEAMING EYES see MacDowell, Edward
Alexander

THY DARK EYES TO MINE see Griffes,
Charles Tomlinson

THY FACE see Schumann, Robert
(Alexander), Dein Angesicht

THY FINGERS MAKE EARLY FLOWERS see
Dougherty, Celius

THY HAND, BELINDA see Purcell, Henry

THY LOVING KINDNESS see Dungan, Olive

THY MERCY, LORD see Handel, George
Frideric

THY PITY I IMPLORE see Rachmaninoff,
Sergey Vassilievitch

THY PRESENCE LORD see Lock

THY SWEET SINGING see Olmstead,
Clarence

THY VOICE IS NEAR see Wrighton, W.T.

THY WILL BE DONE *sac
(Carmichael, Ralph) solo,pno WORD
S-426   (T532)

THY WILL BE DONE see McCann, Leland

THY WORD IS A LAMP see Bone

THYBO, LEIF
Hymn Of Creation *sac
[Eng] S solo,org EGTVED MF 276 s.p.
sc, min sc   (T533)

O Gloriosa Vergine Maria *sac
[It] Mez solo,vln,org sc EGTVED
MF 251 s.p., ipa   (T534)

On His Blindness
[Eng] Mez solo,org EGTVED MF 261
s.p.   (T535)

THYGERSON, ROBERT J.
All Things Are Possible *sac
med solo,pno RICHMOND MI-113 $.35
                              (T536)

With A Little Bit Of Help *sac
med solo,pno RICHMOND MI-100 $.35
                              (T537)

THYME IN MY GARDEN see Lawson, Malcolm

TI COMPRENDO see Schisa, M.

TI GUARDI IL CIEL see Kalman, Emerich

TI NORSKE BARNERIM see Johansen, David
Monrad

TI-RI-TU see Lagerheim-Romare, Margit

TI SENTO see Wolf, Hugo

TIBICINIUM see Farkas, Ferenc

TICHE MILOVANI see Bedrich, Jan

TICHE SVETLO see Pololanik, Zdenek

TIDE RISES, THE TIDE FALLS, THE see
King, Harold C.

TIDES see Shaw, Martin

TIEDE AZUR see Ibert, Jacques

TIEF IM HAINE see Gretchaninov,
Alexander Tikhonovitch, Il S'est
Tu, Le Charmant Rossignol

TIEFEN see Laitenen, Arvo, Syvyyksia

TIEN GEZELLELIEDEREN see Dijk, Jan van

TIEN JAPANSE IMPRESSIES, BD. I see
Bijvanck, Henk

TIEN JAPANSE IMPRESSIES, BD. II see
Bijvanck, Henk

TIEN KERSTLIEDEREN see Tierie, J.F.

TIEN LIEDEREN OP ZUID-AFRIKAANSE TEKST
see Wijdeveld, Wolfgang

TIEN NIEUWE NEDERLANDSE LIEDEREN see
Kruls, A.

TIEN VIVAT EN GAUDEAMUS IGITUR *CC11U
solo,pno ALSBACH s.p.   (T538)

TIERIE, J.F.
Acht Kerstliederen *Op.52, sac,CC8UL
solo,pno/org ALSBACH s.p.   (T539)

Heerlijk Oud Huis *Op.70,No.1
solo,pno ALSBACH s.p.   (T540)

Het Lied Voor De Christelijke
Feestdagen *Op.69, sac,CC6U
solo,pno ALSBACH s.p.   (T541)

Kersthymne En Oud-Jaar *Op.55
solo,pno/org ALSBACH s.p.   (T542)

Nieuwe Lenteliederen *Op.65, sac,
CCU,Lent
solo,pno ALSBACH s.p.   (T543)

O Rijke Heilige Nacht *Op.43
solo,pno ALSBACH s.p.   (T544)

Tien Kerstliederen *Op.31, sac,
CC10UL
solo,pno/org ALSBACH s.p.   (T545)

TIERLIEDER see Krietsch, Georg

TIERLIEDER see Dressel, Erwin

TIERNAPOJAT *CCU,Xmas
   (Marvia) solo,pno FAZER F 3451 s.p.
                                        (T546)

TIERSOT, (JEAN BAPTISTE ELISEE) JULIEN
   (1857-1936)
   Entre Le Boeuf Et L'Ane Gris *sac
      med solo,pno/org HEUGEL s.p. (T547)

   Noel Alsacien *sac,Xmas
      med solo,pno/org HEUGEL s.p. (T548)

   Noel Provencal II *sac
      med solo,pno/org HEUGEL s.p. (T549)

TIESSEN, HEINZ (1887-   )
   Die Amsel
      S solo,orch RIES s.p.   (T550)

   Sechzehn Fruhe Lieder *CC16U
      solo,pno RIES s.p.   (T551)

   Zwanzig Ausgewahlte Lieder *CC20U
      solo,pno RIES s.p.   (T552)

TIGER, THE see Thomson, Virgil

TIGER! WETZE NUR DIE KLAUEN see Mozart,
   Wolfgang Amadeus

TIL ASALI see Nielsen, Carl

TIL DEG, DU HEI see Braein, Edvard
   Fliflet

TIL DEG, HERRE, SET EG MI LIT see
   Nystedt, Knut

'TIL HE APPEARS see Phelps, David

TIL MAIDAG see Peterson-Berger, (Olof)
   Wilhelm

TIL MIN GYLDENLAK see Olsen, Sparre

TIL MOR see Bedinger, Hugo

TIL MOR see Norberg

'TIL THE STORM PASSES BY see Lister,
   Mosie

TILGE, HOCHSTER, MEINE SUNDE see
   Pergolesi, Giovanni Battista,
   Stabat Mater

TILI, TILI TENGAN LOYSIN see Melartin,
   Erkki

TILIM-BOM see Stravinsky, Igor

TILL BRUDEN see Curschmann, F.

TILL BRUDEN see Peterson-Berger, (Olof)
   Wilhelm

TILL DAWN see Loewe, Gilbert

TILL DAWN BREAKS see Ad Or Ha-Boker

TILL DIG see Grafstrom

TILL EARTH OUTWEARS see Finzi, Gerald

TILL ELEKTRA see Kilpinen, Yrio

TILL EN DIKTARE see Kilpinen, Yrio

TILL EN ROS see Stenhammar, Wilhelm

TILL FLYTTFAGLARNA I SODERN see
   Merikanto, Oskar, Kevatlinnuile
   Etelassa

TILL FRIGGA see Sibelius, Jean

TILL HE COMES see Wyrtzen, Don

TILL HE WIPES AWAY MY TEARS see Davis

TILL I KNOW see Wetherington

TILL KRUBBAN GA see Maasalo, Armas, Kay
   Seimen Luo

TILL KVALEN see Sibelius, Jean, Illalle

TILL KVALLEN see Sibelius, Jean,
   Illalle

TILL NAGRA PASKLILJOR see Kilpinen,
   Yrio

TILL ROSORNA see Peterson-Berger,
   (Olof) Wilhelm

TILL SMARTAN see Lundborg, Gosta

TILL THE OLD CAT DIES see Franco, Johan

TILL THE SANDMAN COMES see Menotti,
   Gian Carlo

TILL THE SANDS OF THE DESERT see Ball,
   Ernest R.

TILL THE WHOLE WORLD KNOWS see Hopkins

TILL VASTANVINDEN see Jensen, Adolf

TILL WE WATCH THE LAST LOW STAR see
   Owen, Richard

TILLAGNAN see Schumann, Robert
   (Alexander), Widmung

TILLS DET BLIR SISTA GANG see Larsson,
   Lars-Erik

TIMANTTI HANGELLA see Sibelius, Jean,
   Demanten Pa Marssnon

TIME AND BEYOND see Bassett, Leslie

TIME CANNOT CLAIM THIS HOUR see Bohun,
   Lyle de

TIME DOES NOT BRING RELIEF see Gold,
   Ernest

TIME ENOUGH see Taylor, D.

TIME HAS BIG HANDLES see Linke, Norbert

TIME, I DARE THEE TO DISCOVER see
   Nordoff, Paul

TIME IS A CUNNING THIEF see Ulehla
   Ludmila

TIME LIGHTLY HATH FLOWN OVER ME see
   Schubert, Franz (Peter)

TIME ON TIME IN MIRACLES see Cacioppo,
   G.

TIME, YOU OLD GIPSY MAN see Warren,
   Elinor Remick

TIME, YOU OLD GIPSY MAN see Wheeler

TIMES AND THE SEASONS, THE *sac,CCUL
   (Wyrtzen, Don) solo,kbd SINGSPIR
   $2.95   (T553)

TIME'S GARDEN see Thomas, Arthur Goring

TIME'S ROSES see Barry, Katherine

TIMMEREN see Nieland, H.

TIMON LAULU see Marttinen, Tauno

TINCLER, G.
   La Halte
      solo,pno BROGNEAUX s.p.   (T554)

   Recueillement
      solo,pno BROGNEAUX s.p.   (T555)

TINDRANDE see Anjou, P. d'

TINDRANDE STJARNOR see Anjou, P. d'

TINKER, TAILOR see Greaves, Ralph

TINKER TIM see Johnston, Lyell

TINKER TOM see Buchanan, George

TIO NYA VISOR OM VAREN OCH SOMMAREN see
   Klingendorf

TIO SANGER see Wohlfart, Karl

TIPPETT, MICHAEL (1905-   )
   Boyhood's End *cant
      [Eng] T solo,pno SCHOTTS 10279 s.p.
                                        (T556)
   Heart's Assurance, The *song cycle
      [Eng] high solo,pno SCHOTTS 10158
      s.p.   (T557)

   Songs For Ariel *CCU
      [Eng] solo,pno SCHOTTS 10871 s.p.
                                        (T558)

TIRED see Lindsay, M.

TIRED see Vaughan Williams, Ralph

TIRINDELLI, PIER ADOLFO (1858-1937)
   Canzonetta
      [It] solo,pno SANTIS 104 s.p.
                                        (T559)
   E Lo Mio Amore
      [It] solo,pno SANTIS 107 s.p.
                                        (T560)
   En Stjarna Brann
      solo,pno GEHRMANS 239 s.p.   (T561)
   Mai!
      [It] Mez/Bar solo,pno RICORDI-ARG
      RF 3056 s.p.   (T562)
   Momento
      [It/Eng] Mez/Bar solo,pno RICORDI-
      ENG 108770 s.p.   (T563)

TIRINDELLI, PIER ADOLFO (cont'd.)

   O Primavera!
      [It] S/T solo,pno RICORDI-ARG
      BA 8535 s.p.   (T564)
      [It] Mez/T/Bar solo,pno RICORDI-ENG
      111029 s.p.   (T565)
      "Spring-Time" solo,pno BELWIN $1.50
                                        (T566)
   Parla
      [It] Mez/Bar solo,pno RICORDI-ARG
      RF 3119 s.p.   (T567)
   Sei Tu... Amore
      [It/Eng] S/T solo,pno RICORDI-ENG
      114059 s.p.   (T568)
   So!
      [It] Mez/Bar solo,pno RICORDI-ARG
      108769 s.p.   (T569)

   Spring-Time *see O Primavera!

   Una Fanciulla Parla
      [It] solo,pno SANTIS 106 s.p.
                                        (T570)

TIRITI, TIRITOMBOLA see Longo, Achille

TIRITOMBA *It
   solo,pno ALLANS s.p.   (T571)

TIROOLIN MAASS' JOS RUUSUN SAAN see
   Zeller, Carl

'TIS I see Pinsuti, Ciro

'TIS JUNE see Ronald, Sir Landon

'TIS LOVE THAT KEEPS ME FROM SLEEPING
   see Ferguson, Edwin Earle, Quiero
   Dormir Y No Puedo

'TIS ME O LORD *spir
   (Burleigh, H. T.) med solo,pno BELWIN
   $1.50   (T572)

'TIS SNOWING see Bemberg, Herman, Il
   Neige

'TIS THE DAY see Leoncavallo, Ruggiero,
   Mattinata

'TIS THE END, SO FAREWELL! see Friml,
   Rudolf

'TIS WEARY WAITING see Milkey, E.T.

TISTEL see Salonen, Sulo

TISTEL OCH LAVENDEL see Aner

TISZAN INNEN, DUNAN TUL *CC150U,folk,
   Hung
   (Borsy; Rossa) solo,pno BUDAPEST 459
   s.p.   (T573)

TIT FOR TAT see Britten, Benjamin

TIT FOR TAT see Pontet, Henry

TIT WILLOW see Sullivan, Sir Arthur
   Seymour

TITANIA see Jarnefelt, Armas

TITANIA see Peterson-Berger, (Olof)
   Wilhelm

TITANIA see Wideen, Ivar

TITGADDAL
   see Atta Seter Li

TITO GOBBI ALBUM *CC8L
   [It/Eng] Bar solo,pno RICORDI-ENG
   LD 411 s.p. contains works by: De
   Meglio; Verdi; Puccini; Tosti
                                        (T574)

TITTEL, ERNST (1910-1969)
   Mystisches Triptychon *Op.23, CC3U
      S solo,org DOBLINGER 08 858 s.p.
                                        (T575)

TKALCOVSKA SRDCE see Felix, Vaclav

TO A BIRD AT MY WINDOW see Tomlinson

TO A CACTUS see Rappaport, Eda

TO A CHELSEA CHINA LADY see Hadley

TO A CHILD DANCING IN THE WIND see
   Ruyneman, Daniel

TO A FIREFLY see Stock, Frederick

TO A GIRL ON HER BIRTHDAY see Anderson,
   William H.

TO A HILLTOP see Cox, Ralph

TO A MADONNA see Repper, Charles

TO A MINIATURE see Brahe, May H.

TO A NIGHTINGALE see Sharpe, Evelyn

TO A POET see Finzi, Gerald

TO A SEAGULL see Parker, Kitty

TO A SINISTER POTATO see Beeson, Jack Hamilton

TO A SNOWFLAKE see Tollefsen, Augusta

TO A TREE IN BLOOM see Sherman, H.

TO A TROUT see Shepherd, Arthur

TO A VIOLET see Brahms, Johannes, An Ein Veilchen

TO A VIOLET see LaForge, Frank

TO A WILD ROSE see MacDowell, Edward Alexander

TO ALL THE SEX DECEITFUL see Arne, Thomas Augustine

TO ALTHEA, FROM PRISON see Parry, Charles Hubert Hastings

TO AN ISLE IN THE WATER see Blank, Allan

TO AN OLD COTTAGE see Smith, Herbert Arnold

TO AN OLD LOVE see Flothius, Marius

TO ANTHEA see Hatton, John Liptrot

TO ASTER see Berkeley, Lennox

TO BABY CHRISTINE see Weigl, Karl

TO BE GOD'S PEOPLE see Brown, Charles F.

TO BE NEAR THE FAIR IDOL see Rosa, S., Star Vicino

TO BE OR NOT TO BE see Swanson, Howard

TO BE SUNG UPON THE WATERS see Argento, Dominick

TO BELSHAZZAR see Gerschefski, Edwin

TO BRUNE OJNE see Grieg, Edvard Hagerup

TO BUDE RANO see Mikula, Zdenko

TO CHLOE see Harrison, Julius Allen Greenway

TO CHLOE see Mozart, Wolfgang Amadeus, An Chloe

TO COME, O LORD, TO THEE see Stickles, William

TO DAFFODILS see Delius, Frederick

TO DANCE AND SING see Dunhill, Thomas Frederick

TO-DAY THE FIRST OF MAY see Une Perdriole

TO ELECTRA
see Four Songs From Herrick's 'Hesperides'

TO EVERY THING THERE IS A SEASON see Pinkham, Daniel

TO GET ALONG WITH GIRLS see Beethoven, Ludwig van, Mit Madeln Sich Vertragen

TO GOD SING PRAISE see Handel, George Frideric

TO GOD, WHO MADE THE RADIANT SUN see Handel, George Frideric

TO HELEN see Griffis, E.

TO HELEN see Mourant, Walter

TO IONA *Scot
solo,pno (contains also: Iona Boat Song) PATERSON s.p. see from Hebridean Songs, Vol. IV   (T576)

TO JE VOJNA see Kresanek, Jozef

TO KNOW HIM see Roe, Gloria [Ann]

TO KNOW HIS LOVE see Trued

TO KNOW THOU ART see Sateren, Leland Bernhard

TO LISINSKI see Lang, Ivana

TO LIVE FOR YOU see Ronald, Sir Landon

TO LOVE IS TO GIVE see Smith

TO LUCASTA ON GOING TO THE WARS see Diamond, David

TO LUCUSTA see Lawson, Malcolm

TO MA MAN VAERE see Torjussen, Trygve

TO MRS. ANNA FLAXMAN see Newlin, Dika

TO MUSIC see Bassett, Leslie

TO MUSIC see Gideon, Miriam

TO MUSIC see Schubert, Franz (Peter), An Die Musik

TO MUSIC, TO BECALM HIS FEVER see Hindemith, Paul

TO MY BELOVED, O HASTEN see Mozart, Wolfgang Amadeus, Il Mio Tesoro Intanto

TO MY DEAR LOVE see Lajovic, Aleksander, Misel Na Ljubico

TO MY FIRST LOVE see Lohr, Hermann

TO MY LADY see Buck, Vera

TO MY LADY SINGING see Gilder, Eric

TO OG TYVE SANGE see Moller, Svend-Ove

TO ONE WHO PASSED WHISTLING THROUGH THE NIGHT see Gibbs, Cecil Armstrong

TO PEOPLE WHO HAVE GARDENS
(Kennedy-Fraser, M.; MacLeod, K.) solo,pno (G min) BOOSEY $1.50
(T577)

TO POEMS BY CHILDREN see Uhler, A.

TO SANGE see Borup-Jorgensen, Axel

TO SANGER see Stigen, Fredrik

TO SANGER see Braein, Edvard Fliflet

TO SANGER see Kjeldaas, Arnljot

TO SANGER see Torjussen, Trygve

TO SCENES OF PEACE RETIRING see Mozart, Wolfgang Amadeus, In Diesen Heil'gen Hallen

TO SEA! see Shaw, Martin

TO SINE IN WINTER see Howell, Dorothy

TO SPRING see Gounod, Charles Francois, Au Printemps

TO SPRING see Joubert, John

TO SUNSHINE see Schumann, Robert (Alexander), An Den Sonnenschein

TO THE BELOVED see Schubel, Max

TO THE CHILDREN see Bainton, Edgar Leslie

TO THE CHILDREN see Elgar, Edward

TO THE CHILDREN see Rachmaninoff, Sergey Vassilievitch

TO THE DANCE see Wilson, H. Lane

TO THE DISTANT BELOVED see Beethoven, Ludwig van, An Die Ferne Geliebte

TO THE ENDS OF THE EARTH see Cates, Bill

TO THE EVENING STAR see Wagner, Richard, O Du Mein Holder Abendstern

TO THE FOREST see Tchaikovsky, Piotr Ilyitch

TO THE ISLE OF SKYE *Scot
solo,pno (contains also: The Uncanny Mannikin) PATERSON s.p. see from Hebridean Songs, Vol. IV   (T578)

TO THE LIGHTHOUSE see Bavicchi, John

TO THE LOVED ONE FAR AWAY see Beethoven, Ludwig van, An Die Ferne Geliebte

TO THE NIGHTINGALE see Brahms, Johannes, An Die Nachtigall

TO THE NIGHTINGALE see Gounod, Charles Francois, Au Rossignol

TO THE NIGHTINGALE see Sveinbjornsson, Sveinbjorn

TO THE RIVER see Griffis, E.

TO THE SEA see Nystroem, Gosta, Det Enda

TO THE SONG see Kilpinen, Yrio, Laululle

TO THE THAWING WIND see Duke, John Woods

TO THEE, BEFORE THE CLOSE OF DAY see Pinkham, Daniel, Te Lucis Ante Terminum

TO THEE, DIVINE REDEEMER see Edwards, Clara

TO THINE OWNSELF BE TRUE see Karhu, Edwin T.

TO THIS DARK DUNGEON see Pergolesi, Giovanni Battista, Nel Chiuso Centro

TO THIS WE'VE COME see Menotti, Gian Carlo

TO US A CHILD IS BORN see Schutz, Heinrich

TO US IN BETHLEHEM see Fischer, Gladys W.

TO WET A WIDOW'S EYE see Andriessen, Juriaan

TO WINTER see Joubert, John

TO YOU see Haubiel, Charles

TO YOU see Hope, H. Ashworth

TO YOU see Schat, Peter

TO YOU see Shaw, Clifford

TO YOU see Speaks, Oley

TOAST, A see Overton, Hall

TOBIN, JOHN
Nod
med solo,pno ELKIN 27.2092.02 s.p.
(T579)

TOBY JUG see Arundale, Claude

TOCCANTA see Cowell, Henry Dixon

TOCCATA see Freedman, Harry

TOCCHI, GIAN-LUCA (1901-   )
Canzonetta D'altri Tempi
[It] solo,pno SANTIS 355 s.p.
(T580)

Dodici! Girotondo
see La Stanza Da Giuoco

Eleonora
[It] solo,orch SANTIS rental (T581)
[It] solo,pno SANTIS 668 s.p.
(T582)

Emigranti
[It] solo,orch SANTIS rental (T583)
[It] solo,pno SANTIS 443 s.p.
(T584)

La Colomba
[It] solo,pno SANTIS 473 s.p.
(T585)

La Stanza Da Giuoco
[It] solo,pno cmplt ed SANTIS 476 s.p.
contains: Dodici! Girotondo; Natale Del Bimbo Goloso; Scilinguagnolo   (T586)

Marzo
[It] solo,pno SANTIS 667 s.p.
(T587)

Natale Del Bimbo Goloso
see La Stanza Da Giuoco

Nina Se'l Zielo
[It] solo,pno SANTIS 297 s.p.
(T588)

Quiete
[It] solo,pno SANTIS 315 s.p.
(T589)

Scilinguagnolo
see La Stanza Da Giuoco

TOCH, ERNST (1887-1964)
Nine Songs *Op.41, CC9U
[Eng/Ger] S solo,pno, published with AMP, New York SCHOTTS s.p.
(T590)

TOCHTER ZIONS, FREUE DICH see Handel, George Frideric, Rejoice Greatly, O Daughter Of Zion!

TOD see Lilien, Ignace

TOD DES ZAREN BORIS see Mussorgsky,
   Modest, Death Of Boris, The

TOD EINES KINDES see Schreker, Franz

TOD UND MODER DRINGT HEREIN see
   Telemann, Georg Philipp

TODA, KUNIO (1914-   )
   Sette Canti Dall'antologia Manyoshu
      *CC7U
      solo,pno ONGAKU s.p.   (T591)

TODA MI VIDA OS AME see Milan

TODA MI VIDA OS AME see Milan, Luis

TODAY see Dorsey

TODAY A SHEPHERD AND OUR KIN see
   Berkeley, Lennox

TODAY IS OURS see Buck

TODAY IT CAME see Richter, [Ada]

TODAY'S GONNA BE A BRIGHTER DAY see
   Faye, Linda

TOEKOMST see Mengelberg, Rudolf

TOGETHER see Peterson, John W.

TOGETHER A' THE WAY see Trotere, Henry

TOGLIETEMI LA VITA ANCOR see Scarlatti,
   Alessandro

TOGNI, CAMILLO (1922-   )
   Gesang Zur Nacht
      S solo,12inst sc ZERBONI 5887 s.p.
                                    (T592)
   Helian Di Trakl
      S solo,orch voc sc ZERBONI 5982
      s.p.   (T593)
   Preludes E Rondeaux   *CCU
      solo,pno ZERBONI 6444 s.p.   (T594)
   Rondeaux Per 10
      S solo,9inst min sc ZERBONI 6158
      s.p.   (T595)
   Sei Notturni   *CC6U
      A solo,4inst ZERBONI 6497 rental
                                    (T596)

TOI! see Chaminade, Cecile

TOI see Rabey, Rene

TOI LA PLUS CHERE see Guiraud, Ernest

TOI QUE J'AIME see Bach, J.C.

TOILERS, THE see Piccolomini, Marietta

TOINEN SARJA HAMALAISIA KANSANLAULUJA,
   VOLS. I-II see Hannikainen, Ilmari

TOIVOMUS see Snare, Sigurd, En Onskan

TOKIMEKI see Nakada, Yoshinao

TOLDRA, EDUARDO (1895-1962)
   A L'ombra Del Lledoner   *CC5U
      med-high solo,pno UNION ESP. $2.00
                                    (T597)
   Anacreontica
      [Span] med solo,pno UNION ESP. $.75
                                    (T598)
   As Frolinas Dos Toxos
      [Span] med solo,pno UNION ESP.
      $1.10   (T599)
   Canco De Passar Cantant
      [Span] med-high solo,pno UNION ESP.
      $.75   (T600)
   Canticel
      [Span] med solo,pno UNION ESP. $.75
                                    (T601)
   Els Obercocs I Les Petites Collidores
      [Span] med solo,pno UNION ESP. $.75
                                    (T602)
   Festeig
      [Span] med solo,pno UNION ESP. $.75
                                    (T603)
   La Mar Estava Alegra
      [Span] med solo,pno UNION ESP. $.75
                                    (T604)
   La Rosa Als Llavis
      [Port] med solo,pno UNION ESP.
      $1.75   (T605)
   Les Garbes Domen Al Camp
      [Span] med-high solo,pno UNION ESP.
      $.75   (T606)
   Menta I Farigola
      [Span] med solo,pno UNION ESP. $.60
                                    (T607)
   Seis Canciones   *CC6U
      [Span] med-high solo,pno UNION ESP.
      $2.50   (T608)

TOLDRA, EDUARDO (cont'd.)
   Vinyes Verdes Vora El Mar
      [Span] med-high solo,pno UNION ESP.
      $.75   (T609)

TOLL GATE, THE see Holford, Franz

TOLLEFSEN, AUGUSTA
   Grave Of Love, The
      high solo,pno SEESAW $1.00   (T610)
   To A Snowflake
      high solo,pno SEESAW $1.00   (T611)
   Winter
      med solo,pno SEESAW $1.00   (T612)

TOLONEN, JOUKO (PAAVO KALERVO)
   (1912-   )
   Djupt Till Stillhetens Ljusa Vila
      *see Syvan Aanettomyyden Syliin
   Drei Lieder Der Mignon   *CC3U
      solo,pno FAZER F 5286 s.p.   (T613)
   Liten Karlekssang   *see Pieni
      Rakkauslaulu
   Pieni Rakkauslaulu
      "Liten Karlekssang" see Tre Sanger
   Rukkilaulu
      "Spinnrockssang" see Tre Sanger
   Spinnrockssang   *see Rukkilaulu
   Syvan Aanettomyyden Syliin
      "Djupt Till Stillhetens Ljusa Vila"
      see Tre Sanger
   Tre Sanger
      solo,pno FAZER F 3197 s.p.
         contains: Pieni Rakkauslaulu,
         "Liten Karlekssang";
         Rukkilaulu, "Spinnrockssang";
         Syvan Aanettomyyden Syliin,
         "Djupt Till Stillhetens Ljusa
         Vila"   (T614)

TOLV DUETTER FOR FLICKSKOLORNAS HOGRE
   SANGKLASSER *CC12L
   (Uppling) 2 soli,pno LUNDQUIST s.p.
      contains works by: Pfeil; Myrberg;
      Hallstrom; Andre; Mendelssohn
                                    (T615)

TOM O'BEDLAM'S SONG see Bennett,
   Richard Rodney

TOM TOUGH see Dibdin, Charles

TOMAN, JOSEF (1894-1972)
   Cyklus Pisni O Lasce Na Text J.V.
      Sladka   *song cycle
      "Liederzyklus Von Der Liebe" med
      solo,pno CZECH s.p.   (T616)
   Liederzyklus Von Der Liebe   *see
      Cyklus Pisni O Lasce Na Text J.V.
      Sladka

TOMASEK, JAROSLAV (1896-1970)
   Dem Weibe   *Op.1, song cycle
      solo,pno SUPRAPHON s.p.   (T617)

TOMASEK, V.J.
   Alpsky Lovec
      see Dve Pisne
   Dve Pisne
      solo,pno SUPRAPHON s.p.
         contains: Alpsky Lovec; Plana
         Ruze   (T618)
   Plana Ruze
      see Dve Pisne

TOMASI, H.
   Chants Corses
      solo,orch cmplt ed LEDUC s.p.
         contains & see also: Lamento D'u
         Trenu; Nanna; Serenade
         Complainte; U Mere Pastore
                                    (T619)
   Invocation A La Lune
      solo,pno/inst LEDUC s.p.   (T620)
   Lamento D'u Trenu
      solo,orch LEDUC s.p. see also
      Chants Corses   (T621)
   Le Bonheur Est Dans Le Pre
      solo,pno/inst LEDUC s.p.   (T622)
   Nanna
      solo,orch LEDUC s.p. see also
      Chants Corses   (T623)
   Noa-Noa   *CCU
      T/Bar solo,SATB,orch LEDUC sc s.p.,
      cor pts rental   (T624)
   Serenade Complainte
      solo,orch LEDUC s.p. see also
      Chants Corses   (T625)

TOMASI, H. (cont'd.)
   U Mere Pastore
      solo,orch LEDUC s.p. see also
      Chants Corses   (T626)

TOMASKOVA, M.
   Tricet Snadnych Vocalis   *CC30U,
      vocalise
      solo,pno (easy) SUPRAPHON s.p.
                                    (T627)

TOMBEAU D'AMOUR see Delannoy, Marcel

TOMBEAU DANS UN PARC see Barber, Samuel

TOMBEAU V see Boulez, Pierre

TOMBO, LORRAINE
   Mandy And The Spiders
      med solo,pno (C maj) WILLIS $.60
                                    (T628)

TOMC, MATIJA (1899-   )
   Pomladne Pesmi
      "Spring Songs" solo,pno DRUSTVO
      DSS 205 rental   (T629)
   Sedem Narodnih Pesmi   *CC7U,folk
      solo,pno DRUSTVO DSS 204 rental
                                    (T630)
   Spring Songs   *see Pomladne Pesmi

TOMLINSON
   To A Bird At My Window
      low solo,pno (F maj) ALLANS s.p.
                                    (T631)
      high solo,pno (G maj) ALLANS s.p.
                                    (T632)

TOMMASINI, VINCENZO (1878-1950)
   Due Liriche Sacre   *see O Bone Jesu;
      O Salvador Mundi   (T633)
   O Bone Jesu   *sac
      [It] B solo,pno SANTIS 545 s.p. see
      from Due Liriche Sacre   (T634)
   O Salvador Mundi   *sac
      [It] B solo,pno SANTIS 544 s.p. see
      from Due Liriche Sacre   (T635)

TOMMY, LAD see Margetson, Edward J.

TOMORROW see Strauss, Richard, Morgen

TOMORROW HE MAY COME see Horne, Roger

TOMPKINS
   Revive Our Spirit, O Lord   *sac
      solo,pno LILLENAS SM-871: SN $1.00
                                    (T636)

TON IMAGE see Ropartz, Joseph Guy

TON IMAGE see Schumann, Robert
   (Alexander)

TON MENTON POSE DANS TA MAIN see Rhene-
   Baton

TON NEZ see Delmet, Paul

TON NOM see Kucken, Friedrich Wilhelm

TON SOURIRE see Chaminade, Cecile

TON VISAGE see Schumann, Robert
   (Alexander)

TONAT COELUM CUM FURORE see Piazza,
   Gaetano

TONEN see Palmgren, Selim

TONER see Fordell, Erik (Fritiof)

TONERNA see Dahl

TONERNA see Lagercrantz, Wilhelm

TONERNA see Sjoberg, C.L.

TONERNA see Sjogren, Emil

TONI, ALCEO (1884-1969)
   Canti D'amore   *see Dialogo; Notturno
      Della Luna; O Tardi Venuto   (T637)
   Dialogo
      [It] solo,pno BONGIOVANI 1232 s.p.
      see from Canti D'amore   (T638)
   La Mamma
      [It] solo,pno BONGIOVANI 1544 s.p.
      see from Quattro Liriche
      Romantiche   (T639)
      [Eng] solo,pno BONGIOVANI 1695 s.p.
                                    (T640)
   Notturno Della Luna
      [It] solo,pno BONGIOVANI 1233 s.p.
      see from Canti D'amore   (T641)
   O Bella
      [It] solo,pno BONGIOVANI 1545 s.p.
      see from Quattro Liriche
      Romantiche   (T642)

TONI, ALCEO (cont'd.)

O Tardi Venuto
    [It] solo,pno BONGIOVANI 1231 s.p.
        see from Canti D'amore   (T643)

Oggi Ho Visto Una Rosa
    [It] solo,pno BONGIOVANI 1546 s.p.
        see from Quattro Liriche
        Romantiche   (T644)

Quattro Liriche Romantiche *see La
    Mamma; O Bella; Oggi Ho Visto Una
    Rosa; S'io Ti Vedessi   (T645)

S'io Ti Vedessi
    [It] solo,pno BONGIOVANI 1547 s.p.
        see from Quattro Liriche
        Romantiche   (T646)

TONIGHT I MUST DIE see Pergament,
    Moses, I Natt Skall Jag Do

TONNESSEN, PEDER
    Fast Grunn
        see Tonnessen, Peder, Ransak Meg

    I Heimsems Hjarta
        see Tonnessen, Peder, Via Dolorosa

    Jesus, Lat Meg Likjast Deg *sac
        solo,pno MUSIKK s.p.   (T647)

    Julesalme *Xmas
        solo,pno MUSIKK s.p.   (T648)

    Kristi Kors *sac
        solo,pno MUSIKK s.p.   (T649)

    Ransak Meg
        solo,pno MUSIKK s.p. contains also:
        Fast Grunn   (T650)

    Via Dolorosa *sac
        solo,pno MUSIKK s.p. contains also:
        I Heimsems Hjarta   (T651)

TONY THE TURTLE see Austin, Ernest

TOO LATE TOMORROW see Langenburg

TOO-TOO WAS A DAINTY DOLL see Wright,
    Lawrence

TOP SONGS FOR DUETS *sac,CCUL
    2 soli,pno SINGSPIR 5774 $1.25 (T652)

TOP SONGS FOR HIGH VOICE *CCUL
    (Peterson, John W.) high solo,kbd
    SINGSPIR 5026 $1.25   (T653)

TOP SONGS FOR LOW VOICE SERIES, NOS. 1-
    2 *sac,CCUL
    low solo,kbd SINGSPIR $1.25, ea.
                                      (T654)

TOP SONGS FOR SOLOIST SERIES, NOS. 1-2
    *sac,CCUL
    (Peterson, John W.) med solo,pno
    SINGSPIR $1.25, ea.   (T655)

TOP SONGS FOR TRIOS *sac,CCUL
    (Peterson, John W.) 3 soli,pno
    SINGSPIR 5777 $1.25   (T656)

TOPLIFF, ROBERT
    Consider The Lilies *sac
        med solo,pno (C sharp maj) SCHIRM.G
        $.75   (T657)
        med solo,pno (E flat maj) CENTURY
        703 $.40   (T658)

TOPOLI V JESENI see Ciglic, Zvonimir

TORAH DANCE see Ki Mi-Tziyon

TORCH, THE see Elgar, Edward

TORCHBEARERS, THE see Anu Nosim Lapidim

TOREADOR, HOLA! see Trotere, Henry

TOREADOR SONG see Bizet, Georges, Votre
    Toast, Je Peux Vous Le Rendre

TOREADORENS ARIA see Bizet, Georges,
    Votre Toast, Je Peux Vous Le Rendre

TOREADORENS SANG see Bizet, Georges,
    Votre Toast, Je Peux Vous Rendre

TORJUSSEN, TRYGVE
    Du Kom *Op.55,No.1
        see To Sanger

    Excelsior
        solo,pno MUSIKK s.p.   (T659)

    Hesperia
        solo,pno MUSIKK s.p.   (T660)

    Nirvana
        solo,pno MUSIKK s.p.   (T661)

    To Ma Man Vaere *Op.55,No.2
        see To Sanger

TORJUSSEN, TRYGVE (cont'd.)

    To Sanger
        solo,pno MUSIKK s.p.
            contains: Du Kom, Op.55,No.1; To
            Ma Man Vaere, Op.55,No.2 (T662)

TORLIND
    Biskop Thomas Frihetssang *sac
        solo,pno LUNDQUIST s.p.   (T663)

    Giv
        solo,pno LUNDQUIST s.p.   (T664)

    Lucia
        solo,pno LUNDQUIST s.p.   (T665)

TORLIND, TORE
    Jag Vill Dig Tacka Och Lova
        solo,pno GEHRMANS s.p.   (T666)

    Lucia
        solo&narrator,pno GEHRMANS s.p.
                                      (T667)

TORMODS KVAD see Peterson-Berger,
    (Olof) Wilhelm

TORNA see Denza, Luigi

TORNA AI FELICI DI see Puccini, Giacomo

TORNA PICCINA see Bixio

TORNAMI A DIR CHE M'AMI see Donizetti,
    Gaetano

TORNAN LE STELLE see Cimara, Pietro

TORNET see Sibelius, Jean

TORNQUIST, F.
    O, Honeyed Song *see O, Milda Sang

    O, Milda Sang
        "O, Honeyed Song" [Swed/Eng] med
        solo,kbd NORDISKA s.p.   (T668)

TORPFLICKAN see Collan, Karl

TORRE DE BELEM see Legley, Victor

TORREADOR SONG see Bizet, Georges,
    Votre Toast, Je Peux Vous Le Rendre

TORRENCE, E.
    Smilin' Kitty O'Day
        low solo,pno (D maj) BOOSEY $1.50
                                      (T669)
        high solo,pno (F maj) BOOSEY $1.50
                                      (T670)

TORREZ, S.P.
    Musica Boliviana *CC5U
        [Span] med solo,pno UNION ESP. $.75
                                      (T671)

TORROBA, F.M.
    Canciones Espanolas *CCU
        [Span] med-high solo,pno UNION ESP.
        $3.25, ea. in two volumes   (T672)

    Petenera De La Marchenera
        (Azpiazu) [Span] high solo,gtr
        UNION ESP. $1.00   (T673)

TORSO see Bussotti, Sylvano

TORSO see Hallnas, Hilding

TORTELDUVE see Geraedts, Jaap

TORTOISESHELL CAT see Howell, Dorothy

TORTONE, A.
    Il Calvario
        see Liriche Mistiche Dal Poema Di
        Gesu

    La Crocefissione
        see Liriche Mistiche Dal Poema Di
        Gesu

    La Pecorella Smarrita
        see Liriche Mistiche Dal Poema Di
        Gesu

    L'Ascensione
        see Liriche Mistiche Dal Poema Di
        Gesu

    Liriche Mistiche Dal Poema Di Gesu
        *sac
        [It] solo,pno cmplt ed BONGIOVANI
        2320 s.p.
            contains: Il Calvario; La
            Crocefissione; La Pecorella
            Smarrita; L'Ascensione   (T674)

TOSATTI, VIERI (1920-   )
    Il Giovane Werther
        [It] S/T solo,pno RICORDI-ENG
        128727 s.p.   (T675)

    Il Racconto Del Signore Maillard
        (Dalla Suite) (from Il Sistema
        Della Docezza)
        [It] Bar solo,pno RICORDI-ENG
        128881 s.p.   (T676)

TOSATTI, VIERI (cont'd.)

    Tre Liriche Greche *CC3U
        [It] Mez solo,pno RICORDI-ENG
        128726 s.p.   (T677)

TOSCHI, PIETRO
    Anime Di Campane
        [It] solo,pno BONGIOVANI 1058 s.p.
                                      (T678)

    Ave Maria Dell'Assunta *sac
        [It] solo,pno SANTIS 853 s.p. (T679)

    La Passione Di Mia Madre
        [It] S/Mez solo,pno BONGIOVANI 1059
        s.p.   (T680)

    L'angelo
        [It] S/Mez solo,pno BONGIOVANI 1331
        s.p.   (T681)

    Ninna Nanna A Sera
        [It] S/Mez solo,pno BONGIOVANI 633
        s.p.   (T682)
        [Eng] S/Mez solo,pno BONGIOVANI
        1644 s.p.   (T683)

    Sera Di Festa Dopo Il Ritorno Dalla
        Guerra
        [It] S/Mez solo,pno BONGIOVANI
        634 s.p.   (T684)

TOSELLI, ENRICO (1883-1926)
    Serenade *see Serenata

    Serenata
        high solo,pno (E maj) ALLANS s.p.
                                      (T685)
        2 high soli,pno (E flat maj) ALLANS
        s.p.   (T686)
        med solo,pno (D maj) ALLANS s.p.
                                      (T687)
        low solo,pno (C maj) ALLANS s.p.
                                      (T688)
        2 low soli,pno (C maj) ALLANS s.p.
                                      (T689)
        "Serenade" med-low solo,pno (C maj)
        BOSTON $1.50   (T690)
        "Serenade" low solo,pno (B flat
        maj) BOSTON $1.50   (T691)
        "Serenade" med-high solo,pno (D
        maj) BOSTON $1.50   (T692)

TOSTI, FRANCESCO PAOLO (1846-1916)
    'A Vucchella
        [It] S/T solo,pno RICORDI-ARG
        BA 8622 s.p.   (T693)
        [It] Mez/Bar solo,pno RICORDI-ENG
        112148 s.p.   (T694)
        [It] S/T solo,pno RICORDI-ENG
        112147 s.p.   (T695)

    Addio!
        [It] S/T solo,pno RICORDI-ENG 49616
        s.p.   (T696)
        "Good-By!" med solo,pno (F maj)
        SCHIRM.G $.60   (T697)
        "Good-By!" low solo,pno (E flat
        maj) SCHIRM.G $.60   (T698)

    After *see Dopo!

    Aprile
        [It] S/T solo,pno RICORDI-ARG
        BA 10972 s.p.   (T699)
        [It] S/T solo,pno RICORDI-ENG 48388
        s.p.   (T700)

    Arietta Di Posillipo (from A
        Vucchella)
        low solo,pno BELWIN $1.50   (T701)

    Ave Maria *sac
        [It] S/T solo,pno RICORDI-ARG
        RF 3200 s.p.   (T702)

    Baciami
        [It/Eng] Mez/Bar solo,pno RICORDI-
        ENG s.p.   (T703)

    Cancion De Fortunio *see Chanson De
        Fortunio

    Carmela
        [It] S/T solo,pno RICORDI-ARG 47190
        s.p.   (T704)

    Chanson De Fortunio
        "Cancion De Fortunio" [Fr/Span]
        Mez/Bar solo,pno RICORDI-ARG
        RF 3115 s.p.   (T705)

    Dopo!
        [It] Mez/Bar solo,pno RICORDI-ARG
        s.p.   (T706)
        "After" [It/Eng] S/T solo,pno
        RICORDI-ARG 45229 s.p.   (T707)

    Good-By! *see Addio!

    Ideale
        [It] A/B solo,pno RICORDI-ENG 48406
        s.p.   (T708)
        [It] Mez/Bar solo,pno RICORDI-ENG
        48405 s.p.   (T709)
        [It] S/T solo,pno RICORDI-ENG 48404

TOSTI, FRANCESCO PAOLO (cont'd.)

  s.p.
   [It] Mez/Bar solo,pno RICORDI-ARG
   BA 8166 s.p.   (T711)
   [It] S/T solo,pno RICORDI-ARG
   BA 8766 s.p.   (T712)

  Invano
   [It] S/T solo,pno RICORDI-ARG
   BA 10973 s.p.   (T713)

  La Mia Canzone
   [It/Eng] S/T solo,pno RICORDI-ENG
   104648 s.p.   (T714)

  La Serenata
   [It] S/T solo,pno RICORDI-ARG
   BA 8345 s.p.   (T715)
   [It] Mez/Bar solo,pno RICORDI-ENG
   53247 s.p.   (T716)
   [It] S/T solo,pno RICORDI-ENG 53246
   s.p.   (T717)
   "Serenade" [It/Eng] low solo,pno (C
   maj) SCHIRM.G $.85   (T718)
   "Serenade" [It/Eng] high solo,pno
   (F maj) SCHIRM.G $.85 (T719)

  L'Alba Separa Dalla Luce L'ombra
   [It/Eng] Mez/Bar solo,pno RICORDI-
   ENG LD 372 s.p. see from Quatro
   Canzoni De Amaranta   (T720)
   [It/Eng] S/T solo,pno RICORDI-ENG
   LD 369 s.p. see from Quatro
   Canzoni De Amaranta   (T721)
   [It] S/T solo,pno RICORDI-ENG
   112138 s.p. see from Quatro
   Canzoni De Amaranta   (T722)

  Last Song, The *see L'ultima Canzone

  L'ultima Canzone
   [It] S/T solo,pno RICORDI-ARG
   BA 10974 s.p.   (T723)
   [It] Mez/Bar solo,pno RICORDI-ENG
   111040 s.p.   (T724)
   [It] S/T solo,pno RICORDI-ENG
   111039 s.p.   (T725)
   "Last Song, The" solo,pno (D min)
   BELWIN $1.50   (T726)

  Luna D'estate Stornello
   [It] S/T solo,pno RICORDI-ENG
   114209 s.p.   (T727)

  Malia
   [It] S/T solo,pno RICORDI-ARG
   BA 8344 s.p.   (T728)
   [It] Mez/Bar solo,pno RICORDI-ENG
   52292 s.p.   (T729)
   [It] S/T solo,pno RICORDI-ENG 52291
   s.p.   (T730)

  Marechiare
   [It] S/T solo,pno RICORDI-ENG
   126437 s.p.   (T731)
   [It] S/T solo,pno RICORDI-ARG
   BA 8240 s.p.   (T732)
   [It] Mez/Bar solo,pno RICORDI-ENG
   126438 s.p.   (T733)

  Mattinata, No. 1
   [It] Mez/Bar solo,pno RICORDI-ARG
   RF 3246 s.p.   (T734)

  Mattinata, No. 2
   [It] Mez/Bar solo,pno RICORDI-ARG
   RF 3250 s.p.   (T735)
   [It] S/T solo,pno RICORDI-ARG
   RF 3225 s.p.   (T736)

  Nella Notte D'april
   [It] S/T solo,pno RICORDI-ARG
   110071 s.p.   (T737)

  Ninon
   [Fr] S/T solo,pno RICORDI-ENG 49468
   s.p.   (T738)

  Non M'amate Piu
   [It] S/T solo,pno RICORDI-ARG
   108180 s.p.   (T739)

  Non T'amo Piu
   [It] S/T solo,pno RICORDI-ENG 49519
   s.p.   (T740)

  Nonna, Sorridi?
   [It] S/T solo,pno RICORDI-ARG 47755
   s.p.   (T741)

  Oblio!
   [It] S/T solo,pno RICORDI-ARG
   RF 3025 s.p.   (T742)

  Parla!
   [It] S/T solo,pno RICORDI-ARG
   RF 3224 s.p.   (T743)

  Parted
   [Eng] Mez/Bar solo,pno RICORDI-ENG
   103142 s.p.   (T744)

  Penso!...
   [It] S/T solo,pno RICORDI-ARG
   BA 10975 s.p.   (T745)

TOSTI, FRANCESCO PAOLO (cont'd.)

  Quatro Canzoni De Amaranta *see
   L'Alba Separa Dalla Luce L'ombra
            (T746)

  Segreto
   [It] S/T solo,pno RICORDI-ARG
   BA 10976 s.p.   (T747)

  Serenade *see La Serenata

  Sogno
   [It] S/T solo,pno RICORDI-ARG
   BA 8623 s.p.   (T748)
   [It] Mez/Bar solo,pno RICORDI-ARG
   RF 3257 s.p.   (T749)

  Tristezza
   [It] S/T solo,pno RICORDI-ENG
   112674 s.p.   (T750)

  Vorrei Morire
   [It] S/T solo,pno RICORDI-ARG
   BA 10977 s.p.   (T751)
   [It] S/T solo,pno RICORDI-ENG 46066
   s.p.   (T752)

TOSTO DAL VICIN BOSCO see Legrenzi,
  Giovanni

TOTA PULCHRA ES MARIA see Geraedts,
  Jaap

TOTA PULCHRA EST see Gletle, Johann
  Melchoir

TOTAL ECLIPSE see Handel, George
  Frideric

TOTE TAGE see Oort, H.C.v.

T'OTHER LITTLE TUNE see Lessard, John
  Ayres

TOUCH HANDS see Tedford, John

TOUCH NOT THE NETTLE see Lawson,
  Malcolm

TOUCH OF A VANISHED HAND see Pinsuti,
  Ciro

TOUCH OF HIS HAND, THE see Kerr

TOUCH OF HIS HAND, THE see Lister,
  Mosie

TOUCHED BY HIS NAIL-SCARRED HAND see
  Elliot, Dennis

TOUCHED BY THE HAND OF THE LORD see
  Lister, Mosie

TOUCHING JESUS see Stallings

TOUJOURS see Barbier, Rene

TOUJOURS see Faure, Gabriel-Urbain

TOUJOURS A TOI, SEIGNEUR see Gounod,
  Charles Francois

TOUJOURS DURERONT NOS AMOURS see
  Schumann, Robert (Alexander)

TOUJOURS L'AIMER see Guidon, J.

TOUJOURS L'AMOUR see Langer, Hans-Klaus

TOUJOURS OU JAMAIS see Waldteufel, Emil

TOUJOURS VOUS see Delmet, Paul

TOURAINE *Fr
  (Canteloube, J.) solo,acap DURAND
  s.p. see also Anthologie Des Chants
  Populaires Francais Tome IV (T753)

TOURING THAT CITY see Lane

TOURNEZ S'IL VOUS PLAIT see Schmitt,
  Florent

TOURNIER, MARCEL
  La Lettre Du Jardinier
   solo,harp/pno/orch LEDUC s.p.
            (T754)

TOURNOIEMENT see Saint-Saens, Camille

TOUS LES BOIS see Guiraud, Ernest

TOUS LES BOURGEOIS DE CHATRE see Klerk,
  Albert de

TOUSSAINT DE SUTTER, J.
  Barque D'Or
   solo,pno (med diff) BROGNEAUX s.p.
            (T755)
  Chanson D'Automne
   solo,pno (med diff) BROGNEAUX s.p.
            (T756)
  La Caravane Du Monde
   solo,pno (med diff) BROGNEAUX s.p.
            (T757)

TOUSSAINT DE SUTTER, J. (cont'd.)

  Vous M'avez Dit, Tel Soir
   solo,pno (med diff) BROGNEAUX s.p.
            (T758)

TOUT A L'HEURE see Cuvillier, Charles

TOUT DORT DANS LA NUIT LOURDE see
  Saint-Saens, Camille

TOUT DOUCEMENT see Serpette, Gaston

TOUT DOUX see Legay, Marcel

TOUT EST FINI see Flegier, Ange

TOUT GAI! see Ravel, Maurice

TOUT MON COEUR EST NOUVEAU see Mozart,
  Wolfgang Amadeus

TOUT PASSE! see Berger, Rod.

TOUT PRES DE MOI see Berger, Rod.

TOUT UN SOIR see Dufresne, C.

TOUTAIN-GRUN, J.
  Chanson D'Ete
   solo,pno ENOCH s.p.   (T759)

  Heures Douces
   solo,pno ENOCH s.p.   (T760)

  L'Oiseau Bleu
   solo,pno ENOCH s.p.   (T761)

  Melancolie
   solo,pno ENOCH s.p.   (T762)

  Rondel
   see ALBUM MODERNE

TOUTE ALLEGRESSE see Delage, Maurice

TOUTE MA VIE JE VOUS AI AIMEE see
  Milan, Luis, Toda Mi Vida Os Ame

TOUTE SEULE SILENCE LES YEUX ETEINTS
  see Honegger, Arthur

TOUTE UNE HISTOIRE see Sureau-Bellet,
  J.

TOUTES LES FLEURS see Chabrier,
  Emmanuel

TOUTES LES ROSES see Flegier, Ange

TOVERFLUIT KNABES WUNDERHORN, VOL. I
  see Scholze, J.

TOVERFLUIT KNABES WUNDERHORN, VOL. II
  see Scholze, J.

TOWER OF STRENGTH, A *sac,CC10L
  (Carmichael, Ralph) solo,pno WORD
  37696 $2.50   (T763)

TOWER OF STRENGTH, A see Adair, Tom

TOWN, THE see Hageman, Richard, Die
  Stadt

TOWN TREE see Nelson, H.

TOY-SELLER, THE see Bhatia

TOYE, (JOHN) FRANCIS (1883-1964)
  Inn, The
   solo,pno (C min) ROBERTON 2359 s.p.
            (T764)

TOYLAND see Herbert, Victor

TRA LE FIAMME see Handel, George
  Frideric

TRABADELO, A. DE
  Cherchant D'Amour
   solo,acap (available in 2 keys)
   ENOCH s.p.   (T765)
   solo,pno (available in 2 keys)
   ENOCH s.p.   (T766)

  Dernier Chrysantheme
   solo,acap (available in 2 keys)
   ENOCH s.p.   (T767)
   solo,pno (available in 2 keys)
   ENOCH s.p.   (T768)

  Desir Fou
   solo,acap (available in 2 keys)
   ENOCH s.p.   (T769)
   solo,pno (available in 2 keys)
   ENOCH s.p.   (T770)

  Douleur D'Aimer
   solo,acap (available in 2 keys)
   ENOCH s.p.   (T771)
   solo,pno (available in 2 keys)
   ENOCH s.p.   (T772)

  Extase Langoureuse
   solo,acap (available in 2 keys)
   ENOCH s.p.   (T773)
   solo,pno (available in 2 keys)

TRABADELO, A. DE (cont'd.)

ENOCH s.p. (T774)

Les Chemins
solo,pno (available in 2 keys)
ENOCH s.p. (T775)
solo,acap (available in 2 keys)
ENOCH s.p. (T776)

Marche Basque
solo,acap (available in 2 keys)
ENOCH s.p. (T777)
solo,pno (available in 2 keys)
ENOCH s.p. (T778)

Mon Village
solo,acap (available in 2 keys)
ENOCH s.p. (T779)
solo,opt ob (available in 2 keys)
ENOCH s.p. (T780)

Quand Tu La Verras
solo,acap (available in 2 keys)
ENOCH s.p. (T781)
solo,pno (available in 2 keys)
ENOCH s.p. (T782)

Refrain Printanier
solo,acap (available in 2 keys)
ENOCH s.p. (T783)
solo,pno (available in 2 keys)
ENOCH s.p. (T784)

TRACTUS: QUI HABITAT see Andriessen,
Hendrik

TRAD see Liljefors, Ruben

TRAD see Ryden

TRADE WINDS see Keel, Frederick

TRADGARDSMASTAREN see Wolf, Hugo

TRAEET see Soderman, (Johan) August

TRAETTA, TOMMASO (MICHELE FRANCESCO
SAVERIO) (1727-1779)
Minuetto Cantato
(Gubitosi, E.) solo,2fl,2horn
CARISH s.p. (T785)

TRAFT IHR DAS SCHIFF IM MEERE AN see
Wagner, Richard

TRAGIC TALE, A see Fox, J.B.

TRAGIKOMODIEN see Jirak, Karel Boleslav

TRAGISK BALLAD I YSTAD see Pergament,
Moses

TRAJECTOIRES INTERIEURES see Michel,
Paul-Baudouin

TRAKL-TRILOGIE see Abendroth, Walther

TRAMONTO D'AUTUNNO see Veneziani,
Vittore

TRAMONTO MONTANO see Cantu, M.

TRAMP see Sawyer, Yvonne

TRAMP, THE see Taylor, H. Stanley

TRAMPIN see Boatner, Edward H.

TRANCHANT, J.
Le Roi Marc
solo,acap ENOCH s.p. (T786)
solo,pno ENOCH s.p. (T787)

Quand On Est Dans La Puree
solo,pno ENOCH s.p. (T788)

Soir
solo,pno ENOCH s.p. (T789)
solo,acap ENOCH s.p. (T790)

Sur Le Meme Trottoir
solo,pno ENOCH s.p. (T791)

Un Livre S'ouvre
solo,pno ENOCH s.p. (T792)
solo,acap ENOCH s.p. (T793)

Veux-Tu Ou Ne Veux-Tu Pas
solo,pno ENOCH s.p. (T794)

TRANENDICHTJES see Loots, Ph.

TRANQUIL VALLEY see Birch, Robert
Fairfax

TRANQUILITY see Hinchcliffe, Irvin

TRANSFORMATION see Watts, Wintter

TRAPP, MAX (1887-   )
Dammrung Senkte Sich Von Oben
*Op.39,No.4
see Vier Lieder Nach Goethe

TRAPP, MAX (cont'd.)

Drei Goethelieder
[Ger/Eng/Fr] high solo,pno LEUCKART
s.p.
contains: Fruhzeitiger Fruhling,
Op.38,No.1; Mailied, Op.38,
No.2; Rastlose Liebe, Op.38,
No.3 (T795)

Fruhzeitiger Fruhling *Op.38,No.1
see Drei Goethelieder

Mailied *Op.38,No.2
see Drei Goethelieder

Nachtgesang *Op.39,No.1
see Vier Lieder Nach Goethe

Nahe Des Geliebten *Op.39,No.2
see Vier Lieder Nach Goethe

Rastlose Liebe *Op.38,No.3
see Drei Goethelieder

Vier Lieder Nach Goethe
[Ger/Eng/Fr] med solo,pno LEUCKART
s.p.
contains: Dammrung Senkte Sich
Von Oben, Op.39,No.4;
Nachtgesang, Op.39,No.1; Nahe
Des Geliebten, Op.39,No.2;
Ziehn Die Schafe Von Der Wiese,
Op.39,No.3 (T796)

Ziehn Die Schafe Von Der Wiese
*Op.39,No.3
see Vier Lieder Nach Goethe

TRASTEN I HOSTKVALLEN see Wennerburg,
[Gunnar]

TRAUM DURCH DIE DAMMERUNG see Strauss,
Richard

TRAUMBILD see Landre, Willem

TRAUMDEUTUNG see King, Harold C.

TRAUME see Wagner, Richard

TRAUME DU see Reger, Max

TRAUMEND SINGT DIE STILLE see Borris,
Siegfried

TRAUMEREI see Schumann, Robert
(Alexander)

TRAUMGEKRONT see Marx, Joseph

TRAUMGESICHT see Zagwijn, Henri

TRAUMGEWALTEN see Bordewijk-Roepman,
Johanna

TRAUMLEBEN see Schoenberg, Arnold

TRAUMLIEDCHEN see Lothar, Mark

TRAUMVERKUNDUNG see Weismann, Julius

TRAUMWALD see Bijvanck, Henk

TRAURIGER WIND see Straesser, Joep

TRAUUNGSGESANG see Oort, H.C.v.

TRAUUNGSGESANG NACH DER ARIE "CARO MIO
BEN" see Giordani, Giuseppe, Herr,
Du Und Gott

TRAUUNGSLIED see Welcker, Max

TRAUUNGSLIED VON DIR GESTIFTET IST DIE
EHE see Faisst, Clara

TRAVELLER, THE see Reale, Paul

DE TRAVENET
Pauvre Jacques
see LA MUSIQUE, DEUXIEME CAHIER
solo,acap DURAND s.p. (T797)

TRAVERSEE see Doyen, Albert

TRE ACQUEFORTI see De Angelis, Ruggero

TRE ANDLIGA SANGER see Nordqvist,
Gustaf

TRE ARIE see Mozart, Wolfgang Amadeus

TRE ARIE E QUATTRO DANZE see Panni,
Marcello

TRE BALLATE DI CALENDIMAGGIO see
Cimara, Pietro

TRE BO BERGMAN-DIKTER see Nordqvist,
Gustaf

TRE CANTATE MORALI E STORICHE PER VOCE
E ARCHI see Perti, Giacomo Antonio

TRE CANTI see De Angelis, Ugalberto

TRE CANTI see Scelsi, Giacinto

TRE CANTI ARMENI see Guerrini, Guido

TRE CANTI D'AMORE see Pizzetti,
Ildebrando

TRE CANTI DI FUKUKO see Bizzelli,
Annibale

TRE CANTI DI SHAKESPEARE PER SOPRANO
LEGGERO see Ivanova, Lidia

TRE CANTI DI SHELLEY see Ghedini,
Giorgio Federico

TRE CANTI GRECI see Pizzetti,
Ildebrando

TRE CANTI PER VOCE E CHITARRA see De
Angelis, Ugalberto

TRE CANTI REGIONALI see Porrino, Ennio

TRE CANTI SACRI see Casella, Alfredo

TRE CANTI SAFFICI see Caltabiano, S.

TRE CANTICI see Monnikendam, Marius

TRE CANZONI see Pizzetti, Ildebrando

TRE CANZONI see Pizzetti, Ildebrando

TRE CANZONI TRECENTESCHE see Casella,
Alfredo

TRE DAGAR see Hallnas, Hilding

TRE DIKTER see Korling, August

TRE DIKTER see Wohlfart, Karl

TRE DIKTER AV L. HOLSTEIN see
Nordqvist, Gustaf

TRE DUETTER see Hallen, Andreas

TRE EFTERLAMNADE SANGER see Sjogren,
Emil

TRE EPIGRAMMI GRECI see Margola, Franco

TRE FRAMMENTI DI SAFFO see Prosperi,
Carlo

TRE FRODING-DIKTER see Nordqvist,
Gustaf

TRE GIORNI SON CHE NINA see Pergolesi,
Giovanni Battista

TRE INVOCAZIONI see Vlad, Roman

TRE ITALIENSKE DUETTER see Schierbeck,
Poul

TRE LAUDI see Dallapiccola, Luigi

TRE LIRICHE see Chailly, Luciano

TRE LIRICHE see Peyretti, Alberto

TRE LIRICHE see Alfano, Franco

TRE LIRICHE see Bettinelli, Bruno

TRE LIRICHE see Veretti, Antonio

TRE LIRICHE see Davico, Vincenzo

TRE LIRICHE see Terni, Enrico

TRE LIRICHE see Alfano, Franco

TRE LIRICHE see Petrassi, Goffredo

TRE LIRICHE see Fuga, Sandro

TRE LIRICHE see Geymuller, Margherita

TRE LIRICHE see Labroca, Mario

TRE LIRICHE see Alfano, Franco

TRE LIRICHE see Farina, Guido

TRE LIRICHE CARDUCCIANE see Caltabiano,
S.

TRE LIRICHE DI PASCOLI see Bettarini,
Luciano

TRE LIRICHE DI R. TAGORE see Mortari,
Virgilio

TRE LIRICHE DRAMMATICHE see Pizzetti,
Ildebrando

TRE LIRICHE GIAPPONESI see Platamone,
Stefano

TRE LIRICHE GRECHE see Tosatti, Vieri

TRE LIRICHE HAN see Lorenzini, Danilo

TRE LIRICHE SPAGNOLE see Platamone,
Stefano

TRE LIRICHE SU TESTO CINESE see
Chailly, Luciano

TRE LIRICHE VIETNAMITE *CC3U
(Chailly) Bar solo,pno FORLIVESI s.p.
(T798)

TRE LUSTIGA RIDDARE see Olsson

TRE MADRIGALI see Monteverdi, Claudio

TRE NINNE NANNE POPOLARI see Davico,
Vincenzo

TRE NOUVI POEMI see Alfano, Franco

TRE ORATIONES see Lewkovitch, Bernhard

TRE PEER GYNT SALMER see Saeverud,
Harald

TRE POEMI see Dallapiccola, Luigi

TRE POEMI DA IL GIARDINIERE DI
RABINDRANATH TAGORE see Alfano,
Franco

TRE POEMI DI HERMANN HESSE see Semini,
Carlo Florindo

TRE POEMI DI RILKE see Cortese, Luigi

TRE POEMI IN MUSICA see Usmanbas, Ilkan

TRE POESIE DI ANGELO POLIZIANO see
Malipiero, Gian Francesco

TRE POESIE DI F. GARCIA LORCA see
Caggiano, Roberto

TRE POESIE DI NOVENTA see Bucchi,
Valentino

TRE POESIE DI R. CARRIERI see Caggiano,
Roberto

TRE POESIE MISTICHE DI S. QUASIMODO see
Caggiano, Roberto

TRE POESIE PERSIANE, VOL. I-III see
Santoliquido, Francesco

TRE RELIGIOSE FOLKETONER see Nystedt,
Knut

TRE SALMI PER CONTRALTO E ORGANO see
Kayser, Leif

TRE SANGER see Hallnas, Hilding

TRE SANGER see Korling, August

TRE SANGER see Lundborg, Gosta

TRE SANGER see Hedenblad, Ivar

TRE SANGER see Liljefors, Ruben

TRE SANGER see Milveden, Ingemar

TRE SANGER see Tolonen, Jouko (Paavo
Kalervo)

TRE SANGER see Olsen, Sparre

TRE SANGER see Grafstrom

TRE SANGER see Korling

TRE SANGER see Sjogren, Emil

TRE SANGER see Wohlfart, Karl

TRE SANGER see Lagergren

TRE SANGER see Korling

TRE SANGER I see Merikanto, Oskar

TRE SANGER II see Merikanto, Oskar

TRE SANGER III see Merikanto, Oskar

TRE SMA KINESER OCH NIO ANDRA BARNVISOR
see Karkoff, Maurice Ingvar

TRE SOLDATER see Crome, Fritz

TRE SONETTI A ORFEO see Palester, Roman

TRE SONETTI DEL PETRARCA see Pizzetti,
Ildebrando

TRE SONETTI DI RUSTICO DI FILIPPO see
Bruno, Carlo

TRE SONGAR see Dorumsgaard, Arne

TRE TRALLANDE JANTOR see Wennerberg,
Gunnar

TRE VISOR see Skold

TREACHERY see Brahms, Johannes, Verrath

TREASURE FLOWER see Alcock, Gilbert A.

TREASURES see Medema, Ken

TREASURY OF AMERICAN SONG, A *CC180U,
US
(Siegmeister, Elie) solo,pno MUSIC
040036 $4.95   (T799)

TREBLE TRIOS, NO. 1-6 *sac,CCUL
3 female soli,pno SINGSPIR 5041-5046
$1.25, ea.   (T800)

TREBLE TRIOS, NO. 7 *sac,CCUL
3 female soli,pno SINGSPIR 5091 $1.50
(T801)

TREDE, YNGRE JAN
Five Songs To Texts By Poul Borum
*CC5U
[Dan] Mez solo,fl,vla,pno sc EGTVED
MF 296 s.p., ipa   (T802)

TREDICI ROMANZE see Veneziani, Vittore

TREE, THE see Johansson, Bengt

TREE, THE see Sibelius, Jean

TREE IN THE WOOD, THE see Somervell,
Arthur

TREED IN MIJN HUIS see Clercq, R. de

TREES see Hely-Hutchinson, (Christian)
Victor

TREES see Rasbach, Oscar

TREES see Shaw, Martin

TREES ON THE MOUNTAIN see Floyd,
Carlisle

TREHARNE, BRYCESON (1879-1948)
Corals
med-high solo,pno (F maj) SCHIRM.G
$.85   (T803)

TREI MNESTER
(Carlo, Musi) solo,pno (Bolognese
dialect) BONGIOVANI 2041 s.p. see
from El Mi Canzunett   (T804)

TREINTA AIRES POPULAIRES ALEMANES
*CC30L
(Leuchter) [Ger/Span] solo,pno
RICORDI-ARG BA 10656 s.p.   (T805)

TREINTA CANCIONES POPULAIRES ESPANOLAS
*CC30L,Span
(Grau) [Span] solo,pno RICORDI-ARG
BA 9669 s.p. original and Spanish
texts   (T806)

TREINTAOCHO CANCIONES DEL FOLKLORE
ITALIANO *CC38L,folk,It
[Span] solo,pno RICORDI-ARG BA 9875
s.p. orignal, Italian and Spanish
texts   (T807)

TREINTATRES AIRES ESCANDINAVOS *CC33L
(Jonsson, Dehnow) [Span] solo,pno
RICORDI-ARG BA 9802 s.p. original
and Spanish texts   (T808)

TREINTE LIEDER - AUTORES RUSOS *CC30L
[Fr/Russ/Span] solo,pno RICORDI-ARG
BA 9309 s.p. contains works by:
Alabiev; Arensky; Balakirev;
Borodin; Rimsky-Korsakov; Musorgsky
and others   (T809)

TREMATE, EMPI, TREMATE see Beethoven,
Ludwig van

TREMBLAY, GEORGE (1911-   )
Kekoba
SMezT soli,perc, Ondes Martenot
BERANDOL BER 1141 $10.00   (T810)

TREMISOT, ED.
Air De Concours (from L'Auroele)
solo,orch ENOCH rental   (T811)

Amour Vainqueur
solo,pno (available in 2 keys)
ENOCH s.p. see from Les
Apotheoses   (T812)

Aurore
solo,pno (available in 2 keys)
ENOCH s.p. see from Les
Apotheoses   (T813)

Berceuse (from L'Aureole)
solo,pno (available in 3 keys)
ENOCH s.p.   (T814)

TREMISOT, ED. (cont'd.)

Chanson D'exil
solo,pno (available in 2 keys)
ENOCH s.p.   (T815)

Chanson Du Florero
solo,pno (available in 3 keys)
ENOCH s.p.   (T816)

Chanson Laponne
solo,pno (available in 2 keys)
ENOCH s.p.   (T817)

Crepuscule D'or
solo,pno (available in 2 keys)
ENOCH s.p. see from Les
Apotheoses   (T818)

Fleurs D'Adieu
solo,pno (available in 2 keys)
ENOCH s.p.   (T819)

Fusians *see Le Poete Blesse; Marins
D'Islande   (T820)

Il Etait Une Femme (from L'Aureole)
solo,pno (available in 2 keys)
ENOCH s.p.   (T821)

La Danse De Taia (from L'Aureole)
solo,pno (available in 2 keys)
ENOCH s.p.   (T822)

La Femme Qui Fut (from L'Aureole)
solo,pno (available in 2 keys)
ENOCH s.p.   (T823)

La Legende Des Peagers (from
L'Aureole)
solo,pno (available in 2 keys)
ENOCH s.p.   (T824)

La Noel Des Matelots
solo,pno (available in 2 keys)
ENOCH s.p.   (T825)
solo,acap (available in 2 keys)
ENOCH s.p.   (T826)

La Noel Des Vagabonds
solo,pno (available in 2 keys)
ENOCH s.p.   (T827)
solo,acap (available in 2 keys)
ENOCH s.p.   (T828)

Le Poete Blesse
solo,pno (available in 2 keys)
ENOCH s.p. see from Fusians   (T829)

Le Reveil
solo,pno (available in 2 keys)
ENOCH s.p.   (T830)
solo,acap (available in 2 keys)
ENOCH s.p.   (T831)

Le Sommeil De Leilah
solo,pno (available in 2 keys)
ENOCH s.p.   (T832)

Les Apotheoses *see Amour Vainqueur;
Aurore; Crepuscule D'or   (T833)

Les Lapins
solo,pno ENOCH s.p.   (T834)

Les Yeux
solo,pno (available in 2 keys)
ENOCH s.p.   (T835)

Lied
solo,pno (available in 2 keys)
ENOCH s.p.   (T836)

Ma Vie Est Un Combat Douloureux (from
L'Aureole)
solo,pno (available in 2 keys)
ENOCH s.p.   (T837)

Marins D'Islande
solo,pno (available in 2 keys)
ENOCH s.p. see from Fusians   (T838)

Nausicaa
solo,orch ENOCH rental   (T839)
solo,pno ENOCH s.p.   (T840)

Nids D'oiseaux
solo,pno (available in 2 keys)
ENOCH s.p.   (T841)

Nous Elevons Nos Fils (from
L'Aureole)
solo,pno (available in 2 keys)
ENOCH s.p.   (T842)

Novembre
Mez solo,pno (D maj) ENOCH s.p.
(T843)
S solo,orch ENOCH rental   (T844)
A solo,orch ENOCH rental   (T845)
S solo,pno (E maj) ENOCH s.p.
(T846)
solo,acap solo pt ENOCH s.p.   (T847)
A solo,pno (C maj) ENOCH s.p.
(T848)
Mez solo,orch ENOCH rental   (T849)

TREMISOT, ED. (cont'd.)

Nuit D'Ete
solo,pno (available in 2 keys)
ENOCH s.p. (T850)

Oeillets
solo,pno (available in 2 keys)
ENOCH s.p. (T851)

TRENET, CHARLES
Charles Trenet A New York *CCU,Fr
[Fr] med solo,pno FRANCE $1.25
(T852)

Si Tu Vas A Paris *CC15U
[Fr] med solo,pno FRANCE $1.25
(T853)

TRENNE SANGER see Aulin, Tor

TRENTACINQUE CANTI POPOLARI ITALIANI
see Schinelli, Achille

TRENTE CHANTEFABLES DE R. DESNOS see
Wiener, Jean

TRENTE MELODIE SCELTE see Beethoven,
Ludwig van

TRENTE MELODIES see Liszt, Franz

TRENTE MELODIES see Schubert, Franz
(Peter)

TRENTE MORCEAUX DE CHANT see Godard,
Benjamin Louis Paul

TRENTESEI ARIE ITALIANE DI DIVERSI
AUTORI DEI SECOLI XVII E XVIII
*CC36L,17-18th cent
(Zanon; Dunn, G.) [It/Eng] solo,pno
cmplt ed RICORDI-ENG 129712 s.p.
contains works by: Frescobaldi;
Cavalli; Legrenzi; Freschi;
Agostini; Scarlatti; Caldara;
Ziani; Mancini (T854)

TRENTESEI ARIE NELLO STILE ANTICO, VOL.
I *CCU
(Donaudy) [It] solo,pno RICORDI-ENG
117220 s.p. (T855)

TRENTESEI ARIE NELLO STILE ANTICO, VOL.
II *CCU
(Donaudy) [It] solo,pno RICORDI-ENG
117233 s.p. (T856)

TRENTESEI ARIE NELLO STILE ANTICO, VOL.
III *CCU
(Donaudy) [It] solo,pno RICORDI-ENG
118842 s.p. (T857)

TREPAK see Mussorgsky, Modest

TREPARD, E.
Regardez Passer La Patrie
solo,acap (available in 2 keys)
ENOCH s.p. (T858)
solo,pno (available in 2 keys)
ENOCH s.p. (T859)

TRES ARIAS see Scarlatti, Alessandro

TRES ARIAS see Turina, Joaquin

TRES CANCIONES see Jurafsky, Abraham

TRES CANCIONES see Saenz, Pedro

TRES CANCIONES see Berger, Jean

TRES CANCIONES see Cales Otero, F.

TRES CANCIONES see Romero, A.

TRES CANCIONES ALDEANAS see Egon,
Rodrigo

TRES CANCIONES AMERICANAS, OP. 15 see
Lopez De La Rosa, Horatio

TRES CANCIONES ESPANOLAS see Garcia
Abril, A.

TRES CANCIONES MEDIEVALES *CC2U,Mediev
(Bacarisse) [Span] med solo,pno UNION
ESP. $2.50 (T860)

TRES CANCIONES SOBRE POESIAS DE CERNUDA
see Guastavino, Carlos

TRES CANCIONES SOBRE POESIAS DE
IGLESIAS DE LA CASA see Guastavino,
Carlos

TRES CANCOES see Nobre, Marlos

TRES CANTARES see Surinach, Carlos

TRES CANTIGAS DE ALPHONSE X see Antonio
Jose

TRES CANTOS DE NAVIDAD see Caamano,
Roberto

TRES CANTOS SOBRE TEXTOS DEL SIGLO XIII
see Helm, Theodore Otto

TRES CANTOS URUGUAYOS see Broqua,
Alfonso

TRES ESTAMPAS DE NINEZ see Thomson,
Virgil

TRES ESTROFAS DE AMOR see Casals, Pablo

TRES LIBROS DE MUSICA EN CIFRA PARA
VIHUELA see Mudarra, Alonso de

TRES LIRICAS SOBRE RIMAS DE BECQUER see
Cinque

TRES MELODIAS see Jurafsky, Abraham

TRES MELODIES see Falla, Manuel de

TRES MORILLAS ME ENAMORAN see Anonymous

TRES PASTORALES see Pedrell, F.

TRES PIEZAS see D'Esposito, Salve

TRES POEMAS see Turina, Joaquin

TRES POEMAS DE HILDA BALBIANI see
Lilien, Ignace

TRES POEMAS INDIGENAS see Villa-Lobos,
Heitor

TRES POEMAS NEGROS see Lilien, Ignace

TRES POESIAS DE NEVEUX see Brero,
Cesare

TRES PSALMI see Beekhuis, Hanna

TRES RECUERDOS DEL CIELO see
Bartolozzi, Bruno

TRES SONETOS see Turina, Joaquin

TRES TROVAS see Nobre, Marlos

TRETTON AR see Jarnefelt, Armas

TRETTON AR see Merikanto, Aarre

TREUE LEBE see Brahms, Johannes

TREURIG, TREURIG see Dresden, Sem

TREURZANG see Mortelmans, Lodewijk

TREVALSA, JOAN
My Treasure
solo,pno (F maj) BOOSEY $1.50
(T861)

TREXLER, GEORG (1903-)
Das Lied Des Vollig Arglosen
see Drei Gesange Von Paul Verlaine

Drei Gesange Von Paul Verlaine
S solo,fl,2ob,2clar,2bsn,2horn,
timp,triangle,strings cmplt ed
BREITKOPF-L rental
contains: Das Lied Des Vollig
Arglosen; Mondschein; Und So
Wird Kommen Ein Sommertag
(T862)
Funf Gesange *CC5U
high solo,pno DEUTSCHER 9036 s.p.
(T863)
Mondschein
see Drei Gesange Von Paul Verlaine

Und So Wird Kommen Ein Sommertag
see Drei Gesange Von Paul Verlaine

TRI BALADNE PESMI see Jirim, Frantisek

TRI CANZONY PRO BAS see Kupka, Karel

TRI CHANSONY see Martinu, Bohuslav

TRI CHANSONY see Vackar, Dalibor C.

TRI DOPISY DIVKAM see Vackar, Tomas

TRI DVOJSPEVY see Moyzes, Alexander

TRI LJUDSKE PESMI IZ BENECIJE *CC3U,
folk,It
(Merku, Pavle) S solo,pno DRUSTVO
DSS 343 rental Venetian region
(T864)
TRI LJUDSKE PESMI S TRZASKEGA *CC3U,
folk,It
(Merku, Pavel) B solo,pno DRUSTVO
DSS 347 rental Trieste region
(T865)
TRI MILOSTNE PISNE see Lidl, Vaclav

TRI MINIATURNE PIESNE see Kafenda,
Frico

TRI MURNOVE PESMI see Jirim, Frantisek

TRI NOTTURNA PRO SOLOVY HLAS see
Foerster, Josef Bohuslav

TRI NOVORECKE BASNE see Dvorak, Antonin

TRI PESMI see Lajovic, Anton

TRI PESMI see Ciglic, Zvonimir

TRI PESMI see Koporc, Srecko

TRI PESMI see Kozina, Marijan

TRI PESMI see Magdic, Josip

TRI PESMI see Svetel, Heribert

TRI PESMI see Scek, Ivan

TRI PESMI see Sivic, Pavle

TRI PESMI see Vremsak, Samo

TRI PIESNE Z ORAVY see Urbanec,
Bartolomej

TRI PISNE see Pollack, Bernard

TRI PISNE see Mikoda, Borivoj

TRI PISNE see Slezak, Pavel

TRI PISNE see Pollack, Bernard

TRI PISNE see Suk, Josef

TRI PISNE NA SLOVA FRANCOUZSKE POEZIE
see Bartos, Frantisek

TRI PISNE NA SLOVA K.H. MACHY see
Srnka, Jiri

TRI PISNE NA SLOVA N. GUILLENA see
Raichl, Miroslav

TRI PISNE PRO STREDNI HLAS see Plavec,
Josef

TRI SIVLESONGAR see Beck, Thomas
[Ludvigsen]

TRI SONETY NA SHAKESPEARA see Ferenczy,
Oto

TRI STRAZNICI see Jezek, Jaroslav

TRI TICHE PISNE see Eben, Petr

TRI VESELE PESMI see Kozina, Marijan

TRI VOKALISY see Stepanek, Jiri

TRI ZENSKE DVOJZPEVY see Risinger,
Karel

TRI ZENSKE PESMI see Gregorc, Jurij

TRI ZENSKE PESMI see Sivic, Pavle

TRIAL AND DEATH OF SOCRATES see
Leichtling, Alan

TRIALOGUE NO. 1 see Simons, Netty

TRIALOGUE NO. 2: MYSELVES GRIEVE see
Simons, Netty

TRIALOGUE NO. 3: NOW, SAY NAY see
Simons, Netty

TRIANON see Fontenailles, H. de

TRIBUNES SING, THE *sac,CC10UL
4 soli,pno LILLENAS MB-305 $1.95
(T866)
TRICET SNADNYCH VOCALIS see Tomaskova,
M.

TRIGO LIMPIO see Dublanc, Emilio

TRIJE RECITATIVI see Lovec, Vladimir

TRIJE SAMOSPEVI see Jirim, Frantisek

TRIJE SAMOSPEVI see Lovec, Vladimir

TRIJE SAMOSPEVI see Zebre, Demetrij

TRIJE SPEVI see Svara, Danilo

TRIMBLE, LESTER (1923-)
Four Fragments From The Canterbury
Tales *CC4U
S solo,fl,clar,hpsd sc PETERS
66068P $5.00, ipa (T867)

Petit Concert
med solo,vln,ob,hpsd sc PETERS
66069A $3.00, ipa (T868)

TRINKLIED see Kistenmacher, Arthur

TRINKLIED see Krenek, Ernst

TRINKLIED see Soukup, Vladimir, Pijacka

TRINKLIED see Zipp, Friedrich

TRINKSPRUCH see Schmalstich, Clemens

TRINQUONS see Saint-Saens, Camille

TRIO see Johnson, T.

TRIO see Strauss, Richard

TRIO DES FEMMES MORES see Charpentier, Marc-Antoine

TRIO DES PARQUES see Rameau, Jean-Philippe

TRIO FOR VOICE, PIANO AND PERCUSSION see Steiner, Gitta

TRIO NO. 3 see Bavicchi, John

TRIO OF PRAISE see Koch, Frederick

TRIOLET see Mul, Jan

TRIOMF VAN DEN DOOD see Badings, Henk

TRIOMPHANT DE MULTIPLES EPREUVES see Saint-Saens, Camille

TRIOMPHE QUE J'AIME see Meyerbeer, Giacomo

TRIOS *sac,CCUL
   3 female soli,pno,gtr SINGSPIR 5828
   $1.25   (T869)

TRIP, TRIP, TRIP see Millard, Harrison

TRIPLETT, ROBERT F.
   Two Psalms For High Voice *sac,CC2U
   high solo,pno ABINGDON APM-603
   $2.00   (T870)

TRIPOLI SE, TRIPOLI NO
   (Carlo, Musi) solo,pno (Bolognese
   dialect) BONGIOVANI 2092 s.p. see
   from El Mi Canzunett Seconda Serie
                                      (T871)

TRIPP, LAVERNE
   After Calvary *sac
   solo,pno WORD S-364   (T872)
   solo,pno BENSON S5086-S $1.00
                                      (T873)
   I Know *see Burns

   I'll Get My Reward *sac
   solo,pno BENSON S6240-S $1.00
                                      (T874)
   It's Worth It All *sac
   solo,pno BENSON S6692-S $1.00
                                      (T875)
   solo,pno WORD S-365   (T876)

   That Day Is Almost Here *sac
   solo,pno BENSON S7715-S $1.00
                                      (T877)

TRIPT LUSTIG, MIJN DONZEN DROMEN see
   Adriessen, Willem

TRIPTICO see Turina, Joaquin

TRIPTICO DE CANCIONES see Garcia Leoz, J.

TRIPTICO SACRO see Pardo

TRIPTYCH see Weegenhuise, Johan

TRIPTYCH see Hovhaness, Alan

TRIPTYCHON "SANKT SEBASTIAN see
   Reutter, Hermann

TRISTE see Ginastera, Alberto

TRISTE see Sammartino, Luis

TRISTE EST LA STEPPE see Gretchaninov,
   Alexander Tikhonovitch

TRISTE ESTABA EL REY DAVID see Mudarra,
   Alonso de

TRISTE ME VOY A LOS CAMPOS see
   Perceval, Julio

TRISTE PRIMAVERA see Clementi, F.

TRISTE SERA see Sinigaglia, Leone

TRISTES APPRETS see Rameau, Jean-
   Philippe

TRISTESSE see Albeniz, Isaac

TRISTESSE see Chopin, Frederic

TRISTESSE see Saint-Saens, Camille

TRISTESSE D'ETE see Sauguet, Henri

TRISTESSE DU SOIR see Massenet, Jules

TRISTESSES see Milhaud, Darius

TRISTEZA see Chopin, Frederic,
   Tristesse

TRISTEZA DE HILO BLANCO see Romero, A.

TRISTEZZA see Tosti, Francesco Paolo

TRISTEZZA-SOLITUDINE see Pratella,
   Francesco Balilla

TRISTIZZIA see Bijvanck, Henk

TRITANT, G.
   La Maitrise Moderne, Vol. I *sac,
   CCU,mot
   solo,org voc sc ENOCH   (T878)

   La Maitrise Moderne, Vol. II *sac,
   CCU,mot
   solo,org voc sc ENOCH   (T879)

TRITT AUF DIE GLAUBENSBAHN see Bach,
   Johann Sebastian

TRITTICO LITURGICO PER SOPRANO see
   Hemel, Oscar van

TROCKNE BLUMEN see Schubert, Franz
   (Peter)

TROIS AIRS see Bunge, Sas

TROIS BAISERS see Chaminade, Cecile

TROIS BALLADES DE FRANCOIS VILLON see
   Debussy, Claude

TROIS BALLADES FRANCAISES DE PAUL FORET
   see Roget, H.

TROIS BEAUX OISEAUX DE PARADIS see
   Ravel, Maurice

TROIS BERCEUSES see Szymanowski, Karol

TROIS BERCEUSES CHANTEES see Migot,
   Georges

TROIS CHANSONS see Ravel, Maurice

TROIS CHANSONS see Mulder, Ernest W.

TROIS CHANSONS see Mulder, Ernest W.

TROIS CHANSONS see Manen, Joan

TROIS CHANSONS see Couperin (le Grand),
   Francois

TROIS CHANSONS see Humfrey, Pelham

TROIS CHANSONS see Lawes, Henry

TROIS CHANSONS see Locke, Matthew

TROIS CHANSONS see Mesritz Van
   Velthuysen, Annie

TROIS CHANSONS see Berners, Lord

TROIS CHANSONS 2 see Blow, John

TROIS CHANSONS A DIRE see Charpentier,
   R.

TROIS CHANSONS CELTIQUES see Hennessy,
   Swan

TROIS CHANSONS D'AMOUR see Rosenthal,
   Manuel

TROIS CHANSONS DANS LE CARACTERE
   POPULAIRE see Dupin, Paul

TROIS CHANSONS DANS UN STYLE FRANCAIS
   see Lancen

TROIS CHANSONS DE BILITIS see Debussy,
   Claude

TROIS CHANSONS DE BORD see Jaubert,
   Maurice

TROIS CHANSONS DE CHARLES D'ORLEANS see
   Debussy, Claude

TROIS CHANSONS DE CHARLES VILDRAC see
   Ibert, Jacques

TROIS CHANSONS DE FOUS see Ferroud,
   Pierre-Octave

TROIS CHANSONS DE FRANCE see Debussy,
   Claude

TROIS CHANSONS DE GESTE see Ruzdjak,
   Marko

TROIS CHANSONS DE JULES SUPERVIELLE see
   Ferroud, Pierre-Octave

TROIS CHANSONS DE MARGOT see Migot,
   Georges

TROIS CHANSONS DE SA COMPOSITION see
   Henry VIII, King Of England

TROIS CHANSONS DE SON CHOIX see Pepys,
   Samuel

TROIS CHANSONS DES MAQUISARDS CONDAMNES
   see Ruyneman, Daniel

TROIS CHANSONS ENFANTINES see
   Gradstein, Alfred

TROIS CHANSONS FRANCAIS see Aubert,
   Louis-Francois-Marie

TROIS CHANSONS FRANCAISES see
   Bordewijk-Roepman, Johanna

TROIS CHANSONS NEGRES see Beekhuis,
   Hanna

TROIS CHANSONS POPULAIRES see Kahn,
   Erich Itor

TROIS CHANSONS POPULAIRES ARMENIENNES
   see Gazarossian, Coharik A.

TROIS CHANSONS POUR DANSER see
   Beekhuis, Hanna

TROIS CHANSONS SPIRTUELLES see
   Gagnebin, Henri

TROIS CHANSONS SUR DES POEMES DE
   MAURICE FOMBEURE see Bitsch, Marcel

TROIS CHANSONS TRISTES see Tate,
   Phyllis

TROIS CHANTS see Migot, Georges

TROIS CHANTS see Schmitt, Florent

TROIS CHANTS see Ponse, Luctor

TROIS CHANTS ARABES see Mignan,
   Edouard-Charles-Octave

TROIS CHANTS D'AMOUR see Vermeulen,
   Matthijs

TROIS CHANTS DE FEMMES BERBERES see
   Rosenthal, Manuel

TROIS CHANTS EN L'HONNEUR D'AUGUSTE
   COMTE see Schmitt, Florent

TROIS CHANTS EXTRAITS DU CANTIQUE DES
   CANTIQUES see Canal, Marguerite

TROIS CHANTS HEBRAIQUES see Aubert,
   Louis-Francois-Marie

TROIS CHANTS POPULAIRES SUEDOIS see
   Bagge, G.

TROIS CHANTS POUR TROIS POETES see
   Migot, Georges

TROIS CHANTS SACRES see Pousseur, Henri

TROIS CHANTS SUIVIS D'UN AIR A
   VOCALISES see Migot, Georges

TROIS CHASONNETTES see Orthel, Leon

TROIS CONSEILS see Passani, Emile

TROIS DUOS see Schmitt, Florent

TROIS EPIGRAMMES see Francaix, Jean

TROIS FABLES DE JEAN DE LA FONTAINE see
   Caplet, Andre

TROIS GOELETTES see Schmitt, Florent

TROIS GRANDS EMPEREURS see Georges,
   Alexandre

TROIS HISTOIRES POUR ENFANTS see
   Stravinsky, Igor

TROIS IMPRESSIONS see Sancan, P.

TROIS INTERLUDES see Auric, Georges

TROIS INVOCATIONS see Ryelandt, Joseph

TROIS JOURS DE VENDANGE see Viardot-
   Garcia, Pauline

TROIS LAGU DOLANAN see Simonis, Jean-
   Marie

TROIS LECONS DE TENEBRES see Couperin
   (le Grand), Francois

TROIS LEGENDES see Dupin, Paul

TROIS MADRIGAUX A TROIS VOIX see
   Amezaga, T.H.de

TROIS MELODIES see Busser, H.

TROIS MELODIES see Gallois Montbrun

TROIS MELODIES see Schmitt, Florent

TROIS MELODIES see Beydts, L.

TROIS MELODIES see Delage, Maurice

TROIS MELODIES see Rhene-Baton

TROIS MELODIES see Messiaen, Oliver

TROIS MELODIES see Segond, Pierre

TROIS MELODIES see Tagore

TROIS MELODIES see Ruyneman, Daniel

TROIS MELODIES see Debussy, Claude

TROIS MELODIES see Karjinsky, N.

TROIS MELODIES see Gagnebin, Henri

TROIS MELODIES see Paray, Paul

TROIS MELODIES see Rosenthal, Manuel

TROIS MELODIES see Rougier, A.

TROIS MELODIES (APPOLINAIRE) see Binet, Jean

TROIS MELODIES DE FR. TOUSSAINT see Steenhuis, Francois

TROIS MELODIES DE MAROT see Binet, Jean

TROIS MELODIES, DEUX DUOS ET UN TRIO see Massenet, Jules

TROIS MELODIES POUR UNE VOIX GRAVE see Diepenbrock, Alphons

TROIS MELODIES SUR DES POEMES DE J. DOMINIQUE see Grovlez, Gabriel (Marie)

TROIS MONODIES see Migot, Georges

TROIS NOUVELLES BALLADES FRANCAISES DE PAUL FORT see Gaubert, Philippe

TROIS ODELETTES ANACREONTIQUES see Emmanuel, Maurice

TROIS PASTORALES see Lazar, Filip

TROIS PASTORALES see Andriessen, Hendrik

TROIS PASTORALES see Andriessen, Hendrik

TROIS PETITES CHANSONS-SOUVENIR DE MON ENFANCE see Stravinsky, Igor

TROIS PIECES POUR SOPRANO ET PIANO see Hayama, M

TROIS PIGEONS AIMAIENT see Lacome, Paul

TROIS POEMES see Caplet, Andre

TROIS POEMES see Delage, Maurice

TROIS POEMES see Jongen, Leon

TROIS POEMES see Lacome, Paul

TROIS POEMES see Delannoy, Marcel

TROIS POEMES see Milhaud, Darius

TROIS POEMES see Peyrot

TROIS POEMES D'ALFRED DE MUSSET see Jacob, Dom Clement

TROIS POEMES D'AMOUR see Satie, Erik

TROIS POEMES DE A. RIMBAUD see Nelhybel, Vaclav

TROIS POEMES DE BAUDELAIRE see Bertouille, Gerard

TROIS POEMES DE CECILE SAUVAGE see Daniel-Lesur

TROIS POEMES DE FRANCIS JAMMES see Bernard, R.

TROIS POEMES DE GILLES NORMAND see Migot, Georges

TROIS POEMES DE H. DE REGNIER see Voormolen, Alexander Nicolas

TROIS POEMES DE HENRY CLAIRVAUX see Charpentier, Jean Jacques Beauvarlet

TROIS POEMES DE JULES SUPERVIELLE see Bunge, Sas

TROIS POEMES DE LEON-PAUL FARGUE see Auric, Georges

TROIS POEMES DE LOUIS PARROT see Saguer, Louis

TROIS POEMES DE LOUISE DE VILMORIN see Auric, Georges

TROIS POEMES DE LOUISE DE VILMORIN see Poulenc, Francis

TROIS POEMES DE MAURICE CAREME see Beyerman-Walraven, Jeanne

TROIS POEMES DE PAUL ELUARD see Devries, Ivan

TROIS POEMES DE PAUL VALERY see Ferroud, Pierre-Octave

TROIS POEMES DE PETRONE see Durey, Louis

TROIS POEMES DE R. GANZO see Schmitt, Florent

TROIS POEMES DE RENE CHALUPT see Voormolen, Alexander Nicolas

TROIS POEMES DE STEPHANE MALLARME see Debussy, Claude

TROIS POEMES DE STEPHANE MELLARME see Ravel, Maurice

TROIS POEMES DE TRISTAN KLINGSOR see Absil, Jean

TROIS POEMES D'EDGARD POE see Huybrechts, Albert

TROIS POEMES D'EMILE VERHAEREN see Carion, Fern.

TROIS POEMES DESENCHANTES see Delage, Maurice

TROIS POEMES D'HENRI DE REGNIER see Labey, Marcel

TROIS POEMES FEMININS see Pillois, Jacques

TROIS POEMES INTIMES DE GOETHE see Ferroud, Pierre-Octave

TROIS POEMES PAIENS see Martin, Frank

TROIS PRECIEUSES see Rosenthal, Manuel

TROIS QUATUORS VOCAUX see Busser, Henri-Paul

TROIS REVERENCES A LA MORT see Landowski, M.

TROIS SONNETS POUR HELENE see Duperier, J.

TROIS SONNETS SPIRITUELS see Andriessen, Hendrik

TROIS TANKAS JAPONAIS see Vieu, Jane

TROIS TRIOS see Schmitt, Florent

TROIS VESTALES CHAMPETRES ET TROIS POLICONS see Couperin (le Grand), Francois

TROJAN, VACLAV (1907-   )
Bajaja
  solo,pno SUPRAPHON s.p.   (T880)

Betlem
  solo,pno SUPRAPHON s.p.   (T881)

Broucci
  solo,pno SUPRAPHON s.p.   (T882)

Ceske A Slovenske Lidove Pisne *CCU,
  folk,Czech/Slav
  [Czech/Ger] med solo,pno PANTON
  s.p.   (T883)

Ceske A Slovenske Lidove Pisne *CCU
  [Czech/Eng/Ger] solo,pno PANTON 691
  s.p.   (T884)

Sen Noci Svatojanske
  solo,pno SUPRAPHON s.p.   (T885)

Spalicek
  solo,pno SUPRAPHON s.p.   (T886)

TROLHATTAN see Lindblad, Otto

TROLL- OCH TOMTEHISTORIER see Liljefors, Ruben

TROLLHATTAN see Lindblad, Otto

TROMBLY, PRESTON
O Death, Where Is Thy Sting? *sac,
  Easter
  S solo,pno AM.COMP.AL. $3.30 (T887)

TRONS FRID
  see Andliga Sanger, Heft 3

TROPAR ZA BOGORODICA see Detoni, Dubravko

TROPILLA DE ESTRELLAS see Lasala, Angel

TROPISCHE NACHT see Wall, C. v.d.

TROST see Kahn, Erich Itor

TROST see Trunk, Richard

TROST IM UNGLUCK see Mahler, Gustav

TROTERE, HENRY (1855-1912)
Asthore
  med solo,pno (F min) CRAMER (T888)
  low solo,pno (D min) CRAMER (T889)
  high solo,pno (G min) CRAMER (T890)

For Your Dear Sake
  low solo,pno (F maj) LEONARD-ENG
    (T891)
  high solo,pno (B flat maj) LEONARD-
  ENG (T892)
  med solo,pno (G maj) LEONARD-ENG
    (T893)

I Did Not Know
  2 soli,pno (B flat maj) LEONARD-ENG
    (T894)
  2 soli,pno (A flat maj) LEONARD-ENG
    (T895)
  med solo,pno (B flat maj) LEONARD-
  ENG (T896)
  low solo,pno (A flat maj) LEONARD-
  ENG (T897)
  high solo,pno (C maj) LEONARD-ENG
    (T898)

I Don't Suppose
  low solo,pno (C maj) CRAMER (T899)
  med solo,pno (E flat maj) CRAMER
    (T900)
  med-low solo,pno (D maj) CRAMER
    (T901)
  2 soli,pno CRAMER   (T902)
  high solo,pno (G maj) CRAMER (T903)
  med-high solo,pno (F maj) CRAMER
    (T904)

In Old Madrid
  low solo,pno (B flat maj) CRAMER
    (T905)
  high solo,pno (C maj) CRAMER
    (T906)

In Your Dear Eyes
  med-high solo,pno (F maj) CRAMER
    (T907)
  low solo,pno (D maj) CRAMER (T908)
  high solo,pno (G maj) CRAMER (T909)
  2 soli,pno CRAMER   (T910)
  med solo,pno (E flat maj) CRAMER
    (T911)

Peggy Malone
  med solo,pno (D maj) CRAMER (T912)
  low solo,pno (C maj) CRAMER (T913)
  high solo,pno (F maj) CRAMER (T914)

Piccaninny Mine
  low solo,pno (F maj) CRAMER (T915)
  med-high solo,pno (B flat maj)
  CRAMER (T916)
  med solo,pno (G maj) CRAMER (T917)
  high solo,pno (C maj) CRAMER (T918)

Roses Are Here Again
  solo,pno (B flat maj) CRAMER (T919)

Strolling Player
  solo,pno CRAMER   (T920)

Three Jolly Lightbobs
  low solo,pno (F maj) CRAMER (T921)
  high solo,pno (G maj) CRAMER (T922)

Together A' The Way
  low solo,pno (B flat maj) CRAMER
    (T923)
  high solo,pno (C maj) CRAMER (T924)

Toreador, Hola!
  low solo,pno (F min) CRAMER (T925)
  high solo,pno (G min) CRAMER (T926)

White-Stokin'd Mare
  solo,pno CRAMER   (T927)

Within Your Heart
  high solo,pno (E flat maj) CRAMER
    (T928)
  low solo,pno (E maj) CRAMER (T929)

Zanita
  solo,pno CRAMER   (T930)

TROTTE, TROTTE see Perronnet, Amelie

TROTTIN' TO THE FAIR see Stanford, Charles Villiers

TROUBADOUR SONGS see Stevens, Halsey

TROUBLE see MacGimsey, Robert

TROUT, THE see Schubert, Franz (Peter),
    Die Forelle

TROUVAILLE see Leeuw, Ton de

TROUW see Hullebroeck, Em.

TROVA: "QUIERO ENTONAR A TU OIDO" see
    Gomez Carrillo, Manuel

TROW, KAREL (1930-   )
    Matiere *CC8L
        low solo,fl,bass clar,bsn,vla,vcl
        DONEMUS s.p.   (T931)

TRUBADORSKE ZPEVY see Korte, Oldrich
    Frantisek

TRUE BEAUTY, THE see Mills, Charles

TRUE LOVE see Brahms, Johannes, Treue
    Lebe

TRUE LOVE COMES FROM GOD see Owens,
    Jimmy

TRUE LOVE'S THE GIFT see Chambers, H.A.

TRUE ROMANCE see Rubinstein, Anton

TRUED
    To Know His Love *sac
        med-high solo,pno (A flat maj)
        BOSTON $1.50   (T932)

TRUED, S. CLARENCE (1895-   )
    O God Of Love *sac
        med solo,pno ABINGDON APM-382 $.75
                                        (T933)
        SATB soli,pno ABINGDON APM-382 $.75
                                        (T934)

TRUILLET-SOYER, M.
    Chantons
        solo,pno/inst DURAND s.p. see from
            Pour Les Petits Et Pour Les
            Grands   (T935)

    Clair De Lune
        solo,pno/inst DURAND s.p. see from
            Pour Les Petits Et Pour Les
            Grands   (T936)

    Connais-Tu Mon Beau Village
        solo,pno/inst DURAND s.p. see from
            Pour Les Petits Et Pour Les
            Grands   (T937)

    Dame Souris
        solo,pno/inst DURAND s.p. see from
            Pour Les Petits Et Pour Les
            Grands   (T938)

    Grand'mere
        solo,pno/inst DURAND s.p. see from
            Pour Les Petits Et Pour Les
            Grands   (T939)

    La Berceuse
        solo,pno/inst DURAND s.p. see from
            Pour Les Petits Et Pour Les
            Grands   (T940)

    La Bergeronnette
        solo,pno/inst DURAND s.p. see from
            Pour Les Petits Et Pour Les
            Grands   (T941)

    Le Hanneton
        solo,pno/inst DURAND s.p. see from
            Pour Les Petits Et Pour Les
            Grands   (T942)

    Le Moulin
        solo,pno/inst DURAND s.p. see from
            Pour Les Petits Et Pour Les
            Grands   (T943)

    Le Petit Poulet
        solo,pno/inst DURAND s.p. see from
            Pour Les Petits Et Pour Les
            Grands   (T944)

    Pour Les Petits Et Pour Les Grands
        *see Chantons; Clair De Lune;
        Connais-Tu Mon Beau Village; Dame
        Souris; Grand'mere; La Berceuse;
        La Bergeronnette; Le Hanneton; Le
        Moulin; Le Petit Poulet (T945)

TRULY, TRULY, I SAY TO YOU see Krapf,
    Gerhard

TRUMPET IS CALLING, THE see Handel,
    George Frideric, Un Ombra Di Pace

TRUMPETER see Dix, J. Airlie

TRUMPETER, THE see Dix, J. Airlie

TRUMSLAGAREN see Heland

TRUNK, RICHARD (1879-1968)
    Abendlied *Op.44,No.9
        see Kinderlieder II

    Ammersee *Op.76,No.1
        see Funf Lieder Mit Klavier

    An Die Liebe *Op.40,No.4
        [Ger/Eng] solo,pno ZIMMER. 1414
        s.p.   (T946)

    Aufgepasst *Op.44,No.5
        see Kinderlieder II

    Augen, Meine Lieben Fensterlein
        *Op.48,No.1
        [Ger/Eng] solo,pno ZIMMER. s.p. see
            from Sechs Lieder Nach Gedichten
            Von Gottfried Keller   (T947)

    Brautwerbung *Op.63,No.4
        see Vier Heitere Lieder

    Das Hemd *Op.22,No.3
        [Ger/Eng] solo,pno ZIMMER. 1410
        s.p.   (T948)

    Das Jungfraulein *Op.44,No.3
        see Kinderlieder I

    Das Mauschen *Op.44,No.8
        see Kinderlieder II

    Das Stadtchen *Op.70,No.4
        see Sechs Lieder

    Der Feind *Op.41,No.6
        [Ger/Eng] solo,pno ZIMMER. 1421
        s.p.   (T949)

    Der Handwerksbursche *Op.70,No.6
        see Sechs Lieder

    Der Mann In Mond *Op.44,No.2
        see Kinderlieder I

    Der Sommerfaden *Op.41,No.4
        [Ger/Eng] solo,pno ZIMMER. 1419
        s.p.   (T950)

    Deutsche Volkslieder *Op.72, CC10L
        med-high solo,pno LEUCKART $3.75
                                        (T951)

    Deutschland *Op.70,No.1
        see Sechs Lieder

    Die Allee *Op.42,No.9
        [Ger/Eng] solo,pno ZIMMER. 1422
        s.p. see from ZWOLF GESANGE NACH
            GEDICHTEN VON PAUL VERLAINE
                                        (T952)

    Die Ganse *Op.44,No.1
        see Kinderlieder I

    Die Spinnerin *Op.48,No.5
        [Ger/Eng] solo,pno ZIMMER. s.p. see
            from Sechs Lieder Nach Gedichten
            Von Gottfried Keller   (T953)

    Die Stadt *Op.40,No.3
        [Ger/Eng] solo,pno ZIMMER. 1413
        s.p.   (T954)

    Doppelgleichnis *Op.48,No.2
        [Ger/Eng] solo,pno ZIMMER. s.p. see
            from Sechs Lieder Nach Gedichten
            Von Gottfried Keller   (T955)

    Ecce Homo *Op.40,No.1
        [Ger/Eng] solo,pno ZIMMER. 1411
        s.p.   (T956)

    Ein Brief *Op.47,No.4
        [Ger/Eng] solo,pno ZIMMER. 1429
        s.p.   (T957)

    Ein Gedanke *Op.70,No.5
        see Sechs Lieder

    Erscheinung *Op.76,No.2
        see Funf Lieder Mit Klavier

    Flackre, Ewiges Licht *Op.41,No.1
        [Ger] solo,pno ZIMMER. 1417 s.p.
                                        (T958)

    Flieder Im Mondlicht *Op.47,No.1
        [Ger/Eng] solo,pno ZIMMER. 1426
        s.p.   (T959)

    Fruhlingssonne *Op.9,No.3
        [Ger/Eng] solo,pno ZIMMER. 1406
        s.p.   (T960)

    Funf Lieder Mit Klavier
        [Ger/Eng] med-high solo,pno
            LEUCKART $6.00
            contains: Ammersee, Op.76,No.1;
            Erscheinung, Op.76,No.2;
            Gedankennahe, Op.76,No.4; Von
            Den Tauben, Op.76,No.5; Zweier
            Seelen Lied, Op.76,No.3 (T961)

    Gedankennahe *Op.76,No.4
        see Funf Lieder Mit Klavier

TRUNK, RICHARD (cont'd.)

    Gute Nacht *Op.47,No.6
        solo,pno ZIMMER. 1431 s.p.   (T962)

    Heimatland *Op.70,No.2
        see Sechs Lieder

    Helle Nacht *Op.42,No.8
        [Ger] solo,pno ZIMMER. s.p. see
            from ZWOLF GESANGE NACH GEDICHTEN
            VON PAUL VERLAINE   (T963)

    I Dreamed Once Of A Young Princess
        Fair *see Mir Traumte Von Einem
        Konigskind

    Idyllen *Op.81,No.1-10, CC10L
        [Ger/Eng] S/Bar/SBar soli,pno
            LEUCKART $7.25   (T964)

    In Der Nacht *Op.9,No.1
        [Ger/Eng] solo,pno ZIMMER. 1408
        s.p.   (T965)

    In Stiller Dammerung *Op.42,No.10
        [Ger/Eng] solo,pno ZIMMER. 1423
        s.p. see from ZWOLF GESANGE NACH
            GEDICHTEN VON PAUL VERLAINE
                                        (T966)

    Kinderlieder I
        [Ger/Eng] solo,pno ZIMMER. 1424
        s.p.
            contains: Das Jungfraulein,
            Op.44,No.3; Der Mann In Mond,
            Op.44,No.2; Die Ganse, Op.44,
            No.1; Putzmamsellchen, Op.44,
            No.4   (T967)

    Kinderlieder II
        [Ger] solo,pno ZIMMER. 1425 s.p.
            contains: Abendlied, Op.44,No.9;
            Aufgepasst, Op.44,No.5; Das
            Mauschen, Op.44,No.8;
            Strampelchen Macht Grosse
            Augen, Op.44,No.7; Um Den Ofen
            Herum, Op.44,No.6   (T968)

    Klagen Im Wind *Op.42,No.12
        [Ger] solo,pno ZIMMER. s.p. see
            from ZWOLF GESANGE NACH GEDICHTEN
            VON PAUL VERLAINE   (T969)

    Lenzpassion *Op.47,No.2
        solo,pno ZIMMER. 1427 s.p.   (T970)

    Mandolinen *Op.42,No.3
        [Ger/Eng] solo,pno ZIMMER. s.p. see
            from ZWOLF GESANGE NACH GEDICHTEN
            VON PAUL VERLAINE   (T971)

    Marzlied *Op.70,No.3
        see Sechs Lieder

    Mein Traum *Op.42,No.2
        [Ger/Eng] solo,pno ZIMMER. s.p. see
            from ZWOLF GESANGE NACH GEDICHTEN
            VON PAUL VERLAINE   (T972)

    Meine Mutter Hat's Gewollt *Op.9,
        No.2
        [Ger/Eng] solo,pno ZIMMER. 1409
                                        (T973)

    Menuett *Op.63,No.3
        see Vier Heitere Lieder

    Mir Glanzen Die Augen *Op.48,No.3
        [Ger/Eng] solo,pno ZIMMER. s.p. see
            from Sechs Lieder Nach Gedichten
            Von Gottfried Keller   (T974)

    Mir Traumte Von Einem Konigskind
        *Op.4,No.5
        "I Dreamed Once Of A Young Princess
        Fair" [Ger/Eng] high solo/med
        solo,pno ZIMMER. 1164 $1.25
                                        (T975)

    Mondschein *Op.42,No.1
        [Ger/Eng] solo,pno ZIMMER. s.p. see
            from ZWOLF GESANGE NACH GEDICHTEN
            VON PAUL VERLAINE   (T976)

    Putzmamsellchen *Op.44,No.4
        see Kinderlieder I

    Regen *Op.42,No.4
        [Ger/Eng] solo,pno ZIMMER. s.p. see
            from ZWOLF GESANGE NACH GEDICHTEN
            VON PAUL VERLAINE   (T977)

    Requiem *Op.47,No.3
        solo,pno ZIMMER. 1428 s.p.   (T978)

    Roschen Biss Den Apfel An *Op.48,
        No.4
        [Ger/Eng] solo,pno ZIMMER. s.p. see
            from Sechs Lieder Nach Gedichten
            Von Gottfried Keller   (T979)

    Ruhe *Op.42,No.11
        [Ger/Eng] solo,pno ZIMMER. s.p. see
            from ZWOLF GESANGE NACH GEDICHTEN
            VON PAUL VERLAINE   (T980)

TRUNK, RICHARD (cont'd.)

Schifferlied *Op.48,No.6
[Ger/Eng] solo,pno ZIMMER. s.p. see
from Sechs Lieder Nach Gedichten
Von Gottfried Keller (T981)

Schlafen, Schlafen *Op.41,No.3
[Ger] solo,pno ZIMMER. 1418 s.p.
(T982)

Schlittenfahrt *Op.63,No.1
see Vier Heitere Lieder

Schnitterlied *Op.40,No.6
[Ger/Eng] solo,pno ZIMMER. 1416
s.p. (T983)

Sechs Lieder
med-high solo,pno LEUCKART $4.25
contains: Das Stadtchen, Op.70,
No.4; Der Handwerksbursche,
Op.70,No.6; Deutschland, Op.70,
No.1; Ein Gedanke, Op.70,No.5;
Heimatland, Op.70,No.2;
Marzlied, Op.70,No.3 (T984)

Sechs Lieder Nach Gedichten Von
Gottfried Keller *see Augen,
Meine Lieben Fensterlein, Op.48,
No.1; Die Spinnerin, Op.48,No.5;
Doppelgleichnis, Op.48,No.2; Mir
Glanzen Die Augen, Op.48,No.3;
Roschen Biss Den Apfel An, Op.48,
No.4; Schifferlied, Op.48,No.6
(T985)

Serenade *Op.42,No.7
[Ger/Eng] solo,pno ZIMMER. s.p. see
from ZWOLF GESANGE NACH GEDICHTEN
VON PAUL VERLAINE (T986)

Sieben Eichendorff-Lieder *Op.45,
No.1-7, CC7L
med-high solo,pno LEUCKART $5.00
(T987)

Sieben Lieder *Op.71,No.1-7, CC7L
med-low solo,pno LEUCKART $5.25
(T988)

Sieben Weihnachtslieder *Op.61,No.1-
7, CC7L,Xmas
(Ehrenberg, Carl) [Ger/Eng]
LEUCKART high solo,pno $7.25;
med-low solo,pno $7.25; high
solo,2fl,3ob,2clar,2bsn,3horn,
2trp,timp,harp,cel,5strings
rental (T989)

Sirmione *Op.47,No.5
solo,pno ZIMMER. 1430 s.p. (T990)

Strampelchen Macht Grosse Augen
*Op.44,No.7
see Kinderlieder II

Suleika *Op.40,No.5
[Ger/Eng] solo,pno ZIMMER. 1415
s.p. (T991)

Tanzlied *Op.41,No.5
[Ger] solo,pno ZIMMER. 1420 s.p.
(T992)

Trost *Op.40,No.2
[Ger] solo,pno ZIMMER. 1412 s.p.
(T993)

Um Den Ofen Herum *Op.44,No.6
see Kinderlieder II

Vertrag *Op.63,No.2
see Vier Heitere Lieder

Vier Heitere Lieder
[Ger/Eng] high solo,pno LEUCKART
$3.25
contains: Brautwerbung, Op.63,
No.4; Menuett, Op.63,No.3;
Schlittenfahrt, Op.63,No.1;
Vertrag, Op.63,No.2 (T994)

Von Den Tauben *Op.76,No.5
see Funf Lieder Mit Klavier

Zehn Geistliche Lieder *Op.82,No.1-
10, sac,CC10L
med-high solo,pno/org LEUCKART s.p.
(T995)

Zweier Seelen Lied *Op.76,No.3
see Funf Lieder Mit Klavier

TRUR EG see Dorumsgaard, Arne

TRUST see Sibelius, Jean

TRUST IN HIM see Hamblen, Bernard

TRUST IN THE LORD see Bach, Johann
Sebastian

TRUST IN THE LORD see Davis, Katherine
K.

TRUST IN THE LORD see Handel, George
Frideric, Ombra Mai Fu

TRUST IN THE LORD WITH ALL THINE HEART
see Mehas, Janet Cooper

TRUST YE IN THE LORD see Scott, John
Prindle

TRUSTING EYES see Gartner, Clarence

TRUSTING IS BELIEVING see Price,
Florence B.

TRUTH *sac,CC11L
solo,pno BENSON BO935 $2.50 (T996)

TRY JESUS see Irwin, Lois

TRYGGARE KAN INGEN VARA
see Andliga Sanger, Heft 3

TRYPTYCH FOR HIGH VOICE AND STRING
QUARTET see Shepherd, Arthur

TRYST see Lora, Antonio

TRYST see Mourant, Walter

TRYST, THE see Rachmaninoff, Sergey
Vassilievitch

TRYST, THE see Sibelius, Jean, Flickam
Kom Ifran Sin Alsklings Mote

TRYSTE NOEL see Orr, Charles Wilfred

TSCHASTUSCHKI *CCU
(Ignatieff, Michail; Ignatieff,
Nadia) solo,pno/acord SIKORSKI 748
s.p. (T997)

TSCHUBTSCHIK *folk,Russ
[Ger/Russ] solo,pno ZIMMER. 1850 s.p.
(T998)

TSHEREMISSILAINEN LAULU see Ranta,
Sulho

TSHIRI-BIM-BAM-BAM see Weiner, Lazar, A
Nigun

TSLILIM AL HAGOVA *CCU
solo,pno OR-TAV $3.50 (T999)

TSOUYOPOULOS, GEORGES S. (1930-   )
Serenata Per Voce Da Donna
[It] female solo,fl,gtr,vla MODERN
rental (T1000)

Zwei Madrigale Fur Frauenstimme
*CC2U
female solo,pic,English horn,bass
clar,bsn,2trp,trom,4perc,harp,
cel,vln,vcl MODERN rental (T1001)

TU-BI'SHVAT SONGS see Nardi, Nachum

TU CHE A DIO SPIEGASTI L'ALI see
Donizetti, Gaetano

TU CHE DI GEL SEI CINTA see Puccini,
Giacomo

TU CHE LA VANITA CONOSCESTI DEL MONDO
see Verdi, Giuseppe

TU CH'ODI LO MIO GRIDO see Mascagni,
Pietro

TU E VOI see Novikoff, Sergio

TU ES LE REPOS see Schubert, Franz
(Peter)

TU FAIS LE CASTILLAN SUPERBE see
Cuvillier, Charles

TU FEDEL, TU COSTANTE? see Handel,
George Frideric

TU LO SAI see Scarlatti, Alessandro

TU M'APPARUS see Delmet, Paul

TU M'AS see Leeuw, Ton de

TU M'AS DIT see Rabaud, Henri

TU ME DEMANDES RIEUSE see Tesson, P.

TU ME DIRAIS see Chaminade, Cecile

TU ME TRAHIRAS see Varney, Pierre
Joseph Alphonse

TU METTRAS DANS TES CHEVEUX see
Petitjean, M.

TU NE POURRAS JAMAIS CONNAITRE see
Wagner, Richard

TU NON CANTARE, USIGNOLO! see
Spezzaferri, Giovanni

TU NON STORMIRE, O SEGALA! see
Spezzaferri, Giovanni

TU PASSAIS see Delage, Maurice

TU PASSASTE POR ESTE JARDIM see Villa-
Lobos, Heitor

TU PIE see Espoile, Raoul H.

TU QUI SANTUZZA see Mascagni, Pietro

TU REVIENDRAS see Filipucci, Edm.

TU SAIS QUEL INFAME see Mozart,
Wolfgang Amadeus

TU SAIS TROP BIEN LIRE EN MON AME see
Lefebvre, Channing

TU SCENDI DALLE STELLE see McKinney,
Howard D.

TU SEI PARTITA see Botti, C.

TU SUL LABBRO DE' VEGGENTI see Verdi,
Giuseppe

TU TE NE VAI see Ghedini, Giorgio
Federico

TU, TU PICCOLO IDDIO see Puccini,
Giacomo

TU VAS LE COEUR PLEIN D'ALLEGRESSE see
Saint-Saens, Camille

TU VAS M'ECOUTA see Lacome, Paul

TU VIRGINUM CORONA see Mozart, Wolfgang
Amadeus

TU VOIS LE FEU DU SOIR see Poulenc,
Francis

TUBINGER PSALMEN see Drischner, Max

TUCAPSKY, ANTONIN (1928-   )
Er Ist Alles *see On Je Vse

Hele, Jak Nadherne
"Siehe, Wie Herrlich!" Bar solo,
clar,perc,pno CZECH s.p. (T1002)

Od Stmivani Do Usvitu *CC5U
T solo,fl,bass clar,pno CZECH s.p.
(T1003)

On Je Vse
"Er Ist Alles" Bar solo,clar,perc,
pno CZECH s.p. (T1004)

Siehe, Wie Herrlich! *see Hele, Jak
Nadherne

TUKKIJOELLA I see Merikanto, Oskar

TUKU TUKU LAMPAITANI see Simila, Arpo

TULE see Merikanto, Oskar

TULE ILLALLA see Elokas, Ossi

TULE KANSSANI see Merikanto, Oskar

TULE LUOKSENI HERRA JEESUS see
Hannikainen, Ilmari

TULE, LYKKAAMME LAINEILLE PURREN see
Tuuri, Jaako

TULE MEILLE, TUOMAS-KULTA see Kilpinen,
Yrio

TULE TANNE see Kilpinen, Yrio

TULI TYTTO LUOTA ARMAHANSA see
Sibelius, Jean, Flickan Kom Ifran
Sin Alsklings Mote

TULIP TREE, THE see Rorem, Ned

TULIPAN *CC96U, folk,Hung
(Adam) solo,pno BUDAPEST 1487 s.p.
(T1005)

TUMMA RITVA see Kuusisto, Taneli

TUNA TING see Skold, Sven

TUNC-CATATUNC see Pahissa, Jaime

TUNDER, FRANZ (1614-1667)
Ach Herr, Lass Deine Lieben Engelein
*sac,cant
S solo,strings,org,cembalo
BREITKOPF-L rental (T1006)
[Ger] S solo,strings,cont sc
CONCORDIA 97-4167 $3.00 (T1007)
S solo,strings,org KISTNER cmplt ed
s.p., ipa, voc sc s.p. (T1008)

Ein Kleines Kindelein *sac,Xmas
[Ger] S/T solo,strings sc CONCORDIA
97-4154 $2.50 (T1009)
S solo,strings,org KISTNER cmplt ed
s.p., sc s.p., voc sc s.p., ipa
(T1010)

Wachet Auf! Ruft Uns Die Stimme
*sac,cant
[Ger] S/T solo,strings,cont sc
CONCORDIA 97-4192 $2.65 (T1011)
S solo,strings,org KISTNER cmplt ed
s.p., voc sc s.p., ipa (T1012)
(Guenther, F.) "Wake, Awake" high
solo,pno BELWIN $1.50 (T1013)

TUNDER, FRANZ (cont'd.)

(Guenther, F.) "Wake, Awake" med
solo,pno BELWIN $1.50 (T1014)
(Meyer, Hermann) S solo,4strings,
cont BAREN. 240 $4.75 (T1015)

Wake, Awake *see Wachet Auf! Ruft
Uns Die Stimme

Wake, Awake, For Night Is Flying
*sac
med-high solo,pno oct CONCORDIA
98-1816 $.20 (T1016)

TUNE THY MUSIC TO THY HEART see Davies,
Henry Walford

TUNE YOUR HARPS TO CHEERFUL STRAINS see
Handel, George Frideric

TUNKS, ADA
Dream Vessels
solo,pno CRAMER (T1017)

TUNTURILAHDE see Kilpinen, Yrio

TUNTURILAULU see Kilpinen, Yrio

TUNTURILAULUJA, VOL. I see Kilpinen,
Yrio

TUNTURILAULUJA, VOL. II see Kilpinen,
Yrio

TUNTURILAULUJA, VOL. III see Kilpinen,
Yrio

TUNTURILLE see Kilpinen, Yrio

TUONEN KEHTOLAULU see Marttinen, Tauno

TUONNE, TUONNE KAIPAAN see Soinne,
Aatto

TUPPEN see Korling, Felix

TURCHI, GUIDO (1916-   )
Due Poesie Di Quasimodo *CC2U
solo,pno ZERBONI 5091 s.p. (T1018)

Rapsodia
S solo,orch voc sc ZERBONI 7037
s.p. (T1019)

TURINA, JOAQUIN
Cantares
(Azpiazu) [Span] high solo,gtr
UNION ESP. $1.25 (T1020)

Canto A Sevilla
[Span] high solo,pno UNION ESP.
$4.50 (T1021)

Dos Canciones *CC2U
[Span] high solo,pno UNION ESP.
$1.50 (T1022)

Homenaje A Lope De Vega *Op.90
[Span] high solo,pno UNION ESP.
$1.75 (T1023)

Las Musas De Andalucia *see
Melpomene, Op.93,No.5 (T1024)

Melpomene *Op.93,No.5
[Span] high solo,pno UNION ESP.
$2.00 see from Las Musas De
Andalucia (T1025)

Poema En Forma De Canciones *CCU
[Span] high solo,pno UNION ESP.
$2.25 (T1026)

Saeta, En Forma De Salve
[Span] med solo,pno UNION ESP.
$1.25 (T1027)

Tres Arias *CC3U
[Span] high solo,pno UNION ESP.
$3.00 (T1028)

Tres Poemas *Op.81, CC3U
[Span] high solo,pno UNION ESP.
$2.25 (T1029)

Tres Sonetos *CC3U
[Span] high solo,pno UNION ESP.
$2.75 (T1030)

Triptico *CC3U
[Span] high solo,pno UNION ESP.
$2.25 (T1031)

TURKEY BUZZARD, THE see Beekhuis, Hanna

TURKISCHE LIEDER see Rietz, Johannes

TURN BACK, MY CHILD *sac
(Jennings) solo,pno BENSON S8268-R
$1.00 (T1032)

TURN ME ON! LIGHT ME UP! see Lister,
Mosie

TURN THEE O LORD see Handel, George
Frideric, Verdi Prati

TURN YE TO ME *Scot
high solo,pno (G maj) ALLANS s.p.
(T1033)
low solo,pno (E maj) ALLANS s.p.
(T1034)
med solo,pno (F maj) ALLANS s.p.
(T1035)

TURN YE TO ME see Lawson, Malcolm

TURN YOUR LIFE OVER TO JESUS see
Poglietti, Alessandro

TURN YOUR RADIO ON *sac,gospel
solo,pno ABER.GRP. $1.50 (T1036)

TURN YOUR RADIO ON see Brumley

TURNAND INDRI DA PADEREN!
(Carlo, Musi) solo,pno (Bolognese
dialect) BONGIOVANI 2096 s.p. see
from El Mi Canzunett Seconda Serie
(T1037)

TURNER, J.G.
Enchanted Strings
solo,pno (G maj) BOOSEY $1.50
(T1038)

Music Box
solo,pno (G maj) BOOSEY $1.50
(T1039)

Silent Music
solo,pno (G maj) BOOSEY $1.50
(T1040)

TURNER, OLIVE
Dawn Sprite
low solo,pno (G maj) CRAMER (T1041)
high solo,pno (B flat maj) CRAMER
(T1042)

Little Green Forest, The
solo,pno CRAMER (T1043)

Visitor, The
solo,pno CRAMER (T1044)

TURNER-MALEY, FLORENCE
Fields O' Ballyclare
high solo,pno (G maj) WILLIS $.60
(T1045)
low solo,pno (C maj) WILLIS $.60
(T1046)

Pirate, The
med solo,pno (C maj) WILLIS $.60
(T1047)
high solo,pno (D maj) WILLIS $.60
(T1048)
low solo,pno (B flat maj) WILLIS
$.60 (T1049)

TURNHOUT, GERARD DE (1520-1580)
Sacred And Secular Songs For Three
Voices *sac/sec,CCU
(Wagner, Lavern J.) 3 soli,pno A-R
ED s.p. (T1050)

TUROK, PAUL
Three Songs For Soprano And Flute
*CC3U
S solo,fl SEESAW (T1051)

TURTLE-DOVE, THE see Cardew, Cornelius

TURUNEN, MARTTI (JOHANNES) (1902-   )
Sunnuntai *Op.25,No.1
solo,pno FAZER W 2541 s.p. (T1052)

TUS OJILLOS NEGROS see Falla, Manuel de

TUSCAN SERENADE see Birch, Robert
Fairfax

TUSSCHEN DAM EN REMBRANDTSPLEIN see
Witte, D.

TUSSEN DE LANTAAREN see Kersters,
Willem

TUSSEN DE LANTAARNEN see Kersters,
Willem

TUSSENBROEK, H. VON
Als 'T Kindje Wakker Wordt *Op.35,
No.2
see Op Lichte Vleugelen

Hollandsch Liedje *Op.35,No.5
see Op Lichte Vleugelen

Meidoorn *CC8L
2 soli,pno ALSBACH s.p. (T1053)

Meihoveke *Op.35,No.4
see Op Lichte Vleugelen

Meisje *Op.35,No.3
see Op Lichte Vleugelen

Ons Lied *Op.35,No.1
see Op Lichte Vleugelen

Op Lichte Vleugelen
solo,pno ALSBACH s.p.
contains: Als 'T Kindje Wakker
Wordt, Op.35,No.2; Hollandsch
Liedje, Op.35,No.5; Meihoveke,

TUSSENBROEK, H. VON (cont'd.)

Op.35,No.4; Meisje, Op.35,No.3;
Ons Lied, Op.35,No.1 (T1054)

TUTANKHAMEN see Mack, Hebe

TUTHILL, BURNET CORWIN (1888-   )
Prayer For Those At Home
low solo,pno (F maj) BOOSEY $1.75
(T1055)
high solo,pno (A flat maj) BOOSEY
$1.75 (T1056)

TUTTE LE FESTE AL TEMPIO see Verdi,
Giuseppe

TUTTI I FIORI see Puccini, Giacomo

TUTTO CANGIA E IL DI' CHE VIENE see
Martini, Giambattista

TUTTO E SCIOLTO see Martino, Donald

TUTTO RITORNA see Ferrari-Trecate,
Luigi

TUULAN TEI see Merikanto, Oskar

TUULENHENKI see Merikanto, Oskar

TUULIKIN KEHTOLAULU see Hannikainen,
Ilmari

TUURI, JAAKO
Den Sista Stunden *see Viimeinen
Hetki

Herdeflickans Vaggsang *see
Paimentyton Kehtolaulu

Ole Luonani Silloin *Op.12,No.2
2 soli,pno FAZER F 1021 s.p.
(T1057)
Paimentyton Kehtolaulu *Op.6,No.2
"Herdeflickans Vaggsang" 2 soli,pno
FAZER W 584 s.p. (T1058)

Tule, Lykkaamme Laineille Purren
*Op.12,No.1
2 soli,pno FAZER F 1020 s.p.
(T1059)
Unten Vienot Viljapellot *Op.4
2 soli,pno FAZER F 932 s.p. (T1060)

Viimeinen Hetki *Op.30,No.3
"Den Sista Stunden" 2 soli,pno
FAZER F 2195 s.p. (T1061)

TUUTI LASTA *CC35U
(Sutinen) solo,pno FAZER F 3336 s.p.
(T1062)

TUUTI, TUUTI TUMMAISTANI see Kilpinen,
Yrio

TUUTULAULU see Kilpinen, Yrio

TUXEN-BANG, CARLOS
Nocturnos *CCU
S solo,pno BARRY-ARG BC 2006 $3.00
(T1063)

TUYO ES MI CORAZON see Lehar, Franz,
Dein Ist Mein Ganzes Herz

TVA ANDLIGA SANGER see Nordqvist,
Gustaf

TVA BALLADER see Rangstrom, Ture

TVA DIKTER see Peterson-Berger, (Olof)
Wilhelm

TVA DIKTER AV AUGUST STRINDBERG see
Aulin, Tor

TVA DUETTER see Olson, Daniel

TVA DUETTER see Anjou, P. d'

TVA HOSTDIKTER see Nordqvist, Gustaf

TVA JULSANGER see Sibelius, Jean

TVA JULSANGER see Finnborg

TVA JULSANGER see Heilakka

TVA JULVISOR see Sibelius, Jean

TVA JULVISOR MORMORS TID see Lithenius,
Sofie

TVA KAMMARSANGER TILL DIKTER AV NILS
FERLIN see Milveden, Ingemar

TVA KLARA STJARNOR HAR HIMLEN MIST see
Peterson-Berger, (Olof) Wilhelm

TVA RELIGIOSA SANGER see Nordqvist,
Gustaf

TVA ROMANTISKA VISOR see Peterson-
Berger, (Olof) Wilhelm

TVA ROSENBLAD see Ika

TVA SANGER see Liljefors, Ruben

TVA SANGER see Pergament, Moses

TVA SANGER see Pacius, Fredrik

TVA SANGER see Peterson-Berger, (Olof) Wilhelm

TVA SANGER see Wennerberg, Gunnar

TVA SANGER see Wohlfart, Karl

TVA SANGER FOR MEZZOSOPRAN see Korling, August

TVA SOMMARVISOR see Rangstrom, Ture

TVA VARSANGAR see Fougstedt, Nils-Eric

TVA VISOR see Lyberg, Margot

TVA VISOR I FOLKTON see Nordqvist, Gustaf

TVAR see Mikoda, Borivoj

TVASTAMMIGA SANGER see Wrangel

TVENNE REIGIOSA DIKTER see Palm, Hermann

TVENNE SANGER see Wideen

TVENNE SANGER see Wennerberg, Gunnar

TVO SANGAR see Lie, Harald

TVO SONGAR see Olsen, Sparre

TVUJ HLAS see Mikoda, Borivoj

TWA CORBIES see Lawson, Malcolm

TWA SISTERS O' BINNORIE *folk,Scot solo,pno (C maj) PATERSON FS89 s.p. (T1064)

TWAALF GEDICHTEN, BAND 1 see Andriessen, K.

TWAALF GEUZELIEDJES UIT DEN SPAANASCHEN TIJD *CC12U (Loman, A.D.) solo,pno BREITKOPF-W 57 09094 s.p. (T1065)

TWAALF LIEDEREN, BDS. I & II see Mulder, Herman

TWAALF STUKJES see Ruppe, C.F.

TWAALF STUKJES see Ruppe, C.F.

TWANKYDILLO see Broadwood, Lucy E.

'TWAS IN THE COOL OF EVENTIDE see Bach, Johann Sebastian, Am Abend Da Es Kuhle War

TWAS IN THE MOON OF WINTERTIME see Yon, Pietro Alessandro

TWEE DOODEN see Zagwijn, Henri

TWEE DUETTEN OP TEKST UIT "HET KONINGSGRAF" see Colaco Osorio-Swaab, Reine

TWEE GEDICHTEN VAN JOOST VAN DEN VONDEL see Schouwman, Hans

TWEE GEDICHTEN VAN P. VAN OSTAYEN see Lilien, Ignace

TWEE GEDICHTJES see Loots, Ph.

TWEE GEESTELIJKE LIEDEREN see Mengelberg, Rudolf

TWEE KERSTLIEDEREN see Oort, H.C.v.

TWEE KERSTLIEDEREN see Oort, H.C.v.

TWEE KERSTLIEDEREN UIT HORAE BELGICAE see Boedijn, Gerard H.

TWEE KERSTLIEDJES see Loots, Ph.

TWEE LIEDEREN see Adriessen, Willem

TWEE LIEDEREN see Mulder, Herman

TWEE LIEDEREN see Andriessen, K.

TWEE LIEDEREN see Franco Mendes, H.

TWEE LIEDEREN see Nieland, Jan

TWEE LIEDEREN see Zweers, [Bernard]

TWEE LIEDEREN see Oort, H.C.v.

TWEE LIEDEREN see Cohen, M.J.

TWEE LIEDEREN see Mesritz Van Velthuysen, Annie

TWEE LIEDEREN see Schuurman, Jr.M.

TWEE LIEDEREN see Cohen, M.J.

TWEE LIEDEREN see Wertheim, R.

TWEE LIEDEREN OP DUITSE TEKST see Gilse, Jan van

TWEE LIEDEREN OP OUD-NEDERLANDSCHE TEKSTEN see Nieland, Jan

TWEE LIEDEREN VAN A. VERWEY see Mulder, Herman

TWEE LIEDEREN VAN ALBRECHT RODENBACH see Zagwijn, Henri

TWEE LIEDEREN VAN C. FLEISCHLEIN see Bijvanck, Henk

TWEE LIEDEREN VAN CHARLES VILDRAC see Badings, Henk

TWEE LIEDEREN VAN CHR. MORGENSTERN see Bijvanck, Henk

TWEE LIEDEREN VAN EUGENIE FINK see Bijvanck, Henk

TWEE LIEDEREN VAN F. BASTIAANSE see Mulder, Herman

TWEE LIEDEREN VAN GABRIELA MISTRAL see Leeuw, Ton de

TWEE LIEDEREN VAN GEZELLE see Bijvanck, Henk

TWEE LIEDEREN VAN J. PRINS see Mulder, Herman

TWEE LIEDEREN VAN J. V.D. WAALS see Bijvanck, Henk

TWEE LIEDEREN VAN LI-TAI PO see Bijvanck, Henk

TWEE LIEDEREN VAN MAARTEN MOURIK see Dijk, Jan van

TWEE LIEDEREN VAN P. VAN OSTAYEN see Delden, Lex van

TWEE LIEDEREN VAN R.J. SPITZ see Mulder, Ernest W.

TWEE LIEDEREN VAN RAINER MARIA RILKE see Orthel, Leon

TWEE LIEDEREN VAN RAINER MARIA RILKE see Orthel, Leon

TWEE LIEDEREN VAN RAINER MARIA RILKE see Orthel, Leon

TWEE LIEDEREN VAN SCHAUKAL see Bijvanck, Henk

TWEE LIEDEREN VOOR EEN HUWELIJKSFEEST see Schouwman, Hans

TWEE LIEDERN UIT "KRANS DER MIDDELEEUWEN" see Hemel, Oscar van

TWEE MENSCHEN see Zagwijn, Henri

TWEE NOCTURNES see Hermans, Nico

TWEE NOCTURNES VAN P.C. BOUTENS see Hermans, Nico

TWEE OUDE MELODIEEN EN TWEE VRIJE COMPOSITIES see Beekhuis, Hanna

TWEE REDDELOZEN see Ketting, Otto

TWEE SONNETTEN see Flothius, Marius

TWEE SPREUKEN see Leeuw, Ton de

TWEE SULEIKALIEDEREN see Bijvanck, Henk

TWEE WIJZANGEN see Ruyneman, Daniel

TWELFTH NIGHT see Copley, Ian A.

TWELVE BURNS SONGS see Liddell, Claire

TWELVE CANZONETS see Haydn, (Franz) Joseph

TWELVE CATALAN SONGS, FIRST SERIES see Nin-Culmell, Joaquin

TWELVE DAYS OF CHRISTMAS *sac med solo,pno AMP $1.75 (T1066) (Austin, F.) low solo,pno BELWIN $1.50 (T1067) (Niles, John Jacob) med-low solo,pno (F maj) SCHIRM.G $1.00 (T1068)

TWELVE DAYS OF CHRISTMAS, THE see Austin, Frederick

TWELVE DUETS see Rubinstein, Anton

TWELVE FINNISH FOLK SONGS *CC12U,folk, Finn (Pacius, Fredrik) [Finn/Ger/Eng] solo,pno FAZER W 665 s.p. (T1069)

TWELVE FOLK SONGS FROM JAMAICA *CC12U, folk,Carib (Murray; Gavall) solo,gtr OXFORD 58.608 $.75 (T1070)

TWELVE HEBREW CHILDREN'S SONGS see Alman, Samuel

TWELVE HUMBERT WOLFE SONGS see Holst, Gustav

TWELVE LYRICS see Thomas, Arthur Goring

TWELVE MINIATURES see Somers, Harry Stewart

TWELVE NEW LYRICS see Thomas, Arthur Goring

TWELVE POEMS FROM PIERROT LUNAIRE, VOLUMES I AND II see Kowalski, Max

TWELVE POEMS OF EMILY DICKINSON see Copland, Aaron

TWELVE POPULAR CATALAN SONGS, SECOND SERIES see Nin-Culmell, Joaquin

TWELVE SACRED DUETS FROM CANTATAS, VOL. I see Bach, Johann Sebastian

TWELVE SACRED DUETS FROM CANTATAS, VOL. II see Bach, Johann Sebastian

TWELVE SACRED DUETS FROM CANTATAS, VOL. III see Bach, Johann Sebastian

TWELVE SACRED DUETS FROM CANTATAS, VOL. IV see Bach, Johann Sebastian

TWELVE SACRED SONGS see Speaks, Oley

TWELVE SCOTTISH SONGS see Beethoven, Ludwig van

TWELVE SELECTED SONGS, OP. 4, 14, 21, 26, 34 see Rachmaninoff, Sergey Vassilievitch

TWELVE SONGS see Handel, George Frideric

TWELVE SONGS see Hahn, Reynaldo

TWELVE SONGS see Ives, Charles

TWELVE SONGS see Debussy, Claude

TWELVE SONGS see De Severac, Deodat

TWELVE SONGS see Liszt, Franz

TWELVE SONGS see Kosa, Gyorgy

TWELVE SONGS FOR HELEN AND ONE FOR BILL see Porter, Quincy

TWELVE SONGS FROM THE FOURTH VOLUME see Kennedy-Fraser, Marjory

TWELVE SONGS OF FAITH see Watt, Father Leo

TWELVE SONGS ON WORDS BY EMIL HAGSTROM see Larsson, Lars-Erik

TWELVE SONGS, VOLUME I see Poulenc, Francis

TWELVE SONGS, VOLUME II see Poulenc, Francis

TWELVE TOP OF TOPS *CC12U solo,pno OR-TAV $1.50 (T1071)

TWELVE WISE SAYINGS see Hancocks, B.J.

TWELVE WORDS see Franco, Johan

TWENTIETH CENTURY see Duke, John Woods

TWENTIETH CENTURY ART SONGS *CC27L, 20th cent med solo,pno SCHIRM.G contains works by: Barber; Dougherty; Gold; Weaver and others (T1072)

TWENTY-EIGHT SONGS, VOL. I see Mussorgsky, Modest

TWENTY-EIGHT SONGS, VOL. II see Mussorgsky, Modest

TWENTY-EIGHT SONGS, VOL. III see Mussorgsky, Modest

TWENTY, EIGHTEEN
(Taylor, Deems) med solo,pno BELWIN
$1.50   (T1073)

TWENTY FAVOURITE SONGS see Purcell,
Henry

TWENTY-FIVE FAVORITE LATIN-AMERICAN
SONGS *CC25L,folk,So Am
(Sandoval, Miguel) solo,pno SCHIRM.G
$3.00   (T1074)

TWENTY-FIVE SACRED SONGS see Bach,
Johann Sebastian

TWENTY-FIVE SACRED SONGS FROM THE
SCHEMELLI SONG BOOK see Bach,
Johann Sebastian

TWENTY-FIVE SELECTED SONGS see
Schubert, Franz (Peter)

TWENTY-FIVE SELECTED SONGS see Faure,
Gabriel-Urbain

TWENTY-FIVE SONGS ON LYRICS BY VARIOUS
POETS see Wolf, Hugo

TWENTY-FIVE SONGS, VOL. I see Wolf,
Hugo

TWENTY-FIVE SONGS, VOL. II see Wolf,
Hugo

TWENTY-FOUR CANONS see Haydn, (Franz)
Joseph

TWENTY-FOUR FAVORITE SONGS see
Schubert, Franz (Peter)

TWENTY-FOUR ITALIAN SONGS AND ARIAS OF
THE SEVENTEENTH AND EIGHTEENTH
CENTURIES *CC24L,It,17th cent/18th
cent
[It/Eng] med-high solo,pno SCHIRM.G
1722 $3.50; med-low solo,pno
SCHIRM.G 1723 $3.50   (T1075)

TWENTY-FOUR SONGS, VOL. I see Mahler,
Gustav

TWENTY-FOUR SONGS, VOL. II see Mahler,
Gustav

TWENTY-FOUR SONGS, VOL. III see Mahler,
Gustav

TWENTY-FOUR SONGS, VOL. IV see Mahler,
Gustav

TWENTY HUNGARIAN FOLKSONGS *CC20U,Hung
(Bartok, B.; Kodaly, Z.) [Eng] solo,
pno BUDAPEST $3.50   (T1076)

TWENTY-NINE CHANSONS see Manchicourt,
Pierre de

TWENTY-NINE SELECTED SONGS see Brahms,
Johannes

TWENTY-ONE CONCERT ARIAS FOR SOPRANO,
VOL. I see Mozart, Wolfgang Amadeus

TWENTY-ONE CONCERT ARIAS FOR SOPRANO,
VOL. II see Mozart, Wolfgang
Amadeus

TWENTY-ONE SONGS see Crzellitzer, Fritz

TWENTY POPULAR FRENCH SONGS AND GAMES
*CC20U,Fr
[Fr/Eng] ASHDOWN s.p.   (T1077)

TWENTY SACRED SONGS see Bach, Johann
Sebastian

TWENTY SACRED SONGS FROM THE SCHEMELLI
GESANGBUCH see Bach, Johann
Sebastian

TWENTY SELECTED SONGS see Mendelssohn-
Bartholdy, Felix

TWENTY SELECTED SONGS, VOL. 1 see
Grieg, Edvard Hagerup

TWENTY SONGS see Chausson, Ernest

TWENTY SONGS see Bizet, Georges

TWENTY SONGS see Bemberg, Herman

TWENTY SONGS see Chausson, Ernest

TWENTY SONGS ON POEMS BY EICHENDORFF
see Wolf, Hugo

TWENTY SONGS, VOL. 1 see Gurney, Ivor

TWENTY SONGS, VOL. 2 see Gurney, Ivor

TWENTY SONGS, VOL. 3 see Gurney, Ivor

TWENTY SONGS, VOL. 3, OP. 41 see
Kilpinen, Yrio

TWENTY SONGS, VOL. 4 see Gurney, Ivor

TWENTY-THIRD PSALM see Archer, Violet

22 PAGES see Straesser, Joep

TWENTY-TWO SONGS see Rangstrom, Ture

TWILIGHT see Hengeveld, G.

TWILIGHT see Keel, Frederick

TWILIGHT see Massenet, Jules

TWILIGHT FANCIES see Delius, Frederick

TWILIGHT IN PARIS see Hively, Wells

TWILIGHT PEOPLE see Bainton, Edgar
Leslie

TWILIGHT PEOPLE, THE
A/Bar solo,pno (med) OXFORD 61.725
$1.25   (T1078)

TWINS see Head, Michael (Dewar)

TWINTIG JIDDISCHE VOLKSLIEDEREN
*CC20L,folk
(Millner, Ch.; Nuis, Martien) solo,
pno ALSBACH s.p. Yiddish text
                                         (T1079)

TWINTIG KERSTLIEDEREN see Hengeveld, G.

TWISTED TRINITY, THE see Diamond, David

TWO see Gaburo, Kenneth

TWO ARIAS see Claflin, Avery

TWO ARIAS see Wolf, Hugo

TWO AUSTRALIAN FOLKSONGS see Holford,
Franz

TWO BALLADS see Roselius, Ludwig

TWO BALLADS BY GOETHE see Orland, Henry

TWO BASS SONGS see Strauss, Richard

TWO BELLOC SONGS see Persichetti,
Vincent

TWO BERGERETTE see Riegger, Wallingford

TWO BIRDS see Lecocq, Charles

TWO BROTHERS, THE
see Schirmer's American Folk-Song
Series, Set XXII (American-English
Folk-Ballads From The Southern
Appalachian Mountains)

TWO BROWN EYES see Grieg, Edvard
Hagerup, To Brune Ojne

TWO BY MARIANNE MOORE see Thomson,
Virgil

TWO CANTATAS FOR SOPRANO AND
INSTRUMENTS see Clerambault, Louis-
Nicolas

TWO CELTIC LOVE SONGS see Williams,
W.S.Gwynn

TWO CELTIC SONGS see Williams,
W.S.Gwynn

TWO CHINESE LOVE SONGS see Hurst, G.

TWO CHINESE SONGS see Allbright

TWO CHRISTMAS SONGS see Fulton, Norman

TWO DIALOGUES AND RECITATIVE see
Schuster, Giora

TWO DIVINE HYMNS AND ALLELUIA see
Purcell, Henry

TWO DUETS see Franco, Johan

TWO DYLAN THOMAS SONGS see Whittenberg,
Charles

TWO ENCHANTMENTS OF LI TAI PE see
Dorati, Antal

TWO ENCORE SOLOS BY MARJORIE JONES see
Jones, Marjorie

TWO ENGLISH FOLKSONGS see Stevens,
Halsey

TWO ENGLISH FOLKSONGS see Vaughan
Williams, Ralph

TWO EPIGRAMMES OF MAROT see Ravel,
Maurice

TWO EYES OF GREY see McGeoch, Daisy

TWO FINNISH SONGS see Stout, Alan

TWO FISH see Rawsthorne, Alan

TWO FRENCH FOLK SONGS
(Hopkins, A.) [Fr] med solo,kbd
HANSEN-DEN s.p.
contains: La Bergere Aux Champs; Le
Roi Renard   (T1080)

TWO GOETHE SONGS see Pisk, Paul Amadeus

TWO GRENADIERS, THE see Schumann,
Robert (Alexander), Die Beiden
Grenadiere

TWO GUITARS *Russ
solo,pno ALLANS s.p.   (T1081)

TWO HANNAH SZENESH POEMS see Helfman,
Max

TWO HAZEL EYES see Grieg, Edvard
Hagerup, To Brune Ojne

TWO HEBRIDEAN LOVE SONGS see Henderson,
W.G.

TWO HEINE SONGS see Heller, A.

TWO HOLY WEEK ARIAS see Grimm, Johann
D.

TWO HUMORESKES see Weiner, Lazar

TWO HUMOROUS SONGS FOR BASS AND
ORCHESTRA see Beethoven, Ludwig van

TWO HUNDRED SONGS, VOL. I (CONTAINS ALL
THE CYCLES PLUS 42 SELECTED SONGS)
see Schubert, Franz (Peter)

TWO HUNDRED SONGS, VOL. II see
Schubert, Franz (Peter)

TWO HUNDRED SONGS, VOL. III see
Schubert, Franz (Peter)

TWO HYMNS FOR TENOR AND ORCHESTRA see
Stout, Alan

TWO INVOCATIONS see Joubert, John

TWO IRISH SONGS see Beethoven, Ludwig
van

TWO LITTLE BIRDLINGS see Cate, H.

TWO LITTLE FEET see Arundale, Claude

TWO LITTLE IRISH SONGS see Lohr,
Hermann

TWO LITTLE WOODEN SHOES see Molloy,
James Lyman

TWO LITTLE WORDS see Brahe, May H.

TWO LOVE SONGS see Helm, Everett

TWO LOVE SONGS see Bernstein, Leonard

TWO LOVE SONGS see Mollicone, Henry

TWO MADRIGALS see Schutz, Heinrich

TWO MADRIGALS see Weisgall, Hugo

TWO MELANCHOLIC SONGS see Vidosic,
Tihomil

TWO MEN BETOOK THEMSELVES TO PRAY IN
THE TEMPLE see Schutz, Heinrich

TWO MOTETS see Pinkham, Daniel

TWO NORWEGIAN SONGS see Melby, John

TWO NURSERY RHYMES see Bliss, Sir
Arthur

TWO OLD BIRDS see Avshalomov, Jacob

TWO OLD ENGLISH LOVE LYRICS see Diack,
John Michael

TWO OLD WORLD SONGS see Hope, H.
Ashworth

TWO-PART CANZONETS FOR VOICES AND
RECORDERS (VIOLS) see Morley,
Thomas

TWO PART STYLINGS NO. I *sac,CC9UL
(Boud, Ron) 2 soli,pno LILLENAS
MB-223 $1.50   (T1082)

TWO PART STYLINGS NO. II *sac,CC11UL
(Nelson, Jerry) 2 soli,pno LILLENAS
MB-357 $1.50   (T1083)

TWO PASSIONTIDE SONGS see Wright, Denis

TWO POEMS see Hopkins, B.

TWO POEMS AND THREE JAPANESE LYRICS see Strauss, Richard

TWO POEMS BY A. BESANT see Schouwman, Hans

TWO POEMS BY C. JINARAJADASA see Schouwman, Hans

TWO POEMS BY SHOVE see Vaughan Williams, Ralph

TWO POEMS OF LOUIS ARAGON see Poulenc, Francis

TWO POEMS OF THEODORE ROETHKE see Rorem, Ned

TWO POEMS OF WILLIAM BLAKE see Goldman, Richard Franko

TWO PROVERBS see Leichtling, Alan

TWO PSALMS see Kahn, Erich Itor

TWO PSALMS FOR HIGH VOICE see Triplett, Robert F.

TWO RILKE SONGS see Martino, Donald

TWO SACRED SOLOS see Burns, William K.

TWO SACRED SONGS see Frescobaldi, Girolamo

TWO SACRED SONGS see Starer, Robert

TWO SCENES FOR SOPRANO, TRUMPET AND ORGAN see Plog

TWO SCENES FROM ANTONY AND CLEOPATRA see Barber, Samuel

TWO SELECTED SONGS see Grieg, Edvard Hagerup

TWO SEPHARDIC PRAYERS see Stutschevsky, Joachim

TWO SEVENTEENTH CENTURY POEMS see Orr, Charles Wilfred

TWO SHABBAT SONGS see Zur, Menachem

TWO SHAKESPEARE SONGS see Benton, Daniel

TWO SHAKESPEARE SONGS see Stevens, Halsey

TWO SHAKESPEARE SONNETS see Hovhaness, Alan

TWO SHAKESPEARE SONNETS see Franco, Johan

TWO SHORT SONGS see Hope, H. Ashworth

TWO SOLOS FOR BAPTISM see Bender, Jan

TWO SOLOS FOR GUITAR AND VOICE see Rider, Dale G.

TWO SONGS see Duke, John Woods

TWO SONGS see Van De Water, B.

TWO SONGS see Bedell, Robert Leech

TWO SONGS see Shaw, Martin

TWO SONGS see Chalk, C.

TWO SONGS see Orthel, Leon

TWO SONGS see Strauss, Richard

TWO SONGS see Valen, Fartein

TWO SONGS see Flanagan, William

TWO SONGS see Mompou, Federico

TWO SONGS see Ropartz, Joseph Guy

TWO SONGS see Poulenc, Francis

TWO SONGS see Poulenc, Francis

TWO SONGS see Dowland, John

TWO SONGS see Duke, John Woods

TWO SONGS see Hindemith, Paul

TWO SONGS see Helps, Robert

TWO SONGS see Hoskins, William

TWO SONGS see Whittenberg, Charles

TWO SONGS see Weber, Ben

TWO SONGS see Taylor, Clifford

TWO SONGS see Borodin, Alexander Porfirievitch

TWO SONGS see Ireland, John

TWO SONGS see Wishart

TWO SONGS see Geehl, Henry Ernest

TWO SONGS see Stravinsky, Igor

TWO SONGS see Stravinsky, Igor

TWO SONGS see Mesritz Van Velthuysen, Annie

TWO SONGS see Prister, Bruno

TWO SONGS see Hannikainen, Ilmari

TWO SONGS see Moeran, Ernest J.

TWO SONGS see Tcherepnin, Alexander

TWO SONGS see Teed, Roy

TWO SONGS see Jemnitz, S.

TWO SONGS see Behar, Gy.

TWO SONGS AFTER WILLIAM BLAKE see Hartley, Walter S.

TWO SONGS BETWEEN WALTZES see Rieti, Vittorio

TWO SONGS FOR CONTRALTO see Brahms, Johannes

TWO SONGS FOR CONTRALTO WITH VIOLA AND PIANO see Brahms, Johannes

TWO SONGS FOR MEDIUM VOICE see McAfee, Don

TWO SONGS FOR MEZZOSOPRANO AND GUITAR see Holloway, Robin

TWO SONGS FOR SOPRANO AND PIANO see Steiner, Gitta

TWO SONGS FOR THREE YEARS see Adler, Samuel

TWO SONGS FROM PILGRIM'S PROGRESS see Moore, J. Chris

TWO SONGS FROM " TABLEAUX" see Rochberg, George

TWO SONGS FROM THE FESTIVAL OF BIBLE SONGS   *sac,CC2U,Bibl
solo,pno OR-TAV $.50   (T1084)

TWO SONGS FROM "TWELFTH NIGHT" see Sibelius, Jean

TWO SONGS FROM TWELFTH NIGHT see Cook, John

TWO SONGS FROM ULVENS-SON see Nielsen, Carl

TWO SONGS OF FAITH see Salomon, Karel

TWO SONGS OF FAREWELL see Bissell, Keith W.

TWO SONGS OF JOHN DONNE see Woollen, Russell

TWO SONGS OF SUESKIND VON TIMBERG see Saminsky, Lazare

TWO SONGS OF WILLIAM BLAKE see MacNutt, Walter

TWO SONGS ON A TEXT BY R.M. RILKE see Orthel, Leon

TWO SONGS ON LATIN FRAGMENTS see Pleskow, Raoul

TWO SONGS ON TEXTS BY ROBERT FROST see Ames, W.T.

TWO SONGS (SCULPTURES) see Bijvanck, Henk

TWO SONGS TO POEMS OF MICHELANGELO see Ribari, Antal

TWO SONNETS see Babbit, Milton

TWO SONNETS see Babbit, Milton

TWO SPANISH SONGS see Ferguson, Edwin Earle

TWO THOUSAND YEARS AGO see Wilkin, Marijohn

TWO TOGETHER see Amato, Bruno

TWO WISDOMS see Pisk, Paul Amadeus

TWOFOLD TALE, THE see Ishiketa, M.

TWOHIG
    Lord Is My Captain (composed with
      O'Hara, Geoffrey) *sac,Gen
      high solo,pno (G maj) WILLIS $.75
                                     (T1085)
      low solo,pno (E flat maj) WILLIS
      $.75   (T1086)

TWOIG
    I Walked Today Where Jesus Walked
      (composed with O'Hara, Geoffrey)
      *sac
      solo,pno BENSON S6136-R $1.25
                                     (T1087)

T'Y, QUI DIT, BAH! D'A BOUT D'OU? see Denis, Didier

TYLNAK, IVAN (1910-1969)
    Jesen *CC3U
    [Czech/Ger] B solo,pno CZECH s.p.
                                     (T1088)

TY'S PRISEL ZASE see Marsik, Emanuel

TYSON, MILDRED LUND (1944-   )
    Sea Moods
      low solo,pno (G min) SCHIRM.G $.85
                                     (T1089)

TYST AR SKOGEN OCH NEJDEN ALL see Wideen, Ivar

TYST SOM EN NATT, DJUP SOM ETT HAV see Gotze

TZ'ENA UR'ENA
    (Helfman, Max) "O Daughters Of
    Jerusalem" [Heb] med solo,pno
    TRANSCON. IS 525 $.40   (T1090)

TZU LANG HOB ICH GEVART OIF DIR *Jew
    solo,pno KAMMEN 473 $1.00   (T1091)

TZUBY see Figus-Bystry, Villiam

TZUREISST DIE KAITEN *Jew
    solo,pno KAMMEN 431 $1.00   (T1092)

U

U BACHIANAS BRASILEIRAS, NO. 5 see Villa-Lobos, Heitor

U BRAN STESTI see Foerster, Josef Bohuslav

U MERE PASTORE see Tomasi, H.

UBER ALLEN GIPFELN IST RUH see Liszt, Franz

UBER DEINE AUGENLIDER see Bijvanck, Henk

UBER DEM HAFEN VON LINDOS see Rietz, Johannes

UBER DER ODER see Nick, Edmund

UBER EIN STUNDLEIN see Pfitzner, Hans

UBER NACHT KOMMT STILL DAS LIED see Wolf, Hugo

UBERALL IST WUNDERLAND see Schilling, Otto-Erich

UBI CARITAS see Lege, Gunter

UBUNG AM KLAVIER see Orthel, Leon

UBUNGEN FUR KOLORATURSOPRAN see Kapr, Jan

UCCELLI see Fasullo, P.

UDITE, UDITE, O RUSTICI see Donizetti, Gaetano

UF EM BIBABONEBERG see Vogel, Wladimir

UGALDE, MME
    L'Eleve De Saint-Cyr
      solo,acap ENOCH s.p.   (U1)
      solo,pno ENOCH s.p.   (U2)

UGARTE, FLORO M. (1884-   )
    Naides
      [Span] solo,pno RICORDI-ARG
      BA 11004 s.p.   (U3)

    Revelacion
      [Span] solo,pno RICORDI-ARG
      BA 11663 s.p.   (U4)

UGLY DUCKLING, THE see Prokofiev, Serge

UGOLINI, G.
    De La Justitia E Falsita
      B solo,pno,strings SONZOGNO rental
                    (U5)

UHL, ALFRED (1909-   )
    So Ruhig Geh' Ich Meinen Pfad
      solo,pno DOBLINGER 08 625 s.p. (U6)

UHLER, A.
    To Poems By Children
      med solo,pno SEESAW $3.00   (U7)

UI-I PUITT! PUITT! see Perronnet, Amelie

UIST TRAMPING SONG
    (Roberton, Hugh S.) solo,pno/orch (G
    maj) ROBERTON 2745 s.p. see also
    Songs Of The Isles   (U8)

UIT EEN BRON, VOL. I see Kummer, A.

UIT EEN BRON, VOL. II see Kummer, A.

UIT HET DIEPST VAN MIJN HART see Bordewijk-Roepman, Johanna

UIT "OMAR KHAYAM" see Ruyneman, Daniel

UIT PURE PRET see Hullebroeck, Em.

UITVAART VAN ORPHEUS see Appledoorn, Dina

UKMAR, VILKO (1905-   )
    Astralna Erotika, Bk. 1 *CCU
      solo,pno DRUSTVO DSS 310 rental
                    (U9)
    Astralna Erotika, Bk. 2 *CCU
      solo,pno DRUSTVO DSS 313 rental
                  (U10)

UKOLEBAVKA see Pauer, Jiri

UKOLEBAVKA see Matej, Jozka

UKOLEBAVKA see Sokola, Milos

UKOLEBAVKY see Jirasek, Ivo

UKRAINISCHE VOLKSWEISEN *CC17U, folk, Russ
    (Stingl; Sowiak) solo,gtr SCHOTTS
    6084 s.p.   (U11)

UKRIZOVANE SRDCE see Jirasek, Ivo

ULEHLA LUDMILA
    Three Sonnets From Shakespeare *CC3U
      solo,pno GENERAL 318 $3.00   (U12)

    Time Is A Cunning Thief
      solo,pno GENERAL 319 $1.25   (U13)

ULKOKUORI JA TODELLISUUS see Sipila, Eero, Schein Und Sein

ULM 1592 see Eisler, Hanns

ULTAN, LLOYD
    Silences
      A solo,pno AM.COMP.AL. $2.75 (U14)

ULTIMA ROSA see Zandonai, Riccardo

ULTIMA VERBA see Rhene-Baton

ULTIME AMOUR see Levade, Charles (Gaston)

ULTIME ROSE see Medicus, V.

ULTIMO CANTO see Nacamuli, Guido

ULTIMO CANTO see Persico, Mario

UM BEI DIR ZU SEIN see Bijvanck, Henk

UM DEN OFEN HERUM see Trunk, Richard

UM DIE FLAMME see Handel, George Frideric, Tra Le Fiamme

UM MITTERNACHT see Mahler, Gustav

UM SCHLIMME KINDER see Mahler, Gustav

UMSONST NACH RUHE (from Prince Igor)
    [Russ/Fr/Ger] Bar solo,pno BELAIEFF
    246 s.p.   (U15)

UN ABANICO see Pahissa, Jaime

UN' AURA AMOROSA see Mozart, Wolfgang Amadeus

UN' AVVENTURA A VEGLION!
    (Carlo, Musi) solo,pno (Bolognese
    dialect) BONGIOVANI 2066 s.p. see
    from El Mi Canzunett   (U16)

UN BACIO DI MANO see Mozart, Wolfgang Amadeus

UN BAISER see Fontenailles, H. de

UN BAISER see Lachaume, A.

UN BAL D'ETOILES see Lacome, Paul

UN BAL D'OISEAUX see Lacome, Paul

UN BEL DI VEDREMO see Puccini, Giacomo

UN BEL RISO see Lewkovitch, Bernhard

UN BRUIT DE RAMES see Rhene-Baton

UN CANTO DELLA NOSTALGIA INDIANA see Platamone, Stefano

UN CHANT D'AMOUR see Hermite, M.

UN CONTE see Maeder

UN CYGNE see Barber, Samuel

UN DI ALL'AZZURRO SPAZIO see Giordano, Umberto

UN DI FELICE, ETEREA see Verdi, Giuseppe

UN DINER D'OISEAUX see Wachs, Paul Etienne Victor

UN FIACRE see Arrieu, Claude

UN FINANCIER ET UN POETE see Ravel, Maurice

UN GALLETTO see Mussorgsky, Modest

UN GIORNO AMARO see Ferrari-Trecate, Luigi

UN GRAND SOMMEIL NOIR see Honegger, Arthur

UN GRAND SOMMEIL NOIR see Ravel, Maurice

UN GRAND SOMMEIL NOIR see Varese, Edgar

UN HUMBLE MOINE see Mussorgsky, Modest

UN JOUR see Wellings, M.

UN JOUR AILLEURS see Revel, Peter

UN LAPIN BROUTANT L'HERBETTE see Bernicat, F.

UN LIVRE S'OUVRE see Tranchant, J.

UN MESSAGE DU ROI see Saint-Saens, Camille

UN MOT see Porrino, Ennio

UN MOTO DI GIOIA see Mozart, Wolfgang Amadeus

UN MOTO DI GIOJA see Mozart, Wolfgang Amadeus

UN NOM see Pesse, M.

UN OMBRA DI PACE see Handel, George Frideric

UN ORGANETTO SUONA see Bossi, Renzo

UN PETIT ROSEAU M'A SUFFI see Ropartz, Joseph Guy

UN PETIT ROSEAU M'A SUFFIT see Chapuis, Auguste-Paul-Jean-Baptiste

UN PEU DE BONHEUR see Feraudy, M. de

UN PEU DE VIN see Lacome, Paul

UN POEME see Poulenc, Francis

UN RAMO DI MELO see Venticinque, R.S.

UN RAYON DE TES YEUX see Stigelli, Giorgio

UN RENDEZ-VOUS D'OISEAUX see Gerald, Ed.

UN RESEAU D'OMBRE EMPRISONNE see Messager, Andre

UN REVE see Maurat, Edmond

UN SAPIN ISOLE see Delage, Maurice

UN SIECLE AVANT LE CHRIST see Saint-Saens, Camille

UN SOGNO see Maini, Manlio

UN SOGNO see Respighi, Ottorino

UN SOIR, J'ERRAIS SUR LE RIVAGE see Saint-Saens, Camille

UN SONETTO DI PETRARCA see Dello Joio, Norman

UN SOUFFLE A PASSE see Chaminade, Cecile

UN TRESOR see Perronnet, Amelie

UN VECCHIO PADRE see Pizzetti, Ildebrando

UN VOYAGE EXTRAORDINAIRE see Nell, G.

UNA BONA MEDSEINA
    (Carlo, Musi) solo,pno (Bolognese
    dialect) BONGIOVANI 2068 s.p. see
    from El Mi Canzunett   (U17)

UNA FANCIULLA PARLA see Tirindelli, Pier Adolfo

UNA FONTANA see Cimara, Pietro

UNA FURTIVA LAGRIMA see Donizetti, Gaetano

UNA GRANDE TRISTEZZA see Platamone, Stefano

UNA MESONERA Y UN ARRIERO see Mison, Luis

UNA NOTTE D'INVERNO see Porrino, Ennio

UNA ROSETTA see Gandino, Adolfo

UNA VERGIN, UN ANGEL DI DIO see Donizetti, Gaetano

UNA VOCE POCO FA see Rossini, Gioacchino

UN'ALLODOLA see Pratella, Francesco Balilla

UN'AURA AMOROSA see Mozart, Wolfgang Amadeus

UNBEFANGENHEIT see Weber, Carl Maria von

UNCANNY MANNIKIN, THE *Scot
solo,pno (contains also: To The Isle Of Skye) PATERSON s.p. see from Hebridean Songs, Vol. IV   (U18)

UNCHAINED see Nelson

UNCLE ROME see Homer

UNCLOUDED DAY see Lanier, Gary

UND ALS DER TAG DER PFINGSTEN ERFULLT WAR see Burkhard, Willy

UND ES TRAFEN MICH DORT see Schutz, Heinrich, Invenerunt Me Custodes

UND ES WIRD KOMMEN EON SOMMERTAG see Czernik, W.

UND FAST EIN MADCHEN WARS see Rautavaara, Einojuhani

UND FRIED DEN MENSCHEN AUF DER ERD see Lehner, Walter

UND GESTERN HAT ER MIR ROSEN GEBRACHT see Marx, Joseph

UND HERBSTLAUB UND REGENSCHAUER see Krenek, Ernst

UND ICH FRAGTE DANN NICHT WIEDER see Sibelius, Jean, Se'n Har Jag Ej Fragat Mera

UND OB DIE WOLKE see Weber, Carl Maria von

UND SIEH' see Verhaar, Ary

UND SIEH, ICH HAB, EUCH DENNOCH GERN *folk,Russ
[Ger/Russ] solo,pno ZIMMER. 1512 s.p.   (U19)

UND SIEHE, DER ENGEL DES HERRN see Handel, George Frideric

UND SO WIRD KOMMEN EIN SOMMERTAG see Trexler, Georg

UND WENIG WISSEN see Pezzati, Romano

UND WENN SIE SCHLAFEN see Verhaar, Ary

UND WILLST DU DEINEN LIEBSTEN STERBEN SEHN see Wolf, Hugo

UND WISSE, DASS ICH TIEF UND RAUSCHEND WAR see Bijvanck, Henk

UNDER DE LJUSA LINDAR see Korling, Felix

UNDER RONN OCH SYREN see Palm, Hermann

UNDER STARLIGHT see Debussy, Claude, Nuit D'Etioles

UNDER STJARNORNA see Svedlund, Karl-Erik

UNDER STRANDENS GRAVER see Sibelius, Jean

UNDER THE GREEN-WOOD TREE see Castelnuovo-Tedesco, Mario

UNDER THE GREENWOOD TREE see Bartlet

UNDER THE GREENWOOD TREE see Montgomery, Bruce

UNDER THE GREENWOOD TREE see Russell, Welford

UNDER THE GREENWOOD TREE see Walton, William

UNDER THE PONDWEED see Oldham, Arthur

UNDER THE SHADE OF THE SYCAMORE TREE see Franco, Johan

UNDER THE WILLOW TREE see Barber, Samuel

UNDER THY WINDOW see Thomas, Arthur Goring

UNDER VINTERGATAN see Hallnas, Hilding

UNDER VINTERGATAN see Peterson-Berger, (Olof) Wilhelm

UNDERNEATH THE ABJECT WILLOW see Britten, Benjamin

UNDERSTANDING HEART, AN see Malotte, Albert Hay

UNDINEN see Hallnas, Hilding

UNE BELLE see Delage, Maurice

UNE FABLE see Arensky, Anton Stepanovitch

UNE FACON DE DIRE QUE LES HOMMES DE CENT-VINGT ANS NE CHANTENT PLUS see Bois, Rob du

UNE FEE see Gaubert, Philippe

UNE FEMME see Georges, Alexandre

UNE FEMME QUI PASSE see Delmet, Paul

UNE FLEUR DONNEE A MA FILLE see Roussel, Albert

UNE FLUTE INVISIBLE see Saint-Saens, Camille

UNE GENTILLE FAUVETTE see Messager, Andre

UNE GOUTTE DE PLUIE see Bernard, R.

UNE GOUTTE D'EAU see Schumann, Robert (Alexander)

UNE HERBE PAUVRE see Poulenc, Francis

UNE HEURE VIENDRA see Georges, Alexandre

UNE JEUNE PUCELLE see Klerk, Albert de

UNE MAIN see Middeleer, Jean De

UNE MINUTE see Geraedts, Jaap

UNE NUIT DE MAI see Thomas, Arthur Goring

UNE NUIT QU'ON ENTENDAIT LA MER SANS LA VOIR see Bergmann, R.

UNE PAGE D'AMOUR see Filipucci, Edm.

UNE PERDRIOLE
"To-Day The First Of May" see Crystal Fountain, The

UNE POUPEE AUX YEUX D'EMAIL see Offenbach, Jacques

UNE TABATIERE A MUSIQUE see Liadov, Anatol Konstantinovitch

UNEN MAA see Kaski, Heino

UNFORESEEN, THE see Scott, Cyril Meir

UNG, CHINARY (1942-   )
Mohori
Mez solo,fl,ob,2perc,harp,pno,vcl, gtr PETERS 66630 s.p.   (U20)

Tall Wind
S solo,fl,ob,vcl,gtr sc PETERS 6562 s.p.   (U21)

UNGARISH VOLKSMUSIK, BAND I *CC5U, folk,Hung
(Kodaly, Zoltan) [Hung/Ger/Eng] solo, pno UNIVER. 8480 $4.75   (U22)

UNGARISH VOLKSMUSIK, BAND II *CC5U, folk,Hung
(Kodaly, Zoltan) [Hung/Ger/Eng] solo, pno UNIVER. 8481 $4.75   (U23)

UNGARISH VOLKSMUSIK, BAND III *CC6U, folk,Hung
(Kodaly, Zoltan) [Hung/Ger/Eng] solo, pno UNIVER. 8738 s.p.   (U24)

UNGARISH VOLKSMUSIK, BAND IV *CC8U, folk,Hung
(Kodaly, Zoltan) [Hung/Ger/Eng] solo, pno UNIVER. 9951 $7.50   (U25)

UNGARISH VOLKSMUSIK, BAND V *CC7U, folk,Hung
(Kodaly, Zoltan) [Hung/Ger/Eng] solo, pno UNIVER. 1509 $5.25   (U26)

UNGARISH VOLKSMUSIK, BAND VI: SOLDATENLIEDER *CC5U,folk,Hung
(Kodaly, Zoltan) [Hung/Ger/Eng] solo, pno UNIVER. 7554 $4.25   (U27)

UNGARISH VOLKSMUSIK, BAND VII *CC6U, folk,Hung
(Kodaly, Zoltan) [Hung/Ger/Eng] solo, pno UNIVER. 10008 $4.75   (U28)

UNGARISH VOLKSMUSIK, BAND VIII *CC5U, folk,Hung
(Kodaly, Zoltan) [Hung/Ger/Eng] solo, pno UNIVER. 10009 $4.75   (U29)

UNGARISH VOLKSMUSIK, BAND IX: TRINKLIEDER *CC5U,folk,Hung
(Kodaly, Zoltan) [Hung/Ger/Eng] solo, pno UNIVER. 1508 $4.75   (U30)

UNGARISH VOLKSMUSIK, BAND X *CC5U, folk,Hung
(Kodaly, Zoltan) [Hung/Ger/Eng] solo, pno UNIVER. 10010 $4.25   (U31)

UNGARISH VOLKSMUSIK, BAND XI *CC5U, folk,Hung
(Kodaly, Zoltan) [Hung/Ger/Eng] solo, pno UNIVER. 13499 $3.75   (U32)

UNGEDULD see Schubert, Franz (Peter)

UNGENTLE GUEST see Shaw, Martin

UNGER, MAKSO (1888-   )
Pet Otroskih Pesmi *CC5U
solo,pno DRUSTVO DSS 112 rental   (U33)

UNGEREIMTES see Blacher, Boris

UNGEREIMTES see Blacher, Boris

UNHON MAA see Marvia, Einari

UNI see Sibelius, Jean, Drommen

UNICORN, THE see Corigliano, John

UNITED NATIONS *CC96U
(Cowell) med solo,pno BMI $.50   (U34)

UNIVERS DE RIMBAUD see Escher, Rudolf George

UNIVERSAL PRAYER OF PEACE see Paperte, F.

UNKARILAISIA KANSANLAULUJA VI *CCU
(Aarto; Suonio) solo,pno FAZER F 1184 s.p.   (U35)

UNKNOWN FOSTER, THE see Foster, Stephen Collins

UNKNOWN LAND see Day, Maude Craske

UNKNOWN SEA see Stanford, Charles Villiers

UNO DEI DIECI see Malipiero, Gian Francesco

UNO STABAT, COMUNQUE see Negri, Gino

UNOHTUMATON EHTOO see Sonninen, Ahti

UN'OMBRA see Botti, C.

UNQUIET HEART see Persichetti, Vincent

UNREQUITED LOVE see LaForge, Frank

UNS IST EIN KIND GEBOREN see Schein, Johann Hermann

UNSCHULD KLEINOD REINER SEELEN see Bach, Johann Sebastian

UNSEEN HAND, THE see Sims

UNSER HERR JESUS CHRISTUS see Koler, Martin

UNSER LAND see Vredenburg, Max

UNSER LIEBES FRANZEL see Haas, Joseph

UNSER REBENIU *Jew
solo,pno KAMMEN 42 $1.00   (U36)

UNSER SONNENSCHEIN *CCU
(Moissl) [Ger] med solo,pno OSTER $1.25   (U37)

UNSERE SCHONSTEN WEIHNACHTSLIEDER *CCU,Xmas
(Schwarz-Reiflingen, Erwin) med solo, gtr ZIMMER. s.p.   (U38)

UNSERE WEIHNACHTSLIEDER *CCU,Xmas
(Gotze) solo,gtr SCHOTTS 4361 s.p.   (U39)

UNTAKO VAIN see Sibelius, Jean, Var Det En Drom?

UNTEN VIENOT VILJAPELLOT see Tuuri, Jaako

UNTER DEINEM BEZAUBERNDEN BLICKE *folk,Russ
[Ger/Russ] solo,pno ZIMMER. 1504 s.p.   (U40)

UNTER STERNEN, OP. 54, PART I see Schoeck, Othmar

UNTER STERNEN, OP. 54, PART II see Schoeck, Othmar

UNTER UFERTANNEN SPIELT' DER KNABE see Sibelius, Jean, Under Strandens Graver

UNTERM LINDENBAUM see Eberle, F.

UNTERSCHIED IM ANTWORTEN see Jentsch,
Walter

UNTERWEGS see Jelinek, Hanns

UNTERWEGS see Haas, Joseph

UNTIL see Sanderson, Wilfred

UNTIL AND I HEARD see Dougherty, Celius

UNTIL THE DAY I DIE see Buck

UNTIL THEN see Hamblen

UNTIL YOU FIND THE LORD see Greene

UNTIL YOU WERE THERE see Kirkland,
Terry

UNTIL YOU'VE KNOWN see Goodman

UNTO THE NEW DAY see Wolpe, Stefan

UNTO THEE ALL PRAISE BE GIVEN see Owen,
Laudamus

UNVERGESSEN see Reger, Max

UNWORTHY see Roe, Gloria [Ann]

UNWORTHY see Stanphill, Ira F.

UP FROM SOMERSET see Sanderson, Wilfred

UP IN THE MORNING EARLY *folk,Scot
solo,pno (E min) PATERSON FS88 s.p.
(U41)

UP IN THE SADDLE see Wallace, William

UP IN THE SKY see Arundale, Claude

UP THE GUNS see Bell, Margaret

UP THE RIVER, DOWN THE RIVER
see Three Bohemian Songs

UP WI' THE CARLES O' DYSART *folk,Scot
low solo,pno (C maj) PATERSON FS121
s.p.   (U42)
high solo,pno (D maj) PATERSON FS121
s.p.   (U43)

UPON A CHILD THAT DIED see Birch,
Robert Fairfax

UPON JULIA'S CLOTHES
see Four Songs From Herrick's
'Hesperides'

UPON JULIA'S CLOTHES see Sydeman,
William

UPON MY WORD I DID see Hook, James

UPON THE LOSS OF HIS MISTRESS
see Four Songs From Herrick's
'Hesperides'

UPPBROTT see Madetoja, Leevi, Lahto

UPPLANDSSANGEN see Liljefors, Ruben

UPSIDE-DOWN MAN, THE see Flanagan,
William

UPSTREAM see Dougherty, Celius

UPSTREAM see Kagen, Sergius

UR EN KARLEKSSAGA, HAFTE I see
Peterson-Berger, (Olof) Wilhelm

UR SAUNGBOK GAROARS HOLM see Sveinsson,
Gunnar Reynir

UR STORGARDEN see Wohlfart, Karl

URAY, ERNST LUDWIG (1906-   )
Funf Lieder *CC5U
med solo,pno DOBLINGER 08 605 s.p.
(U44)
Sechs Lieder *CC6U
med solo,pno UNIVER. 12528 $4.75
(U45)

URBANEC, BARTOLOMEJ (1925-   )
Majova Laska
solo,pno SLOV.HUD.FOND s.p. (U46)

Nepises *CCU
solo,pno SLOV.HUD.FOND s.p. (U47)

Piesne O Horach *CCU
T solo,pno SLOV.HUD.FOND s.p. (U48)

Piesne O Vel'kom Priatelstve *CCU
solo,pno SLOV.HUD.FOND s.p.   (U49)

Rozpravka
solo,pno SLOV.HUD.FOND s.p. (U50)

Styri Dvojspevy *CC4U
SA soli,pno SLOV.HUD.FOND s.p.
(U51)

URBANEC, BARTOLOMEJ (cont'd.)

Svadba *CCU
female solo/2 soli,pno
SLOV.HUD.FOND s.p.   (U52)

Tri Piesne Z Oravy *CC3U
solo,pno SLOV.HUD.FOND s.p. (U53)

Vah A Hron
solo,pno SLOV.HUD.FOND s.p. (U54)

URFEY, THOMAS D' (1653-1723)
Songs Of Thomas D'Urfey *CC26U
(Day, Cyrus Lawrence) solo,pno
cloth JOHNSON $17.50   (U55)

URKS, I.J.
Detske Pisnicky *CCU
boy solo/girl solo,pno SUPRAPHON
s.p.   (U56)

Ptaci Znelky *CCU
female solo,pno SUPRAPHON   (U57)

URLICHT see Mahler, Gustav

URNA FATALE DEL MIO DESTINO see Verdi,
Giuseppe

URVAL AV DE MEST OMTYCKTA see Bondeson

USH'AVTEM MAYIM
(Helfman, Max) "Water Dance" [Heb]
med solo,pno TRANSCON. IS 526 $.45
(U58)

USK see Thomas, A.

USMANBAS, ILKAN (1921-   )
Tre Poemi In Musica *CC3U
solo,pno ZERBONI 5306 s.p. (U59)

USODA see Ciglic, Zvonimir

UT MOT HAVET see Braein, Edvard Fliflet

UT SLAER SEG DIN SJELEBLOM see Egge,
Klaus

UTE I SKAREN see Nystroem, Gosta

UTERMOHLEN, C.F.
Gevangen *Op.14
solo,pno ALSBACH s.p.   (U60)

UTI VAR HAGE, DAR VAXA BLA BAR see Berg

UTKIN, V.
In Granite For Ever *song cycle
[Russ] med solo,pno MEZ KNIGA 2.107
s.p.   (U61)

UTVALGTE NORSKE SANGE OG ROMANSER see
Nordsjo, Egil

UUSI ALLADDIN see Kilpinen, Yrio

V

V JESENI see Moyzes, Alexander

V NARODNIM TONU see Dvorak, Antonin

V SLEZSKEM TONU see Burghauser, Jarmil

VA! BRANCARDIER see Wolff, A.

VA, CORSAIRE see Frank, Marcel
[Gustave]

VA, DAL FUROR PORTATA see Mozart,
Wolfgang Amadeus

VA! DIT-ELLE see Meyerbeer, Giacomo

VA MON ADORE see Cuvillier, Charles

VAAN MUN LINTUAIN EI KUULU see
Sibelius, Jean, Men Nin Fagel Marks
Dock Inte

VAARBRUD see Oscarson, Gun

VAARWEL AAN 'T WOUD see Zagwijn, Henri

VACANES see Doyen, Albert

VACATION *sac
high solo,pno ASHLEY $1.00   (V1)
low solo,pno ASHLEY $1.00   (V2)

VACATION see Rappaport, Eda

VACKAR, DALIBOR C. (1906-   )
Tri Chansony *CC3U
solo,pno SUPRAPHON s.p.   (V3)

VACKAR, TOMAS (1945-1963)
Tri Dopisy Divkam *CC3U
[Czech/Ger] med solo,pno PANTON 692
s.p.   (V4)

VACKERT SA see Littmarck

VACKRA BARN DAR VID DITT FONSTER see
Peterson-Berger, (Olof) Wilhelm

VACKRA SKY! see Brolen, Carl A.

VACKRA SMEDEN see Lagerheim-Romare,
Margit

VAD AR KARLEK see Ganz, Rudolph

VAD JAG HAR LOVAT DET SKALL JAG HALLA
see Jag Gick Mig Ut En Aftonstund

VAD SKILJER OSS AT see Nordkvist,
Martin

VAD VISKADE DU? see Myrberg, August M.

VADO, MA DOVE? - OH DEI! see Mozart,
Wolfgang Amadeus

V'ADORO, PUPILLE see Handel, George
Frideric

VAELTAJAN JOULURUKOUS see Ranta, Sulho

VAGA VINN! see Korling

VAGABOND see Vaughan Williams, Ralph

VAGABOND SONG see Head, Michael (Dewar)

VAGABUNDENLIEDER see Mohler, Philipp

VAGANTEN LIEDER see Strategier, Herman

VAGGSANG see Alfven, Hugo

VAGGSANG see Brahms, Johannes,
Wiegenlied

VAGGSANG see Jarnefelt, Armas,
Kehtolaulu

VAGGSANG see Mehler, Friedrich

VAGGVISA see Alfven, Hugo

VAGGVISA see Nyblom, C.G.

VAGGVISA see Palm, Hermann

VAGGVISA see Rangstrom, Ture

VAGGVISA see Runback, Albert

VAGHISSIMA SEMBIANZA see Donaudy,
Stefano

VAGITO see Gandino, Adolfo

VAH A HRON see Urbanec, Bartolomej

VAHA ILO EMOTTOMALLE KAESTA see
  Kilpinen, Yrio

VAIN KAISTA MERTA see Snare, Sigurd, En
  Strimma Hav

VAIN SUIT, THE see Brahms, Johannes,
  Vergebliches Standchen

VAINOS SANGER see Peterson-Berger,
  (Olof) Wilhelm

VAK UPP see Valentin, Karl

VAKTELN see Beethoven, Ludwig van

VALAKINEK MUZSIKALNAK *CC55U,Hung
  solo,pno BUDAPEST 6735 s.p.   (V5)

VALASSKE PISNE see Haba, Karel

VALBORGSMASSAVISA see Korling, Sven

VALCKENOOCHJE see Sigtenhorst-Meyer,
  Bernhard van den

VALDERRABANO, E. DE
  see ENRIQUEZ DE VALDERRABANO, ENRIQUE

VALE see Russell, Kennedy

VALE OF LLANHERNE see Newton, Ernest

VALE OF MONT-MARIE, THE see Morgan,
  Orlando

VALEDICTORY see Melby, John

VALEK, JIRI (1923-   )
  Ani Mracku Na Obzoru
    "Nicht Ein Wolkchen Am Horizont"
    [Czech/Ger] boy solo/girl solo,
    pno CZECH s.p.   (V6)

  Ctyri Pisne Pro Baryton *CC4U
    Bar solo,pno CZECH s.p.   (V7)

  Deset Pohadek Na Motivy Ceskych Pisni
    *CC10U
    med solo,pno/vcl&pno CZECH s.p.
                                        (V8)
  La Partenza Della Primavera *CC4U
    S solo,pno CZECH s.p.   (V9)

  Nicht Ein Wolkchen Am Horizont *see
    Ani Mracku Na Obzoru

  Pet Variaci Na Tema "Veritas" *CC5U
    high solo/low solo,pno CZECH s.p.
                                        (V10)
  Sedm Bajek Podle Ezopa *CC7U
    low solo,pno CZECH s.p.   (V11)

  Sest Monologu O Lasce *CC6U
    Mez solo,4strings,harp,pno CZECH
    s.p.   (V12)

VALEN, FARTEIN (1887-1952)
  Ave Maria *Op.4, sac
    [Lat] S solo,pno LYCHE LY229 s.p.
                                        (V13)
  Sakontala *Op.6,No.1
    see Three Songs

  Suleika *Op.6,No.3
    see Three Songs

  Three Songs
    [Ger] med-high solo,kbd NORSK s.p.
      contains: Sakontala, Op.6,No.1;
      Suleika, Op.6,No.3; Weiss Wie
      Lilien, Op.6,No.2   (V14)

  Two Songs *Op.39,No.1-2, CC2U
    [Ger] S solo,pno LYCHE LY271 s.p.
                                        (V15)
  Weiss Wie Lilien *Op.6,No.2
    see Three Songs

VALENTI COSTA, PEDRO
  Cantar A Un Sauce
    [It] S/T solo,pno RICORDI-ARG
    BA 9340 s.p. contains also:
    Cantar De Amores; Cantar De Una
    Serrana   (V16)

  Cantar De Amores
    see Valenti Costa, Pedro, Cantar A
    Un Sauce

  Cantar De Una Serrana
    see Valenti Costa, Pedro, Cantar A
    Un Sauce

VALENTIN, KARL
  Arabisk Serenad
    solo,pno GEHRMANS s.p.   (V17)

  Den Lycklige
    solo,pno GEHRMANS s.p.   (V18)

  I Midnattstund
    solo,pno GEHRMANS s.p.   (V19)

VALENTIN, KARL (cont'd.)
  Skogen Sover
    solo,pno GEHRMANS s.p.   (V20)

  Vak Upp
    solo,pno GEHRMANS s.p.   (V21)

VALENTINE TO SHERWOOD ANDERSON see
  Flanagan, William

VALENTININ RUKOUS (INVOCATION) see
  Gounod, Charles Francois, Dio
  Possente, Dio D'amor

VALENTINS GEBET see Gounod, Charles
  Francois, Dio Possente, Dio D'amor

VALERIUS GEDENCKKLANK see Lier, Bertus
  van

VALES OF KINTORE
  ABar soli,pno ASHDOWN s.p.   (V22)
  SBar soli,pno ASHDOWN s.p.   (V23)

VALET see Nystedt, Knut

VALET DE COEUR see Delmet, Paul

VALKEAN VAIMON LAULU see Pylkkanen,
  Tauno Kullervo

VALKEAT AAMUT see Marvia, Einari

VALKEAT KAUPUNGIT see Kilpinen, Yrio

VALLARELAT see Wideen

VALLEDOR, J.
  Las Sequidillas Del Apasionado
    (Subira) [Span] high solo,pno UNION
    ESP. $2.25   (V24)

VALLEY OF JEZREEL see Rappaport, Moshe,
  Adam Ki Yamut

VALLEY OF LAUGHTER see Sanderson,
  Wilfred

VALLEY OF MY DREAMS see Gerald

VALLEY OF SILENCE, THE see Bantock,
  Granville

VALLEY WIND, THE see Smith, Hale

VALLFLICKANS VISA see Heijkorn

VALLGOSSENS VISA see Myrberg, August M.

VALLINKORVAN LAULU see Merikanto, Oskar

VALLKULLANS VISA see Soderberg

VALMORE, G.
  Dear Land Of Home
    solo,pno (F maj) LEONARD-ENG (V25)

VALS D'AVRIL see Lachaume, A.

VALS DE CABALLERO DE GRACIA see Chueca,
  Federico

VALS LENTO see Luna, P.

VALS Y CUPLE DE LOS OBREROS see Chueca,
  Federico

VALSE AVEC UNE ETOILE see Middeleer,
  Jean De

VALSE CARESSANTE see Lambert, Fr.

VALSE D'AMOUR see Cuvillier, Charles

VALSE D'AUTOMNE see Lacome, Paul

VALSE D'AVRIL see Lachaume, A.

VALSE DE CYRIL see Caryll, Ivan

VALSE DE POUPEE see Mengelberg, Rudolf

VALSE DES BLANCS JUPONS
  (Emmereshts; Beldent) solo,pno GRAS
  s.p.   (V26)

VALSE DES MOUETTES see Dalcroze,
  Jacques

VALSE DU MIROIR see Messager, Andre

VALSE ENCHANTEE see Berger, Rod.

VALSE ENSORCELEUSE see Filipucci, Edm.

VALSE FLEURIE see Delmet, Paul

VALSE MERVEILLEUSE see Garbaroche, G.

VALSE PRINTANIERE see Schubert, Franz
  (Peter)

VALSE TRISTE see Berger, Rod.

VALSE VENITIENNE see Cristofaro, A. de

VALSE VENTIENNE see Cristofaro, A. de

VALVERDE, JOAQUIN (1846-1910)
  Carnations *see Clavelitos

  Clavelitos
    "Carnations" [Span/Eng] high solo,
      pno (F maj) SCHIRM.G $.75   (V27)
    "Carnations" [Span/Eng] med solo,
      pno (D maj) SCHIRM.G $.75   (V28)
    (Azpiazu) [Span] med solo,gtr UNION
      ESP. $.50   (V29)

  Jota De Los Ratas *see Chueca,
    Federico

  Mazurca *see Chueca, Federico

  Mazurca De Los Paraguas *see Chueca,
    Federico

  Vals De Caballero De Gracia *see
    Chueca, Federico

V'AMO TANTO see Botti, C.

VAMOS A DAR A DESPEDIDA see Camargo
  Guarnieri

VAMOS BEBENDO see Caamano, Roberto

VAN DEN BOEVER see Clercq, R. de

VAN DEN WITTEN EZEL see Hullebroeck,
  Em.

VAN DEN ZANGER see Clercq, R. de

VAN EEN SMEDER see Zagwijn, Henri

VAN JAN DE MOSSELMAN see Hullebroeck,
  Em.

VAN JESUS DE WARE RUSTE see Badings,
  Henk

VAN LANGENDONCK LIEDEREN see Mul, Jan

VAN LI EFFLUVI DE LE ROSE see Respighi,
  Ottorino

VAN LIEFDE EN VERLATENHEID see Wyk,
  Arnold van

VAN 'T SCHOONE WIEDSTERKE see
  Hullebroeck, Em.

VANA ATTESA see Scuderi, Gaspare

VAND ATER TILL HEMMET IDAG see
  Dahlgren, Erland

VAN DE WATER, B.
  Christ Child *sac,Xmas
    solo,pno HARRIS $.75   (V30)

  Death Is The Chilly Night
    see Two Songs

  Good Shepherd
    low solo,pno PRESSER $.75   (V31)
    high solo,pno PRESSER $.75   (V32)

  Loneliness
    see Two Songs

  Night Of Nights *sac,Xmas
    high solo,pno PRESSER $.95   (V33)
    med solo,pno PRESSER $.95   (V34)
    low solo,pno (G maj) HARRIS $.75
                                       (V35)
    high solo,pno (B flat maj) HARRIS
      $.75   (V36)
    med solo,pno (G maj) WATERLOO $.65
                                       (V37)
    high solo,pno (B flat maj) WATERLOO
      $.65   (V38)

  Penitent
    med solo,pno PRESSER $.95   (V39)
    solo,pno (available in 3 keys)
      ASHLEY $.95   (V40)
    high solo,pno PRESSER $.95   (V41)

  Penitent, The *sac
    high solo,pno (E flat maj) SCHIRM.G
      $.85   (V42)
    med solo,pno (C maj) SCHIRM.G $.85
                                       (V43)
  Publican, The
    high solo,pno PRESSER $.95   (V44)
    low solo,pno PRESSER $.95   (V45)

  Two Songs *sec
    solo,pno WATERLOO $1.25
      contains: Death Is The Chilly
      Night; Loneliness   (V46)

VANDOR, IVAN (1932-   )
  Canzone Di Addio
    female solo,5inst sc ZERBONI 6672
    s.p.   (V47)

VANDOR, S.
Songs *CCU
solo,pno BUDAPEST 5699 s.p.   (V48)

VANDRAREN OCH BACKEN see Sibelius,
Jean, Der Wanderer Und Der Bach

VANDRARENS FRIERI see Pesonen, Olavi
(Samuel), Kulkurin Kosinta

VANDRING see Peterson-Berger, (Olof)
Wilhelm

VANDRINGAR see Melartin, Erkki

VANDRINGSSANG see Norlen, Hakan

VANDRINGSSANG see Wohlfart, Karl

VANDRINGSTRALL see Korling

VAN DYKE, MAY
As A Shepherd
low solo,pno (G maj) BOOSEY $1.50
(V49)
high solo,pno (B flat maj) BOOSEY
$1.50   (V50)

Love
high solo,pno (G maj) BOOSEY $1.50
(V51)
low solo,pno (E flat maj) BOOSEY
$1.50   (V52)

Lullaby *sac,Xmas
high solo,pno BELWIN $1.50   (V53)

VAN DYKE, VONDA
Gonna Love *sac
solo,pno WORD S-312   (V54)

I Found A Friend *sac
solo,pno WORD S-324   (V55)

Love Starts With You *sac
solo,pno WORD S-325   (V56)

New Kind Of Happiness *sac
solo,pno WORD S-310   (V57)

Our Lord's Prayer *sac
solo,pno WORD S-326   (V58)

Patches Of Sunlight *sac
solo,pno WORD S-311   (V59)

Reach Up (composed with Gosh, Bobby)
*sac
solo,pno WORD S-329   (V60)

VAN ETTEN, JANE
From The Song Of Songs
high solo/med solo,pno TRANSCON.
TV 457 $.75   (V61)

Passionate Shepherd, The
high solo/med solo,pno TRANSCON.
TV 453 $.50   (V62)

Song For Love, A
high solo,pno TRANSCON. TV 455 $.50
(V63)
Tenor Aria (from Guido Ferranti)
T solo,pno TRANSCON. TV 456 $.50
(V64)
Wynken, Blynken And Nod
med solo,pno TRANSCON. TV 454 $.50
(V65)

VAN GROVE, ISAAC
She Is A Winsome Wee Thing
med solo,pno FITZSIMONS $.40 (V66)

VANHA KIRKKO see Kilpinen, Yrio

VANHA KOTINI KENTUCKYSSA see Foster,
Stephen Collins

VANHA LAULU see Kilpinen, Yrio

VANHA MUMMO see Merikanto, Oskar

VANHA SYYSLAULU see Kuula, Toivo

VAN HULSE, CAMIL
On This Day, O Beautiful Mother
*sac,Marriage
AT soli,pno FITZSIMONS $.60   (V67)

VANISH NOW, YE GLOOMY SHADOWS see Bach,
Johann Sebastian, Weichet Nur,
Betrubte Schatten

VANISHED see Ward, Robert

VANITAS MUNDI see Knab, Armin

VANITY FAIRE see Strange, Allen

VANITY OF HUMAN WISHES, THE see Bush,
Geoffrey

VANITY OF VANITIES see Pinkham, Daniel

VANOCNI KOLEDY see Kricka, Jaroslav

VAN PARYS, G.
La Belle De Paris
solo,pno AMPHION s.p. solo pt, voc
sc   (V68)

VANSKAPENS BLOMMA see Sibelius, Jean

VAN STREEL, R.
Ballade Van Een Verliefde
solo,pno BROGNEAUX s.p.   (V69)

VANWAAR KEN IK UW GELAAT see Baeyens,
August-L.

VAN WYK, ARNOLD
see WYK, ARNOLD VAN

VAPNARENS VISA OM HELIG I ROSENGARD see
Wideen, Ivar

VAR see Runback, Albert

VAR AR MITT VILSNA BARN I KVALL
see Blott En Dag Ett Ogonblick I
Sander

VAR DET EN DROM? see Sibelius, Jean

VAR FORNIMMELSER see Sibelius, Jean

VAR JAG GAR, I SKOGAR, BERG OCH DALAR
see Andliga Sanger, Heft 1

VAR STILLA HJARTA see Kilpinen, Yrio

VARBACKEN see Myrberg, August M.

VARDE LJUS! see Wennerberg, Gunnar

VARDROTTNINGEN see Gluck, Christoph
Willibald Ritter von

VAREN see Grieg, Edvard Hagerup

VAREN FLYKTAR HASTIGT see Sibelius,
Jean

VAREN FLYKTER HASTIGT see Sibelius,
Jean, Varen Flyktar Hastigt

VAREN OCH KARLEKEN see Lassen, Eduard

VARENS FAGEL see Ranta, Sulho,
Kevatlintu

VARENS KAVALJERER see Lagerheim-Romare,
Margit

VARENS OCH HOSTENS SANGER see Pesonen,
Olavi (Samuel)

VARESE, EDGAR (1883-1965)
Chanson De La-Haut
see Offrandes

La Croix Du Sud
see Offrandes

Offrandes
S solo,chamb.orch COLFRANC COL.11
$4.75
contains: Chanson De La-Haut; La
Croix Du Sud   (V70)

Offrandes
S solo,chamb.orch RICORDI-ENG
NY 2074 s.p.   (V71)

Un Grand Sommeil Noir
med solo,pno SALABERT-US $3.50
(V72)

VARFOR? see Chrisander, Nils

VARFOR see Nordqvist, Gustaf

VARFOR HOR JAG KLOCKOR RINGA see Damm,
Svenerik

VARFOR SJUNGER JAG see Merikanto,
Oskar, Miksi Laulan

VARHERRE HAN HVILTE I KRYBBEN SA TRANG
see Beck, Thomas [Ludvigsen]

VARIABLE REALISATIONEN see Beurle,
Jurgen

VARIANTEN ZUR CAVATINE DER ROSINA "UNA
VOCE POCO FA" see Rossini,
Gioacchino

VARIATIONEN UBER EIN ALTES WIENER
STROPHENLIED see Egk, Werner

VARIATIONS ON A THEME BY M.B. TOLSON
see Anderson, Thomas J.

VARIATIONS ON VARIATIONS see Kasemets,
U.

VARIATIONS POUR UNE TROMPETTE DE
CAVALERIE see DuBois, Pierre Max

VARIATIONS SUR "LES CARNEVAL DE VENISE"
(Mortari) solo,pno FORLIVESI 11965
s.p.   (V73)

VARIOUS SONGS AND ARIAS see Beethoven,
Ludwig van

VARJE STEG MIG JESUS LEDER
see Andliga Sanger, Heft 3

VARJO see Pylkkanen, Tauno Kullervo

VARJUBEL see Bengzon

VARJUBEL see Korling, Felix

VARKANNING see Rangstrom, Ture

VARLAAM'S BALLAD see Mussorgsky, Modest

VARLAMM'S SONG see Mussorgsky, Modest

VARLAMOV, A.
Romances And Songs, Vol. IV *CCU
[Russ] solo,pno MEZ KNIGA 57 s.p.
(V74)

VARLAT see Lagergren

VARME OCH LJUS see Josephson, Jacob
Axel

VARMLANNINGARNE see Randel, Andreas

VARNAVA', S.
Canti Nuovi Per La Nuova Liturgia
*sac,CCU,liturg
[It] solo,pno CURCI 9028 s.p. (V75)

VARNEY, PIERRE JOSEPH ALPHONSE
(1881-1879)
Farandole Nocturne
solo,pno ENOCH s.p.   (V76)
solo,acap ENOCH s.p.   (V77)

Franche Ribaude
solo,acap ENOCH s.p.   (V78)
solo,pno ENOCH s.p.   (V79)

La Bachelette
solo,acap ENOCH s.p.   (V80)
solo,pno ENOCH s.p.   (V81)

La Bagatelle
solo,acap ENOCH s.p.   (V82)
solo,pno ENOCH s.p.   (V83)

La Derniere Chanson
solo,acap ENOCH s.p.   (V84)
solo,pno ENOCH s.p.   (V85)

L'Amour Quand Meme
solo,pno ENOCH s.p.   (V86)
solo,acap ENOCH s.p.   (V87)

P'tit Fi! (from L'Amour Mouille)
[Fr] Mez solo,pno CHOUDENS C8 s.p.
(V88)

Regain D'Innocence
solo,pno ENOCH s.p.   (V89)
solo,acap ENOCH s.p.   (V90)

Tu Me Trahiras
solo,pno ENOCH s.p.   (V91)
solo,acap ENOCH s.p.   (V92)

VARNINGEN see Soderman

VARQUES, F.
En Causant D'amour
solo,acap ENOCH s.p.   (V93)
solo,pno ENOCH s.p.   (V94)

Les Femmes Savantes
solo,pno ENOCH s.p.   (V95)
solo,acap ENOCH s.p.   (V96)

VARSANG see Eklof, Einar

VARSANG see Hertzman

VARSANG see Jacobsson

VARSANG see Mendelssohn-Bartholdy,
Felix, Fruhlingslied

VARSANG see Merikanto, Oskar,
Kevatlaulu

VARSANG see Peterson-Berger, (Olof)
Wilhelm

VARSPARVEN see Norman, Ludvig

VART AN DET BAR see Nordqvist, Gustaf

VART LAND see Pacius, Fredrik

VART LIV see Olsen, Sparre

VARTAGEN see Sibelius, Jean

VARTAN DU GAR see Handel, George
Frideric, Where'er You Walk

VARVINDAR FRISKA
see Och Inte Vill Jag Sorja

VARVISA see Nordqvist, Gustaf

VARVISE see Beck, Thomas [Ludvigsen]

VASQUEZ, JUAN
    En La Fuente Del Rosel (composed with
      Pisador, Diego)
      (Pujol) [Span] med solo,gtr ESCHIG
      E1303 $.90   (V97)

    Vos Me Matastes (composed with
      Fuenllana, Miguel de)
      (Pujol) [Span] med solo,gtr ESCHIG
      E1305 $2.00   (V98)

VASS, L.
    Hovering Landscape
      solo,pno BUDAPEST 4740 s.p.   (V99)

VASSEUR, LEON (-FELIX-AUGUSTIN-JOSEPH)
    (1844-1917)
    C'est La Loi Militaire (from Le
      Mariage Au Tambour)
      solo,pno ENOCH s.p.   (V100)

    C'est Le Joyeux Sergent (from Le
      Mariage Au Tambour)
      solo,pno ENOCH s.p.   (V101)

    Du P'tit Tonneau D'la Vivandiere
      (from Le Mariage Au Tambour)
      solo,pno ENOCH s.p.   (V102)

    Place Au Feu, Place A La Chandelle
      (from Le Mariage Au Tambour)
      solo,pno ENOCH s.p.   (V103)

    Pourtant J'ai Garde Dans Mon Coeur
      (from Le Mariage Au Tambour)
      solo,pno ENOCH s.p.   (V104)

VATER ABRAHAM, ERBARME DICH MEIN see
    Schutz, Heinrich

VATER, MUTTER, SCHWESTERN, BRUDER see
    Lortzing, (Gustav) Albert

VATER UND KIND see Stoll, B.

VATER UNSER see Hannikainen, Ilmari,
    Fader Var

VATER UNSER see Krebs, Johann Ludwig

VATER UNSER, DER DU BIST IM HIMMEL see
    Geist, Christian

VATER UNSER IM HIMMELREICH see Schein,
    Johann Hermann

VATERLAND see Pepping, Ernst

VATERLANDISCHER LIEDERKRANZ *CCU
    [Czech] solo,pno SUPRAPHON s.p.
                    (V105)

VATTENE! SE UNA LAGRIMA SOLTANTO see
    Zandonai, Riccardo

VAUCLAIN, CONSTANT
    Miller's Daughter, The
      solo,pno PEER $.85   (V106)

    Proud Maisie
      solo,pno PEER $.85   (V107)

VAUDEVILLE see Badings, Henk

VAUGHAN
    June Is In My Heart
      low solo,pno (C maj) ALLANS s.p.
                    (V108)
      high solo,pno (D maj) ALLANS s.p.
                    (V109)

VAUGHAN WILLIAMS, RALPH (1872-1958)
    Along The Field *CC8L
      T solo,vln (diff) OXFORD 60.806
      $2.25   (V110)

    Amour De Moy
      [Fr/Eng] solo,pno (C maj) BOOSEY
      $1.50   (V111)

    Bright Is The Ring Of Words
      solo,pno (D maj) BOOSEY $1.50
                    (V112)

    Call, The
      solo,pno (E flat maj) STAINER
      3.1400.7 $1.00   (V113)

    Four Hymns *sac,CC4U
      T solo,pno/orch,opt vla BOOSEY
      $4.25   (V114)

    Four Last Songs
      OXFORD 62.219 $2.15
        contains: Hands, Eyes And Heart
        (Mez solo,pno) (easy); Menelaus
        (Mez/Bar solo,pno) (med diff);
        Procris (Mez/Bar solo,pno) (med
        diff); Tired (Mez/Bar solo,pno)
        (med)   (V115)

    Four Nights
      see Two Poems By Shove

    Greensleeves
      Bar solo,pno (very easy) OXFORD
      61.001 $.85   (V116)

VAUGHAN WILLIAMS, RALPH (cont'd.)
      T solo,pno (very easy) OXFORD
      63.047 $.85   (V117)

    Hands, Eyes And Heart
      see Four Last Songs

    Heart's Haven
      high solo,pno (F maj) ASHDOWN s.p.
                    (V118)
      med solo,pno (E maj) ASHDOWN s.p.
                    (V119)
      low solo,pno (D maj) ASHDOWN s.p.
                    (V120)

    Here On My Throne
      solo,pno/orch (A maj) ROBERTON 2350
      s.p.   (V121)

    House Of Life, The *CCU
      med solo,pno ASHDOWN $9.00 (V122)

    How Can The Tree But Wither
      solo,pno OXFORD 61.911 $1.60 (V123)

    Hugh's Song Of The Road
      solo,pno/orch (F min) ROBERTON 2346
      s.p.   (V124)

    I Have Trod The Upward And The
      Downward Slope
      solo,pno (D maj) BOOSEY $1.50
                    (V125)

    It Was A Lover And His Lass
      2 soli,pno/orch ROBERTON 71571 s.p.
                    (V126)

    Lawyer
      see Two English Folksongs

    Linden Lea
      high solo,pno (A maj) BOOSEY $1.50
                    (V127)
      med solo,pno (G maj) BOOSEY $1.50
                    (V128)
      low solo,pno (F maj) BOOSEY $1.50
                    (V129)

    Menelaus
      see Four Last Songs

    Merciless Beauty *CC3U
      high solo,3strings/pno cmplt ed
      FABER C02953 s.p.   (V130)

    Motion And Stillness
      see Two Poems By Shove

    New Ghost, The
      Bar solo,pno (med diff) OXFORD
      62.906 $1.35   (V131)

    On Wenlock Edge *song cycle
      T solo,pno,opt 4strings BOOSEY
      $5.75, ipa   (V132)

    Orpheus With His Lute: No. 1
      solo,pno (F maj) FOX,S   (V133)

    Orpheus With His Lute: No. 2
      solo,pno (G maj) FOX,S   (V134)

    Procris
      see Four Last Songs

    Roadside Fire
      low solo,pno (C maj) BOOSEY $1.50
                    (V135)
      high solo,pno (D flat maj) BOOSEY
      $1.50   (V136)

    Searching For Lambs
      see Two English Folksongs

    Silent Noon
      high solo,pno (G maj) FISCHER,C
      HO 561   (V137)
      med-low solo,pno (E flat maj)
      FISCHER,C HO 563   (V138)
      med-high solo,pno (F maj) FISCHER,C
      HO 562   (V139)
      high solo,orch (G maj) ASHDOWN
      $2.00, ipr   (V140)
      med-high solo,orch (F maj) ASHDOWN
      $2.00, ipr   (V141)
      med solo,orch (E flat maj) ASHDOWN
      $2.00, ipr   (V142)
      low solo,orch (D flat maj) ASHDOWN
      $2.00, ipr   (V143)
      high solo,pno (F maj) WILLIS $.75
                    (V144)
      low solo,pno (D flat maj) WILLIS
      $.75   (V145)
      low solo,pno (D flat maj) FISCHER,C
      HO 564   (V146)

    Sky Above The Roof
      solo,pno (C maj) BOOSEY $1.50
                    (V147)

    Song Of The Leaves Of Life And The
      Waters Of Life
      SS/SA soli,pno (easy) OXFORD 62.206
      $1.50   (V148)

    Songs Of Travel *CCU
      high solo/low solo,pno/orch BOOSEY
      $5.50   (V149)

VAUGHAN WILLIAMS, RALPH (cont'd.)
    Ten Blake Songs *CC10L
      S/T solo,ob OXFORD 60.810 $2.50
                    (V150)

    Three Vocalises *CC3U,vocalise
      S solo,clar (diff) OXFORD 63.052
      $1.50   (V151)

    Tired
      see Four Last Songs

    Two English Folksongs
      Bar solo,vln (easy) OXFORD 61.708
      $1.35
        contains: Lawyer; Searching For
        Lambs   (V152)

    Two Poems By Shove
      OXFORD 62.215 $1.60
        contains: Four Nights (Mez/T
        solo,pno) (med diff); Motion
        And Stillness (Mez/Bar solo,
        pno) (med)   (V153)

    Vagabond
      solo,pno (C min) BOOSEY $1.50
                    (V154)

    Water Mill, The
      Mez/Bar solo,pno (med) OXFORD
      61.732 $1.25   (V155)
      S/T solo,pno (med) OXFORD 63.753
      $1.25   (V156)

    Whither Must I Wander
      solo,pno (C min) BOOSEY $1.50
                    (V157)

VAUGHN
    If I Could Hear My Mother Pray Again
      *see Gerald

VAULLUSLAULU see Pylkkanen, Tauno
    Kullervo

VAXELSANG see Thierfelder

VAY'CHULU see Steinberg, Ben

VAZQUEZ, J.
    De Los Alamos Vengo
      (Azpiazu) [Span] med solo,gtr UNION
      ESP. $.90   (V158)

VDAKA, UJO PARTIZAN see Novak, Milan

VE DEM ATT FRAN MIG DE VIKA see
    Mendelssohn-Bartholdy, Felix

VECCHI, G.
    Medicina E Musica (from Conciliator)
      soli,inst FORNI s.p.   (V159)

VECCHI, H.
    Non Vuo Pregare
      (Pujol) [It] med solo,gtr ESCHIG
      E1316 $2.00   (V160)

VECCHI, ORAZIO (1550-1605)
    Arie, Canzonette E Balli A Tre, A
      Quattro E A Cinque Voci Con Liuto
      *CCU
      (Chilesotti, O.) 3-5 soli,lute
      FORNI s.p.   (V161)

VECCHIA CHITARRA see Cimara, Pietro

VECCHIA ZIMARRA, SENTI see Puccini,
    Giacomo

VECERNI PISNE see Dvorak, Antonin

VED EN UNG HUSTRUS BARE see Grieg,
    Edvard Hagerup

VED NATTETID see Josephson, Jacob Axel

VED RUNDARNE see Grieg, Edvard Hagerup

VED SJOEN DEN MORKE see Kjerulf,
    [Halfdan]

VED SJOEN "HUN GIK LANGS MED STRANDEN"
    see Kjerulf, [Halfdan]

VED SOEN see Wiklund, Adolf

VEDIC HYMNS see Holst, Gustav

VEDO UN CAVALLIN see Oddone, E.

VEDRAI, CARINO, SE SEI BUONIMO see
    Mozart, Wolfgang Amadeus

VEDRAI, CARINO, SE SEI BUONINO see
    Mozart, Wolfgang Amadeus

VEDT KREDSER DU, MIN VILDE FUGL see
    Sjogren, Emil

VEERE see Schouwman, Hans

VEERE see Voormolen, Alexander Nicolas

VEIL, THE see Lora, Antonio

VEILED PICTURE see Gounod, Charles
   Francois

VEILLEE DE NOEL see Sieulle, J.

VEILLEE HEUREUSE see Rhene-Baton

VEILLONS MES SOEURS see Gretry, Andre
   Ernest Modeste

VEINTE CHANTS POPULAIRES ESPAGNOLS
   *CC20U,Span
   (Nin) [Span/Fr] med solo,pno ESCHIG
   $12.00 in two volumes   (V162)

VEINTE LIEDER Y ARIAS RELIGIOSOS see
   Bach, Johann Sebastian

VEINTE Y CINCO CANCIONES POPULARES
   CATALANAS NAVIDENAS *CC25U,Xmas,
   Span
   (Buxo) med solo,pno UNION ESP. $1.25,
   ea. in four volumes, in Spanish and
   Catalan texts   (V163)

VEINTECINCO CANCIONES HEBREAS *CC25L,
   Heb
   (Graetzer) [Span] solo,pno RICORDI-
   ARG BA 9341 s.p. original and
   Spanish texts   (V164)

VEINTECINCO CANCIONES TRADICIONALES
   INGLESAS *CC25L,Eng
   (Fraser) [Eng/Span] solo,pno RICORDI-
   ARG BA 10043 s.p.   (V165)

VEINTEDOS CANCIONES Y DANZAS
   TRADICIONALES ARGENTINAS *CC22L
   (Aretz) [Span] solo,pno RICORDI-ARG
   BA 8748 s.p.   (V166)

VEITCH, WILLIAM
   This Fairy Country
   solo,pno CRAMER   (V167)

VEJVISEREN SYNGER see Kjerulf,
   [Halfdan]

VELAZQUEZ, LEONARDO (1936-   )
   Cuauhtemoc
   [Span] narrator,2fl,pic,2ob,English
   horn,3clar,bass clar,2bsn,
   contrabsn,6horn,4trp,4trom,tuba,
   timp,3perc PETERS 6246 s.p.
                                (V168)

VELDE, H.V.D.
   Voor De Zingende Jeugd, Vol. I *CCU
   solo,pno BROEKMANS 771 s.p. (V169)

   Voor De Zingende Jeugd, Vol. II *CCU
   solo,pno BROEKMANS 772 s.p. (V170)

VELDEN, RENIER VAN DER (1910-   )
   Avondgeluiden
   A/Bar solo,pno CBDM s.p.   (V171)

VELEZ CAMARERO, E.
   Eres Marinerita
   [Span] med solo,pno UNION ESP. $.90
                                (V172)

VELJESPIIRI see Krohn, Felix

VELKOMMEN see Hauger, Kristian

VELLERE, LUCIE
   Berceuse
   see Croquis

   Croquis
   solo,pno cmplt ed BROGNEAUX s.p.
   contains: Berceuse; La Lune;
   L'Automne; Les Canards; Mon
   Petit Chat; Ronde   (V173)

   La Lune
   see Croquis

   L'Automne
   see Croquis

   Les Canards
   see Croquis

   Mon Petit Chat
   see Croquis

   Ronde
   see Croquis

VELLONES, P.
   Chanson
   solo,pno/inst DURAND s.p.   (V174)

   Chanson De Mars Sous La Neige
   see Deux Poemes De P. Fort

   Chansons D'amour De La Veille Chine
   *see La Tchen; Le Collet Bleu; Le
   Gue   (V175)

   Deux Poemes De P. Fort
   MezBar soli,pno cmplt ed DURAND
   s.p.
   contains: Chanson De Mars Sous La
   Neige; Histoire De Chasse
                                (V176)

VELLONES, P. (cont'd.)

   Histoire De Chasse
   see Deux Poemes De P. Fort

   La Tchen
   solo,orch DURAND s.p. see from
   Chansons D'amour De La Veille
   Chine   (V177)

   Le Collet Bleu
   solo,orch DURAND s.p. see from
   Chansons D'amour De La Veille
   Chine   (V178)

   Le Gue
   solo,orch DURAND s.p. see from
   Chansons D'amour De La Veille
   Chine   (V179)

   Le Poisson Volant (from Fables De
   Florian)
   solo,orch DURAND s.p., ipr   (V180)

   Pluies *Op.49
   solo,pno/inst DURAND s.p., ipr
                                (V181)

   Soir D'Idumee *Op.62
   solo,pno/inst DURAND s.p., ipr
                                (V182)

VELLONES, PIERRE
   Cinq Epitaphes
   med solo,pno/orch SALABERT-US $6.50
   contains: ...Du Pauvre Scarron,
   Par Lui-Meme; ...D'un Grand
   Medecin; ...D'un Paresseux;
   ...D'une Devote; ...D'une Femme
   Par Son Mari   (V183)

   ...Du Pauvre Scarron, Par Lui-Meme
   see Cinq Epitaphes

   ...D'un Grand Medecin
   see Cinq Epitaphes

   ...D'un Paresseux
   see Cinq Epitaphes

   ...D'une Devote
   see Cinq Epitaphes

   ...D'une Femme Par Son Mari
   see Cinq Epitaphes

   Fables De Florian *song cycle
   solo,pno DURAND s.p.   (V184)

VELTDEUNTJES see Sigtenhorst-Meyer,
   Bernhard van den

VELVET SHOES see Thompson, Randall

VELVETY RED LIKE see Cimara, Pietro,
   Stornello

VEM AR DU? see Kilpinen, Yrio

VEM KLAPPAR SA SAKTA I AFTONENS FRID
   see Blott En Dag Ett Ogonblick I
   Sander

VEM SPELER I NATTEN see Pergament,
   Moses

VEM STYRDE HIT DIN VAG? see Sibelius,
   Jean

VEN GITANO see Kalman, Emerich, Komm'
   Zigany

VENDEE *Fr
   (Canteloube, J.) solo,acap DURAND
   s.p. see also Anthologie Des Chants
   Populaires Francais Tome III (V185)

VENDEMMIA see Petralia

VENDREDI XIII see Schmitt, Florent

VENE, RUGGERO (1897-1961)
   Notte
   [It/Eng] solo,pno BONGIOVANI 2501
   s.p.   (V186)

   Sento Che T'amo
   [It] solo,pno BONGIOVANI 2502 s.p.
                                (V187)

VENEC PISNI Z MORAVSKEHO SLOVACKA I-II
   see Axmann, Emil

VENEC ZE ZPEVU VLASTENSKYCH *CCU
   solo,pno SUPRAPHON s.p.   (V188)

VENEDIG see Frid, Geza

VENEDIG see Peterson-Berger, (Olof)
   Wilhelm

VENETIA see Lowthian, Caroline

VENETIAN BOAT SONG see Blumenthal,
   Jacob (Jacques)

VENETIAN JOURNAL see Maderna, Bruno

VENEZ MA MIE see Legay, Marcel

VENEZ ME FAIRE DANSER see Migot,
   Georges

VENEZ, PRINCE CHARMANT see Mouton, H.

VENEZIA see Breman, W.F.

VENEZIANA see Gandino, Adolfo

VENEZIANI, VITTORE
   A Due Mani
   [It] solo,pno BONGIOVANI 422 s.p.
   see also Tredici Romanze   (V189)

   All'Amore
   [It] solo,pno BONGIOVANI 417 s.p.
   see also Tredici Romanze   (V190)

   Amore Fidente *see Amour Joyeux

   Amour Joyeux
   "Amore Fidente" [It/Fr] solo,pno
   BONGIOVANI 426 s.p. see also Cinq
   Melodies   (V191)

   Campane Di Festa
   [It] solo,pno BONGIOVANI 423 s.p.
   see also Tredici Romanze   (V192)

   Canto Di Trovatore *see Chant De
   Troubadour

   Canzone Pe 'L Bimbo
   [It] solo,pno BONGIOVANI 619 s.p.
                                (V193)

   Chant De Troubadour
   "Canto Di Trovatore" [It/Fr] solo,
   pno BONGIOVANI 429 s.p. see also
   Cinq Melodies   (V194)

   Cinq Melodies
   [It/Fr] solo,pno cmplt ed
   BONGIOVANI 430 s.p.
   contains & see also: Amour
   Joyeux, "Amore Fidente"; Chant
   De Troubadour, "Canto Di
   Trovatore"; Dans La Rue, "Per
   La Via"; Dans Le Potager,
   "Nell'orto"; Sourires,
   "Sorrisi"   (V195)

   Dans La Rue
   "Per La Via" [It/Fr] solo,pno
   BONGIOVANI 425 s.p. see also Cinq
   Melodies   (V196)

   Dans Le Potager
   "Nell'orto" [It/Fr] solo,pno
   BONGIOVANI 428 s.p. see also Cinq
   Melodies   (V197)

   Ebrezza
   [It] solo,pno BONGIOVANI 418 s.p.
   see also Tredici Romanze   (V198)

   Favola Antica
   [It] solo,pno BONGIOVANI 419 s.p.
   see also Tredici Romanze   (V199)

   Favoletta
   [It] solo,pno BONGIOVANI 420 s.p.
   see also Tredici Romanze   (V200)

   L'addio
   [It] solo,pno BONGIOVANI 413 s.p.
   see also Tredici Romanze   (V201)

   Nell'orto *see Dans Le Potager

   Nenia
   [It] solo,pno BONGIOVANI 411 s.p.
   see also Tredici Romanze   (V202)

   Nostalgia
   [It] solo,pno BONGIOVANI 414 s.p.
   see also Tredici Romanze   (V203)

   Notturno
   [It] solo,pno BONGIOVANI 412 s.p.
   see also Tredici Romanze   (V204)

   Per La Via *see Dans La Rue

   Perche?
   [It] solo,pno BONGIOVANI 416 s.p.
   see also Tredici Romanze   (V205)

   Rimpianto
   [It] solo,pno BONGIOVANI 421 s.p.
   see also Tredici Romanze   (V206)

   Rondo
   [It] solo,pno BONGIOVANI 415 s.p.
   see also Tredici Romanze   (V207)

   Sorrisi *see Sourires

   Sourires
   "Sorrisi" [It/Fr] solo,pno
   BONGIOVANI 427 s.p. see also Cinq
   Melodies   (V208)

VENEZIANI, VITTORE (cont'd.)

Tramonto D'autunno
[It] solo,pno BONGIOVANI 618 s.p.
(V209)

Tredici Romanze
[It] solo,pno cmplt ed BONGIOVANI
424 s.p.
contains & see also: A Due Mani;
All'Amore; Campane Di Festa;
Ebrezza; Favola Antica;
Favoletta; L'addio; Nenia;
Nostalgia; Notturno; Perche?;
Rimpianto; Rondo
(V210)

VENEZIANISCHE NACHT see Czernik, W.

VENEZIANISCHES WIEGENLIED see Marx,
Joseph

VENEZIANSKA VISOR see Merikanto, Oskar

VENGO DE TIERRAS DE ORIENTE see
Maravilla, L.

VENGO, VENGO A STRINGERTI see
Scarlatti, Alessandro

VENHEESSA see Pylkkanen, Tauno Kullervo

VENI DE LIBANO see Schutz, Heinrich

VENI, DILECTE MI see Schutz, Heinrich

VENI, DILECTE, VENI see Caldara,
Antonio

VENI SANCTE SPIRITUS see Dunstable,
John

VENI SANCTE SPIRITUS see Schutz,
Heinrich

VENI, VENI VENIAS see Mul, Jan

VENISE see Godard, Benjamin Louis Paul

VENISE see Gounod, Charles Francois

VENISE see Philippart-Gonzalez, Renee

VENISE LA ROUGE see Philippart-
Gonzalez, Renee

VENITE AD ME see Schutz, Heinrich

VENITE ADORAMUS see Felderhof, Jan

VENITE ADOREMUS see Schrijvers, Jean

VENITE, EXSULTEMUS DOMINO see Morin,
Jean Baptiste

VENITE FILI see Zecca, Giannino

VENITE, PASTORES see Gratiani,
Bonifatio

VENITELO A VEDERE 'I MI' PICCINO see
Respighi, Ottorino

VENNE E MI SEDETTE ACCANTO see Alfano,
Franco

VENNE UNA VECCHIERELLA ALLA MIA CORTE
see Mascagni, Pietro

VENSTERLIEDEKEN see Weegenhuise, Johan

VENT CHANTS DE FRANCE ET D'AILLEURS
*CC20U
(Sanchez) 2-5 soli,gtr CHOUDENS C414
s.p. in various languages (V211)

VENT-CINQ MELODIES CHOISIES see
Schumann, Robert (Alexander)

VENTADORN, BERNART DE (? -1195?)
Amors, E Que-Us Es Vajaire?
see Six Songs In Provencal

Be M'an Perdut
see Six Songs In Provencal

Can L'herba Fresch'
see Six Songs In Provencal

Can Vei La Lauzeta
see Six Songs In Provencal

Era-M Cosselhatz Senhor
see Six Songs In Provencal

Lancan Vei La Folha
see Six Songs In Provencal

Six Songs In Provencal
(Wellesz) S/T solo,vln/vla/rec
(med) OXFORD 68.003 $1.60
contains: Amors, E Que-Us Es
Vajaire?; Be M'an Perdut; Can
L'herba Fresch'; Can Vei La
Lauzeta; Era-M Cosselhatz
Senhor; Lancan Vei La Folha
(V212)

VENTANA FLORIDA see Gutierrez-Ponce, M.

VENTI, FULGURA, PROCELLAE see Mozart,
Wolfgang Amadeus

VENTICINQUE, R.S.
Invito
[It] solo,pno BONGIOVANI 2283 s.p.
(V213)

Nella Neve
[It] solo,pno BONGIOVANI 2284 s.p.
(V214)

Notturnino
[It] solo,pno CURCI 4646 s.p.
(V215)

Un Ramo Di Melo
[It] solo,pno BONGIOVANI 2131 s.p.
(V216)

VENTIQUATRO VECCHIE CANZONI POPULARI
DEL PIEMONTE see Sinigaglia, Leone

VENTIQUATTRO MELODIE see Gandino,
Adolfo

VENTO, MATTIA (1735-1776)
Favourite Songs In The Opera
Demofonte, The (from Demofante)
CCU
FORNI s.p. (V217)

VENTUN CANTI AD UNA, DUE E TRE VOCI
PARI see Ivanova, Lidia

VENUS see Saint-Saens, Camille

VENUS QUI PEUT BRISER see Saint-Saens,
Camille

VERACHTET MIR DIE MEISTER NICHT see
Wagner, Richard

VERACINI, FRANCESCO MARIA (1690-1768)
Favourite Songs In The Opera Call'd
Adriano, The (from Adriano) CCU
solo,pno FORNI s.p. (V218)

Pastoral, A (from Rosalinda)
[It/Eng] T solo,pno (F maj)
SCHIRM.G $.60 (V219)

VERANO see Halffter, Rodolfo

VERBIRG NICHT DEINE HOLDEN STRAHLEN see
Frauenholtz, Johann Christoph

VERBORGENHEIT see Wolf, Hugo

VERBUM CARO FACTUM EST see Schutz,
Heinrich

VERBUM CHRISTI see Forsberg, Roland

VERDE VERDEROL see Garcia Leoz, J.

VERDI, GIUSEPPE (1813-1901)
Addio Del Passato (from La Traviata)
[It] S solo,pno RICORDI-ARG BA 8241
s.p. (V220)
[It] S solo,pno RICORDI-ENG 54374
s.p. (V221)
solo,pno/orch sc KALMUS $3.00
(V222)

Ah Blue Horizon *see O Cieli Azzurri

Ah Che La Moret
[It] high solo,pno (F maj) CRAMER
(V223)
[It] low solo,pno (E flat maj)
CRAMER (V224)

Ah, Fors E Lui (from La Traviata)
[It] S solo,pno RICORDI-ENG 54373
s.p. (V225)
[It] S solo,pno RICORDI-ARG BA 8743
s.p. (V226)
solo,pno ALLANS s.p. (V227)
S solo,pno/orch sc KALMUS $3.00
(V228)
(Liebling) "Is He The One" [It/Eng]
S solo,pno (F min) SCHIRM.G $1.00
(V229)

Ah, La Paterna Mano (from Macbeth)
[It] T solo,pno RICORDI-ENG 109983
s.p. (V230)

Ah Si, Ben Mio (from Il Trovatore)
[It] T solo,pno RICORDI-ENG 54440
s.p. (V231)

Ai Nostri Monti (from Il Trovatore)
"Home To Our Mountains" med solo,
pno (G maj) CENTURY 1568 (V232)
"Home To Our Mountains" [Eng/It]
MezT soli,pno PRESSER $.50 (V233)
"Si La Stanchezza" solo,pno/orch sc
KALMUS $3.00 (V234)

Air De Lenore (from Il Trovatore)
solo,orch HENN s.p. (V235)

Air D'Ulrica (from Un Ballo In
Maschera)
A solo,orch HENN s.p. (V236)

VERDI, GIUSEPPE (cont'd.)

Alla Vita Che T'arride (from Un Ballo
In Maschere)
solo,pno BELWIN $1.50 (V237)
[It] Bar solo,pno RICORDI-ENG 54453
s.p. (V238)

Amor Ti Vieta (from Fedora)
high solo,pno (C maj) SCHIRM.G $.85
(V239)

Aria Album For Baritone *CC20U
[It/Ger] Bar solo,pno PETERS 4249
$7.00 contains arias from:
Aroldo, Attila, Un Ballo In
Maschera, I Due Foscari, Ernani
and others (V240)

Aria Album For Bass *CC13U
[It/Ger] B solo,pno PETERS 4245
$7.00 contains arias from:
Attila, Don Carlos, Ernani, I
Lombardi, Luisa Miller, Macbeth
and others (V241)

Aria Album For Mezzo-Soprano Or Alto
*CC7U
[It/Ger] Mez/A solo,pno PETERS 4247
$7.00 contains arias from: Un
Ballo In Maschera, Don Carlos, La
Forza Del Destino, Il Trovatore
(V242)

Aria Album For Soprano, Vol. I
*CC16U
[It/Ger] S solo,pno PETERS 4246A
$12.00 contains arias from:
Aroldo, Attila, Il Corsaro,
Ernani, I Lombardi and others
(V243)

Aria Album For Soprano, Vol. II
*CC14U
[It/Ger] S solo,pno PETERS 4246B
$12.00 contains arias from: Aida,
Un Ballo Maschera, La Forza Del
Destino, La Traviata and others
(V244)

Aria Album For Tenor *CC23U
[It/Ger] T solo,pno PETERS 4248
$7.00 contains arias from: Aida,
Alzira, Aroldo, Un Ballo In
Maschera, La Battaglia Di
Lagnano, I Due Foscari, Ernani
and others (V245)

Ave Maria
see Quatro Pezzi Sacri
[It] solo,pno RICORDI-ENG 46854
s.p. (V246)

Ave Maria Piena Di Grazie (from
Otello) sac
see Verdi, Giuseppe, Canzone Del
Salice
[Eng/It/Lat] S solo,pno SCHIRM.G
$.75 (V247)
[It] S solo,pno RICORDI-ENG 53539
s.p. (V248)
[It] S solo,pno RICORDI-ARG
BA 11789 s.p. (V249)
solo,pno/orch sc KALMUS $3.00
(V250)

Bella Figlia Dell'amore (from
Rigoletto)
[It] SATBar soli,pno RICORDI-ENG
54750 s.p. (V251)
SATB soli,pno/orch sc KALMUS $3.00
(V252)

Calm Me, O Father *see Pace, Pace,
Mio Dio

Canzone Del Salice (from Otello)
[It/Eng] S solo,pno RICORDI-ARG
BA 11772 s.p. (V253)
[It/Eng] S solo,pno RICORDI-ENG
118145 s.p. (V254)
[It] S solo,pno RICORDI-ENG 51149
s.p. contains also: Ave Maria
Piena Di Grazie (V255)
"Willow Song, The" [It/Eng] high
solo,pno (F sharp maj) SCHIRM.G
$1.00 (V256)

Caro Nome (from Rigoletto)
high solo,pno (E maj) ALLANS s.p.
(V257)
S solo,pno/orch sc KALMUS $3.00
(V258)
[It] S solo,pno RICORDI-ENG 54372
s.p. (V259)
[It] S solo,pno RICORDI-ARG BA 8751
s.p. (V260)

Celeste Aida (from Aida)
high solo,pno (B flat maj) ALLANS
s.p. (V261)
med solo,pno (A maj) ALLANS s.p.
(V262)
T solo,pno/orch sc KALMUS $3.00
(V263)
[It] T solo,pno RICORDI-ENG 42488
s.p. (V264)
[It] T solo,pno RICORDI-ARG BA 8754
s.p. (V265)
T solo,pno/inst LEDUC s.p. (V266)

VERDI, GIUSEPPE (cont'd.)

Col Sangue Sol Cancellasi (from La
  Forza Del Destino)
  [It] TBar soli,pno RICORDI-ENG
  110315 s.p.   (V267)

Come Dal Ciel Precipita (from
  Macbeth)
  [It] B solo,pno RICORDI-ENG 96294
  s.p.   (V268)

Come Rugiada Al Cespite (from Ernani)
  [It] T solo,pno RICORDI-ENG 54432
  s.p.   (V269)

Composizioni Da Camera *CC17L
  [It] solo,pno RICORDI-ENG 123381
  s.p.   (V270)

Condotta Ell'era In Ceppi (from Il
  Trovatore)
  [It] Mez solo,pno RICORDI-ENG 54403
  s.p.   (V271)

Cortigiani, Vil Razza Dannata (from
  Rigoletto)
  [It] Bar solo,pno RICORDI-ENG 96292
  s.p.   (V272)
  [It] Bar solo,pno RICORDI-ARG
  BA 11790 s.p.   (V273)
  med solo,pno (C min) ALLANS s.p.
                                      (V274)

Credo In Un Dio Crudel (from Otello)
  [It] Bar solo,pno RICORDI-ENG 51144
  s.p.   (V275)
  Bar solo,pno/orch sc KALMUS $3.25
                                      (V276)
  solo,pno BELWIN $1.50   (V277)
  "Yes, I Believe" [It/Eng] Bar solo,
  pno SCHIRM.G $.75   (V278)

Dal Labbro Il Canto (from Falstaff)
  [It] T solo,pno RICORDI-ENG 125877
  s.p.   (V279)

D'amor Sull'ali Rosee (from Il
  Trovatore)
  [It] S solo,pno RICORDI-ENG 54376
  s.p.   (V280)

De' Miei Bollenti Spiriti (from La
  Traviata)
  [It] T solo,pno RICORDI-ARG
  BA 11792 s.p.   (V281)
  T solo,pno/orch sc KALMUS $3.00
                                      (V282)
  [It] T solo,pno RICORDI-ENG 54439
  s.p.   (V283)

Deserto Sulla Terra (from Il
  Trovatore)
  [It] T solo,pno RICORDI-ARG
  BA 11794 s.p.   (V284)

Di Provenza Il Mar, Il Suol (from La
  Traviata)
  [It] Bar solo,pno RICORDI-ARG
  BA 8242 s.p.   (V285)
  med solo,pno (D flat maj) ALLANS
  s.p.   (V286)
  Bar solo,pno/orch sc KALMUS $3.00
                                      (V287)
  [It] Bar solo,pno RICORDI-ENG 96293
  s.p.   (V288)
  "Germontin Romanssi" solo,pno FAZER
  F 3421 s.p.   (V289)

Di Quella Pira (from Il Trovatore)
  [It] T solo,pno RICORDI-ARG BA 8658
  s.p.   (V290)
  [It] T solo,pno RICORDI-ENG 119975
  s.p.   (V291)

Di' Tu Se Fedele Il Flutto M'aspetta
  (from Un Ballo In Maschera)
  [It] T solo,pno RICORDI-ENG 54430
  s.p.   (V292)

Dio Di Guida! (from Nabucco)
  [It] Bar solo,pno RICORDI-ENG
  110052 s.p.   (V293)

Dio! Mi Potevi Scagliar Tutti I Mali
  (from Otello)
  [It] T solo,pno RICORDI-ENG 125883
  s.p.   (V294)

Drinking Song *see Libiamo Ne' Lieti
  Calici

Duo Premier Acte (from Otello)
  2 soli,orch HENN s.p.   (V295)

E Sogno? O Realta? (from Falstaff)
  "Nightmare? An Evil Dream?, A" [It/
  Eng] Bar solo,pno (E flat maj)
  SCHIRM.G $1.00   (V296)

Ella Giammai M'amo (from Don Carlo)
  [It] B solo,pno RICORDI-ENG 110100
  s.p.   (V297)
  B solo,pno/orch sc KALMUS $3.00
                                      (V298)
  "I Knew It Long Ago" Bar solo,pno
  (D min) SCHIRM.G $1.00   (V299)

VERDI, GIUSEPPE (cont'd.)

Eri Tu Che Macchiavi (from Un Ballo
  In Maschera)
  [It] Bar solo,pno RICORDI-ARG
  BA 8522 s.p.   (V300)
  [It] Bar solo,pno RICORDI-ENG 54454
  s.p.   (V301)
  "Is It Thou?" [It/Eng] Bar solo,pno
  (F maj) SCHIRM.G $.75   (V302)

Ernani, Ernani, Involami (from
  Ernani)
  [It] S solo,pno RICORDI-ENG 54365
  s.p.   (V303)

Figlia! Mio Padre! (from Rigoletto)
  [It] SBar soli,pno RICORDI-ENG
  110256 s.p.   (V304)

Filli Di Gioia Vuoi Farmi Morir
  see Three Secular Cantatas

Full Of Despair *see Il Lacerato
  Spirito

Germontin Romanssi *see Di Provenza
  Il Mar, Il Suol

Gypsy's Song (from Il Trovatore)
  med solo,pno (E min) CENTURY 1566
                                      (V305)

High Leap The Firetongues *see
  Stride La Vampa

Home To Our Mountains *see Ai Nostri
  Monti

Hour Dark And Solemn, The *see
  Solenne In Quest'ora

I Knew It Long Ago *see Ella Giammai
  M'Amo

Il Balen Del Suo Sorriso (from Il
  Trovatore)
  [It] Bar solo,pno RICORDI-ENG 54459
  s.p.   (V306)
  [It] Bar solo,pno RICORDI-ARG
  BA 11793 s.p.   (V307)

Il Brigidino
  [It] solo,pno SONZOGNO 2906 s.p.
                                      (V308)

Il Lacerato Spirito (from Simon
  Boccanegra)
  [It] B solo,pno RICORDI-ARG
  BA 11750 s.p.   (V309)
  low solo,pno (F sharp min) ALLANS
  s.p.   (V310)
  [It] B solo,pno RICORDI-ENG 110095
  s.p.   (V311)
  med solo,pno (G maj) ALLANS s.p.
                                      (V312)
  "Full Of Despair" [It/Eng] Bar/B
  solo,pno (F sharp maj) SCHIRM.G
  $.85   (V313)

Infelice! E Tuo Credevi (from Ernani)
  [It] B solo,pno RICORDI-ENG 54471
  s.p.   (V314)

Ingemisco (from Manzoni Requiem)
  [Lat/Eng] T solo,pno RICORDI-ENG
  LD 408 s.p.   (V315)

Ingrate Lydia
  see Three Secular Cantatas

Is He The One *see Ah, Fors E Lui

Is It Thou? *see Eri Tu Che
  Macchiavi

King Philip's Aria (from Don Carlos)
  [Russ] low solo,pno MEZ KNIGA 120
  s.p.   (V316)

La Donna E Mobile (from Rigoletto)
  [It] T solo,pno RICORDI-ENG 54438
  s.p.   (V317)
  [It] T solo,pno RICORDI-ARG BA 7586
  s.p.   (V318)
  high solo,pno (B flat maj) ALLANS
  s.p.   (V319)
  med solo,pno (A flat maj) ALLANS
  s.p.   (V320)
  T solo,pno/orch sc KALMUS $3.00
                                      (V321)
  [Eng/It] T solo,pno PRESSER $.75
                                      (V322)
  [It/Eng] low solo,pno (F maj)
  CRAMER   (V323)
  [It/Eng] high solo,pno (B flat maj)
  CRAMER   (V324)
  "Voi Kuinka Hailyva" solo,pno FAZER
  F 3420 s.p.   (V325)

La Mia Letizia Infondere (from I
  Lombardi)
  [It] T solo,pno RICORDI-ENG 54433
  s.p.   (V326)

La Rivedra' Nell'estasi (from Un
  Ballo In Maschera)
  [It] T solo,pno RICORDI-ENG 125868

VERDI, GIUSEPPE (cont'd.)

  s.p.   (V327)

La Vergine Degli Angeli (from La
  Forza Del Destino)
  [It] SB soli,cor,pno RICORDI-ENG
  41327 s.p.   (V328)

Laudi Alla Vergine Maria
  see Quatro Pezzi Sacri

Libiamo Ne' Lieti Calici (from La
  Traviata)
  [It] ST soli,pno RICORDI-ARG
  BA 9081 s.p.   (V329)
  [It] ST soli,pno RICORDI-ENG 25093
  s.p.   (V330)
  "Drinking Song" high solo,pno (A
  flat maj) ALLANS s.p.   (V331)
  "On High Raise Your Glasses" solo,
  pno (A flat maj) ASHDOWN s.p.
                                      (V332)

Ma Dall'arido Stelo Divulsa (from Un
  Ballo In Maschera)
  [It] S solo,pno RICORDI-ENG 54362
  s.p.   (V333)

Ma Se M'e Forza Perderti (from Un
  Ballo In Maschera)
  [It] T solo,pno RICORDI-ENG 54431
  s.p.   (V334)

Madre, Pietosa Vergine (from La Forza
  Del Destino)
  [It] S solo,pno RICORDI-ENG 54921
  s.p.   (V335)

May Laurels Crown Thy Brow *see
  Ritorna Vincitor

Merce', Dilette Amiche (from I Vespri
  Siciliani)
  [It] S solo,pno RICORDI-ENG 54923
  s.p.   (V336)

Miserere (from Il Trovatore)
  solo,pno/orch sc KALMUS $3.00
                                      (V337)
  med solo,pno (F maj) CENTURY 581
                                      (V338)

Morir! Si Pura E Bella (from Aida)
  [It] ST soli,pno RICORDI-ENG 42502
  s.p.   (V339)

Morro, Ma Prima In Grazia (from Un
  Ballo In Maschera)
  [It] S solo,pno RICORDI-ENG 54363
  s.p.   (V340)

Nel Giardin Del Bello (from Don
  Carlo)
  [It] Mez solo,pno RICORDI-ENG
  109906 s.p.   (V341)

Nightmare? An Evil Dream?, A *see E
  Sogno? O Realta?

Niun Mi Tema (from Otello)
  [It] T solo,pno RICORDI-ENG 125889
  s.p.   (V342)

Now The Birds Are Gone To Rest (from
  La Traviata)
  [It/Eng] low solo,pno PRESSER $.75
                                      (V343)

O Cieli Azzurri (from Aida)
  med solo,pno (E flat maj) ALLANS
  s.p.   (V344)
  high solo,pno (F maj) ALLANS s.p.
                                      (V345)
  [It] S solo,pno RICORDI-ENG 42497
  s.p.   (V346)
  [It] S solo,pno RICORDI-ARG
  BA 11786 s.p.   (V347)
  (Ducloux) "Ah Blue Horizon" high
  solo,pno (F maj) SCHIRM.G $1.00
                                      (V348)

O Don Fatale (from Don Carlo)
  [It] Mez solo,pno RICORDI-ARG
  BA 11771 s.p.   (V349)
  [It] Mez solo,pno RICORDI-ENG
  109907 s.p.   (V350)
  "Oh Fatal Gift" [It/Eng] Mez solo,
  pno (F maj) SCHIRM.G $.85 (V351)

O Patria Mia (from Aida)
  solo,pno/orch sc KALMUS $3.00
                                      (V352)

O Tu Che In Seno Agli Angeli (from La
  Forza Del Destino)
  [It] T solo,pno RICORDI-ENG 109982
  s.p.   (V353)

O, Tu, Palermo, Terra Adorata (from I
  Vespri Siciliani)
  [It] B solo,pno RICORDI-ARG BA11775
  s.p.   (V354)
  [It] B solo,pno RICORDI-ENG 110096
  s.p.   (V355)

Oh! De' Verd'anni Miei (from Ernani)
  [It] Bar solo,pno RICORDI-ENG 54456
  s.p.   (V356)

VERDI, GIUSEPPE (cont'd.)

Oh Fatal Gift *see O Don Fatale

On High Raise Your Glasses *see Libiamo Ne' Lieti Calici

Pace, Pace Mio Dio (from La Forza Del Destino)
[It] S solo,pno RICORDI-ARG BA 8832 s.p.   (V357)
high solo,pno (B flat maj) ALLANS s.p.   (V358)
[It] S solo,pno RICORDI-ENG 54922 s.p.   (V359)
"Calm Me, O Father" [It/Eng] S solo,pno (B flat maj) SCHIRM.G $.85   (V360)

Pari Siamo! (from Rigoletto)
[It] Bar solo,pno RICORDI-ARG BA 11773 s.p.   (V361)
med solo,pno (F maj) ALLANS s.p.   (V362)
[It] Bar solo,pno RICORDI-ENG 119472 s.p.   (V363)

Parigi, O Cara (from La Traviata)
ST soli,pno/orch sc KALMUS $3.00   (V364)
[It] ST soli,pno RICORDI-ENG 110212 s.p.   (V365)

Parmi Veder Le Lagrime (from Rigoletto)
[It] T solo,pno RICORDI-ENG 54437 s.p.   (V366)
[It] T solo,pno RICORDI-ARG 11791 s.p.   (V367)

Per Me Giunto E Il Di Supremo (from Don Carlo)
[It] Bar solo,pno RICORDI-ENG 110060 s.p.   (V368)
"Yes, My Life Will Soon Be Ended" [It/Eng] Bar solo,pno SCHIRM.G $.85   (V369)

Piango, Gemo, Sospiro
see Three Secular Cantatas

Pieta, Rispetto, Amore (from Macbeth)
[It] Bar solo,pno RICORDI-ENG 130610 s.p.   (V370)

Pura Siccome Un Angelo (from La Traviata)
[It] SBar soli,pno RICORDI-ENG 110258 s.p.   (V371)

Quando Le Sere Al Placido (from Luisa Miller)
[It] T solo,pno RICORDI-ARG BA 11788 s.p.   (V372)
[It] T solo,pno RICORDI-ENG 54434 s.p.   (V373)

Quatro Pezzi Sacri *sac
[It] solo,pno cmplt ed RICORDI-ENG 101729 s.p.
contains: Ave Maria; Laudi Alla Vergine Maria; Stabat Mater; Te Deum   (V374)

Questa O Quella Per Me Pari Sono (from Rigoletto)
[It] T solo,pno RICORDI-ARG BA 7585 s.p.   (V375)
[It] T solo,pno RICORDI-ENG 54436 s.p.   (V376)

Re Dell'abisso, Affrettati (from Un Ballo In Maschera)
[It] A solo,pno RICORDI-ENG 125916 s.p.   (V377)

Ritorna Vincitor! (from Aida)
S solo,pno/orch sc KALMUS $3.00   (V378)
[It] S solo,pno RICORDI-ENG 42491 s.p.   (V379)
[It] S solo,pno RICORDI-ARG BA 8829 s.p.   (V380)
"May Laurels Crown Thy Brow" low solo,pno (D min) ALLANS s.p.   (V381)
"May Laurels Crown Thy Brow" med solo,pno (A flat maj) ALLANS s.p.   (V382)
"May Laurels Crown Thy Brow" high solo,pno (E min) ALLANS s.p.   (V383)

Rivedrai Le Foreste Imbalsamate (from Aida)
[It] ST soli,pno RICORDI-ENG 42498 s.p.   (V384)

Salce, Salce (from Otello)
solo,pno/orch sc KALMUS $3.00   (V385)

Saper Vorreste (from Un Ballo In Maschera)
[It] S solo,pno RICORDI-ENG 54364 s.p.   (V386)
S solo,pno/orch sc KALMUS $3.00   (V387)

VERDI, GIUSEPPE (cont'd.)

[It/Eng] S solo,pno INTERNAT. $1.00   (V388)

Si La Stanchezza *see Ai Nostri Monti

Signor Ne Principe Io Lo Vorrei (from Rigoletto)
[It] ST soli,pno RICORDI-ENG 110208 s.p.   (V389)

Sleepwalking Scene (from Macbeth)
solo,pno BELWIN $1.25   (V390)

Solenne In Quest'ora (from La Forza Del Destino)
[It] TBar soli,pno RICORDI-ARG BA 8831 s.p.   (V391)
[It] TBar soli,pno RICORDI-ENG 110313 s.p.   (V392)
(Finley) "Hour Dark And Solemn, The" [It/Eng] TBar soli,pno SCHIRM.G $.85   (V393)

Sperate, O Figli (from Nabucco)
[It] B solo,pno RICORDI-ENG 110093 s.p.   (V394)

Stabat Mater
see Quatro Pezzi Sacri

Stride La Vampa (from Il Trovatore)
[It] Mez solo,pno RICORDI-ARG BA 8523 s.p.   (V395)
Mez solo,pno sc KALMUS $3.00 (V396)
[It] Mez solo,pno RICORDI-ENG 109901 s.p.   (V397)
"High Leap The Firetongues" [It/Eng] Mez solo,pno (E min) SCHIRM.G $.75   (V398)

Sul Fil D'un Soffio Etesio (from Falstaff)
[It] S solo,pno RICORDI-ENG 96433 s.p.   (V399)
[It] S solo,pno RICORDI-ARG BA 11785 s.p.   (V400)

Tacea La Notte Placida (from Il Trovatore)
[It] S solo,pno RICORDI-ENG 54375 s.p.   (V401)
[It] S solo,pno RICORDI-ARG BA 11795 s.p.   (V402)
solo,pno ALLANS s.p.   (V403)

Te Deum
see Quatro Pezzi Sacri

Three Secular Cantatas *cant
[It] med solo,pno ZANIBON ZA4194 s.p.
contains: Filli Di Gioia Vuoi Farmi Morir; Ingrate Lydia; Piango, Gemo, Sospiro   (V404)

Tu Che La Vanita Conoscesti Del Mondo (from Don Carlo)
[It] S solo,pno RICORDI-ENG 109875 s.p.   (V405)

Tu Sul Labbro De' Veggenti (from Nabucco)
[It] B solo,pno RICORDI-ENG 110092 s.p.   (V406)

Tutte Le Feste Al Tempio (from Rigoletto)
[It] SBar soli,pno RICORDI-ARG BA 8539 s.p.   (V407)
S solo,pno/orch sc KALMUS $3.00   (V408)
[It] S solo,pno RICORDI-ENG 103361 s.p.   (V409)
[It] SBar soli,pno RICORDI-ENG 110255 s.p.   (V410)

Un Di Felice, Eterea (from La Traviata)
[It] ST soli,pno RICORDI-ARG BA 11774 s.p.   (V411)
[It] ST soli,pno RICORDI-ENG 110211 s.p.   (V412)

Urna Fatale Del Mio Destino (from La Forza Del Destino)
[It] Bar solo,pno RICORDI-ENG 110049 s.p.   (V413)

Vers Nous, Reviens Vainqueur (from Aida)
solo,pno/inst LEDUC s.p.   (V414)

Voi Kuinka Hailyva *see La Donna E Mobile

Volta La Terrea Fronte Alle Stelle (from Un Ballo In Maschera)
[It] S solo,pno RICORDI-ENG 54361 s.p.   (V415)

Willow Song, The *see Canzone Del Salice

VERDI, GIUSEPPE (cont'd.)

Yes, I Believe *see Credo In Un Dio Crudel

Yes, My Life Will Soon Be Ended *see Per Me Giunto E Il Di Supremo

VERDI, RALPH C.
Wedding Song *sac,Marriage
S/T solo,org/pno (easy) GIA G-1809 $1.00   (V416)

VERDI PRATI see Handel, George Frideric

VERDUN see Gallon, Noel

VEREMANS, RENAAT (1894-1969)
Zes Liederen Uit "Adagio" *CC6U
[Dut/Ger] A solo,pno CBDM s.p.   (V417)

VERESS, SANDOR (1907-   )
Canti Ceremissi *CCU
solo,pno ZERBONI 5078 s.p.   (V418)

Elegia
Bar solo,harp,strings min sc ZERBONI 6321 s.p.   (V419)

VERETTI, ANTONIO (1900-   )
Ero E Leandro
[It] solo,pno BONGIOVANI 1293 s.p. see from Tre Liriche   (V420)

Il Canto Dei Cantici
[It] solo,pno BONGIOVANI 1463 s.p.   (V421)

Intermezzo Melico
[It] solo,pno BONGIOVANI 1291 s.p. see from Tre Liriche   (V422)

L'Allegria *CC7U
[It] solo,pno RICORDI-ENG 129786 s.p.   (V423)

Pantomina
[It] solo,pno BONGIOVANI 1292 s.p. see from Tre Liriche   (V424)

Quattro Poesie Di Vigolo *CC4U
S solo,orch voc sc ZERBONI 4746 s.p.   (V425)

Sei Stornelli *CC6U
[It] Mez/Bar solo,pno RICORDI-ENG 120878 s.p.   (V426)

Tre Liriche *see Ero E Leandro; Intermezzo Melico; Pantomina   (V427)

VERGEBLICHES STANDCHEN see Brahms, Johannes

VERGERS see Durey, Louis

VERGERS see Zafred, Mario

VERGERS see King, Harold C.

VERGESSENE WEISEN see Zillig, Winfried

VERGESSENES LIED see Strauss, Johann

VERGIN TUTT'AMOR see Durante, Francesco

VERGISS MEIN MICHT, DASS ICH DEIN NICHT VERGESSE see Bach, Johann Sebastian

VERGISS MEIN NICHT see Jez, Jakob, Spomin

VERGNUGTE PLEISSEN-STADT see Bach, Johann Sebastian

VERGNUGTE RUH, BELIEBTE SEELENLUST see Bach, Johann Sebastian

VERGONNE MIR EIN PAAR MINUTEN see Tchaikovsky, Piotr Ilyitch

VERHAAR, ARY (1900-   )
Auflosung *Op.11,No.2
see Lieder Aus Asien III

Cliqueton, Cliquetis *Op.5, CC7L
A solo,vln,vla,vcl voc sc DONEMUS s.p.   (V428)

Die Verlassene *Op.11,No.3
see Lieder Aus Asien III

Drei Geisha Lieder, O-Sen *CC3U
A solo,fl,clar,pno,strings DONEMUS s.p.   (V429)

Du Bist *Op.11,No.1
see Lieder Aus Asien III

Du, Der Du Weisst *Op.24,No.1
see Von Der Armuth

Incantatio *Op.23,No.4
see Kleine Suite

VERHAAR, ARY (cont'd.)

Kleine Suite
DONEMUS S solo,pno s.p.; S solo,
2fl,2ob,2clar,2bsn,2horn,2trp,
timp,perc,cel,harp,strings rental
contains: Incantatio, Op.23,No.4;
Nocturne, Op.23,No.3;
Pastorale, Op.23,No.2; Prelude,
Op.23,No.1   (V430)

Lieder Aus Asien III
S solo,fl,clar,pno,strings DONEMUS
s.p.
contains: Auflosung, Op.11,No.2;
Die Verlassene, Op.11,No.3; Du
Bist, Op.11,No.1   (V431)

Nocturne *Op.23,No.3
see Kleine Suite

Pastorale *Op.23,No.2
see Kleine Suite

Prelude *Op.23,No.1
see Kleine Suite

Sie Haben Leid *Op.24,No.3
see Von Der Armuth

Sie Sind So Still *Op.24,No.2
see Von Der Armuth

Sie Werden Leben *Op.24,No.6
see Von Der Armuth

Und Sieh' *Op.24,No.5
see Von Der Armuth

Und Wenn Sie Schlafen *Op.24,No.4
see Von Der Armuth

Von Der Armuth
Bar solo,pno DONEMUS s.p.
contains: Du, Der Du Weisst,
Op.24,No.1; Sie Haben Leid,
Op.24,No.3; Sie Sind So Still,
Op.24,No.2; Sie Werden Leben,
Op.24,No.6; Und Sieh', Op.24,
No.5; Und Wenn Sie Schlafen,
Op.24,No.4   (V432)

VERHOEVEN, A.
Priesterwijding
solo,pno ALSBACH s.p.   (V433)

VERIRRT see Bijvanck, Henk

VERIRRT see Borup-Jorgensen, Axel

VERIRRT "WIR LIEFEN WOHL IRRE DEN
ANDERN VORAN" see Sibelius, Jean,
Vilse

VERJAARDAGLIED PRINS BERNHARD see
Frank, A.

VERJAARDAGLIEDJE see Polman, Th.H.

VERJARINGSLIED see Hullebroeck, Em.

VERKKAAN KUIN ILLAN SAMMUVI RUSKO see
Willebrand, F.R. von, Langsamt Som
Kvallskyn

VERKLARTE LIEBE see Weismann, Julius

VERKUNDIGUNG DER GEBURT UNSERES
HEILANDES see Reda, Siegfried

VERLANGEN see Zagwijn, Henri

VERLASSEN see Schoenberg, Arnold

VERLASSEN BIN I see Koschat, Thomas

VERLEIH UNS FRIEDEN see Schutz,
Heinrich

VERLEIH UNS FRIEDEN GENADIGLICH see
Hammerschmidt, Andreas

VERLOREN see Mulder, Herman

VERLORNE MUH'L see Mahler, Gustav

VERLOSSING see Mulder, Ernest W.

VERMEULEN, MATTHIJS (1888-1967)
Dernier Poeme
see Trois Chants D'amour

Hymne
see Trois Chants D'amour

La Maison Dans Le Coeur
see Trois Chants D'amour

La Veille
Mez solo,3fl,3ob,3clar,2bsn,4horn,
3trp,3trom,tuba,timp,perc,harp,
strings DONEMUS s.p.   (V434)
Mez solo,pno DONEMUS s.p.   (V435)

VERMEULEN, MATTHIJS (cont'd.)

Le Balcon
Mez/T solo,pno DONEMUS s.p.   (V436)

Trois Chants D'amour
Mez/T solo,pno DONEMUS s.p.
contains: Dernier Poeme; Hymne;
La Maison Dans Le Coeur   (V437)

VERNAL TRIPTYCH see Obyedov, Yu.

VERNOR, F. DUDLEIGH
Fellowship Song Of Sigma Chi
low solo,pno (C maj) WILLIS $.60
(V438)

VERONICA see Lilien, Ignace

VERONICA TANZT see Lilien, Ignace

VERONICAS TODESGEBET see Lilien, Ignace

VEROVIO, S.
Diletto Spirtuale *sac,CCU
3-4 soli,cembalo,lute FORNI s.p.
(V439)
Lodi Della Musica *CCU
3 soli,cembalo,lute FORNI s.p.
(V440)

VERRAAD see Frid, Geza

VERRALL, JOHN (1908-   )
Lonely Bugle Grieves, The
med solo,pno AM.COMP.AL. $1.37
(V441)
Rose Of The World, The
S solo,fl,pno sc AM.COMP.AL. $2.75
(V442)

VERRASSING see Beekhuis, Hanna

VERRATH see Brahms, Johannes

VERREES, E.
Hij Komt
solo,pno ALSBACH s.p.   (V443)

VERS LE BAL see Ravize, A.

VERS LE CIEL see Delmet, Paul

VERS LE REVE see Vieu, Jane

VERS LES ETOILES see Levade, Charles
(Gaston)

VERS NOUS, REVIENS VAINQUEUR see Verdi,
Giuseppe

VERSE LA GOUTTE see Berger, Rod.

VERSEPUY, MARIUS
Noel Du Patre *sac
med solo,pno/org HEUGEL s.p. (V444)
Sons De Cloches *sac,CC15U
solo,pno/org cmplt ed HEUGEL s.p.
available separetly or in
collection   (V445)

VERSI PER LEI see Oddone, E.

VERSO IL MISTERO see Botti, C.

VERSOHNUNG see Bijvanck, Henk

VERSOS SENCILLOS see Ardevol, Jose

VERSUCH FUR ALLE
SSAATTBB soli,23inst sc GERIG HG 795
s.p., ipa   (V446)

VERTAUS see Merikanto, Oskar, Liknelse

VERTICAL THOUGHTS III see Feldman,
Morton

VERTICAL THOUGHTS V see Feldman, Morton

VERTRAG see Trunk, Richard

VERTRAUEN see Jentsch, Walter

VERWAITES HERZ see Bijvanck, Henk

VERWUNDET AN DEM FLUSS (from Prince
Igor)
[Russ/Fr/Ger] B solo,pno BELAIEFF 247
s.p.   (V447)

VERY SMART!
(Carlo, Musi) solo,pno BONGIOVANI
2060 s.p. see from El Mi Canzunett
(V448)

VERZAMELDE LIEDEREN see Diepenbrock,
Alphons

VERZAUBERTE STUNDE see Bijvanck, Henk

VERZEIH'! *folk,Russ
[Ger/Russ] solo,pno ZIMMER. 1513 s.p.
(V449)

VERZEN see Bosmans, Henriette

VERZI see Lipovsek, Marijan

VESLE JULESTJERNA see Davik, Ingebrigt

VESNICE ZPIVA see Zelinka, Jan
Evangelista

VESPER see Williams, W.S.Gwynn

VESPRO D'AGOSTO see Maini, Manlio

VESTI LA GIUBBA see Leoncavallo,
Ruggiero

VETERAN'S SONG see Adams, Stephen

VE'ULAI
(Sharett, Yehuda) [Heb] solo,pno
TRANSCON. H 1 $.60   (V450)

VEUX-TU? see Chaminade, Cecile

VEUX-TU? see Godard, Benjamin Louis
Paul

VEUX-TU MON REVE see Filipucci, Edm.

VEUX-TU OU NE VEUX-TU PAS see
Tranchant, J.

VEYVODA, GERALD
Through The Looking Glass
A solo,5winds,electronic tape sc
SEESAW $20.00   (V451)

VI ARO LANDET see Nordqvist, Gustaf

VI GA OVER DAGGSTANKTA BERG see
Thunman-Ericson

VI RAVVISO, O LUOGHI AMENI see Bellini,
Vincenzo

VI SES IGEN see Liljefors, Ruben

VI SES IGEN see Norman, Ludvig

VI SKILJAS AT see Donizetti, Gaetano

VI TVA see Lyberg, Margot

VI VANTA VAL ALLA see Nordqvist, Gustaf

VIA DOLOROSA see Tonnessen, Peder

VIA SACRA see Russell, Kennedy

VIADANA, LODOVICO GROSSI DA (1564-1645)
Drei Geistliche Konzerte *sac,CC3U
(Ewerhart, Rudolf) [Lat] B solo,
cont BIELER CS 5 s.p.   (V452)
Drei Geistliche Konzerte *sac,CC3U,
concerto
(Ewerhart, Rudolf) A solo,cont
BIELER CS 40 s.p.   (V453)
Drei Geistliche Konzerte *sac,CC3U,
concerto
(Ewerhart, Rudolf) S solo,cont
BIELER CS 51 s.p.   (V454)

VIAGGIO E FINALE see Bruni, Tedeschi
Alberto

VIANNET, R.
La Niege
solo,acap ENOCH s.p.   (V455)
solo,pno ENOCH s.p.   (V456)

VIARDOT-GARCIA, PAULINE (1821-1910)
Ave Maria *sac
[Lat] solo,pno/org ENOCH s.p.
(V457)
Bonjour Mon Coeur
solo,pno (available in 2 keys)
ENOCH s.p.   (V458)
Chanson De La Pluie
solo,pno (available in 2 keys)
ENOCH s.p.   (V459)
Chanson De Mer
solo,pno (available in 2 keys)
ENOCH s.p.   (V460)
Desespoir
solo,pno ENOCH s.p.   (V461)
Grands Oiseaux Blancs
solo,pno ENOCH s.p.   (V462)
Lamento
solo,pno ENOCH s.p.   (V463)
Les Attraits
solo,pno ENOCH s.p.   (V464)
Mignonne
solo,pno ENOCH s.p.   (V465)
Parme
solo,pno (available in 2 keys)
ENOCH s.p.   (V466)
Rossignol Et Rssognolet
solo,pno (available in 2 keys)
ENOCH s.p.   (V467)

VIARDOT-GARCIA, PAULINE (cont'd.)

Trois Jours De Vendange
solo,pno (available in 2 keys)
ENOCH s.p.   (V468)

VIATIQUE see Chaminade, Cecile

VIBERT, MATHIEU
Du Plus Loin *CC3U
solo,pno HENN 932 s.p.   (V469)

VICAR OF BRAY see Parker, Henry

VICAR'S SONG see Sullivan, Sir Arthur
Seymour

VICINO A TE S'ACQUETA see Giordano,
Umberto

VICK
Come, Ye Sinners
solo,pno SHAWNEE IA5050 $.85 (V470)

VICTOIRE see Saint-Saens, Camille

VICTOR LE MAUVAIS SUJET see Planquette,
Robert

VICTORIA, TOMAS LUIS DE (ca. 1549-1611)
Thomas Ludovici Victoria Abulensis
Opera Omnia (Complete Works)
*sac,CCU
(Pedrell, Felipe) [Lat] vocal works
for various combinations of
performers microfiche
UNIV.MUS.ED. $30.00 reprints of
Breitkopf & Hartel Editions;
contains 8 volumes   (V471)

VICTORIAN GARLAND see Tate, Phyllis

VICTORY, GERARD (1921-   )
Voyelles
S solo,fl,perc,xylo,vibra,glock,
strings NOVELLO rental   (V472)

VID ALVARNA I BABYLON see Berens,
Hermann

VID ALVENS STRAND
solo,pno GEHRMANS 223 s.p. contains
also: Aftonsang   (V473)

VID ASSJORNA see Peterson-Berger,
(Olof) Wilhelm

VID AVFARDEN see Madetoja, Leevi,
Itkisit Joskus Illoin

VID BACKEN see Linko, Ernst (Fredrik),
Purolla

VID DAMMEN see Nordqvist, Gustaf

VID FONSTRET see Stenhammar, Wilhelm

VID FRAGORNAS PORT see Andren, Adolf

VID FROSO KYRKA see Peterson-Berger,
(Olof) Wilhelm

VID JESU HJARTA see Strandsjo, Gote

VID MEDELHAVET see Lidholm, Ingvar

VID MIN LUTAS SILVERTONER see Palmgren,
Selim

VID NATTETID see Rubinstein, Anton

VIDA DE ARTISTA see Strauss, Johann,
Kunsterleben

VIDA, VIDITA, VIDALA see Ginastera,
Alberto

VIDA, VILANDE MIDNATT see Nordqvist,
Gustaf

VIDAL
Le Cordier
see LA MUSIQUE, SEPTIEME CAHIER

VIDAL, PAUL (1863-1931)
La Reine Fiammette *scena
solo,pno ENOCH s.p.   (V474)

VIDALA see De Rogatis, Pascual

VIDALA see Jurafsky, Abraham

VIDALA see Lopez-Buchardo, Carlos

VIDALA DEL REGRESO see Gomez Carrillo,
Manuel

VIDALA SANTIAGUENA see Gilardi, Gilardo

VIDALITA *folk
(Lavie) [Fr/Span] med solo,gtr ESCHIG
$1.10 see from Three Popular Songs
(V475)
(Lavie, Ferandez) [Span/Fr/It] solo,
gtr SCHOTTS GA 196 s.p. see from
Alte Und Neue Werke   (V476)

VIDALITA see Aguirre, Julian

VIDALITA see Boero, Felipe

VIDALITA see Broqua, Alfonso

VIDALITA see Jurafsky, Abraham

VIDALITA see Lopez-Buchardo, Carlos

VIDALITA see Taube, Evert

VIDIT JOANNES JESUM see Hindemith, Paul

VIDOSIC, TIHOMIL (1902-   )
Two Melancholic Songs *CC2U
[Slav] solo,pno CROATICA s.p.
(V477)

VIDSTE DU VEJ see Kjerulf, [Halfdan]

VIE ET MORT see Oboussier, Robert

VIEILLE CHANSON see Bizet, Georges

VIEILLE CHANSON DE MEZIERES
(Travenet) solo,acap DURAND s.p.
(V478)

VIEILLE CHANSON DU JEUNE TEMPS see
Fourdrain, Felix

VIEILLE CHANSON ESPAGNOLE see Aubert,
Louis-Francois-Marie

VIEILLES CARTES, VIEILLES MAINS see
Roussel, Albert

VIEILLES CHANSONS see DuBois, Pierre
Max

VIEILLES CHANSONS DE FRANCE see Pijper,
Willem

VIEL LARM UM NICHTS see Chrennikow,
Tichon

VIEL' OIS VIRITTA TIEOSSANI see
Jarnefelt, Armas

VIEL TRAUME see Sinding, Christian

VIELE MADCHEN KANN ICH ZAHLEN see
Kilpinen, Yrio, Mont' On Mulla
Morsianta

VIELLE ROMANCE see Lacome, Paul

VIELLES CHANSONS ET RONDES FRANCAISES
*CCU
[Fr] solo,pno SCHOTTS 2911 s.p.
(V479)

VIEN, LEONORA, A' PIEDI TUOI see
Donizetti, Gaetano

VIENI! see Denza, Luigi

VIENI A VARASDIN! see Kalman, Emerich

VIENI CHE POI see Gluck, Christoph
Willibald Ritter von

VIENI DI LA, LONTAN LONTANO... see
Respighi, Ottorino

VIENI LA MIA VENDETTA see Donizetti,
Gaetano

VIENI O CARA, AMATA SPOSA see Steffani,
Agostino

VIENI O FIGLIO see Handel, George
Frideric

VIENI OMAI, MINUTO ESTREMO see Bach,
Johann Sebastian, Schlage Doch,
Gewunschte Stunde

VIENI PRODE FEDERICO see Roman, Johan
Helmich

VIENI, VIENI O MIA NINETTA see Mozart,
Wolfgang Amadeus

VIENI, VIENI, O MIO DILETTO see
Vivaldi, Antonio

VIENNA see Wilson, Ernest

VIENS see Dufresne, C.

VIENS! see Godard, Benjamin Louis Paul

VIENS see Saint-Saens, Camille

VIENS AVEC MOI see Rothschild, Mme W.
de

VIENS AVEC NOUS see Godard, Benjamin
Louis Paul

VIENS DANS LES BOIS see Wenzel, L. de

VIENS, DOUCE MORT see Bach, Johann
Sebastian

VIENS FANNY see Busser, Henri-Paul

VIENS ICI! see Chabrier, Emmanuel

VIENS MON BIEN-AIME! see Chaminade,
Cecile

VIENS NOUS AIMER see Lachaume, A.

VIENS, O TOI DONT LE CLAIR VISAGE see
Saint-Saens, Camille

VIENS PRES DE MOI... EFFEUILLEZ LES
ROSES see Nougues, Jean

VIENS, RESPIRONS TOUS DEUX CES TIEDES
BRISES see Wagner, Richard

VIENS TOUT PRES see Chantrier, A.

VIENS, UNE FLUTE INVISIBLE see Caplet,
Andre

VIENS, UNE FLUTE INVISIBLE see Dauly,
G.

VIENS UNE VOIX T'APPELLE see Mozart,
Wolfgang Amadeus

VIER ALTE MARIENLIEDER see Heger,
Robert

VIER ALTFRANZOSISCHE VOLKSLIEDER
*CC4U,Fr,18th cent
(Behrend, Siegfried) solo,gtr
SIKORSKI 475 s.p.   (V480)

VIER AMOUREUZE LIEDEREN UIT HET GROOT
LIEDBOECK see Bunge, Sas

VIER ARIEN see Haydn, (Johann) Michael

VIER BRECHT-LIEDER see Halffter, C.

VIER BRUIDSLIEDEREN see Adriessen,
Willem

VIER CHINESE LIEDEREN NAAR TEKSTEN VAN
LI-TAI-PE EN SCHIN-SCHEN see
Bijvanck, Henk

VIER COPLAS see Mul, Jan

VIER DIALOGE
(Jesson, Roy) (med) cmplt ed PENN
STATE PSM 3 s.p.
contains: Lawes, Henry, On A Kiss
(ST soli,cont); Lawes, Henry,
Shepherd And Nymph (ST soli,
cont); Lawes, William, Charon And
Philomel (TB soli,cont); Lawes,
William, Daphne And Strephon (SB
soli,cont)   (V481)

VIER DRINKLIEDEREN see Strategier,
Herman

VIER DUETTE see Jansen, F. Gustav

VIER DUETTEN see Bijvanck, Henk

VIER DUETTEN see Bijvanck, Henk

VIER ELEVATIONS *sac,CC4U
(Ewerhart, Rudolf) [Lat] S/A/T solo,
cont BIELER CS 26 s.p.   (V482)

VIER ERNSTE GESANGE see Brahms,
Johannes

VIER ERNSTE GESANGE see Brahms,
Johannes

VIER ERNSTE GESANGE see Brahms,
Johannes

VIER ERNSTE GESANGE see Brahms,
Johannes

VIER ERNSTE GESANGE see Brahms,
Johannes

VIER ERNSTE GESANGE see Brahms,
Johannes

VIER ERNSTE GESANGE (FOUR SERIOUS
SONGS) see Brahms, Johannes

VIER FRANZOSISCHE VOLKSLIEDER see
Seiber, Matyas

VIER GEDICHTE VON C.F. MEYER see Gilse,
Jan van

VIER GEDICHTEN see Lilien, Ignace

VIER GEDICHTEN UIT "EXPERIMENTEN" see
Schouwman, Hans

VIER GEDICHTEN UIT "FLUISTERINGEN VAN
DEN AVONDWIND" see Schouwman, Hans

VIER GEDICHTEN VAN REVIUS see
Andriessen, Juriaan

VIER GEDICHTEN VON M. NIJHOFF see
Ketting, Otto

VIER GEESTELIJKE LIEDEREN UIT JEZUS EN
DE ZIEL see Sigtenhorst-Meyer,
Bernhard van den

VIER GEISTLICHE KONZERTE see Becker-
Foss, Jurgen

VIER GEISTLICHE KONZERTE see Dedekind,
Constantine Christian

VIER GEISTLICHE KONZERTE see Vivarino,
Innocentio

VIER GEISTLICHE KONZERTE *sac,CC4U,
concerto
(Grebe) high solo,cont SIKORSKI 236
s.p. contains works by: Viadana,
Ludovico Grossi Da; Cima, Giovanni
Paolo   (V483)

VIER GESANGE *CC4U,spir
(Bresgen, Cesar) Bar solo,clar,bvl,
perc,pno sc GERIG HG 543 s.p., ipa
(V484)

VIER GESANGE see Krenek, Ernst

VIER GESANGE see Kornauth, Egon

VIER GESANGE see Fortner, Wolfgang

VIER GESANGE see Ehrenberg, Carl Emil
Theodor

VIER GESANGE VOM TAGE see Marx, Karl

VIER GOETHE LIEDER see Nielsen,
Riccardo

VIER GOETHE-LIEDEREN see Bijvanck, Henk

VIER GRADNIK-LIEDER see Osterc, Slavko

VIER HEITERE LIEDER see Trunk, Richard

VIER HIRTINNEN see Schutz, Heinrich

VIER HIRTINNEN see Schutz, Heinrich

VIER ITALIENISCHE CANZONETTEN *CC4U,
It,16th cent
(Behrend, Siegfried) solo,gtr
SIKORSKI 673 s.p.   (V485)

VIER KANONISCHE LIEDER see Porena,
Boris

VIER KANTATEN see Eisler, Hanns

VIER KINDERLIEDJES see Geraedts, Jaap

VIER KLEINE WEIHNACHTSLIEDER *Xmas
[Ger] solo,pno BREITKOPF-W EB 5987
$1.00
contains: Alle Fangt An; Lauft, Ihr
Hirten; Lieb Nachtigall; Was Ist
Das Nur Heut   (V486)

VIER KONIG SIND MACHTIG see Horler, A.

VIER LIEBESLIEDER NACH HEBRAISCHEN
TEXTEN see Geissler, Fritz

VIER LIED VOM GOTT DER BETTLER see
Lilien, Ignace

VIER LIEDER see Borris, Siegfried

VIER LIEDER see Westerman, G. von

VIER LIEDER see Wiklund, Adolf

VIER LIEDER see Petzold, Rudolf

VIER LIEDER see Strauss, Richard

VIER LIEDER see Webern, Anton von

VIER LIEDER see Webern, Anton von

VIER LIEDER see Webern, Anton von

VIER LIEDER see Berg, Alban

VIER LIEDER see Salmhofer, Franz

VIER LIEDER see Apostel, Hans Erich

VIER LIEDER see Niggeling, Willi

VIER LIEDER see Siegl, Otto

VIER LIEDER see Blacher, Boris

VIER LIEDER see Blacher, Boris

VIER LIEDER see Pfitzner, Hans

VIER LIEDER see Pfitzner, Hans

VIER LIEDER see Liadov, Anatol
Konstantinovitch

VIER LIEDER see Schumann, Georg

VIER LIEDER see Zipp, Friedrich

VIER LIEDER see Oort, H.C.v.

VIER LIEDER see Oort, H.C.v.

VIER LIEDER see Mixa, Franz

VIER LIEDER see Mixa, Franz

VIER LIEDER see Dvorak, Antonin

VIER LIEDER see Genzmer, Harald

VIER LIEDER see Lothar, Mark

VIER LIEDER see Jentsch, Walter

VIER LIEDER see Schoenberg, Arnold

VIER LIEDER AUF CHINESISCHE TEXTE see
Ringger, Rolf Urs

VIER LIEDER AUF JAPANISCHE LYRIK see
Ringger, Rolf Urs

VIER LIEDER AUS DEM BAROCK see Porena,
Boris

VIER LIEDER (BRENTANO) see Kornauth,
Egon

VIER LIEDER DER ANMUT see Vollerthun,
Georg

VIER LIEDER DER BRAUT see Roetscher,
Konrad

VIER LIEDER DER TRAUER see Bartok, Bela

VIER LIEDER FUR BARITON see Edler,
Robert

VIER LIEDER FUR BASS-STIMME see
Brandts-Buys, H.

VIER LIEDER FUR EINE DUNKLE
FRAUENSTIMME UND KLAVIER see Rietz,
Johannes

VIER LIEDER FUR SOPRAN see Knab, Armin

VIER LIEDER I see Skorzeny, Fritz

VIER LIEDER II see Skorzeny, Fritz

VIER LIEDER (LENAU) see Skorzeny, Fritz

VIER LIEDER NACH C.F. MEYER see
Pfitzner, Hans

VIER LIEDER NACH CHINESISCHEN GEDICHTEN
see David, Thomas Christian

VIER LIEDER NACH GEDICHTEN DES HAFIS
see Wolpert

VIER LIEDER NACH GEDICHTEN VON
FRIEDRICH HOLDERLIN see Klenau,
Paul von

VIER LIEDER NACH GEDICHTEN VON N. SACHS
see Reutter, Hermann

VIER LIEDER NACH GOETHE see Trapp, Max

VIER LIEDER NACH HEINE see Weegenhuise,
Johan

VIER LIEDER NACH PUSCHKIN UND TJUTSCHEW
see Medtner, Nikolai Karlovitch

VIER LIEDER NACH PUSCHKIN UND TJUTSCHEW
see Medtner, Nikolai Karlovitch

VIER LIEDER NACH SCHUBART, KLOPSTOCK,
WEISE UND GUNTHER see Sutermeister,
Heinrich

VIER LIEDER NACH SERBISCHER VOLKSPOESIE
see Dvorak, Antonin

VIER LIEDER NACH TEXTEN
SCHWEIZERIESCHER MINNESANGER see
Sutermeister, Heinrich

VIER LIEDER NACH TEXTEN SCHWEIZERISCHER
MINNESANGER see Sutermeister,
Heinrich

VIER LIEDER NACH TEXTEN VON FRIEDRICH
NIETZSCHE see Pfluger

VIER LIEDER NACH TEXTEN VON PETER
HUCHEL UND CARMEN BERNOS DE
GASZTOLD see Jentsch, Walter

VIER LIEDER VON W. VON DER VOGELWEIDE
see King, Harold C.

VIER LIEDER ZU WORTEN VON AALE TYNNI
see Kuusisto, Ilkka

VIER LIEDEREN see Kersters, Willem

VIER LIEDEREN see Adriessen, Willem

VIER LIEDEREN see Beekhuis, Hanna

VIER LIEDEREN see Bijvanck, Henk

VIER LIEDEREN see Dresden, Sem

VIER LIEDEREN see Lilien, Ignace

VIER LIEDEREN see Mulder, Ernest W.

VIER LIEDEREN see Mulder, Herman

VIER LIEDEREN see Ruyneman, Daniel

VIER LIEDEREN see Weegenhuise, Johan

VIER LIEDEREN see Mulder, Ernest W.

VIER LIEDEREN see Leeuw, Ton de

VIER LIEDEREN see Franco, Johan

VIER LIEDEREN see Kool, B.

VIER LIEDEREN, BAND 1 see Andriessen,
K.

VIER LIEDEREN, BAND 2 see Andriessen,
K.

VIER LIEDEREN NAAR AANL. VAN OUD-
HOLLANDSCHE MELODIEEN see Beekhuis,
Hanna

VIER LIEDEREN OP AFRIKAANSE TEKSTEN see
Mulder, Ernest W.

VIER LIEDEREN OP FRANSE TEKST see
Bosmans, Henriette

VIER LIEDEREN VAN ADAMA VAN SCHELTEMA
see Bijvanck, Henk

VIER LIEDEREN VAN BERTHA DE BRUYN see
Pijper, Willem

VIER LIEDEREN VAN CHR. MORGENSTERN see
Flothius, Marius

VIER LIEDEREN VAN DETLEV VON LILIENCRON
see Gilse, Jan van

VIER LIEDEREN VAN GRETE KORBER see
Bijvanck, Henk

VIER LIEDEREN VAN H. MARSMAN see
Mulder, Herman

VIER LIEDEREN VAN J.H. LEOPOLD see
Ruyneman, Daniel

VIER LIEDEREN VAN JOSSELIN DE JONG see
Schouwman, Hans

VIER LIEDEREN VAN M. VOS see Mulder,
Herman

VIER MADCHENLIEDER see Cuypers, H.

VIER MARIA-ANTIPHONEN see Strategier,
Herman

VIER MINIATUREN see Weegenhuise, Johan

VIER MORGENSTERN LIEDER see Edler,
Robert

VIER MOTETTEN see Nivers, Guillaume
Gabriel

VIER NEUE LIEDER ZUM ADVENT see
Heilbut, P.

VIER ORCHESTERLIEDER see Schoenberg,
Arnold

VIER ORCHESTERLIEDER see Prohaska, Carl

VIER OUD-NEDERLANDSCHE GEDICHTEN see
Voormolen, Alexander Nicolas

VIER OUD-NEDERLANDSCHE LIEDEREN see
Ruyneman, Daniel

VIER REZITATIVE see Gerhard

VIER RILKE-LIEDER see Kronsteiner,
Josef

VIER ROMANZEN see Ippolitov-Ivanov,
Mikhail Mikhailovitch

VIER SAMENZANGEN see Schouwman, Hans

VIER SINTERKLAASLIEDJES see Loots, Ph.

VIER SONETTE see Zillig, Winfried

VIER SONETTE AN ORPHEUS see Steffen,
Wolfgang

VIER SONGS FUR MITTLERE STIMME see
Jelinek, Hanns

VIER TANZLIEDER see Bartok, Bela

VIER VOCALISES see Dresden, Sem

VIER WEEMOEDIGE LIETJIES see Wyk,
Arnold van

VIER WIEGELIEDJES see Badings, Henk

VIER WIEGENLIEDER see Ronnefeld, Peter

VIER WIEGENLIEDJES see Badings, Henk

VIERDANCK, JOHANN (ca. 1610-1646)
Ich Verkundige Euch Grosse Freude
*Xmas,concerto
(Engel, Hans) SS/TT soli,2vln,cont
(med easy) sc BAREN. 468 $5.25,
ipa   (V487)

Lobe Den Herren *sac,concerto
(Erdmann, Hans) SSS/TTT soli,cont
(med easy) cmplt ed BAREN. 453
$5.00   (V488)

Mein Herz Ist Bereit *sac,concerto
(Erdmann, Hans) SS/TT soli,2vln,
cont (med) BAREN. 452 $5.50
(V489)

Siehe, Wie Fein Und Lieblich Ist's
*sac,concerto
(Engel, Hans) SS/TT soli,2vln,cont
(med) sc BAREN. 687 $4.25, ipa
(V490)

VIERGE MARIE see Handel, George
Frideric

VIERGE SAINTE see Missa, Edmond Jean
Louis

VIERGES MORTES see Maurice, Pierre

VIERNE, LOUIS (1870-1937)
Le Rouet
S/T solo,pno/inst DURAND s.p., ipr
(V491)
Mez/Bar solo,pno/inst DURAND s.p.,
ipr   (V492)

L'heure Du Berger
S/T solo,pno/inst DURAND s.p., ipr
(V493)
Mez/Bar solo,pno/inst DURAND s.p.,
ipr   (V494)

O Triste Etait Mon Ame
S/T solo,pno/inst DURAND s.p., ipr
(V495)
Mez/Bar solo,pno/inst DURAND s.p.,
ipr   (V496)

Stances D'amour Et De Reve *Op.29,
CC5UL
high solo,pno/inst cmplt ed DURAND
s.p., ipr   (V497)

VIERUNDFUNFZIG FINNISCHE VOLKSLIEDER,
VOLS. I-II *CC54U
(Maasalo, Armas) [Finn/Ger] solo,pno
FAZER F 2179A; F 2179B s.p., ea.
(V498)

VIERUNDZWANZIG LIEDER UND ARIEN, HEFT I
see Krieger, Johann Philipp

VIERUNDZWANZIG LIEDER UND ARIEN, HEFT
II see Krieger, Johann Philipp

VIERUNDZWANZIG LIEDER UND ROMANZEN see
Tchaikovsky, Piotr Ilyitch

VIERZEHN ARIEN ALTER SPANISCHER MEISTER
*CCU
(Nin, Joaquin) [Span/Fr] solo,pno
SCHOTTS 3056; 3100 s.p., ea. in 2
books   (V499)

VIERZEHN ARIEN, BAND I see Haydn,
(Johann) Michael

VIERZEHN ARIEN, BAND II see Haydn,
(Johann) Michael

VIERZEHN LIEDER see Marx, Karl

VIERZEHN LIEDER see Buhler, W.

VIERZEHN LIEDER AUS "DES KNABEN
WUNDERHORN" see Mahler, Gustav

VIERZEHN LIEDER, HEFT I see Weismann,
Julius

VIERZEHN LIEDER, HEFT II see Weismann,
Julius

VIERZEHN LIEDER UND GESANGE AUS DER
JUGENDZEIT BAND I see Mahler,
Gustav

VIERZEHN LIEDER UND GESANGE AUS DER
JUGENDZEIT, BAND II see Mahler,
Gustav

VIERZEHN LIEDER UND GESANGE AUS DER
JUGENDZEIT, BAND III see Mahler,
Gustav

VIERZEHN VOLKSKINDERLIEDER see Brahms,
Johannes

VIESSANGBOKA *CCU,folk
(Leren; Dramstad) solo,pno NORSK 8717
s.p.   (V500)

VIEU, JANE
A L'Aimee
solo,pno (each available in 2 keys)
ENOCH s.p. see from Trois Tankas
Japonais   (V501)

Aladin
solo,pno ENOCH s.p.   (V502)

Au Pays Parfume
solo,acap ENOCH s.p.   (V503)
solo,pno ENOCH s.p.   (V504)

Carillons Blancs
solo,pno (available in 2 keys)
ENOCH s.p.   (V505)

Chanson Breve
solo,pno ENOCH s.p.   (V506)

Charite
solo,pno ENOCH s.p.   (V507)

La Belle Au Bois Dormant
solo,pno ENOCH s.p.   (V508)
solo,acap ENOCH s.p.   (V509)
solo,pno ENOCH s.p.   (V510)

La Flute De Bambou
solo,pno (each available in 2 keys)
ENOCH s.p. see from Trois Tankas
Japonais   (V511)

La Valse Des Rousses
solo,acap ENOCH s.p.   (V512)
solo,pno ENOCH s.p.   (V513)

Les Deux Baisers
solo,pno (available in 2 keys)
ENOCH s.p.   (V514)

Menuet De La Princesse
solo,pno ENOCH s.p.   (V515)

Monsieur Noel
solo,acap (available in 2 keys)
ENOCH s.p.   (V516)
solo,pno (available in 2 keys)
ENOCH s.p.   (V517)

O Salutaris! *sac
[Lat] solo,org/pno,opt vln/vcl
ENOCH s.p.   (V518)

Pompador
solo,pno (available in 2 keys)
ENOCH s.p.   (V519)

Seduction
solo,acap ENOCH s.p.   (V520)
solo,pno ENOCH s.p.   (V521)

Serenade D'Aladin
solo,acap ENOCH s.p.   (V522)
solo,pno ENOCH s.p.   (V523)

Serenade Japonaise
solo,pno (each available in 2 keys)
ENOCH s.p. see from Trois Tankas
Japonais   (V524)

Sur Le Pont De Bambou
solo,pno ENOCH s.p.   (V525)

Trois Tankas Japonais *see A
L'Aimee; La Flute De Bambou;
Serenade Japonaise   (V526)

Vers Le Reve
solo,pno (available in 2 keys)
ENOCH s.p.   (V527)

VIEUX MADRIGAL see Cuvillier, Charles

VIEUX NOELS DE FRANCE *see Denise;
D'ou Viens-Tu Berger; Noel
Ardennais; Noel De Chalons; Noel De
Stenay; Noel De Troyes; Noel Des
Islettes; Noel Du Doyenne   (V528)

VIEUX PORTRAIT see Chaminade, Cecile

VIGILATE, OCULI MEI see Porpora, Nicola
Antonio

VIGILIA D'AMORE see Bossi, Renzo

VIGILIEN see Jentsch, Walter

VIGLID *folk,Jew
(Roskin) med solo,pno HATIKVAH $.75
(V529)

VIGLID see Weiner, Lazar

VIGNATI, MILOS (1897-1966)
Carovny Kvet
"Zauberblume" med solo,pno CZECH
s.p.   (V530)

Carovny Svet *CCU
boy solo/girl solo,pno SUPRAPHON
s.p.   (V531)

Nenia Eroica
Bar solo,vln,vla,vcl CZECH s.p.
(V532)

Pisne Milostne *CCU
low solo,pno CZECH s.p.   (V533)

Zauberblume *see Carovny Kvet

VIGODA, SAMUEL
Children Of Exile *see Golus Kinder

Golus Kinder
"Children Of Exile" [Heb] high
solo,pno (Yiddish text) TRANSCON.
WJ 416 $.45   (V534)

Shtumer Protest
[Heb] high solo,pno (Yiddish text)
TRANSCON. WJ 417 $.50   (V535)

VIIKON VUOTTELIN KAKEA see Kilpinen,
Yrio

VIIMEINEN HETKI see Tuuri, Jaako

VIIMEINEN KEHTOLAULU see Pylkkanen,
Tauno Kullervo

VIISI KANSANLAULUSOVITUSTA see
Melartin, Erkki

VIISI LAULUA see Marttinen, Tauno

VIISI LAULUA RAAMATUN SANOIHIN see
Sonninen, Ahti

VIJF GEDICHTEN UIT FRENCH EN ANDERE
CANCAN see Baeyens, August-L.

VIJF GEESTELIJKE LIEDEREN VAN JAN
LUYKEN see Sigtenhorst-Meyer,
Bernhard van den

VIJF GEESTSLIJKE MOTETTEN see Mulder,
Ernest W.

VIJF GEZELLELIEDEREN see Dijk, Jan van

VIJF KLEENGEDICHTJES VAN GUIDO GEZELLE
see Dijk, Jan van

VIJF KLEINE VELDEKEN LIEDEREN see
Strategier, Herman

VIJF LIEDEREN see Bijvanck, Henk

VIJF LIEDEREN see Dijk, Jan van

VIJF LIEDEREN see Mulder, Herman

VIJF LIEDEREN OP OUD-NEDERLANDSCHE
TEKSTEN see Mengelberg, Rudolf

VIJF LIEDEREN ROND DE MUIDERKRING see
Paap, Wouter

VIJF LIEDEREN VAN BRUNO ERTLER see
Bijvanck, Henk

VIJF LIEDEREN VAN CHR. V.D. WEYE see
Mulder, Ernest W.

VIJF LIEDEREN VAN F.G. LORCA see Leeuw,
Ton de

VIJF LIEDEREN VAN MORGENSTERN see
Badings, Henk

VIJF LIEDEREN VAN R.M. RILKE see
Franken, Wim

VIJF MINNELIEDEREN OP MIDDELEEUWSE
TEKSTEN see Paap, Wouter

VIJF MINNELIEDEREN UIT "HENRIC VAN
VELDEKEN" see Strategier, Herman

VIJF NAGELDEUNTJES see Andriessen,
Hendrik

VIJF NAGELDEUNTJES see Andriessen,
Juriaan

VIJF NEDERLANDSCHE GEDICHTEN see
Voormolen, Alexander Nicolas

VIJF TEMPELZANGEN see Bordewijk-
Roepman, Johanna

VIJFTIEN HEBREEUWSE LIEDEREN *CC15L,
Heb
(Millner, Ch.; Nuis, Martien) [Heb]
solo,pno ALSBACH s.p.   (V536)

VIKING'S DAUGHTER, THE see Thomas,
Arthur Goring

VILDFAGEL see Andree

VILDMARK see Rangstrom, Ture

VILEC, MICHAL (1902-   )
    Vysoke Letne Nebo *CCU
    med solo,pno SLOV.HUD.FOND s.p.
                                    (V537)
VILF KLEINE MEISJES see Middeleer, Jean
    De, Cinq Petites Filles

VILIA see Lehar, Franz

VILJA-LIED see Lehar, Franz

VILKEN NYTTA AR AV MANNEN see Sonninen,
    Ahti, Munkiksi Joutuva

VILL DU DELA MIN GLADJE see Grafstrom

VILLA CHIUSA see Baldacci, Giov. Bruna

VILLA-LOBOS, HEITOR (1887-1959)
    Adeus Ema
    [Port] med solo,pno ESCHIG $1.75
        see also Characteristic Brazilian
        Songs   (V538)

    Bachianas Brasileiras, No. 5: Aria
    [Fr] S solo,pno ESCHIG $6.00 (V539)
    (Marx) [Port/Eng] S solo,vcl,orch
        AMP $1.25   (V540)
    (Segovia) [Port/Eng] high solo,pno
        AMP $1.50   (V541)

    Cabocla De Caxanga
    [Port] cor,pno ESCHIG $3.50 see
        also Characteristic Brazilian
        Songs   (V542)

    Cancao Das Aguas Claras
    [Port] high solo,orch ESCHIG $7.75
                                    (V543)
    Cancao De Cristal
        "Chanson De Cristal" [Port] med
        solo,pno ESCHIG $2.50   (V544)

    Chanson De Cristal *see Cancao De
        Cristal

    Characteristic Brazilian Songs
        *CC10L,So Am
    [Port] med solo,pno ESCHIG $16.75
        see also: Adeus Ema; Cabocla De
        Caxanga; Estrella E Lua Nova;
        Mokoce Ce-Maka; Nozani-Ha; O'
        Palida Madona; Papae
        Curumiassu; Tu Passaste Por
        Este Jardim; Viola Quebrada;
        Xango   (V545)

    Dos Paysages *CC2U
    [Port] med-high solo,pno ESCHIG
        $6.50   (V546)
    Estrella E Lua Nova
    [Port] med solo,pno ESCHIG $1.25
        sec also Characteristic Brazilian
        Songs   (V547)

    Jardim Fanado
    [Port] med solo,pno ESCHIG $2.25
                                    (V548)
    Modinhas Y Cancoes, Vol. I *CCU
    [Port] med-high solo,pno ESCHIG
        $7.00   (V549)

    Modinhas Y Cancoes, Vol. II *CCU
    [Port] med-high solo,pno ESCHIG
        $7.00   (V550)

    Mokoce Ce-Maka
    [Port] med solo,pno ESCHIG $1.50
        see also Characteristic Brazilian
        Songs   (V551)

    Nozani-Ha
    [Port] med solo,pno ESCHIG $1.25
        see also Characteristic Brazilian
        Songs   (V552)

    O' Palida Madona
    [Port] med solo,pno ESCHIG $2.50
        see also Characteristic Brazilian
        Songs   (V553)

    Papae Curumiassu
    [Port] med solo,pno ESCHIG $.65 see
        also Characteristic Brazilian
        Songs   (V554)

    Poema Da Crianca E Sua Mama
    [Port/Fr] med solo,fl,clar,vcl
        ESCHIG $2.75   (V555)

    Poeme D'Itabira
    [Fr] solo,pno/orch voc sc SCHOTTS
        ME s.p., ipa   (V556)
    [Port] med solo,orch ESCHIG $4.25
                                    (V557)
    Samba-Classico
    [Port] med-high solo,pno ESCHIG
        $2.70   (V558)

VILLA-LOBOS, HEITOR (cont'd.)
    Serenade
    [Port] med solo,pno ESCHIG $7.00
        see from Serestas   (V559)

    Serestas *see Serenade; Voo   (V560)

    Tres Poemas Indigenas *CC3U
    [Port] med solo,pno ESCHIG $5.00
                                    (V561)
    Tu Passaste Por Este Jardim
    [Port] med solo,pno ESCHIG $3.25
        see also Characteristic Brazilian
        Songs   (V562)

    U Bachianas Brasileiras, No. 5
    [Port/Eng] S solo,vcl,orch AMP
        $2.50, ipa   (V563)

    Viola Quebrada
    [Port] med solo,pno ESCHIG $.65 see
        also Characteristic Brazilian
        Songs   (V564)

    Voo
    [Port] med solo,pno ESCHIG $3.50
        see from Serestas   (V565)

    Xango
    [Port] med solo,pno ESCHIG $1.50
        see also Characteristic Brazilian
        Songs   (V566)

VILLAGE BAND, THE see Fryberg, M.,
    Dorfmusik

VILLAGE SWALLOWS IN AUSTRIA see
    Strauss, Johann

VILLANCICO see Lopez De La Rosa,
    Horatio

VILLANCICO see Olazabal, Zirso de

VILLANCICOS see Rodrigo, Joaquin

VILLANCICOS DEL FOLKLORE ESPANOL
    *CC6U,Xmas,Span
    (Gil) [Span] med solo,pno UNION ESP.
        $1.00   (V567)

VILLANCICOS POPULARES *CC6U,Span
    (Benedito) [Span] med solo,pno UNION
        ESP. $1.00   (V568)

VILLANCICOS POPULARES *CCU,Span
    (Angel) [Span] med solo,gtr UNION
        ESP. $1.50, ea. in 3 volumes (V569)

VILLANCICOS TRADICIONALES *CC6U,Xmas
    (Gil) [Span] med solo,pno UNION ESP.
        $1.00   (V570)

VILLANELLE see Berlioz, Hector

VILLANELLE see Costa, G.

VILLANELLE see Dell'Acqua, Eva

VILLANELLE see Mendelssohn-Bartholdy,
    Felix

VILLANELLE see Millot, E.

VILLANELLE see Paray, Paul

VILLANELLE see Saint-Saens, Camille

VILLANELLE see Schumann, Robert
    (Alexander), Landliches Lied

VILLANELLE DES PETITS CANARDS see
    Chabrier, Emmanuel

VILLANESCA see Alderighi, Dante

VILLANESCAS see Berger, Jean

VILLEBICHOT, A. DE
    Je M'en Souviens Toujours
        solo,pno ENOCH s.p.   (V571)
        solo,acap ENOCH s.p.   (V572)

VILLEMO see Peterson-Berger, (Olof)
    Wilhelm

VILLES see Metral, Pierre

VILLONNERIE see Henking, Bernhard

VILSE see Sibelius, Jean

VIN QUI ROUGIS MA TROGNE see Saint-
    Saens, Camille

VINCZE, I.
    Persian Songs *CCU
        solo,pno BUDAPEST 5912 s.p. (V573)

VINDEN BLAES SYNNA - VINDEN BLAES
    NORDA, HEFT I see Beck, Thomas
    [Ludvigsen]

VINDEN BLAES SYNNA - VINDEN BLAES
    NORDA, HEFT II see Beck, Thomas
    [Ludvigsen]

VINDEN BLASER see Nordqvist, Gustaf

VINDEN OCH BACKEN see Korling, Sven

VINDEN SOMNAT I DEN STILLA KVALL see
    Myrberg, August M.

VINDRINGSSANG see Korling, Felix

VINE, JOHN
    Let Him Go
        solo,pno PATERSON s.p.   (V574)

    Ould Lammas Fair, The
        solo,pno PATERSON s.p.   (V575)

VINETA see Palmgren, Selim

VINGT-CINQ MELODIES CELEBRES see
    Schumann, Robert (Alexander)

VINGT-ET-UN CHANSONS, VOL. I see Kosma,
    J.

VINGT MELODIES VOL. 1 see Pierne,
    Gabriel

VINGT MELODIES VOL. 2 see Pierne,
    Gabriel

VINGT MELODIES see Cuvillier, Charles

VINGT MELODIES see Dufresne, C.

VINGT MELODIES ET DOUS, VOL. I see
    Saint-Saens, Camille

VINGT MELODIES ET DOUS, VOL. II see
    Saint-Saens, Camille

VINGT MELODIES, VOL. 1 see Faure,
    Gabriel-Urbain

VINGT MELODIES, VOL. 2 see Faure,
    Gabriel-Urbain

VINGT MELODIES, VOL. 3 see Faure,
    Gabriel-Urbain

VINGT MELODIES, VOL. I see Lacome, Paul

VINGT MELODIES, VOL. I see Chaminade,
    Cecile

VINGT MELODIES, VOL. II see Lacome,
    Paul

VINGT MELODIES, VOL. II see Chaminade,
    Cecile

VINGT MELODIES, VOL. III see Chaminade,
    Cecile

VINGT MELODIES, VOL. IV see Chaminade,
    Cecile

VINGT NOELS FRANCAIS *sac,CC20U,Xmas
    (Tiersot, Julien) med solo,pno/org
    cmplt ed HEUGEL s.p. each title
    available separetly   (V576)

VINGT POEMES DE LA PLEIADE see
    Leguerney, Jacques

VINGT-QUATRE VOCALISES DODECAPHONIQUES
    see Rosseau, Norbert

VINIENDO DE CHILECITO see Guastavino,
    Carlos

VINO, MUJER Y CANTO see Strauss,
    Johann, Wein, Weib Und Gesang

VINTER, GILBERT (1909-   )
    Three Poems *CC3U
        solo,pno CRAMER   (V577)

VINTERMORGON see Kaski, Heino,
    Talviaamu

VINTERNATT see Marvia, Einari, Talviyo

VINYES VERDES VORA EL MAR see Toldra,
    Eduardo

VIOLA *CC93U,folk,Hung
    (Hajdu; Halasz) solo,pno BUDAPEST
        1085 s.p.   (V578)

VIOLA see Bengzon

VIOLA QUEBRADA see Villa-Lobos, Heitor

VIOLE see Paray, Paul

VIOLE PALLIDE see Gandino, Adolfo

VIOLER see Elgar, Edward, Salut D'amour

VIOLET, THE see Mozart, Wolfgang
    Amadeus, Das Veilchen

VIOLET GIRL see Newton, Ernest

VIOLETAS see Guastavino, Carlos

VIOLETTES DE MARS see Schumann, Robert (Alexander)

VIOLON FLEURS see Poulenc, Francis

VIOLONS DANS LE SOIR see Saint-Saens, Camille

VIRAGIM, VIRAGIM *folk
(Adam, J.) [Hung] solo,pno BUDAPEST 1502 (V579)

VIRELAI D'ALSACE see Legay, Marcel

VIRGA JESSE FLORUIT see Bach, Johann Sebastian

VIRGIL see Shepherd, Arthur

VIRGIN, FOUNT OF LOVE see Durante, Francesco, Vergin, Tutt'amor

VIRGIN MARY HAD A BABY BOY see Evans, H.

VIRGINIA see Thomas, A.

VIRGIN'S CRADLE SONG, THE see Brahms, Johannes

VIRGIN'S SLUMBER SONG see Reger, Max, Maria Wiegenlied

VIRGIN'S THREADS, THE see Schmitt, Florent, Fils De La Vierge

VIRGO see Kersters, Willem

VIRTUE see Butt, James

VIS, LUCAS (1947-   )
Music
S solo,vcl DONEMUS s.p. (V580)

VISA see Fougstedt, Nils-Eric

VISA see Kilpinen, Yrio

VISA see Nordqvist, Gustaf

VISA see Sjogren, Emil

VISA I FOLKTON see Nordqvist, Gustaf

VISA I FRAMMANDE LAND see Salonen, Sulo

VISA I JULI see Lundborg, Gosta

VISA "NAR VIKINGEN FOR VIDA" see Hallstrom, Ivar

VISA UR "BROLLOPET PA ULFASA"
(Soderman) solo,pno LUNDQUIST s.p. (V581)

VISA UR MUNTRA FRUARNA see Nicolai

VISE see Nielsen, Carl

VISE I ONNA see Beck, Thomas [Ludvigsen]

VISE TIL SJOLTROST see Beck, Thomas [Ludvigsen]

VISFYND I-II
(Zeland; Sternvall) solo,pno,opt gtr GEHRMANS s.p., ea. assorted sailor songs, love songs and rhymes (V582)

VISION see Dufresne, C.

VISION see Gelli, E.

VISION see Hutchison, W.

VISION, A see Fryxell, Regina Holmen

VISION AND PRAYER see Babbit, Milton

VISION D'AMANT see Delmet, Paul

VISION FUGGITIVA see Massenet, Jules

VISION OF LOVE see Rider, Dale G.

VISION OF TIME AND ETERNITY, A see Mathias, William

VISIONE see De Angelis, Ruggero

VISIONEN see Vycpalek, Ladislav

VISIONS see Balogh

VISIONS see Mulot, M.

VISIONS OF BEASTS AND GODS see Williamson, Malcolm

VISIT FROM THE MOON, A see Dunhill, Thomas Frederick

VISITING WITH JESUS see Greenway

VISITOR, THE see Turner, Olive

VISITS TO ST. ELIZABETH'S see Rorem, Ned

VISOR see Hallen, Andreas

VISOR see Nyblom, C.G.

VISSELULLE NU, BARNLIL! see Nielsen, Carl

VISSI D'ARTE see Puccini, Giacomo

VISTA see Fischer, Irwin

VISTO DE CERCA see De Pablo, Luis

VIT MAN OCH KINAMAN see Taube, Evert

VIT SASOM SNO
see Andliga Sanger, Heft 2

VIT SIPPAN see Sibelius, Jean

VITA BREVE see Cilea, Francesco

VITA ET LES JEUNES FILLES see Indy, Vincent d'

VITA LILJOR see Anjou, P. d'

VITA LILJORNA DOFTA see Rangstrom, Ture

VITEZSTVI BUDE NASE see Nejedly, Vit

VITRAIL see Lachaume, A.

VITSIPPAN see Sibelius, Jean

VITTORIA, VITTORIA see Carissimi, Giacomo

VIVA IL VION SPUMEGGIANTE see Mascagni, Pietro

VIVA LU SULI MIE see Fasullo, P.

VIVALDI, ANTONIO (1678-1741)
All' Ombra Di Sospetto *cant
(Fechner; Franke) "Die Getauschte Liebe" [It/Ger] high solo,fl,cont sc DEUTSCHER 9504 s.p., ipa (V583)

Arie Per Contralto *CC11L
(Corghi, A.) [It] Mez solo,pno cmplt ed RICORDI-ENG 131822 s.p. (V584)

Arie Per Soprano De Opera *CC9L
(Corghi, A.) [It] S solo,pno RICORDI-ENG 131669 s.p. (V585)

Canta In Prato *mot
solo,strings,cont sc CARISH 21863 s.p., ipa, voc sc CARISH 21845 s.p. (V586)

Cessate, Omai Cessate *cant
A solo,pno,strings sc ZERBONI 7146 s.p. (V587)
(Mortari, V.) CARISH s.p. (V588)

Chiare Onde (from Ercole Sul Termodonte)
(Casella, A.) S solo,cembalo, strings sc CARISH 19462 s.p., voc sc CARISH 9825 s.p., ipa contains also: Da Due Venti (V589)

Da Due Venti (from Ercole Sul Termodonte)
see Vivaldi, Antonio, Chiare Onde

Di Due Rai
see Four Arias

Die Getauschte Liebe *see All' Ombra Di Sospetto

Dille Ch'il Vivir Mio
see Four Arias

Four Arias
(Turchi, Guido) [It/Eng] high solo, pno INTERNAT. $2.00 contains: Di Due Rai; Dille Ch'il Vivir Mio; La Pastorella Sul Primo Albore; Vieni, Vieni, O Mio Diletto (V590)

Invicti Bellate
A solo,pno,harp sc ZERBONI 7192 s.p. (V591)

Juditha Triumphans *sac,ora
(Bianchi, Lino) solo,orch SANTIS voc sc s.p., sc rental (V592)

La Gloria E Imeneo
(Blanchard, Roger) SMez soli, strings,cont JOBERT s.p. sc, voc sc (V593)

VIVALDI, ANTONIO (cont'd.)
La Pastorella Sul Primo Albore
see Four Arias

Laudate Pueri (Psalm 112) sac
S solo,orch RICORDI-ENG 131613 s.p. (V594)
A solo,orch sc ZERBONI 7173 s.p. (V595)
(Ephirikian) [Lat/Eng] S solo,orch RICORDI-ENG 131615 s.p. (V596)
(Spinelli, G.) S solo,strings,cont sc CARISH 21835 s.p. (V597)

Motetti A Canto Solo Con Stromenti *sac
SSSSSMez soli,strings HEUGEL L.PUP. 7 s.p. (V598)

Nisi Dominus (Psalm 126) sac
(Bruni, M.) A solo,org,strings sc CARISH 21412 s.p., ipa, voc sc CARISH 21414 s.p. (V599)
(Degrada) [Lat/Eng] A solo,strings, cont RICORDI-ENG 131678 s.p. (V600)

O Qui Coeli Terraeque Serenitas *Op.101,No.6, sac,mot
[Lat] S solo,strings&cembalo/pno sc BROEKMANS B514 rental, ipa, sc BROEKMANS B12 s.p. (V601)
S solo,strings,pno voc sc BROEKMANS 514 s.p., ipa (V602)

Piango Gemo Sospiro *cant
(Mortari, V.) solo,strings,cont sc CARISH 21955 s.p., ipa, voc sc CARISH 21844 s.p. (V603)

Psalm 112 *see Laudate Pueri

Psalm 126 *see Nisi Dominus

Quattro Arie Per Soprano *CC4U
S solo,orch sc SANTIS L. 93 rental (V604)

Qui Coeli Terraeque *mot
solo,pno BROEKMANS 514 s.p. (V605)

Salve Regina *sac
(Ephrikian) [Lat/Eng] A solo,2orch RICORDI-ENG 131686 s.p. (V606)
(Ephrikian, Angelo) A solo,2orch sc RICORDI-ENG 131684 s.p. (V607)
(Negri, Vittorio) A solo,2fl, strings BREITKOPF-W s.p. (V608)

Sei Arie *CC6UL
[It] solo,pno cmplt ed RICORDI-ENG 124325 s.p. (V609)

Stabat Mater *sac
[It] A solo,strings,cont RICORDI-ENG 131565 s.p. (V610)
A solo,strings,cont sc RICORDI-ENG 131563 s.p. (V611)
A solo,pno UNIVER. 27 C 004 s.p. (V612)
(Casella, A.) A solo,org,strings sc CARISH 20760 s.p., ipa, voc sc CARISH 19846 s.p. (V613)

Vieni, Vieni, O Mio Diletto
see Four Arias

VIVAMUS see Cattini, U.

VIVARINO, INNOCENTIO
Vier Geistliche Konzerte *sac,CC4U, concerto
(Ewerhart, Rudolf) S/T solo,cont BIELER CS 66 s.p. (V614)

VIVE HENRY IV *folk
(Lavie) [Fr] med solo,gtr ESCHIG $1.10 see from Three Popular Songs (V615)
(Lavie, Ferandez) [Span/Fr/It] solo, gtr SCHOTTS GA 197 s.p. see from Alte Und Neue Werke (V616)

VIVE LA CANADIENNE!
"Marianna" see Crystal Fountain, The

VIVE LA FRANCE see Saint-Saens, Camille

VIVE L'ANJOU
(Beziade; Verrier) solo,pno GRAS s.p. (V617)

VIVE LE SOLEIL see Ronald, Sir Landon, Sunbeams

VIVE LE VIN DU LAYON
(Gerard, F.; Emmerechts) solo,pno GRAS s.p. (V618)

VIVE L'EAU see Delbruck, J.

VIVES, AMADEO (1871-1932)
Canciones Epigramaticas *CC13U
[Span] med solo,pno ESCHIG $7.75 see also: El Amor Y Los Ojos; El Retrato De Isabela; La Presumida (V619)

VIVES, AMADEO (cont'd.)

El Amor Y Los Ojos
  [Span] med-high solo,pno ESCHIG
  $.75 see also Canciones
  Epigramaticas   (V620)

El Retrato De Isabela
  [Span] med-high solo,pno ESCHIG
  $.75 see also Canciones
  Epigramaticas   (V621)

Joc D'infant
  [Span] med-high solo,pno ESCHIG
  $.75   (V622)

La Presumida
  [Span] med solo,pno ESCHIG $.75 see
  also Canciones Epigramaticas   (V623)

Orentes D'Abril
  [Span] high solo,pno ESCHIG $.75
                                   (V624)

Por El Humo Se Sabe Donde Esta El
  Fuego (from Dona Francisquita)
  [Span] T solo,pno RICORDI-ARG
  BA 8595 s.p.   (V625)

V'LA C'QUE C'EST QU'D'ALLER AU BOIS see
  DuBois, Pierre Max

VLAAMSE KERMIS see Clercq, R. de

VLAAMSE KERMIS see Cuypers, H.

VLAAMSE KERMIS see Hullebroeck, Em.

VLAANDERENS MAAGD see Hullebroeck, Em.

VLAD, ROMAN (1919-   )
  Cadenza Michelangiolesche
  solo,orch sc,quarto RICORDI-ENG
  131028 s.p.   (V626)

  Cinque Elegie Biblici *sac,CC5U,Bibl
  female solo,orch voc sc ZERBONI
  5104 s.p.   (V627)

  Ego Autem
  [It] Bar solo,org RICORDI-ENG
  131982 s.p.   (V628)

  Il Gabbiano
  [It/Ger/Eng] solo,pno RICORDI-ENG
  131484 s.p.   (V629)

  Immer Wieder
  S solo,English horn,clar,bsn,vla,
  vcl,marimba,vibra,harp,pno sc
  UNIVER. 13750 $8.00   (V630)

  Tre Invocazioni *CC3U
  [It] solo,pno SANTIS 842 s.p.;
  solo,orch SANTIS rental   (V631)

VLADERACKEN, G. VON
  Kerstzang
  solo,pno ALSBACH s.p.   (V632)

  Moederdagliedje *CCU
  solo,pno BROEKMANS 91 s.p.   (V633)

  Plange Sion *sac
  high solo,org,opt pno,vla,vln
  ALSBACH s.p.   (V634)

VLETTER, C.
  Begrabe Deine Toten
  solo,pno BROEKMANS 197 s.p.   (V635)

VLIJMEN, JAN VAN (1935-   )
  Aus Stillen Fenstern
  see Drie Morgensterliederen

  Der Zeitungsleser
  see Drie Morgensterliederen

  Drie Morgensterliederen
  Mez solo,pno DONEMUS s.p.
  contains: Aus Stillen Fenstern;
  Der Zeitungsleser; Ein Junger
  Freund   (V636)

  Ein Junger Freund
  see Drie Morgensterliederen

  Mythos
  Mez solo,fl,ob,clar,bsn,horn,2vln,
  vla,vcl DONEMUS s.p.   (V637)

VLINDERLIEDJE see Pijper, Willem

VO' CANTARE see Cimara, Pietro

VOCAL ALBUM see Franz, Robert

VOCAL ALBUM see Schumann, Robert
  (Alexander)

VOCAL ANTHOLOGY: ARIAS, ROMANCES AND
  SONGS *CCU
  [Russ] T solo,pno MEZ KNIGA 102 s.p.
                                   (V638)
VOCAL ANTHOLOGY: SCENES FROM OPERETTAS
  BY SOVIET COMPOSERS *CCU
  [Russ] solo,pno MEZ KNIGA 103 s.p.

                                   (V639)
VOCAL ANTHOLOGY: SONGS, ROMANCES AND
  ARIAS *CCU
  [Russ] solo,pno MEZ KNIGA 104 s.p.
                                   (V640)
VOCAL COMPOSITIONS see Bersa, Blagoje

VOCAL SELECTIONS FROM "DAISY" see
  Harding, B.

VOCAL SOLOS FROM ONE HUNDRED AND TWO
  STRINGS, VOL. 2 see Carmichael,
  Ralph

VOCAL TRIOS, VOL. 1 *sac,CCUL
  3 female soli,pno WORD 10002 $1.25
                                   (V641)
VOCAL WORKS (THIRD EDITION, ENLARGED)
  see Shostakovich, Dmitri

VOCAL WORKS see Falla, Manuel de

VOCAL WORKS see Machavariani, A.

VOCAL WORKS, VOL. II see Prokofiev,
  Serge

VOCAL WORKS WITH SIX-STRINGED OR SEVEN-
  STRINGED GUITAR ACCOMPANIMENT *CCU
  [Russ] solo,gtr MEZ KNIGA 278 s.p.
                                   (V642)
VOCALISE see Boone, Charles

VOCALISE see Copland, Aaron

VOCALISE see Cowell, Henry Dixon

VOCALISE see Delden, Lex van

VOCALISE see D'Haene, Rafael Lodewijk

VOCALISE see Giasson, Paul E.

VOCALISE see Mc Bride, Robert Guyn

VOCALISE see Rachmaninoff, Sergey
  Vassilievitch

VOCALISE see Whittenberg, Charles

VOCALISE NO. 3 ON NONSENSE SYLLABLES
  see Mc Bride, Robert Guyn

VOCALISES see Diamond, David

VOCALITIS see Humphreys

VOCALIZZO see Pizzetti, Ildebrando

VOCALIZZO DA CONCERTO see Ghedini,
  Giorgio Federico

VOCALIZZO PER SOPRANO see Petrassi,
  Goffredo

VOCATIO see Jama, Agnes

VOCCA ADDUROSA see Longo, Achille

VOCE DI DONNA O D'ANGELO see
  Ponchielli, Amilcare

VOCE DI LAGUNA see Recli, Giulia

VOCE II see Gaber, Harley

VOCERO see Perissas, M.

VOCES DE PRIMAVERA see Strauss, Johann,
  Fruhlingsstimmen

VOCI DI FONTANE see Capucci, L.

VODDEN see Witte, D.

VOER MIJ WAAR UW VREDE WENKT see
  Mulder, Ernest W.

VOER MIJ WAAR UW VREDE WENKT see
  Mulder, Herman

VOEU see Ropartz, Joseph Guy

VOEU SUPREME see Chaminade, Cecile

VOEUX see Rabey, Rene

VOGEL, A.
  Ah! Laisse-Moi Le Voir (from La
  Filleule Du Roi)
  solo,pno ENOCH s.p.   (V643)

  Elle Etait Pres De Moi (from La
  Filleule Du Roi)
  solo,pno ENOCH s.p.   (V644)

  La Garbure Bearnaise (from La
  Filleule Du Roi)
  solo,pno ENOCH s.p.   (V645)

  La Jeanneton Pour Dot (from La
  Filleule Du Roi)
  solo,pno ENOCH s.p.   (V646)

VOGEL, A. (cont'd.)
  Maman, Avant De Dire (from La
  Filleule Du Roi)
  solo,pno ENOCH s.p.   (V647)

  Maman, Je Me Rappelle (from La
  Filleule Du Roi)
  solo,pno ENOCH s.p.   (V648)

VOGEL, HANS (1880-1950)
  Stille Nacht, Heilige Nacht *sac
  solo,pno MULLER 439 s.p.   (V649)

VOGEL, HOWARD W.
  Behold, How Fair And Pleasant *sac,
  Marriage
  med solo,pno BELWIN $1.50   (V650)

VOGEL, WLADIMIR (1896-   )
  Alla Memoria Di G.B. Pergolesi
  [It/Ger] solo,pno voc sc RICORDI-
  ENG 129897 s.p.   (V651)

  Chaconne (from Thyl Claes)
  [Fr/Ger] solo,pno RICORDI-ENG
  127957 s.p.   (V652)

  Dal Quaderno Di Francine
  S solo,2inst ZERBONI 5389 rental
                                   (V653)

  Goethe Amphorismen
  S solo,harp voc sc ZERBONI 5525
  s.p.   (V654)

  Introduction (from Thyl Claes)
  [Fr/Ger] solo,pno RICORDI-ENG
  127953 s.p.   (V655)

  Le Supplice De Claes (from Thyl
  Claes)
  [Fr/Ger] solo,pno RICORDI-ENG
  127956 s.p.   (V656)

  Les Adieux De Claes (from Thyl Claes)
  [Fr/Ger] solo,pno RICORDI-ENG
  127955 s.p.   (V657)

  Meditazione Sulla Maschera Di
  Modigliani *cant
  [It] solo,pno RICORDI-ENG 130366
  s.p.   (V658)

  Uf Em Bibaboneberg
  solo,pno HUG s.p.   (V659)

  Wagadu *ora
  [It/Fr/Eng/Ger] solo,pno RICORDI-
  ENG 128392 s.p.   (V660)

VOGELNESTJE see Tetterode, L. Adr. von

VOGELWEIDE see Castelnuovo-Tedesco,
  Mario

VOGGESANG FOR EIN BYTTING see Madsen,
  Age

VOGGSONG see Olsen, Sparre

VOGLEIN SCHWERMUT see Genzmer, Harald

VOGLIATEMI BENE see Puccini, Giacomo

VOGLIO DIRE see Handel, George Frideric

VOGUE, LEGER ZEPHIR see Mendelssohn-
  Bartholdy, Felix

VOGUE, VOGUE LA GALERE see Saint-Saens,
  Camille

V'OHAVTO see Piket, Frederick

VOI AVETE UN COR FEDELE see Mozart,
  Wolfgang Amadeus

VOI CHE SAPETE see Mozart, Wolfgang
  Amadeus

VOI, JOS MIE TOK' MIEHEN SAISIN see
  Kilpinen, Yrio

VOI KUINKA HAILYVA see Verdi, Giuseppe,
  La Donna E Mobile

VOI LO SAPETE see Mascagni, Pietro

VOI MI PIAGASTE, O DIO see Marcello,
  Benedetto

VOI MINUA MIESKULUA see Kilpinen, Yrio

VOI MINUN NUORTA SYDANTANI see
  Merikanto, Oskar

VOICE AND THE FLUTE, THE see Densmore,
  John H.

VOICE IN THE WILDERNESS, THE see Scott,
  John Prindle

VOICE OF GOD, THE see Mourant, Walter

VOICE OF LOVE see Maw, Nicholas

VOICE OF MY BELOVED, THE see Helfman, Max

VOICE OF THE WIND see Gerschefski, Edwin

VOICEPIECE see Hobbs, Christopher

VOICES see Ambrosi, Alearco

VOICES see Birch, Robert Fairfax

VOICES see Wilkinson, M.

VOICES OF SPRING see Strauss, Johann, Frulingsstimmen

VOICES OF SPRING see Thomas, Arthur Goring

VOICES OF THE SKY see Matthews, Harvey Alexander

VOICES OF THE WOODS see Rubinstein, Anton

VOICI COMMENT, SANS DIDACTIQUE see Levade, Charles (Gaston)

VOICI LA DOUCE NUIT DE MAI see Beekhuis, Hanna

VOICI LA DOUCE NUIT DE MAI see Coppola, Piero

VOICI LE PRINTEMPS see Wangermez, Ed.

VOICI LE SOIR see Duvernoy, Victor-Alphonse

VOICI LES TRISTES LIEUX see Rameau, Jean-Philippe

VOICI QUE LE PRINTEMPS see Debussy, Claude

VOICI QUE SE FAIT SI FURTIVE see Gabus, Monique

VOILA L'PLAISIR, MESDAMES see Gerbaud, G.

VOIS DE BELLES FILLES see Roussel, Albert

VOIS MA MISERE, HELAS! see Saint-Saens, Camille

VOIS! PHOEBE ELLE-MEME see Nougues, Jean

VOISINAGE see Chaminade, Cecile

VOIX ANCIENNE see Cerchia, A.

VOIX CLAIRES see Apotheloz, Jean

VOIX DE LA BRISE see Bellenghi, G., Profumi Orientali

VOIX DU LARGE see Chaminade, Cecile

VOIX NOCTURNES see Gretchaninov, Alexander Tikhonovitch

VOJNE SLIKE see Srebotnjak, Alojz F.

VOKALI I see Devcic, Natko

VOKALI II see Devcic, Natko

VOKALWERKE see Shostakovich, Dmitri

VOLA INTANTO L'ORA INSONNE see Menotti, Gian Carlo

VOLA VOLA VOLA see Albanese, Guido

VOLE VO NASCONDER MI see De Grandis, Renato

VOLGA, RIVER VOLGA *CCU,folk,Russ
[Russ] solo,pno MEZ KNIGA 58 s.p.
(V661)

VOLGA, THE DEEP RIVER *folk,Russ
[Russ] high solo,pno MEZ KNIGA 114
s.p. (V662)

VOLGA, VOLGA *CCU
solo,pno FAZER F 1484 s.p. (V663)

VOLKALWERKE (AUS DEM NACHLASS) see
Kappel, Fritz

VOLKMANN, ROBERT (1815-1883)
Naktergalen
low solo,pno GEHRMANS s.p. (V664)
high solo,pno GEHRMANS s.p. (V665)

VOLKONSKY, A.
Les Plaintes De Chtchaza
S solo,English horn,vln,vla,tamb,
vibra,cembalo,xylo sc UNIVER.
14770 $15.00 (V666)

VOLKSLIED
(Soderman) solo,pno LUNDQUIST s.p.
(V667)

VOLKSLIEDBUCHLEIN FUR KLAVIER *CC88U,
folk
(Dietrich, Fritz) (easy) BAREN. 1499
$5.00 (V668)

VOLKSLIEDCHEN see Schumann, Robert
(Alexander)

VOLKSLIEDER AUS ALLER WELT, BOOK I:
ENGLAND *CCU,folk,Eng
(Behrend) [Eng/Ger] med solo,gtr BOTE
$4.25 (V669)

VOLKSLIEDER AUS ALLER WELT, BOOK II:
FRANCE *CCU,folk,Fr
(Behrend) [Fr/Ger] med solo,gtr BOTE
$4.25 (V670)

VOLKSLIEDER AUS ALLER WELT, BOOK III
SPAIN & PORTUGAL *CCU,folk,Port/
Span
(Behrend) [Span/Port/Ger] med solo,
gtr BOTE $5.25 (V671)

VOLKSLIEDER AUS ALLER WELT, BOOK IV:
ITALY *CCU,folk,It
(Behrend) [It/Ger] med solo,gtr BOTE
$3.75 (V672)

VOLKSLIEDER AUS ALLER WELT, BOOK IX:
POLAND *CCU,folk
(Behrend) med solo,gtr BOTE $2.25
Polish and Latvian song, in
original language and German (V673)

VOLKSLIEDER AUS ALLER WELT, BOOK VII:
BALKAN *CCU,folk
(Behrend) med solo,gtr BOTE $4.75 in
Hungarian, Rumanian, Bulgarian,
Yugoslavian and German languages
(V674)

VOLKSLIEDER AUS ALLER WELT, BOOK VIII:
RUSSIA *CCU,folk,Russ
(Behrend) [Russ/Ger] med solo,gtr
BOTE $4.25 (V675)

VOLKSLIEDER AUS ALLER WELT, BOOK X:
GERMANY *CCU,folk,Ger
(Behrend) [Ger] med solo,gtr BOTE
$3.75 (V676)

VOLKSLIEDER AUS ALLER WELT, BOOK XI:
AMERICA *CCU,folk,US
(Behrend) [Eng/Ger] med solo,gtr BOTE
$3.50 (V677)

VOLKSLIEDER AUS ALLER WELT, BOOK XII:
INDONESIA *CCU,folk
(Behrend) med solo,gtr BOTE $4.75
Indonesian songs, in German and
original language (V678)

VOLKSLIEDER AUS OSTPREUSSEN *CC12U,
folk
(Kroll) [Ger] med solo,pno BOTE $2.00
Prussian (V679)

VOLKSLIEDER DES AUSLANDES, BAND I:
SPANISCHE LIEDER *CCU,folk
(Schwarz-Reiflingen, Erwin) [Ger/
Span] med solo,gtr LEUCKART $2.50
(V680)

VOLKSLIEDER DES AUSLANDES, BAND II:
ITALIENISCHE LIEDER *CCU,folk
(Schwarz-Reiflingen, Erwin) [It/Ger]
med solo,gtr LEUCKART $2.50 (V681)

VOLKSLIEDER DES AUSLANDES, BAND III:
RUSSISCHE LIEDER *CCU,folk
(Schwarz-Reiflingen, Erwin) [Ger] med
solo,gtr LEUCKART $2.50 (V682)

VOLKSLIEDERBUCH ZUR GITARRE, BAND 1:
KINDERLIEDER *CCU,folk
(Burkhart, Fr.; Scheit, K.) solo,gtr
DOBLINGER 05 921 s.p. (V683)

VOLKSLIEDERBUCH ZUR GITARRE, BAND 2:
WANDER- UND ABSCHIEDSLIEDER *CCU,
folk
(Burkhart, Fr.; Scheit, K.) solo,gtr
DOBLINGER 05 922 s.p. (V684)

VOLKSWEISE see Bijvanck, Henk

VOLKSWIJZE see Franken, Wim

VOLL JENER SUSSE see Schoenberg, Arnold

VOLLENDUNG see Schubert, Franz (Peter)

VOLLENWYDER, H.
Lieder Nach Dialektgedichten *CCU
solo,pno HUG s.p. (V685)

Liederheft, Heft 1, 2 *CCU
solo,pno HUG s.p., ea. (V686)

VOLLERTHUN, GEORG (1876-1945)
Vier Lieder Der Anmut *Op.24, CC4U
[Ger] med solo,pno BOTE $2.00
(V687)

VOLLMOND AM SEE see Emborg, Jens
Laurson

VOLT MAJN TATE RAJCH GEVEN see Weiner,
Lazar

VOLTA LA TERREA FRONTE ALLE STELLE see
Verdi, Giuseppe

VOLUNTEER ORGANIST see Lamb, Henry

VOLUPTE see Delmet, Paul

VOM AUFGANG DER SONNEN see Schutz,
Heinrich

VOM BAUM DES LEBENS see Taubert, Karl
Heinz

VOM FEBRUAR 1948 see Haba, Alois, Od
Unora 1948

VOM FISCHER UN SYNER FRU see Schoeck,
Othmar

VOM HIMMEL HOCH, DA KOMM ICH HER see
Schop, Johann

VOM HIMMEL HOCH, O ENGLEIN KOMMT see
Metzger, Hans-Arnold

VOM HIMMEL ZUR ERDE *CC3U
solo,pno,opt fl/rec RIES s.p. (V688)

VOM KUSSEN see Reger, Max

VOM MONTE PINCIO see Grieg, Edvard
Hagerup

VOM ROSENBETT see Purcell, Henry

VOM SPASS UND ERNST see Tcherepnin,
Alexander

VOM STRANDE I see Kilpinen, Yrio,
Rannalta I

VOM STRANDE II see Kilpinen, Yrio,
Rannalta II

VOM TIEFINNERN SONG see Baur, Jurg

VOM TODE see Beethoven, Ludwig van

VOM UNENDLICHEN see Schubert, Heinz

VOMACKA, BOLESLAV (1887-1965)
Dve Balady A Pisen *Op.26, CC2U
low solo,orch SUPRAPHON s.p. (V689)

Pisne Letni Noci *Op.34, CCU
high solo,pno SUPRAPHON s.p. (V690)

Ruckkehr Vom Schlachtfeld *Op.13
[Czech/Ger] T solo,pno SUPRAPHON
s.p. (V691)

Sedm Rondeaux Na Basne J. Seifert
*CC7U
Bar solo,pno CZECH s.p. (V692)

Zavata Cesta *Op.1, CC3U
high solo,pno SUPRAPHON s.p. (V693)

Zyklus Von Funf Liedern: "1914"
*Op.11, song cycle
[Czech/Ger/Fr] high solo,pno
SUPRAPHON s.p. (V694)

VON DEINEM HEISZEN KUSSE see Cuypers,
H.

VON DEN HIMMLISCHEN FREUDEN see
Rosenmuller, Johann

VON DEN SIEBEN ZECHBRUDERN see Strauss,
Richard

VON DEN TAUBEN see Trunk, Richard

VON DER ARMUTH see Verhaar, Ary

VON DER DEMUT see Zagwijn, Henri

VON DER LIEBE see Einem, Gottfried von

VON DER LIEBE SUSS UND BITTRER FRUCHT
see Braunfels, Walter

VON DER UNGEORDNETEN VERLASSENSCHAFT
see Weishappel, Rudolf

VON DER VERGANGLICHKEIT see Kraft, Karl

VON EWIGER LIEBE see Brahms, Johannes

VON FRUH BIS SPAT see Bitterauf,
Richard

VON GOTT WILL ICH NICHT LASSEN see
Schutz, Heinrich

VON GUTER ART *CC4U,folk
(Burkhart, Fr.) med solo,ob,gtr
DOBLINGER GKM 57 s.p. (V695)

VON HEISSEM WAHRHEITSDRANG VERZEHRT see
Rimsky-Korsakov, Nikolai

VON JUGEND AUF IM KAMPFGEFILD see
Weber, Carl Maria von

VON JUGEND AUF IM TREUSTEN BUNDE see
Gluck, Christoph Willibald Ritter
von

VON SCHWELLE ZU SCHWELLE see Sivic,
Pavle, Od Praga Do Praga

VONDEL'S VAART NAAR AGRIPPINA see
Diepenbrock, Alphons

VONICKA see Seidel, Jan

VONICKA see Slavicky, Klement

VOO see Villa-Lobos, Heitor

VOOR DE LIEFSTE see Adriessen, Willem

VOOR DE VERRE PRINSES see Godron, Hugo

VOOR DE ZINGENDE JEUGD, VOL. I see
Velde, H.v.d.

VOOR DE ZINGENDE JEUGD, VOL. II see
Velde, H.v.d.

VOOR DEGERAAD see Legley, Victor

VOOR EEN DAG VAN MORGEN see Felderhof,
Jan

VOOR HET KANTKUSSE see Hullebroeck, Em.

VOOR HET KANTKUSSEN see Hullebroeck,
Em.

VOORJAARSBLOEMEN EN BEVRIJDINGSLIED see
Lannoy, K.

VOORJAARSLIED see Mulder, Ernest W.

VOORMOLEN, ALEXANDER NICOLAS
(1895-   )
Amsterdam
    solo,pno DONEMUS s.p.   (V696)
    solo,orch DONEMUS s.p.   (V697)

Angst
    S solo,pno DONEMUS s.p.   (V698)

Appelona
    see Drie Gedichten Van J. Luyken
    see Vijf Nederlandsche Gedichten

Arabeske
    see Vijf Nederlandsche Gedichten

Ave Maria *sac
    B solo,pno/org DONEMUS s.p. (V699)
    low solo,strings DONEMUS s.p.
                                 (V700)
    high solo,strings DONEMUS s.p.
                                 (V701)
    S/T solo,pno/org DONEMUS s.p.
                                 (V702)

Beatrijs
    narrator,pno WAGENAAR s.p.   (V703)

Cecilia
    see Vier Oud-Nederlandsche
    Gedichten

Christmas Song *Xmas
    solo,pno DONEMUS s.p.   (V704)
    solo,orch DONEMUS s.p.   (V705)

Clair De Lune
    med solo,pno DONEMUS s.p.   (V706)

De Zomeravond Op Het Land
    see Vijf Nederlandsche Gedichten

Diana And Her Darlings Deare
    see Three Songs On British Verse

Drie Gedichten Van J. Luyken
    S solo,2fl,ob,2clar,2horn,2bsn,2horn,
    perc,cel,pno,strings DONEMUS s.p.
    contains: Appelona; Spijtig
    Klaartje; Zomerzang   (V707)

Drie Gedichten Van R.M. Rilke
    low solo,pno ALSBACH s.p.
    contains: Ich Geh Jetzt Immer Den
    Gleichen Pfad; Ich War Ein Kind
    Und Traumte Viel; Manchmal
    Geschieht Es In Tiefer Nacht
                                 (V708)

Drie Liederen Van Isoude *CC3U
    A solo,pno ALSBACH s.p.   (V709)

Droom Is 'T Leven, Anders Niet
    see Vijf Nederlandsche Gedichten

Een Nieuwe Lente Op Hollands Erf
    S solo,3fl,2ob,2clar,4horn,
    3trp,3trom,timp,perc,harp,org,
    strings DONEMUS s.p.   (V710)

VOORMOLEN, ALEXANDER NICOLAS (cont'd.)

Eenzame Nacht
    Mez solo,pno ALSBACH s.p.   (V711)

Egidius
    see Vier Oud-Nederlandsche
    Gedichten

Ex Minimis Patet Ipse Deus *see
    Lofsang

Grey Recumbent Tombs
    see Three Songs On British Verse

Had Ick Vloghelen
    see Vier Oud-Nederlandsche
    Gedichten

Herinnering Aan Holland
    Bar solo,pno DONEMUS s.p.   (V712)
    Bar solo,bass clar,strings DONEMUS
    s.p.   (V713)

I Am Confirm'd
    see Three Songs On British Verse

Ich Geh Jetzt Immer Den Gleichen Pfad
    see Drie Gedichten Van R.M. Rilke

Ich War Ein Kind Und Traumte Viel
    see Drie Gedichten Van R.M. Rilke

In Den Nacht
    Mez solo,pno ALSBACH s.p.   (V714)

Kerstliedje *sac
    med solo,pno ALSBACH s.p.   (V715)

Klaartje
    see Vier Oud-Nederlandsche
    Gedichten

La Fille Du Roi De Tartarie
    see Trois Poemes De Rene Chalupt

La Maison De Plaisance
    see Trois Poemes De Rene Chalupt

La Sirene
    S/T solo,2fl,ob,3clar,2horn,trp,
    timp,cel,harp,strings DONEMUS
    s.p.   (V716)

L'adieu
    see Trois Poemes De H. De Regnier

Liedeken
    see Vijf Nederlandsche Gedichten

Lofsang
    "Ex Minimis Patet Ipse Deus" med
    solo,pno/org DONEMUS s.p.   (V717)

Madrigal
    med solo,pno DONEMUS s.p.   (V718)

Manchmal Geschieht Es In Tiefer Nacht
    see Drie Gedichten Van R.M. Rilke

Obsession
    med solo,pno DONEMUS s.p.   (V719)

Odelette
    see Trois Poemes De H. De Regnier

Peau D'ane
    see Trois Poemes De Rene Chalupt

Sonnet
    see Trois Poemes De H. De Regnier

Spijtig
    see Vier Oud-Nederlandsche
    Gedichten

Spijtig Klaartje
    see Drie Gedichten Van J. Luyken

Stanzas Of Charles II *CCU
    Bar solo,fl,English horn,perc,cel,
    strings DONEMUS s.p.   (V720)

Three Songs On British Verse
    [Eng] Bar/B solo,pno DONEMUS D292
    s.p.
    contains: Diana And Her Darlings
    Deare; Grey Recumbent Tombs; I
    Am Confirm'd   (V721)

Trois Poemes De H. De Regnier
    med solo,pno ALSBACH s.p.
    contains: L'adieu; Odelette;
    Sonnet   (V722)

Trois Poemes De Rene Chalupt
    S solo,pno ALSBACH s.p.
    contains: La Fille Du Roi De
    Tartarie; La Maison De
    Plaisance; Peau D'ane   (V723)

Veere
    Mez solo,pno ALSBACH s.p.   (V724)

VOORMOLEN, ALEXANDER NICOLAS (cont'd.)

Vier Oud-Nederlandsche Gedichten
    S solo,pno ALSBACH s.p.
    contains: Cecilia; Egidius; Had
    Ick Vloghelen; Klaartje;
    Spijtig   (V725)

Vijf Nederlandsche Gedichten
    S solo,pno ALBERSEN s.p.
    contains: Appelona; Arabeske; De
    Zomeravond Op Het Land; Droom
    Is 'T Leven, Anders Niet;
    Liedeken   (V726)

Zomerzang
    see Drie Gedichten Van J. Luyken
    high solo,pno ALSBACH s.p.   (V727)

VOORN, JOOP (1932-   )
    Three Lucebert Songs *CC3U
    S solo,pno DONEMUS s.p.   (V728)

    Three Vroman Songs *CC3U
    Bar solo,pno DONEMUS s.p.   (V729)

VOR BILDERN LYONEL FEININGERS, HEFT I
see Koetsier, Jan

VOR BILDERN LYONEL FEININGERS, HEFT II
see Koetsier, Jan

VOR DEM TAG see Crome, Fritz, For Dag

VOR DEM TOD see Krenek, Ernst

VOR DER TUR see Brahms, Johannes

VOR DES LICHTEN TAGES SCHEIN see
Telemann, Georg Philipp

VOR LAUTER LAUSCHEN see Lilien, Ignace

VOR MEINEM AUGE see Sjogren, Emil

VOREBBE DAL TUO COR see Scarlatti,
Domenico

VORFRUHLING see Niggeling, Willi

VORFRUHLING see Peterson-Berger, (Olof)
Wilhelm

VORFRUHLING see Flothius, Marius

VORGEFUHL see Rietz, Johannes

VORGEFUHL see Schoenberg, Arnold

VORIS, W.R.
    Song Of Mothers *sac
    high solo/med solo,pno BELWIN $1.50
                                 (V730)

VORREI MORIRE see Tosti, Francesco
Paolo

VORREI SOGNARE DI TE see Kalman,
Emerich

VORREI SPIEGARVI, OH DIO see Mozart,
Wolfgang Amadeus

VORREI VOLER, SIGNOR QUEL CH'IO NON
VOGLIO see Pizzetti, Ildebrando

VORSPIEL see Zagwijn, Henri

VOS ME MATASTEIS see Rodrigo, Joaquin

VOS ME MATASTES see Vasquez, Juan

VOS PETITS PIEDS see Delmet, Paul

VOS VET SAIN MIT ISROEL? see Dyck,
Vladimir

VOS YEUX see Lonque, Georges

VOSTRAK, ZBYNEK (1920-   )
    Drei Sonette Von Shakespeare *Op.33,
    CC3U
    B solo,chamb.orch sc GERIG HG 578
    s.p.   (V731)

VOTE FOR NAMES see Ives, Charles

VOTRE AME see O'Connolly

VOTRE FEMME M'A DIT JE T'AIME see
Messager, Andre

VOTRE NEZ, MON CHER CAPITAINE see
Messager, Andre

VOTRE SOURIRE see Rabey, Rene

VOTRE TOAST, JE PEUX LE RENDRE see
Bizet, Georges

VOTRE TOAST, JE PEUX VOUS LE RENDRE see
Bizet, Georges

VOTRE TOAST, JE PEUX VOUS RENDRE see
Bizet, Georges

VOU-ME EMBORA see Guarnieri, Camargo
Mozart

VOUDRAIS-TU see Godard, Benjamin Louis
Paul

VOULEZ-VOUS MA TOUTE BELLE! see Raynal,
F.

VOUS, A MES PIEDS see Wagner, Richard

VOUS A QUI LE FLOT OBEIT see Duvernoy,
Victor-Alphonse

VOUS ALLEZ COMPRENDRE see Lacome, Paul

VOUS AUREZ UNE MAISON BLANCHE see
Rhene-Baton

VOUS AVEZ, MADAME see Lacome, Paul

VOUS AVEZ RI! see Delmet, Paul

VOUS ETES JOLIE! see Delmet, Paul

VOUS M'AIMIEZ, JE VOUS AIMAIS see
Rabey, Rene

VOUS M'AVEZ DIT, TEL SOIR see Toussaint
De Sutter, J.

VOUS MON COEUR see Magne, Michel

VOUS NE POURRIEZ SAVIOR see Rhene-Baton

VOUS NE SAVEZ PASOU JE VOUS AI MENEE?
see Debussy, Claude

VOUS N'ECRIVEZ PLUS? see Poulenc,
Francis

VOUS QUE TROUBLAIT NAGUERE L'ECHO DE
MES SOUPIRS see Wagner, Richard

VOUS QUI FAITES L'ENDORMIE see Gounod,
Charles Francois

VOUS QUI ME FUYEZ see Duvernoy, Victor-
Alphonse

VOUS QUI SAVEZ LES CHOSES see Lecocq,
Charles

VOUS RESSEMBLEZ A LA ROSE NAISSANTE see
Gluck, Christoph Willibald Ritter
von

VOUS SOUVIENT-IL? see Mozart, Wolfgang
Amadeus

VOUS SOUVIENT-IL? (ANDANTE ET
VARIATIONS D'UNE SONATE DE MOZART)
see Wekerlin, Jean Baptiste

VOX AMANTIUM see Frid, Geza

VOYAGE see Carter, E.

VOYAGE see Rabey, Rene

VOYAGE, THE see Mills, Charles

VOYAGE D'HIVER RSCYCL see Schubert,
Franz (Peter), Winterreise

VOYAGE EN TORTILLARD see DuBois, Pierre
Max

VOYAGES see Schubert, Franz (Peter)

VOYAGEURS CELESTES see Flegier, Ange

VOYELLES see Victory, Gerard

VRAIMENT ON EN VERRAIT see Lacome, Paul

VRANKEN, JAAP (1897-1956)
Ave Maria *sac
solo,pno BROEKMANS 178 s.p.   (V732)

VRBA, F.
Ctyri Pisne Na Slova Detske Poezie
*CC4U
solo,pno SUPRAPHON s.p.   (V733)

VREDENBURG, MAX (1904-   )
Ah! Beau Rossignol Volage
med solo,pno/cembalo DONEMUS s.p.
(V734)
Akiba
[Heb/Fr] Mez/Bar solo,fl,clar,2bsn,
2horn,trom,harp,cel,strings
DONEMUS rental   (V735)
[Heb/Fr] Mez/Bar solo,pno DONEMUS
s.p.   (V736)
Au Pays Des Vendanges
Mez/Bar solo,pno DONEMUS s.p.
contains: Bon Vin Donne Vigueur;
Chanson A Boire; Odelette
(V737)
Bon Vin Donne Vigueur
see Au Pays Des Vendanges

VREDENBURG, MAX (cont'd.)
Chanson A Boire
see Au Pays Des Vendanges
De Schalmei *Op.16,No.3
see Drie Liederen
De Troubadour *Op.16,No.1
see Drie Liederen
Drie Liederen
ALSBACH high solo,pno s.p.; low
solo,pno s.p.
contains: De Schalmei, Op.16,
No.3; De Troubadour, Op.16,
No.1; Nu Licht Vergeten, Op.16,
No.2   (V738)
Du Printemps
Mez/Bar solo,pno/cembalo DONEMUS
s.p.   (V739)
'N Lied Van De Vrijheid
med solo/low solo,pno BASART s.p.
(V740)
Nu Licht Vergeten *Op.16,No.2
see Drie Liederen
Odelette
see Au Pays Des Vendanges
Unser Land
med solo/low solo,pno LAND s.p.
(V741)

VREMSAK, SAMO (1930-   )
Sest Pesmi *CC6U
solo,pno,vla DRUSTVO DSS 355 rental
(V742)
Tri Pesmi *CC3U
solo,pno DRUSTVO DSS 104 rental
(V743)

VRIES ROBBE, WILLEM DE (1902-   )
Poems By Emily Dickinson *CCU
solo,fl,vibra DONEMUS s.p.   (V744)
Rondeaux
narrator,fl,vibra DONEMUS s.p.
(V745)

VRIJERSLIEDJE see Hullebroeck, Em.

VRIJHEIDSLIED see Hullebroeck, Em.

V'SHOMRU see Freudenthal, Josef

V'SHOMRU see Goldfarb, Samuel E.

VUATAZ
Poemes D'Orient *CC11L
solo,orch HENN s.p.   (V746)

VUES DES ANGES see Kox, Hans

VUGGESANG see Bedinger, Hugo

VUGGEVISE see Olsen, Sparre

VUILLEMIN, L.
Attente
high solo,pno/inst DURAND s.p.
(V747)
Chanson Lasse
solo,pno/inst DURAND s.p.   (V748)
Deux Lieds *see Presents; Retour
(V749)
Il Croit Entendre Pleurer Son Coeur
Dans La Plainte Du Ruisseau
see Rondels Melancoliques
Il Implore La Melancolique Rose
see Rondels Melancoliques
Il Songe Que Nul Ne Saurait Naitre
Pour La Premiere Fois
see Rondels Melancoliques
La Route
solo,vln/vcl DURAND s.p.   (V750)
med solo,vln/vcl DURAND s.p. (V751)
Laissez Venir A Moi *Commun
solo,org&opt harp (E maj) DURAND
(V752)
solo,org&opt harp (F maj) DURAND
s.p.   (V753)
Le Colibri
high solo,pno/inst DURAND s.p.
(V754)
Le Poete Porte Le Deuil Des Joies Pas
Encore Nees
see Rondels Melancoliques
Le Portrait
high solo,pno/inst DURAND s.p.
(V755)
Les Reves
solo,pno/inst (G maj) DURAND s.p.
(V756)
solo,pno/inst (A maj) DURAND s.p.
(V757)
Lied
high solo,pno/inst DURAND s.p.
(V758)

VUILLEMIN, L. (cont'd.)
Ma Cigale (1)
solo,pno/inst (E maj) DURAND s.p.
(V759)
Ma Cigale (2)
solo,pno/inst (D maj) DURAND s.p.
(V760)
Presents
med solo,pno/inst DURAND s.p. see
from Deux Lieds   (V761)
Retour
med solo,pno/inst DURAND s.p. see
from Deux Lieds   (V762)
Romance
high solo,pno/inst DURAND s.p.
(V763)
Rondel Sur Une Joueuse De Flute
med solo,pno/inst DURAND s.p.
(V764)
Rondels Melancoliques
high solo,pno/inst cmplt ed DURAND
s.p.
contains: Il Croit Entendre
Pleurer Son Coeur Dans La
Plainte Du Ruisseau; Il Implore
La Melancolique Rose; Il Songe
Que Nul Ne Saurait Naitre Pour
La Premiere Fois; Le Poete
Porte Le Deuil Des Joies Pas
Encore Nees   (V765)

VUILLERMOZ, EMILE (1878-1960)
Jardin D'amour
med solo,pno SALABERT-US $3.75
(V766)
Le Desir
see Les Dionysies
Les Dionysies
med solo,pno SALABERT-US $6.50
contains: Le Desir; L'Offrande
(V767)
L'Offrande
see Les Dionysies

VULCAN see Bond, Andrews

VULCAN'S SONG see Gounod, Charles
Francois, Au Bruit Des Lourdes

VULNERASTI COR MEUM see Buxtehude,
Dietrich

VUOI CH'IO PARTA see Ariosti, Attilio

VURRIA SCRIVERE NU LIBBRO see Giazotto,
Remo

VUS DU VILST, DUS VIL ICH OICH *Jew
solo,pno KAMMEN 437 $1.00   (V768)

VUS TOIG ES EICH, VUS DARFT IHR ES
*Jew
solo,pno KAMMEN 464 $1.00   (V769)

VYBER Z PISNI see Jindrich, Jindrich

VYCHODOSLOVENSKE SPEVY see Kardos,
Dezider

VYCPALEK, LADISLAV (1882-1969)
Aus Mahren *Op.11a, CC7U
high solo,pno SUPRAPHON s.p. (V770)
Erwachen *Op.17, CC2U
S solo,pno SUPRAPHON s.p.   (V771)
In Gottes Hut *Op.14, song cycle
high solo,pno SUPRAPHON s.p. (V772)
Kladske Pisnicky *CCU
med solo,pno CZECH s.p.   (V773)
Laska, Boze, Laska, Ses. 1-2 *Op.27,
CCU
solo,pno SUPRAPHON s.p., ea. (V774)
Lebensfeste *Op.8, CC4U
med solo,pno SUPRAPHON s.p.   (V775)
Mahrische Ballanden *Op.12, CCU
solo,pno SUPRAPHON s.p.   (V776)
Na Rozloucenou *Op.25, CC6U
solo,pno SUPRAPHON s.p.   (V777)
Pisne Pana Jenika Z Bratric
med solo,pno CZECH s.p.   (V778)
Sonata In D *Op.19
solo,pno SUPRAPHON s.p.   (V779)
Visionen *Op.5, CC5U
med solo,pno SUPRAPHON s.p.   (V780)

VYSOKE LETNE NEBO see Vilec, Michal

VYZNANIA see Holoubek, Ladislav

VZPLANUTI see Goldbach, Stanislav

W

WAAR GAAT GIJ see Dijk, Jan van

WAAR GIJ ZULT HENENGAAN see Oort,
H.C.v.

WAAR STAAT JOUW VADERS HUIS EN HOF see
Nieland, Jan

WACHET AUF, RUFT UNS DIE STIMME see
Bornefeld, Helmut

WACHET AUF! RUFT UNS DIE STIMME see
Lenel, Ludwig

WACHET AUF! RUFT UNS DIE STIMME see
Tunder, Franz

WACHS, F.
    Le Capitaine Cupidon
        solo,pno ENOCH s.p.   (W1)
        solo,acap ENOCH s.p.   (W2)

    Les Dames De Coeur
        solo,pno ENOCH s.p.   (W3)
        solo,acap ENOCH s.p.   (W4)

    Les Plus Presses
        solo,pno ENOCH s.p.   (W5)
        solo,acap ENOCH s.p.   (W6)

    Madelinette
        solo,pno ENOCH s.p.   (W7)
        solo,acap ENOCH s.p.   (W8)

WACHS, PAUL ETIENNE VICTOR (1851-1915)
    La Bien-Aimee
        solo,pno ENOCH s.p.   (W9)
        solo,acap ENOCH s.p.   (W10)

    Un Diner D'Oiseaux
        solo,pno ENOCH s.p.   (W11)
        solo,acap ENOCH s.p.   (W12)

WACHTERLIED see Beekhuis, Hanna

WADE IN DE WATER *spir
    (Burleigh, H. T.) high solo,pno
        BELWIN $1.50   (W13)
    (Burleigh, H. T.) low solo,pno BELWIN
        $1.50   (W14)

WAER IS DIE DOCHTER VAN SEYOEN see
Beuningen, W.v.

WAERMO, EINAR
    It Is Finished *sac
        solo,pno GOSPEL 05 TM 0420 $1.00
                                            (W15)

WAGADU see Vogel, Wladimir

WAGNER, JOSEPH FREDERICK (1900-1974)
    Bewildered Ballade
        solo,orch voc sc PEER $.95, ipr
                                            (W16)
        high solo/med solo/low solo,2fl,
        2ob,3clar,timp,perc,harp,strings
        PEER sc rental, voc sc $.95 (W17)

WAGNER, RICHARD (1813-1883)
    A L'etranger, Enfant, Ton Accueil
        (from Der Fliegende Hollander)
        [Fr] Bar solo,pno/inst DURAND s.p.
                                            (W18)
    Air D'Elisabeth (from Tannhauser Und
        Der Sangerkrieg Auf Wartburg)
        solo,orch HENN s.p.   (W19)

    Air D'Elsa (from Lohengrin)
        solo,orch HENN s.p.   (W20)

    Air Du Baryton (from Die Feen)
        Bar solo,orch HENN s.p.   (W21)

    Allmacht'ge Jungfrau (from
        Tannhauser)
        S solo,3fl,2ob,2clar,2bsn,4horn,
        3trom BREITKOPF-L rental   (W22)
        "Elizabeth's Prayer" S solo,pno
        NOVELLO 17.0047.02 s.p.   (W23)
        "Elizabeth's Prayer" high solo,pno
        (G flat maj) ALLANS s.p.   (W24)

    Angel, The *see Der Engel

    Aria Album For Baritone *CC15U
        [Ger] Bar solo,pno PETERS 4244
        $9.00 contains arias from: Der
        Fliegende Hollander, Tannhauser,
        Lohengrin, Die Meistersinger Von
        Nurenberg and others   (W25)

    Aria Album For Soprano *CC13U
        [Ger] S solo,pno PETERS 4241 $8.50
        contains arias from: Die Feen,
        Das Liebesverbot, Der Fliegende
        Hollander and others   (W26)

WAGNER, RICHARD (cont'd.)
    Aria Album For Tenor *CC19U
        [Ger] T solo,pno PETERS 4243 $9.00
        contains arias from: Rienzi, Der
        Fliegende Hollander, Tannhauser,
        Lohengrin and others   (W27)

    Arrete-Toi *see Stehe Still

    Attente
        Mez/Bar solo,pno/inst DURAND s.p.
                                            (W28)
        S/T solo,pno/inst DURAND s.p. (W29)

    Aux Bords Lointains (from Lohengrin)
        [Fr] solo,acap oct DURAND s.p.
                                            (W30)
    Aux Bords Lointains Dont Nul Mortel
        N'approche (from Lohengrin)
        [Fr] T solo,orch DURAND s.p., ipa
                                            (W31)
        [Fr] Bar solo,orch DURAND s.p.,
                                ipa   (W32)

    Bridal Chorus (from Lohengrin)
        med solo,pno (A flat maj) CENTURY
                                            (W33)

    Chant D'Amour (from Die Walkure)
        see LA MUSIQUE, HUITIEME CAHIER

    Chant De Wolfram (from Tannhauser Und
        Der Sangerkrieg Auf Wartburg)
        solo,orch HENN s.p.   (W34)

    Chant Du Marin (from Tristan Und
        Isolde)
        solo,acap DURAND s.p.   (W35)

    Combien De Fois, Las De Souffrir
        (from Der Fliegende Hollander)
        [Fr] Bar solo,orch DURAND s.p., ipr
                                            (W36)

    Dans Le Serre *see Im Treibhaus

    Das Susse Lied Verhalt (from
        Lohengrin)
        TS soli,3fl,3ob,3clar,3bsn,4horn,
        3trp,3trom,tuba,timp,drums,
        strings BREITKOPF-L rental (W37)

    Deja Se Perd Leur Voix (from
        Lohengrin)
        [Fr] ST soli,pno/inst DURAND s.p.
        contains also: Nous Sommesseuls
                                            (W38)
        [Fr] S/T solo,pno/inst DURAND s.p.
        contains also: Nous Sommesseuls
                                            (W39)
        [Fr] Mez/Bar solo,pno/inst DURAND
        s.p. contains also: Nous
        Sommesseuls   (W40)

    Der Engel
        "Angel, The" see Five Songs
        "El Angel" see Funf Lieder Sobre
        Textos De Wesendonk
        "L'Ange" S solo,pno/inst DURAND
        s.p. see also Funf Gedichte (W41)

    Detente! *see Stehe Still!

    Deux Poemes *see Le Sapin; Les Duex
        Grenadiers   (W42)

    Dich Theure Halle (from Tannhauser)
        S solo,2fl,2ob,2clar,2bsn,4horn,
        timp,strings BREITKOPF-L rental
                                            (W43)
        S solo,pno/orch sc KALMUS $3.00
                                            (W44)
        "Elizabeth's Greeting" S solo,pno
        NOVELLO 17.0046.04 s.p.   (W45)
        "Elizabeth's Greeting" high solo,
        pno (G maj) ALLANS s.p.   (W46)
        "O Vierge Sainte" [Fr/Ger] Mez
        solo,orch DURAND s.p., ipa (W47)
        "O Vierge Sainte" [Fr/Ger] S solo,
        orch DURAND s.p., ipa   (W48)

    Die Frist Ist Um (from Der Fliegende
        Hollander)
        Bar solo,3fl,2ob,2clar,2bsn,4horn,
        2trp,3trom,tuba,timp,strings
        BREITKOPF-L rental   (W49)

    Dieu Tutelaire *see Gerechter Gott

    Dors Mon Enfant
        see LA MUSIQUE, ONZIEME CAHIER
        S/T solo,pno/inst DURAND s.p. (W50)
        Mez/Bar solo,pno/inst DURAND s.p.
                                            (W51)

    Douleurs *see Schmerzen

    Dreams *see Traume

    Einsam In Truben Tagen (from
        Lohengrin)
        S solo,3fl,3ob,3clar,3bsn,2horn,
        3trp,timp,harp,strings BREITKOPF-
        L rental   (W52)

    El Angel *see Der Engel

WAGNER, RICHARD (cont'd.)
    Elisabeth's Arie (from Tannhauser)
        "Salut A Toi, A Noble Demeure" [Fr/
        Ger] S solo,orch DURAND s.p., ipa
                                            (W53)
    Elizabeth's Greeting *see Dich
        Theure Halle

    Elizabeth's Prayer *see Allmacht'ge
        Jungfrau

    En Contemplant Cette Assemblee Imense
        (from Tannhauser)
        [Fr] Bar solo,pno/inst DURAND s.p.,
        ipa   (W54)

    En El Invernaculo *see Im Treibhaus

    Ensuenos *see Traume

    Erhebe Dich, Genossin Meiner Schmach
        (from Lohengrin)
        MezBar soli,3fl,3ob,3clar,3bsn,
        4horn,3trp,3trom,tuba,timp,drums,
        strings BREITKOPF-L rental (W55)

    Euch Luften, Die Meine Klagen (from
        Lohengrin)
        S solo,3fl,3ob,3clar,3bsn,2horn
        BREITKOPF-L rental   (W56)

    Evening Star *see O Du Mein Holder
        Abendstern

    Five Songs
        [Ger/Eng] high solo,pno SCHIRM.G
        1233 $2.00; low solo,pno SCHIRM.G
        1181 $2.00
        contains: Der Engel, "Angel,
        The"; Im Treibhaus, "In A
        Conservatory"; Schmerzen,
        "Tears"; Stehe Still!, "Stand
        Thou Still!"; Traume, "Dreams"
                                            (W57)

    Five Wesendonk Songs *CC5U
        [Ger/Eng] high solo,pno PETERS
        3445A $4.75; low solo,pno PETERS
        3445B $4.75   (W58)

    Fragments D'Operas, Vols. I & II
        *CCU
        S solo,pno/inst DURAND s.p., ea.
                                            (W59)
    Funf Gedichte
        S solo,pno/inst cmplt ed DURAND
        s.p.
        contains & see also: Der Engel,
        "L'Ange"; Im Treibhaus, "Dans
        Le Serre"; Schmerzen,
        "Douleurs"; Stehe Still,
        "Arrete-Toi"; Traume, "Reves"
                                            (W60)

    Funf Gedichte Von Mathilde Wesendonk
        *CC5U
        high solo,pno/orch SCHOTTS 835
        s.p., ipa; low solo,pno/orch
        SCHOTTS 836 s.p., ipa   (W61)

    Funf Lieder Sobre Textos De Wesendonk
        [Ger/Span] solo,pno/inst cmplt ed
        RICORDI-ARG BA 9654 s.p.
        contains: Der Engel, "El Angel";
        Im Treibhaus, "En El
        Invernaculo"; Schmerzen,
        "Penas"; Stehe Still!,
        "Detente!"; Traume, "Ensuenos"
                                            (W62)

    Gerechter Gott (from Rienzi)
        "Dieu Tutelaire" [Fr] Bar solo,orch
        DURAND s.p., ipr   (W63)
        "Dieu Tutelaire" [Fr] T solo,orch
        DURAND s.p., ipr   (W64)

    Hiva (from Der Fliegende Hollander)
        [Fr] S solo,orch DURAND s.p., ipa
                                            (W65)

    Hochstes Vertraun (from Lohengrin)
        T solo,2fl,3ob,3clar,3bsn,4horn,
        3trp,3trom,tuba,timp,strings
        BREITKOPF-L rental   (W66)

    Im Treibhaus
        "En El Invernaculo" see Funf Lieder
        Sobre Textos De Wesendonk
        "In A Conservatory" see Five Songs
        "Dans Le Serre" S solo,pno/inst
        DURAND s.p. see also Funf
        Gedichte   (W67)

    In A Conservatory *see Im Treibhaus

    In Fernem Land, Unnahbar Euren
        Schritten (from Lohengrin)
        TB soli,wom cor,3fl,3ob,3clar,3bsn,
        4horn,3trp,3trom,tuba,timp,perc,
        strings BREITKOPF-L rental (W68)

    Isolde's Liebestod (from Tristan And
        Isolde)
        [Ger/Eng] S solo,pno (A flat maj)
        SCHIRM.G $1.00   (W69)

    Jadis Quand Tu Luttais (from
        Tannhauser)
        [Fr] T solo,pno/inst DURAND s.p.

WAGNER, RICHARD (cont'd.)

(W70)
J'ai Vu Nos Champs (from Rienzi)
[Fr] S solo,pno/inst DURAND s.p.
(W71)

L'Ange *see Der Engel

Le Sapin
S solo,pno/inst DURAND s.p. see
from Deux Poemes   (W72)

Les Duex Grenadiers
S solo,pno/inst DURAND s.p. see
from Deux Poemes   (W73)

Ma Confiance En Toi S'est Bien Montre
(from Lohengrin)
[Fr] T solo,pno/inst DURAND s.p.
(W74)

Malgre Vents Et Tempete (from Der
Fliegende Hollander)
[Fr] T solo,pno/inst DURAND s.p.
(W75)

Mein Lieber Schwan (from Lohengrin)
"Mon Cygne Aime" [Fr] T solo,orch
DURAND s.p., ipa   (W76)
"Mon Cygne Aime" [Fr] Bar solo,orch
DURAND s.p., ipa   (W77)
"Mon Cygne Aime" [Fr] solo,acap oct
DURAND s.p.   (W78)
"Nun Sei Bedankt, Mein Lieber
Schwan" T solo,3fl,3ob,2clar,
2bsn,strings BREITKOPF-L rental (W79)

Merci Cher Peuple (from Lohengrin)
[Fr] Bar solo,pno/inst DURAND s.p.
(W80)

Mignonne
Mez/Bar solo,pno/inst DURAND s.p.
(W81)

Mild Und Leise, Wie Er Lachelt (from
Tristan Und Isolde)
S solo,3fl,3ob,3clar,3bsn,4horn,
3trp,3trom,tuba,timp,harp,strings
BREITKOPF-L rental   (W82)

Mon Cygne Aime *see Mein Lieber
Schwan

Mort D'Isolde (from Tristan Und
Isolde)
[Fr] solo,orch DURAND s.p., ipr
(W83)

Nous Sommesseuls (from Lohengrin)
see Wagner, Richard, Deja Se Perd
Leur Voix
see Wagner, Richard, Deja Se Perd
Leur Voix
see Wagner, Richard, Deja Se Perd
Leur Voix

Nun Sei Bedankt, Mein Lieber Schwan
*see Mein Lieber Schwan

O Ciel, Exauce Ma Piere (from
Tannhauser)
[Fr] Bar solo,pno/inst DURAND s.p.,
ipa   (W84)

O Douce Etoile (from Tannhauser)
[Fr/Ger] S/T solo,orch (A maj)
DURAND s.p., ipa   (W85)
[Fr/Ger] Mez solo,orch (G maj)
DURAND s.p., ipa   (W86)
[Fr/Ger] Bar solo,orch (G maj)
DURAND s.p., ipa   (W87)

O Du Mein Holder Abendstern (from
Tannhauser)
Bar solo,2fl,2ob,2clar,2bsn,3trom,
tuba,harp,strings BREITKOPF-L
rental   (W88)
Bar solo,pno sc KALMUS $3.50 (W89)
"Evening Star" low solo,pno (G maj)
CENTURY 1564   (W90)
"O Star Of Eve" low solo,pno (F
maj) CRAMER   (W91)
"O Star Of Eve" med solo,pno (G
maj) CRAMER   (W92)
"O Star Of Eve" high solo,pno (B
flat maj) CRAMER   (W93)
"Oh Thou Mine Own Dear Evening
Star" solo,pno CRAMER   (W94)
"To The Evening Star" [Ger/It/Eng]
Bar solo,pno (G min) SCHIRM.G
$.75   (W95)
"To The Evening Star" low solo,pno
(F maj) ALLANS s.p.   (W96)
"To The Evening Star" [Ger/It/Eng]
B solo,pno (E flat maj) SCHIRM.G
$.75   (W97)
"To The Evening Star" med solo,pno
(G maj) ALLANS s.p.   (W98)
"To The Evening Star" high solo,pno
(B flat maj) ALLANS s.p.   (W99)

O Star Of Eve *see O Du Mein Holder
Abendstern

O Tendre Reve (from Rienzi)
[Fr] S solo,pno/inst DURAND s.p.
(W100)

O Vierge Sainte *see Dich Theure
Halle

WAGNER, RICHARD (cont'd.)

Oh Thou Mine Own Dear Evening Star
*see O Du Mein Holder Abendstern

Penas *see Schmerzen

Pilgrim's Chorus (from Tannhauser)
med solo,pno (E flat maj) CENTURY
1574   (W101)

Reves *see Traume

Romance De L'etoile (from Tannhauser)
[Fr] solo,acap oct DURAND s.p.
(W102)
solo,orch HENN s.p.   (W103)

Romanza De La Estrella (from
Tannhauser)
[Ger/It] Bar solo,pno RICORDI-ARG
BA 8828 s.p.   (W104)

Sachez Defendre Tous Vos Droits (from
Rienzi)
[Fr] T solo,pno/inst DURAND s.p.
(W105)
[Fr] Bar solo,pno/inst DURAND s.p.
(W106)

Salut A Toi, A Noble Demeure *see
Elisabeth's Arie

Salut A Toi, O Beau Ciel, O Patrie
(from Tannhauser)
[Fr] solo,orch DURAND s.p., ipa
(W107)

Schmerzen
"Penas" see Funf Lieder Sobre
Textos De Wesendonk
"Tears" see Five Songs
"Douleurs" S solo,pno/inst DURAND
s.p. see also Funf Gedichte
(W108)

Seule Dans Ma Misere (from Lohengrin)
[Fr] Mez solo,orch DURAND s.p., ipa
(W109)
[Fr] S solo,orch DURAND s.p., ipa
(W110)

Stand Thou Still! *see Stehe Still!

Stehe Still!
"Detente!" see Funf Lieder Sobre
Textos De Wesendonk
"Stand Thou Still!" see Five Songs
"Arrete-Toi" S solo,pno/inst DURAND
s.p. see also Funf Gedichte
(W111)

Te Souvient-Il Du Jour (from Der
Fliegende Hollander)
[Fr] T solo,pno/inst DURAND s.p.
(W112)
[Fr] Mez/Bar solo,pno/inst DURAND
s.p.   (W113)

Tears *see Schmerzen

To The Evening Star *see O Du Mein
Holder Abendstern

Traft Ihr Das Schiff Im Meere An
(from Der Fliegende Hollander)
S solo,3fl,2ob,2clar,2bsn,4horn,
2trp,3trom,tuba,timp,strings
BREITKOPF-L rental   (W114)

Traume
"Dreams" see Five Songs
"Ensuenos" see Funf Lieder Sobre
Textos De Wesendonk
"Dreams" med solo,pno NOVELLO
17.0042.01 s.p.   (W115)
"Reves" S solo,pno/inst DURAND s.p.
see also Funf Gedichte   (W116)

Tu Ne Pourras Jamais Connaitre (from
Lohengrin)
[Fr] S solo,pno/inst DURAND s.p.
(W117)

Verachtet Mir Die Meister Nicht (from
Die Meistersinger Von Nurnberg)
Bar solo,3fl,2ob,2clar,2bsn,4horn,
3trp,3trom,tuba,timp,perc,strings
BREITKOPF-L rental   (W118)

Viens, Respirons Tous Deux Ces Tiedes
Brises (from Lohengrin)
[Fr] T solo,pno/inst DURAND s.p.
(W119)
[Fr] Bar solo,pno/inst DURAND s.p.
(W120)

Vous, A Mes Pieds (from Tannhauser)
[Fr] ST soli,pno/inst DURAND s.p.
(W121)

Vous Que Troublait Naguere L'echo De
Mes Soupirs (from Lohengrin)
[Fr] S solo,pno/inst DURAND s.p.
(W122)

Weiche, Wotan! Weiche! (from Das
Rheingold)
[Ger/Eng] A solo,orch voc sc
BREITKOPF-W 57 04021 s.p.   (W123)

Willst Jenes Tags Du Dich Nicht Mehr
Entsinnen (from Der Fliegende
Hollander)
T solo,2fl,2ob,2clar,2bsn,4horn,

WAGNER, RICHARD (cont'd.)

strings BREITKOPF-L rental   (W124)

Wolframin Laulu Iltatahdelle *see
Wolframs Lied An Den Abendstern

Wolframs Lied An Den Abendstern (from
Tannhauser)
"Wolframin Laulu Iltatahdelle"
solo,pno FAZER F 2916 s.p.   (W125)

WAGNER-REGENY, RUDOLF (1903-1969)
Acht Zigeunerlieder *CC8U
solo,pno BREITKOPF-L EB 5855 s.p.
(W126)

Dahinter Wird Stille *CC5U
[Ger] med solo,pno BOTE $4.50
(W127)

Hesse-Lieder, Gesange Des Abschieds
*CCU
Bar solo,orch PETERS 9282 $16.00;
Bar solo,pno PETERS 5460 s.p.
(W128)

Lieder *CCU
solo,pno DEUTSCHER 9005 s.p. (W129)

Lieder Der Fruhe *CCU
solo,pno PETERS 5455 $7.50   (W130)

Lieder Des Anglers *CCU
solo,pno PETERS 5047 s.p.   (W131)

Lieder Nach Gedichten Von B. Brecht
*CCU
med solo,pno PETERS 5089 s.p.
(W132)

Liederbuchlein *CCU
solo,pno UNIVER. 10667 s.p. (W133)

WAGON OF LIFE see Pitfield, Thomas
Baron

WAHREND DAS DRAMA DER ZEIT see
Leistner-Mayer, Roland

WAIL FOR OUR DEAD GUITARIST see Mills,
Charles

WAIT FOR ME see Ott, J.

WAITING see Giannini, Vittorio

WAITING FOR THE SPRING see Farkas,
Ferenc

WAKE AND SING *CCU,folk,US
(Jameson) solo,opt cor,pno/vln BMI
$.85   (W134)

WAKE, AWAKE see Tunder, Franz, Wachet
Auf! Ruft Uns Die Stimme

WAKE, AWAKE, FOR NIGHT IS FLYING see
Buxtehude, Dietrich

WAKE, AWAKE, FOR NIGHT IS FLYING see
Lenel, Ludwig, Wachet Auf! Ruft Uns
Die Stimme

WAKE, AWAKE, FOR NIGHT IS FLYING see
Tunder, Franz

WAKE MY TENDER THRILLING FLUTE see Hill

WAKE UP, MY LOVE see Smit, Leo

WAKE WITH THE DAWN see Leoncavallo,
Ruggiero, Mattinata

WAKENING, THE see Hind, John

WAKING see Cory, Eleanor

WAKING, THE see Rorem, Ned

WAKKER see Koetsier, Jan

WALD-SONATE see Siegl, Otto

WALDANDACHT see Abt, Franz

WALDEINSAMKEIT see Bijvanck, Henk

WALDEINSAMKEIT see Reger, Max

WALDER IM RAUHREIF see Bijvanck, Henk

WALDESELIGKEIT see Strauss, Richard

WALDESFAHRT see Strauss, Richard

WALDESGESPRACH see Schumann, Robert
(Alexander)

WALDNACHT see Gilse, Jan van

WALDSONNE see Schoenberg, Arnold

WALDSTEIN, WILHELM (1897-1965)
Acht Ernste Gesange, Heft 1 *CCU
solo,pno DOBLINGER s.p.   (W135)

Acht Ernste Gesange, Heft 2 *CCU
solo,pno DOBLINGER s.p.   (W136)

WALDSTEIN, WILHELM (cont'd.)

Elysium *song cycle
  high solo,pno DOBLINGER $3.25
                                  (W137)

Funf Lieder *CC5U
  solo,pno DOBLINGER s.p.   (W138)

WALDTEUFEL, EMIL (1837-1915)
A Toi
  solo,pno/inst DURAND s.p.   (W139)
  [Fr] solo,acap oct DURAND s.p.
                                  (W140)

Dolores
  [Fr] solo,acap oct DURAND s.p.
                                  (W141)
  solo,pno,acap oct DURAND s.p. (W142)

Les Sirenes
  [Fr] solo,acap oct DURAND s.p.
                                  (W143)
  solo,pno/inst DURAND s.p.   (W144)

Toujours Ou Jamais
  [Fr] solo,acap oct DURAND s.p.
                                  (W145)
  solo,pno/inst DURAND s.p.   (W146)

WALDVOGELEIN see Kowalski, Max

WALES
My Fairy Boat
  med solo,pno ALLANS s.p.   (W147)

WALK A MILE IN MY SHOES see South

WALK IN THE WILDERNESS, THE see
  Fischer, Irwin

WALK ON THE PATHWAY see Hubbard, H.

WALK ON THE WATER see Gaither

WALK WITH ME see Langdon, Al

WALKER, EDWIN
Roses And You
  high solo,pno (C maj) WILLIS $.60
                                  (W148)
  low solo,pno (A flat maj) WILLIS
  $.60   (W149)
  med solo,pno (B flat maj) WILLIS
  $.60   (W150)

WALKER, GEORGE
Bereaved Maid, The
  solo,pno GENERAL 629 $1.50   (W151)

I Went To Heaven
  solo,pno GENERAL 630 $1.25   (W152)

Response
  solo,pno GENERAL 632 $1.25   (W153)

So We'll Go No More A-Roving
  solo,pno GENERAL 631 $1.25   (W154)

Sweet, Let Me Go
  solo,pno GENERAL 633 $1.25   (W155)

With Rue My Heart Is Laden
  solo,pno GENERAL 639 $1.25   (W156)

WALKER, HENRY
Betsy Wareing
  solo,pno CRAMER   (W157)

Bother The Men
  solo,pno CRAMER   (W158)

WALKIN' IN THIS WORLD see Nordeen,
  LaJuana

WALKING THE SEA *sac
  solo,pno STAMPS 7241 $1.00   (W159)

WALKING TO GLORY LAND *sac,gospel
  solo,pno ABER.GRP. $1.50   (W160)

WALKING UP THE KING'S HIGHWAY *sac,
  gospel
  solo,pno ABER.GRP. $1.50   (W161)

WALL, C. V.D.
Kolendragers Van Suez
  see Wall, C. v.d., Schimmenspel

Le Parfum
  solo,pno ALSBACH s.p. contains
    also: Le Portrait   (W162)

Le Portrait
  see Wall, C. v.d., Le Parfum

Maleische Liederen *CCU
  solo,pno ALSBACH s.p.   (W163)

Mohammedaansch Gebed
  solo,pno ALSBACH s.p.   (W164)

Onze Vlag
  solo,pno ALSBACH s.p.   (W165)

Rose Blanche
  solo,pno ALSBACH s.p.   (W166)

WALL, C. V.D. (cont'd.)

Schimmenspel
  solo,pno ALSBACH s.p. contains
    also: Kolendragers Van Suez
                                  (W167)

Tropische Nacht
  solo,pno ALSBACH s.p.   (W168)

WALLACE, WILLIAM (1860-1940)
Freebooter Songs *CCU
  solo,pno CRAMER   (W169)

Rebel, The
  solo,pno CRAMER $.95   (W170)

Son Of Mine
  med solo,pno (E min) CRAMER   (W171)
  low solo,pno (D min) CRAMER $.95
                                  (W172)
  high solo,pno (G min) CRAMER   (W173)

Up In The Saddle
  solo,pno CRAMER   (W174)

WALLACE, WILLIAM VINCENT (1812-1865)
When The Elves At Dawn Do Pass
  high solo,pno (A flat maj) CRAMER
                                  (W175)
  low solo,pno (F maj) CRAMER   (W176)

WALLER, MURPHY
Spinning Wheel
  solo,pno ALLANS s.p.   (W177)

WALLEY, STEVEN
Committed Unto Thee *sac
  solo,pno WORD S-344   (W178)

WALLS CAME TUMBLIN' DOWN, THE *sac
  solo,pno STAMPS 7242 $1.00   (W179)

WALLS CAME TUMBLING DOWN, THE see
  Thacker

WALLS OF ZION see Chajes, Julius, L'chu
  V'nivneh

WALNUT TREE see Schumann, Robert
  (Alexander), Der Nussbaum

WALNUT-TREE, THE see Schumann, Robert
  (Alexander), Der Nussbaum

WALPURGISNAT see Lewkovitch, Bernhard

WALTER, C.
Child's Christmas Song, A
  med solo,pno SEESAW $1.00   (W180)

WALTER, FRIED (1907-   )
Fruhlings-Sonnenschein
  coloratura sop,pno ZIMMER. 1289
  s.p.   (W181)

WALTERS
Poesies Du Soir *CCU
  Mez solo,orch OXFORD rental   (W182)

WALTERS, G.
How Lovely It Is
  solo,pno (G maj) BOOSEY $1.50
                                  (W183)

WALTERS, OSCAR W.
My Love Song To A Tree
  high solo,pno (D maj) ALLANS s.p.
                                  (W184)
  med solo,pno (C maj) ALLANS s.p.
                                  (W185)
  low solo,pno (B flat maj) ALLANS
  s.p.   (W186)

WALTON
Anonymous In Love *CC7L
  (diff) T solo,gtr OXFORD 63.055
  $2.70; T solo,orch OXFORD rental
                                  (W187)

Beatric's Song
  solo,gtr OXFORD 62.235 $1.75   (W188)

Sleep
  Bar solo,4strings,pno (med easy)
  voc sc OXFORD 61.175 $1.25   (W189)

WALTON, K.
If I But Had A Little Coat
  solo,pno (G maj) BOOSEY $1.50
                                  (W190)

WALTON, KENNETH
Knight, The
  low solo,pno BELWIN $1.50   (W191)
  high solo,pno BELWIN $1.50   (W192)

Lost Star, The
  med solo,pno BELWIN $1.50   (W193)

WALTON, WILLIAM (1902-   )
Contrast, The
  see Song For The Lord Mayor's
    Table, A

Daphne
  see Three Songs

WALTON, WILLIAM (cont'd.)

Glide Gently
  see Song For The Lord Mayor's
    Table, A

Holy Thursday
  see Song For The Lord Mayor's
    Table, A

Lord Mayor's Table, The
  see Song For The Lord Mayor's
    Table, A

Old Sir Faulk
  see Three Songs

Rhyme
  see Song For The Lord Mayor's
    Table, A

Song For The Lord Mayor's Table, A
  S solo,pno (diff) OXFORD 63.059
  $3.25
    contains: Contrast, The; Glide
    Gently; Holy Thursday; Lord
    Mayor's Table, The; Rhyme;
    Wapping Old Stairs   (W194)

Three Songs
  S/T solo,pno (med diff) OXFORD
  63.701 $2.40
    contains: Daphne; Old Sir Faulk;
    Through Gilded Trelises   (W195)

Through Gilded Trelises
  see Three Songs

Under The Greenwood Tree
  S/T solo,pno (easy) OXFORD 63.702
  $1.25   (W196)

Wapping Old Stairs
  see Song For The Lord Mayor's
    Table, A

Winds, The
  solo,pno (E min) ROBERTON 2217 s.p.
                                  (W197)

WALTZ SONG see Gounod, Charles
  Francois, Ah! Je Veux Vivre!

WALTZING MATILDA see Cowan

WALVOORD, JOHN
God That Was Real (composed with
  Wyrtzen, Don) *sac
  solo,pno SINGSPIR 7069 $1.00   (W198)

Love Was When (composed with Wyrtzen,
  Don) *sac
  solo,pno SINGSPIR 7065 $1.00   (W199)

On Belief (composed with Wyrtzen,
  Don) *sac
  solo,pno SINGSPIR 7068 $1.00   (W200)

Sandals (composed with Wyrtzen, Don)
  *sac
  solo,pno SINGSPIR 7066 $1.00   (W201)

This World Outside (composed with
  Wyrtzen, Don) *sac
  solo,pno SINGSPIR 7067 $1.00   (W202)

WALZEL, L.M.
Kirschblutenlieder *CCU
  high solo,pno UNIVER. 12367 s.p.
                                  (W203)

WALZERALBUM, BAND I see Koschat, Thomas

WANDER-THIRST see Ronald, Sir Landon

WANDERER, THE see Schubert, Franz
  (Peter), Der Wanderer

WANDERER ERWACHT IN DER HERBERGE see
  Bijvanck, Henk

WANDERER'S PRAYER see Zahavi, David,
  Halicha L'Keysarya

WANDERER'S SONG, THE see Harrison,
  Julius Allen Greenway

WANDERER'S SONGS see Farkas, Ferenc

WANDERING PLAYER, THE see Murray, Alan

WANDERING WILLIE *folk,Scot
  low solo,pno (E flat maj) PATERSON
  FS90 s.p.   (W204)
  high solo,pno (F maj) PATERSON FS90
  s.p.   (W205)

WANDERINGS see Hjorleifsson, Sigguringi
  E.

WANDERLIED see Pylkkanen, Tauno
  Kullervo, Vaulluslaulu

WANDERLIED see Schumann, Robert
  (Alexander)

WANDERLUST see Lora, Antonio

WANDERLUST see Schirmer, Rudolph [E.]

WANDERS GEMUTSRUHE see Foss, Lukas

WANDERSPRUCHE see Schoeck, Othmar

WANDERUNG IM GEBIRGE see Schoeck, Othmar

WANDERUNG ZUR NACHT see Lothar, Mark

WANGERMEZ, ED.
  J'aime Les Cloches
    solo,pno ENOCH s.p.   (W206)
    solo,acap ENOCH s.p.   (W207)

  Nids Et Berceaux
    solo,acap ENOCH s.p.   (W208)
    solo,pno ENOCH s.p.   (W209)

  Oraison Dominicale *sac
    solo,acap ENOCH s.p.   (W210)
    solo,pno ENOCH s.p.   (W211)
    [Fr] solo,pno ENOCH   (W212)

  Souvenez-Vous *sac
    solo,pno ENOCH s.p.   (W213)
    [Fr] solo,pno ENOCH   (W214)
    solo,acap ENOCH s.p.   (W215)

  Voici Le Printemps
    solo,acap ENOCH s.p.   (W216)
    solo,pno ENOCH s.p.   (W217)

WANING MOON, THE see Birch, Robert Fairfax

WANING MOON, THE see Pisk, Paul Amadeus

WANN KOMMT DIE STUNDE? see Melichar

WANN UNSRE AUGEN SCHLAFEN EIN see Schutz, Heinrich

WANNEER GEDENKT GE MIJN see Clercq, R. de

WANNEER NIET MEER see Mulder, Herman

WANSBOROUGH
  Shorn Lamb (composed with Ades)
    med solo,pno SHAWNEE IA5045 $.85
    (W218)

WANTING IS WHAT? see Gerschefski, Edwin

WANTON GALES see Kearton, T. Wilfred

WAPPING OLD STAIRS see Walton, William

WAP VAN PESCH, L.
  Herfstbosch
    solo,pno ALSBACH s.p.   (W219)

WAR ES AUCH NICHTS ALS EIN TRAUM VOM GLUCK see Lehar, Franz

WAR ES EIN TRAUM? see Sibelius, Jean, Var Det En Drom?

WAR ICH NICHT EIN FRISCHES GRASLEIN see Tchaikovsky, Piotr Ilyitch

WAR IS TOIL AND TROUBLE see Handel, George Frideric

WAR PICTURES see Srebotnjak, Alojz F., Vojne Slike

WAR SCENES see Rorem, Ned

WAR SONG OF TYRTAEUS see Sibelius, Jean, Atenarnes Sang

WARBLE FOR LILAC TIME see Carter, Elliott Cook, Jr.

WARD, ROBERT (1917-   )
  As I Watched The Ploughman Ploughing
    solo,pno PEER $.95   (W220)

  Ballad From Pantaloon
    solo,pno HIGHGATE 7.0001.7 $1.50
    (W221)

  Rain Has Fallen All The Day
    solo,pno PEER $.95   (W222)

  Sacred Songs For Pantheists *CCU
    S solo,pno HIGHGATE 7.0038.7 $4.50
    (W223)

  Sorry Of Mydath
    solo,pno PEER $.95   (W224)

  Vanished
    solo,pno PEER $.95   (W225)

WARD, SAMUEL A.
  America, The Beautiful
    low solo,pno (C maj) CENTURY 3568
    (W226)

WARDALE, JOSEPH
  Secret
    solo,pno CRAMER   (W227)

WARE
  Greatest Of These, The *sac
    high solo,pno (E flat maj) BOSTON
    $1.50   (W228)
    low solo,pno (C maj) BOSTON $1.50
    (W229)

  This Day Is Mine
    med solo,pno (C maj) ALLANS s.p.
    (W230)
    low solo,pno (B flat maj) ALLANS
    s.p.   (W231)
    high solo,pno (D maj) ALLANS s.p.
    (W232)

WARE, BROADMAN
  Field Is The World, The *sac
    low solo,pno CRESPUB CP-R 657 $1.00
    (W233)

  Of His Great Love *sac
    med solo,pno CRESPUB CP-S5012 $1.00
    (W234)

WARE, HARRIET (1877-1962)
  Cross, The *sac
    med-low solo,pno (A min) SCHIRM.G
    $.75   (W235)
    high solo,pno (C min) SCHIRM.G $.75
    (W236)

WARFIELD, GERALD
  Study Of Two Pears, A
    S solo,pno sc AM.COMP.AL. $4.95
    (W237)
    Bar solo,pno sc AM.COMP.AL. $4.95
    (W238)
    Bar solo,pno sc AM.COMP.AL. $5.50
    (W239)

WARING, TOM
  Onward For God And My Country *see Dolph

  Songs By Tom Waring *CCU
    solo,pno SHAWNEE IA 65 $7.50 (W240)

WARLAAM'S LIED see Mussorgsky, Modest

WARLOCK, PETER
  see HESELTINE, PHILIP

WARNER, THEODOR (1903)
  Lieder Nach Gedichten Von Ina Seidel
    *CCU
    med solo,pno (med) BAREN. 1893
    $5.50   (W241)

WARNING see Dvorak, Antonin

WARNUNG see Mozart, Wolfgang Amadeus

WARNUNG see Schoenberg, Arnold

WARREN
  Children Of The Moon
    high solo,pno SHAWNEE IA5037 $.60
    (W242)

  Christmas Candle *Xmas
    solo,pno ALLANS s.p.   (W243)

  Magdalene
    high solo&low solo,pno (C maj)
    FISCHER,C V 1981   (W244)

WARREN, BEVERLY
  Song Of Joy, A
    med solo,pno CRESPUB CP-S5048 $1.00
    (W245)

WARREN, CYRIL
  Any Morning Now
    solo,pno (C maj) BOOSEY $1.50
    (W246)

  Paddy Flynns Wedding
    solo,pno CRAMER   (W247)

WARREN, E.
  That's What Love Will Do To You *see Beni, J.

WARREN, ELINOR REMICK (1905-   )
  Christmas Candle *sac
    high solo,pno (F maj) SCHIRM.G $.85
    (W248)
    med-low solo,pno (D maj) SCHIRM.G
    $.85   (W249)

  Dreams
    high solo,pno PRESSER $.75 (W250)
    med solo,pno PRESSER $.75 (W251)

  For You With Love
    med-high solo,pno SCHIRM.G $.85
    (W252)

  God Be In My Heart *sac
    med solo,pno PRESSER $.75 (W253)

  King Arthur's Farewell
    high solo,pno BELWIN $1.50 (W254)
    low solo,pno BELWIN $1.50 (W255)

  More Things Are Wrought By Prayer
    *sac
    high solo,pno BELWIN $1.50 (W256)
    med solo/low solo,pno BELWIN $1.50
    (W257)

  Silent Moon
    high solo,pno PRESSER $.75 (W258)
    low solo,pno PRESSER $.75 (W259)

WARREN, ELINOR REMICK (cont'd.)
  Time, You Old Gipsy Man
    low solo,pno (C sharp min) BOOSEY
    $1.50   (W260)
    high solo,pno (D maj) BOOSEY $1.50
    (W261)

WARREN, RAYMOND (1928-   )
  Drop, Drop, Slow Tears
    Mez solo,pno NOVELLO 17.0043.10
    s.p.   (W262)

  Passion, The
    7 soli,fl,ob,clar,bsn,horn,timp,
    perc,pno,strings NOVELLO rental
    (W263)

  Songs Of Old Age *CC9L
    high solo,pno NOVELLO 17.0280.07
    s.p.   (W264)

WARSHE see Stuchkoff, N.

WARST DU VON STEIN see Herrmann, Hans

WARUM see Othegraven, August J. von

WARUM? see Rietz, Johannes

WARUM? see Tchaikovsky, Piotr Ilyitch

WARUM KAM IN DES ABENDS DAMMERN see Alfano, Franco, Perche Allo Spuntar Del Giorno

WAS BEDEUTET DIE BEWEGUNG see Schubert, Franz (Peter), Suleikas Erster Gesang

WAS BETRUBST DU DICH see Schutz, Heinrich

WAS BETRUBST DU DICH, MEINE SEELE see Bernhard, Christoph

WAS BETRUBST DU DICH, MEINE SEELE see Micheelsen, Hans-Friedrich

WAS BETRUBST DU DICH, MEINE SEELE see Schutz, Heinrich

WAS DAT EEN LIED see Zagwijn, Henri

WAS GOTT TUT, DAS IST WOHLGETAN see Bach, Johann Sebastian

WAS HAST DU VERWIRKET? see Schutz, Heinrich

WAS I HAB' see Bohm, Carl

WAS ICH HAB' see Schmalstich, Clemens

WAS IST DAS NUR HEUT
  see Vier Kleine Weihnachtslieder

WAS IST EIN KUSS see Mana-Zucca, Mme.

WAS IST MIR DENN SO WEHE see Knab, Armin

WAS IST SYLVIA? see Schubert, Franz (Peter), Who Is Sylvia?

WAS IT A DREAM? see Sibelius, Jean, Var Det En Drom?

WAS IT SOME GOLDEN STAR? see Elgar, Edward

WAS KANN ICH TUN see Purcell, Henry

WAS KUMMERT MICH see Kilpinen, Yrio, Mitapa Suren Sanoista

WAS MEIN GOTT WILL, DAS GESCHEH ALLZEIT see Schutz, Heinrich

WAS MICH AUF DIESER WELT BETRUBT see Buxtehude, Dietrich

WAS MIR GEFALLT see Franco Mendes, H.

WAS SCHMERZ SEI UND WAS LEIDEN see Bach, Johann Sebastian, Non Sa Che Sia Dolore

WAS SEH ICH? see Lortzing, (Gustav) Albert

WAS SOLL DEIN WEINEN, LIEBSTER? see Mussorgsky, Modest

WAS THIS FAIR FACE THE CAUSE? see Thomson, Virgil

WAS UNSRE KINDER SINGEN *CC192U
  solo,pno SCHOTTS 600 s.p. (W265)

WAS WILL DIE EINSAME THRANE see Schumann, Robert (Alexander)

WASH DAY AND RAINY DAY see Sherman, H.

WASHBURN, C.
Oh Mo'nah (composed with Weems, J.)
solo,pno LEONARD-ENG   (W266)

WASHED IN SILVER see Mourant, Walter

WASHER OF THE FORD, THE see Bantock,
Granville

WASHINGTON MONUMENT BY NIGHT see
Raphling, Sam

WASSENHOVEN, P. V.
Woudsprookje
solo,pno ALSBACH s.p.   (W267)

WASSERFAHRT see Pfitzner, Hans

WASSERFAL BEI NACHT see Flothius,
Marius

WASSERFALL BEI NACHT see Bijvanck, Henk

WASSERROSE see Strauss, Richard

WASTED YEARS see Fowler

WAT BAET DAT U CORALEN see Bunge, Sas

WAT BEN IK, DAN EEN VOGEL IN DE
SCHEMERING? see Dijk, Jan van

WAT MOEDER SCHREEF see Hullebroeck, Em.

WAT VREUGD' HOOR IK UYT 'S HEMELS
ZAELEN see Horst, Anton van der

WATCH YOUR STEP *Jew
solo,pno KAMMEN 23 $1.00   (W268)

WATCHER see Sheehan, R.

WATCHFUL'S SONG (from Pilgrim's
Progress)
Bar solo,pno (med) OXFORD 62.202
$1.50   (W269)

WATCHING THE WHEAT
high solo,pno (F maj) ASHDOWN s.p.
(W270)
low solo,pno (E flat maj) ASHDOWN
s.p.   (W271)

WATCHMAN, TELL US OF THE NIGHT see
Hovhaness, Alan

WATCHMAN, WHAT OF THE NIGHT? see
Gounod, Charles Francois

WATCHMAN! WHAT OF THE NIGHT see
Sarjeant, J.

WATER BOY see Robinson, A.

WATER COLOURS see Agafonnikov, V.

WATER DANCE see Ush'avtem Mayim

WATER FOLK see Shaw, Martin

WATER LILY, THE see Grieg, Edvard
Hagerup, Med En Vandlilje

WATER MEADOWS see Sharpe, Evelyn

WATER MILL, THE see Vaughan Williams,
Ralph

WATER OF THE MIRROR LAKE, THE see
Bliss, Sir Arthur

WATER OF TYNE see Tate, Phyllis

WATER OT TYNE *folk,Eng
(Whittaker) 2 soli,pno/orch ROBERTON
71662 s.p.   (W272)

WATER SONG see Schubert, Franz (Peter),
Auf Dem Wasser Zu Singen

WATERMAN, CONSTANCE
Ah! With The Grape
solo,pno (D flat maj) LESLIE 7038
(W273)
Lute, The
solo,pno (B flat maj) LESLIE 7039
(W274)

WATERMELON MAN see Atkey, Olive

WATERS
Partners With God (composed with
Stuart) *sac
solo,pno WORD S-52   (W275)

WATERS ARE TROUBLED, THE see Gaither

WATERS, LESLIE
Spring The Travelling Man
solo,pno CRAMER   (W276)

When I Set Out For Lyonnesse
solo,pno CRAMER $1.15   (W277)

WATERS OF SEVERN, THE see Redman,
Reginald

WATERS OF THY LOVE, THE see O'Hara,
Geoffrey

WATERS RIPPLE AND FLOW *Czech
(Taylor, Deems) med solo,pno BELWIN
$1.50   (W278)

WATKINS, MICHAEL BLAKE (1948-   )
Those Dancing Days Are Gone
T solo,clar,vln NOVELLO rental
(W279)
Youth's Dreams And Time's Truth
T solo,trp,harp,strings NOVELLO
rental   (W280)

WATSON, G.
Our Father *sac
solo,pno BERANDOL BER 1294 $1.50
(W281)

WATSON, MICHAEL
Since First I Met Thee
solo,pno (E flat maj) CRAMER   (W282)

WATT, FATHER LEO
Twelve Songs Of Faith *sac,CC12L
solo,pno,gtr ALBERT AE 99 s.p.
(W283)

WATTEAU see Busser, H.

WATTERS, BOB
Jesus Is The Answer (composed with
Watters, Lilian) *sac
solo,pno GOSPEL 05 TM 0408 $1.00
(W284)
Lord Send Me (composed with Watters,
Lilian) *sac
solo,pno GOSPEL 05 TM 0410 $1.00
(W285)

WATTERS, LILIAN
Jesus Is The Answer *see Watters,
Bob

Lord Send Me *see Watters, Bob

WATTS, WINTTER (1884-1962)
Little Shepherd's Song, The
high solo,pno BELWIN $1.50   (W286)
low solo,pno BELWIN $1.50   (W287)

Poet Sings, The
high solo,pno PRESSER $.75   (W288)

Transformation
med-high solo,pno (E flat maj)
SCHIRM.G $.75   (W289)

WAY
Christmas Morn *sac,Xmas
low solo,pno (A maj) FISCHER,C
V 2177   (W290)

WAY A MAN SHOULD GO see Newton, Ernest

WAY OF THE CROSS LED ME HOME, THE see
Lister, Mosie

WAY THAT HE LOVES, THE see Mercer

WAY, THE TRUTH, THE LIFE, THE see Grund

WAY TO EMMAUS see Weinberger, Jaromir

WAYFARER, THE see Borris, Siegfried

WAYFARER'S NIGHT SONG see Martin,
Easthope

WAYFARIN' STRANGER see Mc Bride, Robert
Guyn

WAYFARING PILGRIM, THE *sac,gospel
solo,pno ABER.GRP. $1.50   (W291)

WAYFARING STRANGER see Niles, John
Jacob

WAYNE, BERNIE
Lincoln's Gettysburg Address
solo,pno PEER $.95   (W292)

WAYS, THE see Weber, Ben

WAYSIDE CROSS see Sharpe, Evelyn

WAYSIDE FLOWERS see Griffiths, H.

WE ARE MORE THAN CONQUERORS *sac
(Carmichael, Ralph) solo,pno WORD
S-22   (W293)

WE ARE TOGETHER see Schafmeister

WE CALL ON HIM *sac,gospel
solo,pno ABER.GRP. $1.50   (W294)

WE HAPPY FEW see Cumming, R.

WE HAVE TO FIND A WAY see Reynolds,
William Jensen

WE HEAR YOU, ISRAEL see Miller, Herb

WE LIFT OUR HEARTS TO THEE see
Lovelace, Austin C.

WE LOVE YOU, CALL COLLECT *sac
(Carmichael, Ralph) solo,pno WORD
S-117   (W295)

WE NEVER DO THAT AT SEA see Day, Maude
Craske

WE PRAISE THEE, O GOD *sac,Greg
(Bergen) CONCORDIA 97-6205 $.75
(W296)

WE PRAISE THEE, O GOD see Willan,
Healey

WE SAW HIS GLORY see Mauersberger,
Erhard

WE SHALL ARISE *sac
(Inspirations) solo,pno WORD S-360
(W297)

WE SING TO HIM see Purcell, Henry

WE THREE ARE ONE see Sateren, Leland
Bernhard

WE TRAVEL TOGETHER see Liddell, R.

WE TWO see Diamond, David

WE WERE SLAVES see Weiner, Lazar,
Avodim Hoyinu

WE WILL GO A-SAILING *Scot
solo,pno PATERSON s.p. see from
Hebridean Songs, Vol. IV   (W298)

WE WILL TAKE THE GOOD OLD WAY see
Lawson, Malcolm

WEARY BLUES see Moore, Dorothy Rudd

WEARY FLOWERS see Schubert, Franz
(Peter), Trockne Blumen

WEARY YEARE, THE see Goldman, Richard
Franko

WEATHERLY, F.E.
Danny Boy
low solo,pno (C maj) BOOSEY $1.50
(W299)
2 soli,pno (C maj) BOOSEY $1.75
(W300)
high solo,pno (F maj) BOOSEY $1.50
(W301)
med-high solo,pno (E flat maj)
BOOSEY $1.50   (W302)
med solo,pno (D maj) BOOSEY $1.50
(W303)

WEATHERS see Ireland, John

WEAVER, THE see Wolfe, Lanny

WEAVER, MARY
Heart Of Heaven
med solo,pno GALAXY 1.2048.7 $1.00
(W304)

WEAVER, POWELL (1890-1951)
Bells Of Time
med-high solo,pno GALAXY 1.2086.7
$1.00   (W305)

Build Thee More Stately Mansions
med solo,pno (E flat maj) GALAXY
1.1838.7 $1.00   (W306)

Praise The Lord His Glories Show
high solo,pno GALAXY 1.1666.7 $1.00
(W307)

WEAVING SONG see Lawson, Malcolm

WEBB, MILTON
Those Little Hands
solo,pno (E flat maj) LEONARD-ENG
(W308)

WEBBER, ANDREW LLOYD
Any Dream Will Do (from Joseph And
The Amazing Technicolor
Dreamcoat) (composed with Rice,
Tim)
solo,pno NOVELLO s.p.   (W309)

Close Every Door (from Joseph And The
Amazing Technicolor Dreamcoat)
(composed with Rice, Tim)
solo,pno NOVELLO s.p.   (W310)

WEBBER, LLOYD
Beggar's Song
see Four Bibulous Songs

Four Bibulous Songs
Bar solo,pno ELKIN 27.2231.03 s.p.
contains: Beggar's Song; Strange
Meeting, A; They're Taxing Ale
Again; You Interfering Ladies
(W311)
Oh Lord Spread Thy Wings O'er Me
solo,pno (F maj) ASHDOWN s.p.
(W312)

Strange Meeting, A
see Four Bibulous Songs

They're Taxing Ale Again
see Four Bibulous Songs

WEBBER, LLOYD (cont'd.)

You Interfering Ladies
see Four Bibulous Songs

WEBER
Berceuse
[Ger] solo,pno DURAND s.p.   (W313)

Mourn! Mourn!
high solo,pno EMI s.p.   (W314)

Praise The Lord Ye Heavens Adore Him
*sac
(Park, Dorothy Allan; Bissell,
Keith W.) med solo,pno (C maj)
WATERLOO $.90   (W315)

Selected Songs *CC38U
[Ger] high solo,pno PETERS 278
$9.00   (W316)

WEBER, B.
Four Songs *Op.40,No.1-4, CC4U
S/T solo,vcl,pno MERCURY $1.25
                               (W317)

WEBER, BEN (1916-   )
Bird Came Down The Walk, A
Mez solo,pno AM.COMP.AL. $3.30
                               (W318)

Concert Aria After Solomon *Op.29,
sac,Bibl
S solo,fl,ob,clar,bsn,horn,pno,vln,
vcl AM.COMP.AL. sc $9.35, ipa
voc sc $3.85   (W319)

Five Songs *CC5U
S solo,pno AM.COMP.AL. $3.30 (W320)

Symphony *Op.33
Bar solo,fl,ob,clar,bsn,horn,trom,
harp,cel/pno,perc,vcl sc
AM.COMP.AL. $39.60   (W321)

Two Songs *Op.63, CC2U
med solo,pno AM.COMP.AL. $3.85
                               (W322)

Ways, The
S solo,pno AM.COMP.AL. $8.25 (W323)

WEBER, CARL MARIA VON (1786-1826)
Air De Rezia (from Oberon)
S solo,orch HENN s.p.   (W324)

Ausgewahlte Lieder Fur Gesang Und
Gitarre *CCU
(Scheit, K.) solo,gtr DOBLINGER
GKM 67 s.p.   (W325)

Couplets De Gaspard (from Der
Freischutz)
see LA MUSIQUE, SEPTIEME CAHIER

Der Kleine Fritz An Seine Jungen
Freunde *Op.15,No.3
(Mottl, F.) S solo,fl,2horn,strings
BREITKOPF-L rental   (W326)

Durch Die Walder, Durch Die Auen
(from Der Freischutz)
see Weber, Carl Maria von, Nein,
Langer Trag Ich Nicht Die Qualen

Einst Traumte Meiner Sel'gen Base
(from Der Freischutz)
S solo,2fl,2clar,2bsn,2horn,strings
BREITKOPF-L rental   (W327)
"Romance Et Air D'Annette" solo,
orch HENN s.p.   (W328)

Gitarrelieder *CCU
(Schwarz-Reiflingen, Erwin) solo,
gtr LEUCKART $4.00   (W329)

Hier Im Irdschen Jammertal (from Der
Freischutz)
Bar solo,2fl,2ob,2bsn,strings
BREITKOPF-L rental   (W330)

Invitacion Al Vals *see Invitation
To The Dance

Invitation To The Dance *Op.65
low solo,pno (B flat maj) ALLANS
s.p.   (W331)
high solo,pno (C maj) ALLANS s.p.
                               (W332)
(Pardo) "Invitacion Al Vals" [Span]
S solo,pno,opt fl RICORDI-ARG
BA 8722 s.p.   (W333)

Kommt Ein Schlanker Bursch Geganen
(from Der Freischutz)
S solo,2fl,2ob,2bsn,2horn,strings
BREITKOPF-L rental   (W334)

Leise, Leise, Fromm Weise (from Der
Freischutz)
"Softly Sighs The Voice Of Evening"
solo,pno CRAMER   (W335)
"Softly Sighs The Voice Of Evening"
solo,pno (E maj) ASHDOWN s.p.
                               (W336)
"Softly Sighs The Voice Of Evening"
high solo,pno (E maj) ALLANS s.p.
                               (W337)

WEBER, CARL MARIA VON (cont'd.)

Meine Lieder, Meine Sange *Op.15,
No.1
(Mottl, F.) S solo,ob,2clar,2bsn,
2horn,strings BREITKOPF-L rental
                               (W338)

Nein, Langer Trag Ich Nicht Die
Qualen (from Der Freischutz)
T solo,2fl,2ob,2clar,2bsn,4horn,
timp,strings BREITKOPF-L rental
contains also: Durch Die Walder,
Durch Die Auen   (W339)

Noel *sac,Xmas
Mez solo,pno/org HEUGEL s.p. (W340)

Ozean, Du Ungeheuer (from Oberon)
S solo,2fl,2ob,2clar,2bsn,4horn,
2trp,3trom,timp,strings
BREITKOPF-L rental   (W341)

Romance Et Air D'Annette *see Einst
Traumte Meiner Sel'gen Base

Schelm, Halt Fest (from Der
Freischutz)
SS soli,2fl,2clar,2bsn,2horn,
strings BREITKOPF-L rental (W342)

Schweig, Damit Dich Niemand Warnt
(from Der Freischutz)
Bar solo,4fl,2ob,2clar,2bsn,4horn,
2trp,3trom,timp,strings
BREITKOPF-L rental   (W343)

Softly Sighs The Voice Of Evening
*see Leise, Leise, Fromm Weise

Tho' Clouds By Tempests
solo,pno (A flat maj) ASHDOWN s.p.
                               (W344)

Unbefangenheit *Op.30,No.3
(Reger, Max) Mez solo,2fl,2ob,
2clar,2bsn,2horn,strings sc
BREITKOPF-L PB 957 s.p., ipa
                               (W345)

Und Ob Die Wolke (from Der
Freischutz)
S solo,2clar,2bsn,2horn,strings
BREITKOPF-L rental   (W346)

Von Jugend Auf Im Kampfgefild
T solo,2fl,2ob,2clar,2bsn,4horn,
2trp,trom,timp,strings BREITKOPF-
W s.p.   (W347)

Wie Nahte Mir Der Schlummer (from Der
Freischutz)
S solo,2fl,2ob,2clar,2bsn,4horn,
strings BREITKOPF-L rental (W348)

Wonnig Susses Hoffnungstraumen
[Ger] S solo,2fl,2ob,2clar,2bsn,
2horn,strings MUSIKWISS. 66.5.121
rental   (W349)

WEBERHERZEN see Felix, Vaclav,
Tkalcovska Srdce

WEBERN, ANTON VON (1883-1945)
Drei Geistliche Volkstexte *Op.17,
No.1-3, sac,CC3U
solo,clar,bass clar,vln sc UNIVER.
12272 $4.75, ipa   (W350)

Drei Gesange *Op.23,No.1-3, CC3U
med solo,pno UNIVER. 10255 $3.75
                               (W351)

Drei Lieder *Op.25,No.1-3, CC3U
[Ger/Eng] high solo,pno UNIVER.
12418 $3.75   (W352)

Drei Lieder *Op.18,No.1-3, CC3U
solo,clar,gtr sc UNIVER. 8684 $3.75
                               (W353)

Funf Canons *Op.16,No.1-5, CC5U,
canon
[Lat] S solo,clar,bass clar sc,oct
UNIVER. 9522 $3.75   (W354)

Funf Geistliche Lieder *Op.15,No.1-
5, sac,CC5U
S solo,vln,fl,clar,trp,harp sc
UNIVER. 7629 $7.00, ipa   (W355)

Funf Lieder *Op.4,No.1-5, CC5U
high solo,pno UNIVER. 7395 $3.75
                               (W356)

Funf Lieder *Op.3,No.1-3, CC5U
med solo,pno UNIVER. 6645 s.p.
                               (W357)

Sechs Lieder *Op.14, CC6U
S solo,clar,bass clar,winds,vcl sc
UNIVER. 7578 $7.00, ipa   (W358)

Vier Lieder *Op.12,No.1-4, CC4U
high solo,pno UNIVER. 8257 $4.25
                               (W359)

Vier Lieder *Op.13,No.1-4, CC4U
[Ger/Eng] S solo,pno UNIVER. 12460
$4.25   (W360)

Vier Lieder *Op.13, CC4U
[Ger/Eng] S solo,chamb.grp. sc
UNIVER. 8557 $9.50   (W361)

WEBERN, ANTON VON (cont'd.)

Zwei Lieder *Op.8,No.1-2, CC2U
med solo,clar,horn,trp,cel,harp,
vln,vla,vcl sc UNIVER. 8555 $4.75
                               (W362)

WECHSELLIED ZUM TANZ see Krenek, Ernst

WECHSELRAHMEN see Krenek, Ernst

WECKERLIN, JEAN-BAPTISTE-THEODORE
(1821-1910)
Noel *sac,Xmas
med solo,pno/org HEUGEL s.p. (W363)

WECKMANN, MATTHAIS (1619-1674)
Gegrusset Seist Du, Holdselige *sac
(Schleifer, Karl) ST soli,2fl,2vln,
cont (med) BAREN. 447 s.p. (W364)

Wie Liegt Die Stadt So Wuste *sac
SB soli,strings,org sc CONCORDIA
97-4415 $4.50   (W365)

WEDDED SOULS see Saxe, Serge

WEDDING BENEDICTION, A see Lovelace,
Austin C.

WEDDING BLESSING see Pelz, Walter L.

WEDDING BLESSING, A see Carlson, Dosia

WEDDING BLESSINGS (A COLLECTION OF
SACRED SOLOS AND A DUET) *sac,
CC12L,Marriage
(Bunjes, Paul) med-high solo/2 med-
high soli,pno CONCORDIA 97-9238
$3.00; low solo/2 low soli,pno
CONCORDIA 97-9240 $3.00 contains
works by: Bach; Brahms; Buxtehude;
Helder and others   (W366)

WEDDING BOUQUET *sac,CC17L
(Taylor, Bernard) SCHIRM.G high solo,
pno $2.50; low solo,pno $2.50
contains works by: Bach; Franck;
Grieg; Strauss and others   (W367)

WEDDING CANTATA see Samama

WEDDING GOWN, THE see West, Monica

WEDDING HYMN see France, William E.

WEDDING HYMN see Handel, George
Frideric

WEDDING HYMN see Woollen, Russell

WEDDING IS GREAT JUNO'S CROWN see
Holborne, Antony

WEDDING MUSIC *sac/sec,CC16L,Marriage
BOSTON $4.00 contains works by: Bach;
Franck; Schubert; Browning and
others   (W368)

WEDDING MUSIC FOR THE CHURCH ORGANIST
AND SOLOIST see Lovelace, Austin C.

WEDDING PRAYER see Artman

WEDDING PRAYER see Dunlap, Fern Glasgow

WEDDING PRAYER see Tarner

WEDDING PRAYER, A *sac
solo,pno STAMPS 7250-SN $1.00 (W369)

WEDDING PRAYER, A see Stevens, Halsey

WEDDING PRAYER, A see Williams, David
H.

WEDDING PRAYER, A see Wilson

WEDDING PROCESSIONAL AND AIR see Bach,
Johann Sebastian

WEDDING RING, THE see Haubiel, Charles

WEDDING SONG see Pinkham, Daniel

WEDDING SONG see Schutz, Heinrich

WEDDING SONG see Tesoriero, Gaetano

WEDDING SONG see Verdi, Ralph C.

WEDDING SONG, A see Carroll, J. Robert

WEDDING SONG see Bender, Jan

WEDDING SONGS *CCU,folk,Hung
(Kiss) solo,pno BUDAPEST 2338 s.p.
                               (W370)

WEDDINGTON, MAURICE (1941-   )
Pathogenesis
solo,fl,English horn,bass clar,vla,
vcl,perc MODERN rental   (W371)

WEE FIDDLE MOON see Graham

WEE ROAD FROM CUSHENDALL, THE see
  Thiman, Eric Harding

WEE TOUN CLERK see Roberton, Hugh
  Stevenson

WEE, WEE GERMAN LAIRDIC *folk,Scot
  solo,pno (G min) PATERSON FS91 s.p.
                                    (W372)
WEE WILLIE GRAY *folk,Scot
  solo,pno (E maj) PATERSON FS119 s.p.
                                    (W373)
WEE WILLIE WINKIE see Diack, John
  Michael

WEEGENHUISE, JOHAN (1910-   )
  Abendstandchen
    see Vier Miniaturen

  Als Die Junge Rose Bluhte
    see Vier Lieder Nach Heine

  Altes Minnelied
    see Vier Miniaturen

  Das Gelbe Laub Erzittert
    see Vier Lieder Nach Heine

  Een Lied Van Hertog Jan I Van Barbant
    see Ic En Weet Gheen Schoonder
    Vrouwe

  Egidius, Waer Bestu Bleven?
    see Weegenhuise, Johan, Och Ligdy
    Nu En Slaept
    med solo,4strings DONEMUS s.p.
                                    (W374)
  Ein Grab
    see Vier Miniaturen

  En Begheeft Mi Niet
    see Ic En Weet Gheen Schoonder
    Vrouwe

  Four Boutens Songs *CC4U
    Bar/A solo,pno DONEMUS s.p. (W375)

  Ic En Weet Gheen Schoonder Vrouwe
    A/Bar solo,pno DONEMUS s.p.
      contains: Een Lied Van Hertog Jan
      I Van Barbant; En Begheeft Mi
      Niet; Ic Sech Adieu;
      Vensterliedeken   (W376)

  Ic Sech Adieu
    see Ic En Weet Gheen Schoonder
    Vrouwe

  Ich Sehe Dich In Tausend Bildern
    see Vier Miniaturen

  In Der Fremde
    see Vier Lieder Nach Heine

  In Memoriam
    see Vier Liederen

  Kerstlied *sac
    med solo,pno BANK s.p.   (W377)

  Liedje
    see Vier Liederen

  Mir Traumte Von Einem Schonen Kind
    see Vier Lieder Nach Heine

  O Jesu Vol Genaden
    high solo,org DONEMUS s.p.   (W378)

  Och Ligdy Nu En Slaept
    med solo,4strings DONEMUS s.p.
                                    (W379)
    med solo,org DONEMUS s.p. contains
    also: Egidius, Waer Bestu Bleven?
                                    (W380)
  Tetraptiek *CC4U
    Bar/A solo,pno DONEMUS s.p. (W381)

  Triptych *CC3U
    low solo,pno DONEMUS s.p.   (W382)

  Vensterliedeken
    see Ic En Weet Gheen Schoonder
    Vrouwe

  Vier Lieder Nach Heine
    A/Bar solo,pno DONEMUS s.p.
      contains: Als Die Junge Rose
      Bluhte; Das Gelbe Laub
      Erzittert; In Der Fremde; Mir
      Traumte Von Einem Schonen Kind
                                    (W383)
  Vier Liederen
    A/Bar solo,pno DONEMUS s.p.
      contains: In Memoriam; Liedje;
      Zomeravond; Zomerdag   (W384)

  Vier Miniaturen
    Mez/T solo,pno DONEMUS s.p.
      contains: Abendstandchen; Altes
      Minnelied; Ein Grab; Ich Sehe
      Dich In Tausend Bildern   (W385)

  Zomeravond
    see Vier Liederen

WEEGENHUISE, JOHAN (cont'd.)

  Zomerdag
    see Vier Liederen

WEEMS, J.
  Oh Mo'nah *see Washburn, C.

WEEP EYES, BREAK HEART see Musgrave,
  Thea

WEEP NO MORE see Handel, George
  Frideric

WEEP NO MORE see Raphael, Mark

WEEP NOT FOR FRIENDS DEPARTED see
  Schubert, Franz (Peter)

WEEP YOU NO MORE see Birch, Robert
  Fairfax

WEEP YOU NO MORE see Bush, Geoffrey

WEEP YOU NO MORE see Mourant, Walter

WEEPIN' MARY *spir
  (Burleigh, H. T.) high solo,pno
    BELWIN $1.50   (W386)
  (Burleigh, H. T.) low solo,pno BELWIN
    $1.50   (W387)

WEEPING see Kodaly, Zoltan

WEEPING PLEIADS, THE see Flanagan,
  William

WEG DER LIEBE, I see Brahms, Johannes

WEG DER LIEBE, II see Brahms, Johannes

WEG NACH INNEN see Edler, Robert

WEHE MIR, ACH - LEBEN SOLL ICH see
  Mozart, Wolfgang Amadeus, Misera,
  Dove Son! - Ah! Non Son Io

WEHE MIR! IST'S WAHRHEIT - EILET,
  MITLEID'GE LUFTE see Mozart,
  Wolfgang Amadeus, Misero! O Sogno -
  Aura, Che Intorno Spiri

WEHMUT see Schubert, Franz (Peter)

WEHRLI, WERNER (1892-1944)
  Siebzehn Lieder Nach Gedichten Von
    Sophie Haemmerli-Marti *CC17U
    med solo,pno (diff) BAREN. 2778
    $6.50   (W388)

WEIB see Lilien, Ignace

WEICHE, LUST UND FROHLICHKEIT see
  Telemann, Georg Philipp

WEICHE, WOTAN! WEICHE! see Wagner,
  Richard

WEICHET NUR, BETRUBTE SCHATTEN see
  Bach, Johann Sebastian

WEIDE, WAS NEIGEST see Gretchaninov,
  Alexander Tikhonovitch, Pourquoi Se
  Fanent Tes Feuilles?

WEIGL, KARL (1881-1949)
  And There You Stood
    low solo,pno AM.COMP.AL. $.82
                                    (W389)
  Black Cat
    med solo,pno AM.COMP.AL. $1.37
                                    (W390)
  Blaue Nacht
    "Blue Night" Mez solo,pno
    AM.COMP.AL. $.82   (W391)

  Blue Night *see Blaue Nacht

  Children's Songs *CCU
    high solo,pno AM.COMP.AL. $3.85
                                    (W392)
  Cradle Song, A
    med solo,pno AM.COMP.AL. $.55
                                    (W393)
  Ein Gleiches *Op.1,No.6
    "Similitude" low solo,pno
    AM.COMP.AL. $.27   (W394)

  Five Duets *CC5U
    SBar soli,pno sc AM.COMP.AL. $6.60
                                    (W395)
  Five Songs *Op.8, CC6U
    high solo,pno AM.COMP.AL. $6.60
                                    (W396)
  Five Songs *Op.10, CC5U
    med-low solo,pno AM.COMP.AL. $4.95
                                    (W397)
  Five Songs From "Phantasus" *Op.9,
    CC5U
    high solo,pno AM.COMP.AL. $5.50
                                    (W398)
  Funf Lieder *Op.3,No.1-5, CC5U
    solo,pno UNIVER. 2976 $3.75 (W399)

WEIGL, KARL (cont'd.)

  Funf Lieder *CC5U
    high solo,pno AM.COMP.AL. $5.50
                                    (W400)
  Glorious Hobo, The
    low solo,pno AM.COMP.AL. $1.37
                                    (W401)
  Grey Years
    med solo,pno AM.COMP.AL. $1.37
                                    (W402)
  Invisible Light, The
    high solo,pno AM.COMP.AL. $1.37
                                    (W403)
    low solo,pno AM.COMP.AL. $1.37
                                    (W404)
  Jesus
    Bar solo,pno AM.COMP.AL. $3.30
                                    (W405)
  Liebes-Lieder *Op.22, CCU
    high solo,pno AM.COMP.AL. $6.60
                                    (W406)
  Liebeslied
    high solo,pno AM.COMP.AL. $1.37
                                    (W407)
  Refugee, The
    high solo,pno AM.COMP.AL. $.82
                                    (W408)
  Similitude *see Ein Gleiches

  Six Children's Songs *Op.11, CC6U
    med solo,pno AM.COMP.AL. $3.85
                                    (W409)
  Six Songs *CC6U
    A solo,pno AM.COMP.AL. $4.95 (W410)

  Six Songs On Poems By O. J. Bierbaum
    *CC6U
    high solo,pno AM.COMP.AL. $5.50
                                    (W411)
  Three Songs *Op.1, CC3U
    AM.COMP.AL. Bar solo,acap $3.30;
    Mez/A/Bar solo,acap $3.30   (W412)
  Three Songs *Op.12, CC3U
    S solo,pno AM.COMP.AL. $2.75 (W413)

  Three Songs *CC3U
    Mez solo,4strings AM.COMP.AL. sc
    $5.50, ipa, voc sc $5.50   (W414)
  To Baby Christine
    med solo,pno AM.COMP.AL. $.55
                                    (W415)
  Wiegenlied
    Bar solo,pno AM.COMP.AL. $1.37
                                    (W416)
WEIGL, VALLY
  Beyond Time *song cycle
    high solo,vln,pno sc AM.COMP.AL.
    $5.50, ipa   (W417)
  Christchild's Lullaby
    Mez solo,fl/ob,pno sc AM.COMP.AL.
    $1.37   (W418)
  Christmas Carol, A
    med solo,opt wom cor,pno MERCURY
    $.95   (W419)
  Christmas Lullaby, A *Xmas
    med solo,pno AM.COMP.AL. $.82
                                    (W420)
  Christmas Message, A *Xmas
    med-low solo,pno/org AM.COMP.AL.
    $1.37   (W421)
  City Birds
    Mez solo,fl/clar,pno sc AM.COMP.AL.
    $3.30   (W422)
  Come, Little Leaves
    2 soli&S/2 soli&A solo,rec,pno sc
    AM.COMP.AL. $.82   (W423)
  Conscientious Objector
    male solo,pno sc AM.COMP.AL. $1.37
                                    (W424)
  Dear Earth: A Quintet Of Poems
    med-high solo,horn,vln,vcl,pno sc
    AM.COMP.AL. $7.70, ipa   (W425)
  Dearest, Dearest, Sleepest Thou?
    med solo,pno AM.COMP.AL. $1.10
                                    (W426)
  Death Snips Proud Men By The Nose
    med solo,pno AM.COMP.AL. $1.37
                                    (W427)
  Do Not Awake Me *song cycle
    Mez solo,vln/fl/clar,pno sc
    AM.COMP.AL. $7.70, ipa   (W428)
  Echoes From Poems By Patricia Benton
    *CCU
    med solo,horn/vcl,vln,pno sc
    AM.COMP.AL. $4.95, ipa   (W429)
  Elf And The Doormouse, The
    med solo,pno AM.COMP.AL. $.55
                                    (W430)
  Fairies Have Never A Penny To Spend,
    The
    med solo,pno AM.COMP.AL. $.55
                                    (W431)

WEIGL, VALLY (cont'd.)

Five Songs Of Remembrance *CC5U
AM.COMP.AL. A/Mez solo,4strings sc
$6.60, ipa; Mez solo,fl/vln/clar,
pno sc $6.60, ipa (W432)

Fruhling
"Springtime" med solo,pno
AM.COMP.AL. $.55 (W433)

Glimpse Of Hope
Mez/Bar solo,vln/fl,pno sc
AM.COMP.AL. $.82, ipa (W434)

How Many Nights
med solo,pno sc AM.COMP.AL. $.82
(W435)

Huntsmen, The
med solo,rec,pno sc AM.COMP.AL.
$.82 (W436)

In Springtime
med solo,S rec/fl,pno sc
AM.COMP.AL. $.82 (W437)

In The Meadow
med solo,S rec,pno sc AM.COMP.AL.
$.55 (W438)

Listen
med solo,pno AM.COMP.AL. $.82
(W439)

Little Singers, The
med solo,S rec/fl,pno sc
AM.COMP.AL. $.82 (W440)

Long, Long Ago *Xmas,carol
med solo,S rec/fl,pno sc
AM.COMP.AL. $.82 (W441)

Lullaby From "Native Island"
med solo,pno AM.COMP.AL. $1.37
(W442)

Lyrical Suite *CCU
Mez solo,fl/clar,vcl,pno sc
AM.COMP.AL. $7.70, ipa (W443)

Mice
med solo,pno AM.COMP.AL. $.55
(W444)

Mother's Day
Mez solo,pno AM.COMP.AL. $.27
(W445)

Nature Moods *CCU
high solo,clar/fl,vln sc
AM.COMP.AL. $5.50, ipa (W446)

Night Will Never Stay, The
2 soli,fl,S rec,pno sc AM.COMP.AL.
$.82 (W447)

Pax Hominibus
med solo,pno AM.COMP.AL. $.27
(W448)

Pippa's Song
1-2 soli,pno,S rec sc AM.COMP.AL.
$.82 (W449)

Prayers Of Steel
med solo,pno sc AM.COMP.AL. $1.37
(W450)

Rain At Night *see Regennacht

Rain In Summer
med solo,pno AM.COMP.AL. $.55
(W451)

Regennacht
"Rain At Night" low solo,vla,pno sc
AM.COMP.AL. $1.37, ipa (W452)

Requiem For Allison
S solo,4strings AM.COMP.AL. sc
$1.37, ipa, voc sc $1.37 (W453)

Rock-A-By Lady, The
med solo,rec,pno sc AM.COMP.AL.
$.82 (W454)

Salutation Of The Dawn, The
solo,vln/clar,pno/org (Sanskrit)
sc AM.COMP.AL. $1.37, ipa (W455)

Seeking You
med-low solo,vln/fl,pno sc
AM.COMP.AL. $1.37, ipa (W456)

Seven Songs *CC7U
med solo,pno AM.COMP.AL. $3.30
(W457)

Silver
med solo,rec,pno sc AM.COMP.AL.
$.82 (W458)

Song: The Owl
med solo,pno AM.COMP.AL. $.55
(W459)

Songs For A Child *CCU
1-2 soli,rec/fl,pno sc AM.COMP.AL.
$12.10 (W460)

Songs From "Native Island" *CCU
med-low solo,pno,ob,clar/vln sc
AM.COMP.AL. $3.30, ipa (W461)

WEIGL, VALLY (cont'd.)

Songs From "No Boundary" *CCU
med solo,vln/vla,pno sc AM.COMP.AL.
$6.60, ipa (W462)

Springtime *see Fruhling

Summer's End
med solo,pno AM.COMP.AL. $.82
(W463)

Swiftly Along Flows The River
med solo,pno,horn/vla sc
AM.COMP.AL. $.82 (W464)

Thanks
Mez solo,pno AM.COMP.AL. $.82
(W465)
Bar solo,pno AM.COMP.AL. $.82
(W466)

Thoughts About Grasshoppers
med solo,S rec/fl,pno sc
AM.COMP.AL. $.55 (W467)

When The Vision Dies
med solo,fl/vln/clar,pno sc
AM.COMP.AL. $1.10, ipa (W468)

Where Go The Boats
med solo,rec,pno sc AM.COMP.AL.
$.82 (W469)

Who Has Seen The Wind?
med solo,fl/rec,pno sc AM.COMP.AL.
$.55 (W470)

Winter Night
med solo,S rec,pno sc AM.COMP.AL.
$.82 (W471)

Wynken, Blynken And Nod
med solo/2 med soli,rec,pno sc
AM.COMP.AL. $.82 (W472)

WEIHE NACHT see Zagwijn, Henri

WEIHNACHTEN see Mayer, B.

WEIHNACHTEN see Skorzeny, Fritz

WEIHNACHTEN IM LIED *CC40U,Xmas
[Ger] high solo,pno PETERS 4687A
$11.00; med solo,pno PETERS 4687B
$11.00 (W473)

WEIHNACHTLICHES KRIPPENLIED see
Anonymous

WEIHNACHTS-WEISSAGUNG see Reichard,
Johann Georg

WEIHNACHTSBUCH, HEFT 1: ALTE
WEIHNACHTSLIEDER UND KRIPPENLIEDER
*sac,CCU,Xmas
(Degen, Helmut) solo,pno MULLER 2101
s.p. (W474)

WEIHNACHTSBUCH, HEFT 2: WIEGEN- UND
HIRTENLIEDER *sac,CCU,Xmas
(Degen, Helmut) solo,pno MULLER 2102
s.p. (W475)

WEIHNACHTSBUCH, HEFT 3: DREI-KONIGE-
LIEDER UND WEIHNACHTSCHORALE *sac,
CCU,Xmas
(Degen, Helmut) solo,pno MULLER 2103
s.p. (W476)

WEIHNACHTSBUCHLEIN see Lechthaler,
Josef

WEIHNACHTSGESCHICHTE see Behrend,
Siegfried

WEIHNACHTSKANTILENE see Reutter,
Hermann

WEIHNACHTSKONZERT see Boddecker,
Philipp Friedrich, Natus Est Jesus

WEIHNACHTSLIED see Beck, Reinhold, I.

WEIHNACHTSLIED see Berger, Gustav

WEIHNACHTSLIED see Berners, Lord

WEIHNACHTSLIEDER see Cornelius, Peter

WEIHNACHTSLIEDER see Cornelius, Peter

WEIHNACHTSLIEDER *CC97U,Xmas
solo,pno (med easy) BAREN. 3500 cmplt
ed,pap $5.50, cmplt ed,cloth $8.50
(W477)

WEIHNACHTSLIEDER see Cornelius, Peter

WEIHNACHTSLIEDER see Cornelius, Peter

WEIHNACHTSLIEDER see Cornelius, Peter

WEIHNACHTSLIEDER FUR KLAVIER *CC40U,
Xmas
(Ameln, Konrad) solo,pno (easy)
BAREN. 825 $4.25 (W478)

WEIHNACHTSLIEDER ZUM SINGEN UND SPIELEN
AM KLAVIER *CCU,Xmas
(Dietrich, Fritz) solo,pno,opt S rec
(easy) BAREN. 1303 $5.50 (W479)

WEIHNACHTSLIEDER ZUR GITARRE *CCU,Xmas
(Schwarz-Reiflingen, Erwin) solo,gtr
SIKORSKI 306 s.p. (W480)

WEIHNACHTSWEISE see Sibelius, Jean,
Jouluvirsi

WEIL WIR WISSEN, DASS DER MENSCH DURCH
DES GESETZES WERKE see Rosenmuller,
Johann

WEILAND, JOHANNES JULIUS
(? -ca. 1629)
Amor Jesu *sac,cant
(Langin, Folkmar) high solo,vln,
vcl,cont (med) BAREN. 4339 $3.50
(W481)

Jauchzet Gott, Alle Lande *sac,
Easter,concerto
(Saffe, Ferdinand) S solo,2vln,cont
BAREN. 6455 $5.00 (W482)

WEILL, KURT (1900-1950)
Alabama-Song (from Mahagonny)
solo,pno UNIVER. 8900 $2.75 (W483)

Alle Songs (from Dreigroschenoper)
CC17UL
solo,pno cmplt ed UNIVER. 13832
$6.75
see also: Ballade Vom Angenehmen
Leben (from Dreigroschenoper);
Barbara-Song (from
Dreigroschenoper); Kanonensong
(from Dreigroschenoper);
Liebeslied (from
Dreigroschenoper); Moritat Vom
Mackie Messer (from
Dreigroschenoper); Seerauber-
Jenny (from Dreigroschenoper)
(W484)

Ballade Vom Angenehmen Leben (from
Dreigroschenoper)
solo,pno UNIVER. 9595 $2.75 see
also Alle Songs (W485)

Barbara-Song (from Dreigroschenoper)
solo,pno UNIVER. 9594 $2.75 see
also Alle Songs (W486)

Bilbao-Song (from Happy End)
solo,pno UNIVER. 9892 $2.75 (W487)

Deutsches Lied
med solo,pno UNIVER. 5274 $2.75
(W488)

I Sette Peccati Capitali
[It] solo,pno CURCI 8978 s.p.
(W489)

Kanonensong (from Dreigroschenoper)
solo,pno UNIVER. 8847 $2.75 see
also Alle Songs (W490)

Liebeslied (from Dreigroschenoper)
solo,pno UNIVER. 9596 $2.75 see
also Alle Songs (W491)

Matrosen-Song (from Happy End)
solo,pno UNIVER. 9893 $2.75 (W492)

Moritat Vom Mackie Messer (from
Dreigroschenoper)
solo,pno UNIVER. 9772 $2.75 see
also Alle Songs (W493)

Seerauber-Jenny (from
Dreigroschenoper)
solo,pno UNIVER. 9652 $2.75 see
also Alle Songs (W494)

Surabaya-Jonny (from Happy End)
solo,pno UNIVER. 9862 $2.75 (W495)

WEIN, WEIB UND GESANG see Strauss,
Johann

WEINBERG, JACOB (1883-1956)
Beyn N'har P'rat
see Hebrew Songs, Vol. I

Chayaley Ha-Shalom
"Soldiers Of The Peace" [Heb/Eng]
med solo/low solo,pno (Yiddish
text also included) TRANSCON.
SP 19 $.60 (W496)

Chazak V'emats
see Hebrew Songs, Vol. I

Child's Prayer *sac
high solo,pno TRANSCON. TV 464 $.35
(W497)

El Yivne Ha-Galil
see Hebrew Songs, Vol. I

Haganah
"Song Of Liberation" [Heb/Eng] med
solo,pno (Also with Yiddish text)
TRANSCON. SP 16 $.50 (W498)

WEINBERG, JACOB (cont'd.)

Hebrew Songs, Vol. I
  [Heb] TRANSCON. SP 17 $1.25
    contains: Beyn N'har P'rat;
    Chazak V'emats; El Yivne Ha-
    Galil   (W499)

Hebrew Songs, Vol. II
  [Heb] med solo,pno TRANSCON. SP 18
  $1.25
    contains: Kacha-Kach; Koheleth;
    Yo Adir   (W500)

I Want To Capture
  med solo,pno TRANSCON. TV 466 $.40
                                   (W501)

Indian Summer Day
  high solo/med solo,pno TRANSCON.
  TV 465 $.50   (W502)

Kacha-Kach
  see Hebrew Songs, Vol. II

Koheleth
  see Hebrew Songs, Vol. II

Soldiers Of The Peace *see Chayaley
  Ha-Shalom

Song Of Liberation *see Haganah

Taps *sac
  high solo/med solo,org,opt trp
  TRANSCON. TV 465 $.50   (W503)

Yo Adir
  see Hebrew Songs, Vol. II

WEINBERG, M.
  Singing Baby To Sleep *song cycle
  [Russ] S solo,pno MEZ KNIGA 68 s.p.
                                   (W504)

WEINBERGER, JAROMIR (1896-1967)
  Way To Emmaus *sac,cant
  high solo,org BELWIN $2.00   (W505)

WEINER, LAZAR (1897-   )
  A Gebet
  see Six Yiddish Art Songs

A Maisele
  see Five Yiddish Songs

A Nigun
  "Tshiri-Bim-Bam-Bam" med solo/high
  solo,pno (Yiddish text) TRANSCON.
  WJ 410 $.60   (W506)

Avodim Hoyinu
  "We Were Slaves" med solo/low solo,
  pno (Yiddish text) TRANSCON.
  WJ 423 $.50   (W507)

Bendicho Su Nombre
  "B'rich Sh'meh" solo,pno/org
  TRANSCON. WJ 1409 $2.00   (W508)

B'rich Sh'meh *see Bendicho Su
  Nombre

Di Maise Mit Der Velt
  see Five Yiddish Songs

Di Sun
  see Six Yiddish Art Songs

Ergetz Vait
  see Five Yiddish Songs

Ezekiel
  [Eng] med solo,pno/org TRANSCON.
  TV 541 $1.00   (W509)

Five Jewish Art Songs *CC5U
  solo,pno PRESSER $2.50 Yiddish and
  English   (W510)

Five Yiddish Songs
  [Eng] TRANSCON. WJ 428 $2.25
  Yiddish text
    contains: A Maisele; Di Maise Mit
    Der Velt; Ergetz Vait; Shot'ns;
    Viglid   (W511)

In Feld
  see Six Yiddish Art Songs

Isaiah
  [Eng] med solo,pno TRANSCON. TV 542
  $1.00   (W512)

Mimaamakim
  "Out Of The Depths" [Eng] solo,pno/
  org TRANSCON. TV 543 $1.00   (W513)

Mizmor L'David (Psalm 29)
  solo,fl TRANSCON. WJ 1406 $2.00
                                   (W514)

Out Of The Depths *see Mimaamakim

Psalm 29 *see Mizmor L'David

Ruth
  [Eng] high solo,pno/org TRANSCON.
  TV 540 $1.00   (W515)

WEINER, LAZAR (cont'd.)

Sephardic Kiddush
  solo,fl TRANSCON. WJ 1407 $1.50
                                   (W516)

Seven Songs *CC7U
  solo,pno/org TRANSCON. WJ 1401
  $3.50 Yiddish text   (W517)

Shot'ns
  see Five Yiddish Songs

Shtile Licht
  see Six Yiddish Art Songs

Shtile Tener
  see Six Yiddish Art Songs

Six Yiddish Art Songs
  [Eng] TRANSCON. WJ 408 $2.25 also
  with Yiddish text
    contains: A Gebet; Di Sun; In
    Feld; Shtile Licht; Shtile
    Tener; Volt Majn Tate Rajch
    Geven   (W518)

Song Cycle *song cycle
  solo,pno/org (Yiddish text)
  TRANSCON. WJ 1405 $3.00   (W519)

Three Miniaturn *CC3U
  solo,pno/org TRANSCON. WJ 1403
  $2.00 Yiddish text   (W520)

Tshiri-Bim-Bam-Bam *see A Nigun

Two Humoreskes *CC2U
  solo,pno/org TRANSCON. WJ 1402
  $1.25 Yiddish text   (W521)

Viglid
  see Five Yiddish Songs

Volt Majn Tate Rajch Geven
  see Six Yiddish Art Songs

We Were Slaves *see Avodim Hoyinu

Yom Gila
  solo,pno/org TRANSCON. WJ 1408
  $1.50   (W522)

WEINER-SELA, YEHUDIT
  Present For Chanuka, A *CCU,Hanakkah
  solo,pno OR-TAV $1.00   (W523)

WEINGARTNER, (PAUL) FELIX (1863-1942)
  Abendsonne Am Meer *Op.76,No.3
  solo,2fl,2ob,2clar,2bsn,2horn,trp,
  strings BIRNBACH sc rental, voc
  sc s.p.   (W524)

An Den Schmerz *Op.77, CC4U
  high solo,2ob,2clar,2bsn,2horn,
  strings BIRNBACH sc rental, voc
  sc s.p.   (W525)

Der Traumgott *Op.17,No.2
  solo,2fl,2ob,2clar,2bsn,4horn,harp,
  strings BIRNBACH sc rental, voc
  sc s.p.   (W526)

Die Wallfahrt Nach Kevlaar *Op.12
  low solo,2fl,2ob,2clar,2bsn,4horn,
  2trp,3trom,tuba,timp,harp,strings
  BIRNBACH sc rental, voc sc s.p.
                                   (W527)

Liebe Im Schnee *Op.17,No.3
  solo,2fl,2ob,2clar,2bsn,4horn,trp,
  3trom,tuba,timp,harp,strings
  BIRNBACH sc rental, voc sc s.p.
                                   (W528)

Liebesfeier *Op.16,No.2
  med solo,2fl,2ob,2clar,2bsn,4horn,
  2trp,3trom,timp,harp,strings
  BIRNBACH sc rental, voc sc s.p.
                                   (W529)

Rubezahl *Op.17,No.1
  solo,2fl,2ob,2clar,2bsn,4horn,2trp,
  timp,harp,strings BIRNBACH sc
  rental, voc sc s.p.   (W530)

Schafers Sonntagslied *Op.15,No.1
  high solo,2fl,2ob,2clar,2bsn,4horn,
  2trp,harp,strings BIRNBACH sc
  rental, voc sc s.p.   (W531)

WEISGALL, HUGO (1912-   )
  Four Songs *Op.1,No.1-4, CC4U
  PRESSER med solo,pno $.75; high
  solo,pno $.75   (W532)

Garden Eastward *cant
  high solo,orch voc sc PRESSER
  $3.00, ipr   (W533)

No More I Will Thy Love Importune
  high solo,pno PRESSER $.75 see from
    Two Madrigals   (W534)
  low solo,pno PRESSER $.75 see from
    Two Madrigals   (W535)

Nuptial Song
  high solo,pno PRESSER $.95 see from
    Two Madrigals   (W536)

WEISGALL, HUGO (cont'd.)

Soldier Songs *CCU
  Bar solo,pno MERCURY $3.00   (W537)

Two Madrigals *see No More I Will
  Thy Love Importune; Nuptial Song
                                   (W538)

WEISHAPPEL, RUDOLF (1921-   )
  Von Der Ungeordneten Verlassenschaft
  *cant
  SBar soli,inst sc DOBLINGER 08 814
  s.p., ipr   (W539)

WEISMANN, JULIUS (1879-1950)
  Flieg Dahin *Op.112,No.3
  see Verklarte Liebe

Geweihte Nacht *Op.112,No.5
  see Verklarte Liebe

Orpheus *Op.112,No.1
  see Verklarte Liebe

Traumverkundung *Op.112,No.4
  see Verklarte Liebe

Verklarte Liebe
  high solo,strings BIRNBACH sc
  rental, voc sc s.p.
    contains: Flieg Dahin, Op.112,
    No.3; Geweihte Nacht, Op.112,
    No.5; Orpheus, Op.112,No.1;
    Traumverkundung, Op.112,No.4;
    Zauberische Entfremdung,
    Op.112,No.2   (W540)

Vierzehn Lieder, Heft I *Op.129,
  No.1-7, CC7L
  solo,pno BIRNBACH sc rental, voc sc
  s.p.   (W541)

Vierzehn Lieder, Heft II *Op.129,
  No.8-14, CC7L
  solo,pno voc sc BIRNBACH s.p.
                                   (W542)

Zauberische Entfremdung *Op.112,No.2
  see Verklarte Liebe

WEISMANN, WILHELM (1900-   )
  Acht Gesange *CC8U
  high solo,pno PETERS 5469 $5.50
                                   (W543)

Buch Der Liebe *CC11U
  med solo,pno PETERS 5414 s.p.
                                   (W544)

Das Ferne Lied *CC6U
  solo,pno PETERS 5367 s.p.   (W545)

Drei Gesange Nach Gedichten Von
  Holderlin *CC3U
  Bar solo,pno PETERS 5283 s.p.
                                   (W546)

Es Geht Jetzt Um Die Vesperzeit *sac
  high solo,2S rec,org HANSSLER 5.062
  s.p. see also GESANGE ZUM
  KIRCHENJAHR   (W547)

Hymne An Die Gottin Eos *concerto
  SA soli,pno PETERS 9110 s.p.   (W548)

Sechs Lieder *CC6U
  s.p. high solo,pno PETERS 5021; low
  solo,pno PETERS 9648   (W549)

Zwolf Lieder Und Ballanden Aus "Das
  Knaben Wunderhorn" *CC12U
  med solo,pno PETERS 5250 s.p.
                                   (W550)

WEISS WIE LILIEN see Valen, Fartein

WEISSE AKAZIEN *folk,Russ
  [Ger/Russ] solo,pno ZIMMER. 1535 s.p.
                                   (W551)

WEISSE ORCHIDEEN see Glombig, E.

WEISSE STADTE see Kilpinen, Yrio,
  Valkeat Kaupungit

WEISSE WICKEN IN DER VASE see Apostel,
  Hans Erich

WEISSER JASMIN see Strauss, Richard

WEISSES HAAR IM SPIEGEL see Kox, Hans

WEISST DU, GELIEBTER, ALLABENDLICH see
  Bijvanck, Henk

WEIT HINTER RIO see Girnatis, Walter

WEKERLIN, JEAN BAPTISTE (1821-1910)
  Chanson Du Papillon De Campra
  solo,orch DURAND s.p., ipa   (W552)

Vous Souvient-Il? (Andante Et
  Variations D'une Sonate De
  Mozart)
  solo,pno/inst DURAND s.p.   (W553)

WELCHE DICH SUCHEN see Schoenberg,
  Arnold

WELCKER, MAX
Trauungslied *Op.92,No.10, sac
SBarT soli,org sc BOHM s.p. (W554)

Zur Ersten Heilige Kommunion *Op.92,
No.4, sac
solo,org/harmonium sc BOHM s.p.
(W555)

WELCOME DEATH see Stanley, John

WELCOME HOLY FATHER see Tesoriero,
Gaetano

WELCOME HOME see Diffenderfer

WELCOME HOME, CHILDREN see King

WELKE BLUMEN see Scholz, Erwin
Christian

WELKOM see Loots, Ph.

WELL, THE see B'er Ba-Sadeh

WE'LL CAST OUR CROWNS AT HIS FEET see
Jensen, Gordon

WELL DO YOU KNOW see Mascagni, Pietro,
Voi Lo Sapete

WELL DONE THOU GOOD AND FAITHFUL
SERVANT see Fox, Baynard

WE'LL TALK IT OVER *sac,gospel
solo,pno ABER.GRP. $1.50 (W556)

WE'LL TALK IT OVER see Stanphill, Ira
F.

WE'LL TO THE WOODS NO MORE see Ireland,
John

WELLENFLUSTERN see Sibelius, Jean

WELLESLEY, GRANT
Sing Me A Chantey With A Yo-Heave-Ho
(O'Keefe) Bar solo,pno FOX,S (W557)
(O'Keefe) B solo,pno FOX,S (W558)
(O'Keefe) Bar/B solo,pno FOX,S
(W559)

WELLESZ, EGON (1885-1974)
Lieder Aus Der Fremde *Op.15, CCU
med-high solo,pno DOBLINGER 08 642
$1.50 (W560)

Lieder Aus Wien *Op.82,No.1-5, CC5U
Bar/A solo,chamb.orch/pno DOBLINGER
08 645 $2.00 (W561)

Lieder Nach Dichtungen Von St. George
*Op.22, CCU
solo,pno DOBLINGER 08 643 s.p.
(W562)

On Time *Op.63,No.1-3, CC3U
Bar solo,pno DOBLINGER 08 644 $2.50
(W563)

WELLINGS, M.
C'est Un Reve
solo,acap (available in 2 keys)
ENOCH s.p. (W564)
solo,pno (available in 2 keys)
ENOCH s.p. (W565)

Conseils D'une Grand'Mere
solo,pno ENOCH s.p. (W566)

Le Passeur
solo,pno (available in 2 keys)
ENOCH s.p. (W567)
solo,acap (available in 2 keys)
ENOCH s.p. (W568)

Les Noces D'Or
solo,pno (available in 2 keys)
ENOCH s.p. (W569)
solo,acap (available in 2 keys)
ENOCH s.p. (W570)

Ombre Et Lumiere
solo,pno (available in 2 keys)
ENOCH s.p. (W571)

Pardonne, Oublie
solo,acap (available in 2 keys)
ENOCH s.p. (W572)
solo,pno (available in 2 keys)
ENOCH s.p. (W573)

Un Jour
solo,acap (available in 2 keys)
ENOCH s.p. (W574)
solo,pno (available in 2 keys)
ENOCH s.p. (W575)

WELLS, DANA F.
Three Sacred Solos For Medium Voice
*sac,CC3U,Xmas/Gen/Lent
med solo,pno ABINGDON APM-325 $1.00
(W576)

WELLS, HOWARD
Everyone Sang
med solo,pno (D maj) SCHIRM.G $.75
(W577)

I Know He's Mine *sac
solo,pno WORD S-21 (W578)

WELT, DU KANNST MIR NICHT GEFALLEN see
Lortzing, (Gustav) Albert

WELTER, FRIEDRICH
O Leben, Leben *Op.27,No.1-4, CC4U
A/Bar solo,pno RIES s.p. (W579)

WEN-CHUNG, CHOU
see CHOU, WEN-CHUNG

WEN COLUMBUS GEFINT NIT DUS LAND *Jew
solo,pno KAMMEN 67 $1.00 (W580)

WEN ES FEHLT UNS A MAME'S GEBET see
Meyerowitz, David

WEN TATE-MAME FEHLT *Jew
solo,pno KAMMEN 100 $1.00 (W581)

WENDISCHES MARIENLIED see Holler, Karl

WENIGE WISSEN see Diepenbrock, Alphons

WENN see Strauss, Richard

WENN ABER see Dohl, Friedhelm

WENN DAS VOLLKOMMENE KOMMT see Blarr,
Oskar Gottlieb

WENN DER REGEN FALLT
see Internationale Volklieder, Nol. 3

WENN DES KREUZES BITTERKEITEN MIT DES
FLEISCHES SCHWACHHEIT STREITEN see
Bach, Johann Sebastian

WENN DIE BAUME AM SCHONSTEN BLUHTEN see
Marsik, Emanuel, Kdyz Kvetly Stromy
Nejkrasneji

WENN DIE SANFTEN ABENDWINDE see Mozart,
Wolfgang Amadeus

WENN DU FEIN FROMM BIST see Mozart,
Wolfgang Amadeus

WENN DU ZU DEN BLUMEN GEHST see Wolf,
Hugo

WENN ICH see Kilpinen, Yrio, Voi, Jos
Mie Tok' Miehen Saisin

WENN ICH ABSCHIED NEHME see Schafer,
Dirk

WENN ICH DICH FRAG' see Schmalstich,
Clemens

WENN ICH FURST, WIE IGOR (from Prince
Igor)
[Russ/Fr/Ger] B solo,pno BELAIEFF 251
s.p. (W582)

WENN ICH IHN NUR HABE see Diepenbrock,
Alphons

WENN ICH IN DEINE AUGEN SEH see
Schumann, Robert (Alexander)

WENN ICH MACHT UND GELDE HATTE see
Kilpinen, Yrio, Oisi Mulla Vallan
Miekka

WENN ICH MEIN HUHNCHEN LOCKE see Haas,
Joseph

WENN ICH MIT MENSCHEN-UND MIT
ENGELSZUNGEN see Brahms, Johannes

WENN ICH MIT MENSCHEN- UND MIT
ENGELSZUNGEN REDETE see Micheelsen,
Hans-Friedrich

WENN ICH MIT MENSCHEN- UND MIT
ENGELSZUNGEN REDETE see Roessel,
Louis

WENN ICH MIT MENSCHEN- UND MIT
ENGELZUNGEN REDETE see Brahms,
Johannes

WENN ICH, O KINDLEIN see Hessenberg,
Kurt

WENN ICH TRAUME see Sibelius, Jean, Nar
Jag Drommer

WENN ICH WIEDER KOMM see Schroeder, F.

WENN IHNEN ZWEI BEGEGNEN see Seidel,
Jan, Kdyz Se Dva Setkaji

WENN MEIN LIED ICH BEGINNE see
Kilpinen, Yrio, Jos Ma Laululle
Rupean

WENN NACH DER STURME TOBEN see Bach,
Johann Christian

WENN NACHTS DIE BRUNNEN RAUSCHEN see
Niel, Matty

WENN SANFT DU MIR see Bijvanck, Henk

WENN SEGELND AUF DEN WOGEN see Handel,
George Frideric

WENN SORGEN AUF MICH DRINGEN see Bach,
Johann Sebastian

WENN VOGLEIN KLAGEN see Schoenberg,
Arnold

WENN WEISSE FLOCKEN WALD UND FELD
VERSCHONEN see Jochum, Otto

WENNERBERG, GUNNAR (1817-1901)
En Vintervisa
solo,pno LUNDQUIST s.p. (W583)

Herre Nu Later Du Din Tjanare Fara I
Frid (from Jesu Fodelse) sac
B solo,pno GEHRMANS s.p. (W584)

I Tyst Konvaljeskog
solo,pno LUNDQUIST s.p. see from
Tva Sanger (W585)

Min Ros
solo,pno LUNDQUIST s.p. (W586)

Sommarmorgon
solo,pno LUNDQUIST s.p. see from
Tva Sanger (W587)

Tre Trallande Jantor *CC3U
solo,pno LUNDQUIST s.p. (W588)

Tva Sanger *see I Tyst Konvaljeskog;
Sommarmorgon (W589)

Tvenne Sanger *CC2U
solo,pno LUNDQUIST s.p. (W590)

Varde Ljus!
high solo,pno LUNDQUIST s.p. (W591)
low solo,pno LUNDQUIST s.p. (W592)

WENNERBURG, [GUNNAR]
Avsked
high solo,pno GEHRMANS s.p. (W593)

Davids Psalmer I-II
solo,pno GEHRMANS s.p., ea. (W594)

Gluntarne *CCU
BarB soli,pno GEHRMANS s.p. (W595)

Jatten
B solo,pno GEHRMANS s.p. see from
SANGEN II (W596)
solo,pno GEHRMANS 783 s.p. (W597)

Musikdel *CCU
2 soli,pno GEHRMANS s.p. (W598)

Trasten I Hostkvallen
solo,pno GEHRMANS s.p. (W599)

WENZEL, EBERHARD (1896-)
Jesus Christus, Konig Und Herr *sac
SA soli,2S rec,cont HANSSLER 5.054
s.p. see also GESANGE ZUM
KIRCHENJAHR (W600)

Nun Ist Der Himmel Aufgetan *sac
SA soli,2S rec,cont HANSSLER 5.053
s.p. see also GESANGE ZUM
KIRCHENJAHR (W601)

WENZEL, L. DE
Viens Dans Les Bois
solo,pno ENOCH s.p. (W602)

WER EINMAL VOM DAMON DER LIEBE
VERWUNDET see Handel, George
Frideric

WER FAND IN DIESEM WALDE SO LIEBLICHE
BEUTE see Handel, George Frideric

WER GOTT DAS HERZE GIBET see Jansen, F.
Gustav

WER HAT DAS ERSTE LIED ERDACHT? see
Busoni, Ferruccio Benvenuto

WER HAT DICH HERGEFUHRT *Op.90,No.6
[Swed/Ger] solo,pno BREITKOPF-W
DLV 5636 s.p. see from Sechs Lieder
Nach Texten Von J.L. Runeberg
(W603)

WER HAT DICH HERGEFUHRT? see Hvem
Styrde Hit Din Vag?

WER HAT DICH HERGEFUHRT see Sibelius,
Jean, Vem Styrde Hit Din Vag?

WER HAT DIES LIEDLEIN ERDACHT? see
Mahler, Gustav

WER HOT ASA MEIDELE *Jew
solo,pno KAMMEN 415 $1.00 (W604)

WER IST'S, VON DEM DER RUF ERTONT? see
Saint-Saens, Camille, Qui Donc
Eleve Ici La Voix

WER KENNT DES MENSCHEN HERZ see Handel,
George Frideric

WER LIEBEN WILL, MUSS LEIDEN see
Strauss, Richard

WER NICHT DEM BUGERSTANDE see Haibel,
Jakob J.

WER SEIN HOLDES LIEB VERLOREN see Wolf,
Hugo

WER UNTER DEM SCHIRM DES HOCHSTEN see
Zentner, Johannes

WER UNTER DEM SCHIRM DES HOCHSTEN IST
see Schlenker, Manfred

WER WILL UNS SCHEIDEN see Schutz,
Heinrich

WER WILL UNS SCHEIDEN VON DER LIEBE
GOTTES? see Schutz, Heinrich

WER WILL, WER MAG? *CC27U
    (Poschl; Winkler; Moissl) [Ger] med
    solo,pno/gtr OSTER $1.00   (W605)

WERBA, E.
  Hochzeits-Spruch
    [Ger] med solo,pno OSTER $.50
                                 (W606)

WE'RE ALL GOD'S CHILDREN see Fulmore

WERE I A KING see Thomas, Arthur
Goring, Si J'Etais Roi

WERE MY SONG WITH WINGS PROVIDED see
Hahn, Reynaldo, Si Mes Vers Avaient
Des Ailes

WE'RE NOT HOME YET, CHILDREN see
Bradford

WERE YOU THERE *sac,spir
    solo,pno (available in 3 keys) ASHLEY
    $.95   (W607)
    (Burleigh, H. T.) high solo,pno
    BELWIN $1.50   (W608)
    (Burleigh, H. T.) med solo,pno BELWIN
    $1.50   (W609)
    (Burleigh, H. T.) low solo,pno BELWIN
    $1.50   (W610)
    (Roberton, Hugh S.) 3 soli,pno
    ROBERTON 72114 s.p.   (W611)
    (Washington, B.T.) med solo,pno
    PRESSER $.75   (W612)

WERE YOUR THERE *sac,gospel
    solo,pno ABER.GRP. $1.50   (W613)

WERKELIJKHEID see Andriessen, K.

WERLE, LARS-JOHAN (1926-   )
  Now All The Fingers Of This Tree
    Mez solo,fl,pno,perc,bvl NORDISKA
    10233 s.p.   (W614)

WERNER, E.
  Rabbi Akiba *sac,Jew
    1-2 soli,org/pno SAC.MUS.PR. (W615)

  Rabbi Shimon *sac,Jew
    1-2 soli,org/pno SAC.MUS.PR. (W616)

  Rabbi Tarphon *sac,Jew
    1-2 soli,org/pno SAC.MUS.PR. (W617)

WERNER, GREGOR JOSEPH (1695-1766)
  Salve, Regina *sac,cant
    (Ewerhart, Rudolf) [Lat] B solo,
    2vln,cont sc BIELER DK 8 s.p.,
    ipa   (W618)

WERNER, JEAN-JACQUES (1935-   )
  L'Oiseau Inaugural *cant
    S/T solo,chamb.orch voc sc TRANSAT.
    s.p.   (W619)

  Notes Prises A New York *CCU
    solo,pno TRANSAT. s.p.   (W620)

WERNLUND
  Sveriges Farger
    solo,pno LUNDQUIST s.p.   (W621)

WERT THOU A SLAVE see Kilner, Helen

WERT THOU BUT NEAR see Bach, Johann
Sebastian, Bist Du Bei Mir

WERTHEIM, R.
  Kerstliedje *sac,CCU
    solo,pno BROEKMANS 72 s.p.   (W622)

  Twee Liederen *CC2U
    solo,pno BROEKMANS 188 s.p. (W623)

WERTHER, R.T.
  Music
    [Eng] solo,pno HINRICHSEN H852A
    s.p.   (W624)

WERTHER, RUDOLF
  I Wandered Lonely
    solo,pno ALBERT AE275 s.p.   (W625)

  Serenade
    solo,pno ALBERT AE278 s.p.   (W626)

WESLEY
  Lead Me, Lord *sac
    (Hamlin) med solo,pno (E flat maj)
    BOSTON $1.50   (W627)

  Thou Wilt Keep Him *sac
    (Hamlin) low solo,pno (A maj)
    BOSTON $1.50   (W628)
    (Hamlin) med-high solo,pno (F maj)
    BOSTON $1.50   (W629)

WEST-AWAY see Arundale, Claude

WEST, MONICA
  Little Shepherdess
    high solo,pno (E flat maj) LEONARD-
    ENG   (W630)
    low solo,pno (D maj) LEONARD-ENG
                                 (W631)

  Song Of Joy
    med solo,pno (E flat maj) CRAMER
                                 (W632)
    low solo,pno (A maj) CRAMER (W633)
    high solo,pno (G maj) CRAMER (W634)

  There's A Bonnie House In Ayr
    high solo,pno (F maj) CRAMER (W635)
    med solo,pno (E flat maj) CRAMER
                                 (W636)
    low solo,pno (D maj) CRAMER (W637)

  Wedding Gown, The
    high solo,pno (A flat maj) LEONARD-
    ENG   (W638)
    low solo,pno (G maj) LEONARD-ENG
                                 (W639)

WEST SUSSEX DRINKING SONG see Gow,
David

WEST WIND see Loam, Arthur S.

WEST WIND, THE see Mitchell, Raymond
[Earle]

WESTENDORF
  I'll Take You Home Again Kathleen
    med solo,pno PAXTON P2281 s.p.
                                 (W640)

WESTERGAARD, PETER (1931-   )
  Cantata III *cant
    Mez solo,4inst ARS VIVA s.p. (W641)

WESTERGAARD, RICHARD
  Min Gud Og Min Frelser *Op.19, sac
    solo,pno MUSIKK s.p.   (W642)

WESTERING HOME *folk,Scot
    (Roberton, Hugh S.) solo,pno (A maj)
    ROBERTON 2775 s.p. see also Songs
    Of The Isles   (W643)
    (Roberton, Hugh S.) soli,pno/orch
    ROBERTON 72384 s.p.   (W644)

WESTERING, P. CHR. V.
  Messe De Berceuse *sac,Mass
    S solo,org ALSBACH s.p.   (W645)

WESTERMAN, G. VON
  Drei Lieder *Op.20, CC3U
    [Ger] low solo,4strings/orch BOTE
    $3.00   (W646)

  Landliche Weisen *Op.22, CC4U
    [Ger] med solo,pno BOTE $2.75
                                 (W647)

  Sechs Gesange *Op.13, CC6U
    (Dehmel) [Ger] med-low solo,pno
    BOTE $1.50   (W648)

  Sechs Stimmungsbilder *Op.5, CC6U
    [Ger] med solo,pno BOTE $2.25
                                 (W649)

  Vier Lieder *Op.21, CC4U
    [Ger] high solo,pno BOTE $3.25
                                 (W650)

  Zwei Kaschubische Weihnachtslieder
    *Op.19, CC2U
    [Ger] low solo,pno,orch BOTE $3.00
                                 (W651)

WESTERN PRAISES *sac,CC16UL
    solo,pno,gtr,acord LILLENAS MB-227
    $1.95   (W652)

WESTFALISCHE LIEDER UND TANZE see
Rosenstengel, Albrecht

WESTOVER
  No Greater Love *sac
    solo,pno LILLENAS SM-929: SN $1.00
                                 (W653)

WESTWARD ON THE HIGH-HILLED PLAINS see
Orr, Charles Wilfred

WETHERINGTON
  At The Roll Call *sac
    solo,pno LILLENAS SM-903: SN $1.00
                                 (W654)

WETHERINGTON (cont'd.)

  Better Day, A *sac
    solo,pno LILLENAS SM-901: SN $1.00
                                 (W655)

  Greater Love Hath No Man *sac
    solo,pno LILLENAS SM-907: SN $1.00
                                 (W656)

  He Will Never Let Me Down *sac
    solo,pno LILLENAS SM-910: SN $1.00
                                 (W657)

  I'll Never Be Lonely In Heaven *sac
    solo,pno LILLENAS SM-914: SN $1.00
                                 (W658)

  I'm Going There *sac
    solo,pno LILLENAS SM-916: SN $1.00
                                 (W659)

  Is Your Name Written There? *sac
    solo,pno LILLENAS SM-921: SN $1.00
                                 (W660)

  Little Boy Lost *sac
    solo,pno LILLENAS SM-925: SN $1.00
                                 (W661)

  Lord Accepted Me, The *sac
    solo,pno LILLENAS SM-938: SN $1.00
                                 (W662)

  Lord, I Want To Go Home *sac
    solo,pno LILLENAS SM-926: SN $1.00
                                 (W663)

  Lord, I Want To Go To Heaven *sac
    solo,pno LILLENAS SM-927: SN $1.00
                                 (W664)

  Our Debts Will Be Paid *sac
    solo,pno LILLENAS SM-931: SN $1.00
                                 (W665)

  Samson *sac
    solo,pno LILLENAS SM-933: SN $1.00
                                 (W666)

  Tenderly *sac
    solo,pno LILLENAS SM-936: SN $1.00
                                 (W667)

  This Was Almost Mine *sac
    solo,pno LILLENAS SM-941: SN $1.00
                                 (W668)

  Till I Know *sac
    solo,pno LILLENAS SM-942: SN $1.00
                                 (W669)

WETZEL, JUSTUS HERMANN (1879-   )
  Im Stillen Reich *CC7U
    solo,pno RIES s.p.   (W670)

  Zweiter Liederkreis *Op.11, song
    cycle
    solo,pno RIES s.p.   (W671)

WETZLER, ROBERT PAUL (1932-   )
  God, Hurrah! *sac,song cycle
    Mez solo,English horn,vcl,pno sc
    AMSI $6.50   (W672)

  Good Tidings *sac
    med solo,pno AUGSBURG 11-0740 $2.00
                                 (W673)

  Holy Jesus, Send Your Blessing
    see FIVE WEDDING SONGS

  Psalm 128 *sac
    med solo,pno AUGSBURG 11-0714 $.75
                                 (W674)

WE'VE COME THIS FAR BY FAITH see
Goodson

WEYLAS SANG see Wolf, Hugo

WEYRAUCH, JOHANNES (1897-   )
  Alleluja, Lobet Den Herrn *sac
    med solo,org HANSSLER 5.159 s.p.
                                 (W675)

  Die Herrlichkeit Auf Erden *sac,
    concerto
    S/A solo,org HANSSLER 5.082 s.p.
                                 (W676)

  Kyrie, Gott Vater In Ewigkeit *sac
    med solo,org HANSSLER 5.161 s.p.
                                 (W677)

  Meine Seele Erhebt Den Herrn *sac
    med solo,org HANSSLER 5.081 s.p.
                                 (W678)

  Zeit Ist Wie Ewigkeit *sac
    SA soli,2S rec,cont HANSSLER 5.044
    s.p. see also GESANGE ZUM
    KIRCHENJAHR   (W679)

WHALIN' UP THE LACHLAN see Dawson

WHA'LL BE KING BUT CHARLIE? *folk,Scot
    solo,pno (G maj) PATERSON FS93 s.p.
                                 (W680)

WHAT A BEAUTIFUL DAY FOR THE LORD TO
    COME *sac
    solo,pno BENSON S8359-S $1.00 (W681)

WHAT A DAY THAT WILL BE see Hill

WHAT A DIFFERENCE JESUS MAKES see
Smith, C. Stephen

WHAT A FRIEND WE HAVE IN JESUS *sac,
    gospel
    solo,pno ABER.GRP. $1.50   (W682)

WHAT A FRIEND WE HAVE IN JESUS see
Converse

WHAT A MORNING THAT WILL BE see Smith,
C. Stephen

WHAT A WONDERFUL TIME UP THERE see
Thornehill, Bruce

WHAT ARE THE WILD WAVES SAYING? see
Glover, Stephen

WHAT ARE WORDS see Panetti, Joan

WHAT BLUE EYES ADORN THIS MAIDEN see
Salas, Juan Orrego, Ojos Garcos Ha
La Nina

WHAT CAN WE POOR FEMALES DO? see
Purcell, Henry

WHAT CHILD IS THIS see Greensleeves

WHAT CHRISTMAS MEANS TO ME see Head,
Michael (Dewar)

WHAT DOTH THE LORD REQUIRE OF THEE see
Hart

WHAT GOD ORDAINS IS ALWAYS GOOD see
Pachelbel, Johann

WHAT GOD'S ALMIGHTY POWER HATH MADE see
Bach, Johann Sebastian

WHAT GRANDMA KNEW see Rovics, Howard

WHAT I HAVE see Bohm, Carl, Was I Hab'

WHAT I WANT YOU TO BE see Brown, Aaron

WHAT IS A KISS? see Mana-Zucca, Mme.,
Was Ist Ein Kuss

WHAT IS IN YOUR EYES? see Chalk, C.

WHAT KIND OF MAN IS THIS *sac,gospel
solo,pno ABER.GRP. $1.50   (W683)

WHAT LIPS HAVE KISSED see Alette, C.

WHAT LIPS MY LIPS HAVE KISSED see Fink,
Michael

WHAT LOVE see Fox

WHAT LOVE! see Rushford

WHAT MAKES THE WIND BLOW see Young,
Carlton R.

WHAT MEANS THIS LONELY TEAR? see
Schumann, Robert (Alexander), Was
Will Die Einsame Thrane

WHAT MENYS THYS see Hoag, Charles K.

WHAT OF THY FLOCKS O SHEPHERD! see
Geehl, Henry Ernest

WHAT SHALL HE HAVE THAT KILLED THE
DEER? see Castelnuovo-Tedesco,
Mario

WHAT SHALL HE HAVE THAT KILLED THE
DEER? see Hilton

WHAT SHALL I ASK see Kountz, Richard

WHAT SHALL I DO TO SHOW HOW MUCH I LOVE
HER see Purcell, Henry

WHAT SONGS WERE SUNG see Niles, John
Jacob

WHAT STAR IS THIS? see Greensleeves

WHAT STAR IS THIS? see Ridout, Godfrey

WHAT SWEETER MUSIC see Bennett, Richard
Rodney

WHAT SWEETER MUSICK see Binkerd, Gordon

WHAT THING IS LOVE see Bush, Geoffrey

WHAT THOUGH I TRACE EACH HERB A FLOWER
see Handel, George Frideric

WHAT WERE THEY LIKE? see Heilner, Irwin

WHAT WOULD I DO WITHOUT JESUS see
Harper

WHAT YA GONNA DO see Crouch, Andrae

WHAT YOU ARE see Fischer, Irwin

WHAT'S IN THE AIR TODAY see Eden,
Robert

WHAT'S IN YOUR MIND see Berkeley,
Lennox

WHAT'S NEXT? see Matsudaira, Yori Akki

WHAT'S SWEETER THAN A NEW BLOWN ROSE
see Handel, George Frideric

WHAT'S THE TIME, BLACKBIRD see Oliver

WHEAR, PAUL WILLIAM (1925-   )
From Thoreau
S solo,vln MEDIA 3107 $4.00 (W684)

Renaissance Suite *CCU
S solo,2fl,2ob,2clar,2bsn,4horn,
2trp,3trom,perc,strings LUDWIG
rental   (W685)

Sonnets From Shakespeare *CCU
Bar solo,chamb.orch LUDWIG rental
(W686)

WHEELER
Following Suit *sec
med solo,pno (E flat maj) WATERLOO
$.75   (W687)

Love Triumphant *sac
low solo,pno (C maj) ALLANS s.p.
(W688)
high solo,pno (D maj) ALLANS s.p.
(W689)
med solo,pno (B flat maj) ALLANS
s.p.   (W690)

Time, You Old Gipsy Man
solo,pno ALLANS s.p.   (W691)

WHEELER, ALFRED
Be Thou My Guide *sac
low solo,pno (D flat maj) ALLANS
s.p.   (W692)
high solo,pno (F maj) ALLANS s.p.
(W693)

WHEELER, J.R.
Drake's Drum
solo,pno (F maj) LEONARD-ENG (W694)

WHEN? see Glantz, Yehuda Leib, Matai

WHEN A MAID COMES KNOCKING AT YOUR
HEART see Friml, Rudolf

WHEN A MAIDEN TAKES YOUR FANCY see
Mozart, Wolfgang Amadeus

WHEN ADAM WAS CREATED see Bock, Fred

WHEN ALL THE WORLD WAS GAY see Porter-
Brown, R.

WHEN ANY MORTAL see Clarke, Henry
Leland

WHEN AT MORN see Schumann, Robert
(Alexander), Volksliedchen

WHEN BRIGHT EYES GLANCE see Hedgecock,
Walter William

WHEN CELIA SINGS see Moir, F.L.

WHEN CHILDREN PRAY see Fenner

WHEN CHRIST WAS BORN see Badings, Henk

WHEN DAFFODILS BEGIN TO PEER see Bush,
Geoffrey

WHEN DAFFODILS BEGIN TO PEER see
Castelnuovo-Tedesco, Mario

WHEN DAFFODILS UNFOLD see Dick, Edith

WHEN DAISIES PIED see Arne, Thomas
Augustine

WHEN DAISIES PIED see Castelnuovo-
Tedesco, Mario

WHEN DAISIES PIED see Moeran, Ernest J.

WHEN DE STARS BEGIN TO FALL *spir
(Roberton, Hugh S.) 3 soli,pno
ROBERTON 72107 s.p.   (W695)

WHEN DULL CARE
(Wilson, H.L.) solo,pno (F maj)
BOOSEY $1.50   (W696)

WHEN-E'ER SHE BADE ME CEASE TO PLEAD
see Attwood, Thomas

WHEN FRIENDLY DEATH SHALL GRASP MY HAND
see Franco, Johan

WHEN FROM THE LIPS OF TRUTH see
Fischer, Irwin

WHEN GOD DIPS HIS LOVE IN MY HEART
*sac,gospel
solo,pno ABER.GRP. $1.50   (W697)

WHEN GOD SHALL WIPE ALL MY TEARS AWAY
*sac,gospel
solo,pno ABER.GRP. $1.50   (W698)

WHEN GOD STEPS IN see Fox, Baynard

WHEN GREEN LEAVES COME AGAIN see
Bishop, Sir Henry Rowley

WHEN HEAVEN'S GATES ARE OPEN WIDE see
Croft, Colbert

WHEN I AM DEAD MY DEAREST see
Somervell, Arthur

WHEN I AM LAID IN EARTH see Purcell,
Henry

WHEN I BEHOLD see Dyson, George

WHEN I BRING TO YOU COLOUR'D TOYS see
Carpenter, John Alden

WHEN I COME TO THE END see Lister,
Hovie

WHEN I CONSIDER THE HEAVENS see Scott,
John Prindle

WHEN I FIRST SAW YOU see Guarnieri,
Camargo Mozart

WHEN I GET HOME see Younce, George

WHEN I HAVE FEARS see Hogenhaven, Knud

WHEN I HAVE SUNG MY SONGS see Charles,
Ernest

WHEN I HEARD THE LEARNED ASTRONOMER see
Bairstow, Edward Cuthbert

WHEN I KNEEL DOWN TO PRAY see Ackley,
Bentley D.

WHEN I LOOKED UP AND HE LOOKED DOWN
*sac,gospel
solo,pno ABER.GRP. $1.50   (W699)

WHEN I NEED HIM see Smith

WHEN I SAY JESUS see Johnson, P.

WHEN I SET OUT FOR LYONNESSE see
Heilner, Irwin

WHEN I SET OUT FOR LYONNESSE see
Waters, Leslie

WHEN I SING YOUR SONGS see Dungan,
Olive

WHEN I STEP OFF ON THAT BEAUTIFUL SHORE
see Lambert

WHEN I SURVEY see Goode, George

WHEN I SURVEY THE WONDROUS CROSS see
O'Neill, Charles

WHEN I THINK OF THE CROSS *sac
(Carmichael, Ralph) solo,pno WORD
S-251   (W700)

WHEN I THINK UPON THE MAIDENS see Head,
Michael (Dewar)

WHEN I TOUCHED THE HEM OF HIS GARMENT
*sac,gospel
solo,pno ABER.GRP. $1.50   (W701)

WHEN I WAIT BEFORE HIS THRONE see Davis

WHEN I WAKE UP TO SLEEP NO MORE *sac
solo,pno STAMPS 7237 $1.00   (W702)

WHEN I WAKE UP TO SLEEP NO MORE see
Easterling, Marion W.

WHEN I WALK THROUGH THE VALLEY see
Wilson, Al

WHEN I WAS BORN see Franco, Johan

WHEN I WAS ONE-AND TWENTY see Baksa,
Robert

WHEN I WAS ONE AND TWENTY see Duke,
John Woods

WHEN I WAS ONE-AND-TWENTY see Freed,
Isadore

WHEN I WAS ONE-AND-TWENTY see Gibbs,
Cecil Armstrong

WHEN I WAS ONE AND TWENTY see Orr,
Charles Wilfred

WHEN I WAS ONE AND TWENTY see Peter

WHEN I WAS SEVENTEEN see Kramer, A.
Walter

WHEN I WATCH THE LIVING see Dukelsky,
Vladimir

WHEN I WENT OUT IN THE SPRING MEADOWS
see Sydeman, William

WHEN ICICLES HANG BY THE WALL see
Castelnuovo-Tedesco, Mario

WHEN ICICLES HANG BY THE WALL see Keel,
  Frederick

WHEN ICICLES HANG BY THE WALL see
  Moeran, Ernest J.

WHEN ICICLES HANG BY THE WALL see
  Montgomery, Bruce

WHEN I'M GONE see Horne, Roger

WHEN IN DISGRACE WITH FORTUNE AND MEN'S
  EYES see Hovhaness, Alan

WHEN IN MY HEART see Dungan, Olive

WHEN IN THE CRONICLE see Hogenhaven,
  Knud

WHEN IN THE EARLY MORN see Gounod,
  Charles Francois

WHEN I'VE DONE MY BEST *sac,gospel
  solo,pno ABER.GRP. $1.50   (W703)

WHEN I'VE TRAVELED MY LAST MILE see
  Harper

WHEN JESUS CHRIST WAS FOUR YEARS OLD
  see Fearing, John

WHEN JESUS LEFT HIS FATHER'S THRONE
  *sac,folk
  (Johnson, David N.) med solo,pno
  AUGSBURG 11-0725 $.65   (W704)

WHEN JESUS WALKED ON GALILEE see
  Edwards, Clara

WHEN JESUS WEPT see Billings, William

WHEN KING NIMROD see Cuando El Rey
  Nimrod

WHEN KISSES ARE LIKE STRAWBERRIES see
  Aked, Lindsay

WHEN LONDON WAS A GARDEN see Fraser,
  Dennise

WHEN LOVE GOES THROUGH THE VALLEY see
  Costin, Harold

WHEN LOVE IS KIND
  high solo,pno (A flat maj) ALLANS
  s.p.   (W705)
  med solo,pno (F maj) ALLANS s.p.
                                  (W706)
  (Moore) low solo,pno (F maj) BOOSEY
  $1.50   (W707)
  (Moore) high solo,pno (A flat maj)
  BOOSEY $1.50   (W708)

WHEN LOVE WAS YOUNG see Newton, Ernest

WHEN LOVELY WOMAN STOOPS TO FOLLY see
  Birch, Robert Fairfax

WHEN LOVERS MEET AGAIN see Parry,
  Charles Hubert Hastings

WHEN MA PICCANINNY DIED see Arundale,
  Claude

WHEN MAY WALKS BY see O'Neill, Norman

WHEN MOST I WINK see Delden, Lex van

WHEN MOTHER SAYS "GOODNIGHT" see
  Murray, Alan

WHEN MOTHER WAS MARRIED see Cooke,
  Herbert L.

WHEN MUSIC SOUNDS see Gibbs, Cecil
  Armstrong

WHEN MY LADY GOES A-SHOPPING see
  Norman, Lorna

WHEN MY SHIPS COME SAILING HOME see
  Dorel, F.

WHEN MY SOUL TOUCHES YOURS see
  Bernstein, Leonard

WHEN MYRA SINGS
  (Lehmann, Amelia) low solo,pno (E
  flat maj) ASHDOWN $1.50   (W709)
  (Lehmann, Amelia) high solo,pno (F
  maj) ASHDOWN $1.50   (W710)

WHEN PETER JACKSON PREACHED see
  Snodgrass, Louise

WHEN SHE GIVES HIM A SHAMROCK BLOOM see
  Friml, Rudolf

WHEN SINGING BIRDS WERE MUTE see
  Hamblen, Bernard

WHEN SLIM SOPHIA MOUNTS HER HORSE see
  Duke, John Woods

WHEN SONG IS SWEET see Sans-Souci

WHEN SPARROWS BUILD see Lindsay, M.

WHEN SPRING AND CHERRY BLOSSOM COME see
  Arundale, Claude

WHEN SPRING GOES SHOPPING see Geehl,
  Henry Ernest

WHEN SWEET ANN SINGS see Head, Michael
  (Dewar)

WHEN THAT I WAS A LITTLE TINY BOY
  (Newton, Ernest) 2 soli,pno LEONARD-
  ENG   (W711)

WHEN THAT I WAS AND A LITTLE TINY BOY
  see Castelnuovo-Tedesco, Mario

WHEN THAT I WAS AND A LITTLE TINY BOY
  see Davies, Henry Walford

WHEN THE ELVES AT DAWN DO PASS see
  Wallace, William Vincent

WHEN THE EVENING SHADOWS FALL see
  Lucas, Clarence

WHEN THE FIRST DROP OF BLOOD see
  Younce, George

WHEN THE GREAT RED DAWN IS SHINING see
  Sharpe, Evelyn

WHEN THE HEART IS YOUNG see Bach, D.

WHEN THE HILLS DO see Persichetti,
  Vincent

WHEN THE KING ENJOYS HIS OWN AGAIN see
  Somervell, Arthur

WHEN THE KING WENT FORTH TO WAR see
  Koeneman, T., Quand Le Roi Part Aux
  Combats

WHEN THE KYE COMES HAME *folk,Scot
  low solo,pno (A min) PATERSON FS94
  s.p.   (W712)
  high solo,pno (B min) PATERSON FS94
  s.p.   (W713)

WHEN THE LAD FOR LONGING SIGHS see
  Baksa, Robert

WHEN THE LAD FOR LONGING SIGHS see Orr,
  Charles Wilfred

WHEN THE LORD CALLS FOR HIS OWN *sac,
  gospel
  solo,pno ABER.GRP. $1.50   (W714)

WHEN THE ROBINS SING see Baker, M.

WHEN THE ROSES BLOOM see Reichardt,
  Luise, Hoffnung

WHEN THE SAINTS GO MARCHING IN *sac,
  gospel
  solo,pno ABER.GRP. $1.50   (W715)

WHEN THE SAVIOUR REACHED DOWN FOR ME
  *sac,gospel
  solo,pno ABER.GRP. $1.50   (W716)

WHEN THE SHADOWS FALL TO-NIGHT see
  Lehmann, Liza

WHEN THE SHADOWS OF EVENING FALL see
  Kearton, T. Wilfred

WHEN THE STARS WERE YOUNG see Rubens,
  Paul Alfred

WHEN THE SWALLOW HOMEWARD FLIES see
  Abt, Franz, Agathe

WHEN THE VISION DIES see Weigl, Vally

WHEN THE WIND SIGHS ROUND THE HOUSE see
  Grant, W. Parks

WHEN THEY RING THOSE GOLDEN BELLS
  *sac,gospel
  solo,pno ABER.GRP. $1.50   (W717)

WHEN THROSTLES SING see Oliver, Herbert

WHEN THY BLUE EYES see Lassen, Eduard

WHEN TO THE SESSIONS OF SWEET SILENT
  THOUGHT see Hovhaness, Alan

WHEN TWO THAT LOVE ARE PARTED
  (Marzials) low solo,pno (D flat maj)
  BOOSEY $1.50   (W718)
  (Marzials) high solo,pno (D maj)
  BOOSEY $1.50   (W719)

WHEN WE ARE PARTED see Bartholomew,
  Marshall

WHEN WE SEE CHRIST see Rusthoi, Esther
  Kerr

WHEN WILL THE REDEEMER COME? see Matai
  Yavo Ha-Mashiach

WHEN WITH THINE EYES see Strauss,
  Richard, Mit Deinen Blauen Augen

WHEN YOU ARE NEAR see Mana-Zucca, Mme.,
  Quand Tu Es La

WHEN YOU ARE OLD see Mourant, Walter

WHEN YOU COME HOME see Squire, W.H.

WHEN YOU FIND A MAIDEN CHARMING see
  Mozart, Wolfgang Amadeus

WHEN YOU LOOK IN THE HEART OF A ROSE
  see Methven

WHEN YOU MARRY ME see Handel, George
  Frideric

WHEN YOU WALK see Mourant, Walter

WHEN YOU WALK IN A FIELD see Planten,
  R.

WHEN YOU'RE AWAY see Herbert

WHENAS I WAKE see Orr, Charles Wilfred

WHENAS IN SILKS MY JULIA GOES see
  Lessard, John Ayres

WHENCE see Parry, Charles Hubert
  Hastings

WHENE'ER A SNOWFLAKE LEAVES THE SKY see
  Lehmann, Liza

WHERE ARE THE JOYS? *folk,Scot
  solo,pno (D maj/E maj) PATERSON FS92
  s.p.   (W720)

WHERE ARE YOU GOING? see Beekhuis,
  Hanna

WHERE ARE YOU GOING TO, MY PRETTY MAID
  see Plumstead, Mary

WHERE BE GOING? see Somervell, Arthur

WHERE BE YOU GOING? see Holbrooke,
  Joseph

WHERE BLOSSOMS GROW see Souci, G.S.

WHERE CORALS LIE see Elgar, Edward

WHERE COULD I GO BUT TO THE LORD *sac,
  gospel
  solo,pno ABER.GRP. $1.50   (W721)

WHERE E'ER YOU WALK see Handel, George
  Frideric

WHERE GO THE BOATS see Weigl, Vally

WHERE HE SLEEPS see Thompson, A.

WHERE IS LOVE see York, Sybil

WHERE IS YOUR FAITH? see Ellis

WHERE LILACS BLOW see Repper, Charles

WHERE MORTALS DWELL see Birch, Robert
  Fairfax

WHERE NO ONE STANDS ALONE see Lister,
  Mosie

WHERE NOW see Mozart, Wolfgang Amadeus,
  Dove Sono

WHERE SHALL THE LOVER REST see Parry,
  Charles Hubert Hastings

WHERE THE BEE SUCKS see Arne, Thomas
  Augustine

WHERE THE BEE SUCKS see Castelnuovo-
  Tedesco, Mario

WHERE THE BEE SUCKS see Moeran, Ernest
  J.

WHERE THE CHESTNUTS BLOOM see Newton,
  Ernest

WHERE THE MILESTONES END see Sharpe,
  Evelyn

WHERE THE RIVER SHANNON FLOWS see
  Kennedy, James I.

WHERE THE SEASONS NEVER CHANGE *sac,
  gospel
  solo,pno ABER.GRP. $1.50   (W722)

WHERE THE SPIRIT OF THE LORD IS see
  Adams

WHERE THE TIGRIS FLOWS see Chajes,
  Julius, Beyn N'har P'rat

WHERE THERE IS LOVE see Ellis

WHERE WERE YOU GOING see Hubbard, H.

WHERE'ER THOU GOEST see Hildach, Eugen,
Wo Du Hingehst

WHERE'ER YOU WALK see Handel, George
Frideric

WHEREFORE SEEING WE ARE ALSO COMPASSED
ABOUT see Pinkham, Daniel

WHEREFORES AND WHYS see Eisdell, Hubert

WHERE'S CHRISTMAS see Smith, Tedd

WHERE'S THE COLD HEART SO UNFEELING see
Rossini, Gioacchino, Qui Est Homo

WHETHER I GROW OLD OR NO see Boyce,
William

WHIKEHART, LEWIS W.
O Sing Unto The Lord *sac
high solo,pno BELWIN $1.50 (W723)

WHILE AGES ROLL see Lister, Mosie

WHILE GAZING INTO THY DEAR EYES see
Schumann, Robert (Alexander), Wenn
Ich In Deine Augen Seh

WHILE I WASTE THESE PRECIOUS HOURS see
Menotti, Gian Carlo, Vola Intanto
L'ora Insonne

WHILE SHEPHERDS WATCHED THEIR FLOCKS
see Belcher, Supply

WHILE SUMMER ON IS STEALING see Orr,
Charles Wilfred

WHILST GAZING INTO THY DEAR EYES see
Schumann, Robert (Alexander), Wenn
Ich In Deine Augen Seh

WHIPP, I.M.
Bird Song Away
low solo,pno (A maj) BOOSEY $1.50
(W724)
high solo,pno (B flat maj) BOOSEY
$1.50 (W725)

Feed My Sheep *sac
high solo,pno (G flat maj) FISCHER,
C V 1621 (W726)

WHISPER A PRAYER *sac,gospel
solo,pno ABER.GRP. $1.50 (W727)

WHISPER JESUS see Jensen, Gordon

WHISPERING HOPE *sac,gospel
solo,pno ABER.GRP. $1.50 (W728)

WHISPERING HOPE see Hawthorne, Alice

WHISPERING HOPE *sac,CCU
solo,pno WORD 35050 $2.50 (W729)

WHISP'RINGS OF THE VIENNA WOODS, THE
see Strauss, Johann, G'schicten Aus
Dem Wienerwald

WHISTLE, THE see Kennedy-Fraser,
Marjory

WHISTLIN' THIEF, THE see Hindemith,
Paul

WHIT-MONDAY MORNING see Sharpe, Evelyn

WHITE
Robin's Song
high solo,pno (A flat maj) ALLANS
s.p. (W730)
low solo,pno (F maj) ALLANS s.p.
(W731)

WHITE BIRCH see Birch, Robert Fairfax

WHITE BUTTERFLIES see Bray, Kenneth I.

WHITE COCKADE, THE *folk,Scot
low solo,pno (C maj) PATERSON FS95
s.p. (W732)
high solo,pno (D maj) PATERSON FS95
s.p. (W733)

WHITE DRESS, THE see Duke, John Woods

WHITE FIELDS see Mourant, Walter

WHITE HEATHER see Sveinbjornsson,
Sveinbjorn

WHITE HORSES see Day, Maude Craske

WHITE IN THE MOON see Duke, John Woods

WHITE JADE see Dungan, Olive

WHITE, LOUIE L.
Gloria In Excelsis Deo *sac
"Praise The Lord" med solo,kbd/fl&
hndbl&strings&kbd sc CONCORDIA
97-5259 $2.75, ipa (W734)

Praise The Lord *see Gloria In
Excelsis Deo

This Son So Young *sac,Xmas
S/T solo,harp/pno&org BELWIN $2.00
(W735)

WHITE, MAUDE VALERIE (1855-1937)
Adieu Suzon
solo,pno CRAMER (W736)

It Is Na, Jean, Thy Bonnie Face
med solo,pno (A flat maj) CRAMER
(W737)
low solo,pno (F maj) CRAMER (W738)
2 soli,pno CRAMER (W739)
high solo,pno (B flat maj) CRAMER
(W740)

Widow Bird Sate Mourning
solo,pno CRAMER (W741)

WHITE ROAD, THE see Pratella, Francesco
Balilla, La Strada Bianca

WHITE ROSES see Reif, Paul

WHITE SHEEP, THE see Brumby, Colin

WHITE SKY see Kendrick, Virginia

WHITE-STOKIN'D MARE see Trotere, Henry

WHITE WAVES ON THE WATER see Roberton,
Hugh Stevenson

WHITE WINDOW, THE see Mourant, Walter

WHITEHEAD, PERCY A.
Boating Song Of The Yo Eh
2 soli,pno CRAMER (W742)

Five Little Songs Of Old Japan
*CC5U,Jap
solo,pno CRAMER (W743)

Snail Song
solo,pno CRAMER (W744)

WHITETHROAT AND THE HOLLY, THE see
Holford, Franz

WHITHER? see Schubert, Franz (Peter),
Wohin?

WHITHER AWAY? see Roberton, Hugh
Stevenson

WHITHER MUST I WANDER see Vaughan
Williams, Ralph

WHITHER SHALL I GO FROM THY SPIRIT see
Demarest, A.

WHITHER SHALL I GO FROM THY SPIRIT see
Schinhan, J.P.

WHITHER THOU GOEST *sac,gospel
solo,pno ABER.GRP. $1.50 (W745)

WHITHER THOU GOEST see Cassler, G.
Winston

WHITHER THOU GOEST see Craven, Louise

WHITHER THOU GOEST see Peeters, Flor,
Wo Du Hingehst

WHITMAN CYCLE IV see Stearns, Peter
Pindar

WHITTENBERG, CHARLES
Even Though The World Keeps Changing
Bar solo,fl,vla,vibra sc
AM.COMP.AL. $7.70, ipa (W746)

Two Dylan Thomas Songs *CC2U
S solo,fl,pno sc AM.COMP.AL. $9.35
(W747)

Two Songs *CC2U
Mez solo,pno sc AM.COMP.AL. $3.85
(W748)

Vocalise *vocalise
S solo,vla,perc sc AM.COMP.AL.
$14.85 (W749)

WHITTLE
Do You Know Jesus? *sac
(Edeker) solo,pno LILLENAS
SM-905: SN $1.00 (W750)

WHO AM I? see Goodman

WHO ARE THESE CHILDREN? see Britten,
Benjamin

WHO AT MY DOOR IS STANDING *sac,gospel
solo,pno ABER.GRP. $1.50 (W751)

WHO GOES A-WALKING see Martin, Easthope

WHO GOES WITH FERGUS? see Kauder, Hugo

WHO HAS SEEN THE WIND? see Weigl, Vally

WHO IS SYLVIA? see Amram, David Werner

WHO IS SYLVIA? see Montgomery, Bruce

WHO IS SYLVIA? see Schubert, Franz
(Peter)

WHO IS SYLVIA see Stout, Alan

WHO IS SYLVIAU see Castelnuovo-Tedesco,
Mario

WHO KNOWS see Stickles, William

WHO PLAYS IN THE NIGHT-TIME see
Pergament, Moses, Vem Speler I
Natten

WHO SHALL SEPARATE US FROM THE LOVE OF
CHRIST? see Pinkham, Daniel

WHO SO DWELLETH see Sowerby, Leo

WHO'LL BUY MY LAVENDER see German,
Edward

WHO'S GONNA HOLD YOUR HAND? see Croft,
Colbert

WHO'S THAT CALLING SO SWEET? see
Deveen, T.

WHY? see Moore, John W.

WHY? see Tchaikovsky, Piotr Ilyitch,
Warum?

WHY DID I LAUGH TO-NIGHT? see Saxe,
Serge

WHY DO THE NATIONS SO FURIOUSLY RAGE
TOGETHER? see Handel, George
Frideric

WHY HAVE YOU STOLEN MY DELIGHT see
Head, Michael (Dewar)

WHY HAVE YOU STOLEN MY DELIGHT? see
Methold, Diana

WHY IS MY VERSE see Ruyneman, Daniel

WHY ME? see Kristofferson, Kris

WHY SHOULD I FEAR? see McCann, Leland

WHY SO PALE AND WAN, FOND LOVER? see
Arne, Thomas Augustine

WHY SO PALE THE ROSES? see Tchaikovsky,
Piotr Ilyitch, Warum?

WIANT, BLISS
Great Commission, The *sac
low solo,pno ABINGDON APM-670 $.75
(W752)
high solo,pno ABINGDON APM-669 $.75
(W753)

WIBERGH, OLOF
Kvallen
2 soli,pno LUNDQUIST s.p. (W754)

Kyrkosangarens Album *sac,CCU
solo,pno LUNDQUIST s.p. (W755)

Pa Sangens Jublande Vingar
2 soli,pno LUNDQUIST s.p. (W756)

WIDEEN
Fem Visor
solo,pno LUNDQUIST s.p.
contains: Jag Kande En Trast;
Marianns Visa; Nog Vet Jag En
Mo; Sagan Om Rosalind; Stora
Barnet, Mitt Hjartegull (W757)

Jag Kande En Trast
see Fem Visor

Marianns Visa
see Fem Visor
solo,pno LUNDQUIST s.p. (W758)

Nog Vet Jag En Mo
see Fem Visor

Rod Lyser Stugan
solo,pno LUNDQUIST s.p. (W759)

Sagan Om Rosalind
see Fem Visor
solo,pno LUNDQUIST s.p. (W760)

Stora Barnet, Mitt Hjartegull
see Fem Visor

Tvenne Sanger *CC2U
solo,pno LUNDQUIST s.p. (W761)

Vallarelat
solo,pno LUNDQUIST s.p. (W762)

WIDEEN, IVAR
Det Borde Varit Stjarnor
med solo,pno GEHRMANS s.p.　　(W763)

Det Var En Gang En Jungfru
solo,pno GEHRMANS s.p.　　(W764)

Du Svenska Land
solo,pno GEHRMANS s.p.　　(W765)

Hembygdssang
solo,pno GEHRMANS s.p.　　(W766)

I Sin Vagga I Fager Drom
solo,pno GEHRMANS s.p.　　(W767)

Kung Liljekonvalje Av Dungen
med solo,pno GEHRMANS s.p.　　(W768)

Och Har Ar Dungen Dar Goken Gol
med solo,pno GEHRMANS s.p.　　(W769)

Serenad "Tallarnas Barr"
high solo,pno GEHRMANS s.p.　　(W770)
med solo,pno GEHRMANS s.p.　　(W771)

Spelmansvisa
high solo,pno GEHRMANS s.p.　　(W772)

Titania
med solo,pno GEHRMANS s.p.　　(W773)

Tyst Ar Skogen Och Nejden All
med solo,pno GEHRMANS 765 s.p.
　　(W774)

Vapnarens Visa Om Helig I Rosengard
solo,pno GEHRMANS s.p.　　(W775)

WIDERSTEHE DOCH DER SUNDE see Bach,
Johann Sebastian

WIDMUNG see Franz, Robert

WIDMUNG see Pfitzner, Hans

WIDMUNG see Schumann, Robert
(Alexander)

WIDMUNG see Zipp, Friedrich

WIDOR, CHARLES-MARIE (1844-1937)
Pater Noster　*sac
ST soli,pno/org HEUGEL s.p.　　(W776)

Pourquoi
Mez/Bar solo,pno/inst DURAND s.p.
　　(W777)
S/T solo,pno/inst DURAND s.p.
　　(W778)

Pres D'un Etang
Mez/Bar solo,pno/inst DURAND s.p.
　　(W779)
S/T solo,pno/inst DURAND s.p.
　　(W780)

Silence Ineffable De L'heure
Mez/Bar solo,pno/inst DURAND s.p.
　　(W781)
S/T solo,pno/inst DURAND s.p.
　　(W782)

Soirs D'ete　*Op.63, CC8L
solo,pno DURAND s.p.　　(W783)

WIDOW, THE see Cannon, (Jack) Phillip,
La Veuve

WIDOW BIRD SATE MOURNING see White,
Maude Valerie

WIDOW'S LAMENT IN SPRINGTIME, THE see
Babbit, Milton

WIE BIST DU DENN, O GOTT, IN ZORN
ENTBRANNT see Bach, Johann
Christoph

WIE BIST DU MEINE KONIGIN see Brahms,
Johannes

WIE DER HIRSCH SCHREYET see Pohle,
David

WIE DER KUCKUCK MOCHT' ICH RUFEN see
Kilpinen, Yrio, Saisinko Kaelta
Kielen

WIE EIN RUBIN IN FEINEM GOLDE LEUCHTET
see Schutz, Heinrich

WIE ENTGEHN see Liszt, Franz

WIE ENTGELT' ICH MEINER MUTTER see
Kilpinen, Yrio, Milla Maksan
Maammon Maion

WIE ERHEBET SICH DAS HERZ see Schubert,
Franz (Peter), Dem Unendlichen

WIE FLUCHTIG RINNT DIE STUNDE see
Svedbom, Vilhelm

WIE FREUNDLICHE STRAHLT see Koerppen,
Alfred

WIE FRUHLINSAHNUNG see Pfitzner, Hans

WIE GEORG VON FRUNDSBERG VON SICH
SELBER SANG see Schoenberg, Arnold

WIE HAB ICH EUCH SO GERNE　*folk,Russ
[Ger/Russ] solo,pno ZIMMER. 1537 s.p.
　　(W784)

WIE IST EIN FROHES HERZ see Kilpinen,
Yrio, Erotus Mielilla

WIE KANN EIN TAG... see Bijvanck, Henk

WIE KOSTLICH IST DER HEILIGEN TOD
*sac,CC20U
(Brodde, Otto) med solo,org (med
easy) BAREN. 2949 $7.00　　(W785)

WIE LANG NOCH WELLEN FELKER MIR TREIBEN
*Jew
solo,pno KAMMEN 414 $1.00　　(W786)

WIE LIEGT DIE STADT SO WUSTE see
Weckmann, Matthais

WIE NAHTE MIR DER SCHLUMMER see Weber,
Carl Maria von

WIE SCHON LEUCHTET DER MORGENSTERN see
Bornefeld, Helmut

WIE SHLECHT ES IS OHN GELT　*Jew
solo,pno KAMMEN 407 $1.00　　(W787)

WIE SIE SO SANFT RUH'N　*sac
Mez solo,pno (F maj) LIENAU HOS 158
s.p.　　(W788)

WIE SO STILL ES GEWORDEN see Erdlen,
Hermann

WIE SOLL ICH DICH EMPFANGEN see
Buxtehude, Dietrich

WIE SOLL ICH'S BERGEN see Sjogren, Emil

WIE SUSS ERTONT DES VOGELS SANG see
Galliard, Johann Ernst

WIE WONNIG IST'S AUF BLUMIGEM GEFILD
see Purcell, Henry, How Pleasant Is
This Flowery Plain And Ground

WIE WUNDERSAM see Schilling, M. von

WIE ZWEI VOGELEIN WAREN WIR BEIDE see
Kilpinen, Yrio, Kaks' Oli Meita
Kaunokaista

WIEDER GLANZT DER ABENDSTERN see
Jochum, Otto

WIEDER MOCHT ICH DIR BEGEGNEN see
Liszt, Franz

WIEGELIED see Adriessen, Willem

WIEGELIEDJE see Hullebroeck, Em.

WIEGELIEDJE see Mortelmans, Lodewijk

WIEGELIEDJE see Nieland, Jan

WIEGENLIED see Adriessen, Willem,
Wiegelied

WIEGENLIED see Brahms, Johannes

WIEGENLIED see Flies, J. Bernhard

WIEGENLIED see Gretchaninov, Alexander
Tikhonovitch, Berceuse

WIEGENLIED see Haas, Joseph

WIEGENLIED see Kilpinen, Yrio,
Kehtolaulu

WIEGENLIED see Kilpinen, Yrio,
Tuutulaulu

WIEGENLIED see Kowalski, Max

WIEGENLIED see Mozart, Wolfgang Amadeus

WIEGENLIED see Mussorgsky, Modest

WIEGENLIED see Pfitzner, Hans

WIEGENLIED see Prohaska, Carl

WIEGENLIED see Reger, Max

WIEGENLIED see Ries, Franz

WIEGENLIED see Ruyneman, Daniel

WIEGENLIED see Schneider-Trnavsky,
Mikulas

WIEGENLIED see Schubert, Franz (Peter)

WIEGENLIED see Schumann, Georg

WIEGENLIED see Strauss, Richard

WIEGENLIED see Weigl, Karl

WIEGENLIED see Zipp, Friedrich

WIEGENLIED see Taubert, Karl Heinz

WIEGENLIED DER HIRTEN see Reimann,
Heinrich

WIEGENLIED EINER FROMMEN MAGD see
Lothar, Mark

WIEGENLIEDCHEN see Strauss, Richard

WIEGENLIEDER see Jirasek, Ivo,
Ukolebavky

WIEGENLIEDER see Smetana, Bedrich

WIEGENLIEDER DER WELT　*CCU
(Behrend, Siegfried) med solo,gtr
ZIMMER. 1819 s.p.　　(W789)

WIEMER, WOLFGANG (1934-　　)
Der Herr Ist Mein Hirte　*sac,
concerto
Bar solo,org BREITKOPF-W EB 6429
$2.00　　(W790)

Der Kirschdieb
see Funf Lieder Nach Gedichten Von
Bert Brecht

Der Pflaumenbaum
see Funf Lieder Nach Gedichten Von
Bert Brecht

Der Rauch
see Funf Lieder Nach Gedichten Von
Bert Brecht

Die Maske Des Bosen
see Funf Lieder Nach Gedichten Von
Bert Brecht

Eile Gott, Mich Zu Erretten　*sac,
concerto
high solo,org BREITKOPF-W EB 6524
$3.75　　(W791)

Funf Lieder Nach Gedichten Von Bert
Brecht
[Ger] Bar solo,pno BREITKOPF-W
EB 6501 s.p.
contains: Der Kirschdieb; Der
Pflaumenbaum; Der Rauch; Die
Maske Des Bosen; Lied Der
Starenschwarme　　(W792)

Lied Der Starenschwarme
see Funf Lieder Nach Gedichten Von
Bert Brecht

Lobe Den Herrn, Meine Seele (Psalm
103) sac,concerto
Bar solo,perc,org BREITKOPF-W
EB 8013 s.p.　　(W793)

Psalm 103　*see Lobe Den Herrn, Meine
Seele

WIENER, JEAN
La Fille Du Port
solo,pno ENOCH s.p. see also
Premier Receueil De Chansons
　　(W794)
solo,acap solo pt ENOCH s.p.　(W795)

Les Chantefleurs　*CCU
med solo,pno SALABERT-US $17.00
　　(W796)

Premier Receueil De Chansons　*see La
Fille Du Port　　(W797)

Trente Chantefables De R. Desnos
*CC30L
solo,pno cmplt ed TRANSAT. s.p.
　　(W798)

WIENER KINDER SINGEN GERN see Strauss,
Josef

WIENER WALZER see Lilien, Ignace

WIENERBLUT MUSS WAS EIGENES SEIN see
Strauss, Johann

WIENERWALD LERCHEN see Strauss, Johann

WIENIAWSKI, ADAM (TADEUSZ) (1879-1950)
Le Sommeil De Leilah
solo,pno (available in 2 keys)
ENOCH s.p.　　(W799)

O Joueuse De Flute
solo,pno (available in 2 keys)
ENOCH s.p.　　(W800)

O Joueuse De Tambourin
solo,pno (available in 2 keys)
ENOCH s.p.　　(W801)

WIEROOK see Mortelmans, Lodewijk

WIFE OF WINTER, THE see Lord, Davis

WIFE TROUBLE see Manning, Richard

WIFE WRAPT IN WETHER'S SKIN, THE
see Schirmer's American Folk-Song
Series, Set XXII (American-English
Folk-Ballads From The Southern
Appalachian Mountains)

WIGGERS, A.S.
Barefoot Trail
low solo,pno (F maj) BOOSEY $1.50
(W802)
high solo,pno (B flat maj) BOOSEY
$1.50 (W803)

WIGGERS, W.
Chanson D'amour
solo,pno BROEKMANS 265 s.p. (W804)

WIGGLESWORTH, FRANK (1918-)
Lullaby *folk,Ir
A solo,pno AM.COMP.AL. $1.37 (W805)

Mister Westcott's One Million Dollar
Inheritance
Bar solo,pno AM.COMP.AL. $1.10
(W806)
Song
high solo,pno AM.COMP.AL. $1.37
(W807)

WIJ WILLEN see Hullebroeck, Em.

WIJ ZIJN JONG see Ramshorst, J.D. von

WIJ ZIJN WEER VRIJ see Beek, H. van

WIJ ZINGEN WIJ DE POETEN see
Andriessen, K.

WIJDEVELD, WOLFGANG (1910-)
Liederen Van Walt Whitman
med-low solo,vla,vcl,vln,pno voc sc
DONEMUS s.p.
contains: Old Age And Night; Song
Of The Open Road; Tears; Youth
Day (W808)

Old Age And Night
see Liederen Van Walt Whitman

Song Of The Open Road
see Liederen Van Walt Whitman

Taliesin
MezBar soli,pno DONEMUS s.p. (W809)

Teach Me The Way
med solo,pno DONEMUS s.p. (W810)

Tears
see Liederen Van Walt Whitman

Tien Liederen Op Zuid-Afrikaanse
Tekst *CC10U
[Afr] med solo,pno EIGEN UITGAVE
s.p. (W811)

Youth Day
see Liederen Van Walt Whitman

WIJDING AAN MIJN VADER see Dijk, Jan
van

WIJKER, H.
Drie Gezelle Liederen *CC3U
solo,pno BROEKMANS 204 s.p. (W812)

WIJNKEN, GIJ ZIJT GROENE see
Strategier, Herman

WIJS-MOUTON, J. DE
Zeven Liedjes, Vols. 1-4 & 6-8
*CC49L
solo,pno ALSBACH s.p., ea. contains
seven songs in each vol.; volumes
sold separately (W813)

WIKANDER, DAVID
Det Brinner En Stjarna I Osterland
solo,pno LUNDQUIST s.p. (W814)

Nar Juldagsmorgon Glimmar
solo,pno LUNDQUIST s.p. (W815)

WIKLUND, ADOLF (1879-1950)
Abend *Op.9,No.3
solo,pno GEHRMANS s.p. see from
Vier Lieder (W816)

En Dalmastrall
med solo,pno GEHRMANS s.p. (W817)

Erwartung *Op.9,No.1
solo,pno GEHRMANS s.p. see from
Vier Lieder (W818)

Fyra Sanger *see Pa Floden, Op.12,
No.1; Som Mandelblom, Op.12,No.3;
Sov, Oroliga Hjarta, Op.12,No.2;
Ved Soen, Op.12,No.4 (W819)

Pa Floden *Op.12,No.1
solo,pno GEHRMANS s.p. see from
Fyra Sanger (W820)

WIKLUND, ADOLF (cont'd.)
Som Mandelblom *Op.12,No.3
solo,pno GEHRMANS s.p. see from
Fyra Sanger (W821)

Sov, Oroliga Hjarta *Op.12,No.2
solo,pno GEHRMANS s.p. see from
Fyra Sanger (W822)

Ved Soen *Op.12,No.4
solo,pno GEHRMANS s.p. see from
Fyra Sanger (W823)

Vier Lieder *see Abend, Op.9,No.3;
Erwartung, Op.9,No.1 (W824)

WIKMARK, TORBJORN
Psalm I Ungdomen *sac
solo,pno GEHRMANS s.p. (W825)

WIL JE 'T NIET ZEGGEN? see Loots, Ph.

WILBER, LAWRENCE
Mother On This Blessed Day
med solo,pno GALAXY 1.2159.7 $1.00
(W826)

WILCOCK, F.S.
Are You Coming To My Garden
low solo,pno (B flat maj) LEONARD-
ENG (W827)
high solo,pno (C maj) LEONARD-ENG
(W828)

WILD AMERICAY see Haufrecht, Herbert

WILD ANEMONE, THE see Heilner, Irwin

WILD, ERIC
Eric Wild Folio Of Sacred Music, Vol.
2 *sac,CCU
solo,pno BERANDOL BER 1241 $5.00
(W829)
Goodnight, God Bless You *sac
solo,pno BERANDOL BER 1086 $1.50
(W830)
Sing, Sing, Ev'ryone Sing! *sac
solo,pno BERANDOL BER 1087 $1.50
(W831)
There Is A Time For Everything *sac
solo,pno BERANDOL BER 1088 $2.50
(W832)

WILD FLOWER, THE see Sibelius, Jean, En
Blomma Stad Vid Vagen

WILD FLOWER'S SONG, THE see Hindemith,
Paul

WILD PLUM see Hundley, Richard

WILD ROVER see Dillon, Fannie Charles

WILD SWAN, THE see Peel, Graham

WILDBERGER, JACQUES (1922-)
In My End Is My Beginning
ST soli,fl,ob,clar,bsn,horn,trp,
perc,harp,cel,pno,cembalo,vla,
vcl,bvl sc GERIG HG 504 s.p.
(W833)
La Notte
Mez solo,clar,bass clar,drums,
glock,harp,bvl sc GERIG HG 637
s.p. (W834)

WILDCAT SONGS see Shields, Alice

WILDERNESS AND THE SOLITARY PLACE see
Bantock, Granville

WILDERNESS JOURNAL see Sifler, Paul J.

WILDFLOWER SUITE see Davis

WILDGANS, FRIEDRICH (1913-)
Der Mystische Trompeter *song cycle
high solo,trp,pno DOBLINGER 08 815
$4.25 (W835)

Drei Klavierlieder *CC3U
high solo,pno DOBLINGER 08 641
$2.00 (W836)

Lieder An Den Knaben Elis *CC3U
S solo,clar,vln,vcl DOBLINGER
08 816 $3.50 (W837)

Missa Minima *sac,Mass
[Lat] S solo,clar,vln,vcl DOBLINGER
08 817 $8.25 (W838)

WILHELMUS VAN NASSOUWE
Oorspronkelijke Melodie
solo,pno ALSBACH s.p. (W839)

WILHELMUS VAN NASSOUWE see Rontgen,
[Julius]

WILHELMUS VON NASSAUEN see Kremser,
Edward

WILKIN, MARIJOHN
Behold The Man *sac
solo,pno WORD S-445 (W840)

WILKIN, MARIJOHN (cont'd.)
I Have Returned *sac
solo,pno WORD S-474 (W841)

One Day At A Time (composed with
Kristofferson, Kris) *sac
solo,pno WORD S-430 (W842)
solo,pno BENSON S7282-S $1.00
(W843)
Scars In The Hands Of Jesus, The
*sac
solo,pno WORD S-448 (W844)

Two Thousand Years Ago *sac
solo,pno WORD S-446 (W845)

WILKINSON, M.
Voices
A/Mez solo,fl,clar,bass clar,vcl
sc,oct UNIVER. 12912 $1.50 (W846)

WILL DER HERR GRAF EIN TANZCHEN NUN
WAGEN see Mozart, Wolfgang Amadeus

WILL-O-THE WISP see Spross, Charles
Gilbert

WILL SHE BE WAITING UP? see Bennett,
Sir William Sterndale

WILL YE NO COME BACK AGAIN see
Somervell, Arthur

WILL YOU BE AMONG THE MISSING? see
Jensen, Gordon

WILL YOU RECEIVE THE LORD? see Paris

WILL YOU REMEMBER see Romberg, Sigmund

WILLAN, HEALEY (1880-1968)
"Come, Thou Redeemer Of The Earth"
*sac
med solo,4strings sc CONCORDIA
97-1394 $1.00, ipa, solo pt
CONCORDIA 98-1351 $.20 (W847)

Fairest Lord Jesus *sac,anthem
SS/TT soli,org/pno PETERS 6233 $.30
(W848)
Jesu, Good Above All Others *sac,
anthem
SS/TT soli,org/pno PETERS 6676 $.30
(W849)
King Ascendeth Into Heaven, The *sac
SA soli,pno oct CONCORDIA 98-1381
$.25 (W850)

Let All The World In Every Corner
Sing
SSA soli,org/pno PETERS 6677 $.30
(W851)
Like As The Hart Desireth The
Waterbrooks *sac
med solo,pno oct CONCORDIA 98-1230
$.25 (W852)

Little Red Lark
med-high solo,pno (F maj) BOSTON
$1.50 (W853)

Rejoice Greatly, O Daughter Of Zion
*sac
SA soli,pno oct CONCORDIA 98-1113
$.25 (W854)

We Praise Thee, O God *sac
med solo,pno oct CONCORDIA 98-1059
$.25 (W855)

WILLARD, JAMES
My Heart Sings
solo,pno (F maj) BOOSEY $1.50
(W856)

WILLE, STEWART
Lord I Want To Be
med solo,pno GALAXY 1.0553.7 $1.25
(W857)

WILLEBRAND, F.R. VON
Langsamt Som Kvallskyn
"Verkkaan Kuin Illan Sammuvi Rusko"
solo,pno FAZER W 1061 s.p. (W858)

Verkkaan Kuin Illan Sammuvi Rusko
*see Langsamt Som Kvallskyn

WILLEBY, CHARLES
Biding Still
low solo,pno (B flat maj) ALLANS
s.p. (W859)
high solo,pno (E flat maj) ALLANS
s.p. (W860)
med solo,pno (C maj) ALLANS s.p.
(W861)

I Mind The Day
solo,pno CRAMER (W862)

WILLIAM PENN FRUITS OF SOLITUDE see
Clarke, Henry Leland

WILLIAMS
God Is Everywhere *sac
med solo,pno BELWIN $1.50 (W863)

WILLIAMS (cont'd.)

Someday *see Davis

WILLIAMS, ALICE CRANE
Reverie
med solo,pno PARAGON $.85   (W864)

WILLIAMS, C.
Dream Of Olwen
high solo,pno GEHRMANS s.p.   (W865)
low solo,pno GEHRMANS s.p.   (W866)

WILLIAMS, D.S.
Save Me, O Lord
solo,pno CRAMER   (W867)

WILLIAMS, DAVID H.
Good Bye, My Fancy
med solo,pno BELWIN $1.50   (W868)

In The Bleak Midwinter *sac,Xmas
high solo,pno BELWIN $1.50   (W869)

Jesus, The Very Thought Of Thee *sac
low solo,pno BELWIN $1.50   (W870)
high solo,pno BELWIN $1.50   (W871)

Our Blest Redeemer *sac
high solo,pno BELWIN $1.50   (W872)

Wedding Prayer, A *sac,Marriage
high solo/med solo,pno BELWIN $1.50
                                    (W873)
low solo,pno BELWIN $1.50   (W874)
med solo,pno BELWIN $1.50   (W875)

WILLIAMS, DAVID MCK. (1887-   )
Lullaby Of The Madonna *sac
low solo,pno BELWIN $1.50   (W876)

WILLIAMS, GRACE (1906-   )
Loom, The
A/Bar solo,pno (med easy) OXFORD
61.907 $1.20   (W877)

WILLIAMS, JOAN FRANKS
Await The Wind
S solo,fl,pno sc AM.COMP.AL. $3.85
                                    (W878)

Cassandra
S solo,vln/vla,vcl,fl,trp,perc
(monodrama with film) sc
AM.COMP.AL. $7.70   (W879)

From Paterson
S solo,trp,vcl,pno sc AM.COMP.AL.
$6.60   (W880)

In Celebration
S solo,pno,electronic tape sc
AM.COMP.AL. $5.50   (W881)

WILLIAMS, MEIRION
A Welon Y Mynynn
solo,pno CRAMER   (W882)

Aros Maeir Mynddau Mawr
solo,pno CRAMER   (W883)

Great Hills Remain
solo,pno CRAMER   (W884)

Hwaingerdd
solo,pno CRAMER   (W885)

Mountain Breezes
solo,pno CRAMER   (W886)

Rhosyn Yr Haf.
solo,pno CRAMER   (W887)

Slumber Song
solo,pno CRAMER   (W888)

WILLIAMS, R.H.
By The Cross *sac
SA soli,pno BELWIN $1.50   (W889)

Tell Me, Where Is Fancy Bred
med solo,pno BELWIN $1.50   (W890)

WILLIAMS, W.S.GWYNN
Country Girls
solo,pno LEONARD-ENG   (W891)

Dream Pedlary
solo,pno CRAMER   (W892)

Night Song
solo,pno CRAMER   (W893)

Two Celtic Love Songs
CRAMER $.90 low solo,pno

Two Celtic Songs
CRAMER $.90 high solo,pno

Vesper
low solo,pno (C maj) CRAMER $.95
                                    (W894)
high solo,pno (F maj) CRAMER $.95
                                    (W895)

WILLIAMSON
Lord's Prayer, The
solo,pno GENTRY $1.00   (W896)

WILLIAMSON, MALCOLM
Celebration Of Divine Love
high solo,pno NOVELLO 17.0017.00
s.p.   (W897)

Christmas Carol, A
solo,pno (D maj) WEINBERGER $1.50
                                    (W898)

Four North Country Songs *CC4U
low solo,pno WEINBERGER $2.00
                                    (W899)

From A Child's Garden *song cycle
high solo,pno WEINBERGER $2.50
                                    (W900)

Good Boy, A
high solo,pno PRESSER $.95   (W901)
solo,pno (F maj) WEINBERGER $1.50
                                    (W902)
med solo,pno PRESSER $.95   (W903)

Hasselbacher's Scena (from Our Man In
Havana) scena
Bar solo,pno BOOSEY $1.75   (W904)

Six English Lyrics *CC6U
low solo,pno WEINBERGER $2.00
                                    (W905)

Three Shakespeare Songs *CC3U
high solo,gtr/pno WEINBERGER $4.00
                                    (W906)

Visions Of Beasts And Gods *song
cycle
high solo,pno BOOSEY $7.00   (W907)

WILLIE DROWNED IN YARROW see
Montgomery, Bruce

WILLIE DROWNED IN YARROW see Sampson,
Godfrey

WILLIE WABSTER see Musgrave, Thea

WILLIE WEBSTER see Musgrave, Thea,
Willie Wabster

WILLIE'S GANE TO MELVILLE CASTLE
*folk,Scot
solo,pno (B flat maj/C maj) PATERSON
FS110 s.p.   (W908)

WILLIE'S GANE TO MELVILLE CASTLE see
Lawson, Malcolm

WILLIE'S RARE AND WILLIE'S FAIR *folk,
Scot
solo,pno (A maj/G maj) PATERSON FS98
s.p.   (W909)

WILLIS
Gums
solo,pno ALLANS s.p.   (W910)

WILLKOMM see Carriere, Paul

WILLKOMMEN, SUSSER BRAUTIGAM see
Lubeck, Vincentius

WILLKOMMEN UND ABSCHIED see Pfitzner,
Hans

WILLOW see Birch, Robert Fairfax

WILLOW, THE see Thomas, Arthur Goring

WILLOW BRANCH, THE see Avshalomov,
Aaron

WILLOW BROOK SUITE see Woollen, Russell

WILLOW PATTERN PLATE see Gillington, M.

WILLOW SONG see Sullivan, Sir Arthur
Seymour

WILLOW SONG, THE see Coleridge-Taylor,
Samuel

WILLOW SONG, THE see Verdi, Giuseppe,
Canzone Del Salice

WILLOW TREE, THE see Jongh, George de

WILLOW, WILLOW, WILLOW see Parry,
Charles Hubert Hastings

WILLST DU MEIN LIEBCHEN SEIN see
Mozart, Wolfgang Amadeus, Mandina
Amabile

WILLST DU MIT MIR IN DIE SONNE GEHN?
see Czernik, W.

WILLST JENES TAGS DU DICH NICHT MEHR
ENTSINNEN see Wagner, Richard

WILSON
Beautiful Isle Of Somewhere *see
Fearis, John S.

I Wonder How John Felt (composed with
Taylor; Sherrill, Billy) *sac
solo,pno BENSON S6189-R $1.25

WILSON (cont'd.)
                                    (W911)
Lonesome Valley *sac
SA soli,pno LORENZ $1.00   (W912)

Wedding Prayer, A *sac,Marriage
low solo,pno LORENZ $1.00   (W913)
solo,pno (A flat maj) ALLANS s.p.
                                    (W914)
med solo,pno LORENZ $1.00   (W915)

WILSON, AL
Deep, Deep Waters
med solo,pno CRESPUB CP-S5006 $.95
                                    (W916)

Joy Cometh In The Morning *sac
med solo,pno CRESPUB CP-S5003 $.95
                                    (W917)

Life Really Began *sac
med solo,pno CRESPUB CP-S5007 $.95
                                    (W918)

Miracle Of Grace *sac
med solo,pno CRESPUB CP-S5004 $.95
                                    (W919)

My Heart Sings *sac
med solo,pno CRESPUB CP-S5002 $.95
                                    (W920)

Stumbling Blocks To Stepping Stones
*sac
med solo,pno CRESPUB CP-S5001 $.95
                                    (W921)

There's An Awful Lot Of Glory *sac
med solo,pno CRESPUB CP-S5008 $.95
                                    (W922)

When I Walk Through The Valley *sac
med solo,pno CRESPUB CP-S5005 $.95
                                    (W923)

WILSON, DONALD M.
Space-Out
S solo,electronic tape, jazz lab
band and visuals sc AM.COMP.AL.
$9.35   (W924)

WILSON, ERNEST
Vienna
solo,pno CRAMER   (W925)

WILSON, H. LANE
Carmena
med solo,pno (D maj) SCHIRM.G $.75
                                    (W926)

Somerset Farmer
low solo,pno (C maj) CRAMER   (W927)
high solo,pno (D maj) CRAMER   (W928)

To The Dance
high solo,pno (F maj) CRAMER   (W929)
med solo,pno (D maj) CRAMER   (W930)
low solo,pno (C maj) CRAMER   (W931)

WILSON, HARRY [ROBERT] (1901-   )
I Kneel To Pray
(Wilson, H.L.) low solo,pno (B flat
maj) BOOSEY $1.50   (W932)
(Wilson, H.L.) high solo,pno (D
flat maj) BOOSEY $1.50   (W933)

WILSON, JOHN F.
Just A Mother With A Baby *sac
solo,pno HOPE 553 $.75   (W934)

Lord Of All *sac
solo,pno HOPE 54 $.75   (W935)

My Soul Doth Magnify The Lord *sac
solo,pno HOPE $.75   (W936)

WILSON, R. BARCLAY
If There Be Heart Of Gold
solo,pno CRAMER   (W937)

In Spring
solo,pno CRAMER $1.10   (W938)

WILT THOU BE MY DEARIE? *folk,Scot
solo,pno (F maj/G maj) PATERSON FS96
s.p.   (W939)

WILT THOU LEAVE ME THUS? see Bach,
Johann Sebastian

WILY CUPID see Holford, Franz

WIMBERGER, GERHARD (1923-   )
Acht Chansons Nach Gedichten Von
Erich Kastner *CC8U
med solo,pno SCHOTTS s.p.   (W940)

Drei Lyrische Chansons *CC3U
solo,pno/chamb.orch voc sc SCHOTTS
4978 s.p., ipr   (W941)

Singsang
solo, jazz combo sc SCHOTTS 6502
s.p., ipa   (W942)

WIND, THE see Adler, Samuel

WIND, THE see Bantock, Granville

WIND AND THE SEA, THE see Shaw, Martin

WINDING BANKS OF ERNE see Hughes,
Herbert

WINDING STREAM THROUGH YONDER GLADE see Birch, Robert Fairfax

WINDJAMMER, THE
(Roberton, Hugh S.) solo,pno (F sharp min) ROBERTON 2750 s.p. (W943)

WINDLESS DAY see Klein, Ivy Frances

WINDOW, THE see Medtner, Nikolai Karlovitch

WINDOWS OF HEAVEN *sac,gospel
solo,pno ABER.GRP. $1.50 (W944)

WINDRADER see Marx, Joseph

WINDS, THE see Walton, William

WINDS IN THE SOUTH, THE see Scott, John Prindle

WINDS OF BETHLEHEM see Stanford, Charles Villiers

WINDS WAY see Ashworth-Hope, H.

WIND'S WORK see Benjamin, Arthur

WINDY DAY, A see Hyland, Cyril

WINE OF THE GRAPE see Korte, Karl

WINECOFF, V.D.
Dearest Beloved
low solo,pno BRODT $.60 (W945)
high solo,pno BRODT $.60 (W946)

WINGS OF A DOVE *sac,gospel
solo,pno ABER.GRP. $1.50 (W947)

WINGS OF A DOVE see English, George Phillip

WINGS OF A DOVE see Ferguson

WINKLER, ALEXANDER ADOLFOVITCH (1865-1935)
Air Tzigane
A solo,pno/inst DURAND s.p. (W948)

WINSETT
Jesus Is Coming Soon *sac
solo,pno BENSON S6712-S $1.00 (W949)
Just A Closer Walk With Thee *sac, gospel
solo,pno ABER.GRP. $1.50 (W950)

WINTER *Op.42,No.6
[Ger/Eng] solo,pno ZIMMER. s.p. see from Zwolf Gesange Nach Gedichten Von Paul Verlaine (W951)

WINTER see Bliss, Sir Arthur

WINTER see Tollefsen, Augusta

WINTER AFTERNOON, A see Manning, Kathleen Lockhart

WINTER CHANT see Foss, Hubert James

WINTER IS A COLD THING see Clarke, Henry Leland

WINTER IT IS PAST, THE *folk,Scot
low solo,pno (D maj) PATERSON FS97 s.p. (W952)
high solo,pno (F maj) PATERSON FS97 s.p. (W953)

WINTER NATIVITY see Thiman, Eric Harding

WINTER NIGHT see Medtner, Nikolai Karlovitch

WINTER NIGHT see Strauss, Richard, Winternacht

WINTER NIGHT see Weigl, Vally

WINTER NIGHT IDYLL, A see Goosens, Eugene

WINTER, R.
Auf Ein Schlummerndes Kind Und Voglein Schwermut
[Ger] med solo,pno OSTER $.60 (W954)
Nebel Am Wattenmeer Und Geht Leise
[Ger] high solo,pno OSTER $.60 (W955)

WINTER, SISTER MIRIAM THERESE
I Know The Secret *sac,CC12U
solo,pno,opt gtr VANGUARD V539 $1.95 (W956)

Joy Is Like The Rain *sac,CC12U
solo,pno,opt gtr VANGUARD $1.95 (W957)

Knock, Knock *sac,CC12U
solo,pno,opt gtr VANGUARD V544 $2.00 (W958)

WINTER, SISTER MIRIAM THERESE (cont'd.)
Let The Cosmos Ring! *sac,CC28U
solo,pno,opt gtr VANGUARD V574 $2.00 (W959)

Mass Of A Pilgrim People *sac
solo,pno,opt gtr VANGUARD V532 $1.50 (W960)

Seasons *sac,CC12U
solo,pno,opt gtr VANGUARD V572 $1.95 (W961)

WINTER WAKENETH ALL MY CARE see Sharpe, Evelyn

WINTER WINDS see Fischer, Irwin

WINTER WORDS see Britten, Benjamin

WINTERABEND see Ruyneman, Daniel

WINTERELEGIE see Borup-Jorgensen, Axel

WINTERLICHER MOND see Thomas, Kurt

WINTERLIEBE see Strauss, Richard

WINTERNACHT see Lothar, Mark

WINTERNACHT see Strauss, Richard

WINTERREISE see Schubert, Franz (Peter)

WINTER'S WARMTH see Seyfrit, Michael

WINTERSONG see Mills, Charles

WINTERWALD see Oskam, Izaak J.

WINTERWEIHE see Strauss, Richard

WIR ARMEN, ARMEN MADCHEN see Lortzing, (Gustav) Albert

WIR BESITZEN KEINERLEI FAHIGKEIT, AUS DER KLOSTERNEUBURGERSTRASSE WERZUGEHEN see Krauze, Zygmunt

WIR BITTEN DICH UNENDLICH WESEN see Haydn, (Johann) Michael

WIR EILEN MIT SCHWACHEN, DOCH EMSIGEN SCHRITTEN see Bach, Johann Sebastian

WIR GENIESSEN DIE HIMMLISCHEN FREUDEN see Mahler, Gustav

WIR GLAUBEN ALL AN EINEN GOTT see Schutz, Heinrich

WIR RUHMEN UNS ALLEIN DES KREUZES see Gast, Lothar

WIR TRETEN ZUM BETEN see Kremser, Edward, Dankgebet

WIR WANDELTEN see Beethoven, Ludwig van

WIREN, DAG IVAR (1905-)
Annorstades Vals
solo,pno,opt gtr GEHRMANS s.p. (W962)
Autumn Eve, An *see En Hostens Kvall

En Hostens Kvall (from Hosthorn)
"Autumn Eve, An" [Swed/Eng/Ger] med solo,kbd NORDISKA s.p. (W963)

If O'er The Floor *see Om Till Din Badd

Om Till Din Badd (from Hosthorn)
"If O'er The Floor" [Swed/Eng/Ger] med solo,kbd NORDISKA s.p. (W964)

WIRGES
Dear Friends And Gentle Hearts *see Maxwell

Peace I Leave With You *see Maxwell

WISDOM see Birch, Robert Fairfax

WISE, JESSIE MOORE
Lord Has Given Me A Song, The *see Livingston, Bill

WISE LIVED YESTERDAY, THE see Birch, Robert Fairfax

WISE MEN STILL ADORE HIM see Good, Dwayne

WISEMAN
Tenderly He Watches *sac
solo,pno BENSON S7700-S $1.25 (W965)

WISH, A see Burton, Eldin

WISHART
Dirge
see Two Songs

Mountebank's Song
see Two Songs

Two Songs
T solo,pno OXFORD 62.911 $1.25
contains: Dirge (med); Mountebank's Song (CC,med easy) (W966)

WISHART, PETER (1921-)
June Twilight
[Eng] med solo,pno HINRICHSEN H999 s.p. (W967)

WISHING-CAPS, THE see Binkerd, Gordon

WISSMER, PIERRE (1915-)
Billevesee
see Cinq Poemes De Philippe Monnier

Cinq Poemes De Philippe Monnier
solo,pno AMPHION A 139 $2.25
contains: Billevesee; Jeune Fille; Nuit; Silhouette; Souhait (W968)

Jeune Fille
see Cinq Poemes De Philippe Monnier

La Bonne Fortune *CC6U
S solo,pno AMPHION A 278 $12.50 (W969)

Leonidas
solo,pno AMPHION s.p. solo pt, voc sc (W970)

Nuit
see Cinq Poemes De Philippe Monnier

Silhouette
see Cinq Poemes De Philippe Monnier

Souhait
see Cinq Poemes De Philippe Monnier

WISZNIEWSKI, ZBIGNIEW (1922-)
Deux Ballades *CC2U
A solo,pno MODERN s.p. (W971)

WITH A LITTLE BIT OF HELP see Thygerson, Robert J.

WITH A PAINTED RIBBON see Beethoven, Ludwig van, Mit Einem Gemalten Band

WITH A WATER LILY see Grieg, Edvard Hagerup, Med En Vandlilje

WITH JESUS WILL I GO see Heussenstamm, George

WITH JOYFUL HEART I PRAISE MY SAVIOUR see Bach, Johann Sebastian

WITH LOUDEST REJOICING see Bach, Johann Sebastian

WITH LOVE see Fox, Baynard

WITH MY HEART I FOLLOW YOU see Strickland, Lily Teresa

WITH MYRTLE AND ROSES see Schumann, Robert (Alexander), Mit Myrten Und Rosen

WITH ONE ACCORD see Brandon, George

WITH RUE MY HEART IS LADEN see Barber, Samuel

WITH RUE MY HEART IS LADEN see Dukelsky, Vladimir

WITH RUE MY HEART IS LADEN see Grayson, Richard

WITH RUE MY HEART IS LADEN see Walker, George

WITH SICK AND FAMISH'D EYES see Purcell, Henry

WITH THE DUBLIN FUSILIERS see Stanford, Charles Villiers

WITH THEE ANEAR see Surinach, Carlos

WITH THEE IS PEACE see Schubert, Franz (Peter), Du Bist Die Ruh

WITH THEE ON HIGH *sac,Welsh
med solo,pno (G maj) SCHIRM.G $.60 (W972)

WITH THEE TH' UNSHELTERED MOOR I'D TREAD see Handel, George Frideric

WITH THIS RING see Matesky, T.

WITH VERDURE CLAD see Haydn, (Franz) Joseph

WITH WHAT THEN MAY I BATHE see Rodrigo,
   Joaquin, Con Que La Lavare?

WITHERED FLOWERS see Britain, Radie

WITHIN see Romaine

WITHIN THESE HOLY PORTALS see Mozart,
   Wolfgang Amadeus, In Diesen
   Heil'gen Hallen

WITHIN THINE EYE see Franz, Robert, Ich
   Hab' In Deinem Auge

WITHIN YOUR HEART see Trotere, Henry

WITHOUT HIM see Lefevre

WITHOUT RETURN see Bjelinski, Bruno

WITHOUT SUN see Mussorgsky, Modest

WITHOUT THEE see Gounod, Charles
   Francois, Ce Que Je Suis Sans Toi

WITHOUT, WITHIN see Gagliardi, George

WITHOUT YOU see Oteo, Eres Tu

WITKOWSKI, GEORGES MARTIN (1867-1943)
   Odelette X
      solo,pno/inst DURAND s.p.   (W973)

   Odelettte VIII
      solo,orch DURAND s.p., ipr   (W974)

WITNESS see Johnson

WITTE, D.
   Als De Zondag Komt *Op.25
      solo,pno ALSBACH s.p. see from
      Cabaretliedjes   (W975)

   Asperine *Op.25
      solo,pno ALSBACH s.p. see from
      Cabaretliedjes   (W976)

   Cabaretliedjes *CCUL
      solo,pno cmplt ed ALSBACH s.p.
      see also: De Kleine Soubrette,
      No.7; De Zegen Des
      Vrouwenkiesrechts, No.12; Een
      Liedje Van Verlangen, No.8; Het
      Land Van Noord Scharwou, No.11;
      Lente, No.2; Mensch, Durf Te
      Leven, No.14; M'n Eerste, No.1;
      Nocturne, No.16; Opgang, No.18;
      Oudejaarsavond, No.17; Praters,
      No.19; 'T Portretje, No.6;
      Vodden, No.22   (W977)

   Cabaretliedjes *see Als De Zondag
      Komt, Op.25; Asperine, Op.25; De
      Peren, Op.25; En Toch..., Op.25;
      Halt, Op.25; Laatste Wagen Van
      Lijn Elf, Op.25; Nachtliedje,
      Op.25; Tusschen Dam En
      Rembrandtsplein, Op.25   (W978)

   De Kleine Soubrette *No.7
      solo,pno ALSBACH s.p. see also
      Cabaretliedjes   (W979)

   De Peren *Op.25
      solo,pno ALSBACH s.p. see from
      Cabaretliedjes   (W980)

   De Zegen Des Vrouwenkiesrechts
      *No.12
      solo,pno ALSBACH s.p. see also
      Cabaretliedjes   (W981)

   Een Liedje Van Verlangen *No.8
      solo,pno ALSBACH s.p. see also
      Cabaretliedjes   (W982)

   En Toch... *Op.25
      solo,pno ALSBACH s.p. see from
      Cabaretliedjes   (W983)

   Halt *Op.25
      solo,pno ALSBACH s.p. see from
      Cabaretliedjes   (W984)

   Het Land Van Noord Scharwou *No.11
      solo,pno ALSBACH s.p. see also
      Cabaretliedjes   (W985)

   Laatste Wagen Van Lijn Elf *Op.25
      solo,pno ALSBACH s.p. see from
      Cabaretliedjes   (W986)

   Lente *No.2
      solo,pno ALSBACH s.p. see also
      Cabaretliedjes   (W987)

   Mensch, Durf Te Leven *No.14
      solo,pno ALSBACH s.p. see also
      Cabaretliedjes   (W988)

   M'n Eerste *No.1
      solo,pno ALSBACH s.p. see also
      Cabaretliedjes   (W989)

WITTE, D. (cont'd.)
   Nachtliedje *Op.25
      solo,pno ALSBACH s.p. see from
      Cabaretliedjes   (W990)

   Nocturne *No.16
      solo,pno ALSBACH s.p. see also
      Cabaretliedjes   (W991)

   Opgang *No.18
      solo,pno ALSBACH s.p. see also
      Cabaretliedjes   (W992)

   Oudejaarsavond *No.17
      solo,pno ALSBACH s.p. see also
      Cabaretliedjes   (W993)

   Praters *No.19
      solo,pno ALSBACH s.p. see also
      Cabaretliedjes   (W994)

   'T Portretje *No.6
      solo,pno ALSBACH s.p. see also
      Cabaretliedjes   (W995)

   Tusschen Dam En Rembrandtsplein
      *Op.25
      solo,pno ALSBACH s.p. see from
      Cabaretliedjes   (W996)

   Vodden *No.22
      solo,pno ALSBACH s.p. see also
      Cabaretliedjes   (W997)

WLADLGEROFF, P.
   Lud Gidia *Op.5,No.7
      [Hung] high solo,pno UNIVER. 8258
      $2.75   (W998)

   Sechs Lyrische Lieder *CC6U
      [Ger/Hung] solo,pno UNIVER. 8170
      $4.25   (W999)

WO BIN ICH? NEIN, NICHT EIN OPFER WERD
   ICH'S NENNEN see Gluck, Christoph
   Willibald Ritter von

WO DIE CITRONEN BLUH'N see Strauss,
   Johann

WO DIE SCHONEN TROMPETEN see Mahler,
   Gustav

WO DIE SEELE FLUGELBEBEND SICH OFFNET
   see Woll

WO DU HINGEHST see Becker, R.

WO DU HINGEHST see Hildach, Eugen

WO DU HINGEHST see Peeters, Flor

WO DU HINGEHST see Ries, Franz

WO FIND ICH TROST see Wolf, Hugo

WO GOTT DER HERR NICHT BEI UNS HALT see
   Schutz, Heinrich

WO ICH SEI UND WO MICH HINGEWENDET see
   Schubert, Franz (Peter), Thekla,
   Eine Geisterstimme

WO MAG MEIN SCHATZLEIN WEILEN see
   Kilpinen, Yrio, Missa Armahin

WO SIND SIE HIN? see Grieg, Edvard
   Hagerup, Hvor Er' De Nu?

WO WEILT ER? see Liszt, Franz

WO WILT DU HIN, WEIL'S ABEND IST see
   Krieger, Johann Philipp

WOHER DIESES SEHNEN see Proch, Heinrich

WOHIN? see Schubert, Franz (Peter)

WOHIN FLOHEN DIE WONNESTUNDEN see
   Mozart, Wolfgang Amadeus

WOHL DEM, DER DEN HERREN FURCHTET see
   Bruhns, Nicholaus

WOHL DEM, DER NICHT WANDELT IM RATE DER
   GOTTLOSEN see Schutz, Heinrich

WOHL DENN, DOCH DANN GELIEBTE see
   Mozart, Wolfgang Amadeus, Parto,
   Parto, Ma Tu Ben Mio

WOHL EUCH, IHR AUSERWAHLTEN SEELEN see
   Bach, Johann Sebastian

WOHL WEISS ICH ES see Rimsky-Korsakov,
   Nikolai

WOHLFART, KARL
   Ack, Vad Var Levnad Ar Flyktig Och
      Snar
      solo,pno GEHRMANS s.p. see from Tio
      Sanger   (W1000)

WOHLFART, KARL (cont'd.)
   Angest
      solo,pno GEHRMANS s.p. see from Tio
      Sanger   (W1001)

   Bon
      solo,pno GEHRMANS s.p. see from Tio
      Sanger   (W1002)

   En Gammal Varvisa
      solo,pno GEHRMANS s.p. see from Tio
      Sanger   (W1003)

   Fiolen
      solo,pno GEHRMANS s.p. see from Tio
      Sanger   (W1004)

   Fyra Visor Av Froding *Op.5, CC4U
      solo,pno LUNDQUIST s.p.   (W1005)

   Har Jag Somnat I Doft Av Klover
      solo,pno GEHRMANS s.p. see from Tio
      Sanger   (W1006)

   Morgonsang
      solo,pno GEHRMANS s.p. see from Tio
      Sanger   (W1007)

   Sjofararen Vid Milan *Op.13, CCU
      solo,pno LUNDQUIST s.p.   (W1008)

   Som Ett Blommande Mandeltrad
      solo,pno GEHRMANS s.p. see from Tio
      Sanger   (W1009)

   Spelmansvisa
      solo,pno GEHRMANS s.p. see from Tio
      Sanger   (W1010)

   Tio Sanger *see Ack, Vad Var Levnad
      Ar Flyktig Och Snar; Angest; Bon;
      En Gammal Varvisa; Fiolen; Har
      Jag Somnat I Doft Av Klover;
      Morgonsang; Som Ett Blommande
      Mandeltrad; Spelmansvisa; Ur
      Storgarden   (W1011)

   Tre Dikter *Op.9, CC3U
      solo,pno LUNDQUIST s.p.   (W1012)

   Tre Sanger *Op.11, CC3U
      solo,pno LUNDQUIST s.p.   (W1013)

   Tva Sanger *Op.12, CC2U
      solo,pno LUNDQUIST s.p.   (W1014)

   Ur Storgarden
      solo,pno GEHRMANS s.p. see from Tio
      Sanger   (W1015)

   Vandringssang *Op.14
      solo,pno LUNDQUIST s.p.   (W1016)

WOLCOTT, CH.
   Gebet Von Baha 'U'n9liah
      [Ger/Eng] solo,pno ZIMMER. 1823
      s.p., ea.   (W1017)

WOLF
   Iris
      med solo,pno SHAWNEE IA5030 $.50
                                 (W1018)
      high solo,pno SHAWNEE IA5023 $.50
                                 (W1019)
      low solo,pno SHAWNEE IA5038 $.50
                                 (W1020)

WOLF, ARTUR
   Chatzos
      "Midnight" [Heb/Eng] high solo,pno
      (also with Yiddish text)
      TRANSCON. WJ 403 $.50   (W1021)

   Jacob's Voice *see Kol Yaakov

   Kol Yaakov
      "Jacob's Voice" [Heb/Eng] med solo,
      pno (also with Yiddish text)
      TRANSCON. WJ 404 $.60   (W1022)

   Midnight *see Chatzos

WOLF, HUGO (1860-1903)
   Acht Lieder (from Nachlass) CC8U
      [Ger/Eng] solo,pno (diff) ALKOR 211
      s.p.   (W1023)

   Amato Ben
      see Five Arias

   An Den Schlaf
      [Ger/Eng] solo,2fl,4horn,strings
      PETERS rental   (W1024)

   Anacreon's Grave *see Anakreon's
      Grab

   Anakreon's Grab
      [Ger/Eng] solo,2fl,2clar,2bsn,
      2horn,strings PETERS rental
                                 (W1025)
      "Anacreon's Grave" low solo,pno
      NOVELLO 17.0003.00 s.p.   (W1026)
      (Raphael, Gunter) T solo,2fl,2clar,
      2bsn,2horn,strings BREITKOPF-W
      s.p.   (W1027)

WOLF, HUGO (cont'd.)

Auf Ein Altes Bild
    S solo,2ob,2clar,2bsn BREITKOPF-W
    s.p.   (W1028)
    [Ger/Eng] solo,2ob,2clar,2bsn
    PETERS rental   (W1029)

Book Of Italian Lyrics *CC46UL
    [Ger/Eng] solo,pno INTERNAT. $2.50,
    ea. in 3 volumes   (W1030)

Book Of Spanish Lyrics *CC34UL
    [Ger/Eng] solo,pno INTERNAT. $2.50,
    ea. in 4 volumes   (W1031)

Denk Es, O Seele
    T solo,2ob,2clar,2bsn,2horn,4trp,
    timp,strings BREITKOPF-W s.p.
                                        (W1032)
    [Ger/Eng] solo,2ob,2clar,2bsn,
    2horn,2trp,3trom,timp,strings
    PETERS rental   (W1033)

Der Freund
    (Raphael, Gunter) S solo,2fl,2ob,
    2clar,2bsn,2horn,2trp,timp,
    strings BREITKOPF-W s.p. (W1034)
    (Reger) [Ger/Eng] solo,2fl,2ob,
    2clar,2bsn,2horn,2trp,timp,
    strings PETERS rental   (W1035)

Der Gartner
    (Raphael, Gunter) S solo,fl,ob,
    clar,bsn,horn,strings BREITKOPF-W
    s.p.   (W1036)

Der Rattenfanger
    [Ger] solo,3fl,2ob,2clar,2bsn,
    2horn,2trp,perc,strings PETERS
    rental   (W1037)

Der Tambour
    (Raphael, Gunter) S solo,2clar,
    2bsn,horn,trp,trom,perc,strings
    BREITKOPF-W s.p.   (W1038)

Dreiundzwanzig Gesange In Neuer
    Auswahl *CC23U
    high solo,pno SCHOTTS 114 s.p.
                                        (W1039)

Eichendorff Songs, Vol. I: Nos. 1-10
    *CC10U
    [Eng/Ger] $4.00 solo,pno, original
    keys PETERS 3147A; low solo,pno
    PETERS 3147B   (W1040)

Eichendorff Songs, Vol. II: Nos. 11-
    20 *CC10U
    [Eng/Ger] $4.00 solo,pno, original
    keys PETERS 3148A; low solo,pno
    PETERS 3148B   (W1041)

Elfenlied
    (Raphael, Gunter) A solo,fl,ob,
    clar,horn,trom,harp/pno,strings
    BREITKOPF-W s.p.   (W1042)

Er Ist's
    [Ger/Eng] solo,2fl,2ob,2clar,2bsn,
    4horn,2trp,timp,harp,strings
    PETERS rental   (W1043)
    (Raphael, Gunter) S solo,2fl,2ob,
    2clar,2bsn,2horn,2trp,timp,harp/
    pno,strings BREITKOPF-W s.p.
                                        (W1044)

Feuerreiter *CCU
    [Eng/Ger] high solo,pno PETERS
    3143F $2.50; med solo/low solo,
    pno PETERS 3143G $2.50   (W1045)

Fifty-Two Songs On Poms By Moricke
    *CC52UL
    [Eng/Ger] high solo,pno INTERNAT.
    $2.50, ea. in 4 volumes   (W1046)

Five Arias
    (Kagen, Sergius) [It/Eng] high
    solo,pno INTERNAT. $2.00
    contains: Amato Ben; La
    Farfalletta; Lascera L'amata
    Salma; Sebben Sente; Sento Con
    Quel Diletto   (W1047)

Forty-Eight Songs On Poems By Goethe
    *CC48UL
    [Ger] solo,pno INTERNAT. $2.50, ea.
    in 4 volumes   (W1048)

Fourteen Sacred Songs *sac,CC14U
    (Reger) [Ger] high solo,org PETERS
    3231 $8.00   (W1049)

Funfzehn Lieder *CC15L
    [Ger/Span] solo,pno cmplt ed
    RICORDI-ARG BA 9876 s.p.   (W1050)

Fussreise
    (Raphael, Gunter) A solo,2clar,
    2bsn,2horn,strings BREITKOPF-W
    s.p.   (W1051)

Gebet
    [Ger/Eng] solo,2clar,2bsn,4horn,
    strings PETERS rental   (W1052)
    (Raphael, Gunter) A solo,2clar,

WOLF, HUGO (cont'd.)

    2bsn,4horn/2horn,strings
    BREITKOPF-W s.p.   (W1053)

Gesang Margits
    see Michelangelo Songs

Gesang Weyla's
    [Ger/Eng] solo,clar,horn,harp
    PETERS rental   (W1054)
    S solo,ob,horn,harp/pno BREITKOPF-W
    s.p.   (W1055)

Goethe Songs, Vol. I: Nos. 1-11
    *CC11U
    [Ger] solo,pno PETERS 3156 $4.00
                                        (W1056)

Goethe Songs, Vol. II: Nos. 12-18,
    49-51 *CC10U
    [Ger] solo,pno PETERS 3157 $4.75
                                        (W1057)

Goethe Songs, Vol. III: Nos. 19-33
    *CC15U
    [Ger] solo,pno PETERS 3158 $4.00
                                        (W1058)

Goethe Songs, Vol. IV: Nos. 34-48
    *CC15U
    [Ger] solo,pno PETERS 3159 $4.50
                                        (W1059)

Gudmunds Erste Gesang
    see Michelangelo Songs

Gudmunds Zweite Gesang
    see Michelangelo Songs

Harfenspieler I
    [Ger] solo,2fl,2ob,2clar,2bsn,
    2horn,harp,strings PETERS rental
                                        (W1060)

Harfenspieler II
    [Ger] solo,2ob,clar,2bsn,strings
    PETERS rental   (W1061)

Harfenspieler III
    [Ger] solo,2fl,2ob,2clar,2bsn,
    4horn,harp,strings PETERS rental
                                        (W1062)

Harpist's Songs *CC3U
    [Eng/Ger] med solo/low solo,pno
    PETERS 3156A $2.00   (W1063)

Heimweh
    (Marx) [Ger/Eng] solo,2fl,2ob,
    2clar,2bsn,4horn,trp,timp,strings
    PETERS rental   (W1064)
    (Raphael, Gunter) S solo,2fl,2ob,
    2clar,2bsn,2horn,2trp,strings,
    harp/pno BREITKOPF-W s.p. (W1065)

Heine Lieder *CC7U
    [Ger] high solo,pno PETERS 3161
    $3.25   (W1066)

Hemlangtan
    high solo,pno GEHRMANS s.p. (W1067)

Herr, Schicke Was Du Willt *sac
    Mez solo,pno (E maj) LIENAU HOS 193
    s.p.   (W1068)

Hugo Wolf Album *CC51U
    (Gerhardt, Elena) [Eng/Ger] high
    solo,pno PETERS 4290A $7.50; med
    solo/low solo,pno PETERS 4209B
    $7.50   (W1069)

Hugo Wolf-Album For Baritone Or Bass
    *CC35U
    (Gerhardt, Elena) [Eng/Ger] Bar/B
    solo,pno PETERS 4291 $7.50
                                        (W1070)

I Ensamhet
    low solo,pno GEHRMANS s.p. (W1071)
    solo,pno GEHRMANS 675 s.p. (W1072)
    high solo,pno GEHRMANS s.p. (W1073)

Ich Hab In Penna Einen Liebsten
    Wohnen
    [Ger/Eng] solo,2fl,ob,2clar,2bsn,
    3horn,trp,timp,strings PETERS
    rental   (W1074)

In Der Fruhe
    [Ger/Eng] solo,3ob,2clar,2bsn,
    4horn,3trom,strings PETERS rental
                                        (W1075)
    (Raphael, Gunter) A solo,2English
    horn,2clar,2bsn,4horn,3trom,
    strings BREITKOPF-W s.p. (W1076)

Italian Lyrics, Vol. I: Nos. 1-15
    *CC15U
    [Eng/Ger] solo,pno PETERS 3144
    $4.00   (W1077)

Italian Lyrics, Vol. II: Nos. 16-30
    *CC15U
    [Eng/Ger] solo,pno PETERS 3145
    $4.00   (W1078)

Italian Lyrics, Vol. III: Nos. 31-46
    *CC16U
    [Eng/Ger] solo,pno PETERS 3146
    $4.00   (W1079)

WOLF, HUGO (cont'd.)

Italienisches Liederbuch *CCU
    (Jancik, Hans) solo,pno MUSIKWISS.
    W V s.p.   (W1080)

Karwoche
    [Ger/Eng] solo,3fl,2ob,2clar,2bsn,
    4horn,perc,strings PETERS rental
                                        (W1081)

La Farfalletta
    see Five Arias

Lascera L'amata Salma
    see Five Arias

Lieder-Auswahl *CCU
    s.p. high solo,pno SCHOTTS 5935;
    low solo,pno SCHOTTS 5936 (W1082)

Lieder Nach Gedichten Von E. Morike
    *CCU
    (Jancik, Hans) solo,pno MUSIKWISS.
    W I s.p.   (W1083)

Lieder Nach Gedichten Von Eichendorff
    *CCU
    (Jancik, Hans) solo,pno MUSIKWISS.
    W II s.p.   (W1084)

Lieder Zur Weihnacht *CC8U,Xmas
    [Eng/Ger] med solo,pno PETERS 4289
    $4.00   (W1085)

Liederbuch *CC30U
    [Ger] high solo,pno BREITKOPF-W
    EB 5701 $2.25; low solo,pno
    BREITKOPF-W EB 5702 $2.25 (W1086)

Michelangelo-Lieder *song cycle
    (Borg, Kim) B/Bar solo,2fl,ob,
    2clar,2bsn,2horn,2trp,2trom,timp,
    perc,strings BREITKOPF-W s.p.
                                        (W1087)

Michelangelo Songs
    [Eng/Ger] B solo,pno PETERS 3155
    $2.50
    contains: Gesang Margits;
    Gudmunds Erste Gesang; Gudmunds
    Zweite Gesang   (W1088)

Mignon
    [Ger] solo,2fl,3ob,2clar,3bsn,
    4horn,2trp,3trom,timp,harp,
    strings PETERS rental   (W1089)

Mignon [2]
    [Ger] solo,2fl,3ob,2clar,2bsn,
    4horn,trp,3trom,timp,strings
    PETERS rental   (W1090)

Morike-Lieder *CCU
    (Jancik, Hans) solo,pno (diff)
    BAREN. s.p.   (W1091)

Morike Songs, Vol. I: Nos. 1-12
    *CC12U
    [Eng/Ger] $4.00 solo,pno, original
    keys PETERS 3140A; low solo,pno
    PETERS 3140B   (W1092)

Morike Songs, Vol. II: Nos. 13-24
    *CC12U
    [Eng/Ger] $4.00 solo,pno, original
    keys PETERS 3141A; low solo,pno
    PETERS 3141B   (W1093)

Morike Songs, Vol. III: Nos. 25-39
    *CC15U
    [Eng/Ger] $4.00 solo,pno, original
    keys PETERS 3142A; low solo,pno
    PETERS 3142B   (W1094)

Morike Songs, Vol. IV: Nos. 40-44
    *CC5U
    [Eng/Ger] low solo,pno PETERS 3143B
    $4.00   (W1095)

Morike Songs, Vol. IV: Nos. 40-53
    *CC14U
    [Eng/Ger] solo,pno, original keys
    PETERS 3143A $4.50   (W1096)

Morike Songs, Vol. IV: Nos. 45-51, 53
    *CC8U
    [Eng/Ger] low solo,pno PETERS 3143D
    $4.00   (W1097)

Nachgelassene Lieder II *CCU
    (Jancik, Hans) solo,pno MUSIKWISS.
    W VII-2 s.p.   (W1098)

Neue Liebe
    [Ger/Eng] solo,2fl,2ob,2clar,2bsn,
    4horn,2trp,3trom,timp,strings
    PETERS rental   (W1099)

Par Min Dirti
    see Two Arias

Prometheus
    [Ger] solo,3fl,3ob,2clar,3bsn,
    4horn,3trp,3trom,tuba,perc,
    strings PETERS rental   (W1100)

WOLF, HUGO (cont'd.)

Quinze Lieder, Cahier I *CC8L
(Pittion, Colette Paul) [Ger/Fr]
solo,pno OUVRIERES s.p. (W1101)

Quinze Lieder, Cahier II *CC7L
(Pittion, Colette Paul) [Ger/Fr]
solo,pno OUVRIERES s.p. (W1102)

Schlafendes Jesuskind
[Ger] solo,2fl,2ob,2clar,2bsn,
strings PETERS rental (W1103)
(Raphael, Gunter) S solo,2fl,2ob,
2clar,2bsn,strings BREITKOPF-W
s.p. (W1104)

Sebben Sente
see Five Arias

Sechzehn Lieder Heft I *CC8L
(Wolf, H.; Raphael, G.) S/A/T solo,
2fl,3ob,2clar,2bsn,4horn,2trp,
3trom,timp,harp/pno,strings sc
BREITKOPF-L PB 3440 s.p., ipr in
original keys (W1105)

Sechzehn Lieder Heft II *CC8L
(Wolf, H.; Raphael, G.) S/T solo,
2fl,2ob,2clar,2bsn,2horn,trp,
trom,harp/pno,strings sc
BREITKOPF-L PB 3441 s.p., ipr in
original keys (W1106)

Secrecy *see Verborgenheit

Selected Goethe Songs *CC18U
[Ger] med solo/low solo,pno PETERS
3387 $4.00 (W1107)

Selected Songs From Italian Lyrics
*CC15U
[Eng/Ger] med solo/low solo,pno
PETERS 3184B $4.00 (W1108)

Selected Songs From Spanish Lyrics
(Secular) *sec,CC9U
[Eng/Ger] low solo,pno PETERS 3185B
$4.00 (W1109)

Sento Con Quel Diletto
see Five Arias

Sixty-Five Songs *CC65L
(Kagen, Sergius) [Ger/Eng]
INTERNAT. high solo,pno $7.50;
low solo,pno $7.50 (W1110)

Solitudine *see Verborgenheit

Spanisches Liederbuch *CCU
(Jancik, Hans) solo,pno (diff)
BAREN. s.p. (W1111)

Spanisches Liederbuch *CCU
(Jancik, Hans) solo,pno MUSIKWISS.
W IV s.p. (W1112)

Spanish Lyrics, Vol. I: Nos. 3, 4, 6,
9 *sac,CC4U
[Eng/Ger] low solo,pno PETERS 3185A
$4.00 (W1113)

Spanish Lyrics, Vol. I: Sacred Songs
*sac,CC10U
[Eng/Ger] solo,pno PETERS 3149
$4.00 (W1114)

Spanish Lyrics, Vol. II: Secular
Songs Nos. 1-11 *CC11U
[Eng/Ger] solo,pno PETERS 3150
$4.00 (W1115)

Spanish Lyrics, Vol. III: Secular
Songs Nos. 12-22 *CC11U
[Eng/Ger] solo,pno PETERS 3151
$4.00 (W1116)

Spanish Lyrics, Vol. IV: Secular
Songs Nos. 23-34 *CC12U
[Eng/Ger] solo,pno PETERS 3152
$4.00 (W1117)

Standchen
(Reger) [Ger/Eng] solo,fl,ob,clar,
bsn,horn,timp,strings PETERS
rental (W1118)

Sterb Ich, So Hullt In Blumen Meine
Glieder
(Reger) [Ger/Eng] solo,fl,ob,2clar,
2bsn,2horn,timp,strings PETERS
rental (W1119)

Stum Karlek
low solo,pno GEHRMANS s.p. (W1120)
high solo,pno GEHRMANS s.p. (W1121)

Three Songs On Lyrics By Michelangelo
*CC3U
[Ger/Eng] B solo,pno INTERNAT.
$1.75 (W1122)

Through The Night
low solo,pno (A maj) ASHDOWN s.p.
(W1123)

WOLF, HUGO (cont'd.)

high solo,pno (E flat maj) ASHDOWN
s.p. (W1124)
med solo,pno (C maj) ASHDOWN s.p.
(W1125)

Ti Sento
see Two Arias

Tradgardsmastaren
low solo,pno GEHRMANS s.p. (W1126)
high solo,pno GEHRMANS s.p. (W1127)

Twenty-Five Songs On Lyrics By
Various Poets *CC25UL
[Ger/Eng] solo,pno INTERNAT. $2.50,
ea. in 2 volumes (W1128)

Twenty-Five Songs, Vol. I *CC12U
[Eng/Ger] med solo/low solo,pno
PETERS 3153 $4.50 (W1129)

Twenty-Five Songs, Vol. II *CC13U
[Eng/Ger] med solo/low solo,pno
PETERS 3154 $5.50 (W1130)

Twenty Songs On Poems By Eichendorff
*CC20UL
[Ger/Eng] solo,pno INTERNAT. $2.50,
ea. in 2 volumes (W1131)

Two Arias
(Kagen, Sergius) [It/Eng] med-low
solo,pno INTERNAT. $1.50
contains: Par Min Dirti; Ti Sento
(W1132)

Uber Nacht Kommt Still Das Lied
[Ger/Eng] low solo,pno BOTE $.75
(W1133)
[Ger/Eng] high solo,pno BOTE $.75
(W1134)

Und Willst Du Deinen Liebsten Sterben
Sehn
(Reger) [Ger/Eng] solo,fl,ob,2clar,
2bsn,2horn,timp,strings PETERS
rental (W1135)

Verborgenheit
"Secrecy" med solo,pno NOVELLO
17.0164.09 s.p. (W1136)
"Secrecy" [Eng/Ger] high solo,pno
PRESSER $.75 (W1137)
"Solitudine" solo,2fl,2ob,2clar,
2bsn,2horn CARISH s.p. (W1138)
(Marx) [Ger/Eng] solo,2fl,ob,2clar,
2bsn,3horn,timp,strings PETERS
rental (W1139)
(Raphael, Gunter) S solo,fl,ob,
clar,2bsn,horn,strings BREITKOPF-
W s.p. (W1140)

Wenn Du Zu Den Blumen Gehst
see Zwei Orchesterlieder Aus Dem
Spanischen Liederbuch

Wer Sein Holdes Lieb Verloren
see Zwei Orchesterlieder Aus Dem
Spanischen Liederbuch

Weylas Sang
low solo,pno GEHRMANS s.p. (W1141)
high solo,pno GEHRMANS s.p. (W1142)

Wo Find Ich Trost
[Ger/Eng] solo,2fl,3ob,2clar,2bsn,
4horn,2trp,3trom,timp,strings
PETERS rental (W1143)

Zum Neuen Jahr
(Raphael, Gunter) S solo,2fl,2clar,
2bsn,strings,opt horn BREITKOPF-W
s.p. (W1144)

Zwei Orchesterlieder Aus Dem
Spanischen Liederbuch
(Haas, Robert) [Ger/Eng] T solo,
2fl,2ob,2clar,2bsn,4horn,harp,
strings sc BREITKOPF-L s.p., ipa
contains: Wenn Du Zu Den Blumen
Gehst; Wer Sein Holdes Lieb
Verloren (W1145)

WOLF-FERRARI, ERMANNO (1876-1948)
Aprila, O Bella (from Jewels Of The
Madonna, The)
[It/Eng] Bar solo,pno (G maj)
SCHIRM.G $.75 (W1146)

Bondi, Venezia Casa! (from Il
Campiello)
[It] S solo,pno RICORDI-ENG 127632
s.p. (W1147)

Nella Notturna Selva (from La Vedova
Scaltra)
[It] S solo,pno SONZOGNO 2743 $1.25
(W1148)

Quattro Rispetti *Op.11, CC4U
[It/Ger/Eng] $3.50 high solo,pno
SCHAUR EE 1172; low solo,pno
SCHAUR EE 1173 (W1149)

Quattro Rispetti *Op.12, CC4U
[It/Ger] $3.50 high solo,pno SCHAUR
EE 1174; low solo,pno SCHAUR
EE 1175 (W1150)

WOLFE, JACQUES (1896-   )
Blessed, The *sac
high solo,pno (E min) SCHIRM.G $.75
(W1151)
med-low solo,pno (B min) SCHIRM.G
$.75 (W1152)

De Glory Road
med-low solo,pno (G min) SCHIRM.G
$1.00 (W1153)

Sailormen
solo,pno (D maj) ALLANS s.p.
(W1154)

Shortnin' Bread
low solo,pno (D maj) ALLANS s.p.
(W1155)
high solo,pno (F maj) ALLANS s.p.
(W1156)

WOLFE, LANNY
Before I Found The Lord *sac
solo,pno BENSON S5174-R $1.00 (W1157)

Come On, Let's Praise Him! *sac
solo,pno BENSON S5301-R $1.00 (W1158)

Dawning Of A New Day, The *sac
solo,pno BENSON S7813-R $1.00 (W1159)

Everywhere *sac
solo,pno BENSON S5429-S $1.00
(W1160)

God's Wonderful People *sac
solo,pno BENSON S5578-S $1.00
(W1161)

Greater *sac,CC10UL
solo,pno BENSON BO497 $2.50 (W1162)

Greater Is He That Is In Me *sac
solo,pno BENSON S5600-S $1.00
(W1163)

Heaven For Me *sac
solo,pno BENSON S6751-R $1.00
(W1164)
solo,pno BENSON S6750-S $1.00
(W1165)

I Just Want To Know *sac
solo,pno BENSON S6053-R $1.00
(W1166)

I Love Him Too Much *sac
solo,pno BENSON S6081-R $1.00
(W1167)

Jesus Did It For Me *sac
solo,pno BENSON S6705-R $1.00
(W1168)

Jesus Got Ahold Of My Life *sac
solo,pno BENSON S6706-R $1.00
(W1169)

Jesus Is Still The Answer *sac
solo,pno BENSON S6725-S $1.00
(W1170)

Jesus Made A Believer Out Of Me *sac
solo,pno BENSON S6729-RS $1.00 (W1171)

Joy That Jesus Gives, The *sac
solo,pno BENSON S7910-S $1.00
(W1172)

Let's Sing A Song About Jesus *sac
solo,pno BENSON S6862-R $1.00
(W1173)

Little Taste Of Heaven, A *sac
solo,pno BENSON S5030-R $1.00
(W1174)

One Day Closer *sac
solo,pno BENSON S7285-R $1.00
(W1175)

One Day Too Late *sac
solo,pno BENSON S7289-R $1.00
(W1176)

One Left Behind, The *sac
solo,pno BENSON S8015-S $1.00
(W1177)

Only Jesus Can Satisfy Your Soul
*sac,CC10L
solo,pno BENSON BO496 $2.50 (W1178)

Only Jesus Can Satisfy Your Soul
*sac
solo,pno BENSON S7314-S $1.00
(W1179)

Only One Life *sac
solo,pno BENSON S7315-R $1.00
(W1180)

Race, The *sac
solo,pno BENSON S8019-R $1.00
(W1181)

Someday I'll Walk On Gold *sac
solo,pno BENSON S7534-S $1.00
(W1182)

Sounds Of His Coming, The *sac
solo,pno BENSON S8036-R $1.00
(W1183)

Then Why The Tears? *sac
solo,pno BENSON S8106-S $1.00
(W1184)

There Is Just No Place Like Home
*sac
solo,pno BENSON S8110-R $1.00
(W1185)

There's Something In The Air *sac
solo,pno BENSON S8122-R $1.00
(W1186)

Weaver, The *sac
solo,pno BENSON S8086-R $1.00
(W1187)

WOLFE, LANNY (cont'd.)

Wonderful Feeling, A *sac
solo,pno BENSON S5076-R $1.00
(W1188)

Year When Jesus Comes, The *sac
solo,pno BENSON S8090-R $1.00
(W1189)

You Can't Go Back Now *sac
solo,pno BENSON S8581-R $1.00
(W1190)

WOLFF, A.
Allons, Souvenez-Vous Du Bal (from Le
Marchand De Masques)
high solo,pno ENOCH s.p. (W1191)
low solo,pno ENOCH s.p. (W1192)

Aurore
solo,orch DURAND s.p., ipr see from
Mirages (W1193)

Ce N'est Pas Le Faute A Nous Deux
solo,orch ENOCH rental (W1194)

Eternelle Chanson (from L'Eternelle
Chanson)
solo,orch ENOCH rental (W1195)

Ils Chantent, Tous Ces Masques (from
Le Marchand De Masques)
high solo,pno ENOCH s.p. (W1196)
low solo,pno ENOCH s.p. (W1197)

J'ai Chaud
solo,pno/inst DURAND s.p. see from
Poemes Intimes De Colette (W1198)

Je Veux Pleurer
solo,orch ENOCH rental see also
L'Eternelle Chanson (W1199)
solo,pno ENOCH s.p. see also
L'Eternelle Chanson (W1200)

Je Vous Ai Tellement Mele (from
L'Eternelle Chanson)
solo,pno ENOCH s.p. see also
L'Eternelle Chanson (W1201)
solo,orch ENOCH rental (W1202)

La Chanson De Tyltyl (from L'Oiseau
Bleu)
solo,pno (available in 2 keys)
ENOCH s.p. (W1203)

Les Deux Corteges
solo,orch ENOCH rental (W1204)
solo,pno ENOCH s.p. (W1205)

Les Vierges De Vingt Ans
solo,orch DURAND s.p., ipr see from
Mirages (W1206)

L'Eternelle Chanson *CC12L
cmplt ed ENOCH solo,orch rental;
solo,pno s.p.
see also: Je Veux Pleurer; Je
Vous Ai Tellement Mele; Priere:
Dieu Qui Deroulez (W1207)

Me Taire? Non. J'ai Trop Souffert
(from Le Marchand De Masques)
solo,pno ENOCH s.p. (W1208)

Mirages *see Aurore; Les Vierges De
Vingt Ans; Soir (W1209)

Poemes Intimes De Colette *see J'ai
Chaud; Repit; Sommeil (W1210)

Priere: Dieu Qui Deroulez
solo,pno ENOCH s.p. see also
L'Eternelle Chanson (W1211)
solo,orch ENOCH rental see also
L'Eternelle Chanson (W1212)

Quand Vous Riez (from L'Eternelle
Chanson)
solo,orch ENOCH rental (W1213)

Repit
solo,pno/inst DURAND s.p. see from
Poemes Intimes De Colette (W1214)

Ruines Du Coeur
solo,pno ENOCH s.p. (W1215)

Soir
solo,orch DURAND s.p., ipr see from
Mirages (W1216)

Sommeil (from L'Eternelle Chanson)
solo,pno/inst DURAND s.p. see from
Poemes Intimes De Colette (W1217)
solo,orch ENOCH rental (W1218)

Va, Brancardier
solo,pno ENOCH s.p. (W1219)
solo,orch ENOCH rental (W1220)
solo,acap ENOCH s.p. (W1221)

WOLFRAMIN LAULU ILTATAHDELLE see
Wagner, Richard, Wolframs Lied An
Den Abendstern

WOLFRAMS LIED AN DEN ABENDSTERN see
Wagner, Richard

WOLFSOHN, GEORG
Good Luck, Good Cheer
high solo,pno ISRAELI 210 $2.80
(W1222)

WOLKEROVY PISNE see Jindrich, Jindrich

WOLKONSKIJ, ANDREJ
Spiegel-Suite *song cycle
[Russ/Span/Ger] S solo,fl,perc,org,
vln,gtr SIKORSKI 825 s.p. (W1223)

WOLL
Lieder Der Liebe *CCU
med solo,pno TONGER s.p. (W1224)

Wo Die Seele Flugelbebend Sich Offnet
med solo,pno TONGER s.p. (W1225)

WOLL, E.
Du Hast Uns Gerufen *sac,Mass
solo,inst,org CHRIS 50694 s.p.
(W1226)

WOLPE, STEFAN (1902-1972)
Lazy Andy Ant
solo,2pno sc SEESAW $10.00 (W1227)

O Captain, My Captain
med solo,pno TRANSCON. TV 470 $.50
(W1228)

People's March
med solo,pno TRANSCON. TV 469 $.40
(W1229)

Unto The New Day
med solo,pno TRANSCON. TV 468 $.40
(W1230)

WOLPERT
Das Olgenahrte Lamplein
see Vier Lieder Nach Gedichten Des
Hafis

Das Verschlossene Paradies
see Vier Lieder Nach Gedichten Des
Hafis

Die Nachtigall Und Die Rose
see Vier Lieder Nach Gedichten Des
Hafis

Mondlicht
see Vier Lieder Nach Gedichten Des
Hafis

Vier Lieder Nach Gedichten Des Hafis
[Ger] solo,pno BREITKOPF-W EB 5964
s.p.
contains: Das Olgenahrte
Lamplein; Das Verschlossene
Paradies; Die Nachtigall Und
Die Rose; Mondlicht (W1231)

WOLTERS
Grunt Ein Tannenbaum *Xmas
solo,pno TONGER s.p. (W1232)

WOMAN IS A BRANCHY TREE, A see Mourant,
Walter

WOMAN OF VALOR, A see Adler, Samuel

WOMAN OF VALOR, A see Kosakoff, Reuven

WOMAN OF VIRTUE, A see Clarke, Henry
Leland

WOMAN, WHY WEEPEST THOU? see Schutz,
Heinrich

WOMAN'S ARMOR, A see Kubik, Gail

WOMAN'S KISS, A see Friml, Rudolf

WOMAN'S LIFE see Schumann, Robert
(Alexander), Frauenliebe Und Leben

WOMAN'S LIFE AND LOVE see Schumann,
Robert (Alexander), Frauenliebe Und
Leben

WOMEN ARE A' GANE WUD see Lawson,
Malcolm

WOMEN OF YUEH, THE see Bliss, Sir
Arthur

WONDER ALBUM *CC8L
[It/Eng] S solo,pno RICORDI-ENG
LD 404 s.p. contains works by:
Puccini; Verdi (W1233)

WONDER OF GOD'S LOVE, THE see Baker,
Richard

WONDER OF IT, THE see Shea, George
Beverly

WONDER OF WONDERS see Peterson, John W.

WONDER OF WONDERS, THE
see Songs Of Wonder

WONDERFUL FEELING, A see Wolfe, Lanny

WONDERFUL GRACE OF JESUS *sac,gospel
solo,pno ABER.GRP. $1.50
(W1234)

WONDERFUL WIDOW OF EIGHTEEN SPRINGS,
THE see Cage, John

WOND'ROUS ART THOU, MY LOVELY QUEEN see
Brahms, Johannes, Wie Bist Du Meine
Konigin

WONDROUS LOVE see Rider, Dale G.

WONDROUS MACHINE see Purcell, Henry

WOND'ROUS MONTH OF MAY, THE see
Schumann, Robert (Alexander), Im
Wunderschonen Monat Mai

WONGA DALE see Harrhy, Edith

WONNE DER SEHNSUCHT see Zagwijn, Henri

WONNIG SUSSES HOFFNUNGSTRAUMEN see
Weber, Carl Maria von

WON'T YOU COME ROVING see Bateman,
Ronald

WOO NOT THE WORLD see Birch, Robert
Fairfax

WOOD
This Quiet Night *sac
high solo,pno (A flat maj) BELWIN
$1.50 (W1235)
med solo,pno (F maj) BELWIN
$1.50 (W1236)

Yellow Tree
solo,pno ALLANS s.p. (W1237)

WOOD, CHARLES (1866-1926)
Ethiopia Saluting The Colours
solo,pno (A flat maj) BOOSEY $1.50
(W1238)

Jug Of Punch, The
low solo,pno (F maj) BOOSEY $1.50
(W1239)
high solo,pno (G maj) BOOSEY $1.50
(W1240)

WOOD, DALE
O God Of Love
see FIVE WEDDING SONGS

Slumber, O Holy Jesu *sac,Xmas
low solo,pno ABINGDON APM-373 $.75
(W1241)
high solo,pno ABINGDON APM-370 $.75
(W1242)

WOOD, DANIEL
Garden Of Happiness
low solo,orch (E flat maj) ASHDOWN
$1.50, ipr (W1243)
med-high solo,orch (G maj) ASHDOWN
$1.50, ipr (W1244)
med solo,orch (F maj) ASHDOWN
$1.50, ipr (W1245)
high solo&low solo,pno ASHDOWN
$1.75 (W1246)
med solo&med solo,pno ASHDOWN $1.75
(W1247)
high solo,orch (A flat maj) ASHDOWN
$1.50, ipr (W1248)

Glory Of My Garden, The
low solo,pno (B flat maj) ASHDOWN
s.p. (W1249)
high solo,pno (D maj) ASHDOWN s.p.
(W1250)
med solo,pno (C maj) ASHDOWN s.p.
(W1251)

I Heard You Go By
med solo,orch (E flat maj) ASHDOWN
$2.00, ipr (W1252)
low solo,orch (C maj) ASHDOWN
$2.00, ipr (W1253)
high solo,orch (F maj) ASHDOWN
$2.00, ipr (W1254)

On The Way To You
low solo,orch (B flat maj) ASHDOWN
s.p., ipr (W1255)
high solo,orch (E flat maj) ASHDOWN
s.p., ipr (W1256)
med solo,orch (C maj) ASHDOWN s.p.,
ipr (W1257)

WOOD, DON
Beatitudes *sac
high solo,pno (E flat min) SCHIRM.G
$.75 (W1258)

WOOD, HAYDN (1882-1959)
Bird Of Love Divine
low solo,pno (E flat maj) BOOSEY
$1.50 (W1259)
high solo,pno (G maj) BOOSEY $1.50
(W1260)
med solo,pno (F maj) BOOSEY $1.50
(W1261)

WOOD, JEFF
Side By Side *sac
solo,pno BRIDGE Z 0586 s.p. (W1262)

WOOD, JOSEPH (1915-   )
Chinese Love Poem *Chin
  A solo,pno AM.COMP.AL. $3.57
                              (W1263)

  Lonesome Walls
    high solo,pno AM.COMP.AL. $2.75
                              (W1264)

  Three Songs From The Hebrides *CC3U
    AM.COMP.AL. low solo,pno $3.85; med
    solo,pno $3.85   (W1265)

WOOD FIRES see Hazelhurst, Cecil

WOOD MAGIC see Shaw, Martin

WOOD OF FLOWERS, THE see Klein, Ivy
  Frances

WOODCUTTER'S SONG (from Pilgrim's
  Progress) sac
  S solo,pno/opt inst (easy) OXFORD
  62.208 $1.50   (W1266)

WOODEN SPOON, A see Nakada, Yoshinao

WOODFORDE-FINDEN, AMY
  Florida Love Song
    high solo,pno (A min) LEONARD-ENG
                              (W1267)
    low solo,pno (G min) LEONARD-ENG
                              (W1268)

  Four Indian Love Lyrics *CC4U
    A/Bar solo,pno BOOSEY $3.00 (W1269)

  Kashmiri Song
    med solo,pno (D flat maj) BOOSEY
    $1.50   (W1270)
    low solo,pno (C maj) BOOSEY $1.50
                              (W1271)
    2 soli,pno (B flat maj) BOOSEY
    $1.75   (W1272)
    high solo,pno (F maj) BOOSEY $1.50
                              (W1273)

  Less Than The Dust
    solo,pno (A min) BOOSEY $1.50
                              (W1274)

  Request, A
    low solo,pno (A min) CRAMER (W1275)
    2 soli,pno LEONARD-ENG   (W1276)
    high solo,pno (D min) CRAMER
                              (W1277)
    med-high solo,pno (C min) CRAMER
                              (W1278)
    med solo,pno (B min) CRAMER (W1279)

  Song Of The Lotus-Lily
    solo,pno (B flat maj) CRAMER
                              (W1280)

WOODGATE, LESLIE (1902-1961)
  In Praise Of Cider
    solo,pno CRAMER $.95   (W1281)

  Loveliest Of Trees
    solo,pno CRAMER $1.15   (W1282)

  Wooing Song, A
    solo,pno CRAMER $.95   (W1283)

WOODLAND DELL, A see Goosens, Eugene

WOODLAND MESSAGE, A see Rowley, Alec

WOODLAND SERENADE see Mascheroni,
  Angelo

WOODMAN, RAYMOND HUNTINGTON (1861-1943)
  Birthday, A
    low solo,pno (A flat maj) SCHIRM.G
    $.75   (W1284)

  Open Secret, An
    high solo,pno (D flat maj) SCHIRM.G
    $.75   (W1285)

WOODS SO DENSE see Lully (Lulli), Jean-
  Baptiste, Bois Epais

WOOING OF THE ROSE, THE see Franck,
  Cesar, Le Marriage Des Roses

WOOING SONG, A see Woodgate, Leslie

WOOLER, A.
  Consider And Hear Me *sac
    solo,pno (D maj) ALLANS s.p.
                              (W1286)
    high solo,pno PRESSER $.75 (W1287)

  Lord Is My Shepherd
    high solo,pno (G maj) BOOSEY $1.50
                              (W1288)
    low solo,pno (F maj) BOOSEY $1.50
                              (W1289)

WOOLLEN, RUSSELL
  Farewell, Once My Delight
    high solo,pno AM.COMP.AL. $3.85
                              (W1290)

  Prayer Of St. Francis Of Asissi
    med solo,pno/org AM.COMP.AL. $1.10
                              (W1291)

  Suite For High Voice *CCU
    high solo,pno AM.COMP.AL. $9.35
                              (W1292)

  Three Sonnets Of Dubellay *CC3U
    med solo,pno AM.COMP.AL. $6.60
                              (W1293)

WOOLLEN, RUSSELL (cont'd.)
  Two Songs Of John Donne *CC2U
    med solo,pno AM.COMP.AL. $5.50
                              (W1294)

  Wedding Hymn *Marriage,Bibl
    S solo,org AM.COMP.AL. $3.57
                              (W1295)

  Willow Brook Suite *CCU
    AM.COMP.AL. med solo,pno $12.10;
    low solo,pno $12.10   (W1296)

WORD OF GOD INCARNATE see Gilbert,
  Harry

WORD OF LOVE, THE see Bezanson, Philip

WORD OF THE LORD, THE see Bernstein,
  Leonard

WORDS see Bois, Rob du

WORDS see Hoag, Charles K.

WORK, HENRY CLAY (1832-1884)
  Henry Clay Work Songs *CC39UL
    (Work, Bertram G.) DA CAPO $16.50
                              (W1297)

  My Grandfather's Clock
    med solo,pno PAXTON P2268 s.p.
                              (W1298)

WORK, JOHN [WESLEY] (1901-   )
  Ev'ry Mail Day
    low solo,pno GALAXY 1.1429.7 $1.25
                              (W1299)

  Go Tell It On The Mountain *Xmas
    med solo/high solo,pno (A flat maj)
    GALAXY 1.1928.7 $1.00   (W1300)
    low solo,pno (A flat maj) GALAXY
    1.1929.7 $1.00   (W1301)

  God I Need Thee
    med solo/low solo,pno GALAXY
    1.1762.7 $1.00   (W1302)

  This Little Light O Mine
    med solo,pno GALAXY 1.1489.7 $1.00
                              (W1303)

WORKIN' MAN'S PRAYER see Stanphill, Ira
  F.

WORKS FROM ROEMANIE see D'Haene, Rafael
  Lodewijk

WORLD see Finnessy, Michael

WORLD, THE see Cho-Tung Tang, Jordan

WORLD, THE see Geraedts, Jaap

WORLD FAMOUS SONGS *CC98U
  (Frey, Hugo) solo,pno/gtr MUSIC
  040002 $4.95   (W1304)

WORLD FAMOUS SONGS see Stanphill, Ira
  F.

WORLD OF DREAM, THE see Fischer, Irwin

WORLD SONG, THE *Op.91b
  [Eng/Fr] med solo,kbd HANSEN-DEN s.p.
                              (W1305)

WORLD TODAY IS WILD, THE see Smolanoff,
  Michael

WORLD WILL LAUGH AGAIN, THE see
  Stanton, Louis

WORLDS APART see Peterson, John W.

WORLD'S DELIGHT, THE see Shaw, Martin

WORONOFF, WLADMIR (1903-   )
  Annas Et Le Lepreux *sac
    B solo,pno CBDM s.p.   (W1306)

  D'une Fontaine
    B solo,pno CBDM s.p.   (W1307)

  Les Douze *sac
    [Russ/Fr] B solo,pno CBDM s.p.
                              (W1308)

WORRY, WHO, I? see Moscheo

WORTE DES ALLTAGS see Benguerel,
  Xavier, Paraules De Cada Dia

WORTH
  Midsummer
    low solo,pno (A maj) ALLANS s.p.
                              (W1309)
    high solo,pno (D maj) ALLANS s.p.
                              (W1310)

WORTH, AMY
  Like Frosted Snow The Sheep Lay There
    high solo,pno GALAXY 1.1890.7 $1.00
                              (W1311)

WORTHY IS THE LAMB see Wyrtzen, Don

WORTHY THE LAMB see Gaither

WOUDSPROOKJE see Wassenhoven, P. v.

WOULD YOU see Red, Buryl

WOULD YOU KNOW? see Marshall, L.

WRAGG, RUSSELL
  My Heart Remembers
    med solo,pno (G maj) WILLIS $.60
                              (W1312)

WRANGEL
  Hor Hur Stilla Vinden Susar
    2 soli,pno LUNDQUIST s.p. see from
    Tvastammiga Sanger   (W1313)

  I Skogen
    2 soli,pno LUNDQUIST s.p. see from
    Tvastammiga Sanger   (W1314)

  Tvastammiga Sanger *see Hor Hur
    Stilla Vinden Susar; I Skogen
                              (W1315)

WREFORD, REYNOLD
  Monarchs In Melody *CCU
    solo,pno CRAMER   (W1316)

  Party Games Or Frolics *CCU
    solo,pno CRAMER   (W1317)

WREN, THE see Benedict, Sir Julius

WRIGHT, D.
  O Land Of Hope, America!
    med solo,pno SEESAW $1.00 (W1318)

WRIGHT, DENIS
  Beloved Saviour, Wilt Thou Answer?
    see Two Passiontide Songs

  Jesus, Thou Who Knowest Death
    see Two Passiontide Songs

  Two Passiontide Songs *sac
    s.p. low solo,pno NOVELLO
    17.0207.06; high solo,pno NOVELLO
    17.0206.08
    contains: Beloved Saviour, Wilt
    Thou Answer?; Jesus, Thou Who
    Knowest Death   (W1319)

WRIGHT, GEOFFREY
  Cradle Of Cats, A *song cycle
    [Eng] high solo,kbd CHESTER s.p.
                              (W1320)

WRIGHT, LAWRENCE
  Too-Too Was A Dainty Doll
    solo,pno CRAMER   (W1321)

WRIGHT, NORMAN SORENG (1905-   )
  Psalm 8 *sac,Gen
    low solo,pno (A flat maj) WILLIS
    $.60   (W1322)

WRIGHT, REGINALD
  Love In A Little Child
    low solo,pno (E flat maj) CRAMER
                              (W1323)
    high solo,pno (G maj) CRAMER
                              (W1324)

WRIGHTON, W.T.
  Her Bright Smile Haunts Me Still
    solo,pno CRAMER   (W1325)

  Thy Voice Is Near
    solo,pno (G maj) LEONARD-ENG
                              (W1326)

WRIGHTSON
  Feed My Sheep *sac
    med solo,pno (E flat maj) FISCHER,C
    V 1647   (W1327)
    high solo,pno (G maj) FISCHER,C
    V 1646   (W1328)

WRITING OF HEZEKIAH, THE see Ehrlich,
  Abel

WU NEMT MEN PARNUSSE see Meyerowitz,
  David

WU SANNEN MEINE SIEBEN GUTE YOHR see
  Meyerowitz, David

WUNDER see Kilpinen, Yrio, Ihme

WUNDERBARES HERZ see Micheelsen, Hans-
  Friedrich

WUNDERHORN see Schoenberg, Arnold

WUNDERHORN-LIEDER HEFT I (OP. 12) see
  Petersen, Wilhelm

WUNDERHORN-LIEDER HEFT II (OP.12) see
  Petersen, Wilhelm

WUNDERHORN-LIEDER HEFT III (OP. 12) see
  Petersen, Wilhelm

WUNDERHORN-LIEDER see Zipp, Friedrich

WUNDERHORN SONGS see Mahler, Gustav

WUNDERSAM RAUSCHTE DER WIND see
  Schumann, Georg

WUORINEN, CHARLES (1938-   )
  Door In The Wall, The
    MezMez/MezS soli,pno sc AM.COMP.AL.
    $3.57   (W1329)

WUORINEN, CHARLES (cont'd.)

Madrigale Spirituale *CCU,madrigal
TBar soli,2ob,pno,2vln,vcl
AM.COMP.AL. sc $6.60, voc sc
$2.75   (W1330)

Message To Denmark Hill
Bar solo,fl,vcl,pno PETERS 66384
s.p.   (W1331)

On The Raft
MezMez soli,pno sc AM.COMP.AL.
$1.37   (W1332)

Song To The Lute In Musick, A
S solo,pno PETERS 66452 s.p.
(W1333)

WURM, LOUISE
He Will Not Fail *sac
solo,pno WORD S-49   (W1334)

WURZELN DES WALDES see Knab, Armin

WUS GEVEN IS GEVEN *Jew
solo,pno KAMMEN 459 $1.00   (W1335)

WYATT, E.
Calling To Thee
med solo,pno (D maj) LEONARD-ENG
(W1336)
high solo,pno (F maj) LEONARD-ENG
(W1337)
low solo,pno (C maj) LEONARD-ENG
(W1338)

WYATT, JOHN R.
But Still He Loved Me
med solo,pno CRESPUB CP-S5000 $1.00
(W1339)

WYK, ARNOLD VAN (1916-   )
Van Liefde En Verlatenheid *song
cycle
[Ger/Eng] solo,pno BOOSEY $4.50
(W1340)
Vier Weemoedige Lietjies *CC4U
solo,pno HEUWEKE. 398 s.p. (W1341)

WYNER, YEHUDI (1929-   )
Halleluya (Psalm 66)
med solo,pno PRESSER $.75   (W1342)

May The Words
see Wyner, Yehudi, Silent Devotion

Monkeys
med solo,pno AM.COMP.AL. $1.37
(W1343)
Psalm 66 *see Halleluya

Psalms And Early Songs *CCU
med-low solo,pno AMP $2.00 (W1344)

Silent Devotion *sac,Sab-Eve
med solo,org AM.COMP.AL. $.55
contains also: May The Words
(W1345)
Siz Nito Kain Nechtn
med solo,pno AM.COMP.AL. $1.10
(W1346)

WYNKEN, BLYNKEN AND NOD see Van Etten,
Jane

WYNKEN, BLYNKEN AND NOD see Weigl,
Vally

WYRTZEN, DON
Amazing Grace - Unbounded Grace *see
Newton, John

God That Was Real *see Walvoord,
John

He'll Break Through The Blue *sac
solo,pno SINGSPIR 7126 $1.00
(W1347)
I Wonder If It's Happened Yet To You
*sac
solo,pno SINGSPIR 7124 $1.00
(W1348)
If My People *sac,Bibl
solo,pno SINGSPIR 7288 $1.00
(W1349)
Love Was When *see Walvoord, John

My Home, America *sac
solo,pno SINGSPIR 7287 $1.00
(W1350)
No One Knows This Road Like Jesus
*sac
solo,pno SINGSPIR 7122 $1.00
(W1351)
O Give Me A Soapbox *sac
solo,pno SINGSPIR 7118 $1.00
(W1352)
On Belief *see Walvoord, John

Red, White And Blue, The *see
Peterson, John W.

Sandals *see Walvoord, John

This World Outside *see Walvoord,
John

WYRTZEN, DON (cont'd.)

Till He Comes *sac
solo,pno SINGSPIR 7125 $1.00
(W1353)
Worthy Is The Lamb *sac
solo,pno SINGSPIR 7123 $1.00
(W1354)
Yesterday, Today And Tomorrow *sac,
CCUL
solo,kbd SINGSPIR 5923 $2.95
(W1355)
Yesterday, Today And Tomorrow *sac
solo,pno SINGSPIR 7064 $1.00
(W1356)
WYTON, ALEC (1921-   )
Antiphon *sac
solo,pno HOPE 59 $1.00   (W1357)

X

"X" see Terzakis, Dimitri

XANGO see Villa-Lobos, Heitor

XANROF, LEON (1867-1953)
Les Petites Bonnes D'Hotel
solo,pno ENOCH s.p.   (X1)
solo,acap ENOCH s.p.   (X2)

XILSER, R.
L'amour Enchanteur (from L'Eternelle
Chanson)
solo,pno ENOCH s.p.   (X3)
solo,acap ENOCH s.p.   (X4)

Y

Y AVAIT UN PETIT MAT'LOT see Messager, Andre

YA CABALGA CALAINOS see Enriquez de Valderrabano, Enrique

YA NO PUEDO MAS, SENORA see Garcia Morillo, Roberto

YA-YA see Passani, Emile

YAHRES, SAMUEL C.
  Our Sacred Honor (from Our Sacred Honor)
    med solo,band/orch YAHRES 5011 $.75
                          (Y1)
    high solo,band/orch YAHRES 5012 $.75
                          (Y2)

YAKHNINA, YE.
  Poems Of The Heart *CCU
    [Russ] solo,pno MEZ KNIGA 2.110 s.p.
                          (Y3)

YAKUSHIJI AZUMA-TO see Hayashi, Azusa

YANINA see Rabey, Rene

YANKEE PEDDLER, THE see Agay, Denes

YANNATOS, JAMES
  Four Songs I *song cycle
    high solo,pno AM.COMP.AL. $3.57
                          (Y4)
  Four Songs II *song cycle
    T solo,pno AM.COMP.AL. $3.30
                          (Y5)
  Three Songs *CC3U
    S/T solo,4strings sc AM.COMP.AL. $3.30
                          (Y6)

YANNAY, YEHUDA
  At The End Of The Parade
    Bar solo,vln/vla,bvl,kbd,2perc sc AM.COMP.AL. $18.70
                          (Y7)
  Incantations *CCU
    med solo,pno AM.COMP.AL. $6.60 (Y8)

YANTIS, DAVID
  Goin' Easy *CCUL
    solo,pno,gtr WORD 37755 $1.25 (Y9)

YAR NAZANI see Hovhaness, Alan

YARAVI see Espoile, Raoul H.

YARMOUTH FAIR see Heseltine, Philip

YATOVE, J.
  La Paix, Le Pain, La Liberte (from L'Eternelle Chanson)
    ENOCH s.p. (Y10)

YE BANKS AND BRAES *folk,Scot
  solo,pno (A flat maj/G maj) PATERSON FS100 s.p. (Y11)

YE BANKS AND BRAES see Shaw, Martin

YE BANKS AND BRAES O' BONNIE DOON see Riegger, Wallingford

YE FAUNS AND YE DRYADS see Arne, Thomas Augustine

YE GLOOMY THOUGHTS see Dibdin, Charles

YE OLDE HALL see Crampton, Ernest

YE TWICE TEN HUNDRED DEITIES see Purcell, Henry

YEAR WHEN JESUS COMES, THE see Wolfe, Lanny

YEARNING see Tchaikovsky, Piotr Ilyitch, Nur, Wer Die Sehnsucht Kennt

YEAR'S AT THE SPRING, THE see Beach, Mrs. H.H.A.

YEARS HAVE FLED..., THE *CCU
  [Russ] solo,pno MEZ KNIGA 63 s.p.
                          (Y12)

YELLOW BOREEN, THE see Somervell, Arthur

YELLOW-HAIRED LADDIE, THE *folk,Scot
  solo,pno (B flat maj/C maj) PATERSON FS101 s.p. (Y13)

YELLOW LILY, THE see Pibernik, Zlatko

YELLOW TREE see Wood

Y'ENER
  Chanson
    high solo,pno/inst DURAND s.p.
                          (Y14)
  Douce Fievre
    solo,pno/inst DURAND s.p. (Y15)

YEOMAN'S YARN, A see Geehl, Henry Ernest

YERBA BUENA see Gomez Carrillo, Manuel

YES, AT LENGTH 'TIS THE MOMENT see Mozart, Wolfgang Amadeus, Giunse Alfin Il Momento

YES, GOD IS REAL see Landgrave, Phillip

YES, I BELIEVE see Verdi, Giuseppe, Credo In Un Dio Crudel

YES, I LOVE HIM see Pearson, Albie

YES I'LL KNOW HIM see Hubbard, H.

YES, MY LIFE WILL SOON BE ENDED see Verdi, Giuseppe, Per Me Giunto E Il Di Supremo

YEST' REEN see Needham, Alicia Adelaide

YESTERDAY, TODAY AND TOMORROW see Wyrtzen, Don

YESTERDAY, TODAY AND TOMORROW see Wyrtzen, Don

YESTERDAY'S GONE see Stanphill, Ira F.

YET, LOVE IS BEAUTIFUL INDEED see Surinach, Carlos

YEVARECHECHA *sac
  solo,pno OR-TAV $.50 (Y16)

YIAIS LIED I & II see Madetoja, Leevi

YIBANE HAMIKDASH
  solo,pno OR-TAV $.50 (Y17)

YITZCHOK, LEVY (1740-1809)
  A Dintoire Mit Gott
    (Neumann, Richard J.) [Heb] T solo, orch TRANSCON. rental (Y18)
  A Dudele
    (Neumann, Richard J.) [Heb] T solo, orch TRANSCON. rental (Y19)

YKSIN see Kilpinen, Yrio

YLI HOHTAVAN HANGEN see Kilpinen, Yrio

YNO YN HWYRDDYDD EBRILL see Roberton, Hugh Stevenson

YO see Kuula, Toivo

YO ADIR see Weinberg, Jacob

YO ME ARRIME A UN PINO VERDE see Gianneo, Luis

YO ME PATIERA DE BURGUS see Garcia Morillo, Roberto

YO NACI EN EL VALLE see Ginastera, Alberto

YO ON TYYNI see Sonninen, Ahti

YOBIGOE see Nakada, Yoshinao

YOENG POE TSJOENG see Franken, Wim

YOKEL see Lane-Wilson, H.

YOLLA see Merikanto, Oskar

YOM GILA see Weiner, Lazar

YOME, YOME
  see Six Folk Songs

YON, PIETRO ALESSANDRO (1886-1943)
  Ave Maria *sac
    high solo,pno BELWIN $1.50 (Y20)
    low solo,pno BELWIN $1.50 (Y21)
  Gesu Bambino *sac,Xmas
    med solo,pno (F maj) HARRIS 8867 $1.50 (Y22)
    high solo,pno (G maj) HARRIS 4452 $1.50 (Y23)
    low solo,pno (E maj) HARRIS 4453 $1.50 (Y24)
    low solo,pno BELWIN $1.50 (Y25)
    med solo,pno BELWIN $1.50 (Y26)
    high solo,pno BELWIN $1.50 (Y27)
  Our Paschal Joy *sac
    low solo,pno BELWIN $1.50 (Y28)
    high solo,pno BELWIN $1.50 (Y29)

YON, PIETRO ALESSANDRO (cont'd.)
  They Call Him Jesus *sac
    high solo,pno BELWIN $1.50 (Y30)
    low solo,pno BELWIN $1.50 (Y31)
  Twas In The Moon Of Wintertime
    high solo,pno GALAXY 1.0724.7 $1.00 (Y32)

YON PIIRI see Pylkkanen, Tauno Kullervo

YORK, DANIEL STANLEY
  Lord, Make Me Thine Instrument *sac
    med-high solo,pno MERCURY $1.00 (Y33)

YORK, SYBIL
  Dear David
    med solo,pno CRESPUB CP-S5013 $1.00 (Y34)
  I Love Ordinary Things *sac
    med solo,pno CRESPUB CP-S5014 $1.00 (Y35)
  In Love With Jesus *sac
    med solo,pno CRESPUB CP-S5011 $1.00 (Y36)
  Where Is Love *sac
    med solo,pno CRESPUB CP-S5010 $1.00 (Y37)

YOSSA see Sibelius, Jean, I Natten

YOSSEL, YOSSEL *Jew
  solo,pno KAMMEN 438 $1.00 (Y38)

YOTON YO see Pylkkanen, Tauno Kullervo

YOU ARE MY SOUL'S AWAKENING see Bergman, Erik, Du Bist Die Auferstehung Meiner Seele

YOU ARE THE SONG IN MY HEART see Firestone, Idabelle

YOU CAME TO ME see Beaudrie, M.

YOU CAME TO ME IN MAY see Harrhy, Edith

YOU CAN DEPEND ON ME see Crouch, Andrae

YOU CAN EXPERIENCE see Skillings, Otis

YOU CAN TOUCH HIM IF YOU TRY *sac
  (Carmichael, Ralph) solo,pno WORD S-87 (Y39)

YOU CAN'T GO BACK NOW see Wolfe, Lanny

YOU DIDN'T ASK ME FIRST see Helier, Ivy St.

YOU DON'T HAVE TO GO FAR see Owens, Ron

YOU GONNA REAP see Miller, James

YOU HAVE DESTROYED ME see Rodrigo, Joaquin, Vos Me Matasteis

YOU HAVE HEARD THAT IT WAS SAID see Krapf, Gerhard

YOU INTERFERING LADIES see Webber, Lloyd

YOU LAUGHED ME OUT OF YOUR HEART see Gerald

YOU MAY BURY ME IN DE EAS' *spir
  (Burleigh, H. T.) high solo,pno BELWIN $1.50 (Y40)

YOU NEED HIS HAND *sac,gospel
  solo,pno ABER.GRP. $1.50 (Y41)

YOU NEVER SAW MY GARDEN see Ablett, Norman

YOU SAY 'TIS LOVE see Purcell, Henry

YOU SHOULD HAVE COME SOONER see Mac Kenzie

YOU SHOULD OF DONE IT BLUES, THE see Beeson, Jack Hamilton

YOU SPOTTED SNAKES see Castelnuovo-Tedesco, Mario

YOU WENT AWAY, MY LOVE see Kilpinen, Yrio, Sa Menit

YOU WERE GLAD TONIGHT see Fischer, Irwin

YOU WHO ARE POWERFUL see Mozart, Wolfgang Amadeus, Ihr Machtigen

YOU WON'T BELIEVE THE DIFFERENCE see Redman, Reginald

YOU WROTE TO ME see Tchaikovsky, Piotr Ilyitch, Letter Song, The

YOU'D BETTER ASK ME see Lohr, Hermann

YOUNCE, GEORGE
  I Know He's Mine *sac
    solo,pno WORD S-305   (Y42)

  If I Can Just Hold Out *sac
    solo,pno WORD S-286   (Y43)

  It's All Right *sac
    solo,pno WORD S-304   (Y44)

  Little Deeds *sac
    solo,pno WORD S-338   (Y45)

  My Lord *sac
    solo,pno WORD S-347   (Y46)

  Then I Found Jesus *sac
    solo,pno WORD S-289   (Y47)

  There's A New Name Written Down *sac
    solo,pno WORD S-287   (Y48)

  When I Get Home *sac
    solo,pno WORD S-348   (Y49)

  When The First Drop Of Blood *sac
    solo,pno WORD S-346   (Y50)

YOUNG
  Christmas Morn *sac,Xmas
    high solo,pno (E flat maj) FISCHER,
    C V 1624   (Y51)

  Feed My Sheep *sac
    high solo,pno (E flat maj) FISCHER,
    C V 1626   (Y52)

YOUNG AND LEARNING see Zillner

YOUNG BARTOK, THE, VOL. 1 *CCU
  (Dille) [Hung] solo,pno BUDAPEST 4219
                                  (Y53)
YOUNG, CARLTON R.
  Love Them Now *sac
    solo,pno HOPE 57 $1.00   (Y54)

  What Makes The Wind Blow *sac
    solo,pno HOPE 496 $1.00   (Y55)

YOUNG, GORDON (1919-   )
  Entreat Me Not To Leave Thee
    high solo/med solo,pno (F min)
    GALAXY 1.2217.7 $1.25   (Y56)

  Prayer For This House
    high solo,pno GALAXY 1.1835.7 $1.00
                                  (Y57)
  Reasons Why
    med solo,pno GALAXY 1.1906.7 $1.00
                                  (Y58)
  Requiescat
    med solo,pno GALAXY 1.1988.7 $1.00
                                  (Y59)
  There Will Be Other Summers
    med solo,pno GALAXY 1.1955.7 $1.00
                                  (Y60)

YOUNG HEART see Roe, Gloria [Ann]

YOUNG HERCHARD see Broadwood, Lucy E.

YOUNG HUNTING
    see Schirmer's American Folk-Song
    Series, Set XXII (American-English
    Folk-Ballads From The Southern
    Appalachian Mountains)

YOUNG LOVE see Beaudrie, M.

YOUNG LOVE LIES SLEEPING see Somervell,
  Arthur

YOUNG MAN'S EXHORTATION see Finzi,
  Gerald

YOUNG NUN, THE see Schubert, Franz
  (Peter), Die Junge Nonne

YOUNG SHEPHERD'S SONG see Atkey, Olive

YOUNG SINGER *CCU
  (Row) S solo,pno FISCHER,C RB 81; A
    solo,pno FISCHER,C RB 82; T solo,
    pno FISCHER,C RB 83; Bar solo,pno
    FISCHER,C RB 84   (Y61)

YOUNG SPORTSMAN, THE see Sibelius,
  Jean, Jagargossen

YOUNG, STUART
  Shepherds Sing, The *sac,Xmas
    med solo,opt vln&harp BELWIN $1.50
                                  (Y62)
    low solo,opt vln&harp BELWIN $1.50
                                  (Y63)
YOUNG, VICTOR (1900-1956)
  Don't Talk To Me Of Spring
    high solo,pno (F maj) WILLIS $.50
                                  (Y64)
    low solo,pno (D maj) WILLIS $.50
                                  (Y65)
YOUNGEST SHEPHERD see Brown, Myrtle
  Hare

YOUR CROSS see Deacon, Mary

YOUR ENGLAND AND MINE see Simpson,
  Nellie

YOUR EYES ARE SO NAKED see Bergman,
  Erik, So Nackt Sind Deine Augen

YOUR EYES SHINE IN MY OWN see Strauss,
  Johann

YOUR PHOTO see Friml, Rudolf

YOUR SONG FROM PARADISE see Brown, S.B.

YOUR STEP UPON THE STAIR see Crampton,
  Ernest

YOUR TENDER LOVE see Coleman, Jack

YOUR TINY HAND IS FROZEN see Puccini,
  Giacomo, Che Gelida Manina

YOUR VOICE see Hughes, J. Scott

YOUR VOICE see Scott-Hughes, J.

YOU'RE ALL INVITED TO MY MANSION see
  Stallings

YOU'RE GONNA LOVE YOUR NEW LIFE WITH
  THE LORD see Johnson, P.

YOU'RE IN LOVE see Friml, Rudolf

YOU'RE NOT ALONE see Bartlett, Gene

YOU'RE NOT YOUR OWN see Minkler, Ross

YOUSE, GLAD ROBINSON (1898-   )
  Little Lost Boy, The
    solo,pno PEER $.95   (Y66)

  Red Bird
    high solo,pno (G min) SCHIRM.G $.85
                                  (Y67)
  Splendor Ahead
    med-high solo,pno (D min) SCHIRM.G
    $.85   (Y68)

  Thou Wilt Light My Candle *sac
    med solo,pno (D min) SCHIRM.G $.60
                                  (Y69)
YOUTH DAY see Wijdeveld, Wolfgang

YOUTH, DAY, OLD AGE AND NIGHT see
  Rorem, Ned

YOUTH, THE FIDDLER see Geehl, Henry
  Ernest

YOUTHFUL BARITONE *CCU
  [Ger] Bar solo,pno PRESSER $2.75
                                  (Y70)
YOUTHFUL, CHARMING CHLOE, THE see
  Bantock, Granville

YOUTHFUL SONGS see Moevs, Robert W.

YOUTHFUL TENOR *CCU
  [Ger] T solo,pno PRESSER $2.75   (Y71)

YOUTH'S DREAMS AND TIME'S TRUTH see
  Watkins, Michael Blake

YRADIER, SEBASTIAN (1809-1865)
  Duvan *see La Paloma

  La Paloma
    [It/Span] S/T solo,pno RICORDI-ENG
      127489 s.p.   (Y72)
    low solo,pno (B flat maj) ALLANS
      s.p.   (Y73)
    high solo,pno (D maj) ALLANS s.p.
                                  (Y74)
    low solo,pno (C maj) CENTURY 3636
                                  (Y75)
    [Span] low solo,pno UNION ESP. $.50
                                  (Y76)
    med solo,pno (C maj) ALLANS s.p.
                                  (Y77)
    "Duvan" solo,pno GEHRMANS 574 s.p.
                                  (Y78)
YRESNE M. D'
  J'ai Une Petite Femme
    solo,pno OUVRIERES s.p.   (Y79)

YRTIT TUMMAT see Madetoja, Leevi

YSKIN ALLA TAIVAAN see Bergman, Erik,
  Ensam Under Fastet

YSTAVIEN PIIRI PIENENTYY see Kilpinen,
  Yrio

YTTREHUS, ROLV
  Angstwagen
    S solo,perc sc AM.COMP.AL. $8.25
                                  (Y80)
  Six Haiku *CC6U
    solo,fl,harp,vcl sc AM.COMP.AL.
    $5.50, ipa   (Y81)

YUGOSALV SOLO SONGS, VOL. 2 *CCU
  [Slav] solo,pno CROATICA s.p.   (Y82)

YUGOSLAV SOLO SONGS, VOL. 3 *CCU
  [Slav] solo,pno CROATICA s.p.   (Y83)

YULEI see El-Dabh, Halim

YUNG, ALFRED
  Je Vous Salue Marie *sac
    solo,pno/org (available in 2 keys)
    HEUGEL s.p. contains also: Notre
    Pere   (Y84)

  Notre Pere
    see Yung, Alfred, Je Vous Salue
    Marie

YUNG-YANG see Bantock, Granville

YUOGSLAV SOLO SONGS, VOLS. 1, 2 & 3
  *CCU
  [Slav] solo,pno cmplt ed CROATICA
    s.p.   (Y85)

YVER VOUS N'ESTES QU'UN VILLAIN see
  Debussy, Claude

Z

ZACHARIAS, H.
Geht Nun Zur Ruh
solo,pno SCHAUR s.p.   (Z1)

ZAFRED, MARIO (1922-   )
All'Isonzo
[It] S/T solo,pno RICORDI-ENG
129073 s.p.   (Z2)

Canti Di Novembre *CC7U
[It] solo,pno RICORDI-ENG 128987
s.p.   (Z3)

Epitaphe En Forme De Ballade
Bar solo,orch sc,quarto RICORDI-ENG
131200 s.p.   (Z4)
[It] Bar solo,orch voc sc RICORDI-
ENG 131202 s.p.   (Z5)

Vergers *CC4U
[Fr] solo,pno RICORDI-ENG 128887
s.p.   (Z6)

ZAGATTI, FRANCESCO (ca. 1750?)
Gloria Patri *sac
SA soli,2S rec,cont sc HANSSLER
5.058 s.p., solo pt HANSSLER s.p.
see also GESANGE ZUM KIRCHENJAHR
(Z7)

ZAGE NICHT see Mozart, Wolfgang
Amadeus, Non Temer, Amato Bene

ZAGERS see Clercq, R. de

ZAGWIJN, HENRI (1878-1954)
Aanzoek
see Dichterwijding

Als Ik Van Uw Effen Voorhoofd
see Drie Liedjes Van J. Perk
see Drie Liedjes

Auferstehung *sac,Easter
med solo,pno,harmonium ALSBACH s.p.
contains: Geistliches Lied; Hymne
"Wesen Reiht Sich An Wesen";
Osterglocken; Zwei Zwiegesange
(Z8)

Avond
see Stervend Licht

Avondstemming
see Drie Liederen
see Drie Liederen Van C. Wolfson
solo,pno ALSBACH s.p.   (Z9)

Bezinning
see Stervend Licht
solo,pno ALSBACH s.p.   (Z10)

Blondje
see Drie Liedjes

Bruder!
see Weihe Nacht

Chloe
narrator,pno DONEMUS s.p.   (Z11)

Das Erloschene Altarbild
Mez solo,pno DONEMUS s.p.   (Z12)

Das Karussell
see Drei Rilkelieder

De Fluitspeler
S solo,fl,ob,clar,bsn,horn,pno
DONEMUS s.p.   (Z13)

De Geheime Zee
narrator,pno DONEMUS s.p. contains
also: Minne En Dood; Twee
Menschen; Twee Dooden; Een Lied
Van Den Dood; Het Eiland Der
Beminden   (Z14)

De Kerkerballade
narrator,4fl,3ob,3clar,3bsn,4horn,
3trp,3trom,tuba,timp,perc,cel,
2harp,2mand,strings,gtr DONEMUS
s.p.   (Z15)

De Koelte Neigt
see Eenzame Wake

De Loome Vlerk Gebroken
see Eenzame Wake

De Nachten
see Stervend Licht

De Rozen Droomen
see Eenzame Wake

De Zotte Student
narrator,pno DONEMUS s.p.   (Z16)

Dees Hele Liefde Is Heengegaan
see Eenzame Wake

Dichterleven
Bar solo,pno ALSBACH s.p.   (Z17)

Dichterwijding
Bar solo,pno ALSBACH s.p.
contains: Aanzoek; Eerste
Aanblik; Erato; Kalliope; Was
Dat Een Lied; Zij Komt   (Z18)

Die Fusswaschung
S solo,fl,ob,clar,bsn,horn,timp,
perc,cel,harmonium,pno,strings
DONEMUS s.p.   (Z19)

Die Nacht Van Zelfvernedering
solo,pno ALSBACH s.p.   (Z20)

Die Sonne Schaue
see Weihe Nacht

Die Stille Stadt
Mez solo,pno DONEMUS s.p.   (Z21)
Mez solo,fl,vln,vla,vcl,harp voc sc
DONEMUS s.p.   (Z22)

Drei Rilkelieder
Mez/A solo,pno DONEMUS s.p.
contains: Das Karussell;
Liebeslied; Lied Vom Meer   (Z23)

Drie Liederen
solo,pno ALSBACH s.p.
contains: Avondstemming;
Endymion; Sluimerliedje   (Z24)

Drie Liederen Van C. Wolfson
S solo,pno ALSBACH s.p.
contains: Avondstemming;
Endymion; Sluimerliedje   (Z25)

Drie Liedjes
solo,pno ALSBACH s.p.
contains: Als Ik Van Uw Effen
Voorhoofd; Blondje; 'K Wil U
Eens Wat Zeggen; Leg Uw Beide
Blanke Handjes   (Z26)

Drie Liedjes Van J. Perk
Bar solo,pno ALSBACH s.p.
contains: Als Ik Van Uw Effen
Voorhoofd; 'K Wil U Eens Wat
Zeggen, Blondje; Leg Uw Beide
Blanke Handjes   (Z27)

Drie Smidsliederen
Mez solo,pno ALSBACH s.p.
contains: Ring-King; Smidje-Smee;
Van Een Smeder   (Z28)

Een Lied Van Den Dood
see Zagwijn, Henri, De Geheime Zee

Eenzame Wake
A/Mez solo,pno DONEMUS s.p.
contains: De Koelte Neigt; De
Loome Vlerk Gebroken; De Rozen
Droomen; Dees Hele Liefde Is
Heengegaan; Over Alle Daken
(Z29)

Eerste Aanblik
see Dichterwijding

Endymion
see Drie Liederen
see Drie Liederen Van C. Wolfson

Erato
see Dichterwijding

Es Ist Nacht
Mez solo,pno DONEMUS s.p.   (Z30)

Fantasie
see Twee Liederen Van Albrecht
Rodenbach

Galgenlieder Von Chr. Morgenstern
*CC7L
Bar solo,pno ALSBACH s.p.   (Z31)

Geestelijk Lied *sac
med solo,pno ALSBACH s.p.   (Z32)

Geistliches Lied
see Auferstehung

Geluk
Mez solo,pno DONEMUS s.p.   (Z33)

Ghasel
Mez solo,pno ALSBACH s.p.   (Z34)

Het Avondgebed *Op.5
A solo,pno ALSBACH s.p.   (Z35)

Het Eiland Der Beminden
see Zagwijn, Henri, De Geheime Zee

Het Hooglied Van Salomo
narrator,fl,vla,harp DONEMUS s.p.
(Z36)

Het Klokgebed
S solo,pno ALSBACH s.p.   (Z37)

Het Land Van Utopeia
see Twee Liederen Van Albrecht
Rodenbach

Het Landje Van Kokanje
Bar solo,pno ALSBACH s.p.   (Z38)

Hymne "Wesen Reiht Sich An Wesen"
see Auferstehung

Im Seelenaug
see Weihe Nacht

In Der Fremde
solo,pno ALSBACH s.p.   (Z39)

'K Wil U Eens Wat Zeggen
see Drie Liedjes

'K Wil U Eens Wat Zeggen, Blondje
see Drie Liedjes Van J. Perk

Kalliope
see Dichterwijding

Kleenliedjes Op Kleendichtjes *CCU
S solo,pno ALSBACH s.p.   (Z40)

Laat Mij Nimmermeer
Bar/Mez solo,pno DONEMUS s.p.   (Z41)

L'amour S'effeuille
S solo,pno DONEMUS s.p.   (Z42)

Leeuwerik
S solo,pno DONEMUS s.p.   (Z43)

Leg Uw Beide Blanke Handjes
see Drie Liedjes Van J. Perk
see Drie Liedjes

Lichtend Ontwaken *CC7L
S/Mez solo,pno ALSBACH s.p.   (Z44)

Liebeslied
see Drei Rilkelieder

Lied Der Oudstrijders
Bar solo,pno DONEMUS s.p.   (Z45)

Lied Vom Meer
see Drei Rilkelieder

Minne En Dood
see Zagwijn, Henri, De Geheime Zee

Morgenzang *vocalise
S solo,fl,vln,vla,vcl,harp DONEMUS
s.p.   (Z46)

Naar Droomeland Toe
Mez solo,pno ALSBACH s.p.   (Z47)

Nachtgerausche
A solo,pno DONEMUS s.p.   (Z48)

O Nacht
S solo,pno DONEMUS s.p.   (Z49)

Ochtendbede
solo,pno ALSBACH s.p.   (Z50)

Ode
A solo,2fl,3ob,2clar,2bsn,4horn,
2trp,trom,timp,perc,strings
DONEMUS s.p.   (Z51)

Oerania
A solo,org DONEMUS s.p.   (Z52)

Op! Schroomlijke Reus
high solo&low solo,pno DONEMUS s.p.
(Z53)

Osterglocken
see Auferstehung

Over Alle Daken
see Eenzame Wake

Ring-King
see Drie Smidsliederen

Sluimerliedje
see Drie Liederen Van C. Wolfson
see Drie Liederen
solo,pno ALSBACH s.p.   (Z54)

Smidje-Smee
see Drie Smidsliederen

Soldatenliedje In Volkstoon *CCU
med solo,pno ALSBACH s.p.   (Z55)

Stemming
T solo,vln,pno DONEMUS s.p.   (Z56)

Stervend Licht
Mez solo,pno ALSBACH s.p.
contains: Avond; Bezinning; De
Nachten   (Z57)

ZAGWIJN, HENRI (cont'd.)

Traumgesicht
Mez/A solo,pno DONEMUS s.p. (Z58)

Twee Dooden
see Zagwijn, Henri, De Geheime Zee

Twee Liederen Van Albrecht Rodenbach
Mez/Bar solo,pno ALSBACH s.p.
contains: Fantasie; Het Land Van
Utopeia (Z59)

Twee Menschen
see Zagwijn, Henri, De Geheime Zee

Vaarwel Aan 'T Woud
Bar/Mez solo,pno DONEMUS s.p. (Z60)

Van Een Smeder
see Drie Smidsliederen

Verlangen *CC5U
Mez solo,pno DONEMUS s.p. (Z61)

Von Der Demut
S solo,fl,vln,vla,vcl,harp DONEMUS
s.p. (Z62)

Vorspiel
see Weihe Nacht

Was Dat Een Lied
see Dichterwijding

Weihe Nacht
med solo,pno,harmonium ALSBACH s.p.
contains: Bruder!; Die Sonne
Schaue; Im Seelenaug; Vorspiel;
Zwei Hirtenlieder (Z63)

Wonne Der Sehnsucht
Mez solo,pno ALSBACH s.p. (Z64)

Zangen Der Nacht
Bar solo,pno ALSBACH s.p. (Z65)

Zij Komt
see Dichterwijding

Zwei Hirtenlieder
see Weihe Nacht

Zwei Zwiegesange
see Auferstehung

ZAHAVI, DAVID
Halicha L'Keysarya *sac
"Wanderer's Prayer" [Heb] med solo,
pno TRANSCON. IS 510 $.40 (Z66)

Ten Songs *CC10U
solo,pno OR-TAV $1.00 (Z67)

Wanderer's Prayer *see Halicha
L'Keysarya

ZAHORACKE PESNICKY see Nemeth-
Samorinsky, Stefan

ZAHRADNIK, ZDENEK (1936-)
Ajnyahita *song cycle
S solo,pno/org CZECH s.p. (Z68)

Jedinou Vterinu Jeste *CC3U
low solo,pno CZECH s.p. (Z69)

Pisen O Viktorce *CC3U
S solo,pno,vln CZECH s.p. (Z70)

ZAKLINJANJA see Sivic, Pavle

ZALMY 93 see Blazek, Vilem

ZALMY 100 see Blazek, Vilem

ZALMY 133 see Blazek, Vilem

ZALMY 134 see Blazek, Vilem

ZAMBA see Ginastera, Alberto

ZAMBA DE VARGAS see Gomez Carrillo,
Manuel

ZAMBONA, H.G.
Kanzonetten Und Arie
solo,3pno ZIMMER. 1318 s.p. (Z71)

ZANDONAI, RICCARDO (1883-1944)
Bro, La Chiesetta Triste (from I
Cavalieri Di Ekebu)
[It] T solo,pno RICORDI-ENG 124198
s.p. (Z72)

Donne, Piansi (from Giulietta E
Romeo)
[It] T solo,pno RICORDI-ENG 118801
s.p. (Z73)

Giulietta Sono Io! (from Giulietta E
Romeo)
[It] T solo,pno RICORDI-ENG NY 2391
s.p. (Z74)
solo,pno BELWIN $1.50 (Z75)
[It] T solo,pno BELWIN NY 2391

ZANDONAI, RICCARDO (cont'd.)

$1.00 (Z76)

I Due Tarli
[It] Mez/Bar solo,pno RICORDI-ENG
114833 s.p. see from Sei Melodie
(Z77)

La Serenata
[It] Mez/Bar solo,pno BONGIOVANI 1179 s.p.
see from Sei Liriche (Z78)
[It] Mez/Bar solo,pno RICORDI-ENG
114834 s.p. see from Sei Melodie
(Z79)

L'Assiuolo
[It] Mez/Bar solo,pno RICORDI-ENG
114836 s.p. see from Sei Melodie
(Z80)

Lontana
[It] S/T solo,pno RICORDI-ENG
114835 s.p. see from Sei Melodie
(Z81)

Mistero
[It] solo,pno BONGIOVANI 1174 s.p.
see from Sei Liriche (Z82)

Mistica
[It] solo,pno BONGIOVANI 1176 s.p.
see from Sei Liriche (Z83)

Notte Di Neve
[It] solo,pno BONGIOVANI 1175 s.p.
see from Sei Liriche (Z84)

Occhi Soavi (from Giuliano)
[It] T solo,pno RICORDI-ENG 120824
s.p. (Z85)

Portami Via
[It] solo,pno BONGIOVANI 1177 s.p.
see from Sei Liriche (Z86)

Sei Liriche *see La Serenata;
Mistero; Mistica; Notte Di Neve;
Portami Via; Sotto Il Cielo (Z87)

Sei Melodie *see I Due Tarli; La
Serenata; L'Assiuolo; Lontana;
Ultima Rosa (Z88)

Sotto Il Cielo
[It] solo,pno BONGIOVANI 1178 s.p.
see from Sei Liriche (Z89)

Ultima Rosa
[It] Mez/Bar solo,pno RICORDI-ENG
114832 s.p. see from Sei Melodie
(Z90)

Vattene! Se Una Lagrima Soltanto
(from I Cavalieri Di Ekebu)
[It] S solo,pno RICORDI-ENG 126093
s.p. (Z91)

ZANETTOVICH, DANIELE (1950-)
I Canti Della Pace
Mez solo,bsn,timp,strings SONZOGNO
rental (Z92)

ZANGEN DER NACHT see Zagwijn, Henri

ZANITA see Trotere, Henry

ZARAGOZANA see Chapi

ZARAI
Ballad Of The Red Rock, The
(Darion) solo,pno FOX,S (Z93)

ZARATHUSTRAS RUNDGESANG see Peterson-
Berger, (Olof) Wilhelm

ZASTAVENICKO see Schubert, Franz
(Peter)

ZAUBERBLUME see Vignati, Milos, Carovny
Kvet

ZAUBERISCHE ENTFREMDUNG see Weismann,
Julius

ZAUBERLIEBE see Doubrava, Jaroslav,
Carovna Laska

ZAUBERSPRUCH see Pestalozzi, Heinrich

ZAVAGLIA, FRANCIS L.
Lord The Good Shepherd, The *sac
med solo,pno BELWIN $1.50 (Z94)

ZAVATA CESTA see Vomacka, Boleslav

ZAWSZE, KIEDY CHCE KRZYCZE see Baird,
Tadeusz

ZAZA, PICCOLA ZINGARA see Leoncavallo,
Ruggiero

ZAZNI PISNI VZNESENA II see Gregor, V.

ZBAR, MICHEL (1942-)
Incandescences
solo,narrator,2fl,2ob,2clar,bass
clar,2bsn,4horn,2trp,2trom,bass
trom,tuba,4perc,strings RIDEAU
rental (Z95)

ZBAR, MICHEL (cont'd.)

La Miniature De Sables
S solo,perc,electronic tape,2bvl
RIDEAU rental (Z96)

ZE SRDCE see Novotny, J.

ZE SRDCE see Zich, Otakor

ZEBRE, DEMETRIJ (1912-1970)
Trije Samospevi *CC3U
solo,pno DRUSTVO DSS 495 rental
(Z97)

ZECCA, GIANNINO (1911-)
Venite Fili *sac,mot
S/T solo,org BERBEN 1749 s.p. (Z98)

ZECHLIN, RUTH (1926-)
Die Wolken *see Orchesterstuck No. 1

Drei Liebeslieder (from Carmina
Burana) CC3U
[Lat/Ger] S/T solo,cembalo/pno
DEUTSCHER 9034 s.p. (Z99)

Orchesterstuck No. 1
"Die Wolken" S solo,fl,ob,trp,harp,
perc,strings BREITKOPF-L rental
(Z100)

Sieben Lieder *CC7L
med solo,pno BREITKOPF-L EB 4092
$1.50 (Z101)

ZEFFIRETTI LUSINGHIERI see Mozart,
Wolfgang Amadeus

ZEFIR EN CHLORIS see Schouwman, Hans

ZEGEN, EEN BUNDEL LIEDEREN see King,
Harold C.

ZEHM, FRIEDRICH (1923-)
Ein Bundel Chansons Von Frech Bis
Poco Triste *CCU
solo,pno SCHOTTS 6036 s.p. (Z102)

ZEHN GEISTLICHE LIEDER *sac,CC10U
(Kreutz, Alfred) med solo,pno/org
(med easy) MULLER 1463 $3.50
contains work by: Franck, Johann
Wolfgang and Bohm, Georg (Z103)

ZEHN GEISTLICHE LIEDER see Trunk,
Richard

ZEHN LEIDER see Brahms, Johannes

ZEHN LIEDER see Burkhard, Willy

ZEHN LIEDER see Zillig, Winfried

ZEHN LIEDER see Hessenberg, Kurt

ZEHN LIEDER see Franzson, Bjorn

ZEHN LIEDER AUS DEM QUICKBORN see Ebel,
Arnold

ZEHN LIEDER DER LIEBE see Kilpinen,
Yrio

ZEHN LIEDER IM VOLKSTON NACH GEDICHTEN
VON EMIL GRIMM see Rasch, Hugo

ZEHN LIEDER NACH GEDICHTEN VON HERMANN
HESSE see Schoeck, Othmar

ZEHN LIEDER UND DUETTE see Saint-Saens,
Camille

ZEHN LONS-LIEDER see Graener, Paul

ZEHN MADCHENLIEDER NACH UKRAINISCHEN
VOLKSWEISEN see Schmid, Reinhold

ZEHN WEIHNACHTSLIEDER see Reda,
Siegfried

ZEIT DIE SCHONE VOGT EENS GLOEIEN see
Strategier, Herman

ZEIT DU BIST AVEK FUN MIR *Jew
solo,pno KAMMEN 454 $1.00 (Z104)

ZEIT IST WIE EWIGKEIT see Weyrauch,
Johannes

ZEITUNGSAUSSCHNITTE see Eisler, Hanns

ZELENKA, ISTVAN (1936-)
Requiem Pro Viventibus
S/T solo,vln,vla,vcl MODERN rental
(Z105)

ZELINKA, JAN EVANGELISTA (1893-1969)
Chlapec *CC4U
high solo,pno SUPRAPHON s.p. (Z106)

Das Dorf Singt *see Vesnice Zpiva

Der Knabe
solo,pno SUPRAPHON s.p. (Z107)

Vesnice Zpiva
"Das Dorf Singt" S solo,pno CZECH
s.p. (Z108)

ZELLER
  Dry Your Eyes
    low solo,pno (D maj) ALLANS s.p.
                                              (Z109)
    high solo,pno (E maj) ALLANS s.p.
                                              (Z110)
  Song Of The Nightingale
    solo,pno ALLANS s.p.   (Z111)

ZELLER, CARL (1842-1898)
  Tiroolin Maass' Jos Ruusun Saan
    solo,pno FAZER F 2743 s.p.   (Z112)

ZELTER, CARL FRIEDRICH (1758-1832)
  Funfzig Ausgewahlte Lieder *CC50U/
    CCU,20th cent
    solo,pno SCHOTTS 115 s.p.   (Z113)

ZEMER CHAG
  (Helfman, Max) "Holiday Song" [Heb]
    med solo,pno TRANSCON. IS 527 $.45
                                              (Z114)
ZEMER CHASSIDIM *CCU
  solo,pno OR-TAV $3.50   (Z115)

ZEMIR ET AZOR see Gretry, Andre Ernest
  Modeste

ZENDELINGSBEDE see Hullebroeck, Em.

ZENG see Legley, Victor

ZENTNER, JOHANNES (1903-   )
  Der Lobgesang Der Maria *sac,
    concerto
    A solo,org,4strings sc HANSSLER
    10.105 s.p., ipa   (Z116)

  Wer Unter Dem Schirm Des Hochsten
    *sac,concerto/Psalm
    A solo,vln,org sc HANSSLER 10.130
    s.p., ipa   (Z117)

ZERBINETTA'S RECITATIVE AND ARIA see
  Strauss, Richard

ZERREISS DAS HERZ see Telemann, Georg
  Philipp

ZERSTORUNG MAGDEBURGS see Krenek, Ernst

ZES LIEDEREN see Kersters, Willem

ZES LIEDEREN see Dijk, Jan van

ZES LIEDEREN see Hullebroeck, Em.

ZES LIEDEREN see Hijman, Julius

ZES LIEDEREN see Simon, J.

ZES LIEDEREN UIT "ADAGIO" see Veremans,
  Renaat

ZES OUD-NEDERLANDSE GEDICHTEN see
  Moulaert, Raymond

ZES OUD-NEDERLANDSE LIEDEREN see
  Moulaert, Raymond

ZES TWEESTEMMIGE KINDERLIEDEREN see
  Tetterode, L. Adr. von

ZEVEN ITALIAANSE LIEDEREN see Horst,
  Anton van der

ZEVEN KERSTLIEDEREN see Roos, Robert de

ZEVEN KINDERLIEDJES see Ebbenhorst-
  Tengbergen, M.E. von

ZEVEN LIEDEREN see Hullebroeck, Em.

ZEVEN LIEDEREN see Ommeren, A. v.

ZEVEN LIEDEREN see Reynvaan, M.C.C.

ZEVEN LIEDEREN VAN ADAMA VAN SCHELTEMA
  see Bijvanck, Henk

ZEVEN LIEDEREN VAN GUIDO GEZELLE see
  Bijvanck, Henk

ZEVEN LIEDEREN VAN I.M. GERHARDT see
  Mulder, Herman

ZEVEN LIEDJES, VOLS. 1-4 & 6-8 see
  Wijs-Mouton, J. de

ZIALE A RADOSTI see Figus-Bystry,
  Villiam

ZICH, JAROSLAV (1912-   )
  Dvacet Pet Chodskych Pisni *CC25U
    solo,pno SUPRAPHON s.p.   (Z118)

  Letmy Host *song cycle
    med solo,orch/pno SUPRAPHON s.p.
                                              (Z119)
ZICH, OTAKOR (1879-1934)
  Maticce *song cycle
    med solo,pno SUPRAPHON s.p. (Z120)

  Ze Srdce
    solo,pno SUPRAPHON s.p.   (Z121)

ZICHRON WINE SONG see Lavry, Marc

ZIEHN DIE SCHAFE VON DER WIESE see
  Trapp, Max

ZIEHRER, CARL MICHAEL (1843-1922)
  Das Herz Ist Nur Ein Uhrwerk (from
    Das Dumme Herz)
    solo,pno DOBLINGER 88 516 s.p.
                                              (Z122)
  O Wien, Mein Liebes Wien (from Der
    Fremdenfuhrer)
    solo,pno DOBLINGER 88 515 s.p.
                                              (Z123)
  Sei Gepriesen, Du Lauschige Nacht
    solo,pno DOBLINGER 88 514 s.p.
                                              (Z124)
ZIEMS, H.
  Der Palmgalgen
    (Morgenstern) [Ger] med solo,pno
    BOTE $3.50   (Z125)

ZIERITZ, GRETE VON
  Japanische Lieder *CCU
    solo,pno RIES s.p.   (Z126)

ZIESE KINDER YOHREN *Jew
  solo,pno KAMMEN 80 $1.00   (Z127)

ZIGEUNERLEBEN see Schumann, Robert
  (Alexander)

ZIGEUNERLIED see Busoni, Ferruccio
  Benvenuto

ZIGEUNERLIED see Peterson-Berger,
  (Olof) Wilhelm

ZIGEUNERLIEDER see Brahms, Johannes

ZIGEUNERLIEDER see Brahms, Johannes

ZIGON, MARKO (1929-   )
  Samospevi *CCU
    solo,pno DRUSTVO DSS 359 rental
                                              (Z128)
ZIJ HIELDEN ER WACHT see Loots, Ph.

ZIJ KOMT see Colaco Osorio-Swaab, Reine

ZIJ KOMT see Zagwijn, Henri

ZIJ SLUIMERT see Diepenbrock, Alphons

ZIJT GIJ DOOD DE BESTE BORG see Clercq,
  R. de

ZILCH, MARGOT
  Choose Life *sac
    solo,pno GOSPEL 05 TM 0277 $1.00
                                              (Z129)
  He Is God *sac
    solo,pno GOSPEL 05 TM 0272 $1.00
                                              (Z130)
  May I Never Lose The Wonder *sac
    solo,pno GOSPEL 05 TM 0234 $1.00
                                              (Z131)
  Thou Remainest *sac
    solo,pno GOSPEL 05 TM 0269 $1.00
                                              (Z132)
ZILCHER, HERMANN (1881-1948)
  Aus Dem Hohelied Salomonis *Op.38,
    CCU
    ABar soli,pno,2vln,vla,vcl
    BREITKOPF-W s.p.   (Z133)

  Chiemsee-Terzette *Op.46
    SAA soli solo pt BREITKOPF-W
    PB 2643 s.p.   (Z134)

  Deutsches Volksliederspiel, Heft 2
    *CC7L
    SATB soli,pno BREITKOPF-L rental
                                              (Z135)
  Holderlin *Op.28, song cycle
    T solo,3fl,2English horn,2clar,
    2bsn,4horn,2trp,3trom,timp,perc,
    harp,cel,strings BREITKOPF-W s.p.
                                              (Z136)
  Marienlieder *Op.52a, CCU
    [Ger] high solo,4strings BREITKOPF-
    W $4.50   (Z137)

  Rokoko-Suite *Op.65, CCU
    high solo,vln,vcl,pno BREITKOPF-L
    $3.50, ipr   (Z138)

ZILLIG, WINFRIED (1905-1963)
  Funf Lieder Aus Dem Jahr Der Seele
    *CC5U
    high solo,pno (diff) BAREN. 3867
    s.p.   (Z139)

  Italienisches Liederbuch *CC8U
    high solo,pno (diff) BAREN. 3951
    s.p.   (Z140)

  Lieder Des Abschieds *CCU
    low solo,pno (diff) BAREN. 3954
    rental   (Z141)

  Lieder Des Herbstes *CCU
    low solo,pno (diff) BAREN. 3863
    $5.75   (Z142)

ZILLIG, WINFRIED (cont'd.)

  Nachtwache *CC4U
    Bar solo,pno (diff) BAREN. 3868
    rental   (Z143)

  Nun Die Schatten Dunkeln *CCU
    high solo,pno (diff) BAREN. 3869
    rental   (Z144)

  Sieben Sonette Von Eichendorff *CC7U
    high solo,pno (diff) BAREN. 3865
    s.p.   (Z145)

  Vergessene Weisen
    high solo,pno (diff) BAREN. 3860
    $8.50   (Z146)

  Vier Sonette *CC4U
    high solo,pno (diff) BAREN. 3952
    rental   (Z147)

  Zehn Lieder *CC10U
    high solo,pno (diff) BAREN. 3864
    $9.75   (Z148)

  Zwolf Liebeslieder *CC12U
    high solo,pno (diff) BAREN. 3953
    rental   (Z149)

ZILLNER
  Young And Learning (composed with
    Adams)
    med solo,pno PRESSER $.75   (Z150)

ZILVER see Devreese, Godefroid,
  Beatrice

ZIMMER, JAN (1926-   )
  Jar V Udoli
    S solo,pno SLOV.HUD.FOND s.p.
                                              (Z151)
  Pamiatke Jiriho Wolkra
    B solo,pno SLOV.HUD.FOND s.p.
                                              (Z152)
  Piesne O Jari *CCU
    T solo,pno SLOV.HUD.FOND s.p.
                                              (Z153)
ZIMMERMANN
  Omnia Tempus Habent *sac,cant
    [It/Ger] S solo,17inst sc,oct
    RICORDI-ENG 29994 s.p.   (Z154)

ZIMMERMANN, UDO (1943-   )
  Der Mensch *cant
    S solo,fl,English horn,clar,horn,
    trp,trom,perc,harp,strings
    DEUTSCHER rental   (Z155)

  Funf Gesange Fur Bariton Und
    Kammerorchester *CC5U
    Bar solo,fl,English horn,clar,2sax,
    horn,trp,timp,2vla,vcl,bvl,pno
    DEUTSCHER rental   (Z156)

ZINETTA see Geehl, Henry Ernest

ZING EEN LIEKEN see Saffel, J. de

ZING MAAR BLIJ see Smit, H.J.

ZINGENDE SOLDATEN see Delden, Lex van

ZION, ZION HEILIGE, BLEIBST SHOIN see
  Small, Solomon

ZIONS CHILDREN, COMIN ALONG see Gaul,
  Harvey Bartlet

ZION'S LIEDELE see Meyerowitz, David

ZIPP, FRIEDRICH (1914-   )
  Aufforderung
    see Hafis Songs

  Der Entwurzelte
    see Hafis Songs

  Die Freundin Des Hafis
    see Hafis Songs

  Es Blinken In Der Sonne
    see Vier Lieder

  Hafis Songs
    [Ger] med solo,kbd WILHELM. s.p.
    contains: Aufforderung; Der
    Entwurzelte; Die Freundin Des
    Hafis; In Der Fremde; Trinklied
                                              (Z157)
  In Der Fremde
    see Hafis Songs

  Liebeslied
    see Vier Lieder

  Sechs Alte Minnelieder *CC6U
    med solo,strings,opt fl s.p., ipa
    sc GERIG HG 370, voc sc GERIG
                                              (Z158)
  Sieben Kleine Meisen *CC7U
    solo,fl,rec,2vln,vla,vcl s.p., ipa
    sc GERIG HG 401, voc sc GERIG
    HG 400   (Z159)

ZIPP, FRIEDRICH (cont'd.)

Trinklied
see Hafis Songs

Vier Lieder
med solo,pno LEUCKART s.p.
contains: Es Blinken In Der
Sonne; Liebeslied; Widmung;
Wiegenlied (Z160)

Widmung
see Vier Lieder

Wiegenlied
see Vier Lieder

Wunderhorn-Lieder *Op.5, CCU
med solo,pno (med diff) MULLER 1850
rental (Z161)

Zwei Rilke-Lieder *CC2U
med solo,pno TONOS 5407 s.p. (Z162)

ZITEK, OTAKAR (1892-   )
Pisne Z Vojny *CC4U
solo,pno SUPRAPHON s.p. (Z163)

ZLATA VLNA CERVNA see Kovaricek,
Frantisek

ZMOUDRENI DONA QUICHOTA see Kricka,
Jaroslav

ZO SLNECNEJ GRUZIE see Andrasovan,
Tibor

ZO SRDCA see Schneider-Trnavsky,
Mikulas

ZOBEIDE see Crampton, Ernest

ZOECKLER, DOROTHY A.
Song Of Trust *sac,Gen
med solo,pno (E flat maj) WILLIS
$.60 (Z164)

ZOET JESUSKEN SCHUDT ER ZIJN BEDDEKEN
UIT see Ruyneman, Daniel

ZOET STERREKEN see Clercq, R. de

ZOGRAFSKI, TOMISALV (1934-   )
Bitter Lake *see Gorclivo Ezero

Gorclivo Ezero
"Bitter Lake" S solo,pno,strings
MUSIC INFO rental (Z165)

ZOL ZEIN FREILACH *Jew
solo,pno KAMMEN 14 $1.00 (Z166)

ZOLD A KOKENY see Farkas, Ferenc

ZOLLNER, HEINRICH (1854-1941)
Das Wunderglockenspiel (from Die
Versunkene Glocke)
Bar solo,3fl,2ob,2bass clar,2bsn,
4horn,2trp,3trom,tuba,timp,perc,
harp,strings BREITKOPF-W s.p.
(Z167)

ZOMER see Adriessen, Willem

ZOMERAVOND see Weegenhuise, Johan

ZOMERDAG see Weegenhuise, Johan

ZOMERLIEDJE see Andriessen, K.

ZOMERNACHT see Mulder, Herman

ZOMERNACHT see Schafer, Dirk

ZOMEROCHTENDLIEDJE see Tetterode, L.
Adr. von

ZOMERZANG see Voormolen, Alexander
Nicolas

ZOMPA LLARI LLIRA! see Giannini,
Vittorio

ZONDAARSLIED see Hemel, Oscar van

ZONDAGMORGEN see Nieland, H.

ZONDAGOCHTEND see Schouwman, Hans

ZONN, PAUL
Three Folk Songs *CC3U,folk
A solo,acap AM.COMP.AL. $5.50
(Z168)

ZONNE-KUS see Zweers, [Bernard]

ZONNE SLAPEGAAN see Hullebroeck, Em.

ZONNEDAG see Brucken Fock, G.H.G. van

ZONNEWEELDE see Sigtenhorst-Meyer,
Bernhard van den

ZORONGO GITANO see Azpiazu, Jose de

ZORZAL see Espoile, Raoul H.

ZOT ARTZENU
(Helfman, Max) "This Is Our Land"
[Heb] med solo,pno TRANSCON. IS 528
$.40 (Z169)

ZOUHAR, ZDENEK (1927-   )
Pisnicky O Lasce *CCU
female solo/male solo,pno CZECH
s.p. (Z170)

ZPEV see Kupka, Karel

ZPEV MATKY see Kapr, Jan

ZPEV MINY see Marsik, Emanuel

ZPEV RODNE ZEME see Slavicky, Klement

ZPEV RODNEHO KRAJE see Doubrava,
Jaroslav

ZPEVY ANGLICKYCH HAVIRU see Kubin,
Rudolf

ZPEVY MORAVSKYCH KOPANICARU see Cernik,
Josef

ZPEVY STARE CINY see Palenicek, Josef

ZPIVEJTE S MISOU see Sauer, Frantisek

ZU DEM DONNER EINE WOLKE SPRACH see
Rimsky-Korsakov, Nikolai

ZU DEM SILBERHELLEN BACHE see Schumann,
Georg

ZU GOLDE WARD DIE WELT see Bijvanck,
Henk

ZU SPAT see Edler, Robert

ZU STRASSBURG AUF DER SCHANZ see
Mahler, Gustav

ZU WEM SPRECHE ICH HEUTE? see Bijl,
Theo van der

ZUEIGNUNG see Strauss, Richard

ZUG ES MIR NOCH AMUHL see Ellstein, Abe

ZUG FAR VUS see Ellstein, Abe

ZUGVOGEL see Pfitzner, Hans

ZULLIG, E.
Es Hampfeli Liedli
solo,pno HUG s.p. (Z171)

ZUM see Cugley, Ian

ZUM EINSCHLAFEN ZU SAGEN see Franken,
Wim

ZUM ERNTEKRANZ see Haas, Joseph

ZUM GALLI GALLI *Jew
[Heb/Eng/Jew/Span] solo,pno KAMMEN
486 $1.00 (Z172)

ZUM NEUEN JAHR see Wolf, Hugo

ZUM NEUEN JAHR see Heiss, Hermann

ZUM OSSA SPRACH DER PELION see
Bordewijk-Roepman, Johanna

ZUM SCHLAFEN see Reger, Max

ZUR ERINNERUNG see Kilpinen, Yrio

ZUR ERSTEN HEILIGE KOMMUNION see
Welcker, Max

ZUR, MENACHEM
Affairs, The
S solo,fl,clar,trp,tuba,vla,pno,
2perc sc SEESAW $20.00 (Z173)

Two Shabbat Songs *CC2U
S solo,pno sc SEESAW $2.00 (Z174)

ZUVERSICHT see Ehrenberg, Carl Emil
Theodor

ZUWEILEN DUNKT ES MICH see Oort, H.C.v.

ZVERINCEK see Kowalski, Julius

ZVEROKRUH see Burghauser, Jarmil

ZVIRATKA see Kricka, Jaroslav

ZVIRETNIK see Jirasek, Ivo

ZWANZIG AUSGEWAHLTE LIEDER see Tiessen,
Heinz

ZWANZIG GEISTLICHE LIEDER see Bach,
Johann Sebastian

ZWANZIG KLEINE LIEDER see Brunner, M.

ZWANZIG LIEDER see Beethoven, Ludwig
van

ZWANZIG LIEDER see Bois, Rob du

ZWANZIG LIEDER see Holenia, Hanns

ZWANZIG SPANISCHE VOLKSLIEDER, HEFT I &
II *CCU
(Nin, Joaquin) [Span/Fr] solo,pno
SCHOTTS 3054; 3055 s.p., ea. (Z175)

ZWART, JAN (1877-1937)
O Gij Mijn Troost, Mijn Zoet
Verlangen *sac,hymn
solo,vla,org ALSBACH s.p. (Z176)

ZWEERS, [BERNARD] (1854-1924)
Achter De Wuivende Duinenlijn
solo,pno ALSBACH s.p. (Z177)

De Liereman
solo,pno ALSBACH s.p. (Z178)

De Merel
A solo,pno ALSBACH s.p. (Z179)

De Roos
solo,pno ALSBACH s.p. (Z180)

Diep In Het Dennenbosch
high solo,pno ALSBACH s.p. (Z181)

Een Oud Lied
high solo,pno ALSBACH s.p. (Z182)

Eenmaal Heb Ik U Aanschouwd
high solo,pno ALSBACH s.p. (Z183)

Evangelie Der Natuur
solo,pno/org/harmonium ALSBACH s.p.
(Z184)

'K Wil U Eens Wat Zeggen
high solo,pno ALSBACH s.p. (Z185)

Kind Der Aarde
see Twee Liederen

Laat Mij Nimmermeer
high solo,pno ALSBACH s.p. (Z186)

Leeuwerik
solo,pno ALSBACH s.p. (Z187)

Lof Der Godheid
solo,pno/org/harmonium ALSBACH s.p.
(Z188)

Mei
solo,pno ALSBACH s.p. (Z189)

Mijn Eerste
med solo,pno ALSBACH s.p. (Z190)

Moedertje
med solo,pno ALSBACH s.p. (Z191)

Onder Jonge Bloemen
solo,pno ALSBACH s.p. (Z192)

Rijmpje
solo,pno ALSBACH s.p. (Z193)

Sterren En Heidelied
solo,pno ALSBACH s.p. (Z194)

Twee Liederen
A solo,pno ALSBACH s.p.
contains: Kind Der Aarde; Zonne-
Kus (Z195)

Zonne-Kus
see Twee Liederen

ZWEI ABENDLIEDER see Gilse, Jan van

ZWEI ARIEN see Beethoven, Ludwig van

ZWEI ARIEN DES LYKOMEDES see Scarlatti,
Domenico

ZWEI ARIEN FUR SOPRAN see Beethoven,
Ludwig van

ZWEI BALLADEN see Schoenberg, Arnold

ZWEI BALLADEN VON GOETHE see
Diepenbrock, Alphons

ZWEI DEUTSCHE MARIENLIEDER see Monn,
Georg Matthias

ZWEI DUETTEN see Bijvanck, Henk

ZWEI ELEGIEN see Eisler, Hanns

ZWEI ELEGIEN see Eisler, Hanns

ZWEI ELEVATIONS see Campra, Andre

ZWEI ERNSTE GESANGE see Ehrenberg, Carl
Emil Theodor

ZWEI FRAGMENTE see Staromieyski, J.

ZWEI GEDICHTE VON RICHARD DEHMEL see Prohaska, Carl

ZWEI GEISTLICHE GESANGE see Krenek, Ernst

ZWEI GEISTLICHE GESANGE see Heiller, Anton

ZWEI GEISTLICHE GESANGE see Kropfreiter, Augustinius Franz

ZWEI GEISTLICHE GESANGE see Planyavsky, Peter

ZWEI GEISTLICHE GESANGE see Roselius, Ludwig

ZWEI GEISTLICHE GESANGE see Schutz, Heinrich

ZWEI GEISTLICHE LIEDER see Diepenbrock, Alphons

ZWEI GEISTLICHE LIEDER see Reger, Max

ZWEI GESANGE see Apostel, Hans Erich

ZWEI GESANGE see Brahms, Johannes

ZWEI GESANGE see Siegl, Otto

ZWEI GESANGE see Fibich, Zdenko

ZWEI GESANGE see Schoenberg, Arnold

ZWEI GESANGE AUS DEN "DEUTSCHEN ARIEN" see Handel, George Frideric

ZWEI GESANGE FUR ALT see Brahms, Johannes

ZWEI GITARREN
   see Funf Beruhmte Russische Lieder
   see Russische Volkslieder

ZWEI HIRTENLIEDER see Zagwijn, Henri

ZWEI HYMNEN see Schollum, Robert

ZWEI IN EINER GROSSEN STADT
   see Internationale Volkslieder, Vol. 2

ZWEI KANONS see Salieri, Antonio

ZWEI KASCHUBISCHE WEIHNACHTSLIEDER see Westerman, G. von

ZWEI KLEINE GEISTLICHE KONZERTE see Grimm, Heinrich

ZWEI KLEINE OSTERKONZERTE see Grimm, Heinrich

ZWEI KLEINE WEIHNACHTSKONZERTE see Grimm, Heinrich

ZWEI LIEDER see Schoenberg, Arnold

ZWEI LIEDER see Webern, Anton von

ZWEI LIEDER see Berg, Alban

ZWEI LIEDER see Schoenberg, Arnold

ZWEI LIEDER see Schiske, Karl

ZWEI LIEDER see Andriessen, Hendrik

ZWEI LIEDER see Adriessen, Willem

ZWEI LIEDER see Roos, Robert de

ZWEI LIEDER see Albeniz, Isaac

ZWEI LIEDER see Prado, Almeida

ZWEI LIEDER see Busoni, Ferruccio Benvenuto

ZWEI LIEDER see Crome, Fritz

ZWEI LIEDER NACH GEDICHTEN VON PAUL VERLAINE see Czernik, W.

ZWEI LIEDER NACH GEDICHTEN VON THEODOR STORM see Ehrenberg, Carl Emil Theodor

ZWEI LIEDER NACH GOETHE see Nowak, Lionel

ZWEI LIEDER VON STEFAN ZWEIG see Rontgen, Johannes

ZWEI LIEDER ZUR JAHRESWENDE see Taubert, Karl Heinz

ZWEI LIEDER ZUR PAUKE see Ronnefeld, Peter

ZWEI MADRIGALE FUR FRAUENSTIMME see Tsouyopoulos, Georges S.

ZWEI MINNELIEDER, HEFT 1-2 see Rangstrom, Ture

ZWEI MOTETTEN see Monteverdi, Claudio

ZWEI ORCHESTERLIEDER AUS DEM SPANISCHEN LIEDERBUCH see Wolf, Hugo

ZWEI PSALMEN see Planyavsky, Peter

ZWEI RILKE-LIEDER see Zipp, Friedrich

ZWEI SOLO-KANTATEN see Knab, Armin

ZWEI SONETTE VON MICHELANGELO see Lie, Harald

ZWEI TRAUUNGSGESANGE UND TAUFLIED see Hogner, Friedrich

ZWEI VERLASSENE ITALIENER see Jehring, J.

ZWEI WELTLICHE ARIEN see Bach, Johann Christian

ZWEI WIENER LIEDER see Eysler, Edmund S.

ZWEI ZWIEGESANGE see Zagwijn, Henri

ZWEIER SEELEN LIED see Trunk, Richard

ZWEIERLEI BITTE ICH, HERR, VON DIR see Schutz, Heinrich

ZWEIFELNDE LIEBE see Pfitzner, Hans

ZWEITER LIEDERKREIS see Wetzel, Justus Hermann

ZWERVERS VERZEN see Koetsier, Jan

ZWIEGESANG see Draeger, Walter

ZWIEGESANGE HEFT I: DER JAHRESKREIS see Praetorius, Michael

ZWIEGESANGE HEFT II: DER TAGESKREIS see Praetorius, Michael

ZWISCHEN ABEND UND MORGEN see Herbst, E.

ZWISHENDURCH see Straesser, Joep

ZWOLF ALT-ARIEN AUS OPERN UND ORATORIEN see Handel, George Frideric

ZWOLF BELIEBTE RUSSISCHE ZIGEUNERROMANZEN UND LIEDER
   *CC12U,folk,Russ
   (Ignatieff, Mikail) [Ger/Russ] solo, pno ZIMMER. 1748 $3.50   (Z196)

ZWOLF DUETTE see Albert, Heinrich

ZWOLF EICHENDORFF-LIEDER see Schoeck, Othmar

ZWOLF FJELDLIEDER, OP. 52 see Kilpinen, Yrio

ZWOLF FJELDLIEDER, OP. 53 see Kilpinen, Yrio

ZWOLF FJELDLIEDER, OP. 54 see Kilpinen, Yrio

ZWOLF GEISTLICHE GESANGE see Reger, Max

ZWOLF GEISTLICHE GESANGEN see Schutz, Heinrich

ZWOLF GESANGE see Goldmark, Karl

ZWOLF GESANGE see Hess, W.

ZWOLF GESANGE NACH GEDICHTEN VON NELLY SACHS see Bornefeld, Helmut

ZWOLF GESANGE NACH GEDICHTEN VON PAUL VERLAINE *see Cythere, Op.42,No.5; Winter, Op.42,No.6; Trunk, Richard, Die Allee, Op.42,No.9; Trunk, Richard, Helle Nacht, Op.42,No.8; Trunk, Richard, In Stiller Dammerung, Op.42,No.10; Trunk, Richard, Klagen Im Wind, Op.42, No.12; Trunk, Richard, Mandolinen, Op.42,No.3; Trunk, Richard, Mein Traum, Op.42,No.2; Trunk, Richard, Mondschein, Op.42,No.1; Trunk, Richard, Regen, Op.42,No.4; Trunk, Richard, Ruhe, Op.42,No.11; Trunk, Richard, Serenade, Op.42,No.7
                                                (Z197)

ZWOLF HAFIS-LIEDER see Schoeck, Othmar

ZWOLF LIEBESGESANGE see Pohle, David

ZWOLF LIEBESLIEDER see Zillig, Winfried

ZWOLF LIEDER see Godard, Benjamin Louis Paul

ZWOLF LIEDER see Schumann, Robert (Alexander)

ZWOLF LIEDER see Sixt, Johann Abraham

ZWOLF LIEDER FUR MITTLERE STIMME, OP. 104; ZWEI DUETTE FUR TENOR UND BASS, OP. 106 see Prokofiev, Serge

ZWOLF LIEDER NACH GOETHE see Knab, Armin

ZWOLF LIEDER UND BALLANDEN AUS "DAS KNABEN WUNDERHORN" see Weismann, Wilhelm

ZWOLF LIEDER UND SPRUCHE see Marx, Karl

ZWOLF SOPRAN-ARIEN AUS OPERN UND ORATORIEN see Handel, George Frideric

ZWOLF WUNDERHORN-LIEDER see Handel, George Frideric

ZYKLUS VON FUNF LIEDERN: "1914" see Vomacka, Boleslav

Publishers and Addresses

The list of publishers which follows contains the code assigned for each publisher, the name and address of the publisher, and agents who distribute their publications. This is the master list used for the Music-In-Print series and represents those publishers included in all volumes thus far published. Therefore, all of the publishers do not necessarily occur in the present volume.

Code	Publisher	Agent
ABC	ABC Music Co.	BOURNE
ABER	The Aberbach Group	BIG3
ABINGDON	Abingdon Press 201 Eighth Avenue-Soth Nashville, TN 37202	
ACORD	Edizioni Accordo	CURCI
AGAPE	Agape	HOPE
ALBERSEN	Muziekhandel Albersen & Co.	DONEMUS
ALBERT	J. Albert & Son Pty. Ltd.	BELWIN
ALCOVE	Alcove Music	WESTERN
ALFRED	Alfred Publishing Co., Inc. 75 Channel Drive Port Washington, NY 11050	
ALKOR	Alkor Edition	BAREN.
ALLANS	Allans Music Pty. Ltd. 276 Collins St. Melbourne 3000 Australia	
ALLOWAY	Alloway Publications Box 25 Santa Monica, CA 90406	
ALPHENAAR	W. Alphenaar	DONEMUS
ALSBACH	G. Alsbach & Co.	PETERS
ALSBACH&D	Alsbach & Doyer	PETERS
AM. COMP. AL.	American Composers Alliance 170 West 74th St. New York, NY 10023	
AM. INST. MUS.	American Institute of Musicology	HANSSLER
AM. MUS. ED.	American Music Edition	FISCHER, C
	American Musicological Society	GALAXY
AMICI	Gli Amici della Musica da Camera Via Bocca di Leone 25 Rome, Italy	
AMP	AMP	SCHIRM. G
AMPHION	Editions Amphion	KERBY
AMSI	Art Masters Studios, Inc. 2614 Nicollet Avenue Minneapolis, MN 55408	
ANDEL	Edition Andel Madeliefjeslaan, 26 8400 Oostende Belgium	
APOGEE	Apogee Press, Inc.	WORLD
A-R ED	A-R Editions, Inc. 152 West Johnson St. Madison, WI 53703	

Code	Publisher	Agent
ARCO	Arco Music Publishers	WESTERN
ARION	Coleccion Arion	MEXICANAS
ARNOLD	Edward Arnold Series	NOVELLO
ARS NOVA	Ars Nova	DONEMUS PRESSER
ARS VIVA	Ars Viva Verlag Gmbh.	BELWIN
ARSIS	Arsis Press 1719 Bay St.-Southwest Washington, D.C. 20003	
ARTIA	Artia	BOOSEY
ARTRANSA	Artransa Music	WESTERN
ASCHERBERG	Ascherberg, Hopwood & Crew Ltd.	BELWIN
ASHDOWN	Edwin Ashdown Ltd. 275-281 Cricklewood Broadway London NW2 6QR England	
ASHLEY	Ashley Publications, Inc.	CENTURY
	Associated Music Publishers see AMP	
AUGSBURG	Augsburg Publishing House 426 South Fifth St. Minneapolis, MN 55415	
AULOS	Aulos Music Publishers P.O. Box 411 Montgomery, NY 12547	
AUTRY	Gene Autry's Publishing Companies	BIG3
AVANT	Avant Music	WESTERN
BANK	Annie Bank	DONEMUS WORLD
BANKS MUS	Banks Music, Ltd.	BRODT
BAREN.	Bärenreiter Verlag Heinrich Schütz Allee 29-37 35 Kassel-Wilhelmshöhe Germany	BOONIN MAGNAMUSIC
BARON, M	M. Baron Co. Box 149 Oyster Bay, NY 11771	
BARRY-ARG	Barry & Cia	BOOSEY
BASART	Les Editions Internationales Basart	DONEMUS GENERAL
BEACON HILL	Beacon Hill Music	LILLENAS
BECKEN	Beckenhorst	PRESSER
BEECHWD	Beechwood Music Corp.	BIG3
BELAIEFF	M.P. Belaieff	PETERS

Code	Publisher	Agent
BELMONT	Belmont Music Publishers P.O. Box 49961 Los Angeles, CA 90049	
BELWIN	Belwin-Mills Publishing Corp. 25 Deshon Drive Melville, NY 11746	
BENJ	A. J. Benjamin	SCHAUR
BENSON	John T. Benson 1625 Broadway Nashville, TN 37202	
BERANDOL	Berandol Music Ltd. 11 Saint Joseph St. Toronto, Ontario M4Y 1J8 Canada	
BERBEN	Edizioni Musicali Berben	PRESSER
BERGMANS	W. Bergmans	PETERS
BERLIN	Irving Berlin Music Corp. 1290 Avenue of the Americas New York, NY 10019	
BERNOUILLI	Ed. Bernouilli	DONEMUS
BESSEL	Editions Bessel & Cie	BELWIN
BEZIGE BIJ	De Bezige Bij	DONEMUS
BIELER	Edmund Bieler Musikverlag Zulpicher Strasse 85 5 Cologne-Sulz, West Germany	
BIG3	The Big 3 Music Corp. 729 Seventh Avenue New York, NY 10019	
BIG BELL	Big Bells, Inc. 33 Hovey Avenue Trenton, NJ 08610	
BILLAUDOT	Editions Billaudot	PRESSER
BIRCH	Robert Fairfax Birch	PRESSER
BIRNBACH	Richard Birnbach Dürerstrasse 28a 1000 Berlin 45 Germany	
BMI	Broadcast Music, Inc.	SCHIRM.G
BOETHIUS	Boethius Press 5 Albert Grove Leeds LS6 4DA Yorkshire, England	
BOHM	Anton Böhm & Sohn Postfach 110369 Lange Gasse 26 D-89 Augsburg 11, West Germany	
BOMART	Bomart Music Publications	SCHIRM.G
BONGIOVANI	Casa Musicale Francesco Bongiovani	BELWIN
BOONIN	Joseph Boonin, Inc. P.O. Box 2124 South Hackensack, NJ 07606	
BOOSEY	Boosey & Hawkes, Inc. P.O. Box 130 Oceanside, NY 11572	
BOOSEY-CAN	Boosey & Hawkes Ltd. 279 Yorkland Blvd. Willowdale, Ontario Canada	BOOSEY
BOOSEY-ENG	Boosey & Hawkes	BOOSEY

Code	Publisher	Agent
BORNEMANN	Editions Bornemann	BELWIN
BOSSE	Gustav Bosse Verlag	BOONIN MAGNAMUSIC
BOSTON	Boston Music Company	FRANK
BOSWORTH	Bosworth & Company, Ltd. 14/18 Heddon St. London, W1R 8DP England	
BOTE	Bote & Bock	AMP
BOURNE	Bourne Co. 1212 Avenue of the Americas New York, NY 10036	
BRANDEN	Branden Press, Inc. 221 Columbus Avenue Boston, MA 02116	
BRATFISCH	Musikverlag Georg Bratfisch Trendelstrasse 5 865 Kulmbach, West Germany	
BRAUER	Editions Musicales Herman Brauer 30, Rue Saint Christophe Brussels, Belgium	
BREITKOPF-L	Breitkopf & Härtel, Leipzig	BROUDE, A
BREITKOPF-W	Breitkopf & Härtel, Wiesbaden	AMP
BRIDGE	Bridge Music Publishing Co. 1350 Villa St. Mountain View, CA 94042	
BRIGHT STAR	Bright Star Music Pubications	WESTERN
BR. CONT. MUS.	British and Continental Music Agencies, Ltd.	EMI
	Broadcast Music, Inc. see BMI	
BROADMAN	Broadman Press 127 Ninth Avenue, North Nashville, TN 37203	
BRODT	Brodt Music Co. 1409 E. Independence Blvd. Charlotte, NC 28201	
BROEKMANS	Broekmans & Van Poppel	PETERS
BROGNEAUX	Editions Musicales Brogneaux 73, Avenue Paul Janson 1070 Brussels, Belgium	ELKAN, H
BROUDE, A	Alexander Broude, Inc. 225 West 57th St. New York, NY 10019	
BROUDE BR.	Broude Brothers Ltd. 56 West 45th St. New York, NY 10036	
BROWN	Brown University Choral Series	BOOSEY
BRUZZI	Aldo Bruzzichelli, Editore	AMP
BUDAPEST	Editio Musica Budapest P.O.B. 322 Budapest, Hungary	BOOSEY
CAILLET	Lucien Caillet	SOUTHERN
CAMBIATA	Cambiata Press P.O. Box 1151 Conway, AR 72032	
CANAAN	Canaanland Publications	WORD
CANYON	Canyon Press, Inc.	BOONIN

Code	Publisher	Agent
CAPELLA	Capella Music, Inc.	BOURNE
CARISH	Carish S.p.A.	BOOSEY
CARLTON	Carlton Musikverlag	GERIG
CARUS	Carus-Verlag	HANSSLER
CBDM	Centre Belge De Documentation Musicale	ELKAN, H
CENTURY	Century Music Publishing Co. 263 Veterans Blvd. Carlstadt, NJ 07072	
CENTURY PR	Century Press Publishers 412 North Hudson Oklahoma City, OK 73102	
CHANT	Editions Le Chant Du Monde	MCA
CHANTRY	Chantry Music Press, Inc. Wittenberg University Box 1101 Springfield, OH 45501	
CHAPLET	Chaplet Music Corp.	PARAGON
CHAPPELL	Chappell & Co., Inc. 810 Seventh Avenue New York, NY 10019	
CHAPPELL-ENG	Chappell & Co., Ltd.	CHAPPELL
CHAPPELL-FR	Chappell S.A.	CHAPPELL
CHAR CROS	Charing Cross Music, Inc.	BIG BELL
CHARTER	Charter Publications, Inc. Valley Forge, PA 19481	
CHESTER	J. & W. Chester, Ltd.	BROUDE, A MAGNAMUSIC
CHORISTERS	Choristers Guild 440 Northlake Center P.O. Box 38188 Dallas, TX 75238	
CHOUDENS	Choudens	BARON, M PETERS
CHRIS	Christophorus-Verlag Herder Hermann-Herder-Strasse 4 D-7800 Freiburg/Breisgau, West Germany	
CHURCH	John Church Co.	PRESSER
CIMINO	Cimino Publications P.O. Box 75 1646 New Highway Farmingdale, L.I., NY 11735	
CLARK	Clark and Cruickshank Music Publishers	BERANDOL
COBURN	Coburn Press P.O. Box 75 Sherman, CT 06784	
COLE	M. M. Cole Publishing Co. 251 East Grand Avenue Chicago, IL 60611	
COLFRANC	Colfranc Music Publishing Corp.	KERBY
COLOMBO	Franco Colombo Publications	BELWIN

Code	Publisher	Agent
COMP/PERF	Composer/Performer Edition 2101 22nd St. Sacramento, CA 95818	
COMP. PR	The Composers Press, Inc.	SEESAW
CONCERT	Concert Music Publishing Co.	BOURNE
CONCORD	Concord Music Publishing Co.	ELKAN, H
CONCORDIA	Concordia Publishing House 3558 South Jefferson Avenue St. Louis, MO 63118	
CONGRESS	Congress Music Publications 501 Fagler Federal Bldg. 111 Northeast First St. Miami, FL 33132	
CONSORTIUM	Consortium Musical	ELKAN-V
COSTALL	Editions Costallat	BELWIN
CRAMER	J.B. Cramer & Co., Ltd.	BRODT
CRES.-NETH	Uitg. Crescendo	DONEMUS
CRESCENDO	Crescendo Music Sales Co. Box 395 Naperville, IL 60540	
CRESPUB	Crescendo Publications, Inc. 2580 Gus Thomasson Rd. P.O. Box 28218 Dallas, TX 75228	
CRITERION	Criterion Music Corp. 17 West 60th St. New York, NY 10023	
CROATICA	Croation Music Institute	DRUS. HRVAT. SKLAD.
CURCI	Edizioni Curci Galleria del Corso 4 20122 Milan, Italy	BIG3
CURWEN	J. Curwen & Sons	SCHIRM. G
CZECH	Czechoslovak Music Information Centre Besedni 3 Prague 1, Czechoslovakia	
DA CAPO	Da Capo Press, Inc. 227 West 17th St. New York, NY 10011	
DEAN	Roger Dean Publishing Co. 324 West Jackson Macomb, IL 61455	
DEIRO	Pietro Deiro Publications 133 Seventh Ave. South New York, NY 10014	
DELRIEU	Georges Delrieu & Cie	GALAXY
DESSAIN	Editions Dessain, Belgium	PETERS
DEUTSCHER	Deutscher Verlag für Musik	BROUDE, A
DITSON	Oliver Ditson Co.	PRESSER
DOBLINGER	Ludwig Doblinger Verlag	AMP
DONEMUS	Donemus Foundation	PETERS
DOUBLDAY	Doubleday & Co., Inc. 501 Franklin Avenue Garden City, NY 11530	

Code	Publisher	Agent
DOVER	Dover Publications, Inc. 130 Varick St. New York, NY 10014	
DRUS. HRVAT. SKLAD.	Drustvo Hrvatskih Skladatelja Berislaviceva 9 Zagreb, Yugoslavia	
DRUSTVO	Drustvo Slovenskih Skladateljev Trg Francoske Revolucije 6 61000 Ljubljana, Yugoslavia	
DRZAVNA	Drzavna Zalozba Slovenije	DRUSTVO
DURAND	Durand & Cie	PRESSER
ECK	Van Eck & Zn.	DONEMUS
ECOAM	Editorial Cooperativa Inter-Americana de Compositores	PEER
EGTVED	Edition Egtved Musikhojskolens Forlag ApS DK-6040 Egtved, Denmark	
EIGEN UITGAVE	Eigen Uitgave van de Componist (Self-published by the composer)	DONEMUS
ELITE	Elite Edition	SCHAUR
ELKAN, H	Henri Elkan Music Publisher 1316 Walnut St. Philadelphia, PA 19107	
ELKAN-V	Elkan-Vogel, Inc.	PRESSER
ELKIN	Elkin & Co. Ltd.	NOVELLO
EMI	EMI Music Publishing Ltd. 138/140 Charing Cross Rd. London, WC2H OLD, England	
ENGSTROEM	Engstroem & Soedering	PETERS
ENOCH	Enoch & Cie 27 Boulevard des Italiens Paris 2, France	AMP ASHDOWN BARON, M BRODT PEER
ERDMANN	Rudolf Erdmann, Musikverlag Adolfsallee 34 62 Wiesbaden, Germany	
ERIKS	Eriks Musikhandel & Förlag AB Karlavägen 40 Stockholm Ö, Sweden	
ESCHIG	Editions Max Eschig	AMP
ESSO	Van Esso & Co.	DONEMUS
EULENBURG	Edition Eulenburg	PETERS
EXPERIMENTAL	Experimental Music Catalogue 208 Ladbroke Grove London, W10 5LU England	
FABER	Faber Music Ltd.	SCHIRM. G
FAIR	Fairfield Publishing, Ltd.	NOVELLO
FAITH	Faith Music	LILLENAS
FAR WEST	Far West Music	WESTERN
FARRELL	The Wes Farrell Organization	BIG3
FAZER	Musik Fazer Aleksanterinkatu 11 SF 00100 Helsinki 10 Finland	
FELDMAN, B	B. Feldman & Co., Ltd.	EMI

Code	Publisher	Agent
FEMA	Fema Music Publications	CRESCENDO
FINE ARTS	Fine Arts Music Press P.O. Box 45144 Tulsa, OK 74145	
FISCHER, C	Carl Fischer, Inc. 56-62 Cooper Square New York, NY 10003	
FISCHER, J	J. Fischer & Bro.	BELWIN
FISHER	Fisher Music Co.	PLYMOUTH
FITZSIMONS	H. T. FitzSimons Co., Inc. 615 North LaSalle St. Chicago, IL 60610	
FLAMMER	Harold Flammer, Inc.	SHAWNEE
FMA	Florilegium Musicae Antiquae	HANSSLER
FOETISCH	Foetisch Freres	SCHIRM. EC
FOG	Dan Fog Musikforlag	PETERS
FORBERG	Rob. Forberg-P. Jurgenson, Musikverlag	PETERS SONZOGNO
FORLIVESI	A. Forlivesi & C. Via Roma 4 Florence, Italy	
FORNI	Arnaldo Forni Editore Via Triumvirato 7 40132 Bologna, Italy	
FORTRESS PR	Fortress Press 2900 Queen Lane Philadelphia, PA 19129	
FOSTER	Mark Foster Music Co. Box 4012 Champaign, IL 61820	
FOSTER-HALL	Foster-Hall Publications	PRESSER
FOUR ST	Four Star Publishing Co.	BIG3
FOX	Fox Publications	PRESSER
FOX, S	Sam Fox Publishing Co.	PEPPER
FRANCE	France Music	AMP
FRANCIS	Francis, Day & Hunter, Ltd.	BIG3
FRANK	Frank Distributing Corp. 116 Boylston St. Boston, MA 02116	
FRANTON	Franton Music 4620 Sea Isle Memphis, TN 38117	
FREDONIA	Fredonia Press	SIFLER
FREEMAN, H	H. Freeman & Co., Ltd.	EMI
FURST	Fürstner Ltd.	SCHOTTS SONZOGNO
GALAXY	Galaxy Music Corp. 2121 Broadway New York, NY 10023	
GALLEON	Galleon Press 94 Greenwich Avenue New York, NY 10011	
GALLIARD	Galliard, Ltd.	GALAXY

Code	Publisher	Agent
GEHRMANS	Carl Gehrmans Musikförlag Apelbergsgatan 58 Postfack 505 101 26 Stockholm 1 Sweden	BOOSEY PEER
GENERAL	General Music Publishing Co.	FRANK
GENERAL WDS	General Words and Music Co.	KJOS
GENTRY	Gentry Publications	PRESSER
GERIG	Musikverlage Hans Gerig Drususgasse 7-11 5 Köln 1, Germany	BIG3 MCA
GIA	GIA Publications 7404 S. Mason Avenue Chicago, IL 60638	
GILLMAN	Gillman Publications	PRESSER
GOODWIN	Goodwin & Tabb Publishing, Ltd.	NOVELLO
GORNSTON	David Gornston	FOX, S
GOSPEL	Gospel Publishing House 1445 Boonville Avenue Springfield, MO 65802	
GRAHL	Grahl & Nicklas	PETERS
GRAS	Editions Gras	BARON, M
GRAY	H. W. Gray Co., Inc.	BELWIN
GREENWOOD	Greenwood Press	WORLD
GREGG	Gregg International Publishers, Ltd. 1 Westmead, Farnborough Hants GU14 7RU, England	
	Gregorian Institute of America see GIA	
HAMELLE	Hamelle & Cie	ELKAN-V
HANSEN-DEN	Wilhelm Hansen Edition	BROUDE, A MAGNAMUSIC
HANSEN-ENG	Hansen, London	ALBERT
HANSEN-US	Hansen Press, Inc. 1842 West Avenue Miami Beach, FL 33139	
HANSSLER	Hänssler-Verlag	PETERS
HARMONIA	Harmonia Uitgave	PETERS
HARP PUB	Harp Publications 42 Winship Avenue P.O. Box 972 Ross, CA 94957	
HARRIS	Frederick Harris Music Co., Ltd. P.O. Box 670 Oakville, Ontario Canada	BRODT
HART	F. Pitman Hart & Co., Ltd.	BRODT
HARTH	Harth Musik Verlag	PRO MUSICA
HASTINGS	Hastings Music Corp.	BIG3
HATIKVAH	Hatikvah Publications	TRANSCON.
HAYMOZ	Haydn-Mozart Presse	PRESSER
HEER	Joh. de Heer & Zn.	PETERS
HEIDELBERGER	Heidelberger	BAREN.
HEINRICH.	Heinrichshofen's Verlag	PETERS
HELIOS	Editio Helios	FOSTER

Code	Publisher	Agent
HENLE	G. Henle Verlag Schongauerstrasse 24 8 Munich 55, Germany	BRODT
HENN	Editions Henn 8 rue de Hesse Geneve, Switzerland	
	Editions Henn-Chapuis	HENN
HENREES	Henrees Music Ltd.	EMI
HERITAGE	Heritage Music Press	LORENZ
HERITAGE PUB	Heritage Music Publishing Co.	CENTURY
HEUGEL	Heugel & Cie	PRESSER
HEUWEKE.	Edition Heuwekemeijer	PRESSER
HIEBER	Musikverlag Max Hieber Kaufingerstrasse 23 8000 Munich 33, Germany	
HIGHGATE	Highgate Press	GALAXY
HIGHLAND	Highland Music Co. 1311 North Highland Avenue Hollywood, CA 90028	
HINRICHSEN	Hinrichsen Edition, Ltd.	PETERS
HINSHAW	Hinshaw Music, Inc. P.O. Box 470 Chapel Hill, NC 27514	
HIRSCHS	Abr. Hirschs Förlag	GEHRMANS
HOFMEISTER	Veb Friedrich Hofmeister, Musikverlag, Leipzig	BROUDE, A
HOLLY-PIX	Holly-Pix Music Publishing Co.	WESTERN
HONOUR	Honour Publications	WESTERN
HOPE	Hope Publishing Co. 380 South Main Place Carol Stream, IL 60187	
HUG	Hug & Company	PETERS
HUNTZINGER	R. L. Huntzinger Publications	WILLIS
ICELAND	Iceland Music Information Centre	ELKAN, H
IMPERO	Impero-Verlag	PRESSER
INTERLOCH	Interlochen Press	CRESCENDO
INTERNAT.	International Music Co. 511 Fifth Avenue New York, NY 10017	
INTERNAT. S.	International Music Service Box 66, Ansonia Station New York, NY 10023	
IONE	Ione Press	SCHIRM. EC
ISR. MUS. INST.	Israel Music Institute	BOOSEY
ISR. PUB. AG.	Israel Publishers Agency	SESAC
ISRAELI	Israeli Music Publications, Ltd.	BROUDE, A
JAPAN	Japan Federation of Composers 602 Shinanomachi Bldg. 33 Shinanomachi Shinjuku-ku Tokyo, Japan	
J.B. PUB	J.B. Publications P.O. Box 3 Interlochen, MI 49643	
JEANNETTE	Ed. Jeannette	DONEMUS

Code	Publisher	Agent
JEHLE	Jehle	HANSSLER
JOBERT	Editions Jean Jobert	PRESSER
JOHNSON	Johnson Reprint Corp. 111 Fifth Avenue New York, NY 10003	
JRB	JRB Music Education Materials Distributor	PRESSER
JUS-AUTOR	Jus-Autor, Bulgaria	GERIG
JUSKO	Jusko Publications	WILLIS
KAHNT	C. F. Kahnt, Musikverlag	PETERS
KALMUS	Edwin F. Kalmus Miami-Dade Industrial Park P.O. Box 1007 Opa-Locka, FL 33054	
KAMMEN	J. & J. Kammen Music Co.	CENTURY
KANE	Walter Kane & Son, Inc. 351 West 52nd St. New York, NY 10019	
KENDOR	Kendor Music, Inc. Delevan, NY 14042	
KENYON	Kenyon Publications	PLYMOUTH
KERBY	E. C. Kerby, Ltd.	BOONIN
KING	King Music Publishing Co.	KANE
KING, R	Robert King Music Co. 112 A. Main St. North Easton, MA 02356	
KISTNER	Kistner & Siegel	CONCORD
KJOS	Neil A. Kjos Music Co. 525 Busse Hwy. Park Ridge, IL 60068	
KNUS	Editions Kneusslin	PETERS
KON BOND	Kon Bond van Chr. Zang-en Oratoriumverenigingen	DONEMUS
KONINKLIJK	Koninklijk Nederlands Zangersverbond	DONEMUS
KRENN	Ludwig Krenn Reindorfgasse 42 1150 Wien 15, Austria	
KROMPHOLZ	Krompholz & Co. Spitalgasse 28 3001 Bern, Switzerland	
KRUSEMAN	Ed. Philip Kruseman	DONEMUS
KYSAR	Michael Kysar 1250 South 211th Place Seattle, WA 98148	
LAND	A. Land Ezn, Muziekuitgevers	DONEMUS
LANDES	Landesverbands Evangliche Kirchenchöre in Bayern	HANSSLER
LAUDINELLA	Laudinella Reihe	HANSSLER
LAWSON	Lawson-Gould Music Publishers, Inc.	SCHIRM. G
LEDUC	Alphonse Leduc	BARON, M BRODT ELKAN-V
LEMOINE	Henry Lemoine & Cie	PRESSER
LENGNICK	Alfred Lengnick & Co., Ltd.	HARRIS

Code	Publisher	Agent
LEONARD-ENG	Leonard, Gould & Bolttler	LESLIE
LEONARD-US	Hal Leonard Music 960 East Mark St. Winona, MN 55987	
LESLIE	Leslie Music Supply	BRODT
LEUCKART	F.E.C. Leuckart	AMP
LEXICON	Lexicon Music, Inc.	WORD
LICHTENAUER	W. F. Lichtenauer	DONEMUS
LIENAU	Robert Lienau, Musikverlag	PETERS
LILLENAS	Lillenas Publishing Co. Box 527 Kansas City, MO 64141	
LISTER	Mosie Lister	LILLENAS
LITURGICAL	Liturgical Press St. Johns Abbey Collegeville, MN 56321	
LOOP	Loop Music Co.	KJOS
LORENZ	Lorenz Industries 501 East Third St. Dayton, OH 45401	
LUDWIG	Ludwig Music Publishing Co. 557-67 East 140th St. Cleveland, OH 44110	
LUNDQUIST	Abr. Lundquist AB, Musikförlag Katarina Bangata 17 116 25 Stockholm, Sweden	
LYCHE	Harald Lyche	PETERS
MAGNAMUSIC	Magnamusic-Baton, Inc. 10370 Page Industrial Blvd. St. Louis, MO 63132	
MARCHAND	Marchand, Paap en Strooker	DONEMUS
MARK	Mark Publications	CRESPUB
MARKS	Edward B. Marks Music Corp.	BELWIN
MASTER	Master Music	CRESPUB
MCA	MCA and Mills/MCA Joint Venture Editions	BELWIN
MCAFEE	McAfee Music Corp.	LORENZ
MCGIN-MARX	McGinnis & Marx	DEIRO
MEDIA	Media Press Box 895 Champaign, IL 61820	
MEL BAY	Mel Bay Publications, Inc. 107 West Jefferson Avenue Kirkwood, MO 63122	
MERCURY	Mercury Music Corp.	PRESSER
MERION	Merion Music, Inc.	PRESSER
MERRYMOUNT	Merrymount Music, Inc.	PRESSER
MERSEBURG	Editions Merseburger, Berlin	BAREN. PETERS
METROPOLIS	Editions Metropolis	ELKAN, H
MEXICANAS	Ediciones Mexicanas De Musica	PEER
MEZ KNIGA	Mezhdunarodnaja Kniga Moscow, G-200 USSR	

Code	Publisher	Agent	Code	Publisher	Agent
MILLER	Miller Music Corp.	BIG3	NORSK	Norsk Musikforlag A/S	AMP MAGNAMUSIC
MINKOFF	Minkoff Reprints Chemin de la Mousse 46 1225 Chêne-Bourg Geneva, Switzerland		NORTON	W. W. Norton & Co., Inc. 500 Fifth Avenue New York, NY 10003	
MJQ	MJQ Music, Inc.	FOX, S	NOSKE	A. A. Noske	DONEMUS
MODERN	Edition Modern Musikverlag Hans Wewerka Franz-Joseph-Strasse 2 8 München 13, Germany		NOVELLO	Novello & Co., Ltd. 145 Palisade St. Dobbs Ferry, NY 10522	BELWIN (Rentals)
MOECK	Hermann Moeck Verlag	BELWIN	OAK	Oak Publications	MUSIC
MORAVIAN	Moravian Music Foundation	ABINGDON BELWIN BOOSEY BRODT PETERS	OISEAU	Editons de L'Oiseau-Lyre Les Ramparts Monaco	
			OKRA	Okra Music Corp.	SEESAW
MOSELER	Möseler Verlag Postfach 460 3340 Wolfenbüttel West Germany		OLSCHKI	Casa Editrice, Leo S. Olschki Viuzzo Del Pozzetto Firenze Firenze, 50126, Italy	
MOWBRAY	A. R. Mowbray & Co., Ltd.	BRODT	ONGAKU	Ongaku-No-Tomo Sha Co., Ltd. Kagurazaka 6-30, Shinjuku-ku Tokyo, Japan	PRESSER
MULLER	Willy Müller Süddeutscher Musikverlag	PETERS	OPUS	Opus Music Publishers, Inc. 612 North Michigan Avenue Chicago, IL 60611	
MUNSTER	Van Munster Editie	DONEMUS			
MURPHY	Spud Murphy Publications	WESTERN	OR-TAV	Or-Tav Music Publications P.O. Box 3200 Tel-Aviv, Israel	
MUS. ANT. BOH.	Musica Antiqua Bohemia	BOOSEY			
MUS. RARA	Musica Rara	PETERS	ORGAN	Organ Music Co.	WESTERN
MUS. VIVA HIST.	Musica Viva Historica	BOOSEY	ORLANDO	Orlando-Musikverlag Kaprunerstrasse 1 D-8000 Munich 21 Germany	
MUSIC	Music Sales Corp. 33 West 60th St. New York, NY 10023				
MUSIC INFO	Muzichi Informationi Centar	GERIG	OSTARA	Ostara Press, Inc.	WESTERN
MUSICO	Musico Muziekuitgeverij	DONEMUS	OSTER	Österreichischer Bundesverlag	AMP
MUSICUS	Edition Musicus P.O. Box 1341 Stamford, CT 06904		OTOS	Casa Musicale Otos	BELWIN
			OUVRIERES	Les Editions Ouvrieres	GALAXY
MUSIKAL.	Musikaliska Konstföreningen	NORDISKA	OXFORD	Oxford University Press 200 Madison Avenue New York, NY 10016	
MUSIKHOJ	Musikhojskolens Forlag	BOONIN			
MUSIKK	Musikk-Huset A/S	PETERS	PALLMA	Pallma Music Co.	KJOS
MUSIKWISS.	Musikwissenschaftlicher Verlag	AMP BAREN.	PAN AM	Pan American Union	PEER
			PANTON	Panton	GENERAL
NAGELS	Nagels Verlag	AMP MAGNAMUSIC	PARAGON	Paragon Music Publishers 71 Fourth Avenue New York, NY 10003	
NATIONAL	National Music Publishers P.O. Box 868 Tustin, CA 92680		PARIS	Uitgeverij H.J. Paris	DONEMUS
NEUE	Verlag Neue Musik	BAREN.	PARKS	Parks Music Corp.	KJOS
NEW VALLEY	New Valley Music Press of Smith College Sage Hall 3 Northampton, MA 01060		PATERSON	Paterson's Publications, Ltd.	FISCHER, C
			PAXTON	Paxton Publications	NOVELLO
			PEER	Peer International Corporation 1740 Broadway New York, NY 10019	
NIEUWE	De Nieuwe Musiekhandel	DONEMUS			
NOETZEL	Noetzel Musikverlag	PETERS	PELIKAN	Musikverlag Pelikan	BAREN.
NOORDHOFF	P. Noordhoff	DONEMUS	PENGUIN	Penguin Books 72 Fifth Avenue New York, NY 10011	
NORDISKA	AB Nordiska Musikförlaget	BROUDE, A MAGNAMUSIC			

Code	Publisher	Agent
PENN STATE	Pennsylvania State University Press 215 Wagner Building University Park, PA 16802	
PEPPER	J.W. Pepper and Son, Inc. P.O. Box 850 Valley Forge, PA 19482	
PETERS	C. F. Peters Corp. 373 Park Avenue South New York, NY 10016	
PHILIPPO	Editions Philippo	ELKAN-V
PILLIN	Pillin Music	WESTERN
PIONEER	Pioneer Music Press 975 Southwest Temple St. Salt Lake City, UT 84101	
PLENUM	Plenum Publishing Corp.	DA CAPO
PLYMOUTH	Plymouth Music Co., Inc. 17 West 60th St. New York, NY 10023	
POLSKIE	Polskie Wydawnictwo Muzyczne	MARKS
POLYPHON	Polyphon Musikverlag	GERIG
PORT. MUS.	Portugaliae Musicae	BAREN.
PRESSER	Theodore Presser Co. Presser Place Bryn Mawr, PA 19010	
PRIMAVERA	Editions Primavera	GENERAL
PRO ART	Pro Art Publications, Inc. 469 Union Avenue Westbury, NY 11590	
PRO MUSICA	Pro Musica Verlag Karl-Liebknecht-Strasse 12 701 Leipzig, Germany	
PROSVETNI	Prosvetni Servis	DRUSTVO
PROWSE	Keith Prowse Music Publishing Co.	EMI
PRUETT	Pruett Publishing Co. 3235 Prairie Avenue Boulder, CO 80302	
RAHTER	D. Rahter	SCHAUR
REGENT	Regent Music Corp.	BIG BELL
REN	Les Editions Renaissantes	BOONIN
RICHMOND	Richmond Music Press, Inc. P.O. Box 465 P.P. Sta. Richmond, IN 47374	
RICORDI-ARG	Ricordi Americana S.A.	BELWIN
RICORDI-ENG	G. Ricordi & Company, Ltd.	BELWIN
RICORDI-FR	Societe Anonyme des Editions Ricordi	BELWIN
RIDEAU	Les Editions Rideau Rouge	PRESSER
RIES	Ries & Erler	PETERS
ROBBINS	Robbins Music Corp.	BIG3
ROBERTON	Roberton Publications	SCHIRM. G
ROCHESTER	Rochester Music Publishers, Inc. 358 Aldrich Road Fairport, NY 14450	
RODEHEAVER	Rodeheaver Publications	WORD
RONGWEN	Rongwen Music, Inc.	BROUDE BR.

Code	Publisher	Agent
ROSSUM	Wed. J. R. van Rossum	PETERS
ROUART	Rouart-Lerolle & Cie	SALABERT-US
ROYAL	Royal School of Church Music Addington Place Croydon, Surrey CR9 5AD England	BRODT
ROZSAVO.	Rozsavölgyi & Co.	BUDAPEST
RUBANK	Rubank, Inc. 16215 Northwest 15th Avenue Miami, FL 33169	
SAC. MUS. PR.	Sacred Music Press of Hebrew Union College	PRESSER
SACRED	Sacred Music Press	LORENZ
SACRED SNGS	Sacred Songs, Inc.	WORD
SALABERT-FR	Francis Salabert Editions	SALABERT-US
SALABERT-US	Éditions Salabert, Inc. 575 Madison Avenue New York, NY 10022	
SAMFUNDET	Samfundet til udgivelse af Dansh Musik	PETERS
SANTIS	Edizioni de Santis Via Cassia 13 00191 Rome, Italy	
SAUL AVE	Saul Avenue Publishing Co. 1632 Central Parkway Cincinnati, OH 45210	
SCHAUR	Richard Schauer, Music Publishers	AMP
SCHIRM. EC	E. C. Schirmer Music Co. 112 South St. Boston, MA 02111	
SCHIRM. G	G. Schirmer, Inc. 866 Third Avenue New York, NY 10022	
SCHMITT	Schmitt Music Centers 110 North Fifth St. Minneapolis, MN 55403	
SCHOLA	Editions Musicales de la Schola Cantorium, Paris	PRESSER
SCHOTT	Schott & Co., Ltd.	BELWIN
SCHOTT-FRER	Schott Frères	BELWIN PETERS
SCHOTTS	B. Schotts Söhne	BELWIN
SCHUBERTH	Edward Schuberth & Co., Inc.	ASHLEY
SCHUL	Carl L. Schultheiss Denzenbergstrasse 35 74 Tübingen West Germany	
SCHWANN	Musikverlag Schwann	PETERS
SCHWEIZER.	Schweizerischen Kirchengesangsbundes	HANSSLER
SCOTT	G. Scott Music Publishing Co.	WESTERN
SCREEN	Screen Gems-Columbia Publications 16333 Northwest 54th Avenue Miami, FL 33014	
SEESAW	Seesaw Music Corporation 1966 Broadway New York, NY 10023	

Code	Publisher	Agent	Code	Publisher	Agent
SENART	Ed. Maurice Senart	SALABERT-US	SUMMY	Summy-Birchard Co. 1834 Ridge Avenue Evanston, IL 60204	
SESAC	Sesac, Inc. 10 Columbus Circle New York, NY 10019		SUPRAPHON	Editio Supraphon	BOOSEY
SHAPIRO	Shapiro, Bernstein & Co., Inc.	PLYMOUTH	SYMPHON	Symphonia Verlag	BELWIN
SHATTINGER	Shattinger Music Co. 252 Paul Brown Bldg. St. Louis, MO 63101		THOMP.	Thompson Music House P.O. Box 12463 Nashville, TN 37212	
SHAWNEE	Shawnee Press Delaware Water Gap, PA 18327		THOMP. G	Gordon V. Thompson, Ltd. 29 Birch Avenue Toronto, Ontario M4V 1E2 Canada	BIG3
SHEPPARD	John Sheppard Music Press	BOONIN			
SIDEMTON	Sidemton-Verlag	GERIG	TIEROLFF	Tierolff Muziek Centrale Markt 90-92 Roosendaal, Netherlands	
SIFLER	Paul J. Sifler 3947 Fredonia Drive Hollywood, CA 90028				
SIKORSKI	Hans Sikorski Verlag	BELWIN	TONGER	P. J. Tonger, Musikverlag	PETERS
SIMROCK	N. Simrock	SCHAUR	TONOS	Edition Tonos Ahastrasse 7 6100 Darmstadt, Germany	
SINGSPIR	Singspiration Music The Zondervan Corp. 1415 Lake Dr., S.E. Grand Rapids, MI 49506		TOORTS	Uit. De Toorts	DONEMUS
			TRANSAT.	Editions Transatlantiques	PRESSER
SIRIUS	Sirius-Verlag	PETERS	TRANSCON.	Transcontinental Music Publications 838 Fifth Avenue New York, NY 10021	
SKAND.	Skandinavisk Musikforlag	MAGNAMUSIC			
SLOV. AKA.	Slovenska akademija znanosti in umetnosti	DRUSTVO	TRIGON	Trigon Music Inc.	TRIUNE
SLOV. HUD. FOND.	Slovensky Hudobny Fond Gorkeho 19 Bratislava, Czechoslovakia		TRI-TEN	Tritone Press and Tenuto Publications	PRESSER
			TRIUNE	Triune Music Inc. 824 19th Avenue-South Nashville, TN 37203	
SLOV. MAT.	Slovenska Matica	DRUSTVO			
SOMERSET	Somerset Press	HOPE	TRO	Tro Songways Service, Inc.	PLYMOUTH
SONZOGNO	Casa Musicale Sonzogno	BELWIN	TUSKEGEE	Tuskegee Music Institute Press	KJOS
SOUTHERN	Southern Music Co. 1100 Broadway San Antonio, TX 78215		UNION ESP.	Union Musical Espanola	AMP
			UNITED ART	United Artists Group	BIG3
SOUTHRN PUB	Southern Music Publishing Co., Inc.	PEER	UNITED MUS	United Music Publishers, Ltd. 1 Montague St. London, WC1B 5BS England	
SPIRE	Spire Editions	FISCHER, C WORLD			
SPRATT	Spratt Music Company	PLYMOUTH	UNIV. CAL	University of California Press 2223 Fulton St. Berkeley, CA 94720	
ST. GREG.	St. Gregory Publishing Co. 4 West Hill Road Hoddesdon, Hertfordshire EN1 9DB England		UNIV. CH	University of Chicago Press 5001 South Ellis Avenue Chicago, IL 60637	
ST. MARTIN	St. Martin Music Co., Inc.	ROYAL	UNIV. MUS. ED.	University Music Editions P.O. Box 192—Ft. George Station New York, NY 10040	
STAFF	Staff Music Publishing Co., Inc.	PLYMOUTH			
STAINER	Stainer & Bell, Ltd.	GALAXY			
STAMPS	Stamps-Baxter Music Publications	SINGSPIR	UNIV. NC	University of North Carolina Press Box 2288 Chapel Hill, NC 27514	
STANDARD	Standard Music Publishing, Inc. P.O. Box 1043 Whitman Square Turnersville, NJ 08012		UNIVER.	Universal Edition	BOONIN
			UP WITH	Up With People Music	LORENZ
			VALANDO	Valando Music, Inc.	PLYMOUTH
STEIN	Edition Steingräber Offenbach/M. 62 Wiesbaden, Postfach 471 Germany		VANGUARD	Vanguard Music Corp. 250 West 57th St. New York, NY 10019	
STUDIO	Studio Publications 224 South Lebanon St. Lebanon, IN 46052		VIEWEG	Chr. Friedrich Vieweg	PETERS
			VOLK	Arno Volk Verlag	GERIG

Code	Publisher	Agent	Code	Publisher	Agent
VOLKWEIN	Volkwein Brothers, Inc. 117 Sandusky St. Pittsburgh, PA 15212		WILHELM.	Wilhelmiana Musikverlag	MAGNAMUSIC
WAGENAAR	J. A. H. Wagenaar	ELKAN, H	WILLIS	Willis Music Company 7380 Industrial Highway Florence, KY 41042	
WALTON	Walton Music Corp.	PLYMOUTH	WILLSHIRE	Willshire Press Music Foundation, Inc.	WESTERN
WARNER	Warner Brothers Publications, Inc. 265 Secaucus Rd. Secaucus, NJ 07094		WINGERT	Wingert-Jones Music, Inc. 2026 Broadway P. O. Box 1878 Kansas City, MO 64141	
WATERLOO	Waterloo Music Co., Ltd. 3 Regina St. North Waterloo, Ontario N2J 2Z7 Canada	AMP BRODT	WOLF	Wolf-Mills Music	WESTERN
WEINBERGER	Josef Weinberger, Ltd.	AMP BOOSEY FOX MARKS SCHIRM. G SHAPIRO	WORD	Word, Incorporated 4800 West Waco Drive Waco, TX 76703	
			WORLD	World Library Sacred Music, Inc. 2145 Central Parkway Cincinnati, OH 45214	
WEINTRB	Weintraub Music Co.	MUSIC	YAHRES	Yahres Publications 1315 Vance Avenue Coraopolis, PA 15108	
WESTERN	Western International Music 2859 Holt Avenue Los Angeles, CA 90034		YORKE	Yorke Editions	GALAXY
WESTWOOD	Westwood Press, Inc.	WORLD	ZANIBON	G. Zanibon Edition	PETERS
WHITE, ERN	Ernest White Editions 755 Clinton Avenue Bridgeport, CT 06604		ZENEM.	Zenemükiado Vallalat	BOOSEY GENERAL
			ZENGERINK	Herman Zengerink, Amsterdam	PETERS
WHITE HARV.	White Harvest Publications Box 87 Stewartsville, MO 64490		ZERBONI	Suvini Zerboni	BELWIN
			ZIMMER.	Wilhelm Zimmermann, Musikverlag	PETERS

Publishers' Advertisements